THE CIA WORLD FACTBOOK 2026–2027

CENTRAL INTELLIGENCE AGENCY

Skyhorse Publishing

Skyhorse Publishing books may be purchased in bulk at special discounts for sales promotion, corporate gifts, fundraising, or educational purposes. Special editions can also be created to specifications. For details, contact the Special Sales Department, Skyhorse Publishing, 307 Fifth Avenue, 4th Floor, New York, NY 10016 or info@skyhorsepublishing.com.

Visit our website at www.skyhorsepublishing.com.
Please follow our publisher Tony Lyons on Instagram @tonylyonsisuncertain.

10 9 8 7 6 5 4 3 2

Library of Congress Cataloging-in-Publication Data is available on file.

Cover design by Kai Texel and Brian Peterson

Print ISBN: 978-1-5107-8604-2
Ebook ISBN: 978-1-5107-8605-9

Printed in the United States of America

CONTENTS

COUNTRY PROFILES

A BRIEF HISTORY OF BASIC INTELLIGENCE AND *THE WORLD FACTBOOK*

The Intelligence Cycle is the process of turning raw information into finished intelligence for policymakers. The ***raw information*** *can come from any source and is called* ***open-source information*** *or* ***open-source intelligence*** *when it comes from publicly available sources, such as those used in* The World Factbook. ***Finished intelligence*** *is the product that results from collecting, processing, integrating, analyzing, evaluating, and interpreting information about foreign countries or areas.*

Introduced in 1962, *The World Factbook* evolved from earlier products that were developed to assist US government officials with locating basic facts about the world for use in finished intelligence.

1941

The Japanese attack on Pearl Harbor in 1941 brought home to leaders in the US Congress and the executive branch the need for integrating reports to national policymakers. US government officials realized that multiple government offices produced basic information on countries, resulting in a significant duplication of effort and conflicting information. Detailed and coordinated information was needed not only on major powers such as Germany and Japan, but also on places of little previous interest. In the Pacific Theater, for example, the Navy and Marines had to launch amphibious operations against many islands about which information was unconfirmed or nonexistent. Intelligence authorities resolved that the United States should never again be caught unprepared.

1943–1947

In 1943, Gen. George B. Strong (G-2), Adm. H. C. Train (Office of Naval Intelligence), and Gen. William J. Donovan (Director, Office of Strategic Services) decided that a joint effort should be initiated to coordinate the information, known at the time as "basic intelligence." A steering committee was appointed on 27 April 1943 that recommended the formation of a Joint Intelligence Study Publishing Board to assemble, edit, coordinate, and publish the *Joint Army Navy Intelligence Studies* (JANIS). JANIS was the first interdepartmental basic intelligence program to fulfill the needs of the US government. Between April 1943 and July 1947, the board published 34 JANIS studies. JANIS performed well in the war effort, and numerous letters of commendation were received, including a statement from Adm. Forrest Sherman, Chief of Staff, Pacific Ocean Areas, which said, "JANIS has become the indispensable reference work for the shore-based planners."

1947–48

The Central Intelligence Agency was established on 26 July 1947 and began operating on 18 September 1947. Effective 1 October 1947, the Director of Central Intelligence assumed operational responsibility for JANIS. On 13 January 1948, the National Security Council issued Intelligence Directive (NSCID) No. 3, which authorized the *National Intelligence Survey* (NIS) program as a peacetime replacement for the wartime JANIS program. Before adequate NIS country sections could be produced, government agencies had to develop more comprehensive gazetteers and better maps. The US Board on Geographic Names compiled the names, the Department of the Interior produced the gazetteers, and CIA produced the maps.

1954–73

The Hoover Commission's Clark Committee, set up in 1954 to study CIA's structure and administration, reported to Congress in 1955 that: "The National Intelligence Survey is an invaluable publication which provides the essential elements of basic intelligence on all areas of the world. There will always be a continuing requirement for keeping the Survey up-to-date." The *National Basic Intelligence Factbook* was created in 1962 as an annual summary and update to the encyclopedic NIS studies. The first classified *Factbook* was published in August 1962, and the first unclassified version was published in June 1971. The NIS program was terminated in 1973, except for the *Factbook*, map, and gazetteer components.

1975–95

The 1975 *Factbook* was the first to be made available to the public, with sales through the US Government Printing Office (GPO). The publication was produced semi-annually until 1981, when it became an annual product and was renamed *The World Factbook*. Beginning in 1995, the GPO also offered a CD-ROM version.

1997-present

In June 1997, *The World Factbook* made its internet debut. The hardcopy version ceased publication in 2017.

DEFINITIONS AND NOTES

Abbreviations This information is included in the **Abbreviations** reference guide, which includes all abbreviations and acronyms used in the *Factbook*, with their expansions.

Administrative divisions This entry gives the numbers, designatory terms, and first-order administrative divisions as approved by the US Board on Geographic Names (BGN). Changes that have been reported but not yet acted on by the BGN are noted. Geographic names conform to spellings approved by the BGN with the exception of the omission of diacritical marks and special characters.

Age structure This entry provides the distribution of the population according to age. Information is included by sex and age group as follows: *0–14 years (children)*, *15–64 years (working age)*, and *65 years and over (elderly)*.

Agricultural products This entry provides a list of a country's most important agricultural products, listed by annual tonnage.

Airports This entry gives the total number of active airports or airfields and includes both civilian and military facilities. The runway(s) may be paved (concrete or asphalt surfaces) or unpaved (grass, earth, sand, or gravel surfaces). Airports or airfields that are closed are not included. Note that not all airports have accommodations for refueling, maintenance, or air traffic control.

Alcohol consumption per capita This entry provides information on alcohol consumption per capita (APC), which is the recorded amount of alcohol consumed per capita by persons aged 15 years and over in a calendar year, measured in liters of pure alcohol. APC is broken down further into beer, wine, spirits, and other subfields. Beer includes malt beers, wine includes wine made from grapes, spirits include all distilled beverages, and other includes one or several other alcoholic beverages, such as fermented beverages made from sorghum, maize, millet, rice, or cider, fruit wine, and fortified wine. APC only takes into account the consumption that is recorded from production, import, export, and sales data, primarily derived from taxation.

Area This entry includes three subfields. *Total area* is the sum of all land and water areas delimited by international boundaries and/or coastlines. *Land area* is the aggregate of all surfaces delimited by international boundaries and/or coastlines, excluding inland water bodies (lakes, reservoirs, rivers). *Water area* is the sum of the surfaces of all inland water bodies, such as lakes, reservoirs, or rivers, as delimited by international boundaries and/or coastlines.

Area - comparative This entry provides an area comparison based on total area equivalents. Most entities are compared with the entire US or one of the 50 states based on area measurements (1990 revised) provided by the US Bureau of the Census. The smaller entities are compared with Washington, DC (178 sq km, 69 sq mi) or The Mall in Washington, DC (0.59 sq km, 0.23 sq mi, 146 acres).

Area - rankings This entry, which appears only in the World Geography category, provides rankings for the earth's largest (or smallest) continents, countries, oceans, islands, mountain ranges, or other physical features.

Average household expenditures This entry refers to the average consumer expenditures on food, alcohol, and tobacco for the country specified in a given year. The data is presented as a percentage of all goods and services consumed in private settings for personal or household uses.

Background This entry provides a brief introduction to each country, highlighting information like geographic details, early inhabitants, key leaders, and major historical events.

Bathymetry Bathymetry is the study of the depth and floors of bodies of water. This field describes the major bathymetric features found on the ocean floor. Specific bathymetric features associated with each of the following categories are listed for each ocean.

The *continental shelf* is a rather flat area of the sea floor adjacent to the coast that gradually slopes down from the shore to water depths of about 200 m (660 ft). It is narrow or nearly nonexistent in some places; in others, it extends for hundreds of miles.

The *continental slope* is where the bottom drops off more rapidly until it meets the deep-sea floor (abyssal plain) at about 3,200 m (10,500 ft) water depth. The continental slope can be indented by submarine canyons, often associated with the outflow of major rivers. Another feature of the continental slope are alluvial fans or cones of sediments carried downstream to the ocean by major rivers and deposited down the slope.

The *abyssal plains*, at depths of over 3,000 m (10,000 ft) and covering 70% of the ocean floor, are the largest habitat on earth. Despite their name, these "plains" are not uniformly flat and are interrupted by features like hills, valleys, and seamounts.

The *mid-ocean ridge*, rising up from the abyssal plain, is a continuous range of undersea volcanic mountains that encircles the globe almost entirely underwater. It is the longest mountain range on Earth at over 64,000 km (40,000 mi) long, rising to an average depth of 2,400 m (8,000 ft). Mid-ocean ridges form at divergent plate boundaries where two tectonic plates are moving apart and magma creates new crust.

Seamounts are submarine mountains at least 1,000 m (3,300 ft) high, formed from individual volcanoes on the ocean floor. They are distinct from the plate-boundary volcanic system of the mid-ocean ridges, because seamounts tend to be circular or conical. Flat-topped seamounts are known as "guyots."

Ocean trenches are the deepest parts of the ocean floor and are created by the process of subduction, when tectonic plates move toward each other and one plate sinks (is subducted) under another.

Atolls are the remains of dormant volcanic islands. In warm tropical oceans, coral colonies establish themselves on the margins of the island. Over time, the high elevation of the island collapses and erodes away to sea level, leaving behind an outline of the island in the form of the coral reef. The resulting island typically has a low elevation of sand and coral with an interior shallow lagoon.

Birth rate This entry gives the average annual births during a year per 1,000 persons in the population at midyear, which is also known as "crude birth rate." The birth rate is usually the dominant factor in determining the rate of population growth.

Broadband - fixed subscriptions This entry gives the total number of fixed-broadband subscriptions, as well as the number of subscriptions per 100 inhabitants. Fixed broadband is a physical wired connection to the Internet (e.g., coaxial cable, optical fiber) at speeds equal to or greater than 256 kilobits/second (256 kbit/s).

Broadcast media This entry provides information on the approximate number of public and private TV and radio stations in a country, as well as basic information on the availability of satellite and cable TV services.

Budget This entry includes *revenues* and *expenditures*. *Revenues* include central government receipts from taxes, social contributions, fees, and other income excluding grants. *Expenditures* are payments for operating activities of the central government, including wages for government employees, interest payments, subsidies, social benefits, and other outlays. Figures reported in local currency units have been converted to current US dollars using an average official exchange rate for the year indicated.

Capital This entry gives the *name* of the seat of government, its *geographic coordinates*, the *time difference* relative to **Coordinated Universal Time (UTC)** and the time observed in Washington, DC, and, if applicable, information on *daylight saving time* **(DST)**. Where appropriate, a special *time zone note* has been added to highlight those countries that have multiple time zones. Finally, *etymology* explains how the capital acquired its name.

Carbon dioxide emissions This field refers to the amount of carbon dioxide released in a country by burning coal, petroleum, and natural gas. Data are reported in metric tonnes of CO_2.

Child marriage This entry provides data on the prevalence of child marriage in a country. Data includes the percentage of women aged 20 to 24 years who were first married or in union before age 15, and before age 18; and men aged 20 to 24 years who were first married or in union before age 18.

Children under the age of 5 years underweight This entry gives the percentage of children under five considered to be underweight. Underweight means weight-for-age is less than minus two standard deviations from the median of the World Health Organization Child Growth Standards among children under 5 years of age. This statistic is an indicator of the nutritional status of a community.

Citizenship This entry provides information related to the acquisition and exercise of citizenship; it includes four subfields:

citizenship by birth describes the acquisition of citizenship based on place of birth, known as *Jus soli*, regardless of the citizenship of parents.

citizenship by descent only describes the acquisition of citizenship based on the principle of *Jus sanguinis*, or by descent, where at least one parent is a citizen of the state and being born within the territorial limits of the state is not required. The majority of countries adhere to this practice. In some cases, citizenship is conferred through the father or mother exclusively.

dual citizenship recognized indicates whether a state permits a citizen to simultaneously hold citizenship in another state. Many states do not permit dual citizenship, and the voluntary acquisition of citizenship in another country is grounds for revocation of citizenship. Holding dual citizenship makes an individual legally obligated to more than one state and can negate the normal consular protections afforded to citizens outside their original country of citizenship.

residency requirement for naturalization lists the length of time an applicant is required to live in a country before applying for naturalization. In most countries, citizenship can be acquired through the legal process of naturalization. The requirements for naturalization vary but generally include no criminal record, good health, economic wherewithal, and a period of authorized residency.

Civil aircraft registration country code prefix This entry provides the one- or two-character alphanumeric code indicating the nationality of civil aircraft. An aircraft registration number consists of two parts: this alphanumeric code and a registration suffix of one-to-five characters for the specific aircraft. The prefix codes are based on radio call-signs allocated by the International Telecommunications Union (ITU) to each country. Since 1947, the International Civil Aviation Organization (ICAO) has managed code standards and their allocation.

Climate This entry includes a brief description of typical weather regimes throughout the year; in the World entry only, it includes four subfields that describe climate extremes:

ten driest places on earth (average annual precipitation) describes the annual average precipitation measured in both millimeters and inches for selected countries with climate extremes.

ten wettest places on earth (average annual precipitation) describes the annual average precipitation measured in both millimeters and inches for selected countries with climate extremes.

ten coldest places on earth (lowest average monthly temperature) describes temperature measured in both degrees Celsius and Fahrenheit, as well as the month of the year for selected countries with climate extremes.

ten hottest places on earth (highest average monthly temperature) describes the temperature measured both in degrees Celsius and Fahrenheit, as well the month of the year for selected countries with climate extremes.

Coal This field refers to a country's coal and metallurgical coke *production, consumption, exports, imports,* and *proven reserves.* These energy sources include anthracite, metallurgical, bituminous, subbituminous, lignite coal, and metallurgical coke. *Proven reserves* are the quantities of coal that have been assessed as commercially recoverable in the future based on known reservoirs and assuming current economic conditions. Data are reported in metric tons, and one metric ton is 1,000 kilograms.

Coastline This entry gives the total length of the boundary between the land area (including islands) and the sea.

Communications This category deals with the means of exchanging information and includes entries on telephones (fixed and mobile), telecommunication systems, broadcast media, internet users, and broadband subscriptions.

Communications - note This entry includes miscellaneous communications information not included elsewhere.

Constitution This entry provides information on a country's constitution and includes two subfields, *history* and *amendment process.*

history - the dates of previous constitutions and the main steps and dates in formulating and implementing the latest constitution. For countries with one to three previous constitutions, the years are listed; for those with four to nine previous, the entry is listed as "several previous", and for those with 10 or more, the entry is "many previous."

amendment process - summarizes the process of amending a country's constitution from proposal through passage. Where appropriate, summaries are composed from English-language translations of non-English constitutions, which derive from official or non-official translations or machine translators.

Terms commonly used to describe constitutional changes are "amended", "revised", or "reformed." Sources can differ as to whether changes are stated as new constitutions or are amendments/revisions to existing ones.

A few countries, including Canada, Israel, and the UK, have no single constitution document but have various written and unwritten acts, statutes, common laws, and practices that, when taken together, establish a body of fundamental principles or precedents for governance. Some countries, including Oman and Saudi Arabia, use the term "basic law" instead of constitution.

Coordinated Universal Time (UTC) UTC is the international atomic time scale that serves as the basis of timekeeping for most of the world. The hours, minutes, and seconds represent the time of day at the Prime Meridian (0° longitude) located near Greenwich, England, UK, as reckoned from midnight. UTC is calculated by the Bureau International des Poids et Measures (BIPM) in Sevres, France. UTC is the basis for all civil time, with the world divided into time zones expressed as positive or negative differences from UTC. UTC is also referred to as "Zulu time." See the Standard Time Zones of the World map included with the **Reference Maps**.

Country data codes See **Data codes.**

Country map Maps have been produced from the best information available at the time of preparation. Names and/or boundaries may have subsequently changed.

Country name This entry includes all forms of a country's name approved by the US Board on Geographic Names (Italy is used as an example): *conventional long form* (Italian Republic), *conventional short form* (Italy), *local long form* (Repubblica Italiana), *local short form* (Italia), *former* (Kingdom of Italy), as well as the *abbreviation* (if applicable). Additionally, an *etymology* entry explains how the country acquired its name. See also **Terminology.**

Current account balance This entry records a country's net trade in goods and services, plus net earnings from rents, interest, profits, and dividends and net transfer payments (such as pension funds and worker remittances) to and from the rest of the world during the period specified. These figures are calculated on an exchange rate basis, i.e., not in purchasing power parity (PPP) terms.

Currently married women (ages 15–49) This field provides the percentage of married or in-union women among women of reproductive age (15–49).

Data codes This information is presented in Country Data Codes and Hydrographic Data Codes.

Daylight Saving Time (DST) This entry is included for those entities that have adopted a policy of adjusting the official local time forward, usually one hour, from Standard Time during summer months. Such policies are most common in mid-latitude regions.

Death rate This entry gives the average annual number of deaths during a year per 1,000 persons at midyear, which is also known as "crude death rate." The death rate, while only a rough indicator of the mortality situation in a country, accurately indicates the current mortality impact on population growth. This indicator is significantly affected by age distribution, and most countries will eventually show a rise in the overall death rate, in spite of continued decline in mortality at all ages, as declining fertility and increased lifespans result in an aging population.

Debt - external This entry gives the total public and private debt owed to nonresidents, repayable in internationally accepted currencies, goods, or services. Where indicated, these figures represent the present value of external debt – the sum of short-term debt and discounted outstanding service payments for long-term debt over the lifetime of the loans. Data are in current US dollars for the year indicated.

Dependency ratios Dependency ratios are a measure of the age structure of a population. They calculate the number of individuals that are likely to be economically dependent on the support of others by contrasting the ratio of youths (ages 0–14) and the elderly (ages 65+) to the number of those in the working-age group (ages 15–64). As fertility levels decline, the dependency ratio initially falls because the proportion of youths decreases while the proportion of the population of working age increases. The dependency ratio then increases because the proportion of the population of working age starts to decline as the proportion of elderly persons continues to increase.

total dependency ratio - the ratio of combined youth population (ages 0–14) and elderly population (ages 65+) per 100 people of working age (ages 15–64). A high total dependency ratio indicates that the working-age population and the overall economy face a greater burden to support and provide social services for youth and elderly persons.

youth dependency ratio - the ratio of the youth population (ages 0–14) per 100 people of working age (ages 15–64). A high youth dependency ratio indicates that a country will be spending more on schooling and other services for children.

elderly dependency ratio - the ratio of the elderly population (ages 65+) per 100 people of working age (ages 15–64). Increases in the elderly dependency ratio require more government funding for pensions and healthcare.

potential support ratio - the number of working-age people (ages 15–64) per one elderly person (ages 65+). As a population ages, the potential support ratio tends to fall, meaning there are fewer potential workers to support the elderly.

Dependency status This entry describes the formal relationship between a particular nonindependent entity and an independent state.

Dependent areas This entry contains an alphabetical listing of all nonindependent entities associated in some way with a particular independent state.

Diplomatic representation The US Government has diplomatic relations with 190 independent states, including 188 of the 193 UN members (excluded UN members are Bhutan, Cuba, Iran, North Korea, and the US itself). In addition, the US has diplomatic relations with two independent states that are not in the UN – the Holy See and Kosovo – as well as with the EU.

Diplomatic representation from the US This entry includes the *chief of mission, embassy address, mailing address, telephone number,* FAX *number, email* and *website addresses, branch office* locations, *consulate general* locations, and *consulate* locations.

Diplomatic representation in the US This entry includes the *chief of mission, chancery address, telephone, FAX, email and website addresses, consulate general* locations, and *consulate* locations. The use of the annotated title Appointed Ambassador refers to a new ambassador who has presented his/her credentials to the secretary of state but not the US president. Such ambassadors fulfill all diplomatic functions except meeting with or appearing at functions attended by the president until such time as they formally present their credentials at a White House ceremony.

Drinking water source This entry provides the percentages of a country's population with access to *improved* or *unimproved* drinking water.

improved: water that is free from fecal and chemical contamination and is available in under 30 minutes of travel

unimproved: water collected directly from a river, dam, lake, stream, irrigation canal, unprotected well, or unprotected spring; also includes access to improved water sources available in over 30 minutes of travel

Economic overview This entry summarizes the overall economic status for each country and can include information on domestic markets, public finance, trade, and key partners.

Economy This category includes the entries dealing with the size, development, and management of productive resources such as land, labor, and capital.

Education expenditure This entry is presented both as a percentage of GDP and as a percentage of national budget of current and capital education expenditures.

Electricity

This field refers to a country's installed generating capacities, consumption, exports, imports, and transmission/distribution losses.

installed generating capacity - the total capacity of a country's currently operational electric power generation, expressed in kilowatts (kW). A kilowatt produces one hour of continuously run electricity, commonly referred to as a kilowatt hour (kWh)

consumption - a country's total electricity generated annually plus any imports and minus exports, expressed in kWh

exports - a country's total exported electricity in kWh

imports - a country's total imported electricity in kWh

transmission/distribution losses - the combined difference between the amount of electricity generated and/or imported and the amount consumed and/or exported

Electricity access This entry provides information on access to electricity. Due to differences in definitions and methodology from different sources, data quality may vary from country to country. The data is collected from industry reports, national surveys, and international sources, and it consists of three subfields:

electrification – total population is the percentage of a country's total population with access to electricity

electrification – urban areas is the percentage of a country's urban population with access to electricity

electrification – rural areas is the percentage of a country's rural population with access to electricity

Electricity generation sources This field refers a country's energy portfolio of *fossil fuels, nuclear, solar, wind, hydroelectricity, tide and wave, geothermal,* and *biomass and waste*. Portfolios are expressed as a percentage share of a country's total generating capacity.

Elevation This entry includes the *mean elevation* and the elevation extremes, or *lowest point* and *highest point*.

Energy This category includes entries dealing with the production, consumption, import, and export of various forms of energy, including electricity, crude oil, refined petroleum products, and natural gas.

Energy consumption per capita This entry refers to a country's total energy consumption per capita, including the consumption of petroleum, dry natural gas, coal, net nuclear, hydroelectric, and non-hydroelectric renewable electricity. Data are reported in British thermal units per person (Btu/person).

Entities For this website, "independent state" refers to a people politically organized into a sovereign state with a definite territory. "Dependencies" and "areas of special sovereignty" refer to a broad category of political entities that are associated in some way with an independent state. Country names used in the table of contents or for page headings are usually the short-form names as approved by the US Board on Geographic Names and may include independent states, dependencies, areas of special sovereignty, or other geographic entities. Some of the entities included in this website are not officially recognized by the US Government.

The entities may be categorized as follows:

INDEPENDENT STATES

Afghanistan, Albania, Algeria, Andorra, Angola, Antigua and Barbuda, Argentina, Armenia, Australia, Austria, Azerbaijan, The Bahamas, Bahrain, Bangladesh, Barbados, Belarus, Belgium, Belize, Benin, Bhutan, Bolivia, Bosnia and Herzegovina, Botswana, Brazil,

Brunei, Bulgaria, Burkina Faso, Burma, Burundi, Cambodia, Cameroon, Canada, Cape Verde, Central African Republic, Chad, Chile, China, Colombia, Comoros, Democratic Republic of the Congo, Republic of the Congo, Cook Islands, Costa Rica, Cote d'Ivoire, Croatia, Cuba, Cyprus, Czechia, Denmark, Djibouti, Dominica, Dominican Republic, Ecuador, Egypt, El Salvador, Equatorial Guinea, Eritrea, Estonia, Ethiopia, Fiji, Finland, France, Gabon, The Gambia, Georgia, Germany, Ghana, Greece, Grenada, Guatemala, Guinea, Guinea-Bissau, Guyana, Haiti, Holy See, Honduras, Hungary, Iceland, India, Indonesia, Iran, Iraq, Ireland, Israel, Italy, Jamaica, Japan, Jordan, Kazakhstan, Kenya, Kiribati, North Korea, South Korea, Kosovo, Kuwait, Kyrgyzstan, Laos, Latvia, Lebanon, Lesotho, Liberia, Libya, Liechtenstein, Lithuania, Luxembourg, Macedonia, Madagascar, Malawi, Malaysia, Maldives, Mali, Malta, Marshall Islands, Mauritania, Mauritius, Mexico, Federated States of Micronesia, Moldova, Monaco, Mongolia, Montenegro, Morocco, Mozambique, Namibia, Nauru, Nepal, Netherlands, NZ, Nicaragua, Niger, Nigeria, Niue, Norway, Oman, Pakistan, Palau, Panama, Papua New Guinea, Paraguay, Peru, Philippines, Poland, Portugal, Qatar, Romania, Russia, Rwanda, Saint Kitts and Nevis, Saint Lucia, Saint Vincent and the Grenadines, Samoa, San Marino, Sao Tome and Principe, Saudi Arabia, Senegal, Serbia, Seychelles, Sierra Leone, Singapore, Slovakia, Slovenia, Solomon Islands, Somalia, South Africa, South Sudan, Spain, Sri Lanka, Sudan, Suriname, Swaziland, Sweden, Switzerland, Syria, Tajikistan, Tanzania, Thailand, Timor-Leste, Togo, Tonga, Trinidad and Tobago, Tunisia, Turkey, Turkmenistan, Tuvalu, Uganda, Ukraine, UAE, UK, US, Uruguay, Uzbekistan, Vanuatu, Venezuela, Vietnam, Yemen, Zambia, Zimbabwe

OTHER

Taiwan, European Union

DEPENDENCIES AND AREAS OF SPECIAL SOVEREIGNTY

Australia - Ashmore and Cartier Islands, Christmas Island, Cocos (Keeling) Islands, Coral Sea Islands, Heard Island and McDonald Islands, Norfolk Island
China - Hong Kong, Macau
Denmark - Faroe Islands, Greenland
France - Clipperton Island, French Polynesia, French Southern and Antarctic Lands, New Caledonia, Saint Barthelemy, Saint Martin, Saint Pierre and Miquelon, Wallis and Futuna
Netherlands - Aruba, Curacao, Sint Maarten
New Zealand - Tokelau
Norway - Bouvet Island, Jan Mayen, Svalbard
UK - Akrotiri and Dhekelia, Anguilla, Bermuda, British Indian Ocean Territory, British Virgin Islands, Cayman Islands, Falkland Islands, Gibraltar, Guernsey, Jersey, Isle of Man, Montserrat, Pitcairn Islands, Saint Helena, South Georgia and the South Sandwich Islands, Turks and Caicos Islands
US - American Samoa, Baker Island*, Guam, Howland Island*, Jarvis Island*, Johnston Atoll*, Kingman Reef*, Midway Islands*, Navassa Island, Northern Mariana Islands, Palmyra Atoll*, Puerto Rico, Virgin Islands, Wake Island (* consolidated in United States Pacific Island Wildlife Refuges entry)
Antarctica
Gaza Strip
Paracel Islands
Spratly Islands
West Bank

OTHER ENTITIES

Oceans - Arctic Ocean, Atlantic Ocean, Indian Ocean, Pacific Ocean, Southern Ocean
World

Environmental agreements This information is presented in Selected International Environmental Agreements, which includes the name, abbreviation, date opened for signature, date entered into force, objective, and parties by category.

Environmental issues The following terms and abbreviations are used throughout the entry:

acidification - the lowering of soil and water pH due to acid precipitation and deposition usually through precipitation; this process disrupts ecosystem nutrient flows and may kill freshwater fish and plants dependent on more neutral or alkaline conditions (see acid rain)

acid rain - characterized as containing harmful levels of sulfur dioxide or nitrogen oxide; acid rain is damaging and potentially deadly to the earth's fragile ecosystems; acidity is measured using the pH scale where 7 is neutral, values greater than 7 are considered alkaline, and values below 5.6 are considered acid precipitation; note - a pH of 2.4 (the acidity of vinegar) has been measured in rainfall in New England

biodiversity - also biological diversity; the relative number of species, diverse in form and function, at the genetic, organism, community, and ecosystem level; loss of biodiversity reduces an ecosystem's ability to recover from natural or man-induced disruption

catchments - assemblages used to capture and retain rainwater and runoff; an important water management technique in areas with limited freshwater resources, such as Gibraltar

DDT (dichloro-diphenyl-trichloro-ethane) - a colorless, odorless insecticide that has toxic effects on most animals; the use of DDT was banned in the US in 1972

defoliants - chemicals which cause plants to lose their leaves artificially; often used in agricultural practices for weed control and may have detrimental impacts on human and ecosystem health

deforestation - the destruction of vast areas of forest (e.g., unsustainable forestry practices, agricultural and range land clearing, and the over exploitation of wood products for use as fuel) without planting new growth

desertification - the spread of desert-like conditions in arid or semi-arid areas, due to overgrazing, loss of agriculturally productive soils, or climate change

dredging - the practice of deepening an existing waterway; also, a technique used for collecting bottom-dwelling marine organisms (e.g., shellfish) or harvesting coral, often causing significant destruction of reef and ocean-floor ecosystems

ecosystems - ecological units composed of complex communities of organisms and their specific environments

effluents - waste materials, such as smoke or sewage, that are released into the environment

endangered species - a species that is threatened with extinction through hunting or habitat destruction

freshwater - water with very low soluble mineral content; sources include lakes, streams, rivers, glaciers, and underground aquifers

greenhouse gas - a gas that "traps" infrared radiation in the lower atmosphere causing surface warming; water vapor, carbon dioxide, nitrous oxide, methane, hydrofluorocarbons, and ozone are the primary greenhouse gases in the Earth's atmosphere

groundwater - water sources found below the surface of the earth, often in naturally occurring reservoirs in permeable rock strata; the source for wells and natural springs

metallurgical plants - industries which specialize in the science, technology, and processing of metals; these plants produce highly concentrated and toxic wastes which can contribute to pollution of ground water and air when not properly disposed

overgrazing - permanent plant loss due to too many animals grazing limited range land

ozone shield - a layer of the atmosphere composed of ozone gas (O3) that resides approximately 25 miles above the Earth's surface and absorbs solar ultraviolet radiation that can be harmful to living organisms

poaching - the illegal killing of animals or fish

pollution - the contamination of an environment by man-made waste

potable water - water that is safe to be consumed

salination - the process through which fresh (drinkable) water becomes salt (undrinkable) water; also involves the accumulation of salts in topsoil caused by evaporation of excessive irrigation water, a process that can eventually render soil incapable of supporting crops

siltation - occurs when water channels and reservoirs become clotted with silt and mud, a side effect of deforestation and soil erosion

slash-and-burn agriculture - a rotating cultivation technique in which trees are cut down and burned in order to clear land for temporary agriculture; the land is used until its productivity declines at which point a new plot is selected and the process repeats

soil degradation - damage to the land's productive capacity because of poor agricultural practices such as the excessive use of pesticides or fertilizers, soil compaction from heavy equipment, or erosion of topsoil, eventually resulting in reduced ability to produce agricultural products
soil erosion - the removal of soil by the action of water or wind, compounded by poor agricultural practices, deforestation, overgrazing, and desertification
ultraviolet (UV) radiation - a portion of the electromagnetic energy emitted by the sun and naturally filtered in the upper atmosphere by the ozone layer

Ethnic groups This entry provides an ordered listing of ethnic groups, starting with the largest, and normally includes the percentage of the total population.

Exchange rates This entry provides the average annual price of a country's monetary unit for the time period specified, expressed in units of local currency per US dollar, as determined by international market forces or by official fiat. The International Organization for Standardization (ISO) 4217 alphabetic currency code for the national medium of exchange is presented in parenthesis. Closing daily exchange rates are not presented in *The World Factbook* but are used to convert stock values – e.g., the market value of publicly traded shares – to US dollars as of the specified date.

Executive branch This entry includes seven subentries (when the information is available):
chief of state includes the name, title, and beginning date in office of the leader who represents the state at official and ceremonial functions, but who may not be involved with the day-to-day activities of the government
head of government includes the name and title of the person designated to manage the executive branch, as well as the beginning date in office
cabinet includes the official name and the method of member selection
election/appointment process includes the process for accession to office
most recent election date also notes whether multiple rounds were required
election results includes each candidate's political affiliation and percentage of direct popular vote or indirect legislative/parliamentary vote
expected date of next election notes the year and sometimes the month and day of the next election, which can be subject to change
Most of the world's countries have separate chiefs of state and heads of government; for the remainder, the chief of state is also the head of government. In dependencies, territories, and collectivities of sovereign countries – except those of the United States – representatives are appointed to serve as chiefs of state.

Exports This entry provides the total US dollar amount of merchandise exports on an f.o.b. (free on board) basis. These figures are calculated on an exchange rate basis, i.e., not in purchasing power parity (PPP) terms.

Exports - commodities This entry provides a listing of the highest-valued exported commodities.

Exports - partners This entry provides a rank ordering of trading partners starting with the most important; it sometimes includes the percentage of total dollar value.

Flag This entry provides a written flag description. The flags of independent states are used by their dependencies unless there is an officially recognized local flag. Some disputed entities and other areas do not have flags.

Flag graphic Most country profiles include an image of the country's flag. The flags of independent states are used by their dependencies unless there is an officially recognized local flag. Some disputed entities and other areas do not have flags.

GDP - composition, by end use This entry shows who does the spending in an economy: consumers, businesses, government, and foreigners. Figures may not total 100% due to rounding or gaps in data collection. The percentage contribution to total GDP is shown in the following sub-entries:
household consumption consists of expenditures by resident households – and nonprofit institutions that serve households – on goods and services that individuals consume, including both domestically produced and foreign goods and services
government consumption consists of government expenditures on goods and services and excludes government transfer payments, such as interest on debt, unemployment, and social security
investment in fixed capital consists of total business spending on fixed assets, such as factories, machinery, equipment, dwellings, and raw materials, which provide the basis for future production
investment in inventories consists of net changes to the stock of outputs that are still held by the units that produce them, such as automobiles sitting on a dealer's lot or groceries on the store shelves; the figure may be positive or negative
exports of goods and services consist of sales, barter, gifts, or grants of goods and services from residents to nonresidents
imports of goods and services consist of purchases, barter, or receipts of gifts, or grants of goods and services to residents from nonresidents; imports are treated as a negative to offset the fact that the expenditure figures for consumption, investment, government, and exports also include expenditures on imports; because of this negative offset, the sum of the other five items, excluding imports, will always total more than 100 percent of GDP

GDP - composition, by sector of origin This entry shows where production takes place in an economy. The distribution gives the percentage value-added contribution of *agriculture*, *industry*, and *services* to total GDP after adding outputs and subtracting intermediate inputs. Agriculture includes farming, fishing, hunting, and forestry. Industry includes mining, manufacturing, energy production, and construction. Services cover government activities, communications, transportation, finance, and all other private economic activities that do not produce material goods. Figures may not total 100 percent due to non-allocated consumption, including financial intermediary services indirectly measured (FISIM) not allocated by industry, and taxes less subsidies on products.

GDP (official exchange rate) This entry gives the gross domestic product (GDP) or value of all final goods and services produced within a nation in a given year. A nation's GDP at official exchange rates (OER) is the home-currency-denominated annual GDP figure divided by the bilateral average US exchange rate with that country in that year.

GDP methodology In the **Economy** category, GDP dollar estimates for countries are reported both on a purchasing power parity (PPP) and an official exchange rate (OER) basis.
The PPP method uses standardized international dollar price weights, which are applied to the quantities of final goods and services produced in a given economy. This method probably provides the best starting point for comparisons of economic strength between countries.
The OER method involves a variety of international and domestic financial forces that may not capture the value of domestic output. PPP estimates for OECD countries are reliable, but PPP estimates for developing countries are often rough approximations.
GDP derived using the OER method should be used to calculate the share of items such as exports, imports, military expenditures, external debt, or the current account balance, because the dollar values presented in the *Factbook* for these items have been converted at official exchange rates, not at PPP. Comparison of OER GDP with PPP GDP may also indicate whether a currency is over- or under-valued.
note: The numbers for GDP and other economic data should not be chained together from successive versions of the *Factbook* because of changes in the US dollar measurement, revisions of data from statistical agencies, use of new or different sources of information, and changes in national statistical methods and practices.

Geographic coordinates This entry includes rounded latitude and longitude figures for the center point of a country, expressed in degrees and minutes. It is based on the locations provided in the Geographic Names Server (GNS), maintained by the National Geospatial-Intelligence Agency on behalf of the US Board on Geographic Names.

Geographic names This information is presented in list form in Geographic Names. It includes alternate, former, local, and regional names for one or more related *Factbook* entries. Spellings are usually those approved by the US Board on Geographic Names (BGN). Alternate names and additional information are included in parentheses.

Geographic overview This entry, which appears only in the Geography category under the World entry, provides basic geographic information about the earth's oceans and continents. The entry also lists all of the countries that compose each continent.

Geography This category includes the entries dealing with the natural environment and the effects of human activity on it.

Geography - note This entry includes miscellaneous geographic information of significance that is not included elsewhere.

Geoparks United Nations Educational, Scientific and Cultural Organization (UNESCO) Global Geoparks are geographic areas with sites and landscapes of international geological significance. Global Geoparks use their geological heritage, in connection with all other aspects of the area's natural and cultural heritage, to enhance awareness and understanding of key environmental issues facing society.

Gini Index coefficient - distribution of family income This entry measures the degree of inequality in the distribution of family income in a country. The index is calculated from the Lorenz curve, in which cumulative family income is plotted against the number of families arranged from the poorest to the richest. The index is the ratio of (a) the area between a country's Lorenz curve and the 45-degree helping line to (b) the entire triangular area under the 45-degree line. The more nearly equal a country's income distribution, the closer its Lorenz curve to the 45-degree line and the lower its Gini index, e.g., a Scandinavian country with an index of 25. The more unequal a country's income distribution, the farther its Lorenz curve from the 45-degree line and the higher its Gini index, e.g., a Sub-Saharan country with an index of 50.

GNP Gross national product (GNP) is the value of all final goods and services produced within a nation in a given year, plus income earned by its citizens abroad, minus income earned by foreigners from domestic production. The *Factbook*, following current practice, uses GDP rather than GNP to measure national production. In certain countries, however, net remittances from citizens working abroad may be a significant component of the national economy.

Government This category includes the entries dealing with the system for the adoption and administration of public policy.

Government - note This entry includes miscellaneous government information of significance not included elsewhere.

Government type This entry lists the basic form of government for each country. Definitions of the governmental terms are as follows (note that for some countries more than one definition applies):

absolute monarchy - a form of government where the monarch rules unhindered by laws, constitution, or legally organized opposition
authoritarian - a form of government in which state authority is imposed onto many aspects of citizens' lives
commonwealth - a nation, state, or other political entity founded on law and united by a compact of the people for the common good
communist - a system of government in which the state plans and controls the economy and a single – often authoritarian – party holds power; the state imposes controls and eliminates private ownership of property or capital, while claiming to make progress toward a higher social order in which people equally share all goods in a classless society
constitutional - a government operating under an authoritative document (constitution) that sets forth the system of fundamental laws and principles that determine the nature, functions, and limits of that government
constitutional democracy - a form of government in which the sovereign power of the people is spelled out in a governing constitution
constitutional monarchy - a system of government in which a monarch is guided by a constitution whereby his/her rights, duties, and responsibilities are spelled out in written law or by custom
democracy - a form of government in which the supreme power is retained by the people, but which is usually exercised indirectly through a system of representation and delegated authority periodically renewed
democratic republic - a state in which the supreme power rests in the body of citizens entitled to vote for officers and representatives responsible to them
dictatorship - a form of government in which a ruler or small clique wield absolute power (not restricted by a constitution or laws)
ecclesiastical - a government administrated by a church
emirate - similar to a monarchy or sultanate, but a government in which the supreme power is in the hands of an emir (the ruler of a Muslim state); the emir may be an absolute overlord or a sovereign with constitutionally limited authority
federal (federation) - a form of government in which sovereign power is formally divided – usually by means of a constitution – between a central authority and a number of constituent regions (states, colonies, or provinces), so that each region retains some management of its internal affairs; differs from a confederacy in that the central government exerts influence directly on both individuals and the regional units
federal republic - a state in which the powers of the central government are restricted and in which the component parts (states, colonies, or provinces) retain a degree of self-government; ultimate sovereign power rests with the voters who chose their governmental representatives
monarchy - a government in which the supreme power is in the hands of a monarch who reigns over a state or territory, usually for life and by hereditary right; the monarch may be either a sole absolute ruler or a sovereign – such as a king, queen, or prince – with constitutionally limited authority
oligarchy - a government in which a small group of individuals exercises control
parliamentary democracy - a political system in which the party with the most votes in the legislature (parliament) selects the government – a prime minister, premier, or chancellor and the cabinet ministers; by this system, the government has a responsibility to the people as well as to the parliament
parliamentary government (cabinet-parliamentary government) - a government in which a legislature or parliament nominates members of an executive branch (the cabinet and its leader – a prime minister, premier, or chancellor); this type of government can be dissolved at will by the parliament (legislature) through a no-confidence vote, or the leader of the cabinet may dissolve the parliament if it can no longer function
parliamentary monarchy - a state headed by a monarch who is not actively involved in policy formation or implementation and may have only a ceremonial capacity; governmental leadership is carried out by a cabinet and its head – a prime minister, premier, or chancellor – who are drawn from a legislature (parliament)
presidential - a system of government where the executive branch exists separately from a legislature (to which it is generally not accountable)
republic - a representative democracy in which the people's elected deputies (representatives), not the people themselves, vote on legislation
sultanate - similar to a monarchy, but a government in which the supreme power is in the hands of a sultan (the head of a Muslim state); the sultan may be an absolute ruler or a sovereign with constitutionally limited authority
theocracy - a form of government in which a deity is recognized as the supreme civil ruler, but ecclesiastical authorities interpret (bishops, mullahs, etc.) the deity's laws; a government subject to religious authority

Gross domestic product See GDP

Gross national product See GNP

Gross reproduction rate This entry presents the average number of daughters born alive that a group of women would have in their lifetime if the age-specific fertility rate were to apply to them in a given period, usually a calendar year. It is a measure of replacement fertility that indicates whether the current generation of daughters will replace the preceding generation of women.

Gross world product See **GWP**

GWP This entry gives the gross world product (GWP) or aggregate value of all final goods and services produced worldwide in a given year.

Health expenditure This entry is presented both as a percentage of GDP and as a percentage of national budget. The expenditures are broadly defined as activities performed either by institutions or individuals through the application of medical, paramedical, and/or nursing knowledge and technology, the primary purpose of which is to promote, restore, or maintain health.

Heliports This entry gives the total number of heliports with helicopter pads and no runways available for fixed-wing aircraft.

Hospital bed density This entry provides the number of hospital beds per 1,000 people; it serves as a general measure of inpatient service availability. Hospital beds include inpatient beds available in public, private, general, and specialized hospitals and rehabilitation centers. In most cases, beds for both acute and chronic care are included. The calculation is based on population numbers reported for the year of information.

Household income or consumption by percentage share Data on household income or consumption come from household surveys, with the results adjusted for household size. Nations use different standards and procedures in collecting and adjusting the data. Surveys based on income will normally show a more unequal distribution than surveys based on consumption.

Hydrographic data codes See **Data codes**

Illicit drugs This entry identifies countries that are on at least one of two lists provided in the US State Department's annual International Narcotics Control Strategy Report, which is prepared for the US Congress: 1.) *major illicit drug-producing and/or major drug-transit* countries and 2.) countries that are *major sources of precursor chemicals* used in the production of illicit drugs. The report draws on data from the year prior to the publication date.

major illicit drug-producing country - cultivates or harvests 1,000 hectares or more of illicit opium poppy per year; cultivates or harvests 1,000 hectares or more of illicit coca per year; or cultivates or harvests 5,000 hectares or more of illicit cannabis per year (unless the US President determines that such cannabis production does not significantly affect the United States)

major drug-transit country - a significant direct source of illicit narcotic or psychotropic drugs or other controlled substances significantly affecting the United States, or through which are transported such drugs or substances

major precursor-chemical producer - a significant source of the chemicals required to produce illicit drugs; these chemicals usually have legitimate uses as well

A country's presence on one or both of the lists is not necessarily a reflection of its government's counterdrug efforts or level of cooperation with the United States. The lists are not a sanction or penalty.

Imports This entry provides the total US dollar amount of merchandise imports on a c.i.f. (cost, insurance, and freight) or f.o.b. (free on board) basis. These figures are calculated on an exchange rate basis, i.e., not in purchasing power parity (PPP) terms.

Imports - commodities This entry provides a listing of the highest-valued imported commodities.

Imports - partners This entry provides a rank ordering of trading partners starting with the most important; it sometimes includes the percentage of total dollar value.

Independence For most countries, this entry gives the date that sovereignty was achieved and from which nation, empire, or trusteeship. For the other countries, the date given may not represent "independence" in the strict sense, but rather a significant nationhood event such as the traditional founding date or the date of unification, federation, confederation, establishment, fundamental change in the form of government, or state succession. For a number of countries, the establishment of statehood was a lengthy process occurring over decades or even centuries; in such cases, several significant dates are cited. Dependent areas include the notation "none," followed by the nature of their dependency status. See also **Terminology**.

Industrial production growth rate This entry gives the annual percentage increase in industrial production (includes manufacturing, mining, and construction).

Industries This entry provides a rank ordering of industries starting with the largest by value of annual output.

Infant mortality rate This entry gives the number of deaths of infants under one year old in a given year per 1,000 live births in the same year. Data is provided for the *total* per 1,000 live births, as well as the number of *male* and *female* per 1,000 live births.

Inflation rate (consumer prices) This entry provides the annual inflation rate, as calculated by the percentage change in current consumer prices from the previous year's consumer prices.

International disputes see **Disputes - international**

International environmental agreements This entry separates country participation in international environmental agreements into two levels: *party to* and *signed, but not ratified*. Agreements are listed in alphabetical order by the abbreviated form of the full name.

International law organization participation This entry includes information on a country's acceptance of jurisdiction of the International Court of Justice (ICJ) and of the International Criminal Court (ICCt). Appendix B: International Organizations and Groups explains the differing mandates of the ICJ and ICCt. Consult the online edition of *The World Factbook*.

International organization participation This entry lists in alphabetical order by abbreviation the international organizations in which a country is a member or participates in some other way.

Internet country code This entry includes the two-letter codes maintained by the International Organization for Standardization (ISO) in the ISO 3166 Alpha-2 list and used by the Internet Assigned Numbers Authority (IANA) to establish country-coded top-level domains (ccTLDs).

Internet users This entry gives the *percentage of population* with Internet access. Statistics may include users who access the Internet at least several times a week and those who access it only once within a period of several months.

Introduction This category includes one entry, **Background**.

Irrigated land This entry gives the number of square kilometers of land area that is artificially supplied with water.

Judicial branch This entry includes three subfields. The *highest court(s)* subfield includes the name(s) of a country's highest court(s), the number and titles of the judges, and the types of cases the court hears. A number of countries have separate constitutional courts. The *judge selection and term of office* subfield includes the organizations and associated officials responsible for nominating and appointing judges, and a brief description of the process. Also included are judges' tenures, which can range from a few years to lifelong appointments. The *subordinate courts* subfield lists the lower courts in a country's court system hierarchy. A few countries with federal-style governments also have separate state- or province-level court systems, though generally the systems all interact.

Labor force This entry contains the total labor force figure.

Land boundaries This entry contains the *total* length of all land boundaries and the individual lengths for each of the contiguous *border countries*. When available, official lengths published by national statistical agencies are used. Because surveying methods differ, contiguous countries may report different country border lengths.

Land use This entry lists three different types of land use for a country's total land area: *agricultural land*, *forest*, and *other*.

Agricultural land is further divided into *arable land* (cultivated for crops that are replanted after each harvest), *permanent crops* (crops that are not replanted after each harvest, including land under flowering shrubs, fruit trees, nut trees, and vines), and *permanent pastures and meadows* (used for at least five years to grow herbaceous forage, either cultivated or growing naturally). *Forest* is land spanning more than 0.5 hectare with trees higher than five meters and a canopy cover of more than 10%, including windbreaks, shelterbelts, and corridors of trees greater than 0.5 hectare and at least 20 m wide. Land classified as *other* includes built-up areas, roads and other transportation features, barren land, and wasteland.

Languages This entry provides a listing of languages spoken in each country and specifies any that are official national or regional languages. When data is available, the languages spoken in each country are broken down according to the percentage of the total population speaking each language as a first language, unless otherwise noted. For those countries without available data, languages are listed in rank order based on prevalence, starting with the most-spoken language.

Legal system This entry provides descriptions of countries' legal systems, modeled on elements of five main types: civil law (including French law, the Napoleonic Code, Roman law, Roman-Dutch law, and Spanish law); common law (including United States law); customary law; mixed or pluralistic law; and religious law (including Islamic law). International law, which governs nations' interactions, and a variant known as European Union law are also addressed below.

civil law - the most widespread type, also referred to as European continental law and applied in various forms in approximately 150 countries; derived mainly from the Roman *Corpus Juris Civilus* (Body of Civil Law), compiled under the East Roman (Byzantine) Emperor Justinian I between A.D. 528 and 565; major feature is organization into systematic written codes; legislation – especially codifications in constitutions or government statutes – is considered the primary authority, and secondarily custom

common law - often called "English common law;" England and Wales use the system in the UK; also in force in approximately 80 countries with ties to the former British Empire; has Biblical influences and remnants of early legal systems, including Roman, Anglo-Saxon, and Norman; sometimes attributed to King Henry II (r.1154–1189); foundation is "legal precedent," often referred to as *stare decisis* ("to stand by things decided"), in which judges follow the precedent set by earlier court decisions

customary law - also referred to as primitive law, unwritten law, indigenous law, and folk law; based on the customs of a community; serves as the basis of or has influenced the laws in approximately 40 countries; earliest legal systems were customary and usually developed in small agrarian and hunter-gatherer communities to regulate social relations; seldom written down; if a law is broken, resolution tends to be reconciliatory rather than punitive

European Union (EU) law - also known as community law or supranational law; variant of international law unique to a subset of European countries; the rights of sovereign European nations are limited in relation to one another, with EU law operating in tandem with the member states' legal systems; the European Court of Justice (ECJ) has been largely responsible for its development; fundamental principles include *subsidiarity* (issues handled by the smallest, lowest, or least-centralized competent authority), *proportionality* (the EU may only act to the extent needed to achieve its objectives), *conferral* (EU members grant all its authorities), *legal certainty* (rules must be clear and precise), and *precautionary principle* (burden of proof falls on advocates of an action or policy, if it could cause severe or irreversible harm to the public or the environment)

French law - a type of codified civil law used in France that serves as the basis for or is mixed with other legal systems in approximately 50 countries; distinguishes between "public law," which relates to government, the French Constitution, public administration, and criminal law, and "private law," which covers issues between private citizens or corporations

international law - the body of customary and treaty rules accepted as legally binding for interactions among states; three separate disciplines: *public international law*, which governs the relationship between provinces and international entities and includes treaty law, law of the sea, international criminal law, and international humanitarian law; *private international law*, which addresses legal jurisdiction; and *supranational law*, a legal framework of regional agreements; sources are set out in Article 38–1 of the Statute of the International Court of Justice in the UN Charter

Islamic law - the most widespread type of religious law; used in over 30 countries, particularly in the Near East but also in Central and South Asia, Africa, and Indonesia; often operates in tandem with civil law; is embodied in the *sharia*, an Arabic word meaning "the right path;" sharia covers all aspects of public and private life and organizes them into five categories: obligatory, recommended, permitted, disliked, and forbidden; primary sources are the Qur'an and the Sunnah; traditional Sunni Muslims also recognize *ijmas*, the consensus of Muhammad's companions and Islamic jurists on certain issues, and *qiyas*, various forms of reasoning, including analogy by legal scholars; Shia Muslims reject ijmas and qiyas as legal sources

mixed law - also referred to as pluralistic law; consists of elements of some or all of the other main types of legal systems

Napoleonic Civil Code - also referred to as the Civil Code or *Code Civil des Français;* type of civil law that forms part of the French legal system and underpins the legal systems of Bolivia, Egypt, Lebanon, Poland, and the US state of Louisiana; established under Napoleon Bonaparte in 1804; combined Teutonic civil law tradition of France's northern provinces with Roman law tradition of the south and east; has similarities with the Roman Body of Civil Law (see civil law above); it originally addressed personal status, property, and the acquisition of property, with later additions including civil procedures, commercial law, criminal law, and a penal code

religious law - stems from the sacred text of a religious tradition and in most cases professes to cover all aspects of life as part of devotional obligations; inalterability is implied, because the word of God cannot be amended or legislated, but human elaboration allows for a detailed legal system; main types of religious law are *sharia* in Islam, *halakha* in Judaism, and canon law in some Christian groups; sharia is the most widespread (see Islamic Law) and is the sole system for some countries; no country is fully governed by halakha, but Jewish people may decide to settle disputes through Jewish courts; canon law is considered human law inspired by God and regulates the internal ordering of the Roman Catholic Church, the Eastern Orthodox Church, and the Anglican Communion

Roman law - served as the basis for legal systems developed in a number of continental European countries; developed in ancient Rome and practiced from the time of the city's founding (traditionally 753 B.C.) until the 5th century A.D.; remained the legal system of the Byzantine (Eastern) Empire until 1453; preserved fragments of the first legal text, known as the Law of the Twelve Tables, date from the 5th century B.C. and contain specific provisions designed to change prevailing customary law; basis was the idea that the exact form – not the intention – of words or of actions produced legal consequences

Roman-Dutch law - a type of civil law based on Roman law, as applied in the Netherlands. Roman-Dutch law is the foundation for legal systems in seven African countries, as well as Guyana, Indonesia, and Sri Lanka. It originated in the province of Holland and expanded throughout the Netherlands and was instituted in a number of sub-Saharan African countries during the Dutch colonial period. The Dutch jurist/philosopher Hugo Grotius was the first to attempt to reduce Roman-Dutch civil law into a system in his *Jurisprudence of Holland* (1620–21), and the Dutch historian/lawyer Simon van Leeuwen coined the term "Roman-Dutch law" in 1652. It replaced by the French Civil Code in 1809.

Spanish law - often referred to as the Spanish Civil Code; a type of civil law that is the present legal system of Spain and the basis of legal systems in 12 countries, mostly in Central and South America; mix of customary, Roman, Napoleonic, local, and modern codified law; enacted in 1889 as the Spanish Civil Code, which separates public law (constitutional law, administrative law, criminal law, process law, financial and tax law, and international public law) from private law (civil law, commercial law, labor law, and international private law)

United States law - has several layers, due in part to the division between federal and state law; draws from *constitutional law* (based on the US Constitution, serves as the supreme federal law, with state constitutions governing state law), *statutory law* (federal legislation enacted by the US Congress and codified in the United States Code, or state statutes), *administrative regulation* (the authority delegated to federal and state executive agencies), and *case law* or common law (covers areas where constitutional or statutory law is lacking); case law was originally developed in England and is a collection of judicial decisions, customs, and general principles

Legislative branch This entry is the first of three fields that explain the legislative data for each country, broken down into subfields. The data is now updated monthly, and most election results will be posted after governments certify the vote counts.

The *legislature name* subfield gives the English-language name or translation, with the untranslated name in parentheses. The *legislative structure* explains whether the body is unicameral (one chamber) or bicameral (two chambers). Of the approximately 240 countries or dependencies with legislative bodies, about two-thirds are unicameral and the rest bicameral.

If a legislature is **unicameral**, the following additional information can be found in this field:

Number of seats - the total number of seats in the chamber as established in the country's laws

Electoral system – the method used to elect candidates, whether plurality/majority, proportional representation, mixed system, or other systems; plurality/majority and proportional representation are the two predominant direct voting systems, but many countries use a combination of electoral methods

Scope of elections – whether an election will include all or only some of the seats in the chamber, described as "full renewal" or "partial renewal"

Term of office – length of the legislative term in years

Most recent election date – date or dates of the last election; a date range indicates an election with more than one round of voting on different dates

Parties elected and seats per party – political parties that won seats in the most recent election, with the number of seats each party won in parentheses; only parties with more than 5 percent of the vote are named

Percentage of women in chamber – the proportion of women holding seats in the chamber as of the most recent election

Expected date of next election - the month and year of the next expected election; governments may change the dates at short notice

Countries with **bicameral** legislatures have the subfields for each chamber listed separately under "**Legislative branch – lower chamber**" and "**Legislative branch – upper chamber**."

Legislative branch - lower chamber This entry is the second of three fields that explain the legislative data for each country, broken down into subfields. Of the approximately 240 countries or dependencies with legislative bodies, about two-thirds are unicameral (one chamber) and the rest bicameral (two chambers).

Many countries with bicameral legislatures use different voting systems for each of the two chambers.

Number of seats - the total number of seats in the chamber as established in the country's laws

Electoral system – the method used to elect candidates, whether plurality/majority, proportional representation, mixed system, or other systems; plurality/majority and proportional representation are the two predominant direct voting systems, but many countries use a combination of electoral methods

Scope of elections – whether an election will include all or only some of the seats in the chamber, described as "full renewal" or "partial renewal"

Term of office – length of the legislative term in years

Most recent election date – date or dates of the last election; a date range indicates an election with more than one round of voting on different dates

Parties elected and seats per party – political parties that won seats in the most recent election, with the number of seats each party won in parentheses; only parties with more than 5 percent of the vote are named

Percentage of women in chamber – the proportion of women holding seats in the chamber as of the most recent election

Expected date of next election - the month and year of the next expected election; governments may change the dates at short notice

Legislative branch - upper chamber This entry is the third of three fields that explain the legislative data for each country, broken down into subfields. Of the approximately 240 countries or dependencies with legislative bodies, about two-thirds are unicameral (one chamber) and the rest bicameral (two chambers).

Many countries with bicameral legislatures use different voting systems for each of the two chambers.

Number of seats - the total number of seats in the chamber as established in the country's laws

Electoral system – the method used to elect candidates, whether plurality/majority, proportional representation, mixed system, or other systems; plurality/majority and proportional representation are the two predominant direct voting systems, but many countries use a combination of electoral methods

Scope of elections – whether an election will include all or only some of the seats in the chamber, described as "full renewal" or "partial renewal"

Term of office – length of the legislative term in years

Most recent election date – date or dates of the last election; a date range indicates an election with more than one round of voting on different dates

Parties elected and seats per party – political parties that won seats in the most recent election, with the number of seats each party won in parentheses; only parties with more than 5 percent of the vote are named

Percentage of women in chamber – the proportion of women holding seats in the chamber as of the most recent election

Expected date of next election - the month and year of the next expected election; governments may change the dates at short notice

Life expectancy at birth This entry contains the average number of years a group of people born in the same year will live, if mortality at each age remains constant in the future.

Literacy This entry includes a *definition* of literacy and UNESCO's percentage estimates for populations aged 15 years and over, including *total population*, *males*, and *females*. There are no universal definitions and standards of literacy. Unless otherwise specified, all rates are based on the most common definition, which is the ability to read and write at a specified age.

Location This entry identifies the country's regional location, neighboring countries, and adjacent bodies of water.

Major aquifers This entry lists the major (mega) aquifer system(s) that underlie a country; many of these mega aquifers are so large that they extend under multiple countries. More than 30% of fresh water is held in underground aquifers.

Major lakes (area sq km) This entry describes one of the two major surface hydrological features of a country (the other is rivers). The entry contains a list of major natural lakes, defined as having an area of 500 sq km or greater. Lakes and rivers are the primary sources of surface freshwater.

Major ocean currents This field describes the major ocean currents, or the movement of water from one location to another. Currents are measured in meters per second or in knots (1 knot = 1.85 km per hour or 1.15 mph), and they affect the Earth's climate by driving warm water from the equator and cold water from the poles. Oceanic currents are driven by three main factors:

tides - can create ocean currents that are strongest near the shore but also extend into bays and estuaries along the coast and are called "tidal currents;" change in a very regular pattern and can be predicted; in some locations, strong tidal currents can travel at eight knots or more

winds - drive currents that are at or near the ocean's surface; near coastal areas, tend to drive currents on a localized scale and can result in phenomena like coastal upwelling; on a global scale, can drive currents that circulate water for thousands of miles

thermohaline circulation - a process created by density differences in water due to temperature (thermo) and salinity (haline) variations; these currents can occur at at any ocean depth and move much more slowly than tidal or surface currents

Major rivers (by length in km) This entry describes one of the two major surface hydrological features of a country (the other feature is lakes). The entry includes a list of major rivers, defined as having a length of 1,000 km or greater. These rivers constitute major drainage basins or watersheds that capture the flow of the majority of surface water flow. Rivers and lakes are the primary sources of surface freshwater.

In instances where a river flows through more than one country, a note has been added to the field to indicate the country where the river starts and the country where it ends. An "[s]" after the country name indicates river source; an "[m]" after the country name indicates river mouth.

Major urban areas - population This entry provides the population of the capital and up to six major cities defined as urban agglomerations with populations of at least 750,000 people. An *urban agglomeration* is defined as comprising the city or town proper and also the suburban fringe or thickly settled territory lying outside of, but adjacent to, the boundaries of the city. For smaller countries lacking urban centers of 750,000 or more, only the population of the capital is presented.

Major watersheds (area sq km) This entry lists the major watersheds or catchment areas of major rivers in a country. Most have an area of at least 500,000 sq km, although some smaller but significant watersheds are also included. They are listed by the ocean into which they drain. When they drain into a named body of water other than the ocean, italics are used to identify the constituent part of an ocean (e.g., *Black Sea*). Some watersheds, known as *endorheic basins*, drain internally with no external flow to the ocean. The largest watersheds are frequently located in more than one country.

Map references This entry includes the name of the *Factbook* reference map where a country can be found. Note that boundary representations on these maps are not necessarily authoritative. The entry on Geographic coordinates may be helpful in finding some smaller countries.

Marine fisheries This entry describes the major fisheries in the world's oceans in terms of the area covered, their ranking in global catch, the main producing countries, and the principal species caught.

Maritime claims This entry includes the following claims, excerpted from the UN Convention on the Law of the Sea (UNCLOS), which alone contains the full and definitive descriptions:

territorial sea - the belt of sea adjacent to a coastal state and covered by that state's sovereignty; sovereignty extends to the air space over the territorial sea, as well as its underlying seabed and subsoil; every state has the right to establish the breadth of its territorial sea up to a limit of 12 nautical miles; where the coasts of two states are opposite or adjacent to each other, neither state is entitled to extend its territorial sea beyond the median line

contiguous zone - the zone along a coastal state's territorial sea, where a country may prevent infringement of its customs, fiscal, immigration, or sanitary laws and punish infringement of these laws; may not extend beyond 24 nautical miles from the baselines from which the breadth of the territorial sea is measured; where the coasts of two states are opposite or adjacent to each other, neither state is entitled to extend its contiguous zone beyond the median line

exclusive economic zone (EEZ) - a zone beyond and adjacent to the territorial sea, in which a coastal state has sovereign rights to natural resources and to economic exploitation and exploration; countries have jurisdiction over the establishment and use of artificial islands, installations, and structures, as well as marine scientific research and the protection and preservation of the marine environment; outer limit of the EEZ cannot exceed 200 nautical miles from the baselines from which the breadth of the territorial sea is measured

continental shelf - includes the seabed and subsoil of the submarine areas that extend beyond a country's territorial sea to the outer edge of the continental margin, or to a distance of 200 nautical miles from the baselines from which the breadth of the territorial sea is measured; includes the submerged prolongation of the landmass of the coastal state and consists of the seabed and subsoil of the shelf, the slope, and the rise; if the continental margin extends beyond 200 nautical miles from the baseline, coastal states may extend their claim to a distance of 350 nautical miles or 100 nautical miles from the 2,500-meter isobath

exclusive fishing zone - term is not used in the UNCLOS, but refers to the areas where some states have chosen to claim jurisdiction over the living resources off their coast instead of an EEZ; the breadth of this zone is normally the same as the EEZ, or 200 nautical miles

Maternal mortality ratio The maternal mortality ratio (MMR) is the annual number of female deaths per 100,000 live births, from any cause related to or aggravated by pregnancy or its management (excluding accidental or incidental causes). The MMR includes deaths during pregnancy, childbirth, or within 42 days of termination of pregnancy, irrespective of the duration and site of the pregnancy, for a specified year.

Median age This entry is the age that divides a population into two numerically equal groups; that is, half the people are younger than this age and half are older.

Member states This entry, which appears only in the European Union entry under the Government category, provides a listing of all of the European Union member countries, as well as their associated overseas countries and territories.

Merchant marine This entry provides the total and the number of each type of privately or publicly owned commercial ship for each country; military ships are not included. There are five types of merchant marine ships:

bulk carrier - for cargo such as coal, grain, cement, ores, and gravel

container ship - for loads in truck-size containers (a transportation system called containerization)

general cargo - also referred to as break-bulk containers, for a wide variety of packaged merchandise

oil tanker - for crude oil and petroleum products

other - includes chemical carriers, dredgers, liquefied natural gas (LNG) carriers, refrigerated cargo ships called reefers, tugboats, passenger vessels (cruise and ferry), and offshore supply ships

Methane emissions This entry provides the annual quantity of methane emissions for a country, as measured in megatons. Methane is emitted during the breakdown of organic material from human-influenced and natural processes. Human-influenced sources include the production and transport of coal, natural gas, and oil; the decay of organic waste in landfills; agricultural activities; stationary and mobile combustion; waste-water treatment; and certain industrial processes.

Military This category includes the entries dealing with a country's military structure, manpower, and expenditures.

Military - note This entry includes miscellaneous military information of significance not included elsewhere.

Military and security forces This entry lists the military and security forces subordinate to defense ministries or the equivalent (typically ground, naval, air, and marine forces), as well as those belonging to interior ministries or the equivalent (typically gendarmeries, border/coast guards, paramilitary police, and other internal security forces).

Military and security service personnel strengths This entry provides estimates of military and security service personnel strengths. The numbers are based on a wide range of publicly available information. Unless otherwise noted, military estimates focus on the major services (army, navy, air force, and where applicable, gendarmeries) and do not account for activated reservists or delineate military service members assigned to joint staffs or defense ministries.

Military deployments This entry lists military forces deployed to other countries or territories abroad. *The World Factbook* defines "deployed" as a permanently stationed force or a temporary deployment of greater than six months. Paramilitaries, police, contractors, mercenaries, proxy forces, and deployments smaller than 100 personnel are not included. Numbers provided are estimates only and should be considered paper strengths, not necessarily the current number of troops on the ground. In addition, some estimates, such as those from the US military, are significantly influenced by deployment policies, contingencies, or world events and may change suddenly. Where available, the organization or mission under which at least some of the forces are deployed is listed. The following terms and abbreviations are used throughout the entry:

AMISOM - Africa Union (AU) Mission in Somalia; UN-supported, AU-operated peacekeeping mission

BATUS - British Army Training Unit Suffield, Canada

BATUK - British Army Training Unit, Kenya
CSTO - Collective Security Treaty Organization
ECOMIG - ECOWUS Mission in The Gambia; Africa Union-European Union peacekeeping, stabilization, and training mission in Gambia
EUTM - European Union Training Mission
EUFOR - European Union Force Bosnia and Herzegovina (also known as Operation Althea)
EuroCorps - European multi-national corps headquartered in Strasbourg, France, consisting of troops from Belgium, France, Germany, Luxembourg, and Spain; Greece, Italy, Poland, Romania and Turkey are Associated Nations of EuroCorps
G5 Joint Force - G5 Sahel Cross-Border Joint Force composed of troops from Burkina Faso, Chad, Mali, Mauritania, and Niger
KFOR - the Kosovo Force; a NATO-led international peacekeeping force in Kosovo
MFO - Multinational Force & Observers Sinai, headquartered in Rome
MINUSCA - United Nations Multidimensional Integrated Stabilization Mission in the Central African Republic
MINUSMA - United Nations Multidimensional Integrated Stabilization Mission in Mali
MNJTF - Multinational Joint Task Force Against Boko Haram, composed of troops from Benin, Cameroon, Chad, Niger, and Nigeria with the mission of fighting Boko Haram in the Lake Chad Basin
MONUSCO - United Nations Organization Stabilization Mission in the Democratic Republic of the Congo
NATO - North American Treaty Organization, headquartered in Brussels, Belgium
Operation Barkhane - French-led counterinsurgency and counterterrorism mission in the Sahel alongside the G5 Joint Force; headquartered in N'Djamena, Chad, and supported by Canada, Denmark, Estonia, the European Union, Germany, Spain, the United Kingdom, and the US
Operation Inherent Resolve - US-led coalition to counter the Islamic State in Iraq and Syria and provide assistance and training to Iraqi security forces
UNAFIL - United Nations Interim Force in Lebanon
UNAMID - African Union - United Nations Hybrid Operation in Darfur, Sudan
UNDOF - United Nations Disengagement Observer Force, Golan (Israel-Syria border)
UNFICYP - United Nations Peacekeeping Force in Cyprus
UNISFA - United Nations Interim Security Force for Abyei (Sudan-South Sudan border)
UNMISS - United Nations Mission in the Republic of South Sudan
UNSOM - United Nations Assistance Mission in Somalia

Military equipment inventories and acquisitions This entry provides basic information on each country's military equipment inventories, as well as how they acquire their equipment; it is intended to show broad trends in major military equipment holdings, such as tanks and other armored vehicles, air defense systems, artillery, naval ships, helicopters, and fixed-wing aircraft. Arms acquisition information is an overview of major arms suppliers over a specific period of time, including second-hand arms delivered as aid, with a focus on major weapons systems. It is based on the type and number of weapon systems ordered and delivered and the financial value of the deal. For some countries, general information on domestic defense industry capabilities is provided.

Military expenditures This entry gives estimates for defense-related spending for the most recent year available as a percentage of gross domestic product (GDP). For countries with no military forces, this figure may include expenditures on public security and police.

Military service age and obligation This entry gives the required ages for voluntary or conscript military service and the length of service obligation.

Money figures All money figures are expressed in contemporaneous US dollars unless otherwise indicated.

Mother's mean age at first birth This entry provides the mean (average) age of mothers at the birth of their first child.

National anthem(s) Patriotic musical compositions that evoke and eulogize the history, traditions, or struggles of a nation or its people. National anthems can be officially recognized in a country's constitution or law, or simply through tradition. Some countries have more than one, including local, royal, official, and/or unofficial anthems – where applicable, the second (and in one case, third) anthem is included in the entry.

National coat of arms This field provides descriptive and historical information on each country's official coat of arms.

National color(s) This entry provides the specific colors associated with a country, which are sometimes chosen to represent history, culture, or founding principles. Some are officially designated, and others are widely accepted as the national colors through tradition or popular use.

National heritage The United Nations Educational, Scientific, and Cultural Organization (UNESCO) designates World Heritage Sites as part of its mission to encourage the identification, protection, and preservation of cultural, historic, scientific, and natural heritage sites around the world that are considered to be of outstanding value to humanity. This entry includes two subfields: *total World Heritage Sites* and *selected World Heritage Site locales*. The former is a count of the natural sites (n), cultural sites (c), and mixed (m; natural and cultural) sites in a country; the latter gives a representative sample of the sites found within a country.

National holiday This entry gives the primary national day of celebration, usually an independence day.

National symbol(s) A national symbol is an emblem or object – often flora or fauna – that over time has come to be closely identified with a country or entity. Not all countries have national symbols; a few countries have more than one.

Nationality This entry provides the identifying terms for citizens, both *noun* and *adjective*.

Natural gas This field refers to a country's natural gas *production*, *consumption*, *exports*, *imports*, and *proven reserves*. *Proven reserves* are those quantities of natural gas that have been analyzed as commercially recoverable in the future, based on known reservoirs and assuming current economic conditions. All data reflect only dry natural gas and exclude non-hydrocarbon gases, as well as vented, flared, and reinjected natural gas. Data are reported using cubic meters.

Natural hazards This entry lists potential natural disasters. For countries where volcanic activity is common, a *volcanism* subfield highlights historically active volcanoes.

Natural resources This entry lists a country's mineral, petroleum, hydropower, and other resources of commercial importance, such as rare earth elements (REEs). In general, products appear only if they make a significant contribution to the economy, or are likely to do so in the future.

Net migration rate This entry includes the figure for the difference between the number of persons entering and leaving a country during the year per 1,000 persons (based on midyear population). An excess of persons entering the country is referred to as net immigration (e.g., 3.56 migrants/1,000 population); an excess of persons leaving the country as net emigration (e.g., -9.26 migrants/1,000 population). The net migration rate indicates the contribution of migration to the overall level of population change. The net migration rate does not distinguish between economic migrants, refugees, and other types of migrants, nor does it distinguish between lawful migrants and undocumented migrants.

Nuclear energy This field describes nuclear energy used for production of electricity. The information covers all countries with operational nuclear reactors that are used to produce electricity; the information does not include research reactors. Subfields include the current *number of operational nuclear reactors*, the *number of nuclear reactors under construction*, the *net capacity of operational nuclear reactors* expressed in gigawatts (GW), the *percentage of total electricity production* from nuclear energy, the *percentage of total energy produced* from nuclear energy, and the *number of nuclear reactors permanently shut down*. Watts are a measure of power, describing the rate at which electricity is being used at a specific moment. A gigawatt is 1 billion watts.

Obesity - adult prevalence rate This entry gives the percentage of a country's population considered to be obese. Obesity is defined as an adult having a Body Mass Index (BMI) greater than or equal to 30.0. BMI is calculated by taking a person's weight in kg and dividing it by the person's squared height in meters.

Ocean volume This entry provides the estimated volume of each of the oceans in millions of cubic kilometers and the percentage of the World Ocean total volume.

Particulate matter emissions This entry provides the modeled annual mean concentration of particulate matter of less than 2.5 microns in diameter ($PM_{2.5}$), measured in micrograms per cubic meter of air. Particulate matter is defined as inhalable and respirable particles composed of sulphate, nitrates, ammonia, sodium chloride, black carbon, mineral dust, and water.

People - note This entry includes miscellaneous demographic information of significance not included elsewhere.

People and Society This category includes entries dealing with national identity (including ethnicities, languages, and religions), demography (a variety of population statistics) and societal characteristics (health and education indicators).

Personal names - capitalization The *Factbook* capitalizes the surname or family name of individuals for the convenience of our users, who are faced with a world of different cultures and naming conventions. The following examples illustrate the need for a surname indicator: MAO Zedong, Fidel CASTRO Ruz, George W. BUSH, and TUNKU SALAHUDDIN Abdul Aziz Shah ibni Al-Marhum Sultan Hisammuddin Alam Shah. This capitalization includes the names of leaders with surnames that are not commonly used, such as King CHARLES III. For Vietnamese names, the given name is capitalized because it is used to refer to officials. For example, a former president of Vietnam was Nguyen Xuan PHUC. His surname was Nguyen, but he was referred to by his given name – President PHUC.

Personal names - spelling The transliteration of personal names in the *Factbook* normally follows the US Board on Geographic Names' system for spelling place names. At times, however, a foreign leader expressly indicates a preference for – or the media or official documents regularly use – a spelling that differs from the transliteration derived from the US Government standard. In such cases, the *Factbook* uses the alternative spelling.

Personal names - titles The *Factbook* capitalizes any valid title (or short form of it) immediately preceding a person's name. A title standing alone is not capitalized.

Petroleum This field refers a country's *crude oil production*, *refined petroleum consumption*, *crude oil exports*, *crude oil imports*, and *crude oil proven reserves*.

Crude oil data represent crude oil (including lease condensate), oil sands liquids, natural gas plant liquids, and other liquids. Other liquids include biodiesel, ethanol, liquids produced from coal, gas, and oil shale, Orimulsion, blending components, and other hydrocarbons. Refined petroleum data represent asphalt, petroleum coke, aviation gasoline, lubricants, ethane, naphtha, paraffin wax, petrochemical feedstocks, unfinished oils, white spirits, and direct use of crude oil.

Crude oil production, *refined petroleum consumption*, *crude oil exports*, and *crude oil imports* data are reported in barrels per day (bbl/day), and one barrel of crude oil roughly equates to 42 gallons (roughly 159 liters). *Crude oil proven reserves* data are reported in barrels (bbl) and are those quantities of crude oil that have been analyzed as commercially recoverable in the future based on known reservoirs and assuming current economic conditions.

Petroleum products See entries under **Refined petroleum products**.

Physician density This entry gives the number of medical doctors (physicians), including generalist and specialist medical practitioners, per 1,000 of the population. Medical doctors are defined as doctors that study, diagnose, treat, and prevent illness, disease, injury, and other physical and mental impairments in humans through the application of modern medicine. They also plan, supervise, and evaluate care and treatment plans by other health care providers.

Piracy Piracy is defined by the 1982 United Nations Convention on the Law of the Sea as any illegal act of violence, detention, or depredation directed against a ship, aircraft, persons, or property in a place outside the jurisdiction of any state. Such criminal acts committed in the territorial waters of a littoral state are generally considered to be armed robbery against ships.

Political parties This entry includes a listing of significant political parties, coalitions, and electoral lists **as of each country's last legislative election**, unless otherwise noted. Parties that do not win a seat in national elections are usually not included.

Population This entry gives an estimate from the US Bureau of the Census based on statistics from population censuses, vital statistics registration systems, or sample surveys pertaining to the recent past and based on assumptions about future trends. This annual estimate does not reflect sudden population shifts due to conflicts, natural disasters, or other unexpected events.

Population below poverty line National estimates of the percentage of the population falling below the poverty line are based on surveys of sub-groups, with the results weighted by the number of people in each group. Definitions of poverty vary considerably among nations.

Population distribution This entry provides a summary description of the population dispersion within a country. While it may suggest population density, it does not provide density figures.

Population growth rate The average annual percentage change in the population, resulting from a surplus (or deficit) of births over deaths and the balance of migrants entering and leaving a country. The rate may be positive or negative.

Population pyramid A population pyramid illustrates the age and sex structure of a country's population. The population is distributed along the horizontal axis, with males shown on the left and females on the right. The male and female populations are broken down into five-year age groups represented as horizontal bars along the vertical axis, with the youngest age groups at the bottom and the oldest at the top. The shape of the population pyramid gradually evolves over time based on fertility, mortality, and international migration trends.

Ports This entry gives the number of ports in a country based on harbor size, a classification that is derived from factors such as area, facilities, and wharf space. Ports are usually multi-use, with activities that can include container shipping, military transport, and ferry or cruise ship transit. The total number of oil terminals located at these ports is noted but does not include standalone facilities that may be separate from ports. Liquified natural gas terminals are not listed because they are usually located at a distance from ports for safety reasons.

Preliminary statement This entry, which appears only in the European Union entry under the Introduction, provides an explanation and justification for the inclusion of a separate EU geographic entity.

Principality A sovereign state ruled by a monarch with the title of prince; principalities were common in the past, but today only three remain: Liechtenstein, Monaco, and the co-principality of Andorra.

Public debt This entry records the cumulative total of all government borrowings less repayments that are denominated in a country's home currency. Public debt should not be confused with external debt, which reflects the foreign currency liabilities of both the private and public sector and must be financed out of foreign exchange earnings.

Railways This entry states the *total* route length of the railway network and of its component parts by gauge, which is the measure of the distance between the inner sides of the load-bearing rails. The four typical types of gauges are: *broad*, *standard*, *narrow*, and *dual*. Other gauges are listed in a *note*. Some 60% of the world's railways use the standard gauge of 1.4 m (4.7 ft). Gauges vary by country and sometimes within countries. The choice of gauge during initial construction was mainly in response to local conditions and the intent of the builder. Narrow-gauge railways were cheaper to build and could negotiate sharper curves, broad-gauge railways gave greater stability and permitted higher speeds. Standard-gauge railways were a compromise between narrow and broad gauges.

Rare earth elements Rare earth elements or REEs are 17 chemical elements that are critical in many of today's high-tech industries. They include lanthanum, cerium, praseodymium, neodymium, promethium, samarium, europium, gadolinium, terbium, dysprosium, holmium, erbium, thulium, ytterbium, lutetium, scandium, and yttrium.

Real GDP (purchasing power parity) This entry gives the gross domestic product (GDP) or value of all final goods and services produced within a nation in a given year. A nation's GDP at purchasing power parity (PPP) exchange rates is the sum value of all goods and services produced in the country valued at prices prevailing in the United States in the year noted. This is the measure most economists prefer when looking at per-capita welfare and when comparing living conditions or use of resources across countries. Many countries do not formally participate in the World Bank's PPP project that calculates these measures, so the resulting GDP estimates for these countries may lack precision. For many developing countries, PPP-based GDP measures are multiples of the official exchange rate (OER) measure. The differences between the OER- and PPP-denominated GDP values for most of the wealthy industrialized countries are generally much smaller.

Real GDP growth rate This entry gives a country's real GDP annual growth rate, adjusted for seasonal unemployment and inflation. A country's growth rate is year-over-year, and not compounded.

Real GDP per capita This entry shows real GDP, divided by population as of 1 July for the same year.

Reference maps This section includes world and regional maps.

Refugees and internally displaced persons This entry includes the number of persons residing in the country as *refugees*, *internally displaced persons (IDPs)*, or *stateless persons*.

The UN definition of a *refugee* is "a person who is outside his/her country of nationality or habitual residence; has a well-founded fear of persecution because of his/her race, religion, nationality, membership in a particular social group or political opinion; and is unable or unwilling to avail himself/herself of the protection of that country, or to return there, for fear of persecution."

The term *internally displaced person* is not specifically covered in the 1951 UN Convention Relating to the Status of Refugees; it is used to describe people who have fled their homes for reasons similar to refugees, but who remain within their own national territory and are subject to the laws of that state.

A *stateless person* is defined as someone who is not considered a national by any state, according to the 1954 UN Convention Relating to the Status of Stateless Persons.

Religions This entry is a listing of the religions practiced in a country, sometimes including the percentage of the total population.

Remittances This entry includes personal transfers and employee compensation. Personal transfers consist of all current transfers in cash or in kind made or received by resident households to or from non-resident households. Employee compensation refers to the income of border, seasonal, and other short-term workers who are employed in an economy where they are not resident and of residents employed by nonresident entities.

Reserves of foreign exchange and gold This entry gives the dollar value for the stock of all financial assets that are available to the central monetary authority for use in meeting a country's balance of payments needs as of the end-date of the period specified. This category includes not only foreign currency and gold, but also a country's holdings of Special Drawing Rights in the International Monetary Fund, and its reserve position in the Fund.

Sanitation facility access This entry provides the percentages of a country's population with access to *improved* or *unimproved* sanitation facilities.

improved: facilities that are designed to hygienically separate excreta from human contact and are not shared with other households

unimproved: facilities that use pit latrines without a slab or platform; hanging latrines or bucket latrines; disposal of human waste in open spaces (i.e., bushes, open bodies of water, fields, etc.) or by mixing it with solid waste; open defecation; or shared use of improved facilities among households

School life expectancy (primary to tertiary education) School life expectancy (SLE) is the total number of years of schooling (primary to tertiary) that a child can expect to receive, assuming that the probability of his or her being enrolled in school at any particular future age is equal to the current enrollment ratio at that age. Caution must be maintained when utilizing this indicator in international comparisons, because a year or grade completed in one country is not necessarily the same in terms of educational content or quality as a year or grade completed in another country. SLE represents the expected number of years of schooling that will be completed, including years spent repeating one or more grades.

Sex ratio This entry includes the number of males for each female in five age groups – *at birth, under 15 years, 15–64 years, 65 years and over*, and for the *total population*.

Single Euro Payments Area (SEPA) This entry refers to the payment integration initiative and framework of the European Union (EU) that simplifies non-cash transfers, whether credit or debit, of the euro to both EU and non-EU member states.

Space agency/agencies This field provides the names of national civil space agencies.

Space launch site(s) This field provides the names and locations of identified commercial and government orbital/space launch sites.

Space program overview This field provides a general survey of a country's space program, including areas of expertise and focus, national goals, international cooperation, and commercial space sector activities if applicable.

Stateless person A stateless individual is not considered a national by any country. Estimates of the number of stateless people are inherently imprecise because few countries have procedures to identify them; the UN assesses that there are at least 10 million stateless people worldwide. Stateless people are counted in a country's overall population figure if they have lived there for a year.

Suffrage This entry gives the age at enfranchisement and whether the right to vote is universal or restricted.

Taxes and other revenues This entry records total taxes and other revenues received by the national government during the time period indicated, expressed as a percentage of GDP. Taxes include personal and corporate income taxes, value added taxes, excise taxes, and tariffs. Other revenues include social contributions (such as payments for social security and hospital insurance), grants, and net revenues from public enterprises. Normalizing the data, by dividing total revenues by GDP, enables easy comparisons across countries and provides an average rate at which all income (GDP) is paid to the national-level government for the supply of public goods and services.

Telephone numbers All telephone numbers in *The World Factbook* consist of the country code in brackets, the city or area code (where required) in parentheses, and the local number. The international access code, which varies from country to country, is not included.

Telephones - fixed lines This entry gives the *total* number of fixed telephone lines in use, as well as the number of *subscriptions per 100 inhabitants*.

Telephones - mobile cellular This entry gives the *total* number of mobile cellular telephone subscribers, as well as the number of *subscriptions per 100 inhabitants*. Note that because of the ubiquity of mobile phone use in developed countries, the number of subscriptions per 100 inhabitants can exceed 100.

Terminology Due to the highly structured nature of the *Factbook* database, some collective generic terms have to be used. For example, the word *Country* in the *Country name* entry refers to a wide variety of dependencies, areas of special sovereignty, uninhabited islands, and other entities, in addition to the traditional countries or independent states. *Military* is also used as an umbrella term for various civil defense, security, and defense activities. The *Independence* entry includes colonial independence dates and former ruling states, as well as other significant nationhood dates. These can include the date of founding, unification, federation, confederation, establishment, or state succession. The status of dependent areas is noted.

Terrain This entry contains a brief description of the topography of a country.

Terrorist group(s) This entry lists the US State Department-designated Foreign Terrorist Organizations (FTO) that are assessed to maintain a presence in each country. This includes cases where sympathizers, supporters, or associates of designated FTOs have carried out attacks or been arrested for terrorist-type activities in the country. See Appendix T: Terrorist Organizations for details on each FTO.

Time difference This entry is expressed in *The World Factbook* in two ways. First, it is stated as the difference in hours between the capital of an entity and **Coordinated Universal Time (UTC)** during Standard Time. Additionally, the time difference between the capital of an entity and Washington, D.C., is also provided. Note that the time difference assumes both locations are simultaneously observing Standard Time or Daylight Saving Time.

Time zones Ten countries (Australia, Brazil, Canada, Indonesia, Kazakhstan, Mexico, New Zealand, Russia, Spain, and the United States) and the island of Greenland observe more than one official time depending on the number of designated time zones within their boundaries. An illustration of world and country time zones can be seen in the Standard Time Zones of the World map included in the **World and Regional Maps** section of *The World Factbook*.

Tobacco use This entry provides estimates derived from the most recent survey data on the prevalence of tobacco use, whether smoked or smokeless or both, among persons 15 years of age and older. Estimates are included for the total population in each country, as well as for male and female populations.

Total fertility rate This entry gives a figure for the average number of children that would be born per woman if all women lived to the end of their childbearing years and bore children according to a given fertility rate at each age. The total fertility rate (TFR) is a more direct measure of the level of fertility than the crude birth rate, since it refers to births per woman.

Total renewable water resources This entry provides the long-term average water availability for a country measured in cubic meters per year of precipitation, recharged ground water, and surface inflows from surrounding countries. It does not include water resource totals that have been reserved for upstream or downstream countries through international agreements. Note that these values are averages and do not accurately reflect the total available in any given year, which can vary greatly due to short-term and long-term climatic and weather variations.

Total water withdrawal This entry provides the annual quantity of water in cubic meters withdrawn for municipal, industrial, and agricultural purposes. Municipal sector use refers to the annual quantity of water withdrawn primarily for direct use by the population through the public distribution network. Industrial sector use refers to the annual quantity of self-supplied water withdrawn for industrial purposes. Agricultural sector use refers to the annual quantity of self-supplied water withdrawn for irrigation, livestock, and aquaculture purposes.

Trafficking in persons Trafficking in persons is modern-day slavery, involving victims who are forced, defrauded, or coerced into labor or sexual exploitation. The International Labor Organization (ILO), the UN agency charged with addressing labor standards, employment, and social protection issues, estimated in 2022 that 27.6 million people worldwide were victims of forced labor, bonded labor, forced child labor, sexual servitude, and involuntary servitude. Human trafficking is a multi-dimensional threat, depriving people of their human rights and freedoms, risking global health, promoting social breakdown, inhibiting development by depriving countries of their human capital, and helping fuel the growth of organized crime. In 2000, the US Congress passed the Trafficking Victims Protection Act (TVPA), reauthorized several times (the latest in 2022 became law in January 2023), which provides tools for the US to combat trafficking in persons, both domestically and abroad. One of the law's key components is the creation of the US Department of State's annual *Trafficking in Persons Report*, which assesses the government response in some 185 countries with a significant number of victims trafficked across their borders who are recruited, harbored, transported, provided, or obtained for forced labor or sexual exploitation. Countries in the annual report are rated in three tiers, based on government efforts to combat trafficking. The countries identified in this entry are those listed in the annual *Trafficking in Persons Report* as 'Tier 2 Watch List' or 'Tier 3' based on the following *tier rating* definitions:

Tier 2 Watch List countries do not fully meet the TVPA's minimum standards for the elimination of trafficking but are making significant efforts to do so, and for which:
– the estimated number of victims of severe forms of trafficking is very significant or is significantly increasing and the country is not taking proportional concrete actions; or,
– there is a failure to provide evidence of increasing efforts to combat severe forms of trafficking in persons from the previous year, including increased investigations, prosecutions, and convictions of trafficking crimes, increased assistance to victims, and decreasing evidence of complicity in severe forms of trafficking by government officials

Tier 3 countries do not fully meet the TVPA's minimum standards and are not making significant efforts to do so.

Transnational issues This category includes entries that deal with current issues going beyond national boundaries.

Transportation This category includes the entries dealing with the means for movement of people and goods.

Transportation - note This entry includes miscellaneous transportation information of significance not included elsewhere.

Under-5 mortality rate This entry indicates the probability a newborn would die before reaching exactly 5 years of age, expressed per 1,000 live births. Data is provided for the *total* number of children under 5 per 1,000 live births, as well as for the number of *male* and *female* children under 5 years of age per 1,000 live births.

Unemployment rate This entry contains the percentage of the labor force that is without jobs. Substantial underemployment might be noted.

Union name This entry, which appears only in the European Union entry under the Government category, provides the full name and abbreviation for the European Union.

Urbanization This entry provides two measures of the degree of urbanization of a population. *Urban population* describes the percentage of the total population living in urban areas, as defined by the country. *Rate of urbanization* describes the projected average rate of change of the size of the urban population over the given period of time. It is possible for a country with a 100% urban population to still display a change in the rate of urbanization (up or down). For example, a population of 100,000 that is 100% urban can change in size to 110,000 or 90,000 but remain 100% urban.

Additionally, the World entry includes a list of the *ten largest urban agglomerations*. An *urban agglomeration* is defined as the city or town proper and also the suburban fringe or thickly settled territory lying outside of, but adjacent to, the boundaries of the city.

UTC (Coordinated Universal Time) See entry for **Coordinated Universal Time**.

Waste and recycling This entry provides the amount of municipal solid waste a country produces annually and the amount of that waste that is recycled. Municipal solid waste consists of everyday items that are used and thrown away. Municipal solid waste – often referred to as trash or garbage – comes from homes, schools, hospitals, and businesses. Recycling is the process of collecting and processing materials that would otherwise be thrown away as trash and turning them into new products. This entry includes three subfields: *annual amount of municipal solid waste generated* (tons), *annual amount of municipal solid waste recycled* (tons), and *percentage of municipal solid waste recycled*.

Weights and Measures This information is presented in Weights and Measures and includes mathematical notations (mathematical powers and names), metric interrelationships (prefix; symbol; length, weight, or capacity; area; volume), and standard conversion factors.

Wonders of the World This entry provides an introduction to the Seven Wonders of the Ancient World and the New Seven Wonders of the World.

World biomes A biome is a biogeographical designation describing a biological community of plants and animals that has formed in response to a physical environment and a shared regional climate. Biomes can extend over more than one continent. Different classification systems define different numbers of biomes. *The World Factbook* recognizes the following seven biomes used by NASA: Tundra, Coniferous Forest, Temperate Deciduous Forest, Rainforest, Grassland, Shrubland, and Desert.

Years All year references are for the calendar year (CY) unless indicated as fiscal year (FY). The calendar year is an accounting period of 12 months from 1 January to 31 December. The fiscal year is an accounting period of 12 months other than 1 January to 31 December.

Youth unemployment rate (ages 15–24) This entry gives the percentage of the total labor force aged 15–24 that is unemployed during a specified year.

AFGHANISTAN

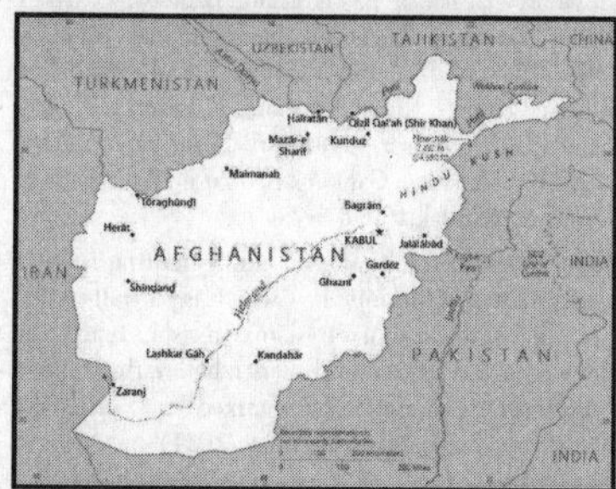

INTRODUCTION

Background: Ahmad Shah DURRANI unified the Pashtun tribes and founded Afghanistan in 1747. The country served as a buffer between the British and Russian Empires until it won independence from notional British control in 1919. A brief experiment in increased democracy ended in a 1973 coup and a 1978 communist countercoup. The Soviet Union invaded in 1979 to support the tottering Afghan communist regime, touching off a long and destructive war. Internationally supported anti-communist mujahidin rebels forced the USSR to withdraw in 1989. A series of subsequent civil wars saw Kabul finally fall in 1996 to the Taliban, a hardline Pakistani-sponsored movement. Following the 11 September 2001 terrorist attacks, a US and Allied military action toppled the Taliban for sheltering Usama BIN LADIN.

A UN-sponsored Bonn Conference in 2001 established a process for political reconstruction that included the adoption of a new constitution, a presidential election in 2004, and National Assembly elections in 2005. In 2004, Hamid KARZAI became the first democratically elected president of Afghanistan, and he was reelected in 2009. Ashraf Ghani AHMADZAI succeeded him as president in 2014 following a disputed election. The Taliban conducted an insurgency for two decades against the Afghan Government and forces from the United States and other countries. In February 2020, the US and the Taliban signed an agreement that led to the withdrawal of international forces in exchange for commitments on counterterrorism and other assurances. The Taliban took over Afghanistan on 15 August 2021.

The Taliban established an all-male interim leadership structure dominated by Pashtun clerics under the leadership of Haivatrullah AKHUNDZADA. The Taliban issued numerous edicts that constrained women's mobility, ability to study and work, and access to education beyond primary school. To date, no country has recognized the Taliban as the government of Afghanistan.

GEOGRAPHY

Location: Southern Asia, north and west of Pakistan, east of Iran

Geographic coordinates: 33 00 N, 65 00 E

Map references: Asia

Area: *total:* 652,230 sq km
land: 652,230 sq km
water: 0 sq km
comparison ranking: total 43

Area - comparative: almost six times the size of Virginia; slightly smaller than Texas

Land boundaries: *total:* 5,987 km
border countries (6): China 91 km; Iran 921 km; Pakistan 2,670 km; Tajikistan 1,357 km; Turkmenistan 804 km; Uzbekistan 144 km

Coastline: 0 km (landlocked)

Maritime claims: none (landlocked)

Climate: arid to semiarid; cold winters and hot summers

Terrain: mostly rugged mountains; plains in north and southwest

Elevation: *highest point:* Noshak 7,492 m
lowest point: Amu Darya 258 m
mean elevation: 1,884 m

Natural resources: natural gas, petroleum, coal, copper, chromite, talc, barites, sulfur, lead, zinc, iron ore, salt, precious and semiprecious stones, arable land

Land use: *agricultural land:* 58.7% (2022 est.)
arable land: 12% (2022 est.)
permanent crops: 0.3% (2022 est.)
permanent pasture: 46.4% (2022 est.)
forest: 1.9% (2022 est.)
other: 39.4% (2022 est.)

Irrigated land: 24,930 sq km (2022)

Major lakes (area sq km): *salt water lake(s):* Ab-e Istadah-ye Muqur (endorheic basin) - 520 sq km

Major rivers (by length in km): Amu Darya (shared with Tajikistan [s], Turkmenistan, and Uzbekistan [m]) - 2,620 km; Helmand river source (shared with Iran) - 1,130 km
note: [s] after country name indicates river source; [m] after country name indicates river mouth

Major watersheds (area sq km): Indian Ocean drainage: Indus (1,081,718 sq km)

Internal (endorheic basin) drainage: Amu Darya (534,739 sq km); Tarim Basin (1,152,448 sq km)

Population distribution: populations tend to cluster in the foothills and periphery of the rugged Hindu Kush range; smaller groups are found in many of the country's interior valleys; in general, the east is more densely settled, while the south is sparsely populated

Natural hazards: damaging earthquakes occur in Hindu Kush mountains; flooding; droughts

Geography - note: landlocked; the Hindu Kush mountains that run northeast to southwest divide the northern provinces from the rest of the country; the highest peaks are in the northern Vakhan (Wakhan Corridor)

PEOPLE AND SOCIETY

Population: *total:* 40,121,552 (2024 est.)
male: 20,301,066
female: 19,820,486
comparison rankings: total 36; male 37; female 37

Nationality: *noun:* Afghan(s)
adjective: Afghan

Ethnic groups: current, reliable statistical data on ethnicity in Afghanistan are not available; Afghanistan's 2004 Constitution cited Pashtun, Tajik, Hazara, Uzbek, Turkman, Baluch, Pashaie, Nuristani, Aymaq, Arab, Qirghiz, Qizilbash, Gujur, and Brahwui ethnicities; Afghanistan has dozens of other small ethnic groups

Languages: Afghan Persian or Dari (official, lingua franca) 77%, Pashto (official) 48%, Uzbeki 11%, English 6%, Turkmani 3%, Urdu 3%, Pashaie 1%, Nuristani 1%, Arabic 1%, Balochi 1%, other <1% (2020 est.)
major-language sample(s):
کتاب حقایق جهان، مرجعی ضروری برای اطلاعات اولیه (Dari)
د دنیا د حقائیقو کتاب، بنیادی معلوماتو لپاره ضروری سرچينه (Pashto)
note 1: percentages sum to more than 100% because many people are multilingual
note 2: Uzbeki, Turkmani, Pashaie, Nuristani, Balochi, and Pamiri are the third official languages in areas where the majority speaks them

Religions: Muslim 99.7% (Sunni 84.7 - 89.7%, Shia 10 - 15%), other <0.3% (2009 est.)

Age structure: *0-14 years:* 39.6% (male 8,062,407/female 7,818,897)
15-64 years: 57.5% (male 11,702,734/female 11,372,249)
65 years and over: 2.9% (2024 est.) (male 535,925/female 629,340)

Dependency ratios: *total dependency ratio:* 82.7 (2024 est.)
youth dependency ratio: 77.5 (2024 est.)
elderly dependency ratio: 5.2 (2024 est.)
potential support ratio: 19.3 (2024 est.)

Median age: *total:* 20 years (2024 est.)
male: 20 years
female: 20.1 years
comparison ranking: total 206

Population growth rate: 2.22% (2024 est.)
comparison ranking: 32

Birth rate: 34.2 births/1,000 population (2024 est.)
comparison ranking: 15

Death rate: 11.8 deaths/1,000 population (2024 est.)
comparison ranking: 19

Net migration rate: -0.1 migrant(s)/1,000 population (2024 est.)
comparison ranking: 99

Population distribution: populations tend to cluster in the foothills and periphery of the rugged Hindu Kush range; smaller groups are found in many of the country's interior valleys; in general, the east is more densely settled, while the south is sparsely populated

Urbanization: *urban population:* 26.9% of total population (2023)
rate of urbanization: 3.34% annual rate of change (2020-25 est.)

Major urban areas - population: 4.589 million KABUL (capital) (2023)

Sex ratio: *at birth:* 1.05 male(s)/female
0-14 years: 1.03 male(s)/female
15-64 years: 1.03 male(s)/female
65 years and over: 0.85 male(s)/female
total population: 1.02 male(s)/female (2024 est.)

Mother's mean age at first birth: 19.9 years (2015 est.)
note: data represents median age at first birth among women 25-49

Maternal mortality ratio: 521 deaths/100,000 live births (2023 est.)
comparison ranking: 7

Infant mortality rate: *total:* 101.3 deaths/1,000 live births (2024 est.)
male: 109.7 deaths/1,000 live births
female: 92.5 deaths/1,000 live births
comparison ranking: total 1

Life expectancy at birth: *total population:* 54.4 years (2024 est.)
male: 52.8 years
female: 56.1 years
comparison ranking: total population 227

Total fertility rate: 4.43 children born/woman (2024 est.)
comparison ranking: 17

Gross reproduction rate: 2.16 (2024 est.)

Drinking water source: *improved: urban:* 99% of population (2022 est.)
rural: 76.1% of population (2022 est.)
total: 82.2% of population (2022 est.)
unimproved: urban: 1% of population (2022 est.)
rural: 23.9% of population (2022 est.)
total: 17.8% of population (2022 est.)

Health expenditure: 21.8% of GDP (2021)
1.1% of national budget (2022 est.)

Physician density: 0.32 physicians/1,000 population (2023)

Hospital bed density: 0.4 beds/1,000 population (2021 est.)

Sanitation facility access: *improved: urban:* 93% of population (2022 est.)
rural: 58.9% of population (2022 est.)
total: 68% of population (2022 est.)
unimproved: urban: 7% of population (2022 est.)
rural: 41.1% of population (2022 est.)
total: 32% of population (2022 est.)

Obesity - adult prevalence rate: 5.5% (2016)
comparison ranking: 177

Alcohol consumption per capita: *total:* 0.01 liters of pure alcohol (2019 est.)
beer: 0 liters of pure alcohol (2019 est.)
wine: 0 liters of pure alcohol (2019 est.)
spirits: 0.01 liters of pure alcohol (2019 est.)
other alcohols: 0 liters of pure alcohol (2019 est.)
comparison ranking: total 183

Tobacco use: *total:* 20.8% (2025 est.)
male: 36.5% (2025 est.)
female: 5.2% (2025 est.)
comparison ranking: total 62

Children under the age of 5 years underweight: 19.1% (2018)
comparison ranking: 17

Currently married women (ages 15-49): 70.3% (2023 est.)

Child marriage: *women married by age 15:* 9.6% (2023)
women married by age 18: 28.7% (2023)
men married by age 18: 7.3% (2015)

Education expenditure: 4.3% of GDP (2017 est.)
8.2% national budget (2017 est.)
comparison ranking: Education expenditure (% GDP) 94

Literacy: *total population:* 37% (2021 est.)
male: 52% (2021 est.)
female: 26.6% (2022 est.)

School life expectancy (primary to tertiary education): *total:* 11 years (2018 est.)
male: 13 years (2018 est.)
female: 8 years (2018 est.)

ENVIRONMENT

Environmental issues: limited natural freshwater resources; inadequate potable water; soil degradation; overgrazing; deforestation (cut down for fuel and building materials); desertification; air and water pollution in urban areas

International environmental agreements: *party to:* Biodiversity, Climate Change, Climate Change-Kyoto Protocol, Climate Change-Paris Agreement, Comprehensive Nuclear Test Ban, Desertification, Endangered Species, Environmental Modification, Hazardous Wastes, Marine Dumping-London Convention, Nuclear Test Ban, Ozone Layer Protection
signed, but not ratified: Law of the Sea, Marine Life Conservation

Climate: arid to semiarid; cold winters and hot summers

Urbanization: *urban population:* 26.9% of total population (2023)
rate of urbanization: 3.34% annual rate of change (2020-25 est.)

Carbon dioxide emissions: 7.757 million metric tonnes of CO2 (2023 est.)
from coal and metallurgical coke: 930,000 metric tonnes of CO2 (2023 est.)
from petroleum and other liquids: 6.827 million metric tonnes of CO2 (2023 est.)
comparison ranking: total emissions 118

Particulate matter emissions: 84 micrograms per cubic meter (2019 est.)

Waste and recycling: *municipal solid waste generated annually:* 5.629 million tons (2024 est.)
percent of municipal solid waste recycled: 11.1% (2022 est.)

Total water withdrawal: *municipal:* 203.4 million cubic meters (2022 est.)
industrial: 169.5 million cubic meters (2022 est.)
agricultural: 20 billion cubic meters (2022 est.)

Total renewable water resources: 65.33 billion cubic meters (2022 est.)

GOVERNMENT

Country name: *conventional long form:* Islamic Republic of Afghanistan (prior to 15 August 2021); current country name disputed
conventional short form: Afghanistan
local long form: Jamhuri-ye Islami-ye Afghanistan (prior to 15 August 2021; current country name is disputed)
local short form: Afghanistan
etymology: the name "Afghan" originally referred to the Pashtun people, but today it is understood to include all the country's ethnic groups; the suffix "-stan" means "place of" or "country," so Afghanistan literally means the "Land of the Afghans"

Government type: theocratic; the United States does not recognize the Taliban Government

Capital: *name:* Kabul
geographic coordinates: 34 31 N, 69 11 E
time difference: UTC+4.5 (9.5 hours ahead of Washington, DC, during Standard Time)
daylight saving time: does not observe daylight savings time
etymology: named for the Kabul River, but the river's name is of unknown origin

Administrative divisions: 34 provinces (*welayat,* singular - *welayat*); Badakhshan, Badghis, Baghlan, Balkh, Bamyan, Daykundi, Farah, Faryab, Ghazni, Ghor, Helmand, Herat, Jowzjan, Kabul, Kandahar, Kapisa, Khost, Kunar, Kunduz, Laghman, Logar, Nangarhar, Nimroz, Nuristan, Paktika, Paktiya, Panjshir, Parwan, Samangan, Sar-e Pul, Takhar, Uruzgan, Wardak, Zabul

Legal system: the Taliban is implementing its own interpretation of Islamic law, which is partially based on the Hanifi school of Islamic jurisprudence and have enforced strict punishments; before the Taliban takeover, Afghanistan had a mixed legal system of civil, customary, and Islamic law (2021)

Constitution: *history:* several previous; latest ratified in 2004, but not currently enforced by the Taliban

International law organization participation: has not submitted an ICJ jurisdiction declaration; formerly accepted ICCt jurisdiction

Citizenship: *citizenship by birth:* no
citizenship by descent only: at least one parent must have been born in - and continuously lived in - Afghanistan
dual citizenship recognized: no
residency requirement for naturalization: 5 years

Suffrage: 18 years of age; universal

Executive branch: *chief of state:* Taliban Leader HAYBATULLAH Akhundzada (since 15 August 2021)
head of government: overall Taliban Leader HAYBATULLAH Akhundzada is the [so-called] Amir-ul Momineen of the Taliban and is seen by them as a head of government
cabinet: the Taliban have announced a "cabinet" for the "caretaker government," including the "acting prime minister," "acting deputy prime ministers," and "ministers" who claim to represent 26 ministries
election/appointment process: the 2004 Afghan constitution directed that the president should be elected by majority popular vote for a 5-year term (eligible for a second term); the Taliban have given no indication that they intend to reinstate elections or any other mechanism of democratic governance
most recent election date: 28 September 2019
note: the United States has not yet made a decision whether to recognize the Taliban or any other entity as the government of Afghanistan

Legislative branch: *note:* Afghanistan's bicameral National Assembly consisted of the House of Elders and House of the People but was dissolved after the Taliban took control of Afghanistan in August 2021

Judicial branch: *highest court(s):* the Taliban are purported to have appointed clerics, including a "Chief Justice," to Afghanistan's Supreme Court
subordinate courts: provincial courts, religious courts, and specialty courts

Political parties: the Taliban Government enforces an authoritarian state and has banned other political parties
the Taliban have banned other political parties but have allowed some party leaders, including the head of Hezb-e-Islami, Gulbuddin Hekmatyar, to continue to live and work in Afghanistan; Hekmatyar likely continues to enjoy some political support from loyalists; leaders of other parties, including Jamiat-e-Islami's Salahuddin Rabbani and Jumbesh's Rashid Dostum, operate from abroad but likely also command some following within Afghanistan

note: before 15 August 2021, the Ministry of Justice had licensed 72 political parties as of April 2019

Diplomatic representation in the US: none
note: the Afghan Embassy closed in March 2022

Diplomatic representation from the US: *embassy:* the United States does not maintain a presence in Afghanistan and its diplomatic mission to Afghanistan has relocated to Doha, Qatar

International organization participation: Afghanistan is a member of the following organizations but Taliban representatives do not participate: ADB, CICA, CP, ECO, EITI (candidate country), FAO, G-77, IAEA, IBRD, ICAO, ICC (NGOs), ICCt, ICRM, IDA, IDB, IFAD, IFC, IFRCS, ILO, IMF, Interpol, IOC, IOM, IPU, ISO (correspondent), ITSO, ITU, ITUC (NGOs), MIGA, NAM, OIC, OPCW, OSCE (partner), SAARC, SACEP, SCO (dialogue member), UN, UNAMA, UNCTAD, UNESCO, UNHCR, UNIDO, UNWTO, UPU, WCO, WFTU (NGOs), WHO, WIPO, WMO, WTO

Independence: 19 August 1919 (from UK control over Afghan foreign affairs)

National holiday: *previous:* Independence Day, 19 August (1919); under the Taliban Government, 15 August (2022) is declared a national holiday, marking the anniversary of the victory of the Afghan jihad

Flag: *description:* three equal vertical bands of black (left), red, and green, with the national emblem in white centered on the red band and slightly overlapping the other bands; the emblem shows a mosque with a pulpit and flags on either side; below the mosque are Eastern Arabic numerals for the solar year 1298 (1919 in the Gregorian calendar, the year of Afghan independence from the UK); a border of wheat sheaves circles the mosque; above the mosque is an Arabic inscription of the Shahada (Muslim creed), with rays of the rising sun over the Takbir (Arabic expression meaning "God is great"); under the mosque is a scroll with the name Afghanistan
meaning: black stands for the past, and red for the blood shed for independence; green can represent hope for the future, agricultural prosperity, or Islam
history: Afghanistan had more changes to its national flag in the 20th century – 19 by one count – than any other country; the colors black, red, and green appeared on most of them
note: the United States has not recognized the Taliban or any other entity as the government of Afghanistan and, accordingly, continues to display the flag of Afghanistan as set forth in the country's constitution of 2004

National symbol(s): lion

National color(s): red, green, black

National anthem(s): *title:* "Milli Surood" (National Anthem)
lyrics/music: Abdul Bari JAHANI/Babrak WASA
history: adopted 2006

National heritage: *total World Heritage Sites:* 2 (both cultural)
selected World Heritage Site locales: Minaret of Jam; Buddhas of Bamyan
note: the monumental 6th- and 7th-century Buddha statues at Bamyan were destroyed by the Taliban in 2001

ECONOMY

Economic overview: low-income South Asian economy; economy stable after major contraction due to Taliban takeover, but recovery remains fragile; widespread poverty and obstacles to human development; import-reliant for food, fuel, and machinery; ongoing sanctions, suspended development aid, and frozen reserve assets

Real GDP (purchasing power parity): $82.238 billion (2023 est.)
$80.416 billion (2022 est.)
$85.768 billion (2021 est.)
note: data in 2021 dollars
comparison ranking: 104

Real GDP growth rate: 2.3% (2023 est.)
-6.2% (2022 est.)
-20.7% (2021 est.)
note: annual GDP % growth based on constant local currency
comparison ranking: 143

Real GDP per capita: $2,000 (2023 est.)
$2,000 (2022 est.)
$2,100 (2021 est.)
note: data in 2021 dollars
comparison ranking: 205

GDP (official exchange rate): $17.152 billion (2023 est.)
note: data in current dollars at official exchange rate

Inflation rate (consumer prices): -6.6% (2024 est.)
-4.6% (2023 est.)
13.7% (2022 est.)
note: annual % change based on consumer prices
comparison ranking: 1

GDP - composition, by sector of origin: *agriculture:* 34.7% (2023 est.)
industry: 13.4% (2023 est.)
services: 46.4% (2023 est.)
note: figures may not total 100% due to non-allocated consumption not captured in sector-reported data
comparison rankings: agriculture 5; industry 170; services 166

GDP - composition, by end use: *household consumption:* 98.1% (2023 est.)
government consumption: 21.2% (2023 est.)
investment in fixed capital: 15.2% (2023 est.)
investment in inventories: 0.1% (2023 est.)
exports of goods and services: 16.9% (2023 est.)
imports of goods and services: -50.7% (2023 est.)
note: figures may not total 100% due to rounding or gaps in data collection

Agricultural products: wheat, milk, grapes, watermelons, potatoes, cantaloupes/melons, vegetables, rice, onions, maize (2023)
note: top ten agricultural products based on tonnage

Industries: small-scale production of bricks, textiles, soap, furniture, shoes, fertilizer, apparel, food products, non-alcoholic beverages, mineral water, cement; handwoven carpets; natural gas, coal, copper

Industrial production growth rate: 1.8% (2023 est.)
note: annual % change in industrial value added based on constant local currency
comparison ranking: 104

Labor force: 9.133 million (2024 est.)
note: number of people ages 15 or older who are employed or seeking work
comparison ranking: 58

Unemployment rate: 13.3% (2024 est.)
14% (2023 est.)
14.1% (2022 est.)
note: % of labor force seeking employment
comparison ranking: 168

Youth unemployment rate (ages 15-24): *total:* 16.7% (2024 est.)
male: 15.8% (2024 est.)
female: 27% (2024 est.)
note: % of labor force ages 15-24 seeking employment
comparison ranking: total 68

Population below poverty line: 54.5% (2016 est.)
note: % of population with income below national poverty line

Remittances: 1.9% of GDP (2023 est.)
2.2% of GDP (2022 est.)
2.2% of GDP (2021 est.)
note: personal transfers and compensation between resident and non-resident individuals/ households/ entities

Budget: *revenues:* $9.093 billion (2017 est.)
expenditures: $7.411 billion (2017 est.)
note: central government revenues (excluding grants) and expenses converted to US dollars at average official exchange rate for year indicated

Taxes and other revenues: 9.9% (of GDP) (2017 est.)
note: central government tax revenue as a % of GDP
comparison ranking: 131

Current account balance: -$3.137 billion (2020 est.)
-$3.792 billion (2019 est.)
-$3.897 billion (2018 est.)
note: balance of payments - net trade and primary/ secondary income in current dollars
comparison ranking: 161

Exports: $1.476 billion (2020 est.)
$1.516 billion (2019 est.)
$1.609 billion (2018 est.)
note: balance of payments - exports of goods and services in current dollars
comparison ranking: 175

Exports - partners: Pakistan 42%, India 40%, China 4%, UAE 2%, Turkey 2% (2023)
note: top five export partners based on percentage share of exports

Exports - commodities: coal, grapes, tropical fruits, gum resins, other nuts (2023)
note: top five export commodities based on value in dollars

Imports: $6.983 billion (2020 est.)
$7.371 billion (2019 est.)
$7.988 billion (2018 est.)
note: balance of payments - imports of goods and services in current dollars
comparison ranking: 140

Imports - partners: UAE 28%, Pakistan 15%, China 15%, Uzbekistan 12%, Kazakhstan 9% (2023)
note: top five import partners based on percentage share of imports

Imports - commodities: wheat flours, tobacco, palm oil, broadcasting equipment, synthetic fabric (2023)
note: top five import commodities based on value in dollars

Reserves of foreign exchange and gold: $9.749 billion (2020 est.)
$8.498 billion (2019 est.)
$8.207 billion (2018 est.)
note: holdings of gold (year-end prices)/foreign exchange/special drawing rights in current dollars
comparison ranking: 79

Debt - external: $2.717 billion (2023 est.)
note: present value of external debt in current US dollars
comparison ranking: 88

Exchange rates: afghanis (AFA) per US dollar -

Exchange rates: 76.814 (2020 est.)

77.738 (2019 est.)
72.083 (2018 est.)
68.027 (2017 est.)
67.866 (2016 est.)

ENERGY

Electricity access: *electrification - total population:* 85.3% (2022 est.)
electrification - urban areas: 95.9%
electrification - rural areas: 81.7%

Electricity: *installed generating capacity:* 627,000 kW (2023 est.)
consumption: 6.468 billion kWh (2023 est.)
imports: 6.221 billion kWh (2023 est.)
transmission/distribution losses: 725.652 million kWh (2023 est.)
comparison rankings: installed generating capacity 147; consumption 122; imports 40; transmission/distribution losses 88

Electricity generation sources: *fossil fuels:* 13.3% of total installed capacity (2023 est.)
solar: 9.7% of total installed capacity (2023 est.)
hydroelectricity: 77% of total installed capacity (2023 est.)

Coal: *production:* 767,000 metric tons (2023 est.)
consumption: 503,000 metric tons (2023 est.)
exports: 265,000 metric tons (2023 est.)
imports: 2,000 metric tons (2023 est.)
proven reserves: 66 million metric tons (2023 est.)

Petroleum: *refined petroleum consumption:* 58,000 bbl/day (2023 est.)

Natural gas: *production:* 80.2 million cubic meters (2020 est.)
consumption: 80.2 million cubic meters (2020 est.)
proven reserves: 49.554 billion cubic meters (2021 est.)

Energy consumption per capita: 3.38 million Btu/person (2023 est.)
comparison ranking: 177

COMMUNICATIONS

Telephones - fixed lines: *total subscriptions:* 182,000 (2023 est.)
subscriptions per 100 inhabitants: (2023 est.) less than 1
comparison ranking: total subscriptions 121

Telephones - mobile cellular: *total subscriptions:* 23 million (2023 est.)
subscriptions per 100 inhabitants: 57 (2021 est.)
comparison ranking: total subscriptions 59

Broadcast media: under the Taliban, independent media outlets have decreased and are probably self-censoring; the Ministry of Information and Culture monitors all mass media; television and radio are key media platforms; only about a fifth of Afghans use the internet, mostly through smartphones (2023)

Internet country code: .af

Internet users: *percent of population:* 18% (2023 est.)

Broadband - fixed subscriptions: *total:* 33,000 (2023 est.)
subscriptions per 100 inhabitants: (2023 est.) less than 1
comparison ranking: total 159

TRANSPORTATION

Civil aircraft registration country code prefix: YA

Airports: 68 (2025)
comparison ranking: 73

Heliports: 8 (2025)
comparison ranking: 80

MILITARY AND SECURITY

Military and security forces: the Taliban claims authority over a Ministry of Defense and a National Army (aka Army of the Islamic Emirate of Afghanistan, Islamic Emirate Army, or Afghan Army); it has also formed police forces under a Ministry of Interior (2025)

Military expenditures: 3.3% of GDP (2019)
3.2% of GDP (2018)
3.3% of GDP (2017)
3.1% of GDP (2016)
2.9% of GDP (2015)

Military and security service personnel strengths: the Taliban claims to have 190,000 under the Ministry of Defense and 215,000 under the Ministry of Interior (2025)

Military equipment inventories and acquisitions: the Taliban military/security forces are armed with weapons and equipment captured in 2021 from the Afghan National Defense and Security Forces, which was largely equipped with Russian/Soviet-era and US material (2024)

Military service age and obligation: service is voluntary; there is no conscription (2023)
note: the Taliban dismissed nearly all women from the former Afghan National Defense and Security Forces, except those serving in detention facilities and assisting with body searches

Military - note: the Taliban's key security priorities are border and internal security; specific issues have included rising tensions with Pakistan along their shared border, armed anti-Taliban resistance elements, and the Islamic State of Iraq and ash-Sham - Khorasan (ISIS-K) terrorist group (2025)

TERRORISM

Terrorist group(s): Terrorist group(s): Haqqani Network; Harakat ul-Mujahidin; Harakat ul-Jihad-i-Islami; Islamic Jihad Union (IJU); Islamic Movement of Uzbekistan (IMU); Islamic State of Iraq and ash-Sham-Khorasan Province (ISIS-K); Islamic Revolutionary Guard Corps (IRGC)/Qods Force; Jaish-e-Mohammed; Jaysh al Adl (Jundallah); Lashkar i Jhangvi; Lashkar-e Tayyiba; alQa'ida; al-Qa'ida in the Indian Subcontinent (AQIS); Tehrik-e-Taliban Pakistan (TTP)
note 1: as of 2024, Afghanistan was assessed to be a place of global significance for terrorism, with approximately 20 designated and non-designated terrorist groups operating in the country
note 2: details about the history, aims, leadership, organization, areas of operation, tactics, targets, weapons, size, and sources of support of the group(s) appear(s) in Appendix T

TRANSNATIONAL ISSUES

Refugees and internally displaced persons: *refugees:* 21,236 (2024 est.)

IDPs: 5,457,183 (2024 est.)

Trafficking in persons: *tier rating:* Tier 3—Afghanistan does not fully meet the minimum standards for the elimination of trafficking and is not making significant efforts to do so, therefore, Afghanistan remained on Tier 3; for more details, go to: https://www.state.gov/reports/2025-trafficking-in-persons-report/afghanistan/

Illicit drugs: USG identification: major illicit drug-producing and/or drug-transit country
major precursor-chemical producer (2025)

AKROTIRI AND DHEKELIA

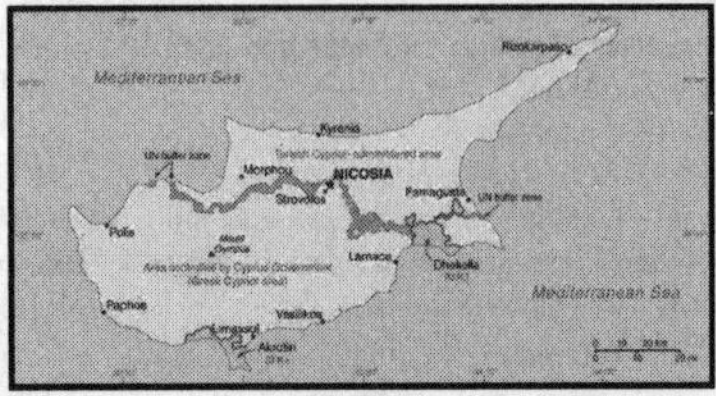

INTRODUCTION

Background: By terms of the 1960 Treaty of Establishment that created the independent Republic of Cyprus, the United Kingdom retained full sovereignty and jurisdiction over two areas of almost 254 sq km (98 sq mi) – Akrotiri and Dhekelia. The southernmost and smaller of the two is Akrotiri Sovereign Base Area, which is also referred to as the Western Sovereign Base Area. The larger area is the Dhekelia Sovereign Base Area, which is also referred to as the Eastern Sovereign Base Area. (2024)

GEOGRAPHY

Location: Eastern Mediterranean; Akrotiri is on a peninsula on the southwest coast of Cyprus; Dhekelia is on the southwest coast of Cyprus near Famagusta

Geographic coordinates: Akrotiri: 34 37 N, 32 58 E

Dhekelia: 34 59 N, 33 45 E

Map references: Middle East

Area: *total:* 254 sq km

Akrotiri: 123 sq km, includes salt and wetlands

Dhekelia: 131 sq km, area surrounds three Cypriot enclaves

comparison ranking: total 213

Area - comparative: Akrotiri: about 0.7 times the size of Washington, D.C.

Dhekelia: about three-quarters the size of Washington, D.C.

Land boundaries: *border countries (1):* Akrotiri: Cyprus 48 km

Dhekelia: Cyprus 108 km

Coastline: Akrotiri: 56.3 km

Dhekelia: 27.5 km

Climate: temperate; Mediterranean with hot, dry summers and cool winters

Geography - note: British extraterritorial rights also extended to several small off-post sites scattered across Cyprus; of the Sovereign Base Area land, 60% is privately owned and farmed, 20% is owned by the UK Ministry of Defense, and 20% is SBA Crown land

PEOPLE AND SOCIETY

Languages: English, Greek
major-language sample(s):
Το Παγκόσμιο Βιβλίο Δεδομένων, η απαραίτητη πηγή βασικών πληροφοριών. (Greek)

ENVIRONMENT

Environmental issues: Akrotiri: hunting around the salt lake; only remaining colony of griffon vultures is on the base

Dhekelia: netting and trapping of small migrant songbirds in the spring and autumn

Climate: temperate; Mediterranean with hot, dry summers and cool winters

GOVERNMENT

Country name: *conventional long form:* none
conventional short form: Akrotiri and Dhekelia
etymology: Akrotiri: named after a village located on a peninsula; the name is derived from the Greek word *akroterion*, meaning "promontory"

Dependency status: both are a special form of UK overseas territory; administered by an administrator who is also the Commander, British Forces Cyprus

Capital: *name:* Episkopi Cantonment in Akrotiri (base administrative center for Akrotiri and Dhekelia)
geographic coordinates: 34 40 N, 32 51 E
time difference: UTC+2 (7 hours ahead of Washington, DC, during Standard Time)
daylight saving time: + 1hr, begins last Sunday in March; ends last Sunday in October
etymology: "Episkopi" means "episcopal" in Greek and may indicate that the site previously served as the bishop's seat of an Orthodox diocese

Legal system: laws applicable to the Cypriot population are, as far as possible, the same as the laws of the Republic of Cyprus (ROC); however, the SBA Administration has its own court system to deal with civil and criminal matters, its own police force for civil law enforcement, and a Cyprus Joint Police Unit for military law enforcement; SBA Police coordinate closely with ROC police and UN Peacekeeping Forces in Cyprus (UNFICYP); the SBA Police force is composed almost entirely of Greek Cypriots in ROC regions of the SBAs, and Turkish Cypriot officers in the small portion of Dhekelia administered by the Turkish Cypriots

Constitution: *history:* presented 3 August 1960, effective 16 August 1960 (The Sovereign Base Areas of Akrotiri and Dhekelia Order in Council 1960 serves as a basic legal document)

Executive branch: *chief of state:* King CHARLES III (since 8 September 2022)
head of government: Administrator Air Vice-Marshall Peter J.M. SQUIRES (since 1 September 2022)
note: administrator reports to the British Ministry of Defense and is also Commander, British Forces Cyprus (BFC); the chief officer, an appointed civilian, is responsible for the day-to-day running of the civil government of the Sovereign Base Areas

Judicial branch: *highest court(s):* Senior Judges' Court (consists of several visiting judges from England and Wales)
judge selection and term of office: see entry for the United Kingdom
subordinate courts: Resident Judges' Court; Courts Martial

Diplomatic representation in the US: none (overseas territory of the UK)

Diplomatic representation from the US: *embassy:* none (overseas territory of the UK)

Flag: the flag of the UK is used

National anthem(s): *title:* "God Save the King"
lyrics/music: unknown
history: official anthem, as a UK area of special sovereignty

ECONOMY

Exchange rates: euros (EUR) per US dollar -
Exchange rates: 0.924 (2024 est.)
0.925 (2023 est.)
0.95 (2022 est.)
0.845 (2021 est.)
0.876 (2020 est.)

COMMUNICATIONS

Broadcast media: British Forces Service (BFBS) provides multi-channel satellite TV service as well as BFBS radio broadcasts to the Akrotiri Sovereign Base Area

MILITARY AND SECURITY

Military - note: defense is the responsibility of the UK

ALBANIA

INTRODUCTION

Background: After declaring independence from the Ottoman Empire in 1912, Albania experienced a period of political upheaval that led to a short-lived monarchy, which ended in 1939 when Italy conquered the country. Germany then occupied Albania in 1943, and communist partisans took over the country in 1944. Albania allied itself first with the USSR (until 1960) and then with China (until 1978). In the early 1990s, Albania ended communist rule and established a multiparty democracy.

Government-endorsed pyramid schemes in 1997 led to economic collapse and civil disorder, which only ended when UN peacekeeping troops intervened. In 1999, some 450,000 ethnic Albanians fled from Kosovo to Albania to escape the war with the Serbs. Albania joined NATO in 2009 and became an official candidate for EU membership in 2014.

GEOGRAPHY

Location: Southeastern Europe, bordering the Adriatic Sea and Ionian Sea, between Greece to the south and Montenegro and Kosovo to the north

Geographic coordinates: 41 00 N, 20 00 E

Map references: Europe

Area: *total:* 28,748 sq km
land: 27,398 sq km
water: 1,350 sq km
comparison ranking: total 144

Area - comparative: slightly smaller than Maryland

Land boundaries: *total:* 691 km
border countries (4): Greece 212 km; Kosovo 112 km; North Macedonia 181 km; Montenegro 186 km

Coastline: 362 km

Maritime claims: *territorial sea:* 12 nm
continental shelf: 200-m depth or to the depth of exploitation

Climate: mild temperate; cool, cloudy, wet winters; hot, clear, dry summers; interior is cooler and wetter

Terrain: mostly mountains and hills; small plains along coast

Elevation: *highest point:* Maja e Korabit (Golem Korab) 2,764 m
lowest point: Adriatic Sea 0 m
mean elevation: 708 m

Natural resources: petroleum, natural gas, coal, bauxite, chromite, copper, iron ore, nickel, salt, timber, hydropower, arable land

Land use: *agricultural land:* 41.4% (2022 est.)
arable land: 21.8% (2022 est.)
permanent crops: 3.2% (2022 est.)
permanent pasture: 16.4% (2022 est.)
forest: 28.8% (2022 est.)
other: 29.8% (2022 est.)

Irrigated land: 1,907 sq km (2022)

Major lakes (area sq km): *fresh water lake(s):* Lake Scutari (shared with Montenegro) - 400 sq km
note - largest lake in the Balkans

Major watersheds (area sq km): Atlantic Ocean drainage: *(Black Sea)* Danube (795,656 sq km)

Population distribution: a fairly even distribution, with somewhat higher concentrations of people in the western and central parts of the country

Natural hazards: destructive earthquakes; tsunamis occur along southwestern coast; floods; drought

Geography - note: strategic location along Strait of Otranto (links Adriatic Sea to Ionian Sea and Mediterranean Sea)

PEOPLE AND SOCIETY

Population: *total:* 3,107,100 (2024 est.)
male: 1,531,063
female: 1,576,037
comparison rankings: total 137; male 138; female 137

Nationality: *noun:* Albanian(s)
adjective: Albanian

Ethnic groups: Albanian 82.6%, Greek 0.9%, other 1% (including Vlach, Romani, Macedonian, Montenegrin, and Egyptian), unspecified 15.5% (2011 est.)
note: data represent population by ethnic and cultural affiliation

Languages: Albanian 98.8% (official - derived from Tosk dialect), Greek 0.5%, other 0.6% (including Macedonian, Romani, Vlach, Turkish, Italian, and Serbo-Croatian), unspecified 0.1% (2011 est.)
major-language sample(s):
Libri i fakteve boterore, burimi i pazevendesueshem per informacione elementare (Albanian)

Religions: Muslim 56.7%, Roman Catholic 10%, Orthodox 6.8%, atheist 2.5%, Bektashi (a Sufi order) 2.1%, other 5.7%, unspecified 16.2% (2011 est.)
note: all mosques and churches were closed in 1967 and religious observances prohibited; in November 1990, Albania began allowing private religious practice

Age structure: *0-14 years:* 18% (male 292,296/female 267,052)
15-64 years: 66.9% (male 1,023,515/female 1,055,388)
65 years and over: 15.1% (2024 est.) (male 215,252/female 253,597)

Dependency ratios: *total dependency ratio:* 47.8 (2024 est.)
youth dependency ratio: 24.3 (2024 est.)
elderly dependency ratio: 23.5 (2024 est.)
potential support ratio: 4.3 (2024 est.)

Median age: *total:* 36.3 years (2024 est.)
male: 34.8 years
female: 37.8 years
comparison ranking: total 91

Population growth rate: 0.16% (2024 est.)
comparison ranking: 181

Birth rate: 12.3 births/1,000 population (2024 est.)
comparison ranking: 141

Death rate: 7.4 deaths/1,000 population (2024 est.)
comparison ranking: 103

Net migration rate: -3.2 migrant(s)/1,000 population (2024 est.)
comparison ranking: 185

Population distribution: a fairly even distribution, with somewhat higher concentrations of people in the western and central parts of the country

Urbanization: *urban population:* 64.6% of total population (2023)
rate of urbanization: 1.29% annual rate of change (2020-25 est.)

Major urban areas - population: 520,000 TIRANA (capital) (2023)

Sex ratio: *at birth:* 1.06 male(s)/female
0-14 years: 1.09 male(s)/female
15-64 years: 0.97 male(s)/female
65 years and over: 0.85 male(s)/female
total population: 0.97 male(s)/female (2024 est.)

Mother's mean age at first birth: 26.6 years (2020 est.)

Maternal mortality ratio: 7 deaths/100,000 live births (2023 est.)
comparison ranking: 160

Infant mortality rate: *total:* 10.3 deaths/1,000 live births (2024 est.)
male: 11.3 deaths/1,000 live births
female: 9.2 deaths/1,000 live births
comparison ranking: total 130

Life expectancy at birth: *total population:* 79.9 years (2024 est.)
male: 77.3 years
female: 82.8 years
comparison ranking: total population 61

Total fertility rate: 1.55 children born/woman (2024 est.)
comparison ranking: 194

Gross reproduction rate: 0.75 (2024 est.)

Drinking water source: *improved: urban:* 95.7% of population (2022 est.)
rural: 94.1% of population (2022 est.)
total: 95.1% of population (2022 est.)
unimproved: urban: 4.3% of population (2022 est.)
rural: 5.9% of population (2022 est.)
total: 4.9% of population (2022 est.)

Health expenditure: 7.3% of GDP (2021)
9.2% of national budget (2022 est.)

Physician density: 1.88 physicians/1,000 population (2020)

Hospital bed density: 2.9 beds/1,000 population (2020 est.)

Sanitation facility access: *improved: urban:* 99.8% of population (2022 est.)
rural: 100% of population (2022 est.)
total: 99.9% of population (2022 est.)
unimproved: urban: 0.2% of population (2022 est.)
rural: 0% of population (2022 est.)
total: 0.1% of population (2022 est.)

Obesity - adult prevalence rate: 21.7% (2016)
comparison ranking: 86

Alcohol consumption per capita: *total:* 4.4 liters of pure alcohol (2019 est.)
beer: 1.75 liters of pure alcohol (2019 est.)
wine: 1.15 liters of pure alcohol (2019 est.)
spirits: 1.43 liters of pure alcohol (2019 est.)
other alcohols: 0.08 liters of pure alcohol (2019 est.)
comparison ranking: total 90

Tobacco use: *total:* 21.4% (2025 est.)
male: 37% (2025 est.)
female: 6.2% (2025 est.)
comparison ranking: total 59

Children under the age of 5 years underweight: 1.5% (2017/18)
comparison ranking: 106

Currently married women (ages 15-49): 67.2% (2023 est.)

Child marriage: *women married by age 15:* 1.4% (2018)
women married by age 18: 11.8% (2018)
men married by age 18: 1.2% (2018)

Education expenditure: 2.9% of GDP (2023 est.)
10.1% national budget (2023 est.)
comparison ranking: Education expenditure (% GDP) 155

Literacy: *total population:* 98.8% (2017 est.)
male: 98.6% (2017 est.)
female: 99% (2017 est.)

School life expectancy (primary to tertiary education): *total:* 15 years (2023 est.)
male: 14 years (2023 est.)
female: 15 years (2023 est.)

ENVIRONMENT

Environmental issues: deforestation; soil erosion; water pollution from industrial and domestic effluents; air pollution from industrial and power plants; loss of biodiversity

International environmental agreements: *party to:* Air Pollution, Air Pollution-Nitrogen_Oxides, Air Pollution-Sulphur 85, Biodiversity, Climate Change, Climate Change-Kyoto Protocol, Climate Change-Paris Agreement, Comprehensive Nuclear Test Ban, Desertification, Endangered Species, Hazardous Wastes, Law of the Sea, Ozone Layer Protection, Ship Pollution, Tropical Timber 2006, Wetlands
signed, but not ratified: none of the selected agreements

Climate: mild temperate; cool, cloudy, wet winters; hot, clear, dry summers; interior is cooler and wetter

Urbanization: *urban population:* 64.6% of total population (2023)
rate of urbanization: 1.29% annual rate of change (2020-25 est.)

Carbon dioxide emissions: 3.392 million metric tonnes of CO2 (2023 est.)
from coal and metallurgical coke: 566,000 metric tonnes of CO2 (2023 est.)
from petroleum and other liquids: 2.734 million metric tonnes of CO2 (2023 est.)
from consumed natural gas: 93,000 metric tonnes of CO2 (2023 est.)
comparison ranking: total emissions 146

Particulate matter emissions: 16.6 micrograms per cubic meter (2019 est.)

Waste and recycling: *municipal solid waste generated annually:* 1.087 million tons (2024 est.)
percent of municipal solid waste recycled: 20.5% (2022 est.)

Total water withdrawal: *municipal:* 221 million cubic meters (2022)
industrial: 11 million cubic meters (2022)
agricultural: 565 million cubic meters (2022)

Total renewable water resources: 30.2 billion cubic meters (2022 est.)

GOVERNMENT

Country name: *conventional long form:* Republic of Albania
conventional short form: Albania
local long form: Republika e Shqiperise
local short form: Shqiperia
former: People's Socialist Republic of Albania
etymology: name may be derived from the pre-Celtic word *alb*, meaning "hill," or from the Indo-European root word *albh*, meaning "white;" the local name "Shqiperia" is derived from the Albanian word *shqiponje* ("eagle") and is popularly interpreted to mean "Land of the Eagles"

Government type: parliamentary republic

Capital: *name:* Tirana (Tirane)
geographic coordinates: 41 19 N, 19 49 E
time difference: UTC+1 (6 hours ahead of Washington, DC, during Standard Time)
daylight saving time: +1hr, begins last Sunday in March; ends last Sunday in October
etymology: the name "Tirana" first appears in a 1418 Venetian document; the origin of the name is unclear

Administrative divisions: 12 counties (*qarqe*, singular - *qark*); Berat, Diber, Durres, Elbasan, Fier, Gjirokaster, Korce, Kukes, Lezhe, Shkoder, Tirane (Tirana), Vlore

Legal system: civil law system except in the northern rural areas where customary law known as the "Code of Leke" is still present

Constitution: *history:* several previous; latest approved by the Assembly 21 October 1998, adopted by referendum 22 November 1998, promulgated 28 November 1998
amendment process: proposed by at least one-fifth of the Assembly membership; passage requires at least a two-thirds majority vote by the Assembly; referendum required only if approved by two-thirds of the Assembly; amendments approved by referendum effective upon declaration by the president of the republic

International law organization participation: has not submitted an ICJ jurisdiction declaration; accepts ICCt jurisdiction

Citizenship: *citizenship by birth:* no
citizenship by descent only: at least one parent must be a citizen of Albania
dual citizenship recognized: yes
residency requirement for naturalization: 5 years

Suffrage: 18 years of age; universal

Executive branch: *chief of state:* President Bajram BEGAJ (since 24 July 2022)
head of government: Prime Minister Edi RAMA (since 10 September 2013)
cabinet: Council of Ministers proposed by the prime minister, nominated by the president, and approved by the Assembly
election/appointment process: president indirectly elected by the Assembly for a 5-year term (eligible for a second term); a candidate needs three-fifths majority vote of the Assembly in 1 of 3 rounds or a simple majority in 2 additional rounds to become president; prime minister appointed by the president on the proposal of the majority party or coalition of parties in the Assembly
most recent election date: held in 4 rounds on 16, 23, and 30 May and 4 June 2022
election results: *2022:* Bajram BEGAJ elected president in the fourth round; Assembly vote - 78-4, opposition parties boycotted
2017: Ilir META elected president in the fourth round; Assembly vote - 87-2
expected date of next election: 2027

Legislative branch: *legislature name:* Albanian Parliament
legislative structure: unicameral
chamber name: Parliament (Kuvendi)
number of seats: 140 (all directly elected)
electoral system: proportional representation
scope of elections: full renewal
term in office: 4 years
most recent election date: 5/11/2025
percentage of women in chamber: 35.7%
expected date of next election: May 2029

Judicial branch: *highest court(s):* Supreme Court (consists of 19 judges, including the chief justice); Constitutional Court (consists of 9 judges, including the chairman)
judge selection and term of office: Supreme Court judges appointed by the High Judicial Council with the consent of the president to serve single 9-year terms; Supreme Court chairman is elected for a single 3-year term by the court members; appointments of Constitutional Court judges are rotated among the president, Parliament, and Supreme Court from a list of pre-qualified candidates (each institution selects 3 judges), to serve single 9-year terms; candidates are pre-qualified by a randomly selected body of experienced judges and prosecutors; Constitutional Court chairman is elected by the court members for a single, renewable 3-year term
subordinate courts: Courts of Appeal; Courts of First Instance; specialized courts: Court for Corruption and Organized Crime, Appeals Court for Corruption and Organized Crime (responsible for corruption, organized crime, and crimes of high officials)

Political parties: Alliance for Change (electoral coalition led by PD)
Democratic Party or PD
Party for Justice, Integration and Unity or PDIU (part of the Alliance for Change)
Social Democratic Party or PSD
Freedom Party of Albania or PL (formerly the Socialist Movement for Integration or LSI)
Socialist Party or PS

Diplomatic representation in the US: *chief of mission:* Ambassador Ervin BUSHATI (since 15 September 2023)
chancery: 2100 S Street NW, Washington, DC 20008
telephone: [1] (202) 223-4942
FAX: [1] (202) 628-7342
email address and website: embassy.washington@mfa.gov.al
http://www.ambasadat.gov.al/usa/en
consulate(s) general: New York

Diplomatic representation from the US: *chief of mission:* Ambassador (vacant); Chargé d'Affaires Nancy VANHORN (since August 2024)
embassy: Rruga Stavro Vinjau, No. 14, Tirana
mailing address: 9510 Tirana Place, Washington DC 20521-9510
telephone: [355] 4 2247-285
FAX: [355] 4 2232-222
email address and website: ACSTirana@state.gov
https://al.usembassy.gov/

International organization participation: BSEC, CD, CE, CEI, EAPC, EBRD, EITI (compliant country), FAO, IAEA, IBRD, ICAO, ICC (national committees), ICCt, ICRM, IDA, IDB, IFAD, IFC, IFRCS, ILO, IMF, IMO, Interpol, IOC, IOM, IPU, ISO (correspondent), ITU, ITUC (NGOs), MIGA, NATO, OAS (observer), OIC, OIF, OPCW, OSCE, PCA, SELEC, UN, UNCTAD, UNESCO, UNHRC, UNIDO, UNOOSA, UNWTO, UPU, WCO, WFTU (NGOs), WHO, WIPO, WMO, WTO
note: Albania is an EU candidate country and must complete accession criteria before being granted full membership

Independence: 28 November 1912 (from the Ottoman Empire)

National holiday: Independence Day, 28 November (1912), also known as Flag Day

Flag: *description:* red with a black two-headed eagle in the center
meaning: Albanians traditionally see themselves as descendants of the eagle; they refer to themselves as "Shqiptare," which translates as "sons of the eagle"
history: the design is said to originate with 15th-century Albanian hero Georgi Kastrioti SKANDERBEG, who led a successful uprising against the Ottoman Turks

National symbol(s): black double-headed eagle

National color(s): red, black

National coat of arms: adopted in 1998 and features the national symbol, the double-headed black eagle, in the national colors of red and black; red represents the courage and strength of the Albanian people, and the golden border represents the country's wealth; the helmet above the eagle is modeled on the helmet of Skanderbeg, a 15th-century Albanian military hero who led a rebellion against the Ottoman Empire; the goat on top of the helmet represents defiance and resistance

National anthem(s): *title:* "Hymni i Flamurit" (Hymn to the Flag)
lyrics/music: Aleksander Stavre DRENOVA/Ciprian PORUMBESCU
history: adopted 1912; only the first two stanzas of the original poem are used, with the second stanza as a chorus

National heritage: *total World Heritage Sites:* 4 (2 cultural, 1 natural, 1 mixed)
selected World Heritage Site locales: Butrint (c); Historic Berat and Gjirokastër (c); Primeval Beech Forests (n); Lake Ohrid Region (m)

ECONOMY

Economic overview: upper-middle-income Balkan economy; EU accession candidate; growth bolstered by tourism, agriculture, mining, construction, and private consumption; fiscal consolidation through revenue collection and tax compliance enhancements to address public debt; challenges include weak governance, corruption, and high emigration rates

Real GDP (purchasing power parity): $51.36 billion (2024 est.)
$49.403 billion (2023 est.)

$47.532 billion (2022 est.)
note: data in 2021 dollars
comparison ranking: 127

Real GDP growth rate: 4% (2024 est.)
3.9% (2023 est.)
4.8% (2022 est.)
note: annual GDP % growth based on constant local currency
comparison ranking: 76

Real GDP per capita: $18,900 (2024 est.)
$18,000 (2023 est.)
$17,100 (2022 est.)
note: data in 2021 dollars
comparison ranking: 106

GDP (official exchange rate): $27.178 billion (2024 est.)
note: data in current dollars at official exchange rate

Inflation rate (consumer prices): 2.2% (2024 est.)
4.8% (2023 est.)
6.7% (2022 est.)
note: annual % change based on consumer prices
comparison ranking: 61

GDP - composition, by sector of origin: *agriculture:* 15.5% (2024 est.)
industry: 22.4% (2024 est.)
services: 48.9% (2024 est.)
note: figures may not total 100% due to non-allocated consumption not captured in sector-reported data
comparison rankings: agriculture 54; industry 116; services 153

GDP - composition, by end use: *household consumption:* 70.2% (2023 est.)
government consumption: 12% (2023 est.)
investment in fixed capital: 24% (2023 est.)
investment in inventories: -1.1% (2023 est.)
exports of goods and services: 38.7% (2023 est.)
imports of goods and services: -43.8% (2023 est.)
note: figures may not total 100% due to rounding or gaps in data collection

Agricultural products: milk, maize, tomatoes, watermelons, potatoes, wheat, grapes, onions, cucumbers/gherkins, olives (2023)
note: top ten agricultural products based on tonnage

Industries: food; footwear, apparel and clothing; lumber, oil, cement, chemicals, mining, basic metals, hydropower

Industrial production growth rate: -0.2% (2024 est.)
note: annual % change in industrial value added based on constant local currency
comparison ranking: 140

Labor force: 1.37 million (2024 est.)
note: number of people ages 15 or older who are employed or seeking work
comparison ranking: 138

Unemployment rate: 10.3% (2024 est.)
10.2% (2023 est.)
10.2% (2022 est.)
note: % of labor force seeking employment
comparison ranking: 150

Youth unemployment rate (ages 15-24): *total:* 25.1% (2024 est.)
male: 23.9% (2024 est.)
female: 26.9% (2024 est.)
note: % of labor force ages 15-24 seeking employment
comparison ranking: total 34

Population below poverty line: 22% (2020 est.)
note: % of population with income below national poverty line

Gini Index coefficient - distribution of family income: 29.4 (2020 est.)
note: index (0-100) of income distribution; higher values represent greater inequality
comparison ranking: 125

Household income or consumption by percentage share: *lowest 10%:* 3.4% (2020 est.)
highest 10%: 22.8% (2020 est.)
note: % share of income accruing to lowest and highest 10% of population

Remittances: 8.4% of GDP (2024 est.)
8.6% of GDP (2023 est.)
9.2% of GDP (2022 est.)
note: personal transfers and compensation between resident and non-resident individuals/households/entities

Budget: *revenues:* $6.636 billion (2023 est.)
expenditures: $6.966 billion (2023 est.)
note: central government revenues (excluding grants) and expenditures converted to US dollars at average official exchange rate for year indicated

Public debt: 81.9% of GDP (2021 est.)
note: central government debt as a % of GDP
comparison ranking: 38

Taxes and other revenues: 17.8% (of GDP) (2023 est.)
note: central government tax revenue as a % of GDP
comparison ranking: 68

Current account balance: -$646.107 million (2024 est.)
-$281.7 million (2023 est.)
-$1.117 billion (2022 est.)
note: balance of payments - net trade and primary/secondary income in current dollars
comparison ranking: 114

Exports: $9.848 billion (2024 est.)
$9.099 billion (2023 est.)
$7.057 billion (2022 est.)
note: balance of payments - exports of goods and services in current dollars
comparison ranking: 117

Exports - partners: Italy 41%, Greece 10%, Germany 5%, Spain 5%, Serbia 4% (2023)
note: top five export partners based on percentage share of exports

Exports - commodities: garments, footwear, electricity, crude petroleum, iron alloys (2023)
note: top five export commodities based on value in dollars

Imports: $11.697 billion (2024 est.)
$10.374 billion (2023 est.)
$9.016 billion (2022 est.)
note: balance of payments - imports of goods and services in current dollars
comparison ranking: 113

Imports - partners: Italy 22%, China 11%, Turkey 9%, Germany 7%, Greece 6% (2023)
note: top five import partners based on percentage share of imports

Imports - commodities: cars, refined petroleum, garments, packaged medicine, iron bars (2023)
note: top five import commodities based on value in dollars

Reserves of foreign exchange and gold: $6.516 billion (2024 est.)
$6.455 billion (2023 est.)
$5.266 billion (2022 est.)
note: holdings of gold (year-end prices)/foreign exchange/special drawing rights in current dollars
comparison ranking: 89

Debt - external: $5.363 billion (2023 est.)
note: present value of external debt in current US dollars
comparison ranking: 71

Exchange rates: leke (ALL) per US dollar -

Exchange rates: 93.123 (2024 est.)
100.645 (2023 est.)
113.042 (2022 est.)
103.52 (2021 est.)
108.65 (2020 est.)

ENERGY

Electricity access: *electrification - total population:* 100% (2022 est.)

Electricity: *installed generating capacity:* 2.857 million kW (2023 est.)
consumption: 7.49 billion kWh (2023 est.)
exports: 2.2 billion kWh (2023 est.)
imports: 1.922 billion kWh (2023 est.)
transmission/distribution losses: 1.238 billion kWh (2023 est.)
comparison rankings: installed generating capacity 111; consumption 116; exports 56; imports 68; transmission/distribution losses 111

Electricity generation sources: *solar:* 3.3% of total installed capacity (2023 est.)
hydroelectricity: 96.7% of total installed capacity (2023 est.)

Coal: *production:* 473,000 metric tons (2023 est.)
consumption: 255,000 metric tons (2023 est.)
exports: 345,000 metric tons (2023 est.)
imports: 180,000 metric tons (2023 est.)
proven reserves: 522 million metric tons (2023 est.)

Petroleum: *total petroleum production:* 14,000 bbl/day (2023 est.)
refined petroleum consumption: 21,000 bbl/day (2023 est.)
crude oil estimated reserves: 150 million barrels (2021 est.)

Natural gas: *production:* 49.977 million cubic meters (2023 est.)
consumption: 49.977 million cubic meters (2023 est.)
proven reserves: 5.692 billion cubic meters (2021 est.)

Energy consumption per capita: 27.407 million Btu/person (2023 est.)
comparison ranking: 120

COMMUNICATIONS

Telephones - fixed lines: *total subscriptions:* 173,000 (2023 est.)
subscriptions per 100 inhabitants: 6 (2023 est.)
comparison ranking: total subscriptions 122

Telephones - mobile cellular: *total subscriptions:* 2.61 million (2023 est.)
subscriptions per 100 inhabitants: 98 (2022 est.)
comparison ranking: total subscriptions 145

Broadcast media: over 65 TV stations, including several that broadcast nationally and are sometimes available to neighboring countries; many viewers have access to Italian and Greek TV via terrestrial reception; TV stations have begun a government-mandated conversion from analog to digital broadcast; cable TV service is available; 2 public radio networks and roughly 78 private radio stations; several international broadcasters are available (2024)

Internet country code: .al

Internet users: *percent of population:* 83% (2023 est.)

Broadband - fixed subscriptions: *total:* 632,000 (2023 est.)
subscriptions per 100 inhabitants: 22 (2023 est.)
comparison ranking: total 89

TRANSPORTATION

Civil aircraft registration country code prefix: ZA

Airports: 3 (2025)
comparison ranking: 185

Heliports: 9 (2025)
comparison ranking: 78

Railways: *total:* 424 km (2017)
2021-All the trains in the country suspended

Merchant marine: *total:* 69 (2023)
by type: general cargo 46, oil tanker 1, other 22
comparison ranking: total 110

Ports: *total ports:* 3 (2024)
large: 0
medium: 0
small: 1
very small: 2
ports with oil terminals: 0
key ports: Durres, Shengjin, Vlores

MILITARY AND SECURITY

Military and security forces: Republic of Albania Armed Forces (Forcat e Armatosura të Republikës së Shqipërisë (FARSH); aka Albanian Armed Forces (AAF)): Land Forces, Naval Force (includes Coast Guard), Air Forces

Ministry of Interior: Guard of the Republic, State Police (includes the Border and Migration Police) (2025)
note: the State Police are primarily responsible for internal security, including counterterrorism, while the Guard of the Republic protects senior state officials, foreign dignitaries, and certain state properties

Military expenditures: 2% of GDP (2025 est.)
1.7% of GDP (2024 est.)
1.7% of GDP (2023 est.)
1.2% of GDP (2022 est.)
1.2% of GDP (2021 est.)

Military and security service personnel strengths: approximately 7,500 active-duty military personnel (2025)

Military equipment inventories and acquisitions: since joining NATO, the military has been in the process of modernizing by retiring its inventory of Soviet-era weapons and replacing them with Western equipment, including donated and second-hand deliveries (2024)

Military service age and obligation: 18-27 (up to 32 in some cases) for voluntary military service for men and women; conscription abolished 2010 (2024)
note: as of 2024, women comprised about 15% of the military's full-time personnel

Military - note: the Albanian Armed Forces (AAF) are responsible for defending the country's independence, sovereignty, and territory, assisting with internal security, providing disaster and humanitarian relief, and participating in international peacekeeping missions; the AAF is a small, lightly armed force that has been undergoing a modernization effort to improve its ability to fulfill NATO missions; the AAF has contributed small numbers of forces to several NATO missions since Albania joined NATO in 2009, including peacekeeping/stability missions in Afghanistan, Kosovo, and Iraq, and multinational battlegroups in Bulgaria and Latvia; it has also contributed to EU and UN missions (2025)

TERRORISM

Terrorist group(s): Terrorist group(s): Islamic Revolutionary Guard Corps/Qods Force; Islamic State of Iraq and ash-Sham (ISIS)
note: details about the history, aims, leadership, organization, areas of operation, tactics, targets, weapons, size, and sources of support of the group(s) appear(s) in Appendix T

TRANSNATIONAL ISSUES

Refugees and internally displaced persons: *refugees:* 9,381 (2024 est.)
stateless persons: 2,203 (2024 est.)

ALGERIA

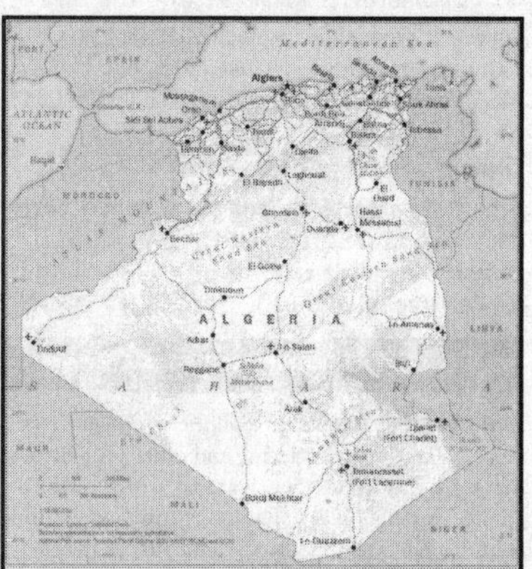

INTRODUCTION

Background: Algeria has known many empires and dynasties, including the ancient Numidians (3rd century B.C.), Phoenicians, Carthaginians, Romans, Vandals, Byzantines, over a dozen different Arab and Amazigh dynasties, Spaniards, and Ottoman Turks. Under the Turks, the Barbary pirates operated from North Africa and preyed on shipping, from about 1500 until the French captured Algiers in 1830. The French southward conquest of Algeria proceeded throughout the 19th century and was marked by many atrocities. A bloody eight-year struggle culminated in Algerian independence in 1962.

Algeria's long-dominant political party, the National Liberation Front (FLN), was established in 1954 as part of the struggle for independence and has since played a large role in politics, though it is falling out of favor with the youth and current President Abdelmadjid TEBBOUNE. The Government of Algeria in 1988 instituted a multi-party system in response to public unrest, but the surprising first-round success of the Islamic Salvation Front (FIS) in the 1991 legislative election led the Algerian military to intervene and postpone the second round of elections to prevent what the secular elite feared would be an extremist-led government from assuming power. An army crackdown on the FIS escalated into an FIS insurgency and intense violence from 1992-98 that resulted in over 100,000 deaths, many of which were attributed to extremist groups massacring villagers. The government gained the upper hand by the late 1990s, and FIS's armed wing, the Islamic Salvation Army, disbanded in 2000. FIS membership is now illegal.

In 1999, Abdelaziz BOUTEFLIKA won the presidency with the backing of the military, in an election that was boycotted by several candidates protesting alleged fraud. He won subsequent elections in 2004, 2009, and 2014. Widespread protests against his decision to seek a fifth term broke out in early 2019. BOUTEFLIKA resigned in April 2019, and in December 2019, Algerians elected former Prime Minister Abdelmadjid TEBBOUNE as the country's new president. A longtime FLN member, TEBBOUNE ran for president as an independent. In 2020, Algeria held a constitutional referendum on governmental reforms, which TEBBOUNE enacted in 2021. Subsequent reforms to the national electoral law introduced open-list voting to curb corruption. The new law also eliminated gender quotas in Parliament, and the 2021 legislative elections saw female representation plummet. The referendum, parliamentary elections, and local elections saw record-low voter turnout.

GEOGRAPHY

Location: Northern Africa, bordering the Mediterranean Sea, between Morocco and Tunisia

Geographic coordinates: 28 00 N, 3 00 E

Map references: Africa

Area: *total:* 2,381,740 sq km
land: 2,381,740 sq km
water: 0 sq km
comparison ranking: total 11

Area - comparative: slightly less than 3.5 times the size of Texas

Land boundaries: *total:* 6,734 km
border countries (6): Libya 989 km; Mali 1,359 km; Mauritania 460 km; Morocco 1,941 km; Niger 951 km; Tunisia 1,034 km

Coastline: 998 km

Maritime claims: *territorial sea:* 12 nm
contiguous zone: 24 nm
exclusive fishing zone: 32-52 nm

Climate: arid to semiarid; mild, wet winters with hot, dry summers along coast; drier with cold winters and hot summers on high plateau; sirocco is a hot, dust/sand-laden wind especially common in summer

Terrain: mostly high plateau and desert; Atlas Mountains in the far north and Hoggar Mountains in the south; narrow, discontinuous coastal plain

Elevation: *highest point:* Tahat 2,908 m
lowest point: Chott Melrhir -40 m
mean elevation: 800 m

Natural resources: petroleum, natural gas, iron ore, phosphates, uranium, lead, zinc

Land use: *agricultural land:* 17.3% (2022 est.)
arable land: 3.2% (2022 est.)
permanent crops: 0.4% (2022 est.)
permanent pasture: 13.8% (2022 est.)
forest: 0.8% (2022 est.)
other: 81.8% (2022 est.)

Irrigated land: 13,819 sq km (2019)

Major watersheds (area sq km): Atlantic Ocean drainage: Niger (2,261,741 sq km)

Internal (endorheic basin) drainage: Lake Chad (2,497,738 sq km)

Major aquifers: Lullemeden-Irhazer Aquifer System, Murzuk-Djado Basin, North Western Sahara Aquifer, Taoudeni-Tanezrouft Basin

Population distribution: the vast majority of the populace is found in the extreme northern part of the country along the Mediterranean Coast

Natural hazards: mountainous areas subject to severe earthquakes; mudslides and floods in rainy season; droughts

Geography - note: largest country in Africa but 80% desert; canyons and caves in the southern Hoggar Mountains and in the barren Tassili n'Ajjer area in the southeast of the country contain numerous examples of prehistoric art – rock paintings and carvings depicting human activities and wild and domestic animals (elephants, giraffes, cattle) – that date to the African Humid Period, roughly 5,000 to 11,000 years ago, when the region was completely vegetated

PEOPLE AND SOCIETY

Population: *total:* 47,022,473 (2024 est.)
male: 23,854,821
female: 23,167,652
comparison rankings: total 33; male 32; female 34

Nationality: *noun:* Algerian(s)
adjective: Algerian

Ethnic groups: Arab-Amazigh 99%, European less than 1%
note: although almost all Algerians are Amazigh in origin and not Arab, only a minority identify themselves as primarily Amazigh, about 15% of the total population; these people live mostly in the mountainous region of Kabylie east of Algiers and in several other communities; the Amazigh are also Muslim but identify with their Amazigh rather than Arab cultural heritage; some Amazigh have long agitated, sometimes violently, for autonomy; the government is unlikely to grant autonomy but has officially recognized Amazigh languages and introduced them into public schools

Languages: Arabic (official), French (lingua franca), Tamazight (official) (dialects include Kabyle (Taqbaylit), Shawiya (Tacawit), Mzab, Tuareg (Tamahaq))
major-language sample(s):
كتاب حقائق العالم، المصدر الذي لا يمكن الاستغناء عنه للمعلومات الأساسية (Arabic)

Religions: Muslim (official; predominantly Sunni) 99%, other (includes Christian, Jewish, Ahmadi Muslim, Shia Muslim, Ibadi Muslim) <1% (2012 est.)

Age structure: *0-14 years:* 30.8% (male 7,411,337/female 7,062,794)
15-64 years: 62.3% (male 14,846,102/female 14,441,034)
65 years and over: 6.9% (2024 est.) (male 1,597,382/female 1,663,824)

Dependency ratios: *total dependency ratio:* 60.6 (2024 est.)
youth dependency ratio: 49.4 (2024 est.)
elderly dependency ratio: 11.1 (2024 est.)
potential support ratio: 9 (2024 est.)

Median age: *total:* 29.1 years (2024 est.)
male: 28.8 years
female: 29.4 years
comparison ranking: total 146

Population growth rate: 1.54% (2024 est.)
comparison ranking: 62

Birth rate: 20.2 births/1,000 population (2024 est.)
comparison ranking: 67

Death rate: 4.4 deaths/1,000 population (2024 est.)
comparison ranking: 208

Net migration rate: -0.5 migrant(s)/1,000 population (2024 est.)
comparison ranking: 122

Population distribution: the vast majority of the populace is found in the extreme northern part of the country along the Mediterranean Coast

Urbanization: *urban population:* 75.3% of total population (2023)
rate of urbanization: 1.99% annual rate of change (2020-25 est.)

Major urban areas - population: 2.902 million ALGIERS (capital), 936,000 Oran (2022)

Sex ratio: *at birth:* 1.05 male(s)/female
0-14 years: 1.05 male(s)/female
15-64 years: 1.03 male(s)/female
65 years and over: 0.96 male(s)/female
total population: 1.03 male(s)/female (2024 est.)

Maternal mortality ratio: 62 deaths/100,000 live births (2023 est.)
comparison ranking: 86

Infant mortality rate: *total:* 18.7 deaths/1,000 live births (2024 est.)
male: 19.8 deaths/1,000 live births
female: 17.5 deaths/1,000 live births
comparison ranking: total 82

Life expectancy at birth: *total population:* 77.9 years (2024 est.)
male: 77.2 years
female: 78.7 years
comparison ranking: total population 85

Total fertility rate: 2.94 children born/woman (2024 est.)
comparison ranking: 49

Gross reproduction rate: 1.43 (2024 est.)

Drinking water source: *improved: urban:* 96.1% of population (2022 est.)
rural: 90.4% of population (2022 est.)
total: 94.7% of population (2022 est.)
unimproved: urban: 3.9% of population (2022 est.)
rural: 9.6% of population (2022 est.)
total: 5.3% of population (2022 est.)

Health expenditure: 5.5% of GDP (2021)
5.4% of national budget (2022 est.)

Physician density: 1.66 physicians/1,000 population (2022)

Hospital bed density: 1.6 beds/1,000 population (2017 est.)

Sanitation facility access: *improved: urban:* 98.3% of population (2022 est.)
rural: 91.7% of population (2022 est.)
total: 96.6% of population (2022 est.)
unimproved: urban: 1.7% of population (2022 est.)
rural: 8.3% of population (2022 est.)
total: 3.4% of population (2022 est.)

Obesity - adult prevalence rate: 27.4% (2016)
comparison ranking: 38

Alcohol consumption per capita: *total:* 0.59 liters of pure alcohol (2019 est.)
beer: 0.31 liters of pure alcohol (2019 est.)
wine: 0.2 liters of pure alcohol (2019 est.)
spirits: 0.08 liters of pure alcohol (2019 est.)
other alcohols: 0 liters of pure alcohol (2019 est.)
comparison ranking: total 160

Tobacco use: *total:* 21.4% (2025 est.)
male: 41.6% (2025 est.)
female: 0.6% (2025 est.)
comparison ranking: total 60

Children under the age of 5 years underweight: 2.7% (2018/19)
comparison ranking: 85

Currently married women (ages 15-49): 56% (2023 est.)

Child marriage: *women married by age 15:* 0% (2019)
women married by age 18: 3.8% (2019)

Education expenditure: 5.6% of GDP (2023 est.)
14.4% national budget (2024 est.)
comparison ranking: Education expenditure (% GDP) 38

Literacy: *female:* 74.2% (2019 est.)

School life expectancy (primary to tertiary education): *total:* 15 years (2023 est.)
male: 15 years (2023 est.)
female: 16 years (2023 est.)

ENVIRONMENT

Environmental issues: air pollution in major cities; soil erosion from overgrazing and other poor farming practices; desertification; river and coastal pollution from dumping of raw sewage, petroleum refining wastes, and other industrial effluents; pollution in Mediterranean Sea from oil wastes, soil erosion, and fertilizer runoff; inadequate potable water

International environmental agreements: *party to:* Biodiversity, Climate Change, Climate Change-Kyoto Protocol, Climate Change-Paris Agreement, Comprehensive Nuclear Test Ban, Desertification, Endangered Species, Environmental Modification, Hazardous Wastes, Law of the Sea, Ozone Layer Protection, Ship Pollution, Wetlands
signed, but not ratified: Nuclear Test Ban

Climate: arid to semiarid; mild, wet winters with hot, dry summers along coast; drier with cold winters and hot summers on high plateau; sirocco is a hot, dust/sand-laden wind especially common in summer

Urbanization: *urban population:* 75.3% of total population (2023)
rate of urbanization: 1.99% annual rate of change (2020-25 est.)

Carbon dioxide emissions: 163.661 million metric tonnes of CO2 (2023 est.)
from coal and metallurgical coke: 741,000 metric tonnes of CO2 (2023 est.)
from petroleum and other liquids: 57.795 million metric tonnes of CO2 (2023 est.)
from consumed natural gas: 105.125 million metric tonnes of CO2 (2023 est.)
comparison ranking: total emissions 34

Particulate matter emissions: 22.4 micrograms per cubic meter (2019 est.)

Methane emissions: *energy:* 2,561.1 kt (2022-2024 est.)
agriculture: 256 kt (2019-2021 est.)
waste: 486.4 kt (2019-2021 est.)
other: 7.6 kt (2019-2021 est.)

Waste and recycling: *municipal solid waste generated annually:* 12.379 million tons (2024 est.)
percent of municipal solid waste recycled: 11% (2022 est.)

Total water withdrawal: *municipal:* 3.389 billion cubic meters (2022)
industrial: 181 million cubic meters (2022)
agricultural: 7.391 billion cubic meters (2022)

Total renewable water resources: 11.667 billion cubic meters (2022 est.)

GOVERNMENT

Country name: *conventional long form:* People's Democratic Republic of Algeria
conventional short form: Algeria
local long form: Al Jumhuriyah al Jaza'iriyah ad Dimuqratiyah ash Sha'biyah
local short form: Al Jaza'ir
etymology: the country name derives from the capital city of Algiers

Government type: presidential republic

Capital: *name:* Algiers
geographic coordinates: 36 45 N, 3 03 E
time difference: UTC+1 (6 hours ahead of Washington, DC, during Standard Time)
etymology: name derives from the Arabic *al-jazair*, meaning "the islands," and refers to the four islands formerly off the coast of the capital but joined to the mainland since 1525

Administrative divisions: 58 provinces (*wilayas*, singular - *wilaya*); Adrar, Ain Defla, Ain Temouchent, Alger (Algiers), Annaba, Batna, Bechar, Bejaia, Beni Abbes, Biskra, Blida, Bordj Badji Mokhtar, Bordj Bou Arreridj, Bouira, Boumerdes, Chlef, Constantine, Djanet, Djelfa, El Bayadh, El Meghaier, El Meniaa, El Oued, El Tarf, Ghardaia, Guelma, Illizi, In Guezzam, In Salah, Jijel, Khenchela, Laghouat, Mascara, Medea, Mila, Mostaganem, M'Sila, Naama, Oran, Ouargla, Ouled Djellal, Oum el Bouaghi, Relizane, Saida, Setif, Sidi Bel Abbes, Skikda, Souk Ahras, Tamanrasset, Tebessa, Tiaret, Timimoun, Tindouf, Tipaza, Tissemsilt, Tizi Ouzou, Tlemcen, Touggourt

Legal system: mixed system of French civil law and Islamic law; judicial review of legislative acts in ad hoc Constitutional Council composed of various public officials including several Supreme Court justices

Constitution: *history:* several previous; latest approved by referendum 1 November 2020
amendment process: proposed by the president of the republic or through the president with the support of three fourths of the members of both houses of Parliament in joint session; passage requires approval by both houses, approval by referendum, and promulgation by the president; the president can forego a referendum if the Constitutional Council determines the proposed amendment does not conflict with basic constitutional principles; articles including the republican form of government, the integrity and unity of the country, and fundamental citizens' liberties and rights cannot be amended

International law organization participation: has not submitted an ICJ jurisdiction declaration; non-party state to the ICCt

Citizenship: *citizenship by birth:* no
citizenship by descent only: the mother must be a citizen of Algeria
dual citizenship recognized: no
residency requirement for naturalization: 7 years

Suffrage: 18 years of age; universal

Executive branch: *chief of state:* President Abdelmadjid TEBBOUNE (since 12 December 2019)
head of government: Prime Minister Sifi GHRIEB (since 28 August 2025)
cabinet: Cabinet of Ministers appointed by the president
election/appointment process: president directly elected by absolute majority popular vote in two rounds if needed for a 5-year term (eligible for a second term); prime minister nominated by the president after consultation with the majority party in Parliament
most recent election date: 7 September 2024
election results: *2024:* Abdelmadjid TEBBOUNE (NLF) 94.7%, Abdelaali Hassani CHERIF (MSP) 3.2%, Youcef AOUCHICHE (FFS) 2.2%
2019: (FLN) 58.1%, Abdelkader BENGRINA (El-Bina) 17.4%, Ali BENFLIS (Talaie El Hurriyet) 10.6%, Azzedine MIHOUBI (RND) 7.3%, Abdelaziz BELAID (Future Front) 6.7%
expected date of next election: 2029

Legislative branch: *legislature name:* Parliament (Barlaman)
legislative structure: bicameral

Legislative branch - lower chamber: *chamber name:* National People's Assembly (Al-Majlis Al-Chaabi Al-Watani)
number of seats: 407 (all directly elected)
electoral system: proportional representation
scope of elections: full renewal
term in office: 5 years
most recent election date: 6/12/2021
parties elected and seats per party: National Liberation Front (FLN) (98); Movement of Society for Peace (MSP) (65); National Democratic Rally (RND) (58); El-Moustakbel Front (Future", FM) (48); El Binaa Movement (39); Independents (84); Other (15)
percentage of women in chamber: 7.9%
expected date of next election: June 2026

Legislative branch - upper chamber: *chamber name:* Council of the Nation (Majlis al-Oumma)
number of seats: 174 (116 indirectly elected; 58 appointed)
electoral system: plurality/majority
scope of elections: partial renewal
term in office: 6 years
most recent election date: 3/9/2025
percentage of women in chamber: 2.5%
expected date of next election: January 2028

Judicial branch: *highest court(s):* Supreme Court or Le Cour Suprême, (consists of 150 judges organized into 8 chambers: Civil, Commercial and Maritime, Criminal, House of Offenses and Contraventions, House of Petitions, Land, Personal Status, and Social; Constitutional Council (consists of 12 members including the court chairman and deputy chairman)
judge selection and term of office: Supreme Court judges appointed by the High Council of Magistracy, an administrative body presided over by the president of the republic, and includes the republic vice-president and several members; judges appointed for life; Constitutional Council members - 4 appointed by the president of the republic, 2 each by the 2 houses of Parliament, 2 by the Supreme Court, and 2 by the Council of State; Council president and members appointed for single 6-year terms with half the membership renewed every 3 years
subordinate courts: appellate or wilaya courts; first instance or daira tribunals
note: Algeria's judicial system does not include sharia courts

Political parties: Algerian National Front or FNA
Algerian Popular Movement or MPA
Algeria's Hope Rally or TAJ
Dignity or El Karama
El-Infitah
El Mostakbal (Future Front)
Ennour El Djazairi Party (Algerian Radiance Party) or PED
Equity and Proclamation Party or PEP
Islamic Renaissance Movement or Ennahda Movement
Justice and Development Front or FJD
Movement for National Reform or El Islah
Movement of Society for Peace or MSP
National Construction Movement or El-Bina (Harakat El-Binaa El-Watani)
National Democratic Rally (Rassemblement National Democratique) or RND
National Front for Social Justice or FNJS
National Liberation Front or FLN
National Militancy Front or FMN
National Party for Solidarity and Development or PNSD
National Republican Alliance or ANR
New Dawn Party (El-Fajr El-Jadid)
New Generation (Jil Jadid)
Oath of 1954 or Ahd 54
Party of Justice and Liberty or PLJ
Rally for Culture and Democracy or RCD
Socialist Forces Front or FFS
Union for Change and Progress or UCP
Union of Democratic and Social Forces or UFDS
Vanguard of Liberties (Talaie El Hurriyet)
Workers Party or PT
Youth Party or PJ
note: a law banning political parties based on religion was enacted in 1997

Diplomatic representation in the US: *chief of mission:* Ambassador Sabri BOUKADOUM (since 27 February 2024)
chancery: 2118 Kalorama Road NW, Washington, DC 20008
telephone: [1] (202) 265-2800
FAX: [1] (202) 986-5906
email address and website: mail@algerianembassy.org
https://www.algerianembassy.org/
consulate(s) general: New York

Diplomatic representation from the US: *chief of mission:* Ambassador Elizabeth Moore AUBIN (since 9 February 2022)
embassy: 05 Chemin Cheikh Bachir, Ibrahimi, El-Biar 16030, Alger
mailing address: 6030 Algiers Place, Washington DC 20521-6030
telephone: [213] (0) 770-08-2000
FAX: [213] (0) 770-08-2299
email address and website: algierspd@state.gov
https://dz.usembassy.gov/

International organization participation: ABEDA, AfDB, AFESD, AMF, AMU, AU, BIS, CAEU, CD, FAO, G-15, G-24, G-77, IAEA, IBRD, ICAO, ICC (national committees), ICRM, IDA, IDB, IFAD, IFC, IFRCS, IHO, ILO, IMF, IMO, IMSO, Interpol, IOC, IOM, IPU, ISO, ITSO, ITU, ITUC (NGOs), LAS, MIGA, MONUSCO, NAM, OAPEC, OAS (observer), OIC, OPCW, OPEC, OSCE (partner), UN, UNCTAD, UNESCO, UNHCR, UNIDO, UNITAR, UNWTO, UPU, WCO, WHO, WIPO, WMO, WTO (observer)

Independence: 5 July 1962 (from France)

National holiday: Independence Day, 5 July (1962); Revolution Day, 1 November (1954)

Flag: *description:* two equal vertical bands of green (left) and white; a red, five-pointed star inside a red crescent, centered over the two-color boundary
meaning: the colors represent Islam (green), purity and peace (white), and liberty (red); the crescent and star are also Islamic symbols, but the crescent is more closed than those of other Muslim countries because Algerians believe the long crescent horns bring happiness

National symbol(s): five-pointed star between the extended horns of a crescent moon; fennec fox

National color(s): green, white, red

National anthem(s): *title:* "Kassaman" (We Pledge)
lyrics/music: Mufdi ZAKARIAH/Mohamed FAWZI
history: adopted 1962; ZAKARIAH wrote "Kassaman" as a poem while imprisoned in Algiers by French colonial forces

National heritage: *total World Heritage Sites:* 7 (6 cultural, 1 mixed)
selected World Heritage Site locales: Beni Hammad Fort (c); Djémila (c); Casbah of Algiers (c); M'zab Valley (c); Tassili n'Ajjer (m); Timgad (c); Tipasa (c)

ECONOMY

Economic overview: suffering oil and gas economy; lack of sector and market diversification; political instability chilling domestic consumption; poor credit access and declines in business confidence; COVID-19 austerity policies; delayed promised socio-economic reforms

Real GDP (purchasing power parity): $722.912 billion (2024 est.)
$699.818 billion (2023 est.)
$672.256 billion (2022 est.)
note: data in 2021 dollars
comparison ranking: 40

Real GDP growth rate: 3.3% (2024 est.)
4.1% (2023 est.)
3.6% (2022 est.)
note: annual GDP % growth based on constant local currency
comparison ranking: 108

Real GDP per capita: $15,400 (2024 est.)
$15,200 (2023 est.)
$14,800 (2022 est.)
note: data in 2021 dollars
comparison ranking: 124

GDP (official exchange rate): $263.62 billion (2024 est.)
note: data in current dollars at official exchange rate

Inflation rate (consumer prices): 4% (2024 est.)
9.3% (2023 est.)
9.3% (2022 est.)
note: annual % change based on consumer prices
comparison ranking: 123

GDP - composition, by sector of origin: *agriculture:* 13.1% (2023 est.)
industry: 37.8% (2023 est.)
services: 45.6% (2023 est.)
note: figures may not total 100% due to non-allocated consumption not captured in sector-reported data
comparison rankings: agriculture 60; industry 25; services 171

GDP - composition, by end use: *household consumption:* 40.8% (2023 est.)
government consumption: 17.9% (2023 est.)
investment in fixed capital: 32.8% (2023 est.)
investment in inventories: 4.9% (2023 est.)
exports of goods and services: 23.6% (2023 est.)
imports of goods and services: -20.1% (2023 est.)
note: figures may not total 100% due to rounding or gaps in data collection

Agricultural products: potatoes, watermelons, wheat, milk, onions, tomatoes, vegetables, oranges, dates, barley (2023)
note: top ten agricultural products based on tonnage

Industries: petroleum, natural gas, light industries, mining, electrical, petrochemical, food processing

Industrial production growth rate: 3.9% (2023 est.)
note: annual % change in industrial value added based on constant local currency
comparison ranking: 63

Labor force: 13.294 million (2024 est.)
note: number of people ages 15 or older who are employed or seeking work
comparison ranking: 46

Unemployment rate: 11.5% (2024 est.)
11.8% (2023 est.)
12.4% (2022 est.)
note: % of labor force seeking employment
comparison ranking: 159

Youth unemployment rate (ages 15-24): *total:* 29.8% (2024 est.)
male: 26.8% (2024 est.)
female: 45.8% (2024 est.)
note: % of labor force ages 15-24 seeking employment
comparison ranking: total 23

Average household expenditures: *on food:* 37.2% of household expenditures (2023 est.)
on alcohol and tobacco: 1% of household expenditures (2023 est.)

Remittances: 0.8% of GDP (2023 est.)
0.8% of GDP (2022 est.)
1% of GDP (2021 est.)
note: personal transfers and compensation between resident and non-resident individuals/households/entities

Budget: *revenues:* $55.185 billion (2019 est.)
expenditures: $64.728 billion (2019 est.)

Public debt: 27.5% of GDP (2017 est.)
note: data cover central government debt as well as debt issued by subnational entities and intra-governmental debt
comparison ranking: 171

Current account balance: $6.359 billion (2023 est.)
$19.433 billion (2022 est.)
-$4.513 billion (2021 est.)
note: balance of payments - net trade and primary/secondary income in current dollars
comparison ranking: 32

Exports: $59.426 billion (2023 est.)
$69.226 billion (2022 est.)
$41.846 billion (2021 est.)
note: balance of payments - exports of goods and services in current dollars
comparison ranking: 63

Exports - partners: Italy 29%, France 14%, Spain 13%, USA 6%, Netherlands 4% (2023)
note: top five export partners based on percentage share of exports

Exports - commodities: natural gas, crude petroleum, refined petroleum, fertilizers, iron bars (2023)
note: top five export commodities based on value in dollars

Imports: $51.131 billion (2023 est.)
$46.613 billion (2022 est.)
$44.287 billion (2021 est.)
note: balance of payments - imports of goods and services in current dollars
comparison ranking: 66

Imports - partners: China 24%, France 12%, Italy 8%, Turkey 7%, Brazil 6% (2023)
note: top five import partners based on percentage share of imports

Imports - commodities: wheat, plastics, cars, milk, corn (2023)
note: top five import commodities based on value in dollars

Reserves of foreign exchange and gold: $83.007 billion (2024 est.)
$81.217 billion (2023 est.)
$71.852 billion (2022 est.)
note: holdings of gold (year-end prices)/foreign exchange/special drawing rights in current dollars
comparison ranking: 32

Debt - external: $4.764 billion (2023 est.)
note: present value of external debt in current US dollars
comparison ranking: 73

Exchange rates: Algerian dinars (DZD) per US dollar -

Exchange rates: 134.053 (2024 est.)
135.843 (2023 est.)
141.995 (2022 est.)
135.064 (2021 est.)
126.777 (2020 est.)

ENERGY

Electricity access: *electrification - total population:* 100% (2022 est.)
electrification - urban areas: 100%
electrification - rural areas: 99.3%

Electricity: *installed generating capacity:* 22.591 million kW (2023 est.)
consumption: 85.687 billion kWh (2023 est.)
exports: 2.753 billion kWh (2023 est.)

imports: 475.8 million kWh (2023 est.)
transmission/distribution losses: 9.237 billion kWh (2023 est.)
comparison rankings: installed generating capacity 47; consumption 37; exports 51; imports 95; transmission/distribution losses 180

Electricity generation sources: *fossil fuels:* 98.1% of total installed capacity (2023 est.)
solar: 0.9% of total installed capacity (2023 est.)
hydroelectricity: 0.9% of total installed capacity (2023 est.)

Coal: *consumption:* 3,000 metric tons (2023 est.)
imports: 241,000 metric tons (2023 est.)
proven reserves: 223 million metric tons (2023 est.)

Petroleum: *total petroleum production:* 1.443 million bbl/day (2023 est.)
refined petroleum consumption: 446,000 bbl/day (2023 est.)
crude oil estimated reserves: 12.2 billion barrels (2021 est.)

Natural gas: *production:* 104.896 billion cubic meters (2023 est.)
consumption: 52.831 billion cubic meters (2023 est.)
exports: 51.566 billion cubic meters (2023 est.)
proven reserves: 4.504 trillion cubic meters (2021 est.)

Energy consumption per capita: 61.843 million Btu/person (2023 est.)
comparison ranking: 81

COMMUNICATIONS

Telephones - fixed lines: *total subscriptions:* 6.324 million (2023 est.)
subscriptions per 100 inhabitants: 14 (2023 est.)
comparison ranking: total subscriptions 25

Telephones - mobile cellular: *total subscriptions:* 51.5 million (2023 est.)
subscriptions per 100 inhabitants: 109 (2022 est.)
comparison ranking: total subscriptions 35

Broadcast media: Radio Algérienne is the state-run radio broadcast; the National Company of Television (Entreprise Nationale de Télévision (ENTV)) is the primary state-run public TV station (2024)

Internet country code: .dz

Internet users: *percent of population:* 77% (2023 est.)

Broadband - fixed subscriptions: *total:* 5.54 million (2023 est.)
subscriptions per 100 inhabitants: 12 (2023 est.)
comparison ranking: total 34

TRANSPORTATION

Civil aircraft registration country code prefix: 7T

Airports: 95 (2025)
comparison ranking: 57

Heliports: 11 (2025)
comparison ranking: 69

Railways: *total:* 4,020 km (2019)

Merchant marine: *total:* 119 (2022)
by type: bulk carrier 1, container ship 4, general cargo 11, oil tanker 14, other 89
comparison ranking: total 83

Ports: *total ports:* 17 (2024)
large: 2
medium: 1
small: 6
very small: 8
ports with oil terminals: 3
key ports: Alger, Annaba, Arzew, Arzew El Djedid, Bejaia, Mers El Kebir, Oran, Port Methanier, Skikda

MILITARY AND SECURITY

Military and security forces: Algerian People's National Army (ANP): Land Forces, Naval Forces (includes Coast Guard), Air Forces, Territorial Air Defense Forces, Republican Guard, National Gendarmerie Ministry of Interior: General Directorate of National Security (national police) (2025)
note: the Republican Guard is subordinate to the ANP, but responsible to the President; the National Gendarmerie performs police functions outside urban areas under the auspices of the Ministry of National Defense and shares responsibility with the General Directorate of National Security for maintaining law and order; it is comprised of territorial, intervention/mobile, border guard, railway, riot control, and air support units

Military expenditures: 8% of GDP (2024 est.)
8% of GDP (2023 est.)
4.8% of GDP (2022 est.)
5.6% of GDP (2021 est.)
6.7% of GDP (2020 est.)

Military and security service personnel strengths: information varies; estimated 200,000 active ANP, including the National Gendarmerie (2025)

Military equipment inventories and acquisitions: the Algerian military has traditionally been armed mostly with Russian and Soviet-era weapons systems and equipment; over the past decade, it has made large investments in acquiring more modern armored vehicles, air defense systems, fighter aircraft, missiles, unmanned aerial vehicles, and warships, largely from Russia, its traditional supplier, but also China and Western European suppliers such as Germany (2024)

Military service age and obligation: 18 is the legal minimum age for voluntary military service for men and women; 19-30 years of age for mandatory national service for men (all Algerian men must register at age 17); service obligation reduced from 18 to 12 months in 2014 (2024)
note: conscripts comprise an estimated 70% of the military

Military - note: the ANP is responsible for external defense but also has some internal security responsibilities; key areas of concern include border and maritime security, terrorism, regional instability, and tensions with Morocco; Algeria supports the pro-independence Polisario Front in Western Sahara and accuses Morocco of supporting the Algerian separatist Movement for the Autonomy of Kabylie (MAK); border security and counterterrorism have received additional focus since the Arab Spring events of 2011 and the rise of terrorist threats emanating from Libya and the Sahel; the Army and Ministry of Defense (MND) paramilitary forces of the Gendarmerie and the border guards have beefed up their presence along the frontiers with Tunisia, Libya, Niger, and Mali to interdict and deter cross-border attacks by Islamist militant groups; the ANP and MND paramilitary forces have also increased counterterrorism cooperation with some neighboring countries, particularly Tunisia, including joint operations
the ANP has also played a large role in the country's politics since independence in 1962, including coups in 1965 and 1991; it was a key backer of BOUTEFLIKA's election in 1999 and remained a center of power during his 20-year rule; the military was instrumental in BOUTEFLIKA's resignation in 2019, when it withdrew support and called for him to be removed from office (2024)

SPACE

Space agency/agencies: Algerian Space Agency (Agence Spatiale Algérienne, ASAL; established 2002) (2025)

Space launch site(s): none; note - in 1947, Algeria began hosting a French military rocket test site known as the Centre Interarmées d'Essais d'Engins Spéciaux (CIEES or Interarmy Special Vehicles Test Center); it was the continent of Africa's first rocket launch site and was in service until 1967

Space program overview: has a national space policy and space research program with stated goals of supporting internal development, managing resources, mastering space technology, and reinforcing national sovereignty; builds and operates communications and remote sensing (RS) satellites; researching and developing a range of space-related capabilities, including satellites and satellite payloads, communications, RS, instrumentation, satellite image processing, and geospatial information; has bilateral relationships with a variety of foreign space agencies and industries, including those of Argentina, China, France, Germany, India, Russia, Slovenia, Ukraine, the UK, and other African countries; member of the African Space Agency and the Arab Space Coordination Group (2025)
note: further details about the key activities, programs, and milestones of the country's space program, as well as government spending estimates on the space sector, appear in the Space Programs reference guide

TERRORISM

Terrorist group(s): Terrorist group(s): al-Qa'ida in the Islamic Maghreb (AQIM); Islamic State of Iraq and ash-Sham (ISIS) – Algeria; al-Mulathamun Battalion (al-Mourabitoun)
note: details about the history, aims, leadership, organization, areas of operation, tactics, targets, weapons, size, and sources of support of the group(s) appear(s) in Appendix T

TRANSNATIONAL ISSUES

Refugees and internally displaced persons: *refugees:* 188,206 (2024 est.)

IDPs: 25 (2024 est.)

Trafficking in persons: *tier rating:* Tier 2 Watch List — Algeria did not demonstrate overall increasing efforts to eliminate trafficking compared with the previous reporting period, therefore Algeria remained on Tier 2 Watch List for the second consecutive year; for more details, go to: https://www.state.gov/reports/2025-trafficking-in-persons-report/algeria/

AMERICAN SAMOA

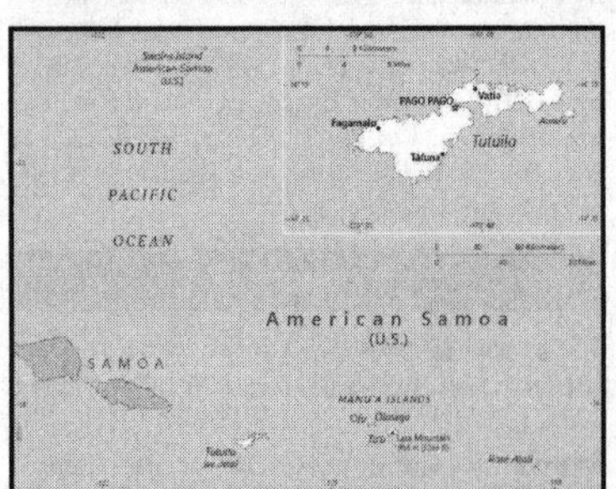

INTRODUCTION

Background: Tutuila – the largest island in American Samoa – was settled by 1000 B.C., and the island served as a refuge for exiled chiefs and defeated warriors from the other Samoan islands. The Manu'a Islands, which are also now part of American Samoa, developed a traditional chiefdom that maintained autonomy by controlling oceanic trade. In 1722, Dutch explorer Jacob ROGGEVEEN was the first European to sail through the Manu'a Islands, and he was followed by French explorer Louis Antoine DE BOUGAINVILLE in 1768. Whalers and missionaries arrived in American Samoa in the 1830s, but American and European traders tended to favor the port in Apia – now in independent Samoa – over the smaller and less-developed Pago Pago on Tutuila. In the mid-1800s, a dispute arose in Samoa over control of the Samoan archipelago, with different chiefs gaining support from Germany, the UK, and the US. In 1872, the high chief of Tutuila offered the US exclusive rights to Pago Pago in return for US protection, but the US rejected this offer. As fighting resumed, the US agreed to the chief's request in 1878 and set up a coaling station at Pago Pago. In 1899, with continued disputes over succession, Germany and the US agreed to divide the Samoan islands, while the UK withdrew its claims in exchange for parts of the Solomon Islands. Local chiefs on Tutuila formally ceded their land to the US in 1900, followed by the chief of Manu'a in 1904. The territory was officially named "American Samoa" in 1911.

The US administered the territory through the Department of the Navy. In 1949, there was an attempt to organize the territory, granting it formal self-government, but local chiefs helped defeat the measure in the US Congress. Administration was transferred to the Department of the Interior in 1951, and in 1967, American Samoa adopted a constitution that provides significant protections for traditional Samoan land-tenure rules, language, and culture. In 1977, after four attempts, voters approved a measure to directly elect their governor. Nevertheless, American Samoa officially remains an unorganized territory, and people born in American Samoa are US nationals rather than US citizens.

GEOGRAPHY

Location: Oceania, group of islands in the South Pacific Ocean, about halfway between Hawaii and New Zealand

Geographic coordinates: 14 20 S, 170 00 W

Map references: Oceania

Area: *total:* 224 sq km
land: 224 sq km
water: 0 sq km
note: includes Rose Atoll and Swains Island
comparison ranking: total 216

Area - comparative: slightly larger than Washington, D.C.

Land boundaries: *total:* 0 km

Coastline: 116 km

Maritime claims: *territorial sea:* 12 nm
exclusive economic zone: 200 nm

Climate: tropical marine, moderated by southeast trade winds; annual rainfall averages about 3 m; rainy season (November to April), dry season (May to October); little seasonal temperature variation

Terrain: five volcanic islands with rugged peaks and limited coastal plains, two coral atolls (Rose Atoll, Swains Island)

Elevation: *highest point:* Lata Mountain 964 m
lowest point: Pacific Ocean 0 m

Natural resources: pumice, pumicite

Land use: *agricultural land:* 14.5% (2022 est.)
arable land: 4.9% (2022 est.)
permanent crops: 9.7% (2022 est.)
permanent pasture: 0% (2022 est.)
forest: 85.4% (2022 est.)
other: 0.2% (2022 est.)

Irrigated land: 0 sq km (2022)

Natural hazards: cyclones common from December to March
volcanism: limited volcanic activity on the Ofu and Olosega Islands; neither has erupted since the 19th century

Geography - note: Pago Pago has one of the best natural deepwater harbors in the South Pacific Ocean, sheltered by shape from rough seas and protected by peripheral mountains from high winds; strategic location in the South Pacific Ocean

PEOPLE AND SOCIETY

Population: *total:* 43,895 (2024 est.)
male: 21,804
female: 22,091
comparison rankings: total 211; male 211; female 211

Nationality: *noun:* American Samoan(s) (US nationals)
adjective: American Samoan

Ethnic groups: Pacific Islander 88.7% (includes Samoan 83.2%, Tongan 2.2%, other 3.3%), Asian 5.8% (includes Filipino 3.4%, other 2.4%), mixed 4.4%, other 1.1% (2020 est.)
note: data represent population by ethnic origin or race

Languages: Samoan 87.9% (closely related to Hawaiian and other Polynesian languages), English 3.3%, Tongan 2.1%, other Pacific Islander 4.1%, Asian languages 2.1%, other 0.5% (2020 est.)
note: most people are bilingual

Religions: Christian 98.3%, other <1%, unaffiliated <1% (2020 est.)

Age structure: *0-14 years:* 25.3% (male 5,738/female 5,387)
15-64 years: 66% (male 14,291/female 14,679)
65 years and over: 8.7% (2024 est.) (male 1,775/female 2,025)

Dependency ratios: *total dependency ratio:* 51.5 (2024 est.)
youth dependency ratio: 38.4 (2024 est.)
elderly dependency ratio: 13.1 (2024 est.)
potential support ratio: 7.6 (2024 est.)

Median age: *total:* 30 years (2024 est.)
male: 29.4 years
female: 30.6 years
comparison ranking: total 141

Population growth rate: -1.54% (2024 est.)
comparison ranking: 235

Birth rate: 15.7 births/1,000 population (2024 est.)
comparison ranking: 102

Death rate: 6.3 deaths/1,000 population (2024 est.)
comparison ranking: 145

Net migration rate: -24.8 migrant(s)/1,000 population (2024 est.)
comparison ranking: 229

Urbanization: *urban population:* 87.2% of total population (2023)
rate of urbanization: 0.26% annual rate of change (2020-25 est.)

Major urban areas - population: 49,000 PAGO PAGO (capital) (2018)

Sex ratio: *at birth:* 1.06 male(s)/female
0-14 years: 1.07 male(s)/female
15-64 years: 0.97 male(s)/female
65 years and over: 0.88 male(s)/female
total population: 0.99 male(s)/female (2024 est.)

Infant mortality rate: *total:* 9.7 deaths/1,000 live births (2024 est.)
male: 11.7 deaths/1,000 live births
female: 7.6 deaths/1,000 live births
comparison ranking: total 136

Life expectancy at birth: *total population:* 75.8 years (2024 est.)
male: 73.4 years
female: 78.5 years
comparison ranking: total population 122

Total fertility rate: 2.06 children born/woman (2024 est.)
comparison ranking: 97

Gross reproduction rate: 1 (2024 est.)

Drinking water source: *improved:* total: 99.8% of population
unimproved: total: 0.2% of population (2020 est.)

Sanitation facility access: *improved:* total: 98.5% of population (2022 est.)
unimproved: total: 1.5% of population (2022 est.)

Currently married women (ages 15-49): 53.5% (2023 est.)

ENVIRONMENT

Environmental issues: limited supply of drinking water; pollution; waste disposal; coastal and stream alteration; soil erosion

Climate: tropical marine, moderated by southeast trade winds; annual rainfall averages about 3 m; rainy season (November to April), dry season (May to October); little seasonal temperature variation

Urbanization: *urban population:* 87.2% of total population (2023)
rate of urbanization: 0.26% annual rate of change (2020-25 est.)

Carbon dioxide emissions: 389,000 metric tonnes of CO2 (2023 est.)
from petroleum and other liquids: 389,000 metric tonnes of CO2 (2023 est.)
comparison ranking: total emissions 192

Waste and recycling: *municipal solid waste generated annually:* 19,000 tons (2024 est.)

GOVERNMENT

Country name: *conventional long form:* American Samoa
conventional short form: American Samoa
former: Eastern Samoa
abbreviation: AS
etymology: the name's meaning is disputed; according to one theory, *sa* means "sacred" and *moa* means "center," so the name can mean "Holy Center"; alternatively, some assert that the name can mean "place of the sacred moa bird" of Polynesian mythology; however, the name may pre-date the Polynesian era (before 1000 B.C.), with *sa'a* meaning "tribe or people" and *moa* meaning "deep sea," or "people of the deep sea"

Government type: unincorporated, unorganized Territory of the US with local self-government; republican form of territorial government with separate executive, legislative, and judicial branches

Dependency status: unincorporated, unorganized Territory of the US; administered by the Office of Insular Affairs, US Department of the Interior

Capital: *name:* Pago Pago
geographic coordinates: 14 16 S, 170 42 W
time difference: UTC-11 (6 hours behind Washington, DC, during Standard Time)
note: pronounced PAHN-go PAHN-go

Administrative divisions: none (territory of the US); no first-order administrative divisions as defined by the US Government, but 3 districts and 2 islands* are considered second-order; Eastern, Manu'a, Rose Island*, Swains Island*, Western

Legal system: mixed legal system of US common law and customary law

Constitution: *history:* adopted 17 October 1960; revised 1 July 1967
amendment process: proposed by either house of the Legislative Assembly; passage requires three-fifths majority vote by the membership of each house, approval by simple majority vote in a referendum, approval by the US Secretary of the Interior, and only by an act of the US Congress

Citizenship: see United States
note: in accordance with US Code Title 8, Section 1408, persons born in American Samoa are US nationals but not US citizens

Suffrage: 18 years of age; universal

Executive branch: *chief of state:* President Donald J. TRUMP (since 20 January 2025)
head of government: Governor Nikolao PULA (since 3 January 2025)
cabinet: Cabinet consists of 12 department directors appointed by the governor with the consent of the Legislature or Fono
election/appointment process: president and vice president indirectly elected on the same ballot by an Electoral College of 'electors' chosen from each state to serve a 4-year term (eligible for a second term); under the US Constitution, residents of unincorporated territories such as American Samoa do not vote in elections for US president and vice president; however, they may vote in Democratic and Republican presidential primary elections; governor and lieutenant governor directly elected on the same ballot by absolute-majority popular vote in 2 rounds, if needed, for a 4-year term (eligible for a second term)
most recent election date: 19 November 2024
election results: Lemanu Peleti MAUGA elected governor in first round; percent of vote - Lemanu Peleti MAUGA (independent) 60.3%, Gaoteote Palaie TOFAU (independent) 21.9%, I'aulualo Fa'afetai TALIA (independent) 12.3%
expected date of next election: November 2028

Legislative branch: *note:* American Samoa elects 1 member by simple majority popular vote to serve a 2-year term as a delegate to the US House of Representatives; the delegate can vote when serving on a committee and when the House meets as the Committee of the Whole House, but not when legislation is submitted for a "full floor" House vote

Judicial branch: *highest court(s):* High Court of American Samoa (consists of the chief justice, associate chief justice, and 6 Samoan associate judges and organized into trial, family, drug, and appellate divisions)
judge selection and term of office: chief justice and associate chief justice appointed by the US Secretary of the Interior to serve for life; Samoan associate judges appointed by the governor to serve for life
subordinate courts: district and village courts
note: American Samoa has no US federal courts

Political parties: Democratic Party
Republican Party

Diplomatic representation in the US: none (territory of the US)

Diplomatic representation from the US: *embassy:* none (territory of the US)

International organization participation: AOSIS (observer), Interpol (subbureau), IOC, PIF (observer), SPC

Independence: none (territory of the US)

National holiday: Flag Day, 17 April (1900)

Flag: *description:* a large white triangle edged in red is based on the right side and extends to the left side, and it is on a dark blue field; a bald eagle holding a Samoan war club (*fa'alaufa'i*) and a coconut-fiber fly whisk (*fue*) sits on the right side of the flag
meaning: the war club and fly whisk are traditional Samoan symbols of authority; the eagle carrying two objects echoes the US Great Seal and reflects the relationship between the United States and American Samoa; the red, white, and blue colors are traditionally used by both countries

National symbol(s): a *fue* (coconut fiber fly whisk that represents wisdom) crossed with a *to'oto'o* (staff that represents authority)

National color(s): red, white, blue

National anthem(s): *title:* "Amerika Samoa" (American Samoa)
lyrics/music: Mariota Tiumalu TUIASOSOPO/ Napoleon Andrew TUITELELEAPAGA
history: local anthem adopted 1950
title: "The Star-Spangled Banner"
lyrics/music: Francis Scott KEY/John Stafford SMITH
history: official anthem, as a US territory

ECONOMY

Economic overview: tourism, tuna, and government services-based territorial economy; sustained economic decline; vulnerable tuna canning industry; large territorial government presence; minimum wage increases to rise to federal standards by 2036

Real GDP (purchasing power parity): $658 million (2016 est.)
$674.9 million (2015 est.)
$666.9 billion (2014 est.)
note: data are in 2016 dollars comparison ranking: 209

Real GDP growth rate: 1.7% (2022 est.)
-0.8% (2021 est.)
4.4% (2020 est.)
note: annual GDP % growth based on constant local currency
comparison ranking: 158

GDP (official exchange rate): $871 million (2022 est.)
note: data in current dollars at official exchange rate

Agricultural products: bananas, coconuts, vegetables, taro, breadfruit, yams, copra, pineapples, papayas; dairy products, livestock

Industries: tuna canneries (largely supplied by foreign fishing vessels), handicrafts

Budget: *revenues:* $249 million (2016 est.)
expenditures: $262.5 million (2016 est.)

Exports: $409 million (2022 est.)
$332 million (2021 est.)
$427 million (2020 est.)
note: GDP expenditure basis - exports of goods and services in current dollars
comparison ranking: 194

Exports - partners: Australia 31%, UK 18%, Tanzania 9%, UAE 7%, Senegal 6% (2023)
note: top five export partners based on percentage share of exports

Exports - commodities: animal meal, aluminum, refined petroleum, gas turbines, broadcasting equipment (2023)
note: top five export commodities based on value in dollars

Imports: $677 million (2022 est.)
$694 million (2021 est.)
$686 million (2020 est.)
note: GDP expenditure basis - imports of goods and services in current dollars comparison ranking: 194

Imports - partners: Singapore 28%, NZ 15%, Fiji 14%, Taiwan 11%, Malaysia 11% (2023)
note: top five import partners based on percentage share of imports

Imports - commodities: refined petroleum, fish, paper containers, wood, construction vehicles (2023)
note: top five import commodities based on value in dollars

Exchange rates: the US dollar is used

ENERGY

Electricity: *installed generating capacity:* 50,000 kW (2023 est.)
consumption: 157.697 million kWh (2023 est.)
transmission/distribution losses: 13.975 million kWh (2023 est.)
comparison rankings: installed generating capacity 196; consumption 192; transmission/distribution losses 21

Electricity generation sources: *fossil fuels:* 97.1% of total installed capacity (2023 est.)
solar: 2.9% of total installed capacity (2023 est.)

Petroleum: *refined petroleum consumption:* 3,000 bbl/day (2023 est.)

Energy consumption per capita: 89.105 million Btu/person (2019 est.)
comparison ranking: 59

COMMUNICATIONS

Telephones - fixed lines: *total subscriptions:* 10,000 (2021 est.)
subscriptions per 100 inhabitants: 20 (2022 est.)
comparison ranking: total subscriptions 187

Telephones - mobile cellular: *total subscriptions:* 2,250 (2009 est.)
subscriptions per 100 inhabitants: 4 (2009 est.)
comparison ranking: total subscriptions 224

Broadcast media: 3 TV stations; multi-channel pay TV services are available; about a dozen radio stations, some of which are repeater stations

Internet country code: .as

Internet users: *percent of population:* 40.3% (1990 est.)

TRANSPORTATION

Airports: 3 (2025)
comparison ranking: 191

Ports: *total ports:* 1 (2024)
large: 0
medium: 0
small: 1
very small: 0
ports with oil terminals: 1
key ports: Pago Pago Harbor

MILITARY AND SECURITY

Military - note: defense is the responsibility of the US

ANDORRA

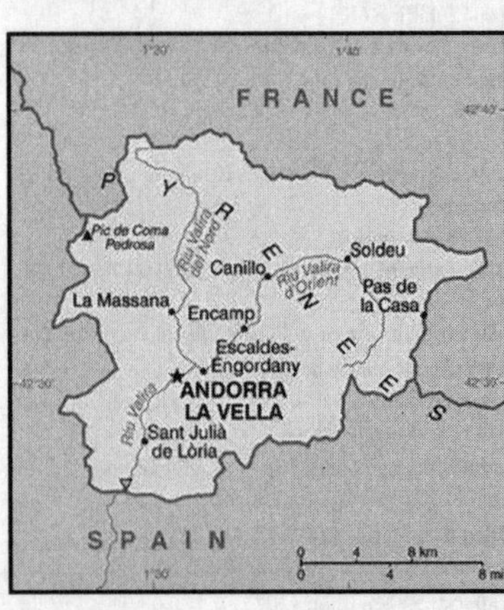

INTRODUCTION

Background: The landlocked Principality of Andorra – one of the smallest states in Europe and nestled high in the Pyrenees between the French and Spanish borders – is the last independent survivor of the Hispanic March states created by Frankish King Charlemagne in 795 after he halted the Moorish invasion of Spain. The March states were a series of buffer states to keep the Muslim Moors from advancing into Christian France. For 715 years, from 1278 to 1993, Andorrans lived under a unique co-principality, ruled by French and Spanish leaders (from 1607 onward, the French chief of state and the Bishop of Urgell). In 1993, this feudal system was modified with the introduction of a modern constitution; the co-princes remained as titular heads of state, but the government transformed into a parliamentary democracy.

Andorra's winter sports, summer climate, and duty-free shopping attract approximately 8 million people each year. Andorra has also become a wealthy international commercial center because of its mature banking sector and low taxes. As part of the effort to modernize its economy, Andorra has opened to foreign investment and engaged in other reforms, such as tax initiatives aimed at supporting broader infrastructure. Although not a member of the EU, Andorra enjoys a special relationship with the bloc that is governed by various customs and cooperation agreements, and Andorra uses the euro as its national currency.

GEOGRAPHY

Location: Southwestern Europe, Pyrenees mountains, on the border between France and Spain

Geographic coordinates: 42 30 N, 1 30 E

Map references: Europe

Area: *total:* 468 sq km
land: 468 sq km
water: 0 sq km
comparison ranking: total 195

Area - comparative: 2.5 times the size of Washington, D.C.

Land boundaries: *total:* 118 km
border countries (2): France 55 km; Spain 63 km

Coastline: 0 km (landlocked)

Maritime claims: none (landlocked)

Climate: temperate; snowy, cold winters and warm, dry summers

Terrain: rugged mountains dissected by narrow valleys

Elevation: *highest point:* Pic de Coma Pedrosa 2,946 m
lowest point: Riu Runer 840 m
mean elevation: 1,996 m

Natural resources: hydropower, mineral water, timber, iron ore, lead

Land use: *agricultural land:* 39.9% (2022 est.)
arable land: 1.6% (2022 est.)
permanent crops: 0% (2022 est.)
permanent pasture: 38.3% (2022 est.)
forest: 34% (2022 est.)
other: 26.1% (2022 est.)

Irrigated land: 0 sq km (2022)

Population distribution: population is unevenly distributed and is concentrated in the seven urbanized valleys that make up the country's parishes (political administrative divisions)

Natural hazards: avalanches

Geography - note: landlocked; straddles a number of important crossroads in the Pyrenees

PEOPLE AND SOCIETY

Population: *total:* 85,370 (2024 est.)
male: 43,652
female: 41,718
comparison rankings: total 199; male 199; female 199

Nationality: *noun:* Andorran(s)
adjective: Andorran

Ethnic groups: Spanish 34.3%, Andorran 32.1%, Portuguese 10%, French 5.6%, other 18% (2024 est.)
note: data represent population by country of birth

Languages: Catalan (official) 44.1%, Castilian 40.3%, Portuguese 13.5%, French 10%, English 3%, other 6.8% (2022 est.)
note: data represent mother tongue

Religions: Christian (predominantly Roman Catholic) 89.5, other 8.8%, unaffiliated 1.7% (2020 est.)

Age structure: *0-14 years:* 12% (male 5,276/female 4,954)
15-64 years: 67.7% (male 29,562/female 28,201)
65 years and over: 20.4% (2024 est.) (male 8,814/female 8,563)

Dependency ratios: *total dependency ratio:* 47.8 (2024 est.)
youth dependency ratio: 17.7 (2024 est.)
elderly dependency ratio: 30.1 (2024 est.)
potential support ratio: 3.3 (2024 est.)

Median age: *total:* 48.8 years (2024 est.)
male: 48.7 years
female: 48.8 years
comparison ranking: total 4

Population growth rate: -0.12% (2024 est.)
comparison ranking: 205

Birth rate: 6.9 births/1,000 population (2024 est.)
comparison ranking: 224

Death rate: 8.1 deaths/1,000 population (2024 est.)
comparison ranking: 85

Net migration rate: 0 migrant(s)/1,000 population (2024 est.)
comparison ranking: 79

Population distribution: population is unevenly distributed and is concentrated in the seven urbanized valleys that make up the country's parishes (political administrative divisions)

Urbanization: *urban population:* 87.8% of total population (2023)
rate of urbanization: 0.11% annual rate of change (2020-25 est.)

Major urban areas - population: 23,000 ANDORRA LA VELLA (capital) (2018)

Sex ratio: *at birth:* 1.06 male(s)/female
0-14 years: 1.06 male(s)/female
15-64 years: 1.05 male(s)/female
65 years and over: 1.03 male(s)/female
total population: 1.05 male(s)/female (2024 est.)

Mother's mean age at first birth: 32.8 years (2019)

Maternal mortality ratio: 11 deaths/100,000 live births (2023 est.)
comparison ranking: 147

Infant mortality rate: *total:* 3.3 deaths/1,000 live births (2024 est.)
male: 3.4 deaths/1,000 live births
female: 3.2 deaths/1,000 live births
comparison ranking: total 200

Life expectancy at birth: *total population:* 83.8 years (2024 est.)
male: 81.6 years
female: 86.2 years
comparison ranking: total population 10

Total fertility rate: 1.47 children born/woman (2024 est.)
comparison ranking: 204

Gross reproduction rate: 0.71 (2024 est.)

Drinking water source: *improved: urban:* 100% of population (2022 est.)
rural: 100% of population (2022 est.)
total: 100% of population (2022 est.)

Health expenditure: 8.3% of GDP (2021)
15.9% of national budget (2022 est.)

Physician density: 5.07 physicians/1,000 population (2023)

Sanitation facility access: *improved: urban:* 100% of population (2022 est.)
rural: 100% of population (2022 est.)
total: 100% of population (2022 est.)

Obesity - adult prevalence rate: 25.6% (2016)
comparison ranking: 50

Alcohol consumption per capita: *total:* 10.99 liters of pure alcohol (2019 est.)
beer: 3.59 liters of pure alcohol (2019 est.)
wine: 4.98 liters of pure alcohol (2019 est.)
spirits: 2.32 liters of pure alcohol (2019 est.)
other alcohols: 0 liters of pure alcohol (2019 est.)
comparison ranking: total 12

Tobacco use: *total:* 33% (2025 est.)
male: 31.7% (2025 est.)
female: 34.4% (2025 est.)
comparison ranking: total 14

Education expenditure: 1.9% of GDP (2023 est.)
12% national budget (2024 est.)
comparison ranking: Education expenditure (% GDP) 187

School life expectancy (primary to tertiary education): *total:* 14 years (2023 est.)
male: 14 years (2023 est.)
female: 15 years (2023 est.)

ENVIRONMENT

Environmental issues: deforestation; soil erosion from overgrazing; air pollution; wastewater treatment and solid waste disposal

International environmental agreements: *party to:* Biodiversity, Climate Change, Climate Change-Paris Agreement, Comprehensive Nuclear Test Ban, Desertification, Hazardous Wastes, Ozone Layer Protection, Wetlands
signed, but not ratified: none of the selected agreements

Climate: temperate; snowy, cold winters and warm, dry summers

Urbanization: *urban population:* 87.8% of total population (2023)
rate of urbanization: 0.11% annual rate of change (2020-25 est.)

Particulate matter emissions: 8.5 micrograms per cubic meter (2019 est.)

Waste and recycling: *municipal solid waste generated annually:* 43,000 tons (2024 est.)

Total renewable water resources: 315.6 million cubic meters (2022 est.)

GOVERNMENT

Country name: *conventional long form:* Principality of Andorra
conventional short form: Andorra
local long form: Principat d'Andorra
local short form: Andorra
etymology: the origin of the country's name is obscure; may originate from the Navarrese word *andurrial*, meaning "shrub-covered land;" alternatively, may derive from the Arabic *addarra* meaning "the forest," a reference to its location; many other theories exist

Government type: parliamentary democracy (since March 1993) that retains its chiefs of state in the form of a co-principality; the two princes are the President of France and Bishop of Seu d'Urgell, Spain

Capital: *name:* Andorra la Vella
geographic coordinates: 42 30 N, 1 31 E
time difference: UTC+1 (6 hours ahead of Washington, DC during Standard Time)
daylight saving time: +1hr, begins last Sunday in March; ends last Sunday in October
etymology: translates as "Andorra the Old" in Catalan

Administrative divisions: 7 parishes (*parroques*, singular - *parroquia*); Andorra la Vella, Canillo, Encamp, Escaldes-Engordany, La Massana, Ordino, Sant Julia de Loria

Legal system: mixed legal system of civil and customary law with the influence of canon (religious) law

Constitution: *history:* drafted 1991, approved by referendum 14 March 1993, effective 28 April 1993
amendment process: proposed by the co-princes jointly or by the General Council; passage requires at least a two-thirds majority vote by the General Council, ratification in a referendum, and sanctioning by the co-princes

International law organization participation: has not submitted an ICJ jurisdiction declaration; accepts ICCt jurisdiction

Citizenship: *citizenship by birth:* no
citizenship by descent only: the mother must be an Andorran citizen or the father must have been born in Andorra and both parents maintain permanent residence in Andorra
dual citizenship recognized: no
residency requirement for naturalization: 25 years

Suffrage: 18 years of age; universal

Executive branch: *chief of state:* Co-prince Emmanuel MACRON (since 14 May 2017); represented by Patrick STROZDA (since 14 May 2017); and Co-prince Archbishop Joan-Enric VIVES i Sicilia (since 12 May 2003); represented by Eduard Ibanez PULIDO (since 27 November 2023)
head of government: Prime Minister Xavier Espot ZAMORA (since 16 May 2019)
cabinet: Executive Council composed of head of government and 11 ministers designated by the head of government
election/appointment process: head of government indirectly elected by the General Council (Andorran parliament), formally appointed by the co-princes for a 4-year term; the leader of the majority party in the General Council is usually elected head of government
most recent election date: 2 April 2023
election results: *2023:* Xaviar Espot ZAMORA (DA) reelected head of government; percent of General Council vote - 57.1%
2019: Xaviar Espot ZAMORA (DA) elected head of government; percent of General Council vote - 60.7
expected date of next election: April 2027

Legislative branch: *legislature name:* General Council (Consell General)
legislative structure: unicameral
number of seats: 28 (all directly elected)
electoral system: mixed system
scope of elections: full renewal
term in office: 4 years
most recent election date: 4/2/2023
parties elected and seats per party: Democrats for Andorra (DA) and its allies (17); Concordia (Concòrdia) and its allies (5); Andorra Forward (Andorra Endavant) (3); Social Democrat Party (PS) - Social Democracy and Progress (SDP) (3)
percentage of women in chamber: 50%
expected date of next election: April 2027
note: voters cast two separate ballots – one for the national election and one for their parish

Judicial branch: *highest court(s):* Supreme Court of Justice of Andorra or Tribunal Superior de la Justicia d'Andorra (consists of the court president and 8 judges organized into civil, criminal, and administrative chambers); Constitutional Court or Tribunal Constitucional (consists of 4 magistrates)
judge selection and term of office: Supreme Court president and judges appointed by the Supreme Council of Justice, a 5-member judicial policy and administrative body appointed 1 each by the co-princes, 1 by the General Council, 1 by the executive council president, and 1 by the courts; judges serve 6-year renewable terms; Constitutional magistrates - 2 appointed by the co-princes and 2 by the General Council; magistrates' appointments limited to 2 consecutive 8-year terms
subordinate courts: Tribunal of Judges or Tribunal de Batlles; Tribunal of the Courts or Tribunal de Corts

Political parties: Action for Andorra or ACCIO
Committed Citizens or CC
Concord or C
Democrats for Andorra or DA
Forward Andorra or AE
Liberals of Andorra or L'A
Social Democratic Party or PS

Social Democracy and Progress or SDP

Diplomatic representation in the US: *chief of mission:* Ambassador Joan FORNER ROVIRA (since 13 January 2025); note - also Permanent Representative to the UN
chancery: 2 United Nations Plaza, 27th Floor, New York, NY 10017
telephone: [1] (212) 750-8064

FAX: [1] (212) 750-6630
email address and website: contact@andorraun.org
https://www.exteriors.ad/en/embassies-of-andorra/andorra-usa-embassy

Diplomatic representation from the US: *embassy:* the US does not have an embassy in Andorra; the US ambassador to Spain is accredited to Andorra; US interests in Andorra are represented by the US Consulate General's office in Barcelona (Spain); mailing address: Paseo Reina Elisenda de Montcada, 23, 08034 Barcelona, Espana; telephone: [34] (93) 280-22-27; FAX: [34] (93) 280-61-75; email address: Barcelonaacs@state.gov

International organization participation: CE, FAO, ICAO, ICC (NGOs), ICCt, ICRM, IFRCS, Interpol, IOC, IPU, ITU, OIF, OPCW, OSCE, UN, UNCTAD, UNESCO, Union Latina, UNWTO, WCO, WHO, WIPO, WTO (observer)

Independence: 1278 (formed under the joint sovereignty of the French Count of Foix and the Spanish Bishop of Urgell)

National holiday: Our Lady of Meritxell Day, 8 September (1278)

Flag: *description:* three vertical bands of blue (left side), yellow, and red, with the national coat of arms centered in the yellow band, which is slightly wider than the other two; the coat of arms features a quartered shield with the emblems of Urgell, Foix, Bearn, and Catalonia; the motto reads VIRTUS UNITA FORTIOR (Strength United is Stronger)
meaning: the flag combines the blue and red French colors with the red and yellow of Spain to symbolize Franco-Spanish protection
note: similar to the flags of Chad and Romania, which do not have a national coat of arms in the center, and the flag of Moldova, which does bear a national emblem

National symbol(s): red cow (breed unspecified)

National color(s): blue, yellow, red

National anthem(s): *title:* "El Gran Carlemany" (The Great Charlemagne)
lyrics/music: Joan BENLLOCH i VIVO/Enric MARFANY BONS
history: adopted 1921; the anthem provides a brief history of Andorra in a first-person narrative

National heritage: *total World Heritage Sites:* 1 (cultural)
selected World Heritage Site locales: Madriu-Perafita-Claror Valley

ECONOMY

Economic overview: high GDP; low unemployment; non-EU Euro user; co-principality duty-free area between Spain and France; tourist hub but hit hard by COVID-19; modern, non-tax haven financial sector; looking for big tech investments; new member of SEPA and IMF

Real GDP (purchasing power parity): $5.402 billion (2024 est.)
$5.226 billion (2023 est.)
$5.094 billion (2022 est.)
note: data in 2021 dollars
comparison ranking: 183

Real GDP growth rate: 3.4% (2024 est.)
2.6% (2023 est.)
9.6% (2022 est.)
note: annual GDP % growth based on constant local currency
comparison ranking: 100

Real GDP per capita: $65,900 (2024 est.)
$64,600 (2023 est.)
$63,900 (2022 est.)
note: data in 2021 dollars
comparison ranking: 23

GDP (official exchange rate): $4.04 billion (2024 est.)
note: data in current dollars at official exchange rate

Inflation rate (consumer prices): 6.2% (2022 est.)
1.7% (2021 est.)
0.1% (2020 est.)
note: annual % change based on consumer prices
comparison ranking: 155

GDP - composition, by sector of origin: *agriculture:* 0.5% (2024 est.)
industry: 12.8% (2024 est.)
services: 77.6% (2024 est.)
note: figures may not total 100% due to non-allocated consumption not captured in sector-reported data
comparison rankings: agriculture 189; industry 172; services 14

Agricultural products: small quantities of rye, wheat, barley, oats, vegetables, tobacco, sheep, cattle

Industries: tourism (particularly skiing), banking, timber, furniture

Industrial production growth rate: 6% (2024 est.)
note: annual % change in industrial value added based on constant local currency
comparison ranking: 32

Remittances: 1.3% of GDP (2023 est.)
1.3% of GDP (2022 est.)
1.6% of GDP (2021 est.)
note: personal transfers and compensation between resident and non-resident individuals/households/entities

Budget: *revenues:* $1.054 billion (2023 est.)
expenditures: $989.38 million (2023 est.)
note: central government revenues (excluding grants) and expenditures converted to US dollars at average official exchange rate for year indicated

Current account balance: $538.287 million (2023 est.)
$393.62 million (2022 est.)
$499.422 million (2021 est.)
note: balance of payments - net trade and primary/secondary income in current dollars
comparison ranking: 65

Exports: $3.169 billion (2023 est.)
$2.736 billion (2022 est.)
$2.446 billion (2021 est.)
note: balance of payments - exports of goods and services in current dollars
comparison ranking: 154

Exports - partners: Spain 39%, USA 21%, France 11%, UK 5%, UAE 3% (2023)
note: top five export partners based on percentage share of exports

Exports - commodities: paintings, integrated circuits, cars, orthopedic appliances, garments (2023)
note: top five export commodities based on value in dollars

Imports: $2.716 billion (2023 est.)
$2.44 billion (2022 est.)
$2.143 billion (2021 est.)
note: balance of payments - imports of goods and services in current dollars
comparison ranking: 166

Imports - partners: Spain 65%, France 11%, Germany 4%, China 3%, Italy 3% (2023)
note: top five import partners based on percentage share of imports

Imports - commodities: cars, refined petroleum, garments, perfumes, electricity (2023)
note: top five import commodities based on value in dollars

Exchange rates: euros (EUR) per US dollar -

Exchange rates: 0.924 (2024 est.)
0.925 (2023 est.)
0.951 (2022 est.)
0.845 (2021 est.)
0.876 (2020 est.)
note: while not an EU member state, Andorra has a 2011 monetary agreement with the EU to produce limited euro coinage—but not banknotes—that began enforcement in April 2012

ENERGY

Electricity access: *electrification - total population:* 100% (2022 est.)

COMMUNICATIONS

Telephones - fixed lines: *total subscriptions:* 52,000 (2023 est.)
subscriptions per 100 inhabitants: 64 (2023 est.)
comparison ranking: total subscriptions 153

Telephones - mobile cellular: *total subscriptions:* 126,000 (2023 est.)
subscriptions per 100 inhabitants: 142 (2022 est.)
comparison ranking: total subscriptions 190

Broadcast media: the media scene is partly shaped by the proximity to France and Spain; Andorrans have access to broadcasts from both countries (2023)

Internet country code: .ad

Internet users: *percent of population:* 95% (2023 est.)

Broadband - fixed subscriptions: *total:* 42,000 (2023 est.)
subscriptions per 100 inhabitants: 52 (2023 est.)
comparison ranking: total 148

TRANSPORTATION

Civil aircraft registration country code prefix: C3

Heliports: 2 (2025)
comparison ranking: 126

MILITARY AND SECURITY

Military and security forces: no regular military forces; Police Corps of Andorra (under the Ministry of Justice and Interior)

Military - note: defense is the responsibility of France and Spain

ANGOLA

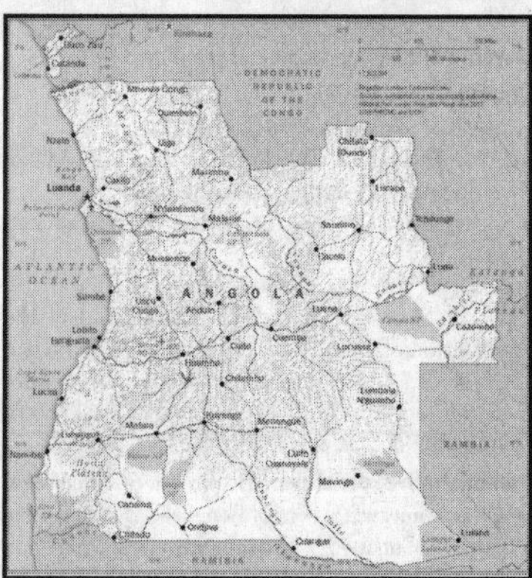

INTRODUCTION

Background: Bantu-speaking people settled in the area now called Angola in 6th century A.D.; by the 10th century various Bantu groups had established kingdoms, of which Kongo became the most powerful. From the late-14th to the mid-19th century, a Kingdom of Kongo stretched across central Africa from present-day northern Angola into the current Congo republics. It traded heavily with the Portuguese who, beginning in the 16th century, established coastal colonies and trading posts and introduced Christianity. Angola became a major hub of the transatlantic slave trade conducted by the Portuguese and other European powers – often in collaboration with local kingdoms, including the Kongo. The Angola area is estimated to have lost as many as 4 million people as a result of the slave trade. The Kingdom of Kongo's main rival was the Kingdom of Ndongo to its south, whose most famous leader was Nzingha Mbande, the 17th century diplomat to the Portuguese and later Queen, who successfully fought off Portuguese encroachment during her nearly 40-year reign. Smaller kingdoms, such as the Matamba and Ngoyo, often came under the control of the Kongo or Ndongo Kingdoms. During the Berlin Conference of 1884-85, Portugal and other European powers set Angola's modern borders, but the Portuguese did not fully control large portions of the territory. Portugal gained control of the Kingdom of Kongo in 1888 when Kongo's King Pedro V sought Portuguese military assistance in exchange for becoming a vassal. After a revolt in 1914, Portugal imposed direct rule over the colony and abolished the Kongo Kingdom.

The Angolan National Revolution began in 1961, and in 1975, Angola won its independence when Portugal's dictatorship fell, a collapse that occurred in part because of growing discontent over conflict in Angola and other colonies. Angola's multiple independence movements soon clashed, with the Popular Movement for Liberation of Angola (MPLA), led by Agostinho NETO, taking power and the National Union for the Total Independence of Angola (UNITA), led by Jonas SAVIMBI, emerging as its main competitor. After NETO's death in 1979, Jose Eduardo DOS SANTOS, also of the MPLA, became president. Over time, the Angolan civil war escalated and became a major Cold War conflict, with the Soviet Union and Cuba supporting the MPLA and the US and South Africa supporting UNITA. Up to 1.5 million lives may have been lost – and 4 million people displaced – during the more than a quarter-century of fighting. SAVIMBI's death in 2002 ended UNITA's insurgency and cemented the MPLA's hold on power. DOS SANTOS did not seek reelection in 2017 and supported Joao LOURENCO's successful bid to become president. LOURENCO was reelected in 2022. Angola scores low on human development indexes despite using its large oil reserves to rebuild since 2002.

GEOGRAPHY

Location: Southern Africa, bordering the South Atlantic Ocean, between Namibia and Democratic Republic of the Congo

Geographic coordinates: 12 30 S, 18 30 E

Map references: Africa

Area: *total:* 1,246,700 sq km
land: 1,246,700 sq km
water: 0 sq km
comparison ranking: total 24

Area - comparative: about eight times the size of Georgia; slightly less than twice the size of Texas

Land boundaries: *total:* 5,369 km
border countries (4): Democratic Republic of the Congo 2,646 km (of which 225 km is the boundary of discontiguous Cabinda Province); Republic of the Congo 231 km; Namibia 1,427 km; Zambia 1,065 km

Coastline: 1,600 km

Maritime claims: *territorial sea:* 12 nm
contiguous zone: 24 nm
exclusive economic zone: 200 nm

Climate: semiarid in south and along coast to Luanda; north has cool, dry season (May to October) and hot, rainy season (November to April)

Terrain: narrow coastal plain rises abruptly to vast interior plateau

Elevation: *highest point:* Moca 2,620 m
lowest point: Atlantic Ocean 0 m
mean elevation: 1,112 m

Natural resources: petroleum, diamonds, iron ore, phosphates, copper, feldspar, gold, bauxite, uranium

Land use: *agricultural land:* 36.8% (2022 est.)
arable land: 4.3% (2022 est.)
permanent crops: 0.3% (2022 est.)
permanent pasture: 32.3% (2022 est.)
forest: 52.5% (2022 est.)
other: 10.6% (2022 est.)

Irrigated land: 860 sq km (2014)

Major rivers (by length in km): Rio Zambeze (Zambezi) (shared with Zambia [s], Namibia, Botswana, Zimbabwe, and Mozambique [m]) - 2,740 km; Rio Cubango (Okavango) river source (shared with Namibia and Botswana [m]) - 1,600 km
note: [s] after country name indicates river source; [m] after country name indicates river mouth

Major watersheds (area sq km): Atlantic Ocean drainage: Congo (3,730,881 sq km)

Indian Ocean drainage: Zambezi (1,332,412 sq km)

Internal (endorheic basin) drainage: Okavango Basin (863,866 sq km)

Major aquifers: Congo Basin, Upper Kalahari-Cuvelai-Upper Zambezi Basin

Population distribution: most people live in the western half of the country; urban areas account for the highest concentrations of people, particularly the capital of Luanda

Natural hazards: locally heavy rainfall causes periodic flooding on the plateau

Geography - note: the province of Cabinda is an exclave, separated from the rest of the country by the Democratic Republic of the Congo

PEOPLE AND SOCIETY

Population: *total:* 37,202,061 (2024 est.)
male: 18,196,058
female: 19,006,003
comparison rankings: total 40; male 42; female 39

Nationality: *noun:* Angolan(s)
adjective: Angolan

Ethnic groups: Ovimbundu 37%, Kimbundu 25%, Bakongo 13%, Mestico (mixed European and native African) 2%, European 1%, other 22%

Languages: Portuguese 71.2% (official), Umbundu 23%, Kikongo 8.2%, Kimbundu 7.8%, Chokwe 6.5%, Nhaneca 3.4%, Nganguela 3.1%, Fiote 2.4%, Kwanhama 2.3%, Muhumbi 2.1%, Luvale 1%, other 3.6% (2014 est.)
note: shares sum to more than 100% because some respondents gave more than one answer on the census

Religions: Roman Catholic 41.1%, Protestant 38.1%, other 8.6%, none 12.3% (2014 est.)

Age structure: *0-14 years:* 46.9% (male 8,752,419/female 8,701,422)
15-64 years: 50.7% (male 9,076,080/female 9,795,035)
65 years and over: 2.4% (2024 est.) (male 367,559/female 509,546)

Dependency ratios: *total dependency ratio:* 96.1 (2024 est.)
youth dependency ratio: 91.1 (2024 est.)
elderly dependency ratio: 5.1 (2024 est.)
potential support ratio: 19.8 (2024 est.)

Median age: *total:* 16.3 years (2024 est.)
male: 15.8 years
female: 16.8 years
comparison ranking: total 227

Population growth rate: 3.33% (2024 est.)
comparison ranking: 3

Birth rate: 41.1 births/1,000 population (2024 est.)
comparison ranking: 2

Death rate: 7.6 deaths/1,000 population (2024 est.)
comparison ranking: 99

Net migration rate: -0.2 migrant(s)/1,000 population (2024 est.)
comparison ranking: 105

Population distribution: most people live in the western half of the country; urban areas account for the highest concentrations of people, particularly the capital of Luanda

Urbanization: *urban population:* 68.7% of total population (2023)
rate of urbanization: 4.04% annual rate of change (2020-25 est.)

Major urban areas - population: 9.292 million LUANDA (capital), 959,000 Lubango, 905,000 Cabinda, 809,000 Benguela, 783,000 Malanje (2023)

Sex ratio: *at birth:* 1.03 male(s)/female
0-14 years: 1.01 male(s)/female
15-64 years: 0.93 male(s)/female
65 years and over: 0.72 male(s)/female
total population: 0.96 male(s)/female (2024 est.)

Mother's mean age at first birth: 19.4 years (2015/16 est.)
note: data represents median age at first birth among women 20-49

Maternal mortality ratio: 183 deaths/100,000 live births (2023 est.)
comparison ranking: 42

Infant mortality rate: *total:* 55.6 deaths/1,000 live births (2024 est.)
male: 60.7 deaths/1,000 live births
female: 50.3 deaths/1,000 live births
comparison ranking: total 13

Life expectancy at birth: *total population:* 62.9 years (2024 est.)
male: 60.8 years
female: 65.1 years
comparison ranking: total population 214

Total fertility rate: 5.7 children born/woman (2024 est.)
comparison ranking: 2

Gross reproduction rate: 2.81 (2024 est.)

Drinking water source: *improved: urban:* 71.7% of population (2022 est.)
rural: 27.8% of population (2022 est.)
total: 57.7% of population (2022 est.)
unimproved: urban: 28.3% of population (2022 est.)
rural: 72.2% of population (2022 est.)
total: 42.3% of population (2022 est.)

Health expenditure: 3% of GDP (2021)
6.7% of national budget (2022 est.)

Physician density: 0.24 physicians/1,000 population (2022)

Hospital bed density: 0.8 beds/1,000 population (2019 est.)

Sanitation facility access: *improved: urban:* 93.7% of population (2022 est.)
rural: 30.3% of population (2022 est.)
total: 73.5% of population (2022 est.)
unimproved: urban: 6.3% of population (2022 est.)
rural: 69.7% of population (2022 est.)
total: 26.5% of population (2022 est.)

Obesity - adult prevalence rate: 8.2% (2016)
comparison ranking: 154

Alcohol consumption per capita: *total:* 5.84 liters of pure alcohol (2019 est.)
beer: 3.78 liters of pure alcohol (2019 est.)
wine: 0.72 liters of pure alcohol (2019 est.)
spirits: 1.27 liters of pure alcohol (2019 est.)
other alcohols: 0.08 liters of pure alcohol (2019 est.)
comparison ranking: total 73

Children under the age of 5 years underweight: 19% (2015/16)
comparison ranking: 18

Currently married women (ages 15-49): 55.7% (2023 est.)

Child marriage: *women married by age 15:* 7.9% (2016)
women married by age 18: 30.3% (2016)
men married by age 18: 6% (2016)

Education expenditure: 2.5% of GDP (2023 est.)
6.5% national budget (2025 est.)
comparison ranking: Education expenditure (% GDP) 173

Literacy: *total population:* 66.2% (2015 est.)
male: 83.8% (2015 est.)
female: 51.9% (2015 est.)

ENVIRONMENT

Environmental issues: overuse of pastures and subsequent soil erosion; desertification; deforestation of tropical rainforest from international demand for timber and domestic use as fuel; loss of biodiversity; soil erosion contributing to water pollution and siltation of rivers and dams; inadequate supplies of potable water

International environmental agreements: *party to:* Biodiversity, Climate Change, Climate Change-Kyoto Protocol, Climate Change-Paris Agreement, Comprehensive Nuclear Test Ban, Desertification, Endangered Species, Hazardous Wastes, Law of the Sea, Marine Dumping-London Protocol, Ozone Layer Protection, Ship Pollution
signed, but not ratified: none of the selected agreements

Climate: semiarid in south and along coast to Luanda; north has cool, dry season (May to October) and hot, rainy season (November to April)

Urbanization: *urban population:* 68.7% of total population (2023)
rate of urbanization: 4.04% annual rate of change (2020-25 est.)

Carbon dioxide emissions: 19.66 million metric tonnes of CO_2 (2023 est.)
from coal and metallurgical coke: 9,000 metric tonnes of CO_2 (2023 est.)
from petroleum and other liquids: 17.21 million metric tonnes of CO_2 (2023 est.)
from consumed natural gas: 2.441 million metric tonnes of CO_2 (2023 est.)
comparison ranking: total emissions 86

Particulate matter emissions: 27.2 micrograms per cubic meter (2019 est.)

Methane emissions: *energy:* 1,009.1 kt (2022-2024 est.)
agriculture: 374.5 kt (2019-2021 est.)
waste: 123 kt (2019-2021 est.)
other: 78.5 kt (2019-2021 est.)

Waste and recycling: *municipal solid waste generated annually:* 4.214 million tons (2024 est.)
percent of municipal solid waste recycled: 19% (2022 est.)

Total water withdrawal: *municipal:* 319.5 million cubic meters (2022 est.)
industrial: 239.6 million cubic meters (2022 est.)
agricultural: 146.7 million cubic meters (2022 est.)

Total renewable water resources: 148.4 billion cubic meters (2022 est.)

GOVERNMENT

Country name: *conventional long form:* Republic of Angola
conventional short form: Angola
local long form: Republica de Angola
local short form: Angola
former: People's Republic of Angola
etymology: in the 15th century, Portuguese explorers derived the name from the title "N'gola," which was held by kings of the Ndongo

Government type: presidential republic

Capital: *name:* Luanda
geographic coordinates: 8 50 S, 13 13 E
time difference: UTC+1 (6 hours ahead of Washington, DC, during Standard Time)
daylight saving time: does not observe daylight savings time
etymology: the Portuguese named the city São Paulo da Assunção de Loanda (Saint Paul of the Assumption of Loanda); over time, it was shortened to "Luanda," which may derive from a Bantu word meaning "tax" or "duty," in reference to local people paying their dues to the king of the Congo

Administrative divisions: 21 provinces (*provincias*, singular - *provincia*); Bengo, Benguela, Bie, Cabinda, Cuando, Cubango, Cuanza-Norte, Cuanza-Sul, Cunene, Huambo, Huila, Icolo e Bengo, Luanda, Lunda-Norte, Lunda-Sul, Malanje, Moxico, Moxico Leste, Namibe, Uige, Zaire

Legal system: civil legal system based on Portuguese civil law; no judicial review of legislation

Constitution: *history:* previous 1975, 1992; latest passed by National Assembly 21 January 2010, adopted 5 February 2010
amendment process: proposed by the president of the republic or supported by at least one third of the National Assembly membership; passage requires at least two-thirds majority vote of the Assembly subject to prior Constitutional Court review if requested by the president of the republic

International law organization participation: has not submitted an ICJ jurisdiction declaration; non-party state to the ICCt

Citizenship: *citizenship by birth:* no
citizenship by descent only: at least one parent must be a citizen of Angola
dual citizenship recognized: no
residency requirement for naturalization: 10 years

Suffrage: 18 years of age; universal

Executive branch: *chief of state:* President Joao Manuel Goncalves LOURENCO (since 26 September 2017)
head of government: President Joao Manuel Goncalves LOURENCO (since 26 September 2017)
cabinet: Council of Ministers appointed by the president
election/appointment process: the candidate of the winning party or coalition in the last legislative election becomes the president; president serves a 5-year term (eligible for a second consecutive or discontinuous term)
most recent election date: 24 August 2022
election results: Joao Manuel Goncalves LOURENCO (MPLA) elected president by then winning party following the 24 August 2022 general election
expected date of next election: 2027

Legislative branch: *legislature name:* National Assembly (Assembleia nacional)
legislative structure: unicameral
number of seats: 220 (all directly elected)
electoral system: proportional representation
scope of elections: full renewal
term in office: 5 years
most recent election date: 8/24/2022

parties elected and seats per party: Popular Movement for the Liberation of Angola (MPLA) (124); National Union for the Total Independence of Angola (UNITA) (90); Other (6)
percentage of women in chamber: 39.1%
expected date of next election: August 2027

Judicial branch: *highest court(s):* Supreme Court or Tribunal Supremo (consists of the court president, vice president, and a minimum of 16 judges); Constitutional Court or Tribunal Constitucional (consists of 11 judges)
judge selection and term of office: Supreme Court judges appointed by the president on recommendation of the Supreme Judicial Council, an 18-member body chaired by the president; judge tenure NA; Constitutional Court judges - 4 nominated by the president, 4 elected by National Assembly, 2 elected by Supreme National Council, 1 elected by competitive submission of curricula; judges serve single 7-year terms
subordinate courts: provincial and municipal courts

Political parties: Broad Convergence for the Salvation of Angola Electoral Coalition or CASA-CE
Humanist Party of Angola or PHI
National Front for the Liberation of Angola or FNLA; note - party has two factions
National Union for the Total Independence of Angola or UNITA (largest opposition party)
Popular Movement for the Liberation of Angola or MPLA; note- ruling party in power since 1975
Social Renewal Party or PRS

Diplomatic representation in the US: *chief of mission:* Ambassador Agostinho de Carvalho dos Santos VAN-DÚNEM (since 30 June 2023)
chancery: 2108 16th Street NW, Washington, DC 20009
telephone: [1] (202) 785-1156

FAX: [1] (202) 822-9049
email address and website: info@angola.org
https://angola.org/
consulate(s) general: Houston, New York

Diplomatic representation from the US: *chief of mission:* Ambassador (vacant); Chargé d'Affaires Ambassador Noah ZARING (since March 2025)
embassy: Rua Houari Boumedienne, #32, Luanda
mailing address: 2550 Luanda Place, Washington, DC 20521-2550
telephone: [244] (222) 64-1000

FAX: [244] (222) 64-1000
email address and website: Consularluanda@state.gov
https://ao.usembassy.gov/

International organization participation: ACP, AfDB, AU, CEMAC, CPLP, FAO, G-77, IAEA, IBRD, ICAO, ICRM, IDA, IFAD, IFC, IFRCS, ILO, IMF, IMO, Interpol, IOC, IOM, IPU, ISO (correspondent), ITSO, ITU, ITUC (NGOs), MIGA, NAM, OAS (observer), SADC, UN, UNCTAD, UNESCO, UNHCR, UNIDO, UNMISS, Union Latina, UNOOSA, UNWTO, UPU, WCO, WFTU (NGOs), WHO, WIPO, WMO, WTO

Independence: 11 November 1975 (from Portugal)

National holiday: Independence Day, 11 November (1975)

Flag: *description:* two equal horizontal bands of red (top) and black with a centered yellow emblem of a five-pointed star inside half a cogwheel, crossed by a machete (in the style of a hammer and sickle)
meaning: red stands for liberty and black for the African continent; the emblem symbolizes workers and peasants

National symbol(s): giant black sable antelope (*Palanca negra gigante*)

National color(s): red, black, yellow

National anthem(s): *title:* "Angola Avante" (Forward Angola)
lyrics/music: Manuel Rui Alves MONTEIRO/Rui Alberto Vieira Dias MINGAO
history: adopted 1975

National heritage: *total World Heritage Sites:* 1 (cultural)
selected World Heritage Site locales: Mbanza-Kongo

ECONOMY

Economic overview: middle-income, oil-dependent African economy; widespread poverty; rising inflation and currency depreciation; seeking diversification through agricultural production; significant corruption in public institutions; major infrastructure investments from China and US; exited OPEC in 2023

Real GDP (purchasing power parity): $278.239 billion (2024 est.)
$266.452 billion (2023 est.)
$263.61 billion (2022 est.)
note: data in 2021 dollars
comparison ranking: 64

Real GDP growth rate: 4.4% (2024 est.)
1.1% (2023 est.)
3% (2022 est.)
note: annual GDP % growth based on constant local currency
comparison ranking: 55

Real GDP per capita: $7,300 (2024 est.)
$7,300 (2023 est.)
$7,400 (2022 est.)
note: data in 2021 dollars
comparison ranking: 154

GDP (official exchange rate): $80.397 billion (2024 est.)
note: data in current dollars at official exchange rate

Inflation rate (consumer prices): 28.2% (2024 est.)
13.6% (2023 est.)
21.4% (2022 est.)
note: annual % change based on consumer prices
comparison ranking: 195

GDP - composition, by sector of origin: *agriculture:* 16.4% (2024 est.)
industry: 44.2% (2024 est.)
services: 39.3% (2024 est.)
note: figures may not total 100% due to non-allocated consumption not captured in sector-reported data
comparison rankings: agriculture 51; industry 14; services 194

GDP - composition, by end use: *household consumption:* 55.3% (2024 est.)
government consumption: 6.3% (2024 est.)
investment in fixed capital: 25% (2024 est.)
investment in inventories: 0% (2024 est.)
exports of goods and services: 37.9% (2024 est.)
imports of goods and services: -24.4% (2024 est.)
note: figures may not total 100% due to rounding or gaps in data collection

Agricultural products: cassava, bananas, maize, sweet potatoes, sugarcane, tomatoes, pineapples, onions, potatoes, citrus fruits (2023)
note: top ten agricultural products based on tonnage

Industries: petroleum; diamonds, iron ore, phosphates, feldspar, bauxite, uranium, and gold; cement; basic metal products; fish processing; food processing, brewing, tobacco products, sugar; textiles; ship repair

Industrial production growth rate: 5% (2024 est.)
note: annual % change in industrial value added based on constant local currency
comparison ranking: 44

Labor force: 15.961 million (2024 est.)
note: number of people ages 15 or older who are employed or seeking work
comparison ranking: 41

Unemployment rate: 14.5% (2024 est.)
14.6% (2023 est.)
14.7% (2022 est.)
note: % of labor force seeking employment
comparison ranking: 172

Youth unemployment rate (ages 15-24): *total:* 27.9% (2024 est.)
male: 30.2% (2024 est.)
female: 25.7% (2024 est.)
note: % of labor force ages 15-24 seeking employment
comparison ranking: total 26

Population below poverty line: 32.3% (2018 est.)
note: % of population with income below national poverty line

Gini Index coefficient - distribution of family income: 51.3 (2018 est.)
note: index (0-100) of income distribution; higher values represent greater inequality
comparison ranking: 7

Average household expenditures: *on food:* 50% of household expenditures (2023 est.)
on alcohol and tobacco: 1.4% of household expenditures (2023 est.)

Household income or consumption by percentage share: *lowest 10%:* 1.3% (2018 est.)
highest 10%: 39.6% (2018 est.)
note: % share of income accruing to lowest and highest 10% of population

Remittances: 0% of GDP (2024 est.)
0% of GDP (2023 est.)
0% of GDP (2022 est.)
note: personal transfers and compensation between resident and non-resident individuals/households/entities

Budget: *revenues:* $18.117 billion (2019 est.)
expenditures: $13.871 billion (2019 est.)
note: central government revenues and expenses (excluding grants/extrabudgetary units/social security funds) converted to US dollars at average official exchange rate for year indicated

Taxes and other revenues: 10.1% (of GDP) (2019 est.)
note: central government tax revenue as a % of GDP
comparison ranking: 127

Current account balance: $6.31 billion (2024 est.)
$4.185 billion (2023 est.)
$11.763 billion (2022 est.)
note: balance of payments - net trade and primary/secondary income in current dollars
comparison ranking: 33

Exports: $36.924 billion (2024 est.)
$36.961 billion (2023 est.)
$50.12 billion (2022 est.)
note: balance of payments - exports of goods and services in current dollars

comparison ranking: 77

Exports - partners: China 40%, India 9%, UAE 6%, Spain 6%, Netherlands 5% (2023)
note: top five export partners based on percentage share of exports

Exports - commodities: crude petroleum, diamonds, natural gas, ships, refined petroleum (2023)
note: top five export commodities based on value in dollars

Imports: $22.683 billion (2024 est.)
$23.688 billion (2023 est.)
$28.564 billion (2022 est.)
note: balance of payments - imports of goods and services in current dollars
comparison ranking: 92

Imports - partners: China 19%, Portugal 10%, UAE 7%, India 6%, USA 5% (2023)
note: top five import partners based on percentage share of imports

Imports - commodities: refined petroleum, wheat, ships, cars, trucks (2023)
note: top five import commodities based on value in dollars

Reserves of foreign exchange and gold: $14.243 billion (2024 est.)
$13.942 billion (2023 est.)
$13.655 billion (2022 est.)
note: holdings of gold (year-end prices)/foreign exchange/special drawing rights in current dollars
comparison ranking: 70

Debt - external: $45.299 billion (2023 est.)
note: present value of external debt in current US dollars
comparison ranking: 16

Exchange rates: kwanza (AOA) per US dollar -

Exchange rates: 869.846 (2024 est.)
685.02 (2023 est.)
460.568 (2022 est.)
631.442 (2021 est.)
578.259 (2020 est.)

ENERGY

Electricity access: *electrification - total population:* 48.5% (2022 est.)
electrification - urban areas: 76.2%
electrification - rural areas: 7.3% (2018 est.)

Electricity: *installed generating capacity:* 7.6 million kW (2023 est.)
consumption: 16.214 billion kWh (2023 est.)
transmission/distribution losses: 1.725 billion kWh (2023 est.)
comparison rankings: installed generating capacity 74; consumption 83; transmission/distribution losses 118

Electricity generation sources: *fossil fuels:* 23.6% of total installed capacity (2023 est.)
solar: 2.2% of total installed capacity (2023 est.)
hydroelectricity: 74% of total installed capacity (2023 est.)
biomass and waste: 0.3% of total installed capacity (2023 est.)

Coal: *imports:* 3,000 metric tons (2023 est.)

Petroleum: *total petroleum production:* 1.175 million bbl/day (2023 est.)
refined petroleum consumption: 121,000 bbl/day (2023 est.)
crude oil estimated reserves: 7.783 billion barrels (2021 est.)

Natural gas: *production:* 5.984 billion cubic meters (2023 est.)
consumption: 1.244 billion cubic meters (2023 est.)
exports: 4.928 billion cubic meters (2023 est.)
proven reserves: 343.002 billion cubic meters (2021 est.)

Energy consumption per capita: 9.146 million Btu/person (2023 est.)
comparison ranking: 151

COMMUNICATIONS

Telephones - fixed lines: *total subscriptions:* 87,000 (2023 est.)
subscriptions per 100 inhabitants: (2023 est.) less than 1
comparison ranking: total subscriptions 138

Telephones - mobile cellular: *total subscriptions:* 25.7 million (2023 est.)
subscriptions per 100 inhabitants: 67 (2022 est.)
comparison ranking: total subscriptions 54

Broadcast media: state-owned media dominate; only four privately owned newspapers still exist in print form; state-run Radio Nacional de Angola (RNA) is the only outlet to offer programs in local languages such as Bantu; private stations operate in cities, including Catholic Radio Ecclesia, but RNA is the only radio broadcaster with near-national coverage (2023)

Internet country code: .ao

Internet users: *percent of population:* 45% (2023 est.)

Broadband - fixed subscriptions: *total:* 137,000 (2023 est.)
subscriptions per 100 inhabitants: (2023 est.) less than 1
comparison ranking: total 126

TRANSPORTATION

Civil aircraft registration country code prefix: D2

Airports: 107 (2025)
comparison ranking: 50

Heliports: 2 (2025)
comparison ranking: 141

Railways: *total:* 2,761 km (2022)
narrow gauge: 2,638 km (2022) 1.067-m gauge
123 km 0.600-mm gauge

Merchant marine: *total:* 64 (2023)
by type: general cargo 13, oil tanker 8, other 43
comparison ranking: total 112

Ports: *total ports:* 21 (2024)
large: 0
medium: 0
small: 8
very small: 13
ports with oil terminals: 17
key ports: Cabinda, Estrela Oil Field, Lobito, Luanda, Malongo Oil Terminal, Namibe, Palanca Terminal, Takula Terminal

MILITARY AND SECURITY

Military and security forces: Angolan Armed Forces (Forcas Armadas Angolanas, FAA): Army, Navy (Marinha de Guerra Angola, MGA), Angolan National Air Force (Forca Aerea Nacional Angolana, FANA)

Ministry of Interior: National Police, Border Guard Police (2025)

Military expenditures: 1% of GDP (2024 est.)
1.3% of GDP (2023 est.)
1.3% of GDP (2022 est.)
1.4% of GDP (2021 est.)
1.7% of GDP (2020 est.)

Military and security service personnel strengths: approximately 100,000 active-duty Armed Forces (2025)

Military equipment inventories and acquisitions: most Angolan military weapons and equipment are of Russian or Soviet-era origin; there are smaller quantities of items originating from such suppliers as China, Brazil, and South Africa (2024)

Military service age and obligation: 20-45 years of age for compulsory and 18-45 years for voluntary military service for men (registration at age 18 is mandatory); 20-45 years of age for voluntary service for women; 24-month conscript service obligation; Angolan citizenship required; the Navy is entirely staffed with volunteers (2023)

Military - note: the Angolan Armed Forces were created in 1991 under the Bicesse Accords signed between the Angolan Government and the National Union for the Total Independence of Angola (UNITA); the current force is responsible for country's external defense but also has some domestic security responsibilities, such as border protection; it participates in multinational exercises, as well as regional peacekeeping operations, including the deployment of several hundred troops to the Democratic Republic of the Congo in 2023; in recent years, the military has placed additional emphasis on maritime security and protecting offshore resources (2025)

SPACE

Space agency/agencies: National Space Program Office (Gabinete de Gestão do Programa Espacial Nacional, GGPEN; established 2013) (2025)

Space program overview: has a national space strategy with a focus on capacity-building, developing space infrastructure, investing in domestic space sector, supporting socioeconomic growth, and establishing cooperation agreements with foreign technical and scientific institutions in the space industry; contracts with foreign companies to build and launch satellites; operates satellites; cooperates with a variety of foreign space agencies and industries, including those of France, Portugal, Russia, the US, and other African countries; member of the African Space Agency (2025)
note: further details about the key activities, programs, and milestones of the country's space program, as well as government spending estimates on the space sector, appear in the Space Programs reference guide

TRANSNATIONAL ISSUES

Refugees and internally displaced persons: *refugees:* 55,542 (2024 est.)

IDPs: 75,308 (2024 est.)

ANGUILLA

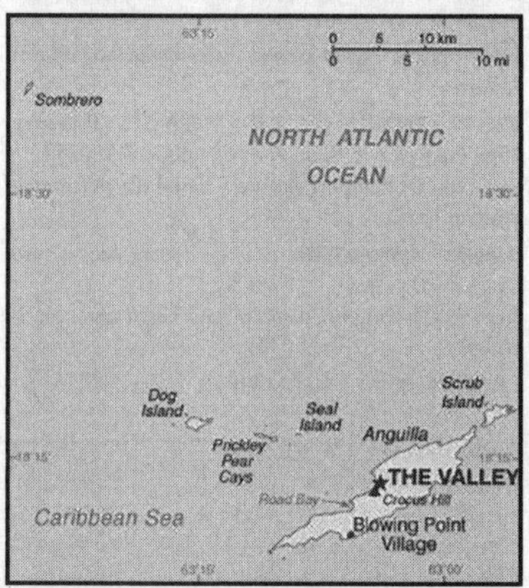

INTRODUCTION

Background: English settlers from Saint Kitts first colonized Anguilla in 1650. Great Britain administered the island until the early 19th century, when – against the wishes of the inhabitants – Anguilla was incorporated into a single British dependency along with Saint Kitts and Nevis. Several attempts at separation failed. In 1971, two years after a revolt, Anguilla was finally allowed to secede; this arrangement was formally recognized in 1980, when Anguilla became a separate British dependency. In 2017, Hurricane Irma caused extensive damage on the island, particularly to communications and residential and business infrastructure.

GEOGRAPHY

Location: Caribbean, islands between the Caribbean Sea and North Atlantic Ocean, east of Puerto Rico

Geographic coordinates: 18 15 N, 63 10 W

Map references: Central America and the Caribbean

Area: *total:* 91 sq km
land: 91 sq km
water: 0 sq km
comparison ranking: total 225

Area - comparative: about one-half the size of Washington, D.C.

Land boundaries: *total:* 0 km

Coastline: 61 km

Maritime claims: *territorial sea:* 12 nm
exclusive economic zone: 200 nm
exclusive fishing zone: 200 nm

Climate: tropical; moderated by northeast trade winds

Terrain: flat and low-lying island of coral and limestone

Elevation: *highest point:* Crocus Hill 73 m
lowest point: Caribbean Sea 0 m

Natural resources: salt, fish, lobster

Land use: *agricultural land:* 0% (2022 est.)
arable land: 0% (2018 est.)
permanent crops: 0% (2018 est.)
permanent pasture: 0% (2018 est.)
forest: 61.1% (2022 est.)
other: 38.9% (2022 est.)

Irrigated land: 0 sq km (2020)

Population distribution: most of the population is concentrated in The Valley in the center of the island; settlement is fairly uniform in the southwest, but rather sparse in the northeast

Natural hazards: frequent hurricanes and other tropical storms (July to October)

Geography - note: the most northerly of the Leeward Islands in the Lesser Antilles

PEOPLE AND SOCIETY

Population: *total:* 19,416 (2024 est.)
male: 9,107
female: 10,309
comparison rankings: total 219; male 219; female 219

Nationality: *noun:* Anguillan(s)
adjective: Anguillan

Ethnic groups: African/Black 85.3%, Hispanic 4.9%, mixed 3.8%, White 3.2%, East Indian/Indian 1%, other 1.6%, unspecified 0.3% (2011 est.)
note: data represent population by ethnic origin

Languages: English (official)

Religions: Protestant 73.2% (includes Anglican 22.7%, Methodist 19.4%, Pentecostal 10.5%, Seventh Day Adventist 8.3%, Baptist 7.1%, Church of God 4.9%, Presbyterian 0.2%, Brethren 0.1%), Roman Catholic 6.8%, Jehovah's Witness 1.1%, other Christian 10.9%, other 3.2%, unspecified 0.3%, none 4.5% (2011 est.)

Age structure: *0-14 years:* 20.8% (male 2,056/female 1,992)
15-64 years: 67.5% (male 5,958/female 7,147)
65 years and over: 11.7% (2024 est.) (male 1,093/female 1,170)

Dependency ratios: *total dependency ratio:* 48.2 (2024 est.)
youth dependency ratio: 30.9 (2024 est.)
elderly dependency ratio: 17.3 (2024 est.)
potential support ratio: 5.8 (2024 est.)

Median age: *total:* 37.1 years (2024 est.)
male: 34.8 years
female: 39 years
comparison ranking: total 83

Population growth rate: 1.74% (2024 est.)
comparison ranking: 53

Birth rate: 11.8 births/1,000 population (2024 est.)
comparison ranking: 154

Death rate: 4.7 deaths/1,000 population (2024 est.)
comparison ranking: 204

Net migration rate: 10.3 migrant(s)/1,000 population (2024 est.)
comparison ranking: 9

Population distribution: most of the population is concentrated in The Valley in the center of the island; settlement is fairly uniform in the southwest, but rather sparse in the northeast

Urbanization: *urban population:* 100% of total population (2023)
rate of urbanization: 0.47% annual rate of change (2020-25 est.)

Major urban areas - population: 1,000 THE VALLEY (capital) (2018)

Sex ratio: *at birth:* 1.03 male(s)/female
0-14 years: 1.03 male(s)/female
15-64 years: 0.83 male(s)/female
65 years and over: 0.93 male(s)/female
total population: 0.88 male(s)/female (2024 est.)

Infant mortality rate: *total:* 3 deaths/1,000 live births (2024 est.)
male: 3.9 deaths/1,000 live births
female: 2.1 deaths/1,000 live births
comparison ranking: total 208

Life expectancy at birth: *total population:* 82.6 years (2024 est.)
male: 80 years
female: 85.3 years
comparison ranking: total population 26

Total fertility rate: 1.72 children born/woman (2024 est.)
comparison ranking: 157

Gross reproduction rate: 0.85 (2024 est.)

Drinking water source: *improved:* total: 97.5% of population

Physician density: 1.51 physicians/1,000 population (2018)

Currently married women (ages 15-49): 46.1% (2023 est.)

Education expenditure: 2.5% of GDP (2022 est.)
10.3% national budget (2024 est.)
comparison ranking: Education expenditure (% GDP) 174

ENVIRONMENT

Environmental issues: inadequate potable water

Climate: tropical; moderated by northeast trade winds

Urbanization: *urban population:* 100% of total population (2023)
rate of urbanization: 0.47% annual rate of change (2020-25 est.)

GOVERNMENT

Country name: *conventional long form:* none
conventional short form: Anguilla
etymology: in 1493, Christopher COLUMBUS named the island Anguilla, meaning "eel" in Spanish, because of the island's elongated shape

Government type: parliamentary democracy (House of Assembly); self-governing overseas territory of the UK

Dependency status: overseas territory of the UK

Capital: *name:* The Valley
geographic coordinates: 18 13 N, 63 03 W
time difference: UTC-4 (1 hour ahead of Washington, DC, during Standard Time)
etymology: name may derive from the capital's location among several hills

Administrative divisions: none (overseas territory of the UK)

Legal system: common law based on the English model

Constitution: *history:* several previous; latest 1 April 1982

Citizenship: see United Kingdom

Suffrage: 18 years of age; universal

Executive branch: *chief of state:* King CHARLES III (since 8 September 2022); represented by Governor Julia CROUCH (since 11 September 2023)
head of government: Premier Cora RICHARDSON-HODGE (since 27 February 2025)
cabinet: Executive Council appointed by the governor from among elected members of the House of Assembly
election/appointment process: the monarchy is hereditary; governor appointed by the monarch; following legislative elections, the governor usually appoints the leader of the majority party or majority coalition as premier

Legislative branch: *legislature name:* House of Assembly
legislative structure: unicameral
number of seats: 11 (7 directly elected, 2 appointed, 2 ex-officio members)
electoral system: plurality/majority
scope of elections: full renewal
term in office: 5 years
most recent election date: 6/29/2020
parties elected and seats per party: APM (7); AUF (4)
percentage of women in chamber: 27.3%

Judicial branch: *highest court(s):* the Eastern Caribbean Supreme Court (ECSC) is the superior court of the Organization of Eastern Caribbean States; the ECSC is headquartered on St. Lucia and consists of the Court of Appeal – headed by the chief justice and 4 judges – and the High Court with 18 judges; the Court of Appeal travels to member states on a schedule to hear appeals from the High Court and subordinate courts
judge selection and term of office: Eastern Caribbean Supreme Court chief justice appointed by the British monarch; other justices and judges appointed by the Judicial and Legal Services Commission; Court of Appeal justices appointed for life with mandatory retirement at age 65; High Court judges appointed for life with mandatory retirement at age 62
subordinate courts: Magistrate's Court; Juvenile Court

Political parties: Anguilla Progressive Movement or APM; (formerly Anguilla United Movement or AUM) Anguilla United Front or AUF

Diplomatic representation in the US: none (overseas territory of the UK)

Diplomatic representation from the US: *embassy:* none (overseas territory of the UK); alternate contact is the US Embassy in Barbados [1] (246) 227-4000

International organization participation: Caricom (associate), CDB, Interpol (subbureau), OECS, UNESCO (associate), UPU

Independence: none (overseas territory of the UK)

National holiday: Anguilla Day, 30 May (1967)

Flag: *description:* blue, with the UK flag in the upper-left quadrant and the Anguillan coat of arms centered on the outer half of the flag; the coat of arms shows three orange dolphins in an interlocking circular design on a white background, with a turquoise-blue field below
meaning: the white on the coat of arms stands for peace; the blue base for the sea, faith, youth, and hope; and the three dolphins for endurance, unity, and strength

National symbol(s): dolphin

National coat of arms: the Anguillan coat of arms features three interlocking dolphins jumping out of seawater; they represent endurance, unity, and strength, and their circular motion stands for continuity; the white background symbolizes peace and tranquility, and the turquoise-blue base represents the sea, as well as faith, youth, and hope

National anthem(s): *title:* "God Bless Anguilla"
lyrics/music: Alex RICHARDSON
history: local anthem, adopted 1981
title: "God Save the King"
lyrics/music: unknown
history: official anthem, as an overseas UK territory

ECONOMY

Economic overview: small, tourism-dependent, territorial-island economy; very high public debt; COVID-19 crippled economic activity; partial recovery underway via tourism, benefitting from its high amount of timeshare residences; considering reopening oil refinery

Real GDP (purchasing power parity): $362.499 million (2024 est.)
$345.238 million (2023 est.)
$336.924 million (2022 est.)
note: data in 2015 dollars
comparison ranking: 213

Real GDP per capita: $31,000 (2024 est.)
$28,900 (2023 est.)
$27,400 (2022 est.)
note: data in 2015 dollars
comparison ranking: 77

GDP (official exchange rate): $452.73 million (2024 est.)
note: data in current dollars at official exchange rate

Inflation rate (consumer prices): 3% (2022 est.)
1.8% (2021 est.)
-0.5% (2020 est.)
note: annual % change based on consumer prices
comparison ranking: 92

Agricultural products: small quantities of tobacco, vegetables; cattle raising

Industries: tourism, boat building, offshore financial services

Budget: *revenues:* $81.925 million (2017 est.)
expenditures: $72.352 million (2017 est.)
note: central government revenues and expenses (excluding grants/extrabudgetary units/social security funds) converted to US dollars at average official exchange rate for year indicated

Exports: $7.9 million (2017 est.)
$3.9 million (2016 est.)
note: Data are in current year dollars and do not include illicit exports or re-exports.
comparison ranking: 212

Exports - partners: Chile 60%, Netherlands 8%, Brazil 5%, Hungary 4%, USA 4% (2023)
note: top five export partners based on percentage share of exports

Exports - commodities: packaged medicine, garments, vehicle parts/accessories, vaccines, cars (2023)
note: top five export commodities based on value in dollars

Imports - partners: Chile 50%, USA 27%, Botswana 15%, Japan 1%, Dominican Republic 1% (2023)
note: top five import partners based on percentage share of imports

Imports - commodities: poultry, copper ore, natural gas, refined petroleum, fish (2023)
note: top five import commodities based on value in dollars

Exchange rates: East Caribbean dollars (XCD) per US dollar -

Exchange rates: 2.7 (2024 est.)
2.7 (2023 est.)
2.7 (2022 est.)
2.7 (2021 est.)
2.7 (2020 est.)

ENERGY

Electricity access: *electrification - total population:* 100% (2020)

COMMUNICATIONS

Telephones - fixed lines: *total subscriptions:* 6,000 (2021 est.)
subscriptions per 100 inhabitants: 38 (2021 est.)
comparison ranking: total subscriptions 198

Telephones - mobile cellular: *total subscriptions:* 26,000 (2021 est.)
subscriptions per 100 inhabitants: 170 (2021 est.)
comparison ranking: total subscriptions 212

Broadcast media: 1 private TV station; multi-channel cable TV subscription services are available; about 10 radio stations, one of which is government-owned (2024)

Internet country code: .ai

Internet users: *percent of population:* 81.6% (2021 est.)

Broadband - fixed subscriptions: *total:* 5,000 (2018 est.)
subscriptions per 100 inhabitants: 35 (2018 est.)
comparison ranking: total 195

TRANSPORTATION

Civil aircraft registration country code prefix: VP-A

Airports: 1 (2025)
comparison ranking: 225

Merchant marine: *total:* 2 (2023)
by type: other 2
comparison ranking: total 176

MILITARY AND SECURITY

Military - note: defense is the responsibility of the UK

ANTARCTICA

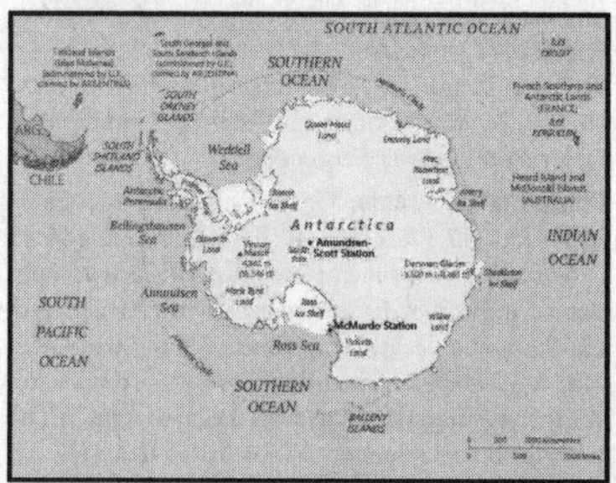

INTRODUCTION

Background: Speculation over the existence of a "southern land" was confirmed in the early 1820s when British and American commercial operators and British and Russian national expeditions began exploring the Antarctic Peninsula region and other areas south of the Antarctic Circle. In 1840, it was finally established that Antarctica was indeed a continent and not merely a group of islands or an area of ocean. Several exploration "firsts" were achieved in the early 20th century, but the area saw little human activity. Following World War II, however, the continent experienced an upsurge in scientific research. A number of countries have set up a range of year-round and seasonal stations, camps, and refuges to support scientific research in Antarctica. Seven have made territorial claims, with two maintaining the basis for a claim, but most countries do not recognize these claims. In order to form a legal framework for countries' activities on the continent, an Antarctic Treaty was negotiated that neither denies nor recognizes existing territorial claims; it was signed in 1959 and entered into force in 1961. Also relevant to Antarctic governance are the Environmental Protocol to the Antarctic Treaty and the Convention on the Conservation of Antarctic Marine Living Resources.

GEOGRAPHY

Location: continent mostly south of the Antarctic Circle

Geographic coordinates: 90 00 S, 0 00 E

Map references: Antarctic Region

Area: *total:* 14.2 million sq km
land: 14.2 million sq km (285,000 sq km ice-free, 13.915 million sq km ice-covered) (est.)
note: fifth-largest continent, following Asia, Africa, North America, and South America, but larger than Australia and the continent of Europe
comparison ranking: total 2

Area - comparative: slightly less than 1.5 times the size of the US

Land boundaries: *note:* see entry on Disputes - international

Coastline: 17,968 km

Maritime claims: Australia, Chile, and Argentina claim Exclusive Economic Zone (EEZ) rights or similar over 200 nm extensions seaward from their continental claims, but like the claims themselves, these zones are not accepted by other countries; 22 of 29 Antarctic Treaty consultative parties have made no claims to Antarctic territory, although Russia and the United States have reserved the right to do so, and no country can make a new claim

Climate: the coldest, windiest, and driest continent on Earth; severe low temperatures vary with latitude, elevation, and distance from the ocean; East Antarctica is colder than West Antarctica because of its higher elevation; Antarctic Peninsula has the most moderate climate; higher temperatures occur in January along the coast and average slightly below freezing; summers characterized by continuous daylight, while winters bring continuous darkness; persistent high pressure over the interior brings dry, subsiding air that results in very little cloud cover

Terrain: about 99% thick continental ice sheet and 1% barren rock, with average elevations between 2,000 and 4,000 m; mountain ranges up to nearly 5,000 m; ice-free coastal areas include parts of southern Victoria Land, Wilkes Land, the Antarctic Peninsula area, and parts of Ross Island on McMurdo Sound; glaciers form ice shelves along about half of the coastline, and floating ice shelves constitute 11% of the area of the continent

Elevation: *highest point:* Vinson Massif 4,892 m
lowest point: Denman Glacier more than -3,500 m (-11,500 ft) below sea level
mean elevation: 2,300 m
note: the lowest known land point in Antarctica is hidden in the Denman Glacier; at its surface is the deepest ice yet discovered and the world's lowest elevation not under seawater

Natural resources: iron ore, chromium, copper, gold, nickel, platinum and other minerals, and coal and hydrocarbons have been found in small noncommercial quantities; mineral exploitation except for scientific research is banned by the Environmental Protocol to the Antarctic Treaty; krill, icefish, toothfish, and crab have been taken by commercial fisheries, which are managed through the Commission for the Conservation of Antarctic Marine Living Resources (CCAMLR)

Land use: *agricultural land:* 0% (2018 est.)

Natural hazards: katabatic (gravity-driven) winds blow coastward from the high interior; frequent blizzards form near the foot of the plateau; cyclonic storms form over the ocean and move clockwise along the coast; large icebergs may calve from ice shelf
volcanism: volcanic activity on Deception Island and isolated areas of West Antarctica; other seismic activity rare and weak

Geography - note: the coldest, windiest, highest (on average), and driest continent; during the summer, more solar radiation reaches the surface at the South Pole than is received at the equator in an equivalent period
mostly uninhabitable, 99% of the land area is covered by the Antarctic ice sheet, the largest single mass of ice on Earth; it covers an area of 14 million sq km (5.4 million sq mi) and contains 26.5 million cu km (6.4 million cu mi) of ice (almost 62% of the world's fresh water)

PEOPLE AND SOCIETY

Population: no permanent inhabitants, but staff is present at year-round and summer-only research stations
note: 56 countries have signed the 1959 Antarctic Treaty; 30 of those operate a number of seasonal-only (summer) and year-round research stations on the continent and its nearby islands; the population varies from approximately 5,000 in summer to 1,100 in winter, with about 1,000 support personnel on ships nearby
as of 2024, peak summer (December-February) maximum capacity in scientific stations - 4,713 total; Argentina 425, Australia 238, Belarus 15, Belgium 55, Brazil 64, Bulgaria 25, Chile 375, China 164, Czechia 32, Ecuador 35, Finland 16, France 136, France and Italy jointly 70, Germany 60, India 72, Italy 150, Japan 130, South Korea 158, New Zealand 85, Norway 60, Peru 30, Poland 41, Russia 211, South Africa 80, Spain 79, Sweden 16, Ukraine 15, United Kingdom 315, United States 1,495, Uruguay 66 (2024)
winter (June-August) maximum capacity in scientific stations - 1,056 total; Argentina 221, Australia 52, Brazil 15, Chile 114, China 32, France 24, France and Italy jointly 13, Germany 9, India 48, Japan 40, Netherlands 10, South Korea 25, NZ 11, Norway 7, Poland 16, Russia 125, South Africa 15, Ukraine 12, UK 44, US 215, Uruguay 8 (2024)

ENVIRONMENT

Environmental issues: size of ozone hole over continent; ice loss

Climate: the coldest, windiest, and driest continent on Earth; severe low temperatures vary with latitude, elevation, and distance from the ocean; East Antarctica is colder than West Antarctica because of its higher elevation; Antarctic Peninsula has the most moderate climate; higher temperatures occur in January along the coast and average slightly below freezing; summers characterized by continuous daylight, while winters bring continuous darkness; persistent high pressure over the interior brings dry, subsiding air that results in very little cloud cover

Carbon dioxide emissions: 15,000 metric tonnes of CO_2 (2023 est.)
from coal and metallurgical coke: 2,000 metric tonnes of CO_2 (2023 est.)
from petroleum and other liquids: 13,000 metric tonnes of CO_2 (2023 est.)
comparison ranking: total emissions 214

GOVERNMENT

Country name: *conventional long form:* none
conventional short form: Antarctica
etymology: name derived from two Greek words, *anti* and *arktikos*, meaning "opposite to the Arctic" or "opposite to the north"

Government type: the Antarctic Treaty and its follow-on agreements govern the use of Antarctica, ensuring it is used only for peaceful purposes and scientific research; signed in 1959 and in force since 1961, the original Treaty bans military activity, weapons testing, and nuclear waste disposal, while

allowing military personnel to assist with research or other peaceful efforts; it promotes international cooperation in science, guarantees the free exchange of research, and freezes territorial claims; the Treaty covers all land and ice south of 60° south latitude, and allows Treaty nations to inspect any station or facility
decisions are made by consensus at annual meetings, and member countries implement these decisions through their national laws (see "Legal system"); additional agreements have strengthened the Treaty system, including conventions to protect seals (1972) and other marine life (1980), as well as an environmental protocol (1991, took effect in 1998); the protocol bans mining and includes strict rules on environmental impact, waste, pollution, wildlife, and protected areas; as of December 2024, there are 58 member nations: 29 consultative members, including the 7 claimant countries (Argentina, Australia, Chile, France, New Zealand, Norway, and the UK), and 29 non-consultative members; a permanent Antarctic Treaty Secretariat, established in 2004 in Buenos Aires, supports the system

Legal system: Antarctica is administered through annual Antarctic Treaty Consultative Meetings that include member nations, observer groups, and experts; decisions are made by consensus and enforced by each country through its own laws, applying to their citizens and operations in the region south of 60° south latitude, including all ice shelves and islands; in the US, the Antarctic Conservation Act prohibits actions like harming native wildlife, introducing non-native species, polluting, or entering protected areas without authorization; the US National Science Foundation and Department of Justice enforce these rules; US expeditions must also notify the Office of Ocean and Polar Affairs at the US Department of State, which informs other Treaty nations, as required under Public Law 95-541

Flag: *description:* two horizontal bands of navy and white, with a stylized white peak at the center; the peak casts a navy shadow in the shape of a compass arrow pointed south
meaning: the bands represent the long days and nights at Antarctica's extreme latitude; the compass arrow is an homage to the continent's legacy of exploration; the peak and the arrow together create a diamond, symbolizing the hope that Antarctica will continue to be a center of peace, discovery, and cooperation
history: the flag is unofficial; created in 2018, the True South flag has quickly become popular for its simple yet elegant design and has been used by national Antarctic programs, Antarctic nonprofits, and expedition teams

ENERGY

Coal: *imports:* 2,000 metric tons (2023 est.)

Petroleum: *refined petroleum consumption:* 79 bbl/day (2023 est.)

COMMUNICATIONS

Internet country code: .aq

Internet users: *percent of population:* 100% (2021 est.)

TRANSPORTATION

Airports: 31 (2025)
comparison ranking: 119

Heliports: 5 (2025)
comparison ranking: 98

Ports: *total ports:* 8 (2024)
large: 0
medium: 0
small: 1
very small: 7
ports with oil terminals: 0
key ports: Admiralty Bay, Andersen Harbor, Ellefsen Harbor, McMurdo Station, Melchior Harbor, Port Foster, Port Lockroy, Scotia Bay

Transportation - note: US coastal stations include McMurdo (77 51 S, 166 40 E) and Palmer (64 43 S, 64 03 W); government use only; all ships are subject to inspection in accordance with Article 7 of the Antarctic Treaty; ships must comply with relevant legal instruments and authorization procedures under the Antarctic Treaty (see "Legal System"); The Hydrographic Commission on Antarctica (HCA), a commission of the International Hydrographic Organization (IHO), coordinates and facilitates provision of accurate and appropriate charts and other aids to navigation; membership in HCA is open to any IHO Member State whose government has acceded to the Antarctic Treaty and which contributes resources or data to IHO Chart coverage of the area

MILITARY AND SECURITY

Military - note: the Antarctic Treaty of 1961 prohibits any measures of a military nature, such as the establishment of military bases and fortifications, the carrying out of military maneuvers, or the testing of any type of weapon; it permits the use of military personnel or equipment for scientific research or for any other peaceful purposes

ANTIGUA AND BARBUDA

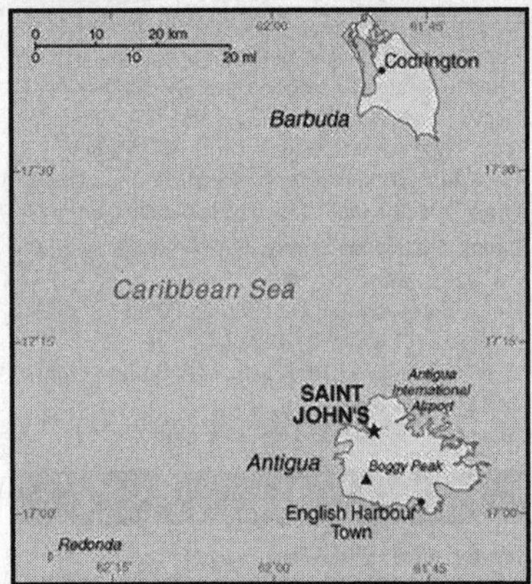

INTRODUCTION

Background: The Siboney were the first people to inhabit the islands of Antigua and Barbuda in 2400 B.C., but the Arawaks populated the islands when Christopher COLUMBUS landed on his second voyage in 1493. Early Spanish and French settlements were succeeded by an English colony in 1667. Slavery, which provided labor on the sugar plantations on Antigua, was abolished in 1834. The islands became an independent state within the British Commonwealth of Nations in 1981. In 2017, Hurricane Irma passed over the island of Barbuda, devastating the island and forcing the evacuation of the population to Antigua. Almost all of the structures on Barbuda were destroyed and the vegetation stripped, but Antigua was spared the worst.

GEOGRAPHY

Location: Caribbean, islands between the Caribbean Sea and the North Atlantic Ocean, east-southeast of Puerto Rico

Geographic coordinates: 17 03 N, 61 48 W

Map references: Central America and the Caribbean

Area: *total:* 443 sq km (Antigua 280 sq km; Barbuda 161 sq km)
land: 443 sq km
water: 0 sq km
note: includes Redonda, 1.6 sq km
comparison ranking: total 200

Area - comparative: 2.5 times the size of Washington, D.C.

Land boundaries: *total:* 0 km

Coastline: 153 km

Maritime claims: *territorial sea:* 12 nm
contiguous zone: 24 nm
exclusive economic zone: 200 nm
continental shelf: 200 nm or to the edge of the continental margin

Climate: tropical maritime; little seasonal temperature variation

Terrain: mostly low-lying limestone and coral islands, with some higher volcanic areas

Elevation: *highest point:* Mount Obama 402 m
lowest point: Caribbean Sea 0 m

Natural resources: NEGL; pleasant climate fosters tourism

Land use: *agricultural land:* 20.5% (2022 est.)
arable land: 9.1% (2022 est.)
permanent crops: 2.3% (2022 est.)
permanent pasture: 9.1% (2022 est.)
forest: 18.2% (2022 est.)
other: 61.4% (2022 est.)

Irrigated land: 1.3 sq km (2012)

Population distribution: the island of Antigua is home to approximately 97% of the population; nearly the entire population of Barbuda lives in Codrington

Natural hazards: hurricanes and tropical storms (July to October); periodic droughts

Geography - note: Antigua has a deeply indented shoreline with many natural harbors and beaches; Barbuda has a large western harbor

PEOPLE AND SOCIETY

Population: *total:* 102,634 (2024 est.)
male: 48,311
female: 54,323
comparison rankings: total 194; male 197; female 192

Nationality: *noun:* Antiguan(s), Barbudan(s)
adjective: Antiguan, Barbudan

Ethnic groups: African descent 87.3%, mixed 4.7%, Hispanic 2.7%, White 1.6%, other 2.7%, unspecified 0.9% (2011 est.)
note: data represent population by ethnic group

Languages: English (official), Antiguan Creole (an English-based creole)

Religions: Protestant 68.3% (Anglican 17.6%, Seventh Day Adventist 12.4%, Pentecostal 12.2%, Moravian 8.3%, Methodist 5.6%, Wesleyan Holiness 4.5%, Church of God 4.1%, Baptist 3.6%), Roman Catholic 8.2%, other 12.2%, unspecified 5.5%, none 5.9% (2011 est.)

Age structure: *0-14 years:* 21.8% (male 11,384/female 11,034)
15-64 years: 67.6% (male 32,312/female 37,094)
65 years and over: 10.5% (2024 est.) (male 4,615/female 6,195)

Dependency ratios: *total dependency ratio:* 47.9 (2024 est.)
youth dependency ratio: 32.3 (2024 est.)
elderly dependency ratio: 15.6 (2024 est.)
potential support ratio: 6.4 (2024 est.)

Median age: *total:* 33.9 years (2024 est.)
male: 31.9 years
female: 35.7 years
comparison ranking: total 109

Population growth rate: 1.11% (2024 est.)
comparison ranking: 83

Birth rate: 14.9 births/1,000 population (2024 est.)
comparison ranking: 113

Death rate: 5.7 deaths/1,000 population (2024 est.)
comparison ranking: 171

Net migration rate: 2 migrant(s)/1,000 population (2024 est.)
comparison ranking: 49

Population distribution: the island of Antigua is home to approximately 97% of the population; nearly the entire population of Barbuda lives in Codrington

Urbanization: *urban population:* 24.3% of total population (2023)
rate of urbanization: 0.87% annual rate of change (2020-25 est.)

Major urban areas - population: 21,000 SAINT JOHN'S (capital) (2018)

Sex ratio: *at birth:* 1.05 male(s)/female
0-14 years: 1.03 male(s)/female
15-64 years: 0.87 male(s)/female
65 years and over: 0.74 male(s)/female
total population: 0.89 male(s)/female (2024 est.)

Maternal mortality ratio: 35 deaths/100,000 live births (2023 est.)
comparison ranking: 110

Infant mortality rate: *total:* 13.6 deaths/1,000 live births (2024 est.)
male: 16.4 deaths/1,000 live births
female: 10.7 deaths/1,000 live births
comparison ranking: total 104

Life expectancy at birth: *total population:* 78.3 years (2024 est.)
male: 76.1 years
female: 80.5 years
comparison ranking: total population 80

Total fertility rate: 1.93 children born/woman (2024 est.)
comparison ranking: 116

Gross reproduction rate: 0.94 (2024 est.)

Drinking water source: *improved: urban:* 98.4% of population (2022 est.)
rural: 98.3% of population (2022 est.)
total: 98.4% of population (2022 est.)
unimproved: urban: 1.6% of population (2022 est.)
rural: 1.7% of population (2022 est.)
total: 1.6% of population (2022 est.)

Health expenditure: 5.9% of GDP (2021)
14% of national budget (2022 est.)

Physician density: 2.92 physicians/1,000 population (2017)

Hospital bed density: 3.3 beds/1,000 population (2020 est.)

Sanitation facility access: *improved: urban:* 95.4% of population (2022 est.)
rural: 98% of population (2022 est.)
total: 97.4% of population (2022 est.)
unimproved: urban: 4.6% of population (2022 est.)
rural: 2% of population (2022 est.)
total: 2.6% of population (2022 est.)

Obesity - adult prevalence rate: 18.9% (2016)
comparison ranking: 115

Alcohol consumption per capita: *total:* 11.88 liters of pure alcohol (2019 est.)
beer: 2.97 liters of pure alcohol (2019 est.)
wine: 3.95 liters of pure alcohol (2019 est.)
spirits: 4.55 liters of pure alcohol (2019 est.)
other alcohols: 0.41 liters of pure alcohol (2019 est.)
comparison ranking: total 6

Currently married women (ages 15-49): 31.5% (2023 est.)

Education expenditure: 3.1% of GDP (2023 est.)
11% national budget (2024 est.)
comparison ranking: Education expenditure (% GDP) 147

ENVIRONMENT

Environmental issues: limited natural freshwater resources; water management hampered by tree-clearing to increase crop production, causing rapid rainfall runoff

International environmental agreements: *party to:* Biodiversity, Climate Change, Climate Change-Kyoto Protocol, Climate Change-Paris Agreement, Comprehensive Nuclear Test Ban, Desertification, Endangered Species, Environmental Modification, Hazardous Wastes, Law of the Sea, Marine Dumping-London Convention, Marine Dumping-London Protocol, Nuclear Test Ban, Ozone Layer Protection, Ship Pollution, Wetlands, Whaling
signed, but not ratified: none of the selected agreements

Climate: tropical maritime; little seasonal temperature variation

Urbanization: *urban population:* 24.3% of total population (2023)
rate of urbanization: 0.87% annual rate of change (2020-25 est.)

Carbon dioxide emissions: 725,000 metric tonnes of CO2 (2023 est.)
from petroleum and other liquids: 725,000 metric tonnes of CO2 (2023 est.)
comparison ranking: total emissions 180

Particulate matter emissions: 8.3 micrograms per cubic meter (2019 est.)

Waste and recycling: *municipal solid waste generated annually:* 30,600 tons (2024 est.)
percent of municipal solid waste recycled: 15.3% (2022 est.)

Total water withdrawal: *municipal:* 7.2 million cubic meters (2022 est.)
industrial: 2.5 million cubic meters (2022 est.)
agricultural: 1.8 million cubic meters (2022 est.)

Total renewable water resources: 52 million cubic meters (2022)

GOVERNMENT

Country name: *conventional long form:* Antigua and Barbuda
conventional short form: Antigua and Barbuda
etymology: *antiguo* is Spanish for "ancient" or "old;" Christopher COLUMBUS named the island in 1493, after the church of Santa Maria la Antigua (Old Saint Mary's) in Seville, Spain; *barbuda* is Spanish for "bearded" and may refer to the island's lichen-covered fig trees

Government type: parliamentary democracy under a constitutional monarchy; a Commonwealth realm

Capital: *name:* Saint John's
geographic coordinates: 17 07 N, 61 51 W
time difference: UTC-4 (1 hour ahead of Washington, DC, during Standard Time)
etymology: named after Saint John the Apostle

Administrative divisions: 6 parishes and 2 dependencies*; Barbuda*, Redonda*, Saint George, Saint John, Saint Mary, Saint Paul, Saint Peter, Saint Philip

Legal system: common law based on the English model

Constitution: *history:* several previous; latest presented 31 July 1981, effective 31 October 1981 (The Antigua and Barbuda Constitution Order 1981)
amendment process: proposed by either house of Parliament; passage of amendments to constitutional sections such as citizenship, fundamental rights and freedoms, the establishment, power, and authority of the executive and legislative branches, the Supreme Court Order, and the procedure for amending the constitution requires approval by at least two-thirds majority vote of the membership of both houses, approval by at least two-thirds majority in a referendum, and assent to by the governor general; passage of other amendments requires only two-thirds majority vote by both houses

International law organization participation: has not submitted an ICJ jurisdiction declaration; accepts ICCt jurisdiction

Citizenship: *citizenship by birth:* yes
citizenship by descent only: yes
dual citizenship recognized: yes
residency requirement for naturalization: 7 years

Suffrage: 18 years of age; universal

Executive branch: *chief of state:* King CHARLES III (since 8 September 2022); represented by Governor General Rodney WILLIAMS (since 14 August 2014)

head of government: Prime Minister Gaston BROWNE (since 13 June 2014)
cabinet: Council of Ministers appointed by the governor general on the advice of the prime minister
election/appointment process: the monarchy is hereditary; governor general appointed by the monarch on the advice of the prime minister; following legislative elections, the governor general usually appoints the leader of the majority party or majority coalition as prime minister

Legislative branch: *legislature name:* Parliament
legislative structure: bicameral

Legislative branch - lower chamber: *chamber name:* House of Representatives
number of seats: 18 (all directly elected)
electoral system: plurality/majority
scope of elections: full renewal
term in office: 5 years
most recent election date: 1/18/2023
parties elected and seats per party: Antigua and Barbuda Labour Party (ABLP) (9); United Progressive Party (UPP) (6); Barbuda People's Movement (BPM) (1); Independents (1)
percentage of women in chamber: 5.6%
expected date of next election: January 2028

Legislative branch - upper chamber: *chamber name:* Senate
number of seats: 17 (all appointed)
scope of elections: full renewal
term in office: 5 years
most recent election date: 2/17/2023
percentage of women in chamber: 41.2%
expected date of next election: February 2028

Judicial branch: *highest court(s):* the Eastern Caribbean Supreme Court (ECSC) is the superior court of the Organization of Eastern Caribbean States; the ECSC is headquartered on St. Lucia and consists of the Court of Appeal – headed by the chief justice and 4 judges – and the High Court with 18 judges; the Court of Appeal travels to member states on a schedule to hear appeals from the High Court and subordinate courts
judge selection and term of office: chief justice of Eastern Caribbean Supreme Court appointed by the British monarch; other justices and judges appointed by the Judicial and Legal Services Commission; Court of Appeal justices appointed for life with mandatory retirement at age 65; High Court judges appointed for life with mandatory retirement at age 62
subordinate courts: Industrial Court; Magistrates' Courts

Political parties: Antigua Labor Party or ABLP
Barbuda People's Movement or BPM
Democratic National Alliance or DNA
Go Green for Life or GGL
United Progressive Party or UPP

Diplomatic representation in the US: *chief of mission:* Ambassador Sir Ronald SANDERS (since 17 September 2015)
chancery: 3216 New Mexico Ave. NW, Washington, DC 20016
telephone: [1] (202) 362-5122
FAX: [1] (202) 362-5225
email address and website: embantbar@aol.com
https://www.antigua-barbuda.org/Aghome01.htm
consulate(s) general: Miami, New York

Diplomatic representation from the US: *embassy:* the US does not have an embassy in Antigua and Barbuda; the US Ambassador to Barbados is accredited to Antigua and Barbuda

International organization participation: ACP, ACS, AOSIS, C, Caricom, CDB, CELAC, FAO, G-77, IBRD, ICAO, ICC (NGOs), ICCt, ICRM, IDA, IFAD, IFC, IFRCS, ILO, IMF, IMO, IMSO, Interpol, IOC, IOM, ISO (subscriber), ITU, ITUC (NGOs), MIGA, NAM (observer), OAS, OECS, OPANAL, OPCW, Petrocaribe, UN, UNCTAD, UNESCO, UPU, WFTU (NGOs), WHO, WIPO, WMO, WTO

Independence: 1 November 1981 (from the UK)

National holiday: Independence Day, 1 November (1981)

Flag: *description:* red, with an inverted isosceles triangle in the center that spans the flag from top to bottom; the triangle contains three horizontal bands of black (top), light blue, and white, with a yellow rising sun in the black band
meaning: the sun stands for the dawn of a new era, black for the African heritage of most of the population, blue for hope, and red for the dynamism of the people; the "V" shape of the triangle stands for victory; the yellow, blue, and white colors are also meant to evoke the country's tourist attractions of sun, sea, and sand

National symbol(s): fallow deer

National color(s): red, white, blue, black, yellow

National anthem(s): *title:* "Fair Antigua, We Salute Thee"
lyrics/music: Novelle Hamilton RICHARDS/Walter Garnet Picart CHAMBERS
history: adopted 1967
title: "God Save the King"
lyrics/music: unknown
history: royal anthem, as a Commonwealth country

National heritage: *total World Heritage Sites:* 1 (cultural)
selected World Heritage Site locales: Antigua Naval Dockyard (Nelson's Dockyard)

ECONOMY

Economic overview: dual island-tourism and construction-driven economy; emerging "blue economy"; limited water supply and susceptibility to hurricanes limit activity; improving road infrastructure; friendly to foreign direct investment; looking at financial innovation in cryptocurrency and blockchain technologies

Real GDP (purchasing power parity): $2.772 billion (2024 est.)
$2.657 billion (2023 est.)
$2.594 billion (2022 est.)
note: data in 2021 dollars
comparison ranking: 193

Real GDP growth rate: 4.3% (2024 est.)
2.4% (2023 est.)
9.1% (2022 est.)
note: annual GDP % growth based on constant local currency
comparison ranking: 59

Real GDP per capita: $29,600 (2024 est.)
$28,500 (2023 est.)
$27,900 (2022 est.)
note: data in 2021 dollars
comparison ranking: 80

GDP (official exchange rate): $2.225 billion (2024 est.)
note: data in current dollars at official exchange rate

Inflation rate (consumer prices): 6.2% (2024 est.)
5.1% (2023 est.)
7.5% (2022 est.)
note: annual % change based on consumer prices
comparison ranking: 156

GDP - composition, by sector of origin: *agriculture:* 1.9% (2023 est.)
industry: 19% (2023 est.)
services: 69.1% (2023 est.)
note: figures may not total 100% due to non-allocated consumption not captured in sector-reported data
comparison rankings: agriculture 154; industry 138; services 41

Agricultural products: tropical fruits, milk, mangoes/guavas, eggs, lemons/limes, pumpkins/squash, sweet potatoes, vegetables, cucumbers/gherkins, yams (2023)
note: top ten agricultural products based on tonnage

Industries: tourism, construction, light manufacturing (clothing, alcohol, household appliances)

Industrial production growth rate: 1% (2023 est.)
note: annual % change in industrial value added based on constant local currency
comparison ranking: 114

Remittances: 1.2% of GDP (2024 est.)
1.7% of GDP (2023 est.)
1.9% of GDP (2022 est.)
note: personal transfers and compensation between resident and non-resident individuals/households/entities

Budget: *revenues:* $251.418 million (2014 est.)
expenditures: $266.044 million (2014 est.)
note: central government revenues and expenses (excluding grants/extrabudgetary units/social security funds) converted to US dollars at average official exchange rate for year indicated

Current account balance: -$181.366 million (2024 est.)
-$271.047 million (2023 est.)
-$291.674 million (2022 est.)
note: balance of payments - net trade and primary/secondary income in current dollars
comparison ranking: 104

Exports: $1.314 billion (2024 est.)
$1.185 billion (2023 est.)
$1.111 billion (2022 est.)
note: balance of payments - exports of goods and services in current dollars
comparison ranking: 178

Exports - partners: Suriname 29%, Poland 21%, USA 8%, Dominican Republic 7%, Australia 5% (2023)
note: top five export partners based on percentage share of exports

Exports - commodities: refined petroleum, ships, soybean meal, shellfish, paintings (2023)
note: top five export commodities based on value in dollars

Imports: $1.282 billion (2024 est.)
$1.273 billion (2023 est.)
$1.227 billion (2022 est.)
note: balance of payments - imports of goods and services in current dollars
comparison ranking: 188

Imports - partners: USA 43%, Poland 6%, China 5%, UK 4%, Germany 4% (2023)
note: top five import partners based on percentage share of imports

Imports - commodities: ships, refined petroleum, cars, plastic products, furniture (2023)
note: top five import commodities based on value in dollars

Reserves of foreign exchange and gold: $358.441 million (2024 est.)
$364.367 million (2023 est.)
$396.506 million (2022 est.)
note: holdings of gold (year-end prices)/foreign exchange/special drawing rights in current dollars
comparison ranking: 167

Exchange rates: East Caribbean dollars (XCD) per US dollar -

Exchange rates: 2.7 (2024 est.)
2.7 (2023 est.)
2.7 (2022 est.)
2.7 (2021 est.)
2.7 (2020 est.)

ENERGY

Electricity access: *electrification - total population:* 100% (2022 est.)

Electricity: *installed generating capacity:* 148,000 kW (2023 est.)
consumption: 322.923 million kWh (2023 est.)
transmission/distribution losses: 38.121 million kWh (2023 est.)
comparison rankings: installed generating capacity 183; consumption 184; transmission/distribution losses 31

Electricity generation sources: *fossil fuels:* 93.6% of total installed capacity (2023 est.)
solar: 6.4% of total installed capacity (2023 est.)

Coal: *imports:* 25 metric tons (2023 est.)

Petroleum: *refined petroleum consumption:* 5,000 bbl/day (2023 est.)

Energy consumption per capita: 110.114 million Btu/person (2023 est.)
comparison ranking: 41

COMMUNICATIONS

Telephones - fixed lines: *total subscriptions:* 27,000 (2021 est.)
subscriptions per 100 inhabitants: 29 (2022 est.)
comparison ranking: total subscriptions 169

Telephones - mobile cellular: *total subscriptions:* 184,000 (2021 est.)
subscriptions per 100 inhabitants: 197 (2021 est.)
comparison ranking: total subscriptions 183

Broadcast media: state-controlled Antigua and Barbuda Broadcasting Service (ABS) operates 1 TV station; multi-channel cable TV subscription services are available; ABS operates 1 radio station; roughly 20 radio stations (2024)

Internet country code: .ag

Internet users: *percent of population:* 78% (2023 est.)

Broadband - fixed subscriptions: *total:* 10,000 (2022 est.)
subscriptions per 100 inhabitants: 11 (2022 est.)
comparison ranking: total 184

TRANSPORTATION

Civil aircraft registration country code prefix: V2

Airports: 4 (2025)
comparison ranking: 182

Heliports: 2 (2025)
comparison ranking: 128

Merchant marine: *total:* 614 (2023)
by type: bulk carrier 24, container ship 109, general cargo 425, oil tanker 6, other 50
comparison ranking: total 36

Ports: *total ports:* 1 (2024)
large: 0
medium: 1
small: 0
very small: 0
ports with oil terminals: 1
key ports: St. John's

MILITARY AND SECURITY

Military and security forces: Antigua and Barbuda Defense Force (ABDF): Antigua and Barbuda Regiment, Air Wing, Coast Guard
Royal Police Force of Antigua and Barbuda (RPFAB) (2025)

Military and security service personnel strengths: approximately 300 active Defense Force personnel (2025)

Military equipment inventories and acquisitions: the ABDF's equipment inventory is limited to small arms, light weapons, and soft-skin vehicles; the Coast Guard maintains ex-US patrol vessels and some smaller boats (2025)

Military service age and obligation: 18-23 years of age for voluntary military service for both men and women; no conscription (2025)

Military - note: the ABDF's responsibilities include providing for internal security and support to the police in maintaining law and order, interdicting narcotics smuggling, responding to natural disasters, and monitoring the country's territorial waters and maritime resources; established in 1981 from colonial forces originally created in 1897, it is one of the world's smallest militaries
the country has been a member of the Caribbean Regional Security System (RSS) since its creation in 1982; RSS signatories (Barbados, Dominica, Grenada, Guyana, Saint Kitts and Nevis, Saint Lucia, and Saint Vincent and the Grenadines) agreed to prepare contingency plans and assist one another, on request, in national emergencies, prevention of smuggling, search and rescue, immigration control, fishery protection, customs and excise control, maritime policing duties, protection of off-shore installations, pollution control, national and other disasters, and threats to national security (2025)

TRANSNATIONAL ISSUES

Refugees and internally displaced persons: *refugees:* 5 (2024 est.)

ARCTIC OCEAN

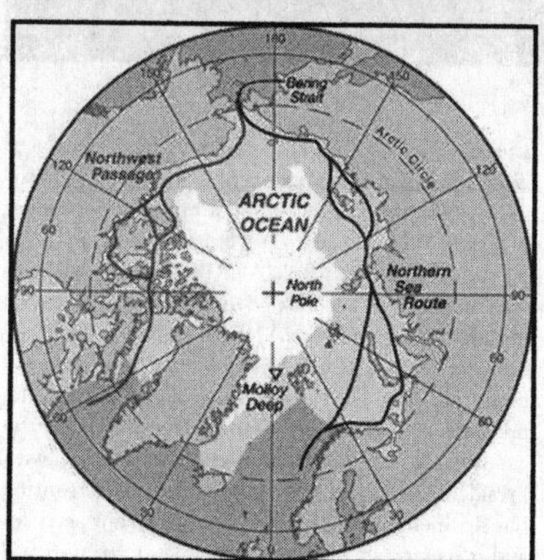

INTRODUCTION

Background: The Arctic Ocean is the smallest of the world's five ocean basins (after the Pacific Ocean, Atlantic Ocean, Indian Ocean, and the Southern Ocean). The Northwest Passage (US and Canada) and Northern Sea Route (Norway and Russia) are two important seasonal waterways. In recent years, the polar ice pack has receded in the summer allowing for increased navigation and raising the possibility of future sovereignty and shipping disputes among the Arctic coastal states affected (Canada, Denmark (Greenland), Iceland, Norway, Russia, US).

GEOGRAPHY

Location: body of water between Europe, Asia, and North America, mostly north of the Arctic Circle

Geographic coordinates: 90 00 N, 0 00 E

Map references: Arctic Region

Area: *total:* 15.558 million sq km
note: includes Barents Sea, Beaufort Sea, Chukchi Sea, East Siberian Sea, Greenland Sea, Kara Sea, Laptev Sea, Northwest Passage, Norwegian Sea, and other tributary water bodies

Area - comparative: slightly less than 1.5 times the size of the US

Coastline: 45,389 km

Climate: polar climate characterized by persistent cold and relatively narrow annual temperature range; winters characterized by continuous darkness, cold and stable weather conditions, and clear skies; summers characterized by continuous daylight, damp and foggy weather, and weak cyclones with rain or snow

Ocean volume: *ocean volume:* 18.75 million cu km
percent of World Ocean total volume: 1.4%

Major ocean currents: *two major, slow-moving, wind-driven currents (drift streams) dominate:* a clockwise drift pattern in the Beaufort Gyre in the western part of the Arctic Ocean and a nearly straight line Transpolar Drift Stream that moves eastward across the ocean from the New Siberian Islands (Russia) to the Fram Strait (between Greenland and Svalbard); sea ice that lies close to the center of the gyre can complete a 360 degree circle in about 2 years, while ice on the gyre periphery will complete the same circle in about 7-8 years; sea ice in the Transpolar Drift crosses the ocean in about 3 years

Bathymetry: *continental shelf:* more than one quarter of the Arctic sea floor; the Eurasian shelf is very wide, extending out 1,500 km (930 mi), and is the largest continental shelf in the world
the following are examples of continental-shelf features in the Arctic Ocean: Barents Shelf
Beaufort Shelf
Davis Sill
Chukchi Shelf
East Siberian Shelf
Kara Shelf
Laptev Shelf
Lincoln Shelf
continental slope: the following are examples of continental-slope features in the Arctic Ocean: Litke Trough
Novaya Zemlya Trough
Svyataya Anna Trough (Saint Anna Trough)
Voronin Trough
abyssal plains: the following are examples of abyssal-plain features in the Arctic Ocean: Baffin Basin
Canada Basin
Fram/Amundsen Basin
Greenland Abyssal Plain
Iceland Basin
Makarov Basin
Molloy Deep (deepest point in the Arctic Ocean)
Nansen Basin
Norwegian Basin
mid-ocean ridge: the following are examples of mid-ocean ridges in the Arctic Ocean: Gakkel Ridge
Mohns Ridge
undersea terrain features: the following are examples of undersea terrain features on the floor of the Arctic Ocean:
Lomonosov Ridge
Gakkel Ridge
Alpha Ridge
Mendeleev Rise
Chukchi Plateau
ocean trenches: none
atolls: none

Elevation: *highest point:* sea level
lowest point: Molloy Deep -5,577 m
mean depth: -1,205 m
ocean zones: the ocean is divided into three zones based on depth and light level; sunlight entering the water may travel about 1,000 m into the oceans under the right conditions, but there is rarely any significant light below 200 m
euphotic zone: the upper 200 m (656 ft) is also called "sunlight" zone; only a small amount of light penetrates beyond this depth
dysphotic zone: between 200 m (656 ft) and 1,000 m (3,280 ft), and also called the twilight zone; the intensity of light rapidly dissipates as depth increases, and photosynthesis is no longer possible
aphotic zone: below 1,000 m (3,280 ft) and also called the midnight zone; sunlight does not penetrate to these depths

Natural resources: sand and gravel aggregates, placer deposits, polymetallic nodules, oil and gas fields, fish, marine mammals (seals and whales)

Natural hazards: ice islands occasionally break away from northern Ellesmere Island; icebergs calved from glaciers in western Greenland and extreme northeastern Canada; permafrost in islands; virtually ice locked from October to June; ships subject to superstructure icing from October to May

Geography - note: major chokepoint is the southern Chukchi Sea (northern access to the Pacific Ocean via the Bering Strait); strategic location between North America and Russia; shortest marine link between the extremes of eastern and western Russia; floating research stations operated by the US and Russia; maximum snow cover in March or April about 20 to 50 centimeters over the frozen ocean; snow cover lasts about 10 months

ENVIRONMENT

Environmental issues: changes in biodiversity and temperature; water pollution from use of toxic chemicals; endangered marine species; ecosystem slow to recover from disruptions or damage; thinning polar icepack

Climate: polar climate characterized by persistent cold and relatively narrow annual temperature range; winters characterized by continuous darkness, cold and stable weather conditions, and clear skies; summers characterized by continuous daylight, damp and foggy weather, and weak cyclones with rain or snow

Marine fisheries: the Arctic fishery region (Region 18) is the smallest in the world with a catch of only 708 mt in 2019, although the Food and Agriculture Organization assesses that some Arctic catches are reported in adjacent regions; Russia and Canada were historically the major producers; in 2017, Canada, Denmark (Greenland), Iceland, Norway, Russia, and the US, along with the People's Republic of China, the European Union, Japan, and the Republic of Korea, agreed to a 16-year ban on fishing in the Central Arctic Ocean to allow for time to study the ecological system of these waters

Regional fisheries bodies: International Council for the Exploration of the Seas; Agreement to Prevent Unregulated High Seas Fisheries in the Central Arctic Ocean

GOVERNMENT

Country name: *etymology:* the name comes from the Greek word *arktikos* meaning "near the bear" or "northern," and that word derives from *arktos*, meaning "bear;" the name refers either to the constellation Ursa Major, the "Great Bear," which is prominent in the northern celestial sphere, or to the constellation Ursa Minor, the "Little Bear," which contains Polaris, the North (Pole) Star

TRANSPORTATION

Transportation - note: sparse network of air, ocean, river, and land routes; the Northwest Passage (North America) and Northern Sea Route (Eurasia) are important seasonal waterways

ARGENTINA

INTRODUCTION

Background: In 1816, the United Provinces of the Río de la Plata declared their independence from Spain. After Bolivia, Paraguay, and Uruguay went their separate ways, the area that remained became Argentina. European immigrants heavily shaped the country's population and culture, with Italy and Spain providing the largest percentage of newcomers from 1860 to 1930. Until about the mid-20th century, much of Argentina's history was dominated by periods of internal political unrest and conflict between civilian and military factions.

After World War II, former President Juan Domingo PERÓN – the founder of the Peronist political movement – introduced an era of populism, serving three non-consecutive terms in office until his death in 1974. Direct and indirect military interference in government throughout the PERÓN years led to a military junta taking power in 1976. In 1982, the junta failed in its bid to seize the Falkland Islands (Islas Malvinas) by force from the United Kingdom. Democracy was reinstated in 1983 and has persisted despite numerous challenges, the most formidable of which was a severe economic crisis in 2001-02 that led to violent public protests and the successive resignations of several presidents. The years 2003-15 saw Peronist rule by Néstor KIRCHNER (2003-07) and his spouse Cristina FERNÁNDEZ DE KIRCHNER (2007-15), who oversaw several years of strong economic growth (2003-11) followed by a gradual deterioration in the government's fiscal situation and eventual economic stagnation and isolation. Argentina underwent a brief period of economic reform and international reintegration under Mauricio MACRI (2015-19), but a recession in 2018-19 and frustration with MACRI's economic policies ushered in a new Peronist government in 2019 led by President Alberto FERNÁNDEZ and Vice President Cristina FERNÁNDEZ DE KIRCHNER. Argentina's high public debts, its pandemic-related inflationary pressures, and systemic monetary woes served as the catalyst for the 2023 elections, culminating with President Javier MILEI's electoral success. Argentina has since eliminated half of its government agencies and is seeking shock therapy to amend taxation and monetary policies.

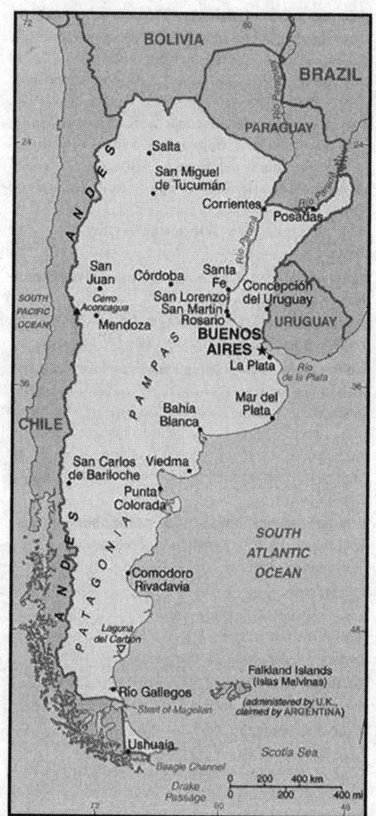

GEOGRAPHY

Location: Southern South America, bordering the South Atlantic Ocean, between Chile and Uruguay

Geographic coordinates: 34 00 S, 64 00 W

Map references: South America

Area: *total:* 2,780,400 sq km
land: 2,736,690 sq km
water: 43,710 sq km
comparison ranking: total 9

Area - comparative: slightly less than three-tenths the size of the US

Land boundaries: *total:* 11,968 km
border countries (5): Bolivia 942 km; Brazil 1,263 km; Chile 6,691 km; Paraguay 2,531 km; Uruguay 541 km

Coastline: 4,989 km

Maritime claims: *territorial sea:* 12 nm
contiguous zone: 24 nm
exclusive economic zone: 200 nm
continental shelf: 200 nm or to the edge of the continental margin

Climate: mostly temperate; arid in southeast; subantarctic in southwest

Terrain: rich plains of the Pampas in northern half, flat to rolling plateau of Patagonia in south, rugged Andes along western border

Elevation: *highest point:* Cerro Aconcagua (located in the northwestern corner of the province of Mendoza; highest point in South America) 6,962 m
lowest point: Laguna del Carbón (located between Puerto San Julián and Comandante Luis Piedra Buena in the province of Santa Cruz) - 105 m
mean elevation: 595 m

Natural resources: fertile plains of the pampas, lead, zinc, tin, copper, iron ore, manganese, petroleum, uranium, arable land

Land use: *agricultural land:* 43.4% (2022 est.)
arable land: 15.7% (2022 est.)
permanent crops: 0.4% (2022 est.)
permanent pasture: 27.3% (2022 est.)
forest: 10.4% (2022 est.)
other: 46.2% (2022 est.)

Irrigated land: 13,910 sq km (2018)

Major lakes (area sq km): *fresh water lake(s):* Lago Buenos Aires (shared with Chile) - 2,240 sq km; Lago Argentino - 1,410 sq km; Lago Viedma - 1,090 sq km; Lago San Martín (shared with Chile) - 1,010 sq km; Lago Colhué Huapi - 800 sq km; Lago Fagnano (shared with Chile) - 590 sq km; Lago Nahuel Huapi - 550 sq km
salt water lake(s): Laguna Mar Chiquita - 1,850 sq km;

Major rivers (by length in km): Río de la Plata/Paraná river mouth (shared with Brazil [s], Paraguay, and Uruguay) - 4,880 km; Paraguay (shared with Brazil [s], and Paraguay [m]) - 2,549 km; Uruguay (shared with Brazil [s] and Uruguay [m]) - 1,610 km
note: [s] after country name indicates river source; [m] after country name indicates river mouth

Major watersheds (area sq km): Atlantic Ocean drainage: Paraná (2,582,704 sq km)

Major aquifers: Guaraní Aquifer System

Population distribution: one third of the population lives in Buenos Aires; pockets of agglomeration occur throughout the northern and central parts of the country; Patagonia to the south remains sparsely populated

Natural hazards: San Miguel de Tucumán and Mendoza areas in the Andes subject to earthquakes; pamperos are violent windstorms that can strike the pampas and northeast; heavy flooding in some areas
volcanism: volcanic activity in the Andes Mountains along the Chilean border; Copahue (2,997 m) last erupted in 2000; other historically active volcanoes include Llullaillaco, Maipo, Planchón-Peteroa, San José, Tromen, Tupungatito, and Viedma

Geography - note: second-largest country in South America (after Brazil); strategic location relative to sea lanes between the South Atlantic and the South Pacific Oceans (Strait of Magellan, Beagle Channel, Drake Passage); diverse geophysical landscapes range from tropical climates in the north to tundra in the far south; Cerro Aconcagua is the Western Hemisphere's tallest mountain, while Laguna del Carbón is the lowest point in the Western Hemisphere; shares Iguazú Falls, the world's largest waterfalls system, with Brazil

PEOPLE AND SOCIETY

Population: *total:* 46,994,384 (2024 est.)
male: 23,274,794
female: 23,719,590
comparison rankings: total 34; male 33; female 33

Nationality: *noun:* Argentine(s)
adjective: Argentine

Ethnic groups: European (mostly Spanish and Italian descent) and Mestizo (mixed European and Indigenous ancestry) 97.2%, Indigenous 2.4%, African descent 0.4% (2010 est.)

Languages: Spanish (official), Italian, English, German, French, indigenous (Quechua, Guarani, Mapudungun)
major-language sample(s):
La Libreta Informativa del Mundo, la fuente indispensable de información básica. (Spanish)

Religions: Roman Catholic 62.9%, Evangelical 15.3% (Pentecostal 13%, other Evangelical 2.3%), Jehovah's Witness and Church of Jesus Christ 1.4%, other 1.2% (includes Muslim, Jewish), none 18.9% (includes agnostic and atheist), unspecified 0.3% (2019 est.)

Age structure: *0-14 years:* 23.3% (male 5,632,983/female 5,301,778)
15-64 years: 63.9% (male 15,071,215/female 14,956,069)
65 years and over: 12.8% (2024 est.) (male 2,570,596/female 3,461,743)

Dependency ratios: *total dependency ratio:* 50.9 (2024 est.)
youth dependency ratio: 31.5 (2024 est.)
elderly dependency ratio: 19.4 (2024 est.)
potential support ratio: 5.1 (2024 est.)

Median age: *total:* 33.3 years (2024 est.)
male: 32.1 years
female: 34.6 years
comparison ranking: total 112

Population growth rate: 0.79% (2024 est.)
comparison ranking: 110

Birth rate: 15.2 births/1,000 population (2024 est.)
comparison ranking: 107

Death rate: 7.3 deaths/1,000 population (2024 est.)
comparison ranking: 107

Net migration rate: -0.1 migrant(s)/1,000 population (2024 est.)
comparison ranking: 98

Population distribution: one third of the population lives in Buenos Aires; pockets of agglomeration occur throughout the northern and central parts of the country; Patagonia to the south remains sparsely populated

Urbanization: *urban population:* 92.5% of total population (2023)
rate of urbanization: 0.97% annual rate of change (2020-25 est.)

Major urban areas - population: 15.490 million BUENOS AIRES (capital), 1.612 million Córdoba, 1.594 million Rosario, 1.226 million Mendoza, 1.027 million San Miguel de Tucumán, 914,000 La Plata (2023)

Sex ratio: *at birth:* 1.07 male(s)/female
0-14 years: 1.06 male(s)/female
15-64 years: 1.01 male(s)/female
65 years and over: 0.74 male(s)/female
total population: 0.98 male(s)/female (2024 est.)

Maternal mortality ratio: 33 deaths/100,000 live births (2023 est.)
comparison ranking: 114

Infant mortality rate: *total:* 9 deaths/1,000 live births (2024 est.)
male: 9.9 deaths/1,000 live births
female: 7.9 deaths/1,000 live births
comparison ranking: total 140

Life expectancy at birth: *total population:* 78.8 years (2024 est.)
male: 75.8 years

female: 82 years
comparison ranking: total population 72

Total fertility rate: 2.15 children born/woman (2024 est.)
comparison ranking: 89

Gross reproduction rate: 1.04 (2024 est.)

Drinking water source: *improved: urban:* 99.8% of population (2022 est.)
unimproved: urban: 0.2% of population (2022 est.)
total: (2020 est.) NA

Health expenditure: 9.7% of GDP (2021)
15.2% of national budget (2022 est.)

Physician density: 5.11 physicians/1,000 population (2023)

Hospital bed density: 3.3 beds/1,000 population (2021 est.)

Sanitation facility access: *improved: urban:* 100% of population (2022 est.)
unimproved: urban: 0% of population (2022 est.)

Obesity - adult prevalence rate: 28.3% (2016)
comparison ranking: 31

Alcohol consumption per capita: *total:* 7.95 liters of pure alcohol (2019 est.)
beer: 3.62 liters of pure alcohol (2019 est.)
wine: 2.88 liters of pure alcohol (2019 est.)
spirits: 0.72 liters of pure alcohol (2019 est.)
other alcohols: 0.72 liters of pure alcohol (2019 est.)
comparison ranking: total 45

Tobacco use: *total:* 21.9% (2025 est.)
male: 26.9% (2025 est.)
female: 17.1% (2025 est.)
comparison ranking: total 54

Children under the age of 5 years underweight: 2% (2018/19)
comparison ranking: 98

Currently married women (ages 15-49): 48.9% (2023 est.)

Child marriage: *women married by age 15:* 2.4% (2020)
women married by age 18: 15.5% (2020)

Education expenditure: 4.8% of GDP (2022 est.)
12.7% national budget (2022 est.)
comparison ranking: Education expenditure (% GDP) 71

School life expectancy (primary to tertiary education): *total:* 19 years (2022 est.)
male: 17 years (2022 est.)
female: 21 years (2022 est.)

ENVIRONMENT

Environmental issues: deforestation; soil degradation (erosion, salinization); desertification; air pollution; water pollution

International environmental agreements: *party to:* Antarctic-Environmental Protection, Antarctic-Marine Living Resources, Antarctic Seals, Antarctic Treaty, Biodiversity, Climate Change, Climate Change-Kyoto Protocol, Climate Change-Paris Agreement, Comprehensive Nuclear Test Ban, Desertification, Endangered Species, Environmental Modification, Hazardous Wastes, Law of the Sea, Marine Dumping-London Convention, Nuclear Test Ban, Ozone Layer Protection, Ship Pollution, Wetlands, Whaling
signed, but not ratified: Marine Dumping-London Protocol, Marine Life Conservation

Climate: mostly temperate; arid in southeast; subantarctic in southwest

Land use: *agricultural land:* 43.4% (2022 est.)
arable land: 15.7% (2022 est.)
permanent crops: 0.4% (2022 est.)
permanent pasture: 27.3% (2022 est.)
forest: 10.4% (2022 est.)
other: 46.2% (2022 est.)

Urbanization: *urban population:* 92.5% of total population (2023)
rate of urbanization: 0.97% annual rate of change (2020-25 est.)

Carbon dioxide emissions: 198.141 million metric tonnes of CO2 (2023 est.)
from coal and metallurgical coke: 5.022 million metric tonnes of CO2 (2023 est.)
from petroleum and other liquids: 102.998 million metric tonnes of CO2 (2023 est.)
from consumed natural gas: 90.122 million metric tonnes of CO2 (2023 est.)
comparison ranking: total emissions 31

Particulate matter emissions: 12 micrograms per cubic meter (2019 est.)

Methane emissions: *energy:* 1,553.3 kt (2022-2024 est.)
agriculture: 3,035.5 kt (2019-2021 est.)
waste: 631 kt (2019-2021 est.)
other: 89.9 kt (2019-2021 est.)

Waste and recycling: *municipal solid waste generated annually:* 17.911 million tons (2024 est.)
percent of municipal solid waste recycled: 9.6% (2022 est.)

Total water withdrawal: *municipal:* 5.85 billion cubic meters (2022 est.)
industrial: 4 billion cubic meters (2022 est.)
agricultural: 27.93 billion cubic meters (2022 est.)

Total renewable water resources: 876.24 billion cubic meters (2022 est.)

GOVERNMENT

Country name: *conventional long form:* Argentine Republic
conventional short form: Argentina
local long form: República Argentina
local short form: Argentina
etymology: the name is derived from one of the Spanish words for "silver," but the origin is unclear; it may have described the land next to the Rio de la Plata ("Silver River"), a major river that forms the boundary between Argentina and Uruguay; another possible source is the Spanish explorers in the 16th century mistakenly believing that the silver ornaments they bought from inhabitants came from a local source of silver

Government type: presidential republic

Capital: *name:* Buenos Aires
geographic coordinates: 34 36 S, 58 22 W
time difference: UTC-3 (2 hours ahead of Washington, DC, during Standard Time)
etymology: the name translates as "fair winds" in Spanish; the full original name, Nuestra Senora Santa Maria de los Buenos Aires, was given only to the port; the city was founded separately from the port in 1536 and was named Ciudad de la Santissima Trinidad (City of the Most Holy Trinity); the shortened version of the port name eventually became the city name

Administrative divisions: 23 provinces (*provincias*, singular - *provincia*) and 1 autonomous city*; Buenos Aires, Catamarca, Chaco, Chubut, Ciudad Autonoma de Buenos Aires*, Cordoba, Corrientes, Entre Rios, Formosa, Jujuy, La Pampa, La Rioja, Mendoza, Misiones, Neuquen, Rio Negro, Salta, San Juan, San Luis, Santa Cruz, Santa Fe, Santiago del Estero, Tierra del Fuego - Antartida e Islas del Atlantico Sur (Tierra del Fuego - Antarctica and the South Atlantic Islands), Tucuman
note: the US does not recognize any claims to Antarctica

Legal system: civil law system based on Western European legal systems
note: in 2015, Argentina adopted a new civil code, replacing the old one in force since 1871

Constitution: *history:* several previous; latest effective 11 May 1853
amendment process: a declaration of proposed amendments requires two-thirds majority vote by both houses of the National Congress followed by approval by an ad hoc, multi-member constitutional convention

International law organization participation: has not submitted an ICJ jurisdiction declaration; accepts ICCt jurisdiction

Citizenship: *citizenship by birth:* yes
citizenship by descent only: yes
dual citizenship recognized: yes
residency requirement for naturalization: 2 years

Suffrage: *18-70 years of age; universal and compulsory; 16-17 years of age:* optional for national elections

Executive branch: *chief of state:* President Javier Gerardo MILEI (since 10 December 2023)
head of government: President Javier Gerardo MILEI (since 10 December 2023)
cabinet: Cabinet appointed by the president
election/appointment process: president and vice president directly elected on the same ballot by qualified majority vote (to win, a candidate must receive at least 45% of votes, or 40% of votes and a 10-point lead over the second-place candidate; if neither occurs, a second round is held); the president serves a 4-year term (eligible for a second consecutive term)
most recent election date: 22 October 2023, with a runoff held 19 November 2023
election results: 2023: Javier Gerardo MILEI elected president in second round; percent vote in first round - Sergio Tomás MASSA (FR) 36.7%, Javier Gerardo MILEI (PL) 30%, Patricia BULLRICH 23.8% (JxC/PRO), Juan SCHIARETTI (PJ) 6.8%, Myriam BREGMAN (PTS) 2.7%; percent of vote in second round - Javier Gerardo MILEI 55.7%, Sergio Tomás MASSA 44.3%
2019: Alberto Ángel FERNÁNDEZ elected president; percent of vote - Alberto Angel FERNÁNDEZ (TODOS) 48.1%, Mauricio MACRI (PRO) 40.4%, Roberto LAVAGNA (independent) 6.2%, other 5.3%
expected date of next election: October 2027

Legislative branch: *legislature name:* National Congress (Congreso de la nación)
legislative structure: bicameral

Legislative branch - lower chamber: *chamber name:* Chamber of Deputies (Cámara de Diputados)
number of seats: 257 (all directly elected)
electoral system: proportional representation
scope of elections: partial renewal
term in office: 4 years

most recent election date: 10/22/2023
parties elected and seats per party: Union for the Homeland (UP) (48); Freedom Advances (LLA) (28); Together for Change (JxC/Juntos) (27); Other (27)
percentage of women in chamber: 42.4%
expected date of next election: October 2025

Legislative branch - upper chamber: *chamber name:* Senate (Senado)
number of seats: 72 (all directly elected)
electoral system: proportional representation
scope of elections: partial renewal
term in office: 6 years
most recent election date: 10/22/2023
parties elected and seats per party: Union for the Homeland (UP) (9); Freedom Advances (LLA) (6); Together for Change (JxC/Juntos) (2); Front for the Renewal of Social Concord – Federal Innovation (2); Federal Renewal (2); For Santa Cruz (2); Other (1)
percentage of women in chamber: 45.8%
expected date of next election: October 2025

Judicial branch: *highest court(s):* Supreme Court or Corte Suprema (consists of the court president, vice president, 2 judges, 1 vacancy)
judge selection and term of office: judges nominated by the president and approved by the Senate; ministers can serve until mandatory retirement at age 75; extensions beyond 75 require renomination by the president and approval by the Senate
subordinate courts: federal-level appellate, district, and territorial courts; provincial-level supreme, appellate, and first-instance courts

Political parties: Avanza Libertad or AL
Civic Coalition ARI or CC-ARI
Consenso Federal (Federal Consensus) or CF
Frente Cívico por Santiago (Civic Front for Santiago)
Frente de Izquierda y de los Trabajadores – Unidad (Workers' Left Front) or FIT-U (coalition of leftist parties in lower house; includes PTS, PO, and MST)
Frente de la Concordia Misionero (Front for the Renewal of Social Concord) or FRCS
Frente Renovador (Renewal Front) or FR
Generación por un Encuentro Nacional (Generation for a National Encounter) or GEN
Hacemos por Córdoba (We do for Cordoba) or HC
Hacemos por Nuestro Pais (We Do For Our Country) or NHP
Juntos por el Cambio (Together for Change) or JxC (includes CC-ARI, PRO, and UCR); note - primary opposition coalition since 2019
Juntos Somos Río Negro (Together We Are Rio Negro) or JSRN
Partido Justicialista (Justicialist Party) or PJ
La Cámpora
La Libertad Avanza (The Liberty Advances) or LLA
Movimiento Popular Neuquino (Neuquén People's Movement) or MPN
Movimiento Socialista de los Trabajadores (Workers' Socialist Movement) or MST
Partido de los Trabajadores Socialistas (Socialist Workers' Party) or PTS
Partido Demócrata (Democratic Party) or PDN
Partido Libertario (Libertarian Party) or PL; note - party is also a founding member of the coalition La Libertad Avanza
Partido Obrero (Workers' Party) or PO
Partido Socialista or PS
Propuesta Republicana (Republican Proposal) or PRO
Unidad Federal (coalition of provencial parties in the lower house; includes FRCS and JSRN)
Unión Cívica Radical (Radical Civic Union) or UCR
Unión por la Patria (Union for the Homeland) or UP *(formerly Frente de Todos (Everyone's Front) or FdT)* (includes FR, La Cámpora, and PJ); note - ruling coalition since 2019; includes several national and provincial Peronist political parties
Vamos con Vos (Let's Go with You) or VcV

Diplomatic representation in the US: *chief of mission:* Ambassador Alejandro (Alec) Carlos Francisco OXENFORD (since 11 June 2025)
chancery: 1600 New Hampshire Avenue NW, Washington, DC 20009
telephone: [1] (202) 238-6400
FAX: [1] (202) 332-3171
email address and website: eeeuu@mrecic.gov.ar
https://eeeuu.cancilleria.gob.ar/en
consulate(s) general: Atlanta, Chicago, Houston, Los Angeles, Miami, New York

Diplomatic representation from the US: *chief of mission:* Ambassador (vacant); Chargé d'Affaires Heidi Gómez RÁPALO (since 11 July 2025)
embassy: Avenida Colombia 4300, (C1425GMN) Buenos Aires
mailing address: 3130 Buenos Aires Place, Washington DC 20521-3130
telephone: [54] (11) 5777-4533
FAX: [54] (11) 5777-4240
email address and website: Buenosairespublicaffairs@state.gov
https://ar.usembassy.gov/

International organization participation: AfDB (nonregional member), Australia Group, BCIE, BIS, CAN (associate), CD, CABEI, CELAC, FAO, FATF, G-15, G-20, G-24, G-77, IADB, IAEA, IBRD, ICAO, ICC (national committees), ICCt, ICRM, IDA, IFAD, IFC, IFRCS, IHO, ILO, IMF, IMO, IMSO, Interpol, IOC, IOM, IPU, ISO, ITSO, ITU, ITUC (NGOs), LAES, LAIA, Mercosur, MIGA, MINURSO, MINUSTAH, NAM (observer), NSG, OAS, OPANAL, OPCW, Paris Club (associate), PCA, PROSUR, SICA (observer), UN, UNASUR, UNCTAD, UNDOF, UNESCO, UNFICYP, UNHCR, UNHRC, UNIDO, Union Latina (observer), UNOOSA, UNTSO, UNWTO, UPU, Wassenaar Arrangement, WCO, WFTU (NGOs), WHO, WIPO, WMO, WTO, ZC

Independence: 9 July 1816 (from Spain)

National holiday: Revolution Day (May Revolution Day), 25 May (1810)

Flag: *description:* three equal horizontal bands of sky blue (top), white, and sky blue; centered in the white band is a radiant yellow sun with a human face that is known as the Sun of May
meaning: the colors represent the clear skies and snow of the Andes Mountains; the sun commemorates the first mass demonstration in favor of independence on 25 May 1810, when the sun broke through the clouds; the sun is designed to look like Inti, the Incan god of the sun

National symbol(s): Sun of May (a sun-with-face symbol)

National color(s): sky blue, white

National anthem(s): *title:* "Himno Nacional Argentino" (Argentine National Anthem)
lyrics/music: Vicente LOPEZ y PLANES/Jose Blas PARERA
history: adopted 1813; Vicente LOPEZ was inspired to write the anthem after watching a play about the 1810 May Revolution against Spain; a 1900 presidential decree declared that only the first and last verses would be considered official, rather than the original nine verses

National heritage: *total World Heritage Sites:* 12 (7 cultural, 5 natural)
selected World Heritage Site locales: Los Glaciares National Park (n); Jesuit Missions of the Guaranis (c); Iguazú National Park (n); Cueva de las Manos (c); Valdés Península (n); Ischigualasto/Talampaya National Parks (n); Jesuit Block and Estancias of Córdoba (c); Quebrada de Humahuaca (c); Qhapaq Ñan/Andean Road System (c)

ECONOMY

Economic overview: large diversified economy; financial risks from debt obligations, rapid inflation, and reduced investor appetites; resource-rich, export-led growth model; increasing trade relations with China; G20 and OAS leader; tendency to nationalize businesses and under-report inflation

Real GDP (purchasing power parity): $1.213 trillion (2024 est.)
$1.234 trillion (2023 est.)
$1.255 trillion (2022 est.)
note: data in 2021 dollars
comparison ranking: 29

Real GDP growth rate: -1.7% (2024 est.)
-1.6% (2023 est.)
5.3% (2022 est.)
note: annual GDP % growth based on constant local currency
comparison ranking: 205

Real GDP per capita: $26,500 (2024 est.)
$27,100 (2023 est.)
$27,600 (2022 est.)
note: data in 2021 dollars
comparison ranking: 88

GDP (official exchange rate): $633.267 billion (2024 est.)
note: data in current dollars at official exchange rate

Inflation rate (consumer prices): 73.1% (2022 est.)
47.1% (2021 est.)
40.5% (2020 est.)
note: annual % change based on consumer prices
comparison ranking: 207

GDP - composition, by sector of origin: *agriculture:* 6% (2024 est.)
industry: 24% (2024 est.)
services: 53.4% (2024 est.)
note: figures may not total 100% due to non-allocated consumption not captured in sector-reported data
comparison rankings: agriculture 102; industry 99; services 129

GDP - composition, by end use: *household consumption:* 68.1% (2024 est.)
government consumption: 15% (2024 est.)
investment in fixed capital: 15.8% (2024 est.)
investment in inventories: -0.1% (2024 est.)
exports of goods and services: 15.3% (2024 est.)
imports of goods and services: -12.8% (2024 est.)
note: figures may not total 100% due to rounding or gaps in data collection

Agricultural products: maize, soybeans, sugarcane, wheat, milk, sunflower seeds, barley, beef, potatoes, chicken (2023)
note: top ten agricultural products based on tonnage

Industries: food processing, motor vehicles, consumer durables, textiles, chemicals and petrochemicals, printing, metallurgy, steel

Industrial production growth rate: -7.2% (2024 est.)
note: annual % change in industrial value added based on constant local currency
comparison ranking: 186

Labor force: 22.286 million (2024 est.)
note: number of people ages 15 or older who are employed or seeking work
comparison ranking: 33

Unemployment rate: 7.9% (2024 est.)
6.2% (2023 est.)
6.9% (2022 est.)
note: % of labor force seeking employment
comparison ranking: 132

Youth unemployment rate (ages 15-24): *total:* 21.2% (2024 est.)
male: 19.8% (2024 est.)
female: 23% (2024 est.)
note: % of labor force ages 15-24 seeking employment
comparison ranking: total 52

Population below poverty line: 41.7% (2023 est.)
note: % of population with income below national poverty line

Gini Index coefficient - distribution of family income: 42.4 (2023 est.)
note: index (0-100) of income distribution; higher values represent greater inequality
comparison ranking: 31

Average household expenditures: *on food:* 23.1% of household expenditures (2023 est.)
on alcohol and tobacco: 1.9% of household expenditures (2023 est.)

Household income or consumption by percentage share: *lowest 10%:* 1.9% (2023 est.)
highest 10%: 31% (2023 est.)
note: % share of income accruing to lowest and highest 10% of population

Remittances: 0.2% of GDP (2024 est.)
0.2% of GDP (2023 est.)
0.2% of GDP (2022 est.)
note: personal transfers and compensation between resident and non-resident individuals/households/entities

Budget: *revenues:* $115.69 billion (2023 est.)
expenditures: $139.037 billion (2023 est.)
note: central government revenues (excluding grants) and expenditures converted to US dollars at average official exchange rate for year indicated

Taxes and other revenues: 10% (of GDP) (2023 est.)
note: central government tax revenue as a % of GDP
comparison ranking: 129

Current account balance: $6.285 billion (2024 est.)
-$20.956 billion (2023 est.)
-$4.055 billion (2022 est.)
note: balance of payments - net trade and primary/secondary income in current dollars
comparison ranking: 34

Exports: $96.899 billion (2024 est.)
$82.947 billion (2023 est.)
$102.928 billion (2022 est.)
note: balance of payments - exports of goods and services in current dollars
comparison ranking: 50

Exports - partners: Brazil 18%, USA 9%, Chile 8%, China 8%, India 4% (2023)
note: top five export partners based on percentage share of exports

Exports - commodities: soybean meal, corn, trucks, soybean oil, crude petroleum (2023)
note: top five export commodities based on value in dollars

Imports: $79.999 billion (2024 est.)
$92.3 billion (2023 est.)
$97.399 billion (2022 est.)
note: balance of payments - imports of goods and services in current dollars
comparison ranking: 51

Imports - partners: Brazil 23%, China 20%, USA 12%, Paraguay 5%, Germany 4% (2023)
note: top five import partners based on percentage share of imports

Imports - commodities: soybeans, vehicle parts/accessories, refined petroleum, natural gas, cars (2023)
note: top five import commodities based on value in dollars

Reserves of foreign exchange and gold: $29.56 billion (2024 est.)
$23.081 billion (2023 est.)
$44.795 billion (2022 est.)
note: holdings of gold (year-end prices)/foreign exchange/special drawing rights in current dollars
comparison ranking: 57

Debt - external: $74.362 billion (2023 est.)
note: present value of external debt in current US dollars
comparison ranking: 13

Exchange rates: Argentine pesos (ARS) per US dollar -

Exchange rates: 914.695 (2024 est.)
296.258 (2023 est.)
130.617 (2022 est.)
94.991 (2021 est.)
70.539 (2020 est.)

ENERGY

Electricity access: *electrification - total population:* 100% (2022 est.)

Electricity: *installed generating capacity:* 47.631 million kW (2023 est.)
consumption: 114.667 billion kWh (2023 est.)
exports: 31 million kWh (2023 est.)
imports: 11.393 billion kWh (2023 est.)
transmission/distribution losses: 27.027 billion kWh (2023 est.)
comparison rankings: installed generating capacity 29; consumption 31; exports 94; imports 20; transmission/distribution losses 195

Electricity generation sources: *fossil fuels:* 61.5% of total installed capacity (2023 est.)
nuclear: 6.9% of total installed capacity (2023 est.)
solar: 2.5% of total installed capacity (2023 est.)
wind: 11% of total installed capacity (2023 est.)
hydroelectricity: 16.5% of total installed capacity (2023 est.)
biomass and waste: 1.7% of total installed capacity (2023 est.)

Nuclear energy: Number of operational nuclear reactors: 3 (2025)

Number of nuclear reactors under construction: 1 (2025)

Net capacity of operational nuclear reactors: 1.64GW (2025 est.)

Percent of total electricity production: 6.3% (2023 est.)

Coal: *production:* 869,000 metric tons (2023 est.)
consumption: 2.534 million metric tons (2023 est.)
exports: 300 metric tons (2023 est.)
imports: 1.936 million metric tons (2023 est.)
proven reserves: 799.999 million metric tons (2023 est.)

Petroleum: *total petroleum production:* 807,000 bbl/day (2023 est.)
refined petroleum consumption: 749,000 bbl/day (2023 est.)
crude oil estimated reserves: 2.483 billion barrels (2021 est.)

Natural gas: *production:* 43.69 billion cubic meters (2023 est.)
consumption: 46.028 billion cubic meters (2023 est.)
exports: 2.344 billion cubic meters (2023 est.)
imports: 5.225 billion cubic meters (2023 est.)
proven reserves: 396.464 billion cubic meters (2021 est.)

Energy consumption per capita: 78.496 million Btu/person (2023 est.)
comparison ranking: 66

COMMUNICATIONS

Telephones - fixed lines: *total subscriptions:* 7.034 million (2023 est.)
subscriptions per 100 inhabitants: 15 (2023 est.)
comparison ranking: total subscriptions 22

Telephones - mobile cellular: *total subscriptions:* 62.7 million (2023 est.)
subscriptions per 100 inhabitants: 132 (2022 est.)
comparison ranking: total subscriptions 29

Broadcast media: one of South America's biggest media markets; dozens of TV networks, hundreds of radio stations, and more than 150 daily newspapers (2023)

Internet country code: .ar

Internet users: *percent of population:* 89% (2023 est.)

Broadband - fixed subscriptions: *total:* 11.5 million (2023 est.)
subscriptions per 100 inhabitants: 25 (2023 est.)
comparison ranking: total 21

TRANSPORTATION

Civil aircraft registration country code prefix: LV

Airports: 764 (2025)
comparison ranking: 10

Heliports: 148 (2025)
comparison ranking: 18

Railways: *total:* 17,866 km (2018)

Merchant marine: *total:* 201 (2023)
by type: container ship 1, bulk carrier 1 general cargo 8, oil tanker 33, other 158
comparison ranking: total 66

Ports: *total ports:* 37 (2024)
large: 1
medium: 2
small: 10
very small: 24
ports with oil terminals: 19
key ports: Buenos Aires, Campana, Concepcion del Uruguay, La Plata, Mar del Plata, Puerto Belgrano, Puerto Ingeniero White, Puerto Madryn, Rosario, San Sebastian Bay, Santa Fe, Ushuaia, Zarate

MILITARY AND SECURITY

Military and security forces: Armed Forces of the Argentine Republic (Fuerzas Armadas de la República Argentina): Argentine Army (Ejercito Argentino, EA), Navy of the Argentine Republic (Armada Republica, ARA; includes naval aviation and naval infantry), Argentine Air Force (Fuerza Aerea Argentina, FAA)

Ministry of Security: Gendarmería Nacional Argentina (National Gendarmerie), Coast Guard (Prefectura Naval) (2025)

note: all federal police forces are under the Ministry of Security

Military expenditures: 0.6% of GDP (2024 est.)
0.5% of GDP (2023 est.)
0.6% of GDP (2022 est.)
0.8% of GDP (2021 est.)
0.8% of GDP (2020 est.)

Military and security service personnel strengths: approximately 75,000 active-duty Armed Forces (45,000 Army; 15,000 Navy, including about 3,500 marines; 15,000 Air Force) (2025)

Military equipment inventories and acquisitions: the inventory of Argentina's armed forces is a mix of domestically-produced and mostly older imported weapons, largely from Europe and the US; in recent years, France and the US have been the leading suppliers of equipment; Argentina has an indigenous defense industry that produces air, land, and naval systems (2024)

Military service age and obligation: 18-24 years of age for voluntary military service for men and women; conscription suspended in 1995; citizens can still be drafted in times of crisis, national emergency, or war, or if the Defense Ministry is unable to fill all vacancies to keep the military functional (2024)

note: as of 2024, women comprised nearly 20% of the active duty military

Military deployments: 325 Cyprus (UNFICYP) (2024)

Military - note: the Argentine military's primary responsibilities are territorial defense and protecting the country's sovereignty; duties also include border security, countering narcotics trafficking, and other internal missions, such as disaster response and infrastructure development; it conducts support operations and has bases in Antarctica to promote an active presence in areas of national territory that are sparsely populated; the military also participates in both bilateral and multinational training exercises and supports UN peacekeeping operations

Argentina participates in the Tripartite Command, an interagency security mechanism created by Argentina, Brazil, and Paraguay to exchange information and combat transnational threats, such as crime and terrorism, in the Tri-Border Area; in addition, Argentina and Chile have a joint peacekeeping force known as the Combined Southern Cross Peacekeeping Force, designed to be made available to the UN; Argentina has Major Non-NATO Ally (MNNA) status with the US, a designation under US law that provides foreign partners with certain benefits in the areas of defense trade and security cooperation

the Army and Navy were both created in 1810 during the Argentine War of Independence, while the Air Force was established in 1945; the military conducted coups d'état in 1930, 1943, 1955, 1962, 1966, and 1976; the 1976 coup, aka the "National Reorganization Process," marked the beginning of the so-called "Dirty War," a period of state-sponsored terrorism that saw the deaths or disappearances of thousands of Argentinians; the defeat in the 1982 Falklands War led to the downfall of the military junta (2025)

SPACE

Space agency/agencies: Argentina National Space Activities Commission (Comision Nacional de Actividades Espaciales, CONAE; formed in 1991); CONAE's predecessor was the National Commission for Space Research (Comisión Nacional de Investigaciones Espaciales, CNIE; formed in 1960) (2025)

Space launch site(s): Manuel Belgrano Space Center (Buenos Aires province); Punta Indio Space Center (Buenos Aires province); Teofilo Tabanera Space Center (CETT; Cordoba Province; testing/mission control) (2025)

Space program overview: has a long history in the development of space-related capabilities, including rockets and satellites; develops, builds, and operates communications, remote sensing (RS), and scientific satellites, often in partnership with other countries; developing additional satellites with more advanced payloads; has a national space plan; contracts with commercial and other government space agencies for launches but has a domestic rocket program and is developing space launch vehicle (SLV) capabilities; cooperates with a broad range of space agencies and industries, including those of Brazil, China, the European Space Agency and its member states (particularly France, Italy), and the US; also has a commercial space industry, which includes efforts to design, build, and launch reusable SLVs (2025)

note: further details about the key activities, programs, and milestones of the country's space program, as well as government spending estimates on the space sector, appear in the Space Programs reference guide

TERRORISM

Terrorist group(s): Terrorist group(s): Hizballah

note: details about the history, aims, leadership, organization, areas of operation, tactics, targets, weapons, size, and sources of support of the group(s) appear(s) in Appendix T

TRANSNATIONAL ISSUES

Refugees and internally displaced persons: *refugees:* 9,175 (2024 est.)

IDPs: 74 (2024 est.)

stateless persons: 34 (2024 est.)

ARMENIA

INTRODUCTION

Background: Armenia prides itself on being the first state to formally adopt Christianity (early 4th century). Armenia has existed as a political entity for centuries, but for much of its history it was under the sway of various empires, including the Roman, Byzantine, Arab, Persian, Ottoman, and Russian. During World War I, the Ottoman Empire instituted a policy of forced resettlement that, coupled with other harsh practices targeting its Armenian subjects, resulted in at least 1 million deaths; these actions have been widely recognized as constituting genocide. During the early 19th century, significant Armenian populations fell under Russian rule. Armenia declared its independence in 1918 in the wake of the Bolshevik Revolution in Russia, but it was conquered by the Soviet Red Army in 1920. Armenia, along with Azerbaijan and Georgia, was initially incorporated into the USSR as part of the Transcaucasian Federated Soviet Socialist Republic; in 1936, the republic was separated into its three constituent entities, which were maintained until the dissolution of the Soviet Union in 1991.

For over three decades, Armenia had a longstanding conflict with neighboring Azerbaijan about the status of the Nagorno-Karabakh region, which historically had a mixed Armenian and Azerbaijani population, although ethnic Armenians have constituted the majority since the late 19th century. In 1921, Moscow placed Nagorno-Karabakh within Soviet Azerbaijan as an autonomous oblast. In the late Soviet period, a separatist movement developed that sought to end Azerbaijani control over the region. Fighting over Nagorno-Karabakh began in 1988 and escalated after Armenia and Azerbaijan declared independence from the Soviet Union in 1991. By the time a cease-fire took effect in 1994, separatists with Armenian support controlled Nagorno-Karabakh and seven surrounding Azerbaijani territories. Armenia and Azerbaijan engaged in a second military conflict over Nagorno-Karabakh in 2020; Armenia lost control over much of the territory it had previously captured, returning the southern part of Nagorno-Karabakh and the territories around it to Azerbaijan. In September 2023, Azerbaijan took military action to regain control over Nagorno-Karabakh; after an armed conflict that lasted only one day, nearly the entire ethnic Armenian population of Nagorno-Karabakh fled to Armenia.

Turkey closed its border with Armenia in 1993 in support of Azerbaijan during the first period of conflict with Armenia and has since maintained a closed border, leaving Armenia with closed borders both in the west (with Turkey) and east (with Azerbaijan). Armenia and Turkey engaged in intensive diplomacy to normalize relations and open the border in 2009, but the signed agreement was not ratified in either country. In 2015, Armenia joined the Eurasian Economic Union alongside Russia, Belarus, Kazakhstan, and Kyrgyzstan. In 2017, Armenia signed a Comprehensive and Enhanced Partnership Agreement (CEPA) with the EU.

In 2018, former President of Armenia (2008-18) Serzh SARGSIAN of the Republican Party of Armenia (RPA) tried to extend his time in power, prompting protests that became known as the "Velvet Revolution." After SARGSIAN resigned, the National Assembly elected the leader of the protests, Civil Contract party chief Nikol PASHINYAN, as the new prime minister. PASHINYAN's party has prevailed in subsequent legislative elections, most recently in 2021.

GEOGRAPHY

Location: Southwestern Asia, between Turkey (to the west) and Azerbaijan; note - Armenia views itself as part of Europe; geopolitically, it can be classified as falling within Europe, the Middle East, or both

Geographic coordinates: 40 00 N, 45 00 E

Map references: Asia

Area: *total:* 29,743 sq km
land: 28,203 sq km
water: 1,540 sq km
comparison ranking: total 142

Area - comparative: slightly smaller than Maryland

Land boundaries: *total:* 1,570 km
border countries (4): Azerbaijan 996 km; Georgia 219 km; Iran 44 km; Turkey 311 km

Coastline: 0 km (landlocked)

Maritime claims: none (landlocked)

Climate: highland continental, hot summers, cold winters

Terrain: Armenian Highland with mountains; little forest land; fast flowing rivers; good soil in Aras River valley

Elevation: *highest point:* Aragats Lerrnagagat' 4,090 m
lowest point: Debed River 400 m
mean elevation: 1,792 m

Natural resources: small deposits of gold, copper, molybdenum, zinc, bauxite

Land use: *agricultural land:* 58.8% (2022 est.)
arable land: 15.6% (2022 est.)
permanent crops: 2.1% (2022 est.)
permanent pasture: 41.1% (2022 est.)
forest: 11.5% (2022 est.)
other: 29.6% (2022 est.)

Irrigated land: 1,559 sq km (2022)

Major lakes (area sq km): *fresh water lake(s):* Lake Sevan - 1,360 sq km

Population distribution: most of the population is located in the northern half of the country; the capital of Yerevan is home to more than five times as many people as Gyumri, the second-largest city in the country

Natural hazards: occasionally severe earthquakes; droughts

Geography - note: landlocked in the Lesser Caucasus Mountains; Sevana Lich (Lake Sevan) is the largest lake in this mountain range

PEOPLE AND SOCIETY

Population: *total:* 2,976,765 (2024 est.)
male: 1,456,415
female: 1,520,350
comparison rankings: total 139; male 139; female 138

Nationality: *noun:* Armenian(s)
adjective: Armenian

Ethnic groups: Armenian 98.1%, Yezidi 1.1%, other 0.8% (2022 est.)

Languages: Armenian (official) 97.9%, Kurmanji (spoken by Yezidi minority) 1%, other 1.1%; note - Russian is widely spoken (2011 est.)
major-language sample(s):
Աշխարհի Փաստագիրք, Անփոխարինելի Աղբյուր Հիմնական Տեղեկատվության. (Armenian)

Religions: Armenian Apostolic Christian 95.2%, other Christian 1.6%, other 0.9%, none 0.6%, unspecified 1.7% (2022 est.)

Age structure: *0-14 years:* 17.7% (male 275,589/female 250,630)
15-64 years: 67% (male 991,490/female 1,004,101)
65 years and over: 15.3% (2024 est.) (male 189,336/female 265,619)

Dependency ratios: *total dependency ratio:* 49.2 (2024 est.)
youth dependency ratio: 26.4 (2024 est.)
elderly dependency ratio: 22.8 (2024 est.)
potential support ratio: 4.4 (2024 est.)

Median age: *total:* 38.9 years (2024 est.)
male: 37.6 years
female: 40.3 years
comparison ranking: total 70

Population growth rate: -0.42% (2024 est.)
comparison ranking: 217

Birth rate: 10.5 births/1,000 population (2024 est.)
comparison ranking: 177

Death rate: 9.6 deaths/1,000 population (2024 est.)
comparison ranking: 42

Net migration rate: -5.2 migrant(s)/1,000 population (2024 est.)
comparison ranking: 204

Population distribution: most of the population is located in the northern half of the country; the capital of Yerevan is home to more than five times as many people as Gyumri, the second-largest city in the country

Urbanization: *urban population:* 63.7% of total population (2023)
rate of urbanization: 0.23% annual rate of change (2020-25 est.)

Major urban areas - population: 1.095 million YEREVAN (capital) (2023)

Sex ratio: *at birth:* 1.07 male(s)/female
0-14 years: 1.1 male(s)/female
15-64 years: 0.99 male(s)/female
65 years and over: 0.71 male(s)/female
total population: 0.96 male(s)/female (2024 est.)

Mother's mean age at first birth: 25.2 years (2019 est.)

Maternal mortality ratio: 19 deaths/100,000 live births (2023 est.)
comparison ranking: 125

Infant mortality rate: *total:* 11.6 deaths/1,000 live births (2024 est.)
male: 13.1 deaths/1,000 live births
female: 10 deaths/1,000 live births
comparison ranking: total 115

Life expectancy at birth: *total population:* 76.7 years (2024 est.)
male: 73.4 years
female: 80.1 years
comparison ranking: total population 102

Total fertility rate: 1.65 children born/woman (2024 est.)
comparison ranking: 172

Gross reproduction rate: 0.8 (2024 est.)

Drinking water source: *improved: urban:* 100% of population (2022 est.)
rural: 100% of population (2022 est.)
total: 100% of population (2022 est.)

Health expenditure: 12.3% of GDP (2021)
6.5% of national budget (2022 est.)

Physician density: 3.36 physicians/1,000 population (2022)

Hospital bed density: 4.6 beds/1,000 population (2020 est.)

Sanitation facility access: *improved: urban:* 100% of population (2022 est.)
rural: 84.6% of population (2022 est.)
total: 94.4% of population (2022 est.)
unimproved: urban: 0% of population (2022 est.)
rural: 15.4% of population (2022 est.)
total: 5.6% of population (2022 est.)

Obesity - adult prevalence rate: 20.2% (2016)
comparison ranking: 101

Alcohol consumption per capita: *total:* 3.77 liters of pure alcohol (2019 est.)
beer: 0.52 liters of pure alcohol (2019 est.)
wine: 0.46 liters of pure alcohol (2019 est.)
spirits: 2.78 liters of pure alcohol (2019 est.)
other alcohols: 0.01 liters of pure alcohol (2019 est.)
comparison ranking: total 99

Tobacco use: *total:* 21.5% (2025 est.)
male: 47.6% (2025 est.)
female: 1.6% (2025 est.)
comparison ranking: total 57

Children under the age of 5 years underweight: 2.6% (2015/16)
comparison ranking: 87

Currently married women (ages 15-49): 64.8% (2023 est.)

Child marriage: *women married by age 15:* 0% (2016)
women married by age 18: 5.3% (2016)
men married by age 18: 0.4% (2016)

Education expenditure: 2.4% of GDP (2023 est.)
10% national budget (2023 est.)
comparison ranking: Education expenditure (% GDP) 176

Literacy: *total population:* 99.8% (2022 est.)
male: 99.7% (2022 est.)
female: 99.9% (2022 est.)

School life expectancy (primary to tertiary education): *total:* 14 years (2023 est.)

male: 14 years (2023 est.)
female: 14 years (2023 est.)

ENVIRONMENT

Environmental issues: soil pollution from toxic chemicals; deforestation; river pollution; threats to drinking water supplies from use of hydropower; nuclear power plant located in earthquake zone

International environmental agreements: *party to:* Air Pollution, Biodiversity, Climate Change, Climate Change-Kyoto Protocol, Climate Change-Paris Agreement, Comprehensive Nuclear Test Ban, Desertification, Endangered Species, Environmental Modification, Hazardous Wastes, Law of the Sea, Nuclear Test Ban, Ozone Layer Protection, Wetlands
signed, but not ratified: Air Pollution-Heavy Metals, Air Pollution-Multi-effect Protocol, Air Pollution-Persistent Organic Pollutants

Climate: highland continental, hot summers, cold winters

Urbanization: *urban population:* 63.7% of total population (2023)
rate of urbanization: 0.23% annual rate of change (2020-25 est.)

Carbon dioxide emissions: 7.144 million metric tonnes of CO2 (2023 est.)
from coal and metallurgical coke: 48,000 metric tonnes of CO2 (2023 est.)
from petroleum and other liquids: 1.934 million metric tonnes of CO2 (2023 est.)
from consumed natural gas: 5.162 million metric tonnes of CO2 (2023 est.)
comparison ranking: total emissions 122

Particulate matter emissions: 28.4 micrograms per cubic meter (2019 est.)

Waste and recycling: *municipal solid waste generated annually:* 492,800 tons (2024 est.)
percent of municipal solid waste recycled: 13.5% (2022 est.)

Total water withdrawal: *municipal:* 542 million cubic meters (2022)
industrial: 150 million cubic meters (2022)
agricultural: 2.38 billion cubic meters (2022)

Total renewable water resources: 7.769 billion cubic meters (2022 est.)

GOVERNMENT

Country name: *conventional long form:* Republic of Armenia
conventional short form: Armenia
local long form: Hayastani Hanrapetut'yun
local short form: Hayastan
former: Armenian Soviet Socialist Republic, Armenian Republic
etymology: the etymology of the country's name remains obscure; according to tradition, the local name for the country, Hayastan, comes from Hayk, the legendary patriarch of the Armenians and the great-great-grandson of Noah; the name Armenia was first recorded in a rock inscription from A.D. 521 in modern-day Iran

Government type: parliamentary democracy; note - constitutional changes adopted in December 2015 transformed the government to a parliamentary system

Capital: *name:* Yerevan
geographic coordinates: 40 10 N, 44 30 E
time difference: UTC+4 (9 hours ahead of Washington, DC, during Standard Time)
etymology: name origin is unclear; it may derive from the name of a local ethnic group, or from the ancient fortress of Erebuni that was built on the current site of Yerevan in 782 B.C.

Administrative divisions: 11 provinces (*marzer*, singular - *marz*); Aragatsotn, Ararat, Armavir, Geghark'unik', Kotayk', Lorri, Shirak, Syunik', Tavush, Vayots' Dzor, Yerevan

Legal system: civil law system

Constitution: *history:* previous 1915, 1978; latest adopted 5 July 1995
amendment process: proposed by the president of the republic or by the National Assembly; passage requires approval by the president, the National Assembly, and a referendum with at least 25% registered-voter participation and more than 50% of votes; constitutional articles on the form of government and democratic procedures are not amendable

International law organization participation: has not submitted an ICJ jurisdiction declaration; non-party state to the ICCt

Citizenship: *citizenship by birth:* no
citizenship by descent only: at least one parent must be a citizen of Armenia
dual citizenship recognized: yes
residency requirement for naturalization: 3 years

Suffrage: 18 years of age; universal

Executive branch: *chief of state:* President Vahagn KHACHATURYAN (since 13 March 2022)
head of government: Prime Minister Nikol PASHINYAN (since 10 September 2021)
cabinet: Council of Ministers appointed by the prime minister
election/appointment process: president indirectly elected by the National Assembly in 3 rounds, if needed, for a single 7-year term; prime minister indirectly elected by majority vote in two rounds, if needed, by the National Assembly
most recent election date: 3 March 2022
election results: *2022:* Vahagn KHACHATURYAN elected president in second round; note - Vahagn KHACHATURYAN (independent) ran unopposed and won the Assembly vote 71-0
2018: Armen SARKISSIAN elected president in first round; note - Armen SARKISSIAN (indpendent) ran unopposed and won the Assembly vote 90-10
expected date of next election: 2029

Legislative branch: *legislature name:* National Assembly (Azgayin Zhoghov)
legislative structure: unicameral
number of seats: 107 (all directly elected)
electoral system: proportional representation
scope of elections: full renewal
term in office: 5 years
most recent election date: 6/20/2021
parties elected and seats per party: Civil Contract Party (71); Armenia Alliance (29); I Have the Honour Alliance (7)
percentage of women in chamber: 38.3%
expected date of next election: June 2026
note 1: additional seats allocated as necessary; the numbers usually change with each parliamentary convocation
note 2: four mandates are reserved for national minorities; no more than 70% of the top membership of a party list can belong to the same sex; political parties must meet a 5% threshold and alliances a 7% threshold to win seats; at least three parties must be seated in the Parliament

Judicial branch: *highest court(s):* Court of Cassation or Appeals Court (consists of the Criminal Chamber with a chairman and 5 judges and the Civil and Administrative Chamber with a chairman and 10 judges – with both civil and administrative specializations); Constitutional Court (consists of 9 judges)
judge selection and term of office: Court of Cassation judges nominated by the Supreme Judicial Council, a 10-member body of selected judges and legal scholars; judges appointed by the president; judges can serve until age 65; Constitutional Court judges - 4 appointed by the president, and 5 elected by the National Assembly; judges can serve until age 70
subordinate courts: criminal and civil appellate courts; administrative appellate court; first instance courts; specialized administrative and bankruptcy courts

Political parties: Armenia Alliance or HD
Armenian National Congress or ANC
Bright Armenia
Civil Contract or KP
Country To Live In
Homeland of Armenians
Homeland Party
I Have Honor Alliance (formerly known as the Republican Party of Armenia) PUD
Liberal Party
National Democratic Party
Prosperous Armenia or BHK
Republic Party (Hanrapetutyun Party)

Diplomatic representation in the US: *chief of mission:* Ambassador Narek MKRTCHYAN (since 19 September 2025)
chancery: 2225 R Street NW, Washington, DC 20008
telephone: [1] (202) 319-1976
FAX: [1] (202) 319-2982
email address and website: armembassyusa@mfa.am
https://usa.mfa.am/en/
consulate(s) general: Glendale (CA)

Diplomatic representation from the US: *chief of mission:* Ambassador Kristina A. KVIEN (since 21 February 2023)
embassy: 1 American Ave., Yerevan 0082
mailing address: 7020 Yerevan Place, Washington, DC 20521-7020
telephone: [374] (10) 464-700
FAX: [374] (10) 464-742
email address and website: acsyerevan@state.gov
https://am.usembassy.gov/

International organization participation: ADB, BSEC, CD, CE, CIS, CSTO, EAEC (observer), EAEU, EAPC, EBRD, FAO, GCTU, IAEA, IBRD, ICAO, ICC, ICRM, IDA, IFAD, IFC, IFRCS, ILO, IMF, Interpol, IOC, IOM, IPU, ISO, ITSO, ITU, MIGA, NAM (observer), OAS (observer), OIF, OPCW, OSCE, PFP, UN, UNCTAD, UNESCO, UNIDO, UNIFIL, UNOOSA, UNWTO, UPU, WCO, WFTU (NGOs), WHO, WIPO, WMO, WTO

Independence: *21 September 1991 (from the Soviet Union); notable earlier dates:* 321 B.C. (Kingdom of Armenia established under the Orontid Dynasty), A.D. 884 (Armenian Kingdom reestablished under the Bagratid Dynasty); 1198 (Cilician Kingdom established); 28 May 1918 (Democratic Republic of Armenia declared)

National holiday: Independence Day, 21 September (1991)

Flag: *description:* three equal horizontal bands of red (top), blue, and orange
meaning: red stands for the blood shed for liberty, blue for the Armenian skies and hope, and orange for the land and the courage of the workers who farm it

National symbol(s): Mount Ararat, eagle, lion

National color(s): red, blue, orange

National anthem(s): *title:* "Mer Hayrenik" (Our Fatherland)
lyrics/music: Mikael NALBANDIAN/Barsegh KANACHYAN
history: adopted 1991; based on the anthem of the Democratic Republic of Armenia (1918-1922), but with different lyrics

National heritage: *total World Heritage Sites:* 3 (3 cultural)
selected World Heritage Site locales: Monasteries of Haghpat and Sanahin; Monastery of Geghard and the Upper Azat Valley; Cathedral and Churches of Echmiatsin

ECONOMY

Economic overview: upper-middle income, fast-growing Caucasus economy; stable fiscal and monetary regime but vulnerable to geopolitical shocks; economic and energy ties to Russia but seeking more EU and US trade; key copper and gold exporter; business-friendly and anti-corruption reforms; persistent unemployment; influx of migrants from Ukraine war easing

Real GDP (purchasing power parity): $60.909 billion (2024 est.)
$57.516 billion (2023 est.)
$53.108 billion (2022 est.)
note: data in 2021 dollars
comparison ranking: 115

Real GDP growth rate: 5.9% (2024 est.)
8.3% (2023 est.)
12.6% (2022 est.)
note: annual GDP % growth based on constant local currency
comparison ranking: 26

Real GDP per capita: $20,100 (2024 est.)
$19,400 (2023 est.)
$17,900 (2022 est.)
note: data in 2021 dollars
comparison ranking: 101

GDP (official exchange rate): $25.787 billion (2024 est.)
note: data in current dollars at official exchange rate

Inflation rate (consumer prices): 0.3% (2024 est.)
2% (2023 est.)
8.6% (2022 est.)
note: annual % change based on consumer prices
comparison ranking: 8

GDP - composition, by sector of origin: *agriculture:* 7.9% (2024 est.)
industry: 23.2% (2024 est.)
services: 61.5% (2024 est.)
note: figures may not total 100% due to non-allocated consumption not captured in sector-reported data
comparison rankings: agriculture 87; industry 106; services 79

GDP - composition, by end use: *household consumption:* 66.5% (2024 est.)
government consumption: 10.7% (2024 est.)
investment in fixed capital: 21.7% (2024 est.)
investment in inventories: 0.5% (2024 est.)
exports of goods and services: 76.3% (2024 est.)
imports of goods and services: -75.8% (2024 est.)
note: figures may not total 100% due to rounding or gaps in data collection

Agricultural products: milk, potatoes, grapes, vegetables, wheat, tomatoes, watermelons, apricots, apples, barley (2023)
note: top ten agricultural products based on tonnage

Industries: brandy, mining, diamond processing, metal-cutting machine tools, forging and pressing machines, electric motors, knitted wear, hosiery, shoes, silk fabric, chemicals, trucks, instruments, microelectronics, jewelry, software, food processing

Industrial production growth rate: 6.2% (2024 est.)
note: annual % change in industrial value added based on constant local currency
comparison ranking: 29

Labor force: 1.51 million (2024 est.)
note: number of people ages 15 or older who are employed or seeking work
comparison ranking: 134

Unemployment rate: 13.4% (2024 est.)
13.3% (2023 est.)
13.4% (2022 est.)
note: % of labor force seeking employment
comparison ranking: 169

Youth unemployment rate (ages 15-24): *total:* 26.2% (2024 est.)
male: 24.8% (2024 est.)
female: 27.9% (2024 est.)
note: % of labor force ages 15-24 seeking employment
comparison ranking: total 31

Population below poverty line: 24.8% (2022 est.)
note: % of population with income below national poverty line

Gini Index coefficient - distribution of family income: 27.2 (2023 est.)
note: index (0-100) of income distribution; higher values represent greater inequality
comparison ranking: 134

Household income or consumption by percentage share: *lowest 10%:* 4% (2023 est.)
highest 10%: 22.9% (2023 est.)
note: % share of income accruing to lowest and highest 10% of population

Remittances: 4.6% of GDP (2024 est.)
6% of GDP (2023 est.)
10.4% of GDP (2022 est.)
note: personal transfers and compensation between resident and non-resident individuals/households/entities

Budget: *revenues:* $5.812 billion (2023 est.)
expenditures: $6.27 billion (2023 est.)
note: central government revenues (excluding grants) and expenditures converted to US dollars at average official exchange rate for year indicated

Public debt: 48.3% of GDP (2023 est.)
note: central government debt as a % of GDP
comparison ranking: 108

Taxes and other revenues: 22.5% (of GDP) (2023 est.)
note: central government tax revenue as a % of GDP
comparison ranking: 34

Current account balance: -$997.086 million (2024 est.)
-$556.329 million (2023 est.)
$64.725 million (2022 est.)
note: balance of payments - net trade and primary/secondary income in current dollars
comparison ranking: 129

Exports: $18.618 billion (2024 est.)
$14.338 billion (2023 est.)
$10.118 billion (2022 est.)
note: balance of payments - exports of goods and services in current dollars
comparison ranking: 93

Exports - partners: Russia 37%, UAE 25%, Hong Kong 7%, China 5%, Georgia 4% (2023)
note: top five export partners based on percentage share of exports

Exports - commodities: gold, diamonds, copper ore, broadcasting equipment, jewelry (2023)
note: top five export commodities based on value in dollars

Imports: $19.087 billion (2024 est.)
$14.532 billion (2023 est.)
$10.265 billion (2022 est.)
note: balance of payments - imports of goods and services in current dollars
comparison ranking: 97

Imports - partners: Russia 29%, China 12%, Vietnam 6%, Georgia 5%, Iran 4% (2023)
note: top five import partners based on percentage share of imports

Imports - commodities: cars, gold, diamonds, broadcasting equipment, natural gas (2023)
note: top five import commodities based on value in dollars

Reserves of foreign exchange and gold: $3.685 billion (2024 est.)
$3.607 billion (2023 est.)
$4.112 billion (2022 est.)
note: holdings of gold (year-end prices)/foreign exchange/special drawing rights in current dollars
comparison ranking: 110

Debt - external: $6.002 billion (2023 est.)
note: present value of external debt in current US dollars
comparison ranking: 67

Exchange rates: drams (AMD) per US dollar -
Exchange rates: 392.73 (2024 est.)
392.476 (2023 est.)
435.666 (2022 est.)
503.77 (2021 est.)
489.009 (2020 est.)

ENERGY

Electricity access: *electrification - total population:* 100% (2022 est.)

Electricity: *installed generating capacity:* 4.265 million kW (2023 est.)
consumption: 7.012 billion kWh (2023 est.)
exports: 1.3 billion kWh (2023 est.)
imports: 194.045 million kWh (2023 est.)
transmission/distribution losses: 530.327 million kWh (2023 est.)
comparison rankings: installed generating capacity 97; consumption 117; exports 64; imports 108; transmission/distribution losses 82

Electricity generation sources: *fossil fuels:* 43% of total installed capacity (2023 est.)
nuclear: 29% of total installed capacity (2023 est.)
solar: 8.9% of total installed capacity (2023 est.)
hydroelectricity: 19% of total installed capacity (2023 est.)

Nuclear energy: Number of operational nuclear reactors: 1 (2025)

Net capacity of operational nuclear reactors: 0.42GW (2025 est.)

Percent of total electricity production: 31.1% (2023 est.)

Number of nuclear reactors permanently shut down: 1 (2025)

Coal: *production:* 300 metric tons (2023 est.)
consumption: 19,000 metric tons (2023 est.)
exports: 24 metric tons (2023 est.)
imports: 23,000 metric tons (2023 est.)
proven reserves: 317 million metric tons (2023 est.)

Petroleum: *refined petroleum consumption:* 15,000 bbl/day (2023 est.)

Natural gas: *consumption:* 2.631 billion cubic meters (2023 est.)
imports: 2.631 billion cubic meters (2023 est.)

Energy consumption per capita: 54.689 million Btu/person (2023 est.)
comparison ranking: 90

COMMUNICATIONS

Telephones - fixed lines: *total subscriptions:* 331,000 (2023 est.)
subscriptions per 100 inhabitants: 11 (2023 est.)
comparison ranking: total subscriptions 103

Telephones - mobile cellular: *total subscriptions:* 3.96 million (2023 est.)
subscriptions per 100 inhabitants: 135 (2022 est.)
comparison ranking: total subscriptions 137

Broadcast media: government-run Public Television network operates alongside 100 privately owned TV stations that provide local to near-nationwide coverage; three Russian TV companies are broadcast under interstate agreements; subscription cable TV services are available in most regions; several major international broadcasters are available, including CNN; Armenian TV completed conversion from analog to digital broadcasting in 2016; Public Radio of Armenia is a national, state-run broadcast network that operates alongside 18 privately owned radio stations (2024)

Internet country code: .am

Internet users: *percent of population:* 80% (2023 est.)

Broadband - fixed subscriptions: *total:* 546,000 (2023 est.)
subscriptions per 100 inhabitants: 19 (2023 est.)
comparison ranking: total 93

TRANSPORTATION

Civil aircraft registration country code prefix: EK

Airports: 11 (2025)
comparison ranking: 154

Heliports: 1 (2025)
comparison ranking: 161

Railways: *total:* 686 km (2017)

MILITARY AND SECURITY

Military and security forces: Armenian Republic Armed Forces: Armenian Army (includes land, air, air defense forces) (2025)
note: the Police of the Republic of Armenia is responsible for internal security, while the National Security Service is responsible for national security, intelligence activities, and border control

Military expenditures: 5.5% of GDP (2024 est.)
5.5% of GDP (2023 est.)
4.3% of GDP (2022 est.)
4.4% of GDP (2021 est.)
5% of GDP (2020 est.)

Military and security service personnel strengths: approximately 40-50,000 active Armenian Armed Forces (2025)

Military equipment inventories and acquisitions: the military's inventory includes mostly Russian and Soviet-era equipment; in recent years however, Armenia has looked to other countries besides Russia to provide military hardware, including France and India (2025)

Military service age and obligation: 18-27 for voluntary (men and women), contract (men and women) or compulsory (men) military service; contract military service is 3-12 months or 3 or 5 years; conscripts serve 24 months; men under the age of 36, who have not previously served as contract servicemen and are registered in the reserve, as well as women, regardless of whether they are registered in the reserve can be enrolled in contractual military service; all citizens aged 27 to 50 are registered in the military reserve and may be called to serve if mobilization is declared (2024)
note: in 2023, Armenia approved six-month voluntary service for women, after which they have the option to switch to a five-year contract; previously, women served on a contract basis; as of 2021, women made up about 10% of the active-duty military

Military - note: the Armenian Armed Forces were officially established in 1992, although their origins go back to 1918; the modern military's missions include deterrence, territorial defense, crisis management, humanitarian assistance, and disaster response, as well as socio-economic development projects; territorial defense is its primary focus, particularly in regards to tensions with neighboring Azerbaijan; Armenia and Azerbaijan engaged in open conflicts over the disputed Nagorno-Karabakh enclave in 1991-94 and 2020; Azerbaijan seized the entire enclave in 2023
Armenia has traditionally had close military ties with Russia; it has been a member of the Russian-led Collective Security Treaty Organization (CSTO) since 1994 and committed troops to CSTO's rapid reaction force until suspending its engagement in 2024; Armenia has relations with NATO going back to 1992 when Armenia joined the North Atlantic Cooperation Council; in 1994, it joined NATO's Partnership for Peace program and has contributed to the NATO force in Kosovo, as well as the former NATO deployment in Afghanistan (2025)

TRANSNATIONAL ISSUES

Refugees and internally displaced persons: *refugees:* 145,354 (2024 est.)
IDPs: 4 (2024 est.)
stateless persons: 373 (2024 est.)

ARUBA

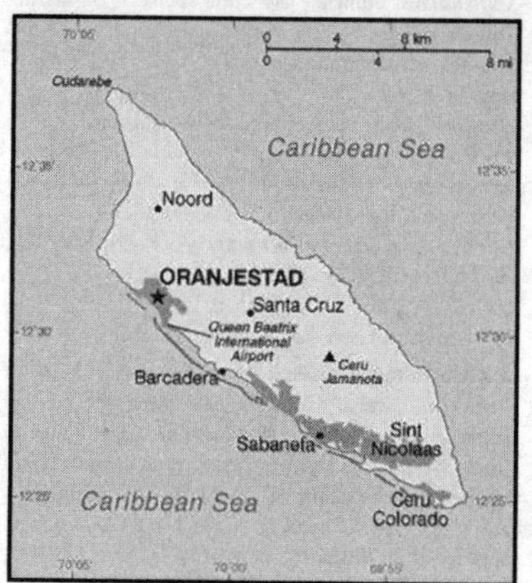

INTRODUCTION

Background: Discovered and claimed for Spain in 1499, Aruba was acquired by the Dutch in 1636. Three main industries have since dominated the island's economy: gold mining, oil refining, and tourism. A 19th-century gold rush was followed by prosperity brought on by the opening of an oil refinery in 1924. The last decades of the 20th century saw a boom in the tourism industry. Aruba seceded from the Netherlands Antilles in 1986 and became a separate, semi-autonomous member of the Kingdom of the Netherlands. Movement toward full independence was halted at Aruba's request in 1990.

GEOGRAPHY

Location: Caribbean, island in the Caribbean Sea, north of Venezuela

Geographic coordinates: 12 30 N, 69 58 W

Map references: Central America and the Caribbean

Area: *total:* 180 sq km
land: 180 sq km
water: 0 sq km
comparison ranking: total 218

Area - comparative: slightly larger than Washington, D.C.

Land boundaries: *total:* 0 km

Coastline: 68.5 km

Maritime claims: *territorial sea:* 12 nm
exclusive economic zone: 200 nm

Climate: tropical marine; little seasonal temperature variation

Terrain: flat with a few hills; scant vegetation

Elevation: *highest point:* Ceru Jamanota 188 m
lowest point: Caribbean Sea 0 m

Natural resources: NEGL; white sandy beaches foster tourism

Land use: *agricultural land:* 11.1% (2022 est.)
arable land: 11.1% (2022 est.)
permanent crops: 0% (2022 est.)
permanent pasture: 0% (2022 est.)
forest: 2.3% (2022 est.)
other: 86.6% (2022 est.)

Irrigated land: NA

Population distribution: most residents live in or around Oranjestad and San Nicolaas; most settlements tend to be located on the less mountainous western side of the island

Natural hazards: hurricanes; lies outside the Caribbean hurricane belt and is rarely threatened

Geography - note: a flat, riverless island known for its white sand beaches; its tropical climate is moderated by constant trade winds from the Atlantic Ocean; the temperature is almost constant at about 27 degrees Celsius (81 degrees Fahrenheit)

PEOPLE AND SOCIETY

Population: *total:* 125,063 (2024 est.)
male: 59,101
female: 65,962
comparison rankings: total 188; male 188; female 188

Nationality: *noun:* Aruban(s)
adjective: Aruban; Dutch

Ethnic groups: Dutch 78.7%, Colombian 6.6%, Venezuelan 5.5%, Dominican 2.8%, Haitian 1.3%, other 5.1% (2020 est.)
note: data represent population by nationality

Languages: Papiamento (official) (a creole language that mixes Portuguese, Spanish, Dutch, English, French, African languages, and Arawak) 69.4%, Spanish 13.7%, English (widely spoken) 7.1%, Dutch (official) 6.1%, Chinese 1.5%, other 1.7%, unspecified 0.4% (2010 est.)

Religions: Roman Catholic 75.3%, Protestant 4.9% (includes Methodist 0.9%, Adventist 0.9%, Anglican 0.4%, other Protestant 2.7%), Jehovah's Witness 1.7%, other 12%, none 5.5%, unspecified 0.5% (2010 est.)

Age structure: *0-14 years:* 17.2% (male 10,815/female 10,747)
15-64 years: 65.7% (male 39,621/female 42,487)
65 years and over: 17.1% (2024 est.) (male 8,665/female 12,728)

Dependency ratios: *total dependency ratio:* 52.3 (2024 est.)
youth dependency ratio: 26.3 (2024 est.)
elderly dependency ratio: 26.1 (2024 est.)
potential support ratio: 3.8 (2024 est.)

Median age: *total:* 40.9 years (2024 est.)
male: 39.3 years
female: 42.4 years
comparison ranking: total 56

Population growth rate: 1.08% (2024 est.)
comparison ranking: 87

Birth rate: 11.6 births/1,000 population (2024 est.)
comparison ranking: 156

Death rate: 8.8 deaths/1,000 population (2024 est.)
comparison ranking: 68

Net migration rate: 8 migrant(s)/1,000 population (2024 est.)
comparison ranking: 11

Population distribution: most residents live in or around Oranjestad and San Nicolaas; most settlements tend to be located on the less mountainous western side of the island

Urbanization: *urban population:* 44.3% of total population (2023)
rate of urbanization: 0.77% annual rate of change (2020-25 est.)

Major urban areas - population: 30,000 ORANJESTAD (capital) (2018)

Sex ratio: *at birth:* 1.02 male(s)/female
0-14 years: 1.01 male(s)/female
15-64 years: 0.93 male(s)/female
65 years and over: 0.68 male(s)/female
total population: 0.9 male(s)/female (2024 est.)

Infant mortality rate: *total:* 11.5 deaths/1,000 live births (2024 est.)
male: 15.6 deaths/1,000 live births
female: 7.3 deaths/1,000 live births
comparison ranking: total 117

Life expectancy at birth: *total population:* 78.5 years (2024 est.)
male: 75.4 years
female: 81.6 years
comparison ranking: total population 78

Total fertility rate: 1.82 children born/woman (2024 est.)
comparison ranking: 137

Gross reproduction rate: 0.9 (2024 est.)

Sanitation facility access: *improved:* total: 98.8% of population (2022 est.)
unimproved: total: 1.2% of population (2022 est.)

Currently married women (ages 15-49): 42.1% (2023 est.)

Education expenditure: 3.6% of GDP (2021 est.)
19.4% national budget (2019 est.)
comparison ranking: Education expenditure (% GDP) 124

ENVIRONMENT

Environmental issues: difficulty in properly disposing waste from tourists; air pollution from waste-burning; water pollution from plastics

Climate: tropical marine; little seasonal temperature variation

Urbanization: *urban population:* 44.3% of total population (2023)
rate of urbanization: 0.77% annual rate of change (2020-25 est.)

Carbon dioxide emissions: 1.163 million metric tonnes of CO_2 (2023 est.)
from petroleum and other liquids: 1.163 million metric tonnes of CO_2 (2023 est.)
comparison ranking: total emissions 170

Waste and recycling: *municipal solid waste generated annually:* 88,100 tons (2024 est.)

GOVERNMENT

Country name: *conventional long form:* Country of Aruba
conventional short form: Aruba
local long form: Land Aruba (Dutch); Pais Aruba (Papiamento)
local short form: Aruba
etymology: the origin of the island's name is unclear; according to tradition, the name comes from the Spanish phrase *oro hubo* ("there was gold"), but no gold was ever found on the island; other possible sources are either the local word *oruba* ("well-situated") or a combination of two Carib Indian words, *ora* and *oubao* ("shell" and "island," respectively)

Government type: parliamentary democracy; part of the Kingdom of the Netherlands

Dependency status: constituent country of the Kingdom of the Netherlands; full autonomy in internal affairs obtained in 1986 upon separation from the Netherlands Antilles; Dutch government responsible for defense and foreign affairs

Capital: *name:* Oranjestad
geographic coordinates: 12 31 N, 70 02 W
time difference: UTC-4 (1 hour ahead of Washington, DC, during Standard Time)
etymology: translates as "orange city" in Dutch; in 1824, the city was named after the royal family of the Netherlands, the House of Orange-Nassau

Administrative divisions: none (part of the Kingdom of the Netherlands)
note: Aruba is one of four constituent countries of the Kingdom of the Netherlands; the other three are the Netherlands, Curacao, and Sint Maarten

Legal system: civil law system based on the Dutch civil code

Constitution: *history:* previous 1947, 1955; latest drafted and approved August 1985, enacted 1 January 1986 (regulates governance of Aruba but is subordinate to the Charter for the Kingdom of the Netherlands); in 1986, Aruba became a semi-autonomous entity within the Kingdom of the Netherlands

Citizenship: see the Netherlands

Suffrage: 18 years of age; universal

Executive branch: *chief of state:* King WILLEM-ALEXANDER of the Netherlands (since 30 April 2013); represented by Governor General Alfonso BOEKHOUDT (since 1 January 2017)
head of government: Prime Minister Mike EMAN (since 28 March 2025)
cabinet: Council of Ministers elected by the Legislature (Staten)
election/appointment process: the monarchy is hereditary; governor general appointed by the monarch for a 6-year term; prime minister and deputy prime minister indirectly elected by the Staten for 4-year term
most recent election date: 6 December 2024
election results: Mike EMAN (AVP) elected prime minister; percent of Staten vote - NA
expected date of next election: by December 2028

Legislative branch: *legislature name:* Legislature (Staten)
legislative structure: unicameral
number of seats: 21
electoral system: proportional representation
scope of elections: full renewal
term in office: 4 years
most recent election date: 6 December 2024
parties elected and seats per party: AVP (9); MEP (8); FUTURO (3); PPA (1)
percentage of women in chamber: 38.1%
expected date of next election: by December 2028

Judicial branch: *highest court(s):* Joint Court of Justice of Aruba, Curacao, Sint Maarten, and of Bonaire, Sint Eustatius and Saba or "Joint Court of Justice" (sits as a 3-judge panel); final appeals heard by the Supreme Court in The Hague, Netherlands
judge selection and term of office: Joint Court judges appointed for life by the monarch
subordinate courts: Court in First Instance

Political parties: Accion21

Aruban People's Party or AVP
Democratic Network or RED
FUTURO
Movimiento Aruba Soberano (Aruban Sovereignty Movement) or MAS
Partido Patriotico di Aruba (Aruban Patriotic Party) or APP
People's Electoral Movement Party or MEP
Pueblo Orguyoso y Respeta or POR
RAIZ (ROOTS)

Diplomatic representation in the US: none (represented by the Kingdom of the Netherlands)

Diplomatic representation from the US: *embassy:* the US does not have an embassy in Aruba; the Consul General to Curacao is accredited to Aruba

International organization participation: ACS (associate), Caricom (observer), FATF, ILO, IMF, Interpol, IOC, ITUC (NGOs), UNESCO (associate), UNWTO (associate), UPU

Independence: none (part of the Kingdom of the Netherlands)

National holiday: National Anthem and Flag Day, 18 March (1976)

Flag: *description:* blue, with two narrow, horizontal yellow stripes across the lower portion and a red four-pointed star outlined in white in the upper-left corner
meaning: the star stands for Aruba's red soil and white beaches, and its four points for the major languages (Papiamento, Dutch, Spanish, English) and the points of a compass, to indicate that its inhabitants come from all over the world; blue symbolizes Caribbean waters and skies; the stripes represent the island's two main industries, tourism and mining

National symbol(s): Hooiberg (Haystack) Hill

National color(s): blue, yellow, red, white

National anthem(s): *title:* "Aruba Deshi Tera" (Aruba Sweet Land)
lyrics/music: Juan Chabaya 'Padu' LAMPE/Rufo Inocencio WEVER
history: national anthem adopted 1976
title: "Het Wilhelmus"
lyrics/music: Philips VAN MARNIX van Sint Aldegonde (presumed)/unknown
history: official anthem, as part of the Kingdom of the Netherlands

ECONOMY

Economic overview: small, tourism-dependent, territorial-island economy; very high public debt; COVID-19 crippled economic activity; partial recovery underway via tourism, benefitting from its high amount of timeshare residences; considering reopening oil refinery

Real GDP (purchasing power parity): $4.35 billion (2023 est.)
$4.172 billion (2022 est.)
$3.844 billion (2021 est.)
note: data in 2021 dollars
comparison ranking: 187

Real GDP growth rate: 4.3% (2023 est.)
8.5% (2022 est.)
24.1% (2021 est.)
note: annual GDP % growth based on constant local currency
comparison ranking: 63

Real GDP per capita: $40,500 (2023 est.)
$38,900 (2022 est.)
$35,700 (2021 est.)
note: data in 2021 dollars
comparison ranking: 59

GDP (official exchange rate): $3.649 billion (2023 est.)
note: data in current dollars at official exchange rate

Inflation rate (consumer prices): 4.3% (2019 est.)
3.6% (2018 est.)
-1% (2017 est.)
note: annual % change based on consumer prices
comparison ranking: 130

GDP - composition, by sector of origin: *agriculture:* 0% (2019 est.)
industry: 11.4% (2019 est.)
services: 78.3% (2019 est.)
note: figures may not total 100% due to non-allocated consumption not captured in sector-reported data
comparison rankings: agriculture 203; industry 179; services 13

GDP - composition, by end use: *household consumption:* 52.1% (2023 est.)
government consumption: 19.6% (2023 est.)
investment in fixed capital: 21.5% (2023 est.)
investment in inventories: 0% (2023 est.)
exports of goods and services: 88.3% (2023 est.)
imports of goods and services: -81.5% (2023 est.)
note: figures may not total 100% due to rounding or gaps in data collection

Agricultural products: aloes; livestock; fish

Industries: tourism, petroleum transshipment facilities, banking

Remittances: 1.1% of GDP (2023 est.)
1.2% of GDP (2022 est.)
1.2% of GDP (2021 est.)
note: personal transfers and compensation between resident and non-resident individuals/households/entities

Budget: *revenues:* $793 million (2019 est.)
expenditures: $782 million (2019 est.)

Current account balance: $194.498 million (2023 est.)
$230.556 million (2022 est.)
$79.257 million (2021 est.)
note: balance of payments - net trade and primary/secondary income in current dollars
comparison ranking: 70

Exports: $3.153 billion (2023 est.)
$2.853 billion (2022 est.)
$2.201 billion (2021 est.)
note: balance of payments - exports of goods and services in current dollars
comparison ranking: 155

Exports - partners: Jordan 34%, Colombia 31%, USA 7%, Guyana 5%, Slovakia 5% (2023)
note: top five export partners based on percentage share of exports

Exports - commodities: tobacco, gas turbines, refined petroleum, steam turbines, heating machinery (2023)
note: top five export commodities based on value in dollars

Imports: $2.565 billion (2023 est.)
$2.429 billion (2022 est.)
$1.947 billion (2021 est.)
note: balance of payments - imports of goods and services in current dollars
comparison ranking: 168

Imports - partners: USA 53%, Netherlands 15%, China 6%, Colombia 3%, Brazil 3% (2023)
note: top five import partners based on percentage share of imports

Imports - commodities: refined petroleum, tobacco, cars, garments, jewelry (2023)
note: top five import commodities based on value in dollars

Reserves of foreign exchange and gold: $1.468 billion (2023 est.)
$1.544 billion (2022 est.)
$1.513 billion (2021 est.)
note: holdings of gold (year-end prices)/foreign exchange/special drawing rights in current dollars
comparison ranking: 135

Exchange rates: Aruban guilders/florins per US dollar -

Exchange rates: 1.79 (2024 est.)
1.79 (2023 est.)
1.79 (2022 est.)
1.79 (2021 est.)
1.79 (2020 est.)

ENERGY

Electricity access: *electrification - total population:* 99.9% (2022 est.)
electrification - urban areas: 100%
electrification - rural areas: 100%

Electricity: *installed generating capacity:* 305,000 kW (2023 est.)
consumption: 824.036 million kWh (2023 est.)
transmission/distribution losses: 166.766 million kWh (2023 est.)
comparison rankings: installed generating capacity 164; consumption 165; transmission/distribution losses 58

Electricity generation sources: *fossil fuels:* 83.6% of total installed capacity (2023 est.)
solar: 2.6% of total installed capacity (2023 est.)
wind: 13.7% of total installed capacity (2023 est.)

Coal: *imports:* 1 metric tons (2023 est.)

Petroleum: *refined petroleum consumption:* 8,000 bbl/day (2023 est.)

Energy consumption per capita: 153.952 million Btu/person (2023 est.)
comparison ranking: 24

COMMUNICATIONS

Telephones - fixed lines: *total subscriptions:* 35,000 (2021 est.)
subscriptions per 100 inhabitants: 32 (2022 est.)
comparison ranking: total subscriptions 164

Telephones - mobile cellular: *total subscriptions:* 141,000 (2021 est.)
subscriptions per 100 inhabitants: 132 (2021 est.)
comparison ranking: total subscriptions 188

Broadcast media: freedom of the press respected, as guaranteed under Dutch law; newspapers are in the Papiamento language; 2 commercial TV stations, with a cable TV subscription service providing access to foreign channels; wide range of commercial radio stations available (2023)

Internet country code: .aw

Internet users: *percent of population:* 97% (2017 est.)

Broadband - fixed subscriptions: *total:* 19,000 (2022 est.)
subscriptions per 100 inhabitants: 17 (2022 est.)
comparison ranking: total 172

TRANSPORTATION

Civil aircraft registration country code prefix: P4

Airports: 1 (2025)
comparison ranking: 221

Merchant marine: *total:* 1 (2023)
by type: other 1
comparison ranking: total 182

Ports: *total ports:* 2 (2024)
large: 0
medium: 0
small: 1
very small: 1
ports with oil terminals: 1
key ports: Paardenbaai (Oranjestad), Sint Nicolaas Baai

MILITARY AND SECURITY

Military and security forces: no regular military forces; Aruban Militia (ARUMIL); Police Department for local law enforcement, supported by the Royal Netherlands Marechaussee (Gendarmerie), the Dutch Caribbean Police Force (Korps Politie Caribisch Nederland, KPCN), and the Dutch Caribbean Coast Guard (DCCG or Kustwacht Caribisch Gebied (KWCARIB)) (2025)

Military - note: defense is the responsibility of the Kingdom of the Netherlands; the Aruba security services focus on organized crime and terrorism; the Dutch Government controls foreign and defense policy; the Dutch Caribbean Coast Guard (DCCG) provides maritime security; the Dutch military maintains a presence on Aruba, including a marine company and a naval base (2024)

ASHMORE AND CARTIER ISLANDS

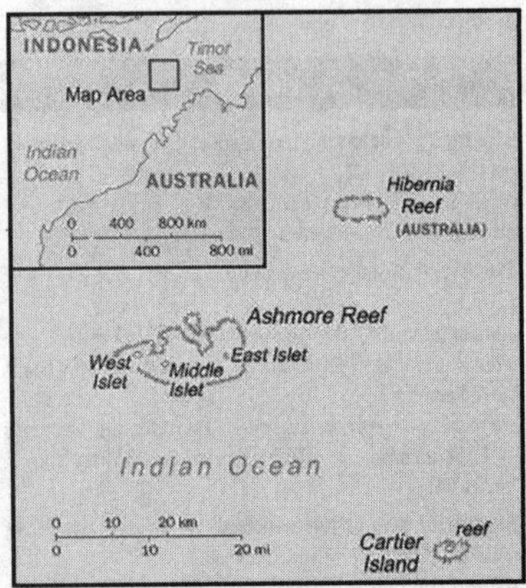

INTRODUCTION

Background: Indonesian fishermen have long fished in the area around Ashmore Reef and Cartier Island. British explorers were the first Europeans to see Cartier Island and Ashmore Reef in 1800 and 1811, respectively. American whalers frequently sailed by the islands in the 1850s and later settled to mine the phosphate deposits on Ashmore Reef, which were exhausted by 1891. The UK disputed US access to Ashmore Reef and formally annexed it in 1878. Cartier Island was annexed in 1909. In 1931, the UK transferred the islands to Australia, which accepted them in 1934 as part of Western Australia. In 1938, Australia transferred governance to the Northern Territory. During World War II, Cartier Island was used as a bombing range. In 1978, governance of Ashmore and Cartier Islands was moved to the federal government. Ashmore Reef and Cartier Island became marine reserves in 1983 and 2000 respectively.

In 1974, Australia and Indonesia signed a memorandum of understanding (MOU) to allow Indonesian fishermen to continue fishing around the islands. The MOU also allows Indonesian fishermen to visit the graves of past fishermen, replenish their fresh water, and shelter in the West Island Lagoon of Ashmore Reef. In the 1990s, Indonesia challenged Australia's claim to the islands, which was settled in a maritime boundary treaty in 1997. The islands were a popular first point of contact for migrants and refugees seeking to enter Australia, so in 2001, Australia declared the islands to be outside the Australian migration zone.

GEOGRAPHY

Location: Southeastern Asia, islands in the Indian Ocean, midway between northwestern Australia and Timor island; Ashmore Reef is 840 km west of Darwin and 610 km north of Broome; Cartier Islet is 70 km east of Ashmore Reef

Geographic coordinates: 12 25 S, 123 20 E
note: Ashmore Reef - 12 14 S, 123 05 E; Cartier Islet - 12 32 S, 123 32 E

Map references: Southeast Asia

Area: *total:* 5 sq km
land: 5 sq km
water: 0 sq km
note: includes Ashmore Reef (West, Middle, and East Islets) and Cartier Island
comparison ranking: total 245

Area - comparative: about eight times the size of the National Mall in Washington, D.C.

Land boundaries: *total:* 0 km

Coastline: 74.1 km

Maritime claims: *territorial sea:* 12 nm
contiguous zone: 24 nm
continental shelf: 200-m depth or to the depth of exploitation
exclusive fishing zone: 200 nm

Climate: tropical

Terrain: low with sand and coral

Elevation: *highest point:* Cartier Island 5 m
lowest point: Indian Ocean 0 m

Natural resources: fish

Land use: *agricultural land:* 0% (2018 est.)

Natural hazards: surrounded by shoals and reefs that can pose maritime hazards

Geography - note: Ashmore Reef National Nature Reserve established in 1983; Cartier Island Marine Reserve established in 2000

PEOPLE AND SOCIETY

Population: *total:* no permanent inhabitants
note: Indonesian fishermen are allowed access to the lagoon and fresh water at Ashmore Reef's West Island; access to East and Middle Islands is by permit only

ENVIRONMENT

Environmental issues: illegal killing of protected wildlife; overfishing; sea-level rise, changes in sea temperature, and ocean acidification; marine debris

Climate: tropical

GOVERNMENT

Country name: *conventional long form:* Territory of Ashmore and Cartier Islands
conventional short form: Ashmore and Cartier Islands
etymology: named after British Captain Samuel ASHMORE, who first sighted the island in 1811, and after the ship *Cartier*, from which the second island was discovered in 1800

Dependency status: territory of Australia; administered from Canberra by the Department of Regional Australia, Local Government, Arts and Sport

Legal system: the laws of the Commonwealth of Australia and the laws of the Northern Territory of Australia, where applicable, apply

Citizenship: see Australia

Diplomatic representation in the US: none (territory of Australia)

Diplomatic representation from the US: *embassy:* none (territory of Australia)

Flag: the flag of Australia is used

MILITARY AND SECURITY

Military - note: defense is the responsibility of Australia

ATLANTIC OCEAN

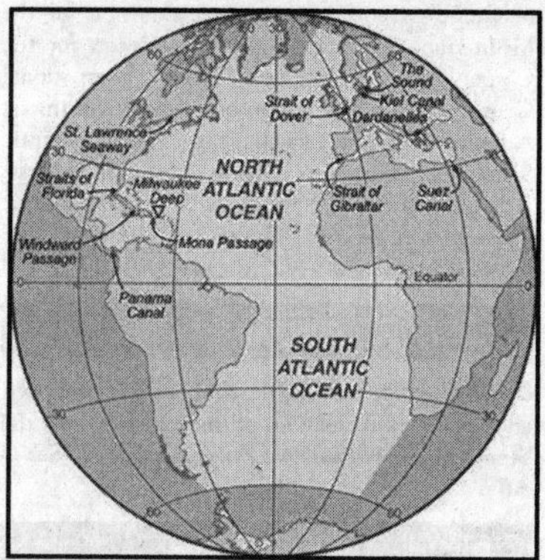

INTRODUCTION

Background: The Atlantic Ocean is the second largest of the world's five ocean basins (after the Pacific Ocean, but larger than the Indian Ocean, Southern Ocean, and Arctic Ocean). The Kiel Canal (Germany), Oresund (Denmark-Sweden), Bosporus (Turkey), Strait of Gibraltar (Morocco-Spain), and the Saint Lawrence Seaway (Canada-US) are important strategic access waterways. The decision by the International Hydrographic Organization in the spring of 2000 to delimit a fifth world ocean basin, the Southern Ocean, removed the portion of the Atlantic Ocean south of 60 degrees south latitude. For convenience and because of its immense size, the Atlantic Ocean is often divided at the Equator and designated as the North Atlantic Ocean and the South Atlantic Ocean.

GEOGRAPHY

Location: body of water between Africa, Europe, the Arctic Ocean, the Americas, and the Southern Ocean

Geographic coordinates: 0 00 N, 25 00 W

Map references: Map of the world oceans

Area: *total:* 85.133 million sq km
note: includes Baffin Bay, Baltic Sea, Black Sea, Caribbean Sea, Davis Strait, Denmark Strait, part of the Drake Passage, Hudson Bay, Hudson Strait, Gulf of America, Labrador Sea, Mediterranean Sea, North Sea, almost all of the Scotia Sea, and other tributary water bodies

Area - comparative: about 7.5 times the size of the US

Coastline: 111,866 km

Climate: tropical cyclones (hurricanes) develop off the coast of Africa near Cabo Verde and move westward into the Caribbean Sea; hurricanes can occur from May to December but are most frequent from August to November

Ocean volume: *ocean volume:* 310,410,900 cu km
percent of World Ocean total volume: 23.3%

Major ocean currents: clockwise North Atlantic Gyre consists of the northward flowing, warm Gulf Stream in the west, the eastward flowing North Atlantic Current in the north, the southward flowing cold Canary Current in the east, and the westward flowing North Equatorial Current in the south; the counterclockwise South Atlantic Gyre composed of the southward flowing warm Brazil Current in the west, the eastward flowing South Atlantic Current in the south, the northward flowing cold Benguela Current in the east, and the westward flowing South Equatorial Current in the north

Bathymetry: *continental shelf:* the passive margins of the Atlantic Ocean provide for wide continental shelves in North America, Northwest Europe, and the southern coast of South America
the following are examples of features on the continental shelf of the Atlantic Ocean: Blake Plateau
Celtic Shelf
Dogger Bank
Flemish Cap
Falkland Plateau
Grand Banks of Newfoundland
Great Bahama Bank
Little Bahama Bank
Tunisian Plateau
Yucatán Shelf
continental slope: the following are examples of features on the continental slope of the Atlantic Ocean: Amazon Cone
Congo Fan
Hudson Canyon
Mississippi Fan
abyssal plains: the following are examples of features on the abyssal plains of the Atlantic Ocean: Angola Basin
Agulhas Basin
Argentine Basin
Brazil Basin
Canary Basin
Cape Basin
Colombia Basin
Labrador Basin
Mexico Basin
Newfoundland Basin
North American Basin
Venezuela Basin
West European Basin
mid-ocean ridge: the Charlie-Gibbs Fracture Zone displaces the mid-ocean ridge 350 km to the west, separating the Mid-Atlantic Ridge from the Reykjanes Ridge; the Romanche Fracture Zone, located near the equator, offsets the Mid-Atlantic Ridge 900 km and is considered the dividing line between the North and South Atlantic Oceans
the following are examples of mid-ocean ridges on the floor of the Atlantic Ocean: East Mediterranean Ridge
Mid-Atlantic Ridge
Reykjanes Ridge
undersea terrain features: the following are examples of undersea terrain features on the floor of the Atlantic Ocean: Bermuda Rise
Cape Verde Plateau
New England Seamounts
Rio Grande Plateau
Rockall Plateau
ocean trenches: the following are examples of ocean trenches on the floor of the Atlantic Ocean: Cayman Trench (Caribbean Sea)
Hellenic Trench (Mediterranean Sea)
Puerto Rico Trench - deepest point in the Atlantic
South Sandwich Trench (South Atlantic)
atolls: Rocas Atoll (Brazil) is the only atoll in the South Atlantic

Elevation: *highest point:* sea level
lowest point: Puerto Rico Trench -8,605 m
mean depth: -3,646 m
ocean zones: the ocean is divided into three zones based on depth and light level; sunlight entering the water may travel about 1,000 m into the oceans under the right conditions, but there is rarely any significant light below 200 m
euphotic zone: the upper 200 m (656 ft) is also called "sunlight" zone; only a small amount of light penetrates beyond this depth
dysphotic zone: between 200 m (656 ft) and 1,000 m (3,280 ft), and also called the twilight zone; the intensity of light rapidly dissipates as depth increases, and photosynthesis is no longer possible
aphotic zone: below 1,000 m (3,280 ft) and also called the midnight zone; sunlight does not penetrate to these depths

Natural resources: oil and gas fields, fish, marine mammals (seals and whales), sand and gravel aggregates, placer deposits, polymetallic nodules, precious stones

Natural hazards: icebergs common in Davis Strait, Denmark Strait, and the northwestern Atlantic Ocean from February to August and have been spotted as far south as Bermuda and the Madeira Islands; ships subject to superstructure icing in extreme northern Atlantic from October to May; persistent fog can be a maritime hazard from May to September; hurricanes (May to December)

Geography - note: major chokepoints include the Dardanelles, Strait of Gibraltar, access to the Panama and Suez Canals; strategic straits include the Strait of Dover, Straits of Florida, Mona Passage, The Sound (Oresund), and Windward Passage; the equator divides the Atlantic Ocean into the North Atlantic Ocean and South Atlantic Ocean

ENVIRONMENT

Environmental issues: endangered marine species; fishery issues (over-fishing, unregulated bottom trawling, drift-net fishing, discards, catch of non-target species); pollution (maritime transport, discharges, offshore drilling, oil spills, improperly disposed waste); municipal sludge pollution off eastern US, southern Brazil, and eastern Argentina; oil pollution in Caribbean Sea, Gulf of America, Lake Maracaibo, Mediterranean Sea, and North Sea; industrial waste and municipal sewage pollution in Baltic Sea, North Sea, and Mediterranean Sea

Climate: tropical cyclones (hurricanes) develop off the coast of Africa near Cabo Verde and move westward into the Caribbean Sea; hurricanes can occur from May to December but are most frequent from August to November

Marine fisheries: *the Atlantic Ocean fisheries are the second most important in the world accounting for 25.8%, or 20,300,000 mt, of the global catch in 2020; of the seven regions delineated by the Food and Agriculture Organization in the Atlantic basin, the most important include the following: Northeast Atlantic* region (Region 27) is the fourth most important in the world, producing 10.5% of the global catch or 8,310,000 mt in 2020; the region encompasses the waters north of 36° North latitude and east of 40° West longitude, with the major producers including Norway (3,528,240 mt), Russia (1,044,153 mt), Iceland (933,019 mt), UK (823,669 mt), and Denmark (641,927 mt); the region includes the historically important fishing grounds of the North Sea, the Baltic Sea, and the Atlantic waters around Greenland, Iceland, and the British Isles; the principal catches include Atlantic cod, haddock, saithe (pollock), blue whiting, herring, and mackerel

Eastern Central Atlantic region (Region 34) is the second most important Atlantic fishery, and seventh largest in the world, producing more than 6.3% of the global catch or 4,950,000 mt in 2020; the region encompasses the waters between 36° North and 6° South latitude and east of 40° West longitude off the west coast of Africa, with the major producers including Morocco (1,419,872 mt), Mauritania (705,850 mt), Senegal (472,571 mt), Nigeria (451,768 mt), Ghana (303,001 mt), Cameroon (265,969 mt), and Sierra Leone (200,000 mt); the principal catches include pilchard, sardinellas, shad, and mackerel

Northwest Atlantic region (Region 21) is the fourth most important Atlantic fishery and eleventh in the world producing 1.9% of the global catch and 1,540,000 mt in 2020; it encompasses the waters north of 35° North latitude and west of 42° West longitude, including major fishing grounds over North America's continental shelf (the Grand Banks, Georges Bank, Flemish Cap, and Baffin Bay); the major producers include the US (927,777 mt), Canada (615,651 mt), and Greenland (179,990 mt); the principal catches include sea scallops, prawns, lobster, herring, and menhaden

Mediterranean and Black Sea region (Region 37) is a minor fishing region representing 1.5% or 1,190,000 mt of the world's total capture in 2020; the region encompasses all waters east of the Strait of Gibraltar, with the major producers including Turkey (686,650 mt), Italy (281,212 mt), Tunisia (129,325 mt), Spain (119,759 mt), and Russia (72,279 mt); the principal catches include European anchovy, European pilchard, gobies, and clams

Regional fisheries bodies: Commission for the Conservation of Southern Bluefin Tuna, Fishery Committee for the Eastern Central Atlantic, Fisheries Committee for the West Central Gulf of Guinea, General Fisheries Commission for the Mediterranean, International Commission for the Conservation of Atlantic Tunas, International Council for the Exploration of the Seas, Northwest Atlantic Fisheries Organization, North Atlantic Salmon Conservation Organization, North East Atlantic Fisheries Commission, Southeast Atlantic Fisheries Organization, Western Central Atlantic Fishery Commission

GOVERNMENT

Country name: *etymology:* name derives from the ancient Greek description of the waters beyond the Strait of Gibraltar, *Atlantis thalassa*, meaning "Sea of Atlas"

TRANSPORTATION

Transportation - note: Kiel Canal and Saint Lawrence Seaway are two important waterways; significant domestic commercial and recreational use of Intracoastal Waterway on central and south Atlantic seaboard and Gulf of America coast of US

AUSTRALIA

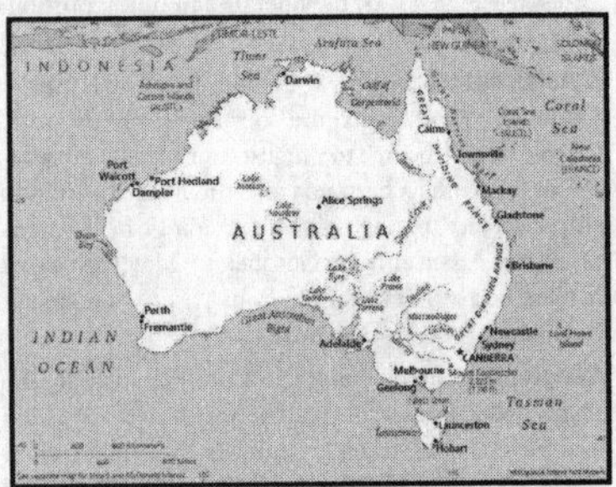

INTRODUCTION

Background: Aboriginal Australians arrived on the continent at least 60,000 years ago and developed complex hunter-gatherer societies and oral histories. Dutch navigators led by Abel TASMAN were the first Europeans to land in Australia in 1606, and they mapped the western and northern coasts. They named the continent New Holland but made no attempts to permanently settle it. In 1770, Englishman James COOK sailed to the east coast of Australia, named it New South Wales, and claimed it for Great Britain. In 1788 and 1825 respectively, Great Britain established New South Wales and then Tasmania as penal colonies. Great Britain and Ireland sent more than 150,000 convicts to Australia before ending the practice in 1868. As Europeans began settling areas away from the coasts, they came into more direct contact with Aboriginal Australians. Europeans also cleared land for agriculture, impacting Aboriginal Australians' ways of life. These issues, along with disease and a policy in the 1900s that forcefully removed Aboriginal children from their parents, reduced the Aboriginal Australian population from more than 700,000 pre-European contact to a low of 74,000 in 1933.

Four additional colonies were established in Australia in the mid-1800s: Western Australia (1829), South Australia (1836), Victoria (1851), and Queensland (1859). Gold rushes beginning in the 1850s brought thousands of new immigrants to New South Wales and Victoria, helping to reorient Australia away from its penal colony roots. In the second half of the 1800s, the colonies were all gradually granted self-government, and in 1901, they federated and became the Commonwealth of Australia. Australia contributed more than 400,000 troops to Allied efforts during World War I, and Australian troops played a large role in the defeat of Japanese troops in the Pacific in World War II. Australia severed most constitutional links with the UK in 1942 but remained part of the British Commonwealth. Australia's post-war economy boomed and by the 1970s, racial policies that prevented most non-Whites from immigrating to Australia were removed, greatly increasing Asian immigration to the country. In recent decades, Australia has become an internationally competitive, advanced market economy due in large part to economic reforms adopted in the 1980s and its proximity to East and Southeast Asia. In the early 2000s, Australian politics became unstable with frequent attempts to oust party leaders, including five changes of prime minister between 2010 and 2018. As a result, both major parties instituted rules to make it harder to remove a party leader.

GEOGRAPHY

Location: Oceania, continent between the Indian Ocean and the South Pacific Ocean

Geographic coordinates: 27 00 S, 133 00 E

Map references: Oceania

Area: *total:* 7,741,220 sq km
land: 7,682,300 sq km
water: 58,920 sq km
note: includes Lord Howe Island and Macquarie Island
comparison ranking: total 7

Area - comparative: slightly smaller than the 48 contiguous US states

Land boundaries: *total:* 0 km

Coastline: 25,760 km

Maritime claims: *territorial sea:* 12 nm
contiguous zone: 24 nm
exclusive economic zone: 200 nm
continental shelf: 200 nm or to the edge of the continental margin

Climate: generally arid to semiarid; temperate in south and east; tropical in north

Terrain: mostly low plateau with deserts; fertile plain in southeast

Elevation: *highest point:* Mount Kosciuszko 2,228 m
lowest point: Lake Eyre -15 m
mean elevation: 330 m

Natural resources: alumina, coal, iron ore, copper, lithium, tin, gold, silver, uranium, nickel, tungsten, rare earth elements, mineral sands, lead, zinc, diamonds, opals, natural gas, petroleum

note 1: Australia is the world's largest net exporter of coal accounting for 26.5% of global coal exports in 2021; coal is the country's most abundant energy resource, and coal ranks as the second-largest export commodity from Australia in terms of revenue; in 2020, Australia held the third-largest recoverable coal reserves in the world behind the United States and Russia
note 2: Australia is by far the world's largest supplier of opals
note 3: Australia holds the largest uranium reserves in the world and was the second-largest global uranium producer behind Kazakhstan in 2020
note 4: Australia was the largest exporter of LNG in the world in 2020

Land use: *agricultural land:* 47.3% (2022 est.)
arable land: 4.1% (2022 est.)
permanent crops: 0.1% (2022 est.)
permanent pasture: 43.1% (2022 est.)
forest: 17.4% (2022 est.)
other: 35.3% (2022 est.)

Irrigated land: 19,450 sq km (2022)

Major lakes (area sq km): *fresh water lake(s):* Lake Alexandrina - 570 sq km
salt water lake(s): Lake Eyre - 9,690 sq km; Lake Torrens (ephemeral) - 5,780 sq km; Lake Gairdner - 4,470 sq km; Lake Mackay (ephemeral) - 3,494 sq km; Lake Frome - 2,410 sq km; Lake Amadeus (ephemeral) - 1,032 sq km

Major rivers (by length in km): River Murray - 2,508 km; Darling River - 1,545 km; Murrumbidgee River - 1,485 km; Lachlan River - 1,339 km; Cooper Creek - 1,113 km; Flinders River - 1,004 km

Major watersheds (area sq km): Indian Ocean drainage: *(Great Australian Bight)* Murray-Darling (1,050,116 sq km)

Internal (endorheic basin) drainage: Lake Eyre (1,212,198 sq km)

Major aquifers: Great Artesian Basin, Canning Basin

Population distribution: population is primarily located on the periphery, with the highest concentration of people residing in the east and southeast; a secondary population center is located in and around Perth in the west; of the states and territories, New South Wales has, by far, the largest population; the interior, or "outback," has a very sparse population

Natural hazards: cyclones along the coast; severe droughts; forest fires
volcanism: volcanic activity on Heard and McDonald Islands

Geography - note: *note 1:* world's smallest continent but sixth-largest country; the largest country in Oceania, the largest country entirely in the Southern Hemisphere, and the largest country without land borders
note 2: the Great Dividing Range that runs along eastern Australia is that continent's longest mountain range and the third-longest land-based range in the world; the term "Great Dividing Range" refers to the fact that the mountains form a watershed crest from which all of the rivers of eastern Australia flow – east, west, north, and south
note 3: Australia is the only continent without glaciers; it is the driest inhabited continent on earth; Perth on the west coast is home to the invigorating sea breeze known as the "Fremantle Doctor," one of the most consistent winds in the world; Australia hosts 10% of the world's biodiversity, and a great number of its flora and fauna exist nowhere else in the world

PEOPLE AND SOCIETY

Population: *total:* 26,768,598 (2024 est.)
male: 13,305,110
female: 13,463,488
comparison rankings: total 54; male 54; female 55

Nationality: *noun:* Australian(s)
adjective: Australian

Ethnic groups: English 33%, Australian 29.9%, Irish 9.5%, Scottish 8.6%, Chinese 5.5%, Italian 4.4%, German 4%, Indian 3.1%, Australian Aboriginal 2.9%, Greek 1.7%, unspecified 4.7% (2021 est.)
note: data represent self-identified ancestry, with the option of reporting two ancestries

Languages: English 72%, Mandarin 2.7%, Arabic 1.4%, Vietnamese 1.3%, Cantonese 1.2%, other 15.7%, unspecified 5.7% (2021 est.)
note: data represent language spoken at home

Religions: Roman Catholic 20%, Protestant 18.1% (Anglican 9.8%, Uniting Church 2.6%, Presbyterian and Reformed 1.6%, Baptist 1.4%, Pentecostal 1%, other Protestant 1.7%), other Christian 3.5%, Muslim 3.2%, Hindu 2.7%, Buddhist 2.4%, Orthodox 2.3% (Eastern Orthodox 2.1%, Oriental Orthodox 0.2%), other 2.1%, none 38.4%, unspecified 7.3% (2021 est.)

Age structure: *0-14 years:* 18.3% (male 2,526,772/female 2,369,425)
15-64 years: 64.7% (male 8,688,023/female 8,640,671)
65 years and over: 17% (2024 est.) (male 2,090,315/female 2,453,392)

Dependency ratios: *total dependency ratio:* 54.5 (2024 est.)
youth dependency ratio: 28.3 (2024 est.)
elderly dependency ratio: 26.2 (2024 est.)
potential support ratio: 3.8 (2024 est.)

Median age: *total:* 38.1 years (2024 est.)
male: 36.9 years
female: 39.2 years
comparison ranking: total 77

Population growth rate: 1.13% (2024 est.)
comparison ranking: 81

Birth rate: 12.2 births/1,000 population (2024 est.)
comparison ranking: 142

Death rate: 6.8 deaths/1,000 population (2024 est.)
comparison ranking: 127

Net migration rate: 5.9 migrant(s)/1,000 population (2024 est.)
comparison ranking: 15

Population distribution: population is primarily located on the periphery, with the highest concentration of people residing in the east and southeast; a secondary population center is located in and around Perth in the west; of the states and territories, New South Wales has, by far, the largest population; the interior, or "outback," has a very sparse population

Urbanization: *urban population:* 86.6% of total population (2023)
rate of urbanization: 1.27% annual rate of change (2020-25 est.)
note: data include Christmas Island, Cocos Islands, and Norfolk Island

Major urban areas - population: 5.235 million Melbourne, 5.121 million Sydney, 2.505 million Brisbane, 2.118 million Perth, 1.367 million Adelaide, 472,000 CANBERRA (capital) (2023)

Sex ratio: *at birth:* 1.06 male(s)/female
0-14 years: 1.07 male(s)/female
15-64 years: 1.01 male(s)/female
65 years and over: 0.85 male(s)/female
total population: 0.99 male(s)/female (2024 est.)

Mother's mean age at first birth: 28.7 years (2019 est.)

Maternal mortality ratio: 2 deaths/100,000 live births (2023 est.)
comparison ranking: 191

Infant mortality rate: *total:* 2.9 deaths/1,000 live births (2024 est.)
male: 3.2 deaths/1,000 live births
female: 2.7 deaths/1,000 live births
comparison ranking: total 211

Life expectancy at birth: *total population:* 83.5 years (2024 est.)
male: 81.3 years
female: 85.7 years
comparison ranking: total population 13

Total fertility rate: 1.73 children born/woman (2024 est.)
comparison ranking: 155

Gross reproduction rate: 0.84 (2024 est.)

Drinking water source: *improved: urban:* 100% of population (2022 est.)
rural: 100% of population (2022 est.)
total: 100% of population (2022 est.)

Health expenditure: 10.5% of GDP (2021)
20.2% of national budget (2022 est.)

Physician density: 4.09 physicians/1,000 population (2022)

Hospital bed density: 3.8 beds/1,000 population (2016 est.)

Sanitation facility access: *improved:* total: 100% of population (2022 est.)
unimproved: total: 0% of population (2022 est.)

Obesity - adult prevalence rate: 29% (2016)
comparison ranking: 27

Alcohol consumption per capita: *total:* 9.51 liters of pure alcohol (2019 est.)
beer: 3.71 liters of pure alcohol (2019 est.)
wine: 3.67 liters of pure alcohol (2019 est.)
spirits: 1.32 liters of pure alcohol (2019 est.)
other alcohols: 0.81 liters of pure alcohol (2019 est.)
comparison ranking: total 27

Tobacco use: *total:* 11.4% (2025 est.)
male: 13.6% (2025 est.)
female: 9.2% (2025 est.)
comparison ranking: total 119

Currently married women (ages 15-49): 55.9% (2023 est.)

Education expenditure: 5.2% of GDP (2022 est.)
13.9% national budget (2022 est.)
comparison ranking: Education expenditure (% GDP) 55

School life expectancy (primary to tertiary education): *total:* 21 years (2023 est.)
male: 20 years (2023 est.)
female: 21 years (2023 est.)

ENVIRONMENT

Environmental issues: soil erosion from overgrazing, deforestation, industrial development, urbanization, and poor farming practices; limited natural freshwater resources; soil salinity from use of poor-quality water, drought, desertification; habitat loss from agricultural clearing; floral extinctions; Great Barrier Reef preservation; overfishing; pollution; invasive species

International environmental agreements: *party to:* Antarctic-Environmental Protection, Antarctic-Marine Living Resources, Antarctic Seals, Antarctic Treaty, Biodiversity, Climate Change, Climate Change-Kyoto Protocol, Climate Change-Paris Agreement, Comprehensive Nuclear Test Ban, Desertification, Endangered Species, Environmental Modification, Hazardous Wastes, Law of the Sea, Marine Dumping-London Convention, Marine Dumping-London Protocol, Marine Life Conservation, Nuclear Test Ban, Ozone Layer Protection, Ship Pollution, Tropical Timber 2006, Wetlands, Whaling
signed, but not ratified: none of the selected agreements

Climate: generally arid to semiarid; temperate in south and east; tropical in north

Urbanization: *urban population:* 86.6% of total population (2023)
rate of urbanization: 1.27% annual rate of change (2020-25 est.)
note: data include Christmas Island, Cocos Islands, and Norfolk Island

Carbon dioxide emissions: 394.653 million metric tonnes of CO2 (2023 est.)
from coal and metallurgical coke: 146.81 million metric tonnes of CO2 (2023 est.)
from petroleum and other liquids: 154.346 million metric tonnes of CO2 (2023 est.)
from consumed natural gas: 93.497 million metric tonnes of CO2 (2023 est.)
comparison ranking: total emissions 16

Particulate matter emissions: 9.1 micrograms per cubic meter (2019 est.)

Methane emissions: *energy:* 2,146 kt (2022-2024 est.)
agriculture: 2,382.2 kt (2019-2021 est.)
waste: 587.8 kt (2019-2021 est.)
other: 144.1 kt (2019-2021 est.)

Waste and recycling: *municipal solid waste generated annually:* 13.345 million tons (2024 est.)
percent of municipal solid waste recycled: 52.9% (2022 est.)

Total water withdrawal: *municipal:* 2.43 billion cubic meters (2022)
industrial: 3.11 billion cubic meters (2022)
agricultural: 11.19 billion cubic meters (2022)

Total renewable water resources: 492 billion cubic meters (2022 est.)

GOVERNMENT

Country name: *conventional long form:* Commonwealth of Australia
conventional short form: Australia
etymology: the name Australia derives from the Latin *australis* meaning "southern;" the Australian landmass was long referred to as "Terra Australis," or the Southern Land

Government type: federal parliamentary democracy under a constitutional monarchy; a Commonwealth realm

Capital: *name:* Canberra
geographic coordinates: 35 16 S, 149 08 E
time difference: UTC+11 (16 hours ahead of Washington, DC, during Standard Time)
daylight saving time: +1hr, begins first Sunday in October; ends first Sunday in April
time zone note: Australia has six time zones, including Lord Howe Island (UTC+11)
etymology: the name may derive from the Aboriginal word *nganbirra*, meaning "meeting place"

Administrative divisions: 6 states and 2 territories*; Australian Capital Territory*, New South Wales, Northern Territory*, Queensland, South Australia, Tasmania, Victoria, Western Australia

Dependent areas: Ashmore and Cartier Islands, Christmas Island, Cocos (Keeling) Islands, Coral Sea Islands, Heard Island and McDonald Islands, Jervis Bay, Norfolk Island (7)

Legal system: common law system based on the English model

Constitution: *history:* approved in a series of referenda from 1898 through 1900 and became law 9 July 1900, effective 1 January 1901
amendment process: proposed by Parliament; passage requires approval of a referendum bill by absolute majority vote in both houses of Parliament, approval in a referendum by a majority of voters in at least four states and in the territories, and Royal Assent; proposals that would reduce a state's representation in either house or change a state's boundaries require that state's approval prior to Royal Assent

International law organization participation: accepts compulsory ICJ jurisdiction with reservations; accepts ICCt jurisdiction

Citizenship: *citizenship by birth:* no
citizenship by descent only: at least one parent must be a citizen or permanent resident of Australia
dual citizenship recognized: yes
residency requirement for naturalization: 4 years

Suffrage: 18 years of age; universal and compulsory

Executive branch: *chief of state:* King CHARLES III (since 8 September 2022); represented by Governor General Samantha (Sam) MOSTYN (since 1 July 2024)
head of government: Prime Minister Anthony ALBANESE (since 23 May 2022)
cabinet: Cabinet nominated by the prime minister from among members of Parliament and sworn in by the governor general
election/appointment process: the monarchy is hereditary; governor general appointed by the monarch on the recommendation of the prime minister; following legislative elections, the leader of the majority party or majority coalition is sworn in as prime minister by the governor general

Legislative branch: *legislature name:* Parliament
legislative structure: bicameral

Legislative branch - lower chamber: *chamber name:* House of Representatives
number of seats: 150 (all directly elected)
electoral system: plurality/majority
scope of elections: full renewal
term in office: 3 years
most recent election date: 5/3/2025
parties elected and seats per party: Australian Labor Party (ALP) (94); Liberal National coalition (43); Independents (10); Other (3)
percentage of women in chamber: 46%
expected date of next election: May 2028

Legislative branch - upper chamber: *chamber name:* Senate
number of seats: 76 (all directly elected)
electoral system: proportional representation
scope of elections: partial renewal
term in office: 6 years
most recent election date: 5/3/2025
parties elected and seats per party: Australian Labor Party (ALP) (16); Liberal (6); The Greens (6); Liberal/Nationals (4); Pauline Hanson's One Nation (3); Liberal National Party of Queensland (2); Other (3)
percentage of women in chamber: 56.6%
expected date of next election: May 2028

Judicial branch: *highest court(s):* High Court of Australia (consists of 7 justices, including the chief justice); each of the 6 states, 2 territories, and Norfolk Island has a Supreme Court; the High Court is the final appellate court
judge selection and term of office: justices appointed by the governor-general in council for life with mandatory retirement at age 70
subordinate courts: subordinate courts: at the federal level: Federal Court; Federal Circuit and Family Court of Australia; *at the state and territory level:* Local Court - New South Wales; Magistrates' Courts – Victoria, Queensland, South Australia, Western Australia, Tasmania, Northern Territory, Australian Capital Territory; District Courts – New South Wales, Queensland, South Australia, Western Australia; County Court – Victoria; Family Court – Western Australia; Court of Petty Sessions – Norfolk Island

Political parties: Australian Greens Party or The Greens
Australian Labor Party or ALP
Centre Alliance (formerly known as the Nick Xenophon Team or NXT)
Jacqui Lambie Network or JLN
Katter's Australian Party (KAP)
Liberal Party of Australia
Liberal National Party of Queensland
The Nationals
One Nation or ONP
United Australia Party
note: the Labor Party is Australia's oldest political party, established federally in 1901; the present Liberal Party was formed in 1944; the Country Party was formed in 1920, renamed the National Country Party in 1975, the National Party of Australia in 1982, and since 2003 has been known as the Nationals; since the general election of 1949, the Liberal Party and the Nationals (under various names) when forming government have done so as a coalition

Diplomatic representation in the US: *chief of mission:* Ambassador Kevin Michael RUDD (since 19 April 2023)
chancery: 1601 Massachusetts Avenue NW, Washington, DC 20036
telephone: [1] (202) 797-3000
FAX: [1] (202) 797-3168
email address and website: info.us@dfat.gov.au
https://usa.embassy.gov.au/
consulate(s) general: Chicago, Honolulu, Houston, Los Angeles, New York, San Francisco

Diplomatic representation from the US: *chief of mission:* Ambassador (vacant); Chargé d'Affaires Erika OLSON (since January 2025)
embassy: Moonah Place, Yarralumla, Australian Capital Territory 2600
mailing address: 7800 Canberra Place, Washington DC 20512-7800
telephone: [61] (02) 6214-5600
FAX: [61] (02) 9373-9184
email address and website: AskEmbassyCanberra@state.gov
https://au.usembassy.gov/
consulate(s) general: Melbourne, Perth, Sydney

International organization participation: ADB, ANZUS, APEC, ARF, ASEAN (dialogue partner), Australia Group, BIS, C, CD, CP, EAS, EBRD, EITI (implementing country), FAO, FATF, G-20, IAEA, IBRD, ICAO, ICC (national committees), ICCt, ICRM, IDA, IEA, IFC, IFRCS, IHO, ILO, IMF, IMO, IMSO, Interpol, IOC, IOM, IPU, ISO, ITSO, ITU, ITUC (NGOs), MIGA, NEA, NSG, OECD, OPCW, OSCE (partner), Pacific Alliance (observer), Paris Club, PCA, PIF, SAARC (observer), Quad, SICA (observer), Sparteca, SPC, UN, UNCTAD, UNESCO, UNHCR, UNMISS, UNMIT, UNRWA, UNTSO, UNWTO, UPU, Wassenaar Arrangement, WCO, WFTU (NGOs), WHO, WIPO, WMO, WTO, ZC

Independence: 1 January 1901 (from the federation of UK colonies)

National holiday: Australia Day (commemorates the arrival of the First Fleet of Australian settlers), 26 January (1788); ANZAC Day (commemorates the anniversary of the landing of troops of the Australian and New Zealand Army Corps during World War I at Gallipoli, Turkey), 25 April (1915)

Flag: *description:* blue, with the UK flag in the upper-left quadrant and a large seven-pointed star in the lower-left quadrant; on the right half is a representation of the Southern Cross constellation in white, with one small five-pointed star and four larger seven-pointed stars
meaning: the largest star is known as the Commonwealth or Federation Star and represents the federation of the Australian colonies in 1901; the star has one point for each of the six original states, plus one representing all of Australia's internal and external territories

National symbol(s): Commonwealth Star (seven-pointed Star of Federation), golden wattle tree (Acacia pycnantha), kangaroo, emu

National color(s): green, gold

National coat of arms: King George V of the United Kingdom granted the current Commonwealth Coat of Arms to Australia on 19 September 1912; the center of the shield has the symbols of Australia's six states; the kangaroo and the emu symbolize a nation moving forward, since neither animal can move backward easily; the gold Commonwealth star sits above the shield, with six points representing the Australian states and the seventh representing the territories; the gold and blue in the wreath under the star are the livery, or identifying, colors for the coat of arms; Australia's floral emblem, the golden wattle, frames the shield

National anthem(s): *title:* Advance Australia Fair
lyrics/music: Peter Dodds McCORMICK
history: adopted 1984; although originally written in the late 19th century, the anthem was not used for all official occasions until 1984
title: "God Save the King"
lyrics/music: unknown
history: royal anthem, as a Commonwealth country
note: the well-known and much-loved bush ballad "Waltzing Matilda" is often referred to as Australia's unofficial national anthem; Australian poet Banjo PATERSON wrote the original lyrics in 1895, and they were first published as sheet music in 1903; since 2012, a Waltzing Matilda Day has been held annually on 6 April, the anniversary of the first performance of the song in 1895

National heritage: *total World Heritage Sites:* 20 (4 cultural, 12 natural, 4 mixed)
selected World Heritage Site locales: Great Barrier Reef (n); Greater Blue Mountains Area (n); Fraser Island (n); Gondwana Rainforests (n); Lord Howe Island Group (n); Royal Exhibition Building and Carlton Gardens (c); Shark Bay (n); Sydney Opera House (c); Uluṟu-Kata Tjuṯa National Park (m); Kakadu National Park (m)
note: includes one site on Heard Island and McDonald Islands

ECONOMY

Economic overview: high-income and globally integrated economy; strong mining, manufacturing, and service sectors driving slow but steady growth; net exporter, driven by commodities to East Asian trade partners; weak productivity and aging population straining labor force participation

Real GDP (purchasing power parity): $1.635 trillion (2024 est.)
$1.611 trillion (2023 est.)
$1.558 trillion (2022 est.)
note: data in 2021 dollars
comparison ranking: 21

Real GDP growth rate: 1.4% (2024 est.)
3.4% (2023 est.)
4.2% (2022 est.)
note: annual GDP % growth based on constant local currency
comparison ranking: 165

Real GDP per capita: $60,100 (2024 est.)
$60,500 (2023 est.)
$59,900 (2022 est.)
note: data in 2021 dollars
comparison ranking: 31

GDP (official exchange rate): $1.752 trillion (2024 est.)
note: data in current dollars at official exchange rate

Inflation rate (consumer prices): 3.2% (2024 est.)
5.6% (2023 est.)
6.6% (2022 est.)
note: annual % change based on consumer prices
comparison ranking: 103

GDP - composition, by sector of origin: *agriculture:* 2.2% (2024 est.)
industry: 26% (2024 est.)
services: 65.5% (2024 est.)
note: figures may not total 100% due to non-allocated consumption not captured in sector-reported data
comparison rankings: agriculture 147; industry 78; services 55

GDP - composition, by end use: *household consumption:* 51.2% (2024 est.)
government consumption: 22.2% (2024 est.)
investment in fixed capital: 24.3% (2024 est.)
investment in inventories: 0.1% (2024 est.)
exports of goods and services: 24.7% (2024 est.)
imports of goods and services: -22.6% (2024 est.)
note: figures may not total 100% due to rounding or gaps in data collection

Agricultural products: wheat, sugarcane, barley, rapeseed, milk, cotton, sorghum, beef, lentils, grapes (2023)
note: top ten agricultural products based on tonnage

Industries: mining, industrial and transportation equipment, food processing, chemicals, steel

Industrial production growth rate: 0.5% (2024 est.)
note: annual % change in industrial value added based on constant local currency
comparison ranking: 124

Labor force: 14.912 million (2024 est.)
note: number of people ages 15 or older who are employed or seeking work
comparison ranking: 43

Unemployment rate: 4.1% (2024 est.)
3.7% (2023 est.)
3.8% (2022 est.)
note: % of labor force seeking employment
comparison ranking: 65

Youth unemployment rate (ages 15-24): *total:* 9.5% (2024 est.)
male: 10.2% (2024 est.)
female: 8.7% (2024 est.)
note: % of labor force ages 15-24 seeking employment
comparison ranking: total 124

Gini Index coefficient - distribution of family income: 34.3 (2018 est.)
note: index (0-100) of income distribution; higher values represent greater inequality
comparison ranking: 83

Average household expenditures: *on food:* 9.9% of household expenditures (2023 est.)
on alcohol and tobacco: 3.6% of household expenditures (2023 est.)

Household income or consumption by percentage share: *lowest 10%:* 2.8% (2018 est.)
highest 10%: 26.2% (2018 est.)
note: % share of income accruing to lowest and highest 10% of population

Remittances: 0.1% of GDP (2024 est.)
0.1% of GDP (2023 est.)
0.1% of GDP (2022 est.)
note: personal transfers and compensation between resident and non-resident individuals/households/entities

Budget: *revenues:* $431.27 billion (2022 est.)
expenditures: $453.105 billion (2022 est.)
note: central government revenues (excluding grants) and expenditures converted to US dollars at average official exchange rate for year indicated

Public debt: 58% of GDP (2022 est.)
note: central government debt as a % of GDP
comparison ranking: 83

Taxes and other revenues: 23.6% (of GDP) (2022 est.)
note: central government tax revenue as a % of GDP
comparison ranking: 25

Current account balance: -$34.402 billion (2024 est.)
-$5.186 billion (2023 est.)
$5.707 billion (2022 est.)
note: balance of payments - net trade and primary/secondary income in current dollars
comparison ranking: 191

Exports: $425.16 billion (2024 est.)

$448.507 billion (2023 est.)
$465.99 billion (2022 est.)
note: balance of payments - exports of goods and services in current dollars
comparison ranking: 24

Exports - partners: China 37%, Japan 16%, S. Korea 6%, India 5%, Taiwan 5% (2023)
note: top five export partners based on percentage share of exports

Exports - commodities: iron ore, coal, natural gas, gold, minerals (2023)
note: top five export commodities based on value in dollars

Imports: $405.336 billion (2024 est.)
$389.211 billion (2023 est.)
$379.981 billion (2022 est.)
note: balance of payments - imports of goods and services in current dollars
comparison ranking: 21

Imports - partners: China 26%, USA 11%, S. Korea 6%, Japan 6%, Thailand 5% (2023)
note: top five import partners based on percentage share of imports

Imports - commodities: refined petroleum, cars, trucks, broadcasting equipment, garments (2023)
note: top five import commodities based on value in dollars

Reserves of foreign exchange and gold: $60.404 billion (2024 est.)
$61.703 billion (2023 est.)
$56.702 billion (2022 est.)
note: holdings of gold (year-end prices)/foreign exchange/special drawing rights in current dollars
comparison ranking: 40

Exchange rates: Australian dollars (AUD) per US dollar -

Exchange rates: 1.515 (2024 est.)
1.505 (2023 est.)
1.442 (2022 est.)
1.331 (2021 est.)
1.453 (2020 est.)

ENERGY

Electricity access: *electrification - total population:* 100% (2022 est.)

Electricity: *installed generating capacity:* 108.193 million kW (2023 est.)
consumption: 267.818 billion kWh (2023 est.)
transmission/distribution losses: 11.455 billion kWh (2023 est.)
comparison rankings: installed generating capacity 15; consumption 19; transmission/distribution losses 184

Electricity generation sources: *fossil fuels:* 64.9% of total installed capacity (2023 est.)
solar: 17.1% of total installed capacity (2023 est.)
wind: 11.5% of total installed capacity (2023 est.)
hydroelectricity: 5.4% of total installed capacity (2023 est.)
biomass and waste: 1.1% of total installed capacity (2023 est.)

Coal: *production:* 445.077 million metric tons (2023 est.)
consumption: 95.667 million metric tons (2023 est.)
exports: 348.32 million metric tons (2023 est.)
imports: 630,000 metric tons (2023 est.)
proven reserves: 149.472 billion metric tons (2023 est.)

Petroleum: *total petroleum production:* 386,000 bbl/day (2023 est.)
refined petroleum consumption: 1.151 million bbl/day (2024 est.)
crude oil estimated reserves: 2.446 billion barrels (2021 est.)

Natural gas: *production:* 151.307 billion cubic meters (2023 est.)
consumption: 48.845 billion cubic meters (2023 est.)
exports: 105.146 billion cubic meters (2023 est.)
imports: 521.034 million cubic meters (2023 est.)
proven reserves: 3.228 trillion cubic meters (2021 est.)

Energy consumption per capita: 223.158 million Btu/person (2023 est.)
comparison ranking: 16

COMMUNICATIONS

Telephones - fixed lines: *total subscriptions:* 6.458 million (2023 est.)
subscriptions per 100 inhabitants: 24 (2023 est.)
comparison ranking: total subscriptions 24

Telephones - mobile cellular: *total subscriptions:* 29.1 million (2023 est.)
subscriptions per 100 inhabitants: 107 (2022 est.)
comparison ranking: total subscriptions 49

Broadcast media: tradition of public broadcasting, but privately owned TV and radio have the biggest audiences; ownership of print and broadcast media is concentrated; Australian Broadcasting Corporation (ABC) runs national and local public radio and TV; other main public broadcaster is the multilingual Special Broadcasting Service (SBS); national commercial TV is dominated by three big free-to-air networks; broadcasters must carry a minimum percentage of Australian-made programs; pay TV via cable, satellite, and IPTV has a strong foothold (2023)

Internet country code: .au

Internet users: *percent of population:* 97% (2023 est.)

Broadband - fixed subscriptions: *total:* 9.63 million (2023 est.)
subscriptions per 100 inhabitants: 36 (2023 est.)
comparison ranking: total 26

TRANSPORTATION

Civil aircraft registration country code prefix: VH

Airports: 2,257 (2025)
comparison ranking: 3

Heliports: 392 (2025)
comparison ranking: 11

Railways: *total:* 32,606 km (2022) 3,448 km electrified
standard gauge: 18,007 km (2022) 1.435 mm
narrow gauge: 11,914 km (2022) 1.067 mm
broad gauge: 2,685 km (2022) 1.600 mm

Merchant marine: *total:* 604 (2023)
by type: bulk carrier 2, general cargo 76, oil tanker 6, other 520
comparison ranking: total 37

Ports: *total ports:* 66 (2024)
large: 5
medium: 8
small: 24
very small: 29
ports with oil terminals: 38
key ports: Brisbane, Dampier, Darwin, Fremantle, Geelong, Hobart, Melbourne, Newcastle, Port Adelaide, Port Dalrymple, Port Kembla, Port Lincoln, Sydney

MILITARY AND SECURITY

Military and security forces: Australian Defense Force (ADF): Australian Army, Royal Australian Navy, Royal Australian Air Force (2025)
note: the Australian Federal Police (AFP) is an independent agency of the Attorney-General's Department; the AFP, state, and territorial police forces are responsible for internal security; the Australian Border Force (ABF) is under the Department of Home Affairs

Military expenditures: 2% of GDP (2024 est.)
2% of GDP (2023 est.)
2% of GDP (2022 est.)
2% of GDP (2021 est.)
2% of GDP (2020 est.)

Military and security service personnel strengths: approximately 60,000 active ADF personnel (2025)

Military equipment inventories and acquisitions: the military's inventory includes a mix of domestically produced and imported Western weapons systems; in recent years, the US has been the largest supplier of arms; the Australian defense industry produces a variety of land and sea weapons platforms; the defense industry also participates in joint development and production ventures with other Western countries, including the US and Canada (2024)
note: in 2023, the Australian defense ministry announced a new strategic review that called for the acquisition of more long-range deterrence capabilities, including missiles, submarines, and cyber tools; in early 2024, Australia announced a 10-year plan to more than double the number of the Navy's major surface combatant ships

Military service age and obligation: 17 years of age (with parental consent; 18 years of age to deploy) for voluntary military service for men and women; no conscription (abolished 1972) (2024)
note 1: as of July 2024, New Zealanders who are permanent residents and have lived in Australia for at least 12 months could apply to join the ADF; from January 2025, eligible permanent residents from Canada, the UK, and the US were also to be allowed to apply
note 2: women have served in all roles, including combat arms, since 2013; in 2024, they comprised slightly more than 20% of the military

Military deployments: *note:* the number of Australian military forces varies by mission; since the 1990s, Australia has deployed more than 30,000 personnel on nearly 100 UN peacekeeping and coalition military operations around the World

Military - note: the ADF's missions include protecting Australia's borders and maritime interests, responding to domestic natural disasters, and deploying overseas for humanitarian, peacekeeping, and other security-related missions; in 2024, it established a cyber command; the ADF regularly participates in bi-lateral and multi-lateral exercises with foreign militaries Australia has been part of the Australia, New Zealand, and US Security (ANZUS) Treaty since 1951; Australia is also a member of the Five Powers Defense Arrangements (FPDA), a series of mutual assistance agreements reached in 1971 embracing Australia, Malaysia, New Zealand, Singapore, and the UK

Australia has long-standing bi-lateral defense and security ties to the UK, including defense and security cooperation treaties in 2024 and 2013; the Australia-UK Ministerial Consultations (AUKMIN) is their premier bilateral forum on foreign policy, defense, and security issues
Australia also has a long-standing military relationship with the US; Australian and US forces first fought together in France in 1918 and have fought together in every major US conflict since; Australia and the US signed an agreement in 2014 that allowed for closer bi-lateral defense and security cooperation, including rotations of US military forces and equipment to Australia; Australian military forces train often with US forces; Australia has Major Non-NATO Ally (MNNA) status with the US, a designation under US law that provides foreign partners with certain benefits in the areas of defense trade and security cooperation
in 2021, Australia, the UK, and the US announced an enhanced trilateral security partnership called "AUKUS" which would build on existing bilateral ties, including deeper integration of defense and security-related science, technology, industrial bases, and supply chains, as well as deeper cooperation on a range of defense and security capabilities (2025)

SPACE

Space agency/agencies: Australian Space Agency (ASA; established 2018; headquarters opened in 2020); Defense Space Command (established 2022) (2025)

Space launch site(s): Whalers Way Orbital Launch Complex (commercial site, South Australia); Arnhem Space Center (commercial site, Northern Territory); Bown Orbital Spaceport (commercial site, North Queensland) (2025)

Space program overview: has a long history of involvement in space-related activities, including astronomy, rockets, satellites, and space tracking; develops, builds, operates, and tracks satellites, including communications, remote sensing (RS), navigational, and scientific/testing/research, often in partnership with other countries; develops other space technologies, including communications, RS capabilities, and telescopes; encouraging growth in domestic commercial space-industry sector, including satellite launch vehicles; cooperates with a variety of foreign space agencies and industries, including those of China, the European Space Agency (ESA), individual ESA member states, India, Japan, New Zealand, South Korea, the UK, and the US; co-leads the Global Earth Observation System of Systems and hosts one of the telescopes for the international Square Kilometer Array radio telescope project (2025)
note: further details about the key activities, programs, and milestones of the country's space program, as well as government spending estimates on the space sector, appear in the Space Programs reference guide

TERRORISM

Terrorist group(s): Terrorist group(s): Islamic State of Iraq and ash-Sham (ISIS)
note: details about the history, aims, leadership, organization, areas of operation, tactics, targets, weapons, size, and sources of support of the group(s) appear(s) in Appendix T

TRANSNATIONAL ISSUES

Refugees and internally displaced persons: *refugees:* 120,789 (2024 est.)

IDPs: 185 (2024 est.)
stateless persons: 6,922 (2024 est.)

AUSTRIA

INTRODUCTION

Background: Once the center of power for the large Austro-Hungarian Empire, Austria was reduced to a small republic after its defeat in World War I. Nazi Germany annexed Austria in 1938, and the victorious Allies then occupied the country in 1945. As a result, Austria's status remained unclear for a decade after World War II, until a State Treaty signed in 1955 ended the occupation, recognized Austria's independence, and forbade unification with Germany. A constitutional law that same year declared the country's "perpetual neutrality" as a condition for Soviet military withdrawal. Austria joined the EU in 1995, but the obligation to remain neutral kept it from joining NATO, although the country became a member of NATO's Partnership for Peace program in 1995. Austria entered the EU Economic and Monetary Union in 1999.

GEOGRAPHY

Location: Central Europe, north of Italy and Slovenia

Geographic coordinates: 47 20 N, 13 20 E

Map references: Europe

Area: *total:* 83,871 sq km
land: 82,445 sq km
water: 1,426 sq km
comparison ranking: total 114

Area - comparative: about the size of South Carolina; slightly more than two-thirds the size of Pennsylvania

Land boundaries: *total:* 2,524 km
border countries (8): Czech Republic 402 km; Germany 801 km; Hungary 321 km; Italy 404 km; Liechtenstein 34 km; Slovakia 105 km; Slovenia 299 km; Switzerland 158 km

Coastline: 0 km (landlocked)

Maritime claims: none (landlocked)

Climate: temperate; continental, cloudy; cold winters with frequent rain and some snow in lowlands and snow in mountains; moderate summers with occasional showers

Terrain: mostly mountains (Alps) in the west and south; mostly flat or gently sloping along the eastern and northern margins

Elevation: *highest point:* Grossglockner 3,798 m
lowest point: Neusiedler See 115 m
mean elevation: 910 m

Natural resources: oil, coal, lignite, timber, iron ore, copper, zinc, antimony, magnesite, tungsten, graphite, salt, hydropower

Land use: *agricultural land:* 31.5% (2022 est.)
arable land: 16% (2022 est.)
permanent crops: 0.8% (2022 est.)
permanent pasture: 14.7% (2022 est.)
forest: 47.2% (2022 est.)
other: 21.3% (2022 est.)

Irrigated land: 382 sq km (2016)

Major lakes (area sq km): *fresh water lake(s):* Lake Constance (shared with Switzerland and Germany) - 540 sq km

Major rivers (by length in km): Donau (Danube) (shared with Germany [s], Slovakia, Hungary, Croatia, Serbia, Bulgaria, Ukraine, Moldova, and Romania [m]) - 2,888 km
note: [s] after country name indicates river source; [m] after country name indicates river mouth

Major watersheds (area sq km): Atlantic Ocean drainage: Rhine-Maas (198,735 sq km), *(Black Sea)* Danube (795,656 sq km)

Population distribution: the northern and eastern portions of the country are more densely populated; nearly two thirds of the populace lives in urban areas

Natural hazards: landslides; avalanches; earthquakes

Geography - note: *note 1:* landlocked; strategic location at the crossroads of central Europe with many easily traversable Alpine passes and valleys; major river is the Danube; population is concentrated on eastern lowlands because of steep slopes, poor soils, and low temperatures elsewhere
note 2: the world's largest and longest ice cave system at 42 km (26 mi) is the Eisriesenwelt (Ice Giants World) inside the Hochkogel mountain near Werfen, about 40 km south of Salzburg; ice caves are bedrock caves that contain year-round ice formations; they differ from glacial caves, which are transient and are formed by melting ice and flowing water within and under glaciers

PEOPLE AND SOCIETY

Population: *total:* 8,967,982 (2024 est.)
male: 4,392,898
female: 4,575,084
comparison rankings: total 100; male 102; female 99

Nationality: *noun:* Austrian(s)
adjective: Austrian

Ethnic groups: Austrian 80.8%, German 2.6%, Bosnian and Herzegovinian 1.9%, Turkish 1.8%, Serbian 1.6%, Romanian 1.3%, other 10% (2018 est.)
note: data represent population by country of birth

Languages: German (official nationwide) 88.6%, Turkish 2.3%, Serbian 2.2%, Croatian (official in Burgenland) 1.6%, other (includes Slovene, official in southern Carinthia, and Hungarian, official in Burgenland) 5.3% (2001 est.)
major-language sample(s): Das World Factbook, die unverzichtbare Quelle für grundlegende Informationen. (German)

Religions: Roman Catholic 55.2%, Muslim 8.3%, Orthodox 4.9%, Evangelical Christian 3.8%, Jewish 0.1%, other 5.4%, none 22.4% (2021 est.)
note: data on Muslim is a 2016 estimate; data on other/none/unspecified are from 2012-2018 estimates

Age structure: *0-14 years:* 14.1% (male 648,639/ female 616,334)
15-64 years: 64.7% (male 2,904,587/female 2,898,339)
65 years and over: 21.2% (2024 est.) (male 839,672/ female 1,060,411)

Dependency ratios: *total dependency ratio:* 53.4 (2024 est.)
youth dependency ratio: 21.7 (2024 est.)
elderly dependency ratio: 31.7 (2024 est.)
potential support ratio: 3.2 (2024 est.)

Median age: *total:* 44.9 years (2024 est.)
male: 43.6 years
female: 46.3 years
comparison ranking: total 24

Population growth rate: 0.3% (2024 est.)
comparison ranking: 167

Birth rate: 9.3 births/1,000 population (2024 est.)
comparison ranking: 194

Death rate: 9.9 deaths/1,000 population (2024 est.)
comparison ranking: 37

Net migration rate: 3.5 migrant(s)/1,000 population (2024 est.)
comparison ranking: 32

Population distribution: the northern and eastern portions of the country are more densely populated; nearly two thirds of the populace lives in urban areas

Urbanization: *urban population:* 59.5% of total population (2023)
rate of urbanization: 0.68% annual rate of change (2020-25 est.)

Major urban areas - population: 1.975 million VIENNA (capital) (2023)

Sex ratio: *at birth:* 1.05 male(s)/female
0-14 years: 1.05 male(s)/female
15-64 years: 1 male(s)/female
65 years and over: 0.79 male(s)/female
total population: 0.96 male(s)/female (2024 est.)

Mother's mean age at first birth: 29.7 years (2020 est.)

Maternal mortality ratio: 6 deaths/100,000 live births (2023 est.)
comparison ranking: 167

Infant mortality rate: *total:* 3.2 deaths/1,000 live births (2024 est.)
male: 3.6 deaths/1,000 live births
female: 2.7 deaths/1,000 live births
comparison ranking: total 201

Life expectancy at birth: *total population:* 82.7 years (2024 est.)
male: 80.1 years
female: 85.4 years
comparison ranking: total population 24

Total fertility rate: 1.52 children born/woman (2024 est.)
comparison ranking: 200

Gross reproduction rate: 0.74 (2024 est.)

Drinking water source: *improved:* *urban:* 100% of population (2022 est.)
rural: 100% of population (2022 est.)
total: 100% of population (2022 est.)

Health expenditure: 12.1% of GDP (2021)
16.3% of national budget (2022 est.)

Physician density: 5.52 physicians/1,000 population (2023)

Hospital bed density: 7.1 beds/1,000 population (2020 est.)

Sanitation facility access: *improved:* *urban:* 100% of population (2022 est.)
rural: 100% of population (2022 est.)
total: 100% of population (2022 est.)

Obesity - adult prevalence rate: 20.1% (2016)
comparison ranking: 105

Alcohol consumption per capita: *total:* 11.9 liters of pure alcohol (2019 est.)
beer: 6.3 liters of pure alcohol (2019 est.)
wine: 3.7 liters of pure alcohol (2019 est.)
spirits: 1.9 liters of pure alcohol (2019 est.)
other alcohols: 0 liters of pure alcohol (2019 est.)
comparison ranking: total 5

Tobacco use: *total:* 19.7% (2025 est.)
male: 21.1% (2025 est.)
female: 18.3% (2025 est.)
comparison ranking: total 72

Currently married women (ages 15-49): 58.7% (2023 est.)

Education expenditure: 4.8% of GDP (2022 est.)
9% national budget (2022 est.)
comparison ranking: Education expenditure (% GDP) 74

School life expectancy (primary to tertiary education): *total:* 16 years (2023 est.)
male: 16 years (2023 est.)
female: 17 years (2023 est.)

ENVIRONMENT

Environmental issues: some forest degradation from air and soil pollution; soil pollution from agricultural chemicals; air pollution from coal- and oil-fired power stations and industrial plants, and from trucks transiting Austria; water pollution

International environmental agreements: *party to:* Air Pollution, Air Pollution-Heavy Metals, Air Pollution-Nitrogen Oxides, Air Pollution-Persistent Organic Pollutants, Air Pollution-Sulphur 85, Air Pollution-Sulphur 94, Air Pollution-Volatile Organic Compounds, Antarctic Treaty, Biodiversity, Climate Change, Climate Change-Kyoto Protocol, Climate Change-Paris Agreement, Comprehensive Nuclear Test Ban, Desertification, Endangered Species, Environmental Modification, Hazardous Wastes, Law of the Sea, Nuclear Test Ban, Ozone Layer Protection, Ship Pollution, Tropical Timber 2006, Wetlands, Whaling
signed, but not ratified: Air Pollution-Multi-effect Protocol, Antarctic-Environmental Protection

Climate: temperate; continental, cloudy; cold winters with frequent rain and some snow in lowlands and snow in mountains; moderate summers with occasional showers

Urbanization: *urban population:* 59.5% of total population (2023)
rate of urbanization: 0.68% annual rate of change (2020-25 est.)

Carbon dioxide emissions: 56.959 million metric tonnes of CO2 (2023 est.)
from coal and metallurgical coke: 10.527 million metric tonnes of CO2 (2023 est.)
from petroleum and other liquids: 33.036 million metric tonnes of CO2 (2023 est.)
from consumed natural gas: 13.397 million metric tonnes of CO2 (2023 est.)
comparison ranking: total emissions 55

Particulate matter emissions: 10.3 micrograms per cubic meter (2019 est.)

Waste and recycling: *municipal solid waste generated annually:* 5.22 million tons (2024 est.)
percent of municipal solid waste recycled: 36% (2022 est.)

Total water withdrawal: *municipal:* 34.36 million cubic meters (2022 est.)
industrial: 2.21 billion cubic meters (2022 est.)
agricultural: 124 million cubic meters (2022 est.)

Total renewable water resources: 77.7 billion cubic meters (2022 est.)

Geoparks: *total global geoparks and regional networks:* 3
global geoparks and regional networks: Ore of the Alps; Styrian Eisenwurzen; Karawanken/Karavanke (includes Slovenia) (2023)

GOVERNMENT

Country name: *conventional long form:* Republic of Austria
conventional short form: Austria
local long form: Republik Oesterreich
local short form: Oesterreich
etymology: the name Oesterreich means "eastern realm" and dates to the 10th century; the designation refers to the fact that Austria was the easternmost extension of Bavaria and the German peoples; the word Austria is a Latinization of the German name

Government type: federal parliamentary republic

Capital: *name:* Vienna
geographic coordinates: 48 12 N, 16 22 E
time difference: UTC+1 (6 hours ahead of Washington, DC, during Standard Time)
daylight saving time: +1hr, begins last Sunday in March; ends last Sunday in October
etymology: the name may have evolved from the Roman name Vindobona, which was taken from the Celtic words *vindo* (white) and *bona* (fort)

Administrative divisions: 9 states (*Bundeslaender*, singular - *Bundesland*); Burgenland, Kaernten (Carinthia), Niederoesterreich (Lower Austria), Oberoesterreich (Upper Austria), Salzburg,

Steiermark (Styria), Tirol (Tyrol), Vorarlberg, Wien (Vienna)

Legal system: civil law system; Constitutional Court reviews legislative acts

Constitution: *history:* several previous; latest adopted 1 October 1920, revised 1929, replaced May 1934, replaced by German Weimar constitution in 1938 following German annexation, reinstated 1 May 1945

amendment process: proposed through laws designated "constitutional laws" or through the constitutional process if the amendment is part of another law; approval required by at least a two-thirds majority vote by the National Assembly and the presence of one-half of the members; a referendum is required only if requested by one-third of the National Council or Federal Council membership; passage by referendum requires absolute majority vote

International law organization participation: accepts compulsory ICJ jurisdiction; accepts ICCt jurisdiction

Citizenship: *citizenship by birth:* no

citizenship by descent only: at least one parent must be a citizen of Austria

dual citizenship recognized: no

residency requirement for naturalization: 10 years

Suffrage: 16 years of age; universal

Executive branch: *chief of state:* President Alexander VAN DER BELLEN (since 26 January 2017)

head of government: Chancellor Christian STOCKER (since 3 March 2025)

cabinet: Council of Ministers proposed by the chancellor and appointed by the president

election/appointment process: president directly elected by absolute-majority popular vote in 2 rounds, if needed, for a 6-year term (eligible for a second term); chancellor appointed by the president but determined by the majority coalition parties in the Federal Assembly; vice chancellor appointed by the president on the advice of the chancellor

most recent election date: 9 October 2022

election results: *2022:* Alexander VAN DER BELLEN reelected in first round; percent of vote - Alexander VAN DER BELLEN (independent) 56.7%, Walter ROSENKRANZ (FPO) 17.7%, Dominik WLAZNY (Beer Party) 8.3%, Tassilo WALLENTIN (independent) 8.1%, Gerald GROSZ (independent) 5.6%

2016: Alexander VAN DER BELLEN elected in second round; percent of vote in first round - Norbert HOFER (FPOe) 35.1%, Alexander VAN DER BELLEN (independent, allied with the Greens) 21.3%, Irmgard GRISS (independent) 18.9%, Rudolf HUNDSTORFER (SPOe) 11.3%, Andreas KHOL (OeVP) 11.1%, Richard LUGNER (independent) 2.3%; percent of vote in second round - Alexander VAN DER BELLEN 53.8%, Norbert HOFER 46.2%

expected date of next election: 2028

Legislative branch: *legislature name:* Parliament (Parlament)

legislative structure: bicameral

Legislative branch - lower chamber: *chamber name:* National Council (Nationalrat)

number of seats: 183 (all directly elected)

electoral system: proportional representation

scope of elections: full renewal

term in office: 5 years

most recent election date: 9/29/2024

parties elected and seats per party: Freedom Party (FPÖ) (57); People's Party (ÖVP) (51); Social Democratic Party (SPÖ) (41); NEOS ("New Austria") (18); Greens (16)

percentage of women in chamber: 36.1%

expected date of next election: September 2029

Legislative branch - upper chamber: *chamber name:* Federal Council (Bundesrat)

number of seats: 60 (all indirectly elected)

parties elected and seats per party: People's Party (OVP) (22); Social Democratic Party (SPO) (18); Freedom Party (16); Greens (3); NEOS (New Austria) (1)

percentage of women in chamber: 46.7%

Judicial branch: *highest court(s):* Supreme Court of Justice or Oberster Gerichtshof (consists of 85 judges organized into 17 senates or panels of 5 judges each); Constitutional Court or Verfassungsgerichtshof (consists of 20 judges including 6 substitutes; Administrative Court or Verwaltungsgerichtshof - 2 judges plus other members depending on the importance of the case)

judge selection and term of office: Supreme Court judges nominated by executive branch departments and appointed by the president; judges serve for life; Constitutional Court judges nominated by several executive branch departments and approved by the president; judges serve for life; Administrative Court judges recommended by executive branch departments and appointed by the president; terms of judges and members determined by the president

subordinate courts: Courts of Appeal (4); Regional Courts (20); district courts (120); county courts

Political parties: Austrian People's Party or OeVP
Freedom Party of Austria or FPOe
The Greens - The Green Alternative
NEOS - The New Austria and Liberal Forum
Social Democratic Party of Austria or SPOe

Diplomatic representation in the US: *chief of mission:* Ambassador Petra SCHNEEBAUER (since 19 APRIL 2023)

chancery: 3524 International Court NW, Washington, DC 20008-3035

telephone: [1] (202) 895-6700

FAX: [1] (202) 895-6750

email address and website: washington-ob@bmeia.gv.at
https://www.austria.org/

consulate(s) general: Los Angeles, New York

consulate(s): Chicago

Diplomatic representation from the US: *chief of mission:* Ambassador (vacant); Chargé d'Affaires Kami A. WITMER (since 20 January 2025)

embassy: Boltzmanngasse 16, 1090, Vienna

mailing address: 9900 Vienna Place, Washington DC 20521-9900

telephone: [43] (1) 31339 0

FAX: [43] (1) 31339 2017

email address and website: ConsulateVienna@state.gov
https://at.usembassy.gov/

International organization participation: ADB (nonregional member), AfDB (nonregional member), Australia Group, BIS, BSEC (observer), CD, CE, CEI, CERN, EAPC, EBRD, ECB, EIB, EMU, ESA, EU, FAO, FATF, G-9, IADB, IAEA, IBRD, ICAO, ICC (national committees), ICCt, ICRM, IDA, IEA, IFAD, IFC, IFRCS, IGAD (partners), ILO, IMF, IMO, Interpol, IOC, IOM, IPU, ISO, ITSO, ITU, ITUC (NGOs), MIGA, MINURSO, NEA, NSG, OAS (observer), OECD, OIF (observer), OPCW, OSCE, Paris Club, PCA, PFP, Schengen Convention, SELEC (observer), UN, UNCTAD, UNESCO, UNFICYP, UNHCR, UNIDO, UNIFIL, UNTSO, UNWTO, UPU, Wassenaar Arrangement, WCO, WFTU (NGOs), WHO, WIPO, WMO, WTO, ZC

Independence: *no official date of independence:* 976 (Margravate of Austria established); 17 September 1156 (Duchy of Austria founded); 6 January 1453 (Archduchy of Austria acknowledged); 11 August 1804 (Austrian Empire proclaimed); 30 March 1867 (Austro-Hungarian dual monarchy established); 12 November 1918 (First Republic proclaimed); 27 April 1945 (Second Republic proclaimed)

National holiday: National Day (commemorates passage of the law on permanent neutrality), 26 October (1955)

Flag: *description:* three equal horizontal bands of red (top), white, and red

history: one of the oldest national flags in the world; according to tradition, after a fierce battle in the Third Crusade in 1191, Duke Leopold V of Austria's white tunic became blood-spattered; when his sash was removed, a white band was revealed, and the red-white-red color combination was adopted as his banner

National symbol(s): eagle, edelweiss, Alpine gentian

National color(s): red, white

National anthem(s): *title:* "Bundeshymne" (Federal Hymn)

lyrics/music: Paula von PRERADOVIC/Wolfgang Amadeus MOZART or Johann HOLZER (disputed)

history: adopted 1947; Austria adopted a new national anthem after World War II to replace the former imperial anthem composed by Franz Josef HAYDN, which Germany had appropriated in 1922 and was thereafter associated with the Nazi regime; the Austrian Federal Assembly adopted a gender-neutral version of the lyrics in 2012

note: the beloved waltz "The Blue Danube" ("An der schoenen, blauen Donau"), composed in 1866 by Johann STRAUSS II, is widely considered Austria's unofficial national anthem

National heritage: *total World Heritage Sites:* 12 (11 cultural, 1 natural)

selected World Heritage Site locales: Historic Salzburg (c); Palace and Gardens of Schönbrunn (c); Halstadt–Dachstein/Salzkammergut Cultural Landscape (c); Semmering railway (c); Historic Graz and Schloss Eggenberg (c); Wachau Cultural Landscape (c); Historic Vienna (c); Fertő/Neusiedlersee Cultural Landscape (c); Baden bei Wien (c); Primeval Beech Forests - Dürrenstein, Kalkalpen (n)

ECONOMY

Economic overview: one of the strongest EU and euro economies; diversified trade portfolios and relations; enormous trade economy; Russian energy dependence, but investing in alternative energy; aging labor force but large refugee population; large government debt

Real GDP (purchasing power parity): $581.131 billion (2024 est.)
$588.031 billion (2023 est.)
$593.701 billion (2022 est.)

note: data in 2021 dollars

comparison ranking: 45

Real GDP growth rate: -1.2% (2024 est.)
-1% (2023 est.)
5.3% (2022 est.)

note: annual GDP % growth based on constant local currency

comparison ranking: 202

Real GDP per capita: $63,300 (2024 est.)
$64,400 (2023 est.)
$65,700 (2022 est.)
note: data in 2021 dollars
comparison ranking: 26

GDP (official exchange rate): $521.642 billion (2024 est.)
note: data in current dollars at official exchange rate

Inflation rate (consumer prices): 2.9% (2024 est.)
7.8% (2023 est.)
8.5% (2022 est.)
note: annual % change based on consumer prices
comparison ranking: 89

GDP - composition, by sector of origin: *agriculture:* 1.2% (2024 est.)
industry: 23.1% (2024 est.)
services: 65.3% (2024 est.)
note: figures may not total 100% due to non-allocated consumption not captured in sector-reported data
comparison rankings: agriculture 169; industry 107; services 57

GDP - composition, by end use: *household consumption:* 52.2% (2023 est.)
government consumption: 20.5% (2023 est.)
investment in fixed capital: 24.9% (2023 est.)
investment in inventories: 0.5% (2023 est.)
exports of goods and services: 59.5% (2023 est.)
imports of goods and services: -57.3% (2023 est.)
note: figures may not total 100% due to rounding or gaps in data collection

Agricultural products: milk, sugar beets, maize, wheat, barley, potatoes, pork, grapes, triticale, soybeans (2023)
note: top ten agricultural products based on tonnage

Industries: construction, machinery, vehicles and parts, food, metals, chemicals, lumber and paper, electronics, tourism

Industrial production growth rate: -5.5% (2024 est.)
note: annual % change in industrial value added based on constant local currency
comparison ranking: 181

Labor force: 4.768 million (2024 est.)
note: number of people ages 15 or older who are employed or seeking work
comparison ranking: 90

Unemployment rate: 5.5% (2024 est.)
5.3% (2023 est.)
5% (2022 est.)
note: % of labor force seeking employment
comparison ranking: 99

Youth unemployment rate (ages 15-24): *total:* 11.7% (2024 est.)
male: 11.4% (2024 est.)
female: 12% (2024 est.)
note: % of labor force ages 15-24 seeking employment
comparison ranking: total 107

Population below poverty line: 14.8% (2021 est.)
note: % of population with income below national poverty line

Gini Index coefficient - distribution of family income: 30.9 (2022 est.)
note: index (0-100) of income distribution; higher values represent greater inequality
comparison ranking: 114

Average household expenditures: *on food:* 10.1% of household expenditures (2023 est.)
on alcohol and tobacco: 3.5% of household expenditures (2023 est.)

Household income or consumption by percentage share: *lowest 10%:* 2.8% (2022 est.)
highest 10%: 24.6% (2022 est.)
note: % share of income accruing to lowest and highest 10% of population

Remittances: 0.7% of GDP (2024 est.)
0.6% of GDP (2023 est.)
0.6% of GDP (2022 est.)
note: personal transfers and compensation between resident and non-resident individuals/households/entities

Budget: *revenues:* $231.132 billion (2023 est.)
expenditures: $241.516 billion (2023 est.)
note: central government revenues (excluding grants) and expenditures converted to US dollars at average official exchange rate for year indicated

Public debt: 78.3% of GDP (2023 est.)
note: central government debt as a % of GDP
comparison ranking: 42

Taxes and other revenues: 25.9% (of GDP) (2023 est.)
note: central government tax revenue as a % of GDP
comparison ranking: 14

Current account balance: $12.642 billion (2024 est.)
$6.783 billion (2023 est.)
-$3.911 billion (2022 est.)
note: balance of payments - net trade and primary/secondary income in current dollars
comparison ranking: 25

Exports: $299.366 billion (2024 est.)
$303.914 billion (2023 est.)
$291.804 billion (2022 est.)
note: balance of payments - exports of goods and services in current dollars
comparison ranking: 33

Exports - partners: Germany 25%, USA 9%, Italy 7%, Switzerland 5%, Hungary 4% (2023)
note: top five export partners based on percentage share of exports

Exports - commodities: cars, packaged medicine, vaccines, vehicle parts/accessories, nitrogen compounds (2023)
note: top five export commodities based on value in dollars

Imports: $284.467 billion (2024 est.)
$293.692 billion (2023 est.)
$294.324 billion (2022 est.)
note: balance of payments - imports of goods and services in current dollars
comparison ranking: 30

Imports - partners: Germany 34%, China 7%, Italy 7%, Switzerland 5%, Czechia 4% (2023)
note: top five import partners based on percentage share of imports

Imports - commodities: cars, garments, vaccines, vehicle parts/accessories, refined petroleum (2023)
note: top five import commodities based on value in dollars

Reserves of foreign exchange and gold: $35.406 billion (2024 est.)
$31.212 billion (2023 est.)
$33.078 billion (2022 est.)
note: holdings of gold (year-end prices)/foreign exchange/special drawing rights in current dollars
comparison ranking: 54

Exchange rates: euros (EUR) per US dollar -

Exchange rates: 0.924 (2024 est.)
0.925 (2023 est.)
0.95 (2022 est.)
0.845 (2021 est.)
0.876 (2020 est.)

ENERGY

Electricity access: *electrification - total population:* 100% (2022 est.)

Electricity: *installed generating capacity:* 33.371 million kW (2023 est.)
consumption: 64.611 billion kWh (2023 est.)
exports: 21.631 billion kWh (2023 est.)
imports: 21.55 billion kWh (2023 est.)
transmission/distribution losses: 3.095 billion kWh (2023 est.)
comparison rankings: installed generating capacity 36; consumption 45; exports 12; imports 10; transmission/distribution losses 141

Electricity generation sources: *fossil fuels:* 14.9% of total installed capacity (2023 est.)
solar: 9% of total installed capacity (2023 est.)
wind: 11.9% of total installed capacity (2023 est.)
hydroelectricity: 56.4% of total installed capacity (2023 est.)
biomass and waste: 7.8% of total installed capacity (2023 est.)

Coal: *production:* 1.288 million metric tons (2023 est.)
consumption: 5.403 million metric tons (2023 est.)
exports: 2,000 metric tons (2022 est.)
imports: 4.179 million metric tons (2023 est.)

Petroleum: *total petroleum production:* 18,000 bbl/day (2023 est.)
refined petroleum consumption: 244,000 bbl/day (2024 est.)
crude oil estimated reserves: 35.2 million barrels (2021 est.)

Natural gas: *production:* 548.976 million cubic meters (2023 est.)
consumption: 6.971 billion cubic meters (2023 est.)
imports: 7.084 billion cubic meters (2023 est.)
proven reserves: 5.04 billion cubic meters (2021 est.)

Energy consumption per capita: 120.211 million Btu/person (2023 est.)
comparison ranking: 35

COMMUNICATIONS

Telephones - fixed lines: *total subscriptions:* 3.604 million (2023 est.)
subscriptions per 100 inhabitants: 40 (2023 est.)
comparison ranking: total subscriptions 34

Telephones - mobile cellular: *total subscriptions:* 11.1 million (2023 est.)
subscriptions per 100 inhabitants: 123 (2022 est.)
comparison ranking: total subscriptions 90

Broadcast media: public broadcaster, Oesterreichischer Rundfunk (ORF), is a major player in the TV and radio markets; private broadcasters, cable, and satellite TV are available in most homes are widely used; some German stations carry programs for Austrian viewers; national and regional newspapers compete fiercely for readers; the print media are owned by a handful of mostly Austrian and German media groups (2023)

Internet country code: .at

Internet users: *percent of population:* 95% (2024 est.)

Broadband - fixed subscriptions: *total:* 2.71 million (2023 est.)
subscriptions per 100 inhabitants: 30 (2023 est.)
comparison ranking: total 52

TRANSPORTATION

Civil aircraft registration country code prefix: OE

Airports: 62 (2025)
comparison ranking: 77

Heliports: 112 (2025)
comparison ranking: 24

Railways: *total:* 6,123 km (2022) 3,523 km electrified

Merchant marine: *total:* 1 (2023)
by type: other 1
comparison ranking: total 181

MILITARY AND SECURITY

Military and security forces: Austrian Armed Forces (Bundesheer): Land Forces, Air Force, Cyber Forces, Special Operations Forces, Militia (reserves) (2025)
note 1: the federal police maintain internal security and report to the Ministry of the Interior
note 2: the militia is comprised of men and women who have done their basic military or training service and continue to perform a task in the armed forces; they are integrated into the military but have civilian jobs and only participate in exercises or operations; missions for the militia may include providing disaster relief, assisting security police, and protecting critical infrastructure (energy, water, etc.), as well as deployments on missions abroad

Military expenditures: 1% of GDP (2024 est.)
0.9% of GDP (2023 est.)
0.7% of GDP (2022 est.)
0.8% of GDP (2021 est.)
0.7% of GDP (2020 est.)

Military and security service personnel strengths: approximately 22,000 active Armed Forces (includes about 14,000 regular troops and around 8,000 reservists/militia undergoing refresher training) (2025)

Military equipment inventories and acquisitions: the military's inventory includes a mix of domestically produced and imported weapons systems from European countries and the US; the Austrian defense industry produces a range of equipment and partners with other countries (2024)

Military service age and obligation: registration requirement at age 17, the legal minimum age for voluntary military service; men above the age of 18 are subject to compulsory military service; women may volunteer; compulsory service is for 6 months, or optionally, alternative civil/community service (Zivildienst) for 9 months (2024)
note 1: as of 2023, women made up about 4% of the military's full-time personnel
note 2: in a January 2013 referendum, a majority of Austrians voted in favor of retaining the system of compulsory military service (with the option of alternative/non-military service) instead of switching to a professional army system

Military deployments: 210 Bosnia-Herzegovina (EUFOR stabilization force); 160 Kosovo (NATO/KFOR); 160 Lebanon (UNIFIL) (2025)

Military - note: the military's primary responsibilities are national defense and protecting Austria's neutrality; it also has some domestic security and disaster response responsibilities; each of the nine federal states has a military command that provides a link between the military and civil authorities; the main tasks of these commands include providing military assistance during disasters and supporting security police operations
the Austrian military contributes to international peacekeeping and humanitarian missions; Austria has been constitutionally militarily non-aligned since 1955 but is an EU member and actively participates in EU peacekeeping and crisis management operations under the EU Common Security and Defense Policy; Austria is not a member of NATO but joined NATO's Partnership for Peace framework in 1995 and participates in some NATO-led crisis management and peacekeeping operations; more than 100,000 Austrian military and civilian personnel have taken part in more than 50 international peace support and humanitarian missions since 1960 (2025)

SPACE

Space agency/agencies: Aeronautics and Space Agency (ALR; established in 1972 as the Austrian Space Agency) (2025)

Space program overview: has a national space program; develops, builds, operates, and tracks satellites, including remote sensing and research/scientific satellites; member of the European Space Agency (ESA) and the EU; works closely with ESA and EU member states and the commercial sector to develop a range of space capabilities and technologies, including applications for satellite payloads, space flight, and space research; also cooperates with other foreign space agencies and industries, including those of China, India, Russia, and the US (2025)
note: further details about the key activities, programs, and milestones of the country's space program, as well as government spending estimates on the space sector, appear in the Space Programs reference guide

TERRORISM

Terrorist group(s): Terrorist group(s): Islamic State of Iraq and ash-Sham (ISIS)
note: details about the history, aims, leadership, organization, areas of operation, tactics, targets, weapons, size, and sources of support of the group(s) appear(s) in Appendix T

TRANSNATIONAL ISSUES

Refugees and internally displaced persons: *refugees:* 313,711 (2024 est.)
stateless persons: 3,919 (2024 est.)

AZERBAIJAN

INTRODUCTION

Background: Azerbaijan – a secular nation with a majority-Turkic and majority-Shia Muslim population – was briefly independent (from 1918 to 1920) following the collapse of the Russian Empire; it was subsequently incorporated into the Soviet Union for seven decades.

Beginning in 1988, Azerbaijan and Armenia fought over the Nagorno-Karabakh region, which was populated largely by ethnic Armenians but incorporated into Soviet Azerbaijan as an autonomous oblast in the early 1920s. In the late Soviet period, an ethnic-Armenian separatist movement sought to end Azerbaijani control over the region. Fighting over Nagorno-Karabakh escalated after Armenia and Azerbaijan gained independence from the Soviet Union in 1991. By the time a ceasefire took effect in 1994, separatists with Armenian support controlled Nagorno-Karabakh and seven surrounding Azerbaijani territories. After decades of cease-fire violations and sporadic flare-ups, a second sustained conflict began in 2020 when Azerbaijan tried to win back the territories it had lost in the 1990s. After significant Azerbaijani gains, Armenia returned the southern part of Nagorno-Karabakh and the surrounding territories to Azerbaijan. In September 2023, Azerbaijan took military action to regain the rest of Nagorno-Karabakh; after a conflict that lasted only one day, nearly the entire ethnic Armenian population of Nagorno-Karabakh fled to Armenia.

Since gaining its independence in 1991, Azerbaijan has significantly reduced the poverty rate and has directed some revenue from its oil and gas production to develop the country's infrastructure. However, corruption remains a burden on the economy, and Western observers and members of the country's political opposition have accused the government of authoritarianism. The country's leadership has remained in the ALIYEV family since

Heydar ALIYEV, the most highly ranked Azerbaijani member of the Communist Party during the Soviet period, became president during the first Nagorno-Karabakh War in 1993.

GEOGRAPHY

Location: Southwestern Asia, bordering the Caspian Sea, between Iran and Russia, with a small European portion north of the Caucasus range

Geographic coordinates: 40 30 N, 47 30 E

Map references: Asia

Area: *total:* 86,600 sq km
land: 82,629 sq km
water: 3,971 sq km
note: includes the exclave of Naxcivan Autonomous Republic and the Nagorno-Karabakh region; the final status of the region has yet to be determined
comparison ranking: total 113

Area - comparative: about three-quarters the size of Pennsylvania; slightly smaller than Maine

Land boundaries: *total:* 2,468 km
border countries (5): Armenia 996 km; Georgia 428 km; Iran 689 km; Russia 338 km; Turkey 17 km

Coastline: 0 km (landlocked)
note: Azerbaijan borders the Caspian Sea (713 km)

Maritime claims: none (landlocked)

Climate: dry, semiarid steppe

Terrain: large, flat Kur-Araz Ovaligi (Kura-Araks Lowland, much of it below sea level) with Great Caucasus Mountains to the north, Qarabag Yaylasi (Karabakh Upland) to the west; Baku lies on Abseron Yasaqligi (Apsheron Peninsula) that juts into Caspian Sea

Elevation: *highest point:* Bazarduzu Dagi 4,466 m
lowest point: Caspian Sea -28 m
mean elevation: 384 m

Natural resources: petroleum, natural gas, iron ore, nonferrous metals, bauxite

Land use: *agricultural land:* 57.8% (2022 est.)
arable land: 25.3% (2022 est.)
permanent crops: 3.3% (2022 est.)
permanent pasture: 29.2% (2022 est.)
forest: 14% (2022 est.)
other: 28.2% (2022 est.)

Irrigated land: 14,693 sq km (2022)

Major lakes (area sq km): *salt water lake(s):* Caspian Sea (shared with Iran, Russia, Turkmenistan, and Kazakhstan) - 374,000 sq km

Population distribution: highest population density is found in the far eastern area of the country, in and around Baku; apart from smaller urbanized areas, the rest of the country has a fairly light and evenly distributed population

Natural hazards: droughts

Geography - note: both the main area of the country and the Naxcivan exclave are landlocked

PEOPLE AND SOCIETY

Population: *total:* 10,650,239 (2024 est.)
male: 5,330,233
female: 5,320,006
comparison rankings: total 88; male 90; female 90

Nationality: *noun:* Azerbaijani(s)
adjective: Azerbaijani

Ethnic groups: Azerbaijani 91.6%, Lezghin 2%, Russian 1.3%, Armenian 1.3%, Talysh 1.3%, other 2.4% (2009 est.)
note: Nagorno-Karabakh, which is part of Azerbaijan on the basis of the borders recognized when the Soviet Union dissolved in 1991, was populated almost entirely by ethnic Armenians; Azerbaijan has over 80 ethnic groups

Languages: Azerbaijani (Azeri) (official) 92.5%, Russian 1.4%, Armenian 1.4%, other 4.7% (2009 est.)
major-language sample(s):
Dünya fakt kitabı, əsas məlumatlar üçün əvəz olunmaz mənbədir (Azerbaijani)
note: Russian is widely spoken

Religions: Muslim 97.3% (predominantly Shia), Christian 2.6%, other <0.1, unaffiliated <0.1 (2020 est.)
note: religious affiliation for the majority of Azerbaijanis is largely nominal, percentages for actual practicing adherents are probably much lower

Age structure: *0-14 years:* 22.3% (male 1,269,241/female 1,104,529)
15-64 years: 68.7% (male 3,659,441/female 3,656,493)
65 years and over: 9% (2024 est.) (male 401,551/female 558,984)

Dependency ratios: *total dependency ratio:* 45.6 (2024 est.)
youth dependency ratio: 32.4 (2024 est.)
elderly dependency ratio: 13.1 (2024 est.)
potential support ratio: 7.6 (2024 est.)

Median age: *total:* 34.3 years (2024 est.)
male: 32.8 years
female: 36 years
comparison ranking: total 104

Population growth rate: 0.43% (2024 est.)
comparison ranking: 156

Birth rate: 11.2 births/1,000 population (2024 est.)
comparison ranking: 161

Death rate: 6.4 deaths/1,000 population (2024 est.)
comparison ranking: 142

Net migration rate: -0.6 migrant(s)/1,000 population (2024 est.)
comparison ranking: 129

Population distribution: highest population density is found in the far eastern area of the country, in and around Baku; apart from smaller urbanized areas, the rest of the country has a fairly light and evenly distributed population

Urbanization: *urban population:* 57.6% of total population (2023)
rate of urbanization: 1.38% annual rate of change (2020-25 est.)
note: data include Nagorno-Karabakh

Major urban areas - population: 2.432 million BAKU (capital) (2023)

Sex ratio: *at birth:* 1.15 male(s)/female
0-14 years: 1.15 male(s)/female
15-64 years: 1 male(s)/female
65 years and over: 0.72 male(s)/female
total population: 1 male(s)/female (2024 est.)

Mother's mean age at first birth: 24 years (2019 est.)

Maternal mortality ratio: 18 deaths/100,000 live births (2023 est.)
comparison ranking: 127

Infant mortality rate: *total:* 10.9 deaths/1,000 live births (2024 est.)
male: 12.6 deaths/1,000 live births
female: 9 deaths/1,000 live births
comparison ranking: total 123

Life expectancy at birth: *total population:* 75.9 years (2024 est.)
male: 73.5 years
female: 78.6 years
comparison ranking: total population 120

Total fertility rate: 1.69 children born/woman (2024 est.)
comparison ranking: 167

Gross reproduction rate: 0.79 (2024 est.)

Drinking water source: *improved: urban:* 100% of population (2022 est.)
rural: 94.5% of population (2022 est.)
total: 97.6% of population (2022 est.)
unimproved: urban: 0% of population (2022 est.)
rural: 5.5% of population (2022 est.)
total: 2.4% of population (2022 est.)

Health expenditure: 4.7% of GDP (2021)
4.6% of national budget (2022 est.)

Physician density: 3.19 physicians/1,000 population (2022)

Hospital bed density: 3.9 beds/1,000 population (2019 est.)

Sanitation facility access: *improved: urban:* 100% of population (2022 est.)
unimproved: urban: 0% of population (2022 est.)

Obesity - adult prevalence rate: 19.9% (2016)
comparison ranking: 107

Alcohol consumption per capita: *total:* 1.38 liters of pure alcohol (2019 est.)
beer: 0.36 liters of pure alcohol (2019 est.)
wine: 0.06 liters of pure alcohol (2019 est.)
spirits: 0.94 liters of pure alcohol (2019 est.)
other alcohols: 0.01 liters of pure alcohol (2019 est.)
comparison ranking: total 143

Tobacco use: *total:* 18.4% (2025 est.)
male: 37.9% (2025 est.)
female: 0.1% (2025 est.)
comparison ranking: total 81

Currently married women (ages 15-49): 62.9% (2023 est.)

Education expenditure: 3.6% of GDP (2023 est.)
10.4% national budget (2022 est.)
comparison ranking: Education expenditure (% GDP) 128

Literacy: *total population:* 100% (2023 est.)
male: 100% (2023 est.)
female: 100% (2023 est.)

School life expectancy (primary to tertiary education): *total:* 13 years (2023 est.)
male: 13 years (2023 est.)
female: 13 years (2023 est.)

ENVIRONMENT

Environmental issues: severe air, soil, and water pollution; soil pollution from oil spills, pesticides, and toxic defoliants used in producing cotton; surface and underground water pollution from untreated municipal and industrial wastewater and agricultural run-off

International environmental agreements: *party to:* Air Pollution, Biodiversity, Climate Change, Climate Change-Kyoto Protocol, Climate

Change-Paris Agreement, Comprehensive Nuclear Test Ban, Desertification, Endangered Species, Hazardous Wastes, Law of the Sea, Marine Dumping-London Convention, Ozone Layer Protection, Ship Pollution, Wetlands
signed, but not ratified: none of the selected agreements

Climate: dry, semiarid steppe

Urbanization: *urban population:* 57.6% of total population (2023)
rate of urbanization: 1.38% annual rate of change (2020-25 est.)
note: data include Nagorno-Karabakh

Carbon dioxide emissions: 38.892 million metric tonnes of CO2 (2023 est.)
from coal and metallurgical coke: 17,000 metric tonnes of CO2 (2023 est.)
from petroleum and other liquids: 13.954 million metric tonnes of CO2 (2023 est.)
from consumed natural gas: 24.921 million metric tonnes of CO2 (2023 est.)
comparison ranking: total emissions 63

Particulate matter emissions: 27.2 micrograms per cubic meter (2019 est.)

Methane emissions: *energy:* 268.8 kt (2022-2024 est.)
agriculture: 188.9 kt (2019-2021 est.)
waste: 93.8 kt (2019-2021 est.)
other: 1 kt (2019-2021 est.)

Waste and recycling: *municipal solid waste generated annually:* 2.93 million tons (2024 est.)
percent of municipal solid waste recycled: 14.4% (2022 est.)

Total water withdrawal: *municipal:* 408 million cubic meters (2022 est.)
industrial: 598 million cubic meters (2022 est.)
agricultural: 11.962 billion cubic meters (2022 est.)

Total renewable water resources: 34.675 billion cubic meters (2022 est.)

GOVERNMENT

Country name: *conventional long form:* Republic of Azerbaijan
conventional short form: Azerbaijan
local long form: Azarbaycan Respublikasi
local short form: Azarbaycan
former: Azerbaijan Soviet Socialist Republic
etymology: the name can be translated as "Fire Keeper" or "The Land of Fire," from the local word *azer*, or "fire," and *baydjan*, a word derived from the Iranian word *baykan*, or "guardian;" may refer to fire worshippers who lived in the region

Government type: presidential republic

Capital: *name:* Baku (Baki, Baky)
geographic coordinates: 40 23 N, 49 52 E
time difference: UTC+4 (9 hours ahead of Washington, DC, during Standard Time)
daylight saving time: does not observe daylight savings time
etymology: the name may derive from the Old Persian word *badkuba*, meaning "windward" and referring to its windy location on the shore of the Caspian Sea
note: at approximately 28 m below sea level, Baku's elevation makes it the lowest capital city in the world

Administrative divisions: 66 districts (*rayonlar*; singular - *rayon*), 11 cities (saharlar; sahar - singular)
districts: Abseron, Agcabadi, Agdam, Agdas, Agstafa, Agsu, Astara, Babak, Balakan, Barda, Beylaqan, Bilasuvar, Cabrayil, Calilabad, Culfa, Daskasan, Fuzuli, Gadabay, Goranboy, Goycay, Goygol, Haciqabul, Imisli, Ismayilli, Kalbacar, Kangarli, Kurdamir, Lacin, Lankaran, Lerik, Masalli, Neftcala, Oguz, Ordubad, Qabala, Qax, Qazax, Qobustan, Quba, Qubadli, Qusar, Saatli, Sabirabad, Sabran, Sadarak, Sahbuz, Saki, Salyan, Samaxi, Samkir, Samux, Sarur, Siyazan, Susa, Tartar, Tovuz, Ucar, Xacmaz, Xizi, Xocali, Xocavand, Yardimli, Yevlax, Zangilan, Zaqatala, Zardab
cities: Baku, Ganca, Lankaran, Mingacevir, Naftalan, Naxcivan (Nakhichevan), Saki, Sirvan, Sumqayit, Xankandi, Yevlax

Legal system: civil law system

Constitution: *history:* several previous; latest adopted 12 November 1995
amendment process: proposed by the president of the republic or by at least 63 members of the National Assembly; passage requires at least 95 votes of Assembly members in two separate readings of the draft amendment six months apart and requires presidential approval after each of the two Assembly votes, followed by presidential signature; constitutional articles on the authority, sovereignty, and unity of the people cannot be amended

International law organization participation: has not submitted an ICJ jurisdiction declaration; non-party state to the ICCt

Citizenship: *citizenship by birth:* yes
citizenship by descent only: yes
dual citizenship recognized: no
residency requirement for naturalization: 5 years

Suffrage: 18 years of age; universal

Executive branch: *chief of state:* President Ilham ALIYEV (since 31 October 2003)
head of government: Prime Minister Ali ASADOV (since 8 October 2019)
cabinet: Council of Ministers appointed by the president and confirmed by the National Assembly
election/appointment process: president directly elected by absolute-majority popular vote in 2 rounds (if needed) for a 7-year term; a single individual is eligible for unlimited terms; prime minister and first deputy prime minister appointed by the president and confirmed by the National Assembly
most recent election date: 7 February 2024
election results: *2024:* Ilham ALIYEV reelected president; percent of vote - Ilham ALIYEV (YAP) 92.1%, Zahid ORUJ (independent) 2.2%; on 16 February 2024, Ali ASADOV reappointed prime minister by parliamentary vote, 105-1
2018: Ilham ALIYEV reelected president in first round; percent of vote - Ilham ALIYEV (YAP) 86%, Zahid ORUJ (independent) 3.1%, other 10.9%
expected date of next election: 2031

Legislative branch: *legislature name:* National Assembly (Milli Majlis)
legislative structure: unicameral
number of seats: 125 (all directly elected)
electoral system: plurality/majority
scope of elections: full renewal
term in office: 5 years
most recent election date: 9/1/2024
parties elected and seats per party: New Azerbaidjan Party (YAP) (68); Independents (44); Other (13)
percentage of women in chamber: 20.8%
expected date of next election: November 2029

Judicial branch: *highest court(s):* Supreme Court (consists of the chairman, vice chairman, and 23 judges in plenum sessions and organized into civil, economic affairs, criminal, and rights violations chambers); Constitutional Court (consists of 9 judges)
judge selection and term of office: Supreme Court judges nominated by the president and appointed by the Milli Majlis; judges appointed for 10 years; Constitutional Court chairman and deputy chairman appointed by the president; other court judges nominated by the president and appointed by the Milli Majlis to serve single 15-year terms
subordinate courts: Courts of Appeal (replaced the Economic Court in 2002); district and municipal courts

Political parties: Civic Solidarity Party or VHP
Democratic Reforms Party DiP
Great Order Party or BQP
Motherland Party or AVP
Party for Democratic Reforms or DIP
Republican Alternative Party or REAL
Unity Party or VƏHDƏT
Whole Azerbaijan Popular Front Party or BAXCP
New Azerbaijan Party (Yeni Azərbaycan Partiyasi) or YAP

Diplomatic representation in the US: *chief of mission:* Ambassador Khazar IBRAHIM (since 15 September 2021)
chancery: 2741 34th Street NW, Washington, DC 20008
telephone: [1] (202) 337-3500
FAX: [1] (202) 337-5911
email address and website: azerbaijan@azembassy.us
https://washington.mfa.gov.az/en
consulate(s) general: Los Angeles

Diplomatic representation from the US: *chief of mission:* Ambassador (vacant); Chargé d'Affaires Amy CARLON (since 23 June 2025)
embassy: 111 Azadlig Avenue, AZ1007 Baku
mailing address: 7050 Baku Place, Washington, DC 20521-7050
telephone: [994] (12) 488-3300
FAX: [994] (12) 488-3330
email address and website: BakuACS@state.gov
https://az.usembassy.gov/

International organization participation: ADB, BSEC, CD, CE, CICA, CIS, EAPC, EBRD, ECO, FAO, GCTU, GUAM, IAEA, IBRD, ICAO, ICC (NGOs), ICRM, IDA, IDB, IFAD, IFC, IFRCS, ILO, IMF, IMO, Interpol, IOC, IOM, IPU, ISO, ITSO, ITU, ITUC (NGOs), MIGA, NAM, OAS (observer), OIC, OPCW, OSCE, PFP, UN, UNCTAD, UNESCO, UNHCR, UNIDO, UNWTO, UPU, WCO, WFTU (NGOs), WHO, WIPO, WMO, WTO (observer)

Independence: 30 August 1991 (declared from the Soviet Union); 18 October 1991 (adopted by the Supreme Council of Azerbaijan)

National holiday: Republic Day (founding of the Democratic Republic of Azerbaijan), 28 May (1918)

Flag: *description:* three equal horizontal bands of sky blue (top), red, and green; a vertical crescent moon and an eight-pointed star in white are centered in the red band
meaning: the blue band stands for Azerbaijan's Turkic heritage, red for modernization and progress, and green for Islam; the crescent moon and star are a Turkic insignia; the eight star points represent the eight Turkic peoples of the world

National symbol(s): flames of fire

National color(s): blue, red, green

National anthem(s): *title:* "Azerbaijan Marsi" (March of Azerbaijan)
lyrics/music: Ahmed JAVAD/Uzeyir HAJIBEYOV
history: adopted 1992; originally written in 1919 during a brief period of independence, but did not become the official anthem until after the dissolution of the Soviet Union

National heritage: *total World Heritage Sites:* 5 (4 cultural, 1 natural)
selected World Heritage Site locales: Walled City of Baku; Gobustan Rock Art Cultural Landscape; Historic Center of Sheki; Cultural Landscape of Khinalig People and "Koc Yolu" Transhumance Route

ECONOMY

Economic overview: upper-middle income, oil-dependent Caucasus economy; minimal economic diversification and dominance of state-owned enterprises; growth and fiscal consolidation supported by oil revenues, but risks remain from demand shocks; potential economic gains from Nagorno-Karabakh ceasefire; education investments to diversify and retain human capital

Real GDP (purchasing power parity): $225.198 billion (2024 est.)
$216.388 billion (2023 est.)
$213.497 billion (2022 est.)
note: data in 2021 dollars
comparison ranking: 73

Real GDP growth rate: 4.1% (2024 est.)
1.4% (2023 est.)
4.7% (2022 est.)
note: annual GDP % growth based on constant local currency
comparison ranking: 71

Real GDP per capita: $22,100 (2024 est.)
$21,300 (2023 est.)
$21,100 (2022 est.)
note: data in 2021 dollars
comparison ranking: 97

GDP (official exchange rate): $74.316 billion (2024 est.)
note: data in current dollars at official exchange rate

Inflation rate (consumer prices): 2.2% (2024 est.)
8.8% (2023 est.)
13.9% (2022 est.)
note: annual % change based on consumer prices
comparison ranking: 62

GDP - composition, by sector of origin: *agriculture:* 5.7% (2024 est.)
industry: 42.6% (2024 est.)
services: 42.3% (2024 est.)
note: figures may not total 100% due to non-allocated consumption not captured in sector-reported data
comparison rankings: agriculture 104; industry 16; services 186

GDP - composition, by end use: *household consumption:* 55.4% (2024 est.)
government consumption: 14.4% (2024 est.)
investment in fixed capital: 16.8% (2024 est.)
investment in inventories: 4.3% (2024 est.)
exports of goods and services: 45.9% (2024 est.)
imports of goods and services: -36.8% (2024 est.)
note: figures may not total 100% due to rounding or gaps in data collection

Agricultural products: milk, wheat, barley, potatoes, tomatoes, watermelons, onions, apples, maize, cotton (2023)
note: top ten agricultural products based on tonnage

Industries: petroleum and petroleum products, natural gas, oilfield equipment; steel, iron ore; cement; chemicals and petrochemicals; textiles

Industrial production growth rate: 2.1% (2024 est.)
note: annual % change in industrial value added based on constant local currency
comparison ranking: 96

Labor force: 5.02 million (2024 est.)
note: number of people ages 15 or older who are employed or seeking work
comparison ranking: 86

Unemployment rate: 5.6% (2024 est.)
5.7% (2023 est.)
5.7% (2022 est.)
note: % of labor force seeking employment
comparison ranking: 106

Youth unemployment rate (ages 15-24): *total:* 13.7% (2024 est.)
male: 12.3% (2024 est.)
female: 15.3% (2024 est.)
note: % of labor force ages 15-24 seeking employment
comparison ranking: total 94

Average household expenditures: *on food:* 42.7% of household expenditures (2023 est.)
on alcohol and tobacco: 2% of household expenditures (2023 est.)

Remittances: 1.8% of GDP (2024 est.)
2.6% of GDP (2023 est.)
5% of GDP (2022 est.)
note: personal transfers and compensation between resident and non-resident individuals/households/entities

Budget: *revenues:* $30.966 billion (2022 est.)
expenditures: $22.95 billion (2022 est.)
note: central government revenues (excluding grants) and expenditures converted to US dollars at average official exchange rate for year indicated

Public debt: 16.8% of GDP (2021 est.)
note: central government debt as a % of GDP
comparison ranking: 187

Taxes and other revenues: 15.4% (of GDP) (2022 est.)
note: central government tax revenue as a % of GDP
comparison ranking: 88

Current account balance: $4.671 billion (2024 est.)
$8.329 billion (2023 est.)
$23.478 billion (2022 est.)
note: balance of payments - net trade and primary/secondary income in current dollars
comparison ranking: 37

Exports: $34.113 billion (2024 est.)
$35.487 billion (2023 est.)
$47.274 billion (2022 est.)
note: balance of payments - exports of goods and services in current dollars
comparison ranking: 80

Exports - partners: Italy 37%, Turkey 19%, Israel 5%, Greece 4%, Russia 4% (2023)
note: top five export partners based on percentage share of exports

Exports - commodities: crude petroleum, natural gas, refined petroleum, plastics, electricity (2023)
note: top five export commodities based on value in dollars

Imports: $27.339 billion (2024 est.)
$25.016 billion (2023 est.)
$21.274 billion (2022 est.)
note: balance of payments - imports of goods and services in current dollars
comparison ranking: 85

Imports - partners: Russia 17%, China 16%, Turkey 14%, Georgia 4%, Germany 4% (2023)
note: top five import partners based on percentage share of imports

Imports - commodities: cars, crude petroleum, refined petroleum, broadcasting equipment, garments (2023)
note: top five import commodities based on value in dollars

Reserves of foreign exchange and gold: $12.699 billion (2024 est.)
$13.749 billion (2023 est.)
$11.338 billion (2022 est.)
note: holdings of gold (year-end prices)/foreign exchange/special drawing rights in current dollars
comparison ranking: 73

Debt - external: $12.378 billion (2023 est.)
note: present value of external debt in current US dollars
comparison ranking: 45

Exchange rates: Azerbaijani manats (AZN) per US dollar -

Exchange rates: 1.7 (2024 est.)
1.7 (2023 est.)
1.7 (2022 est.)
1.7 (2021 est.)
1.7 (2020 est.)

ENERGY

Electricity access: *electrification - total population:* 100% (2022 est.)

Electricity: *installed generating capacity:* 8.383 million kW (2023 est.)
consumption: 23.857 billion kWh (2023 est.)
exports: 3.246 billion kWh (2023 est.)
imports: 212 million kWh (2023 est.)
transmission/distribution losses: 2.197 billion kWh (2023 est.)
comparison rankings: installed generating capacity 70; consumption 71; exports 47; imports 107; transmission/distribution losses 126

Electricity generation sources: *fossil fuels:* 93.5% of total installed capacity (2023 est.)
solar: 0.2% of total installed capacity (2023 est.)
wind: 0.3% of total installed capacity (2023 est.)
hydroelectricity: 5.6% of total installed capacity (2023 est.)
biomass and waste: 0.4% of total installed capacity (2023 est.)

Coal: *consumption:* 6,000 metric tons (2023 est.)
imports: 10,000 metric tons (2023 est.)

Petroleum: *total petroleum production:* 618,000 bbl/day (2023 est.)
refined petroleum consumption: 109,000 bbl/day (2023 est.)
crude oil estimated reserves: 7 billion barrels (2021 est.)

Natural gas: *production:* 35.775 billion cubic meters (2023 est.)
consumption: 12.703 billion cubic meters (2023 est.)
exports: 23.65 billion cubic meters (2023 est.)
imports: 2.173 billion cubic meters (2023 est.)
proven reserves: 1.699 trillion cubic meters (2021 est.)

Energy consumption per capita: 66.467 million Btu/person (2023 est.)
comparison ranking: 75

COMMUNICATIONS

Telephones - fixed lines: *total subscriptions:* 1.635 million (2023 est.)
subscriptions per 100 inhabitants: 16 (2023 est.)
comparison ranking: total subscriptions 55

Telephones - mobile cellular: *total subscriptions:* 11 million (2023 est.)
subscriptions per 100 inhabitants: 107 (2022 est.)
comparison ranking: total subscriptions 91

Broadcast media: TV is the most popular medium; many homes are hooked up to satellite; all Azerbaijan-based channels promote government positions; state-owned AzTV runs three national channels, and state-funded iTV is a national public service broadcaster; 4 national privately-owned stations; Turkish, Russian, and western TV is available on cable; analog terrestrial TV was phased out in 2016-17; radio outlets focus on entertainment, with around a dozen stations on FM in Baku; newspaper distribution is largely limited to Baku (2023)

Internet country code: .az

Internet users: *percent of population:* 89% (2023 est.)

Broadband - fixed subscriptions: *total:* 2.15 million (2023 est.)
subscriptions per 100 inhabitants: 21 (2023 est.)
comparison ranking: total 59

TRANSPORTATION

Civil aircraft registration country code prefix: 4K

Airports: 32 (2025)
comparison ranking: 118

Heliports: 5 (2025)
comparison ranking: 102

Railways: *total:* 2,944.3 km (2017)
broad gauge: 2,944.3 km (2017) 1.520-m gauge (approx. 1,767 km electrified)

Merchant marine: *total:* 312 (2023)
by type: general cargo 40, oil tanker 44, other 228
comparison ranking: total 56

MILITARY AND SECURITY

Military and security forces: Azerbaijan Armed Forces: Land Forces, Air Forces, Navy Forces, Special Forces, State Border Service, Coast Guard

Ministry of Internal Affairs: Internal Troops, local police forces; Special State Protection Service (SSPS): National Guard (2025)
note: the Ministry of Internal Affairs and the State Security Service (intelligence, counterterrorism) are responsible for internal security; the SSPS is under the president and provides protective services to senior officials, foreign missions, significant state assets, government buildings, etc; the National Guard also serves as a reserve for the Army

Military expenditures: 5.1% of GDP (2024 est.)
4.5% of GDP (2023 est.)
4.5% of GDP (2022 est.)
5% of GDP (2021 est.)
5% of GDP (2020 est.)

Military and security service personnel strengths: information varies widely; estimated 100,000 active Armed Forces personnel (2025)

Military equipment inventories and acquisitions: Baku has been actively upgrading its equipment for over a decade with purchases from Belarus, Israel, Russia, and Turkey; while most of the military's equipment was once Soviet-era material, it now fields quantities of advanced equipment, including armored vehicles, artillery systems, air defense systems, tanks, and UAVs (2024)

Military service age and obligation: 18-25 years of age for compulsory military service for men; 18-35 years of age for voluntary/contractual service for men and women; 18 months service for conscripts, 36 months for voluntary/contractual service (2023)

Military - note: the Azerbaijani military was established in 1991, although its origins go back to 1918; much of the military's original equipment was acquired from former Soviet military forces that departed Azerbaijan by 1992; territorial defense is the military's primary focus, particularly with regards to neighboring Armenia; a secondary focus is guarding against Iran; Armenia and Azerbaijan engaged in open conflicts over the Nagorno-Karabakh enclave in 1991-94 and 2020; tensions continued following the 2020 conflict, and Azerbaijan seized the entire enclave in 2023
key bilateral security relationships include Israel, Russia, and Turkiye; Azerbaijan's ties with Turkiye have included weapons transfers, technical advice, bilateral training exercises, and military support during its conflicts with Armenia; Azerbaijan is not part of NATO but has had a cooperative relationship with it dating back to when it joined NATO's Partnership for Peace program in 1994 and has provided troops to NATO-led missions in Kosovo (1999-2008) and Afghanistan (2002-2014) (2025)

SPACE

Space agency/agencies: Space Agency of the Republic of Azerbaijan (Azercosmos; established 2010 as a state-owned satellite operating company); Azerbaijan National Aerospace Agency (NASA; Azərbaycan Milli Aerokosmik Agentliyi, MAKA; established 1992; since 2006, has operated under the Ministry of Defense Industry) (2025)

Space program overview: national space program largely focused on the acquisition and operation of satellites; operates foreign-built communications and remote sensing (RS) satellites; cooperates with a variety of foreign space agencies and commercial entities, including those of China, the European Space Agency (and bilaterally with individual member states such as France), Israel, Russia, Turkey, and the US; Azercosmos is the largest satellite operator in the Caucasus region (2025)
note: further details about the key activities, programs, and milestones of the country's space program, as well as government spending estimates on the space sector, appear in the Space Programs reference guide

TERRORISM

Terrorist group(s): Terrorist group(s): Islamic State of Iraq and ash-Sham (ISIS); Islamic Revolutionary Guard Corps (IRGC)/Qods Force
note: details about the history, aims, leadership, organization, areas of operation, tactics, targets, weapons, size, and sources of support of the group(s) appear(s) in Appendix T

TRANSNATIONAL ISSUES

Refugees and internally displaced persons: *refugees:* 6,698 (2024 est.)

IDPs: 657,996 (2024 est.)
stateless persons: 271 (2024 est.)

BAHAMAS, THE

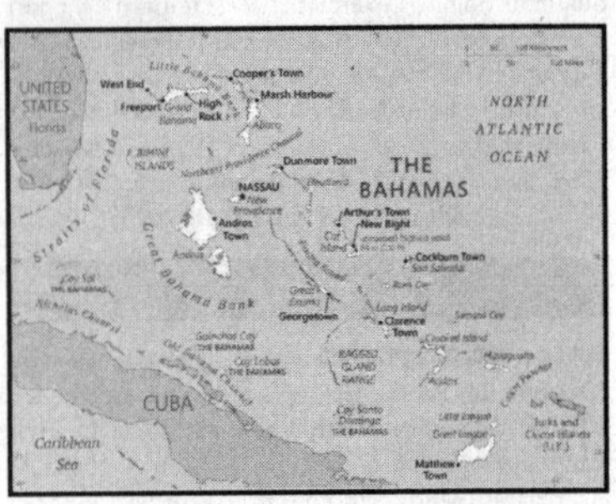

INTRODUCTION

Background: Lucayan Indians inhabited the Bahama islands when Christopher COLUMBUS first set foot in the New World in 1492. British settlement of the islands began in 1647; the islands became a colony in 1783. Piracy thrived in the 17th and 18th centuries because of The Bahamas' close proximity to shipping lanes. Since gaining independence from the UK in 1973, The Bahamas has prospered through tourism, international banking, and investment management, which comprise up to 85% of GDP Because of its proximity to the US – the nearest Bahamian landmass is only 80 km (50 mi) from Florida – the country is a major transshipment point for illicit trafficking to the US mainland, as well as to Europe. US law enforcement agencies cooperate closely with The Bahamas; the Drug Enforcement Administration, US Coast Guard, and US Customs and Border Protection assist Bahamian authorities with maritime security and law enforcement through Operation Bahamas, Turks and Caicos, or OPBAT.

GEOGRAPHY

Location: chain of islands in the North Atlantic Ocean, southeast of Florida, northeast of Cuba; note - although The Bahamas does not border the Caribbean Sea, geopolitically it is often designated as a Caribbean nation

Geographic coordinates: 24 15 N, 76 00 W

Map references: Central America and the Caribbean

Area: *total:* 13,880 sq km
land: 10,010 sq km
water: 3,870 sq km
comparison ranking: total 160

Area - comparative: slightly smaller than Connecticut

Land boundaries: *total:* 0 km

Coastline: 3,542 km

Maritime claims: *territorial sea:* 12 nm
exclusive economic zone: 200 nm

Climate: tropical marine; moderated by warm waters of Gulf Stream

Terrain: long, flat coral formations with some low rounded hills

Elevation: *highest point:* 1.3 km NE of Old Bight on Cat Island 64 m
lowest point: Atlantic Ocean 0 m

Natural resources: salt, aragonite, timber, arable land

Land use: *agricultural land:* 1.3% (2022 est.)
arable land: 0.8% (2022 est.)
permanent crops: 0.3% (2022 est.)
permanent pasture: 0.2% (2022 est.)
forest: 50.9% (2022 est.)
other: 47.8% (2022 est.)

Irrigated land: 10 sq km (2012)

Population distribution: most of the population lives in urban areas, with two thirds living on New Providence Island where Nassau is located

Natural hazards: hurricanes and other tropical storms cause extensive flood and wind damage

Geography - note: strategic location adjacent to US and Cuba; extensive island chain of which 30 are inhabited

PEOPLE AND SOCIETY

Population: *total:* 410,862 (2024 est.)
male: 190,100
female: 220,762
comparison rankings: total 176; male 177; female 175

Nationality: *noun:* Bahamian(s)
adjective: Bahamian

Ethnic groups: African descent 90.6%, White 4.7%, mixed 2.1%, other 1.9%, unspecified 0.7% (2010 est.)
note: data represent population by racial group

Languages: English (official), Creole (among Haitian immigrants)

Religions: Protestant 69.9% (includes Baptist 34.9%, Anglican 13.7%, Pentecostal 8.9% Seventh Day Adventist 4.4%, Methodist 3.6%, Church of God 1.9%, Plymouth Brethren 1.6%, other Protestant 0.9%), Roman Catholic 12%, other Christian 13% (includes Jehovah's Witness 1.1%), other 0.6%, none 1.9%, unspecified 2.6% (2010 est.)

Age structure: *0-14 years:* 21.4% (male 41, 675/ female 46,363)
15-64 years: 70% (male 132,626/female 154,866)
65 years and over: 8.6% (2024 est.) (male 15,799/ female 19,533)

Dependency ratios: *total dependency ratio:* 42.9 (2024 est.)
youth dependency ratio: 30.6 (2024 est.)
elderly dependency ratio: 12.3 (2024 est.)
potential support ratio: 8.1 (2024 est.)

Median age: *total:* 30.7 years (2024 est.)
male: 30.6 years
female: 30.7 years
comparison ranking: total 133

Population growth rate: 1.07% (2024 est.)
comparison ranking: 88

Birth rate: 13.1 births/1,000 population (2024 est.)
comparison ranking: 132

Death rate: 5.6 deaths/1,000 population (2024 est.)
comparison ranking: 175

Net migration rate: 3.2 migrant(s)/1,000 population (2024 est.)
comparison ranking: 34

Population distribution: most of the population lives in urban areas, with two thirds living on New Providence Island where Nassau is located

Urbanization: *urban population:* 83.6% of total population (2023)
rate of urbanization: 1.02% annual rate of change (2020-25 est.)

Major urban areas - population: 280,000 NASSAU (capital) (2018)

Sex ratio: *at birth:* 1.03 male(s)/female
0-14 years: 0.9 male(s)/female
15-64 years: 0.86 male(s)/female
65 years and over: 0.81 male(s)/female
total population: 0.86 male(s)/female (2024 est.)

Maternal mortality ratio: 76 deaths/100,000 live births (2023 est.)
comparison ranking: 75

Infant mortality rate: *total:* 9.4 deaths/1,000 live births (2024 est.)
male: 10.5 deaths/1,000 live births
female: 8.2 deaths/1,000 live births
comparison ranking: total 138

Life expectancy at birth: *total population:* 76.7 years (2024 est.)
male: 75.1 years
female: 78.4 years
comparison ranking: total population 104

Total fertility rate: 1.44 children born/woman (2024 est.)
comparison ranking: 209

Gross reproduction rate: 0.71 (2024 est.)

Drinking water source: *improved:* total: 98.9% of population

Health expenditure: 7.1% of GDP (2021)
15.8% of national budget (2022 est.)

Physician density: 1.9 physicians/1,000 population (2017)

Hospital bed density: 2.7 beds/1,000 population (2021 est.)

Obesity - adult prevalence rate: 31.6% (2016)
comparison ranking: 21

Alcohol consumption per capita: *total:* 9.48 liters of pure alcohol (2019 est.)
beer: 3.66 liters of pure alcohol (2019 est.)
wine: 1.43 liters of pure alcohol (2019 est.)
spirits: 4.08 liters of pure alcohol (2019 est.)
other alcohols: 0.31 liters of pure alcohol (2019 est.)
comparison ranking: total 29

Tobacco use: *total:* 10.8% (2025 est.)
male: 20.8% (2025 est.)
female: 1.9% (2025 est.)
comparison ranking: total 123

Currently married women (ages 15-49): 38.9% (2023 est.)

Education expenditure: 2.8% of GDP (2023 est.)
10.6% national budget (2025 est.)
comparison ranking: Education expenditure (% GDP) 161

ENVIRONMENT

Environmental issues: coral reef decay; solid waste disposal

International environmental agreements: *party to:* Biodiversity, Climate Change, Climate Change-Kyoto Protocol, Climate Change- Paris Agreement, Comprehensive Nuclear Test Ban, Desertification, Endangered Species, Hazardous Wastes, Law of the Sea, Nuclear Test Ban, Ozone Layer Protection, Ship Pollution, Wetlands *signed, but not ratified:* none of the selected agreements

Climate: tropical marine; moderated by warm waters of Gulf Stream

Urbanization: *urban population:* 83.6% of total population (2023)
rate of urbanization: 1.02% annual rate of change (2020-25 est.)

Carbon dioxide emissions: 2.99 million metric tonnes of CO2 (2023 est.)
from coal and metallurgical coke: 2,000 metric tonnes of CO2 (2023 est.)
from petroleum and other liquids: 2.966 million metric tonnes of CO2 (2023 est.)
from consumed natural gas: 23,000 metric tonnes of CO2 (2023 est.)
comparison ranking: total emissions 150

Particulate matter emissions: 5.2 micrograms per cubic meter (2019 est.)

Waste and recycling: *municipal solid waste generated annually:* 264,000 tons (2024 est.)
percent of municipal solid waste recycled: 24.9% (2022 est.)

Total water withdrawal: *municipal:* 31 million cubic meters (2022 est.)

Total renewable water resources: 700 million cubic meters (2022 est.)

GOVERNMENT

Country name: *conventional long form:* Commonwealth of The Bahamas
conventional short form: The Bahamas
etymology: name may be derived from the Spanish *baha mar*, meaning "low sea," which describes the shallow waters of the Bahama Banks; alternatively, it may be a form of the local name Guanahani, which is of unknown origin and meaning

Government type: parliamentary democracy under a constitutional monarchy; a Commonwealth realm

Capital: *name:* Nassau
geographic coordinates: 25 05 N, 77 21 W
time difference: UTC-5 (same time as Washington, DC, during Standard Time)
daylight saving time: +1 hr, begins second Sunday in March; ends first Sunday in November
etymology: named after King WILLIAM III of England (1650-1702), who was a member of the House of Orange-Nassau

Administrative divisions: 31 districts; Acklins Islands, Berry Islands, Bimini, Black Point, Cat Island, Central Abaco, Central Andros, Central Eleuthera, City of Freeport, Crooked Island and Long Cay, East Grand Bahama, Exuma, Grand Cay, Harbour Island, Hope Town, Inagua, Long Island, Mangrove Cay, Mayaguana, Moore's Island, North Abaco, North Andros, North Eleuthera, Ragged Island, Rum Cay, San Salvador, South Abaco, South Andros, South Eleuthera, Spanish Wells, West Grand Bahama

Legal system: common-law system based on the English model

Constitution: *history:* previous 1964 (pre-independence); latest adopted 20 June 1973, effective 10 July 1973
amendment process: proposed as an "Act" by Parliament; passage of amendments to articles such as the organization and composition of the branches of government requires approval by at least two-thirds majority of the membership of both houses of Parliament and majority approval in a referendum; passage of amendments to constitutional articles such as fundamental rights and individual freedoms, the powers, authorities, and procedures of the branches of government, or changes to the Bahamas Independence Act 1973 requires approval by at least three-fourths majority of the membership of both houses and majority approval in a referendum

International law organization participation: has not submitted an ICJ jurisdiction declaration; non-party state to the ICCt

Citizenship: *citizenship by birth:* no
citizenship by descent only: at least one parent must be a citizen of The Bahamas
dual citizenship recognized: no
residency requirement for naturalization: 6-9 years

Suffrage: 18 years of age; universal

Executive branch: *chief of state:* King CHARLES III (since 8 September 2022); represented by Governor-General Cynthia A. PRATT (since 1 September 2023)
head of government: Prime Minister Philip Edward DAVIS (since 17 September 2021)
cabinet: Cabinet appointed by governor-general on recommendation of prime minister
election/appointment process: the monarchy is hereditary; governor-general appointed by the monarch on the advice of the prime minister; following legislative elections, the governor- general appoints the leader of the majority party or majority coalition as prime minister; the prime minister recommends the deputy prime minister

Legislative branch: *legislature name:* Parliament
legislative structure: bicameral
note: Parliament sits for 5 years from the date of the last general election: the government may dissolve the parliament and call elections at any time

Legislative branch - lower chamber: *chamber name:* House of Assembly
number of seats: 39 (all directly elected)
electoral system: plurality/majority
scope of elections: full renewal
term in office: 5 years
most recent election date: 9/16/2021
parties elected and seats per party: Progressive Liberal Party (PLP) (32); Free National Movement (FNM) (7)
percentage of women in chamber: 17.9%
expected date of next election: September 2026

Legislative branch - upper chamber: *chamber name:* Senate
number of seats: 16 (all appointed)
scope of elections: full renewal
term in office: 5 years
most recent election date: 10/6/2021
percentage of women in chamber: 31.3%
expected date of next election: October 2026

Judicial branch: *highest court(s):* Court of Appeal (consists of the court president and 6 justices, organized in 3-member panels); Supreme Court (consists of the chief justice and 19 justices)
judge selection and term of office: Court of Appeal president and Supreme Court chief justice appointed by the governor-general on the advice of the prime minister after consultation with the leader of the opposition party; other Court of Appeal and Supreme Court justices appointed by the governor general upon recommendation of the Judicial and Legal Services Commission, a 5-member body headed by the chief justice; Court of Appeal justices appointed for life with mandatory retirement normally at age 68 but can be extended until age 70; Supreme Court justices appointed for life with mandatory retirement normally at age 65 but can be extended until age 67
subordinate courts: Industrial Tribunal; Magistrates' Courts; Family Island Administrators (can also serve as magistrates)
note: The Bahamas is a member of the 15-member Caribbean Community but is not party to the agreement establishing the Caribbean Court of Justice as its highest appellate court; the Judicial Committee of the Privy Council (in London) serves as the final court of appeal for The Bahamas

Political parties: Coalition of Independents Party or COI
Democratic National Alliance or DNA
Free National Movement or FNM
Progressive Liberal Party or PLP

Diplomatic representation in the US: *chief of mission:* Ambassador Wendall Kermith JONES (since 19 April 2022)
chancery: 600 New Hampshire Ave NW, Suite 530, Washington, DC 20037
telephone: [1] (202) 319-2660
FAX: [1] (202) 319-2668
email address and website: embassy@bahamasembdc.org
https://www.bahamasembdc.org/
consulate(s) general: Atlanta, Miami, New York

Diplomatic representation from the US: *chief of mission:* Ambassador (vacant); Charge d'Affaires Kimberly FURNISH (since June 2024)
embassy: 42 Queen Street, Nassau
mailing address: 3370 Nassau Place, Washington, DC 20521-3370
telephone: [1] (242) 322-1181
FAX: [1] (242) 356-7174
email address and website: acsnassau@state.gov
https://bs.usembassy.gov/

International organization participation: ACP, ACS, AOSIS, C, Caricom, CDB, CELAC, FAO, G-77, IADB, IAEA, IBRD, ICAO, ICC (NGOs), ICRM, IDA, IFAD, IFC, IFRCS, ILO, IMF, IMO, IMSO, Interpol, IOC, IOM, ISO (correspondent), ITSO, ITU, LAES, MIGA, NAM, OAS, OPANAL, OPCW, Petrocaribe, UN, UNCTAD, UNESCO, UNIDO, UNWTO, UPU, WCO, WHO, WIPO, WMO, WTO (observer)

Independence: 10 July 1973 (from the UK)

National holiday: Independence Day, 10 July (1973)

Flag: *description:* three equal horizontal bands of aquamarine (top), gold, and aquamarine, with a black equilateral triangle based on the left side
meaning: the band colors represent the islands' golden beaches surrounded by the aquamarine sea; black stands for the vigor and force of a united people, and the triangle for the people's enterprise and determination

National symbol(s): blue marlin, flamingo, yellow elderflower

National color(s): aquamarine, yellow, black

National coat of arms: the motto on the Bahamas coat of arms is "Forward, Upward, Onward Together;" the flamingo and marlin supporting the shield are national animals that represent respectively the land and sea; the pink conch shell symbolizes the marine life of the islands, and the green palm fronds represent the natural vegetation; the *Santa Maria*, Christopher Columbus's flagship, also appears; the sun signifies the world-famous climate and the bright future of the islands

National anthem(s): *title:* "March On, Bahamaland!"
lyrics/music: Timothy GIBSON
history: adopted 1973
title: "God Save the King"
lyrics/music: unknown
history: royal anthem, as a Commonwealth country

ECONOMY

Economic overview: high-income tourism and financial services economy; major income inequality; strong US bilateral relations; several tax relief programs; targeted investment in agriculture, energy, light manufacturing, and technology industries

Real GDP (purchasing power parity): $14.544 billion (2024 est.)
$14.069 billion (2023 est.)
$13.653 billion (2022 est.)
note: data in 2021 dollars
comparison ranking: 159

Real GDP growth rate: 3.4% (2024 est.)
3% (2023 est.)
10.9% (2022 est.)
note: annual GDP % growth based on constant local currency
comparison ranking: 106

Real GDP per capita: $36,200 (2024 est.)
$35,200 (2023 est.)
$34,300 (2022 est.)
note: data in 2021 dollars
comparison ranking: 65

GDP (official exchange rate): $15.833 billion (2024 est.)
note: data in current dollars at official exchange rate

Inflation rate (consumer prices): 0.4% (2024 est.)
3.1% (2023 est.)
5.6% (2022 est.)
note: annual % change based on consumer prices
comparison ranking: 10

GDP - composition, by sector of origin: *agriculture:* 0.5% (2024 est.)
industry: 9.6% (2024 est.)
services: 77.2% (2024 est.)
note: figures may not total 100% due to non-allocated consumption not captured in sector- reported data
comparison rankings: agriculture 188; industry 190; services 1

GDP - composition, by end use: *household consumption:* 64.3% (2024 est.)
government consumption: 12.9% (2024 est.)
investment in fixed capital: 25.7% (2024 est.)
investment in inventories: 1.1% (2024 est.)
exports of goods and services: 37.8% (2024 est.)
imports of goods and services: -41.5% (2024 est.)
note: figures may not total 100% due to rounding or gaps in data collection

Agricultural products: sugarcane, grapefruits, vegetables, bananas, tomatoes, chicken, tropical fruits, oranges, coconuts, mangoes/guavas (2023)
note: top ten agricultural products based on tonnage

Industries: tourism, banking, oil bunkering, maritime industries, transshipment and logistics, salt, aragonite, pharmaceuticals

Industrial production growth rate: 12.5% (2024 est.)
note: annual % change in industrial value added based on constant local currency
comparison ranking: 3

Labor force: 237,100 (2024 est.)
note: number of people ages 15 or older who are employed or seeking work
comparison ranking: 174

Unemployment rate: 8.5% (2024 est.)
8.7% (2023 est.)
9.3% (2022 est.)
note: % of labor force seeking employment
comparison ranking: 139

Youth unemployment rate (ages 15-24): *total:* 17.8% (2024 est.)
male: 17.8% (2024 est.)
female: 17.8% (2024 est.)
note: % of labor force ages 15-24 seeking employment
comparison ranking: total 64

Remittances: 0.4% of GDP (2024 est.)
0.4% of GDP (2023 est.)
0.4% of GDP (2022 est.)
note: personal transfers and compensation between resident and non-resident individuals/ households/ entities

Budget: *revenues:* $2.855 billion (2023 est.)
expenditures: $3.389 billion (2023 est.)
note: central government revenues and expenses (excluding grants/extrabudgetary units/ social security funds) converted to US dollars at average official exchange rate for year indicated

Public debt: 73.7% of GDP (2023 est.)
note: central government debt as a % of GDP
comparison ranking: 49

Taxes and other revenues: 16.2% (of GDP) (2023 est.)
note: central government tax revenue as a % of GDP
comparison ranking: 83

Current account balance: -$1.053 billion (2024 est.)
-$1.069 billion (2023 est.)
-$1.233 billion (2022 est.)
note: balance of payments - net trade and primary/ secondary income in current dollars
comparison ranking: 132

Exports: $6.771 billion (2024 est.)
$6.011 billion (2023 est.)
$5.425 billion (2022 est.)
note: balance of payments - exports of goods and services in current dollars
comparison ranking: 129

Exports - partners: USA 36%, Zimbabwe 16%, Cote d'Ivoire 14%, Germany 8%, Guyana 8% (2023)
note: top five export partners based on percentage share of exports

Exports - commodities: refined petroleum, ships, aluminum, shellfish, plastics (2023)
note: top five export commodities based on value in dollars

Imports: $7.069 billion (2024 est.)
$6.273 billion (2023 est.)
$5.843 billion (2022 est.)
note: balance of payments - imports of goods and services in current dollars
comparison ranking: 139

Imports - partners: USA 60%, Germany 13%, China 5%, Japan 3%, Brazil 2% (2023)
note: top five import partners based on percentage share of imports

Imports - commodities: refined petroleum, ships, aircraft, cars, crude petroleum (2023)
note: top five import commodities based on value in dollars

Reserves of foreign exchange and gold: $2.512 billion (2023 est.)
$2.609 billion (2022 est.)
$2.433 billion (2021 est.)
note: holdings of gold (year-end prices)/foreign exchange/special drawing rights in current dollars
comparison ranking: 122

Exchange rates: Bahamian dollars (BSD) per US dollar -

Exchange rates: 1 (2024 est.)
1 (2023 est.)
1 (2022 est.)
1 (2021 est.)
1 (2020 est.)

ENERGY

Electricity access: *electrification - total population:* 100% (2022 est.)

Electricity: *installed generating capacity:* 608,000 kW (2023 est.)
consumption: 2.036 billion kWh (2023 est.)
transmission/distribution losses: 10 million kWh (2023 est.)
comparison rankings: installed generating capacity 148; consumption 149; transmission/distribution losses 15

Electricity generation sources: *fossil fuels:* 99.1% of total installed capacity (2023 est.)
solar: 0.9% of total installed capacity (2023 est.)

Coal: *imports:* 600 metric tons (2023 est.)

Petroleum: *refined petroleum consumption:* 20,000 bbl/ day (2023 est.)

Natural gas: *consumption:* 14.13 million cubic meters (2023 est.)
imports: 14.13 million cubic meters (2023 est.)

Energy consumption per capita: 104.409 million Btu/ person (2023 est.)
comparison ranking: 45

COMMUNICATIONS

Telephones - fixed lines: *total subscriptions:* 97,000 (2023 est.)
subscriptions per 100 inhabitants: 24 (2023 est.)
comparison ranking: total subscriptions 135

Telephones - mobile cellular: *total subscriptions:* 400,000 (2023 est.)
subscriptions per 100 inhabitants: 99 (2022 est.)
comparison ranking: total subscriptions 177

Broadcast media: 4 major TV providers; 1 TV station is operated by government-owned, commercially run Broadcasting Corporation of the Bahamas (BCB) and competes with 4 privately owned TV stations; multi-channel cable TV subscription service is widely available; 32 licensed broadcast (radio) service providers, with 31 privately owned FM radio stations; the BCB operates a multi-channel radio network with national coverage; the sector is regulated by the Utilities Regulation and Competition Authority (2019)

Internet country code: .bs

Internet users: *percent of population:* 95% (2023 est.)

Broadband - fixed subscriptions: *total:* 95,000 (2023 est.)
subscriptions per 100 inhabitants: 24 (2023 est.)
comparison ranking: total 136

TRANSPORTATION

Civil aircraft registration country code prefix: C6

Airports: 54 (2025)
comparison ranking: 86

Heliports: 9 (2025)
comparison ranking: 77

Merchant marine: *total:* 1,274 (2023)
by type: bulk carrier 345, container ship 39, general cargo 58, oil tanker 193, other 639
comparison ranking: total 19

Ports: *total ports:* 6 (2024)
large: 0
medium: 1
small: 1
very small: 4
ports with oil terminals: 4
key ports: Clifton Pier, Cockburn Town, Freeport, Matthew Town, Nassau, South Riding Point

MILITARY AND SECURITY

Military and security forces: Royal Bahamas Defense Force (RBDF): includes land, air, maritime elements; Royal Bahamas Police Force (RBPF) (2025)

note: the RBPF maintains internal security; both the RBDF and the RBPF, as well as the Department of Corrections, report to the Minister of National Security

Military expenditures: 0.7% of GDP (2024 est.)
0.8% of GDP (2023 est.)
0.8% of GDP (2022 est.)
0.9% of GDP (2021 est.)
0.9% of GDP (2020 est.)

Military and security service personnel strengths: approximately 1,700 active RBDF (2024)

Military equipment inventories and acquisitions: most of the RBDF's major equipment inventory has been acquired from the Netherlands or the US (2024)

Military service age and obligation: 18-30 years of age for voluntary service for men and women (18-60 for Reserves); no conscription (2025)

Military - note: the RBDF was established in 1980; its primary responsibilities are maritime security and safeguarding the territorial integrity of the Bahamas, providing disaster relief and humanitarian assistance, and supporting internal law and order in cooperation with other law enforcement agencies; the RBDF is a naval force with a few light aircraft, coastal patrol craft, and patrol boats, as well as a lightly-armed marine infantry/commando squadron for base and internal security; the RBDF has training relationships with the UK and the US (2025)

TRANSNATIONAL ISSUES

Refugees and internally displaced persons: *refugees:* 30 (2024 est.)

IDPs: 30 (2024 est.)

Illicit drugs: USG identification: major illicit drug-producing and/or drug-transit country (2025)

BAHRAIN

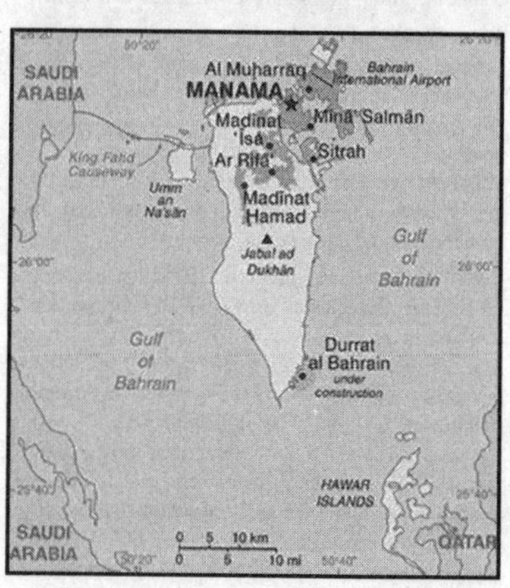

INTRODUCTION

Background: In 1783, the Sunni AL-KHALIFA family took power in Bahrain. In order to secure these holdings, it entered into a series of treaties with the UK during the 19th century that made Bahrain a British protectorate. The archipelago attained its independence in 1971. A steady decline in oil production and reserves since 1970 prompted Bahrain to take steps to diversify its economy, in the process developing petroleum processing and refining, aluminum production, and hospitality and retail sectors. It has also endeavored to become a leading regional banking center, especially with respect to Islamic finance. Bahrain's small size, central location among Gulf countries, economic dependence on Saudi Arabia, and proximity to Iran require it to play a delicate balancing act in foreign affairs among its larger neighbors. Its foreign policy activities usually fall in line with Saudi Arabia and the UAE. In 2022, the United States designated Bahrain as a major non-NATO ally.

The Sunni royal family has long struggled to manage relations with its Shia-majority population. In 2011, amid Arab uprisings elsewhere in the region, the Bahraini Government responded to similar pro-democracy and reform protests at home with police and military action, including deploying Gulf Cooperation Council security forces. Ongoing dissatisfaction with the political status quo continues to factor into sporadic clashes between demonstrators and security forces. In 2020, Bahrain and the United Arab Emirates signed the US-brokered Abraham Accords with Israel. In 2023, Bahrain and the United States signed the Comprehensive Security Integration and Prosperity Agreement to enhance cooperation across a wide range of areas, from defense and security to emerging technology, trade, and investment.

GEOGRAPHY

Location: Middle East, archipelago in the Persian Gulf, east of Saudi Arabia

Geographic coordinates: 26 00 N, 50 33 E

Map references: Middle East

Area: *total:* 760 sq km
land: 760 sq km
water: 0 sq km
comparison ranking: total 187

Area - comparative: 3.5 times the size of Washington, D.C.

Land boundaries: *total:* 0 km

Coastline: 161 km

Maritime claims: *territorial sea:* 12 nm
contiguous zone: 24 nm
continental shelf: extending to boundaries to be determined

Climate: arid; mild, pleasant winters; very hot, humid summers

Terrain: mostly low desert plain rising gently to low central escarpment

Elevation: *highest point:* Jabal ad Dukhan 135 m
lowest point: Persian Gulf 0 m

Natural resources: oil, associated and nonassociated natural gas, fish, pearls

Land use: *agricultural land:* 10.3% (2022 est.)
arable land: 2.7% (2022 est.)
permanent crops: 2.5% (2022 est.)
permanent pasture: 5.1% (2022 est.)
forest: 0.9% (2022 est.)
other: 88.8% (2022 est.)

Irrigated land: 40 sq km (2012)

Major aquifers: Arabian Aquifer System

Population distribution: smallest population of the Gulf States, but urbanization rate exceeds 90%; largest settlement concentration is found on the far northern end of the island in and around Manamah and Al Muharraq

Natural hazards: periodic droughts; dust storms

Geography - note: close to primary Middle Eastern petroleum sources; strategic location in Persian Gulf, through which much of the Western world's petroleum must transit to reach open ocean

PEOPLE AND SOCIETY

Population: *total:* 1,566,888 (2024 est.)
male: 940,022
female: 626,866
comparison rankings: total 155; male 154; female 159

Nationality: *noun:* Bahraini(s)
adjective: Bahraini

Ethnic groups: Bahraini 47.4%, Asian 43.4%, other Arab 4.9%, African 1.4%, North American 1.1%, Gulf Co-operative countries 0.9%, European 0.8%, other 0.1% (2020 est.)

Languages: Arabic (official), English, Farsi, Urdu
major-language sample(s):
العالم، المصدر الذي لا يمكن الاستغناء عنه للمعلومات الأساسية كتاب حقائق (Arabic)

Religions: Muslim 74.2%, other (includes Christian, Jewish, Hindu, Baha'i) 25.8% (2020 est.)

Age structure: *0-14 years:* 18.1% (male 143,399/ female 139,667)
15-64 years: 77.7% (male 762,190/female 454,616)
65 years and over: 4.3% (2024 est.) (male 34,433/ female 32,583)

Dependency ratios: *total dependency ratio:* 28.8 (2024 est.)
youth dependency ratio: 23.3 (2024 est.)
elderly dependency ratio: 5.5 (2024 est.)
potential support ratio: 18.2 (2024 est.)

Median age: *total:* 33.4 years (2024 est.)
male: 34.6 years
female: 31.2 years
comparison ranking: total 111

Population growth rate: 0.82% (2024 est.)
comparison ranking: 109

Birth rate: 12.2 births/1,000 population (2024 est.)
comparison ranking: 146

Death rate: 2.8 deaths/1,000 population (2024 est.)
comparison ranking: 226

Net migration rate: -1.2 migrant(s)/1,000 population (2024 est.)
comparison ranking: 151

Population distribution: smallest population of the Gulf States, but urbanization rate exceeds 90%; largest settlement concentration is found on the far northern end of the island in and around Manamah and Al Muharraq

Urbanization: *urban population:* 89.9% of total population (2023)
rate of urbanization: 1.99% annual rate of change (2020-25 est.)

Major urban areas - population: 709,000 MANAMA (capital) (2023)

Sex ratio: *at birth:* 1.03 male(s)/female
0-14 years: 1.03 male(s)/female
15-64 years: 1.68 male(s)/female
65 years and over: 1.06 male(s)/female
total population: 1.5 male(s)/female (2024 est.)

Maternal mortality ratio: 17 deaths/100,000 live births (2023 est.)
comparison ranking: 129

Infant mortality rate: *total:* 9.7 deaths/1,000 live births (2024 est.)
male: 11.3 deaths/1,000 live births
female: 8 deaths/1,000 live births
comparison ranking: total 135

Life expectancy at birth: *total population:* 80.4 years (2024 est.)
male: 78.1 years
female: 82.7 years
comparison ranking: total population 52

Total fertility rate: 1.65 children born/woman (2024 est.)
comparison ranking: 171

Gross reproduction rate: 0.81 (2024 est.)

Drinking water source: *improved:* total: 99.9% of population (2022 est.)
unimproved: total: 0.1% of population (2022 est.)

Health expenditure: 4.3% of GDP (2021)
8.6% of national budget (2022 est.)

Physician density: 0.74 physicians/1,000 population (2020)

Hospital bed density: 1.7 beds/1,000 population (2019 est.)

Sanitation facility access: *improved:* total: 100% of population (2022 est.)

Obesity - adult prevalence rate: 29.8% (2016)
comparison ranking: 25

Alcohol consumption per capita: *total:* 1.18 liters of pure alcohol (2019 est.)
beer: 0.4 liters of pure alcohol (2019 est.)
wine: 0.11 liters of pure alcohol (2019 est.)
spirits: 0.66 liters of pure alcohol (2019 est.)
other alcohols: 0.01 liters of pure alcohol (2019 est.)
comparison ranking: total 148

Tobacco use: *total:* 17.3% (2025 est.)
male: 24.3% (2025 est.)
female: 4.8% (2025 est.)
comparison ranking: total 89

Currently married women (ages 15-49): 43.8% (2023 est.)

Education expenditure: 2% of GDP (2022 est.)
7.7% national budget (2022 est.)
comparison ranking: Education expenditure (% GDP) 183

Literacy: *total population:* 98% (2023 est.)
male: 99% (2023 est.)
female: 96% (2023 est.)

School life expectancy (primary to tertiary education): *total:* 16 years (2023 est.)
male: 15 years (2023 est.)
female: 17 years (2023 est.)

ENVIRONMENT

Environmental issues: desertification; drought; coastal degradation from oil spills and other discharges from large tankers, oil refineries, and distribution stations; lack of freshwater resources; saline contamination from lowered water table

International environmental agreements: *party to:* Biodiversity, Climate Change, Climate Change-Kyoto Protocol, Climate Change- Paris Agreement, Comprehensive Nuclear Test Ban, Desertification, Endangered Species, Hazardous Wastes, Law of the Sea, Ozone Layer Protection, Ship Pollution, Wetlands
signed, but not ratified: none of the selected agreements

Climate: arid; mild, pleasant winters; very hot, humid summers

Urbanization: *urban population:* 89.9% of total population (2023)
rate of urbanization: 1.99% annual rate of change (2020-25 est.)

Carbon dioxide emissions: 47.818 million metric tonnes of CO2 (2023 est.)
from coal and metallurgical coke: -1,401 metric tonnes of CO2 (2023 est.)
from petroleum and other liquids: 8.825 million metric tonnes of CO2 (2023 est.)
from consumed natural gas: 38.995 million metric tonnes of CO2 (2023 est.)
comparison ranking: total emissions 57

Particulate matter emissions: 51.8 micrograms per cubic meter (2019 est.)

Methane emissions: *energy:* 165.3 kt (2022-2024 est.)
agriculture: 0.6 kt (2019-2021 est.)
waste: 163.6 kt (2019-2021 est.)
other: 1.2 kt (2019-2021 est.)

Waste and recycling: *municipal solid waste generated annually:* 951,900 tons (2024 est.)
percent of municipal solid waste recycled: 14.1% (2022 est.)

Total water withdrawal: *municipal:* 275.6 million cubic meters (2022 est.)
industrial: 14.1 million cubic meters (2022 est.)
agricultural: 144.7 million cubic meters (2022 est.)

Total renewable water resources: 116 million cubic meters (2022 est.)

GOVERNMENT

Country name: *conventional long form:* Kingdom of Bahrain
conventional short form: Bahrain
local long form: Mamlakat al Bahrayn
local short form: Al Bahrayn
former: Dilmun, Tylos, Awal, Mishmahig, Bahrayn, State of Bahrain
etymology: the name means "the two seas" in Arabic and refers to the water bodies on each side of the archipelago

Government type: constitutional monarchy

Capital: *name:* Manama
geographic coordinates: 26 14 N, 50 34 E
time difference: UTC+3 (8 hours ahead of Washington, DC, during Standard Time)
etymology: name derives from the Arabic word *al-manama*, meaning "place of rest" or "place of dreams"

Administrative divisions: 4 governorates (*muhafazat*, singular - *muhafazah*); Asimah (Capital), Janubiyah (Southern), Muharraq, Shamaliyah (Northern)
note: each governorate administered by an appointed governor

Legal system: mixed legal system of Islamic (sharia) law, English common law, Egyptian civil, criminal, and commercial codes; customary law

Constitution: *history:* previous 1973; latest adopted 14 February 2002, entry into force 14 February 2002
amendment process: proposed by the king or by at least 15 members of either chamber of the National Assembly followed by submission to an Assembly committee for review and, if approved, submitted to the government for restatement as drafts; passage requires a two- thirds majority vote by the membership of both chambers and validation by the king; constitutional articles on the state religion (Islam), state language (Arabic), and the monarchy and "inherited rule" cannot be amended

International law organization participation: has not submitted an ICJ jurisdiction declaration; non-party state to the ICCt

Citizenship: *citizenship by birth:* no
citizenship by descent only: the father must be a citizen of Bahrain
dual citizenship recognized: no
residency requirement for naturalization: 25 years; 15 years for Arab nationals

Suffrage: 20 years of age; universal

Executive branch: *chief of state:* King HAMAD bin Isa Al-Khalifa (since 6 March 1999)
head of government: Prime Minister Crown Prince SALMAN bin Hamad Al-Khalifa (since 11 November 2020)
cabinet: Cabinet appointed by the monarch
election/appointment process: the monarchy is hereditary; prime minister appointed by the monarch

Legislative branch: *legislature name:* National Assembly (Al-Majlis Al-Watani)
legislative structure: bicameral
Legislative branch - lower chamber
chamber name: Council of Representatives (Majlis Al-Nuwab)

number of seats: 40 (all directly elected)
electoral system: plurality/majority
scope of elections: full renewal
term in office: 4 years
most recent election date: 11 /12/2022 to 11/19/2022
percentage of women in chamber: 20%
expected date of next election: November 2026

Legislative branch - upper chamber: *chamber name:* Shura Council (Majlis Al-Shura)
number of seats: 40 (all appointed)
scope of elections: full renewal
term in office: 4 years
most recent election date: 11/27/2022
percentage of women in chamber: 25%
expected date of next election: November 2026

Judicial branch: *highest court(s):* Court of Cassation (consists of the chairman and 3 judges); Supreme Court of Appeal (consists of the chairman and 3 judges); Constitutional Court (consists of the president and 6 members); High Sharia Court of Appeal (court sittings include the president and at least one judge)
judge selection and term of office: Court of Cassation judges appointed by royal decree and serve for a specified tenure; Constitutional Court president and members appointed by the Higher Judicial Council, a body chaired by the monarch and includes judges from the Court of Cassation, sharia law courts, and Civil High Courts of Appeal; members serve 9-year terms; High Sharia Court of Appeal member appointments by royal decree for a specified tenure
subordinate courts: Civil High Courts of Appeal; middle and lower civil courts; High Sharia Court of Appeal; Senior Sharia Court; Administrative Courts of Appeal; military courts
note: the judiciary of Bahrain is divided into civil law courts and sharia law courts; sharia courts (involving personal status and family law) are further divided into Sunni Muslim and Shia Muslim; the Courts are supervised by the Supreme Judicial Council.

Political parties: *note:* political parties are prohibited, but political societies were legalized under a July 2005 law

Diplomatic representation in the US: *chief of mission:* Ambassador Abdulla bin Rashed AL KHALIFA (since 21 July 2017)
chancery: 3502 International Drive NW, Washington, DC 20008
telephone: [1] (202) 342-1111
FAX: [1] (202) 362-2192
email address and website: ambsecretary@bahrainembassy.org
https://www.mofa.gov.bh/Default.aspx?language=en-US&tabid=7702
consulate(s) general: New York

Diplomatic representation from the US: *chief of mission:* Ambassador Steven C. BONDY (since 9 February 2022)
embassy: Building 979, Road 3119, Block 331, Zinj District, P.O. Box 26431, Manama
mailing address: 6210 Manama Place, Washington DC 20521-6210
telephone: [973] 17-242700
FAX: [973] 17-272594
email address and website: ManamaConsular@state.gov
https://bh.usembassy.gov/

International organization participation: ABEDA, AFESD, AMF, CAEU, CICA, FAO, G-77, GCC, IAEA, IBRD, ICAO, ICC (national committees), ICRM, IDA, IDB, IFC, IFRCS, IHO, ILO, IMF, IMO, IMSO, Interpol, IOC, IOM (observer), IPU, ISO, ITSO, ITU, ITUC (NGOs), LAS, MIGA, NAM, OAPEC, OIC, OPCW, PCA, UN, UNCTAD, UNESCO, UNIDO, UNOOSA, UNWTO, UPU, WCO, WFTU (NGOs), WHO, WIPO, WMO, WTO

Independence: 15 August 1971 (from the UK)

National holiday: National Day, 16 December (1971)
note: 15 August 1971 was the date of independence from the UK, 16 December 1971 was the date of independence from British protection

Flag: *description:* red, with a white serrated band of five white points on the left side
meaning: red is the traditional color for flags of Persian Gulf states; the five points represent the five pillars of Islam
history: until 2002, the flag had eight white points, but this was reduced to five to avoid confusion with the Qatari flag

National symbol(s): a white serrated band with five white points on top of a red field

National color(s): red, white

National anthem(s): *title:* "Bahrainona" (Our Bahrain)
lyrics/music: unknown
history: adopted 1971; Mohamed Sudqi AYYASH wrote the original lyrics, but they were changed in 2002 after Bahrain became a kingdom

National heritage: *total World Heritage Sites:* 3 (all cultural)
selected World Heritage Site locales: Dilmun Burial Mounds; Qal'at al-Bahrain - Ancient Harbor and Capital of Dilmun; Bahrain Pearling Path

ECONOMY

Economic overview: high-income, growing Middle Eastern island economy; oil and aluminum exporter with diversification led by services, construction and manufacturing; regional finance and tourism hub; high public debt linked to oil revenue dependence and limited tax base; vulnerable to water reservoir depletion

Real GDP (purchasing power parity): $93.937 billion (2024 est.)
$91.185 billion (2023 est.)
$87.781 billion (2022 est.)
note: data in 2021 dollars
comparison ranking: 99

Real GDP growth rate: 3% (2024 est.)
3.9% (2023 est.)
6.2% (2022 est.)
note: annual GDP % growth based on constant local currency
comparison ranking: 118

Real GDP per capita: $59,100 (2024 est.)
$57,800 (2023 est.)
$57,600 (2022 est.)
note: data in 2021 dollars
comparison ranking: 32

GDP (official exchange rate): $47.737 billion (2024 est.)
note: data in current dollars at official exchange rate

Inflation rate (consumer prices): 0.9% (2024 est.)
0.1% (2023 est.)
3.6% (2022 est.)
note: annual % change based on consumer prices
comparison ranking: 18

GDP - composition, by sector of origin: *agriculture:* 0.3% (2023 est.)
industry: 43.4% (2023 est.)
services: 51.9% (2023 est.)
note: figures may not total 100% due to non-allocated consumption not captured in sector-reported data
comparison rankings: agriculture 195; industry 15; services 135

GDP - composition, by end use: *household consumption:* 38.9% (2023 est.)
government consumption: 14.6% (2023 est.)
investment in fixed capital: 27.5% (2023 est.)
investment in inventories: 1.8% (2023 est.)
exports of goods and services: 87.4% (2023 est.)
imports of goods and services: -70.1% (2023 est.)
note: figures may not total 100% due to rounding or gaps in data collection

Agricultural products: lamb/mutton, dates, milk, tomatoes, chicken, eggs, sheep offal, sheepskins, eggplants, chillies/peppers (2023)
note: top ten agricultural products based on tonnage

Industries: petroleum processing and refining, aluminum smelting, iron pelletization, fertilizers, Islamic and offshore banking, insurance, ship repairing, tourism

Industrial production growth rate: 0.1% (2023 est.)
note: annual % change in industrial value added based on constant local currency
comparison ranking: 133

Labor force: 913,300 (2024 est.)
note: number of people ages 15 or older who are employed or seeking work
comparison ranking: 147

Unemployment rate: 1.2% (2024 est.)
1.2% (2023 est.)
1.4% (2022 est.)
note: % of labor force seeking employment
comparison ranking: 7

Youth unemployment rate (ages 15-24): *total:* 5.2% (2024 est.)
male: 2.5% (2024 est.)
female: 12.4% (2024 est.)
note: % of labor force ages 15-24 seeking employment
comparison ranking: total 162

Average household expenditures: *on food:* 13.6% of household expenditures (2023 est.)
on alcohol and tobacco: 0.4% of household expenditures (2023 est.)

Remittances: 0% of GDP (2023 est.)
0% of GDP (2022 est.)
0% of GDP (2021 est.)
note: personal transfers and compensation between resident and non-resident individuals/ households/ entities

Budget: *revenues:* $5.538 billion (2020 est.)
expenditures: $9.982 billion (2020 est.)
note: central government revenues and expenses (excluding grants/extrabudgetary units/ social security funds) converted to US dollars at average official exchange rate for year indicated

Public debt: 111.6% of GDP (2020 est.)
note: central government debt as a % of GDP
comparison ranking: 13

Taxes and other revenues: 2.8% (of GDP) (2020 est.)
note: central government tax revenue as a % of GDP
comparison ranking: 150

Current account balance: $2.282 billion (2024 est.)
$2.699 billion (2023 est.)
$6.839 billion (2022 est.)

note: balance of payments - net trade and primary/secondary income in current dollars
comparison ranking: 44

Exports: $41.303 billion (2024 est.)
$40.344 billion (2023 est.)
$44.58 billion (2022 est.)
note: balance of payments - exports of goods and services in current dollars
comparison ranking: 72

Exports - partners: UAE 16%, Saudi Arabia 15%, South Africa 8%, USA 6%, India 4% (2023)
note: top five export partners based on percentage share of exports

Exports - commodities: refined petroleum, aluminum, iron ore, aluminum wire, jewelry (2023)
note: top five export commodities based on value in dollars

Imports: $33.044 billion (2024 est.)
$32.374 billion (2023 est.)
$33.066 billion (2022 est.)
note: balance of payments - imports of goods and services in current dollars
comparison ranking: 79

Imports - partners: China 13%, Saudi Arabia 12%, UAE 11%, Brazil 8%, Australia 7% (2023) note: top five import partners based on percentage share of imports

Imports - commodities: iron ore, aluminum oxide, ships, cars, gold (2023)
note: top five import commodities based on value in dollars

Reserves of foreign exchange and gold: $4.949 billion (2024 est.)
$5.118 billion (2023 est.)
$4.775 billion (2022 est.)
note: holdings of gold (year-end prices)/foreign exchange/special drawing rights in current dollars
comparison ranking: 101

Exchange rates: Bahraini dinars (BHD) per US dollar -

Exchange rates: 0.376 (2024 est.)
0.376 (2023 est.)
0.376 (2022 est.)
0.376 (2021 est.)
0.376 (2020 est.)

ENERGY

Electricity access: *electrification - total population:* 100% (2022 est.)

Electricity: *installed generating capacity:* 7.031 million kW (2023 est.)
consumption: 35.09 billion kWh (2023 est.)
exports: 467.898 million kWh (2023 est.)
imports: 480.883 million kWh (2023 est.)
transmission/distribution losses: 1.093 billion kWh (2023 est.)
comparison rankings: installed generating capacity 77; consumption 63; exports 76; imports 94; transmission/distribution losses 102

Electricity generation sources: *fossil fuels:* 99.7% of total installed capacity (2023 est.)
solar: 0.2% of total installed capacity (2023 est.)

Coal: *exports:* 600 metric tons (2023 est.)
imports: 300 metric tons (2023 est.)

Petroleum: *total petroleum production:* 190,000 bbl/day (2023 est.)
refined petroleum consumption: 72,000 bbl/day (2023 est.)
crude oil estimated reserves: 186.5 million barrels (2021 est.)

Natural gas: *production:* 19.55 billion cubic meters (2023 est.)
consumption: 19.878 billion cubic meters (2023 est.)
imports: 81.98 million cubic meters (2020 est.)
proven reserves: 81.383 billion cubic meters (2021 est.)

Energy consumption per capita: 554.202 million Btu/person (2023 est.)
comparison ranking: 3

COMMUNICATIONS

Telephones - fixed lines: *total subscriptions:* 246,000 (2023 est.)
subscriptions per 100 inhabitants: 16 (2023 est.)
comparison ranking: total subscriptions 113

Telephones - mobile cellular: *total subscriptions:* 2.42 million (2023 est.)
subscriptions per 100 inhabitants: 145 (2022 est.)
comparison ranking: total subscriptions 147

Broadcast media: state-run Bahrain Radio and Television Corporation (BRTC) operates 6 terrestrial TV networks and several radio stations; satellite TV systems provide access to international broadcasts; 1 private FM station has broadcasts for Indian listeners; radio and TV broadcasts from countries in the region are available (2023)

Internet country code: .bh

Internet users: *percent of population:* 100% (2023 est.)

Broadband - fixed subscriptions: *total:* 268,000 (2023 est.)
subscriptions per 100 inhabitants: 17 (2023 est.)
comparison ranking: total 117

TRANSPORTATION

Civil aircraft registration country code prefix: A9C

Airports: 3 (2025)
comparison ranking: 189

Heliports: 8 (2025)
comparison ranking: 85

Merchant marine: *total:* 184 (2023)
by type: general cargo 12, oil tanker 3, other 169
comparison ranking: total 71

Ports: *total ports:* 4 (2024)
large: 0
medium: 3
small: 1
very small: 0
ports with oil terminals: 1
key ports: Al Manamah, Khalifa Bin Salman, Mina Salman, Sitrah

MILITARY AND SECURITY

Military and security forces: Bahrain Defense Force (BDF): Royal Bahraini Army (includes the Royal Guard), Royal Bahraini Navy, Royal Bahraini Air Force

Ministry of Interior: National Guard, Special Security Forces Command (SSFC), Coast Guard (2025)
note 1: the Royal Guard is officially under the command of the Army, but exercises considerable autonomy
note 2: the Ministry of Interior is responsible for internal security and oversees police and specialized security units responsible for maintaining internal order; the National Guard's primary mission is to guard critical infrastructure such as the airport and oil fields and is a back-up to the police; the Guard is under the Ministry of Interior but reports directly to the king

Military expenditures: 3% of GDP (2024 est.)
3.2% of GDP (2023 est.)
3.2% of GDP (2022 est.)
3.6% of GDP (2021 est.)
4.2% of GDP (2020 est.)

Military and security service personnel strengths: information varies; approximately 10,000 active Bahrain Defense Force; approximately 3,000 National Guard (2025)

Military equipment inventories and acquisitions: the military's inventory consists of a mix of equipment acquired from a wide variety of suppliers; in recent years, the US has been the leading supplier of arms to Bahrain (2024)

Military service age and obligation: 18 years of age for voluntary military service; 18-55 to voluntarily join the reserves; no compulsory service (2024)

Military - note: the BDF (established 1968) is responsible for territorial defense and support to internal security; its primary concern is Iran, both the conventional military threat and Tehran's support to regional terrorist groups; the BDF participates in multinational exercises and has conducted small deployments outside of the country; in 2015, for example, Bahrain joined the Saudi Arabia-led military intervention in Yemen, supplying a few hundred troops and combat aircraft
Bahrain's closest security partners are Saudi Arabia and the US; Bahraini leaders have said that the security ties of Bahrain and Saudi Arabia are "indivisible"; Saudi Arabia sent forces to Bahrain to assist with internal security following the 2011 uprising; Bahrain hosts the US Naval Forces Central Command (USNAVCENT; established 1983), which includes the US 5th Fleet and the Combined Maritime Forces (established 2002), a coalition of more than 30 nations providing maritime security for regional shipping lanes; in 2003, the US granted Bahrain Major Non-NATO Ally status, a designation under US law that provides foreign partners with certain benefits in the areas of defense trade and security cooperation; Bahrain also has close security ties with the UK, which maintains a naval support facility there
Bahrain hosts the Gulf Cooperation Council's (GCC) Unified Maritime Operations Center and is a member of the Peninsula Shield Forces, a joint military force established by the GCC countries with the aim of maintaining security and stability in the region (2025)

SPACE

Space agency/agencies: Bahrain Space Agency (BSA; established 2014) (2025)

Space program overview: has a national space program with a focus on promoting space research and science, applying space-related technologies, and building capacity in the fields of satellite manufacturing, tracking, control, data processing and analysis, and remote sensing; cooperates with a variety of foreign agencies and commercial entities, including those of India, Italy, Japan, Oman, Saudi Arabia, the UK, the UAE, and the US; also a member of the Arab Space Coordination Group (2025)
note: further details about the key activities, programs, and milestones of the country's space program,

as well as government spending estimates on the space sector, appear in the Space Programs reference guide

TERRORISM

Terrorist group(s): Terrorist group(s): al-Ashtar Brigades; Islamic Revolutionary Guard Corps/Qods Force

note 1: details about the history, aims, leadership, organization, areas of operation, tactics, targets, weapons, size, and sources of support of the group(s) appear(s) in Appendix T

note 2: in addition to the al-Ashtar Brigades and the IRGC/Qods Force, Saraya al-Mukhtar (aka The Mukhtar Brigade) is an Iran-backed terrorist organization based in Bahrain, reportedly receiving financial and logistic support from the IRGC; Saraya al-Mukhtar's self-described goal is to depose the Bahraini Government with the intention of paving the way for Iran to exert greater influence in Bahrain; the group was designated by the US as a Specially Designated Global Terrorist in Dec 2020

TRANSNATIONAL ISSUES

Refugees and internally displaced persons: *refugees:* 371 (2024 est.)

BANGLADESH

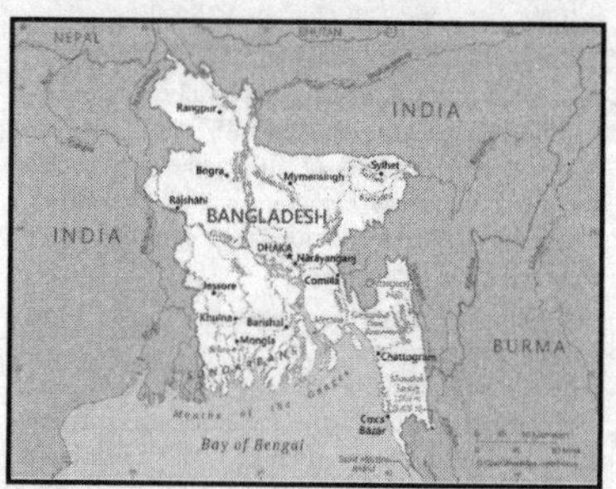

INTRODUCTION

Background: The huge delta region at the confluence of the Ganges and Brahmaputra River systems – now referred to as Bangladesh – was a loosely incorporated outpost of various empires for much of the first millennium A.D. Muslim conversions and settlement in the region began in the 10th century, primarily from Arab and Persian traders and preachers. Europeans established trading posts in the area in the 16th century. Eventually the area known as Bengal, which is primarily Hindu in the western section and mostly Muslim in the eastern half, became part of British India. After the partition of India in 1947, the Muslim-majority area became East Pakistan. Calls for greater autonomy and animosity between the eastern and western areas of Pakistan led to a Bengali independence movement. That movement, led by the Awami League (AL) and supported by India, won the independence war for Bangladesh in 1971.

The military overthrew the post-independence AL government in 1975, the first of a series of military coups that resulted in a military-backed government and the subsequent creation of the Bangladesh Nationalist Party (BNP) that took power in 1979. That government also ended in a coup in 1981, followed by military-backed rule until democratic elections were held in 1991. The BNP and AL alternated in power from 1991 to 2008, with the exception of a military-backed, emergency caretaker regime in 2007. The country returned to fully democratic rule in 2008 with the election of the AL and Prime Minister Sheikh HASINA. With the help of international development assistance, Bangladesh is on track to graduate from the UN's Least Developed Countries (LDC) list in 2026.

The economy has grown at an annual average of about 6.25% for the last two decades. Poverty declined from 11.8 percent in 2010 to 5.0 percent in 2022, based on the international poverty line of $2.15 a day (using 2017 Purchasing Power Parity exchange rate). The country made a rapid recovery from the COVID-19 pandemic, but still faces economic challenges.

GEOGRAPHY

Location: Southern Asia, bordering the Bay of Bengal, between Burma and India

Geographic coordinates: 24 00 N, 90 00 E

Map references: Asia

Area: *total:* 148,460 sq km
land: 130,170 sq km
water: 18,290 sq km
comparison ranking: total 94

Area - comparative: slightly larger than Pennsylvania and New Jersey combined; slightly smaller than Iowa

Land boundaries: *total:* 4,413 km
border countries (2): Burma 271 km; India 4,142 km

Coastline: 580 km

Maritime claims: *territorial sea:* 12 nm
contiguous zone: 18 nm
exclusive economic zone: 200 nm
continental shelf: to the outer limits of the continental margin

Climate: tropical; mild winter (October to March); hot, humid summer (March to June); humid, warm rainy monsoon (June to October)

Terrain: mostly flat alluvial plain; hilly in southeast

Elevation: *highest point:* Mowdok Taung 1,060 m
lowest point: Bay of Bengal 0 m
mean elevation: 85 m

Natural resources: natural gas, arable land, timber, coal

Land use: *agricultural land:* 72.4% (2022 est.)
arable land: 60.5% (2022 est.)
permanent crops: 7.2% (2022 est.)
permanent pasture: 4.6% (2022 est.)
forest: 14.5% (2022 est.)
other: 13.2% (2022 est.)

Irrigated land: 83,690 sq km (2022)

Major rivers (by length in km): Brahmaputra river mouth (shared with China [s] and India) - 3,969 km; Ganges river mouth (shared with India [s]) - 2,704 km
note: [s] after country name indicates river source; [m] after country name indicates river mouth

Major watersheds (area sq km): Indian Ocean drainage: Brahmaputra (651,335 sq km), Ganges (1,016,124 sq km)

Major aquifers: Indus-Ganges-Brahmaputra Basin

Natural hazards: droughts; cyclones; much of the country routinely inundated during the summer monsoon season

Geography - note: *most of the country is situated on deltas of large rivers flowing from the Himalayas:* the Ganges unites with the Jamuna (main channel of the Brahmaputra) and later joins the Meghna to eventually empty into the Bay of Bengal

PEOPLE AND SOCIETY

Population: *total:* 168,697,184 (2024 est.)
male: 82,708,252
female: 85,988,932
comparison rankings: total 8; male 8; female 8

Nationality: *noun:* Bangladeshi(s)
adjective: Bangladeshi

Ethnic groups: Bengali at least 99%, other indigenous ethnic groups 1% (2022 est.)
note: Bangladesh's government recognizes 27 indigenous ethnic groups under the 2010 Cultural Institution for Small Anthropological Groups Act; other sources estimate there are about 75 ethnic groups

Languages: Bangla 98.8% (official, also known as Bengali), other 1.2% (2011 est.)
major-language sample(s):
বিশ্ব ফেসবুক, মৌলিক তথ্যের অপরিহার্য উৎস (Bangla)

Religions: Muslim 91%, Hindu 8%, other 1% (2022 est.)

Age structure: *0-14 years:* 25.1% (male 21,540,493/female 20,800,712)
15-64 years: 67.1% (male 55,071,592/female 58,180,322)
65 years and over: 7.8% (2024 est.) (male 6,096,167/female 7,007,898)

Dependency ratios: *total dependency ratio:* 49 (2024 est.)
youth dependency ratio: 37.4 (2024 est.)
elderly dependency ratio: 11.6 (2024 est.)
potential support ratio: 8.6 (2024 est.)

Median age: *total:* 29.6 years (2024 est.)
male: 28.7 years
female: 30.4 years
comparison ranking: total 144

Population growth rate: 0.89% (2024 est.)
comparison ranking: 103

Birth rate: 17.3 births/1,000 population (2024 est.)
comparison ranking: 88

Death rate: 5.5 deaths/1,000 population (2024 est.)
comparison ranking: 179

Net migration rate: -2.9 migrant(s)/1,000 population (2024 est.)
comparison ranking: 178

Urbanization: *urban population:* 40.5% of total population (2023)
rate of urbanization: 2.88% annual rate of change (2020-25 est.)

Major urban areas - population: 23.210 million DHAKA (capital), 5.380 million Chittagong, 955,000 Khulna, 962,000 Rajshahi, 964,000 Sylhet, 906,000 Bogra (2023)

Sex ratio: *at birth:* 1.04 male(s)/female
0-14 years: 1.04 male(s)/female
15-64 years: 0.95 male(s)/female
65 years and over: 0.87 male(s)/female
total population: 0.96 male(s)/female (2024 est.)

Mother's mean age at first birth: 18.6 years (2017/18 est.)
note: data represents median age at first birth among women 20-49

Maternal mortality ratio: 115 deaths/100,000 live births (2023 est.)
comparison ranking: 63

Infant mortality rate: *total:* 28.8 deaths/1,000 live births (2024 est.)
male: 31.3 deaths/1,000 live births
female: 26.3 deaths/1,000 live births
comparison ranking: total 52

Life expectancy at birth: *total population:* 75.2 years (2024 est.)
male: 73.1 years
female: 77.5 years
comparison ranking: total population 129

Total fertility rate: 2.07 children born/woman (2024 est.)
comparison ranking: 96

Gross reproduction rate: 1.01 (2024 est.)

Drinking water source: *improved: urban:* 98.3% of population (2022 est.)
rural: 98.5% of population (2022 est.)
total: 98.4% of population (2022 est.)
unimproved: urban: 1.7% of population (2022 est.)
rural: 1.5% of population (2022 est.)
total: 1.6% of population (2022 est.)

Health expenditure: 2.4% of GDP (2021)
1.2% of national budget (2022 est.)

Physician density: 0.72 physicians/1,000 population (2023)

Hospital bed density: 0.9 beds/1,000 population (2019 est.)

Sanitation facility access: *improved: urban:* 90.3% of population (2022 est.)
rural: 81.4% of population (2022 est.)
total: 84.9% of population (2022 est.)
unimproved: urban: 9.7% of population (2022 est.)
rural: 18.6% of population (2022 est.)
total: 15.1% of population (2022 est.)

Obesity - adult prevalence rate: 3.6% (2016)
comparison ranking: 191

Alcohol consumption per capita: *total:* 0 liters of pure alcohol (2019 est.)
beer: 0 liters of pure alcohol (2019 est.)
wine: 0 liters of pure alcohol (2019 est.)
spirits: 0 liters of pure alcohol (2019 est.)
other alcohols: 0 liters of pure alcohol (2019 est.)
comparison ranking: total 187

Tobacco use: *total:* 29.7% (2025 est.)
male: 47.6% (2025 est.)
female: 12.5% (2025 est.)
comparison ranking: total 22

Children under the age of 5 years underweight: 22.6% (2019)
comparison ranking: 9

Currently married women (ages 15-49): 80.1% (2023 est.)

Child marriage: *women married by age 15:* 15.5% (2019)
women married by age 18: 51.4% (2019)

Education expenditure: 2% of GDP (2024 est.)
11.6% national budget (2024 est.)
comparison ranking: Education expenditure (% GDP) 184

Literacy: *total population:* 79% (2022 est.)
male: 81% (2022 est.)
female: 77% (2022 est.)

School life expectancy (primary to tertiary education): *total:* 11 years (2023 est.)
male: 11 years (2023 est.)
female: 12 years (2023 est.)

ENVIRONMENT

Environmental issues: flooding; water pollution, especially of fishing areas, from the use of commercial pesticides; groundwater pollution from naturally occurring arsenic; falling water tables in the northern and central parts of the country; soil degradation and erosion; deforestation; destruction of wetlands; severe overpopulation with noise pollution

International environmental agreements: *party to:* Biodiversity, Climate Change, Climate Change-Kyoto Protocol, Climate Change-Paris Agreement, Comprehensive Nuclear Test Ban, Desertification, Endangered Species, Environmental Modification, Hazardous Wastes, Law of the Sea, Nuclear Test Ban, Ozone Layer Protection, Ship Pollution, Wetlands
signed, but not ratified: none of the selected agreements

Climate: tropical; mild winter (October to March); hot, humid summer (March to June); humid, warm rainy monsoon (June to October)

Urbanization: *urban population:* 40.5% of total population (2023)
rate of urbanization: 2.88% annual rate of change (2020-25 est.)

Carbon dioxide emissions: 125.956 million metric tonnes of CO2 (2023 est.)
from coal and metallurgical coke: 26.967 million metric tonnes of CO2 (2023 est.)
from petroleum and other liquids: 42.083 million metric tonnes of CO2 (2023 est.)
from consumed natural gas: 56.906 million metric tonnes of CO2 (2023 est.)
comparison ranking: total emissions 37

Particulate matter emissions: 42.5 micrograms per cubic meter (2019 est.)

Methane emissions: *energy:* 544 kt (2022-2024 est.)
agriculture: 2,391.4 kt (2019-2021 est.)
waste: 693 kt (2019-2021 est.)
other: 38.6 kt (2019-2021 est.)

Waste and recycling: *municipal solid waste generated annually:* 14.778 million tons (2024 est.)
percent of municipal solid waste recycled: 15.7% (2022 est.)

Total water withdrawal: *municipal:* 3.6 billion cubic meters (2022 est.)
industrial: 770 million cubic meters (2022 est.)
agricultural: 31.5 billion cubic meters (2022 est.)

Total renewable water resources: 1.227 trillion cubic meters (2022 est.)

GOVERNMENT

Country name: *conventional long form:* People's Republic of Bangladesh
conventional short form: Bangladesh
local long form: Gana Prajatantri Bangladesh
local short form: Bangladesh
former: East Bengal, East Pakistan
etymology: the name is a compound of the Bengali words *Bangla* (Bengali) and *desh* (country)

Government type: parliamentary republic

Capital: *name:* Dhaka
geographic coordinates: 23 43 N, 90 24 E
time difference: UTC+6 (11 hours ahead of Washington, DC, during Standard Time)
etymology: the origins of the name are unclear, but it may be derived from either the dhak tree or Dhakeshwari, a goddess with a shrine in the city

Administrative divisions: 8 divisions; Barishal, Chattogram, Dhaka, Khulna, Mymensingh, Rajshahi, Rangpur, Sylhet

Legal system: common law, incorporating elements of English common law; since independence, statutory law has been the primary form of legislation; Islamic law applies to Muslims in family and inheritance laws, with Hindu personal law applying to Hindus and Buddhists

Constitution: *history:* previous 1935, 1956, 1962 (pre-independence); latest enacted 4 November 1972, effective 16 December 1972, suspended March 1982, restored November 1986
amendment process: proposed by the House of the Nation; approval requires at least two-thirds majority vote of the House membership and assent of the president of the republic

International law organization participation: has not submitted an ICJ jurisdiction declaration; accepts ICCt jurisdiction

Citizenship: *citizenship by birth:* no
citizenship by descent only: at least one parent must be a citizen of Bangladesh
dual citizenship recognized: yes, but limited to select countries
residency requirement for naturalization: 5 years

Suffrage: 18 years of age; universal

Executive branch: *chief of state:* President Mohammad SHAHABUDDIN Chuppi (since 24 April 2023)
head of government: Interim Prime Minister Muhammad YUNUS (since 8 August 2024)
cabinet: Cabinet selected by the prime minister, appointed by the president
election/appointment process: president indirectly elected by the National Parliament for a 5-year term (eligible for a second term); the president appoints as prime minister the majority party leader in the National Parliament
most recent election date: 13 February 2023
election results: President Mohammad SHAHABUDDIN Chuppi (AL) elected unopposed by the National Parliament; Sheikh HASINA reappointed prime minister for a fifth term following the 7 January 2024 parliamentary election; note - Sheikh HASINA resigned and fled the country on 5 August 2024 following mass protests against her government in July and August 2024, and Mohammad YUNIS

was appointed as interim Prime Minister on 8 August 2024
expected date of next election: 2028

Legislative branch: *expected date of next election:* February 2026
note: the Parliament (House of the Nation) was dissolved on 6 August 2024 by President Mohammad SHAHABUDDIN Chuppi following the resignation of Prime Minister Sheikh HASINA Wazed on 5 August 2024; new national elections will be held in February 2026

Judicial branch: *highest court(s):* Supreme Court of Bangladesh (organized into the Appellate Division with 7 justices and the High Court Division with 99 justices)
judge selection and term of office: chief justice and justices appointed by the president; justices serve until retirement at age 67
subordinate courts: civil courts include: Assistant Judge's Court; Joint District Judge's Court; Additional District Judge's Court; District Judge's Court; criminal courts include: Court of Sessions; Court of Metropolitan Sessions; Metropolitan Magistrate Courts; Magistrate Court; special courts/tribunals

Political parties: Awami League or AL
Bangladesh Jamaat-i-Islami or JIB
Bangladesh Nationalist Party or BNP
Islami Andolan Bangladesh
Jatiya Party or JP (Ershad faction)
Jatiya Party or JP (Manju faction)
National Socialist Party (Jatiya Samajtantrik Dal) or JSD
Workers Party or WP

Diplomatic representation in the US: *chief of mission:* Ambassador Tareq Md Ariful ISLAM (since 5 September 2025)
chancery: 3510 International Drive NW, Washington, DC 20008
telephone: [1] (202) 244-0183
FAX: [1] (202) 244-2771
email address and website: mission.washington@mofa.gov.bd
Embassy of the People's Republic of Bangladesh, Washington, DC (mofa.gov.bd)
consulate(s) general: Los Angeles, Miami, New York

Diplomatic representation from the US: *chief of mission:* Ambassador (vacant); Chargé d'Affaires Ambassador Tracey Ann JACOBSEN (since 11 January 2025)
embassy: Madani Avenue, Baridhara, Dhaka - 1212
mailing address: 6120 Dhaka Place, Washington DC 20521-6120
telephone: [880] (2) 5566-2000
FAX: [880] (2) 5566-2907
email address and website: DhakaACS@state.gov
https://bd.usembassy.gov/

International organization participation: ADB, ARF, BIMSTEC, C, CD, CICA (observer), CP, D-8, FAO, G-77, IAEA, IBRD, ICAO, ICC (national committees), ICRM, IDA, IDB, IFAD, IFC, IFRCS, IHO, ILO, IMF, IMO, IMSO, Interpol, IOC, IOM, IPU, ISO, ITSO, ITU, ITUC (NGOs), MIGA, MINURSO, MINUSCA, MONUSCO, NAM, OIC, OPCW, PCA, SAARC, SACEP, UN, UNAMID, UNCTAD, UNESCO, UNHCR, UNIDO, UNISFA, UNIFIL, UNMISS, UNOOSA, UNWTO, UPU, WCO, WFTU (NGOs), WHO, WIPO, WMO, WTO

Independence: 16 December 1971 (from Pakistan)

National holiday: Independence Day, 26 March (1971); Victory Day, 16 December (1971)
note: 26 March 1971 is the date of the Awami League's declaration of an independent Bangladesh, and 16 December (Victory Day) memorializes the military victory over Pakistan and the official creation of the state of Bangladesh

Flag: *description:* green field with a large red disk shifted slightly to the left
meaning: the red disk represents the rising sun and the sacrifice to achieve independence; the green field symbolizes the lush vegetation of Bangladesh

National symbol(s): Bengal tiger, water lily

National color(s): green, red

National coat of arms: the water lily is the national flower and symbolizes promise, aesthetics, and elegance; the water under the lily, the rice sheaves on the sides, and the jute leaves at the top represent the Bangladeshi landscape and economy; the four stars represent the aims and ambition of the nation

National anthem(s): *title:* "Amar Shonar Bangla" (My Golden Bengal)
lyrics/music: Rabindranath TAGORE
history: adopted 1971; Rabindranath TAGORE, a Nobel laureate, also wrote India's national anthem

National heritage: *total World Heritage Sites:* 3 (2 cultural, 1 natural)
selected World Heritage Site locales: Bagerhat Historic Mosque (c); Ruins of the Buddhist Vihara at Paharpur (c); Sundarbans (n)

ECONOMY

Economic overview: one of the fastest growing emerging market economies; strong economic rebound following COVID-19; significant poverty reduction; exports dominated by textile industry; weakened exports and remittances resulted in declining foreign exchange reserves and 2022 IMF loan request

Real GDP (purchasing power parity): $1.473 trillion (2024 est.)
$1.413 trillion (2023 est.)
$1.336 trillion (2022 est.)
note: data in 2021 dollars
comparison ranking: 24

Real GDP growth rate: 4.2% (2024 est.)
5.8% (2023 est.)
7.1% (2022 est.)
note: annual GDP % growth based on constant local currency
comparison ranking: 68

Real GDP per capita: $8,500 (2024 est.)
$8,200 (2023 est.)
$7,900 (2022 est.)
note: data in 2021 dollars
comparison ranking: 152

GDP (official exchange rate): $450.119 billion (2024 est.)
note: data in current dollars at official exchange rate

Inflation rate (consumer prices): 10.5% (2024 est.)
9.9% (2023 est.)
7.7% (2022 est.)
note: annual % change based on consumer prices
comparison ranking: 179

GDP - composition, by sector of origin: *agriculture:* 11.2% (2024 est.)
industry: 34.1% (2024 est.)
services: 51.4% (2024 est.)
note: figures may not total 100% due to non-allocated consumption not captured in sector-reported data
comparison rankings: agriculture 68; industry 36; services 140

GDP - composition, by end use: *household consumption:* 70.1% (2024 est.)
government consumption: 5.9% (2024 est.)
investment in fixed capital: 30.7% (2024 est.)
investment in inventories: 0% (2024 est.)
exports of goods and services: 10.5% (2024 est.)
imports of goods and services: -16.3% (2024 est.)
note: figures may not total 100% due to rounding or gaps in data collection

Agricultural products: rice, milk, potatoes, maize, sugarcane, onions, jute, vegetables, mangoes/guavas, tropical fruits (2023)
note: top ten agricultural products based on tonnage

Industries: cotton, textiles and clothing, jute, tea, paper, cement, fertilizer, sugar, light engineering

Industrial production growth rate: 3.5% (2024 est.)
note: annual % change in industrial value added based on constant local currency
comparison ranking: 69

Labor force: 77.355 million (2024 est.)
note: number of people ages 15 or older who are employed or seeking work
comparison ranking: 8

Unemployment rate: 4.7% (2024 est.)
4.5% (2023 est.)
4.6% (2022 est.)
note: % of labor force seeking employment
comparison ranking: 82

Youth unemployment rate (ages 15-24): *total:* 11.5% (2024 est.)
male: 13.7% (2024 est.)
female: 9.2% (2024 est.)
note: % of labor force ages 15-24 seeking employment
comparison ranking: total 110

Population below poverty line: 18.7% (2022 est.)
note: % of population with income below national poverty line

Gini Index coefficient - distribution of family income: 33.4 (2022 est.)
note: index (0-100) of income distribution; higher values represent greater inequality
comparison ranking: 97

Average household expenditures: *on food:* 52.8% of household expenditures (2023 est.)
on alcohol and tobacco: 2.1% of household expenditures (2023 est.)

Household income or consumption by percentage share: *lowest 10%:* 3.5% (2022 est.)
highest 10%: 27.4% (2022 est.)
note: % share of income accruing to lowest and highest 10% of population

Remittances: 6% of GDP (2024 est.)
5.1% of GDP (2023 est.)
4.7% of GDP (2022 est.)
note: personal transfers and compensation between resident and non-resident individuals/households/entities

Budget: *revenues:* $39.849 billion (2021 est.)
expenditures: $51.558 billion (2021 est.)
note: central government revenues and expenses (excluding grants/extrabudgetary units/social security funds) converted to US dollars at average official exchange rate for year indicated

Taxes and other revenues: 7.6% (of GDP) (2021 est.)

note: central government tax revenue as a % of GDP
comparison ranking: 139

Current account balance: $1.87 billion (2024 est.)
$4.388 billion (2023 est.)
-$14.438 billion (2022 est.)
note: balance of payments - net trade and primary/secondary income in current dollars
comparison ranking: 48

Exports: $53.848 billion (2024 est.)
$58.885 billion (2023 est.)
$60.066 billion (2022 est.)
note: balance of payments - exports of goods and services in current dollars
comparison ranking: 67

Exports - partners: USA 16%, Germany 15%, UK 8%, Spain 7%, Poland 6% (2023)
note: top five export partners based on percentage share of exports

Exports - commodities: garments, footwear, fabric, textiles, trunks and cases (2023)
note: top five export commodities based on value in dollars

Imports: $74.96 billion (2024 est.)
$73.172 billion (2023 est.)
$93.635 billion (2022 est.)
note: balance of payments - imports of goods and services in current dollars
comparison ranking: 53

Imports - partners: China 34%, India 17%, Indonesia 5%, Singapore 5%, Malaysia 4% (2023)
note: top five import partners based on percentage share of imports

Imports - commodities: refined petroleum, cotton fabric, natural gas, cotton, fabric (2023)
note: top five import commodities based on value in dollars

Reserves of foreign exchange and gold: $21.395 billion (2024 est.)
$21.86 billion (2023 est.)
$33.747 billion (2022 est.)
note: holdings of gold (year-end prices)/foreign exchange/special drawing rights in current dollars
comparison ranking: 63

Debt - external: $58.02 billion (2023 est.)
note: present value of external debt in current US dollars
comparison ranking: 15

Exchange rates: taka (BDT) per US dollar -

Exchange rates: 115.604 (2024 est.)
106.309 (2023 est.)
91.745 (2022 est.)
85.084 (2021 est.)
84.871 (2020 est.)

ENERGY

Electricity access: *electrification - total population:* 99.4% (2022 est.)
electrification - urban areas: 100%
electrification - rural areas: 99.3%

Electricity: *installed generating capacity:* 22.699 million kW (2023 est.)
consumption: 107.285 billion kWh (2023 est.)
imports: 9.407 billion kWh (2023 est.)
transmission/distribution losses: 8.279 billion kWh (2023 est.)
comparison rankings: installed generating capacity 45; consumption 33; imports 28; transmission/distribution losses 177

Electricity generation sources: *fossil fuels:* 98.4% of total installed capacity (2023 est.)
solar: 1% of total installed capacity (2023 est.)
hydroelectricity: 0.6% of total installed capacity (2023 est.)

Nuclear energy: Number of nuclear reactors under construction: 2 (2025)

Coal: *production:* 767,000 metric tons (2023 est.)
consumption: 14.05 million metric tons (2023 est.)
imports: 13.305 million metric tons (2023 est.)
proven reserves: 3.26 billion metric tons (2023 est.)

Petroleum: *total petroleum production:* 13,000 bbl/day (2023 est.)
refined petroleum consumption: 263,000 bbl/day (2023 est.)
crude oil estimated reserves: 28 million barrels (2021 est.)

Natural gas: *production:* 22.334 billion cubic meters (2023 est.)
consumption: 29.119 billion cubic meters (2023 est.)
imports: 6.785 billion cubic meters (2023 est.)
proven reserves: 126.293 billion cubic meters (2021 est.)

Energy consumption per capita: 11.472 million Btu/person (2023 est.)
comparison ranking: 146

COMMUNICATIONS

Telephones - fixed lines: *total subscriptions:* 302,000 (2023 est.)
subscriptions per 100 inhabitants: (2023 est.) less than 1
comparison ranking: total subscriptions 108

Telephones - mobile cellular: *total subscriptions:* 191 million (2023 est.)
subscriptions per 100 inhabitants: 105 (2022 est.)
comparison ranking: total subscriptions 9

Broadcast media: state-owned Bangladesh Television (BTV) broadcasts nationally; some channels operate via satellite; the government also owns a medium-wave radio channel and some private FM radio news channels; of the 41 approved TV stations, 26 are currently being used to broadcast, and 23 operate under private management via cable distribution

Internet country code: .bd

Internet users: *percent of population:* 45% (2023 est.)

Broadband - fixed subscriptions: *total:* 12.9 million (2023 est.)
subscriptions per 100 inhabitants: 8 (2023 est.)
comparison ranking: total 20

TRANSPORTATION

Civil aircraft registration country code prefix: S2

Airports: 17 (2025)
comparison ranking: 145

Heliports: 36 (2025)
comparison ranking: 44

Railways: *total:* 2,460 km (2014)
narrow gauge: 1,801 km (2014) 1.000-m gauge
broad gauge: 659 km (2014) 1.676-m gauge

Merchant marine: *total:* 558 (2023)
by type: bulk carrier 68, container ship 10, general cargo 170, oil tanker 162, other 148
comparison ranking: total 40

Ports: *total ports:* 2 (2024)
large: 0
medium: 1
small: 1
very small: 0
ports with oil terminals: 0
key ports: Chittagong, Mongla

MILITARY AND SECURITY

Military and security forces: Armed Forces of Bangladesh (aka Bangladesh Defense Force): Bangladesh Army, Bangladesh Navy, Bangladesh Air Force

Ministry of Home Affairs: Bangladesh Police, Border Guard Bangladesh (BGB), Bangladesh Coast Guard, Rapid Action Battalion (RAB), Ansars, Village Defense Party (VDP) (2025)
note 1: the Armed Forces of Bangladesh are jointly administered by the Ministry of Defense (MOD) and the Armed Forces Division (AFD), both under the Prime Minister's Office; the AFD has ministerial status and parallel functions with MOD; the AFD is a joint coordinating headquarters for the three services and also functions as a joint command center during wartime; to coordinate policy, the prime minister and the president are advised by a six-member board, which includes the three service chiefs of staff, the principal staff officer of the AFD, and the military secretaries to the prime minister and president
note 2: the RAB, Ansars, and VDP are paramilitary organizations for internal security; the RAB is a joint task force comprised of Police, Army, Navy, Air Force, and Border Guards personnel seconded to the RAB; its mandate includes internal security, intelligence gathering related to criminal activities, and government-directed investigations

Military expenditures: 0.9% of GDP (2024 est.)
1% of GDP (2023 est.)
1.1% of GDP (2022 est.)
1.2% of GDP (2021 est.)
1.3% of GDP (2020 est.)

Military and security service personnel strengths: information varies; approximately 170,000 active Armed Forces (2025)

Military equipment inventories and acquisitions: much of the military's inventory is comprised of Chinese- and Russian-origin equipment; in recent years, China has been the leading provider of arms to Bangladesh (2024)

Military service age and obligation: generally 17-21 for voluntary military service; length of service varies by military service (2024)

Military deployments: approximately 1,400 Central African Republic (MINUSCA); 1,650 Democratic Republic of the Congo (MONUSCO; plus about 200 police); 120 Lebanon (UNIFIL); 100 Mali (MINUSMA; plus about 150 police); 1,600 South Sudan (UNMISS); 500 Sudan (UNISFA) (2024)
note: as of early 2024, Bangladesh had nearly 6,000 total military and police personnel deployed on UN missions

Military - note: the military's primary responsibility is external defense but it also has a domestic security role; following widespread domestic protests in September 2024, the Army was given law enforcement powers, including making arrests, conducting searches, and dispersing unlawful assemblies; the military has traditionally been a significant player in the country's politics and has commercial business interests in such areas as banking, food, hotels,

manufacturing, real estate, and shipbuilding, and manages government infrastructure and construction projects
the military has a long history of participating in UN peacekeeping missions, which has provided operational experience and a source of funding; it runs an international institute for the training of peacekeepers; the military also conducts multinational and bilateral exercises with foreign partners, particularly India (2025)

SPACE

Space agency/agencies: Bangladesh Space Research and Remote Sensing Organization (SPARRSO; established as a statutory body in 1991 and designated as the country's national focal point for space-related activities in 1995) (2025)

Space program overview: has a modest space program focused on designing, building, and operating satellites, particularly those with remote sensing (RS) capabilities; SPARSSO's mandate is to use space and RS technology in such areas as agriculture, education, environmental studies, fisheries, forestry, geology, land use, mapping, meteorology, oceanography, and water resources; has a government-owned company for acquiring and operating satellites (Bangladesh Satellite Company Limited or BSCL, established in 2017); has relations with several foreign space agencies and commercial entities, including those of France, Japan, Russia, and the US; member of several international space organizations, such as the Asia-Pacific Space Cooperation Organization (2025)
note: further details about the key activities, programs, and milestones of the country's space program, as well as government spending estimates on the space sector, appear in the Space Programs reference guide

TERRORISM

Terrorist group(s): Terrorist group(s): Harakat ul-Jihad-i-Islami/Bangladesh (HUJI-B); Islamic State of Iraq and ash-Sham (ISIS) in Bangladesh (ISB); al-Qa'ida; al-Qa'ida in the Indian Subcontinent (AQIS)
note: details about the history, aims, leadership, organization, areas of operation, tactics, targets, weapons, size, and sources of support of the group(s) appear(s) in Appendix T

TRANSNATIONAL ISSUES

Refugees and internally displaced persons: *refugees:* 1,005,637 (2024 est.)

IDPs: 756,743 (2024 est.)
stateless persons: 1,005,520 (2024 est.)

BARBADOS

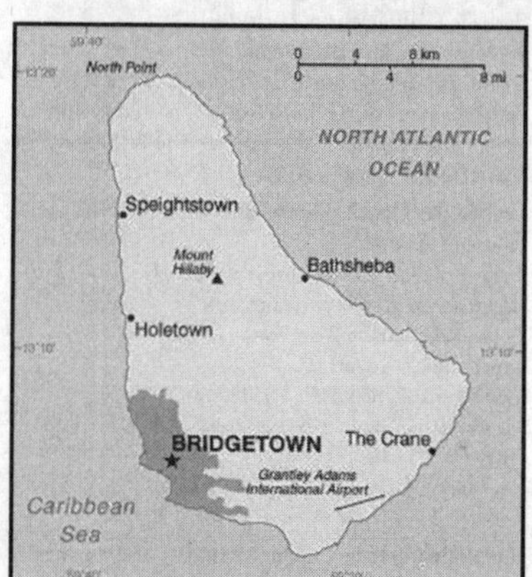

INTRODUCTION

Background: Barbados was uninhabited when first settled by the British in 1627. Enslaved Africans worked the sugar plantations established on the island, which initially dominated the Caribbean sugar industry. By 1720, Barbados was no longer a dominant force within the sugar industry, having been surpassed by the Leeward Islands and Jamaica. Slavery was abolished in 1834. The Barbadian economy remained heavily dependent on sugar, rum, and molasses production through most of the 20th century. The gradual introduction of social and political reforms in the 1940s and 1950s led to independence from the UK in 1966. In the 1990s, tourism and manufacturing surpassed the sugar industry in economic importance. Barbados became a republic in 2021, with the former Governor-General Sandra MASON elected as the first president.

GEOGRAPHY

Location: Caribbean, island in the North Atlantic Ocean, northeast of Venezuela

Geographic coordinates: 13 10 N, 59 32 W

Map references: Central America and the Caribbean

Area: *total:* 430 sq km
land: 430 sq km
water: 0 sq km
comparison ranking: total 201

Area - comparative: 2.5 times the size of Washington, D.C.

Land boundaries: *total:* 0 km

Coastline: 97 km

Maritime claims: *territorial sea:* 12 nm
exclusive economic zone: 200 nm

Climate: tropical; rainy season (June to October)

Terrain: relatively flat; rises gently to central highland region

Elevation: *highest point:* Mount Hillaby 336 m
lowest point: Atlantic Ocean 0 m

Natural resources: petroleum, fish, natural gas

Land use: *agricultural land:* 23.3% (2022 est.)
arable land: 16.3% (2022 est.)
permanent crops: 2.3% (2022 est.)
permanent pasture: 4.7% (2022 est.)
forest: 14.7% (2022 est.)
other: 62.1% (2022 est.)

Irrigated land: 50 sq km (2012)

Population distribution: most densely populated country in the eastern Caribbean; approximately one third of the population lives in urban areas

Natural hazards: infrequent hurricanes; periodic landslides

Geography - note: easternmost Caribbean island

PEOPLE AND SOCIETY

Population: *total:* 304,139 (2024 est.)
male: 146,587
female: 157,552
comparison rankings: total 181; male 182; female 180

Nationality: *noun:* Barbadian(s) or Bajan (colloquial)
adjective: Barbadian or Bajan (colloquial)

Ethnic groups: African descent 92.4%, mixed 3.1%, White 2.7%, East Indian 1.3%, other 0.2%, unspecified 0.3% (2010 est.)

Languages: English (official), Bajan (English-based creole language, widely spoken in informal settings)

Religions: Protestant 66.4% (includes Anglican 23.9%, other Pentecostal 19.5%, Adventist 5.9%, Methodist 4.2%, Wesleyan 3.4%, Nazarene 3.2%, Church of God 2.4%, Baptist 1.8%, Moravian 1.2%, other Protestant 0.9%), Roman Catholic 3.8%, other Christian 5.4% (includes Jehovah's Witness 2.0%, other 3.4%), Rastafarian 1%, other 1.5%, none 20.6%, unspecified 1.2% (2010 est.)

Age structure: *0-14 years:* 16.6% (male 25,273/female 25,284)
15-64 years: 67% (male 100,328/female 103,536)
65 years and over: 16.3% (2024 est.) (male 20,986/female 28,732)

Dependency ratios: *total dependency ratio:* 49.2 (2024 est.)
youth dependency ratio: 24.8 (2024 est.)
elderly dependency ratio: 24.4 (2024 est.)
potential support ratio: 4.1 (2024 est.)

Median age: *total:* 41.4 years (2024 est.)
male: 40.3 years
female: 42.5 years
comparison ranking: total 50

Population growth rate: 0.23% (2024 est.)
comparison ranking: 173

Birth rate: 10.7 births/1,000 population (2024 est.)
comparison ranking: 172

Death rate: 8.1 deaths/1,000 population (2024 est.)
comparison ranking: 83

Net migration rate: -0.3 migrant(s)/1,000 population (2024 est.)
comparison ranking: 112

Population distribution: most densely populated country in the eastern Caribbean; approximately one third of the population lives in urban areas

Urbanization: *urban population:* 31.4% of total population (2023)

rate of urbanization: 0.46% annual rate of change (2020-25 est.)
Major urban areas - population: 89,000 BRIDGETOWN (capital) (2018)
Sex ratio: *at birth:* 1.01 male(s)/female
0-14 years: 1 male(s)/female
15-64 years: 0.97 male(s)/female
65 years and over: 0.73 male(s)/female
total population: 0.93 male(s)/female (2024 est.)

Maternal mortality ratio: 35 deaths/100,000 live births (2023 est.)
comparison ranking: 112

Infant mortality rate: *total:* 9.6 deaths/1,000 live births (2024 est.)
male: 11.1 deaths/1,000 live births
female: 8.1 deaths/1,000 live births
comparison ranking: total 137

Life expectancy at birth: *total population:* 79 years (2024 est.)
male: 76.3 years
female: 81.8 years
comparison ranking: total population 68

Total fertility rate: 1.7 children born/woman (2024 est.)
comparison ranking: 163

Gross reproduction rate: 0.85 (2024 est.)

Drinking water source: *improved:* total: 98.5% of population (2022 est.)
unimproved: total: 1.5% of population (2022 est.)

Health expenditure: 8.1% of GDP (2021)
8.7% of national budget (2022 est.)

Physician density: 2.96 physicians/1,000 population (2022)

Hospital bed density: 5.7 beds/1,000 population (2020 est.)

Sanitation facility access: *improved:* total: 100% of population (2022 est.)

Obesity - adult prevalence rate: 23.1% (2016)
comparison ranking: 69

Alcohol consumption per capita: *total:* 9.94 liters of pure alcohol (2019 est.)
beer: 3.66 liters of pure alcohol (2019 est.)
wine: 1.36 liters of pure alcohol (2019 est.)
spirits: 4.75 liters of pure alcohol (2019 est.)
other alcohols: 0.17 liters of pure alcohol (2019 est.)
comparison ranking: total 22

Tobacco use: *total:* 6.2% (2025 est.)
male: 11.4% (2025 est.)
female: 1.5% (2025 est.)
comparison ranking: total 157

Currently married women (ages 15-49): 57.1% (2023 est.)

Education expenditure: 4% of GDP (2023 est.)
12.5% national budget (2023 est.)
comparison ranking: Education expenditure (% GDP) 106

ENVIRONMENT

Environmental issues: pollution of coastal waters from waste disposal by ships; soil erosion; illegal solid-waste disposal

International environmental agreements: *party to:* Biodiversity, Climate Change, Climate Change-Kyoto Protocol, Climate Change-Paris Agreement, Comprehensive Nuclear Test Ban, Desertification, Endangered Species, Hazardous Wastes, Law of the Sea, Marine Dumping-London Convention, Marine Dumping-London Protocol, Ozone Layer Protection, Ship Pollution, Wetlands
signed, but not ratified: none of the selected agreements

Climate: tropical; rainy season (June to October)

Urbanization: *urban population:* 31.4% of total population (2023)
rate of urbanization: 0.46% annual rate of change (2020-25 est.)

Carbon dioxide emissions: 1.348 million metric tonnes of CO2 (2023 est.)
from coal and metallurgical coke: 2 metric tonnes of CO2 (2023 est.)
from petroleum and other liquids: 1.284 million metric tonnes of CO2 (2023 est.)
from consumed natural gas: 64,000 metric tonnes of CO2 (2023 est.)
comparison ranking: total emissions 166

Particulate matter emissions: 9.8 micrograms per cubic meter (2019 est.)

Waste and recycling: *municipal solid waste generated annually:* 174,800 tons (2024 est.)
percent of municipal solid waste recycled: 10.6% (2022 est.)

Total water withdrawal: *municipal:* 20 million cubic meters (2022 est.)
industrial: 6.2 million cubic meters (2022 est.)
agricultural: 54.8 million cubic meters (2022 est.)
Total renewable water resources: 80 million cubic meters (2022 est.)

GOVERNMENT

Country name: *conventional long form:* none
conventional short form: Barbados
etymology: the name is the plural of the Spanish word *barbado* and means "the bearded ones," which could refer either to the beard-like leaves of the island's fig trees or to the beards of Carib inhabitants

Government type: parliamentary republic; a Commonwealth realm
Capital: *name:* Bridgetown
geographic coordinates: 13 06 N, 59 37 W
time difference: UTC-4 (1 hour ahead of Washington, DC, during Standard Time)
etymology: originally named Indian Bridge in 1628 for a bridge built beside Carlisle Bay, then called St. Michael's Town until the 19th century; now named after a bridge built over the Constitution River that flows through the center of the city

Administrative divisions: 11 parishes and 1 city*; Bridgetown*, Christ Church, Saint Andrew, Saint George, Saint James, Saint John, Saint Joseph, Saint Lucy, Saint Michael, Saint Peter, Saint Philip, Saint Thomas

Legal system: English common law; no judicial review of legislative acts
Constitution: *history:* adopted 22 November 1966, effective 30 November 1966; Constitution (Amendment) (No. 2) Bill, 2021 establishes Barbados as a republic and revokes the earlier Order in Council
amendment process: proposed by Parliament; passage of amendments to constitutional sections such as citizenship, fundamental rights and freedoms, and the organization and authorities of the branches of government requires two-thirds majority vote by the membership of both houses of Parliament; passage of other amendments only requires a majority vote of both houses

International law organization participation: accepts compulsory ICJ jurisdiction with reservations; accepts ICCt jurisdiction
Citizenship: *citizenship by birth:* yes
citizenship by descent only: yes
dual citizenship recognized: yes
residency requirement for naturalization: 5 years

Suffrage: 18 years of age; universal

Executive branch: *chief of state:* President Sandra MASON (since 30 November 2021)
head of government: Prime Minister Mia MOTTLEY (since 25 May 2018)
cabinet: Cabinet appointed by the president on the advice of the prime minister
election/appointment process: president elected by an electoral college of both Houses of Parliament for a 4-year renewable term; following legislative elections, the president usually appoints the leader of the majority party or leader of the majority coalition as prime minister; the prime minister recommends the deputy prime minister
most recent election date: 20 October 2021
election results: Sandra MASON elected as first president on 20 October 2021
expected date of next election: by January 2027
Legislative branch: *legislature name:* Parlement de Barbade (Parliament of Barbados)
legislative structure: bicameral
note: tradition dictates that the next election is held within 5 years of the last election, but constitutionally it is 5 years from the first seating of Parliament plus a 90-day grace period

Legislative branch - lower chamber: *chamber name:* House of Assembly
number of seats: 30 (all directly elected)
electoral system: plurality/majority
scope of elections: full renewal
term in office: 5 years
most recent election date: 1/19/2022
parties elected and seats per party: Barbados Labour Party (BLP) (30)
percentage of women in chamber: 26.7%
expected date of next election: January 2027

Legislative branch - upper chamber: *chamber name:* Senate
number of seats: 21 (all appointed)
scope of elections: full renewal
term in office: 5 years
most recent election date: 2/4/2022
percentage of women in chamber: 33.3%
expected date of next election: February 2027

Judicial branch: *highest court(s):* Supreme Court (consists of the High Court with 8 justices) and the Court of Appeal (consists of the High Court chief justice and president of the court and 4 justices; Caribbean Court of Justice is the final court of appeal
judge selection and term of office: Supreme Court chief justice appointed by the president on the recommendation of the prime minister and opposition leader of Parliament; other justices appointed by the president on the recommendation of the Judicial and Legal Service Commission, a 5-member independent body consisting of the Supreme Court chief justice, the commission head, and presidential appointees recommended by the prime minister; justices serve until mandatory retirement at age 65
subordinate courts: Magistrates' Courts

Political parties: Alliance Party for Progress or APP
Barbados Labor Party or BLP
Democratic Labor Party or DLP

Diplomatic representation in the US: *chief of mission:* Ambassador Victor Anthony FERNANDES (since 18 September 2024)
chancery: 2144 Wyoming Avenue NW, Washington, DC 20008
telephone: [1] (202) 939-9200
FAX: [1] (202) 332-7467
email address and website: washington@foreign.gov.bb https://www.foreign.gov.bb/embassies-high-commissions-and-permanent-missions/
consulate(s) general: Miami, New York

Diplomatic representation from the US: *chief of mission:* Ambassador (vacant); Chargé d'Affaires Karin B. SULLIVAN (since January 2025); note - also accredited to Antigua and Barbuda, Dominica, Grenada, Saint Kitts and Nevis, Saint Lucia, and Saint Vincent and the Grenadines
embassy: Wildey Business Park, St. Michael BB 14006, Barbados, W.I.
mailing address: 3120 Bridgetown Place, Washington DC 20521-3120
telephone: (246) 227-4000
FAX: (246) 431-0179
email address and website: bridgetownpublicaffairs@state.gov
https://bb.usembassy.gov/

International organization participation: ACP, ACS, AOSIS, C, Caricom, CDB, CELAC, FAO, G-77, IADB, IBRD, ICAO, ICCt, ICRM, IDA, IFAD, IFC, IFRCS, ILO, IMF, IMO, Interpol, IOC, ISO, ITSO, ITU, ITUC (NGOs), LAES, MIGA, NAM, OAS, OPANAL, OPCW, UN, UNCTAD, UNESCO, UNHCR, UNIDO, UPU, WCO, WFTU (NGOs), WHO, WIPO, WMO, WTO

Independence: 30 November 1966 (from the UK)

National holiday: Independence Day, 30 November (1966)

Flag: *description:* three equal vertical bands of ultramarine blue (left side), gold, and ultramarine blue with a black trident head centered on the gold band
meaning: blue stands for the sea and sky, and gold for the beaches; the trident head represents independence and a break with the past

National symbol(s): Neptune's trident, pelican, red bird of paradise flower (also known as "Pride of Barbados")

National color(s): blue, yellow, black

National anthem(s): *title:* "The National Anthem of Barbados"
lyrics/music: Irving BURGIE/C. Van Roland EDWARDS
history: adopted 1966

National heritage: *total World Heritage Sites:* 1 (cultural)
selected World Heritage Site locales: Historic Bridgetown and its Garrison

ECONOMY

Economic overview: high-income Eastern Caribbean economy; high standard of living among regional peers; key tourism, construction, and financial sectors driving recent GDP growth; declining but still very high public debt leading to IMF support programs; susceptible to natural disasters and reliance on import partners

Real GDP (purchasing power parity): $5.634 billion (2024 est.)
$5.428 billion (2023 est.)
$5.214 billion (2022 est.)
note: data in 2021 dollars *comparison ranking:* 180

Real GDP growth rate: 3.8% (2024 est.)
4.1% (2023 est.)
17.8% (2022 est.)
note: annual GDP % growth based on constant local currency
comparison ranking: 84

Real GDP per capita: $19,900 (2024 est.)
$19,200 (2023 est.)
$18,500 (2022 est.)
note: data in 2021 dollars
comparison ranking: 102

GDP (official exchange rate): $7.165 billion (2024 est.)
note: data in current dollars at official exchange rate

Inflation rate (consumer prices): -0.5% (2024 est.)
9.8% (2023 est.)
4.1% (2019 est.)
note: annual % change based on consumer prices
comparison ranking: 2

GDP - composition, by sector of origin: *agriculture:* 1.9% (2023 est.)
industry: 13.2% (2023 est.)
services: 75.4% (2023 est.)
note: figures may not total 100% due to non-allocated consumption not captured in sector-reported data
comparison rankings: agriculture 153; industry 171; services 22

GDP - composition, by end use: *household consumption:* 75.6% (2022 est.)
government consumption: 11.8% (2022 est.)
investment in fixed capital: 16.5% (2022 est.)
investment in inventories: 0.2% (2022 est.)
exports of goods and services: 34.3% (2022 est.)
imports of goods and services: -42.2% (2022 est.)
note: figures may not total 100% due to rounding or gaps in data collection

Agricultural products: sugarcane, chicken, vegetables, milk, eggs, sweet potatoes, pork, coconuts, tropical fruits, pulses (2023)
note: top ten agricultural products based on tonnage

Industries: tourism, sugar, light manufacturing, component assembly for export

Industrial production growth rate: -1.3% (2023 est.)
note: annual % change in industrial value added based on constant local currency
comparison ranking: 152

Labor force: 147,200 (2024 est.)
note: number of people ages 15 or older who are employed or seeking work
comparison ranking: 178

Unemployment rate: 7.6% (2024 est.)
7.9% (2023 est.)
8.4% (2022 est.)
note: % of labor force seeking employment
comparison ranking: 130

Youth unemployment rate (ages 15-24): *total:* 23.7% (2024 est.)
male: 27.5% (2024 est.)
female: 19.6% (2024 est.)
note: % of labor force ages 15-24 seeking employment
comparison ranking: total 39

Gini Index coefficient - distribution of family income: 34.1 (2016 est.)
note: index (0-100) of income distribution; higher values represent greater inequality
comparison ranking: 84

Household income or consumption by percentage share: *lowest 10%:* 2.5% (2016 est.)
highest 10%: 25.8% (2016 est.)
note: % share of income accruing to lowest and highest 10% of population

Remittances: 1.3% of GDP (2023 est.)
1.4% of GDP (2022 est.)
1.6% of GDP (2021 est.)
note: personal transfers and compensation between resident and non-resident individuals/households/entities

Budget: *revenues:* $1.269 billion (2015 est.)
expenditures: $1.664 billion (2015 est.)
note: central government revenues and expenses (excluding grants/extrabudgetary units/social security funds) converted to US dollars at average official exchange rate for year indicated

Public debt: 133.2% of GDP (2016 est.)
note: central government debt as a % of GDP
comparison ranking: 6

Taxes and other revenues: 24.9% (of GDP) (2016 est.)
note: central government tax revenue as a % of GDP
comparison ranking: 17

Current account balance: -$296.396 million (2017 est.)
-$452.39 million (2016 est.)
-$98.732 million (2015 est.)
note: balance of payments - net trade and primary/secondary income in current dollars
comparison ranking: 106

Exports: $2.228 billion (2017 est.)
$2.41 billion (2016 est.)
$2.358 billion (2015 est.)
note: balance of payments - exports of goods and services in current dollars
comparison ranking: 163

Exports - partners: USA 22%, Jamaica 17%, Trinidad & Tobago 8%, Canada 6%, Guyana 6% (2023)
note: top five export partners based on percentage share of exports

Exports - commodities: liquor, refined petroleum, packaged medicine, margarine, baked goods (2023)
note: top five export commodities based on value in dollars

Imports: $2.12 billion (2021 est.)
$2.213 billion (2017 est.)
$2.238 billion (2016 est.)
note: balance of payments - imports of goods and services in current dollars
comparison ranking: 176

Imports - partners: USA 32%, Trinidad & Tobago 19%, Netherlands 6%, UK 6%, Guyana 5% (2023)
note: top five import partners based on percentage share of imports

Imports - commodities: refined petroleum, crude petroleum, cars, plastic products, ships (2023)
note: top five import commodities based on value in dollars

Reserves of foreign exchange and gold: $1.606 billion (2023 est.)
$1.52 billion (2022 est.)
$1.673 billion (2021 est.)
note: holdings of gold (year-end prices)/foreign exchange/special drawing rights in current dollars
comparison ranking: 132

Exchange rates: Barbadian dollars (BBD) per US dollar -

Exchange rates: 2 (2024 est.)
2 (2023 est.)
2 (2022 est.)

2 (2021 est.)
2 (2020 est.)
note: the Barbadian dollar is pegged to the US dollar

ENERGY

Electricity access: *electrification - total population*: 100% (2022 est.)

Electricity: *installed generating capacity*: 320,000 kW (2023 est.)
consumption: 1.025 billion kWh (2023 est.)
transmission/distribution losses: 64.586 million kWh (2023 est.)
comparison rankings: installed generating capacity 163; consumption 161; transmission/distribution losses 40

Electricity generation sources: *fossil fuels*: 91.9% of total installed capacity (2023 est.)
solar: 7.9% of total installed capacity (2023 est.)
biomass and waste: 0.2% of total installed capacity (2023 est.)

Coal: *exports*: 4 metric tons (2023 est.)
imports: 57 metric tons (2023 est.)

Petroleum: *total petroleum production*: 2,000 bbl/day (2023 est.)
refined petroleum consumption: 8,000 bbl/day (2023 est.)
crude oil estimated reserves: 1.978 million barrels (2021 est.)

Natural gas: *production*: 7.957 million cubic meters (2023 est.)
consumption: 32.593 million cubic meters (2023 est.)
imports: 24.636 million cubic meters (2023 est.)
proven reserves: 113.267 million cubic meters (2021 est.)

Energy consumption per capita: 68.293 million Btu/person (2023 est.)
comparison ranking: 72

COMMUNICATIONS

Telephones - fixed lines: *total subscriptions*: 121,000 (2022 est.)
subscriptions per 100 inhabitants: 43 (2022 est.)
comparison ranking: total subscriptions 132

Telephones - mobile cellular: *total subscriptions*: 323,000 (2022 est.)
subscriptions per 100 inhabitants: 115 (2022 est.)
comparison ranking: total subscriptions 179

Broadcast media: government-owned Caribbean Broadcasting Corporation (CBC) operates the lone terrestrial TV station; CBC also has a multi-channel cable TV subscription service; roughly a dozen CBC-operated radio stations operate alongside privately owned radio stations (2019)

Internet country code: .bb

Internet users: *percent of population*: 80% (2023 est.)

Broadband - fixed subscriptions: *total*: 106,000 (2022 est.)
subscriptions per 100 inhabitants: 37 (2022 est.)
comparison ranking: total 131

TRANSPORTATION

Civil aircraft registration country code prefix: 8P

Airports: 1 (2025)
comparison ranking: 212

Heliports: 1 (2025)
comparison ranking: 166

Merchant marine: *total*: 272 (2023)
by type: bulk carrier 90, general cargo 149, oil tanker 5, other 28
comparison ranking: total 59

Ports: *total ports*: 1 (2024)
large: 0: *medium*: 0: *small*: 1
very small: 0: *ports with oil terminals*: 1: *key ports*: Bridgetown

MILITARY AND SECURITY

Military and security forces: Barbados Defense Force (BDF): The Barbados Regiment, The Barbados Coast Guard (2025)
note 1: the Barbados Police Service (TBPS) is the national police force; it is modeled after London's Metropolitan Police Service and divided into three territorial divisions
note 2: the Barbados Cadet Corps is a national youth organization affiliated with the BDF; membership is open to all school children in Barbados between the ages of 11 and 18

Military expenditures: 0.7% of GDP (2024 est.)
0.7% of GDP (2023 est.)
0.8% of GDP (2022 est.)
0.9% of GDP (2021 est.)
0.9% of GDP (2020 est.)

Military and security service personnel strengths: approximately 600 active BDF personnel (2025)

Military equipment inventories and acquisitions: the BDF's major equipment inventory is comprised mostly of donated items from China, the Netherlands, and the US (2024)

Military service age and obligation: voluntary service only (men and women); 17 years, 9 months to 17 years, 11 months with letter of consent from a parent or guardian, or be in the age range of 18-25 years (18-30 for the Reserves) at the start of recruit training; citizens of Barbados by descent or naturalization (2024)

Military - note: formed in 1979, the Barbados Defense Force (BDF) is responsible for protecting national security, but it may also be called up to maintain internal public order in times of crisis, emergency, or other specific needs, such as special joint patrols with the police; it also provides humanitarian assistance and disaster response operations both domestically and regionally; other duties include assisting with national development, such as through the training of the country's youth with the units of the Barbados Cadet Corps
Barbados has been a member of the Caribbean Regional Security System (RSS) since its creation in 1982; RSS signatories (Antigua and Barbuda, Dominica, Grenada, Guyana, Saint Kitts and Nevis, Saint Lucia, and Saint Vincent and the Grenadines) agreed to prepare contingency plans and assist one another, on request, in national emergencies, prevention of smuggling, search and rescue, immigration control, fishery protection, customs and excise control, maritime policing duties, protection of off-shore installations, pollution control, national and other disasters, and threats to national security; the RSS is headquartered in Barbados (2025)

TRANSNATIONAL ISSUES

Refugees and internally displaced persons: *refugees*: 13 (2024 est.)

Trafficking in persons: *tier rating*: Tier 2 Watch List — Barbados did not demonstrate overall increasing efforts to eliminate trafficking compared with the previous reporting period and was downgraded to Tier 2 Watch List; for more details, go to: https://www.state.gov/reports/2025-trafficking-in-persons-report/barbados/

BELARUS

INTRODUCTION

Background: After seven decades as a constituent republic of the USSR, Belarus attained its independence in 1991. It has retained closer political and economic ties to Russia than any of the other former Soviet republics. In 1999, Belarus and Russia signed a treaty on a two-state union, envisioning greater political and economic integration. Although Belarus agreed to a framework to carry out the accord, serious implementation has yet to take place and negotiations on further integration have been contentious. Since taking office in 1994 as the country's first and only directly elected president, Alyaksandr LUKASHENKA has steadily consolidated his power through authoritarian means and a centralized economic system. Government restrictions on political and civil freedoms, freedom of speech and the press, peaceful assembly, and religion have remained in place. Restrictions on political freedoms have tightened in the wake of the disputed presidential election in 2020. The election results sparked large-scale protests as members of the opposition and civil society criticized the election's validity. LUKASHENKA has remained in power as the disputed winner of the presidential election after quelling protests in 2020. Since 2022, Belarus has facilitated Russia's war in

Ukraine, which was launched in part from Belarusian territory.

GEOGRAPHY

Location: Eastern Europe, east of Poland

Geographic coordinates: 53 00 N, 28 00 E

Map references: Europe

Area: *total:* 207,600 sq km
land: 202,900 sq km
water: 4,700 sq km
comparison ranking: total 86

Area - comparative: slightly less than twice the size of Kentucky; slightly smaller than Kansas

Land boundaries: *total:* 3,599 km
border countries (5): Latvia 161 km; Lithuania 640 km; Poland 375 km; Russia 1,312 km; Ukraine 1,111 km

Coastline: 0 km (landlocked)

Maritime claims: none (landlocked)

Climate: cold winters, cool and moist summers; transitional between continental and maritime

Terrain: generally flat with much marshland

Elevation: *highest point:* Dzyarzhynskaya Hara 346 m
lowest point: Nyoman River 90 m
mean elevation: 160 m

Natural resources: timber, peat deposits, small quantities of oil and natural gas, granite, dolomitic limestone, marl, chalk, sand, gravel, clay

Land use: *agricultural land:* 39.9% (2022 est.)
arable land: 27.6% (2022 est.)
permanent crops: 0.4% (2022 est.)
permanent pasture: 11.8% (2022 est.)
forest: 43.3% (2022 est.)
other: 16.8% (2022 est.)

Irrigated land: 260 sq km (2022)

Major rivers (by length in km): Dnyapro (Dnieper) (shared with Russia [s] and Ukraine [m]) - 2,287 km
note: [s] after country name indicates river source; [m] after country name indicates river mouth

Major watersheds (area sq km): Atlantic Ocean drainage: ***(Black Sea)*** Dnieper (533,966 sq km)

Population distribution: a fairly even distribution throughout most of the country, with urban areas attracting larger and denser populations

Natural hazards: large tracts of marshy land

Geography - note: landlocked; glacial scouring accounts for the flatness of Belarusian terrain and for its 11,000 lakes

PEOPLE AND SOCIETY

Population: *total:* 9,501,451 (2024 est.)
male: 4,433,839
female: 5,067,612
comparison rankings: total 97; male 99; female 93

Nationality: *noun:* Belarusian(s)
adjective: Belarusian

Ethnic groups: Belarusian 83.7%, Russian 8.3%, Polish 3.1%, Ukrainian 1.7%, other 2.4%, unspecified 0.9% (2009 est.)

Languages: Russian (official) 71.4%, Belarusian (official) 26%, other 0.3% (includes small Polish- and Ukrainian-speaking minorities), unspecified 2.3% (2019 est.)
major-language sample(s):
Книга фактов о мире – незаменимый источник базовой информации. (Russian)

Religions: Orthodox 48.3%, Catholic 7.1%, other 3.5%, non-believers 41.1% (2011 est.)

Age structure: *0-14 years:* 16.1% (male 787,849/female 741,293)
15-64 years: 66.1% (male 3,073,507/female 3,204,088)
65 years and over: 17.8% (2024 est.) (male 572,483/female 1,122,231)

Dependency ratios: *total dependency ratio:* 51.4 (2024 est.)
youth dependency ratio: 24.4 (2024 est.)
elderly dependency ratio: 27 (2024 est.)
potential support ratio: 3.7 (2024 est.)

Median age: *total:* 42.1 years (2024 est.)
male: 39.5 years
female: 45 years
comparison ranking: total 46

Population growth rate: -0.42% (2024 est.)
comparison ranking: 216

Birth rate: 8.3 births/1,000 population (2024 est.)
comparison ranking: 210

Death rate: 13.3 deaths/1,000 population (2024 est.)
comparison ranking: 10

Net migration rate: 0.8 migrant(s)/1,000 population (2024 est.)
comparison ranking: 67

Population distribution: a fairly even distribution throughout most of the country, with urban areas attracting larger and denser populations

Urbanization: *urban population:* 80.7% of total population (2023)
rate of urbanization: 0.28% annual rate of change (2020-25 est.)

Major urban areas - population: 2.057 million MINSK (capital) (2023)

Sex ratio: *at birth:* 1.06 male(s)/female
0-14 years: 1.06 male(s)/female
15-64 years: 0.96 male(s)/female
65 years and over: 0.51 male(s)/female
total population: 0.88 male(s)/female (2024 est.)

Mother's mean age at first birth: 26.8 years (2019 est.)

Maternal mortality ratio: 1 deaths/100,000 live births (2023 est.)
comparison ranking: 194

Infant mortality rate: *total:* 2.1 deaths/1,000 live births (2024 est.)
male: 2.5 deaths/1,000 live births
female: 1.7 deaths/1,000 live births
comparison ranking: total 219

Life expectancy at birth: *total population:* 74.7 years (2024 est.)
male: 69.8 years
female: 80 years
comparison ranking: total population 138

Total fertility rate: 1.45 children born/woman (2024 est.)
comparison ranking: 208

Gross reproduction rate: 0.7 (2024 est.)

Drinking water source: *improved:* *urban:* 99.5% of population (2022 est.)
rural: 98.1% of population (2022 est.)
total: 99.2% of population (2022 est.)
unimproved: *urban:* 0.5% of population (2022 est.)
rural: 1.9% of population (2022 est.)
total: 0.8% of population (2022 est.)

Health expenditure: 6.6% of GDP (2021)
12.3% of national budget (2022 est.)

Physician density: 4.72 physicians/1,000 population (2023)

Hospital bed density: 9.7 beds/1,000 population (2019 est.)

Sanitation facility access: *improved:* *urban:* 99.9% of population (2022 est.)
rural: 98.3% of population (2022 est.)
total: 99.6% of population (2022 est.)
unimproved: *urban:* 0.1% of population (2022 est.)
rural: 1.7% of population (2022 est.)
total: 0.4% of population (2022 est.)

Obesity - adult prevalence rate: 24.5% (2016)
comparison ranking: 58

Alcohol consumption per capita: *total:* 10.57 liters of pure alcohol (2019 est.)
beer: 2.26 liters of pure alcohol (2019 est.)
wine: 0.98 liters of pure alcohol (2019 est.)
spirits: 4.67 liters of pure alcohol (2019 est.)
other alcohols: 2.66 liters of pure alcohol (2019 est.)
comparison ranking: total 18

Tobacco use: *total:* 26.4% (2025 est.)
male: 44.5% (2025 est.)
female: 11.6% (2025 est.)
comparison ranking: total 36

Currently married women (ages 15-49): 66.6% (2023 est.)

Child marriage: *women married by age 15:* 0.1% (2019)
women married by age 18: 4.7% (2019)
men married by age 18: 1.6% (2019)

Education expenditure: 5% of GDP (2023 est.)
12.8% national budget (2023 est.)
comparison ranking: Education expenditure (% GDP) 64

Literacy: *total population:* 100% (2019 est.)
male: 100% (2019 est.)
female: 100% (2019 est.)

School life expectancy (primary to tertiary education): *total:* 14 years (2023 est.)
male: 14 years (2023 est.)
female: 15 years (2023 est.)

ENVIRONMENT

Environmental issues: soil pollution from pesticide use; southern part of the country contaminated with fallout from 1986 nuclear reactor accident at Chornobyl' in northern Ukraine

International environmental agreements: *party to:* Air Pollution, Air Pollution-Nitrogen Oxides, Air Pollution-Sulphur 85, Antarctic-Environmental Protection, Antarctic Treaty, Biodiversity, Climate Change, Climate Change-Kyoto Protocol, Climate Change-Paris Agreement, Comprehensive Nuclear Test Ban, Desertification, Endangered Species, Environmental Modification, Hazardous Wastes, Law of the Sea, Marine Dumping-London Convention, Nuclear Test Ban, Ozone Layer Protection, Ship Pollution, Wetlands
signed, but not ratified: none of the selected agreements

Climate: cold winters, cool and moist summers; transitional between continental and maritime

Urbanization: *urban population:* 80.7% of total population (2023)
rate of urbanization: 0.28% annual rate of change (2020-25 est.)

Carbon dioxide emissions: 46.709 million metric tonnes of CO_2 (2023 est.)
from coal and metallurgical coke: 1.497 million metric tonnes of CO_2 (2023 est.)
from petroleum and other liquids: 15.884 million metric tonnes of CO_2 (2023 est.)
from consumed natural gas: 29.328 million metric tonnes of CO_2 (2023 est.)
comparison ranking: total emissions 58

Particulate matter emissions: 13.4 micrograms per cubic meter (2019 est.)

Waste and recycling: *municipal solid waste generated annually:* 4.28 million tons (2024 est.)
percent of municipal solid waste recycled: 19% (2022 est.)

Total water withdrawal: *municipal:* 600 million cubic meters (2022)
industrial: 430 million cubic meters (2022)
agricultural: 385 million cubic meters (2022)

Total renewable water resources: 57.9 billion cubic meters (2022 est.)

GOVERNMENT

Country name: *conventional long form:* Republic of Belarus
conventional short form: Belarus
local long form: Respublika Byelarus' (Belarusian)/ Respublika Belarus' (Russian)
local short form: Byelarus' (Belarusian)/ Belarus' (Russian)
former: Belorussian (Byelorussian) Soviet Socialist Republic
etymology: the name is a compound of the Slavic words "bel" (white) and "Rus" (the Old East Slavic ethnic designation) to form the meaning White Rusian or White Ruthenian

Government type: presidential republic in name, although in fact a dictatorship

Capital: *name:* Minsk
geographic coordinates: 53 54 N, 27 34 E
time difference: UTC+3 (8 hours ahead of Washington, DC, during Standard Time)
etymology: the origin of the name is disputed; it may be derived from the Menka River

Administrative divisions: 6 regions (*voblastsi*, singular - *voblasts'*) and 1 municipality* (*horad*); Brest, Homyel' (Gomel'), Horad Minsk* (Minsk City), Hrodna (Grodno), Mahilyow (Mogilev), Minsk, Vitsyebsk (Vitebsk)
note: administrative divisions have the same names as their administrative centers; Russian spelling provided for reference when different from Belarusian

Legal system: civil law system
note: nearly all major codes (civil, civil procedure, criminal, criminal procedure, family, and labor) were revised and came into force in 1999 and 2000

Constitution: *history:* several previous; latest drafted between late 1991 and early 1994, signed 15 March 1994
amendment process: proposed by the president of the republic through petition to the National Assembly or by petition of least 150,000 eligible voters; approval required by at least two-thirds majority vote in both chambers or by simple majority of votes cast in a referendum
note: one of several amendments passed in the February 2022 referendum – the presidential 5-year, two-term limit – will be imposed after the 2025 election

International law organization participation: has not submitted an ICJ jurisdiction declaration; non-party state to the ICCt

Citizenship: *citizenship by birth:* no
citizenship by descent only: at least one parent must be a citizen of Belarus
dual citizenship recognized: no
residency requirement for naturalization: 7 years

Suffrage: 18 years of age; universal

Executive branch: *chief of state:* President Alyaksandr LUKASHENKA (since 20 July 1994)
head of government: Prime Minister Alyaksandr TURCHYN (since 10 March 2025)
cabinet: Council of Ministers appointed by the president
election/appointment process: president directly elected by absolute-majority popular vote in 2 rounds, if needed, for a 5-year term (no term limits); prime minister and deputy prime ministers appointed by the president and approved by the National Assembly
most recent election date: first election held on 23 June and 10 July 1994; the 1994 constitution set the next election for 1999, but Alyaksandr LUKASHENKA extended his term to 2001 via a referendum; subsequent election held in 2001; a 2004 referendum ended presidential term limits and allowed LUKASHENKA to run and win a third term (19 March 2006), fourth term (19 December 2010), fifth term (11 October 2015), sixth term (9 August 2020), and seventh term (26 January 2025)
election results: 2025: Alyaksandr LUKASHENKA reelected president; percent of vote - Alyaksandr LUKASHENKA (independent) 86.8%, Sergey Syrankov (Communist Party) 3.2%, 3.6% voting against all
2020: Alyaksandr LUKASHENKA reelected president; percent of vote - Alyaksandr LUKASHENKA (independent) 80.1%, Svyatlana TSIKHANOWSKAYA (independent) 10.1%, other 9.8%; note - widespread street protests erupted following announcement of the election results amid allegations of voter fraud
2015: Alyaksandr LUKASHENKA elected president; percent of vote - Alyaksandr LUKASHENKA (independent) 84.1%, Tatsyana KARATKEVIC (BSDPH) 4.4%, Sergey GAYDUKEVICH (LDP) 3.3%, other 8.2%.
expected date of next election: 2030

Legislative branch: *legislature name:* National Assembly (Natsionalnoye Sobranie)
legislative structure: bicameral
Legislative branch - lower chamber
chamber name: House of Representatives (Palata Predstaviteley)
number of seats: 110 (all directly elected)
electoral system: plurality/majority
scope of elections: full renewal
term in office: 5 years
most recent election date: 2/25/2024
parties elected and seats per party: Belaya Rus party (51); Republican Party of Labour and Justice (8); Communist Party of Belarus (7); Non-partisans (40); Other (4)
percentage of women in chamber: 33.9%
expected date of next election: February 2029

Legislative branch - upper chamber: *chamber name:* Council of the Republic (Soviet Respubliki)
number of seats: 65 (56 indirectly elected; 8 appointed)
scope of elections: full renewal
term in office: 5 years
most recent election date: 4/4/2024
percentage of women in chamber: 30.5%
expected date of next election: March 2029

Judicial branch: *highest court(s):* Supreme Court (consists of the chairman and deputy chairman and organized into several specialized panels, including economic and military; number of judges set by the president of the republic and the court chairman); Constitutional Court (consists of 12 judges, including a chairman and deputy chairman)
judge selection and term of office: Supreme Court judges appointed by the president with the consent of the Council of the Republic; judges initially appointed for 5 years and evaluated for life appointment; Constitutional Court judges - 6 appointed by the president and 6 elected by the Council of the Republic; the presiding judge directly elected by the president and approved by the Council of the Republic; judges can serve for 11 years with an age limit of 70
subordinate courts: oblast courts; Minsk City Court; town courts; Minsk city and oblast economic courts

Political parties: Belaya Rus or BR
Republican Party of Labour and Justice or RPTS
Communist Party of Belarus or CBP
Liberal Democratic Party of Belarus or LDPB

Diplomatic representation in the US: *chief of mission:* Ambassador (vacant; recalled by Belarus in 2008); Chargé d'Affaires Pavel SHIDLOWSKI (since 9 August 2022)
chancery: 1619 New Hampshire Avenue NW, Washington, DC 20009
telephone: [1] (202) 986-1606
FAX: [1] (202) 986-1805
email address and website: usa@mfa.gov.by
Embassy of the Republic of Belarus in the United States of America (mfa.gov.by)

Diplomatic representation from the US: *chief of mission:* Ambassador (vacant); Chargé d'Affaires Michael KREIDLER (since July 2025)
embassy: 46 Starovilenskaya Street, Minsk 220002
mailing address: 7010 Minsk Place, Washington DC 20521-7010
telephone: [375] (17) 210-12-83
FAX: [375] (17) 334-78-53
email address and website: ConsularMinsk@state.gov
https://by.usembassy.gov/

International organization participation: BSEC (observer), CBSS (observer), CEI, CIS, CSTO, EAEC, EAEU, EAPC, EBRD, FAO, GCTU, IAEA, IBRD, ICAO, ICC (NGOs), ICRM, IDA, IFC, IFRCS, ILO, IMF, IMSO, Interpol, IOC, IOM, IPU, ISO, ITU, ITUC (NGOs), MIGA, NAM, NSG, OPCW, OSCE, PCA, PFP, SCO (dialogue member), UN, UNCTAD, UNESCO, UNIDO, UNIFIL, UNWTO, UPU, WCO, WFTU (NGOs), WHO, WIPO, WMO, WTO (observer), ZC

Independence: 25 August 1991 (from the Soviet Union)

National holiday: Independence Day, 3 July (1944)
note: 3 July 1944 was the date Minsk was liberated from German troops, 25 August 1991 was the date of independence from the Soviet Union

Flag: *description:* red horizontal band (top), with a green horizontal band below that is half the width of the red band; a white vertical stripe on the left side has traditional Belarusian designs in red
meaning: the red stands for past struggles to escape oppression, and the green for hope and the country's forests

National symbol(s): no official symbol; the mounted knight known as Pahonia (the Chaser) is the traditional symbol

National color(s): green, red, white

National anthem(s): *title:* "My, Bielarusy" (We Belarusians)
lyrics/music: Mikhas KLIMKOVICH and Uladzimir KARYZNA/Nester SAKALOUSKI
history: music adopted 1955, lyrics adopted 2002; after the fall of the Soviet Union, Belarus kept the music of its Soviet-era anthem but adopted new lyrics; also known as "Dziarzauny himn Respubliki Bielarus" (State Anthem of the Republic of Belarus)

National heritage: *total World Heritage Sites:* 4 (3 cultural, 1 natural)
selected World Heritage Site locales: Białowieża Forest (n); Mir Castle Complex (c); Architectural, Residential, and Cultural Complex of the Radziwill Family at Nesvizh (c)

ECONOMY

Economic overview: declining Russian energy subsidies will end in 2024; growing public debt; strong currency pressures have led to higher inflation; recent price controls on basic food and drugs; public sector wage increases and fragile private sector threaten household income gains and economic growth

Real GDP (purchasing power parity): $265.22 billion (2024 est.)
$254.995 billion (2023 est.)
$244.89 billion (2022 est.)
note: data in 2021 dollars
comparison ranking: 66

Real GDP growth rate: 4% (2024 est.)
4.1% (2023 est.)
-4.7% (2022 est.)
note: annual GDP % growth based on constant local currency
comparison ranking: 77

Real GDP per capita: $29,000 (2024 est.)
$27,800 (2023 est.)
$26,500 (2022 est.)
note: data in 2021 dollars
comparison ranking: 82

GDP (official exchange rate): $75.962 billion (2024 est.)
note: data in current dollars at official exchange rate

Inflation rate (consumer prices): 5.8% (2024 est.)
5% (2023 est.)
15.2% (2022 est.)
note: annual % change based on consumer prices
comparison ranking: 150

GDP - composition, by sector of origin: *agriculture:* 6.9% (2024 est.)
industry: 30.7% (2024 est.)
services: 49.7% (2024 est.)
note: figures may not total 100% due to non-allocated consumption not captured in sector-reported data
comparison rankings: agriculture 94; industry 52; services 148

GDP - composition, by end use: *household consumption:* 56.8% (2024 est.)
government consumption: 19% (2024 est.)
investment in fixed capital: 23.8% (2024 est.)
investment in inventories: 2% (2024 est.)
exports of goods and services: 65.1% (2024 est.)
imports of goods and services: -66.9% (2024 est.)
note: figures may not total 100% due to rounding or gaps in data collection

Agricultural products: milk, sugar beets, potatoes, wheat, triticale, barley, maize, rapeseed, rye, chicken (2023)
note: top ten agricultural products based on tonnage

Industries: metal-cutting machine tools, tractors, trucks, earthmovers, motorcycles, synthetic fibers, fertilizer, textiles, refrigerators, washing machines and other household appliances

Industrial production growth rate: 6% (2024 est.)
note: annual % change in industrial value added based on constant local currency
comparison ranking: 33

Labor force: 4.817 million (2024 est.)
note: number of people ages 15 or older who are employed or seeking work
comparison ranking: 89

Unemployment rate: 3.4% (2024 est.)
3.5% (2023 est.)
3.6% (2022 est.)
note: % of labor force seeking employment
comparison ranking: 55

Youth unemployment rate (ages 15-24): *total:* 10.1% (2024 est.)
male: 11.7% (2024 est.)
female: 8.4% (2024 est.)
note: % of labor force ages 15-24 seeking employment
comparison ranking: total 117

Population below poverty line: 3.9% (2022 est.)
note: % of population with income below national poverty line

Gini Index coefficient - distribution of family income 24.4 (2020 est.)
note: index (0-100) of income distribution; higher values represent greater inequality
comparison ranking: 147

Average household expenditures: *on food:* 29.5% of household expenditures (2023 est.)
on alcohol and tobacco: 7.6% of household expenditures (2023 est.)

Household income or consumption by percentage share: *lowest 10%:* 4.5% (2020 est.)
highest 10%: 20.7% (2020 est.)
note: % share of income accruing to lowest and highest 10% of population

Remittances: 1.8% of GDP (2024 est.)
1.7% of GDP (2023 est.)
2% of GDP (2022 est.)
note: personal transfers and compensation between resident and non-resident individuals/households/entities

Budget: *revenues:* $22.876 billion (2023 est.)
expenditures: $21.912 billion (2023 est.)
note: central government revenues (excluding grants) and expenditures converted to US dollars at average official exchange rate for year indicated

Public debt: 33.2% of GDP (2019 est.)
note: central government debt as a % of GDP
comparison ranking: 160

Taxes and other revenues: 12.7% (of GDP) (2023 est.)
note: central government tax revenue as a % of GDP
comparison ranking: 107

Current account balance: -$1.925 billion (2024 est.)
-$1.104 billion (2023 est.)
$2.628 billion (2022 est.)
note: balance of payments - net trade and primary/secondary income in current dollars
comparison ranking: 146

Exports: $49.386 billion (2024 est.)
$47.714 billion (2023 est.)
$47.124 billion (2022 est.)
note: balance of payments - exports of goods and services in current dollars
comparison ranking: 68

Exports - partners: China 34%, Kazakhstan 10%, Uzbekistan 7%, Poland 6%, Brazil 5% (2023)
note: top five export partners based on percentage share of exports

Exports - commodities: fertilizers, rapeseed oil, wood, poultry, beef (2023)
note: top five export commodities based on value in dollars

Imports: $50.679 billion (2024 est.)
$47.459 billion (2023 est.)
$42.438 billion (2022 est.)
note: balance of payments - imports of goods and services in current dollars
comparison ranking: 67

Imports - partners: China 33%, Poland 16%, Germany 11%, Lithuania 10%, Turkey 9% (2023)
note: top five import partners based on percentage share of imports

Imports - commodities: cars, broadcasting equipment, fabric, plastic products, video displays (2023)
note: top five import commodities based on value in dollars

Reserves of foreign exchange and gold: $8.912 billion (2024 est.)
$8.118 billion (2023 est.)
$7.923 billion (2022 est.)
note: holdings of gold (year-end prices)/foreign exchange/special drawing rights in current dollars
comparison ranking: 83

Debt - external: $18.01 billion (2023 est.)
note: present value of external debt in current US dollars
comparison ranking: 36

Exchange rates: Belarusian rubles (BYB/BYR) per US dollar -

Exchange rates: 3.246 (2024 est.)
3.007 (2023 est.)
2.626 (2022 est.)
2.539 (2021 est.)
2.44 (2020 est.)

ENERGY

Electricity access: *electrification - total population:* 100% (2022 est.)

Electricity: *installed generating capacity:* 12.653 million kW (2023 est.)
consumption: 39.883 billion kWh (2023 est.)
exports: 4.553 billion kWh (2023 est.)
imports: 4 billion kWh (2023 est.)
transmission/distribution losses: 3.149 billion kWh (2023 est.)
comparison rankings: installed generating capacity 61; consumption 60; exports 41; imports 51; transmission/distribution losses 143

Electricity generation sources: *fossil fuels:* 70% of total installed capacity (2023 est.)
nuclear: 26.9% of total installed capacity (2023 est.)
solar: 0.5% of total installed capacity (2023 est.)
wind: 0.4% of total installed capacity (2023 est.)
hydroelectricity: 0.9% of total installed capacity (2023 est.)
biomass and waste: 1.2% of total installed capacity (2023 est.)

Nuclear energy: Number of operational nuclear reactors: 2 (2025)

Net capacity of operational nuclear reactors: 2.22GW (2025 est.)

Percent of total electricity production: 28.6% (2023 est.)

Coal: *consumption:* 710,000 metric tons (2023 est.)
exports: 966,000 metric tons (2023 est.)
imports: 1.635 million metric tons (2023 est.)

Petroleum: *total petroleum production:* 30,000 bbl/day (2023 est.)
refined petroleum consumption: 125,000 bbl/day (2023 est.)
crude oil estimated reserves: 198 million barrels (2021 est.)

Natural gas: *production:* 68.494 million cubic meters (2023 est.)
consumption: 15.094 billion cubic meters (2023 est.)
imports: 15.433 billion cubic meters (2023 est.)
proven reserves: 2.832 billion cubic meters (2021 est.)

Energy consumption per capita: 104.821 million Btu/person (2023 est.)
comparison ranking: 43

COMMUNICATIONS

Telephones - fixed lines: *total subscriptions:* 4.173 million (2023 est.)
subscriptions per 100 inhabitants: 46 (2023 est.)
comparison ranking: total subscriptions 32

Telephones - mobile cellular: *total subscriptions:* 11.8 million (2023 est.)
subscriptions per 100 inhabitants: 123 (2022 est.)
comparison ranking: total subscriptions 86

Broadcast media: 7 state-controlled national TV channels; Polish and Russian TV broadcasts are available in some areas; state-run Belarusian Radio operates 5 national networks and an external service; Russian and Polish radio broadcasts are available (2019)

Internet country code: .by

Internet users: *percent of population:* 92% (2023 est.)

Broadband - fixed subscriptions: *total:* 3.2 million (2023 est.)
subscriptions per 100 inhabitants: 35 (2023 est.)
comparison ranking: total 48

TRANSPORTATION

Civil aircraft registration country code prefix: EW

Airports: 46 (2025)
comparison ranking: 92
Heliports: 4 (2025)
comparison ranking: 110

Railways: *total:* 5,528 km (2014)
standard gauge: 25 km (2014) 1.435-m gauge
broad gauge: 5,503 km (2014) 1.520-m gauge (874 km electrified)

Merchant marine: *total:* 4 (2023)
by type: other 4
comparison ranking: total 171

MILITARY AND SECURITY

Military and security forces: Belarus Armed Forces: Army, Air and Air Defense Force, Special Operations Force, Special Troops, Territorial Defense Forces

Ministry of Interior: State Border Troops, Militia, Internal Troops (2025)
note: in early 2023, President LUKASHENKA ordered the formation of a new volunteer paramilitary territorial defense force to supplement the Army

Military expenditures: 2% of GDP (2024 est.)
1.8% of GDP (2023 est.)
1.7% of GDP (2022 est.)
1.4% of GDP (2021 est.)
1.5% of GDP (2020 est.)

Military and security service personnel strengths: approximately 50-60,000 active-duty military personnel (2025)

Military equipment inventories and acquisitions: the military's inventory is comprised mostly of Russian and Soviet-origin equipment; Belarus's defense industry manufactures some equipment (mostly modernized Soviet designs), including vehicles, guided weapons, and electronic warfare systems (2024)

Military service age and obligation: 18-27 years of age for compulsory military or alternative service; conscript service obligation is 12-18 months, depending on academic qualifications, and 24-36 months for alternative service, also depending on academic qualifications; 17-year-olds are eligible to become cadets at military higher education institutes, where they are classified as military personnel (2023)
note: conscripts can be assigned to the military, to the Ministry of Interior, or to the Ministry of Labor and Social Protection (alternative service)

Military - note: the military of Belarus is responsible for territorial defense; Russia is the country's closest security partner, and the military conducts joint training exercises with Russian forces; in 2022, Belarus allowed the Russian military to stage on its territory for their invasion of Ukraine; in 2023, Belarus agreed to permit Russia to deploy nuclear weapons on its soil
Belarus has been a member of the Collective Security Treaty Organization (CSTO) since 1994 and has committed an airborne brigade to CSTO's rapid reaction force; the military trains regularly with other CSTO members (2025)

TRANSNATIONAL ISSUES

Refugees and internally displaced persons: *refugees:* 44,621 (2024 est.)
stateless persons: 5,620 (2024 est.)

Trafficking in persons: *tier rating:* Tier 3 — Belarus does not fully meet the minimum standards for the elimination of trafficking and is not making significant efforts to do so, therefore, Belarus remained on Tier 3; for more details, go to: https://www.state.gov/reports/2025-trafficking-in-persons-report/belarus/

BELGIUM

INTRODUCTION

Background: Belgium became independent from the Netherlands in 1830; it was occupied by Germany during World Wars I and II. The country prospered as a modern, technologically advanced European state and member of NATO and the EU. In recent years, longstanding tensions between the Dutch-speaking Flemish of the north and the French-speaking Walloons of the south have led to constitutional amendments granting these regions formal recognition and autonomy. The capital city of Brussels is home to numerous international organizations, including the EU and NATO.

GEOGRAPHY

Location: Western Europe, bordering the North Sea, between France and the Netherlands
Geographic coordinates: 50 50 N, 4 00 E

Map references: Europe

Area: *total:* 30,528 sq km
land: 30,278 sq km
water: 250 sq km
comparison ranking: total 140

Area - comparative: about the size of Maryland

Land boundaries: *total:* 1,297 km
border countries (4): France 556 km; Germany 133 km; Luxembourg 130 km; Netherlands 478 km

Coastline: 66.5 km

Maritime claims: *territorial sea:* 12 nm
contiguous zone: 24 nm
exclusive economic zone: geographic coordinates define outer limit
continental shelf: median line with neighbors

Climate: temperate; mild winters, cool summers; rainy, humid, cloudy

Terrain: flat coastal plains in northwest, central rolling hills, rugged mountains of Ardennes Forest in southeast

Elevation: *highest point:* Botrange 694 m
lowest point: North Sea 0 m
mean elevation: 181 m

Natural resources: construction materials, silica sand, carbonates, arable land

Land use: *agricultural land:* 44.6% (2022 est.)
arable land: 28.3% (2022 est.)
permanent crops: 0.8% (2022 est.)
permanent pasture: 15.5% (2022 est.)
forest: 22.6% (2022 est.)
other: 32.8% (2022 est.)

Irrigated land: 57 sq km (2013)

Major watersheds (area sq km): Atlantic Ocean drainage: Seine (78,919 sq km), Rhine-Maas (198,735 sq km)

Population distribution: most of the population is concentrated in the northern two thirds of the country; the southeast is more thinly populated; considered to have one of the highest population densities in the world, with approximately 97% living in urban areas

Natural hazards: flooding is a threat along rivers and in areas of reclaimed coastal land, protected from the sea by concrete dikes

Geography - note: crossroads of Western Europe; most West European capitals are within 1,000 km of Brussels, the seat of both the EU and NATO

PEOPLE AND SOCIETY

Population: *total:* 11,977,634 (2024 est.)
male: 5,909,057
female: 6,068,577
comparison rankings: total 82; male 83; female 82

Nationality: *noun:* Belgian(s)
adjective: Belgian

Ethnic groups: Belgian 75.2%, Italian 4.1%, Moroccan 3.7%, French 2.4%, Turkish 2%, Dutch 2%, other 10.6% (2012 est.)

Languages: Dutch (official) 60%, French (official) 40%, German (official) less than 1%
major-language sample(s):
Het Wereld Feitenboek, een onmisbare bron van informatie. (Dutch)
The World Factbook, une source indispensable d'informations de base. (French)

Religions: Roman Catholic 57.1%, Protestant 2.3%, other Christian, 2.8%, Muslim 6.8%, other 1.7%, atheist 9.1%, nonbeliever/agnostic 20.2% (2018 est.)

Age structure: *0-14 years:* 16.9% (male 1,038,578/female 990,215)
15-64 years: 62.8% (male 3,796,844/female 3,730,784)
65 years and over: 20.2% (2024 est.) (male 1,073,635/female 1,347,578)

Dependency ratios: *total dependency ratio:* 57.3 (2024 est.)
youth dependency ratio: 25.3 (2024 est.)
elderly dependency ratio: 32.1 (2024 est.)
potential support ratio: 3.1 (2024 est.)

Median age: *total:* 42 years (2024 est.)
male: 40.8 years
female: 43.1 years
comparison ranking: total 47

Population growth rate: 0.53% (2024 est.)
comparison ranking: 148

Birth rate: 10.8 births/1,000 population (2024 est.)
comparison ranking: 169

Death rate: 9.5 deaths/1,000 population (2024 est.)
comparison ranking: 46

Net migration rate: 4 migrant(s)/1,000 population (2024 est.)
comparison ranking: 27

Population distribution: most of the population is concentrated in the northern two thirds of the country; the southeast is more thinly populated; considered to have one of the highest population densities in the world, with approximately 97% living in urban areas

Urbanization: *urban population:* 98.2% of total population (2023)
rate of urbanization: 0.38% annual rate of change (2020-25 est.)

Major urban areas - population: 2.122 million BRUSSELS (capital), 1.057 million Antwerp (2023)

Sex ratio: *at birth:* 1.05 male(s)/female
0-14 years: 1.05 male(s)/female
15-64 years: 1.02 male(s)/female
65 years and over: 0.8 male(s)/female
total population: 0.97 male(s)/female (2024 est.)

Mother's mean age at first birth: 29.2 years (2020 est.)

Maternal mortality ratio: 4 deaths/100,000 live births (2023 est.)
comparison ranking: 177

Infant mortality rate: *total:* 3.1 deaths/1,000 live births (2024 est.)
male: 3.5 deaths/1,000 live births
female: 2.7 deaths/1,000 live births
comparison ranking: total 205

Life expectancy at birth: *total population:* 82.3 years (2024 est.)
male: 79.7 years
female: 85 years
comparison ranking: total population 30

Total fertility rate: 1.76 children born/woman (2024 est.)
comparison ranking: 145

Gross reproduction rate: 0.86 (2024 est.)

Drinking water source: *improved: urban:* 100% of population (2022 est.)
rural: 100% of population (2022 est.)
total: 100% of population (2022 est.)

Health expenditure: 11% of GDP (2021)
15.2% of national budget (2022 est.)

Physician density: 6.53 physicians/1,000 population (2023)

Hospital bed density: 5.5 beds/1,000 population (2021 est.)

Sanitation facility access: *improved: urban:* 100% of population (2022 est.)
rural: 100% of population (2022 est.)
total: 100% of population (2022 est.)

Obesity - adult prevalence rate: 22.1% (2016)
comparison ranking: 82

Alcohol consumption per capita: *total:* 9.15 liters of pure alcohol (2019 est.)
beer: 4.35 liters of pure alcohol (2019 est.)
wine: 3.41 liters of pure alcohol (2019 est.)
spirits: 1.09 liters of pure alcohol (2019 est.)
other alcohols: 0.3 liters of pure alcohol (2019 est.)
comparison ranking: total 34

Tobacco use: *total:* 24.1% (2025 est.)
male: 26.4% (2025 est.)
female: 22% (2025 est.)
comparison ranking: total 41

Children under the age of 5 years underweight: 1% (2014/15)
comparison ranking: 109

Currently married women (ages 15-49): 43.2% (2023 est.)

Child marriage: *women married by age 15:* 0% (2020)
women married by age 18: 0.1% (2020)

Education expenditure: 6.4% of GDP (2021 est.)
11.3% national budget (2021 est.)
comparison ranking: Education expenditure (% GDP) 26

School life expectancy (primary to tertiary education): *total:* 19 years (2022 est.)
male: 18 years (2022 est.)
female: 20 years (2022 est.)

ENVIRONMENT

Environmental issues: urbanization; possible risks from industry and intensive farming; air and water pollution

International environmental agreements: *party to:* Air Pollution, Air Pollution-Heavy Metals, Air Pollution-Multi-effect Protocol, Air Pollution-Nitrogen Oxides, Air Pollution-Persistent Organic Pollutants, Air Pollution-Sulphur 85, Air Pollution-Sulphur 94, Air Pollution-Volatile Organic Compounds, Antarctic-Environmental Protection, Antarctic-Marine Living Resources, Antarctic Seals, Antarctic Treaty, Biodiversity, Climate Change, Climate Change-Kyoto Protocol, Climate Change-Paris Agreement, Comprehensive Nuclear Test Ban, Desertification, Endangered Species, Environmental Modification, Hazardous Wastes, Law of the Sea, Marine Dumping-London Convention, Marine Dumping-London Protocol, Marine Life Conservation, Nuclear Test Ban, Ozone Layer Protection, Ship Pollution, Tropical Timber 2006, Wetlands, Whaling
signed, but not ratified: none of the selected agreements

Climate: temperate; mild winters, cool summers; rainy, humid, cloudy

Urbanization: *urban population:* 98.2% of total population (2023)
rate of urbanization: 0.38% annual rate of change (2020-25 est.)

Carbon dioxide emissions: 112.083 million metric tonnes of CO_2 (2023 est.)
from coal and metallurgical coke: 8.166 million metric tonnes of CO_2 (2023 est.)
from petroleum and other liquids: 76.635 million metric tonnes of CO_2 (2023 est.)
from consumed natural gas: 27.282 million metric tonnes of CO_2 (2023 est.)
comparison ranking: total emissions 39

Particulate matter emissions: 12.3 micrograms per cubic meter (2019 est.)

Waste and recycling: *municipal solid waste generated annually:* 4.766 million tons (2024 est.)
percent of municipal solid waste recycled: 31.7% (2022 est.)

Total water withdrawal: *municipal:* 740.19 million cubic meters (2022 est.)
industrial: 4.14 billion cubic meters (2022 est.)
agricultural: 41.97 million cubic meters (2022 est.)

Total renewable water resources: 18.3 billion cubic meters (2022 est.)

Geoparks: *total global geoparks and regional networks:* 2 (2024)

global geoparks and regional networks: Famenne-Ardenne; Schelde Delta (includes Netherlands) (2024)

GOVERNMENT

Country name: *conventional long form:* Kingdom of Belgium
conventional short form: Belgium
local long form: Royaume de Belgique (French)/ Koninkrijk Belgie (Dutch)/Koenigreich Belgien (German)
local short form: Belgique/Belgie/Belgien
etymology: the name derives from the Belgae, an ancient Celtic tribal confederation that inhabited an area between the English Channel and the west bank of the Rhine in the first centuries B.C.

Government type: federal parliamentary democracy under a constitutional monarchy
Capital: *name:* Brussels
geographic coordinates: 50 84 N, 4 35 E
time difference: UTC+1 (6 hours ahead of Washington, DC, during Standard Time) daylight saving time: +1hr, begins last Sunday in March; ends last Sunday in October
etymology: the name is of Germanic origin, from *broca* (marsh) and *sali* (room or building)
Administrative divisions: 3 *regions* (French: *régions*, singular - *région*; Dutch: *gewesten*, singular - *gewest*); Brussels-Capital Region, also known as Brussels Hoofdstedelijk Gewest (Dutch), Region de Bruxelles-Capitale (French long form), Bruxelles-Capitale (French short form); Flemish Region (Flanders), also known as Vlaams Gewest (Dutch long form), Vlaanderen (Dutch short form), Région Flamande (French long form), Flandre (French short form); Walloon Region (Wallonia), also known as Région Wallonne (French long form), Wallonie (French short form), Waals Gewest (Dutch long form), Wallonie (Dutch short form)
note: as a result of the 1993 constitutional revision that furthered devolution into a federal state, there are now three levels of government (federal, regional, and linguistic community) with a complex division of responsibilities; the 2012 sixth state reform transferred additional competencies from the federal state to the regions and linguistic communities

Legal system: civil law system based on the French Civil Code; judicial review of legislative acts
Constitution: *history:* drafted 25 November 1830, approved 7 February 1831, entered into force 26 July 1831, revised 14 July 1993 (creating a federal state)
amendment process: "revisions" proposed as declarations by the federal government in accord with the king or by Parliament followed by dissolution of Parliament and new elections; adoption requires two-thirds majority vote of a two-thirds quorum in both houses of the next elected Parliament

International law organization participation: accepts compulsory ICJ jurisdiction with reservations; accepts ICCt jurisdiction
Citizenship: *citizenship by birth:* no
citizenship by descent only: at least one parent must be a citizen of Belgium
dual citizenship recognized: yes
residency requirement for naturalization: 5 years

Suffrage: 18 years of age; universal and compulsory
Executive branch: *chief of state:* King PHILIPPE (since 21 July 2013)
head of government: Prime Minister Bart DE WEVER (since 3 February 2025)
cabinet: Council of Ministers formally appointed by the monarch
election/appointment process: the monarchy is hereditary and constitutional; following legislative elections, the monarch usually appoints the leader of the majority party or majority coalition as prime minister, which the legislature approves
Legislative branch: *legislature name:* Federal Parliament (Parlement fédéral - Federaal Parlement - Föderales Parlament)
legislative structure: bicameral
note: the 1993 constitutional revision that further devolved Belgium into a federal state created three levels of government (federal, regional, and linguistic community) with a complex division of responsibilities; this results in six governments, each with its own legislative assembly

Legislative branch - lower chamber: *chamber name:* House of Representatives (Chambre des Représentants)
number of seats: 150 (all directly elected)
electoral system: proportional representation
scope of elections: full renewal
term in office: 5 years
most recent election date: 6/9/2024
parties elected and seats per party: New Flemish Alliance (N-VA) (24); Vlaams Belang (Flemish Interest) (20); Movement for Reform (MR) (20); Socialist Party in Wallonia (PS) (16); Workers' Party of Belgium (PTB*PVDA) (15); LES ENGAGÉS (14); Vooruit (13); Christian Democratic and Flemish (CD&V) (11); Other (17)
percentage of women in chamber: 41.3%
expected date of next election: June 2029

Legislative branch - upper chamber: *chamber name:* Senate (Sénat - Senaat - Senat)
number of seats: 60 (all indirectly elected)
scope of elections: full renewal
term in office: 5 years
most recent election date: 7/18/2024
percentage of women in chamber: 47.5%
expected date of next election: July 2029

Judicial branch: *highest court(s):* Constitutional Court or Grondwettelijk Hof (in Dutch) and Cour Constitutionelle (in French) (consists of 12 judges - 6 Dutch-speaking and 6 French-speaking); Supreme Court of Justice or Hof van Cassatie (in Dutch) and Cour de Cassation (in French) (court organized into 3 chambers: civil and commercial; criminal; social, fiscal, and armed forces; each chamber includes a Dutch division and a French division, each with a chairperson and 5-6 judges)
judge selection and term of office: Constitutional Court judges appointed by the monarch from candidates submitted by Parliament; judges appointed for life with mandatory retirement at age 70; Supreme Court judges appointed by the monarch from candidates submitted by the High Council of Justice, a 44-member independent body of judicial and non-judicial members; judges appointed for life
subordinate courts: Courts of Appeal; regional courts; specialized courts for administrative, commercial, labor, immigration, and audit issues; magistrate's courts; justices of the peace

Political parties: Flemish parties: Christian Democratic and Flemish or CD&V
Vooruit or Forward (formerly Social Progressive Alternative or SP.A)
Groen or Green (formerly AGALEV, Flemish Greens)
New Flemish Alliance or N-VA
Open Flemish Liberals and Democrats or Open VLD
Vlaams Belang (Flemish Interest) or VB
Francophone parties: Ecolo (Francophone Greens)
Francophone Federalist Democrats or Defi
Les Engages (formerly Humanist and Democratic Center or CDH)
Reform Movement or MR
Socialist Party or PS
Workers' Party or PVDA-PTB

Diplomatic representation in the US: *chief of mission:* Ambassador Frédéric BERNARD (since 25 February 2025)
chancery: 1430 K Street NW, Washington DC 20005
telephone: [1] (202) 333-6900
FAX: [1] (202) 338-4960
email address and website: Washington@diplobel.fed.be
https://unitedstates.diplomatie.belgium.be/en
consulate(s) general: Atlanta, Los Angeles, New York
Diplomatic representation from the US: *chief of mission:* Ambassador (vacant); Chargé d'Affaires Kathleen LIVELY (since July 2025)
embassy: Regentlaan 27 Boulevard du Regent, B-1000 Brussels
mailing address: 7600 Brussels Place, Washington DC 20521-7600
telephone: [32] (2) 811-4000
FAX: [32] (2) 811-4500
email address and website: uscitizenBrussels@state.gov
https://be.usembassy.gov/

International organization participation: ADB (nonregional members), AfDB (nonregional members), Australia Group, Benelux, BIS, CD, CE, CERN, EAPC, EBRD, ECB, EIB, EITI (implementing country), EMU, ESA, EU, FAO, FATF, G-9, G-10, IADB, IAEA, IBRD, ICAO, ICC (national committees), ICCt, ICRM, IDA, IEA, IFAD, IFC, IFRCS, IGAD (partners), IHO, ILO, IMF, IMO, IMSO, Interpol, IOC, IOM, IPU, ISO, ITSO, ITU, ITUC (NGOs), MIGA, MONUSCO, NATO, NEA, NSG, OAS (observer), OECD, OIF, OPCW, OSCE, Pacific Alliance (observer), Paris Club, PCA, Schengen Convention, SELEC (observer), UN, UNCTAD, UNESCO, UNHCR, UNIDO, UNIFIL, UNRWA, UNTSO, UPU, Wassenaar Arrangement, WCO, WHO, WIPO, WMO, WTO, ZC

Independence: 4 October 1830 (a provisional government declared independence from the Netherlands); 21 July 1831 (King LEOPOLD I ascended to the throne)

National holiday: Belgian National Day (ascension to the throne of King LEOPOLD I), 21 July (1831)

Flag: *description:* three equal vertical bands of black (left side), yellow, and red
history: the vertical design was based on the flag of France; the colors are from the arms of the duchy of Brabant (yellow lion with red claws and tongue on a black field)

National symbol(s): golden rampant lion

National color(s): red, black, yellow

National anthem(s): *title:* "La Brabançonne" (The Song of Brabant)
lyrics/music: Louis-Alexandre DECHET [French] and Victor CEULEMANS [Dutch]/Francois VAN CAMPENHOUT
history: adopted 1830; according to legend Louis-Alexandre DECHET, an actor at the theater where the revolution against the Netherlands began, wrote

the lyrics with a group of young people in a Brussels cafe

National heritage: *total World Heritage Sites:* 16 (15 cultural, 1 natural)
selected World Heritage Site locales: Belfries of Belgium (c); Historic Brugge (c); The Grand Place, Brussels (c); Major Town Houses of Victor Horta (c); Notre-Dame Cathedral, Tournai (c); Spa, Liege (c); Primeval Beech Forests - Sonian Wood (n); Stoclet Palace (c)

ECONOMY

Economic overview: high-income, core EU and eurozone economy; slow growth with weakened domestic consumption and export demand; high public debt and structural deficits linked to social spending; aging workforce with weak productivity growth and participation rates

Real GDP (purchasing power parity): $749.229 billion (2024 est.)
$741.672 billion (2023 est.)
$732.865 billion (2022 est.)
note: data in 2021 dollars
comparison ranking: 36

Real GDP growth rate: 1% (2024 est.)
1.2% (2023 est.)
4.3% (2022 est.)
note: annual GDP % growth based on constant local currency
comparison ranking: 178

Real GDP per capita: $63,100 (2024 est.)
$62,900 (2023 est.)
$62,700 (2022 est.)
note: data in 2021 dollars
comparison ranking: 27

GDP (official exchange rate): $664.564 billion (2024 est.)
note: data in current dollars at official exchange rate

Inflation rate (consumer prices): 3.1% (2024 est.)
4% (2023 est.)
9.6% (2022 est.)
note: annual % change based on consumer prices
comparison ranking: 97

GDP - composition, by sector of origin: *agriculture:* 0.8% (2024 est.)
industry: 17.6% (2024 est.)
services: 72.1% (2024 est.)
note: figures may not total 100% due to non-allocated consumption not captured in sector-reported data
comparison rankings: agriculture 179; industry 148; services 30

GDP - composition, by end use: *household consumption:* 50.4% (2023 est.)
government consumption: 23.8% (2023 est.)
investment in fixed capital: 24.4% (2023 est.)
investment in inventories: 1% (2023 est.)
exports of goods and services: 84.2% (2023 est.)
imports of goods and services: -84.8% (2023 est.)
note: figures may not total 100% due to rounding or gaps in data collection

Agricultural products: sugar beets, milk, potatoes, wheat, pork, lettuce, maize, chicken, barley, pears (2023)
note: top ten agricultural products based on tonnage

Industries: engineering and metal products, motor vehicle assembly, transportation equipment, scientific instruments, processed food and beverages, chemicals, pharmaceuticals, base metals, textiles, glass, petroleum

Industrial production growth rate: -0.6% (2024 est.)
note: annual % change in industrial value added based on constant local currency
comparison ranking: 143

Labor force: 5.416 million (2024 est.)
note: number of people ages 15 or older who are employed or seeking work
comparison ranking: 81

Unemployment rate: 5.5% (2024 est.)
5.6% (2023 est.)
5.6% (2022 est.)
note: % of labor force seeking employment
comparison ranking: 102

Youth unemployment rate (ages 15-24): *total:* 16.8% (2024 est.)
male: 18.6% (2024 est.)
female: 14.7% (2024 est.)
note: % of labor force ages 15-24 seeking employment
comparison ranking: total 67

Population below poverty line: 12.3% (2022 est.)
note: % of population with income below national poverty line
Gini Index coefficient - distribution of family income 26.4 (2022 est.)
note: index (0-100) of income distribution; higher values represent greater inequality
comparison ranking: 139

Average household expenditures: *on food:* 12.2% of household expenditures (2023 est.)
on alcohol and tobacco: 4% of household expenditures (2023 est.)

Household income or consumption by percentage share: *lowest 10%:* 3.8% (2022 est.)
highest 10%: 22.2% (2022 est.)
note: % share of income accruing to lowest and highest 10% of population

Remittances: 2.3% of GDP (2024 est.)
2.3% of GDP (2023 est.)
2.3% of GDP (2022 est.)
note: personal transfers and compensation between resident and non-resident individuals/households/entities

Budget: *revenues:* $220.657 billion (2022 est.)
expenditures: $235.767 billion (2022 est.)
note: central government revenues (excluding grants) and expenditures converted to US dollars at average official exchange rate for year indicated

Public debt: 92.5% of GDP (2022 est.)
note: central government debt as a % of GDP
comparison ranking: 28

Taxes and other revenues: 22.7% (of GDP) (2022 est.)
note: central government tax revenue as a % of GDP
comparison ranking: 32

Current account balance: -$5.679 billion (2024 est.)
-$4.503 billion (2023 est.)
-$7.031 billion (2022 est.)
note: balance of payments - net trade and primary/secondary income in current dollars
comparison ranking: 175

Exports: $525.458 billion (2024 est.)
$542.508 billion (2023 est.)
$565.233 billion (2022 est.)
note: balance of payments - exports of goods and services in current dollars
comparison ranking: 19

Exports - partners: France 20%, Netherlands 15%, Germany 14%, Italy 6%, USA 5% (2023)
note: top five export partners based on percentage share of exports

Exports - commodities: refined petroleum, natural gas, vaccines, cars, packaged medicine (2023)
note: top five export commodities based on value in dollars

Imports: $531.029 billion (2024 est.)
$546.426 billion (2023 est.)
$573.192 billion (2022 est.)
note: balance of payments - imports of goods and services in current dollars
comparison ranking: 18

Imports - partners: Netherlands 20%, Germany 13%, France 11%, USA 7%, Ireland 4% (2023)
note: top five import partners based on percentage share of imports

Imports - commodities: cars, natural gas, vaccines, packaged medicine, crude petroleum (2023)
note: top five import commodities based on value in dollars

Reserves of foreign exchange and gold: $41.449 billion (2024 est.)
$40.813 billion (2023 est.)
$41.274 billion (2022 est.)
note: holdings of gold (year-end prices)/foreign exchange/special drawing rights in current dollars
comparison ranking: 50

Exchange rates: euros (EUR) per US dollar -

Exchange rates: 0.924 (2024 est.)
0.925 (2023 est.)
0.95 (2022 est.)
0.845 (2021 est.)
0.876 (2020 est.)

ENERGY

Electricity access: *electrification - total population:* 100% (2022 est.)

Electricity: *installed generating capacity:* 28.248 million kW (2023 est.)
consumption: 74.537 billion kWh (2023 est.)
exports: 18.279 billion kWh (2023 est.)
imports: 18.626 billion kWh (2023 est.)
transmission/distribution losses: 3.147 billion kWh (2023 est.)
comparison rankings: installed generating capacity 39; consumption 43; exports 16; imports 14; transmission/distribution losses 142

Electricity generation sources: *fossil fuels:* 24.1% of total installed capacity (2023 est.)
nuclear: 40.4% of total installed capacity (2023 est.)
solar: 9.4% of total installed capacity (2023 est.)
wind: 20% of total installed capacity (2023 est.)
hydroelectricity: -0.1% of total installed capacity (2023 est.) note: Belgium has negative net hydroelectric power generation based on losses from use of pumped storage hydropower
biomass and waste: 6.2% of total installed capacity (2023 est.)

Nuclear energy: Number of operational nuclear reactors: 4 (2025)

Net capacity of operational nuclear reactors: 3.46GW (2025 est.)

Percent of total electricity production: 41.2% (2023 est.)

Number of nuclear reactors permanently shut down: 3 (2025)

Coal: *production:* 1.269 million metric tons (2023 est.)

consumption: 4.372 million metric tons (2023 est.)
exports: 184,000 metric tons (2023 est.)
imports: 4.046 million metric tons (2023 est.)
proven reserves: 4.1 billion metric tons (2023 est.)

Petroleum: *total petroleum production:* 11,000 bbl/day (2023 est.)
refined petroleum consumption: 596,000 bbl/day (2024 est.)

Natural gas: *production:* 12.938 million cubic meters (2023 est.)
consumption: 14.382 billion cubic meters (2023 est.)
exports: 8.461 billion cubic meters (2023 est.)
imports: 23.007 billion cubic meters (2023 est.)

Energy consumption per capita: 190.416 million Btu/person (2023 est.)
comparison ranking: 19

COMMUNICATIONS

Telephones - fixed lines: *total subscriptions:* 2.667 million (2023 est.)
subscriptions per 100 inhabitants: 23 (2023 est.)
comparison ranking: total subscriptions 42

Telephones - mobile cellular: *total subscriptions:* 12.1 million (2023 est.)
subscriptions per 100 inhabitants: 102 (2022 est.)
comparison ranking: total subscriptions 83

Broadcast media: a segmented market with the three major linguistic communities (Flemish-, French-, and German-speaking) each responsible for their own broadcast media; multiple TV channels exist for each community; over 90% of households are connected to cable and can access TV broadcasts from neighboring countries; each community has a public radio network coexisting with private broadcasters

Internet country code: .be

Internet users: *percent of population:* 95% (2023 est.)

Broadband - fixed subscriptions: *total:* 5.12 million (2023 est.)
subscriptions per 100 inhabitants: 44 (2023 est.)
comparison ranking: total 35

TRANSPORTATION

Civil aircraft registration country code prefix: OO

Airports: 48 (2025)
comparison ranking: 90

Heliports: 112 (2025)
comparison ranking: 25

Railways: *total:* 3,602 km (2020) 3,160 km electrified

Merchant marine: *total:* 198 (2023)
by type: bulk carrier 17, container ship 2, general cargo 16, oil tanker 21, other 142
comparison ranking: total 68

Ports: *total ports:* 7 (2024)
large: 1
medium: 2
small: 2
very small: 2
ports with oil terminals: 5
key ports: Antwerpen, Bruxelles, Ghent, Oostende, Zeebrugge

MILITARY AND SECURITY

Military and security forces: Belgian Armed Forces (Defensie or La Défense): Land Component, Marine (Naval) Component, Air Component, Medical Component, Cyber Command (2025)
note: the Belgian Federal Police is the national police force and responsible for internal security and nationwide law and order, including migration and border enforcement

Military expenditures: 2% of GDP (2025 est.)
1.3% of GDP (2024 est.)
1.2% of GDP (2023 est.)
1.2% of GDP (2022 est.)
1.1% of GDP (2021 est.)

Military and security service personnel strengths: approximately 23,000 active-duty military personnel (2025)

Military equipment inventories and acquisitions: the armed forces have a mix of weapons systems from European countries, Israel, and the US; Belgium has an export-focused defense industry that focuses on components and subcontracting (2024)

Military service age and obligation: 18 years of age for voluntary military service for men and women; conscription abolished in 1995 (2024)
note 1: in 2024, women comprised about 11% of the military's full-time personnel
note 2: foreign nationals 18-34 years of age who speak Dutch or French and are citizens of EU countries, Iceland, Lichtenstein, Norway, and Switzerland may apply to join the military

Military deployments: has about 1,000 personnel deployed on foreign missions, including more than 300 ground forces deployed in Eastern Europe, as well as air and naval assets, supporting NATO missions for the defense of NATO's eastern flank (2024)

Military - note: the Belgian military's responsibilities include territorial defense, humanitarian/disaster relief, assistance to the police if required, international peacekeeping missions, and support to its NATO and EU security commitments, which Belgium considers vital components of its national security policy; outside of the country, the military operates almost always within an international organization or a coalition; Belgium was one of the original 12 countries to sign the North Atlantic Treaty (also known as the Washington Treaty) establishing NATO in 1949; it hosts the NATO headquarters in Brussels; Belgium also cooperates bilaterally with neighboring countries, such as Luxembourg and the Netherlands, in conducting joint patrols of their respective air spaces and in a composite combined special operations command with Denmark and the Netherlands (2025)

SPACE

Space agency/agencies: Royal Belgian Institute for Space Aeronomy-Interfederal Space Agency of Belgium (BIRA-IASB; established 1964; IASB added 2017); Belgium Federal Science Policy Office (BELSPO) (2025)

Space program overview: founding member of the European Space Agency (ESA), which acts as the de facto Belgian space agency; builds satellites, particularly research/science/technology and remote sensing platforms; researches, develops, and produces a wide variety of space technologies, including telecommunications, optics, robotics, scientific instruments, and space launch vehicle (SLV) components; provides funding for the ESA's SLV program, as well as legal, scientific, and technological expertise; works closely with the EU on space; hosts the European Space Security and Education Center (established 1968); participates in international astronomy efforts, particularly through the European Southern Observatory (ESO); in addition to the ESA, EU, and their members states, has cooperated bi-laterally with a variety foreign space agencies and commercial entities, including those of Argentina, China, India, Russia, South Africa, UAE, Vietnam, and the US (2025)
note: further details about the key activities, programs, and milestones of the country's space program, as well as government spending estimates on the space sector, appear in the Space Programs reference guide

TERRORISM

Terrorist group(s): Terrorist group(s): Islamic Revolutionary Guard Corps/Qods Force; Islamic State of Iraq and ash-Sham (ISIS)
note: details about the history, aims, leadership, organization, areas of operation, tactics, targets, weapons, size, and sources of support of the group(s) appear(s) in Appendix T

TRANSNATIONAL ISSUES

Refugees and internally displaced persons: *refugees:* 236,689 (2024 est.)
stateless persons: 849 (2024 est.)

Illicit drugs: USG identification: major precursor-chemical producer (2025)

BELIZE

INTRODUCTION

Background: Belize was the site of several Mayan city states until their decline at the end of the first millennium A.D. The British and Spanish disputed the region in the 17th and 18th centuries; it formally became the colony of British Honduras in 1862. Territorial disputes between the UK and Guatemala delayed the independence of Belize until 1981. Guatemala refused to recognize the new nation until 1992, and the two countries are still involved in an ongoing border dispute. Tourism has become the mainstay of the economy. Current concerns include the country's heavy foreign debt burden, high crime rates, high unemployment combined with a majority youth population, growing involvement in the Mexican and South American drug trade, and one of the highest HIV/AIDS prevalence rates in Central America.

GEOGRAPHY

Location: Central America, bordering the Caribbean Sea, between Guatemala and Mexico

Geographic coordinates: 17 15 N, 88 45 W

Map references: Central America and the Caribbean

Area: *total:* 22,966 sq km
land: 22,806 sq km
water: 160 sq km
comparison ranking: total 151

Area - comparative: slightly smaller than Massachusetts

Land boundaries: *total:* 542 km
border countries (2): Guatemala 266 km; Mexico 276 km

Coastline: 386 km

Maritime claims: *territorial sea:* 12 nm in the north, 3 nm in the south
exclusive economic zone: 200 nm
note: from the mouth of the Sarstoon River to Ranguana Cay, Belize's territorial sea is 3 nm; according to Belize's Maritime Areas Act (1992), the purpose of this limit is to provide a framework for negotiating a definitive agreement on territorial differences with Guatemala

Climate: tropical; very hot and humid; rainy season (May to November); dry season (February to May)

Terrain: flat, swampy coastal plain; low mountains in south

Elevation: *highest point:* Doyle's Delight 1,124 m
lowest point: Caribbean Sea 0 m
mean elevation: 173 m

Natural resources: arable land potential, timber, fish, hydropower

Land use: *agricultural land:* 8% (2022 est.)
arable land: 4.4% (2022 est.)
permanent crops: 1.4% (2022 est.)
permanent pasture: 2.2% (2022 est.)
forest: 55% (2022 est.)
other: 37% (2022 est.)

Irrigated land: 35 sq km (2012)

Population distribution: approximately 25% to 30% of the population lives in the former capital, Belize City; over half of the overall population is rural; population density is slightly higher in the north and east

Natural hazards: frequent, devastating hurricanes (June to November) and coastal flooding (especially in south)

Geography - note: only country in Central America without a coastline on the North Pacific Ocean

PEOPLE AND SOCIETY

Population: *total:* 415,789 (2024 est.)
male: 205,895
female: 209,894
comparison rankings: total 175; male 175; female 176

Nationality: *noun:* Belizean(s)
adjective: Belizean

Ethnic groups: Mestizo 52.9%, Creole 25.9%, Maya 11.3%, Garifuna 6.1%, East Indian 3.9%, Mennonite 3.6%, White 1.2%, Asian 1%, other 1.2%, unknown 0.3% (2010 est.)
note: percentages add up to more than 100% because respondents were able to identify more than one ethnic origin

Languages: English 62.9% (official), Spanish 56.6%, Creole 44.6%, Maya 10.5%, German 3.2%, Garifuna 2.9%, other 1.8%, unknown 0.5% (2010 est.)
major-language sample(s):
La Libreta Informativa del Mundo, la fuente indispensable de información básica. (Spanish)
note: shares sum to more than 100% because some respondents gave more than one answer on the census

Religions: Roman Catholic 40.1%, Protestant 31.5% (includes Pentecostal 8.4%, Seventh Day Adventist 5.4%, Anglican 4.7%, Mennonite 3.7%, Baptist 3.6%, Methodist 2.9%, Nazarene 2.8%), Jehovah's Witness 1.7%, other 10.5% (includes Baha'i, Buddhist, Hindu, Church of Jesus Christ, Muslim, Rastafarian, Salvation Army), unspecified 0.6%, none 15.5% (2010 est.)

Age structure: *0-14 years:* 27.7% (male 58,529/female 56,811)
15-64 years: 66.7% (male 135,903/female 141,503)
65 years and over: 5.5% (2024 est.) (male 11,463/female 11,580)

Dependency ratios: *total dependency ratio:* 49.9 (2024 est.)
youth dependency ratio: 41.6 (2024 est.)
elderly dependency ratio: 8.3 (2024 est.)
potential support ratio: 12 (2024 est.)

Median age: *total:* 26.8 years (2024 est.)
male: 26.4 years
female: 27.2 years
comparison ranking: total 162

Population growth rate: 1.47% (2024 est.)
comparison ranking: 67

Birth rate: 17.7 births/1,000 population (2024 est.)
comparison ranking: 81

Death rate: 5 deaths/1,000 population (2024 est.)
comparison ranking: 194

Net migration rate: 2 migrant(s)/1,000 population (2024 est.)
comparison ranking: 50

Population distribution: approximately 25% to 30% of the population lives in the former capital, Belize City; over half of the overall population is rural; population density is slightly higher in the north and east

Urbanization: *urban population:* 46.6% of total population (2023)
rate of urbanization: 2.3% annual rate of change (2020-25 est.)

Major urban areas - population: 23,000 BELMOPAN (capital) (2018)

Sex ratio: *at birth:* 1.05 male(s)/female
0-14 years: 1.03 male(s)/female
15-64 years: 0.96 male(s)/female
65 years and over: 0.99 male(s)/female
total population: 0.98 male(s)/female (2024 est.)

Maternal mortality ratio: 67 deaths/100,000 live births (2023 est.)
comparison ranking: 80

Infant mortality rate: *total:* 11.3 deaths/1,000 live births (2024 est.)
male: 12.4 deaths/1,000 live births
female: 10.1 deaths/1,000 live births
comparison ranking: total 120

Life expectancy at birth: *total population:* 74.3 years (2024 est.)
male: 72.6 years
female: 76.1 years
comparison ranking: total population 143

Total fertility rate: 2.05 children born/woman (2024 est.)
comparison ranking: 100

Gross reproduction rate: 1 (2024 est.)

Drinking water source: *improved: urban:* 98.9% of population (2022 est.)
rural: 98% of population (2022 est.)
total: 98.4% of population (2022 est.)
unimproved: urban: 1.1% of population (2022 est.)
rural: 2% of population (2022 est.)
total: 1.6% of population (2022 est.)

Health expenditure: 5% of GDP (2021)
11.5% of national budget (2022 est.)

Physician density: 1.09 physicians/1,000 population (2018)

Hospital bed density: 1 beds/1,000 population (2018 est.)

Sanitation facility access: *improved: urban:* 99.1% of population (2022 est.)
rural: 95.7% of population (2022 est.)
total: 97.3% of population (2022 est.)
unimproved: urban: 0.9% of population (2022 est.)
rural: 4.3% of population (2022 est.)
total: 2.7% of population (2022 est.)

Obesity - adult prevalence rate: 24.1% (2016)
comparison ranking: 60

Alcohol consumption per capita: *total:* 5.93 liters of pure alcohol (2019 est.)
beer: 3.88 liters of pure alcohol (2019 est.)
wine: 0.68 liters of pure alcohol (2019 est.)
spirits: 1.19 liters of pure alcohol (2019 est.)
other alcohols: 0.17 liters of pure alcohol (2019 est.)
comparison ranking: total 72

Tobacco use: *total:* 8.3% (2025 est.)
male: 14.8% (2025 est.)
female: 1.8% (2025 est.)
comparison ranking: total 141

Children under the age of 5 years underweight: 4.6% (2015/16)
comparison ranking: 67

Currently married women (ages 15-49): 64.3% (2023 est.)

Child marriage: *women married by age 15:* 6.3% (2016)
women married by age 18: 33.5% (2016)
men married by age 18: 22.2% (2016)

Education expenditure: 4.6% of GDP (2024 est.)
18.9% national budget (2024 est.)
comparison ranking: Education expenditure (% GDP) 81

Literacy: *total population:* 90.9% (2015 est.)
male: 90.2% (2015 est.)
female: 91.6% (2015 est.)

School life expectancy (primary to tertiary education): *total:* 12 years (2023 est.)
male: 12 years (2023 est.)
female: 12 years (2023 est.)

ENVIRONMENT

Environmental issues: deforestation; water pollution from sewage, industrial effluents, agricultural runoff; inability to properly dispose of solid waste

International environmental agreements: *party to:* Biodiversity, Climate Change, Climate Change-Kyoto Protocol, Climate Change-Paris Agreement, Comprehensive Nuclear Test Ban, Desertification, Endangered Species, Hazardous Wastes, Law of the Sea, Ozone Layer Protection, Ship Pollution, Wetlands, Whaling
signed, but not ratified: none of the selected agreements

Climate: tropical; very hot and humid; rainy season (May to November); dry season (February to May)

Urbanization: *urban population:* 46.6% of total population (2023)
rate of urbanization: 2.3% annual rate of change (2020-25 est.)

Carbon dioxide emissions: 662,000 metric tonnes of CO2 (2023 est.)
from coal and metallurgical coke: 3 metric tonnes of CO2 (2023 est.)
from petroleum and other liquids: 662,000 metric tonnes of CO2 (2023 est.)
comparison ranking: total emissions 184

Particulate matter emissions: 10.5 micrograms per cubic meter (2019 est.)

Waste and recycling: *municipal solid waste generated annually:* 101,400 tons (2024 est.)
percent of municipal solid waste recycled: 10.4% (2022 est.)

Total water withdrawal: *municipal:* 11.4 million cubic meters (2022 est.)
industrial: 21.2 million cubic meters (2022 est.)
agricultural: 68.4 million cubic meters (2022 est.)

Total renewable water resources: 21.734 billion cubic meters (2022 est.)

GOVERNMENT

Country name: *conventional long form:* none
conventional short form: Belize
former: British Honduras
etymology: traditionally believed to be derived from the Spanish pronunciation of the last name of Scottish explorer Peter Wallace, who settled in the area in 1638; alternatively, may be named for the Belize River, whose name possibly derives from the Maya word "belix," meaning "muddy-watered"

Government type: parliamentary democracy (National Assembly) under a constitutional monarchy; a Commonwealth realm

Capital: *name:* Belmopan
geographic coordinates: 17 15 N, 88 46 W
time difference: UTC-6 (1 hour behind Washington, DC, during Standard Time)
etymology: the name is formed from two words: "Belize," the name of the longest river in the country, and "Mopan," one of the rivers in the area that empties into the Belize River

Administrative divisions: 6 districts; Belize, Cayo, Corozal, Orange Walk, Stann Creek, Toledo

Legal system: English common law

Constitution: *history:* previous 1954, 1963 (pre-independence); latest signed and entered into force 21 September 1981
amendment process: proposed and adopted by two-thirds majority vote of the National Assembly House of Representatives except for amendments relating to rights and freedoms, changes to the Assembly, and to elections and judiciary matters, which require at least three-quarters majority vote of the House; both types of amendments require assent of the governor general

International law organization participation: has not submitted an ICJ jurisdiction declaration; accepts ICCt jurisdiction

Citizenship: *citizenship by birth:* yes
citizenship by descent only: yes
dual citizenship recognized: yes
residency requirement for naturalization: 5 years

Suffrage: 18 years of age; universal

Executive branch: *chief of state:* King CHARLES III (since 8 September 2022); represented by Governor-General Froyla TZALAM (since 27 May 2021)
head of government: Prime Minister John BRICEÑO (since 12 November 2020)
cabinet: governor general appoints Cabinet from among members of the National Assembly, on the advice of the prime minister
election/appointment process: the monarchy is hereditary; governor-general appointed by the monarch; following legislative elections, the leader of the majority party or majority coalition usually appointed prime minister by the governor-general; prime minister recommends the deputy prime minister

Legislative branch: *legislature name:* National Assembly
legislative structure: bicameral

Legislative branch - lower chamber: *chamber name:* House of Representatives
number of seats: 32 (all directly elected)
electoral system: plurality/majority
scope of elections: full renewal
term in office: 5 years
most recent election date: 3/12/2025
parties elected and seats per party: People's United Party (PUP) (26); United Democratic Party (UDP) (5)
percentage of women in chamber: 12.5%
expected date of next election: March 2030

Legislative branch - upper chamber: *chamber name:* Senate
number of seats: 13 (all appointed)
scope of elections: full renewal
term in office: 5 years
most recent election date: 5/9/2025
percentage of women in chamber: 35.7%
expected date of next election: May 2030

Judicial branch: *highest court(s):* Supreme Court of Judicature (consists of the Court of Appeal with the court president and 3 justices, and the Supreme Court with the chief justice and 10 justices); the Caribbean Court of Justice is the final court of appeal
judge selection and term of office: Court of Appeal president and justices appointed by the governor-general upon advice of the prime minister after consultation with the National Assembly opposition leader; justices' tenures vary by terms of appointment; Supreme Court chief justice appointed by the governor-general upon the advice of the prime minister and the National Assembly opposition leader; other judges appointed by the governor-general upon the advice of the Judicial and Legal Services Section of the Public Services Commission and with the concurrence of the prime minister after consultation with the National Assembly opposition leader; judges can be appointed beyond age 65 but must retire by age 75
subordinate courts: Magistrates' Courts; Family Court

Political parties: Belize People's Front or BPF
Belize Progressive Party or BPP (formed in 2015 from a merger of the People's National Party, elements of the Vision Inspired by the People, and other smaller political groups)
People's United Party or PUP
United Democratic Party or UDP
Vision Inspired by the People or VIP

Diplomatic representation in the US: *chief of mission:* Ambassador Lynn Raymond YOUNG (since 7 July 2021)
chancery: 2535 Massachusetts Avenue NW, Washington, DC 20008-2826
telephone: [1] (202) 332-9636
FAX: [1] (202) 332-6888
email address and website: reception.usa@mfa.gov.bz
https://www.belizeembassyusa.mfa.gov.bz/
consulate(s) general: Chicago, Los Angeles, Miami, New York

Diplomatic representation from the US: *chief of mission:* Ambassador (vacant); Chargé d'Affaires Katharine BEAMER (since 23 August 2025)
embassy: 4 Floral Park Road, Belmopan, Cayo
mailing address: 3050 Belmopan Place, Washington DC 20521-3050
telephone: (501) 822-4011
FAX: (501) 822-4012
email address and website: ACSBelize@state.gov
https://bz.usembassy.gov/

International organization participation: ACP, ACS, AOSIS, C, Caricom, CD, CDB, CELAC, FAO, G-77, IADB, IAEA, IBRD, ICAO, ICC (NGOs), ICRM, IDA, IFAD, IFC, IFRCS, ILO, IMF, IMO, Interpol, IOC, IOM, ITU, LAES, MIGA, NAM, OAS, OPANAL, OPCW, PCA, Petrocaribe, SICA, UN, UNCTAD, UNESCO, UNIDO, UPU, WCO, WHO, WIPO, WMO, WTO

Independence: 21 September 1981 (from the UK)

National holiday: Battle of St. George's Caye Day (National Day), 10 September (1798); Independence Day, 21 September (1981)

Flag: *description:* royal blue with a narrow red stripe along the top and the bottom edges; the coat of arms is on a large white disk at the center and shows a shield flanked by two workers in front of a mahogany tree, with the motto SUB UMBRA FLOREO (I Flourish in the Shade) on a scroll at the bottom; a green garland of 50 mahogany leaves rings the coat of arms
meaning: the figures, the mahogany tree, and the garland refer to the logging industry that led the British to settle Belize; blue and red are the colors of the two main political parties
note: Belize has the only national flag that depicts humans; the flags of two British overseas territories, Montserrat and the British Virgin Islands, also depict humans

National symbol(s): Baird's tapir (a large forest-dwelling mammal), keel-billed toucan, black orchid

National color(s): red, blue

National anthem(s): *title:* "Land of the Free"
lyrics/music: Samuel Alfred HAYNES/Selwyn Walford YOUNG
history: adopted 1981

title: "God Save the King"
lyrics/music: unknown
history: royal anthem, as a Commonwealth country

National heritage: *total World Heritage Sites:* 1 (natural)
selected World Heritage Site locales: Belize Barrier Reef Reserve System

ECONOMY

Economic overview: tourism- and agriculture-driven economy; strong post-pandemic rebound; innovative and ecological bond restructuring that significantly lowered public debt and expanded marine protections; central bank offering USD-denominated treasury notes; high mobility across borders

Real GDP (purchasing power parity): $5.538 billion (2024 est.)
$5.12 billion (2023 est.)
$5.062 billion (2022 est.)
note: data in 2021 dollars
comparison ranking: 182

Real GDP growth rate: 8.2% (2024 est.)
1.1% (2023 est.)
9.7% (2022 est.)
note: annual GDP % growth based on constant local currency
comparison ranking: 11

Real GDP per capita: $13,300 (2024 est.)
$12,500 (2023 est.)
$12,600 (2022 est.)
note: data in 2021 dollars
comparison ranking: 132

GDP (official exchange rate): $3.516 billion (2024 est.)
note: data in current dollars at official exchange rate

Inflation rate (consumer prices): 3.3% (2024 est.)
4.4% (2023 est.)
6.3% (2022 est.)
note: annual % change based on consumer prices
comparison ranking: 108

GDP - composition, by sector of origin: *agriculture:* 8.1% (2023 est.)
industry: 14.3% (2023 est.)
services: 62.4% (2023 est.)
note: figures may not total 100% due to non-allocated consumption not captured in sector-reported data
comparison rankings: agriculture 85; industry 166; services 73

GDP - composition, by end use: *household consumption:* 62.9% (2023 est.)
government consumption: 15.7% (2023 est.)
investment in fixed capital: 20.6% (2023 est.)
investment in inventories: -2.3% (2023 est.)
exports of goods and services: 55.3% (2023 est.)
imports of goods and services: -51.2% (2023 est.)
note: figures may not total 100% due to rounding or gaps in data collection

Agricultural products: sugarcane, maize, bananas, sorghum, soybeans, chicken, rice, oranges, fruits, plantains (2023)
note: top ten agricultural products based on tonnage

Industries: garment production, food processing, tourism, construction, oil

Industrial production growth rate: 4.8% (2024 est.)
note: annual % change in industrial value added based on constant local currency
comparison ranking: 48

Labor force: 190,000 (2024 est.)
note: number of people ages 15 or older who are employed or seeking work
comparison ranking: 177

Unemployment rate: 7% (2024 est.)
8.3% (2023 est.)
8.8% (2022 est.)
note: % of labor force seeking employment
comparison ranking: 124

Youth unemployment rate (ages 15-24): *total:* 16.3% (2024 est.)
male: 10.6% (2024 est.)
female: 25.6% (2024 est.)
note: % of labor force ages 15-24 seeking employment
comparison ranking: total 72

Gini Index coefficient - distribution of family income: 39.9 (2018 est.)
note: index (0-100) of income distribution; higher values represent greater inequality
comparison ranking: 41

Household income or consumption by percentage share: *lowest 10%:* 2.2% (2018 est.)
highest 10%: 30% (2018 est.)
note: % share of income accruing to lowest and highest 10% of population

Remittances: 4.4% of GDP (2024 est.)
4.9% of GDP (2023 est.)
5% of GDP (2022 est.)
note: personal transfers and compensation between resident and non-resident individuals/households/entities

Budget: *revenues:* $554.405 million (2017 est.)
expenditures: $506.316 million (2017 est.)
note: central government revenues and expenses (excluding grants/extrabudgetary units/social security funds) converted to US dollars at average official exchange rate for year indicated

Public debt: 99% of GDP (2017 est.)
note: central government debt as a % of GDP
comparison ranking: 23

Taxes and other revenues: 21.3% (of GDP) (2017 est.)
note: central government tax revenue as a % of GDP
comparison ranking: 43

Current account balance: -$51.762 million (2024 est.)
-$19.761 million (2023 est.)
-$235.566 million (2022 est.)
note: balance of payments - net trade and primary/secondary income in current dollars
comparison ranking: 90

Exports: $1.64 billion (2024 est.)
$1.536 billion (2023 est.)
$1.369 billion (2022 est.)
note: balance of payments - exports of goods and services in current dollars
comparison ranking: 168

Exports - partners: USA 22%, UK 14%, Spain 9%, Guatemala 7%, Portugal 5% (2023)
note: top five export partners based on percentage share of exports

Exports - commodities: raw sugar, bananas, fish, shellfish, refined petroleum (2023)
note: top five export commodities based on value in dollars

Imports: $1.724 billion (2024 est.)
$1.573 billion (2023 est.)
$1.574 billion (2022 est.)
note: balance of payments - imports of goods and services in current dollars
comparison ranking: 179

Imports - partners: USA 37%, China 17%, Guatemala 10%, Mexico 8%, Costa Rica 6% (2023)
note: top five import partners based on percentage share of imports

Imports - commodities: refined petroleum, orthopedic appliances, ships, garments, tobacco (2023)
note: top five import commodities based on value in dollars

Reserves of foreign exchange and gold: $498.087 million (2024 est.)
$473.729 million (2023 est.)
$482.146 million (2022 est.)
note: holdings of gold (year-end prices)/foreign exchange/special drawing rights in current dollars
comparison ranking: 158

Debt - external: $1.235 billion (2023 est.)
note: present value of external debt in current US dollars
comparison ranking: 103

Exchange rates: Belizean dollars (BZD) per US dollar -

Exchange rates: 2 (2024 est.)
2 (2023 est.)
2 (2022 est.)
2 (2021 est.)
2 (2020 est.)

ENERGY

Electricity access: *electrification - total population:* 98.6% (2022 est.)
electrification - urban areas: 98.4%
electrification - rural areas: 97.1%

Electricity: *installed generating capacity:* 220,000 kW (2023 est.)
consumption: 595.389 million kWh (2023 est.)
imports: 283.8 million kWh (2023 est.)
transmission/distribution losses: 140.519 million kWh (2023 est.)
comparison rankings: installed generating capacity 170; consumption 170; imports 103; transmission/distribution losses 53

Electricity generation sources: *fossil fuels:* 12% of total installed capacity (2023 est.)
solar: 2.4% of total installed capacity (2023 est.)
hydroelectricity: 52.9% of total installed capacity (2023 est.)
biomass and waste: 32.7% of total installed capacity (2023 est.)

Coal: *imports:* 32 metric tons (2023 est.)

Petroleum: *total petroleum production:* 800 bbl/day (2023 est.)
refined petroleum consumption: 5,000 bbl/day (2023 est.)
crude oil estimated reserves: 6.7 million barrels (2021 est.)

Energy consumption per capita: 30.752 million Btu/person (2023 est.)
comparison ranking: 115

COMMUNICATIONS

Telephones - fixed lines: *total subscriptions:* 19,000 (2021 est.)
subscriptions per 100 inhabitants: 4 (2022 est.)
comparison ranking: total subscriptions 173

Telephones - mobile cellular: *total subscriptions:* 264,000 (2021 est.)
subscriptions per 100 inhabitants: 66 (2021 est.)
comparison ranking: total subscriptions 180

Broadcast media: 8 privately owned TV stations; multi-channel cable TV provides access to foreign stations; about 25 radio stations broadcasting on roughly 50 different frequencies; state-run radio was privatized in 1998 (2019)

Internet country code: .bz

Internet users: *percent of population:* 72% (2023 est.)

Broadband - fixed subscriptions: *total:* 39,000 (2022 est.)
subscriptions per 100 inhabitants: 10 (2022 est.)
comparison ranking: total 152

TRANSPORTATION

Civil aircraft registration country code prefix: V3

Airports: 27 (2025)
comparison ranking: 124

Heliports: 5 (2025)
comparison ranking: 99

Merchant marine: *total:* 774 (2023)
by type: bulk carrier 49, general cargo 410, oil tanker 64, other 251
comparison ranking: total 31

Ports: *total ports:* 2 (2024)
large: 0
medium: 0
small: 1
very small: 0
size unknown: 1
ports with oil terminals: 1
key ports: Belize City, Big Creek

MILITARY AND SECURITY

Military and security forces: Belize Defense Force (BDF): Army, Air Wing; Belize Coast Guard (BCG) (2025)
note: the Ministry of National Defense and Border Security is responsible for oversight of the BDF and the Coast Guard, while the Ministry of Home Affairs and New Growth Industries has responsibility for the Belize Police Department (BPD) and prisons

Military expenditures: 1% of GDP (2024 est.)
0.9% of GDP (2023 est.)
1.1% of GDP (2022 est.)
1.3% of GDP (2021 est.)
1.5% of GDP (2020 est.)

Military and security service personnel strengths: approximately 1,500 BDF personnel (2025)

Military equipment inventories and acquisitions: the military has a small inventory consisting mostly of UK- and US-origin equipment (2024)

Military service age and obligation: 18-23 years of age for voluntary military service; laws allow for conscription only if volunteers are insufficient, but conscription has never been implemented; initial service obligation is 12 years (2024)

Military - note: the Belize Defense Force (BDF) is responsible for external security but also provides some support to civilian authorities; it has limited powers of arrest within land and shoreline areas, while the Coast Guard has arrest powers and jurisdiction within coastal and maritime areas; the BDF traces its history back to the Prince Regent Royal Honduras Militia, a volunteer force established in 1817; the BDF was established in 1978 from the disbanded Police Special Force and the Belize Volunteer Guard to assist the resident British forces with the defense of Belize against Guatemala
the British Army has maintained a presence in Belize since its independence; the presence consists of a small training support unit that provides jungle training to troops from the UK and international partners (2025)

TRANSNATIONAL ISSUES

Refugees and internally displaced persons: *refugees:* 2,287 (2024 est.)

IDPs: 8 (2024 est.)

Illicit drugs: USG identification: major illicit drug-producing and/or drug-transit country (2025)

BENIN

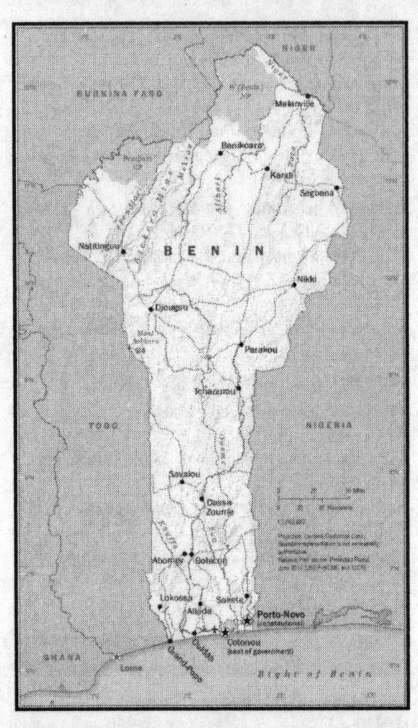

INTRODUCTION

Background: Present-day Benin is comprised of about 42 ethnic groups, including the Yoruba in the southeast, who migrated from what is now Nigeria in the 12th century; the Dendi in the north-central area, who came from Mali in the 16th century; the Bariba and the Fula in the northeast; the Ottamari in the Atakora mountains; the Fon in the area around Abomey in the south-central area; and the Mina, Xueda, and Aja, who came from Togo, on the coast. The Kingdom of Dahomey emerged on the Abomey plateau in the 17th century and was a regional power for much of the 18th and 19th centuries. The growth of Dahomey coincided with the growth of the Atlantic slave trade, and it became known as a major source of enslaved people. France began to control the coastal areas of Dahomey in the second half of the 19th century; the entire kingdom was conquered by 1894. French Dahomey achieved independence in 1960, and it changed its name to the Republic of Benin in 1975.

A succession of military governments ended in 1972 with the rise to power of Mathieu KEREKOU and a Marxist-Leninist government. A move to representative government began in 1989. Two years later, free elections ushered in former Prime Minister Nicephore SOGLO as president, marking the first successful transfer of power in Africa from a dictatorship to a democracy. KEREKOU returned to power after elections in 1996 and 2001. He stepped down in 2006 and was succeeded by Thomas YAYI Boni, a political outsider and independent, who won a second term in 2011. Patrice TALON, a wealthy businessman, took office in 2016; the space for pluralism, dissent, and free expression has narrowed under his administration. TALON won a second term in 2021.

GEOGRAPHY

Location: Western Africa, bordering the Bight of Benin, between Nigeria and Togo

Geographic coordinates: 9 30 N, 2 15 E

Map references: Africa

Area: *total:* 112,622 sq km
land: 110,622 sq km
water: 2,000 sq km
comparison ranking: total 102

Area - comparative: slightly smaller than Pennsylvania

Land boundaries: *total:* 2,123 km
border countries (4): Burkina Faso 386 km; Niger 277 km; Nigeria 809 km; Togo 651 km

Coastline: 121 km

Maritime claims: *territorial sea:* 200 nm; note: the US does not recognize this claim
continental shelf: 200 nm
exclusive fishing zone: 200 nm

Climate: tropical; hot, humid in south; semiarid in north

Terrain: mostly flat to undulating plain; some hills and low mountains

Elevation: *highest point:* unnamed elevation 675 m; located 2.5 km southeast of the town of Kotopounga
lowest point: Atlantic Ocean 0 m
mean elevation: 273 m

Natural resources: small offshore oil deposits, limestone, marble, timber

Land use: *agricultural land:* 43.1% (2022 est.)
arable land: 31.4% (2022 est.)
permanent crops: 6.7% (2022 est.)
permanent pasture: 4.9% (2022 est.)

forest: 26.9% (2022 est.)
other: 30% (2022 est.)
Irrigated land: 530 sq km (2019)

Major watersheds (area sq km): Atlantic Ocean drainage: Niger (2,261,741 sq km), Volta (410,991 sq km)

Population distribution: the population is primarily located in the south, with the highest concentration of people residing in and around the cities on the Atlantic coast; most of the north remains sparsely populated with higher concentrations of residents in the west, as shown in this population distribution map

Natural hazards: hot, dry, dusty harmattan wind may affect north from December to March
Geography - note: sandbanks create difficult access to a coast with no natural harbors, river mouths, or islands

PEOPLE AND SOCIETY

Population: *total:* 14,697,052 (2024 est.)
male: 7,253,258
female: 7,443,794
comparison rankings: total 74; male 74; female 74
Nationality: *noun:* Beninese (singular and plural)
adjective: Beninese
Ethnic groups: Fon and related 38.4%, Adja and related 15.1%, Yoruba and related 12%, Bariba and related 9.6%, Fulani and related 8.6%, Ottamari and related 6.1%, Yoa-Lokpa and related 4.3%, Dendi and related 2.9%, other 0.9%, foreigner 1.9% (2013 est.)

Languages: 55 languages; French (official); Fon (a Gbe language), Yom (a Gur language) and Yoruba are the most important indigenous languages in the south; half a dozen regionally important languages in the north, including Bariba and Fulfulde

Religions: Muslim 27.7%, Roman Catholic 25.5%, Protestant 13.5% (Celestial 6.7%, Methodist 3.4%, other Protestant 3.4%), Vodoun 11.6%, other Christian 9.5%, other traditional religions 2.6%, other 2.6%, none 5.8% (2013 est.)

Age structure: *0-14 years:* 45.3% (male 3,360,027/female 3,294,201)
15-64 years: 52.2% (male 3,727,040/female 3,951,786)
65 years and over: 2.5% (2024 est.) (male 166,191/female 197,807)

Dependency ratios: *total dependency ratio:* 91.4 (2024 est.)
youth dependency ratio: 86.7 (2024 est.)
elderly dependency ratio: 4.7 (2024 est.)
potential support ratio: 21.1 (2024 est.)

Median age: *total:* 17.2 years (2024 est.)
male: 16.6 years
female: 17.7 years
comparison ranking: total 223

Population growth rate: 3.29% (2024 est.)
comparison ranking: 4

Birth rate: 40.3 births/1,000 population (2024 est.)
comparison ranking: 3

Death rate: 7.6 deaths/1,000 population (2024 est.)
comparison ranking: 97

Net migration rate: 0.2 migrant(s)/1,000 population (2024 est.)
comparison ranking: 75

Population distribution: the population is primarily located in the south, with the highest concentration of people residing in and around the cities on the Atlantic coast; most of the north remains sparsely populated with higher concentrations of residents in the west, as shown in this population distribution map

Urbanization: *urban population:* 50.1% of total population (2023)
rate of urbanization: 3.74% annual rate of change (2020-25 est.)

Major urban areas - population: 285,000 PORTO-NOVO (capital) (2018); 1.253 million Abomey-Calavi, 722,000 COTONOU (seat of government) (2022)

Sex ratio: *at birth:* 1.05 male(s)/female
0-14 years: 1.02 male(s)/female
15-64 years: 0.94 male(s)/female
65 years and over: 0.84 male(s)/female
total population: 0.97 male(s)/female (2024 est.)

Mother's mean age at first birth: 20.5 years (2017/18 est.)
note: data represents median age at first birth among women 25-49

Maternal mortality ratio: 518 deaths/100,000 live births (2023 est.)
comparison ranking: 8

Infant mortality rate: *total:* 52.9 deaths/1,000 live births (2024 est.)
male: 57.8 deaths/1,000 live births
female: 47.8 deaths/1,000 live births
comparison ranking: total 16

Life expectancy at birth: *total population:* 63 years (2024 est.)
male: 61.1 years
female: 65 years
comparison ranking: total population 213

Total fertility rate: 5.34 children born/woman (2024 est.)
comparison ranking: 5

Gross reproduction rate: 2.61 (2024 est.)

Drinking water source: *improved: urban:* 74.1% of population (2022 est.)
rural: 60.8% of population (2022 est.)
total: 67.4% of population (2022 est.)
unimproved: urban: 25.9% of population (2022 est.)
rural: 39.2% of population (2022 est.)
total: 32.6% of population (2022 est.)

Health expenditure: 2.6% of GDP (2021)
2.6% of national budget (2022 est.)

Physician density: 0.22 physicians/1,000 population (2023)

Hospital bed density: 0.4 beds/1,000 population (2021 est.)

Sanitation facility access: *improved: urban:* 58.5% of population (2022 est.)
rural: 20.8% of population (2022 est.)
total: 39.5% of population (2022 est.)
unimproved: urban: 41.5% of population (2022 est.)
rural: 79.2% of population (2022 est.)
total: 60.5% of population (2022 est.)

Obesity - adult prevalence rate: 9.6% (2016)
comparison ranking: 142

Alcohol consumption per capita: *total:* 1.25 liters of pure alcohol (2019 est.)
beer: 0.81 liters of pure alcohol (2019 est.)
wine: 0.02 liters of pure alcohol (2019 est.)
spirits: 0.2 liters of pure alcohol (2019 est.)
other alcohols: 0.22 liters of pure alcohol (2019 est.)
comparison ranking: total 145

Tobacco use: *total:* 4.8% (2025 est.)
male: 8.3% (2025 est.)
female: 1.5% (2025 est.)
comparison ranking: total 163

Children under the age of 5 years underweight: 16.8% (2017/18)
comparison ranking: 26

Currently married women (ages 15-49): 68.3% (2023 est.)

Child marriage: *women married by age 15:* 5.9% (2022)
women married by age 18: 27.5% (2022)
men married by age 18: 4.6% (2022)

Education expenditure: 3.7% of GDP (2023 est.)
18% national budget (2025 est.)
comparison ranking: Education expenditure (% GDP) 122

Literacy: *total population:* 51.4% (2022 est.)
male: 62.6% (2022 est.)
female: 41.5% (2022 est.)

School life expectancy (primary to tertiary education): *total:* 10 years (2022 est.)
male: 11 years (2022 est.)
female: 9 years (2022 est.)

ENVIRONMENT

Environmental issues: inadequate supplies of potable water; water pollution; poaching; deforestation; desertification; droughts

International environmental agreements: *party to:* Biodiversity, Climate Change, Climate Change-Kyoto Protocol, Climate Change-Paris Agreement, Comprehensive Nuclear Test Ban, Desertification, Endangered Species, Environmental Modification, Hazardous Wastes, Law of the Sea, Marine Dumping-London Convention, Nuclear Test Ban, Ozone Layer Protection, Ship Pollution, Tropical Timber 2006, Wetlands, Whaling
signed, but not ratified: none of the selected agreements
Climate: tropical; hot, humid in south; semiarid in north

Urbanization: *urban population:* 50.1% of total population (2023)
rate of urbanization: 3.74% annual rate of change (2020-25 est.)

Carbon dioxide emissions: 5.948 million metric tonnes of CO2 (2023 est.)
from coal and metallurgical coke: 379,000 metric tonnes of CO2 (2023 est.)
from petroleum and other liquids: 5.263 million metric tonnes of CO2 (2023 est.)
from consumed natural gas: 306,000 metric tonnes of CO2 (2023 est.)
comparison ranking: total emissions 130

Particulate matter emissions: 32.6 micrograms per cubic meter (2019 est.)

Methane emissions: *energy:* 63.4 kt (2022-2024 est.)
agriculture: 106.1 kt (2019-2021 est.)
waste: 34.3 kt (2019-2021 est.)
other: 43.5 kt (2019-2021 est.)

Waste and recycling: *municipal solid waste generated annually:* 685,900 tons (2024 est.)
percent of municipal solid waste recycled: 56.9% (2022 est.)

Total water withdrawal: *municipal:* 145 million cubic meters (2022 est.)
industrial: 30 million cubic meters (2022 est.)
agricultural: 59 million cubic meters (2022 est.)

Total renewable water resources: 26.39 billion cubic meters (2022 est.)

GOVERNMENT

Country name: *conventional long form:* Republic of Benin
conventional short form: Benin
local long form: République du Benin
local short form: Benin
former: Dahomey, People's Republic of Benin
etymology: the current name comes from a local ethnic group, the Bini, whose name may be related to the Arabic word *bani,* meaning "sons;" the former name, Dahomey, comes from a previous kingdom in the area called Dan Homé

Government type: presidential republic

Capital: *name:* Porto-Novo (constitutional capital); Cotonou (seat of government)
geographic coordinates: 6 29 N, 2 37 E
time difference: UTC+1 (6 hours ahead of Washington, DC, during Standard Time)
etymology: the name Porto-Novo is Portuguese for "new port"; Cotonou means "mouth of the river of death" in the native Fon language

Administrative divisions: 12 departments; Alibori, Atacora, Atlantique, Borgou, Collines, Couffo, Donga, Littoral, Mono, Oueme, Plateau, Zou

Legal system: civil law system modeled largely on the French system and some customary law

Constitution: *history:* previous 1946, 1958 (pre-independence); latest adopted by referendum 2 December 1990, promulgated 11 December 1990
amendment process: proposed concurrently by the president of the republic (after a decision in the Council of Ministers) and the National Assembly; consideration of drafts or proposals requires at least three-fourths majority vote of the Assembly membership; passage requires approval in a referendum unless approved by at least four-fifths majority vote of the Assembly membership; constitutional articles affecting territorial sovereignty, the republican form of government, and secularity of Benin cannot be amended

International law organization participation: has not submitted an ICJ jurisdiction declaration; accepts ICCt jurisdiction

Citizenship: *citizenship by birth:* no
citizenship by descent only: at least one parent must be a citizen of Benin
dual citizenship recognized: yes
residency requirement for naturalization: 10 years

Suffrage: 18 years of age; universal

Executive branch: *chief of state:* President Patrice TALON (since 6 April 2016)
head of government: President Patrice TALON (since 6 April 2016)
cabinet: Council of Ministers appointed by the president
election/appointment process: president directly elected by absolute-majority popular vote in 2 rounds, if needed, for a 5-year term (eligible for a second term)
most recent election date: 11 April 2021
election results: *2021:* Patrice TALON reelected president in the; percent of vote - Patrice TALON (independent) 86.3%, Alassane SOUMANOU (FCBE) 11.4%, Corentin KOHOUE (The Democrats) 2.3%
2016: Patrice TALON elected president in second round; percent of vote in first round - Lionel ZINSOU (FCBE) 28.4%, Patrice TALON (independent) 24.8%, Sebastien AJAVON (independent) 23%, Abdoulaye Bio TCHANE (ABT) 8.8%, Pascal KOUPAKI (NC) 5.9%, other 9.1%; percent of vote in second round - Patrice TALON 65.4%, Lionel ZINSOU 34.6%
expected date of next election: 12 April 2026
note: the president is both head of state and head of government

Legislative branch: *legislature name:* National Assembly (Assemblée nationale)
legislative structure: unicameral
number of seats: 109 (all directly elected)
electoral system: proportional representation
scope of elections: full renewal
term in office: 4 years
most recent election date: 1/8/2023
parties elected and seats per party: Progressive Union for Renewal (53); Republican Block (BR) (28); Democrats (28)
percentage of women in chamber: 26.6%
expected date of next election: January 2026
note: seat total includes 24 seats reserved for women

Judicial branch: *highest court(s):* Supreme Court or Cour Supreme (consists of the chief justice and 16 justices organized into an administrative division, judicial chamber, and chamber of accounts); Constitutional Court or Cour Constitutionnelle (consists of 7 members, including the court president); High Court of Justice (consists of the Constitutional Court members, 6 members appointed by the National Assembly, and the Supreme Court president)
judge selection and term of office: Supreme Court president and judges appointed by the president of the republic on the advice of the National Assembly; judges appointed for single renewable 5-year terms; Constitutional Court members - 4 appointed by the National Assembly and 3 by the president of the republic; members appointed for single renewable 5-year terms; other members of the High Court of Justice elected by the National Assembly; member tenure NA
subordinate courts: Court of Appeal or Cour d'Appel; Court for the Repression of Economic and Terrorism Infractions (CRIET) or Cour de Répression des Infractions Economiques et du Terrorisme; district courts; village courts; Assize courts
note: jurisdiction of the High Court of Justice is limited to cases of high treason by the national president or members of the government while in office

Political parties: African Movement for Development and Progress or MADEP
Benin Renaissance or RB
Cowrie Force for an Emerging Benin or FCBE
Democratic Renewal Party or PRD
Progressive Union for Renewal
Republican Bloc
Sun Alliance or AS
The Democrats
Union Makes the Nation or UN (includes PRD, MADEP)
note: approximately 20 additional minor parties

Diplomatic representation in the US: *chief of mission:* Ambassador Agniola AHOUANMENOU (since 24 July 2025)
chancery: 2124 Kalorama Road NW, Washington, DC 20008
telephone: [1] (202) 232-6656
FAX: [1] (202) 265-1996
email address and website: ambassade.washington@gouv.bj
https://beninembassy.us/

Diplomatic representation from the US: *chief of mission:* Ambassador Brian SHUKAN (since 5 May 2022)
embassy: 01BP 2012, Cotonou
mailing address: 2120 Cotonou Place, Washington DC 20521-2120
telephone: [229] 21-36-75-00
FAX: [229] 21-30-03-84
email address and website: ACSCotonou@state.gov
https://bj.usembassy. gov/

International organization participation: ACP, AfDB, AU, CD, ECOWAS, Entente, FAO, FZ, G-77, IAEA, IBRD, ICAO, ICCt, ICRM, IDA, IDB, IFAD, IFC, IFRCS, ILO, IMF, IMO, Interpol, IOC, IOM, IPU, ISO, ITSO, ITU, ITUC (NGOs), MIGA, MNJTF, MONUSCO, NAM, OAS (observer), OIC, OIF, OPCW, PCA, UN, UNAMID, UNCTAD, UNESCO, UNHCR, UNHRC, UNIDO, UNISFA, UNMIL, UNMISS, UNOCI, UNOOSA, UNWTO, UPU, WADB (regional), WAEMU, WCO, WFTU (NGOs), WHO, WIPO, WMO, WTO

Independence: 1 August 1960 (from France)

National holiday: Independence Day, 1 August (1960)

Flag: *description:* two equal horizontal bands of yellow (top) and red (bottom) to the right, with a vertical green band on the left side
meaning: green stands for hope and revival, yellow for wealth, and red for courage
history: uses the colors of the Pan-African movement

National symbol(s): leopard

National color(s): green, yellow, red

National anthem(s): *title:* "L'Aube Nouvelle" (The Dawn of a New Day)
lyrics/music: Gilbert Jean DAGNON
history: adopted 1960

National heritage: *total World Heritage Sites:* 3 (2 cultural, 1 natural)
selected World Heritage Site locales: Royal Palaces of Abomey (c); W-Arly-Pendjari Complex (n); Koutammakou, the Land of the Batammariba (c)

ECONOMY

Economic overview: robust economic growth; slightly declining but still widespread poverty; strong trade relations with Nigeria; cotton exporter; COVID-19 has led to capital outflows and border closures; WAEMU member with currency pegged to the euro; recent fiscal deficit and debt reductions

Real GDP (purchasing power parity): $56.424 billion (2024 est.)
$52.51 billion (2023 est.)
$49.374 billion (2022 est.)
note: data in 2021 dollars
comparison ranking: 122

Real GDP growth rate: 7.5% (2024 est.)
6.4% (2023 est.)
6.3% (2022 est.)
note: annual GDP % growth based on constant local currency
comparison ranking: 13

Real GDP per capita: $3,900 (2024 est.)
$3,700 (2023 est.)
$3,600 (2022 est.)
note: data in 2021 dollars
comparison ranking: 182

GDP (official exchange rate): $21.483 billion (2024 est.)
note: data in current dollars at official exchange rate

Inflation rate (consumer prices): 1.2% (2024 est.)
2.7% (2023 est.)
1.4% (2022 est.)
note: annual % change based on consumer prices
comparison ranking: 28

GDP - composition, by sector of origin: *agriculture:* 24.2% (2024 est.)
industry: 17.4% (2024 est.)
services: 48.9% (2024 est.)
note: figures may not total 100% due to non-allocated consumption not captured in sector-reported data
comparison rankings: agriculture 22; industry 151; services 154

GDP - composition, by end use: *household consumption:* 58.9% (2024 est.)
government consumption: 9% (2024 est.)
investment in fixed capital: 34.7% (2024 est.)
investment in inventories: 0.4% (2024 est.)
exports of goods and services: 18.8% (2024 est.)
imports of goods and services: -21.8% (2024 est.)
note: figures may not total 100% due to rounding or gaps in data collection

Agricultural products: cassava, yams, maize, oil palm fruit, cotton, soybeans, rice, pineapples, tomatoes, chillies/peppers (2023)
note: top ten agricultural products based on tonnage

Industries: textiles, food processing, construction materials, cement

Industrial production growth rate: 9.7% (2024 est.)
note: annual % change in industrial value added based on constant local currency
comparison ranking: 13

Labor force: 6.397 million (2024 est.)
note: number of people ages 15 or older who are employed or seeking work
comparison ranking: 73

Unemployment rate: 1.8% (2024 est.)
1.7% (2023 est.)
1.7% (2022 est.)
note: % of labor force seeking employment
comparison ranking: 14

Youth unemployment rate (ages 15-24): *total:* 3.3% (2024 est.)
male: 3.6% (2024 est.)
female: 2.9% (2024 est.)
note: % of labor force ages 15-24 seeking employment
comparison ranking: total 179

Population below poverty line: 38.5% (2018 est.)
note: % of population with income below national poverty line
Gini Index coefficient - distribution of family income 34.4 (2021 est.)
note: index (0-100) of income distribution; higher values represent greater inequality
comparison ranking: 81

Household income or consumption by percentage share: *lowest 10%:* 3.1% (2021 est.)
highest 10%: 27.2% (2021 est.)
note: % share of income accruing to lowest and highest 10% of population

Remittances: 1.7% of GDP (2023 est.)
1.4% of GDP (2022 est.)
1.3% of GDP (2021 est.)
note: personal transfers and compensation between resident and non-resident individuals/households/entities

Budget: *revenues:* $2.024 billion (2019 est.)
expenditures: $2.101 billion (2019 est.)

Current account balance: -$1.609 billion (2023 est.)
-$991.005 million (2022 est.)
-$734.659 million (2021 est.)
note: balance of payments - net trade and primary/secondary income in current dollars
comparison ranking: 140

Exports: $4.511 billion (2023 est.)
$4.271 billion (2022 est.)
$4.154 billion (2021 est.)
note: balance of payments - exports of goods and services in current dollars
comparison ranking: 143

Exports - partners: UAE 42%, Bangladesh 20%, India 11%, China 5%, Togo 3% (2023)
note: top five export partners based on percentage share of exports

Exports - commodities: gold, cotton, coconuts/brazil nuts/cashews, soybeans, wood (2023)
note: top five export commodities based on value in dollars

Imports: $6.189 billion (2023 est.)
$5.296 billion (2022 est.)
$4.925 billion (2021 est.)
note: balance of payments - imports of goods and services in current dollars
comparison ranking: 144

Imports - partners: China 21%, India 15%, USA 6%, France 6%, Nigeria 4% (2023)
note: top five import partners based on percentage share of imports

Imports - commodities: rice, refined petroleum, palm oil, poultry, cars (2023)
note: top five import commodities based on value in dollars

Debt - external: $6.309 billion (2023 est.)
note: present value of external debt in current US dollars
comparison ranking: 66

Exchange rates: Communaute Financiere Africaine francs (XOF) per US dollar -

Exchange rates: 606.345 (2024 est.)
606.655 (2023 est.)
622.912 (2022 est.)
554.608 (2021 est.)
574.295 (2020 est.)

ENERGY

Electricity access: *electrification - total population:* 56.5% (2022 est.)
electrification - urban areas: 71.1%
electrification - rural areas: 45.5%

Electricity: *installed generating capacity:* 505,000 kW (2023 est.)
consumption: 1.459 billion kWh (2023 est.)
exports: 2 million kWh (2023 est.)
imports: 844.888 million kWh (2023 est.)
transmission/distribution losses: 385 million kWh (2023 est.)
comparison rankings: installed generating capacity 151; consumption 156; exports 101; imports 81; transmission/distribution losses 76

Electricity generation sources: *fossil fuels:* 96.7% of total installed capacity (2023 est.)
solar: 3.3% of total installed capacity (2023 est.)

Coal: *consumption:* 164,000 metric tons (2023 est.)
imports: 164,000 metric tons (2023 est.)

Petroleum: *refined petroleum consumption:* 40,000 bbl/day (2023 est.)
crude oil estimated reserves: 8 million barrels (2021 est.)

Natural gas: *consumption:* 157.25 million cubic meters (2023 est.)
imports: 157.25 million cubic meters (2023 est.)
proven reserves: 1.133 billion cubic meters (2021 est.)

Energy consumption per capita: 6.472 million Btu/person (2023 est.)
comparison ranking: 165

COMMUNICATIONS

Telephones - fixed lines: *total subscriptions:* 1,000 (2023 est.)
subscriptions per 100 inhabitants: (2023 est.) less than 1
comparison ranking: total subscriptions 217

Telephones - mobile cellular: *total subscriptions:* 16.4 million (2023 est.)
subscriptions per 100 inhabitants: 109 (2022 est.)
comparison ranking: total subscriptions 70

Broadcast media: state-run Office de Radiodiffusion et de Télévision du Benin (ORTB) operates a TV station with a wide broadcast reach; several privately owned TV stations broadcast from Cotonou; satellite TV subscription service is available; state-owned radio, under ORTB control, includes a national station supplemented by a number of regional stations; substantial number of privately owned radio stations; transmissions of a few international broadcasters are available on FM in Cotonou (2019)

Internet country code: .bj

Internet users: *percent of population:* 32% (2023 est.)

Broadband - fixed subscriptions: *total:* 24,000 (2023 est.)
subscriptions per 100 inhabitants: (2023 est.) less than 1
comparison ranking: total 163

TRANSPORTATION

Civil aircraft registration country code prefix: TY

Airports: 10 (2025)
comparison ranking: 159

Railways: *total:* 438 km (2014)
narrow gauge: 438 km (2014) 1.000-m gauge

Merchant marine: *total:* 6 (2023)
by type: other 6
comparison ranking: total 165

Ports: *total ports:* 1 (2024)
large: 0
medium: 1
small: 0
very small: 0
ports with oil terminals: 1
key ports: Cotonou

MILITARY AND SECURITY

Military and security forces: Beninese Armed Forces (Forces Armees Beninoises, FAB; aka Benin Defense Forces): Army, Air Force, National Navy, National Guard (aka Republican Guard)

Ministry of Interior and Public Security: Republican Police (Police Republicaine, DGPR) (2025)
note: FAB is under the Ministry of Defense and is responsible for external security and supporting the DGPR in maintaining internal security, which has

primary responsibility for enforcing law and maintaining order; the DGPR was formed in 2018 through a merger of police and gendarmes

Military expenditures: 0.7% of GDP (2024 est.)
0.5% of GDP (2023 est.)
0.7% of GDP (2022 est.)
0.7% of GDP (2021 est.)
0.5% of GDP (2020 est.)

Military and security service personnel strengths: estimated 10,000 active-duty Armed Forces (including National Guard) (2025)

Military equipment inventories and acquisitions: the FAB is equipped with a small mix of mostly older or secondhand French, Soviet-era, and US equipment; in recent years, the EU, France, and the US have provided it with limited amounts of newer military hardware such as armored vehicles and helicopters (2024)

Military service age and obligation: 18-30 years of age for voluntary and selective compulsory military service for men and women; conscript service is 18 months (2024)

Military - note: the Beninese Armed Forces (FAB) are responsible for defense against external aggression and may be required to assist in maintaining public order and internal security under conditions defined by the country's president; it may also participate in economic development projects
a key focus for the security forces of Benin is countering infiltrations into the country by terrorist groups tied to al-Qa'ida and the Islamic State of Iraq and ash-Sham (ISIS) operating just over the border from northern Benin in Burkina Faso and Niger; in 2022, the Benin Government said it was "at war" after suffering a series of attacks from these groups; later that same year, President TALON pledged to increase the size of the military, modernize military equipment, and establish forward operating bases; the military since 2022 has also deployed thousands of additional troops to the north of the country to better secure the border region; in addition, the FAB participates in the Multinational Joint Task Force (MNJTF) against Boko Haram and ISIS-West Africa in the general area of the Lake Chad Basin and along Nigeria's northeastern border (2025)

TERRORISM

Terrorist group(s): Terrorist group(s): Jama'at Nusrat al Islam wal Muslimeen (JNIM); Islamic State in the Greater Sahara (ISIS-GS); Boko Haram
note: details about the history, aims, leadership, organization, areas of operation, tactics, targets, weapons, size, and sources of support of the group(s) appear(s) in Appendix T

TRANSNATIONAL ISSUES

Refugees and internally displaced persons: *refugees:* 23,225 (2024 est.)

IDPs: 12,501 (2024 est.)

BERMUDA

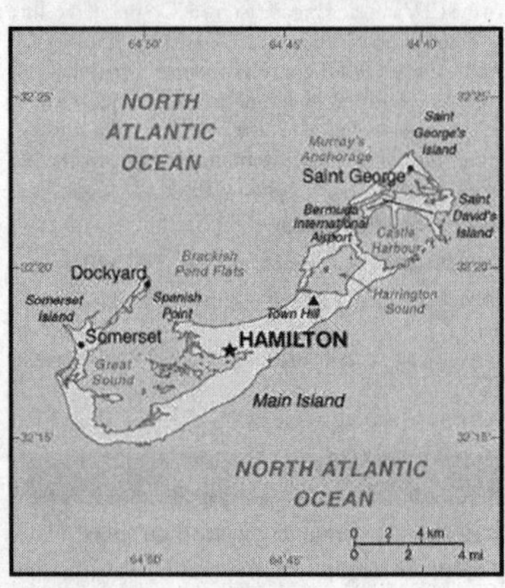

INTRODUCTION

Background: Bermuda was first settled in 1609 by shipwrecked English colonists heading for Virginia. Self-governing since 1620, Bermuda is the oldest and most populous of the British Overseas Territories. Vacationing on the island to escape North American winters first developed in Victorian times. Tourism continues to be important for the island's economy, although international business has overtaken it in recent years as Bermuda has developed into a highly successful offshore financial center. A referendum on independence from the UK was soundly defeated in 1995.

GEOGRAPHY

Location: North America, group of islands in the North Atlantic Ocean, east of South Carolina (US)

Geographic coordinates: 32 20 N, 64 45 W

Map references: North America

Area: *total:* 54 sq km
land: 54 sq km
water: 0 sq km
comparison ranking: total 229

Area - comparative: about one-third the size of Washington, D.C.

Land boundaries: *total:* 0 km

Coastline: 103 km

Maritime claims: *territorial sea:* 12 nm
exclusive economic zone: 200 nm
exclusive fishing zone: 200 nm

Climate: subtropical; mild, humid; gales, strong winds common in winter

Terrain: low hills separated by fertile depressions

Elevation: *highest point:* Town Hill 79 m
lowest point: Atlantic Ocean 0 m

Natural resources: limestone, pleasant climate fostering tourism

Land use: *agricultural land:* 5.6% (2022 est.)
arable land: 5.6% (2022 est.)
permanent crops: 0% (2022 est.)
permanent pasture: 0% (2022 est.)
forest: 18.5% (2022 est.)
other: 75.9% (2022 est.)

Irrigated land: NA

Population distribution: relatively even population distribution throughout

Natural hazards: hurricanes (June to November)

Geography - note: the archipelago consists of over 170 coral islands and islets with ample rainfall, as well as thousands of cays, but no rivers or freshwater lakes; some land was leased by the US Government from 1941 to 1995

PEOPLE AND SOCIETY

Population: *total:* 72,800 (2024 est.)
male: 35,401
female: 37,399
comparison rankings: total 202; male 202; female 201

Nationality: *noun:* Bermudian(s)
adjective: Bermudian

Ethnic groups: African descent 52%, White 31%, mixed 9%, Asian 4%, other 4% (2010 est.)

Languages: English (official), Portuguese

Religions: Protestant 46.2% (includes Anglican 15.8%, African Methodist Episcopal 8.6%, Seventh Day Adventist 6.7%, Pentecostal 3.5%, Methodist 2.7%, Presbyterian 2.0%, Church of God 1.6%, Baptist 1.2%, Salvation Army 1.1%, Brethren 1.0%, other Protestant 2.0%), Roman Catholic 14.5%, Jehovah's Witness 1.3%, other Christian 9.1%, Muslim 1%, other 3.9%, none 17.8%, unspecified 6.2% (2010 est.)

Age structure: *0-14 years:* 16.4% (male 6,133/female 5,817)
15-64 years: 60.9% (male 22,247/female 22,113)
65 years and over: 22.7% (2024 est.) (male 7,021/female 9,469)

Dependency ratios: *total dependency ratio:* 64.1 (2024 est.)
youth dependency ratio: 26.9 (2024 est.)
elderly dependency ratio: 37.2 (2024 est.)
potential support ratio: 2.7 (2024 est.)

Median age: *total:* 43.8 years (2024 est.)
male: 41.5 years
female: 46.3 years
comparison ranking: total 34

Population growth rate: 0.3% (2024 est.)
comparison ranking: 165

Birth rate: 10.9 births/1,000 population (2024 est.)
comparison ranking: 167

Death rate: 9.3 deaths/1,000 population (2024 est.)
comparison ranking: 50

Net migration rate: 1.4 migrant(s)/1,000 population (2024 est.)
comparison ranking: 59

Population distribution: relatively even population distribution throughout

Urbanization: *urban population:* 100% of total population (2023)
rate of urbanization: -0.2% annual rate of change (2020-25 est.)

Major urban areas - population: 10,000 HAMILTON (capital) (2018)

Sex ratio: *at birth:* 1.05 male(s)/female

0-14 years: 1.05 male(s)/female
15-64 years: 1.01 male(s)/female
65 years and over: 0.74 male(s)/female
total population: 0.95 male(s)/female (2024 est.)

Infant mortality rate: *total:* 2.1 deaths/1,000 live births (2024 est.)
male: 2.5 deaths/1,000 live births
female: 1.8 deaths/1,000 live births
comparison ranking: total 220

Life expectancy at birth: *total population:* 82.5 years (2024 est.)
male: 79.4 years
female: 85.7 years
comparison ranking: total population 29

Total fertility rate: 1.88 children born/woman (2024 est.)
comparison ranking: 125

Gross reproduction rate: 0.92 (2024 est.)

Drinking water source: *improved: urban:* 99.9% of population (2022 est.)
total: 99.9% of population (2022 est.)
unimproved: urban: 0.1% of population (2022 est.)
total: 0.1% of population (2022 est.)

Sanitation facility access: *improved: urban:* 99.9% of population (2022 est.)
total: 99.9% of population (2022 est.)
unimproved: urban: 0.1% of population (2022 est.)
total: 0.1% of population (2022 est.)

Currently married women (ages 15-49): 47.6% (2023 est.)

Education expenditure: 1.9% of GDP (2023 est.)
11.6% national budget (2024 est.)
comparison ranking: Education expenditure (% GDP) 185

School life expectancy (primary to tertiary education): *total:* 12 years (2023 est.)
male: 11 years (2023 est.)
female: 12 years (2023 est.)

ENVIRONMENT

Environmental issues: air pollution from vehicle emissions; scarce water resources; solid waste disposal; hazardous waste disposal; sewage disposal; overfishing; oil spills

Climate: subtropical; mild, humid; gales, strong winds common in winter

Urbanization: *urban population:* 100% of total population (2023)
rate of urbanization: -0.2% annual rate of change (2020-25 est.)

Carbon dioxide emissions: 577,000 metric tonnes of CO_2 (2023 est.)
from coal and metallurgical coke: 9 metric tonnes of CO_2 (2023 est.)
from petroleum and other liquids: 577,000 metric tonnes of CO_2 (2023 est.)
comparison ranking: total emissions 187

Waste and recycling: *municipal solid waste generated annually:* 82,000 tons (2024 est.)
percent of municipal solid waste recycled: 2% (2012 est.)

GOVERNMENT

Country name: *conventional long form:* none
conventional short form: Bermuda
former: Somers Islands
etymology: named after Juan de BERMUDEZ, an early 16th-century Spanish sea captain and the first European explorer of the archipelago

Government type: Overseas Territory of the UK with limited self-government; parliamentary democracy

Dependency status: overseas territory of the UK

Capital: *name:* Hamilton
geographic coordinates: 32 17 N, 64 47 W
time difference: UTC-4 (1 hour ahead of Washington, DC, during Standard Time)
daylight saving time: +1hr, begins second Sunday in March; ends first Sunday in November
etymology: named after Henry HAMILTON, who served as governor of Bermuda from 1788 to 1794

Administrative divisions: 9 parishes and 2 municipalities*; Devonshire, Hamilton, Hamilton*, Paget, Pembroke, Saint George*, Saint George's, Sandys, Smith's, Southampton, Warwick

Legal system: English common law

Constitution: *history:* several previous (dating to 1684); latest entered into force 8 June 1968 (Bermuda Constitution Order 1968)
amendment process: proposal procedure - NA; passage by an Order in Council in the UK

International law organization participation: has not submitted an ICJ jurisdiction declaration; non-party state to the ICCt

Citizenship: *citizenship by birth:* no
citizenship by descent only: at least one parent must be a citizen of the UK
dual citizenship recognized: yes
residency requirement for naturalization: 10 years

Suffrage: 18 years of age; universal

Executive branch: *chief of state:* King CHARLES III (since 8 September 2022); represented by Governor Andrew MURDOCH (since 23 January 2025)
head of government: Premier David BURT (since 19 July 2017)
cabinet: Cabinet nominated by the premier, approved by the governor
election/appointment process: the monarchy is hereditary; governor appointed by the monarch; following legislative elections, the governor usually appoints the leader of the majority party or majority coalition as the premier

Legislative branch: *legislature name:* Parliament
legislative structure: bicameral

Legislative branch - lower chamber: *chamber name:* House of Assembly
number of seats: 36 (directly elected)
electoral system: plurality/majority
scope of elections: full renewal
term in office: 5 years
most recent election date: 10/1/2020
parties elected and seats per party: PLP (30); OBA (6)
percentage of women in chamber: 20%
expected date of next election: 2025

Legislative branch - upper chamber: *chamber name:* Senate
number of seats: 11 (appointed)
term in office: 5 years
most recent election date: 2022
percentage of women in chamber: 63.6%
expected date of next election: 2027

Judicial branch: *highest court(s):* Court of Appeal (consists of the court president and at least 2 justices); Supreme Court (consists of the chief justice, 4 puisne judges, and 1 associate justice); the Judicial Committee of the Privy Council (in London) is the court of final appeal
judge selection and term of office: Court of Appeal justice appointed by the governor; justice tenure by individual appointment; Supreme Court judges nominated by the Judicial and Legal Services Commission and appointed by the governor; judge tenure based on terms of appointment
subordinate courts: commercial court (began in 2006); magistrates' courts

Political parties: Free Democratic Movement or FDM
One Bermuda Alliance or OBA
Progressive Labor Party or PLP

Diplomatic representation in the US: none (overseas territory of the UK)

Diplomatic representation from the US: *chief of mission:* Consul General Antoinette HURTADO (since 27 March 2025)
embassy: US Consulate Bermuda, 16 Middle Road, Devonshire, DV 03, Bermuda
mailing address: 5300 Hamilton Place, Washington, DC 20520-5300
telephone: (441) 295-1342
FAX: (441) 295-1592
email address and website: HamiltonConsulate@state.gov
https://bm.usconsulate.gov/
consulate(s) general: 16 Middle Road, Devonshire DV O3

International organization participation: Caricom (associate), ICC (NGOs), Interpol (subbureau), IOC, ITUC (NGOs), UPU, WCO

Independence: none (overseas territory of the UK)

National holiday: Bermuda Day, 24 May
note: formerly known as Victoria Day, Empire Day, and Commonwealth Day

Flag: *description:* a red field with the UK flag in the upper-left quadrant and the Bermudian coat of arms centered on the right half of the flag; the coat of arms is a white shield with a red lion on a green field, holding a scroll showing the sinking of the ship "Sea Venture"
history: the 1609 shipwreck of the "Sea Venture" led to the settling of Bermuda
note: Bermuda is the only British overseas territory that uses a red field on its flag; all others use blue

National symbol(s): red lion

National coat of arms: Bermuda's coat of arms was formally granted by Royal Warrant on 4 October 1910 but has been in use since at least 1624; the red lion is a symbol of Great Britain; the Latin motto under the coat of arms, *Quo Fata Ferunt*, means "Whither the Fates Carry [Us];" the ship is the *Sea Venture*, an English ship that was wrecked on then-uninhabited Bermuda in 1609

National anthem(s): *title:* "Hail to Bermuda"
lyrics/music: Bette JOHNS
history: serves as a local anthem
title: "God Save the King"
lyrics/music: unknown
history: official anthem, as a UK territory

National heritage: *total World Heritage Sites:* 1 (cultural); note - excerpted from the UK entry
selected World Heritage Site locales: Historic Town of St. George and Related Fortifications

ECONOMY

Economic overview: small, tourism- and construction-based, territorial-island economy; American import and tourist destination; known offshore banking hub; increasing inflation; major re-exportation and re-importation area

Real GDP (purchasing power parity): $6.808 billion (2024 est.)
$6.667 billion (2023 est.)
$6.355 billion (2022 est.)
note: data in 2021 dollars
comparison ranking: 172

Real GDP growth rate: 2.1% (2024 est.)
4.9% (2023 est.)
6.5% (2022 est.)
note: annual GDP % growth based on constant local currency
comparison ranking: 148

Real GDP per capita: $105,300 (2024 est.)
$103,100 (2023 est.)
$98,100 (2022 est.)
note: data in 2021 dollars
comparison ranking: 8

GDP (official exchange rate): $8.98 billion (2024 est.)
note: data in current dollars at official exchange rate

Inflation rate (consumer prices): 2.8% (2022 est.)
1.4% (2021 est.)
0% (2020 est.)
note: annual % change based on consumer prices
comparison ranking: 79

GDP - composition, by sector of origin: *agriculture:* 0.2% (2023 est.)
industry: 4.6% (2023 est.)
services: 91.5% (2023 est.)
note: figures may not total 100% due to non-allocated consumption not captured in sector-reported data
comparison rankings: agriculture 197; industry 205; services 2

GDP - composition, by end use: *household consumption:* 45.6% (2024 est.)
government consumption: 11% (2024 est.)
investment in fixed capital: 11.3% (2024 est.)
investment in inventories: 0% (2024 est.)
exports of goods and services: 56.3% (2024 est.)
imports of goods and services: -24.2% (2024 est.)
note: figures may not total 100% due to rounding or gaps in data collection

Agricultural products: bananas, vegetables, citrus, flowers; dairy products, honey

Industries: international business, tourism, light manufacturing

Industrial production growth rate: -3.6% (2023 est.)
note: annual % change in industrial value added based on constant local currency
comparison ranking: 172

Remittances: 23.7% of GDP (2023 est.)
22.3% of GDP (2022 est.)
22.7% of GDP (2021 est.)
note: personal transfers and compensation between resident and non-resident individuals/households/entities

Budget: *revenues:* $999.2 million (2017 est.)
expenditures: $1.176 billion (2017 est.)

Current account balance: $1.32 billion (2023 est.)
$1.135 billion (2022 est.)
$962.258 million (2021 est.)
note: balance of payments - net trade and primary/secondary income in current dollars
comparison ranking: 56

Exports: $1.599 billion (2023 est.)
$1.425 billion (2022 est.)
$1.136 billion (2021 est.)
note: balance of payments - exports of goods and services in current dollars
comparison ranking: 172

Exports - partners: Germany 40%, South Africa 38%, Netherlands 15%, USA 2%, Angola 2% (2023)
note: top five export partners based on percentage share of exports

Exports - commodities: crude petroleum, ships, aircraft, liquor, railway cargo containers (2023)
note: top five export commodities based on value in dollars

Imports: $2.3 billion (2023 est.)
$2.235 billion (2022 est.)
$1.925 billion (2021 est.)
note: balance of payments - imports of goods and services in current dollars
comparison ranking: 172

Imports - partners: USA 38%, Cyprus 31%, UK 6%, China 6%, Canada 4% (2023)
note: top five import partners based on percentage share of imports

Imports - commodities: ships, refined petroleum, railway cargo containers, packaged medicine, cars (2023)
note: top five import commodities based on value in dollars

Exchange rates: Bermudian dollars (BMD) per US dollar -

Exchange rates: 1 (2024 est.)
1 (2023 est.)
1 (2022 est.)
1 (2021 est.)
1 (2020 est.)

ENERGY

Electricity access: *electrification - total population:* 100% (2022 est.)

Electricity: *installed generating capacity:* 172,000 kW (2023 est.)
consumption: 590.38 million kWh (2023 est.)
transmission/distribution losses: 43.172 million kWh (2023 est.)
comparison rankings: installed generating capacity 177; consumption 171; transmission/distribution losses 36

Electricity generation sources: *fossil fuels:* 99% of total installed capacity (2023 est.)
biomass and waste: 1% of total installed capacity (2023 est.)

Coal: *consumption:* 4 metric tons (2023 est.)
imports: 4 metric tons (2023 est.)

Petroleum: *refined petroleum consumption:* 4,000 bbl/day (2023 est.)

Energy consumption per capita: 122.737 million Btu/person (2023 est.)
comparison ranking: 32

COMMUNICATIONS

Telephones - fixed lines: *total subscriptions:* 25,000 (2021 est.)
subscriptions per 100 inhabitants: 39 (2022 est.)
comparison ranking: total subscriptions 170

Telephones - mobile cellular: *total subscriptions:* 68,000 (2021 est.)
subscriptions per 100 inhabitants: 106 (2021 est.)
comparison ranking: total subscriptions 201

Broadcast media: 3 TV stations; cable and satellite TV subscription services are available; roughly 13 radio stations operating

Internet country code: .bm

Internet users: *percent of population:* 98% (2017 est.)

Broadband - fixed subscriptions: *total:* 23,000 (2022 est.)
subscriptions per 100 inhabitants: 36 (2022 est.)
comparison ranking: total 167

TRANSPORTATION

Civil aircraft registration country code prefix: VP-B

Airports: 1 (2025)
comparison ranking: 232

Merchant marine: *total:* 122 (2023)
by type: container ship 15, oil tanker 8, other 99
comparison ranking: total 81

Ports: *total ports:* 4 (2024)
large: 0
medium: 1
small: 2
very small: 0
size unknown: 1
ports with oil terminals: 3
key ports: Freeport, Hamilton, Ireland Island, St. George

MILITARY AND SECURITY

Military and security forces: Royal Bermuda Regiment; Bermuda Police Service (2025)
note: the Royal Bermuda Regiment (aka "The Regiment") includes the Royal Bermuda Regiment Coast Guard

Military and security service personnel strengths: the Royal Bermuda Regiment has about 350 troops (2025)

Military equipment inventories and acquisitions: the Regiment is equipped with small arms (2024)

Military service age and obligation: men and women who are Commonwealth citizens and 18-45 years of age can volunteer for the Bermuda Regiment; service is for a minimum period of three years and two months from the date of enlistment; after completing their initial service, soldiers in the Regiment can choose to extend their service (2025)

Military - note: defense is the responsibility of the UK; the Royal Bermuda Regiment's responsibilities include maritime security of Bermuda's inshore waters, search and rescue, ceremonial duties, humanitarian/disaster assistance, security of key installations, and assisting the Bermuda Police with maintaining public order; it includes explosive ordnance disposal, diver, maritime, security police, and support units (2025)

BHUTAN

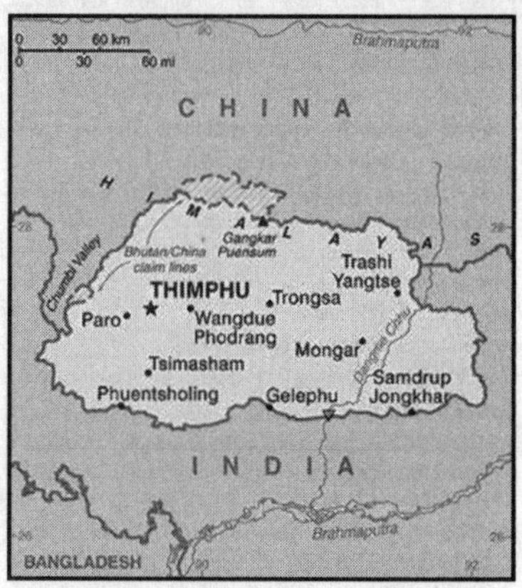

INTRODUCTION

Background: After Britain's victory in the 1865 Duar War, Britain and Bhutan signed the Treaty of Sinchulu, under which Bhutan would receive an annual subsidy in exchange for ceding land to British India. Ugyen WANGCHUCK – who had served as the de facto ruler of an increasingly unified Bhutan and had improved relations with the British toward the end of the 19th century – was named king in 1907. Three years later, a treaty was signed whereby the British agreed not to interfere in Bhutanese internal affairs, and Bhutan allowed Britain to direct its foreign affairs. Bhutan negotiated a similar arrangement with independent India in 1949. The Indo-Bhutanese Treaty of Friendship returned to Bhutan a small piece of the territory annexed by the British, formalized the annual subsidies the country received, and defined India's responsibilities in defense and foreign relations. Under a succession of modernizing monarchs beginning in the 1950s, Bhutan joined the UN in 1971 and slowly continued its engagement beyond its borders.

In 2005, King Jigme Singye WANGCHUCK unveiled the draft of Bhutan's first constitution – which introduced major democratic reforms – and held a national referendum for its approval. The King abdicated the throne in 2006 in favor of his son, Jigme Khesar Namgyel WANGCHUCK. In 2007, India and Bhutan renegotiated their treaty, eliminating the clause that stated that Bhutan would be "guided by" India in conducting its foreign policy, although Thimphu continues to coordinate closely with New Delhi. In 2008, Bhutan held its first parliamentary election in accordance with the constitution. Bhutan experienced a peaceful turnover of power following a parliamentary election in 2013, which resulted in the defeat of the incumbent party. In 2018, the incumbent party again lost the parliamentary election. In 2024, of the more than 100,000 ethnic Nepali – predominantly Lhotshampa – refugees who fled or were forced out of Bhutan in the 1990s, about 6,500 remain displaced in Nepal.

GEOGRAPHY

Location: Southern Asia, between China and India

Geographic coordinates: 27 30 N, 90 30 E

Map references: Asia

Area: *total:* 38,394 sq km
land: 38,394 sq km
water: 0 sq km
comparison ranking: total 136

Area - comparative: slightly larger than Maryland; about one-half the size of Indiana

Land boundaries: *total:* 1,136 km
border countries (2): China 477 km; India 659 km

Coastline: 0 km (landlocked)

Maritime claims: none (landlocked)

Climate: varies; tropical in southern plains; cool winters and hot summers in central valleys; severe winters and cool summers in Himalayas

Terrain: mostly mountainous with some fertile valleys and savanna

Elevation: *highest point:* Gangkar Puensum 7,570 m
lowest point: Drangeme Chhu 97 m
mean elevation: 2,220 m

Natural resources: timber, hydropower, gypsum, calcium carbonate

Land use: *agricultural land:* 12.8% (2022 est.)
arable land: 1.8% (2022 est.)
permanent crops: 0.2% (2022 est.)
permanent pasture: 10.8% (2022 est.)
forest: 71.6% (2022 est.)
other: 15.6% (2022 est.)

Irrigated land: 320 sq km (2012)

Natural hazards: violent storms from the Himalayas are the source of the country's Bhutanese name, which translates as Land of the Thunder Dragon; frequent landslides during the rainy season

Geography - note: landlocked; strategic location between China and India; controls several key Himalayan mountain passes

PEOPLE AND SOCIETY

Population: *total:* 884,546 (2024 est.)
male: 457,665
female: 426,881
comparison rankings: total 165; male 163; female 165

Nationality: *noun:* Bhutanese (singular and plural)
adjective: Bhutanese

Ethnic groups: Ngalop (also known as Bhote) 50%, ethnic Nepali 35% (predominantly Lhotshampas), indigenous or migrant tribes 15%

Languages: Sharchopkha 28%, Dzongkha (official) 24%, Lhotshamkha 22%, other 26% (includes foreign languages) (2005 est.)

Religions: Lamaistic Buddhist 75.3%, Indian- and Nepali-influenced Hinduism 22.1%, other 2.6% (2005 est.)

Age structure: *0-14 years:* 23.1% (male 104,771/female 99,981)
15-64 years: 70.2% (male 322,497/female 298,324)
65 years and over: 6.7% (2024 est.) (male 30,397/female 28,576)

Dependency ratios: *total dependency ratio:* 42.5 (2024 est.)
youth dependency ratio: 33 (2024 est.)
elderly dependency ratio: 9.5 (2024 est.)
potential support ratio: 10.5 (2024 est.)

Median age: *total:* 30.7 years (2024 est.)
male: 31.1 years
female: 30.3 years
comparison ranking: total 134

Population growth rate: 0.95% (2024 est.)
comparison ranking: 98

Birth rate: 15.3 births/1,000 population (2024 est.)
comparison ranking: 106

Death rate: 5.9 deaths/1,000 population (2024 est.)
comparison ranking: 158

Net migration rate: 0 migrant(s)/1,000 population (2024 est.)
comparison ranking: 92

Urbanization: *urban population:* 44.4% of total population (2023)
rate of urbanization: 2.52% annual rate of change (2020-25 est.)

Major urban areas - population: 203,000 THIMPHU (capital) (2018)

Sex ratio: *at birth:* 1.05 male(s)/female
0-14 years: 1.05 male(s)/female
15-64 years: 1.08 male(s)/female
65 years and over: 1.06 male(s)/female
total population: 1.07 male(s)/female (2024 est.)

Maternal mortality ratio: 47 deaths/100,000 live births (2023 est.)
comparison ranking: 97

Infant mortality rate: *total:* 24.3 deaths/1,000 live births (2024 est.)
male: 24.6 deaths/1,000 live births
female: 23.9 deaths/1,000 live births
comparison ranking: total 63

Life expectancy at birth: *total population:* 73.7 years (2024 est.)
male: 72.5 years
female: 75 years
comparison ranking: total population 147

Total fertility rate: 1.76 children born/woman (2024 est.)
comparison ranking: 147

Gross reproduction rate: 0.86 (2024 est.)

Drinking water source: *improved: urban:* 99.5% of population (2022 est.)
rural: 98.8% of population (2022 est.)
total: 99.1% of population (2022 est.)
unimproved: urban: 0.5% of population (2022 est.)
rural: 1.2% of population (2022 est.)
total: 0.9% of population (2022 est.)

Health expenditure: 3.8% of GDP (2021)
6.7% of national budget (2022 est.)

Physician density: 0.55 physicians/1,000 population (2022)

Hospital bed density: 2.2 beds/1,000 population (2021 est.)

Sanitation facility access: *improved: urban:* 91.1% of population (2022 est.)
rural: 85.5% of population (2022 est.)

total: 87.9% of population (2022 est.)
unimproved: urban: 8.9% of population (2022 est.)
rural: 14.5% of population (2022 est.)
total: 12.1% of population (2022 est.)

Obesity - adult prevalence rate: 6.4% (2016)
comparison ranking: 168

Alcohol consumption per capita: *total:* 0.07 liters of pure alcohol (2019 est.)
beer: 0.01 liters of pure alcohol (2019 est.)
wine: 0.05 liters of pure alcohol (2019 est.)
spirits: 0 liters of pure alcohol (2019 est.)
other alcohols: 0 liters of pure alcohol (2019 est.)
comparison ranking: total 179

Tobacco use: *total:* 18.5% (2025 est.)
male: 26.1% (2025 est.)
female: 9.8% (2025 est.)
comparison ranking: total 80

Currently married women (ages 15-49): 62.8% (2023 est.)

Education expenditure: 5.8% of GDP (2023 est.)
17.2% national budget (2024 est.)
comparison ranking: Education expenditure (% GDP) 34

Literacy: *total population:* 67% (2017 est.)
male: 75% (2017 est.)
female: 57% (2017 est.)

School life expectancy (primary to tertiary education): *total:* 13 years (2022 est.)
male: 12 years (2022 est.)
female: 14 years (2022 est.)

ENVIRONMENT

Environmental issues: soil erosion; limited access to potable water; wildlife conservation; industrial pollution; waste disposal

International environmental agreements: *party to:* Biodiversity, Climate Change, Climate Change-Kyoto Protocol, Climate Change-Paris Agreement, Desertification, Endangered Species, Hazardous Wastes, Nuclear Test Ban, Ozone Layer Protection, Wetlands
signed, but not ratified: Law of the Sea

Climate: varies; tropical in southern plains; cool winters and hot summers in central valleys; severe winters and cool summers in Himalayas

Urbanization: *urban population:* 44.4% of total population (2023)
rate of urbanization: 2.52% annual rate of change (2020-25 est.)

Carbon dioxide emissions: 733,000 metric tonnes of CO2 (2023 est.)
from coal and metallurgical coke: 241,000 metric tonnes of CO2 (2023 est.)
from petroleum and other liquids: 492,000 metric tonnes of CO2 (2023 est.)
comparison ranking: total emissions 178

Particulate matter emissions: 26.4 micrograms per cubic meter (2019 est.)

Waste and recycling: *municipal solid waste generated annually:* 111,300 tons (2024 est.)
percent of municipal solid waste recycled: 1.7% (2022 est.)

Total water withdrawal: *municipal:* 17 million cubic meters (2022 est.)
industrial: 3 million cubic meters (2022 est.)
agricultural: 318 million cubic meters (2022 est.)

Total renewable water resources: 78 billion cubic meters (2022 est.)

GOVERNMENT

Country name: *conventional long form:* Kingdom of Bhutan
conventional short form: Bhutan
local long form: Druk Gyalkhap
local short form: Druk Yul
etymology: name may derive from the Sanskrit words *bhota*, the name for Tibet, and *anta*, meaning "end" – a reference to Bhutan's location at the southernmost end of Tibet; the local Dzongkha name Druk Yul means "Land of the Dragon"

Government type: constitutional monarchy

Capital: *name:* Thimphu
geographic coordinates: 27 28 N, 89 38 E
time difference: UTC+6 (11 hours ahead of Washington, DC, during Standard Time)
etymology: the origins of the name are unclear; the traditional explanation, dating to the 14th century, is that *thim* means "dissolve" and *phu* means "rock," in reference to a local deity who dissolved before a traveler's eyes, becoming a part of the rock on which the present city stands

Administrative divisions: 20 districts (*dzongkhag*, singular and plural); Bumthang, Chhukha, Dagana, Gasa, Haa, Lhuentse, Mongar, Paro, Pemagatshel, Punakha, Samdrup Jongkhar, Samtse, Sarpang, Thimphu, Trashigang, Trashi Yangtse, Trongsa, Tsirang, Wangdue Phodrang, Zhemgang

Legal system: civil law based on Buddhist religious law

Constitution: *history:* previous governing documents were various royal decrees; first constitution drafted November 2001 to March 2005, ratified 18 July 2008
amendment process: proposed as a motion by simple majority vote in a joint session of Parliament; passage requires at least a three-fourths majority vote in a joint session of the next Parliament and assent by the king

International law organization participation: has not submitted an ICJ jurisdiction declaration; non-party state to the ICCt

Citizenship: *citizenship by birth:* no
citizenship by descent only: the father must be a citizen of Bhutan
dual citizenship recognized: no
residency requirement for naturalization: 10 years

Suffrage: 18 years of age; universal

Executive branch: *chief of state:* King Jigme Khesar Namgyel WANGCHUCK (since 14 December 2006)
head of government: Prime Minister Tshering TOBGAY (since 28 January 2024)
cabinet: Council of Ministers or Lhengye Zhungtshog members nominated by the monarch in consultation with the prime minister and approved by the National Assembly; members serve 5-year terms
election/appointment process: the monarchy is hereditary but can be removed by a two-thirds vote of Parliament; leader of the majority party in Parliament is nominated as the prime minister, appointed by the monarch

Legislative branch: *legislature name:* Parliament (Chi Tshog)
legislative structure: bicameral

Legislative branch - lower chamber: *chamber name:* National Assembly (Tshogdu)
number of seats: 47 (all directly elected)
electoral system: plurality/majority
scope of elections: full renewal
term in office: 5 years
most recent election date: 1/9/2024
parties elected and seats per party: People's Democratic Party (PDP) (30); Bhutan Tendrel Party (BTP) (17)
percentage of women in chamber: 4.3%
expected date of next election: January 2029

Legislative branch - upper chamber: *chamber name:* National Council (Gyelyong Tshogde)
number of seats: 25 (20 directly elected; 5 appointed)
electoral system: plurality/majority
scope of elections: full renewal
term in office: 5 years
most recent election date: 4/20/2023
percentage of women in chamber: 12%
expected date of next election: April 2028

Judicial branch: *highest court(s):* Supreme Court (consists of the chief justice and 4 associate justices)
judge selection and term of office: Supreme Court chief justice appointed by the monarch on the advice of the National Judicial Commission, a 4-member body to include the Legislative Committee of the National Assembly, the attorney general, the Chief Justice of Bhutan and the senior Associate Justice of the Supreme Court; other judges (drangpons) appointed by the monarch from among the High Court judges selected by the National Judicial Commission; chief justice serves a 5-year term or until reaching age 65 years, whichever is earlier; the 4 other judges serve 10-year terms or until age 65, whichever is earlier
subordinate courts: High Court (first appellate court); District or Dzongkhag Courts; sub-district or Dungkhag Courts
note: the Supreme Court has sole jurisdiction in constitutional matters

Political parties: Bhutan Peace and Prosperity Party (Druk Phuensum Tshogpa) or DPT
Bhutan Tendrel Party or BTP
Druk Thuendrel Tshogpa or DTT
People's Democratic Party or PDP
United Party of Bhutan (Druk Nyamrup Tshogpa) or DNT

Diplomatic representation in the US: *consulate(s) general:* 343 East, 43rd Street, New York, NY 10017
telephone: [1] (212) 682-2371
FAX: [1] (212) 661-0551
email address and website: consulate.pmbny@mfa.gov.bt
https://www.mfa.gov. bt/pmbny/
note: Bhutan and the United States do not have diplomatic relations, but the two countries established consular relations on 23 July 1986; the Consulate General of the Kingdom of Bhutan was established in New York with an officer from the Permanent Mission of the Kingdom of Bhutan to the United Nations holding dual accreditation as the Consul General with consular jurisdiction in the US; Phuntsho NORBU has served as the Consul General since October 2022 and is the Deputy Permanent Representative to the UN

Diplomatic representation from the US: *note:* Although Bhutan and the United States have never established formal diplomatic relations, the two countries maintain informal relations via the U.S. Embassy in New Delhi, India, and Bhutan's Mission to the United Nations in New York

International organization participation: ADB, BIMSTEC, CP, FAO, G-77, IBRD, ICAO, IDA, IFAD, IFC, IMF, Interpol, IOC, IOM (observer), IPU, ISO (correspondent), ITSO, ITU, MIGA,

NAM, OPCW, SAARC, SACEP, UN, UNCTAD, UNESCO, UNIDO, UNISFA, UNTSO, UNWTO, UPU, WCO, WHO, WIPO, WMO, WTO (observer)

Independence: 17 December 1907 (became a unified kingdom under its first hereditary king); 8 August 1949 (Treaty of Friendship with India maintains Bhutanese independence)

National holiday: National Day (Ugyen WANGCHUCK became first hereditary king), 17 December (1907)

Flag: *description:* divided diagonally from the lower-left corner to the upper-right corner; the upper triangle is yellow, and the lower triangle is dark orange; centered along the dividing line is a large, stylized black-and-white dragon facing to the right; the dragon is called the Druk (Thunder Dragon) and is the national emblem
meaning: white stands for purity, and the jewels in the dragon's claws symbolize wealth; the background colors represent the spiritual and secular powers in Bhutan, with orange standing for Buddhism and yellow for the ruling dynasty

National symbol(s): mythical thunder dragon *(druk)*

National color(s): orange, yellow

National anthem(s): *title:* "Druk tsendhen" (The Thunder Dragon Kingdom)
lyrics/music: Gyaldun Dasho Thinley DORJI/Aku TONGMI
history: adopted 1953

ECONOMY

Economic overview: hydropower investments spurring economic development; Gross National Happiness economy; sharp poverty declines; low inflation; strong monetary and fiscal policies; stable currency; fairly resilient response to COVID-19; key economic and strategic relations with India; climate vulnerabilities

Real GDP (purchasing power parity): $11.517 billion (2023 est.)
$10.981 billion (2022 est.)
$10.437 billion (2021 est.)
note: data in 2021 dollars
comparison ranking: 165

Real GDP growth rate: 4.9% (2023 est.)
5.2% (2022 est.)
4.4% (2021 est.)
note: annual GDP % growth based on constant local currency
comparison ranking: 48

Real GDP per capita: $14,600 (2023 est.)
$14,100 (2022 est.)
$13,500 (2021 est.)
note: data in 2021 dollars
comparison ranking: 125

GDP (official exchange rate): $3.019 billion (2023 est.)
note: data in current dollars at official exchange rate

Inflation rate (consumer prices): 2.8% (2024 est.)
4.2% (2023 est.)
5.6% (2022 est.)
note: annual % change based on consumer prices
comparison ranking: 78

GDP - composition, by sector of origin: *agriculture:* 15% (2023 est.)
industry: 29.6% (2023 est.)
services: 52.7% (2023 est.)
note: figures may not total 100% due to non-allocated consumption not captured in sector-reported data
comparison rankings: agriculture 56; industry 59; services 130

GDP - composition, by end use: *household consumption:* 59.4% (2023 est.)
government consumption: 20.3% (2023 est.)
investment in fixed capital: 44.5% (2023 est.)
investment in inventories: 0.7% (2023 est.)
exports of goods and services: 28.3% (2023 est.)
imports of goods and services: -53.2% (2023 est.)
note: figures may not total 100% due to rounding or gaps in data collection

Agricultural products: rice, milk, potatoes, root vegetables, maize, oranges, areca nuts, chillies/peppers, pumpkins/squash, carrots/turnips (2023)
note: top ten agricultural products based on tonnage

Industries: cement, wood products, processed fruits, alcoholic beverages, calcium carbide, tourism

Industrial production growth rate: 0% (2023 est.)
note: annual % change in industrial value added based on constant local currency
comparison ranking: 137

Labor force: 406,500 (2024 est.)
note: number of people ages 15 or older who are employed or seeking work
comparison ranking: 161

Unemployment rate: 2.9% (2024 est.)
3.2% (2023 est.)
6% (2022 est.)
note: % of labor force seeking employment
comparison ranking: 35

Youth unemployment rate (ages 15-24): *total:* 13.8% (2024 est.)
male: 11.2% (2024 est.)
female: 16.5% (2024 est.)
note: % of labor force ages 15-24 seeking employment
comparison ranking: total 90

Population below poverty line: 12.4% (2022 est.)
note: % of population with income below national poverty line

Gini Index coefficient - distribution of family income: 28.5 (2022 est.)
note: index (0-100) of income distribution; higher values represent greater inequality
comparison ranking: 131

Household income or consumption by percentage share: *lowest 10%:* 3.6% (2022 est.)
highest 10%: 22.7% (2022 est.)
note: % share of income accruing to lowest and highest 10% of population

Remittances: 3.6% of GDP (2023 est.)
3.3% of GDP (2022 est.)
2.6% of GDP (2021 est.)
note: personal transfers and compensation between resident and non-resident individuals/households/entities

Budget: *revenues:* $740.328 million (2020 est.)
expenditures: $802.177 million (2020 est.)
note: central government revenues and expenses (excluding grants/extrabudgetary units/social security funds) converted to US dollars at average official exchange rate for year indicated

Public debt: 111% of GDP (2020 est.)
note: central government debt as a % of GDP
comparison ranking: 14

Taxes and other revenues: 12.3% (of GDP) (2020 est.)
note: central government tax revenue as a % of GDP
comparison ranking: 112

Current account balance: -$669.766 million (2024 est.)
-$963.122 million (2023 est.)
-$805.723 million (2022 est.)
note: balance of payments - net trade and primary/secondary income in current dollars
comparison ranking: 118

Exports: $944.391 million (2024 est.)
$867.871 million (2023 est.)
$791.342 million (2022 est.)
note: balance of payments - exports of goods and services in current dollars
comparison ranking: 184

Exports - partners: India 92%, Italy 4%, Indonesia 1%, China 1%, Singapore 0% (2023)
note: top five export partners based on percentage share of exports

Exports - commodities: iron alloys, aircraft, dolomite, semi-finished iron, cement (2023)
note: top five export commodities based on value in dollars

Imports: $1.513 billion (2024 est.)
$1.77 billion (2023 est.)
$1.581 billion (2022 est.)
note: balance of payments - imports of goods and services in current dollars
comparison ranking: 183

Imports - partners: India 82%, Singapore 8%, China 5%, Thailand 2%, Indonesia 1% (2023)
note: top five import partners based on percentage share of imports

Imports - commodities: refined petroleum, gold, plastics, broadcasting equipment, iron reductions (2023)
note: top five import commodities based on value in dollars

Reserves of foreign exchange and gold: $941.018 million (2024 est.)
$654.481 million (2023 est.)
$825.755 million (2022 est.)
note: holdings of gold (year-end prices)/foreign exchange/special drawing rights in current dollars
comparison ranking: 145

Debt - external: $2.827 billion (2023 est.)
note: present value of external debt in current US dollars
comparison ranking: 87

Exchange rates: ngultrum (BTN) per US dollar -

Exchange rates: 83.669 (2024 est.)
82.599 (2023 est.)
78.604 (2022 est.)
73.918 (2021 est.)
74.1 (2020 est.)

ENERGY

Electricity access: *electrification - total population:* 100% (2022 est.)

Electricity: *installed generating capacity:* 2.344 million kW (2023 est.)
consumption: 11.914 billion kWh (2023 est.)
exports: 6 billion kWh (2020 est.)
imports: 834.7 million kWh (2023 est.)
transmission/distribution losses: 86.681 million kWh (2023 est.)
comparison rankings: installed generating capacity 116; consumption 100; exports 38; imports 82; transmission/distribution losses 43

Electricity generation sources: *hydroelectricity:* 100% of total installed capacity (2023 est.)

Coal: *production:* 4,000 metric tons (2023 est.)
consumption: 105,000 metric tons (2023 est.)
exports: 54 metric tons (2023 est.)
imports: 122,000 metric tons (2023 est.)

Petroleum: *refined petroleum consumption:* 4,000 bbl/day (2023 est.)

Energy consumption per capita: 64.082 million Btu/person (2023 est.)
comparison ranking: 79

COMMUNICATIONS

Telephones - fixed lines: *total subscriptions:* 18,000 (2023 est.)
subscriptions per 100 inhabitants: 2 (2023 est.)
comparison ranking: total subscriptions 174

Telephones - mobile cellular: *total subscriptions:* 752,000 (2023 est.)
subscriptions per 100 inhabitants: 95 (2022 est.)
comparison ranking: total subscriptions 169

Broadcast media: state-owned TV station established in 1999; cable TV service offers dozens of Indian and other international channels; first radio station, privately launched in 1973, is now state-owned; 5 private radio stations are currently broadcasting (2012)

Internet country code: .bt

Internet users: *percent of population:* 88% (2023 est.)

Broadband - fixed subscriptions: *total:* 10,000 (2023 est.)
subscriptions per 100 inhabitants: 1 (2023 est.)
comparison ranking: total 183

TRANSPORTATION

Civil aircraft registration country code prefix: A5

Airports: 4 (2025)
comparison ranking: 180

Heliports: 8 (2025)
comparison ranking: 84

MILITARY AND SECURITY

Military and security forces: Royal Bhutan Army (RBA; includes Royal Bodyguard of Bhutan, or RBG, and an air wing); National Militia

Ministry of Home and Cultural Affairs: Royal Bhutan Police (2025)

Military and security service personnel strengths: estimated 7-8,000 active Royal Bhutan Army (2025)

Military equipment inventories and acquisitions: the Royal Bhutan Army is lightly armed; it has a small amount of heavy equipment, such as armored cars and helicopters, originating from India and Thailand (2024)

Military service age and obligation: 18 years of age for voluntary military service for men and women; no conscription; militia training is compulsory for males aged 20-25, over a 3-year period (2023)
note: in 2021, the Royal Bhutan Army graduated from a year-long training course the first batch of 150 women to be allowed to serve in combat roles; previously, women were allowed to serve in medical and other non-combat roles

Military deployments: 190 Central African Republic (MINUSCA) (2024)

Military - note: the Army is responsible for external threats but also has some internal security functions such as conducting counterinsurgency operations, guarding forests, and providing security for prominent persons; Bhutan's closest security partner is India; under the 2007 India-Bhutan Friendship Treaty, both countries agreed to cooperate closely on issues relating to their national interests (2025)

TRANSNATIONAL ISSUES

Refugees and internally displaced persons: IDPs: 138 (2024 est.)

BOLIVIA

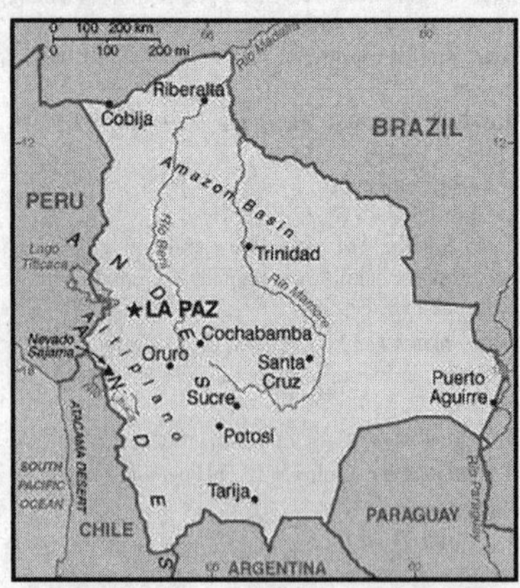

INTRODUCTION

Background: Bolivia, named after independence fighter Simón BOLÍVAR, broke away from Spanish rule in 1825. Much of its subsequent history has consisted of a series of coups and countercoups, with the last coup occurring in 1980. Democratic civilian rule was established in 1982, but leaders have faced problems of deep-seated poverty, social unrest, and illegal drug production.

In 2005, Bolivians elected Movement Toward Socialism leader Evo MORALES as president – by the widest margin of any leader since 1982 – after he ran on a promise to change the country's traditional political class and empower the poor and indigenous majority. In 2009 and 2014, MORALES easily won reelection, and his party maintained control of the legislative branch. In 2016, MORALES narrowly lost a referendum to approve a constitutional amendment that would have allowed him to compete in the 2019 presidential election. A subsequent Supreme Court ruling stating that term limits violate human rights provided the justification for MORALES to run despite the referendum, but rising violence, pressure from the military, and widespread allegations of electoral fraud ultimately forced him to flee the country. An interim government, led by President Jeanine AÑEZ Chávez, held new elections in 2020, and Luis Alberto ARCE Catacora was elected president.

GEOGRAPHY

Location: Central South America, southwest of Brazil

Geographic coordinates: 17 00 S, 65 00 W

Map references: South America

Area: *total:* 1,098,581 sq km
land: 1,083,301 sq km
water: 15,280 sq km
comparison ranking: total 29

Area - comparative: slightly less than three times the size of Montana

Land boundaries: *total:* 7,252 km
border countries (5): Argentina 942 km; Brazil 3,403 km; Chile 942 km; Paraguay 753 km; Peru 1,212 km

Coastline: 0 km (landlocked)

Maritime claims: none (landlocked)

Climate: varies with altitude; humid and tropical to cold and semiarid

Terrain: rugged Andes Mountains with a highland plateau (Altiplano), hills, lowland plains of the Amazon Basin

Elevation: *highest point:* Nevado Sajama 6,542 m
lowest point: Rio Paraguay 90 m
mean elevation: 1,192 m

Natural resources: lithium, tin, natural gas, petroleum, zinc, tungsten, antimony, silver, iron, lead, gold, timber, hydropower

Land use: *agricultural land:* 35.8% (2022 est.)
arable land: 5.1% (2022 est.)
permanent crops: 0.2% (2022 est.)
permanent pasture: 30.5% (2022 est.)
forest: 46.5% (2022 est.)
other: 17.6% (2022 est.)

Irrigated land: 2,972 sq km (2017)

Major lakes (area sq km): *fresh water lake(s):* Lago Titicaca (shared with Peru) - 8,030 sq km
salt water lake(s): Lago Poopo - 1,340 sq km

Major watersheds (area sq km): Atlantic Ocean drainage: Amazon (6,145,186 sq km), Paraná (2,582,704 sq km)

Major aquifers: Amazon Basin

Population distribution: a high-altitude plain in the west between two cordillera of the Andes, known as the Altiplano, is the focal area for most of the population; a dense settlement pattern is also found in and around the city of Santa Cruz, located on the eastern side of the Andes

Natural hazards: flooding in the northeast (March to April)
volcanism: volcanic activity in Andes Mountains on the border with Chile; historically active volcanoes in this region are Irruputuncu (5,163 m), which last erupted in 1995, and the Olca-Paruma volcanic complex (5,762 m to 5,167 m)

Geography - note: landlocked; shares control of Lago Titicaca, world's highest navigable lake (elevation 3,805 m), with Peru

PEOPLE AND SOCIETY

Population: *total:* 12,311,974 (2024 est.)
male: 6,192,774
female: 6,119,200
comparison rankings: total 80; male 81; female 80

Nationality: *noun:* Bolivian(s)
adjective: Bolivian

Ethnic groups: Mestizo (mixed White and Indigenous ancestry) 68%, Indigenous 20%, White 5%, Cholo/Chola 2%, African descent 1%, other 1%, unspecified 3%; 44% other Indigenous group, predominantly Quechua or Aymara (2009 est.)
note: results among surveys vary based on the wording of the ethnicity question and the available response choices; the 2001 national census did not provide "Mestizo" as a response choice, resulting in a much higher proportion of respondents identifying themselves as belonging to one of the available indigenous ethnicity choices; the use of "Mestizo" and "Cholo" varies among response choices in surveys, with surveys using the terms interchangeably, providing one or the other as a response choice, or providing the two as separate response choices

Languages: Spanish (official) 68.1%, Quechua (official) 17.2%, Aymara (official) 10.5%, Guarani (official) 0.6%, other 1.5%, unspecified 2.1%; note - Spanish and all Indigenous languages are official (2012 est.)
major-language sample(s):
La Libreta Informativa del Mundo, la fuente indispensable de información básica. (Spanish)

Religions: Roman Catholic 65%, Protestant 19.6% (Evangelical (non-specific) 11.9%, Evangelical Baptist 2.1%, Evangelical Pentecostal 1.8%, Evangelical Methodist 0.7%, Adventist 2.8%, Protestant (non-specific) 0.3%), Believer (not belonging to the church) 0.9%, other 4.8%, atheist 1.7%, agnostic 0.6%, none 6.1%, unspecified 1.3% (2023 est.)

Age structure: *0-14 years:* 28.5% (male 1,792,803/female 1,718,081)
15-64 years: 64.5% (male 4,002,587/female 3,937,953)
65 years and over: 7% (2024 est.) (male 397,384/female 463,166)

Dependency ratios: *total dependency ratio:* 55.1 (2024 est.)
youth dependency ratio: 44.2 (2024 est.)
elderly dependency ratio: 10.8 (2024 est.)
potential support ratio: 9.2 (2024 est.)

Median age: *total:* 26.6 years (2024 est.)
male: 26.2 years
female: 27 years
comparison ranking: total 163

Population growth rate: 1% (2024 est.)
comparison ranking: 92

Birth rate: 17.6 births/1,000 population (2024 est.)
comparison ranking: 84

Death rate: 6.6 deaths/1,000 population (2024 est.)
comparison ranking: 130

Net migration rate: -1 migrant(s)/1,000 population (2024 est.)
comparison ranking: 143

Population distribution: a high-altitude plain in the west between two cordillera of the Andes, known as the Altiplano, is the focal area for most of the population; a dense settlement pattern is also found in and around the city of Santa Cruz, located on the eastern side of the Andes

Urbanization: *urban population:* 71.2% of total population (2023)
rate of urbanization: 1.87% annual rate of change (2020-25 est.)

Major urban areas - population: 1.936 million LA PAZ (capital), 1.820 million Santa Cruz, 1.400 million Cochabamba (2022); 278,000 Sucre (constitutional capital) (2018)

Sex ratio: *at birth:* 1.05 male(s)/female
0-14 years: 1.04 male(s)/female
15-64 years: 1.02 male(s)/female
65 years and over: 0.86 male(s)/female
total population: 1.01 male(s)/female (2024 est.)

Mother's mean age at first birth: 21.1 years (2008 est.)
note: data represents median age at first birth among women 25-49

Maternal mortality ratio: 146 deaths/100,000 live births (2023 est.)
comparison ranking: 51

Infant mortality rate: *total:* 22.3 deaths/1,000 live births (2024 est.)
male: 24.5 deaths/1,000 live births
female: 20 deaths/1,000 live births
comparison ranking: total 68

Life expectancy at birth: *total population:* 72.5 years (2024 est.)
male: 71 years
female: 74 years
comparison ranking: total population 161

Total fertility rate: 2.2 children born/woman (2024 est.)
comparison ranking: 85

Gross reproduction rate: 1.07 (2024 est.)

Drinking water source: *improved:* *urban:* 99.5% of population (2022 est.)
rural: 81% of population (2022 est.)
total: 94.1% of population (2022 est.)
unimproved: *urban:* 0.5% of population (2022 est.)
rural: 19% of population (2022 est.)
total: 5.9% of population (2022 est.)

Health expenditure: 8.2% of GDP (2021)
16.4% of national budget (2022 est.)

Physician density: 1.28 physicians/1,000 population (2021)

Hospital bed density: 1.4 beds/1,000 population (2021 est.)

Sanitation facility access: *improved:* *urban:* 100% of population (2022 est.)
rural: 51.4% of population (2022 est.)
total: 85.8% of population (2022 est.)
unimproved: *urban:* 0% of population (2022 est.)
rural: 48.6% of population (2022 est.)
total: 14.2% of population (2022 est.)

Obesity - adult prevalence rate: 20.2% (2016)
comparison ranking: 103

Alcohol consumption per capita: *total:* 2.98 liters of pure alcohol (2019 est.)
beer: 2.22 liters of pure alcohol (2019 est.)
wine: 0.14 liters of pure alcohol (2019 est.)
spirits: 0.54 liters of pure alcohol (2019 est.)
other alcohols: 0.08 liters of pure alcohol (2019 est.)
comparison ranking: total 115

Tobacco use: *total:* 11% (2025 est.)
male: 18.9% (2025 est.)
female: 3.2% (2025 est.)
comparison ranking: total 122

Children under the age of 5 years underweight: 3.4% (2016)
comparison ranking: 77

Currently married women (ages 15-49): 57.1% (2023 est.)

Child marriage: *women married by age 15:* 3.4% (2016)
women married by age 18: 19.7% (2016)
men married by age 18: 5.2% (2016)

Education expenditure: 8.3% of GDP (2023 est.)
23.1% national budget (2021 est.)
comparison ranking: Education expenditure (% GDP) 10

Literacy: *total population:* 94% (2020 est.)
male: 97% (2020 est.)
female: 91% (2020 est.)

ENVIRONMENT

Environmental issues: deforestation from agricultural clearing and international demand for timber; soil erosion from overgrazing and poor cultivation methods (including slash-and-burn agriculture); desertification; loss of biodiversity; industrial pollution of water supplies used for drinking and irrigation

International environmental agreements: *party to:* Biodiversity, Climate Change, Climate Change-Kyoto Protocol, Climate Change-Paris Agreement, Comprehensive Nuclear Test Ban, Desertification, Endangered Species, Hazardous Wastes, Law of the Sea, Marine Dumping-London Convention, Nuclear Test Ban, Ozone Layer Protection, Ship Pollution, Wetlands,
signed, but not ratified: Environmental Modification, Marine Life Conservation

Climate: varies with altitude; humid and tropical to cold and semiarid

Urbanization: *urban population:* 71.2% of total population (2023)
rate of urbanization: 1.87% annual rate of change (2020-25 est.)

Carbon dioxide emissions: 21.552 million metric tonnes of CO2 (2023 est.)
from coal and metallurgical coke: 24,000 metric tonnes of CO2 (2023 est.)
from petroleum and other liquids: 13.647 million metric tonnes of CO2 (2023 est.)
from consumed natural gas: 7.881 million metric tonnes of CO2 (2023 est.)
comparison ranking: total emissions 82

Particulate matter emissions: 24.6 micrograms per cubic meter (2019 est.)

Methane emissions: *energy:* 122.8 kt (2022-2024 est.)
agriculture: 673.4 kt (2019-2021 est.)
waste: 73.1 kt (2019-2021 est.)
other: 150.3 kt (2019-2021 est.)

Waste and recycling: *municipal solid waste generated annually:* 2.219 million tons (2024 est.)
percent of municipal solid waste recycled: 34.4% (2022 est.)

Total water withdrawal: *municipal:* 252.91 million cubic meters (2022 est.)
industrial: 32 million cubic meters (2022 est.)

agricultural: 1.92 billion cubic meters (2022 est.)
Total renewable water resources: 574 billion cubic meters (2022 est.)

GOVERNMENT

Country name: *conventional long form:* Plurinational State of Bolivia
conventional short form: Bolivia
local long form: Estado Plurinacional de Bolivia
local short form: Bolivia
former: Upper Peru
etymology: the country is named in honor of Simón BOLÍVAR, a 19th-century leader in the South American wars for independence

Government type: presidential republic

Capital: *name:* La Paz (administrative capital); Sucre (constitutional [legislative and judicial] capital)
geographic coordinates: 16 30 S, 68 09 W
time difference: UTC-4 (1 hour ahead of Washington, DC, during Standard Time)
etymology: La Paz is a shortening of the original name of the city, Pueblo Nuevo de Nuestra Señora de La Paz (New Town of Our Lady of Peace); Sucre is named after Antonio José de SUCRE (1795-1830), the second president of Bolivia
note: at approximately 3,630 m above sea level, La Paz's elevation makes it the highest capital city in the world

Administrative divisions: 9 departments *(departamentos*, singular - *departamento)*; Beni, Chuquisaca, Cochabamba, La Paz, Oruro, Pando, Potosi, Santa Cruz, Tarija

Legal system: civil law system with influences from Roman, Spanish, canon (religious), French, and ethnic groups' pre-colonial law

Constitution: *history:* many previous; latest drafted 6 August 2006 to 9 December 2008, approved by referendum 25 January 2009, effective 7 February 2009
amendment process: proposed through public petition by at least 20% of voters or by the Plurinational Legislative Assembly; passage requires approval by at least two-thirds majority vote of the total membership of the Assembly and approval in a referendum

International law organization participation: has not submitted an ICJ jurisdiction declaration; accepts ICCt jurisdiction

Citizenship: *citizenship by birth:* yes
citizenship by descent only: yes
dual citizenship recognized: yes
residency requirement for naturalization: 3 years

Suffrage: 18 years of age; universal and compulsory

Executive branch: *chief of state:* President Luis Alberto ARCE Catacora (since 8 November 2020)
head of government: President Luis Alberto ARCE Catacora (since 8 November 2020)
cabinet: Cabinet appointed by the president
election/appointment process: president and vice president directly elected on the same ballot one of 3 ways: candidate wins at least 50% of the vote, or at least 40% of the vote and 10% more than the next highest candidate; otherwise, a second round is held and the winner determined by simple majority vote; president and vice president are elected by majority vote to serve a 5-year term; no term limits
most recent election date: 17 August 2025
election results: *2025:* First round election results: percent of vote - Rodrigo PAZ Pereira (PDC) 32.1%, Jorge Fernando QUIROGA Ramírez (LIBRE) 26.7%, Samuel DORIA MEDINA Auza (UN) 19.7%, Andrónico RODRÌGUEZ Ledezma (AP) 8.5%, Manfred REYES Villa (APB Súmate) 6.8%, Eduardo DEL CASTILLO (MAS) 3.2%, other 3%; note - PAZ and QUIROGA advance to a run-off election set for 19 October 2025
2020: Luis Alberto ARCE Catacora elected president; percent of vote - Luis Alberto ARCE Catacora (MAS) 55.1%; Carlos Diego MESA Gisbert (CC) 28.8%; Luis Fernando CAMACHO Vaca (Creemos) 14%; other 2.1%
2019: Juan Evo MORALES Ayma reelected president; percent of vote - Juan Evo MORALES Ayma (MAS) 61%; Samuel DORIA MEDINA Arana (UN) 24.5%; Jorge QUIROGA Ramirez (POC) 9.1%; other 5.4%
expected date of next election: 2030
note: the president is both chief of state and head of government
note: elections were held in successive years in 2019 and 2020 because Juan Evo MORALES resigned from office on 10 November 2019 over alleged election rigging; Jeanine ANEZ Chavez served as interim president until the 8 November 2020 inauguration of Luis Alberto ARCE Catacora, who won the 18 October 2020 presidential election

Legislative branch: *legislature name:* Plurinational Legislative Assembly (Asamblea Legislativa Plurinacional)
legislative structure: bicameral
Legislative branch - lower chamber
chamber name: Chamber of Deputies (Cámara de Diputados)
number of seats: 130 (all directly elected)
electoral system: mixed system
scope of elections: full renewal
term in office: 5 years
most recent election date: 8/17/2025
parties elected and seats per party: Movement for Socialism (MAS-IPSP) (75); Civic Community (C.C) (39); Creemos (16)
percentage of women in chamber: 46.2%
expected date of next election: August 2030

Legislative branch - upper chamber: *chamber name:* Chamber of Senators (Cámara de Senadores)
number of seats: 36 (all directly elected)
electoral system: proportional representation
scope of elections: full renewal
term in office: 5 years
most recent election date: 8/17/2025
parties elected and seats per party: Movement for Socialism (MAS-IPSP) (21); Civic Community (C.C) (11); Creemos (4)
percentage of women in chamber: 55.6%
expected date of next election: August 2030

Judicial branch: *highest court(s):* Supreme Court or Tribunal Supremo de Justicia (consists of 12 judges organized into civil, penal, social, and administrative chambers); Plurinational Constitutional Tribunal (consists of 7 primary and 7 alternate magistrates); Plurinational Electoral Organ (consists of 7 members and 6 alternates); National Agro-Environment Court (consists of 5 primary and 5 alternate judges; Council of the Judiciary (consists of 3 primary and 3 alternate judges)
judge selection and term of office: Supreme Court, Plurinational Constitutional Tribunal, National Agro-Environmental Court, and Council of the Judiciary candidates pre-selected by the Plurinational Legislative Assembly and elected by direct popular vote; judges elected for 6-year terms; Plurinational Electoral Organ judges appointed - 6 by the Legislative Assembly and 1 by the president of the republic; members serve single 6-year terms
subordinate courts: National Electoral Court; District Courts (in each of the 9 administrative departments); agro-environmental lower courts

Political parties: Autonomy for Bolivia – Súmate or APB Súmate
Christian Democratic Party or PDC
Community Citizen Alliance or ACC
Freedom and Democracy or LIBRE
Front for Victory or FPV
Movement Toward Socialism or MAS
National Unity or UN
Popular Alliance or AP
Revolutionary Left Front or FRI
Revolutionary Nationalist Movement or MNR
Social Democrat Movement or MDS
Third System Movement or MTS
We Believe or Creemos
note: We Believe or Creemos [Luis Fernando CAMACHO Vaca] is a coalition comprised of several opposition parties that participated in the 2020 election, which includes the Christian Democratic Party (PDC) and Solidarity Civic Unity (UCS)

Diplomatic representation in the US: *chief of mission:* Ambassador (vacant); Chargé d'Affaires Henry BALDELOMAR CHÁVEZ (since 11 October 2023)
chancery: 3014 Massachusetts Ave., NW, Washington, DC 20008
telephone: [1] (202) 483-4410
FAX: [1] (202) 328-3712
email address and website: embolivia.wdc@gmail.com
https://www.boliviawdc.org/en-us/
consulate(s) general: Houston, Los Angeles, Miami, New York

Diplomatic representation from the US: *chief of mission:* Ambassador (vacant); Chargé d'Affaires Debra HEVIA (since September 2023)
embassy: Avenida Arce 2780, Casilla 425, La Paz
mailing address: 3220 La Paz Place, Washington DC 20512-3220
telephone: [591] (2) 216-8000
FAX: [591] (2) 216-8111
email address and website: ConsularLaPazACS@state.gov
https://bo.usembassy.gov/
note: in September 2008, the Bolivian Government expelled the US Ambassador to Bolivia, Philip GOLDBERG, and both countries have yet to reinstate their ambassadors

International organization participation: CAN, CD, CELAC, FAO, G-77, IADB, IAEA, IBRD, ICAO, ICC (national committees), ICCt, ICRM, IDA, IFAD, IFC, IFRCS, ILO, IMF, IMO, Interpol, IOC, IOM, IPU, ISO (correspondent), ITSO, ITU, LAES, LAIA, Mercosur (associate), MIGA, MINUSTAH, MONUSCO, NAM, OAS, OPANAL, OPCW, PCA, UN, UN Security Council (temporary), UNAMID, UNASUR, UNCTAD, UNESCO, UNIDO, Union Latina, UNISFA, UNMIL, UNMISS, UNOCI, UNOOSA, UNWTO, UPU, WCO, WFTU (NGOs), WHO, WIPO, WMO, WTO

Independence: 6 August 1825 (from Spain)

National holiday: Independence Day, 6 August (1825)

Flag: *description:* three equal horizontal bands of red (top), yellow, and green, with the coat of arms centered on the yellow band

meaning: red stands for bravery and the blood of national heroes, yellow for the nation's mineral resources, and green for the land's fertility
history: in 2009, a presidential decree made it mandatory for a *wiphala* – a square, multi-colored flag representing the country's ethnic groups – to be used alongside the national flag
note: similar to the flag of Ghana, which has a large, five-pointed black star centered in the yellow band

National symbol(s): llama, Andean condor; two national flowers, the cantuta and the patuju

National color(s): red, yellow, green

National anthem(s): *title:* "Cancion Patriotica" (Patriotic Song)
lyrics/music: Jose Ignacio de SANJINES/Leopoldo Benedetto VINCENTI
history: adopted 1852

National heritage: *total World Heritage Sites:* 7 (6 cultural, 1 natural)
selected World Heritage Site locales: City of Potosi (c); El Fuerte de Samaipata (c); Historic Sucre (c); Jesuit Missions of Chiquitos (c); Noel Kempff Mercado National Park (n); Tiahuanacu (c); Qhapaq Ñan/Andean Road System (c)

ECONOMY

Economic overview: resource-rich economy benefits during commodity booms; has bestowed juridical rights to Mother Earth, impacting extraction industries; increasing Chinese lithium mining trade relations; hard hit by COVID-19; increased fiscal spending amid poverty increases; rampant banking and finance corruption

Real GDP (purchasing power parity): $122.2 billion (2024 est.)
$120.531 billion (2023 est.)
$116.927 billion (2022 est.)
note: data in 2021 dollars
comparison ranking: 91

Real GDP growth rate: 1.4% (2024 est.)
3.1% (2023 est.)
3.6% (2022 est.)
note: annual GDP % growth based on constant local currency
comparison ranking: 167

Real GDP per capita: $9,800 (2024 est.)
$9,800 (2023 est.)
$9,700 (2022 est.)
note: data in 2021 dollars
comparison ranking: 147

GDP (official exchange rate): $49.668 billion (2024 est.)
note: data in current dollars at official exchange rate

Inflation rate (consumer prices): 5.1% (2024 est.)
2.6% (2023 est.)
1.7% (2022 est.)
note: annual % change based on consumer prices
comparison ranking: 146

GDP - composition, by sector of origin: *agriculture:* 13.5% (2023 est.)
industry: 24.2% (2023 est.)
services: 51.1% (2023 est.)
note: figures may not total 100% due to non-allocated consumption not captured in sector-reported data
comparison rankings: agriculture 59; industry 96; services 141

GDP - composition, by end use: *household consumption:* 68.5% (2023 est.)
government consumption: 19.3% (2023 est.)
investment in fixed capital: 17.5% (2023 est.)
investment in inventories: 0.1% (2023 est.)
exports of goods and services: 25.5% (2023 est.)
imports of goods and services: -30.9% (2023 est.)
note: figures may not total 100% due to rounding or gaps in data collection

Agricultural products: sugarcane, soybeans, maize, potatoes, sorghum, rice, milk, chicken, plantains, beef (2023)
note: top ten agricultural products based on tonnage

Industries: mining, smelting, electricity, petroleum, food and beverages, handicrafts, clothing, jewelry

Industrial production growth rate: 1.1% (2023 est.)
note: annual % change in industrial value added based on constant local currency
comparison ranking: 112

Labor force: 6.859 million (2024 est.)
note: number of people ages 15 or older who are employed or seeking work
comparison ranking: 69

Unemployment rate: 3.1% (2024 est.)
3.1% (2023 est.)
3.6% (2022 est.)
note: % of labor force seeking employment
comparison ranking: 43

Youth unemployment rate (ages 15-24): *total:* 5.2% (2024 est.)
male: 4.8% (2024 est.)
female: 5.8% (2024 est.)
note: % of labor force ages 15-24 seeking employment
comparison ranking: total 163

Population below poverty line: 37.7% (2022 est.)
note: % of population with income below national poverty line
Gini Index coefficient - distribution of family income 42.1 (2023 est.)
note: index (0-100) of income distribution; higher values represent greater inequality
comparison ranking: 33

Average household expenditures: *on food:* 29.3% of household expenditures (2023 est.)
on alcohol and tobacco: 2.2% of household expenditures (2023 est.)

Household income or consumption by percentage share: *lowest 10%:* 1.8% (2023 est.)
highest 10%: 31.3% (2023 est.)
note: % share of income accruing to lowest and highest 10% of population

Remittances: 3.2% of GDP (2023 est.)
3.3% of GDP (2022 est.)
3.5% of GDP (2021 est.)
note: personal transfers and compensation between resident and non-resident individuals/households/entities

Budget: *revenues:* $11.796 billion (2019 est.)
expenditures: $14.75 billion (2019 est.)

Public debt: 49% of GDP (2017 est.)
note: data cover general government debt and includes debt instruments issued by government entities other than the treasury; the data include treasury debt held by foreign entities; the data include debt issued by subnational entities
comparison ranking: 105

Current account balance: -$1.15 billion (2023 est.)
$939.084 million (2022 est.)
$1.581 billion (2021 est.)
note: balance of payments - net trade and primary/secondary income in current dollars
comparison ranking: 134

Exports: $11.905 billion (2023 est.)
$14.465 billion (2022 est.)
$11.594 billion (2021 est.)
note: balance of payments - exports of goods and services in current dollars
comparison ranking: 109

Exports - partners: Brazil 15%, India 13%, China 11%, Argentina 11%, UAE 8% (2023)
note: top five export partners based on percentage share of exports

Exports - commodities: gold, natural gas, precious metal ore, zinc ore, soybean meal (2023)
note: top five export commodities based on value in dollars

Imports: $12.988 billion (2023 est.)
$13.462 billion (2022 est.)
$10.187 billion (2021 est.)
note: balance of payments - imports of goods and services in current dollars
comparison ranking: 111

Imports - partners: China 22%, Brazil 18%, Chile 13%, USA 7%, Peru 5% (2023)
note: top five import partners based on percentage share of imports

Imports - commodities: refined petroleum, cars, pesticides, trucks, plastics (2023)
note: top five import commodities based on value in dollars

Reserves of foreign exchange and gold: $1.977 billion (2024 est.)
$1.8 billion (2023 est.)
$3.752 billion (2022 est.)
note: holdings of gold (year-end prices)/foreign exchange/special drawing rights in current dollars
comparison ranking: 127

Debt - external: $11.174 billion (2023 est.)
note: present value of external debt in current US dollars
comparison ranking: 47

Exchange rates: bolivianos (BOB) per US dollar -

Exchange rates: 6.91 (2024 est.)
6.91 (2023 est.)
6.91 (2022 est.)
6.91 (2021 est.)
6.91 (2020 est.)

ENERGY

Electricity access: *electrification - total population:* 99.9% (2022 est.)
electrification - urban areas: 100%
electrification - rural areas: 95.6%

Electricity: *installed generating capacity:* 4.375 million kW (2023 est.)
consumption: 10.863 billion kWh (2023 est.)
transmission/distribution losses: 1.079 billion kWh (2023 est.)
comparison rankings: installed generating capacity 96; consumption 103; transmission/distribution losses 101

Electricity generation sources: *fossil fuels:* 65% of total installed capacity (2023 est.)
solar: 2.9% of total installed capacity (2023 est.)
wind: 3.7% of total installed capacity (2023 est.)
hydroelectricity: 24.9% of total installed capacity (2023 est.)
biomass and waste: 3.5% of total installed capacity (2023 est.)

Coal: *consumption:* 9,000 metric tons (2023 est.)
imports: 7,000 metric tons (2023 est.)

proven reserves: 1 million metric tons (2023 est.)

Petroleum: *total petroleum production:* 58,000 bbl/day (2023 est.)
refined petroleum consumption: 100,000 bbl/day (2023 est.)
crude oil estimated reserves: 240.9 million barrels (2021 est.)

Natural gas: *production:* 12.302 billion cubic meters (2023 est.)
consumption: 4.025 billion cubic meters (2023 est.)
exports: 7.816 billion cubic meters (2023 est.)
proven reserves: 302.99 billion cubic meters (2021 est.)

Energy consumption per capita: 29.34 million Btu/person (2023 est.)
comparison ranking: 117

COMMUNICATIONS

Telephones - fixed lines: *total subscriptions:* 550,000 (2021 est.)
subscriptions per 100 inhabitants: 4 (2022 est.)
comparison ranking: total subscriptions 89

Telephones - mobile cellular: *total subscriptions:* 12 million (2021 est.)
subscriptions per 100 inhabitants: 100 (2021 est.)
comparison ranking: total subscriptions 85

Broadcast media: large number of radio and TV stations broadcasting with private media outlets dominating; state-owned and private radio and TV stations generally operating freely, although both pro-government and anti-government groups have attacked media outlets in response to their reporting (2019)

Internet country code: .bo

Internet users: *percent of population:* 70% (2023 est.)

Broadband - fixed subscriptions: *total:* 1.33 million (2022 est.)
subscriptions per 100 inhabitants: 11 (2022 est.)
comparison ranking: total 72

TRANSPORTATION

Civil aircraft registration country code prefix: CP

Airports: 201 (2025)
comparison ranking: 32

Heliports: 3 (2025)
comparison ranking: 118

Railways: *total:* 3,960 km (2019)
narrow gauge: 3,960 km (2014) 1.000-m gauge

Merchant marine: *total:* 50 (2023)
by type: general cargo 30, oil tanker 2, other 18
comparison ranking: total 121

MILITARY AND SECURITY

Military and security forces: Bolivian Armed Forces (Fuerzas Armadas de Bolivia or FAB): Bolivian Army (Ejercito de Boliviano), Bolivian Navy (Armada Boliviana), Bolivian Air Force (Fuerza Aerea Boliviana)

Ministry of Government: National Police (Policía Nacional de Bolivia, PNB) (2025)
note: the PNB is part of the reserves for the Armed Forces; the police and military share responsibility for border enforcement

Military expenditures: 1.2% of GDP (2024 est.)
1.2% of GDP (2023 est.)
1.3% of GDP (2022 est.)
1.4% of GDP (2021 est.)
1.4% of GDP (2020 est.)

Military and security service personnel strengths: approximately 30-35,000 active-duty Armed Forces (2025)

Military equipment inventories and acquisitions: the military is equipped with a mix of mostly older Brazilian, Chinese, European, and US equipment (2024)

Military service age and obligation: compulsory for all men between the ages of 18 and 22; men can volunteer from the age of 16, women from 18; service is for 12 months; Search and Rescue service can be substituted for citizens who have reached the age of compulsory military service; duration of this service is 24 months (2024)
note 1: foreign nationals 18-22 residing in Bolivia may join the armed forces; joining speeds the process of acquiring Bolivian citizenship by naturalization
note 2: as of 2022, women comprised about 8% of the Bolivian military's personnel

Military - note: the Bolivian Armed Forces (FAB) are responsible for territorial defense but also have some internal security duties, particularly counternarcotics and border security; the FAB shares responsibility for border enforcement with the National Police (PNB), and it may be called out to assist the PNB with maintaining public order in critical situations
land-locked Bolivia has a naval force for patrolling some 5,000 miles of navigable rivers to combat narcotics trafficking and smuggling, provide disaster relief, and deliver supplies to remote rural areas, as well as for maintaining a presence on Lake Titicaca; the Navy also exists in part to cultivate a maritime tradition and as a reminder of Bolivia's defeat at the hands of Chile in the War of the Pacific (1879-1883), and its desire to regain access to the Pacific Ocean; every year on 23 March, the Navy participates in parades and government ceremonies commemorating the Día Del Mar (Day of the Sea) holiday that remembers the loss (2025)

SPACE

Space agency/agencies: Bolivian Space Agency (la Agencia Boliviana Espacial, ABE; established 2010 as a national public company under Ministry of Public Works, Services and Housing) (2025)

Space program overview: has a small space program focused on acquiring and operating satellites; operates a telecommunications satellite and ground stations; has cooperated with China and India and member states of the Latin American and Caribbean Space Agency (ALCE) (2025)
note: further details about the key activities, programs, and milestones of the country's space program, as well as government spending estimates on the space sector, appear in the Space Programs reference guide

TERRORISM

Terrorist group(s): Terrorist group(s): Tren de Aragua (TdA)
note: details about the history, aims, leadership, organization, areas of operation, tactics, targets, weapons, size, and sources of support of the group(s) appear(s) in Appendix T

TRANSNATIONAL ISSUES

Refugees and internally displaced persons: *refugees:* 1,163 (2024 est.)

IDPs: 12,070 (2024 est.)

Trafficking in persons: *tier rating:* Tier 2 Watch List — Bolivia did not demonstrate overall increasing efforts to eliminate trafficking compared with the previous reporting period and was downgraded to Tier 2 Watch List; for more details, go to: https://www.state.gov/reports/2025-trafficking-in-persons-report/bolivia/

Illicit drugs: USG identification: major illicit drug-producing and/or drug-transit country
major precursor-chemical producer (2025)

BOSNIA AND HERZEGOVINA

INTRODUCTION

Background: After four centuries of Ottoman rule over Bosnia and Herzegovina, Austria-Hungary took control in 1878 and held the region until 1918, when it was incorporated into the newly created Kingdom of Serbs, Croats, and Slovenes. After World War II, Bosnia and Herzegovina joined the Socialist Federal Republic of Yugoslavia (SFRY).

Bosnia and Herzegovina declared sovereignty in October 1991 and independence from the SFRY on 3 March 1992 after a referendum boycotted by ethnic Serbs. Bosnian Serb militias, with the support of Serbia and Croatia, then tried to take control of territories they claimed as their own. From 1992 to 1995, ethnic cleansing campaigns killed thousands and displaced more than two million people. On 21 November 1995, in Dayton, Ohio, the warring parties initialed a peace agreement, and the final agreement was signed in Paris on 14 December 1995.

The Dayton Accords retained Bosnia and Herzegovina's international boundaries and created a multiethnic and democratic government composed of two entities roughly equal in size: the predominantly Bosniak-Bosnian Croat Federation of Bosnia and Herzegovina and the predominantly Bosnian Serb-led Republika Srpska (RS). The Dayton Accords also established the Office of the High Representative to oversee the agreement's implementation. In 1996, the NATO-led Stabilization Force (SFOR) took over responsibility for enforcing the peace. In 2004, European Union peacekeeping troops (EUFOR) replaced SFOR. As of 2022, EUFOR deploys around 1,600 troops in Bosnia in a peacekeeping capacity. Bosnia and Herzegovina became an official candidate for EU membership in 2022.

GEOGRAPHY

Location: Southeastern Europe, bordering the Adriatic Sea and Croatia

Geographic coordinates: 44 00 N, 18 00 E

Map references: Europe

Area: *total:* 51,197 sq km
land: 51,187 sq km
water: 10 sq km
comparison ranking: total 128

Area - comparative: slightly smaller than West Virginia

Land boundaries: *total:* 1,543 km
border countries (3): Croatia 956 km; Montenegro 242 km; Serbia 345 km

Coastline: 20 km

Maritime claims: NA

Climate: hot summers and cold winters; areas of high elevation have short, cool summers and long, severe winters; mild, rainy winters along coast

Terrain: mountains and valleys

Elevation: *highest point:* Maglic 2,386 m
lowest point: Adriatic Sea 0 m
mean elevation: 500 m

Natural resources: coal, iron ore, antimony, bauxite, copper, lead, zinc, chromite, cobalt, manganese, nickel, clay, gypsum, salt, sand, timber, hydropower

Land use: *agricultural land:* 44.2% (2022 est.)
arable land: 19.7% (2022 est.)
permanent crops: 2.1% (2022 est.)
permanent pasture: 22.4% (2022 est.)
forest: 42.7% (2022 est.)
other: 13.1% (2022 est.)

Irrigated land: 30 sq km (2012)

Major watersheds (area sq km): Atlantic Ocean drainage: ***(Black Sea)*** Danube (795,656 sq km)

Population distribution: the northern and central areas of the country are the most densely populated

Natural hazards: destructive earthquakes

Geography - note: within Bosnia and Herzegovina's recognized borders, the country is divided into a joint Bosniak/Croat Federation (about 51% of the territory) and the Bosnian Serb-led Republika Srpska or RS (about 49% of the territory); the region called Herzegovina is contiguous to Croatia and Montenegro

PEOPLE AND SOCIETY

Population: *total:* 3,798,671 (2024 est.)
male: 1,852,164
female: 1,946,507
comparison rankings: total 131; male 132; female 130

Nationality: *noun:* Bosnian(s), Herzegovinian(s)
adjective: Bosnian, Herzegovinian

Ethnic groups: Bosniak 50.1%, Serb 30.8%, Croat 15.4%, other 2.7%, not declared/no answer 1% (2013 est.)
note: Republika Srpska authorities dispute the methodology and refuse to recognize the results; Bosniak has replaced Muslim as an ethnic term in part to avoid confusion with the religious term Muslim - an adherent of Islam

Languages: Bosnian (official) 52.9%, Serbian (official) 30.8%, Croatian (official) 14.6%, other 1.6%, no answer 0.2% (2013 est.)
major-language sample(s):
Knjiga svjetskih činjenica, neophodan izvor osnovnih informacija. (Bosnian)
Knjiga svetskih činjenica, neophodan izvor osnovnih informacija. (Serbian)
Knjiga svjetskih činjenica, nužan izvor osnovnih informacija. (Croatian)

Religions: Muslim 50.7%, Orthodox 30.7%, Roman Catholic 15.2%, atheist 0.8%, agnostic 0.3%, other 1.2%, undeclared/no answer 1.1% (2013 est.)

Age structure: *0-14 years:* 13.1% (male 257,444/female 240,209)
15-64 years: 68.3% (male 1,305,271/female 1,290,920)
65 years and over: 18.6% (2024 est.) (male 289,449/female 415,378)

Dependency ratios: *total dependency ratio:* 43.5 (2024 est.)
youth dependency ratio: 16.8 (2024 est.)
elderly dependency ratio: 26.7 (2024 est.)
potential support ratio: 3.7 (2024 est.)

Median age: *total:* 44.8 years (2024 est.)
male: 43.1 years
female: 46.5 years
comparison ranking: total 28

Population growth rate: -0.25% (2024 est.)
comparison ranking: 211

Birth rate: 8.2 births/1,000 population (2024 est.)
comparison ranking: 213

Death rate: 10.3 deaths/1,000 population (2024 est.)
comparison ranking: 32

Net migration rate: -0.4 migrant(s)/1,000 population (2024 est.)
comparison ranking: 118

Population distribution: the northern and central areas of the country are the most densely populated

Urbanization: *urban population:* 50.3% of total population (2023)
rate of urbanization: 0.61% annual rate of change (2020-25 est.)

Major urban areas - population: 346,000 SARAJEVO (capital) (2023)

Sex ratio: *at birth:* 1.07 male(s)/female
0-14 years: 1.07 male(s)/female
15-64 years: 1.01 male(s)/female
65 years and over: 0.7 male(s)/female
total population: 0.95 male(s)/female (2024 est.)

Mother's mean age at first birth: 27.7 years (2019 est.)

Maternal mortality ratio: 6 deaths/100,000 live births (2023 est.)
comparison ranking: 164

Infant mortality rate: *total:* 5 deaths/1,000 live births (2024 est.)
male: 5.1 deaths/1,000 live births
female: 4.9 deaths/1,000 live births
comparison ranking: total 176

Life expectancy at birth: *total population:* 78.5 years (2024 est.)
male: 75.5 years
female: 81.6 years
comparison ranking: total population 77

Total fertility rate: 1.38 children born/woman (2024 est.)
comparison ranking: 214

Gross reproduction rate: 0.67 (2024 est.)

Drinking water source: *improved: urban:* 94.8% of population (2022 est.)
rural: 97.3% of population (2022 est.)
total: 96.1% of population (2022 est.)
unimproved: urban: 5.2% of population (2022 est.)
rural: 2.7% of population (2022 est.)
total: 3.9% of population (2022 est.)

Health expenditure: 9.6% of GDP (2021)
14.8% of national budget (2022 est.)

Physician density: 2.58 physicians/1,000 population (2019)

Hospital bed density: 2.3 beds/1,000 population (2019 est.)

Sanitation facility access: *improved: urban:* 99.5% of population (2022 est.)
unimproved: urban: 0.5% of population (2022 est.)

Obesity - adult prevalence rate: 17.9% (2016)
comparison ranking: 118

Alcohol consumption per capita: *total:* 5.46 liters of pure alcohol (2019 est.)
beer: 4.19 liters of pure alcohol (2019 est.)
wine: 0.47 liters of pure alcohol (2019 est.)
spirits: 0.62 liters of pure alcohol (2019 est.)
other alcohols: 0.17 liters of pure alcohol (2019 est.)
comparison ranking: total 81

Tobacco use: *total:* 34% (2025 est.)
male: 39.2% (2025 est.)
female: 29% (2025 est.)
comparison ranking: total 11

Currently married women (ages 15-49): 63.8% (2023 est.)

Education expenditure: 3% of GDP (2022 est.)
10.4% national budget (2021 est.)
comparison ranking: Education expenditure (% GDP) 153

School life expectancy (primary to tertiary education): *total:* 14 years (2023 est.)
male: 14 years (2023 est.)
female: 15 years (2023 est.)

ENVIRONMENT

Environmental issues: air pollution; deforestation and illegal logging; inadequate wastewater treatment and flood management facilities; urban waste disposal; uncleared land mines from the 1990s

International environmental agreements: *party to:* Air Pollution, Biodiversity, Climate Change, Climate Change-Kyoto Protocol, Climate Change-Paris Agreement, Comprehensive Nuclear Test Ban, Desertification, Endangered Species, Hazardous

Wastes, Law of the Sea, Marine Life Conservation, Nuclear Test Ban, Ozone Layer Protection, Wetlands
signed, but not ratified: none of the selected agreements

Climate: hot summers and cold winters; areas of high elevation have short, cool summers and long, severe winters; mild, rainy winters along coast

Urbanization: *urban population:* 50.3% of total population (2023)
rate of urbanization: 0.61% annual rate of change (2020-25 est.)

Carbon dioxide emissions: 24.513 million metric tonnes of CO2 (2023 est.)
from coal and metallurgical coke: 19.292 million metric tonnes of CO2 (2023 est.)
from petroleum and other liquids: 4.785 million metric tonnes of CO2 (2023 est.)
from consumed natural gas: 436,000 metric tonnes of CO2 (2023 est.)
comparison ranking: total emissions 78

Particulate matter emissions: 26.2 micrograms per cubic meter (2019 est.)

Waste and recycling: *municipal solid waste generated annually:* 1.249 million tons (2024 est.)
percent of municipal solid waste recycled: 23.8% (2022 est.)

Total water withdrawal: *municipal:* 320 million cubic meters (2022)
industrial: 475 million cubic meters (2022)

Total renewable water resources: 37.5 billion cubic meters (2022 est.)

GOVERNMENT

Country name: *conventional long form:* none
conventional short form: Bosnia and Herzegovina
local long form: none
local short form: Bosna i Hercegovina
former: People's Republic of Bosnia and Herzegovina, Socialist Republic of Bosnia and Herzegovina
abbreviation: BiH
etymology: the larger northern territory is named for the Bosna River; the smaller southern section takes its name from the Old Serbian word *herceg*, meaning "duke," combined with the possessive *-ov* and the suffix *-ina*, meaning "country," to denote "dukedom"

Government type: parliamentary republic

Capital: *name:* Sarajevo
geographic coordinates: 43 52 N, 18 25 E
time difference: UTC+1 (6 hours ahead of Washington, DC, during Standard Time)
daylight saving time: +1hr, begins last Sunday in March; ends last Sunday in October
etymology: the name derives from the Turkish word *saray*, meaning "palace" or "mansion"

Administrative divisions: 3 first-order administrative divisions - Brcko District (Brcko Distrikt) (ethnically mixed), Federation of Bosnia and Herzegovina (Federacija Bosne i Hercegovine) (predominantly Bosniak-Croat), Republika Srpska (predominantly Serb)

Legal system: civil law system; Constitutional Court review of legislative acts

Constitution: *history:* 14 December 1995 (constitution included as part of the Dayton Peace Accords)
amendment process: decided by the Parliamentary Assembly, including a two-thirds majority vote of members present in the House of Representatives; the constitutional article on human rights and fundamental freedoms cannot be amended
note: each of the political entities has its own constitution

International law organization participation: has not submitted an ICJ jurisdiction declaration; accepts ICCt jurisdiction

Citizenship: *citizenship by birth:* no
citizenship by descent only: at least one parent must be a citizen of Bosnia and Herzegovina
dual citizenship recognized: yes, provided there is a bilateral agreement with the other state
residency requirement for naturalization: 8 years

Suffrage: 18 years of age, 16 if employed; universal

Executive branch: *chief of state:* Chairperson of the Presidency Zeljko KOMSIC (chairperson since 16 July 2025; presidency member since 20 November 2018 - Croat seat); Denis BECIROVIC (presidency member since 16 November 2022 - Bosniak seat); Zeljka CVIJANOVIC (presidency member since 16 November 2022 - Serb seat)
head of government: Chairperson of the Council of Ministers Borjana KRISTO (since 25 January 2023)
cabinet: Council of Ministers nominated by the council chairperson, approved by the state-level House of Representatives
election/appointment process: 3-member presidency (1 Bosniak and 1 Croat elected from the Federation of Bosnia and Herzegovina and 1 Serb elected from the Republika Srpska) directly elected by simple-majority popular vote for a 4-year term (eligible for a second term but then ineligible for 4 years); the presidency chairpersonship rotates every 8 months, with the new member of the presidency elected with the highest number of votes starting the new mandate as chair; the chairperson of the Council of Ministers appointed by the presidency and confirmed by the state-level House of Representatives
most recent election date: 2 October 2022
election results: *2022:* percent of vote - Denis BECIROVIC - (SDP BiH) 57.4% - Bosniak seat; Zeljko KOMSIC (DF) 55.8% - Croat seat; Zeljka CVIJANOVIC (SNSD) 51.7% - Serb seat
2018: percent of vote - Milorad DODIK (SNSD) 53.9% - Serb seat; Zeljko KOMSIC (DF) 52.6% - Croat seat; Sefik DZAFEROVIC (SDA) 36.6% - Bosniak seat
expected date of next election: October 2026
note: President of the Federation of Bosnia and Herzegovina Lidiia BRADARA (since 28 February 2023)

Legislative branch: *legislature name:* Parliamentary Assembly (Skupstina)
legislative structure: bicameral

Legislative branch - lower chamber: *chamber name:* House of Representatives (Predstavnicki dom)
number of seats: 42 (all directly elected)
electoral system: proportional representation
scope of elections: full renewal
term in office: 4 years
most recent election date: 10/2/2022
parties elected and seats per party: Party of Democratic Action (SDA) (9); Alliance of Independent Social Democrats (SNSD) (6); Social Democratic Party of Bosnia and Herzegovina (SDP) (5); HDZ BiH, HSS, HSP BiH, HKDU, HSPAS, HDU, HSPHB, HRAST (4); Democratic Front (DF) - Civic Alliance (GS) (3); People and Justice (NAROD I PRAVDA) (3); Other (12)
percentage of women in chamber: 19%
expected date of next election: October 2026

Legislative branch - upper chamber: *chamber name:* House of Peoples (Dom Naroda)
number of seats: 15 (all appointed)
scope of elections: full renewal
term in office: 4 years
most recent election date: 2/16/2023
percentage of women in chamber: 6.7%
expected date of next election: February 2027

Judicial branch: *highest court(s):* Bosnia and Herzegovina (BiH) Constitutional Court (consists of 9 members); Court of BiH (consists of 44 national judges and 7 international judges organized into 3 divisions - Administrative, Appellate, and Criminal, which includes a War Crimes Chamber)
judge selection and term of office: BiH Constitutional Court judges - 4 selected by the Federation of Bosnia and Herzegovina House of Representatives, 2 selected by the Republika Srpska's National Assembly, and 3 non-Bosnian judges selected by the president of the European Court of Human Rights; Court of BiH president and national judges appointed by the High Judicial and Prosecutorial Council; Court of BiH president appointed for renewable 6-year term; other national judges appointed to serve until age 70; international judges recommended by the president of the Court of BiH and appointed by the High Representative for Bosnia and Herzegovina; international judges appointed to serve until age 70
subordinate courts: the Federation has 10 cantonal courts plus a number of municipal courts; the Republika Srpska has a supreme court, 5 district courts, and a number of municipal courts

Political parties: Alliance of Independent Social Democrats or SNSD
Bosnian-Herzegovinian Initiative or BHI KF
Civic Alliance or GS
Croatian Democratic Union of Bosnia and Herzegovina or HDZ-BiH
Democratic Front or DF
Democratic Union or DEMOS
For Justice and Order
Our Party or NS/HC
Party for Democratic Action or SDA
Party of Democratic Progress or PDP
People and Justice Party or NiP
People's European Union of Bosnia and Herzegovina or NES
Serb Democratic Party or SDS
Social Democratic Party or SDP
United Srpska or US

Diplomatic representation in the US: *chief of mission:* Ambassador Sven ALKALAJ (since 30 June 2023)
chancery: 2109 E Street NW, Washington, DC 20037
telephone: [1] (202) 337-1500
FAX: [1] (202) 337-1502
email address and website: info@bhembassy.org
http://www.bhembassy.org/index.html
consulate(s) general: Chicago

Diplomatic representation from the US: *chief of mission:* Ambassador (vacant); Chargé d'Affaires Daniel KOSKI (since February 2025)
embassy: 1 Robert C. Frasure Street, 71000 Sarajevo
mailing address: 7130 Sarajevo Place, Washington DC 20521-7130
telephone: [387] (33) 704-000
FAX: [387] (33) 659-722
email address and website: sarajevoACS@state.gov
https://ba.usembassy.gov/
branch office(s): Banja Luka, Mostar

International organization participation: BIS, CD, CE, CEI, EAPC, EBRD, FAO, G-77, IAEA, IBRD, ICAO, ICC (NGOs), ICCt, ICRM, IDA, IFAD, IFC, IFRCS, ILO, IMF, IMO, IMSO, Interpol, IOC, IOM, IPU, ISO, ITSO, ITU, ITUC (NGOs), MIGA, MONUSCO, NAM (observer), OAS (observer), OIC (observer), OIF (observer), OPCW, OSCE, PFP, SELEC, UN, UNCTAD, UNESCO, UNIDO, UNWTO, UPU, WCO, WHO, WIPO, WMO, WTO (observer)
note: Bosnia-Herzegovina is an EU candidate country whose satisfactory completion of accession criteria is required before being granted full EU membership

Independence: 1 March 1992 (from Yugoslavia)
note: referendum for independence completed on 1 March 1992; independence declared on 3 March 1992

National holiday: Independence Day, 1 March (1992) and Statehood Day, 25 November (1943) - both observed in the Federation of Bosnia and Herzegovina entity; Victory Day, 9 May (1945) and Dayton Agreement Day, 21 November (1995) - both observed in the Republika Srpska entity
note: there is no national-level holiday

Flag: *description:* a wide blue vertical band on the right side, with a large yellow isosceles triangle in the middle of the flag, based at the top; the rest of the flag is blue, with seven five-pointed white stars and two half-stars along the triangle's hypotenuse
meaning: the triangle approximates the country's shape, and its three points stand for the Bosniaks, Croats, and Serbs; the stars represent Europe; the colors (white, blue, and yellow) are traditional and are also associated with neutrality and peace
note: one of four national flags that reflect the shape of the country in the flag design; the others are Brazil, Eritrea, and Vanuatu

National symbol(s): golden lily

National color(s): blue, yellow, white

National anthem(s): *title:* "Drzavna himna Bosne i Hercegovine" (The National Anthem of Bosnia and Herzegovina)
lyrics/music: none officially/Dusan SESTIC
history: music adopted 1999; lyrics proposed in 2009 were accepted by a parliamentary commission but are still awaiting adoption, so the anthem remains officially wordless

National heritage: *total World Heritage Sites:* 5 (3 cultural, 2 natural)
selected World Heritage Site locales: Old Bridge Area of Mostar (c); Mehmed Paša Sokolović Bridge in Višegrad (c); Stećci Medieval Tombstones Graveyards (c); Ancient and Primeval Beech Forests of the Carpathians and Other Regions of Europe - Janj Forest (n); Vjetrenica Cave, Ravno (n)

ECONOMY

Economic overview: import-dominated economy; remains consumption-heavy; lack of private sector investments and diversification; jointly addressing structural economic challenges; Chinese energy infrastructure investments; high unemployment; tourism industry impacted by COVID-19

Real GDP (purchasing power parity): $64.641 billion (2024 est.)
$63.077 billion (2023 est.)
$61.843 billion (2022 est.)
note: data in 2021 dollars
comparison ranking: 114

Real GDP growth rate: 2.5% (2024 est.)
2% (2023 est.)
4.2% (2022 est.)
note: annual GDP % growth based on constant local currency
comparison ranking: 137

Real GDP per capita: $20,400 (2024 est.)
$19,800 (2023 est.)
$19,300 (2022 est.)
note: data in 2021 dollars
comparison ranking: 100

GDP (official exchange rate): $28.343 billion (2024 est.)
note: data in current dollars at official exchange rate

Inflation rate (consumer prices): 1.7% (2024 est.)
6.1% (2023 est.)
14% (2022 est.)
note: annual % change based on consumer prices
comparison ranking: 42

GDP - composition, by sector of origin: *agriculture:* 4.3% (2024 est.)
industry: 22% (2024 est.)
services: 58% (2024 est.)
note: figures may not total 100% due to non-allocated consumption not captured in sector-reported data
comparison rankings: agriculture 117; industry 120; services 106

GDP - composition, by end use: *household consumption:* 68.3% (2023 est.)
government consumption: 19.1% (2023 est.)
investment in fixed capital: 23.1% (2023 est.)
investment in inventories: 3.2% (2023 est.)
exports of goods and services: 43.9% (2023 est.)
imports of goods and services: -55.7% (2023 est.)
note: figures may not total 100% due to rounding or gaps in data collection

Agricultural products: maize, milk, vegetables, potatoes, plums, wheat, apples, barley, chicken, tomatoes (2023)
note: top ten agricultural products based on tonnage

Industries: steel, coal, iron ore, lead, zinc, manganese, bauxite, aluminum, motor vehicle assembly, textiles, tobacco products, wooden furniture, ammunition, domestic appliances, oil refining

Industrial production growth rate: -2.4% (2024 est.)
note: annual % change in industrial value added based on constant local currency
comparison ranking: 163

Labor force: 1.356 million (2024 est.)
note: number of people ages 15 or older who are employed or seeking work
comparison ranking: 140

Unemployment rate: 10.8% (2024 est.)
10.7% (2023 est.)
12.7% (2022 est.)
note: % of labor force seeking employment
comparison ranking: 152

Youth unemployment rate (ages 15-24): *total:* 27.3% (2024 est.)
male: 25.4% (2024 est.)
female: 30.9% (2024 est.)
note: % of labor force ages 15-24 seeking employment
comparison ranking: total 27

Population below poverty line: 16.9% (2015 est.)
note: % of population with income below national poverty line

Average household expenditures: *on food:* 32.1% of household expenditures (2023 est.)
on alcohol and tobacco: 7.1% of household expenditures (2023 est.)

Remittances: 11% of GDP (2024 est.)
10.2% of GDP (2023 est.)
10.5% of GDP (2022 est.)
note: personal transfers and compensation between resident and non-resident individuals/households/entities

Budget: *revenues:* $10.196 billion (2023 est.)
expenditures: $10.463 billion (2023 est.)
note: central government revenues (excluding grants) and expenditures converted to US dollars at average official exchange rate for year indicated

Public debt: 40.3% of GDP (2023 est.)
note: central government debt as a % of GDP
comparison ranking: 131

Taxes and other revenues: 19.1% (of GDP) (2023 est.)
note: central government tax revenue as a % of GDP
comparison ranking: 57

Current account balance: -$1.176 billion (2024 est.)
-$638.769 million (2023 est.)
-$1.078 billion (2022 est.)
note: balance of payments - net trade and primary/secondary income in current dollars
comparison ranking: 135

Exports: $12.141 billion (2024 est.)
$12.126 billion (2023 est.)
$11.838 billion (2022 est.)
note: balance of payments - exports of goods and services in current dollars
comparison ranking: 107

Exports - partners: Germany 15%, Croatia 14%, Serbia 12%, Austria 10%, Slovenia 9% (2023)
note: top five export partners based on percentage share of exports

Exports - commodities: footwear, electricity, garments, plastic products, insulated wire (2023)
note: top five export commodities based on value in dollars

Imports: $16.202 billion (2024 est.)
$15.37 billion (2023 est.)
$15.166 billion (2022 est.)
note: balance of payments - imports of goods and services in current dollars
comparison ranking: 105

Imports - partners: Italy 13%, Germany 11%, Serbia 11%, China 9%, Croatia 8% (2023)
note: top five import partners based on percentage share of imports

Imports - commodities: refined petroleum, cars, garments, plastic products, packaged medicine (2023)
note: top five import commodities based on value in dollars

Reserves of foreign exchange and gold: $9.419 billion (2024 est.)
$9.205 billion (2023 est.)
$8.762 billion (2022 est.)
note: holdings of gold (year-end prices)/foreign exchange/special drawing rights in current dollars
comparison ranking: 80

Debt - external: $5.359 billion (2023 est.)
note: present value of external debt in current US dollars
comparison ranking: 72

Exchange rates: konvertibilna markas (BAM) per US dollar -

Exchange rates: 1.808 (2024 est.)

1.809 (2023 est.)
1.859 (2022 est.)
1.654 (2021 est.)
1.717 (2020 est.)

ENERGY

Electricity access: *electrification - total population:* 100% (2022 est.)

Electricity: *installed generating capacity:* 4.682 million kW (2023 est.)
consumption: 12.867 billion kWh (2023 est.)
exports: 7.104 billion kWh (2023 est.)
imports: 3.6 billion kWh (2023 est.)
transmission/distribution losses: 1.339 billion kWh (2023 est.)
comparison rankings: installed generating capacity 93; consumption 94; exports 33; imports 55; transmission/distribution losses 113

Electricity generation sources: *fossil fuels:* 64% of total installed capacity (2023 est.)
solar: 0.9% of total installed capacity (2023 est.)
wind: 2.2% of total installed capacity (2023 est.)
hydroelectricity: 31.1% of total installed capacity (2023 est.)
biomass and waste: 1.8% of total installed capacity (2023 est.)

Coal: *production:* 12.311 million metric tons (2023 est.)
consumption: 12.304 million metric tons (2023 est.)
exports: 1.254 million metric tons (2023 est.)
imports: 1.327 million metric tons (2023 est.)
proven reserves: 2.264 billion metric tons (2023 est.)

Petroleum: *refined petroleum consumption:* 34,000 bbl/day (2023 est.)

Natural gas: *consumption:* 228.855 million cubic meters (2023 est.)
imports: 228.855 million cubic meters (2023 est.)

Energy consumption per capita: 91.227 million Btu/person (2023 est.)
comparison ranking: 58

COMMUNICATIONS

Telephones - fixed lines: *total subscriptions:* 614,000 (2023 est.)
subscriptions per 100 inhabitants: 19 (2023 est.)
comparison ranking: total subscriptions 85

Telephones - mobile cellular: *total subscriptions:* 3.87 million (2023 est.)
subscriptions per 100 inhabitants: 118 (2022 est.)
comparison ranking: total subscriptions 139

Broadcast media: *3 public TV broadcasters:* Radio and TV of Bosnia and Herzegovina, Federation TV (operating 2 networks), and Republika Srpska Radio-TV; a local commercial network of 5 TV stations; 3 private, near-national TV stations and dozens of small independent TV stations; 3 large public radio broadcasters and many private radio stations (2019)

Internet country code: .ba

Internet users: *percent of population:* 83% (2023 est.)

Broadband - fixed subscriptions: *total:* 908,000 (2023 est.)
subscriptions per 100 inhabitants: 29 (2023 est.)
comparison ranking: total 80

TRANSPORTATION

Civil aircraft registration country code prefix: T9

Airports: 20 (2025)
comparison ranking: 139

Heliports: 3 (2025)
comparison ranking: 114

Railways: *total:* 965 km (2014)
standard gauge: 965 km (2014) 1.435-m gauge (565 km electrified)

Ports: *total ports:* 1 (2024)
large: 0
medium: 0
small: 1
very small: 0
ports with oil terminals: 0
key ports: Neum

MILITARY AND SECURITY

Military and security forces: Armed Forces of Bosnia and Herzegovina (AFBiH or Oruzanih Snaga Bosne i Hercegovine, OSBiH): Army, Air, Air Defense forces organized into an Operations Command and a Support Command

Ministry of Security: Border Police (2025)

Military expenditures: 0.8% of GDP (2024 est.)
0.8% of GDP (2023 est.)
0.8% of GDP (2022 est.)
0.9% of GDP (2021 est.)
0.9% of GDP (2020 est.)

Military and security service personnel strengths: approximately 10,000 active-duty Armed Forces (2024)

Military equipment inventories and acquisitions: the military's inventory of weapons and equipment is a combination of material originating from the former Soviet Union/former Yugoslavia and secondhand deliveries from Western suppliers such as the UK and especially the US (2024)

Military service age and obligation: 18 years of age for voluntary military service; conscription abolished in 2005 (2024)
note: as of 2024, women made up about 9% of the military's full-time personnel

Military - note: the Armed Forces of Bosnia and Herzegovina (AFBiH) are responsible for territorial defense, providing assistance to civil authorities during disasters or other emergencies, and participating in collective security and peace support operations; each of the AFBiH's three combat brigades are headquartered inside of their respective ethnicity territory, while its main headquarters is in Sarajevo; Bosnia and Herzegovina aspires to join NATO; Bosnia and Herzegovina joined NATO's Partnership for Peace (PfP) program in 2006 and was invited to join NATO's Membership Action Plan in 2010; the AFBiH is undergoing a 10-year (2017-2027) defense modernization and reform program for preparing to join and integrate with NATO; it has contributed small numbers of troops to EU, NATO, and UN missions
NATO maintains a military headquarters in Sarajevo with the mission of assisting Bosnia and Herzegovina with the PfP program and promoting closer integration with NATO, as well as providing logistics and other support to the EU Force Bosnia and Herzegovina (EUFOR), which has operated in the country to oversee implementation of the Dayton/Paris Agreement since taking over from NATO's Stabilization Force (SFOR) in 2004 (2025)

TERRORISM

Terrorist group(s): Terrorist group(s): Islamic Revolutionary Guard Corps/Qods Force
note: details about the history, aims, leadership, organization, areas of operation, tactics, targets, weapons, size, and sources of support of the group(s) appear(s) in Appendix T

TRANSNATIONAL ISSUES

Refugees and internally displaced persons: *refugees:* 685 (2024 est.)

IDPs: 94,796 (2024 est.)
stateless persons: 23 (2024 est.)

BOTSWANA

INTRODUCTION

Background: In the early 1800s, multiple political entities in what is now Botswana were destabilized or destroyed by a series of conflicts and population movements in southern Africa. By the end of this period, the Tswana ethnic group, who also live across the border in South Africa, had become the most prominent group in the area. In 1852, Tswana forces halted the expansion of white Afrikaner settlers who were seeking to expand their territory northwards into what is now Botswana. In 1885, Great Britain claimed territory that roughly corresponds with modern day Botswana as a protectorate called Bechuanaland. Upon independence in 1966, the British protectorate of Bechuanaland adopted the new name of Botswana, which means "land of the Tswana."

More than five decades of uninterrupted civilian leadership, progressive social policies, and significant capital investment have created an enduring democracy and upper-middle-income economy. The ruling Botswana Democratic Party has won every national election since independence; President Mokgweetsi Eric Keabetswe MASISI assumed the presidency in 2018 after the retirement of former President Ian KHAMA due to constitutional term limits. MASISI won his first election as president in 2019, and he is Botswana's fifth president since independence. Mineral extraction, principally diamond mining, dominates economic activity, though tourism is a growing sector due to the country's conservation practices and extensive nature preserves. Botswana

has one of the world's highest rates of HIV/AIDS infection but also one of Africa's most progressive and comprehensive programs for dealing with the disease.

GEOGRAPHY

Location: Southern Africa, north of South Africa

Geographic coordinates: 22 00 S, 24 00 E

Map references: Africa

Area: *total:* 581,730 sq km
land: 566,730 sq km
water: 15,000 sq km
comparison ranking: total 50

Area - comparative: slightly smaller than Texas; almost four times the size of Illinois

Land boundaries: *total:* 4,347.15 km
border countries (4): Namibia 1,544 km; South Africa 1,969 km; Zambia 0.15 km; Zimbabwe 834 km

Coastline: 0 km (landlocked)

Maritime claims: none (landlocked)

Climate: semiarid; warm winters and hot summers

Terrain: predominantly flat to gently rolling tableland; Kalahari Desert in southwest

Elevation: *highest point:* Manyelanong Hill 1,495 m
lowest point: junction of the Limpopo and Shashe Rivers 513 m
mean elevation: 1,013 m

Natural resources: diamonds, copper, nickel, salt, soda ash, potash, coal, iron ore, silver

Land use: *agricultural land:* 45.6% (2022 est.)
arable land: 0.5% (2022 est.)
permanent crops: 0% (2022 est.)
permanent pasture: 45.2% (2022 est.)
forest: 26.5% (2022 est.)
other: 27.9% (2022 est.)

Irrigated land: 25 sq km (2014)

Major rivers (by length in km): Zambezi (shared with Zambia [s]), Angola, Namibia, Zimbabwe, and Mozambique [m]) - 2,740 km; Limpopo (shared with South Africa [s], Zimbabwe, and Mozambique [m]) - 1,800 km; Okavango river mouth (shared with Angola [s], and Namibia) - 1,600 km
note: [s] after country name indicates river source; [m] after country name indicates river mouth

Major watersheds (area sq km): Atlantic Ocean drainage: Orange (941,351 sq km)

Indian Ocean drainage: Zambezi (1,332,412 sq km)

Internal (endorheic basin) drainage: Okavango Basin (863,866 sq km)

Major aquifers: Lower Kalahari-Stampriet Basin, Upper Kalahari-Cuvelai-Upper Zambezi Basin

Population distribution: the population is primarily concentrated in the east, with a focus in and around the capital of Gaborone and the eastern city of Francistown; population density remains low in other areas in the country, especially in the Kalahari Desert to the west.

Natural hazards: periodic droughts; seasonal August winds blow from the west, carrying sand and dust across the country, which can obscure visibility

Geography - note: landlocked; sparsely populated with most settlement concentrated in the southern and eastern parts of the country; geography dominated by the Kalahari Desert, which covers about 70% of the country, although the Okavango Delta brings considerable biodiversity as one of the largest inland deltas in the World

PEOPLE AND SOCIETY

Population: *total:* 2,450,668 (2024 est.)
male: 1,174,306
female: 1,276,362
comparison rankings: total 146; male 146; female 143

Nationality: *noun:* Motswana (singular), Batswana (plural)
adjective: Motswana (singular), Batswana (plural)

Ethnic groups: Tswana (or Setswana) 79%, Kalanga 11%, Basarwa 3%, other, including Kgalagadi and people of European ancestry 7%

Languages: Setswana 77.3%, Sekalanga 7.4%, Shekgalagadi 3.4%, English (official) 2.8%, Zezuru/Shona 2%, Sesarwa 1.7%, Sembukushu 1.6%, Ndebele 1%, other 2.8% (2011 est.)

Religions: Christian 79.1%, Badimo 4.1%, other 1.4% (includes Baha'i, Hindu, Muslim, Rastafarian), none 15.2%, unspecified 0.3% (2011 est.)

Age structure: *0-14 years:* 28.7% (male 355,583/female 348,863)
15-64 years: 65.2% (male 759,210/female 837,752)
65 years and over: 6.1% (2024 est.) (male 59,513/female 89,747)

Dependency ratios: *total dependency ratio:* 53.5 (2024 est.)
youth dependency ratio: 44.1 (2024 est.)
elderly dependency ratio: 9.3 (2024 est.)
potential support ratio: 10.7 (2024 est.)

Median age: *total:* 27.1 years (2024 est.)
male: 26 years
female: 28.3 years
comparison ranking: total 161

Population growth rate: 1.34% (2024 est.)
comparison ranking: 72

Birth rate: 19.6 births/1,000 population (2024 est.)
comparison ranking: 72

Death rate: 8.9 deaths/1,000 population (2024 est.)
comparison ranking: 62

Net migration rate: 2.7 migrant(s)/1,000 population (2024 est.)
comparison ranking: 42

Population distribution: the population is primarily concentrated in the east, with a focus in and around the capital of Gaborone and the eastern city of Francistown; population density remains low in other areas in the country, especially in the Kalahari Desert to the west.

Urbanization: *urban population:* 72.9% of total population (2023)
rate of urbanization: 2.47% annual rate of change (2020-25 est.)

Major urban areas - population: 269,000 GABORONE (capital) (2018)

Sex ratio: *at birth:* 1.03 male(s)/female
0-14 years: 1.02 male(s)/female
15-64 years: 0.91 male(s)/female
65 years and over: 0.66 male(s)/female
total population: 0.92 male(s)/female (2024 est.)

Maternal mortality ratio: 155 deaths/100,000 live births (2023 est.)
comparison ranking: 50

Infant mortality rate: *total:* 23.7 deaths/1,000 live births (2024 est.)
male: 25.9 deaths/1,000 live births
female: 21.4 deaths/1,000 live births
comparison ranking: total 65

Life expectancy at birth: *total population:* 66.4 years (2024 est.)
male: 64.4 years
female: 68.6 years
comparison ranking: total population 201

Total fertility rate: 2.34 children born/woman (2024 est.)
comparison ranking: 75

Gross reproduction rate: 1.15 (2024 est.)

Drinking water source: *improved: urban:* 97.5% of population (2022 est.)
rural: 79.6% of population (2022 est.)
total: 92.6% of population (2022 est.)
unimproved: urban: 2.5% of population (2022 est.)
rural: 20.4% of population (2022 est.)
total: 7.4% of population (2022 est.)

Health expenditure: 6.3% of GDP (2021)
14.6% of national budget (2022 est.)

Physician density: 0.38 physicians/1,000 population (2023)

Hospital bed density: 2.2 beds/1,000 population (2021 est.)

Sanitation facility access: *improved: urban:* 94.9% of population (2022 est.)
rural: 63% of population (2022 est.)
total: 86% of population (2022 est.)
unimproved: urban: 5.1% of population (2022 est.)
rural: 37% of population (2022 est.)
total: 14% of population (2022 est.)

Obesity - adult prevalence rate: 18.9% (2016)
comparison ranking: 114

Alcohol consumption per capita: *total:* 5.98 liters of pure alcohol (2019 est.)
beer: 2.93 liters of pure alcohol (2019 est.)
wine: 0.46 liters of pure alcohol (2019 est.)
spirits: 0.96 liters of pure alcohol (2019 est.)
other alcohols: 1.64 liters of pure alcohol (2019 est.)
comparison ranking: total 71

Tobacco use: *total:* 17.1% (2025 est.)
male: 29.2% (2025 est.)
female: 5.5% (2025 est.)
comparison ranking: total 92

Children under the age of 5 years underweight: NA

Currently married women (ages 15-49): 45% (2023 est.)

Education expenditure: 8.1% of GDP (2020 est.)
21.5% national budget (2020 est.)
comparison ranking: Education expenditure (% GDP) 11

School life expectancy (primary to tertiary education): *total:* 12 years (2021 est.)
male: 12 years (2021 est.)
female: 13 years (2021 est.)

ENVIRONMENT

Environmental issues: overgrazing; desertification; limited freshwater resources; air pollution

International environmental agreements: *party to:* Biodiversity, Climate Change, Climate Change-Kyoto Protocol, Climate Change-Paris Agreement, Desertification, Endangered Species, Hazardous Wastes, Law of the Sea, Nuclear Test Ban, Ozone Layer Protection, Wetlands
signed, but not ratified: none of the selected agreements

Climate: semiarid; warm winters and hot summers

Urbanization: *urban population:* 72.9% of total population (2023)
rate of urbanization: 2.47% annual rate of change (2020-25 est.)

Carbon dioxide emissions: 5.897 million metric tonnes of CO_2 (2023 est.)
from coal and metallurgical coke: 2.818 million metric tonnes of CO_2 (2023 est.)
from petroleum and other liquids: 3.079 million metric tonnes of CO_2 (2023 est.)
comparison ranking: total emissions 131

Particulate matter emissions: 12.5 micrograms per cubic meter (2019 est.)

Methane emissions: *energy:* 26 kt (2022-2024 est.)
agriculture: 144 kt (2019-2021 est.)
waste: 841.4 kt (2019-2021 est.)
other: 1.7 kt (2019-2021 est.)

Waste and recycling: *municipal solid waste generated annually:* 210,900 tons (2024 est.)
percent of municipal solid waste recycled: 21% (2022 est.)

Total water withdrawal: *municipal:* 129.327 million cubic meters (2022)
industrial: 24.295 million cubic meters (2022)
agricultural: 59.661 million cubic meters (2022)

Total renewable water resources: 12.24 billion cubic meters (2022 est.)

GOVERNMENT

Country name: *conventional long form:* Republic of Botswana
conventional short form: Botswana
local long form: Republic of Botswana
local short form: Botswana
former: Bechuanaland
etymology: the name Botswana means "Land of the Tswana," referring to the country's largest ethnic group

Government type: parliamentary republic

Capital: *name:* Gaborone
geographic coordinates: 24 38 S, 25 54 E
time difference: UTC+2 (7 hours ahead of Washington, DC, during Standard Time)
etymology: named after GABORONE (ca. 1825-1931), a chief of the Tlokwa tribe, whose name means "it is not unbecoming"

Administrative divisions: 10 districts and 6 town councils*; Central, Chobe, Francistown*, Gaborone*, Ghanzi, Jwaneng*, Kgalagadi, Kgatleng, Kweneng, Lobatse*, North East, North West, Selebi-Phikwe*, South East, Southern, Sowa Town*

Legal system: mixed legal system of civil law influenced by the Roman-Dutch model, including customary and common law

Constitution: *history:* previous 1960 (pre-independence); latest adopted March 1965, effective 30 September 1966
amendment process: proposed by the National Assembly; passage requires approval in two successive Assembly votes with at least two-thirds majority in the final vote; proposals to amend constitutional provisions on fundamental rights and freedoms, the structure and branches of government, and public services also requires approval by majority vote in a referendum and assent by the president of the republic

International law organization participation: accepts compulsory ICJ jurisdiction with reservations; accepts ICCt jurisdiction

Citizenship: *citizenship by birth:* no
citizenship by descent only: at least one parent must be a citizen of Botswana
dual citizenship recognized: no
residency requirement for naturalization: 10 years

Suffrage: 18 years of age; universal

Executive branch: *chief of state:* President Duma BOKO (since 1 November 2024)
head of government: President Duma BOKO (since 1 November 2024)
cabinet: Cabinet appointed by the president
election/appointment process: president indirectly elected by the National Assembly for a 5-year term (eligible for a second term); vice president appointed by the president
most recent election date: 31 October 2024
election results: BOKO's UDC won 35 seats in the National Assembly, which then selected BOKO as president
expected date of next election: October 2029

Legislative branch: *legislature name:* Parliament
legislative structure: unicameral
chamber name: National Assembly
number of seats: 69 (61 directly elected; 6 indirectly elected)
electoral system: plurality/majority
scope of elections: full renewal
term in office: 5 years
most recent election date: 10/30/2024
parties elected and seats per party: Umbrella for Democratic Change (UDC) (36); Botswana Congress Party (BCP) (15); Botswana Patriotic Front (BPF) (5); Botswana Democratic Party (BDP) (4); Other (1)
percentage of women in chamber: 9%
expected date of next election: October 2029
note: the House of Chiefs (Ntlo ya Dikgosi), an advisory body to the National Assembly, consists of 35 members – 8 hereditary chiefs from Botswana's principal tribes, 22 indirectly elected by the chiefs, and 5 appointed by the president; the House of Chiefs consults on issues including powers of chiefs, customary courts, customary law, tribal property, and constitutional amendments

Judicial branch: *highest court(s):* Court of Appeal, High Court (each consists of a chief justice and a number of other judges as prescribed by the Parliament)
judge selection and term of office: Court of Appeal and High Court chief justices appointed by the president and other judges appointed by the president upon the advice of the Judicial Service Commission; all judges appointed to serve until age 70
subordinate courts: Industrial Court (with circuits scheduled monthly in the capital city and in 3 districts); Magistrates Courts (1 in each district); Customary Court of Appeal; Paramount Chief's Court/Urban Customary Court; Senior Chief's Representative Court; Chief's Representative's Court; Headman's Court

Political parties: Alliance of Progressives or AP
Botswana Congress Party or BCP
Botswana Democratic Party or BDP
Botswana National Front or BNF [Duma BOKO]
Botswana Patriotic Front or BPF
Botswana Peoples Party or BPP
Botswana Republic Party or BRP
Umbrella for Democratic Change or UDC (various times the coalition has included the BPP, BCP, BNF and other parties)

Diplomatic representation in the US: *chief of mission:* Ambassador Mpho Churchill MOPHUTING (since 18 September 2024)
chancery: 1531-1533 New Hampshire Avenue NW, Washington, DC 20036
telephone: [1] (202) 244-4990
FAX: [1] (202) 244-4164
email address and website: info@ botswanaembassy.org
http://www.botswanaembassy.org/

Diplomatic representation from the US: *chief of mission:* Ambassador Howard A. VAN VRANKEN (since 24 May 2023)
embassy: Embassy Drive, Government Enclave (off Khama Crescent), Gaborone
mailing address: 2170 Gaborone Place, Washington DC 20521-2170
telephone: [267] 395-3982
FAX: [267] 318-0232
email address and website: ConsularGaborone@state.gov
https://bw.usembassy.gov/

International organization participation: ACP, AfDB, AU, C, CD, FAO, G-77, IAEA, IBRD, ICAO, ICCt, ICRM, IDA, IFAD, IFC, IFRCS, ILO, IMF, Interpol, IOC, IOM, IPU, ISO, ITSO, ITU, ITUC (NGOs), MIGA, MONUSCO, NAM, OPCW, SACU, SADC, UN, UNCTAD, UNESCO, UNIDO, UNWTO, UPU, WCO, WFTU (NGOs), WHO, WIPO, WMO, WTO

Independence: 30 September 1966 (from the UK)

National holiday: Independence Day (Botswana Day), 30 September (1966)

Flag: *description:* light blue with a horizontal white-edged black stripe across the middle
meaning: the blue symbolizes rainwater, and the black and white bands represent racial harmony

National symbol(s): zebra

National color(s): light blue, white, black

National coat of arms: *the two zebras, the country's national symbol, support an elephant tusk that represents the country's fauna and a head of sorghum that signifies agriculture; the three wavy blue bands stand for the country's reliance on water, the cog wheels for industry, and the bull's head for the cattle industry; the coat of arms also features the national colors of light blue, white, and black; the motto reflects the scarcity of rain in the country: pula* means "let there be rain" in Setswana, the national language

National anthem(s): *title:* "Fatshe leno la rona" (Our Land)
lyrics/music: Kgalemang Tumedisco MOTSETE
history: adopted 1966

National heritage: *total World Heritage Sites:* 2 (1 cultural, 1 natural)
selected World Heritage Site locales: Tsodilo Hills (c); Okavango Delta (n)

ECONOMY

Economic overview: good economic governance and financial management; diamond-driven growth model declining; rapid poverty reductions; high unemployment, particularly among youth; COVID-19 sharply contracted the economy and recovery is slow; public sector wages have posed fiscal challenges

Real GDP (purchasing power parity): $45.553 billion (2024 est.)
$46.957 billion (2023 est.)
$45.498 billion (2022 est.)
note: data in 2021 dollars
comparison ranking: 134

Real GDP growth rate: -3% (2024 est.)
3.2% (2023 est.)
5.5% (2022 est.)
note: annual GDP % growth based on constant local currency
comparison ranking: 210

Real GDP per capita: $18,100 (2024 est.)
$18,900 (2023 est.)
$18,600 (2022 est.)
note: data in 2021 dollars
comparison ranking: 111

GDP (official exchange rate): $19.401 billion (2024 est.)
note: data in current dollars at official exchange rate

Inflation rate (consumer prices): 2.8% (2024 est.)
5.1% (2023 est.)
11.7% (2022 est.)
note: annual % change based on consumer prices
comparison ranking: 83

GDP - composition, by sector of origin: *agriculture:* 1.7% (2024 est.)
industry: 29.4% (2024 est.)
services: 63.5% (2024 est.)
note: figures may not total 100% due to non-allocated consumption not captured in sector-reported data
comparison rankings: agriculture 159; industry 60; services 65

GDP - composition, by end use: *household consumption:* 45.3% (2024 est.)
government consumption: 32.1% (2024 est.)
investment in fixed capital: 28.5% (2024 est.)
investment in inventories: 7.7% (2024 est.)
exports of goods and services: 26% (2024 est.)
imports of goods and services: -40.9% (2024 est.)
note: figures may not total 100% due to rounding or gaps in data collection

Agricultural products: root vegetables, beef, vegetables, sorghum, maize, game meat, milk, watermelons, goat milk, sunflower seeds (2023)
note: top ten agricultural products based on tonnage

Industries: diamonds, copper, nickel, salt, soda ash, potash, coal, iron ore, silver; beef processing; textiles

Industrial production growth rate: -13.5% (2024 est.)
note: annual % change in industrial value added based on constant local currency
comparison ranking: 190

Labor force: 1.173 million (2024 est.)
note: number of people ages 15 or older who are employed or seeking work
comparison ranking: 142

Unemployment rate: 23.2% (2024 est.)
23.4% (2023 est.)
23.7% (2022 est.)
note: % of labor force seeking employment
comparison ranking: 185

Youth unemployment rate (ages 15-24): *total:* 43.9% (2024 est.)
male: 39.8% (2024 est.)
female: 48.6% (2024 est.)
note: % of labor force ages 15-24 seeking employment
comparison ranking: total 5

Population below poverty line: 16.1% (2015 est.)
note: % of population with income below national poverty line

Gini Index coefficient - distribution of family income 54.9 (2015 est.)
note: index (0-100) of income distribution; higher values represent greater inequality
comparison ranking: 2

Household income or consumption by percentage share: *lowest 10%:* 1.4% (2015 est.)
highest 10%: 42.9% (2015 est.)
note: % share of income accruing to lowest and highest 10% of population

Remittances: 0.4% of GDP (2023 est.)
0.3% of GDP (2022 est.)
0.3% of GDP (2021 est.)
note: personal transfers and compensation between resident and non-resident individuals/households/entities

Budget: *revenues:* $5.474 billion (2024 est.)
expenditures: $6.296 billion (2024 est.)
note: central government revenues and expenses (excluding grants/extrabudgetary units/social security funds) converted to US dollars at average official exchange rate for year indicated

Public debt: 19.6% of GDP (2020 est.)
note: central government debt as a % of GDP
comparison ranking: 183

Taxes and other revenues: 19.6% (of GDP) (2022 est.)
note: central government tax revenue as a % of GDP
comparison ranking: 53

Current account balance: -$116.727 million (2023 est.)
-$232.122 million (2022 est.)
-$314.583 million (2021 est.)
note: balance of payments - net trade and primary/secondary income in current dollars
comparison ranking: 96

Exports: $6.398 billion (2023 est.)
$8.914 billion (2022 est.)
$7.861 billion (2021 est.)
note: balance of payments - exports of goods and services in current dollars
comparison ranking: 130

Exports - partners: UAE 27%, India 17%, Belgium 16%, South Africa 8%, USA 7% (2023)
note: top five export partners based on percentage share of exports

Exports - commodities: diamonds, copper ore, insulated wire, carbonates, cattle (2023)
note: top five export commodities based on value in dollars

Imports: $7.228 billion (2023 est.)
$8.826 billion (2022 est.)
$9.25 billion (2021 est.)
note: balance of payments - imports of goods and services in current dollars
comparison ranking: 137

Imports - partners: South Africa 65%, Namibia 8%, Canada 5%, China 3%, India 3% (2023)
note: top five import partners based on percentage share of imports

Imports - commodities: refined petroleum, diamonds, cars, flavored water, electricity (2023)
note: top five import commodities based on value in dollars

Reserves of foreign exchange and gold: $3.456 billion (2024 est.)
$4.756 billion (2023 est.)
$4.279 billion (2022 est.)
note: holdings of gold (year-end prices)/foreign exchange/special drawing rights in current dollars
comparison ranking: 112

Debt - external: $1.761 billion (2023 est.)
note: present value of external debt in current US dollars
comparison ranking: 98

Exchange rates: pulas (BWP) per US dollar -

Exchange rates: 13.563 (2024 est.)
13.596 (2023 est.)
12.369 (2022 est.)
11.087 (2021 est.)
11.456 (2020 est.)

ENERGY

Electricity access: *electrification - total population:* 75.9% (2022 est.)
electrification - urban areas: 95.5%
electrification - rural areas: 25%

Electricity: *installed generating capacity:* 758,000 kW (2023 est.)
consumption: 3.879 billion kWh (2023 est.)
exports: 2 million kWh (2023 est.)
imports: 1.923 billion kWh (2023 est.)
transmission/distribution losses: 625.694 million kWh (2023 est.)
comparison rankings: installed generating capacity 143; consumption 137; exports 102; imports 67; transmission/distribution losses 87

Electricity generation sources: *fossil fuels:* 99.8% of total installed capacity (2023 est.)
solar: 0.2% of total installed capacity (2023 est.)

Coal: *production:* 2.242 million metric tons (2023 est.)
consumption: 1.351 million metric tons (2023 est.)
exports: 891,000 metric tons (2023 est.)
imports: 300 metric tons (2023 est.)
proven reserves: 1.66 billion metric tons (2023 est.)

Petroleum: *refined petroleum consumption:* 22,000 bbl/day (2023 est.)

Energy consumption per capita: 32.443 million Btu/person (2023 est.)
comparison ranking: 113

COMMUNICATIONS

Telephones - fixed lines: *total subscriptions:* 90,000 (2023 est.)
subscriptions per 100 inhabitants: 4 (2023 est.)
comparison ranking: total subscriptions 137

Telephones - mobile cellular: *total subscriptions:* 4.44 million (2023 est.)
subscriptions per 100 inhabitants: 165 (2022 est.)
comparison ranking: total subscriptions 131

Broadcast media: 2 TV stations, 1 state-owned and 1 privately owned; privately owned satellite TV subscription service is available; 2 state-owned national radio stations; 4 privately owned radio stations broadcast locally (2019)

Internet country code: .bw

Internet users: *percent of population:* 81% (2023 est.)

Broadband - fixed subscriptions: *total:* 85,000 (2023 est.)
subscriptions per 100 inhabitants: 3 (2023 est.)
comparison ranking: total 138

TRANSPORTATION

Civil aircraft registration country code prefix: A2

Airports: 122 (2025)
comparison ranking: 42

Railways: *total:* 888 km (2014)
narrow gauge: 888 km (2014) 1.067-m gauge

MILITARY AND SECURITY

Military and security forces: Botswana Defense Force (BDF): Ground Forces Command, Air Arm Command, Defense Logistics Command (2025)
note 1: both the BDF and the Botswana Police Service (BPS) report to the Ministry of Defense, Justice and Security; the BPS has primary responsibility for internal security
note 2: the Ground Force Command includes a marine unit with boats and river craft for patrolling Botswana's internal waterways and supporting anti-poaching operations

Military expenditures: 2.9% of GDP (2024 est.)
2.6% of GDP (2023 est.)
2.8% of GDP (2022 est.)
3% of GDP (2021 est.)
3% of GDP (2020 est.)

Military and security service personnel strengths: estimated 10,000 active Botswana Defense Force (2025)

Military equipment inventories and acquisitions: the BDF has a mix of mostly older weapons and equipment, largely of Western/European origin; in recent years, it has received limited amounts of material from several European countries and the US (2024)

Military service age and obligation: 18 is the legal minimum age for voluntary military service for men and women; no conscription (2024)

Military - note: the key responsibilities of the Botswana Defense Force (BDF) are defending the country's sovereignty and territorial integrity on land and in the air, ensuring national security and stability, and aiding civil authorities in support of domestic missions such as disaster relief and anti-poaching; the BDF also participates in regional and international security operations
Bechuanaland/Botswana did not have a permanent military during colonial times, with the British colonial administrators relying instead on small, lightly armed constabularies such as the Bechuanaland Mounted Police, the Bechuanaland Border Police, and by the early 1960s, the Police Mobile Unit (PMU); after independence in 1966, Botswana militarized the PMU and gave it responsibility for the country's defense rather than create a conventional military force; however, turmoil in neighboring countries and numerous cross-border incursions by Rhodesian and South African security forces in the 1960s and 1970s demonstrated that the PMU was inadequate for defending the country and led to the establishment of the BDF in 1977 (2025)

TRANSNATIONAL ISSUES

Refugees and internally displaced persons: *refugees:* 823 (2024 est.)

IDPs: 99 (2023 est.)

BOUVET ISLAND

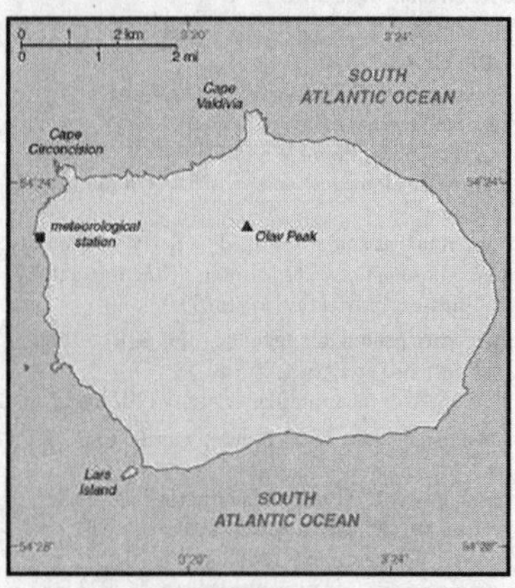

INTRODUCTION

Background: This uninhabited volcanic island in Antarctica is almost entirely covered by glaciers, making it difficult to approach. Bouvet Island is recognized as the most remote island on Earth because it is furthest from any other point of land (1,639 km from Antarctica). The island was named after the French naval officer who discovered it in 1739, although no country laid claim to it until 1825, when the British flag was raised. A few expeditions visited the island in the late 19th century. In 1929, the UK waived its claim in favor of Norway, which had occupied the island two years previously. In 1971, Norway designated Bouvet Island and the adjacent territorial waters as a nature reserve. Since 1977, Norway has run an automated meteorological station and studied foraging strategies and distribution of fur seals and penguins on the island. In 2006, an earthquake weakened the station's foundation, causing it to be blown out to sea in a winter storm. Norway erected a new research station in 2014 that can hold six people for periods of two to four months.

GEOGRAPHY

Location: island in the South Atlantic Ocean, southwest of the Cape of Good Hope (South Africa)

Geographic coordinates: 54 26 S, 3 24 E

Map references: Antarctic Region

Area: *total:* 49 sq km
land: 49 sq km
water: 0 sq km
comparison ranking: total 231

Area - comparative: about 0.3 times the size of Washington, D.C.

Land boundaries: *total:* 0 km

Coastline: 29.6 km

Maritime claims: *territorial sea:* 4 nm

Climate: antarctic

Terrain: volcanic; coast is mostly inaccessible

Elevation: *highest point:* Olavtoppen (Olav Peak) 780 m
lowest point: South Atlantic Ocean 0 m

Natural resources: none

Land use: *agricultural land:* 0% (2018 est.)
arable land: 0% (2018 est.)
permanent crops: 0% (2018 est.)
permanent pasture: 0% (2018 est.)
forest: 0% (2018 est.)
other: 100% (2018 est.)

Natural hazards: occasional volcanism, rock slides; harsh climate, surrounded by pack ice in winter

Geography - note: almost entirely covered by glacial ice (93%); declared a nature reserve by Norway; the distance from Bouvet Island to Norway is 12,776 km, which is almost one-third the circumference of the earth

PEOPLE AND SOCIETY

Population: *total:* uninhabited
note: a small, seasonal research station is located in the northwest corner of Bouvet Island

ENVIRONMENT

Climate: antarctic

GOVERNMENT

Country name: *conventional long form:* none
conventional short form: Bouvet Island
etymology: named after the French naval officer Jean-Baptiste Charles BOUVET who discovered the island in 1739
note: pronounced boo-vay i-land

Dependency status: territory of Norway; administered by the Polar Department of the Ministry of Justice and Oslo Police

Legal system: the laws of Norway apply

Flag: the flag of Norway is used

COMMUNICATIONS

Internet country code: .bv

BRAZIL

INTRODUCTION

Background: After more than three centuries under Portuguese rule, Brazil gained its independence in 1822, maintaining a monarchical system of government until the abolition of slavery in 1888 and the subsequent proclamation of a republic by the military in 1889. Brazilian coffee exporters politically dominated the country until populist leader Getúlio VARGAS rose to power in 1930. VARGAS governed through various versions of democratic and authoritarian regimes from 1930 to 1945. Democratic rule returned in 1945 – including a democratically elected VARGAS administration from 1951 to 1954 – and lasted until 1964, when the military overthrew President João GOULART. The military regime censored journalists and repressed and tortured dissidents in the late 1960s and early 1970s. The dictatorship lasted until 1985, when the military regime peacefully ceded power to civilian rulers, and the Brazilian Congress passed its current constitution in 1988.

By far the largest and most populous country in South America, Brazil continues to pursue industrial and agricultural growth and development of its interior. Having successfully weathered a period of global financial difficulty in the late 20th century, Brazil was soon seen as one of the world's strongest emerging markets and a contributor to global growth under President Luiz Inácio LULA da Silva (2003-2010). The awarding of the 2014 FIFA World Cup and 2016 Summer Olympic Games – the first ever to be held in South America – to Brazil was symbolic of the country's rise. However, from about 2013 to 2016, Brazil was plagued by a sagging economy, high unemployment, and high inflation, only emerging from recession in 2017. Congress removed then-President Dilma ROUSSEFF (2011-2016) from office in 2016 for having committed impeachable acts against Brazil's budgetary laws, and her vice president, Michel TEMER, served the remainder of her second term. A money-laundering investigation, Operation Lava Jato, uncovered a vast corruption scheme and prosecutors charged several high-profile Brazilian politicians with crimes. Former President LULA was convicted of accepting bribes and served jail time (2018-19), although his conviction was overturned in 2021. LULA's revival became complete in 2022 when he narrowly defeated incumbent Jair BOLSONARO (2019-2022) in the presidential election. Positioning Brazil as an independent global leader on climate change and promoting sustainable development, LULA took on the 2024 G20 presidency, balancing the fight against deforestation with sustainable energy and other projects designed to alleviate poverty and promote economic growth, such as expanding fossil fuel exploration.

GEOGRAPHY

Location: Eastern South America, bordering the Atlantic Ocean

Geographic coordinates: 10 00 S, 55 00 W

Map references: South America

Area: *total:* 8,515,770 sq km
land: 8,358,140 sq km
water: 157,630 sq km
note: includes Arquipelago de Fernando de Noronha, Atol das Rocas, Ilha da Trindade, Ilhas Martin Vaz, and Penedos de Sao Pedro e Sao Paulo
comparison ranking: total 6

Area - comparative: slightly smaller than the US

Land boundaries: *total:* 16,145 km
border countries (10): Argentina 1,263 km; Bolivia 3,403 km; Colombia 1,790 km; French Guiana 649 km; Guyana 1,308 km; Paraguay 1,371 km; Peru 2,659 km; Suriname 515 km; Uruguay 1,050 km; Venezuela 2,137 km

Coastline: 7,491 km

Maritime claims: *territorial sea:* 12 nm
contiguous zone: 24 nm
exclusive economic zone: 200 nm
continental shelf: 200 nm or to edge of the continental margin

Climate: mostly tropical, but temperate in south

Terrain: mostly flat to rolling lowlands in north; some plains, hills, mountains, and narrow coastal belt

Elevation: *highest point:* Pico da Neblina 2,994 m
lowest point: Atlantic Ocean 0 m
mean elevation: 320 m

Natural resources: alumina, bauxite, beryllium, gold, iron ore, manganese, nickel, niobium, phosphates, platinum, tantalum, tin, rare earth elements, uranium, petroleum, hydropower, timber

Land use: *agricultural land:* 26.7% (2022 est.)
arable land: 6.7% (2022 est.)
permanent crops: 0.9% (2022 est.)
permanent pasture: 19.1% (2022 est.)
forest: 59.1% (2022 est.)
other: 14.2% (2022 est.)

Irrigated land: 91,833 sq km (2022)

Major lakes (area sq km): *fresh water lake(s):* Lagoa dos Patos - 10,140 sq km
salt water lake(s): Lagoa Mirim (shared with Uruguay) - 2,970 sq km

Major rivers (by length in km): Amazon river mouth (shared with Peru [s]) - 6,400 km; Río de la Plata/ Paraná river source (shared with Paraguay, Argentina, and Uruguay [m]) - 4,880 km; Tocantins - 3,650 km; São Francisco - 3,180 km; Paraguay river source (shared with Argentina and Paraguay [m]) - 2,549 km; Rio Negro river mouth (shared with Colombia [s] and Venezuela) - 2,250 km; Uruguay river source (shared with Argentina and Uruguay [m]) - 1,610 km
note: [s] after country name indicates river source; [m] after country name indicates river mouth

Major watersheds (area sq km): Atlantic Ocean drainage: Amazon (6,145,186 sq km), Orinoco (953,675 sq km), Paraná (2,582,704 sq km), São Francisco (617,814 sq km), Tocantins (764,213 sq km)

Major aquifers: Amazon Basin, Guarani Aquifer System, Maranhao Basin

Population distribution: the vast majority of people live along or near the Atlantic coast in the east; the population core is in the southeast, anchored by the cities of São Paolo, Brasília, and Rio de Janeiro

Natural hazards: recurring droughts in northeast; floods and occasional frost in south

Geography - note: *note 1:* largest country in South America and in the Southern Hemisphere; shares common boundaries with every South American country except Chile and Ecuador; most of the Pantanal, the world's largest tropical wetland, extends through the west central part of the country; shares Iguaçu Falls (Iguazú Falls), the world's largest waterfalls system, with Argentina
note 2: Rocas Atoll, located off the northeast coast of Brazil, is the only atoll in the South Atlantic

PEOPLE AND SOCIETY

Population: *total:* 220,051,512 (2024 est.)
male: 108,166,491
female: 111,885,021
comparison rankings: total 7; male 7; female 7

Nationality: *noun:* Brazilian(s)
adjective: Brazilian

Ethnic groups: mixed 45.3%, White 43.5%, Black 10.2%, Indigenous 0.6%, Asian 0.4% (2022 est.)

Languages: Portuguese (official and most widely spoken language); less common languages include Spanish (border areas and schools), German, Italian, Japanese, English, and many minor Amerindian languages
major-language sample(s):
O Livro de Fatos Mundiais, a fonte indispensável para informação básica. (Brazilian Portuguese)

Religions: Roman Catholic 56.8%, Evangelical 26.9%, none 9.3%, other 4%, Spirtism (Espírita) 1.8%, unspecified 1.4%, Umbanda and Candomblé 1.1%, Indigenous religions.06%, undeclared 0.2% (2022)

Age structure: *0-14 years:* 19.6% (male 22,025,593/ female 21,088,398)
15-64 years: 69.5% (male 75,889,089/female 77,118,722)
65 years and over: 10.9% (2024 est.) (male 10,251,809/female 13,677,901)

Dependency ratios: *total dependency ratio:* 43.8 (2024 est.)
youth dependency ratio: 28.2 (2024 est.)
elderly dependency ratio: 15.6 (2024 est.)

potential support ratio: 6.4 (2024 est.)

Median age: *total:* 35.1 years (2024 est.)
male: 34 years
female: 36.1 years
comparison ranking: total 101

Population growth rate: 0.61% (2024 est.)
comparison ranking: 138

Birth rate: 13.2 births/1,000 population (2024 est.)
comparison ranking: 131

Death rate: 7 deaths/1,000 population (2024 est.)
comparison ranking: 119

Net migration rate: -0.2 migrant(s)/1,000 population (2024 est.)
comparison ranking: 103

Population distribution: the vast majority of people live along or near the Atlantic coast in the east; the population core is in the southeast, anchored by the cities of São Paolo, Brasília, and Rio de Janeiro

Urbanization: *urban population:* 87.8% of total population (2023)
rate of urbanization: 0.87% annual rate of change (2020-25 est.)

Major urban areas - population: 22.620 million São Paulo, 13.728 million Rio de Janeiro, 6.248 million Belo Horizonte, 4.873 million BRASÍLIA (capital), 4.264 million Recife, 4.212 million Porto Alegre (2023)

Sex ratio: *at birth:* 1.05 male(s)/female
0-14 years: 1.04 male(s)/female
15-64 years: 0.98 male(s)/female
65 years and over: 0.75 male(s)/female
total population: 0.97 male(s)/female (2024 est.)

Maternal mortality ratio: 67 deaths/100,000 live births (2023 est.)
comparison ranking: 83

Infant mortality rate: *total:* 12.9 deaths/1,000 live births (2024 est.)
male: 14.6 deaths/1,000 live births
female: 11.1 deaths/1,000 live births
comparison ranking: total 107

Life expectancy at birth: *total population:* 76.3 years (2024 est.)
male: 72.6 years
female: 80.1 years
comparison ranking: total population 113

Total fertility rate: 1.74 children born/woman (2024 est.)
comparison ranking: 151

Gross reproduction rate: 0.85 (2024 est.)

Drinking water source: *improved:* *urban:* 99.8% of population (2022 est.)
rural: 98% of population (2022 est.)
total: 99.6% of population (2022 est.)
unimproved: *urban:* 0.2% of population (2022 est.)
rural: 2% of population (2022 est.)
total: 0.4% of population (2022 est.)

Health expenditure: 9.9% of GDP (2021)
9% of national budget (2022 est.)

Physician density: 2.36 physicians/1,000 population (2023)

Hospital bed density: 2.5 beds/1,000 population (2021 est.)

Sanitation facility access: *improved:* *urban:* 94.7% of population (2022 est.)
rural: 65% of population (2022 est.)
total: 91% of population (2022 est.)
unimproved: *urban:* 5.3% of population (2022 est.)
rural: 35% of population (2022 est.)
total: 9% of population (2022 est.)

Obesity - adult prevalence rate: 22.1% (2016)
comparison ranking: 81

Alcohol consumption per capita: *total:* 6.12 liters of pure alcohol (2019 est.)
beer: 3.84 liters of pure alcohol (2019 est.)
wine: 0.24 liters of pure alcohol (2019 est.)
spirits: 2 liters of pure alcohol (2019 est.)
other alcohols: 0.04 liters of pure alcohol (2019 est.)
comparison ranking: total 68

Tobacco use: *total:* 11.2% (2025 est.)
male: 14.4% (2025 est.)
female: 8.3% (2025 est.)
comparison ranking: total 121

Children under the age of 5 years underweight: 3.1% (2019)
comparison ranking: 79

Currently married women (ages 15-49): 55.9% (2023 est.)

Education expenditure: 5.5% of GDP (2021 est.)
12.8% national budget (2021 est.)
comparison ranking: Education expenditure (% GDP) 40

Literacy: *total population:* 93% (2022 est.)
male: 92.5% (2022 est.)
female: 93.5% (2022 est.)

School life expectancy (primary to tertiary education): *total:* 16 years (2022 est.)
male: 15 years (2022 est.)
female: 17 years (2022 est.)

ENVIRONMENT

Environmental issues: deforestation in Amazon Basin; illegal wildlife trade; illegal poaching; air and water pollution in Rio de Janeiro, Sao Paulo, and other large cities; land degradation and water pollution from mining; wetland degradation; oil spills

International environmental agreements: *party to:* Antarctic-Environmental Protection, Antarctic-Marine Living Resources, Antarctic Seals, Antarctic Treaty, Biodiversity, Climate Change, Climate Change-Kyoto Protocol, Climate Change-Paris Agreement, Comprehensive Nuclear Test Ban, Desertification, Endangered Species, Environmental Modification, Hazardous Wastes, Law of the Sea, Marine Dumping-London Convention, Nuclear Test Ban, Ozone Layer Protection, Ship Pollution, Tropical Timber 2006, Wetlands, Whaling
signed, but not ratified: Marine Dumping-London Protocol

Climate: mostly tropical, but temperate in south

Urbanization: *urban population:* 87.8% of total population (2023)
rate of urbanization: 0.87% annual rate of change (2020-25 est.)

Carbon dioxide emissions: 437.769 million metric tonnes of CO_2 (2023 est.)
from coal and metallurgical coke: 53.664 million metric tonnes of CO_2 (2023 est.)
from petroleum and other liquids: 331.079 million metric tonnes of CO_2 (2023 est.)
from consumed natural gas: 53.026 million metric tonnes of CO_2 (2023 est.)
comparison ranking: total emissions 14

Particulate matter emissions: 10.9 micrograms per cubic meter (2019 est.)

Methane emissions: *energy:* 1,759.1 kt (2022-2024 est.)
agriculture: 13,761.9 kt (2019-2021 est.)
waste: 3,361.8 kt (2019-2021 est.)
other: 382.6 kt (2019-2021 est.)

Waste and recycling: *municipal solid waste generated annually:* 79.07 million tons (2024 est.)
percent of municipal solid waste recycled: 2.8% (2022 est.)

Total water withdrawal: *municipal:* 16.397 billion cubic meters (2022)
industrial: 10.2 billion cubic meters (2022)
agricultural: 41.336 billion cubic meters (2022)

Total renewable water resources: 8.647 trillion cubic meters (2022 est.)

Geoparks: *total global geoparks and regional networks:* 6: *global geoparks and regional networks:* Araripe; Cacapava; Quarta Colonia; Serido; Southern Canyons Pathways; Uberaba (2024)

GOVERNMENT

Country name: *conventional long form:* Federative Republic of Brazil
conventional short form: Brazil
local long form: República Federativa do Brasil
local short form: Brasil
etymology: the country name derives from the brazil tree that used to grow plentifully along the coast of Brazil and that was used to produce a deep red dye

Government type: federal presidential republic

Capital: *name:* Brasília
geographic coordinates: 15 47 S, 47 55 W
time difference: UTC-3 (2 hours ahead of Washington, DC, during Standard Time)
time zone note: Brazil has four time zones, including one for the Fernando de Noronha Islands
etymology: the name is the Latinized form of the country name, bestowed on the new capital of Brazil in 1960; previous Brazilian capitals were Salvador (1549-1763) and Rio de Janeiro (1763 to 1960)

Administrative divisions: 26 states (*estados*, singular - *estado*) and 1 federal district* (distrito federal); Acre, Alagoas, Amapa, Amazonas, Bahia, Ceara, Distrito Federal*, Espirito Santo, Goias, Maranhao, Mato Grosso, Mato Grosso do Sul, Minas Gerais, Para, Paraiba, Parana, Pernambuco, Piaui, Rio de Janeiro, Rio Grande do Norte, Rio Grande do Sul, Rondonia, Roraima, Santa Catarina, São Paulo, Sergipe, Tocantins

Legal system: civil law
note: a new civil-law code in 2002 replaced the 1916 code

Constitution: *history:* several previous; latest ratified 5 October 1988
amendment process: proposed by at least one third of either house of the National Congress, by the president of the republic, or by simple majority vote by more than half of the state legislative assemblies; passage requires at least three-fifths majority vote by both houses in each of two readings; constitutional provisions affecting the federal form of government, separation of powers, suffrage, or individual rights and guarantees cannot be amended

International law organization participation: has not submitted an ICJ jurisdiction declaration; accepts ICCt jurisdiction

Citizenship: *citizenship by birth:* yes
citizenship by descent only: yes
dual citizenship recognized: yes
residency requirement for naturalization: 4 years

Suffrage: voluntary between 16 to 18 years of age, over 70, and if illiterate; compulsory between 18 to 70 years of age
note: military conscripts by law cannot vote

Executive branch: *chief of state:* President Luiz Inácio LULA da Silva (since 1 January 2023)
head of government: President Luiz Inácio LULA da Silva (since 1 January 2023)
cabinet: Cabinet appointed by the president
election/appointment process: president and vice president directly elected on the same ballot by absolute-majority popular vote in 2 rounds, if needed, for a 4-year term (eligible for a single consecutive term and additional terms after at least one term has elapsed)
most recent election date: 2 October 2022, with runoff on 30 October 2022
election results: *2022:* Luiz Inácio LULA da Silva elected president in second round; percent of vote in first round - Luiz Inácio LULA da Silva (PT) 48.4%, Jair BOLSONARO (PSL) 43.2%, Simone Nassar TEBET (MDB) 4.2%, Ciro GOMES (PDT) 3%, other 1.2%; percent of vote in second round - Luiz Inácio LULA da Silva (PT) 50.9%, Jair BOLSONARO (PSL) 49.1%
2018: Jair BOLSONARO elected president in second round; percent of vote in first round - Jair BOLSONARO (PSL) 46%, Fernando HADDAD (PT) 29.3%, Ciro GOMEZ (PDT) 12.5%, Geraldo ALCKMIN (PSDB) 4.8%, other 7.4%; percent of vote in second round - Jair BOLSONARO (PSL) 55.1%, Fernando HADDAD (PT) 44.9%
expected date of next election: 4 October 2026
note: the president is both chief of state and head of government

Legislative branch: *legislature name:* National Congress (Congresso nacional)
legislative structure: bicameral
Legislative branch - lower chamber
chamber name: Chamber of Deputies (Câmara dos Deputados)
number of seats: 513 (all directly elected)
electoral system: proportional representation
scope of elections: full renewal
term in office: 4 years
most recent election date: 10/2/2022
parties elected and seats per party: Liberal Party (PL) (99); Workers' Party (PT) (69); Brazil Union (União) (59); Progressive Party (PP) (47); Brazilian Democratic Movement (MDB) (42); Social Democratic Party (PSD) (42); Republicans (Republicanos) (40); Other (115)
percentage of women in chamber: 18.1%
expected date of next election: October 2026

Legislative branch - upper chamber: *chamber name:* Federal Senate (Senado Federal)
number of seats: 81 (all directly elected)
electoral system: plurality/majority
scope of elections: partial renewal
term in office: 8 years
most recent election date: 10/2/2022
parties elected and seats per party: Liberal Party (PL) (8); Brazil Union (União) (5); Workers' Party (PT) (4); Progressive Party (PP) (3); Social Democratic Party (PSD) (2); Republicans (Republicanos) (2); Other (3)
percentage of women in chamber: 19.8%
expected date of next election: October 2026

Judicial branch: *highest court(s):* Supreme Federal Court or Supremo Tribunal Federal (consists of 11 justices)
judge selection and term of office: justices appointed by the president and approved by absolute majority by the Federal Senate; justices appointed to serve until mandatory retirement at age 75
subordinate courts: Tribunal of the Union, Federal Appeals Court, Superior Court of Justice, Superior Electoral Court, regional federal courts; state court system

Political parties: Act (Agir) (formerly Christian Labor Party or PTC)
Avante (formerly Labor Party of Brazil or PTdoB)
Brazil Union (União Brasil); note - founded from a merger between the Democrats (DEM) and the Social Liberal Party (PSL)
Brazilian Communist Party or PCB
Brazilian Democratic Movement or MDB
Brazilian Labor Party or PTB
Brazilian Renewal Labor Party or PRTB
Brazilian Labor Party or PTB
Brazilian Social Democracy Party or PSDB
Brazilian Socialist Party or PSB
Christian Democracy or DC (formerly Christian Social Democratic Party)
Cidadania (formerly Popular Socialist Party or PPS)
Communist Party of Brazil or PCdoB
Democratic Labor Party or PDT
Democratic Party or PSDC
Democrats or DEM (formerly Liberal Front Party or PFL); note - dissolved in February 2022
Green Party or PV
Liberal Party or PL [Valdemar Costa Neto] (formerly Party of the Republic or PR)
National Mobilization Party or PMN
New Party or NOVO
Patriota (formerly National Ecologic Party or PEN)
Podemos (formerly National Labor Party or PTN)
Progressive Party (Progressistas) or PP
Republican Social Order Party or PROS
Republicans (Republicanos) (formerly Brazilian Republican Party or PRB)
Social Christian Party or PSC
Social Democratic Party or PSD
Social Liberal Party or PSL
Socialism and Freedom Party or PSOL
Solidarity or SD
Sustainability Network or REDE
United Socialist Workers' Party or PSTU
Workers' Cause Party or PCO
Workers' Party or PT

Diplomatic representation in the US: *chief of mission:* Ambassador Maria Luiza Ribeiro VIOTTI (since 30 June 2023)
chancery: 3006 Massachusetts Avenue NW, Washington, DC 20008
telephone: [1] (202) 238-2700
FAX: [1] (202) 238-2827
email address and website: contact.washington@itamaraty.gov.br
https://www.gov.br/mre/pt-br/embaixada-washington
consulate(s) general: Atlanta, Boston, Chicago, Hartford (CT), Houston, Los Angeles, Miami, New York, Orlando, San Francisco

Diplomatic representation from the US: *chief of mission:* Ambassador (vacant); Chargé d'Affaires Gabriel ESCOBAR (since 21 January 2025)
embassy: SES - Avenida das Nações, Quadra 801, Lote 03, 70403-900 - Brasília, DF
mailing address: 7500 Brasilia Place, Washington DC 20521-7500
telephone: [55] (61) 3312-7000
FAX: [55] (61) 3225-9136
email address and website: BrasilliaACS@state.gov
https://br.usembassy.gov/
consulate(s) general: Recife, Porto Alegre, Rio de Janeiro, São Paulo
branch office(s): Belo Horizonte

International organization participation: AfDB (nonregional member), BIS, BRICS, CAN (associate), CD, CELAC, CPLP, FAO, FATF, G-15, G-20, G-24, G-5, G-77, IADB, IAEA, IBRD, ICAO, ICC (national committees), ICCt, ICRM, IDA, IFAD, IFC, IFRCS, IHO, ILO, IMF, IMO, IMSO, Interpol, IOC, IOM, IPU, ISO, ITSO, ITU, ITUC (NGOs), LAES, LAIA, LAS (observer), Mercosur, MIGA, MINURSO, MINUSTAH, MONUSCO, NAM (observer), NSG, OAS, OECD (enhanced engagement), OPANAL, OPCW, Paris Club (associate), PCA, PROSUR, SICA (observer), UN, UNASUR, UNCTAD, UNESCO, UNFICYP, UNHCR, UNHRC, UNIDO, UNISFA, UNIFIL, Union Latina, UNISFA, UNITAR, UNMIL, UNMISS, UNOCI, UNOOSA, UNRWA, UNWTO, UPU, WCO, WFTU (NGOs), WHO, WIPO, WMO, WTO

Independence: 7 September 1822 (from Portugal)

National holiday: Independence Day, 7 September (1822)

Flag: *description:* green with a large yellow diamond in the center, showing a blue celestial globe with 27 five-pointed white stars; the globe has a white equatorial band with the motto ORDEM E PROGRESSO (Order and Progress)
meaning: green stands for the country's forests, and yellow for its mineral wealth, with the diamond representing the country's shape; the blue globe and stars depict the sky over Rio de Janeiro on the morning of 15 November 1889, the day the Republic of Brazil was declared; the number of stars has risen with the creation of new states, from 21 to 27 (one for each state and the Federal District)
history: the flag was inspired by the former Empire of Brazil's flag (1822-1889)
note: one of four national flags that reflect the shape of the country in the flag design; the others are Bosnia and Herzegovina, Eritrea, and Vanuatu

National symbol(s): Southern Cross constellation
National color(s): green, yellow, blue
National anthem(s): *title:* "Hino Nacional Brasileiro" (Brazilian National Anthem)
lyrics/music: Joaquim Osorio Duque ESTRADA/ Francisco Manoel DA SILVA
history: music adopted 1890, lyrics adopted 1922; the anthem's music, composed in 1822, was used unofficially for many years

National heritage: *total World Heritage Sites:* 24 (15 cultural, 8 natural, 1 mixed)
selected World Heritage Site locales: Brasilia (c); Historic Salvador de Bahia (c); Historic Ouro Preto (c); Historic Center of the Town of Olinda (c); Iguaçu National Park (n); Jesuit Missions of the Guaranis (c); Rio de Janeiro: Carioca Landscapes

(c); Central Amazon Conservation Complex (n); Atlantic Forest South-East Reserves (n); Historic Center of Salvador de Bahia (c); Sanctuary of Bom Jesus do Congonhas (c); Brasilia (c); Serra da Capivara National Park (c); Historic Center of Sao Luis(c); Discovery Coast Atlantic Forest Reserves (n); Historic Center of the Town of Diamantina (c); Pantanal Conservation Area (n); Brazilian Atlantic Islands: Fernando de Noronha and Atol das Rocas Reserves (n); Cerrado Protected Areas: Chapada dos Veadeiros and Emas National Parks (n); Historic Centre of the Town of Goiás (c); São Francisco Square in the Town of São Cristóvão (c); Rio de Janeiro: Carioca Landscapes between the Mountain and the Sea (c); Pampulha Modern Ensemble (c); Valongo Wharf Archaeological Site (c); Paraty and Ilha Grande – Culture and Biodiversity (m); Sítio Roberto Burle Marx (c); Lençóis Maranhenses National Park (n)

ECONOMY

Economic overview: upper-middle-income, largest Latin American economy; Mercosur, BRICS, G20 member and OECD accession candidate; growth driven by strong domestic consumption; monetary tightening helping curb inflation rate; high inequality in income and access to health and education

Real GDP (purchasing power parity): $4.165 trillion (2024 est.)
$4.029 trillion (2023 est.)
$3.902 trillion (2022 est.)
note: data in 2021 dollars
comparison ranking: 7

Real GDP growth rate: 3.4% (2024 est.)
3.2% (2023 est.)
3% (2022 est.)
note: annual GDP % growth based on constant local currency
comparison ranking: 101

Real GDP per capita: $19,600 (2024 est.)
$19,100 (2023 est.)
$18,600 (2022 est.)
note: data in 2021 dollars
comparison ranking: 103

GDP (official exchange rate): $2.179 trillion (2024 est.)
note: data in current dollars at official exchange rate

Inflation rate (consumer prices): 4.4% (2024 est.)
4.6% (2023 est.)
9.3% (2022 est.)
note: annual % change based on consumer prices
comparison ranking: 132

GDP - composition, by sector of origin: *agriculture:* 5.6% (2024 est.)
industry: 21.3% (2024 est.)
services: 59.3% (2024 est.)
note: figures may not total 100% due to non-allocated consumption not captured in sector-reported data
comparison rankings: agriculture 106; industry 124; services 94

GDP - composition, by end use: *household consumption:* 63.8% (2024 est.)
government consumption: 18.8% (2024 est.)
investment in fixed capital: 17% (2024 est.)
investment in inventories: -0.1% (2024 est.)
exports of goods and services: 18% (2024 est.)
imports of goods and services: -17.5% (2024 est.)
note: figures may not total 100% due to rounding or gaps in data collection

Agricultural products: sugarcane, soybeans, maize, milk, cassava, oranges, chicken, beef, rice, wheat (2023)
note: top ten agricultural products based on tonnage

Industries: textiles, shoes, chemicals, cement, lumber, iron ore, tin, steel, aircraft, motor vehicles and parts, other machinery and equipment

Industrial production growth rate: 3.3% (2024 est.)
note: annual % change in industrial value added based on constant local currency
comparison ranking: 75

Labor force: 106.79 million (2024 est.)
note: number of people ages 15 or older who are employed or seeking work
comparison ranking: 6

Unemployment rate: 7.7% (2024 est.)
8% (2023 est.)
9.3% (2022 est.)
note: % of labor force seeking employment
comparison ranking: 131

Youth unemployment rate (ages 15-24): *total:* 18% (2024 est.)
male: 15.7% (2024 est.)
female: 20.9% (2024 est.)
note: % of labor force ages 15-24 seeking employment
comparison ranking: total 63

Population below poverty line: 4.2% (2016 est.)
note: approximately 4% of the population are below the "extreme" poverty line
Gini Index coefficient - distribution of family income 51.6 (2023 est.)
note: index (0-100) of income distribution; higher values represent greater inequality
comparison ranking: 5

Average household expenditures: *on food:* 16.2% of household expenditures (2023 est.)
on alcohol and tobacco: 1.7% of household expenditures (2023 est.)

Household income or consumption by percentage share: *lowest 10%:* 1.3% (2023 est.)
highest 10%: 40.8% (2023 est.)
note: % share of income accruing to lowest and highest 10% of population

Remittances: 0.2% of GDP (2024 est.)
0.2% of GDP (2023 est.)
0.3% of GDP (2022 est.)
note: personal transfers and compensation between resident and non-resident individuals/households/entities

Budget: *revenues:* $556.303 billion (2023 est.)
expenditures: $706.816 billion (2023 est.)
note: central government revenues (excluding grants) and expenditures converted to US dollars at average official exchange rate for year indicated

Public debt: 83% of GDP (2023 est.)
note: central government debt as a % of GDP
comparison ranking: 34

Taxes and other revenues: 14% (of GDP) (2023 est.)
note: central government tax revenue as a % of GDP
comparison ranking: 98

Current account balance: -$61.194 billion (2024 est.)
-$27.933 billion (2023 est.)
-$42.157 billion (2022 est.)
note: balance of payments - net trade and primary/secondary income in current dollars
comparison ranking: 192

Exports: $388.333 billion (2024 est.)
$389.192 billion (2023 est.)
$380.492 billion (2022 est.)
note: balance of payments - exports of goods and services in current dollars
comparison ranking: 25

Exports - partners: China 30%, USA 10%, Argentina 5%, Netherlands 3%, Chile 2% (2023)
note: top five export partners based on percentage share of exports

Exports - commodities: soybeans, crude petroleum, iron ore, raw sugar, corn (2023)
note: top five export commodities based on value in dollars

Imports: $377.05 billion (2024 est.)
$340.195 billion (2023 est.)
$369.861 billion (2022 est.)
note: balance of payments - imports of goods and services in current dollars
comparison ranking: 24

Imports - partners: China 23%, USA 16%, Germany 5%, Argentina 5%, Russia 4% (2023)
note: top five import partners based on percentage share of imports

Imports - commodities: refined petroleum, fertilizers, crude petroleum, vehicle parts/accessories, gas turbines (2023)
note: top five import commodities based on value in dollars

Reserves of foreign exchange and gold: $329.732 billion (2024 est.)
$355.021 billion (2023 est.)
$324.673 billion (2022 est.)
note: holdings of gold (year-end prices)/foreign exchange/special drawing rights in current dollars
comparison ranking: 12

Debt - external: $198.582 billion (2023 est.)
note: present value of external debt in current US dollars
comparison ranking: 5

Exchange rates: reals (BRL) per US dollar -

Exchange rates: 5.389 (2024 est.)
4.994 (2023 est.)
5.164 (2022 est.)
5.394 (2021 est.)
5.155 (2020 est.)

ENERGY

Electricity access: *electrification - total population:* 100% (2022 est.)
electrification - urban areas: 100%
electrification - rural areas: 97.3%

Electricity: *installed generating capacity:* 240.251 million kW (2023 est.)
consumption: 608.451 billion kWh (2023 est.)
exports: 7.186 billion kWh (2023 est.)
imports: 22.294 billion kWh (2023 est.)
transmission/distribution losses: 106.916 billion kWh (2023 est.)
comparison rankings: installed generating capacity 7; consumption 6; exports 32; imports 8; transmission/distribution losses 208

Electricity generation sources: *fossil fuels:* 8.9% of total installed capacity (2023 est.)
nuclear: 2.1% of total installed capacity (2023 est.)
solar: 6.9% of total installed capacity (2023 est.)
wind: 13.5% of total installed capacity (2023 est.)
hydroelectricity: 60.2% of total installed capacity (2023 est.)

biomass and waste: 8.3% of total installed capacity (2023 est.)

Nuclear energy: Number of operational nuclear reactors: 2 (2025)

Number of nuclear reactors under construction: 1 (2025)

Net capacity of operational nuclear reactors: 1.88GW (2025 est.)

Percent of total electricity production: 2.2% (2023 est.)

Coal: *production:* 15.556 million metric tons (2023 est.)
consumption: 32.223 million metric tons (2023 est.)
exports: 5,000 metric tons (2023 est.)
imports: 18.257 million metric tons (2023 est.)
proven reserves: 6.596 billion metric tons (2023 est.)

Petroleum: *total petroleum production:* 4.221 million bbl/day (2023 est.)
refined petroleum consumption: 3.163 million bbl/day (2023 est.)
crude oil estimated reserves: 12.715 billion barrels (2021 est.)

Natural gas: *production:* 22.702 billion cubic meters (2023 est.)
consumption: 29.065 billion cubic meters (2023 est.)
exports: 101.203 million cubic meters (2023 est.)
imports: 6.356 billion cubic meters (2023 est.)
proven reserves: 363.985 billion cubic meters (2021 est.)

Energy consumption per capita: 48.889 million Btu/person (2023 est.)
comparison ranking: 95

COMMUNICATIONS

Telephones - fixed lines: *total subscriptions:* 25.574 million (2023 est.)
subscriptions per 100 inhabitants: 12 (2023 est.)
comparison ranking: total subscriptions 10

Telephones - mobile cellular: *total subscriptions:* 213 million (2023 est.)
subscriptions per 100 inhabitants: 99 (2022 est.)
comparison ranking: total subscriptions 8

Broadcast media: state-run Radiobras operates a radio and a TV network; more than 1,000 radio stations and more than 100 TV channels operating, mostly privately owned; private media ownership highly concentrated (2022)

Internet country code: .br

Internet users: *percent of population:* 84% (2023 est.)

Broadband - fixed subscriptions: *total:* 48.4 million (2023 est.)
subscriptions per 100 inhabitants: 23 (2023 est.)
comparison ranking: total 3

TRANSPORTATION

Civil aircraft registration country code prefix: PP

Airports: 5,297 (2025)
comparison ranking: 2

Heliports: 1,871 (2025)
comparison ranking: 3

Railways: *total:* 29,849.9 km (2014)
standard gauge: 194 km (2014) 1.435-m gauge
narrow gauge: 23,341.6 km (2014) 1.000-m gauge (24 km electrified)
broad gauge: 5,822.3 km (2014) 1.600-m gauge (498.3 km electrified)
dual gauge: 492 km (2014) 1.600-1.000-m gauge

Merchant marine: *total:* 888 (2023)
by type: bulk carrier 13, container ship 20, general cargo 38, oil tanker 27, other 790
comparison ranking: total 26

Ports: *total ports:* 45 (2024)
large: 4
medium: 7
small: 19
very small: 15
ports with oil terminals: 31
key ports: Belem, DTSE/Gegua Oil Terminal, Itajai, Port de Salvador, Porto Alegre, Recife, Rio de Janeiro, Rio Grande, Santos, Tubarao, Vitoria

MILITARY AND SECURITY

Military and security forces: Brazilian Armed Forces (Forças Armadas Brasileiras): Brazilian Army (Exercito Brasileiro, EB), Brazilian Navy (Marinha do Brasil; includes Naval Aviation (Aviacao Naval Brasileira) and Marine Corps (Corpo de Fuzileiros Navais)), Brazilian Air Force (Forca Aerea Brasileira) (2025)
note: the three national police forces – the Federal Police, Federal Highway Police, and Federal Railway Police – have domestic security responsibilities and report to the Ministry of Justice and Public Security (Ministry of Justice)

Military expenditures: 1.1% of GDP (2024 est.)
1.1% of GDP (2023 est.)
1.2% of GDP (2022 est.)
1.3% of GDP (2021 est.)
1.4% of GDP (2020 est.)

Military and security service personnel strengths: approximately 360,000 active Armed Forces (220,000 Army; 70,000 Navy; 70,000 Air Force) (2025)

Military equipment inventories and acquisitions: the Brazilian military's inventory consists of a mix of domestically produced and imported weapons, largely from Europe and the US; Brazil's defense industry designs and manufactures equipment for all three military services and for export; it also jointly produces equipment with other countries (2024)

Military service age and obligation: 18-45 years of age for compulsory military service for men (women exempted); only 5-10% of those inducted are required to serve; conscript service obligation is 10-12 months; 17-45 (18 for women) years of age for voluntary service (2024)
note: in 2024, women were reported to comprise approximately 10% of the Brazilian military

Military - note: the Brazilian Armed Forces (BAF) are the second largest military in the Western Hemisphere behind the US; they are responsible for external security and protecting the country's sovereignty but also have an internal security role; the BAF's missions include patrolling and protecting the country's long borders and coastline and extensive territorial waters and river network, assisting with internal security, providing domestic disaster response and humanitarian assistance, and participating in multinational peacekeeping missions; it also cooperates with neighboring countries such as Argentina and Paraguay to combat cross-border smuggling and trafficking
Brazil has Major Non-NATO Ally (MNNA) status with the US, a designation under US law that provides foreign partners with certain benefits in the areas of defense trade and security cooperation
the origins of Brazil's military stretch back to the 1640s; Brazil provided a 25,000-man expeditionary force with air and ground units to fight with the Allies in the Mediterranean Theater during World War II; the Navy participated in the Battle of the Atlantic (2025)

SPACE

Space agency/agencies: Brazilian Space Agency (Agência Espacial Brasileira, AEB; established in 1994 when Brazil's space program was transferred from the military to civilian control); National Institute for Space Research (INPE, under the Ministry of Science, Technology and Innovations); Department of Aerospace Science and Technology (DCTA, under the Aeronautics Command (COMAER) of the Ministry of Defense) (2025)

Space launch site(s): Alcantara Launch Center (Maranhão state); Barreira do Inferno Launch Center (Rio Grande do Norte state) (2025)

Space program overview: has an active program with a long history; develops, builds, operates, and tracks satellites, including communications, remote sensing (RS), multi-mission, navigational, and scientific/testing/research; satellites are launched by foreign partners, but Brazil has a long-standing sounding (research) rocket and space launch vehicle (SLV) program and rocket launch facilities; cooperates with a variety of foreign space agencies and commercial entities, including those of Argentina, Canada, the European Space Agency and individual member states (particularly France and Germany), India, Japan, Russia, South Africa, South Korea, Ukraine, and the US; has a state-controlled communications company that operates Brazil's communications satellites and a growing commercial space sector with expertise in satellite technology (2025)
note: further details about the key activities, programs, and milestones of the country's space program, as well as government spending estimates on the space sector, appear in the Space Programs reference guide

TERRORISM

Terrorist group(s): Terrorist group(s): Hizballah; Tren de Aragua (TdA)
note: details about the history, aims, leadership, organization, areas of operation, tactics, targets, weapons, size, and sources of support of the group(s) appear(s) in Appendix T

TRANSNATIONAL ISSUES

Refugees and internally displaced persons: *refugees:* 331,097 (2024 est.)

IDPs: 19,043 (2024 est.)
stateless persons: 27 (2024 est.)

Trafficking in persons: *tier rating:* Tier 2 Watch List — Brazil did not demonstrate overall increasing efforts to eliminate trafficking compared with the previous reporting period and was downgraded to Tier 2 Watch List; for more details, go to: https://www.state.gov/reports/2025-trafficking-in-persons-report/brazil/

Illicit drugs: USG identification: major precursor-chemical producer (2025)

BRITISH INDIAN OCEAN TERRITORY

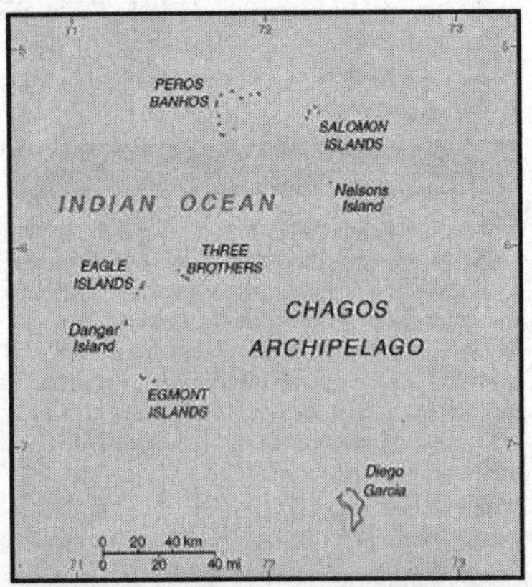

INTRODUCTION

Background: Formerly administered as part of the British Crown Colony of Mauritius, the British Indian Ocean Territory (BIOT) was established as an overseas territory of the UK in 1965. A number of the islands in the territory were later transferred to the Seychelles when it gained independence in 1976. Subsequently, BIOT has consisted of the six main island groups that make up the Chagos Archipelago. Only Diego Garcia, the largest and most southerly of the islands, is inhabited. It contains a joint UK-US naval support facility and hosts one of four dedicated ground antennas that assist in the operation of the Global Positioning System (GPS) navigation system – the others are on Kwajalein (Marshall Islands); at Cape Canaveral, Florida (US); and on Ascension Island (Saint Helena, Ascension, and Tristan da Cunha). The US Air Force also operates a telescope array on Diego Garcia as part of the Ground-Based Electro-Optical Deep Space Surveillance System (GEODSS) for tracking orbital debris, which can be a hazard to spacecraft and astronauts.

Between 1967 and 1973, the former agricultural workers who lived on the islands were relocated, primarily to Mauritius but also to the Seychelles. Negotiations with the UK between 1971 and 1982 resulted in the establishment of a trust fund to compensate the displaced islanders, known as Chagossians. Beginning in 1998, the islanders pursued a series of lawsuits against the British Government, seeking further compensation and the right to return to the territory. British court rulings in 2006 and 2007 invalidated immigration policies that had excluded the islanders from the archipelago, but in 2008, the House of Lords – the final court of appeal in the UK – ruled in favor of the British Government by overturning the lower court rulings and finding no right of return for the Chagossians. In 2015, the Permanent Court of Arbitration unanimously held that the marine protected area that the UK declared around the Chagos Archipelago in 2010 violated the UN Convention on the Law of the Sea.

In 2019, the International Court of Justice ruled in an advisory opinion that Britain's decolonization of Mauritius was not lawful because of continued Chagossian claims. A non-binding 2019 UN General Assembly vote demanded that Britain end its "colonial administration" of the Chagos Archipelago and that it be returned to Mauritius. On 22 May 2025, the United Kingdom and Mauritius signed an agreement that will lead to the transfer of sovereignty of the Chagos Archipelago to Mauritius. Under the agreement, the United Kingdom will lease Diego Garcia from Mauritius for 99 years and maintain full operational control of the joint UK-US military base.

GEOGRAPHY

Location: archipelago in the Indian Ocean, south of India, about halfway between Africa and Indonesia

Geographic coordinates: 6 00 S, 71 30 E
note: Diego Garcia 7 20 S, 72 25 E

Map references: Political Map of the World

Area: *total:* 60 sq km
land: 60 sq km (44 Diego Garcia)
water: 54,340 sq km
note: includes the entire Chagos Archipelago of 55 islands
comparison ranking: total 228

Area - comparative: land area is about one-third the size of Washington, D.C.

Land boundaries: *total:* 0 km

Coastline: 698 km

Maritime claims: *territorial sea:* 12 nm

Environment (Protection and Preservation) Zone: 200 nm

Climate: tropical marine; hot, humid, moderated by trade winds

Terrain: flat and low coral atolls (most areas do not exceed 2 m, or 6.6 ft, in elevation); sits atop the submarine volcanic Chagos-Laccadive Ridge

Elevation: *highest point:* ocean-side dunes on Diego Garcia 9 m
lowest point: Indian Ocean 0 m

Natural resources: coconuts, fish, sugarcane

Land use: *agricultural land:* 0% (2018 est.)
arable land: 0% (2018 est.)
permanent crops: 0% (2018 est.)
permanent pasture: 0% (2018 est.)
forest: 0% (2018 est.)
other: 100% (2018 est.)

Natural hazards: none; located outside routes of Indian Ocean cyclones

Geography - note: *note 1:* archipelago of 55 islands; Diego Garcia, the largest and southernmost island, occupies a strategic location in the central Indian Ocean
note 2: Diego Garcia is the only inhabited island of the BIOT

PEOPLE AND SOCIETY

Population: *total:* no permanent inhabitants
note: Diego Garcia, the largest of the 58 islands, hosts a joint UK-US military facility

ENVIRONMENT

Environmental issues: wastewater discharge into the lagoon on Diego Garcia

Climate: tropical marine; hot, humid, moderated by trade winds

GOVERNMENT

Country name: *conventional long form:* British Indian Ocean Territory
conventional short form: none
abbreviation: BIOT
etymology: self-descriptive name specifying the territory's affiliation and location

Dependency status: overseas territory of the UK; administered by a commissioner, resident in the Foreign, Commonwealth, and Development Office in London

Capital: *name:* administered from London; often regarded as being on Diego Garcia
geographic coordinates: 7 18S, 12 24E
time difference: UTC+6 (12 hours ahead of Washington, DC, during Standard Time)

Legal system: the laws of the UK apply

Constitution: *history:* British Indian Ocean Territory (Constitution) Order 2004

Executive branch: *chief of state:* King CHARLES III (since 8 September 2022)
head of government: Commissioner Nishi DHOLAKIA (since 16 December 2024); Administrator Bob FAIRWEATHER; both reside in the UK and are represented by Commander Andrew WILLIAMS, RN, the officer commanding British Forces on Diego Garcia (since January 2025)
cabinet: NA
election/appointment process: the monarchy is hereditary; commissioner and administrator appointed by the monarch

Diplomatic representation in the US: none (overseas territory of the UK)

Diplomatic representation from the US: *embassy:* none (overseas territory of the UK)

International organization participation: UPU

Flag: *description:* white with six wavy blue horizontal stripes; the UK flag is in the upper-left quadrant; the striped section has a palm tree and yellow crown (the territory's symbols) centered on the right half of the flag
meaning: the wavy stripes represent the Indian Ocean; the six blue stripes may stand for the six main atolls of the archipelago

National anthem(s): *title:* "God Save the King"
lyrics/music: unknown
history: official anthem, as a UK overseas territory

ECONOMY

Economic overview: small island territory economy; economic activity mainly on Diego Garcia with national military installations; recently settled disputes with Mauritius have increased oil exports; established marine reserve has limited commercial fishing

Exports - partners: Singapore 86%, Pakistan 8%, USA 1%, South Africa 1%, Czechia 1% (2023)
note: top five export partners based on percentage share of exports

Exports - commodities: fish (2023)

note: top export commodities based on value in dollars over $500,000

Imports - partners: Greece 52%, Singapore 38%, USA 4%, Panama 2%, UAE 2% (2023)
note: top five import partners based on percentage share of imports

Imports - commodities: refined petroleum, animal products, aluminum structures, insulated wire, prefabricated buildings (2023)
note: top five import commodities based on value in dollars

Exchange rates: the US dollar is used

COMMUNICATIONS

Broadcast media: Armed Forces Radio and Television Service (AFRTS) broadcasts over 3 frequencies for US and UK military personnel stationed on the islands

Internet country code: .io

Communications - note: Diego Garcia hosts one of four dedicated ground antennas that assist in the operation of the Global Positioning System (GPS) navigation system (the others are on Kwajalein (Marshall Islands), at Cape Canaveral, Florida (US), and on Ascension Island (Saint Helena, Ascension, and Tristan da Cunha))

TRANSPORTATION

Airports: 1 (2025)
comparison ranking: 228

Ports: *total ports:* 1 (2024)
large: 0
medium: 0
small: 0
very small: 1
ports with oil terminals: 1
key ports: Diego Garcia

MILITARY AND SECURITY

Military and security forces: no regular military forces

Military - note: defense is the responsibility of the UK; on 22 May 2025, the United Kingdom and Mauritius signed an agreement that will lead to the transfer of sovereignty of the Chagos Archipelago to Mauritius; under the agreement, the United Kingdom will lease Diego Garcia from Mauritius for 99 years and maintain full operational control of the joint UK-US military base

BRITISH VIRGIN ISLANDS

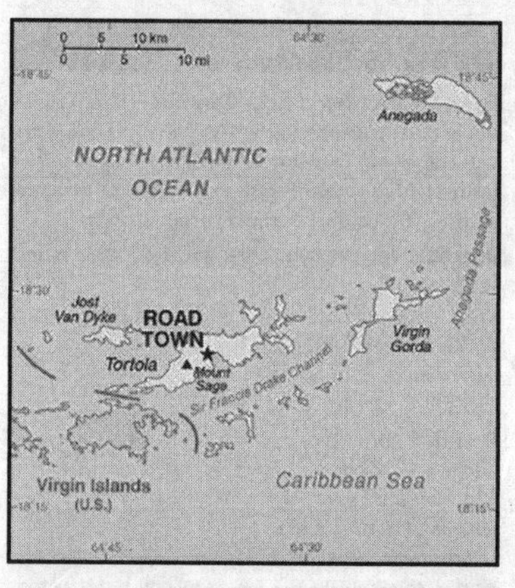

INTRODUCTION

Background: First inhabited by Arawak and later by Carib Indians, the Virgin Islands were settled by the Dutch in 1648 and then annexed by the English in 1672. The islands were part of the British colony of the Leeward Islands (1872-1960); they were granted autonomy in 1967. The economy is closely tied to the larger and more populous US Virgin Islands to the west, and the US dollar is the legal currency. In 2017, Hurricane Irma devastated the island of Tortola. An estimated 80% of residential and business structures were destroyed or damaged, communications disrupted, and local roads rendered impassable.

GEOGRAPHY

Location: Caribbean, between the Caribbean Sea and the North Atlantic Ocean, east of Puerto Rico

Geographic coordinates: 18 30 N, 64 30 W

Map references: Central America and the Caribbean

Area: *total:* 151 sq km
land: 151 sq km
water: 0 sq km
note: comprised of 16 inhabited and more than 20 uninhabited islands; includes the islands of Tortola, Anegada, Virgin Gorda, Jost van Dyke
comparison ranking: total 220

Area - comparative: about 0.9 times the size of Washington, D.C.

Land boundaries: *total:* 0 km

Coastline: 80 km

Maritime claims: *territorial sea:* 12 nm
exclusive fishing zone: 200 nm

Climate: subtropical; humid; temperatures moderated by trade winds

Terrain: coral islands relatively flat; volcanic islands steep, hilly

Elevation: *highest point:* Mount Sage 521 m
lowest point: Caribbean Sea 0 m

Natural resources: NEGL; pleasant climate, beaches foster tourism

Land use: *agricultural land:* 46.7% (2022 est.)
arable land: 6.7% (2022 est.)
permanent crops: 6.7% (2022 est.)
permanent pasture: 33.3% (2022 est.)
forest: 24.1% (2022 est.)
other: 29.2% (2022 est.)

Irrigated land: NA

Population distribution: a fairly even distribution throughout the inhabited islands, with the largest islands of Tortola, Anegada, Virgin Gorda, and Jost Van Dyke having the largest populations

Natural hazards: hurricanes and tropical storms (July to October)

Geography - note: strong ties to nearby US Virgin Islands and Puerto Rico

PEOPLE AND SOCIETY

Population: *total:* 40,102 (2024 est.)
male: 19,042
female: 21,060
comparison rankings: total 213; male 213; female 212

Nationality: *noun:* British Virgin Islander(s)
adjective: British Virgin Islander

Ethnic groups: African/Black 76.3%, Latino 5.5%, White 5.4%, mixed 5.3%, Indian 2.1%, East Indian 1.6%, other 3%, unspecified 0.8% (2010 est.)

Languages: English (official), Virgin Islands Creole

Religions: Protestant 70.2% (Methodist 17.6%, Church of God 10.4%, Anglican 9.5%, Seventh Day Adventist 9.0%, Pentecostal 8.2%, Baptist 7.4%, New Testament Church of God 6.9%, other Protestant 1.2%), Roman Catholic 8.9%, Jehovah's Witness 2.5%, Hindu 1.9%, other 6.2%, none 7.9%, unspecified 2.4% (2010 est.)

Age structure: *0-14 years:* 16.6% (male 3,298/female 3,351)
15-64 years: 71.3% (male 13,455/female 15,152)
65 years and over: 12.1% (2024 est.) (male 2,289/female 2,557)

Dependency ratios: *total dependency ratio:* 40.2 (2024 est.)
youth dependency ratio: 23.2 (2024 est.)
elderly dependency ratio: 16.9 (2024 est.)
potential support ratio: 5.9 (2024 est.)

Median age: *total:* 38.5 years (2024 est.)
male: 38.1 years
female: 38.9 years
comparison ranking: total 74

Population growth rate: 1.82% (2024 est.)
comparison ranking: 47

Birth rate: 10.9 births/1,000 population (2024 est.)
comparison ranking: 168

Death rate: 5.5 deaths/1,000 population (2024 est.)
comparison ranking: 183

Net migration rate: 12.9 migrant(s)/1,000 population (2024 est.)
comparison ranking: 4

Population distribution: a fairly even distribution throughout the inhabited islands, with the largest islands of Tortola, Anegada, Virgin Gorda, and Jost Van Dyke having the largest populations

Urbanization: *urban population:* 49.7% of total population (2023)
rate of urbanization: 1.73% annual rate of change (2020-25 est.)

Major urban areas - population: 15,000 ROAD TOWN (capital) (2018)

Sex ratio: *at birth:* 1.05 male(s)/female
0-14 years: 0.98 male(s)/female
15-64 years: 0.89 male(s)/female
65 years and over: 0.9 male(s)/female
total population: 0.9 male(s)/female (2024 est.)

Infant mortality rate: *total:* 13.4 deaths/1,000 live births (2024 est.)
male: 16 deaths/1,000 live births
female: 10.7 deaths/1,000 live births
comparison ranking: total 105

Life expectancy at birth: *total population:* 80.1 years (2024 est.)
male: 78.6 years
female: 81.7 years
comparison ranking: total population 57

Total fertility rate: 1.38 children born/woman (2024 est.)
comparison ranking: 213

Gross reproduction rate: 0.67 (2024 est.)

Drinking water source: *improved:* total: 99.9% of population (2022 est.)
unimproved: total: 0.1% of population (2022 est.)

Currently married women (ages 15-49): 46.6% (2023 est.)

Education expenditure: 2.5% of GDP (2022 est.)
13.6% national budget (2025 est.)
comparison ranking: Education expenditure (% GDP) 172

School life expectancy (primary to tertiary education): *total:* 11 years (2022 est.)
male: 11 years (2022 est.)
female: 11 years (2022 est.)

ENVIRONMENT

Environmental issues: limited natural freshwater resources; water pollution from sewage and mining/industry waste; coral reef preservation

Climate: subtropical; humid; temperatures moderated by trade winds

Urbanization: *urban population:* 49.7% of total population (2023)
rate of urbanization: 1.73% annual rate of change (2020-25 est.)

Carbon dioxide emissions: 188,000 metric tonnes of CO_2 (2023 est.)
from petroleum and other liquids: 188,000 metric tonnes of CO_2 (2023 est.)
comparison ranking: total emissions 203

Waste and recycling: *municipal solid waste generated annually:* 21,100 tons (2024 est.)

GOVERNMENT

Country name: *conventional long form:* none
conventional short form: British Virgin Islands
abbreviation: BVI
etymology: the islets, cays, and rocks surrounding the major islands reminded explorer Christopher COLUMBUS in 1493 of Saint Ursula and her 11,000 virgin followers (Santa Ursula y las Once Mil Virgenes), which over time was shortened to the Virgins (las Virgenes)

Government type: Overseas Territory of the UK with limited self-government; parliamentary democracy

Dependency status: overseas territory of the UK; internal self-governing

Capital: *name:* Road Town
geographic coordinates: 18 25 N, 64 37 W
time difference: UTC-4 (1 hour ahead of Washington, DC, during Standard Time)
etymology: name refers to the nautical term "roadstead" or "roads," a body of water less sheltered than a harbor but where ships can still lie at anchor

Administrative divisions: none (overseas territory of the UK)

Legal system: English common law

Constitution: *history:* several previous; latest effective 15 June 2007 (The Virgin Islands Constitution Order 2007)
amendment process: initiated by any elected member of the House of Assembly; passage requires simple majority vote by the elected members of the Assembly and assent by the governor on behalf of the monarch

Citizenship: see United Kingdom

Suffrage: 18 years of age; universal

Executive branch: *chief of state:* King CHARLES III (since 8 September 2022); represented by Governor Daniel PRUCE (since 29 January 2024)
head of government: Premier Dr. Natalio WHEATLEY (since 5 May 2022)
cabinet: Executive Council appointed by the governor from members of the House of Assembly
election/appointment process: the monarchy is hereditary; governor appointed by the monarch; following legislative elections, the governor usually appoints the leader of the majority party or majority coalition as premier
note: on 5 May 2022, Premier Andrew FAHIE was removed from office by a no-confidence vote in the House of Assembly after his arrest on drug-trafficking and money-laundering charges; Premier Dr. Natalio WHEATLEY was sworn in as premier on 5 May 2022

Legislative branch: *legislature name:* House of Assembly
legislative structure: unicameral
number of seats: 15 (directly elected and appointed)
scope of elections: full renewal
term in office: 4 years
most recent election date: 4/24/2023
parties elected and seats per party: VIP (6); NDP (3); PVIM (3); PU (1)
expected date of next election: 2027

Judicial branch: *highest court(s):* the Eastern Caribbean Supreme Court (ECSC) is the superior court of the Organization of Eastern Caribbean States; the ECSC is headquartered on St. Lucia and consists of the Court of Appeal – headed by the chief justice and 4 judges – and the High Court with 18 judges; the Court of Appeal travels to member states on a schedule to hear appeals from the High Court and subordinate courts
judge selection and term of office: Eastern Caribbean Supreme Court chief justice appointed by the British monarch; other justices and judges appointed by the Judicial and Legal Services Commission; Court of Appeal justices appointed for life with mandatory retirement at age 65; High Court judges appointed for life with mandatory retirement at age 62
subordinate courts: Magistrates' Courts

Political parties: National Democratic Party or NDP
Progressive Virgin Islands Movement or PVIM
Progressives United or PU
Virgin Islands Party or VIP

Diplomatic representation in the US: none (overseas territory of the UK)

Diplomatic representation from the US: *embassy:* none (overseas territory of the UK)

International organization participation: ACS (associate), Caricom (associate), CDB, Interpol (subbureau), IOC, OECS, UNESCO (associate), UPU

Independence: none (overseas territory of the UK)

National holiday: Territory Day, 1 July (1956)

Flag: *description:* blue with the UK flag in the upper-left quadrant and the Virgin Islander coat of arms centered on the right half of the flag; the coat of arms depicts a woman between two columns of six oil lamps, above a scroll with the Latin word VIGILATE (Be Watchful)
meaning: Christopher COLUMBUS named the islands in 1493 in honor of Saint Ursula and her virgin followers, and the figure holding a lamp represents the saint, with the other lamps symbolizing her followers

National symbol(s): zenaida dove, white cedar flower

National color(s): yellow, green, red, white, blue

National anthem(s): *title:* "God Save the King"
lyrics/music: unknown
history: official anthem, as a UK overseas territory

ECONOMY

Economic overview: British Caribbean island territorial economy; strong tourism and services industries; vulnerable to hurricanes; navigating public debt insolvency since 2008 Crisis; considered a tax haven; high electrification costs; major rum exporter

Real GDP (purchasing power parity): $1.634 billion (2024 est.)
$1.579 billion (2023 est.)
$1.537 billion (2022 est.)
note: data in 2015 dollars
comparison ranking: 200

Real GDP per capita: $40,500 (2024 est.)
$38,600 (2023 est.)
$38,400 (2022 est.)
note: data in 2015 dollars
comparison ranking: 58

GDP (official exchange rate): $1.598 billion (2024 est.)
note: data in current dollars at official exchange rate

Inflation rate (consumer prices): 8.5% (2022 est.)
2.8% (2021 est.)
1.4% (2020 est.)
note: annual % change based on consumer prices
comparison ranking: 169

Agricultural products: fruits, vegetables; livestock, poultry; fish

Industries: tourism, light industry, construction, rum, concrete block, offshore banking center

Budget: *revenues:* $400 million (2017 est.)
expenditures: $400 million (2017 est.)

Exports - partners: Malta 33%, Guyana 22%, Greece 11%, Germany 7%, Indonesia 4% (2023)

Exports - commodities: ships, refined petroleum, aircraft, molasses, precious stones (2023)

Imports - partners: USA 34%, Italy 10%, France 9%, China 8%, Luxembourg 5% (2023)

Imports - commodities: ships, refined petroleum, aircraft, railway cargo containers, jewelry (2023)

Exchange rates: the US dollar is used

ENERGY

Electricity access: *electrification - total population:* 100% (2022 est.)

Electricity: *installed generating capacity:* 63,000 kW (2023 est.)
consumption: 163.82 million kWh (2023 est.)
transmission/distribution losses: 10.18 million kWh (2023 est.)
comparison rankings: installed generating capacity 190; consumption 191; transmission/distribution losses 18

Electricity generation sources: *fossil fuels:* 97.7% of total installed capacity (2023 est.)
solar: 1.1% of total installed capacity (2023 est.)
wind: 1.1% of total installed capacity (2023 est.)

Coal: *imports:* 20 metric tons (2023 est.)

Petroleum: *refined petroleum consumption:* 1,000 bbl/day (2023 est.)

Energy consumption per capita: 66.998 million Btu/person (2023 est.)
comparison ranking: 74

COMMUNICATIONS

Telephones - fixed lines: *total subscriptions:* 23,000 (2021 est.)
subscriptions per 100 inhabitants: 17 (2022 est.)
comparison ranking: total subscriptions 171

Telephones - mobile cellular: *total subscriptions:* 38,000 (2021 est.)
subscriptions per 100 inhabitants: 121 (2021 est.)
comparison ranking: total subscriptions 210

Broadcast media: 1 private TV station; multi-channel TV is available from cable and satellite subscription services; about a half-dozen private radio stations

Internet country code: .vg

Internet users: *percent of population:* 78% (2017 est.)

Broadband - fixed subscriptions: *total:* 7,000 (2022 est.)
subscriptions per 100 inhabitants: 18 (2022 est.)
comparison ranking: total 190

TRANSPORTATION

Civil aircraft registration country code prefix: VP-L

Airports: 3 (2025)
comparison ranking: 194

Heliports: 2 (2025)
comparison ranking: 127

Merchant marine: *total:* 29 (2023)
by type: general cargo 3, other 26
comparison ranking: total 137

Ports: *total ports:* 1 (2024)
large: 0
medium: 1
small: 0
very small: 0
ports with oil terminals: 1
key ports: Road Harbor

MILITARY AND SECURITY

Military - note: defense is the responsibility of the UK

TRANSNATIONAL ISSUES

Refugees and internally displaced persons: *refugees:* 41 (2024 est.)

BRUNEI

INTRODUCTION

Background: The Sultanate of Brunei's influence peaked between the 15th and 17th centuries, when its control extended over coastal areas of northwest Borneo and the southern Philippines. Internal strife over royal succession, colonial expansion of European powers, and piracy subsequently brought on a period of decline. In 1888, Brunei became a British protectorate; independence was achieved in 1984. The same family has ruled Brunei for over six centuries, and in 2017, the country celebrated the 50th anniversary of Sultan Hassanal BOLKIAH's accession to the throne. Brunei has one of the highest per-capita GDPs in the world, thanks to extensive petroleum and natural gas fields.

GEOGRAPHY

Location: Southeastern Asia, along the northern coast of the island of Borneo, bordering the South China Sea and Malaysia

Geographic coordinates: 4 30 N, 114 40 E

Map references: Southeast Asia

Area: *total:* 5,765 sq km
land: 5,265 sq km
water: 500 sq km
comparison ranking: total 172

Area - comparative: slightly smaller than Delaware

Land boundaries: *total:* 266 km
border countries (1): Malaysia 266 km

Coastline: 161 km

Maritime claims: *territorial sea:* 12 nm
exclusive economic zone: 200 nm or to median line

Climate: tropical; hot, humid, rainy

Terrain: flat coastal plain rises to mountains in east; hilly lowland in west

Elevation: *highest point:* Bukit Pagon 1,850 m
lowest point: South China Sea 0 m
mean elevation: 478 m

Natural resources: petroleum, natural gas, timber

Land use: *agricultural land:* 2.5% (2022 est.)
arable land: 0.8% (2022 est.)
permanent crops: 1.1% (2022 est.)
permanent pasture: 0.6% (2022 est.)
forest: 72.1% (2022 est.)
other: 25.4% (2022 est.)

Irrigated land: 10 sq km (2012)

Population distribution: the vast majority of the population is found along the coast in the western part of Brunei, which is separated from the eastern portion by Malaysia; the largest population concentration is in the far north on the western side of the Brunei Bay, in and around the capital of Bandar Seri Begawan

Natural hazards: typhoons, earthquakes, and severe flooding are rare

Geography - note: close to vital sea lanes through South China Sea linking Indian and Pacific Oceans; two parts physically separated by Malaysia; the eastern part, the Temburong district, is an exclave and is almost an enclave within Malaysia

PEOPLE AND SOCIETY

Population: *total:* 491,900 (2024 est.)
male: 239,140
female: 252,760
comparison rankings: total 173; male 173; female 173

Nationality: *noun:* Bruneian(s)
adjective: Bruneian

Ethnic groups: Malay 67.4%, Chinese 9.6%, other 23% (2021 est.)

Languages: Malay (Bahasa Melayu) (official), English, Chinese dialects
major-language sample(s):
Buku Fakta Dunia, sumber yang diperlukan untuk maklumat asas. (Malay)

Religions: Muslim (official) 82.1%, Christian 6.7%, Buddhist 6.3%, other 4.9% (2021 est.)

Age structure: *0-14 years:* 21.7% (male 54,924/female 51,710)
15-64 years: 70.8% (male 166,289/female 182,011)
65 years and over: 7.5% (2024 est.) (male 17,927/female 19,039)

Dependency ratios: *total dependency ratio:* 41.2 (2024 est.)
youth dependency ratio: 30.6 (2024 est.)
elderly dependency ratio: 10.6 (2024 est.)
potential support ratio: 9.4 (2024 est.)

Median age: *total:* 32.3 years (2024 est.)
male: 31.4 years
female: 33.1 years

comparison ranking: total 117

Population growth rate: 1.4% (2024 est.)
comparison ranking: 71

Birth rate: 15.8 births/1,000 population (2024 est.)
comparison ranking: 101

Death rate: 3.9 deaths/1,000 population (2024 est.)
comparison ranking: 218

Net migration rate: 2.1 migrant(s)/1,000 population (2024 est.)
comparison ranking: 48

Population distribution: the vast majority of the population is found along the coast in the western part of Brunei, which is separated from the eastern portion by Malaysia; the largest population concentration is in the far north on the western side of the Brunei Bay, in and around the capital of Bandar Seri Begawan

Urbanization: *urban population:* 79.1% of total population (2023)
rate of urbanization: 1.44% annual rate of change (2020-25 est.)

Major urban areas - population: 266,682 BANDAR SERI BEGAWAN (capital) (2021)
note: the boundaries of the capital city were expanded in 2007, greatly increasing the city area; the population of the capital increased tenfold

Sex ratio: *at birth:* 1.05 male(s)/female
0-14 years: 1.06 male(s)/female
15-64 years: 0.91 male(s)/female
65 years and over: 0.94 male(s)/female
total population: 0.95 male(s)/female (2024 est.)

Maternal mortality ratio: 36 deaths/100,000 live births (2023 est.)
comparison ranking: 109

Infant mortality rate: *total:* 10 deaths/1,000 live births (2024 est.)
male: 12.2 deaths/1,000 live births
female: 7.7 deaths/1,000 live births
comparison ranking: total 132

Life expectancy at birth: *total population:* 78.9 years (2024 est.)
male: 76.5 years
female: 81.3 years
comparison ranking: total population 71

Total fertility rate: 1.73 children born/woman (2024 est.)
comparison ranking: 153

Gross reproduction rate: 0.85 (2024 est.)

Drinking water source: *improved:* total: 99.9% of population (2022 est.)
unimproved: urban: 0.4% of population
rural: 0% of population
total: 0.1% of population (2022 est.)

Health expenditure: 2.2% of GDP (2021)
6.4% of national budget (2022 est.)

Physician density: 1.89 physicians/1,000 population (2021)

Hospital bed density: 3.9 beds/1,000 population (2021 est.)

Sanitation facility access: *improved:* total: 99.5% of population (2022 est.)
unimproved: total: 0.5% of population (2022 est.)

Obesity - adult prevalence rate: 14.1% (2016)
comparison ranking: 129

Alcohol consumption per capita: *total:* 0.69 liters of pure alcohol (2019 est.)
beer: 0.66 liters of pure alcohol (2019 est.)
wine: 0.04 liters of pure alcohol (2019 est.)
spirits: 0 liters of pure alcohol (2019 est.)
other alcohols: 0 liters of pure alcohol (2019 est.)
comparison ranking: total 157

Tobacco use: *total:* 17% (2025 est.)
male: 31.2% (2025 est.)
female: 1.9% (2025 est.)
comparison ranking: total 93

Currently married women (ages 15-49): 54.3% (2023 est.)

Education expenditure: 4.4% of GDP (2016 est.)
11.4% national budget (2016 est.)
comparison ranking: Education expenditure (% GDP) 87

School life expectancy (primary to tertiary education): *total:* 14 years (2023 est.)
male: 13 years (2023 est.)
female: 14 years (2023 est.)

ENVIRONMENT

Environmental issues: air pollution, including seasonal haze from forest fires in Indonesia

International environmental agreements: *party to:* Biodiversity, Climate Change, Climate Change-Kyoto Protocol, Climate Change-Paris Agreement, Comprehensive Nuclear Test Ban, Desertification, Endangered Species, Hazardous Wastes, Law of the Sea, Ozone Layer Protection, Ship Pollution
signed, but not ratified: none of the selected agreements

Climate: tropical; hot, humid, rainy

Urbanization: *urban population:* 79.1% of total population (2023)
rate of urbanization: 1.44% annual rate of change (2020-25 est.)

Carbon dioxide emissions: 10.823 million metric tonnes of CO2 (2023 est.)
from coal and metallurgical coke: 998,000 metric tonnes of CO2 (2023 est.)
from petroleum and other liquids: 2.175 million metric tonnes of CO2 (2023 est.)
from consumed natural gas: 7.65 million metric tonnes of CO2 (2023 est.)
comparison ranking: total emissions 104

Particulate matter emissions: 7.4 micrograms per cubic meter (2019 est.)

Methane emissions: *energy:* 50.5 kt (2022-2024 est.)
agriculture: 0.9 kt (2019-2021 est.)
waste: 9.2 kt (2019-2021 est.)
other: 0.3 kt (2019-2021 est.)

Waste and recycling: *municipal solid waste generated annually:* 216,300 tons (2024 est.)
percent of municipal solid waste recycled: 20% (2022 est.)

Total water withdrawal: *municipal:* 151.5 million cubic meters (2022 est.)
agricultural: 5.3 million cubic meters (2022 est.)

Total renewable water resources: 8.5 billion cubic meters (2022 est.)

GOVERNMENT

Country name: *conventional long form:* Brunei Darussalam
conventional short form: Brunei
local long form: Negara Brunei Darussalam
local short form: Brunei
etymology: derivation of the name is unclear; the name may come from the Sanskrit word *bhumi*, meaning "land" or "region"

Government type: absolute monarchy or sultanate

Capital: *name:* Bandar Seri Begawan
geographic coordinates: 4 53 N, 114 56 E
time difference: UTC+8 (13 hours ahead of Washington, DC, during Standard Time)
etymology: named in 1970 after Sultan Omar Ali SAIFUDDIEN III (1914-1986), who adopted the title of "Seri Begawan" (approximately meaning "honored lord") when he abdicated in 1967; "bandar" means "city" or "port" in Malay; the capital had previously been called Bandar Brunei (Brunei City)

Administrative divisions: 4 districts (*daerah-daerah*, singular - *daerah*); Belait, Brunei dan Muara, Temburong, Tutong

Legal system: mixed legal system based on English common law and Islamic law
note: in 2019, sharia penal codes came into force and apply to Muslims and partly to non-Muslims in parallel with common law codes

Constitution: *history:* drafted 1954 to 1959, signed 29 September 1959
amendment process: proposed by the monarch; passage requires submission to the Privy Council for Legislative Council review and finalization takes place by proclamation; the monarch can accept or reject changes to the original proposal provided by the Legislative Council
note: some constitutional provisions suspended since 1962 under a state of emergency, others suspended since independence in 1984

International law organization participation: has not submitted an ICJ jurisdiction declaration; non-party state to the ICC

Citizenship: *citizenship by birth:* no
citizenship by descent only: the father must be a citizen of Brunei
dual citizenship recognized: no
residency requirement for naturalization: 12 years

Suffrage: 18 years of age for village elections; universal

Executive branch: *chief of state:* Sultan and Prime Minister Sir HASSANAL Bolkiah (since 5 October 1967)
head of government: Sultan and Prime Minister Sir HASSANAL Bolkiah (since 5 October 1967)
cabinet: Council of Ministers appointed and presided over by the monarch
election/appointment process: none; the monarchy is hereditary
note 1: the monarch is both chief of state and head of government, as well as Minister of Finance, Defense, and Foreign Affairs and Trade
note 2: 4 additional advisory councils appointed by the monarch are the Religious Council, Privy Council for Constitutional Issues, Council of Succession, and Legislative Council

Legislative branch: *legislature name:* Legislative Council (Majlis Mesyuarat Negara)
legislative structure: unicameral
number of seats: 45 (all appointed)
electoral system: plurality/majority
scope of elections: full renewal
term in office: 5 years
most recent election date: 1/20/2023
percentage of women in chamber: 11.8%
expected date of next election: January 2028

Judicial branch: *highest court(s):* Supreme Court (consists of the Court of Appeal and the High Court, each with a chief justice and 2 judges); Sharia Court (consists the Court of Appeals and the High Court)
judge selection and term of office: Supreme Court judges appointed by the monarch to serve until age 65, and older if approved by the monarch; Sharia Court judges appointed by the monarch for life
subordinate courts: Intermediate Court; Magistrates' Courts; Juvenile Court; small claims courts; lower sharia courts
note: Brunei has a dual judicial system of secular and sharia (religious) courts; the Judicial Committee of Privy Council (in London) serves as the final appellate court for civil cases only

Political parties: National Development Party or NDP
note: the NDP is Brunei's only registered party, but does not have representation in the Legislative Council, which is appointed

Diplomatic representation in the US: *chief of mission:* Ambassador (vacant); Chargé d'Affaires IZZATI Baharuddin (since 6 May 2025)
chancery: 3520 International Court NW, Washington, DC 20008
telephone: [1] (202) 237-1838

FAX: [1] (202) 885-0560
email address and website: info@bruneiembassy.org
http://www.bruneiembassy.org/index.html
consulate(s): New York

Diplomatic representation from the US: *chief of mission:* Ambassador Caryn R. McCLELLAND (since December 2021)
embassy: Simpang 336-52-16-9, Jalan Duta, Bandar Seri Begawan, BC4115
mailing address: 4020 Bandar Seri Begawan Place, Washington DC 20521-4020
telephone: (673) 238-7400

FAX: (673) 238-7533
email address and website: ConsularBrunei@state.gov
https://bn.usembassy.gov/

International organization participation: ADB, APEC, ARF, ASEAN, C, CP, EAS, FAO, G-77, IAEA, IBRD, ICAO, ICC (NGOs), ICRM, IDA, IFRCS, ILO, IMF, IMO, IMSO, Interpol, IOC, ISO (correspondent), ITSO, ITU, NAM, OIC, OPCW, UN, UNCTAD, UNESCO, UNIFIL, UNWTO, UPU, WCO, WHO, WIPO, WMO, WTO

Independence: 1 January 1984 (from the UK)

National holiday: National Day, 23 February (1984)
note: 1 January 1984 was the date of independence from the UK, 23 February 1984 was the date of independence from British protection; the Sultan's birthday, 15 June

Flag: *description:* yellow with a diagonal white band and second below it in black, both starting from the upper left; the national emblem in red is at the center; the state motto, "Always render service with God's guidance," appears in yellow Arabic script on the emblem's crescent; a ribbon below the crescent reads "Brunei, the Abode of Peace"
meaning: yellow symbolizes the sultanate, and the white and black bands stand for the chief ministers; the emblem includes a royal umbrella (the monarchy), two wings with four feathers (justice, tranquility, prosperity, and peace), two upraised hands (the government's pledge to preserve and promote the people's welfare), and the crescent moon of Islam (the state religion)

National symbol(s): royal parasol

National color(s): yellow, white, black

National anthem(s): *title:* "Allah Peliharakan Sultan" (God Bless His Majesty)
lyrics/music: Pengiran Haji Mohamed YUSUF bin Pengiran Abdul Rahim/Awang Haji BESAR bin Sagap
history: adopted 1951

ECONOMY

Economic overview: almost exclusively an oil and gas economy; high income country; expansive and robust welfare system; the majority of the population works for the government; promulgating a nationalized halal brand; considering establishment of a bond market and stock exchange

Real GDP (purchasing power parity): $36.64 billion (2024 est.)
$35.163 billion (2023 est.)
$34.771 billion (2022 est.)
note: data in 2021 dollars
comparison ranking: 140

Real GDP growth rate: 4.2% (2024 est.)
1.1% (2023 est.)
-1.6% (2022 est.)
note: annual GDP % growth based on constant local currency
comparison ranking: 66

Real GDP per capita: $79,200 (2024 est.)
$76,600 (2023 est.)
$76,400 (2022 est.)
note: data in 2021 dollars
comparison ranking: 11

GDP (official exchange rate): $15.463 billion (2024 est.)
note: data in current dollars at official exchange rate

Inflation rate (consumer prices): -0.4% (2024 est.)
0.4% (2023 est.)
3.7% (2022 est.)
note: annual % change based on consumer prices
comparison ranking: 4

GDP - composition, by sector of origin: *agriculture:* 1.2% (2024 est.)
industry: 61.7% (2024 est.)
services: 38.7% (2024 est.)
note: figures may not total 100% due to non-allocated consumption not captured in sector-reported data
comparison rankings: agriculture 171; industry 3; services 195

GDP - composition, by end use: *household consumption:* 28.5% (2024 est.)
government consumption: 23% (2024 est.)
investment in fixed capital: 28.2% (2024 est.)
investment in inventories: 0.2% (2024 est.)
exports of goods and services: 74.3% (2024 est.)
imports of goods and services: -58.9% (2024 est.)
note: figures may not total 100% due to rounding or gaps in data collection

Agricultural products: chicken, eggs, fruits, vegetables, rice, bananas, beans, cucumbers/gherkins, pineapples, beef (2023)
note: top ten agricultural products based on tonnage

Industries: petroleum, petroleum refining, liquefied natural gas, construction, agriculture, aquaculture, transportation

Industrial production growth rate: 5.7% (2024 est.)
note: annual % change in industrial value added based on constant local currency
comparison ranking: 34

Labor force: 233,500 (2024 est.)
note: number of people ages 15 or older who are employed or seeking work
comparison ranking: 175

Unemployment rate: 5.2% (2024 est.)
5.2% (2023 est.)
5.2% (2022 est.)
note: % of labor force seeking employment
comparison ranking: 92

Youth unemployment rate (ages 15-24): *total:* 18.5% (2024 est.)
male: 16.5% (2024 est.)
female: 21.6% (2024 est.)
note: % of labor force ages 15-24 seeking employment
comparison ranking: total 61

Remittances: 0% of GDP (2023 est.)
0% of GDP (2022 est.)
0% of GDP (2021 est.)
note: personal transfers and compensation between resident and non-resident individuals/households/entities

Budget: *revenues:* $1.058 billion (2020 est.)
expenditures: $3.189 billion (2020 est.)

Public debt: 2.8% of GDP (2017 est.)
note: central government debt as a % of GDP
comparison ranking: 199

Current account balance: $2.23 billion (2024 est.)
$1.944 billion (2023 est.)
$3.256 billion (2022 est.)
note: balance of payments - net trade and primary/secondary income in current dollars
comparison ranking: 45

Exports: $11.483 billion (2024 est.)
$11.573 billion (2023 est.)
$14.405 billion (2022 est.)
note: balance of payments - exports of goods and services in current dollars
comparison ranking: 112

Exports - partners: Australia 21%, Japan 17%, China 17%, Singapore 16%, Malaysia 6% (2023)
note: top five export partners based on percentage share of exports

Exports - commodities: refined petroleum, natural gas, crude petroleum, hydrocarbons, fertilizers (2023)
note: top five export commodities based on value in dollars

Imports: $9.11 billion (2024 est.)
$9.077 billion (2023 est.)
$10.099 billion (2022 est.)
note: balance of payments - imports of goods and services in current dollars
comparison ranking: 126

Imports - partners: Malaysia 23%, UAE 10%, China 10%, UK 10%, Australia 6% (2023)
note: top five import partners based on percentage share of imports

Imports - commodities: crude petroleum, gold, refined petroleum, coal, cars (2023)
note: top five import commodities based on value in dollars

Reserves of foreign exchange and gold: $4.414 billion (2024 est.)
$4.483 billion (2023 est.)
$5.035 billion (2022 est.)

note: holdings of gold (year-end prices)/foreign exchange/special drawing rights in current dollars
comparison ranking: 105

Exchange rates: Bruneian dollars (BND) per US dollar -

Exchange rates: 1.336 (2024 est.)
1.343 (2023 est.)
1.379 (2022 est.)
1.344 (2021 est.)
1.38 (2020 est.)

ENERGY

Electricity access: *electrification - total population:* 100% (2022 est.)

Electricity: *installed generating capacity:* 904,000 kW (2023 est.)
consumption: 5.081 billion kWh (2023 est.)
transmission/distribution losses: 502.188 million kWh (2023 est.)
comparison rankings: installed generating capacity 136; consumption 130; transmission/distribution losses 81

Electricity generation sources: *fossil fuels:* 99.9% of total installed capacity (2023 est.)
solar: 0.1% of total installed capacity (2023 est.)

Coal: *consumption:* 841,000 metric tons (2023 est.)
imports: 841,000 metric tons (2023 est.)

Petroleum: *total petroleum production:* 95,000 bbl/day (2023 est.)
refined petroleum consumption: 15,000 bbl/day (2023 est.)
crude oil estimated reserves: 1.1 billion barrels (2021 est.)

Natural gas: *production:* 10.093 billion cubic meters (2023 est.)
consumption: 3.911 billion cubic meters (2023 est.)
exports: 5.733 billion cubic meters (2023 est.)
proven reserves: 260.515 billion cubic meters (2021 est.)

Energy consumption per capita: 403.365 million Btu/person (2023 est.)
comparison ranking: 5

COMMUNICATIONS

Telephones - fixed lines: *total subscriptions:* 122,000 (2023 est.)
subscriptions per 100 inhabitants: 26 (2023 est.)
comparison ranking: total subscriptions 131

Telephones - mobile cellular: *total subscriptions:* 541,000 (2023 est.)
subscriptions per 100 inhabitants: 118 (2022 est.)
comparison ranking: total subscriptions 174

Broadcast media: state-controlled Radio Television Brunei (RTB) operates 5 channels; 3 Malaysian TV stations are available; foreign TV broadcasts are available via satellite systems; RTB operates 5 radio networks and broadcasts on multiple frequencies; British Forces Broadcast Service (BFBS) provides radio broadcasts on 2 FM stations; some radio broadcast stations from Malaysia are available via repeaters

Internet country code: .bn

Internet users: *percent of population:* 99% (2023 est.)

Broadband - fixed subscriptions: *total:* 93,000 (2023 est.)
subscriptions per 100 inhabitants: 20 (2023 est.)
comparison ranking: total 137

TRANSPORTATION

Civil aircraft registration country code prefix: V8

Airports: 2 (2025)
comparison ranking: 198

Heliports: 14 (2025)
comparison ranking: 62

Merchant marine: *total:* 97 (2023)
by type: general cargo 18, oil tanker 2, other 77
comparison ranking: total 90

Ports: *total ports:* 5 (2024)
large: 0: *medium:* 0: *small:* 2
very small: 3
ports with oil terminals: 5
key ports: Bandar Seri Begawan, Kuala Belait, Lumut, Muara Harbor, Seria Oil Loading Terminal

MILITARY AND SECURITY

Military and security forces: Royal Brunei Armed Forces (RBAF) or Angkatan Bersenjata Diraja Brunei (ABDB): Royal Brunei Land Force (RBLF), Royal Brunei Navy (RBN), Royal Brunei Air Force (RBAirF) (2025)
note 1: the Gurkha Security Unit under the Ministry of Defense is a special guard force for the Sultan, the royal family, and the country's oil installations
note 2: the Royal Brunei Police Force (RBPF) is under the Prime Minister's Office

Military expenditures: 3% of GDP (2023 est.)
2.6% of GDP (2022 est.)
3.1% of GDP (2021 est.)
3.7% of GDP (2020 est.)
3.1% of GDP (2019 est.)

Military and security service personnel strengths: approximately 7,000 active Armed Forces (2025)

Military equipment inventories and acquisitions: the military's s inventory includes equipment and weapons systems from a wide variety of suppliers from Asia, Europe, and the US (2024)

Military service age and obligation: 17 years of age for voluntary military service; non-Malays are ineligible to serve (2024)
note: the Gurkha Reserve Unit (GRU) employs hundreds of Gurkhas from Nepal, the majority of whom are veterans of the British Army and the Singapore Police Force who have joined the GRU as a second career

Military - note: the Royal Brunei Armed Forces (RBAF) are responsible for ensuring the country's sovereignty and territorial integrity, as well as countering outside aggression, terrorism, and insurgency
Brunei has a long-standing defense relationship with the UK and hosts a British Army garrison, which includes a Gurkha battalion and a jungle warfare school; Brunei also has close security ties with Singapore and hosts a Singaporean military training detachment
the RBAF was formed in 1961 with British support as the Brunei Malay Regiment; "Royal" was added as an honorary title in 1965 and its current name was given in 1984 (2025)

TRANSNATIONAL ISSUES

Refugees and internally displaced persons: *stateless persons:* 20,863 (2024 est.)

Trafficking in persons: *tier rating:* Tier 2 Watch List — Brunei does not fully meet the minimum standards for the elimination of trafficking but is making significant efforts to do so, therefore Brunei was upgraded to Tier 2 Watch List; for more details, go to: https://www.state.gov/reports/2025-trafficking-in-persons-report/brunei/

BULGARIA

INTRODUCTION

Background: The Bulgars, a Central Asian Turkic tribe, merged with the local Slavic inhabitants in the late 7th century to form the first Bulgarian state. In succeeding centuries, Bulgaria struggled with the Byzantine Empire to assert its place in the Balkans, but by the end of the 14th century, the Ottoman Turks overran the country. Northern Bulgaria attained autonomy in 1878, and all of Bulgaria became independent from the Ottoman Empire in 1908. Having fought on the losing side in both World Wars, Bulgaria fell within the Soviet sphere of influence and became a People's Republic in 1946. Communist domination ended in 1990, when Bulgaria held its first multiparty election since World War II and began the contentious process of moving toward political democracy and a market economy while combating inflation, unemployment, corruption, and crime. The country joined NATO in 2004, the EU in 2007, and the Schengen Area for air and sea travel in 2024.

GEOGRAPHY

Location: Southeastern Europe, bordering the Black Sea, between Romania and Turkey

Geographic coordinates: 43 00 N, 25 00 E

Map references: Europe

Area: *total:* 110,879 sq km
land: 108,489 sq km
water: 2,390 sq km
comparison ranking: total 105

Area - comparative: almost identical in size to Virginia; slightly larger than Tennessee

Land boundaries: *total:* 1,806 km
border countries (5): Greece 472 km; Macedonia 162 km; Romania 605 km; Serbia 344 km; Turkey 223 km

Coastline: 354 km

Maritime claims: *territorial sea:* 12 nm
contiguous zone: 24 nm
exclusive economic zone: 200 nm

Climate: temperate; cold, damp winters; hot, dry summers

Terrain: mostly mountains with lowlands in north and southeast

Elevation: *highest point:* Musala 2,925 m
lowest point: Black Sea 0 m
mean elevation: 472 m

Natural resources: bauxite, copper, lead, zinc, coal, timber, arable land

Land use: *agricultural land:* 46.3% (2022 est.)
arable land: 31.9% (2022 est.)
permanent crops: 1.3% (2022 est.)
permanent pasture: 13% (2022 est.)
forest: 36.1% (2022 est.)
other: 17.6% (2022 est.)

Irrigated land: 929 sq km (2016)

Major rivers (by length in km): Dunav (Danube) (shared with Germany [s], Austria, Slovakia, Hungary, Croatia, Serbia, Ukraine, Moldova, and Romania [m]) - 2,888 km
note: [s] after country name indicates river source; [m] after country name indicates river mouth

Major watersheds (area sq km): Atlantic Ocean drainage: *(Black Sea)* Danube (795,656 sq km)

Population distribution: a fairly even distribution throughout most of the country, with urban areas attracting larger populations

Natural hazards: earthquakes; landslides

Geography - note: strategic location near Turkish Straits; controls key land routes from Europe to Middle East and Asia

PEOPLE AND SOCIETY

Population: *total:* 6,782,659 (2024 est.)
male: 3,303,491
female: 3,479,168
comparison rankings: total 107; male 107; female 106

Nationality: *noun:* Bulgarian(s)
adjective: Bulgarian

Ethnic groups: Bulgarian 78.5%, Turkish 7.8%, Roma 4.1%, other 1.2%, unspecified 9.4% (2021 est.)
note: Romani populations are usually underestimated in official statistics and may represent 9–11% of Bulgaria's population

Languages: Bulgarian (official) 77.3%, Turkish 7.9%, Romani 3.5%, other 1%, unspecified 10.4% (2021 est.)
major-language sample(s):
Световен Алманах, незаменимият източник за основна информация. (Bulgarian)

Religions: Christian 64.7%, Muslim 9.8%, other 0.1%, none 4.7%, unspecified 20.7% (2021 est.)

Age structure: *0-14 years:* 13.8% (male 479,586/ female 453,423)
15-64 years: 65.2% (male 2,250,962/female 2,171,279)
65 years and over: 21% (2024 est.) (male 572,943/ female 854,466)

Dependency ratios: *total dependency ratio:* 53.4 (2024 est.)
youth dependency ratio: 21.1 (2024 est.)
elderly dependency ratio: 32.3 (2024 est.)
potential support ratio: 3.1 (2024 est.)

Median age: *total:* 45.1 years (2024 est.)
male: 43.3 years
female: 47 years
comparison ranking: total 19

Population growth rate: -0.66% (2024 est.)
comparison ranking: 226

Birth rate: 7.9 births/1,000 population (2024 est.)
comparison ranking: 216

Death rate: 14.2 deaths/1,000 population (2024 est.)
comparison ranking: 7

Net migration rate: -0.3 migrant(s)/1,000 population (2024 est.)
comparison ranking: 111

Population distribution: a fairly even distribution throughout most of the country, with urban areas attracting larger populations

Urbanization: *urban population:* 76.7% of total population (2023)
rate of urbanization: -0.28% annual rate of change (2020-25 est.)

Major urban areas - population: 1.288 million SOFIA (capital) (2023)

Sex ratio: *at birth:* 1.06 male(s)/female
0-14 years: 1.06 male(s)/female
15-64 years: 1.04 male(s)/female
65 years and over: 0.67 male(s)/female
total population: 0.95 male(s)/female (2024 est.)

Mother's mean age at first birth: 26.4 years (2020 est.)

Maternal mortality ratio: 6 deaths/100,000 live births (2023 est.)
comparison ranking: 168

Infant mortality rate: *total:* 7.7 deaths/1,000 live births (2024 est.)
male: 8.7 deaths/1,000 live births
female: 6.6 deaths/1,000 live births
comparison ranking: total 149

Life expectancy at birth: *total population:* 76.1 years (2024 est.)
male: 72.9 years
female: 79.4 years
comparison ranking: total population 118

Total fertility rate: 1.51 children born/woman (2024 est.)
comparison ranking: 202

Gross reproduction rate: 0.73 (2024 est.)

Drinking water source: *improved: urban:* 99.6% of population (2022 est.)
rural: 97.3% of population (2022 est.)
total: 99.1% of population (2022 est.)
unimproved: urban: 0.4% of population (2022 est.)
rural: 2.7% of population (2022 est.)
total: 0.9% of population (2022 est.)

Health expenditure: 8.6% of GDP (2021)
11.6% of national budget (2022 est.)

Physician density: 4.33 physicians/1,000 population (2022)

Hospital bed density: 7.8 beds/1,000 population (2020 est.)

Sanitation facility access: *improved: urban:* 100% of population (2022 est.)
rural: 100% of population (2022 est.)
total: 100% of population (2022 est.)
unimproved: urban: 0% of population (2022 est.)
rural: 0% of population (2022 est.)
total: 0% of population (2022 est.)

Obesity - adult prevalence rate: 25% (2016)
comparison ranking: 53

Alcohol consumption per capita: *total:* 11.18 liters of pure alcohol (2019 est.)
beer: 4.44 liters of pure alcohol (2019 est.)
wine: 1.72 liters of pure alcohol (2019 est.)
spirits: 4.96 liters of pure alcohol (2019 est.)
other alcohols: 0.06 liters of pure alcohol (2019 est.)
comparison ranking: total 9

Tobacco use: *total:* 33.1% (2025 est.)
male: 36.2% (2025 est.)
female: 30.3% (2025 est.)
comparison ranking: total 12

Children under the age of 5 years underweight: 1.6% (2014)
comparison ranking: 104

Currently married women (ages 15-49): 57.3% (2023 est.)

Education expenditure: 3.9% of GDP (2022 est.)
9.4% national budget (2022 est.)
comparison ranking: Education expenditure (% GDP) 115

School life expectancy (primary to tertiary education): *total:* 15 years (2023 est.)
male: 15 years (2023 est.)
female: 16 years (2023 est.)

ENVIRONMENT

Environmental issues: air pollution from industrial emissions; rivers polluted from raw sewage, heavy metals, detergents; deforestation; forest damage from air pollution and acid rain; soil contamination from heavy metals from metallurgical plants and industrial wastes

International environmental agreements: *party to:* Air Pollution, Air Pollution-Heavy Metals, Air Pollution-Multi-effect Protocol, Air Pollution-Nitrogen Oxides, Air Pollution-Persistent Organic Pollutants, Air Pollution-Sulphur 85, Air Pollution-Sulphur 94, Air Pollution-Volatile Organic Compounds, Antarctic-Environmental Protection, Antarctic-Marine Living Resources, Antarctic Treaty, Biodiversity, Climate Change, Climate Change-Kyoto Protocol, Climate Change-Paris Agreement, Comprehensive Nuclear Test Ban, Desertification, Endangered Species, Environmental Modification, Hazardous Wastes, Law of the Sea, Marine Dumping-London Convention, Marine Dumping-London Protocol, Nuclear Test Ban, Ozone Layer Protection, Ship Pollution, Tropical Timber 2006, Wetlands, Whaling
signed, but not ratified: none of the selected agreements

Climate: temperate; cold, damp winters; hot, dry summers

Urbanization: *urban population:* 76.7% of total population (2023)

rate of urbanization: -0.28% annual rate of change (2020-25 est.)

Carbon dioxide emissions: 33.465 million metric tonnes of CO2 (2023 est.)
from coal and metallurgical coke: 14.486 million metric tonnes of CO2 (2023 est.)
from petroleum and other liquids: 13.958 million metric tonnes of CO2 (2023 est.)
from consumed natural gas: 5.021 million metric tonnes of CO2 (2023 est.)
comparison ranking: total emissions 71

Particulate matter emissions: 18.6 micrograms per cubic meter (2019 est.)

Waste and recycling: *municipal solid waste generated annually:* 2.859 million tons (2024 est.)
percent of municipal solid waste recycled: 29.8% (2022 est.)

Total water withdrawal: *municipal:* 838 million cubic meters (2022)
industrial: 3.879 billion cubic meters (2022)
agricultural: 726.434 million cubic meters (2022)

Total renewable water resources: 21.3 billion cubic meters (2022 est.)

GOVERNMENT

Country name: *conventional long form:* Republic of Bulgaria
conventional short form: Bulgaria
local long form: Republika Bulgaria
local short form: Bulgaria
former: Kingdom of Bulgaria, People's Republic of Bulgaria
etymology: named after the Bulgar tribes who settled the lower Balkan region in the 7th century A.D.; the tribal name may come from the Turkic word *bulga*, or "mixed," referring to the blend of Turkic and Slavic ethnicities in the tribes

Government type: parliamentary republic

Capital: *name:* Sofia
geographic coordinates: 42 41 N, 23 19 E
time difference: UTC+2 (7 hours ahead of Washington, DC, during Standard Time)
daylight saving time: +1hr, begins last Sunday in March; ends last Sunday in October
etymology: named after the Church of Saint Sofia in the city, parts of which may date to the 4th century

Administrative divisions: 28 provinces (*oblasti*, singular - *oblast*); Blagoevgrad, Burgas, Dobrich, Gabrovo, Haskovo, Kardzhali, Kyustendil, Lovech, Montana, Pazardzhik, Pernik, Pleven, Plovdiv, Razgrad, Ruse, Shumen, Silistra, Sliven, Smolyan, Sofia, Sofia-Grad (Sofia City), Stara Zagora, Targovishte, Varna, Veliko Tarnovo, Vidin, Vratsa, Yambol

Legal system: civil law

Constitution: *history:* several previous; latest drafted between late 1990 and early 1991, adopted 13 July 1991
amendment process: proposed by the National Assembly or by the president of the republic; passage requires three-fourths majority vote of National Assembly members in three ballots; signed by the National Assembly chairperson; note - under special circumstances, a "Grand National Assembly" is elected with the authority to write a new constitution and amend certain articles of the constitution, including those affecting basic civil rights and national sovereignty; passage requires at least two-thirds majority vote in each of several readings

International law organization participation: accepts compulsory ICJ jurisdiction with reservations; accepts ICCt jurisdiction

Citizenship: *citizenship by birth:* no
citizenship by descent only: at least one parent must be a citizen of Bulgaria
dual citizenship recognized: yes
residency requirement for naturalization: 5 years

Suffrage: 18 years of age; universal

Executive branch: *chief of state:* President Rumen RADEV (since 22 January 2017)
head of government: Prime Minister Rosen ZHELYAZKOV (since 16 January 2025)
cabinet: Council of Ministers nominated by the prime minister, elected by the National Assembly
election/appointment process: president and vice president elected on the same ballot by absolute-majority popular vote in 2 rounds, if needed, for a 5-year term (eligible for a second term); chairman of the Council of Ministers (prime minister) elected by the National Assembly; deputy prime ministers nominated by the prime minister, elected by the National Assembly
most recent election date: 14 and 21 November 2021
election results: 2021: Rumen RADEV reelected president in second round; percent of vote in the first round - Rumen RADEV (independent) 49.4%, Anastas GERDZHIKOV (independent) 22.8%, Mustafa KARADAYI (DPS) 11.6%, Kostadin KOSTADINOV (Revival) 3.9%, Lozan PANOV (independent) 3.7%, other 8.6%; percent of vote in the second round - Rumen RADEV 66.7%, Anastas GERDZHIKOV 31.8%, neither 1.5%
2016: Rumen RADEV elected president in second round; percent of vote - Rumen RADEV (independent, supported by Bulgarian Socialist Party) 59.4%, Tsetska TSACHEVA (GERB) 36.2%, neither 4.5%
expected date of next election: fall 2026

Legislative branch: *legislature name:* National Assembly (Narodno sabranie)
legislative structure: unicameral
number of seats: 240 (all directly elected)
electoral system: proportional representation
scope of elections: full renewal
term in office: 4 years
most recent election date: 10/27/2024
parties elected and seats per party: Citizens for European Development of Bulgaria Party (GERB) - Union of Democratic Forces (UDF) (69); We Continue the Change - Democratic Bulgaria (37); Revival (Vuzrazhdane) (35); Movement for Rights and Freedoms (DPS) - New Beginning (30); Bulgarian Socialist Party (BSP) - United Left (20); Alliance for Rights and Freedoms (APS) (19); There is Such a People (PP-ITN) (18); Political Party Morality, Unity, Honour (PP MECh) (12)
percentage of women in chamber: 21.3%
expected date of next election: October 2028

Judicial branch: *highest court(s):* Supreme Court of Cassation consists of a chairman and approximately 72 judges organized into penal, civil, and commercial colleges; Supreme Administrative Court is organized into 2 colleges with various panels of 5 judges each; Constitutional Court consists of 12 justices) and resides outside the judiciary
judge selection and term of office: Supreme Court of Cassation and Supreme Administrative judges elected by the Supreme Judicial Council or SJC (consists of 25 members with extensive legal experience) and appointed by the president; judges can serve until mandatory retirement at age 65; Constitutional Court justices elected by the National Assembly and appointed by the president and the SJC; justices appointed for 9-year terms with renewal of 4 justices every 3 years
subordinate courts: appeals courts; regional and district courts; administrative courts; courts martial

Political parties: BSP for Bulgaria (electoral alliance of BSP, PKT, Ecoglasnost)
Bulgarian Rise or BV
Bulgarian Socialist Party or BSP
Citizens for the European Development of Bulgaria or GERB (alliance with SDS)
Democratic Bulgaria or DB (electoral alliance of Yes! Bulgaria, DSB, and The Greens) Democrats for a Strong Bulgaria or DSB
Ecoglasnost
Green Movement or The Greens
Movement for Rights and Freedoms or DPS
Political Club Thrace or PKT
Revival
Stand Up.BG or IS.BG
There is Such a People or ITN
Union of Democratic Forces or SDS (alliance with GERB)
Yes! Bulgaria
We Continue the Change or PP
We Continue the Change and Democratic Bulgaria or PP-DB (electoral alliance of PP, DB, Yes! Bulgaria)

Diplomatic representation in the US: *chief of mission:* Ambassador (vacant); Chargé d'Affaires Stefka YOVCHEVA (since 7 May 2025)
chancery: 1621 22nd Street NW, Washington, DC 20008
telephone: [1] (202) 387 5770
FAX: [1] (202) 234-7973
email address and website: office@bulgaria-embassy.org https://www.bulgaria-embassy.org/en/homepage/:
consulate(s) general: Chicago, Los Angeles, New York

Diplomatic representation from the US: *chief of mission:* Ambassador (vacant); Chargé d'Affaires H. Martin McDOWELL (since May 2025)
embassy: 16, Kozyak Street, Sofia 1408
mailing address: 5740 Sofia Place, Washington, DC 20521-5740
telephone: [359] (2) 937-5100
FAX: [359] (2) 937-5209
email address and website: acs_sofia@state.gov https://bg.usembassy.gov/: International organization participation: Australia Group, BIS, BSEC, CD, CE, CEI, CERN, EAPC, EBRD, ECB, EIB, EU, FAO, G- 9, IAEA, IBRD, ICAO, ICC (national committees), ICCt, ICRM, IDA, IFC, IFRCS, IHO (pending member), ILO, IMF, IMO, IMSO, Interpol, IOC, IOM, IPU, ISO, ITU, ITUC (NGOs), MIGA, NATO, NSG, OAS (observer), OIF, OPCW, OSCE, PCA, SELEC, UN, UNCTAD, UNESCO, UNHCR, UNHRC, UNIDO, UNMIL, UNOOSA, UNWTO, UPU, Wassenaar Arrangement, WCO, WFTU (NGOs), WHO, WIPO, WMO, WTO, ZC

Independence: 3 March 1878 (as an autonomous principality within the Ottoman Empire); 22 September 1908 (complete independence from the Ottoman Empire)

National holiday: Liberation Day, 3 March (1878)

Flag: *description:* three equal horizontal bands of white (top), green, and red
meaning: white stands for peace, love, and freedom; green for the country's agricultural wealth; red for the independence struggle and military courage

history: originally adopted in 1879 as a modified version of the Russian tricolor flag, using green instead of blue; the communist coat of arms was added to the flag in various forms between 1948 and 1990, when it was removed after the communist government collapsed

National symbol(s): lion

National color(s): white, green, red

National coat of arms: Bulgaria's coat of arms in the national colors of white, green, and red was adopted in 1997; the three lions are a national symbol for strength, courage, and leadership that was used during the country's liberation movement in the 1870s and the kingdom period in the early 20th century; above the shield is the crown of Bulgaria (originally the crown of the medieval Bulgarian tsars) with a gold cross on top; a white scroll over the oak branches bears the Bulgarian national motto, "United we stand strong"

National anthem(s): *title:* "Mila Rodino" (Dear Homeland)
lyrics/music: Tsvetan RADOSLAVOV
history: adopted 1964; composed in 1885 by a student en route to fight in the Serbo-Bulgarian War

National heritage: *total World Heritage Sites:* 10 (7 cultural, 3 natural)
selected World Heritage Site locales: Boyana Church (c); Madara Rider (c); Thracian Tomb of Kazanlak (c); Rock-Hewn Churches of Ivanovo (c); Rila Monastery (c); Ancient City of Nessebar (c); Thracian Tomb of Sveshtari (c); Srebarna Nature Reserve (n); Pirin National Park (n); Primeval Beech Forests of the Carpathians (n)

ECONOMY

Economic overview: upper-middle-income EU economy; currency pegged to the euro, with eurozone accession pending; declining energy prices helping lower inflation rate; EU structural funds contributing to investment recovery; skilled labor shortage driven by emigration and aging population

Real GDP (purchasing power parity): $219.645 billion (2024 est.)
$213.64 billion (2023 est.)
$209.683 billion (2022 est.)
note: data in 2021 dollars
comparison ranking: 74

Real GDP growth rate: 2.8% (2024 est.)
1.9% (2023 est.)
4% (2022 est.)
note: annual GDP % growth based on constant local currency
comparison ranking: 127

Real GDP per capita: $34,100 (2024 est.)
$33,100 (2023 est.)
$32,400 (2022 est.)
note: data in 2021 dollars
comparison ranking: 70

GDP (official exchange rate): $112.212 billion (2024 est.)
note: data in current dollars at official exchange rate

Inflation rate (consumer prices): 2.4% (2024 est.)
9.4% (2023 est.)
15.3% (2022 est.)
note: annual % change based on consumer prices
comparison ranking: 68

GDP - composition, by sector of origin: *agriculture:* 2.1% (2024 est.)
industry: 22.5% (2024 est.)
services: 62.6% (2024 est.)
note: figures may not total 100% due to non-allocated consumption not captured in sector-reported data
comparison rankings: agriculture 148; industry 114; services 71

GDP - composition, by end use: *household consumption:* 57.6% (2024 est.)
government consumption: 19.7% (2024 est.)
investment in fixed capital: 17.9% (2024 est.)
investment in inventories: 2.5% (2024 est.)
exports of goods and services: 55.8% (2024 est.)
imports of goods and services: -53.5% (2024 est.)
note: figures may not total 100% due to rounding or gaps in data collection

Agricultural products: wheat, maize, sunflower seeds, barley, milk, rapeseed, grapes, potatoes, triticale, tomatoes (2023)
note: top ten agricultural products based on tonnage

Industries: electricity, gas, water; food, beverages, tobacco; machinery and equipment, automotive parts, base metals, chemical products, coke, refined petroleum, nuclear fuel; outsourcing centers

Industrial production growth rate: 1.9% (2024 est.)
note: annual % change in industrial value added based on constant local currency
comparison ranking: 102

Labor force: 3.124 million (2024 est.)
note: number of people ages 15 or older who are employed or seeking work
comparison ranking: 107

Unemployment rate: 4.2% (2024 est.)
4.4% (2023 est.)
4.3% (2022 est.)
note: % of labor force seeking employment
comparison ranking: 68

Youth unemployment rate (ages 15-24): *total:* 12.1% (2024 est.)
male: 12.4% (2024 est.)
female: 11.8% (2024 est.)
note: % of labor force ages 15-24 seeking employment
comparison ranking: total 102

Population below poverty line: 20.6% (2022 est.)
note: % of population with income below national poverty line

Gini Index coefficient - distribution of family income: 38.2 (2022 est.)
note: index (0-100) of income distribution; higher values represent greater inequality
comparison ranking: 52

Average household expenditures: *on food:* 20.7% of household expenditures (2023 est.)
on alcohol and tobacco: 4.8% of household expenditures (2023 est.)

Household income or consumption by percentage share: *lowest 10%:* 2.1% (2022 est.)
highest 10%: 30.1% (2022 est.)
note: % share of income accruing to lowest and highest 10% of population

Remittances: 2.4% of GDP (2024 est.)
2.2% of GDP (2023 est.)
2.3% of GDP (2022 est.)
note: personal transfers and compensation between resident and non-resident individuals/ households/ entities

Budget: *revenues:* $35.615 billion (2023 est.)
expenditures: $37.546 billion (2023 est.)
note: central government revenues (excluding grants) and expenditures converted to US dollars at average official exchange rate for year indicated

Public debt: 30.1% of GDP (2023 est.)
note: central government debt as a % of GDP
comparison ranking: 166

Taxes and other revenues: 20.5% (of GDP) (2023 est.)
note: central government tax revenue as a % of GDP
comparison ranking: 48

Current account balance: -$2.014 billion (2024 est.)
-$894.86 million (2023 est.)
-$2.43 billion (2022 est.)
note: balance of payments - net trade and primary/secondary income in current dollars
comparison ranking: 148

Exports: $62.661 billion (2024 est.)
$63.415 billion (2023 est.)
$63.246 billion (2022 est.)
note: balance of payments - exports of goods and services in current dollars
comparison ranking: 60

Exports - partners: Germany 14%, Romania 11%, Italy 8%, Greece 6%, Turkey 5% (2023)
note: top five export partners based on percentage share of exports

Exports - commodities: refined petroleum, garments, refined copper, wheat, natural gas (2023)
note: top five export commodities based on value in dollars

Imports: $60.029 billion (2024 est.)
$59.158 billion (2023 est.)
$62.261 billion (2022 est.)
note: balance of payments - imports of goods and services in current dollars
comparison ranking: 61

Imports - partners: Germany 12%, Turkey 8%, Romania 8%, Russia 7%, Italy 6% (2023)
note: top five import partners based on percentage share of imports

Imports - commodities: crude petroleum, copper ore, cars, packaged medicine, electricity (2023)
note: top five import commodities based on value in dollars

Reserves of foreign exchange and gold: $43.698 billion (2024 est.)
$46.334 billion (2023 est.)
$40.989 billion (2022 est.)
note: holdings of gold (year-end prices)/foreign exchange/special drawing rights in current dollars
comparison ranking: 48

Debt - external: $14.277 billion (2022 est.)
note: present value of external debt in current US dollars
comparison ranking: 42

Exchange rates: leva (BGN) per US dollar -

Exchange rates: 1.808 (2024 est.)
1.809 (2023 est.)
1.86 (2022 est.)
1.654 (2021 est.)
1.716 (2020 est.)

ENERGY

Electricity access: *electrification - total population:* 100% (2022 est.)
electrification - urban areas: 100%
electrification - rural areas: 99.6%

Electricity: *installed generating capacity:* 12.939 million kW (2023 est.)
consumption: 34.221 billion kWh (2023 est.)
exports: 7.748 billion kWh (2023 est.)
imports: 4.415 billion kWh (2023 est.)
transmission/distribution losses: 1.972 billion kWh (2023 est.)
comparison rankings: installed generating capacity 59; consumption 65; exports 30; imports 48;
transmission/distribution losses 123: Electricity generation sources: *fossil fuels:* 35.2% of total installed capacity (2023 est.)
nuclear: 40.9% of total installed capacity (2023 est.)
solar: 8.2% of total installed capacity (2023 est.)
wind: 4% of total installed capacity (2023 est.)
hydroelectricity: 7.5% of total installed capacity (2023 est.)
biomass and waste: 4.1% of total installed capacity (2023 est.)

Nuclear energy: Number of operational nuclear reactors: 2 (2025)

Net capacity of operational nuclear reactors: 2.01GW (2025 est.)

Percent of total electricity production: 40.3% (2023 est.)

Number of nuclear reactors permanently shut down: 4 (2025)

Coal: *production:* 20.97 million metric tons (2023 est.)
consumption: 20.557 million metric tons (2023 est.)
exports: 1.091 million metric tons (2023 est.)
imports: 753,000 metric tons (2023 est.)
proven reserves: 2.174 billion metric tons (2023 est.)

Petroleum: *total petroleum production:* 4,000 bbl/day (2023 est.)
refined petroleum consumption: 101,000 bbl/day (2023 est.)
crude oil estimated reserves: 15 million barrels (2021 est.)

Natural gas: *production:* 10.444 million cubic meters (2023 est.)
consumption: 2.607 billion cubic meters (2023 est.)
exports: 2.75 million cubic meters (2020 est.)
imports: 2.544 billion cubic meters (2023 est.)
proven reserves: 5.663 billion cubic meters (2021 est.)

Energy consumption per capita: 102.171 million Btu/person (2023 est.)
comparison ranking: 47

COMMUNICATIONS

Telephones - fixed lines: *total subscriptions:* 619,000 (2023 est.)
subscriptions per 100 inhabitants: 9 (2023 est.)
comparison ranking: total subscriptions 84

Telephones - mobile cellular: *total subscriptions:* 8.01 million (2023 est.)
subscriptions per 100 inhabitants: 117 (2022 est.)
comparison ranking: total subscriptions 102

Broadcast media: 4 national terrestrial TV stations with 1 state-owned and 3 privately owned; a vast array of TV stations are available from cable and satellite TV providers; state-owned national radio broadcasts over 3 networks; large number of private radio stations, especially in urban areas

Internet country code: .bg

Internet users: *percent of population:* 80% (2023 est.)

Broadband - fixed subscriptions: *total:* 2.45 million (2023 est.)
subscriptions per 100 inhabitants: 36 (2023 est.)
comparison ranking: total 56

TRANSPORTATION

Civil aircraft registration country code prefix: LZ

Airports: 107 (2025)
comparison ranking: 49

Heliports: 8 (2025)
comparison ranking: 86

Railways: *total:* 4,029 km (2020) 2,871 km electrified

Merchant marine: *total:* 78 (2023)
by type: bulk carrier 2, general cargo 13, oil tanker 8, other 55
comparison ranking: total 100

Ports: *total ports:* 2 (2024)
large: 1
medium: 0
small: 1
very small: 0
ports with oil terminals: 2
key ports: Burgas, Varna

MILITARY AND SECURITY

Military and security forces: Bulgarian Armed Forces (aka Bulgarian Army): Land Forces, Air Force, Navy

Ministry of Interior: General Directorate National Police (GDNP), General Directorate Border Police (GDBP), Special Unit for Combating Terrorism (SOBT) (2025)
note 1: the Bulgarian military also has a Joint Special Operations Command, a Logistic Support Command, and a Communications and Information Support and Cyber Defence Command
note 2: the GDNP includes the Gendarmerie, a special police force with military status deployed to secure important facilities, buildings and infrastructure, respond to riots, and counter militant threats

Military expenditures: 2.1% of GDP (2025 est.)
2% of GDP (2024 est.)
1.9% of GDP (2023 est.)
1.6% of GDP (2022 est.)
1.6% of GDP (2021 est.)

Military and security service personnel strengths: approximately 27,000 active-duty Armed Forces (17,000 Army; 3,000 Navy; 7,000 Air Force) (2024)
note: in 2021, Bulgaria released a 10-year defense plan which called for an active military strength of 43,000

Military equipment inventories and acquisitions: the military's inventory consists largely of Soviet-era equipment, although in recent years Bulgaria has procured some more modern Western weapons systems in an effort to modernize and achieve NATO interoperability (2024)

Military service age and obligation: 18-40 years of age for voluntary military service; conscription ended in 2007; service obligation 6-9 months (2023)
note 1: in 2021, women comprised about 17% of the Bulgarian military's full-time personnel
note 2: in 2020, Bulgaria announced a program to allow every citizen up to the age of 40 to join the armed forces for 6 months of military service in the voluntary reserve

Military - note: the Bulgarian military is responsible for guaranteeing Bulgaria's independence, sovereignty, and territorial integrity, providing support to international peace and security missions, and contributing to national security in peacetime, including such missions as responding to disasters or assisting with border security; the military trains regularly including in multinational exercises with regional partners and with NATO since Bulgaria joined the organization in 2004; it also participates in overseas peacekeeping and other security missions under the EU, NATO, and the UN; in 2022, Bulgaria established and began leading a NATO multinational battlegroup as part of an effort to boost NATO defenses in Eastern Europe following Russia's invasion of Ukraine; in 2021, Bulgaria approved a 10-year defense development program, which included calls for equipment upgrades and procurements, boosts in manpower, organizational reforms, and greater focus on such areas as cyber defense, communications, logistics support, and research and development
the Bulgarian military has participated in several significant conflicts since its establishment in 1878, including the Serbo-Bulgarian War (1885), the First Balkan War (1912-13), the Second Balkan War (1913), World War I (1915-1918), and World War II (1941-45); during the Cold War it was one of the Warsaw Pact's largest militaries with over 150,000 personnel and more than 200 Soviet-made combat aircraft (2025)

SPACE

Space agency/agencies: Space Research and Technology Institute - Bulgarian Academy of Sciences (SRTI-BAS; formed in 1987 but originated from the Central Laboratory for Space Research and the Bulgarian Aerospace Agency, which was established in 1969) (2025)

Space program overview: has a long history of involvement in space-related activities going back to the 1960s; develops, produces, and operates satellites; researches, develops, and produces other space technologies, including those related to astrophysics, remote sensing, data exploitation, optics, and electronics; has specialized in producing scientific instruments for space research; has more than 20 research institutes; Cooperating State of the European Space Agency (ESA) since 2015; cooperates with a variety of foreign space agencies and commercial entities, including those of the ESA and EU (and bi-laterally with their member states), India, Japan, Russia, and the US (2025)
note: further details about the key activities, programs, and milestones of the country's space program, as well as government spending estimates on the space sector, appear in the Space Programs reference guide

TERRORISM

Terrorist group(s): Terrorist group(s): Islamic State of Iraq and ash-Sham (ISIS); Islamic Revolutionary Guard Corps/Qods Force
note: details about the history, aims, leadership, organization, areas of operation, tactics, targets, weapons, size, and sources of support of the group(s) appear(s) in Appendix T

TRANSNATIONAL ISSUES

Refugees and internally displaced persons: *refugees:* 114,728 (2024 est.)
stateless persons: 862 (2024 est.)

BURKINA FASO

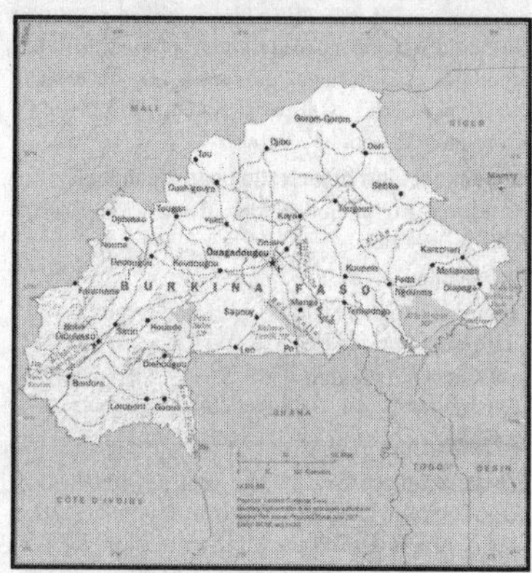

INTRODUCTION

Background: Many of Burkina Faso's ethnic groups arrived in the region between the 12th and 15th centuries. The Gurma and Mossi peoples established several of the largest kingdoms in the area and used horse-mounted warriors in military campaigns. Of the various Mossi kingdoms, the most powerful were Ouagadougou and Yatenga. In the late 19th century, European states competed for control of the region. France eventually conquered the area and established it as a French protectorate.

The country achieved independence from France in 1960 and changed its name to Burkina Faso in 1984. Repeated military coups were common in the country's first few decades. In 1987 Blaise COMPAORE deposed the president, established a government, and ruled for 27 years. In 2014, COMPAORE resigned after protests against his repeated efforts to amend the constitution's two-term presidential limit. An interim administration led a year-long transition, organizing presidential and legislative elections. In 2015, Roch Marc Christian KABORE was elected president, and he was reelected in 2020. In 2022, the military conducted two takeovers: In January, army colonel Paul Henri DAMIBA overthrew KABORE in a coup d'etat, and then in September, army captain Ibrahim TRAORE deposed DAMIBA and declared himself transition president. The transition government planned to hold elections by July 2024, but they may be delayed due to security concerns.

Terrorist groups – including groups affiliated with Al-Qa'ida and the Islamic State – began attacks in the country in 2016 and conducted attacks in the capital in 2016, 2017, and 2018. By early 2023, insecurity in Burkina Faso had displaced more than 2 million people and led to significant jumps in humanitarian needs and food insecurity. In addition to terrorism, the country faces a myriad of problems including high population growth, recurring drought, pervasive and perennial food insecurity, and limited natural resources. It is one of the world's poorest countries.

GEOGRAPHY

Location: Western Africa, north of Ghana

Geographic coordinates: 13 00 N, 2 00 W

Map references: Africa

Area: *total:* 274,200 sq km
land: 273,800 sq km
water: 400 sq km
comparison ranking: total 76

Area - comparative: slightly larger than Colorado

Land boundaries: *total:* 3,611 km
border countries (6): Benin 386 km; Cote d'Ivoire 545 km; Ghana 602 km; Mali 1325 km; Niger 622 km; Togo 131 km

Coastline: 0 km (landlocked)

Maritime claims: none (landlocked)

Climate: three climate zones including a hot tropical savanna with a short rainy season in the southern half, a tropical hot semi-arid steppe climate typical of the Sahel region in the northern half, and small area of hot desert in the very north of the country bordering the Sahara Desert

Terrain: mostly flat to dissected, undulating plains; hills in the west and southeast; occupies an extensive plateau with savanna that is grassy in the north and gradually gives way to sparse forests in the south

Elevation: *highest point:* Tena Kourou 749 m
lowest point: Mouhoun (Black Volta) River 200 m
mean elevation: 297 m

Natural resources: gold, manganese, zinc, limestone, marble, phosphates, pumice, salt

Land use: *agricultural land:* 53.2% (2022 est.)
arable land: 28.9% (2022 est.)
permanent crops: 2.4% (2022 est.)
permanent pasture: 21.9% (2022 est.)
forest: 22.4% (2022 est.)
other: 24.4% (2022 est.)

Irrigated land: 550 sq km (2016)

Major rivers (by length in km): Volta river source (shared with Ghana [m]) - 1,600 km
note: [s] after country name indicates river source; [m] after country name indicates river mouth

Major watersheds (area sq km): Atlantic Ocean drainage: Niger (2,261,741 sq km), Volta (410,991 sq km)

Population distribution: most of the population is located in the center and south; nearly one third lives in cities, including the capital city of Ouagadougou (Ouaga), as shown in this population distribution map (2019)

Natural hazards: recurring droughts

Geography - note: landlocked savanna cut by the three principal rivers, the Black, Red, and White Voltas

PEOPLE AND SOCIETY

Population: *total:* 23,042,199 (2024 est.)
male: 11,297,749
female: 11,744,450
comparison rankings: total 59; male 59; female 59

Nationality: *noun:* Burkinabe (singular and plural)
adjective: Burkinabe

Ethnic groups: Mossi 53.7%, Fulani (Peuhl) 6.8%, Gurunsi 5.9%, Bissa 5.4%, Gurma 5.2%, Bobo 3.4%, Senufo 2.2%, Bissa 1.5%, Lobi 1.5%, Tuareg/Bella 0.1%, other 12.8%, foreign 0.7% (2021 est.)

Languages: Mossi 52.9%, Fula 7.8%, Gourmantche 6.8%, Dyula 5.7%, Bissa 3.3%, Gurunsi 3.2%, French (official) 2.2%, Bwamu 2%, Dagara 2%, San 1.7%, Marka 1.6%, Bobo 1.5%, Senufo 1.5%, Lobi 1.2%, other 6.6% (2019 est.)

Religions: Muslim 63.8%, Roman Catholic 20.1%, Animiste 9%, Protestant 6.2%, other 0.2%, none 0.7% (2019 est.)

Age structure: *0-14 years:* 41.6% (male 4,868,488/female 4,727,316)
15-64 years: 55.1% (male 6,116,674/female 6,590,775)
65 years and over: 3.2% (2024 est.) (male 312,587/female 426,359)

Dependency ratios: *total dependency ratio:* 80.7 (2024 est.)
youth dependency ratio: 74.9 (2024 est.)
elderly dependency ratio: 5.8 (2024 est.)
potential support ratio: 17.2 (2024 est.)

Median age: *total:* 18.7 years (2024 est.)
male: 17.9 years
female: 19.5 years
comparison ranking: total 218

Population growth rate: 2.4% (2024 est.)
comparison ranking: 22

Birth rate: 31.9 births/1,000 population (2024 est.)
comparison ranking: 22

Death rate: 7.3 deaths/1,000 population (2024 est.)
comparison ranking: 110

Net migration rate: -0.6 migrant(s)/1,000 population (2024 est.)
comparison ranking: 123

Population distribution: most of the population is located in the center and south; nearly one third lives in cities, including the capital city of Ouagadougou (Ouaga), as shown in this population distribution map (2019)

Urbanization: *urban population:* 32.5% of total population (2023)
rate of urbanization: 4.75% annual rate of change (2020-25 est.)

Major urban areas - population: 3.204 million OUAGADOUGOU (capital), 1.129 million Bobo-Dioulasso (2023)

Sex ratio: *at birth:* 1.03 male(s)/female
0-14 years: 1.03 male(s)/female
15-64 years: 0.93 male(s)/female
65 years and over: 0.73 male(s)/female
total population: 0.96 male(s)/female (2024 est.)

Mother's mean age at first birth: 20.1 years (2021 est.)
note: data represents median age at first birth among women 25-49

Maternal mortality ratio: 242 deaths/100,000 live births (2023 est.)
comparison ranking: 30

Infant mortality rate: *total:* 47 deaths/1,000 live births (2024 est.)
male: 51.1 deaths/1,000 live births
female: 42.7 deaths/1,000 live births
comparison ranking: total 20

Life expectancy at birth: *total population:* 64.2 years (2024 est.)
male: 62.3 years
female: 66.1 years
comparison ranking: total population 208

Total fertility rate: 4.02 children born/woman (2024 est.)
comparison ranking: 23

Gross reproduction rate: 1.98 (2024 est.)

Drinking water source: *improved: urban:* 80.9% of population (2022 est.)
rural: 34.8% of population (2022 est.)
total: 49.5% of population (2022 est.)
unimproved: urban: 19.1% of population (2022 est.)
rural: 65.2% of population (2022 est.)
total: 50.5% of population (2022 est.)

Health expenditure: 6.4% of GDP (2021)
8.4% of national budget (2022 est.)

Physician density: 0.15 physicians/1,000 population (2022)

Hospital bed density: 0.2 beds/1,000 population (2020 est.)

Sanitation facility access: *improved: urban:* 91.2% of population (2022 est.)
rural: 42.6% of population (2022 est.)
total: 58.1% of population (2022 est.)
unimproved: urban: 8.8% of population (2022 est.)
rural: 57.4% of population (2022 est.)
total: 41.9% of population (2022 est.)

Obesity - adult prevalence rate: 5.6% (2016)
comparison ranking: 175

Alcohol consumption per capita: *total:* 7.28 liters of pure alcohol (2019 est.)
beer: 1 liters of pure alcohol (2019 est.)
wine: 0.08 liters of pure alcohol (2019 est.)
spirits: 0.31 liters of pure alcohol (2019 est.)
other alcohols: 5.88 liters of pure alcohol (2019 est.)
comparison ranking: total 57

Tobacco use: *total:* 12.4% (2025 est.)
male: 20.4% (2025 est.)
female: 4.6% (2025 est.)
comparison ranking: total 110

Children under the age of 5 years underweight: 17.5% (2021)
comparison ranking: 25

Currently married women (ages 15-49): 73.5% (2023)

Child marriage: *women married by age 15:* 8.9% (2015)
women married by age 18: 51.3% (2015)
men married by age 18: 1.6% (2015)

Education expenditure: 5.3% of GDP (2023 est.)
20.3% national budget (2023 est.)
comparison ranking: Education expenditure (% GDP) 52

Literacy: *total population:* 40.9% (2022 est.)
male: 49.8% (2022 est.)
female: 33.7% (2022 est.)

School life expectancy (primary to tertiary education): *total:* 7 years (2023 est.)
male: 7 years (2023 est.)
female: 7 years (2023 est.)

ENVIRONMENT

Environmental issues: droughts; desertification; overgrazing; soil degradation; deforestation (2019)

International environmental agreements: *party to:* Biodiversity, Climate Change, Climate Change-Kyoto Protocol, Climate Change-Paris Agreement, Comprehensive Nuclear Test Ban, Desertification, Endangered Species, Hazardous Wastes, Law of the Sea, Marine Life Conservation, Ozone Layer Protection, Wetlands
signed, but not ratified: Nuclear Test Ban

Climate: three climate zones including a hot tropical savanna with a short rainy season in the southern half, a tropical hot semi-arid steppe climate typical of the Sahel region in the northern half, and small area of hot desert in the very north of the country bordering the Sahara Desert

Urbanization: *urban population:* 32.5% of total population (2023)
rate of urbanization: 4.75% annual rate of change (2020-25 est.)

Carbon dioxide emissions: 5.243 million metric tonnes of CO2 (2023 est.)
from coal and metallurgical coke: 7 metric tonnes of CO2 (2023 est.)
from petroleum and other liquids: 5.243 million metric tonnes of CO2 (2023 est.)
comparison ranking: total emissions 136

Particulate matter emissions: 38.5 micrograms per cubic meter (2019 est.)

Waste and recycling: *municipal solid waste generated annually:* 2.575 million tons (2024 est.)
percent of municipal solid waste recycled: 23% (2022 est.)

Total water withdrawal: *municipal:* 375.6 million cubic meters (2022 est.)
industrial: 21.7 million cubic meters (2022 est.)
agricultural: 420.7 million cubic meters (2022 est.)

Total renewable water resources: 13.5 billion cubic meters (2022 est.)

GOVERNMENT

Country name: *conventional long form:* none
conventional short form: Burkina Faso
local long form: none
local short form: Burkina Faso
former: Upper Volta, Republic of Upper Volta
etymology: name translates as "Land of the Worthy Men," from the Dyula words *burkina*,or "worthy," and *faso*, which means "land" or literally "father village," from *fa*, or "father," and *so*, or "village"

Government type: presidential republic

Capital: *name:* Ouagadougou
geographic coordinates: 12 22 N, 1 31 W
time difference: UTC 0 (5 hours ahead of Washington, DC, during Standard Time)
etymology: Ouagadougou is a Francophone spelling of the native name "Wogodogo," which may come from the personal name "Waga" or "Woga" and the Dyula word "dugu," meaning "village"

Administrative divisions: 13 regions; Boucle du Mouhoun, Cascades, Centre, Centre-Est, Centre-Nord, Centre-Ouest, Centre-Sud, Est, Hauts-Bassins, Nord, Plateau-Central, Sahel, Sud-Ouest

Legal system: civil law based on the French model and customary law

Constitution: *history:* several previous; latest approved by referendum 2 June 1991, adopted 11 June 1991, temporarily suspended late October to mid-November 2014; initial draft of a new constitution to usher in the new republic was completed in January 2017 and a final draft was submitted to the government in December 2017; a constitutional referendum originally scheduled for adoption in March 2019 was postponed; on 1 March 2022 a transition charter was adopted, allowing military authorities to rule for three years and barring the transitional president from being an electoral candidate after the transition
amendment process: proposed by the president, by a majority of National Assembly membership, or by petition of at least 30,000 eligible voters submitted to the Assembly; passage requires at least three-fourths majority vote in the Assembly; failure to meet that threshold requires majority voter approval in a referendum; constitutional provisions on the form of government, the multiparty system, and national sovereignty cannot be amended

International law organization participation: has not submitted an ICJ jurisdiction declaration; accepts ICCt jurisdiction

Citizenship: *citizenship by birth:* no
citizenship by descent only: at least one parent must be a citizen of Burkina Faso
dual citizenship recognized: yes
residency requirement for naturalization: 10 years

Suffrage: 18 years of age; universal

Executive branch: *chief of state:* Transitional President Capt. Ibrahim TRAORE (since 30 September 2022)
head of government: Prime Minister Joachim KYLEM DE TAMBELA (since 21 October 2022)
cabinet: prior to the 2022 coups and ad hoc suspension of laws and constitutional provisions, Council of Ministers appointed by the president on the recommendation of the prime minister
election/appointment process: prior to the 2022 coups and ad hoc suspension of laws and constitutional provisions, president directly elected by absolute-majority popular vote in 2 rounds, if needed, for a 5-year term (eligible for a second term); prime minister appointed by the president with consent of the National Assembly
most recent election date: 22 November 2020
election results: *2020:* Roch Marc Christian KABORE reelected president in first round; percent of vote - Roch Marc Christian KABORE (MPP) 57.9%, Eddie KOMBOIGO (CDP) 15.5%, Zephirin DIABRE (UPC) 12.5%, other 14.1%
2015: Roch Marc Christian KABORE elected president in first round; percent of vote - Roch Marc Christian KABORE (MPP) 53.5%, Zephirin DIABRE (UPC) 29.6%, Tahirou BARRY (PAREN) 3.1%, Benewende Stanislas SANKARA (UNIR-MS) 2.8%, other 10.9%
expected date of next election: were to be held by July 2024, but were delayed
note: on 30 September 2022, a military junta led by TRAORE took power and ousted Transition President Lt. Col. Paul-Henri Sandaogo DAMIBA

Legislative branch: *legislature name:* Parliament (Parlement)
legislative structure: unicameral
chamber name: Transitional Legislative Assembly (Assemblée législative de la transition)
number of seats: 71
electoral system: proportional representation
most recent election date: 11/11/2022
percentage of women in chamber: 18.3%
expected date of next election: June 2029
note: a series of coups in 2022 led to the ad hoc suspension of laws and constitutional provisions, including the unicameral National Assembly; a military junta in 2022 appointed the 71-member Transnational Legislative Assembly (ALT); a Transitional Charter, adopted in October 2022, provided for a transitional period that was extended in May 2024 until July 2029

Judicial branch: *highest court(s):* Supreme Court of Appeals or Cour de Cassation (consists of NA judges); Council of State (consists of NA judges); Constitutional Council or Conseil Constitutionnel (consists of the council president and 9 members)

judge selection and term of office: Supreme Court judge appointments mostly controlled by the president of Burkina Faso; judges have no term limits; Council of State judge appointment and tenure NA; Constitutional Council judges appointed by the president of Burkina Faso after a proposal from the minister of justice and the president of the National Assembly; judges appointed for 9-year terms with one-third of membership renewed every 3 years
subordinate courts: Appeals Court; High Court; first instance tribunals; district courts; specialized courts relating to issues of labor, children, and juveniles; village (customary) courts

Political parties: Act Together
African Democratic Rally/Alliance for Democracy and Federation or ADF/RDA
Congress for Democracy and Progress or CDP
Convergence for Progress and Solidarity-Generation 3 or CPS-G3
Movement for the Future Burkina Faso or MBF
National Convention for Progress or CNP
New Era for Democracy or NTD
Pan-African Alliance for Refoundation or APR
Party for Democracy and Socialism/Metba or PDS/Metba
Party for Development and Change or PDC
Patriotic Rally for Integrity or RPI
Peoples Movement for Progress or MPP
Progressives United for Renewal or PUR
Union for Progress and Reform or UPC
Union for Rebirth - Sankarist Party or UNIR-PS

Diplomatic representation in the US: *chief of mission:* Ambassador Kassoum COULIBALY (since 24 July 2025)
chancery: 2340 Massachusetts Avenue NW, Washington, DC 20008
telephone: [1] (202) 332-5577
FAX: [1] (202) 667-1882
email address and website: contact@burkina-usa.org
https://burkina-usa.org/

Diplomatic representation from the US: *chief of mission:* Ambassador Joann M. LOCKARD (since 28 June 2024)
embassy: Secteur 15, Ouaga 2000, Avenue Sembene Ousmane, Rue 15.873, Ouagadougou
mailing address: 2440 Ouagadougou Place, Washington, DC 20521-2440
telephone: (226) 25-49-53-00
FAX: (226) 25-49-56-23
email address and website: AmembOuaga@state.gov
https://bf.usembassy.gov/

International organization participation: ACP, AfDB, AU (suspended), CD, EITI (compliant country), Entente, FAO, FZ, G-77, IAEA, IBRD, ICAO, ICC (NGOs), ICCt, ICRM, IDA, IDB, IFAD, IFC, IFRCS, ILO, IMF, Interpol, IOC, IOM, IPU, ISO, ITSO, ITU, ITUC (NGOs), MIGA, MINUSCA, MONUSCO, NAM, OIC, OIF, OPCW, PCA, UN, UNCTAD, UNESCO, UNIDO, UNISFA, UNITAR, UNMISS, UNOOSA, UNWTO, UPU, WADB (regional), WAEMU, WCO, WFTU (NGOs), WHO, WIPO, WMO, WTO

Independence: 5 August 1960 (from France)

National holiday: Republic Day, 11 December (1958)
note: commemorates the day that Upper Volta became an autonomous republic in the French Community

Flag: *description:* two equal horizontal bands of red (top) and green, with a five-pointed yellow star in the center
meaning: red stands for the country's struggle for independence, green for hope and abundance, and yellow for the country's mineral wealth
history: uses the colors of the Pan-African movement

National symbol(s): white stallion

National color(s): red, yellow, green

National anthem(s): *title:* "Le Ditanye" (Anthem of Victory)
lyrics/music: Thomas SANKARA
history: adopted 1974; also known as "Une Seule Nuit"(One Single Night); written by the country's former president, an avid guitar player

National heritage: *total World Heritage Sites:* 4 (3 cultural, 1 natural)
selected World Heritage Site locales: Ruins of Loropéni (c); Ancient Ferrous Metallurgy Sites of Burkina Faso (c); W-Arly-Pendjari Complex (n); Royal Court of Tiébélé (c)

ECONOMY

Economic overview: highly agrarian, low-income economy; limited natural resources; widespread poverty; terrorism disrupting potential economic activity; improving trade balance via increases in gold exports; economy inflating after prior deflation; growing public debt but still manageable

Real GDP (purchasing power parity): $60.001 billion (2024 est.)
$57.152 billion (2023 est.)
$55.508 billion (2022 est.)
note: data in 2021 dollars
comparison ranking: 116

Real GDP growth rate: 5% (2024 est.)
3% (2023 est.)
1.5% (2022 est.)
note: annual GDP % growth based on constant local currency
comparison ranking: 46

Real GDP per capita: $2,500 (2024 est.)
$2,500 (2023 est.)
$2,500 (2022 est.)
note: data in 2021 dollars
comparison ranking: 204

GDP (official exchange rate): $23.25 billion (2024 est.)
note: data in current dollars at official exchange rate

Inflation rate (consumer prices): 4.2% (2024 est.)
0.7% (2023 est.)
14.3% (2022 est.)
note: annual % change based on consumer prices
comparison ranking: 128

GDP - composition, by sector of origin: *agriculture:* 18.6% (2024 est.)
industry: 29.7% (2024 est.)
services: 40.2% (2024 est.)
note: figures may not total 100% due to non-allocated consumption not captured in sector-reported data
comparison rankings: agriculture 37; industry 57; services 193

GDP - composition, by end use: *household consumption:* 60.6% (2024 est.)
government consumption: 18.8% (2024 est.)
investment in fixed capital: 16.5% (2024 est.)
investment in inventories: 10.6% (2024 est.)
exports of goods and services: 28.5% (2024 est.)
imports of goods and services: -34.9% (2024 est.)
note: figures may not total 100% due to rounding or gaps in data collection

Agricultural products: maize, sorghum, fruits, vegetables, millet, cowpeas, cotton, groundnuts, sugarcane, rice (2023)
note: top ten agricultural products based on tonnage

Industries: cotton lint, beverages, agricultural processing, soap, cigarettes, textiles, gold

Industrial production growth rate: -5.4% (2024 est.)
note: annual % change in industrial value added based on constant local currency
comparison ranking: 180

Labor force: 6.461 million (2024 est.)
note: number of people ages 15 or older who are employed or seeking work
comparison ranking: 72

Unemployment rate: 5.2% (2024 est.)
5.4% (2023 est.)
5.4% (2022 est.)
note: % of labor force seeking employment
comparison ranking: 91

Youth unemployment rate (ages 15-24): *total:* 8.1% (2024 est.)
male: 7.8% (2024 est.)
female: 8.5% (2024 est.)
note: % of labor force ages 15-24 seeking employment
comparison ranking: total 138

Population below poverty line: 43.2% (2021 est.)
note: % of population with income below national poverty line

Gini Index coefficient - distribution of family income: 37.4 (2021 est.)
note: index (0-100) of income distribution; higher values represent greater inequality
comparison ranking: 59

Household income or consumption by percentage share: *lowest 10%:* 3% (2021 est.)
highest 10%: 30.2% (2021 est.)
note: % share of income accruing to lowest and highest 10% of population

Remittances: 2.9% of GDP (2023 est.)
2.8% of GDP (2022 est.)
2.9% of GDP (2021 est.)
note: personal transfers and compensation between resident and non-resident individuals/households/entities

Budget: *revenues:* $5.174 billion (2023 est.)
expenditures: $6.308 billion (2023 est.)
note: central government revenues (excluding grants) and expenditures converted to US dollars at average official exchange rate for year indicated

Public debt: 61.3% of GDP (2023 est.)
note: central government debt as a % of GDP
comparison ranking: 74

Taxes and other revenues: 18.4% (of GDP) (2023 est.)
note: central government tax revenue as a % of GDP
comparison ranking: 62

Current account balance: -$1.017 billion (2023 est.)
-$1.404 billion (2022 est.)
$77.255 million (2021 est.)
note: balance of payments - net trade and primary/secondary income in current dollars
comparison ranking: 130

Exports: $5.912 billion (2023 est.)
$5.814 billion (2022 est.)
$6.234 billion (2021 est.)
note: balance of payments - exports of goods and services in current dollars
comparison ranking: 133

Exports - partners: Switzerland 72%, UAE 10%, India 3%, Mali 3%, Cote d'Ivoire 2% (2023)
note: top five export partners based on percentage share of exports

Exports - commodities: gold, cotton, oil seeds, coconuts/brazil nuts/cashews, cement (2023)
note: top five export commodities based on value in dollars

Imports: $6.834 billion (2023 est.)
$6.761 billion (2022 est.)
$5.835 billion (2021 est.)
note: balance of payments - imports of goods and services in current dollars
comparison ranking: 142

Imports - partners: Cote d'Ivoire 14%, China 13%, Ghana 9%, Russia 9%, France 7% (2023)
note: top five import partners based on percentage share of imports

Imports - commodities: refined petroleum, plastic products, cement, electricity, packaged medicine (2023)
note: top five import commodities based on value in dollars

Debt - external: $3.565 billion (2023 est.)
note: present value of external debt in current US dollars
comparison ranking: 82

Exchange rates: Communaute Financiere Africaine francs (XOF) per US dollar -

Exchange rates: 606.345 (2024 est.)
606.57 (2023 est.)
623.76 (2022 est.)
554.531 (2021 est.)
575.586 (2020 est.)

ENERGY

Electricity access: *electrification - total population:* 19.5% (2022 est.)
electrification - urban areas: 60.5%
electrification - rural areas: 3.4%

Electricity: *installed generating capacity:* 749,000 kW (2023 est.)
consumption: 3.096 billion kWh (2023 est.)
imports: 1.577 billion kWh (2023 est.)
transmission/distribution losses: 212.254 million kWh (2023 est.)
comparison rankings: installed generating capacity 144; consumption 141; imports 70; transmission/distribution losses 67

Electricity generation sources: *fossil fuels:* 82.9% of total installed capacity (2023 est.)
solar: 5.4% of total installed capacity (2023 est.)
hydroelectricity: 6.7% of total installed capacity (2023 est.)
biomass and waste: 5.1% of total installed capacity (2023 est.)

Coal: *exports:* 1 metric tons (2023 est.)
imports: 74 metric tons (2023 est.)

Petroleum: *refined petroleum consumption:* 37,000 bbl/day (2023 est.)

Energy consumption per capita: 3.481 million Btu/person (2023 est.)
comparison ranking: 176

COMMUNICATIONS

Telephones - fixed lines: *total subscriptions:* 81,000 (2021 est.)
subscriptions per 100 inhabitants: (2022 est.) less than 1
comparison ranking: total subscriptions 141

Telephones - mobile cellular: *total subscriptions:* 24.7 million (2021 est.)
subscriptions per 100 inhabitants: 112 (2021 est.)
comparison ranking: total subscriptions 56

Broadcast media: 14 digital TV channels, of which 2 are state-owned; over 140 national radio stations (commercial, religious, community), including a national and regional state-owned network; state-owned Radio Burkina and private Radio Omega are among the most widely available and broadcast in both French and local languages (2019)

Internet country code: .bf

Internet users: *percent of population:* 17% (2023 est.)

Broadband - fixed subscriptions: *total:* 15,000 (2022 est.)
subscriptions per 100 inhabitants: (2022 est.) less than 1
comparison ranking: total 177

TRANSPORTATION

Civil aircraft registration country code prefix: XT

Airports: 49 (2025)
comparison ranking: 89

Railways: *total:* 622 km (2014)
narrow gauge: 622 km (2014) 1.000-m gauge
note: another 660 km of this railway extends into Cote d'Ivoire

MILITARY AND SECURITY

Military and security forces: Armed Forces of Burkina Faso (FABF; aka National Armed Forces (FAN), aka Defense and Security Forces (Forces de Défense et de Sécurité or FDS)): Army of Burkina Faso (L'Armee de Terre), Air Force of Burkina Faso (Force Aerienne de Burkina Faso), National Gendarmerie, National Fire Brigade (Brigade Nationale de Sapeurs-Pompiers or BNSP); Homeland Defense Volunteers (Forcés de Volontaires de Défense pour la Patrie or VDP)

Ministry of Territorial Administration, Decentralization and Security (Ministère de l'Administration Territoriale, de la Décentralisation et de la Sécurité): National Police of Burkina Faso (includes Border Police, Judicial Police, and Intervention Units, as well as State and Public Security forces) (2025)
note 1: the National Gendarmerie is under the Ministry of Defense, but usually operates in support of the Ministry of Territorial Administration, Decentralization, and Security; the Gendarmerie's primary mission is counterterrorism
note 2: the VDP is a lightly armed civilian defense/militia force established in 2019 to act as auxiliaries to the Army; the volunteers receive two weeks of training and typically assist with carrying out surveillance, information-gathering, and escort duties, as well as local defense; they are based in each of the country's more than 300 municipalities

Military expenditures: 4.5% of GDP (2024 est.)
4% of GDP (2023 est.)
2.9% of GDP (2022 est.)
2.4% of GDP (2021 est.)
2.4% of GDP (2020 est.)

Military and security service personnel strengths: estimated 20,000 Armed Forces; estimated 50,000 Homeland Defense Volunteers (2025)

Military equipment inventories and acquisitions: the FABF has a mix of older, secondhand, and some modern equipment from a variety of suppliers, including China, Egypt, France, Russia, South Africa, Turkey, the UK, and the US (2024)

Military service age and obligation: 18-26 years of age for voluntary military service for men and women; citizens 18-77 years of age are eligible to volunteer for the VDP (2023)
note: the military government implemented an emergency law in 2023 that allows the president extensive powers to combat terrorist groups operating in the country, including conscripting citizens into the security services

Military deployments: *note:* in 2024, Burkina Faso, Mali, and Niger announced they were forming joint force of 5,000 troops to combat extremist groups in the Sahel

Military - note: the Armed Forces of Burkina Faso (FABF) are responsible for external defense but also have an internal security role and can be called out to assist internal security forces in restoring public order, combating crime, securing the border, and conducting counterterrorism/ counterinsurgency/internal defense operations
the FABF's primary focus is combatting militants affiliated with the al-Qa'ida and Islamic State of Iraq and ash-Sham (ISIS) terrorist groups, which have operated in the country for more than a decade and are estimated to control at least 30 percent of Burkina Faso as of 2025; Jama'at Nusrat al-Islam wal-Muslimin (JNIM), a coalition of al-Qa'ida linked militant groups that act as al-Qa'ida in the Land of the Islamic Magreb's (AQIM) arm in the Sahel, is strongest in the north but active in nearly all of the country's 13 provinces, while ISIS in the Greater Sahara (aka ISIS-Sahel) operates in the eastern part of the country
the FABF has a history of involvement in the country's politics, having conducted eight coups since its formation in 1960-61, including the most recent in September 2022; several combat units were disbanded in 2011 following mutinies (2025)

TERRORISM

Terrorist group(s): Terrorist group(s): Ansarul Islam; Islamic State of Iraq and ash-Sham in the Greater Sahara (ISIS-GS); al-Mulathamun Battalion (al-Mourabitoun); Jama'at Nusrat al-Islam wal-Muslimin (JNIM)
note: details about the history, aims, leadership, organization, areas of operation, tactics, targets, weapons, size, and sources of support of the group(s) appear(s) in Appendix T

TRANSNATIONAL ISSUES

Refugees and internally displaced persons: *refugees:* 41,408 (2024 est.)

IDPs: 2,065,358 (2024 est.)

Trafficking in persons: *tier rating:* Tier 2 Watch List — the government did not demonstrate overall increasing efforts to eliminate trafficking compared with the previous reporting period, therefore Burkina Faso remained on Tier 2 Watch List for the second consecutive year; for more details, go to: https://www.state.gov/reports/2025-trafficking-in-persons-report/burkina-faso/

BURMA

INTRODUCTION

Background: Burma is home to ethnic Burmans and scores of other ethnic and religious minority groups that have resisted external efforts to consolidate control of the country throughout its history. Britain conquered Burma over a period extending from the 1820s to the 1880s and administered it as a province of India until 1937, when Burma became a self-governing colony. Burma gained full independence in 1948. In 1962, General NE WIN seized power and ruled the country until 1988 when a new military regime took control.

In 1990, the military regime permitted an election but then rejected the results after the main opposition National League for Democracy (NLD) and its leader AUNG SAN SUU KYI (ASSK) won in a landslide. The military regime placed ASSK under house arrest until 2010. In 2007, rising fuel prices in Burma led pro-democracy activists and Buddhist monks to launch a "Saffron Revolution" consisting of large protests against the regime, which violently suppressed the movement. The regime prevented new elections until it had drafted a constitution designed to preserve the military's political control; it passed the new constitution in its 2008 referendum. The regime conducted an election in 2010, but the NLD boycotted the vote, and the military's political proxy, the Union Solidarity and Development Party, easily won; international observers denounced the election as flawed.

Burma nonetheless began a halting process of political and economic reforms. ASSK's return to government in 2012 eventually led to the NLD's sweeping victory in the 2015 election. With ASSK as the de facto head of state, Burma's first credibly elected civilian government drew international criticism for blocking investigations into Burma's military operations – which the US Department of State determined constituted genocide – against its ethnic Rohingya population. When the 2020 elections resulted in further NLD gains, the military denounced the vote as fraudulent. In 2021, the military's senior leader General MIN AUNG HLAING launched a coup that returned Burma to authoritarian rule, with military crackdowns that undid reforms and resulted in the detention of ASSK and thousands of pro-democracy actors.

Pro-democracy organizations have formed in the wake of the coup, including the National Unity Government (NUG). Members of the NUG include representatives from the NLD, ethnic minority groups, and civil society. In 2021, the NUG announced the formation of armed militias called the People's Defense Forces (PDF) and an insurgency against the military junta. As of 2024, PDF units across the country continued to fight the regime with varying levels of support from and cooperation with the NUG and other anti-regime organizations, including armed ethnic groups that have been fighting the central government for decades.

GEOGRAPHY

Location: Southeastern Asia, bordering the Andaman Sea and the Bay of Bengal, between Bangladesh and Thailand

Geographic coordinates: 22 00 N, 98 00 E

Map references: Southeast Asia

Area: *total:* 676,578 sq km
land: 653,508 sq km
water: 23,070 sq km
comparison ranking: total 42

Area - comparative: slightly smaller than Texas

Land boundaries: *total:* 6,522 km
border countries (5): Bangladesh 271 km; China 2,129 km; India 1,468 km; Laos 238 km; Thailand 2,416 km

Coastline: 1,930 km

Maritime claims: *territorial sea:* 12 nm
contiguous zone: 24 nm
exclusive economic zone: 200 nm
continental shelf: 200 nm or to the edge of the continental margin

Climate: tropical monsoon; cloudy, rainy, hot, humid summers (southwest monsoon, June to September); less cloudy, scant rainfall, mild temperatures, lower humidity during winter (northeast monsoon, December to April)

Terrain: central lowlands ringed by steep, rugged highlands

Elevation: *highest point:* Gamlang Razi 5,870 m
lowest point: Andaman Sea/Bay of Bengal 0 m
mean elevation: 702 m

Natural resources: petroleum, timber, tin, antimony, zinc, copper, tungsten, lead, coal, marble, limestone, precious stones, natural gas, hydropower, arable land

Land use: *agricultural land:* 19.9% (2022 est.)
arable land: 16.8% (2022 est.)
permanent crops: 2.3% (2022 est.)
permanent pasture: 0.7% (2022 est.)
forest: 42.8% (2022 est.)
other: 37.3% (2022 est.)

Irrigated land: 17,140 sq km (2020)

Major rivers (by length in km): Mekong (shared with China [s], Laos, Thailand, Cambodia, and Vietnam [m]) - 4,350 km; Salween river mouth (shared with China [s] and Thailand) - 3,060 km; Irrawaddy river mouth (shared with China [s]) - 2,809 km; Chindwin - 1,158 km
note: [s] after country name indicates river source; [m] after country name indicates river mouth

Major watersheds (area sq km): Indian Ocean drainage: Brahmaputra (651,335 sq km), Ganges (1,016,124 sq km), Irrawaddy (413,710 sq km), Salween (271,914 sq km)

Pacific Ocean drainage: Mekong (805,604 sq km)

Population distribution: population concentrated along coastal areas and in general proximity to the shores of the Irrawaddy River; the extreme north is relatively underpopulated

Natural hazards: destructive earthquakes and cyclones; flooding and landslides common during rainy season (June to September); periodic droughts

Geography - note: strategic location near major Indian Ocean shipping lanes; the north-south flowing Irrawaddy River is the country's largest and most important commercial waterway

PEOPLE AND SOCIETY

Population: *total:* 57,527,139 (2024 est.)
male: 28,387,831
female: 29,139,308
comparison rankings: total 27; male 27; female 27

Nationality: *noun:* Burmese (singular and plural)
adjective: Burmese

Ethnic groups: Burman (Bamar) 68%, Shan 9%, Karen 7%, Rakhine 4%, Chinese 3%, Indian 2%, Mon 2%, other 5%
note: the largest ethnic group — the Burman (or Bamar) — dominate politics, and the military ranks are largely drawn from this ethnic group; the Burman mainly populate the central parts of the country, while various ethnic minorities have traditionally lived in the peripheral regions that surround the plains in a horseshoe shape; the government recognizes 135 indigenous ethnic groups

Languages: Burmese (official)
major-language sample(s):
ကမ္ဘာ့အချက်အလက်စာအုပ်- အခြေခံအချက်အလက်တွေအတွက် မရှိမဖြစ်တဲ့ အရင်းအမြစ်
(Burmese)
note: minority ethnic groups use their own languages

Religions: Buddhist 87.9%, Christian 6.2%, Muslim 4.3%, Animist 0.8%, Hindu 0.5%, other 0.2%, none 0.1% (2014 est.)
note: religion estimate is based on the 2014 national census, including an estimate for the non-enumerated population of Rakhine State, which is

assumed to mainly affiliate with the Islamic faith; as of December 2019, Muslims probably make up less than 3% of Burma's total population due to the large outmigration of the Rohingya population since 2017

Age structure: *0-14 years:* 24.4% (male 7,197,177/female 6,843,879)
15-64 years: 68.5% (male 19,420,361/female 19,998,625)
65 years and over: 7.1% (2024 est.) (male 1,770,293/female 2,296,804)

Dependency ratios: *total dependency ratio:* 45.9 (2024 est.)
youth dependency ratio: 35.6 (2024 est.)
elderly dependency ratio: 10.3 (2024 est.)
potential support ratio: 9.7 (2024 est.)

Median age: *total:* 30.8 years (2024 est.)
male: 29.9 years
female: 31.6 years
comparison ranking: total 131

Population growth rate: 0.71% (2024 est.)
comparison ranking: 123

Birth rate: 15.7 births/1,000 population (2024 est.)
comparison ranking: 103

Death rate: 7.3 deaths/1,000 population (2024 est.)
comparison ranking: 108

Net migration rate: -1.4 migrant(s)/1,000 population (2024 est.)
comparison ranking: 155

Population distribution: population concentrated along coastal areas and in general proximity to the shores of the Irrawaddy River; the extreme north is relatively underpopulated

Urbanization: *urban population:* 32.1% of total population (2023)
rate of urbanization: 1.85% annual rate of change (2020-25 est.)

Major urban areas - population: 5.610 million RANGOON (Yangon) (capital), 1.532 million Mandalay (2023)

Sex ratio: *at birth:* 1.06 male(s)/female
0-14 years: 1.05 male(s)/female
15-64 years: 0.97 male(s)/female
65 years and over: 0.77 male(s)/female
total population: 0.97 male(s)/female (2024 est.)

Mother's mean age at first birth: 24.7 years (2015/16 est.)
note: data represents median age at first birth among women 25-49

Maternal mortality ratio: 185 deaths/100,000 live births (2023 est.)
comparison ranking: 41

Infant mortality rate: *total:* 32.1 deaths/1,000 live births (2024 est.)
male: 35.4 deaths/1,000 live births
female: 28.5 deaths/1,000 live births
comparison ranking: total 42

Life expectancy at birth: *total population:* 70.3 years (2024 est.)
male: 68.5 years
female: 72.1 years
comparison ranking: total population 177

Total fertility rate: 1.97 children born/woman (2024 est.)
comparison ranking: 109

Gross reproduction rate: 0.96 (2024 est.)

Drinking water source: *improved: urban:* 93.7% of population (2022 est.)
rural: 77.1% of population (2022 est.)
total: 82.4% of population (2022 est.)
unimproved: urban: 6.3% of population (2022 est.)
rural: 22.9% of population (2022 est.)
total: 17.6% of population (2022 est.)

Health expenditure: 5.6% of GDP (2021)
2.5% of national budget (2022 est.)

Physician density: 0.76 physicians/1,000 population (2019)

Hospital bed density: 1.1 beds/1,000 population (2020 est.)

Sanitation facility access: *improved: urban:* 94.1% of population (2022 est.)
rural: 82% of population (2022 est.)
total: 85.9% of population (2022 est.)
unimproved: urban: 5.9% of population (2022 est.)
rural: 18% of population (2022 est.)
total: 14.1% of population (2022 est.)

Obesity - adult prevalence rate: 5.8% (2016)
comparison ranking: 173

Alcohol consumption per capita: *total:* 2.06 liters of pure alcohol (2019 est.)
beer: 0.5 liters of pure alcohol (2019 est.)
wine: 0.02 liters of pure alcohol (2019 est.)
spirits: 1.55 liters of pure alcohol (2019 est.)
other alcohols: 0 liters of pure alcohol (2019 est.)
comparison ranking: total 128

Tobacco use: *total:* 42.2% (2025 est.)
male: 68.1% (2025 est.)
female: 17.1% (2025 est.)
comparison ranking: total 2

Children under the age of 5 years underweight: 19.1% (2018)
comparison ranking: 16

Currently married women (ages 15-49): 57.5% (2023 est.)

Child marriage: *women married by age 15:* 1.9% (2016)
women married by age 18: 16% (2016)
men married by age 18: 5% (2016)

Education expenditure: 2% of GDP (2019 est.)
9.8% national budget (2019 est.)
comparison ranking: Education expenditure (% GDP) 182

Literacy: *total population:* 89% (2019 est.)
male: 92% (2019 est.)
female: 86% (2019 est.)

School life expectancy (primary to tertiary education): *total:* 12 years (2018 est.)
male: 11 years (2018 est.)
female: 12 years (2018 est.)

ENVIRONMENT

Environmental issues: deforestation; industrial pollution of air, soil, and water; inadequate sanitation and water treatment; rapid depletion of the country's natural resources

International environmental agreements: *party to:* Biodiversity, Climate Change, Climate Change-Kyoto Protocol, Climate Change-Paris Agreement, Comprehensive Nuclear Test Ban, Desertification, Endangered Species, Hazardous Wastes, Law of the Sea, Nuclear Test Ban, Ozone Layer Protection, Ship Pollution, Tropical Timber 2006, Wetlands
signed, but not ratified: none of the selected agreements

Climate: tropical monsoon; cloudy, rainy, hot, humid summers (southwest monsoon, June to September); less cloudy, scant rainfall, mild temperatures, lower humidity during winter (northeast monsoon, December to April)

Urbanization: *urban population:* 32.1% of total population (2023)
rate of urbanization: 1.85% annual rate of change (2020-25 est.)

Carbon dioxide emissions: 27.005 million metric tonnes of CO_2 (2023 est.)
from coal and metallurgical coke: 1.24 million metric tonnes of CO_2 (2023 est.)
from petroleum and other liquids: 17.39 million metric tonnes of CO_2 (2023 est.)
from consumed natural gas: 8.376 million metric tonnes of CO_2 (2023 est.)
comparison ranking: total emissions 76

Particulate matter emissions: 27.2 micrograms per cubic meter (2019 est.)

Waste and recycling: *municipal solid waste generated annually:* 4.677 million tons (2024 est.)
percent of municipal solid waste recycled: 12.3% (2022 est.)

Total water withdrawal: *municipal:* 3.323 billion cubic meters (2022 est.)
industrial: 498.4 million cubic meters (2022 est.)
agricultural: 29.57 billion cubic meters (2022 est.)

Total renewable water resources: 1.168 trillion cubic meters (2022 est.)

GOVERNMENT

Country name: *conventional long form:* Union of Burma
conventional short form: Burma
local long form: Pyidaungzu Thammada Myanma Naingngandaw (translated as the Republic of the Union of Myanmar)
local short form: Myanma Naingngandaw
former: Socialist Republic of the Union of Burma, Union of Myanmar
etymology: both "Burma" and "Myanmar" derive from the name of the majority Burman (Bamar) ethnic group, with the term *myanma*, or "the strong," being the group's name for itself
note: since 1989 the military authorities in Burma and the deposed parliamentary government have promoted the name Myanmar as a conventional name for their state; the US Government has not officially adopted the name

Government type: military regime

Capital: *name:* Rangoon (aka Yangon, continues to be recognized as the primary Burmese capital by the US Government); Nay Pyi Taw is the administrative capital
geographic coordinates: 16 48 N, 96 10 E
time difference: UTC+6.5 (11.5 hours ahead of Washington, DC, during Standard Time)
etymology: Rangoon/Yangon derives from the Burmese words *yan* and *koun*, commonly translated as "end of strife"; Nay Pyi Taw translates as "abode of kings"

Administrative divisions: 7 regions (*taing-myar*, singular - *taing*), 7 states (*pyi ne-myar*, singular - *pyi ne*), 1 union territory
regions: Ayeyarwady (Irrawaddy), Bago, Magway, Mandalay, Sagaing, Tanintharyi, Yangon (Rangoon)
states: Chin, Kachin, Kayah, Karen, Mon, Rakhine, Shan
union territory: Nay Pyi Taw

Legal system: mixed legal system of English common law (as introduced in codifications designed for colonial India) and customary law

Constitution: *history:* previous 1947, 1974 (suspended until 2008); latest drafted 9 April 2008, approved by referendum 29 May 2008
amendment process: proposals require at least 20% approval by the Assembly of the Union membership; passage of amendments to sections of the constitution on basic principles, government structure, branches of government, state emergencies, and amendment procedures requires 75% approval by the Assembly and approval in a referendum by absolute majority of registered voters; passage of amendments to other sections requires only 75% Assembly approval; military granted 25% of parliamentary seats by default

International law organization participation: has not submitted an ICJ jurisdiction declaration; non-party state to the ICCt

Citizenship: *citizenship by birth:* no
citizenship by descent only: both parents must be citizens of Burma
dual citizenship recognized: no
residency requirement for naturalization: none
note: an applicant for naturalization must be the child or spouse of a citizen

Suffrage: 18 years of age; universal

Executive branch: *chief of state:* Acting President Sr. Gen. MIN AUNG HLAING (since 31 July 2025)
head of government: Prime Minister NYO SAW (since 31 July 2025)
cabinet: Cabinet appointments shared by the president and the commander-in-chief
election/appointment process: prior to the military takeover in 2021, president was indirectly elected by simple majority vote by the full Assembly of the Union from among 3 vice-presidential candidates nominated by the Presidential Electoral College (consists of members of the lower and upper houses and military members); the other 2 candidates became vice presidents (president elected for a 5-year term)
most recent election date: 8 November 2020
election results: *2020:* the National League for Democracy (NLD) won 396 seats across both houses – well above the 322 required for a parliamentary majority – but on 1 February 2021, the military claimed the results of the election were illegitimate and deposed State Counsellor AUNG SAN SUU KYI and President WIN MYINT of the NLD, causing military-affiliated Vice President MYINT SWE (USDP) to become acting president; MYINT SWE subsequently handed power to coup leader MIN AUNG HLAING; WIN MYINT and other key leaders of the ruling NLD party were placed under arrest after the military takeover
2018: WIN MYINT elected president in an indirect by-election held on 28 March 2018 after the resignation of HTIN KYAW; Assembly of the Union vote for president - WIN MYINT (NLD) 403, MYINT SWE (USDP) 211, HENRY VAN THIO (NLD) 18, 4 votes canceled (636 votes cast)
expected date of next election: on 31 July 2025, the military government announced that it was preparing for elections to be held in December 2025
state counsellor: State Counselor AUNG SAN SUU KYI (since 6 April 2016); note - under arrest since 1 February 2021
note 1: on 31 July 2025, the military ended the state of emergency that had been in place since taking over the government in February 2021, although martial law continues to exist in parts of the country; at the same time, the military dissolved the State Administrative Council (SAC), which had been the official name of the military government in Burma, and replaced it with the National Security and Peace Commission (NSPC), chaired by Sr. Gen. MIN AUNG HLAING, who also retains his position as chief of the armed forces
note 2: prior to the military takeover, the state counsellor served the equivalent term of the president and was similar to a prime minister

Legislative branch: *legislature name:* Assembly of the Union (Pyidaungsu Hluttaw)
legislative structure: bicameral
most recent election date: 8 November 2020
expected date of next election: on 31 July 2025, the military government announced that it was preparing for elections to be held in late December 2025
note: on 1 February 2021, the Burmese military claimed the results of the 2020 general election were illegitimate and launched a coup led by Sr. General MIN AUNG HLAING; the military subsequently dissolved the Assembly of the Union and replaced it with the military-led State Administration Council

Judicial branch: *highest court(s):* Supreme Court of the Union (consists of the chief justice and 7-11 judges)
judge selection and term of office: chief justice and judges nominated by the president, with approval of the Lower House, and appointed by the president; judges normally serve until mandatory retirement at age 70
subordinate courts: High Courts of the Region; High Courts of the State; Court of the Self-Administered Division; Court of the Self-Administered Zone; district and township courts; special courts (for juvenile, municipal, and traffic offenses); courts martial

Political parties: Arakan National Party or ANP
Democratic Party or DP
Kayah State Democratic Party or KySDP
Kayin People's Party or KPP
Kokang Democracy and Unity Party or KDUP
La Hu National Development Party or LHNDP
Lisu National Development Party or LNDP
Mon Unity Party (formed in 2019 from the All Mon Region Democracy Party and Mon National Party)
National Democratic Force or NDF
National League for Democracy or NLD
National Unity Party or NUP
Pa-O National Organization or PNO
People's Party
Shan Nationalities Democratic Party or SNDP
Shan Nationalities League for Democracy or SNLD
Ta'ang National Party or TNP
Tai-Leng Nationalities Development Party or TNDP
Union Solidarity and Development Party or USDP
Unity and Democracy Party of Kachin State or UDPKS
Wa Democratic Party or WDP
Wa National Unity Party or WNUP
Zomi Congress for Democracy or ZCD
note: more than 90 political parties participated in the 2020 elections; political parties continued to function after the 2021 coup, although some political leaders have been arrested by the military regime; in 2023, the regime announced a new law with several rules and restrictions on political parties and their ability to participate in elections; dozens of parties refused to comply with the new rules; the regime's election commission has subsequently banned more than 80 political parties, including the National League for Democracy

Diplomatic representation in the US: *chief of mission:* Ambassador (vacant); Chargé d'Affaires Soe Thet NAUNG (since 24 June 2025)
chancery: 2300 S Street NW, Washington, DC 20008
telephone: [1] (202) 332-3344
FAX: [1] (202) 332-4351
email address and website: washington-embassy@mofa.gov.mm
https://www.mewashingtondc.org/
consulate(s) general: Los Angeles

Diplomatic representation from the US: *chief of mission:* Ambassador (vacant); Chargé d'Affaires Susan STEVENSON (since 10 July 2023)
embassy: 110 University Avenue, Kamayut Township, Rangoon
mailing address: 4250 Rangoon Place, Washington DC 20521-4250
telephone: [95] (1) 753-6509
FAX: [95] (1) 751-1069
email address and website: ACSRangoon@state.gov
https://mm.usembassy.gov/

International organization participation: ADB, ARF, ASEAN, BIMSTEC, CP, EAS, EITI (candidate country), FAO, G-77, IAEA, IBRD, ICAO, ICRM, IDA, IFAD, IFC, IFRCS, IHO, ILO, IMF, IMO, Interpol, IOC, IOM, IPU, ISO (correspondent), ITU, ITUC (NGOs), NAM, OPCW (signatory), SAARC (observer), UN, UNCTAD, UNESCO, UNIDO, UNWTO, UPU, WCO, WHO, WIPO, WMO, WTO

Independence: 4 January 1948 (from the UK)

National holiday: Independence Day, 4 January (1948); Union Day, 12 February (1947)

Flag: *description:* three equal horizontal stripes of yellow (top), green, and red; centered on the green band is a five-pointed white star that overlaps onto the yellow and red stripes
history: the design revives the triband colors that Burma used from 1943 to 1945, during the Japanese occupation

National symbol(s): chinthe (mythical lion)

National color(s): yellow, green, red, white

National anthem(s): *title:* "Kaba Ma Kyei" (Till the End of the World)
lyrics/music: SAYA TIN
history: adopted 1948

National heritage: *total World Heritage Sites:* 2 (both cultural)
selected World Heritage Site locales: Pyu Ancient Cities; Bagan

ECONOMY

Economic overview: prior to COVID-19 and the February 2021 military coup, massive declines in poverty, rapid economic growth, and improving social welfare; underdevelopment, climate change, and unequal investment threaten progress and sustainability planning; since coup, foreign assistance has ceased from most funding sources

Real GDP (purchasing power parity): $287.559 billion (2024 est.)
$290.381 billion (2023 est.)
$287.624 billion (2022 est.)
note: data in 2021 dollars
comparison ranking: 63

Real GDP growth rate: -1% (2024 est.)
1% (2023 est.)
4% (2022 est.)

note: annual GDP % growth based on constant local currency
comparison ranking: 200

Real GDP per capita: $5,300 (2024 est.)
$5,400 (2023 est.)
$5,400 (2022 est.)
note: data in 2021 dollars
comparison ranking: 172

GDP (official exchange rate): $74.08 billion (2024 est.)
note: data in current dollars at official exchange rate

Inflation rate (consumer prices): 8.8% (2019 est.)
6.9% (2018 est.)
4.6% (2017 est.)
note: annual % change based on consumer prices
comparison ranking: 172

GDP - composition, by sector of origin: *agriculture:* 20.8% (2024 est.)
industry: 37.8% (2024 est.)
services: 41.4% (2024 est.)
note: figures may not total 100% due to non-allocated consumption not captured in sector-reported data
comparison rankings: agriculture 32; industry 24; services 191

Agricultural products: rice, sugarcane, vegetables, beans, maize, groundnuts, plantains, fruits, coconuts, onions (2023)
note: top ten agricultural products based on tonnage

Industries: agricultural processing; wood and wood products; copper, tin, tungsten, iron; cement, construction materials; pharmaceuticals; fertilizer; oil and natural gas; garments; jade and gems

Industrial production growth rate: -0.2% (2024 est.)
note: annual % change in industrial value added based on constant local currency
comparison ranking: 138

Labor force: 22.742 million (2024 est.)
note: number of people ages 15 or older who are employed or seeking work
comparison ranking: 32

Unemployment rate: 3.1% (2024 est.)
3.1% (2023 est.)
3.1% (2022 est.)
note: % of labor force seeking employment
comparison ranking: 42

Youth unemployment rate (ages 15-24): *total:* 10% (2024 est.)
male: 10.5% (2024 est.)
female: 9.4% (2024 est.)
note: % of labor force ages 15-24 seeking employment
comparison ranking: total 119

Population below poverty line: 24.8% (2017 est.)
note: % of population with income below national poverty line

Gini Index coefficient - distribution of family income: 30.7 (2017 est.)
note: index (0-100) of income distribution; higher values represent greater inequality
comparison ranking: 116

Average household expenditures: *on food:* 53.9% of household expenditures (2023 est.)
on alcohol and tobacco: 0.5% of household expenditures (2023 est.)

Household income or consumption by percentage share: *lowest 10%:* 3.8% (2017 est.)
highest 10%: 25.5% (2017 est.)
note: % share of income accruing to lowest and highest 10% of population

Remittances: 1.6% of GDP (2023 est.)
2% of GDP (2022 est.)
1.9% of GDP (2021 est.)
note: personal transfers and compensation between resident and non-resident individuals/households/entities

Budget: *revenues:* $10.945 billion (2019 est.)
expenditures: $10.22 billion (2019 est.)
note: central government revenues (excluding grants) and expenses converted to US dollars at average official exchange rate for year indicated

Taxes and other revenues: 6% (of GDP) (2019 est.)
note: central government tax revenue as a % of GDP
comparison ranking: 147

Current account balance: $67.72 million (2019 est.)
-$2.561 billion (2018 est.)
-$4.917 billion (2017 est.)
note: balance of payments - net trade and primary/secondary income in current dollars
comparison ranking: 79

Exports: $20.4 billion (2021 est.)
$17.523 billion (2019 est.)
$15.728 billion (2018 est.)
note: balance of payments - exports of goods and services in current dollars
comparison ranking: 91

Exports - partners: China 32%, Thailand 16%, Japan 7%, Germany 6%, India 5% (2023)
note: top five export partners based on percentage share of exports

Exports - commodities: garments, natural gas, dried legumes, rare-earth metal compounds, precious stones (2023)
note: top five export commodities based on value in dollars

Imports: $23.1 billion (2021 est.)
$17.356 billion (2019 est.)
$18.664 billion (2018 est.)
note: balance of payments - imports of goods and services in current dollars
comparison ranking: 90

Imports - partners: China 40%, Thailand 18%, Singapore 15%, Indonesia 4%, Malaysia 4% (2023)
note: top five import partners based on percentage share of imports

Imports - commodities: refined petroleum, synthetic fabric, fertilizers, crude petroleum, fabric (2023)
note: top five import commodities based on value in dollars

Reserves of foreign exchange and gold: $9.338 billion (2023 est.)
$8.182 billion (2022 est.)
$9.103 billion (2021 est.)
note: holdings of gold (year-end prices)/foreign exchange/special drawing rights in current dollars
comparison ranking: 82

Debt - external: $8.748 billion (2023 est.)
note: present value of external debt in current US dollars
comparison ranking: 53

Exchange rates: kyats (MMK) per US dollar -
Exchange rates: 2,100 (2023 est.)
1,932.543 (2022 est.)
1,615.367 (2021 est.)
1,381.619 (2020 est.)
1,518.255 (2019 est.)

ENERGY

Electricity access: *electrification - total population:* 73.7% (2022 est.)
electrification - urban areas: 93.9%
electrification - rural areas: 62.8%

Electricity: *installed generating capacity:* 7.419 million kW (2023 est.)
consumption: 23.625 billion kWh (2023 est.)
exports: 200 million kWh (2023 est.)
transmission/distribution losses: 1.855 billion kWh (2023 est.)
comparison rankings: installed generating capacity 75; consumption 72; exports 85; transmission/distribution losses 120

Electricity generation sources: *fossil fuels:* 61.8% of total installed capacity (2023 est.)
solar: 0.4% of total installed capacity (2023 est.)
hydroelectricity: 36.7% of total installed capacity (2023 est.)
biomass and waste: 1% of total installed capacity (2023 est.)

Coal: *production:* 1.031 million metric tons (2023 est.)
consumption: 907,000 metric tons (2023 est.)
exports: 221,000 metric tons (2023 est.)
imports: 67,000 metric tons (2023 est.)
proven reserves: 252 million metric tons (2023 est.)

Petroleum: *total petroleum production:* 7,000 bbl/day (2023 est.)
refined petroleum consumption: 122,000 bbl/day (2023 est.)
crude oil estimated reserves: 139 million barrels (2021 est.)

Natural gas: *production:* 13.549 billion cubic meters (2023 est.)
consumption: 4.241 billion cubic meters (2023 est.)
exports: 9.29 billion cubic meters (2023 est.)
imports: 219.822 million cubic meters (2021 est.)
proven reserves: 637.129 billion cubic meters (2021 est.)

Energy consumption per capita: 8.384 million Btu/person (2023 est.)
comparison ranking: 156

COMMUNICATIONS

Telephones - fixed lines: *total subscriptions:* 588,000 (2023 est.)
subscriptions per 100 inhabitants: 1 (2023 est.) less than 1
comparison ranking: total subscriptions 86

Telephones - mobile cellular: *total subscriptions:* 65.5 million (2023 est.)
subscriptions per 100 inhabitants: 107 (2022 est.)
comparison ranking: total subscriptions 28

Broadcast media: government controls all domestic broadcast media; 2 state-controlled TV stations, with 1 controlled by the armed forces; 2 pay-TV stations are joint state-private ventures; 1 state-controlled radio station; 9 FM stations are joint state-private ventures; several international broadcasts are available in some areas; the Voice of America (VOA), Radio Free Asia (RFA), BBC Burmese service, the Democratic Voice of Burma (DVB), and Radio Australia use shortwave to broadcast; VOA, RFA, and DVB produce daily TV news programs that are transmitted by satellite; in 2017, the government granted licenses to 5 private broadcasters for digital free-to-air TV channels to be operated in partnership with government-owned Myanmar Radio and Television (MRTV); after the 2021 military coup, the regime revoked the media licenses of most independent outlets, including the free-to-air licenses for DVB and Mizzima (2022)

Internet country code: .mm

Internet users: *percent of population:* 59% (2023 est.)

Broadband - fixed subscriptions: *total:* 1.51 million (2023 est.)
subscriptions per 100 inhabitants: 3 (2023 est.)
comparison ranking: total 70

TRANSPORTATION

Civil aircraft registration country code prefix: XY

Airports: 74 (2025)
comparison ranking: 70

Heliports: 6 (2025)
comparison ranking: 93

Railways: *total:* 5,031 km (2008)
narrow gauge: 5,031 km (2008) 1.000-m gauge

Merchant marine: *total:* 101 (2023)
by type: bulk carrier 1, general cargo 44, oil tanker 5, other 51
comparison ranking: total 89

Ports: *total ports:* 7 (2024)
large: 0
medium: 0
small: 5
very small: 2
ports with oil terminals: 3
key ports: Bassein, Mergui, Moulmein Harbor, Rangoon, Sittwe

MILITARY AND SECURITY

Military and security forces: Burmese Defense Service (aka Armed Forces of Burma, Myanmar Army, Royal Armed Forces, the Tatmadaw, or the Sit-Tat): Army (Tatmadaw Kyi), Navy (Tatmadaw Yay), Air Force (Tatmadaw Lay); People's Militia

Ministry of Home Affairs: Burma (People's) Police Force, Border Guard Forces/Police (2025)
note 1: under the 2008 constitution, the Tatmadaw was given control over the appointments of senior officials to lead the Ministry of Defense, the Ministry of Border Affairs, and the Ministry of Home Affairs; in 2022, a new law gave the commander-in-chief of the Tatmadaw the authority to appoint or remove the head of the police force
note 2: the military is supported by pro-government militias; some are integrated within the Tatmadaw's command structure as Border Guard Forces, which are organized as battalions with a mix of militia forces, ethnic armed groups, and government soldiers that are armed, supplied, and paid by the Tatmadaw; other pro-military government militias are not integrated within the Tatmadaw command structure but receive direction and some support from the military and are recognized as government militias; a third type of pro-government militias are small community-based units that are armed, coordinated, and trained by local Tatmadaw forces and activated as needed

Military expenditures: 3.9% of GDP (2023 est.)
3.6% of GDP (2022 est.)
3.5% of GDP (2021 est.)
3% of GDP (2020 est.)
4.1% of GDP (2019 est.)

Military and security service personnel strengths: information varies; estimated 150,000 active military personnel (2025)
note: the Tatmadaw has reportedly suffered heavy personnel losses in the ongoing fighting against anti-regime forces

Military equipment inventories and acquisitions: the Burmese military's inventory is comprised mostly of older Chinese and Russian/Soviet-era weapons and equipment with a smaller mix of more modern acquisitions, mostly from China and Russia; Burma's defense industry is involved in shipbuilding and the production of ground force equipment based largely on Chinese and Russian designs (2024)

Military service age and obligation: 18-35 years of age (men) and 18-27 years of age (women) for voluntary and conscripted military service; 24-month service obligation; conscripted professional men (ages 18-45) and women (ages 18-35), including doctors, engineers, and mechanics, serve up to 36 months; service terms may be extended to 60 months in an officially declared emergency (2024)
note: in February 2024, the military government announced that the People's Military Service Law requiring mandatory military service would go into effect; the Service Law was first introduced in 2010 but had not previously been enforced; the military government also said that it intended to call up about 60,000 men and women annually for mandatory service; during the ongoing insurgency, the military has recruited men 18-60 to serve in local militias

Military - note: since the country's founding, the Tatmadaw has been deeply involved in domestic politics and the national economy; it ran the country for five decades following a military coup in 1962; prior to the most recent coup in 2021, the military already controlled three key security ministries (Defense, Border, and Home Affairs), one of two vice presidential appointments, 25% of the parliamentary seats, and had a proxy political party, the Union Solidarity and Development Party (USDP); it owns and operates two business conglomerates that have over 100 subsidiaries; the business activities of these conglomerates include banking and insurance, hotels, tourism, jade and ruby mining, timber, construction, real estate, and the production of palm oil, sugar, soap, cement, beverages, drinking water, coal, and gas; some of the companies supply goods and services to the military, such as food, clothing, insurance, and cellphone service; the military also manages a film industry, publishing houses, and television stations
the Tatmadaw's primary operational focus is internal security, and it is conducting counterinsurgency operations against anti-regime forces that launched an armed rebellion following the 2021 coup and an array of ethnic armed groups (EAGs), some of which have considerable conventional military capabilities; as of 2024, the Tatmadaw was reportedly engaged in combat operations in 10 of its 14 regional commands
EAGs have been fighting for self-rule against the Burmese Government since 1948; they range in strength from a few hundred fighters up to an estimated 30,000; some are organized along military lines with "brigades" and "divisions" and armed with heavy weaponry, including artillery; they control large tracts of the country's territory, primarily in the border regions; key groups include the United Wa State Army, Karen National Union, Kachin Independence Army, Arakan Army, Ta'ang National Liberation Army, and the Myanmar Nationalities Democratic Alliance Army
the opposition National Unity Government claims its armed wing, the People's Defense Force (PDF), has more than 60,000 fighters loosely organized into battalions; in addition, several EAGs have cooperated with the NUG and supported local PDF groups (2024)

TRANSNATIONAL ISSUES

Refugees and internally displaced persons: IDPs: 3,646,658 (2024 est.)
stateless persons: 619,429 (2024 est.)

Trafficking in persons: *tier rating:* Tier 3 — Burma does not fully meet the minimum standards for the elimination of trafficking and is not making significant efforts to do so, therefore, Burma remained on Tier 3; for more details, go to: https://www.state.gov/reports/2025-trafficking-in-persons-report/burma/

Illicit drugs: USG identification: major illicit drug-producing and/or drug-transit country
major precursor-chemical producer (2025)

BURUNDI

INTRODUCTION

Background: Established in the 1600s, the Burundi Kingdom has had borders similar to those of modern Burundi since the 1800s. Burundi's two major ethnic groups, the majority Hutu and minority Tutsi, share a common language and culture and largely lived in peaceful cohabitation under Tutsi monarchs in pre-colonial Burundi. Regional, class, and clan distinctions contributed to social status in the Burundi Kingdom, yielding a complex class structure. German colonial rule in the late 19th and early 20th centuries and Belgian rule after World War I preserved Burundi's monarchy. Seeking to simplify administration, Belgian colonial officials reduced the number of chiefdoms and eliminated most Hutu chiefs from positions of power. In 1961, the Burundian Tutsi king's oldest son, Louis RWAGASORE, was murdered by a competing political faction shortly before he was set to become prime minister, triggering increased political competition that contributed to later instability.

Burundi gained its independence from Belgium in 1962 as the Kingdom of Burundi. Revolution in neighboring Rwanda stoked ethnic polarization as the Tutsi increasingly feared violence and loss of political power. A failed Hutu-led coup in 1965 triggered a purge of Hutu officials and set the stage for Tutsi officers to overthrow the monarchy in 1966 and establish a Tutsi-dominated republic. A

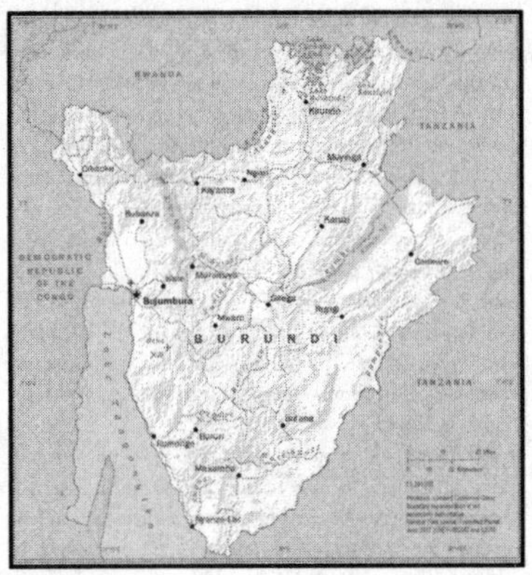

Hutu rebellion in 1972 resulted in the deaths of several thousand Tutsi civilians and sparked brutal Tutsi-led military reprisals against Hutu civilians which ultimately killed 100,000-200,000 people. International pressure led to a new constitution in 1992 and democratic elections in 1993. Tutsi military officers feared Hutu domination and assassinated Burundi's first democratically elected president, Hutu Melchior NDADAYE, in 1993 after only 100 days in office, sparking a civil war. In 1994, his successor, Cyprien NTARYAMIRA, died when the Rwandan president's plane he was traveling on was shot down, which triggered the Rwandan genocide and further entrenched ethnic conflict in Burundi. The internationally brokered Arusha Agreement, signed in 2000, and subsequent cease-fire agreements with armed movements ended the 1993-2005 civil war. Burundi's second democratic elections were held in 2005, resulting in the election of Pierre NKURUNZIZA as president. He was reelected in 2010 and again in 2015 after a controversial court decision allowed him to circumvent a term limit. President Evariste NDAYISHIMIYE – from NKURUNZIZA's ruling party – was elected in 2020.

GEOGRAPHY

Location: Central Africa, east of the Democratic Republic of the Congo, west of Tanzania

Geographic coordinates: 3 30 S, 30 00 E

Map references: Africa

Area: *total:* 27,830 sq km
land: 25,680 sq km
water: 2,150 sq km
comparison ranking: total 146

Area - comparative: slightly smaller than Maryland

Land boundaries: *total:* 1,140 km
border countries (3): Democratic Republic of the Congo 236 km; Rwanda 315 km; Tanzania 589 km

Coastline: 0 km (landlocked)

Maritime claims: none (landlocked)

Climate: equatorial; high plateau with considerable altitude variation (772 m to 2,670 m above sea level); average annual temperature varies with altitude from 23 to 17 degrees Celsius but is generally moderate; average annual rainfall is about 150 cm with two wet seasons (February to May and September to November) and two dry seasons (June to August and December to January)

Terrain: hilly and mountainous, dropping to a plateau in east, some plains

Elevation: *highest point:* unnamed elevation on Mukike Range 2,685 m
lowest point: Lake Tanganyika 772 m
mean elevation: 1,504 m

Natural resources: nickel, uranium, rare earth oxides, peat, cobalt, copper, platinum, vanadium, arable land, hydropower, niobium, tantalum, gold, tin, tungsten, kaolin, limestone

Land use: *agricultural land:* 82.8% (2022 est.)
arable land: 50.4% (2022 est.)
permanent crops: 13.6% (2022 est.)
permanent pasture: 18.8% (2022 est.)
forest: 10.9% (2022 est.)
other: 6.3% (2022 est.)

Irrigated land: 230 sq km (2012)

Major lakes (area sq km): *fresh water lake(s):* Lake Tanganyika (shared with Democratic Republic of Congo, Tanzania, and Zambia) - 32,000 sq km

Major watersheds (area sq km): Atlantic Ocean drainage: Congo (3,730,881 sq km), *(Mediterranean Sea)* Nile (3,254,853 sq km)

Population distribution: one of Africa's most densely populated countries; concentrations tend to be in the north and along the northern shore of Lake Tanganyika in the west; most people live on farms near areas of fertile volcanic soil, as shown in this population distribution map

Natural hazards: flooding; landslides; drought

Geography - note: landlocked; straddles crest of the Nile-Congo watershed; the Kagera, which drains into Lake Victoria, is the most remote headstream of the White Nile

PEOPLE AND SOCIETY

Population: *total:* 13,590,102 (2024 est.)
male: 6,755,456
female: 6,834,646
comparison rankings: total 77; male 77; female 77

Nationality: *noun:* Burundian(s)
adjective: Burundian

Ethnic groups: Hutu, Tutsi, Twa, South Asian

Languages: Kirundi (official), French (official), English (official, least spoken), Swahili (2008 est.)
major-language sample(s):
Igitabo Mpuzamakungu c'ibimenyetso bifatika, isoko ntabanduka ku nkuru z'urufatiro. (Kirundi)
note: data represent languages read and written by people 10 years of age or older; spoken Kirundi is nearly universal

Religions: Christian 93.9% (Roman Catholic 58.6%, Protestant 35.3% [includes Adventist 2.7% and other Protestant religions 32.6%]), Muslim 3.4%, other 1.3%, none 1.3% (2016-17 est.)

Age structure: *0-14 years:* 42.3% (male 2,895,275/female 2,848,286)
15-64 years: 54.4% (male 3,662,688/female 3,727,022)
65 years and over: 3.4% (2024 est.) (male 197,493/female 259,338)

Dependency ratios: *total dependency ratio:* 83.9 (2024 est.)
youth dependency ratio: 77.7 (2024 est.)
elderly dependency ratio: 6.2 (2024 est.)
potential support ratio: 16.2 (2024 est.)

Median age: *total:* 18.4 years (2024 est.)
male: 18 years
female: 18.7 years
comparison ranking: total 220

Population growth rate: 2.81% (2024 est.)
comparison ranking: 11

Birth rate: 34.6 births/1,000 population (2024 est.)
comparison ranking: 14

Death rate: 5.7 deaths/1,000 population (2024 est.)
comparison ranking: 174

Net migration rate: -0.7 migrant(s)/1,000 population (2024 est.)
comparison ranking: 137

Population distribution: one of Africa's most densely populated countries; concentrations tend to be in the north and along the northern shore of Lake Tanganyika in the west; most people live on farms near areas of fertile volcanic soil, as shown in this population distribution map

Urbanization: *urban population:* 14.8% of total population (2023)
rate of urbanization: 5.43% annual rate of change (2020-25 est.)

Major urban areas - population: 1.207 million BUJUMBURA (capital) (2023)

Sex ratio: *at birth:* 1.03 male(s)/female
0-14 years: 1.02 male(s)/female
15-64 years: 0.98 male(s)/female .
65 years and over: 0.76 male(s)/female
total population: 0.99 male(s)/female (2024 est.)

Mother's mean age at first birth: 21.5 years (2016/17 est.)
note: data represents median age at first birth among women 25-49

Maternal mortality ratio: 392 deaths/100,000 live births (2023 est.)
comparison ranking: 14

Infant mortality rate: *total:* 35.7 deaths/1,000 live births (2024 est.)
male: 39.7 deaths/1,000 live births
female: 31.5 deaths/1,000 live births
comparison ranking: total 36

Life expectancy at birth: *total population:* 68.1 years (2024 est.)
male: 66 years
female: 70.3 years
comparison ranking: total population 192

Total fertility rate: 4.9 children born/woman (2024 est.)
comparison ranking: 10

Gross reproduction rate: 2.41 (2024 est.)

Drinking water source: *improved: urban:* 90.7% of population (2022 est.)
rural: 57.7% of population (2022 est.)
total: 62.4% of population (2022 est.)
unimproved: urban: 9.3% of population (2022 est.)
rural: 42.3% of population (2022 est.)
total: 37.6% of population (2022 est.)

Health expenditure: 9.1% of GDP (2021)
4.7% of national budget (2022 est.)

Physician density: 0.08 physicians/1,000 population (2022)

Sanitation facility access: *improved: urban:* 87.4% of population (2022 est.)
rural: 53.7% of population (2022 est.)
total: 58.6% of population (2022 est.)
unimproved: urban: 12.6% of population (2022 est.)
rural: 46.3% of population (2022 est.)
total: 41.4% of population (2022 est.)

Obesity - adult prevalence rate: 5.4% (2016)
comparison ranking: 178

Alcohol consumption per capita: *total:* 4.07 liters of pure alcohol (2019 est.)
beer: 1.84 liters of pure alcohol (2019 est.)
wine: 0 liters of pure alcohol (2019 est.)
spirits: 0 liters of pure alcohol (2019 est.)
other alcohols: 2.23 liters of pure alcohol (2019 est.)
comparison ranking: total 95

Tobacco use: *total:* 9.1% (2025 est.)
male: 14% (2025 est.)
female: 4.3% (2025 est.)
comparison ranking: total 134

Children under the age of 5 years underweight: 27.6% (2022)
comparison ranking: 5

Currently married women (ages 15-49): 54.1% (2023 est.)

Child marriage: *women married by age 15:* 2.8% (2017)
women married by age 18: 19% (2017)
men married by age 18: 1.4% (2017)

Education expenditure: 4.4% of GDP (2022 est.)
20.6% national budget (2022 est.)
comparison ranking: Education expenditure (% GDP) 88

Literacy: *total population:* 68% (2017 est.)
male: 76% (2017 est.)
female: 61% (2017 est.)

School life expectancy (primary to tertiary education): *total:* 10 years (2018 est.)
male: 10 years (2018 est.)
female: 10 years (2018 est.)

ENVIRONMENT

Environmental issues: soil erosion from overgrazing and agricultural expansion; deforestation; wildlife habitat loss

International environmental agreements: *party to:* Biodiversity, Climate Change, Climate Change-Kyoto Protocol, Climate Change-Paris Agreement, Comprehensive Nuclear Test Ban, Desertification, Endangered Species, Hazardous Wastes, Ozone Layer Protection, Wetlands
signed, but not ratified: Law of the Sea, Nuclear Test Ban

Climate: equatorial; high plateau with considerable altitude variation (772 m to 2,670 m above sea level); average annual temperature varies with altitude from 23 to 17 degrees Celsius but is generally moderate; average annual rainfall is about 150 cm with two wet seasons (February to May and September to November) and two dry seasons (June to August and December to January)

Urbanization: *urban population:* 14.8% of total population (2023)
rate of urbanization: 5.43% annual rate of change (2020-25 est.)

Carbon dioxide emissions: 838,000 metric tonnes of CO_2 (2023 est.)
from coal and metallurgical coke: 32,000 metric tonnes of CO_2 (2023 est.)
from petroleum and other liquids: 806,000 metric tonnes of CO_2 (2023 est.)
comparison ranking: total emissions 174

Particulate matter emissions: 26.3 micrograms per cubic meter (2019 est.)

Waste and recycling: *municipal solid waste generated annually:* 1.872 million tons (2024 est.)
percent of municipal solid waste recycled: 7.1% (2022 est.)

Total water withdrawal: *municipal:* 43.1 million cubic meters (2022 est.)
industrial: 15 million cubic meters (2022 est.)
agricultural: 222 million cubic meters (2022 est.)

Total renewable water resources: 12.536 billion cubic meters (2022 est.)

GOVERNMENT

Country name: *conventional long form:* Republic of Burundi
conventional short form: Burundi
local long form: République du Burundi (French)/ Republika y'u Burundi (Kirundi)
local short form: Burundi
former: Urundi, German East Africa, Ruanda-Urundi, Kingdom of Burundi
etymology: name dates from 1966 and is derived from the name of the local Bantu people, the Rundi or Barundi; *ba-* is the prefix for the people, and *bu-* is the prefix for the country; the former name, Urundi, is the Swahili version

Government type: presidential republic

Capital: *name:* Gitega (political capital), Bujumbura (commercial capital)
geographic coordinates: 3 25 S, 29 55 E
time difference: UTC+2 (7 hours ahead of Washington, DC, during Standard Time)
etymology: the origin of the name Bujumbura is unclear, but "bu-" is a Bantu prefix meaning "place"
note: in January 2019, the Burundian parliament voted to make Gitega the political capital of the country while Bujumbura would remain its economic capital; as of 2023, the government's move to Gitega remains incomplete

Administrative divisions: 5 *provinces:* Buhumuza, Bujumbura, Burunga, Butanyerera, Gitega

Legal system: mixed legal system of Belgian civil law and customary law

Constitution: *history:* several previous, ratified by referendum 28 February 2005
amendment process: proposed by the president of the republic after consultation with the government or by absolute majority support of the membership in both houses of Parliament; passage requires at least two-thirds majority vote by the Senate membership and at least four-fifths majority vote by the National Assembly; the president can opt to submit amendment bills to a referendum; constitutional articles including those on national unity, the secularity of Burundi, its democratic form of government, and its sovereignty cannot be amended

International law organization participation: has not submitted an ICJ jurisdiction declaration; withdrew from ICCt in October 2017

Citizenship: *citizenship by birth:* no
citizenship by descent only: the father must be a citizen of Burundi
dual citizenship recognized: no
residency requirement for naturalization: 10 years

Suffrage: 18 years of age; universal

Executive branch: *chief of state:* President Evariste NDAYISHIMIYE (since 18 June 2020)
head of government: Prime Minister Nestor NTAHONTUYE (since 5 August 2025)
cabinet: Council of Ministers appointed by president
election/appointment process: president directly elected by absolute-majority popular vote in 2 rounds, if needed, for a 7-year term (eligible for a second term); vice presidents nominated by the president, endorsed by Parliament
most recent election date: 20 May 2020
election results: *2020:* Evariste NDAYISHIMIYE elected president; percent of vote - Evariste NDAYISHIMIYE (CNDD-FDD) 71.5%, Agathon RWASA (CNL) 25.2%, Gaston SINDIMWO (UPRONA) 1.7%, other 1.6%
2015: Pierre NKURUNZIZA reelected president; percent of vote - Pierre NKURUNZIZA (CNDD-FDD) 69.4%, Agathon RWASA (Hope of Burundians - Amizerio y'ABARUNDI) 19%, other 11.6%
expected date of next election: May 2027

Legislative branch: *legislature name:* Parliament (Parlement)
legislative structure: bicameral

Legislative branch - lower chamber: *chamber name:* National Assembly (Inama Nshingamateka)
number of seats: 111 (all directly elected)
electoral system: proportional representation
scope of elections: full renewal
term in office: 5 years
most recent election date: 6/5/2025
parties elected and seats per party: National Council for the Defense of Democracy - Front for the Defense of Democracy (CNDD-FDD) (108); Other (3)
percentage of women in chamber: 39.6%
expected date of next election: June 2030
note: 60% of seats in the National Assembly are allocated to Hutus and 40% to Tutsis; 3 seats are reserved for Twas; 30% of total seats are reserved for women

Legislative branch - upper chamber: *chamber name:* Senate (Inama Nkenguzamateka)
number of seats: 13 (all indirectly elected)
scope of elections: full renewal
term in office: 5 years
most recent election date: 7/23/2025
parties elected and seats per party: National Council for the Defense of Democracy - Front for the Defense of Democracy (CNDD-FDD) (10)
percentage of women in chamber: 46.2%
expected date of next election: July 2030
note: 3 seats in the Senate are reserved for Twas, and 30% of all votes are reserved for women

Judicial branch: *highest court(s):* Supreme Court (consists of 9 judges and organized into judicial, administrative, and cassation chambers); Constitutional Court (consists of 7 members)
judge selection and term of office: Supreme Court judges nominated by the Judicial Service Commission, a 15-member body of judicial and legal profession officials), appointed by the president and confirmed by the Senate; judge tenure NA; Constitutional Court judges appointed by the president and confirmed by the Senate and serve 6-year nonrenewable terms
subordinate courts: Courts of Appeal; County Courts; Courts of Residence; Martial Court; Commercial Court

Political parties: Council for Democracy and the Sustainable Development of Burundi or CODEBU
Front for Democracy in Burundi-Sahwanya or FRODEBU-Sahwanya
National Council for the Defense of Democracy - Front for the Defense of Democracy or CNDD-FDD
National Congress for Liberty or CNL
National Liberation Forces or FNL
Union for National Progress (Union pour le Progress Nationale) or UPRONA

Diplomatic representation in the US: *chief of mission:* Ambassador Jean Bosco BAREGE (since 27 February 2024)
chancery: 2233 Wisconsin Avenue NW, Washington, DC 20007
telephone: [1] (202) 342-2574
FAX: [1] (202) 342-2578
email address and website: burundiembusadc@gmail.com
Burundi Embassy Washington D.C. (burundiembassy-usa.com)

Diplomatic representation from the US: *chief of mission:* Ambassador Lisa PETERSON (since 27 June 2024)
embassy: No 50 Avenue Des Etats-Unis, 110-01-02, Bujumbura
mailing address: 2100 Bujumbura Place, Washington DC 20521-2100
telephone: [257] 22-207-000
FAX: [257] 22-222-926
email address and website: BujumburaC@state.gov
https://bi.usembassy.gov/

International organization participation: ACP, AfDB, ATMIS, AU, CEMAC, CEPGL, CICA, COMESA, EAC, FAO, G-77, IBRD, ICAO, ICGLR, ICRM, IDA, IFAD, IFC, IFRCS, ILO, IMF, Interpol, IOC, IOM, IPU, ISO (correspondent), ITU, ITUC (NGOs), MIGA, NAM, OIF, OPCW, UN, UNCTAD, UNESCO, UNHRC, UNIDO, UNISFA, UNMISS, UNWTO, UPU, WCO, WHO, WIPO, WMO, WTO

Independence: 1 July 1962 (from UN trusteeship under Belgian administration)

National holiday: Independence Day, 1 July (1962)

Flag: *description:* divided by a white diagonal cross into red triangles (top and bottom) and green triangles (on each side) with a white disk at the center bearing three six-pointed red stars outlined in green and arranged in a triangular design
meaning: green stands for hope and optimism, white for purity and peace, and red for the blood shed in the struggle for independence; the three stars represent the major ethnic groups (Hutu, Twa, Tutsi), as well as unity, work, and progress

National symbol(s): lion

National color(s): red, white, green

National anthem(s): *title:* "Burundi Bwacu" (Our Beloved Burundi)
lyrics/music: Jean-Baptiste NTAHOKAJA/Marc BARENGAYABO
history: adopted 1962

ECONOMY

Economic overview: highly agrarian, low-income Sub-Saharan economy; declining foreign assistance; increasing fiscal insolvencies; dense and still growing population; COVID-19 weakened economic recovery and flipped two years of deflation

Real GDP (purchasing power parity): $11.739 billion (2024 est.)
$11.343 billion (2023 est.)
$11.048 billion (2022 est.)
note: data in 2021 dollars
comparison ranking: 164

Real GDP growth rate: 3.5% (2024 est.)
2.7% (2023 est.)
1.8% (2022 est.)
note: annual GDP % growth based on constant local currency
comparison ranking: 99

Real GDP per capita: $800 (2024 est.)
$800 (2023 est.)
$800 (2022 est.)
note: data in 2021 dollars
comparison ranking: 215

GDP (official exchange rate): $2.162 billion (2024 est.)
note: data in current dollars at official exchange rate

Inflation rate (consumer prices): 20.2% (2024 est.)
26.9% (2023 est.)
18.8% (2022 est.)
note: annual % change based on consumer prices
comparison ranking: 190

GDP - composition, by sector of origin: *agriculture:* 25.3% (2023 est.)
industry: 9.6% (2023 est.)
services: 49% (2023 est.)
note: figures may not total 100% due to non-allocated consumption not captured in sector-reported data
comparison rankings: agriculture 18; industry 189; services 151

GDP - composition, by end use: *household consumption:* 75.9% (2023 est.)
government consumption: 30.7% (2023 est.)
investment in fixed capital: 13.1% (2023 est.)
investment in inventories: 0% (2023 est.)
exports of goods and services: 5.3% (2023 est.)
imports of goods and services: -24.4% (2023 est.)
note: figures may not total 100% due to rounding or gaps in data collection

Agricultural products: cassava, bananas, sweet potatoes, beans, maize, vegetables, potatoes, rice, sugarcane, fruits (2023)
note: top ten agricultural products based on tonnage

Industries: light consumer goods (sugar, shoes, soap, beer); cement, assembly of imported components; public works construction; food processing (fruits)

Industrial production growth rate: -0.2% (2024 est.)
note: annual % change in industrial value added based on constant local currency
comparison ranking: 139

Labor force: 6.107 million (2024 est.)
note: number of people ages 15 or older who are employed or seeking work
comparison ranking: 75

Unemployment rate: 1% (2024 est.)
1% (2023 est.)
1% (2022 est.)
note: % of labor force seeking employment
comparison ranking: 5

Youth unemployment rate (ages 15-24): *total:* 1.6% (2024 est.)
male: 2.1% (2024 est.)
female: 1.2% (2024 est.)
note: % of labor force ages 15-24 seeking employment
comparison ranking: total 185

Population below poverty line: 51% (2020 est.)
note: % of population with income below national poverty line

Gini Index coefficient - distribution of family income: 37.5 (2020 est.)
note: index (0-100) of income distribution; higher values represent greater inequality
comparison ranking: 57

Household income or consumption by percentage share: *lowest 10%:* 2.9% (2020 est.)
highest 10%: 29.9% (2020 est.)
note: % share of income accruing to lowest and highest 10% of population

Remittances: 7.5% of GDP (2023 est.)
4.9% of GDP (2022 est.)
6.1% of GDP (2021 est.)
note: personal transfers and compensation between resident and non-resident individuals/households/entities

Budget: *revenues:* $713.694 million (2021 est.)
expenditures: $737.898 million (2021 est.)
note: central government revenues and expenses (excluding grants/extrabudgetary units/social security funds) converted to US dollars at average official exchange rate for year indicated

Taxes and other revenues: 15.6% (of GDP) (2021 est.)
note: central government tax revenue as a % of GDP
comparison ranking: 87

Current account balance: -$625.597 million (2023 est.)
-$621.969 million (2022 est.)
-$393.88 million (2021 est.)
note: balance of payments - net trade and primary/secondary income in current dollars
comparison ranking: 112

Exports: $378.229 million (2023 est.)
$333.637 million (2022 est.)
$302.752 million (2021 est.)
note: balance of payments - exports of goods and services in current dollars
comparison ranking: 196

Exports - partners: UAE 59%, Uganda 8%, China 5%, Germany 5%, USA 3% (2023)
note: top five export partners based on percentage share of exports

Exports - commodities: gold, coffee, tea, tin ores, iron bars (2023)
note: top five export commodities based on value in dollars

Imports: $1.433 billion (2023 est.)
$1.42 billion (2022 est.)
$1.166 billion (2021 est.)
note: balance of payments - imports of goods and services in current dollars
comparison ranking: 187

Imports - partners: Tanzania 26%, China 15%, Uganda 10%, Kenya 10%, India 6% (2023)
note: top five import partners based on percentage share of imports

Imports - commodities: fertilizers, cement, packaged medicine, plastic products, cars (2023)
note: top five import commodities based on value in dollars

Reserves of foreign exchange and gold: $90.35 million (2023 est.)
$158.53 million (2022 est.)
$266.164 million (2021 est.)
note: holdings of gold (year-end prices)/foreign exchange/special drawing rights in current dollars
comparison ranking: 176

Debt - external: $805.174 million (2023 est.)
note: present value of external debt in current US dollars
comparison ranking: 109

Exchange rates: Burundi francs (BIF) per US dollar -

Exchange rates: 2,574.052 (2023 est.)
2,034.307 (2022 est.)
1,975.951 (2021 est.)
1,915.046 (2020 est.)
1,845.623 (2019 est.)

ENERGY

Electricity access: *electrification - total population:* 10.3% (2022 est.)
electrification - urban areas: 64%
electrification - rural areas: 1.7%

Electricity: *installed generating capacity:* 131,000 kW (2023 est.)
consumption: 444.018 million kWh (2023 est.)
imports: 100 million kWh (2023 est.)
transmission/distribution losses: 39.994 million kWh (2023 est.)
comparison rankings: installed generating capacity 185; consumption 177; imports 112; transmission/distribution losses 33

Electricity generation sources: *fossil fuels:* 31.2% of total installed capacity (2023 est.)
solar: 0.5% of total installed capacity (2023 est.)
hydroelectricity: 66.7% of total installed capacity (2023 est.)
biomass and waste: 1.6% of total installed capacity (2023 est.)

Coal: *consumption:* 1,000 metric tons (2023 est.)
imports: 10,000 metric tons (2023 est.)

Petroleum: *refined petroleum consumption:* 6,000 bbl/day (2023 est.)

Energy consumption per capita: 946,000 Btu/person (2023 est.)
comparison ranking: 194

COMMUNICATIONS

Telephones - fixed lines: *total subscriptions:* 14,000 (2023 est.)
subscriptions per 100 inhabitants: (2023 est.) less than 1
comparison ranking: total subscriptions 182

Telephones - mobile cellular: *total subscriptions:* 8.65 million (2023 est.)
subscriptions per 100 inhabitants: 58 (2022 est.)
comparison ranking: total subscriptions 98

Broadcast media: state-controlled Radio Television Nationale de Burundi (RTNB) operates a TV station and a national radio network; 3 private TV stations and about 10 privately owned radio stations;transmissions of several international broadcasters are available in Bujumbura (2019)

Internet country code: .bi

Internet users: *percent of population:* 11% (2023 est.)

Broadband - fixed subscriptions: *total:* 3,000 (2023 est.)
subscriptions per 100 inhabitants: (2023 est.) less than 1
comparison ranking: total 198

TRANSPORTATION

Civil aircraft registration country code prefix: 9U

Airports: 6 (2025)
comparison ranking: 173

MILITARY AND SECURITY

Military and security forces: Burundi National Defense Force (BNDF; Force de Defense Nationale du Burundi, FDNB): Land Force (Army), Naval Force, Air Force, Specialized Units

Ministry of Interior, Community Development, and Public Security: Burundi National Police (Police Nationale du Burundi, PNB) (2024)
note: the Naval Force is responsible for monitoring Burundi's 175-km shoreline on Lake Tanganyika; the Specialized Units include a special security brigade for the protection of institutions (aka BSPI), commandos, special forces, and military police

Military expenditures: 3.5% of GDP (2024 est.)
3% of GDP (2023 est.)
2.6% of GDP (2022 est.)
2% of GDP (2021 est.)
2.1% of GDP (2020 est.)

Military and security service personnel strengths: limited available information; estimated 25-30,000 active-duty Defense Force troops (2025)

Military equipment inventories and acquisitions: the military has a mix of mostly older weapons and equipment typically of French, Russian, and Soviet origin, and a smaller selection of more modern secondhand equipment from such countries as China, South Africa, and the US (2024)

Military service age and obligation: 18 years of age for voluntary military service for men and women (2023)

Military deployments: 770 Central African Republic (MINUSCA) (2025)
note: Burundi has deployed several thousand military troops to the Democratic Republic of the Congo (DRC) since 2022 to assist the DRC Government in combating armed anti-government rebel groups; as of 2025, a contingent remained in the DRC

Military - note: the National Defense Force (FDNB) is responsible for defending Burundi's territorial integrity and protecting its sovereignty; it has an internal security role, including maintaining and restoring public order if required; the FDNB also participates in providing humanitarian/disaster assistance, countering terrorism, narcotics trafficking, piracy, and illegal arms trade, and protecting the country's environment; the FDNB conducts limited training with foreign partners such as Russia and participates in regional peacekeeping missions, most recently in the Central African Republic, the Democratic Republic of the Congo (DRC), and Somalia; in recent years the FDNB has conducted operations against anti-government rebel groups based in the neighboring DRC that have carried out sporadic attacks in Burundi, such as the such as National Forces of Liberation (FNL), the Resistance for the Rule of Law-Tabara (aka RED Tabara), and Popular Forces of Burundi (FPB or FOREBU); Burundi has accused Rwanda of supporting the RED-Tabara
the Arusha Accords that ended the 1993-2005 civil war created a unified military by balancing the predominantly Tutsi ex-Burundi Armed Forces (ex-FAB) and the largely Hutu dominated armed movements and requiring the military to have a 50/50 ethnic mix of Tutsis and Hutus (2025)

TRANSNATIONAL ISSUES

Refugees and internally displaced persons: *refugees:* 91,164 (2024 est.)

IDPs: 92,174 (2024 est.)
stateless persons:.791 (2024 est.)

CABO VERDE

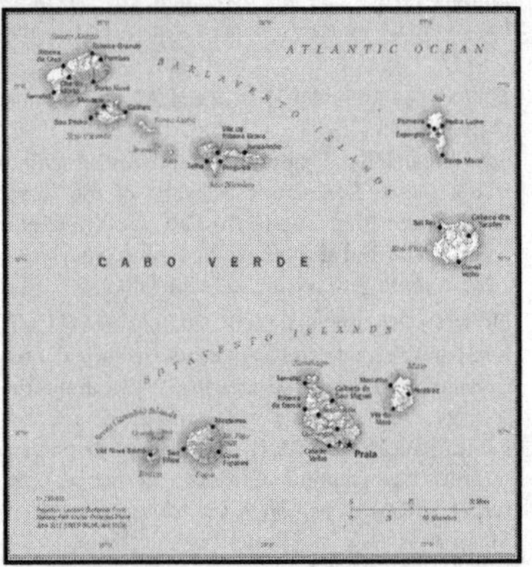

INTRODUCTION

Background: The Portuguese discovered and colonized the uninhabited islands of Cabo Verde in the 15th century; Cabo Verde subsequently became a trading center for African slaves and later an important coaling and resupply stop for whaling and transatlantic shipping. The fusing of European and various African cultural traditions is reflected in Cabo Verde's Crioulo language, music, and pano textiles. After gaining independence in 1975, a one-party system was established and maintained until multi-party elections were held in 1990. Cabo Verde continues to sustain one of Africa's most stable democratic governments and relatively stable economies, maintaining a currency pegged first to the Portuguese escudo and then to the euro since 1998. Repeated droughts during the second half of the 20th century caused significant hardship and prompted heavy emigration. As a result, Cabo Verde's expatriate population – concentrated in Boston, Massachusetts and Western Europe – is greater than its domestic one.

Most Cabo Verdeans have both African and Portuguese antecedents. Cabo Verde's population descends from its first permanent inhabitants in the late 15th-century – a preponderance of West African slaves, a small share of Portuguese colonists, and even fewer Italians and Spaniards. Among the nine inhabited islands, population distribution is varied. The islands in the east are very dry and are home to the country's growing tourism industry. The more western islands receive more precipitation and support larger populations, but agriculture and livestock grazing have damaged their soil fertility and vegetation. For centuries, the country's overall population size has fluctuated significantly, as recurring periods of famine and epidemics have caused high death tolls and emigration.

GEOGRAPHY

Location: Western Africa, group of islands in the North Atlantic Ocean, west of Senegal

Geographic coordinates: 16 00 N, 24 00 W

Map references: Africa

Area: *total:* 4,033 sq km
land: 4,033 sq km
water: 0 sq km
comparison ranking: total 175

Area - comparative: slightly larger than Rhode Island

Land boundaries: *total:* 0 km

Coastline: 965 km

Maritime claims: *territorial sea:* 12 nm
contiguous zone: 24 nm
exclusive economic zone: 200 nm
note: measured from claimed archipelagic baselines

Climate: temperate; warm, dry summer; precipitation meager and erratic

Terrain: steep, rugged, rocky, volcanic

Elevation: *highest point:* Mt. Fogo (a volcano on Fogo Island) 2,829 m
lowest point: Atlantic Ocean 0 m

Natural resources: salt, basalt rock, limestone, kaolin, fish, clay, gypsum

Land use: *agricultural land:* 19.6% (2022 est.)
arable land: 12.4% (2022 est.)
permanent crops: 1% (2022 est.)
permanent pasture: 6.2% (2022 est.)
forest: 11.5% (2022 est.)
other: 68.9% (2022 est.)

Irrigated land: 35 sq km (2012)

Population distribution: among the nine inhabited islands, population distribution is variable; islands in the east are very dry and are only sparsely settled; the more southerly islands receive more precipitation and support larger populations; approximately half of the population lives on Sao Tiago Island, which is the location of the capital of Praia; Mindelo, on the northern island of Sao Vicente, also has a large urban population, as shown in this population distribution map

Natural hazards: prolonged droughts; seasonal harmattan wind produces obscuring dust; volcanically and seismically active
volcanism: Fogo (2,829 m), which last erupted in 1995, is Cabo Verde's only active volcano

Geography - note: strategic location 500 km from west coast of Africa near major north-south sea routes; one of four North Atlantic archipelagos that make up Macaronesia; the others are Azores (Portugal), Canary Islands (Spain), and Madeira (Portugal)

PEOPLE AND SOCIETY

Population: *total:* 611,014 (2024 est.)
male: 297,106
female: 313,908
comparison rankings: total 171; male 171; female 171

Nationality: *noun:* Cabo Verdean(s)
adjective: Cabo Verdean

Ethnic groups: Creole (Mulatto) 71%, African 28%, European 1%

Languages: Portuguese (official), Crioulo (a Portuguese-based creole language with two main dialects)

Religions: Roman Catholic 72.5%, Protestant 4% (includes Adventist 1.9%, Nazarene 1.8%, Assembly of God 0.2%, God is Love 0.1%), Christian Rationalism 1.7%, Muslim 1.3%, Jehovah's Witness 1.2%, Church of Jesus Christ 1%, other Christian 1.3%, other 1.2%, none 15.6%, no response 0.4% (2021 est.)

Age structure: *0-14 years:* 26.4% (male 80,973/female 80,129)
15-64 years: 67.2% (male 201,084/female 209,676)
65 years and over: 6.4% (2024 est.) (male 15,049/female 24,103)

Dependency ratios: *total dependency ratio:* 48.8 (2024 est.)
youth dependency ratio: 39.2 (2024 est.)
elderly dependency ratio: 9.5 (2024 est.)
potential support ratio: 10.5 (2024 est.)

Median age: *total:* 28.8 years (2024 est.)
male: 27.9 years
female: 29.6 years
comparison ranking: total 149

Population growth rate: 1.16% (2024 est.)
comparison ranking: 78

Birth rate: 17.9 births/1,000 population (2024 est.)
comparison ranking: 79

Death rate: 5.7 deaths/1,000 population (2024 est.)
comparison ranking: 168

Net migration rate: -0.6 migrant(s)/1,000 population (2024 est.)
comparison ranking: 124

Population distribution: among the nine inhabited islands, population distribution is variable; islands in the east are very dry and are only sparsely settled; the more southerly islands receive more precipitation and support larger populations; approximately half of the population lives on Sao Tiago Island, which is the location of the capital of Praia; Mindelo, on the northern island of Sao Vicente, also has a large urban population, as shown in this population distribution map

Urbanization: *urban population:* 68% of total population (2023)
rate of urbanization: 1.83% annual rate of change (2020-25 est.)

Major urban areas - population: 168,000 PRAIA (capital) (2018)

Sex ratio: *at birth:* 1.03 male(s)/female
0-14 years: 1.01 male(s)/female
15-64 years: 0.96 male(s)/female
65 years and over: 0.62 male(s)/female
total population: 0.95 male(s)/female (2024 est.)

Maternal mortality ratio: 40 deaths/100,000 live births (2023 est.)
comparison ranking: 104

Infant mortality rate: *total:* 22.4 deaths/1,000 live births (2024 est.)
male: 26.3 deaths/1,000 live births
female: 18.4 deaths/1,000 live births
comparison ranking: total 67

Life expectancy at birth: *total population:* 74.3 years (2024 est.)
male: 72 years
female: 76.7 years
comparison ranking: total population 144

Total fertility rate: 2.1 children born/woman (2024 est.)
comparison ranking: 95

Gross reproduction rate: 1.03 (2024 est.)

Drinking water source: *improved: urban:* 93.2% of population (2022 est.)
rural: 82.9% of population (2022 est.)
total: 89.9% of population (2022 est.)
unimproved: urban: 6.8% of population (2022 est.)
rural: 17.1% of population (2022 est.)
total: 10.1% of population (2022 est.)

Health expenditure: 6.9% of GDP (2021)
16.1% of national budget (2022 est.)

Physician density: 0.73 physicians/1,000 population (2023)

Hospital bed density: 2 beds/1,000 population (2018 est.)

Sanitation facility access: *improved: urban:* 95.6% of population (2022 est.)
rural: 77.8% of population (2022 est.)
total: 89.8% of population (2022 est.)
unimproved: urban: 4.4% of population (2022 est.)
rural: 22.2% of population (2022 est.)
total: 10.2% of population (2022 est.)

Obesity - adult prevalence rate: 11.8% (2016)
comparison ranking: 134

Alcohol consumption per capita: *total:* 4.7 liters of pure alcohol (2019 est.)
beer: 2.28 liters of pure alcohol (2019 est.)
wine: 1.82 liters of pure alcohol (2019 est.)
spirits: 0.6 liters of pure alcohol (2019 est.)
other alcohols: 0 liters of pure alcohol (2019 est.)
comparison ranking: total 86

Tobacco use: *total:* 9.8% (2025 est.)
male: 15.3% (2025 est.)
female: 4.5% (2025 est.)
comparison ranking: total 128

Currently married women (ages 15-49): 46.9% (2023 est.)

Child marriage: *women married by age 15:* 1.8% (2018)
women married by age 18: 8.4% (2018)
men married by age 18: 1.5% (2018)

Education expenditure: 4.3% of GDP (2023 est.)
13.4% national budget (2024 est.)
comparison ranking: Education expenditure (% GDP) 92

Literacy: *total population:* 87% (2015 est.)
male: 92% (2015 est.)
female: 82% (2015 est.)

School life expectancy (primary to tertiary education): *total:* 13 years (2018 est.)
male: 13 years (2018 est.)
female: 14 years (2018 est.)

ENVIRONMENT

Environmental issues: deforestation due to demand for firewood; water shortages; droughts; desertification; soil erosion; illegal beach sand extraction; overfishing

International environmental agreements: *party to:* Biodiversity, Climate Change, Climate Change-Kyoto Protocol, Climate Change-Paris Agreement, Comprehensive Nuclear Test Ban, Desertification, Endangered Species, Environmental Modification, Hazardous Wastes, Law of the Sea, Marine Dumping-London Convention, Nuclear Test Ban, Ozone Layer Protection, Ship Pollution, Wetlands
signed, but not ratified: none of the selected agreements

Climate: temperate; warm, dry summer; precipitation meager and erratic

Urbanization: *urban population:* 68% of total population (2023)
rate of urbanization: 1.83% annual rate of change (2020-25 est.)

Carbon dioxide emissions: 714,000 metric tonnes of CO2 (2023 est.)
from petroleum and other liquids: 714,000 metric tonnes of CO2 (2023 est.)
comparison ranking: total emissions 181

Particulate matter emissions: 27.4 micrograms per cubic meter (2019 est.)

Waste and recycling: *municipal solid waste generated annually:* 132,600 tons (2024 est.)
percent of municipal solid waste recycled: 17.4% (2022 est.)

Total water withdrawal: *municipal:* 155.895 million cubic meters (2022)
industrial: 5.614 million cubic meters (2022)
agricultural: 103.217 million cubic meters (2022)

Total renewable water resources: 300 million cubic meters (2022 est.)

GOVERNMENT

Country name: *conventional long form:* Republic of Cabo Verde
conventional short form: Cabo Verde
local long form: Republica de Cabo Verde
local short form: Cabo Verde
etymology: the name derives from the Cape Verde (Green Cape) peninsula on the Senegalese coast, the westernmost point of Africa and the nearest mainland to the islands

Government type: parliamentary republic

Capital: *name:* Praia
geographic coordinates: 14 55 N, 23 31 W
time difference: UTC-1 (4 hours ahead of Washington, DC, during Standard Time)
etymology: the earlier Portuguese name was Villa de Praia ("Village of the Beach"); it was shortened to Praia in 1974

Administrative divisions: 22 municipalities (*concelhos*, singular - *concelho*); Boa Vista, Brava, Maio, Mosteiros, Paul, Porto Novo, Praia, Ribeira Brava, Ribeira Grande, Ribeira Grande de Santiago, Sal, Santa Catarina, Santa Catarina do Fogo, Santa Cruz, São Domingos, São Filipe, São Lourenco dos Orgaos, São Miguel, São Salvador do Mundo, São Vicente, Tarrafal, Tarrafal de São Nicolau

Legal system: civil law system of Portugal

Constitution: *history:* previous 1981; latest effective 25 September 1992
amendment process: proposals require support of at least four fifths of the active National Assembly membership; amendment drafts require sponsorship of at least one third of the active Assembly membership; passage requires at least two-thirds majority vote by the Assembly membership; constitutional sections, including those on national independence, form of government, political pluralism, suffrage, and human rights and liberties, cannot be amended

International law organization participation: has not submitted an ICJ jurisdiction declaration; accepts ICCt jurisdiction

Citizenship: *citizenship by birth:* no
citizenship by descent only: at least one parent must be a citizen of Cabo Verde
dual citizenship recognized: yes
residency requirement for naturalization: 5 years

Suffrage: 18 years of age; universal

Executive branch: *chief of state:* President Jose Maria Pereira NEVES (since 9 November 2021)
head of government: Prime Minister Jose Ulisses CORREIA e SILVA (since 22 April 2016)
cabinet: Council of Ministers appointed by the president on the recommendation of the prime minister
election/appointment process: president directly elected by absolute-majority popular vote in 2 rounds, if needed, for a 5-year term (eligible for a second term); prime minister nominated by the National Assembly and appointed by the president
most recent election date: 17 October 2021
election results: *2020:* Jose Maria Pereira NEVES elected president; percent of vote - Jose Maria Pereira NEVES (PAICV) 51.7%, Carlos VEIGA (MPD) 42.4%, Casimiro DE PINA (independent) 1.8%, Fernando Rocha DELGADO (independent) 1.4%, Helio SANCHES (independent) 1.14%, Gilson ALVES (independent) 0.8%, Joaquim MONTEIRO (independent) 3.4%
2016: Jorge Carlos FONSECA reelected president; percent of vote - Jorge Carlos FONSECA (MPD) 74.1%, Albertino GRACA (independent) 22.5%, other 3.4%
expected date of next election: October 2026

Legislative branch: *legislature name:* National Assembly (Assembleia Nacional)
legislative structure: unicameral
number of seats: 72 (all directly elected)
electoral system: proportional representation
scope of elections: full renewal
term in office: 5 years
most recent election date: 4/18/2021
parties elected and seats per party: Movement for Democracy (MpD) (38); African Party for the Independence of Cabo Verde (PAICV) (30); Union for an Independent Democratic Cape Verde (UCID) (4)
percentage of women in chamber: 44.4%
expected date of next election: April 2026

Judicial branch: *highest court(s):* Supreme Court of Justice (consists of the chief justice and at least 7 judges and organized into civil, criminal, and administrative sections)
judge selection and term of office: judge appointments - 1 by the president of the republic, 1 elected by the National Assembly, and 3 by the Superior Judicial Council (SJC), a 16-member independent body chaired by the chief justice and includes the attorney general, 8 private citizens, 2 judges, 2 prosecutors, the senior legal inspector of the Attorney General's office, and a representative of the Ministry of Justice; chief justice appointed by the president of the republic from among peers of the Supreme Court of Justice and in consultation with the SJC; judges appointed for life
subordinate courts: appeals courts, first instance (municipal) courts; audit, military, and fiscal and customs courts

Political parties: African Party for Independence of Cabo Verde or PAICV
Democratic and Independent Cabo Verdean Union or UCID
Democratic Christian Party or PDC
Democratic Renewal Party or PRD
Movement for Democracy or MPD
Party for Democratic Convergence or PCD
Party of Work and Solidarity or PTS
Social Democratic Party or PSD

Diplomatic representation in the US: *chief of mission:* Ambassador Jose Luis do Livramento MONTEIRO ALVES DE BRITO (since 23 December 2020)
chancery: 3415 Massachusetts Avenue NW, Washington, DC 20007
telephone: [1] (202) 965-6820

FAX: [1] (202) 965-1207
email address and website: embassy.wdc@mnec.gov.cv
https://www.embcv-usa.gov.cv/
consulate(s) general: Boston

Diplomatic representation from the US: *chief of mission:* Ambassador Jennifer ADAMS (since 10 September 2024)
embassy: Rua Abilio Macedo 6, Praia
mailing address: 2460 Praia Place, Washington DC 20521-2460
telephone: [238] 260-8900

FAX: [238] 261-1355
email address and website: PraiaConsular@state.gov
https://cv.usembassy.gov/

International organization participation: ACP, AfDB, AOSIS, AU, CD, CPLP, ECOWAS, FAO, G-77, IAEA, IBRD, ICAO, ICCt (signatory), ICRM, IDA, IFAD, IFC, IFRCS, ILO, IMF, IMO, Interpol, IOC, IOM, IPU, ITSO, ITU, ITUC (NGOs), MIGA, NAM, OIF, OPCW, UN, UNCTAD, UNESCO, UNIDO, Union Latina, UNWTO, UPU, WCO, WHO, WIPO, WMO, WTO

Independence: 5 July 1975 (from Portugal)

National holiday: Independence Day, 5 July (1975)

Flag: *description:* five unequal horizontal bands; the top band of blue is half the height of the flag; under it are three narrow bands of white, red, and white, and a bottom stripe of blue; a circle of 10 five-pointed yellow stars is centered on the red stripe and sits toward the left side of the flag
meaning: blue stands for the sea and sky; the stripes symbolize the country's formation through peace (white) and effort (red); the stars represent the 10 major islands

National symbol(s): ten five-pointed yellow stars

National color(s): blue, white, red, yellow

National anthem(s): *title:* "Cantico da Liberdade" (Song of Freedom)
lyrics/music: Amilcar Spencer LOPES/Adalberto Higino Tavares SILVA
history: adopted 1996

National heritage: *total World Heritage Sites:* 1 (cultural)
selected World Heritage Site locales: Cidade Velha; Historic Center of Ribeira Grande

ECONOMY

Economic overview: stable, middle-income, developing island economy; strong GDP growth led by tourism sector recovery; sustained poverty reduction through PEDS II development plan; high reliance on foreign remittances and aid to finance external debt

Real GDP (purchasing power parity): $5.2 billion (2024 est.)
$4.848 billion (2023 est.)
$4.6 billion (2022 est.)
note: data in 2021 dollars
comparison ranking: 184

Real GDP growth rate: 7.3% (2024 est.)
5.4% (2023 est.)
15.8% (2022 est.)
note: annual GDP % growth based on constant local currency
comparison ranking: 14

Real GDP per capita: $9,900 (2024 est.)
$9,300 (2023 est.)
$8,900 (2022 est.)
note: data in 2021 dollars
comparison ranking: 146

GDP (official exchange rate): $2.768 billion (2024 est.)
note: data in current dollars at official exchange rate

Inflation rate (consumer prices): 1% (2024 est.)
3.7% (2023 est.)
7.9% (2022 est.)
note: annual % change based on consumer prices
comparison ranking: 21

GDP - composition, by sector of origin: *agriculture:* 4.7% (2024 est.)
industry: 10.5% (2024 est.)
services: 69.4% (2024 est.)
note: figures may not total 100% due to non-allocated consumption not captured in sector-reported data
comparison rankings: agriculture 112; industry 184; services 38

GDP - composition, by end use: *household consumption:* 74.7% (2024 est.)
government consumption: 20.7% (2024 est.)
investment in fixed capital: 16% (2024 est.)
investment in inventories: 0% (2024 est.)
exports of goods and services: 41.9% (2024 est.)
imports of goods and services: -53.2% (2024 est.)
note: figures may not total 100% due to rounding or gaps in data collection

Agricultural products: sugarcane, tomatoes, coconuts, pulses, goat milk, milk, vegetables, bananas, cabbages, onions (2023)
note: top ten agricultural products based on tonnage

Industries: food and beverages, fish processing, shoes and garments, salt mining, ship repair

Industrial production growth rate: 4.4% (2024 est.)
note: annual % change in industrial value added based on constant local currency
comparison ranking: 54

Labor force: 224,500 (2024 est.)
note: number of people ages 15 or older who are employed or seeking work
comparison ranking: 176

Unemployment rate: 11.9% (2024 est.)
12% (2023 est.)
12.3% (2022 est.)
note: % of labor force seeking employment
comparison ranking: 163

Youth unemployment rate (ages 15-24): *total:* 28.2% (2024 est.)
male: 24.6% (2024 est.)
female: 33.8% (2024 est.)
note: % of labor force ages 15-24 seeking employment
comparison ranking: total 25

Population below poverty line: 35.2% (2015 est.)
note: % of population with income below national poverty line

Gini Index coefficient - distribution of family income: 42.4 (2015 est.)
note: index (0-100) of income distribution; higher values represent greater inequality
comparison ranking: 30

Household income or consumption by percentage share: *lowest 10%:* 2.2% (2015 est.)
highest 10%: 32.3% (2015 est.)
note: % share of income accruing to lowest and highest 10% of population

Remittances: 12.1% of GDP (2024 est.)
12.5% of GDP (2023 est.)
14% of GDP (2022 est.)
note: personal transfers and compensation between resident and non-resident individuals/households/entities

Budget: *revenues:* $453.182 million (2020 est.)
expenditures: $623.816 million (2020 est.)
note: central government revenues and expenses (excluding grants/extrabudgetary units/social security funds) converted to US dollars at average official exchange rate for year indicated

Taxes and other revenues: 18.4% (of GDP) (2020 est.)
note: central government tax revenue as a % of GDP
comparison ranking: 61

Current account balance: $101.072 million (2024 est.)
-$64.439 million (2023 est.)
-$78.271 million (2022 est.)
note: balance of payments - net trade and primary/secondary income in current dollars
comparison ranking: 76

Exports: $1.158 billion (2024 est.)
$972.636 million (2023 est.)
$851.907 million (2022 est.)
note: balance of payments - exports of goods and services in current dollars
comparison ranking: 181

Exports - partners: Spain 46%, Portugal 9%, Togo 7%, Italy 7%, India 6% (2023)
note: top five export partners based on percentage share of exports

Exports - commodities: fish, refined petroleum, railway cargo containers, shellfish, garments (2023)
note: top five export commodities based on value in dollars

Imports: $1.473 billion (2024 est.)
$1.428 billion (2023 est.)
$1.31 billion (2022 est.)
note: balance of payments - imports of goods and services in current dollars
comparison ranking: 185

Imports - partners: Portugal 29%, Saudi Arabia 11%, Netherlands 9%, Spain 8%, China 7% (2023)
note: top five import partners based on percentage share of imports

Imports - commodities: refined petroleum, aircraft, cars, fish, railway cargo containers (2023)
note: top five import commodities based on value in dollars

Reserves of foreign exchange and gold: $783.106 million (2024 est.)
$837.881 million (2023 est.)
$729.566 million (2022 est.)
note: holdings of gold (year-end prices)/foreign exchange/special drawing rights in current dollars
comparison ranking: 147

Debt - external: $1.385 billion (2023 est.)
note: present value of external debt in current US dollars
comparison ranking: 101

Exchange rates: Cabo Verdean escudos (CVE) per US dollar -

Exchange rates: 101.922 (2024 est.)
101.805 (2023 est.)
104.863 (2022 est.)

93.218 (2021 est.)
96.796 (2020 est.)

ENERGY

Electricity access: *electrification - total population:* 97.1% (2022 est.)
electrification - urban areas: 95.3%
electrification - rural areas: 96.9%

Electricity: *installed generating capacity:* 200,000 kW (2023 est.)
consumption: 400 million kWh (2023 est.)
transmission/distribution losses: 106 million kWh (2023 est.)
comparison rankings: installed generating capacity 172; consumption 180; transmission/distribution losses 49

Electricity generation sources: *fossil fuels:* 71.1% of total installed capacity (2023 est.)
solar: 14.2% of total installed capacity (2023 est.)
wind: 14.6% of total installed capacity (2023 est.)

Petroleum: *refined petroleum consumption:* 5,000 bbl/day (2023 est.)

Energy consumption per capita: 19.999 million Btu/person (2023 est.)
comparison ranking: 132

COMMUNICATIONS

Telephones - fixed lines: *total subscriptions:* 60,000 (2023 est.)
subscriptions per 100 inhabitants: 12 (2023 est.)
comparison ranking: total subscriptions 151

Telephones - mobile cellular: *total subscriptions:* 590,000 (2023 est.)
subscriptions per 100 inhabitants: 99 (2022 est.)
comparison ranking: total subscriptions 172

Broadcast media: state-run TV and radio network, plus a growing number of private broadcasters; Portuguese public TV and radio services for Africa are available; transmissions of a few international broadcasters are available (2019)

Internet country code: .cv

Internet users: *percent of population:* 74% (2023 est.)

Broadband - fixed subscriptions: *total:* 38,000 (2023 est.)
subscriptions per 100 inhabitants: 7 (2023 est.)
comparison ranking: total 153

TRANSPORTATION

Civil aircraft registration country code prefix: D4

Airports: 10 (2025)
comparison ranking: 158

Merchant marine: *total:* 44 (2023)
by type: general cargo 14, oil tanker 2, other 28
comparison ranking: total 122

Ports: *total ports:* 2 (2024)
large: 0
medium: 0
small: 1
very small: 1
ports with oil terminals: 1
key ports: Porto da Praia, Porto Grande

MILITARY AND SECURITY

Military and security forces: Cabo Verdean Armed Forces (FACV): National Guard (GN), Cabo Verde Coast Guard (Guardia Costeira de Cabo Verde, GCCV) (2025)
note: the National Police are under the Ministry of Internal Affairs

Military expenditures: 0.6% of GDP (2024 est.)
0.6% of GDP (2023 est.)
0.5% of GDP (2022 est.)
0.5% of GDP (2021 est.)
0.5% of GDP (2020 est.)

Military and security service personnel strengths: the FACV has approximately 1,000-1,500 active personnel (2025)

Military equipment inventories and acquisitions: the FACV has a limited amount of mostly dated or second-hand equipment, largely from China, some European countries, and the former Soviet Union (2024)

Military service age and obligation: 18-35 years of age for male and female selective compulsory military service; 24-month conscript service obligation; 17 years of age for voluntary service (with parental consent) (2024)

Military - note: the FACV is responsible for external defense; it also has an internal security role in collaboration with the police if required; its duties include monitoring and patrolling the country's air and maritime spaces, participating in training exercises, conducting search and rescue, countering narcotics and other forms of illicit trafficking, and supporting the police and civil society (2025)

TRANSNATIONAL ISSUES

Refugees and internally displaced persons: *stateless persons:* 115 (2024 est.)

Trafficking in persons: *tier rating:* Tier 2 Watch List — Cabo Verde did not demonstrate overall increasing efforts to eliminate trafficking compared with the previous reporting period and was downgraded to Tier 2 Watch List; for more details, go to: https://www.state.gov/reports/2025-trafficking-in-persons-report/cabo-verde/

CAMBODIA

INTRODUCTION

Background: Most Cambodians consider themselves to be Khmers, descendants of the Angkor Empire that extended over much of Southeast Asia and reached its zenith between the 10th and 13th centuries. Attacks by the Thai and Cham (from present-day Vietnam) weakened the empire, ushering in a long period of decline. The king placed the country under French protection in 1863, and it became part of French Indochina in 1887. Following Japanese occupation in World War II, Cambodia gained full independence from France in 1953. In 1975, after a seven-year struggle, communist Khmer Rouge forces captured Phnom Penh and evacuated all cities and towns. At least 1.5 million Cambodians died from execution, forced hardships, or starvation during the Khmer Rouge regime under POL POT. A 1978 Vietnamese invasion drove the Khmer Rouge into the countryside, began a 10-year Vietnamese occupation, and touched off 13 years of internecine warfare in which a coalition of Khmer Rouge, Cambodian nationalists, and royalist insurgents, with assistance from China, fought the Vietnamese-backed People's Republic of Kampuchea (PRK).

The 1991 Paris Agreements ended the country's civil war and mandated democratic elections, which took place in 1993 and ushered in a period of multi-party democracy with a constitutional monarchy. King Norodom SIHANOUK was reinstated as head of state, and the Cambodian People's Party (CPP) and the royalist FUNCINPEC party formed a coalition government. Nevertheless, the power-sharing arrangement proved fractious and fragile, and in 1997, a coup led by CPP leader and former PRK prime minister HUN SEN dissolved the coalition and sidelined FUNCINPEC. Despite further attempts at coalition governance, the CPP has since remained in power through elections criticized for lacking fairness, political and judicial corruption, media control, and influence over labor unions, all of which have been enforced with violence and intimidation. HUN SEN remained as prime minister until 2023, when he transferred power to his son, HUN MANET. HUN SEN has subsequently maintained considerable influence as the leader of the CPP and the Senate. The CPP has also placed limits on civil society, press freedom, and freedom of expression. Despite some economic growth and considerable investment from China over the past decade, Cambodia remains one of East Asia's poorest countries.

The remaining elements of the Khmer Rouge surrendered in 1999. A UN-backed special tribunal established in Cambodia in 1997 tried some of the surviving Khmer Rouge leaders for crimes against humanity and genocide. The tribunal concluded in 2022 with three convictions.

GEOGRAPHY

Location: Southeastern Asia, bordering the Gulf of Thailand, between Thailand, Vietnam, and Laos

Geographic coordinates: 13 00 N, 105 00 E

Map references: Southeast Asia

Area: *total:* 181,035 sq km
land: 176,515 sq km
water: 4,520 sq km
comparison ranking: total 90

Area - comparative: 1.5 times the size of Pennsylvania; slightly smaller than Oklahoma

Land boundaries: *total:* 2,530 km
border countries (3): Laos 555 km; Thailand 817 km; Vietnam 1158 km

Coastline: 443 km

Maritime claims: *territorial sea:* 12 nm
contiguous zone: 24 nm
exclusive economic zone: 200 nm
continental shelf: 200 nm

Climate: tropical; rainy, monsoon season (May to November); dry season (December to April); little seasonal temperature variation

Terrain: mostly low, flat plains; mountains in southwest and north

Elevation: *highest point:* Phnum Aoral 1,810 m
lowest point: Gulf of Thailand 0 m
mean elevation: 126 m

Natural resources: oil and gas, timber, gemstones, iron ore, manganese, phosphates, hydropower potential, arable land

Land use: *agricultural land:* 34.6% (2022 est.)
arable land: 23.3% (2022 est.)
permanent crops: 2.8% (2022 est.)
permanent pasture: 8.5% (2022 est.)
forest: 43.9% (2022 est.)
other: 21.4% (2022 est.)

Irrigated land: 3,540 sq km (2012)

Major lakes (area sq km): *fresh water lake(s):* Tonle Sap - 2,700-16,000 sq km

Major rivers (by length in km): Mekong (shared with China [s], Burma, Thailand, Laos, and Vietnam [m]) - 4,350 km
note: [s] after country name indicates river source; [m] after country name indicates river mouth

Major watersheds (area sq km): Pacific Ocean drainage: Mekong (805,604 sq km)

Population distribution: population concentrated in the southeast, particularly in and around the capital of Phnom Penh; further distribution is linked closely to the Tonle Sap and Mekong Rivers

Natural hazards: monsoonal rains (June to November); flooding; occasional droughts

Geography - note: a land of paddies and forests dominated by the Mekong River and Tonle Sap (Southeast Asia's largest freshwater lake)

PEOPLE AND SOCIETY

Population: *total:* 17,063,669 (2024 est.)
male: 8,277,588
female: 8,786,081
comparison rankings: total 73; male 73; female 73

Nationality: *noun:* Cambodian(s)
adjective: Cambodian

Ethnic groups: Khmer 95.4%, Cham 2.4%, Chinese 1.5%, other 0.7% (2019-20 est.)

Languages: Khmer (official) 95.8%, minority languages 2.9%, Chinese 0.6%, Vietnamese 0.5%, other 0.2% (2019 est.)
major-language sample(s):
សៀវភៅហេតុការណ៍នៅលើពិភពលោក។
ទីតាំងពត៌មានមូលដ្ឋានគ្រឹះយ៉ាងសំខាន់។. (Khmer)

Religions: Buddhist (official) 97.1%, Muslim 2%, Christian 0.3%, other 0.5% (2019 est.)

Age structure: *0-14 years:* 28.9% (male 2,497,056/female 2,436,618)
15-64 years: 65.8% (male 5,456,941/female 5,765,206)
65 years and over: 5.3% (2024 est.) (male 323,591/female 584,257)

Dependency ratios: *total dependency ratio:* 52.1 (2024 est.)
youth dependency ratio: 44 (2024 est.)
elderly dependency ratio: 8.1 (2024 est.)
potential support ratio: 12.4 (2024 est.)

Median age: *total:* 27.9 years (2024 est.)
male: 26.9 years
female: 28.9 years
comparison ranking: total 154

Population growth rate: 0.99% (2024 est.)
comparison ranking: 93

Birth rate: 18.2 births/1,000 population (2024 est.)
comparison ranking: 77

Death rate: 5.7 deaths/1,000 population (2024 est.)
comparison ranking: 173

Net migration rate: -2.6 migrant(s)/1,000 population (2024 est.)
comparison ranking: 173

Population distribution: population concentrated in the southeast, particularly in and around the capital of Phnom Penh; further distribution is linked closely to the Tonle Sap and Mekong Rivers

Urbanization: *urban population:* 25.6% of total population (2023)
rate of urbanization: 3.06% annual rate of change (2020-25 est.)

Major urban areas - population: 2.281 million PHNOM PENH (capital) (2023)

Sex ratio: *at birth:* 1.04 male(s)/female
0-14 years: 1.02 male(s)/female
15-64 years: 0.95 male(s)/female
65 years and over: 0.55 male(s)/female
total population: 0.94 male(s)/female (2024 est.)

Mother's mean age at first birth: 23.3 years (2021-22 est.)
note: data represents median age at first birth among women 25-49

Maternal mortality ratio: 137 deaths/100,000 live births (2023 est.)
comparison ranking: 55

Infant mortality rate: *total:* 27.9 deaths/1,000 live births (2024 est.)
male: 31.3 deaths/1,000 live births
female: 24.4 deaths/1,000 live births
comparison ranking: total 54

Life expectancy at birth: *total population:* 71.4 years (2024 est.)
male: 69.6 years
female: 73.3 years
comparison ranking: total population 169

Total fertility rate: 2.17 children born/woman (2024 est.)
comparison ranking: 88

Gross reproduction rate: 1.06 (2024 est.)

Drinking water source: *improved: urban:* 93.6% of population (2022 est.)
rural: 72.8% of population (2022 est.)
total: 78% of population (2022 est.)
unimproved: urban: 6.4% of population (2022 est.)
rural: 27.2% of population (2022 est.)
total: 22% of population (2022 est.)

Health expenditure: 7.5% of GDP (2021)
7% of national budget (2022 est.)

Physician density: 0.21 physicians/1,000 population (2019)

Hospital bed density: 0.7 beds/1,000 population (2018 est.)

Sanitation facility access: *improved: urban:* 100% of population (2022 est.)
rural: 79.6% of population (2022 est.)
total: 84.7% of population (2022 est.)
unimproved: urban: 0% of population (2022 est.)
rural: 20.4% of population (2022 est.)
total: 15.3% of population (2022 est.)

Obesity - adult prevalence rate: 3.9% (2016)
comparison ranking: 188

Alcohol consumption per capita: *total:* 4.56 liters of pure alcohol (2019 est.)
beer: 4.12 liters of pure alcohol (2019 est.)
wine: 0.03 liters of pure alcohol (2019 est.)
spirits: 0.41 liters of pure alcohol (2019 est.)
other alcohols: 0 liters of pure alcohol (2019 est.)
comparison ranking: total 87

Tobacco use: *total:* 14.5% (2025 est.)
male: 24.9% (2025 est.)
female: 4.7% (2025 est.)
comparison ranking: total 104

Children under the age of 5 years underweight: 16.3% (2022)
comparison ranking: 27

Currently married women (ages 15-49): 66.4% (2023 est.)

Child marriage: *women married by age 15:* 1.9% (2022)
women married by age 18: 17.9% (2022)
men married by age 18: 3.3% (2022)

Education expenditure: 3% of GDP (2023 est.)
11.5% national budget (2023 est.)
comparison ranking: Education expenditure (% GDP) 151

Literacy: *total population:* 71.9% (2021 est.)
male: 81.5% (2021 est.)
female: 63.6% (2021 est.)

School life expectancy (primary to tertiary education): *total:* 11 years (2023 est.)
male: 11 years (2023 est.)
female: 11 years (2023 est.)

ENVIRONMENT

Environmental issues: habitat and biodiversity loss from illegal logging and strip mining; destruction of mangrove swamps; soil erosion; limited access to potable water in rural areas; illegal fishing and overfishing; deforestation leading to sediment build-up in coastal ecosystems

International environmental agreements: *party to:* Biodiversity, Climate Change, Climate Change-Kyoto Protocol, Climate Change-Paris Agreement, Comprehensive Nuclear Test Ban, Desertification, Endangered Species, Hazardous Wastes, Marine

Life Conservation, Ozone Layer Protection, Ship Pollution, Tropical Timber 2006, Wetlands, Whaling
signed, but not ratified: Law of the Sea

Climate: tropical; rainy, monsoon season (May to November); dry season (December to April); little seasonal temperature variation

Urbanization: *urban population:* 25.6% of total population (2023)
rate of urbanization: 3.06% annual rate of change (2020-25 est.)

Carbon dioxide emissions: 18.779 million metric tonnes of CO2 (2023 est.)
from coal and metallurgical coke: 8.026 million metric tonnes of CO2 (2023 est.)
from petroleum and other liquids: 10.753 million metric tonnes of CO2 (2023 est.)
comparison ranking: total emissions 91

Particulate matter emissions: 18.4 micrograms per cubic meter (2019 est.)

Waste and recycling: *municipal solid waste generated annually:* 1.089 million tons (2024 est.)
percent of municipal solid waste recycled: 12.4% (2022 est.)

Total water withdrawal: *municipal:* 98 million cubic meters (2022 est.)
industrial: 33 million cubic meters (2022 est.)
agricultural: 2.053 billion cubic meters (2022 est.)

Total renewable water resources: 476.1 billion cubic meters (2022 est.)

GOVERNMENT

Country name: *conventional long form:* Kingdom of Cambodia
conventional short form: Cambodia
local long form: Preahreacheanachakr Kampuchea (phonetic transliteration)
local short form: Kampuchea
former: Khmer Republic, Democratic Kampuchea, People's Republic of Kampuchea, State of Cambodia
etymology: the name is derived from Kambu, a legendary ancestor of the Cambodian people

Government type: parliamentary constitutional monarchy

Capital: *name:* Phnom Penh
geographic coordinates: 11 33 N, 104 55 E
time difference: UTC+7 (12 hours ahead of Washington, DC, during Standard Time)
etymology: the name means "mountain of plenty," from the Cambodian words *phnom* (mountain or hill) and *penh* (full)

Administrative divisions: 24 provinces (*khett*, singular and plural) and 1 municipality (*krong*, singular and plural)
provinces: Banteay Meanchey, Battambang, Kampong Cham, Kampong Chhnang, Kampong Speu, Kampong Thom, Kampot, Kandal, Kep, Koh Kong, Kratie, Mondolkiri, Oddar Meanchey, Pailin, Preah Sihanouk, Preah Vihear, Prey Veng, Pursat, Ratanakiri, Siem Reap, Stung Treng, Svay Rieng, Takeo, Tbong Khmum
municipalities: Phnom Penh (Phnum Penh)

Legal system: civil law system (influenced by the UN Transitional Authority in Cambodia), customary law, Communist legal theory, and common law

Constitution: *history:* previous 1947; latest promulgated 21 September 1993
amendment process: proposed by the monarch, by the prime minister, or by the president of the National Assembly if supported by one fourth of the Assembly membership; passage requires two-thirds majority of the Assembly membership; constitutional articles on the multiparty democratic form of government and the monarchy cannot be amended

International law organization participation: accepts compulsory ICJ jurisdiction with reservations; accepts ICCt jurisdiction

Citizenship: *citizenship by birth:* no
citizenship by descent only: at least one parent must be a citizen of Cambodia
dual citizenship recognized: yes
residency requirement for naturalization: 7 years

Suffrage: 18 years of age; universal

Executive branch: *chief of state:* King Norodom SIHAMONI (since 29 October 2004)
head of government: Prime Minister HUN MANET (since 22 August 2023)
cabinet: Council of Ministers named by the prime minister and appointed by the monarch
election/appointment process: monarch chosen by the 9-member Royal Council of the Throne from among all eligible males of royal descent; after legislative elections, a member of the majority party or majority coalition is named prime minister by the Chairman of the National Assembly and appointed by the monarch
note: MANET succeeded his father, HUN SEN, who had been prime minister since 1985

Legislative branch: *legislature name:* Parliament
legislative structure: bicameral

Legislative branch - lower chamber: *chamber name:* National Assembly (Radhsphea Ney Preah Recheanachakr Kampuchea)
number of seats: 125 (all directly elected)
electoral system: proportional representation
scope of elections: full renewal
term in office: 5 years
most recent election date: 7/23/2023
parties elected and seats per party: Cambodian People's Party (CPP) (120); Other (5)
percentage of women in chamber: 13.6%
expected date of next election: July 2028

Legislative branch - upper chamber: *chamber name:* Senate
number of seats: 62 (60 indirectly elected; 2 appointed)
scope of elections: full renewal
term in office: 6 years
most recent election date: 2/25/2024
percentage of women in chamber: 19.4%
expected date of next election: February 2030

Judicial branch: *highest court(s):* Supreme Council (organized into 5- and 9-judge panels and includes a court chief and deputy chief); Constitutional Court (consists of 9 members)
judge selection and term of office: Supreme Court and Constitutional Council judge candidates recommended by the Supreme Council of Magistracy, a 17-member body chaired by the monarch and includes other high-level judicial officers; judges of both courts appointed by the monarch; Supreme Court judges appointed for life; Constitutional Council judges appointed for 9-year terms with one third of the court renewed every 3 years
subordinate courts: Appellate Court; provincial and municipal courts; Military Court

Political parties: Candlelight Party or CP
Cambodian People's Party or CPP
Khmer Will Party or KWP
note 1: 18 parties registered to run in the 2023 parliamentary election
note 2: the Cambodian Government disqualified the Candlelight Party, the main opposition party, from the July 2023 election

Diplomatic representation in the US: *chief of mission:* Ambassador Koy KUONG (since 11 June 2025)
chancery: 4530 16th Street NW, Washington, DC 20011
telephone: [1] (202) 726-7742
FAX: [1] (202) 726-8381
email address and website: camemb.usa@mfaic.gov.kh
https://www.embassyofcambodiadc.org/

Diplomatic representation from the US: *chief of mission:* Ambassador (vacant); Chargé d'Affaires Bridgette L. WALKER (since August 2024)
embassy: #1, Street 96, Sangkat Wat Phnom, Khan Daun Penh, Phnom Penh
mailing address: 4540 Phnom Penh Place, Washington DC 20521-4540
telephone: [855] (23) 728-000
FAX: [855] (23) 728-700
email address and website: ACSPhnomPenh@state.gov
https://kh.usembassy.gov/

International organization participation: ADB, ARF, ASEAN, CICA, EAS, FAO, G-77, IAEA, IBRD, ICAO, ICRM, IDA, IFAD, IFC, IFRCS, ILO, IMF, IMO, Interpol, IOC, IOM, IPU, ISO (correspondent), ITU, MIGA, NAM, OIF, OPCW, PCA, UN, UNAMID, UNCTAD, UNESCO, UNIDO, UNIFIL, UNISFA, UNMISS, UNWTO, UPU, WCO, WFTU (NGOs), WHO, WIPO, WMO, WTO

Independence: 9 November 1953 (from France)

National holiday: Independence Day, 9 November (1953)

Flag: *description:* three horizontal bands of blue (top), red (double-width), and blue; a three-towered, stylized white temple outlined in black is in the center of the red band, representing Angkor Wat
meaning: red and blue are traditional Cambodian colors
note: only national flag to prominently incorporate an identifiable building into its design; Afghanistan, San Marino, Portugal, and Spain show small generic buildings as part of their coats of arms on the flag

National symbol(s): Angkor Wat temple, kouprey (wild ox)

National color(s): red, blue

National coat of arms: Cambodia's coat of arms is also the Royal Arms of Cambodia; the lions symbolize strength, courage, and the divine protection of the monarchs; the lion on the left is a gajasingha (a lion with an elephant's trunk), and the lion on the right is a rajasingha (royal lion); both hold five-tiered umbrellas representing the king and queen, and they stand on a blue ribbon that says "Preah Chao Krung Kampuche'" (King of the Kingdom of Cambodia); between the lions is a crown with the Unalome, the Buddhist and Hindu symbol for the spiritual path to enlightenment, under it and a ray of light on top

National anthem(s): *title:* "Nokoreach" (Royal Kingdom)
lyrics/music: CHUON NAT/F. PERRUCHOT and J. JEKYLL
history: adopted 1941, restored 1993; the anthem, based on a Cambodian folk tune, was restored after the defeat of the Communist regime

National heritage: *total World Heritage Sites:* 4 (all cultural)
selected World Heritage Site locales: Angkor; Temple of Preah Vihear; Sambor Prei Kuk; Koh Ker: Archaeological Site of Ancient Lingapora or Chok Gargyar

ECONOMY

Economic overview: one of the fastest growing economies; tourism and clothing exports; substantial manufacturing and construction sectors; COVID-19 declines and the suspension of EU market preferential access; massive reductions in poverty, but rural areas remain disproportionately poor

Real GDP (purchasing power parity): $123.676 billion (2024 est.)
$116.658 billion (2023 est.)
$111.095 billion (2022 est.)
note: data in 2021 dollars
comparison ranking: 90

Real GDP growth rate: 6% (2024 est.)
5% (2023 est.)
5.1% (2022 est.)
note: annual GDP % growth based on constant local currency
comparison ranking: 25

Real GDP per capita: $7,000 (2024 est.)
$6,700 (2023 est.)
$6,500 (2022 est.)
note: data in 2021 dollars
comparison ranking: 159

GDP (official exchange rate): $46.353 billion (2024 est.)
note: data in current dollars at official exchange rate

Inflation rate (consumer prices): 2.1% (2023 est.)
5.3% (2022 est.)
2.9% (2021 est.)
note: annual % change based on consumer prices
comparison ranking: 52

GDP - composition, by sector of origin: *agriculture:* 16.6% (2024 est.)
industry: 41.8% (2024 est.)
services: 35.6% (2024 est.)
note: figures may not total 100% due to non-allocated consumption not captured in sector-reported data
comparison rankings: agriculture 49; industry 17; services 201

GDP - composition, by end use: *household consumption:* 59.8% (2024 est.)
government consumption: 5.8% (2024 est.)
investment in fixed capital: 31.6% (2024 est.)
investment in inventories: 0.6% (2024 est.)
exports of goods and services: 71.4% (2024 est.)
imports of goods and services: -72.1% (2024 est.)
note: figures may not total 100% due to rounding or gaps in data collection

Agricultural products: cassava, rice, maize, sugarcane, vegetables, oil palm fruit, rubber, bananas, jute, pork (2023)
note: top ten agricultural products based on tonnage

Industries: tourism, garments, construction, rice milling, fishing, wood and wood products, rubber, cement, gem mining, textiles

Industrial production growth rate: 9.5% (2024 est.)
note: annual % change in industrial value added based on constant local currency
comparison ranking: 14

Labor force: 9.904 million (2024 est.)
note: number of people ages 15 or older who are employed or seeking work
comparison ranking: 57

Unemployment rate: 0.3% (2024 est.)
0.3% (2023 est.)
0.3% (2022 est.)
note: % of labor force seeking employment
comparison ranking: 2

Youth unemployment rate (ages 15-24): *total:* 0.8% (2024 est.)
male: 0.7% (2024 est.)
female: 0.9% (2024 est.)
note: % of labor force ages 15-24 seeking employment
comparison ranking: total 187

Average household expenditures: *on food:* 40.7% of household expenditures (2023 est.)
on alcohol and tobacco: 1.9% of household expenditures (2023 est.)

Remittances: 6.1% of GDP (2024 est.)
6.6% of GDP (2023 est.)
6.5% of GDP (2022 est.)
note: personal transfers and compensation between resident and non-resident individuals/households/entities

Budget: *revenues:* $7.076 billion (2023 est.)
expenditures: $8.285 billion (2023 est.)
note: central government revenues (excluding grants) and expenditures converted to US dollars at average official exchange rate for year indicated

Public debt: 50.3% of GDP (2023 est.)
note: central government debt as a % of GDP
comparison ranking: 102

Taxes and other revenues: 12.2% (of GDP) (2023 est.)
note: central government tax revenue as a % of GDP
comparison ranking: 113

Current account balance: $222.108 million (2024 est.)
$552.346 million (2023 est.)
-$7.582 billion (2022 est.)
note: balance of payments - net trade and primary/secondary income in current dollars
comparison ranking: 69

Exports: $31.712 billion (2024 est.)
$27.753 billion (2023 est.)
$25.497 billion (2022 est.)
note: balance of payments - exports of goods and services in current dollars
comparison ranking: 82

Exports - partners: USA 36%, Germany 6%, China 6%, Japan 6%, Thailand 5% (2023)
note: top five export partners based on percentage share of exports

Exports - commodities: garments, semiconductors, trunks and cases, footwear, gold (2023)
note: top five export commodities based on value in dollars

Imports: $34.329 billion (2024 est.)
$29.421 billion (2023 est.)
$34.759 billion (2022 est.)
note: balance of payments - imports of goods and services in current dollars
comparison ranking: 74

Imports - partners: China 39%, Thailand 20%, Vietnam 12%, Singapore 6%, Indonesia 3% (2023)
note: top five import partners based on percentage share of imports

Imports - commodities: refined petroleum, fabric, gold, plastic products, synthetic fabric (2023)
note: top five import commodities based on value in dollars

Reserves of foreign exchange and gold: $22.506 billion (2024 est.)
$19.984 billion (2023 est.)
$17.801 billion (2022 est.)
note: holdings of gold (year-end prices)/foreign exchange/special drawing rights in current dollars
comparison ranking: 60

Debt - external: $8.019 billion (2023 est.)
note: present value of external debt in current US dollars
comparison ranking: 56

Exchange rates: riels (KHR) per US dollar -

Exchange rates: 4,072.397 (2024 est.)
4,110.653 (2023 est.)
4,102.038 (2022 est.)
4,098.723 (2021 est.)
4,092.783 (2020 est.)

ENERGY

Electricity access: *electrification - total population:* 92.3% (2022 est.)
electrification - urban areas: 99%
electrification - rural areas: 88%

Electricity: *installed generating capacity:* 3.673 million kW (2023 est.)
consumption: 16.998 billion kWh (2023 est.)
imports: 5.096 billion kWh (2023 est.)
transmission/distribution losses: 1.882 billion kWh (2023 est.)
comparison rankings: installed generating capacity 104; consumption 81; imports 45; transmission/distribution losses 122

Electricity generation sources: *fossil fuels:* 55.5% of total installed capacity (2023 est.)
solar: 5.8% of total installed capacity (2023 est.)
hydroelectricity: 38.6% of total installed capacity (2023 est.)
biomass and waste: 0.1% of total installed capacity (2023 est.)

Coal: *production:* 27,000 metric tons (2023 est.)
consumption: 4.39 million metric tons (2023 est.)
imports: 4.36 million metric tons (2023 est.)

Petroleum: *refined petroleum consumption:* 77,000 bbl/day (2023 est.)

Energy consumption per capita: 15.664 million Btu/person (2023 est.)
comparison ranking: 138

COMMUNICATIONS

Telephones - fixed lines: *total subscriptions:* 38,000 (2022 est.)
subscriptions per 100 inhabitants: (2022 est.) less than 1
comparison ranking: total subscriptions 162

Telephones - mobile cellular: *total subscriptions:* 19.5 million (2022 est.)
subscriptions per 100 inhabitants: 116 (2022 est.)
comparison ranking: total subscriptions 66

Broadcast media: mix of state-owned, joint public-private, and privately owned broadcast media; 27 TV stations, with most operating on multiple channels, including 1 state-operated station with multiple locations and 11 stations either jointly operated or privately owned, some with several locations; multi-channel cable and satellite systems; 84 radio stations, including 1 state-owned broadcaster with multiple stations and a mix of public and private broadcasters; one international broadcaster is available, as well as one TV station that is jointly run by China and the Ministry of Interior; several TV and radio operators broadcast online only (often via Facebook) (2019)

Internet country code: .kh

Internet users: *percent of population:* 61% (2023 est.)

Broadband - fixed subscriptions: *total:* 510,000 (2022 est.) Slowly increase as focus is on mobile internet
subscriptions per 100 inhabitants: 3 (2022 est.)
comparison ranking: total 96

TRANSPORTATION

Civil aircraft registration country code prefix: XU

Airports: 12 (2025)
comparison ranking: 153

Heliports: 1 (2025)
comparison ranking: 151

Railways: *total:* 642 km (2014)
narrow gauge: 642 km (2014) 1.000-m gauge
note: under restoration

Merchant marine: *total:* 195 (2023)
by type: container ship 2, general cargo 123, oil tanker 18, other 52
comparison ranking: total 69

Ports: *total ports:* 2 (2024)
large: 0
medium: 1
small: 0
very small: 1
ports with oil terminals: 1
key ports: Kampong Saom, Phsar Ream

MILITARY AND SECURITY

Military and security forces: Royal Cambodian Armed Forces (RCAF): Royal Cambodian Army, Royal Khmer Navy, Royal Cambodian Air Force, Royal Gendarmerie (Military Police); National Committee for Maritime Security (2025)
note 1: the National Committee for Maritime Security performs coast guard functions and has representation from military and civilian agencies
note 2: the Cambodian National Police are under the Ministry of Interior

Military expenditures: 1.5% of GDP (2024 est.)
1.5% of GDP (2023 est.)
2.1% of GDP (2022 est.)
2.3% of GDP (2021 est.)
2.3% of GDP (2020 est.)

Military and security service personnel strengths: information varies; estimated 200,000 Armed Forces, including Gendarmerie (2025)

Military equipment inventories and acquisitions: the RCAF is armed largely with older Chinese and Russian-origin equipment; in recent years it has received limited amounts of more modern equipment from several suppliers, particularly China (2024)
note: in December 2021, the US Government halted arms-related trade with Cambodia, citing deepening Chinese military influence, corruption, and human rights abuses by the government and armed forces; the policy of denial applied to licenses or other approvals for exports and imports of defense articles and defense services destined for or originating in Cambodia, with exceptions (on a case-by-case basis) related to conventional weapons destruction and humanitarian demining activities

Military service age and obligation: 18 is the legal minimum age for military service for men and women (2025)
note: in 2006, Cambodia's parliament approved a law requiring all Cambodians aged 18 to 30 to serve in the military for 18 months, although the law has never been enforced (service was to be voluntary for women); in 2025, the Cambodian Government announced that the 2006 conscription law would be enforced beginning in 2026 and have a 24-month service requirement

Military deployments: 340 Central African Republic (MINUSCA); 180 Lebanon (UNIFIL) (2024)

Military - note: the primary responsibilities of the Royal Cambodian Armed Forces (RCAF) are border, coastal, and internal security; key security partners include China and Vietnam; in July 2025, following months of rising tensions, the RCAF and the military forces of Thailand clashed in multiple locations along their disputed border; both sides blamed the other for provoking the five-day conflict, which included cross-border artillery shelling by both sides and air attacks by RTARF fighter aircraft and drones
the RCAF was re-established in 1993 under the first coalition government from the merger of the Cambodian Government's military forces (Cambodian People's Armed Forces) and the two non-communist resistance forces (Sihanoukist National Army, aka National Army for Khmer Independence, and the Khmer People's National Liberation Armed Forces); thousands of communist Khmer Rouge fighters began surrendering by 1994 under a government amnesty program and the last of the Khmer Rouge forces (National Army of Democratic Kampuchea) were demobilized or absorbed into the RCAF in 1999 (2025)

TRANSNATIONAL ISSUES

Refugees and internally displaced persons: *refugees:* 28 (2024 est.)

IDPs: 2,526 (2024 est.)
stateless persons: 75,000 (2024 est.)

Trafficking in persons: *tier rating:* Tier 3 — Cambodia does not fully meet the minimum standards for the elimination of trafficking and is not making significant efforts to do so, therefore, Cambodia remained on Tier 3; for more details, go to: https://www.state.gov/reports/2025-trafficking-in-persons-report/cambodia/

CAMEROON

INTRODUCTION

Background: Powerful chiefdoms ruled much of the area of present-day Cameroon before it became a German colony known as Kamerun in 1884. After World War I, the territory was divided between France and the UK as League of Nations mandates. French Cameroon became independent in 1960 as the Republic of Cameroon. The following year, the southern portion of neighboring British Cameroon voted to merge with the new country to form the Federal Republic of Cameroon. In 1972, a new constitution replaced the federation with a unitary state, the United Republic of Cameroon. The country has generally enjoyed stability, which has enabled the development of agriculture, roads, and railways, as well as a petroleum industry. Nonetheless, unrest and violence in the country's two western, English-speaking regions have persisted since 2016. Movement toward democratic reform is slow, and political power remains firmly in the hands of President Paul BIYA.

GEOGRAPHY

Location: Central Africa, bordering the Bight of Biafra, between Equatorial Guinea and Nigeria

Geographic coordinates: 6 00 N, 12 00 E

Map references: Africa

Area: *total:* 475,440 sq km
land: 472,710 sq km
water: 2,730 sq km
comparison ranking: total 56

Area - comparative: slightly larger than California; about four times the size of Pennsylvania

Land boundaries: *total:* 5,018 km
border countries (6): Central African Republic 901 km; Chad 1,116 km; Republic of the Congo 494 km; Equatorial Guinea 183 km; Gabon 349 km; Nigeria 1975 km

Coastline: 402 km

Maritime claims: *territorial sea:* 12 nm
contiguous zone: 24 nm

Climate: varies with terrain, from tropical along coast to semiarid and hot in north

Terrain: diverse, with coastal plain in southwest, dissected plateau in center, mountains in west, plains in north

Elevation: *highest point:* Fako on Mont Cameroun 4,045 m
lowest point: Atlantic Ocean 0 m
mean elevation: 667 m

Natural resources: petroleum, bauxite, iron ore, timber, hydropower

Land use: *agricultural land:* 20.6% (2022 est.)
arable land: 13.1% (2022 est.)
permanent crops: 3.3% (2022 est.)
permanent pasture: 4.2% (2022 est.)
forest: 42.8% (2022 est.)
other: 36.6% (2022 est.)

Irrigated land: 290 sq km (2012)

Major lakes (area sq km): *fresh water lake(s):* Lake Chad (endorheic lake shared with Niger, Nigeria, and Chad) - 10,360-25,900 sq km
note - area varies by season and year to year

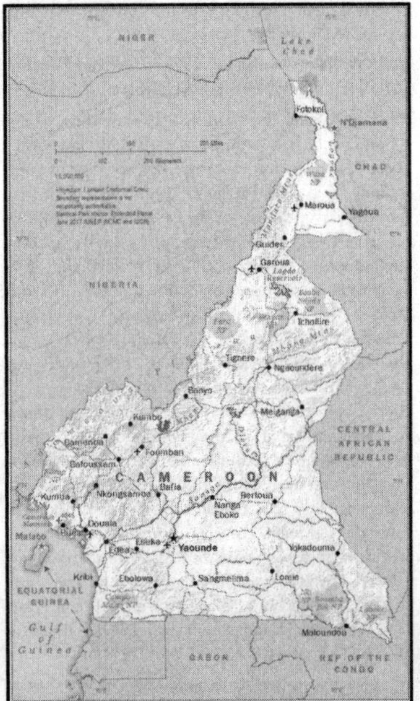

Major watersheds (area sq km): Atlantic Ocean drainage: Congo (3,730,881 sq km), Niger (2,261,741 sq km)

Internal (endorheic basin) drainage: Lake Chad (2,497,738 sq km)

Major aquifers: Lake Chad Basin

Population distribution: population concentrated in the west and north, with the interior of the country sparsely populated, as shown in this population distribution map

Natural hazards: volcanic activity with periodic releases of poisonous gases from Lake Nyos and Lake Monoun volcanoes
volcanism: Mt. Cameroon (4,095 m), which last erupted in 2000, is the most frequently active volcano in West Africa; lakes in the Oku volcanic field sometimes release fatal levels of gas, which killed about 1,700 people in 1986

Geography - note: sometimes referred to as the hinge of Africa because of its central location on the continent and its position at the west-south juncture of the Gulf of Guinea; areas of thermal springs and indications of current or prior volcanic activity; Mount Cameroon, the highest mountain in Sub-Saharan west Africa, is an active volcano

PEOPLE AND SOCIETY

Population: *total:* 30,966,105 (2024 est.)
male: 15,429,588
female: 15,536,517
comparison rankings: total 51; male 50; female 51

Nationality: *noun:* Cameroonian(s)
adjective: Cameroonian

Ethnic groups: Bamileke-Bamu 22.2%, Biu-Mandara 16.4%, Arab-Choa/Hausa/Kanuri 13.5%, Beti/Bassa, Mbam 13.1%, Grassfields 9.9%, Adamawa-Ubangi, 9.8%, Cotier/Ngoe/Oroko 4.6%, Southwestern Bantu 4.3%, Kako/Meka 2.3%, foreign/other ethnic group 3.8% (2022 est.)

Languages: 24 major African language groups, English (official), French (official)
major-language sample(s):
The World Factbook, une source indispensable d'informations de base. (French)

Religions: Roman Catholic 33.1%, Muslim 30.6%, Protestant 27.1% other Christian 6.1%, animist 1.3%, other 0.7%, none 1.2% (2022 est.)

Age structure: *0-14 years:* 41.5% (male 6,477,438/female 6,364,987)
15-64 years: 55.3% (male 8,488,522/female 8,638,519)
65 years and over: 3.2% (2024 est.) (male 463,628/female 533,011)

Dependency ratios: *total dependency ratio:* 80.8 (2024 est.)
youth dependency ratio: 75 (2024 est.)
elderly dependency ratio: 5.8 (2024 est.)
potential support ratio: 17.2 (2024 est.)

Median age: *total:* 18.9 years (2024 est.)
male: 18.6 years
female: 19.2 years
comparison ranking: total 216

Population growth rate: 2.71% (2024 est.)
comparison ranking: 14

Birth rate: 34.7 births/1,000 population (2024 est.)
comparison ranking: 13

Death rate: 7.4 deaths/1,000 population (2024 est.)
comparison ranking: 102

Net migration rate: -0.3 migrant(s)/1,000 population (2024 est.)
comparison ranking: 114

Population distribution: population concentrated in the west and north, with the interior of the country sparsely populated, as shown in this population distribution map

Urbanization: *urban population:* 59.3% of total population (2023)
rate of urbanization: 3.43% annual rate of change (2020-25 est.)

Major urban areas - population: 4.509 million YAOUNDE (capital), 4.063 million Douala (2023)

Sex ratio: *at birth:* 1.03 male(s)/female
0-14 years: 1.02 male(s)/female
15-64 years: 0.98 male(s)/female
65 years and over: 0.87 male(s)/female
total population: 0.99 male(s)/female (2024 est.)

Mother's mean age at first birth: 20.1 years (2018 est.)
note: data represents median age at first birth among women 25-49

Maternal mortality ratio: 258 deaths/100,000 live births (2023 est.)
comparison ranking: 28

Infant mortality rate: *total:* 46.1 deaths/1,000 live births (2024 est.)
male: 50.8 deaths/1,000 live births
female: 41.3 deaths/1,000 live births
comparison ranking: total 23

Life expectancy at birth: *total population:* 64.2 years (2024 est.)
male: 62.3 years
female: 66.1 years
comparison ranking: total population 209

Total fertility rate: 4.44 children born/woman (2024 est.)
comparison ranking: 16

Gross reproduction rate: 2.19 (2024 est.)

Drinking water source: *improved: urban:* 81.6% of population (2022 est.)
rural: 52.5% of population (2022 est.)
total: 69.6% of population (2022 est.)
unimproved: urban: 18.4% of population (2022 est.)
rural: 47.5% of population (2022 est.)
total: 30.4% of population (2022 est.)

Health expenditure: 3.8% of GDP (2021)
3.9% of national budget (2022 est.)

Physician density: 0.14 physicians/1,000 population (2022)

Hospital bed density: 2.6 beds/1,000 population (2016 est.)

Sanitation facility access: *improved: urban:* 83.2% of population (2022 est.)
rural: 27.4% of population (2022 est.)
total: 60.2% of population (2022 est.)
unimproved: urban: 16.8% of population (2022 est.)
rural: 72.6% of population (2022 est.)
total: 39.8% of population (2022 est.)

Obesity - adult prevalence rate: 11.4% (2016)
comparison ranking: 135

Alcohol consumption per capita: *total:* 4.09 liters of pure alcohol (2019 est.)
beer: 2.36 liters of pure alcohol (2019 est.)
wine: 0.16 liters of pure alcohol (2019 est.)
spirits: 0.01 liters of pure alcohol (2019 est.)
other alcohols: 1.56 liters of pure alcohol (2019 est.)
comparison ranking: total 94

Tobacco use: *total:* 5% (2025 est.)
male: 9.2% (2025 est.)
female: 0.9% (2025 est.)
comparison ranking: total 160

Children under the age of 5 years underweight: 11% (2018/19)
comparison ranking: 48

Currently married women (ages 15-49): 54.2% (2023 est.)

Child marriage: *women married by age 15:* 10.7% (2018)
women married by age 18: 29.8% (2018)
men married by age 18: 2.9% (2018)

Education expenditure: 2.8% of GDP (2023 est.)
13.1% national budget (2023 est.)
comparison ranking: Education expenditure (% GDP) 163

Literacy: *total population:* 72.5% (2018 est.)
male: 79.7% (2018 est.)
female: 66.2% (2018 est.)

School life expectancy (primary to tertiary education): *total:* 11 years (2023 est.)
male: 12 years (2023 est.)
female: 10 years (2023 est.)

ENVIRONMENT

Environmental issues: deforestation; overgrazing; soil erosion; desertification; poaching; overfishing; overhunting

International environmental agreements: *party to:* Biodiversity, Climate Change, Climate Change-Kyoto Protocol, Climate Change-Paris Agreement, Comprehensive Nuclear Test Ban, Desertification, Endangered Species, Environmental Modification, Hazardous Wastes, Law of the Sea, Ozone Layer Protection, Ship Pollution, Tropical Timber 2006, Wetlands, Whaling
signed, but not ratified: Nuclear Test Ban

Climate: varies with terrain, from tropical along coast to semiarid and hot in north

Urbanization: *urban population:* 59.3% of total population (2023)
rate of urbanization: 3.43% annual rate of change (2020-25 est.)

Carbon dioxide emissions: 6.707 million metric tonnes of CO2 (2023 est.)
from coal and metallurgical coke: 200 metric tonnes of CO2 (2023 est.)
from petroleum and other liquids: 5.658 million metric tonnes of CO2 (2023 est.)
from consumed natural gas: 1.049 million metric tonnes of CO2 (2023 est.)
comparison ranking: total emissions 127

Particulate matter emissions: 62 micrograms per cubic meter (2019 est.)

Methane emissions: *energy:* 293.3 kt (2022-2024 est.)
agriculture: 278.2 kt (2019-2021 est.)
waste: 166.4 kt (2019-2021 est.)
other: 24 kt (2019-2021 est.)

Waste and recycling: *municipal solid waste generated annually:* 3.271 million tons (2024 est.)
percent of municipal solid waste recycled: 4.6% (2022 est.)

Total water withdrawal: *municipal:* 246.8 million cubic meters (2022 est.)
industrial: 104.6 million cubic meters (2022 est.)
agricultural: 737 million cubic meters (2022 est.)

Total renewable water resources: 283.15 billion cubic meters (2022 est.)

GOVERNMENT

Country name: *conventional long form:* Republic of Cameroon
conventional short form: Cameroon
local long form: République du Cameroun (French)/ Republic of Cameroon (English)
local short form: Cameroun/Cameroon
former: Kamerun, French Cameroon, British Cameroon, Federal Republic of Cameroon, United Republic of Cameroon
etymology: in the 16th century, Portuguese explorers named an estuary near the mouth of the Wouri River the Rio dos Camaroes (River of Prawns) after the abundant shrimp in the water; the name Camaroes evolved into "Cameroon"

Government type: presidential republic

Capital: *name:* Yaounde
geographic coordinates: 3 52 N, 11 31 E
time difference: UTC+1 (6 hours ahead of Washington, DC, during Standard Time)
etymology: Germans founded the city in 1888, but the name comes from the native Ewondo people; the meaning of the name is unclear

Administrative divisions: 10 regions (*régions*, singular - *région*); Adamaoua, Centre, East (Est), Far North (Extrême-Nord), Littoral, North (Nord), North-West (Nord-Ouest), West (Ouest), South (Sud), South-West (Sud-Ouest)

Legal system: mixed system of English common law, French civil law, and customary law

Constitution: *history:* several previous; latest effective 18 January 1996
amendment process: proposed by the president of the republic or by Parliament; amendment drafts require approval of at least one third of the membership in either house of Parliament; passage requires absolute majority vote of the Parliament membership; passage of drafts requested by the president for a second reading in Parliament requires two-thirds majority vote of its membership; the president can opt to submit drafts to a referendum, in which case passage requires a simple majority; constitutional articles on Cameroon's unity and territorial integrity and its democratic principles cannot be amended

International law organization participation: accepts compulsory ICJ jurisdiction; non-party state to the ICCt

Citizenship: *citizenship by birth:* no
citizenship by descent only: at least one parent must be a citizen of Cameroon
dual citizenship recognized: no
residency requirement for naturalization: 5 years

Suffrage: 20 years of age; universal

Executive branch: *chief of state:* President Paul BIYA (since 6 November 1982)
head of government: Prime Minister Joseph NGUTE (since 4 January 2019)
cabinet: Cabinet proposed by the prime minister, appointed by the president
election/appointment process: president directly elected by simple-majority popular vote for a 7-year term (no term limits); prime minister appointed by the president
most recent election date: 7 October 2018
election results: *2018:* Paul BIYA reelected president; percent of vote - Paul BIYA (CPDM) 71.3%, Maurice KAMTO (MRC) 14.2%, Cabral LIBII (Univers) 6.3%, other 8.2%
2011: Paul BIYA reelected president; percent of vote - Paul BIYA (CPDM) 78.0%, John FRU NDI (SDF) 10.7%, Garga Haman ADJI 3.2%, other 8.1% (2018)
expected date of next election: October 2025

Legislative branch: *legislature name:* Parlement - Parliament
legislative structure: bicameral

Legislative branch - lower chamber: *chamber name:* National Assembly (Assemblée nationale - National Assembly)
number of seats: 180 (all directly elected)
electoral system: proportional representation
scope of elections: full renewal
term in office: 5 years
most recent election date: 2/9/2020 to 3/22/2020
parties elected and seats per party: Cameroon People's Democratic Movement (RDPC/CPDM) (152); Other (28)
percentage of women in chamber: 33.9%
expected date of next election: February 2026

Legislative branch - upper chamber: *chamber name:* Senate (Sénat - Senate)
number of seats: 100 (70 indirectly elected; 30 appointed)
scope of elections: full renewal
term in office: 5 years
most recent election date: 3/12/2023
percentage of women in chamber: 33%
expected date of next election: March 2027

Judicial branch: *highest court(s):* Supreme Court of Cameroon (consists of 9 titular and 6 surrogate judges and organized into judicial, administrative, and audit chambers); Constitutional Council (consists of 11 members)
judge selection and term of office: Supreme Court judges appointed by the president with the advice of the Higher Judicial Council of Cameroon, a body chaired by the president and includes the minister of justice, selected magistrates, and representatives of the National Assembly; judge term NA; Constitutional Council members appointed by the president for renewable 6-year terms
subordinate courts: Parliamentary Court of Justice (jurisdiction limited to cases involving the president and prime minister); appellate and first instance courts; circuit and magistrates' courts

Political parties: Alliance for Democracy and Development
Cameroon People's Democratic Movement or CPDM
Cameroon People's Party or CPP
Cameroon Renaissance Movement or MRC
Cameroonian Democratic Union or UDC
Cameroonian Party for National Reconciliation or PCRN
Front for the National Salvation of Cameroon or FSNC
Movement for the Defense of the Republic or MDR
Movement for the Liberation and Development of Cameroon or MLDC
National Union for Democracy and Progress or UNDP
Progressive Movement or MP
Social Democratic Front or SDF
Union of Peoples of Cameroon or UPC
Union of Socialist Movements

Diplomatic representation in the US: *chief of mission:* Ambassador Henri ETOUNDI ESSOMBA (since 27 June 2016)
chancery: 2349 Massachusetts Avenue NW, Washington, DC 20008
telephone: [1] (202) 265-8790
FAX: [1] (202) 387-3826
email address and website: mail@cameroonembassyusa
Cameroon Embassy in Washington DC, USA (cameroonembassyusa.org)

Diplomatic representation from the US: *chief of mission:* Ambassador Christopher J. LAMORA (since 21 March 2022)
embassy: Avenue Rosa Parks, Yaoundé
mailing address: 2520 Yaounde Place, Washington, DC 20521-2520
telephone: [237] 22251-4000
FAX: [237] 22251-4000, Ext. 4531
email address and website: YaoundeACS@state.gov
https://cm.usembassy.gov/
branch office(s): Douala

International organization participation: ACP, AfDB, AU, BDEAC, C, CEMAC, EITI (compliant country), FAO, FZ, G-77, IAEA, IBRD, ICAO, ICRM, IDA, IDB, IFAD, IFC, IFRCS, IHO, ILO, IMF, IMO, IMSO, Interpol, IOC, IOM, IPU, ISO, ITSO, ITU, ITUC (NGOs), LCBC, MIGA, MNJTF, MONUSCO, NAM, OIC, OIF, OPCW, PCA, UN, UNCTAD, UNESCO, UNHRC, UNIDO, UNMISS, UNWTO, UPU, WCO, WFTU (NGOs), WHO, WIPO, WMO, WTO

Independence: 1 January 1960 (from French-administered UN trusteeship)

National holiday: State Unification Day (National Day), 20 May (1972)

Flag: *description:* three equal vertical bands of green (left side), red, and yellow, with a small five-pointed yellow star centered in the red band
meaning: red stands for unity; yellow for the sun, happiness, and the northern savannahs; green for hope and the southern forests; the star is called the "star of unity;" the vertical tricolor design is similar to the French flag
history: uses the colors of the Pan-African movement

National symbol(s): lion

National color(s): green, red, yellow

National anthem(s): *title:* "O Cameroun, Berceau de Nos Ancêtres" (O Cameroon, Cradle of Our Forefathers)
lyrics/music: Rene Djam AFAME, Samuel Minkio BAMBA, Moise Nyatte NKO'O [French], Benard Nsokika FONLON [English]/Rene Djam AFAME
history: adopted 1957; lyrics were changed slightly to the current version in 1978

National heritage: *total World Heritage Sites:* 2 (both natural)
selected World Heritage Site locales: Dja Faunal Reserve; Sangha Trinational Forest

ECONOMY

Economic overview: largest CEMAC economy with many natural resources; recent political instability and terrorism reducing economic output; systemic corruption; poor property rights enforcement; increasing poverty in northern regions

Real GDP (purchasing power parity): $143.264 billion (2024 est.)
$138.191 billion (2023 est.)
$133.843 billion (2022 est.)
note: data in 2021 dollars
comparison ranking: 85

Real GDP growth rate: 3.7% (2024 est.)
3.2% (2023 est.)
3.7% (2022 est.)
note: annual GDP % growth based on constant local currency
comparison ranking: 87

Real GDP per capita: $4,900 (2024 est.)
$4,900 (2023 est.)
$4,800 (2022 est.)
note: data in 2021 dollars
comparison ranking: 174

GDP (official exchange rate): $51.327 billion (2024 est.)
note: data in current dollars at official exchange rate

Inflation rate (consumer prices): 4.5% (2024 est.)
7.4% (2023 est.)
6.2% (2022 est.)
note: annual % change based on consumer prices
comparison ranking: 137

GDP - composition, by sector of origin: *agriculture:* 17.4% (2024 est.)
industry: 25.6% (2024 est.)
services: 49.9% (2024 est.)
note: figures may not total 100% due to non-allocated consumption not captured in sector-reported data
comparison rankings: agriculture 43; industry 81; services 147

GDP - composition, by end use: *household consumption:* 74.5% (2024 est.)
government consumption: 10.5% (2024 est.)
investment in fixed capital: 21.4% (2024 est.)
investment in inventories: 0% (2024 est.)
exports of goods and services: 14.7% (2024 est.)
imports of goods and services: -21.1% (2024 est.)
note: figures may not total 100% due to rounding or gaps in data collection

Agricultural products: cassava, plantains, oil palm fruit, maize, taro, tomatoes, sorghum, sugarcane, bananas, vegetables (2023)
note: top ten agricultural products based on tonnage

Industries: petroleum production and refining, aluminum production, food processing, light consumer goods, textiles, lumber, ship repair

Industrial production growth rate: 1.9% (2024 est.)
note: annual % change in industrial value added based on constant local currency
comparison ranking: 101

Labor force: 11.119 million (2024 est.)
note: number of people ages 15 or older who are employed or seeking work
comparison ranking: 51

Unemployment rate: 3.6% (2024 est.)
3.7% (2023 est.)
3.7% (2022 est.)
note: % of labor force seeking employment
comparison ranking: 58

Youth unemployment rate (ages 15-24): *total:* 6.2% (2024 est.)
male: 5.9% (2024 est.)
female: 6.7% (2024 est.)
note: % of labor force ages 15-24 seeking employment
comparison ranking: total 155

Gini Index coefficient - distribution of family income: 42.2 (2021 est.)
note: index (0-100) of income distribution; higher values represent greater inequality
comparison ranking: 32

Average household expenditures: *on food:* 45.8% of household expenditures (2023 est.)
on alcohol and tobacco: 2.9% of household expenditures (2023 est.)

Household income or consumption by percentage share: *lowest 10%:* 2.1% (2021 est.)
highest 10%: 31.1% (2021 est.)
note: % share of income accruing to lowest and highest 10% of population

Remittances: 1.6% of GDP (2023 est.)
1.3% of GDP (2022 est.)
1% of GDP (2021 est.)
note: personal transfers and compensation between resident and non-resident individuals/households/entities

Budget: *revenues:* $6.385 billion (2021 est.)
expenditures: $7.624 billion (2021 est.)
note: central government revenues and expenses (excluding grants/extrabudgetary units/social security funds) converted to US dollars at average official exchange rate for year indicated

Taxes and other revenues: 11.3% (of GDP) (2021 est.)
note: central government tax revenue as a % of GDP
comparison ranking: 123

Current account balance: -$2.019 billion (2023 est.)
-$1.505 billion (2022 est.)
-$1.794 billion (2021 est.)
note: balance of payments - net trade and primary/secondary income in current dollars
comparison ranking: 149

Exports: $8.353 billion (2023 est.)
$8.641 billion (2022 est.)
$7.447 billion (2021 est.)
note: balance of payments - exports of goods and services in current dollars
comparison ranking: 123

Exports - partners: Netherlands 21%, France 14%, UAE 13%, India 9%, China 8% (2023)
note: top five export partners based on percentage share of exports

Exports - commodities: crude petroleum, natural gas, gold, cocoa beans, wood (2023)
note: top five export commodities based on value in dollars

Imports: $10.294 billion (2023 est.)
$9.759 billion (2022 est.)
$9.025 billion (2021 est.)
note: balance of payments - imports of goods and services in current dollars
comparison ranking: 121

Imports - partners: China 43%, France 6%, India 6%, Belgium 4%, UAE 4% (2023)
note: top five import partners based on percentage share of imports

Imports - commodities: garments, refined petroleum, plastic products, wheat, rice (2023)
note: top five import commodities based on value in dollars

Reserves of foreign exchange and gold: $4.882 billion (2023 est.)
$5.133 billion (2022 est.)
$4.3 billion (2021 est.)
note: holdings of gold (year-end prices)/foreign exchange/special drawing rights in current dollars
comparison ranking: 102

Debt - external: $11.112 billion (2023 est.)
note: present value of external debt in current US dollars
comparison ranking: 48

Exchange rates: Cooperation Financiere en Afrique Centrale francs (XAF) per US dollar -

Exchange rates: 606.345 (2024 est.)
606.57 (2023 est.)
623.76 (2022 est.)
554.531 (2021 est.)
575.586 (2020 est.)

ENERGY

Electricity access: *electrification - total population:* 71% (2022 est.)
electrification - urban areas: 94%
electrification - rural areas: 25%

Electricity: *installed generating capacity:* 1.798 million kW (2023 est.)
consumption: 6.161 billion kWh (2023 est.)
imports: 60 million kWh (2023 est.)
transmission/distribution losses: 2.238 billion kWh (2023 est.)
comparison rankings: installed generating capacity 123; consumption 124; imports 115; transmission/distribution losses 128

Electricity generation sources: *fossil fuels:* 36.1% of total installed capacity (2023 est.)
solar: 0.3% of total installed capacity (2023 est.)
hydroelectricity: 63.1% of total installed capacity (2023 est.)
biomass and waste: 0.5% of total installed capacity (2023 est.)

Coal: *imports:* 300 metric tons (2023 est.)

Petroleum: *total petroleum production:* 64,000 bbl/day (2023 est.)
refined petroleum consumption: 41,000 bbl/day (2023 est.)
crude oil estimated reserves: 200 million barrels (2021 est.)

Natural gas: *production:* 2.356 billion cubic meters (2023 est.)

consumption: 534.691 million cubic meters (2023 est.)
exports: 1.821 billion cubic meters (2023 est.)
proven reserves: 135.071 billion cubic meters (2021 est.)

Energy consumption per capita: 4.271 million Btu/person (2023 est.)
comparison ranking: 173

COMMUNICATIONS

Telephones - fixed lines: *total subscriptions:* 896,000 (2022 est.)
subscriptions per 100 inhabitants: 3 (2022 est.)
comparison ranking: total subscriptions 70

Telephones - mobile cellular: *total subscriptions:* 26.2 million (2023 est.)
subscriptions per 100 inhabitants: 83 (2022 est.)
comparison ranking: total subscriptions 51

Broadcast media: government maintains tight control over broadcast media; state-owned Cameroon Radio Television (CRTV), with both TV and radio broadcasts, was the only officially recognized and fully licensed broadcaster until 2007, when the government issued licenses to 2 private TV broadcasters and 1 private radio broadcaster; about 70 privately owned, unlicensed radio stations operate under "administrative tolerance," meaning the stations could be subject to closure at any time (2023)

Internet country code: .cm

Internet users: *percent of population:* 42% (2023 est.)

Broadband - fixed subscriptions: *total:* 603,000 (2022 est.)
subscriptions per 100 inhabitants: 2 (2022 est.)
comparison ranking: total 90

TRANSPORTATION

Civil aircraft registration country code prefix: TJ

Airports: 37 (2025)
comparison ranking: 108

Heliports: 1 (2025)
comparison ranking: 153

Railways: *total:* 987 km (2014)
narrow gauge: 987 km (2014) 1.000-m gauge
note: railway connections generally efficient but limited; rail lines connect major cities of Douala, Yaounde, Ngaoundere, and Garoua; passenger and freight service provided by CAMRAIL

Merchant marine: *total:* 198 (2023)
by type: bulk carrier 2, general cargo 91, oil tanker 42, other 63
comparison ranking: total 67

Ports: *total ports:* 7 (2024)
large: 0
medium: 1
small: 0
very small: 5
size unknown: 1
ports with oil terminals: 5
key ports: Douala, Ebome Marine Terminal, Kole Oil Terminal, Kome Kribi 1 Marine Terminal, Kribi Deep Sea Port, Limboh Terminal, Moudi Marine Terminal

MILITARY AND SECURITY

Military and security forces: Cameroon Armed Forces (Forces Armees Camerounaises, FAC): Army, Cameroon Navy (includes naval infantry or fusiliers marin), Air Force, National Gendarmerie, National Firefighting Corps

General Delegation for National Security (Délégation Générale à la Sûreté Nationale or DGSN): Cameroon Police (2025)
note 1: the Army includes the Rapid Intervention Brigade (Brigade d'Intervention Rapide or BIR), which maintains its own command and control structure and reports directly to the Chief of Defense staff and the Presidency; the BIR includes airborne/airmobile, amphibious, armored reconnaissance, artillery, and counterterrorism forces, as well as support elements, such as intelligence
note 2: the Cameroon Police and the National Gendarmerie are responsible for internal security; the Gendarmerie conducts administrative, criminal, and military investigative functions; other missions include customs, air and maritime surveillance, and road traffic control; in times of conflict, it participates in internal defense

Military expenditures: 1% of GDP (2024 est.)
1% of GDP (2023 est.)
1% of GDP (2022 est.)
1% of GDP (2021 est.)
1% of GDP (2020 est.)

Military and security service personnel strengths: estimated 40-50,000 active FAC, including the Gendarmerie (2025)

Military equipment inventories and acquisitions: the FAC inventory is comprised of weapons and equipment from a variety of countries, including China, Israel, Russia/former Soviet Union, South Africa, the US, and some Western European countries, particularly France (2024)

Military service age and obligation: 18-24 years of age for voluntary military service for men and women; no conscription; high school graduation required; service obligation 4 years (2024)

Military deployments: 750 (plus about 350 police) Central African Republic (MINUSCA) (2024)
note: Cameroon has committed approximately 2,000-2,500 troops to the Multinational Joint Task Force (MNJTF) against Boko Haram and other terrorist groups operating in the general area of the Lake Chad Basin and along Nigeria's northeast border; national MNJTF troop contingents are deployed within their own country territories, although cross-border operations occur occasionally

Military - note: the Cameroon Armed Forces (FAC) are responsible for defending the country's territorial integrity, providing humanitarian assistance, supporting regional peacekeeping operations, and contributing to internal security; key areas of focus are the threat from the terrorist groups Boko Haram and ISIS-West Africa along its frontiers with Nigeria and Chad (Far North region) and, since 2016, an insurgency from armed Anglophone separatist groups in the North-West and South-West regions; in addition, the FAC often deploys ground units to the border region with the Central African Republic to counter intrusions from armed militias and bandits; the Navy's missions include protecting Cameroon's oil installations, combatting crime and piracy in the Gulf of Guinea, and patrolling the country's lakes and rivers; the FAC's small Air Force supports both the ground and naval forces (2025)

TERRORISM

Terrorist group(s): Terrorist group(s): Boko Haram; Islamic State of Iraq and ash-Sham – West Africa
note: details about the history, aims, leadership, organization, areas of operation, tactics, targets, weapons, size, and sources of support of the group(s) appear(s) in Appendix T

TRANSNATIONAL ISSUES

Refugees and internally displaced persons: *refugees:* 443,740 (2024 est.)

IDPs: 1,058,405 (2024 est.)

CANADA

INTRODUCTION

Background: A land of vast distances and rich natural resources, Canada became a self-governing dominion in 1867, while retaining ties to the British crown. Canada gained legislative independence from Britain in 1931 and formalized its constitutional independence from the UK when it passed the Canada Act in 1982. Economically and technologically, the nation has developed in parallel with the US, its neighbor to the south across the world's longest international border. Canada faces the political challenges of meeting public demands for quality improvements in health care, education, social services, and economic competitiveness, as well as responding to the particular concerns of predominantly francophone Quebec. Canada also aims to develop its diverse energy resources while maintaining its commitment to the environment.

GEOGRAPHY

Location: Northern North America, bordering the North Atlantic Ocean on the east, North Pacific Ocean on the west, and the Arctic Ocean on the north, north of the conterminous US

Geographic coordinates: 60 00 N, 95 00 W

Map references: North America

Area: *total:* 9,984,670 sq km
land: 9,093,507 sq km
water: 891,163 sq km
comparison ranking: total 3

Area - comparative: slightly larger than the US

Land boundaries: *total:* 8,892 km
border countries (2): US 8,891 km (includes 2,475 km with Alaska); Denmark (Greenland) 1.3 km

Coastline: 202,080 km
note: the Canadian Arctic Archipelago – consisting of 36,563 islands, several of them among the world's

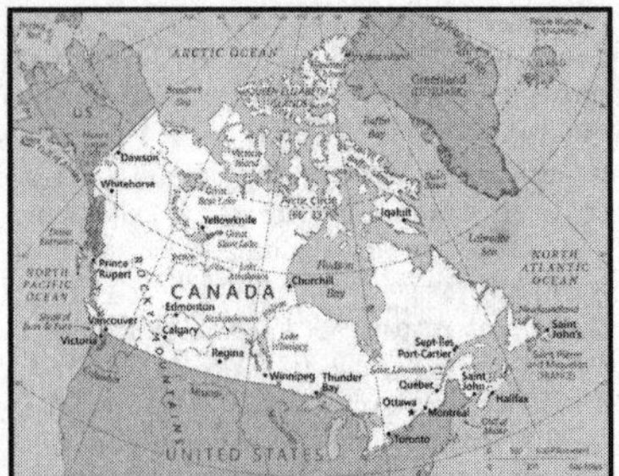

largest – gives Canada the longest coastline in the world

Maritime claims: *territorial sea:* 12 nm
contiguous zone: 24 nm
exclusive economic zone: 200 nm
continental shelf: 200 nm or to the edge of the continental margin

Climate: varies from temperate in south to subarctic and arctic in north

Terrain: mostly plains with mountains in west, lowlands in southeast

Elevation: *highest point:* Mount Logan 5,959 m
lowest point: Atlantic/Pacific/Arctic Oceans 0 m
mean elevation: 487 m

Natural resources: bauxite, iron ore, nickel, zinc, copper, gold, lead, uranium, rare earth elements, molybdenum, potash, diamonds, silver, fish, timber, wildlife, coal, petroleum, natural gas, hydropower

Land use: *agricultural land:* 6.5% (2022 est.)
arable land: 4.4% (2022 est.)
permanent crops: 0% (2022 est.)
permanent pasture: 2.1% (2022 est.)
forest: 39.5% (2022 est.)
other: 54% (2022 est.)

Irrigated land: 9,045 sq km (2015)

Major lakes (area sq km): *fresh water lake(s):* Huron* - 35,972 sq km; Great Bear Lake - 31,328 sq km; Superior* - 28,754 sq km; Great Slave Lake - 28,568 sq km; Lake Winnipeg - 24,387 sq km; Erie* - 12,776 sq km; Ontario* - 9,790 sq km; Lake Athabasca - 7,935 sq km; Reindeer Lake - 6,650 sq km; Nettilling Lake - 5,542 sq km
note - Great Lakes* area shown as Canadian waters

Major rivers (by length in km): Mackenzie - 4,241 km; Yukon river source (shared with the US [m]) - 3,185 km; Saint Lawrence river mouth (shared with US) - 3,058 km; Nelson - 2,570 km; Columbia river source (shared with the US [m]) - 1,953 km; Churchill - 1,600 km; Fraser - 1,368 km; Ottawa - 1,271 km; Athabasca - 1,231 km; North Saskatchewan - 1,220 km; Liard - 1,115 km
note: [s] after country name indicates river source; [m] after country name indicates river mouth

Major watersheds (area sq km): Arctic Ocean drainage: Mackenzie (1,706,388 sq km)

Atlantic Ocean drainage: Mississippi* *(Gulf of America)* (3,202,185 sq km, Canada only 32,000 sq km), Nelson *(Hudson Bay)* (1,093,141 sq km), Saint Lawrence* (1,049,636 sq km, Canada only 839,200 sq km)

Pacific Ocean drainage: Yukon* (847,620 sq km, Canada only 823,800 sq km), Columbia* (657,501 sq km, Canada only 103,000 sq km)
note: watersheds shared with the US shown with *

Major aquifers: Northern Great Plains Aquifer

Population distribution: vast majority of the population lives in a discontinuous band within approximately 300 km (186 mi) of the southern border with the United States; the most populated province is Ontario, followed by Quebec and British Columbia

Natural hazards: continuous permafrost in north is a serious obstacle to development; cyclonic storms form east of the Rocky Mountains, a result of the mixing of air masses from the Arctic, Pacific, and North American interior, and produce most of the country's rain and snow east of the mountains
volcanism: the vast majority of volcanoes in Western Canada's Coast Mountains remain dormant

Geography - note: *note 1:* second-largest country in the world (after Russia) and largest in the Americas; strategic location between Russia and US via north polar route; approximately 90% of the population is concentrated within 160 km (100 mi) of the US border
note 2: Canada has more fresh water than any other country, and almost 9% of Canadian territory is water; Canada has at least 2 million and possibly over 3 million lakes, more than all other countries combined

PEOPLE AND SOCIETY

Population: *total:* 38,794,813 (2024 est.)
male: 19,234,729
female: 19,560,084
comparison rankings: total 37; male 38; female 38

Nationality: *noun:* Canadian(s)
adjective: Canadian

Ethnic groups: Canadian 15.6%, English 14.7%, Scottish 12.1%, French 11%, Irish 12.1%, German 8.1%, Chinese 4.7%, Italian 4.3%, First Nations 1.7%, Indian 3.7%, Ukrainian 3.5%, Metis 1.5% (2021 est.)
note: percentages add up to more than 100% because respondents were able to identify more than one ethnic origin

Languages: English (official) 87.1%, French (official) 29.1%, Chinese languages 4.2%, Spanish 3.2%, Punjabi 2.6%, Arabic 2.4%, Tagalog 2.3%, Italian 1.5% (2022 est.)
major-language sample(s):
The World Factbook, une source indispensable d'informations de base. (French)

Religions: Christian 53.3%, Muslim 4.9%, Hindu 2.3%, Sikh 2.1%, Buddhist 1%, Jewish 0.9%, Traditional (North American Indigenous) 0.2%, other religions and traditional spirituality 0.6%, none 34.6% (2021 est.)

Age structure: *0-14 years:* 15.5% (male 3,098,478/female 2,929,148)
15-64 years: 63.4% (male 12,382,422/female 12,227,512)
65 years and over: 21% (2024 est.) (male 3,753,829/female 4,403,424)

Dependency ratios: *total dependency ratio:* 56.8 (2024 est.)
youth dependency ratio: 23.9 (2024 est.)
elderly dependency ratio: 32.9 (2024 est.)
potential support ratio: 3 (2024 est.)

Median age: *total:* 42.6 years (2024 est.)
male: 41.4 years
female: 43.8 years
comparison ranking: total 40

Population growth rate: 0.71% (2024 est.)
comparison ranking: 125

Birth rate: 10 births/1,000 population (2024 est.)
comparison ranking: 186

Death rate: 8.2 deaths/1,000 population (2024 est.)
comparison ranking: 82

Net migration rate: 5.3 migrant(s)/1,000 population (2024 est.)
comparison ranking: 19

Population distribution: vast majority of the population lives in a discontinuous band within approximately 300 km (186 mi) of the southern border with the United States; the most populated province is Ontario, followed by Quebec and British Columbia

Urbanization: *urban population:* 81.9% of total population (2023)
rate of urbanization: 0.95% annual rate of change (2020-25 est.)

Major urban areas - population: 6.372 million Toronto, 4.308 million Montreal, 2.657 million Vancouver, 1.640 million Calgary, 1.544 million Edmonton, 1.437 million OTTAWA (capital) (2023)

Sex ratio: *at birth:* 1.05 male(s)/female
0-14 years: 1.06 male(s)/female
15-64 years: 1.01 male(s)/female
65 years and over: 0.85 male(s)/female
total population: 0.98 male(s)/female (2024 est.)

Mother's mean age at first birth: 29.4 years (2019 est.)

Maternal mortality ratio: 12 deaths/100,000 live births (2023 est.)
comparison ranking: 143

Infant mortality rate: *total:* 4.3 deaths/1,000 live births (2024 est.)
male: 4.5 deaths/1,000 live births
female: 4 deaths/1,000 live births
comparison ranking: total 185

Life expectancy at birth: *total population:* 84.2 years (2024 est.)
male: 81.9 years
female: 86.6 years
comparison ranking: total population 5

Total fertility rate: 1.58 children born/woman (2024 est.)
comparison ranking: 189

Gross reproduction rate: 0.77 (2024 est.)

Drinking water source: *improved: urban:* 99.3% of population (2022 est.)
rural: 99.1% of population (2022 est.)
total: 99.2% of population (2022 est.)
unimproved: urban: 0.7% of population (2022 est.)
rural: 0.9% of population (2022 est.)
total: 0.8% of population (2022 est.)

Health expenditure: 11.2% of GDP (2022)
19.5% of national budget (2022 est.)

Physician density: 2.82 physicians/1,000 population (2023)

Hospital bed density: 2.6 beds/1,000 population (2020 est.)

Sanitation facility access: *improved: urban:* 98.6% of population (2022 est.)
rural: 98.8% of population (2022 est.)
total: 98.6% of population (2022 est.)
unimproved: urban: 1.4% of population (2022 est.)
rural: 1.2% of population (2022 est.)
total: 1.4% of population (2022 est.)

Obesity - adult prevalence rate: 29.4% (2016)
comparison ranking: 26

Alcohol consumption per capita: *total:* 8 liters of pure alcohol (2019 est.)

beer: 3.5 liters of pure alcohol (2019 est.)
wine: 2 liters of pure alcohol (2019 est.)
spirits: 2.1 liters of pure alcohol (2019 est.)
other alcohols: 0.4 liters of pure alcohol (2019 est.)
comparison ranking: total 44

Tobacco use: *total:* 10.1% (2025 est.)
male: 12.3% (2025 est.)
female: 8% (2025 est.)
comparison ranking: total 126

Currently married women (ages 15-49): 52.2% (2023 est.)

Education expenditure: 4.5% of GDP (2023 est.)
11.2% national budget (2023 est.)
comparison ranking: Education expenditure (% GDP) 86

School life expectancy (primary to tertiary education): *total:* 16 years (2022 est.)
male: 15 years (2022 est.)
female: 17 years (2022 est.)

ENVIRONMENT

Environmental issues: air pollution and acid rain from vehicle emissions, coal-burning, and metal smelting severely affecting lakes and forests; seawater pollution from agriculture, industry, mining, and forestry

International environmental agreements: *party to:* Air Pollution, Air Pollution-Heavy Metals, Air Pollution-Multi-effect Protocol, Air Pollution-Nitrogen Oxides, Air Pollution-Persistent Organic Pollutants, Air Pollution-Sulphur 85, Air Pollution-Sulphur 94, Antarctic-Environmental Protection, Antarctic-Marine Living Resources, Antarctic Treaty, Biodiversity, Climate Change, Climate Change-Paris Agreement, Comprehensive Nuclear Test Ban, Desertification, Endangered Species, Environmental Modification, Hazardous Wastes, Law of the Sea, Marine Dumping-London Convention, Marine Dumping-London Protocol, Nuclear Test Ban, Ozone Layer Protection, Ship Pollution, Wetlands
signed, but not ratified: Air Pollution-Volatile Organic Compounds, Marine Life Conservation

Climate: varies from temperate in south to subarctic and arctic in north

Urbanization: *urban population:* 81.9% of total population (2023)
rate of urbanization: 0.95% annual rate of change (2020-25 est.)

Carbon dioxide emissions: 585.853 million metric tonnes of CO2 (2023 est.)
from coal and metallurgical coke: 32.486 million metric tonnes of CO2 (2023 est.)
from petroleum and other liquids: 294.196 million metric tonnes of CO2 (2023 est.)
from consumed natural gas: 259.171 million metric tonnes of CO2 (2023 est.)
comparison ranking: total emissions 11

Particulate matter emissions: 6.7 micrograms per cubic meter (2019 est.)

Methane emissions: *energy:* 2,787.3 kt (2022-2024 est.)
agriculture: 1,049.8 kt (2019-2021 est.)
waste: 816.7 kt (2019-2021 est.)
other: 39.3 kt (2019-2021 est.)

Waste and recycling: *municipal solid waste generated annually:* 25.103 million tons (2024 est.)
percent of municipal solid waste recycled: 23.1% (2022 est.)

Total water withdrawal: *municipal:* 4.869 billion cubic meters (2022 est.)
industrial: 27.357 billion cubic meters (2022 est.)
agricultural: 3.859 billion cubic meters (2022 est.)

Total renewable water resources: 2.902 trillion cubic meters (2022 est.)

Geoparks: *total global geoparks and regional networks:* 5
global geoparks and regional networks: Perce; Stonehammer; Tumbler Ridge; Cliffs of Fundy; Discovery (2023)

GOVERNMENT

Country name: *conventional long form:* none
conventional short form: Canada
etymology: the name is probably derived from the Huron or Iroquois word *kanata*, meaning village or camp

Government type: federal parliamentary democracy (Parliament of Canada) under a constitutional monarchy; a Commonwealth realm; federal and state authorities and responsibilities regulated in constitution

Capital: *name:* Ottawa
geographic coordinates: 45 25 N, 75 42 W
time difference: UTC-5 (same time as Washington, DC, during Standard Time)
daylight saving time: +1hr, begins second Sunday in March; ends first Sunday in November
time zone note: Canada has six time zones
etymology: the city lies on the south bank of the Ottawa River, from which it derives its name; the river name comes from the Algonquin word *adawe*, meaning "to trade"

Administrative divisions: 10 provinces and 3 territories*; Alberta, British Columbia, Manitoba, New Brunswick, Newfoundland and Labrador, Northwest Territories*, Nova Scotia, Nunavut*, Ontario, Prince Edward Island, Québec, Saskatchewan, Yukon*

Legal system: common law system except in Quebec, where civil law based on the French civil code prevails

Constitution: *history:* consists of unwritten and written acts, customs, judicial decisions, and traditions dating from 1763; the written part of the constitution consists of the Constitution Act of 29 March 1867, which created a federation of four provinces, and the Constitution Act of 17 April 1982
amendment process: proposed by either house of Parliament or by the provincial legislative assemblies; there are 5 methods for passage though most require approval by both houses of Parliament, approval of at least two thirds of the provincial legislative assemblies and assent and formalization as a proclamation by the governor general in council; the most restrictive method is reserved for amendments affecting fundamental sections of the constitution, such as the office of the monarch or the governor general, and the constitutional amendment procedures, which require unanimous approval by both houses and by all the provincial assemblies, and assent of the governor general in council

International law organization participation: accepts compulsory ICJ jurisdiction with reservations; accepts ICCt jurisdiction

Citizenship: *citizenship by birth:* yes
citizenship by descent only: yes
dual citizenship recognized: yes
residency requirement for naturalization: minimum of 3 of last 5 years resident in Canada

Suffrage: 18 years of age; universal

Executive branch: *chief of state:* King CHARLES III (since 8 September 2022); represented by Governor General Mary SIMON (since 26 July 2021)
head of government: Prime Minister Mark CARNEY (since 14 March 2025)
cabinet: Federal Ministry chosen by the prime minister usually from among members of his/her own party sitting in Parliament
election/appointment process: the monarchy is hereditary; governor general appointed by the monarch on the advice of the prime minister for a 5-year term; after legislative elections, the governor general usually designates the leader of the majority party or majority coalition in the House of Commons as prime minister
note: the governor general position is largely ceremonial

Legislative branch: *legislature name:* Parliament of Canada - Parlement du Canada
legislative structure: bicameral

Legislative branch - lower chamber: *chamber name:* House of Commons
number of seats: 343 (all directly elected)
electoral system: plurality/majority
scope of elections: full renewal
term in office: 4 years
most recent election date: 4/28/2025
parties elected and seats per party: Liberal Party (169); Conservative Party (144); Bloc Québécois (BQ) (22); Other (8)
percentage of women in chamber: 30.3%
expected date of next election: October 2029

Legislative branch - upper chamber: *chamber name:* Senate
number of seats: 105 (all appointed)
percentage of women in chamber: 54.8%

Judicial branch: *highest court(s):* Supreme Court of Canada (consists of the chief justice and 8 judges)
judge selection and term of office: chief justice and judges appointed by the prime minister in council; all judges appointed for life with mandatory retirement at age 75
subordinate courts: federal level: Federal Court of Appeal; Federal Court; Tax Court; federal administrative tribunals; Courts Martial; provincial/territorial level: provincial superior, appeals, first instance, and specialized courts
note: in 1999, the Nunavut Court – a circuit court with the power of a provincial superior court, as well as a territorial court – was established to serve isolated settlements

Political parties: Bloc Quebecois
Conservative Party of Canada or CPC
Green Party
Liberal Party
New Democratic Party or NDP
People's Party of Canada

Diplomatic representation in the US: *chief of mission:* Ambassador Kirsten HILLMAN (since 17 July 2020)
chancery: 501 Pennsylvania Avenue NW, Washington, DC 20001
telephone: [1] (844) 880-6519

FAX: [1] (202) 682-7738
email address and website: ccs.scc@international.gc.ca
https://www.international.gc.ca/country-pays/us-eu/washington.aspx?lang=eng
consulate(s) general: Atlanta, Boston, Chicago, Dallas, Denver, Detroit, Los Angeles, Miami, Minneapolis, New York, San Francisco, Seattle

trade office(s): Houston, Palo Alto (CA), San Diego; note - there are trade offices in the Consulates General

Diplomatic representation from the US: *chief of mission:* Ambassador Pete HOEKSTRA (since 29 April 2025)
embassy: 490 Sussex Drive, Ottawa, Ontario K1N 1G8
mailing address: 5480 Ottawa Place, Washington DC 20521-5480
telephone: [1] (613) 688-5335
FAX: [1] (613) 241-7845
email address and website: OttawaNIV@state.gov
https://ca.usembassy.gov/
consulate(s) general: Calgary, Halifax, Montreal, Quebec City, Toronto, Vancouver
consulate(s): Winnipeg

International organization participation: ADB (nonregional member), AfDB (nonregional member), APEC, Arctic Council, ARF, ASEAN (dialogue partner), Australia Group, BIS, C, CD, CDB, CE (observer), EAPC, EBRD, EITI (implementing country), FAO, FATF, G-7, G-8, G-10, G-20, IADB, IAEA, IBRD, ICAO, ICC (national committees), ICCt, ICRM, IDA, IEA, IFAD, IFC, IFRCS, IGAD (partners), IHO, ILO, IMF, IMO, IMSO, Interpol, IOC, IOM, IPU, ISO, ITSO, ITU, ITUC (NGOs), MIGA, MINUSTAH, MONUSCO, NAFTA, NATO, NEA, NSG, OAS, OECD, OIF, OPCW, OSCE, Pacific Alliance (observer), Paris Club, PCA, PIF (partner), UN, UNCTAD, UNESCO, UNFICYP, UNHCR, UNMISS, UNRWA, UNTSO, UPU, USMCA, Wassenaar Arrangement, WCO, WFTU (NGOs), WHO, WIPO, WMO, WTO, ZC

Independence: 1 July 1867 (union of British North American colonies); 11 December 1931 (recognized by UK per Statute of Westminster)

National holiday: Canada Day, 1 July (1867)

Flag: *description:* two vertical bands of red on each side, with a white square between them; a large 11-pointed red maple leaf is centered in the white square
meaning: the maple leaf is a national symbol

National symbol(s): maple leaf, beaver

National color(s): red, white

National anthem(s): *title:* "O Canada"
lyrics/music: Adolphe-Basile ROUTHIER [French], Robert Stanley WEIR [English]/Calixa LAVALLEE
history: adopted 1980; originally written in 1880, it served as an unofficial anthem for many years; the original version had four verses, but the anthem today officially consists of one verse in French and one in English
title: "God Save the King"
lyrics/music: unknown
history: royal anthem, as a Commonwealth country

National heritage: *total World Heritage Sites:* 22 (10 cultural, 11 natural, 1 mixed) (2021)
selected World Heritage Site locales: L'Anse aux Meadows (c); Canadian Rocky Mountain Parks (n); Dinosaur Provincial Park (n); Historic District of Old Quebec (c); Old Town Lunenburg (c); Wood Buffalo National Park (n); Head-Smashed-In Buffalo Jump (c); Gros Morne National Park (n); Pimachiowin Aki (m)

ECONOMY

Economic overview: high-income economy and second-largest US trading partner; key timber, oil, and gas industries; trade uncertainties and weak business investments contributing to economic slowdown; high and growing public debt; inflation moderating but remains above target range

Real GDP (purchasing power parity): $2.341 trillion (2024 est.)
$2.305 trillion (2023 est.)
$2.271 trillion (2022 est.)
note: data in 2021 dollars
comparison ranking: 16

Real GDP growth rate: 1.5% (2024 est.)
1.5% (2023 est.)
4.2% (2022 est.)
note: annual GDP % growth based on constant local currency
comparison ranking: 163

Real GDP per capita: $56,700 (2024 est.)
$57,500 (2023 est.)
$58,300 (2022 est.)
note: data in 2021 dollars
comparison ranking: 33

GDP (official exchange rate): $2.241 trillion (2024 est.)
note: data in current dollars at official exchange rate

Inflation rate (consumer prices): 2.4% (2024 est.)
3.9% (2023 est.)
6.8% (2022 est.)
note: annual % change based on consumer prices
comparison ranking: 69

GDP - composition, by sector of origin: *agriculture:* 1.6% (2021 est.)
industry: 25.3% (2021 est.)
services: 66.4% (2021 est.)
note: figures may not total 100% due to non-allocated consumption not captured in sector-reported data
comparison rankings: agriculture 162; industry 87; services 48

GDP - composition, by end use: *household consumption:* 54.4% (2023 est.)
government consumption: 20.9% (2023 est.)
investment in fixed capital: 22.9% (2023 est.)
investment in inventories: 1% (2023 est.)
exports of goods and services: 33.3% (2023 est.)
imports of goods and services: -33.3% (2023 est.)
note: figures may not total 100% due to rounding or gaps in data collection

Agricultural products: wheat, rapeseed, maize, milk, barley, soybeans, potatoes, peas, oats, pork (2023)
note: top ten agricultural products based on tonnage

Industries: transportation equipment, chemicals, processed and unprocessed minerals, food products, wood and paper products, fish products, petroleum, natural gas

Industrial production growth rate: 0% (2024 est.)
note: annual % change in industrial value added based on constant local currency
comparison ranking: 136

Labor force: 22.868 million (2024 est.)
note: number of people ages 15 or older who are employed or seeking work
comparison ranking: 30

Unemployment rate: 6.5% (2024 est.)
5.5% (2023 est.)
5.3% (2022 est.)
note: % of labor force seeking employment
comparison ranking: 120

Youth unemployment rate (ages 15-24): *total:* 13% (2024 est.)
male: 13.8% (2024 est.)
female: 12.1% (2024 est.)
note: % of labor force ages 15-24 seeking employment
comparison ranking: total 96

Gini Index coefficient - distribution of family income: 29.9 (2020 est.)
note: index (0-100) of income distribution; higher values represent greater inequality
comparison ranking: 121

Average household expenditures: *on food:* 9.7% of household expenditures (2023 est.)
on alcohol and tobacco: 3.5% of household expenditures (2023 est.)

Household income or consumption by percentage share: *lowest 10%:* 3.5% (2020 est.)
highest 10%: 23.4% (2020 est.)
note: % share of income accruing to lowest and highest 10% of population

Remittances: 0% of GDP (2024 est.)
0% of GDP (2023 est.)
0% of GDP (2022 est.)
note: personal transfers and compensation between resident and non-resident individuals/households/entities

Budget: *revenues:* $428.312 billion (2023 est.)
expenditures: $417.421 billion (2023 est.)
note: central government revenues (excluding grants) and expenditures converted to US dollars at average official exchange rate for year indicated

Public debt: 61.3% of GDP (2023 est.)
note: central government debt as a % of GDP
comparison ranking: 75

Taxes and other revenues: 13.8% (of GDP) (2023 est.)
note: central government tax revenue as a % of GDP
comparison ranking: 101

Current account balance: -$10.349 billion (2024 est.)
-$13.764 billion (2023 est.)
-$6.318 billion (2022 est.)
note: balance of payments - net trade and primary/secondary income in current dollars
comparison ranking: 183

Exports: $727.831 billion (2024 est.)
$724.754 billion (2023 est.)
$743.782 billion (2022 est.)
note: balance of payments - exports of goods and services in current dollars
comparison ranking: 14

Exports - partners: USA 71%, China 5%, UK 3%, Japan 2%, Mexico 2% (2023)
note: top five export partners based on percentage share of exports

Exports - commodities: crude petroleum, cars, gold, natural gas, refined petroleum (2023)
note: top five export commodities based on value in dollars

Imports: $733.778 billion (2024 est.)
$723.399 billion (2023 est.)
$731.058 billion (2022 est.)
note: balance of payments - imports of goods and services in current dollars
comparison ranking: 11

Imports - partners: USA 51%, China 11%, Mexico 6%, Germany 3%, Japan 3% (2023)
note: top five import partners based on percentage share of imports

Imports - commodities: cars, trucks, vehicle parts/accessories, refined petroleum, crude petroleum (2023)
note: top five import commodities based on value in dollars

Reserves of foreign exchange and gold: $119.778 billion (2024 est.)
$117.551 billion (2023 est.)
$106.952 billion (2022 est.)
note: holdings of gold (year-end prices)/foreign exchange/special drawing rights in current dollars
comparison ranking: 24

Exchange rates: Canadian dollars (CAD) per US dollar -

Exchange rates: 1.369 (2024 est.)
1.35 (2023 est.)
1.302 (2022 est.)
1.254 (2021 est.)
1.341 (2020 est.)

ENERGY

Electricity access: *electrification - total population:* 100% (2022 est.)

Electricity: *installed generating capacity:* 161.988 million kW (2023 est.)
consumption: 555.683 billion kWh (2023 est.)
exports: 49.444 billion kWh (2023 est.)
imports: 21.77 billion kWh (2023 est.)
transmission/distribution losses: 31.784 billion kWh (2023 est.)
comparison rankings: installed generating capacity 8; consumption 8; exports 3; imports 9; transmission/distribution losses 199

Electricity generation sources: *fossil fuels:* 18.9% of total installed capacity (2023 est.)
nuclear: 13.7% of total installed capacity (2023 est.)
solar: 1.4% of total installed capacity (2023 est.)
wind: 6% of total installed capacity (2023 est.)
hydroelectricity: 58.6% of total installed capacity (2023 est.)
biomass and waste: 1.4% of total installed capacity (2023 est.)

Nuclear energy: Number of operational nuclear reactors: 17 (2025)

Net capacity of operational nuclear reactors: 12.71GW (2025 est.)

Percent of total electricity production: 13.7% (2023 est.)

Number of nuclear reactors permanently shut down: 8 (2025)

Coal: *production:* 50.687 million metric tons (2023 est.)
consumption: 20.092 million metric tons (2023 est.)
exports: 35.447 million metric tons (2023 est.)
imports: 7.03 million metric tons (2023 est.)
proven reserves: 6.582 billion metric tons (2023 est.)

Petroleum: *total petroleum production:* 5.688 million bbl/day (2023 est.)
refined petroleum consumption: 2.377 million bbl/day (2024 est.)
crude oil estimated reserves: 170.3 billion barrels (2021 est.)

Natural gas: *production:* 194.105 billion cubic meters (2023 est.)
consumption: 131.887 billion cubic meters (2023 est.)
exports: 82.537 billion cubic meters (2023 est.)
imports: 29.058 billion cubic meters (2023 est.)
proven reserves: 2.067 trillion cubic meters (2021 est.)

Energy consumption per capita: 311.599 million Btu/person (2023 est.)
comparison ranking: 8

COMMUNICATIONS

Telephones - fixed lines: *total subscriptions:* 10.897 million (2023 est.)
subscriptions per 100 inhabitants: 28 (2023 est.)
comparison ranking: total subscriptions 16

Telephones - mobile cellular: *total subscriptions:* 36.5 million (2023 est.)
subscriptions per 100 inhabitants: 91 (2022 est.)
comparison ranking: total subscriptions 44

Broadcast media: 2 public TV broadcasting networks, 1 in English and 1 in French, each with a large number of network affiliates; several private commercial networks, also with multiple network affiliates; a total of about 150 TV stations, accessible via multi-channel satellite and cable systems; mix of public and commercial radio, with over 1,000 licensed stations; public broadcaster Canadian Broadcasting Corporation (CBC) provides 4 radio networks, Radio Canada International, and radio services to ethnic populations in the north (2016)

Internet country code: .ca

Internet users: *percent of population:* 94% (2023 est.)

Broadband - fixed subscriptions: *total:* 17 million (2023 est.)
subscriptions per 100 inhabitants: 43 (2023 est.)
comparison ranking: total 16

TRANSPORTATION

Civil aircraft registration country code prefix: C

Airports: 1,459 (2025)
comparison ranking: 5

Heliports: 506 (2025)
comparison ranking: 5

Railways: *total:* 49,422 km (2021) note: 129 km electrified (2021)
standard gauge: 49,422 km (2021) 1.435-m gauge

Merchant marine: *total:* 716 (2023)
by type: bulk carrier 22, container ship 1, general cargo 78, oil tanker 15, other 600
comparison ranking: total 32

Ports: *total ports:* 284 (2024)
large: 4
medium: 14
small: 58
very small: 149
size unknown: 59
ports with oil terminals: 59
key ports: Argentia, Canaport (St. John), Halifax, Hamilton, Montreal, New Westminster, Pond Inlet, Prince Rupert, Quebec, Sept Iles, St. John, Sydney, Thunder Bay, Toronto, Trois Rivieres, Vancouver, Victoria Harbor, Windsor

MILITARY AND SECURITY

Military and security forces: Canadian Forces: Canadian Army, Royal Canadian Navy, Royal Canadian Air Force (2025)
note 1: the CAF is comprised of both a Regular Force and a Reserve Force; the Reserve Force is comprised of the Primary Reserve, Canadian Rangers, Cadet Organizations Administration and Training Service, and the Supplementary Reserve; the Canadian Rangers are part of the Army Reserve Force and provide a limited presence in Canada's northern, coastal, and isolated areas for sovereignty, public safety, and surveillance roles
note 2: the Royal Canadian Mounted Police (RCMP or "Mounties") is under the Department of Public Safety; the Coast Guard is under the Department of Fisheries and Oceans

Military expenditures: 2% of GDP (2025 est.)
1.5% of GDP (2024 est.)
1.3% of GDP (2023 est.)
1.2% of GDP (2022 est.)
1.3% of GDP (2021 est.)

Military and security service personnel strengths: approximately 75,000 active-duty military personnel (2025)

Military equipment inventories and acquisitions: the CAF's inventory is a mix of domestically produced equipment and imported weapons systems from Australia, Europe, Israel, and the US; in recent years, the leading supplier has been the US; Canada's defense industry develops, maintains, and produces a range of equipment, including aircraft, combat vehicles, naval vessels, and associated components (2024)

Military service age and obligation: 17 years of age for voluntary male and female military service (with parental consent); 16 years of age for Reserve and Military College applicants; Canadian citizenship or permanent residence status required; maximum 34 years of age; service obligation 3-9 years (2023)
note 1: Canada opened up all military occupations to women in 2001; women in 2023 comprised about 16% of the CAF
note 2: the CAF offers waivers to foreign nationals applying for military service only in exceptional cases — to individuals on international military exchanges, for example, or to candidates who have specialized skills in high demand

Military deployments: the CAF has approximately 1,000 military personnel forward deployed for NATO air, land, and sea missions in the European theater, including a ground task force in Latvia; it also contributes smaller numbers of air, ground, and naval forces to a variety of other NATO and international missions (2024)
note: in 2024, Canada announced plans to have a full 2,000-person brigade deployed to Latvia by 2026

Military - note: the Canadian Armed Forces (CAF) are responsible for external security; the CAF's core missions include detecting, deterring, and defending against threats to or attacks on Canada; the military also provides assistance to civil authorities and law enforcement as needed for such missions as counterterrorism, search and rescue, and responding to natural disasters or other major emergencies; it regularly participates in bilateral and multinational training exercises with a variety of partners, including NATO (Canada is one of the original members) and the US; the CAF also contributes to international peacekeeping, stability, humanitarian, combat, and capacity building operations, principally through NATO, but also with the UN and other security partners
Canada is part of the North American Aerospace Defense Command (NORAD; established 1958); NORAD is a Canada/US bi-national military command responsible for monitoring and defending North American airspace; traditionally, a CAF officer has served as the deputy commander of NORAD; Canada's defense relationship with the US extends back to the Ogdensburg Declaration of 1940, when the two countries formally agreed on military

cooperation, including the establishment of the Permanent Joint Board on Defense (PJBD), which continues to be the highest-level bilateral defense forum between Canada and the US
British troops withdrew from Canada in 1871 as part of the US-UK Treaty of Washington; following the withdrawal, the first Canadian militia, known as the Royal Canadian Regiment, was organized in 1883 to protect Canadian territory and defend British interests abroad, which it did in the South African War (1899-1902), Canada's first overseas conflict; militia units formed the backbone of the more than 425,000 Canadian soldiers that went to Europe during World War I in what was called the Canadian Expeditionary Force; the Royal Canadian Navy was created in 1910, while the Canadian Air Force was established in 1920 and became the Royal Canadian Air Force in 1924; the Canadian Army was officially founded in 1942; a unified Canadian Armed Forces was created in 1968 (2025)

SPACE

Space agency/agencies: Canadian Space Agency (CSA; established 1989) (2025)

Space launch site(s): developing commercial space port sites in Nova Scotia and Newfoundland (2025)
note: the Churchill Rocket Research Range in Manitoba was used for rocket testing from 1956-1985

Space program overview: has a substantial program, a national space strategy, and a long history of developing space-related technologies; designs, builds, operates, and tracks communications, remote sensing (RS), multi-mission, and scientific/testing satellites; has an astronaut program; designs, builds, or contributes to a variety of other space-related programs, including space telescopes, planetary probes, lunar rovers, sensors, and robotic systems (such as the Canadian-made robotic arms used on the US Space Shuttle and the International Space Station); participates in international space efforts and cooperates with a variety of foreign space agencies and commercial entities, including those of Argentina, Brazil, the European Space Agency (ESA)/EU (and their member states), India, and particularly the US; ESA Cooperating State since 1979; has a robust commercial space sector that is involved in navigation, optics, satellite communications, space exploration, and space science (2025)
note: further details about the key activities, programs, and milestones of the country's space program, as well as government spending estimates on the space sector, appear in the Space Programs reference guide

TERRORISM

Terrorist group(s): Terrorist group(s): Hizballah; Islamic State of Iraq and ash-Sham (ISIS)
note: details about the history, aims, leadership, organization, areas of operation, tactics, targets, weapons, size, and sources of support of the group(s) appear(s) in Appendix T

TRANSNATIONAL ISSUES

Refugees and internally displaced persons: *refugees:* 561,551 (2024 est.)

IDPs: 1,981 (2024 est.)
stateless persons: 8,166 (2024 est.)

Illicit drugs: USG identification: major precursor-chemical producer (2025)

CAYMAN ISLANDS

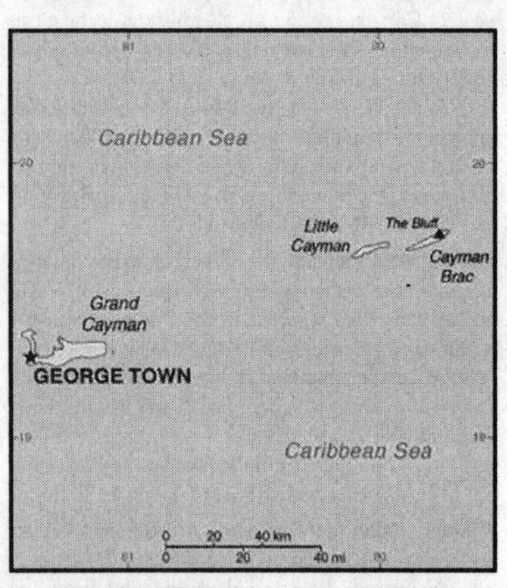

INTRODUCTION

Background: The British colonized the Cayman Islands during the 18th and 19th centuries, and Jamaica – also a British colony at the time – administered the islands after 1863. In 1959, the islands became a territory within the Federation of the West Indies. When the Federation dissolved in 1962, the Cayman Islands chose to remain a British dependency. The territory has transformed itself into a significant offshore financial center.

GEOGRAPHY

Location: Caribbean, three-island group (Grand Cayman, Cayman Brac, Little Cayman) in Caribbean Sea, 240 km south of Cuba and 268 km northwest of Jamaica

Geographic coordinates: 19 30 N, 80 30 W

Map references: Central America and the Caribbean

Area: *total:* 264 sq km
land: 264 sq km
water: 0 sq km
comparison ranking: total 210

Area - comparative: 1.5 times the size of Washington, D.C.

Land boundaries: *total:* 0 km

Coastline: 160 km

Maritime claims: *territorial sea:* 12 nm
exclusive economic zone: 200 nm
exclusive fishing zone: 200 nm

Climate: tropical marine; warm, rainy summers (May to October) and cool, relatively dry winters (November to April)

Terrain: low-lying limestone base surrounded by coral reefs

Elevation: *highest point:* 1 km SW of The Bluff on Cayman Brac 50 m
lowest point: Caribbean Sea 0 m

Natural resources: fish, climate and beaches that foster tourism

Land use: *agricultural land:* 11.3% (2022 est.)
arable land: 0.8% (2022 est.)
permanent crops: 2.1% (2022 est.)
permanent pasture: 8.3% (2022 est.)
forest: 52.7% (2022 est.)
other: 36.1% (2022 est.)

Irrigated land: NA

Population distribution: majority of the population resides on Grand Cayman

Natural hazards: hurricanes (July to November)

Geography - note: important location between Cuba and Central America

PEOPLE AND SOCIETY

Population: *total:* 66,653 (2024 est.)
male: 32,379
female: 34,274
comparison rankings: total 204; male 204; female 203

Nationality: *noun:* Caymanian(s)
adjective: Caymanian

Ethnic groups: Cayman Islander 35.4%, Jamaican 24.8%, Filipino 5.5%, British 5.3%, American 5.2%, Honduran 4.2%, Canadian 3.3%, Indian 2.1%, Cuban 1.6%, Nicaraguan 1%, other 11.1%, unspecified 0.5% (2021 est.)
note: data represent population by country of birth

Languages: English (official) 88.8%, Spanish 3.9%, Filipino 3.8%, other 2.8%, unspecified 0.7% (2021 est.)
note: data represent main language spoken at home

Religions: Protestant 60.8% (includes Church of God 19.5%, Seventh Day Adventist 8.7%, non-denominational 8.3%, Baptist 6.9%, Pentecostal 6.8%, Presbyterian/United Church 5.7%, Anglican 2.8%, Wesleyan Holiness 1.5%, Methodist 0.5%), Roman Catholic 13.6%, Hindu 1.7%, Jehovah's Witness 0.9%, other 4.8%, none 16.7%, unspecified 1.4% (2021 est.)

Age structure: *0-14 years:* 17.4% (male 5,845/female 5,767)
15-64 years: 65.9% (male 21,480/female 22,456)
65 years and over: 16.7% (2024 est.) (male 5,054/female 6,051)

Dependency ratios: *total dependency ratio:* 51.7 (2024 est.)
youth dependency ratio: 26.4 (2024 est.)
elderly dependency ratio: 25.3 (2024 est.)
potential support ratio: 4 (2024 est.)

Median age: *total:* 41.2 years (2024 est.)
male: 40.3 years
female: 42 years
comparison ranking: total 51

Population growth rate: 1.75% (2024 est.)
comparison ranking: 51

Birth rate: 11.5 births/1,000 population (2024 est.)

comparison ranking: 158

Death rate: 6.1 deaths/1,000 population (2024 est.)
comparison ranking: 149

Net migration rate: 12.1 migrant(s)/1,000 population (2024 est.)
comparison ranking: 5

Population distribution: majority of the population resides on Grand Cayman

Urbanization: *urban population:* 100% of total population (2023)
rate of urbanization: 1.13% annual rate of change (2020-25 est.)

Major urban areas - population: 35,000 GEORGE TOWN (capital) (2018)

Sex ratio: *at birth:* 1.02 male(s)/female
0-14 years: 1.01 male(s)/female
15-64 years: 0.96 male(s)/female
65 years and over: 0.84 male(s)/female
total population: 0.95 male(s)/female (2024 est.)

Infant mortality rate: *total:* 7.3 deaths/1,000 live births (2024 est.)
male: 8.8 deaths/1,000 live births
female: 5.7 deaths/1,000 live births
comparison ranking: total 154

Life expectancy at birth: *total population:* 82.5 years (2024 est.)
male: 79.8 years
female: 85.2 years
comparison ranking: total population 27

Total fertility rate: 1.82 children born/woman (2024 est.)
comparison ranking: 136

Gross reproduction rate: 0.9 (2024 est.)

Drinking water source: *improved: urban:* 95.5% of population (2022 est.)
total: 95.5% of population (2022 est.)
unimproved: urban: 4.5% of population (2022 est.)
total: 4.5% of population (2022 est.)

Sanitation facility access: *improved: urban:* 93.5% of population (2022 est.)
total: 93.5% of population (2022 est.)
unimproved: urban: 6.5% of population (2022 est.)
total: 6.5% of population (2022 est.)

Currently married women (ages 15-49): 51.4% (2023 est.)

Education expenditure: 1.5% of GDP (2022 est.)
15% national budget (2019 est.)
comparison ranking: Education expenditure (% GDP) 192

ENVIRONMENT

Environmental issues: no natural freshwater resources; trash washing up or being deposited on beaches; no recycling or waste-treatment facilities; deforestation

Climate: tropical marine; warm, rainy summers (May to October) and cool, relatively dry winters (November to April)

Urbanization: *urban population:* 100% of total population (2023)
rate of urbanization: 1.13% annual rate of change (2020-25 est.)

Carbon dioxide emissions: 737,000 metric tonnes of CO_2 (2023 est.)
from petroleum and other liquids: 737,000 metric tonnes of CO_2 (2023 est.)
comparison ranking: total emissions 177

Waste and recycling: *municipal solid waste generated annually:* 60,000 tons (2024 est.)

GOVERNMENT

Country name: *conventional long form:* none
conventional short form: Cayman Islands
etymology: Spanish explorers named the islands in the early 16th century, using the Carib word for marine crocodiles, *caiman*

Government type: parliamentary democracy; self-governing overseas territory of the UK

Dependency status: overseas territory of the UK

Capital: *name:* George Town (on Grand Cayman)
geographic coordinates: 19 18 N, 81 23 W
time difference: UTC-5 (same time as Washington, DC, during Standard Time)
etymology: originally named Hogstyes, the town was renamed in honor of English King GEORGE III (1738-1820) around 1800

Administrative divisions: 6 districts; Bodden Town, Cayman Brac and Little Cayman, East End, George Town, North Side, West Bay

Legal system: English common law and local statutes

Constitution: *history:* several previous; latest approved 10 June 2009, entered into force 6 November 2009 (The Cayman Islands Constitution Order 2009)

Citizenship: see United Kingdom

Suffrage: 18 years of age; universal

Executive branch: *chief of state:* King CHARLES III (since 8 September 2022); represented by Governor Jane OWEN (since 21 April 2023)
head of government: Premier André Martin EBANKS (since 6 May 2025)
cabinet: Cabinet selected from the Parliament and appointed by the governor on the advice of the premier
election/appointment process: the monarchy is hereditary; governor appointed by the monarch; following legislative elections, the governor appoints the leader of the majority party or majority coalition as premier

Legislative branch: *legislature name:* Parliament
legislative structure: unicameral
number of seats: 21 (directly elected and appointed)
scope of elections: full renewal
term in office: 4 years
most recent election date: 4/14/2021
parties elected and seats per party: independent (12); PPM (7)
percentage of women in chamber: 23.8%
expected date of next election: 2025

Judicial branch: *highest court(s):* Court of Appeal (consists of the court president and at least 2 judges); Grand Court (consists of the court president and at least 2 judges)
judge selection and term of office: Court of Appeal and Grand Court judges appointed by the governor on the advice of the Judicial and Legal Services Commission, an 8-member independent body consisting of governor appointees, Court of Appeal president, and attorneys; Court of Appeal judges' tenure based on their individual instruments of appointment; Grand Court judges normally appointed until retirement at age 65 but can be extended until age 70
subordinate courts: Summary Court
note: appeals beyond the Court of Appeal are heard by the Judicial Committee of the Privy Council (in London)

Political parties: Cayman Islands Peoples Party or CIPP
People's Progressive Movement or PPM

Diplomatic representation in the US: none (overseas territory of the UK)

Diplomatic representation from the US: *embassy:* none (overseas territory of the UK); consular services provided through the US Embassy in Jamaica

International organization participation: Caricom (associate), CDB, Interpol (subbureau), IOC, UNESCO (associate), UPU

Independence: none (overseas territory of the UK)

National holiday: Constitution Day, the first Monday in July (1959)

Flag: *description:* a blue field with the UK flag in the upper-left quadrant and the Caymanian coat of arms centered on the right half of the flag; the coat of arms has a pineapple, a turtle, a shield with a golden lion and three green stars, and a scroll below the shield with the motto HE HATH FOUNDED IT UPON THE SEAS
meaning: the pineapple represents ties to Jamaica; the turtle represents the Caymans' seafaring tradition; the lion symbolizes Great Britain; the green stars represent the three islands; the white and blue wavy lines on the coat of arms represent the sea

National symbol(s): green sea turtle

National coat of arms: the Queen of England approved the Cayman Islands' coat of arms – which was designed with input from the public – in 1958; the shield features the lion of England and three green stars that symbolize the three islands of Grand Cayman, Cayman Brac, and Little Cayman; the green turtle stands for the islands' seafaring history, the rope under it for the thatch-rope industry, and the pineapple for historical ties with Jamaica; the motto comes from Psalms 24, acknowledging the Caymans' Christian heritage

National anthem(s): *title:* "Beloved Isle Cayman"
lyrics/music: Leila E. ROSS
history: adopted 1960; served as an unofficial anthem since 1930
title: "God Save the King"
lyrics/music: unknown
history: official anthem, as an overseas UK territory

ECONOMY

Economic overview: dominant offshore banking territory; services sector accounts for over 85% of economic activity; recently adopted a fiscal responsibility framework to combat tax evasion and money laundering; large tourism sector; does not have any welfare system; high standard of living

Real GDP (purchasing power parity): $5.705 billion (2023 est.)
$5.467 billion (2022 est.)
$5.199 billion (2021 est.)
note: data in 2021 dollars
comparison ranking: 179

Real GDP growth rate: 4.4% (2023 est.)
5.2% (2022 est.)
4.9% (2021 est.)
note: annual GDP % growth based on constant local currency
comparison ranking: 56

Real GDP per capita: $78,100 (2023 est.)
$76,400 (2022 est.)
$74,200 (2021 est.)

note: data in 2021 dollars
comparison ranking: 12

GDP (official exchange rate): $7.139 billion (2023 est.)
note: data in current dollars at official exchange rate

Inflation rate (consumer prices): 2% (2017 est.)
-0.6% (2016 est.)
-2.3% (2015 est.)
note: annual % change based on consumer prices
comparison ranking: 49

GDP - composition, by sector of origin: *agriculture:* 0.5% (2022 est.)
industry: 8.2% (2022 est.)
services: 85.4% (2022 est.)
note: figures may not total 100% due to non-allocated consumption not captured in sector-reported data
comparison rankings: agriculture 191; industry 197; services 9

Agricultural products: vegetables, fruit; livestock; turtle farming

Industries: tourism, banking, insurance and finance, construction, construction materials, furniture

Industrial production growth rate: 3.4% (2022 est.)
note: annual % change in industrial value added based on constant local currency
comparison ranking: 72

Remittances: 0.2% of GDP (2023 est.)
0.2% of GDP (2022 est.)
0.2% of GDP (2021 est.)
note: personal transfers and compensation between resident and non-resident individuals/households/entities

Budget: *revenues:* $874.5 million (2017 est.)
expenditures: $766.6 million (2017 est.)

Current account balance: -$712.684 million (2023 est.)
-$749.482 million (2022 est.)
-$794.205 million (2021 est.)
note: balance of payments - net trade and primary/secondary income in current dollars
comparison ranking: 120

Exports: $4.6 billion (2023 est.)
$4.215 billion (2022 est.)
$3.542 billion (2021 est.)
note: balance of payments - exports of goods and services in current dollars
comparison ranking: 141

Exports - partners: UK 40%, Cyprus 21%, Germany 9%, Grenada 8%, Italy 5% (2023)
note: top five export partners based on percentage share of exports

Exports - commodities: aircraft, ships, refined petroleum, natural gas, broadcasting equipment (2023)
note: top five export commodities based on value in dollars

Imports: $3.444 billion (2023 est.)
$3.287 billion (2022 est.)
$2.808 billion (2021 est.)
note: balance of payments - imports of goods and services in current dollars
comparison ranking: 161

Imports - partners: Germany 30%, USA 29%, Italy 20%, Turkey 5%, China 5% (2023)
note: top five import partners based on percentage share of imports

Imports - commodities: ships, refined petroleum, cars, furniture, jewelry (2023)
note: top five import commodities based on value in dollars

Reserves of foreign exchange and gold: $234 million (2023 est.)
$225.4 million (2022 est.)
$228.3 million (2021 est.)
note: holdings of gold (year-end prices)/foreign exchange/special drawing rights in current dollars
comparison ranking: 172

Exchange rates: Caymanian dollars (KYD) per US dollar -

Exchange rates: 0.833 (2024 est.)
0.833 (2023 est.)
0.833 (2022 est.)
0.833 (2021 est.)
0.833 (2020 est.)

ENERGY

Electricity access: *electrification - total population:* 100% (2022 est.)

Electricity: *installed generating capacity:* 176,000 kW (2023 est.)
consumption: 698.767 million kWh (2023 est.)
transmission/distribution losses: 2.117 million kWh (2023 est.)
comparison rankings: installed generating capacity 176; consumption 167; transmission/distribution losses 6

Electricity generation sources: *fossil fuels:* 96.7% of total installed capacity (2023 est.)
solar: 3.1% of total installed capacity (2023 est.)
wind: 0.1% of total installed capacity (2023 est.)

Petroleum: *refined petroleum consumption:* 5,000 bbl/day (2023 est.)

Energy consumption per capita: 143.149 million Btu/person (2023 est.)
comparison ranking: 26

COMMUNICATIONS

Telephones - fixed lines: *total subscriptions:* 36,000 (2021 est.)
subscriptions per 100 inhabitants: 50 (2022 est.)
comparison ranking: total subscriptions 163

Telephones - mobile cellular: *total subscriptions:* 100,000 (2021 est.)
subscriptions per 100 inhabitants: 147 (2021 est.)
comparison ranking: total subscriptions 194

Broadcast media: 4 TV stations; cable and satellite subscription services offer international programming; government-owned Radio Cayman operates 2 networks broadcasting on 5 stations; 10 privately owned radio stations operate alongside Radio Cayman

Internet country code: .ky

Internet users: *percent of population:* 81% (2017 est.)

Broadband - fixed subscriptions: *total:* 40,000 (2022 est.)
subscriptions per 100 inhabitants: 56 (2022 est.)
comparison ranking: total 149

TRANSPORTATION

Civil aircraft registration country code prefix: VP-C

Airports: 3 (2025)
comparison ranking: 187

Heliports: 5 (2025)
comparison ranking: 100

Merchant marine: *total:* 130 (2023)
by type: bulk carrier 29, container ship 3, general cargo 1, oil tanker 20, other 77
comparison ranking: total 77

Ports: *total ports:* 2 (2024)
large: 0
medium: 0
small: 0
very small: 2
ports with oil terminals: 2
key ports: Cayman Brac, Georgetown

MILITARY AND SECURITY

Military and security forces: no regular military forces; Royal Cayman Islands Police Service

Military - note: defense is the responsibility of the UK

TRANSNATIONAL ISSUES

Refugees and internally displaced persons: *refugees:* 65 (2024 est.)

CENTRAL AFRICAN REPUBLIC

INTRODUCTION

Background: The Central African Republic (CAR) is a perennially weak state that sits at the crossroads of ethnic and linguistic groups in the center of the African continent. Among the last areas of Sub-Saharan Africa to be drawn into the world economy, its introduction into trade networks around the early 1700s fostered significant competition among its population. The local population sought to benefit from the lucrative Atlantic, trans-Saharan, and Indian Ocean trade in enslaved people and ivory. Slave raids aided by the local populations fostered animosity between ethnic groups that remains today. The territory was established as a French colony named Ubangui-Shari in 1903, and France modeled its administration of the colony after the Belgian Congo, subcontracting control of the territory to private companies that collected rubber and ivory. Although France banned the domestic slave trade in CAR in the 1910s, the private companies continued to exploit the population through forced labor. The colony of Ubangi-Shari gained independence from France as the Central African Republic in 1960, but the death of independence leader Barthelemy BOGANDA six months prior led to an immediate struggle for power.

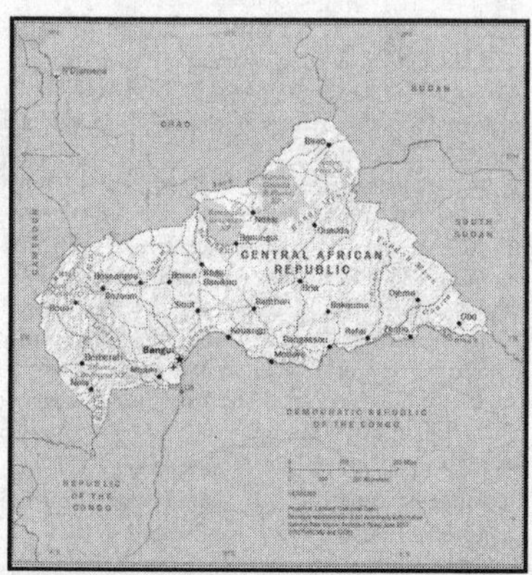

CAR's political history has since been marred by a series of coups, the first of which brought Jean-Bedel BOKASSA to power in 1966. Widespread corruption and intolerance for any political opposition characterized his regime. In an effort to prolong his mandate, BOKASSA named himself emperor in 1976 and changed the country's name to the Central African Empire. His regime's economic mismanagement culminated in widespread student protests in 1979 that were violently suppressed by security forces. BOKASSA fell out of favor with the international community and was overthrown in a French-backed coup in 1979. After BOKASSA's departure, the country's name once again became the Central African Republic.

CAR's fifth coup in 2013 unseated President Francois BOZIZE after the Seleka, a mainly Muslim rebel coalition, seized the capital and forced BOZIZE to flee the country. The Seleka's widespread abuses spurred the formation of mainly Christian self-defense groups that called themselves the anti-Balaka, which have also committed human rights abuses against Muslim populations in retaliation. Since the rise of these groups, conflict in CAR has become increasingly ethnoreligious, although focused on identity rather than religious ideology. Elections in 2016 installed independent candidate Faustin-Archange TOUADERA as president; he was reelected in 2020. A peace agreement signed in 2019 between the government and the main armed factions has had little effect, and armed groups remain in control of large swaths of the country's territory. TOUADERA's United Hearts Movement has governed the country since 2016, and a new constitution approved by referendum on 30 July 2023 effectively ended term limits, creating the potential for TOUADERA to extend his rule.

GEOGRAPHY

Location: Central Africa, north of Democratic Republic of the Congo

Geographic coordinates: 7 00 N, 21 00 E

Map references: Africa

Area: *total:* 622,984 sq km
land: 622,984 sq km
water: 0 sq km
comparison ranking: total 47

Area - comparative: slightly smaller than Texas; about four times the size of Georgia

Land boundaries: *total:* 5,920 km
border countries (5): Cameroon 901 km; Chad 1556 km; Democratic Republic of the Congo 1,747 km, Republic of the Congo 487 km; South Sudan 1055 km; Sudan 174 km

Coastline: 0 km (landlocked)

Maritime claims: none (landlocked)

Climate: tropical; hot, dry winters; mild to hot, wet summers

Terrain: vast, flat to rolling plateau; scattered hills in northeast and southwest

Elevation: *highest point:* Mont Ngaoui 1,410 m
lowest point: Oubangui River 335 m
mean elevation: 635 m

Natural resources: diamonds, uranium, timber, gold, oil, hydropower

Land use: *agricultural land:* 9% (2022 est.)
arable land: 2.9% (2022 est.)
permanent crops: 1.3% (2022 est.)
permanent pasture: 4.8% (2022 est.)
forest: 35.7% (2022 est.)
other: 55.3% (2022 est.)

Irrigated land: 10 sq km (2012)

Major rivers (by length in km): Oubangui (Ubangi) river [s] (shared with Democratic Republic of Congo and Republic of Congo [m]) - 2,270 km
note: [s] after country name indicates river source; [m] after country name indicates river mouth

Major watersheds (area sq km): Atlantic Ocean drainage: Congo (3,730,881 sq km), *(Mediterranean Sea)* Nile (3,254,853 sq km)

Internal (endorheic basin) drainage: Lake Chad (2,497,738 sq km)

Major aquifers: Congo Basin, Lake Chad Basin

Population distribution: majority of residents live in the western and central areas of the country, especially in and around the capital of Bangui, as shown in this population distribution map

Natural hazards: hot, dry, dusty harmattan winds affect northern areas; floods are common

Geography - note: landlocked; almost the precise center of Africa

PEOPLE AND SOCIETY

Population: *total:* 5,650,957 (2024 est.)
male: 2,814,497
female: 2,836,460
comparison rankings: total 117; male 117; female 119

Nationality: *noun:* Central African(s)
adjective: Central African

Ethnic groups: Baya 28.8%, Banda 22.9%, Mandjia 9.9%, Sara 7.9%, M'Baka-Bantu 7.9%, Arab-Fulani (Peuhl) 6%, Mbum 6%, Ngbanki 5.5%, Zande-Nzakara 3%, other Central African Republic ethnic groups 2%, non-Central African Republic ethnic groups.1% (2003 est.)

Languages: French (official), Sangho (lingua franca and national language), tribal languages

Religions: Roman Catholic 34.6%, Protestant 15.7%, other Christian 22.9%, Muslim 13.8%, ethnic religionist 12%, Baha'i 0.2%, agnostic/atheist 0.7% (2020 est.)
note: animistic beliefs and practices strongly influence the Christian majority

Age structure: *0-14 years:* 38.5% (male 1,113,795/ female 1,063,971)
15-64 years: 58% (male 1,613,770/female 1,662,522)
65 years and over: 3.5% (2024 est.) (male 86,932/ female 109,967)

Dependency ratios: *total dependency ratio:* 72.5 (2024 est.)
youth dependency ratio: 66.5 (2024 est.)
elderly dependency ratio: 6 (2024 est.)
potential support ratio: 16.6 (2024 est.)

Median age: *total:* 20.4 years (2024 est.)
male: 19.7 years
female: 21.2 years
comparison ranking: total 202

Population growth rate: 1.76% (2024 est.)
comparison ranking: 50

Birth rate: 31.9 births/1,000 population (2024 est.)
comparison ranking: 21

Death rate: 11.3 deaths/1,000 population (2024 est.)
comparison ranking: 21

Net migration rate: -3.1 migrant(s)/1,000 population (2024 est.)
comparison ranking: 180

Population distribution: majority of residents live in the western and central areas of the country, especially in and around the capital of Bangui, as shown in this population distribution map

Urbanization: *urban population:* 43.6% of total population (2023)
rate of urbanization: 3.32% annual rate of change (2020-25 est.)

Major urban areas - population: 958,000 BANGUI (capital) (2023)

Sex ratio: *at birth:* 1.03 male(s)/female
0-14 years: 1.05 male(s)/female
15-64 years: 0.97 male(s)/female
65 years and over: 0.79 male(s)/female
total population: 0.99 male(s)/female (2024 est.)

Maternal mortality ratio: 692 deaths/100,000 live births (2023 est.)
comparison ranking: 4

Infant mortality rate: *total:* 80.5 deaths/1,000 live births (2024 est.)
male: 86.4 deaths/1,000 live births
female: 74.5 deaths/1,000 live births
comparison ranking: total 3

Life expectancy at birth: *total population:* 56.4 years (2024 est.)
male: 55.1 years
female: 57.7 years
comparison ranking: total population 226

Total fertility rate: 3.94 children born/woman (2024 est.)
comparison ranking: 25

Gross reproduction rate: 1.94 (2024 est.)

Drinking water source: *improved: urban:* 48.1% of population (2022 est.)
rural: 27.4% of population (2022 est.)
total: 36.3% of population (2022 est.)
unimproved: urban: 51.9% of population (2022 est.)
rural: 72.6% of population (2022 est.)
total: 63.7% of population (2022 est.)

Health expenditure: 9.1% of GDP (2021)
9% of national budget (2022 est.)

Physician density: 0.07 physicians/1,000 population (2023)

Sanitation facility access: *improved: urban:* 53.5% of population (2022 est.)
rural: 12.4% of population (2022 est.)
total: 30.2% of population (2022 est.)

unimproved: urban: 46.5% of population (2022 est.)
rural: 87.6% of population (2022 est.)
total: 69.8% of population (2022 est.)

Obesity - adult prevalence rate: 7.5% (2016)
comparison ranking: 159

Alcohol consumption per capita: *total:* 0.94 liters of pure alcohol (2019 est.)
beer: 0.55 liters of pure alcohol (2019 est.)
wine: 0.04 liters of pure alcohol (2019 est.)
spirits: 0.02 liters of pure alcohol (2019 est.)
other alcohols: 0.33 liters of pure alcohol (2019 est.)
comparison ranking: total 152

Children under the age of 5 years underweight: 20.5% (2019)
comparison ranking: 13

Currently married women (ages 15-49): 64.7% (2023 est.)

Child marriage: *women married by age 15:* 25.8% (2019)
women married by age 18: 61% (2019)
men married by age 18: 17.1% (2019)

Education expenditure: 1.8% of GDP (2023 est.)
10% national budget (2023 est.)
comparison ranking: Education expenditure (% GDP) 189

Literacy: *total population:* 42.4% (2019 est.)
male: 59.8% (2019 est.)
female: 27.1% (2019 est.)

ENVIRONMENT

Environmental issues: water pollution; tap water not potable; poaching; wildlife mismanagement; desertification; deforestation; soil erosion

International environmental agreements: *party to:* Biodiversity, Climate Change, Climate Change-Kyoto Protocol, Climate Change-Paris Agreement, Comprehensive Nuclear Test Ban, Desertification, Endangered Species, Hazardous Wastes, Nuclear Test Ban, Ozone Layer Protection, Tropical Timber 2006, Wetlands
signed, but not ratified: Law of the Sea

Climate: tropical; hot, dry winters; mild to hot, wet summers

Urbanization: *urban population:* 43.6% of total population (2023)
rate of urbanization: 3.32% annual rate of change (2020-25 est.)

Carbon dioxide emissions: 313,000 metric tonnes of CO_2 (2023 est.)
from petroleum and other liquids: 313,000 metric tonnes of CO_2 (2023 est.)
comparison ranking: total emissions 197

Particulate matter emissions: 25.5 micrograms per cubic meter (2019 est.)

Waste and recycling: *municipal solid waste generated annually:* 1.106 million tons (2024 est.)
percent of municipal solid waste recycled: 9.1% (2022 est.)

Total water withdrawal: *municipal:* 60.1 million cubic meters (2022 est.)
industrial: 12 million cubic meters (2022 est.)
agricultural: 400,000 cubic meters (2022 est.)

Total renewable water resources: 141 billion cubic meters (2022 est.)

GOVERNMENT

Country name: *conventional long form:* Central African Republic
conventional short form: none
local long form: République centrafricaine
local short form: none
former: Ubangi-Shari, Central African Empire
abbreviation: CAR
etymology: self-descriptive name specifying the country's location on the continent; "Africa" is derived from the Roman designation of the area corresponding to present-day Tunisia, "Africa terra," which meant "Land of the Afri" (the tribe resident in that area), but which eventually came to mean the entire continent

Government type: presidential republic

Capital: *name:* Bangui
geographic coordinates: 4 22 N, 18 35 E
time difference: UTC+1 (6 hours ahead of Washington, DC, during Standard Time)
etymology: established as a French military post in 1889; the name means "rapids" in the local Bobangui language, because of the city's location above the first great rapid on the Ubangi River

Administrative divisions: 14 prefectures (*préfectures*, singular - *préfecture*), 2 economic prefectures* (*préfectures économiques*, singular - *préfecture économique*), and 1 commune**; Bamingui-Bangoran, Bangui**, Basse-Kotto, Haute-Kotto, Haut-Mbomou, Kemo, Lobaye, Mambere-Kadei, Mbomou, Nana-Grebizi*, Nana-Mambere, Ombella-Mpoko, Ouaka, Ouham, Ouham-Pende, Sangha-Mbaere*, Vakaga

Legal system: civil law system based on the French model

Constitution: *history:* several previous; latest constitution passed by a national referendum on 30 July 2023 and validated by the Constitutional Court on 30 August 2023
amendment process: proposals require support of the government, two thirds of the National Council of Transition, and assent by the "Mediator of the Central African" crisis; passage requires at least three-fourths majority vote by the National Council membership; non-amendable constitutional provisions include those on the secular and republican form of government, fundamental rights and freedoms, amendment procedures, or changes to the authorities of various high-level executive, parliamentary, and judicial officials

International law organization participation: has not submitted an ICJ jurisdiction declaration; accepts ICCt jurisdiction

Citizenship: *citizenship by birth:* no
citizenship by descent only: least one parent must be a citizen of the Central African Republic
dual citizenship recognized: yes
residency requirement for naturalization: 35 years

Suffrage: 18 years of age; universal

Executive branch: *chief of state:* President Faustin-Archange TOUADÉRA (since 30 March 2016)
head of government: Prime Minister Félix MOLOUA (since 7 February 2022)
cabinet: Council of Ministers appointed by the president
election/appointment process: current president was directly elected for 5-year term; constitutional referendum in July 2023 removed term limits and instituted 7-year terms
most recent election date: 27 December 2020
election results: *2020:* Faustin-Archange TOUADÉRA reelected president in first round; percent of vote - Faustin-Archange TOUADÉRA (independent) 53.9%, Anicet Georges DOLOGUELE (URCA) 21%, other 25.1%
2015: Faustin-Archange TOUADÉRA elected president in the second round; percent of vote in first round - Anicet-Georges DOLOGUELE (URCA) 23.7%, Faustin-Archange TOUADÉRA (independent) 19.1%, Desire KOLINGBA (RDC) 12%, Martin ZIGUELE (MLPC) 11.4%, other 33.8%; percent of vote in second round - Faustin-Archange TOUADÉRA 62.7%, Anicet-Georges DOLOGUELE 37.3%
expected date of next election: December 2025

Legislative branch: *legislature name:* National Assembly (Assemblée nationale)
legislative structure: unicameral
number of seats: 140 (all directly elected)
electoral system: plurality/majority
scope of elections: full renewal
term in office: 5 years
most recent election date: 12/27/2020 to 7/25/2021
parties elected and seats per party: United Hearts Movement (MCU) (61); National Movement of Independents (MOUNI) (9); Union for Central African Renewal (URCA) (7); Independents (17); Other (39)
percentage of women in chamber: 11.4%
expected date of next election: December 2025
note 1: on 27 December 2020, the day of first round elections, voting in many electoral areas was disrupted by armed groups; on 13 February 2021, President TOUADERA announced that new first round elections would be held on 27 February 2021 for those areas controlled by armed groups and the second round on 14 March 2021; ultimately, two additional rounds were held on 23 May and 25 July 2021 in areas that continued to suffer from election security problems
note 2: in accordance with article 98 of the constitution published in August 2023, the parliamentary term has increased from five to seven years and will be first applied to the legislature due to be elected in late 2025

Judicial branch: *highest court(s):* Supreme Court or Cour Supreme (number of judges unknown); Constitutional Court (consists of 9 judges, at least 3 of whom are women)
judge selection and term of office: Supreme Court judges appointed by the president; Constitutional Court judge appointments - 2 by the president, 1 by the speaker of the National Assembly, 2 elected by their peers, 2 are advocates elected by their peers, and 2 are law professors elected by their peers; judges serve 7-year non-renewable terms
subordinate courts: high courts; magistrates' courts

Political parties: Action Party for Development or PAD
African Party for Radical Transformation and Integration of States or PATRIE
Alliance for Democracy and Progress or ADP
Be Africa ti e Kwe (also known as Central Africa for Us All or BTK)
Central African Democratic Rally or RDC
Central African Party for Integrated Development or PCDI
Democratic Movement for the Renewal and Evolution of Central Africa or MDREC
Kodro Ti Mo Kozo Si Movement or MKMKS
Movement for Democracy and Development or MDD

Movement for the Liberation of the Central African People or MLPC
National Convergence (also known as Kwa Na Kwa or KNK)
National Movement of Independents or MOUNI
National Union for Democracy and Progress or UNDP
National Union of Republican Democrats or UNADER
New Impetus for Central Africa or CANE
Party for Democracy and Solidarity - Kélémba or KPDS
Party for Democratic Governance or PGD
Path of Hope or CDE
Renaissance for Sustainable Development or RDD
Socialist Party or PS
Transformation Through Action Initiative or ITA
Union for Central African Renewal or URCA
Union for Renaissance and Development or URD
United Hearts Movement or MCU

Diplomatic representation in the US: *chief of mission:* Ambassador Martial NDOUBOU (since 17 September 2018)
chancery: 2704 Ontario Road NW, Washington, DC 20009
telephone: [1] (202) 483-7800
FAX: [1] (202) 332-9893
email address and website: centrafricwashington@yahoo.com
https://www.usrcaembassy.org/

Diplomatic representation from the US: *chief of mission:* Ambassador (vacant); Chargé d'Affaires Melanie Anne ZIMMERMAN (since July 2025)
embassy: Avenue David Dacko, Bangui
mailing address: 2060 Bangui Place, Washington DC 20521-2060
telephone: [236] 2161-0200
FAX: [236] 2161-4494
email address and website: https://cf.usembassy.gov/

International organization participation: ACP, AfDB, AU, BDEAC, CEMAC, EITI (compliant country) (suspended), FAO, FZ, G-77, IAEA, IBRD, ICAO, ICCt, ICRM, IDA, IFAD, IFC, IFRCS, ILO, IMF, Interpol, IOC, IOM, ITSO, ITU, ITUC (NGOs), LCBC, MIGA, NAM, OIC (observer), OIF, OPCW, UN, UNCTAD, UNESCO, UNIDO, UNWTO, UPU, WCO, WHO, WIPO, WMO, WTO

Independence: 13 August 1960 (from France)

National holiday: Republic Day, 1 December (1958)

Flag: *description:* four equal horizontal bands of blue (top), white, green, and yellow with a vertical red band in the center; a five-pointed yellow star sits in the top left corner of the flag, on the blue band
meaning: combines the pan-African and French flag colors; red stands for blood spilled in the struggle for independence, blue for the sky and freedom, white for peace and dignity, green for hope and faith, and yellow for tolerance; the star represents aspiring to a vibrant future

National symbol(s): elephant

National color(s): blue, white, green, yellow, red

National anthem(s): *title:* "La Renaissance" (The Renaissance)
lyrics/music: Barthelemy BOGANDA/Herbert PEPPER
history: adopted 1960; BOGANDA wrote the anthem's lyrics and was the first prime minister of the autonomous French territory

National heritage: *total World Heritage Sites:* 2 (natural)
selected World Heritage Site locales: Manovo-Gounda St. Floris National Park; Sangha Trinational Forest

ECONOMY

Economic overview: enormous natural resources; extreme poverty; weak public institutions and infrastructure; political and gender-based violence have led to displacement of roughly 25% of population; Bangui-Douala corridor blockade reduced activity and tax collection; strong agricultural performance offset COVID-19 downturn

Real GDP (purchasing power parity): $5.926 billion (2024 est.)
$5.836 billion (2023 est.)
$5.795 billion (2022 est.)
note: data in 2021 dollars
comparison ranking: 176

Real GDP growth rate: 1.5% (2024 est.)
0.7% (2023 est.)
0.5% (2022 est.)
note: annual GDP % growth based on constant local currency
comparison ranking: 161

Real GDP per capita: $1,100 (2024 est.)
$1,100 (2023 est.)
$1,100 (2022 est.)
note: data in 2021 dollars
comparison ranking: 214

GDP (official exchange rate): $2.752 billion (2024 est.)
note: data in current dollars at official exchange rate

Inflation rate (consumer prices): 3% (2023 est.)
5.6% (2022 est.)
4.3% (2021 est.)
note: annual % change based on consumer prices
comparison ranking: 93

GDP - composition, by sector of origin: *agriculture:* 32.5% (2024 est.)
industry: 17.8% (2024 est.)
services: 40.5% (2024 est.)
note: figures may not total 100% due to non-allocated consumption not captured in sector-reported data
comparison rankings: agriculture 10; industry 146; services 192

GDP - composition, by end use: *household consumption:* 94.7% (2024 est.)
government consumption: 9.7% (2024 est.)
investment in fixed capital: 15.4% (2024 est.)
investment in inventories: 0% (2024 est.)
exports of goods and services: 15.5% (2024 est.)
imports of goods and services: -32.4% (2024 est.)
note: figures may not total 100% due to rounding or gaps in data collection

Agricultural products: cassava, groundnuts, yams, coffee, maize, sesame seeds, taro, sugarcane, beef, milk (2023)
note: top ten agricultural products based on tonnage

Industries: gold and diamond mining, logging, brewing, sugar refining

Industrial production growth rate: 9.7% (2024 est.)
note: annual % change in industrial value added based on constant local currency
comparison ranking: 11

Labor force: 2 million (2024 est.)
note: number of people ages 15 or older who are employed or seeking work
comparison ranking: 126

Unemployment rate: 5.9% (2024 est.)
5.9% (2023 est.)
6% (2022 est.)
note: % of labor force seeking employment
comparison ranking: 111

Youth unemployment rate (ages 15-24): *total:* 9.5% (2024 est.)
male: 8.5% (2024 est.)
female: 10.6% (2024 est.)
note: % of labor force ages 15-24 seeking employment
comparison ranking: total 125

Population below poverty line: 68.8% (2021 est.)
note: % of population with income below national poverty line

Gini Index coefficient - distribution of family income: 43 (2021 est.)
note: index (0-100) of income distribution; higher values represent greater inequality
comparison ranking: 28

Household income or consumption by percentage share: *lowest 10%:* 2.1% (2021 est.)
highest 10%: 33.1% (2021 est.)
note: % share of income accruing to lowest and highest 10% of population

Remittances: 0% of GDP (2023 est.)
0% of GDP (2022 est.)
0% of GDP (2021 est.)
note: personal transfers and compensation between resident and non-resident individuals/households/entities

Budget: *revenues:* $360.48 million (2021 est.)
expenditures: $462.104 million (2021 est.)
note: central government revenues and expenses (excluding grants/extrabudgetary units/social security funds) converted to US dollars at average official exchange rate for year indicated

Taxes and other revenues: 8.2% (of GDP) (2021 est.)
note: central government tax revenue as a % of GDP
comparison ranking: 136

Exports: $425.306 million (2024 est.)
$369.034 million (2023 est.)
$293.074 million (2022 est.)
note: GDP expenditure basis - exports of goods and services in current dollars
comparison ranking: 192

Exports - partners: UAE 54%, China 14%, France 6%, Turkey 5%, Belgium 4% (2023)
note: top five export partners based on percentage share of exports

Exports - commodities: gold, wood, diamonds, vehicle parts/accessories, cotton (2023)
note: top five export commodities based on value in dollars

Imports: $890.572 million (2024 est.)
$742.108 million (2023 est.)
$784.669 million (2022 est.)
note: GDP expenditure basis - imports of goods and services in current dollars
comparison ranking: 191

Imports - partners: China 16%, Cameroon 14%, France 8%, Belgium 6%, Cote d'Ivoire 5% (2023)
note: top five import partners based on percentage share of imports

Imports - commodities: refined petroleum, cars, packaged medicine, vaccines, tanks and armored vehicles (2023)
note: top five import commodities based on value in dollars

Reserves of foreign exchange and gold: $479.593 million (2023 est.)
$374.405 million (2022 est.)
$483.872 million (2021 est.)
note: holdings of gold (year-end prices)/foreign exchange/special drawing rights in current dollars
comparison ranking: 162

Debt - external: $724.179 million (2023 est.)
note: present value of external debt in current US dollars
comparison ranking: 111

Exchange rates: Cooperation Financiere en Afrique Centrale francs (XAF) per US dollar -

Exchange rates: 606.345 (2024 est.)
606.57 (2023 est.)
623.76 (2022 est.)
554.531 (2021 est.)
575.586 (2020 est.)

ENERGY

Electricity access: *electrification - total population:* 15.7% (2022 est.)
electrification - urban areas: 34.7%
electrification - rural areas: 1.6%

Electricity: *installed generating capacity:* 63,000 kW (2023 est.)
consumption: 132.105 million kWh (2023 est.)
transmission/distribution losses: 10 million kWh (2023 est.)
comparison rankings: installed generating capacity 191; consumption 196; transmission/distribution losses 17

Electricity generation sources: *fossil fuels:* 0.8% of total installed capacity (2023 est.)
hydroelectricity: 99.2% of total installed capacity (2023 est.)

Coal: *imports:* 1 metric tons (2023 est.)
proven reserves: 3 million metric tons (2023 est.)

Petroleum: *refined petroleum consumption:* 2,000 bbl/day (2023 est.)

Energy consumption per capita: 954,000 Btu/person (2023 est.)
comparison ranking: 193

COMMUNICATIONS

Telephones - fixed lines: *total subscriptions:* 2,000 (2021 est.)
subscriptions per 100 inhabitants: (2022 est.) less than 1
comparison ranking: total subscriptions 213

Telephones - mobile cellular: *total subscriptions:* 1.83 million (2021 est.)
subscriptions per 100 inhabitants: 34 (2021 est.)
comparison ranking: total subscriptions 153

Broadcast media: government-owned network, Radiodiffusion Télévision Centrafricaine, provides limited TV broadcasting; state-owned radio network is supplemented by a small number of privately owned broadcast stations, as well as a few community radio stations; transmissions of at least 2 international broadcasters are available (2017)

Internet country code: .cf

Internet users: *percent of population:* 8% (2019 est.)

Broadband - fixed subscriptions: *total:* 1,000 (2022 est.) Data available for 2019 only.
subscriptions per 100 inhabitants: (2022 est.) less than 1
comparison ranking: total 206

TRANSPORTATION

Civil aircraft registration country code prefix: TL

Airports: 43 (2025)
comparison ranking: 98

MILITARY AND SECURITY

Military and security forces: Central African Armed Forces (Forces Armees Centrafricaines, FACA): Army (includes an air squadron, Escadrille Centrafricaine)

Ministry of Interior: National Gendarmerie (Gendarmerie Nationale), National Police (2025)
note: the Special Republican Protection Group (Groupement Spécial Chargé de la Protection Républicaine or GSPR) provides protection to the head of state; it is part of the Army but reports to the president

Military expenditures: 2.5% of GDP (2024 est.)
1.8% of GDP (2023 est.)
1.7% of GDP (2022 est.)
1.8% of GDP (2021 est.)
1.8% of GDP (2020 est.)

Military and security service personnel strengths: estimated 10-15,000 active FACA (2025)

Military equipment inventories and acquisitions: most of the military's heavy weapons and equipment were destroyed or captured during the 2012–2014 civil war; prior to the war, most of its equipment was of French, Russian, or Soviet origin; in recent years, it has received some secondhand equipment from China and Russia, including light weapons, as well as some armored vehicles, unmanned aerial vehicles, and helicopters (2024)
note: the CAR was under a UNSC arms embargo from 2013-July 2024

Military service age and obligation: 18 years of age for military service; no conscription although the constitution provides for the possibility of conscription in the event of an imminent threat to the country (2023)

Military - note: the Central African Armed Forces (FACA) are focused on internal security; since the 2013 coup, multiple armed groups have been active in the country, carrying out attacks, controlling territory, and undermining security; the coup resulted in the institutional collapse of the FACA; its forces were overwhelmed and forced to flee to neighboring countries; it has been estimated that only 10% of the FACA returned afterwards; over the past decade, the FACA has sought to rebuild with considerable foreign assistance, including from France, the EU, Russia, Rwanda, and the UN; Russian private military contractors and bilateral Rwandan military forces are assisting the FACA in its operations against rebel groups
the UN Multidimensional Integrated Stabilization Mission in the Central African Republic (MINUSCA) has operated in the country since 2014; its mission includes providing security, protecting civilians, facilitating humanitarian assistance, disarming and demobilizing armed groups, and supporting the country's transitional government; MINUSCA has more than 18,000 personnel (2025)

TRANSNATIONAL ISSUES

Refugees and internally displaced persons: *refugees:* 53,378 (2024 est.)

IDPs: 469,342 (2024 est.)

CHAD

INTRODUCTION

Background: Chad emerged from a collection of powerful states that controlled the Sahelian belt starting around the 9th century. These states focused on controlling trans-Saharan trade routes and profited mostly from the slave trade. The Kanem-Bornu Empire, centered around the Lake Chad Basin, existed between the 9th and 19th centuries, and at its peak, the empire controlled territory stretching from southern Chad to southern Libya and included portions of modern-day Algeria, Cameroon, Niger, Nigeria, and Sudan. The Sudanese warlord Rabih AZ-ZUBAYR used an army comprised largely of slaves to conquer the Kanem-Bornu Empire in the late 19th century. In southeastern Chad, the Bagirmi and Ouaddai (Wadai) kingdoms emerged in the 15th and 16th centuries and lasted until the arrival of the French in the 19th and 20th centuries. France began moving into the region in the late 1880s and defeated the Bagirmi kingdom in 1897, Rabih AZ-ZUBAYR in 1900, and the Ouddai kingdom in 1909. In the arid regions of northern Chad and southern Libya, an Islamic order called the Sanusiyya (Sanusi) relied heavily on the trans-Saharan slave trade and had upwards of 3 million followers by the 1880s. The French defeated the Sanusiyya in 1910 after years of intermittent war. By 1910, France had incorporated the northern arid region, the Lake Chad Basin, and southeastern Chad into French Equatorial Africa.

Chad achieved its independence in 1960 and then saw three decades of instability, oppressive rule, civil war, and a Libyan invasion. With the help of the French military and several African countries, Chadian leaders expelled Libyan forces during the 1987 "Toyota War," so named for the use of Toyota pickup trucks as fighting vehicles. In 1990, Chadian general Idriss DEBY led a rebellion against President Hissene HABRE. Under DEBY, Chad approved a constitution and held elections in 1996. Shortly after DEBY was killed during a rebel incursion in 2021, a group of military officials – led by DEBY's son, Mahamat Idriss DEBY – took control of the government. The military officials dismissed the National Assembly, suspended the Constitution, and formed a

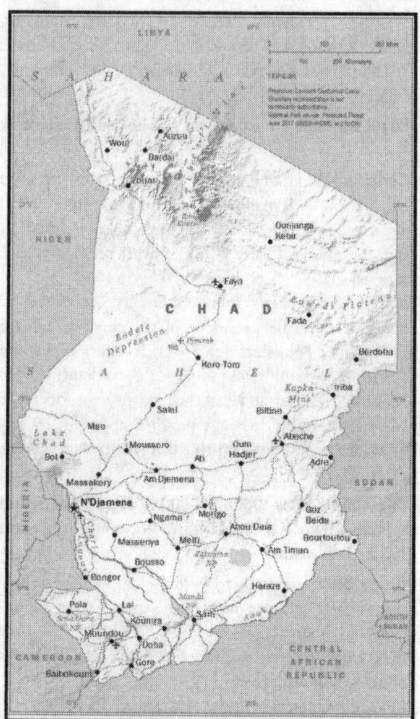

Transitional Military Council (TMC), while pledging to hold democratic elections by October 2022. A national dialogue in August-October 2022 culminated in decisions to extend the transition for up to two years, dissolve the TMC, and appoint Mahamat DEBY as Transitional President; the transitional authorities held a constitutional referendum in December 2023 and claimed 86 percent of votes were in favor of the new constitution. The transitional authorities have announced plans to hold elections by October 2024.

Chad has faced widespread poverty, an economy severely weakened by volatile international oil prices, terrorist-led insurgencies in the Lake Chad Basin, and several waves of rebellions in northern and eastern Chad. In 2015, the government imposed a state of emergency in the Lake Chad Basin following multiple attacks by the terrorist group Boko Haram, now known as ISIS-West Africa. The same year, Boko Haram conducted bombings in N'Djamena. In 2019, the Chadian government also declared a state of emergency in the Sila and Ouaddai regions bordering Sudan and in the Tibesti region bordering Niger, where rival ethnic groups are still fighting. The army has suffered heavy losses to Islamic terror groups in the Lake Chad Basin.

GEOGRAPHY

Location: Central Africa, south of Libya

Geographic coordinates: 15 00 N, 19 00 E

Map references: Africa

Area: *total:* 1.284 million sq km
land: 1,259,200 sq km
water: 24,800 sq km
comparison ranking: total 22

Area - comparative: almost nine times the size of New York state; slightly more than three times the size of California

Land boundaries: *total:* 6,406 km
border countries (6): Cameroon 1,116 km; Central African Republic 1,556 km; Libya 1,050 km; Niger 1,196 km; Nigeria 85 km; Sudan 1,403 km

Coastline: 0 km (landlocked)

Maritime claims: none (landlocked)

Climate: tropical in south, desert in north

Terrain: broad, arid plains in center, desert in north, mountains in northwest, lowlands in south

Elevation: *highest point:* Emi Koussi 3,445 m
lowest point: Djourab 160 m
mean elevation: 543 m

Natural resources: petroleum, uranium, natron, kaolin, fish (Lake Chad), gold, limestone, sand and gravel, salt

Land use: *agricultural land:* 40% (2022 est.)
arable land: 4.2% (2022 est.)
permanent crops: 0% (2022 est.)
permanent pasture: 35.7% (2022 est.)
forest: 3.2% (2022 est.)
other: 56.8% (2022 est.)

Irrigated land: 300 sq km (2012)

Major lakes (area sq km): *fresh water lake(s):* Lake Chad (endorheic lake shared with Niger, Nigeria, and Cameroon) - 10,360-25,900 sq km
note - area varies by season and year to year

Major watersheds (area sq km): Atlantic Ocean drainage: Niger (2,261,741 sq km)

Internal (endorheic basin) drainage: Lake Chad (2,497,738 sq km)

Major aquifers: Lake Chad Basin, Nubian Aquifer System

Population distribution: the population is unevenly distributed due to contrasts in climate and physical geography; the highest density is found in the southwest, particularly around Lake Chad and points south; the dry Saharan zone to the north is the least densely populated, as shown in this population distribution map

Natural hazards: hot, dry, dusty harmattan winds occur in north; periodic droughts; locust plagues

Geography - note: *note 1:* Chad is the largest of Africa's 16 landlocked countries
note 2: a wide variety of animals lived in modern-day Chad during the African Humid Period, including elephants, giraffes, hippos, and antelope; the last remnant of this "Green Sahara" exists in the Lakes of Ounianga in northern Chad, a series of 18 interconnected freshwater, saline, and hypersaline lakes
note 3: Lake Chad, the most significant water body in the Sahel, is a remnant of a former inland sea, paleolake Mega-Chad; at its greatest extent, sometime before 5000 B.C., Lake Mega-Chad was the largest of four Saharan paleolakes that existed during the African Humid Period; it covered an area of about 400,000 sq km (150,000 sq mi), roughly the size of today's Caspian Sea

PEOPLE AND SOCIETY

Population: *total:* 19,093,595 (2024 est.)
male: 9,464,699
female: 9,628,896
comparison rankings: total 65; male 65; female 65

Nationality: *noun:* Chadian(s)
adjective: Chadian

Ethnic groups: Sara (Ngambaye/Sara/Madjingaye/Mbaye) 30.5%, Kanembu/Bornu/Buduma 9.8%, Arab 9.7%, Wadai/Maba/Masalit/Mimi 7%, Gorane 5.8%, Masa/Musseye/Musgum 4.9%, Bulala/Medogo/Kuka 3.7%, Marba/Lele/Mesme 3.5%, Mundang 2.7%, Bidiyo/Migaama/Kenga/Dangleat 2.5%, Dadjo/Kibet/Muro 2.4%, Tupuri/Kera 2%, Gabri/Kabalaye/Nanchere/Somrai 2%, Fulani/Fulbe/Bodore 1.8%, Karo/Zime/Peve 1.3%, Baguirmi/Barma 1.2%, Zaghawa/Bideyat/Kobe 1.1%, Tama/Assongori/Mararit 1.1%, Mesmedje/Massalat/Kadjakse 0.8%, other 4.6%, unspecified 1.7% (2014-15 est.)

Languages: French (official), Arabic (official), Sara (in south), more than 120 languages and dialects
major-language sample(s):
The World Factbook, une source indispensable d'informations de base. (French)
كتاب حقائق العالم، المصدر الذي لا يمكن الاستغناء عنه للمعلومات الأساسية
(Arabic)

Religions: Muslim 52.1%, Protestant 23.9%, Roman Catholic 20%, animist 0.3%, other Christian 0.2%, none 2.8%, unspecified 0.7% (2014-15 est.)

Age structure: *0-14 years:* 45.8% (male 4,428,132/female 4,323,398)
15-64 years: 51.7% (male 4,831,744/female 5,031,383)
65 years and over: 2.5% (2024 est.) (male 204,823/female 274,115)

Dependency ratios: *total dependency ratio:* 93.6 (2024 est.)
youth dependency ratio: 88.7 (2024 est.)
elderly dependency ratio: 4.9 (2024 est.)
potential support ratio: 20.6 (2024 est.)

Median age: *total:* 16.7 years (2024 est.)
male: 16.3 years
female: 17.2 years
comparison ranking: total 225

Population growth rate: 3.01% (2024 est.)
comparison ranking: 8

Birth rate: 39.2 births/1,000 population (2024 est.)
comparison ranking: 7

Death rate: 9 deaths/1,000 population (2024 est.)
comparison ranking: 60

Net migration rate: -0.1 migrant(s)/1,000 population (2024 est.)
comparison ranking: 101

Population distribution: the population is unevenly distributed due to contrasts in climate and physical geography; the highest density is found in the southwest, particularly around Lake Chad and points south; the dry Saharan zone to the north is the least densely populated, as shown in this population distribution map

Urbanization: *urban population:* 24.4% of total population (2023)
rate of urbanization: 4.1% annual rate of change (2020-25 est.)

Major urban areas - population: 1.592 million N'DJAMENA (capital) (2023)

Sex ratio: *at birth:* 1.04 male(s)/female
0-14 years: 1.02 male(s)/female
15-64 years: 0.96 male(s)/female
65 years and over: 0.75 male(s)/female
total population: 0.98 male(s)/female (2024 est.)

Mother's mean age at first birth: 18.1 years (2014/15 est.)
note: data represents median age at first birth among women 20-49

Maternal mortality ratio: 748 deaths/100,000 live births (2023 est.)
comparison ranking: 2

Infant mortality rate: *total:* 62.5 deaths/1,000 live births (2024 est.)
male: 68.1 deaths/1,000 live births
female: 56.7 deaths/1,000 live births
comparison ranking: total 7

Life expectancy at birth: *total population:* 60 years (2024 est.)
male: 58.1 years
female: 62 years
comparison ranking: total population 222

Total fertility rate: 5.24 children born/woman (2024 est.)
comparison ranking: 6

Gross reproduction rate: 2.57 (2024 est.)

Drinking water source: *improved: urban:* 77.9% of population (2022 est.)
rural: 43.8% of population (2022 est.)
total: 52% of population (2022 est.)
unimproved: urban: 22.1% of population (2022 est.)
rural: 56.2% of population (2022 est.)
total: 48% of population (2022 est.)

Health expenditure: 5.2% of GDP (2021)
7.3% of national budget (2022 est.)

Physician density: 0.09 physicians/1,000 population (2023)

Hospital bed density: 0.4 beds/1,000 population (2017 est.)

Sanitation facility access: *improved: urban:* 56.4% of population (2022 est.)
rural: 6.3% of population (2022 est.)
total: 18.4% of population (2022 est.)
unimproved: urban: 43.6% of population (2022 est.)
rural: 93.7% of population (2022 est.)
total: 81.6% of population (2022 est.)

Obesity - adult prevalence rate: 6.1% (2016)
comparison ranking: 171

Alcohol consumption per capita: *total:* 0.55 liters of pure alcohol (2019 est.)
beer: 0.37 liters of pure alcohol (2019 est.)
wine: 0.01 liters of pure alcohol (2019 est.)
spirits: 0.01 liters of pure alcohol (2019 est.)
other alcohols: 0.16 liters of pure alcohol (2019 est.)
comparison ranking: total 162

Tobacco use: *total:* 6.5% (2025 est.)
male: 11.8% (2025 est.)
female: 1.3% (2025 est.)
comparison ranking: total 154

Children under the age of 5 years underweight: 18.9% (2022)
comparison ranking: 19

Currently married women (ages 15-49): 70.6% (2023 est.)

Child marriage: *women married by age 15:* 24.2% (2019)
women married by age 18: 60.6% (2019)
men married by age 18: 8.1% (2019)

Education expenditure: 3.2% of GDP (2023 est.)
16.5% national budget (2023 est.)
comparison ranking: Education expenditure (% GDP) 145

Literacy: *total population:* 30.6% (2019 est.)
male: 44.5% (2019 est.)
female: 18.6% (2019 est.)

School life expectancy (primary to tertiary education): *total:* 7 years (2015 est.)
male: 9 years (2015 est.)
female: 6 years (2015 est.)

ENVIRONMENT

Environmental issues: inadequate supplies of potable water; soil and water pollution from improper waste disposal in rural areas and poor farming practices; desertification

International environmental agreements: *party to:* Biodiversity, Climate Change, Climate Change-Kyoto Protocol, Climate Change-Paris Agreement, Comprehensive Nuclear Test Ban, Desertification, Endangered Species, Hazardous Wastes, Law of the Sea, Nuclear Test Ban, Ozone Layer Protection, Wetlands
signed, but not ratified: Marine Dumping-London Convention

Climate: tropical in south, desert in north

Urbanization: *urban population:* 24.4% of total population (2023)
rate of urbanization: 4.1% annual rate of change (2020-25 est.)

Carbon dioxide emissions: 2.054 million metric tonnes of CO2 (2023 est.)
from coal and metallurgical coke: 2 metric tonnes of CO2 (2023 est.)
from petroleum and other liquids: 2.054 million metric tonnes of CO2 (2023 est.)
comparison ranking: total emissions 159

Particulate matter emissions: 41.2 micrograms per cubic meter (2019 est.)

Methane emissions: *energy:* 101.8 kt (2022-2024 est.)
agriculture: 1,282.9 kt (2019-2021 est.)
waste: 60.3 kt (2019-2021 est.)
other: 12 kt (2019-2021 est.)

Waste and recycling: *municipal solid waste generated annually:* 1.359 million tons (2024 est.)
percent of municipal solid waste recycled: 11.1% (2022 est.)

Total water withdrawal: *municipal:* 103.7 million cubic meters (2022 est.)
industrial: 103.7 million cubic meters (2022 est.)
agricultural: 672.2 million cubic meters (2022 est.)

Total renewable water resources: 45.7 billion cubic meters (2022 est.)

GOVERNMENT

Country name: *conventional long form:* Republic of Chad
conventional short form: Chad
local long form: République du Tchad/Jumhuriyat Tshad
local short form: Tchad/Tshad
etymology: named for Lake Chad, which lies along the country's western border; taken from a local word meaning "large body of water" or "lake"
note: the only country whose name is composed of a single syllable with a single vowel

Government type: presidential republic

Capital: *name:* N'Djamena
geographic coordinates: 12 06 N, 15 02 E
time difference: UTC+1 (6 hours ahead of Washington, DC, during Standard Time)
etymology: said to derive its name from a local word meaning "place of rest"

Administrative divisions: 23 provinces; Barh-El-Gazel, Batha, Borkou, Chari-Baguirmi, Ennedi-Est, Ennedi-Ouest, Guera, Hadjer-Lamis, Kanem, Lac, Logone Occidental, Logone Oriental, Mandoul, Mayo-Kebbi-Est, Mayo-Kebbi-Ouest, Moyen-Chari, N'Djamena, Ouaddai, Salamat, Sila, Tandjile, Tibesti, Wadi-Fira

Legal system: mixed system of civil and customary law

Constitution: *history:* several previous; latest adopted by National Transitional Council 27 June 2023, approved by referendum 17 December, verified by Chad Supreme Court 28 December, promulgated 1 January 2024
amendment process: previous process: proposed as a revision by the president of the republic after a Council of Ministers (cabinet) decision or by the National Assembly; approval for consideration of a revision requires at least three-fifths majority vote by the Assembly; passage requires approval by referendum or at least two-thirds majority vote by the Assembly

International law organization participation: has not submitted an ICJ jurisdiction declaration; accepts ICCt jurisdiction

Citizenship: *citizenship by birth:* no
citizenship by descent only: both parents must be citizens of Chad
dual citizenship recognized: Chadian law does not address dual citizenship
residency requirement for naturalization: 15 years

Suffrage: 18 years of age; universal

Executive branch: *chief of state:* President Mahamat Idriss DÉBY (since 6 May 2024)
head of government: Prime Minister Allamaye HALINA (since 23 May 2024)
cabinet: Council of Ministers
election/appointment process: president directly elected by absolute-majority popular vote in 2 rounds, if needed, for a 5-year term (no term limits)
most recent election date: 6 May 2024
election results: 2024: Mahamat Idriss DÉBY elected president; percent of vote - Mahamat Idriss DÉBY (MPS) 61%, Succes MASRA (Transformers) 18.5%, Albert PADACKE 16.9%, other 3.6%
2021: Lt. Gen. Idriss DÉBY reelected transitional president; percent of vote - Lt. Gen. Idriss DÉBY (MPS) 79.3%, Pahimi PADACKET Albert (RNDT) 10.3%, Lydie BEASSEMDA (Party for Democracy and Independence) 3.2%, other 7.2%

Legislative branch: *legislature name:* Parliament
legislative structure: bicameral

Legislative branch - lower chamber: *chamber name:* National Assembly (Conseil national de transition)
number of seats: 188 (all directly elected)
electoral system: mixed system
scope of elections: full renewal
term in office: 5 years
most recent election date: 12/29/2024
parties elected and seats per party: Patriotic Salvation Movement (MPS) (124); Rally of Chadian Nationalists/Awakening (RNDT/ Le Réveil) (12); Others (27); Other (25)
percentage of women in chamber: 33.5%
expected date of next election: December 2029

Legislative branch - upper chamber: *chamber name:* Senate (Senate)
number of seats: 69 (46 indirectly elected; 23 appointed)
scope of elections: full renewal
term in office: 6 years
most recent election date: 2/25/2025

percentage of women in chamber: 36.2%
expected date of next election: February 2031

Judicial branch: *highest court(s):* Supreme Court (consists of the chief justice, 3 chamber presidents, and 12 judges or councilors and divided into 3 chambers); Supreme Council of the Judiciary (consists of the Judiciary president, vice president and 13 members)
judge selection and term of office: Supreme Court chief justice selected by the president; councilors - 8 designated by the president and 7 by the speaker of the National Assembly; chief justice and councilors appointed for life; Supreme Council of the Judiciary - with the exception of the Judiciary president and vice president, members are elected for single renewable 4-year terms
subordinate courts: High Court of Justice; Courts of Appeal; tribunals; justices of the peace

Political parties: Chadian Convention for Peace and Development or CTPD
Federation Action for the Republic or FAR
National Rally for Development and Progress or Viva-RNDP
National Union for Democracy and Renewal or UNDR
Party for Unity and Reconstruction or PUR
Patriotic Salvation Movement or MPS
Rally for Democracy and Progress or RDP
Rally of Chadian Nationalists/Awakening or RNDT/Le Reveil
Social Democratic Party for a Change-over of Power or PDSA
Union for Democracy and the Republic or UDR
Union for Renewal and Democracy or URD
Transformers
note 1: 19 additional parties each contributed one member
note 2: on 5 October 2021, Interim President Mahamat Idriss DEBY appointed 93 members to the interim National Transitional Council (NTC); 30% of the NTC members were retained from parties previously represented in the National Assembly

Diplomatic representation in the US: *chief of mission:* Ambassador (vacant); Chargé d'Affaires ANWAR SADAT Fatahalbab (since 30 July 2025)
chancery: 2401 Massachusetts Avenue NW, Washington, DC 20008
telephone: [1] (202) 652-1312
FAX: [1] (202) 578-0431
email address and website: info@chadembassy.us
https://chadembassy.us/

Diplomatic representation from the US: *chief of mission:* Ambassador (vacant); Chargé d'Affaires William FLENS (since July 2025)
embassy: Rond-Point Chagoua, B.P. 413, N'Djamena
mailing address: 2410 N'Djamena Place, Washington DC 20521-2410
telephone: [235] 6885-1065
FAX: [235] 2253-9102
email address and website: NdjamenaACS@state.gov
https://td.usembassy.gov/

International organization participation: ACP, AfDB, AU, BDEAC, CEMAC, EITI (compliant country), FAO, FZ, G-77, IAEA, IBRD, ICAO, ICCt, ICRM, IDA, IDB, IFAD, IFC, IFRCS, ILO, IMF, Interpol, IOC, IOM, IPU, ITSO, ITU, ITUC (NGOs), LCBC, MIGA, MNJTF, NAM, OIC, OIF, OPCW, UN, UNCTAD, UNESCO, UNIDO, UNOCI, UNOOSA, UNWTO, UPU, WCO, WHO, WIPO, WMO, WTO

Independence: 11 August 1960 (from France)

National holiday: Independence Day, 11 August (1960)

Flag: *description:* three equal vertical bands of blue (left side), gold, and red
meaning: combines the blue and red French (former colonial) colors with the red and yellow Pan-African colors; blue stands for the sky, hope, and the south of the country; gold for the sun and the desert in the north; red for progress, unity, and sacrifice
note: almost identical to the flag of Romania, but with a darker shade of blue; also similar to the flags of Andorra and Moldova, both of which have a national coat of arms centered in the yellow band; design based on France's flag

National symbol(s): goat (north), lion (south)

National color(s): blue, yellow, red

National anthem(s): *title:* "La Tchadienne" (The Chadian)
lyrics/music: Louis GIDROL and his students/Paul VILLARD
history: adopted 1960

National heritage: *total World Heritage Sites:* 2 (1 natural, 1 mixed)
selected World Heritage Site locales: Lakes of Ounianga (n); Ennedi Massif: Natural and Cultural Landscape (m)

ECONOMY

Economic overview: oil-dependent economy challenged by market fluctuations, regional instability, refugee influx, and climate vulnerability; high levels of extreme poverty and food insecurity; recent growth driven by oil and agricultural recovery; debt-restructuring agreement under G20 Common Framework

Real GDP (purchasing power parity): $52.895 billion (2024 est.)
$51.03 billion (2023 est.)
$49.012 billion (2022 est.)
note: data in 2021 dollars
comparison ranking: 125

Real GDP growth rate: 3.7% (2024 est.)
4.1% (2023 est.)
12.9% (2022 est.)
note: annual GDP % growth based on constant local currency
comparison ranking: 89

Real GDP per capita: $2,600 (2024 est.)
$2,600 (2023 est.)
$2,700 (2022 est.)
note: data in 2021 dollars
comparison ranking: 202

GDP (official exchange rate): $20.626 billion (2024 est.)
note: data in current dollars at official exchange rate

Inflation rate (consumer prices): 8.9% (2024 est.)
10.8% (2023 est.)
5.8% (2022 est.)
note: annual % change based on consumer prices
comparison ranking: 173

GDP - composition, by sector of origin: *agriculture:* 32.2% (2024 est.)
industry: 29.7% (2024 est.)
services: 31.6% (2024 est.)
note: figures may not total 100% due to non-allocated consumption not captured in sector-reported data
comparison rankings: agriculture 12; industry 56; services 205

GDP - composition, by end use: *household consumption:* 61.3% (2024 est.)
government consumption: 8.7% (2024 est.)
investment in fixed capital: 14.4% (2024 est.)
investment in inventories: 3.4% (2024 est.)
exports of goods and services: 28.1% (2024 est.)
imports of goods and services: -17.2% (2024 est.)
note: figures may not total 100% due to rounding or gaps in data collection

Agricultural products: sorghum, groundnuts, millet, beef, cereals, yams, sugarcane, maize, cassava, milk (2023)
note: top ten agricultural products based on tonnage

Industries: oil, cotton textiles, brewing, natron (sodium carbonate), soap, cigarettes, construction materials

Industrial production growth rate: 5.1% (2024 est.)
note: annual % change in industrial value added based on constant local currency
comparison ranking: 43

Labor force: 6.6 million (2024 est.)
note: number of people ages 15 or older who are employed or seeking work
comparison ranking: 71

Unemployment rate: 1.1% (2024 est.)
1.1% (2023 est.)
1.1% (2022 est.)
note: % of labor force seeking employment
comparison ranking: 6

Youth unemployment rate (ages 15-24): *total:* 1.5% (2024 est.)
male: 2.1% (2024 est.)
female: 0.7% (2024 est.)
note: % of labor force ages 15-24 seeking employment
comparison ranking: total 186

Population below poverty line: 44.8% (2022 est.)
note: % of population with income below national poverty line

Gini Index coefficient - distribution of family income: 37.4 (2022 est.)
note: index (0-100) of income distribution; higher values represent greater inequality
comparison ranking: 58

Household income or consumption by percentage share: *lowest 10%:* 2.8% (2022 est.)
highest 10%: 29.5% (2022 est.)
note: % share of income accruing to lowest and highest 10% of population

Remittances: 0% of GDP (2023 est.)
0% of GDP (2022 est.)
0% of GDP (2021 est.)
note: personal transfers and compensation between resident and non-resident individuals/households/entities

Budget: *revenues:* $2.129 billion (2020 est.)
expenditures: $2.15 billion (2020 est.)
note: central government revenues and expenses (excluding grants/extrabudgetary units/social security funds) converted to US dollars at average official exchange rate for year indicated

Exports: $5.799 billion (2024 est.)
$5.7 billion (2023 est.)
$5.658 billion (2022 est.)

note: GDP expenditure basis - exports of goods and services in current dollars
comparison ranking: 136

Exports - partners: UAE 26%, China 19%, Germany 17%, Netherlands 13%, France 10% (2023)
note: top five export partners based on percentage share of exports

Exports - commodities: crude petroleum, gold, oil seeds, gum resins, cotton (2023)
note: top five export commodities based on value in dollars

Imports: $3.557 billion (2024 est.)
$3.271 billion (2023 est.)
$2.898 billion (2022 est.)
note: GDP expenditure basis - imports of goods and services in current dollars
comparison ranking: 160

Imports - partners: China 28%, UAE 23%, Turkey 10%, France 9%, India 5% (2023)
note: top five import partners based on percentage share of imports

Imports - commodities: jewelry, broadcasting equipment, packaged medicine, cars, refined petroleum (2023)
note: top five import commodities based on value in dollars

Reserves of foreign exchange and gold: $1.05 billion (2023 est.)
$1.013 billion (2022 est.)
$211.591 million (2021 est.)
note: holdings of gold (year-end prices)/foreign exchange/special drawing rights in current dollars
comparison ranking: 142

Debt - external: $2.286 billion (2023 est.)
note: present value of external debt in current US dollars
comparison ranking: 93

Exchange rates: Cooperation Financiere en Afrique Centrale francs (XAF) per US dollar -

Exchange rates: 606.345 (2024 est.)
606.57 (2023 est.)
623.76 (2022 est.)
554.531 (2021 est.)
575.586 (2020 est.)

ENERGY

Electricity access: *electrification - total population:* 11.7% (2022 est.)
electrification - urban areas: 46.3%
electrification - rural areas: 1.3%

Electricity: *installed generating capacity:* 167,000 kW (2023 est.)
consumption: 282.103 million kWh (2023 est.)
transmission/distribution losses: 109.04 million kWh (2023 est.)
comparison rankings: installed generating capacity 178; consumption 185; transmission/distribution losses 50

Electricity generation sources: *fossil fuels:* 94.3% of total installed capacity (2023 est.)
solar: 0.8% of total installed capacity (2023 est.)
wind: 2.3% of total installed capacity (2023 est.)
biomass and waste: 2.6% of total installed capacity (2023 est.)

Coal: *imports:* 20 metric tons (2023 est.)

Petroleum: *total petroleum production:* 124,000 bbl/day (2023 est.)
refined petroleum consumption: 15,000 bbl/day (2023 est.)
crude oil estimated reserves: 1.5 billion barrels (2021 est.)

Energy consumption per capita: 1.502 million Btu/person (2023 est.)
comparison ranking: 191

COMMUNICATIONS

Telephones - fixed lines: *total subscriptions:* 5,000 (2022 est.)
subscriptions per 100 inhabitants: (2022 est.) less than 1
comparison ranking: total subscriptions 203

Telephones - mobile cellular: *total subscriptions:* 12.1 million (2022 est.)
subscriptions per 100 inhabitants: 68 (2022 est.)
comparison ranking: total subscriptions 84

Broadcast media: 1 state-owned TV station; 2 privately-owned TV stations; state-owned radio network, Radiodiffusion Nationale Tchadienne (RNT), operates national and regional stations; over 10 private radio stations; some stations rebroadcast programs from international broadcasters (2017)

Internet country code: .td

Internet users: *percent of population:* 13% (2023 est.)

Broadband - fixed subscriptions: *total:* 0 (2022 est.)
subscriptions per 100 inhabitants: (2022 est.) less than 1
comparison ranking: total 213

TRANSPORTATION

Civil aircraft registration country code prefix: TT

Airports: 44 (2025)
comparison ranking: 96

MILITARY AND SECURITY

Military and security forces: Chadian National Army (Armee Nationale du Tchad, ANT): Ground Forces (l'Armee de Terre, AdT), Chadian Air Force (l'Armee de l'Air Tchadienne, AAT), Chadian National Gendarmerie; General Direction of the Security Services of State Institutions (Direction Generale des Services de Securite des Institutions de l'Etat, GDSSIE)

Ministry of Public Security and Immigration: National Nomadic Guard of Chad (GNNT) (2025)
note 1: the GDSSIE is the presidential guard force and is considered to be Chad's elite military unit; it is reportedly a division-sized force with infantry, armor, and special forces/anti-terrorism regiments (known as the Special Anti-Terrorist Group or SATG, aka Division of Special Anti-Terrorist Groups or DGSAT); it reports directly to the president
note 2: the Chadian National Police are under the Ministry of Public Security and Immigration; border security duties are shared by the ANT, Customs (Ministry of Public Security and Immigration), the National Gendarmerie, and the GNNT

Military expenditures: 3% of GDP (2024 est.)
2.9% of GDP (2023 est.)
2.6% of GDP (2022 est.)
2.5% of GDP (2021 est.)
2.9% of GDP (2020 est.)

Military and security service personnel strengths: estimated 35-40,000 active Chadian National Army (2025)
note: in 2021, Chad pledged to increase the size of the military to 60,000

Military equipment inventories and acquisitions: the ANT is armed with a mix of older, secondhand, and some more modern weapons and equipment from a wide variety of suppliers, including Brazil, China, France, Russia/former Soviet Union, Turkey, Ukraine, and the US (2024)

Military service age and obligation: 20 is the legal minimum age for compulsory military service for men with an 18-36 month service obligation (information varies); women are subject to 12 months of compulsory military or civic service at age 21; 18-35 for voluntary service (18-25 for officer recruits); soldiers released from active duty are in the reserves until the age of 50 (2023)

Military deployments: Chad has committed approximately 1,000-1,500 troops to the Multinational Joint Task Force (MNJTF) against Boko Haram and other terrorist groups operating in the general area of the Lake Chad Basin and along Nigeria's northeast border; national MNJTF troop contingents are deployed within their own territories, although cross-border operations are conducted periodically (2024)

Military - note: internal security is the primary focus of the Chadian National Army, and it is actively engaged in counterinsurgency operations against multiple terrorist and rebel groups; the terrorist groups Boko Haram and Islamic State of Iraq and ash-Sham in West Africa operate in the Lake Chad Basin area; meanwhile, a number of anti-government militias operate in northern Chad, some from bases in southern Libya, including the FACT (Front pour le Changement et la Concorde au Tchad), the Military Command Council for the Salvation of the Republic (le Conseil de Commandement Militaire pour le salut de la République or CCSMR), the Union of Forces for Democracy and Development (le Union des Forces pour la Démocratie et le Développement or UFDD), and the Union of Resistance Forces (le Union des Forces de la Résistance UFR); former Chadian President Idriss DEBY was killed in April 2021 during fighting between the FACT and government forces (2025)

TERRORISM

Terrorist group(s): Terrorist group(s): Boko Haram; Islamic State of Iraq and ash-Sham - West Africa (ISIS-WA)
note: details about the history, aims, leadership, organization, areas of operation, tactics, targets, weapons, size, and sources of support of the group(s) appear(s) in Appendix T

TRANSNATIONAL ISSUES

Refugees and internally displaced persons: *refugees:* 1,286,645 (2024 est.)

IDPs: 1,542,532 (2024 est.)

Trafficking in persons: *tier rating:* Tier 3 — Chad does not fully meet the minimum standards for the elimination of trafficking and is not making significant efforts to do so, therefore, Chad was downgraded to Tier 3; for more details, go to: https://www.state.gov/reports/2025-trafficking-in-persons-report/chad/

CHILE

INTRODUCTION

Background: Indigenous groups inhabited central and southern Chile for several thousand years, living in mixed pastoralist and settled communities. The Inca then ruled the north of the country for nearly a century prior to the arrival of the Spanish in the 16th century. In 1541, the Spanish established the Captaincy General of Chile, which lasted until Chile declared its independence in 1810. The subsequent struggle with the Spanish became tied to other South American independence conflicts, with a decisive victory not being achieved until 1818. In the War of the Pacific (1879-83), Chile defeated Peru and Bolivia to win its current northernmost regions. By the 1880s, the Chilean central government cemented its control over the central and southern regions inhabited by Mapuche Indigenous peoples. Between 1891 and 1973, a series of elected governments succeeded each other until the Marxist government of Salvador ALLENDE was overthrown in 1973 in a military coup led by General Augusto PINOCHET, who ruled until a democratically elected president was inaugurated in 1990. Economic reforms that were maintained consistently since the 1980s contributed to steady growth, reduced poverty rates by over half, and helped secure the country's commitment to democratic and representative government. Chile has increasingly assumed regional and international leadership roles befitting its status as a stable, democratic nation.

GEOGRAPHY

Location: Southern South America, bordering the South Pacific Ocean, between Argentina and Peru

Geographic coordinates: 30 00 S, 71 00 W

Map references: South America

Area: *total:* 756,102 sq km
land: 743,812 sq km
water: 12,290 sq km
note: includes Easter Island (Isla de Pascua) and Isla Sala y Gomez
comparison ranking: total 39

Area - comparative: slightly smaller than twice the size of Montana

Land boundaries: *total:* 7,801 km
border countries (3): Argentina 6,691 km; Bolivia 942 km; Peru 168 km

Coastline: 6,435 km

Maritime claims: *territorial sea:* 12 nm
contiguous zone: 24 nm
exclusive economic zone: 200 nm
continental shelf: 200/350 nm

Climate: temperate; desert in north; Mediterranean in central region; cool and damp in south

Terrain: low coastal mountains, fertile central valley, rugged Andes in east

Elevation: *highest point:* Nevado Ojos del Salado 6,893 m (highest volcano in the world)
lowest point: Pacific Ocean 0 m
mean elevation: 1,871 m

Natural resources: copper, timber, iron ore, nitrates, precious metals, molybdenum, hydropower

Land use: *agricultural land:* 14.3% (2022 est.)
arable land: 1.7% (2022 est.)
permanent crops: 0.7% (2022 est.)
permanent pasture: 11.8% (2022 est.)
forest: 24.8% (2022 est.)
other: 60.9% (2022 est.)

Irrigated land: 9,094 sq km (2022)

Major lakes (area sq km): *fresh water lake(s):* Lago General Carrera (shared with Argentina) - 2,240 sq km; Lago O'Higgins (shared with Argentina) - 1,010 sq km; Lago Llanquihue - 800 sq km; Lago Fagnano (shared with Argentina) - 590 sq km

Population distribution: 90% of the population is located in the middle third of the country around the capital of Santiago; the far north, including the Atacama Desert, and the extreme south are relatively underpopulated

Natural hazards: severe earthquakes; active volcanism; tsunamis
volcanism: significant volcanic activity due to more than three-dozen active volcanoes along the Andes Mountains; Lascar (5,592 m), which last erupted in 2007, is the most active volcano in the northern Chilean Andes; Llaima (3,125 m) in central Chile, which last erupted in 2009, is another of the country's most active; Chaiten's 2008 eruption forced major evacuations; other notable historically active volcanoes include Cerro Hudson, Calbuco, Copahue, Guallatiri, Llullaillaco, Nevados de Chillan, Puyehue, San Pedro, and Villarrica; see note 2 under "Geography - note"

Geography - note: *note 1:* Chile is the longest country north-to-south in the world, extending across 39 degrees of latitude
note 2: Chile is one of the countries along the Ring of Fire, which is a belt bordering the Pacific Ocean that contains about 75% of the world's volcanoes and up to 90% of the world's earthquakes
note 3: the Atacama Desert in the north of Chile is the driest desert in the world; Ojos del Salado (6,893 m) in the Atacama Desert is the highest active volcano in the world, Chile's tallest mountain, and the second-highest in the Western Hemisphere and the Southern Hemisphere; the volcano's small crater lake is the world's highest lake at 6,390 m

PEOPLE AND SOCIETY

Population: *total:* 18,664,652 (2024 est.)
male: 9,169,736
female: 9,494,916
comparison rankings: total 67; male 67; female 67

Nationality: *noun:* Chilean(s)
adjective: Chilean

Ethnic groups: White and non-Indigenous 88.9%, Mapuche 9.1%, Aymara 0.7%, other Indigenous groups 1% (includes Rapa Nui, Likan Antai, Quechua, Colla, Diaguita, Kawesqar, Yagan or Yamana), unspecified 0.3% (2012 est.)

Languages: Spanish 99.5% (official), English 10.2%, Indigenous 1% (includes Mapudungun, Aymara, Quechua, Rapa Nui), other 2.3%, unspecified 0.2% (2012 est.)
major-language sample(s):
La Libreta Informativa del Mundo, la fuente indispensable de información básica. (Spanish)
note: shares sum to more than 100% because some respondents gave more than one answer on the census

Religions: Catholic 57%, none 25.7%, Evangelical or Protestant 16.2%, other Christians and traditions related to Christ 1.3%; less than 1%: Buddhist, Catholic Orthodox, Church of Jesus Christ of Latter-Day Saints, Islam, Judaism, other religions, no religion (2024)

Age structure: *0-14 years:* 19.2% (male 1,822,908/female 1,751,528)
15-64 years: 67.3% (male 6,274,620/female 6,278,467)
65 years and over: 13.6% (2024 est.) (male 1,072,208/female 1,464,921)

Dependency ratios: *total dependency ratio:* 44.9 (2024 est.)
youth dependency ratio: 24.8 (2024 est.)
elderly dependency ratio: 20 (2024 est.)
potential support ratio: 5 (2024 est.)

Median age: *total:* 36.9 years (2024 est.)
male: 35.8 years
female: 38.2 years
comparison ranking: total 85

Population growth rate: 0.61% (2024 est.)
comparison ranking: 136

Birth rate: 12.4 births/1,000 population (2024 est.)

comparison ranking: 140

Death rate: 6.6 deaths/1,000 population (2024 est.)
comparison ranking: 133

Net migration rate: 0.3 migrant(s)/1,000 population (2024 est.)
comparison ranking: 74

Population distribution: 90% of the population is located in the middle third of the country around the capital of Santiago; the far north, including the Atacama Desert, and the extreme south are relatively underpopulated

Urbanization: *urban population:* 88% of total population (2023)
rate of urbanization: 0.78% annual rate of change (2020-25 est.)

Major urban areas - population: 6.903 million SANTIAGO (capital), 1.009 million Valparaiso, 912,000 Concepcion (2023)

Sex ratio: *at birth:* 1.04 male(s)/female
0-14 years: 1.04 male(s)/female
15-64 years: 1 male(s)/female
65 years and over: 0.73 male(s)/female
total population: 0.97 male(s)/female (2024 est.)

Maternal mortality ratio: 10 deaths/100,000 live births (2023 est.)
comparison ranking: 150

Infant mortality rate: *total:* 6.3 deaths/1,000 live births (2024 est.)
male: 6.9 deaths/1,000 live births
female: 5.7 deaths/1,000 live births
comparison ranking: total 166

Life expectancy at birth: *total population:* 80.3 years (2024 est.)
male: 77.3 years
female: 83.3 years
comparison ranking: total population 55

Total fertility rate: 1.75 children born/woman (2024 est.)
comparison ranking: 148

Gross reproduction rate: 0.85 (2024 est.)

Drinking water source: *improved: urban:* 100% of population (2022 est.)
rural: 100% of population (2022 est.)
total: 100% of population (2022 est.)
unimproved: urban: 0% of population (2022 est.)
rural: 0% of population (2022 est.)
total: 0% of population (2022 est.)

Health expenditure: 9% of GDP (2022)
19% of national budget (2022 est.)

Physician density: 3.33 physicians/1,000 population (2023)

Hospital bed density: 2 beds/1,000 population (2021 est.)

Sanitation facility access: *improved: urban:* 100% of population (2022 est.)
rural: 100% of population (2022 est.)
total: 100% of population (2022 est.)
unimproved: urban: 0% of population (2022 est.)
rural: 0% of population (2022 est.)
total: 0% of population (2022 est.)

Obesity - adult prevalence rate: 28% (2016)
comparison ranking: 32

Alcohol consumption per capita: *total:* 7.8 liters of pure alcohol (2019 est.)
beer: 2.76 liters of pure alcohol (2019 est.)
wine: 2.61 liters of pure alcohol (2019 est.)
spirits: 2.43 liters of pure alcohol (2019 est.)
other alcohols: 0 liters of pure alcohol (2019 est.)
comparison ranking: total 47

Tobacco use: *total:* 26.2% (2025 est.)
male: 28.4% (2025 est.)
female: 24.1% (2025 est.)
comparison ranking: total 37

Currently married women (ages 15-49): 46.3% (2023 est.)

Education expenditure: 5% of GDP (2021 est.)
14.9% national budget (2021 est.)
comparison ranking: Education expenditure (% GDP) 63

Literacy: *total population:* 96% (2017 est.)
male: 96% (2017 est.)
female: 96% (2017 est.)

School life expectancy (primary to tertiary education): *total:* 17 years (2023 est.)
male: 17 years (2023 est.)
female: 17 years (2023 est.)

ENVIRONMENT

Environmental issues: air pollution from industrial and vehicle emissions; water pollution from raw sewage; noise pollution; improper garbage disposal; soil degradation; widespread deforestation; pollution and ecosystem degradation from mining; wildlife conservation

International environmental agreements: *party to:* Antarctic-Environmental Protection, Antarctic-Marine Living Resources, Antarctic Seals, Antarctic Treaty, Biodiversity, Climate Change, Climate Change-Kyoto Protocol, Climate Change-Paris Agreement, Comprehensive Nuclear Test Ban, Desertification, Endangered Species, Environmental Modification, Hazardous Wastes, Law of the Sea, Marine Dumping-London Convention, Marine Dumping-London Protocol, Nuclear Test Ban, Ozone Layer Protection, Ship Pollution, Wetlands, Whaling
signed, but not ratified: none of the selected agreements

Climate: temperate; desert in north; Mediterranean in central region; cool and damp in south

Urbanization: *urban population:* 88% of total population (2023)
rate of urbanization: 0.78% annual rate of change (2020-25 est.)

Carbon dioxide emissions: 83.058 million metric tonnes of CO2 (2023 est.)
from coal and metallurgical coke: 14.773 million metric tonnes of CO2 (2023 est.)
from petroleum and other liquids: 55.504 million metric tonnes of CO2 (2023 est.)
from consumed natural gas: 12.781 million metric tonnes of CO2 (2023 est.)
comparison ranking: total emissions 46

Particulate matter emissions: 18.8 micrograms per cubic meter (2019 est.)

Waste and recycling: *municipal solid waste generated annually:* 6.517 million tons (2024 est.)
percent of municipal solid waste recycled: 1% (2022 est.)

Total water withdrawal: *municipal:* 1.29 billion cubic meters (2022 est.)
industrial: 1.66 billion cubic meters (2022 est.)
agricultural: 29.42 billion cubic meters (2022 est.)

Total renewable water resources: 923.06 billion cubic meters (2022 est.)

Geoparks: *total global geoparks and regional networks:* 1
global geoparks and regional networks: Kutralkura (2023)

GOVERNMENT

Country name: *conventional long form:* Republic of Chile
conventional short form: Chile
local long form: República de Chile
local short form: Chile
etymology: derivation of the name is unclear; it may come from a local word meaning either "land's end" or "cold," or a local word that was confused with the Mexican Spanish word *chili*, meaning a chili pepper, in reference to the area's shape

Government type: presidential republic

Capital: *name:* Santiago; note - Valparaiso is the seat of the national legislature
geographic coordinates: 33 27 S, 70 40 W
time difference: UTC-3 (2 hours ahead of Washington, DC, during Standard Time)
daylight saving time: +1hr, begins second Sunday in August; ends second Sunday in May; note - Punta Arenas observes DST throughout the year
time zone note: Chile has three time zones: the continental portion at UTC-3; the southern Magallanes region, which does not use daylight savings time and remains at UTC-3 for the summer months; and Easter Island at UTC-5
etymology: Santiago is named after Saint James, the patron saint of Spain (Santo Iago in Spanish); Valparaiso derives from the Spanish words *valle* (valley) and *paraíso* (paradise)

Administrative divisions: 16 regions (*regiones*, singular - *region*); Aysen, Antofagasta, Araucania, Arica y Parinacota, Atacama, Biobio, Coquimbo, Libertador General Bernardo O'Higgins, Los Lagos, Los Rios, Magallanes y de la Antartica Chilena (Magallanes and Chilean Antarctica), Maule, Nuble, Region Metropolitana (Santiago), Tarapaca, Valparaiso
note: the US does not recognize any claims to Antarctica

Legal system: civil law system influenced by several Western European civil legal systems; Constitutional Tribunal reviews legislative acts

Constitution: *history:* many previous; latest adopted 11 September 1980, effective 11 March 1981; in September 2022 and again in December 2023, referendums presented for a new constitution were both defeated, and the September 1980 constitution remains in force
amendment process: proposed by members of either house of the National Congress or by the president of the republic; passage requires at least four-sevenths majority vote of the membership in both houses and approval by the president; passage of amendments to constitutional articles, such as the republican form of government, basic rights and freedoms, the Constitutional Tribunal, electoral justice, the Council of National Security, or the constitutional amendment process, requires at least four-sevenths majority vote by both houses of Congress and approval by the president; the president can opt to hold a referendum when Congress and the president disagree on an amendment

International law organization participation: has not submitted an ICJ jurisdiction declaration; accepts ICCt jurisdiction

Citizenship: *citizenship by birth:* yes
citizenship by descent only: yes

dual citizenship recognized: yes
residency requirement for naturalization: 5 years

Suffrage: 18 years of age; universal

Executive branch: *chief of state:* President Gabriel BORIC (since 11 March 2022)
head of government: President Gabriel BORIC (since 11 March 2022)
cabinet: Cabinet appointed by the president
election/appointment process: president directly elected by absolute-majority popular vote in 2 rounds, if needed, for a single 4-year term
most recent election date: 21 November 2021, with a runoff held on 19 December 2021
election results: *2021:* Gabriel BORIC elected president in second round; percent of vote in first round - Jose Antonio KAST (FSC) 27.9%; Gabriel BORIC (AD) 25.8%; Franco PARISI (PDG) 12.8%; Sebastian SICHEL (ChP+) 12.8%; Yasna PROVOSTE (New Social Pact) 11.6%; other 9.1%; percent of vote in second round - Gabriel BORIC 55.9%; Jose Antonio KAST 44.1%
2017: Sebastian PINERA Echenique elected president in second round; percent of vote in first round - Sebastian PINERA Echenique (independent) 36.6%; Alejandro GUILLIER (independent) 22.7%; Beatriz SANCHEZ (independent) 20.3%; Jose Antonio KAST (independent) 7.9%; Carolina GOIC (PDC) 5.9%; Marco ENRIQUEZ-OMINAMI (PRO) 5.7%; other 0.9%; percent of vote in second round - Sebastian PINERA Echenique 54.6%, Alejandro GUILLIER 45.4%
expected date of next election: 23 November 2025 (a runoff, if needed, will take place on 20 December 2025)
note: the president is both chief of state and head of government

Legislative branch: *legislature name:* National Congress (Congreso Nacional)
legislative structure: bicameral

Legislative branch - lower chamber: *chamber name:* Chamber of Deputies (Cámara de Diputados)
number of seats: 155 (all directly elected)
electoral system: proportional representation
scope of elections: full renewal
term in office: 4 years
most recent election date: 11/21/2021
parties elected and seats per party: Chile Podemos (Empowering Chile", CP +) (53); New Social Pact (NPS) (37); Approving Dignity (AD) (37); Christian Social Front (FSC) (15); Other (13)
percentage of women in chamber: 35.1%
expected date of next election: November 2025

Legislative branch - upper chamber: *chamber name:* Senate (Senado)
number of seats: 50 (all directly elected)
electoral system: proportional representation
scope of elections: partial renewal
term in office: 8 years
most recent election date: 11/21/2021
parties elected and seats per party: Chile Podemos (Empowering Chile", CP +) (12); New Social Pact (NPS) (8); Approving Dignity (AD) (4); Independents (2); Other (1)
percentage of women in chamber: 26%
expected date of next election: November 2025

Judicial branch: *highest court(s):* Supreme Court or Corte Suprema (consists of a court president and 20 members); Constitutional Court (consists of 10 members and is independent of the rest of the judiciary); Elections Qualifying Court (consists of 5 members)
judge selection and term of office: Supreme Court president and judges (ministers) appointed by the president of the republic and ratified by the Senate from lists of candidates provided by the court itself; judges appointed for life with mandatory retirement at age 70; Constitutional Court members appointed - 3 by the Supreme Court, 3 by the president of the republic, 2 by the Chamber of Deputies, and 2 by the Senate; members serve 9-year terms with partial membership replacement every 3 years (the court reviews constitutionality of legislation); Elections Qualifying Court members appointed by lottery - 1 by the former president or vice president of the Senate and 1 by the former president or vice president of the Chamber of Deputies, 2 by the Supreme Court, and 1 by the Appellate Court of Valparaiso; members appointed for 4-year terms
subordinate courts: Courts of Appeal; oral criminal tribunals; military tribunals; local police courts; specialized tribunals and courts in matters such as family, labor, customs, taxes, and electoral affairs

Political parties: Approve Dignity (Apruebo Dignidad) coalition or AD (included PC, FA, and FREVS); note - dissolved 2023
Broad Front Coalition (Frente Amplio) or FA (includes RD, CS, and Comunes)
Chile We Can Do More (Chile Podemos Más) or ChP+ (coalition includes EVOPOLI, PRI, RN, UDI)
Christian Democratic Party or PDC
Common Sense Party or SC
Commons (Comunes)
Communist Party of Chile or PCCh
Democratic Revolution or RD
Democrats or PD
Equality Party or PI
Green Ecological Party or PEV (dissolved 7 February 2022)
Green Popular Alliance or AVP
Humanist Action Party or PAH
Humanist Party or PH
Independent Democratic Union or UDI
Liberal Party (Partido Liberal de Chile) or PL
National Renewal or RN
New Social Pact or NPS (includes PDC, PL, PPD, PRSD, PS)
Party for Democracy or PPD
Party of the People or PDG
Political Evolution or EVOPOLI
Popular Party or PP
Progressive Homeland Party or PRO
Radical Party or PR
Republican Party or PLR
Social Christian Party or PSC
Social Convergence or CS
Social Green Regionalist Federation or FREVS
Socialist Party or PS
Yellow Movement for Chile or AMAR

Diplomatic representation in the US: *chief of mission:* Ambassador Juan Gabriel VALDES Soublette (since 7 June 2022)
chancery: 1732 Massachusetts Avenue NW, Washington, DC 20036
telephone: [1] (202) 785-1746
FAX: [1] (202) 887-5579
email address and website: echile.eeuu@minrel.gob.cl
https://chile.gob.cl/estados-unidos/en/
consulate(s) general: Chicago, Houston, Los Angeles, Miami, New York, San Francisco

Diplomatic representation from the US: *chief of mission:* Ambassador (vacant); Chargé d'Affaires Richard T. (Rick) YONEOKA (since January 2025)
embassy: Avenida Andres Bello 2800, Las Condes, Santiago
mailing address: 3460 Santiago Place, Washington DC 20521-3460
telephone: [56] (2) 2330-3000
FAX: [56] (2) 2330-3710
email address and website: SantiagoUSA@state.gov
https://cl.usembassy.gov/

International organization participation: APEC, BIS, CAN (associate), CD, CELAC, FAO, G-15, G-77, IADB, IAEA, IBRD, ICAO, ICC (national committees), ICCt, ICRM, IDA, IFAD, IFC, IFRCS, IHO, ILO, IMF, IMO, IMSO, Interpol, IOC, IOM, IPU, ISO, ITSO, ITU, ITUC (NGOs), LAES, LAIA, Mercosur (associate), MIGA, MINUSTAH, NAM, OAS, OECD (enhanced engagement), OPANAL, OPCW, Pacific Alliance, PCA, PROSUR, SICA (observer), UN, UNASUR, UNCTAD, UNESCO, UNFICYP, UNHCR, UNIDO, Union Latina, UNMOGIP, UNTSO, UNWTO, UPU, WCO, WFTU (NGOs), WHO, WIPO, WMO, WTO

Independence: 18 September 1810 (from Spain)

National holiday: Independence Day, 18 September (1810)

Flag: *description:* two equal horizontal bands of white (top) and red; a blue square sits in the top left corner of the flag, the same height as the white band; the square has a five-pointed white star in the center
meaning: the star represents a guide to progress and honor; blue stands for the sky, white for the Andes Mountains, and red for the blood spilled to achieve independence
note: design influenced by the US flag

National symbol(s): huemul (mountain deer), Andean condor

National color(s): red, white, blue

National anthem(s): *title:* "Himno Nacional de Chile" (National Anthem of Chile)
lyrics/music: Eusebio LILLO Robles and Bernardo DE VERA y Pintado/Ramon CARNICER y Battle
history: music adopted 1828, original lyrics adopted 1818, adapted lyrics adopted 1847; under Augusto PINOCHET's military rule, a verse glorifying the army was added; some citizens refused to sing this verse as a protest, and it was removed when democracy was restored in 1990

National heritage: *total World Heritage Sites:* 7 (all cultural)
selected World Heritage Site locales: Rapa Nui National Park; Churches of Chiloe; Historic Valparaiso; Humberstone and Santa Laura Saltpeter Works; Sewell Mining Town; Qhapaq Ñan/Andean Road System; Chinchorro archeological sites

ECONOMY

Economic overview: export-driven economy; leading copper producer; though hit by COVID-19, fairly quick rebound from increased liquidity and rapid vaccine rollouts; decreasing poverty but still lingering inequality; public debt rising but still manageable; recent political violence has had negative economic consequences

Real GDP (purchasing power parity): $596.556 billion (2024 est.)
$581.187 billion (2023 est.)
$578.173 billion (2022 est.)
note: data in 2021 dollars
comparison ranking: 43

Real GDP growth rate: 2.6% (2024 est.)
0.5% (2023 est.)
2.2% (2022 est.)
note: annual GDP % growth based on constant local currency
comparison ranking: 133

Real GDP per capita: $30,200 (2024 est.)
$29,600 (2023 est.)
$29,600 (2022 est.)
note: data in 2021 dollars
comparison ranking: 78

GDP (official exchange rate): $330.267 billion (2024 est.)
note: data in current dollars at official exchange rate

Inflation rate (consumer prices): 4.3% (2024 est.)
7.6% (2023 est.)
11.6% (2022 est.)
note: annual % change based on consumer prices
comparison ranking: 129

GDP - composition, by sector of origin: *agriculture:* 3.9% (2024 est.)
industry: 30.1% (2024 est.)
services: 56.1% (2024 est.)
note: figures may not total 100% due to non-allocated consumption not captured in sector-reported data
comparison rankings: agriculture 121; industry 55; services 115

GDP - composition, by end use: *household consumption:* 58.1% (2024 est.)
government consumption: 15.1% (2024 est.)
investment in fixed capital: 23.5% (2024 est.)
investment in inventories: -0.3% (2024 est.)
exports of goods and services: 33.7% (2024 est.)
imports of goods and services: -30.1% (2024 est.)
note: figures may not total 100% due to rounding or gaps in data collection

Agricultural products: grapes, milk, apples, wheat, tomatoes, potatoes, chicken, maize, sugar beets, pork (2023)
note: top ten agricultural products based on tonnage

Industries: copper, lithium, other minerals, foodstuffs, fish processing, iron and steel, wood and wood products, transport equipment, cement, textiles

Industrial production growth rate: 3.5% (2024 est.)
note: annual % change in industrial value added based on constant local currency
comparison ranking: 70

Labor force: 10.088 million (2024 est.)
note: number of people ages 15 or older who are employed or seeking work
comparison ranking: 56

Unemployment rate: 9.1% (2024 est.)
9.1% (2023 est.)
8.3% (2022 est.)
note: % of labor force seeking employment
comparison ranking: 143

Youth unemployment rate (ages 15-24): *total:* 22.3% (2024 est.)
male: 20.3% (2024 est.)
female: 24.9% (2024 est.)
note: % of labor force ages 15-24 seeking employment
comparison ranking: total 47

Population below poverty line: 6.5% (2022 est.)
note: % of population with income below national poverty line

Gini Index coefficient - distribution of family income: 43 (2022 est.)
note: index (0-100) of income distribution; higher values represent greater inequality
comparison ranking: 27

Average household expenditures: *on food:* 19.4% of household expenditures (2023 est.)
on alcohol and tobacco: 3.5% of household expenditures (2023 est.)

Household income or consumption by percentage share: *lowest 10%:* 2.3% (2022 est.)
highest 10%: 34.5% (2022 est.)
note: % share of income accruing to lowest and highest 10% of population

Remittances: 0% of GDP (2024 est.)
0% of GDP (2023 est.)
0% of GDP (2022 est.)
note: personal transfers and compensation between resident and non-resident individuals/households/entities

Budget: *revenues:* $77.003 billion (2023 est.)
expenditures: $85.024 billion (2023 est.)
note: central government revenues (excluding grants) and expenditures converted to US dollars at average official exchange rate for year indicated

Taxes and other revenues: 17.7% (of GDP) (2023 est.)
note: central government tax revenue as a % of GDP
comparison ranking: 70

Current account balance: -$4.853 billion (2024 est.)
-$10.497 billion (2023 est.)
-$26.656 billion (2022 est.)
note: balance of payments - net trade and primary/secondary income in current dollars
comparison ranking: 171

Exports: $111.123 billion (2024 est.)
$103.256 billion (2023 est.)
$107.039 billion (2022 est.)
note: balance of payments - exports of goods and services in current dollars
comparison ranking: 45

Exports - partners: China 39%, USA 16%, Japan 7%, S. Korea 6%, Brazil 4% (2023)
note: top five export partners based on percentage share of exports

Exports - commodities: copper ore, refined copper, fish, carbonates, pitted fruits (2023)
note: top five export commodities based on value in dollars

Imports: $99.239 billion (2024 est.)
$100.082 billion (2023 est.)
$118.928 billion (2022 est.)
note: balance of payments - imports of goods and services in current dollars
comparison ranking: 47

Imports - partners: China 23%, USA 20%, Brazil 10%, Argentina 7%, Germany 5% (2023)
note: top five import partners based on percentage share of imports

Imports - commodities: refined petroleum, crude petroleum, cars, garments, trucks (2023)
note: top five import commodities based on value in dollars

Reserves of foreign exchange and gold: $44.403 billion (2024 est.)
$46.377 billion (2023 est.)
$39.102 billion (2022 est.)
note: holdings of gold (year-end prices)/foreign exchange/special drawing rights in current dollars
comparison ranking: 46

Exchange rates: Chilean pesos (CLP) per US dollar -

Exchange rates: 943.572 (2024 est.)
840.067 (2023 est.)
873.314 (2022 est.)
758.955 (2021 est.)
792.727 (2020 est.)

ENERGY

Electricity access: *electrification - total population:* 100% (2022 est.)

Electricity: *installed generating capacity:* 39.238 million kW (2023 est.)
consumption: 83.295 billion kWh (2023 est.)
transmission/distribution losses: 4.384 billion kWh (2023 est.)
comparison rankings: installed generating capacity 33; consumption 38; transmission/distribution losses 158

Electricity generation sources: *fossil fuels:* 35.6% of total installed capacity (2023 est.)
solar: 20.6% of total installed capacity (2023 est.)
wind: 10.8% of total installed capacity (2023 est.)
hydroelectricity: 26.6% of total installed capacity (2023 est.)
geothermal: 0.5% of total installed capacity (2023 est.)
biomass and waste: 5.9% of total installed capacity (2023 est.)

Coal: *production:* 474,000 metric tons (2023 est.)
consumption: 8.087 million metric tons (2023 est.)
exports: 63,000 metric tons (2023 est.)
imports: 7.589 million metric tons (2023 est.)
proven reserves: 1.181 billion metric tons (2023 est.)

Petroleum: *total petroleum production:* 11,000 bbl/day (2023 est.)
refined petroleum consumption: 404,000 bbl/day (2024 est.)
crude oil estimated reserves: 150 million barrels (2021 est.)

Natural gas: *production:* 1.362 billion cubic meters (2023 est.)
consumption: 6.5 billion cubic meters (2023 est.)
exports: 39.009 million cubic meters (2023 est.)
imports: 5.196 billion cubic meters (2023 est.)
proven reserves: 97.976 billion cubic meters (2021 est.)

Energy consumption per capita: 71.42 million Btu/person (2023 est.)
comparison ranking: 70

COMMUNICATIONS

Telephones - fixed lines: *total subscriptions:* 1.978 million (2023 est.)
subscriptions per 100 inhabitants: 10 (2023 est.)
comparison ranking: total subscriptions 48

Telephones - mobile cellular: *total subscriptions:* 26.7 million (2023 est.)
subscriptions per 100 inhabitants: 135 (2022 est.)
comparison ranking: total subscriptions 50

Broadcast media: national and local terrestrial TV channels, coupled with extensive cable TV networks; the state-owned Television Nacional de Chile (TVN) network is self-financed through commercial advertising and is not under direct government control; large number of privately owned TV stations; about 250 radio stations

Internet country code: .cl

Internet users: *percent of population:* 95% (2023 est.)

Broadband - fixed subscriptions: *total:* 4.52 million (2023 est.)
subscriptions per 100 inhabitants: 23 (2023 est.)
comparison ranking: total 38

TRANSPORTATION

Civil aircraft registration country code prefix: CC

Airports: 379 (2025)
comparison ranking: 18

Heliports: 115 (2025)
comparison ranking: 22

Railways: *total:* 7,281.5 km (2014)
narrow gauge: 3,853.5 km (2014) 1.000-m gauge
broad gauge: 3,428 km (2014) 1.676-m gauge (1,691 km electrified)

Merchant marine: *total:* 249 (2023)
by type: bulk carrier 3, container ship 5, general cargo 66, oil tanker 14, other 161
comparison ranking: total 64

Ports: *total ports:* 39 (2024)
large: 0
medium: 2
small: 10
very small: 27
ports with oil terminals: 25
key ports: Antofagasta, Bahia de Valdivia, Bahia de Valparaiso, Coronel, Iquique, Mejillones, Puerto Montt, Puerto San Antonio, Rada de Arica, Rada Punta Arenas, Talcahuano, Tocopilla

MILITARY AND SECURITY

Military and security forces: Armed Forces of Chile (Fuerzas Armadas de Chile): Chilean Army (Ejército de Chile), Chilean Navy (Armada de Chile, includes Marine Corps and Maritime Territory and Merchant Marine Directorate or Directemar), Chilean Air Force (Fuerza Aerea de Chile, FACh) (2025)
note 1: the Directemar is the country's coast guard
note 2: the National Police Force (Carabineros de Chile) is responsible to both the Ministry of Defense and the Ministry of the Interior and Public Security

Military expenditures: 1.5% of GDP (2024 est.)
1.5% of GDP (2023 est.)
1.6% of GDP (2022 est.)
2% of GDP (2021 est.)
2% of GDP (2020 est.)

Military and security service personnel strengths: approximately 70,000 active Armed Forces (40,000 Army; 20,000 Navy; 10,000 Air Force); approximately 50,000 Carabineros (2025)

Military equipment inventories and acquisitions: the Chilean military inventory is comprised of a broad mix of older foreign supplied weapons and equipment and some domestically produced systems; significant foreign suppliers have included Australia, Brazil, France, Germany, Israel, the Netherlands, Spain, the UK, and the US; Chile's defense industry is active in the production of military aircraft, ships, and vehicles (2024)

Military service age and obligation: 17 or 18 for voluntary military service for men and women; selective compulsory service (there are usually enough volunteers to make compulsory service unnecessary); service obligation is a minimum of 12 months for Army and 22 months for Navy and Air Force (2024)
note: as of 2024, women comprised approximately 20% of the armed forces

Military - note: the Chilean military's responsibilities are territorial defense, ensuring the country's sovereignty, assisting with disaster and humanitarian relief, and providing some internal security duties such as border security or maintaining public order if required; a key focus in recent years has been assisting with securing the border area with Bolivia and Peru; it trains regularly and participates in bilateral and multinational training exercises, as well as international peacekeeping operations
Chile and Argentina have a joint peacekeeping force known as the Combined Southern Cross Peacekeeping Force (FPC), designed to be made available to the UN; the FPC is made up of air, ground, and naval components, as well as a combined logistics support unit
the Chilean Army was founded in 1810, but traces its origins back to the Army of the Kingdom of Chile, which was established by the Spanish Crown in the early 1600s; Chile's military aviation was inaugurated in 1913 with the creation of a military aviation school; the Navy traces its origins to 1817; it was first led by a British officer and the first ships were largely crewed by American, British, and Irish sailors; by the 1880s, the Chilean Navy was one of the most powerful in the Americas, and included the world's first protected cruiser (a ship with an armored deck to protect vital machine spaces) (2025)

SPACE

Space agency/agencies: the Chilean Space Agency was established in 2001 and dissolved in 2014, at which time the space program became part of the Ministry of Defense; the Ministry of Science also participates in Chile's space program (2025)

Space program overview: space program focused on the acquisition and operation of satellites; operates foreign-built satellites and satellite ground stations; building small remote sensing (RS) satellites; researching and developing additional capabilities and technologies for the production of satellites and satellite sub-systems; is a world leader in astronomy and astrophysics; the Atacama Desert is home to more than a dozen astronomical observatories, including the Cerro Tololo Inter-American Observatory, the Las Campanas Observatory, and the European Southern Observatory; Chile is also home to several astronomy institutes; has established relations with space agencies and industries of Canada, China, France, India, Israel, Mexico, Russia, the UK, and the US (2025)
note: further details about the key activities, programs, and milestones of the country's space program, as well as government spending estimates on the space sector, appear in the Space Programs reference guide

TERRORISM

Terrorist group(s): Terrorist group(s): Tren de Aragua (TdA)
note: details about the history, aims, leadership, organization, areas of operation, tactics, targets, weapons, size, and sources of support of the group(s) appear(s) in Appendix T

TRANSNATIONAL ISSUES

Refugees and internally displaced persons: *refugees:* 15,788 (2024 est.)

IDPs: 8,323 (2024 est.)
stateless persons: 1,688 (2024 est.)

CHINA

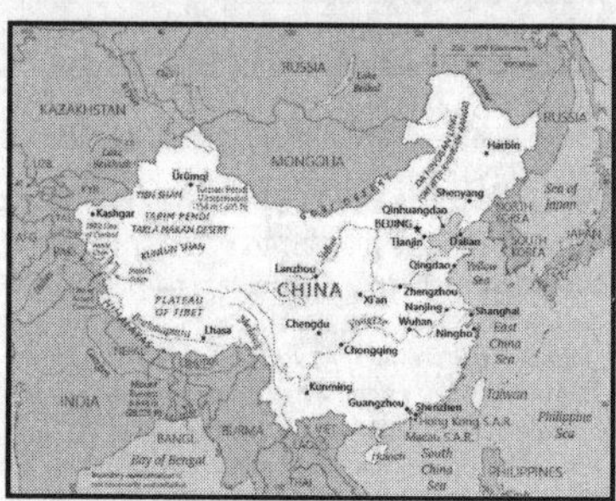

INTRODUCTION

Background: China's historical civilization dates to at least the 13th century B.C., first under the Shang (to 1046 B.C.) and then the Zhou (1046-221 B.C.) dynasties. The imperial era of China began in 221 B.C. under the Qin Dynasty and lasted until the fall of the Qing Dynasty in 1912. During this period, China alternated between periods of unity and disunity under a succession of imperial dynasties. In the 19 century, the Qing Dynasty suffered heavily from overextension by territorial conquest, insolvency, civil war, imperialism, military defeats, and foreign expropriation of ports and infrastructure. It collapsed following the Revolution of 1911, and China became a republic under SUN Yat-sen of the Kuomintang (KMT or Nationalist) Party. However, the republic was beset by division, warlordism, and continued foreign intervention. In the late 1920s, a civil war erupted between the ruling KMT-controlled government, led by CHIANG Kai-shek, and the Chinese Communist Party (CCP). Japan occupied much of northeastern China in the early 1930s, and then launched a full-scale invasion of the country in 1937. The resulting eight years of warfare devastated the country and cost up to 20 million Chinese lives by the time of Japan's defeat in 1945. The Nationalist-Communist civil war continued with renewed intensity after the end of World War II and culminated with a CCP victory in 1949, under the leadership of MAO Zedong.

MAO and the CCP established an autocratic socialist system that, while ensuring the PRC's sovereignty, imposed strict controls over everyday life and launched agricultural, economic, political, and social policies – such as the Great Leap Forward (1958-1962) and the Cultural Revolution (1966-1976) – that cost the lives of millions of people. MAO died in 1976. Beginning in 1978, leaders DENG Xiaoping, JIANG Zemin, and HU Jintao focused on market-oriented economic development and opening up the country to foreign trade, while maintaining the rule of the CCP. Since the change, China has been among the world's fastest growing economies, with real gross domestic product averaging over 9% growth annually through 2021, lifting an estimated 800 million people out of poverty and dramatically improving overall living standards. By 2011, the PRC's economy was the second largest in the world. Current leader XI Jinping has continued these policies but has also maintained tight political controls. Over the past decade, China has increased its global outreach, including military deployments, participation in international organizations, and a global connectivity plan in 2013 called the "Belt and Road Initiative" (BRI). Many nations have signed on to BRI agreements to attract PRC investment, but others have expressed concerns about such issues as the opaque nature of the projects, financing, and potentially unsustainable debt obligations. XI Jinping assumed the positions of General Secretary of the Chinese Communist Party and Chairman of the Central Military Commission in 2012 and President in 2013. In 2018, the PRC's National People's Congress passed an amendment abolishing presidential term limits, which allowed XI to gain a third five-year term in 2023.

GEOGRAPHY

Location: Eastern Asia, bordering the East China Sea, Korea Bay, Yellow Sea, and South China Sea, between North Korea and Vietnam

Geographic coordinates: 35 00 N, 105 00 E

Map references: Asia

Area: *total:* 9,596,960 sq km
land: 9,326,410 sq km
water: 270,550 sq km
comparison ranking: total 5

Area - comparative: slightly smaller than the US

Land boundaries: *total:* 22,457 km
border countries (14): Afghanistan 91 km; Bhutan 477 km; Burma 2,129 km; India 2,659 km; Kazakhstan 1,765 km; North Korea 1,352 km; Kyrgyzstan 1,063 km; Laos 475 km; Mongolia 4,630 km; Nepal 1,389 km; Pakistan 438 km; Russia (northeast) 4,133 km and Russia (northwest) 46 km; Tajikistan 477 km; Vietnam 1,297 km

Coastline: 14,500 km

Maritime claims: *territorial sea:* 12 nm
contiguous zone: 24 nm
exclusive economic zone: 200 nm
continental shelf: 200 nm or to the edge of the continental margin

Climate: extremely diverse; tropical in south to subarctic in north

Terrain: mostly mountains, high plateaus, deserts in west; plains, deltas, and hills in east

Elevation: *highest point:* Mount Everest (highest peak in Asia and highest point on earth above sea level) 8,849 m
lowest point: Turpan Pendi (Turfan Depression) -154 m
mean elevation: 1,840 m

Natural resources: coal, iron ore, helium, petroleum, natural gas, arsenic, bismuth, cobalt, cadmium, ferrosilicon, gallium, germanium, hafnium, indium, lithium, mercury, tantalum, tellurium, tin, titanium, tungsten, antimony, manganese, magnesium, molybdenum, selenium, strontium, vanadium, magnetite, aluminum, lead, zinc, rare earth elements, uranium, hydropower potential (world's largest), arable land

Land use: *agricultural land:* 55.3% (2022 est.)
arable land: 11.5% (2022 est.)
permanent crops: 2.1% (2022 est.)
permanent pasture: 41.7% (2022 est.)
forest: 23.7% (2022 est.)
other: 21% (2022 est.)

Irrigated land: 690,070 sq km (2012)

Major lakes (area sq km): *fresh water lake(s):* Dongting Hu - 3,100 sq km; Poyang Hu - 3,350 sq km; Hongze Hu - 2,700 sq km; Tai Hu - 2,210 sq km; Hulun Nur - 1,590
salt water lake(s): Quinghai Hu - 4,460 sq km; Nam Co - 2,500 sq km; Siling Co - 1,860 sq km; Tangra Yumco - 1,400 sq km; Bosten Hu 1,380 sq km

Major rivers (by length in km): Yangtze - 6,300 km; Huang He - 5,464 km; Amur river source (shared with Mongolia and Russia [m]) - 4,444 km; Lancang Jiang (Mekong) river source (shared with Burma, Laos, Thailand, Cambodia, and Vietnam [m]) - 4,350 km; Yarlung Zangbo Jiang (Brahmaputra) river source (shared with India and Bangladesh [m]) - 3,969 km; Yin-tu Ho (Indus) river source (shared with India and Pakistan [m]) - 3,610 km; Nu Jiang (Salween) river source (shared with Thailand and Burma [m]) - 3,060 km; Irrawaddy river source (shared with Burma [m]) - 2,809 km; Zhu Jiang (Pearl) (shared with Vietnam [s]) - 2,200 km; Yuan Jiang (Red river) source (shared with Vietnam [m]) - 1,149 km
note: [s] after country name indicates river source; [m] after country name indicates river mouth

Major watersheds (area sq km): Arctic Ocean drainage: Ob (2,972,493 sq km)

Indian Ocean drainage: Brahmaputra (651,335 sq km), Ganges (1,016,124 sq km), Indus (1,081,718 sq km), Irrawaddy (413,710 sq km), Salween (271,914 sq km)

Pacific Ocean drainage: Amur (1,929,955 sq km), Huang He (944,970 sq km), Mekong (805,604 sq km), Yangtze (1,722,193 sq km)

Internal (endorheic basin) drainage: Tarim Basin (1,152,448 sq km), Amu Darya (534,739 sq km), Syr Darya (782,617 sq km), Lake Balkash (510,015 sq km)

Major aquifers: North China Aquifer System (Huang Huai Hai Plain), Song-Liao Plain, Tarim Basin

Population distribution: overwhelming majority of the population is found in the eastern half of the country; the west, with its vast mountainous and desert areas, remains sparsely populated; though ranked first in the world in total population, overall density is less than that of many Asian and European countries; high population density is found along the Yangtze and Yellow River valleys, the Xi Jiang River delta, the Sichuan Basin (around Chengdu), in and around Beijing, and the industrial area around Shenyang

Natural hazards: frequent typhoons (about five per year along southern and eastern coasts); damaging floods; tsunamis; earthquakes; droughts; land subsidence
volcanism: China contains some historically active volcanoes including Changbaishan (also known as Baitoushan, Baegdu, or P'aektu-san), Hainan Dao, and Kunlun although most have been relatively inactive in recent centuries

Geography - note: *note 1:* world's fourth largest country (after Russia, Canada, and the US) and largest country situated entirely in Asia; Mount Everest, on the border with Nepal, is the world's tallest peak above sea level
note 2: the largest cave chamber in the world is the Miao Room, in the Gebihe cave system at China's Ziyun Getu He Chuandong National Park, which encloses about 10.78 million cu m (380.7 million cu ft); the world's largest sinkhole is the Xiaoxhai Tiankeng sinkhole in Chongqing Municipality, which is 660 m deep, with a volume of 130 million cu m

PEOPLE AND SOCIETY

Population: *total:* 1,416,043,270 (2024 est.)
male: 722,201,504
female: 693,841,766
comparison rankings: total 1; male 2; female 1

Nationality: *noun:* Chinese (singular and plural)
adjective: Chinese

Ethnic groups: Han Chinese 91.1%, ethnic minorities 8.9% (includes Zhang, Hui, Manchu, Uighur, Miao, Yi, Tujia, Tibetan, Mongol, Dong, Buyei, Yao, Bai, Korean, Hani, Li, Kazakh, Dai, and other nationalities) (2021 est.)
note: the PRC officially recognizes 56 ethnic groups

Languages: Standard Chinese or Mandarin (official; Putonghua, based on the Beijing dialect), Yue (Cantonese), Wu (Shanghainese), Minbei (Fuzhou), Minnan (Hokkien-Taiwanese), Xiang, Gan, Hakka dialects, minority languages; note - Zhuang is official in Guangxi Zhuang, Yue is official in Guangdong, Mongolian is official in Nei Mongol, Uyghur is official in Xinjiang Uygur, Kyrgyz is official in Xinjiang Uyghur, and Tibetan is official in Xizang (Tibet)
major-language sample(s):
世界概況 – 不可缺少的基本消息來源 (Standard Chinese)

Religions: folk religion 21.9%, Buddhist 18.2%, Christian 5.1%, Muslim 1.8%, Hindu < 0.1%, Jewish < 0.1%, other 0.7% (includes Daoist (Taoist)), unaffiliated 52.1% (2021 est.)
note: officially atheist

Age structure: *0-14 years:* 16.3% (male 122,644,111/female 107,926,176)
15-64 years: 69.3% (male 505,412,555/female 476,599,793)
65 years and over: 14.4% (2024 est.) (male 94,144,838/female 109,315,797)

Dependency ratios: *total dependency ratio:* 43.9 (2024 est.)
youth dependency ratio: 23.2 (2024 est.)
elderly dependency ratio: 20.7 (2024 est.)
potential support ratio: 4.8 (2024 est.)
note: data do not include Hong Kong, Macau, and Taiwan

Median age: *total:* 40.2 years (2024 est.)
male: 39 years

female: 41.5 years
comparison ranking: total 61

Population growth rate: 0.23% (2024 est.)
comparison ranking: 172

Birth rate: 10.2 births/1,000 population (2024 est.)
comparison ranking: 183

Death rate: 7.7 deaths/1,000 population (2024 est.)
comparison ranking: 95

Net migration rate: -0.1 migrant(s)/1,000 population (2024 est.)
comparison ranking: 100

Population distribution: overwhelming majority of the population is found in the eastern half of the country; the west, with its vast mountainous and desert areas, remains sparsely populated; though ranked first in the world in total population, overall density is less than that of many Asian and European countries; high population density is found along the Yangtze and Yellow River valleys, the Xi Jiang River delta, the Sichuan Basin (around Chengdu), in and around Beijing, and the industrial area around Shenyang

Urbanization: *urban population:* 64.6% of total population (2023)
rate of urbanization: 1.78% annual rate of change (2020-25 est.)
note: data do not include Hong Kong and Macau

Major urban areas - population: 29.211 million Shanghai, 21.766 million BEIJING (capital), 17.341 million Chongqing, 14.284 million Guangzhou, 14.239 million Tianjin, 13.073 million Shenzhen (2023)

Sex ratio: *at birth:* 1.09 male(s)/female
0-14 years: 1.14 male(s)/female
15-64 years: 1.06 male(s)/female
65 years and over: 0.86 male(s)/female
total population: 1.04 male(s)/female (2024 est.)

Maternal mortality ratio: 16 deaths/100,000 live births (2023 est.)
comparison ranking: 131

Infant mortality rate: *total:* 6.2 deaths/1,000 live births (2024 est.)
male: 6.7 deaths/1,000 live births
female: 5.7 deaths/1,000 live births
comparison ranking: total 167

Life expectancy at birth: *total population:* 78.7 years (2024 est.)
male: 76 years
female: 81.7 years
comparison ranking: total population 75

Total fertility rate: 1.55 children born/woman (2024 est.)
comparison ranking: 193

Gross reproduction rate: 0.74 (2024 est.)

Drinking water source: *improved: urban:* 98.4% of population (2022 est.)
rural: 96.4% of population (2022 est.)
total: 97.6% of population (2022 est.)
unimproved: urban: 1.6% of population (2022 est.)
rural: 3.6% of population (2022 est.)
total: 2.4% of population (2022 est.)

Health expenditure: 5.4% of GDP (2021)
8.8% of national budget (2022 est.)

Physician density: 3.11 physicians/1,000 population (2022)

Hospital bed density: 5 beds/1,000 population (2020 est.)

Sanitation facility access: *improved: urban:* 99.5% of population (2022 est.)
rural: 95.3% of population (2022 est.)
total: 98% of population (2022 est.)
unimproved: urban: 0.5% of population (2022 est.)
rural: 4.7% of population (2022 est.)
total: 2% of population (2022 est.)

Obesity - adult prevalence rate: 6.2% (2016)
comparison ranking: 169

Alcohol consumption per capita: *total:* 4.48 liters of pure alcohol (2019 est.)
beer: 1.66 liters of pure alcohol (2019 est.)
wine: 0.18 liters of pure alcohol (2019 est.)
spirits: 2.63 liters of pure alcohol (2019 est.)
other alcohols: 0 liters of pure alcohol (2019 est.)
comparison ranking: total 89

Tobacco use: *total:* 24.5% (2025 est.)
male: 46.6% (2025 est.)
female: 1.9% (2025 est.)
comparison ranking: total 40

Children under the age of 5 years underweight: 2.4% (2013)
comparison ranking: 92

Currently married women (ages 15-49): 75.9% (2023 est.)

Child marriage: *women married by age 15:* 0.1% (2020)
women married by age 18: 2.8% (2020)
men married by age 18: 0.7% (2020)

Education expenditure: 4% of GDP (2022 est.)
10.5% national budget (2022 est.)
comparison ranking: Education expenditure (% GDP) 108

Literacy: *total population:* 97% (2020 est.)
male: 98% (2020 est.)
female: 95% (2020 est.)

People - note: in October 2015, the Chinese Government announced that it would change its rules to allow all couples to have two children, loosening a 1979 mandate that restricted many couples to one child; the new policy was implemented on 1 January 2016 to address China's rapidly aging population and future economic needs

ENVIRONMENT

Environmental issues: air pollution and acid rain from reliance on coal; carbon dioxide emissions from the burning of fossil fuels; water shortages, particularly in the north; water pollution from untreated wastes; coastal destruction due to land reclamation, industrial development, and aquaculture; deforestation and habitat destruction; poor land management leading to soil erosion, landslides, floods, droughts, dust storms, and desertification; trade in endangered species

International environmental agreements: *party to:* Antarctic-Environmental Protection, Antarctic-Marine Living Resources, Antarctic Treaty, Biodiversity, Climate Change, Climate Change-Kyoto Protocol, Climate Change-Paris Agreement, Desertification, Endangered Species, Environmental Modification, Hazardous Wastes, Law of the Sea, Marine Dumping-London Convention, Marine Dumping-London Protocol, Ozone Layer Protection, Ship Pollution, Tropical Timber 2006, Wetlands, Whaling
signed, but not ratified: Comprehensive Nuclear Test Ban

Climate: extremely diverse; tropical in south to subarctic in north

Urbanization: *urban population:* 64.6% of total population (2023)
rate of urbanization: 1.78% annual rate of change (2020-25 est.)
note: data do not include Hong Kong and Macau

Carbon dioxide emissions: 12.196 billion metric tonnes of CO2 (2023 est.)
from coal and metallurgical coke: 9.575 billion metric tonnes of CO2 (2023 est.)
from petroleum and other liquids: 1.847 billion metric tonnes of CO2 (2023 est.)
from consumed natural gas: 774.076 million metric tonnes of CO2 (2023 est.)
comparison ranking: total emissions 1

Particulate matter emissions: 41.4 micrograms per cubic meter (2019 est.)

Methane emissions: *energy:* 27,832.7 kt (2022-2024 est.)
agriculture: 18,177.8 kt (2019-2021 est.)
waste: 9,402.4 kt (2019-2021 est.)
other: 1,186.9 kt (2019-2021 est.)

Waste and recycling: *municipal solid waste generated annually:* 395.081 million tons (2024 est.)
percent of municipal solid waste recycled: 24.4% (2022 est.)

Total water withdrawal: *municipal:* 117.01 billion cubic meters (2022 est.)
industrial: 103.04 billion cubic meters (2022 est.)
agricultural: 361.24 billion cubic meters (2022 est.)

Total renewable water resources: 2.84 trillion cubic meters (2022 est.)

Geoparks: *total global geoparks and regional networks:* 49 (2025)
global geoparks and regional networks: Alxa; Arxan; Dali-Cangshan; Danxiashan; Dunhuang; Enshi Grand Canyon-Tenglongdong; Fangshan; Funiushan; Guangwushan-Noushuihe; Hexigten; Hong Kong; Huanggang Dabieshan; Huangshan; Jingpohu; Jiuhuashan; Kanbula; Keketuohai; Leiqiong; Leye Fengshan; Linxia; Longhushan; Longyan; Lushan; Mount Changbaishan; Mount Kunlun; Ningde; Qinling Zhongnanshan; Sanqingshan; Shennongjia; Shilin; Songshan; Taining; Taishan; Tianzhushan; Wangwushan-Daimeishan; Wudalianchi; Wugongshan; Xiangxi; Xingwen; Yingyi; Yandangshan; Yanqing; Yimengshan; Yuntaishan; Yunyang: Zhangjlajle; Zhangye; Zhijingdong Cave; Zigong (2025)

GOVERNMENT

Country name: *conventional long form:* People's Republic of China
conventional short form: China
local long form: Zhonghua Renmin Gongheguo
local short form: Zhongguo
abbreviation: PRC
etymology: English name could be derived from the Qin (Chin, Ts'in) rulers in the 3rd century B.C., or from the province of Shaanxi (Shensi) with its capital of Xi'an (Sian); the Chinese name Zhongguo translates as "Central Nation" or "Middle Country"

Government type: communist party-led state

Capital: *name:* Beijing
geographic coordinates: 39 55 N, 116 23 E
time difference: UTC+8 (13 hours ahead of Washington, DC, during Standard Time)
time zone note: China is the largest country (in terms of area) with just one time zone; before 1949 it was divided into five
etymology: the name comes from the Chinese words *bei* (north) and *jing* (capital)

Administrative divisions: 23 provinces (*sheng*, singular and plural), 5 autonomous regions (*zizhiqu*, singular and plural), 4 municipalities (*shi*, singular and plural), and two special administrative regions (*tebie xingzhengqu*, singular and plural)
provinces: Anhui, Fujian, Gansu, Guangdong, Guizhou, Hainan, Hebei, Heilongjiang, Henan, Hubei, Hunan, Jiangsu, Jiangxi, Jilin, Liaoning, Qinghai, Shaanxi, Shandong, Shanxi, Sichuan, Yunnan, Zhejiang; (see note on Taiwan)
autonomous regions: Guangxi, Nei Mongol (Inner Mongolia), Ningxia, Xinjiang Uyghur, Xizang (Tibet)
municipalities: Beijing, Chongqing, Shanghai, Tianjin
special administrative regions: Hong Kong, Macau
note: China considers Taiwan its 23rd province; see separate entries for the special administrative regions of Hong Kong and Macau
Legal system: civil law influenced by Soviet and continental European civil law systems; legislature retains power to interpret statutes
note: in 2020, the National People's Congress adopted the PRC Civil Code, which codifies personal relations and property relations
Constitution: *history:* several previous; latest promulgated 4 December 1982
amendment process: proposed by the Standing Committee of the National People's Congress or supported by more than one fifth of the National People's Congress membership; passage requires more than two-thirds majority vote of the Congress membership
International law organization participation: has not submitted an ICJ jurisdiction declaration; non-party state to the ICCt
Citizenship: *citizenship by birth:* no
citizenship by descent only: least one parent must be a citizen of China
dual citizenship recognized: no
residency requirement for naturalization: while naturalization is theoretically possible, in practical terms it is extremely difficult; residency is required but not specified
Suffrage: 18 years of age; universal
Executive branch: *chief of state:* President XI Jinping (since 14 March 2013)
head of government: Premier LI Qiang (since 11 March 2023)
cabinet: State Council appointed by National People's Congress
election/appointment process: president and vice president indirectly elected by National People's Congress; premier nominated by president, confirmed by National People's Congress
most recent election date: 10 March 2023
election results: *2023:* XI Jinping reelected president; National People's Congress vote - 2,952 (unanimously); HAN Zheng elected vice president with 2,952 votes; LI Qiang elected premier with 2,936 votes
2018: XI Jinping reelected president; National People's Congress vote - 2,970 (unanimously); WANG Qishan elected vice president with 2,969 votes
expected date of next election: March 2028
note: ultimate authority rests with the Communist Party Central Committee's 25-member Political Bureau (Politburo) and its seven-member Standing Committee; XI Jinping holds the three most powerful positions as party general secretary, state president, and chairman of the Central Military Commission
Legislative branch: *legislature name:* National People's Congress (Quanguo Renmin Daibiao Dahui)
legislative structure: unicameral
number of seats: 3000 (all indirectly elected)
scope of elections: full renewal
term in office: 5 years
most recent election date: 3/5/2023
percentage of women in chamber: 26.5%
expected date of next election: March 2028
note: in practice, only members of the Chinese Communist Party (CCP), its 8 allied independent parties, and CCP-approved independent candidates are elected
Judicial branch: *highest court(s):* Supreme People's Court (consists of over 340 judges, including the chief justice and 13 grand justices organized into a civil committee and tribunals for civil, economic, administrative, complaint and appeal, and communication and transportation cases)
judge selection and term of office: chief justice appointed by the People's National Congress (NPC); limited to 2 consecutive 5-year-terms; other justices and judges nominated by the chief justice and appointed by the Standing Committee of the NPC; term of other justices and judges determined by the NPC
subordinate courts: Higher People's Courts; Intermediate People's Courts; District and County People's Courts; Autonomous Region People's Courts; International Commercial Courts; Special People's Courts for military, maritime, transportation, and forestry issues
Political parties: Chinese Communist Party or CCP
note: China has 8 nominally independent small parties controlled by the CCP
Diplomatic representation in the US: *chief of mission:* Ambassador XIE Feng (since 30 June 2023)
chancery: 3505 International Place NW, Washington, DC 20008
telephone: [1] (202) 495-2266
FAX: [1] (202) 495-2138
email address and website: chinaemppress_us@mfa.gov.cn
http://www.china-embassy.org/eng/
consulate(s) general: Chicago, Los Angeles, New York, San Francisco
Diplomatic representation from the US: *chief of mission:* Ambassador David PERDUE (since 25 July 2025)
embassy: 55 Anjialou Road, Chaoyang District, Beijing 100600
mailing address: 7300 Beijing Place, Washington DC 20521-7300
telephone: [86] (10) 8531-3000
FAX: [86] (10) 8531-4200
email address and website: BeijingACS@state.gov
https://china.usembassy-china.org.cn/
consulate(s) general: Guangzhou, Shanghai, Shenyang, Wuhan; note - the Chinese Government ordered closure of the US consulate in Chengdu in late July 2020
International organization participation: ADB, AfDB (nonregional member), APEC, Arctic Council (observer), ARF, ASEAN (dialogue partner), BIS, BRICS, CDB, CICA, EAS, FAO, FATF, G-20, G-24 (observer), G-5, G-77, IADB, IAEA, IBRD, ICAO, ICC (national committees), ICRM, IDA, IFAD, IFC, IFRCS, IHO, ILO, IMF, IMO, IMSO, Interpol, IOC, IOM (observer), IPU, ISO, ITSO, ITU, LAIA (observer), MIGA, MINURSO, MONUSCO, NAM (observer), NSG, OAS (observer), OPCW, Pacific Alliance (observer), PCA, PIF (partner), SAARC (observer), SCO, SICA (observer), UN, UNAMID, UNCTAD, UNESCO, UNFICYP, UNHCR, UNHRC, UNIDO, UNIFIL, UNISFA, UNMIL, UNMISS, UNOCI, UNOOSA, UN Security Council (permanent), UNTSO, UNWTO, UPU, WCO, WHO, WIPO, WMO, WTO, ZC
Independence: *1 October 1949 (People's Republic of China established); notable earlier dates:* 221 B.C. (unification under the Qin Dynasty); 1 January 1912 (Qing Dynasty replaced by the Republic of China)
National holiday: National Day (anniversary of the founding of the People's Republic of China), 1 October (1949)
Flag: *description:* red with a large five-pointed yellow star and four smaller ones in the upper-left corner; the small stars are arranged in a vertical arc around the large one
meaning: red represents revolution; the stars symbolize the four social classes – the working class, the peasantry, the urban petty bourgeoisie, and the national bourgeoisie (capitalists) – united under the Communist Party of China
National symbol(s): dragon, giant panda
National color(s): red, yellow
National anthem(s): *title:* "Yiyongjun Jinxingqu" (The March of the Volunteers)
lyrics/music: TIAN Han/NIE Er
history: adopted 1982; the anthem, which was banned during the Cultural Revolution, is more commonly known as "Zhongguo Guoge" (Chinese National Song)
National heritage: *total World Heritage Sites:* 59 (40 cultural, 15 natural, 4 mixed)
selected World Heritage Site locales: Imperial Palaces of the Ming and Qing Dynasties (c); Mausoleum of the First Qin Emperor (c); The Great Wall (c); Summer Palace, an Imperial Garden in Beijing (c); Jiuzhaigou Valley Scenic and Historic Interest Area (n); Historic Ensemble of the Potala Palace, Lhasa (c); Ancient Ancient City of Ping Yao (c); Historic Center of Macau (c); Historic Monuments of Dengfeng in "The Centre of Heaven and Earth" (c); The Grand Canal (c); Mount Huangshan (m); Mogao Caves (c); Mount Taishan (m); Peking Man Site at Zhoukoudian(c); Huanglong Scenic and Historic Interest Area (n);Wulingyuan Scenic and Historic Interest Area (n); Ancient Building Complex in the Wudang Mountains (c); Mountain Resort and its Outlying Temples, Chengde (c); Temple and Cemetery of Confucius and the Kong Family Mansion in Qufu (c); Lushan National Park (c); Mount Emei Scenic Area, including Leshan Giant Buddha Scenic Area (m); Classical Gardens of Suzhou (c); Old Town of Lijiang (c); Temple of Heaven: an Imperial Sacrificial Altar in Beijing (c); Dazu Rock Carvings (c); Mount Wuyi (m); Ancient Villages in Southern Anhui – Xidi and Hongcun (c); Imperial Tombs of the Ming and Qing Dynasties (c); Longmen Grottoes (c); Mount Qingcheng and the Dujiangyan Irrigation System (c); Yungang Grottoes (c); Three Parallel Rivers of Yunnan Protected Areas (n); Capital Cities and Tombs of the Ancient Koguryo Kingdom (c); Sichuan Giant Panda Sanctuaries - Wolong, Mt. Siguniang, and Jiajin Mountains (c); Yin Xu (c); Kaiping Diaolou and Villages (c); South China Karst (n); Fujian Tulou (c); Mount Sanqingshan National Park (n); Mount Wutai (c); China Danxia (n); West Lake Cultural Landscape of Hangzhou (c); Chengjiang Fossil Site (n); Site of Xanadu (c); Cultural Landscape of Honghe Hani

Rice Terraces(c); Xinjiang Tianshan (n); Silk Roads: the Routes Network of Chang'an-Tianshan Corridor (c); Tusi Sites (c); Hubei Shennongjia (n); Zuojiang Huashan Rock Art Cultural Landscape (c); Kulangsu, a Historic International Settlement (c); Qinghai Hoh Xil (n); Fanjingshan (n); Archaeological Ruins of Liangzhu City (c); Migratory Bird Sanctuaries along the Coast of Yellow Sea-Bohai Gulf of China (n); Quanzhou: Emporium of the World in Song-Yuan China (c); Cultural Landscape of Old Tea Forests of the Jingmai Mountain in Pu'er (c); Badain Jaran Desert - Towers of Sand and Lakes (n); Beijing Central Axis: A Building Ensemble Exhibiting the Ideal Order of the Chinese Capital (c)

ECONOMY

Economic overview: world's second-largest economy by nominal GDP; global leader in exports and manufacturing; historically strong growth slowing; challenges of aging workforce, weak productivity, rising youth unemployment, struggling property sector, and public debt; state-sponsored economic controls and infrastructure investments

Real GDP (purchasing power parity): $33.598 trillion (2024 est.)
$32.005 trillion (2023 est.)
$30.361 trillion (2022 est.)
note: data in 2021 dollars
comparison ranking: 1

Real GDP growth rate: 5% (2024 est.)
5.4% (2023 est.)
3.1% (2022 est.)
note: annual GDP % growth based on constant local currency
comparison ranking: 42

Real GDP per capita: $23,800 (2024 est.)
$22,700 (2023 est.)
$21,500 (2022 est.)
note: data in 2021 dollars
comparison ranking: 93

GDP (official exchange rate): $18.744 trillion (2024 est.)
note: data in current dollars at official exchange rate

Inflation rate (consumer prices): 0.2% (2024 est.)
0.2% (2023 est.)
2% (2022 est.)
note: annual % change based on consumer prices
comparison ranking: 7

GDP - composition, by sector of origin: *agriculture:* 6.8% (2024 est.)
industry: 36.5% (2024 est.)
services: 56.7% (2024 est.)
note: figures may not total 100% due to non-allocated consumption not captured in sector-reported data
comparison rankings: agriculture 95; industry 32; services 112

GDP - composition, by end use: *household consumption:* 39.6% (2023 est.)
government consumption: 17.2% (2023 est.)
investment in fixed capital: 40.5% (2023 est.)
investment in inventories: 0.6% (2023 est.)
exports of goods and services: 19.1% (2023 est.)
imports of goods and services: -17% (2023 est.)
note: figures may not total 100% due to rounding or gaps in data collection

Agricultural products: maize, rice, vegetables, wheat, sugarcane, potatoes, cucumbers/gherkins, tomatoes, watermelons, pork (2023)
note: top ten agricultural products based on tonnage

Industries: world leader in gross value of industrial output; mining and ore processing, iron, steel, aluminum, and other metals, coal; machine building; armaments; textiles and apparel; petroleum; cement; chemicals; fertilizer; consumer products (including footwear, toys, and electronics); food processing; transportation equipment, including automobiles, railcars and locomotives, ships, aircraft; telecommunications equipment, commercial space launch vehicles, satellites

Industrial production growth rate: 5.3% (2024 est.)
note: annual % change in industrial value added based on constant local currency
comparison ranking: 40

Labor force: 773.88 million (2024 est.)
note: number of people ages 15 or older who are employed or seeking work
comparison ranking: 1

Unemployment rate: 4.6% (2024 est.)
4.7% (2023 est.)
5% (2022 est.)
note: % of labor force seeking employment
comparison ranking: 80

Youth unemployment rate (ages 15-24): *total:* 15.2% (2024 est.)
male: 16.5% (2024 est.)
female: 13.5% (2024 est.)
note: % of labor force ages 15-24 seeking employment
comparison ranking: total 79

Population below poverty line: 0% (2020 est.)
note: % of population with income below national poverty line

Gini Index coefficient - distribution of family income: 35.7 (2021 est.)
note: index (0-100) of income distribution; higher values represent greater inequality
comparison ranking: 69

Average household expenditures: *on food:* 21.2% of household expenditures (2023 est.)
on alcohol and tobacco: 3.2% of household expenditures (2023 est.)

Household income or consumption by percentage share: *lowest 10%:* 3.2% (2021 est.)
highest 10%: 28.2% (2021 est.)
note: % share of income accruing to lowest and highest 10% of population

Remittances: 0.2% of GDP (2024 est.)
0.2% of GDP (2023 est.)
0.1% of GDP (2022 est.)
note: personal transfers and compensation between resident and non-resident individuals/households/entities

Budget: *revenues:* $2.684 trillion (2022 est.) note: central government revenues (excluding grants) converted to US dollars at average official exchange rate for year indicated
expenditures: $4.893 trillion (2019 est.)

Public debt: 47% of GDP (2017 est.)
note: *official data; data cover both central and local government debt, including debt officially recognized by China's National Audit Office report in 2011; data exclude policy bank bonds, Ministry of Railway debt, and China Asset Management Company debt comparison ranking:* 112

Taxes and other revenues: 7.6% (of GDP) (2023 est.)
note: central government tax revenue as a % of GDP
comparison ranking: 138

Current account balance: $423.919 billion (2024 est.)
$263.382 billion (2023 est.)
$443.374 billion (2022 est.)
note: balance of payments - net trade and primary/secondary income in current dollars
comparison ranking: 1

Exports: $3.793 trillion (2024 est.)
$3.508 trillion (2023 est.)
$3.719 trillion (2022 est.)
note: balance of payments - exports of goods and services in current dollars
comparison ranking: 1

Exports - partners: USA 13%, Hong Kong 8%, Japan 5%, Germany 5%, S. Korea 4% (2023)
note: top five export partners based on percentage share of exports

Exports - commodities: broadcasting equipment, computers, integrated circuits, garments, machine parts (2023)
note: top five export commodities based on value in dollars

Imports: $3.254 trillion (2024 est.)
$3.122 trillion (2023 est.)
$3.142 trillion (2022 est.)
note: balance of payments - imports of goods and services in current dollars
comparison ranking: 2

Imports - partners: S. Korea 7%, USA 7%, Japan 6%, Australia 6%, Russia 6% (2023)
note: top five import partners based on percentage share of imports

Imports - commodities: crude petroleum, integrated circuits, iron ore, gold, natural gas (2023)
note: top five import commodities based on value in dollars

Reserves of foreign exchange and gold: $3.456 trillion (2024 est.)
$3.45 trillion (2023 est.)
$3.307 trillion (2022 est.)
note: holdings of gold (year-end prices)/foreign exchange/special drawing rights in current dollars
comparison ranking: 1

Debt - external: $488.114 billion (2023 est.)
note: present value of external debt in current US dollars
comparison ranking: 1

Exchange rates: Renminbi yuan (RMB) per US dollar -

Exchange rates: 7.197 (2024 est.)
7.084 (2023 est.)
6.737 (2022 est.)
6.449 (2021 est.)
6.901 (2020 est.)

ENERGY

Electricity access: *electrification - total population:* 100% (2022 est.)

Electricity: *installed generating capacity:* 2.949 billion kW (2023 est.)
consumption: 8.894 trillion kWh (2023 est.)
exports: 20.577 billion kWh (2023 est.)
imports: 7.195 billion kWh (2023 est.)
transmission/distribution losses: 325.352 billion kWh (2023 est.)
comparison rankings: installed generating capacity 1; consumption 1; exports 13; imports 36; transmission/distribution losses 211

Electricity generation sources: *fossil fuels:* 64.2% of total installed capacity (2023 est.)
nuclear: 4.7% of total installed capacity (2023 est.)
solar: 6.3% of total installed capacity (2023 est.)
wind: 9.6% of total installed capacity (2023 est.)

hydroelectricity: 13.3% of total installed capacity (2023 est.)
biomass and waste: 1.9% of total installed capacity (2023 est.)

Nuclear energy: Number of operational nuclear reactors: 57 (2025)

Number of nuclear reactors under construction: 28 (2025)

Net capacity of operational nuclear reactors: 55.32GW (2025 est.)

Percent of total electricity production: 4.9% (2023 est.)

Coal: *production:* 4.805 billion metric tons (2023 est.)
consumption: 5.191 billion metric tons (2023 est.)
exports: 13.239 million metric tons (2023 est.)
imports: 401.517 million metric tons (2023 est.)
proven reserves: 157.041 billion metric tons (2023 est.)

Petroleum: *total petroleum production:* 4.984 million bbl/day (2023 est.)
refined petroleum consumption: 16.189 million bbl/day (2023 est.)
crude oil estimated reserves: 26.023 billion barrels (2021 est.)

Natural gas: *production:* 239.402 billion cubic meters (2023 est.)
consumption: 395.341 billion cubic meters (2023 est.)
exports: 6.025 billion cubic meters (2023 est.)
imports: 161.808 billion cubic meters (2023 est.)
proven reserves: 6.654 trillion cubic meters (2021 est.)

Energy consumption per capita: 113.805 million Btu/person (2023 est.)
comparison ranking: 38

COMMUNICATIONS

Telephones - fixed lines: *total subscriptions:* 173.326 million (2023 est.)
subscriptions per 100 inhabitants: 12 (2023 est.)
comparison ranking: total subscriptions 1

Telephones - mobile cellular: *total subscriptions:* 1.81 billion (2023 est.)
subscriptions per 100 inhabitants: 125 (2022 est.)
comparison ranking: total subscriptions 1

Broadcast media: all broadcast media are owned by, or affiliated with, the Chinese Communist Party (CCP) or a government agency; no privately owned TV or radio stations; state-run Chinese Central TV, provincial, and municipal stations offer more than 2,000 channels; the Central Propaganda Department and local (provincial, municipal) officials direct news reporting and approve all programming; foreign-made TV programs must be approved/censored prior to broadcast; widespread use of online platforms (Bilibili, Tencent Video, iQiyi, etc) to access domestic and international films and TV shows; Cyberspace Administration of China (CAC) regulates video platforms (2022)

Internet country code: .cn

Internet users: *percent of population:* 78% (2023 est.)

Broadband - fixed subscriptions: *total:* 636 million (2023 est.)
subscriptions per 100 inhabitants: 45 (2023 est.)
comparison ranking: total 1

TRANSPORTATION

Civil aircraft registration country code prefix: B

Airports: 552 (2025)
comparison ranking: 16

Heliports: 120 (2025)
comparison ranking: 21

Railways: *total:* 150,000 km (2021) 1.435-m gauge (100,000 km electrified); 104,0000 traditional, 40,000 high-speed

Merchant marine: *total:* 8,314 (2023)
by type: bulk carrier 1,831, container ship 419, general cargo 1,392, oil tanker 1,196, other 3,476
comparison ranking: total 2

Ports: *total ports:* 66 (2024)
large: 5
medium: 9
small: 25
very small: 27
ports with oil terminals: 48
key ports: Chaozhou, Dalian, Fang-Cheng, Guangzhou, Hankow, Lon Shui Terminal, Qingdao Gang, Qinhuangdao, Shanghai, Shekou, Tianjin Xin Gang, Weihai, Wenzhou, Xiamen

MILITARY AND SECURITY

Military and security forces: People's Liberation Army (PLA): Ground Forces or People's Liberation Army Army (PLAA), Navy (PLAN, includes Marine Corps (PLANMC)), Air Force (PLAAF), Rocket Force (PLARF), Aerospace Force (ASF), Cyberspace Force (CSF), Information Support Force (ISF), Joint Logistics Support Force (JLSF); People's Armed Police (PAP, includes Coast Guard, Border Defense Force, Internal Security Forces); PLA Reserve Force (2025)
note 1: the PAP is a paramilitary police component of China's armed forces that is under the dual authority of the Central Committee of the Communist Party and the Central Military Commission; the China Coast Guard (CCG) is subordinate to the PAP
note 2: the PLA (established 1927) is the military arm of the ruling Chinese Communist Party (CCP), which oversees the PLA through its Central Military Commission (CMC); the CMC is China's top military decision making body

Military expenditures: 1.5% of GDP (2024 est.)
1.5% of GDP (2023 est.)
1.5% of GDP (2022 est.)
1.5% of GDP (2021 est.)
1.7% of GDP (2020 est.)

Military and security service personnel strengths: approximately 2 million active-duty PLA (950,000-1 million Ground; 250,000 Navy, including about 50,000 Marines; 350-400,000 Air Force; 120,000 Rocket Forces; 150-175,000 other forces) (2024)

Military equipment inventories and acquisitions: the PLA has a mix of mostly modern domestically produced and imported weapons and equipment; most of its imported weaponry has come from Russia; China has one of the world's largest defense-industrial sectors and is capable of producing advanced weapons systems across all military domains (2024)
note: the PLA is in the midst of a decades-long modernization effort to achieve a "world-class" military by 2049

Military service age and obligation: 18-22 years of age for men for selective compulsory military service, with a 2-year service obligation; women 18-19 years of age who are high school graduates and meet requirements for specific military jobs are subject to conscription (2024)
note: the PLA's conscription system functions as a levy; the PLA establishes the number of enlistees needed, which produces quotas for the provinces; each province provides a set number of soldiers or sailors; if the number of volunteers fails to meet quotas, the local governments may compel individuals to enter military service

Military deployments: 400 Lebanon (UNIFIL); 1,030 South Sudan (UNMISS); 150 Sudan/South Sudan (UNISFA); up to 2,000 Djibouti (2024)

Military - note: the People's Liberation Army (PLA) is the world's largest military; the PLA's primary responsibility is external security but it also has some domestic security duties; China's stated defense policy includes safeguarding sovereignty, security, and development interests while emphasizing a greater global role for the PLA; the PLA conducts air, counterspace, cyber, electronic warfare, joint, land, maritime, missile, nuclear, and space operations; it trains regularly, including multinational and multiservice exercises, deploys overseas, and participates in international peacekeeping missions
the PRC's internal security forces consist primarily of the Ministry of Public Security (MPS), the Ministry of State Security (MSS), the People's Armed Police (PAP), and the militia; the PLA support the internal security forces as necessary: –the MPS controls the civilian national police, which serves as the first-line force for public order; its primary mission is domestic law enforcement and maintaining order, including anti-rioting and anti-terrorism
–the MSS is the PRC's main civilian intelligence and counterintelligence service
–the PAP is a paramilitary component (or adjunct) of the PLA; its primary missions include internal security, maintaining public order, maritime security, and assisting the PLA in times of war; the China Coast Guard (CCG) administratively falls under the PAP and has a variety of missions, such as maritime sovereignty enforcement, surveillance, resource protection, anti-smuggling, and general law enforcement; it is the largest maritime law enforcement fleet in the world
–the militia is an armed reserve of civilians which serves as an auxiliary and reserve force for the PLA upon mobilization, although it is distinct from the PLA's reserve forces; militia units are organized around towns, villages, urban sub-districts, and enterprises, and vary widely in composition and mission; they have dual civilian-military command structures; a key component of the militia are the local maritime forces, commonly referred to as the People's Armed Forces Maritime Militia (PAFMM); the PAFMM consists of mariners (and their vessels) who receive training, equipment, and other forms of support from the Navy and CCG (although the PAFMM remains separate from both) to perform tasks such as maritime patrolling, surveillance and reconnaissance, emergency/disaster response, transportation, search and rescue, and auxiliary tasks in support of naval operations in wartime; the PAFMM's tasks are often conducted in conjunction or coordination with the Navy and the CCG; it has been used to assert Beijing's maritime claims in the Sea of Japan and South China Sea (2024)

SPACE

Space agency/agencies: China National Space Administration (CNSA; established in 1993); Administration for Science, Technology, and Industry for National Defense (SASTIND; subordinate to the Ministry of Industry and Information Technology); People's Liberation Army (PLA) Aerospace Force (2025)

note: in 2024, the PLA created the Aerospace Force from the former Strategic Support Force, which had included the Space Systems Department and the China Manned Space Engineering Office or CMSEO)
Space launch site(s): Jiuquan Launch Center (Inner Mongolia); Xichang Launch Center (Sichuan); Wenchang Launch Center (Hainan; Wenchang includes a commercial launch pad, the Hainan Commercial Space Launch Site, which became operational in December 2024); Taiyuan Launch Center (Shanxi); Eastern Spaceport (Shandong; a coastal spaceport designed to facilitate maritime launches) (2025)
Space program overview: has a large, comprehensive, and ambitious space program and is considered one of the world's leading space powers; capable of manufacturing and operating the full spectrum of space launch vehicles (SLVs) and spacecraft, including human-crewed, lunar/inter-planetary/asteroid probes, satellites (communications, remote sensing, navigational, scientific, etc.), space stations, and reusable space transportation systems such as orbital space planes/shuttles; has an astronaut/taikonaut program; researches and develops a range of space-related capabilities, including advanced telecommunications, optics, spacecraft components, and satellite payloads; participates in international space programs and co-leads (with Australia and Japan) the Global Earth Observation System of Systems; has signed space cooperation agreements with more than 45 national space agencies, including those of Brazil, Canada, France, and Russia, as well several international organizations; it has also cooperated with the European Space Agency; has a space industry dominated by two state-owned aerospace enterprises, but has developed a substantial commercial space sector, including launch services (2025)
note 1: further details about the key activities, programs, and milestones of the country's space program, as well as government spending estimates on the space sector, appear in the Space Programs reference guide
note 2: the US NASA is barred by a 2011 law from cooperating with the Chinese bilaterally in space unless approved by the US Congress; the US objected to China's participation in the International Space Station program

TRANSNATIONAL ISSUES

Refugees and internally displaced persons: *refugees:* 814 (2024 est.)
IDPs: 198,400 (2024 est.)
Trafficking in persons: *tier rating:* Tier 3 — China does not fully meet the minimum standards for elimination of trafficking and is not making significant efforts to do so, therefore, China remained on Tier 3; for more details, go to: https://www.state.gov/reports/2025-trafficking-in-persons-report/china/
Illicit drugs: USG identification: major illicit drug-producing and/or drug-transit country
major precursor-chemical producer (2025)

CHRISTMAS ISLAND

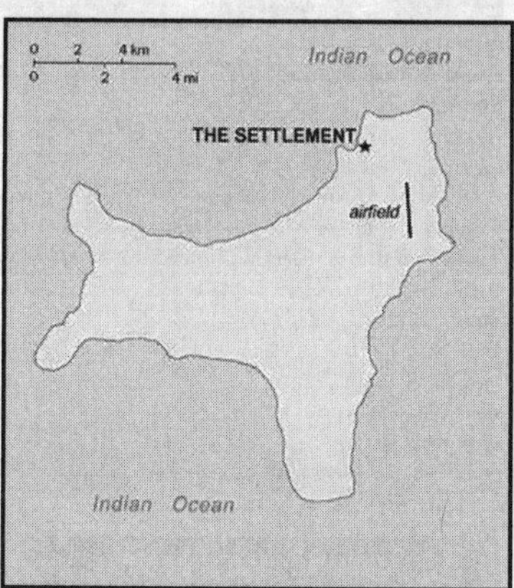

INTRODUCTION

Background: Although Europeans sighted Christmas Island in 1615, it was named for the day of its rediscovery in 1643. Steep cliffs and dense jungle hampered attempts to explore the island over the next two centuries. The discovery of phosphate on the island in 1887 led to the UK annexing it the following year. In 1898, 200 Chinese indentured servants were brought in to work the mines, along with Malays, Sikhs, and a small number of Europeans. The UK administered Christmas Island from Singapore.
Japan invaded the island in 1942, but islanders sabotaged Japanese mining operations, making the mines relatively unproductive. After World War II, Australia and New Zealand bought the company mining the phosphate, and in 1958, the UK transferred sovereignty from Singapore to Australia in exchange for $20 million to compensate for the loss of future phosphate income. In 1980, Australia set up the Christmas Island National Park and expanded its boundaries throughout the 1980s until it covered more than 60% of the island's territory. The phosphate mine was closed in 1987 because of environmental concerns, and Australia has rejected several efforts to reopen it.

In the 1980s, boats of asylum seekers started landing on Christmas Island, and the migrants claimed refugee status because they were on Australian territory. In 2001, Australia declared Christmas Island to be outside the Australian migration zone and built an immigration detention center on the island. Completed in 2008, the controversial detention center was closed in 2018 but then reopened in 2019. In 2020, the center served as a coronavirus quarantine facility for Australian citizens evacuated from China.

GEOGRAPHY

Location: Southeastern Asia, island in the Indian Ocean, south of Indonesia
Geographic coordinates: 10 30 S, 105 40 E
Map references: Southeast Asia
Area: *total:* 135 sq km
land: 135 sq km
water: 0 sq km
comparison ranking: total 222
Area - comparative: about three-quarters the size of Washington, D.C.
Land boundaries: *total:* 0 km
Coastline: 138.9 km
Maritime claims: *territorial sea:* 12 nm
contiguous zone: 12 nm
exclusive fishing zone: 200 nm
Climate: tropical with a wet season (December to April) and dry season; heat and humidity moderated by trade winds
Terrain: steep cliffs along coast rise abruptly to central plateau
Elevation: *highest point:* Murray Hill 361 m
lowest point: Indian Ocean 0 m
Natural resources: phosphate, beaches
Land use: *agricultural land:* 0% (2018 est.)
other: 100% (2018 est.)
Irrigated land: NA
Population distribution: majority of the population lives on the northern tip of the island
Natural hazards: the narrow fringing reef surrounding the island can be a maritime hazard
Geography - note: located along major sea lanes of the Indian Ocean

PEOPLE AND SOCIETY

Population: *total:* 1,692 (2021 est.)
male: 1,007
female: 685
comparison rankings: total 234; male 231; female 233
Nationality: *noun:* Christmas Islander(s)
adjective: Christmas Island
Ethnic groups: Chinese 70%, European 20%, Malay 10% (2001)
note: no indigenous population
Languages: English (official) 27.6%, Mandarin 17.2%, Malay 17.1%, Cantonese 3.9%, Min Nan 1.6%, Tagalog 1%, other 4.5%, unspecified 27.1% (2016 est.)
note: data represent language spoken at home
Religions: Muslim 19.4%, Buddhist 18.3%, Roman Catholic 8.8%, Protestant 6.5% (includes Anglican 3.6%, Uniting Church 1.2%, other 1.7%), other Christian 3.3%, other 0.6%, none 15.3%, unspecified 27.7% (2016 est.)
Age structure: *0-14 years:* 16.6%
15-64 years: 70.4%
65 years and over: 13% (2021)
Median age: *total:* 38 years (2021 est.)
comparison ranking: total 78
Population growth rate: 1.11% (2014 est.)
comparison ranking: 84
Population distribution: majority of the population lives on the northern tip of the island

ENVIRONMENT

Environmental issues: loss of rainforest; impact of phosphate mining

Climate: tropical with a wet season (December to April) and dry season; heat and humidity moderated by trade winds

GOVERNMENT

Country name: *conventional long form:* Territory of Christmas Island
conventional short form: Christmas Island
etymology: named by English Captain William MYNORS for the day of its rediscovery, Christmas Day (25 December 1643); Europeans had sighted the island as early as 1615
Government type: non-self-governing overseas territory of Australia
Dependency status: non-self-governing territory of Australia; administered from Canberra by the Department of Infrastructure, Transport, Cities & Regional Development
Capital: *name:* The Settlement (Flying Fish Cove)
geographic coordinates: 10 25 S, 105 43 E
time difference: UTC+7 (12 hours ahead of Washington, DC, during Standard Time)
etymology: Flying Fish Cove was named after a British explorer's ship in 1886
Administrative divisions: none (territory of Australia)
Legal system: system is under the authority of the governor general of Australia and Australian law
Constitution: *history:* 1 October 1958 (Christmas Island Act 1958)
Citizenship: see Australia
Suffrage: 18 years of age
Executive branch: *chief of state:* King CHARLES III (since 8 September 2022); represented by Governor-General of the Commonwealth of Australia General Sam MOSTYN (since 1 July 2024)
head of government: Administrator Farzian ZAINAL (since 11 May 2023)
cabinet: NA
election/appointment process: the monarchy is hereditary; governor general appointed by the monarch on the recommendation of the Australian prime minister; administrator appointed by the governor-general of Australia for a 2-year term and represents the monarch and Australia
Legislative branch: *legislature name:* Christmas Island Shire Council
legislative structure: unicameral
number of seats: 9 (directly elected)
electoral system: plurality/majority
scope of elections: partial renewal
term in office: 4 years
most recent election date: 10/2023
parties elected and seats per party: independent (9)
percentage of women in chamber: 13%
expected date of next election: October 2025
Judicial branch: *highest court(s):* under the terms of the Territorial Law Reform Act 1992, Western Australia provides court services as needed for the island, including the Supreme Court and subordinate courts (District Court, Magistrate Court, Family Court, Children's Court, and Coroners' Court)
Political parties: none
Diplomatic representation in the US: none (territory of Australia)
Diplomatic representation from the US: *embassy:* none (territory of Australia)
International organization participation: none
Independence: none (territory of Australia)
National holiday: Australia Day (commemorates the arrival of the First Fleet of Australian settlers), 26 January (1788)
Flag: *description:* territorial flag; divided diagonally from upper left to lower right; the upper triangle is green with a yellow silhouette of the golden bosun bird; the lower triangle is blue and shows the Southern Cross constellation, representing Australia; a centered yellow disk displays a green outline of the island
note: the flag of Australia is used for official purposes
National symbol(s): golden bosun bird
National anthem(s): *title:* "Advance Australia Fair"
lyrics/music: Peter Dodds McCORMICK
history: national anthem, as an Australian territory
title: "God Save the King"
lyrics/music: unknown
history: royal anthem, as an Australian territory

ECONOMY

Economic overview: high-income Australian territorial economy; development through government services and phosphate mining; operates Australia's Immigration Detention Centre; increasing tourism and government investments; sustained environmental protections
Industries: tourism, phosphate extraction (near depletion)
Exports - partners: Indonesia 30%, USA 26%, Malaysia 12%, Ireland 8%, UK 7% (2023)
note: top five export partners based on percentage share of exports
Exports - commodities: fertilizers, paintings, amine compounds (2023)
note: top export commodities based on value in dollars over $500,000
Imports - partners: USA 58%, Australia 40%, Malaysia 1%, Fiji 0%, Singapore 0% (2023)
note: top five import partners based on percentage share of imports
Imports - commodities: aircraft, refined petroleum, cars, air conditioners, plastic products (2023)
note: top five import commodities based on value in dollars
Exchange rates: Australian dollars (AUD) per US dollar -
Exchange rates: 1.515 (2024 est.)
1.505 (2023 est.)
1.442 (2022 est.)
1.331 (2021 est.)
1.453 (2020 est.)

COMMUNICATIONS

Broadcast media: 1 community radio station; satellite broadcasts of several Australian radio and TV stations (2017)
Internet country code: .cx
Internet users: *percent of population:* 78.6% (2016 est.)

TRANSPORTATION

Airports: 1 (2025)
comparison ranking: 230
Railways: *total:* 18 km (2017)
standard gauge: 18 km (2017) 1.435-m (not in operation)
note: the 18-km Christmas Island Phosphate Company Railway between Flying Fish Cove and South Point was decommissioned in 1987; some tracks and scrap remain in place
Ports: *total ports:* 1 (2024)
large: 0
medium: 1
small: 0
very small: 0
ports with oil terminals: 0
key ports: Flying Fish Cove

MILITARY AND SECURITY

Military - note: defense is the responsibility of Australia

CLIPPERTON ISLAND

INTRODUCTION

Background: This isolated atoll was named for John CLIPPERTON, an English pirate who was rumored to have made it his hideout early in the 18th century. Annexed by France in 1855 and claimed by the US, it was seized by Mexico in 1897. Arbitration eventually awarded the island to France in 1931, which took possession in 1935.

GEOGRAPHY

Location: Middle America, atoll in the North Pacific Ocean, 1,120 km southwest of Mexico
Geographic coordinates: 10 17 N, 109 13 W
Map references: Political Map of the World
Area: *total:* 6 sq km
land: 6 sq km
water: 0 sq km
comparison ranking: total 244
Area - comparative: about 12 times the size of the National Mall in Washington, D.C.
Land boundaries: *total:* 0 km
Coastline: 11.1 km
Maritime claims: *territorial sea:* 12 nm
exclusive economic zone: 200 nm
Climate: tropical; humid, average temperature 20-32 degrees Celsius, wet season (May to October)
Terrain: coral atoll
Elevation: *highest point:* Rocher Clipperton 29 m
lowest point: Pacific Ocean 0 m

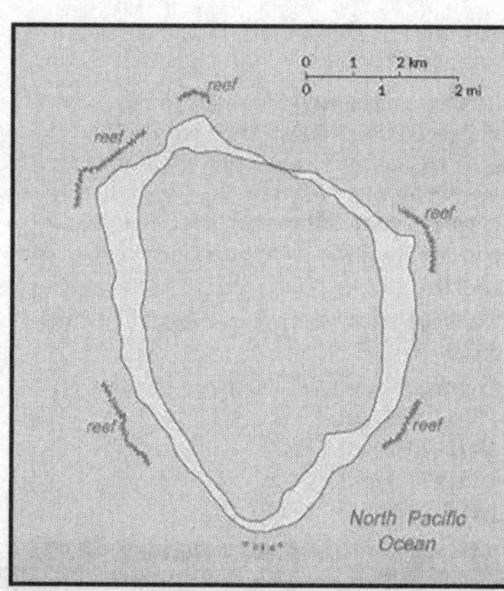

Natural resources: fish
Land use: *agricultural land:* 0% (2018 est.)
forest: 0% (2018 est.)
other: 100% (2018 est.)
Natural hazards: subject to tropical storms and hurricanes from May to October
Geography - note: the atoll reef is approximately 12 km (7.5 mi) in circumference

PEOPLE AND SOCIETY

Population: *total:* uninhabited

ENVIRONMENT

Environmental issues: no natural resources, guano deposits depleted; stagnant fresh-water lagoon
Climate: tropical; humid, average temperature 20-32 degrees Celsius, wet season (May to October)

GOVERNMENT

Country name: *conventional long form:* none
conventional short form: Clipperton Island
local long form: none
local short form: Ile Clipperton
former: sometimes referred to as Ile de la Passion or Atoll Clipperton
etymology: named after an 18th-century English pirate who is alleged to have used the island as a base starting in 1705
Dependency status: possession of France; administered directly by the Minister of Overseas France
Legal system: the laws of France apply
Flag: the flag of France is used

MILITARY AND SECURITY

Military - note: defense is the responsibility of France

COCOS (KEELING) ISLANDS

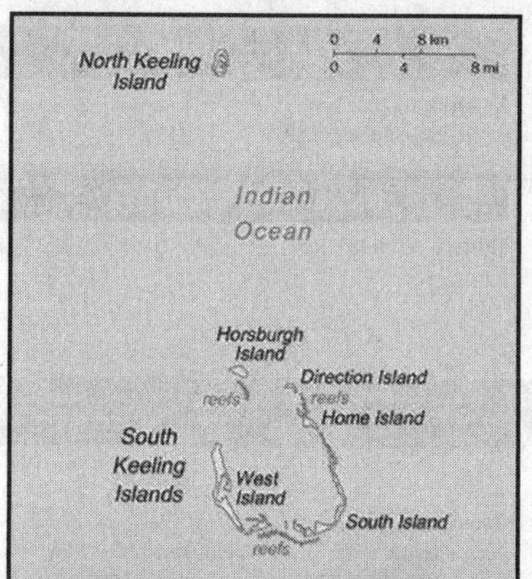

INTRODUCTION

Background: British sea captain William KEELING discovered the Cocos (Keeling) Islands in 1609, and they were named for their coconut trees in 1622. Some maps began referring to them as the Keeling Islands in 1703. In 1825, Scottish trader John CLUNIES-ROSS was trying to get to Christmas Island but was blown off course and landed on Cocos (Keeling) Islands. The next year, a British trader hired CLUNIES-ROSS's brother to bring slaves and a harem of Malay women to create the first permanent settlement on the island. By the 1830s, the Clunies-Ross family had firmly established themselves as the leaders of the islands, and they ruled Cocos (Keeling) Islands in a feudal style until 1978.

The UK annexed the islands in 1857 and administered them from Ceylon after 1878 and from Singapore after 1886. The Cocos (Keeling) Islands hosted a cable relaying station and was attacked by the Germans in World War I. The Japanese similarly attacked the islands in World War II. The UK transferred the islands to Australia in 1955, when they were officially named the Cocos (Keeling) Islands, and in 1978, Australia bought all the land held by the Clunies-Ross family, ending their control of the islands. In a referendum in 1984, most islanders voted to integrate with Australia, and Western Australian laws have applied on the islands since 1992.

GEOGRAPHY

Location: Southeastern Asia, group of islands in the Indian Ocean, southwest of Indonesia, about halfway between Australia and Sri Lanka
Geographic coordinates: 12 30 S, 96 50 E
Map references: Southeast Asia
Area: *total:* 14 sq km
land: 14 sq km
water: 0 sq km
note: includes the two main islands of West Island and Home Island
comparison ranking: total 239
Area - comparative: about 24 times the size of the National Mall in Washington, D.C.
Land boundaries: *total:* 0 km
Coastline: 26 km
Maritime claims: *territorial sea:* 12 nm
exclusive fishing zone: 200 nm
Climate: tropical with high humidity, moderated by the southeast trade winds for about nine months of the year
Terrain: flat, low-lying coral atolls
Elevation: *highest point:* South Point on South Island 9 m
lowest point: Indian Ocean 0 m
Natural resources: fish
Land use: *agricultural land:* 0% (2018 est.)
forest: 0% (2018 est.)
other: 100% (2018 est.)
Irrigated land: NA
Population distribution: only Home Island and West Island are populated
Natural hazards: cyclone season is October to April
Geography - note: there are 27 coral islands in the group; apart from North Keeling Island, which lies 30 km north of the main group, the islands form a horseshoe-shaped atoll around a lagoon

PEOPLE AND SOCIETY

Population: *total:* 593 (2021 est.)
male: 301
female: 292
comparison rankings: total 236; male 234; female 234
Nationality: *noun:* Cocos Islander(s)
adjective: Cocos Islander
Ethnic groups: Europeans, Cocos Malays
Languages: Malay (Cocos dialect) 68.8%, English 22.3%, unspecified 8.9%; note - data represent language spoken at home (2016 est.)
major-language sample(s):
Buku Fakta Dunia, sumber yang diperlukan untuk maklumat asas. (Malay)
Religions: Muslim (predominantly Sunni) 75%, Anglican 3.5%, Roman Catholic 2.2%, none 12.9%, unspecified 6.3% (2016 est.)
Age structure: *0-14 years:* 21.2%
15-64 years: 61.5%
65 years and over: 17.3% (2021)
Median age: *total:* 40 years (2021 est.)
comparison ranking: total 62
Death rate: 8.89 deaths/1,000 population (2021 est.)
comparison ranking: 66
Population distribution: only Home Island and West Island are populated

ENVIRONMENT

Environmental issues: limited freshwater resources; illegal fishing
Climate: tropical with high humidity, moderated by the southeast trade winds for about nine months of the year

GOVERNMENT

Country name: *conventional long form:* Territory of Cocos (Keeling) Islands
conventional short form: Cocos (Keeling) Islands
etymology: the name refers to the abundant coconut trees on the islands and to English Captain William KEELING, the first European to sight the islands in 1609
Government type: non-self-governing overseas territory of Australia
Dependency status: non-self-governing territory of Australia; administered from Canberra by the Department of Infrastructure, Transport, Cities & Regional Development

Capital: *name:* West Island
geographic coordinates: 12 10 S, 96 50 E
time difference: UTC+6.5 (11.5 hours ahead of Washington, DC, during Standard Time)
Administrative divisions: none (territory of Australia)
Legal system: common law based on the Australian model
Constitution: *history:* 23 November 1955 (Cocos (Keeling) Islands Act 1955)
Citizenship: see Australia
Suffrage: 18 years of age
Executive branch: *chief of state:* King CHARLES III (since 8 September 2022); represented by Governor-General of the Commonwealth of Australia General Sam MOSTYN (since 1 July 2024)
head of government: Administrator Farzian ZAINAL (since 11 May 2023)
cabinet: NA
election/appointment process: the monarchy is hereditary; governor general appointed by the monarch on the recommendation of the Australian prime minister; administrator appointed by the governor-general for a 2-year term and represents the monarch and Australia
Legislative branch: *legislature name:* Cocos (Keeling) Islands Shire Council
legislative structure: unicameral
number of seats: 7 (directly elected)
electoral system: plurality/majority
scope of elections: partial renewal
term in office: 4 years
most recent election date: 10/21/2023
percentage of women in chamber: 16.7%
expected date of next election: October 2025
Judicial branch: *highest court(s):* under the terms of the Territorial Law Reform Act 1992, Western Australia provides court services as needed for the island including the Supreme Court and subordinate courts (District Court, Magistrate Court, Family Court, Children's Court, and Coroners' Court)
Political parties: none
Diplomatic representation in the US: none (territory of Australia)
Diplomatic representation from the US: *embassy:* none (territory of Australia)
International organization participation: none
Independence: none (territory of Australia)
National holiday: Australia Day (commemorates the arrival of the First Fleet of Australian settlers), 26 January (1788)
Flag: the flag of Australia is used
National anthem(s): *title:* "Advance Australia Fair"
lyrics/music: Peter Dodds McCORMICK
history: national anthem, as an Australian territory
title: "God Save the King"
lyrics/music: unknown
history: royal anthem, as an Australian territory

ECONOMY

Agricultural products: vegetables, bananas, pawpaws, coconuts
Industries: copra products, tourism
Exports - partners: USA 31%, Singapore 29%, UK 12%, Australia 3%, Brazil 3% (2023)
note: top five export partners based on percentage share of exports
Exports - commodities: ships (2023)
note: top export commodities based on value in dollars over $500,000
Imports - partners: Australia 87%, USA 3%, Philippines 2%, Sweden 2%, Brazil 1% (2023)
note: top five import partners based on percentage share of imports
Imports - commodities: iron structures, special purpose motor vehicles, cars, ships, aluminum structures (2023)
Exchange rates: Australian dollars (AUD) per US dollar -
Exchange rates: 1.515 (2024 est.)
1.505 (2023 est.)
1.442 (2022 est.)
1.331 (2021 est.)
1.453 (2020 est.)

COMMUNICATIONS

Broadcast media: 1 local radio station staffed by community volunteers; satellite broadcasts of several Australian radio and TV stations available (2017)
Internet country code: .cc
Internet users: *percent of population:* 13.4% (2021 est.)

TRANSPORTATION

Airports: 1 (2025)
comparison ranking: 219

MILITARY AND SECURITY

Military - note: defense is the responsibility of Australia

COLOMBIA

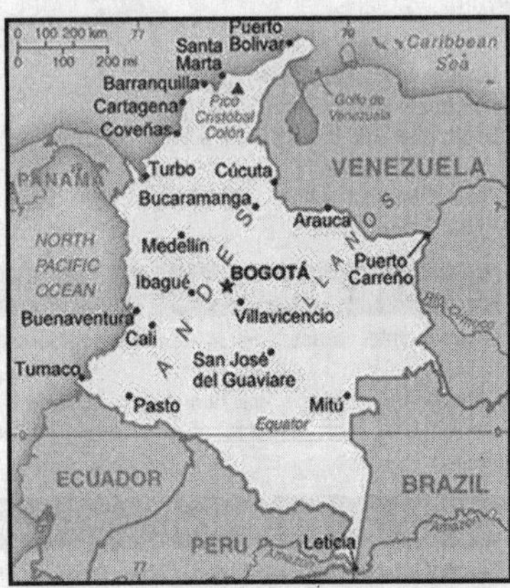

INTRODUCTION

Background: Colombia was one of three countries that emerged after the dissolution of Gran Colombia in 1830 – the others are Ecuador and Venezuela. A decades-long conflict among government forces, paramilitaries, and antigovernment insurgent groups heavily funded by the drug trade – principally the Revolutionary Armed Forces of Colombia (FARC) – escalated during the 1990s. In the wake of the paramilitary demobilization in the 2000s, new criminal groups arose that included some former paramilitaries. After four years of formal peace negotiations, the Colombian Government signed a final accord with the FARC in 2016 that called for its members to demobilize, disarm, and reincorporate into society and politics. The accord also committed the Colombian Government to create three new institutions to form a 'comprehensive system for truth, justice, reparation, and non-repetition,' including a truth commission, a special unit to coordinate the search for those who disappeared during the conflict, and a 'Special Jurisdiction for Peace' to administer justice for conflict-related crimes. Despite decades of internal conflict and drug-trade-related security challenges, Colombia maintains relatively strong and independent democratic institutions characterized by peaceful, transparent elections and the protection of civil liberties.

GEOGRAPHY

Location: Northern South America, bordering the Caribbean Sea, between Panama and Venezuela, and bordering the North Pacific Ocean, between Ecuador and Panama
Geographic coordinates: 4 00 N, 72 00 W
Map references: South America
Area: *total:* 1,138,910 sq km
land: 1,038,700 sq km
water: 100,210 sq km
note: includes Isla de Malpelo, Roncador Cay, and Serrana Bank
comparison ranking: total 27
Area - comparative: slightly less than twice the size of Texas
Land boundaries: *total:* 6,672 km
border countries (5): Brazil 1,790 km; Ecuador 708 km; Panama 339 km; Peru 1,494 km; Venezuela 2,341 km
Coastline: 3,208 km (Caribbean Sea 1,760 km, North Pacific Ocean 1,448 km)
Maritime claims: *territorial sea:* 12 nm
exclusive economic zone: 200 nm
continental shelf: 200-m depth or to the depth of exploitation
Climate: tropical along coast and eastern plains; cooler in highlands
Terrain: flat coastal lowlands, central highlands, high Andes Mountains, eastern lowland plains (Llanos)
Elevation: *highest point:* Pico Cristobal Colon 5,730 m
lowest point: Pacific Ocean 0 m
mean elevation: 593 m
Natural resources: petroleum, natural gas, coal, iron ore, nickel, gold, copper, emeralds, hydropower
Land use: *agricultural land:* 37.6% (2022 est.)
arable land: 2.2% (2022 est.)
permanent crops: 2.2% (2022 est.)
permanent pasture: 33.2% (2022 est.)

forest: 52.9% (2022 est.)
other: 9.4% (2022 est.)

Irrigated land: 6,506 sq km (2013)

Major rivers (by length in km): Rio Negro river source (shared with Venezuela and Brazil [m]) - 2,250 km; Orinoco (shared with Venezuela [s]) - 2,101 km
note: [s] after country name indicates river source; [m] after country name indicates river mouth

Major watersheds (area sq km): Atlantic Ocean drainage: Amazon (6,145,186 sq km), Orinoco (953,675 sq km)

Major aquifers: Amazon Basin

Population distribution: the majority of people live in the north and west, where agricultural opportunities and natural resources are found; the vast grasslands of the llanos to the south and east, which make up approximately 60% of the country, are sparsely populated

Natural hazards: highlands subject to volcanic eruptions; occasional earthquakes; periodic droughts
volcanism: Galeras (4,276 m) is one of Colombia's most active volcanoes; it has been deemed a Decade Volcano by the International Association of Volcanology and Chemistry of the Earth's Interior, worthy of study due to its explosive history and close proximity to human populations; Nevado del Ruiz (5,321 m), 129 km (80 mi) west of Bogota, erupted in 1985, producing lahars (mudflows) that killed 23,000 people; the volcano last erupted in 1991; after 500 years of dormancy, Nevado del Huila reawakened in 2007 and has experienced frequent eruptions since then; other historically active volcanoes include Cumbal, Dona Juana, Nevado del Tolima, and Purace

Geography - note: only South American country with coastlines on both the North Pacific Ocean and Caribbean Sea

PEOPLE AND SOCIETY

Population: *total:* 49,588,357 (2024 est.)
male: 24,206,371
female: 25,381,986
comparison rankings: total 30; male 30; female 29

Nationality: *noun:* Colombian(s)
adjective: Colombian

Ethnic groups: Mestizo and White 87.6%, Afro-Colombian (includes Mulatto, Raizal, and Palenquero) 6.8%, Indigenous 4.3%, unspecified 1.4% (2018 est.)

Languages: Spanish (official) 98.9%, indigenous 1%, Portuguese 0.1%; 65 indigenous languages exist (2023 est.)
major-language sample(s):
La Libreta Informativa del Mundo, la fuente indispensable de información básica. (Spanish)

Religions: Roman Catholic 63.6%, Protestant 17.2% (Evangelical 16.7%, Adventist 0.3%, other Protestant 0.2%), Jehovah's Witness 0.6%, Church of Jesus Christ 0.1%, other 0.3%, believer, 0.2%. agnostic 1%, atheist 1%, none 14.2%, unspecified 1.8% (2023 est.)

Age structure: *0-14 years:* 22.3% (male 5,643,995/female 5,394,147)
15-64 years: 66.5% (male 16,127,377/female 16,859,161)
65 years and over: 11.2% (2024 est.) (male 2,434,999/female 3,128,678)

Dependency ratios: *total dependency ratio:* 50.3 (2024 est.)
youth dependency ratio: 33.5 (2024 est.)
elderly dependency ratio: 16.9 (2024 est.)
potential support ratio: 5.9 (2024 est.)

Median age: *total:* 32.7 years (2024 est.)
male: 31.5 years
female: 34 years
comparison ranking: total 114

Population growth rate: 0.48% (2024 est.)
comparison ranking: 152

Birth rate: 14.9 births/1,000 population (2024 est.)
comparison ranking: 112

Death rate: 8 deaths/1,000 population (2024 est.)
comparison ranking: 91

Net migration rate: -2.1 migrant(s)/1,000 population (2024 est.)
comparison ranking: 168

Population distribution: the majority of people live in the north and west, where agricultural opportunities and natural resources are found; the vast grasslands of the llanos to the south and east, which make up approximately 60% of the country, are sparsely populated

Urbanization: *urban population:* 82.4% of total population (2023)
rate of urbanization: 1.01% annual rate of change (2020-25 est.)

Major urban areas - population: 11.508 million BOGOTA (capital), 4.102 million Medellin, 2.864 million Cali, 2.349 million Barranquilla, 1.381 million Bucaramanga, 1.088 million Cartagena (2023)

Sex ratio: *at birth:* 1.05 male(s)/female
0-14 years: 1.05 male(s)/female
15-64 years: 0.96 male(s)/female
65 years and over: 0.78 male(s)/female
total population: 0.95 male(s)/female (2024 est.)

Mother's mean age at first birth: 21.7 years (2015 est.)
note: data represents median age at first birth among women 25-49

Maternal mortality ratio: 59 deaths/100,000 live births (2023 est.)
comparison ranking: 88

Infant mortality rate: *total:* 11.7 deaths/1,000 live births (2024 est.)
male: 13.1 deaths/1,000 live births
female: 10.2 deaths/1,000 live births
comparison ranking: total 114

Life expectancy at birth: *total population:* 74.9 years (2024 est.)
male: 71.3 years
female: 78.7 years
comparison ranking: total population 134

Total fertility rate: 1.94 children born/woman (2024 est.)
comparison ranking: 114

Gross reproduction rate: 0.95 (2024 est.)

Drinking water source: *improved:* *urban:* 99.9% of population (2022 est.)
rural: 86.7% of population (2022 est.)
total: 97.5% of population (2022 est.)
unimproved: *urban:* 0.1% of population (2022 est.)
rural: 13.3% of population (2022 est.)
total: 2.5% of population (2022 est.)

Health expenditure: 9% of GDP (2021)
15.7% of national budget (2022 est.)

Physician density: 2.54 physicians/1,000 population (2023)

Hospital bed density: 1.7 beds/1,000 population (2020 est.)

Sanitation facility access: *improved:* *urban:* 98.9% of population (2022 est.)
rural: 88.2% of population (2022 est.)
total: 97% of population (2022 est.)
unimproved: *urban:* 1.1% of population (2022 est.)
rural: 11.8% of population (2022 est.)
total: 3% of population (2022 est.)

Obesity - adult prevalence rate: 22.3% (2016)
comparison ranking: 78

Alcohol consumption per capita: *total:* 4.09 liters of pure alcohol (2019 est.)
beer: 3.09 liters of pure alcohol (2019 est.)
wine: 0.06 liters of pure alcohol (2019 est.)
spirits: 0.92 liters of pure alcohol (2019 est.)
other alcohols: 0.02 liters of pure alcohol (2019 est.)
comparison ranking: total 93

Tobacco use: *total:* 7.6% (2025 est.)
male: 11.2% (2025 est.)
female: 4.1% (2025 est.)
comparison ranking: total 146

Children under the age of 5 years underweight: 3.7% (2015/16)
comparison ranking: 72

Currently married women (ages 15-49): 55.3% (2023 est.)

Child marriage: *women married by age 15:* 4.9% (2015)
women married by age 18: 23.4% (2015)
men married by age 18: 6.7% (2015)

Education expenditure: 5.3% of GDP (2020 est.)
comparison ranking: Education expenditure (% GDP) 51

Literacy: *total population:* 96% (2020 est.)
male: 95% (2020 est.)
female: 96% (2020 est.)

School life expectancy (primary to tertiary education): *total:* 14 years (2022 est.)
male: 14 years (2022 est.)
female: 15 years (2022 est.)

ENVIRONMENT

Environmental issues: deforestation from timber exploitation in the Amazon and the Chocó region; soil erosion; soil and water pollution from overuse of pesticides; air pollution, especially in Bogota, from vehicle emissions

International environmental agreements: *party to:* Antarctic-Environmental Protection, Antarctic Treaty, Biodiversity, Climate Change, Climate Change-Kyoto Protocol, Climate Change-Paris Agreement, Comprehensive Nuclear Test Ban, Desertification, Endangered Species, Hazardous Wastes, Marine Life Conservation, Nuclear Test Ban, Ozone Layer Protection, Ship Pollution, Tropical Timber 2006, Wetlands, Whaling
signed, but not ratified: Law of the Sea

Climate: tropical along coast and eastern plains; cooler in highlands

Urbanization: *urban population:* 82.4% of total population (2023)
rate of urbanization: 1.01% annual rate of change (2020-25 est.)

Carbon dioxide emissions: 85.878 million metric tonnes of CO2 (2023 est.)
from coal and metallurgical coke: 15.463 million metric tonnes of CO2 (2023 est.)

from petroleum and other liquids: 49.727 million metric tonnes of CO_2 (2023 est.)
from consumed natural gas: 20.688 million metric tonnes of CO_2 (2023 est.)
comparison ranking: total emissions 44

Particulate matter emissions: 13.1 micrograms per cubic meter (2019 est.)

Methane emissions: *energy:* 814.5 kt (2022-2024 est.)
agriculture: 1,791.5 kt (2019-2021 est.)
waste: 600.8 kt (2019-2021 est.)
other: 18.9 kt (2019-2021 est.)

Waste and recycling: *municipal solid waste generated annually:* 12.15 million tons (2024 est.)
percent of municipal solid waste recycled: 28.5% (2022 est.)

Total water withdrawal: *municipal:* 3.405 billion cubic meters (2022)
industrial: 1.033 billion cubic meters (2022)
agricultural: 20.46 billion cubic meters (2022)

Total renewable water resources: 2.36 trillion cubic meters (2022 est.)

GOVERNMENT

Country name: *conventional long form:* Republic of Colombia
conventional short form: Colombia
local long form: República de Colombia
local short form: Colombia
etymology: named after explorer Christopher COLUMBUS

Government type: presidential republic

Capital: *name:* Bogotá
geographic coordinates: 4 36 N, 74 05 W
time difference: UTC-5 (same time as Washington, DC, during Standard Time)
etymology: originally named Santa Fe de Bacatá in 1538, after the Chibcha people's nearby settlement of Bacatá; the name was later corrupted to Bogotá

Administrative divisions: 32 departments (*departamentos*, singular - *departamento*) and 1 capital district* (*distrito capital*); Amazonas, Antioquia, Arauca, Atlántico, Bogota*, Bolivar, Boyacá, Caldas, Caqueta, Casanare, Cauca, Cesar, Choco, Cordoba, Cundinamarca, Guainía, Guaviare, Huila, La Guajira, Magdalena, Meta, Nariño, Norte de Santander, Putumayo, Quindío, Risaralda, Archipielago de San Andres, Providencia y Santa Catalina (colloquially San Andres y Providencia), Santander, Sucre, Tolima, Valle del Cauca, Vaupes, Vichada

Legal system: civil law system influenced by the Spanish and French civil codes

Constitution: *history:* several previous; latest promulgated 4 July 1991
amendment process: proposed by the government, by Congress, by a constituent assembly, or by public petition; passage requires a majority vote by Congress in each of two consecutive sessions; passage of amendments to constitutional articles on citizen rights, guarantees, and duties also require approval in a referendum by over one half of voters and participation of over one fourth of citizens registered to vote

International law organization participation: has not submitted an ICJ jurisdiction declaration; accepts ICCt jurisdiction

Citizenship: *citizenship by birth:* no
citizenship by descent only: least one parent must be a citizen or permanent resident of Colombia
dual citizenship recognized: yes
residency requirement for naturalization: 5 years

Suffrage: 18 years of age; universal

Executive branch: *chief of state:* President Gustavo Francisco PETRO Urrego (since 7 August 2022)
head of government: President Gustavo Francisco PETRO Urrego (since 7 August 2022)
cabinet: Cabinet appointed by the president
election/appointment process: president directly elected by absolute majority vote in 2 rounds, if needed, for a single 4-year term
most recent election date: 29 May 2022, with a runoff held on 19 June 2022
election results: *2022:* Gustavo Francisco PETRO Urrego elected president in second round; percent of vote in first round - Gustavo Francisco PETRO Urrego (PHxC) 40.3%, Rodolfo HERNÁNDEZ Suárez (LIGA) 28.2%, Federico GUTIÉRREZ Zuluaga (Team for Colombia / CREEMOS) 23.9%, other 7.6%; percent of vote in second round - Gustavo Francisco PETRO Urrego 50.4%, Rodolfo HERNÁNDEZ Suarez 47.3%, blank 2.3%
2018: Iván DUQUE Márquez elected president in second round; percent of vote - Iván DUQUE Márquez (CD) 54%, Gustavo Francisco PETRO Urrego (Humane Colombia) 41.8%, other/blank/invalid 4.2%
expected date of next election: 31 May 2026
note 1: the president is both chief of state and head of government
note 2: reforms in 2015 eliminated presidential reelection

Legislative branch: *legislature name:* Congress (Congreso)
legislative structure: bicameral

Legislative branch - lower chamber: *chamber name:* House of Representatives (Cámara de Representantes)
number of seats: 187 (all directly elected)
electoral system: proportional representation
scope of elections: full renewal
term in office: 4 years
most recent election date: 3/13/2022
parties elected and seats per party: Liberal Party (PL) (32); Historic Pact (27); Conservative Party (CP) (25); Democratic Centre (CD) (16); Radical Change (CR) (16); Union Party for the People "Partido de la U" (15); Green Alliance - Hope Centre coalition (11); Seats reserved for victims of the armed conflict (Citrep) (16); Other (28)
percentage of women in chamber: 29.4%
expected date of next election: March 2026

Legislative branch - upper chamber: *chamber name:* Senate (Senado de la República)
number of seats: 108 (all directly elected)
electoral system: proportional representation
scope of elections: full renewal
term in office: 4 years
most recent election date: 3/13/2022
parties elected and seats per party: Historic Pact (20); Conservative Party (CP) (15); Liberal Party (PL) (14); Green Alliance - Hope Centre coalition (13); Democratic Centre (CD) (13); Radical Change (CR) (11); Union Party for the People "Partido de la U" (10); Other (4)
percentage of women in chamber: 31.4%
expected date of next election: March 2026

Judicial branch: *highest court(s):* Supreme Court of Justice or Corte Suprema de Justicia (consists of the Civil-Agrarian and Labor Chambers each with 7 judges, and the Penal Chamber with 9 judges); Constitutional Court (consists of 9 magistrates); Council of State (consists of 27 judges); Superior Judiciary Council (consists of 13 magistrates)
judge selection and term of office: Supreme Court judges appointed by the Supreme Court members from candidates submitted by the Superior Judiciary Council; judges elected for individual 8-year terms; Constitutional Court magistrates - nominated by the president, by the Supreme Court, and elected by the Senate; judges elected for individual 8-year terms; Council of State members appointed by the State Council plenary from lists nominated by the Superior Judiciary Council
subordinate courts: Superior Tribunals (appellate courts for each of the judicial districts); regional courts; civil municipal courts; Superior Military Tribunal; first instance administrative courts

Political parties: Alternative Democratic Pole or PDA
Citizens Option (Opcion Ciudadana) or OC (formerly known as the National Integration Party or PIN)
The Commons (formerly People's Alternative Revolutionary Force or FARC)
Conservative Party or PC
Democratic Center Party or CD
Fair and Free Colombia (Colombia Justa Libres)
Green Alliance
Historic Pact for Colombia or PHxC (coalition composed of several left-leaning political parties and social movements)
Humane Colombia
Independent Movement of Absolute Renovation or MIRA
League of Anti-Corruption Rulers or LIGA
Liberal Party or PL
People's Alternative Revolutionary Force or FARC
Radical Change or CR
Team for Colombia - also known as the Experience Coalition or Coalition of the Regions (coalition composed of center-right and right-wing parties)
Union Party for the People or U Party
We Believe Colombia or CREEMOS
note: Colombia has numerous smaller political parties and movements

Diplomatic representation in the US: *chief of mission:* Ambassador Daniel GARCÍA-PEÑA JARAMILLO (since 18 September 2024)
chancery: 1724 Massachusetts Avenue NW, Washington, DC 20036
telephone: [1] (202) 387-8338
FAX: [1] (202) 232-8643
email address and website: eestadosunidos@cancilleria.gov.co
https://www.colombiaemb.org/
consulate(s) general: Atlanta, Boston, Chicago, Houston, Los Angeles, Miami, New York, Newark (NJ), Orlando, San Francisco, San Juan (Puerto Rico)

Diplomatic representation from the US: *chief of mission:* Ambassador (vacant); Chargé d'Affaires John McNAMARA (since 1 February 2025)
embassy: Carrera 45, No. 24B-27, Bogota
mailing address: 3030 Bogota Place, Washington DC 20521-3030
telephone: [57] (601) 275-2000
FAX: [57] (601) 275-4600
email address and website: ACSBogota@state.gov
https://co.usembassy.gov/

International organization participation: ACS, BCIE, BIS, CABEI, CAN, Caricom (observer), CD, CDB, CELAC, EITI (candidate country), FAO, G-3, G-24,

G-77, IADB, IAEA, IBRD, ICAO, ICC (national committees), ICCt, ICRM, IDA, IFAD, IFC, IFRCS, IHO, ILO, IMF, IMO, IMSO, Interpol, IOC, IOM, IPU, ISO, ITSO, ITU, ITUC (NGOs), LAES, LAIA, Mercosur (associate), MIGA, NAM, OAS, OPANAL, OPCW, Pacific Alliance, PCA, PROSUR, UN, UNASUR, UNCTAD, UNESCO, UNHCR, UNIDO, Union Latina, UNOOSA, UNWTO, UPU, WCO, WFTU (NGOs), WHO, WIPO, WMO, WTO

Independence: 20 July 1810 (from Spain)

National holiday: Independence Day, 20 July (1810)

Flag: *description:* three horizontal bands of yellow (top, double-width), blue, and red
meaning: various interpretations of the colors exist; one has yellow for the gold in Colombia's land, blue for the sea, and red for the blood spilled in attaining freedom; another describes them as representing sovereignty and justice (yellow), loyalty and vigilance (blue), and valor and generosity (red); another has the colors standing for liberty, equality, and fraternity
note: similar to the flag of Ecuador, which is wider and has the Ecuadorian coat of arms in the center

National symbol(s): Andean condor

National color(s): yellow, blue, red

National anthem(s): *title:* "Himno Nacional de la Republica de Colombia" (National Anthem of the Republic of Colombia)
lyrics/music: Rafael NUNEZ/Oreste SINDICI
history: adopted 1920; the anthem comes from an inspirational poem written by President Rafael NUNEZ; the anthem always starts with the chorus

National heritage: *total World Heritage Sites:* 9 (6 cultural, 2 natural, 1 mixed)
selected World Heritage Site locales: Chiribiquete National Park (m); Coffee Cultural Landscape of Colombia (c); Historic Center of Santa Cruz de Mompox (c); Los Katíos National Park (n); Malpelo Fauna and Flora Sanctuary (n); Tierradentro National Archeological Park (c); San Agustín Archaeological Park (c); Colonial Cartagena (c); Qhapaq Ñan/Andean Road System (c)

ECONOMY

Economic overview: prior to COVID-19, one of the most consistent growth economies; declining poverty; large stimulus package has mitigated economic fallout, but delayed key infrastructure investments; successful inflation management; sound flexible exchange rate regime; domestic economy suffers from lack of trade integration and infrastructure

Real GDP (purchasing power parity): $978.592 billion (2024 est.)
$961.82 billion (2023 est.)
$955.016 billion (2022 est.)
note: data in 2021 dollars
comparison ranking: 32

Real GDP growth rate: 1.7% (2024 est.)
0.7% (2023 est.)
7.3% (2022 est.)
note: annual GDP % growth based on constant local currency
comparison ranking: 159

Real GDP per capita: $18,500 (2024 est.)
$18,400 (2023 est.)
$18,500 (2022 est.)
note: data in 2021 dollars
comparison ranking: 110

GDP (official exchange rate): $418.542 billion (2024 est.)
note: data in current dollars at official exchange rate

Inflation rate (consumer prices): 6.6% (2024 est.)
11.7% (2023 est.)
10.2% (2022 est.)
note: annual % change based on consumer prices
comparison ranking: 160

GDP - composition, by sector of origin: *agriculture:* 9.3% (2024 est.)
industry: 23.1% (2024 est.)
services: 58.2% (2024 est.)
note: figures may not total 100% due to non-allocated consumption not captured in sector-reported data
comparison rankings: agriculture 78; industry 108; services 105

GDP - composition, by end use: *household consumption:* 73.1% (2024 est.)
government consumption: 14.7% (2024 est.)
investment in fixed capital: 16.5% (2024 est.)
investment in inventories: 0.6% (2024 est.)
exports of goods and services: 16% (2024 est.)
imports of goods and services: -20.9% (2024 est.)
note: figures may not total 100% due to rounding or gaps in data collection

Agricultural products: sugarcane, oil palm fruit, milk, rice, plantains, potatoes, bananas, maize, chicken, avocados (2023)
note: top ten agricultural products based on tonnage

Industries: textiles, food processing, oil, clothing and footwear, beverages, chemicals, cement; gold, coal, emeralds

Industrial production growth rate: -1.3% (2024 est.)
note: annual % change in industrial value added based on constant local currency
comparison ranking: 154

Labor force: 26.822 million (2024 est.)
note: number of people ages 15 or older who are employed or seeking work
comparison ranking: 26

Unemployment rate: 9.7% (2024 est.)
9.6% (2023 est.)
10.6% (2022 est.)
note: % of labor force seeking employment
comparison ranking: 146

Youth unemployment rate (ages 15-24): *total:* 19.8% (2024 est.)
male: 16.5% (2024 est.)
female: 24.3% (2024 est.)
note: % of labor force ages 15-24 seeking employment
comparison ranking: total 56

Population below poverty line: 33% (2023 est.)
note: % of population with income below national poverty line

Gini Index coefficient - distribution of family income: 53.9 (2023 est.)
note: index (0-100) of income distribution; higher values represent greater inequality
comparison ranking: 4

Average household expenditures: *on food:* 20.6% of household expenditures (2023 est.)
on alcohol and tobacco: 3.6% of household expenditures (2023 est.)

Household income or consumption by percentage share: *lowest 10%:* 1.1% (2023 est.)
highest 10%: 42.7% (2023 est.)
note: % share of income accruing to lowest and highest 10% of population

Remittances: 2.8% of GDP (2024 est.)
2.8% of GDP (2023 est.)
2.7% of GDP (2022 est.)
note: personal transfers and compensation between resident and non-resident individuals/households/entities

Budget: *revenues:* $116.49 billion (2023 est.)
expenditures: $123.966 billion (2023 est.)
note: central government revenues (excluding grants) and expenditures converted to US dollars at average official exchange rate for year indicated

Public debt: 71.3% of GDP (2023 est.)
note: central government debt as a % of GDP
comparison ranking: 56

Taxes and other revenues: 17.6% (of GDP) (2023 est.)
note: central government tax revenue as a % of GDP
comparison ranking: 71

Current account balance: -$7.412 billion (2024 est.)
-$8.285 billion (2023 est.)
-$20.879 billion (2022 est.)
note: balance of payments - net trade and primary/secondary income in current dollars
comparison ranking: 180

Exports: $68.866 billion (2024 est.)
$68.674 billion (2023 est.)
$73.514 billion (2022 est.)
note: balance of payments - exports of goods and services in current dollars
comparison ranking: 55

Exports - partners: USA 27%, Panama 9%, India 5%, China 5%, Netherlands 4% (2023)
note: top five export partners based on percentage share of exports

Exports - commodities: crude petroleum, coal, gold, coffee, refined petroleum (2023)
note: top five export commodities based on value in dollars

Imports: $78.633 billion (2024 est.)
$76.449 billion (2023 est.)
$89.608 billion (2022 est.)
note: balance of payments - imports of goods and services in current dollars
comparison ranking: 52

Imports - partners: USA 26%, China 22%, Brazil 6%, Mexico 5%, Germany 4% (2023)
note: top five import partners based on percentage share of imports

Imports - commodities: refined petroleum, cars, broadcasting equipment, aircraft, packaged medicine (2023)
note: top five import commodities based on value in dollars

Reserves of foreign exchange and gold: $61.898 billion (2024 est.)
$59.041 billion (2023 est.)
$56.704 billion (2022 est.)
note: holdings of gold (year-end prices)/foreign exchange/special drawing rights in current dollars
comparison ranking: 39

Debt - external: $108.027 billion (2023 est.)
note: present value of external debt in current US dollars
comparison ranking: 9

Exchange rates: Colombian pesos (COP) per US dollar -

Exchange rates: 4,074.434 (2024 est.)
4,325.955 (2023 est.)
4,256.194 (2022 est.)
3,744.244 (2021 est.)
3,693.276 (2020 est.)

ENERGY

Electricity access: *electrification - total population:* 100% (2022 est.)

Electricity: *installed generating capacity:* 21.053 million kW (2023 est.)
consumption: 82.309 billion kWh (2023 est.)
exports: 1.293 billion kWh (2023 est.)
imports: 407.788 million kWh (2023 est.)
transmission/distribution losses: 7.232 billion kWh (2023 est.)
comparison rankings: installed generating capacity 49; consumption 39; exports 65; imports 98; transmission/distribution losses 172

Electricity generation sources: *fossil fuels:* 34% of total installed capacity (2023 est.)
solar: 1.3% of total installed capacity (2023 est.)
wind: 0.1% of total installed capacity (2023 est.)
hydroelectricity: 62.1% of total installed capacity (2023 est.)
biomass and waste: 2.5% of total installed capacity (2023 est.)

Coal: *production:* 52.376 million metric tons (2023 est.)
consumption: 9.72 million metric tons (2023 est.)
exports: 46.425 million metric tons (2023 est.)
imports: 1,000 metric tons (2023 est.)
proven reserves: 4.554 billion metric tons (2023 est.)

Petroleum: *total petroleum production:* 800,000 bbl/day (2023 est.)
refined petroleum consumption: 374,000 bbl/day (2023 est.)
crude oil estimated reserves: 2.036 billion barrels (2021 est.)

Natural gas: *production:* 10.927 billion cubic meters (2023 est.)
consumption: 11.885 billion cubic meters (2023 est.)
imports: 958.724 million cubic meters (2023 est.)
proven reserves: 87.782 billion cubic meters (2021 est.)

Energy consumption per capita: 29.305 million Btu/person (2023 est.)
comparison ranking: 118

COMMUNICATIONS

Telephones - fixed lines: *total subscriptions:* 7.277 million (2023 est.)
subscriptions per 100 inhabitants: 14 (2023 est.)
comparison ranking: total subscriptions 21

Telephones - mobile cellular: *total subscriptions:* 87.4 million (2023 est.)
subscriptions per 100 inhabitants: 156 (2022 est.)
comparison ranking: total subscriptions 20

Broadcast media: combination of state-owned and privately owned broadcast media provide service; more than 500 radio stations and many national, regional, and local TV stations (2019)

Internet country code: .co

Internet users: *percent of population:* 77% (2023 est.)

Broadband - fixed subscriptions: *total:* 8.91 million (2023 est.)
subscriptions per 100 inhabitants: 17 (2023 est.)
comparison ranking: total 27

TRANSPORTATION

Civil aircraft registration country code prefix: HJ, HK

Airports: 661 (2025)
comparison ranking: 11

Heliports: 57 (2025)
comparison ranking: 35

Railways: *total:* 2,141 km (2019)
standard gauge: 150 km (2019) 1.435-m gauge
narrow gauge: 1,991 km (2019) 0.914-m gauge

Merchant marine: *total:* 153 (2023)
by type: general cargo 28, oil tanker 13, other 112
comparison ranking: total 74

Ports: *total ports:* 14 (2024)
large: 0
medium: 2
small: 8
very small: 3
size unknown: 1
ports with oil terminals: 10
key ports: Barranquilla, Buenaventura, Cartagena, Covenas, El Bosque, Mamonal, Pozos Colorados, Puerto Bolivar, Puerto Prodeco, Santa Marta

MILITARY AND SECURITY

Military and security forces: Military Forces of Colombia (Fuerzas Militares de Colombia): National Army (Ejercito Nacional), Colombian Aerospace Force (Fuerza Aeroespacial Colombiana, FAC), Colombian Navy (Armada de Colombia; includes Coast Guard); National Police of Colombia (Policia Nacional de Colombia, PNC) (2025)
note: the PNC is a civilian force under the jurisdiction of the Ministry of Defense

Military expenditures: 3.4% of GDP (2024 est.)
3% of GDP (2023 est.)
3% of GDP (2022 est.)
3.2% of GDP (2021 est.)
3.4% of GDP (2020 est.)

Military and security service personnel strengths: information varies; approximately 260,000 active Military Forces; approximately 150,000 National Police (2025)

Military equipment inventories and acquisitions: the military's inventory includes a wide mix of equipment from a variety of suppliers, including Canada, Germany, Israel, South Korea, and especially the US; Colombia's defense industry is active in producing air, land, and naval platforms (2024)

Military service age and obligation: 18-24 years of age for compulsory (men) and voluntary (men and women) military (and police) service; conscript service obligation is 18 months or 12 months for those with a college degree; conscripted soldiers reportedly include regular soldiers (conscripts without a high school degree), drafted high school graduates (bachilleres), and rural (campesino) soldiers who serve in their home regions (2024)
note: the Colombian military first incorporated women in 1976 in administrative positions; women were incorporated as non-commissioned officers in 1983 and officers in 2009; as of 2023, about 6,000 women served in the uniformed military while more than 30,000 served in the National Police

Military deployments: 275 Egypt (MFO) (2025)

Military - note: the Colombian military is responsible for defending and maintaining the country's independence, national sovereignty, and territorial integrity but also has a considerable internal security role, which includes protecting the civilian population, as well as private and state-owned assets, and ensuring a secure environment; the military's primary focus is the conduct of counterinsurgency and counter-narcotics operations against domestic illegal armed groups, including drug traffickers, several factions of the former Revolutionary Armed Forces of Colombia (FARC) terrorist group, and the insurgent/terrorist group National Liberation Army (ELN)
border security is also a focus, particularly with Venezuela where economic and political instability has brought refugees and attracted narcotics trafficking and other cross-border crime; both the ELN and FARC dissidents operate openly in the border region; ELN and FARC insurgents have also used neighboring Ecuador to rest, resupply, and shelter
Colombia has close security ties with the US, including joint training, military assistance, and designation in 2022 as a Major Non-NATO Ally, which provides foreign partners with certain benefits in the areas of defense, trade, and security cooperation; it also has close security ties with regional neighbors, such as Argentina, Brazil, Chile, and Peru; Colombian military and security forces have training programs with their counterparts from a variety of countries, mostly those from Mexico, Central America, and the Caribbean (2025)

SPACE

Space agency/agencies: Colombian Space Commission (Comision Colombiana Del Espacio, CCE; established 2006); Air and Space Operations Command (Colombian military); note – the Colombian Space Agency (Agencia Espacial Del Colombia, AEC) is a private, non-profit agency established in 2017 (2025)

Space program overview: has a small program focused on acquiring satellites, particularly remote sensing (RS) satellites; operates satellites and produces nanosatellites; researches other space technologies, including astronautics, satellite navigation, and telecommunications; has relations with a variety of foreign space agencies or commercial space industries, including those of Denmark, India, Russia, Sweden, the US, and some members of the Latin American and Caribbean Space Agency (ALCE) (2025)
note: further details about the key activities, programs, and milestones of the country's space program, as well as government spending estimates on the space sector, appear in the Space Programs reference guide

TERRORISM

Terrorist group(s): Terrorist group(s): National Liberation Army (ELN); Revolutionary Armed Forces of Colombia - People's Army (FARC-EP); Segunda Marquetalia (SM); Tren de Aragua (TdA)
note: details about the history, aims, leadership, organization, areas of operation, tactics, targets, weapons, size, and sources of support of the group(s) appear(s) in Appendix T

TRANSNATIONAL ISSUES

Refugees and internally displaced persons: *refugees:* 30,611 (2024 est.)

IDPs: 7,264,767 (2024 est.)
stateless persons: 5 (2024 est.)

Illicit drugs: USG identification: major illicit drug-producing and/or drug-transit country
major precursor-chemical producer (2025)

COMOROS

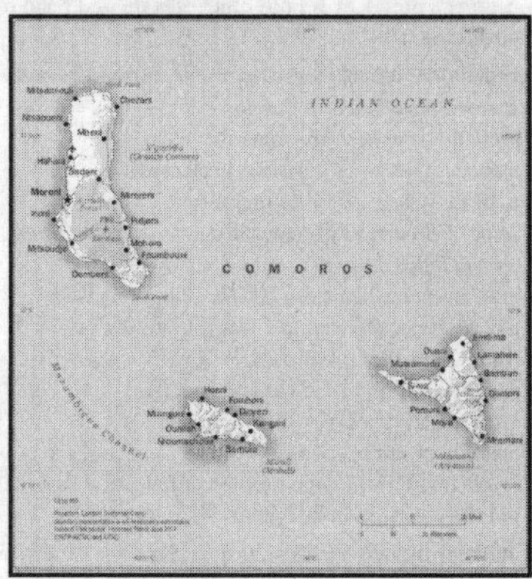

INTRODUCTION

Background: For centuries prior to colonization in the 19th century, the Comoros archipelago in the Indian Ocean served as a key node in maritime trade networks that connected the Middle East, India, and eastern African regions. Composed of the islands of Anjouan, Mayotte, Moheli, and Grande Comore, Comoros spent most of the 20th century as a colonial outpost until it declared independence from France on 6 July 1975. Residents of Mayotte, however, voted to remain in France, and the French Government has since classified it as a French Overseas Department.

Since independence, Comoros has weathered approximately 20 successful and attempted coups, mostly between 1975 and 2000, resulting in prolonged political instability and stunted economic development. In 2002, President AZALI Assoumani became the first elected president following the completion of the Fomboni Accords, in which the islands of Grande Comore, Anjouan, and Moheli agreed to rotate the presidency among the islands every five years. This power-sharing agreement also included provisions allowing each island to maintain its local government. In 2007, Mohamed BACAR effected Anjouan's de-facto secession from the Union of the Comoros, refusing to step down when Comoros' other islands held legitimate elections. The African Union (AU) initially attempted to resolve the political crisis with sanctions and a naval blockade of Anjouan, but in 2008, the AU and Comoran soldiers seized the island. The island's inhabitants generally welcomed the move. In 2011, Ikililou DHOININE won the presidency in peaceful elections widely deemed to be free and fair. In closely contested elections in 2016, AZALI won a second term, when the rotating presidency returned to Grande Comore. In 2018, a referendum – which the opposition parties boycotted – approved a new constitution that extended presidential term limits and abolished the requirement for the presidency to rotate between the three main islands. AZALI formed a new government later that year, and he subsequently ran and was reelected in 2019. AZALI was reelected again in January 2024 in an election that the opposition disputed but the Supreme Court validated.

GEOGRAPHY

Location: Southern Africa, group of islands at the northern mouth of the Mozambique Channel, about two-thirds of the way between northern Madagascar and northern Mozambique

Geographic coordinates: 12 10 S, 44 15 E

Map references: Africa

Area: *total:* 2,235 sq km
land: 2,235 sq km
water: 0 sq km
comparison ranking: total 179

Area - comparative: slightly more than 12 times the size of Washington, D.C.

Land boundaries: *total:* 0 km

Coastline: 340 km

Maritime claims: *territorial sea:* 12 nm
exclusive economic zone: 200 nm

Climate: tropical marine; rainy season (November to May)

Terrain: volcanic islands, interiors vary from steep mountains to low hills

Elevation: *highest point:* Karthala 2,360 m
lowest point: Indian Ocean 0 m

Natural resources: fish

Land use: *agricultural land:* 71.5% (2022 est.)
arable land: 34.9% (2022 est.)
permanent crops: 28.5% (2022 est.)
permanent pasture: 8.1% (2022 est.)
forest: 17.2% (2022 est.)
other: 11.3% (2022 est.)

Irrigated land: 1.3 sq km (2012)

Population distribution: the capital city of Maroni, on the western side of the island of Grande Comore, is the country's largest city; however, Anjouan is the most densely populated of the three islands that comprise Comoros, as shown in this population distribution map

Natural hazards: cyclones possible during rainy season (December to April); volcanic activity on Grand Comore
volcanism: Karthala (2,361 m) on Grand Comore Island last erupted in 2007; a 2005 eruption forced thousands of people to be evacuated and produced a large ash cloud

Geography - note: important location at northern end of Mozambique Channel; the only Arab League country that lies entirely in the Southern Hemisphere

PEOPLE AND SOCIETY

Population: *total:* 900,141 (2024 est.)
male: 435,758
female: 464,383
comparison rankings: total 164; male 165; female 164

Nationality: *noun:* Comoran(s)
adjective: Comoran

Ethnic groups: Antalote, Cafre, Makoa, Oimatsaha, Sakalava

Languages: Arabic (official), French (official), Shikomoro (official; similar to Swahili), Comorian

Religions: Muslim 98.1% (overwhelmingly Sunni Muslim, small Shia Muslim and Ahmadiyya Muslim populations), ethnic religionist 1.1%, Christian 0.6%, other 0.3% (2020 est.)
note: Sunni Islam is the state religion

Age structure: *0-14 years:* 32.6% (male 146,480/female 146,626)
15-64 years: 62.8% (male 271,139/female 294,231)
65 years and over: 4.6% (2024 est.) (male 18,139/female 23,526)

Dependency ratios: *total dependency ratio:* 59.2 (2024 est.)
youth dependency ratio: 51.8 (2024 est.)
elderly dependency ratio: 7.4 (2024 est.)
potential support ratio: 13.6 (2024 est.)

Median age: *total:* 22.7 years (2024 est.)
male: 22.1 years
female: 23.3 years
comparison ranking: total 183

Population growth rate: 1.3% (2024 est.)
comparison ranking: 73

Birth rate: 21.6 births/1,000 population (2024 est.)
comparison ranking: 58

Death rate: 6.4 deaths/1,000 population (2024 est.)
comparison ranking: 140

Net migration rate: -2.2 migrant(s)/1,000 population (2024 est.)
comparison ranking: 170

Population distribution: the capital city of Maroni, on the western side of the island of Grande Comore, is the country's largest city; however, Anjouan is the most densely populated of the three islands that comprise Comoros, as shown in this population distribution map

Urbanization: *urban population:* 30.1% of total population (2023)
rate of urbanization: 2.97% annual rate of change (2020-25 est.)

Major urban areas - population: 62,000 MORONI (capital) (2018)

Sex ratio: *at birth:* 1.03 male(s)/female
0-14 years: 1 male(s)/female
15-64 years: 0.92 male(s)/female
65 years and over: 0.77 male(s)/female
total population: 0.94 male(s)/female (2024 est.)

Mother's mean age at first birth: 23 years (2012 est.)
note: data represents median age at first birth among women 25-49

Maternal mortality ratio: 179 deaths/100,000 live births (2023 est.)
comparison ranking: 43

Infant mortality rate: *total:* 54.9 deaths/1,000 live births (2024 est.)
male: 64.9 deaths/1,000 live births
female: 44.7 deaths/1,000 live births
comparison ranking: total 14

Life expectancy at birth: *total population:* 67.8 years (2024 est.)
male: 65.5 years
female: 70.2 years
comparison ranking: total population 193

Total fertility rate: 2.61 children born/woman (2024 est.)

comparison ranking: 65

Gross reproduction rate: 1.28 (2024 est.)

Drinking water source: *improved: urban:* 97.4% of population
rural: 88.5% of population
total: 91% of population
unimproved: urban: 2.6% of population
rural: 11.5% of population
total: 8.9% of population (2017 est.)

Health expenditure: 6.3% of GDP (2021)
4.7% of national budget (2022 est.)

Physician density: 0.42 physicians/1,000 population (2022)

Obesity - adult prevalence rate: 7.8% (2016)
comparison ranking: 157

Alcohol consumption per capita: *total:* 0.18 liters of pure alcohol (2019 est.)
beer: 0.04 liters of pure alcohol (2019 est.)
wine: 0.07 liters of pure alcohol (2019 est.)
spirits: 0.07 liters of pure alcohol (2019 est.)
other alcohols: 0 liters of pure alcohol (2019 est.)
comparison ranking: total 173

Tobacco use: *total:* 14.7% (2025 est.)
male: 24.8% (2025 est.)
female: 4.7% (2025 est.)
comparison ranking: total 103

Currently married women (ages 15-49): 61.2% (2023 est.)

Child marriage: *women married by age 15:* 4.9% (2022)
women married by age 18: 20.7% (2022)
men married by age 18: 6.9% (2022)

Education expenditure: 2.3% of GDP (2023 est.)
11.5% national budget (2025 est.)
comparison ranking: Education expenditure (% GDP) 179

ENVIRONMENT

Environmental issues: deforestation; soil degradation and erosion from forest loss and crop cultivation on slopes without proper terracing; silting of coral reefs

International environmental agreements: *party to:* Biodiversity, Climate Change, Climate Change-Kyoto Protocol, Climate Change-Paris Agreement, Comprehensive Nuclear Test Ban, Desertification, Endangered Species, Hazardous Wastes, Law of the Sea, Ozone Layer Protection, Ship Pollution, Wetlands
signed, but not ratified: none of the selected agreements

Climate: tropical marine; rainy season (November to May)

Urbanization: *urban population:* 30.1% of total population (2023)
rate of urbanization: 2.97% annual rate of change (2020-25 est.)

Carbon dioxide emissions: 436,000 metric tonnes of CO_2 (2023 est.)
from petroleum and other liquids: 436,000 metric tonnes of CO_2 (2023 est.)
comparison ranking: total emissions 191

Particulate matter emissions: 14.5 micrograms per cubic meter (2019 est.)

Waste and recycling: *municipal solid waste generated annually:* 91,000 tons (2024 est.)
percent of municipal solid waste recycled: 10.1% (2022 est.)

Total water withdrawal: *municipal:* 4.8 million cubic meters (2022 est.)
industrial: 500,000 cubic meters (2022 est.)
agricultural: 4.7 million cubic meters (2022 est.)

Total renewable water resources: 1.2 billion cubic meters (2022 est.)

GOVERNMENT

Country name: *conventional long form:* Union of the Comoros
conventional short form: Comoros
local long form: Udzima wa Komori (Comorian)/Union des Comores (French)/Al Ittihad al Qumuri (Arabic)
local short form: Komori (Comorian)/Les Comores (French)/Juzur al Qamar (Arabic)
former: Comorian State, Federal Islamic Republic of the Comoros
etymology: name derives from the Arabic *al qamar*, meaning "the moon"

Government type: federal presidential republic

Capital: *name:* Moroni
geographic coordinates: 11 42 S, 43 14 E
time difference: UTC+3 (8 hours ahead of Washington, DC, during Standard Time)
etymology: the name means "at the place of fire," referring to the capital's location below the active volcano Mt. Karthala

Administrative divisions: 3 islands; Anjouan (Ndzuwani), Grande Comore (N'gazidja), Moheli (Mwali)

Legal system: mixed legal system of Islamic religious law, the French civil code of 1975, and customary law

Constitution: *history:* previous 1996, 2001; newest adopted 30 July 2018
amendment process: proposed by the president of the union or supported by at least one third of the Assembly of the Union membership; adoption requires approval by at least three-quarters majority of the total Assembly membership or approval in a referendum

International law organization participation: has not submitted an ICJ jurisdiction declaration; accepts ICCt jurisdiction

Citizenship: *citizenship by birth:* no
citizenship by descent only: at least one parent must be a citizen of the Comoros
dual citizenship recognized: no
residency requirement for naturalization: 10 years

Suffrage: 18 years of age; universal

Executive branch: *chief of state:* President AZALI Assoumani (since 26 May 2016)
head of government: President AZALI Assoumani (since 26 May 2016)
cabinet: Council of Ministers appointed by the president
election/appointment process: president directly elected by absolute majority vote in 2 rounds, if needed, for a 5-year term
most recent election date: 14 January 2024
election results: 2024: AZALI Assoumani reelected president in first round - AZALI Assoumani (CRC) 63%, SALIM ISSA Abdallah (PJ) 20.3%, DAOUDOU Abdallah Mohamed (Orange Party) 5.9%, Bourhane HAMIDOU (independent) 5.1%
2019: AZALI Assoumani elected president in first round - AZALI Assoumani (CRC) 60.8%, Ahamada MAHAMOUDOU (PJ) 14.6%, Mouigni Baraka Said SOILIHI (independent) 5.6%, other 19%
expected date of next election: 2029
note: the president is both chief of state and head of government

Legislative branch: *legislature name:* Assembly of the Union (Assemblée de l'Union)
legislative structure: unicameral
number of seats: 33 (all directly elected)
electoral system: plurality/majority
scope of elections: full renewal
term in office: 5 years
most recent election date: 1/12/2025 to 2/16/2025
parties elected and seats per party: Convention for the Renewal of the Comoros (CRC) (31); Other (2)
percentage of women in chamber: 15.2%
expected date of next election: January 2030
note: opposition parties, which claimed there was "gross fraud" during the most recent election, boycotted the elections in 2020 and 2025

Judicial branch: *highest court(s):* Supreme Court or Cour Supreme (consists of 7 judges)
judge selection and term of office: Supreme Court judges - selection and term of office NA
subordinate courts: Court of Appeals (in Moroni); Tribunal de première instance; island village (community) courts; religious courts

Political parties: Convention for the Renewal of the Comoros or CRC
Juwa Party (Parti Juwa) or PJ
Orange Party (2020)

Diplomatic representation in the US: *chief of mission:* Ambassador Issimail CHANFI (since 23 December 2020); note - also Permanent Representative to the UN
chancery: Permanent Mission to the UN, 866 United Nations Plaza, Suite 495, New York, NY 10017
telephone: [1] (212) 750-1637

FAX: [1] (212) 750-1657
email address and website: comoros@un.int
https://www.un.int/comoros/

Diplomatic representation from the US: *embassy:* the US does not have an embassy in Comoros; the US Ambassador to Madagascar is accredited to Comoros

International organization participation: ACP, AfDB, AMF, AOSIS, AU, CAEU (candidates), COMESA, FAO, FZ, G-77, IBRD, ICAO, ICCt, ICRM, IDA, IDB, IFAD, IFC, IFRCS, ILO, IMF, IMO, IMSO, InOC, Interpol, IOC, IOM, ITSO, ITU, ITUC (NGOs), LAS, MIGA, NAM, OIC, OIF, OPCW, UN, UNCTAD, UNESCO, UNIDO, UPU, WCO, WHO, WIPO, WMO, WTO (observer)

Independence: 6 July 1975 (from France)

National holiday: Independence Day, 6 July (1975)

Flag: *description:* four equal horizontal bands of yellow (top), white, red, and blue, with a green isosceles triangle based on the left; a vertical white crescent moon is centered in the triangle, with four five-pointed white stars placed vertically in a line between the points of the crescent
meaning: the horizontal bands and the stars represent the four main islands of the archipelago – Mwali, N'gazidja, Ndzuwani, and Mahore (Mayotte is a department of France, but claimed by Comoros)
note: the crescent, stars, and color green are traditional symbols of Islam

National symbol(s): four five-pointed stars and crescent moon

National color(s): green, white

National coat of arms: *the coat of arms is in the national colors of green and white; was adopted in 1978; the crescent and stars represent Islam, with the four stars also symbolizing the archipelago's four main islands:* Grande Comore, Mohéli, Anjouan, and Mayotte (the last of which is a French department claimed by Comoros); above and below the sun's rays is the name of the nation written in French and Arabic; two olive branches, representing peace, are connected by a banner with the national motto in French, which translates as "Unity, Solidarity, Development"

National anthem(s): *title:* "Udzima wa ya Masiwa" (The Union of the Great Islands)
lyrics/music: Said Hachim SIDI ABDEREMANE/ Said Hachim SIDI ABDEREMANE and Kamildine ABDALLAH
history: adopted 1978

ECONOMY

Economic overview: small trade-based island economy; declining remittances; new structural and fiscal reforms; adverse cyclone and COVID-19 impacts; manageable debts; fragile liquidity environment; large foreign direct investment; state-owned enterprises suffering

Real GDP (purchasing power parity): $3.092 billion (2024 est.)
$2.99 billion (2023 est.)
$2.901 billion (2022 est.)
note: data in 2021 dollars
comparison ranking: 192

Real GDP growth rate: 3.4% (2024 est.)
3.1% (2023 est.)
2.8% (2022 est.)
note: annual GDP % growth based on constant local currency
comparison ranking: 105

Real GDP per capita: $3,600 (2024 est.)
$3,500 (2023 est.)
$3,500 (2022 est.)
note: data in 2021 dollars
comparison ranking: 188

GDP (official exchange rate): $1.546 billion (2024 est.)
note: data in current dollars at official exchange rate

Inflation rate (consumer prices): 1% (2017 est.)
1.8% (2016 est.)
note: annual % change based on consumer prices
comparison ranking: 19

GDP - composition, by sector of origin: *agriculture:* 36.6% (2024 est.)
industry: 9.6% (2024 est.)
services: 50.1% (2024 est.)
note: figures may not total 100% due to non-allocated consumption not captured in sector-reported data
comparison rankings: agriculture 3; industry 191; services 145

GDP - composition, by end use: *household consumption:* 103.6% (2024 est.)
government consumption: 9.2% (2024 est.)
investment in fixed capital: 11.7% (2024 est.)
investment in inventories: 0% (2024 est.)
exports of goods and services: 9.9% (2024 est.)
imports of goods and services: -34.5% (2024 est.)
note: figures may not total 100% due to rounding or gaps in data collection

Agricultural products: bananas, coconuts, cassava, yams, maize, taro, milk, tomatoes, sweet potatoes, pulses (2023)
note: top ten agricultural products based on tonnage

Industries: fishing, tourism, perfume distillation

Industrial production growth rate: 3.8% (2024 est.)
note: annual % change in industrial value added based on constant local currency
comparison ranking: 64

Labor force: 276,400 (2024 est.)
note: number of people ages 15 or older who are employed or seeking work
comparison ranking: 168

Unemployment rate: 3.9% (2024 est.)
3.8% (2023 est.)
3.9% (2022 est.)
note: % of labor force seeking employment
comparison ranking: 62

Youth unemployment rate (ages 15-24): *total:* 8.9% (2024 est.)
male: 8.3% (2024 est.)
female: 9.6% (2024 est.)
note: % of labor force ages 15-24 seeking employment
comparison ranking: total 131

Population below poverty line: 44.8% (2020 est.)
note: % of population with income below national poverty line

Remittances: 21.4% of GDP (2023 est.)
22% of GDP (2022 est.)
22.2% of GDP (2021 est.)
note: personal transfers and compensation between resident and non-resident individuals/households/ entities

Budget: *revenues:* $212.551 million (2023 est.)
expenditures: $230.338 million (2023 est.)
note: central government revenues and expenses (excluding grants/extrabudgetary units/social security funds) converted to US dollars at average official exchange rate for year indicated

Current account balance: -$24.621 million (2023 est.)
-$5.248 million (2022 est.)
-$4.076 million (2021 est.)
note: balance of payments - net trade and primary/ secondary income in current dollars
comparison ranking: 89

Exports: $148.455 million (2023 est.)
$166.032 million (2022 est.)
$128.331 million (2021 est.)
note: balance of payments - exports of goods and services in current dollars
comparison ranking: 204

Exports - partners: Indonesia 25%, India 23%, Turkey 16%, UAE 11%, USA 3% (2023)
note: top five export partners based on percentage share of exports

Exports - commodities: cloves, ships, essential oils, vanilla, scrap iron (2023)
note: top five export commodities based on value in dollars

Imports: $504.036 million (2023 est.)
$480.268 million (2022 est.)
$415.965 million (2021 est.)
note: balance of payments - imports of goods and services in current dollars
comparison ranking: 201

Imports - partners: China 24%, UAE 21%, Tanzania 12%, France 7%, India 6% (2023)
note: top five import partners based on percentage share of imports

Imports - commodities: refined petroleum, poultry, rice, flavored water, additive manufacturing machines (2023)
note: top five import commodities based on value in dollars

Reserves of foreign exchange and gold: $323.946 million (2024 est.)
$324.561 million (2023 est.)
$283.746 million (2022 est.)
note: holdings of gold (year-end prices)/foreign exchange/special drawing rights in current dollars
comparison ranking: 169

Debt - external: $267.652 million (2023 est.)
note: present value of external debt in current US dollars
comparison ranking: 119

Exchange rates: Comoran francs (KMF) per US dollar -

Exchange rates: 454.524 (2024 est.)
454.991 (2023 est.)
467.184 (2022 est.)
415.956 (2021 est.)
430.721 (2020 est.)

ENERGY

Electricity access: *electrification - total population:* 89.9% (2022 est.)
electrification - urban areas: 100%
electrification - rural areas: 82.9%

Electricity: *installed generating capacity:* 32,000 kW (2023 est.)
consumption: 113.052 million kWh (2023 est.)
transmission/distribution losses: 22.1 million kWh (2023 est.)
comparison rankings: installed generating capacity 201; consumption 198; transmission/distribution losses 26

Electricity generation sources: *fossil fuels:* 100% of total installed capacity (2023 est.)

Coal: *imports:* 2,000 metric tons (2023 est.)

Petroleum: *refined petroleum consumption:* 3,000 bbl/ day (2023 est.)

Energy consumption per capita: 7.139 million Btu/ person (2023 est.)
comparison ranking: 162

COMMUNICATIONS

Telephones - fixed lines: *total subscriptions:* 9,000 (2023 est.)
subscriptions per 100 inhabitants: 1 (2023 est.) less than 1
comparison ranking: total subscriptions 189

Telephones - mobile cellular: *total subscriptions:* 934,000 (2023 est.)
subscriptions per 100 inhabitants: 100 (2022 est.)
comparison ranking: total subscriptions 166

Broadcast media: national state-owned TV station and a TV station run by Anjouan regional government; national state-owned radio; regional governments on the islands of Grande Comore and Anjouan each operate a radio station; a few independent and small community radio stations operate on the islands of Grande Comore and Moheli, and these two islands have access to Mayotte Radio and French TV

Internet country code: .km

Internet users: *percent of population:* 36% (2023 est.)

Broadband - fixed subscriptions: *total:* 3,000 (2023 est.)
subscriptions per 100 inhabitants: (2023 est.) less than 1
comparison ranking: total 199

TRANSPORTATION

Civil aircraft registration country code prefix: D6

Airports: 3 (2025)
comparison ranking: 190

Merchant marine: *total:* 273 (2023)
by type: bulk carrier 17, container ship 7, general cargo 125, oil tanker 36, other 88
comparison ranking: total 58

Ports: *total ports:* 4 (2024)
large: 0
medium: 0
small: 0
very small: 4
ports with oil terminals: 3
key ports: Dzaoudzi, Fomboni, Moroni, Moutsamoudu

MILITARY AND SECURITY

Military and security forces: National Army for Development (l'Armee Nationale de Developpement, AND): Comoran Defense Force (Force Comorienne de Defense or FCD; includes Comoran National Gendarmerie); Ministry of Interior: Coast Guard, Federal Police, National Directorate of Territorial Safety (customs and immigration) (2024)
note 1: when the Gendarmerie serves as the judicial police, it reports to the Minister of Justice; the Gendarmerie also has an intervention platoon that may act under the authority of the Interior Minister
note 2: the FCD is also known as the Comoran Security Force

Military and security service personnel strengths: estimated 600 Defense Force; estimated 500 Federal Police (2023)

Military equipment inventories and acquisitions: the AND is lightly armed and equipped with small arms and a few light aircraft (2023)

Military service age and obligation: 18-25 years of age for 2-year voluntary military service for men and women; no conscription (2021)

Military - note: the focus for the security forces is search and rescue operations and maintaining internal security; a defense treaty with France provides naval resources for the protection of territorial waters, training of Comoran military personnel, and air surveillance; France maintains a small maritime base and a Foreign Legion contingent on neighboring Mayotte (2024)

TRANSNATIONAL ISSUES

Refugees and internally displaced persons: *refugees:* 18 (2024 est.)

IDPs: 38 (2024 est.)

CONGO, DEMOCRATIC REPUBLIC OF THE

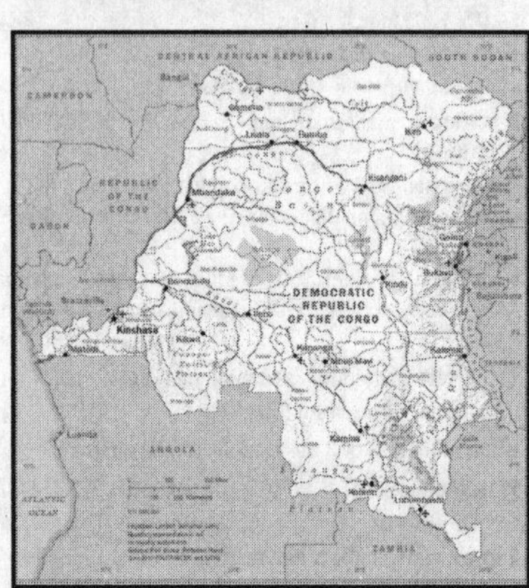

INTRODUCTION

Background: Bantu, Sudanic, and other migrants from West and Northeastern Africa arrived in the Congo River Basin between 2000 B.C. and A.D. 500. The territory that is now the Democratic Republic of the Congo has more than 200 ethnic groups that trace their histories to many communal organizations and kingdoms. The Kingdom of Kongo, for example, ruled the area around the mouth of the Congo River from the 14th to 19th centuries. Meanwhile, the Kingdoms of Luba and Lunda, located to the south and east, were also notable political groupings in the territory and ruled from the 16th and 17th centuries to the 19th century. European prospectors in the Congo Basin invaded and splintered these kingdoms in the late 1800's, sponsored by King LEOPOLD II of Belgium, and the kingdoms were eventually forced to grant Leopold the rights to the Congo territory as his private property. During this period, known as the Congo Free State, the king's private colonial military forced the local population to produce rubber. From 1885 to 1908, millions of Congolese people died as a result of disease and inhumane treatment. International condemnation finally forced LEOPOLD to cede the land to the state of Belgium, creating the Belgian Congo.

The Republic of the Congo gained its independence from Belgium in 1960, but its early years were marred by instability. Col. Joseph MOBUTU seized power and declared himself president in a 1965 coup. He subsequently changed his name to MOBUTU Sese Seko and the country's name to Zaire. MOBUTU retained his position for 32 years, using sham elections and brute force. In 1994, a massive inflow of refugees from conflict in neighboring Rwanda and Burundi sparked ethnic strife and civil war. A rebellion backed by Rwanda and Uganda and fronted by Laurent KABILA toppled the MOBUTU regime in 1997. KABILA renamed the country the Democratic Republic of the Congo (DRC). In 1998, another insurrection – again backed by Rwanda and Uganda – challenged the KABILA regime, but troops from Angola, Chad, Namibia, Sudan, and Zimbabwe helped quell the uprising.

In 2001, KABILA was assassinated, and his son, Joseph KABILA, was named head of state. In 2002, the new president negotiated the withdrawal of Rwandan forces occupying the eastern DRC; the remaining warring parties subsequently signed the Pretoria Accord to end the fighting and establish a government of national unity. KABILA was elected as president in 2006 and 2011. The DRC constitution barred him from running for a third term, so in 2016, the DRC Government delayed national elections for two years. This fueled significant civil and political unrest, with sporadic street protests and exacerbation of tensions in the eastern DRC regions.

The results of the 2018 elections were disputed, but opposition candidate Felix TSHISEKEDI, son of long-time opposition leader Etienne TSHISEKEDI, was announced as the election winner. This was the first transfer of power to an opposition candidate without significant violence or a coup since 1960. In 2023, the DRC held its fourth electoral cycle since independence; TSHISEKEDI was proclaimed the winner despite some allegations of fraud, with his Sacred Union alliance retaining a large parliamentary majority.

The DRC continues to experience violence – particularly in the East – perpetrated by more than 100 armed groups active in the region, including the March 23 (M23) rebel group, the ISIS-affiliated Allied Democratic Forces (ADF, or ISIS-DRC), the Democratic Forces for the Liberation of Rwanda (FDLR), and assorted local militias known as Mai Mai militias. The UN Organization Stabilization Mission in the DRC (MONUSCO) has operated in the region since 1999 and is the largest and most expensive UN peacekeeping mission in the world.

GEOGRAPHY

Location: Central Africa, northeast of Angola

Geographic coordinates: 0 00 N, 25 00 E

Map references: Africa

Area: *total:* 2,344,858 sq km
land: 2,267,048 sq km
water: 77,810 sq km
comparison ranking: total 12

Area - comparative: slightly less than one-fourth the size of the US

Land boundaries: *total:* 11,027 km
border countries (9): Angola 2,646 km (of which 225 km is the boundary of Angola's discontiguous Cabinda Province); Burundi 236 km; Central African Republic 1,747 km; Republic of the Congo 1,775 km; Rwanda 221 km; South Sudan 714 km; Tanzania 479 km; Uganda 877 km; Zambia 2,332 km

Coastline: 37 km

Maritime claims: *territorial sea:* 12 nm
exclusive economic zone: since 2011, the DRC has had a Common Interest Zone agreement with Angola for the mutual development of off-shore resources

Climate: tropical; hot and humid in equatorial river basin; cooler and drier in southern highlands; cooler and wetter in eastern highlands; north of Equator - wet season (April to October), dry season (December to February); south of Equator - wet season (November to March), dry season (April to October)

Terrain: vast central basin is a low-lying plateau; mountains in east

Elevation: *highest point:* Pic Marguerite on Mont Ngaliema (Mount Stanley) 5,110 m
lowest point: Atlantic Ocean 0 m
mean elevation: 726 m

Natural resources: cobalt, copper, niobium, tantalum, petroleum, industrial and gem diamonds, gold, silver, zinc, manganese, tin, uranium, coal, hydropower, timber
note 1: coltan, the industrial name for a columbite–tantalite mineral from which niobium and tantalum are extracted, is mainly artisanal and small-scale; tantalum, tin, tungsten, and gold extracted from central Africa are considered "conflict minerals" and as such are subject to international monitoring
note 2: the DROC is the World's leading producer of cobalt, accounting for as much as 70% of the World's supply; between 20-30% of this cobalt is produced in artisanal and small-scale mining operations

Land use: *agricultural land:* 15.5% (2022 est.)
arable land: 6.6% (2022 est.)
permanent crops: 0.9% (2022 est.)
permanent pasture: 8% (2022 est.)
forest: 54.7% (2022 est.)
other: 29.8% (2022 est.)

Irrigated land: 110 sq km (2012)

Major lakes (area sq km): *fresh water lake(s):* Lake Tanganyika (shared with Burundi, Tanzania, and Zambia) - 32,000 sq km; Lake Albert (shared with Uganda) - 5,590 sq km; Lake Mweru (shared with Zambia) - 4,350 sq km; Lac Mai-Ndombe - 2,300 sq km; Lake Kivu (shared with Rwanda) - 2,220 sq km; Lake Edward (shared with Uganda) - 2,150 sq km; Lac Tumba - 500 sq km; Lac Upemba - 530 sq km

Major rivers (by length in km): Zaïre (Congo) river mouth (shared with Zambia [s], Angola, and Republic of Congo) - 2,920 km; Ubangi river mouth (shared with Central African Republic [s] and Republic of Congo) - 2,270 km note: [s] after country name indicates river source; [m] after country name indicates river mouth

Major watersheds (area sq km): Atlantic Ocean drainage: Congo (3,730,881 sq km), *(Mediterranean Sea)* Nile (3,254,853 sq km)

Indian Ocean drainage: Zambezi (1,332,412 sq km)

Major aquifers: Congo Basin

Population distribution: urban clusters are spread throughout the country, particularly in the northeast along the border with Uganda, Rwanda, and Burundi; the largest city is the capital, Kinshasha, located in the west along the Congo River; the south is least densely populated, as shown in this population distribution map

Natural hazards: periodic droughts in south; Congo River floods (seasonal); active volcanoes in the east along the Great Rift Valley
volcanism: the active volcano Nyiragongo (3,470 m) poses a major threat to the city of Goma, home to a quarter of a million people; it produces unusually fast-moving lava, known to travel up to 100 km/hr; Nyiragongo has been deemed a Decade Volcano by the International Association of Volcanology and Chemistry of the Earth's Interior, worthy of study due to its explosive history and close proximity to human populations; its neighbor Nyamuragira is Africa's most active volcano; Visoke is the only other historically active volcano

Geography - note: *note 1:* second-largest country in Africa (after Algeria) and largest country in sub-Saharan Africa; straddles the equator; dense tropical rainforest in central river basin and eastern highlands; the narrow strip of land that controls the lower Congo River is the DRC's only outlet to the South Atlantic Ocean
note 2: the Congo River, most of which flows through the DRC, has never been accurately measured along much of its length because of its speed, cataracts, rapids, and turbulence; nonetheless, it is conceded to be the deepest river in the world, with estimates of the point of greatest depth varying between 220 and 250 meters

PEOPLE AND SOCIETY

Population: *total:* 115,403,027 (2024 est.)
male: 57,688,160
female: 57,714,867
comparison rankings: total 14; male 14; female 14

Nationality: *noun:* Congolese (singular and plural)
adjective: Congolese or Congo

Ethnic groups: more than 200 African ethnic groups of which the majority are Bantu; the four largest groups - Mongo, Luba, Kongo (all Bantu), and the Mangbetu-Azande (Hamitic) - make up about 45% of the population

Languages: French (official), Lingala (a trade language), Kingwana (a dialect of Kiswahili or Swahili), Kikongo, Tshiluba
major-language sample(s):
Buku oyo ya bosembo ya Mokili Mobimba Ezali na Makanisi ya Liboso Mpenza. (Lingala)

Religions: Christian 93/1% (Roman Catholic 29.9%, Protestant 26.7%, other Christian 36.5%), Kimbanguist 2.8%, Muslim 1.3%, other (includes syncretic sects and indigenous beliefs) 1.2%, none 1.3%, unspecified 0.2% (2014 est.)

Age structure: *0-14 years:* 45.7% (male 26,584,268/female 26,208,891)
15-64 years: 51.8% (male 29,845,450/female 29,884,958)
65 years and over: 2.5% (2024 est.) (male 1,258,442/female 1,621,018)

Dependency ratios: *total dependency ratio:* 93.2 (2024 est.)
youth dependency ratio: 88.4 (2024 est.)
elderly dependency ratio: 4.8 (2024 est.)
potential support ratio: 20.7 (2024 est.)

Median age: *total:* 16.9 years (2024 est.)
male: 16.7 years
female: 17 years
comparison ranking: total 224

Population growth rate: 3.11% (2024 est.)
comparison ranking: 7

Birth rate: 39.2 births/1,000 population (2024 est.)
comparison ranking: 6

Death rate: 7.6 deaths/1,000 population (2024 est.)
comparison ranking: 98

Net migration rate: -0.6 migrant(s)/1,000 population (2024 est.)
comparison ranking: 127

Population distribution: urban clusters are spread throughout the country, particularly in the northeast along the border with Uganda, Rwanda, and Burundi; the largest city is the capital, Kinshasha, located in the west along the Congo River; the south is least densely populated, as shown in this population distribution map

Urbanization: *urban population:* 47.4% of total population (2023)
rate of urbanization: 4.33% annual rate of change (2020-25 est.)

Major urban areas - population: 16.316 million KINSHASA (capital), 2.892 million Mbuji-Mayi, 2.812 million Lubumbashi, 1.664 million Kananga, 1.423 million Kisangani, 1.249 million Bukavu (2023)

Sex ratio: *at birth:* 1.03 male(s)/female
0-14 years: 1.01 male(s)/female
15-64 years: 1 male(s)/female
65 years and over: 0.78 male(s)/female
total population: 1 male(s)/female (2024 est.)

Mother's mean age at first birth: 19.9 years (2013/14 est.)
note: data represents median age at first birth among women 20-49

Maternal mortality ratio: 427 deaths/100,000 live births (2023 est.)
comparison ranking: 13

Infant mortality rate: *total:* 57.4 deaths/1,000 live births (2024 est.)
male: 62.9 deaths/1,000 live births
female: 51.9 deaths/1,000 live births
comparison ranking: total 11

Life expectancy at birth: *total population:* 62.6 years (2024 est.)
male: 60.7 years
female: 64.6 years
comparison ranking: total population 215

Total fertility rate: 5.49 children born/woman (2024 est.)
comparison ranking: 3

Gross reproduction rate: 2.7 (2024 est.)

Drinking water source: *improved: urban:* 59.3% of population (2022 est.)
rural: 13.8% of population (2022 est.)
total: 35.1% of population (2022 est.)
unimproved: urban: 40.7% of population (2022 est.)
rural: 86.2% of population (2022 est.)
total: 64.9% of population (2022 est.)

Health expenditure: 3.8% of GDP (2021)
4% of national budget (2022 est.)

Physician density: 0.21 physicians/1,000 population (2022)

Sanitation facility access: *improved: urban:* 48.8% of population (2022 est.)
rural: 20.5% of population (2022 est.)
total: 33.7% of population (2022 est.)
unimproved: urban: 51.2% of population (2022 est.)
rural: 79.5% of population (2022 est.)
total: 66.3% of population (2022 est.)

Obesity - adult prevalence rate: 6.7% (2016)
comparison ranking: 164

Alcohol consumption per capita: *total:* 0.56 liters of pure alcohol (2019 est.)
beer: 0.5 liters of pure alcohol (2019 est.)
wine: 0.01 liters of pure alcohol (2019 est.)
spirits: 0.05 liters of pure alcohol (2019 est.)
other alcohols: 0 liters of pure alcohol (2019 est.)
comparison ranking: total 161

Tobacco use: *total:* 10.4% (2025 est.)
male: 18.8% (2025 est.)
female: 2.3% (2025 est.)

comparison ranking: total 125

Children under the age of 5 years underweight: 23.1% (2017/18)
comparison ranking: 6

Currently married women (ages 15-49): 55.3% (2023 est.)

Child marriage: *women married by age 15:* 8.4% (2018)
women married by age 18: 29.1% (2018)
men married by age 18: 5.6% (2018)

Education expenditure: 2.8% of GDP (2022 est.)
18.4% national budget (2022 est.)
comparison ranking: Education expenditure (% GDP) 164

Literacy: *total population:* 73.6% (2018 est.)
male: 87.5% (2018 est.)
female: 61.6% (2018 est.)

ENVIRONMENT

Environmental issues: poaching; water pollution; deforestation from agriculture and wood used for fuel; soil erosion; damage from mining

International environmental agreements: *party to:* Biodiversity, Climate Change, Climate Change-Kyoto Protocol, Climate Change-Paris Agreement, Comprehensive Nuclear Test Ban, Desertification, Endangered Species, Hazardous Wastes, Law of the Sea, Marine Dumping-London Convention, Nuclear Test Ban, Ozone Layer Protection, Tropical Timber 2006, Wetlands
signed, but not ratified: Environmental Modification

Climate: tropical; hot and humid in equatorial river basin; cooler and drier in southern highlands; cooler and wetter in eastern highlands; north of Equator - wet season (April to October), dry season (December to February); south of Equator - wet season (November to March), dry season (April to October)

Urbanization: *urban population:* 47.4% of total population (2023)
rate of urbanization: 4.33% annual rate of change (2020-25 est.)

Carbon dioxide emissions: 5.883 million metric tonnes of CO2 (2023 est.)
from coal and metallurgical coke: 731,000 metric tonnes of CO2 (2023 est.)
from petroleum and other liquids: 5.152 million metric tonnes of CO2 (2023 est.)
comparison ranking: total emissions 132

Particulate matter emissions: 33.7 micrograms per cubic meter (2019 est.)

Methane emissions: *energy:* 780.6 kt (2022-2024 est.)
agriculture: 567.3 kt (2019-2021 est.)
waste: 499.2 kt (2019-2021 est.)
other: 214.3 kt (2019-2021 est.)

Waste and recycling: *municipal solid waste generated annually:* 14.385 million tons (2024 est.)
percent of municipal solid waste recycled: 6.4% (2022 est.)

Total water withdrawal: *municipal:* 464.9 million cubic meters (2022 est.)
industrial: 146.8 million cubic meters (2022 est.)
agricultural: 71.9 million cubic meters (2022 est.)

Total renewable water resources: 1.283 trillion cubic meters (2022 est.)

GOVERNMENT

Country name: *conventional long form:* Democratic Republic of the Congo
conventional short form: DRC
local long form: République démocratique du Congo
local short form: RDC
former: Congo Free State, Belgian Congo, Congo/Leopoldville, Congo/Kinshasa, Zaire
abbreviation: DRC (or DROC)
etymology: named for the Congo River, most of which lies within the DRC; the river name derives from Kongo, a Bantu kingdom in the area

Government type: semi-presidential republic

Capital: *name:* Kinshasa
geographic coordinates: 4 19 S, 15 18 E
time difference: UTC+1 (6 hours ahead of Washington, DC, during Standard Time)
time zone note: the DRC has two time zones
etymology: founded as a trading post in 1881 and named Leopoldville in honor of King LEOPOLD II of the Belgians; in 1966, Leopoldville was renamed Kinshasa, a Bantu name of unknown meaning

Administrative divisions: 26 provinces; Bas-Uele (Lower Uele), Equateur, Haut-Katanga (Upper Katanga), Haut-Lomami (Upper Lomami), Haut-Uele (Upper Uele), Ituri, Kasai, Kasai-Central, Kasai-Oriental (East Kasai), Kinshasa, Kongo Central, Kwango, Kwilu, Lomami, Lualaba, Mai-Ndombe, Maniema, Mongala, Nord-Kivu (North Kivu), Nord-Ubangi (North Ubangi), Sankuru, Sud-Kivu (South Kivu), Sud-Ubangi (South Ubangi), Tanganyika, Tshopo, Tshuapa

Legal system: civil law system primarily based on Belgian law, but also customary and tribal law

Constitution: *history:* several previous; latest adopted 13 May 2005, approved by referendum 18-19 December 2005, promulgated 18 February 2006
amendment process: proposed by the president of the republic, by the government, by either house of Parliament, or by public petition; agreement on the substance of a proposed bill requires absolute majority vote in both houses; passage requires a referendum only if both houses in joint meeting fail to achieve three-fifths majority vote; constitutional articles, including the form of government, universal suffrage, judicial independence, political pluralism, and personal freedoms, cannot be amended

International law organization participation: accepts compulsory ICJ jurisdiction with reservations; accepts ICCt jurisdiction

Citizenship: *citizenship by birth:* no
citizenship by descent only: at least one parent must be a citizen of the Democratic Republic of the Congo
dual citizenship recognized: no
residency requirement for naturalization: 5 years

Suffrage: 18 years of age; universal and compulsory

Executive branch: *chief of state:* President Felix TSHISEKEDI (since 20 January 2024)
head of government: Prime Minister Judith SUMINWA Tuluka (since 29 May 2024)
cabinet: Ministers of State appointed by the president
election/appointment process: president directly elected by simple majority vote for a 5-year term (eligible for a second term); prime minister appointed by the president
most recent election date: 20 December 2023
election results: *2023:* Felix TSHISEKEDI reelected president; percent of vote - Felix TSHISEKEDI (UDPS) 73.3%, Moise KATUMBI (Ensemble) 18.8%, Martin FAYULU (ECIDE) 5.3%, other 2.6%
2018: Felix TSHISEKEDI elected president; percent of vote - Felix TSHISEKEDI (UDPS) 38.6%, Martin FAYULU (Lamuka coalition) 34.8%, Emmanuel Ramazani SHADARY (PPRD) 23.9%, other 2.7%
expected date of next election: 20 December 2028

Legislative branch: *legislature name:* Parlement (Parliament)
legislative structure: bicameral

Legislative branch - lower chamber: *chamber name:* National Assembly (Assemblée nationale)
number of seats: 500 (all directly elected)
electoral system: mixed system
scope of elections: full renewal
term in office: 5 years
most recent election date: 12/20/2023
parties elected and seats per party: Union for Democracy and Social Progress/TSHISEKEDI (UDPS/TSHISEKEDI) (69); Action of Allies and Union for the Congolese Nation (A/A-UNC) (35); Alliance of Democratic Forces of Congo and Allies (AFDC-A) (35); Act and Build (AB) (26); Other (312)
percentage of women in chamber: 12.8%
expected date of next election: December 2028

Legislative branch - upper chamber: *chamber name:* Senate (Sénat)
number of seats: 109 (all indirectly elected)
scope of elections: full renewal
term in office: 5 years
most recent election date: 4/29/2024 to 5/26/2024
percentage of women in chamber: 15.8%
expected date of next election: April 2029

Judicial branch: *highest court(s):* Court of Cassation or Cour de Cassation (consists of 26 justices and organized into legislative and judiciary sections); Constitutional Court (consists of 9 judges)
judge selection and term of office: Court of Cassation judges nominated by the Judicial Service Council, an independent body of public prosecutors and selected judges of the lower courts; judge tenure NA; Constitutional Court judges - 3 nominated by the president, 3 by the Judicial Service Council, and 3 by the legislature; judges appointed by the president to serve 9-year non-renewable terms with one third of the membership renewed every 3 years
subordinate courts: State Security Court; Court of Appeals (organized into administrative and judiciary sections); Tribunal de Grande Instance; magistrates' courts; customary courts

Political parties: Christian Democrat Party or PDC
Congolese Rally for Democracy or RCD
Convention of Christian Democrats or CDC
Engagement for Citizenship and Development or ECIDE
Forces of Renewal or FR
Movement for the Liberation of the Congo or MLC
Nouvel Elan
Our Congo or CNB ("Congo Na Biso")
People's Party for Reconstruction and Democracy or PPRD
Social Movement for Renewal or MSR
Together for Change ("Ensemble")
Unified Lumumbist Party or PALU
Union for the Congolese Nation or UNC
Union for Democracy and Social Progress or UDPS

Diplomatic representation in the US: *chief of mission:* Ambassador (vacant); Chargé d'Affaires Michael SHAKU YUMI (since 1 August 2024)

chancery: 1100 Connecticut Avenue NW, Suite 725, Washington DC 20036
telephone: [1] (202) 234-7690
FAX: [1] (202) 234-2609
email address and website: ambassade@ambardcusa.org
https://www.ambardcusa.org/
representative office: New York

Diplomatic representation from the US: *chief of mission:* Ambassador Lucy TAMLYN (since 6 February 2023)
embassy: 310 Avenue des Aviateurs, Kinshasa, Gombe
mailing address: 2220 Kinshasa Place, Washington DC 20521-2220
telephone: [243] 081 556-0151
FAX: [243] 81 556-0175
email address and website: ACSKinshasa@state.gov
https://cd.usembassy.gov/

International organization participation: ACP, AfDB, AU, CEMAC, CEPGL, COMESA, EITI (compliant country), FAO, G-24, G-77, IAEA, IBRD, ICAO, ICC (NGOs), ICCt, ICRM, IDA, IFAD, IFC, IFRCS, IHO, ILO, IMF, IMO, Interpol, IOC, IOM, IPU, ISO, ITSO, ITU, ITUC (NGOs), LCBC (observer), MIGA, NAM, OIF, OPCW, PCA, SADC, UN, UNCTAD, UNESCO, UNHCR, UNIDO, UNWTO, UPU, WCO, WFTU (NGOs), WHO, WIPO, WMO, WTO

Independence: 30 June 1960 (from Belgium)

National holiday: Independence Day, 30 June (1960)

Flag: *description:* sky-blue field divided diagonally from the lower-left corner to the upper-right corner by a red stripe bordered with two narrow yellow stripes; a five-pointed yellow star is in the upper-left corner
meaning: blue stands for peace and hope, red for the blood of the country's martyrs, and yellow for the country's wealth and prosperity; the star symbolizes unity and a brilliant future for the country

National symbol(s): leopard

National color(s): sky blue, red, yellow

National anthem(s): *title:* "Debout Congolaise" (Arise, Congolese)
lyrics/music: Joseph LUTUMBA/Simon-Pierre BOKA di Mpasi Londi
history: adopted 1960; replaced when the country was known as Zaire, but readopted in 1997

National heritage: *total World Heritage Sites:* 5 (all natural)
selected World Heritage Site locales: Garamba National Park; Kahuzi-Biega National Park; Okapi Wildlife Reserve; Salonga National Park; Virunga National Park

ECONOMY

Economic overview: very poor, large, natural resource-rich sub-Saharan country; possesses the world's second largest rainforest; increasing Chinese extractive sector trade; massive decrease in government investments; increasing current account deficit and public debts

Real GDP (purchasing power parity): $164.367 billion (2024 est.)
$154.081 billion (2023 est.)
$141.867 billion (2022 est.)
note: data in 2021 dollars
comparison ranking: 81

Real GDP growth rate: 6.7% (2024 est.)
8.6% (2023 est.)
8.9% (2022 est.)
note: annual GDP % growth based on constant local currency
comparison ranking: 18

Real GDP per capita: $1,500 (2024 est.)
$1,500 (2023 est.)
$1,400 (2022 est.)
note: data in 2021 dollars
comparison ranking: 212

GDP (official exchange rate): $70.749 billion (2024 est.)
note: data in current dollars at official exchange rate

Inflation rate (consumer prices): 41.5% (2017 est.)
2.9% (2016 est.)
0.7% (2015 est.)
note: annual % change based on consumer prices
comparison ranking: 202

GDP - composition, by sector of origin: *agriculture:* 17.1% (2024 est.)
industry: 46.6% (2024 est.)
services: 33% (2024 est.)
note: figures may not total 100% due to non-allocated consumption not captured in sector-reported data
comparison rankings: agriculture 45; industry 11; services 204

GDP - composition, by end use: *household consumption:* 62.7% (2024 est.)
government consumption: 8.1% (2024 est.)
investment in fixed capital: 32.9% (2024 est.)
investment in inventories: 0.5% (2024 est.)
exports of goods and services: 46.6% (2024 est.)
imports of goods and services: -50.9% (2024 est.)
note: figures may not total 100% due to rounding or gaps in data collection

Agricultural products: cassava, plantains, sugarcane, maize, oil palm fruit, rice, root vegetables, bananas, sweet potatoes, groundnuts (2023)
note: top ten agricultural products based on tonnage

Industries: mining (copper, cobalt, gold, diamonds, coltan, zinc, tin, tungsten), mineral processing, consumer products (textiles, plastics, footwear, cigarettes), metal products, processed foods and beverages, timber, cement, commercial ship repair

Industrial production growth rate: 10.1% (2024 est.)
note: annual % change in industrial value added based on constant local currency
comparison ranking: 8

Labor force: 38.546 million (2024 est.)
note: number of people ages 15 or older who are employed or seeking work
comparison ranking: 17

Unemployment rate: 4.6% (2024 est.)
4.5% (2023 est.)
4.6% (2022 est.)
note: % of labor force seeking employment
comparison ranking: 76

Youth unemployment rate (ages 15-24): *total:* 8.5% (2024 est.)
male: 10.8% (2024 est.)
female: 6.6% (2024 est.)
note: % of labor force ages 15-24 seeking employment
comparison ranking: total 134

Population below poverty line: 56.2% (2020 est.)
note: % of population with income below national poverty line

Gini Index coefficient - distribution of family income: 44.7 (2020 est.)
note: index (0-100) of income distribution; higher values represent greater inequality
comparison ranking: 18

Household income or consumption by percentage share: *lowest 10%:* 2.1% (2020 est.)
highest 10%: 35.7% (2020 est.)
note: % share of income accruing to lowest and highest 10% of population

Remittances: 4.9% of GDP (2023 est.)
5% of GDP (2022 est.)
2.4% of GDP (2021 est.)
note: personal transfers and compensation between resident and non-resident individuals/households/entities

Budget: *revenues:* $11.568 billion (2022 est.)
expenditures: $13.026 billion (2022 est.)
note: central government revenues and expenses (excluding grants/extrabudgetary units/social security funds) converted to US dollars at average official exchange rate for year indicated

Public debt: 16% of GDP (2022 est.)
note: central government debt as a % of GDP
comparison ranking: 188

Taxes and other revenues: 11.4% (of GDP) (2022 est.)
note: central government tax revenue as a % of GDP
comparison ranking: 122

Current account balance: -$3.883 billion (2023 est.)
-$3.148 billion (2022 est.)
-$587.407 million (2021 est.)
note: balance of payments - net trade and primary/secondary income in current dollars
comparison ranking: 165

Exports: $29.65 billion (2023 est.)
$28.753 billion (2022 est.)
$22.354 billion (2021 est.)
note: balance of payments - exports of goods and services in current dollars
comparison ranking: 83

Exports - partners: China 69%, UAE 7%, India 3%, Spain 3%, Egypt 3% (2023)
note: top five export partners based on percentage share of exports

Exports - commodities: refined copper, cobalt, copper ore, raw copper, crude petroleum (2023)
note: top five export commodities based on value in dollars

Imports: $33.68 billion (2023 est.)
$31.699 billion (2022 est.)
$22.193 billion (2021 est.)
note: balance of payments - imports of goods and services in current dollars
comparison ranking: 77

Imports - partners: China 35%, Zambia 12%, South Africa 12%, India 5%, Belgium 4% (2023)
note: top five import partners based on percentage share of imports

Imports - commodities: trucks, refined petroleum, stone processing machines, plastic products, sulphur (2023)
note: top five import commodities based on value in dollars

Reserves of foreign exchange and gold: $5.104 billion (2023 est.)
$4.378 billion (2022 est.)
$3.467 billion (2021 est.)

note: holdings of gold (year-end prices)/foreign exchange/special drawing rights in current dollars
comparison ranking: 98

Debt - external: $7.926 billion (2023 est.)
note: present value of external debt in current US dollars
comparison ranking: 57

Exchange rates: Congolese francs (CDF) per US dollar -

Exchange rates: 2,340.036 (2023 est.)
2,006.708 (2022 est.)
1,989.391 (2021 est.)
1,851.122 (2020 est.)
1,647.76 (2019 est.)

ENERGY

Electricity access: *electrification - total population:* 21.5% (2022 est.)
electrification - urban areas: 45.3%
electrification - rural areas: 1%

Electricity: *installed generating capacity:* 3.229 million kW (2023 est.)
consumption: 16.069 billion kWh (2023 est.)
exports: 62 million kWh (2023 est.)
imports: 1.473 billion kWh (2023 est.)
transmission/distribution losses: 1.242 billion kWh (2023 est.)
comparison rankings: installed generating capacity 107; consumption 84; exports 92; imports 72; transmission/distribution losses 112

Electricity generation sources: *solar:* 13.8% of total installed capacity (2023 est.)
hydroelectricity: 86% of total installed capacity (2023 est.)
biomass and waste: 0.2% of total installed capacity (2023 est.)

Coal: *consumption:* 304,000 metric tons (2023 est.)
imports: 304,000 metric tons (2023 est.)
proven reserves: 987.999 million metric tons (2023 est.)

Petroleum: *total petroleum production:* 19,000 bbl/day (2023 est.)
refined petroleum consumption: 35,000 bbl/day (2023 est.)
crude oil estimated reserves: 180 million barrels (2021 est.)

Natural gas: *production:* 380,000 cubic meters (2019 est.)
consumption: 380,000 cubic meters (2019 est.)
proven reserves: 991.09 million cubic meters (2021 est.)

Energy consumption per capita: 1.305 million Btu/person (2023 est.)
comparison ranking: 192

COMMUNICATIONS

Telephones - fixed lines: *total subscriptions:* 0 (2021 est.) less than 1
subscriptions per 100 inhabitants: (2022 est.) less than 1
comparison ranking: total subscriptions 226

Telephones - mobile cellular: *total subscriptions:* 49.8 million (2022 est.)
subscriptions per 100 inhabitants: 50 (2022 est.)
comparison ranking: total subscriptions 38

Broadcast media: state-owned TV station with near-national coverage; more than a dozen privately owned TV stations, including 2 with near-national coverage; 2 state-owned radio stations and over 100 private radio stations; transmissions of at least 2 international broadcasters are available

Internet country code: .cd

Internet users: *percent of population:* 31% (2023 est.)

Broadband - fixed subscriptions: *total:* 33,000 (2022 est.)
subscriptions per 100 inhabitants: (2022 est.) less than 1
comparison ranking: total 158

TRANSPORTATION

Civil aircraft registration country code prefix: 9Q

Airports: 273 (2025)
comparison ranking: 25

Heliports: 1 (2025)
comparison ranking: 160

Railways: *total:* 4,007 km (2014)
narrow gauge: 3,882 km (2014) 1.067-m gauge (858 km electrified)
125 1.000-mm gauge

Merchant marine: *total:* 24 (2023)
by type: general cargo 5, oil tanker 2, other 17
comparison ranking: total 143

Ports: *total ports:* 3 (2024)
large: 0
medium: 0
small: 2
very small: 1
ports with oil terminals: 2
key ports: Banana, Boma, Matadi

MILITARY AND SECURITY

Military and security forces: Armed Forces of the Democratic Republic of the Congo (Forces d'Armees de la Republique Democratique du Congo, FARDC): Land Forces (Forces Terrestres), National Navy (La Marine Nationale), Congolese Air Force (Force Aerienne Congolaise, FAC); Republican Guard (Garde Républicaine, GR)

Ministry of Interior: Congolese National Police (Police Nationale Congolaise, PNC) (2025)
note: the Republican Guard is overseen by the office of the presidency rather than the FARDC; it focuses on protecting the president and government institutions and enforcing internal security
note 2: community-based self-defense groups, known as Wazalendo militias, are also active in areas contested by illegal armed groups, such as M23

Military expenditures: 1.2% of GDP (2024 est.)
1.2% of GDP (2023 est.)
0.7% of GDP (2022 est.)
0.7% of GDP (2021 est.)
0.7% of GDP (2020 est.)

Military and security service personnel strengths: estimated 100-150,000 active FARDC (2025)

Military equipment inventories and acquisitions: the FARDC is equipped mostly with Soviet-era and older French weapons and equipment; in 2024, the DRC signed an agreement with China for the provision of military equipment (2024)

Military service age and obligation: 18-35 years of age for voluntary military service for men and women; 18-45 years of age for compulsory military service for men; it is unclear how much conscription is used (2024)
note: in eastern Congo, fighters from armed groups, including some associated with government security forces, have been accused of forced recruitment of child soldiers

Military - note: the FARDC's primary focus is internal security and conducting operations against rebels and other illegal armed groups (IOGs) operating in the DRC, particularly in the eastern provinces of Ituri, North Kivu, and South Kivu, where more than 15 significant and cohesive IOGs operate; there is also IOG-related violence in Maniema, Kasai, Kasai Central, and Tanganyika provinces; some estimates place over 100 IOGs operating in the country, including organized militias, such as the Nduma Defense of Congo-Renewal (NDC-R), which controls a large portion of North Kivu; Mai Mai groups (local militias that operate variously as self-defense networks and criminal rackets); and foreign-origin groups seeking safe haven and resources, such as the Ugandan-origin Allied Democratic Forces (ADF; aka Islamic State of Iraq and ash-Sham in the DRC), the Democratic Forces for the Liberation of Rwanda (FDLR), multiple groups originating from Burundi, the Lords Resistance Army (LRA), and the March 23 Movement (aka M23 or Congolese Revolutionary Army), which Rwanda has been accused of supporting militarily; the FARDC incorporates some non-state armed groups and has been accused of collaborating with some IOGs, such as the NDC-R
the UN Organization Stabilization Mission in the Democratic Republic of the Congo (MONUSCO) has operated in the central and eastern parts of the country since 1999; it has nearly 14,000 personnel assigned, and its mandate had been extended to the end of 2025; MONUSCO includes a Force Intervention Brigade (FIB), the first ever UN peacekeeping force specifically tasked to carry out targeted offensive operations to neutralize and disarm groups considered a threat to state authority and civilian security (2025)

TERRORISM

Terrorist group(s): Terrorist group(s): Islamic State of Iraq and ash-Sham – Democratic Republic of the Congo (ISIS-DRC)
note: details about the history, aims, leadership, organization, areas of operation, tactics, targets, weapons, size, and sources of support of the group(s) appear(s) in Appendix T

TRANSNATIONAL ISSUES

Refugees and internally displaced persons: *refugees:* 518,445 (2024 est.)

IDPs: 6,895,648 (2024 est.)

Trafficking in persons: *tier rating:* Tier 2 Watch List — the Democratic Republic of the Congo did not demonstrate overall increasing efforts to eliminate trafficking compared with the previous reporting period and was downgraded to Tier 2 Watch List; for more details, go to: https://www.state.gov/reports/2025-trafficking-in-persons-report/democratic-republic-of-the-congo/

CONGO, REPUBLIC OF THE

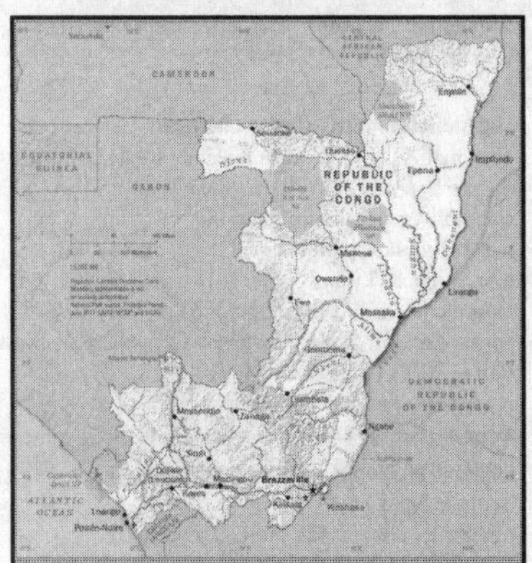

INTRODUCTION

Background: Upon independence in 1960, the former French region of Middle Congo became the Republic of the Congo. From 1968 to 1992, the country was named the People's Republic of the Congo. A quarter-century of experimentation with Marxism was abandoned in 1990, and a democratically elected government took office in 1992, at which time the country reverted to "the Republic of the Congo" name. A two-year civil war that ended in 1999 restored to power former President Denis SASSOU-Nguesso, who had ruled from 1979 to 1992. A new constitution adopted three years later provided for a multi-party system and a seven-year presidential term, and the next elections retained SASSOU-Nguesso. After a year of renewed fighting, SASSOU-Nguesso and southern-based rebel groups agreed to a final peace accord in 2003. SASSOU-Nguesso was reelected in 2009 and, after passing a constitutional referendum allowing him to run for additional terms, was reelected again in 2016 and 2021. The Republic of the Congo is one of Africa's largest petroleum producers.

GEOGRAPHY

Location: Central Africa, bordering the South Atlantic Ocean, between Angola and Gabon

Geographic coordinates: 1 00 S, 15 00 E

Map references: Africa

Area: *total:* 342,000 sq km
land: 341,500 sq km
water: 500 sq km
comparison ranking: total 65

Area - comparative: slightly smaller than Montana; about twice the size of Florida

Land boundaries: *total:* 5,554 km
border countries (5): Angola 231 km; Cameroon 494 km; Central African Republic 487 km; Democratic Republic of the Congo 1,775 km; Gabon 2,567 km

Coastline: 169 km

Maritime claims: *territorial sea:* 12 nm
contiguous zone: 24 nm
exclusive economic zone: 200 nm

Climate: tropical; rainy season (March to June); dry season (June to October); persistent high temperatures and humidity; particularly enervating climate astride the Equator

Terrain: coastal plain, southern basin, central plateau, northern basin

Elevation: *highest point:* Mont Nabeba 1,020 m
lowest point: Atlantic Ocean 0 m
mean elevation: 430 m

Natural resources: petroleum, timber, potash, lead, zinc, uranium, copper, phosphates, gold, magnesium, natural gas, hydropower

Land use: *agricultural land:* 31.3% (2022 est.)
arable land: 1.6% (2022 est.)
permanent crops: 0.4% (2022 est.)
permanent pasture: 29.3% (2022 est.)
forest: 64.2% (2022 est.)
other: 4.5% (2022 est.)

Irrigated land: 20 sq km (2012)

Major rivers (by length in km): Oubangui (Ubangi) (shared with Central African Republic [s] and Democratic Republic of Congo [m]) - 2,270 km
note: [s] after country name indicates river source; [m] after country name indicates river mouth

Major watersheds (area sq km): Atlantic Ocean drainage: Congo (3,730,881 sq km)

Major aquifers: Congo Basin

Population distribution: the population is primarily located in the south, in and around the capital of Brazzaville, as shown in this population distribution map

Natural hazards: seasonal flooding

Geography - note: about 70% of the population lives in Brazzaville, Pointe-Noire, or along the railroad between them

PEOPLE AND SOCIETY

Population: *total:* 6,097,665 (2024 est.)
male: 3,045,973
female: 3,051,692
comparison rankings: total 113; male 112; female 113

Nationality: *noun:* Congolese (singular and plural)
adjective: Congolese or Congo

Ethnic groups: Kongo (Bakongo) 40.5%, Teke 16.9%, Mbochi 13.1%, foreigner 8.2%, Sangha 5.6%, Mbere/Mbeti/Kele 4.4%, Punu 4.3%, Pygmy 1.6%, Oubanguiens 1.6%, Duma 1.5%, Makaa 1.3%, other and unspecified 1% (2014-15 est.)

Languages: French (official), French Lingala and Monokutuba (trade languages), many local languages and dialects (of which Kikongo is the most widespread)
major-language sample(s):
Buku oyo ya bosembo ya Mokili Mobimba Ezali na Makanisi ya Liboso Mpenza. (Lingala)

Religions: Roman Catholic 33.1%, Awakening Churches/Christian Revival 22.3%, Protestant 19.9%, Salutiste 2.2%, Muslim 1.6%, Kimbanguist 1.5%, other 8.1%, none 11.3% (2007 est.)

Age structure: *0-14 years:* 37.8% (male 1,162,298/female 1,143,668)
15-64 years: 57.8% (male 1,770,337/female 1,756,925)
65 years and over: 4.3% (2024 est.) (male 113,338/female 151,099)

Dependency ratios: *total dependency ratio:* 72.9 (2024 est.)
youth dependency ratio: 65.4 (2024 est.)
elderly dependency ratio: 7.5 (2024 est.)
potential support ratio: 13.3 (2024 est.)

Median age: *total:* 20.7 years (2024 est.)
male: 20.5 years
female: 20.9 years
comparison ranking: total 200

Population growth rate: 2.38% (2024 est.)
comparison ranking: 23

Birth rate: 28.7 births/1,000 population (2024 est.)
comparison ranking: 30

Death rate: 4.8 deaths/1,000 population (2024 est.)
comparison ranking: 203

Net migration rate: -0.1 migrant(s)/1,000 population (2024 est.)
comparison ranking: 97

Population distribution: the population is primarily located in the south, in and around the capital of Brazzaville, as shown in this population distribution map

Urbanization: *urban population:* 69.2% of total population (2023)
rate of urbanization: 3.19% annual rate of change (2020-25 est.)

Major urban areas - population: 2.638 million BRAZZAVILLE (capital), 1.336 million Pointe-Noire (2023)

Sex ratio: *at birth:* 1.03 male(s)/female
0-14 years: 1.02 male(s)/female
15-64 years: 1.01 male(s)/female
65 years and over: 0.75 male(s)/female
total population: 1 male(s)/female (2024 est.)

Mother's mean age at first birth: 19.6 years (2011/12 est.)
note: data represents median age at first birth among women 20-49

Maternal mortality ratio: 241 deaths/100,000 live births (2023 est.)
comparison ranking: 31

Infant mortality rate: *total:* 30.6 deaths/1,000 live births (2024 est.)
male: 33.5 deaths/1,000 live births
female: 27.7 deaths/1,000 live births
comparison ranking: total 48

Life expectancy at birth: *total population:* 72.9 years (2024 est.)
male: 71.5 years
female: 74.3 years
comparison ranking: total population 156

Total fertility rate: 3.79 children born/woman (2024 est.)
comparison ranking: 29

Gross reproduction rate: 1.87 (2024 est.)

Health expenditure: 3.9% of GDP (2021)
3.5% of national budget (2022 est.)

Physician density: 0.17 physicians/1,000 population (2022)

Obesity - adult prevalence rate: 9.6% (2016)
comparison ranking: 143

Alcohol consumption per capita: *total:* 5.74 liters of pure alcohol (2019 est.)
beer: 5.11 liters of pure alcohol (2019 est.)
wine: 0.1 liters of pure alcohol (2019 est.)
spirits: 0.52 liters of pure alcohol (2019 est.)
other alcohols: 0.01 liters of pure alcohol (2019 est.)
comparison ranking: total 75

Tobacco use: *total:* 15.8% (2025 est.)
male: 30% (2025 est.)
female: 1.7% (2025 est.)
comparison ranking: total 99

Currently married women (ages 15-49): 51.8% (2023 est.)

Child marriage: *women married by age 15:* 6.9% (2015)
women married by age 18: 27.3% (2015)
men married by age 18: 5.6% (2018 est.)

Education expenditure: 3.3% of GDP (2023 est.)
14.7% national budget (2023 est.)
comparison ranking: Education expenditure (% GDP) 138

ENVIRONMENT

Environmental issues: air pollution from vehicle emissions; water pollution from raw sewage; tap water not potable; deforestation; wildlife protection

International environmental agreements: *party to:* Biodiversity, Climate Change, Climate Change-Kyoto Protocol, Climate Change-Paris Agreement, Desertification, Endangered Species, Hazardous Wastes, Law of the Sea, Marine Dumping-London Protocol, Ozone Layer Protection, Ship Pollution, Tropical Timber 2006, Wetlands
signed, but not ratified: none of the selected agreements

Climate: tropical; rainy season (March to June); dry season (June to October); persistent high temperatures and humidity; particularly enervating climate astride the Equator

Urbanization: *urban population:* 69.2% of total population (2023)
rate of urbanization: 3.19% annual rate of change (2020-25 est.)

Carbon dioxide emissions: 2.66 million metric tonnes of CO2 (2023 est.)
from petroleum and other liquids: 1.826 million metric tonnes of CO2 (2023 est.)
from consumed natural gas: 834,000 metric tonnes of CO2 (2023 est.)
comparison ranking: total emissions 153

Particulate matter emissions: 36.5 micrograms per cubic meter (2019 est.)

Methane emissions: *energy:* 308.8 kt (2022-2024 est.)
agriculture: 19.7 kt (2019-2021 est.)
waste: 25.3 kt (2019-2021 est.)
other: 11.4 kt (2019-2021 est.)

Waste and recycling: *municipal solid waste generated annually:* 451,200 tons (2024 est.)
percent of municipal solid waste recycled: 17.2% (2022 est.)

Total water withdrawal: *municipal:* 63.7 million cubic meters (2022 est.)
industrial: 24 million cubic meters (2022 est.)
agricultural: 4 million cubic meters (2022 est.)

Total renewable water resources: 832 billion cubic meters (2022 est.)

GOVERNMENT

Country name: *conventional long form:* Republic of the Congo
conventional short form: Congo (Brazzaville)
local long form: République du Congo
local short form: Congo
former: French Congo, Middle Congo, People's Republic of the Congo, Congo/Brazzaville
etymology: named for the Congo River, which makes up much of the country's eastern border; the river name derives from Kongo, a Bantu kingdom in the area

Government type: presidential republic

Capital: *name:* Brazzaville
geographic coordinates: 4 15 S, 15 17 E
time difference: UTC+1 (6 hours ahead of Washington, DC, during Standard Time)
etymology: named after the Italian-born French explorer and humanitarian, Pierre Savorgnan de BRAZZA (1852-1905), who founded the town in 1883

Administrative divisions: 15 departments; Bouenza, Brazzaville, Congo-Oubangui, Cuvette, Cuvette-Ouest, Djoue-Lefini, Kouilou, Lekoumou, Likouala, Niari, Nkeni-Alima, Plateaux, Pointe-Noire, Pool, Sangha

Legal system: mixed system of French civil law and customary law

Constitution: *history:* several previous; latest approved by referendum 25 October 2015
amendment process: proposed by the president of the republic or by Parliament; passage of presidential proposals requires Supreme Court review followed by approval in a referendum; such proposals may also be submitted directly to Parliament, in which case passage requires at least three-quarters majority vote of both houses in joint session; proposals by Parliament require three-fourths majority vote of both houses in joint session; constitutional articles including those affecting the country's territory, republican form of government, and secularity of the state are not amendable

International law organization participation: has not submitted an ICJ jurisdiction declaration; accepts ICCt jurisdiction

Citizenship: *citizenship by birth:* no
citizenship by descent only: at least one parent must be a citizen of the Republic of the Congo
dual citizenship recognized: no
residency requirement for naturalization: 10 years

Suffrage: 18 years of age; universal

Executive branch: *chief of state:* President Denis SASSOU-Nguesso (since 1997)
head of government: Prime Minister Anatole Collinet MAKOSSO (since 12 May 2021)
cabinet: Council of Ministers appointed by the president
election/appointment process: president directly elected by absolute majority popular vote in 2 rounds, if needed, for a 5-year term (eligible for 2 additional terms)
most recent election date: 21 March 2021
election results: *2021:* Denis SASSOU-Nguesso reelected president in the first round; percent of vote - Denis SASSOU-Nguesso (PCT) 88.4%, Guy Price Parfait KOLELAS (MCDDI) 8.0%, other 3.6%
2016: Denis SASSOU-Nguesso reelected president in the first round; percent of vote - Denis SASSOU-Nguesso (PCT) 60.4%, Guy Price Parfait KOLELAS (MCDDI) 15.1%, Jean-Marie MOKOKO (independent) 13.9%, Pascal Tsaty MABIALA (UPADS) 4.4%, other 6.2%
expected date of next election: 21 March 2026

Legislative branch: *legislature name:* Parliament (Parlement)
legislative structure: bicameral

Legislative branch - lower chamber: *chamber name:* National Assembly (Assemblée nationale)
number of seats: 151 (all directly elected)
electoral system: plurality/majority
scope of elections: full renewal
term in office: 5 years
most recent election date: 7/10/2022 to 7/31/2022
parties elected and seats per party: Congolese Workers Party (PCT) (112); Other (39)
percentage of women in chamber: 14.6%
expected date of next election: July 2026

Legislative branch - upper chamber: *chamber name:* Senate (Sénat)
number of seats: 72 (all indirectly elected)
scope of elections: full renewal
term in office: 6 years
most recent election date: 8/20/2023
percentage of women in chamber: 31.9%
expected date of next election: August 2029

Judicial branch: *highest court(s):* Supreme Court or Cour Supreme (consists of NA judges); Constitutional Court (consists of 9 members)
judge selection and term of office: Supreme Court judges elected by Parliament and serve until age 65; Constitutional Court members appointed by the president of the republic - 3 directly by the president and 6 nominated by Parliament; members appointed for renewable 9-year terms with one third of the membership renewed every 3 years
subordinate courts: Court of Audit and Budgetary Discipline; courts of appeal; regional and district courts; employment tribunals; juvenile courts
note: a High Court of Justice, outside the judicial authority, tries cases involving treason by the President of the Republic

Political parties: Alliance of the Presidential Majority or AMP
Action Movement for Renewal or MAR
Citizen's Rally or RC
Congolese Labour Party or PCT
Congolese Movement for Democracy and Integral Development or MCDDI
Congo on the Move or LCEM
Movement for Unity, Solidarity, and Work or MUST
Pan-African Union for Social Development or UPADS
Club 2002-Party for the Unity and the Republic or Club 2002
Patriotic Union for Democracy and Progress or UPDP
Perspectives and Realities Club or CPR
Rally for Democracy and Social Progress or RDPS
Republican and Liberal Party or PRL
Union of Democratic Forces or UDF
Union for Democracy and Republic or UDR
Union of Humanist Democrats or UDH-YUKI
Union for the Republic or UR

Diplomatic representation in the US: *chief of mission:* Ambassador (vacant); Chargé d'Affaires Firmine BOUITY (since 6 September 2025)
chancery: 1720 16th Street NW, Washington, DC 20009
telephone: [1] (202) 726-5500
FAX: [1] (202) 726-1860

email address and website: info@ambacongo-us.org http://www.ambacongo-us.org/en-us/home.aspx

Diplomatic representation from the US: *chief of mission:* Ambassador (vacant); Chargé d'Affaires Amanda S. JACOBSEN (since 18 July 2025)
embassy: 70-83 Section D, Boulevard Denis Sassou N'Guesso, Brazzaville
mailing address: 2090 Brazzaville Place, Washington DC 20521-2090
telephone: [242] 06 612-2000, [242] 05 387-9700
email address and website: BrazzavilleACS@state.gov https://cg.usembassy.gov/

International organization participation: ACP, AfDB, AU, BDEAC, CEMAC, EITI (compliant country), FAO, FZ, G-77, IAEA, IBRD, ICAO, ICCt, ICRM, IDA, IFAD, IFC, IFRCS, ILO, IMF, IMO, Interpol, IOC, IOM, IPU, ISO (correspondent), ITSO, ITU, ITUC (NGOs), LCBC (observer), MIGA, NAM, OIF, OPCW, UN, UNCTAD, UNESCO, UNHCR, UNIDO, UNWTO, UPU, WCO, WFTU (NGOs), WHO, WIPO, WMO, WTO

Independence: 15 August 1960 (from France)

National holiday: Independence Day, 15 August (1960)

Flag: *description:* divided diagonally from the lower-left side by a wide yellow band; the upper triangle (left side) is green, and the lower triangle is red
meaning: green stands for agriculture and forests, and yellow for the people's friendship and nobility; the meaning of the red color is not noted but has been associated with the struggle for independence
history: uses the colors of the Pan-African movement

National symbol(s): lion, elephant

National color(s): green, yellow, red

National anthem(s): *title:* "La Congolaise" (The Congolese)
lyrics/music: Jacques TONDRA and Georges KIBANGHI/Jean ROYER and Joseph SPADILIERE
history: originally adopted 1959, restored 1991

National heritage: *total World Heritage Sites:* 2 (natural)
selected World Heritage Site locales: Sangha Trinational Forest; Forest Massif of Odzala-Kokoua

ECONOMY

Economic overview: primarily an oil- and natural resources-based economy; recovery from mid-2010s oil devaluation has been slow and curtailed by COVID-19; extreme poverty increasing, particularly in southern rural regions; attempting to implement recommended CEMAC reforms; increasing likelihood of debt default

Real GDP (purchasing power parity): $39.147 billion (2024 est.)
$38.163 billion (2023 est.)
$37.448 billion (2022 est.)
note: data in 2021 dollars
comparison ranking: 139

Real GDP growth rate: 2.6% (2024 est.)
1.9% (2023 est.)
1.5% (2022 est.)
note: annual GDP % growth based on constant local currency
comparison ranking: 130

Real GDP per capita: $6,200 (2024 est.)
$6,200 (2023 est.)
$6,200 (2022 est.)
note: data in 2021 dollars
comparison ranking: 165

GDP (official exchange rate): $15.72 billion (2024 est.)
note: data in current dollars at official exchange rate

Inflation rate (consumer prices): 3.1% (2024 est.)
4.3% (2023 est.)
3% (2022 est.)
note: annual % change based on consumer prices
comparison ranking: 96

GDP - composition, by sector of origin: *agriculture:* 9.4% (2024 est.)
industry: 40.1% (2024 est.)
services: 45% (2024 est.)
note: figures may not total 100% due to non-allocated consumption not captured in sector-reported data
comparison rankings: agriculture 76; industry 19; services 174

GDP - composition, by end use: *household consumption:* 47.4% (2024 est.)
government consumption: 13.4% (2024 est.)
investment in fixed capital: 26.5% (2024 est.)
investment in inventories: 0.3% (2024 est.)
exports of goods and services: 52.8% (2024 est.)
imports of goods and services: -40.4% (2024 est.)
note: figures may not total 100% due to rounding or gaps in data collection

Agricultural products: cassava, sugarcane, oil palm fruit, bananas, plantains, root vegetables, game meat, vegetables, mangoes/guavas, fruits (2023)
note: top ten agricultural products based on tonnage

Industries: petroleum extraction, cement, lumber, brewing, sugar, palm oil, soap, flour, cigarettes

Industrial production growth rate: 0.3% (2024 est.)
note: annual % change in industrial value added based on constant local currency
comparison ranking: 128

Labor force: 2.563 million (2024 est.)
note: number of people ages 15 or older who are employed or seeking work
comparison ranking: 121

Unemployment rate: 19.7% (2024 est.)
19.9% (2023 est.)
20.2% (2022 est.)
note: % of labor force seeking employment
comparison ranking: 183

Youth unemployment rate (ages 15-24): *total:* 40% (2024 est.)
male: 41% (2024 est.)
female: 39% (2024 est.)
note: % of labor force ages 15-24 seeking employment
comparison ranking: total 9

Remittances: 0.3% of GDP (2023 est.)
0.3% of GDP (2022 est.)
0.3% of GDP (2021 est.)
note: personal transfers and compensation between resident and non-resident individuals/households/entities

Budget: *revenues:* $2.393 billion (2020 est.)
expenditures: $3.231 billion (2020 est.)
note: central government revenues (excluding grants) and expenditures converted to US dollars at average official exchange rate for year indicated

Taxes and other revenues: 6.5% (of GDP) (2021 est.)
note: central government tax revenue as a % of GDP
comparison ranking: 146

Current account balance: $1.716 billion (2021 est.)
$1.441 billion (2020 est.)
$1.632 billion (2019 est.)
note: balance of payments - net trade and primary/secondary income in current dollars
comparison ranking: 51

Exports: $7.752 billion (2021 est.)
$4.67 billion (2020 est.)
$7.855 billion (2019 est.)
note: balance of payments - exports of goods and services in current dollars
comparison ranking: 125

Exports - partners: China 46%, UAE 23%, India 6%, Saudi Arabia 5%, Portugal 3% (2023)
note: top five export partners based on percentage share of exports

Exports - commodities: crude petroleum, refined copper, gold, wood, refined petroleum (2023)
note: top five export commodities based on value in dollars

Imports: $4.487 billion (2021 est.)
$3.279 billion (2020 est.)
$4.945 billion (2019 est.)
note: balance of payments - imports of goods and services in current dollars
comparison ranking: 154

Imports - partners: China 24%, Angola 20%, Gabon 9%, France 6%, UAE 5% (2023)
note: top five import partners based on percentage share of imports

Imports - commodities: ships, poultry, garments, iron pipes, refined petroleum (2023)
note: top five import commodities based on value in dollars

Reserves of foreign exchange and gold: $715.391 million (2023 est.)
$835.649 million (2022 est.)
$828.56 million (2021 est.)
note: holdings of gold (year-end prices)/foreign exchange/special drawing rights in current dollars
comparison ranking: 150

Debt - external: $6.36 billion (2023 est.)
note: present value of external debt in current US dollars
comparison ranking: 65

Exchange rates: Cooperation Financiere en Afrique Centrale francs (XAF) per US dollar -

Exchange rates: 606.345 (2024 est.)
606.57 (2023 est.)
623.76 (2022 est.)
554.531 (2021 est.)
575.586 (2020 est.)

ENERGY

Electricity access: *electrification - total population:* 50.6% (2022 est.)
electrification - urban areas: 67.5%
electrification - rural areas: 12.4%

Electricity: *installed generating capacity:* 842,000 kW (2023 est.)
consumption: 2.832 billion kWh (2023 est.)
exports: 31 million kWh (2023 est.)
imports: 30.588 million kWh (2023 est.)
transmission/distribution losses: 2.335 billion kWh (2023 est.)
comparison rankings: installed generating capacity 137; consumption 144; exports 95; imports 120; transmission/distribution losses 129

Electricity generation sources: *fossil fuels:* 79.4% of total installed capacity (2023 est.)
solar: 0.2% of total installed capacity (2023 est.)
hydroelectricity: 20.2% of total installed capacity (2023 est.)

biomass and waste: 0.2% of total installed capacity (2023 est.)

Coal: *imports:* 65 metric tons (2023 est.)

Petroleum: *total petroleum production:* 267,000 bbl/day (2023 est.)
refined petroleum consumption: 13,000 bbl/day (2023 est.)
crude oil estimated reserves: 2.882 billion barrels (2021 est.)

Natural gas: *production:* 425 million cubic meters (2023 est.)
consumption: 425 million cubic meters (2023 est.)
proven reserves: 283.99 billion cubic meters (2021 est.)

Energy consumption per capita: 7.351 million Btu/person (2023 est.)
comparison ranking: 161

COMMUNICATIONS

Telephones - fixed lines: *total subscriptions:* 17,000 (2020 est.)
subscriptions per 100 inhabitants: (2022 est.) less than 1
comparison ranking: total subscriptions 177

Telephones - mobile cellular: *total subscriptions:* 5.87 million (2023 est.)
subscriptions per 100 inhabitants: 97 (2021 est.)
comparison ranking: total subscriptions 122

Broadcast media: 1 state-owned TV and 3 state-owned radio stations; several privately owned TV and radio stations; satellite TV service is available; rebroadcasts of several international broadcasters are available

Internet country code: .cg

Internet users: *percent of population:* 38% (2023 est.)

Broadband - fixed subscriptions: *total:* 78,000 (2023 est.)
subscriptions per 100 inhabitants: 1 (2023 est.)
comparison ranking: total 140

TRANSPORTATION

Civil aircraft registration country code prefix: TN

Airports: 56 (2025)
comparison ranking: 81

Railways: *total:* 510 km (2014)
narrow gauge: 510 km (2014) 1.067-m gauge

Merchant marine: *total:* 11 (2023)
by type: oil tanker 1, other 10
comparison ranking: total 159

Ports: *total ports:* 5 (2024)
large: 0
medium: 0
small: 1
very small: 4
ports with oil terminals: 4
key ports: Djeno Terminal, Dussafu Terminal, N'kossa Terminal, Pointe Noire, Yombo Terminal

MILITARY AND SECURITY

Military and security forces: Congolese Armed Forces (Forces Armees Congolaises, FAC): Army, Navy, Congolese Air Force, National Gendarmerie

Ministry of Interior: National Police (2025)
note: the National Gendarmerie (GN) is a paramilitary force with domestic law enforcement and security responsibilities; it is under the Ministry of Defense, but also reports to the Ministry of Interior; the GN nominally includes the Republican Guard (GR), which is responsible for presidential security and has a separate command structure

Military expenditures: 1.2% of GDP (2024 est.)
2% of GDP (2023 est.)
1.8% of GDP (2022 est.)
2.4% of GDP (2021 est.)
2.8% of GDP (2020 est.)

Military and security service personnel strengths: approximately 12-14,000 active FAC, including Gendarmerie (2025)

Military equipment inventories and acquisitions: the FAC has mostly Soviet-era armaments, with a small mix of Chinese, French, and South African equipment (2024)

Military service age and obligation: 18-25 years of age for voluntary military service for men and women; conscription ended in 1969 (2024)

Military deployments: has about 190 mostly police personnel deployed to the Central African Republic (MINUSCA) (2024)

Military - note: the FAC's primary focuses are internal and maritime security; since its creation in 1961, the FAC has had a turbulent history; it has been sidelined by some national leaders in favor of personal militias, endured an internal rebellion (1996), and clashed with various rebel groups and political or ethnic militias (1993-1996, 2002-2005, 2017); during the 1997-1999 civil war, the military generally split along ethnic lines, with most northern officers supporting eventual winner SASSOU-Nguesso, and most southerners backing the rebels; others joined ethnic-based factions loyal to regional warlords; forces backing SASSOU-Nguesso were supported by Angolan troops and received some French assistance; the FAC also has undergone at least three reorganizations that included the incorporation of former rebel combatants and various ethnic and political militias; in recent years, France has provided some advice and training, and a military cooperation agreement was signed with Russia in 2019 (2025)

TRANSNATIONAL ISSUES

Refugees and internally displaced persons: *refugees:* 69,766 (2024 est.)

Trafficking in persons: *tier rating:* Tier 2 Watch List — the Republic of the Congo does not fully meet the minimum standards for the elimination of trafficking, but the government has devoted sufficient resources to a written plan that, if implemented, would constitute significant efforts to meet the minimum standards; therefore, the Republic of the Congo was granted a waiver per the Trafficking Victims Protection Act from an otherwise required downgrade to Tier 3 and remained on Tier 2 Watch List for the third consecutive year; for more details, go to: https://www.state.gov/reports/2025-trafficking-in-persons-report/republic-of-the-congo/

COOK ISLANDS

INTRODUCTION

Background: Polynesians from Tahiti were probably the first people to settle Rarotonga – the largest of the Cook Islands – around A.D. 900. Over time, Samoans and Tongans also settled in Rarotonga, and Rarotongans voyaged to the northern Cook Islands, settling Manihiki and Rakahanga. Pukapuka and Penrhyn in the northern Cook Islands were settled directly from Samoa. Prior to European contact, there was considerable travel and trade between inhabitants of the different islands and atolls, but they were not united in a single political entity. Spanish navigators were the first Europeans to spot the northern Cook Islands in 1595, followed by the first landing in 1606, but no further European contact occurred until the 1760s. In 1773, British explorer James COOK spotted Manuae in the southern Cook Islands, and Russian mapmakers named the islands after COOK in the 1820s.

Fearing France would militarily occupy the islands as it did in Tahiti, Rarotongans asked the UK for protectorate status in the 1840s and 1860s, a request the UK ignored. In 1888, Queen MAKEA TAKAU of Rarotonga formally petitioned for protectorate status, to which the UK reluctantly agreed. In 1901, the UK placed Rarotonga and the rest of the islands in the New Zealand Colony, and in 1915, the Cook Islands Act organized the islands into one political entity. It remained a protectorate until 1965, when New Zealand granted the Cook Islands self-governing status. The Cook Islands has a great deal of local autonomy and is an independent member of international organizations, but it is in free association with New Zealand, which is responsible for its defense and foreign affairs. In September 2023, the US recognized the Cook Islands as a sovereign and independent state.

GEOGRAPHY

Location: Oceania, group of islands in the South Pacific Ocean, about halfway between Hawaii and New Zealand

Geographic coordinates: 21 14 S, 159 46 W

Map references: Oceania

Area: *total:* 236 sq km
land: 236 sq km
water: 0 sq km
comparison ranking: total 215

Area - comparative: 1.3 times the size of Washington, D.C.

Land boundaries: *total:* 0 km

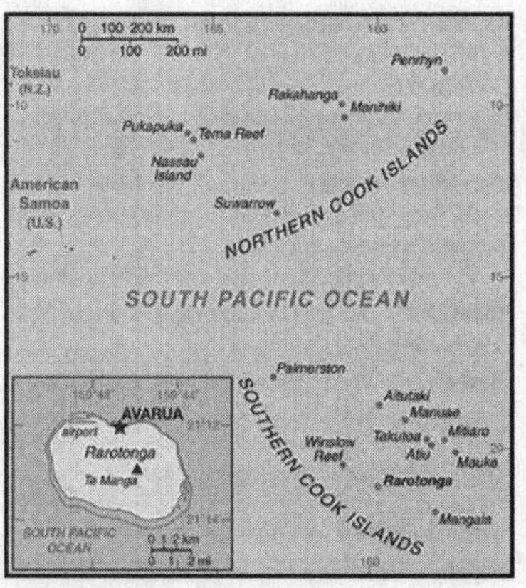

Coastline: 120 km

Maritime claims: *territorial sea:* 12 nm
exclusive economic zone: 200 nm
continental shelf: 200 nm or to the edge of the continental margin

Climate: tropical oceanic; moderated by trade winds; a dry season from April to November and a more humid season from December to March

Terrain: low coral atolls in north; volcanic, hilly islands in south

Elevation: *highest point:* Te Manga 652 m
lowest point: Pacific Ocean 0 m

Natural resources: coconuts (copra)

Land use: *agricultural land:* 7.9% (2022 est.)
arable land: 2.1% (2022 est.)
permanent crops: 5.8% (2022 est.)
permanent pasture: 0% (2022 est.)
forest: 65% (2022 est.)
other: 27.1% (2022 est.)

Irrigated land: NA

Population distribution: most of the population is found on the island of Rarotonga

Natural hazards: tropical cyclones (November to March)

Geography - note: the northern Cook Islands are seven low-lying, sparsely populated, coral atolls; the southern Cook Islands, where most of the population lives, consist of eight elevated, fertile, volcanic isles, including the largest, Rarotonga, at 67 sq km

PEOPLE AND SOCIETY

Population: *total:* 7,761 (2024 est.)
male: 3,980
female: 3,781
comparison rankings: total 224; male 223; female 224

Nationality: *noun:* Cook Islander(s)
adjective: Cook Islander

Ethnic groups: Cook Island Maori 77.4%, part Cook Island Maori 8.3%, Fijian 3.6%, New Zealand Maori/European 3.4%, Filipino 2.9%, other Pacific Islands 1.8%, other 2.6% (2021 est.)

Languages: English (official) 86.4%, Cook Islands Maori (Rarotongan) (official) 76.2%, other 8.3% (2011 est.)
note: shares sum to more than 100% because some respondents gave more than one answer on the census

Religions: Protestant 55% (Cook Islands Christian Church 43.1%, Seventh Day Adventist 8.3%, Assemblies of God 3.6%), Roman Catholic 16.7%, Church of Jesus Christ 3.9%, Jehovah's Witness 2.2%, Apostolic Church 2.1%, other 4.5%, none/unspecified 15.6% (2021 est.)

Age structure: *0-14 years:* 18.2% (male 738/female 671)
15-64 years: 65.9% (male 2,634/female 2,479)
65 years and over: 16% (2024 est.) (male 608/female 631)

Dependency ratios: *total dependency ratio:* 51.8 (2024 est.)
youth dependency ratio: 27.6 (2024 est.)
elderly dependency ratio: 24.2 (2024 est.)
potential support ratio: 4.1 (2024 est.)

Median age: *total:* 41.1 years (2024 est.)
male: 40.7 years
female: 41.4 years
comparison ranking: total 53

Population growth rate: -2.24% (2024 est.)
comparison ranking: 236

Birth rate: 12.1 births/1,000 population (2024 est.)
comparison ranking: 147

Death rate: 9.4 deaths/1,000 population (2024 est.)
comparison ranking: 48

Net migration rate: -25.1 migrant(s)/1,000 population (2024 est.)
comparison ranking: 230

Population distribution: most of the population is found on the island of Rarotonga

Urbanization: *urban population:* 76.2% of total population (2023)
rate of urbanization: 0.52% annual rate of change (2020-25 est.)

Sex ratio: *at birth:* 1.04 male(s)/female
0-14 years: 1.1 male(s)/female
15-64 years: 1.06 male(s)/female
65 years and over: 0.96 male(s)/female
total population: 1.05 male(s)/female (2024 est.)

Maternal mortality ratio: 0 deaths/100,000 live births (2023 est.)
comparison ranking: 196

Infant mortality rate: *total:* 15.1 deaths/1,000 live births (2024 est.)
male: 19 deaths/1,000 live births
female: 11.1 deaths/1,000 live births
comparison ranking: total 95

Life expectancy at birth: *total population:* 77.6 years (2024 est.)
male: 74.8 years
female: 80.6 years
comparison ranking: total population 88

Total fertility rate: 2.02 children born/woman (2024 est.)
comparison ranking: 104

Gross reproduction rate: 0.99 (2024 est.)

Drinking water source: *improved: urban:* NA
rural: NA
total: 100% of population (2022 est.)
unimproved: urban: NA
rural: NA
total: 0% of population (2022 est.)

Health expenditure: 3.2% of GDP (2020)
11.9% of national budget (2022 est.)

Physician density: 1.67 physicians/1,000 population (2020)

Hospital bed density: 8.2 beds/1,000 population (2021 est.)

Sanitation facility access: *improved:* total: 96.8% of population (2022 est.)
unimproved: total: 3.2% of population (2022 est.)

Obesity - adult prevalence rate: 55.9% (2016)
comparison ranking: 2

Alcohol consumption per capita: *total:* 12.97 liters of pure alcohol (2019 est.)
beer: 3.62 liters of pure alcohol (2019 est.)
wine: 2.28 liters of pure alcohol (2019 est.)
spirits: 7.07 liters of pure alcohol (2019 est.)
other alcohols: 0 liters of pure alcohol (2019 est.)
comparison ranking: total 1

Tobacco use: *total:* 24% (2025 est.)
male: 28.6% (2025 est.)
female: 20.1% (2025 est.)
comparison ranking: total 44

Currently married women (ages 15-49): 42.6% (2023 est.)

Education expenditure: 4.6% of GDP (2023 est.)
8.7% national budget (2024 est.)
comparison ranking: Education expenditure (% GDP) 79

School life expectancy (primary to tertiary education): *total:* 15 years (2023 est.)
male: 15 years (2023 est.)
female: 15 years (2023 est.)

ENVIRONMENT

Environmental issues: solid- and liquid-waste disposal; soil degradation; deforestation; use of pesticides; improper disposal of pollutants; overfishing and destructive fishing practices; over-dredging of lagoons and coral rubble beds; unregulated building

International environmental agreements: *party to:* Antarctic-Marine Living Resources, Biodiversity, Climate Change, Climate Change-Kyoto Protocol, Climate Change-Paris Agreement, Comprehensive Nuclear Test Ban, Desertification, Hazardous Wastes, Law of the Sea, Ozone Layer Protection, Ship Pollution
signed, but not ratified: none of the selected agreements

Climate: tropical oceanic; moderated by trade winds; a dry season from April to November and a more humid season from December to March

Urbanization: *urban population:* 76.2% of total population (2023)
rate of urbanization: 0.52% annual rate of change (2020-25 est.)

Carbon dioxide emissions: 103,000 metric tonnes of CO2 (2023 est.)
from petroleum and other liquids: 103,000 metric tonnes of CO2 (2023 est.)
comparison ranking: total emissions 208

Particulate matter emissions: 7.8 micrograms per cubic meter (2019 est.)

GOVERNMENT

Country name: *conventional long form:* none
conventional short form: Cook Islands
former: Hervey Islands
etymology: named after Captain James COOK, the British explorer who visited the islands in 1773 and 1777

Government type: parliamentary democracy

Dependency status: self-governing in free association with New Zealand; Cook Islands is fully responsible for internal affairs and conducts its own international relations, including establishing diplomatic relationships with foreign countries; New Zealand has a constitutional responsibility to respond to requests for assistance with foreign affairs, disasters, and defense

Capital: *name:* Avarua
geographic coordinates: 21 12 S, 159 46 W
time difference: UTC-10 (5 hours behind Washington, DC, during Standard Time)
etymology: translates as "two harbors" in Maori

Administrative divisions: none

Legal system: common law similar to New Zealand common law

Constitution: *history:* 4 August 1965 (Cook Islands Constitution Act 1964)
amendment process: proposed by Parliament; passage requires at least two-thirds majority vote by the Parliament membership in each of several readings and assent of the chief of state's representative; passage of amendments relating to the chief of state also requires two-thirds majority approval in a referendum

International law organization participation: has not submitted an ICJ jurisdiction declaration (New Zealand normally retains responsibility for external affairs); accepts ICCt jurisdiction

Suffrage: 18 years of age; universal

Executive branch: *chief of state:* King CHARLES III (since 8 September 2022); represented by Sir Tom J. MARSTERS (since 9 August 2013); New Zealand High Commissioner Catherine GRAHAM (since 8 September 2024)
head of government: Prime Minister Mark BROWN (since 1 October 2020)
cabinet: Cabinet chosen by the prime minister
election/appointment process: the monarchy is hereditary; UK representative appointed by the monarch; New Zealand high commissioner appointed by the New Zealand Government; following legislative elections, the leader of the majority party or majority coalition usually becomes prime minister

Legislative branch: *legislature name:* Parliament
legislative structure: unicameral
number of seats: 24 (directly elected)
electoral system: plurality/majority
scope of elections: full renewal
term in office: 4 years
most recent election date: 8/1/2022
parties elected and seats per party: CIP (12); Demo (5); Cook Islands United Party (3); OCI (1); independent (3)
percentage of women in chamber: 25%
expected date of next election: 2026
note: the House of Ariki, a 24-member parliamentary body of traditional leaders appointed by the King's representative, serves as a consultative body to the Parliament

Judicial branch: *highest court(s):* Court of Appeal (consists of the chief justice and 3 judges of the High Court); High Court (consists of the chief justice and at least 4 judges and organized into civil, criminal, and land divisions)
judge selection and term of office: High Court chief justice appointed by the Queen's Representative on the advice of the Executive Council tendered by the prime minister; other judges appointed by the Queen's Representative, on the advice of the Executive Council tendered by the chief justice, High Court chief justice, and the minister of justice; chief justice and judges appointed for 3-year renewable terms
subordinate courts: justices of the peace
note: appeals beyond the Cook Islands Court of Appeal are heard by the Judicial Committee of the Privy Council (in London)

Political parties: Cook Islands Party or CIP
Cook Islands United Party
Democratic Party or Demo
One Cook Islands Movement or OCI

Diplomatic representation in the US: none (self-governing in free association with New Zealand)

Diplomatic representation from the US: *embassy:* none (self-governing in free association with New Zealand)
note: on 25 September 2023, the US officially established diplomatic relations with Cook Islands

International organization participation: ACP, ADB, AOSIS, FAO, ICAO, ICCt, ICRM, IFAD, IFRCS, IMO, IMSO, IOC, ITUC (NGOs), OPCW, PIF, Sparteca, SPC, UNESCO, UPU, WHO, WMO

Independence: 4 August 1965 (Cook Islands became self-governing state in free association with New Zealand)

National holiday: Constitution Day, the first Monday in August (1965)

Flag: *description:* blue with the UK flag in the upper-left quadrant and a large circle of 15 five-pointed white stars (one for each island) centered in the right half of the flag

National symbol(s): a circle of 15 five-pointed white stars on a blue field, tiare maori flower (*Gardenia taitensis*)

National color(s): green, white

National anthem(s): *title:* "Te Atua Mou E" (To God Almighty)
lyrics/music: Tepaeru Te RITO/Thomas DAVIS
history: adopted 1982; as prime minister, Sir Thomas DAVIS composed the anthem; Pa Tepaeru Terito Ariki, his wife and a tribal chief, wrote the lyrics
title: "God Save the King"
lyrics/music: unknown
history: royal anthem

ECONOMY

Economic overview: high-income self-governing New Zealand territorial economy; tourism-based activity but diversifying; severely curtailed by COVID-19 pandemic; copra and tropical fruit exporter; Asian Development Bank aid recipient

Real GDP (purchasing power parity): $401.155 million (2024 est.)
$364.686 million (2023 est.)
$306.285 million (2022 est.)
note: data are in 2015 dollars
comparison ranking: 212

Real GDP growth rate: 10.5% (2022 est.)
-24.5% (2021 est.)
-5.2% (2020 est.)
comparison ranking: 3

Real GDP per capita: $29,800 (2024 est.)
$25,700 (2023 est.)
$19,700 (2022 est.)
note: data in 2015 dollars
comparison ranking: 79

GDP (official exchange rate): $409.077 million (2024 est.)
note: data in current dollars at official exchange rate

Inflation rate (consumer prices): 10.6% (2022 est.)
1.9% (2021 est.)
1% (2020 est.)
note: annual % change based on consumer prices
comparison ranking: 180

Agricultural products: coconuts, vegetables, papayas, pork, sweet potatoes, tomatoes, fruits, mangoes/guavas, watermelons, chicken (2023)
note: top ten agricultural products based on tonnage

Industries: fishing, fruit processing, tourism, clothing, handicrafts

Budget: *revenues:* $113.687 million (2022 est.)
expenditures: $143.391 million (2022 est.)
note: central government revenues and expenses (excluding grants/extrabudgetary units/social security funds) converted to US dollars at average official exchange rate for year indicated

Exports - partners: Japan 33%, Thailand 15%, Greece 15%, France 11%, China 8% (2023)
note: top five export partners based on percentage share of exports

Exports - commodities: fish, ships, garments, shellfish (2023)
note: top export commodities based on value in dollars over $500,000

Imports - partners: NZ 44%, Italy 26%, Fiji 9%, China 7%, Australia 3% (2023)
note: top five import partners based on percentage share of imports

Imports - commodities: ships, refined petroleum, cars, plastic products, additive manufacturing machines (2023)
note: top five import commodities based on value in dollars

Exchange rates: New Zealand dollars (NZD) per US dollar -

Exchange rates: 1.652 (2024 est.)
1.628 (2023 est.)
1.577 (2022 est.)
1.414 (2021 est.)
1.542 (2020 est.)

ENERGY

Electricity: *installed generating capacity:* 17,000 kW (2023 est.)
consumption: 37.5 million kWh (2023 est.)
transmission/distribution losses: 3.2 million kWh (2023 est.)
comparison rankings: installed generating capacity 206; consumption 206; transmission/distribution losses 7

Electricity generation sources: *fossil fuels:* 60.9% of total installed capacity (2023 est.)
solar: 39.1% of total installed capacity (2023 est.)

Coal: *imports:* 1 metric tons (2022 est.)

Petroleum: *refined petroleum consumption:* 700 bbl/day (2023 est.)

COMMUNICATIONS

Telephones - fixed lines: *total subscriptions:* 7,000 (2021 est.)
subscriptions per 100 inhabitants: 41 (2021 est.)
comparison ranking: total subscriptions 192

Telephones - mobile cellular: *total subscriptions:* 17,000 (2021 est.)
subscriptions per 100 inhabitants: 100 (2021 est.)
comparison ranking: total subscriptions 217

Broadcast media: 1 privately owned TV station in Rarotonga provides a mix of local news and overseas-sourced programs (2019)

Internet country code: .ck

Internet users: *percent of population:* 64.8% (2021 est.)

Broadband - fixed subscriptions: *total:* 2,700 (2018 est.)
subscriptions per 100 inhabitants: 15 (2018 est.)
comparison ranking: total 200

TRANSPORTATION

Civil aircraft registration country code prefix: E5

Airports: 10 (2025)
comparison ranking: 162

Merchant marine: *total:* 190 (2023)
by type: bulk carrier 19, general cargo 44, oil tanker 58, other 69
comparison ranking: total 70

Ports: *total ports:* 1 (2024)
large: 0
medium: 0
small: 0
very small: 1
ports with oil terminals: 1
key ports: Avatiu

MILITARY AND SECURITY

Military and security forces: no regular military forces; Cook Islands Police Service

Military - note: defense is the responsibility of New Zealand in consultation with the Cook Islands and at its request
the Cook Islands have a "shiprider" agreement with the US, which allows local maritime law enforcement officers to embark on US Coast Guard (USCG) and US Navy (USN) vessels, including to board and search vessels suspected of violating laws or regulations within its designated exclusive economic zone (EEZ) or on the high seas; "shiprider" agreements also enable USCG personnel and USN vessels with embarked USCG law enforcement personnel to work with host nations to protect critical regional resources (2025)

CORAL SEA ISLANDS

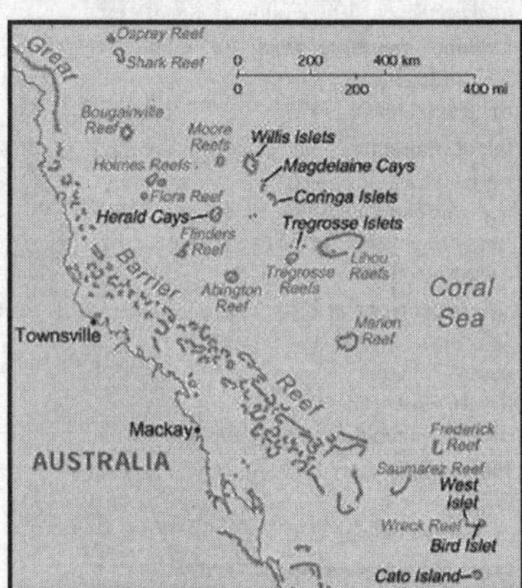

INTRODUCTION

Background: The widely scattered Coral Sea Islands were first charted in 1803, but they were too small to host permanent human habitation. The 1870s and 1880s saw attempts at guano mining, but these were soon abandoned. The islands became an Australian territory in 1969, and the boundaries were extended in 1997. A small meteorological staff has operated on the Willis Islets since 1921, and several other islands host unmanned weather stations, beacons, and lighthouses. Much of the territory lies within national marine nature reserves.

GEOGRAPHY

Location: Oceania, islands in the Coral Sea, northeast of Australia

Geographic coordinates: 18 00 S, 152 00 E

Map references: Oceania

Area: *total:* 3 sq km less than
land: 3 sq km less than
water: 0 sq km
note: includes numerous small islands and reefs scattered over a sea area of about 780,000 sq km (300,000 sq mi), with the Willis Islets the most important
comparison ranking: total 248

Area - comparative: about four times the size of the National Mall in Washington, D.C.

Land boundaries: *total:* 0 km

Coastline: 3,095 km

Maritime claims: *territorial sea:* 3 nm
exclusive fishing zone: 200 nm

Climate: tropical

Terrain: sand and coral reefs and islands (cays)

Elevation: *highest point:* unnamed location on Cato Island 9 m
lowest point: Pacific Ocean 0 m

Natural resources: fish

Land use: *agricultural land:* 0% (2018 est.)
other: 100% (2018 est.)

Natural hazards: occasional tropical cyclones

Geography - note: important nesting area for birds and turtles

PEOPLE AND SOCIETY

Population: *total:* no permanent inhabitants
note: Willis Island is inhabited by meteorological staff

ENVIRONMENT

Environmental issues: no permanent freshwater resources; damaging activities include coral mining, fishing practices (overfishing, blast fishing)

Climate: tropical

GOVERNMENT

Country name: *conventional long form:* Coral Sea Islands Territory
conventional short form: Coral Sea Islands
etymology: self-descriptive name to reflect the islands' position in the Coral Sea off the northeastern coast of Australia

Dependency status: territory of Australia; administered from Canberra by the Department of Regional Australia, Local Government, Arts and Sport

Legal system: the common law system of Australia applies

Citizenship: see Australia

Diplomatic representation in the US: none (territory of Australia)

Diplomatic representation from the US: *embassy:* none (territory of Australia)

Flag: the flag of Australia is used

MILITARY AND SECURITY

Military - note: defense is the responsibility of Australia

COSTA RICA

INTRODUCTION

Background: Although explored by the Spanish early in the 16th century, initial attempts at colonizing Costa Rica proved unsuccessful due to a combination of factors, including disease from mosquito-infested swamps, brutal heat, resistance from Indigenous populations, and pirate raids. It was not until 1563 that a permanent settlement of Cartago was established in the cooler, fertile central highlands. The area remained a colony for some two-and-a-half centuries. In 1821, Costa Rica was one of several

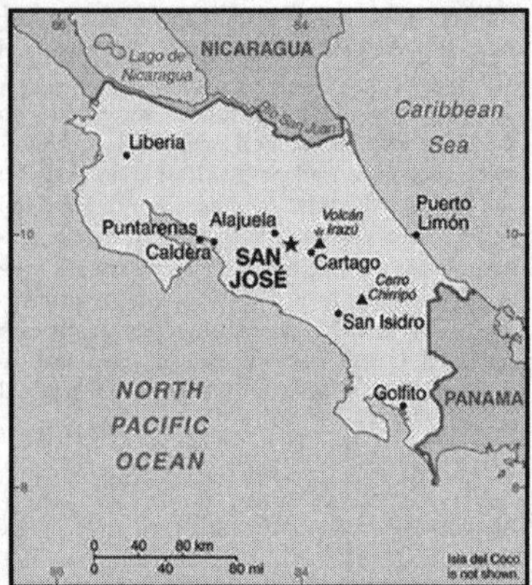

Central American provinces that jointly declared independence from Spain. Two years later it joined the United Provinces of Central America, but this federation disintegrated in 1838, at which time Costa Rica proclaimed its sovereignty and independence.

Since the late 19th century, only two brief periods of violence have marred the country's democratic development. General Federico TINOCO Granados led a coup in 1917, but the threat of US intervention pushed him to resign in 1919. In 1948, landowner Jose FIGUERES Ferrer raised his own army and rebelled against the government. The brief civil war ended with an agreement to allow FIGUERES to remain in power for 18 months, then step down in favor of the previously elected Otilio ULATE. FIGUERES was later elected twice in his own right, in 1953 and 1970.

Costa Rica experienced destabilizing waves of refugees from Central American civil wars in the 1970s and 1980s, but peace in the region has since helped the economy rebound. Although it still maintains a large agricultural sector, Costa Rica has expanded its economy to include strong technology and tourism industries.

GEOGRAPHY

Location: Central America, bordering both the Caribbean Sea and the North Pacific Ocean, between Nicaragua and Panama

Geographic coordinates: 10 00 N, 84 00 W

Map references: Central America and the Caribbean

Area: *total:* 51,100 sq km
land: 51,060 sq km
water: 40 sq km
note: includes Isla del Coco
comparison ranking: total 129

Area - comparative: slightly smaller than West Virginia

Land boundaries: *total:* 661 km
border countries (2): Nicaragua 313 km; Panama 348 km

Coastline: 1,290 km

Maritime claims: *territorial sea:* 12 nm
exclusive economic zone: 200 nm
continental shelf: 200 nm

Climate: tropical and subtropical; dry season (December to April); rainy season (May to November); cooler in highlands

Terrain: coastal plains separated by rugged mountains including over 100 volcanic cones, of which several are major active volcanoes

Elevation: *highest point:* Cerro Chirripo 3,819 m
lowest point: Pacific Ocean 0 m
mean elevation: 746 m

Natural resources: hydropower

Land use: *agricultural land:* 34.7% (2022 est.)
arable land: 3.8% (2022 est.)
permanent crops: 6.4% (2022 est.)
permanent pasture: 24.4% (2022 est.)
forest: 60.1% (2022 est.)
other: 5.3% (2022 est.)

Irrigated land: 1,015 sq km (2012)

Population distribution: roughly half of the nation's population resides in urban areas; the capital of San Jose is the largest city and home to approximately one fifth of the population

Natural hazards: occasional earthquakes, hurricanes along Atlantic coast; frequent flooding of lowlands at onset of rainy season and landslides; active volcanoes
volcanism: Arenal (1,670 m) is the most active volcano in Costa Rica; a 1968 eruption destroyed the town of Tabacon; Irazu (3,432 m), situated just east of San Jose, has the potential to spew ash over the capital city, as it did between 1963 and 1965; other historically active volcanoes include Miravalles, Poas, Rincon de la Vieja, and Turrialba

Geography - note: four volcanoes, two of them active, rise near the capital of San Jose in the center of the country; one of the volcanoes, Irazu, erupted destructively in 1963-65

PEOPLE AND SOCIETY

Population: *total:* 5,265,575 (2024 est.)
male: 2,635,481
female: 2,630,094
comparison rankings: total 123; male 123; female 124

Nationality: *noun:* Costa Rican(s)
adjective: Costa Rican

Ethnic groups: White or Mestizo 83.6%, Mulatto 6.7%, Indigenous 2.4%, Black or African descent 1.1%, other 1.1%, none 2.9%, unspecified 2.2% (2011 est.)

Languages: Spanish (official), English
major-language sample(s):
La Libreta Informativa del Mundo, la fuente indispensable de información básica. (Spanish)

Religions: Roman Catholic 47.5%, Evangelical and Pentecostal 19.8%, Jehovah's Witness 1.4%, other Protestant 1.2%, other 3.1%, none 27% (2021 est.)

Age structure: *0-14 years:* 18.8% (male 506,041/female 482,481)
15-64 years: 70.2% (male 1,862,872/female 1,832,024)
65 years and over: 11.1% (2024 est.) (male 266,568/female 315,589)

Dependency ratios: *total dependency ratio:* 42.5 (2024 est.)
youth dependency ratio: 26.8 (2024 est.)
elderly dependency ratio: 15.8 (2024 est.)
potential support ratio: 6.3 (2024 est.)

Median age: *total:* 35.5 years (2024 est.)
male: 34.9 years
female: 36.1 years
comparison ranking: total 96

Population growth rate: 0.74% (2024 est.)
comparison ranking: 119

Birth rate: 10.8 births/1,000 population (2024 est.)
comparison ranking: 171

Death rate: 5.3 deaths/1,000 population (2024 est.)
comparison ranking: 188

Net migration rate: 1.9 migrant(s)/1,000 population (2024 est.)
comparison ranking: 52

Population distribution: roughly half of the nation's population resides in urban areas; the capital of San Jose is the largest city and home to approximately one fifth of the population

Urbanization: *urban population:* 82.6% of total population (2023)
rate of urbanization: 1.5% annual rate of change (2020-25 est.)

Major urban areas - population: 1.462 million SAN JOSE (capital) (2023)

Sex ratio: *at birth:* 1.05 male(s)/female
0-14 years: 1.05 male(s)/female
15-64 years: 1.02 male(s)/female
65 years and over: 0.84 male(s)/female
total population: 1 male(s)/female (2024 est.)

Maternal mortality ratio: 24 deaths/100,000 live births (2023 est.)
comparison ranking: 120

Infant mortality rate: *total:* 6.7 deaths/1,000 live births (2024 est.)
male: 7 deaths/1,000 live births
female: 6.3 deaths/1,000 live births
comparison ranking: total 158

Life expectancy at birth: *total population:* 80.3 years (2024 est.)
male: 77.7 years
female: 82.9 years
comparison ranking: total population 54

Total fertility rate: 1.43 children born/woman (2024 est.)
comparison ranking: 210

Gross reproduction rate: 0.7 (2024 est.)

Drinking water source: *improved: urban:* 99.8% of population (2022 est.)
rural: 99.6% of population (2022 est.)
total: 99.8% of population (2022 est.)
unimproved: urban: 0.2% of population (2022 est.)
rural: 0.4% of population (2022 est.)
total: 0.2% of population (2022 est.)

Health expenditure: 7.6% of GDP (2021)
25.8% of national budget (2022 est.)

Physician density: 2.69 physicians/1,000 population (2022)

Hospital bed density: 1.2 beds/1,000 population (2021 est.)

Sanitation facility access: *improved: urban:* 99.2% of population (2022 est.)
rural: 97.6% of population (2022 est.)
total: 98.9% of population (2022 est.)
unimproved: urban: 0.8% of population (2022 est.)
rural: 2.4% of population (2022 est.)
total: 1.1% of population (2022 est.)

Obesity - adult prevalence rate: 25.7% (2016)
comparison ranking: 48

Alcohol consumption per capita: *total:* 3.07 liters of pure alcohol (2019 est.)
beer: 2.17 liters of pure alcohol (2019 est.)
wine: 0.15 liters of pure alcohol (2019 est.)
spirits: 0.36 liters of pure alcohol (2019 est.)
other alcohols: 0.39 liters of pure alcohol (2019 est.)
comparison ranking: total 113

Tobacco use: *total:* 8.1% (2025 est.)
male: 12.2% (2025 est.)
female: 4.1% (2025 est.)
comparison ranking: total 142

Children under the age of 5 years underweight: 2.9% (2018)
comparison ranking: 82

Currently married women (ages 15-49): 48.4% (2023 est.)

Child marriage: *women married by age 15:* 2% (2018)
women married by age 18: 17.1% (2018)

Education expenditure: 6.2% of GDP (2021 est.)
31.2% national budget (2021 est.)
comparison ranking: Education expenditure (% GDP) 29

School life expectancy (primary to tertiary education): *total:* 16 years (2019 est.)
male: 15 years (2019 est.)
female: 16 years (2019 est.)

ENVIRONMENT

Environmental issues: deforestation, largely from clearing land for cattle ranching and agriculture; soil erosion; coastal marine pollution; fisheries protection; solid waste management; air pollution

International environmental agreements: *party to:* Biodiversity, Climate Change, Climate Change-Kyoto Protocol, Climate Change-Paris Agreement, Comprehensive Nuclear Test Ban, Desertification, Endangered Species, Environmental Modification, Hazardous Wastes, Law of the Sea, Marine Dumping-London Convention, Nuclear Test Ban, Ozone Layer Protection, Tropical Timber 2006, Wetlands, Whaling
signed, but not ratified: Marine Life Conservation

Climate: tropical and subtropical; dry season (December to April); rainy season (May to November); cooler in highlands

Urbanization: *urban population:* 82.6% of total population (2023)
rate of urbanization: 1.5% annual rate of change (2020-25 est.)

Carbon dioxide emissions: 7.91 million metric tonnes of CO2 (2023 est.)
from coal and metallurgical coke: 58,000 metric tonnes of CO2 (2023 est.)
from petroleum and other liquids: 7.852 million metric tonnes of CO2 (2023 est.)
comparison ranking: total emissions 116

Particulate matter emissions: 15.1 micrograms per cubic meter (2019 est.)

Waste and recycling: *municipal solid waste generated annually:* 1.46 million tons (2024 est.)
percent of municipal solid waste recycled: 5.4% (2022 est.)

Total water withdrawal: *municipal:* 1.109 billion cubic meters (2022 est.)
industrial: 245.34 million cubic meters (2022 est.)
agricultural: 2.093 billion cubic meters (2022 est.)

Total renewable water resources: 113 billion cubic meters (2022 est.)

GOVERNMENT

Country name: *conventional long form:* Republic of Costa Rica
conventional short form: Costa Rica
local long form: República de Costa Rica
local short form: Costa Rica
etymology: the name means "rich coast" in Spanish; Christopher COLUMBUS named it in 1502, referring to the region's abundant vegetation and water

Government type: presidential republic

Capital: *name:* San José
geographic coordinates: 9 56 N, 84 05 W
time difference: UTC-6 (1 hour behind Washington, DC, during Standard Time)
etymology: Spanish settlers originally named the city Villa Nueva in 1736; it was later renamed for Saint Joseph

Administrative divisions: 7 provinces (*provincias*, singular - *provincia*); Alajuela, Cartago, Guanacaste, Heredia, Limon, Puntarenas, San Jose

Legal system: civil law system based on Spanish civil code; Supreme Court reviews legislative acts

Constitution: *history:* many previous; latest effective 8 November 1949
amendment process: proposals require the signatures of at least 10 Legislative Assembly members or petition of at least 5% of qualified voters; consideration of proposals requires two-thirds majority approval in each of three readings by the Assembly, followed by preparation of the proposal as a legislative bill and its approval by simple majority of the Assembly; passage requires at least two-thirds majority vote of the Assembly membership; a referendum is required only if approved by at least two thirds of the Assembly

International law organization participation: accepts compulsory ICJ jurisdiction; accepts ICCt jurisdiction

Citizenship: *citizenship by birth:* yes
citizenship by descent only: yes
dual citizenship recognized: yes
residency requirement for naturalization: 7 years

Suffrage: 18 years of age; universal and compulsory

Executive branch: *chief of state:* President Rodrigo CHAVES Robles (since 8 May 2022)
head of government: President Rodrigo CHAVES Robles (since 8 May 2022)
cabinet: Cabinet selected by the president
election/appointment process: president and vice presidents directly elected on the same ballot by modified majority popular vote (40% threshold) for a 4-year term (eligible for non-consecutive terms)
most recent election date: 6 February 2022, with a runoff on 3 April 2022
election results: *2022:* Rodrigo CHAVES Robles elected president in second round; percent of vote in first round - Jose Maria FIGUERES Olsen (PLN) 27.3%, Rodrigo CHAVES Robles (PPSD) 16.8%, Fabricio ALVARADO Munoz (PNR) 14.9%, Eliecer FEINZAIG Mintz (PLP) 12.4%, Lineth SABORIO Chaverri (PUSC) 12.4%, Jose Maria VILLALTA Florez-Estrada 8.7% (PFA), other 7.5%; percent of vote in second round - Rodrigo CHAVES Robles (PPSD) 52.8%, Jose Maria FIGUERES Olsen (PLN) 47.2%
2018: Carlos ALVARADO Quesada elected president in second round; percent of vote in first round - Fabricio ALVARADO Munoz (PRN) 25%; Carlos ALVARADO Quesada (PAC) 21.6%; Antonio ALVAREZ (PLN) 18.6%; Rodolfo PIZA (PUSC) 16%; Juan Diego CASTRO (PIN) 9.5%; Rodolfo HERNANDEZ (PRSC) 4.9%, other 4.4%; percent of vote in second round - Carlos ALVARADO Quesada (PAC) 60.7%; Fabricio ALVARADO Munoz (PRN) 39.3%
expected date of next election: February 2026 (a runoff, if needed, will take place in April 2026)
note: the president is both chief of state and head of government

Legislative branch: *legislature name:* Legislative Assembly (Asamblea Legislativa)
legislative structure: unicameral
number of seats: 57 (all directly elected)
electoral system: proportional representation
scope of elections: full renewal
term in office: 4 years
most recent election date: 2/6/2022
parties elected and seats per party: National Liberation Party (PLN) (19); Democratic Social Progress Party (PPSD) (10); Christian Social Unity Party (USC) (9); New Republic Party (NR) (7); Broad Front (FA) (6); Progressive Liberal Party (LP) (6)
percentage of women in chamber: 49.1%
expected date of next election: February 2026

Judicial branch: *highest court(s):* Supreme Court of Justice (consists of 22 judges organized into 3 cassation chambers each with 5 judges and the Constitutional Chamber with 7 judges)
judge selection and term of office: Supreme Court of Justice judges elected by the National Assembly for 8-year terms with renewal decided by the National Assembly
subordinate courts: appellate courts; trial courts; first instance and justice of the peace courts; Superior Electoral Tribunal

Political parties: Accessibility Without Exclusion or PASE
Broad Front (Frente Amplio) or PFA
Citizen Action Party or PAC
Costa Rican Renewal Party or PRC
Here Costa Rica Commands Party or ACRM
Liberal Progressive Party or PLP
Libertarian Movement Party or ML
National Integration Party or PIN
National Liberation Party or PLN
National Restoration Party or PRN
New Generation or PNG
New Republic Party or PNR
Social Christian Republican Party or PRSC
Social Christian Unity Party or PUSC of UNIDAD
Social Democratic Progress Party or PPSD

Diplomatic representation in the US: *chief of mission:* Ambassador Catalina CRESPO SANCHO (since 19 April 2023)
chancery: 2114 S Street NW, Washington, DC 20008
telephone: [1] (202) 499-2980
FAX: [1] (202) 265-4795
email address and website: embcr-us@rree.go.cr
https://www.embassycr.org/
consulate(s) general: Atlanta, Houston, Los Angeles, Miami, New York, Washington DC

Diplomatic representation from the US: *chief of mission:* Ambassador (vacant); Chargé d'Affaires Jennifer SAVAGE (since August 2025)
embassy: Calle 98 Via 104, Pavas, San Jose
mailing address: 3180 St. George's Place, Washington DC 20521-3180
telephone: [506] 2519-2000
FAX: [506] 2519-2305
email address and website: acssanjose@state.gov
https://cr.usembassy.gov/

International organization participation: ACS, BCIE, CACM, CD, CELAC, FAO, G-77, IADB, IAEA, IBRD, ICAO, ICC (national committees), ICCt, ICRM, IDA, IFAD, IFC, IFRCS, ILO, IMF, IMO, IMSO, Interpol, IOC, IOM, IPU, ISO, ITSO, ITU, ITUC (NGOs), LAES, LAIA (observer), MIGA, NAM (observer), OAS, OIF (observer), OPANAL,

OPCW, Pacific Alliance (observer), PCA, SICA, UN, UNCTAD, UNESCO, UNHCR, UNIDO, Union Latina, UNOOSA, UNWTO, UPU, WCO, WFTU (NGOs), WHO, WIPO, WMO, WTO

Independence: 15 September 1821 (from Spain)

National holiday: Independence Day, 15 September (1821)

Flag: *description:* five horizontal bands of blue (top), white, red (double-width), white, and blue, with the coat of arms in a white elliptical disk placed toward the left side of the red band
meaning: the blue is said to stand for the sky, opportunity, and perseverance; the white for peace, happiness, and wisdom; and the red for the blood shed for freedom, as well as Costa Ricans' generosity and vibrancy
history: Costa Rica retained the earlier blue-white-blue flag of Central America until 1848 when, in response to revolutions in Europe, it was decided to incorporate the French colors by adding a central red stripe
note: somewhat resembles the flag of North Korea; similar to the flag of Thailand, but with the blue and red colors reversed

National symbol(s): yiguirro (clay-colored thrush)

National color(s): blue, white, red

National coat of arms: the Costa Rican coat of arms highlights the country's natural beauty and history; three volcanoes, each topped with a white cloud, are surrounded with water, symbolizing the seaports of the Pacific and Atlantic Oceans; the rising sun in the background stands for the birth of a new nation, and the seven white stars for the country's provinces; the two merchant ships carrying Costa Rica's flag are a reminder of the maritime trade that shaped the country's history

National anthem(s): *title:* "Himno Nacional de Costa Rica" (National Anthem of Costa Rica)
lyrics/music: Jose Maria ZELEDON Brenes/Manuel Maria GUTIERREZ
history: adopted 1949; the music was originally written for a welcome ceremony in 1852 for the US and UK diplomatic missions; the lyrics were added in 1900

National heritage: *total World Heritage Sites:* 4 (1 cultural, 3 natural)
selected World Heritage Site locales: Guanacaste Conservation Area (n); Cocos Island National Park (n); Precolumbian Stone Spheres (c); La Amistad International Park (n)

ECONOMY

Economic overview: trade-based upper middle-income economy; green economy leader, having reversed deforestation; investing in blue economy infrastructure; declining poverty until hard impacts of COVID-19; lingering inequality and growing government debts have prompted a liquidity crisis

Real GDP (purchasing power parity): $138.371 billion (2024 est.)
$132.64 billion (2023 est.)
$126.189 billion (2022 est.)
note: data in 2021 dollars
comparison ranking: 87

Real GDP growth rate: 4.3% (2024 est.)
5.1% (2023 est.)
4.6% (2022 est.)
note: annual GDP % growth based on constant local currency
comparison ranking: 60

Real GDP per capita: $27,000 (2024 est.)
$26,000 (2023 est.)
$24,800 (2022 est.)
note: data in 2021 dollars
comparison ranking: 86

GDP (official exchange rate): $95.35 billion (2024 est.)
note: data in current dollars at official exchange rate

Inflation rate (consumer prices): -0.4% (2024 est.)
0.5% (2023 est.)
8.3% (2022 est.)
note: annual % change based on consumer prices
comparison ranking: 3

GDP - composition, by sector of origin: *agriculture:* 3.6% (2024 est.)
industry: 19.7% (2024 est.)
services: 68.8% (2024 est.)
note: figures may not total 100% due to non-allocated consumption not captured in sector-reported data
comparison rankings: agriculture 123; industry 133; services 43

GDP - composition, by end use: *household consumption:* 63.9% (2024 est.)
government consumption: 14.7% (2024 est.)
investment in fixed capital: 15.8% (2024 est.)
investment in inventories: -0.1% (2024 est.)
exports of goods and services: 38.5% (2024 est.)
imports of goods and services: -32.8% (2024 est.)
note: figures may not total 100% due to rounding or gaps in data collection

Agricultural products: sugarcane, pineapples, bananas, oil palm fruit, milk, fruits, oranges, chicken, cassava, beef (2023)
note: top ten agricultural products based on tonnage

Industries: medical equipment, food processing, textiles and clothing, construction materials, fertilizer, plastic products

Industrial production growth rate: 4.1% (2024 est.)
note: annual % change in industrial value added based on constant local currency
comparison ranking: 60

Labor force: 2.357 million (2024 est.)
note: number of people ages 15 or older who are employed or seeking work
comparison ranking: 123

Unemployment rate: 7.9% (2024 est.)
8.4% (2023 est.)
11.4% (2022 est.)
note: % of labor force seeking employment
comparison ranking: 133

Youth unemployment rate (ages 15-24): *total:* 23% (2024 est.)
male: 20.7% (2024 est.)
female: 26.2% (2024 est.)
note: % of labor force ages 15-24 seeking employment
comparison ranking: total 42

Population below poverty line: 24.4% (2023 est.)
note: % of population with income below national poverty line

Gini Index coefficient - distribution of family income: 45.8 (2024 est.)
note: index (0-100) of income distribution; higher values represent greater inequality
comparison ranking: 15

Average household expenditures: *on food:* 21.3% of household expenditures (2023 est.)
on alcohol and tobacco: 1.7% of household expenditures (2023 est.)

Household income or consumption by percentage share: *lowest 10%:* 1.7% (2024 est.)
highest 10%: 34.2% (2024 est.)
note: % share of income accruing to lowest and highest 10% of population

Remittances: 0.8% of GDP (2024 est.)
0.8% of GDP (2023 est.)
0.9% of GDP (2022 est.)
note: personal transfers and compensation between resident and non-resident individuals/households/entities

Budget: *revenues:* $26.333 billion (2023 est.)
expenditures: $25.953 billion (2023 est.)
note: central government revenues (excluding grants) and expenditures converted to US dollars at average official exchange rate for year indicated

Taxes and other revenues: 13.9% (of GDP) (2023 est.)
note: central government tax revenue as a % of GDP
comparison ranking: 100

Current account balance: -$1.291 billion (2024 est.)
-$1.239 billion (2023 est.)
-$2.272 billion (2022 est.)
note: balance of payments - net trade and primary/secondary income in current dollars
comparison ranking: 137

Exports: $36.77 billion (2024 est.)
$33.683 billion (2023 est.)
$29.392 billion (2022 est.)
note: balance of payments - exports of goods and services in current dollars
comparison ranking: 78

Exports - partners: USA 40%, Netherlands 6%, China 5%, Guatemala 4%, Belgium 3% (2023)
note: top five export partners based on percentage share of exports

Exports - commodities: medical instruments, integrated circuits, orthopedic appliances, bananas, tropical fruits (2023)
note: top five export commodities based on value in dollars

Imports: $30.459 billion (2024 est.)
$28.413 billion (2023 est.)
$27.095 billion (2022 est.)
note: balance of payments - imports of goods and services in current dollars
comparison ranking: 82

Imports - partners: USA 38%, China 15%, Mexico 6%, Brazil 3%, Guatemala 3% (2023)
note: top five import partners based on percentage share of imports

Imports - commodities: refined petroleum, plastic products, cars, medical instruments, broadcasting equipment (2023)
note: top five import commodities based on value in dollars

Reserves of foreign exchange and gold: $14.177 billion (2024 est.)
$13.225 billion (2023 est.)
$8.554 billion (2022 est.)
note: holdings of gold (year-end prices)/foreign exchange/special drawing rights in current dollars
comparison ranking: 71

Debt - external: $15.574 billion (2023 est.)
note: present value of external debt in current US dollars
comparison ranking: 40

Exchange rates: Costa Rican colones (CRC) per US dollar -

Exchange rates: 515.11 (2024 est.)
544.051 (2023 est.)
647.136 (2022 est.)
620.785 (2021 est.)
584.901 (2020 est.)

ENERGY

Electricity access: *electrification - total population:* 100% (2022 est.)

Electricity: *installed generating capacity:* 3.751 million kW (2023 est.)
consumption: 9.957 billion kWh (2023 est.)
exports: 774 million kWh (2023 est.)
imports: 54 million kWh (2023 est.)
transmission/distribution losses: 1.039 billion kWh (2023 est.)
comparison rankings: installed generating capacity 103; consumption 105; exports 72; imports 116; transmission/distribution losses 100

Electricity generation sources: *fossil fuels:* 0.1% of total installed capacity (2023 est.)
solar: 0.7% of total installed capacity (2023 est.)
wind: 12.7% of total installed capacity (2023 est.)
hydroelectricity: 72.9% of total installed capacity (2023 est.)
geothermal: 13.1% of total installed capacity (2023 est.)
biomass and waste: 0.5% of total installed capacity (2023 est.)

Coal: *consumption:* 23,000 metric tons (2023 est.)
imports: 24,000 metric tons (2023 est.)

Petroleum: *total petroleum production:* 400 bbl/day (2023 est.)
refined petroleum consumption: 60,000 bbl/day (2023 est.)

Energy consumption per capita: 30.725 million Btu/person (2023 est.)
comparison ranking: 116

COMMUNICATIONS

Telephones - fixed lines: *total subscriptions:* 678,000 (2023 est.)
subscriptions per 100 inhabitants: 13 (2023 est.)
comparison ranking: total subscriptions 81

Telephones - mobile cellular: *total subscriptions:* 7.44 million (2023 est.)
subscriptions per 100 inhabitants: 152 (2022 est.)
comparison ranking: total subscriptions 109

Broadcast media: over two dozen privately owned TV stations and 1 publicly owned TV station; cable network services are widely available; more than 100 privately owned radio stations and a public radio network (2022)

Internet country code: .cr

Internet users: *percent of population:* 85% (2023 est.)

Broadband - fixed subscriptions: *total:* 1.15 million (2023 est.)
subscriptions per 100 inhabitants: 23 (2023 est.)
comparison ranking: total 75

TRANSPORTATION

Civil aircraft registration country code prefix: TI

Airports: 132 (2025)
comparison ranking: 39

Heliports: 8 (2025)
comparison ranking: 79

Railways: *total:* 278 km (2014)
narrow gauge: 278 km (2014) 1.067-m gauge
note: the entire rail network fell into disrepair and out of use at the end of the 20th century; since 2005, certain sections of rail have been rehabilitated

Merchant marine: *total:* 11 (2023)
by type: other 11
comparison ranking: total 157

Ports: *total ports:* 6 (2024)
large: 0
medium: 0
small: 1
very small: 5
ports with oil terminals: 4
key ports: Golfito, Puerto Caldera, Puerto Limon, Puerto Moin, Puerto Quepos, Puntarenas

MILITARY AND SECURITY

Military and security forces: Ministry of Public Security (Ministerio de Seguridad Pública de Costa Rica): National Police (Fuerza Pública), Air Surveillance Service (Servicio de Vigilancia Aérea), National Coast Guard Service (Servicio Nacional de Guardacostas), Drug Control Police (Policía Control de Drogas), Border Police (Policia de Fronteras), Professional Migration Police (Policía Profesional de Migración)

Ministry of Presidency: Directorate of Intelligence and Security (DIS), Special Intervention Unit (UEI) (2025)
note: Costa Rica's armed forces were constitutionally abolished in 1949

Military expenditures: 0.6% of GDP (2024 est.)
0.6% of GDP (2023 est.)
0.6% of GDP (2022 est.)
0.7% of GDP (2021 est.)
0.7% of GDP (2020 est.)

Military and security service personnel strengths: approximately 10-15,000 Ministry of Public Security personnel (2025)

Military equipment inventories and acquisitions: the National Police are lightly armed although small special units are trained and equipped for tactical operations; the US has provided equipment and support to forces such the Coast Guard, including secondhand US vessels and aircraft (2024)

Military - note: Costa Rica relies on specialized paramilitary units within the Ministry of Public Security (MPS) for internal security missions and countering transnational threats such as narcotics smuggling and organized crime, as well as for participating in regional security operations and exercises; MPS forces have received advisory and training support from the US (2025)

SPACE

Space agency/agencies: Costa Rican Space Agency (ACE; established by legislation in 2021); ACE is a non-state, public entity subject to guidelines issued by the Ministry of Science, Technology, and Telecommunications (2025)

Space program overview: has a small, recently established program focused on using space to develop the country's economy and industry, including acquiring and utilizing satellites; has built a remote sensing (RS) cube satellite; has relations with the space agencies and commercial space industries of the US, the European Space Agency, and the Latin American and Caribbean Space Agency (2025)
note: further details about the key activities, programs, and milestones of the country's space program, as well as government spending estimates on the space sector, appear in the Space Programs reference guide

TRANSNATIONAL ISSUES

Refugees and internally displaced persons: *refugees:* 249,521 (2024 est.)

IDPs: 58 (2024 est.)
stateless persons: 345 (2024 est.)

Illicit drugs: USG identification: major illicit drug-producing and/or drug-transit country
major precursor-chemical producer (2025)

COTE D'IVOIRE

INTRODUCTION

Background: Various small kingdoms ruled the area of Cote d'Ivoire between the 15th and 19th centuries, when European explorers arrived and then began to expand their presence. In 1844, France established a protectorate. During this period, many of these kingdoms and tribes fought to maintain their cultural identities – some well into the 20th century. For example, the Sanwi kingdom – originally founded in the 17th century – tried to break away from Cote d'Ivoire and establish an independent state in 1969. Cote d'Ivoire achieved independence from France in 1960 but has maintained close ties. Foreign investment and the export and production of cocoa drove economic growth that led Cote d'Ivoire to become one of the most prosperous states in West Africa. Then in 1999, a military coup overthrew the government, and a year later, junta leader Robert GUEI held rigged elections and declared himself the winner. Popular protests forced him to step aside, and Laurent GBAGBO was elected. Ivoirian dissidents and members of the military launched a failed coup in 2002 that developed into a civil war. In 2003, a cease-fire resulted in rebels holding the north, the government holding the south, and peacekeeping forces occupying a buffer zone in the middle. In 2007, President GBAGBO and former rebel leader Guillaume SORO signed an agreement in which SORO joined GBAGBO's government as prime minister. The two agreed to reunite the country by dismantling the buffer zone, integrating rebel forces into the national armed forces, and holding elections.

In 2010, Alassane Dramane OUATTARA won the presidential election, but GBAGBO refused to hand over power, resulting in five months of violent

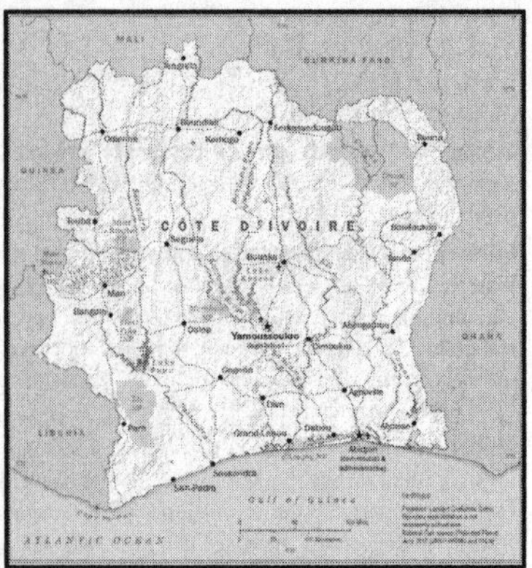

conflict. Armed OUATTARA supporters and UN and French troops eventually forced GBAGBO to step down in 2011. OUATTARA won a second term in 2015 and a controversial third term in 2020 – despite the two-term limit in the Ivoirian constitution – in an election boycotted by the opposition. Through political compromise with OUATTARA, the opposition participated peacefully in 2021 legislative elections and won a substantial minority of seats. Also in 2021, the International Criminal Court in The Hague ruled on a final acquittal for GBAGBO, who was on trial for crimes against humanity, paving the way for GBAGBO's return to Abidjan the same year. GBAGBO has publicly met with OUATTARA since his return as a demonstration of political reconciliation.

GEOGRAPHY

Location: Western Africa, bordering the North Atlantic Ocean, between Ghana and Liberia

Geographic coordinates: 8 00 N, 5 00 W

Map references: Africa

Area: *total:* 322,463 sq km
land: 318,003 sq km
water: 4,460 sq km
comparison ranking: total 70

Area - comparative: slightly larger than New Mexico

Land boundaries: *total:* 3,458 km
border countries (5): Burkina Faso 545 km; Ghana 720 km; Guinea 816 km; Liberia 778 km; Mali 599 km
Coastline 515 km

Maritime claims: *territorial sea:* 12 nm
exclusive economic zone: 200 nm
continental shelf: 200 nm

Climate: tropical along coast, semiarid in far north; three seasons - warm and dry (November to March), hot and dry (March to May), hot and wet (June to October)

Terrain: mostly flat to undulating plains; mountains in northwest

Elevation: *highest point:* Monts Nimba 1,752 m
lowest point: Gulf of Guinea 0 m
mean elevation: 250 m

Natural resources: petroleum, natural gas, diamonds, manganese, iron ore, cobalt, bauxite, copper, gold, nickel, tantalum, silica sand, clay, cocoa beans, coffee, palm oil, hydropower

Land use: *agricultural land:* 84.2% (2022 est.)
arable land: 13.5% (2022 est.)
permanent crops: 29.1% (2022 est.)
permanent pasture: 41.5% (2022 est.)
forest: 8.2% (2022 est.)
other: 7.6% (2022 est.)

Irrigated land: 730 sq km (2012)

Major lakes (area sq km): *salt water lake(s):* Lagune Aby - 780 sq km

Major watersheds (area sq km): Atlantic Ocean drainage: Niger (2,261,741 sq km), Volta (410,991 sq km)

Population distribution: the population is primarily located in the forested south, with the highest concentration of people residing in and around the cities on the Atlantic coast; most of the northern savanna remains sparsely populated, with higher concentrations located along transportation corridors, as shown in this population distribution map

Natural hazards: coast has heavy surf and no natural harbors; during the rainy season torrential flooding is possible

Geography - note: most of the inhabitants live along the sandy coastal region; apart from the capital area, the forested interior is sparsely populated

PEOPLE AND SOCIETY

Population: *total:* 29,981,758 (2024 est.)
male: 15,040,032
female: 14,941,726
comparison rankings: total 52; male 52; female 52

Nationality: *noun:* Ivoirian(s)
adjective: Ivoirian

Ethnic groups: Akan 38%, Voltaique or Gur 22%, Northern Mande 22%, Kru 9.1%, Southern Mande 8.6%, other 0.3% (2021 est.)

Languages: French (official), 60 native dialects of which Dioula is the most widely spoken
major-language sample(s):

Religions: Muslim 42.9%, Catholic 17.2%, Evangelical 11.8%, Methodist 1.7%, other Christian 3.2%, animist 3.6%, other religion 0.5%, none 19.1% (2014 est.)
note: the majority of foreign migrant workers are Muslim (72.7%) and Christian (17.7%)

Age structure: *0-14 years:* 36.1% (male 5,437,108/female 5,390,782)
15-64 years: 60.9% (male 9,200,957/female 9,060,748)
65 years and over: 3% (2024 est.) (male 401,967/female 490,196)

Dependency ratios: *total dependency ratio:* 73.6 (2024 est.)
youth dependency ratio: 68.8 (2024 est.)
elderly dependency ratio: 4.7 (2024 est.)
potential support ratio: 21.1 (2024 est.)

Median age: *total:* 21.2 years (2024 est.)
male: 21.2 years
female: 21.2 years
comparison ranking: total 195

Population growth rate: 2.13% (2024 est.)
comparison ranking: 36

Birth rate: 27.5 births/1,000 population (2024 est.)
comparison ranking: 35

Death rate: 7.3 deaths/1,000 population (2024 est.)
comparison ranking: 109

Net migration rate: 1.1 migrant(s)/1,000 population (2024 est.)
comparison ranking: 62

Population distribution: the population is primarily located in the forested south, with the highest concentration of people residing in and around the cities on the Atlantic coast; most of the northern savanna remains sparsely populated, with higher concentrations located along transportation corridors, as shown in this population distribution map

Urbanization: *urban population:* 53.1% of total population (2023)
rate of urbanization: 3.38% annual rate of change (2020-25 est.)

Major urban areas - population: 231,000 YAMOUSSOUKRO (capital) (2018), 5.686 million ABIDJAN (seat of government) (2023)

Sex ratio: *at birth:* 1.03 male(s)/female
0-14 years: 1.01 male(s)/female
15-64 years: 1.02 male(s)/female
65 years and over: 0.82 male(s)/female
total population: 1.01 male(s)/female (2024 est.)

Mother's mean age at first birth: 19.6 years (2011/12 est.)
note: data represents median age at first birth among women 20-49

Maternal mortality ratio: 359 deaths/100,000 live births (2023 est.)
comparison ranking: 18

Infant mortality rate: *total:* 52.5 deaths/1,000 live births (2024 est.)
male: 59.5 deaths/1,000 live births
female: 45.2 deaths/1,000 live births
comparison ranking: total 17

Life expectancy at birth: *total population:* 63.2 years (2024 est.)
male: 60.9 years
female: 65.4 years
comparison ranking: total population 212

Total fertility rate: 3.4 children born/woman (2024 est.)
comparison ranking: 39

Gross reproduction rate: 1.67 (2024 est.)

Drinking water source: *improved: urban:* 86.2% of population (2022 est.)
rural: 58% of population (2022 est.)
total: 72.9% of population (2022 est.)
unimproved: urban: 13.8% of population (2022 est.)
rural: 42% of population (2022 est.)
total: 27.1% of population (2022 est.)

Health expenditure: 3.1% of GDP (2021)
6.2% of national budget (2022 est.)

Physician density: 0.17 physicians/1,000 population (2023)

Sanitation facility access: *improved: urban:* 84.6% of population (2022 est.)
rural: 41.5% of population (2022 est.)
total: 64.2% of population (2022 est.)
unimproved: urban: 15.4% of population (2022 est.)
rural: 58.5% of population (2022 est.)
total: 35.8% of population (2022 est.)

Obesity - adult prevalence rate: 10.3% (2016)
comparison ranking: 139

Alcohol consumption per capita: *total:* 1.7 liters of pure alcohol (2019 est.)
beer: 1.13 liters of pure alcohol (2019 est.)
wine: 0.33 liters of pure alcohol (2019 est.)
spirits: 0.2 liters of pure alcohol (2019 est.)
other alcohols: 0.04 liters of pure alcohol (2019 est.)
comparison ranking: total 133

Tobacco use: *total:* 7.8% (2025 est.)

male: 14.9% (2025 est.)
female: 0.6% (2025 est.)
comparison ranking: total 144

Children under the age of 5 years underweight: 14% (2021)
comparison ranking: 37

Currently married women (ages 15-49): 60.3% (2023 est.)

Child marriage: *women married by age 15:* 7.4% (2021)
women married by age 18: 25.8% (2021)
men married by age 18: 1.9% (2021)

Education expenditure: 3.4% of GDP (2023 est.)
15.9% national budget (2023 est.)
comparison ranking: Education expenditure (% GDP) 133

Literacy: *total population:* 50% (2021 est.)
male: 60.2% (2021 est.)
female: 40.3% (2021 est.)

School life expectancy (primary to tertiary education): *total:* 11 years (2023 est.)
male: 11 years (2023 est.)
female: 11 years (2023 est.)

ENVIRONMENT

Environmental issues: deforestation; water pollution from sewage and from industrial, mining, and agricultural effluents

International environmental agreements: *party to:* Biodiversity, Climate Change, Climate Change-Kyoto Protocol, Climate Change-Paris Agreement, Comprehensive Nuclear Test Ban, Desertification, Endangered Species, Hazardous Wastes, Law of the Sea, Marine Dumping-London Convention, Nuclear Test Ban, Ozone Layer Protection, Ship Pollution, Tropical Timber 2006, Wetlands, Whaling
signed, but not ratified: none of the selected agreements

Climate: tropical along coast, semiarid in far north; three seasons - warm and dry (November to March), hot and dry (March to May), hot and wet (June to October)

Urbanization: *urban population:* 53.1% of total population (2023)
rate of urbanization: 3.38% annual rate of change (2020-25 est.)

Carbon dioxide emissions: 16.28 million metric tonnes of CO2 (2023 est.)
from petroleum and other liquids: 11.641 million metric tonnes of CO2 (2023 est.)
from consumed natural gas: 4.639 million metric tonnes of CO2 (2023 est.)
comparison ranking: total emissions 98

Particulate matter emissions: 36 micrograms per cubic meter (2019 est.)

Methane emissions: *energy:* 187.7 kt (2022-2024 est.)
agriculture: 192 kt (2019-2021 est.)
waste: 199.9 kt (2019-2021 est.)
other: 28.9 kt (2019-2021 est.)

Waste and recycling: *municipal solid waste generated annually:* 4.441 million tons (2024 est.)
percent of municipal solid waste recycled: 13.3% (2022 est.)

Total water withdrawal: *municipal:* 320 million cubic meters (2022 est.)
industrial: 242 million cubic meters (2022 est.)
agricultural: 600 million cubic meters (2022 est.)

Total renewable water resources: 84.14 billion cubic meters (2022 est.)

GOVERNMENT

Country name: *conventional long form:* Republic of Côte d'Ivoire
conventional short form: Côte d'Ivoire
local long form: République de Côte d'Ivoire
local short form: Cote d'Ivoire
former: Ivory Coast
etymology: name, which means "Ivory Coast" in French, reflects the ivory trade in the region from the 15th to 17th centuries; the French version of the name has been used internationally since 1986, at the country's request
note: pronounced coat-div-whar

Government type: presidential republic

Capital: *name:* Yamoussoukro (legislative capital), Abidjan (administrative and economic capital); note - the US Embassy is in Abidjan
geographic coordinates: 6 49 N, 5 16 W
time difference: UTC 0 (5 hours ahead of Washington, DC, during Standard Time)
etymology: formerly a village named N'Gokro, Yamoussoukro is named after Queen YAMOUSSOU, who ruled during the early 20th century; Abidjan's name may have come from a misunderstanding when a French explorer asked a group of women the name of the village – thinking it was a question about what they were doing, they replied "t'chan m'bi djan," which in the Ebrie language means "I return from cutting leaves," so the explorer recorded the name of the locale as Abidjan

Administrative divisions: 12 districts and 2 autonomous districts*; Abidjan*, Bas-Sassandra, Comoe, Denguele, Goh-Djiboua, Lacs, Lagunes, Montagnes, Sassandra-Marahoue, Savanes, Vallée du Bandama, Woroba, Yamoussoukro*, Zanzan

Legal system: civil law system based on the French civil code; Constitutional Chamber of the Supreme Court reviews legislation

Constitution: *history:* previous 1960, 2000; latest draft completed 24 September 2016, approved by the National Assembly 11 October 2016, approved by referendum 30 October 2016, promulgated 8 November 2016
amendment process: proposed by the president of the republic or by Parliament; consideration of drafts or proposals requires an absolute majority vote by the parliamentary membership; passage of amendments affecting presidential elections, presidential term of office and vacancies, and amendment procedures requires approval by absolute majority in a referendum; passage of other proposals by the president requires at least four-fifths majority vote by Parliament; constitutional articles on the sovereignty of the state and its republican and secular form of government cannot be amended

International law organization participation: accepts compulsory ICJ jurisdiction with reservations; accepts ICCt jurisdiction

Citizenship: *citizenship by birth:* no
citizenship by descent only: at least one parent must be a citizen of Cote d'Ivoire
dual citizenship recognized: no
residency requirement for naturalization: 5 years

Suffrage: 18 years of age; universal

Executive branch: *chief of state:* President Alassane Dramane OUATTARA (since 4 December 2010)
head of government: Prime Minister Robert BREUGRE MAMBE (since 17 October 2023)
cabinet: Council of Ministers appointed by the president
election/appointment process: president directly elected by absolute-majority popular vote in 2 rounds, if needed, for a single renewable 5-year term; vice president elected on same ballot as president; prime minister appointed by the president
most recent election date: 31 October 2020
election results: *2020:* Alassane OUATTARA reelected president; percent of vote - Alassane OUATTARA (RDR) 94.3%, Kouadio Konan BERTIN (PDCI-RDA) 2.0%, other 3.7%
2015: Alassane OUATTARA reelected president; percent of vote - Alassane OUATTARA (RDR) 83.7%, Pascal Affi N'GUESSAN (FPI) 9.3%, Konan Bertin KOUADIO (independent) 3.9%, other 3.1%
expected date of next election: October 2025
note: because President OUATTARA promulgated the new constitution in 2016, he has claimed that the clock is reset on term limits, allowing him to run for up to two additional terms

Legislative branch: *legislature name:* Parliament (Parlement)
legislative structure: bicameral

Legislative branch - lower chamber: *chamber name:* National Assembly (Assemblée nationale)
number of seats: 255 (all directly elected)
electoral system: plurality/majority
scope of elections: full renewal
term in office: 5 years
most recent election date: 3/6/2021 to 6/12/2021
parties elected and seats per party: Rally of Houphouetists for Democracy and Peace (RHDP) (139); Democratic Party of Côte d'Ivoire-African Democratic Rally (PDCI-RDA)-Together for Democracy and Sovereignty (EDS) (49); Democratic Party of Côte d'Ivoire-African Democratic Rally (PDCI-RDA) (23); Independents (26); Other (18)
percentage of women in chamber: 13.4%
expected date of next election: December 2025

Legislative branch - upper chamber: *chamber name:* Senate (Sénat)
number of seats: 99 (66 indirectly elected; 33 appointed)
scope of elections: full renewal
term in office: 5 years
most recent election date: 9/16/2023
percentage of women in chamber: 24.5%
expected date of next election: September 2028

Judicial branch: *highest court(s):* Supreme Court or Cour Supreme (organized into Judicial, Audit, Constitutional, and Administrative Chambers; consists of the court president, 3 vice presidents for the Judicial, Audit, and Administrative chambers, and 9 associate justices or magistrates)
judge selection and term of office: judges nominated by the Superior Council of the Magistrature, a 7-member body consisting of the national president (chairman), 3 "bench" judges, and 3 public prosecutors; judges appointed for life
subordinate courts: Courts of Appeal (organized into civil, criminal, and social chambers); first instance courts; peace courts

Political parties: African Peoples' Party-Cote d'Ivoire or PPA-CI
Democratic Party of Cote d'Ivoire or PDCI
Ivorian Popular Front or FPI
Liberty and Democracy for the Republic or LIDER
Movement of the Future Forces or MFA

Pan-African Congress for People's Justice and Equality or COJEP
Rally of Houphouetists for Democracy and Peace or RHDP
Rally of the Republicans or RDR
Together for Democracy and Sovereignty or EDS
Together to Build (UDPCI, FPI,and allies)
Union for Cote d'Ivoire or UPCI
Union for Democracy and Peace in Cote d'Ivoire or UDPCI

Diplomatic representation in the US: *chief of mission:* Ambassador Ibrahima TOURE (since 13 January 2022)
chancery: 2424 Massachusetts Avenue NW, Washington, DC 20008
telephone: [1] (202) 797-0300

FAX: [1] (202) 204-3967
email address and website: info@ambacidc.org
Ambassade de Cote D'ivoire aux USA (ambaciusa.org)

Diplomatic representation from the US: *chief of mission:* Ambassador Jessica Davis BA (since 2 March 2023)
embassy: B.P. 730 Abidjan Cidex 03
mailing address: 2010 Abidjan Place, Washington DC 20521-2010
telephone: [225] 27-22-49-40-00

FAX: [225] 27-22-49-43-23
email address and website: AbjAmCit@state.gov
https://ci.usembassy.gov/

International organization participation: ACP, AfDB, AU, ECOWAS, EITI (compliant country), Entente, FAO, FZ, G-24, G-77, IAEA, IBRD, ICAO, ICC, ICCt, ICRM, IDA, IDB, IFAD, IFC, IFRCS, ILO, IMF, IMO, Interpol, IOC, IOM, IPU, ISO, ITSO, ITU, ITUC (NGOs), MIGA, MINUSCA, MONUSCO, NAM, OIC, OIF, OPCW, UN, UNCTAD, UNESCO, UNHCR, UNHRC, UNIDO, UNMISS, Union Latina, UNWTO, UPU, WADB (regional), WAEMU, WCO, WFTU (NGOs), WHO, WIPO, WMO, WTO

Independence: 7 August 1960 (from France)

National holiday: Independence Day, 7 August (1960)

Flag: *description:* three equal vertical bands of orange (left side), white, and green
meaning: orange stands for the savannah and fertility, white for peace and unity, green for the forests of the south and the hope for a bright future; design based on France's flag
note: similar to the flag of Ireland, which is wider and has the colors reversed – green (left side), white, and orange; also similar to the flag of Italy, which is green (left side), white, and red

National symbol(s): elephant

National color(s): orange, white, green

National anthem(s): *title:* "L'Abidjanaise" (Song of Abidjan)
lyrics/music: Mathieu EKRA, Joachim BONY, and Pierre Marie COTY/Pierre Marie COTY and Pierre Michel PANGO
history: adopted 1960; named after the former capital city of Abidjan

National heritage: *total World Heritage Sites:* 5 (2 cultural, 3 natural)
selected World Heritage Site locales: Comoé National Park (n); Historic Grand-Bassam (c); Mount Nimba Strict Nature Reserve (n); Sudanese-style Mosques (c); Taï National Park (n)

ECONOMY

Economic overview: one of West Africa's most influential, stable, and rapidly developing economies; poverty declines in urban but increases in rural areas; strong construction sector and increasingly diverse economic portfolio; increasing but manageable public debt; large labor force in agriculture

Real GDP (purchasing power parity): $215.018 billion (2024 est.)
$202.943 billion (2023 est.)
$190.645 billion (2022 est.)
note: data in 2021 dollars
comparison ranking: 76

Real GDP growth rate: 6% (2024 est.)
6.5% (2023 est.)
6.4% (2022 est.)
note: annual GDP % growth based on constant local currency
comparison ranking: 23

Real GDP per capita: $6,700 (2024 est.)
$6,500 (2023 est.)
$6,300 (2022 est.)
note: data in 2021 dollars
comparison ranking: 162

GDP (official exchange rate): $86.538 billion (2024 est.)
note: data in current dollars at official exchange rate

Inflation rate (consumer prices): 3.5% (2024 est.)
4.4% (2023 est.)
5.3% (2022 est.)
note: annual % change based on consumer prices
comparison ranking: 111

GDP - composition, by sector of origin: *agriculture:* 17.9% (2024 est.)
industry: 22.1% (2024 est.)
services: 53.9% (2024 est.)
note: figures may not total 100% due to non-allocated consumption not captured in sector-reported data
comparison rankings: agriculture 41; industry 119; services 126

GDP - composition, by end use: *household consumption:* 66% (2024 est.)
government consumption: 9% (2024 est.)
investment in fixed capital: 24.5% (2024 est.)
investment in inventories: 0% (2024 est.)
exports of goods and services: 27.6% (2024 est.)
imports of goods and services: -27.1% (2024 est.)
note: figures may not total 100% due to rounding or gaps in data collection

Agricultural products: yams, cassava, oil palm fruit, cocoa beans, sugarcane, plantains, rice, rubber, maize, cashews (2023)
note: top ten agricultural products based on tonnage

Industries: foodstuffs, beverages; wood products, oil refining, gold mining, truck and bus assembly, textiles, fertilizer, building materials, electricity

Industrial production growth rate: 2.8% (2024 est.)
note: annual % change in industrial value added based on constant local currency
comparison ranking: 86

Labor force: 12.595 million (2024 est.)
note: number of people ages 15 or older who are employed or seeking work
comparison ranking: 47

Unemployment rate: 2.3% (2024 est.)
2.3% (2023 est.)
2.4% (2022 est.)
note: % of labor force seeking employment
comparison ranking: 21

Youth unemployment rate (ages 15-24): *total:* 3.9% (2024 est.)
male: 3.5% (2024 est.)
female: 4.4% (2024 est.)
note: % of labor force ages 15-24 seeking employment
comparison ranking: total 172

Population below poverty line: 37.5% (2021 est.)
note: % of population with income below national poverty line

Gini Index coefficient - distribution of family income: 35.3 (2021 est.)
note: index (0-100) of income distribution; higher values represent greater inequality
comparison ranking: 72

Average household expenditures: *on food:* 37.7% of household expenditures (2023 est.)
on alcohol and tobacco: 3.2% of household expenditures (2023 est.)

Household income or consumption by percentage share: *lowest 10%:* 3.1% (2021 est.)
highest 10%: 27.8% (2021 est.)
note: % share of income accruing to lowest and highest 10% of population

Remittances: 1.3% of GDP (2023 est.)
1.5% of GDP (2022 est.)
0.6% of GDP (2021 est.)
note: personal transfers and compensation between resident and non-resident individuals/households/entities

Budget: *revenues:* $12.351 billion (2023 est.)
expenditures: $16.03 billion (2023 est.)
note: central government revenues (excluding grants) and expenditures converted to US dollars at average official exchange rate for year indicated

Taxes and other revenues: 13.2% (of GDP) (2023 est.)
note: central government tax revenue as a % of GDP
comparison ranking: 104

Current account balance: -$5.394 billion (2022 est.)
-$2.874 billion (2021 est.)
-$1.974 billion (2020 est.)
note: balance of payments - net trade and primary/secondary income in current dollars
comparison ranking: 173

Exports: $17.211 billion (2022 est.)
$16.23 billion (2021 est.)
$13.232 billion (2020 est.)
note: balance of payments - exports of goods and services in current dollars
comparison ranking: 97

Exports - partners: Switzerland 17%, Netherlands 9%, Mali 7%, USA 5%, Malaysia 4% (2023)
note: top five export partners based on percentage share of exports

Exports - commodities: gold, cocoa beans, rubber, refined petroleum, coconuts/brazil nuts/cashews (2023)
note: top five export commodities based on value in dollars

Imports: $19.948 billion (2022 est.)
$16.191 billion (2021 est.)
$12.66 billion (2020 est.)

note: balance of payments - imports of goods and services in current dollars
comparison ranking: 95

Imports - partners: China 16%, Nigeria 12%, France 6%, India 5%, USA 4% (2023)
note: top five import partners based on percentage share of imports

Imports - commodities: crude petroleum, ships, refined petroleum, fish, rice (2023)
note: top five import commodities based on value in dollars

Debt - external: $26.576 billion (2023 est.)
note: present value of external debt in current US dollars
comparison ranking: 28

Exchange rates: Communaute Financiere Africaine francs (XOF) per US dollar -

Exchange rates: 606.345 (2024 est.)
606.57 (2023 est.)
623.76 (2022 est.)
554.531 (2021 est.)
575.586 (2020 est.)

ENERGY

Electricity access: *electrification - total population:* 70.4% (2022 est.)
electrification - urban areas: 95%
electrification - rural areas: 45.3%

Electricity: *installed generating capacity:* 2.315 million kW (2023 est.)
consumption: 8.746 billion kWh (2023 est.)
exports: 971 million kWh (2023 est.)
imports: 222.79 million kWh (2023 est.)
transmission/distribution losses: 1.638 billion kWh (2023 est.)
comparison rankings: installed generating capacity 117; consumption 111; exports 70; imports 105; transmission/distribution losses 116

Electricity generation sources: *fossil fuels:* 68.9% of total installed capacity (2023 est.)
solar: 0.2% of total installed capacity (2023 est.)
hydroelectricity: 30.1% of total installed capacity (2023 est.)
biomass and waste: 0.8% of total installed capacity (2023 est.)

Petroleum: *total petroleum production:* 29,000 bbl/day (2023 est.)
refined petroleum consumption: 87,000 bbl/day (2023 est.)
crude oil estimated reserves: 100 million barrels (2021 est.)

Natural gas: *production:* 2.474 billion cubic meters (2023 est.)
consumption: 2.474 billion cubic meters (2023 est.)
proven reserves: 28.317 billion cubic meters (2021 est.)

Energy consumption per capita: 8.489 million Btu/person (2023 est.)
comparison ranking: 155

COMMUNICATIONS

Telephones - fixed lines: *total subscriptions:* 244,000 (2023 est.)
subscriptions per 100 inhabitants: 1 (2023 est.) less than 1
comparison ranking: total subscriptions 114

Telephones - mobile cellular: *total subscriptions:* 53.6 million (2023 est.)
subscriptions per 100 inhabitants: 174 (2022 est.)
comparison ranking: total subscriptions 32

Broadcast media: state-controlled Radiodiffusion Télévision Ivoirienne (RTI) is made up of 2 radio stations (Radio Cote d'Ivoire and Fréquence2) and 2 TV stations (RTI1 and RTI2) with nationwide coverage, broadcasting mainly in French; 178 proximity radio stations, 16 religious radio stations, 5 commercial radio stations, and 5 international radio stations; government now runs radio station UNOCIFM, previously owned by the UN Operation in Cote d'Ivoire; in 2016, 4 media companies were granted licenses: Live TV, Optimum Media Cote d'Ivoire, the Audiovisual Company of Cote d'Ivoire (Sedaci), and Sorano-CI (2019)

Internet country code: .ci

Internet users: *percent of population:* 41% (2023 est.)

Broadband - fixed subscriptions: *total:* 425,000 (2023 est.)
subscriptions per 100 inhabitants: 1 (2023 est.)
comparison ranking: total 105

TRANSPORTATION

Civil aircraft registration country code prefix: TU

Airports: 29 (2025)
comparison ranking: 122

Heliports: 1 (2025)
comparison ranking: 146

Railways: *total:* 660 km (2008)
narrow gauge: 660 km (2008) 1.000-m gauge
note: an additional 622 km of this railroad extends into Burkina Faso

Merchant marine: *total:* 25 (2023)
by type: oil tanker 2, other 23
comparison ranking: total 140

Ports: *total ports:* 5 (2024)
large: 1
medium: 0
small: 0
very small: 4
ports with oil terminals: 5
key ports: Abidjan, Baobab Marine Terminal, Espoir Marine Terminal, Port Bouet, San Pedro

MILITARY AND SECURITY

Military and security forces: Armed Forces of Cote d'Ivoire (Forces Armees de Cote d'Ivoire, FACI; aka Republican Forces of Ivory Coast, FRCI): Army, National Navy, Air Force, Special Forces; National Gendarmerie

Ministry of Security and Civil Protection: National Police (2025)
note: the National Gendarmerie is a paramilitary force under the Ministry of Defense that is responsible for ensuring public safety, maintaining order, enforcing laws, and protecting institutions, people, and property; it is organized into mobile and territorial components; the Mobile Gendarmerie is responsible for maintaining and restoring order and is considered the backbone of the country's domestic security; the Territorial Gendarmerie is responsible for the administrative, judicial, and military police; the Gendarmerie also has separate specialized units for security, intervention (counterterrorism, hostage rescue, etc), VIP protection, and surveillance

Military expenditures: 0.8% of GDP (2024 est.)
0.9% of GDP (2023 est.)
0.9% of GDP (2022 est.)
1.1% of GDP (2021 est.)
1.1% of GDP (2020 est.)

Military and security service personnel strengths: approximately 25-30,000 active FACI, including Gendarmerie personnel (2025)

Military equipment inventories and acquisitions: the inventory of the FACI consists mostly of older or second-hand equipment, typically of French or Soviet-era origin; Cote d'Ivoire was under a partial UN arms embargo from 2004 to 2016; in recent years it has received some new and secondhand equipment from a variety of suppliers, including Bulgaria, China, France, South Africa, and Turkey (2024)

Military service age and obligation: 18-26 years of age for compulsory and voluntary military service for men and women; conscription is reportedly not enforced (2023)

Military deployments: 180 Central African Republic (MINUSCA) (2024)

Military - note: the military (FACI) is responsible for external defense but also has a considerable internal role supporting the National Gendarmerie and other internal security forces; key areas of focus for the FACI are the country's porous international borders and the threat posed by Islamic militants associated with the al-Qa'ida in the Islamic Maghreb (AQIM) terrorist group operating across the border in Burkina Faso and Mali; AQIM militants conducted attacks in the country in 2016 and 2020; Côte d'Ivoire since 2016 has stepped up border security and completed building a joint counter-terrorism training center with France near Abidjan in 2020; Cote d'Ivoire has long maintained a close security relationship with France
the FACI has mutinied several times since the late 1990s, most recently in 2017, and has had a large role in the country's political turmoil; it was established in 1960 from home defense units the French colonial government began standing up in 1950 (2025)

SPACE

Space agency/agencies: National Office for Technical Studies and Development (Bureau d'Études Techniques et de Développement or BNETD) (2025)
note: in mid-2025, Côte d'Ivoire announced that it would establish the Space Agency of Côte d'Ivoire (ASCI) in 2026 under the Minister of Higher Education and Scientific Research

Space program overview: has a small, nascent program with a focus on satellite technology and geospatial information systems for effective national planning, resource management, addressing environmental challenges, supporting the agricultural sector and scientific research, promoting domestic expertise, and national security issues (2025)
note: further details about the key activities, programs, and milestones of the country's space program, as well as government spending estimates on the space sector, appear in the Space Programs reference guide

TERRORISM

Terrorist group(s): Terrorist group(s): al-Qa'ida in the Islamic Maghreb (AQIM); Jama'at Nusrat al Islam wal Muslimeen (JNIM)
note: details about the history, aims, leadership, organization, areas of operation, tactics, targets, weapons, size, and sources of support of the group(s) appear(s) in Appendix T

TRANSNATIONAL ISSUES

Refugees and internally displaced persons: *refugees:* 69,176 (2024 est.)
stateless persons: 930,978 (2024 est.)

CROATIA

INTRODUCTION

Background: The lands that today comprise Croatia were part of the Austro-Hungarian Empire until the end of World War I. In 1918, the Croats, Serbs, and Slovenes formed a kingdom known after 1929 as Yugoslavia. Following World War II, Yugoslavia became a federal independent communist state consisting of six socialist republics, including Croatia, under the strong hand of Josip Broz, aka TITO. Although Croatia declared its independence from Yugoslavia in 1991, it took four years of sporadic, but often bitter, fighting before Yugoslav forces were cleared from Croatian lands, along with a majority of Croatia's ethnic Serb population. Under UN supervision, the last Serb-held enclave in eastern Slavonia was returned to Croatia in 1998. The country joined NATO in 2009 and the EU in 2013. In January 2023, Croatia further integrated into the EU by joining the Eurozone and the Schengen Area.

GEOGRAPHY

Location: Southeastern Europe, bordering the Adriatic Sea, between Bosnia and Herzegovina and Slovenia

Geographic coordinates: 45 10 N, 15 30 E

Map references: Europe

Area: *total:* 56,594 sq km
land: 55,974 sq km
water: 620 sq km
comparison ranking: total 127

Area - comparative: slightly smaller than West Virginia

Land boundaries: *total:* 2,237 km
border countries (5): Bosnia and Herzegovina 956 km; Hungary 348 km; Montenegro 19 km; Serbia 314 km; Slovenia 600 km

Coastline: 5,835 km (mainland 1,777 km; islands 4,058 km)

Maritime claims: *territorial sea:* 12 nm
continental shelf: 200-m depth or to the depth of exploitation

Climate: Mediterranean and continental; continental climate predominant with hot summers and cold winters; mild winters, dry summers along coast

Terrain: geographically diverse; flat plains along Hungarian border, low mountains and highlands near Adriatic coastline and islands

Elevation: *highest point:* Dinara 1,831 m
lowest point: Adriatic Sea 0 m
mean elevation: 331 m

Natural resources: oil, some coal, bauxite, low-grade iron ore, calcium, gypsum, natural asphalt, silica, mica, clays, salt, hydropower

Land use: *agricultural land:* 25.9% (2022 est.)
arable land: 15.2% (2022 est.)
permanent crops: 1.4% (2022 est.)
permanent pasture: 9.2% (2022 est.)
forest: 34.7% (2022 est.)
other: 39.4% (2022 est.)

Irrigated land: 170 sq km (2022)

Major rivers (by length in km): Dunav (Danube) (shared with Germany [s], Austria, Slovakia, Hungary, Serbia, Bulgaria, Ukraine, Moldova, and Romania [m]) - 2,888 km
note: [s] after country name indicates river source; [m] after country name indicates river mouth

Major watersheds (area sq km): Atlantic Ocean drainage: *(Black Sea)* Danube (795,656 sq km)

Population distribution: more of the population lives in the northern half of the country, with approximately a quarter of the populace residing in and around the capital of Zagreb; many of the islands are sparsely populated

Natural hazards: destructive earthquakes

Geography - note: controls most land routes from Western Europe to the Aegean Sea and Turkish Straits; most Adriatic Sea islands lie off the coast of Croatia – some 1,200 islands, islets, ridges, and rocks

PEOPLE AND SOCIETY

Population: *total:* 4,150,116 (2024 est.)
male: 2,003,431
female: 2,146,685
comparison rankings: total 129; male 130; female 129

Nationality: *noun:* Croat(s), Croatian(s)
adjective: Croatian
note: the French designation of "Croate" to Croatian mercenaries in the 17th century eventually became "Cravate" and later came to be applied to the soldiers' scarves - the cravat; Croatia celebrates Cravat Day every 18 October

Ethnic groups: Croat 91.6%, Serb 3.2%, other 3.9% (including Bosniak, Romani, Albanian, Italian, and Hungarian), unspecified 1.3% (2021 est.)

Languages: Croatian (official) 95.2%, Serbian 1.2%, other 3.1% (including Bosnian, Romani, Albanian, and Italian) unspecified 0.5% (2021 est.)
major-language sample(s):
Knjiga svjetskih činjenica, nužan izvor osnovnih informacija. (Croatian)

Religions: Roman Catholic 79%, Orthodox 3.3%, Protestant 0.3%, other Christian 4.8%, Muslim 1.3%, other 1.1%, agnostic 1.7%, none or atheist 4.7%, unspecified 3.9% (2021 est.)

Age structure: *0-14 years:* 13.8% (male 296,527/female 278,236)
15-64 years: 63.1% (male 1,307,814/female 1,309,394)
65 years and over: 23.1% (2024 est.) (male 399,090/female 559,055)

Dependency ratios: *total dependency ratio:* 55.2 (2024 est.)
youth dependency ratio: 21.6 (2024 est.)
elderly dependency ratio: 33.6 (2024 est.)
potential support ratio: 3 (2024 est.)

Median age: *total:* 45.1 years (2024 est.)
male: 43.2 years
female: 47 years
comparison ranking: total 20

Population growth rate: -0.46% (2024 est.)
comparison ranking: 220

Birth rate: 8.5 births/1,000 population (2024 est.)
comparison ranking: 205

Death rate: 13.1 deaths/1,000 population (2024 est.)
comparison ranking: 13

Net migration rate: 0 migrant(s)/1,000 population (2024 est.)
comparison ranking: 86

Population distribution: more of the population lives in the northern half of the country, with approximately a quarter of the populace residing in and around the capital of Zagreb; many of the islands are sparsely populated

Urbanization: *urban population:* 58.6% of total population (2023)
rate of urbanization: 0.05% annual rate of change (2020-25 est.)

Major urban areas - population: 684,000 ZAGREB (capital) (2023)

Sex ratio: *at birth:* 1.06 male(s)/female
0-14 years: 1.07 male(s)/female
15-64 years: 1 male(s)/female
65 years and over: 0.71 male(s)/female
total population: 0.93 male(s)/female (2024 est.)

Mother's mean age at first birth: 29 years (2020 est.)

Maternal mortality ratio: 3 deaths/100,000 live births (2023 est.)

comparison ranking: 188

Infant mortality rate: *total:* 8.4 deaths/1,000 live births (2024 est.)
male: 8.2 deaths/1,000 live births
female: 8.7 deaths/1,000 live births
comparison ranking: total 143

Life expectancy at birth: *total population:* 77.7 years (2024 est.)
male: 74.6 years
female: 81 years
comparison ranking: total population 86

Total fertility rate: 1.46 children born/woman (2024 est.)
comparison ranking: 206

Gross reproduction rate: 0.71 (2024 est.)

Drinking water source: *improved: urban:* 100% of population (2022 est.)
unimproved: urban: 0% of population (2022 est.)

Health expenditure: 8.1% of GDP (2021)
13.7% of national budget (2022 est.)

Physician density: 3.91 physicians/1,000 population (2022)

Hospital bed density: 5.6 beds/1,000 population (2020 est.)

Obesity - adult prevalence rate: 24.4% (2016)
comparison ranking: 59

Alcohol consumption per capita: *total:* 9.64 liters of pure alcohol (2019 est.)
beer: 4.75 liters of pure alcohol (2019 est.)
wine: 3.52 liters of pure alcohol (2019 est.)
spirits: 1.37 liters of pure alcohol (2019 est.)
other alcohols: 0.36 liters of pure alcohol (2019 est.)
comparison ranking: total 25

Tobacco use: *total:* 32.8% (2025 est.)
male: 33.6% (2025 est.)
female: 32.1% (2025 est.)
comparison ranking: total 15

Currently married women (ages 15-49): 50.8% (2023 est.)

Education expenditure: 4.8% of GDP (2022 est.)
10.7% national budget (2022 est.)
comparison ranking: Education expenditure (% GDP) 73

School life expectancy (primary to tertiary education): *total:* 16 years (2022 est.)
male: 15 years (2022 est.)
female: 17 years (2022 est.)

ENVIRONMENT

Environmental issues: air pollution in urban areas, as well as emissions from neighboring countries; surface water pollution in the Danube River Basin

International environmental agreements: *party to:* Air Pollution, Air Pollution-Heavy Metals, Air Pollution-Multi-effect Protocol, Air Pollution-Nitrogen Oxides, Air Pollution-Persistent Organic Pollutants, Air Pollution-Sulphur 94, Air Pollution-Volatile Organic Compounds, Biodiversity, Climate Change, Climate Change-Kyoto Protocol, Climate Change-Paris Agreement, Comprehensive Nuclear Test Ban, Desertification, Endangered Species, Hazardous Wastes, Law of the Sea, Marine Dumping-London Convention, Nuclear Test Ban, Ozone Layer Protection, Ship Pollution, Tropical Timber 2006, Wetlands, Whaling
signed, but not ratified: none of the selected agreements

Climate: Mediterranean and continental; continental climate predominant with hot summers and cold winters; mild winters, dry summers along coast

Urbanization: *urban population:* 58.6% of total population (2023)
rate of urbanization: 0.05% annual rate of change (2020-25 est.)

Carbon dioxide emissions: 16.467 million metric tonnes of CO2 (2023 est.)
from coal and metallurgical coke: 1.335 million metric tonnes of CO2 (2023 est.)
from petroleum and other liquids: 9.858 million metric tonnes of CO2 (2023 est.)
from consumed natural gas: 5.275 million metric tonnes of CO2 (2023 est.)
comparison ranking: total emissions 97

Particulate matter emissions: 15.2 micrograms per cubic meter (2019 est.)

Waste and recycling: *municipal solid waste generated annually:* 1.81 million tons (2024 est.)
percent of municipal solid waste recycled: 20% (2022 est.)

Total water withdrawal: *municipal:* 465 million cubic meters (2022)
industrial: 475 million cubic meters (2022)
agricultural: 76 million cubic meters (2022)

Total renewable water resources: 105.5 billion cubic meters (2022 est.)

Geoparks: *total global geoparks and regional networks:* 3 (2024)
global geoparks and regional networks: Biokovo-Imotski Lakes; Papuk; Vis Archipelago (2024)

GOVERNMENT

Country name: *conventional long form:* Republic of Croatia
conventional short form: Croatia
local long form: Republika Hrvatska
local short form: Hrvatska
former: People's Republic of Croatia, Socialist Republic of Croatia
etymology: name probably derives from the Croats, a Slavic tribe who migrated to the Balkans in the 7th century A.D., but that name may be related to the Russian word *khrebet*, meaning "mountain chain"

Government type: parliamentary republic

Capital: *name:* Zagreb
geographic coordinates: 45 48 N, 16 00 E
time difference: UTC+1 (6 hours ahead of Washington, DC, during Standard Time)
daylight saving time: +1hr, begins last Sunday in March; ends last Sunday in October
etymology: the city's name means "beyond the bank (or ditch)"; *za* in Old Croat means "beyond," and *greb* means "bank" or "ditch," relating to the city's original site above the Sava River

Administrative divisions: 20 counties (*zupanije*, singular - *zupanija*) and 1 city* (*grad* - singular) with special county status; Bjelovarsko-Bilogorska (Bjelovar-Bilogora), Brodsko-Posavska (Brod-Posavina), Dubrovacko-Neretvanska (Dubrovnik-Neretva), Istarska (Istria), Karlovacka (Karlovac), Koprivnicko-Krizevacka (Koprivnica-Krizevci), Krapinsko-Zagorska (Krapina-Zagorje), Licko-Senjska (Lika-Senj), Medimurska (Medimurje), Osjecko-Baranjska (Osijek-Baranja), Pozesko-Slavonska (Pozega-Slavonia), Primorsko-Goranska (Primorje-Gorski Kotar), Sibensko-Kninska (Sibenik-Knin), Sisacko-Moslavacka (Sisak-Moslavina), Splitsko-Dalmatinska (Split-Dalmatia), Varazdinska (Varazdin), Viroviticko-Podravska (Virovitica-Podravina), Vukovarsko-Srijemska (Vukovar-Syrmia), Zadarska (Zadar), Zagreb*, Zagrebacka (Zagreb county)

Legal system: civil law system influenced by legal heritage of Austria-Hungary

Constitution: *history:* several previous; latest adopted 22 December 1990
amendment process: proposed by at least one fifth of the Assembly membership, by the president of the republic, by the Government of Croatia, or through petition by at least 10% of the total electorate; proceedings to amend require majority vote by the Assembly; passage requires two-thirds majority vote by the Assembly; passage by petition requires a majority vote in a referendum and promulgation by the Assembly

International law organization participation: has not submitted an ICJ jurisdiction declaration; accepts ICCt jurisdiction

Citizenship: *citizenship by birth:* no
citizenship by descent only: at least one parent must be a citizen of Croatia
dual citizenship recognized: yes
residency requirement for naturalization: 5 years

Suffrage: 18 years of age; universal

Executive branch: *chief of state:* President Zoran MILANOVIC (since 18 February 2020)
head of government: Prime Minister Andrej PLENKOVIC (since 19 October 2016)
cabinet: Council of Ministers named by the prime minister and approved by the Assembly
election/appointment process: president directly elected by absolute-majority popular vote in 2 rounds, if needed, for a 5-year term (eligible for a second term); the leader of the majority party or majority coalition is usually appointed prime minister by the president and approved by the Assembly
most recent election date: December 2024 (first round) and January 2025 (second round)
election results: *2025:* Zoran MILANOVIC elected president in second round; percent of vote in second round - Zoran MILANOVIC (SDP) 74.6%, Dragan PRIMORAC (independent) 25.3%
2019: Zoran MILANOVIC elected president in second round; percent of vote in second round - Zoran MILANOVIC (SDP) 52.7%, Kolinda GRABAR-KITAROVIC (HDZ) 47.3%
expected date of next election: 2029

Legislative branch: *legislature name:* Croatian Parliament (Hrvatski Sabor)
legislative structure: unicameral
number of seats: 151 (all directly elected)
electoral system: proportional representation
scope of elections: full renewal
term in office: 4 years
most recent election date: 4/17/2024
parties elected and seats per party: Croatian Democratic Union (HDZ) (55); Social Democratic Party of Croatia (SDP) (37); Homeland Movement (DP) (11); We Can! – Political Platform (Možemo!) (10); Independent (NZ) (10); Other (28)
percentage of women in chamber: 33.1%
expected date of next election: April 2028
note: of the 151 seats, 140 members come from 10 multi-seat constituencies, with 3 members in a constituency for Croatian diaspora; voters belonging to recognized minorities elect an additional 8 members from a nationwide constituency: the Serb minority elects 3 members, the

Hungarian and Italian minorities elect 1 each, the Czech and Slovak minorities elect 1 jointly, and all other minorities elect 2

Judicial branch: *highest court(s):* Supreme Court (consists of the court president and vice president, 25 civil department justices, and 16 criminal department justices)
judge selection and term of office: president of Supreme Court nominated by the president of Croatia and elected by the Sabor for a 4-year term; other Supreme Court justices appointed by the National Judicial Council; all judges serve until age 70
subordinate courts: Administrative Court; county, municipal, and specialized courts
note: an 11-member Constitutional Court has jurisdiction limited to constitutional issues, but it is outside the judicial system

Political parties: Bosniaks Together
The Bridge or MOST (formerly the Bridge of Independent Lists)
Croatia Romani Union Kali Sara (SRRH)
Croatian Democratic Union or HDZ Democratic Union of Hungarians in Croatia (DZMH)
Focus or Fokus
Homeland Movement or DP (also known as Miroslav Škoro Homeland Movement or DPMS)
Independent Democratic Serb Party or SDSS
Independent Platform of the North (NPS)
Istrian Democratic Assembly or IDS
Social Democratic Party of Croatia or SDP
We Can! or Mozemo!

Diplomatic representation in the US: *chief of mission:* Ambassador Pjer ŠIMUNOVIĆ (since 8 September 2017)
chancery: 2343 Massachusetts Avenue NW, Washington, DC 20008
telephone: [1] (202) 588-5899
FAX: [1] (202) 588-8937
email address and website: washington@mvep.hr
https://mvep.gov.hr/embassy-114969/114969
consulate(s) general: Chicago, Los Angeles, New York, Seattle (WA)
consulate(s): Anchorage (AL), Houston, Kansas City (MO),Minneapolis/St. Paul (MN), New Orleans, Pittsburgh (PA)

Diplomatic representation from the US: *chief of mission:* Ambassador (vacant); Chargé d'Affaires Trey LYONS (since January 2025)
embassy: Ulica Thomasa Jeffersona 2, 10010 Zagreb
mailing address: 5080 Zagreb Place, Washington DC 20521-5080
telephone: [385] (1) 661-2200
FAX: [385] (1) 665-8933
email address and website: ZagrebACS@state.gov
https://hr.usembassy.gov/

International organization participation: AIIB, Australia Group, BIS, BSEC (observer), CD, CE, CEI, EAPC, EBRD, ECB, EMU, EU, FAO, G-11, IADB, IAEA, IBRD, ICAO, ICC (national committees), ICCt, ICRM, IDA, IFAD, IFC, IFRCS, IHO, ILO, IMF, IMO, IMSO, Interpol, IOC, IOM, IPU, ISO, ITSO, ITU, ITUC (NGOs), MIGA, MINURSO, NAM (observer), NATO, NSG, OAS (observer), OIF (observer), OPCW, OSCE, PCA, Schengen Convention, SELEC, UN, UNCTAD, UNESCO, UNFICYP, UNHCR, UNIDO, UNIFIL, UNMIL, UNMOGIP, UNWTO, UPU, Wassenaar Arrangement, WCO, WHO, WIPO, WMO, WTO, ZC

Independence: *25 June 1991 (from Yugoslavia); notable earlier dates:* ca. 925 (Kingdom of Croatia established), 1 December 1918 (Kingdom of Serbs, Croats, and Slovenes established, later became Yugoslavia)
note: 25 June 1991 was the day the Croatian parliament voted for independence; the legislature adopted a decision on 8 October 1991 to sever constitutional relations with Yugoslavia

National holiday: Statehood Day (National Day), 30 May (1990)
note: marks the day in 1990 that the first modern multi-party Croatian parliament convened

Flag: *description:* three equal horizontal bands of red (top), white, and blue – the pan-Slav colors – with the Croatian coat of arms in the center, which consists of a main shield (a checkerboard of 13 red and 12 silver fields) with five smaller shields that form a crown over the main shield
meaning: the small shields represent the five historic regions (from left to right): Croatia, Dubrovnik, Dalmatia, Istria, and Slavonia
history: Russia's 19th-century flag inspired the pan-Slav colors

National symbol(s): red-and-white checkerboard

National color(s): red, white, blue

National anthem(s): *title:* "Lijepa nasa domovino" (Our Beautiful Homeland)
lyrics/music: Antun MIHANOVIC/Josip RUNJANIN
history: adopted in 1972 while still part of Yugoslavia; the lyrics were written in 1835, and it served as an unofficial anthem beginning in 1891

National heritage: *total World Heritage Sites:* 10 (8 cultural, 2 natural)
selected World Heritage Site locales: Plitvice Lakes National Park (n); Historic Split (c); Old City of Dubrovnik (c); Euphrasian Basilica; Historic Trogir (c); Šibenik Cathedral (c); Stari Grad Plain (c); Zadar and Fort St. Nikola Venetian Defense Works (c); Primeval Beech Forests (n); Stećci Medieval Tombstones Graveyards (c)

ECONOMY

Economic overview: upper-middle-income Balkan economy; newest euro user (introduced in 2023); increased investments from EU structural funds and tourism sector contributing to strong but moderating economic growth; declining energy prices and restrictive monetary policy easing inflation; historically low unemployment rate with labor shortages within services and manufacturing sectors

Real GDP (purchasing power parity): $164.825 billion (2024 est.)
$158.769 billion (2023 est.)
$153.693 billion (2022 est.)
note: data in 2021 dollars
comparison ranking: 79

Real GDP growth rate: 3.8% (2024 est.)
3.3% (2023 est.)
7.3% (2022 est.)
note: annual GDP % growth based on constant local currency
comparison ranking: 83

Real GDP per capita: $42,600 (2024 est.)
$41,100 (2023 est.)
$39,900 (2022 est.)
note: data in 2021 dollars
comparison ranking: 52

GDP (official exchange rate): $92.526 billion (2024 est.)
note: data in current dollars at official exchange rate

Inflation rate (consumer prices): 3% (2024 est.)
7.9% (2023 est.)
10.8% (2022 est.)
note: annual % change based on consumer prices
comparison ranking: 94

GDP - composition, by sector of origin: *agriculture:* 3.4% (2024 est.)
industry: 19.8% (2024 est.)
services: 59.7% (2024 est.)
note: figures may not total 100% due to non-allocated consumption not captured in sector-reported data
comparison rankings: agriculture 126; industry 131; services 91

GDP - composition, by end use: *household consumption:* 57% (2024 est.)
government consumption: 22.6% (2024 est.)
investment in fixed capital: 23.7% (2024 est.)
investment in inventories: -0.2% (2024 est.)
exports of goods and services: 49.8% (2024 est.)
imports of goods and services: -52.9% (2024 est.)
note: figures may not total 100% due to rounding or gaps in data collection

Agricultural products: maize, wheat, sugar beets, milk, barley, soybeans, sunflower seeds, potatoes, pork, grapes (2023)
note: top ten agricultural products based on tonnage

Industries: chemicals and plastics, machine tools, fabricated metal, electronics, pig iron and rolled steel products, aluminum, paper, wood products, construction materials, textiles, shipbuilding, petroleum and petroleum refining, food and beverages, tourism

Industrial production growth rate: 2.1% (2024 est.)
note: annual % change in industrial value added based on constant local currency
comparison ranking: 99

Labor force: 1.733 million (2024 est.)
note: number of people ages 15 or older who are employed or seeking work
comparison ranking: 130

Unemployment rate: 5.3% (2024 est.)
6.1% (2023 est.)
7% (2022 est.)
note: % of labor force seeking employment
comparison ranking: 93

Youth unemployment rate (ages 15-24): *total:* 16.6% (2024 est.)
male: 15.5% (2024 est.)
female: 18.2% (2024 est.)
note: % of labor force ages 15-24 seeking employment
comparison ranking: total 70

Population below poverty line: 18% (2021 est.)
note: % of population with income below national poverty line

Gini Index coefficient - distribution of family income: 30 (2022 est.)
note: index (0-100) of income distribution; higher values represent greater inequality
comparison ranking: 119

Average household expenditures: *on food:* 18.5% of household expenditures (2023 est.)
on alcohol and tobacco: 7.9% of household expenditures (2023 est.)

Household income or consumption by percentage share: *lowest 10%:* 2.9% (2022 est.)
highest 10%: 23% (2022 est.)

note: % share of income accruing to lowest and highest 10% of population

Remittances: 7.3% of GDP (2024 est.)
7.2% of GDP (2023 est.)
7.5% of GDP (2022 est.)
note: personal transfers and compensation between resident and non-resident individuals/households/entities

Budget: *revenues:* $32.487 billion (2023 est.)
expenditures: $33.715 billion (2023 est.)
note: central government revenues (excluding grants) and expenditures converted to US dollars at average official exchange rate for year indicated

Public debt: 75.6% of GDP (2023 est.)
note: central government debt as a % of GDP
comparison ranking: 46

Taxes and other revenues: 21.5% (of GDP) (2023 est.)
note: central government tax revenue as a % of GDP
comparison ranking: 40

Current account balance: -$1.049 billion (2024 est.)
$635.97 million (2023 est.)
-$2.621 billion (2022 est.)
note: balance of payments - net trade and primary/secondary income in current dollars
comparison ranking: 131

Exports: $46.601 billion (2024 est.)
$45.064 billion (2023 est.)
$41.907 billion (2022 est.)
note: balance of payments - exports of goods and services in current dollars
comparison ranking: 69

Exports - partners: Italy 14%, Germany 11%, Slovenia 11%, Bosnia & Herzegovina 6%, Austria 6% (2023)
note: top five export partners based on percentage share of exports

Exports - commodities: ships, garments, electricity, packaged medicine, wood (2023)
note: top five export commodities based on value in dollars

Imports: $49.86 billion (2024 est.)
$46.811 billion (2023 est.)
$46.769 billion (2022 est.)
note: balance of payments - imports of goods and services in current dollars
comparison ranking: 68

Imports - partners: Italy 14%, Germany 14%, Slovenia 11%, Hungary 6%, Austria 5% (2023)
note: top five import partners based on percentage share of imports

Imports - commodities: refined petroleum, cars, garments, natural gas, crude petroleum (2023)
note: top five import commodities based on value in dollars

Reserves of foreign exchange and gold: $3.336 billion (2024 est.)
$3.176 billion (2023 est.)
$29.726 billion (2022 est.)
note: holdings of gold (year-end prices)/foreign exchange/special drawing rights in current dollars
comparison ranking: 115

Exchange rates: euros (EUR) per US dollar -

Exchange rates: 0.924 (2024 est.)
0.925 (2023 est.)
0.95 (2022 est.)
0.845 (2021 est.)
0.876 (2020 est.)
note: Croatia used the kuna prior to conversion to the euro on 1 January 2023. During the transition period the exchange rate was fixed at 7.53450 kuna to 1 euro.

ENERGY

Electricity access: *electrification - total population:* 100% (2022 est.)

Electricity: *installed generating capacity:* 5.518 million kW (2023 est.)
consumption: 16.408 billion kWh (2023 est.)
exports: 8.461 billion kWh (2023 est.)
imports: 10.038 billion kWh (2023 est.)
transmission/distribution losses: 2.053 billion kWh (2023 est.)
comparison rankings: installed generating capacity 87; consumption 82; exports 28; imports 26; transmission/distribution losses 125

Electricity generation sources: *fossil fuels:* 31.2% of total installed capacity (2023 est.)
solar: 1.7% of total installed capacity (2023 est.)
wind: 14.8% of total installed capacity (2023 est.)
hydroelectricity: 48.5% of total installed capacity (2023 est.)
geothermal: 0.1% of total installed capacity (2023 est.)
biomass and waste: 3.7% of total installed capacity (2023 est.)

Coal: *consumption:* 596,000 metric tons (2023 est.)
exports: 1,000 metric tons (2022 est.)
imports: 663,000 metric tons (2023 est.)

Petroleum: *total petroleum production:* 11,000 bbl/day (2023 est.)
refined petroleum consumption: 70,000 bbl/day (2023 est.)
crude oil estimated reserves: 71 million barrels (2021 est.)

Natural gas: *production:* 722.231 million cubic meters (2023 est.)
consumption: 2.689 billion cubic meters (2023 est.)
exports: 1.119 billion cubic meters (2023 est.)
imports: 2.995 billion cubic meters (2023 est.)
proven reserves: 24.919 billion cubic meters (2021 est.)

Energy consumption per capita: 79.907 million Btu/person (2023 est.)
comparison ranking: 65

COMMUNICATIONS

Telephones - fixed lines: *total subscriptions:* 1.203 million (2023 est.)
subscriptions per 100 inhabitants: 31 (2023 est.)
comparison ranking: total subscriptions 64

Telephones - mobile cellular: *total subscriptions:* 4.56 million (2023 est.)
subscriptions per 100 inhabitants: 111 (2022 est.)
comparison ranking: total subscriptions 130

Broadcast media: the national state-owned public broadcaster, Croatian Radiotelevision, operates 4 terrestrial TV networks, a satellite channel that rebroadcasts programs for Croatians overseas, and 6 regional TV centers; 2 private broadcasters with national terrestrial networks; 29 privately owned regional TV stations; multi-channel cable and satellite TV subscription services are available; state-owned public broadcaster operates 4 national radio networks and 23 regional radio stations; 2 privately owned national radio networks and 117 local radio stations (2019)

Internet country code: .hr

Internet users: *percent of population:* 83% (2023 est.)

Broadband - fixed subscriptions: *total:* 1.11 million (2023 est.)
subscriptions per 100 inhabitants: 28 (2023 est.)
comparison ranking: total 76

TRANSPORTATION

Civil aircraft registration country code prefix: 9A

Airports: 45 (2025)
comparison ranking: 95

Heliports: 7 (2025)
comparison ranking: 90

Railways: *total:* 2,617 km (2020) 980 km electrified

Merchant marine: *total:* 384 (2023)
by type: bulk carrier 10, general cargo 32, oil tanker 14, other 328
comparison ranking: total 50

Ports: *total ports:* 16 (2024)
large: 2
medium: 0
small: 6
very small: 8
ports with oil terminals: 8
key ports: Bakar, Dubrovnik, Omisalj, Rijeka Luka, Rovinj, Sibenik, Split, Zadar

MILITARY AND SECURITY

Military and security forces: Armed Forces of the Republic of Croatia (Oruzane Snage Republike Hrvatske, OSRH): Croatian Army (Hrvatska Kopnena Vojska, HKoV), Croatian Navy (Hrvatska Ratna Mornarica, HRM; includes Coast Guard), Croatian Air Force (Hrvatsko Ratno Zrakoplovstvo, HRZ) (2025)
note: the Ministry of the Interior is responsible for internal security, including law enforcement (Croatia Police) and border security

Military expenditures: 2% of GDP (2025 est.)
1.9% of GDP (2024 est.)
1.7% of GDP (2023 est.)
1.8% of GDP (2022 est.)
2% of GDP (2021 est.)

Military and security service personnel strengths: approximately 15,000 active-duty military personnel (2025)

Military equipment inventories and acquisitions: the military's inventory is a mix of Soviet-era (largely from the former Yugoslavia) equipment and a growing amount of more modern, NATO-compatible weapon systems from suppliers such as France, Germany, Turkey, and the US (2024)

Military service age and obligation: 18-27 years of age for voluntary military service; conscription abolished in 2008 but slated to be reinstated in January 2025 (2024)
note: as of 2024, women comprised about 14% of the military's full-time personnel

Military deployments: 150 Kosovo (KFOR/NATO); 175 Lithuania (NATO; Croatia also has a few hundred personnel participating in several other EU, NATO, and UN missions (2024)

Military - note: the Armed Forces of Croatia (OSRH) are responsible for the defense of Croatia's sovereignty and territory, contributing to international

humanitarian, peacekeeping, and security missions, and providing assistance to civil authorities for such missions as responding to disasters, search and rescue, anti-terrorism, and internal security in times of crisis if called upon by the prime minister or the president; Croatia joined NATO in 2009, and the OSRH participates in NATO missions, including its peacekeeping force in Kosovo and the Enhanced Forward Presence mission in Eastern Europe; it also contributes to EU and UN missions; the OSRH trains regularly with NATO and regional partners
the OSRH was established in 1991 from the Croatian National Guard during the Croatian War of Independence (1991-95); during the war, the ground forces grew to as many as 60 brigades and dozens of independent battalions, and a single military offensive against Serbian forces in 1995 included some 100,000 Croatian troops; in 2000, Croatia initiated an effort to modernize and reform the OSRH into a small, professional military capable of meeting the challenges of NATO membership (2025)

TRANSNATIONAL ISSUES

Refugees and internally displaced persons: *refugees:* 29,927 (2024 est.)
stateless persons: 758 (2024 est.)

CUBA

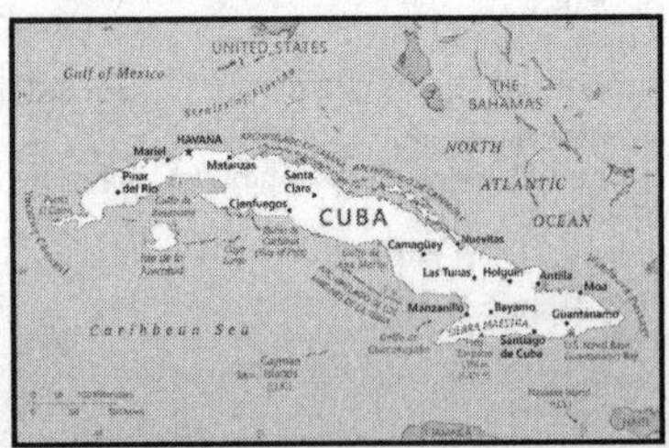

INTRODUCTION

Background: The native Amerindian population of Cuba began to decline after the arrival of Christopher COLUMBUS in 1492, as the country was developed as a Spanish colony during the next several centuries. Large numbers of African slaves were imported to work the coffee and sugar plantations, and Havana became the launching point for the annual treasure fleets bound for Spain from Mexico and Peru. Spanish rule eventually provoked an independence movement, and occasional rebellions were harshly suppressed. US intervention during the Spanish-American War in 1898 assisted the Cubans in overthrowing Spanish rule. The Treaty of Paris established Cuban independence from Spain in 1898, and after three-and-a-half years of subsequent US military rule, Cuba became an independent republic in 1902.

Cuba then experienced a string of governments mostly dominated by the military and corrupt politicians. Fidel CASTRO led a rebel army to victory in 1959; his authoritarian rule held the subsequent regime together for nearly five decades. He handed off the presidency to his younger brother Raul CASTRO in 2008. Cuba's communist revolution, with Soviet support, was exported throughout Latin America and Africa during the 1960s, 1970s, and 1980s. Miguel DIAZ-CANEL Bermudez, hand-picked by Raul CASTRO to succeed him, was approved as president by the National Assembly and took office in 2018. DIAZ-CANEL was appointed First Secretary of the Communist Party in 2021 after the retirement of Raul CASTRO and continues to serve as both president and first secretary.

Cuba traditionally and consistently portrays the US embargo, in place since 1961, as the source of its socioeconomic difficulties. As a result of efforts begun in 2014 to reestablish diplomatic relations, the US and Cuba reopened embassies in their respective countries in 2015. The embargo remains in place, however, and the relationship between the US and Cuba remains tense. Illicit migration of Cuban nationals to the US via maritime and overland routes has been a longstanding challenge. In 2017, the US and Cuba signed a Joint Statement ending the so-called "wet-foot, dry-foot" policy, by which Cuban nationals who reached US soil were permitted to stay. Irregular Cuban maritime migration has dropped significantly since 2016, when migrant interdictions at sea topped 5,000, but land border crossings continue.

GEOGRAPHY

Location: Caribbean, island between the Caribbean Sea and the North Atlantic Ocean, 150 km south of Key West, Florida

Geographic coordinates: 21 30 N, 80 00 W

Map references: Central America and the Caribbean

Area: *total:* 110,860 sq km
land: 109,820 sq km
water: 1,040 sq km
comparison ranking: total 106

Area - comparative: slightly smaller than Pennsylvania

Land boundaries: *total:* 28.5 km
border countries (1): US Naval Base at Guantanamo Bay 28.5 km
note: Guantanamo Naval Base is leased by the US and remains part of Cuba

Coastline: 3,735 km

Maritime claims: *territorial sea:* 12 nm
contiguous zone: 24 nm
exclusive economic zone: 200 nm

Climate: tropical; moderated by trade winds; dry season (November to April); rainy season (May to October)

Terrain: mostly flat to rolling plains, with rugged hills and mountains in the southeast

Elevation: *highest point:* Pico Turquino 1,974 m
lowest point: Caribbean Sea 0 m
mean elevation: 108 m

Natural resources: cobalt, nickel, iron ore, chromium, copper, salt, timber, silica, petroleum, arable land

Land use: *agricultural land:* 61.7% (2022 est.)
arable land: 28% (2022 est.)
permanent crops: 6.3% (2022 est.)
permanent pasture: 27.4% (2022 est.)
forest: 31.2% (2022 est.)
other: 7.1% (2022 est.)

Irrigated land: 8,700 sq km (2012)

Population distribution: large population clusters found throughout the country, the more significant ones being in the larger towns and cities, particularly the capital of Havana

Natural hazards: the east coast is subject to hurricanes from August to November (in general, the country averages about one hurricane every other year); droughts are common

Geography - note: largest country in Caribbean and westernmost island of the Greater Antilles

PEOPLE AND SOCIETY

Population: *total:* 10,966,038 (2024 est.)
male: 5,441,507
female: 5,524,531
comparison rankings: total 85; male 87; female 84

Nationality: *noun:* Cuban(s)
adjective: Cuban

Ethnic groups: White 64.1%, Mulatto or mixed 26.6%, Black 9.3% (2012 est.)
note: data represent racial self-identification from Cuba's 2012 national census

Languages: Spanish (official)
major-language sample(s):
La Libreta Informativa del Mundo, la fuente indispensable de información básica. (Spanish)

Religions: Christian 58.9%, folk religion 17.6%, Buddhist <1%, Hindu <1%, Jewish <1%, Muslim <1%, other <1%, none 23.2% (2020 est.)
note: folk religions include religions of African origin, spiritualism, and others intermingled with Catholicism or Protestantism; data is estimative because no authoritative source on religious affiliation exists for Cuba

Age structure: *0-14 years:* 16.3% (male 918,066/female 866,578)
15-64 years: 66.5% (male 3,670,531/female 3,623,658)
65 years and over: 17.2% (2024 est.) (male 852,910/female 1,034,295)

Dependency ratios: *total dependency ratio:* 49.6 (2024 est.)
youth dependency ratio: 23 (2024 est.)
elderly dependency ratio: 26.5 (2024 est.)
potential support ratio: 3.8 (2024 est.)

Median age: *total:* 42.6 years (2024 est.)
male: 41 years
female: 44.4 years
comparison ranking: total 42

Population growth rate: -0.17% (2024 est.)
comparison ranking: 209

Birth rate: 9.9 births/1,000 population (2024 est.)
comparison ranking: 188

Death rate: 9.5 deaths/1,000 population (2024 est.)
comparison ranking: 45

Net migration rate: -2.1 migrant(s)/1,000 population (2024 est.)
comparison ranking: 169

Population distribution: large population clusters found throughout the country, the more significant ones being in the larger towns and cities, particularly the capital of Havana

Urbanization: *urban population:* 77.5% of total population (2023)
rate of urbanization: 0.19% annual rate of change (2020-25 est.)

Major urban areas - population: 2.149 million HAVANA (capital) (2023)

Sex ratio: *at birth:* 1.06 male(s)/female
0-14 years: 1.06 male(s)/female
15-64 years: 1.01 male(s)/female
65 years and over: 0.82 male(s)/female
total population: 0.99 male(s)/female (2024 est.)

Maternal mortality ratio: 35 deaths/100,000 live births (2023 est.)
comparison ranking: 111

Infant mortality rate: *total:* 4 deaths/1,000 live births (2024 est.)
male: 4.5 deaths/1,000 live births
female: 3.5 deaths/1,000 live births
comparison ranking: total 187

Life expectancy at birth: *total population:* 80.1 years (2024 est.)
male: 77.8 years
female: 82.6 years
comparison ranking: total population 58

Total fertility rate: 1.71 children born/woman (2024 est.)
comparison ranking: 162

Gross reproduction rate: 0.83 (2024 est.)

Drinking water source: *improved: urban:* 95.5% of population (2022 est.)
rural: 91.8% of population (2022 est.)
total: 94.7% of population (2022 est.)
unimproved: urban: 4.5% of population (2022 est.)
rural: 8.2% of population (2022 est.)
total: 5.3% of population (2022 est.)

Health expenditure: 13.8% of GDP (2021)
21% of national budget (2022 est.)

Physician density: 9.54 physicians/1,000 population (2021)

Hospital bed density: 4.2 beds/1,000 population (2021 est.)

Sanitation facility access: *improved: urban:* 98.4% of population (2022 est.)
rural: 95.7% of population (2022 est.)
total: 97.8% of population (2022 est.)
unimproved: urban: 1.6% of population (2022 est.)
rural: 4.3% of population (2022 est.)
total: 2.2% of population (2022 est.)

Obesity - adult prevalence rate: 24.6% (2016)
comparison ranking: 56

Alcohol consumption per capita: *total:* 4.7 liters of pure alcohol (2019 est.)
beer: 1.77 liters of pure alcohol (2019 est.)
wine: 0.23 liters of pure alcohol (2019 est.)
spirits: 2.69 liters of pure alcohol (2019 est.)
other alcohols: 0.01 liters of pure alcohol (2019 est.)
comparison ranking: total 85

Tobacco use: *total:* 16.7% (2025 est.)
male: 24.7% (2025 est.)
female: 9% (2025 est.)
comparison ranking: total 95

Children under the age of 5 years underweight: 2.4% (2019)
comparison ranking: 91

Currently married women (ages 15-49): 58% (2023 est.)

Child marriage: *women married by age 15:* 4.8% (2019)
women married by age 18: 29.4% (2019)
men married by age 18: 5.9% (2019)

Education expenditure: 8.4% of GDP (2022 est.)
17% national budget (2022 est.)
comparison ranking: Education expenditure (% GDP) 8

Literacy: *total population:* 97.7% (2019 est.)
male: 99% (2019 est.)
female: 96.4% (2019 est.)

School life expectancy (primary to tertiary education): *total:* 14 years (2023 est.)
male: 13 years (2023 est.)
female: 15 years (2023 est.)

People - note: illicit emigration is a continuing problem; Cubans attempt to depart the island and enter the US using homemade rafts, alien smugglers, direct flights, or falsified visas; Cubans also use non-maritime routes to enter the US including direct flights to Miami and overland via the southwest border; the number of Cubans migrating to the US surged after the announcement of normalization of US-Cuban relations in late December 2014 but has decreased since the end of the so-called "wet-foot, dry-foot" policy on 12 January 2017

ENVIRONMENT

Environmental issues: soil degradation and desertification (brought on by poor farming techniques and natural disasters); biodiversity loss; deforestation; air and water pollution

International environmental agreements: *party to:* Antarctic Treaty, Biodiversity, Climate Change, Climate Change-Kyoto Protocol, Climate Change-Paris Agreement, Comprehensive Nuclear Test Ban, Desertification, Endangered Species, Environmental Modification, Hazardous Wastes, Law of the Sea, Marine Dumping-London Convention, Ozone Layer Protection, Ship Pollution, Wetlands
signed, but not ratified: Marine Life Conservation

Climate: tropical; moderated by trade winds; dry season (November to April); rainy season (May to October)

Urbanization: *urban population:* 77.5% of total population (2023)
rate of urbanization: 0.19% annual rate of change (2020-25 est.)

Carbon dioxide emissions: 19.716 million metric tonnes of CO2 (2023 est.)
from coal and metallurgical coke: 16,000 metric tonnes of CO2 (2023 est.)
from petroleum and other liquids: 18.12 million metric tonnes of CO2 (2023 est.)
from consumed natural gas: 1.58 million metric tonnes of CO2 (2023 est.)
comparison ranking: total emissions 85

Particulate matter emissions: 13.3 micrograms per cubic meter (2019 est.)

Methane emissions: *energy:* 23 kt (2022-2024 est.)
agriculture: 249.7 kt (2019-2021 est.)
waste: 146.4 kt (2019-2021 est.)
other: 2.2 kt (2019-2021 est.)

Waste and recycling: *municipal solid waste generated annually:* 2.693 million tons (2024 est.)
percent of municipal solid waste recycled: 25.7% (2022 est.)

Total water withdrawal: *municipal:* 1.7 billion cubic meters (2022 est.)
industrial: 740 million cubic meters (2022 est.)
agricultural: 4.519 billion cubic meters (2022 est.)

Total renewable water resources: 38.12 billion cubic meters (2022 est.)

GOVERNMENT

Country name: *conventional long form:* Republic of Cuba
conventional short form: Cuba
local long form: República de Cuba
local short form: Cuba
etymology: the origin of the name is disputed; it could be derived from a local Taino word, either *cubao*, meaning "where fertile land is abundant," or coabana, meaning "great place"

Government type: communist state

Capital: *name:* Havana
geographic coordinates: 23 07 N, 82 21 W
time difference: UTC-5 (same time as Washington, DC, during Standard Time)
daylight saving time: +1hr, begins second Sunday in March; ends first Sunday in November; note - Cuba has been known to alter the schedule of DST on short notice in an attempt to conserve electricity for lighting
etymology: Spanish soldier Diego VELAZQUEZ named the city San Cristobal de la Habana, or Saint Christopher of the Habana; "Habana" may have been the name of a local ethnic group, but the meaning of the word is unknown

Administrative divisions: 15 provinces (*provincias*, singular - *provincia*) and 1 special municipality* (*municipio especial*); Artemisa, Camaguey, Ciego de Avila, Cienfuegos, Granma, Guantanamo, Holguin, Isla de la Juventud*, La Habana (Havana), Las Tunas, Matanzas, Mayabeque, Pinar del Río, Sancti Spiritus, Santiago de Cuba, Villa Clara

Legal system: civil law system based on Spanish civil code

Constitution: *history:* several previous; latest drafted 14 July 2018, approved by the National Assembly 22 December 2018, approved by referendum 24 February 2019
amendment process: proposed by the National Assembly of People's Power; passage requires approval of at least two-thirds majority of the National Assembly membership; amendments to constitutional articles on the authorities of the National Assembly, Council of State, or any rights and duties in the constitution also require approval in a referendum; constitutional articles on the Cuban political, social, and economic system cannot be amended

International law organization participation: has not submitted an ICJ jurisdiction declaration; non-party state to the ICCt

Citizenship: *citizenship by birth:* yes
citizenship by descent only: yes
dual citizenship recognized: no
residency requirement for naturalization: unknown

Suffrage: 16 years of age; universal

Executive branch: *chief of state:* President Miguel DIAZ-CANEL Bermudez (since 19 April 2018)

head of government: Prime Minister Manuel MARRERO Cruz (since 21 December 2019)
cabinet: Council of Ministers proposed by the president and appointed by the National Assembly
election/appointment process: president and vice president indirectly elected by the National Assembly for a 5-year term (eligible for a second term)
most recent election date: 19 April 2023
election results: *2023:* Miguel DIAZ-CANEL Bermudez (PCC) reelected president; percent of National Assembly vote - 97.7%; Salvador Antonio VALDES Mesa (PCC) reelected vice president; percent of National Assembly vote - 93.4%
2018: Miguel DIAZ-CANEL Bermudez (PCC) elected president; percent of National Assembly vote - 98.8%; Salvador Antonio VALDES Mesa (PCC) elected vice president; percent of National Assembly vote - 98.1%
expected date of next election: 2028

Legislative branch: *legislature name:* National Assembly of the People's Power (Asamblea nacional del Poder popular)
legislative structure: unicameral
number of seats: 470 (all directly elected)
electoral system: other systems
scope of elections: full renewal
term in office: 5 years
most recent election date: 3/26/2023
percentage of women in chamber: 55.7%
expected date of next election: March 2028
note: the National Candidature Commission submits a slate of approved candidates; to be elected, candidates must receive more than 50% of valid votes, otherwise the seat remains vacant or the Council of State can declare another election

Judicial branch: *highest court(s):* People's Supreme Court (consists of court president, vice president, 41 professional justices, and NA lay judges); organization includes the State Council, criminal, civil, administrative, labor, crimes against the state, and military courts)
judge selection and term of office: professional judges elected by the National Assembly are not subject to a specific term; lay judges nominated by workplace collectives and neighborhood associations and elected by municipal or provincial assemblies; lay judges appointed for 5-year terms and serve up to 30 days per year
subordinate courts: People's Provincial Courts; People's Regional Courts; People's Courts

Political parties: Cuban Communist Party or PCC

Diplomatic representation in the US: *chief of mission:* Ambassador (vacant); Chargé d'Affaires Lianys TORRES RIVERA (since 14 January 2021)
chancery: 2630 16th Street NW, Washington, DC 20009
telephone: [1] (202) 797-8515
FAX: [1] (202) 797-8521
email address and website: recepcion@usadc.embacuba.cu
https://misiones.cubaminrex.cu/en/usa/embassy-cuba-usa

Diplomatic representation from the US: *chief of mission:* Ambassador (vacant); Chargé d'Affaires Mike HAMMER (since 14 November 2024)
embassy: Calzada between L & M Streets, Vedado, Havana
mailing address: 3200 Havana Place, Washington DC 20521-3200
telephone: [53] (7) 839-4100
FAX: [53] (7) 839-4247
email address and website: acshavana@state.gov
https://cu.usembassy.gov/

International organization participation: ACP, ACS, ALBA, AOSIS, CABEI, CELAC, EAEU (observer), FAO, G-77, IAEA, ICAO, ICC (national committees), ICRM, IFAD, IFRCS, IHO, ILO, IMO, IMSO, Interpol, IOC, IOM (observer), IPU, ISO, ITSO, ITU, LAES, LAIA, NAM, OAS (excluded from formal participation since 1962), OPANAL, OPCW, PCA, Petrocaribe, PIF (partner), UN, UNCTAD, UNESCO, UNHRC, UNIDO, Union Latina, UNOOSA, UNWTO, UPU, WCO, WFTU (NGOs), WHO, WIPO, WMO, WTO

Independence: 20 May 1902 (from US administration); 10 December 1898 (from Spain); not acknowledged by the Cuban Government as days of independence

National holiday: Triumph of the Revolution (Liberation Day), 1 January (1959)

Flag: *description:* five equal horizontal bands of blue (top, center, and bottom) alternating with white; a red equilateral triangle based on the left side has a five-pointed white star in the center
meaning: the blue bands stand for the islands' three former departments: Central, Occidental, and Oriental; the white bands for the purity of the independence ideal; the triangle for liberty, equality, and fraternity; the red color for the blood shed in the independence struggle; the white star, called "La Estrella Solitaria" (the Lone Star), lights the way to freedom and was inspired by the state flag of Texas
note: design similar to the Puerto Rican flag, with the colors of the bands and triangle reversed

National symbol(s): royal palm

National color(s): red, white, blue

National anthem(s): *title:* "La Bayamesa" (The Bayamo Song)
lyrics/music: Pedro FIGUEREDO
history: adopted 1940; Pedro FIGUEREDO first performed it in 1868 during the Ten Years War against the Spanish; a leading figure in the uprising, FIGUEREDO was captured in 1870 and executed by a firing squad; just before being shot, he is said to have shouted, "Morir por la Patria es vivir" (To die for the country is to live), a line from the anthem

National heritage: *total World Heritage Sites:* 9 (7 cultural, 2 natural)
selected World Heritage Site locales: Old Havana (c); Trinidad and the Valley de los Ingenios (c); San Pedro de la Roca Castle (c); Desembarco del Granma National Park (n); Viñales Valley (c); Archaeological Landscape of the First Coffee Plantations (c); Alejandro de Humboldt National Park (n); Historic Cienfuegos (c); Historic Camagüey (c)

ECONOMY

Economic overview: still largely state-run planned economy, although privatization increasing under new constitution; widespread protests due to lack of basic necessities and electricity; massive foreign investment increases recently; known tobacco exporter; unique oil-for-doctors relationship with Venezuela; widespread corruption

Real GDP (purchasing power parity): $81.165 billion (2024 est.)
$81.985 billion (2023 est.)
$83.597 billion (2022 est.)
note: data in 2015 dollars
comparison ranking: 105

Real GDP growth rate: -1.9% (2023 est.)
1.8% (2022 est.)
1.3% (2021 est.)
note: annual GDP % growth based on constant local currency
comparison ranking: 206

Real GDP per capita: $23,700 (2024 est.)
$18,300 (2023 est.)
$13,300 (2022 est.)
note: data in 2015 dollars
comparison ranking: 94

GDP (official exchange rate): $259.781 billion (2024 est.)
note: data in current dollars at official exchange rate

Inflation rate (consumer prices): 76.1% (2022 est.)
151.9% (2021 est.)
11.9% (2020 est.)
note: annual % change based on consumer prices
comparison ranking: 208

GDP - composition, by sector of origin: *agriculture:* 1.3% (2023 est.)
industry: 27.5% (2023 est.)
services: 70% (2023 est.)
note: figures may not total 100% due to non-allocated consumption not captured in sector-reported data
comparison rankings: agriculture 168; industry 71; services 36

GDP - composition, by end use: *household consumption:* 73.3% (2023 est.)
government consumption: 25.5% (2023 est.)
investment in fixed capital: 12.3% (2023 est.)
investment in inventories: 10% (2023 est.)
exports of goods and services: 43.5% (2023 est.)
imports of goods and services: -64.6% (2023 est.)
note: figures may not total 100% due to rounding or gaps in data collection

Agricultural products: sugarcane, cassava, plantains, vegetables, mangoes/guavas, milk, tomatoes, pumpkins/squash, sweet potatoes, bananas (2023)
note: top ten agricultural products based on tonnage

Industries: petroleum, nickel, cobalt, pharmaceuticals, tobacco, construction, steel, cement, agricultural machinery, sugar

Industrial production growth rate: -0.9% (2023 est.)
note: annual % change in industrial value added based on constant local currency
comparison ranking: 146

Labor force: 4.859 million (2024 est.)
note: number of people ages 15 or older who are employed or seeking work
comparison ranking: 88

Unemployment rate: 1.6% (2024 est.)
1.8% (2023 est.)
1.9% (2022 est.)
note: % of labor force seeking employment
comparison ranking: 12

Youth unemployment rate (ages 15-24): *total:* 3.9% (2024 est.)
male: 4.1% (2024 est.)
female: 3.5% (2024 est.)
note: % of labor force ages 15-24 seeking employment
comparison ranking: total 171

Budget: *revenues:* $54.52 billion (2017 est.)
expenditures: $64.64 billion (2017 est.)

Exports: $8.768 billion (2020 est.)
$12.632 billion (2019 est.)

$14.53 billion (2018 est.)
note: GDP expenditure basis - exports of goods and services in current dollars
comparison ranking: 122

Exports - partners: China 34%, Spain 12%, Germany 6%, Switzerland 5%, Hong Kong 4% (2023)
note: top five export partners based on percentage share of exports

Exports - commodities: tobacco, nickel, liquor, zinc ore, precious metal ore (2023)
note: top five export commodities based on value in dollars

Imports: $8.067 billion (2020 est.)
$10.971 billion (2019 est.)
$12.567 billion (2018 est.)
note: GDP expenditure basis - imports of goods and services in current dollars
comparison ranking: 132

Imports - partners: Spain 24%, China 13%, Netherlands 10%, USA 9%, Canada 6% (2023)
note: top five import partners based on percentage share of imports

Imports - commodities: beer, poultry, rice, plastic products, soybean oil (2023)
note: top five import commodities based on value in dollars

Exchange rates: Cuban pesos (CUP) per US dollar -

Exchange rates: 24 (2024 est.)
24 (2023 est.)
24 (2022 est.)
24 (2021 est.)
1 (2020 est.)
note: official exchange rate of 24 Cuban pesos per US dollar effective 1 January 2021

ENERGY

Electricity access: *electrification - total population:* 100% (2022 est.)

Electricity: *installed generating capacity:* 7.264 million kW (2023 est.)
consumption: 11.951 billion kWh (2023 est.)
transmission/distribution losses: 3.352 billion kWh (2023 est.)
comparison rankings: installed generating capacity 76; consumption 99; transmission/distribution losses 146

Electricity generation sources: *fossil fuels:* 95.2% of total installed capacity (2023 est.)
solar: 1.4% of total installed capacity (2023 est.)
wind: 0.4% of total installed capacity (2023 est.)
hydroelectricity: 0.8% of total installed capacity (2023 est.)
biomass and waste: 2.2% of total installed capacity (2023 est.)

Coal: *consumption:* 1,000 metric tons (2023 est.)
exports: 25 metric tons (2023 est.)
imports: 8,000 metric tons (2023 est.)

Petroleum: *total petroleum production:* 34,000 bbl/day (2023 est.)
refined petroleum consumption: 118,000 bbl/day (2023 est.)
crude oil estimated reserves: 124 million barrels (2021 est.)

Natural gas: *production:* 850.133 million cubic meters (2023 est.)
consumption: 850.133 million cubic meters (2023 est.)
proven reserves: 70.792 billion cubic meters (2021 est.)

Energy consumption per capita: 26.07 million Btu/person (2023 est.)
comparison ranking: 121

COMMUNICATIONS

Telephones - fixed lines: *total subscriptions:* 1.589 million (2023 est.)
subscriptions per 100 inhabitants: 14 (2023 est.)
comparison ranking: total subscriptions 56

Telephones - mobile cellular: *total subscriptions:* 7.67 million (2023 est.)
subscriptions per 100 inhabitants: 68 (2022 est.)
comparison ranking: total subscriptions 106

Broadcast media: *government owns and controls all broadcast media:* 8 national TV channels (Cubavision, Cubavision Plus, Tele Rebelde, Multivision, Educational Channel 1 and 2, Canal Clave, Canal Habana), 2 international channels (Cubavision Internacional and Canal Caribe), multiple regional TV stations, 7 national radio networks, and multiple regional radio stations; the government uses the Radio-TV Marti signal; private ownership of electronic media is officially prohibited, with several online independent news sites tolerated but blocked if critical of the government; YouTube popular; Christian denominations create original video content to distribute via social media (2023)

Internet country code: .cu

Internet users: *percent of population:* 71% (2023 est.)
note: private citizens are prohibited from buying computers or accessing the Internet without special authorization; foreigners may access the Internet in large hotels but are subject to firewalls; some Cubans buy illegal passwords on the black market or take advantage of public outlets to access limited email and the government-controlled "intranet"; issues relating to COVID-19 impact research into internet adoption, so actual internet user figures may be different than published numbers suggest

Broadband - fixed subscriptions: *total:* 327,000 (2023 est.)
subscriptions per 100 inhabitants: 3 (2023 est.)
comparison ranking: total 114

TRANSPORTATION

Civil aircraft registration country code prefix: CU

Airports: 120 (2025)
comparison ranking: 43

Heliports: 4 (2025)
comparison ranking: 113

Railways: *total:* 8,367 km (2017)
standard gauge: 8,195 km (2017) 1.435-m gauge (124 km electrified)
narrow gauge: 172 km (2017) 1.000-m gauge
note: As of 2013, 70 km of standard gauge and 12 km of narrow gauge track were not for public use

Merchant marine: *total:* 65 (2023)
by type: general cargo 13, oil tanker 10, other 42
comparison ranking: total 111

Ports: *total ports:* 34 (2024)
large: 6
medium: 3
small: 10
very small: 6
size unknown: 9
ports with oil terminals: 14
key ports: Antilla, Bahai de la Habana, Bahia de Sagua de Tanamo, Cabanas, Casilda, Cienfuegos, Nuevitas Bay, Puerto Guantanamo, Santiago de Cuba

MILITARY AND SECURITY

Military and security forces: Revolutionary Armed Forces (Fuerzas Armadas Revolucionarias, FAR): Ground Troops (Tropas Terrestres), Revolutionary Navy (Marina de Guerra Revolucionaria, MGR), Revolutionary Air and Air Defense Forces (Defensas Anti-Aereas y Fuerza Aerea Revolucionaria, DAAFAR)

Paramilitary forces under the FAR: Youth Labor Army (Ejercito Juvenil del Trabajo, EJT), Territorial Militia Troops (Milicia de Tropas de Territoriales, MTT), Defense and Production Brigades (Brigadas de Producción y Defensa, BPD), Civil Defense Organization (Defensa Civil de Cuba)

Ministry of Interior: National Revolutionary Police (Policía Nacional Revolucionaria, PNR), Directorate of Border Guard Troops (Dirección de Tropas de Guardia Fronteriza, TGF), Department of State Security (Departamento de Seguridad del Estado, DSE) (2025)

Military expenditures: 4.2% of GDP (2020 est.)
3.2% of GDP (2019 est.)
2.9% of GDP (2018 est.)
2.9% of GDP (2017 est.)
3.1% of GDP (2016 est.)

Military and security service personnel strengths: limited available information; estimated 50,000 active Armed Forces (2025)

Military equipment inventories and acquisitions: the military's inventory is comprised of Russian and Soviet-era equipment (2024)

Military service age and obligation: 17-28 years of age for compulsory (men) and voluntary (men and women) military service; conscripts serve for 18-24 months (2025)

Military - note: the Cuban military is largely focused on protecting territorial integrity and the state; it perceives the US as its primary threat; the military is a central pillar of the Cuban regime and viewed as the guardian of the Cuban revolution; it has a large role in the country's politics and economy; many senior government posts are held by military officers, and the FAR reportedly has interests in agriculture, banking and finance, construction, import/export, ports, industry, real estate, retail, shipping, transportation, and tourism (2025)

TRANSNATIONAL ISSUES

Refugees and internally displaced persons: *refugees:* 171 (2024 est.)

IDPs: 37,171 (2024 est.)

Trafficking in persons: *tier rating:* Tier 3 — Cuba does not fully meet the minimum standards for the elimination of trafficking and is not making significant efforts to do so, therefore, Cuba remained on Tier 3; for more details, go to: https://www.state.gov/reports/2025-trafficking-in-persons-report/cuba/

CURAÇAO

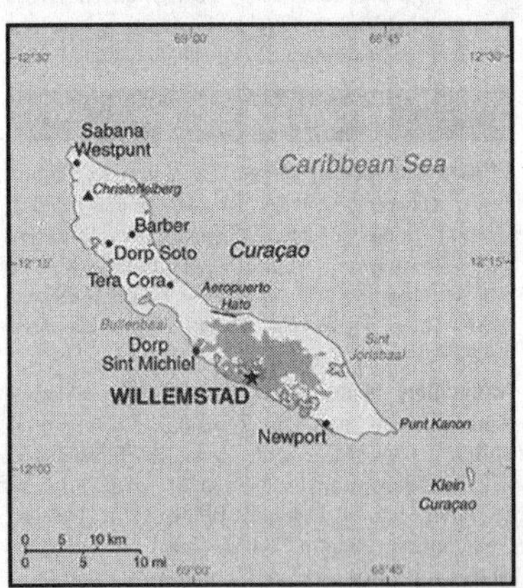

INTRODUCTION

Background: The original Arawak Indian settlers who arrived on Curaçao from South America in about A.D. 1000 were largely enslaved by the Spanish early in the 16th century and forcibly relocated to other colonies where labor was needed. The Dutch seized Curaçao from the Spanish in 1634. Once the center of the Caribbean slave trade, Curaçao was hard hit economically when the Dutch abolished slavery in 1863. Its prosperity (and that of neighboring Aruba) was restored in the early 20th century with the construction of the Isla Refineria to service the newly discovered Venezuelan oilfields. In 1954, Curaçao and several other Dutch Caribbean colonies were reorganized as the Netherlands Antilles, part of the Kingdom of the Netherlands. In referenda in 2005 and 2009, the citizens of Curaçao voted to become a self-governing country within the Kingdom of the Netherlands. The change in status became effective in 2010 with the dissolution of the Netherlands Antilles.

GEOGRAPHY

Location: Caribbean, an island in the Caribbean Sea, 55 km off the coast of Venezuela

Geographic coordinates: 12 10 N, 69 00 W

Map references: Central America and the Caribbean

Area: *total:* 444 sq km
land: 444 sq km
water: 0 sq km
comparison ranking: total 199

Area - comparative: more than twice the size of Washington, D.C.

Land boundaries: *total:* 0 km

Coastline: 364 km

Maritime claims: *territorial sea:* 12 nm
exclusive economic zone: 200 nm

Climate: tropical marine climate, ameliorated by northeast trade winds, results in mild temperatures; semiarid with average rainfall of 60 cm/year

Terrain: generally low, hilly terrain

Elevation: *highest point:* Mt. Christoffel 372 m
lowest point: Caribbean Sea 0 m

Natural resources: calcium phosphates, protected harbors, hot springs

Land use: *agricultural land:* 0% (2022 est.)
arable land: 10% (2018)
forest: 0.2% (2022 est.)
other: 99.8% (2022 est.)

Irrigated land: NA

Population distribution: largest concentration on the island is Willemstad; smaller settlements near the coast can be found throughout the island, particularly in the northwest

Natural hazards: Curaçao is south of the Caribbean hurricane belt and is rarely threatened

Geography - note: Curaçao is a part of the Windward Islands (southern) group in the Lesser Antilles

PEOPLE AND SOCIETY

Population: *total:* 153,289 (2024 est.)
male: 73,755
female: 79,534
comparison rankings: total 187; male 187; female 187

Nationality: *noun:* Curacaoan
adjective: Curacaoan; Dutch

Ethnic groups: Curacaoan 75.4%, Dutch 6%, Dominican 3.6%, Colombian 3%, Bonairean, Sint Eustatian, Saban 1.5%, Haitian 1.2%, Surinamese 1.2%, Venezuelan 1.1%, Aruban 1.1%, other 5%, unspecified 0.9% (2011 est.)

Languages: Papiamento (official) (a creole language that is a mixture of Portuguese, Spanish, Dutch, English, and, to a lesser extent, French, as well as elements of African languages and the language of the Arawak) 80%, Dutch (official) 8.8%, Spanish 5.6%, English (official) 3.1%, other 2.3%, unspecified 0.3% (2011 est.)
note: data represent most spoken language in household

Religions: Roman Catholic 72.8%, Pentecostal 6.6%, Protestant 3.2%, Adventist 3%, Jehovah's Witness 2%, Evangelical 1.9%, other 3.8%, none 6%, unspecified 0.6% (2011 est.)

Age structure: *0-14 years:* 19.2% (male 15,069/female 14,337)
15-64 years: 62.3% (male 47,258/female 48,217)
65 years and over: 18.5% (2024 est.) (male 11,428/female 16,980)

Dependency ratios: *total dependency ratio:* 60.6 (2024 est.)
youth dependency ratio: 30.8 (2024 est.)
elderly dependency ratio: 29.8 (2024 est.)
potential support ratio: 3.4 (2024 est.)

Median age: *total:* 37.8 years (2024 est.)
male: 35.5 years
female: 40.2 years
comparison ranking: total 81

Population growth rate: 0.28% (2024 est.)
comparison ranking: 168

Birth rate: 12.9 births/1,000 population (2024 est.)
comparison ranking: 135

Death rate: 8.9 deaths/1,000 population (2024 est.)
comparison ranking: 64

Net migration rate: -1.3 migrant(s)/1,000 population (2024 est.)
comparison ranking: 152

Population distribution: largest concentration on the island is Willemstad; smaller settlements near the coast can be found throughout the island, particularly in the northwest

Urbanization: *urban population:* 89% of total population (2023)
rate of urbanization: 0.57% annual rate of change (2020-25 est.)

Major urban areas - population: 144,000 WILLEMSTAD (capital) (2018)

Sex ratio: *at birth:* 1.05 male(s)/female
0-14 years: 1.05 male(s)/female
15-64 years: 0.98 male(s)/female
65 years and over: 0.67 male(s)/female
total population: 0.93 male(s)/female (2024 est.)

Infant mortality rate: *total:* 7.5 deaths/1,000 live births (2024 est.)
male: 8.3 deaths/1,000 live births
female: 6.7 deaths/1,000 live births
comparison ranking: total 152

Life expectancy at birth: *total population:* 79.9 years (2024 est.)
male: 77.6 years
female: 82.3 years
comparison ranking: total population 59

Total fertility rate: 1.96 children born/woman (2024 est.)
comparison ranking: 111

Gross reproduction rate: 0.96 (2024 est.)

Currently married women (ages 15-49): 49.7% (2023 est.)

Education expenditure: 7.4% of GDP (2020 est.)
comparison ranking: Education expenditure (% GDP) 14

ENVIRONMENT

Environmental issues: waste management, including pollution of marine areas from domestic sewage, inadequate sewage treatment facilities, industrial effluents, agricultural runoff, mismanagement of toxic substances, and ineffective regulations; damage from neglect and a lack of controls at major refinery

Climate: tropical marine climate, ameliorated by northeast trade winds, results in mild temperatures; semiarid with average rainfall of 60 cm/year

Urbanization: *urban population:* 89% of total population (2023)
rate of urbanization: 0.57% annual rate of change (2020-25 est.)

Waste and recycling: *municipal solid waste generated annually:* 24,700 tons (2024 est.)

GOVERNMENT

Country name: *conventional long form:* Country of Curacao
conventional short form: Curacao
local long form: Land Curacao (Dutch)/Pais Korsou (Papiamento)
local short form: Curacao (Dutch)/ Korsou (Papiamento)
former: Netherlands Antilles; Curacao and Dependencies

etymology: the origin of the name is disputed; many historians now agree that the name derives from a similar-sounding word the original inhabitants used to describe themselves

Government type: parliamentary democracy

Dependency status: constituent country of the Kingdom of the Netherlands; full autonomy in internal affairs granted in 2010; Dutch government responsible for defense and foreign affairs

Capital: *name:* Willemstad
geographic coordinates: 12 06 N, 68 55 W
time difference: UTC-4 (1 hour ahead of Washington, DC, during Standard Time)
etymology: the name means "William's Town" in Dutch; named after Prince WILLEM of Orange (1533-84), the first stadtholder of the United Provinces of the Netherlands

Administrative divisions: none (part of the Kingdom of the Netherlands)
note: Curaçao is one of four constituent countries of the Kingdom of the Netherlands; the other three are the Netherlands, Aruba, and Sint Maarten

Legal system: based on Dutch civil law

Constitution: *history:* previous 1947, 1955; latest adopted 5 September 2010, entered into force 10 October 2010 (regulates governance of Curacao but is subordinate to the Charter for the Kingdom of the Netherlands)

Citizenship: see the Netherlands

Suffrage: 18 years of age; universal

Executive branch: *chief of state:* King WILLEM-ALEXANDER of the Netherlands (since 30 April 2013); represented by Governor Lucille A. GEORGE-WOUT (since 4 November 2013)
head of government: Prime Minister Gilmar PISAS (since 14 June 2021)
cabinet: Cabinet sworn-in by the governor
election/appointment process: the monarch is hereditary; governor appointed by the monarch; following legislative elections, the legislature usually elects the leader of the majority party as prime minister
most recent election date: 21 March 2025
expected date of next election: 2029

Legislative branch: *legislature name:* Parliament of Curacao
legislative structure: unicameral
number of seats: 21 (directly elected)
electoral system: proportional representation
scope of elections: full renewal
term in office: 4 years
most recent election date: 3/19/2021
parties elected and seats per party: MFK (9); PAR (4); PNP (4); MAN (2); KEM (1); TPK (1)
percentage of women in chamber: 28.6%
expected date of next election: 2025

Judicial branch: *highest court(s):* Joint Court of Justice of Aruba, Curacao, Sint Maarten, and of Bonaire, Sint Eustatius and Saba or "Joint Court of Justice" (sits as a 3-judge panel); final appeals heard by the Supreme Court in The Hague, Netherlands
judge selection and term of office: Joint Court judges appointed by the monarch for life
subordinate courts: first instance courts, appeals court; specialized courts

Political parties: Korsou di Nos Tur or KdnT
Korsou Esun Miho or KEM
Movementu Futuro Korsou or MFK
Movementu Progresivo or MP
Movishon Antia Nobo or MAN
Partido Antia Restruktura or PAR
Partido Inovashon Nashonal or PIN
Partido Nashonal di Pueblo or PNP
Pueblo Soberano or PS
Trabou pa Kòrsou or TPK
Un Korsou Hustu

Diplomatic representation in the US: none (represented by the Kingdom of the Netherlands)

Diplomatic representation from the US: *chief of mission:* Consul General Ramón "Chico" NEGRÓN (since 9 June 2025); note - also accredited to Aruba and Sint Maarten
embassy: P.O. Box 158, J.B. Gorsiraweg 1
mailing address: 3160 Curacao Place, Washington DC 20521-3160
telephone: [599] (9) 461-3066
FAX: [599] (9) 461-6489
email address and website: ACSCuracao@state.gov
https://cw.usconsulate.gov/

International organization participation: ACS (associate), Caricom (observer), FATF, ILO, ITU, UNESCO (associate), UPU

Independence: none (part of the Kingdom of the Netherlands)

National holiday: King's Day (birthday of King WILLEM-ALEXANDER), 27 April (1967)
note: King's or Queen's Day are observed on the ruling monarch's birthday; celebrated on 26 April if 27 April is a Sunday

Flag: *description:* on a blue field, a horizontal yellow band divides the flag below the center; two five-pointed white stars – the smaller above and to the left of the larger – appear in the upper left
meaning: the blue stands for the sky and sea, and yellow for the sun; the stars symbolize Curacao and its uninhabited sister island of Klein Curacao (Little Curacao); the star points represent the five continents from which Curacao's inhabitants originate

National symbol(s): laraha (citrus tree)

National color(s): blue, yellow, white

National anthem(s): *title:* "Himmo di Korsou" (Anthem of Curacao)
lyrics/music: Guillermo ROSARIO, Mae HENRIQUEZ, Enrique MULLER, Betty DORAN/ Frater Candidus NOWENS, Errol "El Toro" COLINA
history: adapted 1978; the lyrics, originally written in 1899, were rewritten in 1978 to remove colonial references

National heritage: *total World Heritage Sites:* 1 (cultural); note - excerpted from the Netherlands entry
selected World Heritage Site locales: Historic Willemstad

ECONOMY

Economic overview: high-income island economy; developed infrastructure; tourism and financial services-based economy; investing in information technology incentives; oil refineries service Venezuela and China

Real GDP (purchasing power parity): $4.312 billion (2023 est.)
$4.138 billion (2022 est.)
$3.834 billion (2021 est.)
note: data in 2021 dollars
comparison ranking: 188

Real GDP growth rate: 4.2% (2023 est.)
7.9% (2022 est.)
4.2% (2021 est.)
note: annual GDP % growth based on constant local currency
comparison ranking: 65

Real GDP per capita: $27,700 (2023 est.)
$27,600 (2022 est.)
$25,200 (2021 est.)
note: data in 2021 dollars
comparison ranking: 84

GDP (official exchange rate): $3.281 billion (2023 est.)
note: data in current dollars at official exchange rate

Inflation rate (consumer prices): 2.6% (2019 est.)
2.6% (2018 est.)
1.6% (2017 est.)
note: annual % change based on consumer prices
comparison ranking: 74

GDP - composition, by sector of origin: *agriculture:* 0.3% (2023 est.)
industry: 11.7% (2023 est.)
services: 73.3% (2023 est.)
note: figures may not total 100% due to non-allocated consumption not captured in sector-reported data
comparison rankings: agriculture 194; industry 175; services 24

GDP - composition, by end use: *household consumption:* 73.2% (2018 est.)
government consumption: 14.5% (2018 est.)
investment in fixed capital: 34% (2018 est.)
investment in inventories: 7.1% (2018 est.)
exports of goods and services: 63.2% (2018 est.)
imports of goods and services: -92% (2018 est.)
note: figures may not total 100% due to rounding or gaps in data collection

Agricultural products: aloe, sorghum, peanuts, vegetables, tropical fruit

Industries: tourism, petroleum refining, petroleum transshipment, light manufacturing, financial and business services

Remittances: 5.4% of GDP (2023 est.)
5.2% of GDP (2022 est.)
5.2% of GDP (2021 est.)
note: personal transfers and compensation between resident and non-resident individuals/households/ entities

Current account balance: -$654.688 million (2023 est.)
-$822.667 million (2022 est.)
-$508.758 million (2021 est.)
note: balance of payments - net trade and primary/ secondary income in current dollars
comparison ranking: 117

Exports: $2.107 billion (2023 est.)
$2.046 billion (2022 est.)
$1.363 billion (2021 est.)
note: balance of payments - exports of goods and services in current dollars
comparison ranking: 165

Exports - partners: Armenia 57%, USA 15%, Guyana 5%, Dominican Republic 4%, Netherlands 2% (2023)
note: top five export partners based on percentage share of exports

Exports - commodities: diamonds, refined petroleum, crude petroleum, gold, petroleum coke (2023)
note: top five export commodities based on value in dollars

Imports: $2.764 billion (2023 est.)
$2.891 billion (2022 est.)

$1.91 billion (2021 est.)
note: balance of payments - imports of goods and services in current dollars
comparison ranking: 165

Imports - partners: USA 39%, Netherlands 24%, China 6%, Colombia 5%, Brazil 3% (2023)
note: top five import partners based on percentage share of imports

Imports - commodities: refined petroleum, cars, garments, plastic products, packaged medicine (2023)
note: top five import commodities based on value in dollars

Exchange rates: Netherlands Antillean guilders (ANG) per US dollar -

Exchange rates: 1.79 (2024 est.)
1.79 (2023 est.)
1.79 (2022 est.)
1.79 (2021 est.)
1.79 (2020 est.)

ENERGY

Electricity access: *electrification - total population:* 100% (2022 est.)

COMMUNICATIONS

Telephones - fixed lines: *total subscriptions:* 51,000 (2022 est.)
subscriptions per 100 inhabitants: 27 (2022 est.)
comparison ranking: total subscriptions 154

Telephones - mobile cellular: *total subscriptions:* 172,000 (2022 est.)
subscriptions per 100 inhabitants: 88 (2021 est.)
comparison ranking: total subscriptions 185

Broadcast media: government-run TeleCuracao operates a TV station and a radio station; 2 other privately owned TV stations and several privately owned radio stations (2019)

Internet country code: .cw

Internet users: *percent of population:* 68% (2017 est.)

Broadband - fixed subscriptions: *total:* 61,000 (2022 est.)
subscriptions per 100 inhabitants: 33 (2022 est.)
comparison ranking: total 144

TRANSPORTATION

Civil aircraft registration country code prefix: PJ

Airports: 1 (2025)
comparison ranking: 222

Merchant marine: *total:* 57 (2023)
by type: general cargo 5, oil tanker 1, other 51
comparison ranking: total 116

Ports: *total ports:* 4 (2024)
large: 0
medium: 2
small: 1
very small: 1
ports with oil terminals: 3
key ports: Bullenbaai, Caracasbaai, Sint Michelsbaai, Willemstad

MILITARY AND SECURITY

Military and security forces: Curaçao Militia (CURMIL); Curaçao Volunteer Corps; Curacao Police Force (Korps Politie Curacao) (2025)

Military - note: defense is the responsibility of the Kingdom of the Netherlands; the Dutch Government controls foreign and defense policy; local security forces are supported by the Royal Netherlands Marechaussee (Gendarmerie), the Dutch Caribbean Police Force (Korps Politie Caribisch Nederland, KPCN), and the Dutch Caribbean Coast Guard (DCCG or Kustwacht Caribisch Gebied (KWCARIB)); there are two Dutch naval bases on Curaçao, and the Dutch Army maintains a small unit on a rotational basis (2025)

CYPRUS

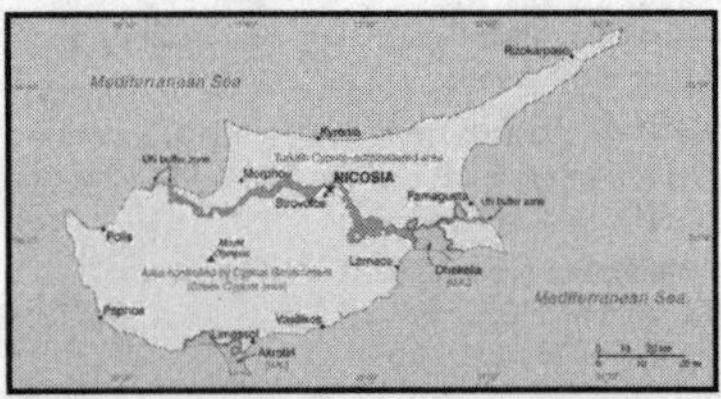

INTRODUCTION

Background: A former British colony, Cyprus became independent in 1960 after years of resistance to British rule. Tensions between the Greek Cypriot majority and Turkish Cypriot minority came to a head in December 1963, when violence broke out in the capital of Nicosia. Despite the deployment of UN peacekeepers in 1964, sporadic intercommunal violence continued and forced most Turkish Cypriots into enclaves throughout the island. In 1974, a Greek Government-sponsored attempt to overthrow the elected president of Cyprus was met by military intervention from Turkey, which soon controlled more than a third of the island. In 1983, the Turkish Cypriot administered area declared itself the "Turkish Republic of Northern Cyprus" (TRNC), but it is recognized only by Turkey. A UN-mediated agreement to reunite Cyprus, the Annan Plan, failed to win approval from both communities in 2004. The most recent round of reunification negotiations was suspended in 2017 after failure to achieve a breakthrough.

The entire island joined the EU in 2004, although the EU acquis – the body of common rights and obligations – applies only to the areas under the internationally recognized government and is suspended in the TRNC. However, individual Turkish Cypriots able to document their eligibility for Republic of Cyprus citizenship have the same legal rights accorded to citizens of other EU states.

GEOGRAPHY

Location: Middle East, island in the Mediterranean Sea, south of Turkey; note - Cyprus views itself as part of Europe; geopolitically, it can be classified as falling within Europe, the Middle East, or both

Geographic coordinates: 35 00 N, 33 00 E

Map references: Middle East

Area: *total:* 9,251 sq km (of which 3,355 sq km are in north Cyprus)
land: 9,241 sq km
water: 10 sq km
comparison ranking: total 169

Area - comparative: about 0.6 times the size of Connecticut

Land boundaries: *total:* 156 km
border sovereign base areas: Akrotiri 48 km; Dhekelia 108 km

Coastline: 648 km

Maritime claims: *territorial sea:* 12 nm
contiguous zone: 24 nm
continental shelf: 200-m depth or to the depth of exploitation

Climate: temperate; Mediterranean with hot, dry summers and cool winters

Terrain: central plain with mountains to north and south; scattered but significant plains along southern coast

Elevation: *highest point:* Mount Olympus 1,951 m
lowest point: Mediterranean Sea 0 m
mean elevation: 91 m

Natural resources: copper, pyrites, asbestos, gypsum, timber, salt, marble, clay earth pigment

Land use: *agricultural land:* 13.3% (2022 est.)
arable land: 10.3% (2022 est.)
permanent crops: 2.8% (2022 est.)
permanent pasture: 0.2% (2022 est.)
forest: 18.7% (2022 est.)
other: 68% (2022 est.)

Irrigated land: 269 sq km (2020)

Population distribution: *population concentrated in central Nicosia and in the major cities of the south:* Paphos, Limassol, and Larnaca

Natural hazards: moderate earthquake activity; droughts

Geography - note: the third largest island in the Mediterranean Sea (after Sicily and Sardinia)

PEOPLE AND SOCIETY

Population: *total:* 1,320,525 (2024 est.)
male: 675,196
female: 645,329
comparison rankings: total 158; male 158; female 157

Nationality: *noun:* Cypriot(s)
adjective: Cypriot

Ethnic groups: Greek 98.8%, other 1% (includes Maronite, Armenian, Turkish-Cypriot), unspecified 0.2% (2011 est.)
note: data represent only the Greek-Cypriot citizens in the Republic of Cyprus

Languages: Greek (official) 80.9%, Turkish (official) 0.2%, English 4.1%, Romanian 2.9%, Russian 2.5%,

Bulgarian 2.2%, Arabic 1.2%, Filipino 1.1%, other 4.3%, unspecified 0.6% (2011 est.)
major-language sample(s):
Το Παγκόσμιο Βιβλίο Δεδομένων, η απαραίτητη πηΥή βασικών πληροφοριών. (Greek)
note: data represent only the Republic of Cyprus

Religions: Eastern Orthodox Christian 89.1%, Roman Catholic 2.9%, Protestant/Anglican 2%, Muslim 1.8%, Buddhist 1%, other (includes Maronite Catholic, Armenian Apostolic, Hindu) 1.4%, unknown 1.1%, none/atheist 0.6% (2011 est.)
note: data represent only the government-controlled area of Cyprus

Age structure: *0-14 years:* 15.6% (male 105,533/ female 100,099)
15-64 years: 70% (male 486,569/female 437,651)
65 years and over: 14.4% (2024 est.) (male 83,094/ female 107,579)

Dependency ratios: *total dependency ratio:* 42.9 (2024 est.)
youth dependency ratio: 22.2 (2024 est.)
elderly dependency ratio: 20.6 (2024 est.)
potential support ratio: 4.8 (2024 est.)
note: data represent the whole country

Median age: *total:* 39.5 years (2024 est.)
male: 38.2 years
female: 41 years
comparison ranking: total 67

Population growth rate: 0.95% (2024 est.)
comparison ranking: 95

Birth rate: 10.2 births/1,000 population (2024 est.)
comparison ranking: 182

Death rate: 7 deaths/1,000 population (2024 est.)
comparison ranking: 123

Net migration rate: 6.3 migrant(s)/1,000 population (2024 est.)
comparison ranking: 13

Population distribution: *population concentrated in central Nicosia and in the major cities of the south:* Paphos, Limassol, and Larnaca

Urbanization: *urban population:* 67% of total population (2023)
rate of urbanization: 0.76% annual rate of change (2020-25 est.)

Major urban areas - population: 269,000 NICOSIA (capital) (2018)

Sex ratio: *at birth:* 1.05 male(s)/female
0-14 years: 1.05 male(s)/female
15-64 years: 1.11 male(s)/female
65 years and over: 0.77 male(s)/female
total population: 1.05 male(s)/female (2024 est.)

Mother's mean age at first birth: 30 years (2020 est.)
note: data represents only government-controlled areas

Maternal mortality ratio: 14 deaths/100,000 live births (2023 est.)
comparison ranking: 140

Infant mortality rate: *total:* 8.1 deaths/1,000 live births (2024 est.)
male: 9.7 deaths/1,000 live births
female: 6.4 deaths/1,000 live births
comparison ranking: total 144

Life expectancy at birth: *total population:* 80.2 years (2024 est.)
male: 77.4 years
female: 83.1 years
comparison ranking: total population 56

Total fertility rate: 1.49 children born/woman (2024 est.)
comparison ranking: 203

Gross reproduction rate: 0.73 (2024 est.)

Drinking water source: *improved: urban:* 99.7% of population (2022 est.)
rural: 99.8% of population (2022 est.)
total: 99.8% of population (2022 est.)
unimproved: urban: 0.3% of population (2022 est.)
rural: 0.2% of population (2022 est.)
total: 0.2% of population (2022 est.)

Health expenditure: 9.4% of GDP (2021)
18.3% of national budget (2022 est.)

Physician density: 3.56 physicians/1,000 population (2022)

Hospital bed density: 2.2 beds/1,000 population (2019 est.)

Sanitation facility access: *improved: urban:* 99.7% of population (2022 est.)
rural: 98.8% of population (2022 est.)
total: 99.4% of population (2022 est.)
unimproved: urban: 0.3% of population (2022 est.)
rural: 1.2% of population (2022 est.)
total: 0.6% of population (2022 est.)

Obesity - adult prevalence rate: 21.8% (2016)
comparison ranking: 84

Alcohol consumption per capita: *total:* 9.59 liters of pure alcohol (2019 est.)
beer: 2.85 liters of pure alcohol (2019 est.)
wine: 2.72 liters of pure alcohol (2019 est.)
spirits: 4.02 liters of pure alcohol (2019 est.)
other alcohols: 0 liters of pure alcohol (2019 est.)
comparison ranking: total 26

Tobacco use: *total:* 33.1% (2025 est.)
male: 44.1% (2025 est.)
female: 22.2% (2025 est.)
comparison ranking: total 13

Currently married women (ages 15-49): 54.5% (2023 est.)

Education expenditure: 5.1% of GDP (2022 est.)
13.2% national budget (2022 est.)
comparison ranking: Education expenditure (% GDP) 59

School life expectancy (primary to tertiary education): *total:* 16 years (2022 est.)
male: 16 years (2022 est.)
female: 17 years (2022 est.)

People - note: demographic data for Cyprus represent the population of the government-controlled area and the area administered by Turkish Cypriots, unless otherwise indicated

ENVIRONMENT

Environmental issues: scarce water resources; salination; water pollution from sewage, industrial wastes, and pesticides; coastal degradation; erosion; loss of wildlife habitats from urbanization

International environmental agreements: *party to:* Air Pollution, Air Pollution-Heavy Metals, Air Pollution-Multi-effect Protocol, Air Pollution-Nitrogen Oxides, Air Pollution-Persistent Organic Pollutants, Air Pollution-Sulphur 94, Biodiversity, Climate Change, Climate Change-Kyoto Protocol, Climate Change-Paris Agreement, Comprehensive Nuclear Test Ban, Desertification, Endangered Species, Environmental Modification, Hazardous Wastes, Law of the Sea, Marine Dumping-London Convention, Nuclear Test Ban, Ozone Layer Protection, Ship Pollution, Tropical Timber 2006, Wetlands, Whaling
signed, but not ratified: none of the selected agreements

Climate: temperate; Mediterranean with hot, dry summers and cool winters

Urbanization: *urban population:* 67% of total population (2023)
rate of urbanization: 0.76% annual rate of change (2020-25 est.)

Carbon dioxide emissions: 6.837 million metric tonnes of CO2 (2023 est.)
from coal and metallurgical coke: 100,000 metric tonnes of CO2 (2023 est.)
from petroleum and other liquids: 6.737 million metric tonnes of CO2 (2023 est.)
comparison ranking: total emissions 126

Particulate matter emissions: 14.5 micrograms per cubic meter (2019 est.)

Waste and recycling: *municipal solid waste generated annually:* 769,500 tons (2024 est.)
percent of municipal solid waste recycled: 17.6% (2022 est.)

Total water withdrawal: *municipal:* 112 million cubic meters (2022)
industrial: 17 million cubic meters (2022 est.)
agricultural: 177 million cubic meters (2022)

Total renewable water resources: 780 million cubic meters (2022 est.)

Geoparks: *total global geoparks and regional networks:* 1
global geoparks and regional networks: Troodos (2023)

GOVERNMENT

Country name: *conventional long form:* Republic of Cyprus
conventional short form: Cyprus
local long form: Kypriaki Dimokratia (Greek)/ Kibris Cumhuriyeti (Turkish)
local short form: Kypros (Greek)/ Kibris (Turkish)
etymology: the Greek name for the island is Kupros, which is probably derived from the Sumerian *kabar*, meaning "copper" or "bronze;" copper mines were located on the island in antiquity
note: the Turkish Cypriot community, which administers the northern part of the island, refers to itself as the "Turkish Republic of Northern Cyprus" or "TRNC" ("Kuzey Kibris Turk Cumhuriyeti" or "KKTC")

Government type: Republic of Cyprus - presidential republic; self-declared "Turkish Republic of Northern Cyprus" (TRNC) - parliamentary republic with enhanced presidency
note: a separation of the two main ethnic communities inhabiting the island began following the outbreak of communal strife in 1963; this separation was further solidified when a Greek military-junta-supported coup attempt prompted the Turkish military intervention in July 1974 that gave the Turkish Cypriots de facto control in the north; Greek Cypriots control the only internationally recognized government on the island; on 15 November 1983, then Turkish Cypriot "President" Rauf DENKTAS declared independence and the formation of the "TRNC," which is recognized only by Turkey

Capital: *name:* Nicosia (Lefkosia/Lefkosa)
geographic coordinates: 35 10 N, 33 22 E
time difference: UTC+2 (7 hours ahead of Washington, DC, during Standard Time)
daylight saving time: +1hr, begins last Sunday in March; ends last Sunday in October

etymology: may have been named after Nike, the Greek goddess of victory; the Greek name for the city, Lefkosia, and the Turkish name, Lefkosa, both mean "White City"

Administrative divisions: 6 districts; Ammochostos (Famagusta; all but a small part located in the Turkish Cypriot community), Keryneia (Kyrenia; the only district located entirely in the Turkish Cypriot community), Larnaka (Larnaca; with a small part located in the Turkish Cypriot community), Lefkosia (Nicosia; a small part administered by Turkish Cypriots), Lemesos (Limassol), Pafos (Paphos)
note: the 5 "districts" of the "Turkish Republic of Northern Cyprus" are Gazimagusa (Famagusta), Girne (Kyrenia), Guzelyurt (Morphou), Iskele (Trikomo), Lefkosa (Nicosia)

Legal system: mixed system of English common law and civil law, with European law supremacy

Constitution: *history:* ratified 16 August 1960
amendment process: constitution of the Republic of Cyprus – proposed by the House of Representatives; passage requires at least two-thirds majority vote of the total membership of the "Greek Community" and the "Turkish Community"; however, all seats of Turkish Cypriot members have remained vacant since 1964
constitution of the "Turkish Republic of Northern Cyprus" – proposed by at least 10 members of the "Assembly of the Republic"; passage requires at least two-thirds majority vote of the total Assembly membership and approval by referendum
note: in 1963, the constitution was partly suspended as Turkish Cypriots withdrew from the government; Turkish-held territory in 1983 was declared the "Turkish Republic of Northern Cyprus" ("TRNC"); in 1985, the "TRNC" approved its own constitution

International law organization participation: accepts compulsory ICJ jurisdiction with reservations; accepts ICCt jurisdiction

Citizenship: *citizenship by birth:* no
citizenship by descent only: at least one parent must be a citizen of Cyprus
dual citizenship recognized: yes
residency requirement for naturalization: 7 years

Suffrage: 18 years of age; universal

Executive branch: *chief of state:* President Nikos CHRISTODOULIDIS (since 28 February 2023)
head of government: President Nikos CHRISTODOULIDIS (since 28 February 2023)
cabinet: Council of Ministers appointed by the president
election/appointment process: president directly elected by absolute-majority popular vote in 2 rounds, if needed, for a 5-year term (limited to 2 consecutive terms)
most recent election date: 5 February 2023, with a run-off on 12 February 2023
election results: *2023:* Nikos CHRISTODOULIDIS elected president in second round; percent of vote in first round - Nikos CHRISTODOULIDIS (independent) 32%, Andreas MAVROGIANNIS (independent) 29.6%, Averof NEOFYTOU (DISY) 26.1%, Christos CHRISTOU (ELAM) 6%, other 6.3%; percent of vote in second round - Nikos CHRISTODOULIDS 52%, Andreas MAVROGIANNIS 48%
2018: Nikos ANASTASIADIS reelected president in second round; percent of vote in first round - Nikos ANASTASIADIS (DISY) 35.5%, Stavros MALAS (AKEL) 30.2%, Nicolas PAPADOPOULOS (DIKO) 25.7%, other 8.6%; percent of vote in second round - Nikos ANASTASIADIS 56%, Stavros MALAS 44%
expected date of next election: 2028
note 1: vice presidency reserved for a Turkish Cypriot, but the post has been vacant since 1974 because Turkish Cypriots do not participate in the Republic of Cyprus Government
note 2: under the 1960 constitution, 3 ministerial posts are reserved for Turkish Cypriots, appointed by the vice president, but Greek Cypriots currently hold the positions

Legislative branch: *legislature name:* House of Representatives (Vouli Antiprosopon)
legislative structure: unicameral
number of seats: 80 (all directly elected)
electoral system: proportional representation
scope of elections: full renewal
term in office: 5 years
most recent election date: 5/30/2021
parties elected and seats per party: Democratic Rally (DISY) (17); Progressive Party of the Working People (AKEL) (15); Democratic Party (DIKO) (9); National Popular Front (ELAM) (4); Movement of Social Democrats (EDEK) (4); Democratic Alignment (DIPA) (4); Cyprus Green Party (KOP) (3)
percentage of women in chamber: 14.3%
expected date of next election: May 2026
note: the area of Cyprus that Turkish Cypriots administer has a separate unicameral Assembly of the Republic, or Cumhuriyet Meclisi (50 seats); members are directly elected in multi-seat constituencies by proportional representation vote

Judicial branch: *highest court(s):* Supreme Court of Cyprus (consists of 13 judges, including the court president)
judge selection and term of office: Republic of Cyprus Supreme Court judges appointed by the president of the republic on the recommendation of the Supreme Court judges; judges can serve until age 68; "TRNC Supreme Court" judges appointed by the "Supreme Council of Judicature," a 12-member body of judges, the attorney general, appointees by the president of the "TRNC," and by the "Legislative Assembly," and members elected by the bar association; judge tenure NA
subordinate courts: Republic of Cyprus district courts; Assize Courts; Administrative Court; specialized courts for issues relating to family, industrial disputes, the military, and rent control; "TRNC Assize Courts"; "TNRC district and family courts"
note: the highest court in the TRNC is the Supreme Court (consists of 8 judges, including the court president)

Political parties: *area under government control:*
Democratic Front or DIPA
Democratic Party or DIKO
Democratic Rally or DISY
Movement of Ecologists - Citizens' Alliance
Movement of Social Democrats EDEK
National Popular Front or ELAM
Progressive Party of the Working People or AKEL (Communist Party)
Solidarity Movement
area administered by Turkish Cypriots: Communal Democracy Party or TDP
Communal Liberation Party - New Forces or TKP-YG
Cyprus Socialist Party or KSP
Democratic Party or DP
National Democratic Party or NDP
National Unity Party or UBP
New Cyprus Party or YKP
People's Party or HP
Rebirth Party or YDP
Republican Turkish Party or CTP
United Cyprus Party or BKP

Diplomatic representation in the US: *chief of mission:* Ambassador Evangelos SAVVA (since 15 September 2023)
chancery: 2211 R Street NW, Washington, DC 20008
telephone: [1] (202) 462-5772
FAX: [1] (202) 483-6710
email address and website: info@cyprusembassy.net
https://www.cyprusembassy.net/
consulate(s) general: New York
honorary consulate(s): Atlanta, Chicago, Houston, Kirkland (WA), Los Angeles, New Orleans, San Francisco

Diplomatic representation from the US: *chief of mission:* Ambassador Julie Davis FISHER (since 21 February 2023); note - Ambassador FISHER is temporarily assigned to the U.S. Embassy in Kyiv, Ukraine as Chargé d' Affaires ad interim; she remains fully accredited in Cyprus
embassy: Metochiou and Ploutarchou Street, 2407, Engomi, Nicosia
mailing address: 5450 Nicosia Place, Washington DC 20521-5450
telephone: [357] (22) 393939
FAX: [357] (22) 780944
email address and website: ACSNicosia@state.gov
https://cy.usembassy.gov/

International organization participation: Australia Group, C, CD, CE, EBRD, ECB, EIB, EMU, EU, FAO, IAEA, IBRD, ICAO, ICC (national committees), ICCt, ICRM, IDA, IFAD, IFC, IFRCS, IHO, ILO, IMF, IMO, IMSO, Interpol, IOC, IOM, IPU, ISO, ITSO, ITU, ITUC (NGOs), MIGA, NAM, NSG, OAS (observer), OIF, OPCW, OSCE, PCA, UN, UNCTAD, UNESCO, UNHCR, UNIDO, UNIFIL, UNWTO, UPU, WCO, WFTU (NGOs), WHO, WIPO, WMO, WTO

Independence: 16 August 1960 (from the UK)
note: Turkish Cypriots proclaimed self-rule on 13 February 1975 and independence in 1983, but only Turkey recognizes these proclamations

National holiday: Independence Day, 1 October (1960)
note: Turkish Cypriots celebrate 15 November (1983) as "Republic Day"

Flag: *description:* a copper-colored silhouette of the island is centered on a white field above two crossed green olive branches
meaning: the olive branches symbolize hope for peace and reconciliation between the Greek and Turkish communities
note 1: one of two national flags that uses a map as a design element; the flag of Kosovo is the other
note 2: the "Turkish Republic of Northern Cyprus" flag retains the white field of the Cyprus national flag but has narrow horizontal red stripes near the top and bottom edges, with a red crescent and a five-pointed red star between them; the banner is modeled on the Turkish national flag, but with the colors reversed

National symbol(s): Cypriot mouflon (wild sheep), white dove

National color(s): blue, white

National anthem(s): *title:* "Ymnos eis tin Eleftherian" (Hymn to Freedom)
lyrics/music: Dionysios SOLOMOS/Nikolaos MANTZAROS
history: adopted 1966; Cyprus uses the Greek national anthem; the Turkish Cypriot community in Cyprus uses Turkey's national anthem

National heritage: *total World Heritage Sites:* 3 (all cultural)
selected World Heritage Site locales: Paphos; Painted Churches in the Troodos Region; Choirokoitia

ECONOMY

Economic overview: services-based, high-income EU island economy; heavy tourism; sustained growth between recovery of national banking system and COVID-19 trade restrictions; high living standards; a known financial hub, its stock exchange functions as an investment bridge between EU-and EEU-member countries
note: Even though the whole of the island is part of the EU, implementation of the EU "acquis communautaire" has been suspended in the area administered by Turkish Cypriots, known locally as the Turkish Republic of Northern Cyprus, until political conditions permit the reunification of the island. Its market-based economy is roughly one-fifth the size of its southern neighbor and is likewise dominated by the service sector with a large portion of the population employed by the government. Manufacturing is limited mainly to food and beverages, furniture and fixtures, construction materials, metal and non-metal products, textiles and clothing. Little trade exists with the Republic of Cyprus outside of construction, historically relying heavily upon Turkey for financial aid, defense, telecommunications, utilities, and postal services. The Turkish Lira is the preferred currency, though foreign currencies are widely accepted in business transactions.

Real GDP (purchasing power parity): $50.055 billion (2024 est.)
$48.386 billion (2023 est.)
$47.085 billion (2022 est.)
note: data in 2021 dollars
comparison ranking: 130

Real GDP growth rate: 3.4% (2024 est.)
2.8% (2023 est.)
7.2% (2022 est.)
note: annual GDP % growth based on constant local currency
comparison ranking: 103

Real GDP per capita: $53,300 (2024 est.)
$52,200 (2023 est.)
$51,600 (2022 est.)
note: data in 2021 dollars
comparison ranking: 36

GDP (official exchange rate): $36.333 billion (2024 est.)
note: data in current dollars at official exchange rate

Inflation rate (consumer prices): 1.8% (2024 est.)
3.5% (2023 est.)
8.4% (2022 est.)
note: annual % change based on consumer prices
comparison ranking: 47

GDP - composition, by sector of origin: *agriculture:* 1.2% (2024 est.)
industry: 10.3% (2024 est.)
services: 76.9% (2024 est.)
note: figures may not total 100% due to non-allocated consumption not captured in sector-reported data
comparison rankings: agriculture 170; industry 185; services 16

GDP - composition, by end use: *household consumption:* 58.9% (2024 est.)
government consumption: 18.6% (2024 est.)
investment in fixed capital: 20.5% (2024 est.)
investment in inventories: -1.6% (2024 est.)
exports of goods and services: 96.7% (2024 est.)
imports of goods and services: -93.1% (2024 est.)
note: figures may not total 100% due to rounding or gaps in data collection

Agricultural products: milk, potatoes, sheep milk, pork, goat milk, wheat, chicken, olives, grapes, barley (2023)
note: top ten agricultural products based on tonnage

Industries: tourism, food and beverage processing, cement and gypsum, ship repair and refurbishment, textiles, light chemicals, metal products, wood, paper, stone and clay products
note: area administered by Turkish Cypriots - foodstuffs, textiles, clothing, ship repair, clay, gypsum, copper, furniture

Industrial production growth rate: 4.6% (2024 est.)
note: annual % change in industrial value added based on constant local currency
comparison ranking: 52

Labor force: 772,300 (2024 est.)
note: number of people ages 15 or older who are employed or seeking work
comparison ranking: 153

Unemployment rate: 5.7% (2024 est.)
6.1% (2023 est.)
6.9% (2022 est.)
note: % of labor force seeking employment
comparison ranking: 110

Youth unemployment rate (ages 15-24): *total:* 15.6% (2024 est.)
male: 17.4% (2024 est.)
female: 13.7% (2024 est.)
note: % of labor force ages 15-24 seeking employment
comparison ranking: total 76

Population below poverty line: *13.9% (2021 est.)*
note: % of population with income below national poverty line

Gini Index coefficient - distribution of family income: 31.5 (2022 est.)
note: index (0-100) of income distribution; higher values represent greater inequality
comparison ranking: 110

Household income or consumption by percentage share: *lowest 10%:* 3.6% (2022 est.)
highest 10%: 26.2% (2022 est.)
note: % share of income accruing to lowest and highest 10% of population

Remittances: 1.8% of GDP (2023 est.)
1.7% of GDP (2022 est.)
2.1% of GDP (2021 est.)
note: personal transfers and compensation between resident and non-resident individuals/households/entities

Budget: *revenues:* $14.39 billion (2023 est.)
expenditures: $13.733 billion (2023 est.)
note: central government revenues (excluding grants) and expenditures converted to US dollars at average official exchange rate for year indicated

Public debt: 97.5% of GDP (2017 est.)
note: data cover general government debt and include debt instruments issued (or owned) by government entities other than the treasury; the data include treasury debt held by foreign entities; the data exclude debt issued by subnational entities, as well as intragovernmental debt; intragovernmental debt consists of treasury borrowings from surpluses in the social funds, such as for retirement, medical care, and unemployment
comparison ranking: 25

Taxes and other revenues: 24.1% (of GDP) (2023 est.)
note: central government tax revenue as a % of GDP
comparison ranking: 21

Current account balance: -$3.05 billion (2024 est.)
-$3.831 billion (2023 est.)
-$2.178 billion (2022 est.)
note: balance of payments - net trade and primary/secondary income in current dollars
comparison ranking: 160

Exports: $35.12 billion (2024 est.)
$32.922 billion (2023 est.)
$32.563 billion (2022 est.)
note: balance of payments - exports of goods and services in current dollars
comparison ranking: 79

Exports - partners: Libya 14%, Greece 11%, Lebanon 8%, Bermuda 7%, Marshall Islands 5% (2023)
note: top five export partners based on percentage share of exports

Exports - commodities: ships, refined petroleum, packaged medicine, cheese, scented mixtures (2023)
note: top five export commodities based on value in dollars

Imports: $33.802 billion (2024 est.)
$32.556 billion (2023 est.)
$31.486 billion (2022 est.)
note: balance of payments - imports of goods and services in current dollars
comparison ranking: 76

Imports - partners: Greece 20%, UK 10%, Italy 7%, Turkey 6%, Spain 6% (2023)
note: top five import partners based on percentage share of imports

Imports - commodities: refined petroleum, ships, cars, packaged medicine, coal tar oil (2023)
note: top five import commodities based on value in dollars

Reserves of foreign exchange and gold: $2.088 billion (2024 est.)
$1.789 billion (2023 est.)
$1.671 billion (2022 est.)
note: holdings of gold (year-end prices)/foreign exchange/special drawing rights in current dollars
comparison ranking: 124

Exchange rates: euros (EUR) per US dollar -
Exchange rates: 0.924 (2024 est.)
0.925 (2023 est.)
0.95 (2022 est.)
0.845 (2021 est.)
0.876 (2020 est.)

ENERGY

Electricity access: *electrification - total population:* 100% (2022 est.)

Electricity: *installed generating capacity:* 2.288 million kW (2023 est.)
consumption: 5.197 billion kWh (2023 est.)

transmission/distribution losses: 146.11 million kWh (2023 est.)
comparison rankings: installed generating capacity 118; consumption 129; transmission/distribution losses 55

Electricity generation sources: *fossil fuels:* 79.1% of total installed capacity (2023 est.)
solar: 16% of total installed capacity (2023 est.)
wind: 3.9% of total installed capacity (2023 est.)
biomass and waste: 1% of total installed capacity (2023 est.)

Coal: *consumption:* 46,000 metric tons (2023 est.)
exports: 71.6 metric tons (2022 est.)
imports: 22,000 metric tons (2023 est.)

Petroleum: *refined petroleum consumption:* 45,000 bbl/day (2023 est.)

Energy consumption per capita: 107.188 million Btu/person (2023 est.)
comparison ranking: 42

COMMUNICATIONS

Telephones - fixed lines: *total subscriptions:* 270,000 (2023 est.)
subscriptions per 100 inhabitants: 29 (2023 est.)
comparison ranking: total subscriptions 110

Telephones - mobile cellular: *total subscriptions:* 1.43 million (2023 est.)
subscriptions per 100 inhabitants: 149 (2021 est.)
comparison ranking: total subscriptions 160

Broadcast media: mix of state and privately run TV and radio; the public broadcaster operates 2 TV channels and 4 radio stations; 6 private TV broadcasters, satellite and cable TV services (including from Greece and Turkey), and a number of private radio stations; in areas administered by Turkish Cypriots, there are 2 public TV stations, 4 public radio stations, 7 privately owned TV stations and 21 privately owned radio stations, 6 radio and 4 TV channels at local universities, 1 military radio station, and 1 radio station for civil defense cooperation, as well as relay stations from Turkey (2019)

Internet country code: .cy

Internet users: *percent of population:* 91% (2023 est.)

Broadband - fixed subscriptions: *total:* 357,000 (2023 est.)
subscriptions per 100 inhabitants: 39 (2023 est.)
comparison ranking: total 110

TRANSPORTATION

Civil aircraft registration country code prefix: 5B

Airports: 14 (2025)
comparison ranking: 150

Heliports: 68 (2025)
comparison ranking: 30

Merchant marine: *total:* 1,005 (2023)
by type: bulk carrier 243, container ship 154, general cargo 211, oil tanker 47, other 350
comparison ranking: total 23

Ports: *total ports:* 6 (2024)
large: 0
medium: 0
small: 3
very small: 3
ports with oil terminals: 4
key ports: Dhekelia, Famagusta, Kyrenia, Larnaca, Limassol, Xeros

MILITARY AND SECURITY

Military and security forces: Cypriot National Guard (Ethniki Froura, EF): Army, Navy, Air Force (2025)

Military expenditures: 1.7% of GDP (2024 est.)
1.8% of GDP (2023 est.)
1.8% of GDP (2022 est.)
1.8% of GDP (2021 est.)
1.8% of GDP (2020 est.)

Military and security service personnel strengths: approximately 12-15,000 active Cypriot National Guard (2025)

Military equipment inventories and acquisitions: the military's inventory includes mostly Russian and Soviet-era weapons and equipment along with a smaller mix of largely older Brazilian, European, Israeli, and US armaments; in 2023, Cyprus announced a 5-year modernization program to replace its Russian-made weapon systems with modern equipment from the West; the country had been under an arms embargo by the US since 1987 but the embargo was lifted in 2022 with conditions that require certifying each year (2024)

Military service age and obligation: Cypriot National Guard (CNG): 18-50 years of age for compulsory military service for all Greek Cypriot males; 17 years of age for voluntary service; 14-month service obligation (2023)
note: the CNG accepts all foreign nationals of at least partial Cypriot descent under age 32 as volunteers; dual citizenship Cypriot origin citizens, who were born in Cyprus or abroad, have the obligation to serve in the CNG on repatriation, regardless of whether or not they possess a foreign citizenship; a person is considered as having Cypriot origin where a grandparent or parent was/is a Cypriot citizen

Military - note: established in 1964, the National Guard (EF) is responsible for ensuring Cyprus's territorial integrity and sovereignty; its primary focus is Turkey, which invaded Cyprus in 1974 and maintains a large military presence in the unrecognized Turkish Republic of Northern Cyprus; the majority of the force is deployed along the "Green Line" that separates the Greek Cypriots from the Turkish Cypriots; the EF also participates in some internal missions, such as providing assistance during natural disasters; Greece is its primary security partner and maintains a military presence on Cyprus; the EF has conducted training exercises with other militaries including France, Israel, and the US; since Cyprus joined the EU in 2004, the EF has actively participated in the EU's Common Security and Defense Policy and has sent small numbers of personnel to some EU and missions; Cyprus is also part of the Organization for Security and Cooperation in Europe
the UN Peacekeeping Force in Cyprus (UNFICYP) has been deployed in Cyprus since 1964; its mandate includes supervising the de facto ceasefire that came into effect in August 1974 and maintaining a buffer zone between the lines of the Cypriot National Guard and of the Turkish and Turkish Cypriot forces; UNFICYP has about 1,100 personnel assigned (2025)

TERRORISM

Terrorist group(s): Terrorist group(s): Islamic State of Iraq and ash-Sham (ISIS)
note: details about the history, aims, leadership, organization, areas of operation, tactics, targets, weapons, size, and sources of support of the group(s) appear(s) in Appendix T

TRANSNATIONAL ISSUES

Refugees and internally displaced persons: *refugees:* 73,303 (2024 est.)

IDPs: 244,944 (2024 est.)
stateless persons: 130 (2024 est.)

CZECHIA

INTRODUCTION

Background: At the close of World War I, the Czechs and Slovaks of the former Austro-Hungarian Empire merged to form Czechoslovakia, a parliamentarian democracy. During the interwar years, having rejected a federal system, the new country's predominantly Czech leaders were frequently preoccupied with meeting the increasingly strident demands of other ethnic minorities within the republic, most notably the Slovaks, the Sudeten Germans, and the Ruthenians (Ukrainians). On the eve of World War II, Nazi Germany occupied the territory that today comprises Czechia, and Slovakia became an independent state allied with Germany. After the war, a reunited but truncated Czechoslovakia (less Ruthenia) fell within the Soviet sphere of influence when the pro-Soviet Communist party staged a coup in February 1948. In 1968, an invasion by fellow Warsaw Pact troops ended the efforts of the country's leaders to liberalize communist rule and create "socialism with a human face," ushering in a period of repression known as "normalization." The peaceful "Velvet Revolution" swept the Communist Party from power at the end of 1989 and inaugurated a return to democratic rule and a market economy. On 1 January 1993, the country underwent a nonviolent "velvet divorce" into its two national components, the Czech Republic and Slovakia. The Czech Republic joined NATO in 1999 and the European Union in 2004. The country formally added the short-form name Czechia in 2016, while also continuing to use the full form name, the Czech Republic.

GEOGRAPHY

Location: Central Europe, between Germany, Poland, Slovakia, and Austria

Geographic coordinates: 49 45 N, 15 30 E

Map references: Europe

Area: *total:* 78,867 sq km
land: 77,247 sq km
water: 1,620 sq km

comparison ranking: total 116

Area - comparative: about two-thirds the size of Pennsylvania; slightly smaller than South Carolina

Land boundaries: *total:* 2,046 km
border countries (4): Austria 402 km; Germany 704 km; Poland 699 km; Slovakia 241 km

Coastline: 0 km (landlocked)

Maritime claims: none (landlocked)

Climate: temperate; cool summers; cold, cloudy, humid winters

Terrain: Bohemia in the west consists of rolling plains, hills, and plateaus surrounded by low mountains; Moravia in the east consists of very hilly country

Elevation: *highest point:* Snezka 1,602 m
lowest point: Labe (Elbe) River 115 m
mean elevation: 433 m

Natural resources: hard coal, soft coal, kaolin, clay, graphite, timber, arable land

Land use: *agricultural land:* 45.7% (2022 est.)
arable land: 32.1% (2022 est.)
permanent crops: 0.6% (2022 est.)
permanent pasture: 13% (2022 est.)
forest: 34.7% (2022 est.)
other: 19.5% (2022 est.)

Irrigated land: 220 sq km (2022)

Major rivers (by length in km): Labe (Elbe) river source (shared with Germany [m]) - 1,252 km
note: [s] after country name indicates river source; [m] after country name indicates river mouth

Major watersheds (area sq km): Atlantic Ocean drainage: *(Black Sea)* Danube (795,656 sq km)

Population distribution: a fairly even distribution throughout most of the country, but the northern and eastern regions tend to have larger urban concentrations

Natural hazards: flooding

Geography - note: *note 1:* landlocked; strategically located on some of oldest and most significant land routes in Europe; Moravian Gate is a traditional military corridor between the North European Plain and the Danube in central Europe
note 2: the Hranice Abyss in Czechia is the world's deepest surveyed freshwater cave at 519 m (1,703 ft); its survey is not complete, and it may be up to 800-1,200 m (2,625-3,937 ft) deep

PEOPLE AND SOCIETY

Population: *total:* 10,837,890 (2024 est.)
male: 5,335,737
female: 5,502,153
comparison rankings: total 86; male 88; female 85

Nationality: *noun:* Czech(s)
adjective: Czech

Ethnic groups: Czech 57.3%, Moravian 3.4%, other 7.7%, unspecified 31.6% (2021 est.)
note: includes only persons with one ethnicity

Languages: Czech (official) 88.4%, Slovak 1.5%, other 2.6%, unspecified 7.2% (2021 est.)
major-language sample(s):
World Factbook, nepostradatelný zdroj základních informací. (Czech)
note: includes only persons with one mother tongue

Religions: Roman Catholic 7%, other believers belonging to a church or religious society 6% (includes Evangelical United Brethren Church and Czechoslovak Hussite Church), believers unaffiliated with a religious society 9.1%, none 47.8%, unspecified 30.1% (2021 est.)

Age structure: *0-14 years:* 15.7% (male 871,303/female 826,896)
15-64 years: 63.8% (male 3,542,298/female 3,373,127)
65 years and over: 20.5% (2024 est.) (male 922,136/female 1,302,130)

Dependency ratios: *total dependency ratio:* 56.7 (2024 est.)
youth dependency ratio: 24.6 (2024 est.)
elderly dependency ratio: 32.2 (2024 est.)
potential support ratio: 3.1 (2024 est.)

Median age: *total:* 44.2 years (2024 est.)
male: 42.7 years
female: 45.7 years
comparison ranking: total 31

Population growth rate: 0.04% (2024 est.)
comparison ranking: 190

Birth rate: 9.8 births/1,000 population (2024 est.)
comparison ranking: 190

Death rate: 12 deaths/1,000 population (2024 est.)
comparison ranking: 17

Net migration rate: 2.7 migrant(s)/1,000 population (2024 est.)
comparison ranking: 40

Population distribution: a fairly even distribution throughout most of the country, but the northern and eastern regions tend to have larger urban concentrations

Urbanization: *urban population:* 74.6% of total population (2023)
rate of urbanization: 0.2% annual rate of change (2020-25 est.)

Major urban areas - population: 1.323 million PRAGUE (capital) (2023)

Sex ratio: *at birth:* 1.05 male(s)/female
0-14 years: 1.05 male(s)/female
15-64 years: 1.05 male(s)/female
65 years and over: 0.71 male(s)/female
total population: 0.97 male(s)/female (2024 est.)

Mother's mean age at first birth: 28.5 years (2020 est.)

Maternal mortality ratio: 3 deaths/100,000 live births (2023 est.)
comparison ranking: 187

Infant mortality rate: *total:* 2.6 deaths/1,000 live births (2024 est.)
male: 2.7 deaths/1,000 live births
female: 2.4 deaths/1,000 live births
comparison ranking: total 214

Life expectancy at birth: *total population:* 78.6 years (2024 est.)
male: 75.6 years
female: 81.8 years
comparison ranking: total population 76

Total fertility rate: 1.73 children born/woman (2024 est.)
comparison ranking: 154

Gross reproduction rate: 0.85 (2024 est.)

Drinking water source: *improved: urban:* 99.9% of population (2022 est.)
rural: 99.8% of population (2022 est.)
total: 99.9% of population (2022 est.)
unimproved: urban: 0.1% of population (2022 est.)
rural: 0.2% of population (2022 est.)
total: 0.1% of population (2022 est.)

Health expenditure: 9.5% of GDP (2021)
16.7% of national budget (2022 est.)

Physician density: 4.35 physicians/1,000 population (2022)

Hospital bed density: 6.6 beds/1,000 population (2020 est.)

Sanitation facility access: *improved: urban:* 100% of population (2022 est.)
rural: 100% of population (2022 est.)
total: 100% of population (2022 est.)
unimproved: urban: 0% of population (2022 est.)
rural: 0% of population (2022 est.)
total: 0% of population (2022 est.)

Obesity - adult prevalence rate: 26% (2016)
comparison ranking: 46

Alcohol consumption per capita: *total:* 12.73 liters of pure alcohol (2019 est.)
beer: 6.77 liters of pure alcohol (2019 est.)
wine: 2.73 liters of pure alcohol (2019 est.)
spirits: 3.24 liters of pure alcohol (2019 est.)
other alcohols: 0 liters of pure alcohol (2019 est.)
comparison ranking: total 3

Tobacco use: *total:* 26.8% (2025 est.)
male: 30.8% (2025 est.)
female: 23% (2025 est.)
comparison ranking: total 32

Currently married women (ages 15-49): 48.4% (2023 est.)

Education expenditure: 4.7% of GDP (2022 est.)
11.1% national budget (2022 est.)
comparison ranking: Education expenditure (% GDP) 75

School life expectancy (primary to tertiary education): *total:* 17 years (2022 est.)
male: 16 years (2022 est.)
female: 18 years (2022 est.)

ENVIRONMENT

Environmental issues: air and water pollution (including acid rain) in areas of northwest Bohemia and in northern Moravia around Ostrava; pollution from industry, mining, and agriculture

International environmental agreements: *party to:* Air Pollution, Air Pollution-Heavy Metals, Air Pollution-Multi-effect Protocol, Air Pollution-Nitrogen Oxides, Air Pollution-Persistent Organic Pollutants, Air Pollution-Sulphur 85, Air Pollution-Sulphur 94, Air Pollution-Volatile Organic Compounds, Antarctic-Environmental Protection, Antarctic Treaty, Biodiversity, Climate Change, Climate Change-Kyoto Protocol, Climate

Change-Paris Agreement, Comprehensive Nuclear Test Ban, Desertification, Endangered Species, Environmental Modification, Hazardous Wastes, Law of the Sea, Nuclear Test Ban, Ozone Layer Protection, Ship Pollution, Tropical Timber 2006, Wetlands, Whaling
signed, but not ratified: none of the selected agreements

Climate: temperate; cool summers; cold, cloudy, humid winters

Urbanization: *urban population:* 74.6% of total population (2023)
rate of urbanization: 0.2% annual rate of change (2020-25 est.)

Carbon dioxide emissions: 79.901 million metric tonnes of CO2 (2023 est.)
from coal and metallurgical coke: 41.667 million metric tonnes of CO2 (2023 est.)
from petroleum and other liquids: 25.707 million metric tonnes of CO2 (2023 est.)
from consumed natural gas: 12.527 million metric tonnes of CO2 (2023 est.)
comparison ranking: total emissions 47

Particulate matter emissions: 15 micrograms per cubic meter (2019 est.)

Waste and recycling: municipal solid waste generated annually:5.335 million tons (2024 est.)
percent of municipal solid waste recycled: 37.3% (2022 est.)

Total water withdrawal: *municipal:* 626 million cubic meters (2022)
industrial: 776 million cubic meters (2022)
agricultural: 44 million cubic meters (2022)

Total renewable water resources: 13.15 billion cubic meters (2022 est.)

Geoparks: *total global geoparks and regional networks:* 1
global geoparks and regional networks: Bohemian Paradise (2023)

GOVERNMENT

Country name: *conventional long form:* Czech Republic
conventional short form: Czechia
local long form: Ceska republika
local short form: Cesko
etymology: name derives from the Czechs, a West Slavic tribe who rose to prominence in the late 9th century A.D.; the tribal name is said to come from an ancestral chief

Government type: parliamentary republic

Capital: *name:* Prague
geographic coordinates: 50 05 N, 14 28 E
time difference: UTC+1 (6 hours ahead of Washington, DC, during Standard Time)
daylight saving time: +1hr, begins last Sunday in March; ends last Sunday in October
etymology: the name may derive from the old Slavic word "praga" or "prah," meaning "threshold;" it could also be related to the same Slavic root word as the modern Czech "pražiti," a term for woodland cleared by burning

Administrative divisions: 13 regions (*kraje*, singular - *kraj*) and 1 capital city* (*hlavni mesto*); Jihocesky (South Bohemia), Jihomoravsky (South Moravia), Karlovarsky (Karlovy Vary), Kralovehradecky (Hradec Kralove), Liberecky (Liberec), Moravskoslezsky (Moravia-Silesia), Olomoucky (Olomouc), Pardubicky (Pardubice), Plzensky (Pilsen), Praha (Prague)*, Stredocesky (Central Bohemia), Ustecky (Usti), Vysocina (Highlands), Zlinsky (Zlin)

Legal system: new civil code enacted in 2014, replacing civil code of 1964 based on former Austro-Hungarian civil codes and socialist theory

Constitution: *history:* previous 1960; latest ratified 16 December 1992, effective 1 January 1993
amendment process: passage requires at least three-fifths concurrence of members present in both houses of Parliament

International law organization participation: has not submitted an ICJ jurisdiction declaration; accepts ICCt jurisdiction

Citizenship: *citizenship by birth:* no
citizenship by descent only: at least one parent must be a citizen of Czechia
dual citizenship recognized: no
residency requirement for naturalization: 5 years

Suffrage: 18 years of age; universal

Executive branch: *chief of state:* President Petr PAVEL (since 9 March 2023)
head of government: Prime Minister Petr FIALA (since 17 December 2021)
cabinet: Cabinet appointed by the president on the recommendation of the prime minister
election/appointment process: president directly elected by absolute-majority popular vote in 2 rounds, if needed, for a 5-year term (limited to 2 consecutive terms); prime minister appointed by the president for a 4-year term
most recent election date: 13-14 January 2023, with a second round on 27-28 January 2023
election results: *2023:* Petr PAVEL elected in the second round; percent of vote in the first round - Petr PAVEL (independent) 35.4%, Andrej BABIS (ANO) 35%, Danuse NERUDOVA (Mayors and Independents) 13.9%, Pavel FISCHER (independent) 6.8%; percent of vote in the second round - Petr PAVEL 58.3%, Andrej BABIS 41.6%
2018: Milos ZEMAN reelected president in the second round; percent of vote - Milos ZEMAN (SPO) 51.4%, Jiri DRAHOS (independent) 48.6%
expected date of next election: by January 2028

Legislative branch: *legislature name:* Parliament (Parlament)
legislative structure: bicameral

Legislative branch - lower chamber: *chamber name:* Chamber of Deputies (Poslanecka Snemovna)
number of seats: 200 (all directly elected)
electoral system: proportional representation
scope of elections: full renewal
term in office: 4 years
most recent election date: 10/8/2021 to 10/9/2021
parties elected and seats per party: ANO (72); SPOLU (71); Pirate Party (Pirati) - Mayors and independents (STAN) (37); Freedom and Direct Democracy (SPD) (20)
percentage of women in chamber: 25.5%
expected date of next election: October 2025

Legislative branch - upper chamber: *chamber name:* Senate (Senat)
number of seats: 81 (all directly elected)
electoral system: plurality/majority
scope of elections: partial renewal
term in office: 6 years
most recent election date: 9/20/2024 to 9/28/2024
parties elected and seats per party: Civic Democratic Party (ODS) (8); Christian Democratic Union - Czechoslovak People's Party (KDU - CSL) (7); TOP 09 (3); ANO 2011 (3); Independents (2); Other (4)
percentage of women in chamber: 21.3%
expected date of next election: September 2026

Judicial branch: *highest court(s):* Supreme Court (organized into Civil Law and Commercial Division, and Criminal Division each with a court chief justice, vice justice, and several judges); Constitutional Court (consists of 15 justices); Supreme Administrative Court (consists of 36 judges, including the court president and vice president, and organized into 6-, 7-, and 9-member chambers)
judge selection and term of office: Supreme Court judges proposed by the Chamber of Deputies and appointed by the president; judges appointed for life; Constitutional Court judges appointed by the president and confirmed by the Senate; judges appointed for 10-year, renewable terms; Supreme Administrative Court judges selected by the president of the Court; unlimited terms
subordinate courts: High Court; regional and district courts

Political parties: Action of Dissatisfied Citizens or ANO (*Akce nespokojených občanů*)
Christian and Democratic Union - Czechoslovak People's Party or *KDU-ČSL*
Civic Democratic Party or ODS
Communist Party of Bohemia and Moravia or KSČM
Czech Pirate Party or Piráti
ForMOST or ProMOST
Freedom and Direct Democracy or SPD
Independents or NEZ
Mayors and Independents or STAN
Mayors for the Liberec Region or SLK
Ostravak
Přísaha
Senator 21 or SEN 21
Social Democracy SOCDEM
Svobodni
Tradition Responsibility Prosperity 09 or TOP 09
Tábor 2020 or T2020
United Democrats - Association of Independents or SD-SN

Diplomatic representation in the US: *chief of mission:* Ambassador Miloslav STAŠEK (since 16 September 2022)
chancery: 3900 Spring of Freedom Street NW, Washington, DC 20008-3803
telephone: [1] (202) 274-9100
FAX: [1] (202) 966-8540
email address and website: washington@embassy.mzv.cz
https://www.mzv.cz/washington/
consulate(s) general: Chicago, Los Angeles, New York

Diplomatic representation from the US: *chief of mission:* Ambassador (vacant); Chargé d'Affaires David WISNER (since June 2025)
embassy: Trziste 15, 118 01 Praha 1 - Mala Strana
mailing address: 5630 Prague Place, Washington DC 20521-5630
telephone: [420] 257-022-000
FAX: [420] 257-022-809
email address and website: ACSPrg@state.gov
https://cz.usembassy.gov/

International organization participation: Australia Group, BIS, BSEC (observer), CD, CE, CEI, CERN, EAPC, EBRD, ECB, EIB, ESA, EU, FAO, IAEA, IBRD, ICAO, ICC (national committees), ICCt, ICRM, IDA, IEA, IFC, IFRCS, ILO, IMF, IMO, IMSO, Interpol, IOC, IOM, IPU, ISO, ITSO, ITU, ITUC (NGOs), MIGA, MONUSCO, NATO, NEA, NSG, OAS (observer), OECD, OIF (observer), OPCW, OSCE, PCA, Schengen Convention,

SELEC, UN, UNCTAD, UNESCO, UNHCR, UNIDO, UNOOSA, UNWTO, UPU, Wassenaar Arrangement, WCO, WFTU (NGOs), WHO, WIPO, WMO, WTO, ZC

Independence: 1 January 1993 (Czechoslovakia split into the Czech Republic and Slovakia)
note: although 1 January is the day the Czech Republic came into being, the Czechs commemorate 28 October 1918, the day the former Czechoslovakia declared its independence from the Austro-Hungarian Empire, as their independence day

National holiday: Czechoslovak Founding Day, 28 October (1918)

Flag: *description:* two equal horizontal bands of white (top) and red with a blue isosceles triangle based on the left side
note: combines the white and red of Bohemia with blue from the arms of Moravia; identical to the flag of the former Czechoslovakia

National symbol(s): silver (or white) double-tailed rampant lion

National color(s): white, red, blue

National anthem(s): *title:* "Kde domov muj?" (Where is My Home?)
lyrics/music: Josef Kajetan TYL/Frantisek Jan SKROUP
history: adopted 1993; the anthem was originally written as incidental music for the play "Fidlovacka" (1834), but it soon became popular as an unofficial anthem of the Czech nation; its first verse served as the official Czechoslovak anthem beginning in 1918, and the second verse (Slovak) was dropped after Czechoslovakia was dissolved in 1993

National heritage: *total World Heritage Sites:* 17 (16 cultural, 1 natural)
selected World Heritage Site locales: Historic Prague (c); Historic Telč (c); Historic Český Krumlov (c); Lednice-Valtice Cultural Landscape (c); Historic Kutná Hora (c); Holy Trinity Column, Olomouc (c); Karlovy Vary Spa (c); Zatec and the Landscape of Saaz Hops; Žatec and the Landscape of Saaz Hops (n)

ECONOMY

Economic overview: high-income, diversified EU economy; manufacturing-oriented exporter led by automotive industry; moderate growth driven by household consumption and investments, despite negative contribution from net exports; tight labor market with low unemployment; gained energy independence from Russian oil in April 2025

Real GDP (purchasing power parity): $521.928 billion (2024 est.)
$516.145 billion (2023 est.)
$516.431 billion (2022 est.)
note: data in 2021 dollars
comparison ranking: 48

Real GDP growth rate: 1.1% (2024 est.)
-0.1% (2023 est.)
2.8% (2022 est.)
note: annual GDP % growth based on constant local currency
comparison ranking: 173

Real GDP per capita: $48,000 (2024 est.)
$47,500 (2023 est.)
$48,400 (2022 est.)
note: data in 2021 dollars
comparison ranking: 43

GDP (official exchange rate): $345.037 billion (2024 est.)
note: data in current dollars at official exchange rate

Inflation rate (consumer prices): 2.4% (2024 est.)
10.7% (2023 est.)
15.1% (2022 est.)
note: annual % change based on consumer prices
comparison ranking: 66

GDP - composition, by sector of origin: *agriculture:* 1.5% (2024 est.)
industry: 30.2% (2024 est.)
services: 59.5% (2024 est.)
note: figures may not total 100% due to non-allocated consumption not captured in sector-reported data
comparison rankings: agriculture 163; industry 54; services 93

GDP - composition, by end use: *household consumption:* 44% (2023 est.)
government consumption: 19.7% (2023 est.)
investment in fixed capital: 27.3% (2023 est.)
investment in inventories: 0.7% (2023 est.)
exports of goods and services: 69% (2023 est.)
imports of goods and services: -64% (2023 est.)
note: figures may not total 100% due to rounding or gaps in data collection

Agricultural products: wheat, sugar beets, milk, barley, rapeseed, potatoes, maize, triticale, pork, chicken (2023)
note: top ten agricultural products based on tonnage

Industries: motor vehicles, metallurgy, machinery and equipment, glass, armaments

Industrial production growth rate: -1% (2024 est.)
note: annual % change in industrial value added based on constant local currency
comparison ranking: 148

Labor force: 5.541 million (2024 est.)
note: number of people ages 15 or older who are employed or seeking work
comparison ranking: 79

Unemployment rate: 2.6% (2024 est.)
2.6% (2023 est.)
2.3% (2022 est.)
note: % of labor force seeking employment
comparison ranking: 25

Youth unemployment rate (ages 15-24): *total:* 8.4% (2024 est.)
male: 8.2% (2024 est.)
female: 8.6% (2024 est.)
note: % of labor force ages 15-24 seeking employment
comparison ranking: total 135

Population below poverty line: 10.2% (2021 est.)
note: % of population with income below national poverty line

Gini Index coefficient - distribution of family income: 25.9 (2022 est.)
note: index (0-100) of income distribution; higher values represent greater inequality
comparison ranking: 143

Average household expenditures: *on food:* 15.7% of household expenditures (2023 est.)
on alcohol and tobacco: 7.7% of household expenditures (2023 est.)

Household income or consumption by percentage share: *lowest 10%:* 3.8% (2022 est.)
highest 10%: 21.8% (2022 est.)
note: % share of income accruing to lowest and highest 10% of population

Remittances: 1.2% of GDP (2024 est.)
1.2% of GDP (2023 est.)
1.4% of GDP (2022 est.)
note: personal transfers and compensation between resident and non-resident individuals/households/entities

Budget: *revenues:* $94.01 billion (2022 est.)
expenditures: $106.07 billion (2022 est.)
note: central government revenues (excluding grants) and expenditures converted to US dollars at average official exchange rate for year indicated

Taxes and other revenues: 12.6% (of GDP) (2022 est.)
note: central government tax revenue as a % of GDP
comparison ranking: 108

Current account balance: $6.047 billion (2024 est.)
-$432.727 million (2023 est.)
-$13.644 billion (2022 est.)
note: balance of payments - net trade and primary/secondary income in current dollars
comparison ranking: 35

Exports: $239.259 billion (2024 est.)
$236.103 billion (2023 est.)
$219.419 billion (2022 est.)
note: balance of payments - exports of goods and services in current dollars
comparison ranking: 34

Exports - partners: Germany 29%, Slovakia 7%, Poland 6%, France 5%, UK 5% (2023)
note: top five export partners based on percentage share of exports

Exports - commodities: cars, vehicle parts/accessories, broadcasting equipment, computers, plastic products (2023)
note: top five export commodities based on value in dollars

Imports: $216.741 billion (2024 est.)
$219.09 billion (2023 est.)
$216.042 billion (2022 est.)
note: balance of payments - imports of goods and services in current dollars
comparison ranking: 34

Imports - partners: Germany 22%, China 17%, Poland 8%, Slovakia 5%, Italy 4% (2023)
note: top five import partners based on percentage share of imports

Imports - commodities: broadcasting equipment, vehicle parts/accessories, cars, plastic products, computers (2023)
note: top five import commodities based on value in dollars

Reserves of foreign exchange and gold: $146.281 billion (2024 est.)
$148.379 billion (2023 est.)
$139.981 billion (2022 est.)
note: holdings of gold (year-end prices)/foreign exchange/special drawing rights in current dollars
comparison ranking: 23

Exchange rates: koruny (CZK) per US dollar -

Exchange rates: 23.217 (2024 est.)
22.198 (2023 est.)
23.357 (2022 est.)
21.678 (2021 est.)
23.21 (2020 est.)

ENERGY

Electricity access: *electrification - total population:* 100% (2022 est.)

Electricity: *installed generating capacity:* 21.802 million kW (2023 est.)
consumption: 63.628 billion kWh (2023 est.)

exports: 22.648 billion kWh (2023 est.)
imports: 13.465 billion kWh (2023 est.)
transmission/distribution losses: 3.012 billion kWh (2023 est.)
comparison rankings: installed generating capacity 48; consumption 47; exports 11; imports 17; transmission/distribution losses 138

Electricity generation sources: *fossil fuels:* 45.1% of total installed capacity (2023 est.)
nuclear: 40.1% of total installed capacity (2023 est.)
solar: 4.2% of total installed capacity (2023 est.)
wind: 0.9% of total installed capacity (2023 est.)
hydroelectricity: 2.6% of total installed capacity (2023 est.)
biomass and waste: 7% of total installed capacity (2023 est.)

Nuclear energy: Number of operational nuclear reactors: 6 (2025)

Net capacity of operational nuclear reactors: 3.96GW (2025 est.)

Percent of total electricity production: 40% (2023 est.)

Coal: *production:* 31.946 million metric tons (2023 est.)
consumption: 33.239 million metric tons (2023 est.)
exports: 2.128 million metric tons (2023 est.)
imports: 4.09 million metric tons (2023 est.)
proven reserves: 3.595 billion metric tons (2023 est.)

Petroleum: *total petroleum production:* 4,000 bbl/day (2023 est.)
refined petroleum consumption: 219,000 bbl/day (2024 est.)
crude oil estimated reserves: 15 million barrels (2021 est.)

Natural gas: *production:* 163.333 million cubic meters (2023 est.)
consumption: 6.499 billion cubic meters (2023 est.)
imports: 6.812 billion cubic meters (2023 est.)
proven reserves: 3.964 billion cubic meters (2021 est.)

Energy consumption per capita: 136.306 million Btu/person (2023 est.)
comparison ranking: 28

COMMUNICATIONS

Telephones - fixed lines: *total subscriptions:* 1.197 million (2023 est.)
subscriptions per 100 inhabitants: 11 (2023 est.)
comparison ranking: total subscriptions 65

Telephones - mobile cellular: *total subscriptions:* 13.6 million (2023 est.)
subscriptions per 100 inhabitants: 128 (2022 est.)
comparison ranking: total subscriptions 79

Broadcast media: 22 national TV stations, with 17 privately owned; publicly operated Czech Television has 5 national channels; over 350 TV channels, many through cable, satellite, and IPTV subscription services; 63 radio broadcasters operate over 80 radio stations, including 7 multiregional radio stations or networks; publicly owned broadcaster Czech Radio operates 4 national, 14 regional, and 4 Internet stations; both Czech Radio and Czech Television are partly financed through a license fee (2019)

Internet country code: .cz

Internet users: *percent of population:* 86% (2023 est.)

Broadband - fixed subscriptions: *total:* 4.1 million (2023 est.)
subscriptions per 100 inhabitants: 38 (2023 est.)
comparison ranking: total 42

TRANSPORTATION

Civil aircraft registration country code prefix: OK

Airports: 252 (2025)
comparison ranking: 28

Heliports: 107 (2025)
comparison ranking: 26

Railways: *total:* 9,548 km (2020) 3,242 km electrified

MILITARY AND SECURITY

Military and security forces: Czech Armed Forces: Land Forces, Air Force, Special Forces (2025)
also has Cyber Command, Territorial Command, Operations Command, plus commands for Land Forces and Air Forces

Military expenditures: 2% of GDP (2025 est.)
2.1% of GDP (2024 est.)
1.5% of GDP (2023 est.)
1.3% of GDP (2022 est.)
1.4% of GDP (2021 est.)

Military and security service personnel strengths: approximately 30,000 active-duty military personnel (2025)

Military equipment inventories and acquisitions: the Czech military has a mix of domestically produced, Soviet-era, and more recently acquired modern weapons and equipment from such suppliers as Austria, Germany, Sweden, and the US; its domestic defense industry has produced such items as armored combat vehicles and light attack aircraft; during the Cold War, Czechoslovakia was a major producer of tanks, armored personnel carriers, military trucks, and trainer aircraft (2024)
note: in 2019, Czechia announced a modernization plan to acquire more Western equipment that was compliant with NATO standards, including armored vehicles, fighter aircraft, and helicopters

Military service age and obligation: 18-28 years of age for voluntary military service for men and women; conscription abolished 2004 (2024)
note: as of 2023, women comprised nearly 14% of the military's full-time personnel

Military deployments: up to 130 Lithuania (NATO); 130 Slovakia (NATO) (2024)

Military - note: the Czech military is responsible for national and territorial defense, assisting civil authorities during natural disasters or other emergencies, boosting border security alongside the police, participating in international peacekeeping operations, and supporting its collective security commitments to the EU and NATO, both of which Czechia considers pillars of its national security strategy; Czechia is a member of the Organization for Security and Cooperation in Europe, contributes to UN peacekeeping operations, and actively participates in EU military and security missions under the EU Common Security and Defense Policy; the Czech military has been an active member of NATO since the country joined in 2009 and participates in a variety of NATO's collective defense missions, including contributing to the Enhanced Forward Presence in Eastern Europe, Baltic Air Policing operations, rapid response forces, and operations in Kosovo; it also exercises regularly with NATO partners and maintains close bilateral ties to a number of militaries particularly partner members of the Visegrad Group (Hungary, Poland, and Slovakia) and Germany
the military has commands for its land, air, cyber/information operations, and territorial forces, as well as a joint operations command and a separate special forces directorate; the Territorial Command is responsible for the active reserves and regional military commands that align with each of Czechia's 13 regions and the capital, Prague (2025)

TRANSNATIONAL ISSUES

Refugees and internally displaced persons: *refugees:* 392,198 (2024 est.)

IDPs: 5 (2024 est.)
stateless persons: 588 (2024 est.)

DENMARK

INTRODUCTION

Background: Once the seat of Viking raiders and later a major north European power, Denmark has evolved into a modern, prosperous nation that is part of the general political and economic integration of Europe. It joined NATO in 1949 and the EEC (now the EU) in 1973. The country has opted out of certain elements of the EU's Maastricht Treaty, including the European Economic and Monetary Union and justice and home affairs issues. a 2022 referendum resulted in the removal of Denmark's 30-year opt-out on defense issues, now allowing Denmark to participate fully in the EU's Common Security and Defense Policy.

GEOGRAPHY

Location: Northern Europe, bordering the Baltic Sea and the North Sea, on a peninsula north of Germany (Jutland); also includes several major islands (Sjaelland, Fyn, and Bornholm)

Geographic coordinates: 56 00 N, 10 00 E

Map references: Europe

Area: *total:* 43,094 sq km
land: 42,434 sq km
water: 660 sq km
note: includes the island of Bornholm in the Baltic Sea and the rest of metropolitan Denmark (the Jutland Peninsula, and the major islands of Sjaelland and Fyn) but excludes the Faroe Islands and Greenland
comparison ranking: total 133

Area - comparative: slightly less than twice the size of Massachusetts; about two-thirds the size of West Virginia

Land boundaries: *total:* 141 km
border countries (2): Germany 140 km; Canada 1.3 km

Coastline: 7,314 km

Maritime claims: *territorial sea:* 12 nm
contiguous zone: 24 nm
exclusive economic zone: 200 nm
continental shelf: 200-m depth or to the depth of exploitation

Climate: temperate; humid and overcast; mild, windy winters and cool summers

Terrain: low and flat to gently rolling plains

Elevation: *highest point:* Store Mollehoj 171 m
lowest point: Lammefjord -7 m
mean elevation: 34 m

Natural resources: petroleum, natural gas, fish, arable land, salt, limestone, chalk, stone, gravel and sand

Land use: *agricultural land:* 65.6% (2022 est.)
arable land: 59% (2022 est.)
permanent crops: 0.8% (2022 est.)
permanent pasture: 5.8% (2022 est.)
forest: 15.8% (2022 est.)
other: 18.6% (2022 est.)

Irrigated land: 2,420 sq km (2022)

Population distribution: population centers tend to be along coastal areas, particularly in Copenhagen and the eastern side of the country's mainland

Natural hazards: flooding is a threat in some areas of the country (e.g., parts of Jutland, along the southern coast of the island of Lolland) that are protected from the sea by a system of dikes

Geography - note: composed of the Jutland Peninsula and a group of more than 400 islands (Danish Archipelago); controls Danish Straits (Skagerrak and Kattegat) linking Baltic and North Seas; about one-quarter of the population lives in greater Copenhagen

PEOPLE AND SOCIETY

Population: *total:* 5,973,136 (2024 est.)
male: 2,975,261
female: 2,997,875
comparison rankings: total 115; male 115; female 115

Nationality: *noun:* Dane(s)
adjective: Danish

Ethnic groups: Danish (includes Greenlandic (who are predominantly Inuit) and Faroese) 84.2%, Turkish 1.1%, other 14.7% (largest groups are Polish, Romanian, Syrian, Ukrainian, German, and Iraqi) (2023 est.)
note: data represent population by country of origin

Languages: Danish, Faroese, Greenlandic (an Inuit dialect), German (small minority); note - English is the predominant second language
major-language sample(s):
Verdens Faktabog, den uundværlig kilde til grundlæggende oplysninger. (Danish)

Religions: Evangelical Lutheran (official) 71.4%, Muslim 4.3%, other/none/unspecified (denominations include Roman Catholic, Jehovah's Witness, Serbian Orthodox Christian, Jewish, Baptist, Buddhist, Church of Jesus Christ, Pentecostal, and nondenominational Christian) 24.3% (2024 est.)

Age structure: *0-14 years:* 16.2% (male 496,793/female 471,018)
15-64 years: 62.9% (male 1,903,315/female 1,856,615)
65 years and over: 20.8% (2024 est.) (male 575,153/female 670,242)

Dependency ratios: *total dependency ratio:* 57.2 (2024 est.)
youth dependency ratio: 24.7 (2024 est.)
elderly dependency ratio: 32.5 (2024 est.)
potential support ratio: 3.1 (2024 est.)

Median age: *total:* 42.2 years (2024 est.)
male: 41 years
female: 43.4 years
comparison ranking: total 45

Population growth rate: 0.44% (2024 est.)
comparison ranking: 155

Birth rate: 11.3 births/1,000 population (2024 est.)
comparison ranking: 160

Death rate: 9.6 deaths/1,000 population (2024 est.)
comparison ranking: 41

Net migration rate: 2.7 migrant(s)/1,000 population (2024 est.)
comparison ranking: 41

Population distribution: population centers tend to be along coastal areas, particularly in Copenhagen and the eastern side of the country's mainland

Urbanization: *urban population:* 88.5% of total population (2023)
rate of urbanization: 0.54% annual rate of change (2020-25 est.)

Major urban areas - population: 1.381 million COPENHAGEN (capital) (2023)

Sex ratio: *at birth:* 1.07 male(s)/female
0-14 years: 1.05 male(s)/female
15-64 years: 1.03 male(s)/female
65 years and over: 0.86 male(s)/female
total population: 0.99 male(s)/female (2024 est.)

Mother's mean age at first birth: 29.8 years (2020 est.)

Maternal mortality ratio: 4 deaths/100,000 live births (2023 est.)
comparison ranking: 178

Infant mortality rate: *total:* 3 deaths/1,000 live births (2024 est.)
male: 3.4 deaths/1,000 live births
female: 2.5 deaths/1,000 live births
comparison ranking: total 210

Life expectancy at birth: *total population:* 82.1 years (2024 est.)
male: 80.2 years
female: 84.1 years
comparison ranking: total population 35

Total fertility rate: 1.77 children born/woman (2024 est.)
comparison ranking: 144

Gross reproduction rate: 0.86 (2024 est.)

Drinking water source: *improved: urban:* 100% of population (2022 est.)
rural: 100% of population (2022 est.)
total: 100% of population (2022 est.)
unimproved: urban: 0% of population (2022 est.)
rural: 0% of population (2022 est.)
total: 0% of population (2022 est.)

Health expenditure: 9.5% of GDP (2022)
17.7% of national budget (2022 est.)

Physician density: 7.24 physicians/1,000 population (2021)

Hospital bed density: 2.5 beds/1,000 population (2021 est.)

Sanitation facility access: *improved: urban:* 100% of population (2022 est.)
rural: 100% of population (2022 est.)
total: 100% of population (2022 est.)
unimproved: urban: 0% of population (2022 est.)
rural: 0% of population (2022 est.)
total: 0% of population (2022 est.)

Obesity - adult prevalence rate: 19.7% (2016)
comparison ranking: 109

Alcohol consumption per capita: *total:* 9.16 liters of pure alcohol (2019 est.)

beer: 3.42 liters of pure alcohol (2019 est.)
wine: 4.08 liters of pure alcohol (2019 est.)
spirits: 1.66 liters of pure alcohol (2019 est.)
other alcohols: 0 liters of pure alcohol (2019 est.)
comparison ranking: total 33

Tobacco use: *total:* 14.3% (2025 est.)
male: 14.4% (2025 est.)
female: 14.3% (2025 est.)
comparison ranking: total 106

Currently married women (ages 15-49): 59.6% (2023 est.)

Child marriage: *women married by age 18:* 0.7% (2021)

Education expenditure: 5.3% of GDP (2022 est.)
11.8% national budget (2022 est.)
comparison ranking: Education expenditure (% GDP) 50

School life expectancy (primary to tertiary education): *total:* 18 years (2023 est.)
male: 18 years (2023 est.)
female: 19 years (2023 est.)

ENVIRONMENT

Environmental issues: air pollution, principally from vehicle and power-plant emissions; nitrogen and phosphorus pollution of the North Sea; water pollution from animal wastes and pesticides

International environmental agreements: *party to:* Air Pollution, Air Pollution-Heavy Metals, Air Pollution-Multi-effect Protocol, Air Pollution-Nitrogen Oxides, Air Pollution-Persistent Organic Pollutants, Air Pollution-Sulphur 85, Air Pollution-Sulphur 94, Air Pollution-Volatile Organic Compounds, Antarctic Treaty, Biodiversity, Climate Change, Climate Change-Kyoto Protocol, Climate Change-Paris Agreement, Comprehensive Nuclear Test Ban, Desertification, Endangered Species, Environmental Modification, Hazardous Wastes, Law of the Sea, Marine Dumping-London Convention, Marine Dumping-London Protocol, Marine Life Conservation, Nuclear Test Ban, Ozone Layer Protection, Ship Pollution, Tropical Timber 2006, Wetlands, Whaling
signed, but not ratified: Antarctic-Environmental Protection

Climate: temperate; humid and overcast; mild, windy winters and cool summers

Urbanization: *urban population:* 88.5% of total population (2023)
rate of urbanization: 0.54% annual rate of change (2020-25 est.)

Carbon dioxide emissions: 29.915 million metric tonnes of CO2 (2023 est.)
from coal and metallurgical coke: 2.54 million metric tonnes of CO2 (2023 est.)
from petroleum and other liquids: 22.535 million metric tonnes of CO2 (2023 est.)
from consumed natural gas: 4.841 million metric tonnes of CO2 (2023 est.)
comparison ranking: total emissions 74

Particulate matter emissions: 10.1 micrograms per cubic meter (2019 est.)

Methane emissions: *energy:* 49.7 kt (2022-2024 est.)
agriculture: 236.5 kt (2019-2021 est.)
waste: 54.4 kt (2019-2021 est.)
other: 5.3 kt (2019-2021 est.)

Waste and recycling: *municipal solid waste generated annually:* 4.911 million tons (2024 est.)
percent of municipal solid waste recycled: 35.4% (2022 est.)

Total water withdrawal: *municipal:* 382.787 million cubic meters (2022)
industrial: 45.076 million cubic meters (2022)
agricultural: 506.487 million cubic meters (2022)

Total renewable water resources: 6 billion cubic meters (2022 est.)

Geoparks: *total global geoparks and regional networks:* 3 (2024)
global geoparks and regional networks: Odsherred; South Fyn Archipelago; Vestjylland (2024)

GOVERNMENT

Country name: *conventional long form:* Kingdom of Denmark
conventional short form: Denmark
local long form: Kongeriget Danmark
local short form: Danmark
etymology: the name derives from the words *Dane*, a tribal name with unclear Germanic origins, and *mark*, a Danish word that refers to a march (borderland)

Government type: parliamentary constitutional monarchy

Capital: *name:* Copenhagen
geographic coordinates: 55 40 N, 12 35 E
time difference: UTC+1 (6 hours ahead of Washington, DC, during Standard Time)
daylight saving time: +1hr, begins last Sunday in March; ends last Sunday in October; note - applies to continental Denmark only, not to its North Atlantic components
etymology: name derives from the Danish words *køber* (merchant or buyer) and *havn* (harbor or port)

Administrative divisions: metropolitan Denmark - 5 regions (*regioner*, singular - *region*); Hovedstaden (Capital), Midtjylland (Central Jutland), Nordjylland (North Jutland), Sjaelland (Zealand), Syddanmark (Southern Denmark)

Legal system: civil law; judicial review of legislative acts

Constitution: *history:* several previous; latest adopted 5 June 1953
amendment process: proposed by the Folketing (Parliament) with consent of the government; passage requires approval by the next Folketing following a general election, approval by simple majority vote of at least 40% of voters in a referendum, and assent of the chief of state

International law organization participation: accepts compulsory ICJ jurisdiction with reservations; accepts ICCt jurisdiction

Citizenship: *citizenship by birth:* no
citizenship by descent only: at least one parent must be a citizen of Denmark
dual citizenship recognized: yes
residency requirement for naturalization: 7 years

Suffrage: 18 years of age; universal

Executive branch: *chief of state:* King FREDERIK X (since 14 January 2024)
head of government: Prime Minister Mette FREDERIKSEN (since 27 June 2019)
cabinet: Council of State appointed by the monarch
election/appointment process: the monarchy is hereditary; following legislative elections, the monarch usually appoints the leader of the majority party or majority coalition as prime minister
note: Queen MARGRETHE II abdicated on 14 January 2024, the first Danish monarch to voluntarily abdicate since King ERIC III in 1146

Legislative branch: *legislature name:* Parliament (Folketinget)
legislative structure: unicameral
chamber name: The Danish Parliament (Folketinget)
number of seats: 179 (all directly elected)
electoral system: proportional representation
scope of elections: full renewal
term in office: 4 years
most recent election date: 11/1/2022
parties elected and seats per party: Social Democratic Party (50); Liberal Party (Venstre) (23); Moderates (M) (16); Socialist People's Party (SF) (15); Danish Democrats (Æ) (14); Liberal Alliance (14); Conservative People's Party (10); Unity List-Red-Green Alliance (9); Other (24)
percentage of women in chamber: 43.6%
expected date of next election: October 2026

Judicial branch: *highest court(s):* Supreme Court (consists of the court president and 18 judges)
judge selection and term of office: judges appointed by the monarch upon the recommendation of the Minister of Justice, with the advice of the Judicial Appointments Council, a 6-member independent body of judges and lawyers; judges appointed for life with retirement at age 70
subordinate courts: Special Court of Indictment and Revision; 2 High Courts; Maritime and Commercial Court; county courts

Political parties: The Alternative or AP
Conservative People's Party or DKF or C
Danish People's Party or DF or O
Denmark Democrats or E
Green Left or SF or F (formerly Socialist People's Party or SF or F)
Liberal Alliance or LA or I
Liberal Party (Venstre) or V
Moderates or M
New Right Party or NB or D
Red-Green Alliance (Unity List) or EL
Social Democrats or SDP or A
Social Liberal Party or SLP or B

Diplomatic representation in the US: *chief of mission:* Ambassador Jesper Møller SØRENSEN (since 15 September 2023)
chancery: 3200 Whitehaven Street NW, Washington, DC 20008
telephone: [1] (202) 234-4300
FAX: [1] (202) 328-1470
email address and website: wasamb@um.dk
https://usa.um.dk/en
consulate(s) general: Chicago, Houston, New York, Silicon Valley (CA)

Diplomatic representation from the US: *chief of mission:* Ambassador (vacant); Chargé d'Affaires Mark STROH (since June 2025)
embassy: Dag Hammarskjolds Alle 24, 2100 Kobenhavn 0
mailing address: 5280 Copenhagen Place, Washington DC 20521-5280
telephone: [45] 33-41-71-00
FAX: [45] 35-43-02-23
email address and website: CopenhagenACS@state.gov
https://dk.usembassy.gov/

International organization participation: ADB (nonregional member), AfDB (nonregional member), Arctic Council, Australia Group, BIS, CBSS,

CD, CE, CERN, EAPC, EBRD, ECB, EIB, EITI (implementing country), ESA, EU, FAO, FATF, G-9, IADB, IAEA, IBRD, ICAO, ICC (national committees), ICCt, ICRM, IDA, IEA, IFAD, IFC, IFRCS, IGAD (partners), IHO, ILO, IMF, IMO, IMSO, Interpol, IOC, IOM, IPU, ISO, ITSO, ITU, ITUC (NGOs), MIGA, NATO, NC, NEA, NIB, NSG, OAS (observer), OECD, OPCW, OSCE, Paris Club, PCA, Schengen Convention, UN, UNCTAD, UNESCO, UNHCR, UNIDO, UNMIL, UNMISS, UNOOSA, UNRWA, UNTSO, UPU, Wassenaar Arrangement, WCO, WHO, WIPO, WMO, WTO, ZC

Independence: ca. 965 (unified and Christianized under Harald I GORMSSON); 5 June 1849 (became a parliamentary constitutional monarchy)

National holiday: Constitution Day, 5 June (1849)
note: closest equivalent to a national holiday

Flag: *description:* red field with a white cross that extends to the edges of the flag; the vertical part of the cross is shifted to the left
history: referred to as the Dannebrog (Danish flag) and is one of the oldest national flags in the world; the origin of the design is unclear; one legend says that the banner fell from the sky during an early-13th-century battle and inspired the royal army to victory; in actuality, the flag may derive from a crusade banner
note: Finland, Iceland, Norway, Sweden, and the Faroe Islands subsequently adopted the shifted-cross design

National symbol(s): lion, mute swan

National color(s): red, white

National coat of arms: Denmark's King Frederick VI adopted the national coat of arms in 1819; the crown of King Christian V, who ruled Denmark and Norway from 1670 to 1699, sits atop the shield, symbolizing royal and national authority; the three lions represent a strong and powerful country, with red lily pads in the shape of hearts that stand for strength, valor, and joy

National anthem(s): *title:* "Der er et yndigt land" (There is a Lovely Country)
lyrics/music: Adam Gottlob OEHLENSCHLAGER/ Hans Ernst KROYER; Johannes EWALD/unknown
history: adopted 1844; national anthem
title: "Kong Christian stod ved højen mast" (King Christian Stood by the Lofty Mast)
lyrics/music: Johannes EWALD/unknown
history: adopted 1780; one of the oldest royal anthems in the world; used for events when Danish royalty is present; anthem has equal status with the national anthem
note: Denmark is one of only two countries that has two national anthems of equal status (New Zealand is the other)

National heritage: *total World Heritage Sites:* 11 (8 cultural, 3 natural)
selected World Heritage Site locales: Denmark: Mounds, Runic Stones, and Church at Jelling (c); Roskilde Cathedral (c); Kronborg Castle (c); Wadden Sea (n); Stevns Klint (n); Christiansfeld, Moravian Church Settlement (c); Par force hunting landscape, North Zealand (c); Greenland: Ilulissat Icefjord (n); Kujataa, Norse and Inuit Farming (c); Aasivissuit–Nipisat, Inuit Hunting Ground (c); Viking-Age Ring Fortresses (c)
note: includes three sites in Greenland

ECONOMY

Economic overview: high-income, EU-member, trade-oriented Nordic economy; growth driven by pharmaceuticals, energy, and services; large share of employment in public sector; fixed exchange rate pegged to euro; strong fiscal position and declining public debt; tight labor market mitigated by migrant workers and higher retirement age

Real GDP (purchasing power parity): $440.558 billion (2024 est.)
$424.937 billion (2023 est.)
$414.592 billion (2022 est.)
note: data in 2021 dollars
comparison ranking: 53

Real GDP growth rate: 3.7% (2024 est.)
2.5% (2023 est.)
1.5% (2022 est.)
note: annual GDP % growth based on constant local currency
comparison ranking: 90

Real GDP per capita: $73,700 (2024 est.)
$71,500 (2023 est.)
$70,200 (2022 est.)
note: data in 2021 dollars
comparison ranking: 14

GDP (official exchange rate): $429.457 billion (2024 est.)
note: data in current dollars at official exchange rate

Inflation rate (consumer prices): 1.4% (2024 est.)
3.3% (2023 est.)
7.7% (2022 est.)
note: annual % change based on consumer prices
comparison ranking: 34

GDP - composition, by sector of origin: *agriculture:* 0.7% (2024 est.)
industry: 24% (2024 est.)
services: 64% (2024 est.)
note: figures may not total 100% due to non-allocated consumption not captured in sector-reported data
comparison rankings: agriculture 182; industry 98; services 62

GDP - composition, by end use: *household consumption:* 45.5% (2023 est.)
government consumption: 22.5% (2023 est.)
investment in fixed capital: 22.6% (2023 est.)
investment in inventories: 0.2% (2023 est.)
exports of goods and services: 68% (2023 est.)
imports of goods and services: -59.8% (2023 est.)
note: figures may not total 100% due to rounding or gaps in data collection

Agricultural products: milk, wheat, potatoes, barley, sugar beets, pork, rapeseed, rye, oats, chicken (2023)
note: top ten agricultural products based on tonnage

Industries: wind turbines, pharmaceuticals, medical equipment, shipbuilding and refurbishment, iron, steel, nonferrous metals, chemicals, food processing, machinery and transportation equipment, textiles and clothing, electronics, construction, furniture and other wood products

Industrial production growth rate: 12% (2024 est.)
note: annual % change in industrial value added based on constant local currency
comparison ranking: 5

Labor force: 3.21 million (2024 est.)
note: number of people ages 15 or older who are employed or seeking work
comparison ranking: 105

Unemployment rate: 5.6% (2024 est.)
5.1% (2023 est.)
4.5% (2022 est.)
note: % of labor force seeking employment
comparison ranking: 109

Youth unemployment rate (ages 15-24): *total:* 12.1% (2024 est.)
male: 12.3% (2024 est.)
female: 11.9% (2024 est.)
note: % of labor force ages 15-24 seeking employment
comparison ranking: total 101

Population below poverty line: 12.4% (2021 est.)
note: % of population with income below national poverty line

Gini Index coefficient - distribution of family income: 29.3 (2022 est.)
note: index (0-100) of income distribution; higher values represent greater inequality
comparison ranking: 127

Average household expenditures: *on food:* 11.9% of household expenditures (2023 est.)
on alcohol and tobacco: 3.5% of household expenditures (2023 est.)

Household income or consumption by percentage share: *lowest 10%:* 3.6% (2022 est.)
highest 10%: 24.5% (2022 est.)
note: % share of income accruing to lowest and highest 10% of population

Remittances: 0.4% of GDP (2024 est.)
0.4% of GDP (2023 est.)
0.3% of GDP (2022 est.)
note: personal transfers and compensation between resident and non-resident individuals/households/entities

Budget: *revenues:* $149.393 billion (2023 est.)
expenditures: $136.662 billion (2023 est.)
note: central government revenues (excluding grants) and expenditures converted to US dollars at average official exchange rate for year indicated

Public debt: 35.3% of GDP (2017 est.)
note: data cover general government debt and include debt instruments issued (or owned) by government entities other than the treasury; the data include treasury debt held by foreign entities; the data include debt issued by subnational entities, as well as intra-governmental debt; intragovernmental debt consists of treasury borrowings from surpluses in the social funds, such as for retirement, medical care, and unemployment; debt instruments for the social funds are not sold at public auctions
comparison ranking: 152

Taxes and other revenues: 31.4% (of GDP) (2023 est.)
note: central government tax revenue as a % of GDP
comparison ranking: 3

Current account balance: $55.901 billion (2024 est.)
$40.061 billion (2023 est.)
$46.488 billion (2022 est.)
note: balance of payments - net trade and primary/secondary income in current dollars
comparison ranking: 10

Exports: $299.405 billion (2024 est.)
$276.646 billion (2023 est.)
$283.37 billion (2022 est.)
note: balance of payments - exports of goods and services in current dollars
comparison ranking: 32

Exports - partners: Germany 13%, USA 10%, Sweden 9%, Netherlands 7%, China 5% (2023)

note: top five export partners based on percentage share of exports

Exports - commodities: packaged medicine, fish, vaccines, refined petroleum, pork (2023)
note: top five export commodities based on value in dollars

Imports: $252.954 billion (2024 est.)
$243.478 billion (2023 est.)
$245.07 billion (2022 est.)
note: balance of payments - imports of goods and services in current dollars
comparison ranking: 33

Imports - partners: Germany 18%, Sweden 11%, Norway 10%, Netherlands 9%, China 7% (2023)
note: top five import partners based on percentage share of imports

Imports - commodities: natural gas, cars, garments, packaged medicine, refined petroleum (2023)
note: top five import commodities based on value in dollars

Reserves of foreign exchange and gold: $108.405 billion (2024 est.)
$109.371 billion (2023 est.)
$96.073 billion (2022 est.)
note: holdings of gold (year-end prices)/foreign exchange/special drawing rights in current dollars
comparison ranking: 26

Exchange rates: Danish kroner (DKK) per US dollar -

Exchange rates: 6.894 (2024 est.)
6.89 (2023 est.)
7.076 (2022 est.)
6.287 (2021 est.)
6.542 (2020 est.)

ENERGY

Electricity access: *electrification - total population:* 100% (2022 est.)

Electricity: *installed generating capacity:* 20.794 million kW (2023 est.)
consumption: 35.253 billion kWh (2023 est.)
exports: 16.698 billion kWh (2023 est.)
imports: 19.831 billion kWh (2023 est.)
transmission/distribution losses: 1.825 billion kWh (2023 est.)
comparison rankings: installed generating capacity 50; consumption 62; exports 17; imports 12; transmission/distribution losses 119

Electricity generation sources: *fossil fuels:* 11.3% of total installed capacity (2023 est.)
solar: 9.9% of total installed capacity (2023 est.)
wind: 57.6% of total installed capacity (2023 est.)
hydroelectricity: 0.1% of total installed capacity (2023 est.)
biomass and waste: 21.2% of total installed capacity (2023 est.)

Coal: *consumption:* 1.135 million metric tons (2023 est.)
exports: 124,000 metric tons (2023 est.)
imports: 1.296 million metric tons (2023 est.)

Petroleum: *total petroleum production:* 63,000 bbl/day (2023 est.)
refined petroleum consumption: 151,000 bbl/day (2024 est.)
crude oil estimated reserves: 441 million barrels (2021 est.)

Natural gas: *production:* 2.021 billion cubic meters (2023 est.)
consumption: 2.309 billion cubic meters (2023 est.)
exports: 8.388 billion cubic meters (2023 est.)
imports: 8.612 billion cubic meters (2023 est.)
proven reserves: 29.534 billion cubic meters (2021 est.)

Energy consumption per capita: 98.513 million Btu/person (2023 est.)
comparison ranking: 52

COMMUNICATIONS

Telephones - fixed lines: *total subscriptions:* 755,000 (2023 est.)
subscriptions per 100 inhabitants: 13 (2023 est.)
comparison ranking: total subscriptions 78

Telephones - mobile cellular: *total subscriptions:* 7.5 million (2023 est.)
subscriptions per 100 inhabitants: 127 (2022 est.)
comparison ranking: total subscriptions 108

Broadcast media: strong public-sector TV presence, with Danmarks Radio (DR) operating 6 channels and TV2 operating roughly a half-dozen channels; private stations are available via satellite and cable feed; DR operates 4 FM radio stations, 10 digital audio stations, and 14 web-based radio stations; 140 commercial and 187 community (non-commercial) radio stations (2019)

Internet country code: .dk

Internet users: *percent of population:* 100% (2024 est.)

Broadband - fixed subscriptions: *total:* 2.65 million (2023 est.)
subscriptions per 100 inhabitants: 44 (2023 est.)
comparison ranking: total 54

TRANSPORTATION

Civil aircraft registration country code prefix: OY

Airports: 102 (2025)
comparison ranking: 53

Heliports: 29 (2025)
comparison ranking: 47

Railways: *total:* 2,682 km (2020) 876 km electrified

Merchant marine: *total:* 715 (2023)
by type: bulk carrier 15, container ship 132, general cargo 69, oil tanker 107, other 392
comparison ranking: total 33

Ports: *total ports:* 69 (2024)
large: 1
medium: 2
small: 30
very small: 36
ports with oil terminals: 33
key ports: Abenra, Alborg, Arhus, Assens, Augustenborg, Bandholm, Esbjerg, Faborg, Fredericia, Frederikshavn, Haderslev, Holstebro-Stuer, Kalundborg, Kobenhavn, Kolding, Korsor, Marstal, Middelfart, Naestved, Nakskov, Nyborg, Nykobing, Odense, Randers, Ronne, Rudkobing, Sakskobing, Skagen Havn, Sonderborg, Stubbekobing, Studstrup, Svendborg, Vejle

MILITARY AND SECURITY

Military and security forces: Danish Armed Forces (Forsvaret): Royal Danish Army, Royal Danish Navy, Royal Danish Air Force (2025)

Military expenditures: 3.2% of GDP (2025 est.)
2.3% of GDP (2024 est.)
2% of GDP (2023 est.)
1.4% of GDP (2022 est.)
1.3% of GDP (2021 est.)

Military and security service personnel strengths: approximately 17,000 active-duty military personnel (2025)

Military equipment inventories and acquisitions: the Danish military inventory is comprised of modern European, US, and domestically produced weapons and equipment; the Danish defense industry is active in the production of naval vessels, defense electronics, and subcomponents of larger weapons systems, such as the US F-35 fighter aircraft; the major warships of the Royal Danish Navy were all produced domestically (2024)

Military service age and obligation: 18 years of age for compulsory and voluntary military service for men and women; conscripts serve 11 months, including five months of basic training, followed by six months in an operational unit (2025)
note 1: Denmark has had compulsory military service since 1849; conscripts are chosen by lottery (about 4,700 were selected in 2024); conscientious objectors can choose to instead serve 6 months in a non-military position, for example in Beredskabsstyrelsen (dealing with non-military disasters like fires, flood, pollution, etc.) or overseas foreign aid work
note 2: women have been able serve in all military occupations, including combat arms, since 1988; as of 2022, they made up about 9% of the military's full-time personnel; military conscription was extended to women in June 2025
note 3: foreigners who have lived in Denmark for at least one year or in another EU country for six years may apply to join the armed forces, provided they are fluent in Danish

Military deployments: approximately 800 Latvia (NATO); Denmark contributes small numbers of air, ground, and naval forces to a variety of other NATO and international missions (2024)

Military - note: the Danish Armed Forces (Forsvaret) have a variety of missions, including enforcing the country's sovereignty, monitoring Danish waters and airspace, search and rescue, environmental protection, host nation support for alliance partners, international peacekeeping, fulfilling Denmark's commitments to NATO, and providing assistance to the police for border control, guard tasks, air surveillance, and during national disasters and other emergencies
NATO has been a cornerstone of Danish security and defense police since it joined in 1949 as one of the organization's original members under the North Atlantic Treaty (also known as the Washington Treaty); the Forsvaret regularly exercises with NATO allies and participates in a number of NATO missions, including its Enhanced Forward Presence in Eastern Europe, air policing in the Baltics, naval operations in the Baltic Sea and North Atlantic, and an advisory mission in Iraq; the Forsvaret leads NATO's Multinational Division – North (inaugurated 2019), a headquarters based in Latvia that supports the defense planning of Estonia, Latvia, and Lithuania, and the coordination of regional military activities, including NATO's forward deployed forces; it also takes part in other international missions for Europe and the UN ranging from peacekeeping in Africa to protecting Europe's external borders by patrolling the Mediterranean Sea in support of the European Border and Coast Guard Agency; Denmark is a member of the EU and voted to join the EU's Common Defense and Security Policy in a 2022 referendum; the Forsvaret cooperates closely with

the militaries of other Nordic countries through the Nordic Defense Cooperation (NORDEFCO; established 2009), which consists of Denmark, Finland, Iceland, Norway, and Sweden in such areas as armaments, training and exercises, and operations; it also has a joint composite special operations command with Belgium and the Netherlands

the Forsvaret has an Arctic Command to protect the sovereignty of Denmark in the Arctic region, including the Faroe Islands and Greenland, and conducts maritime pollution prevention, environmental monitoring, fishery inspections, search and rescue, and hydrographical surveys, plus support to governmental science missions; there is also a joint service Special Operations Command (SOKOM), which includes the Sirius Dog Sled Patrol, an elite unit that patrols the most remote parts of northeast Greenland (2025)

TERRORISM

Terrorist group(s): Terrorist group(s): Islamic State of Iraq and ash-Sham (ISIS); Islamic Revolutionary Guard Corps (IRGC)/Qods Force

note: details about the history, aims, leadership, organization, areas of operation, tactics, targets, weapons, size, and sources of support of the group(s) appear(s) in Appendix T

TRANSNATIONAL ISSUES

Refugees and internally displaced persons: *refugees:* 100,832 (2024 est.)
stateless persons: 8,566 (2024 est.)

DJIBOUTI

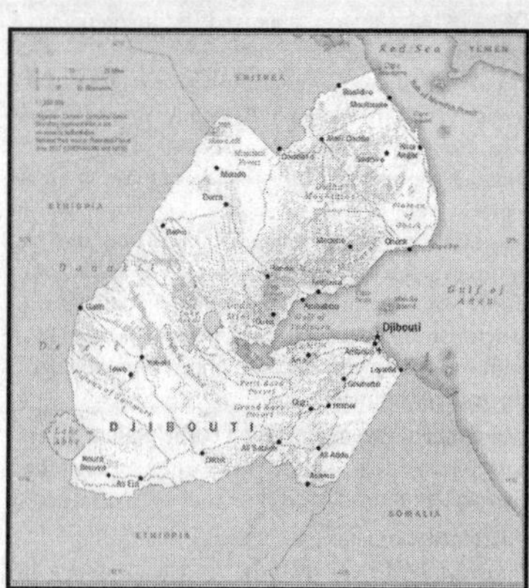

INTRODUCTION

Background: Present-day Djibouti was the site of the medieval Ifat and Adal Sultanates. In the late 19th century, the Afar sultans signed treaties with the French that allowed the latter to establish the colony of French Somaliland in 1862. The French signed additional treaties with the ethnic Somali in 1885.

Tension between the ethnic Afar and Somali populations increased over time, as the ethnic Somalis perceived that the French unfairly favored the Afar and gave them disproportionate influence in local governance. In 1958, the French held a referendum that provided residents of French Somaliland the option to either continue their association with France or to join neighboring Somalia as it established its independence. Ethnic Somali protested the vote, because French colonial leaders did not recognize many Somali as residents, which gave the Afar outsized influence in the decision to uphold ties with France. After a second referendum in 1967, the French changed the territory's name to the French Territory of the Afars and the Issas, in part to underscore their relationship with the ethnic Afar and downplay the significance of the ethnic Somalis. A final referendum in 1977 established Djibouti as an independent nation and granted ethnic Somalis Djiboutian nationality, formally resetting the balance of power between the majority ethnic Somalis and minority ethnic Afar residents. Upon independence, the country was named after its capital city of Djibouti. Hassan Gouled APTIDON, an ethnic Somali leader, installed an authoritarian one-party state and served as president until 1999. Unrest between the Afar minority and Somali majority culminated in a civil war during the 1990s that ended in 2001 with a peace accord between Afar rebels and the Somali Issa-dominated government. In 1999, Djibouti's first multiparty presidential election resulted in the election of Ismail Omar GUELLEH as president; he was reelected to a second term in 2005 and extended his tenure in office via a constitutional amendment, which allowed him to serve his third and fourth terms, and to begin a fifth term in 2021.

Djibouti occupies a strategic geographic location at the intersection of the Red Sea and the Gulf of Aden. Its ports handle 95% of Ethiopia's trade. Djibouti's ports also service transshipments between Europe, the Middle East, and Asia. The government has longstanding ties to France, which maintains a military presence in the country, as do the US, Japan, Italy, Germany, Spain, and China.

GEOGRAPHY

Location: Eastern Africa, bordering the Gulf of Aden and the Red Sea, between Eritrea and Somalia

Geographic coordinates: 11 30 N, 43 00 E

Map references: Africa

Area: *total:* 23,200 sq km
land: 23,180 sq km
water: 20 sq km
comparison ranking: total 150

Area - comparative: slightly smaller than New Jersey

Land boundaries: *total:* 528 km
border countries (3): Eritrea 125 km; Ethiopia 342 km; Somalia 61 km

Coastline: 314 km

Maritime claims: *territorial sea:* 12 nm
contiguous zone: 24 nm
exclusive economic zone: 200 nm

Climate: desert; torrid, dry

Terrain: coastal plain and plateau separated by central mountains

Elevation: *highest point:* Moussa Ali 2,021 m
lowest point: Lac Assal -155 m
mean elevation: 430 m

Natural resources: potential geothermal power, gold, clay, granite, limestone, marble, salt, diatomite, gypsum, pumice, petroleum

Land use: *agricultural land:* 73.5% (2022 est.)
arable land: 0.1% (2022 est.)
permanent crops: 0% (2022 est.)
permanent pasture: 73.3% (2022 est.)
forest: 0.3% (2022 est.)
other: 26.2% (2022 est.)

Irrigated land: 10 sq km (2012)

Major lakes (area sq km): *salt water lake(s):* Abhe Bad/Abhe Bid Hayk (shared with Ethiopia) - 780 sq km

Population distribution: most densely populated areas are in the east; the largest city is Djibouti, and the other cities in the country are a fraction of its size, as shown in this population distribution map

Natural hazards: earthquakes; droughts; occasional cyclonic disturbances from the Indian Ocean bring heavy rains and flash floods
volcanism: experiences limited volcanic activity; Ardoukoba (298 m) last erupted in 1978;
Manda-Inakir, located along the Ethiopian border, is also historically active

Geography - note: strategic location near world's busiest shipping lanes and close to Arabian oilfields; Lac Assal (Lake Assal) is the lowest point in Africa and the saltiest lake in the world

PEOPLE AND SOCIETY

Population: *total:* 994,974 (2024 est.)
male: 450,796
female: 544,178
comparison rankings: total 162; male 164; female 162

Nationality: *noun:* Djiboutian(s)
adjective: Djiboutian

Ethnic groups: Somali 60%, Afar 35%, other 5% (mostly Yemeni Arab, also French, Ethiopian, and Italian)

Languages: French (official), Arabic (official), Somali, Afar

Religions: Sunni Muslim 94% (nearly all Djiboutians), other 6% (mainly foreign-born residents - Shia Muslim, Christian, Hindu, Jewish, Baha'i, and atheist)

Age structure: *0-14 years:* 28.4% (male 141,829/female 140,696)
15-64 years: 67.4% (male 290,654/female 379,778)
65 years and over: 4.2% (2024 est.) (male 18,313/female 23,704)

Dependency ratios: *total dependency ratio:* 48.4 (2024 est.)
youth dependency ratio: 42.1 (2024 est.)
elderly dependency ratio: 6.3 (2024 est.)
potential support ratio: 16 (2024 est.)

Median age: *total:* 26.3 years (2024 est.)
male: 24.4 years
female: 27.9 years
comparison ranking: total 164

Population growth rate: 1.89% (2024 est.)
comparison ranking: 45

Birth rate: 21.8 births/1,000 population (2024 est.)
comparison ranking: 56

Death rate: 7 deaths/1,000 population (2024 est.)
comparison ranking: 120

Net migration rate: 4.2 migrant(s)/1,000 population (2024 est.)
comparison ranking: 23

Population distribution: most densely populated areas are in the east; the largest city is Djibouti, and the other cities in the country are a fraction of its size, as shown in this population distribution map

Urbanization: *urban population:* 78.6% of total population (2023)
rate of urbanization: 1.56% annual rate of change (2020-25 est.)

Major urban areas - population: 600,000 DJIBOUTI (capital) (2023)

Sex ratio: *at birth:* 1.03 male(s)/female
0-14 years: 1.01 male(s)/female
15-64 years: 0.77 male(s)/female
65 years and over: 0.77 male(s)/female
total population: 0.83 male(s)/female (2024 est.)

Maternal mortality ratio: 162 deaths/100,000 live births (2023 est.)
comparison ranking: 47

Infant mortality rate: *total:* 45.2 deaths/1,000 live births (2024 est.)
male: 52.1 deaths/1,000 live births
female: 38 deaths/1,000 live births
comparison ranking: total 25

Life expectancy at birth: *total population:* 65.9 years (2024 est.)
male: 63.4 years
female: 68.5 years
comparison ranking: total population 202

Total fertility rate: 2.11 children born/woman (2024 est.)
comparison ranking: 94

Gross reproduction rate: 1.04 (2024 est.)

Drinking water source: *improved:* *urban:* 84.1% of population (2022 est.)
rural: 47.3% of population (2022 est.)
total: 76.2% of population (2022 est.)
unimproved: *urban:* 15.9% of population (2022 est.)
rural: 52.7% of population (2022 est.)
total: 23.8% of population (2022 est.)

Health expenditure: 2.9% of GDP (2021)
5.2% of national budget (2022 est.)

Physician density: 0.21 physicians/1,000 population (2022)

Hospital bed density: 1.4 beds/1,000 population (2018 est.)

Sanitation facility access: *improved:* *urban:* 87.7% of population (2022 est.)
rural: 24.2% of population (2022 est.)
total: 74% of population (2022 est.)
unimproved: *urban:* 12.3% of population (2022 est.)
rural: 75.8% of population (2022 est.)
total: 26% of population (2022 est.)

Obesity - adult prevalence rate: 13.5% (2016)
comparison ranking: 131

Alcohol consumption per capita: *total:* 0.21 liters of pure alcohol (2019 est.)
beer: 0.05 liters of pure alcohol (2019 est.)
wine: 0.02 liters of pure alcohol (2019 est.)
spirits: 0.14 liters of pure alcohol (2019 est.)
other alcohols: 0 liters of pure alcohol (2019 est.)
comparison ranking: total 172

Children under the age of 5 years underweight: 16.2% (2019)
comparison ranking: 29

Currently married women (ages 15-49): 50.6% (2023 est.)

Child marriage: *women married by age 15:* 1.4% (2019)
women married by age 18: 6.5% (2019)

Education expenditure: 3.8% of GDP (2018 est.)
14.5% national budget (2018 est.)
comparison ranking: Education expenditure (% GDP) 118

ENVIRONMENT

Environmental issues: inadequate supplies of potable water; water pollution; limited arable land; deforestation (forests threatened by agriculture and the use of wood for fuel); desertification; endangered species

International environmental agreements: *party to:* Biodiversity, Climate Change, Climate Change-Kyoto Protocol, Climate Change-Paris Agreement, Comprehensive Nuclear Test Ban, Desertification, Endangered Species, Hazardous Wastes, Law of the Sea, Ozone Layer Protection, Ship Pollution, Wetlands
signed, but not ratified: none of the selected agreements

Climate: desert; torrid, dry

Urbanization: *urban population:* 78.6% of total population (2023)
rate of urbanization: 1.56% annual rate of change (2020-25 est.)

Carbon dioxide emissions: 685,000 metric tonnes CO_2 (2023 est.)
from coal and metallurgical coke: 45,000 metric tonnes of CO_2 (2023 est.)
from petroleum and other liquids: 640,000 metric tonnes of CO_2 (2023 est.)
comparison ranking: total emissions 182

Particulate matter emissions: 21 micrograms per cubic meter (2019 est.)

Waste and recycling: *municipal solid waste generated annually:* 115,000 tons (2024 est.)
percent of municipal solid waste recycled: 14.9% (2022 est.)

Total water withdrawal: *municipal:* 16 million cubic meters (2022 est.)
industrial: 0 cubic meters (2022 est.)
agricultural: 3 million cubic meters (2022 est.)

Total renewable water resources: 300 million cubic meters (2022 est.)

GOVERNMENT

Country name: *conventional long form:* Republic of Djibouti
conventional short form: Djibouti
local long form: République de Djibouti (French)/ Jumhuriyat Jibuti (Arabic)
local short form: Djibouti (French)/ Jibuti (Arabic)
former: French Somaliland, French Territory of the Afars and Issas
etymology: the country name derives from the capital city of Djibouti

Government type: presidential republic

Capital: *name:* Djibouti
geographic coordinates: 11 35 N, 43 09 E
time difference: UTC+3 (8 hours ahead of Washington, DC, during Standard Time)
etymology: the name is said to derive from the Afar word *gabouri*, meaning "plate," in reference to a palm-fiber plate used for ceremonial purposes

Administrative divisions: 6 districts (*cercles*, singular - *cercle*); Ali Sabieh, Arta, Dikhil, Djibouti, Obock, Tadjourah

Legal system: mixed system based primarily on the French civil code (as it existed in 1997), Islamic religious law (in matters of family law and successions), and customary law

Constitution: *history:* approved by referendum 4 September 1992
amendment process: proposed by the president of the republic or by the National Assembly; Assembly consideration of proposals requires assent of at least one third of the membership; passage requires a simple majority vote by the Assembly and approval by simple majority vote in a referendum; the president can opt to bypass a referendum if adopted by at least two-thirds majority vote of the Assembly; constitutional articles on the sovereignty of Djibouti, its republican form of government, and its pluralist form of democracy cannot be amended

International law organization participation: accepts compulsory ICJ jurisdiction with reservations; accepts ICCt jurisdiction

Citizenship: *citizenship by birth:* no
citizenship by descent only: the mother must be a citizen of Djibouti
dual citizenship recognized: no
residency requirement for naturalization: 10 years

Suffrage: 18 years of age; universal

Executive branch: *chief of state:* President Ismail Omar GUELLEH (since 8 May 1999)
head of government: Prime Minister Abdoulkader Kamil MOHAMED (since 1 April 2013)
cabinet: Council of Ministers appointed by the prime minister
election/appointment process: president directly elected by absolute-majority popular vote in 2 rounds, if needed, for a 5-year term; prime minister appointed by the president
most recent election date: 9 April 2021
election results: *2021:* Ismail Omar GUELLEH reelected president for a fifth term; percent of vote - Ismail Omar GUELLEH (RPP) 97.4%, Zakaria Ismael FARAH (MDEND) 2.7%
2016: Ismail Omar GUELLEH reelected president for a fourth term; percent of vote - Ismail Omar GUELLEH (RPP) 87%, Omar Elmi KHAIREH (CDU) 7.3%, other 5.6%
expected date of next election: April 2026

Legislative branch: *legislature name:* National Assembly (Assemblée nationale)
legislative structure: unicameral
number of seats: 65 (all directly elected)
electoral system: mixed system
scope of elections: full renewal
term in office: 5 years
most recent election date: 2/24/2023
parties elected and seats per party: Union for the Presidential Majority (UMP) (58); Union for Democracy and Justice (UDJ) (7)

percentage of women in chamber: 26.2%
expected date of next election: February 2028
note: most opposition parties boycotted the 2023 polls, stating the elections were "not free, not transparent, and not democratic"

Judicial branch: *highest court(s):* Supreme Court or Cour Suprême (consists of NA magistrates); Constitutional Council (consists of 6 magistrates)
judge selection and term of office: Supreme Court magistrates appointed by the president with the advice of the Superior Council of the Magistracy (CSM), a 10-member body consisting of 4 judges, 3 members (non-parliamentarians and judges) appointed by the president, and 3 appointed by the National Assembly president or speaker; magistrates appointed for life with retirement at age 65; Constitutional Council magistrate appointments - 2 by the president of the republic, 2 by the president of the National Assembly, and 2 by the CSM; magistrates appointed for 8-year, non-renewable terms
subordinate courts: High Court of Appeal; Courts of First Instance; customary courts; State Court (replaced sharia courts in 2003)

Political parties: Front for Restoration of Unity and Democracy (Front pour la Restauration de l'Unite Democratique) or FRUD
National Democratic Party or PND
People's Rally for Progress or RPP
Peoples Social Democratic Party or PPSD
Union for Democracy and Justice or UDJ
Union for the Presidential Majority coalition or UMP
Union of Reform Partisans or UPR

Diplomatic representation in the US: *chief of mission:* Ambassador Mohamed Siad DOUALEH (28 January 2016)
chancery: 1156 15th Street NW, Suite 515, Washington, DC 20005
telephone: [1] (202) 331-0270
FAX: [1] (202) 331-0302
email address and website: info@djiboutiembassyus.org
https://www.djiboutiembassyus.org/

Diplomatic representation from the US: *chief of mission:* Ambassador Cynthia KIERSCHT (since 17 October 2024)
embassy: Lot 350-B Haramouss, B.P. 185
mailing address: 2150 Djibouti Place, Washington DC 20521-2150
telephone: [253] 21-45-30-00
FAX: [253] 21-45-31-29
email address and website: DjiboutiACS@state.gov
https://dj.usembassy.gov/

International organization participation: ACP, AfDB, AFESD, AMF, ATMIS, AU, CAEU (candidates), COMESA, FAO, G-77, IBRD, ICAO, ICCt, ICRM, IDA, IDB, IFAD, IFC, IFRCS, IGAD, ILO, IMF, IMO, Interpol, IOC, IOM, IPU, ITU, ITUC (NGOs), LAS, MIGA, MINURSO, NAM, OIC, OIF, OPCW, UN, UNCTAD, UNESCO, UNHCR, UNIDO, UNWTO, UPU, WCO, WFTU (NGOs), WHO, WIPO, WMO, WTO

Independence: 27 June 1977 (from France)

National holiday: Independence Day, 27 June (1977)

Flag: *description:* two equal horizontal bands of light blue (top) and light green, with a white isosceles triangle based on the left side that has a five-pointed red star in the center
meaning: blue stands for sea, sky, and the Issa Somali people, green for earth and the Afar people, and white for peace; the red star stands for the struggle for independence and unity

National symbol(s): red star

National color(s): light blue, green, white, red

National anthem(s): *title:* "Jabuuti" (Djibouti)
lyrics/music: Aden ELMI/Abdi ROBLEH
history: adopted 1977

ECONOMY

Economic overview: food import-dependent Horn of Africa economy driven by various national military bases and port-based trade; fairly resilient from COVID-19 disruptions; major re-exporter; increasing Ethiopian and Chinese trade relations; investing in infrastructure

Real GDP (purchasing power parity): $7.995 billion (2024 est.)
$7.546 billion (2023 est.)
$7.028 billion (2022 est.)
note: data in 2021 dollars
comparison ranking: 170

Real GDP growth rate: 6% (2024 est.)
7.4% (2023 est.)
5.2% (2022 est.)
note: annual GDP % growth based on constant local currency
comparison ranking: 24

Real GDP per capita: $6,800 (2024 est.)
$6,500 (2023 est.)
$6,200 (2022 est.)
note: data in 2021 dollars
comparison ranking: 161

GDP (official exchange rate): $4.086 billion (2024 est.)
note: data in current dollars at official exchange rate

Inflation rate (consumer prices): 2.1% (2024 est.)
1.5% (2023 est.)
5.2% (2022 est.)
note: annual % change based on consumer prices
comparison ranking: 54

GDP - composition, by sector of origin: *agriculture:* 2.6% (2024 est.)
industry: 15.4% (2024 est.)
services: 75.5% (2024 est.)
note: figures may not total 100% due to non-allocated consumption not captured in sector-reported data
comparison rankings: agriculture 139; industry 163; services 21

GDP - composition, by end use: *household consumption:* 73% (2024 est.)
government consumption: 18.8% (2024 est.)
investment in fixed capital: 26.3% (2024 est.)
investment in inventories: -30.1% (2024 est.)
exports of goods and services: 160.8% (2024 est.)
imports of goods and services: -148.3% (2024 est.)
note: figures may not total 100% due to rounding or gaps in data collection

Agricultural products: vegetables, beans, milk, beef, camel milk, lemons/limes, goat meat, lamb/mutton, tomatoes, beef offal (2023)
note: top ten agricultural products based on tonnage

Industries: construction, agricultural processing, shipping

Industrial production growth rate: 9.7% (2024 est.)
note: annual % change in industrial value added based on constant local currency
comparison ranking: 12

Labor force: 265,200 (2024 est.)
note: number of people ages 15 or older who are employed or seeking work
comparison ranking: 170

Unemployment rate: 25.9% (2024 est.)
26.2% (2023 est.)
26.4% (2022 est.)
note: % of labor force seeking employment
comparison ranking: 188

Youth unemployment rate (ages 15-24): *total:* 76.3% (2024 est.)
male: 75.3% (2024 est.)
female: 77.9% (2024 est.)
note: % of labor force ages 15-24 seeking employment
comparison ranking: total 1

Population below poverty line: 21.1% (2017 est.)
note: % of population with income below national poverty line

Gini Index coefficient - distribution of family income: 41.6 (2017 est.)
note: index (0-100) of income distribution; higher values represent greater inequality
comparison ranking: 35

Household income or consumption by percentage share: *lowest 10%:* 1.9% (2017 est.)
highest 10%: 32.3% (2017 est.)
note: % share of income accruing to lowest and highest 10% of population

Remittances: 1.4% of GDP (2024 est.)
1.5% of GDP (2023 est.)
1.6% of GDP (2022 est.)
note: personal transfers and compensation between resident and non-resident individuals/households/entities

Budget: *revenues:* $725 million (2019 est.)
expenditures: $754 million (2019 est.)

Current account balance: $610.124 million (2024 est.)
$721.349 million (2023 est.)
$656.207 million (2022 est.)
note: balance of payments - net trade and primary/secondary income in current dollars
comparison ranking: 63

Exports: $5.25 billion (2024 est.)
$5.877 billion (2023 est.)
$5.674 billion (2022 est.)
note: balance of payments - exports of goods and services in current dollars
comparison ranking: 139

Exports - partners: Ethiopia 77%, UAE 5%, China 3%, Singapore 2%, France 2% (2023)
note: top five export partners based on percentage share of exports

Exports - commodities: raw sugar, seed oils, cars, palm oil, rice (2023)
note: top five export commodities based on value in dollars

Imports: $4.765 billion (2024 est.)
$5.269 billion (2023 est.)
$5.096 billion (2022 est.)
note: balance of payments - imports of goods and services in current dollars
comparison ranking: 153

Imports - partners: China 32%, India 12%, UAE 10%, Turkey 6%, Morocco 5% (2023)
note: top five import partners based on percentage share of imports

Imports - commodities: refined petroleum, palm oil, fertilizers, cars, seed oils (2023)
note: top five import commodities based on value in dollars

Reserves of foreign exchange and gold: $348.725 million (2024 est.)

$502.034 million (2023 est.)
$589.437 million (2022 est.)
note: holdings of gold (year-end prices)/foreign exchange/special drawing rights in current dollars
comparison ranking: 168

Debt - external: $2.531 billion (2023 est.)
note: present value of external debt in current US dollars
comparison ranking: 92

Exchange rates: Djiboutian francs (DJF) per US dollar -

Exchange rates: 177.721 (2024 est.)
177.721 (2023 est.)
177.721 (2022 est.)
177.721 (2021 est.)
177.721 (2020 est.)

ENERGY

Electricity access: *electrification - total population:* 65% (2022 est.)
electrification - urban areas: 72.8%
electrification - rural areas: 36.6%

Electricity: *installed generating capacity:* 210,000 kW (2023 est.)
consumption: 584.997 million kWh (2023 est.)
imports: 512 million kWh (2023 est.)
transmission/distribution losses: 128.74 million kWh (2023 est.)
comparison rankings: installed generating capacity 171; consumption 172; imports 90; transmission/distribution losses 51

Electricity generation sources: *fossil fuels:* 65.3% of total installed capacity (2023 est.)
solar: 0.5% of total installed capacity (2023 est.)
wind: 34.2% of total installed capacity (2023 est.)

Coal: *exports:* 8 metric tons (2023 est.)
imports: 19,000 metric tons (2023 est.)

Petroleum: *refined petroleum consumption:* 5,000 bbl/day (2023 est.)

Energy consumption per capita: 10.428 million Btu/person (2023 est.)
comparison ranking: 150

COMMUNICATIONS

Telephones - fixed lines: *total subscriptions:* 29,000 (2023 est.)
subscriptions per 100 inhabitants: 2 (2023 est.)
comparison ranking: total subscriptions 167

Telephones - mobile cellular: *total subscriptions:* 574,000 (2023 est.)
subscriptions per 100 inhabitants: 46 (2022 est.)
comparison ranking: total subscriptions 173

Broadcast media: state-owned Radiodiffusion-Télévision de Djibouti operates the sole terrestrial TV station, as well as the 2 domestic radio networks; no private TV or radio stations; transmissions of several international broadcasters are available (2019)

Internet country code: .dj

Internet users: *percent of population:* 65% (2023 est.)

Broadband - fixed subscriptions: *total:* 17,000 (2023 est.)
subscriptions per 100 inhabitants: 1 (2023 est.)
comparison ranking: total 175

TRANSPORTATION

Civil aircraft registration country code prefix: J2

Airports: 10 (2025)
comparison ranking: 161

Heliports: 6 (2025)
comparison ranking: 97

Railways: *total:* 97 km (2017) (Djibouti segment of the 756 km Addis Ababa-Djibouti railway)
standard gauge: 97 km (2017) 1.435-m gauge

Merchant marine: *total:* 40 (2023)
by type: bulk carrier 1, container ship 1, general cargo 4, oil tanker 13, other 21
comparison ranking: total 126

Ports: *total ports:* 2 (2024)
large: 0
medium: 0
small: 2
very small: 0
ports with oil terminals: 2
key ports: Djibouti, Doraleh

MILITARY AND SECURITY

Military and security forces: Djibouti Armed Forces (Forces Armées Djiboutiennes or FAD): Djiboutian (or National) Army, Djiboutian Navy (includes Djiboutian Coast Guard), Djiboutian Air Force; Djiboutian National Gendarmerie

Ministry of Interior: National Police (Police Nationale) (2025)
note 1: the National Gendarmerie is a security force with military status under the FAD and the Ministry of Defense, but also has responsibilities to the Ministry of Interior; the Gendarmerie's duties include providing security outside of Djibouti City and protecting critical infrastructure within the city, such as the international airport
note 2: the National Police is responsible for security within Djibouti City and has primary control over immigration and customs procedures for all land border-crossing points

Military expenditures: 3.5% of GDP (2019 est.)
3.5% of GDP (2018 est.)
3.3% of GDP (2017 est.)
2.7% of GDP (2016 est.)
2.5% of GDP (2015 est.)

Military and security service personnel strengths: estimated 10-12,000 active Armed Forces, including Gendarmerie (2025)

Military equipment inventories and acquisitions: the FAD's inventory is a mix of mostly older or secondhand equipment from a wide variety of suppliers, including China, France, Italy, Japan, Russia/former Soviet Union, South Africa, Turkey, and the US (2024)

Military service age and obligation: 18 years of age for voluntary military service for men and women; 16-25 years of age for voluntary military training; no conscription (2023)

Military deployments: approximately 1,500 Somalia (AUSSOM) (2025)

Military - note: Djibouti's military forces are largely focused on border, coastal, and internal security duties, such as counterterrorism; as recently as February 2025, Djiboutian forces have conducted operations near its border with Ethiopia against members of the Armed Front for the Restoration of Unity and Democracy (FRUD A), which Djibouti considers a terrorist group
China, France, Italy, Japan, and the US maintain bases in Djibouti for regional military missions, including counterterrorism, counter-piracy, crisis response, and security assistance; other countries, such as Germany and Spain, have smaller military contingents; the EU and NATO also maintain a presence in Djibouti to support multinational naval counter-piracy operations and maritime training efforts (2025)

TERRORISM

Terrorist group(s): Terrorist group(s): al-Shabaab
note: details about the history, aims, leadership, organization, areas of operation, tactics, targets, weapons, size, and sources of support of the group(s) appear(s) in Appendix T

TRANSNATIONAL ISSUES

Refugees and internally displaced persons: *refugees:* 32,636 (2024 est.)

Trafficking in persons: *tier rating:* Tier 2 Watch List — Djibouti does not fully meet the minimum standards for the elimination of trafficking but is making significant efforts to do so, therefore Djibouti was upgraded to Tier 2 Watch List; for more details, go to: https://www.state.gov/reports/2025-trafficking-in-persons-report/djibouti/

DOMINICA

INTRODUCTION

Background: Dominica was the last of the Caribbean islands to be colonized by Europeans, due chiefly to the fierce resistance of the native Caribs. France ceded possession to Britain in 1763, and Dominica became a British colony in 1805. Slavery ended in 1833, and in 1835, the first three men of African descent were elected to the legislative assembly of Dominica. In 1871, Dominica became first part of the British Leeward Islands and then the British Windward Islands until 1958. In 1967, Dominica became an associated state of the UK, formally taking responsibility for its internal affairs, and the country gained its independence in 1978. In 1980, Dominica's fortunes improved when Mary Eugenia CHARLES – the first female prime minister in the Caribbean – replaced a corrupt and tyrannical administration, and she served for the next 15 years. In 2017, Hurricane Maria passed over the island, causing extensive damage to structures, roads, communications, and the power supply, and largely destroying critical agricultural areas.

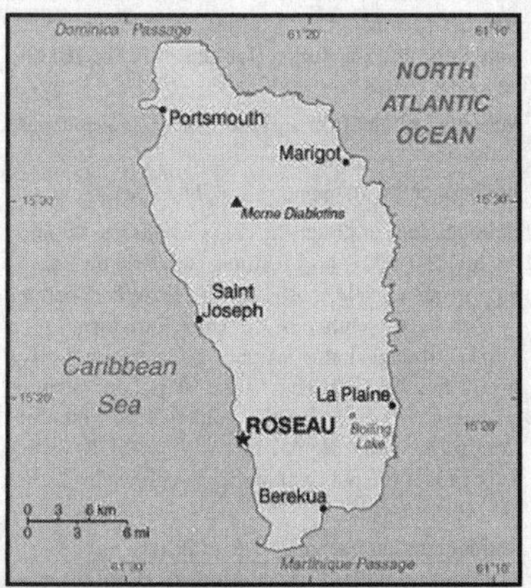

GEOGRAPHY

Location: Caribbean, island between the Caribbean Sea and the North Atlantic Ocean, about halfway between Puerto Rico and Trinidad and Tobago

Geographic coordinates: 15 25 N, 61 20 W

Map references: Central America and the Caribbean

Area: *total:* 751 sq km
land: 751 sq km
water: NEGL
comparison ranking: total 188

Area - comparative: slightly more than four times the size of Washington, D.C.

Land boundaries: *total:* 0 km

Coastline: 148 km

Maritime claims: *territorial sea:* 12 nm
contiguous zone: 24 nm
exclusive economic zone: 200 nm

Climate: tropical; moderated by northeast trade winds; heavy rainfall

Terrain: rugged mountains of volcanic origin

Elevation: *highest point:* Morne Diablotins 1,447 m
lowest point: Caribbean Sea 0 m

Natural resources: timber, hydropower, arable land

Land use: *agricultural land:* 33.3% (2022 est.)
arable land: 8% (2022 est.)
permanent crops: 22.7% (2022 est.)
permanent pasture: 2.7% (2022 est.)
forest: 63.8% (2022 est.)
other: 2.8% (2022 est.)

Irrigated land: NA

Population distribution: population is mostly clustered along the coast, with roughly a third living in the parish of St. George, in or around the capital of Roseau; the volcanic interior is sparsely populated

Natural hazards: flash floods are a constant threat; destructive hurricanes can be expected during the late summer months
volcanism: Dominica lies in the middle of the volcanic-island arc of the Lesser Antilles that extends from the island of Saba in the north to Grenada in the south; of the 16 volcanoes that make up this arc, five are located on Dominica, more than any other island in the Caribbean: Morne aux Diables (861 m), Morne Diablotins (1,430 m), Morne Trois Pitons (1,387 m), Watt Mountain (1,224 m), which last erupted in 1997, and Morne Plat Pays (940 m); the two best-known volcanic features on Dominica, the Valley of Desolation and the Boiling Lake thermal areas, lie on the flanks of Watt Mountain, and both are popular tourist destinations

Geography - note: known as "The Nature Island of the Caribbean" due to its lush and varied flora and fauna, which are protected by an extensive natural park system; the most mountainous of the Lesser Antilles, its volcanic peaks are cones of lava craters and include Boiling Lake, the second-largest thermally active lake in the world

PEOPLE AND SOCIETY

Population: *total:* 74,661 (2024 est.)
male: 37,753
female: 36,908
comparison rankings: total 201; male 201; female 202

Nationality: *noun:* Dominican(s)
adjective: Dominican

Ethnic groups: African descent 84.5%, mixed 9%, Indigenous 3.8%, other 2.1%, unspecified 0.6% (2011 est.)

Languages: English (official), French patois

Religions: Roman Catholic 52.7%, Protestant 29.7% (includes Seventh Day Adventist 6.7%, Pentecostal 6.1%, Baptist 5.2%, Christian Union Church 3.9%, Methodist 2.6%, Gospel Mission 2.1%, other Protestant 3.1%), Jehovah's Witness 1.3%, Rastafarian 1.1%, other 4.3%, none 9.4%, unspecified 1.4% (2011 est.)

Age structure: *0-14 years:* 20.7% (male 7,891/female 7,530)
15-64 years: 65.6% (male 25,000/female 24,009)
65 years and over: 13.7% (2024 est.) (male 4,862/female 5,369)

Dependency ratios: *total dependency ratio:* 52.3 (2024 est.)
youth dependency ratio: 31.5 (2024 est.)
elderly dependency ratio: 20.9 (2024 est.)
potential support ratio: 4.8 (2024 est.)

Median age: *total:* 37 years (2024 est.)
male: 36.5 years
female: 37.6 years
comparison ranking: total 84

Population growth rate: -0.01% (2024 est.)
comparison ranking: 196

Birth rate: 13.3 births/1,000 population (2024 est.)
comparison ranking: 129

Death rate: 8.1 deaths/1,000 population (2024 est.)
comparison ranking: 87

Net migration rate: -5.3 migrant(s)/1,000 population (2024 est.)
comparison ranking: 205

Population distribution: population is mostly clustered along the coast, with roughly a third living in the parish of St. George, in or around the capital of Roseau; the volcanic interior is sparsely populated

Urbanization: *urban population:* 72% of total population (2023)
rate of urbanization: 0.84% annual rate of change (2020-25 est.)

Major urban areas - population: 15,000 ROSEAU (capital) (2018)

Sex ratio: *at birth:* 1.05 male(s)/female
0-14 years: 1.05 male(s)/female
15-64 years: 1.04 male(s)/female
65 years and over: 0.91 male(s)/female
total population: 1.02 male(s)/female (2024 est.)

Maternal mortality ratio: 36 deaths/100,000 live births (2023 est.)
comparison ranking: 107

Infant mortality rate: *total:* 10.7 deaths/1,000 live births (2024 est.)
male: 14.5 deaths/1,000 live births
female: 6.8 deaths/1,000 live births
comparison ranking: total 127

Life expectancy at birth: *total population:* 78.7 years (2024 est.)
male: 75.8 years
female: 81.8 years
comparison ranking: total population 74

Total fertility rate: 2.01 children born/woman (2024 est.)
comparison ranking: 106

Gross reproduction rate: 0.98 (2024 est.)

Health expenditure: 6.5% of GDP (2021)
6.2% of national budget (2022 est.)

Physician density: 1.16 physicians/1,000 population (2018)

Hospital bed density: 3 beds/1,000 population (2021 est.)

Obesity - adult prevalence rate: 27.9% (2016)
comparison ranking: 34

Alcohol consumption per capita: *total:* 6.32 liters of pure alcohol (2019 est.)
beer: 1.64 liters of pure alcohol (2019 est.)
wine: 0.29 liters of pure alcohol (2019 est.)
spirits: 4.39 liters of pure alcohol (2019 est.)
other alcohols: 0 liters of pure alcohol (2019 est.)
comparison ranking: total 67

Currently married women (ages 15-49): 40.3% (2023 est.)

Education expenditure: 5.4% of GDP (2024 est.)
5.8% national budget (2025 est.)
comparison ranking: Education expenditure (% GDP) 44

People - note: 3,000-3,500 Kalinago (Carib) still living on Dominica are the only pre-Columbian population remaining in the Caribbean; only 70-100 may be "pure" Kalinago because of years of integration into the broader population

ENVIRONMENT

Environmental issues: pollution from agrochemicals and from untreated sewage; forests endangered by the expansion of farming; soil erosion; pollution of the coastal zone from agricultural/industrial chemicals and untreated sewage

International environmental agreements: *party to:* Biodiversity, Climate Change, Climate Change-Kyoto Protocol, Climate Change-Paris Agreement, Desertification, Endangered Species, Environmental Modification, Hazardous Wastes, Law of the Sea, Ozone Layer Protection, Ship Pollution, Whaling
signed, but not ratified: none of the selected agreements

Climate: tropical; moderated by northeast trade winds; heavy rainfall

Urbanization: *urban population:* 72% of total population (2023)
rate of urbanization: 0.84% annual rate of change (2020-25 est.)

Carbon dioxide emissions: 168,000 metric tonnes of CO2 (2023 est.)
from petroleum and other liquids: 168,000 metric tonnes of CO2 (2023 est.)
comparison ranking: total emissions 205

Particulate matter emissions: 7.9 micrograms per cubic meter (2019 est.)

Waste and recycling: *municipal solid waste generated annually:* 13,200 tons (2024 est.)
percent of municipal solid waste recycled: 12.6% (2022 est.)

Total water withdrawal: *municipal:* 19 million cubic meters (2022 est.)
industrial: 0 cubic meters (2022 est.)
agricultural: 1 million cubic meters (2022 est.)

Total renewable water resources: 200 million cubic meters (2022 est.)

GOVERNMENT

Country name: *conventional long form:* Commonwealth of Dominica
conventional short form: Dominica
etymology: the island was named by explorer Christopher COLUMBUS for the day of the week on which he spotted it, Sunday (*Domingo* in Spanish, *dominica dies* in Latin), 3 November 1493

Government type: parliamentary republic

Capital: *name:* Roseau
geographic coordinates: 15 18 N, 61 24 W
time difference: UTC-4 (1 hour ahead of Washington, DC, during Standard Time)
etymology: the name is French for "reed;" the first settlement was named after the river reeds that grew in the area

Administrative divisions: 10 parishes; Saint Andrew, Saint David, Saint George, Saint John, Saint Joseph, Saint Luke, Saint Mark, Saint Patrick, Saint Paul, Saint Peter

Legal system: common law based on the English model

Constitution: *history:* previous 1967 (pre-independence); latest presented 25 July 1978, entered into force 3 November 1978
amendment process: proposed by the House of Assembly; passage of amendments to constitutional sections such as fundamental rights and freedoms, the government structure, and constitutional amendment procedures requires approval by three fourths of the Assembly membership in the final reading of the amendment bill, approval by simple majority in a referendum, and assent of the president

International law organization participation: accepts compulsory ICJ jurisdiction; accepts ICCt jurisdiction

Citizenship: *citizenship by birth:* yes
citizenship by descent only: yes
dual citizenship recognized: yes
residency requirement for naturalization: 5 years

Suffrage: 18 years of age; universal

Executive branch: *chief of state:* President Sylvanie BURTON (since 2 October 2023)
head of government: Prime Minister Roosevelt SKERRIT (since 8 January 2004)
cabinet: Cabinet appointed by the president on the advice of the prime minister
election/appointment process: president nominated by the prime minister and leader of the opposition party and elected by the House of Assembly for a 5-year term (eligible for a second term); prime minister appointed by the president
most recent election date: 27 September 2023
election results: *2023:* parliament elects Sylvanie BURTON (DLP) with 20 votes for and five against
2018: Charles A. SAVARIN (DLP) reelected president unopposed
expected date of next election: October 2028

Legislative branch: *legislature name:* House of Assembly
legislative structure: unicameral
number of seats: 32 (21 directly elected; 9 appointed)
electoral system: proportional representation
scope of elections: full renewal
term in office: 5 years
most recent election date: 12/6/2022
parties elected and seats per party: Dominica Labor Party (DLP) (19); Independents (2)
percentage of women in chamber: 40.6%
expected date of next election: December 2027

Judicial branch: *highest court(s):* the Eastern Caribbean Supreme Court (ECSC) is the superior court of the Organization of Eastern Caribbean States; the ECSC is headquartered on St. Lucia and consists of the Court of Appeal – headed by the chief justice and 4 judges – and the High Court with 18 judges; the Court of Appeal travels to member states on a schedule to hear appeals from the High Court and subordinate courts; the Caribbean Court of Justice is the final court of appeal
judge selection and term of office: chief justice of Eastern Caribbean Supreme Court appointed by the British monarch; other justices and judges appointed by the Judicial and Legal Services Commission, an independent body of judicial officials; Court of Appeal justices appointed for life with mandatory retirement at age 65; High Court judges appointed for life with mandatory retirement at age 62
subordinate courts: Court of Summary Jurisdiction; magistrates' courts

Political parties: Dominica Freedom Party or DFP
Dominica Labor Party or DLP
Dominica United Workers Party or UWP

Diplomatic representation in the US: *chief of mission:* Ambassador Steve FERROL (since 15 September 2023)
chancery: 3216 New Mexico Ave NW Washington, DC 20016
telephone: [1] (202) 364-6781
FAX: [1] (202) 364-6791
email address and website: embdomdc@gmail.com
consulate(s) general: New York

Diplomatic representation from the US: *embassy:* the US does not have an embassy in Dominica; the US Ambassador to Barbados is accredited to Dominica

International organization participation: ACP, ACS, AOSIS, C, Caricom, CD, CDB, CELAC, Commonwealth of Nations, ECCU, FAO, G-77, IAEA, IBRD, ICCt, ICRM, IDA, IFAD, IFC, IFRCS, ILO, IMF, IMO, Interpol, IOC, ISO (correspondent), ITU, ITUC (NGOs), MIGA, NAM, OAS, OECS, OIF, OPANAL, OPCW, Petrocaribe, UN, UNCTAD, UNESCO, UNIDO, UPU, WFTU, WHO, WIPO, WMO, WTO

Independence: 3 November 1978 (from the UK)

National holiday: Independence Day, 3 November (1978)

Flag: *description:* green with a centered cross of three equal bands in yellow, black, and white; in the center of the cross is a red disk with a Sisserou parrot surrounded by 10 five-pointed green stars edged in yellow
meaning: the stars represent the 10 administrative divisions (parishes); green symbolizes the island's lush vegetation; the tricolor cross represents the Christian Trinity; yellow stands for sunshine, the primary agricultural products (citrus and bananas), and the Carib people; black for the rich soil and the African heritage of most citizens; white for rivers, waterfalls, and the purity of aspirations; the red disc for social justice

National symbol(s): sisserou parrot, Carib wood flower

National color(s): green, yellow, black, white, red

National coat of arms: the coat of arms was adopted on July 21, 1961, and features two sisserou parrots supporting a shield that is divided into four sections by a cross, a reference to the island's discovery on a Sunday; the quadrants feature a palm tree, a banana tree, a frog that is native to the island, and a canoe on the Caribbean Sea; the golden lion symbolizes Dominica's past colonial ties with the UK; below the shield is the national motto, which means "After God is the Earth"

National anthem(s): *title:* "Isle of Beauty"
lyrics/music: Wilfred Oscar Morgan POND/Lemuel McPherson CHRISTIAN
history: adopted 1967

ECONOMY

Economic overview: highly agrarian OECS island economy; ECCU-member state; large banana exporter; improved oversight of its citizenship-by-investment program; emerging ecotourism, information and communications, and education industries

Real GDP (purchasing power parity): $1.241 billion (2024 est.)
$1.216 billion (2023 est.)
$1.173 billion (2022 est.)
note: data in 2021 dollars
comparison ranking: 206

Real GDP growth rate: 2.1% (2024 est.)
3.7% (2023 est.)
10.4% (2022 est.)
note: annual GDP % growth based on constant local currency
comparison ranking: 145

Real GDP per capita: $18,700 (2024 est.)
$18,300 (2023 est.)
$17,600 (2022 est.)
note: data in 2021 dollars
comparison ranking: 108

GDP (official exchange rate): $688.881 million (2024 est.)
note: data in current dollars at official exchange rate

Inflation rate (consumer prices): 2.6% (2024 est.)
5.1% (2023 est.)
2.9% (2022 est.)
note: annual % change based on consumer prices
comparison ranking: 75

GDP - composition, by sector of origin: *agriculture:* 12.2% (2024 est.)
industry: 13.9% (2024 est.)
services: 56.9% (2024 est.)
note: figures may not total 100% due to non-allocated consumption not captured in sector-reported data
comparison rankings: agriculture 64; industry 168; services 110

GDP - composition, by end use: *household consumption:* 87.7% (2018 est.)
government consumption: 27.4% (2018 est.)
investment in fixed capital: 32.7% (2018 est.)
investment in inventories: 0% (2018 est.)
exports of goods and services: 29.2% (2018 est.)
imports of goods and services: -77.8% (2018 est.)
note: figures may not total 100% due to rounding or gaps in data collection

Agricultural products: taro, grapefruits, yams, bananas, coconuts, plantains, milk, yautia, sugarcane, oranges (2023)
note: top ten agricultural products based on tonnage

Industries: soap, coconut oil, tourism, copra, furniture, cement blocks, shoes

Industrial production growth rate: 8.8% (2024 est.)
note: annual % change in industrial value added based on constant local currency
comparison ranking: 18

Remittances: 5.6% of GDP (2024 est.)
5.2% of GDP (2023 est.)
6.1% of GDP (2022 est.)
note: personal transfers and compensation between resident and non-resident individuals/households/entities

Budget: *revenues:* $233.831 million (2017 est.)
expenditures: $164.673 million (2017 est.)
note: central government revenues and expenses (excluding grants/extrabudgetary units/social security funds) converted to US dollars at average official exchange rate for year indicated

Current account balance: -$160.12 million (2024 est.)
-$223.632 million (2023 est.)
-$163.746 million (2022 est.)
note: balance of payments - net trade and primary/secondary income in current dollars
comparison ranking: 101

Exports: $212.753 million (2024 est.)
$188.818 million (2023 est.)
$173.93 million (2022 est.)
note: balance of payments - exports of goods and services in current dollars
comparison ranking: 201

Exports - partners: Bahamas, The 13%, Saudi Arabia 11%, Iceland 10%, Guyana 7%, Antigua & Barbuda 7% (2023)
note: top five export partners based on percentage share of exports

Exports - commodities: iron blocks, medical instruments, excavation machinery, power equipment, soap (2023)
note: top five export commodities based on value in dollars

Imports: $387.532 million (2024 est.)
$417.164 million (2023 est.)
$354.27 million (2022 est.)
note: balance of payments - imports of goods and services in current dollars
comparison ranking: 204

Imports - partners: USA 24%, China 11%, Indonesia 8%, Trinidad & Tobago 7%, Italy 7% (2023)
note: top five import partners based on percentage share of imports

Imports - commodities: refined petroleum, ships, plastic products, semi-finished iron, cars (2023)
note: top five import commodities based on value in dollars

Reserves of foreign exchange and gold: $155.971 million (2024 est.)
$183.53 million (2023 est.)
$204.343 million (2022 est.)
note: holdings of gold (year-end prices)/foreign exchange/special drawing rights in current dollars
comparison ranking: 175

Debt - external: $301.191 million (2023 est.)
note: present value of external debt in current US dollars
comparison ranking: 116

Exchange rates: East Caribbean dollars (XCD) per US dollar -

Exchange rates: 2.7 (2024 est.)
2.7 (2023 est.)
2.7 (2022 est.)
2.7 (2021 est.)
2.7 (2020 est.)

ENERGY

Electricity access: *electrification - total population:* 100% (2022 est.)

Electricity: *installed generating capacity:* 41,000 kW (2023 est.)
consumption: 145.827 million kWh (2023 est.)
transmission/distribution losses: 8 million kWh (2023 est.)
comparison rankings: installed generating capacity 197; consumption 193; transmission/distribution losses 14

Electricity generation sources: *fossil fuels:* 84.3% of total installed capacity (2023 est.)
solar: 0.1% of total installed capacity (2023 est.)
wind: 0.7% of total installed capacity (2023 est.)
hydroelectricity: 15% of total installed capacity (2023 est.)

Petroleum: *refined petroleum consumption:* 1,000 bbl/day (2023 est.)

Energy consumption per capita: 36.395 million Btu/person (2023 est.)
comparison ranking: 106

COMMUNICATIONS

Telephones - fixed lines: *total subscriptions:* 7,000 (2021 est.)
subscriptions per 100 inhabitants: 11 (2021 est.)
comparison ranking: total subscriptions 195

Telephones - mobile cellular: *total subscriptions:* 57,000 (2022 est.)
subscriptions per 100 inhabitants: 86 (2021 est.)
comparison ranking: total subscriptions 205

Broadcast media: no terrestrial TV service; subscription cable TV provider offers some locally produced programming, plus channels from the US, Latin America, and the Caribbean; state-operated radio broadcasts on 6 stations; privately owned radio broadcasts on about 15 stations (2019)

Internet country code: .dm

Internet users: *percent of population:* 84% (2023 est.)

Broadband - fixed subscriptions: *total:* 14,000 (2022 est.)
subscriptions per 100 inhabitants: 21 (2022 est.)
comparison ranking: total 179

TRANSPORTATION

Civil aircraft registration country code prefix: J7

Airports: 2 (2025)
comparison ranking: 200

Merchant marine: *total:* 77 (2023)
by type: general cargo 26, oil tanker 10, other 41
comparison ranking: total 101

Ports: *total ports:* 2 (2024)
large: 0
medium: 0
small: 0
very small: 2
ports with oil terminals: 1
key ports: Portsmouth, Roseau

MILITARY AND SECURITY

Military and security forces: no regular military forces; Commonwealth of Dominica Police Force (CDPF) under the Ministry of National Security and Legal Affairs (2025)

Military - note: Dominica has been a member of the Caribbean Regional Security System (RSS) since its creation in 1982; RSS signatories (Antigua and Barbuda, Barbados, Grenada, Guyana, St. Kitts and Nevis, St. Lucia, and St. Vincent and the Grenadines) agreed to prepare contingency plans and assist one another, on request, in national emergencies, prevention of smuggling, search and rescue, immigration control, fishery protection, customs and excise control, maritime policing duties, protection of off-shore installations, pollution control, national and other disasters, and threats to national security (2025)

TRANSNATIONAL ISSUES

Refugees and internally displaced persons: *refugees:* 5 (2024 est.)

DOMINICAN REPUBLIC

INTRODUCTION

Background: The Taino – indigenous inhabitants of Hispaniola prior to the arrival of Europeans – divided the island now known as the Dominican Republic and Haiti into five chiefdoms and territories. Christopher COLUMBUS explored and claimed the island on his first voyage in 1492; it became a springboard for Spanish conquest of the Caribbean and the American mainland. In 1697, Spain recognized French dominion over the western third of the island, which in 1804 became Haiti. The remainder of the island, by then known as Santo Domingo, sought to gain its own independence in 1821, but the Haitians conquered and ruled it for 22 years; it finally attained independence as the Dominican Republic in 1844. In 1861, the Dominicans voluntarily returned to the Spanish Empire, but two years later, they launched a war that restored independence in 1865.

A legacy of unsettled and mostly non-representative rule followed, capped by the dictatorship of Rafael Leonidas TRUJILLO from 1930 to 1961. Juan BOSCH was elected president in 1962 but was deposed in a military coup in 1963. In 1965, the US

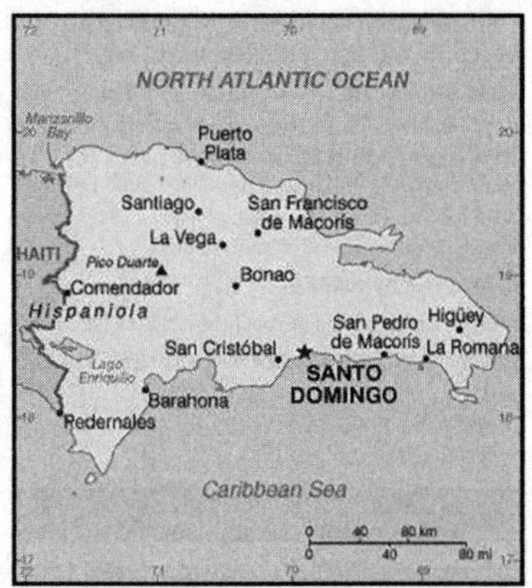

led an intervention in the midst of a civil war sparked by an uprising to restore BOSCH. In 1966, Joaquin BALAGUER defeated BOSCH in the presidential election. BALAGUER maintained a tight grip on power for most of the next 30 years, until international reaction to flawed elections forced him to curtail his term in 1996. Since then, regular competitive elections have been held.

GEOGRAPHY

Location: Caribbean, eastern two-thirds of the island of Hispaniola, between the Caribbean Sea and the North Atlantic Ocean, east of Haiti

Geographic coordinates: 19 00 N, 70 40 W

Map references: Central America and the Caribbean

Area: *total:* 48,670 sq km
land: 48,320 sq km
water: 350 sq km
comparison ranking: total 131

Area - comparative: slightly more than twice the size of New Jersey

Land boundaries: *total:* 376 km
border countries (1): Haiti 376 km

Coastline: 1,288 km

Maritime claims: *territorial sea:* 12 nm
contiguous zone: 24 nm
exclusive economic zone: 200 nm
continental shelf: 200 nm or to the edge of the continental margin
note: measured from claimed archipelagic straight baselines

Climate: tropical maritime; little seasonal temperature variation; seasonal variation in rainfall

Terrain: rugged highlands and mountains interspersed with fertile valleys

Elevation: *highest point:* Pico Duarte 3,098 m
lowest point: Lago Enriquillo -46 m
mean elevation: 424 m

Natural resources: nickel, bauxite, gold, silver, arable land

Land use: *agricultural land:* 50.6% (2022 est.)
arable land: 18.2% (2022 est.)
permanent crops: 7.6% (2022 est.)
permanent pasture: 24.8% (2022 est.)
forest: 44.8% (2022 est.)
other: 4.6% (2022 est.)

Irrigated land: 2,981 sq km (2018)

Major lakes (area sq km): *salt water lake(s):* Lago de Enriquillo - 500 sq km

Population distribution: coastal development is significant, especially in the southern coastal plains and the Cibao Valley, where population density is highest; smaller population clusters exist in the interior mountains (Cordillera Central)

Natural hazards: lies in the middle of the hurricane belt and subject to severe storms from June to October; occasional flooding; periodic droughts

Geography - note: shares island of Hispaniola with Haiti (eastern two-thirds makes up the Dominican Republic, western one-third is Haiti); the second largest country in the Antilles (after Cuba); geographically diverse with the Caribbean's tallest mountain, Pico Duarte, and lowest elevation and largest lake, Lago Enriquillo

PEOPLE AND SOCIETY

Population: *total:* 10,815,857 (2024 est.)
male: 5,465,776
female: 5,350,081
comparison rankings: total 87; male 86; female 87

Nationality: *noun:* Dominican(s)
adjective: Dominican

Ethnic groups: mixed 70.4% (Mestizo/Indio 58%, Mulatto 12.4%), Black 15.8%, White 13.5%, other 0.3% (2014 est.)
note: respondents self-identified their race; the term "indio" in the Dominican Republic is not associated with people of indigenous ancestry but people of mixed ancestry or skin color between light and dark

Languages: Spanish (official)
major-language sample(s):
La Libreta Informativa del Mundo, la fuente indispensable de información básica. (Spanish)

Religions: Evangelical 50.2%, Roman Catholic 30.1%, none 18.5%, unspecified 1.2% (2023 est.)

Age structure: *0-14 years:* 25.5% (male 1,402,847/female 1,358,833)
15-64 years: 66.9% (male 3,667,584/female 3,563,848)
65 years and over: 7.6% (2024 est.) (male 395,345/female 427,400)

Dependency ratios: *total dependency ratio:* 49.6 (2024 est.)
youth dependency ratio: 38.2 (2024 est.)
elderly dependency ratio: 11.4 (2024 est.)
potential support ratio: 8.8 (2024 est.)

Median age: *total:* 29.2 years (2024 est.)
male: 29.1 years
female: 29.4 years
comparison ranking: total 145

Population growth rate: 0.76% (2024 est.)
comparison ranking: 115

Birth rate: 17.3 births/1,000 population (2024 est.)
comparison ranking: 87

Death rate: 7.1 deaths/1,000 population (2024 est.)
comparison ranking: 118

Net migration rate: -2.7 migrant(s)/1,000 population (2024 est.)
comparison ranking: 175

Population distribution: coastal development is significant, especially in the southern coastal plains and the Cibao Valley, where population density is highest; smaller population clusters exist in the interior mountains (Cordillera Central)

Urbanization: *urban population:* 84.4% of total population (2023)
rate of urbanization: 1.64% annual rate of change (2020-25 est.)

Major urban areas - population: 3.524 million SANTO DOMINGO (capital) (2023)

Sex ratio: *at birth:* 1.04 male(s)/female
0-14 years: 1.03 male(s)/female
15-64 years: 1.03 male(s)/female
65 years and over: 0.93 male(s)/female
total population: 1.02 male(s)/female (2024 est.)

Mother's mean age at first birth: 20.9 years (2013 est.)
note: data represents median age at first birth among women 25-49

Maternal mortality ratio: 124 deaths/100,000 live births (2023 est.)
comparison ranking: 58

Infant mortality rate: *total:* 21.7 deaths/1,000 live births (2024 est.)
male: 24.3 deaths/1,000 live births
female: 19 deaths/1,000 live births
comparison ranking: total 74

Life expectancy at birth: *total population:* 72.6 years (2024 est.)
male: 71 years
female: 74.3 years
comparison ranking: total population 160

Total fertility rate: 2.15 children born/woman (2024 est.)
comparison ranking: 92

Gross reproduction rate: 1.06 (2024 est.)

Drinking water source: *improved: urban:* 97.8% of population (2022 est.)
rural: 91.4% of population (2022 est.)
total: 96.8% of population (2022 est.)
unimproved: urban: 2.2% of population (2022 est.)
rural: 8.6% of population (2022 est.)
total: 3.2% of population (2022 est.)

Health expenditure: 4.9% of GDP (2021)
14.4% of national budget (2022 est.)

Physician density: 2.43 physicians/1,000 population (2023)

Hospital bed density: 1.4 beds/1,000 population (2020 est.)

Sanitation facility access: *improved: urban:* 97.4% of population (2022 est.)
rural: 91.9% of population (2022 est.)
total: 96.5% of population (2022 est.)
unimproved: urban: 2.6% of population (2022 est.)
rural: 8.1% of population (2022 est.)
total: 3.5% of population (2022 est.)

Obesity - adult prevalence rate: 27.6% (2016)
comparison ranking: 37

Alcohol consumption per capita: *total:* 5.56 liters of pure alcohol (2019 est.)
beer: 3.15 liters of pure alcohol (2019 est.)
wine: 0.17 liters of pure alcohol (2019 est.)
spirits: 2.18 liters of pure alcohol (2019 est.)
other alcohols: 0.06 liters of pure alcohol (2019 est.)
comparison ranking: total 78

Tobacco use: *total:* 9.7% (2025 est.)
male: 13.5% (2025 est.)
female: 5.9% (2025 est.)
comparison ranking: total 130

Children under the age of 5 years underweight: 3% (2019)
comparison ranking: 80

Currently married women (ages 15-49): 52.1% (2023 est.)

Child marriage: *women married by age 15:* 9.4% (2019)
women married by age 18: 31.5% (2019)

Education expenditure: 4.3% of GDP (2023 est.)
21.9% national budget (2024 est.)
comparison ranking: Education expenditure (% GDP) 89

Literacy: *total population:* 94% (2016 est.)
male: 94% (2016 est.)
female: 87.4% (2019 est.)

School life expectancy (primary to tertiary education): *total:* 14 years (2022 est.)
male: 13 years (2022 est.)
female: 15 years (2022 est.)

ENVIRONMENT

Environmental issues: soil eroding into the sea damages coral reefs; deforestation

International environmental agreements: *party to:* Biodiversity, Climate Change, Climate Change-Kyoto Protocol, Climate Change-Paris Agreement, Comprehensive Nuclear Test Ban, Desertification, Endangered Species, Hazardous Wastes, Law of the Sea, Marine Dumping-London Convention, Marine Life Conservation, Nuclear Test Ban, Ozone Layer Protection, Ship Pollution, Wetlands, Whaling
signed, but not ratified: none of the selected agreements

Climate: tropical maritime; little seasonal temperature variation; seasonal variation in rainfall

Urbanization: *urban population:* 84.4% of total population (2023)
rate of urbanization: 1.64% annual rate of change (2020-25 est.)

Carbon dioxide emissions: 29.713 million metric tonnes of CO2 (2023 est.)
from coal and metallurgical coke: 5.374 million metric tonnes of CO2 (2023 est.)
from petroleum and other liquids: 19.872 million metric tonnes of CO2 (2023 est.)
from consumed natural gas: 4.467 million metric tonnes of CO2 (2023 est.)
comparison ranking: total emissions 75

Particulate matter emissions: 8 micrograms per cubic meter (2019 est.)

Waste and recycling: *municipal solid waste generated annually:* 4.064 million tons (2024 est.)
percent of municipal solid waste recycled: 11.6% (2022 est.)

Total water withdrawal: *municipal:* 855 million cubic meters (2022 est.)
industrial: 659.9 million cubic meters (2022 est.)
agricultural: 7.563 billion cubic meters (2022 est.)

Total renewable water resources: 23.5 billion cubic meters (2022 est.)

GOVERNMENT

Country name: *conventional long form:* Dominican Republic
conventional short form: The Dominican
local long form: República Dominicana
local short form: La Dominicana
former: Santo Domingo (the capital city's name formerly applied to the entire country)
etymology: the name is a latinized form of the Spanish term *Santo Domingo*, meaning "holy Sunday;" Spanish explorers originally settled the island on a Sunday in 1496, and the name was first given to the island of Hispaniola as a whole in 1697

Government type: presidential republic

Capital: *name:* Santo Domingo
geographic coordinates: 18 28 N, 69 54 W
time difference: UTC-4 (1 hour ahead of Washington, DC, during Standard Time)
etymology: named after Saint Domingo de GUZMAN (1170-1221), founder of the Dominican Order; the city's full name was originally Santo Domingo de Guzman

Administrative divisions: 31 provinces (*provincias*, singular - *provincia*), 1 district* (*distrito*); Azua, Baoruco, Barahona, Dajabón, Distrito Nacional*, Duarte, Elías Piña, El Seibo, Espaillat, Hato Mayor, Hermanas Mirabal, Independencia, La Altagracia, La Romana, La Vega, María Trinidad Sánchez, Monseñor Nouel, Monte Cristi, Monte Plata, Pedernales, Peravia, Puerto Plata, Samaná, Sánchez Ramírez, San Cristóbal, San José de Ocoa, San Juan, San Pedro de Macorís, Santiago, Santiago Rodríguez, Santo Domingo, Valverde

Legal system: civil law system based on the French civil code; Criminal Procedures Code modified in 2004 to include important elements of an accusatory system

Constitution: *history:* many previous (38 total); latest proclaimed 13 June 2015
amendment process: proposed by a special session of the National Congress called the National Revisory Assembly; passage requires at least two-thirds majority approval by at least one half of those present in both houses of the Assembly; passage of amendments to constitutional articles, such as fundamental rights and guarantees, territorial composition, nationality, or the procedures for constitutional reform, also requires approval in a referendum

International law organization participation: accepts compulsory ICJ jurisdiction; accepts ICCt jurisdiction

Citizenship: *citizenship by birth:* no
citizenship by descent only: at least one parent must be a citizen of the Dominican Republic
dual citizenship recognized: yes
residency requirement for naturalization: 2 years

Suffrage: 18 years of age; universal and compulsory; married persons can vote, regardless of age
note: members of the armed forces and national police by law cannot vote

Executive branch: *chief of state:* President Luis Rodolfo ABINADER Corona (since 16 August 2020)
head of government: President Luis Rodolfo ABINADER Corona (since 16 August 2020)
cabinet: Cabinet nominated by the president
election/appointment process: president and vice president directly elected on the same ballot by absolute vote in 2 rounds, if needed, for a 4-year term (eligible for a maximum of two consecutive terms)
most recent election date: 19 May 2024
election results: *2024:* Luis Rodolfo ABINADER Corona reelected president; percent of vote - Luis Rodolfo ABINADER Corona (PRM) 57.5%, Leonel Antonio FERNÁNDEZ Reyna (FP) 28.8%, Abel MARTÍNEZ (PLD) 10.4%, other 3.3%
2020: Luis Rodolfo ABINADER Corona elected president in first round; percent of vote - Luis Rodolfo ABINADER Corona (PRM) 52.5%, Gonzalo CASTILLO Terrero (PLD) 37.5%, Leonel Antonio FERNÁNDEZ Reyna (FP) 8.9%, other 1.1%
expected date of next election: 21 May 2028
note: the president is both chief of state and head of government

Legislative branch: *legislature name:* National Congress of the Republic (Congreso Nacional de la República)
legislative structure: bicameral

Legislative branch - lower chamber: *chamber name:* Chamber of Deputies (Cámara de Diputados)
number of seats: 190 (all directly elected)
electoral system: proportional representation
scope of elections: full renewal
term in office: 4 years
most recent election date: 5/19/2024
parties elected and seats per party: Modern Revolutionary Party (PRM) and its allies (146); People's Force (FP) and its allies (28); Other (16)
percentage of women in chamber: 36.8%
expected date of next election: May 2028

Legislative branch - upper chamber: *chamber name:* Senate (Senado)
number of seats: 32 (all directly elected)
electoral system: proportional representation
scope of elections: full renewal
term in office: 4 years
most recent election date: 5/19/2024
parties elected and seats per party: Modern Revolutionary Party (PRM) and its allies (24); People's Force (FP) and its allies (3); Other (5)
percentage of women in chamber: 12.5%
expected date of next election: May 2028

Judicial branch: *highest court(s):* Supreme Court of Justice or Suprema Corte de Justicia (consists of a minimum of 16 magistrates); Constitutional Court or Tribunal Constitucional (consists of 13 judges)
judge selection and term of office: Supreme Court and Constitutional Court judges appointed by the National Council of the Judiciary composed of the president, the leaders of both chambers of congress, the president of the Supreme Court, and a non-governing party congressional representative; Supreme Court judges appointed for 7-year terms; Constitutional Court judges appointed for 9-year terms
subordinate courts: courts of appeal; courts of first instance; justices of the peace; special courts for juvenile, labor, and land cases; Contentious Administrative Court for cases filed against the government

Political parties: Alliance for Democracy or APD
Broad Front (Frente Amplio)
Country Alliance or AP
Dominican Liberation Party or PLD
Dominican Revolutionary Party or PRD
Dominicans For Change or DXC
Independent Revolutionary Party or PRI
Institutional Social Democratic Bloc or BIS
Liberal Reformist Party or PRL (formerly the Liberal Party of the Dominican Republic or PLRD)
Modern Revolutionary Party or PRM
National Progressive Front or FNP
People's First Party or PPG
People's Force or FP
Social Christian Reformist Party or PRSC

Diplomatic representation in the US: *chief of mission:* Ambassador María Isabel CASTILLO BÁEZ (since 11 June 2025)
chancery: 1715 22nd Street NW, Washington, DC 20008
telephone: [1] (202) 332-6280

FAX: [1] (202) 265-8057
email address and website: embassy@drembassyusa.org
http://drembassyusa.org/
consulate(s) general: Boston, Chicago, Houston, Los Angelos, Miami, New Jersey, New Orleans, New York, Orlando, Philadelphia

Diplomatic representation from the US: *chief of mission:* Ambassador (vacant); Chargé d'Affaires Patricia AGUILERA (since 1 October 2023)
embassy: Av. Republica de Colombia #57, Santo Domingo
mailing address: 3470 Santo Domingo Place, Washington DC 20521-3470
telephone: (809) 567-7775
email address and website: SDOAmericans@state.gov
https://do.usembassy.gov/

International organization participation: ACP, ACS, AOSIS, BCIE, Caricom (observer), CD, CELAC, FAO, G-77, IADB, IAEA, IBRD, ICAO, ICC (national committees), ICCt, ICRM, IDA, IFAD, IFC, IFRCS, IHO, ILO, IMF, IMO, Interpol, IOC, IOM, IPU, ISO (correspondent), ITSO, ITU, ITUC (NGOs), LAES, LAIA, MIGA, MINUSMA, NAM, OAS, OIF (observer), OPANAL, OPCW, Pacific Alliance (observer), PCA, Petrocaribe, SICA (associated member), UN, UNCTAD, UNESCO, UNHRC, UNIDO, Union Latina, UNOOSA, UNWTO, UPU, WCO, WFTU (NGOs), WHO, WIPO, WMO, WTO

Independence: 27 February 1844 (from Haiti)

National holiday: Independence Day, 27 February (1844)

Flag: *description:* a centered white cross extends to the edges and divides the flag into four rectangles; the top ones are ultramarine blue (left side) and vermilion red, and the bottom ones are vermilion red (left side) and ultramarine blue; a small coat of arms with a shield supported by a laurel branch and a palm branch is at the center of the cross; above the shield, a blue ribbon displays the motto DIOS, PATRIA, LIBERTAD (God, Fatherland, Liberty); below the shield, REPUBLICA DOMINICANA is on a red ribbon; on the shield, a Bible is opened to a verse that reads "Y la verdad nos hara libre" (And the truth shall set you free)
meaning: blue stands for liberty, white for salvation, and red for the blood of heroes

National symbol(s): palmchat (bird)

National color(s): red, white, blue

National anthem(s): *title:* "Himno Nacional" (National Anthem)
lyrics/music: Emilio PRUD'HOMME/Jose REYES
history: adopted 1934; also known as "Quisqueyanos valientes" (Valiant Sons of Quisqueye); the anthem refers to the Dominican people as Quisqueyanos, which comes from the ethnic name for the island

National heritage: *total World Heritage Sites:* 1 (cultural)
selected World Heritage Site locales: Colonial City of Santo Domingo

ECONOMY

Economic overview: surging middle-income tourism, construction, mining, and telecommunications OECS economy; major foreign US direct investment and free-trade zones; developing local financial markets; improving debt management; declining poverty

Real GDP (purchasing power parity): $276.884 billion (2024 est.)
$263.82 billion (2023 est.)
$258.16 billion (2022 est.)
note: data in 2021 dollars
comparison ranking: 65

Real GDP growth rate: 5% (2024 est.)
2.2% (2023 est.)
5.2% (2022 est.)
note: annual GDP % growth based on constant local currency
comparison ranking: 44

Real GDP per capita: $24,200 (2024 est.)
$23,300 (2023 est.)
$23,000 (2022 est.)
note: data in 2021 dollars
comparison ranking: 92

GDP (official exchange rate): $124.282 billion (2024 est.)
note: data in current dollars at official exchange rate

Inflation rate (consumer prices): 3.3% (2024 est.)
4.8% (2023 est.)
8.8% (2022 est.)
note: annual % change based on consumer prices
comparison ranking: 104

GDP - composition, by sector of origin: *agriculture:* 4.5% (2024 est.)
industry: 28.7% (2024 est.)
services: 59.8% (2024 est.)
note: figures may not total 100% due to non-allocated consumption not captured in sector-reported data
comparison rankings: agriculture 114; industry 65; services 90

GDP - composition, by end use: *household consumption:* 67.7% (2024 est.)
government consumption: 11.5% (2024 est.)
investment in fixed capital: 26.1% (2024 est.)
investment in inventories: 0.9% (2024 est.)
exports of goods and services: 22.8% (2024 est.)
imports of goods and services: -29% (2024 est.)
note: figures may not total 100% due to rounding or gaps in data collection

Agricultural products: sugarcane, bananas, papayas, plantains, avocados, rice, milk, watermelons, vegetables, pineapples (2023)
note: top ten agricultural products based on tonnage

Industries: tourism, sugar processing, gold mining, textiles, cement, tobacco, electrical components, medical devices

Industrial production growth rate: 3% (2024 est.)
note: annual % change in industrial value added based on constant local currency
comparison ranking: 80

Labor force: 5.413 million (2024 est.)
note: number of people ages 15 or older who are employed or seeking work
comparison ranking: 82

Unemployment rate: 5.5% (2024 est.)
5.6% (2023 est.)
5.6% (2022 est.)
note: % of labor force seeking employment
comparison ranking: 100

Youth unemployment rate (ages 15-24): *total:* 11.7% (2024 est.)
male: 9.2% (2024 est.)
female: 15.5% (2024 est.)
note: % of labor force ages 15-24 seeking employment
comparison ranking: total 106

Population below poverty line: 23% (2023 est.)
note: % of population with income below national poverty line

Gini Index coefficient - distribution of family income: 38.4 (2023 est.)
note: index (0-100) of income distribution; higher values represent greater inequality
comparison ranking: 51

Average household expenditures: *on food:* 28.1% of household expenditures (2023 est.)
on alcohol and tobacco: 3.8% of household expenditures (2023 est.)

Household income or consumption by percentage share: *lowest 10%:* 2.3% (2023 est.)
highest 10%: 29.1% (2023 est.)
note: % share of income accruing to lowest and highest 10% of population

Remittances: 9% of GDP (2024 est.)
8.8% of GDP (2023 est.)
9.1% of GDP (2022 est.)
note: personal transfers and compensation between resident and non-resident individuals/households/entities

Budget: *revenues:* $20.418 billion (2023 est.)
expenditures: $24.348 billion (2023 est.)
note: central government revenues (excluding grants) and expenditures converted to US dollars at average official exchange rate for year indicated

Taxes and other revenues: 14.5% (of GDP) (2023 est.)
note: central government tax revenue as a % of GDP
comparison ranking: 94

Current account balance: -$4.167 billion (2024 est.)
-$4.418 billion (2023 est.)
-$6.549 billion (2022 est.)
note: balance of payments - net trade and primary/secondary income in current dollars
comparison ranking: 167

Exports: $28.563 billion (2024 est.)
$25.79 billion (2023 est.)
$25.169 billion (2022 est.)
note: balance of payments - exports of goods and services in current dollars
comparison ranking: 85

Exports - partners: USA 52%, Switzerland 7%, Haiti 6%, China 5%, India 3% (2023)
note: top five export partners based on percentage share of exports

Exports - commodities: medical instruments, tobacco, gold, garments, power equipment (2023)
note: top five export commodities based on value in dollars

Imports: $36.144 billion (2024 est.)
$34.45 billion (2023 est.)
$36.838 billion (2022 est.)
note: balance of payments - imports of goods and services in current dollars
comparison ranking: 72

Imports - partners: USA 40%, China 18%, Brazil 4%, Spain 4%, Mexico 3% (2023)
note: top five import partners based on percentage share of imports

Imports - commodities: refined petroleum, cars, natural gas, plastic products, crude petroleum (2023)
note: top five import commodities based on value in dollars

Reserves of foreign exchange and gold: $13.471 billion (2024 est.)
$15.547 billion (2023 est.)
$14.523 billion (2022 est.)
note: holdings of gold (year-end prices)/foreign exchange/special drawing rights in current dollars

comparison ranking: 72

Debt - external: $35.044 billion (2023 est.)
note: present value of external debt in current US dollars
comparison ranking: 24

Exchange rates: Dominican pesos (DOP) per US dollar -

Exchange rates: 59.565 (2024 est.)
56.158 (2023 est.)
55.141 (2022 est.)
57.221 (2021 est.)
56.525 (2020 est.)

ENERGY

Electricity access: *electrification - total population:* 98.1% (2022 est.)
electrification - urban areas: 98.8%
electrification - rural areas: 95%

Electricity: *installed generating capacity:* 6.581 million kW (2023 est.)
consumption: 22.193 billion kWh (2023 est.)
transmission/distribution losses: 2.369 billion kWh (2023 est.)
comparison rankings: installed generating capacity 81; consumption 74; transmission/distribution losses 131

Electricity generation sources: *fossil fuels:* 82.7% of total installed capacity (2023 est.)
solar: 5.5% of total installed capacity (2023 est.)
wind: 4.9% of total installed capacity (2023 est.)
hydroelectricity: 6% of total installed capacity (2023 est.)
biomass and waste: 0.9% of total installed capacity (2023 est.)

Coal: *consumption:* 2.356 million metric tons (2023 est.)
imports: 2.356 million metric tons (2023 est.)

Petroleum: *refined petroleum consumption:* 146,000 bbl/day (2023 est.)

Natural gas: *consumption:* 2.277 billion cubic meters (2023 est.)
exports: 1.997 million cubic meters (2023 est.)
imports: 2.279 billion cubic meters (2023 est.)

Energy consumption per capita: 39.329 million Btu/person (2023 est.)
comparison ranking: 103

COMMUNICATIONS

Telephones - fixed lines: *total subscriptions:* 1.144 million (2023 est.)
subscriptions per 100 inhabitants: 10 (2023 est.)
comparison ranking: total subscriptions 68

Telephones - mobile cellular: *total subscriptions:* 10.4 million (2023 est.)
subscriptions per 100 inhabitants: 90 (2022 est.)
comparison ranking: total subscriptions 93

Broadcast media: combination of state-owned and privately owned broadcast media; 1 state-owned TV network and a number of private TV networks; networks operate repeaters to extend signals throughout country; over 300 state-owned and privately owned radio stations (2019)

Internet country code: .do

Internet users: *percent of population:* 85% (2023 est.)

Broadband - fixed subscriptions: *total:* 1.26 million (2023 est.)
subscriptions per 100 inhabitants: 11 (2023 est.)
comparison ranking: total 74

TRANSPORTATION

Civil aircraft registration country code prefix: HI

Airports: 32 (2025)
comparison ranking: 117

Heliports: 8 (2025)
comparison ranking: 81

Railways: *total:* 496 km (2014)
standard gauge: 354 km (2014) 1.435-m gauge
narrow gauge: 142 km (2014) 0.762-m gauge

Merchant marine: *total:* 40 (2023)
by type: container ship 1, general cargo 2, oil tanker 1, other 36
comparison ranking: total 124

Ports: *total ports:* 17 (2024)
large: 0
medium: 2
small: 7
very small: 6
size unknown: 2
ports with oil terminals: 7
key ports: Andres (Andres Lng Terminal), Las Calderas, Puerto de Haina, Puerto Plata, Punta Nizao Oil Terminal, San Pedro de Macoris, Santa Barbara de Samana, Santa Cruz de Barahona, Santo Domingo

MILITARY AND SECURITY

Military and security forces: Armed Forces of the Dominican Republic: Army of the Dominican Republic (Ejercito de la República Dominicana, ERD), Navy (Armada de República Dominicana or ARD; includes naval infantry), Dominican Air Force (Fuerza Aerea de la República Dominicana, FARD) (2025)
note 1: in addition to the three main branches of the military, the Ministry of Defense directs the Specialized Border Security Corps (CESFRONT), the Specialized Corps in Port Security (CESEP), and the Specialized Corps in Airport and Civil Aviation Safety (CESAC); these specialized corps are joint forces, made up of personnel from all military branches in addition to civilian personnel; they may also assist in overall citizen security working together with the National Police, which is under the Ministry of Interior

Military expenditures: 0.8% of GDP (2024 est.)
0.7% of GDP (2023 est.)
0.7% of GDP (2022 est.)
0.7% of GDP (2021 est.)
0.8% of GDP (2020 est.)

Military and security service personnel strengths: approximately 55-60,000 Armed Forces; up to 35,000 National Police (2025)

Military equipment inventories and acquisitions: the military's equipment inventory comes largely from the US, with smaller quantities from such suppliers vas Brazil and Spain (2024)

Military service age and obligation: 16-23 years of age for voluntary military service for men and women (ages vary slightly according to the military service; under 18 admitted with permission of parents); recruits must have completed primary school and be Dominican Republic citizens (2024)
note: as of 2023, women made up approximately 18% of the active duty military

Military - note: the military is responsible for defending the independence, integrity, and sovereignty of the Dominican Republic; it also has an internal security role, which includes assisting with airport, border, port, tourism, and urban security, supporting the police in maintaining or restoring public order, countering transnational crime, and providing disaster or emergency relief/management; a key area of focus is securing the country's 217-mile (350-kilometer) long border with Haiti, where the Army in recent years has assigned thousands of troops to assist with security; these forces complement the personnel of the Border Security Corps permanently deployed along the border; the Air Force and Navy also provide support to the Haitian border mission; the Army has a brigade dedicated to managing and providing relief during natural disasters; the military also contributes personnel to the National Drug Control Directorate, and both the Air Force and Navy devote assets to detecting and interdicting narcotics trafficking; the Navy conducts regular bilateral maritime interdiction exercises with the US Navy (2025)

TRANSNATIONAL ISSUES

Refugees and internally displaced persons: *refugees:* 1,004 (2024 est.)

IDPs: 390 (2023 est.)

Illicit drugs: USG identification: major illicit drug-producing and/or drug-transit country (2025)

E

ECUADOR

INTRODUCTION

Background: What is now Ecuador formed part of the northern Inca Empire until the Spanish conquest in 1533. Quito – the traditional name for the area – became a seat of Spanish colonial government in 1563 and part of the Viceroyalty of New Granada in 1717. The territories of the Viceroyalty – New Granada (Colombia), Venezuela, and Quito – gained their independence between 1819 and 1822 and formed a federation known as Gran Colombia. When Quito withdrew to become an independent republic in 1830, the traditional name was changed to the "Republic of the Equator." Between 1904 and 1942, Ecuador lost territories in a series of conflicts with its neighbors. A border war with Peru that flared in 1995 was resolved in 1999. Although Ecuador has had nearly 50 years of civilian governance, the period has been marked by political instability.

GEOGRAPHY

Location: Western South America, bordering the Pacific Ocean at the Equator, between Colombia and Peru

Geographic coordinates: 2 00 S, 77 30 W

Map references: South America

Area: *total:* 283,561 sq km
land: 276,841 sq km
water: 6,720 sq km
note: includes Galapagos Islands
comparison ranking: total 75

Area - comparative: slightly smaller than Nevada

Land boundaries: *total:* 2,237 km
border countries (2): Colombia 708 km; Peru 1529 km

Coastline: 2,237 km

Maritime claims: *territorial sea:* 12 nm
exclusive economic zone: 200 nm
continental shelf: 200 nm
note: Ecuador has declared its right to extend its continental shelf to 350 nm, measured from the baselines of the Galapagos Archipelago

Climate: tropical along coast, becoming cooler inland at higher elevations; tropical in Amazonian jungle lowlands

Terrain: coastal plain (costa), inter-Andean central highlands (sierra), and flat to rolling eastern jungle (oriente)

Elevation: *highest point:* Chimborazo 6,267
lowest point: Pacific Ocean 0 m
mean elevation: 1,117 m
note: because the earth is not a perfect sphere and has an equatorial bulge, the highest point on the planet farthest from its center is Mount Chimborazo not Mount Everest, which is merely the highest peak above sea level

Natural resources: petroleum, fish, timber, hydropower

Land use: *agricultural land:* 21.5% (2022 est.)
arable land: 3.9% (2022 est.)
permanent crops: 5.5% (2022 est.)
permanent pasture: 12.1% (2022 est.)
forest: 49.8% (2022 est.)
other: 28.7% (2022 est.)

Irrigated land: 12,520 sq km (2022)

Major watersheds (area sq km): Atlantic Ocean drainage: Amazon (6,145,186 sq km)

Population distribution: nearly half of the population is concentrated in the interior, with large concentrations also found along the western coastal strip; the rainforests of the east remain sparsely populated

Natural hazards: frequent earthquakes; landslides; volcanic activity; floods; periodic droughts
volcanism: volcanic activity concentrated along the Andes Mountains; Sangay (5,230 m) is mainland Ecuador's most active volcano; other historically active volcanoes in the Andes include Antisana, Cayambe, Chacana, Cotopaxi, Guagua Pichincha, Reventador, Sumaco, and Tungurahua; Fernandina (1,476 m), a shield volcano, is the most active of the many Galapagos volcanoes; other historically active Galapagos volcanoes include Wolf, Sierra Negra, Cerro Azul, Pinta, Marchena, and Santiago

Geography - note: Cotopaxi in the Andes is highest active volcano in world

PEOPLE AND SOCIETY

Population: *total:* 18,309,984 (2024 est.)
male: 9,023,170
female: 9,286,814
comparison rankings: total 68; male 69; female 69

Nationality: *noun:* Ecuadorian(s)
adjective: Ecuadorian

Ethnic groups: Mestizo (mixed Indigenous and White) 77.5%, Montubio 7.7%, Indigenous 7.7%, White 2.2%, Afroecuadorian 2%, Mulatto 1.4%, Black 1.3%, other 0.1% (2022 est.)

Languages: Spanish (Castilian; official) 98.6%, indigenous 3.9% (Quechua 3.2%, other indigenous 0.7%), foreign 2.8%, other 0.6% (includes Ecuadorian sign language) (2022 est.)
major-language sample(s):
La Libreta Informativa del Mundo, la fuente indispensable de información básica. (Spanish)
note 1: shares sum to more than 100% because some respondents gave more than one answer on the census
note 2: Quechua and Shuar are official languages of intercultural relations; other indigenous languages are in official use by indigenous peoples in the areas they inhabit

Religions: Roman Catholic 68.2%, Protestant 19% (Evangelical 18.3%, Adventist 0.6%, other Protestant 0.2%), Jehovah's Witness 1.4%, other 2.3%, none 8.2% don't know/no response 1% (2023 est.)

Age structure: *0-14 years:* 26.8% (male 2,505,729/ female 2,395,198)
15-64 years: 64.1% (male 5,771,234/female 5,972,938)
65 years and over: 9.1% (2024 est.) (male 746,207/ female 918,678)

Dependency ratios: *total dependency ratio:* 55.9 (2024 est.)
youth dependency ratio: 41.7 (2024 est.)
elderly dependency ratio: 14.2 (2024 est.)
potential support ratio: 7.1 (2024 est.)

Median age: *total:* 28 years (2024 est.)
male: 27 years
female: 28.9 years
comparison ranking: total 153

Population growth rate: 0.94% (2024 est.)
comparison ranking: 99

Birth rate: 17.7 births/1,000 population (2024 est.)
comparison ranking: 83

Death rate: 7.2 deaths/1,000 population (2024 est.)
comparison ranking: 113

Net migration rate: -1.1 migrant(s)/1,000 population (2024 est.)
comparison ranking: 150

Population distribution: nearly half of the population is concentrated in the interior, with large concentrations also found along the western coastal strip; the rainforests of the east remain sparsely populated

Urbanization: *urban population:* 64.8% of total population (2023)
rate of urbanization: 1.62% annual rate of change (2020-25 est.)

Major urban areas - population: 3.142 million Guayaquil, 1.957 million QUITO (capital) (2023)

Sex ratio: *at birth:* 1.05 male(s)/female
0-14 years: 1.05 male(s)/female
15-64 years: 0.97 male(s)/female
65 years and over: 0.81 male(s)/female
total population: 0.97 male(s)/female (2024 est.)

Maternal mortality ratio: 55 deaths/100,000 live births (2023 est.)
comparison ranking: 92

Infant mortality rate: *total:* 11.2 deaths/1,000 live births (2024 est.)
male: 12.2 deaths/1,000 live births
female: 10.2 deaths/1,000 live births
comparison ranking: total 121

Life expectancy at birth: *total population:* 74.9 years (2024 est.)
male: 69.7 years
female: 80.4 years
comparison ranking: total population 135

Total fertility rate: 2.21 children born/woman (2024 est.)
comparison ranking: 83

Gross reproduction rate: 1.08 (2024 est.)

Drinking water source: *improved: urban:* 100% of population (2022 est.)
rural: 87.9% of population (2022 est.)
total: 95.7% of population (2022 est.)
unimproved: urban: 0% of population (2022 est.)
rural: 12.1% of population (2022 est.)
total: 4.3% of population (2022 est.)

Health expenditure: 8.3% of GDP (2021)
11.9% of national budget (2022 est.)

Physician density: 2.31 physicians/1,000 population (2020)

Hospital bed density: 1.3 beds/1,000 population (2021 est.)

Sanitation facility access: *improved: urban:* 100% of population (2022 est.)
rural: 98.2% of population (2022 est.)
total: 99.4% of population (2022 est.)
unimproved: urban: 0% of population (2022 est.)
rural: 1.8% of population (2022 est.)
total: 0.6% of population (2022 est.)

Obesity - adult prevalence rate: 19.9% (2016)
comparison ranking: 106

Alcohol consumption per capita: *total:* 3.05 liters of pure alcohol (2019 est.)
beer: 2.32 liters of pure alcohol (2019 est.)
wine: 0.09 liters of pure alcohol (2019 est.)
spirits: 0.61 liters of pure alcohol (2019 est.)
other alcohols: 0.03 liters of pure alcohol (2019 est.)
comparison ranking: total 114

Tobacco use: *total:* 9.7% (2025 est.)
male: 17.2% (2025 est.)
female: 2.4% (2025 est.)
comparison ranking: total 131

Children under the age of 5 years underweight: 5.2% (2018/19)
comparison ranking: 65

Currently married women (ages 15-49): 55.1% (2023 est.)

Child marriage: *women married by age 15:* 3.8% (2018)
women married by age 18: 22.2% (2018)

Education expenditure: 3.9% of GDP (2023 est.)
9.7% national budget (2023 est.)
comparison ranking: Education expenditure (% GDP) 113

Literacy: *total population:* 94% (2022 est.)
male: 95% (2022 est.)
female: 93% (2022 est.)

School life expectancy (primary to tertiary education): *total:* 15 years (2022 est.)
male: 14 years (2022 est.)
female: 15 years (2022 est.)

ENVIRONMENT

Environmental issues: deforestation; soil erosion; desertification; water pollution; pollution from oil production wastes in areas of the Amazon Basin and Galapagos Islands

International environmental agreements: *party to:* Antarctic-Environmental Protection, Antarctic Treaty, Biodiversity, Climate Change, Climate Change-Kyoto Protocol, Climate Change-Paris Agreement, Comprehensive Nuclear Test Ban, Desertification, Endangered Species, Hazardous Wastes, Law of the Sea, Nuclear Test Ban, Ozone Layer Protection, Ship Pollution, Tropical Timber 2006, Wetlands, Whaling
signed, but not ratified: none of the selected agreements

Climate: tropical along coast, becoming cooler inland at higher elevations; tropical in Amazonian jungle lowlands

Urbanization: *urban population:* 64.8% of total population (2023)
rate of urbanization: 1.62% annual rate of change (2020-25 est.)

Carbon dioxide emissions: 38.286 million metric tonnes of CO2 (2023 est.)
from coal and metallurgical coke: 39,000 metric tonnes of CO2 (2023 est.)
from petroleum and other liquids: 37.711 million metric tonnes of CO2 (2023 est.)
from consumed natural gas: 536,000 metric tonnes of CO2 (2023 est.)
comparison ranking: total emissions 65

Particulate matter emissions: 17.3 micrograms per cubic meter (2019 est.)

Methane emissions: *energy:* 454.3 kt (2022-2024 est.)
agriculture: 346.3 kt (2019-2021 est.)
waste: 210.1 kt (2019-2021 est.)
other: 2.6 kt (2019-2021 est.)

Waste and recycling: *municipal solid waste generated annually:* 5.297 million tons (2024 est.)
percent of municipal solid waste recycled: 28% (2022 est.)

Total water withdrawal: *municipal:* 1.293 billion cubic meters (2022 est.)
industrial: 549 million cubic meters (2022 est.)
agricultural: 8.076 billion cubic meters (2022 est.)

Total renewable water resources: 442.4 billion cubic meters (2022 est.)

Geoparks: *total global geoparks and regional networks:* 3 (2025)
global geoparks and regional networks: Imbabura: Napo Sumaco; Tungurahua (2025)

GOVERNMENT

Country name: *conventional long form:* Republic of Ecuador
conventional short form: Ecuador
local long form: República del Ecuador
local short form: Ecuador
former: Quito
etymology: the name is the Spanish word for "equator," referring to its geographic position

Government type: presidential republic

Capital: *name:* Quito
geographic coordinates: 0 13 S, 78 30 W
time difference: UTC-5 (same time as Washington, DC, during Standard Time)
time zone note: Ecuador has two time zones, including the Galapagos Islands (UTC-6)
etymology: named after the Quitu, a Pre-Columbian people who lived in the area; the meaning of their name is unknown

Administrative divisions: 24 provinces (*provincias*, singular - *provincia*); Azuay, Bolivar, Canar, Carchi, Chimborazo, Cotopaxi, El Oro, Esmeraldas, Galapagos, Guayas, Imbabura, Loja, Los Rios, Manabi, Morona Santiago, Napo, Orellana, Pastaza, Pichincha, Santa Elena, Santo Domingo de los Tsachilas, Sucumbios, Tungurahua, Zamora Chinchipe

Legal system: civil law based on the Chilean civil code with modifications; traditional law in ethnic communities

Constitution: *history:* many previous; latest approved 20 October 2008
amendment process: proposed by the president of the republic through a referendum, by public petition of at least 1% of registered voters, or by agreement of at least one-third membership of the National Assembly; passage requires two separate readings a year apart and approval by at least two-thirds majority vote of the Assembly, and approval by absolute majority in a referendum; amendments such as changes to the structure of the state, constraints on personal rights and guarantees, or constitutional amendment procedures are not allowed

International law organization participation: has not submitted an ICJ jurisdiction declaration; accepts ICCt jurisdiction

Citizenship: *citizenship by birth:* yes
citizenship by descent only: yes
dual citizenship recognized: no
residency requirement for naturalization: 3 years

Suffrage: 18-65 years of age; universal and compulsory; voluntary for 16-18, over 65, and other eligible voters

Executive branch: *chief of state:* President Daniel NOBOA Azin (since 23 November 2023)
head of government: President Daniel NOBOA Azin (since 23 November 2023)
cabinet: Cabinet appointed by the president
election/appointment process: president and vice president directly elected on the same ballot by absolute-majority popular vote in 2 rounds, if needed, for a 4-year term (eligible for a second term)
most recent election date: 9 February 2025, with a runoff on 13 April 2025
election results: 2025: Daniel NOBOA Azin reelected president; percent of vote in the first round - Daniel NOBOA Azin (ADN) 44.2%, Luisa GONZÁLEZ Alcivar (MRC) 44%, Leonidas IZA (MUPP) 5.3%, other 6.5%; percent of vote in the second round - Daniel NOBOA Azin 55.6%, Luisa GONZÁLEZ Alcivar 44.4%
2023: Daniel NOBOA Azin elected president; percent of vote in the first round - Luisa GONZÁLEZ Alcivar (MRC) 33.6%, Daniel NOBOA Azin (ADN) 23.5%, Christian Gustavo ZURITA Ron (Construye) 16.4%, Jan Tomislav TOPIC Feraud (Por Un País Sin Miedo) 14.7%, Otto Ramón SONNENHOLZNER Sper (Avanza) 7.1%, other 4.7%; percent of vote in the second round - Daniel NOBOA Azin 51.8%, Luisa GONZÁLEZ Alcivar 48.2%
2021: Guillermo LASSO Mendoza elected president; percent of vote in the first round - Andres ARAUZ (UNES) 32.7%, Guillermo LASSO Mendoza (CREO) 19.7%, Yaku PEREZ Guartambel (MUPP) 19.4%, Xavier HERVAS Mora (ID) 15.7%, other 12.5%; percent of vote in the second round - Guillermo LASSO Mendoza (CREO) 52.5%, Andres ARAUZ (UNES) 47.5%
expected date of next election: 28 February 2029
note 1: the president is both chief of state and head of government
note 2: though eligible for a second term, former president Guillermo LASSO announced that he would not run in the 2023 election; President Daniel NOBOA Azin is serving out the remainder of the presidential term (2021–2025)

Legislative branch: *legislature name:* National Assembly (Asamblea Nacional)
legislative structure: unicameral
number of seats: 151 (all directly elected)

electoral system: proportional representation
scope of elections: full renewal
term in office: 4 years
most recent election date: 2/9/2025
parties elected and seats per party: Citizen Revolution Movement (RC) - Renewal Movement (RETO) (67); National Democratic Action (ADN) (66); Pachakutik (9); Other (9)
percentage of women in chamber: 45%
expected date of next election: February 2029
note 1: all Assembly members have alternates from the same party who cast votes when a primary member is absent, resigns, or is removed from office
note 2: on 18 May 2023, Ecuador's National Electoral Council announced that the legislative and presidential elections - originally scheduled for February 2025 - would be held on 20 August 2023 after President Guillermo LASSO dissolved the National Assembly by decree on 17 May 2023; a return to a regular election cycle will occur in February 2025

Judicial branch: *highest court(s):* National Court of Justice or Corte Nacional de Justicia (consists of 21 judges, including the chief justice and organized into 5 specialized chambers); Constitutional Court or Corte Constitucional (consists of the court president and 8 judges)
judge selection and term of office: candidates for the National Court of Justice evaluated and appointed justices by the Judicial Council, a 9-member independent body of law professionals; justices elected for 9-year, non-renewable terms, with one third of the membership renewed every 3 years; candidates for the Constitutional Court evaluated and appointed judges by a 6-member independent body of law professionals; judges appointed for 4-year renewable terms
subordinate courts: provincial courts (one for each province except Galapagos); fiscal, criminal, and administrative tribunals; Election Dispute Settlement Courts; cantonal courts

Political parties: Actuemos Ecuador or Actuemos
AMIGO movement, Independent Mobilizing Action Generating Opportunities (Movimiento AMIGO (Acción Movilizadora Independiente Generando Oportunidades)) or AM16O
Avanza Party or AVANZA
Central Democratic Movement or CD
Citizen Revolution Movement or MRC or RC5
Creating Opportunities Movement or CREO
Democratic Left or ID
Democracy Yes Movement (Movimiento Democracia Si)
For A Country Without Fear (Por Un País Sin Miedo) (an alliance including PSC, CD, and PSP)
Green Movement (Movimiento Verde)
Movimiento Construye or Construye
National Democratic Action (Acción Democrática Nacional) or ADN
Pachakutik Plurinational Unity Movement or MUPP
Patriotic Society Party or PSP
People, Equality, and Democracy Party (Partido Pueblo, Igualdad y Democracia) or PID
Popular Unity Party (Partido Unidad Popular) or UP
Revolutionary and Democratic Ethical Green Movement (Movimiento Verde Ético Revolucionario y Democrático) or MOVER
Social Christian Party or PSC
Socialist Party
Society United for More Action or SUMA
Total Renovation Movement (Movimiento Renovacion Total) or RETO

Diplomatic representation in the US: *chief of mission:* Ambassador Pablo Agustín ZAMBRANO Albuja (since 24 July 2025)
chancery: 2535 15th Street NW, Washington, DC 20009
telephone: [1] (202) 234-7200
FAX: [1] (202) 333-2893
email address and website: eecuusanotifications@mmrree.gob.ec
Contact – Washington (cancilleria.gob.ec)
consulate(s) general: Atlanta, Chicago, Houston, Los Angeles, Miami, Minneapolis (MN), New Haven (CT), New York, Newark (NJ), Phoenix, San Juan (PR)

Diplomatic representation from the US: *chief of mission:* Ambassador (vacant); Chargé d'Affaires Lawrence PETRONI (since 17 April 2025)
embassy: E12-170 Avenida Avigiras y Avenida Eloy Alfaro, Quito
mailing address: 3420 Quito Place, Washington DC 20521-3420
telephone: [593] (2) 398-5000
email address and website: ACSQuito@state.gov
https://ec.usembassy.gov/
consulate(s) general: Guayaquil

International organization participation: CAN, CD, CELAC, FAO, G-11, G-77, IADB, IAEA, IBRD, ICAO, ICC (national committees), ICCt, ICRM, IDA, IFAD, IFC, IFRCS, IHO, ILO, IMF, IMO, Interpol, IOC, IOM, IPU, ISO, ITSO, ITU, ITUC (NGOs), LAES, LAIA, Mercosur (associate), MIGA, MINUSTAH, NAM, OAS, OPANAL, OPCW, OPEC, Pacific Alliance (observer), PCA, PROSUR, SICA (observer), UN, UNCTAD, UNESCO, UNHCR, UNIDO, Union Latina, UNISFA, UNMIL, UNMISS, UNOCI, UNWTO, UPU, WCO, WFTU (NGOs), WHO, WIPO, WMO, WTO

Independence: 24 May 1822 (from Spain)

National holiday: Independence Day (independence of Quito), 10 August (1809)

Flag: *description:* three horizontal bands of yellow (top, double-width), blue, and red, with the coat of arms at the center of the flag
meaning: yellow stands for sunshine, grain, and mineral wealth; blue for the sky, sea, and rivers; red for patriots' blood spilled in the struggle for freedom and justice
note: similar to the flag of Colombia, which is shorter and does not have a coat of arms

National symbol(s): Andean condor

National color(s): yellow, blue, red

National anthem(s): *title:* "Salve, O Patria!" (We Salute You, Our Homeland)
lyrics/music: Juan Leon MERA/Antonio NEUMANE
history: adopted 1948; MERA wrote the lyrics in 1865; only the chorus and second verse are sung

National heritage: *total World Heritage Sites:* 5 (3 cultural, 2 natural)
selected World Heritage Site locales: Historic Quito (c); Galápagos Islands (n); Historic Cuenca (c); Qhapaq Ñan/Andean Road System (c); Sangay National Park (n)

ECONOMY

Economic overview: highly informal South American economy; USD currency user; major banana exporter; hard hit by COVID-19; macroeconomic fragility from oil dependency; successful debt restructuring; China funding budget deficits; social unrest hampering economic activity

Real GDP (purchasing power parity): $252.728 billion (2024 est.)
$257.889 billion (2023 est.)
$252.861 billion (2022 est.)
note: data in 2021 dollars
comparison ranking: 68

Real GDP growth rate: -2% (2024 est.)
2% (2023 est.)
5.9% (2022 est.)
note: annual GDP % growth based on constant local currency
comparison ranking: 207

Real GDP per capita: $13,900 (2024 est.)
$14,300 (2023 est.)
$14,200 (2022 est.)
note: data in 2021 dollars
comparison ranking: 129

GDP (official exchange rate): $124.676 billion (2024 est.)
note: data in current dollars at official exchange rate

Inflation rate (consumer prices): 1.5% (2024 est.)
2.2% (2023 est.)
3.5% (2022 est.)
note: annual % change based on consumer prices
comparison ranking: 36

GDP - composition, by sector of origin: *agriculture:* 9.5% (2024 est.)
industry: 26.5% (2024 est.)
services: 57.2% (2024 est.)
note: figures may not total 100% due to non-allocated consumption not captured in sector-reported data
comparison rankings: agriculture 75; industry 73; services 109

GDP - composition, by end use: *household consumption:* 64.9% (2024 est.)
government consumption: 13.3% (2024 est.)
investment in fixed capital: 18.4% (2024 est.)
investment in inventories: 0.1% (2024 est.)
exports of goods and services: 30.3% (2024 est.)
imports of goods and services: -26.9% (2024 est.)
note: figures may not total 100% due to rounding or gaps in data collection

Agricultural products: bananas, sugarcane, milk, oil palm fruit, maize, rice, plantains, chicken, pineapples, cocoa beans (2023)
note: top ten agricultural products based on tonnage

Industries: petroleum, food processing, textiles, wood products, chemicals

Industrial production growth rate: -3.7% (2024 est.)
note: annual % change in industrial value added based on constant local currency
comparison ranking: 173

Labor force: 8.821 million (2024 est.)
note: number of people ages 15 or older who are employed or seeking work
comparison ranking: 60

Unemployment rate: 4.8% (2024 est.)
3.6% (2023 est.)
3.8% (2022 est.)
note: % of labor force seeking employment
comparison ranking: 83

Youth unemployment rate (ages 15-24): *total:* 10.1% (2024 est.)
male: 8.3% (2024 est.)
female: 13% (2024 est.)
note: % of labor force ages 15-24 seeking employment
comparison ranking: total 118

Population below poverty line: 26% (2023 est.)
note: % of population with income below national poverty line

Gini Index coefficient - distribution of family income: 44.6 (2023 est.)
note: index (0-100) of income distribution; higher values represent greater inequality
comparison ranking: 19

Average household expenditures: *on food:* 25.9% of household expenditures (2023 est.)
on alcohol and tobacco: 0.9% of household expenditures (2023 est.)

Household income or consumption by percentage share: *lowest 10%:* 1.6% (2023 est.)
highest 10%: 33.2% (2023 est.)
note: % share of income accruing to lowest and highest 10% of population

Remittances: 5.2% of GDP (2024 est.)
4.5% of GDP (2023 est.)
4.1% of GDP (2022 est.)
note: personal transfers and compensation between resident and non-resident individuals/households/entities

Budget: *revenues:* $35.962 billion (2022 est.)
expenditures: $35.969 billion (2022 est.)
note: central government revenues (excluding grants) and expenditures converted to US dollars at average official exchange rate for year indicated

Taxes and other revenues: 13.1% (of GDP) (2022 est.)
note: central government tax revenue as a % of GDP
comparison ranking: 105

Current account balance: $7.082 billion (2024 est.)
$2.217 billion (2023 est.)
$2.136 billion (2022 est.)
note: balance of payments - net trade and primary/secondary income in current dollars
comparison ranking: 29

Exports: $38.468 billion (2024 est.)
$35.687 billion (2023 est.)
$36.588 billion (2022 est.)
note: balance of payments - exports of goods and services in current dollars
comparison ranking: 74

Exports - partners: USA 22%, China 21%, Panama 12%, Japan 3%, Peru 3% (2023)
note: top five export partners based on percentage share of exports

Exports - commodities: crude petroleum, shellfish, bananas, fish, gold (2023)
note: top five export commodities based on value in dollars

Imports: $33.97 billion (2024 est.)
$35.421 billion (2023 est.)
$36.644 billion (2022 est.)
note: balance of payments - imports of goods and services in current dollars
comparison ranking: 75

Imports - partners: USA 27%, China 20%, Colombia 7%, Brazil 4%, Peru 4% (2023)
note: top five import partners based on percentage share of imports

Imports - commodities: refined petroleum, coal tar oil, cars, packaged medicine, plastics (2023)
note: top five import commodities based on value in dollars

Reserves of foreign exchange and gold: $6.908 billion (2024 est.)
$4.442 billion (2023 est.)
$8.459 billion (2022 est.)
note: holdings of gold (year-end prices)/foreign exchange/special drawing rights in current dollars
comparison ranking: 87

Debt - external: $39.658 billion (2023 est.)
note: present value of external debt in current US dollars
comparison ranking: 21

Exchange rates: the US dollar became Ecuador's currency in 2001

ENERGY

Electricity access: *electrification - total population:* 100% (2022 est.)

Electricity: *installed generating capacity:* 8.438 million kW (2023 est.)
consumption: 29.305 billion kWh (2023 est.)
exports: 192 million kWh (2023 est.)
imports: 466 million kWh (2023 est.)
transmission/distribution losses: 5.119 billion kWh (2023 est.)
comparison rankings: installed generating capacity 69; consumption 68; exports 86; imports 96; transmission/distribution losses 163

Electricity generation sources: *fossil fuels:* 23.2% of total installed capacity (2023 est.)
solar: 0.1% of total installed capacity (2023 est.)
wind: 0.2% of total installed capacity (2023 est.)
hydroelectricity: 75.4% of total installed capacity (2023 est.)
biomass and waste: 1.1% of total installed capacity (2023 est.)

Coal: *consumption:* 14,000 metric tons (2023 est.)
exports: 200 metric tons (2023 est.)
imports: 14,000 metric tons (2023 est.)
proven reserves: 24 million metric tons (2023 est.)

Petroleum: *total petroleum production:* 480,000 bbl/day (2023 est.)
refined petroleum consumption: 272,000 bbl/day (2023 est.)
crude oil estimated reserves: 8.273 billion barrels (2021 est.)

Natural gas: *production:* 271.053 million cubic meters (2023 est.)
consumption: 271.053 million cubic meters (2023 est.)
proven reserves: 10.902 billion cubic meters (2021 est.)

Energy consumption per capita: 35.7 million Btu/person (2023 est.)
comparison ranking: 107

COMMUNICATIONS

Telephones - fixed lines: *total subscriptions:* 1.434 million (2023 est.)
subscriptions per 100 inhabitants: 8 (2023 est.)
comparison ranking: total subscriptions 58

Telephones - mobile cellular: *total subscriptions:* 18.2 million (2023 est.)
subscriptions per 100 inhabitants: 97 (2022 est.)
comparison ranking: total subscriptions 68

Broadcast media: 956 media outlets, of which 89% are private, 5% are public, and 6% belong to small communities; government controls most of the 44 public media stations, including national media and multiple local radio stations; most media outlets are concentrated in Guayas and Pichincha (2022)

Internet country code: .ec

Internet users: *percent of population:* 77% (2024 est.)
according to 2021 statistics from Ecuador's Ministry of Telecommunications and Information Society, 50% of homes do not have access to fixed internet

Broadband - fixed subscriptions: *total:* 2.89 million (2023 est.)
subscriptions per 100 inhabitants: 16 (2023 est.)
comparison ranking: total 50

TRANSPORTATION

Civil aircraft registration country code prefix: HC

Airports: 317 (2025)
comparison ranking: 22

Heliports: 28 (2025)
comparison ranking: 48

Railways: *total:* 965 km (2022)
narrow gauge: 965 km (2022) 1.067-m gauge
note: passenger service limited to certain sections of track, mostly for tourist trains

Merchant marine: *total:* 154 (2023)
by type: container ship 1, general cargo 8, oil tanker 28, other 117
comparison ranking: total 73

Ports: *total ports:* 6 (2024)
large: 0
medium: 0
small: 2
very small: 4
ports with oil terminals: 5
key ports: Esmeraldas, Guayaquil, La Libertad, Manta, Puerto Bolivar, Puerto Maritimo de Guayaquil

MILITARY AND SECURITY

Military and security forces: Ecuadorian Armed Forces (Fuerzas Armadas del Ecuador): Ground Force (Fuerza Terrestre), Naval Force (Fuerza Naval; includes naval infantry, naval aviation, coast guard), Ecuadorian Air Force (Fuerza Aérea Ecuatoriana) (2025)
note: the National Police of Ecuador (Policía Nacional del Ecuador) is under the Ministry of Government/Interior

Military expenditures: 2.2% of GDP (2024 est.)
2.3% of GDP (2023 est.)
2.2% of GDP (2022 est.)
2.4% of GDP (2021 est.)
2.3% of GDP (2020 est.)

Military and security service personnel strengths: approximately 40,000 active Ecuadorian Armed Forces (2025)

Military equipment inventories and acquisitions: the military's inventory includes a diverse mix of older and smaller quantities of more modern equipment derived from a variety of sources such as Brazil, China, France, Italy, Germany, Russia/Soviet-Union, Spain, Turkey, the UK, and the US (2024)

Military service age and obligation: 18-22 years of age for selective conscript military service for men, although conscription was suspended in 2008; 18 years of age for voluntary military service for men and women; 12-month service obligation (2023)
note: in 2022, women made up an estimated 3-4% of the military

Military - note: the military is responsible for preserving Ecuador's national sovereignty and defending the integrity of the state; it also has some domestic security responsibilities and may complement police operations in maintaining public order if required;

the military shares responsibility for border enforcement with the National Police; it participates in bilateral and multinational training exercises and has sent troops on UN peacekeeping missions; the military has defense ties to regional countries, such as Chile, Colombia, and Peru

border conflicts with Peru dominated the military's focus until the late 1990s and border security remains a priority, but in more recent years, security challenges have included counterinsurgency and counternarcotics operations, particularly in the northern border area where violence and other criminal activity related to terrorism, insurgency, and narco-trafficking in Colombia, as well as refugees from Venezuela, have spilled over the border; the military has established a joint service task force for counterinsurgency and counternarcotics operations and boosted troop deployments along those borders; other missions include countering illegal mining, smuggling, and maritime piracy; since 2012, the Ecuadorian Government has expanded the military's role in general public security and domestic crime operations, in part due to rising violence, police corruption, and police ineffectiveness; in 2024, Ecuador passed a constitutional amendment formally authorizing the military to participate in complementary security roles such as supporting law enforcement in high-risk areas, conducting joint operations against organized crime, and providing logistical assistance in maintaining public order

the military ruled the country from 1963-1966 and 1972-1979, and supported a dictatorship in 1970-1972; during the 1980s, the military remained loyal to the civilian government, but civilian-military relations were at times tenuous, and the military had considerable autonomy from civilian oversight; it was involved in coup attempts in 2000 and 2010 (2025)

SPACE

Space agency/agencies: Ecuadorian Civilian Space Agency (EXA; a civilian independent research and development institution in charge of the administration and execution of Ecuador's space program, established 2007) (2025)

Space program overview: has a small program focused on acquiring or manufacturing satellites; builds scientific satellites; conducts research and develops some space-related technologies; has relationships with China and Russia's space agencies and industries, as well as the Latin American and Caribbean Space Agency (ALCE) and its member states (2025)

note: further details about the key activities, programs, and milestones of the country's space program, as well as government spending estimates on the space sector, appear in the Space Programs reference guide

TRANSNATIONAL ISSUES

Refugees and internally displaced persons: *refugees:* 30,241 (2024 est.)

IDPs: 57,402 (2024 est.)

Illicit drugs: USG identification: major illicit drug-producing and/or drug-transit country

major precursor-chemical producer (2025)

EGYPT

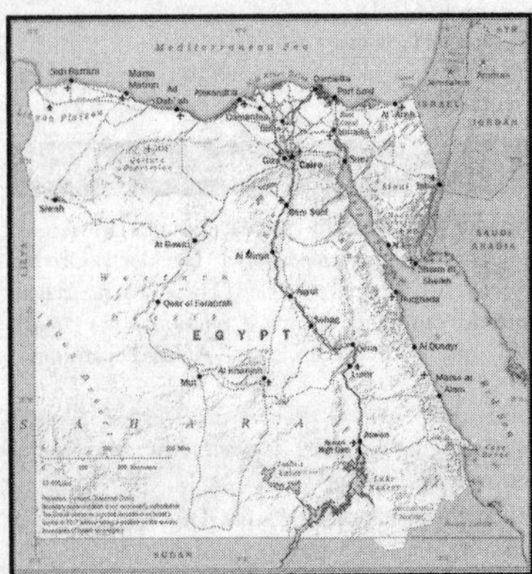

INTRODUCTION

Background: The regularity and richness of the annual Nile River flood, coupled with semi-isolation provided by deserts to the east and west, allowed for the development of one of the world's great civilizations in Egypt. A unified kingdom arose circa 3200 B.C., and a series of dynasties ruled in Egypt for the next three millennia. The last native dynasty fell to the Persians in 341 B.C., who in turn were replaced by the Greeks, Romans, and Byzantines. Arab conquerors introduced Islam and the Arabic language in the 7th century and ruled for the next six centuries. The Mamluks, a local military caste, took control around 1250 and continued to govern after the Ottoman Turks conquered Egypt in 1517.

Completion of the Suez Canal in 1869 elevated Egypt as an important world transportation hub. Ostensibly to protect its investments, Britain seized control of Egypt's government in 1882, but the country's nominal allegiance to the Ottoman Empire continued until 1914. Egypt gained partial independence from the UK in 1922 and full sovereignty in 1952. British forces evacuated the Suez Canal Zone in 1956. The completion of the Aswan High Dam in 1971 and the resultant Lake Nasser have reaffirmed the time-honored place of the Nile River in the agriculture and ecology of Egypt. A rapidly growing population (the largest in the Arab world), limited arable land, and dependence on the Nile all continue to overtax resources and stress society. The government has struggled to meet the demands of Egypt's fast-growing population as it implements large-scale infrastructure projects, energy cooperation, and foreign direct investment appeals.

Inspired by the 2010 Tunisian revolution, Egyptian opposition groups led demonstrations and labor strikes countrywide, culminating in President Hosni MUBARAK's ouster in 2011. Egypt's military assumed national leadership until a new legislature was in place in early 2012; later that same year, Muslim Brotherhood candidate Mohamed MORSI won the presidential election. Following protests throughout the spring of 2013 against MORSI's government and the Muslim Brotherhood, the Egyptian Armed Forces intervened and removed MORSI from power in July 2013 and replaced him with interim president Adly MANSOUR. Simultaneously, the government began enacting laws to limit freedoms of assembly and expression. In 2014, voters approved a new constitution by referendum and then elected former defense minister Abdel Fattah EL-SISI president. EL-SISI was reelected to a second four-year term in 2018 and a third term in December 2023.

GEOGRAPHY

Location: Northern Africa, bordering the Mediterranean Sea, between Libya and the Gaza Strip, and the Red Sea north of Sudan, and includes the Asian Sinai Peninsula

Geographic coordinates: 27 00 N, 30 00 E

Map references: Africa

Area: *total:* 1,001,450 sq km
land: 995,450 sq km
water: 6,000 sq km
comparison ranking: total 31

Area - comparative: more than eight times the size of Ohio; slightly more than three times the size of New Mexico

Land boundaries: *total:* 2,612 km
border countries (4): Gaza Strip 13 km; Israel 208 km; Libya 1,115 km; Sudan 1,276 km

Coastline: 2,450 km

Maritime claims: *territorial sea:* 12 nm
contiguous zone: 24 nm
exclusive economic zone: 200 nm or the equidistant median line with Cyprus
continental shelf: 200 nm

Climate: desert; hot, dry summers with moderate winters

Terrain: vast desert plateau interrupted by Nile valley and delta

Elevation: *highest point:* Mount Catherine 2,629 m
lowest point: Qattara Depression -133 m
mean elevation: 321 m

Natural resources: petroleum, natural gas, iron ore, phosphates, manganese, limestone, gypsum, talc, asbestos, lead, rare earth elements, zinc

Land use: *agricultural land:* 4.1% (2022 est.)
arable land: 3.1% (2022 est.)
permanent crops: 1% (2022 est.)
permanent pasture: 0% (2022 est.)
forest: 0% (2022 est.)
other: 95.9% (2022 est.)

Irrigated land: 36,500 sq km (2012)

Major lakes (area sq km): *salt water lake(s):* Lake Manzala - 1,360 sq km
note - largest of Nile Delta lakes

Major rivers (by length in km): An Nīl (Nile) river mouth (shared with Rwanda [s], Tanzania, Uganda, South Sudan, and Sudan) - 6,650 km
note: [s] after country name indicates river source; [m] after country name indicates river mouth

Major watersheds (area sq km): Atlantic Ocean drainage: *(Mediterranean Sea)* Nile (3,254,853 sq km)

Major aquifers: Nubian Aquifer System

Population distribution: approximately 95% of the population lives within 20 km (12 mi) of the Nile River and its delta; vast areas of the country remain sparsely populated or uninhabited, as shown in this population distribution map

Natural hazards: periodic droughts; frequent earthquakes; flash floods; landslides; hot, driving windstorms called khamsin occur in spring; dust storms; sandstorms

Geography - note: controls Sinai Peninsula, the only land bridge between Africa and remainder of Eastern Hemisphere; controls Suez Canal, a sea link between Indian Ocean and Mediterranean Sea

PEOPLE AND SOCIETY

Population: *total:* 111,247,248 (2024 est.)
male: 57,142,484
female: 54,104,764
comparison rankings: total 15; male 15; female 15

Nationality: *noun:* Egyptian(s)
adjective: Egyptian

Ethnic groups: Egyptian 99.7%, other 0.3% (2006 est.)
note: data represent respondents by nationality

Languages: Arabic (official); English and French widely understood by educated classes
major-language sample(s):
كتاب حقائق العالم، أفضل مصدر للمعلومات الأساسية (Arabic)

Religions: Muslim (predominantly Sunni) 90%, Christian (majority Coptic Orthodox, other Christians include Armenian Apostolic, Catholic, Maronite, Orthodox, and Anglican) 10%

Age structure: *0-14 years:* 33.8% (male 19,349,395/female 18,243,571)
15-64 years: 60.6% (male 34,646,369/female 32,792,151)
65 years and over: 5.6% (2024 est.) (male 3,146,720/female 3,069,042)

Dependency ratios: *total dependency ratio:* 65 (2024 est.)
youth dependency ratio: 55.7 (2024 est.)
elderly dependency ratio: 9.2 (2024 est.)
potential support ratio: 10.8 (2024 est.)

Median age: *total:* 24.4 years (2024 est.)
male: 24.3 years
female: 24.4 years
comparison ranking: total 177

Population growth rate: 1.49% (2024 est.)
comparison ranking: 65

Birth rate: 19.5 births/1,000 population (2024 est.)
comparison ranking: 73

Death rate: 4.3 deaths/1,000 population (2024 est.)
comparison ranking: 212

Net migration rate: -0.3 migrant(s)/1,000 population (2024 est.)
comparison ranking: 115

Population distribution: approximately 95% of the population lives within 20 km (12 mi) of the Nile River and its delta; vast areas of the country remain sparsely populated or uninhabited, as shown in this population distribution map

Urbanization: *urban population:* 43.1% of total population (2023)
rate of urbanization: 1.9% annual rate of change (2020-25 est.)

Major urban areas - population: 22.183 million CAIRO (capital), 5.588 million Alexandria, 778,000 Bur Sa'id (2023)

Sex ratio: *at birth:* 1.06 male(s)/female
0-14 years: 1.06 male(s)/female
15-64 years: 1.06 male(s)/female
65 years and over: 1.03 male(s)/female
total population: 1.06 male(s)/female (2024 est.)

Mother's mean age at first birth: 22.6 years (2014 est.)
note: data represents median age at first birth among women 25-49

Maternal mortality ratio: 17 deaths/100,000 live births (2023 est.)
comparison ranking: 128

Infant mortality rate: *total:* 16.8 deaths/1,000 live births (2024 est.)
male: 17.8 deaths/1,000 live births
female: 15.9 deaths/1,000 live births
comparison ranking: total 88

Life expectancy at birth: *total population:* 75 years (2024 est.)
male: 73.8 years
female: 76.2 years
comparison ranking: total population 132

Total fertility rate: 2.65 children born/woman (2024 est.)
comparison ranking: 63

Gross reproduction rate: 1.28 (2024 est.)

Drinking water source: *improved: urban:* 99.3% of population (2022 est.)
rural: 98.4% of population (2022 est.)
total: 98.8% of population (2022 est.)
unimproved: urban: 0.7% of population (2022 est.)
rural: 1.6% of population (2022 est.)
total: 1.2% of population (2022 est.)

Health expenditure: 4.6% of GDP (2021)
7.2% of national budget (2022 est.)

Physician density: 0.67 physicians/1,000 population (2020)

Hospital bed density: 1.1 beds/1,000 population (2020 est.)

Sanitation facility access: *improved: urban:* 99.9% of population (2022 est.)
rural: 98.5% of population (2022 est.)
total: 99.1% of population (2022 est.)
unimproved: urban: 0.1% of population (2022 est.)
rural: 1.5% of population (2022 est.)
total: 0.9% of population (2022 est.)

Obesity - adult prevalence rate: 32% (2016)
comparison ranking: 19

Alcohol consumption per capita: *total:* 0.14 liters of pure alcohol (2019 est.)
beer: 0.09 liters of pure alcohol (2019 est.)
wine: 0.01 liters of pure alcohol (2019 est.)
spirits: 0.04 liters of pure alcohol (2019 est.)
other alcohols: 0 liters of pure alcohol (2019 est.)
comparison ranking: total 175

Tobacco use: *total:* 25.8% (2025 est.)
male: 51% (2025 est.)
female: 0.3% (2025 est.)
comparison ranking: total 39

Currently married women (ages 15-49): 71.1% (2023 est.)

Child marriage: *women married by age 15:* 1.8% (2021)
women married by age 18: 15.8% (2021)

Education expenditure: 3.9% of GDP (2015 est.)
12% national budget (2015 est.)
comparison ranking: Education expenditure (% GDP) 114

Literacy: *total population:* 71% (2017 est.)
male: 76% (2017 est.)
female: 66% (2017 est.)

School life expectancy (primary to tertiary education): *total:* 13 years (2023 est.)
male: 13 years (2023 est.)
female: 13 years (2023 est.)

ENVIRONMENT

Environmental issues: rapid growth in population straining natural resources; increasing soil salination below Aswan High Dam; desertification; oil pollution in coastal ecosystems; water pollution from agricultural pesticides, raw sewage, and industrial effluents; limited natural freshwater resources away from the Nile

International environmental agreements: *party to:* Biodiversity, Climate Change, Climate Change-Kyoto Protocol, Climate Change-Paris Agreement, Desertification, Endangered Species, Environmental Modification, Hazardous Wastes, Law of the Sea, Marine Dumping-London Convention, Marine Dumping-London Protocol, Nuclear Test Ban, Ozone Layer Protection, Ship Pollution, Wetlands
signed, but not ratified: Comprehensive Nuclear Test Ban

Climate: desert; hot, dry summers with moderate winters

Urbanization: *urban population:* 43.1% of total population (2023)
rate of urbanization: 1.9% annual rate of change (2020-25 est.)

Carbon dioxide emissions: 236.618 million metric tonnes of CO2 (2023 est.)
from coal and metallurgical coke: 6.966 million metric tonnes of CO2 (2023 est.)
from petroleum and other liquids: 114.507 million metric tonnes of CO2 (2023 est.)
from consumed natural gas: 115.144 million metric tonnes of CO2 (2023 est.)
comparison ranking: total emissions 29

Particulate matter emissions: 66.4 micrograms per cubic meter (2019 est.)

Methane emissions: *energy:* 690.8 kt (2022-2024 est.)
agriculture: 548.9 kt (2019-2021 est.)
waste: 874 kt (2019-2021 est.)
other: 9.2 kt (2019-2021 est.)

Waste and recycling: *municipal solid waste generated annually:* 21 million tons (2024 est.)
percent of municipal solid waste recycled: 26.6% (2022 est.)

Total water withdrawal: *municipal:* 10.75 billion cubic meters (2022 est.)
industrial: 5.4 billion cubic meters (2022 est.)
agricultural: 61.35 billion cubic meters (2022 est.)

Total renewable water resources: 57.5 billion cubic meters (2022 est.)

GOVERNMENT

Country name: *conventional long form:* Arab Republic of Egypt
conventional short form: Egypt
local long form: Jumhuriyat Misr al-Arabiyah
local short form: Misr
former: United Arab Republic (short-lived unification with Syria)
etymology: the English name Egypt derives from the ancient Greek name for the country, "Aguptos," and the ancient Roman name, "Aegyptus," with the Greek form coming from the words *aia gupos*, or "land of the vulture;" the Arabic name for the country, Misr, can be traced to the Assyrian word *misir*, meaning "fort"

Government type: presidential republic

Capital: *name:* Cairo
geographic coordinates: 30 03 N, 31 15 E
time difference: UTC+2 (7 hours ahead of Washington, DC, during Standard Time)
daylight saving time: +1hr, begins last Friday in April; ends last Friday in October
etymology: the ancient Egyptian name of the original city was Khere-ohe or Kheri-aha; the modern city's name may also derive from the Arabic *al-qahir*, meaning "the victorious;" this is an Arabic name for the planet Mars, which was in the ascendant on the day in 969 A.D. when construction on the new part of the city began

Administrative divisions: 27 governorates (*muhafazat*, singular - *muhafazat*); Ad Daqahliyah, Al Bahr al Ahmar (Red Sea), Al Buhayrah, Al Fayyum, Al Gharbiyah, Al Iskandariyah (Alexandria), Al Isma'iliyah (Ismailia), Al Jizah (Giza), Al Minufiyah, Al Minya, Al Qahirah (Cairo), Al Qalyubiyah, Al Uqsur (Luxor), Al Wadi al Jadid (New Valley), As Suways (Suez), Ash Sharqiyah, Aswan, Asyut, Bani Suwayf, Bur Sa'id (Port Said), Dumyat (Damietta), Janub Sina' (South Sinai), Kafr ash Shaykh, Matruh, Qina, Shamal Sina' (North Sinai), Suhaj

Legal system: mixed system based on Napoleonic civil and penal law, Islamic religious law, and vestiges of colonial-era laws; Supreme Constitutional Court reviews laws

Constitution: *history:* several previous; latest approved by a constitutional committee in December 2013, approved by referendum held on 14-15 January 2014, ratified by interim president on 19 January 2014
amendment process: proposed by the president of the republic or by one fifth of the House of Representatives members; a decision to accept the proposal requires majority vote by House members; passage of amendment requires a two-thirds majority vote by House members and passage by majority vote in a referendum; articles of reelection of the president and principles of freedom are not amendable unless the amendment "brings more guarantees"

International law organization participation: accepts compulsory ICJ jurisdiction with reservations; non-party state to the ICCt

Citizenship: *citizenship by birth:* no
citizenship by descent only: if the father was born in Egypt
dual citizenship recognized: only with prior permission from the government
residency requirement for naturalization: 10 years

Suffrage: 18 years of age; universal and compulsory

Executive branch: *chief of state:* President Abdel Fattah EL-SISI (since 8 June 2014)
head of government: Prime Minister Mostafa MADBOULY (since 7 June 2018)
cabinet: Cabinet ministers nominated by the executive branch and approved by the House of Representatives
election/appointment process: president elected by absolute-majority popular vote in 2 rounds, if needed, for a 6-year term (eligible for 3 consecutive terms); prime minister appointed by the president, approved by the House of Representatives
most recent election date: 10-12 December 2023
election results: 2023: Abdel Fattah EL-SISI reelected president in first round; percent of valid votes cast - Abdel Fattah EL-SISI (independent) 89.6%, Hazam OMAR (Republican People's Party) 4.5%, Farid ZAHRAN (Egyptian Social Democratic Party 4%, Abdel-Samad YAMAMA 1.9%
2018: Abdelfattah ELSISI reelected president in first round; percent of valid votes cast - Abdelfattah ELSISI (independent) 97.1%, Moussa Mostafa MOUSSA (El Ghad Party) 2.9%; note - more than 7% of ballots cast were deemed invalid
expected date of next election: 2029

Legislative branch: *legislative structure:* bicameral

Legislative branch - lower chamber: *chamber name:* House of Representatives (Majlis Al-Nuwab)
number of seats: 596 (568 directly elected; 28 appointed)
electoral system: mixed system
scope of elections: full renewal
term in office: 5 years
most recent election date: 10/24/2020 to 12/8/2020
parties elected and seats per party: Future of the Nation (Mostakbal Watan) (317); Republican People's party (El Shaab el Gomhory) (49); Independents (117); Other (109)
percentage of women in chamber: 27.7%
expected date of next election: October 2025

Legislative branch - upper chamber: *chamber name:* Senate (Majlis Al-Shiyoukh)
number of seats: 300 (200 directly elected; 100 appointed)
electoral system: mixed system
scope of elections: full renewal
term in office: 5 years
most recent election date: 8/4/2025 to 8/28/2025
parties elected and seats per party: Future of the Nation (Mostakbal Watan) (148); Republican People's party (17); Independents (88); Other (47)
percentage of women in chamber: 13.7%
expected date of next election: July 2030

Judicial branch: *highest court(s):* Supreme Constitutional Court (SCC) (consists of the court president and 10 justices); the SCC serves as the final court of arbitration on the constitutionality of laws and conflicts between lower courts regarding jurisdiction and rulings; Court of Cassation (CC) (consists of the court president and 550 judges organized in circuits with cases heard by panels of 5 judges); the CC is the highest appeals body for civil and criminal cases, also known as "ordinary justices"; Supreme Administrative Court (SAC) (consists of the court president and NA judges and organized in circuits with cases heard by panels of 5 judges); the SAC is the highest court of the State Council
judge selection and term of office: under the 2014 constitution, all judges and justices selected and appointed by the Supreme Judiciary Council and approved as a formality by the president of the Republic; judges appointed for life; under the 2019 amendments, the president has the power to appoint heads of judiciary authorities and courts, the prosecutor general, and the head of the Supreme Constitutional Court
subordinate courts: Courts of Appeal; Courts of First Instance; courts of limited jurisdiction; Family Court (established in 2004)

Political parties: Al-Nour
Arab Democratic Nasserist Party
Congress Party
Conservative Party
Democratic Peace Party
Egyptian National Movement Party
Egyptian Social Democratic Party
El Ghad Party
El Serh El Masry el Hor
Eradet Geel Party
Free Egyptians Party
Freedom Party
Justice Party
Homeland's Protector Party
Modern Egypt Party
My Homeland Egypt Party
Nation's Future Party (Mostaqbal Watan)
National Progressive Unionist (Tagammu) Party
Reform and Development Party
Republican People's Party
Revolutionary Guards Party
Wafd Party

Diplomatic representation in the US: *chief of mission:* Ambassador Motaz Mounir ZAHRAN (since 17 September 2020)
chancery: 3521 International Court NW, Washington, DC 20008
telephone: [1] (202) 895-5400
FAX: (202) 244-4319
email address and website: embassy@egyptembassy.net
https://www.egyptembassy.net/
consulate(s) general: Chicago, Houston, Los Angeles, New York

Diplomatic representation from the US: *chief of mission:* Ambassador Herro MUSTAFA GARG (since 15 November 2023)
embassy: 5 Tawfik Diab St., Garden City, Cairo
mailing address: 7700 Cairo Place, Washington DC 20512-7700
telephone: [20-2] 2797-3300
FAX: [20-2] 2797-3200
email address and website: ConsularCairoACS@state.gov
https://eg.usembassy.gov/
consulate(s) general: Alexandria

International organization participation: ABEDA, AfDB, AFESD, AMF, AU, BRICS, BSEC (observer), CAEU, CD, CICA, COMESA, D-8, EBRD, FAO, G-15, G-24, G-77, IAEA, IBRD, ICAO, ICC (national committees), ICRM, IDA, IDB, IFAD, IFC, IFRCS, IHO, ILO, IMF, IMO, IMSO, Interpol, IOC, IOM, IPU, ISO, ITSO, ITU, LAS, LCBC (observer), MIGA, MINURSO, MONUSCO, NAM, OAPEC, OAS (observer), OIC, OIF, OSCE (partner), PCA, UN, UNAMID, UNCTAD, UNESCO, UNHCR, UNIDO, UNISFA, UNMISS, UNOCI, UNOOSA, UNRWA, UNWTO, UPU, WCO, WFTU (NGOs), WHO, WIPO, WMO, WTO

Independence: 28 February 1922 (from UK protectorate status; the military-led revolution that began on 23 July 1952 led to a republic being declared on 18 June 1953 and all British troops withdrawn on 18 June 1956)

note: the Two Lands of Upper (southern) and Lower (northern) Egypt were first united politically around 3200 B.C.

National holiday: Revolution Day, 23 July (1952)

Flag: *description:* three equal horizontal bands of red (top), white, and black; centered in the white band is the national emblem, a gold Eagle of Saladin; it faces the left side, with a shield on its chest, above a scroll with the country's name in Arabic
meaning: the band colors derive from the Arab Liberation flag and represent oppression (black) overcome through bloody struggle (red), to be replaced by a bright future (white)
note: similar to the flags of Syria (two green stars in the white band), Iraq (an Arabic inscription centered in the white band), and Yemen (plain white band)

National symbol(s): golden eagle, white lotus

National color(s): red, white, black

National anthem(s): *title:* "Bilady, Bilady, Bilady" (My Homeland, My Homeland, My Homeland)
lyrics/music: Younis-al QADI/Sayed DARWISH
history: adopted 1979; the current anthem was written after the 1979 peace treaty with Israel; the composer is considered the father of modern Egyptian music; of the three verses, only the first verse is sung, preceded and followed by the chorus

National heritage: *total World Heritage Sites:* 7 (6 cultural, 1 natural)
selected World Heritage Site locales: Memphis and its Necropolis (c); Ancient Thebes with its Necropolis (c); Nubian Monuments (c); Saint Catherine Area (c); Abu Mena (c); Historic Cairo (c); Wadi Al-Hitan (Whale Valley) (n)

ECONOMY

Economic overview: Africa's second-largest economy; 2030 Vision to diversify markets and energy infrastructure; improving fiscal, external, and current accounts; underperforming private sector; poor labor force participation; expanded credit access

Real GDP (purchasing power parity): $1.958 trillion (2024 est.)
$1.912 trillion (2023 est.)
$1.842 trillion (2022 est.)
note: data in 2021 dollars
comparison ranking: 18

Real GDP growth rate: 2.4% (2024 est.)
3.8% (2023 est.)
6.6% (2022 est.)
note: annual GDP % growth based on constant local currency
comparison ranking: 140

Real GDP per capita: $16,800 (2024 est.)
$16,700 (2023 est.)
$16,400 (2022 est.)
note: data in 2021 dollars
comparison ranking: 114

GDP (official exchange rate): $389.06 billion (2024 est.)
note: data in current dollars at official exchange rate

Inflation rate (consumer prices): 28.3% (2024 est.)
33.9% (2023 est.)
13.9% (2022 est.)
note: annual % change based on consumer prices
comparison ranking: 196

GDP - composition, by sector of origin: *agriculture:* 13.7% (2024 est.)
industry: 32.6% (2024 est.)
services: 48.9% (2024 est.)
note: figures may not total 100% due to non-allocated consumption not captured in sector-reported data
comparison rankings: agriculture 58; industry 40; services 152

GDP - composition, by end use: *household consumption:* 87.6% (2024 est.)
government consumption: 6.3% (2024 est.)
investment in fixed capital: 11.7% (2024 est.)
investment in inventories: 1.3% (2024 est.)
exports of goods and services: 16.4% (2024 est.)
imports of goods and services: -23.2% (2024 est.)
note: figures may not total 100% due to rounding or gaps in data collection

Agricultural products: sugarcane, sugar beets, wheat, maize, potatoes, tomatoes, rice, milk, onions, oranges (2023)
note: top ten agricultural products based on tonnage

Industries: textiles, food processing, tourism, chemicals, pharmaceuticals, hydrocarbons, construction, cement, metals, light manufactures

Industrial production growth rate: -1.9% (2024 est.)
note: annual % change in industrial value added based on constant local currency
comparison ranking: 159

Labor force: 33.749 million (2024 est.)
note: number of people ages 15 or older who are employed or seeking work
comparison ranking: 20

Unemployment rate: 7.2% (2024 est.)
7.4% (2023 est.)
7.4% (2022 est.)
note: % of labor force seeking employment
comparison ranking: 125

Youth unemployment rate (ages 15-24): *total:* 18.7% (2024 est.)
male: 12.4% (2024 est.)
female: 47.1% (2024 est.)
note: % of labor force ages 15-24 seeking employment
comparison ranking: total 59

Population below poverty line: 29.7% (2019 est.)
note: % of population with income below national poverty line

Gini Index coefficient - distribution of family income: 28.5 (2021 est.)
note: index (0-100) of income distribution; higher values represent greater inequality
comparison ranking: 130

Average household expenditures: *on food:* 36.9% of household expenditures (2023 est.)
on alcohol and tobacco: 4.6% of household expenditures (2023 est.)

Household income or consumption by percentage share: *lowest 10%:* 4.2% (2021 est.)
highest 10%: 24.6% (2021 est.)
note: % share of income accruing to lowest and highest 10% of population

Remittances: 4.9% of GDP (2023 est.)
5.9% of GDP (2022 est.)
7.4% of GDP (2021 est.)
note: personal transfers and compensation between resident and non-resident individuals/households/entities

Budget: *revenues:* $69.999 billion (2015 est.)
expenditures: $96.057 billion (2015 est.)
note: central government revenues (excluding grants) and expenses converted to US dollars at average official exchange rate for year indicated

Public debt: 103% of GDP (2017 est.)
note: data cover central government debt and include debt instruments issued (or owned) by government entities other than the treasury; the data include treasury debt held by foreign entities; the data include debt issued by subnational entities, as well as intragovernmental debt; intragovernmental debt consists of treasury borrowings from surpluses in the social funds, such as for retirement, medical care, and unemployment; debt instruments for the social funds are sold at public auctions
comparison ranking: 18

Taxes and other revenues: 12.5% (of GDP) (2015 est.)
note: central government tax revenue as a % of GDP
comparison ranking: 110

Current account balance: -$12.564 billion (2023 est.)
-$10.537 billion (2022 est.)
-$18.611 billion (2021 est.)
note: balance of payments - net trade and primary/secondary income in current dollars
comparison ranking: 184

Exports: $68.218 billion (2023 est.)
$76.295 billion (2022 est.)
$58.339 billion (2021 est.)
note: balance of payments - exports of goods and services in current dollars
comparison ranking: 56

Exports - partners: Saudi Arabia 10%, Turkey 9%, Italy 6%, USA 5%, UAE 5% (2023)
note: top five export partners based on percentage share of exports

Exports - commodities: refined petroleum, natural gas, fertilizers, garments, crude petroleum (2023)
note: top five export commodities based on value in dollars

Imports: $82.265 billion (2023 est.)
$97.144 billion (2022 est.)
$94.039 billion (2021 est.)
note: balance of payments - imports of goods and services in current dollars
comparison ranking: 49

Imports - partners: China 16%, Saudi Arabia 6%, Russia 6%, USA 6%, Germany 5% (2023)
note: top five import partners based on percentage share of imports

Imports - commodities: refined petroleum, wheat, plastics, natural gas, packaged medicine (2023)
note: top five import commodities based on value in dollars

Reserves of foreign exchange and gold: $44.921 billion (2024 est.)
$33.07 billion (2023 est.)
$32.144 billion (2022 est.)
note: holdings of gold (year-end prices)/foreign exchange/special drawing rights in current dollars
comparison ranking: 45

Debt - external: $117.272 billion (2023 est.)
note: present value of external debt in current US dollars
comparison ranking: 8

Exchange rates: Egyptian pounds (EGP) per US dollar -

Exchange rates: 45.299 (2024 est.)
30.626 (2023 est.)
19.16 (2022 est.)
15.645 (2021 est.)
15.759 (2020 est.)

ENERGY

Electricity access: *electrification - total population:* 100% (2022 est.)

Electricity: *installed generating capacity:* 59.68 million kW (2023 est.)
consumption: 162.026 billion kWh (2023 est.)
exports: 1.785 billion kWh (2023 est.)
imports: 187 million kWh (2023 est.)
transmission/distribution losses: 45.67 billion kWh (2023 est.)
comparison rankings: installed generating capacity 26; consumption 25; exports 62; imports 109; transmission/distribution losses 205

Electricity generation sources: *fossil fuels:* 87.9% of total installed capacity (2023 est.)
solar: 2.2% of total installed capacity (2023 est.)
wind: 2.8% of total installed capacity (2023 est.)
hydroelectricity: 7% of total installed capacity (2023 est.)
biomass and waste: 0.2% of total installed capacity (2023 est.)

Nuclear energy: Number of nuclear reactors under construction: 4 (2025)

Coal: *production:* 69,000 metric tons (2023 est.)
consumption: 3.262 million metric tons (2023 est.)
exports: 68,000 metric tons (2023 est.)
imports: 3.263 million metric tons (2023 est.)
proven reserves: 182 million metric tons (2023 est.)

Petroleum: *total petroleum production:* 667,000 bbl/day (2023 est.)
refined petroleum consumption: 830,000 bbl/day (2023 est.)
crude oil estimated reserves: 3.3 billion barrels (2021 est.)

Natural gas: *production:* 57.181 billion cubic meters (2023 est.)
consumption: 58.695 billion cubic meters (2023 est.)
exports: 5.344 billion cubic meters (2023 est.)
imports: 9.126 billion cubic meters (2023 est.)
proven reserves: 1.784 trillion cubic meters (2021 est.)

Energy consumption per capita: 34.975 million Btu/person (2023 est.)
comparison ranking: 109

COMMUNICATIONS

Telephones - fixed lines: *total subscriptions:* 12.475 million (2023 est.)
subscriptions per 100 inhabitants: 11 (2023 est.)
comparison ranking: total subscriptions 15

Telephones - mobile cellular: *total subscriptions:* 106 million (2023 est.)
subscriptions per 100 inhabitants: 93 (2022 est.)
comparison ranking: total subscriptions 17

Broadcast media: mix of state-run and private broadcast media; state-run TV operates 2 national and 6 regional terrestrial networks, as well as a few satellite channels; dozens of private satellite channels and a large number of Arabic satellite channels are available for free; some limited satellite services are also available via subscription; state-run radio operates about 30 stations belonging to 8 networks; privately-owned radio includes 8 major stations (2019)

Internet country code: .eg

Internet users: *percent of population:* 73% (2023 est.)

Broadband - fixed subscriptions: *total:* 13.6 million (2023 est.)
subscriptions per 100 inhabitants: 12 (2023 est.)
comparison ranking: total 18

TRANSPORTATION

Civil aircraft registration country code prefix: SU

Airports: 73 (2025)
comparison ranking: 71

Heliports: 60 (2025)
comparison ranking: 33

Railways: *total:* 5,085 km (2014)
standard gauge: 5,085 km (2014) 1.435-m gauge (62 km electrified)

Merchant marine: *total:* 441 (2023)
by type: bulk carrier 14, container ship 6, general cargo 23, oil tanker 42, other 356
comparison ranking: total 45

Ports: *total ports:* 31 (2024)
large: 5
medium: 1
small: 8
very small: 16
size unknown: 1
ports with oil terminals: 17
key ports: Ain Sukhna Terminal, Al Iskandariyh (Alexandria), As Suways, Bur Sa'id, Damietta, Ras Shukhier

MILITARY AND SECURITY

Military and security forces: Egyptian Armed Forces (EAF): Army (includes Republican Guard), Navy (includes Coast Guard), Air Force, Air Defense Forces, Border Guard Forces

Interior Ministry: Public Security Sector Police, the Central Security Force, National Security Agency (2024)
note: the Public Security Sector Police are responsible for law enforcement nationwide; the Central Security Force protects infrastructure and is responsible for crowd control; the National Security Agency is responsible for internal security threats and counterterrorism along with other security services

Military expenditures: 0.8% of GDP (2024 est.)
1% of GDP (2023 est.)
1.2% of GDP (2022 est.)
1.3% of GDP (2021 est.)
1.3% of GDP (2020 est.)

Military and security service personnel strengths: estimated 450,000 active Armed Forces (2025)

Military equipment inventories and acquisitions: the EAF's inventory is comprised of a mix of domestically produced, Soviet-era, and more modern, particularly Western, weapons systems; in recent years, the EAF has embarked on an equipment modernization program with significant purchases from foreign suppliers; major suppliers have included China, France, Germany, Italy, Russia, and the US; Egypt has an established defense industry that produces a range of products from small arms to armored vehicles and naval vessels; it also has licensed and co-production agreements with several countries, including Germany and the US (2024)

Military service age and obligation: voluntary enlistment possible from age 16 for men and 17 for women; 18-30 years of age for conscript service for men; service obligation 14-36 months, followed by a 9-year reserve obligation; active service length depends on education; high school drop-outs serve for the full 36 months, while college graduates serve for lesser periods of time, depending on their education level (2023)
note: conscripts make up a considerable portion of the military and the Central Security Force

Military deployments: 1,000 (plus nearly 200 police) Central African Republic (MINUSCA); also has about 350 police deployed to the Democratic Republic of the Congo under MONUSCO; slated to have about 1,100 personnel in Somalia under AUSSOM in 2025 (2024)

Military - note: the Egyptian Armed Forces (EAF) are responsible for external defense but also have an internal role assisting police and paramilitary security forces during emergencies and in anti-terrorism operations; the EAF also participates in foreign peacekeeping and other security missions, as well as both bilateral and multinational exercises; the military has considerable political power and independence; it has long had a crucial role in Egypt's politics and has a large stake in the civilian economy, including running banks, businesses, gas stations, shipping lines, and utilities, and producing consumer and industrial goods, importing commodities, and building and managing infrastructure projects, such as bridges, roads, hospitals, and housing
key areas of concern for the EAF include Islamist militant groups operating out of the Sinai Peninsula, regional challenges such as ongoing conflicts and instability, and maritime security; since 2011, the EAF has been conducting operations alongside other security forces in the North Sinai governorate against several militant groups, particularly the Islamic State of Iraq and ash-Sham (ISIS); over the past decade, it has deployed additional units along the border with Libya, provided air support to the Saudi-led coalition's intervention in Yemen, and most recently boosted its presence on the border with Gaza in response to the HAMAS-Israel conflict; the Navy in recent years has sought to modernize and expand its capabilities and profile in the Eastern Mediterranean and Red Sea, including the acquisition of helicopter carriers, modern frigates, and attack submarines, as well as the establishment of a joint service military base on the Red Sea
the Multinational Force & Observers (MFO) has operated in the Sinai since 1982 as a peacekeeping and monitoring force to supervise the implementation of the security provisions of the 1979 Egyptian-Israeli Treaty of Peace; the MFO is an independent international organization, created by agreement between Egypt and Israel; it has about 1,150 troops from 13 countries; Colombia, Fiji, and the US are the leading providers of troops to the MFO (2025)

SPACE

Space agency/agencies: Egyptian Space Agency (EgSA; established 2019); National Authority for Remote Sensing and Space Science (NARSS; formed in 1994 from the Remote Sensing Center, which was established in 1971) (2025)

Space program overview: has a growing space program and seeks to become a regional space power; operates satellites; builds satellites jointly with foreign partners but developing localized satellite manufacturing capabilities and associated support infrastructure; acquiring other space-related technologies through transfers and domestic development, including on communications, Earth imaging/remote sensing (RS), and satellite payloads and components;

cooperating on space-related issues with a variety of foreign governments and commercial space companies, including those of Belarus, Canada, China, the European Space Agency and its member states (particularly France, Germany, Italy), Ghana, India, Japan, Kazakhstan, Kenya, Nigeria, Russia, South Africa, Sudan, Uganda, Ukraine, the UAE, and the US; also a member of the Arab Space Coordination Group; has a commercial space sector that focuses on satellite communications, satellite design and production, RS capabilities, and space applications (2025)

note: further details about the key activities, programs, and milestones of the country's space program, as well as government spending estimates on the space sector, appear in the Space Programs reference guide

TERRORISM

Terrorist group(s): Terrorist group(s): Army of Islam; Harakat Sawa'd Misr (HASM); Islamic State of Iraq and ash-Sham – Sinai Province (ISIS-SP); al-Qa'ida

note: details about the history, aims, leadership, organization, areas of operation, tactics, targets, weapons, size, and sources of support of the group(s) appear(s) in Appendix T

TRANSNATIONAL ISSUES

Refugees and internally displaced persons: *refugees:* 876,962 (2024 est.)
stateless persons: 5 (2024 est.)

EL SALVADOR

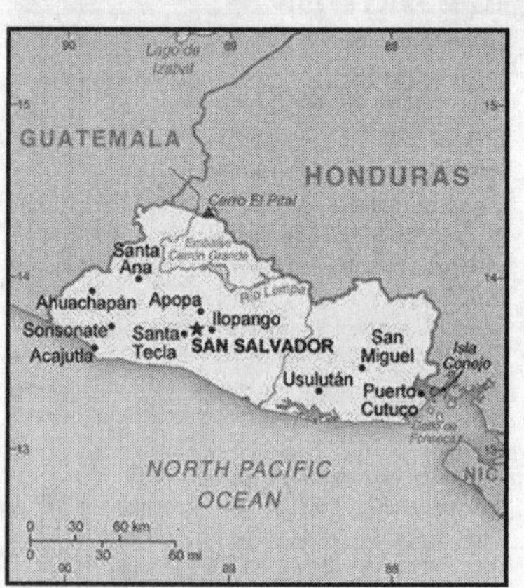

INTRODUCTION

Background: El Salvador achieved independence from Spain in 1821 and from the Central American Federation in 1839. A 12-year civil war, which cost about 75,000 lives, was brought to a close in 1992 when the government and leftist rebels signed a treaty that provided for military and political reforms. El Salvador is beset by one of the world's highest homicide rates and pervasive criminal gangs.

GEOGRAPHY

Location: Central America, bordering the North Pacific Ocean, between Guatemala and Honduras

Geographic coordinates: 13 50 N, 88 55 W

Map references: Central America and the Caribbean

Area: *total:* 21,041 sq km
land: 20,721 sq km
water: 320 sq km
comparison ranking: total 153

Area - comparative: about the same size as New Jersey

Land boundaries: *total:* 590 km
border countries (2): Guatemala 199 km; Honduras 391 km

Coastline: 307 km

Maritime claims: *territorial sea:* 12 nm
contiguous zone: 24 nm
exclusive economic zone: 200 nm

Climate: tropical; rainy season (May to October); dry season (November to April); tropical on coast; temperate in uplands

Terrain: mostly mountains with narrow coastal belt and central plateau

Elevation: *highest point:* Cerro El Pital 2,730 m
lowest point: Pacific Ocean 0 m
mean elevation: 442 m

Natural resources: hydropower, geothermal power, petroleum, arable land

Land use: *agricultural land:* 57.7% (2022 est.)
arable land: 34.8% (2022 est.)
permanent crops: 7.7% (2022 est.)
permanent pasture: 15.2% (2022 est.)
forest: 27.7% (2022 est.)
other: 14.5% (2022 est.)

Irrigated land: 240 sq km (2022)

Population distribution: high population density country-wide, with particular concentration around the capital of San Salvador

Natural hazards: known as the Land of Volcanoes; frequent and sometimes destructive earthquakes and volcanic activity; extremely susceptible to hurricanes
volcanism: significant volcanic activity; San Salvador (1,893 m), which last erupted in 1917, has the potential to cause major harm to the country's capital, which lies just below the volcano's slopes; San Miguel (2,130 m) is one of the most active volcanoes in the country; other historically active volcanoes include Conchaguita, Ilopango, Izalco, and Santa Ana

Geography - note: smallest Central American country and only one without a coastline on the Caribbean Sea

PEOPLE AND SOCIETY

Population: *total:* 6,628,702 (2024 est.)
male: 3,172,244
female: 3,456,458
comparison rankings: total 110; male 110; female 107

Nationality: *noun:* Salvadoran(s)
adjective: Salvadoran

Ethnic groups: Mestizo 86.3%, White 12.7%, Indigenous 0.2% (includes Lenca, Kakawira, Nahua-Pipil), Black 0.1%, other 0.6% (2007 est.)

Languages: Spanish (official), Nawat (among some indigenous)
major-language sample(s):
La Libreta Informativa del Mundo, la fuente indispensable de información básica. (Spanish)

Religions: Roman Catholic 43.9%, Protestant 39.6% (Evangelical - unspecified 38.2%, Evangelical - Methodist 1.3%, Evangelical - Baptist 0.1%), none 16.3%, unspecified 0.2% (2023 est.)

Age structure: *0-14 years:* 25.3% (male 855,841/female 818,642)
15-64 years: 66.3% (male 2,077,745/female 2,317,416)
65 years and over: 8.4% (2024 est.) (male 238,658/female 320,400)

Dependency ratios: *total dependency ratio:* 47.6 (2024 est.)
youth dependency ratio: 35 (2024 est.)
elderly dependency ratio: 12.5 (2024 est.)
potential support ratio: 8 (2024 est.)

Median age: *total:* 29.7 years (2024 est.)
male: 28.2 years
female: 31.2 years
comparison ranking: total 143

Population growth rate: 0.34% (2024 est.)
comparison ranking: 163

Birth rate: 17.1 births/1,000 population (2024 est.)
comparison ranking: 90

Death rate: 5.9 deaths/1,000 population (2024 est.)
comparison ranking: 161

Net migration rate: -7.7 migrant(s)/1,000 population (2024 est.)
comparison ranking: 219

Population distribution: high population density country-wide, with particular concentration around the capital of San Salvador

Urbanization: *urban population:* 75.4% of total population (2023)
rate of urbanization: 1.33% annual rate of change (2020-25 est.)

Major urban areas - population: 1.116 million SAN SALVADOR (capital) (2023)

Sex ratio: *at birth:* 1.05 male(s)/female
0-14 years: 1.05 male(s)/female
15-64 years: 0.9 male(s)/female
65 years and over: 0.74 male(s)/female
total population: 0.92 male(s)/female (2024 est.)

Mother's mean age at first birth: 20.8 years (2008 est.)
note: data represents median age at first birth among women 25-29

Maternal mortality ratio: 39 deaths/100,000 live births (2023 est.)
comparison ranking: 105

Infant mortality rate: *total:* 11.7 deaths/1,000 live births (2024 est.)
male: 13.3 deaths/1,000 live births
female: 10 deaths/1,000 live births
comparison ranking: total 112

Life expectancy at birth: *total population:* 75.9 years (2024 est.)
male: 72.4 years
female: 79.5 years
comparison ranking: total population 121

Total fertility rate: 2.02 children born/woman (2024 est.)
comparison ranking: 105

Gross reproduction rate: 0.98 (2024 est.)

Drinking water source: *improved: urban:* 100% of population (2022 est.)
rural: 94.4% of population (2022 est.)
total: 98.6% of population (2022 est.)
unimproved: urban: 0% of population (2022 est.)
rural: 5.6% of population (2022 est.)
total: 1.4% of population (2022 est.)

Health expenditure: 9.7% of GDP (2021)
21.2% of national budget (2022 est.)

Physician density: 1.62 physicians/1,000 population (2023)

Hospital bed density: 1.2 beds/1,000 population (2021 est.)

Sanitation facility access: *improved: urban:* 100% of population (2022 est.)
rural: 98.3% of population (2022 est.)
total: 99.6% of population (2022 est.)
unimproved: urban: 0% of population (2022 est.)
rural: 1.7% of population (2022 est.)
total: 0.4% of population (2022 est.)

Obesity - adult prevalence rate: 24.6% (2016)
comparison ranking: 57

Alcohol consumption per capita: *total:* 2.94 liters of pure alcohol (2019 est.)
beer: 1.5 liters of pure alcohol (2019 est.)
wine: 0.06 liters of pure alcohol (2019 est.)
spirits: 1.37 liters of pure alcohol (2019 est.)
other alcohols: 0 liters of pure alcohol (2019 est.)
comparison ranking: total 116

Tobacco use: *total:* 7.8% (2025 est.)
male: 14.7% (2025 est.)
female: 1.7% (2025 est.)
comparison ranking: total 145

Currently married women (ages 15-49): 55% (2023 est.)

Child marriage: *women married by age 15:* 4.3% (2021)
women married by age 18: 19.7% (2021)

Education expenditure: 3.2% of GDP (2023 est.)
12.5% national budget (2023 est.)
comparison ranking: Education expenditure (% GDP) 144

Literacy: *total population:* 90% (2023 est.)
male: 92% (2023 est.)
female: 88% (2023 est.)

School life expectancy (primary to tertiary education): *total:* 11 years (2023 est.)
male: 11 years (2023 est.)
female: 12 years (2023 est.)

ENVIRONMENT

Environmental issues: deforestation; soil erosion; water pollution; contamination of soils from disposal of toxic wastes

International environmental agreements: *party to:* Biodiversity, Climate Change, Climate Change-Kyoto Protocol, Climate Change-Paris Agreement, Comprehensive Nuclear Test Ban, Desertification, Endangered Species, Hazardous Wastes, Nuclear Test Ban, Ozone Layer Protection, Ship Pollution, Wetlands
signed, but not ratified: Law of the Sea

Climate: tropical; rainy season (May to October); dry season (November to April); tropical on coast; temperate in uplands

Urbanization: *urban population:* 75.4% of total population (2023)
rate of urbanization: 1.33% annual rate of change (2020-25 est.)

Carbon dioxide emissions: 8.694 million metric tonnes of CO2 (2023 est.)
from coal and metallurgical coke: 1,000 metric tonnes of CO2 (2023 est.)
from petroleum and other liquids: 7.745 million metric tonnes of CO2 (2023 est.)
from consumed natural gas: 948,000 metric tonnes of CO2 (2023 est.)
comparison ranking: total emissions 113

Particulate matter emissions: 23.8 micrograms per cubic meter (2019 est.)

Waste and recycling: *municipal solid waste generated annually:* 1.649 million tons (2024 est.)
percent of municipal solid waste recycled: 15.2% (2022 est.)

Total water withdrawal: *municipal:* 433.229 million cubic meters (2022)
industrial: 94.316 million cubic meters (2022)
agricultural: 1.411 billion cubic meters (2022)

Total renewable water resources: 26.27 billion cubic meters (2022 est.)

GOVERNMENT

Country name: *conventional long form:* Republic of El Salvador
conventional short form: El Salvador
local long form: República de El Salvador
local short form: El Salvador
etymology: means "the Savior" in Spanish and is a shortened form of "the Divine Savior of the World" (el Divino Salvador del Mundo), referring to Jesus Christ; 16th-century Spanish colonists gave the name "San Salvador" to the fort located where the country's capital of San Salvador now stands, and the name was later used for the city and the surrounding region; the country was officially named El Salvador in 1824

Government type: presidential republic

Capital: *name:* San Salvador
geographic coordinates: 13 42 N, 89 12 W
time difference: UTC-6 (1 hour behind Washington, DC, during Standard Time)
etymology: Spanish colonists founded the city in 1526 on the feast day of the Transfiguration of the Savior (Jesus Christ), and the name means "Holy Savior" in Spanish

Administrative divisions: 14 departments (*departamentos*, singular - *departamento*); Ahuachapan, Cabanas, Chalatenango, Cuscatlan, La Libertad, La Paz, La Union, Morazan, San Miguel, San Salvador, San Vicente, Santa Ana, Sonsonate, Usulutan

Legal system: civil law system with minor common law influence; Supreme Court reviews legislative acts

Constitution: *history:* many previous; latest drafted 16 December 1983, enacted 23 December 1983
amendment process: proposals require agreement by absolute majority of the Legislative Assembly membership; passage requires at least two-thirds majority vote of the Assembly; constitutional articles on basic principles, and citizen rights and freedoms cannot be amended

International law organization participation: has not submitted an ICJ jurisdiction declaration; non-party state to the ICCt

Citizenship: *citizenship by birth:* yes
citizenship by descent only: yes
dual citizenship recognized: yes
residency requirement for naturalization: 5 years

Suffrage: 18 years of age; universal

Executive branch: *chief of state:* President Nayib Armando BUKELE Ortez (since 1 June 2019)
head of government: President Nayib Armando BUKELE Ortez (since 1 June 2019)
cabinet: Council of Ministers selected by the president
election/appointment process: president and vice president directly elected on the same ballot by absolute-majority popular vote for a 6-year term (no term limits)
most recent election date: 4 February 2024
election results: *2024:* Nayib Armando BUKELE Ortez reelected president - Nayib Armando BUKELE Ortez (Nuevas Ideas) 84.7%, Manuel FLORES (FMLN) 6.4%, Joel SANCHEZ (ARENA) 5.6%, Luis PARADA (NT) 2%, other 1.3%
2019: Nayib Armando BUKELE Ortez elected president - Nayib Armando BUKELE Ortez (GANA) 53.1%, Carlos CALLEJA Hakker (ARENA) 31.7%, Hugo MARTINEZ (FMLN) 14.4%, other 0.8%
expected date of next election: 28 February 2027; note - on 31 July 2025, the Legislative Assembly voted to move the date of the next presidential election from 2029 to 2027 to bring the presidential election cycle in line with the three-year legislative and municipal election cycle
note: the president is both chief of state and head of government

Legislative branch: *legislature name:* Legislative Assembly (Asamblea legislativa)
legislative structure: unicameral
number of seats: 60 (all directly elected)
electoral system: proportional representation
scope of elections: full renewal
term in office: 3 years
most recent election date: 2/4/2024
parties elected and seats per party: New Ideas (N) (54); Other (6)
percentage of women in chamber: 31.7%
expected date of next election: February 2027

Judicial branch: *highest court(s):* Supreme Court or Corte Suprema de Justicia (consists of 15 judges, including its president, and 15 substitute judges organized into Constitutional, Civil, Penal, and Administrative Conflict Chambers)
judge selection and term of office: judges elected by the Legislative Assembly on the recommendation of

both the National Council of the Judicature, an independent body elected by the Legislative Assembly, and the Bar Association; judges elected for 9-year terms, with renewal of one third of membership every 3 years; consecutive reelection is allowed
subordinate courts: Appellate Courts; Courts of First Instance; Courts of Peace

Political parties: Christian Democratic Party or PDC
Farabundo Marti National Liberation Front or FMLN
Great Alliance for National Unity or GANA
National Coalition Party or PCN
Nationalist Republican Alliance or ARENA
New Ideas (Nuevas Ideas) or NI
Our Time (Nuestro Tiempo) or NT
Vamos or V

Diplomatic representation in the US: *chief of mission:* Ambassador Carmen Milena MAYORGA VALERA (since 23 December 2020)
chancery: 1400 16th Street NW, Suite 100, Washington, DC 20036
telephone: [1] (202) 595-7500
FAX: [1] (202) 232-3763
email address and website: infoEEUU@rree.gob.sv
https://rree.gob.sv/embajadas-consulados-y-misiones-permanentes-de-la-republica-de-el-salvador/
consulate(s) general: Aurora (CO), Boston, Charlotte (NC), Chicago, Dallas, Doral (FL), Duluth (GA), El Paso (TX), Elizabeth (NJ), Fresno (CA), Houston, Las Vegas (NV), Laredo (TX), Long Island (NY), Los Angeles, McAllen (TX), New York, Omaha (NE), San Bernardino (CA), San Francisco, Salt Lake City, Seattle, Silver Spring (MD), Springdale (AR), St. Paul (MN), Tucson (AZ), Woodbridge (VA)

Diplomatic representation from the US: *chief of mission:* Ambassador (vacant); Chargé d'Affaires Naomi C. FELLOWS (since August 2025)
embassy: Final Boulevard Santa Elena, Antiguo Cuscatlan, La Libertad, San Salvador
mailing address: 3450 San Salvador Place, Washington, DC 20521-3450
telephone: [503] 2501-2999
FAX: [503] 2501-2150
email address and website: ACSSanSal@state.gov
https://sv.usembassy.gov/

International organization participation: ACS, BCIE, CACM, CD, CELAC, FAO, G-11, G-77, IADB, IAEA, IBRD, ICAO, ICC (national committees), ICRM, IDA, IFAD, IFC, IFRCS, ILO, IMF, IMO, Interpol, IOC, IOM, IPU, ISO (correspondent), ITSO, ITU, ITUC (NGOs), LAES, LAIA (observer), MIGA, MINURSO, MINUSTAH, NAM (observer), OAS, OPANAL, OPCW, Pacific Alliance (observer), PCA, Petrocaribe, SICA, UN, UNCTAD, UNESCO, UNIDO, UNIFIL, Union Latina, UNISFA, UNMISS, UNOCI, UNOOSA, UNWTO, UPU, WCO, WFTU (NGOs), WHO, WIPO, WMO, WTO

Independence: 15 September 1821 (from Spain)

National holiday: Independence Day, 15 September (1821)

Flag: *description:* three equal horizontal bands of cobalt blue (top), white, and cobalt blue, with the national coat of arms centered in the white band; the coat of arms has a round emblem with the words REPUBLICA DE EL SALVADOR EN LA AMERICA CENTRAL around it
meaning: the blue bands stand for the Pacific Ocean and the Caribbean Sea, and the white for the land, as well as peace and prosperity
history: the banner is based on the former blue-white-blue flag of the Federal Republic of Central America
note: similar to the flag of Nicaragua, which has a different coat of arms centered in the white band; also similar to the flag of Honduras, which has five blue stars arranged in an "X" pattern and centered in the white band

National symbol(s): turquoise-browed motmot (bird)

National color(s): blue, white

National anthem(s): *title:* "Himno Nacional de El Salvador" (National Anthem of El Salvador)
lyrics/music: Juan Jose CANAS/Juan ABERLE
history: officially adopted 1953, in use since 1879; at four minutes and 20 seconds, the anthem is one of the world's longest

National heritage: *total World Heritage Sites:* 1 (cultural)
selected World Heritage Site locales: Joya de Cerén Archaeological Site

ECONOMY

Economic overview: upper-middle-income, dollarized Central American economy; reliant on remittances from US; recent growth linked to infrastructure investment, consumption, and crime reduction; $1.3 billion IMF loan to address fiscal imbalances; Bitcoin adopted as legal tender; persistent poverty and large informal sector

Real GDP (purchasing power parity): $73.961 billion (2024 est.)
$72.085 billion (2023 est.)
$69.621 billion (2022 est.)
note: data in 2021 dollars
comparison ranking: 108

Real GDP growth rate: 2.6% (2024 est.)
3.5% (2023 est.)
3% (2022 est.)
note: annual GDP % growth based on constant local currency
comparison ranking: 131

Real GDP per capita: $11,700 (2024 est.)
$11,400 (2023 est.)
$11,100 (2022 est.)
note: data in 2021 dollars
comparison ranking: 138

GDP (official exchange rate): $35.365 billion (2024 est.)
note: data in current dollars at official exchange rate

Inflation rate (consumer prices): 0.9% (2024 est.)
4% (2023 est.)
7.2% (2022 est.)
note: annual % change based on consumer prices
comparison ranking: 17

GDP - composition, by sector of origin: *agriculture:* 4.4% (2024 est.)
industry: 22.4% (2024 est.)
services: 61% (2024 est.)
note: figures may not total 100% due to non-allocated consumption not captured in sector-reported data
comparison rankings: agriculture 115; industry 115; services 81

GDP - composition, by end use: *household consumption:* 79.6% (2024 est.)
government consumption: 19.2% (2024 est.)
investment in fixed capital: 22.2% (2024 est.)
investment in inventories: -1.9% (2024 est.)
exports of goods and services: 32.8% (2024 est.)
imports of goods and services: -51.9% (2024 est.)
note: figures may not total 100% due to rounding or gaps in data collection

Agricultural products: sugarcane, maize, milk, chicken, sorghum, beans, oranges, coconuts, eggs, mangoes/guavas (2023)
note: top ten agricultural products based on tonnage

Industries: food processing, beverages, petroleum, chemicals, fertilizer, textiles, furniture, light metals

Industrial production growth rate: 0.4% (2024 est.)
note: annual % change in industrial value added based on constant local currency
comparison ranking: 125

Labor force: 2.89 million (2024 est.)
note: number of people ages 15 or older who are employed or seeking work
comparison ranking: 113

Unemployment rate: 2.9% (2024 est.)
3% (2023 est.)
3% (2022 est.)
note: % of labor force seeking employment
comparison ranking: 36

Youth unemployment rate (ages 15-24): *total:* 6.7% (2024 est.)
male: 5.2% (2024 est.)
female: 9.5% (2024 est.)
note: % of labor force ages 15-24 seeking employment
comparison ranking: total 151

Population below poverty line: 26.6% (2022 est.)
note: % of population with income below national poverty line

Gini Index coefficient - distribution of family income: 39.8 (2023 est.)
note: index (0-100) of income distribution; higher values represent greater inequality
comparison ranking: 43

Average household expenditures: *on food:* 26.7% of household expenditures (2023 est.)
on alcohol and tobacco: 0.5% of household expenditures (2023 est.)

Household income or consumption by percentage share: *lowest 10%:* 1.9% (2023 est.)
highest 10%: 29.7% (2023 est.)
note: % share of income accruing to lowest and highest 10% of population

Remittances: 24% of GDP (2024 est.)
24.5% of GDP (2023 est.)
24.6% of GDP (2022 est.)
note: personal transfers and compensation between resident and non-resident individuals/households/entities

Budget: *revenues:* $9.359 billion (2023 est.)
expenditures: $10.313 billion (2023 est.)
note: central government revenues (excluding grants) and expenditures converted to US dollars at average official exchange rate for year indicated

Public debt: 102.2% of GDP (2023 est.)
note: central government debt as a % of GDP
comparison ranking: 20

Taxes and other revenues: 20.7% (of GDP) (2023 est.)
note: central government tax revenue as a % of GDP
comparison ranking: 47

Current account balance: -$632.549 million (2024 est.)
-$367.831 million (2023 est.)
-$2.144 billion (2022 est.)

note: balance of payments - net trade and primary/secondary income in current dollars
comparison ranking: 113

Exports: $11.586 billion (2024 est.)
$10.629 billion (2023 est.)
$10.164 billion (2022 est.)
note: balance of payments - exports of goods and services in current dollars
comparison ranking: 111

Exports - partners: USA 36%, Guatemala 17%, Honduras 15%, Nicaragua 8%, Costa Rica 5% (2023)
note: top five export partners based on percentage share of exports

Exports - commodities: garments, plastic products, electrical capacitors, raw sugar, toilet paper (2023)
note: top five export commodities based on value in dollars

Imports: $18.354 billion (2024 est.)
$17.034 billion (2023 est.)
$18.181 billion (2022 est.)
note: balance of payments - imports of goods and services in current dollars
comparison ranking: 102

Imports - partners: USA 28%, China 15%, Guatemala 11%, Mexico 8%, Honduras 5% (2023)
note: top five import partners based on percentage share of imports

Imports - commodities: refined petroleum, natural gas, garments, packaged medicine, plastics (2023)
note: top five import commodities based on value in dollars

Reserves of foreign exchange and gold: $3.705 billion (2024 est.)
$3.079 billion (2023 est.)
$2.695 billion (2022 est.)
note: holdings of gold (year-end prices)/foreign exchange/special drawing rights in current dollars
comparison ranking: 109

Debt - external: $12.668 billion (2023 est.)
note: present value of external debt in current US dollars
comparison ranking: 44

Exchange rates: the US dollar is used as a medium of exchange and circulates freely in the economy

ENERGY

Electricity access: *electrification - total population:* 100% (2022 est.)

Electricity: *installed generating capacity:* 2.803 million kW (2023 est.)
consumption: 6.335 billion kWh (2023 est.)
exports: 140 million kWh (2023 est.)
imports: 750.096 million kWh (2023 est.)
transmission/distribution losses: 770.613 million kWh (2023 est.)
comparison rankings: installed generating capacity 113; consumption 123; exports 89; imports 86; transmission/distribution losses 90

Electricity generation sources: *fossil fuels:* 9.3% of total installed capacity (2023 est.)
solar: 19.1% of total installed capacity (2023 est.)
wind: 2.1% of total installed capacity (2023 est.)
hydroelectricity: 31% of total installed capacity (2023 est.)
geothermal: 24.5% of total installed capacity (2023 est.)
biomass and waste: 14% of total installed capacity (2023 est.)

Coal: *consumption:* 500 metric tons (2022 est.)
imports: 2,000 metric tons (2023 est.)

Petroleum: *total petroleum production:* 3 bbl/day (2023 est.)
refined petroleum consumption: 56,000 bbl/day (2023 est.)

Natural gas: *consumption:* 486.291 million cubic meters (2023 est.)
imports: 486.291 million cubic meters (2023 est.)

Energy consumption per capita: 24.421 million Btu/person (2023 est.)
comparison ranking: 125

COMMUNICATIONS

Telephones - fixed lines: *total subscriptions:* 863,000 (2022 est.)
subscriptions per 100 inhabitants: 14 (2022 est.)
comparison ranking: total subscriptions 72

Telephones - mobile cellular: *total subscriptions:* 11.5 million (2022 est.)
subscriptions per 100 inhabitants: 182 (2022 est.)
comparison ranking: total subscriptions 88

Broadcast media: multiple privately owned national terrestrial TV networks, supplemented by cable TV networks that carry international channels; hundreds of commercial radio stations and 2 government-owned radio stations; transition to digital transmission was set to begin in 2018, along with adoption of the Japanese-Brazilian Digital Standard (ISDB-T) (2022)

Internet country code: .sv

Internet users: *percent of population:* 68% (2023 est.)

Broadband - fixed subscriptions: *total:* 671,000 (2022 est.)
subscriptions per 100 inhabitants: 11 (2022 est.)
comparison ranking: total 88

TRANSPORTATION

Civil aircraft registration country code prefix: YS

Airports: 27 (2025)
comparison ranking: 126

Railways: *total:* 12.5 km (2014)
narrow gauge: 12.5 km (2014) 0.914-mm gauge

Merchant marine: *total:* 5 (2023)
by type: other 5
comparison ranking: total 169

Ports: *total ports:* 3 (2024)
large: 0
medium: 0
small: 0
very small: 3
ports with oil terminals: 3
key ports: Acajutla, Acajutla Offshore Terminal, La Union

MILITARY AND SECURITY

Military and security forces: The Armed Forces of El Salvador (La Fuerza Armada de El Salvador, FAES): Army of El Salvador (Ejercito de El Salvador, ES), Naval Force of El Salvador (Fuerza Naval de El Salvador, FNES), Salvadoran Air Force (Fuerza Aérea Salvadoreña, FAS)

Ministry of Justice and Public Safety: National Civil Police (Policia Nacional Civil, PNC) (2025)

Military expenditures: 1.2% of GDP (2024 est.)
1.2% of GDP (2023 est.)
1.3% of GDP (2022 est.)
1.2% of GDP (2021 est.)
1.4% of GDP (2020 est.)

Military and security service personnel strengths: approximately 25,000 active FAES (2025)
note: El Salvador has pledged to increase the size of the military to 40,000 troops by 2026

Military equipment inventories and acquisitions: the FAES is lightly armed with an inventory of mostly older imported arms and equipment, largely from the US (2023)

Military service age and obligation: 18-30 years of age for selective compulsory military service; 16-22 years of age for voluntary military service for men and women; service obligation is 12 months, with 11 months for officers and non-commissioned officers (2023)

Military - note: the Armed Force of El Salvador (FAES) is responsible for defending national sovereignty and ensuring territorial integrity but also has considerable domestic security responsibilities; while the National Civil Police (PNC) are responsible for maintaining public security, the country's constitution allows the president to use the FAES "in exceptional circumstances" to maintain internal peace and public security; in 2016, the government created a special joint unit of Army commandos and police to fight criminal gangs; more military personnel were devoted to internal security beginning in 2019 when President BUKELE signed a decree authorizing military involvement in police duties to combat rising gang violence, organized crime, and narcotics trafficking, as well as assisting with border security
the military led the country for much of the 20th century; from 1980 to 1992, it fought a bloody civil war against guerrillas from the Farabundo Martí National Liberation Front or FMLN, the paramilitary arm of the Democratic Revolutionary Front (Frente Democrático Revolucionario), a coalition of left-wing dissident political groups backed by Cuba and the Soviet Union; the FAES received considerable US support during the conflict; significant human rights violations occurred during the war and approximately 75,000 Salvadorans, mostly civilians, were killed (2025)

TERRORISM

Terrorist group(s): Terrorist group(s): La Mara Salvatrucha (MS-13)
note: details about the history, aims, leadership, organization, areas of operation, tactics, targets, weapons, size, and sources of support of the group(s) appear(s) in Appendix T

TRANSNATIONAL ISSUES

Refugees and internally displaced persons: *refugees:* 392 (2024 est.)

IDPs: 35,391 (2024 est.)

Illicit drugs: USG identification: major illicit drug-producing and/or drug-transit country
major precursor-chemical producer (2025)

EQUATORIAL GUINEA

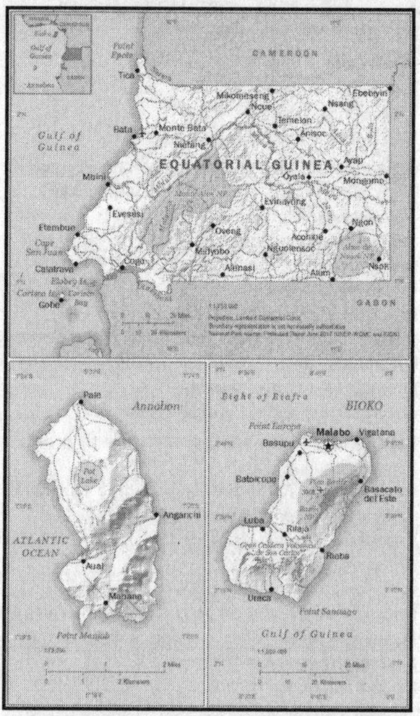

INTRODUCTION

Background: Equatorial Guinea consists of a continental territory and five inhabited islands; it is one of the smallest countries by area and population in Africa. The mainland region was most likely predominantly inhabited by Pygmy ethnic groups prior to the migration of various Bantu-speaking ethnic groups around the second millennium BC. The island of Bioko, the largest of Equatorial Guinea's five inhabited islands and the location of the country's capital of Malabo, has been occupied since at least 1000 B.C. In the early 1470s, Portuguese explorers landed on Bioko Island, and Portugal soon after established control of the island and other areas of modern Equatorial Guinea. In 1778, Portugal ceded its colonial hold over present-day Equatorial Guinea to Spain in the Treaty of El Pardo. The borders of modern-day Equatorial Guinea would evolve between 1778 and 1968 as the area remained under European colonial rule.

In 1968, Equatorial Guinea was granted independence from Spain and elected Francisco MACIAS NGUEMA as its first president. MACIAS consolidated power soon after his election and ruled brutally for over a decade. Under his regime, Equatorial Guinea experienced mass suppression, purges, and killings. Some estimates indicate that a third of the population either went into exile or was killed under MACIAS' rule. In 1979, present-day President OBIANG Nguema Mbasogo, then a senior military officer, deposed MACIAS in a violent coup. OBIANG has ruled since and has been elected in non-competitive contests several times, most recently in 2022. The president exerts near-total control over the political system.

Equatorial Guinea experienced rapid economic growth in the early years of the 21st century due to the discovery of large offshore oil reserves in 1996. Production peaked in 2004 and has declined since. The country's economic windfall from oil production resulted in massive increases in government revenue, a significant portion of which was earmarked for infrastructure development. Systemic corruption, however, has hindered socio-economic development, and the population has seen only limited improvements to living standards. Equatorial Guinea continues to seek to diversify its economy, increase foreign investment, and assume a greater role in regional and international affairs.

GEOGRAPHY

Location: Central Africa, bordering the Bight of Biafra, between Cameroon and Gabon

Geographic coordinates: 2 00 N, 10 00 E

Map references: Africa

Area: *total:* 28,051 sq km
land: 28,051 sq km
water: 0 sq km
comparison ranking: total 145

Area - comparative: slightly smaller than Maryland

Land boundaries: *total:* 528 km
border countries (2): Cameroon 183 km; Gabon 345 km

Coastline: 296 km

Maritime claims: *territorial sea:* 12 nm
exclusive economic zone: 200 nm

Climate: tropical; always hot, humid

Terrain: coastal plains rise to interior hills; islands are volcanic

Elevation: *highest point:* Pico Basile 3,008 m
lowest point: Atlantic Ocean 0 m
mean elevation: 577 m

Natural resources: petroleum, natural gas, timber, gold, bauxite, diamonds, tantalum, sand and gravel, clay

Land use: *agricultural land:* 3.7% (2022 est.)
arable land: 1.9% (2022 est.)
permanent crops: 1.7% (2022 est.)
permanent pasture: 0.2% (2022 est.)
forest: 86.7% (2022 est.)
other: 9.6% (2022 est.)

Irrigated land: NA

Population distribution: the two large cities are Bata on the mainland and the capital Malabo on the island of Bioko; small communities are scattered throughout the mainland and the five inhabited islands, as shown in this population distribution map

Natural hazards: violent windstorms; flash floods
volcanism: Santa Isabel (3,007 m), which last erupted in 1923, is the country's only historically active volcano; Santa Isabel and two dormant volcanoes form Bioko Island in the Gulf of Guinea

Geography - note: insular and continental regions widely separated; despite its name, no part of the equator passes through Equatorial Guinea – the mainland part of the country is located just north of the equator

PEOPLE AND SOCIETY

Population: *total:* 1,795,834 (2024 est.)
male: 962,385
female: 833,449
comparison rankings: total 154; male 153; female 153

Nationality: *noun:* Equatorial Guinean(s) or Equatoguinean(s)
adjective: Equatorial Guinean or Equatoguinean

Ethnic groups: Fang 78.1%, Bubi 9.4%, Ndowe 2.8%, Nanguedambo 2.7%, Bisio 0.9%, foreigner 5.3%, other 0.7%, unspecified 0.2% (2011 est.)

Languages: Spanish (official) 67.6%, other (includes Fang, Bubi, Portuguese (official), French (official), Fa d'Ambo spoken in Annobon) 32.4% (1994 est.)
major-language sample(s):
La Libreta Informativa del Mundo, la fuente indispensable de información básica. (Spanish)

Religions: Roman Catholic 88%, Protestant 5%, Muslim 2%, other 5% (animist, Baha'i, Jewish) (2015 est.)

Age structure: *0-14 years:* 35.6% (male 330,636/female 309,528)
15-64 years: 59.4% (male 585,139/female 481,121)
65 years and over: 5% (2024 est.) (male 46,610/female 42,800)

Dependency ratios: *total dependency ratio:* 68.4 (2024 est.)
youth dependency ratio: 60 (2024 est.)
elderly dependency ratio: 8.4 (2024 est.)
potential support ratio: 11.9 (2024 est.)

Median age: *total:* 22.1 years (2024 est.)
male: 22.7 years
female: 21.5 years
comparison ranking: total 186

Population growth rate: 3.23% (2024 est.)
comparison ranking: 5

Birth rate: 29 births/1,000 population (2024 est.)
comparison ranking: 28

Death rate: 8.9 deaths/1,000 population (2024 est.)
comparison ranking: 61

Net migration rate: 12.1 migrant(s)/1,000 population (2024 est.)
comparison ranking: 6

Population distribution: the two large cities are Bata on the mainland and the capital Malabo on the island of Bioko; small communities are scattered throughout the mainland and the five inhabited islands, as shown in this population distribution map

Urbanization: *urban population:* 74.4% of total population (2023)
rate of urbanization: 3.62% annual rate of change (2020-25 est.)

Major urban areas - population: 297,000 MALABO (capital) (2018)

Sex ratio: *at birth:* 1.03 male(s)/female
0-14 years: 1.07 male(s)/female
15-64 years: 1.22 male(s)/female
65 years and over: 1.09 male(s)/female
total population: 1.16 male(s)/female (2024 est.)

Maternal mortality ratio: 174 deaths/100,000 live births (2023 est.)
comparison ranking: 44

Infant mortality rate: *total:* 77.4 deaths/1,000 live births (2024 est.)
male: 83.3 deaths/1,000 live births
female: 71.3 deaths/1,000 live births
comparison ranking: total 4

Life expectancy at birth: *total population:* 63.9 years (2024 est.)
male: 61.6 years
female: 66.2 years
comparison ranking: total population 210

Total fertility rate: 4.12 children born/woman (2024 est.)
comparison ranking: 21

Gross reproduction rate: 2.03 (2024 est.)

Health expenditure: 3.4% of GDP (2021)
4.4% of national budget (2022 est.)

Physician density: 0.15 physicians/1,000 population (2022)

Obesity - adult prevalence rate: 8% (2016)
comparison ranking: 156

Alcohol consumption per capita: *total:* 6.11 liters of pure alcohol (2019 est.)
beer: 3.83 liters of pure alcohol (2019 est.)
wine: 1.24 liters of pure alcohol (2019 est.)
spirits: 0.99 liters of pure alcohol (2019 est.)
other alcohols: 0.05 liters of pure alcohol (2019 est.)
comparison ranking: total 69

Currently married women (ages 15-49): 60.2% (2023 est.)

ENVIRONMENT

Environmental issues: deforestation (agricultural expansion, fires, and grazing); desertification; water pollution; tap water non-potable; wildlife preservation

International environmental agreements: *party to:* Biodiversity, Climate Change, Climate Change-Kyoto Protocol, Climate Change-Paris Agreement, Desertification, Endangered Species, Hazardous Wastes, Law of the Sea, Marine Dumping-London Convention, Nuclear Test Ban, Ozone Layer Protection, Ship Pollution, Wetlands
signed, but not ratified: Comprehensive Nuclear Test Ban

Climate: tropical; always hot, humid

Urbanization: *urban population:* 74.4% of total population (2023)
rate of urbanization: 3.62% annual rate of change (2020-25 est.)

Carbon dioxide emissions: 5.471 million metric tonnes of CO2 (2023 est.)
from coal and metallurgical coke: 1 metric tonnes of CO2 (2023 est.)
from petroleum and other liquids: 896,000 metric tonnes of CO2 (2023 est.)
from consumed natural gas: 4.575 million metric tonnes of CO2 (2023 est.)
comparison ranking: total emissions 135

Particulate matter emissions: 26.5 micrograms per cubic meter (2019 est.)

Methane emissions: *energy:* 129.8 kt (2022-2024 est.)
agriculture: 0.4 kt (2019-2021 est.)
waste: 10 kt (2019-2021 est.)
other: 2.2 kt (2019-2021 est.)

Waste and recycling: *municipal solid waste generated annually:* 198,400 tons (2024 est.)
percent of municipal solid waste recycled: 23.9% (2022 est.)

Total water withdrawal: *municipal:* 15.8 million cubic meters (2022 est.)
industrial: 3 million cubic meters (2022 est.)
agricultural: 1 million cubic meters (2022 est.)

Total renewable water resources: 26 billion cubic meters (2022 est.)

GOVERNMENT

Country name: *conventional long form:* Republic of Equatorial Guinea
conventional short form: Equatorial Guinea
local long form: Republica de Guinea Ecuatorial (Spanish)/ République de Guinée équatoriale (French)
local short form: Guinea Ecuatorial (Spanish)/Guinée équatoriale (French)
former: Spanish Guinea
etymology: the country is named for the Guinea region of West Africa that lies along the Gulf of Guinea and stretches north to the Sahel; the "equatorial" refers to the fact that the country lies just north of the Equator

Government type: presidential republic

Capital: *name:* Malabo; note - Malabo is on the island of Bioko; some months of the year, the government operates out of Bata on the mainland region.
geographic coordinates: 3 45 N, 8 47 E
time difference: UTC+1 (6 hours ahead of Washington, DC, during Standard Time)
etymology: English settlers who founded the city in 1827 named it Port Clarence after the Duke of CLARENCE; the Spanish renamed it Santa Isabel in 1843, for Queen ISABELLA II of Spain; it was renamed again in 1973 after King MALABO (1837–1937), the last king of the Bubi (local ethnic group)

Administrative divisions: 8 provinces (*provincias*, singular - *provincia*); Annobon, Bioko Norte, Bioko Sur, Centro Sur, Djibloho, Kie-Ntem, Litoral, Wele-Nzas

Legal system: mixed system of civil and customary law

Constitution: *history:* previous 1968, 1973, 1982; approved by referendum 17 November 1991
amendment process: proposed by the president of the republic or supported by three fourths of the membership in either house of the National Assembly; passage requires three-fourths majority vote by both houses of the Assembly and approval in a referendum if requested by the president

International law organization participation: accepts compulsory ICJ jurisdiction; accepts ICCt jurisdiction

Citizenship: *citizenship by birth:* no
citizenship by descent only: at least one parent must be a citizen of Equatorial Guinea
dual citizenship recognized: no
residency requirement for naturalization: 10 years

Suffrage: 18 years of age; universal

Executive branch: *chief of state:* President OBIANG Nguema Mbasogo (since 3 August 1979)
head of government: Prime Minister Manuel Osa Nsue Nsua (since 17 August 2024)
cabinet: Council of Ministers appointed by the president and overseen by the prime minister
election/appointment process: president directly elected by simple-majority popular vote for a 7-year term (eligible for a second term); prime minister and deputy prime ministers appointed by the president
most recent election date: 20 November 2022
election results: 2022: OBIANG Nguema Mbasogo reelected president; percent of vote - OBIANG Nguema Mbasogo (PDGE) 95%, other 6.1%
2016: OBIANG Nguema Mbasogo reelected president; percent of vote - OBIANG Nguema Mbasogo (PDGE) 93.5%, other 6.5%
expected date of next election: 2029

Legislative branch: *legislature name:* Parliament (Parlamento)
legislative structure: bicameral

Legislative branch - lower chamber: *chamber name:* Chamber of Deputies (Cámara de los Diputados)
number of seats: 100 (all directly elected)
electoral system: proportional representation
scope of elections: full renewal
term in office: 5 years
most recent election date: 11/20/2022
parties elected and seats per party: Democratic Party of Equatorial Guinea (PDGE) and its allies (100)
percentage of women in chamber: 31%
expected date of next election: November 2027

Legislative branch - upper chamber: *chamber name:* Senate (Senado)
number of seats: 70 (55 directly elected; 15 appointed)
electoral system: proportional representation
scope of elections: full renewal
term in office: 5 years
most recent election date: 11/20/2022
parties elected and seats per party: Democratic Party of Equatorial Guinea (PDGE) and its allies (55)
percentage of women in chamber: 25%
expected date of next election: November 2027

Judicial branch: *highest court(s):* Supreme Court of Justice (consists of the President of the Supreme Court and nine judges organized into civil, criminal, commercial, labor, administrative, and customary sections); Constitutional Court (consists of the court president and 4 members)
judge selection and term of office: Supreme Court judges appointed by the president for five-year terms; Constitutional Court members appointed by the president, 2 of whom are nominated by the Chamber of Deputies
subordinate courts: Court of Guarantees; military courts; Courts of Appeal; first instance tribunals; district and county tribunals

Political parties: Center Right Union or UCD
Convergence Party for Social Democracy or CPDS
Democratic Party for Equatorial Guinea or PDGE
Liberal Democratic Convention or CLD
Liberal Party or PL
National Congress of Equatorial Guinea (CNGE)
National Democratic Party (PNDGE)
National Democratic Union or UDENA
National Union for Democracy PUNDGE
Popular Action of Equatorial Guinea or APGE
Popular Union or UP
Progressive Democratic Alliance or ADP
Social and Popular Convergence Party or CSDP
Social Democratic Coalition Party (PCSD)
Social Democratic Party of Equatorial Guinea or PSDGE
Social Democratic Union or UDS
Socialist Party of Equatorial Guinea

Diplomatic representation in the US: *chief of mission:* Ambassador Dr. Crisantos OBAMA ONDO (since 27 February 2024)
chancery: 2020 16th Street NW, Washington, DC 20009
telephone: [1] (202) 518-5700

FAX: [1] (202) 518-5252
email address and website: info@egembassydc.com
https://www.egembassydc.com/
consulate(s) general: Houston

Diplomatic representation from the US: *chief of mission:* Ambassador David R. GILMOUR (since 24 May 2022)
embassy: Malabo II Highway (between the Headquarters of Sonagas and the offices of the United Nations), Malabo
mailing address: 2320 Malabo Place, Washington, DC 20521-2520
telephone: [240] 333 09-57-41
email address and website: Malaboconsular@state.gov
https://gq.usembassy.gov/

International organization participation: ACP, AfDB, AU, BDEAC, CEMAC, CPLP, FAO, Francophonie, FZ, G-77, IBRD, ICAO, ICRM, IDA, IFAD, IFC, IFRCS, ILO, IMF, IMO, Interpol, IOC, IPU, ITSO, ITU, MIGA, NAM, OAS (observer), OIF, OPCW, UN, UNCTAD, UNESCO, UNIDO, UNWTO, UPU, WHO, WIPO, WTO (observer)

Independence: 12 October 1968 (from Spain)

National holiday: Independence Day, 12 October (1968)

Flag: *description:* three equal horizontal bands of green (top), white, and red, with a blue isosceles triangle based on the left side and the coat of arms centered in the white band; the coat of arms has six six-pointed yellow stars (representing the mainland and five offshore islands) above a gray shield with a silk-cotton tree; below is a scroll with the motto UNIDAD, PAZ, JUSTICIA (Unity, Peace, Justice)
meaning: green stands for the jungle and natural resources, blue for the sea, white for peace, and red for the fight for independence

National symbol(s): silk cotton tree

National color(s): green, white, red, blue

National coat of arms: the national symbol, the silk cotton tree, is in the center of the coat of arms; the tree represents the location where the first treaty was signed between local rulers and the Portuguese; the stars above the tree symbolize the mainland and the five offshore islands; a ribbon below the shield displays the national motto, "Unidad, Paz, Justicia" (Unity, Peace, Justice)

National anthem(s): *title:* "Caminemos pisando la senda" (Let Us Tread the Path)
lyrics/music: Atanasio Ndongo MIYONO/Atanasio Ndongo MIYONO or Ramiro Sanchez LOPEZ (disputed)
history: adopted 1968

ECONOMY

Economic overview: growing CEMAC economy and new OPEC member; large oil and gas reserves; targeting economic diversification and poverty reduction; still recovering from CEMAC crisis; improving public financial management; persistent poverty; hard-hit by COVID-19

Real GDP (purchasing power parity): $29.248 billion (2024 est.)
$28.985 billion (2023 est.)
$30.539 billion (2022 est.)
note: data in 2021 dollars
comparison ranking: 147

Real GDP growth rate: 0.9% (2024 est.)
-5.1% (2023 est.)
3.2% (2022 est.)
note: annual GDP % growth based on constant local currency
comparison ranking: 181

Real GDP per capita: $15,500 (2024 est.)
$15,700 (2023 est.)
$16,900 (2022 est.)
note: data in 2021 dollars
comparison ranking: 123

GDP (official exchange rate): $12.766 billion (2024 est.)
note: data in current dollars at official exchange rate

Inflation rate (consumer prices): 4.8% (2022 est.)
-0.1% (2021 est.)
4.8% (2020 est.)
note: annual % change based on consumer prices
comparison ranking: 144

GDP - composition, by sector of origin: *agriculture:* 3.1% (2024 est.)
industry: 45.8% (2024 est.)
services: 51.1% (2024 est.)
note: figures may not total 100% due to non-allocated consumption not captured in sector-reported data
comparison rankings: agriculture 130; industry 12; services 142

GDP - composition, by end use: *household consumption:* 52.9% (2024 est.)
government consumption: 28.3% (2024 est.)
investment in fixed capital: 9.1% (2024 est.)
investment in inventories: -0.1% (2024 est.)
exports of goods and services: 35.2% (2024 est.)
imports of goods and services: -25.4% (2024 est.)
note: figures may not total 100% due to rounding or gaps in data collection

Agricultural products: sweet potatoes, cassava, plantains, oil palm fruit, root vegetables, bananas, coconuts, coffee, cocoa beans, chicken (2023)
note: top ten agricultural products based on tonnage

Industries: petroleum, natural gas, sawmilling

Industrial production growth rate: 0.8% (2024 est.)
note: annual % change in industrial value added based on constant local currency
comparison ranking: 120

Labor force: 715,000 (2024 est.)
note: number of people ages 15 or older who are employed or seeking work
comparison ranking: 155

Unemployment rate: 7.9% (2024 est.)
8.4% (2023 est.)
8.5% (2022 est.)
note: % of labor force seeking employment
comparison ranking: 134

Youth unemployment rate (ages 15-24): *total:* 14.7% (2024 est.)
male: 13.9% (2024 est.)
female: 15.7% (2024 est.)
note: % of labor force ages 15-24 seeking employment
comparison ranking: total 80

Gini Index coefficient - distribution of family income: 38.5 (2022 est.)
note: index (0-100) of income distribution; higher values represent greater inequality
comparison ranking: 50

Household income or consumption by percentage share: *lowest 10%:* 2.6% (2022 est.)
highest 10%: 29.1% (2022 est.)
note: % share of income accruing to lowest and highest 10% of population

Remittances: 0% of GDP (2023 est.)
0% of GDP (2022 est.)
0% of GDP (2021 est.)
note: personal transfers and compensation between resident and non-resident individuals/households/entities

Budget: *revenues:* $3.62 billion (2022 est.)
expenditures: $2.051 billion (2022 est.)
note: central government revenues and expenses (excluding grants/extrabudgetary units/social security funds) converted to US dollars at average official exchange rate for year indicated

Taxes and other revenues: 6.6% (of GDP) (2022 est.)
note: central government tax revenue as a % of GDP
comparison ranking: 145

Exports: $4.489 billion (2024 est.)
$4.516 billion (2023 est.)
$7.25 billion (2022 est.)
note: GDP expenditure basis - exports of goods and services in current dollars
comparison ranking: 145

Exports - partners: China 27%, Netherlands 12%, Spain 10%, Italy 7%, Germany 6% (2023)
note: top five export partners based on percentage share of exports

Exports - commodities: crude petroleum, natural gas, alcohols, wood, scrap iron (2023)
note: top five export commodities based on value in dollars

Imports: $3.24 billion (2024 est.)
$3.065 billion (2023 est.)
$3.948 billion (2022 est.)
note: GDP expenditure basis - imports of goods and services in current dollars
comparison ranking: 163

Imports - partners: China 20%, Spain 17%, USA 10%, Gabon 5%, UK 5% (2023)
note: top five import partners based on percentage share of imports

Imports - commodities: ships, poultry, plastic products, beer, valves (2023)
note: top five import commodities based on value in dollars

Reserves of foreign exchange and gold: $1.538 billion (2023 est.)
$1.458 billion (2022 est.)
$44.271 million (2021 est.)
note: holdings of gold (year-end prices)/foreign exchange/special drawing rights in current dollars
comparison ranking: 134

Exchange rates: Cooperation Financiere en Afrique Centrale francs (XAF) per US dollar -

Exchange rates: 606.345 (2024 est.)
606.57 (2023 est.)
623.76 (2022 est.)
554.531 (2021 est.)
575.586 (2020 est.)

ENERGY

Electricity access: *electrification - total population:* 67% (2022 est.)
electrification - urban areas: 89.8%
electrification - rural areas: 1.4%

Electricity: *installed generating capacity:* 349,000 kW (2023 est.)
consumption: 1.402 billion kWh (2023 est.)
transmission/distribution losses: 170.527 million kWh (2023 est.)

comparison rankings: installed generating capacity 159; consumption 157; transmission/distribution losses 61

Electricity generation sources: *fossil fuels:* 68.6% of total installed capacity (2023 est.)
hydroelectricity: 31.4% of total installed capacity (2023 est.)

Coal: *imports:* 8 metric tons (2023 est.)

Petroleum: *total petroleum production:* 98,000 bbl/day (2023 est.)
refined petroleum consumption: 6,000 bbl/day (2023 est.)
crude oil estimated reserves: 1.1 billion barrels (2021 est.)

Natural gas: *production:* 6.013 billion cubic meters (2023 est.)
consumption: 2.332 billion cubic meters (2023 est.)
exports: 3.63 billion cubic meters (2023 est.)
proven reserves: 139.007 billion cubic meters (2021 est.)

Energy consumption per capita: 54.509 million Btu/person (2023 est.)
comparison ranking: 91

COMMUNICATIONS

Telephones - fixed lines: *total subscriptions:* 11,000 (2022 est.)
subscriptions per 100 inhabitants: 1 (2022 est.) less than 1
comparison ranking: total subscriptions 184

Telephones - mobile cellular: *total subscriptions:* 893,000 (2022 est.)
subscriptions per 100 inhabitants: 53 (2022 est.)
comparison ranking: total subscriptions 167

Broadcast media: the state maintains control of broadcast media; 1 state-owned TV station, 1 private TV station owned by the president's eldest son, 1 state-owned radio station, and 1 private radio station owned by the president's eldest son; satellite TV service is available; transmissions of multiple international broadcasters are generally accessible (2019)

Internet country code: .gq

Internet users: *percent of population:* 60% (2023 est.)

Broadband - fixed subscriptions: *total:* 2,000 (2022 est.)
subscriptions per 100 inhabitants: (2022 est.) less than 1
comparison ranking: total 202

TRANSPORTATION

Civil aircraft registration country code prefix: 3C

Airports: 7 (2025)
comparison ranking: 171

Merchant marine: *total:* 53 (2023)
by type: bulk carrier 1, general cargo 16, oil tanker 7, other 29
comparison ranking: total 118

Ports: *total ports:* 7 (2024)
large: 0
medium: 0
small: 1
very small: 6
ports with oil terminals: 6
key ports: Bata, Ceiba Terminal, Cogo, Luba, Malabo, Punta Europa Terminal, Serpentina Terminal

MILITARY AND SECURITY

Military and security forces: Equatorial Guinea Armed Forces (Fuerzas Armadas de Guinea Ecuatorial, FAGE): Army, Navy, Air Force, Gendarmerie (Guardia Civil) (2025)
note: the National Police report to the Ministry of National Security, while the Gendarmerie reports to the Ministry of National Defense; police generally are responsible for maintaining law and order in the cities, while gendarmes are responsible for security outside cities and for special events

Military expenditures: 1% of GDP (2024)
1.6% of GDP (2023 est.)
1.3% of GDP (2022 est.)
1.3% of GDP (2021 est.)
1.6% of GDP (2020 est.)

Military and security service personnel strengths: estimated 2,000 active Armed Forces, including Gendarmerie (2025)

Military equipment inventories and acquisitions: the FAGE is armed with mostly older (typically Soviet-era) and second-hand weapons systems; in recent years, it has sought to modernize its naval inventory with purchases of vessels from several countries, including Bulgaria and Israel; China and Russia have also supplied some equipment to the FAGE (2024)

Military service age and obligation: 18 years of age for selective compulsory military service, although conscription is rare in practice; 24-month service obligation (2023)

Military - note: the Armed Forces of Equatorial Guinea (FAGE) are responsible for defending the territory and sovereignty of the country; the FAGE also has some internal security duties, including fulfilling some police functions in border areas, sensitive sites, and high-traffic areas; maritime security, particularly protecting offshore oil installations and combating piracy and crime in the Gulf of Guinea, is a key priority (2024)

TRANSNATIONAL ISSUES

Refugees and internally displaced persons: *refugees:* 5 (2024 est.)

ERITREA

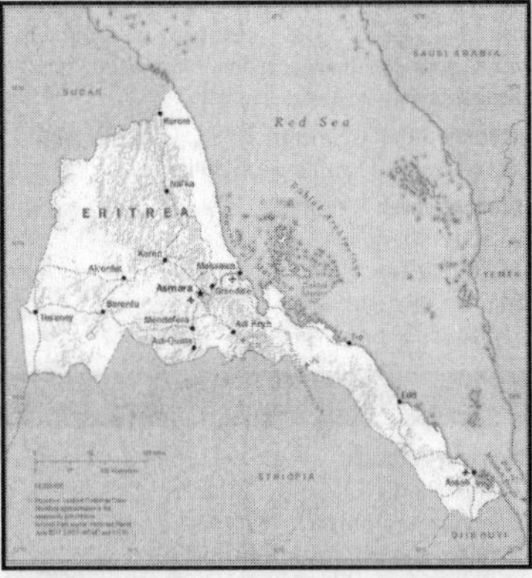

INTRODUCTION

Background: Eritrea won independence from Italian colonial control in 1941, but the UN only established it as an autonomous region within the Ethiopian federation in 1952, after a decade of British administrative control. Ethiopia's full annexation of Eritrea as a province 10 years later sparked a violent 30-year conflict for independence that ended in 1991 with Eritrean fighters defeating government forces. Eritreans overwhelmingly approved independence in a 1993 referendum. ISAIAS Afwerki has been Eritrea's only president since independence; his rule, particularly since 2001, has been characterized by highly autocratic and repressive actions. His government has created a highly militarized society by instituting an unpopular program of mandatory conscription into national service – divided between military and civilian service – of indefinite length.

A two-and-a-half-year border war with Ethiopia that erupted in 1998 ended under UN auspices in 2000. Ethiopia rejected a subsequent 2007 Eritrea-Ethiopia Boundary Commission (EEBC) demarcation. More than a decade of a tense "no peace, no war" stalemate ended in 2018 when the newly elected Ethiopian prime minister accepted the EEBC's 2007 ruling, and the two countries signed declarations of peace and friendship. Eritrean leaders then engaged in intensive diplomacy around the Horn of Africa, bolstering regional peace, security, and cooperation, as well as brokering rapprochements between governments and opposition groups. In 2018, the UN Security Council lifted an arms embargo that had been imposed on Eritrea since 2009, after the UN Somalia-Eritrea Monitoring Group reported they had not found evidence of Eritrean support in recent years for al-Shabaab. The country's rapprochement with Ethiopia led to a resumption of economic ties, but the level of air transport, trade, and tourism have remained roughly the same since late 2020.

The Eritrean economy remains agriculture-dependent, and the country is still one of Africa's poorest nations. Eritrea faced new international condemnation and US sanctions in mid-2021 for its participation in the war in Ethiopia's Tigray Regional State, where Eritrean forces were found to have committed war crimes and crimes against humanity. As most Eritrean troops were departing northern Ethiopia in January 2023, ISAIAS began a series of diplomatic engagements aimed at bolstering Eritrea's foreign partnerships and regional influence. Despite the country's improved relations with its neighbors, ISAIAS has not let up on repression, and conscription and militarization continue.

GEOGRAPHY

Location: Eastern Africa, bordering the Red Sea, between Djibouti and Sudan

Geographic coordinates: 15 00 N, 39 00 E

Map references: Africa

Area: *total:* 117,600 sq km
land: 101,000 sq km
water: 16,600 sq km
comparison ranking: total 101

Area - comparative: slightly smaller than Pennsylvania

Land boundaries: *total:* 1,840 km
border countries (3): Djibouti 125 km; Ethiopia 1,033 km; Sudan 682 km

Coastline: 2,234 km (mainland on Red Sea 1,151 km; islands in Red Sea 1,083 km)

Maritime claims: *territorial sea:* 12 nm

Climate: hot, dry desert strip along Red Sea coast; cooler and wetter in the central highlands (up to 61 cm of rainfall annually, heaviest June to September); semiarid in western hills and lowlands

Terrain: dominated by extension of Ethiopian north-south trending highlands, descending on the east to a coastal desert plain, on the northwest to hilly terrain and on the southwest to flat-to-rolling plains

Elevation: *highest point:* Soira 3,018 m
lowest point: near Kulul within the Danakil Depression -75 m
mean elevation: 853 m

Natural resources: gold, potash, zinc, copper, salt, possibly oil and natural gas, fish

Land use: *agricultural land:* 62.7% (2022 est.)
arable land: 5.7% (2022 est.)
permanent crops: 0% (2022 est.)
permanent pasture: 57% (2022 est.)
forest: 8.7% (2022 est.)
other: 28.6% (2022 est.)

Irrigated land: 210 sq km (2012)

Population distribution: density is highest in the center of the country, in and around the cities of Asmara (capital) and Keren; smaller settlements exist in the north and south, as shown in this population distribution map

Natural hazards: frequent droughts, rare earthquakes and volcanoes; locust swarms
volcanism: Dubbi (1,625 m), which last erupted in 1861, was the country's only historically
active volcano until Nabro (2,218 m) came to life in 2011

Geography - note: strategic geopolitical position along world's busiest shipping lanes

PEOPLE AND SOCIETY

Population: *total:* 6,343,956 (2024 est.)
male: 3,122,433
female: 3,221,523
comparison rankings: total 111; male 111; female 110

Nationality: *noun:* Eritrean(s)
adjective: Eritrean

Ethnic groups: Tigrinya 50%, Tigre 30%, Saho 4%, Afar 4%, Kunama 4%, Bilen 3%, Hedareb/Beja 2%, Nara 2%, Rashaida 1% (2021 est.)
note: data represent Eritrea's nine recognized ethnic groups

Languages: Tigrinya (official), Arabic (official), English (official), Tigre, Kunama, Afar, other Cushitic languages

Religions: Eritrean Orthodox, Roman Catholic, Evangelical Lutheran, Sunni Muslim

Age structure: *0-14 years:* 35.7% (male 1,138,382/female 1,123,925)
15-64 years: 60.3% (male 1,882,547/female 1,944,266)
65 years and over: 4% (2024 est.) (male 101,504/female 153,332)

Dependency ratios: *total dependency ratio:* 65.8 (2024 est.)
youth dependency ratio: 59.1 (2024 est.)
elderly dependency ratio: 6.7 (2024 est.)
potential support ratio: 15 (2024 est.)

Median age: *total:* 21.3 years (2024 est.)
male: 20.8 years
female: 21.8 years
comparison ranking: total 192

Population growth rate: 1.12% (2024 est.)
comparison ranking: 82

Birth rate: 26.3 births/1,000 population (2024 est.)
comparison ranking: 41

Death rate: 6.5 deaths/1,000 population (2024 est.)
comparison ranking: 139

Net migration rate: -8.7 migrant(s)/1,000 population (2024 est.)
comparison ranking: 220

Population distribution: density is highest in the center of the country, in and around the cities of Asmara (capital) and Keren; smaller settlements exist in the north and south, as shown in this population distribution map

Urbanization: *urban population:* 43.3% of total population (2023)
rate of urbanization: 3.67% annual rate of change (2020-25 est.)

Major urban areas - population: 1.073 million ASMARA (capital) (2023)

Sex ratio: *at birth:* 1.03 male(s)/female
0-14 years: 1.01 male(s)/female
15-64 years: 0.97 male(s)/female
65 years and over: 0.66 male(s)/female
total population: 0.97 male(s)/female (2024 est.)

Mother's mean age at first birth: 21.3 years (2010 est.)
note: data represents median age at first birth among women 25-29

Maternal mortality ratio: 291 deaths/100,000 live births (2023 est.)
comparison ranking: 25

Infant mortality rate: *total:* 39.8 deaths/1,000 live births (2024 est.)
male: 46.6 deaths/1,000 live births
female: 32.8 deaths/1,000 live births
comparison ranking: total 29

Life expectancy at birth: *total population:* 67.5 years (2024 est.)
male: 64.9 years
female: 70.2 years
comparison ranking: total population 197

Total fertility rate: 3.43 children born/woman (2024 est.)
comparison ranking: 37

Gross reproduction rate: 1.69 (2024 est.)

Health expenditure: 4.2% of GDP (2021)
2.4% of national budget (2022 est.)

Physician density: 0.09 physicians/1,000 population (2022)

Hospital bed density: 1 beds/1,000 population (2020 est.)

Obesity - adult prevalence rate: 5% (2016)
comparison ranking: 183

Alcohol consumption per capita: *total:* 0.93 liters of pure alcohol (2019 est.)
beer: 0.42 liters of pure alcohol (2019 est.)
wine: 0 liters of pure alcohol (2019 est.)
spirits: 0 liters of pure alcohol (2019 est.)
other alcohols: 0.51 liters of pure alcohol (2019 est.)
comparison ranking: total 153

Tobacco use: *total:* 7.5% (2020 est.)
male: 14.7% (2020 est.)
female: 0.2% (2020 est.)
comparison ranking: total 148

Currently married women (ages 15-49): 52.3% (2023 est.)

School life expectancy (primary to tertiary education): *total:* 8 years (2015 est.)
male: 9 years (2015 est.)
female: 7 years (2015 est.)

ENVIRONMENT

Environmental issues: deforestation; desertification; soil erosion; overgrazing

International environmental agreements: *party to:* Biodiversity, Climate Change, Climate Change-Kyoto Protocol, Comprehensive Nuclear Test Ban, Desertification, Endangered Species, Hazardous Wastes, Ozone Layer Protection, Whaling
signed, but not ratified: Climate Change-Paris Agreement

Climate: hot, dry desert strip along Red Sea coast; cooler and wetter in the central highlands (up to 61 cm of rainfall annually, heaviest June to September); semiarid in western hills and lowlands

Urbanization: *urban population:* 43.3% of total population (2023)
rate of urbanization: 3.67% annual rate of change (2020-25 est.)

Carbon dioxide emissions: 733,000 metric tonnes of CO_2 (2023 est.)
from petroleum and other liquids: 733,000 metric tonnes of CO_2 (2023 est.)
comparison ranking: total emissions 179

Particulate matter emissions: 22.7 micrograms per cubic meter (2019 est.)

Methane emissions: *energy:* 15.7 kt (2022-2024 est.)
agriculture: 117.4 kt (2019-2021 est.)
waste: 20.5 kt (2019-2021 est.)
other: 2.8 kt (2019-2021 est.)

Waste and recycling: *municipal solid waste generated annually:* 727,000 tons (2024 est.)
percent of municipal solid waste recycled: 6.8% (2022 est.)

Total water withdrawal: *municipal:* 31 million cubic meters (2022 est.)
industrial: 1 million cubic meters (2022 est.)
agricultural: 550 million cubic meters (2022 est.)

Total renewable water resources: 7.315 billion cubic meters (2022 est.)

GOVERNMENT

Country name: *conventional long form:* State of Eritrea
conventional short form: Eritrea
local long form: Hagere Ertra
local short form: Ertra
former: Eritrea Autonomous Region in Ethiopia
etymology: the country name derives from the ancient Greek name *Erythra Thalassa*, meaning "Red Sea," the body of water that borders the country

Government type: presidential republic

Capital: *name:* Asmara
geographic coordinates: 15 20 N, 38 56 E
time difference: UTC+3 (8 hours ahead of Washington, DC, during Standard Time)
etymology: the name's origin is unclear; according to Tigrinya oral tradition, the name is part of a phrase meaning "the women made them unite," referring to a group of women who made four clans unite to defeat a common enemy; *asmara* also means "flowery wood" in the Tigrinya language

Administrative divisions: 6 regions (*zobatat*, singular - *zoba*); 'Anseba, Debub (South), Debubawi K'eyyih Bahri (Southern Red Sea), Gash-Barka, Ma'ikel (Central), Semienawi K'eyyih Bahri (Northern Red Sea)

Legal system: mixed system of civil, customary, and Islamic religious law

Constitution: *history:* ratified by the Constituent Assembly 23 May 1997 (never implemented)
amendment process: proposed by the president of Eritrea or by assent of at least one half of the National Assembly membership; passage requires at least an initial three-quarters majority vote by the Assembly and, after one year, final passage by at least four-fifths majority vote by the Assembly

International law organization participation: has not submitted an ICJ jurisdiction declaration; non-party state to the ICCt

Citizenship: *citizenship by birth:* no
citizenship by descent only: at least one parent must be a citizen of Eritrea
dual citizenship recognized: no
residency requirement for naturalization: 20 years

Suffrage: 18 years of age; universal

Executive branch: *chief of state:* President ISAIAS Afwerki (since 24 May 1993)
head of government: President ISAIAS Afwerki (since 8 June 1993)
cabinet: State Council appointed by the president
election/appointment process: president indirectly elected by the National Assembly for a 5-year term (eligible for a second term), according to the constitution
most recent election date: 24 May 1993, following independence from Ethiopia
election results: *1993:* ISAIAS Afwerki elected president by the transitional National Assembly; percent of National Assembly vote - ISAIAS Afwerki (PFDJ) 95%, other 5%
expected date of next election: postponed indefinitely
note: the president is both chief of state and head of government and is head of the State Council and National Assembly

Legislative branch: *legislature name:* National Assembly (Hagerawi Baito)
legislative structure: unicameral
number of seats: 150 (all indirectly elected)
scope of elections: full renewal
term in office: 4 years
most recent election date: 2/1/1994
note: in 1997, after the new constitution was adopted, the government formed a Transitional National Assembly to serve as the country's legislative body until countrywide elections to form a National Assembly could be held; the constitution stipulates that once past the transition stage, all National Assembly members will be elected by secret ballot of all eligible voters; National Assembly elections scheduled for December 2001 were postponed indefinitely due to the war with Ethiopia; as of 2025, no sitting legislative body exists

Judicial branch: *highest court(s):* High Court (consists of 20 judges and organized into civil, commercial, criminal, labor, administrative, and customary sections)
judge selection and term of office: High Court judges appointed by the president
subordinate courts: regional/zonal courts; community courts; special courts; sharia courts (for issues dealing with Muslim marriage, inheritance, and family); military courts

Political parties: People's Front for Democracy and Justice or PFDJ (the only party recognized by the government)

Diplomatic representation in the US: *chief of mission:* Ambassador (vacant); Chargé d'Affaires Berhane Gebrehiwet SOLOMON (since 15 March 2011)
chancery: 1708 New Hampshire Avenue NW, Washington, DC 20009
telephone: [1] (202) 319-1991
FAX: [1] (202) 319-1304
email address and website: embassyeritrea@embassyeritrea.org
https://us.embassyeritrea.org/

Diplomatic representation from the US: *chief of mission:* Ambassador (vacant); Chargé d'Affaires Christine E. MEYER (since July 2025)
embassy: 179 Alaa Street, Asmara
mailing address: 7170 Asmara Place, Washington DC 20521-7170
telephone: [291] (1) 12-00-04
FAX: [291] (1) 12-75-84
email address and website: consularasmara@state.gov
https://er.usembassy.gov/

International organization participation: ACP, AfDB, AU, COMESA, FAO, G-77, IAEA, IBRD, ICAO, ICC (NGOs), IDA, IFAD, IFC, IFRCS (observer), IGAD, ILO, IMF, IMO, Interpol, IOC, ISO (correspondent), ITU, ITUC (NGOs), LAS (observer), MIGA, NAM, OPCW, PCA, UN, UNCTAD, UNESCO, UNHRC, UNIDO, UNWTO, UPU, WCO, WFTU (NGOs), WHO, WIPO, WMO

Independence: 24 May 1993 (from Ethiopia)

National holiday: Independence Day, 24 May (1991)

Flag: *description:* a red isosceles triangle (based on the left side) divides the flag into two right triangles; the upper triangle is green, the lower is blue; a gold wreath around a gold olive branch is on the left side of the red triangle
meaning: green stands for the country's agriculture economy, red for the blood shed in the fight for freedom, and blue for the sea's bounty; the shape of the red triangle mimics the country's shape
note: one of four national flags that reflect the country's shape in the flag design; the others are Bosnia and Herzegovina, Brazil, and Vanuatu

National symbol(s): camel

National color(s): green, red, blue

National coat of arms: Eritrea adopted its coat of arms on May 24, 1993, when it won independence from Ethiopia; the camel was used to transport supplies and goods during the war, and it became a symbol of the country's success; the olive wreath represents peace, reconciliation, and harmony; under the camel is name of the country in its three official languages: Tigrinya, English, and Arabic

National anthem(s): *title:* "Ertra, Ertra, Ertra" (Eritrea, Eritrea, Eritrea)
lyrics/music: SOLOMON Tsehaye Beraki/Isaac Abraham MEHAREZGI and ARON Tekle Tesfatsion
history: adopted 1993, after gaining independence from Ethiopia

National heritage: *total World Heritage Sites:* 1 (cultural)
selected World Heritage Site locales: Asmara: A Modernist African City

ECONOMY

Economic overview: largely agrarian economy with a significant mining sector; substantial fiscal surplus due to tight controls; high and vulnerable debts; increased Ethiopian trade and shared port usage decreasing prices; financial and economic data integrity challenges

Real GDP (purchasing power parity): $2.534 billion (2024 est.)
$2.465 billion (2023 est.)
$2.398 billion (2022 est.)
note: data in 2015 dollars
comparison ranking: 194

Real GDP growth rate: 5% (2017 est.)
1.9% (2016 est.)
2.6% (2015 est.)
comparison ranking: 45

Real GDP per capita: $700 (2024 est.)
$700 (2023 est.)
$700 (2022 est.)
note: data in 2015 dollars
comparison ranking: 216

GDP (official exchange rate): $2.535 billion (2024 est.)
note: data in current dollars at official exchange rate

Inflation rate (consumer prices): 7.4% (2022 est.)
6.6% (2021 est.)
5.6% (2020 est.)
note: annual % change based on consumer prices
comparison ranking: 166

Agricultural products: sorghum, milk, barley, vegetables, root vegetables, cereals, pulses, wheat, beef, maize (2023)
note: top ten agricultural products based on tonnage

Industries: food processing, beverages, clothing and textiles, light manufacturing, salt, cement

Labor force: 1.71 million (2024 est.)
note: number of people ages 15 or older who are employed or seeking work
comparison ranking: 131

Unemployment rate: 5.6% (2024 est.)
5.6% (2023 est.)
5.7% (2022 est.)
note: % of labor force seeking employment
comparison ranking: 108

Youth unemployment rate (ages 15-24): *total:* 9.4% (2024 est.)

male: 8.5% (2024 est.)
female: 10.5% (2024 est.)
note: % of labor force ages 15-24 seeking employment
comparison ranking: total 127

Budget: *revenues:* $633 million (2018 est.)
expenditures: $549 million (2018 est.)

Exports: $624.3 million (2017 est.)
$485.4 million (2016 est.)
$374.898 million (2011 est.)
comparison ranking: 189

Exports - partners: China 67%, UAE 26%, Philippines 5%, Italy 1%, Croatia 1% (2023)
note: top five export partners based on percentage share of exports

Exports - commodities: copper ore, zinc ore, gold, garments, liquor (2023)
note: top five export commodities based on value in dollars

Imports: $494.229 million (2010 est.)
$435.275 million (2009 est.)
comparison ranking: 202

Imports - partners: China 32%, UAE 27%, Turkey 9%, USA 7%, Italy 5% (2023)
note: top five import partners based on percentage share of imports

Imports - commodities: trucks, sorghum, construction vehicles, wheat flours, other foods (2023)
note: top five import commodities based on value in dollars

Reserves of foreign exchange and gold: $191.694 million (2019 est.)
$163.034 million (2018 est.)
$143.412 million (2017 est.)
note: holdings of gold (year-end prices)/foreign exchange/special drawing rights in current dollars
comparison ranking: 173

Debt - external: $461.376 million (2023 est.)
note: present value of external debt in current US dollars
comparison ranking: 113

Exchange rates: nakfa (ERN) per US dollar -

Exchange rates: 15.075 (2024 est.)
15.075 (2023 est.)
15.075 (2022 est.)
15.075 (2021 est.)
15.075 (2020 est.)

ENERGY

Electricity access: *electrification - total population:* 55.4% (2022 est.)
electrification - urban areas: 75.5%
electrification - rural areas: 36%

Electricity: *installed generating capacity:* 243,000 kW (2023 est.)
consumption: 388.987 million kWh (2023 est.)
transmission/distribution losses: 51.528 million kWh (2023 est.)
comparison rankings: installed generating capacity 169; consumption 182; transmission/distribution losses 39

Electricity generation sources: *fossil fuels:* 89.1% of total installed capacity (2023 est.)
solar: 10.7% of total installed capacity (2023 est.)
wind: 0.2% of total installed capacity (2023 est.)

Petroleum: *refined petroleum consumption:* 5,000 bbl/day (2023 est.)

Energy consumption per capita: 2.977 million Btu/person (2023 est.)
comparison ranking: 179

COMMUNICATIONS

Telephones - fixed lines: *total subscriptions:* 66,000 (2021 est.)
subscriptions per 100 inhabitants: 2 (2022 est.)
comparison ranking: total subscriptions 149

Telephones - mobile cellular: *total subscriptions:* 1.8 million (2021 est.)
subscriptions per 100 inhabitants: 50 (2021 est.)
comparison ranking: total subscriptions 154

Broadcast media: government controls broadcast media, with private ownership prohibited; 1 state-owned TV station; 2 state-owned radio networks; purchases of satellite dishes and subscriptions to international broadcast media are permitted (2023)

Internet country code: .er

Internet users: *percent of population:* 20% (2023 est.)

Broadband - fixed subscriptions: *total:* 6,000 (2022 est.)
subscriptions per 100 inhabitants: (2022 est.) less than 1
comparison ranking: total 194

TRANSPORTATION

Civil aircraft registration country code prefix: E3

Airports: 11 (2025)
comparison ranking: 155

Railways: *total:* 306 km (2018)
narrow gauge: 306 km (2018) 0.950-m gauge

Merchant marine: *total:* 9 (2023)
by type: general cargo 4, oil tanker 1, other 4
comparison ranking: total 161

Ports: *total ports:* 2 (2024)
large: 0
medium: 0
small: 2
very small: 0
ports with oil terminals: 2
key ports: Assab, Mitsiwa Harbor

MILITARY AND SECURITY

Military and security forces: Eritrean Defense Forces (EDF): Eritrean Ground Forces, Eritrean Navy, Eritrean Air Force; People's Militia (aka People's Army or Hizbawi Serawit) (2024)
note: police are responsible for maintaining internal security, but the government sometimes uses the armed forces, reserves, demobilized soldiers, or civilian militia to meet domestic as well as external security requirements; the armed forces have authority to arrest and detain civilians

Military expenditures: 10% of GDP (2019 est.)
10.2% of GDP (2018 est.)
10.3% of GDP (2017 est.)
10.4% of GDP (2016 est.)
10.6% of GDP (2015 est.)

Military and security service personnel strengths: available information varies widely; estimated 150,000-200,000 active Defense Forces (2025)

Military equipment inventories and acquisitions: the EDF's inventory is comprised primarily of Soviet-era weapons and equipment (2024)

Military service age and obligation: Eritrea mandates military service for all citizens age 18-40; 18-month conscript service obligation, which reportedly includes 4-6 months of military training and 12 months of military or other national service (military service is most common); in practice, military and national service is often extended indefinitely; citizens up to the age of 59 eligible for recall during mobilization (2024)

Military - note: the military's primary responsibilities are external defense, border security, and providing the regime a vehicle for national cohesion; the conscript-based Army is the dominant service
since the country's independence in 1991, the Eritrean military has participated in numerous conflicts, including the Hanish Island Crisis with Yemen (1995), the First Congo War (1996-1997), the Second Sudanese Civil War (1996-1998), the Eritrea-Ethiopia War (1998-2000), the Djiboutian-Eritrean border conflict (2008), and the Tigray conflict in Ethiopia (2020-2022); during the Tigray conflict, the Eritrean Defense Forces were accused of human rights abuses; in recent years, it has provided training support to the military of Somalia (2025)

TRANSNATIONAL ISSUES

Refugees and internally displaced persons: *refugees:* 119 (2024 est.)

Trafficking in persons: *tier rating:* Tier 3 — Eritrea does not fully meet the minimum standards for the elimination of trafficking and is not making significant efforts to do so, therefore Eritrea remained on Tier 3; for more details, go to: https://www.state.gov/reports/2025-trafficking-in-persons-report/eritrea/

ESTONIA

INTRODUCTION

Background: After centuries of Danish, Swedish, German, and Russian rule, Estonia attained independence in 1918. Forcibly incorporated into the USSR in 1940 – an action never recognized by the US and many other countries – it regained its freedom in 1991 with the collapse of the Soviet Union. Since the last Russian troops left in 1994, Estonia has been free to promote economic and political ties with the West. It joined both NATO and the EU in 2004, formally joined the OECD in 2010, and adopted the euro as its official currency in 2011.

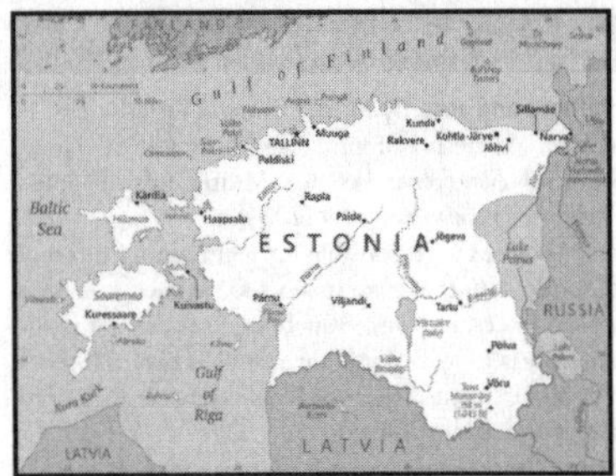

GEOGRAPHY

Location: Eastern Europe, bordering the Baltic Sea and Gulf of Finland, between Latvia and Russia

Geographic coordinates: 59 00 N, 26 00 E

Map references: Europe

Area: *total:* 45,228 sq km
land: 42,388 sq km
water: 2,840 sq km
note: includes 1,520 islands in the Baltic Sea
comparison ranking: total 132

Area - comparative: about twice the size of New Jersey

Land boundaries: *total:* 657 km
border countries (2): Latvia 333 km; Russia 324 km

Coastline: 3,794 km

Maritime claims: *territorial sea:* 12 nm
exclusive economic zone: limits as agreed to by Estonia, Finland, Latvia, Sweden, and Russia

Climate: maritime; wet, moderate winters, cool summers

Terrain: marshy, lowlands; flat in the north, hilly in the south

Elevation: *highest point:* Suur Munamagi 318 m
lowest point: Baltic Sea 0 m
mean elevation: 61 m

Natural resources: oil shale, peat, rare earth elements, phosphorite, clay, limestone, sand, dolomite, arable land, sea mud

Land use: *agricultural land:* 23.1% (2022 est.)
arable land: 16.5% (2022 est.)
permanent crops: 0.1% (2022 est.)
permanent pasture: 6.4% (2022 est.)
forest: 57.1% (2022 est.)
other: 19.9% (2022 est.)

Irrigated land: 20 sq km (2016)

Major lakes (area sq km): *fresh water lake(s):* Lake Peipus - 4,300 sq km (shared with Russia); Lake Võrtsjärv - 270 sq km

Population distribution: a fairly even distribution throughout most of the country, with urban areas attracting larger and denser populations

Natural hazards: sometimes flooding occurs in the spring

Geography - note: the mainland terrain is flat, boggy, and partly wooded; over 1,500 islands lie offshore

PEOPLE AND SOCIETY

Population: *total:* 1,193,791 (2024 est.)
male: 563,079
female: 630,712
comparison rankings: total 160; male 160; female 158

Nationality: *noun:* Estonian(s)
adjective: Estonian

Ethnic groups: Estonian 69.1%, Russian 23.7%, Ukrainian 2.1%, other 4.6%, unspecified 0.5% (2021 est.)

Languages: Estonian (official) 67.2%, Russian 28.5%, other 3.7%, unspecified 0.6% (2021est.)

Religions: Orthodox 16.5%, Protestant 9.2% (Lutheran 7.7%, other Protestant 1.5%), other 3% (includes Roman Catholic, Muslim, Jehovah's Witness, Pentecostal, Buddhist, and Taara Believer), none 58.4%, unspecified 12.9% (2021 est.)

Age structure: *0-14 years:* 15.2% (male 92,980/female 88,753)
15-64 years: 62.2% (male 373,989/female 368,113)
65 years and over: 22.6% (2024 est.) (male 96,110/female 173,846)

Dependency ratios: *total dependency ratio:* 57.6 (2024 est.)
youth dependency ratio: 25.4 (2024 est.)
elderly dependency ratio: 32.2 (2024 est.)
potential support ratio: 3.1 (2024 est.)

Median age: *total:* 45 years (2024 est.)
male: 41.9 years
female: 48.2 years
comparison ranking: total 22

Population growth rate: -0.76% (2024 est.)
comparison ranking: 228

Birth rate: 8.2 births/1,000 population (2024 est.)
comparison ranking: 212

Death rate: 13.2 deaths/1,000 population (2024 est.)
comparison ranking: 12

Net migration rate: -2.7 migrant(s)/1,000 population (2024 est.)
comparison ranking: 174

Population distribution: a fairly even distribution throughout most of the country, with urban areas attracting larger and denser populations

Urbanization: *urban population:* 69.8% of total population (2023)
rate of urbanization: -0.03% annual rate of change (2020-25 est.)

Major urban areas - population: 454,000 TALLINN (capital) (2023)

Sex ratio: *at birth:* 1.05 male(s)/female
0-14 years: 1.05 male(s)/female
15-64 years: 1.02 male(s)/female
65 years and over: 0.55 male(s)/female
total population: 0.89 male(s)/female (2024 est.)

Mother's mean age at first birth: 28.2 years (2020 est.)

Maternal mortality ratio: 5 deaths/100,000 live births (2023 est.)
comparison ranking: 170

Infant mortality rate: *total:* 3.3 deaths/1,000 live births (2024 est.)
male: 3.2 deaths/1,000 live births
female: 3.4 deaths/1,000 live births
comparison ranking: total 196

Life expectancy at birth: *total population:* 78.4 years (2024 est.)
male: 73.8 years
female: 83.2 years
comparison ranking: total population 79

Total fertility rate: 1.62 children born/woman (2024 est.)
comparison ranking: 178

Gross reproduction rate: 0.79 (2024 est.)

Drinking water source: *improved: urban:* 100% of population (2022 est.)
rural: 100% of population (2022 est.) NA
total: 100% of population (2022 est.)
unimproved: urban: 0% of population (2022 est.)
rural: 0% of population (2022 est.) NA
total: 0% of population (2022 est.)

Health expenditure: 6.9% of GDP (2022)
13.2% of national budget (2022 est.)

Physician density: 3.47 physicians/1,000 population (2022)

Hospital bed density: 4.5 beds/1,000 population (2020 est.)

Sanitation facility access: *improved: urban:* 99.7% of population (2022 est.)
rural: 100% of population (2022 est.)
total: 99.8% of population (2022 est.)
unimproved: urban: 0.3% of population (2022 est.)
rural: 0% of population (2022 est.)
total: 0.2% of population (2022 est.)

Obesity - adult prevalence rate: 21.2% (2016)
comparison ranking: 93

Alcohol consumption per capita: *total:* 11.65 liters of pure alcohol (2019 est.)
beer: 4 liters of pure alcohol (2019 est.)
wine: 1.92 liters of pure alcohol (2019 est.)
spirits: 4.6 liters of pure alcohol (2019 est.)
other alcohols: 1.13 liters of pure alcohol (2019 est.)
comparison ranking: total 7

Tobacco use: *total:* 23.7% (2025 est.)
male: 29.9% (2025 est.)
female: 18.3% (2025 est.)
comparison ranking: total 46

Currently married women (ages 15-49): 52.3% (2023 est.)

Education expenditure: 5.7% of GDP (2022 est.)
14.6% national budget (2022 est.)
comparison ranking: Education expenditure (% GDP) 37

School life expectancy (primary to tertiary education): *total:* 16 years (2023 est.)
male: 15 years (2023 est.)
female: 16 years (2023 est.)

ENVIRONMENT

Environmental issues: air pollution from sulfur dioxide from oil-shale-burning power plants; coastal seawater pollution

International environmental agreements: *party to:* Air Pollution, Air Pollution-Heavy Metals, Air Pollution-Nitrogen Oxides, Air Pollution-Persistent Organic Pollutants, Air Pollution-Sulphur 85, Air Pollution-Volatile Organic Compounds, Antarctic Treaty, Biodiversity, Climate Change, Climate Change-Kyoto Protocol, Climate Change-Paris Agreement, Comprehensive Nuclear Test Ban, Desertification, Endangered Species, Environmental Modification, Hazardous Wastes, Law of the Sea, Marine Dumping-London Protocol, Ozone Layer Protection, Ship Pollution, Tropical Timber 2006, Wetlands, Whaling
signed, but not ratified: none of the selected agreements

Climate: maritime; wet, moderate winters, cool summers

Urbanization: *urban population:* 69.8% of total population (2023)

rate of urbanization: -0.03% annual rate of change (2020-25 est.)

Carbon dioxide emissions: 4.607 million metric tonnes of CO2 (2023 est.)
from coal and metallurgical coke: -19,814 metric tonnes of CO2 (2023 est.)
from petroleum and other liquids: 3.977 million metric tonnes of CO2 (2023 est.)
from consumed natural gas: 649,000 metric tonnes of CO2 (2023 est.)
comparison ranking: total emissions 139

Particulate matter emissions: 6.6 micrograms per cubic meter (2019 est.)

Methane emissions: *energy:* 11.9 kt (2022-2024 est.)
agriculture: 27.3 kt (2019-2021 est.)
waste: 23.7 kt (2019-2021 est.)
other: 2.2 kt (2019-2021 est.)

Waste and recycling: *municipal solid waste generated annually:* 489,500 tons (2024 est.)
percent of municipal solid waste recycled: 39.1% (2022 est.)

Total water withdrawal: *municipal:* 64.998 million cubic meters (2022)
industrial: 1.135 billion cubic meters (2022)
agricultural: 5 million cubic meters (2022)

Total renewable water resources: 12.806 billion cubic meters (2022 est.)

GOVERNMENT

Country name: *conventional long form:* Republic of Estonia
conventional short form: Estonia
local long form: Eesti Vabariik
local short form: Eesti
former: Estonian Soviet Socialist Republic (while occupied by the USSR)
etymology: derives from the name of the people who lived along the eastern Baltic Sea in the first centuries A.D., which came from the Baltic word *aueist*, meaning "waterside dwellers"

Government type: parliamentary republic

Capital: *name:* Tallinn
geographic coordinates: 59 26 N, 24 43 E
time difference: UTC+2 (7 hours ahead of Washington, DC, during Standard Time)
daylight saving time: +1hr, begins last Sunday in March; ends last Sunday in October
etymology: the name derives from the Old Estonian term *tan-linn*, meaning "Danish fort," a reference to Danish King VALDEMAR II founding the city in 1219

Administrative divisions: 15 urban municipalities (*linnad*, singular - *linn*), 64 rural municipalities (*vallad*, singular - *vald*)
urban municipalities: Haapsalu, Keila, Kohtla-Jarve, Loksa, Maardu, Narva, Narva-Joesuu, Paide, Parnu, Rakvere, Sillamae, Tallinn, Tartu, Viljandi, Voru
rural municipalities: Alutaguse, Anija, Antsla, Elva, Haademeeste, Haljala, Harku, Hiiumaa, Jarva, Joelahtme, Jogeva, Johvi, Kadrina, Kambja, Kanepi, Kastre, Kehtna, Kihnu, Kiili, Kohila, Kose, Kuusalu, Laane-Harju, Laane-Nigula, Laaneranna, Luganuse, Luunja, Marjamaa, Muhu, Mulgi, Mustvee, Noo, Otepaa, Peipsiaare, Pohja-Parnumaa, Pohja-Sakala, Poltsamaa, Polva, Raasiku, Rae, Rakvere, Räpina, Rapla, Rouge, Ruhnu, Saarde, Saaremaa, Saku, Saue, Setomaa, Tapa, Tartu, Toila, Tori, Torva, Turi, Vaike-Maarja, Valga, Viimsi, Viljandi, Vinni, Viru-Nigula, Vormsi, Voru

Legal system: civil law system

Constitution: *history:* several previous; latest adopted 28 June 1992, entered into force 3 July 1992
amendment process: proposed by at least one-fifth of Parliament members or by the president of the republic; passage requires three readings of the proposed amendment and a simple majority vote in two successive memberships of Parliament; passage of amendments to the "General Provisions" and "Amendment of the Constitution" chapters requires at least three-fifths majority vote by Parliament to conduct a referendum and majority vote in a referendum

International law organization participation: accepts compulsory ICJ jurisdiction with reservations; accepts ICCt jurisdiction

Citizenship: *citizenship by birth:* no
citizenship by descent only: at least one parent must be a citizen of Estonia
dual citizenship recognized: no
residency requirement for naturalization: 5 years

Suffrage: 18 years of age; universal; age 16 for local elections

Executive branch: *chief of state:* President Alar KARIS (since 11 October 2021)
head of government: Prime Minister Kristen MICHAL (since 23 July 2024)
cabinet: Cabinet appointed by the prime minister, approved by Parliament
election/appointment process: president indirectly elected by Parliament for a 5-year term (eligible for a second term); if a candidate does not secure two thirds of the votes after 3 rounds of balloting, then an electoral college consisting of Parliament members and local council members elects the president, choosing between the 2 candidates with the most votes; if a president is still not elected, the process begins again; prime minister nominated by the president and approved by Parliament
most recent election date: 30-31 August 2021
election results: *2021:* Alar KARIS (independent) elected president; won second round of voting in parliament with 72 of 101 votes
2016: Kersti KALJULAID elected president; won sixth round of voting in parliament with 81 of 98 votes (17 ballots blank); KALJULAID sworn in on 10 October 2016 - first female head of state of Estonia
expected date of next election: 2026

Legislative branch: *legislature name:* The Estonian Parliament (Riigikogu)
legislative structure: unicameral
number of seats: 101 (all directly elected)
electoral system: proportional representation
scope of elections: full renewal
term in office: 4 years
most recent election date: 3/5/2023
parties elected and seats per party: Reform Party (37); Conservative People's Party
(EKRE) (17); Centre Party (16); Estonia 200 (Eesti 200) (14); Social Democratic Party (9); Pro Patria (Isamaa) (8)
percentage of women in chamber: 28.7%
expected date of next election: March 2027

Judicial branch: *highest court(s):* Supreme Court (consists of 19 justices, including the chief justice, and organized into civil, criminal, administrative, and constitutional review chambers)
judge selection and term of office: the chief justice is proposed by the president of the republic and appointed by the Riigikogu; other justices proposed by the chief justice and appointed by the Riigikogu; justices appointed for life
subordinate courts: circuit (appellate) courts; administrative, county, city, and specialized courts

Political parties: Conservative People's Party (Konservatiivne Rahvaerakond) or EKRE
Estonia 200 or E200
Estonia Centre Party of (Keskerakond) or KE
Estonian Free Party or VAP
Estonian Greens or EER
Estonian Nationalists and Conservatives or ERK
Estonian Reform Party (Reformierakond) or RE
Estonian United Left Party or EÜVP
Fatherland or I
Pro Patria (Isamaa)
The Right or PP
Social Democratic Party or SDE

Diplomatic representation in the US: *chief of mission:* Ambassador Kristjan PRIKK (since 7 July 2021)
chancery: 2131 Massachusetts Ave, NW Washington, DC, 20008
telephone: [1] (202) 588-0101

FAX: [1] (202) 588-0108
email address and website: Embassy.Washington@mfa.ee
https://washington.mfa.ee/
consulate(s) general: New York, San Francisco

Diplomatic representation from the US: *chief of mission:* Ambassador (vacant); Chargé d'Affaires Matthew E. WALL (since January 2025)
embassy: Kentmanni 20, 15099 Tallinn
mailing address: 4530 Tallinn Place, Washington DC 20521-4530
telephone: [372] 668-8100

FAX: [372] 668-8265
email address and website: acstallinn@state.gov
https://ee.usembassy.gov/

International organization participation: Australia Group, BA, BIS, CBSS, CD, CE, EAPC, EBRD, ECB, EIB, EMU, ESA (cooperating state), EU, FAO, IAEA, IBRD, ICAO, ICC (national committees), ICCt, ICRM, IDA, IEA, IFAD, IFC, IFRCS, IHO, ILO, IMF, IMO, Interpol, IOC, IOM, IPU, ISO, ITSO, ITU, ITUC (NGOs), MIGA, NATO, NIB, NSG, OAS (observer), OECD, OIF (observer), OPCW, OSCE, PCA, Schengen Convention, UN, UNCTAD, UNESCO, UNHCR, UNTSO, UPU, Wassenaar Arrangement, WCO, WHO, WIPO, WMO, WTO

Independence: 24 February 1918 (from Soviet Russia); 20 August 1991 (declared from the Soviet Union); 6 September 1991 (recognized by the Soviet Union)

National holiday: Independence Day, 24 February (1918)
note: 24 February 1918 was the date Estonia declared its independence from Soviet Russia and established its statehood; 20 August 1991 was the date it declared its independence from the Soviet Union and restored its statehood

Flag: *description:* three equal horizontal bands of blue (top), black, and white
meaning: blue stands for faith, loyalty, and devotion, and also the sky, sea, and lakes; black for the country's soil and the Estonian people's past suffering; white for striving for enlightenment and virtue and also for birch bark, snow, and summer nights illuminated by the midnight sun

National symbol(s): barn swallow, cornflower

National color(s): blue, black, white

National anthem(s): *title:* "Mu isamaa, mu onn ja room" (My Native Land, My Pride and Joy)
lyrics/music: Johann Voldemar JANNSEN/Fredrik PACIUS
history: adopted 1920, but banned between 1940 and 1990 under Soviet occupation; unofficially in use since 1869, it has the same melody as Finland's anthem, but with different lyrics

National heritage: *total World Heritage Sites:* 2 (both cultural)
selected World Heritage Site locales: Historic Center (Old Town) of Tallinn; Struve Geodetic Arc

ECONOMY

Economic overview: high-income, service-based EU and eurozone economy; rebound in exports playing a role in economic recovery; rising food prices contributing to inflation; decrease in labor force participation and rising unemployment rate; recovery depends on boosting private investment and productivity rates

Real GDP (purchasing power parity): $57.001 billion (2024 est.)
$57.15 billion (2023 est.)
$58.931 billion (2022 est.)
note: data in 2021 dollars
comparison ranking: 121

Real GDP growth rate: -0.3% (2024 est.)
-3% (2023 est.)
0.1% (2022 est.)
note: annual GDP % growth based on constant local currency
comparison ranking: 195

Real GDP per capita: $41,500 (2024 est.)
$41,700 (2023 est.)
$43,700 (2022 est.)
note: data in 2021 dollars
comparison ranking: 55

GDP (official exchange rate): $42.765 billion (2024 est.)
note: data in current dollars at official exchange rate

Inflation rate (consumer prices): 3.5% (2024 est.)
9.2% (2023 est.)
19.4% (2022 est.)
note: annual % change based on consumer prices
comparison ranking: 110

GDP - composition, by sector of origin: *agriculture:* 1.9% (2024 est.)
industry: 20.5% (2024 est.)
services: 65.1% (2024 est.)
note: figures may not total 100% due to non-allocated consumption not captured in sector-reported data
comparison rankings: agriculture 155; industry 127; services 60

GDP - composition, by end use: *household consumption:* 52.3% (2023 est.)
government consumption: 20.6% (2023 est.)
investment in fixed capital: 27.9% (2023 est.)
investment in inventories: -0.2% (2023 est.)
exports of goods and services: 77.9% (2023 est.)
imports of goods and services: -77% (2023 est.)
note: figures may not total 100% due to rounding or gaps in data collection

Agricultural products: milk, wheat, barley, rapeseed, peas, oats, potatoes, rye, pork, triticale (2023)
note: top ten agricultural products based on tonnage

Industries: food, engineering, electronics, wood and wood products, textiles; information technology, telecommunications

Industrial production growth rate: -7% (2024 est.)
note: annual % change in industrial value added based on constant local currency
comparison ranking: 185

Labor force: 756,200 (2024 est.)
note: number of people ages 15 or older who are employed or seeking work
comparison ranking: 154

Unemployment rate: 7.9% (2024 est.)
6.4% (2023 est.)
5.6% (2022 est.)
note: % of labor force seeking employment
comparison ranking: 135

Youth unemployment rate (ages 15-24): *total:* 20.9% (2024 est.)
male: 21.9% (2024 est.)
female: 20% (2024 est.)
note: % of labor force ages 15-24 seeking employment
comparison ranking: total 53

Population below poverty line: 22.5% (2022 est.)
note: % of population with income below national poverty line

Gini Index coefficient - distribution of family income: 32.3 (2022 est.)
note: index (0-100) of income distribution; higher values represent greater inequality
comparison ranking: 106

Average household expenditures: *on food:* 19.9% of household expenditures (2023 est.)
on alcohol and tobacco: 6.7% of household expenditures (2023 est.)

Household income or consumption by percentage share: *lowest 10%:* 2.8% (2022 est.)
highest 10%: 24.4% (2022 est.)
note: % share of income accruing to lowest and highest 10% of population

Remittances: 1.2% of GDP (2024 est.)
1.2% of GDP (2023 est.)
1.2% of GDP (2022 est.)
note: personal transfers and compensation between resident and non-resident individuals/households/entities

Budget: *revenues:* $15.784 billion (2023 est.)
expenditures: $16.721 billion (2023 est.)
note: central government revenues (excluding grants) and expenditures converted to US dollars at average official exchange rate for year indicated

Public debt: 28.3% of GDP (2023 est.)
note: central government debt as a % of GDP
comparison ranking: 167

Taxes and other revenues: 21.4% (of GDP) (2023 est.)
note: central government tax revenue as a % of GDP
comparison ranking: 42

Current account balance: -$489.659 million (2024 est.)
-$722.668 million (2023 est.)
-$1.496 billion (2022 est.)
note: balance of payments - net trade and primary/secondary income in current dollars
comparison ranking: 108

Exports: $32.637 billion (2024 est.)
$32.147 billion (2023 est.)
$33.178 billion (2022 est.)
note: balance of payments - exports of goods and services in current dollars
comparison ranking: 81

Exports - partners: Finland 14%, Latvia 10%, Lithuania 9%, Sweden 7%, Russia 6% (2023)
note: top five export partners based on percentage share of exports

Exports - commodities: cars, wood, broadcasting equipment, refined petroleum, prefabricated buildings (2023)
note: top five export commodities based on value in dollars

Imports: $32.375 billion (2024 est.)
$31.796 billion (2023 est.)
$33.655 billion (2022 est.)
note: balance of payments - imports of goods and services in current dollars
comparison ranking: 80

Imports - partners: Finland 11%, Germany 11%, China 10%, Lithuania 6%, Poland 6% (2023)
note: top five import partners based on percentage share of imports

Imports - commodities: cars, refined petroleum, broadcasting equipment, natural gas, packaged medicine (2023)
note: top five import commodities based on value in dollars

Reserves of foreign exchange and gold: $2.075 billion (2024 est.)
$2.593 billion (2023 est.)
$2.217 billion (2022 est.)
note: holdings of gold (year-end prices)/foreign exchange/special drawing rights in current dollars
comparison ranking: 125

Exchange rates: euros (EUR) per US dollar -

Exchange rates: 0.924 (2024 est.)
0.925 (2023 est.)
0.95 (2022 est.)
0.845 (2021 est.)
0.876 (2020 est.)

ENERGY

Electricity access: *electrification - total population:* 100% (2022 est.)

Electricity: *installed generating capacity:* 3.225 million kW (2023 est.)
consumption: 8.636 billion kWh (2023 est.)
exports: 4.355 billion kWh (2023 est.)
imports: 7.66 billion kWh (2023 est.)
transmission/distribution losses: 1.164 billion kWh (2023 est.)
comparison rankings: installed generating capacity 108; consumption 112; exports 42; imports 33; transmission/distribution losses 107

Electricity generation sources: *fossil fuels:* 52.2% of total installed capacity (2023 est.)
solar: 9.7% of total installed capacity (2023 est.)
wind: 10.5% of total installed capacity (2023 est.)
hydroelectricity: 0.4% of total installed capacity (2023 est.)
biomass and waste: 27.2% of total installed capacity (2023 est.)

Coal: *consumption:* 800 metric tons (2023 est.)
exports: 7,000 metric tons (2023 est.)
imports: 800 metric tons (2023 est.)

Petroleum: *total petroleum production:* 24,000 bbl/day (2023 est.)
refined petroleum consumption: 27,000 bbl/day (2024 est.)

Natural gas: *consumption:* 334.748 million cubic meters (2023 est.)
exports: 675.708 million cubic meters (2023 est.)
imports: 1.01 billion cubic meters (2023 est.)

Energy consumption per capita: 73.679 million Btu/person (2023 est.)
comparison ranking: 68

COMMUNICATIONS

Telephones - fixed lines: *total subscriptions:* 238,000 (2023 est.)
subscriptions per 100 inhabitants: 17 (2023 est.)
comparison ranking: total subscriptions 115

Telephones - mobile cellular: *total subscriptions:* 2.05 million (2023 est.)
subscriptions per 100 inhabitants: 155 (2022 est.)
comparison ranking: total subscriptions 150

Broadcast media: the publicly owned broadcaster, Eesti Rahvusringhaaling (ERR), operates 3 TV channels and 5 radio networks; growing number of private commercial radio stations broadcasting nationally, regionally, and locally; fully transitioned to digital television in 2010; national private TV channels expanding service, with a range of channels aimed at Russian-speaking viewers; in 2016, there were 42 on-demand services available in Estonia, including 19 pay TVOD and SVOD services; roughly 85% of households accessed digital television services

Internet country code: .ee

Internet users: *percent of population:* 93% (2023 est.)

Broadband - fixed subscriptions: *total:* 516,000 (2023 est.)
subscriptions per 100 inhabitants: 38 (2023 est.)
comparison ranking: total 94

TRANSPORTATION

Civil aircraft registration country code prefix: ES

Airports: 34 (2025)
comparison ranking: 115

Heliports: 10 (2025)
comparison ranking: 76

Railways: *total:* 1,441 km (2020) 225 km electrified

Merchant marine: *total:* 72 (2023)
by type: general cargo 3, oil tanker 3, other 66
comparison ranking: total 108

Ports: *total ports:* 20 (2024)
large: 4
medium: 1
small: 4
very small: 11
ports with oil terminals: 5
key ports: Muuga - Port of Tallin, Paldiski Lounasadam, Paljassaare, Sillamae, Vanasadam - Port of Tallinn

MILITARY AND SECURITY

Military and security forces: Estonian Defense Forces: Land Forces, Navy, Air Force; Estonian Defense League

Ministry of Interior: Police and Border Guard Board, Internal Security Service (2025)
note: the Estonian Defense League is a voluntary national defense organization that operates under the Estonian Ministry of Defense

Military expenditures: 3.4% of GDP (2025 est.)
3.4% of GDP (2024 est.)
3% of GDP (2023 est.)
2.2% of GDP (2022 est.)
2% of GDP (2021 est.)

Military and security service personnel strengths: approximately 7,500 active-duty military personnel (2025)
note: the Estonian Defense Forces rely largely on reservists who have completed compulsory conscription in the previous 10 years to fill out its active duty and Territorial Defense units during a crisis; there are more than 40,000 trained reservists, and approximately 230,000 Estonians are enrolled in the mobilization registry

Military equipment inventories and acquisitions: the Estonian military has a mix of weapons and equipment from western European suppliers, as well as Israel, South Korea, Turkey, and the US (2024)

Military service age and obligation: 18-27 for compulsory military or governmental service for men; conscript service requirement 8-11 months depending on education; non-commissioned officers, reserve officers, and specialists serve 11 months; women can volunteer, and as of 2018 could serve in any military branch (2025)
note 1: conscripts comprise approximately 3,000-3,300 of the Estonian military's active-duty personnel and serve in all branches, except for the Air Force; after conscript service, reservists are called up for training every 5 years; Estonia has had conscription since 1991
note 2: in 2021, women comprised about 10% of the full-time professional military force; the Defense League includes a Women's Voluntary Defense Organization

Military - note: Estonia's defense policy aims to guarantee the country's independence and sovereignty, protect its territorial integrity, including waters and airspace, and preserve constitutional order; Estonia's main defense goals are developing and maintaining a credible deterrent to outside aggression and ensuring the Estonian Defense Forces (EDF) can fulfill their commitments to NATO and interoperate with the armed forces of NATO and EU member states; the EDF's primary external focus is Russia; since Russia's full-scale invasion of Ukraine in 2022, Estonia has boosted defense spending, sent arms to Ukraine, and sought to boost the EDF's capabilities in such areas as air defense, artillery, personnel readiness, and surveillance
Estonia has been a member of NATO since 2004, is fully integrated within the NATO structure, and relies on its NATO partners for defense; since 2017, Estonia has hosted a UK-led multinational NATO ground force battlegroup as part of the Alliance's Enhanced Forward Presence initiative; as the EDF Air Force does not have any combat aircraft, NATO has provided airspace protection for Estonia since 2004 through its Baltic Air Policing mission; NATO member countries that possess air combat capabilities voluntarily contribute to the mission on four-month rotations; NATO fighter aircraft have been hosted at Estonia's Ämari Air Base since 2014; Estonia also hosts a NATO cyber security center; it cooperates closely with the EU on defense issues through the EU Common Security and Defense Policy and is a member of the UK-led Joint Expeditionary Force, a pool of high-readiness military forces from 10 Baltic and Scandinavian countries designed to respond to a wide range of contingencies in the North Atlantic, Baltic Sea, and High North regions; Estonia also has close defense ties with its Baltic neighbors and has bilateral military agreements with a number of European countries, as well as Canada and the US (2025)

TRANSNATIONAL ISSUES

Refugees and internally displaced persons: *refugees:* 42,439 (2024 est.)
stateless persons: 63,944 (2024 est.)

ESWATINI

INTRODUCTION

Background: A Swazi kingdom was founded in the mid-18th century and ruled by a series of kings, including MSWATI II, a 19th century ruler whose name was adopted for the country and its predominant ethnic group. European countries defined the kingdom's modern borders during the late-19th century, and Swaziland (as it became known) was administered as a UK high commission territory from 1903 until its independence in 1968. A new constitution that came into effect in 2005 included provisions for a more independent parliament and judiciary, but the legal status of political parties remains unclear, and the kingdom is still considered an absolute monarchy. King MSWATI III renamed the country from Swaziland to Eswatini in 2018 to reflect the name most commonly used by its citizens.

In 2021, MSWATI III used security forces to suppress prodemocracy protests. A national dialogue and reconciliation process agreed to in the wake of violence has not materialized. In November 2023, King MSWATI III appointed a new prime minister following peaceful national elections. Despite its classification as a lower-middle income country, Eswatini suffers from severe poverty, corruption, and high unemployment. Eswatini has the world's highest HIV/AIDS prevalence rate, although recent years have shown marked declines in new infections. Eswatini is the only country in Africa that recognizes Taiwan.

GEOGRAPHY

Location: Southern Africa, between Mozambique and South Africa

Geographic coordinates: 26 30 S, 31 30 E

Map references: Africa

Area: *total:* 17,364 sq km
land: 17,204 sq km

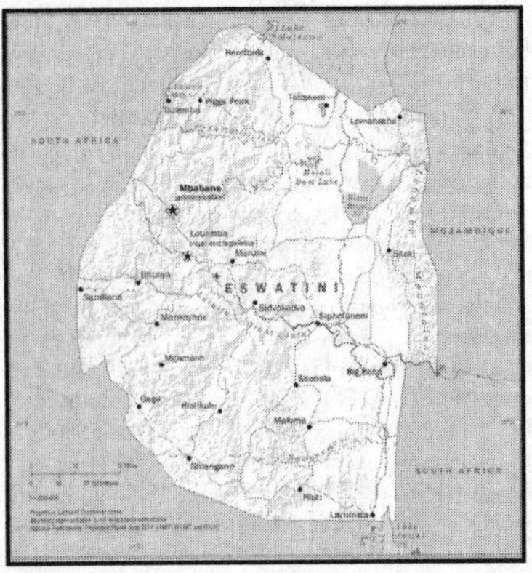

water: 160 sq km
comparison ranking: total 158

Area - comparative: slightly smaller than New Jersey

Land boundaries: *total*: 546 km
border countries (2): Mozambique 108 km; South Africa 438 km

Coastline: 0 km (landlocked)

Maritime claims: none (landlocked)

Climate: varies from tropical to near temperate

Terrain: mostly mountains and hills; some moderately sloping plains

Elevation: *highest point*: Emlembe 1,862 m
lowest point: Great Usutu River 21 m
mean elevation: 305 m

Natural resources: asbestos, coal, clay, cassiterite, hydropower, forests, small gold and diamond deposits, quarry stone, and talc

Land use: *agricultural land*: 69.5% (2022 est.)
arable land: 10.3% (2022 est.)
permanent crops: 1% (2022 est.)
permanent pasture: 58.1% (2022 est.)
forest: 29.1% (2022 est.)
other: 1.5% (2022 est.)

Irrigated land: 500 sq km (2012)

Population distribution: because of its mountainous terrain, the population distribution is uneven throughout the country, concentrating primarily in valleys and plains as shown in this population distribution map

Natural hazards: drought

Geography - note: landlocked; almost completely surrounded by South Africa

PEOPLE AND SOCIETY

Population: *total*: 1,138,089 (2024 est.)
male: 538,600
female: 599,489
comparison rankings: total 161; male 161; female 160

Nationality: *noun*: liSwati (singular), emaSwati (plural); note - former term, Swazi(s), still used among English speakers
adjective: Swati; note - former term, Swazi, still used among English speakers

Ethnic groups: predominantly Swazi; smaller populations of other African ethnic groups, including the Zulu, as well as people of European ancestry

Languages: English (official, used for government business), siSwati (official)

Religions: Christian 90% (Zionist - a blend of Christianity and traditional African religions - 40%, Roman Catholic 20%, other Christian 30% - includes Anglican, Methodist, Church of Jesus Christ, Jehovah's Witness), Muslim 2%, other 8% (includes Baha'i, Buddhist, Hindu, indigenous, Jewish) (2015 est.)

Age structure: *0-14 years*: 31.6% (male 180,328/female 179,840)
15-64 years: 64.3% (male 341,298/female 390,884)
65 years and over: 4% (2024 est.) (male 16,974/female 28,765)

Dependency ratios: *total dependency ratio*: 55.4 (2024 est.)
youth dependency ratio: 49.2 (2024 est.)
elderly dependency ratio: 6.2 (2024 est.)
potential support ratio: 16 (2024 est.)

Median age: *total*: 24.6 years (2024 est.)
male: 23.4 years
female: 25.8 years
comparison ranking: total 175

Population growth rate: 0.7% (2024 est.)
comparison ranking: 127

Birth rate: 22.3 births/1,000 population (2024 est.)
comparison ranking: 51

Death rate: 9.4 deaths/1,000 population (2024 est.)
comparison ranking: 49

Net migration rate: -6 migrant(s)/1,000 population (2024 est.)
comparison ranking: 209

Population distribution: because of its mountainous terrain, the population distribution is uneven throughout the country, concentrating primarily in valleys and plains as shown in this population distribution map

Urbanization: *urban population*: 24.8% of total population (2023)
rate of urbanization: 2.42% annual rate of change (2020-25 est.)

Major urban areas - population: 68,000 MBABANE (capital) (2018)

Sex ratio: *at birth*: 1.03 male(s)/female
0-14 years: 1 male(s)/female
15-64 years: 0.87 male(s)/female
65 years and over: 0.59 male(s)/female
total population: 0.9 male(s)/female (2024 est.)

Maternal mortality ratio: 118 deaths/100,000 live births (2023 est.)
comparison ranking: 61

Infant mortality rate: *total*: 36.7 deaths/1,000 live births (2024 est.)
male: 40.7 deaths/1,000 live births
female: 32.5 deaths/1,000 live births
comparison ranking: total 33

Life expectancy at birth: *total population*: 60.7 years (2024 est.)
male: 58.7 years
female: 62.8 years
comparison ranking: total population 219

Total fertility rate: 2.37 children born/woman (2024 est.)
comparison ranking: 73

Gross reproduction rate: 1.17 (2024 est.)

Drinking water source: *improved*: *urban*: 98% of population (2022 est.)
rural: 65.5% of population (2022 est.)
total: 73.5% of population (2022 est.)
unimproved: *urban*: 2% of population (2022 est.)
rural: 34.5% of population (2022 est.)
total: 26.5% of population (2022 est.)

Health expenditure: 7% of GDP (2021)
11.3% of national budget (2022 est.)

Physician density: 0.56 physicians/1,000 population (2023)

Sanitation facility access: *improved*: *urban*: 92.4% of population (2022 est.)
rural: 84.2% of population (2022 est.)
total: 86.2% of population (2022 est.)
unimproved: *urban*: 7.6% of population (2022 est.)
rural: 15.8% of population (2022 est.)
total: 13.8% of population (2022 est.)

Obesity - adult prevalence rate: 16.5% (2016)
comparison ranking: 124

Alcohol consumption per capita: *total*: 7.68 liters of pure alcohol (2019 est.)
beer: 2.45 liters of pure alcohol (2019 est.)
wine: 0.06 liters of pure alcohol (2019 est.)
spirits: 0 liters of pure alcohol (2019 est.)
other alcohols: 5.17 liters of pure alcohol (2019 est.)
comparison ranking: total 50

Tobacco use: *total*: 8.5% (2025 est.)
male: 16.1% (2025 est.)
female: 1.2% (2025 est.)
comparison ranking: total 138

Currently married women (ages 15-49): 37.1% (2023 est.)

Child marriage: *women married by age 15*: 0.1% (2022)
women married by age 18: 1.9% (2022)
men married by age 18: 0% (2022)

Education expenditure: 6% of GDP (2024 est.)
19.2% national budget (2025 est.)
comparison ranking: Education expenditure (% GDP) 31

Literacy: *total population*: 90.7% (2022 est.)
male: 91.1% (2022 est.)
female: 90.4% (2022 est.)

ENVIRONMENT

Environmental issues: limited supplies of potable water; overhunting depleting wildlife; population growth, deforestation, and overgrazing lead to soil erosion and soil degradation

International environmental agreements: *party to*: Biodiversity, Climate Change, Climate Change-Kyoto Protocol, Climate Change-Paris Agreement, Comprehensive Nuclear Test Ban, Desertification, Endangered Species, Hazardous Wastes, Law of the Sea, Nuclear Test Ban, Ozone Layer Protection, Wetlands
signed, but not ratified: none of the selected agreements

Climate: varies from tropical to near temperate

Urbanization: *urban population*: 24.8% of total population (2023)
rate of urbanization: 2.42% annual rate of change (2020-25 est.)

Carbon dioxide emissions: 1.326 million metric tonnes of CO2 (2023 est.)
from coal and metallurgical coke: 410,000 metric tonnes of CO2 (2023 est.)
from petroleum and other liquids: 916,000 metric tonnes of CO2 (2023 est.)
comparison ranking: total emissions 168

Particulate matter emissions: 16.4 micrograms per cubic meter (2019 est.)

Waste and recycling: *municipal solid waste generated annually:* 218,200 tons (2024 est.)
percent of municipal solid waste recycled: 17.3% (2022 est.)

Total water withdrawal: *municipal:* 41.3 million cubic meters (2022 est.)
industrial: 20.7 million cubic meters (2022 est.)
agricultural: 1.006 billion cubic meters (2022 est.)

Total renewable water resources: 4.51 billion cubic meters (2022 est.)

GOVERNMENT

Country name: *conventional long form:* Kingdom of Eswatini
conventional short form: Eswatini
local long form: Umbuso weSwatini
local short form: eSwatini
former: Swaziland
etymology: the country name derives from 19th century King MSWATI II, under whose rule Swati territory was expanded and unified
note: pronounced ay-swatini or eh-swatini

Government type: absolute monarchy

Capital: *name:* Mbabane (administrative capital); Lobamba (royal and legislative capital)
geographic coordinates: 26 19 S, 31 08 E
time difference: UTC+2 (7 hours ahead of Washington, DC, during Standard Time)
etymology: the origin of the name is unclear; it may come from the Mbabane River next to the city, whose name is said to derive from the word *lubabe*, a type of shrub; another theory cites a local chief, Mbabane KUNENE, as the source of the name

Administrative divisions: 4 regions; Hhohho, Lubombo, Manzini, Shiselweni

Legal system: mixed system of civil, common, and customary law

Constitution: *history:* previous 1968, 1978; latest signed by the king 26 July 2005, effective 8 February 2006
amendment process: proposed at a joint sitting of both houses of Parliament; passage requires majority vote by both houses and/or majority vote in a referendum, and assent of the king; passage of amendments affecting "specially entrenched" constitutional provisions requires at least three-fourths majority vote by both houses, passage by simple majority vote in a referendum, and assent of the king; passage of "entrenched" provisions requires at least two-thirds majority vote of both houses, passage in a referendum, and assent of the king

International law organization participation: accepts compulsory ICJ jurisdiction with reservations; non-party state to the ICCt

Citizenship: *citizenship by birth:* no
citizenship by descent only: both parents must be citizens of Eswatini
dual citizenship recognized: no
residency requirement for naturalization: 5 years

Suffrage: 18 years of age

Executive branch: *chief of state:* King MSWATI III (since 25 April 1986)
head of government: Prime Minister Russell DLAMINI (since 6 November 2023)
cabinet: Cabinet recommended by the prime minister, confirmed by the monarch; at least one-half of the cabinet membership must be appointed from among elected members of the House of Assembly
election/appointment process: the monarchy is hereditary; prime minister appointed by the monarch from among members of the House of Assembly

Legislative branch: *legislature name:* Parliament (Libandla)
legislative structure: bicameral

Legislative branch - lower chamber: *chamber name:* House of Assembly
number of seats: 74 (59 directly elected; 4 indirectly elected; 10 appointed)
electoral system: plurality/majority
scope of elections: full renewal
term in office: 5 years
most recent election date: 9/29/2023
percentage of women in chamber: 21.6%
expected date of next election: September 2028
note: four women, one representing each region, elected by the members if representation of elected women is less than 30%

Legislative branch - upper chamber: *chamber name:* Senate
number of seats: 30 (10 indirectly elected; 20 appointed)
scope of elections: full renewal
term in office: 5 years
most recent election date: 11/6/2023
percentage of women in chamber: 46.7%
expected date of next election: November 2028

Judicial branch: *highest court(s):* Supreme Court (consists of the chief justice and at least 4 justices) and the High Court (consists of the chief justice ex officio and 4 justices)
judge selection and term of office: justices of the Supreme Court and High Court appointed by the monarch on the advice of the Judicial Service Commission (JSC), a judicial advisory body consisting of the Supreme Court Chief Justice, 4 members appointed by the monarch, and the chairman of the Civil Service Commission; justices of both courts eligible for retirement at age 65 with mandatory retirement at age 75
subordinate courts: magistrates' courts; National Swazi Courts for administering customary/traditional laws (jurisdiction restricted to customary law for Swazi citizens)
note: the Supreme Court has jurisdiction in all constitutional matters

Political parties: *political parties exist but conditions for their operations, particularly in elections, are undefined, legally unclear, or culturally restricted; the following are considered political associations:* African United Democratic Party or AUDP
Ngwane National Liberatory Congress or NNLC
People's United Democratic Movement or PUDEMO
Swazi Democratic Party or SWADEPA

Diplomatic representation in the US: *chief of mission:* Ambassador Kennedy Fitzgerald GROENING (7 June 2022)
chancery: 1712 New Hampshire Avenue NW, Washington, DC 20009
telephone: [1] (202) 234-5002
FAX: [1] (202) 234-8254
email address and website: swaziland@compuserve.com

Diplomatic representation from the US: *chief of mission:* Ambassador (vacant) Chargé d'Affaires Marc WEINSTOCK (since August 2025)
embassy: Corner of MR 103 and Cultural Center Drive, Ezulwini, P.O. Box D202, The Gables, H106
mailing address: 2350 Mbabane Place, Washington DC 20521-2350
telephone: (268) 2417-9000
FAX: [268] 2416-3344
email address and website: ConsularMbabane@state.gov

Homepage - U.S. Embassy in Eswatini (usembassy.gov): International organization participation: ACP, AfDB, AU, C, COMESA, FAO, G-77, IAEA, IBRD, ICAO, ICRM, IDA, IFAD, IFC, IFRCS, ILO, IMF, IMO, Interpol, IOC, IOM, ISO (correspondent), ITSO, ITU, ITUC (NGOs), MIGA, NAM, OPCW, PCA, SACU, SADC, UN, UNCTAD, UNESCO, UNIDO, UNWTO, UPU, WCO, WHO, WIPO, WMO, WTO

Independence: 6 September 1968 (from the UK)

National holiday: Independence Day (Somhlolo Day), 6 September (1968)

Flag: *description:* three horizontal bands of blue (top), red (triple-width), and blue; the red band is edged in yellow, with a large black-and-white shield in the center that covers two horizontal spears and a staff with feather tassels
meaning: blue stands for peace and stability, red for past struggles, and yellow for the mineral resources of the country; the shield, spears, and staff symbolize protection from enemies, and the shield colors stand for ethnic groups living in peaceful coexistence

National symbol(s): lion, elephant

National color(s): blue, yellow, red

National coat of arms: the national coat of arms was adopted in 1968 after independence from the United Kingdom; two national symbols, the lion (representing the king of Eswatini) and the elephant (representing the queen mother), support a traditional Nguni shield; above the shield is the king's *lidlabe*, or crown of feathers, and at the bottom is Eswatini's motto, *Siyinqaba*, or "We are the fortress"

National anthem(s): *title:* "Nkulunkulu Mnikati wetibusiso temaSwati" (O God, Bestower of the Blessings of the Swazi)
lyrics/music: Andrease Enoke Fanyana SIMELANE/David Kenneth RYCROFT
history: adopted 1968; uses elements of both ethnic Swazi and Western music styles

ECONOMY

Economic overview: landlocked southern African economy; South African trade dependent and currency pegging; CMA and SACU member state; COVID-19 economic slowdown; growing utilities inflation; persistent poverty and unemployment; HIV/AIDS labor force disruptions

Real GDP (purchasing power parity): $12.885 billion (2024 est.)
$12.553 billion (2023 est.)
$12.135 billion (2022 est.)
note: data in 2021 dollars
comparison ranking: 161

Real GDP growth rate: 2.6% (2024 est.)
3.4% (2023 est.)
1.1% (2022 est.)
note: annual GDP % growth based on constant local currency
comparison ranking: 132

Real GDP per capita: $10,400 (2024 est.)
$10,200 (2023 est.)
$10,000 (2022 est.)
note: data in 2021 dollars
comparison ranking: 142

GDP (official exchange rate): $4.892 billion (2024 est.)
note: data in current dollars at official exchange rate

Inflation rate (consumer prices): 2.6% (2019 est.)
4.8% (2018 est.)
6.2% (2017 est.)
note: annual % change based on consumer prices
comparison ranking: 73

GDP - composition, by sector of origin: *agriculture:* 6.8% (2023 est.)
industry: 34.7% (2023 est.)
services: 51.7% (2023 est.)
note: figures may not total 100% due to non-allocated consumption not captured in sector-reported data
comparison rankings: agriculture 96; industry 35; services 137

GDP - composition, by end use: *household consumption:* 64% (2023 est.)
government consumption: 19.5% (2023 est.)
investment in fixed capital: 16.1% (2023 est.)
investment in inventories: 3.1% (2023 est.)
exports of goods and services: 48.7% (2023 est.)
imports of goods and services: -51.4% (2023 est.)
note: figures may not total 100% due to rounding or gaps in data collection

Agricultural products: sugarcane, maize, root vegetables, grapefruits, oranges, milk, pineapples, bananas, beef, sweet potatoes (2023)
note: top ten agricultural products based on tonnage

Industries: soft drink concentrates, coal, forestry, sugar processing, textiles, and apparel

Industrial production growth rate: 0.5% (2023 est.)
note: annual % change in industrial value added based on constant local currency
comparison ranking: 122

Labor force: 390,600 (2024 est.)
note: number of people ages 15 or older who are employed or seeking work
comparison ranking: 162

Unemployment rate: 34.4% (2024 est.)
35.1% (2023 est.)
35.4% (2022 est.)
note: % of labor force seeking employment
comparison ranking: 190

Youth unemployment rate (ages 15-24): *total:* 58.2% (2024 est.)
male: 56% (2024 est.)
female: 60.3% (2024 est.)
note: % of labor force ages 15-24 seeking employment
comparison ranking: total 3

Population below poverty line: 58.9% (2016 est.)
note: % of population with income below national poverty line

Gini Index coefficient - distribution of family income: 54.6 (2016 est.)
note: index (0-100) of income distribution; higher values represent greater inequality
comparison ranking: 3

Household income or consumption by percentage share: *lowest 10%:* 1.4% (2016 est.)
highest 10%: 42.7% (2016 est.)
note: % share of income accruing to lowest and highest 10% of population

Remittances: 1.7% of GDP (2023 est.)
2.7% of GDP (2022 est.)
2.8% of GDP (2021 est.)
note: personal transfers and compensation between resident and non-resident individuals/households/entities

Budget: *revenues:* $1.217 billion (2021 est.)
expenditures: $1.439 billion (2021 est.)
note: central government revenues and expenses (excluding grants/extrabudgetary units/social security funds) converted to US dollars at average official exchange rate for year indicated

Public debt: 35.9% of GDP (2021 est.)
note: central government debt as a % of GDP
comparison ranking: 149

Taxes and other revenues: 24.5% (of GDP) (2021 est.)
note: central government tax revenue as a % of GDP
comparison ranking: 20

Current account balance: $107.534 million (2023 est.)
-$140.972 million (2022 est.)
$125.318 million (2021 est.)
note: balance of payments - net trade and primary/secondary income in current dollars
comparison ranking: 75

Exports: $2.174 billion (2023 est.)
$2.095 billion (2022 est.)
$2.132 billion (2021 est.)
note: balance of payments - exports of goods and services in current dollars
comparison ranking: 164

Exports - partners: South Africa 61%, Ireland 4%, Mozambique 4%, Kenya 4%, Nigeria 3% (2023)
note: top five export partners based on percentage share of exports

Exports - commodities: scented mixtures, raw sugar, industrial acids/oils/alcohols, garments, wood (2023)
note: top five export commodities based on value in dollars

Imports: $2.351 billion (2023 est.)
$2.288 billion (2022 est.)
$2.173 billion (2021 est.)
note: balance of payments - imports of goods and services in current dollars
comparison ranking: 171

Imports - partners: South Africa 71%, China 8%, India 4%, USA 2%, Mozambique 1% (2023)
note: top five import partners based on percentage share of imports

Imports - commodities: refined petroleum, electricity, plastic products, cotton fabric, garments (2023)
note: top five import commodities based on value in dollars

Reserves of foreign exchange and gold: $479.261 million (2023 est.)
$452.352 million (2022 est.)
$572.282 million (2021 est.)
note: holdings of gold (year-end prices)/foreign exchange/special drawing rights in current dollars
comparison ranking: 163

Debt - external: $923.266 million (2023 est.)
note: present value of external debt in current US dollars
comparison ranking: 105

Exchange rates: emalangeni per US dollar -

Exchange rates: 18.318 (2024 est.)
18.454 (2023 est.)
16.362 (2022 est.)
14.783 (2021 est.)
16.47 (2020 est.)

ENERGY

Electricity access: *electrification - total population:* 82.3% (2022 est.)
electrification - urban areas: 86.1%
electrification - rural areas: 81.6%

Electricity: *installed generating capacity:* 285,000 kW (2023 est.)
consumption: 1.308 billion kWh (2023 est.)
imports: 928.237 million kWh (2023 est.)
transmission/distribution losses: 167.476 million kWh (2023 est.)
comparison rankings: installed generating capacity 166; consumption 158; imports 78; transmission/distribution losses 59

Electricity generation sources: *fossil fuels:* 3.1% of total installed capacity (2023 est.)
solar: 4.9% of total installed capacity (2023 est.)
hydroelectricity: 54.4% of total installed capacity (2023 est.)
biomass and waste: 37.6% of total installed capacity (2023 est.)

Coal: *production:* 253,000 metric tons (2023 est.)
consumption: 202,000 metric tons (2023 est.)
exports: 4,000 metric tons (2023 est.)
imports: 201,000 metric tons (2023 est.)
proven reserves: 4.644 billion metric tons (2023 est.)

Petroleum: *refined petroleum consumption:* 6,000 bbl/day (2023 est.)

Energy consumption per capita: 18.823 million Btu/person (2023 est.)
comparison ranking: 133

COMMUNICATIONS

Telephones - fixed lines: *total subscriptions:* 42,000 (2023 est.)
subscriptions per 100 inhabitants: 3 (2023 est.)
comparison ranking: total subscriptions 161

Telephones - mobile cellular: *total subscriptions:* 1.52 million (2023 est.)
subscriptions per 100 inhabitants: 122 (2022 est.)
comparison ranking: total subscriptions 159

Broadcast media: 1 state-owned TV station; satellite dishes can access South African providers; state-owned radio network with 3 channels; 1 private radio station (2019)

Internet country code: .sz

Internet users: *percent of population:* 58% (2023 est.)

Broadband - fixed subscriptions: *total:* 34,000 (2023 est.)
subscriptions per 100 inhabitants: 3 (2023 est.)
comparison ranking: total 157

TRANSPORTATION

Civil aircraft registration country code prefix: 3DC

Airports: 16 (2025)
comparison ranking: 147

Heliports: 1 (2025)
comparison ranking: 156

Railways: *total:* 301 km (2014)
narrow gauge: 301 km (2014) 1.067-m gauge

MILITARY AND SECURITY

Military and security forces: Umbutfo Eswatini Defense Force (UEDF): Army (includes a small air wing); the Royal Eswatini Police Service (REPS) (2025)

Military expenditures: 1.4% of GDP (2024 est.)
1.4% of GDP (2023 est.)
1.6% of GDP (2022 est.)
1.7% of GDP (2021 est.)
1.8% of GDP (2020 est.)

Military and security service personnel strengths: approximately 3,000 active-duty Defense Force (2023)

Military equipment inventories and acquisitions: the UEDF has a light and small inventory of mostly older equipment originating from Europe, South Africa, and the US (2024)

Military service age and obligation: 18-35 years of age for voluntary military service for men and women; no conscription (2023)

Military - note: the UEDF's primary mission is external defense, which includes mostly securing the borders; it also has domestic security responsibilities, including protecting members of the royal family; the king is the UEDF commander in chief and holds the position of minister of defense, although the UEDF reports to the Army commander and principal under-secretary of defense for day-to-day operations; the Royal Eswatini Police Service (REPS) is responsible for maintaining internal security as well as migration and border crossing enforcement; it is under the prime minister, although the king is the force's titular commissioner in chief; the UEDF was originally created in 1973 as the Royal Swaziland Defense Force (2024)

TRANSNATIONAL ISSUES

Refugees and internally displaced persons: *refugees:* 4,459 (2024 est.)

IDPs: 56 (2024 est.)

ETHIOPIA

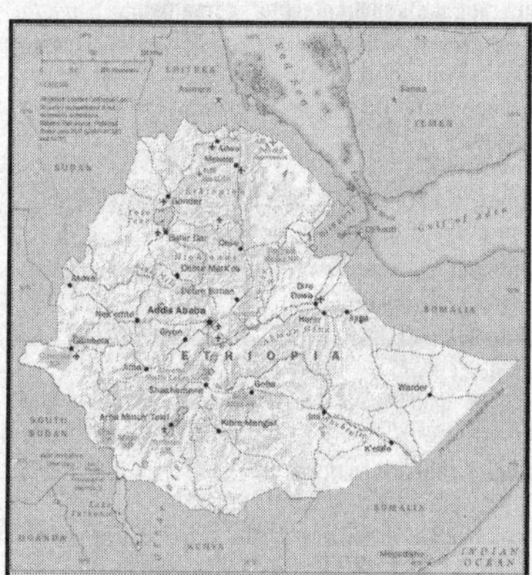

INTRODUCTION

Background: The area that is modern-day Ethiopia is rich in cultural and religious diversity with more than 80 ethnic groups. The oldest hominid yet found comes from Ethiopia, and Ethiopia was the second country to officially adopt Christianity in the 4th century A.D. A series of monarchies ruled the area that is now Ethiopia from 980 B.C. to 1855, when the Amhara kingdoms of northern Ethiopia united in an empire under Tewodros II. Many Ethiopians still speak reverently about the Battle of Adwa in 1896, when they defeated Italian forces and won their freedom from colonial rule.

Emperor Haile SELASSIE became an internationally renowned figure in 1935, when he unsuccessfully appealed to the League of Nations to prevent Italy from occupying Ethiopia from 1936 to 1941. SELASSIE survived an attempted coup in 1960, annexed modern-day Eritrea in 1962, and played a leading role in establishing the Organization of African Unity in 1963. However, in 1974, a military junta called the Derg deposed him and established a socialist state. Torn by bloody coups, uprisings, drought, and massive displacement, the Derg regime was toppled in 1991 by a coalition of opposing forces, the Ethiopian People's Revolutionary Democratic Front (EPRDF). The EPRDF became an ethno-federalist political coalition that ruled Ethiopia from 1991 until its dissolution in 2019. Ethiopia adopted its constitution in 1994 and held its first multiparty elections in 1995.

A two-and-a-half-year border war with Eritrea in the late 1990s ended with a peace treaty in 2000. Ethiopia subsequently rejected the 2007 Eritrea-Ethiopia Boundary Commission demarcation. This resulted in more than a decade of a tense "no peace, no war" stalemate between the two countries. In 2012, longtime Prime Minister MELES Zenawi died in office and was replaced by his Deputy Prime Minister HAILEMARIAM Desalegn, marking the first peaceful transition of power in decades. Following a wave of popular dissent and anti-government protest that began in 2015, HAILEMARIAM resigned in 2018, and ABIY Ahmed Ali took office the same year as Ethiopia's first ethnic Oromo prime minister. In 2018, ABIY promoted a rapprochement between Ethiopia and Eritrea that was marked with a peace agreement and a reopening of their shared border. In 2019, Ethiopia's nearly 30-year ethnic-based ruling coalition, the EPRDF, merged into a single unity party called the Prosperity Party; however, the lead coalition party, the Tigray People's Liberation Front (TPLF), declined to join. In 2020, a military conflict erupted between forces aligned with the TPLF and the Ethiopian military. The conflict – which was marked by atrocities committed by all parties – ended in 2022 with a cessation of hostilities agreement between the TPLF and the Ethiopian Government. However, Ethiopia continues to experience ethnic-based violence as other groups – including the Oromo Liberation Army (OLA) and Amhara militia Fano – seek concessions from the Ethiopian Government.

GEOGRAPHY

Location: Eastern Africa, west of Somalia

Geographic coordinates: 8 00 N, 38 00 E

Map references: Africa

Area: *total:* 1,104,300 sq km
land: 1,096,570 sq km
water: 7,730 sq km
note: area numbers are approximate since a large portion of the Ethiopia-Somalia border is undefined
comparison ranking: total 28

Area - comparative: slightly less than twice the size of Texas

Land boundaries: *total:* 5,925 km
border countries (6): Djibouti 342 km; Eritrea 1,033 km; Kenya 867 km; Somalia 1,640 km; South Sudan 1,299 km; Sudan 744 km

Coastline: 0 km (landlocked)

Maritime claims: none (landlocked)

Climate: tropical monsoon with wide topographic-induced variation

Terrain: high plateau with central mountain range divided by Great Rift Valley

Elevation: *highest point:* Ras Dejen 4,550 m
lowest point: Danakil Depression -125 m
mean elevation: 1,330 m

Natural resources: small reserves of gold, platinum, copper, potash, natural gas, hydropower

Land use: *agricultural land:* 34.1% (2022 est.)
arable land: 14.5% (2022 est.)
permanent crops: 1.8% (2022 est.)
permanent pasture: 17.7% (2022 est.)
forest: 15% (2022 est.)
other: 50.9% (2022 est.)

Irrigated land: 1,814 sq km (2020)

Major lakes (area sq km): *fresh water lake(s):* Lake Tana - 3,600 sq km; Abaya Hayk - 1,160 sq km; Ch'amo Hayk - 550 sq km
salt water lake(s): Lake Turkana (shared with Kenya) - 6,400 sq km; Abhe Bid Hayk/Abhe Bad (shared with Djibouti) - 780 sq km;

Major rivers (by length in km): Blue Nile river source (shared with Sudan [m]) - 1,600 km
note: [s] after country name indicates river source; [m] after country name indicates river mouth

Major watersheds (area sq km): Atlantic Ocean drainage: *(Mediterranean Sea)* Nile (3,254,853 sq km)

Major aquifers: Ogaden-Juba Basin, Sudd Basin (Umm Ruwaba Aquifer)

Population distribution: highest density is found in the highlands of the north and middle areas of the country, particularly around the centrally located capital city of Addis Ababa; the far east and southeast are sparsely populated, as shown in this population distribution map

Natural hazards: geologically active Great Rift Valley susceptible to earthquakes, volcanic eruptions; frequent droughts
volcanism: volcanic activity in the Great Rift Valley; Erta Ale (613 m) is the country's most active volcano; Dabbahu became active in 2005, forcing evacuations;

other historically active volcanoes include Alayta, Dalaffilla, Dallol, Dama Ali, Fentale, Kone, Manda Hararo, and Manda-Inakir

Geography - note: the most populous landlocked country in the world; the Blue Nile, the chief head-stream of the Nile by water volume, rises in T'ana Hayk (Lake Tana) in northwest Ethiopia

PEOPLE AND SOCIETY

Population: *total:* 118,550,298 (2024 est.)
male: 59,062,093
female: 59,488,205
comparison rankings: total 12; male 13; female 12

Nationality: *noun:* Ethiopian(s)
adjective: Ethiopian

Ethnic groups: Oromo 35.8%, Amhara 24.1%, Somali 7.2%, Tigray 5.7%, Sidama 4.1%, Guragie 2.6%, Welaita 2.3%, Afar 2.2%, Silte 1.3%, Kefficho 1.2%, other 13.5% (2022 est.)

Languages: Oromo (official regional working language) 33.8%, Amharic (official national language) 29.3%, Somali (official regional working language) 6.2%, Tigrigna (Tigrinya) (official regional working language) 5.9%, Sidamo 4%, Wolaytta 2.2%, Gurage 2%, Afar (official regional working language) 1.7%, Hadiyya 1.7%, Gamo 1.5%, Gedeo 1.3%, Opuuo 1.2%, Kafa 1.1%, other 8.1%, English (2007 est.)
major-language sample(s):
Kitaaba Addunyaa Waan Qabataamaatiif - Kan Madda Odeeffannoo bu'uraawaatiif baay'ee barbaachisaa ta'e. (Oromo)
የአለም እውነታ መጽሐፍ፣ ለመሠረታዊ መረጃ እጅግ አስፈላጊ የሆነ ምንጭ:: (Amharic)

Religions: Ethiopian Orthodox 43.8%, Muslim 31.3%, Protestant 22.8%, Catholic 0.7%, traditional 0.6%, other 0.8% (2016 est.)

Age structure: *0-14 years:* 38.7% (male 23,092,496/female 22,765,882)
15-64 years: 58% (male 34,175,328/female 34,536,238)
65 years and over: 3.4% (2024 est.) (male 1,794,269/female 2,186,085)

Dependency ratios: *total dependency ratio:* 72.5 (2024 est.)
youth dependency ratio: 66.7 (2024 est.)
elderly dependency ratio: 5.8 (2024 est.)
potential support ratio: 17.3 (2024 est.)

Median age: *total:* 20.4 years (2024 est.)
male: 20.2 years
female: 20.7 years
comparison ranking: total 203

Population growth rate: 2.37% (2024 est.)
comparison ranking: 26

Birth rate: 29.6 births/1,000 population (2024 est.)
comparison ranking: 27

Death rate: 5.8 deaths/1,000 population (2024 est.)
comparison ranking: 164

Net migration rate: -0.1 migrant(s)/1,000 population (2024 est.)
comparison ranking: 96

Population distribution: highest density is found in the highlands of the north and middle areas of the country, particularly around the centrally located capital city of Addis Ababa; the far east and southeast are sparsely populated, as shown in this population distribution map

Urbanization: *urban population:* 23.2% of total population (2023)
rate of urbanization: 4.4% annual rate of change (2020-25 est.)

Major urban areas - population: 5.461 million ADDIS ABABA (capital) (2023)

Sex ratio: *at birth:* 1.03 male(s)/female
0-14 years: 1.01 male(s)/female
15-64 years: 0.99 male(s)/female
65 years and over: 0.82 male(s)/female
total population: 0.99 male(s)/female (2024 est.)

Mother's mean age at first birth: 19.3 years (2019 est.)
note: data represents median age at first birth among women 20-49

Maternal mortality ratio: 195 deaths/100,000 live births (2023 est.)
comparison ranking: 38

Infant mortality rate: *total:* 32.6 deaths/1,000 live births (2024 est.)
male: 37.4 deaths/1,000 live births
female: 27.6 deaths/1,000 live births
comparison ranking: total 40

Life expectancy at birth: *total population:* 67.7 years (2024 est.)
male: 65.4 years
female: 70 years
comparison ranking: total population 196

Total fertility rate: 3.84 children born/woman (2024 est.)
comparison ranking: 27

Gross reproduction rate: 1.89 (2024 est.)

Drinking water source: *improved: urban:* 83.2% of population (2022 est.)
rural: 42.2% of population (2022 est.)
total: 51.5% of population (2022 est.)
unimproved: urban: 16.8% of population (2022 est.)
rural: 57.8% of population (2022 est.)
total: 48.5% of population (2022 est.)

Health expenditure: 3.2% of GDP (2021)
5.7% of national budget (2022 est.)

Physician density: 0.14 physicians/1,000 population (2023)

Hospital bed density: 0.3 beds/1,000 population (2016 est.)

Sanitation facility access: *improved: urban:* 50.8% of population (2022 est.)
rural: 8.2% of population (2022 est.)
total: 17.8% of population (2022 est.)
unimproved: urban: 49.2% of population (2022 est.)
rural: 91.8% of population (2022 est.)
total: 82.2% of population (2022 est.)

Obesity - adult prevalence rate: 4.5% (2016)
comparison ranking: 185

Alcohol consumption per capita: *total:* 1.16 liters of pure alcohol (2019 est.)
beer: 0.92 liters of pure alcohol (2019 est.)
wine: 0 liters of pure alcohol (2019 est.)
spirits: 0.2 liters of pure alcohol (2019 est.)
other alcohols: 0.03 liters of pure alcohol (2019 est.)
comparison ranking: total 149

Tobacco use: *total:* 4.5% (2025 est.)
male: 7.7% (2025 est.)
female: 1.4% (2025 est.)
comparison ranking: total 164

Children under the age of 5 years underweight: 21.2% (2019)
comparison ranking: 11

Currently married women (ages 15-49): 67.5% (2023 est.)

Child marriage: *women married by age 15:* 14.1% (2016)
women married by age 18: 40.3% (2016)
men married by age 18: 5% (2016)

Education expenditure: 2.3% of GDP (2024 est.)
16.7% national budget (2024 est.)
comparison ranking: Education expenditure (% GDP) 180

Literacy: *total population:* 47.5% (2016 est.)
male: 62.6% (2016 est.)
female: 40.4% (2019 est.)

ENVIRONMENT

Environmental issues: deforestation; overgrazing; soil erosion; desertification; loss of biodiversity; water shortages in some areas from water-intensive farming and poor management; industrial pollution and pesticides contribute to air, water, and soil pollution

International environmental agreements: *party to:* Biodiversity, Climate Change, Climate Change-Kyoto Protocol, Climate Change-Paris Agreement, Comprehensive Nuclear Test Ban, Desertification, Endangered Species, Hazardous Wastes, Ozone Layer Protection
signed, but not ratified: Environmental Modification, Law of the Sea, Nuclear Test Ban

Climate: tropical monsoon with wide topographic-induced variation

Urbanization: *urban population:* 23.2% of total population (2023)
rate of urbanization: 4.4% annual rate of change (2020-25 est.)

Carbon dioxide emissions: 18.519 million metric tonnes of CO_2 (2023 est.)
from coal and metallurgical coke: 3.427 million metric tonnes of CO_2 (2023 est.)
from petroleum and other liquids: 15.092 million metric tonnes of CO_2 (2023 est.)
comparison ranking: total emissions 93

Particulate matter emissions: 23.5 micrograms per cubic meter (2019 est.)

Methane emissions: *energy:* 1,108.5 kt (2022-2024 est.)
agriculture: 1,948.6 kt (2019-2021 est.)
waste: 356.3 kt (2019-2021 est.)
other: 143.9 kt (2019-2021 est.)

Waste and recycling: *municipal solid waste generated annually:* 6.533 million tons (2024 est.)
percent of municipal solid waste recycled: 12.8% (2022 est.)

Total water withdrawal: *municipal:* 810 million cubic meters (2022 est.)
industrial: 51.1 million cubic meters (2022 est.)
agricultural: 9.687 billion cubic meters (2022 est.)

Total renewable water resources: 122 billion cubic meters (2022 est.)

GOVERNMENT

Country name: *conventional long form:* Federal Democratic Republic of Ethiopia
conventional short form: Ethiopia
local long form: YeItyop'iya Federalawi Demokrasiyawi Ripeblik
local short form: Ityop'iya
former: Abyssinia, Italian East Africa
abbreviation: FDRE

etymology: the country name derives from the ancient Greek word used to describe the inhabitants, *aithiops*, meaning "burnt appearance"

Government type: federal parliamentary republic

Capital: *name:* Addis Ababa
geographic coordinates: 9 02 N, 38 42 E
time difference: UTC+3 (8 hours ahead of Washington, DC, during Standard Time)
etymology: the name in Amharic means "new flower;" Empress TAITU gave the name to the new capital city in 1887

Administrative divisions: 12 ethnically based regional states (*kililoch*, singular - *kilil*) and 2 chartered cities* (*astedader akabibiwach*, singular - *astedader akabibi*); Adis Abeba* (Addis Ababa), Afar, Amara (Amhara), Binshangul Gumuz, Dire Dawa*, Gambela Hizboch (Gambela), Hareri Hizb (Harari), Oromia, Sidama, Sumale, Tigray, YeDebub Biheroch Bihereseboch na Hizboch (Southern Nations, Nationalities and Peoples), YeDebub M'irab Ityop'iya Hizboch (Southwest Ethiopia Peoples), Southern Ethiopia Peoples

Legal system: civil law system

Constitution: *history:* several previous; latest drafted June 1994, adopted 8 December 1994, entered into force 21 August 1995
amendment process: proposals submitted for discussion require two-thirds majority approval in either house of Parliament or majority approval of one-third of the State Councils; passage of amendments other than constitutional articles on fundamental rights and freedoms and the initiation and amendment of the constitution requires two-thirds majority vote in a joint session of Parliament and majority vote by two thirds of the State Councils; passage of amendments affecting rights and freedoms and amendment procedures requires two-thirds majority vote in each house of Parliament and majority vote by all the State Councils

International law organization participation: has not submitted an ICJ jurisdiction declaration; non-party state to the ICCt

Citizenship: *citizenship by birth:* no
citizenship by descent only: at least one parent must be a citizen of Ethiopia
dual citizenship recognized: no
residency requirement for naturalization: 4 years

Suffrage: 18 years of age; universal

Executive branch: *chief of state:* President TAYE Atske Selassie (since 7 October 2024)
head of government: Prime Minister ABIY Ahmed Ali (since April 2018)
cabinet: Council of Ministers selected by the prime minister and approved by the House of People's Representatives
election/appointment process: president indirectly elected by both chambers of Parliament for a 6-year term (eligible for a second term); prime minister designated by the majority party following legislative elections
most recent election date: 21 June 2021 and 30 September 2021 (scheduled 29 August 2020 election was postponed due to the COVID-19 pandemic)
election results: *2021:* SAHLE-WORK Zewde reelected president during joint session of Parliament, vote - 659 (unanimous); ABIY confirmed Prime Minister by House of Peoples' Representatives (4 October 2021)
2018: SAHLE-WORK Zewde elected president during joint session of Parliament, vote - 659 (unanimous); snap election held on 25 October 2018 due to resignation of President MULATA Teshome

Legislative branch: *legislative structure:* bicameral
note: the House of Federation is responsible for interpreting the constitution and federal-regional issues, and the House of People's Representatives is responsible for passing legislation

Legislative branch - lower chamber: *chamber name:* House of Peoples' Representatives (Yehizb Tewokayoch Mekir Bete)
number of seats: 547 (all directly elected)
electoral system: plurality/majority
scope of elections: full renewal
term in office: 5 years
most recent election date: 6/21/2021 to 9/30/2021
parties elected and seats per party: Prosperity Party (448); Other (22)
percentage of women in chamber: 41.9%
expected date of next election: June 2026
note: only 470 of the 547 seats in the House of People's Representatives were filled during the 2021 elections due to security issues in the Tigray State and other areas

Legislative branch - upper chamber: *chamber name:* House of the Federation (Yefedereshein Mekir Bete)
number of seats: 153 (all indirectly elected)
scope of elections: full renewal
term in office: 5 years
most recent election date: 10/4/2021
percentage of women in chamber: 29.7%
expected date of next election: October 2026

Judicial branch: *highest court(s):* Federal Supreme Court (consists of 11 judges)
judge selection and term of office: president and vice president of Federal Supreme Court recommended by the prime minister and appointed by the House of People's Representatives; other Supreme Court judges nominated by the Federal Judicial Administrative Council (a 10-member body chaired by the president of the Federal Supreme Court) and appointed by the House of People's Representatives; judges serve until retirement at age 60
subordinate courts: federal high courts and federal courts of first instance; state court systems (mirror structure of federal system); sharia courts and customary and traditional courts
note: the House of Federation has jurisdiction for all constitutional issues

Political parties: Ethiopian Citizens for Social Justice and Democracy or EZEMA
Gedeo People's Democratic Party
Independent
Kucha People Democratic Party
National Movement of Amhara or NAMA
Prosperity Party or PP

Diplomatic representation in the US: *chief of mission:* Ambassador BINALF Andualem Ashenef (since 25 February 2025)
chancery: 3506 International Drive NW, Washington, DC 20008
telephone: [1] (202) 364-1200
FAX: [1] (202) 587-0195
email address and website: ethiopia@ethiopianembassy.org
https://ethiopianembassy.org/
consulate(s) general: Los Angeles, St. Paul (MN)

Diplomatic representation from the US: *chief of mission:* Ambassador Ervin MASSINGA (since 4 October 2023)
embassy: Entoto Street, P.O. Box 1014, Addis Ababa
mailing address: 2030 Addis Ababa Place, Washington DC 20521-2030
telephone: [251] 111-30-60-00
FAX: [251] 111-24-24-01
email address and website: AddisACS@state.gov
https://et.usembassy.gov/

International organization participation: ACP, AfDB, ATMIS, AU, BRICS, COMESA, EITI, FAO, G-24, G-77, IAEA, IBRD, ICAO, ICRM, IDA, IFAD, IFC, IFRCS, IGAD, ILO, IMF, IMO, Interpol, IOC, IOM, IPU, ISO, ITSO, ITU, ITUC (NGOs), MIGA, NAM, OPCW, PCA, UN, UNCTAD, UNESCO, UNHCR, UNIDO, UNMISS, UNOOSA, UNWTO, UPU, WCO, WFTU (NGOs), WHO, WIPO, WMO, WTO (accession candidate)

Independence: oldest independent country in Africa and one of the oldest in the world, at least 2,000 years; may be traced to the Aksumite Kingdom, which appeared in the first century B.C.

National holiday: Derg Downfall Day (defeat of MENGISTU regime), 28 May (1991)

Flag: *description:* three equal horizontal bands of green (top), yellow, and red, with a light blue disk centered on the three bands; on the disk is a yellow pentagram with single yellow rays emanating from the angles between the points
meaning: green stands for hope and the land's fertility, yellow for justice and harmony, and red for sacrifice and heroism; the blue of the disk symbolizes peace, and the pentagram represents the Ethiopian people's unity and equality
history: the emblem in the center of the current flag was added in 1996
note: Ethiopia is the oldest independent country in Africa, and newly independent African countries often adopted the Ethiopian flag's colors, which were later known as the Pan-African movement's colors

National symbol(s): Abyssinian lion (traditional), yellow pentagram with five rays of light on a blue field (promoted by government)

National color(s): green, yellow, red

National anthem(s): *title:* "Whedefit Gesgeshi Woud Enat Ethiopia" (March Forward, Dear Mother Ethiopia)
lyrics/music: DEREJE Melaku Mengesha/SOLOMON Lulu
history: adopted 1992

National heritage: *total World Heritage Sites:* 12 (10 cultural, 2 natural)
selected World Heritage Site locales: Rock-Hewn Churches, Lalibela (c); Simien National Park (n); Fasil Ghebbi, Gondar Region (c); Aksum (c); Lower Valley of the Awash (c); Lower Valley of the Omo (c); Tiya (c); Harar Jugol, the Fortified Historic Town (c); Konso Cultural Landscape (c); Gedeo Cultural Landscape (c); Bale Mountains National Park (n); Melka Kunture and Balchit: Archaeological and Palaeontological Sites in the Highland Area of Ethiopia (c)

ECONOMY

Economic overview: low-income, fast-growing Horn of Africa economy; widespread poverty and food insecurity worsened by conflict and environmental factors; landlocked with tensions over seaport access; development aid supporting reforms to boost private-sector growth and financial stability; challenge of creating jobs for growing labor force

Real GDP (purchasing power parity): $380.895 billion (2024 est.)
$354.926 billion (2023 est.)
$332.97 billion (2022 est.)
note: data in 2021 dollars
comparison ranking: 56

Real GDP growth rate: 7.3% (2024 est.)
6.6% (2023 est.)
5.3% (2022 est.)
note: annual GDP % growth based on constant local currency
comparison ranking: 15

Real GDP per capita: $2,900 (2024 est.)
$2,800 (2023 est.)
$2,700 (2022 est.)
note: data in 2021 dollars
comparison ranking: 195

GDP (official exchange rate): $126.773 billion (2022 est.)
note: data in current dollars at official exchange rate

Inflation rate (consumer prices): 21% (2024 est.)
30.2% (2023 est.)
33.9% (2022 est.)
note: annual % change based on consumer prices
comparison ranking: 191

GDP - composition, by sector of origin: *agriculture:* 34.9% (2024 est.)
industry: 25.4% (2024 est.)
services: 37.6% (2024 est.)
note: figures may not total 100% due to non-allocated consumption not captured in sector-reported data
comparison rankings: agriculture 4; industry 84; services 197

GDP - composition, by end use: *household consumption:* 80.2% (2024 est.)
government consumption: 5.5% (2024 est.)
investment in fixed capital: 20.5% (2024 est.)
investment in inventories: 0% (2024 est.)
exports of goods and services: 5.6% (2024 est.)
imports of goods and services: -11.8% (2024 est.)
note: figures may not total 100% due to rounding or gaps in data collection

Agricultural products: maize, cereals, wheat, milk, sorghum, barley, taro, beans, sweet potatoes, potatoes (2023)
note: top ten agricultural products based on tonnage

Industries: food processing, beverages, textiles, leather, garments, chemicals, metals processing, cement

Industrial production growth rate: 9.2% (2024 est.)
note: annual % change in industrial value added based on constant local currency
comparison ranking: 16

Labor force: 54.47 million (2024 est.)
note: number of people ages 15 or older who are employed or seeking work
comparison ranking: 13

Unemployment rate: 3.4% (2024 est.)
3.5% (2023 est.)
3.5% (2022 est.)
note: % of labor force seeking employment
comparison ranking: 53

Youth unemployment rate (ages 15-24): *total:* 5.4% (2024 est.)
male: 4% (2024 est.)
female: 7.2% (2024 est.)
note: % of labor force ages 15-24 seeking employment
comparison ranking: total 160

Population below poverty line: 23.5% (2015 est.)
note: % of population with income below national poverty line

Gini Index coefficient - distribution of family income: 31.1 (2021 est.)
note: index (0-100) of income distribution; higher values represent greater inequality
comparison ranking: 113

Average household expenditures: *on food:* 37.9% of household expenditures (2023 est.)
on alcohol and tobacco: 3.1% of household expenditures (2023 est.)

Household income or consumption by percentage share: *lowest 10%:* 3.5% (2021 est.)
highest 10%: 24.8% (2021 est.)
note: % share of income accruing to lowest and highest 10% of population

Remittances: 0.33% of GDP (2023 est.)
0.4% of GDP (2022 est.)
0.4% of GDP (2021 est.)
note: personal transfers and compensation between resident and non-resident individuals/households/entities

Budget: *revenues:* $8.808 billion (2023 est.)
expenditures: $12.49 billion (2023 est.)
note: central government revenues and expenses (excluding grants/extrabudgetary units/social security funds) converted to US dollars at average official exchange rate for year indicated

Public debt: 31.4% of GDP (2019 est.)
note: central government debt as a % of GDP
comparison ranking: 165

Taxes and other revenues: 3.9% (of GDP) (2023 est.)
note: central government tax revenue as a % of GDP
comparison ranking: 149

Current account balance: -$4.788 billion (2023 est.)
-$5.16 billion (2022 est.)
-$4.507 billion (2021 est.)
note: balance of payments - net trade and primary/secondary income in current dollars
comparison ranking: 170

Exports: $10.865 billion (2023 est.)
$10.971 billion (2022 est.)
$9.496 billion (2021 est.)
note: balance of payments - exports of goods and services in current dollars
comparison ranking: 115

Exports - partners: USA 12%, China 10%, UAE 8%, Saudi Arabia 8%, Netherlands 5% (2023)
note: top five export partners based on percentage share of exports

Exports - commodities: coffee, garments, dried legumes, cut flowers, oil seeds (2023)
note: top five export commodities based on value in dollars

Imports: $22.951 billion (2023 est.)
$24.187 billion (2022 est.)
$20.859 billion (2021 est.)
note: balance of payments - imports of goods and services in current dollars
comparison ranking: 91

Imports - partners: China 26%, Djibouti 16%, India 7%, Kuwait 7%, Saudi Arabia 6% (2023)
note: top five import partners based on percentage share of imports

Imports - commodities: refined petroleum, fertilizers, plastics, raw sugar, cars (2023)
note: top five import commodities based on value in dollars

Reserves of foreign exchange and gold: $3.784 billion (2024 est.)
$2.028 billion (2023 est.)
$1.192 billion (2022 est.)
note: holdings of gold (year-end prices)/foreign exchange/special drawing rights in current dollars
comparison ranking: 108

Debt - external: $25.426 billion (2023 est.)
note: present value of external debt in current US dollars
comparison ranking: 31

Exchange rates: birr (ETB) per US dollar -

Exchange rates: 54.601 (2023 est.)
51.756 (2022 est.)
43.734 (2021 est.)
34.927 (2020 est.)
29.07 (2019 est.)

ENERGY

Electricity access: *electrification - total population:* 55% (2022 est.)
electrification - urban areas: 94%
electrification - rural areas: 43%

Electricity: *installed generating capacity:* 5.69 million kW (2023 est.)
consumption: 12.298 billion kWh (2023 est.)
exports: 1.762 billion kWh (2023 est.)
transmission/distribution losses: 4.194 billion kWh (2023 est.)
comparison rankings: installed generating capacity 84; consumption 97; exports 63; transmission/distribution losses 155

Electricity generation sources: *solar:* 0.2% of total installed capacity (2023 est.)
wind: 3.1% of total installed capacity (2023 est.)
hydroelectricity: 96.5% of total installed capacity (2023 est.)
geothermal: 0.2% of total installed capacity (2023 est.)

Coal: *production:* 456,000 metric tons (2023 est.)
consumption: 1.653 million metric tons (2023 est.)
exports: 1,000 metric tons (2022 est.)
imports: 1.153 million metric tons (2023 est.)

Petroleum: *refined petroleum consumption:* 102,000 bbl/day (2023 est.)
crude oil estimated reserves: 428,000 barrels (2021 est.)

Natural gas: *proven reserves:* 24.919 billion cubic meters (2021 est.)

Energy consumption per capita: 2.366 million Btu/person (2023 est.)
comparison ranking: 181

COMMUNICATIONS

Telephones - fixed lines: *total subscriptions:* 862,000 (2022 est.)
subscriptions per 100 inhabitants: 1 (2022 est.) less than 1
comparison ranking: total subscriptions 73

Telephones - mobile cellular: *total subscriptions:* 71.4 million (2022 est.)
subscriptions per 100 inhabitants: 56 (2022 est.)
comparison ranking: total subscriptions 25

Broadcast media: 10 public/state broadcasters; 9 public/state radio stations; 13 commercial FM radio stations; 18 commercial TV stations; 45 community radio stations; 5 community TV stations (2023)

Internet country code: .et

Internet users: *percent of population:* 17% (2021 est.)

Broadband - fixed subscriptions: *total:* 566,000 (2022 est.)
subscriptions per 100 inhabitants: (2022 est.) less than 1
comparison ranking: total 91

TRANSPORTATION

Civil aircraft registration country code prefix: ET

Airports: 58 (2025)
comparison ranking: 78

Heliports: 1 (2025)
comparison ranking: 145

Railways: *total:* 659 km (2017) (Ethiopian segment of the 756 km Addis Ababa-Djibouti railroad)
standard gauge: 659 km (2017) 1.435-m gauge
note: electric railway with redundant power supplies; under joint control of Djibouti and Ethiopia and managed by a Chinese contractor

Merchant marine: *total:* 12 (2023)
by type: general cargo 10, oil tanker 2
comparison ranking: total 156

MILITARY AND SECURITY

Military and security forces: Ethiopian National Defense Force (ENDF; aka Federal Defense Force of Ethiopia, FDRE): Army, Air Force, Naval Force, Defense Cyber Main Directorate (2025)
note 1: national and regional police forces are responsible for law enforcement and maintenance of order, with the ENDF sometimes providing internal security support; the Ethiopian Federal Police (EFP) report to the Prime Minister's Office
note 2: the regional governments control regional security forces, including "special" paramilitary forces, which generally operate independently from the federal government and in some cases operate as regional defense forces maintaining national borders; in April 2023, the federal government ordered the integration of these regional special forces into the EFP or ENDF; in some cases, the regional governments have maintained former members of the special forces for "crowd control/Adma Bitena" as a separate unit within their security structures; local militias also operate across the country in loose and varying coordination with regional security and police forces, the ENDF, and the EFP
note 3: in 2018, Ethiopia established a Republican Guard military unit as a separate command operationally under the Office of the Prime Minister and administratively accountable to the Ministry of Defense; it is responsible for protecting senior officials and government institutions and conducting some military operations

Military expenditures: 0.7% of GDP (2024 est.)
1% of GDP (2023 est.)
1.7% of GDP (2022 est.)
0.5% of GDP (2021 est.)
0.5% of GDP (2020 est.)

Military and security service personnel strengths: available information varies widely; estimated 150-300,000 active-duty Defense Force (2025)

Military equipment inventories and acquisitions: the ENDF's major weapons and equipment inventory has traditionally been comprised of Russian, Soviet, and Eastern bloc material; it suffered considerable equipment losses during the 2020-2022 Tigray conflict; in more recent years, Ethiopia has diversified its arms sources to include weapons from China, Israel, Turkey, Ukraine, and the UAE; Ethiopia has a modest industrial defense base centered on small arms and production of armored vehicles under license (2024)

Military service age and obligation: 18-22 years of age for voluntary military service (although the military may, when necessary, recruit a person more than 22 years old); no compulsory military service, but the military can conduct callups when necessary and compliance is compulsory (2023)

Military deployments: as many as 10,000 troops Somalia (approximately 2,500 under the AU; the remainder under a bilateral agreement with the Somali Government); 1,500 South Sudan (UNMISS) (2024)

Military - note: the Ethiopian National Defense Force (ENDF) is focused on both external threats emanating from its neighbors and internal threats from multiple internal armed groups; since 1998, the ENDF has engaged in several conventional and counterinsurgency operations, including border wars with Eritrea (1998-2000) and Somalia (2006-2008) and internal conflicts with the Tigray regional state (2020-2022), multiple insurgent groups and ethnic militias, and the al-Shabaab terrorist group; as of 2025, the ENDF was actively conducting counterinsurgency operations against anti-government militants in several states, including the Amhara militia Fano and the Oromo Liberation Army (OLA), as well as al-Shabaab in Somalia (2025)

SPACE

Space agency/agencies: Ethiopian Space Science and Geospatial Institute (ESSGI; formed in 2022 from the joining of the Ethiopian Space Science and Technology Institute or ESSTI and the Ethiopian Geospatial Information Institute or EGII) (2025)

Space program overview: has a small space program focused on acquiring and operating satellites, as well as conducting research; jointly builds satellites with foreign partners and operates and exploits remote sensing (RS) satellites; developing the ability to manufacture satellites and their associated payloads; involved in astronomy and in the construction of space observatories; cooperates on space-related issues with a variety of countries, including China, France, India, Russia, and multiple African countries, particularly Kenya, Rwanda, Sudan, Tanzania, and Uganda; shares RS data with neighboring countries (2025)
note: further details about the key activities, programs, and milestones of the country's space program, as well as government spending estimates on the space sector, appear in the Space Programs reference guide

TERRORISM

Terrorist group(s): Terrorist group(s): al-Shabaab
note: details about the history, aims, leadership, organization, areas of operation, tactics, targets, weapons, size, and sources of support of the group(s) appear(s) in Appendix T

TRANSNATIONAL ISSUES

Refugees and internally displaced persons: *refugees:* 1,071,881 (2024 est.)

IDPs: 3,134,600 (2024 est.)

EUROPEAN UNION

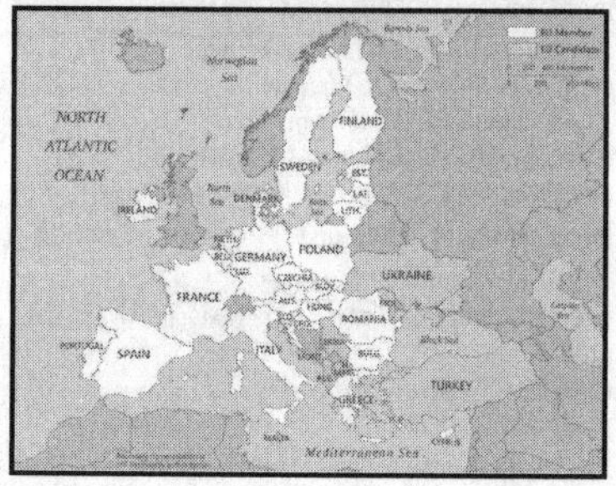

INTRODUCTION

Preliminary statement: The European Union's (EU) evolution is unprecedented in history, transforming from a regional economic agreement among six neighboring states in 1951 to today's hybrid intergovernmental and supranational organization of 27 countries across the European continent. Such a large number of nation-states ceding some of their sovereignty to an overarching entity is unique. Dynastic unions for territorial consolidation were long the norm in Europe, although country-level unions were sometimes arranged, such as the Polish-Lithuanian Commonwealth and the Austro-Hungarian Empire.

The EU is not a federation in the strict sense, but it is far more than a free-trade association such as ASEAN or Mercosur. It has certain attributes associated with independent nations: its own flag, currency (for some members), and law-making abilities, as well as diplomatic representation and a common foreign and security policy in its dealings with external partners.

For these reasons, *The World Factbook* includes basic information on the EU as a separate entity.

Background: In the aftermath and devastation of the two World Wars, a number of far-sighted European leaders in the late 1940s sought to respond to the overwhelming desire for peace and reconciliation on the continent. In 1950, French Foreign Minister Robert SCHUMAN proposed pooling the production of coal and steel in Western Europe, which would bring France and West Germany together and be open to other countries as well. The following year, the European Coal and Steel Community (ECSC) was set up when six members – Belgium, France, West Germany, Italy, Luxembourg, and the Netherlands – signed the Treaty of Paris.

Within a few years, the ECSC was so successful that member states decided to further integrate their economies. In 1957, envisioning an "ever closer union," the Treaties of Rome created the European Economic Community (EEC) and the European Atomic Energy Community (Euratom), which eliminated trade barriers among the six member states to create a common market. In 1967, the institutions of all three communities were formally merged into the European Community (EC), creating a single Commission, a single Council of Ministers, and a legislative body known today as the European Parliament. Members of the European Parliament were initially selected by national parliaments, but direct elections began in 1979 and have been held every five years since.

In 1973, the first enlargement of the EC added Denmark, Ireland, and the UK. The 1980s saw further membership expansion, with Greece joining in 1981 and Spain and Portugal in 1986. The 1992 Treaty of Maastricht laid the basis for further cooperation in foreign and defense policy and judicial and internal affairs, as well as the creation of an economic and monetary union – including a common currency. The Maastricht Treaty created the European Union (EU), at the time standing alongside the EC. In 1995, Austria, Finland, and Sweden joined the EU/EC, raising the total number of member states to 15. On 1 January 1999, the new euro currency was launched in world markets and became the unit of exchange for all EU member states except Denmark, Sweden, and the UK. In 2002, citizens of the 12 participating member states began using euro banknotes and coins.

In an effort to ensure that the EU could function efficiently with an expanded membership, the Treaty of Nice in 2000 set forth rules to streamline the size and procedures of the EU's institutions. An effort to establish a "Constitution for Europe," growing out of a Convention held in 2002-2003, foundered when it was rejected in referenda in France and the Netherlands in 2005. A subsequent effort in 2007 incorporated many features of the rejected draft Constitutional Treaty, while also making a number of substantive as well as symbolic changes. The new treaty, referred to as the Treaty of Lisbon, sought to amend existing treaties rather than replace them. The treaty was approved at a conference of member states, and after all member states ratified, the Lisbon Treaty came into force on 1 December 2009, at which point the EU officially replaced and succeeded the EC.

Ten new countries joined the EU in 2004 – Cyprus, the Czech Republic, Estonia, Hungary, Latvia, Lithuania, Malta, Poland, Slovakia, and Slovenia. Bulgaria and Romania joined in 2007 and Croatia in 2013. UK citizens on 23 June 2016 narrowly voted to leave the EU; the formal exit, widely known as "Brexit," took place on 31 January 2020. The EU and the UK negotiated a withdrawal agreement that included a status quo transition period through December 2020, when the follow-on EU-UK Trade and Cooperation Agreement was concluded. Current EU membership stands at 27. Eight of the newer member states – Croatia, Cyprus, Estonia, Latvia, Lithuania, Malta, Slovakia, and Slovenia – have now adopted the euro, bringing total euro-zone membership to 20.

GEOGRAPHY

Location: Europe between the North Atlantic Ocean in the west and Russia, Belarus, and Ukraine to the east

Map references: Europe

Area: *total:* 4,236,351 sq km
rank by area (sq km):
1. France (includes five overseas regions) 643,801
2. Spain 505,370
3. Sweden 450,295
4. Germany 357,022
5. Finland 338,145
6. Poland 312,685
7. Italy 301,340
8. Romania 238,391
9. Greece 131,957
10. Bulgaria 110,879
11. Hungary 93,028
12. Portugal 92,090
13. Austria 83,871
14. Czechia 78,867
15. Ireland 70,273
16. Lithuania 65,300
17. Latvia 64,589
18. Croatia 56,594
19. Slovakia 49,035
20. Estonia 45,228
21. Denmark 43,094
22. Netherlands 41,543
23. Belgium 30,528
24. Slovenia 20,273
25. Cyprus 9,251
26. Luxembourg 2,586
27. Malta 316

Area - comparative: less than one-half the size of the United States

Land boundaries: *total:* 13,770 km
border countries (18): Albania 212 km; Andorra 118 km; Belarus 1,176 km; Bosnia and Herzegovina 956 km; Holy See 3 km; Liechtenstein 34 km; North Macedonia 396 km; Moldova 683 km; Monaco 6 km; Montenegro 19 km; Norway 2,375 km; Russia 2,435 km; San Marino 37 km; Serbia 1,353 km; Switzerland 1,729 km; Turkey 415 km; United Kingdom 499 km; Ukraine 1,324 km
note: data for European continent only

Coastline: 53,563.9 km

Climate: cold temperate; potentially subarctic in the north to temperate; mild wet winters; hot dry summers in the south

Terrain: fairly flat along Baltic and Atlantic coasts; mountainous in the central and southern areas

Elevation: *highest point:* Mont Blanc, France 4,810 m
lowest point: Zuidplaspolder, Netherlands -7 m

Natural resources: iron ore, natural gas, petroleum, coal, copper, lead, zinc, bauxite, uranium, potash, salt, hydropower, arable land, timber, fish

Irrigated land: 154,539.82 sq km (2011 est.)

Population distribution: population distribution varies considerably from country to country but tends to follow a pattern of coastal and river settlement, with urban agglomerations forming large hubs; the area in and around the Netherlands, Belgium, and Luxembourg (known collectively as Benelux), is the most densely populated area in the EU

Natural hazards: flooding along coasts; avalanches in mountainous area; earthquakes in the south; volcanic eruptions in Italy; periodic droughts in Spain; ice floes in the Baltic Sea region

PEOPLE AND SOCIETY

Population: *total:* 451,815,312 (2024 est.)
male: 220,631,332
female: 231,183,980

Languages: Bulgarian, Croatian, Czech, Danish, Dutch, English, Estonian, Finnish, French, German, Greek, Hungarian, Irish, Italian, Latvian, Lithuanian, Maltese, Polish, Portuguese, Romanian, Slovak, Slovene, Spanish, Swedish
note: only the 24 official languages are listed; German, the major language of Germany and Austria, is the most widely spoken mother tongue - about 16% of the EU population; English is the most widely spoken foreign language - about 29% of the EU population is conversant with it; English is an official language in Ireland and Malta and thus remained an official EU language after the UK left the bloc (2020)

Religions: Roman Catholic 41%, Orthodox 10%, Protestant 9%, other Christian 4%, Muslim 2%, other 4% (includes Jewish, Sikh, Buddhist, Hindu), atheist 10%, non-believer/agnostic 17%, unspecified 3% (2019 est.)

Age structure: *0-14 years:* 14.5% (male 33,606,273/female 31,985,118)
15-64 years: 63.5% (male 143,874,460/female 143,104,994)
65 years and over: 22% (2024 est.) (male 43,150,599/female 56,093,868)

Dependency ratios: *total dependency ratio:* 57.2 (2024)
youth dependency ratio: 22.8 (2024)
elderly dependency ratio: 34.5 (2024)
potential support ratio: 3 (2024)

Median age: *total:* 44 years (2020)
male: 42.6 years
female: 45.5 years

Population growth rate: 0.1% (2021 est.)

Birth rate: 8.9 births/1,000 population (2024 est.)

Death rate: 11.2 deaths/1,000 population (2024 est.)

Net migration rate: -2.85 migrant(s)/1,000 population

Population distribution: population distribution varies considerably from country to country but tends to follow a pattern of coastal and river settlement, with urban agglomerations forming large hubs; the area in and around the Netherlands, Belgium, and Luxembourg (known collectively as Benelux), is the most densely populated area in the EU

Sex ratio: *at birth:* 1.05 male(s)/female
0-14 years: 1.05 male(s)/female
15-64 years: 1.01 male(s)/female
65 years and over: 0.77 male(s)/female
total population: 0.95 male(s)/female (2024 est.)

Infant mortality rate: *total:* 3.4 deaths/1,000 live births (2024 est.)

Life expectancy at birth: *total population:* 77.63 years (2021)
male: 72.98 years
female: 82.51 years

Total fertility rate: 1.54 children born/woman (2024 est.)

Gross reproduction rate: 0.75 (2024 est.)

Health expenditure: 10.9% of GDP (2021)

Education expenditure: 5% of GDP (2020 est.)

ENVIRONMENT

Environmental issues: various forms of air, soil, and water pollution; see individual country entries

International environmental agreements: *party to:* Air Pollution, Air Pollution-Heavy Metals, Air Pollution-Multi-effect Protocol, Air Pollution-Nitrogen Oxides, Air Pollution-Persistent Organic Pollutants, Air Pollution-Sulphur 94, Antarctic-Marine Living Resources, Biodiversity, Climate Change, Climate Change-Kyoto Protocol, Climate Change-Paris Agreement, Desertification, Endangered Species, Hazardous Wastes, Law of the Sea, Ozone Layer Protection, Tropical Timber 2006

signed, but not ratified: Air Pollution-Volatile Organic Compounds

Climate: cold temperate; potentially subarctic in the north to temperate; mild wet winters; hot dry summers in the south

Carbon dioxide emissions: 2.651 billion metric tonnes of CO2 (2023 est.)

from coal and metallurgical coke: 518.857 million metric tonnes of CO2 (2023 est.)

from petroleum and other liquids: 1.489 billion metric tonnes of CO2 (2023 est.)

from consumed natural gas: 643.8 million metric tonnes of CO2 (2023 est.)

Total renewable water resources: 1.7 trillion cubic meters (2019)

GOVERNMENT

Union name: *conventional long form:* European Union

abbreviation: EU

Government type: a hybrid and unique intergovernmental and supranational organization

Capital: *name:* Brussels (Belgium), Strasbourg (France), Luxembourg, Frankfurt (Germany)

geographic coordinates: (Brussels) 50 50 N, 4 20 E

time difference: UTC+1 (6 hours ahead of Washington, DC, during Standard Time)

daylight saving time: +1 hr, begins last Sunday in March; ends last Sunday in October

time zone note: the 27 European Union member states are spread across three time zones

note: the European Council and the Council of the European Union meet in Brussels, Belgium, except for Council of the EU meetings held in Luxembourg in April, June, and October; the European Parliament meets in Brussels and Strasbourg, France, and has administrative offices in Luxembourg; the Court of Justice of the European Union is located in Luxembourg; and the European Central Bank is located in Frankfurt, Germany

Member states

27 countries: Austria, Belgium, Bulgaria, Croatia, Cyprus, Czechia, Denmark, Estonia, Finland, France, Germany, Greece, Hungary, Ireland, Italy, Latvia, Lithuania, Luxembourg, Malta, Netherlands, Poland, Portugal, Romania, Slovakia, Slovenia, Spain, Sweden

13 overseas countries and territories: 1 with Denmark (Greenland), 6 with France (French Polynesia, French Southern and Antarctic Lands, New Caledonia, Saint Barthelemy, Saint Pierre and Miquelon, Wallis and Futuna), and 6 with the Netherlands (Aruba, Bonaire, Curacao, Saba, Sint Eustatius, Sint Maarten); all are part of the Overseas Countries and Territories Association (OCTA)

note 1: the 9 EU candidate countries include Albania, Bosnia and Herzegovina, Georgia, Moldova, Montenegro, North Macedonia, Serbia, Turkey, and Ukraine

note 2: several non-European overseas countries and territories (OCTs) have special relations with Denmark, France, and the Netherlands (list is annexed to the Treaty on the Functioning of the European Union) and are associated with the EU to promote their economic and social development; member states apply the same treatment to their trade with OCTs as they accord each other; OCT nationals are in principle EU citizens, but OCTs are not part of or subject to the EU

Legal system: unique supranational system in which EU treaties and EU law have primacy over member-state law

Constitution: *history:* none; the EU legal order relies primarily on the Treaty on European Union (TEU) and the Treaty on the Functioning of the EU (TFEU)

amendment process: EU treaties can be amended in several ways: 1) Ordinary Revision Procedure (for key amendments to the treaties); initiated by an EU member state, the European Parliament, or the European Commission; after the proposal is adopted by the European Council, a conference of national government representatives then reviews the proposal; passage requires ratification by all EU member states

2) Simplified Revision Procedure (for amendment of EU internal policies and actions); passage of a proposal requires unanimous European Council vote after European Council consultation with the European Commission, the European Parliament, and the European Central Bank (if the amendment concerns monetary matters) and requires ratification by all EU member states

3) Passerelle Clause; allows the alteration of a legislative procedure without a formal amendment of the treaties

4) Flexibility Clause; permits the EU to decide in subject areas where EU competences have not been explicitly granted in the treaties but are necessary to the attainment of treaty objectives

Suffrage: 18 years of age (16 years in Austria); universal; voting for the European Parliament occurs in each member state

Executive branch: *three EU institutions have functions that can be regarded as executive in nature: European Council* - composed of member-state heads of state or government, along with the president of the European Commission; meets at least four times a year to issue general policy guidance; the president of the European Council is appointed by leaders of the EU member states for a 2 1/2 year term, renewable once

president: António Costa (since 1 December 2024)

Council of the European Union - consists of member-state officials, ranging from working-level diplomats to cabinet ministers in specific policy fields such as foreign affairs, agriculture, or economy; has policymaking, coordinating, and legislative functions

president: the six-month presidency rotates among the member states

European Commission - composed of 27 commissioners (one from each member state), including the president; the president assigns each commissioner one or more policy areas, called portfolios; the Commission has the sole right to initiate EU legislation, except for foreign and security/defense policy, and is responsible for monitoring the application of EU law, implementing/executing the EU budget, negotiating in certain policy areas, and ensuring the EU's external representation in some policy areas; the president is nominated for a 5-year term by the European Council and confirmed by the European Parliament; the European Parliament also confirms the entire Commission for a 5-year term

president: Ursula von der Leyen (since 1 December 2019)

note: for external representation and foreign policy, member-state leaders appoint a High Representative of the Union for Foreign Affairs and Security Policy; the High Representative's concurrent appointment as Vice President of the European Commission is meant to bring more coherence to the EU's foreign policy; the High Representative helps develop and implement the EU's Common Foreign and Security Policy and Common Security and Defense Policy, chairs the Council of the EU's meetings of member-state foreign ministers, represents and acts for the EU in many international contexts, and oversees the European External Action Service, the EU's diplomatic corps

Legislative branch: *legislature name:* Council of the European Union (Council) and the European Parliament (EP) (separate legislative bodies; *see note 2*)

number of seats: Council - 27; EP - 720

electoral system: Council - none, composed of ministers from EU member states; EP - proportional representation

scope of elections: EP - full renewal

term in office: 5 years *note:* for the EP

most recent election date: EP - 6/9/2024

parties elected and seats per party: EP - PP (188); S&D (136); PfE (84); ECR (78); Renew (77); Greens/EFA (53); GUE-NGL (46); ESN (25); non-attached (12); other (21)

percentage of women in chamber: 39.8% *note:* for the EP

expected date of next election: EP - June 2029

note 1: the European Parliament (EP) President, Roberta METSOLA, was elected in January 2022 and reelected in July 2024 by a majority of EP members (MEPs)

note 2: the EP and the Council of the EU share responsibilities for adopting the bulk of EU legislation; the European Commission proposes legislation, and the two other bodies have to agree for the proposal to become law – except in the area of Common Foreign and Security Policy, which is governed by consensus of the EU member-state governments

Judicial branch: *highest court(s):* Court of Justice of the European Union, which includes the Court of Justice (informally known as the European Court of Justice or ECJ, includes 11 advocates general) and the General Court (consists of 27 judges, one drawn from each member state; can include additional judges); both the ECJ and the General Court sit in chambers of 3 to 5 judges but may sit in a Grand Chamber of 15 judges in special cases

judge selection and term of office: judges appointed by the common consent of the member states to serve 6-year renewable terms

Political parties: The Left or GUE/NGL

European Conservatives and Reformists or ECR

Greens/European Free Alliance or Greens/EFA

European People's Party or EPP

Europe of Sovereign Nations or ESN

Patriots for Europe or PfE

Progressive Alliance of Socialists and Democrats or S&D
Renew Europe or Renew (formerly Alliance of Liberals and Democrats for Europe or ALDE)

Diplomatic representation in the US: *chief of mission:* Ambassador Jovita NELIUPŠIENĖ, Head of Delegation (since 27 February 2024)
chancery: 2175 K Street NW, Washington, DC 20037
telephone: [1] (202) 862-9500

FAX: [1] (202) 429-1766
email address and website: delegation-usa-info@eeas.europa.eu
Delegation of the European Union to the United States of America | EEAS (europa.eu)

Diplomatic representation from the US: *chief of mission:* Ambassador Andrew PUZDER (since 11 September 2025)
embassy: Zinnerstraat - 13 - Rue Zinner, B-1000 Brussels
mailing address: use embassy street address
telephone: [32] (2) 811-4100
email address and website: https://useu.usmission.gov/

International organization participation: ARF, ASEAN (dialogue member), Australian Group, BIS, BSEC (observer), CBSS, CERN, EBRD, FAO, FATF, G-7, G-10, G-20, IDA, IEA, IGAD (partners), LAIA (observer), NSG (observer), OAS (observer), OECD, PIF (partner), SAARC (observer), SICA (observer), UN (observer), UNRWA (observer), wCo, WTO, ZC (observer)

Independence: 7 February 1992 (Maastricht Treaty signed establishing the European Union); 1 November 1993 (Maastricht Treaty entered into force)
note: the Treaties of Rome, signed on 25 March 1957 and entered into force on 1 January 1958, created the European Economic Community and the European Atomic Energy Community; a series of subsequent treaties increased efficiency and transparency, prepared for new member states, and introduced new areas of cooperation such as a single currency; the Treaty of Lisbon, signed on 13 December 2007 and entered into force on 1 December 2009, is the most recent

National holiday: Europe Day (also known as Schuman Day), 9 May (1950)

Flag: *description:* a blue field with 12 five-pointed gold stars arranged in a circle in the center; blue stands for the sky of the Western world, and the stars for unity, solidarity, and harmony
meaning: the number of stars is fixed and does not correspond to the number of member states

National symbol(s): a circle of 12 five-pointed golden-yellow stars on a blue field

National color(s): blue, yellow

National anthem(s): *title:* "European Anthem" (Ode to Joy)
lyrics/music: no lyrics/Ludwig VAN BEETHOVEN, arranged by Herbert VON KARAJAN
history: adopted 1985; the anthem is meant to represent all of Europe rather than just the organization, conveying the ideals of peace, freedom, and unity

ECONOMY

Real GDP (purchasing power parity): $24.441 trillion (2024 est.)
$24.17 trillion (2023 est.)
$24.036 trillion (2022 est.)
note: data in 2021 dollars

Real GDP growth rate: 1% (2024 est.)
0.5% (2023 est.)
3.5% (2022 est.)
note: annual GDP % growth based on constant local currency

Real GDP per capita: $54,300 (2024 est.)
$53,800 (2023 est.)
$53,700 (2022 est.)
note: data in 2021 dollars

GDP (official exchange rate): $19.423 trillion (2024 est.)
note: data in current dollars at official exchange rate

Inflation rate (consumer prices): 2.4% (2024 est.)
6.3% (2023 est.)
8.8% (2022 est.)
note: annual % change based on consumer prices

GDP - composition, by sector of origin: *agriculture:* 1.6% (2024 est.)
industry: 22.1% (2024 est.)
services: 66.1% (2024 est.)
note: figures may not total 100% due to non-allocated consumption not captured in sector-reported data

GDP - composition, by end use: *household consumption:* 51.6% (2023 est.)
government consumption: 20.8% (2023 est.)
investment in fixed capital: 22% (2023 est.)
investment in inventories: 0.4% (2023 est.)
exports of goods and services: 51.9% (2023 est.)
imports of goods and services: -48.3% (2023 est.)
note: figures may not total 100% due to rounding or gaps in data collection

Agricultural products: milk, wheat, sugar beets, maize, potatoes, barley, grapes, pork, rapeseed, tomatoes (2022)
note: top ten agricultural products based on tonnage for all EU member states

Industries: *among the world's largest and most technologically advanced regions, the EU industrial base includes:* ferrous and non-ferrous metal production and processing, metal products, petroleum, coal, cement, chemicals, pharmaceuticals, aerospace, rail transportation equipment, passenger and commercial vehicles, construction equipment, industrial equipment, shipbuilding, electrical power equipment, machine tools and automated manufacturing systems, electronics and telecommunications equipment, fishing, food and beverages, furniture, paper, textiles

Industrial production growth rate: -0.7% (2024 est.)
note: annual % change in industrial value added based on constant local currency

Labor force: 221.391 million (2024 est.)
note: number of people ages 15 or older who are employed or seeking work

Unemployment rate: 6% (2024 est.)
6.1% (2023 est.)
6.2% (2022 est.)
note: % of labor force seeking employment

Youth unemployment rate (ages 15-24): *total:* 15.9% (2024 est.)
male: 16% (2024 est.)
female: 16% (2024 est.)
note: % of labor force ages 15-24 seeking employment
Gini Index coefficient - distribution of family income 31 (2015 est.)

Remittances: 0.8% of GDP (2024 est.)
0.8% of GDP (2023 est.)
0.8% of GDP (2022 est.)
note: personal transfers and compensation between resident and non-resident individuals/households/entities

Taxes and other revenues: 19.8% (of GDP) (2022 est.)
note: central government tax revenue as a % of GDP

Exports: $9.783 trillion (2024 est.)
$9.689 trillion (2023 est.)
$9.425 trillion (2022 est.)
note: balance of payments - exports of goods and services in current dollars

Exports - partners: US 20%, UK 12%, China 10%, Switzerland 7%, Turkey 4% (2023)
note: top five non-EU export partners based on percentage share of external exports; does not include internal trade among EU member states

Exports - commodities: cars, packaged medicine, refined petroleum, vehicle parts/accessories, vaccines (2023)
note: top five export commodities based on value in dollars; includes both exports to external partners and internal trade among EU member states

Imports: $8.953 trillion (2024 est.)
$8.978 trillion (2023 est.)
$9.072 trillion (2022 est.)
note: balance of payments - imports of goods and services in current dollars

Imports - partners: China 21%, US 14%, UK 7%, Switzerland 6%, Norway 5% (2023)
note: top five non-EU import partners based on percentage share of external imports; does not include internal trade among EU member states

Imports - commodities: cars, crude petroleum, natural gas, refined petroleum, vehicle parts/accessories (2023)
note: top five import commodities based on value in dollars; includes both imports from external partners and internal trade among EU member states

Exchange rates: euros (EUR) per US dollar -

Exchange rates: 0.924 (2024 est.)
0.925 (2023 est.)
0.95 (2022 est.)
0.845 (2021 est.)
0.876 (2020 est.)

ENERGY

Electricity access: *electrification - total population:* 100% (2022 est.)

Electricity: *installed generating capacity:* 1.142 billion kW (2023 est.)
consumption: 2.511 trillion kWh (2023 est.)
exports: 407.824 billion kWh (2023 est.)
imports: 405.154 billion kWh (2023 est.)
transmission/distribution losses: 169.694 billion kWh (2023 est.)

Electricity generation sources: *fossil fuels:* 33.1% of total installed capacity (2023 est.)
nuclear: 22.1% of total installed capacity (2023 est.)
solar: 9.2% of total installed capacity (2023 est.)
wind: 17.7% of total installed capacity (2023 est.)
hydroelectricity: 11.7% of total installed capacity (2023 est.)
geothermal: 0.2% of total installed capacity (2023 est.)
biomass and waste: 6% of total installed capacity (2023 est.)

Nuclear energy: Number of operational nuclear reactors: 100 (2025)

Number of nuclear reactors under construction: 1 (2025)

Net capacity of operational nuclear reactors: 97.63GW (2025 est.)

Number of nuclear reactors permanently shut down: 75 (2025)

Coal: *production:* 304.827 million metric tons (2023 est.)
consumption: 398.817 million metric tons (2023 est.)
exports: 32.326 million metric tons (2023 est.)
imports: 127.304 million metric tons (2023 est.)
proven reserves: 84.193 billion metric tons (2023 est.)

Petroleum: *total petroleum production:* 748,000 bbl/day (2023 est.)
refined petroleum consumption: 11.022 million bbl/day (2023 est.)

Natural gas: *production:* 40.239 billion cubic meters (2023 est.)
consumption: 335.326 billion cubic meters (2023 est.)
exports: 100.238 billion cubic meters (2023 est.)
imports: 396.993 billion cubic meters (2023 est.)

Energy consumption per capita: 114.309 million Btu/person (2023 est.)

COMMUNICATIONS

Telephones - fixed lines: *total subscriptions:* 155.005 million (2022 est.)
subscriptions per 100 inhabitants: 36 (2022 est.)

Telephones - mobile cellular: *total subscriptions:* 552.316 million (2022 est.)
subscriptions per 100 inhabitants: 124 (2022 est.)

Internet country code: .eu
note: see country entries of member states for individual country codes

Internet users: *percent of population:* 90% (2023 est.)

Broadband - fixed subscriptions: *total:* 172.888 million (2022 est.)
subscriptions per 100 inhabitants: 39 (2022 est.)

TRANSPORTATION

Airports: 5,211 (2025)

Heliports: 2,069 (2025)

Railways: *total:* 4,894,173 km (2019)

MILITARY AND SECURITY

Military and security forces: the EU's Common Security and Defense Policy (CSDP) provides the civilian, military, and political structures for EU crisis management and security issues; the highest bodies are: the Political and Security Committee (PSC), which meets at the ambassadorial level as a preparatory body for the Council of the EU; it assists with defining policies and preparing a crisis response
the European Union Military Committee (EUMC) is the EU's highest military body; it is composed of the chiefs of defense (CHODs) of the Member States, who are regularly represented by their permanent Military Representatives; the EUMC provides the PSC with advice and recommendations on all military matters within the EU
the Committee for Civilian Aspects of Crisis Management (CIVCOM) provides advice and recommendations to the PSC in parallel with the EUMC on civilian aspects of crisis management
the Politico-Military Group (PMG) provides advice and recommendations to the PSC on political aspects of EU military and civil-military issues, including concepts, capabilities and operations and missions, and monitors implementation
other bodies set up under the CSDP include the Security and Defense Policy Directorate (SECDEFPOL), the Integrated approach for Security and Peace Directorate (ISP), the EU Military Staff (EUMS), the Civilian Planning and Conduct Capability (CPCC), the Civilian Operations Headquarters (CivOpsHQ), the Military Planning and Conduct Capability (MPCC), the European Defense Agency (EDA), the European Security and Defense College (ESDC), the EU Institute for Security Studies, the EU Satellite Center, the Peace, Partnerships and Crisis Management Directorate (PCM) (2025)
note 1: Frontex is the European Border and Coast Guard Agency that supports EU Member States and Schengen-associated countries in the management of the EU's external borders and the fight against cross-border crime; it has a standing corps of uniformed border guard officers directly employed by Frontex as staff members and regularly deployed to border guarding missions, plus thousands of other officers seconded by EU member states
note 2: in 2017, the EU set up the Permanent Structured Cooperation on Defense (PESCO), a mechanism for deepening defense cooperation amongst member states through binding commitments and collaborative programs on a variety of military-related capabilities such as cyber, maritime surveillance, medical support, operational readiness, procurement, and training

Military expenditures: 1.9% of GDP (2024 est.)
1.8% of GDP (2023 est.)
1.6% of GDP (2022 est.)
1.6% of GDP (2021 est.)
1.6% of GDP (2020 est.)
note 1: the European Defense Fund (EDF) has a budget of approximately $8 billion for 2021-2027; about $2.7 billion is devoted to funding collaborative defense research while about $5.3 billion is allocated for collaborative capability development projects that complement national contributions; the EDF identifies critical defense domains that it will support
note 2: NATO is separate from the EU and is resourced through the direct and indirect contributions of its members; NATO's common funds are direct contributions to collective budgets, capabilities and programs, which equate to only 0.3% of total NATO defense spending (approximately $3.3 billion for 2023) to develop capabilities and run NATO, its military commands, capabilities, and infrastructure; NATO's 2014 Defense Investment Pledge called for NATO members to meet the 2% of GDP guideline for defense spending and the 20% of annual defense expenditure on major new equipment by 2024
note 3: average spending for all NATO countries was 2.5% of GDP in 2023 and 2.7% of GDP in 2024

Military and security service personnel strengths: the combined countries of the EU had an estimated 1.4 m active military personnel in 2024; the largest EU country military forces belong to France, Germany, and Italy (2024)
note: the combined countries of NATO had an estimated 3.4 million active military personnel in 2024

Military deployments: since 2003, the EU has launched more than 30 civilian and military crisis-management, advisory, and training missions in Africa, Asia, Europe, and the Middle East, as well as counter-piracy operations off the coast of Somalia and a naval operation in the Mediterranean to disrupt human smuggling and trafficking networks and prevent the loss of life at sea (2024)
note: in response to the 2022 Russian invasion of Ukraine, the EU announced that it would develop a rapid deployment force consisting of up to 5,000 troops by 2025

Military - note: the EU partners with the North Atlantic Treaty Organization (NATO); NATO is an alliance of 32 countries from North America and Europe; its role is to safeguard the security of its member countries by political and military means; NATO conducts crisis management and peacekeeping missions; member countries that participate in the military aspect of the Alliance contribute forces and equipment, which remain under national command and control until a time when they are required by NATO for a specific purpose (i.e., conflict or crisis, peacekeeping); NATO, however, does possess some common capabilities owned and operated by the Alliance, such as some early warning radar aircraft; relations between NATO and the EU were institutionalized in the early 2000s, building on steps taken during the 1990s to promote greater European responsibility in defense matters; cooperation and coordination covers a broad array of issues, including crisis management, defense and political consultations, civil preparedness, capacity building, military capabilities, maritime security, planning, cyber defense, countering hybrid threats, information sharing, logistics, defense industry, counterterrorism, etc.; since Russia's invasion of Ukraine in February 2022, the EU and NATO have intensified their work and cooperation; NATO and the EU have 23 member countries in common
there are no permanent standing EU forces, but Europe has a variety of multinational military organizations that may be deployed through the EU, in a NATO environment, upon the mandate of the participating countries, or upon the mandate of other international organizations, such as the UN or OSCE including: the EU Rapid Deployment Capacity (EU RDC) was declared operational in May 2025; the RDC's purpose is to enable the EU to respond to different crisis scenarios by providing a flexible and scalable military instrument of up to 5,000 troops that can be deployed in a swift manner; missions could include capacity building, conflict prevention, humanitarian assistance and disaster relief, rescue and evacuation, or stabilization; the use of the RDC is subject to a unanimous decision by the EU Member States
EU Battlegroups (BGs) are rapid reaction multinational army units that form a key part of the EU's capacity to respond to crises and conflicts; their deployment is subject to a unanimous decision by the European Council; BGs typically consists of 1,500-2,000 troops organized around an infantry battalion depending on the mission; the troops and equipment are drawn from EU member states and under the direction of a lead nation; two BGs are always on standby for a period of six months; the BGs were declared operational in 2007 but have never been used operationally due to political and financial obstacles
the European Corps (Eurocorps) is an independent multinational land force corps headquarters composed of personnel from six framework nations and five associated nations; the corps has no standing operational units; during a crisis, units would be drawn from participating states, and the corps would be placed at the service of the EU and NATO; Eurocorps was established in 1992 by France and Germany; Belgium (1993), Spain (1994), and Luxembourg (1996) joined over the next few years;

Poland joined in 2022; Greece and Turkey (since 2002), Italy, Romania, and Austria (since 2009, 2016, and 2021 respectively) participate as associated nations; Eurocorps is headquartered in France

the European Gendarmerie Force (EURGENDFOR) is an operational, pre-organized, and rapidly deployable European gendarmerie/police force; it is not established at the EU level, but is capable of performing police tasks, including law enforcement, stability operations, and training in support of the EU, the UN, OSCE, NATO, and other international organizations or ad hoc coalitions; member state gendarmeries include those of France, Italy, the Netherlands, Poland, Portugal, Romania, and Spain; the Lithuanian Public Security Service is a partner, while Turkey's Gendarmerie is an observer force

the European Medical Corps (EMC) was set up in the aftermath of the Ebola crisis in West Africa in 2014 to enable the deployment of teams and equipment from EU member states to provide medical assistance and public health expertise in response to emergencies inside and outside the EU; as of 2024, 12 European states had committed teams and equipment to the EMC

the European Medical Command (EMC) was formed to provide a standing EU medical capability, increase medical operational readiness, and improve interoperability amongst the participating EU members; it operates closely with the NATO Framework Nations Concept's Multinational Medical Coordination Center (MMCC) under a single administrative and infrastructural framework (MMCC/EMC); the EMC was declared operational in May 2022

the European Air Transport Command (EATC) is a single multinational command for more than 150 military air mobility assets from seven member states, including transport, air-to-air refueling, and aeromedical evacuation; the EATC headquarters is located in the Netherlands, but the air assets remain located at member national air bases; the EATC was established in 2010

the European Air Group (EAG) is an independent organization formed by the air forces of its seven member nations (Belgium, France, Germany, Italy, Netherlands, Spain, and the UK) that is focused on improving interoperability between the air forces of EAG members and its 14 partner and associate nations; it was established in the late 1990s and is headquartered in the UK

the European Maritime Force (EUROMARFOR or EMF) is a four-nation (France, Italy, Portugal, and Spain), non-standing naval force with the ability to carry out naval, air, and amphibious operations; EUROMARFOR was formed in 1995 to conduct missions such as crisis response, humanitarian missions, peacekeeping, peace enforcement, and sea control; it can deploy under EU, NATO, or UN mandate, but also as long as the four partner nations agree

the Combined Joint Expeditionary Force (CJEF) is a deployable, combined France-UK military force of up to 10,000 personnel for use in a wide range of crisis scenarios, up to and including high intensity combat operations; the CJEF has no standing forces but would be available at short notice for French-UK bilateral, NATO, EU, UN, or other operations; it was established in 2010 and declared operational in 2020

the 1st German/Netherlands (Dutch) Corps is a combined army corps headquarters that has the ability to conduct operations under the command and control of Germany and the Netherlands, NATO, or the EU; in peacetime, approximately 1,100 Dutch and German soldiers are assigned, but during a crisis up to 80,000 troops may be assigned; it was formed in 1995 and is headquartered in Germany

the Lithuanian-Polish-Ukrainian Brigade (LITPOLUKRBRIG) is comprised of an international staff, three battalions, and specialized units; units affiliated with the multinational brigade remain within the structures of the armed forces of their respective countries until the brigade is activated for participation in an international operation; it was formed in 2014 and is headquartered in Poland (2025)

SPACE

Space agency/agencies: the only EU agency dedicated to space is the EU Agency for the Space Program (EUSPA; established in 2021); the EUSPA originated with the Galileo Joint Undertaking (GJU) set up in 2002 by the European Community (EC) and the European Space Agency (ESA) to manage the development phase of Europe's Galileo satellite navigation program; the GJU's responsibilities were assumed by the European Global Navigation Satellite System Supervisory Authority (GSA) in 2007

the ESA (established 1975 from the European Launcher Development Organization and the European Space Research Organization, which were established in the early 1960s) is an independent organization although it maintains close ties with the EU through an ESA/EC Framework Agreement; the ESA and EC share a joint European Strategy for Space and have together developed a European Space Policy

the ESA has 23 member states; the national bodies responsible for space in these countries sit on ESA's governing Council: Austria, Belgium, Czechia, Denmark, Estonia, Finland, France, Germany, Greece, Hungary, Ireland, Italy, Luxembourg, the Netherlands, Norway, Poland, Portugal, Romania, Slovenia, Spain, Sweden, Switzerland, and the UK; Canada also sits on the Council and takes part in some projects under a Cooperation Agreement; Latvia, Lithuania, and Slovakia are Associate Members; Bulgaria, Croatia, Cyprus, and Malta have cooperation agreements with ESA; ESA has established formal cooperation with all member states of the EU that are not ESA members (2025)

Space launch site(s): ESA's spaceport is located in Kourou, French Guiana; EU members Norway and Sweden have operational commercial space ports; the UK, non-EU member, has two operational commercial space ports (2025)

Space program overview: EU member states have a large and advanced commercial space sector capable of developing and producing a full range of capabilities and technologies; a key focus for both the EU Agency for the Space Program (EUSPA) and the European Space Agency (ESA) is encouraging the European commercial space sector; Europe is a global leader in satellite-based communications and hosts the headquarters of three of the world's major satellite communications companies

ESA is comprehensive space agency that is active across the space sector except for launching humans into space including producing and operating satellites with a full spectrum of capabilities (communications, multipurpose, navigational, remote sensing, science/ technology), satellite launch vehicles (SLVs), space launches, human space flight (has an astronaut training program), space transportation/ automated transfer vehicles, reusable spacecraft, space station modules, spacecraft components, robotic space labs, lunar/ planetary surface rovers, interplanetary space probes and exploration, space telescopes, and research; ESA participates in international space programs such as the International Space Station and works closely with Europe's commercial space industry; it also cooperates with a broad range of space agencies and industries of non-member countries, including China, Japan, Russia, and the US; many of its programs are conducted jointly, particularly with the US space program

the EUSPA is responsible for the operational management of the European Geostationary Navigation Overlay Service (EGNOS) and Galileo satellite navigation programs; the EU space strategy includes encouraging investment in and the use of space services and data, fostering competition and innovation, developing space technologies, and reinforcing Europe's autonomy in accessing space (2025)

note: further details about the key activities, programs, and milestones of the country's space program, as well as government spending estimates on the space sector, appear in the Space Programs reference guide

TERRORISM

Terrorist group(s): Terrorist group(s): see individual EU member states

FALKLAND ISLANDS (ISLAS MALVINAS)

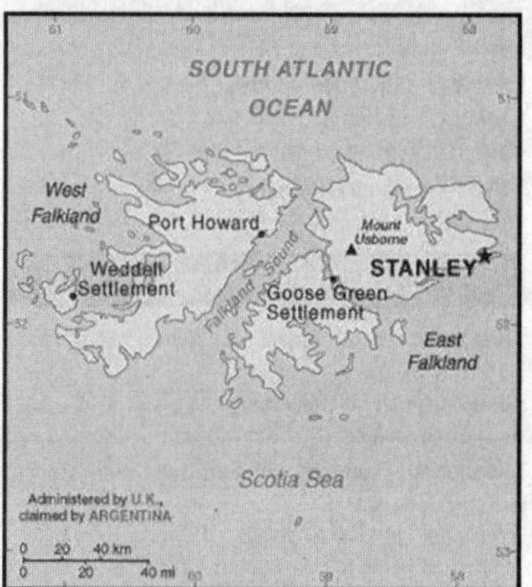

INTRODUCTION

Background: Although first sighted by an English navigator in 1592, the first landing (English) did not occur until almost a century later in 1690, and the first settlement (French) was not established until 1764. The colony was turned over to Spain two years later, and the islands have since been the subject of a territorial dispute, first between Britain and Spain, then between Britain and Argentina. The UK asserted its claim to the islands by establishing a naval garrison there in 1833. Argentina invaded the islands in 1982. The British responded with an expeditionary force and after fierce fighting forced an Argentine surrender on 14 June 1982. With hostilities ended and Argentine forces withdrawn, UK administration resumed. In response to renewed calls from Argentina for Britain to relinquish control of the islands, a referendum was held in 2013 that resulted in 99.8% of the population voting to remain a part of the UK.

GEOGRAPHY

Location: Southern South America, islands in the South Atlantic Ocean, about 500 km east of southern Argentina

Geographic coordinates: 51 45 S, 59 00 W

Map references: South America

Area: *total:* 12,173 sq km
land: 12,173 sq km
water: 0 sq km
note: includes the two main islands of East and West Falkland and about 200 small islands
comparison ranking: total 163

Area - comparative: slightly smaller than Connecticut

Land boundaries: *total:* 0 km

Coastline: 1,288 km

Maritime claims: *territorial sea:* 12 nm
continental shelf: 200 nm
exclusive fishing zone: 200 nm

Climate: cold marine; strong westerly winds, cloudy, humid; rain occurs on more than half of days in year; average annual rainfall is 60 cm in Stanley; occasional snow all year, except in January and February, but typically does not accumulate

Terrain: rocky, hilly, mountainous with some boggy, undulating plains

Elevation: *highest point:* Mount Usborne 705 m
lowest point: Atlantic Ocean 0 m

Natural resources: fish, squid, wildlife, calcified seaweed, sphagnum moss

Land use: *agricultural land:* 93.5% (2022 est.)
arable land: 0% (2022 est.)
permanent crops: 0% (2022 est.)
permanent pasture: 93.5% (2022 est.)
forest: 0% (2022 est.)
other: 6.5% (2022 est.)

Irrigated land: NA

Population distribution: a very small population, with most residents living in and around Stanley

Natural hazards: strong winds persist throughout the year

Geography - note: deeply indented coast provides good natural harbors; short growing season

PEOPLE AND SOCIETY

Population: *total:* 3,142 (2021)
male: 1,645
female: 1,497
note: data include all persons usually resident in the islands at the time of the 2021 census
comparison rankings: total 228; male 228; female 228

Nationality: *noun:* Falkland Islander(s)
adjective: Falkland Island

Ethnic groups: Falkland Islander 48.3%, British 23.1%, St. Helenian 7.5%, Chilean 4.6%, mixed 6%, other 8.5%, unspecified 2% (2016 est.)
note: data represent population by national identity

Languages: English 89%, Spanish 7.7%, other 3.3% (2006 est.)

Religions: Christian 57.1%, other 1.6%, none 35.4%, unspecified 6% (2016 est.)

Dependency ratios: *total dependency ratio:* 38.4 (2021)
youth dependency ratio: 21.8 (2021)
elderly dependency ratio: 16.6 (2021)
potential support ratio: 6 (2021)

Population growth rate: 0.01% (2014 est.)
comparison ranking: 193

Birth rate: 10.9 births/1,000 population (2012 est.)
comparison ranking: 166

Death rate: 4.9 deaths/1,000 population (2012 est.)
comparison ranking: 201

Population distribution: a very small population, with most residents living in and around Stanley

Urbanization: *urban population:* 79.7% of total population (2023)
rate of urbanization: 0.53% annual rate of change (2020-25 est.)

Major urban areas - population: 2,000 STANLEY (capital) (2018)

Sex ratio: *total population:* 1.12 male(s)/female (2016 est.)

Life expectancy at birth: *total population:* (2017 est.) 77.9
male: 75.6
female: 79.6

Drinking water source: *improved:* *urban:* 100% of population (2022 est.)
unimproved: *urban:* 0% of population (2022 est.)
rural: 21.8% of population

Sanitation facility access: *improved:* *urban:* 100% of population (2022 est.)
rural: 100% of population (2022 est.)
total: 100% of population (2022 est.)
unimproved: *urban:* 0% of population (2022 est.)
rural: 0% of population (2022 est.)
total: 0% of population (2022 est.)

Currently married women (ages 15-49): 44.8% (2023 est.)

ENVIRONMENT

Environmental issues: overfishing by unlicensed vessels; grazing threatens important habitats; soil erosion from fires

Climate: cold marine; strong westerly winds, cloudy, humid; rain occurs on more than half of days in year; average annual rainfall is 60 cm in Stanley; occasional snow all year, except in January and February, but typically does not accumulate

Urbanization: *urban population:* 79.7% of total population (2023)
rate of urbanization: 0.53% annual rate of change (2020-25 est.)

Carbon dioxide emissions: 36,000 metric tonnes of CO_2 (2023 est.)
from petroleum and other liquids: 36,000 metric tonnes of CO_2 (2023 est.)
comparison ranking: total emissions 212

GOVERNMENT

Country name: *conventional long form:* none
conventional short form: Falkland Islands (Islas Malvinas)
etymology: the archipelago takes its name from the Falkland Sound, the strait separating the two main islands; the channel was named after the Fifth Viscount of FALKLAND, who sponsored an expedition to the islands in 1690; the Spanish name for the archipelago derives from the French "Iles Malouines," meaning Islands of Malo, the name French explorer Louis-Antoine de BOUGAINVILLE gave the islands in 1764 in honor of the French port of Saint-Malo

Government type: parliamentary democracy (Legislative Assembly); self-governing overseas territory of the UK

Dependency status: overseas territory of the UK; also claimed by Argentina

Capital: *name:* Stanley
geographic coordinates: 51 42 S, 57 51 W
time difference: UTC-3 (2 hour ahead of Washington, DC, during Standard Time)
etymology: named in 1844 after Edward SMITH-STANLEY, the 14th Earl of Derby

Administrative divisions: none (administered by the UK; claimed by Argentina)

Legal system: English common law and local statutes

Constitution: *history:* previous 1985; latest entered into force 1 January 2009 (The Falkland Islands Constitution Order 2008)

Citizenship: see United Kingdom

Suffrage: 18 years of age; universal

Executive branch: *chief of state:* King CHARLES III (since 8 September 2022); represented by Governor Alison BLAKE (since 23 July 2022)
head of government: Chief Executive Andy KEELING (since April 2021)
cabinet: Executive Council elected by the Legislative Council
election/appointment process: the monarchy is hereditary; monarch appoints the governor, who appoints the chief executive

Legislative branch: *legislature name:* Legislative Assembly
legislative structure: unicameral
number of seats: 10 (8 directly elected, 2 appointed)
electoral system: plurality/majority
scope of elections: full renewal
term in office: 4 years
most recent election date: 11/4/2021
percentage of women in chamber: 25% *note:* does not include the speaker
expected date of next election: November 2025

Judicial branch: *highest court(s):* Court of Appeal (consists of the court president, the chief justice as an ex officio non-resident member, and 2 justices of appeal); Supreme Court (consists of the chief justice)
judge selection and term of office: chief justice, court of appeal president, and justices appointed by the governor; tenure specified in each justice's instrument of appointment
subordinate courts: Magistrate's Court (senior magistrate presides over civil and criminal divisions); Court of Summary Jurisdiction
note: appeals beyond the Court of Appeal are referred to the Judicial Committee of the Privy Council (in London)

Political parties: none; all independents

Diplomatic representation in the US: none (administered by the UK; claimed by Argentina)

Diplomatic representation from the US: *embassy:* none (administered by the UK; claimed by Argentina)

International organization participation: UPU

Independence: none (overseas territory of the UK; also claimed by Argentina)

National holiday: Liberation Day, 14 June (1982)

Flag: *description:* blue with the UK flag in the upper-left quadrant and the Falkland Island coat of arms centered on the right half of the flag; the coat of arms has a white ram above the ship "Desire" (whose crew discovered the islands), with a scroll at the bottom bearing the motto DESIRE THE RIGHT

National symbol(s): ram

National color(s): red, white, blue

National coat of arms: the Falkland Islands adopted its coat of arms in 1948; the shield highlights the national symbol, the ram, which represents the country's agricultural industry and stands on native tussock grass; English navigator John Davis's sailing vessel, the *Desire*, is shown, referencing his sighting of the islands in 1592; below the shield is the national motto, "Desire the Right"

National anthem(s): *title:* "Song of the Falklands"
lyrics/music: Christopher LANHAM
history: adopted unknown
title: "God Save the King"
lyrics/music: unknown
history: official anthem, as a UK territory

ECONOMY

Economic overview: British South American territorial economy; longstanding fishing industry; surging tourism prior to COVID-19 and Brexit; recent offshore hydrocarbon discoveries threaten ecotourism industries; no central bank and must have British approval on currency shifts

Real GDP per capita: $70,800 (2015 est.)
$63,000 (2014 est.)
comparison ranking: 18

GDP (official exchange rate): $206.4 million (2015 est.)

Agricultural products: fodder and vegetable crops; venison, sheep, dairy products; fish, squid

Industries: fish and wool processing; tourism

Exports - partners: Spain 68%, Morocco 10%, USA 8%, Namibia 3%, Germany 2% (2023)
note: top five export partners based on percentage share of exports

Exports - commodities: shellfish, fish, wool, sheep and goat meat (2023)
note: top export commodities based on value in dollars over $500,000

Imports - partners: UK 68%, Greece 19%, Spain 11%, Netherlands 1%, NZ 0% (2023)
note: top five import partners based on percentage share of imports

Imports - commodities: refined petroleum, aircraft parts, prefabricated buildings, plastic products, surveying equipment (2023)
note: top five import commodities based on value in dollars

Exchange rates: Falkland pounds (FKP) per US dollar -

Exchange rates: 0.78 (2024 est.)
0.805 (2023 est.)
0.811 (2022 est.)
0.727 (2021 est.)
0.78 (2020 est.)

ENERGY

Electricity: *installed generating capacity:* 10,000 kW (2023 est.)
consumption: 18.257 million kWh (2023 est.)
transmission/distribution losses: 900,000 kWh (2023 est.)
comparison rankings: installed generating capacity 208; consumption 208; transmission/distribution losses 3

Electricity generation sources: *fossil fuels:* 73.9% of total installed capacity (2023 est.)
wind: 26.1% of total installed capacity (2023 est.)

Petroleum: *refined petroleum consumption:* 200 bbl/day (2023 est.)

COMMUNICATIONS

Telephones - fixed lines: *total subscriptions:* 2,000 (2021 est.)
subscriptions per 100 inhabitants: 53 (2021 est.)
comparison ranking: total subscriptions 215

Telephones - mobile cellular: *total subscriptions:* 6,000 (2021 est.)
subscriptions per 100 inhabitants: 160 (2021 est.)
comparison ranking: total subscriptions 221

Broadcast media: TV service provided by a multi-channel service provider; radio provided by public broadcaster Falkland Islands Radio Service and the British Forces Broadcasting Service (2007)

Internet country code: .fk

Internet users: *percent of population:* 99% (2021 est.)

Broadband - fixed subscriptions: *total:* 1,000 (2020 est.)
subscriptions per 100 inhabitants: 33 (2020 est.)
comparison ranking: total 211

TRANSPORTATION

Civil aircraft registration country code prefix: VP-F

Airports: 34 (2025)
comparison ranking: 113

Merchant marine: *total:* 2 (2023)
by type: general cargo 1, other 1
comparison ranking: total 180

Ports: *total ports:* 1 (2024)
large: 0
medium: 1
small: 0
very small: 0
ports with oil terminals: 1
key ports: Stanley

MILITARY AND SECURITY

Military and security forces: no regular military forces

Military - note: defense is the responsibility of the UK, which maintains a military presence on the islands

FAROE ISLANDS

INTRODUCTION

Background: The Faroe Islands were already populated by about A.D. 500, but whether the original settlers were Celtic or early Norse (or someone else) has yet to be determined. Viking settlers arrived on the islands in the 9th century, and the islands served as an important stepping stone for medieval Viking exploration of the North Atlantic. The islands have been connected politically to Denmark since the 14th century, and today the Faroe Islands are a self-governing dependency of Denmark. The Home Rule Act of 1948 granted a high degree of self-government to the Faroese, who have autonomy over most internal affairs and external trade, while

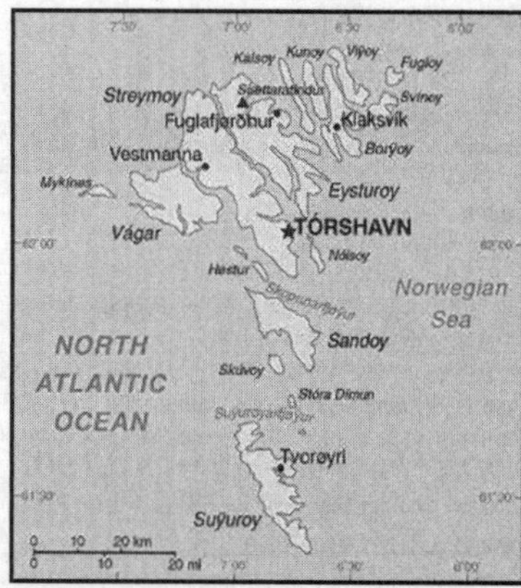

Denmark is responsible for justice, defense, and some foreign affairs. The Faroe Islands are not part of the European Union.

GEOGRAPHY

Location: Northern Europe, island group between the Norwegian Sea and the North Atlantic Ocean, about halfway between Iceland and Norway

Geographic coordinates: 62 00 N, 7 00 W

Map references: Europe

Area: *total:* 1,393 sq km
land: 1,393 sq km
water: 0 sq km (some lakes and streams)
comparison ranking: total 182

Area - comparative: eight times the size of Washington, D.C.

Land boundaries: *total:* 0 km

Coastline: 1,117 km

Maritime claims: *territorial sea:* 12 nm
continental shelf: 200 nm or agreed boundaries or median line
exclusive fishing zone: 200 nm or agreed boundaries or median line

Climate: mild winters, cool summers; usually overcast; foggy, windy

Terrain: rugged, rocky, some low peaks; cliffs along most of coast

Elevation: *highest point:* Slaettaratindur 882 m
lowest point: Atlantic Ocean 0 m

Natural resources: fish, whales, hydropower, possible oil and gas

Land use: *agricultural land:* 70.1% (2022 est.)
arable land: 0.1% (2022 est.)
permanent crops: 0% (2022 est.)
permanent pasture: 70.1% (2022 est.)
forest: 0.1% (2022 est.)
other: 29.8% (2022 est.)

Population distribution: the island of Streymoy is by far the most populous with over 40% of the population; it has approximately twice as many inhabitants as Eysturoy, the second most populous island; seven of the inhabited islands have fewer than 100 people

Natural hazards: strong winds and heavy rains can occur throughout the year

Geography - note: archipelago of 17 inhabited islands, one uninhabited island, and a few uninhabited islets; strategically located along important sea lanes in northeastern Atlantic; precipitous terrain limits habitation to small coastal lowlands

PEOPLE AND SOCIETY

Population: *total:* 52,933 (2024 est.)
male: 27,400
female: 25,533
comparison rankings: total 208; male 208; female 208

Nationality: *noun:* Faroese (singular and plural)
adjective: Faroese

Ethnic groups: Faroese 83.8% (Scandinavian and Anglo-Saxon descent), Danish 8.3%, Filipino 1.2%, other Nordic 0.9%, other 4.5% (includes Polish and Romanian) (2024 est.)
note: data represent respondents by country of birth

Languages: Faroese 93.8% (derived from Old Norse), Danish 3.2%, other 3% (2011 est.)
note: data represent population by primary language

Religions: Christian 87% (predominantly Evangelical Lutheran), other 0.9%, none 3.7%, unspecified 8.9% (2011 est.)

Age structure: *0-14 years:* 20% (male 5,489/female 5,122)
15-64 years: 61.5% (male 17,188/female 15,346)
65 years and over: 18.5% (2024 est.) (male 4,723/female 5,065)

Dependency ratios: *total dependency ratio:* 62.7 (2024 est.)
youth dependency ratio: 32.6 (2024 est.)
elderly dependency ratio: 30.1 (2024 est.)
potential support ratio: 3.3 (2024 est.)

Median age: *total:* 36.8 years (2024 est.)
male: 36.9 years
female: 36.8 years
comparison ranking: total 86

Population growth rate: 0.63% (2024 est.)
comparison ranking: 135

Birth rate: 14.9 births/1,000 population (2024 est.)
comparison ranking: 114

Death rate: 8.6 deaths/1,000 population (2024 est.)
comparison ranking: 70

Net migration rate: 0 migrant(s)/1,000 population (2024 est.)
comparison ranking: 93

Population distribution: the island of Streymoy is by far the most populous with over 40% of the population; it has approximately twice as many inhabitants as Eysturoy, the second most populous island; seven of the inhabited islands have fewer than 100 people

Urbanization: *urban population:* 43% of total population (2023)
rate of urbanization: 0.89% annual rate of change (2020-25 est.)

Major urban areas - population: 21,000 TORSHAVN (capital) (2018)

Sex ratio: *at birth:* 1.07 male(s)/female
0-14 years: 1.07 male(s)/female
15-64 years: 1.12 male(s)/female
65 years and over: 0.93 male(s)/female
total population: 1.07 male(s)/female (2024 est.)

Infant mortality rate: *total:* 5.7 deaths/1,000 live births (2024 est.)
male: 6.3 deaths/1,000 live births
female: 5.1 deaths/1,000 live births
comparison ranking: total 171

Life expectancy at birth: *total population:* 81.7 years (2024 est.)
male: 79.2 years
female: 84.4 years
comparison ranking: total population 42

Total fertility rate: 2.27 children born/woman (2024 est.)
comparison ranking: 79

Gross reproduction rate: 1.09 (2024 est.)

Drinking water source: *improved:* *urban:* NA
rural: NA
total: 100% of population (2022 est.)
unimproved: *urban:* NA
rural: NA
total: 0% of population (2022 est.)

Physician density: 2.62 physicians/1,000 population (2016)

Currently married women (ages 15-49): 34.8% (2023 est.)

Education expenditure: 7.6% of GDP (2019 est.)
comparison ranking: Education expenditure (% GDP) 12

ENVIRONMENT

Environmental issues: coastal erosion, landslides and rockfalls, flash flooding, wind storms; oil spills

Climate: mild winters, cool summers; usually overcast; foggy, windy

Urbanization: *urban population:* 43% of total population (2023)
rate of urbanization: 0.89% annual rate of change (2020-25 est.)

Carbon dioxide emissions: 742,000 metric tonnes of CO2 (2023 est.)
from petroleum and other liquids: 742,000 metric tonnes of CO2 (2023 est.)
comparison ranking: total emissions 176

Waste and recycling: *municipal solid waste generated annually:* 61,000 tons (2024 est.)
percent of municipal solid waste recycled: 67% (2012 est.)

GOVERNMENT

Country name: *conventional long form:* none
conventional short form: Faroe Islands
local long form: none
local short form: Foroyar
etymology: the archipelago's name derives from the Old Norse name Faeroyar, meaning "sheep islands;" *faer* means "sheep," and *-oyar* means "islands"

Government type: parliamentary democracy (Faroese Parliament); part of the Kingdom of Denmark

Dependency status: part of the Kingdom of Denmark; self-governing overseas administrative division of Denmark since 1948

Capital: *name:* Torshavn
geographic coordinates: 62 00 N, 6 46 W
time difference: UTC 0 (5 hours ahead of Washington, DC, during Standard Time)
daylight saving time: +1hr, begins last Sunday in March; ends last Sunday in October
etymology: the name means "Thor's harbor" in Danish

Administrative divisions: part of the Kingdom of Denmark; self-governing overseas administrative division of Denmark; there are 29 first-order municipalities *(kommunur,* singular - *kommuna)* Eidhi, Eystur, Famjin, Fuglafjordhur, Fugloy, Hov, Husavik, Hvalba, Hvannasund, Klaksvik, Kunoy, Kvivik, Nes, Porkeri, Runavik, Sandur, Sjovar, Skalavik, Skopun, Skuvoy, Sorvagur, Sumba, Sunda, Torshavn, Tvoroyri, Vagar, Vagur, Vestmanna, Vidhareidhi

Legal system: the laws of Denmark apply

Constitution: *history:* 5 June 1953 (Danish Constitution), 23 March 1948 (Home Rule Act), and 24 June 2005 (Takeover Act) serve as the Faroe Islands' constitutional position in the Unity of the Realm
amendment process: see entry for Denmark

Citizenship: see Denmark

Suffrage: 18 years of age; universal

Executive branch: *chief of state:* King FREDERIK X of Denmark (since 14 January 2024), represented by High Commissioner Lene Moyell JOHANSEN, chief administrative officer (since 15 May 2017) (2024)
head of government: Prime Minister Aksel V. JOHANNESEN (since 22 December 2022)
cabinet: Landsstyri appointed by the prime minister
election/appointment process: the monarchy is hereditary; high commissioner appointed by the monarch; following legislative elections, the Parliament usually elects the leader of the majority party or majority coalition as the prime minister
most recent election date: 8 December 2022
expected date of next election: 2026

Legislative branch: *legislature name:* Faroese Parliament (Logting)
legislative structure: unicameral
number of seats: 33 (directly elected)
electoral system: proportional representation
scope of elections: full renewal
term in office: 4 years
most recent election date: 12/8/2022
parties elected and seats per party: JF (9); B (7); A (6); E (6); F (3); H (2)
percentage of women in chamber: 27.3%
expected date of next election: 2026
note: the Faroe Islands elect 2 members to the Danish Parliament to serve 4-year terms

Judicial branch: *highest court(s):* Faroese Court or Raett (Rett in Danish) decides both civil and criminal cases; the Court is part of the Danish legal system
subordinate courts: Court of the First Instance or Tribunal de Première Instance; Court of Administrative Law or Tribunal Administratif; Mixed Commercial Court; Land Court

Political parties: Center Party or H (Midflokkurin)
People's Party or A (Folkaflokkurin)
Progress Party or F (Framsokn)
Republic or E (Tjodveldi) (formerly the Republican Party)
Self-Government Party or D (Sjalvstyri or Sjalvstyrisflokkurin)
Social Democratic Party or JF (Javnadarflokkurin) or JF
Union Party or B (Sambandsflokkurin)

Diplomatic representation in the US: none (self-governing overseas administrative division of Denmark)

Diplomatic representation from the US: *embassy:* none (self-governing overseas administrative division of Denmark)

International organization participation: Arctic Council, IMO (associate), NC, NIB, UNESCO (associate), UPU

Independence: none (self-governing overseas administrative division of Denmark)

National holiday: Olaifest (Olavsoka), 29 July (1030)
note: commemorates the death in battle of King OLAF II of Norway, later St. OLAF

Flag: *description:* white with a red cross outlined in blue that extends to the edges of the flag; the cross is shifted toward the left side in the style of the Dannebrog (Danish flag)
meaning: white represents waves breaking on the shore; red and blue are traditional Faroese colors
history: the flag is referred to as Merkid, meaning "the banner" or "the mark;" a group of students designed it in 1919, although it wasn't officially adopted until 1940
note: resembles the flags of Iceland and Norway; uses the same three colors in a different sequence and with a lighter blue

National symbol(s): ram

National anthem(s): *title:* "Mitt alfagra land" (My Fairest Land)
lyrics/music: Simun av SKAROI/Peter ALBERG
history: adopted 1948; the anthem is also known as "Tu alfagra land mitt" (Thou Fairest Land of Mine); as a self-governing overseas administrative division of Denmark, the Faroe Islands are permitted to have their own national anthem

ECONOMY

Economic overview: high-income Danish territorial economy; party neither to the EU nor the Schengen Area; associate Nordic Council member; very low unemployment; unique foreign ownership allowance in fishing industry; known salmon exporter; growing IT industries

Real GDP (purchasing power parity): $3.834 billion (2023 est.)
$3.741 billion (2022 est.)
$3.613 billion (2021 est.)
note: data in 2021 dollars
comparison ranking: 190

Real GDP growth rate: 2.5% (2023 est.)
3.6% (2022 est.)
5.5% (2021 est.)
note: annual GDP % growth based on constant local currency
comparison ranking: 134

Real GDP per capita: $70,400 (2023 est.)
$69,400 (2022 est.)
$67,800 (2021 est.)
note: data in 2021 dollars
comparison ranking: 19

GDP (official exchange rate): $3.907 billion (2023 est.)
note: data in current dollars at official exchange rate

GDP - composition, by sector of origin: *agriculture:* 18.2% (2023 est.)
industry: 19.7% (2023 est.)
services: 52% (2023 est.)
note: figures may not total 100% due to non-allocated consumption not captured in sector-reported data
comparison rankings: agriculture 39; industry 132; services 133

GDP - composition, by end use: *household consumption:* 40.6% (2023 est.)
government consumption: 27.3% (2023 est.)
investment in fixed capital: 31% (2023 est.)
investment in inventories: 0% (2023 est.)
exports of goods and services: 57.7% (2023 est.)
imports of goods and services: -56.6% (2023 est.)
note: figures may not total 100% due to rounding or gaps in data collection

Agricultural products: milk, potatoes, lamb/mutton, sheepskins, sheep offal, beef, sheep fat, beef offal, cattle hides, beef suet (2023)
note: top ten agricultural products based on tonnage

Industries: fishing, fish processing, tourism, small ship repair and refurbishment, handicrafts

Remittances: 4.1% of GDP (2023 est.)
4.4% of GDP (2022 est.)
4.3% of GDP (2021 est.)
note: personal transfers and compensation between resident and non-resident individuals/households/entities

Exports: $2.255 billion (2023 est.)
$2.219 billion (2022 est.)
$1.923 billion (2021 est.)
note: GDP expenditure basis - exports of goods and services in current dollars
comparison ranking: 162

Exports - partners: Russia 26.4%, UK 14.1%, Germany 8.4%, China 7.9%, Spain 6.8%, Denmark 6.2%, US 4.7%, Poland 4.4%, Norway 4.1% (2017)

Exports - commodities: fish and fish products (2021)

Imports: $2.212 billion (2023 est.)
$2.223 billion (2022 est.)
$1.906 billion (2021 est.)
note: GDP expenditure basis - imports of goods and services in current dollars
comparison ranking: 175

Imports - partners: Denmark 33%, China 10.7%, Germany 7.6%, Poland 6.8%, Norway 6.7%, Ireland 5%, Chile 4.3% (2017)

Imports - commodities: goods for household consumption, machinery and transport equipment, fuels, raw materials and semi-manufactures, cars

Exchange rates: Danish kroner (DKK) per US dollar -

Exchange rates: 6.894 (2024 est.)
6.89 (2023 est.)
7.076 (2022 est.)
6.287 (2021 est.)
6.542 (2020 est.)

ENERGY

Electricity access: *electrification - total population:* 100% (2022 est.)
electrification - urban areas: 99.9%
electrification - rural areas: 100%

Electricity: *installed generating capacity:* 180,000 kW (2023 est.)
consumption: 463.285 million kWh (2023 est.)
transmission/distribution losses: 25.115 million kWh (2023 est.)
comparison rankings: installed generating capacity 175; consumption 176; transmission/distribution losses 28

Electricity generation sources: *fossil fuels:* 53.7% of total installed capacity (2023 est.)
wind: 18.4% of total installed capacity (2023 est.)
hydroelectricity: 26.8% of total installed capacity (2023 est.)
biomass and waste: 1% of total installed capacity (2023 est.)

Coal: *imports:* 1 metric tons (2023 est.)

Petroleum: *refined petroleum consumption:* 5,000 bbl/day (2023 est.)

COMMUNICATIONS

Telephones - fixed lines: *total subscriptions:* 15,000 (2021 est.)
subscriptions per 100 inhabitants: 28 (2022 est.)
comparison ranking: total subscriptions 181

Telephones - mobile cellular: *total subscriptions:* 59,000 (2021 est.)

subscriptions per 100 inhabitants: 112 (2021 est.)
comparison ranking: total subscriptions 204

Broadcast media: 1 publicly owned TV station; the Faroese telecommunications company distributes local and international channels through its digital terrestrial network; publicly owned radio station supplemented by 3 privately owned stations broadcasting over multiple frequencies

Internet country code: .fo

Internet users: *percent of population:* 98% (2017 est.)

Broadband - fixed subscriptions: *total:* 19,000 (2022 est.)
subscriptions per 100 inhabitants: 35 (2022 est.)
comparison ranking: total 173

TRANSPORTATION

Civil aircraft registration country code prefix: OY-H

Airports: 1 (2025)
comparison ranking: 229

Heliports: 12 (2025)
comparison ranking: 67

Merchant marine: *total:* 91 (2023)
by type: container ships 6, general cargo 45, other 40
comparison ranking: total 95

Ports: *total ports:* 9 (2024)
large: 0
medium: 0
small: 0
very small: 9
ports with oil terminals: 5
key ports: Fuglafjordur, Klaksvik, Kongshavn, Runavik, Sorvagur, Torshavn, Tvoroyri, Vagur, Vestmanna

MILITARY AND SECURITY

Military and security forces: no regular military forces or conscription

Military - note: the Government of Denmark has responsibility for defense; as such, the Danish military's Joint Arctic Command in Nuuk, Greenland is responsible for coordinating the defense of the Faroe Islands; the Joint Arctic Command has a contact element in the capital of Torshavn

FIJI

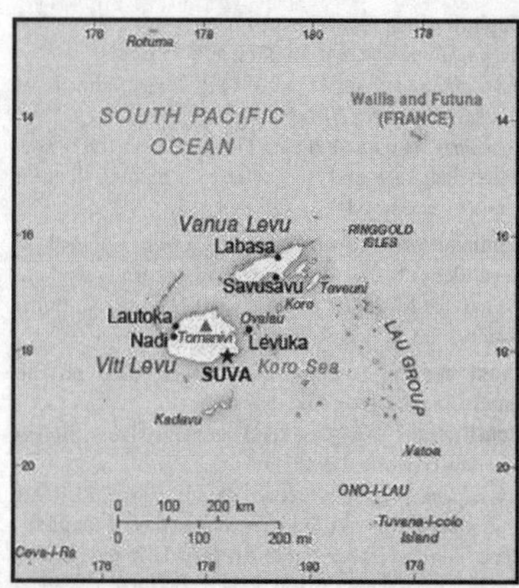

INTRODUCTION

Background: Austronesians settled Fiji around 1000 B.C., followed by successive waves of Melanesians starting around the first century A.D. Fijians traded with Polynesian groups in Samoa and Tonga, and by about 900, much of Fiji was in the Tu'i Tongan Empire's sphere of influence. The Tongan influence declined significantly by 1200, while Melanesian seafarers continued to periodically arrive in Fiji, further mixing Melanesian and Polynesian cultural traditions. The first European spotted Fiji in 1643 and by the 1800s, European merchants, missionaries, traders, and whalers frequented the islands. Rival kings and chiefs competed for power, at times aided by Europeans, and in 1865, Seru Epenisa CAKOBAU united many groups into the Confederacy of Independent Kingdoms of Viti. The arrangement proved weak, however, and in 1871 CAKOBAU formed the Kingdom of Fiji in an attempt to centralize power. Fearing a hostile takeover by a foreign power as the kingdom's economy began to falter, CAKOBAU ceded Fiji to the UK in 1874.

The first British governor set up a plantation-style economy and brought in more than 60,000 Indians as indentured laborers, most of whom chose to stay in Fiji rather than return to India when their contracts expired. In the early 1900s, society was divided along ethnic lines, with iTaukei (indigenous Fijians), Europeans, and Indo-Fijians living in separate areas and maintaining their own languages and traditions. ITaukei fears of an Indo-Fijian takeover of government delayed independence through the 1960s; Fiji achieved independence in 1970 with agreements to allocate parliamentary seats by ethnic groups. After two coups in 1987, a new constitution in 1990 cemented iTaukei control of politics, leading thousands of Indo-Fijians to leave. A reformed constitution in 1997 was more equitable and led to the election of an Indo-Fijian prime minister in 1999, who was ousted in a coup the following year. In 2005, the new prime minister put forward a bill that would grant pardons to the coup perpetrators, leading Josaia Voreqe "Frank" BAINIMARAMA to launch a coup in 2006. BAINIMARAMA appointed himself prime minister in 2007 and retained the position after elections in 2014 and 2018 that international observers deemed credible. BAINIMARAMA's party lost control of the prime minister position after elections in 2022 with former opposition leader Sitiveni Ligamamada RABUKA winning the office by a narrow margin.

GEOGRAPHY

Location: Oceania, island group in the South Pacific Ocean, about two-thirds of the way from Hawaii to New Zealand

Geographic coordinates: 18 00 S, 175 00 E

Map references: Oceania

Area: *total:* 18,274 sq km
land: 18,274 sq km
water: 0 sq km
comparison ranking: total 156

Area - comparative: slightly smaller than New Jersey

Land boundaries: *total:* 0 km

Coastline: 1,129 km

Maritime claims: *territorial sea:* 12 nm
contiguous zone: 24 nm
exclusive economic zone: 200 nm
continental shelf: 200-m depth or to the depth of exploitation
note: measured from claimed archipelagic straight baselines

Climate: tropical marine; only slight seasonal temperature variation

Terrain: mostly mountains of volcanic origin

Elevation: *highest point:* Tomanivi 1,324 m
lowest point: Pacific Ocean 0 m

Natural resources: timber, fish, gold, copper, offshore oil potential, hydropower

Land use: *agricultural land:* 17.1% (2022 est.)
arable land: 4.2% (2022 est.)
permanent crops: 3.4% (2022 est.)
permanent pasture: 9.5% (2022 est.)
forest: 63.1% (2022 est.)
other: 19.8% (2022 est.)

Irrigated land: 40 sq km (2012)

Population distribution: approximately 70% of the population lives on the island of Viti Levu; roughly half of the population lives in urban areas

Natural hazards: cyclonic storms can occur from November to January

Geography - note: consists of 332 islands, approximately 110 of which are inhabited, and more than 500 islets

PEOPLE AND SOCIETY

Population: *total:* 951,611 (2024 est.)
male: 482,304
female: 469,307
comparison rankings: total 163; male 162; female 163

Nationality: *noun:* Fijian(s)
adjective: Fijian

Ethnic groups: iTaukei 56.8% (predominantly Melanesian with a Polynesian admixture), Indo-Fijian 37.5%, Rotuman 1.2%, other 4.5% (European, part European, other Pacific Islanders, Chinese) (2007 est.)
note: a 2010 law replaces 'Fijian' with 'iTaukei' when referring to the original and native settlers of Fiji

Languages: English (official), iTaukei (official), Fiji Hindi (official)

Religions: Protestant 45% (Methodist 34.6%, Assembly of God 5.7%, Seventh Day Adventist 3.9%, and Anglican 0.8%), Hindu 27.9%, other

Christian 10.4%, Roman Catholic 9.1%, Muslim 6.3%, Sikh 0.3%, other 0.3%, none 0.8% (2007 est.)

Age structure: *0-14 years:* 24.7% (male 119,910/ female 114,904)
15-64 years: 66.4% (male 323,339/female 308,921)
65 years and over: 8.9% (2024 est.) (male 39,055/ female 45,482)

Dependency ratios: *total dependency ratio:* 50.5 (2024 est.)
youth dependency ratio: 37.1 (2024 est.)
elderly dependency ratio: 13.4 (2024 est.)
potential support ratio: 7.5 (2024 est.)

Median age: *total:* 31.6 years (2024 est.)
male: 31.4 years
female: 31.8 years
comparison ranking: total 124

Population growth rate: 0.4% (2024 est.)
comparison ranking: 157

Birth rate: 15.9 births/1,000 population (2024 est.)
comparison ranking: 99

Death rate: 6.5 deaths/1,000 population (2024 est.)
comparison ranking: 135

Net migration rate: -5.5 migrant(s)/1,000 population (2024 est.)
comparison ranking: 206

Population distribution: approximately 70% of the population lives on the island of Viti Levu; roughly half of the population lives in urban areas

Urbanization: *urban population:* 58.7% of total population (2023)
rate of urbanization: 1.37% annual rate of change (2020-25 est.)

Major urban areas - population: 178,000 SUVA (capital) (2018)

Sex ratio: *at birth:* 1.05 male(s)/female
0-14 years: 1.04 male(s)/female
15-64 years: 1.05 male(s)/female
65 years and over: 0.86 male(s)/female
total population: 1.03 male(s)/female (2024 est.)

Maternal mortality ratio: 30 deaths/100,000 live births (2023 est.)
comparison ranking: 117

Infant mortality rate: *total:* 9.7 deaths/1,000 live births (2024 est.)
male: 11.1 deaths/1,000 live births
female: 8.1 deaths/1,000 live births
comparison ranking: total 133

Life expectancy at birth: *total population:* 74.8 years (2024 est.)
male: 72.2 years
female: 77.6 years
comparison ranking: total population 136

Total fertility rate: 2.21 children born/woman (2024 est.)
comparison ranking: 84

Gross reproduction rate: 1.08 (2024 est.)

Drinking water source: *improved: urban:* 98.7% of population (2022 est.)
rural: 91.1% of population (2022 est.)
total: 95.5% of population (2022 est.)
unimproved: urban: 1.3% of population (2022 est.)
rural: 8.9% of population (2022 est.)
total: 4.5% of population (2022 est.)

Health expenditure: 5.4% of GDP (2021)
10.3% of national budget (2022 est.)

Physician density: 0.81 physicians/1,000 population (2015)

Hospital bed density: 1.9 beds/1,000 population (2017 est.)

Sanitation facility access: *improved: urban:* 100% of population (2022 est.)
rural: 100% of population (2022 est.)
total: 100% of population (2022 est.)
unimproved: urban: 0% of population (2022 est.)
rural: 0% of population (2022 est.)
total: 0% of population (2022 est.)

Obesity - adult prevalence rate: 30.2% (2016)
comparison ranking: 24

Alcohol consumption per capita: *total:* 2.71 liters of pure alcohol (2019 est.)
beer: 1.64 liters of pure alcohol (2019 est.)
wine: 0.29 liters of pure alcohol (2019 est.)
spirits: 0.79 liters of pure alcohol (2019 est.)
other alcohols: 0 liters of pure alcohol (2019 est.)
comparison ranking: total 120

Tobacco use: *total:* 26.8% (2025 est.)
male: 40.8% (2025 est.)
female: 12.9% (2025 est.)
comparison ranking: total 31

Children under the age of 5 years underweight: 4.6% (2021)
comparison ranking: 68

Currently married women (ages 15-49): 58.8% (2023 est.)

Child marriage: *women married by age 15:* 0.2% (2021)
women married by age 18: 4% (2021)
men married by age 18: 1.7% (2021)

Education expenditure: 4.2% of GDP (2023 est.)
11.6% national budget (2024 est.)
comparison ranking: Education expenditure (% GDP) 95

Literacy: *female:* 92.4% (2021 est.)

ENVIRONMENT

Environmental issues: air pollution from waste incineration and vehicle emissions; deforestation and soil erosion; soil erosion from clearing land by bush burning

International environmental agreements: *party to:* Biodiversity, Climate Change, Climate Change-Kyoto Protocol, Climate Change-Paris Agreement, Comprehensive Nuclear Test Ban, Desertification, Endangered Species, Law of the Sea, Marine Life Conservation, Nuclear Test Ban, Ozone Layer Protection, Ship Pollution, Tropical Timber 2006, Wetlands
signed, but not ratified: none of the selected agreements

Climate: tropical marine; only slight seasonal temperature variation

Urbanization: *urban population:* 58.7% of total population (2023)
rate of urbanization: 1.37% annual rate of change (2020-25 est.)

Carbon dioxide emissions: 1.432 million metric tonnes of CO2 (2023 est.)
from coal and metallurgical coke: 12 metric tonnes of CO2 (2023 est.)
from petroleum and other liquids: 1.432 million metric tonnes of CO2 (2023 est.)
comparison ranking: total emissions 165

Particulate matter emissions: 8.1 micrograms per cubic meter (2019 est.)

Waste and recycling: *municipal solid waste generated annually:* 189,400 tons (2024 est.)
percent of municipal solid waste recycled: 16.1% (2022 est.)

Total water withdrawal: *municipal:* 25.3 million cubic meters (2022 est.)
industrial: 9.6 million cubic meters (2022 est.)
agricultural: 50 million cubic meters (2022 est.)

Total renewable water resources: 28.55 billion cubic meters (2022 est.)

GOVERNMENT

Country name: *conventional long form:* Republic of Fiji
conventional short form: Fiji
local long form: Republic of Fiji (English)/ Matanitu ko Viti (Fijian)
local short form: Fiji (English)/ Viti (Fijian)
etymology: the Fijians called their home Viti, but the neighboring Tongans called it Fisi; in the Anglicized spelling of the Tongan pronunciation – promulgated by explorer Captain James COOK – the designation became Fiji

Government type: parliamentary republic

Capital: *name:* Suva (on Viti Levu)
geographic coordinates: 18 08 S, 178 25 E
time difference: UTC+12 (17 hours ahead of Washington, DC, during Standard Time)
etymology: the name means "little hill" in the native Fijian language and may refer to a mound where a temple once stood

Administrative divisions: 14 provinces and 1 dependency*; Ba, Bua, Cakaudrove, Kadavu, Lau, Lomaiviti, Macuata, Nadroga and Navosa, Naitasiri, Namosi, Ra, Rewa, Rotuma*, Serua, Tailevu

Legal system: common law system based on the English model

Constitution: *history:* several previous; latest signed into law 6 September 2013
amendment process: proposed as a bill by Parliament and supported by at least three quarters of its members, followed by referral to the president and then to the Electoral Commission, which conducts a referendum; passage requires approval by at least three-quarters of registered voters and assent by the president

International law organization participation: has not submitted an ICJ jurisdiction declaration; accepts ICCt jurisdiction

Citizenship: *citizenship by birth:* no
citizenship by descent only: at least one parent must be a citizen of Fiji
dual citizenship recognized: yes
residency requirement for naturalization: at least 5 years residency out of the 10 years preceding application

Suffrage: 18 years of age; universal

Executive branch: *chief of state:* President Ratu Naiqama LALABALAVU (since 12 November 2024)
head of government: Prime Minister Sitiveni Ligamamada RABUKA (since 24 December 2022)
cabinet: Cabinet appointed by the prime minister from among members of Parliament and is responsible to Parliament
election/appointment process: president elected by Parliament for a 3-year term (eligible for a second term); prime minister endorsed by the president
most recent election date: 31 October 2024
election results: *2024:* Ratu Naiqama LALABALAVU elected president (People's Alliance) 35 votes, Meli Tora TAVAIQIA (Fiji First) 14 votes

2021: Ratu Wiliame KATONIVERE elected president; Wiliame KATONIVERE (People's Alliance) 28 votes, Teimumu KEPA (SODELPA) 23 votes
expected date of next election: 2027

Legislative branch: *legislature name:* Parliament
legislative structure: unicameral
number of seats: 55 (all directly elected)
electoral system: proportional representation
scope of elections: full renewal
term in office: 4 years
most recent election date: 12/14/2022
parties elected and seats per party: FijiFirst (26); People's Alliance (21); National Federation Party (NFP) (5); Social Democratic Liberal Party (Soldelpa) (3)
percentage of women in chamber: 9.1%
expected date of next election: December 2026

Judicial branch: *highest court(s):* Supreme Court (consists of the chief justice, all justices of the Court of Appeal, and judges appointed specifically as Supreme Court judges); Court of Appeal (consists of the court president, all puisne judges of the High Court, and judges specifically appointed to the Court of Appeal); High Court (chaired by the chief justice and includes a minimum of 10 puisne judges; High Court organized into civil, criminal, family, employment, and tax divisions)
judge selection and term of office: chief justice appointed by the president of Fiji on the advice of the prime minister following consultation with the parliamentary leader of the opposition; judges of the Supreme Court, the president of the Court of Appeal, the justices of the Court of Appeal, and puisne judges of the High Court appointed by the president of Fiji on the nomination of the Judicial Service Commission after consulting with the cabinet minister and the House of Representatives committee responsible for the administration of justice; the chief justice, Supreme Court judges, and justices of Appeal generally required to retire at age 70, but this requirement may be waived for one or more sessions of the court; puisne judges appointed for not less than 4 years or more than 7 years, with mandatory retirement at age 65
subordinate courts: Magistrates' Court (organized into civil, criminal, juvenile, and small claims divisions)

Political parties: Fiji First
Fiji Labor Party or FLP
Freedom Alliance (formerly Fiji United Freedom Party or FUFP)
National Federation Party or NFP
People's Alliance
Peoples Democratic Party or PDP
Social Democratic Liberal Party or SODELPA
Unity Fiji

Diplomatic representation in the US: *chief of mission:* Ambassador Ilisoni VUIDREKETI (since 17 June 2024)
chancery: 1707 L Street NW, Suite 200, Washington, DC 20036
telephone: [1] (917) 208-4560
FAX: [1] (202) 466-8325
email address and website: info@FijiEmbassyDC.com
https://www.fijiembassydc.com/

Diplomatic representation from the US: *chief of mission:* Ambassador Marie DAMOUR (since 24 November 2022); note - also accredited to Kiribati, Nauru, Tonga, and Tuvalu
embassy: 158 Princes Road, Tamavua, Suva
mailing address: 4290 Suva Place, Washington DC 20521-4290
telephone: [679] 331-4466
FAX: [679] 330-2267
email address and website: SuvaACS@state.gov
https://fj.usembassy.gov/

International organization participation: ACP, ADB, AOSIS, C, CP, FAO, G-77, IAEA, IBRD, ICAO, ICCt, ICRM, IDA, IFAD, IFC, IFRCS, IHO, ILO, IMF, IMO, Interpol, IOC, IOM, ISO, ITSO, ITU, ITUC (NGOs), MIGA, OPCW, PCA, PIF, Sparteca (suspended), SPC, UN, UNCTAD, UNDOF, UNESCO, UNIDO, UNISFA, UNMISS, UNWTO, UPU, WCO, WFTU (NGOs), WHO, WIPO, WMO, WTO

Independence: 10 October 1970 (from the UK)

National holiday: Fiji (Independence) Day, 10 October (1970)

Flag: *description:* light blue with the UK flag in the upper-left quadrant and the Fijian shield centered on the right half of the flag; the shield shows a yellow lion holding a coconut above a white field quartered by the cross of Saint George; the four quarters depict sugarcane, a palm tree, a banana bunch, and a white dove
meaning: blue symbolizes the Pacific Ocean

National symbol(s): Fijian canoe

National color(s): light blue

National anthem(s): *title:* "God Bless Fiji" (Let Us Show Pride)
lyrics/music: Michael Francis Alexander PRESCOTT/C. Austin MILES (adapted by Michael Francis Alexander PRESCOTT)
history: adopted 1970; known in Fijian as "Meda Dau Doka" (Let Us Show Pride); adapted from the hymn, "Dwelling in Beulah Land," the anthem's English lyrics are usually used, although they differ in meaning from the official Fijian lyrics

National heritage: *total World Heritage Sites:* 1 (cultural)
selected World Heritage Site locales: Levuka Historical Port Town

ECONOMY

Economic overview: upper-middle income, tourism-based Pacific island economy; susceptible to ocean rises; key energy and infrastructure investments; post-pandemic tourism resurgence; improved debt standing; limited workforce

Real GDP (purchasing power parity): $13.1 billion (2024 est.)
$12.617 billion (2023 est.)
$11.734 billion (2022 est.)
note: data in 2021 dollars
comparison ranking: 160

Real GDP growth rate: 3.8% (2024 est.)
7.5% (2023 est.)
19.8% (2022 est.)
note: annual GDP % growth based on constant local currency
comparison ranking: 82

Real GDP per capita: $14,100 (2024 est.)
$13,700 (2023 est.)
$12,800 (2022 est.)
note: data in 2021 dollars
comparison ranking: 128

GDP (official exchange rate): $5.841 billion (2024 est.)
note: data in current dollars at official exchange rate

Inflation rate (consumer prices): 4.5% (2024 est.)
2.3% (2023 est.)
4.3% (2022 est.)
note: annual % change based on consumer prices
comparison ranking: 136

GDP - composition, by sector of origin: *agriculture:* 8.4% (2024 est.)
industry: 14.1% (2024 est.)
services: 56.2% (2024 est.)
note: figures may not total 100% due to non-allocated consumption not captured in sector-reported data
comparison rankings: agriculture 82; industry 167; services 114

GDP - composition, by end use: *household consumption:* 71.7% (2023 est.)
government consumption: 20.8% (2023 est.)
investment in fixed capital: 18.6% (2023 est.)
investment in inventories: 1.2% (2023 est.)
exports of goods and services: 57% (2023 est.)
imports of goods and services: -69.2% (2023 est.)
note: figures may not total 100% due to rounding or gaps in data collection

Agricultural products: sugarcane, cassava, taro, vegetables, chicken, coconuts, eggs, ginger, milk, sweet potatoes (2023)
note: top ten agricultural products based on tonnage

Industries: tourism, sugar processing, clothing, copra, gold, silver, lumber

Industrial production growth rate: 7.3% (2024 est.)
note: annual % change in industrial value added based on constant local currency
comparison ranking: 22

Labor force: 387,800 (2024 est.)
note: number of people ages 15 or older who are employed or seeking work
comparison ranking: 163

Unemployment rate: 4.4% (2024 est.)
4.4% (2023 est.)
4.5% (2022 est.)
note: % of labor force seeking employment
comparison ranking: 71

Youth unemployment rate (ages 15-24): *total:* 15.5% (2024 est.)
male: 11.8% (2024 est.)
female: 22.5% (2024 est.)
note: % of labor force ages 15-24 seeking employment
comparison ranking: total 77

Population below poverty line: 24.1% (2019 est.)
note: % of population with income below national poverty line

Gini Index coefficient - distribution of family income 30.7 (2019 est.)
note: index (0-100) of income distribution; higher values represent greater inequality
comparison ranking: 115

Household income or consumption by percentage share: *lowest 10%:* 3.5% (2019 est.)
highest 10%: 24.2% (2019 est.)
note: % share of income accruing to lowest and highest 10% of population

Remittances: 9.2% of GDP (2023 est.)
9.2% of GDP (2022 est.)
9.1% of GDP (2021 est.)
note: personal transfers and compensation between resident and non-resident individuals/households/entities

Budget: *revenues:* $1.345 billion (2023 est.)
expenditures: $1.562 billion (2023 est.)

note: central government revenues and expenses (excluding grants/extrabudgetary units/social security funds) converted to US dollars at average official exchange rate for year indicated

Taxes and other revenues: 20.7% (of GDP) (2023 est.)
note: central government tax revenue as a % of GDP
comparison ranking: 45

Current account balance: -$865.665 million (2022 est.)
-$686.577 million (2021 est.)
-$614.13 million (2020 est.)
note: balance of payments - net trade and primary/secondary income in current dollars
comparison ranking: 125

Exports: $2.376 billion (2022 est.)
$1.171 billion (2021 est.)
$1.23 billion (2020 est.)
note: balance of payments - exports of goods and services in current dollars
comparison ranking: 160

Exports - partners: USA 32%, Australia 12%, Tonga 6%, NZ 6%, Samoa 4% (2023)
note: top five export partners based on percentage share of exports

Exports - commodities: water, fish, raw sugar, refined petroleum, garments (2023)
note: top five export commodities based on value in dollars

Imports: $3.434 billion (2022 est.)
$2.344 billion (2021 est.)
$1.977 billion (2020 est.)
note: balance of payments - imports of goods and services in current dollars
comparison ranking: 162

Imports - partners: Singapore 25%, China 16%, Australia 15%, NZ 14%, USA 5% (2023)
note: top five import partners based on percentage share of imports

Imports - commodities: refined petroleum, medical instruments, cars, broadcasting equipment, plastics (2023)
note: top five import commodities based on value in dollars

Reserves of foreign exchange and gold: $1.6 billion (2024 est.)
$1.548 billion (2023 est.)
$1.557 billion (2022 est.)
note: holdings of gold (year-end prices)/foreign exchange/special drawing rights in current dollars
comparison ranking: 133

Debt - external: $1.397 billion (2023 est.)
note: present value of external debt in current US dollars
comparison ranking: 100

Exchange rates: Fijian dollars (FJD) per US dollar -

Exchange rates: 2.268 (2024 est.)
2.25 (2023 est.)
2.201 (2022 est.)
2.071 (2021 est.)
2.169 (2020 est.)

ENERGY

Electricity access: *electrification - total population:* 92% (2022 est.)
electrification - urban areas: 97.6%
electrification - rural areas: 86.8%

Electricity: *installed generating capacity:* 427,000 kW (2023 est.)
consumption: 1.048 billion kWh (2023 est.)
transmission/distribution losses: 102.047 million kWh (2023 est.)
comparison rankings: installed generating capacity 154; consumption 160; transmission/distribution losses 46

Electricity generation sources: *fossil fuels:* 36.3% of total installed capacity (2023 est.)
solar: 1.1% of total installed capacity (2023 est.)
wind: 0.2% of total installed capacity (2023 est.)
hydroelectricity: 52.3% of total installed capacity (2023 est.)
biomass and waste: 10% of total installed capacity (2023 est.)

Coal: *consumption:* 6 metric tons (2023 est.)
imports: 2 metric tons (2022 est.)

Petroleum: *refined petroleum consumption:* 10,000 bbl/day (2023 est.)

Energy consumption per capita: 25.375 million Btu/person (2023 est.)
comparison ranking: 123

COMMUNICATIONS

Telephones - fixed lines: *total subscriptions:* 49,000 (2021 est.)
subscriptions per 100 inhabitants: 4 (2022 est.)
comparison ranking: total subscriptions 155

Telephones - mobile cellular: *total subscriptions:* 992,000 (2021 est.)
subscriptions per 100 inhabitants: 107 (2021 est.)
comparison ranking: total subscriptions 163

Broadcast media: Fiji TV, a publicly traded company, operates a free-to-air channel; Digicel Fiji operates the Sky Fiji and Sky Pacific multi-channel pay-TV services; state-owned commercial company, Fiji Broadcasting Corporation, Ltd, operates 6 radio stations, including 2 public broadcasters and 4 commercial broadcasters with multiple repeaters; 5 radio stations with repeaters operated by Communications Fiji, Ltd; transmissions of multiple international broadcasters are available

Internet country code: fj

Internet users: *percent of population:* 79% (2023 est.)

Broadband - fixed subscriptions: *total:* 23,000 (2022 est.)
subscriptions per 100 inhabitants: 3 (2022 est.)
comparison ranking: total 166

TRANSPORTATION

Civil aircraft registration country code prefix: DQ

Airports: 26 (2025)
comparison ranking: 128

Heliports: 2 (2025)
comparison ranking: 138

Railways: *total:* 597 km (2008)
narrow gauge: 597 km (2008) 0.600-m gauge
note: belongs to the government-owned Fiji Sugar Corporation; used to haul sugarcane during the harvest season, which runs from May to December

Merchant marine: *total:* 74 (2023)
by type: general cargo 21, oil tanker 4, other 49
comparison ranking: total 105

Ports: *total ports:* 5 (2024)
large: 0
medium: 0
small: 2
very small: 3
ports with oil terminals: 4
key ports: Lautoka Harbor, Levuka, Malai, Savusavu Bay, Suva Harbor

MILITARY AND SECURITY

Military and security forces: Republic of Fiji Military Forces (RFMF): Land Force, Republic of Fiji Navy (2025)

Military expenditures: 1.4% of GDP (2024 est.)
1.1% of GDP (2023 est.)
1.2% of GDP (2022 est.)
1.5% of GDP (2021 est.)
1.4% of GDP (2020 est.)

Military and security service personnel strengths: approximately 4,000 active Republic of Fiji Military Forces (2025)

Military equipment inventories and acquisitions: the RFMF is lightly armed and equipped; Australia has provided patrol boats and a few armored personnel carriers; it also provides logistical support for RFMF regional or UN operations; in recent years, China and the US have provided small amounts of equipment (2025)

Military service age and obligation: 18-25 years of age for voluntary military service for men and women (2024)
note: as of 2024, women comprised approximately 8% of the Fiji Military Forces

Military deployments: 170 Egypt (MFO); 160 Iraq (UNAMI); 150 Golan Heights (UNDOF) (2024)

Military - note: the Fiji Military Forces (RFMF) are responsible for external security but can be assigned some domestic security responsibilities in specific circumstances; the RFMF has a history of intervening in the country's politics, and it continues to have significant political power; it also has a tradition of participating in UN peacekeeping operations, which have offered experience and a source of financial support; Fiji has sent troops on nearly 20 such missions since first deploying personnel to South Lebanon in 1978
Fiji has a "shiprider" agreement with the US, which allows local maritime law enforcement officers to embark on US Coast Guard (USCG) and US Navy (USN) vessels, including to board and search vessels suspected of violating laws or regulations within Fiji's designated exclusive economic zone (EEZ) or on the high seas; "shiprider" agreements also enable USCG personnel and USN vessels with embarked USCG law enforcement personnel to work with host nations to protect critical regional resources (2025)

TRANSNATIONAL ISSUES

Refugees and internally displaced persons: *refugees:* 25 (2024 est.)

IDPs: 259 (2024 est.)

Trafficking in persons: *tier rating:* Tier 2 Watch List — the government did not demonstrate overall increasing efforts to eliminate trafficking compared with the previous reporting period, therefore Fiji remained on Tier 2 Watch List for the second consecutive year; for more details, go to: https://www.state.gov/reports/2025-trafficking-in-persons-report/fiji/

FINLAND

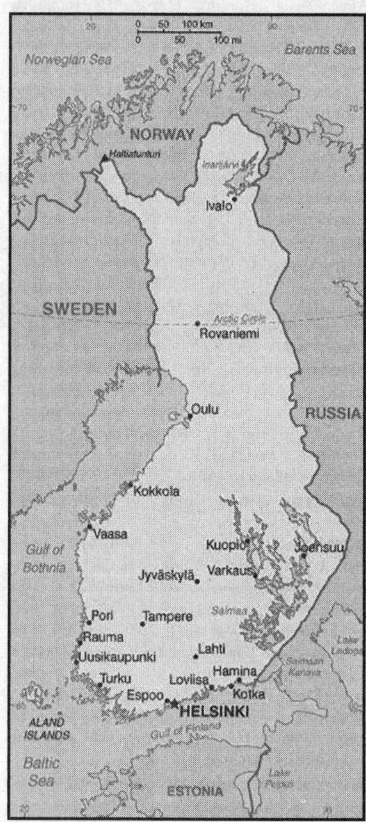

INTRODUCTION

Background: Finland was a province and then a grand duchy under Sweden from the 12th to the 19th centuries and an autonomous grand duchy of Russia after 1809. It gained complete independence in 1917. During World War II, Finland successfully defended its independence through cooperation with Germany and resisted subsequent invasions by the Soviet Union, albeit with some loss of territory. During the next half-century, Finland transformed from a farm/forest economy to a diversified modern industrial economy; per-capita income is among the highest in Western Europe. A member of the EU since 1995, Finland was the only Nordic state to join the euro single currency at its initiation in January 1999. In the 21st century, the key features of Finland's modern welfare state are high-quality education, promotion of equality, and a national social welfare system, although the system is currently facing the challenges of an aging population and the fluctuations of an export-driven economy. Following Russia's invasion of Ukraine in 2022, Finland opted to join NATO; it became the organization's 31st member in April 2023.

GEOGRAPHY

Location: Northern Europe, bordering the Baltic Sea, Gulf of Bothnia, and Gulf of Finland, between Sweden and Russia

Geographic coordinates: 64 00 N, 26 00 E

Map references: Europe

Area: *total:* 338,145 sq km
land: 303,815 sq km
water: 34,330 sq km
comparison ranking: total 66

Area - comparative: slightly more than two times the size of Georgia; slightly smaller than Montana

Land boundaries: *total:* 2,563 km
border countries (3): Norway 709 km; Sweden 545 km; Russia 1,309 km

Coastline: 1,250 km

Maritime claims: *territorial sea:* 12 nm (in the Gulf of Finland - 3 nm)
contiguous zone: 24 nm
continental shelf: 200 m depth or to the depth of exploitation
exclusive fishing zone: 12 nm; extends to continental shelf boundary with Sweden, Estonia, and Russia

Climate: cold temperate; potentially subarctic but comparatively mild because of moderating influence of the North Atlantic Current, Baltic Sea, and more than 60,000 lakes

Terrain: mostly low, flat to rolling plains interspersed with lakes and low hills

Elevation: *highest point:* Halti (alternatively Haltia, Haltitunturi, Haltiatunturi) 1,328 m
lowest point: Baltic Sea 0 m
mean elevation: 164 m

Natural resources: timber, iron ore, copper, lead, zinc, chromite, nickel, gold, silver, limestone

Land use: *agricultural land:* 7.5% (2022 est.)
arable land: 7.4% (2022 est.)
permanent crops: 0% (2022 est.)
permanent pasture: 0.1% (2022 est.)
forest: 73.7% (2022 est.)
other: 18.8% (2022 est.)

Irrigated land: 80 sq km (2016)

Major lakes (area sq km): *fresh water lake(s):* Saimaa - 1,760 sq km; Paijanne - 1,090 sq km; Inarijarvi - 1,000 sq km; Oulujarvi - 900 sq km; Pielinen - 850 sq km

Population distribution: the vast majority of people are found in the south; the northern interior areas remain sparsely populated

Natural hazards: severe winters in the north

Geography - note: long boundary with Russia; Helsinki is northernmost national capital on European continent; population concentrated on small southwestern coastal plain

PEOPLE AND SOCIETY

Population: *total:* 5,626,414 (2024 est.)
male: 2,773,656
female: 2,852,758
comparison rankings: total 118; male 119; female 118

Nationality: *noun:* Finn(s)
adjective: Finnish

Ethnic groups: Finnish, Swedish, Russian, Estonian, Romani, Sami
note: 90.9% of the population has a Finnish background (2022 est.)

Languages: Finnish (official) 85.9%, Swedish (official) 5.2%, Russian 1.7%, other 7.2% (2022 est.)
major-language sample(s):
World Factbook, korvaamaton perustietolähde. (Finnish)

Religions: Lutheran 66.6%, Greek Orthodox 1.1%, other 1.7%, none 30.6% (2022 est.)

Age structure: *0-14 years:* 16.2% (male 464,939/female 444,585)
15-64 years: 60.3% (male 1,725,072/female 1,668,604)
65 years and over: 23.5% (2024 est.) (male 583,645/female 739,569)

Dependency ratios: *total dependency ratio:* 62.4 (2024 est.)
youth dependency ratio: 23.8 (2024 est.)
elderly dependency ratio: 38.5 (2024 est.)
potential support ratio: 2.6 (2024 est.)

Median age: *total:* 43.3 years (2024 est.)
male: 41.8 years
female: 44.9 years
comparison ranking: total 36

Population growth rate: 0.2% (2024 est.)
comparison ranking: 178

Birth rate: 10.2 births/1,000 population (2024 est.)
comparison ranking: 184

Death rate: 10.4 deaths/1,000 population (2024 est.)
comparison ranking: 30

Net migration rate: 2.2 migrant(s)/1,000 population (2024 est.)
comparison ranking: 47

Population distribution: the vast majority of people are found in the south; the northern interior areas remain sparsely populated

Urbanization: *urban population:* 85.8% of total population (2023)
rate of urbanization: 0.42% annual rate of change (2020-25 est.)

Major urban areas - population: 1.338 million HELSINKI (capital) (2023)

Sex ratio: *at birth:* 1.05 male(s)/female
0-14 years: 1.05 male(s)/female
15-64 years: 1.03 male(s)/female
65 years and over: 0.79 male(s)/female
total population: 0.97 male(s)/female (2024 est.)

Mother's mean age at first birth: 29.5 years (2020 est.)

Maternal mortality ratio: 8 deaths/100,000 live births (2023 est.)
comparison ranking: 156

Infant mortality rate: *total:* 2.1 deaths/1,000 live births (2024 est.)
male: 2.3 deaths/1,000 live births
female: 1.9 deaths/1,000 live births
comparison ranking: total 221

Life expectancy at birth: *total population:* 82.2 years (2024 est.)
male: 79.3 years

female: 85.2 years
comparison ranking: total population 31

Total fertility rate: 1.74 children born/woman (2024 est.)
comparison ranking: 150

Gross reproduction rate: 0.85 (2024 est.)

Drinking water source: *improved: urban:* 100% of population (2022 est.)
rural: 100% of population (2022 est.)
total: 100% of population (2022 est.)
unimproved: urban: 0% of population (2022 est.)
rural: 0% of population (2022 est.)
total: 0% of population (2022 est.)

Health expenditure: 10.2% of GDP (2021)
14.8% of national budget (2022 est.)

Physician density: 3.61 physicians/1,000 population (2021)

Hospital bed density: 2.8 beds/1,000 population (2020 est.)

Sanitation facility access: *improved: urban:* 100% of population (2022 est.)
rural: 100% of population (2022 est.)
total: 100% of population (2022 est.)
unimproved: urban: 0% of population (2022 est.)
rural: 0% of population (2022 est.)
total: 0% of population (2022 est.)

Obesity - adult prevalence rate: 22.2% (2016)
comparison ranking: 80

Alcohol consumption per capita: *total:* 8.23 liters of pure alcohol (2019 est.)
beer: 3.76 liters of pure alcohol (2019 est.)
wine: 1.59 liters of pure alcohol (2019 est.)
spirits: 1.96 liters of pure alcohol (2019 est.)
other alcohols: 0.91 liters of pure alcohol (2019 est.)
comparison ranking: total 41

Tobacco use: *total:* 18% (2025 est.)
male: 21.7% (2025 est.)
female: 14.3% (2025 est.)
comparison ranking: total 85

Currently married women (ages 15-49): 57.2% (2023 est.)

Child marriage: *women married by age 18:* 0.1% (2017)

Education expenditure: 6.5% of GDP (2021 est.)
10.2% national budget (2021 est.)
comparison ranking: Education expenditure (% GDP) 25

School life expectancy (primary to tertiary education): *total:* 20 years (2023 est.)
male: 18 years (2023 est.)
female: 21 years (2023 est.)

ENVIRONMENT

Environmental issues: limited air pollution in urban centers; some water pollution from industrial wastes, agricultural chemicals; habitat loss threatens wildlife populations

International environmental agreements: *party to:* Air Pollution, Air Pollution-Heavy Metals, Air Pollution-Multi-effect Protocol, Air Pollution-Nitrogen Oxides, Air Pollution-Persistent Organic Pollutants, Air Pollution-Sulphur 85, Air Pollution-Sulphur 94, Air Pollution-Volatile Organic Compounds, Antarctic- Environmental Protection, Antarctic-Marine Living Resources, Antarctic Treaty, Biodiversity, Climate Change, Climate Change-Kyoto Protocol, Climate Change-Paris Agreement, Comprehensive Nuclear Test Ban, Desertification, Endangered Species, Environmental Modification, Hazardous Wastes, Law of the Sea, Marine Dumping-London Convention, Marine Dumping-London Protocol, Marine Life Conservation, Nuclear Test Ban, Ozone Layer Protection, Ship Pollution, Tropical Timber 2006, Wetlands, Whaling
signed, but not ratified: none of the selected agreements

Climate: cold temperate; potentially subarctic but comparatively mild because of moderating influence of the North Atlantic Current, Baltic Sea, and more than 60,000 lakes

Urbanization: *urban population:* 85.8% of total population (2023)
rate of urbanization: 0.42% annual rate of change (2020-25 est.)

Carbon dioxide emissions: 33.594 million metric tonnes of CO2 (2023 est.)
from coal and metallurgical coke: 7.536 million metric tonnes of CO2 (2023 est.)
from petroleum and other liquids: 23.069 million metric tonnes of CO2 (2023 est.)
from consumed natural gas: 2.989 million metric tonnes of CO2 (2023 est.)
comparison ranking: total emissions 69

Particulate matter emissions: 6 micrograms per cubic meter (2019 est.)

Waste and recycling: *municipal solid waste generated annually:* 3.124 million tons (2024 est.)
percent of municipal solid waste recycled: 35.4% (2022 est.)

Total water withdrawal: *municipal:* 500 million cubic meters (2022 est.)
industrial: 1.299 billion cubic meters (2022 est.)
agricultural: 1 billion cubic meters (2022 est.)

Total renewable water resources: 110 billion cubic meters (2022 est.)

Geoparks: *total global geoparks and regional networks:* 4 (2024)
global geoparks and regional networks: Impact Crater Lake - Lappajarvi; Rokua; Lauhanvuori-Haemeenkangas; Saimaa; Salpausselka (2024)

GOVERNMENT

Country name: *conventional long form:* Republic of Finland
conventional short form: Finland
local long form: Suomen tasavalta (Finnish)/ Republiken Finland (Swedish)
local short form: Suomi (Finnish)/ Finland (Swedish)
etymology: name derives from the Finns, an ethnic group in northeastern Europe; their name comes from the Germanic word finna, meaning "fish scale;" the local name, Suomi, may come from two local words: suo, meaning "marsh," and *maa,* meaning "land"

Government type: parliamentary republic

Capital: *name:* Helsinki
geographic coordinates: 60 10 N, 24 56 E
time difference: UTC+2 (7 hours ahead of Washington, DC, during Standard Time)
daylight saving time: +1hr, begins last Sunday in March; ends last Sunday in October
etymology: the modern name is a Finnish derivation; King Gustav VASA of Sweden founded the city in 1550 as Helsingfors; the name came from *Helsing*, the Old Norwegian name for a local people, and the word *fors*, or "waterfall," referring to a waterfall at the city's original location on the Vantaa River

Administrative divisions: 19 regions (*maakunnat*, singular - *maakunta* (Finnish); *landskapen*, singular - *landskapet* (Swedish)); Aland (Swedish), Ahvenanmaa (Finnish); Etela-Karjala (Finnish), Sodra Karelen (Swedish) [South Karelia]; Etela-Pohjanmaa (Finnish), Sodra Osterbotten (Swedish) [South Ostrobothnia]; Etela-Savo (Finnish), Sodra Savolax (Swedish) [South Savo]; Kanta-Hame (Finnish), Egentliga Tavastland (Swedish); Kainuu (Finnish), Kajanaland (Swedish); Keski- Pohjanmaa (Finnish), Mellersta Osterbotten (Swedish) [Central Ostrobothnia]; Keski-Suomi (Finnish), Mellersta Finland (Swedish) [Central Finland]; Kymenlaakso (Finnish), Kymmenedalen (Swedish); Lappi (Finnish), Lappland (Swedish); Paijat-Hame (Finnish), Paijanne-Tavastland (Swedish); Pirkanmaa (Finnish), Birkaland (Swedish) [Tampere]; Pohjanmaa (Finnish), Osterbotten (Swedish) [Ostrobothnia]; Pohjois-Karjala (Finnish), Norra Karelen (Swedish) [North Karelia]; Pohjois-Pohjanmaa (Finnish), Norra Osterbotten (Swedish) [North Ostrobothnia]; Pohjois-Savo (Finnish), Norra Savolax (Swedish) [North Savo]; Satakunta (Finnish and Swedish); Uusimaa (Finnish), Nyland (Swedish) [Newland]; Varsinais-Suomi (Finnish), Egentliga Finland (Swedish) [Southwest Finland]

Legal system: civil law system based on the Swedish model

Constitution: *history:* previous 1906, 1919; latest drafted 17 June 1997, approved by Parliament 11 June 1999, entered into force 1 March 2000
amendment process: proposed by Parliament; passage normally requires simple majority vote in two readings in the first parliamentary session and at least two-thirds majority vote in a single reading by the newly elected Parliament; proposals declared "urgent" by five-sixths of Parliament members can be passed by at least two-thirds majority vote in the first parliamentary session only

International law organization participation: accepts compulsory ICJ jurisdiction with reservations; accepts ICCt jurisdiction

Citizenship: *citizenship by birth:* no
citizenship by descent only: at least one parent must be a citizen of Finland
dual citizenship recognized: yes
residency requirement for naturalization: 6 years

Suffrage: 18 years of age; universal

Executive branch: *chief of state:* President Alexander STUBB (since 1 March 2024)
head of government: Prime Minister Petteri ORPO (since 20 June 2023)
cabinet: Council of State or Valtioneuvosto appointed by the president, responsible to Parliament
election/appointment process: president directly elected by absolute-majority popular vote in 2 rounds, if needed, for a 6-year term (eligible for a second term); prime minister appointed by Parliament
most recent election date: 28 January 2024, with a run-off on 11 February 2024
election results: 2024: Alexander STUBB elected in the second round; percent of vote in the first round - Alexander STUBB (KoK) 27.2%, Pekka HAAVISTO (Vihr) 25.8%, Jussi HALLA-AHO (PS) 19.0%, Olli REHN (Kesk) 15.3%; percent of vote in second round - STUBB 51.6%, HAAVISTO 48.4%
2018: Sauli NIINISTO reelected president; percent of vote - Sauli NIINISTO (independent) 62.7%, Pekka HAAVISTO (Vihr) 12.4%, Laura

HUHTASAARI (PS) 6.9%, Paavo VAYRYNEN (independent) 6.2%, Matti VANHANEN (Kesk) 4.1%, other 7.7%
expected date of next election: by 28 January 2030

Legislative branch: *legislature name:* Parliament (Eduskunta - Riksdagen)
legislative structure: unicameral
number of seats: 200 (all directly elected)
electoral system: proportional representation
scope of elections: full renewal
term in office: 4 years
most recent election date: 4/2/2023
parties elected and seats per party: National Coalition Party (KOK) (48); The Finns Party (PS) (46); Social Democratic Party (SDP) (43); Center Party (KESK) (23); The Greens (13); Left Alliance (Vas) (11); Other (16)
percentage of women in chamber: 45.5%
expected date of next election: April 2027

Judicial branch: *highest court(s):* Supreme Court or Korkein Oikeus (consists of the court president and 18 judges); Supreme Administrative Court (consists of 21 judges, including the court president; organized into 3 chambers)
judge selection and term of office: Supreme Court and Supreme Administrative Court judges appointed by the president of the republic; judges serve until mandatory retirement at age 68
subordinate courts: 6 Courts of Appeal; 8 regional administrative courts; 27 district courts; special courts for issues relating to markets, labor, insurance, impeachment, land, tenancy, and water rights
note: Finland has a dual judicial system; courts with civil and criminal jurisdiction, and administrative courts with jurisdiction for litigation between individuals and administrative organs of the state and communities

Political parties: Aland Coalition (a coalition of several political parties on the Aland Islands)
Center Party or Kesk
Christian Democrats or KD
Finns Party or PS
Green League or Vihr
Left Alliance or Vas
Movement Now or Liike Nyt
National Coalition Party or Kok
Social Democratic Party or SDP
Swedish People's Party or RKP or SFP

Diplomatic representation in the US: *chief of mission:* Ambassador Leena-Kaisa MIKKOLA (since 18 September 2024)
chancery: 3301 Massachusetts Avenue NW, Washington, DC 20008
telephone: [1] (202) 298-5800
FAX: [1] (202) 298-6030
email address and website: sanomat.WAS@gov.fi
https://finlandabroad.fi/web/usa/mission
consulate(s) general: Los Angeles, New York

Diplomatic representation from the US: *chief of mission:* Ambassador (vacant); Chargé d'Affaires J. Chris KARBER (since July 2025)
embassy: Itainen Puistotie 14 B, 00140 Helsinki
mailing address: 5310 Helsinki Place, Washington DC 20521-5310
telephone: [358] (9) 616-250
FAX: [358] (9) 174-681
email address and website: HelsinkiACS@state.gov
https://fi.usembassy. gov/

International organization participation: ADB (nonregional member), AfDB (nonregional member), Arctic Council, Australia Group, BIS, CBSS, CD, CE, CERN, EAPC, EBRD, ECB, EIB, EITI (implementing country), EMU, ESA, EU, FAO, FATF, G-9, IADB, IAEA, IBRD, ICAO, ICC (national committees), ICCt, ICRM, IDA, IEA, IFAD, IFC, IFRCS, IHO, ILO, IMF, IMO, IMSO, Interpol, IOC, IOM, IPU, ISO, ITSO, ITU, ITUC (NGOs), MIGA, NATO, NC, NEA, NIB, NSG, OAS (observer), OECD, OPCW, OSCE, Pacific Alliance (observer), Paris Club, PCA, PFP, Schengen Convention, UN, UNCTAD, UNESCO, UNHCR, UNHRC, UNIDO, UNIFIL, UNMIL, UNMOGIP, UNOOSA, UNRWA, UNSOM, UNTSO, UPU, Wassenaar Arrangement, WCO, WFTU (NGOs), WHO, WIPO, WMO, WTO, ZC

Independence: 6 December 1917 (from Russia)

National holiday: Independence Day, 6 December (1917)

Flag: *description:* white with a blue cross extending to the edges of the flag; the cross is shifted to the left in the style of the Dannebrog (Danish flag)
meaning: the blue stands for the country's thousands of lakes, and the white for snow

National symbol(s): lion

National color(s): blue, white

National anthem(s): *title:* "Maamme" (Our Land)
lyrics/music: Paavo Eemil KAJANDER, Johan Ludvig RUNEBERG/Fredrik PACIUS
history: in use since 1848; although never officially adopted, the anthem has been popular since a student group first sang it in 1848

National heritage: *total World Heritage Sites:* 7 (6 cultural, 1 natural)
selected World Heritage Site locales: Fortress of Suomenlinna (c); Old Rauma (c); Petäjävesi Old Church (c); Verla Groundwood and Board Mill (c); Bronze Age Burial Site of Sammallahdenmäki (c); High Coast / Kvarken Archipelago (n); Struve Geodetic Arc (c)

ECONOMY

Economic overview: high-income, export-based EU and eurozone economy; major timber, metals, engineering, telecom, and electronics industries; emerging from recession triggered by inflation, weak consumer and export demand, and lower private investment; labor market reform plan to address structural rigidities

Real GDP (purchasing power parity): $313.591 billion (2024 est.)
$314.075 billion (2023 est.)
$317.078 billion (2022 est.)
note: data in 2021 dollars
comparison ranking: 61

Real GDP growth rate: -0.2% (2024 est.)
-0.9% (2023 est.)
0.8% (2022 est.)
note: annual GDP % growth based on constant local currency
comparison ranking: 194

Real GDP per capita: $55,600 (2024 est.)
$56,200 (2023 est.)
$57,100 (2022 est.)
note: data in 2021 dollars
comparison ranking: 34

GDP (official exchange rate): $299.836 billion (2024 est.)
note: data in current dollars at official exchange rate

Inflation rate (consumer prices): 1.6% (2024 est.)
6.3% (2023 est.)
7.1% (2022 est.)
note: annual % change based on consumer prices
comparison ranking: 38

GDP - composition, by sector of origin: *agriculture:* 2.5% (2024 est.)
industry: 22.1% (2024 est.)
services: 62.9% (2024 est.)
note: figures may not total 100% due to non-allocated consumption not captured in sector-reported data
comparison rankings: agriculture 142; industry 118; services 68

GDP - composition, by end use: *household consumption:* 53.4% (2023 est.)
government consumption: 25.6% (2023 est.)
investment in fixed capital: 23.4% (2023 est.)
investment in inventories: -0.4% (2023 est.)
exports of goods and services: 43.1% (2023 est.)
imports of goods and services: -42.8% (2023 est.)
note: figures may not total 100% due to rounding or gaps in data collection

Agricultural products: milk, barley, oats, wheat, potatoes, sugar beets, pork, chicken, peas, rye (2023)
note: top ten agricultural products based on tonnage

Industries: metals and metal products, electronics, machinery and scientific instruments, shipbuilding, pulp and paper, foodstuffs, chemicals, textiles, clothing

Industrial production growth rate: -2.2% (2024 est.)
note: annual % change in industrial value added based on constant local currency
comparison ranking: 160

Labor force: 2.898 million (2024 est.)
note: number of people ages 15 or older who are employed or seeking work
comparison ranking: 112

Unemployment rate: 8.3% (2024 est.)
7.2% (2023 est.)
6.8% (2022 est.)
note: % of labor force seeking employment
comparison ranking: 136

Youth unemployment rate (ages 15-24): *total:* 19.2% (2024 est.)
male: 20% (2024 est.)
female: 18.3% (2024 est.)
note: % of labor force ages 15-24 seeking employment
comparison ranking: total 57

Population below poverty line: 12.2% (2022 est.)
note: % of population with income below national poverty line
Gini Index coefficient - distribution of family income 27.9 (2022 est.)
note: index (0-100) of income distribution; higher values represent greater inequality
comparison ranking: 132

Average household expenditures: *on food:* 12.3% of household expenditures (2023 est.)
on alcohol and tobacco: 4.4% of household expenditures (2023 est.)

Household income or consumption by percentage share: *lowest 10%:* 3.8% (2022 est.)
highest 10%: 23.1% (2022 est.)
note: % share of income accruing to lowest and highest 10% of population

Remittances: 0.2% of GDP (2024 est.)
0.3% of GDP (2023 est.)
0.2% of GDP (2022 est.)

note: personal transfers and compensation between resident and non-resident individuals/households/entities

Budget: *revenues:* $126.337 billion (2023 est.)
expenditures: $131.978 billion (2023 est.)
note: central government revenues (excluding grants) and expenditures converted to US dollars at average official exchange rate for year indicated

Public debt: 61.3% of GDP (2017 est.)
note: data cover general government debt and include debt instruments issued (or owned) by government entities other than the treasury; the data include treasury debt held by foreign entities; the data include debt issued by subnational entities, as well as intragovernmental debt; intragovernmental debt consists of treasury borrowings from surpluses in the social funds, such as for retirement, medical care, and unemployment; debt instruments for the social funds are not sold at public auctions
comparison ranking: 76

Taxes and other revenues: 25.4% (of GDP) (2023 est.)
note: central government tax revenue as a % of GDP
comparison ranking: 16

Current account balance: $930.393 million (2024 est.)
-$1.58 billion (2023 est.)
-$7.026 billion (2022 est.)
note: balance of payments - net trade and primary/secondary income in current dollars
comparison ranking: 58

Exports: $124.531 billion (2024 est.)
$127.098 billion (2023 est.)
$129.389 billion (2022 est.)
note: balance of payments - exports of goods and services in current dollars
comparison ranking: 43

Exports - partners: USA 11%, Germany 11%, Sweden 10%, Netherlands 7%, China 5% (2023)
note: top five export partners based on percentage share of exports

Exports - commodities: paper, refined petroleum, steel, wood pulp, ships (2023)
note: top five export commodities based on value in dollars

Imports: $122.644 billion (2024 est.)
$126.175 billion (2023 est.)
$135.119 billion (2022 est.)
note: balance of payments - imports of goods and services in current dollars
comparison ranking: 42

Imports - partners: Germany 14%, Sweden 12%, China 9%, Norway 8%, Netherlands 5% (2023)
note: top five import partners based on percentage share of imports

Imports - commodities: crude petroleum, cars, refined petroleum, packaged medicine, broadcasting equipment (2023)
note: top five import commodities based on value in dollars

Reserves of foreign exchange and gold: $17.993 billion (2024 est.)
$16.929 billion (2023 est.)
$16.036 billion (2022 est.)
note: holdings of gold (year-end prices)/foreign exchange/special drawing rights in current dollars
comparison ranking: 66

Exchange rates: euros (EUR) per US dollar -

Exchange rates: 0.924 (2024 est.)
0.925 (2023 est.)
0.95 (2022 est.)
0.845 (2021 est.)
0.876 (2020 est.)

ENERGY

Electricity access: *electrification - total population:* 100% (2022 est.)

Electricity: *installed generating capacity:* 26.782 million kW (2023 est.)
consumption: 77.419 billion kWh (2023 est.)
exports: 7.883 billion kWh (2023 est.)
imports: 9.644 billion kWh (2023 est.)
transmission/distribution losses: 2.721 billion kWh (2023 est.)
comparison rankings: installed generating capacity 41; consumption 41; exports 29; imports 27; transmission/distribution losses 136

Electricity generation sources: *fossil fuels:* 5.6% of total installed capacity (2023 est.)
nuclear: 41.8% of total installed capacity (2023 est.)
solar: 0.8% of total installed capacity (2023 est.)
wind: 18.7% of total installed capacity (2023 est.)
hydroelectricity: 19.4% of total installed capacity (2023 est.)
biomass and waste: 13.7% of total installed capacity (2023 est.)

Nuclear energy: Number of operational nuclear reactors: 5 (2025)

Net capacity of operational nuclear reactors: 4.37GW (2025 est.)

Percent of total electricity production: 42% (2025 est.)

Coal: *production:* 811,000 metric tons (2023 est.)
consumption: 3.933 million metric tons (2023 est.)
exports: 113,000 metric tons (2023 est.)
imports: 2.624 million metric tons (2023 est.)

Petroleum: *total petroleum production:* 8,000 bbl/day (2023 est.)
refined petroleum consumption: 172,000 bbl/day (2024 est.)

Natural gas: *consumption:* 1.55 billion cubic meters (2023 est.)
exports: 479.457 million cubic meters (2023 est.)
imports: 2.112 billion cubic meters (2023 est.)

Energy consumption per capita: 183.54 million Btu/person (2023 est.)
comparison ranking: 21

COMMUNICATIONS

Telephones - fixed lines: *total subscriptions:* 158,000 (2023 est.)
subscriptions per 100 inhabitants: 3 (2023 est.)
comparison ranking: total subscriptions 124

Telephones - mobile cellular: *total subscriptions:* 7.14 million (2023 est.)
subscriptions per 100 inhabitants: 129 (2022 est.)
comparison ranking: total subscriptions 112

Broadcast media: 3 publicly operated TV stations and numerous privately owned TV stations; several free and special-interest pay-TV channels; cable and satellite multi-channel subscription services are available; all TV signals are digital; 13 national and 25 regional public radio stations; a large number of private radio broadcasters

Internet country code: .fi
note: Aland Islands assigned.ax

Internet users: *percent of population:* 94% (2023 est.)

Broadband - fixed subscriptions: *total:* 1.98 million (2023 est.)
subscriptions per 100 inhabitants: 35 (2023 est.)
comparison ranking: total 62

TRANSPORTATION

Civil aircraft registration country code prefix: OH

Airports: 98 (2025)
comparison ranking: 56

Heliports: 17 (2025)
comparison ranking: 56

Railways: *total:* 5,918 km (2020) 3,349 km electrified

Merchant marine: *total:* 282 (2023)
by type: bulk carrier 9, general cargo 75, oil tanker 4, other 194
comparison ranking: total 57

Ports: *total ports:* 37 (2024)
large: 5
medium: 7
small: 11
very small: 14
ports with oil terminals: 21
key ports: Helsinki, Kaskinen, Kokkola, Kotka, Kristinestad, Mantyluoto, Oulu, Pietarsaari, Pori, Rauma, Turku, Vaasa

MILITARY AND SECURITY

Military and security forces: Finnish Defense Forces (FDF; Puolustusvoimat): Army (Maavoimat), Navy (Merivoimat), Air Force (Ilmavoimat) (2025)
note: the Border Guard (Rajavartiolaitos) and National Police are under the Ministry of the Interior; the Border Guard becomes part of the FDF in wartime

Military expenditures: 2.8% of GDP (2025 est.)
2.4% of GDP (2024 est.)
2.1% of GDP (2023 est.)
1.7% of GDP (2022 est.)
1.4% of GDP (2021 est.)

Military and security service personnel strengths: approximately 31,000 active-duty military personnel (2025)
note: active-duty figures include about 21,000 conscripts carrying out their obligated military service

Military equipment inventories and acquisitions: the military's inventory consists of a wide mix of modern US, European, Israeli, South Korean, and domestically produced weapons systems; the Finnish defense industry produces a variety of military equipment, including wheeled armored vehicles and naval vessels; Finland also cooperates with other European countries and the US in the joint production of arms (2024)

Military service age and obligation: all Finnish men are obligated to serve 5.5-12 months of service within a branch of the military or the Border Guard upon reaching the age of 18 (length of service depends on the type of duty); women 18-29 may volunteer for service; there is also an option to perform non-military service which lasts for 8.5 or 11.5 months; after completing their initial conscript obligation, individuals enter the reserves and remain eligible for mobilization until the age of 50 for rank-and-file and 60 for non-commissioned and commissioned officers (2025)
note 1: Finland has had conscription since 1951; each year, the military inducts and active-duty units train

approximately 21,000 conscripts; the resulting pool of trained reservists gives the FDF a wartime strength of approximately 280,000 and a total reserve of some 900,000 citizens with military service
note 2: women have served on a voluntary basis since 1995, and as of 2022 made up about 19% of the military's full-time personnel

Military deployments: 165 Lebanon (UNIFIL) (2024)

Military - note: the Finnish Defense Forces (FDF) are focused primarily on territorial defense, which is based on having a large, trained reserve force created by general conscription; other FDF responsibilities include support to international peacekeeping operations and some domestic security duties, such as assisting the National Police in maintaining law and order in crises
the FDF is also focused on fulfilling its commitment to NATO; following Russia's full-scale invasion of Ukraine in 2022, Finland applied for NATO membership, gaining entry in April 2023; Finland had been part of NATO's Partnership for Peace program since 1994 and participated in NATO-led military missions in the Balkans, Afghanistan, and Iraq; in 2024, it joined NATO's Air Policing mission in Eastern Europe
Finland is a signatory of the EU's Common Security and Defense Policy and actively participates in EU crisis management missions and operations; the FDF also cooperates closely with the militaries of other Nordic countries through the Nordic Defense Cooperation structure (NORDEFCO; established 2009), which consists of Denmark, Finland, Iceland, Norway, and Sweden and involves cooperation in such areas as armaments, education, human resources, training and exercises, and operations; Sweden, the UK, and the US are close bi-lateral defense partners; in 2022, Finland signed a mutual security agreement with the UK, and since 2014 has been part of the UK-led Joint Expeditionary Force, a pool of high-readiness military forces from 10 Baltic and Scandinavian countries designed to respond to a wide range of contingencies in the North Atlantic, Baltic Sea, and High North regions (2025)

TERRORISM

Terrorist group(s): Terrorist group(s): Islamic State of Iraq and ash-Sham (ISIS)

TRANSNATIONAL ISSUES

Refugees and internally displaced persons: *refugees:* 97,568 (2024 est.)
stateless persons: 1,326 (2024 est.)

FRANCE

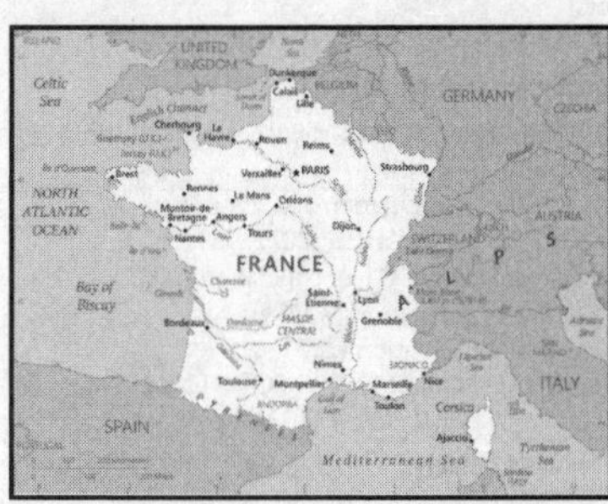

INTRODUCTION

Background: France today is one of the most modern countries in the world and is a leader among European nations. It plays an influential global role as a permanent member of the United Nations Security Council, NATO, the G-7, the G-20, the EU, and other multilateral organizations. France rejoined NATO's integrated military command structure in 2009, reversing then President Charles DE GAULLE's 1966 decision to withdraw French forces from NATO. Since 1958, it has constructed a hybrid presidential-parliamentary governing system resistant to the instabilities experienced in earlier, more purely parliamentary administrations. In recent decades, its reconciliation and cooperation with Germany have proved central to the economic integration of Europe, including the introduction of a common currency, the euro, in January 1999. In the early 21st century, five French overseas entities – French Guiana, Guadeloupe, Martinique, Mayotte, and Reunion – became French regions and were made part of France proper.

GEOGRAPHY

Location: *metropolitan France:* Western Europe, bordering the Bay of Biscay and English Channel, between Belgium and Spain, southeast of the UK; bordering the Mediterranean Sea, between Italy and Spain

French Guiana: Northern South America, bordering the North Atlantic Ocean, between Brazil and Suriname

Guadeloupe: Caribbean, islands between the Caribbean Sea and the North Atlantic Ocean, southeast of Puerto Rico

Martinique: Caribbean, island between the Caribbean Sea and North Atlantic Ocean, north of Trinidad and Tobago

Mayotte: Southern Indian Ocean, island in the Mozambique Channel, about halfway between northern Madagascar and northern Mozambique

Reunion: Southern Africa, island in the Indian Ocean, east of Madagascar

Geographic coordinates: *metropolitan France:* 46 00 N, 2 00 E

French Guiana: 4 00 N, 53 00 W

Guadeloupe: 16 15 N, 61 35 W

Martinique: 14 40 N, 61 00 W

Mayotte: 12 50 S, 45 10 E

Reunion: 21 06 S, 55 36 E

Map references: *metropolitan France:* Europe

French Guiana: South America

Guadeloupe: Central America and the Caribbean

Martinique: Central America and the Caribbean

Mayotte: Africa

Reunion: World

Area: *total:* 643,801 sq km; 551,500 sq km (metropolitan France)
land: 640,427 sq km; 549,970 sq km (metropolitan France)
water: 3,374 sq km; 1,530 sq km (metropolitan France)
note: the first numbers include the overseas regions of French Guiana, Guadeloupe, Martinique, Mayotte, and Reunion
comparison ranking: total 45

Area - comparative: slightly more than four times the size of Georgia; slightly less than the size of Texas

Land boundaries: *total:* 3,956 km
border countries (8): Andorra 55 km; Belgium 556 km; Germany 418 km; Italy 476 km; Luxembourg 69 km; Monaco 6 km; Spain 646 km; Switzerland 525 km
metropolitan France - total: 2751 km

French Guiana - total: 1205 km

Coastline: 4,853 km
metropolitan France: 3,427 km

Maritime claims: *territorial sea:* 12 nm
contiguous zone: 24 nm
exclusive economic zone: 200 nm (does not apply to the Mediterranean Sea)
continental shelf: 200m depth or to the depth of exploitation

Climate: *metropolitan France:* generally cool winters and mild summers, but mild winters and hot summers along the Mediterranean; occasional strong, cold, dry, north-to-northwesterly wind known as the mistral

French Guiana: tropical; hot, humid; little seasonal temperature variation

Guadeloupe and Martinique: subtropical tempered by trade winds; moderately high humidity; rainy season (June to October); vulnerable to devastating cyclones (hurricanes) every eight years on average

Mayotte: tropical; marine; hot, humid, rainy season during northeastern monsoon (November to May); dry season is cooler (May to November)

Reunion: tropical, but temperature moderates with elevation; cool and dry (May to November), hot and rainy (November to April)

Terrain: *metropolitan France:* mostly flat plains or gently rolling hills in north and west; remainder is mountainous, especially Pyrenees in south, Alps in east

French Guiana: low-lying coastal plains rising to hills and small mountains

Guadeloupe: Basse-Terre is volcanic in origin with interior mountains; Grande-Terre is low limestone formation; most of the seven other islands are volcanic in origin

Martinique: mountainous with indented coastline; dormant volcano

Mayotte: generally undulating, with deep ravines and ancient volcanic peaks

Reunion: mostly rugged and mountainous; fertile lowlands along coast

Elevation: *highest point:* Mont Blanc 4,810
lowest point: Rhone River delta -2 m
mean elevation: 375 m
note: to assess the possible effects of climate change on the ice and snow cap of Mont Blanc, its surface and peak have been extensively measured in recent years; these new peak measurements have exceeded the traditional height of 4,807 m and have varied between 4,808 m and 4,811 m; the actual rock summit is 4,792 m and is 40 m away from the ice-covered summit

Natural resources: *metropolitan France:* coal, iron ore, bauxite, zinc, uranium, antimony, arsenic, potash, feldspar, fluorspar, gypsum, timber, arable land, fish; *French Guiana:*gold deposits, petroleum, kaolin, niobium, tantalum, clay

Land use: *agricultural land:* 51.7% (2022 est.)
arable land: 34.1% (2022 est.)
permanent crops: 1.9% (2022 est.)
permanent pasture: 15.7% (2022 est.)
forest: 31.8% (2022 est.)
other: 16.5% (2022 est.)

Irrigated land: 14,236 sq km (2020)

Major lakes (area sq km): *fresh water lake(s):* Lake Geneva (shared with Switzerland) - 580 sq km

Major rivers (by length in km): Rhin (Rhine) (shared with Switzerland [s], Germany, and Netherlands [m]) - 1,233 km; Loire - 1,012 km
note: [s] after country name indicates river source; [m] after country name indicates river mouth

Major watersheds (area sq km): Atlantic Ocean drainage: Loire (115,282 sq km), Seine (78,919 sq km), Rhine-Maas (198,735 sq km), *(Adriatic Sea)* Po (76,997 sq km), *(Mediterranean Sea)* Rhone (100,543 sq km)

Major aquifers: Paris Basin

Population distribution: much of the population is concentrated in the north and southeast; although there are many urban agglomerations throughout the country, Paris is by far the largest city, with Lyon ranked a distant second

Natural hazards: *metropolitan France:* flooding; avalanches; midwinter windstorms; drought; forest fires in south
overseas departments: hurricanes (cyclones); flooding
volcanism: Montagne Pelée (1,394 m) on the island of Martinique in the Caribbean is the most active volcano of the Lesser Antilles arc, although it last erupted in 1932; a catastrophic eruption in 1902 destroyed the city of St. Pierre, killing an estimated 30,000 people; La Soufrière (1,467 m) on the island of Guadeloupe has also had explosive eruptions in recent years

Geography - note: largest Western European nation; most major French rivers – the Meuse, Seine, Loire, Charente, Dordogne, and Garonne – flow northward or westward into the Atlantic Ocean, only the Rhone flows southward into the Mediterranean Sea

PEOPLE AND SOCIETY

Population: *total:* 68,374,591 (2024 est.)
male: 33,557,094
female: 34,817,497
comparison rankings: total 22; male 23; female 21

Nationality: *noun:* Frenchman(men), Frenchwoman(women)
adjective: French

Ethnic groups: Celtic and Latin with Teutonic, Slavic, North African (Algerian, Moroccan, Tunisian), Indochinese, Basque minorities
note: overseas departments: Black, White, Mulatto, East Indian, Chinese, Indigenous

Languages: French (official) 100%, declining regional dialects and languages (Provençal, Breton, Alsatian, Corsican, Catalan, Basque, Flemish, Occitan, Picard)
major-language sample(s):
The World Factbook, une source indispensable d'informations de base. (French)
note: overseas departments - French, Creole patois, Mahorian (a Swahili dialect)

Religions: Roman Catholic 47%, Muslim 4%, Protestant 2%, Buddhist 2%, Orthodox 1%, Jewish 1%, other 1%, none 33%, unspecified 9% (2021 est.)
note: France maintains a tradition of secularism and has not officially collected data on religious affiliation since the 1872 national census, which complicates assessments of France's religious composition; an 1872 law prohibiting state authorities from collecting data on individuals' ethnicity or religious beliefs was reaffirmed by a 1978 law emphasizing the prohibition of the collection or exploitation of personal data revealing an individual's race, ethnicity, or political, philosophical, or religious opinions; a 1905 law codified France's separation of church and state

Age structure: *0-14 years:* 17.3% (male 6,060,087/female 5,792,805)
15-64 years: 60.7% (male 20,875,861/female 20,615,847)
65 years and over: 22% (2024 est.) (male 6,621,146/female 8,408,845)

Dependency ratios: *total dependency ratio:* 64.8 (2024 est.)
youth dependency ratio: 28.6 (2024 est.)
elderly dependency ratio: 36.2 (2024 est.)
potential support ratio: 2.8 (2024 est.)

Median age: *total:* 42.6 years (2024 est.)
male: 41 years
female: 44.2 years
comparison ranking: total 41

Population growth rate: 0.2% (2024 est.)
comparison ranking: 177

Birth rate: 10.9 births/1,000 population (2024 est.)
comparison ranking: 164

Death rate: 10 deaths/1,000 population (2024 est.)
comparison ranking: 35

Net migration rate: 1.1 migrant(s)/1,000 population (2024 est.)
comparison ranking: 65

Population distribution: much of the population is concentrated in the north and southeast; although there are many urban agglomerations throughout the country, Paris is by far the largest city, with Lyon ranked a distant second

Urbanization: *urban population:* 81.8% of total population (2023)
rate of urbanization: 0.67% annual rate of change (2020-25 est.)

Major urban areas - population: 11.208 million PARIS (capital), 1.761 million Lyon, 1.628 million Marseille-Aix-en-Provence, 1.079 million Lille, 1.060 million Toulouse, 1.000 million Bordeaux (2023)

Sex ratio: *at birth:* 1.05 male(s)/female
0-14 years: 1.05 male(s)/female
15-64 years: 1.01 male(s)/female
65 years and over: 0.79 male(s)/female
total population: 0.96 male(s)/female (2024 est.)

Mother's mean age at first birth: 28.9 years (2020 est.)

Maternal mortality ratio: 7 deaths/100,000 live births (2023 est.)
comparison ranking: 159

Infant mortality rate: *total:* 3.1 deaths/1,000 live births (2024 est.)
male: 3.4 deaths/1,000 live births
female: 2.8 deaths/1,000 live births
comparison ranking: total 204

Life expectancy at birth: *total population:* 82.6 years (2024 est.)
male: 79.8 years
female: 85.5 years
comparison ranking: total population 25

Total fertility rate: 1.9 children born/woman (2024 est.)
comparison ranking: 121

Gross reproduction rate: 0.93 (2024 est.)

Drinking water source: *improved: urban:* 100% of population (2022 est.)
rural: 100% of population (2022 est.)
total: 100% of population (2022 est.)
unimproved: urban: 0% of population (2022 est.)
rural: 0% of population (2022 est.)
total: 0% of population (2022 est.)

Health expenditure: 12.3% of GDP (2021)
15.3% of national budget (2022 est.)

Physician density: 3.28 physicians/1,000 population (2022)

Hospital bed density: 6 beds/1,000 population (2020 est.)

Sanitation facility access: *improved: urban:* 100% of population (2022 est.)
rural: 100% of population (2022 est.)
total: 100% of population (2022 est.)
unimproved: urban: 0% of population (2022 est.)
rural: 0% of population (2022 est.)
total: 0% of population (2022 est.)

Obesity - adult prevalence rate: 21.6% (2016)
comparison ranking: 87

Alcohol consumption per capita: *total:* 11.44 liters of pure alcohol (2019 est.)
beer: 2.52 liters of pure alcohol (2019 est.)
wine: 6.44 liters of pure alcohol (2019 est.)
spirits: 2.3 liters of pure alcohol (2019 est.)
other alcohols: 0.18 liters of pure alcohol (2019 est.)
comparison ranking: total 8

Tobacco use: *total:* 28.9% (2025 est.)
male: 30.7% (2025 est.)
female: 27.3% (2025 est.)
comparison ranking: total 24

Currently married women (ages 15-49): 54.8% (2023 est.)

Education expenditure: 5.4% of GDP (2021 est.)
8.9% national budget (2021 est.)
comparison ranking: Education expenditure (% GDP) 43

School life expectancy (primary to tertiary education): *total:* 16 years (2022 est.)

male: 16 years (2022 est.)
female: 17 years (2022 est.)

ENVIRONMENT

Environmental issues: air pollution and acid rain from industrial and vehicle emissions; water pollution from urban wastes, agricultural runoff

International environmental agreements: *party to:* Air Pollution, Air Pollution-Heavy Metals, Air Pollution-Multi-effect Protocol, Air Pollution-Nitrogen Oxides, Air Pollution-Persistent Organic Pollutants, Air Pollution-Sulphur 85, Air Pollution-Sulphur 94, Air Pollution-Volatile Organic Compounds, Antarctic- Environmental Protection, Antarctic-Marine Living Resources, Antarctic Seals, Antarctic Treaty, Biodiversity, Climate Change, Climate Change-Kyoto Protocol, Climate Change-Paris Agreement, Comprehensive Nuclear Test Ban, Desertification, Endangered Species, Hazardous Wastes, Law of the Sea, Marine Dumping-London Convention, Marine Dumping-London Protocol, Marine Life Conservation, Ozone Layer Protection, Ship Pollution, Tropical Timber 2006, Wetlands, Whaling
signed, but not ratified: none of the selected agreements

Climate: *metropolitan France:* generally cool winters and mild summers, but mild winters and hot summers along the Mediterranean; occasional strong, cold, dry, north-to-northwesterly wind known as the mistral

French Guiana: tropical; hot, humid; little seasonal temperature variation

Guadeloupe and Martinique: subtropical tempered by trade winds; moderately high humidity; rainy season (June to October); vulnerable to devastating cyclones (hurricanes) every eight years on average

Mayotte: tropical; marine; hot, humid, rainy season during northeastern monsoon (November to May); dry season is cooler (May to November)

Reunion: tropical, but temperature moderates with elevation; cool and dry (May to November), hot and rainy (November to April)

Urbanization: *urban population:* 81.8% of total population (2023)
rate of urbanization: 0.67% annual rate of change (2020-25 est.)

Carbon dioxide emissions: 303.779 million metric tonnes of CO2 (2023 est.)
from coal and metallurgical coke: 25.355 million metric tonnes of CO2 (2023 est.)
from petroleum and other liquids: 209.4 million metric tonnes of CO2 (2023 est.)
from consumed natural gas: 69.025 million metric tonnes of CO2 (2023 est.)
comparison ranking: total emissions 21

Particulate matter emissions: 9 micrograms per cubic meter (2019 est.)

Methane emissions: *energy:* 232 kt (2022-2024 est.)
agriculture: 1,496.1 kt (2019-2021 est.)
waste: 550.9 kt (2019-2021 est.)
other: 37.7 kt (2019-2021 est.)

Waste and recycling: *municipal solid waste generated annually:* 36.749 million tons (2024 est.)
percent of municipal solid waste recycled: 31.6% (2022 est.)

Total water withdrawal: *municipal:* 5.271 billion cubic meters (2022 est.)
industrial: 16.641 billion cubic meters (2022 est.)
agricultural: 2.515 billion cubic meters (2022 est.)

Total renewable water resources: 211 billion cubic meters (2022 est.)

Geoparks: *total global geoparks and regional networks:* 9 (2024)
global geoparks and regional networks: Armorique; Beaujolais; Causses du Quersey; Chablais; Haute-Provence; Luberon; Massif des Bauges; Monts d'Ardèche; Normandie-Maine (2024)

GOVERNMENT

Country name: *conventional long form:* French Republic
conventional short form: France
local long form: République française
local short form: France
etymology: derives from the Latin name *Francia*, meaning "Land of the Franks"; the Franks were a group of Germanic tribes located along the middle and lower Rhine River in the 3rd century A.D.; the origin of the tribal name is unclear but may come from the Old German word *franka*, meaning "brave," or from a personal name such as Francio or Francus

Government type: semi-presidential republic

Capital: *name:* Paris
geographic coordinates: 48 52 N, 2 20 E
time difference: UTC+1 (6 hours ahead of Washington, DC, during Standard Time)
daylight saving time: +1hr, begins last Sunday in March; ends last Sunday in October
time zone note: applies to metropolitan France only; for its overseas regions the time difference is UTC-4 for Guadeloupe and Martinique, UTC-3 for French Guiana, UTC+3 for Mayotte, and UTC+4 for Reunion
etymology: name derives from the Parisii, a Celtic tribe that inhabited the area from the 3rd century B.C.; the Celtic settlement became the Roman town of Lutetia Parisiorum (Lutetia of the Parisii); over subsequent centuries it became Parisium and then Paris

Administrative divisions: 18 regions (*régions*, singular - *région*); Auvergne-Rhône-Alpes, Bourgogne-Franche-Comté, Bretagne (Brittany), Centre-Val de Loire (Center-Loire Valley), Corse (Corsica), Grand Est (Grand East), Guadeloupe, Guyane (French Guiana), Hauts-de-France (Upper France), Ile-de-France, Martinique, Mayotte, Normandie (Normandy), Nouvelle-Aquitaine (New Aquitaine), Occitanie (Occitania), Pays de la Loire (Lands of the Loire), Provence-Alpes-Côte d'Azur, Reunion
note: France is divided into 13 metropolitan regions (including the "collectivity" of Corse, or Corsica) and 5 overseas regions (French Guiana, Guadeloupe, Martinique, Mayotte, and Réunion) and is subdivided into 96 metropolitan departments and 5 overseas departments (which are the same as the overseas regions)

Dependent areas: Clipperton Island, French Polynesia, French Southern and Antarctic Lands, New Caledonia, Saint Barthelemy, Saint Martin, Saint Pierre and Miquelon, Wallis and Futuna (8)
note: the US Government does not recognize claims to Antarctica; New Caledonia has been considered a "sui generis" collectivity of France since 1998, a unique status falling between that of an independent country and a French overseas department

Legal system: civil law; review of administrative but not legislative acts

Constitution: *history:* many previous; latest effective 4 October 1958
amendment process: proposed by the president of the republic (upon recommendation of the prime minister and Parliament) or by Parliament; proposals submitted by Parliament members require passage by both houses followed by approval in a referendum; passage of proposals submitted by the government can bypass a referendum if submitted by the president to Parliament and passed by at least three-fifths majority vote by Parliament's National Assembly

International law organization participation: has not submitted an ICJ jurisdiction declaration; accepts ICCt jurisdiction

Citizenship: *citizenship by birth:* no
citizenship by descent only: at least one parent must be a citizen of France
dual citizenship recognized: yes
residency requirement for naturalization: 5 years

Suffrage: 18 years of age; universal

Executive branch: *chief of state:* President Emmanuel MACRON (since 14 May 2017)
head of government: Sébastien LECORNU (since 10 September 2025)
cabinet: Council of Ministers appointed by the president at the suggestion of the prime minister
election/appointment process: president directly elected by absolute-majority popular vote in 2 rounds, if needed, for a 5-year term (eligible for a second term); prime minister appointed by the president
most recent election date: 10 April 2022, with a runoff held on 24 April 2022
election results: *2022:* Emmanuel MACRON reelected in second round; percent of vote in first round - Emmanuel MACRON (LREM) 27.8%, Marine LE PEN (RN) 23.2%, Jean-Luc MELENCHON (LFI) 22%, Eric ZEMMOUR (Reconquête) 7.1%, Valerie PECRESSE (LR) 4.8%, Yannick JADOT (EELV) 4.6%, other 10.6%; percent of vote in second round - MACRON 58.5%, LE PEN 41.5%
2017: Emmanuel MACRON elected president in second round; percent of vote in first round - Emmanuel MACRON (EM) 24%, Marine LE PEN (FN) 21.3%, Francois FILLON (LR) 20%, Jean-Luc MELENCHON (FI) 19.6%, Benoit HAMON (PS) 6.4%, other 8.7%; percent of vote in second round - MACRON 66.1%, LE PEN 33.9%
expected date of next election: April 2027

Legislative branch: *legislature name:* Parliament (Parlement)
legislative structure: bicameral

Legislative branch - lower chamber: *chamber name:* National Assembly (Assemblée nationale)
number of seats: 577 (all directly elected)
electoral system: plurality/majority
scope of elections: full renewal
term in office: 5 years
most recent election date: 6/30/2024 to 7/7/2024
parties elected and seats per party: New Popular Front (NFP)/UG (178); Ensemble (presidential majority) (150); National Rally (RN) (125); The Republicans (LR) (39); Other (85)
percentage of women in chamber: 36.2%
expected date of next election: June 2029

Legislative branch - upper chamber: *chamber name:* Senate (Sénat)
number of seats: 348 (all indirectly elected)
scope of elections: partial renewal
term in office: 6 years
most recent election date: 9/24/2023

percentage of women in chamber: 37.1%
expected date of next election: September 2026
note 1: of the 348 Senate seats, 328 seats are for metropolitan France, overseas departments, and regions of Guadeloupe, Martinique, French Guiana, Reunion, and Mayotte; the remainder of the seats include 2 for New Caledonia, 2 for French Polynesia, 1 for Saint-Pierre and Miquelon, 1 for Saint-Barthelemy, 1 for Saint-Martin, 1 for Wallis and Futuna, and 12 for French nationals abroad
note 2: Senate members are indirectly elected by departmental electoral colleges, using absolute majority vote in two rounds if needed for departments with 1-3 members, and proportional representation vote in departments with 4 or more members

Judicial branch: *highest court(s):* Court of Cassation or Cour de Cassation (consists of the court president, 6 divisional presiding judges, 120 trial judges, and 70 deputy judges organized into 6 divisions – 3 civil, 1 commercial, 1 labor, and 1 criminal); Constitutional Council (consists of 9 members)
judge selection and term of office: Court of Cassation judges appointed by the president of the republic from nominations from the High Council of the Judiciary, presided over by the Court of Cassation and 15 appointed members; judges appointed for life; Constitutional Council has 3 members appointed by the president of the republic and 3 each by the National Assembly and Senate presidents; members serve 9-year, non-renewable terms with one third of the membership renewed every 3 years
subordinate courts: appellate courts or cours d'appel; regional courts or tribunaux judiciaires; first instance courts or tribunaux de proximité; administrative courts

Political parties: Citizen and Republican Movement or MRC
Debout la France or DLF
Democratic Movement or MoDem
Ensemble or ENS (electoral coalition including RE, MoDem, Horizons, PRV, UDI)
The Ecologists - the Greens or EELV
French Communist Party or PCF
Horizons
La France Insoumise or FI
Liberties, Independents, Overseas and Territories or LIOT
Movement of Progressives or MDP
National Rally or RN (formerly National Front or FN)
New Democrats or LND (formerly Ecology Democracy Solidarity or EDS)
New Popular Front or NFP (electoral coalition including FI, EELV, PS, PCF)
Radical Party of the Left or PRV
Reconquete or REC
Renaissance or RE
Résistons!
Socialist Party or PS
The Republicans or LR
Union of Democrats and Independents or UDI
Union of Far Right or UXD (electoral coalition of LR, RN)

Diplomatic representation in the US: *chief of mission:* Ambassador Laurent BILI (since 19 April 2023)
chancery: 4101 Reservoir Road NW, Washington, DC 20007
telephone: [1] (202) 944-6000
FAX: [1] (202) 944-6166
email address and website: info@ambafrance-us.org
https://franceintheus.org/
consulate(s) general: Atlanta, Boston, Chicago, Houston, Los Angeles, Miami, New Orleans, New York, San Francisco

Diplomatic representation from the US: *chief of mission:* Ambassador Charles KUSHNER (since 11 July 2025); note - also accredited to Monaco
embassy: 2 avenue Gabriel, 75008 Paris
mailing address: 9200 Paris Place, Washington DC 20521-9200
telephone: [33] (1) 43-12-22-22, [33] (1) 42-66-97-83
FAX: [33] (1) 42-66-97-83
email address and website: Citizeninfo@state.gov
https://fr.usembassy. gov/
consulate(s) general: Marseille, Strasbourg
consulate(s): Bordeaux, Lyon, Rennes

International organization participation: ADB (nonregional member), AfDB (nonregional member), Arctic Council (observer), Australia Group, BDEAC, BIS, BSEC (observer), CBSS (observer), CE, CERN, EAPC, EBRD, ECB, EIB, EITI (implementing country), EMU, ESA, EU, FAO, FATF, FZ, G-5, G-7, G-8, G-10, G-20, IADB, IAEA, IBRD, ICAO, ICC (national committees), ICCt, ICRM, IDA, IEA, IFAD, IFC, IFRCS, IGAD (partners), IHO, ILO, IMF, IMO, IMSO, InOC, Interpol, IOC, IOM, IPU, ISO, ITSO, ITU, ITUC (NGOs), MIGA, MINURSO, MINUSTAH, MONUSCO, NATO, NEA, NSG, OAS (observer), OECD, OIF, OPCW, OSCE, Pacific Alliance (observer), Paris Club, PCA, PIF (partner), Schengen Convention, SELEC (observer), SPC, UN, UNCTAD, UNESCO, UNHCR, UNHRC, UNIDO, UNIFIL, Union Latina, UNMIL, UNOCI, UNOOSA, UNRWA, UN Security Council (permanent), UNTSO, UNWTO, UPU, Wassenaar Arrangement, WCO, WFTU (NGOs), WHO, WIPO, WMO, WTO, ZC

Independence: *no official date of independence:* 486 (Frankish tribes unified under Merovingian kingship); 10 August 843 (Western Francia established from the division of the Carolingian Empire); 14 July 1789 (French monarchy overthrown); 22 September 1792 (First French Republic established); 4 October 1958 (Fifth French Republic established)

National holiday: Fête de la Fédération, 14 July (1790)
note: often incorrectly referred to as Bastille Day, the celebration commemorates the storming of the Bastille prison on 14 July 1789 and the establishment of a constitutional monarchy; other names for the holiday are *la Fête nationale* (National Holiday) and *le Quatorze Juillet* (14th of July)

Flag: *description:* three equal vertical bands of blue (left side), white, and red
history: known as the *le tricolore* (tricolor), the flag dates to 1790 and the French Revolution, when the traditional color of white was combined with the blue and red of the Paris militia; for the first four years of the flag's use (1790-94), the order of colors was reversed (red-white-blue)
note 1: serves as the official flag for all French dependencies
note 2: the design and colors are similar to a number of other flags, including those of Belgium, Chad, Cote d'Ivoire, Ireland, Italy, Luxembourg, and Netherlands

National symbol(s): Gallic rooster, fleur-de-lis, Marianne (female personification of the country)

National color(s): blue, white, red

National anthem(s): *title:* "La Marseillaise" (The Song of Marseille)
lyrics/music: Claude-Joseph ROUGET de Lisle
history: adopted 1795, restored 1870; acquired its name when the National Guard of Marseille sang the song while marching into Paris in 1792 during the French Revolution; one of the most recognized anthems in the world

National heritage: *total World Heritage Sites:* 53 (45 cultural, 7 natural, 1 mixed); note - includes one site in New Caledonia and one site in French Polynesia
selected World Heritage Site locales: Chartres Cathedral (c); Palace and Park of Versailles (c); Mont-Saint-Michel and its Bay (c); Prehistoric Sites and Decorated Caves of the Vézère Valley (c); Pyrénées - Mont Perdu (m); Cistercian Abbey of Fontenay (c); Paris, Banks of the Seine (c); The Loire Valley between Sully-sur-Loire and Chalonnes (c); Pont du Gard (Roman Aqueduct) (c); Amiens Cathedral (c); Palace and Park of Fontainebleau (c); Historic Fortified City of Carcassonne (c); The Maison Carrée of Nîmes (c); Gulf of Porto: Calanche of Piana, Gulf of Girolata, Scandola Reserve (Corsica) (n)

ECONOMY

Economic overview: high-income, advanced EU economy and eurozone member; strong tourism, aircraft manufacturing, pharmaceuticals, and industrial sectors; high public debt; ongoing pension reform efforts; transitioning to a green economy via "France 2030" strategy

Real GDP (purchasing power parity): $3.732 trillion (2024 est.)
$3.689 trillion (2023 est.)
$3.655 trillion (2022 est.)
note: data in 2021 dollars
comparison ranking: 9

Real GDP growth rate: 1.2% (2024 est.)
0.9% (2023 est.)
2.6% (2022 est.)
note: annual GDP % growth based on constant local currency
comparison ranking: 170

Real GDP per capita: $54,500 (2024 est.)
$54,000 (2023 est.)
$53,700 (2022 est.)
note: data in 2021 dollars
comparison ranking: 35

GDP (official exchange rate): $3.162 trillion (2024 est.)
note: data in current dollars at official exchange rate

Inflation rate (consumer prices): 2% (2024 est.)
4.9% (2023 est.)
5.2% (2022 est.)
note: annual % change based on consumer prices
comparison ranking: 51

GDP - composition, by sector of origin: *agriculture:* 1.4% (2024 est.)
industry: 17.5% (2024 est.)
services: 70.4% (2024 est.)
note: figures may not total 100% due to non-allocated consumption not captured in sector-reported data
comparison rankings: agriculture 165; industry 149; services 33

GDP - composition, by end use: *household consumption:* 53.4% (2023 est.)
government consumption: 23.1% (2023 est.)
investment in fixed capital: 23.1% (2023 est.)
investment in inventories: 0.1% (2023 est.)

exports of goods and services: 34.3% (2023 est.)
imports of goods and services: -36.3% (2023 est.)
note: figures may not total 100% due to rounding or gaps in data collection

Agricultural products: wheat, sugar beets, milk, maize, barley, potatoes, grapes, rapeseed, pork, sunflower seeds (2023)
note: top ten agricultural products based on tonnage

Industries: machinery, chemicals, automobiles, metallurgy, aircraft, electronics, textiles, food processing, tourism

Industrial production growth rate: 0.7% (2024 est.)
note: annual % change in industrial value added based on constant local currency
comparison ranking: 121

Labor force: 31.725 million (2024 est.)
note: number of people ages 15 or older who are employed or seeking work
comparison ranking: 22

Unemployment rate: 7.4% (2024 est.)
7.4% (2023 est.)
7.4% (2022 est.)
note: % of labor force seeking employment
comparison ranking: 127

Youth unemployment rate (ages 15-24): *total:* 16.6% (2024 est.)
male: 17.1% (2024 est.)
female: 16% (2024 est.)
note: % of labor force ages 15-24 seeking employment
comparison ranking: total 69

Population below poverty line: 15.6% (2021 est.)
note: % of population with income below national poverty line
Gini Index coefficient - distribution of family income 31.2 (2022 est.)
note: index (0-100) of income distribution; higher values represent greater inequality
comparison ranking: 112

Average household expenditures: *on food:* 12.6% of household expenditures (2023 est.)
on alcohol and tobacco: 3.5% of household expenditures (2023 est.)

Household income or consumption by percentage share: *lowest 10%:* 3% (2022 est.)
highest 10%: 24.6% (2022 est.)
note: % share of income accruing to lowest and highest 10% of population

Remittances: 1.2% of GDP (2024 est.)
1.2% of GDP (2023 est.)
1.2% of GDP (2022 est.)
note: personal transfers and compensation between resident and non-resident individuals/households/entities

Budget: *revenues:* $1.29 trillion (2023 est.)
expenditures: $1.447 trillion (2023 est.)
note: central government revenues (excluding grants) and expenditures converted to US dollars at average official exchange rate for year indicated

Public debt: 98.5% of GDP (2023 est.)
note: central government debt as a % of GDP
comparison ranking: 24

Taxes and other revenues: 23.1% (of GDP) (2023 est.)
note: central government tax revenue as a % of GDP
comparison ranking: 29

Current account balance: $12.382 billion (2024 est.)
-$30.334 billion (2023 est.)
-$33.069 billion (2022 est.)
note: balance of payments - net trade and primary/secondary income in current dollars
comparison ranking: 26

Exports: $1.071 trillion (2024 est.)
$1.05 trillion (2023 est.)
$1.021 trillion (2022 est.)
note: balance of payments - exports of goods and services in current dollars
comparison ranking: 5

Exports - partners: Germany 11%, Italy 9%, USA 8%, Belgium 8%, Spain 7% (2023)
note: top five export partners based on percentage share of exports

Exports - commodities: aircraft, cars, packaged medicine, gas turbines, vehicle parts/accessories (2023)
note: top five export commodities based on value in dollars

Imports: $1.074 trillion (2024 est.)
$1.094 trillion (2023 est.)
$1.092 trillion (2022 est.)
note: balance of payments - imports of goods and services in current dollars
comparison ranking: 5

Imports - partners: Germany 15%, Belgium 11%, Netherlands 9%, Spain 8%, Italy 8% (2023)
note: top five import partners based on percentage share of imports

Imports - commodities: cars, natural gas, crude petroleum, refined petroleum, garments (2023)
note: top five import commodities based on value in dollars

Reserves of foreign exchange and gold: $282.857 billion (2024 est.)
$240.792 billion (2023 est.)
$242.416 billion (2022 est.)
note: holdings of gold (year-end prices)/foreign exchange/special drawing rights in current dollars
comparison ranking: 14

Exchange rates: euros (EUR) per US dollar -

Exchange rates: 0.924 (2024 est.)
0.925 (2023 est.)
0.95 (2022 est.)
0.845 (2021 est.)
0.876 (2020 est.)

ENERGY

Electricity access: *electrification - total population:* 100% (2022 est.)

Electricity: *installed generating capacity:* 151.463 million kW (2023 est.)
consumption: 415.542 billion kWh (2023 est.)
exports: 76.207 billion kWh (2023 est.)
imports: 25.107 billion kWh (2023 est.)
transmission/distribution losses: 35.282 billion kWh (2023 est.)
comparison rankings: installed generating capacity 9; consumption 10; exports 1; imports 7; transmission/distribution losses 200

Electricity generation sources: *fossil fuels:* 7.9% of total installed capacity (2023 est.)
nuclear: 63.9% of total installed capacity (2023 est.)
solar: 4.5% of total installed capacity (2023 est.)
wind: 10.4% of total installed capacity (2023 est.)
hydroelectricity: 10.8% of total installed capacity (2023 est.)
tide and wave: 0.1% of total installed capacity (2023 est.)
biomass and waste: 2.3% of total installed capacity (2023 est.)

Nuclear energy: Number of operational nuclear reactors: 57 (2025)

Net capacity of operational nuclear reactors: 61.37GW (2025 est.)

Percent of total electricity production: 64.8% (2023 est.)

Number of nuclear reactors permanently shut down: 14 (2025)

Coal: *production:* 2.157 million metric tons (2023 est.)
consumption: 12.57 million metric tons (2023 est.)
exports: 64,000 metric tons (2023 est.)
imports: 10.347 million metric tons (2023 est.)
proven reserves: 160 million metric tons (2023 est.)

Petroleum: *total petroleum production:* 80,000 bbl/day (2023 est.)
refined petroleum consumption: 1.536 million bbl/day (2024 est.)
crude oil estimated reserves: 61.719 million barrels (2021 est.)

Natural gas: *production:* 17.928 million cubic meters (2023 est.)
consumption: 33.238 billion cubic meters (2023 est.)
exports: 13.584 billion cubic meters (2023 est.)
imports: 46.909 billion cubic meters (2023 est.)
proven reserves: 7.787 billion cubic meters (2021 est.)

Energy consumption per capita: 123.526 million Btu/person (2023 est.)
comparison ranking: 31

COMMUNICATIONS

Telephones - fixed lines: *total subscriptions:* 37.22 million (2023 est.)
subscriptions per 100 inhabitants: 56 (2023 est.)
comparison ranking: total subscriptions 5

Telephones - mobile cellular: *total subscriptions:* 77.4 million (2023 est.)
subscriptions per 100 inhabitants: 119 (2022 est.)
comparison ranking: total subscriptions 24

Broadcast media: a mix of both publicly operated and privately owned TV stations; state-owned TV stations operate 4 networks and have part-interest in several thematic cable/satellite channels and international channels; large number of privately owned regional and local TV stations; multichannel satellite and cable services; public broadcaster Radio France operates 7 national networks, a series of regional networks, and services for overseas territories and foreign audiences; Radio France Internationale, under the Ministry of Foreign Affairs, is a leading international broadcaster; large number of commercial FM stations

Internet country code: metropolitan France -.fr; French Guiana -.gf; Guadeloupe -.gp; Martinique -.mq; Mayotte -.yt; Reunion -.re

Internet users: *percent of population:* 87% (2023 est.)

Broadband - fixed subscriptions: *total:* 32.3 million (2023 est.)
subscriptions per 100 inhabitants: 49 (2023 est.)
comparison ranking: total 8

TRANSPORTATION

Civil aircraft registration country code prefix: F

Airports: 1,218 (2025)

note: Includes 29 airports in French overseas departments (French Guiana, Guadeloupe, Martinique, Mayotte, Reunion)
comparison ranking: 6
Heliports: 405 (2025)
note: Includes 11 heliports in French overseas departments (French Guiana, Guadeloupe, Martinique, Mayotte, Reunion)
comparison ranking: 10
Railways: *total:* 27,860 km (2020) 16,660 km electrified
narrow gauge: -5 km
Merchant marine: *total:* 553 (2023)
by type: container ship 32, general cargo 48, oil tanker 25, other 448
note: includes Monaco
comparison ranking: total 41
Ports: *total ports:* 66 (2024)
large: 6
medium: 12
small: 22
very small: 26
ports with oil terminals: 31
key ports: Bayonne, Bordeaux, Boulogne-sur-Mer, Dunkerque Port Est, Dunkerque Port Ouest, La Pallice, La Rochelle, Les Sables d'Olonne, Lorient, Montoir, Nantes, Le Havre, Rouen, Rade de Brest, Rade de Cherbourg, Rochefort, St. Nazaire, Toulon
Transportation - note: begun in 1988 and completed in 1994, the Channel Tunnel (nicknamed the Chunnel) is a 50.5-km (31.4-mi) rail tunnel under the English Channel at the Strait of Dover; it runs from Folkestone, Kent, in England to Coquelles, Pas-de-Calais, in northern France and is the only fixed link between the island of Great Britain and mainland Europe

MILITARY AND SECURITY

Military and security forces: French Armed Forces (Forces Armées Françaises): Army (l'Armee de Terre; includes Foreign Legion), Navy (Marine Nationale), Air and Space Force (l'Armee de l'Air et de l'Espace); includes Air Defense), National Guard (Garde Nationale), National Gendarmerie (Gendarmerie Nationale) (2025)
note 1: under the direction of the Ministry of the Interior, the civilian National Police and the National Gendarmerie maintain internal security; the National Gendarmerie is a paramilitary police force that is a branch of the Armed Forces and therefore part of the Ministry of Defense but under the jurisdiction of the Ministry of the Interior; it also has additional duties to the Ministry of Justice
note 2: the French Foreign Legion, established in 1831, is a military force that is open to foreign recruits willing to serve in the French military for service in France and abroad; the Foreign Legion is an integrated part of the French Army; its combat units are a mix of armored cavalry and airborne, light, mechanized, and motorized infantry regiments
Military expenditures: 2.1% of GDP (2025 est.)
2% of GDP (2024 est.)
1.9% of GDP (2023 est.)
1.9% of GDP (2022 est.)
1.9% of GDP (2021 est.)
Military and security service personnel strengths: approximately 205,000 active duty Armed Forces; approximately 100,000 National Gendarmerie; approximately 75,000 National Guard (2024)
Military equipment inventories and acquisitions: the French military's inventory consists mostly of domestically produced weapons systems, including some jointly produced with other European countries; there is a smaller mix of armaments from other Western countries, particularly the US; France has a large and sophisticated defense industry capable of manufacturing the full spectrum of air, land, and naval military weapons systems (2024)
note: two major future acquisition programs for the French military included the Franco- German-Spanish Future Combat Air System, or FCAS (known in France as the système combat aérien du futur, or SCAF) and a next-generation tank development project with Germany known as the Main Ground Combat System, or MGCS
Military service age and obligation: generally 17-30 years of age for both men and women with some variations by service, position, and enlisted versus officer; basic service contract is for 12 months; no conscription (abolished 2001) (2025)
note 1: in 2023, women comprised more than 16% of the uniformed armed forces
note 2: French citizens can also volunteer for the Voluntary Military Service (VMS), which allows unemployed youth aged 18-25 to learn a trade or gain work experience while receiving basic military training and sports activities; VMS terms are 3-12 months; French citizens may also join the military operational reserve up to age 72
note 3: men between the ages of 17.5 and 39.5 years of age, of any nationality, may join the French Foreign Legion; those volunteers selected for service sign five-year contracts
Military deployments: France typically has up to 30,000 total air, ground, and naval forces deployed on permanent or temporary foreign missions; up to 10,000 are permanently deployed, including Djibouti (1,500); French Guyana (2,600); French Polynesia (1,000); French West Indies (1,000); Reunion Island (2,100); UAE (800)
other non-permanent deployments include military missions under NATO, the EU, and the UN, as well as some unilateral operations, in such places as Europe, Africa, and the Middle East and adjacent waters (2025)
Military - note: the French military has a global footprint and a wide range of missions and responsibilities, to include protecting French territory, population, and interests, and fulfilling France's commitments to NATO, European security, and international peacekeeping operations under the UN; it is the largest military in the EU and has a leading role in the EU security framework, as well as in NATO; in recent years, it has actively participated in coalition peacekeeping and other security operations in regions such as Africa, the Middle East, and the Balkans, often in a lead role; the military regularly conducts large-scale exercises and participates in a variety of bi-lateral and multinational exercises; it also has a domestic security mission, including providing enhanced security at sensitive sites and large events and support during national crises or disasters, such as fighting forest fires; in recent years, defense responsibilities have expanded to include cyber and space domains
in 2010, France and the UK signed a declaration on defense and security cooperation that included greater military interoperability and a Combined Joint Expeditionary Force (CJEF), a deployable, combined Anglo-French military force for use in a wide range of crisis scenarios, including high intensity operations, peacekeeping, disaster relief, and humanitarian assistance; the CJEF has no standing forces, but would be available at short notice for French-UK bilateral, NATO, EU, UN, or other operations (2025)

SPACE

Space agency/agencies: National Center for Space Studies (Centre National d'Etudes Spatiales, CNES; established 1961) (2025)
Space launch site(s): Guiana Space Center (Kourou, French Guiana; also serves as the spaceport for the ESA); note – prior to the completion of the Guiana Space Center in 1969, France launched rockets from Algeria (2025)
Space program overview: has one of Europe's largest space programs and is a key member of the European Space Agency (ESA), as well as one of its largest contributors; has independent capabilities in all areas of space categories except for autonomous manned space flight; can build, launch, and operate a range of space/satellite launch vehicles (SLVs) and spacecraft, including exploratory probes and a full spectrum of satellites; trained astronauts until training mission shifted to ESA in 2001; develops a wide range of space-related technologies; hosts the ESA headquarters and its space launch facility; participates in international space programs such as the Square Kilometer Array Project (world's largest radio telescope) and International Space Station (ISS); cooperates with a broad range of space agencies and commercial space companies, including those of China, Egypt, individual ESA and EU member countries, India, Indonesia, Israel, Japan, Mexico, Russia, the UAE, the US, and several African countries; has a large commercial space sector involved in such areas as satellite construction and payloads, launch capabilities, and a range of other space-related capabilities and technologies (2025)
note: further details about the key activities, programs, and milestones of the country's space program, as well as government spending estimates on the space sector, appear in the Space Programs reference guide

TERRORISM

Terrorist group(s): Terrorist group(s): Islamic Revolutionary Guard Corps/Qods Force; Islamic State of Iraq and ash-Sham (ISIS); al-Qa'ida
note: details about the history, aims, leadership, organization, areas of operation, tactics, targets, weapons, size, and sources of support of the group(s) appear(s) in Appendix T

TRANSNATIONAL ISSUES

Refugees and internally displaced persons: *refugees:* 810,325 (2024 est.)
IDPs: 59 (2024 est.)
stateless persons: 2,634 (2024 est.)

FRENCH POLYNESIA

INTRODUCTION

Background: French Polynesia consists of five archipelagos – the Austral Islands, the Gambier Islands, the Marquesas Islands, the Society Islands, and the Tuamotu Archipelago. The Marquesas were first settled around 200 B.C. and the Society Islands around A.D. 300. Raiatea in the Society Islands became a center for religion and culture. Exploration of the other islands emanated from Raiatea, and by 1000, there were small permanent settlements in all the island groups. Ferdinand MAGELLAN was the first European to see the islands of French Polynesia in 1520. In 1767, British explorer Samuel WALLIS was the first European to visit Tahiti, followed by French navigator Louis Antoine de BOUGAINVILLE in 1768 and British explorer James COOK in 1769. King POMARE I united Tahiti and surrounding islands into the Kingdom of Tahiti in 1788. Protestant missionaries arrived in 1797, and POMARE I's successor converted in the 1810s, along with most Tahitians. In the 1830s, Queen POMARE IV refused to allow French Catholic missionaries to operate, leading France to declare a protectorate over Tahiti and fight the French-Tahitian War of the 1840s in an attempt to annex the islands.

In 1880, King POMARE V ceded Tahiti and its possessions to France, changing its status into a colony. France then claimed the Gambier Islands and Tuamotu Archipelago and by 1901 had incorporated all five island groups into its establishments in Oceania. A Tahitian nationalist movement formed in 1940, leading France to grant French citizenship to the islanders in 1946 and change it to an overseas territory. In 1957, the islands' name was changed to French Polynesia, and the following year, 64% of voters chose to stay part of France when they approved a new constitution. Uninhabited Mururoa Atoll was established as a French nuclear test site in 1962, and tests were conducted between 1966 and 1992 (underground beginning in 1975). France also conducted tests at Fangataufa Atoll, including its last nuclear test in 1996.

France granted French Polynesia partial internal autonomy in 1977 and expanded autonomy in 1984. French Polynesia was converted into an overseas collectivity in 2003 and renamed an overseas territory in 2004. Pro-independence politicians won a surprise majority in local elections that same year, but in subsequent elections, they have been relegated to a vocal minority. In 2013, French Polynesia was relisted on the UN List of Non-Self-Governing Territories.

GEOGRAPHY

Location: Oceania, five archipelagoes (Archipel des Tuamotu, Iles Gambier, Iles Marquises, Iles Tubuai, Society Islands) in the South Pacific Ocean about halfway between South America and Australia

Geographic coordinates: 15 00 S, 140 00 W

Map references: Oceania

Area: *total:* 4,167 sq km (118 islands and atolls; 67 are inhabited)
land: 3,827 sq km
water: 340 sq km
comparison ranking: total 174

Area - comparative: slightly less than one-third the size of Connecticut

Land boundaries: *total:* 0 km

Coastline: 2,525 km

Maritime claims: *territorial sea:* 12 nm
exclusive economic zone: 200 nm

Climate: tropical, but moderate

Terrain: mixture of rugged high islands and low islands with reefs

Elevation: *highest point:* Mont Orohena 2,241 m
lowest point: Pacific Ocean 0 m

Natural resources: timber, fish, cobalt, hydropower

Land use: *agricultural land:* 14% (2022 est.)
arable land: 0.7% (2022 est.)
permanent crops: 7.5% (2022 est.)
permanent pasture: 5.8% (2022 est.)
forest: 43.1% (2022 est.)
other: 43% (2022 est.)

Irrigated land: 10 sq km (2012)

Population distribution: the majority of the population lives in the Society Islands, one of five archipelagos that includes the most populous island, Tahiti, with approximately 70% of the nation's population

Natural hazards: occasional cyclonic storms in January

Geography - note: *includes five archipelagoes:* four volcanic (Iles Gambier, Iles Marquises, Iles Tubuai, Society Islands) and one coral (Archipel des Tuamotu); the Tuamotu Archipelago forms the largest group of atolls in the world – 78 in total, 48 inhabited; Makatea in the Tuamotu Archipelago is one of the three great phosphate rock islands in the Pacific Ocean – the others are Banaba (Ocean Island) in Kiribati and Nauru

PEOPLE AND SOCIETY

Population: *total:* 303,540 (2024 est.)
male: 155,138
female: 148,402
comparison rankings: total 182; male 180; female 182

Nationality: *noun:* French Polynesian(s)
adjective: French Polynesian

Ethnic groups: Polynesian 78%, Chinese 12%, local French 6%, metropolitan French 4%

Languages: French (official) 73.5%, Tahitian 20.1%, Marquesan 2.6%, Austral languages 1.2%, Paumotu 1%, other 1.6% (2017 est.)
major-language sample(s):
The World Factbook, une source indispensable d'informations de base. (French)

Religions: Protestant 54%, Roman Catholic 30%, other 10%, no religion 6%

Age structure: *0-14 years:* 20.3% (male 31,659/female 30,006)
15-64 years: 68.7% (male 107,162/female 101,228)
65 years and over: 11% (2024 est.) (male 16,317/female 17,168)

Dependency ratios: *total dependency ratio:* 45.7 (2024 est.)
youth dependency ratio: 29.6 (2024 est.)
elderly dependency ratio: 16.1 (2024 est.)
potential support ratio: 6.2 (2024 est.)

Median age: *total:* 35.3 years (2024 est.)
male: 35 years
female: 35.6 years
comparison ranking: total 98

Population growth rate: 0.66% (2024 est.)
comparison ranking: 133

Birth rate: 13 births/1,000 population (2024 est.)
comparison ranking: 134

Death rate: 5.8 deaths/1,000 population (2024 est.)
comparison ranking: 167

Net migration rate: -0.6 migrant(s)/1,000 population (2024 est.)
comparison ranking: 126

Population distribution: the majority of the population lives in the Society Islands, one of five archipelagos that includes the most populous island, Tahiti, with approximately 70% of the nation's population

Urbanization: *urban population:* 62.3% of total population (2023)
rate of urbanization: 0.65% annual rate of change (2020-25 est.)

Major urban areas - population: 136,000 PAPEETE (capital) (2018)

Sex ratio: *at birth:* 1.05 male(s)/female
0-14 years: 1.06 male(s)/female
15-64 years: 1.06 male(s)/female
65 years and over: 0.95 male(s)/female
total population: 1.05 male(s)/female (2024 est.)

Infant mortality rate: *total:* 4.3 deaths/1,000 live births (2024 est.)
male: 5.2 deaths/1,000 live births
female: 3.4 deaths/1,000 live births
comparison ranking: total 184

Life expectancy at birth: *total population:* 78.9 years (2024 est.)
male: 76.6 years
female: 81.3 years
comparison ranking: total population 69

Total fertility rate: 1.79 children born/woman (2024 est.)
comparison ranking: 143

Gross reproduction rate: 0.87 (2024 est.)

Drinking water source: *improved:* total: 100% of population (2022 est.)
unimproved: *total:* 0% of population (2022 est.)

Physician density: 0.02 physicians/1,000 population (2023)

Sanitation facility access: *improved:* total: 97% of population (2022 est.)
unimproved: total: 3% of population (2022 est.)

Currently married women (ages 15-49): 27.2% (2023 est.)

ENVIRONMENT

Environmental issues: sea-level rise; cyclones, storms, and tsunamis producing floods, landslides, erosion, and reef damage; droughts; fresh water scarcity

Climate: tropical, but moderate

Urbanization: *urban population:* 62.3% of total population (2023)
rate of urbanization: 0.65% annual rate of change (2020-25 est.)

Carbon dioxide emissions: 1.01 million metric tonnes of CO2 (2023 est.)
from petroleum and other liquids: 1.01 million metric tonnes of CO2 (2023 est.)
comparison ranking: total emissions 172

Waste and recycling: *municipal solid waste generated annually:* 147,000 tons (2024 est.)

GOVERNMENT

Country name: *conventional long form:* Overseas Lands of French Polynesia
conventional short form: French Polynesia
local long form: Pays d'outre-mer de la Polynésie française
local short form: Polynésie Française
former: Establishments in Oceania, French Establishments in Oceania
etymology: the term "Polynesia" is an 18th-century construct composed of two Greek words, *poly* (many) and *nesoi* (islands), and refers to the more than 1,000 islands scattered over the central and southern Pacific Ocean

Government type: parliamentary democracy (Assembly of French Polynesia); an overseas collectivity of France

Dependency status: overseas country of France
note: overseas territory of France from 1946-2003; overseas collectivity of France since 2003, but it is often referred to as an overseas country due to its degree of autonomy

Capital: *name:* Papeete (located on Tahiti)
geographic coordinates: 17 32 S, 149 34 W
time difference: UTC-10 (5 hours behind Washington, DC, during Standard Time)
etymology: the name derives from the Tahitian words *pape* (water) and *ete* (basket), referring to a place where people came to get water

Administrative divisions: 5 *administrative subdivisions (subdivisions administratives, singular - subdivision administrative):* Iles Australes (Austral Islands), Iles du Vent (Windward Islands), Iles Marquises (Marquesas Islands), Iles Sous-le-Vent (Leeward Islands), Iles Tuamotu-Gambier
note: the Leeward Islands and the Windward Islands together make up the Society Islands (Iles de la Société)

Legal system: the laws of France apply

Constitution: *history:* 4 October 1958 (French Constitution)
amendment process: French constitution amendment procedures apply

Citizenship: see France

Suffrage: 18 years of age; universal

Executive branch: *chief of state:* President Emmanuel MACRON (since 14 May 2017), represented by High Commissioner of the Republic Alexander ROCHATTE (since 1 September 2025)
head of government: President of French Polynesia Moetai BROTHERSON (since 12 May 2023)
cabinet: Council of Ministers approved by the Assembly from a list of its members submitted by the president
election/appointment process: French president directly elected by absolute-majority popular vote in 2 rounds, if needed, for a 5-year term (eligible for a second term); high commissioner appointed by the French president on the advice of the French Ministry of Interior; French Polynesia president indirectly elected by Assembly of French Polynesia for a 5-year term (no term limits)

Legislative branch: *legislature name:* Assembly of French Polynesia (Assemblée de la Polynésie française)
legislative structure: unicameral
number of seats: 57 (directly elected)
electoral system: proportional representation
scope of elections: full renewal
term in office: 5 years
most recent election date: 4/30/2023
parties elected and seats per party: People's Servant People (38); List of the People (15); I Love Polynesia (3); Rally of the Mahoi People (1)
percentage of women in chamber: 49.1%
expected date of next election: 2028
note 1: elections held in two rounds; in the second round, 38 members are directly elected in multi-seat constituencies by a closed-list proportional representation vote; the party receiving the most votes gets an additional 19 seats
note 2: French Polynesia indirectly elects 2 senators to the French Senate for 6-year terms with one-half the membership renewed every 3 years and directly elects 3 deputies to the French National Assembly for 5-year terms

Judicial branch: *highest court(s):* Court of Appeal or Cour d'Appel (composition NA)
judge selection and term of office: judges assigned from France for 3 years
subordinate courts: Court of the First Instance or Tribunal de Première Instance; Court of Administrative Law or Tribunal Administratif
note: appeals beyond the French Polynesia Court of Appeal are heard by the Court of Cassation (in Paris)

Political parties: I Love Polynesia (A here la Porinetia)
List of the People (Tapura Huiraatira)
People's Servant Party (Tavini Huiraatira)
Rally of the Maohi People (Amuitahira'a o te Nuna'a Maohi) (formerly known as Popular Rally (Tahoeraa Huiraatira))

Diplomatic representation in the US: none (overseas lands of France)

Diplomatic representation from the US: *embassy:* none (overseas lands of France)

International organization participation: ITUC (NGOs), PIF, SPC, UPU, WMO

Independence: none (overseas land of France)

National holiday: Fête de la Fédération, 14 July (1790)
note 1: the local holiday is Internal Autonomy Day, 29 June (1880)
note 2: often incorrectly referred to as Bastille Day, France's national celebration commemorates the storming of the Bastille prison on 14 July 1789 and the establishment of a constitutional monarchy; other names for the holiday are *la Fête nationale* (National Holiday) and *le Quatorze Juillet* (14th of July)

Flag: *description:* two horizontal red bands flank a wide white band in a 1:2:1 ratio; centered on the white band is a disk with a blue-and-white wave pattern depicting the sea on the lower half and a gold-and-white ray pattern depicting the sun on the upper half; a stylized red Polynesian canoe on the disk has a crew of five, represented by five stars
meaning: the stars symbolize the five island groups; red and white are traditional Polynesian colors
note 1: similar to the red-white-red flag of Tahiti, the largest and most populous of the French Polynesian islands, but the Tahitian flag has no emblem on the white band
note 2: the flag of France is used for official occasions

National symbol(s): outrigger canoe, Tahitian gardenia flower (*Gardenia taitensis*)

National color(s): red, white

National anthem(s): *title:* "Ia Ora 'O Tahiti Nui" (Long Live Tahiti Nui)
lyrics/music: Maeva BOUGES, Irmine TEHEI, Angele TEROROTUA, Johanna NOUVEAU, Patrick AMARU, Louis MAMATUI, and Jean-Pierre CELESTIN (created both the lyrics and music)
history: adopted 1993; serves as a local anthem
title: "La Marseillaise" (The Song of Marseille)
lyrics/music: Claude-Joseph ROUGET de Lisle
history: official anthem, as a French territory

National heritage: *total World Heritage Sites:* 2 (1 cultural, 1 mixed); note - excerpted from the France entry
selected World Heritage Site locales: Taputapuatea (c); Te Henua Enata – The Marquesas Islands (m)

Government - note: French Polynesia has acquired autonomy from France in all areas except those relating to police, monetary policy, tertiary education, immigration, and defense and foreign affairs; the duties of its president are similar to those of the French prime minister

ECONOMY

Economic overview: small, territorial-island tourism-based economy; large French financing; lower EU import duties; Pacific Islands Forum member; fairly resilient from COVID-19; oil-dependent infrastructure

Real GDP (purchasing power parity): $6.007 billion (2024 est.)
$5.935 billion (2023 est.)
$5.892 billion (2022 est.)
note: data in 2015 dollars
comparison ranking: 175

Real GDP growth rate: 3% (2023 est.)
4.5% (2022 est.)
2.1% (2021 est.)
note: annual GDP % growth based on constant local currency
comparison ranking: 115

Real GDP per capita: $23,300 (2024 est.)
$22,800 (2023 est.)
$20,700 (2022 est.)
note: data in 2015 dollars

comparison ranking: 96

GDP (official exchange rate): $6.563 billion (2024 est.)
note: data in current dollars at official exchange rate

Inflation rate (consumer prices): 6.4% (2022 est.)
0.5% (2021 est.)
-0.1% (2020 est.)
note: annual % change based on consumer prices
comparison ranking: 158

GDP - composition, by sector of origin: *agriculture:* 2.2% (2020 est.)
industry: 10.6% (2020 est.)
services: 75.9% (2020 est.)
note: figures may not total 100% due to non-allocated consumption not captured in sector-reported data
comparison rankings: agriculture 146; industry 183; services 20

GDP - composition, by end use: *household consumption:* 70.4% (2023 est.)
government consumption: 30.5% (2023 est.)
investment in fixed capital: 21.7% (2023 est.)
investment in inventories: 0% (2023 est.)
exports of goods and services: 23.1% (2023 est.)
imports of goods and services: -45.6% (2023 est.)
note: figures may not total 100% due to rounding or gaps in data collection

Agricultural products: coconuts, fruits, cassava, sugarcane, pineapples, eggs, tropical fruits, watermelons, tomatoes, pork (2023)
note: top ten agricultural products based on tonnage

Industries: tourism, pearls, agricultural processing, handicrafts, phosphates

Labor force: 119,100 (2024 est.)
note: number of people ages 15 or older who are employed or seeking work
comparison ranking: 180

Unemployment rate: 11.8% (2024 est.)
11.8% (2023 est.)
11.9% (2022 est.)
note: % of labor force seeking employment
comparison ranking: 162

Youth unemployment rate (ages 15-24): *total:* 36.9% (2024 est.)
male: 33.5% (2024 est.)
female: 41.5% (2024 est.)
note: % of labor force ages 15-24 seeking employment
comparison ranking: total 12

Remittances: 9.1% of GDP (2023 est.)
10% of GDP (2022 est.)
9.5% of GDP (2021 est.)
note: personal transfers and compensation between resident and non-resident individuals/households/entities

Current account balance: $411.963 million (2016 est.)
$291.182 million (2015 est.)
$264.32 million (2014 est.)
note: balance of payments - net trade and primary/secondary income in current dollars
comparison ranking: 66

Exports: $162 million (2021 est.)
$94.4 million (2020 est.)
$184 million (2019 est.)
note: balance of payments - exports of goods and services in current dollars
comparison ranking: 202

Exports - partners: Japan 44%, USA 15%, France 12%, Netherlands 9%, China 5% (2023)
note: top five export partners based on percentage share of exports

Exports - commodities: pearls, fish, aircraft parts, gas turbines, vanilla (2023)
note: top five export commodities based on value in dollars

Imports: $1.66 billion (2021 est.)
$1.75 billion (2020 est.)
$2.24 billion (2019 est.)
note: balance of payments - imports of goods and services in current dollars
comparison ranking: 181

Imports - partners: France 26%, China 11%, USA 10%, NZ 7%, Malaysia 4% (2023)
note: top five import partners based on percentage share of imports

Imports - commodities: cars, packaged medicine, refined petroleum, poultry, broadcasting equipment (2023)
note: top five import commodities based on value in dollars

Exchange rates: Comptoirs Francais du Pacifique francs (XPF) per US dollar -

Exchange rates: 110.306 (2024 est.)
110.347 (2023 est.)
113.474 (2022 est.)
100.88 (2021 est.)
104.711 (2020 est.)

ENERGY

Electricity access: *electrification - total population:* 100% (2022 est.)

Electricity: *installed generating capacity:* 345,000 kW (2023 est.)
consumption: 669.5 million kWh (2023 est.)
transmission/distribution losses: 42.663 million kWh (2023 est.)
comparison rankings: installed generating capacity 160; consumption 168; transmission/distribution losses 35

Electricity generation sources: *fossil fuels:* 66% of total installed capacity (2023 est.)
solar: 7% of total installed capacity (2023 est.)
hydroelectricity: 27% of total installed capacity (2023 est.)

Coal: *imports:* 1 metric tons (2023 est.)

Petroleum: *refined petroleum consumption:* 7,000 bbl/day (2023 est.)

COMMUNICATIONS

Telephones - fixed lines: *total subscriptions:* 139,000 (2022 est.)
subscriptions per 100 inhabitants: 50 (2022 est.)
comparison ranking: total subscriptions 128

Telephones - mobile cellular: *total subscriptions:* 328,000 (2022 est.)
subscriptions per 100 inhabitants: 107 (2022 est.)
comparison ranking: total subscriptions 178

Broadcast media: French public overseas broadcaster Réseau Outre-Mer provides 2 TV channels and 1 radio station; 1 government-owned TV station; a small number of privately owned radio stations (2019)

Internet country code: .pf

Internet users: *percent of population:* 73% (2017 est.)

Broadband - fixed subscriptions: *total:* 78,000 (2022 est.)
subscriptions per 100 inhabitants: 28 (2022 est.)
comparison ranking: total 141

TRANSPORTATION

Civil aircraft registration country code prefix: F-OH

Airports: 54 (2025)
comparison ranking: 85

Merchant marine: *total:* 24 (2023)
by type: general cargo 14
comparison ranking: total 145

Ports: *total ports:* 6 (2024)
large: 0
medium: 0
small: 1
very small: 5
ports with oil terminals: 1
key ports: Atuona, Baie Taiohae, Papeete, Port Rikitea, Uturoa, Vaitape

MILITARY AND SECURITY

Military and security forces: no regular military forces

Military - note: defense is the responsibility of France, and it maintains a military garrison in French Polynesia (Forces Armées en Polynésie Française, FAPF)

FRENCH SOUTHERN AND ANTARCTIC LANDS

INTRODUCTION

Background: In 2007, the Iles Eparses became an integral part of the French Southern and Antarctic Lands (TAAF). The Southern Lands are now divided into five administrative districts, two of which are archipelagos, the Iles Crozet and Iles Kerguelen; the third is a district composed of two volcanic islands, Ile Saint-Paul and Ile Amsterdam; the fourth, Iles Eparses, consists of five scattered tropical islands around Madagascar. They contain no permanent inhabitants and are visited only by researchers studying the native fauna, scientists at the various scientific stations, fishermen, and military personnel. The fifth district is the Antarctic portion, which consists of "Adelie Land," a thin slice of the Antarctic continent discovered and claimed by the French in 1840.

Ile Amsterdam: Discovered but not named in 1522 by the Spanish, the island subsequently received the appellation of Nieuw Amsterdam from a Dutchman; it was claimed by France in 1843. A short-lived

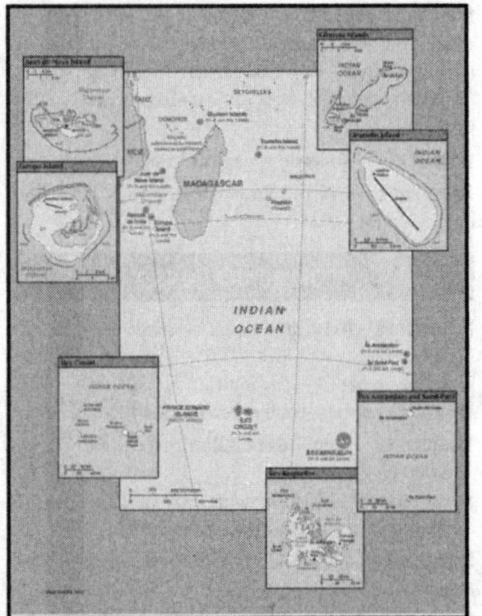

attempt at cattle farming began in 1871. A French meteorological station established on the island in 1949 is still in use.

Ile Saint Paul: Claimed by France since 1893, the island was a fishing industry center from 1843 to 1914. In 1928, a spiny lobster cannery was established, but when the company went bankrupt in 1931, seven workers were abandoned. Only two survived until 1934 when rescue finally arrived.

Iles Crozet: A large archipelago formed from the Crozet Plateau, Iles Crozet is divided into two main groups: L'Occidental (the West), which includes Ile aux Cochons, Ilots des Apotres, Ile des Pingouins, and the reefs Brisants de l'Heroine; and L'Oriental (the East), which includes Ile d'Est and Ile de la Possession, the largest island of the Crozets. Discovered and claimed by France in 1772, the islands were used for seal hunting and as a base for whaling. Originally administered as a dependency of Madagascar, they became part of the TAAF in 1955.

Iles Kerguelen: This island group, discovered in 1772, consists of one large island (Ile Kerguelen) and about 300 smaller islands. A permanent group of 50 to 100 scientists resides at the main base at Port-aux-Francais.

Adelie Land: The only non-insular district of the TAAF is the Antarctic claim known as "Adelie Land." The US Government does not recognize it as a French dependency.

Bassas da India: A French possession since 1897, this atoll is a volcanic rock surrounded by reefs and is awash at high tide.

Europa Island: This heavily wooded island has been a French possession since 1897; it is the site of a small military garrison that staffs a weather station.

Glorioso Islands: A French possession since 1892, the Glorioso Islands are composed of two lushly vegetated coral islands (Ile Glorieuse and Ile du Lys) and three rock islets. A military garrison operates a weather and radio station on Ile Glorieuse.

Juan de Nova Island: Named after a famous 15th-century Spanish navigator and explorer, the island has been a French possession since 1897. It has been exploited for its guano and phosphate. Presently a small military garrison oversees a meteorological station.

Tromelin Island: First explored by the French in 1776, the island came under the jurisdiction of Reunion in 1814. At present, it serves as a sea turtle sanctuary and is the site of an important meteorological station.

GEOGRAPHY

Location: southeast and east of Africa, islands in the southern Indian Ocean, some near Madagascar and others about equidistant between Africa, Antarctica, and Australia; note - French Southern and Antarctic Lands include Ile Amsterdam, Ile Saint-Paul, Iles Crozet, Iles Kerguelen, Bassas da India, Europa Island, Glorioso Islands, Juan de Nova Island, and Tromelin Island in the southern Indian Ocean, along with the French-claimed sector of Antarctica, "Adelie Land"; the US does not recognize the French claim to "Adelie Land"

Geographic coordinates: Ile Amsterdam (Ile Amsterdam et Ile Saint-Paul): 37 50 S, 77 32 E

Ile Saint-Paul (Ile Amsterdam et Ile Saint-Paul): 38 72 S, 77 53 E

Iles Crozet: 46 25 S, 51 00 E

Iles Kerguelen: 49 15 S, 69 35 E

Bassas da India (Iles Eparses): 21 30 S, 39 50 E

Europa Island (Iles Eparses): 22 20 S, 40 22 E

Glorioso Islands (Iles Eparses): 11 30 S, 47 20 E

Juan de Nova Island (Iles Eparses): 17 03 S, 42 45 E

Tromelin Island (Iles Eparses): 15 52 S, 54 25 E

Map references: Antarctic Region
Africa

Area: Ile Amsterdam (Ile Amsterdam et Ile Saint-Paul): total - 55 sq km; land - 55 sq km; water - 0 sq km

Ile Saint-Paul (Ile Amsterdam et Ile Saint-Paul): total - 7 sq km; land - 7 sq km; water - 0 sq km

Iles Crozet: total - 352 sq km; land - 352 sq km; water - 0 sq km

Iles Kerguelen: total - 7,215 sq km; land - 7,215 sq km; water - 0 sq km

Bassas da India (Iles Eparses): total - 80 sq km; land - 0.2 sq km; water - 79.8 sq km (lagoon)

Europa Island (Iles Eparses): total - 28 sq km; land - 28 sq km; water - 0 sq km

Glorioso Islands (Iles Eparses): total - 5 sq km; land - 5 sq km; water - 0 sq km

Juan de Nova Island (Iles Eparses): total - 4.4 sq km; land - 4.4 sq km; water - 0 sq km

Tromelin Island (Iles Eparses): total - 1 sq km; land - 1 sq km; water - 0 sq km
note: excludes "Adelie Land" claim of about 500,000 sq km in Antarctica that is not recognized by the US

Area - comparative: Ile Amsterdam (Ile Amsterdam et Ile Saint-Paul): less than one-half the size of Washington, D.C.

Ile Saint-Paul (Ile Amsterdam et Ile Saint-Paul): more than 10 times the size of the National Mall in Washington, D.C.

Iles Crozet: about twice the size of Washington, D.C.

Iles Kerguelen: slightly larger than Delaware

Bassas da India (Iles Eparses): land area about one-third the size of the National Mall in Washington, D.C.

Europa Island (Iles Eparses): about one-sixth the size of Washington, D.C.

Glorioso Islands (Iles Eparses): about eight times the size of the National Mall in Washington, D.C.

Juan de Nova Island (Iles Eparses): about seven times the size of the National Mall in Washington, D.C.

Tromelin Island (Iles Eparses): about 1.7 times the size of the National Mall in Washington, D.C.

Land boundaries: *total:* 0 km

Coastline: Ile Amsterdam (Ile Amsterdam et Ile Saint-Paul): 28 km

Ile Saint-Paul (Ile Amsterdam et Ile Saint-Paul): Iles Kerguelen: 2,800 km

Bassas da India (Iles Eparses): 35.2 km

Europa Island (Iles Eparses): 22.2 km

Glorioso Islands (Iles Eparses): 35.2 km

Juan de Nova Island (Iles Eparses): 24.1 km

Tromelin Island (Iles Eparses): 3.7 km

Maritime claims: *territorial sea:* 12 nm
exclusive economic zone: 200 nm from Iles Kerguelen and Iles Eparses (does not include the rest of French Southern and Antarctic Lands); Juan de Nova Island and Tromelin Island claim a continental shelf of 200-m depth or to the depth of exploitation

Climate: Ile Amsterdam et Ile Saint-Paul: oceanic with persistent westerly winds and high humidity

Iles Crozet: windy, cold, wet, and cloudy

Iles Kerguelen: oceanic, cold, overcast, windy

Iles Eparses: tropical

Terrain: Ile Amsterdam (Ile Amsterdam et Ile Saint-Paul): a volcanic island with steep coastal cliffs; the center floor of the volcano is a large plateau

Ile Saint-Paul (Ile Amsterdam et Ile Saint-Paul): triangular in shape, the island is the top of a volcano, rocky with steep cliffs on the eastern side; has active thermal springs

Iles Crozet: a large archipelago formed from the Crozet Plateau is divided into two groups of islands

Iles Kerguelen: the interior of the large island of Ile Kerguelen is composed of high mountains, hills, valleys, and plains with peninsulas stretching off its coasts

Bassas da India (Iles Eparses): atoll, awash at high tide; shallow (15 m) lagoon

Europa Island, Glorioso Islands, Juan de Nova Island: low, flat, and sandy

Tromelin Island (Iles Eparses): low, flat, sandy; likely volcanic seamount

Elevation: *highest point:* Mont de la Dives on Ile Amsterdam (Ile Amsterdam et Ile Saint-Paul) 867 m
lowest point: Indian Ocean 0 m
highest points throughout the French Southern and Antarctic Lands: Crête de la Novara on Ile Saint-Paul (Ile Amsterdam et Ile Saint-Paul) 284 m; Pic Marion-Dufresne in Iles Crozet 1090 m; Mont Ross in Iles Kerguelen 1850 m; unnamed location on Bassas de India (Iles Eparses) 2.4 m; 24 unnamed location on Europa Island (Iles Eparses) 6 m; unnamed location on Glorioso Islands (Iles Eparses) 12 m; unnamed location on Juan de Nova Island (Iles Eparses) 10 m; unnamed location on Tromelin Island (Iles Eparses) 7 m

Natural resources: fish, crayfish, note, Glorioso Islands and Tromelin Island (Iles Eparses) have guano, phosphates, and coconuts
note: in the 1950's and 1960's, several species of trout were introduced to Iles Kerguelen of which

two, brown trout and brook trout, survived to establish wild populations; reindeer were also introduced to Iles Kerguelen in 1956 as a source of fresh meat for whaling crews – the herd today, one of two in the Southern Hemisphere, is estimated to number around 4,000

Natural hazards: Ile Amsterdam and Ile Saint-Paul are inactive volcanoes; Iles Éparses are subject to periodic cyclones; Bassas da India is a maritime hazard because it is under water for three hours before and after high tide

volcanism: Reunion Island - Piton de la Fournaise (2,632 m), which has erupted many times in recent years, is one of the world's most active volcanoes; although rare, eruptions outside the volcano's caldera could threaten nearby cities

Geography - note: islands are widely scattered across remote locations in the southern Indian Ocean

Bassas da India (Iles Éparses): atoll is a circular reef on top of a long-extinct, submerged volcano

Europa Island and Juan de Nova Island (Iles Éparses): wildlife sanctuary for seabirds and sea turtles

Glorioso Island (Iles Éparses): an extensive reef system surrounds the island

Tromelin Island (Iles Éparses): climatologically important location for forecasting cyclones in the western Indian Ocean; wildlife sanctuary (seabirds, tortoises)

PEOPLE AND SOCIETY

Population: *total:* no permanent inhabitants

Ile Amsterdam (Ile Amsterdam et Ile Saint-Paul): uninhabited but has a meteorological station

Ile Saint-Paul (Ile Amsterdam et Ile Saint-Paul): uninhabited but is visited by fishermen and researchers

Iles Crozet: uninhabited except for staff of the Alfred Faure research station on Ile del la Possession

Iles Kerguelen: researchers are located at the main base at Port-aux-Francais on Ile Kerguelen

Bassas da India (Iles Eparses): uninhabitable

Europa Island, Glorioso Islands, Juan de Nova Island (Iles Eparses): a small French military garrison and a few meteorologists on each possession; visited by researchers

Tromelin Island (Iles Eparses): uninhabited, visited by researchers

ENVIRONMENT

Environmental issues: problems from introduction of foreign species on Iles Crozet; overfishing of Patagonian toothfish around Iles Crozet and Iles Kerguelen

Climate: Ile Amsterdam et Ile Saint-Paul: oceanic with persistent westerly winds and high humidity

Iles Crozet: windy, cold, wet, and cloudy

Iles Kerguelen: oceanic, cold, overcast, windy

Iles Eparses: tropical

GOVERNMENT

Country name: *conventional long form:* Territory of the French Southern and Antarctic Lands

conventional short form: French Southern and Antarctic Lands

local long form: Terres australes et antarctiques françaises

local short form: Terres Australes et Antarctiques Françaises

abbreviation: TAAF

etymology: self-descriptive name specifying the territories' affiliation and location in the Southern Hemisphere

Dependency status: overseas territory of France since 1955

Administrative divisions: none (overseas territory of France); no first-order administrative divisions as defined by the US government, but the 5 administrative districts are Iles Crozet, Iles Éparses, Iles Kerguelen, Ile Saint-Paul et Ile Amsterdam, and "Adelie Land," a claim in Antarctica that the US does not recognize

Legal system: the laws of France apply

Citizenship: see France

Executive branch: *chief of state:* President Emmanuel MACRON (since 14 May 2017), represented by Prefect Florence JEANBLANC-RISLER (since 5 October 2022)

Diplomatic representation in the US: none (overseas territory of France)

Diplomatic representation from the US: *embassy:* none (overseas territory of France)

International organization participation: UPU

Flag: the flag of France is used

National anthem(s): *title:* "La Marseillaise" (The Song of Marseille)

lyrics/music: Claude-Joseph ROUGET de Lisle

history: official anthem, as a French territory

ECONOMY

Economic overview: very small, fishing-based, domestic economic activity; military base servicing

Exports - partners: France 47%, USA 34%, Poland 9%, Singapore 3%, Saudi Arabia 2% (2023)

note: top five export partners based on percentage share of exports

Exports - commodities: fish (2023)

note: top export commodities based on value in dollars over $500,000

Imports - partners: France 41%, Ireland 15%, Germany 11%, Poland 7%, Netherlands 7% (2023)

note: top five import partners based on percentage share of imports

Imports - commodities: scented mixtures, industrial acids/oils/alcohols, surveying equipment, fish, refined petroleum (2023)

note: top five import commodities based on value in dollars

COMMUNICATIONS

Internet country code: .tf

TRANSPORTATION

Airports: 4 (2025)

comparison ranking: 184

Heliports: 3 (2025)

comparison ranking: 116

Merchant marine: *total:* 2 (2023)

by type: other 2

comparison ranking: total 179

MILITARY AND SECURITY

Military - note: defense is the responsibility of France; the French military maintains a Foreign Legion detachment on Mayotte to maintain France's presence in the region and support French forces operating in the southern zone of the Indian Ocean and the east coast of Africa; the detachment regularly deploys to the outlying Glorioso Islands

GABON

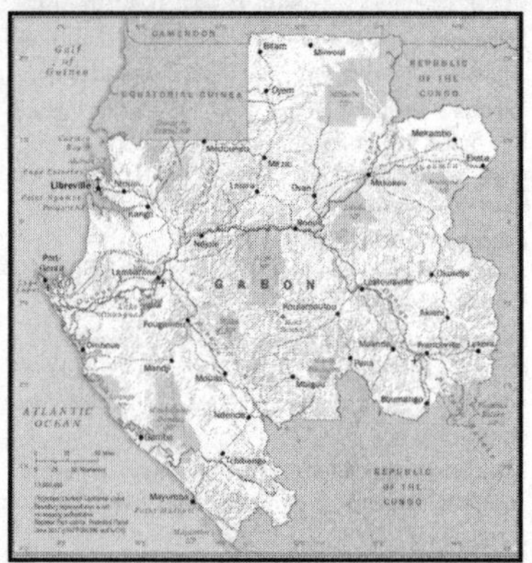

INTRODUCTION

Background: Gabon, a sparsely populated country known for its dense rainforests and vast petroleum reserves, is one of the most prosperous and stable countries in central Africa. Approximately 40 ethnic groups are represented, the largest of which is the Fang, a group that covers the northern third of Gabon and expands north into Equatorial Guinea and Cameroon. From about the early 1300s, various kingdoms emerged in present-day Gabon and the surrounding area, including the Kingdoms of Loango and Orungu. Because most early Bantu languages spoken in these kingdoms did not have a written form, much of Gabon's early history was lost over time. Portuguese traders who arrived in the mid-1400s gave the area its name of Gabon. At that time, indigenous trade networks began to engage with European traders, exchanging goods such as ivory and wood. For a century beginning in the 1760s, trade came to focus mostly on enslaved people. While many groups in Gabon participated in the slave trade, the Fang were a notable exception. As the slave trade declined in the late 1800s, France colonized the country and directed a widespread extraction of Gabonese resources. Anti-colonial rhetoric by Gabon's educated elites increased significantly in the early 1900s, but no widespread rebellion materialized. French decolonization after World War II led to the country's independence in 1960.

Within a year of independence, the government changed from a parliamentary to a presidential system, and Leon M'BA won the first presidential election in 1961. El Hadj Omar BONGO Ondimba was M'BA's vice president and assumed the presidency after M'BA's death in 1967. BONGO went on to dominate the country's political scene for four decades (1967-2009). In 1968, he declared Gabon a single-party state and created the still-dominant Parti Democratique Gabonais (PDG). In the early 1990s, he reintroduced a multiparty system under a new constitution in response to growing political opposition. He was reelected by wide margins in 1995, 1998, 2002, and 2005 against a divided opposition and amidst allegations of fraud. After BONGO's death in 2009, a new election brought his son, Ali BONGO Ondimba, to power, and he was reelected in 2016. He won a third term in the August 2023 election but was overthrown in a military coup a few days later. Gen. Brice OLIGUI Nguema led a military group called the Committee for the Transition and Restoration of Institutions that arrested BONGO, canceled the election results, and dissolved state institutions. In September 2023, OLIGUI was sworn in as transitional president of Gabon.

GEOGRAPHY

Location: Central Africa, bordering the Atlantic Ocean at the Equator, between Republic of the Congo and Equatorial Guinea

Geographic coordinates: 1 00 S, 11 45 E

Map references: Africa

Area: *total:* 267,667 sq km
land: 257,667 sq km
water: 10,000 sq km
comparison ranking: total 78

Area - comparative: slightly smaller than Colorado

Land boundaries: *total:* 3,261 km
border countries (3): Cameroon 349 km; Republic of the Congo 2,567 km; Equatorial Guinea 345 km

Coastline: 885 km

Maritime claims: *territorial sea:* 12 nm
contiguous zone: 24 nm
exclusive economic zone: 200 nm

Climate: tropical; always hot, humid

Terrain: narrow coastal plain; hilly interior; savanna in east and south

Elevation: *highest point:* Mont Bengoue 1,050 m
lowest point: Atlantic Ocean 0 m
mean elevation: 377 m

Natural resources: petroleum, natural gas, diamond, niobium, manganese, uranium, gold, timber, iron ore, hydropower

Land use: *agricultural land:* 8.4% (2022 est.)
arable land: 1.3% (2022 est.)
permanent crops: 0.7% (2022 est.)
permanent pasture: 6.4% (2022 est.)
forest: 91.2% (2022 est.)
other: 0.4% (2022 est.)

Irrigated land: 40 sq km (2012)

Major watersheds (area sq km): Atlantic Ocean drainage: Congo (3,730,881 sq km)

Major aquifers: Congo Basin

Population distribution: the relatively small population is spread in pockets throughout the country; the largest urban center is the capital of Libreville, located along the Atlantic coast in the northwest, as shown in this population distribution map

Natural hazards: none

Geography - note: the country has maintained its pristine rain forest and rich biodiversity

PEOPLE AND SOCIETY

Population: *total:* 2,455,105 (2024 est.)
male: 1,270,023
female: 1,185,082
comparison rankings: total 145; male 143; female 145

Nationality: *noun:* Gabonese (singular and plural)
adjective: Gabonese

Ethnic groups: Fang 23.5%, Shira-Punu'Vii 20.6%, Nzabi-Duma 11.2%, Mbede-Teke 5.6%, Myene 4.4%, Kota-Kele 4.3%, Okande-Tsogho 1.6%, other 12.6%, foreigner 16.2% (2021 est.)

Languages: French (official), Fang, Myene, Nzebi, Bapounou/Eschira, Bandjabi

Religions: Protestant 46.4% (Revival Church 37%, other Protestant 9.4%), Roman Catholic 29.8%, other Christian 4%, Muslim 10.8%, traditional/animist 1.1%, other 0.9%, none 7% (2019-21 est.)

Age structure: *0-14 years:* 34.6% (male 429,133/female 421,120)
15-64 years: 61.1% (male 787,480/female 711,913)
65 years and over: 4.3% (2024 est.) (male 53,410/female 52,049)

Dependency ratios: *total dependency ratio:* 63.7 (2024 est.)
youth dependency ratio: 56.7 (2024 est.)
elderly dependency ratio: 7 (2024 est.)
potential support ratio: 14.2 (2024 est.)

Median age: *total:* 22 years (2024 est.)
male: 22.5 years
female: 21.5 years
comparison ranking: total 187

Population growth rate: 2.37% (2024 est.)
comparison ranking: 25

Birth rate: 25.7 births/1,000 population (2024 est.)
comparison ranking: 43

Death rate: 5.5 deaths/1,000 population (2024 est.)
comparison ranking: 181

Net migration rate: 3.5 migrant(s)/1,000 population (2024 est.)
comparison ranking: 31

Population distribution: the relatively small population is spread in pockets throughout the country; the largest urban center is the capital of Libreville, located along the Atlantic coast in the northwest, as shown in this population distribution map

Urbanization: *urban population:* 91% of total population (2023)
rate of urbanization: 2.27% annual rate of change (2020-25 est.)

Major urban areas - population: 870,000 LIBREVILLE (capital) (2023)

Sex ratio: *at birth:* 1.03 male(s)/female
0-14 years: 1.02 male(s)/female
15-64 years: 1.11 male(s)/female
65 years and over: 1.03 male(s)/female
total population: 1.07 male(s)/female (2024 est.)

Mother's mean age at first birth: 19.6 years (2012 est.)
note: data represents median age at first birth among women 20-49

Maternal mortality ratio: 233 deaths/100,000 live births (2023 est.)
comparison ranking: 34

Infant mortality rate: *total:* 26.9 deaths/1,000 live births (2024 est.)
male: 29.7 deaths/1,000 live births
female: 24 deaths/1,000 live births
comparison ranking: total 57

Life expectancy at birth: *total population:* 70.4 years (2024 est.)
male: 68.6 years
female: 72.1 years
comparison ranking: total population 175

Total fertility rate: 3.21 children born/woman (2024 est.)
comparison ranking: 43

Gross reproduction rate: 1.58 (2024 est.)

Drinking water source: *improved:* *urban:* 90.2% of population (2022 est.)
rural: 54.9% of population (2022 est.)
total: 86.9% of population (2022 est.)
unimproved: *urban:* 9.8% of population (2022 est.)
rural: 45.1% of population (2022 est.)
total: 13.1% of population (2022 est.)

Health expenditure: 2.7% of GDP (2021)
9.6% of national budget (2022 est.)

Physician density: 0.52 physicians/1,000 population (2022)

Sanitation facility access: *improved:* *urban:* 81.3% of population (2022 est.)
rural: 55.1% of population (2022 est.)
total: 78.9% of population (2022 est.)
unimproved: *urban:* 18.7% of population (2022 est.)
rural: 44.9% of population (2022 est.)
total: 21.1% of population (2022 est.)

Obesity - adult prevalence rate: 15% (2016)
comparison ranking: 127

Alcohol consumption per capita: *total:* 6.47 liters of pure alcohol (2019 est.)
beer: 5.31 liters of pure alcohol (2019 est.)
wine: 0.62 liters of pure alcohol (2019 est.)
spirits: 0.5 liters of pure alcohol (2019 est.)
other alcohols: 0.04 liters of pure alcohol (2019 est.)
comparison ranking: total 64

Children under the age of 5 years underweight: 5.4% (2020)
comparison ranking: 63

Currently married women (ages 15-49): 49.7% (2023 est.)

Child marriage: *women married by age 15:* 2.9% (2021)
women married by age 18: 13.3% (2021)
men married by age 18: 4.8% (2021)

Education expenditure: 2.3% of GDP (2023 est.)
13.6% national budget (2023 est.)
comparison ranking: Education expenditure (% GDP) 177

Literacy: *total population:* 88.9% (2021 est.)
male: 90.8% (2021 est.)
female: 87.1% (2021 est.)

ENVIRONMENT

Environmental issues: deforestation from logging; solid-waste disposal; water pollution from oil industry; wildlife poaching

International environmental agreements: *party to:* Biodiversity, Climate Change, Climate Change-Kyoto Protocol, Climate Change-Paris Agreement, Comprehensive Nuclear Test Ban, Desertification, Endangered Species, Hazardous Wastes, Law of the Sea, Marine Dumping-London Convention, Nuclear Test Ban, Ozone Layer Protection, Ship Pollution, Tropical Timber 2006, Wetlands, Whaling
signed, but not ratified: none of the selected agreements

Climate: tropical; always hot, humid

Urbanization: *urban population:* 91% of total population (2023)
rate of urbanization: 2.27% annual rate of change (2020-25 est.)

Carbon dioxide emissions: 3.144 million metric tonnes of CO2 (2023 est.)
from coal and metallurgical coke: 230,000 metric tonnes of CO2 (2023 est.)
from petroleum and other liquids: 2.005 million metric tonnes of CO2 (2023 est.)
from consumed natural gas: 908,000 metric tonnes of CO2 (2023 est.)
comparison ranking: total emissions 147

Particulate matter emissions: 29.6 micrograms per cubic meter (2019 est.)

Methane emissions: *energy:* 272.4 kt (2022-2024 est.)
agriculture: 4.9 kt (2019-2021 est.)
waste: 18.6 kt (2019-2021 est.)
other: 5.4 kt (2019-2021 est.)

Waste and recycling: *municipal solid waste generated annually:* 238,100 tons (2024 est.)
percent of municipal solid waste recycled: 22.4% (2022 est.)

Total water withdrawal: *municipal:* 84.7 million cubic meters (2022 est.)
industrial: 14.1 million cubic meters (2022 est.)
agricultural: 40.3 million cubic meters (2022 est.)

Total renewable water resources: 166 billion cubic meters (2022 est.)

GOVERNMENT

Country name: *conventional long form:* Gabonese Republic
conventional short form: Gabon
local long form: République Gabonaise
local short form: Gabon
etymology: name originates from the Portuguese word *gabão*, meaning "cloak," possibly used by early explorers to describe the shape of the Komo River estuary

Government type: presidential republic

Capital: *name:* Libreville
geographic coordinates: 0 23 N, 9 27 E
time difference: UTC+1 (6 hours ahead of Washington, DC, during Standard Time)
etymology: the city was founded in 1849 by freed slaves, and the name means "free town" in French

Administrative divisions: 9 provinces; Estuaire, Haut-Ogooue, Moyen-Ogooue, Ngounie, Nyanga, Ogooue-Ivindo, Ogooue-Lolo, Ogooue-Maritime, Woleu-Ntem

Legal system: mixed system of French civil law and customary law

Constitution: *history:* previous 1961, 1991; latest approved in November 2024 referendum
amendment process: proposed by the president of the republic, by the Council of Ministers, or by one third of either house of Parliament; passage requires Constitutional Court evaluation, at least two-thirds majority vote of two thirds of the Parliament membership convened in joint session, and approval in a referendum; constitutional articles on Gabon's democratic form of government cannot be amended

International law organization participation: has not submitted an ICJ jurisdiction declaration; accepts ICCt jurisdiction

Citizenship: *citizenship by birth:* no
citizenship by descent only: at least one parent must be a citizen of Gabon
dual citizenship recognized: no
residency requirement for naturalization: 10 years

Suffrage: 18 years of age; universal

Executive branch: *chief of state:* President Brice OLIGUI Nguema (since 3 May 2025)
head of government: President Brice OLIGUI Nguema (since 3 May 2025)
cabinet: cabinet appointed by president
election/appointment process: the president directly elected by plurality vote to a 7-year term (no term limits)
most recent election date: 12 April 2025
election results: *2025:* Brice OLIGUI Nguema elected president; percent of vote - Brice OLIGUI Nguema (Ind.) 90.35%, Alain Claude Bilie By Nze (EPG) 3.02%, other 6.63%
2016: Ali BONGO Ondimba reelected president; percent of vote - Ali BONGO Ondimba (PDG) 49.8%, Jean PING (UFC) 48.2%, other 2.0%

Legislative branch: *legislature name:* Transitional Parlement (Parliament de la transition)
legislative structure: bicameral

Legislative branch - lower chamber: *chamber name:* Transitional National Assembly (Assemblée nationale de la transition)
number of seats: 98 (all appointed)
scope of elections: full renewal
most recent election date: 10/6/2023
percentage of women in chamber: 25.5%
expected date of next election: September 2025

Legislative branch - upper chamber: *chamber name:* Transitional Senate (Sénat de la transition)
number of seats: 70 (all appointed)
scope of elections: full renewal
most recent election date: 10/6/2023
percentage of women in chamber: 20.3%
expected date of next election: August 2025

Judicial branch: *highest court(s):* Supreme Court (consists of 4 permanent specialized supreme courts - Supreme Court or Cour de Cassation, Administrative Supreme Court or Conseil d'Etat, Accounting Supreme Court or Cour des Comptes, Constitutional Court or Cour Constitutionnelle, and the non-permanent Court of State Security, initiated only for cases of high treason by the president and criminal activity by executive branch officials)
judge selection and term of office: appointment and tenure of Supreme, Administrative, Accounting, and State Security courts NA; Constitutional Court judges appointed - 3 by the national president, 3 by the president of the Senate, and 3 by the president of the National Assembly; judges serve single renewable 7-year terms
subordinate courts: Courts of Appeal; county courts; military courts

Political parties: Gabonese Democratic Party or PDG
Restoration of Republican Values or RV
The Democrats or LD
Paul Mba Abessole

Diplomatic representation in the US: *chief of mission:* Ambassador Noël Nelson MESSONE (12 December 2022)
chancery: 2034 20th Street NW, Suite 200, Washington, DC 20009
telephone: [1] (202) 797-1000

FAX: [1] (301) 332-0668

email address and website: info@gaboneembassyusa.org https://gabonembassyusa.org/en/
consulate(s) general: New York

Diplomatic representation from the US: *chief of mission:* Ambassador Vernelle Trim FITZPATRICK (since 26 January 2024); note - also accredited to Sao Tome and Principe
embassy: Sabliere, B.P. 4000, Libreville
mailing address: 2270 Libreville Place, Washington, DC 20521-2270
telephone: [241] 011-45-71-00

FAX: [241] 011-45-71-05
email address and website: ACSLibreville@state.gov https://ga.usembassy.gov/

International organization participation: ACP, AfDB, AU (suspended), BDEAC, CEMAC, FAO, FZ, G-24, G-77, IAEA, IBRD, ICAO, ICCt, ICRM, IDA, IDB, IFAD, IFC, IFRCS, ILO, IMF, IMO, IMSO, Interpol, IOC, IOM, IPU, ISO, ITSO, ITU, ITUC (NGOs), MIGA, MINUSCA, NAM, OIC, OIF, OPCW, UN, UNCTAD, UNESCO, UNIDO, UNWTO, UPU, WCO, WHO, WIPO, WMO, WTO

Independence: 17 August 1960 (from France)

National holiday: Independence Day, 17 August (1960)

Flag: *description:* three equal horizontal bands of green (top), yellow, and blue
meaning: green stands for the country's forests and natural resources, gold for the equator and the sun, and blue for the sea

National symbol(s): black panther

National color(s): green, yellow, blue

National coat of arms: the panthers represent vigilance and courage, and they support a shield with a ship and an okoume tree, which is a symbol of the timber trade; the ribbon below the shield has the national motto in French, *Union, Travail, Justice* ("Union, Work, Justice"), and the ribbon above the shield has the Latin phrase *Uniti Progrediemur* ("We shall go forward united")

National anthem(s): *title:* "La Concorde" (The Concorde)
lyrics/music: Georges Aleka DAMAS
history: adopted 1960

National heritage: *total World Heritage Sites:* 2 (1 natural, 1 mixed)
selected World Heritage Site locales: Ecosystem and Relict Cultural Landscape of Lopé-Okanda (m); Ivindo National Park (n)

ECONOMY

Economic overview: natural-resource-rich, upper-middle-income, Central African economy; significant reliance on oil and mineral exports; highly urbanized population; high levels of poverty and unemployment; uncertainty on institutional and development reform progress following 2023 military coup

Real GDP (purchasing power parity): $48.045 billion (2024 est.)
$46.472 billion (2023 est.)
$45.363 billion (2022 est.)
note: data in 2021 dollars
comparison ranking: 131

Real GDP growth rate: 3.4% (2024 est.)
2.4% (2023 est.)
3% (2022 est.)
note: annual GDP % growth based on constant local currency
comparison ranking: 104

Real GDP per capita: $18,900 (2024 est.)
$18,700 (2023 est.)
$18,700 (2022 est.)
note: data in 2021 dollars
comparison ranking: 107

GDP (official exchange rate): $20.867 billion (2024 est.)
note: data in current dollars at official exchange rate

Inflation rate (consumer prices): 1.2% (2024 est.)
3.6% (2023 est.)
4.2% (2022 est.)
note: annual % change based on consumer prices
comparison ranking: 30

GDP - composition, by sector of origin: *agriculture:* 6.2% (2024 est.)
industry: 50.9% (2024 est.)
services: 37.5% (2024 est.)
note: figures may not total 100% due to non-allocated consumption not captured in sector-reported data
comparison rankings: agriculture 99; industry 8; services 198

GDP - composition, by end use: *household consumption:* 33.7% (2024 est.)
government consumption: 12.2% (2024 est.)
investment in fixed capital: 18.1% (2024 est.)
investment in inventories: 0% (2024 est.)
exports of goods and services: 65.3% (2024 est.)
imports of goods and services: -29.2% (2024 est.)
note: figures may not total 100% due to rounding or gaps in data collection

Agricultural products: oil palm fruit, plantains, cassava, sugarcane, yams, taro, vegetables, maize, groundnuts, game meat (2023)
note: top ten agricultural products based on tonnage

Industries: petroleum extraction and refining; manganese, gold; chemicals, ship repair, food and beverages, textiles, lumbering and plywood, cement

Industrial production growth rate: 2.8% (2024 est.)
note: annual % change in industrial value added based on constant local currency
comparison ranking: 85

Labor force: 824,400 (2024 est.)
note: number of people ages 15 or older who are employed or seeking work
comparison ranking: 150

Unemployment rate: 20.1% (2024 est.)
20.3% (2023 est.)
20.4% (2022 est.)
note: % of labor force seeking employment
comparison ranking: 184

Youth unemployment rate (ages 15-24): *total:* 36% (2024 est.)
male: 31.1% (2024 est.)
female: 42.3% (2024 est.)
note: % of labor force ages 15-24 seeking employment
comparison ranking: total 15

Population below poverty line: 33.4% (2017 est.)
note: % of population with income below national poverty line

Gini Index coefficient - distribution of family income: 38 (2017 est.)
note: index (0-100) of income distribution; higher values represent greater inequality
comparison ranking: 53

Household income or consumption by percentage share: *lowest 10%:* 2.2% (2017 est.)
highest 10%: 27.7% (2017 est.)
note: % share of income accruing to lowest and highest 10% of population

Remittances: 0.1% of GDP (2023 est.)
0.1% of GDP (2022 est.)
0.1% of GDP (2021 est.)
note: personal transfers and compensation between resident and non-resident individuals/households/entities

Budget: *revenues:* $2.939 billion (2021 est.)
expenditures: $3.226 billion (2021 est.)
note: central government revenues and expenses (excluding grants/extrabudgetary units/social security funds) converted to US dollars at average official exchange rate for year indicated

Taxes and other revenues: 9.5% (of GDP) (2021 est.)
note: central government tax revenue as a % of GDP
comparison ranking: 133

Current account balance: $140.996 million (2015 est.)
$1.112 billion (2014 est.)
$1.463 billion (2013 est.)
note: balance of payments - net trade and primary/secondary income in current dollars
comparison ranking: 72

Exports: $13.622 billion (2024 est.)
$12.869 billion (2023 est.)
$13.814 billion (2022 est.)
note: GDP expenditure basis - exports of goods and services in current dollars
comparison ranking: 103

Exports - partners: China 26%, Indonesia 8%, Spain 7%, Israel 6%, Congo, Republic of the 5% (2023)
note: top five export partners based on percentage share of exports

Exports - commodities: crude petroleum, ships, manganese ore, refined petroleum, wood (2023)
note: top five export commodities based on value in dollars

Imports: $6.094 billion (2024 est.)
$5.38 billion (2023 est.)
$5.005 billion (2022 est.)
note: GDP expenditure basis - imports of goods and services in current dollars
comparison ranking: 145

Imports - partners: France 14%, China 13%, S. Korea 13%, USA 7%, India 4% (2023)
note: top five import partners based on percentage share of imports

Imports - commodities: ships, refined petroleum, iron pipes, cars, packaged medicine (2023)
note: top five import commodities based on value in dollars

Reserves of foreign exchange and gold: $1.447 billion (2023 est.)
$1.415 billion (2022 est.)
$1.304 billion (2021 est.)
note: holdings of gold (year-end prices)/foreign exchange/special drawing rights in current dollars
comparison ranking: 136

Debt - external: $6.442 billion (2023 est.)
note: present value of external debt in current US dollars
comparison ranking: 64

Exchange rates: Coopération Financière en Afrique Centrale francs (XAF) per US dollar -

Exchange rates: 606.345 (2024 est.)
606.57 (2023 est.)
623.76 (2022 est.)

554.531 (2021 est.)
575.586 (2020 est.)

ENERGY

Electricity access: *electrification - total population:* 93.5% (2022 est.)
electrification - urban areas: 98.5%
electrification - rural areas: 29%

Electricity: *installed generating capacity:* 785,000 kW (2023 est.)
consumption: 3.173 billion kWh (2023 est.)
imports: 584.039 million kWh (2023 est.)
transmission/distribution losses: 604 million kWh (2023 est.)
comparison rankings: installed generating capacity 140; consumption 140; imports 89; transmission/distribution losses 86

Electricity generation sources: *fossil fuels:* 51.9% of total installed capacity (2023 est.)
hydroelectricity: 47.7% of total installed capacity (2023 est.)
biomass and waste: 0.3% of total installed capacity (2023 est.)

Coal: *imports:* 75,000 metric tons (2023 est.)

Petroleum: *total petroleum production:* 204,000 bbl/day (2023 est.)
refined petroleum consumption: 14,000 bbl/day (2023 est.)
crude oil estimated reserves: 2 billion barrels (2021 est.)

Natural gas: *production:* 463 million cubic meters (2023 est.)
consumption: 463 million cubic meters (2023 est.)
proven reserves: 25.995 billion cubic meters (2021 est.)

Energy consumption per capita: 22.101 million Btu/person (2023 est.)
comparison ranking: 130

COMMUNICATIONS

Telephones - fixed lines: *total subscriptions:* 43,000 (2022 est.)
subscriptions per 100 inhabitants: 2 (2022 est.)
comparison ranking: total subscriptions 160

Telephones - mobile cellular: *total subscriptions:* 3 million (2022 est.)
subscriptions per 100 inhabitants: 125 (2022 est.)
comparison ranking: total subscriptions 141

Broadcast media: 2 state-run TV stations and 2 state-run radio stations; a few private radio and TV stations; transmissions of at least 2 international broadcasters are accessible; satellite service subscriptions are available

Internet country code: .ga

Internet users: *percent of population:* 72% (2023 est.)

Broadband - fixed subscriptions: *total:* 80,000 (2022 est.)
subscriptions per 100 inhabitants: 3 (2022 est.)
comparison ranking: total 139

TRANSPORTATION

Civil aircraft registration country code prefix: TR

Airports: 42 (2025)
comparison ranking: 101

Railways: *total:* 649 km (2014)
standard gauge: 649 km (2014) 1.435-m gauge

Merchant marine: *total:* 87 (2023)
by type: bulk carrier 1, general cargo 19, oil tanker 30, other 37
comparison ranking: total 96

Ports: *total ports:* 9 (2024)
large: 0
medium: 2
small: 2
very small: 5
ports with oil terminals: 7
key ports: Libreville, Oguendjo Terminal, Port Gentil, Port Owendo

MILITARY AND SECURITY

Military and security forces: Gabonese Armed Forces (Force Armées Gabonaise or FAG; aka National Defense and Security Forces of Gabon or des Forces Nationales de Défense et de Sécurité (FNDS) du Gabon): Army (Armée de Terre, AT), Navy (Marine Nationale, MN), Air Force (l'Armée de l'Air, AA), Light Aviation (L'Aviation Légère des Armées, ALA), Fire Brigade (du Corps des Sapeurs-Pompiers); National Gendarmerie (Gendarmerie Gabonaise, GENA); Republican Guard (Garde Républicaine, GR); Military Health Service (Service de Santé Militaire, SSM); Military Engineering (Génie Militaire) (2025)
note 1: the National Police Forces, under the Ministry of Interior, and the National Gendarmerie (GENA), under the Ministry of Defense, are responsible for law enforcement and public security; elements of the armed forces and the Republican Guard, an elite unit that protects the president under his direct authority, sometimes perform internal security functions
note 2: the GENA is organized into regionally-based "legions," mobile forces, a national parks security unit, and a special intervention group

Military expenditures: 1.5% of GDP (2024 est.)
1.3% of GDP (2023 est.)
1.3% of GDP (2022 est.)
1.7% of GDP (2021 est.)
1.8% of GDP (2020 est.)

Military and security service personnel strengths: approximately 7,000 active-duty Armed Forces including the Republican Guard and Gendarmerie (2025)

Military equipment inventories and acquisitions: the Gabonese military has a mix of older and more modern weapons and equipment from a variety of suppliers including Brazil, China, France, Germany, Russia/former Soviet Union, and South Africa (2024)

Military service age and obligation: 18-24 years of age for voluntary military service; no conscription (2024)

Military - note: the Gabonese military is a small and lightly armed force that is responsible for both external and internal security; the military may also participate in the economic and social development work of the nation; key defense priorities include securing the country's borders and maritime domain; it has contributed to regional peacekeeping and joint security operations; in August 2023, officers from the Republican Guard seized control of the government and placed the president under arrest (2025)

SPACE

Space agency/agencies: Gabonese Studies and Space Observations Agency (Agence Gabonaise d'Etudes et d'Observations Spatiales or AGEOS; established 2015) (2025)

Space program overview: has a small space program focused on the acquisition, processing, analysis, and furnishing of data from remote sensing (RS) satellites for environmental management, mapping, natural resources, land use planning, and maritime surveillance, as well as research and innovation; member of the African Space Agency; has relationships with Brazil, China, the European Space Agency and its member states (particularly France), and the US, as well as African countries such as Kenya, Niger, Rwanda, and South Africa; shares RS data with neighboring countries (2025)
note: further details about the key activities, programs, and milestones of the country's space program, as well as government spending estimates on the space sector, appear in the Space Programs reference guide

TRANSNATIONAL ISSUES

Refugees and internally displaced persons: *refugees:* 261 (2024 est.)

GAMBIA, THE

INTRODUCTION

Background: In the 10th century, Muslim merchants established some of The Gambia's earliest large settlements as trans-Saharan trade hubs. These settlements eventually grew into major export centers sending slaves, gold, and ivory across the Sahara. Between the 16th and 17th centuries, European colonial powers began establishing trade with The Gambia. In 1664, the United Kingdom established a colony in The Gambia focused on exporting enslaved people across the Atlantic. During the roughly 300 years of the trans-Atlantic slave trade, the UK and other European powers may have exported as many as 3 million people from The Gambia.

The Gambia gained its independence from the UK in 1965. Geographically surrounded by Senegal, it formed the short-lived confederation of Senegambia between 1982 and 1989. In 1994, Yahya JAMMEH led a military coup overthrowing the president and banning political activity. He subsequently won every presidential election until 2016, when he lost to Adama BARROW, who headed an opposition

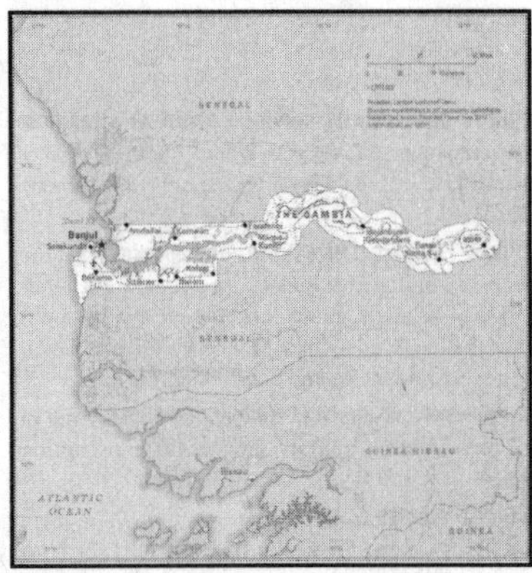

coalition during free and fair elections. BARROW won reelection in 2021. The Gambia is the only member of the Economic Community of West African States that does not have presidential term limits. Since the 2016 election, The Gambia and the US have enjoyed improved relations. US assistance to the country has supported democracy-strengthening activities, capacity building, economic development, and security sector education and training programs.

GEOGRAPHY

Location: Western Africa, bordering the North Atlantic Ocean and Senegal

Geographic coordinates: 13 28 N, 16 34 W

Map references: Africa

Area: *total:* 11,300 sq km
land: 10,120 sq km
water: 1,180 sq km
comparison ranking: total 165

Area - comparative: slightly less than twice the size of Delaware

Land boundaries: *total:* 749 km
border countries (1): Senegal 749 km

Coastline: 80 km

Maritime claims: *territorial sea:* 12 nm
contiguous zone: 18 nm
continental shelf: extent not specified
exclusive fishing zone: 200 nm

Climate: tropical; hot, rainy season (June to November); cooler, dry season (November to May)

Terrain: flood plain of the Gambia River flanked by some low hills

Elevation: *highest point:* unnamed elevation 63 m; 3 km southeast of the town of Sabi
lowest point: Atlantic Ocean 0 m
mean elevation: 34 m

Natural resources: fish, clay, silica sand, titanium (rutile and ilmenite), tin, zircon

Land use: *agricultural land:* 62.6% (2022 est.)
arable land: 43.5% (2022 est.)
permanent crops: 0.7% (2022 est.)
permanent pasture: 18.5% (2022 est.)
forest: 22.8% (2022 est.)
other: 14.5% (2022 est.)

Irrigated land: 50 sq km (2012)

Major rivers (by length in km): Gambia river mouth (shared with Senegal and Guinea [s]) - 1,094 km
note: [s] after country name indicates river source; [m] after country name indicates river mouth

Major aquifers: Senegalo-Mauritanian Basin

Population distribution: settlements are found scattered along the Gambia River; the largest communities, including the capital of Banjul and the country's largest city, Serekunda, are found at the mouth of the Gambia River along the Atlantic coast, as shown in this population distribution map

Natural hazards: droughts

Geography - note: almost an enclave of Senegal; smallest country on the African mainland

PEOPLE AND SOCIETY

Population: *total:* 2,523,327 (2024 est.)
male: 1,250,490
female: 1,272,837
comparison rankings: total 144; male 144; female 144

Nationality: *noun:* Gambian(s)
adjective: Gambian

Ethnic groups: Mandinka/Jahanka 33.3%, Fulani/Tukulur/Lorobo 18.2%, Wolof 12.9%, Jola/Karoninka 11%, Serahuleh 7.2%, Serer 3.5%, other 4%, non-Gambian 9.9% (2019-20 est.)

Languages: English (official), Mandinka, Wolof, Fula, other indigenous vernaculars

Religions: Muslim 96.4%, Christian 3.5%, other or none 0.1% (2019-20 est.)

Age structure: *0-14 years:* 38.2% (male 486,472/female 477,309)
15-64 years: 58.1% (male 723,360/female 743,127)
65 years and over: 3.7% (2024 est.) (male 40,658/female 52,401)

Dependency ratios: *total dependency ratio:* 72.1 (2024 est.)
youth dependency ratio: 65.7 (2024 est.)
elderly dependency ratio: 6.3 (2024 est.)
potential support ratio: 15.8 (2024 est.)

Median age: *total:* 20.2 years (2024 est.)
male: 19.8 years
female: 20.6 years
comparison ranking: total 205

Population growth rate: 2.16% (2024 est.)
comparison ranking: 34

Birth rate: 27.3 births/1,000 population (2024 est.)
comparison ranking: 36

Death rate: 5.6 deaths/1,000 population (2024 est.)
comparison ranking: 177

Net migration rate: 0 migrant(s)/1,000 population (2024 est.)
comparison ranking: 80

Population distribution: settlements are found scattered along the Gambia River; the largest communities, including the capital of Banjul and the country's largest city, Serekunda, are found at the mouth of the Gambia River along the Atlantic coast, as shown in this population distribution map

Urbanization: *urban population:* 64.5% of total population (2023)
rate of urbanization: 3.75% annual rate of change (2020-25 est.)

Major urban areas - population: 481,000 BANJUL (capital) (2023)
note: includes the local government areas of Banjul and Kanifing

Sex ratio: *at birth:* 1.03 male(s)/female
0-14 years: 1.02 male(s)/female
15-64 years: 0.97 male(s)/female
65 years and over: 0.78 male(s)/female
total population: 0.98 male(s)/female (2024 est.)

Mother's mean age at first birth: 20.7 years (2019/20 est.)
note: data represents median age at first birth among women 25-49

Maternal mortality ratio: 354 deaths/100,000 live births (2023 est.)
comparison ranking: 20

Infant mortality rate: *total:* 35.7 deaths/1,000 live births (2024 est.)
male: 39.1 deaths/1,000 live births
female: 32.2 deaths/1,000 live births
comparison ranking: total 35

Life expectancy at birth: *total population:* 68.4 years (2024 est.)
male: 66.7 years
female: 70.1 years
comparison ranking: total population 189

Total fertility rate: 3.52 children born/woman (2024 est.)
comparison ranking: 33

Gross reproduction rate: 1.74 (2024 est.)

Drinking water source: *improved: urban:* 90.9% of population (2022 est.)
rural: 76.4% of population (2022 est.)
total: 85.6% of population (2022 est.)
unimproved: urban: 9.1% of population (2022 est.)
rural: 23.6% of population (2022 est.)
total: 14.4% of population (2022 est.)

Health expenditure: 3.2% of GDP (2021)
7.5% of national budget (2022 est.)

Physician density: 0.09 physicians/1,000 population (2023)

Hospital bed density: 1.2 beds/1,000 population (2021 est.)

Sanitation facility access: *improved: urban:* 74.9% of population (2022 est.)
rural: 32% of population (2022 est.)
total: 59.4% of population (2022 est.)
unimproved: urban: 25.1% of population (2022 est.)
rural: 68% of population (2022 est.)
total: 40.6% of population (2022 est.)

Obesity - adult prevalence rate: 10.3% (2016)
comparison ranking: 138

Alcohol consumption per capita: *total:* 2.67 liters of pure alcohol (2019 est.)
beer: 0.21 liters of pure alcohol (2019 est.)
wine: 0 liters of pure alcohol (2019 est.)
spirits: 0.02 liters of pure alcohol (2019 est.)
other alcohols: 2.44 liters of pure alcohol (2019 est.)
comparison ranking: total 121

Tobacco use: *total:* 8.6% (2025 est.)
male: 17% (2025 est.)
female: 0.5% (2025 est.)
comparison ranking: total 137

Children under the age of 5 years underweight: 11.6% (2020)
comparison ranking: 45

Currently married women (ages 15-49): 60.9% (2023 est.)

Child marriage: *women married by age 15:* 5.6% (2020)
women married by age 18: 23.1% (2020)
men married by age 18: 0.2% (2020)

Education expenditure: 2.7% of GDP (2023 est.)
17.5% national budget (2023 est.)

comparison ranking: Education expenditure (% GDP) 168

Literacy: *total population:* 51.6% (2021 est.)
male: 65.3% (2021 est.)
female: 40.5% (2021 est.)

ENVIRONMENT

Environmental issues: deforestation due to slash-and-burn agriculture; desertification; water pollution; water-borne diseases

International environmental agreements: *party to:* Biodiversity, Climate Change, Climate Change-Kyoto Protocol, Climate Change-Paris Agreement, Desertification, Endangered Species, Hazardous Wastes, Law of the Sea, Nuclear Test Ban, Ozone Layer Protection, Ship Pollution, Wetlands, Whaling
signed, but not ratified: Comprehensive Nuclear Test Ban

Climate: tropical; hot, rainy season (June to November); cooler, dry season (November to May)

Urbanization: *urban population:* 64.5% of total population (2023)
rate of urbanization: 3.75% annual rate of change (2020-25 est.)

Carbon dioxide emissions: 537,000 metric tonnes of CO2 (2023 est.)
from petroleum and other liquids: 537,000 metric tonnes of CO2 (2023 est.)
comparison ranking: total emissions 188

Particulate matter emissions: 34.9 micrograms per cubic meter (2019 est.)

Waste and recycling: *municipal solid waste generated annually:* 193,400 tons (2024 est.)
percent of municipal solid waste recycled: 13% (2022 est.)

Total water withdrawal: *municipal:* 41.2 million cubic meters (2022 est.)
industrial: 21.2 million cubic meters (2022 est.)
agricultural: 39.2 million cubic meters (2022 est.)

Total renewable water resources: 8 billion cubic meters (2022 est.)

GOVERNMENT

Country name: *conventional long form:* Republic of The Gambia
conventional short form: The Gambia
etymology: named for the Gambia River that flows through the country; Portuguese explorers in the 15th century derived the name for the river from its local name, Ba-Dimma, meaning "the river"

Government type: presidential republic

Capital: *name:* Banjul
geographic coordinates: 13 27 N, 16 34 W
time difference: UTC 0 (5 hours ahead of Washington, DC, during Standard Time)
etymology: the name derives from a misunderstanding between Portuguese colonists and inhabitants in the 15th century; when asked what the area was called, the inhabitants thought they were being asked what they were doing and replied, "*bangjulo*," or "rope making"

Administrative divisions: 5 regions, 1 city*, and 1 municipality**; Banjul*, Central River, Kanifing**, Lower River, North Bank, Upper River, West Coast

Legal system: mixed system of English common law, Islamic law, and customary law

Constitution: *history:* previous 1965 (Independence Act), 1970; latest adopted 8 April 1996, approved by referendum 8 August 1996, effective 16 January 1997
amendment process: proposed by the National Assembly; passage requires at least three-fourths majority vote by the Assembly membership in each of several readings and approval by the president of the republic; a referendum is required for amendments affecting national sovereignty, fundamental rights and freedoms, government structures and authorities, taxation, and public funding; passage by referendum requires participation of at least 50% of eligible voters and approval by at least 75% of votes cast
note: in 2024, The Gambian government announced its commitment to adopting a new constitution

International law organization participation: accepts compulsory ICJ jurisdiction with reservations; accepts ICCt jurisdiction

Citizenship: *citizenship by birth:* yes
citizenship by descent only: yes
dual citizenship recognized: no
residency requirement for naturalization: 5 years

Suffrage: 18 years of age; universal

Executive branch: *chief of state:* President Adama BARROW (since 19 January 2022)
head of government: Vice President Mohammed JALLOW (since 23 February 2024)
cabinet: Cabinet appointed by the president
election/appointment process: president directly elected by simple-majority popular vote for a 5-year term (no term limits); vice president appointed by the president
most recent election date: 4 December 2021
election results: *2021:* Adama BARROW reelected president; percent of vote - Adama BARROW (NPP) 53.2%, Ousainou DARBOE (UDP) 27.7%, Mamma KANDEH (GDC) 12.3%, other 6.8%
2016: Adama BARROW elected president; percent of vote - Adama BARROW (Coalition 2016) 43.3%, Yahya JAMMEH (APRC) 39.6%, Mamma KANDEH (GDC) 17.1%
expected date of next election: 2026

Legislative branch: *legislature name:* National Assembly
legislative structure: unicameral
number of seats: 58 (53 directly elected; 5 appointed)
electoral system: plurality/majority
scope of elections: full renewal
term in office: 5 years
most recent election date: 4/9/2022
parties elected and seats per party: National People's Party (NPP) (18); United Democratic Party (UDP) (15); National Reconciliation Party (NRP) (4); Independents (12); Other (4)
percentage of women in chamber: 8.6%
expected date of next election: April 2027

Judicial branch: *highest court(s):* Supreme Court of The Gambia (consists of the chief justice and 6 justices; court sessions held with 5 justices)
judge selection and term of office: justices appointed by the president after consultation with the Judicial Service Commission, a 6-member independent body of high-level judicial officials, a presidential appointee, and a National Assembly appointee; justices appointed for life or until mandatory retirement at age 75
subordinate courts: Court of Appeal; High Court; Special Criminal Court; Khadis or Muslim courts; district tribunals; magistrates courts; cadi courts

Political parties: Alliance for Patriotic Reorientation and Construction or APRC
Gambia Democratic Congress or GDC
Gambia Moral Congress or GMC
National People's Party or NPP
People's Progressive Party or PPP
United Democratic Party or UDP

Diplomatic representation in the US: *chief of mission:* Ambassador Momodou Lamin BAH (12 December 2022)
chancery: 5630 16th Street NW, Washington, DC 20011
telephone: [1] (202) 785-1399
FAX: [1] (202) 785-1430
email address and website: info@gambiaembassydc.us
https://www.gambiaembassydc.us/home

Diplomatic representation from the US: *chief of mission:* Ambassador (vacant); Chargé d'Affaires Robert ANDERSON (since 22 August 2025)
embassy: Kairaba Avenue, Fajara, P.M.B. 19, Banjul
mailing address: 2070 Banjul Place, Washington DC 20521-2070
telephone: [220] 439-2856
FAX: [220] 439-2475
email address and website: ConsularBanjul@state.gov
https://gm.usembassy.gov/

International organization participation: ACP, AfDB, AU, ECOWAS, FAO, G-77, IBRD, ICAO, ICCt, ICRM, IDA, IDB, IFAD, IFC, IFRCS, ILO, IMF, IMO, Interpol, IOC, IOM, IPU, ISO (correspondent), ITSO, ITU, ITUC (NGOs), MIGA, NAM, OIC, OPCW, UN, UNAMID, UNCTAD, UNESCO, UNHRC, UNIDO, UNISFA, UNMIL, UNOCI, UNWTO, UPU, WCO, WFTU (NGOs), WHO, WIPO, WMO, WTO

Independence: 18 February 1965 (from the UK)

National holiday: Independence Day, 18 February (1965)

Flag: *description:* three equal horizontal bands of red (top), blue with white edges, and green
meaning: red stands for the sun and the savannah, blue for the Gambia River, and green for forests and agriculture; the white stripes denote unity and peace

National symbol(s): lion

National color(s): red, blue, green, white

National anthem(s): *title:* "For The Gambia, Our Homeland"
lyrics/music: Virginia Julie HOWE/adapted by Jeremy Frederick HOWE
history: adopted 1965; the music is an adaptation of the traditional Mandinka song "Foday Kaba Dumbuya"

National heritage: *total World Heritage Sites:* 2 (both cultural)
selected World Heritage Site locales: Kunta Kinteh Island and Related Sites; Stone Circles of Senegambia

ECONOMY

Economic overview: low-income West African economy; agriculture-dominant; high poverty rate; heightened inflation; dependent on foreign assistance and remittances; structural reforms conditioned by IMF Extended Credit Facility program

Real GDP (purchasing power parity): $8.365 billion (2024 est.)
$7.911 billion (2023 est.)
$7.549 billion (2022 est.)

note: data in 2021 dollars
comparison ranking: 169

Real GDP growth rate: 5.7% (2024 est.)
4.8% (2023 est.)
5.5% (2022 est.)
note: annual GDP % growth based on constant local currency
comparison ranking: 29

Real GDP per capita: $3,000 (2024 est.)
$2,900 (2023 est.)
$2,900 (2022 est.)
note: data in 2021 dollars
comparison ranking: 194

GDP (official exchange rate): $2.508 billion (2024 est.)
note: data in current dollars at official exchange rate

Inflation rate (consumer prices): 11.6% (2024 est.)
17% (2023 est.)
11.5% (2022 est.)
note: annual % change based on consumer prices
comparison ranking: 185

GDP - composition, by sector of origin: *agriculture:* 24.1% (2024 est.)
industry: 14.7% (2024 est.)
services: 53.9% (2024 est.)
note: figures may not total 100% due to non-allocated consumption not captured in sector-reported data
comparison rankings: agriculture 23; industry 165; services 127

GDP - composition, by end use: *household consumption:* 83.2% (2024 est.)
government consumption: 8.5% (2024 est.)
investment in fixed capital: 39% (2024 est.)
investment in inventories: 0% (2024 est.)
exports of goods and services: 6.6% (2024 est.)
imports of goods and services: -37.2% (2024 est.)
note: figures may not total 100% due to rounding or gaps in data collection

Agricultural products: rice, groundnuts, milk, millet, oil palm fruit, maize, vegetables, cassava, fruits, sorghum (2023)
note: top ten agricultural products based on tonnage

Industries: peanuts, fish, hides, tourism, beverages, agricultural machinery assembly, woodworking, metalworking, clothing

Industrial production growth rate: 2.4% (2024 est.)
note: annual % change in industrial value added based on constant local currency
comparison ranking: 92

Labor force: 783,100 (2024 est.)
note: number of people ages 15 or older who are employed or seeking work
comparison ranking: 151

Unemployment rate: 6.5% (2024 est.)
6.5% (2023 est.)
6.1% (2022 est.)
note: % of labor force seeking employment
comparison ranking: 119

Youth unemployment rate (ages 15-24): *total:* 10.9% (2024 est.)
male: 10.9% (2024 est.)
female: 10.9% (2024 est.)
note: % of labor force ages 15-24 seeking employment
comparison ranking: total 114

Population below poverty line: 53.4% (2020 est.)
note: % of population with income below national poverty line

Gini Index coefficient - distribution of family income: 38.8 (2020 est.)
note: index (0-100) of income distribution; higher values represent greater inequality
comparison ranking: 47

Household income or consumption by percentage share: *lowest 10%:* 2.6% (2020 est.)
highest 10%: 30.5% (2020 est.)
note: % share of income accruing to lowest and highest 10% of population

Remittances: 21.1% of GDP (2024 est.)
21.5% of GDP (2023 est.)
22.8% of GDP (2022 est.)
note: personal transfers and compensation between resident and non-resident individuals/households/entities

Budget: *revenues:* $308.887 million (2018 est.)
expenditures: $221.137 million (2018 est.)
note: central government revenues and expenses (excluding grants/extrabudgetary units/social security funds) converted to US dollars at average official exchange rate for year indicated

Current account balance: -$74.374 million (2024 est.)
-$120.064 million (2023 est.)
-$90.251 million (2022 est.)
note: balance of payments - net trade and primary/secondary income in current dollars
comparison ranking: 93

Exports: $838.409 million (2024 est.)
$717.774 million (2023 est.)
$267.377 million (2022 est.)
note: balance of payments - exports of goods and services in current dollars
comparison ranking: 186

Exports - partners: Kazakhstan 92%, Guinea-Bissau 2%, China 1%, India 1%, Greece 1% (2023)
note: top five export partners based on percentage share of exports

Exports - commodities: packaged medicine, cars, harvesting machinery, refined petroleum, trailers (2023)
note: top five export commodities based on value in dollars

Imports: $1.549 billion (2024 est.)
$1.353 billion (2023 est.)
$829.516 million (2022 est.)
note: balance of payments - imports of goods and services in current dollars
comparison ranking: 182

Imports - partners: Kazakhstan 26%, China 18%, Senegal 8%, India 7%, Brazil 4% (2023)
note: top five import partners based on percentage share of imports

Imports - commodities: crude petroleum, refined petroleum, cotton fabric, iron alloys, rice (2023)
note: top five import commodities based on value in dollars

Reserves of foreign exchange and gold: $577.028 million (2023 est.)
$568.244 million (2022 est.)
$652.671 million (2021 est.)
note: holdings of gold (year-end prices)/foreign exchange/special drawing rights in current dollars
comparison ranking: 156

Debt - external: $902.421 million (2023 est.)
note: present value of external debt in current US dollars
comparison ranking: 106

Exchange rates: dalasis (GMD) per US dollar -

Exchange rates: 61.096 (2023 est.)
54.923 (2022 est.)
51.484 (2021 est.)
51.502 (2020 est.)
50.062 (2019 est.)

ENERGY

Electricity access: *electrification - total population:* 65.4% (2022 est.)
electrification - urban areas: 82.8%
electrification - rural areas: 31.2%

Electricity: *installed generating capacity:* 162,000 kW (2023 est.)
consumption: 410.824 million kWh (2023 est.)
transmission/distribution losses: 104.176 million kWh (2023 est.)
comparison rankings: installed generating capacity 179; consumption 179; transmission/distribution losses 48

Electricity generation sources: *fossil fuels:* 99% of total installed capacity (2023 est.)
solar: 0.6% of total installed capacity (2023 est.)
wind: 0.4% of total installed capacity (2023 est.)

Petroleum: *refined petroleum consumption:* 3,000 bbl/day (2023 est.)

Energy consumption per capita: 2.731 million Btu/person (2023 est.)
comparison ranking: 180

COMMUNICATIONS

Telephones - fixed lines: *total subscriptions:* 60,000 (2021 est.)
subscriptions per 100 inhabitants: 2 (2022 est.)
comparison ranking: total subscriptions 150

Telephones - mobile cellular: *total subscriptions:* 2.68 million (2021 est.)
subscriptions per 100 inhabitants: 101 (2021 est.)
comparison ranking: total subscriptions 144

Broadcast media: 1 state-run TV-channel; one privately owned TV station; 1 online TV station; 3 state-owned and 31 privately owned radio stations; 8 community radio stations; transmissions of multiple international broadcasters are available; cable and satellite TV subscription services in some parts of the country (2019)

Internet country code: .gm

Internet users: *percent of population:* 46% (2023 est.)

Broadband - fixed subscriptions: *total:* 6,000 (2022 est.)
subscriptions per 100 inhabitants: (2022 est.) less than 1
comparison ranking: total 193

TRANSPORTATION

Civil aircraft registration country code prefix: C5

Airports: 1 (2025)
comparison ranking: 223

Merchant marine: *total:* 15 (2023)
by type: general cargo 5, other 10
comparison ranking: total 151

Ports: *total ports:* 1 (2024)
large: 0
medium: 0
small: 0
very small: 1
ports with oil terminals: 1
key ports: Banjul

MILITARY AND SECURITY

Military and security forces: Gambian Armed Forces (GAF; aka Armed Forces of the Gambia): *the Gambian National Army (GNA), Gambia Navy, Gambia Air Force, Republican National Guard (RNG)*
Ministry of Interior: Gambia Police Force (GPF) (2025)
note: the RNG is responsible for VIP protection, riot control, and presidential security, while the GPF maintains internal security

Military expenditures: 0.6% of GDP (2024 est.)
0.6% of GDP (2023 est.)
0.7% of GDP (2022 est.)
0.8% of GDP (2021 est.)
0.8% of GDP (2020 est.)

Military and security service personnel strengths: estimated 3,000-4,000 active Gambian Armed Forces (2025)

Military equipment inventories and acquisitions: the military of Gambia has a limited inventory of mostly older, obsolescent, or donated equipment originating from several suppliers, including Taiwan, Turkey, the UK, and the US (2024)

Military service age and obligation: 18-25 years of age for voluntary service for men and women (18-22 for officers); no conscription; service obligation six months (2024)

Military - note: the Gambian Armed Forces (GAF) are responsible for external defense and aiding civil authorities in internal emergencies and natural disaster relief; they participate in multinational peacekeeping missions, as well as domestic support activities such as agricultural development, construction, education, and health services; the Gambian security forces have a history of involvement in domestic politics, including multiple coup attempts and mutinies, with the latest being an attempted coup in 2022
since January 2017, several members of the Economic Community of West African States (ECOWAS) have provided security forces for Gambia's stability, plus assistance and training for the GAF and other Gambian security forces through the ECOWAS Mission in the Gambia (ECOMIG); as of 2025, Ghana, Nigeria, and Senegal were providing military and gendarmerie personnel for ECOMIG (2025)

TRANSNATIONAL ISSUES

Refugees and internally displaced persons: *refugees:* 4,411 (2024 est.)
IDPs: 7,462 (2024 est.)

GAZA STRIP

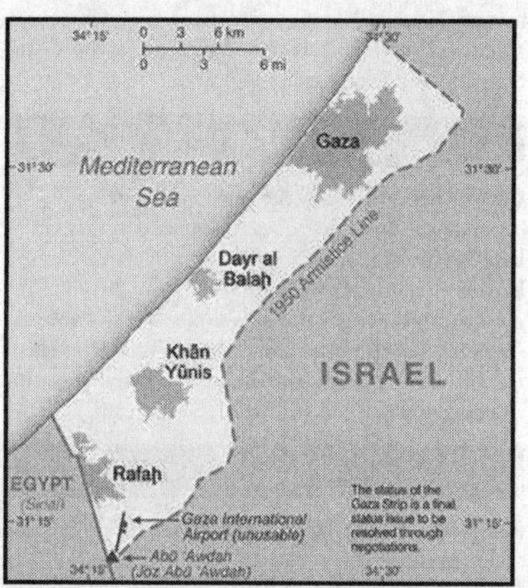

INTRODUCTION

Background: The Gaza Strip has been under the de facto governing authority of the Islamic Resistance Movement (HAMAS) since 2007 and has faced years of conflict, poverty, and humanitarian crises. Inhabited since at least the 15th century B.C., the Gaza Strip area has been dominated by many different peoples and empires throughout its history; it was incorporated into the Ottoman Empire in the early 16th century. The Gaza Strip fell to British forces during World War I, becoming a part of the British Mandate of Palestine. Following the 1948 Arab-Israeli War, Egypt administered the newly formed Gaza Strip; Israel captured it in the Six-Day War in 1967. Under a series of agreements known as the Oslo Accords signed between 1993 and 1999, Israel transferred to the newly-created Palestinian Authority (PA) security and civilian responsibility for many Palestinian-populated areas of the Gaza Strip, as well as the West Bank.

In 2000, a violent intifada or uprising began in response to perceived Israeli provocations, and in 2001, negotiations to determine the permanent status of the West Bank, East Jerusalem, and Gaza Strip stalled. Subsequent attempts to re-start negotiations have not resulted in progress toward determining final status and resolving the Israeli-Palestinian conflict. Israel in 2005 unilaterally withdrew all of its settlers and soldiers and dismantled its military facilities in the Gaza Strip, but it continues to control the Gaza Strip's land borders, maritime territorial waters, cyberspace, telecommunications, and airspace. In 2006, HAMAS won a majority in the Palestinian Legislative Council election. Fatah, the dominant Palestinian political faction in the West Bank, and HAMAS failed to maintain a unity government, leading to violent clashes between their respective supporters and HAMAS's violent seizure of all PA military and governmental institutions in the Gaza Strip in 2007. Since HAMAS's takeover, Israel and Egypt have enforced tight restrictions on movement and access of goods and individuals into and out of the territory. Fatah and HAMAS have since negotiated a series of agreements aimed at restoring political unity between the Gaza Strip and the West Bank but have struggled to enact them.

Palestinian militants in the Gaza Strip and the Israel Defense Forces periodically exchange projectiles and air strikes, respectively, threatening broader conflict. In 2021, HAMAS launched rockets into Israel, sparking an 11-day conflict that also involved other Gaza-based militant groups. Egypt, Qatar, and the UN Special Coordinator for the Middle East Peace Process negotiated ceasefires, averting a broader conflict. Since 2018, HAMAS has coordinated demonstrations along the Gaza-Israel security fence. HAMAS has also stood by while other militant groups, such as Palestinian Islamic Jihad, fought brief conflicts with Israel, most recently in August 2022 and May 2023.

On 7 October 2023, HAMAS militants inside the Gaza Strip launched a combined unguided rocket and ground attack into Israel. The attack began with a barrage of more than 3,000 rockets fired toward Israel from Gaza, and included thousands of terrorists infiltrating Israel by land, sea, and air via paragliders. Militants attacked military bases, clashed with security forces mostly in southern Israel, and simultaneously infiltrated civilian communities. During the attack, terrorists carried out massacres and murdered civilians, including torture, acts of abuse and rape, a massacre at the Supernova music festival near Kibbutz Re'im, as well as kidnapping approximately 240 civilians, including men, women, children, and soldiers. These attacks were followed soon after by Israeli Defense Forces (IDF) air strikes inside Gaza. The next day, Israeli Prime Minister NETANYAHU formally declared war on Gaza. The IDF on 28 October launched a large-scale ground assault inside Gaza that is ongoing as of April 2024.

GEOGRAPHY

Location: Middle East, bordering the Mediterranean Sea, between Egypt and Israel

Geographic coordinates: 31 25 N, 34 20 E

Map references: Middle East

Area: *total:* 360 sq km
land: 360 sq km
water: 0 sq km
comparison ranking: total 206

Area - comparative: slightly more than twice the size of Washington, D.C.

Land boundaries: *total:* 72 km
border countries (2): Egypt 13 km; Israel 59 km

Coastline: 40 km

Maritime claims: see entry for Israel

Climate: temperate, mild winters, dry and warm to hot summers

Terrain: flat to rolling, sand- and dune-covered coastal plain

Elevation: *highest point:* Abu 'Awdah (Joz Abu 'Awdah) 105 m
lowest point: Mediterranean Sea 0 m

Natural resources: arable land, natural gas

Land use: *agricultural land:* 64.9% (2022 est.)
arable land: 7% (2022 est.)
permanent crops: 11.8% (2022 est.)
permanent pasture: 46.1% (2022 est.)
forest: 1.7% (2022 est.)
other: 33.4% (2022 est.)

Irrigated land: (2013) 151 sq km; note - includes the West Bank

Population distribution: population concentrated in major cities, particularly Gaza City in the north

Natural hazards: droughts

Geography - note: once a strategic strip of land along Mideast-North African trade routes

PEOPLE AND SOCIETY

Population: *total:* 2,141,643 (2024 est.)
male: 1,086,340
female: 1,055,303
comparison rankings: total 148; male 148; female 149

Ethnic groups: Palestinian Arab

Languages: Arabic, Hebrew (spoken by many Palestinians), English (widely understood)
major-language sample(s):

يمكن الاستغناء عنه للمعلومات الأساسية

كتاب حقائق العالم، المصدر الذي لا

(Arabic)

Religions: Muslim 98.0 - 99.0% (predominantly Sunni), Christian <1.0%, other, unaffiliated, unspecified <1.0% (2012 est.)
note: Israel dismantled its settlements in September 2005; Gaza has had no Jewish population since then

Age structure: *0-14 years:* 38.8% (male 427,450/female 404,288)
15-64 years: 58.3% (male 627,235/female 620,903)
65 years and over: 2.9% (2024 est.) (male 31,655/female 30,112)

Dependency ratios: *total dependency ratio:* 71.6 (2024 est.)
youth dependency ratio: 66.6 (2024 est.)
elderly dependency ratio: 4.9 (2024 est.)
potential support ratio: 20.2 (2024 est.)

Median age: *total:* 19.5 years (2024 est.)
male: 19.3 years
female: 19.8 years
comparison ranking: total 208

Population growth rate: 2.02% (2024 est.)
comparison ranking: 40

Birth rate: 26.8 births/1,000 population (2024 est.)
comparison ranking: 38

Death rate: 2.9 deaths/1,000 population (2024 est.)
comparison ranking: 225

Net migration rate: -3.7 migrant(s)/1,000 population (2024 est.)
comparison ranking: 190

Population distribution: population concentrated in major cities, particularly Gaza City in the north

Urbanization: *urban population:* 77.6% of total population (2023)
rate of urbanization: 2.85% annual rate of change (2020-25 est.)
note: data represent Gaza Strip and the West Bank

Major urban areas - population: 778,000 Gaza (2023)

Sex ratio: *at birth:* 1.06 male(s)/female
0-14 years: 1.06 male(s)/female
15-64 years: 1.01 male(s)/female
65 years and over: 1.05 male(s)/female
total population: 1.03 male(s)/female (2024 est.)

Maternal mortality ratio: 16 deaths/100,000 live births (2023 est.)
note: data represent Gaza Strip and the West Bank
comparison ranking: 133

Infant mortality rate: *total:* 15.1 deaths/1,000 live births (2024 est.)
male: 16.3 deaths/1,000 live births
female: 13.8 deaths/1,000 live births
comparison ranking: total 91

Life expectancy at birth: *total population:* 75.5 years (2024 est.)
male: 73.7 years
female: 77.4 years
comparison ranking: total population 126

Total fertility rate: 3.26 children born/woman (2024 est.)
comparison ranking: 42

Gross reproduction rate: 1.58 (2024 est.)

Drinking water source: *improved:* total: 98.9% of population
unimproved: total: 1.1% of population (2022 est.)
note: includes Gaza Strip and the West Bank

Health expenditure: 13.5% of national budget (2022 est.)
note: includes Gaza Strip and the West Bank

Physician density: 2.17 physicians/1,000 population (2020)

Hospital bed density: 1.3 beds/1,000 population (2019 est.)

Sanitation facility access: *improved: urban:* 100% of population (2022 est.)
rural: 99% of population (2022 est.)
total: 99.8% of population
unimproved: urban: 0% of population (2022 est.)
rural: 1% of population (2022 est.)
total: 0.2% of population (2022 est.)
note: includes Gaza Strip and the West Bank

Children under the age of 5 years underweight: 2.1% (2019/20)
note: estimate is for Gaza Strip and the West Bank
comparison ranking: 94

Currently married women (ages 15-49): 62.4% (2023 est.)
note: data includes Gaza and the West Bank

Child marriage: *women married by age 15:* 0.7% (2020)
women married by age 18: 13.4% (2020)
note: includes both the Gaza Strip and the West Bank

Education expenditure: 5.4% of GDP (2021 est.)
note: includes Gaza Strip and the West Bank
comparison ranking: Education expenditure (% GDP) 47

Literacy: *total population:* 98% (2022 est.)
male: 99% (2022 est.)
female: 97% (2022 est.)
note: estimates are for Gaza Strip and the West Bank

School life expectancy (primary to tertiary education): *total:* 13 years (2023 est.)
male: 12 years (2023 est.)
female: 14 years (2023 est.)
note: data represent Gaza Strip and the West Bank

ENVIRONMENT

Environmental issues: soil degradation; desertification; water pollution from chemicals and pesticides; salination of fresh water; improper sewage treatment; depletion and contamination of underground water resources

Climate: temperate, mild winters, dry and warm to hot summers

Urbanization: *urban population:* 77.6% of total population (2023)
rate of urbanization: 2.85% annual rate of change (2020-25 est.)
note: data represent Gaza Strip and the West Bank

Carbon dioxide emissions: 3.913 million metric tonnes of CO_2 (2023 est.)
from petroleum and other liquids: 3.913 million metric tonnes of CO_2 (2023 est.)
note: includes the West Bank and the Gaza Strip
comparison ranking: total emissions 142

Particulate matter emissions: 31.3 micrograms per cubic meter (2019 est.)

Waste and recycling: *municipal solid waste generated annually:* 1.387 million tons (2024 est.)
note: data represent combined total from the Gaza Strip and the West Bank.

Total water withdrawal: *municipal:* 251 million cubic meters (2022)
industrial: 37 million cubic meters (2022)
agricultural: 158 million cubic meters (2022)
note: data represent combined total from the Gaza Strip and the West Bank.

Total renewable water resources: 837 million cubic meters (2022 est.)
note: data represent combined total from the Gaza Strip and the West Bank.

GOVERNMENT

Country name: *conventional long form:* none
conventional short form: Gaza, Gaza Strip
local long form: none
local short form: Qita' Ghazzah
etymology: named for the largest city in the enclave, Gaza, whose settlement can be traced back to at least the 15th century B.C. (as "Ghazzat"); "Strip" refers to its elongated shape along the Mediterranean

ECONOMY

Real GDP (purchasing power parity): $20.339 billion (2024 est.)
$27.694 billion (2023 est.)
$29.016 billion (2022 est.)
note: data in 2021 dollars; entry includes West Bank and Gaza Strip
comparison ranking: 155

Real GDP growth rate: -26.6% (2024 est.)
-4.6% (2023 est.)
4.1% (2022 est.)
note: annual GDP % growth based on constant local currency; entry includes West Bank and Gaza Strip
comparison ranking: 217

Real GDP per capita: $3,800 (2024 est.)
$5,400 (2023 est.)
$5,800 (2022 est.)
note: data in 2021 dollars; entry includes West Bank and Gaza Strip
comparison ranking: 184

GDP (official exchange rate): $13.711 billion (2024 est.)
note: data in current dollars at official exchange rate; entry includes West Bank and Gaza Strip

Inflation rate (consumer prices): 53.7% (2024 est.)
5.9% (2023 est.)
3.7% (2022 est.)
note: annual % change based on consumer prices; entry includes West Bank and Gaza Strip
comparison ranking: 205

GDP - composition, by sector of origin: *agriculture:* 5.7% (2022 est.)
industry: 17.4% (2022 est.)
services: 58.3% (2022 est.)
note: figures may not total 100% due to non-allocated consumption not captured in sector-reported data
comparison rankings: agriculture 103; industry 150; services 100

GDP - composition, by end use: *household consumption:* 95.5% (2024 est.)
government consumption: 20.7% (2024 est.)
investment in fixed capital: 21.8% (2024 est.)
investment in inventories: 1.7% (2024 est.)
exports of goods and services: 21% (2024 est.)
imports of goods and services: -60.3% (2024 est.)
note: figures may not total 100% due to rounding or gaps in data collection

Agricultural products: tomatoes, milk, cucumbers/gherkins, olives, potatoes, sheep milk, eggplants, pumpkins/squash, grapes, goat milk (2023)
note: top ten agricultural products based on tonnage

Industries: textiles, food processing, furniture

Industrial production growth rate: -32.2% (2024 est.)
note: annual % change in industrial value added based on constant local currency; entry includes West Bank and Gaza Strip
comparison ranking: 195

Labor force: 1.391 million (2022 est.)
note: number of people ages 15 or older who are employed or seeking work; entry includes West Bank and Gaza Strip
comparison ranking: 136

Unemployment rate: 24.5% (2022 est.)
26.4% (2021 est.)
25.9% (2020 est.)
note: % of labor force seeking employment; entry includes West Bank and Gaza Strip
comparison ranking: 187

Youth unemployment rate (ages 15-24): *total:* 36.1% (2022 est.)
male: 31.6% (2022 est.)
female: 56.6% (2022 est.)
note: % of labor force ages 15-24 seeking employment
comparison ranking: total 14

Population below poverty line: 29.2% (2016 est.)
note: % of population with income below national poverty line; entry includes West Bank and Gaza Strip

Gini Index coefficient - distribution of family income: 36.4 (2023 est.)
note: index (0-100) of income distribution; higher values represent greater inequality; entry includes West Bank and Gaza Strip
comparison ranking: 63

Household income or consumption by percentage share: *lowest 10%:* 2.5% (2023 est.)
highest 10%: 27.1% (2023 est.)
note: % share of income accruing to lowest and highest 10% of population; entry includes West Bank and Gaza Strip

Remittances: 5.4% of GDP (2024 est.)
18.2% of GDP (2023 est.)
24% of GDP (2022 est.)
note: personal transfers and compensation between resident and non-resident individuals/households/entities; entry includes West Bank and Gaza Strip

Budget: see entry for the West Bank

Taxes and other revenues: 21.5% (of GDP) (2021 est.)
note: central government tax revenue as a % of GDP; entry includes West Bank and Gaza Strip
comparison ranking: 38

Current account balance: -$2.899 billion (2024 est.)
-$2.895 billion (2023 est.)
-$2.037 billion (2022 est.)
note: balance of payments - net trade and primary/secondary income in current dollars; entry includes West Bank and Gaza Strip
comparison ranking: 156

Exports: $2.885 billion (2024 est.)
$3.413 billion (2023 est.)
$3.533 billion (2022 est.)
note: balance of payments - exports of goods and services in current dollars; entry includes West Bank and Gaza Strip
comparison ranking: 157

Exports - partners: Jordan 51%, Turkey 12%, UAE 8%, Saudi Arabia 5%, UK 4% (2023)
note: top five export partners based on percentage share of exports; entry includes the West Bank and the Gaza Strip

Exports - commodities: scrap iron, tropical fruits, olive oil, building stone, prepared meat (2023)
note: top five export commodities based on value in dollars; entry includes the West Bank and the Gaza Strip

Imports: $8.264 billion (2024 est.)
$11.637 billion (2023 est.)
$12.257 billion (2022 est.)
note: balance of payments - imports of goods and services in current dollars; entry includes West Bank and Gaza Strip
comparison ranking: 130

Imports - partners: Egypt 25%, Jordan 17%, China 8%, Germany 7%, UAE 7% (2023)
note: top five import partners based on percentage share of imports; entry includes the West Bank and the Gaza Strip

Imports - commodities: cement, raw sugar, cars, baked goods, perfumes (2023)
note: top five import commodities based on value in dollars; entry includes the West Bank and the Gaza Strip

Reserves of foreign exchange and gold: $1.328 billion (2024 est.)
$1.323 billion (2023 est.)
$896.9 million (2022 est.)
note: holdings of gold (year-end prices)/foreign exchange/special drawing rights in current dollars; entry includes West Bank and Gaza Strip
comparison ranking: 139

Exchange rates: see entry for the West Bank

ENERGY

Electricity access: *electrification - total population:* 100% (2022 est.)
note: includes the West Bank and the Gaza Strip

Electricity: *installed generating capacity:* 352,000 kW (2023 est.)
consumption: 6.956 billion kWh (2023 est.)
imports: 6.925 billion kWh (2023 est.)
transmission/distribution losses: 988 million kWh (2023 est.)
note: includes the West Bank and the Gaza Strip
comparison rankings: installed generating capacity 158; consumption 119; imports 38; transmission/distribution losses 98

Electricity generation sources: *fossil fuels:* 66.5% of total installed capacity (2023 est.)
solar: 33.5% of total installed capacity (2023 est.)
note: includes the West Bank and the Gaza Strip

Coal: *exports:* 1 metric tons (2023 est.)
note: includes the West Bank and the Gaza Strip

Petroleum: *refined petroleum consumption:* 29,000 bbl/day (2023 est.)
note: includes the West Bank and the Gaza Strip

Energy consumption per capita: 14.991 million Btu/person (2023 est.)
note: includes the West Bank and the Gaza Strip
comparison ranking: 139

COMMUNICATIONS

Telephones - fixed lines: *total subscriptions:* 384,000 (2023 est.)
subscriptions per 100 inhabitants: 7 (2023 est.)
note: entry includes the West Bank and the Gaza Strip
comparison ranking: total subscriptions 101

Telephones - mobile cellular: *total subscriptions:* 4.15 million (2023 est.)
subscriptions per 100 inhabitants: 78 (2021 est.)
note: entry includes the West Bank and the Gaza Strip
comparison ranking: total subscriptions 134

Broadcast media: 1 TV station and about 10 radio stations; satellite TV accessible

Internet country code: .ps
note: IANA has designated.ps for the Gaza Strip, same as the West Bank

Internet users: *percent of population:* 87% (2023 est.)
note: includes the West Bank

Broadband - fixed subscriptions: *total:* 431,000 (2023 est.)
subscriptions per 100 inhabitants: 8 (2023 est.)
note: includes the West Bank
comparison ranking: total 103

MILITARY AND SECURITY

Military and security forces: HAMAS maintains security forces inside Gaza in addition to its military wing, the 'Izz al-Din al-Qassam Brigades; the military wing ostensibly reports to the HAMAS Political Bureau but operates with considerable autonomy; there are several other militant groups operating in the Gaza Strip, most notably the Al-Quds Brigades of Palestinian Islamic Jihad, which are usually but not always beholden to HAMAS's authority (2024)

Military expenditures: not available

Military and security service personnel strengths: prior to the start of the 2023-2025 conflict with Israel, the military wing of HAMAS was estimated to have 20-30,000 fighters (2024)

Military equipment inventories and acquisitions: the military wing is armed with light weapons, including an inventory of rocket, anti-tank, anti-aircraft, indirect fire (typically mortars), and armed UAV capabilities; HAMAS acquires its weapons through smuggling or local construction and receives significant military support from Iran (2024)

TERRORISM

Terrorist group(s): Terrorist group(s): Army of Islam; Abdallah Azzam Brigades; al-Aqsa Martyrs Brigade; HAMAS; Islamic Revolutionary Guard Corps/Qods Force; Palestine Islamic Jihad (PIJ); Palestine Liberation Front; Popular Front for the Liberation of Palestine (PFLP); PFLP-General Command
note: details about the history, aims, leadership, organization, areas of operation, tactics, targets, weapons, size, and sources of support of the group(s) appear(s) in Appendix T

TRANSNATIONAL ISSUES

Refugees and internally displaced persons: IDPs: 2,032,011 (2024 est.)

GEORGIA

INTRODUCTION

Background: The region of present-day Georgia once contained the ancient kingdoms of Colchis (known as Egrisi locally) and Kartli-Iberia. The area came under Roman influence in the first centuries A.D., and Christianity became the state religion in the 330s. Persian, Arab, and Turk domination was followed by a Georgian golden age (11th-13th centuries) that was cut short when the Mongols invaded in 1236. Subsequently, the Ottoman and Persian empires competed for influence in the region. Georgia was absorbed into the Russian Empire in the 19th century. Independent for three years (1918-1921) following the Russian revolution, it was forcibly incorporated into the USSR in 1921 and regained its independence when the Soviet Union dissolved in 1991.

In 2003, mounting public discontent over rampant corruption, ineffective government services, and a government attempt to manipulate parliamentary elections touched off widespread protests that led to the resignation of Eduard SHEVARDNADZE, who had been president since 1995. In the aftermath of this "Rose Revolution," new elections in 2004 swept Mikheil SAAKASHVILI and his United National Movement (UNM) party into power. SAAKASHVILI made progress on market reforms and governance, but he faced accusations of abuse of office. Progress was further complicated when Russian support for the separatist regions of Abkhazia and South Ossetia led to a five-day conflict between Russia and Georgia in August 2008, which included Russia invading large portions of Georgian territory. Russia initially pledged to pull back from most Georgian territory but then unilaterally recognized the independence of Abkhazia and South Ossetia, and Russian military forces have remained in those regions.

Billionaire Bidzina IVANISHVILI's unexpected entry into politics in 2011 brought the divided opposition together under his Georgian Dream coalition, which won a majority of seats in the 2012 parliamentary elections and removed UNM from power. Conceding defeat, SAAKASHVILI named IVANISHVILI as prime minister and left the country after his presidential term ended in 2013. IVANISHVILI voluntarily resigned from office after the presidential succession, and in the years since, the prime minister position has seen frequent turnover. In 2021, SAAKASHVILI returned to Georgia, where he was immediately arrested to serve six years in prison on outstanding abuse-of-office convictions. Popular support for integration with the West is high in Georgia. Joining the EU and NATO are among the country's top foreign policy goals, and Georgia applied for EU membership in 2022, becoming a candidate country in December 2023. Georgia and the EU have a Deep and Comprehensive Free Trade Agreement, and since 2017, Georgian citizens have been able to travel to the Schengen area without a visa.

GEOGRAPHY

Location: Southwestern Asia, bordering the Black Sea, between Turkey and Russia, with a sliver of land north of the Caucasus extending into Europe; note - Georgia views itself as part of Europe; geopolitically, it can be classified as falling within Europe, the Middle East, or both

Geographic coordinates: 42 00 N, 43 30 E

Map references: Asia

Area: *total:* 69,700 sq km
land: 69,700 sq km
water: 0 sq km
note: approximately 12,560 sq km, or about 18% of Georgia's area, is Russian-occupied; the seized area includes all of Abkhazia and the breakaway region of South Ossetia, which consists of the northern part of Shida Kartli, eastern slivers of the Imereti region, Racha-Lechkhumi, Kvemo Svaneti, and part of western Mtskheta-Mtianeti
comparison ranking: total 121

Area - comparative: slightly smaller than South Carolina; slightly larger than West Virginia

Land boundaries: *total:* 1,814 km
border countries (4): Armenia 219 km; Azerbaijan 428 km; Russia 894 km; Turkey 273 km

Coastline: 310 km

Maritime claims: *territorial sea:* 12 nm
exclusive economic zone: 200 nm

Climate: warm and pleasant; Mediterranean-like on Black Sea coast

Terrain: largely mountainous with Great Caucasus Mountains in the north and Lesser Caucasus Mountains in the south; Kolkhet'is Dablobi (Kolkhida Lowland) opens to the Black Sea in the west; Mtkvari River Basin in the east; fertile soils in river valley flood plains and foothills of Kolkhida Lowland

Elevation: *highest point:* Mt'a Shkhara 5,193 m
lowest point: Black Sea 0 m
mean elevation: 1,432 m

Natural resources: timber, hydropower, manganese deposits, iron ore, copper, minor coal and oil deposits; coastal climate and soils allow for important tea and citrus growth

Land use: *agricultural land:* 34.3% (2022 est.)
arable land: 4.5% (2022 est.)
permanent crops: 1.8% (2022 est.)
permanent pasture: 27.9% (2022 est.)
forest: 40.6% (2022 est.)
other: 25.1% (2022 est.)

Irrigated land: 4,330 sq km (2012)

Population distribution: settlement concentrated in the central valley, particularly in the capital city of Tbilisi in the east; smaller urban agglomerations dot the Black Sea coast, with Bat'umi being the largest

Natural hazards: earthquakes

Geography - note: *note 1:* strategically located east of the Black Sea, Georgia controls much of the Caucasus Mountains and the routes through them
note 2: the world's four deepest caves are all in Georgia, including two that are the only known caves on earth deeper than 2,000 m: Krubera Cave at -2,197 m (-7,208 ft; reached in 2012) and Veryovkina Cave at -2,212 (-7,257 ft; reached in 2018)

PEOPLE AND SOCIETY

Population: *total:* 4,900,961 (2024 est.)
male: 2,343,068
female: 2,557,893
comparison rankings: total 126; male 126; female 126

Nationality: *noun:* Georgian(s)
adjective: Georgian

Ethnic groups: Georgian 86.8%, Azeri 6.3%, Armenian 4.5%, other 2.3% (includes Russian, Ossetian, Yazidi, Ukrainian, Kist, Greek) (2014 est.)

Languages: Georgian (official) 87.6%, Azeri 6.2%, Armenian 3.9%, Russian 1.2%, other 1% (including Abkhaz, the official language in Abkhazia) (2014 est.)
major-language sample(s):

მსოფლიო ფაქტების წიგნი, ძირითადი ინფორმაციის აუცილებელი წყარო.
(Georgian)

Religions: Eastern Orthodox Christian (official) 83.4%, Muslim 10.7%, Armenian Apostolic Christian 2.9%, other 1.2% (includes Roman Catholic Christian, Jehovah's Witness, Yazidi, Protestant Christian, Jewish), none 0.5%, unspecified/no answer 1.2% (2014 est.)

Age structure: *0-14 years:* 20.6% (male 520,091/female 489,882)

15-64 years: 62.7% (male 1,500,036/female 1,572,637)
65 years and over: 16.7% (2024 est.) (male 322,941/ female 495,374)

Dependency ratios: *total dependency ratio:* 59.5 (2024 est.)
youth dependency ratio: 32.9 (2024 est.)
elderly dependency ratio: 26.6 (2024 est.)
potential support ratio: 3.8 (2024 est.)

Median age: *total:* 38.3 years (2024 est.)
male: 35.9 years
female: 40.6 years
comparison ranking: total 75

Population growth rate: -0.5% (2024 est.)
comparison ranking: 222

Birth rate: 12 births/1,000 population (2024 est.)
comparison ranking: 148

Death rate: 13.3 deaths/1,000 population (2024 est.)
comparison ranking: 11

Net migration rate: -3.8 migrant(s)/1,000 population (2024 est.)
comparison ranking: 193

Population distribution: settlement concentrated in the central valley, particularly in the capital city of Tbilisi in the east; smaller urban agglomerations dot the Black Sea coast, with Bat'umi being the largest

Urbanization: *urban population:* 60.7% of total population (2023)
rate of urbanization: 0.35% annual rate of change (2020-25 est.)
note: data include Abkhazia and South Ossetia

Major urban areas - population: 1.082 million TBILISI (capital) (2023)

Sex ratio: *at birth:* 1.07 male(s)/female
0-14 years: 1.06 male(s)/female
15-64 years: 0.95 male(s)/female
65 years and over: 0.65 male(s)/female
total population: 0.92 male(s)/female (2024 est.)

Mother's mean age at first birth: 25.9 years (2019 est.)
note: data does not cover Abkhazia and South Ossetia

Maternal mortality ratio: 20 deaths/100,000 live births (2023 est.)
comparison ranking: 121

Infant mortality rate: *total:* 21.7 deaths/1,000 live births (2024 est.)
male: 23.6 deaths/1,000 live births
female: 19.7 deaths/1,000 live births
comparison ranking: total 72

Life expectancy at birth: *total population:* 72.8 years (2024 est.)
male: 68.7 years
female: 77.2 years
comparison ranking: total population 158

Total fertility rate: 1.95 children born/woman (2024 est.)
comparison ranking: 112

Gross reproduction rate: 0.94 (2024 est.)

Drinking water source: *improved: urban:* 99.2% of population (2022 est.)
rural: 88.5% of population (2022 est.)
total: 95% of population (2022 est.)
unimproved: urban: 0.8% of population (2022 est.)
rural: 11.5% of population (2022 est.)
total: 5% of population (2022 est.)

Health expenditure: 7.4% of GDP (2022)
10.5% of national budget (2022 est.)

Physician density: 5.64 physicians/1,000 population (2023)

Hospital bed density: 4.9 beds/1,000 population (2020 est.)

Sanitation facility access: *improved: urban:* 96.6% of population (2022 est.)
rural: 72.5% of population (2022 est.)
total: 87.1% of population (2022 est.)
unimproved: urban: 3.4% of population (2022 est.)
rural: 27.5% of population (2022 est.)
total: 12.9% of population (2022 est.)

Obesity - adult prevalence rate: 21.7% (2016)
comparison ranking: 85

Alcohol consumption per capita: *total:* 7.45 liters of pure alcohol (2019 est.)
beer: 1.71 liters of pure alcohol (2019 est.)
wine: 3.19 liters of pure alcohol (2019 est.)
spirits: 2.52 liters of pure alcohol (2019 est.)
other alcohols: 0.02 liters of pure alcohol (2019 est.)
comparison ranking: total 53

Tobacco use: *total:* 28.7% (2025 est.)
male: 53.9% (2025 est.)
female: 7.5% (2025 est.)
comparison ranking: total 27

Children under the age of 5 years underweight: 2.1% (2018)
comparison ranking: 96

Currently married women (ages 15-49): 67.1% (2023 est.)

Child marriage: *women married by age 15:* 0.3% (2018)
women married by age 18: 13.9% (2018)
men married by age 18: 0.5% (2018)

Education expenditure: 3.7% of GDP (2023 est.)
14.1% national budget (2023 est.)
comparison ranking: Education expenditure (% GDP) 121

Literacy: *total population:* 99.6% (2023 est.)
male: 99.5% (2023 est.)
female: 99.6% (2023 est.)

School life expectancy (primary to tertiary education): *total:* 16 years (2023 est.)
male: 16 years (2023 est.)
female: 17 years (2023 est.)

ENVIRONMENT

Environmental issues: air pollution, particularly in Rust'avi; heavy water pollution of Mtkvari River and the Black Sea; inadequate supplies of potable water; soil pollution from toxic chemicals; land and forest degradation; biodiversity loss; waste management

International environmental agreements: *party to:* Air Pollution, Biodiversity, Climate Change, Climate Change-Kyoto Protocol, Climate Change-Paris Agreement, Comprehensive Nuclear Test Ban, Desertification, Endangered Species, Hazardous Wastes, Law of the Sea, Marine Dumping-London Protocol, Ozone Layer Protection, Ship Pollution, Wetlands
signed, but not ratified: none of the selected agreements

Climate: warm and pleasant; Mediterranean-like on Black Sea coast

Urbanization: *urban population:* 60.7% of total population (2023)
rate of urbanization: 0.35% annual rate of change (2020-25 est.)
note: data include Abkhazia and South Ossetia

Carbon dioxide emissions: 10.7 million metric tonnes of CO2 (2023 est.)
from coal and metallurgical coke: 812,000 metric tonnes of CO2 (2023 est.)
from petroleum and other liquids: 4.469 million metric tonnes of CO2 (2023 est.)
from consumed natural gas: 5.419 million metric tonnes of CO2 (2023 est.)
comparison ranking: total emissions 106

Particulate matter emissions: 18.6 micrograms per cubic meter (2019 est.)

Waste and recycling: *municipal solid waste generated annually:* 800,000 tons (2024 est.)
percent of municipal solid waste recycled: 19.6% (2022 est.)

Total water withdrawal: *municipal:* 504.96 million cubic meters (2022)
industrial: 354.46 million cubic meters (2022)
agricultural: 433.96 million cubic meters (2022)

Total renewable water resources: 63.33 billion cubic meters (2022 est.)

GOVERNMENT

Country name: *conventional long form:* none
conventional short form: Georgia
local long form: Republic of Georgia
local short form: Sak'art'velo
former: Georgian Soviet Socialist Republic
etymology: the Western name probably derives from the name of the local people, the Gurz, whose name origin is uncertain; the native name "Sak'art'velo" means "Land of the Kartvelians" and refers to the core central Georgian region of Kartli

Government type: semi-presidential republic

Capital: *name:* Tbilisi
geographic coordinates: 41 41 N, 44 50 E
time difference: UTC+4 (9 hours ahead of Washington, DC, during Standard Time)
etymology: the name comes from the Georgian word *tbili*, meaning "warm" and referring to the hot sulfur springs in the area

Administrative divisions: 9 regions (*mkharebi*, singular - *mkhare*), 1 city (*kalaki*), and 2 autonomous republics (*avtomnoy respubliki*, singular - *avtom respublika*)
regions: Guria, Imereti, Kakheti, Kvemo Kartli, Mtskheta Mtianeti, Racha-Lechkhumi and Kvemo Svaneti, Samegrelo and Zemo Svaneti, Samtskhe-Javakheti, Shida Kartli; note - the breakaway region of South Ossetia consists of the northern part of Shida Kartli, eastern slivers of the Imereti region and Racha-Lechkhumi and Kvemo Svaneti, and part of western Mtskheta-Mtianeti
city: Tbilisi
autonomous republics: Abkhazia or Ap'khazet'is Avtonomiuri Respublika (Sokhumi), Ajaria or Acharis Avtonomiuri Respublika (Bat'umi)
note 1: the administrative centers of the two autonomous republics are shown in parentheses
note 2: the United States recognizes the breakaway regions of Abkhazia and South Ossetia as part of Georgia

Legal system: civil law system

Constitution: *history:* previous 1921, 1978 (based on 1977 Soviet Union constitution); latest approved 24 August 1995, effective 17 October 1995
amendment process: proposed as a draft law supported by more than one half of the Parliament membership or by petition of at least 200,000 voters; passage

requires support by at least three fourths of the Parliament membership in two successive sessions three months apart and the signature and promulgation by the president of Georgia

International law organization participation: accepts compulsory ICJ jurisdiction; accepts ICCt jurisdiction

Citizenship: *citizenship by birth:* no
citizenship by descent only: at least one parent must be a citizen of Georgia
dual citizenship recognized: no
residency requirement for naturalization: 10 years

Suffrage: 18 years of age; universal

Executive branch: *chief of state:* President Mikheil KAVELASHVILI (since 29 December 2024)
head of government: Prime Minister Irakli KOBAKHIDZE (since 8 February 2024)
cabinet: Cabinet of Ministers
election/appointment process: president elected by a 300-member College of Electors; prime minister nominated by Parliament, appointed by the president
most recent election date: 14 December 2024
election results: *2024:* Mikheil KAVELASHVILI (Georgian Dream Party) was formally inaugurated on 29 December 2024
2024: Irakli KOBAKHIDZE approved as prime minister by Parliamentary vote 84-10
2018: Salome ZOURABICHVILI elected president in second round; percent of vote in second round - Salome ZOURABICHVILI (independent, backed by Georgian Dream) 59.5%, Grigol VASHADZE (UNM) 40.5%; Irakli GARIBASHVILI approved as prime minister by Parliamentary vote 89-2
expected date of next election: 2029

Legislative branch: *legislature name:* Parliament (Sakartvelos Parlamenti)
legislative structure: unicameral
number of seats: 150 (all directly elected)
electoral system: proportional representation
scope of elections: full renewal
term in office: 4 years
most recent election date: 10/26/2024
parties elected and seats per party: Georgian Dream (89); Coalition for Changes (19); Unity - National Movement (16); Strong Georgia – Lelo, For people, For Liberty! (14); For Georgia (12)
percentage of women in chamber: 12.4%
expected date of next election: October 2028

Judicial branch: *highest court(s):* Supreme Court (consists of 28 judges organized into several specialized judicial chambers; number of judges determined by the president of Georgia); Constitutional Court (consists of 9 judges)
judge selection and term of office: Supreme Court judges nominated by the High Council of Justice (a 14-member body consisting of the Supreme Court chairperson, common court judges, and appointees of the president of Georgia) and appointed by Parliament; judges appointed for life; Constitutional Court judges appointed 3 each by the president, by Parliament, and by the Supreme Court judges; judges appointed for 10-year terms
subordinate courts: Courts of Appeal; regional (town) and district courts
note: the Abkhazian and Ajarian Autonomous republics each have a supreme court and a hierarchy of lower courts

Political parties: Citizens
European Socialists
For Georgia
Georgian Dream
Girchi
Law and Justice
Lelo for Georgia
National Democratic Party
People's Power
Progress and Freedom
Republican Party
State for the People
Strategy Aghmashenebeli
United National Movement or UNM
Victorious Georgia

Diplomatic representation in the US: *chief of mission:* Ambassador Tamar TALIASHVILI (since 24 July 2025)
chancery: 1824 R Street NW, Washington, DC 20009
telephone: [1] (202) 387-2390
FAX: [1] (202) 387-0864
email address and website: embgeo.usa@mfa.gov.ge
https://georgiaembassyusa.org/contact/
consulate(s) general: New York, San Francisco

Diplomatic representation from the US: *chief of mission:* Ambassador Robin L. DUNNIGAN (since 12 October 2023)
embassy: 29 Georgian-American Friendship Avenue, Didi Dighomi, Tbilisi, 0131
mailing address: 7060 Tbilisi Place, Washington, DC 20521-7060
telephone: [995] (32) 227-70-00
FAX: [995] (32) 253-23-10
email address and website: askconsultbilisi@state.gov
https://ge.usembassy.gov/

International organization participation: ADB, BSEC, CD, CE, CPLP (associate), EAPC, EBRD, FAO, G-11, GCTU, GUAM, IAEA, IBRD, ICAO, ICC (national committees), ICCt, ICRM, IDA, IFAD, IFC, IFRCS, ILO, IMF, IMO, Interpol, IOC, IOM, IPU, ISO (correspondent), ITSO, ITU, ITUC (NGOs), MIGA, OAS (observer), OIF (observer), OPCW, OSCE, PFP, SELEC (observer), UN, UNCTAD, UNESCO, UNIDO, UNWTO, UPU, WCO, WHO, WIPO, WMO, WTO

Independence: 9 April 1991 *(from the Soviet Union)*; *notable earlier date:* A.D. 1008 (Georgia unified under King BAGRAT III)

National holiday: Independence Day, 26 May (1918)
note: 26 May 1918 was the date of independence from Soviet Russia; 9 April 1991 was the date of independence from the Soviet Union

Flag: *description:* white rectangle with a central red cross extending to all four sides of the flag; each of the four quadrants displays a small red *bolnur-katskhuri* cross (also known as Bolnisi cross), which has equal-length arms that are slightly wider at the end than in the center
history: sometimes referred to as the Five-Cross Flag, the design is based on a 14th-century banner of the Kingdom of Georgia

National symbol(s): Saint George, lion

National color(s): red, white

National anthem(s): *title:* "Tavisupleba" (Liberty)
lyrics/music: Davit MAGRADSE/ Zakaria PALIASHVILI (adapted by Joseb KETSCHAKMADSE)
history: adopted 2004, after the Rose Revolution; based on music from the operas "Abesalom da Eteri" and "Daisi"

National heritage: *total World Heritage Sites:* 4 (3 cultural, 1 natural)
selected World Heritage Site locales: Gelati Monastery (c); Historical Monuments of Mtskheta (c); Upper Svaneti (c); Colchic Rainforests and Wetlands (n)

ECONOMY

Economic overview: upper-middle income, fast-growing South Caucasus economy; regionally focused exporter of cars, metal ores, and energy; financial and migrant inflows resulting from Ukraine conflict; EU accession talks suspended over disputed election and foreign influence law; low inflation but persistent high unemployment

Real GDP (purchasing power parity): $91.849 billion (2024 est.)
$83.935 billion (2023 est.)
$77.838 billion (2022 est.)
note: data in 2021 dollars
comparison ranking: 100

Real GDP growth rate: 9.4% (2024 est.)
7.8% (2023 est.)
11% (2022 est.)
note: annual GDP % growth based on constant local currency
comparison ranking: 4

Real GDP per capita: $25,000 (2024 est.)
$22,600 (2023 est.)
$21,000 (2022 est.)
note: data in 2021 dollars
comparison ranking: 89

GDP (official exchange rate): $33.776 billion (2024 est.)
note: data in current dollars at official exchange rate

Inflation rate (consumer prices): 1.1% (2024 est.)
2.5% (2023 est.)
11.9% (2022 est.)
note: annual % change based on consumer prices
comparison ranking: 25

GDP - composition, by sector of origin: *agriculture:* 5.4% (2024 est.)
industry: 19.1% (2024 est.)
services: 62.8% (2024 est.)
note: figures may not total 100% due to non-allocated consumption not captured in sector-reported data
comparison rankings: agriculture 109; industry 137; services 69

GDP - composition, by end use: *household consumption:* 71.3% (2024 est.)
government consumption: 13.4% (2024 est.)
investment in fixed capital: 22% (2024 est.)
investment in inventories: 0.8% (2024 est.)
exports of goods and services: 48.4% (2024 est.)
imports of goods and services: -56% (2024 est.)
note: figures may not total 100% due to rounding or gaps in data collection

Agricultural products: milk, grapes, potatoes, maize, wheat, tangerines/mandarins, tomatoes, barley, apples, eggs (2023)
note: top ten agricultural products based on tonnage

Industries: steel, machine tools, electrical appliances, mining (manganese, copper, gold), chemicals, wood products, wine

Industrial production growth rate: 5.4% (2024 est.)
note: annual % change in industrial value added based on constant local currency
comparison ranking: 39

Labor force: 1.833 million (2024 est.)
note: number of people ages 15 or older who are employed or seeking work
comparison ranking: 128

Unemployment rate: 11.5% (2024 est.)
11.6% (2023 est.)
11.7% (2022 est.)
note: % of labor force seeking employment
comparison ranking: 158

Youth unemployment rate (ages 15-24): *total:* 29.9% (2024 est.)
male: 28.4% (2024 est.)
female: 32.4% (2024 est.)
note: % of labor force ages 15-24 seeking employment
comparison ranking: total 22

Population below poverty line: 11.8% (2023 est.)
note: % of population with income below national poverty line

Gini Index coefficient - distribution of family income: 34.8 (2023 est.)
note: index (0-100) of income distribution; higher values represent greater inequality
comparison ranking: 78

Average household expenditures: *on food:* 39% of household expenditures (2023 est.)
on alcohol and tobacco: 3.8% of household expenditures (2023 est.)

Household income or consumption by percentage share: *lowest 10%:* 2.7% (2023 est.)
highest 10%: 26.9% (2023 est.)
note: % share of income accruing to lowest and highest 10% of population

Remittances: 11.8% of GDP (2024 est.)
13.7% of GDP (2023 est.)
15.4% of GDP (2022 est.)
note: personal transfers and compensation between resident and non-resident individuals/households/entities

Budget: *revenues:* $8.686 billion (2023 est.)
expenditures: $9.307 billion (2023 est.)
note: central government revenues (excluding grants) and expenditures converted to US dollars at average official exchange rate for year indicated

Public debt: 43.4% of GDP (2023 est.)
note: central government debt as a % of GDP
comparison ranking: 122

Taxes and other revenues: 23.6% (of GDP) (2023 est.)
note: central government tax revenue as a % of GDP
comparison ranking: 26

Current account balance: -$1.491 billion (2024 est.)
-$1.709 billion (2023 est.)
-$1.105 billion (2022 est.)
note: balance of payments - net trade and primary/secondary income in current dollars
comparison ranking: 139

Exports: $16.321 billion (2024 est.)
$15.173 billion (2023 est.)
$13.24 billion (2022 est.)
note: balance of payments - exports of goods and services in current dollars
comparison ranking: 98

Exports - partners: Azerbaijan 13%, Turkey 11%, Armenia 11%, Russia 10%, Kyrgyzstan 8% (2023)
note: top five export partners based on percentage share of exports

Exports - commodities: cars, copper ore, electricity, garments, wine (2023)
note: top five export commodities based on value in dollars

Imports: $18.915 billion (2024 est.)
$17.816 billion (2023 est.)
$15.665 billion (2022 est.)
note: balance of payments - imports of goods and services in current dollars
comparison ranking: 98

Imports - partners: Turkey 16%, USA 13%, Russia 11%, China 8%, Germany 6% (2023)
note: top five import partners based on percentage share of imports

Imports - commodities: cars, refined petroleum, packaged medicine, natural gas, garments (2023)
note: top five import commodities based on value in dollars

Reserves of foreign exchange and gold: $4.447 billion (2024 est.)
$5.002 billion (2023 est.)
$4.886 billion (2022 est.)
note: holdings of gold (year-end prices)/foreign exchange/special drawing rights in current dollars
comparison ranking: 104

Debt - external: $9.085 billion (2023 est.)
note: present value of external debt in current US dollars
comparison ranking: 52

Exchange rates: laris (GEL) per US dollar -

Exchange rates: 2.721 (2024 est.)
2.628 (2023 est.)
2.916 (2022 est.)
3.222 (2021 est.)
3.109 (2020 est.)

ENERGY

Electricity access: *electrification - total population:* 100% (2022 est.)

Electricity: *installed generating capacity:* 4.526 million kW (2023 est.)
consumption: 12.569 billion kWh (2023 est.)
exports: 4.913 billion kWh (2023 est.)
imports: 4.234 billion kWh (2023 est.)
transmission/distribution losses: 1.148 billion kWh (2023 est.)
comparison rankings: installed generating capacity 94; consumption 96; exports 40; imports 49; transmission/distribution losses 106

Electricity generation sources: *fossil fuels:* 23.9% of total installed capacity (2023 est.)
wind: 0.6% of total installed capacity (2023 est.)
hydroelectricity: 75.5% of total installed capacity (2023 est.)

Coal: *production:* 148,000 metric tons (2023 est.)
consumption: 384,000 metric tons (2023 est.)
exports: 80 metric tons (2023 est.)
imports: 223,000 metric tons (2023 est.)
proven reserves: 900.999 million metric tons (2023 est.)

Petroleum: *total petroleum production:* 300 bbl/day (2023 est.)
refined petroleum consumption: 34,000 bbl/day (2023 est.)
crude oil estimated reserves: 35 million barrels (2021 est.)

Natural gas: *production:* 10.77 million cubic meters (2023 est.)
consumption: 2.775 billion cubic meters (2023 est.)
imports: 2.764 billion cubic meters (2023 est.)
proven reserves: 8.495 billion cubic meters (2021 est.)

Energy consumption per capita: 56.076 million Btu/person (2023 est.)
comparison ranking: 88

COMMUNICATIONS

Telephones - fixed lines: *total subscriptions:* 278,000 (2023 est.)
subscriptions per 100 inhabitants: 7 (2023 est.)
comparison ranking: total subscriptions 109

Telephones - mobile cellular: *total subscriptions:* 5.91 million (2023 est.)
subscriptions per 100 inhabitants: 156 (2022 est.)
comparison ranking: total subscriptions 121

Broadcast media: state-owned Georgian Public Broadcaster (GPB) includes Channel 1, Channel 2, and Adjara TV; independent commercial TV broadcasters include Imedi, Rustavi 2, Pirveli TV, Maestro, Kavkasia, Georgian Dream Studios (GDS), Obiektivi, Mtavari Arkhi, and TOK TV (Russian language); Tabula and Post TV are web-based TV outlets; Georgian Orthodox Church operates a satellite-based television station called Unanimity; 26 regional TV broadcasters; TV shifted to digital in 2015; several dozen private radio stations; GPB operates 2 radio stations (2019)

Internet country code: .ge

Internet users: *percent of population:* 82% (2023 est.)

Broadband - fixed subscriptions: *total:* 1.1 million (2023 est.)
subscriptions per 100 inhabitants: 29 (2023 est.)
comparison ranking: total 77

TRANSPORTATION

Civil aircraft registration country code prefix: 4L

Airports: 21 (2025)
comparison ranking: 132

Heliports: 4 (2025)
comparison ranking: 111

Railways: *total:* 1,363 km (2014)
narrow gauge: 37 km (2014) 0.912-m gauge (37 km electrified)
broad gauge: 1,326 km (2014) 1.520-m gauge (1,251 km electrified)

Merchant marine: *total:* 26 (2023)
by type: general cargo 3, other 23
comparison ranking: total 139

Ports: *total ports:* 3 (2024)
large: 0
medium: 0
small: 1
very small: 2
ports with oil terminals: 2
key ports: Batumi, Sokhumi, Supsa Marine Terminal

MILITARY AND SECURITY

Military and security forces: Georgian Defense Forces (GDF; aka Defense Forces of Georgia, DFG): Ground Forces, Air Force, Special Operations Forces, National Guard

Ministry of Internal Affairs: Police, Border Police of Georgia, Coast Guard of Georgia (includes naval forces, which were merged with the Coast Guard in 2009) (2025)

Military expenditures: 1.7% of GDP (2024 est.)
1.7% of GDP (2023 est.)
1.6% of GDP (2022 est.)
1.5% of GDP (2021 est.)
1.6% of GDP (2020 est.)

Military and security service personnel strengths: the Georgia Defense Forces are authorized up to 37,000 personnel (2025)

Military equipment inventories and acquisitions: the majority of the military's inventory consists of Soviet-era weapons and equipment, some of which has been upgraded; it has smaller quantities of mostly second-hand material from such countries as Israel, Turkey, and the US, as well as some domestically produced equipment; Georgia has a small defense industry which produces such items as small arms and light armored vehicles (2024)

Military service age and obligation: 18-35 years of age for voluntary military service for men and women; conscription was abolished in 2016, but reinstated in 2017 for men 18-27 years of age; conscript service obligation is up to 11 months (six months of service in a combat unit; or eight months of service in another security organization; or 11 months of service in junior command positions and predetermined specialties (2024)
note 1: approximately 6-7,000 individuals are called up annually for conscription for service; conscripts serve in the Defense Forces, the Ministry of Internal Affairs, or the Ministry of Corrections
note 2: as of 2022, women made up about 8% of the military's full-time personnel

Military - note: the Defense Forces of Georgia (DFG) are responsible for protecting the independence, sovereignty, and territorial integrity of the country; the DFG also provides units for multinational military operations abroad and supports the Border Police in border protection and civil authorities in counter-terrorist operations, if requested; it is focused primarily on Russia, which maintains military bases and troops in occupied Abkhazia and South Ossetia; a five-day conflict with Russian forces in 2008 resulted in the defeat and expulsion of Georgian forces from the breakaway regions
Georgia is not a member of NATO but has had a relationship with the Alliance since 1992 and declared its aspiration to join in 2002; the military is working to make itself more compatible with NATO and has participated in multinational exercises and security operations abroad with NATO, such as Afghanistan, where it was one of the top non-NATO contributors, and Kosovo; the DFG has also contributed troops to EU and UN missions (2025)

TRANSNATIONAL ISSUES

Refugees and internally displaced persons: *refugees*: 31,791 (2024 est.)

IDPs: 347,754 (2024 est.)
stateless persons: 488 (2024 est.)

GERMANY

INTRODUCTION

Background: As Europe's largest economy and second most-populous nation (after Russia), Germany is a key member of the continent's economic, political, and defense organizations. European power struggles immersed Germany in two devastating world wars in the first half of the 20th century and left the country occupied by the victorious Allied powers of the US, UK, France, and the Soviet Union in 1945. With the advent of the Cold War, two German states were formed in 1949: the western Federal Republic of Germany (FRG) and the eastern German Democratic Republic (GDR). The democratic FRG embedded itself in key western economic and security organizations, including the EC (now the EU) and NATO, while the communist GDR was on the front line of the Soviet-led Warsaw Pact. The decline of the Soviet Union and the end of the Cold War allowed German reunification to occur in 1990. Since then, Germany has expended considerable funds to bring eastern productivity and wages up to western standards. In January 1999, Germany and 10 other EU countries introduced a common European exchange currency, the euro.

GEOGRAPHY

Location: Central Europe, bordering the Baltic Sea and the North Sea, between the Netherlands and Poland, south of Denmark

Geographic coordinates: 51 00 N, 9 00 E

Map references: Europe

Area: *total*: 357,022 sq km
land: 348,672 sq km
water: 8,350 sq km
comparison ranking: total 64

Area - comparative: three times the size of Pennsylvania; slightly smaller than Montana

Land boundaries: *total*: 3,694 km
border countries (9): Austria 801 km; Belgium 133 km; Czechia 704 km; Denmark 140 km; France 418 km; Luxembourg 128 km; Netherlands 575 km; Poland 447 km; Switzerland 348 km

Coastline: 2,389 km

Maritime claims: *territorial sea*: 12 nm
exclusive economic zone: 200 nm
continental shelf: 200-m depth or to the depth of exploitation

Climate: temperate and marine; cool, cloudy, wet winters and summers; occasional warm mountain (foehn) wind

Terrain: lowlands in north, uplands in center, Bavarian Alps in south

Elevation: *highest point*: Zugspitze 2,963 m
lowest point: Neuendorf bei Wilster -3.5 m
mean elevation: 263 m

Natural resources: coal, lignite, natural gas, iron ore, copper, nickel, uranium, potash, salt, construction materials, timber, arable land

Land use: *agricultural land*: 47.5% (2022 est.)
arable land: 33.4% (2022 est.)
permanent crops: 0.6% (2022 est.)
permanent pasture: 13.5% (2022 est.)
forest: 32.7% (2022 est.)
other: 19.8% (2022 est.)

Irrigated land: 5,065 sq km (2020)

Major lakes (area sq km): *fresh water lake(s)*: Lake Constance (shared with Switzerland and Austria) - 540 sq km
salt water lake(s): Stettiner Haff/Zalew Szczecinski (shared with Poland) - 900 sq km

Major rivers (by length in km): Donau (Danube) river source (shared with Austria, Slovakia, Hungary, Croatia, Serbia, Bulgaria, Ukraine, Moldova, and Romania [m]) - 2,888 km; Elbe river mouth (shared with Czechia [s]) - 1,252 km; Rhein (Rhine) (shared with Switzerland [s], France, and Netherlands [m]) - 1,233 km
note: [s] after country name indicates river source; [m] after country name indicates river mouth

Major watersheds (area sq km): Atlantic Ocean drainage: Rhine-Maas (198,735 sq km), *(Black Sea)* Danube (795,656 sq km)

Population distribution: second most populous country in Europe; a fairly even distribution throughout most of the country, with urban areas attracting larger and denser populations, particularly in the far-western part of the industrial state of North Rhine-Westphalia

Natural hazards: flooding

Geography - note: strategic location on North European Plain and along the entrance to the Baltic Sea; most major rivers in Germany – the Rhine, Weser, Oder, Elbe – flow northward; the Danube, which originates in the Black Forest, flows eastward

PEOPLE AND SOCIETY

Population: *total*: 84,119,100 (2024 est.)
male: 41,572,702
female: 42,546,398
comparison rankings: total 19; male 19; female 18

Nationality: *noun*: German(s)
adjective: German

Ethnic groups: German 85.4%, Turkish 1.8%, Ukrainian 1.4%, Syrian 1.1%, Romanian 1%, Poland 1%, other/stateless/unspecified 8.3% (2022 est.)
note: data represent population by nationality

Languages: German (official); note - Danish, Frisian, Sorbian, and Romani are official minority languages; Low German, Danish, North Frisian, Sater Frisian, Lower Sorbian, Upper Sorbian, and Romani are recognized as regional languages
major-language sample(s):

Das World Factbook, die unverzichtbare Quelle für grundlegende Informationen. (German)

Religions: Roman Catholic 24.8%, Protestant 22.6%, Muslim 3.7%, other 5.1%, none 43.8% (2022 est.)

Age structure: *0-14 years:* 13.8% (male 5,925,800/ female 5,688,603)
15-64 years: 62.5% (male 26,705,657/female 25,875,865)
65 years and over: 23.7% (2024 est.) (male 8,941,245/ female 10,981,930)

Dependency ratios: *total dependency ratio:* 60 (2024 est.)
youth dependency ratio: 22.1 (2024 est.)
elderly dependency ratio: 37.9 (2024 est.)
potential support ratio: 2.6 (2024 est.)

Median age: *total:* 46.8 years (2024 est.)
male: 45.5 years
female: 48.3 years
comparison ranking: total 9

Population growth rate: -0.12% (2024 est.)
comparison ranking: 206

Birth rate: 8.9 births/1,000 population (2024 est.)
comparison ranking: 200

Death rate: 12 deaths/1,000 population (2024 est.)
comparison ranking: 15

Net migration rate: 1.8 migrant(s)/1,000 population (2024 est.)
comparison ranking: 53

Population distribution: second most populous country in Europe; a fairly even distribution throughout most of the country, with urban areas attracting larger and denser populations, particularly in the far-western part of the industrial state of North Rhine-Westphalia

Urbanization: *urban population:* 77.8% of total population (2023)
rate of urbanization: 0.13% annual rate of change (2020-25 est.)

Major urban areas - population: 3.574 million BERLIN (capital), 1.788 million Hamburg, 1.576 million Munich, 1.144 million Cologne, 796,000 Frankfurt (2023)

Sex ratio: *at birth:* 1.05 male(s)/female
0-14 years: 1.04 male(s)/female
15-64 years: 1.03 male(s)/female
65 years and over: 0.81 male(s)/female
total population: 0.98 male(s)/female (2024 est.)

Mother's mean age at first birth: 29.9 years (2020 est.)

Maternal mortality ratio: 4 deaths/100,000 live births (2023 est.)
comparison ranking: 182

Infant mortality rate: *total:* 3.1 deaths/1,000 live births (2024 est.)
male: 3.5 deaths/1,000 live births
female: 2.7 deaths/1,000 live births
comparison ranking: total 206

Life expectancy at birth: *total population:* 81.9 years (2024 est.)
male: 79.6 years
female: 84.4 years
comparison ranking: total population 38

Total fertility rate: 1.58 children born/woman (2024 est.)
comparison ranking: 190

Gross reproduction rate: 0.77 (2024 est.)

Drinking water source: *improved: urban:* 100% of population (2022 est.)
rural: 100% of population (2022 est.)
total: 100% of population (2022 est.)
unimproved: urban: 0% of population (2022 est.)
rural: 0% of population (2022 est.)
total: 0% of population (2022 est.)

Health expenditure: 12.7% of GDP (2022)
20.5% of national budget (2022 est.)

Physician density: 4.53 physicians/1,000 population (2022)

Hospital bed density: 7.8 beds/1,000 population (2020 est.)

Sanitation facility access: *improved: urban:* 100% of population (2022 est.)
rural: 100% of population (2022 est.)
total: 100% of population (2022 est.)
unimproved: urban: 0% of population (2022 est.)
rural: 0% of population (2022 est.)
total: 0% of population (2022 est.)

Obesity - adult prevalence rate: 22.3% (2016)
comparison ranking: 79

Alcohol consumption per capita: *total:* 10.56 liters of pure alcohol (2019 est.)
beer: 5.57 liters of pure alcohol (2019 est.)
wine: 3.02 liters of pure alcohol (2019 est.)
spirits: 1.97 liters of pure alcohol (2019 est.)
other alcohols: 0 liters of pure alcohol (2019 est.)
comparison ranking: total 19

Tobacco use: *total:* 17.2% (2025 est.)
male: 19.4% (2025 est.)
female: 15% (2025 est.)
comparison ranking: total 91

Children under the age of 5 years underweight: 0.5% (2014/17)
comparison ranking: 112

Currently married women (ages 15-49): 54.4% (2023 est.)

Education expenditure: 4.5% of GDP (2023 est.)
9.3% national budget (2023 est.)
comparison ranking: Education expenditure (% GDP) 85

School life expectancy (primary to tertiary education): *total:* 17 years (2023 est.)
male: 17 years (2023 est.)
female: 17 years (2023 est.)

ENVIRONMENT

Environmental issues: air pollution and acid rain from coal-burning utilities and industries; water pollution from raw sewage and industrial effluents; hazardous waste disposal

International environmental agreements: *party to:* Air Pollution, Air Pollution-Heavy Metals, Air Pollution-Multi-effect Protocol, Air Pollution-Nitrogen Oxides, Air Pollution-Persistent Organic Pollutants, Air Pollution-Sulphur 85, Air Pollution-Sulphur 94, Air Pollution-Volatile Organic Compounds, Antarctic-Environmental Protection, Antarctic-Marine Living Resources, Antarctic Seals, Antarctic Treaty, Biodiversity, Climate Change, Climate Change-Kyoto Protocol, Climate Change-Paris Agreement, Comprehensive Nuclear Test Ban, Desertification, Endangered Species, Environmental Modification, Hazardous Wastes, Law of the Sea, Marine Dumping-London Convention, Marine Dumping-London Protocol, Nuclear Test Ban, Ozone Layer Protection, Ship Pollution, Tropical Timber 2006, Wetlands, Whaling
signed, but not ratified: none of the selected agreements

Climate: temperate and marine; cool, cloudy, wet winters and summers; occasional warm mountain (foehn) wind

Urbanization: *urban population:* 77.8% of total population (2023)
rate of urbanization: 0.13% annual rate of change (2020-25 est.)

Carbon dioxide emissions: 600.192 million metric tonnes of CO2 (2023 est.)
from coal and metallurgical coke: 163.407 million metric tonnes of CO2 (2023 est.)
from petroleum and other liquids: 277.688 million metric tonnes of CO2 (2023 est.)
from consumed natural gas: 159.097 million metric tonnes of CO2 (2023 est.)
comparison ranking: total emissions 10

Particulate matter emissions: 10.6 micrograms per cubic meter (2019 est.)

Methane emissions: *energy:* 476.2 kt (2022-2024 est.)
agriculture: 1,197.8 kt (2019-2021 est.)
waste: 459 kt (2019-2021 est.)
other: 110 kt (2019-2021 est.)

Waste and recycling: *municipal solid waste generated annually:* 50.628 million tons (2024 est.)
percent of municipal solid waste recycled: 49.8% (2022 est.)

Total water withdrawal: *municipal:* 10.713 billion cubic meters (2022 est.)
industrial: 14.005 billion cubic meters (2022 est.)
agricultural: 1.075 billion cubic meters (2022 est.)

Total renewable water resources: 154 billion cubic meters (2022 est.)

Geoparks: *total global geoparks and regional networks:* 8
global geoparks and regional networks: Bergstraße-Odenwald; Harz, Braunschweiger Land; Swabian Alb; TERRA.vita; Vulkaneifel; Thuringia Inselsberg -Drei Gleichen; Muskauer Faltenbogen /Łuk Mużakowa (includes Poland); Ries (2023)

GOVERNMENT

Country name: *conventional long form:* Federal Republic of Germany
conventional short form: Germany
local long form: Bundesrepublik Deutschland
local short form: Deutschland
former: German Reich
etymology: the origin of the name is unclear; it may come from Celtic words meaning "neighboring people," or it may derive from Germanic words meaning either "spear man" or "head man;" the native designation "Deutsch" comes from the Old High German "diutisc" meaning "national"

Government type: federal parliamentary republic

Capital: *name:* Berlin
geographic coordinates: 52 31 N, 13 24 E
time difference: UTC+1 (6 hours ahead of Washington, DC, during Standard Time)
daylight saving time: +1hr, begins last Sunday in March; ends last Sunday in October
etymology: the origin of the name is unclear but may be related to the Old Slavic (Polabian) word *berl* or *birl*, meaning "swamp" and referring to the original settlement site by the Spree River

Administrative divisions: 16 states (*Laender*, singular - *Land*); Baden-Wuerttemberg, Bayern (Bavaria), Berlin, Brandenburg, Bremen, Hamburg, Hessen (Hesse), Mecklenburg-Vorpommern (Mecklenburg-Western Pomerania), Niedersachsen (Lower Saxony), Nordrhein-Westfalen (North Rhine-Westphalia), Rheinland-Pfalz (Rhineland-Palatinate), Saarland, Sachsen (Saxony), Sachsen-Anhalt (Saxony-Anhalt), Schleswig-Holstein, Thueringen (Thuringia)
note: Bayern, Sachsen, and Thueringen refer to themselves as free states (*Freistaaten*, singular - *Freistaat*), while Bremen calls itself a Free Hanseatic City (*Freie Hansestadt*) and Hamburg considers itself a Free and Hanseatic City (*Freie und Hansestadt*)

Legal system: civil law system

Constitution: *history:* previous 1919 (Weimar Constitution); latest drafted 10-23 August 1948, approved 12 May 1949, promulgated 23 May 1949, entered into force 24 May 1949
amendment process: proposed by Parliament; passage and enactment into law require two-thirds majority vote by both the Bundesrat (upper house) and the Bundestag (lower house) of Parliament; articles including those on basic human rights and freedoms cannot be amended

International law organization participation: accepts compulsory ICJ jurisdiction with reservations; accepts ICCt jurisdiction

Citizenship: *citizenship by birth:* no
citizenship by descent only: at least one parent must be a German citizen or a resident alien who has lived in Germany at least 8 years
dual citizenship recognized: yes, but requires prior permission from government
residency requirement for naturalization: 8 years

Suffrage: 18 years of age; universal; age 16 for some state and municipal elections

Executive branch: *chief of state:* President Frank-Walter STEINMEIER (since 19 March 2017)
head of government: Chancellor Friedrich MERZ (since 6 May 2025)
cabinet: Cabinet or Bundesminister (Federal Ministers) recommended by the chancellor, appointed by the president
election/appointment process: president indirectly elected by a Federal Convention consisting of all members of the Federal Parliament (Bundestag) and an equivalent number of delegates indirectly elected by the state parliaments; president serves a 5-year term (eligible for a second term); following the most recent Federal Parliament election, the party or coalition with the most representatives usually elects the chancellor, who is appointed by the president to serve a renewable 4-year term
most recent election date: president: 13 February 2022
chancellor: 6 May 2025
election results: 2025: Friedrich MERZ (CDU) elected chancellor in second round; Federal Parliament vote -325 to 289
2022: Frank-Walter STEINMEIER reelected president; Federal Convention vote count -Frank-Walter STEINMEIER (SPD) 1,045, Max OTTE (CDU) 140, Gerhard TRABERT (The Left) 96, Stefanie GEBAUER (Free Voters) 58, abstentions 86
expected date of next election: president: February 2027

Legislative branch: *legislative structure:* bicameral
note: due to Germany's recognition of the concepts of "overhang" (when a party's share of the nationwide votes would entitle it to fewer seats than the number of individual constituency seats won in an election under Germany's mixed member proportional system) and "leveling" (whereby additional seats are elected to supplement the members directly elected by each constituency in order to ensure that each party's share of the total seats is roughly proportional to the party's overall shares of votes at the national level), the 20th Bundestag is the largest to date

Legislative branch - lower chamber: *chamber name:* German Bundestag (Deutscher Bundestag)
number of seats: 630 (all directly elected)
electoral system: mixed system
scope of elections: full renewal
term in office: 4 years
most recent election date: 2/23/2025
parties elected and seats per party: Christian Democratic Union (CDU) (164); Alternative for Germany (AfD) (152); Social Democratic Party (SPD) (120); Green Party (85); Left Party (Die Linke) (64); Christian Social Union of Bavaria (CSU) (44); Other (1)
percentage of women in chamber: 32.4%
expected date of next election: February 2029
note 1: total seats can vary each electoral term; currently includes 4 seats for independent members; approximately one-half of members directly elected in multi-seat constituencies by proportional representation vote and approximately one-half directly elected in single-seat constituencies by simple majority vote; members' terms vary depending on the states they represent
note 2: the 20th Bundestag is the largest to date, due to Germany's recognition of "overhang" (when a party's share of the nationwide votes would entitle it to fewer seats than the number of individual constituency seats won in an election) and "leveling" (when additional seats are elected to supplement the members directly elected in order to ensure that each party's share of the total seats is roughly proportional to its overall share of votes at the national level)

Legislative branch - upper chamber: *chamber name:* Federal Council (Bundesrat)
number of seats: 69 (all appointed)
parties elected and seats per party: SPD 23; CDU 17; Green Party 15; Left Party 4; CSU 3; FW 3; FDP 2; other 2
percentage of women in chamber: 34.8%

Judicial branch: *highest court(s):* Federal Court of Justice (court consists of 127 judges, including the court president, vice presidents, presiding judges, other judges; organized into 25 Senates subdivided into 12 civil panels, 5 criminal panels, and 8 special panels); Federal Constitutional Court or Bundesverfassungsgericht (consists of 2 Senates each subdivided into 3 chambers, each with a chairman and 8 members)
judge selection and term of office: Federal Court of Justice judges selected by the Judges Election Committee, which consists of the Secretaries of Justice from each of the 16 federated states and 16 members appointed by the Federal Parliament; judges appointed by the president; judges serve until mandatory retirement at age 65; half of Federal Constitutional Court judges are elected by the House of Representatives and half by the Senate; judges appointed for 12-year terms with mandatory retirement at age 68
subordinate courts: Federal Administrative Court; Federal Finance Court; Federal Labor Court; Federal Social Court; each of the 16 federated states or Land has its own constitutional court and a hierarchy of ordinary (civil, criminal, family) and specialized (administrative, finance, labor, social) courts; two English-speaking commercial courts opened in 2020 in the state of Baden-Wuerttemberg – the Stuttgart Commercial Court and the Mannheim Commercial Court

Political parties: Alliance '90/Greens
Alternative for Germany or AfD
Christian Democratic Union or CDU
Christian Social Union or CSU
Free Democratic Party or FDP
Free Voters or FW
The Left or Die Linke
Social Democratic Party or SPD

Diplomatic representation in the US: *chief of mission:* Ambassador Jens HANEFELD (since 5 September 2025)
chancery: 4645 Reservoir Road NW, Washington, DC 20007
telephone: [1] (202) 298-4000
FAX: [1] (202) 298-4261
email address and website: info@washington.diplo.de
https://www.germany.info/us-en
consulate(s) general: Atlanta, Boston, Chicago, Houston, Los Angeles, Miami, New York, San Francisco

Diplomatic representation from the US: *chief of mission:* Ambassador (vacant); Chargé d'Affaires Alan MELTZER (since July 2024)
embassy: Pariser Platz 2, 10117 Berlin
Clayallee 170, 14191 Berlin (administrative services)
mailing address: 5090 Berlin Place, Washington DC 20521-5090
telephone: [49] (30) 8305-0
FAX: [49] (30) 8305-1215
email address and website: BerlinPCO@state.gov
https://de.usembassy.gov/
consulate(s) general: Dusseldorf, Frankfurt am Main, Hamburg, Leipzig, Munich

International organization participation: ADB (nonregional member), AfDB (nonregional member), Arctic Council (observer), Australia Group, BIS, BSEC (observer), CBSS, CD, CDB, CE, CERN, EAPC, EBRD, ECB, EIB, EITI (implementing country), EMU, ESA, EU, FAO, FATF, G-5, G-7, G-8, G-10, G-20, IADB, IAEA, IBRD, ICAO, ICC (national committees), ICCt, ICRM, IDA, IEA, IFAD, IFC, IFRCS, IGAD (partners), IHO, ILO, IMF, IMO, IMSO, Interpol, IOC, IOM, IPU, ISO, ITSO, ITU, ITUC (NGOs), MIGA, MINURSO, NATO, NEA, NSG, OAS (observer), OECD, OPCW, OSCE, Pacific Alliance (observer), Paris Club, PCA, Schengen Convention, SELEC (observer), SICA (observer), UN, UNAMID, UNCTAD, UNESCO, UNHCR, UNHRC, UNIDO, UNIFIL, UNMISS, UNOOSA, UNRWA, UNSOM, UNWTO, UPU, Wassenaar Arrangement, WCO, WHO, WIPO, WMO, WTO, ZC

Independence: 18 January 1871 (establishment of the German Empire); divided into four zones of occupation (UK, US, USSR, and France) in 1945 after World War II; Federal Republic of Germany (FRG or West Germany) proclaimed on 23 May 1949 and included the former UK, US, and French zones; German Democratic Republic (GDR or East Germany) proclaimed on 7 October 1949 and included the former USSR zone; West Germany and East Germany unified on 3 October 1990, with all four powers formally relinquishing rights on 15 March 1991; notable earlier dates: 10 August 843 (Eastern Francia established from the division of the Carolingian Empire); 2 February 962 (crowning of OTTO I, recognized as the first Holy Roman Emperor)

National holiday: German Unity Day, 3 October (1990)

Flag: *description:* three equal horizontal bands of black (top), red, and gold
history: the colors can be traced back to the medieval banner of the Holy Roman Emperor –a black eagle with red claws and beak on a gold field

National symbol(s): eagle

National color(s): black, red, yellow

National coat of arms: Germany's coat of arms is the world's oldest, said to date back to 1200, and uses the country's national colors; it features the oldest European national symbol, an eagle known as the *Bundesadler* (Federal Eagle); the coat of arms has varied over time for military or political reasons, but the eagle has always been part of the design; the Federal Republic of Germany adopted this version in 1950

National anthem(s): *title:* "Lied der Deutschen"(Song of the Germans)
lyrics/music: August Heinrich HOFFMANN VON FALLERSLEBEN/Franz Joseph HAYDN
history: first adopted 1922; the anthem, also known as "Deutschlandlied" (Song of Germany), was originally adopted for its connection to the March 1848 liberal revolution; the Nazis later appropriated the first verse – specifically the phrase "Deutschland, Deutschland ueber alles" (Germany, Germany above all) – to promote nationalism, and the anthem was banned after 1945; in 1952, West Germany adopted the third verse as its national anthem; in 1990, it became the national anthem for the reunited Germany

National heritage: *total World Heritage Sites:* 55 (53 cultural, 2 natural)
selected World Heritage Site locales: Museumsinsel (Museum Island), Berlin (c); Palaces and Parks of Potsdam and Berlin (c); Speyer Cathedral (c); Aachen Cathedral (c); Bauhaus and its Sites in Weimar, Dessau, and Bernau (c); Caves and Ice Age Art in the Swabian Jura (c); Roman Monuments, Cathedral of St. Peter, and Church of Our Lady in Trier (c); Hanseatic City of Lübeck (c); Old Town of Regensburg with Stadtamhof (c); Würzburg Residence with the Court Gardens and Residence Square (c); Pilgrimage Church of Wies (c); Castles of Augustusburg and Falkenlust at Brühl (c); St Mary's Cathedral and St Michael's Church at Hildesheim (c); Abbey and Altenmünster of Lorsch (c); Maulbronn Monastery Complex (c); Collegiate Church, Castle and Old Town of Quedlinburg (c); Cologne Cathedral (c); Castle Church in Wittenberg (c); Classical Weimar (c); Wartburg Castle (c); Garden Kingdom of Dessau-Wörlitz (c); Monastic Island of Reichenau (c); Berlin Modernism Housing Estates (c); Prehistoric Pile Dwellings around the Alps (c); Moravian Church Settlements (c); Speicherstadt and Kontorhaus District with Chilehaus (c); The Architectural Work of Le Corbusier, an Outstanding Contribution to the Modern Movement (c); Archaeological Border complex of Hedeby and the Danevirke (c); Naumburg Cathedral (c); Mathildenhöhe Darmstadt (c); ShUM Sites of Speyer, Worms and Mainz (c); The Great Spa Towns of Europe (c); Jewish-Medieval Heritage of Erfurt (c); Schwerin Residence Ensemble (c); The Palaces of King Ludwig II of Bavaria: Neuschwanstein, Linderhof, Schachen and Herrenchiemsee (c)

ECONOMY

Economic overview: leading export-driven, core EU and eurozone economy; key automotive, chemical, engineering, finance, and green energy industries; growth stalled by energy crisis and declining exports; tight labor market with falling working-age population; fiscal rebalancing with phaseout of energy price supports

Real GDP (purchasing power parity): $5.247 trillion (2024 est.)
$5.26 trillion (2023 est.)
$5.274 trillion (2022 est.)
note: data in 2021 dollars
comparison ranking: 6

Real GDP growth rate: -0.2% (2024 est.)
-0.3% (2023 est.)
1.4% (2022 est.)
note: annual GDP % growth based on constant local currency
comparison ranking: 193

Real GDP per capita: $62,800 (2024 est.)
$62,700 (2023 est.)
$62,900 (2022 est.)
note: data in 2021 dollars
comparison ranking: 28

GDP (official exchange rate): $4.66 trillion (2024 est.)
note: data in current dollars at official exchange rate

Inflation rate (consumer prices): 2.3% (2024 est.)
5.9% (2023 est.)
6.9% (2022 est.)
note: annual % change based on consumer prices
comparison ranking: 65

GDP - composition, by sector of origin: *agriculture:* 0.8% (2024 est.)
industry: 25.8% (2024 est.)
services: 63.9% (2024 est.)
note: figures may not total 100% due to non-allocated consumption not captured in sector-reported data
comparison rankings: agriculture 180; industry 80; services 63

GDP - composition, by end use: *household consumption:* 49.9% (2023 est.)
government consumption: 21.2% (2023 est.)
investment in fixed capital: 21.5% (2023 est.)
investment in inventories: 0.2% (2023 est.)
exports of goods and services: 43.4% (2023 est.)
imports of goods and services: -39.4% (2023 est.)
note: figures may not total 100% due to rounding or gaps in data collection

Agricultural products: milk, sugar beets, wheat, potatoes, barley, maize, rapeseed, pork, rye, triticale (2023)
note: top ten agricultural products based on tonnage

Industries: iron, steel, coal, cement, chemicals, machinery, vehicles, machine tools, electronics, automobiles, food and beverages, shipbuilding, textiles

Industrial production growth rate: -3% (2024 est.)
note: annual % change in industrial value added based on constant local currency
comparison ranking: 171

Labor force: 43.772 million (2024 est.)
note: number of people ages 15 or older who are employed or seeking work
comparison ranking: 15

Unemployment rate: 3.5% (2024 est.)
3.1% (2023 est.)
3.2% (2022 est.)
note: % of labor force seeking employment
comparison ranking: 57

Youth unemployment rate (ages 15-24): *total:* 6.7% (2024 est.) male: 7.4% (2024 est.)
female: 5.9% (2024 est.)
note: % of labor force ages 15-24 seeking employment
comparison ranking: total 150

Population below poverty line: 14.8% (2021 est.)
note: % of population with income below national poverty line

Gini Index coefficient - distribution of family income: 32.4 (2020 est.)
note: index (0-100) of income distribution; higher values represent greater inequality
comparison ranking: 101

Average household expenditures: *on food:* 11.6% of household expenditures (2023 est.)
on alcohol and tobacco: 3.1% of household expenditures (2023 est.)

Household income or consumption by percentage share: *lowest 10%:* 2.9% (2020 est.)
highest 10%: 25% (2020 est.)
note: % share of income accruing to lowest and highest 10% of population

Remittances: 0.5% of GDP (2024 est.)
0.5% of GDP (2023 est.)
0.5% of GDP (2022 est.)
note: personal transfers and compensation between resident and non-resident individuals/ households/ entities

Budget: *revenues:* $1.279 trillion (2023 est.)
expenditures: $1.369 trillion (2023 est.)
note: central government revenues (excluding grants) and expenditures converted to US dollars at average official exchange rate for year indicated

Public debt: 63.9% of GDP (2017 est.)
note: general government gross debt is defined in the Maastricht Treaty as consolidated general government gross debt at nominal value, outstanding at the end of the year in the following categories of government liabilities (as defined in ESA95): currency and deposits (AF.2), securities other than shares excluding financial derivatives (AF.3, excluding AF.34), and loans (AF.4); the general government sector comprises the sub-sectors of central government, state government, local government and social security funds; the series are presented as a percentage of GDP and in millions of euros; GDP used as a denominator is the gross domestic product at current market prices; data expressed in national currency are converted into euro using end-of-year exchange rates provided by the European Central Bank
comparison ranking: 68

Taxes and other revenues: 11% (of GDP) (2022 est.)
note: central government tax revenue as a % of GDP
comparison ranking: 124

Current account balance: $267.056 billion (2024 est.)
$251.479 billion (2023 est.)
$161.759 billion (2022 est.)

note: balance of payments - net trade and primary/secondary income in current dollars
comparison ranking: 2

Exports: $1.949 trillion (2024 est.)
$1.958 trillion (2023 est.)
$1.917 trillion (2022 est.)
note: balance of payments - exports of goods and services in current dollars
comparison ranking: 3

Exports - partners: USA 10%, France 8%, Netherlands 7%, China 7%, Italy 6% (2023)
note: top five export partners based on percentage share of exports

Exports - commodities: cars, vehicle parts/accessories, packaged medicine, plastic products, vaccines (2023)
note: top five export commodities based on value in dollars

Imports: $1.774 trillion (2024 est.)
$1.781 trillion (2023 est.)
$1.808 trillion (2022 est.)
note: balance of payments - imports of goods and services in current dollars
comparison ranking: 3

Imports - partners: China 12%, Netherlands 7%, USA 7%, Poland 6%, France 5% (2023)
note: top five import partners based on percentage share of imports

Imports - commodities: cars, vehicle parts/accessories, garments, natural gas, vaccines (2023)
note: top five import commodities based on value in dollars

Reserves of foreign exchange and gold: $377.936 billion (2024 est.) $322.7 billion (2023 est.) $293.914 billion (2022 est.)
note: holdings of gold (year-end prices)/foreign exchange/special drawing rights in current dollars
comparison ranking: 11

Exchange rates: euros (EUR) per US dollar -

Exchange rates: 0.924 (2024 est.)
0.925 (2023 est.)
0.95 (2022 est.)
0.845 (2021 est.)
0.876 (2020 est.)

ENERGY

Electricity access: *electrification - total population:* 100% (2022 est.)

Electricity: *installed generating capacity:* 275.658 million kW (2023 est.)
consumption: 519.691 billion kWh (2023 est.)
exports: 60.316 billion kWh (2023 est.)
imports: 69.353 billion kWh (2023 est.)
transmission/distribution losses: 25.774 billion kWh (2023 est.)
comparison rankings: installed generating capacity 6; consumption 9; exports 2; imports 1; transmission/distribution losses 192

Electricity generation sources: *fossil fuels:* 49% of total installed capacity (2023 est.)
nuclear: 1.3% of total installed capacity (2023 est.)
solar: 11.1% of total installed capacity (2023 est.)
wind: 25.9% of total installed capacity (2023 est.)
hydroelectricity: 3.2% of total installed capacity (2023 est.)
biomass and waste: 9.4% of total installed capacity (2023 est.)

Nuclear energy: Percent of total electricity production: 1.4% (2023 est.)

Number of nuclear reactors permanently shut down: 33 (2025)

Coal: *production:* 109.741 million metric tons (2023 est.)
consumption: 140.994 million metric tons (2023 est.)
exports: 1.68 million metric tons (2023 est.)
imports: 32.933 million metric tons (2023 est.)
proven reserves: 35.4 billion metric tons (2023 est.)

Petroleum: *total petroleum production:* 131,000 bbl/day (2023 est.)
refined petroleum consumption: 2.062 million bbl/day (2024 est.)
crude oil estimated reserves: 115.2 million barrels (2021 est.)

Natural gas: *production:* 4.337 billion cubic meters (2023 est.)
consumption: 82.371 billion cubic meters (2023 est.)
imports: 74.989 billion cubic meters (2023 est.)
proven reserves: 23.39 billion cubic meters (2021 est.)

Energy consumption per capita: 120.457 million Btu/person (2023 est.)
comparison ranking: 34

COMMUNICATIONS

Telephones - fixed lines: *total subscriptions:* 38.8 million (2023 est.)
subscriptions per 100 inhabitants: 46 (2023 est.)
comparison ranking: total subscriptions 4

Telephones - mobile cellular: *total subscriptions:* 105 million (2023 est.)
subscriptions per 100 inhabitants: 125 (2022 est.)
comparison ranking: total subscriptions 18

Broadcast media: a mix of publicly operated and privately owned TV and radio stations; 70 national and regional public broadcasters compete with nearly 400 privately owned national and regional TV stations; more than 90% of households have cable or satellite TV; hundreds of radio stations, including national and regional networks and a large number of local stations

Internet country code: .de

Internet users: *percent of population:* 94% (2024 est.)

Broadband - fixed subscriptions: *total:* 38.4 million (2023 est.)
subscriptions per 100 inhabitants: 45 (2023 est.)
comparison ranking: total 6

TRANSPORTATION

Civil aircraft registration country code prefix: D

Airports: 840 (2025)
comparison ranking: 9

Heliports: 449 (2025)
comparison ranking: 8

Railways: *total:* 39,379 km (2020) 20,942 km electrified 15 km 0.900-mm gauge, 24 km 0.750-mm gauge (2015)

Merchant marine: *total:* 595 (2023)
by type: bulk carrier 1, container ship 69, general cargo 82, oil tanker 32, other 411
comparison ranking: total 38

Ports: *total ports:* 35 (2024)
large: 5
medium: 4
small: 11
very small: 15
ports with oil terminals: 12
key ports: Brake, Bremen, Bremerhaven, Cuxhaven, Emden, Hamburg, Kiel, Lubeck, Rostock

MILITARY AND SECURITY

Military and security forces: Federal Armed Forces (Bundeswehr): German Army (Deutsche Heer), German Navy (Deutsche Marine, includes naval air arm), German Air Force (Deutsche Luftwaffe, includes air defense), Cyber and Information Space (Cyber und Informationsraum) (2025)
note: responsibility for internal and border security is shared by the police forces of the 16 states, the Federal Criminal Police Office, and the Federal Police; the states' police forces report to their respective interior ministries while the Federal Police forces report to the Federal Ministry of the Interior

Military expenditures: 2% of GDP (2024 est.)
1.6% of GDP (2023 est.)
1.5% of GDP (2022 est.)
1.4% of GDP (2021 est.)
1.5% of GDP (2020 est.)

Military and security service personnel strengths: approximately 185,000 active-duty military personnel (2025)

Military equipment inventories and acquisitions: the inventory of Federal Armed Forces is comprised of weapons systems produced domestically or jointly with other European countries and Western imports, particularly from the US; Germany's defense industry is capable of manufacturing the full spectrum of air, land, and naval military weapons systems, and Germany is one of the world's leading arms exporters; it also participates in joint defense production projects with the US and European partners (2024)

Military service age and obligation: 17-23 years of age for voluntary military service for men and women (must have completed compulsory full-time education and have German citizenship); conscription ended July 2011; service obligation 7-23 months or 12 years; in July 2020, the government launched a new voluntary conscript initiative focused on homeland security tasks; volunteers serve for 7 months plus 5 months as reservists over a 6 year period (2024)
note: women have been eligible for voluntary service in all military branches and positions since 2001 and accounted for about 12% of the active-duty German military in 2023

Military deployments: 100 Estonia; up to 500 Iraq (NATO); Lebanon 170 (UNIFIL); up to 1,700 Lithuania (NATO); 100 Romania (NATO); 280 Slovakia (NATO) (2024)
note: the German military has over 2,000 ground forces, plus air and naval contingents deployed on some 18 foreign missions

Military - note: the Bundeswehr's core mission is the defense of Germany and its NATO partners; it has a wide range of peacetime duties, including crisis management, cyber security, deterrence, homeland security, humanitarian and disaster relief, and international peacekeeping and stability operations; as a key member of NATO and the EU, the Bundeswehr typically operates in a coalition environment, and its capabilities are largely based on NATO and EU planning goals and needs; it has participated in a range of NATO and EU missions in Europe, Africa,

and Asia, as well as global maritime operations; the Bundeswehr has close bilateral defense ties with a number of EU countries, including the Czechia, France, the Netherlands, and Romania, as well as the UK and the US; it also contributes forces to UN peacekeeping missions
the Bundeswehr was established in 1955; at the height of the Cold War in the 1980s, it had nearly 600,000 personnel, over 7,000 tanks, and 1,000 combat aircraft; in addition, over 400,000 soldiers from other NATO countries—including about 200,000 US military personnel —were stationed in West Germany; in the years following the collapse of the Soviet Union and the end of the Cold War, the Bundeswehr shrank by more than 60% in size (over 90% in tanks and about 80% in aircraft), while funding fell from nearly 3% of GDP and over 4% of government spending in the mid-1980s to 1.2% and 1.6% respectively; by the 2010s, the Bundeswehr's ability to fulfill its regional security commitments had deteriorated; the Russian annexation of Crimea in 2014 and full-scale assault on Ukraine in 2022 led to renewed emphasis on Germany's leadership role in European defense and NATO and efforts to boost funding for the Bundeswehr to improve readiness, modernize, and expand (2025)

SPACE

Space agency/agencies: German Aerospace Center (Deutsches Zentrum für Luft- und Raumfahrt, DLR; established 1997); predecessor organization, German Test and Research Institute for Aviation and Space Flight, was established in 1969; note – the Federal Republic of Germany was allowed to research space flight after gaining sovereignty in 1955 (2025)

Space launch site(s): a commercial offshore launch platform that will operate from the North Sea is under development with both government and private funding (2025)

Space program overview: has one of Europe's largest space programs; is a key member of the European Space Agency (ESA) and one of its largest contributors; builds and operates satellites, satellite/space launch vehicles (SLVs), space probes, and unmanned orbiters; conducts research and develops a range of other space-related capabilities and technologies, including reusable space planes, satellite payloads (cameras, remote sensing, communications, optics, sensors, etc.), rockets and rocket propulsion, propulsion assisted landing technologies, and aeronautics; participates in ESA's astronaut training program and human space flight operations and hosts the European Astronaut Center; participates in other international space programs, such as the International Space Station (ISS); hosts the mission control centers for the ISS and the ESA, as well as the European Organization for the Exploitation of Meteorological Satellites (EUMETSAT); in addition to ESA/EU and their member states, has ties to a range of foreign space programs, including those of China, Japan, Russia, and the US; has a robust commercial space industry sector that develops a broad range of space capabilities, including satellite launchers and reusable space craft, and cooperates closely with DLR, ESA, and other international commercial entities and government agencies (2025)
note: further details about the key activities, programs, and milestones of the country's space program, as well as government spending estimates on the space sector, appear in the Space Programs reference guide

TERRORISM

Terrorist group(s): Terrorist group(s): Islamic Revolutionary Guard Corps/Qods Force; Islamic State of Iraq and ash-Sham (ISIS); al-Qa'ida
note: details about the history, aims, leadership, organization, areas of operation, tactics, targets, weapons, size, and sources of support of the group(s) appear(s) in Appendix T

TRANSNATIONAL ISSUES

Refugees and internally displaced persons: *refugees:* 3,098,169 (2024 est.)

IDPs: 100 (2023 est.)
stateless persons: 28,813 (2024 est.)

Illicit drugs: USG identification: major precursor-chemical producer (2025)

GHANA

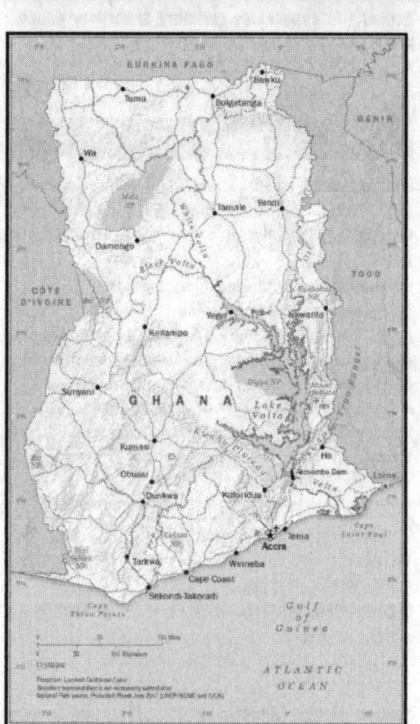

INTRODUCTION

Background: Ghana is a multiethnic country rich in natural resources and is one of the most stable and democratic countries in West Africa. Ghana has been inhabited for at least several thousand years, but little is known about its early inhabitants. By the 12th century, the gold trade started to boom in Bono (Bonoman) state in what is today southern Ghana, and it became the genesis of the Akan people's power and wealth in the region. Beginning in the 15th century, the Portuguese, followed by other European powers, arrived and competed for trading rights. Numerous kingdoms and empires emerged in the area, among the most powerful were the Kingdom of Dagbon in the north and the Asante (Ashanti) Empire in the south. By the mid-18th century, Asante was a highly organized state with immense wealth; it provided enslaved people for the Atlantic slave trade, and in return received firearms that facilitated its territorial expansion. The Asante resisted increasing British influence in the coastal areas, engaging in a series of wars during the 19th century before ultimately falling under British control. Formed from the merger of the British colony of the Gold Coast and the Togoland trust territory, Ghana in 1957 became the first Sub-Saharan country in colonial Africa to gain its independence, with Kwame NKRUMAH as its first leader.

Ghana endured a series of coups before Lt. Jerry RAWLINGS took power in 1981 and banned political parties. After approving a new constitution and restoring multiparty politics in 1992, RAWLINGS won presidential elections in 1992 and 1996 but was constitutionally prevented from running for a third term in 2000. John KUFUOR of the opposition New Patriotic Party (NPP) succeeded him and was reelected in 2004. John Atta MILLS of the National Democratic Congress won the 2008 presidential election and took over as head of state. MILLS died in 2012 and was constitutionally succeeded by his vice president, John Dramani MAHAMA, who subsequently won the 2012 presidential election. In 2016, Nana Addo Dankwa AKUFO-ADDO of the NPP defeated MAHAMA, marking the third time that Ghana's presidency had changed parties since the return to democracy. AKUFO-ADDO was reelected in 2020. In recent years, Ghana has taken an active role in promoting regional stability and is highly integrated in international affairs.

GEOGRAPHY

Location: Western Africa, bordering the Gulf of Guinea, between Cote d'Ivoire and Togo

Geographic coordinates: 8 00 N, 2 00 W

Map references: Africa

Area: *total:* 238,533 sq km
land: 227,533 sq km
water: 11,000 sq km
comparison ranking: total 82

Area - comparative: slightly smaller than Oregon

Land boundaries: *total:* 2,420 km
border countries (3): Burkina Faso 602 km; Cote d'Ivoire 720 km; Togo 1098 km

Coastline: 539 km

Maritime claims: *territorial sea:* 12 nm
contiguous zone: 24 nm
exclusive economic zone: 200 nm
continental shelf: 200 nm

Climate: tropical; warm and comparatively dry along southeast coast; hot and humid in southwest; hot and dry in north

Terrain: mostly low plains with dissected plateau in south-central area

Elevation: *highest point:* Mount Afadjato 885 m
lowest point: Atlantic Ocean 0 m
mean elevation: 190 m

Natural resources: gold, timber, industrial diamonds, bauxite, manganese, fish, rubber, hydropower, petroleum, silver, salt, limestone

Land use: *agricultural land:* 55.4% (2022 est.)
arable land: 20.7% (2022 est.)
permanent crops: 11.9% (2022 est.)
permanent pasture: 22.8% (2022 est.)
forest: 35.2% (2022 est.)
other: 9.4% (2022 est.)

Irrigated land: 360 sq km (2013)

Major rivers (by length in km): Volta river mouth (shared with Burkina Faso [s]) - 1,600 km
note: [s] after country name indicates river source; [m] after country name indicates river mouth

Major watersheds (area sq km): Atlantic Ocean drainage: Volta (410,991 sq km)

Population distribution: population is concentrated in the southern half of the country, with the highest concentrations on or near the Atlantic coast, as shown in this population distribution map

Natural hazards: dry, dusty, northeastern harmattan winds from January to March; droughts

Geography - note: Lake Volta is the world's largest artificial lake (manmade reservoir) by surface area (8,482 sq km; 3,275 sq mi); the lake was created after the Akosombo Dam was completed in 1965

PEOPLE AND SOCIETY

Population: *total:* 34,589,092 (2024 est.)
male: 16,902,073
female: 17,687,019
comparison rankings: total 44; male 45; female 43

Nationality: *noun:* Ghanaian(s)
adjective: Ghanaian

Ethnic groups: Akan 45.7%, Mole-Dagbani 18.5%, Ewe 12.8%, Ga-Dangme 7.1%, Gurma 6.4%, Guan 3.2%, Grusi 2.7%, Mande 2%, other 1.6% (2021 est.)

Languages: Asante 16%, Ewe 14%, Fante 11.6%, Boron (Brong) 4.9%, Dagomba 4.4%, Dangme 4.2%, Dagarte (Dagaba) 3.9%, Kokomba 3.5%, Akyem 3.2%, Ga 3.1%, other 31.2% (2010 est.)
note: English is the official language

Religions: Christian 71.3% (Pentecostal/Charismatic 31.6%, Protestant 17.4%, Catholic 10%, other 12.3%), Muslim 19.9%, traditionalist 3.2%, other 4.5%, none 1.1% (2021 est.)

Age structure: *0-14 years:* 37.4% (male 6,527,386/female 6,400,245)
15-64 years: 58.2% (male 9,690,498/female 10,444,197)
65 years and over: 4.4% (2024 est.) (male 684,189/female 842,577)

Dependency ratios: *total dependency ratio:* 71.8 (2024 est.)
youth dependency ratio: 64.2 (2024 est.)
elderly dependency ratio: 7.6 (2024 est.)
potential support ratio: 13.2 (2024 est.)

Median age: *total:* 21.4 years (2024 est.)
male: 20.6 years
female: 22.3 years
comparison ranking: total 191

Population growth rate: 2.15% (2024 est.)
comparison ranking: 35

Birth rate: 27.6 births/1,000 population (2024 est.)
comparison ranking: 33

Death rate: 5.9 deaths/1,000 population (2024 est.)
comparison ranking: 162

Net migration rate: -0.2 migrant(s)/1,000 population (2024 est.)
comparison ranking: 107

Population distribution: population is concentrated in the southern half of the country, with the highest concentrations on or near the Atlantic coast, as shown in this population distribution map

Urbanization: *urban population:* 59.2% of total population (2023)
rate of urbanization: 3.06% annual rate of change (2020-25 est.)

Major urban areas - population: 3.768 million Kumasi, 2.660 million ACCRA (capital), 1.078 million Sekondi Takoradi (2023)

Sex ratio: *at birth:* 1.03 male(s)/female
0-14 years: 1.02 male(s)/female
15-64 years: 0.93 male(s)/female
65 years and over: 0.81 male(s)/female
total population: 0.96 male(s)/female (2024 est.)

Mother's mean age at first birth: 22.1 years (2022 est.)
note: data represents median age at first birth among women 25-49

Maternal mortality ratio: 234 deaths/100,000 live births (2023 est.)
comparison ranking: 33

Infant mortality rate: *total:* 31.2 deaths/1,000 live births (2024 est.)
male: 34.5 deaths/1,000 live births
female: 27.8 deaths/1,000 live births
comparison ranking: total 46

Life expectancy at birth: *total population:* 70.1 years (2024 est.)
male: 68.4 years
female: 71.8 years
comparison ranking: total population 180

Total fertility rate: 3.56 children born/woman (2024 est.)
comparison ranking: 32

Gross reproduction rate: 1.75 (2024 est.)

Drinking water source: *improved: urban:* 98.4% of population (2022 est.)
rural: 74.1% of population (2022 est.)
total: 88.4% of population (2022 est.)
unimproved: urban: 1.6% of population (2022 est.)
rural: 25.9% of population (2022 est.)
total: 11.6% of population (2022 est.)

Health expenditure: 4.2% of GDP (2021)
7.4% of national budget (2022 est.)

Physician density: 0.27 physicians/1,000 population (2023)

Hospital bed density: 0.7 beds/1,000 population (2015 est.)

Sanitation facility access: *improved: urban:* 85.7% of population (2022 est.)
rural: 55.3% of population (2022 est.)
total: 73.1% of population (2022 est.)
unimproved: urban: 14.3% of population (2022 est.)
rural: 44.7% of population (2022 est.)
total: 26.9% of population (2022 est.)

Obesity - adult prevalence rate: 10.9% (2016)
comparison ranking: 136

Alcohol consumption per capita: *total:* 1.59 liters of pure alcohol (2019 est.)
beer: 0.53 liters of pure alcohol (2019 est.)
wine: 0.05 liters of pure alcohol (2019 est.)
spirits: 0.39 liters of pure alcohol (2019 est.)
other alcohols: 0.61 liters of pure alcohol (2019 est.)
comparison ranking: total 137

Tobacco use: *total:* 2.8% (2025 est.)
male: 5.4% (2025 est.)
female: 0.3% (2025 est.)
comparison ranking: total 167

Children under the age of 5 years underweight: 12.6% (2017/18)
comparison ranking: 38

Currently married women (ages 15-49): 54.3% (2023 est.)

Child marriage: *women married by age 15:* 3.3% (2022)
women married by age 18: 16.1% (2022)
men married by age 18: 2.4% (2022)

Education expenditure: 2.9% of GDP (2022 est.)
13.2% national budget (2022 est.)
comparison ranking: Education expenditure (% GDP) 158

Literacy: *total population:* 76.5% (2021 est.)
male: 81.3% (2021 est.)
female: 72.1% (2021 est.)

School life expectancy (primary to tertiary education): *total:* 12 years (2022 est.)
male: 12 years (2022 est.)
female: 12 years (2022 est.)

ENVIRONMENT

Environmental issues: drought in north; deforestation; overgrazing; soil erosion; poaching and habitat destruction; water pollution; inadequate potable water

International environmental agreements: *party to:* Biodiversity, Climate Change, Climate Change-Kyoto Protocol, Climate Change-Paris Agreement, Comprehensive Nuclear Test Ban, Desertification, Endangered Species, Environmental Modification, Hazardous Wastes, Law of the Sea, Marine Dumping-London Protocol, Nuclear Test Ban, Ozone Layer Protection, Ship Pollution, Tropical Timber 2006, Wetlands, Whaling
signed, but not ratified: Marine Life Conservation

Climate: tropical; warm and comparatively dry along southeast coast; hot and humid in southwest; hot and dry in north

Urbanization: *urban population:* 59.2% of total population (2023)
rate of urbanization: 3.06% annual rate of change (2020-25 est.)

Carbon dioxide emissions: 20.822 million metric tonnes of CO_2 (2023 est.)
from coal and metallurgical coke: 107,000 metric tonnes of CO_2 (2023 est.)
from petroleum and other liquids: 13.349 million metric tonnes of CO_2 (2023 est.)
from consumed natural gas: 7.366 million metric tonnes of CO_2 (2023 est.)

comparison ranking: total emissions 83

Particulate matter emissions: 43.4 micrograms per cubic meter (2019 est.)

Methane emissions: *energy:* 164.9 kt (2022-2024 est.)
agriculture: 166.7 kt (2019-2021 est.)
waste: 134 kt (2019-2021 est.)
other: 28.1 kt (2019-2021 est.)

Waste and recycling: *municipal solid waste generated annually:* 3.538 million tons (2024 est.)
percent of municipal solid waste recycled: 13.3% (2022 est.)

Total water withdrawal: *municipal:* 299.6 million cubic meters (2022 est.)
industrial: 95 million cubic meters (2022 est.)
agricultural: 1.07 billion cubic meters (2022 est.)

Total renewable water resources: 56.2 billion cubic meters (2022 est.)

GOVERNMENT

Country name: *conventional long form:* Republic of Ghana
conventional short form: Ghana
former: Gold Coast
etymology: named for a tribal chieftain who ruled a large part of the region prior to the 13th century, even though his territory was northwest of modern-day Ghana; the former name, Gold Coast, came from the gold that Portuguese explorers discovered in the region in the late 15th century

Government type: presidential republic

Capital: *name:* Accra
geographic coordinates: 5 33 N, 0 13 W
time difference: UTC 0 (5 hours ahead of Washington, DC, during Standard Time)
etymology: the name derives from the Akan word *nkran*, meaning "ant," and may refer to the nickname local forest dwellers gave to the Nigerian tribes who settled in the area in the 16th century

Administrative divisions: 16 regions; Ahafo, Ashanti, Bono, Bono East, Central, Eastern, Greater Accra, North East, Northern, Oti, Savannah, Upper East, Upper West, Volta, Western, Western North

Legal system: mixed system of English common law and customary law

Constitution: *history:* several previous; latest drafted 31 March 1992, approved and promulgated 28 April 1992, entered into force 7 January 1993
amendment process: proposed by Parliament; consideration requires prior referral to the Council of State, a body of prominent citizens who advise the president of the republic; passage of amendments to "entrenched" constitutional articles (including those on national sovereignty, fundamental rights and freedoms, the structure and authorities of the branches of government, and amendment procedures) requires approval in a referendum by at least 40% participation of eligible voters and at least 75% of votes cast, followed by at least two-thirds majority vote in Parliament, and assent of the president; amendments to non-entrenched articles do not require referenda

International law organization participation: has not submitted an ICJ jurisdiction declaration; accepts ICCt jurisdiction

Citizenship: *citizenship by birth:* no
citizenship by descent only: at least one parent or grandparent must be a citizen of Ghana
dual citizenship recognized: yes
residency requirement for naturalization: 5 years

Suffrage: 18 years of age; universal

Executive branch: *chief of state:* President John Dramani MAHAMA (since 7 January 2025)
head of government: President John Dramani MAHAMA (since 7 January 2025)
cabinet: Council of Ministers; nominated by the president, approved by Parliament
election/appointment process: president and vice president directly elected on the same ballot by absolute-majority popular vote in 2 rounds, if needed, for a 4-year term (eligible for a second term); the president is both chief of state and head of government
most recent election date: 7 December 2024
election results: *2024:* John Dramani MAHAMA elected president in the first round; percent of vote-John Dramani MAHAMA (NDC) 56.5%, Mahamudu BAWUMIA (NPC) 41%, other 2.5%
2020: Nana Addo Dankwa AKUFO-ADDO reelected president in the first round; percent of vote - Nana Addo Dankwa AKUFO-ADDO (NPP) 51.3%, John Dramani MAHAMA (NDC) 47.4%, other 1.3% (2020)
expected date of next election: 7 December 2028

Legislative branch: *legislature name:* Parliament
legislative structure: unicameral
number of seats: 276 (all directly elected)
electoral system: plurality/majority
scope of elections: full renewal
term in office: 4 years
most recent election date: 12/7/2024
parties elected and seats per party: National Democratic Congress (NDC) (183); New Patriotic Party (NPP) (88); Other (4)
percentage of women in chamber: 14.5%
expected date of next election: December 2028

Judicial branch: *highest court(s):* Supreme Court (consists of the chief justice and 13 justices)
judge selection and term of office: chief justice appointed by the president in consultation with the Council of State (a small advisory body of prominent citizens) and with the approval of Parliament; other justices appointed by the president on the advice of the Judicial Council (an 18-member independent body of judicial, military and police officials, and presidential nominees) and on the advice of the Council of State; justices can retire at age 60, with compulsory retirement at age 70
subordinate courts: Court of Appeal; High Court; Circuit Court; District Court; regional tribunals

Political parties: All Peoples Congress or APC
Convention People's Party or CPP
Ghana Freedom Party or GFP
Ghana Union Movement or GUM
Great Consolidated Popular Party or GCPP
Liberal Party of Ghana or LPG
National Democratic Congress or NDC
National Democratic Party or NDP
New Patriotic Party or NPP
People's National Convention or PNC
Progressive People's Party or PPP
United Front Party or UFP
United Progressive Party or UPP

Diplomatic representation in the US: *chief of mission:* Ambassador Victor Emmanuel SMITH (since 19 September 2025)
chancery: 3512 International Drive NW, Washington, DC 20008
telephone: [1] (202) 686-4520
FAX: [1] (202) 686-4527
email address and website: info.washington@mfa.gov.gh
https://washington.mfa.gov.gh/
consulate(s) general: New York

Diplomatic representation from the US: *chief of mission:* Ambassador (vacant); Chargé d'Affaires Rolf OLSON (since 29 May 2025)
embassy: No. 24, Fourth Circular Road, Cantonments, Accra, P.O. Box 2288, Accra
mailing address: 2020 Accra Place, Washington DC 20521-2020
telephone: [233] (0) 30-274-1000
email address and website: ACSAccra@state.gov
https://gh.usembassy.gov/

International organization participation: ACP, AfDB, ATMIS, AU, C, ECOWAS, EITI (compliant country), FAO, G-24, G-77, IAEA, IBRD, ICAO, ICC (national committees), ICCt, ICRM, IDA, IFAD, IFC, IFRCS, ILO, IMF, IMO, IMSO, Interpol, IOC, IOM, IPU, ISO, ITSO, ITU, ITUC (NGOs), MIGA, MINURSO, MONUSCO, NAM, OAS (observer), OIF, OPCW, UN, UNAMID, UNCTAD, UNESCO, UNHCR, UNHRC, UNIDO, UNIFIL, UNISFA, UNMIL, UNMISS, UNOCI, UNOOSA, UNSOM, UNWTO, UPU, WCO, WFTU (NGOs), WHO, WIPO, WMO, WTO

Independence: 6 March 1957 (from the UK)

National holiday: Independence Day, 6 March (1957)

Flag: *description:* three equal horizontal bands of red (top), yellow, and green, with a large five-pointed black star centered in the yellow band
meaning: red stands for the blood shed for independence, yellow for the country's mineral wealth, and green for its forests and natural wealth; the black star is said to be the lodestar of African freedom
history: uses the colors of the Pan-African movement
note: similar to the flag of Bolivia, which has a coat of arms centered in the yellow band

National symbol(s): black star, golden eagle

National color(s): red, yellow, green, black

National anthem(s): *title:* "God Bless Our Homeland Ghana"
lyrics/music: unknown/Philip GBEHO
history: music adopted 1957, lyrics adopted 1966; the lyrics were changed twice, in 1960 when a republic was declared and after a 1966 coup

National heritage: *total World Heritage Sites:* 2 (both cultural)
selected World Heritage Site locales: Forts and Castles, Volta, Greater Accra, Central and Western Regions; Asante Traditional Buildings

ECONOMY

Economic overview: West African lower-middle income economy; major gold, oil and cocoa exporter; macroeconomic challenges following nearly four decades of sustained growth; recent progress in debt restructuring, fiscal reforms, financial stability, and curbing runaway inflation under 2023-26 IMF credit facility program

Real GDP (purchasing power parity): $243.124 billion (2024 est.)
$230.046 billion (2023 est.)
$223.043 billion (2022 est.)
note: data in 2021 dollars
comparison ranking: 70

Real GDP growth rate: 5.7% (2024 est.)
3.1% (2023 est.)
3.8% (2022 est.)
note: annual GDP % growth based on constant local currency

comparison ranking: 30

Real GDP per capita: $7,100 (2024 est.)
$6,800 (2023 est.)
$6,700 (2022 est.)
note: data in 2021 dollars
comparison ranking: 157

GDP (official exchange rate): $82.825 billion (2024 est.)
note: data in current dollars at official exchange rate

Inflation rate (consumer prices): 22.8% (2024 est.)
38.1% (2023 est.)
31.3% (2022 est.)
note: annual % change based on consumer prices
comparison ranking: 192

GDP - composition, by sector of origin: *agriculture:* 20.7% (2024 est.)
industry: 28.8% (2024 est.)
services: 43.9% (2024 est.)
note: figures may not total 100% due to non-allocated consumption not captured in sector-reported data
comparison rankings: agriculture 33; industry 63; services 179

GDP - composition, by end use: *household consumption:* 84.1% (2024 est.)
government consumption: 4.8% (2024 est.)
investment in fixed capital: 9.8% (2024 est.)
investment in inventories: 0.2% (2024 est.)
exports of goods and services: 35.3% (2024 est.)
imports of goods and services: -34.1% (2024 est.)
note: figures may not total 100% due to rounding or gaps in data collection

Agricultural products: cassava, yams, plantains, maize, oil palm fruit, taro, rice, oranges, pineapples, cocoa beans (2023)
note: top ten agricultural products based on tonnage

Industries: mining, lumbering, light manufacturing, aluminum smelting, food processing, cement, small commercial ship building, petroleum

Industrial production growth rate: 7.1% (2024 est.)
note: annual % change in industrial value added based on constant local currency
comparison ranking: 25

Labor force: 13.928 million (2024 est.)
note: number of people ages 15 or older who are employed or seeking work
comparison ranking: 45

Unemployment rate: 3.1% (2024 est.)
3.1% (2023 est.)
3.1% (2022 est.)
note: % of labor force seeking employment
comparison ranking: 44

Youth unemployment rate (ages 15-24): *total:* 5.4% (2024 est.)
male: 5.5% (2024 est.)
female: 5.3% (2024 est.)
note: % of labor force ages 15-24 seeking employment
comparison ranking: total 161

Population below poverty line: 23.4% (2016 est.)
note: % of population with income below national poverty line

Gini Index coefficient - distribution of family income: 43.5 (2016 est.)
note: index (0-100) of income distribution; higher values represent greater inequality
comparison ranking: 26

Average household expenditures: *on food:* 39.1% of household expenditures (2023 est.)
on alcohol and tobacco: 0.4% of household expenditures (2023 est.)

Household income or consumption by percentage share: *lowest 10%:* 1.6% (2016 est.)
highest 10%: 32.2% (2016 est.)
note: % share of income accruing to lowest and highest 10% of population

Remittances: 3% of GDP (2023 est.)
2.8% of GDP (2022 est.)
2.4% of GDP (2021 est.)
note: personal transfers and compensation between resident and non-resident individuals/households/entities

Budget: *revenues:* $11.684 billion (2022 est.)
expenditures: $19.102 billion (2022 est.)
note: central government revenues and expenses (excluding grants/extrabudgetary units/social security funds) converted to US dollars at average official exchange rate for year indicated

Taxes and other revenues: 12.3% (of GDP) (2022 est.)
note: central government tax revenue as a % of GDP
comparison ranking: 111

Current account balance: $1.407 billion (2023 est.)
-$1.741 billion (2022 est.)
-$2.541 billion (2021 est.)
note: balance of payments - net trade and primary/secondary income in current dollars
comparison ranking: 54

Exports: $25.365 billion (2023 est.)
$25.52 billion (2022 est.)
$23.901 billion (2021 est.)
note: balance of payments - exports of goods and services in current dollars
comparison ranking: 88

Exports - partners: Switzerland 24%, UAE 18%, India 8%, South Africa 7%, China 7% (2023)
note: top five export partners based on percentage share of exports

Exports - commodities: gold, crude petroleum, cocoa beans, manganese ore, cocoa paste (2023)
note: top five export commodities based on value in dollars

Imports: $26.024 billion (2023 est.)
$26.329 billion (2022 est.)
$25.967 billion (2021 est.)
note: balance of payments - imports of goods and services in current dollars
comparison ranking: 86

Imports - partners: China 30%, Netherlands 8%, India 5%, USA 5%, Russia 5% (2023)
note: top five import partners based on percentage share of imports

Imports - commodities: refined petroleum, cars, plastics, plastic products, footwear (2023)
note: top five import commodities based on value in dollars

Reserves of foreign exchange and gold: $3.624 billion (2023 est.)
$5.205 billion (2022 est.)
$9.917 billion (2021 est.)
note: holdings of gold (year-end prices)/foreign exchange/special drawing rights in current dollars
comparison ranking: 111

Debt - external: $29.241 billion (2023 est.)
note: present value of external debt in current US dollars
comparison ranking: 27

Exchange rates: cedis (GHC) per US dollar -
Exchange rates: 11.02 (2023 est.)
8.272 (2022 est.)
5.806 (2021 est.)
5.596 (2020 est.)
5.217 (2019 est.)

ENERGY

Electricity access: *electrification - total population:* 85.1% (2022 est.)
electrification - urban areas: 95%
electrification - rural areas: 71.6%

Electricity: *installed generating capacity:* 5.519 million kW (2023 est.)
consumption: 19.534 billion kWh (2023 est.)
exports: 2 billion kWh (2023 est.)
imports: 48.449 million kWh (2023 est.)
transmission/distribution losses: 2.796 billion kWh (2023 est.)
comparison rankings: installed generating capacity 86; consumption 78; exports 58; imports 117; transmission/distribution losses 137

Electricity generation sources: *fossil fuels:* 61.5% of total installed capacity (2023 est.)
solar: 0.6% of total installed capacity (2023 est.)
hydroelectricity: 37.8% of total installed capacity (2023 est.)
biomass and waste: 0.1% of total installed capacity (2023 est.)

Coal: *consumption:* 51,000 metric tons (2023 est.)
exports: 21 metric tons (2023 est.)
imports: 52,000 metric tons (2023 est.)

Petroleum: *total petroleum production:* 176,000 bbl/day (2023 est.)
refined petroleum consumption: 96,000 bbl/day (2023 est.)
crude oil estimated reserves: 660 million barrels (2021 est.)

Natural gas: *production:* 3.116 billion cubic meters (2023 est.)
consumption: 3.755 billion cubic meters (2023 est.)
imports: 639.204 million cubic meters (2023 est.)
proven reserves: 22.653 billion cubic meters (2021 est.)

Energy consumption per capita: 10.493 million Btu/person (2023 est.)
comparison ranking: 149

COMMUNICATIONS

Telephones - fixed lines: *total subscriptions:* 320,000 (2023 est.)
subscriptions per 100 inhabitants: 1 (2023 est.) less than 1
comparison ranking: total subscriptions 104

Telephones - mobile cellular: *total subscriptions:* 33.4 million (2023 est.)
subscriptions per 100 inhabitants: 120 (2022 est.)
comparison ranking: total subscriptions 46

Broadcast media: state-owned TV station, 2 state-owned radio networks; several privately owned TV stations and a large number of privately owned radio stations; transmissions of multiple international broadcasters are accessible; several cable and satellite TV subscription services are obtainable

Internet country code: .gh

Internet users: *percent of population:* 70% (2023 est.)

Broadband - fixed subscriptions: *total:* 223,000 (2023 est.)
subscriptions per 100 inhabitants: 1 (2023 est.)
comparison ranking: total 120

TRANSPORTATION

Civil aircraft registration country code prefix: 9G

Airports: 11 (2025)
comparison ranking: 156

Heliports: 7 (2025)
comparison ranking: 88

Railways: *total:* 947 km (2022)
narrow gauge: 947 km (2022) 1.067-m gauge

Merchant marine: *total:* 52 (2023)
by type: general cargo 8, oil tanker 3, other 41
comparison ranking: total 119

Ports: *total ports:* 4 (2024)
large: 0
medium: 1
small: 1
very small: 2
ports with oil terminals: 3
key ports: Saltpond, Sekondi, Takoradi, Tema

MILITARY AND SECURITY

Military and security forces: Ghana Armed Forces (GAF): Army, Air Force, Ghana Navy

Ministry of Interior: Ghana Police Service (2025)
note: the GAF also has a Medical Service/Corps

Military expenditures: 0.4% of GDP (2024 est.)
0.4% of GDP (2023 est.)
0.4% of GDP (2022 est.)
0.5% of GDP (2021 est.)
0.4% of GDP (2020 est.)

Military and security service personnel strengths: estimated 15-20,000 active Armed Forces (2025)
note: over the past decade, Ghana has sought to increase the size of the GAF, particularly the Army, which has added a number of new units

Military equipment inventories and acquisitions: the military's inventory is a mix of older and some newer Chinese, Russian, and Western equipment, including US, which has donated items such as patrol boats; the government in recent years has committed to an increase in funding for equipment acquisitions, including armor, mechanized, and special forces capabilities for the Army, light attack aircraft for the Air Force, and more modern coastal patrol vessels for the Navy (2024)

Military service age and obligation: 18-27 years of age for voluntary military service, with basic education certificate; no conscription (2024)
note: as of 2024, women comprised approximately 15% of the military; Ghanaian women first began serving in the late 1950s

Military deployments: 875 Lebanon (UNIFIL); 725 (plus about 275 police) South Sudan (UNMISS); 670 Sudan (UNISFA) (2025)
note: since sending a contingent of troops to the Congo in 1960, the military has been a regular contributor to African- and UN-sponsored peacekeeping missions

Military - note: the military's primary missions are border defense, assisting with internal security, peacekeeping, and protecting the country's territorial waters, particularly its offshore oil and gas infrastructure; it has benefited from cooperation with foreign partners, such as the UK and the US, and experience gained from participation in multiple international peacekeeping missions
in recent years, Ghana has expanded the Army and reinforced its presence in the northern part of the country to shore up porous borders, interdict smuggling routes, and counter threats from the terrorist organization Jama'at Nasr al-Islam wal Muslimin (JNIM), a coalition of al-Qa'ida linked militant groups which has a considerable presence in Burkina Faso and has conducted attacks in Cote d'Ivoire and Togo; Ghana has also made efforts to increase the Navy's capabilities to protect its maritime claims and counter threats such as piracy and illegal fishing (2025)

SPACE

Space agency/agencies: Ghana Space Science and Technology Institute (GSSTI; established 2011); note – the GSSTI is eventually slated to become the Ghana Space Agency (2025)

Space program overview: has nascent space program focused on earth observation, space science education, and telecommunications; seeks to exploit remote sensing (RS) technology for agriculture, natural resource management, weather forecasting, and national security issues; relies on foreign imagery for analysis but seeks to develop its own RS satellite capabilities; has established cooperative relationships with China and Japan, as well as a number of regional states, particularly South Africa; cooperating with Egypt, Kenya, Nigeria, Sudan, and Uganda to establish a joint satellite to monitor climate changes in the African continent; member of the African Space Agency; partner of the Square Kilometer Array (SKA) international astronomy initiative (2025)
note: further details about the key activities, programs, and milestones of the country's space program, as well as government spending estimates on the space sector, appear in the Space Programs reference guide

TRANSNATIONAL ISSUES

Refugees and internally displaced persons: *refugees:* 17,334 (2024 est.)

IDPs: 4,937 (2024 est.)

GIBRALTAR

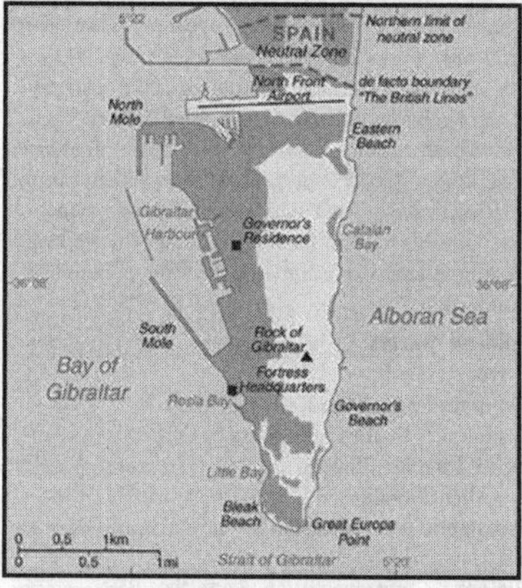

INTRODUCTION

Background: Spain reluctantly ceded the strategically important Gibraltar to Great Britain in the 1713 Treaty of Utrecht, and the British garrison at Gibraltar was formally declared a colony in 1830. In a referendum held in 1967, Gibraltarians voted overwhelmingly to remain a British dependency. After the UK granted Gibraltar autonomy in 1969, Spain closed the border and severed all communication links. Between 1997 and 2002, the UK and Spain held a series of talks on establishing temporary joint sovereignty over Gibraltar. In response to these talks, the Gibraltar Government called a referendum in 2002 in which the majority of citizens voted overwhelmingly against sharing sovereignty with Spain. Since 2004, Spain, the UK, and Gibraltar have held tripartite talks to resolve problems that affect the local population, and work continues on cooperation agreements in areas such as taxation and financial services, communications and maritime security, legal and customs services, environmental protection, and education and visa services. A new noncolonial constitution came into force in 2007, and the European Court of First Instance recognized Gibraltar's right to regulate its own tax regime in 2008. The UK retains responsibility for defense, foreign relations, internal security, and financial stability.

Spain and the UK continue to spar over the territory. In 2009, for example, a dispute over Gibraltar's claim to territorial waters extending out three miles gave rise to periodic non-violent maritime confrontations between Spanish and UK naval patrols. Spain renewed its demands for an eventual return of Gibraltar to Spanish control after the UK's 2016 vote to leave the EU, but London has dismissed any connection between the vote and its sovereignty over Gibraltar.

GEOGRAPHY

Location: Southwestern Europe, bordering the Strait of Gibraltar, which links the Mediterranean Sea and the North Atlantic Ocean, on the southern coast of Spain

Geographic coordinates: 36 08 N, 5 21 W

Map references: Europe

Area: *total:* 7 sq km
land: 6.5 sq km
water: 0 sq km
comparison ranking: total 243

Area - comparative: more than 10 times the size of the National Mall in Washington, D.C.

Land boundaries: *total:* 1.2 km
border countries (1): Spain 1.2 km

Coastline: 12 km

Maritime claims: *territorial sea:* 3 nm

Climate: Mediterranean with mild winters and warm summers

Terrain: a narrow coastal lowland borders the Rock of Gibraltar
Elevation: *highest point:* Rock of Gibraltar 426 m
lowest point: Mediterranean Sea 0 m
Natural resources: none
Land use: *agricultural land:* 0% (2022 est.)
forest: 0% (2022 est.)
other: 100% (2022 est.)
Irrigated land: NA
Natural hazards: occasional droughts; no streams or large bodies of water on the peninsula (all potable water comes from desalination)
Geography - note: strategic location on Strait of Gibraltar that links the North Atlantic Ocean and Mediterranean Sea

PEOPLE AND SOCIETY

Population: *total:* 29,683 (2024 est.)
male: 14,919
female: 14,764
comparison rankings: total 217; male 217; female 217
Nationality: *noun:* Gibraltarian(s)
adjective: Gibraltar
Ethnic groups: Gibraltarian 79%, other British 13.2%, Spanish 2.1%, Moroccan 1.6%, other EU 2.4%, other 1.6% (2012 est.)
note: data represent population by nationality
Languages: English (used in schools and for official purposes), Spanish, Italian, Portuguese
Religions: Roman Catholic 72.1%, Church of England 7.7%, other Christian 3.8%, Muslim 3.6%, Jewish 2.4%, Hindu 2%, other 1.1%, none 7.1%, unspecified 0.1% (2012 est.)
Age structure: *0-14 years:* 20% (male 3,045/female 2,895)
15-64 years: 62.5% (male 9,383/female 9,179)
65 years and over: 17.5% (2024 est.) (male 2,491/ female 2,690)
Dependency ratios: *total dependency ratio:* 59.9 (2024 est.)
youth dependency ratio: 32 (2024 est.)
elderly dependency ratio: 27.9 (2024 est.)
potential support ratio: 3.6 (2024 est.)
Median age: *total:* 36.8 years (2024 est.)
male: 36.2 years
female: 37.5 years
comparison ranking: total 88
Population growth rate: 0.17% (2024 est.)
comparison ranking: 179
Birth rate: 13.7 births/1,000 population (2024 est.)
comparison ranking: 124
Death rate: 8.7 deaths/1,000 population (2024 est.)
comparison ranking: 69
Net migration rate: -3.2 migrant(s)/1,000 population (2024 est.)
comparison ranking: 186
Urbanization: *urban population:* 100% of total population (2023)
rate of urbanization: 0.45% annual rate of change (2015-20 est.)
Major urban areas - population: 35,000 GIBRALTAR (capital) (2018)
Sex ratio: *at birth:* 1.05 male(s)/female
0-14 years: 1.05 male(s)/female
15-64 years: 1.02 male(s)/female
65 years and over: 0.93 male(s)/female
total population: 1.01 male(s)/female (2024 est.)
Infant mortality rate: *total:* 6 deaths/1,000 live births (2024 est.)
male: 6.8 deaths/1,000 live births
female: 5.2 deaths/1,000 live births
comparison ranking: total 169
Life expectancy at birth: *total population:* 80.9 years (2024 est.)
male: 78.1 years
female: 83.8 years
comparison ranking: total population 48
Total fertility rate: 1.89 children born/woman (2024 est.)
comparison ranking: 123
Gross reproduction rate: 0.92 (2024 est.)
Drinking water source: *improved: urban:* 100% of population (2022 est.)
total: 100% of population (2022 est.)
unimproved: urban: 0% of population (2022 est.)
total: 0% of population (2022 est.)
Sanitation facility access: *improved: urban:* 100% of population (2022 est.)
total: 100% of population (2022 est.)
unimproved: urban: 0% of population (2022 est.)
total: 0% of population (2022 est.)
Currently married women (ages 15-49): 40.7% (2023 est.)
Education expenditure: 8.8% national budget (2023 est.)

ENVIRONMENT

Environmental issues: limited natural freshwater resources
Climate: Mediterranean with mild winters and warm summers
Urbanization: *urban population:* 100% of total population (2023)
rate of urbanization: 0.45% annual rate of change (2015-20 est.)
Carbon dioxide emissions: 15.608 million metric tonnes of CO2 (2023 est.)
from petroleum and other liquids: 15.458 million metric tonnes of CO2 (2023 est.)
from consumed natural gas: 150,000 metric tonnes of CO2 (2023 est.)
comparison ranking: total emissions 99
Waste and recycling: *municipal solid waste generated annually:* 17,000 tons (2024 est.)

GOVERNMENT

Country name: *conventional long form:* none
conventional short form: Gibraltar
etymology: from the Spanish derivation of the Arabic *jabal tariq*, which means "Mountain of Tariq" and refers to the Berber chief who captured the peninsula in A.D. 711
Government type: parliamentary democracy (Parliament); self-governing overseas territory of the UK
Dependency status: overseas territory of the UK
Capital: *name:* Gibraltar
geographic coordinates: 36 08 N, 5 21 W
time difference: UTC+1 (6 hours ahead of Washington, DC, during Standard Time)
daylight saving time: +1hr, begins last Sunday in March; ends last Sunday in October
etymology: from the Spanish derivation of the Arabic *jabal tariq*, which means "Mountain of Tariq" and refers to the Berber chief who captured the peninsula in A.D. 711
Administrative divisions: none (overseas territory of the UK)
Legal system: the laws of the UK apply
Constitution: *history:* previous 1969; latest passed by referendum 30 November 2006, entered into effect 14 December 2006, entered into force 2 January 2007
amendment process: proposed by Parliament and requires prior consent of the British monarch (through the Secretary of State); passage requires at least three-fourths majority vote in Parliament followed by simple majority vote in a referendum; note – only sections 1 through 15 in Chapter 1 (Protection of Fundamental Rights and Freedoms) can be amended by Parliament
Citizenship: see United Kingdom
Suffrage: 18 years of age; universal; and British citizens with six months residence or more
Executive branch: *chief of state:* King CHARLES III (since 8 September 2022); represented by Governor Sir David STEEL (since 11 June 2020)
head of government: Chief Minister Fabian PICARDO (since 9 December 2011)
cabinet: Council of Ministers appointed from among the 17 elected members of Parliament by the governor, in consultation with the chief minister
election/appointment process: the monarchy is hereditary; governor appointed by the monarch; following legislative elections, the governor usually appoints the leader of the majority party or majority coalition as chief minister
Legislative branch: *legislature name:* Parliament
legislative structure: unicameral
number of seats: 18 (17 directly elected, 1 appointed)
electoral system: plurality/majority
scope of elections: full renewal
term in office: 4 years
most recent election date: 10/12/2023
parties elected and seats per party: GSLP-Liberal Alliance (9) (GSLP 7, LPG 2); GSD (8)
percentage of women in chamber: 38.5%
expected date of next election: October 2027
Judicial branch: *highest court(s):* Court of Appeal (consists of at least 3 judges, including the court president); Supreme Court of Gibraltar (consists of the chief justice and 3 judges)
judge selection and term of office: Court of Appeal and Supreme Court judges appointed by the governor upon the advice of the Judicial Service Commission, a 7-member body of judges and appointees of the governor; tenure of the Court of Appeal president based on terms of appointment; Supreme Court chief justice and judges normally appointed until retirement at age 67, but tenure can be extended 3 years
subordinate courts: Court of First Instance; Magistrates' Court; specialized tribunals for issues relating to social security, taxes, and employment
note: appeals beyond the Court of Appeal are heard by the Judicial Committee of the Privy Council (in London)
Political parties: Gibraltar Liberal Party or Liberal Party of Gibraltar or LPG
Gibraltar Social Democrats or GSD
Gibraltar Socialist Labor Party or GSLP
GSLP-Liberal Alliance
Together Gibraltar or TG
Diplomatic representation in the US: none (overseas territory of the UK)
Diplomatic representation from the US: *embassy:* none (overseas territory of the UK)
International organization participation: ICC (NGOs), Interpol (subbureau), UPU
Independence: none (overseas territory of the UK)
National holiday: National Day, 10 September (1967)

note: day of the national referendum to decide whether to remain with the UK or join Spain

Flag: *description:* two horizontal bands of white (top, double-width) and red with a three-towered red castle in the center of the white band; a gold key hangs from the castle gate and is centered in the red band
meaning: the castle symbolizes Gibraltar as a fortress, and the key represents Gibraltar's strategic importance – the key to the Mediterranean
history: the design comes from Gibraltar's coat of arms, which King Ferdinand and Queen Isabella of Spain granted on 10 July 1502

National symbol(s): Barbary partridge

National color(s): red, white, yellow

National coat of arms: King Ferdinand and Queen Isabella of Spain granted this coat of arms to Gibraltar in 1502; the castle in the center of the shield represents Gibraltar as a fortress, and the gold key represents its strategic position as the gateway to the Mediterranean; below the shield is the national motto, *Montis Insignia Calpe* ("Badge of the Rock of Gibraltar"); the coat of arms uses the national colors of red, white, and yellow

National anthem(s): *title:* "Gibraltar Anthem"
lyrics/music: Peter EMBERLEY
history: adopted 1994; serves as a local anthem
title: "God Save the King"
lyrics/music: unknown
history: official anthem, as an overseas UK territory

ECONOMY

Economic overview: British territorial high-income economy; Brexit caused significant economic disruption to longstanding financial services, shipping, and tourism industries; ongoing negotiations to rejoin EU Schengen Area; independent taxation authority

GDP (official exchange rate): $2.044 billion (2014 est.)

Agricultural products: none

Industries: tourism, banking and finance, ship repairing, tobacco

Exports - partners: Netherlands 38%, France 26%, Cyprus 7%, Poland 7%, Sweden 6% (2023)
note: top five export partners based on percentage share of exports

Exports - commodities: refined petroleum, natural gas, ships, cars, scrap iron (2023)
note: top five export commodities based on value in dollars

Imports - partners: Italy 26%, Greece 12%, Spain 10%, Netherlands 9%, India 9% (2023)
note: top five import partners based on percentage share of imports

Imports - commodities: refined petroleum, crude petroleum, coal tar oil, natural gas, ships (2023)
note: top five import commodities based on value in dollars

Exchange rates: Gibraltar pounds (GIP) per US dollar -

Exchange rates: 0.782 (2024 est.)
0.805 (2023 est.)
0.811 (2022 est.)
0.727 (2021 est.)
0.78 (2020 est.)

ENERGY

Electricity access: *electrification - total population:* 100% (2022 est.)

Electricity: *installed generating capacity:* 50,000 kW (2023 est.)
consumption: 213.744 million kWh (2023 est.)
transmission/distribution losses: 6.256 million kWh (2023 est.)
comparison rankings: installed generating capacity 195; consumption 189; transmission/distribution losses 13

Electricity generation sources: *fossil fuels:* 100% of total installed capacity (2023 est.)

Petroleum: *refined petroleum consumption:* 91,000 bbl/day (2023 est.)

Natural gas: *consumption:* 77.196 million cubic meters (2023 est.)
imports: 77.196 million cubic meters (2023 est.)

COMMUNICATIONS

Telephones - fixed lines: *total subscriptions:* 17,000 (2022 est.)
subscriptions per 100 inhabitants: 46 (2022 est.)
comparison ranking: total subscriptions 178

Telephones - mobile cellular: *total subscriptions:* 37,000 (2022 est.)
subscriptions per 100 inhabitants: 112 (2022 est.)
comparison ranking: total subscriptions 211

Broadcast media: Gibraltar Broadcasting Corporation (GBC) provides TV and radio services via 1 TV station and 4 radio stations; British Forces Broadcasting Service (BFBS) operates 1 radio station; broadcasts from Spanish radio and TV stations are accessible

Internet country code: .gi

Internet users: *percent of population:* 94% (2016 est.)

Broadband - fixed subscriptions: *total:* 23,000 (2022 est.)
subscriptions per 100 inhabitants: 61 (2022 est.)
comparison ranking: total 165

TRANSPORTATION

Civil aircraft registration country code prefix: VP-G

Airports: 1 (2025)
comparison ranking: 217

Merchant marine: *total:* 129 (2023)
by type: bulk carrier 8, container ship 5, general cargo 31, oil tanker 16, other 69
comparison ranking: total 78

Ports: *total ports:* 1 (2024)
large: 0
medium: 1
small: 0
very small: 0
ports with oil terminals: 1
key ports: Europa Point

MILITARY AND SECURITY

Military and security forces: Royal Gibraltar Regiment (2025)

Military - note: defense is the responsibility of the UK

GREECE

INTRODUCTION

Background: Greece won independence from the Ottoman Empire in 1830 and became a kingdom. During the second half of the 19th century and the first half of the 20th century, it gradually added neighboring islands and territories, most with Greek-speaking populations. In World War II, Greece was first invaded by Italy (1940) and subsequently occupied by Germany (1941-44); fighting endured in a protracted civil war between supporters of the king and other anti-communist and communist rebels. The communists were defeated in 1949, and Greece joined NATO in 1952. In 1967, a military coup forced the king to flee the country. The ensuing military dictatorship collapsed in 1974, and Greece abolished the monarchy to become a parliamentary republic.

In 1981, Greece joined the EC (now the EU); it became the 12th member of the European Economic and Monetary Union in 2001. From 2009 until 2019, Greece suffered a severe economic crisis due to nearly a decade of chronic overspending and structural rigidities. Beginning in 2010, Greece entered three bailout agreements – the first two with the European Commission, the European Central Bank, and the IMF; and the third in 2015 with the European Stability Mechanism – worth in total about $300 billion. The Greek Government formally exited the third bailout in 2018, and Greece's economy has since improved significantly. In 2022, the country finalized its early repayment to the IMF and graduated on schedule from the EU's enhanced surveillance framework.

GEOGRAPHY

Location: Southern Europe, bordering the Aegean Sea, Ionian Sea, and the Mediterranean Sea, between Albania and Turkey

Geographic coordinates: 39 00 N, 22 00 E

Map references: Europe

Area: *total:* 131,957 sq km
land: 130,647 sq km
water: 1,310 sq km
comparison ranking: total 97

Area - comparative: slightly smaller than Alabama

Land boundaries: *total:* 1,110 km
border countries (4): Albania 212 km; Bulgaria 472 km; North Macedonia 234 km; Turkey 192 km

Coastline: 13,676 km

Maritime claims: *territorial sea:* 6 nm
continental shelf: 200-m depth or to the depth of exploitation

Climate: temperate; mild, wet winters; hot, dry summers

Terrain: mountainous with ranges extending into the sea as peninsulas or chains of islands

Elevation: *highest point:* Mount Olympus 2,917
lowest point: Mediterranean Sea 0 m
mean elevation: 498 m
note: Mount Olympus actually has 52 peaks but its highest point, Mytikas (meaning "nose"), rises to 2,917 meters; in Greek mythology, Olympus' Mytikas peak was the home of the Greek gods

Natural resources: lignite, petroleum, iron ore, bauxite, lead, zinc, nickel, magnesite, marble, salt, hydropower potential

Land use: *agricultural land:* 44.3% (2022 est.)
arable land: 14.1% (2022 est.)
permanent crops: 8% (2022 est.)
permanent pasture: 22.3% (2022 est.)
forest: 30.3% (2022 est.)
other: 25.4% (2022 est.)

Irrigated land: 12,191 sq km (2021)

Population distribution: one third of the population lives in and around metropolitan Athens; the remainder of the country has moderate population density mixed with sizeable urban clusters

Natural hazards: severe earthquakes
volcanism: Santorini (367 m) has been deemed a Decade Volcano by the International Association of Volcanology and Chemistry of the Earth's Interior, worthy of study due to its explosive history and close proximity to human populations; Methana and Nisyros in the Aegean are also classified as historically active

Geography - note: strategic location dominating the Aegean Sea and southern approach to Turkish Straits; a peninsular country, with an archipelago of about 2,000 islands

PEOPLE AND SOCIETY

Population: *total:* 10,461,091 (2024 est.)
male: 5,117,862
female: 5,343,229
comparison rankings: total 90; male 92; female 88

Nationality: *noun:* Greek(s)
adjective: Greek

Ethnic groups: Greek 91.6%, Albanian 4.4%, other 4% (2011 est.)
note: data represent citizenship; Greece does not collect data on ethnicity

Languages: Greek (official) 99%, other (includes English and French) 1%
major-language sample(s): Παγκόσμιο Βιβλίο Δεδομένων, η απαραίτητη πηγή βασικών πληροφοριών. (Greek)

Religions: Greek Orthodox 81-90%, Muslim 2%, other 3%, none 4-15%, unspecified 1% (2015 est.)

Age structure: *0-14 years:* 13.8% (male 742,131/female 699,079)
15-64 years: 62.6% (male 3,278,906/female 3,267,140)
65 years and over: 23.6% (2024 est.) (male 1,096,825/female 1,377,010)

Dependency ratios: *total dependency ratio:* 59.8 (2024 est.)
youth dependency ratio: 22 (2024 est.)
elderly dependency ratio: 37.8 (2024 est.)
potential support ratio: 2.6 (2024 est.)

Median age: *total:* 46.5 years (2024 est.)
male: 44.6 years
female: 48.3 years
comparison ranking: total 10

Population growth rate: -0.35% (2024 est.)
comparison ranking: 215

Birth rate: 7.4 births/1,000 population (2024 est.)
comparison ranking: 219

Death rate: 12 deaths/1,000 population (2024 est.)
comparison ranking: 16

Net migration rate: 1.1 migrant(s)/1,000 population (2024 est.)
comparison ranking: 63

Population distribution: one third of the population lives in and around metropolitan Athens; the remainder of the country has moderate population density mixed with sizeable urban clusters

Urbanization: *urban population:* 80.7% of total population (2023)
rate of urbanization: 0.11% annual rate of change (2020-25 est.)

Major urban areas - population: 3.154 million ATHENS (capital), 815,000 Thessaloniki (2023)

Sex ratio: *at birth:* 1.07 male(s)/female
0-14 years: 1.06 male(s)/female
15-64 years: 1 male(s)/female
65 years and over: 0.8 male(s)/female
total population: 0.96 male(s)/female (2024 est.)

Mother's mean age at first birth: 30.7 years (2020 est.)

Maternal mortality ratio: 5 deaths/100,000 live births (2023 est.)
comparison ranking: 171

Infant mortality rate: *total:* 3.4 deaths/1,000 live births (2024 est.)
male: 3.8 deaths/1,000 live births
female: 3 deaths/1,000 live births
comparison ranking: total 195

Life expectancy at birth: *total population:* 81.9 years (2024 est.)
male: 79.4 years
female: 84.6 years
comparison ranking: total population 40

Total fertility rate: 1.41 children born/woman (2024 est.)
comparison ranking: 211

Gross reproduction rate: 0.68 (2024 est.)

Drinking water source: *improved: urban:* 100% of population (2022 est.)
rural: 100% of population (2022 est.)
total: 100% of population (2022 est.)
unimproved: urban: 0% of population (2022 est.)
rural: 0% of population (2022 est.)
total: 0% of population (2022 est.)

Health expenditure: 9.2% of GDP (2021)
8.7% of national budget (2022 est.)

Physician density: 6.58 physicians/1,000 population (2022)

Hospital bed density: 4.2 beds/1,000 population (2019 est.)

Sanitation facility access: *improved: urban:* 100% of population (2022 est.)
rural: 100% of population (2022 est.)
total: 100% of population (2022 est.)
unimproved: urban: 0% of population (2022 est.)
rural: 0% of population (2022 est.)
total: 0% of population (2022 est.)

Obesity - adult prevalence rate: 24.9% (2016)
comparison ranking: 54

Alcohol consumption per capita: *total:* 6.33 liters of pure alcohol (2019 est.)
beer: 2.13 liters of pure alcohol (2019 est.)
wine: 2.66 liters of pure alcohol (2019 est.)
spirits: 1.45 liters of pure alcohol (2019 est.)
other alcohols: 0.08 liters of pure alcohol (2019 est.)
comparison ranking: total 66

Tobacco use: *total:* 27.3% (2025 est.)
male: 30.3% (2025 est.)
female: 24.6% (2025 est.)
comparison ranking: total 30

Currently married women (ages 15-49): 54.1% (2023 est.)

Education expenditure: 3.8% of GDP (2022 est.)
7.2% national budget (2022 est.)
comparison ranking: Education expenditure (% GDP) 119

School life expectancy (primary to tertiary education): *total:* 21 years (2022 est.)
male: 21 years (2022 est.)
female: 21 years (2022 est.)

ENVIRONMENT

Environmental issues: air pollution; air emissions from transport and electricity power stations; water pollution; degradation of coastal zones; loss of biodiversity; municipal and industrial waste disposal

International environmental agreements: *party to:* Air Pollution, Air Pollution-Nitrogen Oxides, Air Pollution-Sulphur 94, Antarctic-Environmental Protection, Antarctic-Marine Living Resources, Antarctic Treaty, Biodiversity, Climate Change, Climate Change-Kyoto Protocol, Climate Change-Paris Agreement, Comprehensive Nuclear Test Ban, Desertification, Endangered Species, Environmental Modification, Hazardous Wastes, Law of the Sea, Marine Dumping-London Convention, Nuclear Test Ban, Ozone Layer Protection, Ship Pollution, Tropical Timber 2006, Wetlands
signed, but not ratified: Air Pollution-Heavy Metals, Air Pollution-Multi-effect Protocol, Air Pollution-Persistent Organic Pollutants, Air Pollution-Volatile Organic Compounds

Climate: temperate; mild, wet winters; hot, dry summers

Urbanization: *urban population:* 80.7% of total population (2023)
rate of urbanization: 0.11% annual rate of change (2020-25 est.)

Carbon dioxide emissions: 62.06 million metric tonnes of CO2 (2023 est.)
from coal and metallurgical coke: 10.794 million metric tonnes of CO2 (2023 est.)
from petroleum and other liquids: 44.649 million metric tonnes of CO2 (2023 est.)
from consumed natural gas: 6.617 million metric tonnes of CO2 (2023 est.)
comparison ranking: total emissions 51

Particulate matter emissions: 14.6 micrograms per cubic meter (2019 est.)

Waste and recycling: *municipal solid waste generated annually:* 5.615 million tons (2024 est.)
percent of municipal solid waste recycled: 22.4% (2022 est.)

Total water withdrawal: *municipal:* 1.687 billion cubic meters (2022)
industrial: 279.8 million cubic meters (2022)
agricultural: 8.107 billion cubic meters (2022)

Total renewable water resources: 68 billion cubic meters (2022 est.)

Geoparks: *total global geoparks and regional networks:* 9 (2024)
global geoparks and regional networks: Chelmos Vouraikos; Grevena - Kozani; Kefalonia-Ithaca; Lavreotiki; Lesvos Island; Meteora Pyli; Psiloritis; Sitia; Vikos - Aoos (2024)

GOVERNMENT

Country name: *conventional long form:* Hellenic Republic
conventional short form: Greece
local long form: Elliniki Dimokratia
local short form: Ellas or Ellada
former: Hellenic State, Kingdom of Greece
etymology: the English name derives from the Roman (Latin) designation *Graecia*, meaning "Land of the Greeks"; the Greeks call their country Ellas or Ellada, which is probably derived from Hellas, the name of the mythical son of Deucalian

Government type: parliamentary republic

Capital: *name:* Athens
geographic coordinates: 37 59 N, 23 44 E
time difference: UTC+2 (7 hours ahead of Washington, DC, during Standard Time)
daylight saving time: +1hr, begins last Sunday in March; ends last Sunday in October
etymology: the origin of the name is uncertain; according to tradition, the city is named after Athena, the Greek goddess of wisdom, but the name is probably pre-Hellenic

Administrative divisions: 13 regions (*perifereies*, singular - *perifereia*) and 1 autonomous monastic state* (*aftonomi monastiki politeia*); Agion Oros* (Mount Athos), Anatoliki Makedonia kai Thraki (East Macedonia and Thrace), Attiki (Attica), Dytiki Ellada (West Greece), Dytiki Makedonia (West Macedonia), Ionia Nisia (Ionian Islands), Ipeiros (Epirus), Kentriki Makedonia (Central Macedonia), Kriti (Crete), Notio Aigaio (South Aegean), Peloponnisos (Peloponnese), Sterea Ellada (Central Greece), Thessalia (Thessaly), Voreio Aigaio (North Aegean)

Legal system: civil legal system based on Roman law

Constitution: *history:* many previous; latest entered into force 11 June 1975
amendment process: proposed by at least 50 members of Parliament and agreed by three-fifths majority vote in two separate ballots at least 30 days apart; passage requires absolute majority vote by the next elected Parliament; entry into force finalized through a "special parliamentary resolution"; articles on human rights and freedoms and the form of government cannot be amended

International law organization participation: accepts compulsory ICJ jurisdiction with reservations; accepts ICCt jurisdiction

Citizenship: *citizenship by birth:* no
citizenship by descent only: at least one parent must be a citizen of Greece
dual citizenship recognized: yes
residency requirement for naturalization: 10 years

Suffrage: 17 years of age; universal and compulsory

Executive branch: *chief of state:* President Konstantinos TASOULAS (since 13 March 2025)
head of government: Prime Minister Kyriakos MITSOTAKIS (since 26 June 2023)
cabinet: Cabinet appointed by the president on the recommendation of the prime minister
election/appointment process: president elected by Hellenic Parliament for a 5-year term (eligible for a second term); president appoints as prime minister the leader of the majority party or coalition in the Hellenic Parliament
most recent election date: 12 February 2025
election results: *2025:* Konstantinos TASOULAS (ND) elected president by Parliament - 160 of 300 votes
2020: Katerina SAKELLAROPOULOU (independent) elected president by Parliament - 261 of 300 votes
expected date of next election: 2030

Legislative branch: *legislature name:* Hellenic Parliament (Vouli Ton Ellinon)
legislative structure: unicameral
number of seats: 300 (all directly elected)
electoral system: proportional representation
scope of elections: full renewal
term in office: 4 years
most recent election date: 6/25/2023
parties elected and seats per party: New Democracy (ND) (158); Coalition of the Radical Left (SYRIZA) (47); Panhellenic Socialist Movement - Movement for Change (PASOK-KINAL) (32); Communist Party (KKE) (21); Other (42)
percentage of women in chamber: 22.9%
expected date of next election: June 2027
note: only parties surpassing a 3% vote threshold are entitled to parliamentary seats; parties need 10 seats to become formal parliamentary groups but can retain that status if the party participated in the last election and received the minimum 3% threshold

Judicial branch: *highest court(s):* Supreme Civil and Criminal Court or Areios Pagos (consists of 56 judges, including the court presidents); Council of State (supreme administrative court) consists of the president, 7 vice presidents, 42 privy councilors, 48 associate councilors and 50 reporting judges, organized into six 5- and 7-member chambers; Court of Audit (government audit and enforcement) consists of the president, 5 vice presidents, 20 councilors, and 90 associate and reporting judges
judge selection and term of office: Supreme Court judges appointed by presidential decree on the advice of the Supreme Judicial Council (SJC), which includes the president of the Supreme Court, other judges, and the prosecutor of the Supreme Court; judges appointed for life after a 2-year probationary period; Council of State president appointed by the Greek Cabinet to serve a 4-year term; other judge appointments and tenure NA; Court of Audit president appointed by decree of the president of the republic on the advice of the SJC; court president serves a 4-year term or until age 67; tenure of vice presidents, councilors, and judges NA
subordinate courts: Courts of Appeal and Courts of First Instance (district courts)

Political parties: Coalition of the Radical Left-Progressive Alliance or SYRIZA-PS
Communist Party of Greece or KKE
Course of Freedom
Democratic Patriotic Movement-Victory or NIKI
Greek Solution
New Democracy or ND
PASOK - Movement for Change or PASOK-KINAL
Spartans

Diplomatic representation in the US: *chief of mission:* Ambassador Ekaterini NASSIKA (since 27 February 2024)
chancery: 2217 Massachusetts Avenue NW, Washington, DC 20008
telephone: [1] (202) 939-1300
FAX: [1] (202) 939-1324
email address and website: gremb.was@mfa.gr
https://www.mfa.gr/usa/en/the-embassy/
consulate(s) general: Boston, Chicago, Los Angeles, New York, Tampa (FL), San Francisco
consulate(s): Atlanta, Houston

Diplomatic representation from the US: *chief of mission:* Ambassador (vacant); Chargé d'Affaires Josh HUCK (since 1 August 2025)
embassy: 91 Vasillisis Sophias Avenue, 10160 Athens
mailing address: 7100 Athens Place, Washington DC 20521-7100
telephone: [30] (210) 721-2951
FAX: [30] (210) 724-5313
email address and website: athensamericancitizenservices@state.gov
https://gr.usembassy.gov/
consulate(s) general: Thessaloniki

International organization participation: Australia Group, BIS, BSEC, CD, CE, CERN, EAPC, EBRD, ECB, EIB, EMU, ESA, EU, FAO, FATF, IAEA, IBRD, ICAO, ICC (national committees), ICCt, ICRM, IDA, IEA, IFAD, IFC, IFRCS, IGAD (partners), IHO, ILO, IMF, IMO, IMSO, Interpol, IOC, IOM, IPU, ISO, ITSO, ITU, ITUC (NGOs), MIGA, NATO, NEA, NSG, OAS (observer), OECD, OIF, OPCW, OSCE, PCA, Schengen Convention, SELEC, UN, UNCTAD, UNESCO, UNHCR, UNIDO, UNIFIL, UNWTO, UPU, Wassenaar Arrangement, WCO, WFTU (NGOs), WHO, WIPO, WMO, WTO, ZC

Independence: 3 February 1830 (from the Ottoman Empire)
note: the national revolt against the Ottomans began on 25 March 1821; the London Protocol recognizing Greek independence was signed on 3 February 1830 by Great Britain, France, and Russia

National holiday: Independence Day, 25 March (1821)

Flag: *description:* nine equal horizontal stripes of blue alternating with white; a blue square with a white cross is in the upper-left corner
meaning: the cross symbolizes Greek Orthodoxy, the established religion; there is no set meaning for the stripes and colors

note: Greek legislation states that the flag colors are cyan and white, but cyan can mean "blue" in Greek, so the exact shade of blue has never been set and has varied from a light to a dark blue over time; the blue is now usually an azure

National symbol(s): Greek cross (white cross on a blue field)

National color(s): blue, white

National coat of arms: the coat of arms was designed by Greek artist Kostas Grammatopoulos and has been in use since 1975; depicted in the national colors of blue and white; the white cross represents the country's primary religion, Greek Orthodoxy, and the laurel branches symbolize victory

National anthem(s): *title:* "Ymnos eis tin Eleftherian" (Hymn to Freedom)
lyrics/music: Dionysios SOLOMOS/Nikolaos MANTZAROS
history: adopted 1864; the anthem is based on a 158-stanza poem by the same name, which was inspired by the Greek Revolution of 1821 against the Ottomans (only the first two stanzas are used); Cyprus also uses "Hymn to Freedom" as its anthem

National heritage: *total World Heritage Sites:* 19 (17 cultural, 2 mixed)
selected World Heritage Site locales: Acropolis, Athens (c); Archaeological site of Delphi (c); Meteora (m); Medieval City of Rhodes (c); Archaeological site of Olympia (c); Archaeological site of Mycenae and Tiryns (c); Old Town of Corfu (c); Mount Athos (m); Delos (c); Archaeological Site of Philippi (c)

ECONOMY

Economic overview: high-income EU and eurozone economy; growth above euro average, supported by private consumption and EU fund investments; structural reforms strengthening public finances and enhancing resilience within banking system; declining unemployment but low labor productivity and skill shortages

Real GDP (purchasing power parity): $392.205 billion (2024 est.)
$383.493 billion (2023 est.)
$374.753 billion (2022 est.)
note: data in 2021 dollars
comparison ranking: 54

Real GDP growth rate: 2.3% (2024 est.)
2.3% (2023 est.)
5.7% (2022 est.)
note: annual GDP % growth based on constant local currency
comparison ranking: 142

Real GDP per capita: $37,800 (2024 est.)
$36,900 (2023 est.)
$35,900 (2022 est.)
note: data in 2021 dollars
comparison ranking: 62

GDP (official exchange rate): $257.145 billion (2024 est.)
note: data in current dollars at official exchange rate

Inflation rate (consumer prices): 2.7% (2024 est.)
3.5% (2023 est.)
9.6% (2022 est.)
note: annual % change based on consumer prices
comparison ranking: 76

GDP - composition, by sector of origin: *agriculture:* 3.3% (2024 est.)
industry: 15.4% (2024 est.)
services: 68% (2024 est.)
note: figures may not total 100% due to non-allocated consumption not captured in sector-reported data
comparison rankings: agriculture 127; industry 162; services 44

GDP - composition, by end use: *household consumption:* 66.9% (2023 est.)
government consumption: 19.3% (2023 est.)
investment in fixed capital: 15.2% (2023 est.)
investment in inventories: 1.5% (2023 est.)
exports of goods and services: 43.7% (2023 est.)
imports of goods and services: -48.4% (2023 est.)
note: figures may not total 100% due to rounding or gaps in data collection

Agricultural products: maize, wheat, sheep milk, oranges, tomatoes, milk, peaches/nectarines, grapes, watermelons, barley (2023)
note: top ten agricultural products based on tonnage

Industries: tourism, food and tobacco processing, textiles, chemicals, metal products; mining, petroleum

Industrial production growth rate: 6.1% (2024 est.)
note: annual % change in industrial value added based on constant local currency
comparison ranking: 30

Labor force: 4.655 million (2024 est.)
note: number of people ages 15 or older who are employed or seeking work
comparison ranking: 92

Unemployment rate: 10.2% (2024 est.)
11.1% (2023 est.)
12.5% (2022 est.)
note: % of labor force seeking employment
comparison ranking: 149

Youth unemployment rate (ages 15-24): *total:* 24.7% (2024 est.)
male: 23.2% (2024 est.)
female: 26.6% (2024 est.)
note: % of labor force ages 15-24 seeking employment
comparison ranking: total 35

Population below poverty line: 18.8% (2021 est.)
note: % of population with income below national poverty line

Gini Index coefficient - distribution of family income: 33.4 (2022 est.)
note: index (0-100) of income distribution; higher values represent greater inequality
comparison ranking: 95

Average household expenditures: *on food:* 16.4% of household expenditures (2023 est.)
on alcohol and tobacco: 4.4% of household expenditures (2023 est.)

Household income or consumption by percentage share: *lowest 10%:* 2.7% (2022 est.)
highest 10%: 25.7% (2022 est.)
note: % share of income accruing to lowest and highest 10% of population

Remittances: 0.2% of GDP (2024 est.)
0.2% of GDP (2023 est.)
0.3% of GDP (2022 est.)
note: personal transfers and compensation between resident and non-resident individuals/households/entities

Budget: *revenues:* $111.938 billion (2023 est.)
expenditures: $114.497 billion (2023 est.)
note: central government revenues (excluding grants) and expenditures converted to US dollars at average official exchange rate for year indicated

Public debt: 190.6% of GDP (2023 est.)
note: central government debt as a % of GDP
comparison ranking: 2

Taxes and other revenues: 26.6% (of GDP) (2023 est.)
note: central government tax revenue as a % of GDP
comparison ranking: 11

Current account balance: -$16.399 billion (2024 est.)
-$15.008 billion (2023 est.)
-$22.623 billion (2022 est.)
note: balance of payments - net trade and primary/secondary income in current dollars
comparison ranking: 187

Exports: $108.424 billion (2024 est.)
$107.218 billion (2023 est.)
$106.189 billion (2022 est.)
note: balance of payments - exports of goods and services in current dollars
comparison ranking: 46

Exports - partners: Italy 12%, Germany 6%, Cyprus 6%, Bulgaria 4%, USA 4% (2023)
note: top five export partners based on percentage share of exports

Exports - commodities: refined petroleum, packaged medicine, aluminum, olive oil, tobacco (2023)
note: top five export commodities based on value in dollars

Imports: $122.408 billion (2024 est.)
$119.234 billion (2023 est.)
$127.82 billion (2022 est.)
note: balance of payments - imports of goods and services in current dollars
comparison ranking: 43

Imports - partners: Germany 10%, China 10%, Italy 8%, Iraq 7%, Netherlands 6% (2023)
note: top five import partners based on percentage share of imports

Imports - commodities: crude petroleum, refined petroleum, natural gas, cars, packaged medicine (2023)
note: top five import commodities based on value in dollars

Reserves of foreign exchange and gold: $15.222 billion (2024 est.)
$13.608 billion (2023 est.)
$12.061 billion (2022 est.)
note: holdings of gold (year-end prices)/foreign exchange/special drawing rights in current dollars
comparison ranking: 68

Exchange rates: euros (EUR) per US dollar -
Exchange rates: 0.924 (2024 est.)
0.925 (2023 est.)
0.95 (2022 est.)
0.845 (2021 est.)
0.876 (2020 est.)

ENERGY

Electricity access: *electrification - total population:* 100% (2022 est.)

Electricity: *installed generating capacity:* 24.169 million kW (2023 est.)
consumption: 46.929 billion kWh (2023 est.)
exports: 3.24 billion kWh (2023 est.)
imports: 8.152 billion kWh (2023 est.)
transmission/distribution losses: 5.346 billion kWh (2023 est.)
comparison rankings: installed generating capacity 44; consumption 55; exports 48; imports 31; transmission/distribution losses 166

Electricity generation sources: *fossil fuels:* 48.9% of total installed capacity (2023 est.)

solar: 17.5% of total installed capacity (2023 est.)
wind: 23.3% of total installed capacity (2023 est.)
hydroelectricity: 9.8% of total installed capacity (2023 est.)
biomass and waste: 0.6% of total installed capacity (2023 est.)

Coal: *production:* 10.469 million metric tons (2023 est.)
consumption: 10.091 million metric tons (2023 est.)
exports: 5 metric tons (2023 est.)
imports: 49,000 metric tons (2023 est.)
proven reserves: 2.876 billion metric tons (2023 est.)

Petroleum: *total petroleum production:* 5,000 bbl/day (2023 est.)
refined petroleum consumption: 308,000 bbl/day (2024 est.)
crude oil estimated reserves: 10 million barrels (2021 est.)

Natural gas: *production:* 1.323 million cubic meters (2023 est.)
consumption: 3.344 billion cubic meters (2023 est.)
exports: 8.362 billion cubic meters (2023 est.)
imports: 11.619 billion cubic meters (2023 est.)
proven reserves: 991.09 million cubic meters (2021 est.)

Energy consumption per capita: 92.693 million Btu/person (2023 est.)
comparison ranking: 56

COMMUNICATIONS

Telephones - fixed lines: *total subscriptions:* 4.962 million (2023 est.)
subscriptions per 100 inhabitants: 48 (2023 est.)
comparison ranking: total subscriptions 29

Telephones - mobile cellular: *total subscriptions:* 11.3 million (2023 est.)
subscriptions per 100 inhabitants: 109 (2022 est.)
comparison ranking: total subscriptions 89

Broadcast media: broadcast media dominated by the private sector; roughly 150 private TV channels, about 10 of which broadcast nationwide; 1 state-owned terrestrial TV channel with national coverage; 3 privately owned satellite channels; multi-channel satellite and cable TV services available; over 1,500 radio stations, all privately owned; state-owned broadcaster has 2 national radio stations

Internet country code: .gr

Internet users: *percent of population:* 85% (2023 est.)

Broadband - fixed subscriptions: *total:* 4.48 million (2023 est.)
subscriptions per 100 inhabitants: 44 (2023 est.)
comparison ranking: total 39

TRANSPORTATION

Civil aircraft registration country code prefix: SX

Airports: 82 (2025)
comparison ranking: 64

Heliports: 59 (2025)
comparison ranking: 34

Railways: *total:* 2,345 km (2020) 731 km electrified

Merchant marine: *total:* 1,215 (2023)
by type: bulk carrier 132, container ship 4, general cargo 79, oil tanker 299, other 701 comparison ranking: total 20

Ports: *total ports:* 57 (2024)
large: 1
medium: 7
small: 7
very small: 42
ports with oil terminals: 13
key ports: Alexandroupoli, Iraklion, Kerkira, Ormos Aliveriou, Piraievs, Soudha, Thessaloniki, Volos

MILITARY AND SECURITY

Military and security forces: Hellenic Armed Forces (HAF; Ellinikes Enoples Dynamis, EED): Hellenic Army (Ellinikos Stratos, ES; includes National Guard), Hellenic Navy (Elliniko Polemiko Navtiko, EPN), Hellenic Air Force (Elliniki Polemiki Aeroporia, EPA; includes air defense) (2025)
note 1: the police (under the Ministry of Citizen Protection) and the armed forces (Ministry of National Defense) share law enforcement duties in certain border areas; the Greek Coast Guard is under the Ministry of Shipping Affairs and Island Policy
note 2: the National Guard was established in 1982 as an official part of the Army to help protect Greece and provide reinforcements and support to the Army in peacetime and in times of mobilization and war

Military expenditures: 2.9% of GDP (2025 est.)
2.7% of GDP (2024 est.)
2.8% of GDP (2023 est.)
3.9% of GDP (2022 est.)
3.7% of GDP (2021 est.)

Military and security service personnel strengths: approximately 112,000 active-duty military personnel (2025)

Military equipment inventories and acquisitions: the military's inventory consists of a mix of domestically produced and imported weapons and equipment from Europe and the US; in recent years, France, Germany, and the US have been major suppliers; Greece's defense industry is capable of producing a range of military hardware, including naval vessels and associated subsystems (2024)
note: Greece is in the midst of a military modernization program which includes acquisitions of fighter aircraft and naval ships from France and armored vehicles and tanks from Germany; it has also boosted purchases of US equipment, including fighter aircraft upgrades, helicopters, and naval patrol craft

Military service age and obligation: 19-45 years of age for compulsory military service for men; 12-month obligation for all services (note - as an exception, the duration of the full military service is 9 instead of 12 months if conscripts, after the initial training, serve the entire remaining time in certain areas of the eastern borders, in Cyprus, or in certain military units); 18 years of age for voluntary military service for men and women (2023)
note 1: compulsory service applies to any individual whom the Greek authorities consider to be Greek, regardless of whether the individual considers himself Greek, has a foreign citizenship and passport, or was born or lives outside of Greece; Greek citizens living permanently outside of Greece have the right to postpone their conscription; they are permanently exempted from their military obligations when they reach the age of 45 years old
note 2: as of 2023, women comprised nearly 17% of the military's full-time personnel

Military deployments: approximately 1,000 Cyprus; 110 Kosovo (NATO); 120 Lebanon (UNIFIL) (2024)

Military - note: the Hellenic Armed Forces (HAF) are responsible for protecting Greece's independence, sovereignty, and territorial integrity; the HAF also maintains a presence on Cyprus (the Hellenic Force in Cyprus or ELDYK) to assist and support the Cypriot National Guard; as a member of the EU, NATO, and other international organizations, the HAF participates in multinational peacekeeping and other security missions abroad, taking a particular interest in missions occurring in the near regions, such as the Balkans, the Mediterranean and Aegean seas, the Middle East, and North Africa; areas of focus for the HAF include instability in the Balkans, territorial disputes with Turkey, and support to European security through the EU and NATO
Greece's NATO membership is a key component of its security; it became a NATO member in 1952 and occupies a strategic location in the Eastern Mediterranean on NATO's southern flank; Greece is host to several NATO facilities, including the Deployable Corps Greece (NDCGR) headquarters in Thessaloniki, the Combined Air Operations Center in Larissa, the Multinational Peace Support Operations Training Center in Kilkis, the Multinational Sealift Coordination Center in Athens, and the Naval Base, Maritime Interdiction Operational Training Centre, and NATO Missile Firing Installation at Souda, Crete (2025)

SPACE

Space agency/agencies: Hellenic Space Center (HSC; aka Hellenic Space Agency; established 2018) (2025)

Space program overview: space program focused on building and operating satellites for communications and remote sensing (RS); researches and develops technologies in a variety of space sectors, including such areas agricultural areas, defense, environmental studies, RS, and telecommunications; has a national space strategy; as a member of the European Space Agency (ESA), it contributes to, participates in, and benefits from ESA capabilities and programs; cooperates with space agencies and commercial space sectors of ESA and EU member states, as well as the US; has a commercial space sector that researches, develops, and produces a variety of space technologies and capabilities, including satellite components, electronics, sensors, and telecommunications (2025)
note: further details about the key activities, programs, and milestones of the country's space program, as well as government spending estimates on the space sector, appear in the Space Programs reference guide

TERRORISM

Terrorist group(s): Terrorist group(s): Islamic State of Iraq and ash-Sham (ISIS); Revolutionary Struggle (RS); Revolutionary People's Liberation Party/Front (DHKP/C)
note: details about the history, aims, leadership, organization, areas of operation, tactics, targets, weapons, size, and sources of support of the group(s) appear(s) in the Terrorism reference guide

TRANSNATIONAL ISSUES

Refugees and internally displaced persons: *refugees:* 144,694 (2024 est.)
stateless persons: 3,743 (2024 est.)

GREENLAND

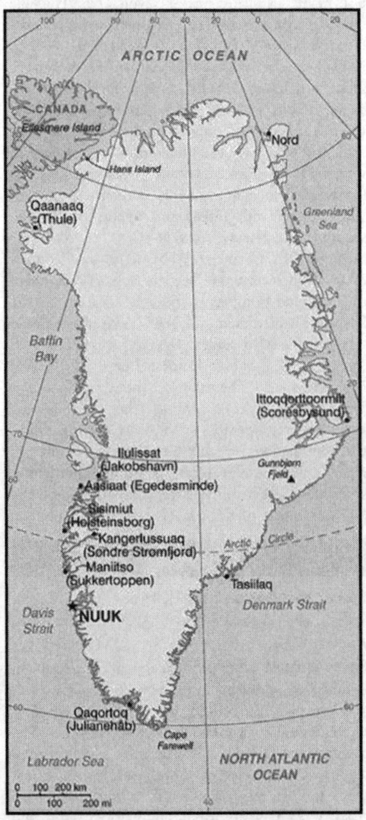

INTRODUCTION

Background: Greenland, the world's largest island, is about 80% ice capped. The Inuit came to Greenland from North America in a series of migrations that stretched from 2500 BC to the11th century. Vikings reached the island in the 10th century from Iceland; Danish colonization began in the 18th century, and Greenland became part of the Kingdom of Denmark in 1953. It joined the European Community (now the EU) with Denmark in 1973 but withdrew in 1985 over a dispute centered on stringent fishing quotas. Greenland remains a member of the EU's Overseas Countries and Territories Association. The Danish parliament granted Greenland home rule in 1979; the law went into effect the following year. Greenland voted in favor of self-government in 2008 and acquired greater responsibility for internal affairs when the Act on Greenland Self-Government was signed into law in 2009. The Kingdom of Denmark, however, continues to exercise control over several policy areas on behalf of Greenland, including foreign affairs, security, and financial policy, in consultation with Greenland's Self-Rule Government.

GEOGRAPHY

Location: Northern North America, island between the Arctic Ocean and the North Atlantic Ocean, northeast of Canada

Geographic coordinates: 72 00 N, 40 00 W

Map references: Arctic Region

Area: *total:* 2,166,086 sq km
land: 2,166,086 sq km (approximately 1,710,000 sq km ice-covered)
comparison ranking: total 13

Area - comparative: slightly more than three times the size of Texas

Land boundaries: *total:* 0 km

Coastline: 44,087 km

Maritime claims: *territorial sea:* 3 nm
continental shelf: 200 nm or agreed boundaries or median line
exclusive fishing zone: 200 nm or agreed boundaries or median line

Climate: arctic to subarctic; cool summers, cold winters

Terrain: flat to gradually sloping icecap covers all but a narrow, mountainous, barren, rocky coast

Elevation: *highest point:* Gunnbjorn Fjeld 3,694 m
lowest point: Atlantic Ocean 0 m
mean elevation: 1,792 m

Natural resources: coal, iron ore, lead, zinc, molybdenum, diamonds, gold, platinum, niobium, tantalite, uranium, fish, seals, whales, hydropower, possible oil and gas

Land use: *agricultural land:* 0.6% (2022 est.)
arable land: 0% (2022 est.)
permanent crops: 0% (2022 est.)
permanent pasture: 0.6% (2022 est.)
forest: 0% (2022 est.)
other: 99.4% (2022 est.)

Irrigated land: NA

Population distribution: settlement concentrated on the southwest shoreline, with limited settlements scattered along the remaining coast; interior is uninhabited

Natural hazards: continuous permafrost over northern two-thirds of the island

Geography - note: dominates North Atlantic Ocean between North America and Europe; sparse population confined to small settlements along coast; close to one-quarter of the population lives in the capital, Nuuk; world's second largest ice sheet after that of Antarctica, covering an area of 1.71 million sq km (660,000 sq mi), or about 79% of the island, and containing 2.85 million cu km (684 thousand cu mi) of ice (almost 7% of the world's fresh water)

PEOPLE AND SOCIETY

Population: *total:* 57,751 (2024 est.)
male: 29,843
female: 27,908
comparison rankings: total 206; male 206; female 206

Nationality: *noun:* Greenlander(s)
adjective: Greenlandic

Ethnic groups: Greenlandic 88.1%, Danish 7.1%, Filipino 1.6%, other Nordic peoples 0.9%, and other 2.3% (2024 est.)
note: data represent population by country of birth

Languages: Greenlandic, Danish, English
note: West Greenlandic or Kalaallisut is the official language; Tunumiisut (East Greenlandic) and Inuktun (Polar Inuit Greenlandic) are considered dialects of Kalaallisut and spoken by about 10% of Greenlanders

Religions: Evangelical Lutheran, traditional Inuit spiritual beliefs

Age structure: *0-14 years:* 20.4% (male 5,964/female 5,798)
15-64 years: 67.1% (male 20,050/female 18,711)
65 years and over: 12.5% (2024 est.) (male 3,829/female 3,399)

Dependency ratios: *total dependency ratio:* 49 (2024 est.)
youth dependency ratio: 30.3 (2024 est.)
elderly dependency ratio: 18.6 (2024 est.)
potential support ratio: 5.4 (2024 est.)

Median age: *total:* 35.3 years (2024 est.)
male: 35.9 years
female: 34.7 years
comparison ranking: total 100

Population growth rate: -0.05% (2024 est.)
comparison ranking: 200

Birth rate: 13.5 births/1,000 population (2024 est.)
comparison ranking: 126

Death rate: 9.2 deaths/1,000 population (2024 est.)
comparison ranking: 51

Net migration rate: -4.9 migrant(s)/1,000 population (2024 est.)
comparison ranking: 202

Population distribution: settlement concentrated on the southwest shoreline, with limited settlements scattered along the remaining coast; interior is uninhabited

Urbanization: *urban population:* 87.9% of total population (2023)
rate of urbanization: 0.41% annual rate of change (2020-25 est.)

Major urban areas - population: 18,000 NUUK (capital) (2018)

Sex ratio: *at birth:* 1.05 male(s)/female
0-14 years: 1.03 male(s)/female
15-64 years: 1.07 male(s)/female
65 years and over: 1.13 male(s)/female
total population: 1.07 male(s)/female (2024 est.)

Infant mortality rate: *total:* 8.5 deaths/1,000 live births (2024 est.)
male: 9.9 deaths/1,000 live births
female: 6.9 deaths/1,000 live births
comparison ranking: total 142

Life expectancy at birth: *total population:* 74.5 years (2024 est.)
male: 71.8 years
female: 77.3 years
comparison ranking: total population 141

Total fertility rate: 1.88 children born/woman (2024 est.)

comparison ranking: 124

Gross reproduction rate: 0.92 (2024 est.)

Drinking water source: *improved:* total: 100% of population (2022 est.)
unimproved: total: 0% of population (2022 est.)

Physician density: 1.87 physicians/1,000 population (2016)

Sanitation facility access: *improved:* total: 62.5% of population (2022 est.)
unimproved: urban: 0% of population
rural: 0% of population
total: 37.5% of population (2022 est.)

Currently married women (ages 15-49): 39.4% (2023 est.)

Education expenditure: 10.2% of GDP (2019 est.)
comparison ranking: Education expenditure (% GDP) 5

ENVIRONMENT

Environmental issues: changes in sea levels and other disruptions in the Arctic environment

Climate: arctic to subarctic; cool summers, cold winters

Urbanization: *urban population:* 87.9% of total population (2023)
rate of urbanization: 0.41% annual rate of change (2020-25 est.)

Carbon dioxide emissions: 527,000 metric tonnes of CO2 (2023 est.)
from coal and metallurgical coke: 12 metric tonnes of CO2 (2023 est.)
from petroleum and other liquids: 527,000 metric tonnes of CO2 (2023 est.)
comparison ranking: total emissions 189

Waste and recycling: *municipal solid waste generated annually:* 50,000 tons (2024 est.)

GOVERNMENT

Country name: *conventional long form:* none
conventional short form: Greenland
local long form: none
local short form: Kalaallit Nunaat
etymology: named by Norse navigator Erik THORVALDSSON (Erik the Red) in A.D. 985 to attract settlers to the island; the original Greenlandic name, Kalaallit Nunaat, means "land of the people"

Government type: parliamentary democracy (Parliament of Greenland or Inatsisartut)

Dependency status: part of the Kingdom of Denmark; self-governing overseas administrative division of Denmark since 1979

Capital: *name:* Nuuk
geographic coordinates: 64 11 N, 51 45 W
time difference: UTC-2 (3 hours ahead of Washington, DC, during Standard Time)
daylight saving time: +1hr, begins last Sunday in March; ends last Sunday in October
time zone note: Greenland has three time zones
etymology: *nuuk* is the Inuit word for "cape;" until 1979, the name was Godthab, from the Danish words meaning "good hope"

Administrative divisions: 5 municipalities (*kommuner*, singular - *kommune*); Avannaata, Kujalleq, Qeqertalik, Qeqqata, Sermersooq
note: Northeast Greenland National Park (Kalaallit Nunaanni Nuna Eqqissisimatitaq) and the Pituffik Space Base (formerly known as Thule Air Base) in northwest Greenland are two unincorporated areas; the national park's 972,000 sq km – about 46% of the island – makes it the largest national park in the world and also the most northerly

Legal system: Denmark's laws apply in some areas, and Greenland's law for the remainder

Constitution: *history:* previous 1953 (Greenland established as a constituency in the Danish constitution), 1979 (Greenland Home Rule Act); latest 21 June 2009 (Greenland Self-Government Act)

Citizenship: see Denmark

Suffrage: 18 years of age; universal

Executive branch: *chief of state:* King FREDERIK X of Denmark (since 14 January 2024), represented by High Commissioner Julie Praest WILCHE (since May 2022) (2024)
head of government: Prime Minister Jens-Frederik NIELSEN (since 28 March 2025)
cabinet: Self-rule Government (Naalakkersuisut) elected by the Parliament (Inatsisartut)
election/appointment process: the monarchy is hereditary; high commissioner appointed by the monarch; premier indirectly elected by Parliament for a 4-year term
election results: 2025: Jens-Frederik NIELSEN (D) elected premier
2021: Mute B. EGEDE elected premier; Parliament vote - Mute B. EGEDE (Inuit Ataqatigiit) unanimous
2014: Kim KIELSEN elected premier; Parliament vote - Kim KIELSEN (S) 27.2%, Sara OLSVIG (IA) 25.5%, Randi Vestergaard EVALDSEN (D) 19.5%, other 27.8%

Legislative branch: *legislature name:* Parliament (Inatsisartut)
legislative structure: unicameral
number of seats: 31 (directly elected)
electoral system: proportional representation
scope of elections: full renewal
term in office: 4 years
most recent election date: 4/6/2021
parties elected and seats per party: IA (12); S (10); N (4); D (3); A (2)
percentage of women in chamber: 35%
expected date of next election: 2025
note: Greenland elects 2 members to the Danish Parliament to serve 4-year terms

Judicial branch: *highest court(s):* High Court of Greenland (consists of the presiding professional judge and 2 lay assessors)
judge selection and term of office: judges appointed by the monarch on the recommendation of the Judicial Appointments Council, a 6-member independent body of judges and lawyers; judges appointed for life with retirement at age 70
subordinate courts: Court of Greenland; 18 district or magistrates' courts
note: appeals beyond the High Court of Greenland can be heard by the Supreme Court (in Copenhagen)

Political parties: Democrats Party (Demokraatit) or D
Fellowship Party (Atassut) or A
Forward Party (Siumut) or S
Inuit Community (Inuit Ataqatigiit) or IA
Signpost Party (Naleraq) or N (formerly Partii Naleraq)

Diplomatic representation in the US: *chief of mission:* Kenneth HØEGH, Head of Representation (since 1 August 2021)
chancery: 3200 Whitehaven Street, NW Washington, DC 20008
telephone: [1] (202) 234-4300
FAX: [1] (202) 328-1470
email address and website: washington@nanoq.gl

All Greenlandic Representations | GrÃ¸nlands RÃ¦prÃ¦sentation (grl-rep.dk); https://naalakkersuisut.gl/en/Naalakkersuisut/Groenlands-repraesentation-Washington
note: Greenland also has offices in the Danish consulates in Chicago and New York

Diplomatic representation from the US: *chief of mission:* Consul Monica BLAND (since July 2023)
embassy: Aalisartut Aqqutaa 47
Nuuk 3900
Greenland
telephone: (+299) 384100
email address and website: USConsulateNuuk@state.gov
Homepage - U.S. Embassy & Consulate in the Kingdom of Denmark (usembassy.gov)

International organization participation: Arctic Council, ICC, NC, NIB, UPU

Independence: none (extensive self-rule as part of the Kingdom of Denmark)

National holiday: National Day, June 21
note: marks the summer solstice and the longest day of the year in the Northern Hemisphere

Flag: *description:* two equal horizontal bands of white (top) and red, with a large disk set slightly to the left; the top half of the disk is red, and the bottom is white
meaning: the design represents the sun reflecting off a field of ice; the colors are the same as the Danish flag and symbolize Greenland's links to the Kingdom of Denmark

National symbol(s): polar bear

National color(s): red, white

National anthem(s): *title:* "Nunarput utoqqarsuanngoravit" (Our Country, Who's Become So Old)
lyrics/music: Henrik LUND/Jonathan PETERSEN
history: adopted 1916
title: "Nuna asiilasooq" (The Land of Great Length)
lyrics/music: unknown
history: adopted 1979, when home rule was granted; the Greenlandic government recognizes this local Kalaallit song as a secondary anthem

National heritage: *total World Heritage Sites:* 3 (2 cultural, 1 natural); note - excerpted from the Denmark entry
selected World Heritage Site locales: Ilulissat Icefjord (n); Kujataa, Norse, and Inuit Farming (c); Aasivissuit–Nipisat, Inuit Hunting Ground (c)

ECONOMY

Economic overview: high-income, self-governing Danish territorial economy; non-EU member but preferential market access; dependent on Danish financial support; exports led by fishing industry; growing tourism and interest in untapped mineral deposits; relies on hydropower for fuel

Real GDP (purchasing power parity): $4.04 billion (2023 est.)
$4.005 billion (2022 est.)
$3.926 billion (2021 est.)
note: data in 2021 dollars
comparison ranking: 189

Real GDP growth rate: 0.9% (2023 est.)
2% (2022 est.)
1.6% (2021 est.)

note: annual GDP % growth based on constant local currency
comparison ranking: 180

Real GDP per capita: $71,000 (2023 est.)
$70,700 (2022 est.)
$69,300 (2021 est.)
note: data in 2021 dollars
comparison ranking: 15

GDP (official exchange rate): $3.327 billion (2023 est.)
note: data in current dollars at official exchange rate

Inflation rate (consumer prices): 1.2% (2022 est.)
0% (2021 est.)
2.1% (2020 est.)
note: annual % change based on consumer prices
comparison ranking: 27

GDP - composition, by sector of origin: *agriculture:* 16.6% (2023 est.)
industry: 18.4% (2023 est.)
services: 61% (2023 est.)
note: figures may not total 100% due to non-allocated consumption not captured in sector-reported data
comparison rankings: agriculture 48; industry 142; services 82

GDP - composition, by end use: *household consumption:* 32.6% (2023 est.)
government consumption: 41.7% (2023 est.)
investment in fixed capital: 34.7% (2023 est.)
investment in inventories: 1.3% (2023 est.)
exports of goods and services: 40.8% (2023 est.)
imports of goods and services: -51.1% (2023 est.)
note: figures may not total 100% due to rounding or gaps in data collection

Agricultural products: sheep, cattle, reindeer, fish, shellfish

Industries: fish processing (mainly shrimp and Greenland halibut), anorthosite and ruby mining, handicrafts, hides and skins, small shipyards

Industrial production growth rate: -1.3% (2023 est.)
note: annual % change in industrial value added based on constant local currency
comparison ranking: 151

Budget: *revenues:* $1.719 billion (2016 est.)
expenditures: $1.594 billion (2016 est.)

Exports: $1.357 billion (2023 est.)
$1.286 billion (2022 est.)
$1.122 billion (2021 est.)
note: GDP expenditure basis - exports of goods and services in current dollars
comparison ranking: 177

Exports - partners: Denmark 50%, China 23%, UK 5%, Japan 5%, Germany 3% (2023)
note: top five export partners based on percentage share of exports

Exports - commodities: fish, shellfish, processed crustaceans, ships, precious stones (2023)
note: top five export commodities based on value in dollars

Imports: $1.7 billion (2023 est.)
$1.657 billion (2022 est.)
$1.635 billion (2021 est.)
note: GDP expenditure basis - imports of goods and services in current dollars
comparison ranking: 180

Imports - partners: Denmark 58%, Sweden 19%, Spain 8%, Iceland 7%, Canada 2% (2023)
note: top five import partners based on percentage share of imports

Imports - commodities: refined petroleum, ships, garments, plastic products, furniture (2023)
note: top five import commodities based on value in dollars

Exchange rates: Danish kroner (DKK) per US dollar -

Exchange rates: 6.894 (2024 est.)
6.89 (2023 est.)
7.076 (2022 est.)
6.287 (2021 est.)
6.542 (2020 est.)

ENERGY

Electricity access: *electrification - total population:* 100% (2022 est.)

Electricity: *installed generating capacity:* 190,000 kW (2023 est.)
consumption: 534.5 million kWh (2023 est.)
transmission/distribution losses: 10 million kWh (2023 est.)
comparison rankings: installed generating capacity 174; consumption 175; transmission/distribution losses 16

Electricity generation sources: *fossil fuels:* 13.6% of total installed capacity (2023 est.)
solar: 0.2% of total installed capacity (2023 est.)
hydroelectricity: 85.8% of total installed capacity (2023 est.)
biomass and waste: 0.5% of total installed capacity (2023 est.)

Coal: *imports:* 5 metric tons (2023 est.)
proven reserves: 383 million metric tons (2023 est.)

Petroleum: *refined petroleum consumption:* 4,000 bbl/day (2023 est.)

COMMUNICATIONS

Telephones - fixed lines: *total subscriptions:* 6,000 (2020 est.)
subscriptions per 100 inhabitants: 9 (2022 est.)
comparison ranking: total subscriptions 197

Telephones - mobile cellular: *total subscriptions:* 67,000 (2021 est.)
subscriptions per 100 inhabitants: 118 (2021 est.)
comparison ranking: total subscriptions 202

Broadcast media: Greenland Broadcasting Company provides public radio and TV, with a broadcast station and a series of repeaters; a few private local TV and radio stations; Danish public radio rebroadcasts are available (2019)

Internet country code: .gl

Internet users: *percent of population:* 70% (2017 est.)

Broadband - fixed subscriptions: *total:* 18,000 (2022 est.)
subscriptions per 100 inhabitants: 32 (2022 est.)
comparison ranking: total 174

TRANSPORTATION

Civil aircraft registration country code prefix: OY-H

Airports: 25 (2025)
comparison ranking: 129

Heliports: 54 (2025)
comparison ranking: 37

Merchant marine: *total:* 10 (2023)
by type: other 10
comparison ranking: total 160

Ports: *total ports:* 23 (2024)
large: 0
medium: 0
small: 7
very small: 10
size unknown: 6
ports with oil terminals: 5
key ports: Aasiaat, Ilulissat (Jakobshavn), Kusanartoq, Nuuk, Paamuit (Frederikshab), Qeqertarsuaq, Sisimiut

MILITARY AND SECURITY

Military and security forces: no regular military forces

Military - note: the Danish military's Joint Arctic Command in Nuuk is responsible for coordinating Denmark's defense of Greenland
the US Space Force maintains a base on Greenland's northwest coast, about 750 miles from the North Pole

GRENADA

INTRODUCTION

Background: The indigenous Carib people inhabited Grenada when Christopher COLUMBUS landed on the island in 1498, but it remained uncolonized for more than a century. The French settled Grenada in the 17th century, established sugar estates, and imported large numbers of African slaves. Britain took the island in 1762 and vigorously expanded sugar production. In the 19th century, cacao eventually surpassed sugar as the main export crop; in the 20th century, nutmeg became the leading export. In 1967, Britain gave Grenada autonomy over its internal affairs. Full independence was attained in 1974, making Grenada one of the smallest independent countries in the Western Hemisphere. In 1979, a leftist New Jewel Movement seized power under Maurice BISHOP, ushering in the Grenada Revolution. On 19 October 1983, factions within the revolutionary government overthrew and killed BISHOP and members of his party. Six days later, US forces and those of six other Caribbean nations intervened, quickly capturing the ringleaders and their hundreds of Cuban advisers. Rule of law was restored, and democratic elections were reinstituted the following year and have continued since.

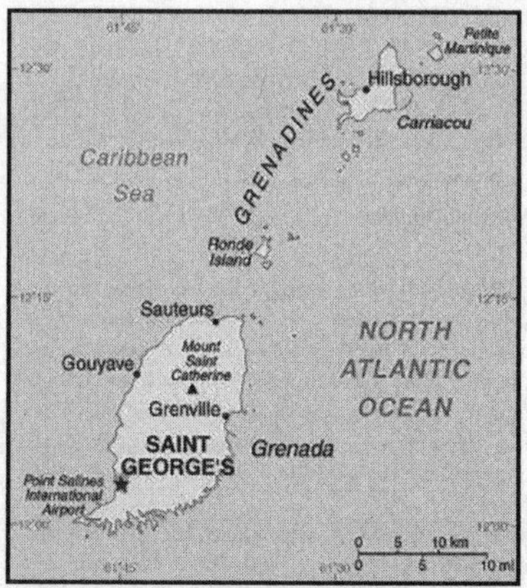

GEOGRAPHY

Location: Caribbean, island between the Caribbean Sea and Atlantic Ocean, north of Trinidad and Tobago

Geographic coordinates: 12 07 N, 61 40 W

Map references: Central America and the Caribbean

Area: *total:* 344 sq km
land: 344 sq km
water: 0 sq km
comparison ranking: total 207

Area - comparative: twice the size of Washington, D.C.

Land boundaries: *total:* 0 km

Coastline: 121 km

Maritime claims: *territorial sea:* 12 nm
exclusive economic zone: 200 nm

Climate: tropical; tempered by northeast trade winds

Terrain: volcanic in origin with central mountains

Elevation: *highest point:* Mount Saint Catherine 840 m
lowest point: Caribbean Sea 0 m

Natural resources: timber, tropical fruit

Land use: *agricultural land:* 23.5% (2022 est.)
arable land: 8.8% (2022 est.)
permanent crops: 11.8% (2022 est.)
permanent pasture: 2.9% (2022 est.)
forest: 52.1% (2022 est.)
other: 24.4% (2022 est.)

Irrigated land: 20 sq km (2012)

Population distribution: approximately one third of the population is found in the capital of St. George's; the island's population is concentrated along the coast

Natural hazards: lies on edge of hurricane belt; hurricane season lasts from June to November
volcanism: Mount Saint Catherine (840 m) is on the island of Grenada; Kick 'em Jenny, an active submarine volcano (seamount) on the Caribbean Sea floor, lies about 8 km (5 mi) north of Grenada; these two volcanoes are at the southern end of the volcanic island arc of the Lesser Antilles that extends to the Dutch dependency of Saba in the north

PEOPLE AND SOCIETY

Population: *total:* 114,621 (2024 est.)
male: 58,168
female: 56,453
comparison rankings: total 190; male 189; female 190

Nationality: *noun:* Grenadian(s)
adjective: Grenadian

Ethnic groups: African descent 82.4%, mixed 13.3%, East Indian 2.2%, other 1.3%, unspecified 0.9% (2011 est.)

Languages: English (official), French patois

Religions: Protestant 49.2% (includes Pentecostal 17.2%, Seventh Day Adventist 13.2%, Anglican 8.5%, Baptist 3.2%, Church of God 2.4%, Evangelical 1.9%, Methodist 1.6%, other 1.2%), Roman Catholic 36%, Jehovah's Witness 1.2%, Rastafarian 1.2%, other 5.5%, none 5.7%, unspecified 1.3% (2011 est.)

Age structure: *0-14 years:* 21.9% (male 13,095/female 12,003)
15-64 years: 65.3% (male 38,129/female 36,726)
65 years and over: 12.8% (2024 est.) (male 6,944/female 7,724)

Dependency ratios: *total dependency ratio:* 53.1 (2024 est.)
youth dependency ratio: 33.5 (2024 est.)
elderly dependency ratio: 19.6 (2024 est.)
potential support ratio: 5.1 (2024 est.)

Median age: *total:* 35.4 years (2024 est.)
male: 35.2 years
female: 35.7 years
comparison ranking: total 97

Population growth rate: 0.27% (2024 est.)
comparison ranking: 169

Birth rate: 13.3 births/1,000 population (2024 est.)
comparison ranking: 128

Death rate: 8.4 deaths/1,000 population (2024 est.)
comparison ranking: 76

Net migration rate: -2.2 migrant(s)/1,000 population (2024 est.)
comparison ranking: 171

Population distribution: approximately one third of the population is found in the capital of St. George's; the island's population is concentrated along the coast

Urbanization: *urban population:* 37.1% of total population (2023)
rate of urbanization: 0.86% annual rate of change (2020-25 est.)

Major urban areas - population: 39,000 SAINT GEORGE'S (capital) (2018)

Sex ratio: *at birth:* 1.1 male(s)/female
0-14 years: 1.09 male(s)/female
15-64 years: 1.04 male(s)/female
65 years and over: 0.9 male(s)/female
total population: 1.03 male(s)/female (2024 est.)

Maternal mortality ratio: 48 deaths/100,000 live births (2023 est.)
comparison ranking: 95

Infant mortality rate: *total:* 9 deaths/1,000 live births (2024 est.)
male: 8.6 deaths/1,000 live births
female: 9.5 deaths/1,000 live births
comparison ranking: total 139

Life expectancy at birth: *total population:* 76.3 years (2024 est.)
male: 73.7 years
female: 79.1 years
comparison ranking: total population 112

Total fertility rate: 1.9 children born/woman (2024 est.)
comparison ranking: 118

Gross reproduction rate: 0.91 (2024 est.)

Health expenditure: 5.7% of GDP (2021)
6.3% of national budget (2022 est.)

Physician density: 1.38 physicians/1,000 population (2018)

Hospital bed density: 3.2 beds/1,000 population (2018 est.)

Obesity - adult prevalence rate: 21.3% (2016)
comparison ranking: 91

Alcohol consumption per capita: *total:* 8.62 liters of pure alcohol (2019 est.)
beer: 3.54 liters of pure alcohol (2019 est.)
wine: 0.56 liters of pure alcohol (2019 est.)
spirits: 4.21 liters of pure alcohol (2019 est.)
other alcohols: 0.31 liters of pure alcohol (2019 est.)
comparison ranking: total 37

Currently married women (ages 15-49): 41.3% (2023 est.)

Education expenditure: 5.1% of GDP (2023 est.)
14.5% national budget (2024 est.)
comparison ranking: Education expenditure (% GDP) 61

School life expectancy (primary to tertiary education): *total:* 18 years (2018 est.)
male: 17 years (2018 est.)
female: 18 years (2018 est.)

ENVIRONMENT

Environmental issues: deforestation causing habitat and species loss; coastal erosion and contamination; pollution and sedimentation; inadequate solid waste management

International environmental agreements: *party to:* Biodiversity, Climate Change, Climate Change-Kyoto Protocol, Climate Change-Paris Agreement, Comprehensive Nuclear Test Ban, Desertification, Endangered Species, Law of the Sea, Ozone Layer Protection, Ship Pollution, Wetlands, Whaling
signed, but not ratified: none of the selected agreements

Climate: tropical; tempered by northeast trade winds

Urbanization: *urban population:* 37.1% of total population (2023)
rate of urbanization: 0.86% annual rate of change (2020-25 est.)

Carbon dioxide emissions: 348,000 metric tonnes of CO2 (2023 est.)
from petroleum and other liquids: 348,000 metric tonnes of CO2 (2023 est.)
comparison ranking: total emissions 194

Particulate matter emissions: 10.2 micrograms per cubic meter (2019 est.)

Waste and recycling: *municipal solid waste generated annually:* 29,500 tons (2024 est.)
percent of municipal solid waste recycled: 15.1% (2022 est.)

Total water withdrawal: *municipal:* 12 million cubic meters (2022 est.)

industrial: 0 cubic meters (2022 est.)
agricultural: 2.1 million cubic meters (2022 est.)

Total renewable water resources: 200 million cubic meters (2022 est.)

GOVERNMENT

Country name: *conventional long form:* none
conventional short form: Grenada
etymology: origin of the name remains obscure; some sources attribute the designation to Spanish influence (most likely named for the Spanish city of Granada); in Spanish *granada* means "pomegranate"

Government type: parliamentary democracy under a constitutional monarchy; a Commonwealth realm

Capital: *name:* Saint George's
geographic coordinates: 12 03 N, 61 45 W
time difference: UTC-4 (1 hour ahead of Washington, DC, during Standard Time)
etymology: originally named Ville de Fort Royal (Fort Royal Town), the name was changed to Saint George's Town in 1764, in honor of the patron saint of England, when the English took over Grenada from the French; the name was eventually shortened to Saint George's

Administrative divisions: 6 parishes and 1 dependency*; Carriacou and Petite Martinique*, Saint Andrew, Saint David, Saint George, Saint John, Saint Mark, Saint Patrick

Legal system: common law based on English model

Constitution: *history:* previous 1967; latest presented 19 December 1973, effective 7 February 1974, suspended 1979 following a revolution but restored in 1983
amendment process: proposed by either house of Parliament; passage requires two-thirds majority vote by the membership in both houses and assent of the governor general; passage of amendments to constitutional sections, such as personal rights and freedoms, the structure, authorities, and procedures of the branches of government, the delimitation of electoral constituencies, or the procedure for amending the constitution, also requires two-thirds majority approval in a referendum

International law organization participation: has not submitted an ICJ jurisdiction declaration; accepts ICCt jurisdiction

Citizenship: *citizenship by birth:* yes
citizenship by descent only: yes
dual citizenship recognized: yes
residency requirement for naturalization: 7 years for persons from a non-Caribbean state and 4 years for a person from a Caribbean state

Suffrage: 18 years of age; universal

Executive branch: *chief of state:* King CHARLES III (since 8 September 2022); represented by Governor General Cecile LA GRENADE (since 7 May 2013)
head of government: Prime Minister Dickon MITCHELL (since 24 June 2022)
cabinet: Cabinet appointed by the governor general on the advice of the prime minister
election/appointment process: the monarchy is hereditary; governor general appointed by the monarch; following legislative elections, the governor general usually appoints the leader of the majority party or majority coalition as prime minister

Legislative branch: *legislature name:* Parliament
legislative structure: bicameral

Legislative branch - lower chamber: *chamber name:* House of Representatives
number of seats: 15 (all directly elected)
electoral system: plurality/majority
scope of elections: full renewal
term in office: 5 years
most recent election date: 6/23/2022
parties elected and seats per party: National Democratic Congress (NDC) (9); New National Party (NNP) (6)
percentage of women in chamber: 31.3%
expected date of next election: June 2027

Legislative branch - upper chamber: *chamber name:* Senate
number of seats: 13 (all appointed)
scope of elections: full renewal
term in office: 5 years
most recent election date: 8/31/2022
percentage of women in chamber: 30.8%
expected date of next election: August 2027

Judicial branch: *highest court(s):* regionally, the Eastern Caribbean Supreme Court (ECSC) is the superior court of the Organization of Eastern Caribbean States; the ECSC is headquartered on St. Lucia and consists of the Court of Appeal – headed by the chief justice and 4 judges – and the High Court with 18 judges; the Court of Appeal travels to member states on a schedule to hear appeals from the High Court and subordinate courts
judge selection and term of office: chief justice of Eastern Caribbean Supreme Court appointed by the British monarch; other justices and judges appointed by the Judicial and Legal Services Commission, and independent body of judicial officials; Court of Appeal justices appointed for life with mandatory retirement at age 65; High Court judges appointed for life with mandatory retirement at age 62
subordinate courts: magistrates' courts; Court of Magisterial Appeals
note: appeals beyond the ECSC in civil and criminal matters are heard by the Judicial Committee of the Privy Council (in London)

Political parties: National Democratic Congress or NDC
New National Party or NNP

Diplomatic representation in the US: *chief of mission:* Ambassador Tarlie FRANCIS (since 15 September 2023)
chancery: 1701 New Hampshire Avenue NW, Washington, DC 20009
telephone: [1] (202) 265-2561

FAX: [1] (202) 265-2468
email address and website: embassy@grenadaembassy-usa.org
https://grenadaembassyusa.org/
consulate(s) general: Miami, New York

Diplomatic representation from the US: *chief of mission:* the US does not have an official embassy in Grenada; the Chargé d'Affaires to Barbados, Karin B. SULLIVAN, is accredited to Grenada
embassy: Lance-aux-Epines, Saint George's
mailing address: 3180 Grenada Place, Washington DC 20521-3180
telephone: [1] (473) 444-1173

FAX: [1] (473) 444-4820
email address and website: StgeorgesACS@state.gov
https://bb.usembassy.gov/embassy/grenada/

International organization participation: ACP, ACS, AOSIS, CARIFORUM, CARIBCAN, Caricom, CBI, CDB, CELAC, CSME, ECCU, EPA, FAO, G-77, IBRD, ICAO, ICCt (signatory), ICRM, IDA, IFAD, IFC, IFRCS, ILO, IMF, IMO, Interpol, IOC, ITU, ITUC, LAES, MIGA, NAM, OAS, OECS, OPANAL, OPCW, Petrocaribe, UN, UNCTAD, UNESCO, UNIDO, UPU, WHO, WIPO, WTO

Independence: 7 February 1974 (from the UK)

National holiday: Independence Day, 7 February (1974)

Flag: *description:* a rectangle divided diagonally into yellow triangles (top and bottom) and green triangles (left and right), with a wide red border around the flag; three five-pointed yellow stars are centered on the top and bottom of the red border, with one larger yellow star on a red disk at the center of the flag; a small yellow-and-red nutmeg pod is on the left triangle
meaning: the seven stars stand for the country's administrative divisions, with the central star symbolizing the capital, St. George's; yellow stands for the sun and the warmth of the people, green for vegetation and agriculture, and red for harmony, unity, and courage

National symbol(s): Grenada dove, bougainvillea flower

National color(s): red, yellow, green

National coat of arms: Grenada's coat of arms shows Grand Etang Lake, a crater lake on the volcano that formed Grenada; in the center of the shield is Christopher Columbus's ship, the Santa Maria, which landed on the island in 1498; the gold cross dividing the shield, the two Madonna lilies, and the national motto signal the importance of religion; two lions symbolize past UK rule (1762-1974), as well as Grenada's current status as a Commonwealth country; the corn stalk and banana plant represent agriculture; the armadillo and Grenada dove next to the shield are native to the island, and the roses in the bougainvillea flower garland represent Grenada's seven communities

National anthem(s): *title:* "Hail Grenada"
lyrics/music: Irva Merle BAPTISTE/Louis Arnold MASANTO
history: adopted 1974
title: "God Save the King"
lyrics/music: unknown
history: royal anthem, as a Commonwealth country

ECONOMY

Economic overview: small OECS service-based economy; large tourism, construction, transportation, and education sectors; major spice exporter; shrinking but still high public debt; vulnerable to hurricanes; emerging blue economy incentives

Real GDP (purchasing power parity): $2.08 billion (2024 est.)
$2.005 billion (2023 est.)
$1.916 billion (2022 est.)
note: data in 2021 dollars
comparison ranking: 196

Real GDP growth rate: 3.7% (2024 est.)
4.7% (2023 est.)
7.3% (2022 est.)
note: annual GDP % growth based on constant local currency
comparison ranking: 88

Real GDP per capita: $17,700 (2024 est.)
$17,100 (2023 est.)
$16,400 (2022 est.)

note: data in 2021 dollars
comparison ranking: 113

GDP (official exchange rate): $1.391 billion (2024 est.)
note: data in current dollars at official exchange rate

Inflation rate (consumer prices): 1.1% (2024 est.)
2.7% (2023 est.)
2.6% (2022 est.)
note: annual % change based on consumer prices
comparison ranking: 24

GDP - composition, by sector of origin: *agriculture:* 2.7% (2024 est.)
industry: 14.8% (2024 est.)
services: 65.2% (2024 est.)
note: figures may not total 100% due to non-allocated consumption not captured in sector-reported data
comparison rankings: agriculture 135; industry 164; services 59

Agricultural products: sugarcane, coconuts, eggs, vegetables, fruits, bananas, plantains, grapefruits, avocados, mangoes/guavas (2023)
note: top ten agricultural products based on tonnage

Industries: food and beverages, textiles, light assembly operations, tourism, construction, education, call-center operations

Industrial production growth rate: 2.9% (2024 est.)
note: annual % change in industrial value added based on constant local currency
comparison ranking: 83

Population below poverty line: 25% (2018 est.)
note: % of population with income below national poverty line

Gini Index coefficient - distribution of family income: 43.8 (2018 est.)
note: index (0-100) of income distribution; higher values represent greater inequality
comparison ranking: 23

Household income or consumption by percentage share: *lowest 10%:* 2.1% (2018 est.)
highest 10%: 33.7% (2018 est.)
note: % share of income accruing to lowest and highest 10% of population

Remittances: 5% of GDP (2024 est.)
5.3% of GDP (2023 est.)
5.1% of GDP (2022 est.)
note: personal transfers and compensation between resident and non-resident individuals/households/entities

Budget: *revenues:* $288.404 million (2017 est.)
expenditures: $222.475 million (2017 est.)
note: central government revenues and expenses (excluding grants/extrabudgetary units/social security funds) converted to US dollars at average official exchange rate for year indicated

Current account balance: -$270.771 million (2024 est.)
-$243.473 million (2023 est.)
-$148.445 million (2022 est.)
note: balance of payments - net trade and primary/secondary income in current dollars
comparison ranking: 105

Exports: $858.949 million (2024 est.)
$828.529 million (2023 est.)
$706.195 million (2022 est.)
note: balance of payments - exports of goods and services in current dollars
comparison ranking: 185

Exports - partners: USA 24%, Antigua & Barbuda 13%, St. Vincent & the Grenadines 8%, Dominica 6%, Trinidad & Tobago 5% (2023)
note: top five export partners based on percentage share of exports

Exports - commodities: nutmeg/cardamons, fish, wheat flours, frozen fruits and nuts, aqueous paints (2023)
note: top five export commodities based on value in dollars

Imports: $990.587 million (2024 est.)
$924.688 million (2023 est.)
$785.022 million (2022 est.)
note: balance of payments - imports of goods and services in current dollars
comparison ranking: 190

Imports - partners: USA 37%, Trinidad & Tobago 13%, Cayman Islands 10%, China 4%, UK 3% (2023)
note: top five import partners based on percentage share of imports

Imports - commodities: refined petroleum, cars, poultry, ships, plastic products (2023)
note: top five import commodities based on value in dollars

Reserves of foreign exchange and gold: $423.263 million (2024 est.)
$404.13 million (2023 est.)
$371.767 million (2022 est.)
note: holdings of gold (year-end prices)/foreign exchange/special drawing rights in current dollars
comparison ranking: 164

Debt - external: $501.371 million (2023 est.)
note: present value of external debt in current US dollars
comparison ranking: 112

Exchange rates: East Caribbean dollars (XCD) per US dollar -

Exchange rates: 2.7 (2024 est.)
2.7 (2023 est.)
2.7 (2022 est.)
2.7 (2021 est.)
2.7 (2020 est.)

ENERGY

Electricity access: *electrification - total population:* 94.2% (2022 est.)

Electricity: *installed generating capacity:* 60,000 kW (2023 est.)
consumption: 221.453 million kWh (2023 est.)
transmission/distribution losses: 18 million kWh (2023 est.)
comparison rankings: installed generating capacity 192; consumption 187; transmission/distribution losses 24

Electricity generation sources: *fossil fuels:* 98.2% of total installed capacity (2023 est.)
solar: 1.7% of total installed capacity (2023 est.)
wind: 0.1% of total installed capacity (2023 est.)

Coal: *imports:* 1 metric tons (2023 est.)

Petroleum: *refined petroleum consumption:* 2,000 bbl/day (2023 est.)

Energy consumption per capita: 41.703 million Btu/person (2023 est.)
comparison ranking: 101

COMMUNICATIONS

Telephones - fixed lines: *total subscriptions:* 17,000 (2022 est.)
subscriptions per 100 inhabitants: 14 (2022 est.)
comparison ranking: total subscriptions 176

Telephones - mobile cellular: *total subscriptions:* 112,000 (2022 est.)
subscriptions per 100 inhabitants: 81 (2021 est.)
comparison ranking: total subscriptions 192

Broadcast media: multiple publicly and privately owned TV and radio stations; state-owned Grenada Information Service (GIS) provides TV and radio; the Grenada Broadcasting Network, jointly owned by the government and the Caribbean Communications Network of Trinidad and Tobago, operates a TV station and 2 radio stations; multi-channel cable TV subscription service is provided by Columbus Communications Grenada (FLOW GRENADA); approximately 25 private radio stations (2019)

Internet country code: .gd

Internet users: *percent of population:* 74% (2023 est.)

Broadband - fixed subscriptions: *total:* 35,000 (2022 est.)
subscriptions per 100 inhabitants: 30 (2022 est.)
comparison ranking: total 155

TRANSPORTATION

Civil aircraft registration country code prefix: J3

Airports: 2 (2025)
comparison ranking: 203

Merchant marine: *total:* 6 (2023)
by type: general cargo 3, other 3
comparison ranking: total 166

Ports: *total ports:* 1 (2024)
large: 0
medium: 0
small: 1
very small: 0
ports with oil terminals: 1
key ports: St. George's

MILITARY AND SECURITY

Military and security forces: no regular military forces; the Royal Grenada Police Force (under the Ministry of National Security) includes a Coast Guard and a paramilitary Special Services Unit (2025)

Military - note: Grenada joined the Caribbean Regional Security System (RSS) in 1985; RSS signatories (Antigua and Barbuda, Barbados, Dominica, Guyana, Saint Kitts and Nevis, Saint Lucia, and Saint Vincent and the Grenadines) agreed to prepare contingency plans and assist one another, on request, in national emergencies, prevention of smuggling, search and rescue, immigration control, fishery protection, customs and excise control, maritime policing duties, protection of off-shore installations, pollution control, national and other disasters, and threats to national security (2024)

TRANSNATIONAL ISSUES

Refugees and internally displaced persons: IDPs: 383 (2024 est.)

GUAM

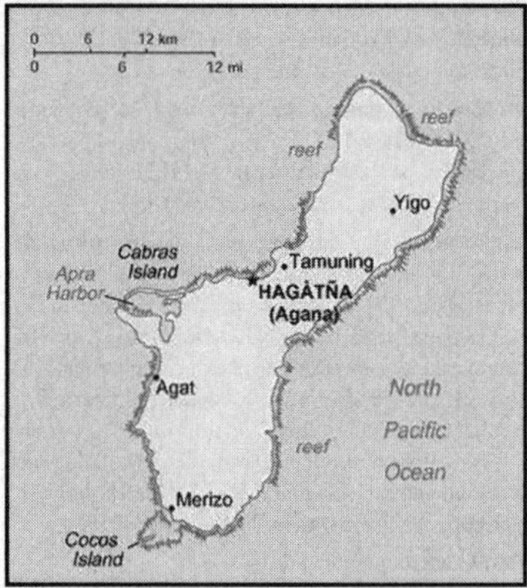

INTRODUCTION

Background: Guam was settled by Austronesian people around 1500 B.C. These people became the indigenous Chamorro and were influenced by later migrations, including the Micronesians in the first millennium A.D., and island Southeast Asians around 900. Society was stratified, with higher classes living along the coast and lower classes living inland. Spanish explorer Ferdinand MAGELLAN was the first European to see Guam in 1521, and Spain claimed the island in 1565 because it served as a refueling stop for ships between Mexico and the Philippines. Spain formally colonized Guam in 1668. Spain's brutal repression of the Chamorro, along with new diseases and intermittent warfare, reduced the indigenous population from more than 100,000 to less than 5,000 by the 1700s. Spain tried to repopulate the island by forcing people from nearby islands to settle on Guam and preventing them from escaping.

Guam became a hub for whalers and traders in the western Pacific in the early 1800s. During the 1898 Spanish-American War, the US Navy occupied Guam and set up a military administration. The US Navy opposed local control of government despite repeated petitions from the Chamorro. Japan invaded Guam in 1941 and instituted a repressive regime. During the US recapture of Guam in 1944, the island's two largest villages were destroyed. After World War II, political pressure from local Chamorro leaders led to Guam being established as an unincorporated organized US territory in 1950, with US citizenship granted to all Chamorro. In a referendum in 1982, more than 75% of voters chose closer relations with the US over independence, although no change in status was made because of disagreements on the future right of Chamorro self-determination. The US military holds about 29% of Guam's land and stations several thousand troops on the island. The installations are some of the most strategically important US bases in the Pacific; they also constitute the island's most important source of income and economic stability.

GEOGRAPHY

Location: Oceania, island in the North Pacific Ocean, about three-quarters of the way from Hawaii to the Philippines

Geographic coordinates: 13 28 N, 144 47 E

Map references: Oceania

Area: *total:* 544 sq km
land: 544 sq km
water: 0 sq km
comparison ranking: total 194

Area - comparative: three times the size of Washington, D.C.

Land boundaries: *total:* 0 km

Coastline: 125.5 km

Maritime claims: *territorial sea:* 12 nm
exclusive economic zone: 200 nm

Climate: tropical marine; generally warm and humid, moderated by northeast trade winds; dry season (January to June), rainy season (July to December); little seasonal temperature variation

Terrain: volcanic origin, surrounded by coral reefs; relatively flat coralline limestone plateau (source of most fresh water), with steep coastal cliffs and narrow coastal plains in north, low hills in center, mountains in south

Elevation: *highest point:* Mount Lamlam 406 m
lowest point: Pacific Ocean 0 m

Natural resources: aquatic wildlife (supporting tourism), fishing (largely undeveloped)

Land use: *agricultural land:* 29.6% (2022 est.)
arable land: 1.9% (2022 est.)
permanent crops: 13% (2022 est.)
permanent pasture: 14.8% (2022 est.)
forest: 51.9% (2022 est.)
other: 18.5% (2022 est.)

Irrigated land: 2 sq km (2012)

Population distribution: no large cities exist on the island; large villages (municipalities) attract much of the population; the largest of these is Dededo

Natural hazards: frequent squalls during rainy season; relatively rare but potentially destructive typhoons (June to December)

Geography - note: largest and southernmost island in the Mariana Islands archipelago and the largest island in Micronesia; strategic location in western North Pacific Ocean

PEOPLE AND SOCIETY

Population: *total:* 169,532 (2024 est.)
male: 87,345
female: 82,187
comparison rankings: total 185; male 185; female 186

Nationality: *noun:* Guamanian(s) (US citizens)
adjective: Guamanian

Ethnic groups: Native Hawaiian and other Pacific Islander 46.1% (Chamorro 32.8%, Chuukese 6.7%, Palauan 1.4%, Pohnpeian 1.4%, Yapese 1%, other Native Hawaiian and other Pacific Islander 2.8%), Asian 35.5% (Filipino 29.1%, Korean 2.2%, Japanese 1.4%, Chinese (except Taiwanese) 1.3%, other Asian 1.5%), White 6.8%, African descent or African-American 0.9%, Indigenous 0.1%, other 0.6%, mixed 10% (2020 est.)

Languages: English 43.3%, Filipino 24.9%, Chamorro 16%, other Pacific Island languages 9.4%, Asian languages 6.5% (2020 est.)

Religions: Christian (predominantly Roman Catholic) 94.2%, folk religions 1.5%, Buddhist 1.1%, other 1.6%, unaffiliated 1.7% (2020 est.)

Age structure: *0-14 years:* 26.4% (male 23,139/ female 21,632)
15-64 years: 62.7% (male 55,591/female 50,741)
65 years and over: 10.9% (2024 est.) (male 8,615/ female 9,814)

Dependency ratios: *total dependency ratio:* 59.4 (2024 est.)
youth dependency ratio: 42.1 (2024 est.)
elderly dependency ratio: 17.3 (2024 est.)
potential support ratio: 5.8 (2024 est.)

Median age: *total:* 30.3 years (2024 est.)
male: 29.6 years
female: 31.1 years
comparison ranking: total 137

Population growth rate: 0.11% (2024 est.)
comparison ranking: 184

Birth rate: 18.1 births/1,000 population (2024 est.)
comparison ranking: 78

Death rate: 6.1 deaths/1,000 population (2024 est.)
comparison ranking: 150

Net migration rate: -10.9 migrant(s)/1,000 population (2024 est.)
comparison ranking: 224

Population distribution: no large cities exist on the island; large villages (municipalities) attract much of the population; the largest of these is Dededo

Urbanization: *urban population:* 95.2% of total population (2022)
rate of urbanization: 0.84% annual rate of change (2020-25 est.)

Major urban areas - population: 147,000 HAGATNA (capital) (2018)

Sex ratio: *at birth:* 1.07 male(s)/female
0-14 years: 1.07 male(s)/female
15-64 years: 1.1 male(s)/female
65 years and over: 0.88 male(s)/female
total population: 1.06 male(s)/female (2024 est.)

Infant mortality rate: *total:* 10.9 deaths/1,000 live births (2024 est.)
male: 11 deaths/1,000 live births
female: 10.9 deaths/1,000 live births
comparison ranking: total 124

Life expectancy at birth: *total population:* 78 years (2024 est.)
male: 75.6 years
female: 80.5 years
comparison ranking: total population 83

Total fertility rate: 2.73 children born/woman (2024 est.)
comparison ranking: 59

Gross reproduction rate: 1.32 (2024 est.)

Drinking water source: *improved:* total: 99.7% of population (2022 est.)
unimproved: total: 0.3% of population (2022 est.)

Sanitation facility access: *improved:* total: 99.2% of population (2022 est.)
unimproved: *total:* 0.8% of population (2022 est.)

Currently married women (ages 15-49): 37% (2023 est.)

ENVIRONMENT

Environmental issues: freshwater scarcity; reef damage; inadequate sewage treatment; rapid proliferation of the non-native brown tree snake

Climate: tropical marine; generally warm and humid, moderated by northeast trade winds; dry season (January to June), rainy season (July to December); little seasonal temperature variation

Urbanization: *urban population:* 95.2% of total population (2022)
rate of urbanization: 0.84% annual rate of change (2020-25 est.)

Carbon dioxide emissions: 1.819 million metric tonnes of CO2 (2023 est.)
from petroleum and other liquids: 1.819 million metric tonnes of CO2 (2023 est.)
comparison ranking: total emissions 161

Waste and recycling: *municipal solid waste generated annually:* 141,500 tons (2024 est.)
percent of municipal solid waste recycled: 17.9% (2011 est.)

GOVERNMENT

Country name: *conventional long form:* none
conventional short form: Guam
local long form: none
local short form: Guahan
abbreviation: GU
etymology: the native Chamorro name for the island, Guahan (meaning "we have"), was changed to Guam in the 1898 Treaty of Paris, when Spain relinquished Guam, Cuba, Puerto Rico, and the Philippines to the US

Government type: unincorporated organized territory of the US with local self-government; republican form of territorial government with separate executive, legislative, and judicial branches

Dependency status: unincorporated, organized territory of the US, with policy relations between Guam and the Federal government under the jurisdiction of the Office of Insular Affairs, US Department of the Interior

Capital: *name:* Hagatna (Agana)
geographic coordinates: 13 28 N, 144 44 E
time difference: UTC+10 (15 hours ahead of Washington, DC, during Standard Time)
etymology: the name Hagatna is derived from the Chamorro word *haga*, meaning "life's blood" and referring to the town's role as the center of government for the island

Administrative divisions: none (territory of the US)

Legal system: common law modeled on US system; US federal laws apply

Constitution: *history:* effective 1 July 1950 (Guam Act of 1950 serves as a constitution)

Citizenship: see United States

Suffrage: 18 years of age; universal
note: Guamanians are US citizens but do not vote in US presidential elections

Executive branch: *chief of state:* President Donald J. TRUMP (since 20 January 2025)
head of government: Governor Lourdes LEON GUERRERO (since 7 January 2019)
cabinet: Cabinet appointed by the governor with the consent of the Legislature
election/appointment process: president and vice president indirectly elected on the same ballot by an Electoral College of electors chosen from each state to serve a 4-year term (eligible for a second term); under the US Constitution, residents of unincorporated territories, such as Guam, do not vote in elections for US president and vice president, but they can vote in Democratic and Republican presidential primary elections; governor and lieutenant governor elected on the same ballot by absolute majority vote in 2 rounds, if needed, for a 4-year term (eligible for 2 consecutive terms)
most recent election date: *gubernatorial:* 8 November 2022
election results: *2022:* Lourdes LEON GUERRERO reelected governor; percent of vote - Lourdes LEON GUERRERO (Democratic Party) 55%, Felix CAMACHO (Republican Party) 44%; Josh TENORIO (Democratic Party) elected lieutenant governor
2018: Lourdes LEON GUERRERO elected governor; percent of vote - Lourdes LEON GUERRERO (Democratic Party) 50.7%, Ray TENORIO (Republican Party) 26.4%; Josh TENORIO (Democratic Party) elected lieutenant governor
expected date of next election: *gubernatorial:* 3 November 2026

Legislative branch: *legislature name:* Legislature of Guam (Liheslaturan Guahan)
legislative structure: unicameral
number of seats: 15 (directly elected)
electoral system: plurality/majority
scope of elections: full renewal
term in office: 2 years
most recent election date: 11/8/2022
parties elected and seats per party: Democratic Party (9); Republican Party (6)
percentage of women in chamber: 40%
expected date of next election: November 2024
note: Guam directly elects 1 member by simple majority vote to serve a 2-year term as delegate to the US House of Representatives; the delegate can vote when serving on a committee and when the House meets as the Committee of the Whole House, but not when legislation is submitted for a "full floor" House vote

Judicial branch: *highest court(s):* Supreme Court of Guam (consists of 3 justices)
judge selection and term of office: justices appointed by the governor and confirmed by the Guam legislature; justices appointed for life but subject to retention election every 10 years
subordinate courts: Superior Court of Guam (includes several divisions); US Federal District Court for the District of Guam (a US territorial court; appeals beyond this court are heard before the US Court of Appeals for the Ninth Circuit)
note: appeals beyond the Supreme Court of Guam are referred to the US Supreme Court

Political parties: Democratic Party
Republican Party

Diplomatic representation in the US: none (territory of the US)

Diplomatic representation from the US: *embassy:* none (territory of the US)

International organization participation: AOSIS (observer), IOC, PIF (observer), SPC, UPU

Independence: none (territory of the US)

National holiday: Discovery Day (or Magellan Day), first Monday in March (1521)

Flag: *description:* territorial flag is dark blue with a narrow red border on all four sides; centered is a red-bordered, pointed, vertical ellipse containing a beach scene, a *proa* (outrigger canoe with sail), and a palm tree; the word GUAM in red is centered in the ellipse; the proa is sailing in Agana Bay with the promontory of Puntan Dos Amantes in the background
meaning: blue stands for the sea and red for the blood shed in the fight against oppression; the central emblem is shaped like a Chamorro sling stone (a weapon for defense or hunting)
note: the US flag is the national flag

National symbol(s): coconut tree

National color(s): deep blue, red

National anthem(s): *title:* "Fanohge Chamoru" (Stand, Ye Guamanians)
lyrics/music: Ramon Manalisay SABLAN [English], Lagrimas UNTALAN [Chamoru]/Ramon Manalisay SABLAN
history: adopted 1919; the local anthem is also known as "Guam Hymn"
title: "The Star-Spangled Banner"
lyrics/music: Francis Scott KEY/John Stafford SMITH
history: official anthem, as a US territory; played before "Stand, Ye Guamanians"

ECONOMY

Economic overview: small Pacific island US territorial economy; upper income, tourism-based economy; hard-hit by COVID-19 disruptions; relaunched many industries via vaccination tourism; domestic economy relies on multiple military bases; environmentally fragile economy

Real GDP growth rate: 5.1% (2022 est.)
2.1% (2021 est.)
-10.5% (2020 est.)
note: annual GDP % growth based on constant local currency
comparison ranking: 38

Real GDP per capita: $35,600 (2016 est.)
$35,200 (2015 est.)
$34,400 (2014 est.)
comparison ranking: 67

GDP (official exchange rate): $6.91 billion (2022 est.)
note: data in current dollars at official exchange rate

Agricultural products: fruits, copra, vegetables; eggs, pork, poultry, beef

Industries: national defense, tourism, construction, transshipment services, concrete products, printing and publishing, food processing, textiles

Labor force: 77,700 (2024 est.)
note: number of people ages 15 or older who are employed or seeking work
comparison ranking: 185

Unemployment rate: 5.6% (2024 est.)
5.4% (2023 est.)
5.5% (2022 est.)
note: % of labor force seeking employment
comparison ranking: 107

Youth unemployment rate (ages 15-24): *total:* 13.7% (2024 est.)
male: 13.3% (2024 est.)

female: 14.1% (2024 est.)
note: % of labor force ages 15-24 seeking employment
comparison ranking: total 93

Average household expenditures: *on food:* 34.6% of household expenditures (2021 est.)
on alcohol and tobacco: 1.3% of household expenditures (2021 est.)

Budget: *revenues:* $1.24 billion (2016 est.)
expenditures: $1.299 billion (2016 est.)

Exports: $545 million (2022 est.)
$193 million (2021 est.)
$379 million (2020 est.)
note: GDP expenditure basis - exports of goods and services in current dollars
comparison ranking: 190

Exports - partners: Taiwan 42%, Hong Kong 12%, Philippines 11%, Italy 8%, Australia 6% (2023)
note: top five export partners based on percentage share of exports

Exports - commodities: scrap iron, scrap copper, trunks and cases (2023)
note: top export commodities based on value in dollars over $500,000

Imports: $4.421 billion (2022 est.)
$3.662 billion (2021 est.)
$3.388 billion (2020 est.)
note: GDP expenditure basis - imports of goods and services in current dollars
comparison ranking: 156

Imports - partners: Singapore 52%, Japan 15%, Malaysia 6%, Taiwan 4%, Greece 4% (2023)
note: top five import partners based on percentage share of imports

Imports - commodities: refined petroleum, cars, trunks and cases, gas turbines, flavored water (2023)
note: top five import commodities based on value in dollars

Exchange rates: the US dollar is used

ENERGY

Electricity access: *electrification - total population:* 100% (2022 est.)

Electricity: *installed generating capacity:* 525,000 kW (2023 est.)
consumption: 1.715 billion kWh (2023 est.)
transmission/distribution losses: 90.023 million kWh (2023 est.)
comparison rankings: installed generating capacity 150; consumption 152; transmission/distribution losses 44

Electricity generation sources: *fossil fuels:* 92.1% of total installed capacity (2023 est.)
solar: 7.8% of total installed capacity (2023 est.)
wind: 0.1% of total installed capacity (2023 est.)

Petroleum: *refined petroleum consumption:* 11,000 bbl/day (2023 est.)

Energy consumption per capita: 150.555 million Btu/person (2019 est.)
comparison ranking: 25

COMMUNICATIONS

Telephones - fixed lines: *total subscriptions:* 70,000 (2021 est.)
subscriptions per 100 inhabitants: 43 (2022 est.)
comparison ranking: total subscriptions 146

Telephones - mobile cellular: *total subscriptions:* 98,000 (2009 est.)
subscriptions per 100 inhabitants: 62 (2009 est.)
comparison ranking: total subscriptions 195

Broadcast media: about a dozen TV channels, including digital; multi-channel cable TV services are available; roughly 20 radio stations

Internet country code: .gu

Internet users: *percent of population:* 81% (2017 est.)

Broadband - fixed subscriptions: *total:* 3,000 (2022 est.)
subscriptions per 100 inhabitants: 2 (2022 est.)
comparison ranking: total 197

TRANSPORTATION

Civil aircraft registration country code prefix: N

Airports: 3 (2025)
comparison ranking: 186

Heliports: 2 (2025)
comparison ranking: 136

Merchant marine: *total:* 3 (2023)
by type: other 3
comparison ranking: total 173

Ports: *total ports:* 1 (2024)
large: 0
medium: 1
small: 0
very small: 0
ports with oil terminals: 1
key ports: Apra Harbor

MILITARY AND SECURITY

Military and security forces: Guam Police Department (GPD); Guam (US) National Guard

Military - note: defense is the responsibility of the US; the US military maintains about 8,000 active-duty uniformed personnel and several bases and installations

GUATEMALA

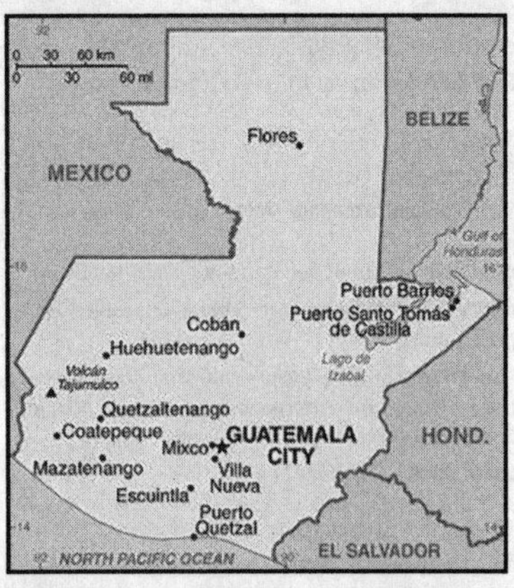

INTRODUCTION

Background: The Maya civilization flourished in Guatemala and surrounding regions during the first millennium A.D. After almost three centuries as a Spanish colony, Guatemala won its independence in 1821. During the second half of the 20th century, it experienced a variety of military and civilian governments, as well as a 36-year guerrilla war. In 1996, the government signed a peace agreement formally ending the internal conflict.

GEOGRAPHY

Location: Central America, bordering the North Pacific Ocean, between El Salvador and Mexico, and bordering the Gulf of Honduras (Caribbean Sea) between Honduras and Belize

Geographic coordinates: 15 30 N, 90 15 W

Map references: Central America and the Caribbean

Area: *total:* 108,889 sq km
land: 107,159 sq km
water: 1,730 sq km
comparison ranking: total 107

Area - comparative: slightly smaller than Pennsylvania

Land boundaries: *total:* 1,667 km
border countries (4): Belize 266 km; El Salvador 199 km; Honduras 244 km; Mexico 958 km

Coastline: 400 km

Maritime claims: *territorial sea:* 12 nm
exclusive economic zone: 200 nm
continental shelf: 200-m depth or to the depth of exploitation

Climate: tropical; hot, humid in lowlands; cooler in highlands

Terrain: *two east-west trending mountain chains divide the country into three regions:* the mountainous highlands, the Pacific coast south of mountains, and the vast northern Peten lowlands

Elevation: *highest point:* Volcan Tajumulco (highest point in Central America) 4,220 m
lowest point: Pacific Ocean 0 m
mean elevation: 759 m

Natural resources: petroleum, nickel, rare woods, fish, chicle, hydropower

Land use: *agricultural land:* 43% (2022 est.)
arable land: 14.5% (2022 est.)
permanent crops: 11% (2022 est.)
permanent pasture: 17.5% (2022 est.)
forest: 32.7% (2022 est.)
other: 24.3% (2022 est.)

Irrigated land: 3,375 sq km (2012)

Major lakes (area sq km): *fresh water lake(s):* Lago de Izabal - 590 sq km

Population distribution: the vast majority of the populace resides in the southern half of the country, particularly in the mountainous regions; more than half of the population lives in rural areas

Natural hazards: numerous volcanoes in mountains, with occasional violent earthquakes; Caribbean coast extremely susceptible to hurricanes and other tropical storms
volcanism: significant volcanic activity in the Sierra Madre range; Santa Maria (3,772 m) has been deemed a Decade Volcano by the International Association of Volcanology and Chemistry of the Earth's Interior, worthy of study due to its explosive history and close proximity to human populations; Pacaya (2,552 m) is one of the country's most active volcanoes, with frequent eruptions since 1965; other historically active volcanoes include Acatenango, Almolonga, Atitlan, Fuego, and Tacana; see note 2 under "Geography - note"

Geography - note: *note 1:* despite having both eastern and western coastlines (Caribbean Sea and Pacific Ocean), there are no natural harbors on the west coast
note 2: Guatemala is one of the countries along the Ring of Fire, which is a belt bordering the Pacific Ocean that contains about 75% of the world's volcanoes and up to 90% of the world's earthquakes

PEOPLE AND SOCIETY

Population: *total:* 18,255,216 (2024 est.)
male: 9,050,684
female: 9,204,532
comparison rankings: total 69; male 68; female 70

Nationality: *noun:* Guatemalan(s)
adjective: Guatemalan

Ethnic groups: Mestizo (mixed Indigenous-Spanish - in local Spanish called Ladino) 56%, Maya 41.7%, Xinca (Indigenous, non-Maya) 1.8%, African descent 0.2%, Garifuna (mixed West and Central African, Island Carib, and Arawak) 0.1%, foreign 0.2% (2018 est.)

Languages: Spanish (official) 69.9%, Maya languages 29.7% (Q'eqchi' 8.3%, K'iche 7.8%, Mam 4.4%, Kaqchikel 3%, Q'anjob'al 1.2%, Poqomchi' 1%, other 4%), other 0.4% (includes Xinca and Garifuna) (2018 est.)
major-language sample(s):
La Libreta Informativa del Mundo, la fuente indispensable de información básica. (Spanish)
note: the 2003 Law of National Languages officially recognized 23 indigenous languages, including 21 Maya languages, Xinca, and Garifuna

Religions: Evangelical 45.7%, Roman Catholic 42.4%, none 11%, unspecified 0.9% (2023 est.)

Age structure: *0-14 years:* 31.5% (male 2,925,079/female 2,819,927)
15-64 years: 63.2% (male 5,688,500/female 5,839,958)
65 years and over: 5.4% (2024 est.) (male 437,105/female 544,647)

Dependency ratios: *total dependency ratio:* 58.3 (2024 est.)
youth dependency ratio: 49.8 (2024 est.)
elderly dependency ratio: 8.5 (2024 est.)
potential support ratio: 11.7 (2024 est.)

Median age: *total:* 24.8 years (2024 est.)
male: 24.2 years
female: 25.4 years
comparison ranking: total 174

Population growth rate: 1.49% (2024 est.)
comparison ranking: 64

Birth rate: 21.4 births/1,000 population (2024 est.)
comparison ranking: 59

Death rate: 4.9 deaths/1,000 population (2024 est.)
comparison ranking: 200

Net migration rate: -1.6 migrant(s)/1,000 population (2024 est.)
comparison ranking: 161

Population distribution: the vast majority of the populace resides in the southern half of the country, particularly in the mountainous regions; more than half of the population lives in rural areas

Urbanization: *urban population:* 53.1% of total population (2023)
rate of urbanization: 2.59% annual rate of change (2020-25 est.)

Major urban areas - population: 3.095 million GUATEMALA CITY (capital) (2023)

Sex ratio: *at birth:* 1.05 male(s)/female
0-14 years: 1.04 male(s)/female
15-64 years: 0.97 male(s)/female
65 years and over: 0.8 male(s)/female
total population: 0.98 male(s)/female (2024 est.)

Mother's mean age at first birth: 20.6 years (2014/15 est.)
note: data represents median age at first birth among women 25-49

Maternal mortality ratio: 94 deaths/100,000 live births (2023 est.)
comparison ranking: 67

Infant mortality rate: *total:* 25 deaths/1,000 live births (2024 est.)
male: 28.1 deaths/1,000 live births
female: 21.7 deaths/1,000 live births
comparison ranking: total 59

Life expectancy at birth: *total population:* 73.5 years (2024 est.)
male: 71.5 years
female: 75.6 years
comparison ranking: total population 149

Total fertility rate: 2.52 children born/woman (2024 est.)
comparison ranking: 70

Gross reproduction rate: 1.23 (2024 est.)

Drinking water source: *improved: urban:* 97.8% of population (2022 est.)
rural: 91% of population (2022 est.)
total: 94.6% of population (2022 est.)
unimproved: urban: 2.2% of population (2022 est.)
rural: 9% of population (2022 est.)
total: 5.4% of population (2022 est.)

Health expenditure: 6.9% of GDP (2021)
16.9% of national budget (2022 est.)

Physician density: 1.28 physicians/1,000 population (2020)

Hospital bed density: 0.4 beds/1,000 population (2021 est.)

Sanitation facility access: *improved: urban:* 91.4% of population (2022 est.)
rural: 68.9% of population (2022 est.)
total: 80.8% of population (2022 est.)
unimproved: urban: 8.6% of population (2022 est.)
rural: 31.1% of population (2022 est.)
total: 19.2% of population (2022 est.)

Obesity - adult prevalence rate: 21.2% (2016)
comparison ranking: 92

Alcohol consumption per capita: *total:* 1.63 liters of pure alcohol (2019 est.)
beer: 0.9 liters of pure alcohol (2019 est.)
wine: 0.05 liters of pure alcohol (2019 est.)
spirits: 0.68 liters of pure alcohol (2019 est.)
other alcohols: 0.01 liters of pure alcohol (2019 est.)
comparison ranking: total 135

Tobacco use: *total:* 11.8% (2025 est.)
male: 22.5% (2025 est.)
female: 1.5% (2025 est.)
comparison ranking: total 115

Children under the age of 5 years underweight: 14.4% (2021/22)
comparison ranking: 34

Currently married women (ages 15-49): 57.2% (2023 est.)

Child marriage: *women married by age 15:* 6.2% (2015)
women married by age 18: 29.5% (2015)
men married by age 18: 9.6% (2015)

Education expenditure: 3.2% of GDP (2023 est.)
18.9% national budget (2022 est.)
comparison ranking: Education expenditure (% GDP) 146

Literacy: *total population:* 83% (2022 est.)
male: 88.4% (2022 est.)
female: 78.6% (2022 est.)

School life expectancy (primary to tertiary education): *total:* 11 years (2023 est.)
male: 10 years (2023 est.)
female: 11 years (2023 est.)

ENVIRONMENT

Environmental issues: deforestation in the Peten rainforest; soil erosion; water pollution

International environmental agreements: *party to:* Antarctic Treaty, Biodiversity, Climate Change, Climate Change-Kyoto Protocol, Climate Change-Paris Agreement, Comprehensive Nuclear Test Ban, Desertification, Endangered Species, Environmental Modification, Hazardous Wastes, Law of the Sea, Marine Dumping-London Convention, Marine Dumping-London Protocol, Nuclear Test Ban, Ozone Layer Protection, Ship Pollution, Tropical Timber 2006, Wetlands
signed, but not ratified: none of the selected agreements

Climate: tropical; hot, humid in lowlands; cooler in highlands

Urbanization: *urban population:* 53.1% of total population (2023)
rate of urbanization: 2.59% annual rate of change (2020-25 est.)

Carbon dioxide emissions: 18.546 million metric tonnes of CO_2 (2023 est.)
from coal and metallurgical coke: 2.31 million metric tonnes of CO_2 (2023 est.)
from petroleum and other liquids: 16.232 million metric tonnes of CO_2 (2023 est.)
from consumed natural gas: 4,000 metric tonnes of CO_2 (2023 est.)
comparison ranking: total emissions 92

Particulate matter emissions: 21.8 micrograms per cubic meter (2019 est.)

Waste and recycling: *municipal solid waste generated annually:* 2.757 million tons (2024 est.)
percent of municipal solid waste recycled: 10.4% (2022 est.)

Total water withdrawal: *municipal:* 835 million cubic meters (2022 est.)
industrial: 603.1 million cubic meters (2022 est.)
agricultural: 1.886 billion cubic meters (2022 est.)

Total renewable water resources: 127.91 billion cubic meters (2022 est.)

GOVERNMENT

Country name: *conventional long form:* Republic of Guatemala
conventional short form: Guatemala
local long form: República de Guatemala
local short form: Guatemala
etymology: the Spanish conquistadors' first capital (established in 1524) was a former Mayan settlement called "Quauhtemallan" by their Nahuatl-speaking Mexican allies, a name that means "land of the eagle" but that the Spanish probably pronounced "Guatemala"

Government type: presidential republic

Capital: *name:* Guatemala City
geographic coordinates: 14 37 N, 90 31 W
time difference: UTC-6 (1 hour behind Washington, DC, during Standard Time)
etymology: the Spanish conquistadors' first capital (established in 1524) was a former Mayan settlement called "Quauhtemallan" by their Nahuatl-speaking Mexican allies, a name that means "land of the eagle" but that the Spanish probably pronounced "Guatemala"

Administrative divisions: 22 departments (*departamentos*, singular - *departamento*); Alta Verapaz, Baja Verapaz, Chimaltenango, Chiquimula, El Progreso, Escuintla, Guatemala, Huehuetenango, Izabal, Jalapa, Jutiapa, Peten, Quetzaltenango, Quiche, Retalhuleu, Sacatepequez, San Marcos, Santa Rosa, Solola, Suchitepequez, Totonicapan, Zacapa

Legal system: civil law system; judicial review of legislative acts

Constitution: *history:* several previous; latest adopted 31 May 1985, effective 14 January 1986; suspended and reinstated in 1994
amendment process: proposed by the president of the republic, by agreement of 10 or more deputies of Congress, by the Constitutional Court, or by public petition of at least 5,000 citizens; passage requires at least two-thirds majority vote by the Congress membership and approval by public referendum, referred to as "popular consultation"; constitutional articles such as national sovereignty, the republican form of government, limitations on those seeking the presidency, or presidential tenure cannot be amended

International law organization participation: has not submitted an ICJ jurisdiction declaration; accepts ICCt jurisdiction

Citizenship: *citizenship by birth:* yes
citizenship by descent only: yes
dual citizenship recognized: yes
residency requirement for naturalization: 5 years with no absences of six consecutive months or longer or absences totaling more than a year

Suffrage: 18 years of age; universal
note: active-duty members of the armed forces and police by law cannot vote and are restricted to their barracks on election day

Executive branch: *chief of state:* President Bernardo ARÉVALO de León (since 15 January 2024)
head of government: President Bernardo ARÉVALO de León (since 15 January 2024)
cabinet: Council of Ministers appointed by the president
election/appointment process: president and vice president directly elected on the same ballot by absolute-majority popular vote in 2 rounds, if needed, for a 4-year term (not eligible for consecutive terms)
most recent election date: 25 June 2023, with a runoff on 20 August 2023
election results: *2023:* Bernardo ARÉVALO de León elected president in second round; percent of vote in first round - Sandra TORRES (UNE) 21%; Bernardo ARÉVALO de León (SEMILLA) 15.6%, Manuel CONDE Orellana (VAMOS) 10.4%; Armando CASTILLO Alvarado (VIVA) 9.6%, other 43.4%; percent of vote in second round - Bernardo ARÉVALO de León 60.9%, Sandra TORRES 39.1%
2019: Alejandro GIAMMATTEI elected president; percent of vote in first round - Sandra TORRES (UNE) 25.5%, Alejandro GIAMMATTEI (VAMOS) 14%, Edmond MULET (PHG) 11.2%, Thelma CABRERA (MLP) 10.4%, Roberto ARZU (PAN-PODEMOS) 6.1%, other 32.8%; percent of vote in second round - Alejandro GIAMMATTEI 58%, Sandra TORRES 42%
expected date of next election: June 2027
note: the president is both chief of state and head of government

Legislative branch: *legislature name:* Congress of the Republic (Congreso de la República)
legislative structure: unicameral
number of seats: 160 (all directly elected)
electoral system: mixed system
scope of elections: full renewal
term in office: 4 years
most recent election date: 6/25/2023
parties elected and seats per party: Let's Go for a Different Guatemala (Vamos) (39); National Unity of Hope Party (UNE) (28); Seed Movement (Semilla) (23); Cabal (18); Vision with Values (VIVA) (11); Other (41)
percentage of women in chamber: 20%
expected date of next election: June 2027

Judicial branch: *highest court(s):* Supreme Court of Justice or Corte Suprema de Justicia (consists of 13 magistrates, including the court president and organized into 3 chambers)
judge selection and term of office: Supreme Court magistrates elected by the Congress of the Republic from candidates proposed by the Postulation Committee, an independent body of deans of the country's university law schools, representatives of the country's law associations, and representatives of the Courts of Appeal; magistrates elected for concurrent, renewable 5-year terms; Constitutional Court judges - 1 elected by the Congress of the Republic, 1 by the Supreme Court, 1 by the president of the republic, 1 by the (public) University of San Carlos, and 1 by the Assembly of the College of Attorneys and Notaries; judges elected for renewable, consecutive 5-year terms; the presidency of the court rotates among the magistrates for a single 1-year term
subordinate courts: Appellate Courts of Accounts, Contentious Administrative Tribunal, courts of appeal, first instance courts, child and adolescence courts, minor or peace courts
note 1: the Supreme Court of Justice president also supervises trial judges countrywide
note 2: the Constitutional Court or Corte de Constitucionalidad of Guatemala resides outside the country's judicial system; its sole purpose is the interpretation of the constitution and to see that the laws and regulations are not superior to the constitution (consists of 5 titular magistrates and 5 substitute magistrates)

Political parties: Bienestar Nacional or BIEN
Blue Party (Partido Azul) or Blue
CABAL
Cambio
Citizen Prosperity or PC
Commitment, Renewal, and Order or CREO
Elephant Community (Comunidad Elefante) or Elephant
Everyone Together for Guatemala or TODOS
Guatemalan National Revolutionary Unity or URNG-MAIZ or URNG
Humanist Party of Guatemala or PHG
Movement for the Liberation of Peoples or MLP
Movimiento Semilla or SEMILLA
National Advancement Party or PAN
National Convergence Front or FCN-NACION
National Unity for Hope or UNE
Nationalist Change Union or UCN (dissolved 16 December 2021)
Nosotros or PPN
PODEMOS
Political Movement Winaq or Winaq
TODOS
Value or VALOR
Vamos por una Guatemala Diferente or VAMOS
Victory or VICTORIA
Vision with Values or VIVA
Will, Opportunity and Solidarity (Voluntad, Oportunidad y Solidaridad) or VOS

Diplomatic representation in the US: *chief of mission:* Ambassador Hugo Eduardo BETETA (since 17 June 2024)
chancery: 2220 R Street NW, Washington, DC 20008
telephone: [1] (202) 745-4953
FAX: [1] (202) 745-1908
email address and website: embestadosunidos@minex.gob.gt
https://estadosunidos.minex.gob.gt/home/home.aspx
consulate(s) general: Atlanta, Chicago, Columbus (OH), Denver, Houston, Los Angeles, Miami, Nashville (TN), New York, Oklahoma City, Omaha (NE), Philadelphia, Phoenix, Providence (RI), Raleigh (NC), Rockville (MD), San Francisco, Seattle
consulate(s): Dallas, Del Rio (TX), Lake Worth (FL), McAllen (TX), Riverhead (NY), San Bernardino (CA), Tucson (AZ)

Diplomatic representation from the US: *chief of mission:* Ambassador Tobin BRADLEY (since 12 February 2024)
embassy: Boulevard Austriaco 11-51, Zone 16, Guatemala City
mailing address: 3190 Guatemala Place, Washington DC 20521-3190
telephone: [502] 2354-0000
FAX: [502] 2326-4654
email address and website: AmCitsGuatemala@state.gov
https://gt.usembassy.gov/

International organization participation: ACS, BCIE, CACM, CD, CELAC, EITI (compliant country), FAO, G-24, G-77, IADB, IAEA, IBRD, ICAO, ICC (national committees), ICCt (signatory), ICRM, IDA, IFAD, IFC, IFRCS, IHO, ILO, IMF, IMO, Interpol, IOC, IOM, IPU, ISO (correspondent), ITSO, ITU, ITUC (NGOs), LAES, LAIA (observer), MIGA, MINUSTAH, MONUSCO, NAM, OAS, OPANAL, OPCW, Pacific Alliance (observer), PCA, Petrocaribe, SICA, UN, UNCTAD, UNESCO, UNHCR, UNIDO, UNIFIL, Union Latina, UNISFA, UNITAR, UNMISS, UNOCI, UNOOSA, UNWTO, UPU, WCO, WFTU (NGOs), WHO, WIPO, WMO, WTO

Independence: 15 September 1821 (from Spain)

National holiday: Independence Day, 15 September (1821)

Flag: *description:* three equal vertical bands of light blue (left side), white, and light blue, with the coat of arms centered in the white band; the coat of arms includes a green-and-red quetzal (the national bird), a scroll with the inscription LIBERTAD 15 DE SEPTIEMBRE DE 1821 (the original date of independence from Spain), a pair of crossed rifles, and a pair of crossed swords; a laurel wreath frames the objects
meaning: the rifles stand for Guatemala's willingness to defend itself, the swords for honor, and the laurel wreath for victory; blue stands for the Pacific Ocean and Caribbean Sea, and white for peace and purity
note: one of two national flags featuring a firearm – the other is Mozambique

National symbol(s): quetzal (bird)

National color(s): blue, white

National anthem(s): *title:* "Himno Nacional de Guatemala" (National Anthem of Guatemala)
lyrics/music: Jose Joaquin PALMA/Rafael Alvarez OVALLE
history: adopted 1897, modified lyrics adopted 1934; Cuban poet Jose Joaquin PALMA anonymously submitted lyrics to a public contest calling for a national anthem and it was not discovered until 1911; anthem has four verses with four separate choruses at the end of each verse – all are official, and the anthem is sung in its entirety when performed in Guatemala

National heritage: *total World Heritage Sites:* 4 (3 cultural, 1 mixed)
selected World Heritage Site locales: Antigua Guatemala (c); Tikal National Park (m); Archaeological Park and Ruins of Quirigua (c); National Archaeological Park Tak'alik Ab'aj (c)

ECONOMY

Economic overview: developing Central American economy; steady economic growth fueled by remittances; high poverty and income inequality; limited government services, lack of employment opportunities, and frequent natural disasters impede human development efforts and drive emigration

Real GDP (purchasing power parity): $232.673 billion (2024 est.)
$224.475 billion (2023 est.)
$216.815 billion (2022 est.)
note: data in 2021 dollars
comparison ranking: 71

Real GDP growth rate: 3.7% (2024 est.)
3.5% (2023 est.)
4.2% (2022 est.)
note: annual GDP % growth based on constant local currency
comparison ranking: 93

Real GDP per capita: $12,600 (2024 est.)
$12,400 (2023 est.)
$12,100 (2022 est.)
note: data in 2021 dollars
comparison ranking: 136

GDP (official exchange rate): $113.2 billion (2024 est.)
note: data in current dollars at official exchange rate

Inflation rate (consumer prices): 2.9% (2024 est.)
6.2% (2023 est.)
6.9% (2022 est.)
note: annual % change based on consumer prices
comparison ranking: 86

GDP - composition, by sector of origin: *agriculture:* 9.8% (2024 est.)
industry: 21.7% (2024 est.)
services: 61.8% (2024 est.)
note: figures may not total 100% due to non-allocated consumption not captured in sector-reported data
comparison rankings: agriculture 73; industry 121; services 77

GDP - composition, by end use: *household consumption:* 88% (2024 est.)
government consumption: 10.9% (2024 est.)
investment in fixed capital: 16.1% (2024 est.)
investment in inventories: 0.6% (2024 est.)
exports of goods and services: 15.9% (2024 est.)
imports of goods and services: -31.5% (2024 est.)
note: figures may not total 100% due to rounding or gaps in data collection

Agricultural products: sugarcane, bananas, oil palm fruit, maize, cantaloupes/melons, potatoes, milk, tomatoes, chicken, pineapples (2023)
note: top ten agricultural products based on tonnage

Industries: sugar, textiles and clothing, furniture, chemicals, petroleum, metals, rubber, tourism

Industrial production growth rate: 2% (2024 est.)
note: annual % change in industrial value added based on constant local currency
comparison ranking: 100

Labor force: 7.575 million (2024 est.)
note: number of people ages 15 or older who are employed or seeking work
comparison ranking: 66

Unemployment rate: 2.3% (2024 est.)
2.4% (2023 est.)
3.1% (2022 est.)
note: % of labor force seeking employment
comparison ranking: 20

Youth unemployment rate (ages 15-24): *total:* 4.2% (2024 est.)
male: 4% (2024 est.)
female: 4.7% (2024 est.)
note: % of labor force ages 15-24 seeking employment
comparison ranking: total 167

Population below poverty line: 56% (2023 est.)
note: % of population with income below national poverty line

Gini Index coefficient - distribution of family income: 45.2 (2023 est.)
note: index (0-100) of income distribution; higher values represent greater inequality
comparison ranking: 16

Average household expenditures: *on food:* 35.1% of household expenditures (2023 est.)
on alcohol and tobacco: 1.3% of household expenditures (2023 est.)

Household income or consumption by percentage share: *lowest 10%:* 1.6% (2023 est.)
highest 10%: 34.1% (2023 est.)
note: % share of income accruing to lowest and highest 10% of population

Remittances: 19.1% of GDP (2024 est.)
19.1% of GDP (2023 est.)
19% of GDP (2022 est.)
note: personal transfers and compensation between resident and non-resident individuals/households/entities

Budget: *revenues:* $16.603 billion (2023 est.)
expenditures: $17.349 billion (2023 est.)
note: central government revenues (excluding grants) and expenditures converted to US dollars at average official exchange rate for year indicated

Public debt: 31.56% of GDP (2020 est.)
note: central government debt as a % of GDP
comparison ranking: 164

Taxes and other revenues: 11.6% (of GDP) (2023 est.)
note: central government tax revenue as a % of GDP
comparison ranking: 119

Current account balance: $3.333 billion (2024 est.)
$3.212 billion (2023 est.)
$1.116 billion (2022 est.)
note: balance of payments - net trade and primary/secondary income in current dollars
comparison ranking: 39

Exports: $17.997 billion (2024 est.)
$17.342 billion (2023 est.)
$18.141 billion (2022 est.)
note: balance of payments - exports of goods and services in current dollars
comparison ranking: 94

Exports - partners: USA 33%, El Salvador 11%, Honduras 9%, Nicaragua 6%, Mexico 4% (2023)
note: top five export partners based on percentage share of exports

Exports - commodities: garments, bananas, coffee, palm oil, raw sugar (2023)
note: top five export commodities based on value in dollars

Imports: $35.576 billion (2024 est.)
$33.056 billion (2023 est.)
$33.943 billion (2022 est.)
note: balance of payments - imports of goods and services in current dollars
comparison ranking: 73

Imports - partners: USA 30%, China 19%, Mexico 11%, El Salvador 4%, Costa Rica 3% (2023)
note: top five import partners based on percentage share of imports

Imports - commodities: refined petroleum, video displays, cars, trucks, packaged medicine (2023)
note: top five import commodities based on value in dollars

Reserves of foreign exchange and gold: $24.412 billion (2024 est.)
$21.311 billion (2023 est.)
$20.415 billion (2022 est.)
note: holdings of gold (year-end prices)/foreign exchange/special drawing rights in current dollars
comparison ranking: 59

Debt - external: $11.862 billion (2023 est.)
note: present value of external debt in current US dollars
comparison ranking: 46

Exchange rates: quetzales (GTQ) per US dollar -
Exchange rates: 7.759 (2024 est.)
7.832 (2023 est.)
7.748 (2022 est.)
7.734 (2021 est.)
7.722 (2020 est.)

ENERGY

Electricity access: *electrification - total population:* 99.1% (2022 est.)
electrification - urban areas: 97.7%
electrification - rural areas: 98.2%

Electricity: *installed generating capacity:* 4.995 million kW (2023 est.)
consumption: 12.222 billion kWh (2023 est.)
exports: 1.104 billion kWh (2023 est.)
imports: 1.573 billion kWh (2023 est.)
transmission/distribution losses: 1.716 billion kWh (2023 est.)
comparison rankings: installed generating capacity 91; consumption 98; exports 68; imports 71; transmission/distribution losses 117

Electricity generation sources: *fossil fuels:* 25.4% of total installed capacity (2023 est.)
solar: 1.8% of total installed capacity (2023 est.)
wind: 2.6% of total installed capacity (2023 est.)
hydroelectricity: 42% of total installed capacity (2023 est.)
geothermal: 2.5% of total installed capacity (2023 est.)
biomass and waste: 25.7% of total installed capacity (2023 est.)

Coal: *consumption:* 1.012 million metric tons (2023 est.)
exports: 20 metric tons (2023 est.)
imports: 808,000 metric tons (2023 est.)

Petroleum: *total petroleum production:* 6,000 bbl/day (2023 est.)
refined petroleum consumption: 117,000 bbl/day (2023 est.)
crude oil estimated reserves: 86.11 million barrels (2021 est.)

Natural gas: *production:* 2.016 million cubic meters (2023 est.)
consumption: 1.991 million cubic meters (2023 est.)

Energy consumption per capita: 17.096 million Btu/person (2023 est.)
comparison ranking: 135

COMMUNICATIONS

Telephones - fixed lines: *total subscriptions:* 1.94 million (2023 est.)
subscriptions per 100 inhabitants: 11 (2023 est.)
comparison ranking: total subscriptions 51

Telephones - mobile cellular: *total subscriptions:* 20.6 million (2023 est.)
subscriptions per 100 inhabitants: 115 (2022 est.)
comparison ranking: total subscriptions 64

Broadcast media: 4 privately owned national terrestrial TV channels dominate TV broadcasting; multi-channel satellite and cable services are available; 1 government-owned radio station and hundreds of privately owned radio stations (2019)

Internet country code: .gt

Internet users: *percent of population:* 56% (2023 est.)

Broadband - fixed subscriptions: *total:* 921,000 (2023 est.)
subscriptions per 100 inhabitants: 5 (2023 est.)
comparison ranking: total 79

TRANSPORTATION

Civil aircraft registration country code prefix: TG

Airports: 58 (2025)
comparison ranking: 79

Heliports: 2 (2025)
comparison ranking: 123

Railways: *total:* 800 km (2018)
narrow gauge: 800 km (2018) 0.914-m gauge
note: despite the existence of a railway network, all rail service was suspended in 2007 and no passenger or freight train currently runs in the country (2018)

Merchant marine: *total:* 9 (2023)
by type: oil tanker 1, other 8
comparison ranking: total 162

Ports: *total ports:* 3 (2024)
large: 0
medium: 0
small: 2
very small: 1
ports with oil terminals: 2
key ports: Puerto Barrios, Puerto Quetzal, Santo Tomas de Castilla

MILITARY AND SECURITY

Military and security forces: Army of Guatemala (Ejercito de Guatemala; aka Armed Forces of Guatemala or Fuerzas Armadas de Guatemala): Land Forces (Fuerzas de Tierra), Naval Forces (Fuerzas de Mar), and Air Force (Fuerza de Aire) (2025)
note: the National Civil Police (Policia Nacional Civil or PNC) are under the Ministry of Government (Interior)

Military expenditures: 0.4% of GDP (2024 est.)
0.4% of GDP (2023 est.)
0.4% of GDP (2022 est.)
0.4% of GDP (2021 est.)
0.4% of GDP (2020 est.)

Military and security service personnel strengths: approximately 20,000 active Armed Forces (2025)

Military equipment inventories and acquisitions: the military is lightly armed with an inventory mostly comprised of older US equipment; in recent years, Guatemala has received small amounts of equipment from several countries, including Colombia, Spain, and the US (2024)

Military service age and obligation: all male citizens 18-50 are eligible for military service; most of the force is volunteer; a selective draft system is employed, resulting in a small portion of 17-21 year-olds being conscripted; conscript service obligation varies from 12-24 months; women may volunteer (2023)

Military deployments: 180 Democratic Republic of the Congo (MONUSCO) (2025)

Military - note: the military is responsible for maintaining the independence, sovereignty, territorial integrity, and the honor of Guatemala, but has long focused on internal security; since the 2000s, the Guatemalan Government has used the military to support the National Civil Police in internal security operations (as permitted by the constitution) to combat organized crime, gang violence, and narco-trafficking; other responsibilities include border security, cybersecurity, and providing humanitarian assistance; it also participates in UN missions on a small scale and has a peacekeeping operations training command that offers training to regional countries; the military has security ties with regional partners such as Brazil, Colombia, El Salvador, and Honduras; cooperation with El Salvador and Honduras has included a combined police-military anti-gang task force to patrol border areas; it also has ties with the US, including joint training exercises and material assistance the military held power during most of Guatemala's 36-year civil war (1960-1996) and conducted a campaign of widespread violence and repression, particularly against the country's majority indigenous population; more than 200,000 people were estimated to have been killed or disappeared during the conflict (2025)

TERRORISM

Terrorist group(s): Terrorist group(s): La Mara Salvatrucha (MS-13)
note: details about the history, aims, leadership, organization, areas of operation, tactics, targets, weapons, size, and sources of support of the group(s) appear(s) in Appendix T

TRANSNATIONAL ISSUES

Refugees and internally displaced persons: *refugees:* 4,676 (2024 est.)

IDPs: 572,813 (2024 est.)

Illicit drugs: USG identification: major illicit drug-producing and/or drug-transit country
major precursor-chemical producer (2025)

GUERNSEY

INTRODUCTION

Background: Guernsey and the other Channel Islands represent the last remnants of the medieval Duchy of Normandy, which held sway in both France and England. The islands were the only British soil that Germany occupied in World War II. The Bailiwick of Guernsey consists of the main island of Guernsey and a number of smaller islands, including Alderney, Sark, Herm, Jethou, Brecqhou, and Lihou. The Bailiwick is a self-governing British Crown dependency that is not part of the UK. However, the UK Government is constitutionally responsible for its defense and international representation.

GEOGRAPHY

Location: Western Europe, islands in the English Channel, northwest of France

Geographic coordinates: 49 28 N, 2 35 W

Map references: Europe

Area: *total:* 78 sq km
land: 78 sq km
water: 0 sq km
note: includes Alderney, Guernsey, Herm, Sark, and some other smaller islands
comparison ranking: total 226

Area - comparative: about one-half the size of Washington, D.C.

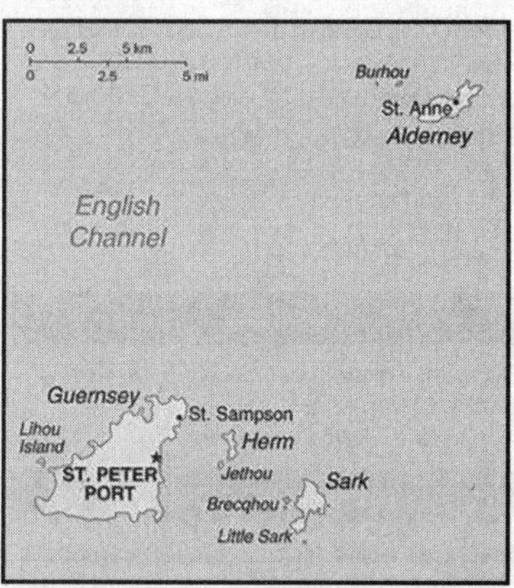

Land boundaries: *total:* 0 km

Coastline: 50 km

Maritime claims: *territorial sea:* 12 nm
exclusive fishing zone: 12 nm

Climate: temperate with mild winters and cool summers; about 50% of days are overcast

Terrain: mostly flat with low hills in southwest

Elevation: *highest point:* Le Moulin on Sark 114 m
lowest point: English Channel 0 m

Natural resources: cropland

Land use: *agricultural land:* 43.3% (2022 est.)
arable land: 18.3% (2022 est.)
permanent crops: 0% (2022 est.)
permanent pasture: 24.9% (2022 est.)
forest: 5.2% (2022 est.)
other: 51.6% (2022 est.)

Irrigated land: NA

Natural hazards: very large tidal variation and fast currents can make local waters dangerous

Geography - note: large, deepwater harbor at Saint Peter Port

PEOPLE AND SOCIETY

Population: *total:* 67,787 (2024 est.)
male: 33,712
female: 34,075
comparison rankings: total 203; male 203; female 204

Nationality: *noun:* Channel Islander(s)
adjective: Channel Islander

Ethnic groups: Guernsey 53.5%, UK and Ireland 23.8%, Portugal 2.1%, Latvia 1.4%, other Europe 2.7%, other Crown Dependencies 0.7%, other 5.3%, unspecified 10.5% (2022 est.)
note: data represent population by country of birth; the native population is of British and Norman-French descent

Languages: English, French, Norman-French dialect spoken in country districts

Religions: Protestant (Anglican, Presbyterian, Baptist, Congregational, Methodist), Roman Catholic

Age structure: *0-14 years:* 14.3% (male 4,999/female 4,717)
15-64 years: 64.1% (male 21,937/female 21,547)
65 years and over: 21.5% (2024 est.) (male 6,776/female 7,811)

Dependency ratios: *total dependency ratio:* 55.9 (2024 est.)
youth dependency ratio: 22.3 (2024 est.)
elderly dependency ratio: 33.5 (2024 est.)
potential support ratio: 3 (2024 est.)

Median age: *total:* 45 years (2024 est.)
male: 43.8 years
female: 46.2 years
comparison ranking: total 23

Population growth rate: 0.21% (2024 est.)
comparison ranking: 176

Birth rate: 9.7 births/1,000 population (2024 est.)
comparison ranking: 192

Death rate: 9.2 deaths/1,000 population (2024 est.)
comparison ranking: 54

Net migration rate: 1.6 migrant(s)/1,000 population (2024 est.)
comparison ranking: 55

Urbanization: *urban population:* 31.2% of total population (2023)
rate of urbanization: 0.68% annual rate of change (2020-25 est.)
note: data include Guernsey and Jersey

Major urban areas - population: 16,000 SAINT PETER PORT (capital) (2018)

Sex ratio: *at birth:* 1.05 male(s)/female
0-14 years: 1.06 male(s)/female
15-64 years: 1.02 male(s)/female
65 years and over: 0.87 male(s)/female
total population: 0.99 male(s)/female (2024 est.)

Infant mortality rate: *total:* 3.3 deaths/1,000 live births (2024 est.)
male: 3.7 deaths/1,000 live births
female: 2.7 deaths/1,000 live births
comparison ranking: total 197

Life expectancy at birth: *total population:* 83.6 years (2024 est.)
male: 80.9 years
female: 86.4 years
comparison ranking: total population 11

Total fertility rate: 1.59 children born/woman (2024 est.)
comparison ranking: 188

Gross reproduction rate: 0.77 (2024 est.)

ENVIRONMENT

Environmental issues: coastal erosion, coastal flooding; declining biodiversity

Climate: temperate with mild winters and cool summers; about 50% of days are overcast

Urbanization: *urban population:* 31.2% of total population (2023)
rate of urbanization: 0.68% annual rate of change (2020-25 est.)
note: data include Guernsey and Jersey

Waste and recycling: *municipal solid waste generated annually:* 178,900 tons (2024 est.)
percent of municipal solid waste recycled: 28.4% (2016 est.)
note: data include combined totals for Guernsey and Jersey.

GOVERNMENT

Country name: *conventional long form:* Bailiwick of Guernsey
conventional short form: Guernsey
former: Norman Isles
etymology: the name is of Old Norse origin; the meaning of the root "Guern(s)" is unclear but may refer to a person's name, Grani, or to the color green; the "-ey" ending means "island"

Government type: parliamentary democracy (States of Deliberation)

Dependency status: British crown dependency

Capital: *name:* Saint Peter Port
geographic coordinates: 49 27 N, 2 32 W
time difference: UTC 0 (5 hours ahead of Washington, DC, during Standard Time)
daylight saving time: +1hr, begins last Sunday in March; ends last Sunday in October
etymology: named for the patron saint of fishermen; "port" distinguishes it from the Saint Peter (sometimes called Saint Peter in the Wood) on the other side of the island

Administrative divisions: *none (British Crown dependency); no first-order administrative divisions as defined by the US government, but 10 parishes:* Castel, Forest, Saint Andrew, Saint Martin, Saint Peter Port, Saint Pierre du Bois, Saint Sampson, Saint Saviour, Torteval, Vale
note: two additional parishes for Guernsey are sometimes listed – Saint Anne on the island of Alderney and Saint Peter on the island of Sark

Legal system: customary system based on Norman customary law; includes elements of the French civil code and English common law

Constitution: *history:* unwritten; includes royal charters, statutes, and common law and practice
amendment process: new laws or changes to existing laws are initiated by the States of Deliberation; passage requires majority vote

Citizenship: see United Kingdom

Suffrage: 16 years of age; universal

Executive branch: *chief of state:* King CHARLES III (since 8 September 2022); represented by Lieutenant-Governor Richard CRIPWELL (since 15 February 2022)
head of government: Chief Minister Lindsay de SAUSMAREZ (since 1 July 2025)
cabinet: none
election/appointment process: the monarchy is hereditary; lieutenant governor and bailiff appointed by the monarch; chief minister, who is the president of the Policy and Resources Committee, indirectly elected by the States of Deliberation for a 4-year term
most recent election date: 7/1/2025
election results: *2025:* Lindsay de SAUSMAREZ (independent) elected president of the Policy and Resources Committee and chief minister
2020: Peter FERBRACHE (independent) elected president of the Policy and Resources Committee and chief minister: percent of States of Guernsey vote - 57.5%
2016: Gavin ST. PIER (independent) elected president of the Policy and Resources Committee and chief minister
expected date of next election: 2029
note: the chief minister is the president of the Policy and Resources Committee and is the de facto head of government; the Policy and Resources Committee, elected by the States of Deliberation, functions as the executive; the 5 members all have equal voting rights

Legislative branch: *legislature name:* States of Deliberation
legislative structure: unicameral
number of seats: 38 (directly elected)
electoral system: plurality/majority

scope of elections: full renewal
term in office: 4 years
most recent election date: 7/1/2025
parties elected and seats per party: independent (35); Forward Guernsey (3)
percentage of women in chamber: 20%
expected date of next election: 2030
note: non-voting members include the bailiff (presiding officer), attorney-general, and solicitor-general

Judicial branch: *highest court(s):* Guernsey Court of Appeal (consists of the Bailiff of Guernsey, who is the ex-officio president of the Guernsey Court of Appeal, and at least 12 judges); Royal Court (organized into 3 divisions - Full Court sits with 1 judge and 7 to 12 jurats acting as judges of fact, Ordinary Court sits with 1 judge and normally 3 jurats, and Matrimonial Causes Division sits with 1 judge and 4 jurats)
judge selection and term of office: Royal Court Bailiff, Deputy Bailiff, and Court of Appeal justices appointed by the British Crown and hold office at Her Majesty's pleasure; jurats elected by the States of Election, a body chaired by the Bailiff and a number of jurats
subordinate courts: Court of Alderney; Court of the Seneschal of Sark; Magistrates' Court (includes Juvenile Court); Contracts Court; Ecclesiastical Court; Court of Chief Pleas
note: appeals beyond Guernsey courts are heard by the Judicial Committee of the Privy Council (in London)

Political parties: Forward Guernsey

Diplomatic representation in the US: none (British crown dependency)

Diplomatic representation from the US: *embassy:* none (British crown dependency)

International organization participation: UPU

Independence: none (British Crown dependency)

National holiday: Liberation Day, 9 May (1945)

Flag: *description:* white with the red cross of Saint George (patron saint of England) extending to the edges of the flag and a yellow equal-armed cross of William the Conqueror on top of the Saint George cross
meaning: the red cross represents Guernsey's status as a British Crown dependency
history: the gold cross is a replica of the one William the Conqueror carried at the Battle of Hastings in 1066

National symbol(s): Guernsey cow, donkey

National color(s): red, white, yellow

National anthem(s): *title:* "Sarnia Cherie" (Guernsey Dear)
lyrics/music: George DEIGHTON/Domencio SANTANGELO
history: adopted 1911; serves as a local anthem
title: "God Save the King"
lyrics/music: unknown
history: official anthem, as a British crown dependency

ECONOMY

Economic overview: high-income English Channel island economy; strong financial sector but stressed due to COVID-19 disruptions; manufacturing, tourism, and construction industries suffered but expected to recover; stable inflation; maintains independent taxation authority

Real GDP growth rate: 3.7% (2023 est.)
5.3% (2022 est.)
9.9% (2021 est.)
note: annual GDP % growth based on constant local currency; entry includes Jersey and Guernsey
comparison ranking: 86

GDP (official exchange rate): $12.508 billion (2023 est.)
note: data in current dollars at official exchange rate; entry includes Jersey and Guernsey

GDP - composition, by sector of origin: *agriculture:* 0.6% (2023 est.)
industry: 8.2% (2023 est.)
services: 91.2% (2023 est.)
note: figures may not total 100% due to non-allocated consumption not captured in sector-reported data
comparison rankings: agriculture 187; industry 196; services 6

Agricultural products: tomatoes, greenhouse flowers, sweet peppers, eggplant, fruit; Guernsey cattle

Industries: tourism, banking

Industrial production growth rate: 1.3% (2023 est.)
note: annual % change in industrial value added based on constant local currency; entry includes Jersey and Guernsey
comparison ranking: 109

Labor force: 82,400 (2024 est.)
note: number of people ages 15 or older who are employed or seeking work;entry includes Jersey and Guernsey
comparison ranking: 183

Unemployment rate: 6.3% (2024 est.)
6.2% (2023 est.)
6.2% (2022 est.)
note: % of labor force seeking employment; entry includes Jersey and Guernsey
comparison ranking: 117

Youth unemployment rate (ages 15-24): *total:* 14.1% (2024 est.)
male: 14.2% (2024 est.)
female: 13.9% (2024 est.)
note: % of labor force ages 15-24 seeking employment
comparison ranking: total 87

Exports - partners: almost entirely United Kingdom (2022)

Exports - commodities: aircraft, photo lab equipment, clocks, ships, paintings (2022)
top five export commodities based on value in dollars

Imports - partners: almost entirely United Kingdom (2022)

Imports - commodities: ships, aircraft, refined petroleum, mineral manufactures, beverages (2022)

Exchange rates: Guernsey pound per US dollar

Exchange rates: 0.782 (2024 est.)
0.805 (2023 est.)
0.811 (2022 est.)
0.727 (2021 est.)
0.78 (2020 est.)

ENERGY

Electricity access: *electrification - total population:* 100% (2022 est.)
note: includes Guernsey and Jersey

COMMUNICATIONS

Telephones - fixed lines: *total subscriptions:* 33,930 (2021 est.)
subscriptions per 100 inhabitants: 53 (2021 est.)
comparison ranking: total subscriptions 165

Telephones - mobile cellular: *total subscriptions:* 71,485 (2021 est.)
subscriptions per 100 inhabitants: 112 (2021 est.)
comparison ranking: total subscriptions 197

Broadcast media: multiple UK terrestrial TV broadcasts are received via a transmitter in Jersey with relays in Jersey, Guernsey, and Alderney; satellite packages are available; BBC Radio Guernsey and 1 other radio station

Internet country code: .gg

Internet users: *percent of population:* 86.6% (2021 est.)

Broadband - fixed subscriptions: *total:* 25,336 (2020 est.)
subscriptions per 100 inhabitants: 40 (2020 est.)
comparison ranking: total 162

TRANSPORTATION

Civil aircraft registration country code prefix: 2

Airports: 2 (2025)
comparison ranking: 206

Heliports: 1 (2025)
comparison ranking: 154

Ports: *total ports:* 3 (2024)
large: 0
medium: 0
small: 1
very small: 2
ports with oil terminals: 2
key ports: Alderney Harbour, Saint Peter Port, Saint Sampson

MILITARY AND SECURITY

Military - note: defense is the responsibility of the UK

GUINEA

INTRODUCTION

Background: Guinea's deep Muslim heritage arrived via the neighboring Almoravid Empire in the 11th century. Following Almoravid decline, Guinea existed on the fringe of several African kingdoms, all competing for regional dominance. In the 13th century, the Mali Empire took control of Guinea and encouraged its already growing Muslim faith. After the fall of the West African empires, various smaller kingdoms controlled Guinea. In the 18th century, Fulani Muslims established an Islamic state in central

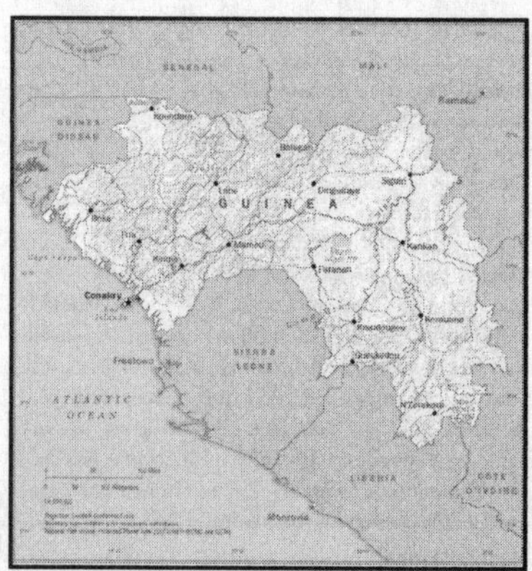

Guinea that provided one of the earliest examples of a written constitution and alternating leadership. European traders first arrived in the 16th century, and the French secured colonial rule in the 19th century.

In 1958, Guinea achieved independence from France. Sekou TOURE became Guinea's first post-independence president; he established a dictatorial regime and ruled until his death in 1984, after which General Lansana CONTE staged a coup and seized the government. He too established an authoritarian regime and manipulated presidential elections until his death in 2008, when Captain Moussa Dadis CAMARA led a military coup, seized power, and suspended the constitution. In 2009, CAMARA was wounded in an assassination attempt and was exiled to Burkina Faso. In 2010 and 2013 respectively, the country held its first free and fair presidential and legislative elections. Alpha CONDE won the 2010 and 2015 presidential elections, and his first cabinet was the first all-civilian government in Guinean history. CONDE won a third term in 2020 after a constitutional change to term limits. In 2021, Col Mamady DOUMBOUYA led another successful military coup, establishing the National Committee for Reconciliation and Development (CNRD), suspending the constitution, and dissolving the government and the legislature. DOUMBOUYA was sworn in as transition president and appointed Mohamed BEAVOGUI as transition prime minister. The National Transition Council (CNT), which acts as the legislative body for the transition, was formed in 2022 and consists of appointed members representing a broad swath of Guinean society.

GEOGRAPHY

Location: Western Africa, bordering the North Atlantic Ocean, between Guinea-Bissau and Sierra Leone

Geographic coordinates: 11 00 N, 10 00 W

Map references: Africa

Area: *total:* 245,857 sq km
land: 245,717 sq km
water: 140 sq km
comparison ranking: total 79

Area - comparative: slightly smaller than Oregon; slightly larger than twice the size of Pennsylvania

Land boundaries: *total:* 4,046 km
border countries (6): Cote d'Ivoire 816 km; Guinea-Bissau 421 km; Liberia 590 km; Mali 1062 km; Senegal 363 km; Sierra Leone 794 km

Coastline: 320 km

Maritime claims: *territorial sea:* 12 nm
exclusive economic zone: 200 nm

Climate: generally hot and humid; monsoonal-type rainy season (June to November) with southwesterly winds; dry season (December to May) with northeasterly harmattan winds

Terrain: generally flat coastal plain, hilly to mountainous interior

Elevation: *highest point:* Mont Nimba 1,752 m
lowest point: Atlantic Ocean 0 m
mean elevation: 472 m

Natural resources: bauxite, iron ore, diamonds, gold, uranium, hydropower, fish, salt

Land use: *agricultural land:* 70% (2022 est.)
arable land: 20.7% (2022 est.)
permanent crops: 5.8% (2022 est.)
permanent pasture: 43.5% (2022 est.)
forest: 24.9% (2022 est.)
other: 5.2% (2022 est.)

Irrigated land: 949 sq km (2017)

Major rivers (by length in km): Niger river source (shared with Mali, and Nigeria [m]) - 4,200 km; Gambie (Gambia) river source (shared with Senegal and The Gambia [m]) - 1,094 km
note: [s] after country name indicates river source; [m] after country name indicates river mouth

Major watersheds (area sq km): Atlantic Ocean drainage: Niger (2,261,741 sq km), Senegal (456,397 sq km)

Population distribution: areas of highest density are in the west and south; interior is sparsely populated, as shown in this population distribution map

Natural hazards: hot, dry, dusty harmattan haze may reduce visibility during dry season

Geography - note: the Niger and its important tributary, the Milo River, have their sources in the Guinean highlands

PEOPLE AND SOCIETY

Population: *total:* 13,986,179 (2024 est.)
male: 6,985,606
female: 7,000,573
comparison rankings: total 75; male 75; female 75

Nationality: *noun:* Guinean(s)
adjective: Guinean

Ethnic groups: Fulani (Peuhl) 33.4%, Malinke 29.4%, Susu 21.2%, Guerze 7.8%, Kissi 6.2%, Toma 1.6%, other/foreign 0.4% (2018 est.)

Languages: French (official), Pular, Maninka, Susu, other native languages
note: about 40 languages are spoken; each ethnic group has its own language

Religions: Muslim 85.2%, Christian 13.4%, animist 0.2%, none 1.2% (2018 est.)

Age structure: *0-14 years:* 40.9% (male 2,884,146/female 2,835,794)
15-64 years: 55.1% (male 3,846,852/female 3,856,366)
65 years and over: 4% (2024 est.) (male 254,608/female 308,413)

Dependency ratios: *total dependency ratio:* 81.6 (2024 est.)
youth dependency ratio: 74.3 (2024 est.)
elderly dependency ratio: 7.3 (2024 est.)
potential support ratio: 13.7 (2024 est.)

Median age: *total:* 19.4 years (2024 est.)
male: 19.2 years
female: 19.6 years
comparison ranking: total 209

Population growth rate: 2.74% (2024 est.)
comparison ranking: 12

Birth rate: 35.3 births/1,000 population (2024 est.)
comparison ranking: 12

Death rate: 7.8 deaths/1,000 population (2024 est.)
comparison ranking: 92

Net migration rate: 0 migrant(s)/1,000 population (2024 est.)
comparison ranking: 89

Population distribution: areas of highest density are in the west and south; interior is sparsely populated, as shown in this population distribution map

Urbanization: *urban population:* 38.1% of total population (2023)
rate of urbanization: 3.64% annual rate of change (2020-25 est.)

Major urban areas - population: 2.111 million CONAKRY (capital) (2023)

Sex ratio: *at birth:* 1.03 male(s)/female
0-14 years: 1.02 male(s)/female
15-64 years: 1 male(s)/female
65 years and over: 0.83 male(s)/female
total population: 1 male(s)/female (2024 est.)

Mother's mean age at first birth: 19.9 years (2018 est.)
note: data represents median age at first birth among women 20-49

Maternal mortality ratio: 494 deaths/100,000 live births (2023 est.)
comparison ranking: 10

Infant mortality rate: *total:* 47 deaths/1,000 live births (2024 est.)
male: 51.6 deaths/1,000 live births
female: 42.3 deaths/1,000 live births
comparison ranking: total 21

Life expectancy at birth: *total population:* 64.6 years (2024 est.)
male: 62.7 years
female: 66.6 years
comparison ranking: total population 206

Total fertility rate: 4.78 children born/woman (2024 est.)
comparison ranking: 11

Gross reproduction rate: 2.36 (2024 est.)

Drinking water source: *improved: urban:* 92% of population (2022 est.)
rural: 59% of population (2022 est.)
total: 71.5% of population (2022 est.)
unimproved: urban: 8% of population (2022 est.)
rural: 41% of population (2022 est.)
total: 28.5% of population (2022 est.)

Health expenditure: 3.8% of GDP (2021)
5% of national budget (2022 est.)

Physician density: 0.21 physicians/1,000 population (2022)

Sanitation facility access: *improved: urban:* 95.6% of population (2022 est.)
rural: 39.4% of population (2022 est.)
total: 60.6% of population (2022 est.)
unimproved: urban: 4.4% of population (2022 est.)
rural: 60.6% of population (2022 est.)
total: 39.4% of population (2022 est.)

Obesity - adult prevalence rate: 7.7% (2016)
comparison ranking: 158

Alcohol consumption per capita: *total:* 0.33 liters of pure alcohol (2019 est.)

beer: 0.29 liters of pure alcohol (2019 est.)
wine: 0.01 liters of pure alcohol (2019 est.)
spirits: 0.03 liters of pure alcohol (2019 est.)
other alcohols: 0 liters of pure alcohol (2019 est.)
comparison ranking: total 168

Children under the age of 5 years underweight: 16.3% (2018)
comparison ranking: 28

Currently married women (ages 15-49): 68.7% (2023 est.)

Child marriage: *women married by age 15:* 17% (2018)
women married by age 18: 46.5% (2018)
men married by age 18: 1.9% (2018)

Education expenditure: 1.7% of GDP (2023 est.)
9.3% national budget (2024 est.)
comparison ranking: Education expenditure (% GDP) 190

Literacy: *total population:* 40% (2018 est.)
male: 54% (2018 est.)
female: 28% (2018 est.)

School life expectancy (primary to tertiary education): *total:* 9 years (2021 est.)
male: 9 years (2021 est.)
female: 8 years (2021 est.)

ENVIRONMENT

Environmental issues: deforestation; inadequate potable water; desertification; soil contamination and erosion; overfishing, overpopulation in forest region; poor mining practices; water pollution; improper waste disposal

International environmental agreements: *party to:* Biodiversity, Climate Change, Climate Change-Kyoto Protocol, Climate Change-Paris Agreement, Comprehensive Nuclear Test Ban, Desertification, Endangered Species, Hazardous Wastes, Law of the Sea, Ozone Layer Protection, Ship Pollution, Wetlands, Whaling
signed, but not ratified: none of the selected agreements

Climate: generally hot and humid; monsoonal-type rainy season (June to November) with southwesterly winds; dry season (December to May) with northeasterly harmattan winds

Urbanization: *urban population:* 38.1% of total population (2023)
rate of urbanization: 3.64% annual rate of change (2020-25 est.)

Carbon dioxide emissions: 4.505 million metric tonnes of CO2 (2023 est.)
from coal and metallurgical coke: 1,000 metric tonnes of CO2 (2023 est.)
from petroleum and other liquids: 4.504 million metric tonnes of CO2 (2023 est.)
comparison ranking: total emissions 140

Particulate matter emissions: 34.2 micrograms per cubic meter (2019 est.)

Waste and recycling: *municipal solid waste generated annually:* 596,900 tons (2024 est.)
percent of municipal solid waste recycled: 23.9% (2022 est.)

Total water withdrawal: *municipal:* 230 million cubic meters (2022 est.)
industrial: 60 million cubic meters (2022 est.)
agricultural: 600 million cubic meters (2022 est.)

Total renewable water resources: 226 billion cubic meters (2022 est.)

GOVERNMENT

Country name: *conventional long form:* Republic of Guinea
conventional short form: Guinea
local long form: République de Guinée
local short form: Guinée
former: French Guinea
etymology: the country is named after the Guinea region of West Africa that lies along the Gulf of Guinea, but the name itself derives from the Tuareg word *aginaw*, meaning "black people"

Government type: presidential republic

Capital: *name:* Conakry
geographic coordinates: 9 30 N, 13 42 W
time difference: UTC 0 (5 hours ahead of Washington, DC, during Standard Time)
etymology: the name derives from *konakri*, a Susu word meaning "over the water" and referring to the city's location on a peninsula; it was originally the name of a local village

Administrative divisions: 7 administrative regions (*régions administratives*, singular - *région administrative*) and 1 governorate (*gouvenorat*)*; Boke, Conakry*, Faranah, Kankan, Kindia, Labe, Mamou, N'Zerekore

Legal system: civil law system based on the French model

Constitution: *history:* previous 1958, 1990; 2010 and a referendum in 2020, which was suspended on 5 September 2021 via a coup d'état; on 27 September, the Transitional Charter was released, which supersedes the constitution until a new constitution is promulgated

International law organization participation: accepts compulsory ICJ jurisdiction with reservations; accepts ICCt jurisdiction

Citizenship: *citizenship by birth:* no
citizenship by descent only: at least one parent must be a citizen of Guinea
dual citizenship recognized: no
residency requirement for naturalization: na

Suffrage: 18 years of age; universal

Executive branch: *chief of state:* Interim President Col. Mamady DOUMBOUYA (since 1 October 2021)
head of government: Prime Minister Amadou Oury BAH (since 27 February 2024)
cabinet: formerly the Council of Ministers appointed by the president
election/appointment process: formerly, the president was directly elected by absolute-majority popular vote in 2 rounds, if needed, for a 5-year term (eligible for a second term), and the prime minister was appointed by the president
most recent election date: 18 October 2020
election results: *2020:* Alpha CONDE reelected president in the first round; percent of vote - Alpha CONDE (RPG) 59.5%, Cellou Dalein DIALLO (UFDG) 33.5%, other 7%
2015: Alpha CONDE reelected president in the first round; percent of vote - Alpha CONDE (RPG) 57.8%, Cellou Dalein DIALLO (UFDG) 31.4%, other 10.8%
note 1: in 2021, the military arrested and detained the president, suspended the constitution, and dissolved the government and legislature
note 2: the transitional government has not announced a new election timetable

Legislative branch: *legislature name:* Transitional National Council (Conseil national de transition)
legislative structure: unicameral
number of seats: 81 (all appointed)
electoral system: mixed system
scope of elections: full renewal
most recent election date: 1/22/2022
percentage of women in chamber: 29.6%
expected date of next election: December 2025
note: on 5 September 2021, Col. Mamady DOUMBOUYA led a military coup in which President CONDE was arrested and detained, the constitution suspended, and the government and People's National Assembly dissolved; in January 2022, an 81-member Transitional National Council was installed; in February 2024, Guinea's military leaders dissolved the government

Judicial branch: *highest court(s):* Supreme Court or Cour Suprême (organized into Administrative Chamber and Civil, Penal, and Social Chamber; court consists of the first president, 2 chamber presidents, 10 councilors, the solicitor general, and NA deputies); Constitutional Court - suspended on 5 September 2021
judge selection and term of office: Supreme Court first president appointed by the national president after consultation with the National Assembly; other members appointed by presidential decree; members serve 9-year terms until age 65
subordinate courts: Court of Appeal or Cour d'Appel; High Court of Justice or Cour d'Assises; Court of Account (Court of Auditors); Courts of First Instance (Tribunal de Première Instance); labor court; military tribunal; justices of the peace; specialized courts

Political parties: African Congress for Democracy and Renewal or CADRE
Alliance for National Renewal or ARN
Alliance for National Renewal or ARENA
Bloc Liberal or BL
Citizen Generation or GECI
Citizen Party for the Defense of Collective Interests or PCDIC
Democratic Alliance for Renewal or ADR
Democratic National Movement or MND
Democratic Union for Renewal and Progress or UDRP
Democratic Union of Guinea or UDG
Democratic People's Movement of Guinea or MPDG
Democratic Workers' Party of Guinea or PDTG
Front for the National Alliance or FAN
Generation for Reconciliation Union and Prosperity or GRUP
Guinea for Democracy and Balance or GDE
Guinean Party for Peaceful Coexistence and Development or PGCD
Guinean Party for Solidarity and Democracy or PGSD
Guinean Union for Democracy and Development or UGDD
Guinean Rally for Development or RGD
Guinean Rally for Unity and Development or RGUD
Guinean Renaissance Party or PGR
Modern Guinea
Movement for Solidarity and Development or MSD
National Committee for Reconciliation and Development
National Front for Development or FND
National Union for Prosperity or UNP
National Party for Hope and Development or PEDN
New Democratic Forces or NFD
New Generation for the Republic or NGR

New Guinea or NG
New Political Generation or NGP
Party for Progress and Change or PPC
Party of Citizen Action through Labor or PACT
Party of Democrats for Hope or PADES
Party of Freedom and Progress or PLP
Party of Hope for National Development or PEDN
Rally for Renaissance and Development or RRD
Rally for the Guinean People or RPG
Rally for the Integrated Development of Guinea or RDIG
Rally for the Republic or RPR
Union of Democratic Forces of Guinea or UFDG
Union for Progress and Renewal or UPR
Union for the Defense of Republican Interests or UDIR
Union for the Progress of Guinea or UPG
Union of Democratic Forces or UFD a or UFDG
Union of Democrats for the Renaissance of Guinea or UDRG
Union of Republican Forces or UFR
Unity and Progress Party or PUP

Diplomatic representation in the US: *chief of mission:* Ambassador Fatoumata KABA (since 19 April 2023)
chancery: 2112 Leroy Place NW, Washington, DC 20008
telephone: [1] (202) 986-4300
FAX: [1] (202) 986-3800
email address and website: http://guineaembassyusa.org/en/welcome-to-the-embassy-of-guinea-washington-usa/
consulate(s): Los Angelos

Diplomatic representation from the US: *chief of mission:* Ambassador (vacant); Chargé d'Affaires Mary E. DASCHBACH (since 15 July 2025)
embassy: Transversale No. 2, Centre Administratif de Koloma, Commune de Ratoma, Conakry
mailing address: 2110 Conakry Place, Washington DC 20521-2110
telephone: [224] 65-10-40-00
FAX: [224] 65-10-42-97
email address and website: ConakryACS@state.gov https://gn.usembassy.gov/

International organization participation: ACP, AfDB, EITI (compliant country), FAO, G-77, IBRD, ICAO, ICCt, ICRM, IDA, IDB, IFAD, IFC, IFRCS, ILO, IMF, IMO, Interpol, IOC, IOM, IPU, ISO (correspondent), ITSO, ITU, ITUC (NGOs), MIGA, MINURSO, MONUSCO, NAM, OIC, OIF, OPCW, UN, UNCTAD, UNESCO, UNHCR, UNIDO, UNISFA, UNMISS, UNOCI, UNWTO, UPU, WCO, WFTU (NGOs), WHO, WIPO, WMO, WTO

Independence: 2 October 1958 (from France)

National holiday: Independence Day, 2 October (1958)

Flag: *description:* three equal vertical bands of red (left side), yellow, and green
meaning: red stands for the people's sacrifice for liberation and work; yellow for the sun, the riches of the earth, and justice; green for the country's vegetation and unity
history: uses the colors of the Pan-African movement
note: the colors from left to right are the reverse of those on the flags of neighboring Mali and Senegal

National symbol(s): elephant

National color(s): red, yellow, green

National anthem(s): *title:* "Liberté" (Liberty)
lyrics/music: unknown/Fodeba KEITA
history: adopted 1958

National heritage: *total World Heritage Sites:* 1 (natural)
selected World Heritage Site locales: Mount Nimba Strict Nature Reserve

ECONOMY

Economic overview: growing but primarily agrarian West African economy; major mining sector; improving fiscal and debt balances prior to COVID-19; economy increasingly vulnerable to climate change; slow infrastructure improvements; gender wealth and human capital gaps

Real GDP (purchasing power parity): $59.439 billion (2024 est.)
$56.251 billion (2023 est.)
$53.297 billion (2022 est.)
note: data in 2021 dollars
comparison ranking: 117

Real GDP growth rate: 5.7% (2024 est.)
5.5% (2023 est.)
4% (2022 est.)
note: annual GDP % growth based on constant local currency
comparison ranking: 27

Real GDP per capita: $4,000 (2024 est.)
$3,900 (2023 est.)
$3,800 (2022 est.)
note: data in 2021 dollars
comparison ranking: 181

GDP (official exchange rate): $25.334 billion (2024 est.)
note: data in current dollars at official exchange rate

Inflation rate (consumer prices): 8.1% (2024 est.)
7.8% (2023 est.)
10.5% (2022 est.)
note: annual % change based on consumer prices
comparison ranking: 168

GDP - composition, by sector of origin: *agriculture:* 29.6% (2024 est.)
industry: 25.3% (2024 est.)
services: 37.5% (2024 est.)
note: figures may not total 100% due to non-allocated consumption not captured in sector-reported data
comparison rankings: agriculture 13; industry 86; services 199

GDP - composition, by end use: *household consumption:* 67.4% (2024 est.)
government consumption: 13.4% (2024 est.)
investment in fixed capital: 32.1% (2024 est.)
investment in inventories: -0.9% (2024 est.)
exports of goods and services: 44% (2024 est.)
imports of goods and services: -56.1% (2024 est.)
note: figures may not total 100% due to rounding or gaps in data collection

Agricultural products: rice, cassava, maize, groundnuts, oil palm fruit, plantains, potatoes, fonio, yams, sweet potatoes (2023)
note: top ten agricultural products based on tonnage

Industries: bauxite, gold, diamonds, iron ore; light manufacturing, agricultural processing

Industrial production growth rate: 7.1% (2024 est.)
note: annual % change in industrial value added based on constant local currency
comparison ranking: 24

Labor force: 4.534 million (2024 est.)
note: number of people ages 15 or older who are employed or seeking work
comparison ranking: 93

Unemployment rate: 5.3% (2024 est.)
5.3% (2023 est.)
5.3% (2022 est.)
note: % of labor force seeking employment comparison ranking: 94

Youth unemployment rate (ages 15-24): *total:* 7.1% (2024 est.)
male: 6.2% (2024 est.)
female: 8% (2024 est.)
note: % of labor force ages 15-24 seeking employment
comparison ranking: total 145

Population below poverty line: 43.7% (2018 est.)
note: % of population with income below national poverty line

Gini Index coefficient - distribution of family income: 29.6 (2018 est.)
note: index (0-100) of income distribution; higher values represent greater inequality
comparison ranking: 124

Household income or consumption by percentage share: *lowest 10%:* 3.5% (2018 est.)
highest 10%: 23.1% (2018 est.)
note: % share of income accruing to lowest and highest 10% of population

Remittances: 2.2% of GDP (2023 est.)
2.6% of GDP (2022 est.)
2% of GDP (2021 est.)
note: personal transfers and compensation between resident and non-resident individuals/households/entities

Budget: *revenues:* $1.949 billion (2019 est.)
expenditures: $2.014 billion (2019 est.)

Current account balance: $2.288 billion (2023 est.)
$3.35 billion (2022 est.)
$4.639 billion (2021 est.)
note: balance of payments - net trade and primary/secondary income in current dollars
comparison ranking: 43

Exports: $12.008 billion (2023 est.)
$8.898 billion (2022 est.)
$10.266 billion (2021 est.)
note: balance of payments - exports of goods and services in current dollars
comparison ranking: 108

Exports - partners: UAE 50%, China 36%, India 8%, Switzerland 1%, Spain 1% (2023)
note: top five export partners based on percentage share of exports

Exports - commodities: gold, aluminum ore, cocoa beans, crude petroleum, coconuts/brazil nuts/cashews (2023)
note: top five export commodities based on value in dollars

Imports: $8.365 billion (2023 est.)
$5.749 billion (2022 est.)
$5.353 billion (2021 est.)
note: balance of payments - imports of goods and services in current dollars
comparison ranking: 129

Imports - partners: China 39%, India 9%, Netherlands 7%, Belgium 6%, UAE 4% (2023)
note: top five import partners based on percentage share of imports

Imports - commodities: refined petroleum, rice, garments, construction vehicles, cars (2023)
note: top five import commodities based on value in dollars

Reserves of foreign exchange and gold: $1.887 billion (2023 est.)
$2.11 billion (2022 est.)
$2.183 billion (2021 est.)
note: holdings of gold (year-end prices)/foreign exchange/special drawing rights in current dollars
comparison ranking: 128

Debt - external: $3.764 billion (2023 est.)
note: present value of external debt in current US dollars
comparison ranking: 77

Exchange rates: Guinean francs (GNF) per US dollar -

Exchange rates: 9,565.082 (2020 est.)
9,183.876 (2019 est.)
9,011.134 (2018 est.)
9,088.319 (2017 est.)
8,967.927 (2016 est.)

ENERGY

Electricity access: *electrification - total population:* 47.7% (2022 est.)
electrification - urban areas: 91%
electrification - rural areas: 21.3%

Electricity: *installed generating capacity:* 1.06 million kW (2023 est.)
consumption: 3.624 billion kWh (2023 est.)
transmission/distribution losses: 424.356 million kWh (2023 est.)
comparison rankings: installed generating capacity 134; consumption 138; transmission/distribution losses 77

Electricity generation sources: *fossil fuels:* 25.3% of total installed capacity (2023 est.)
solar: 0.6% of total installed capacity (2023 est.)
hydroelectricity: 74.1% of total installed capacity (2023 est.)

Coal: *imports:* 400 metric tons (2023 est.)

Petroleum: *refined petroleum consumption:* 32,000 bbl/day (2023 est.)

Energy consumption per capita: 5.235 million Btu/person (2023 est.)
comparison ranking: 170

COMMUNICATIONS

Telephones - fixed lines: *total subscriptions:* 0 (2021 est.)
subscriptions per 100 inhabitants: (2022 est.) less than 1
comparison ranking: total subscriptions 221

Telephones - mobile cellular: *total subscriptions:* 13.8 million (2021 est.)
subscriptions per 100 inhabitants: 102 (2021 est.)
comparison ranking: total subscriptions 77

Broadcast media: government maintains control over broadcast media; single state-run TV station; state-run radio also operates several stations in rural areas; a dozen private TV stations; many privately owned radio stations, nearly all in Conakry, and about a dozen community radio stations; foreign TV programming available via satellite and cable subscription services (2022)

Internet country code: .gn

Internet users: *percent of population:* 27% (2023 est.)

Broadband - fixed subscriptions: *total:* 1,000 (2022 est.)
subscriptions per 100 inhabitants: (2022 est.) less than 1
comparison ranking: total 205

TRANSPORTATION

Civil aircraft registration country code prefix: 3X

Airports: 16 (2025)
comparison ranking: 148

Heliports: 1 (2025)
comparison ranking: 144

Railways: *total:* 1,086 km (2017)
standard gauge: 279 km (2017) 1.435-m gauge
narrow gauge: 807 km (2017) 1.000-m gauge

Merchant marine: *total:* 2 (2023)
by type: other 2
comparison ranking: total 175

Ports: *total ports:* 4 (2024)
large: 0
medium: 1
small: 0
very small: 3
ports with oil terminals: 2
key ports: Benti, Conakry, Kamsar, Victoria

MILITARY AND SECURITY

Military and security forces: Guinean (or National) Armed Forces (Forces Armées Guinéennes): Army, Air Force, Navy, National Gendarmerie

Ministry of Security: National Police (2024)
note: the Gendarmerie and National Police share responsibility for internal security; Guinea's military and security forces are sometimes collectively referred to as the Defense and Security Forces

Military expenditures: 2.1% of GDP (2024 est.)
2.1% of GDP (2023 est.)
1.8% of GDP (2022 est.)
1.5% of GDP (2021 est.)
1.4% of GDP (2020 est.)

Military and security service personnel strengths: estimated 10-12,000 active Armed Forces (2025)

Military equipment inventories and acquisitions: the Guinean military's inventory consists almost entirely of Soviet-era weapons and equipment along with small amounts of secondhand material from China, France, Russia, and South Africa (2024)

Military service age and obligation: 18 years of age for voluntary and selective conscripted service; 9-12 months of service (2023)

Military - note: the Guinean military is responsible for territorial defense, but also has some domestic security responsibilities and has historically been involved in suppressing public protests; in 2021 the Army's special forces led a military overthrow of the government; the military-led government has since been accused of cracking down on dissent, the media, and political opposition; border security is a key focus for the Guinean military, particularly a territorial dispute with Sierra Leone that dates back to 2001 (2025)

TRANSNATIONAL ISSUES

Refugees and internally displaced persons: *refugees:* 2,343 (2024 est.)

IDPs: 5,160 (2024 est.)

GUINEA-BISSAU

INTRODUCTION

Background: For much of its history, Guinea-Bissau was under the control of the Mali Empire and the Kaabu Kingdom. In the 16th century, Portugal began establishing trading posts along Guinea-Bissau's shoreline. Initially, the Portuguese were restricted to the coastline and islands. However, the slave and gold trades were lucrative to local African leaders, and the Portuguese were slowly able to expand their power and influence inland. Starting in the 18th century, the Mali Empire and Kingdom of Kaabu slowly disintegrated into smaller local entities. By the 19th century, Portugal had fully incorporated Guinea-Bissau into its empire.

Since gaining independence in 1974, Guinea-Bissau has experienced considerable political and military upheaval. In 1980, a military coup established General Joao Bernardo 'Nino' VIEIRA as president. VIEIRA's regime suppressed political opposition and purged political rivals. Several coup attempts through the 1980s and early 1990s failed to unseat him, but a military mutiny and civil war in 1999 led to VIEIRA's ouster. In 2000, a transitional government turned over power to opposition leader Kumba YALA. In 2003, a bloodless military coup overthrew YALA and installed businessman Henrique ROSA as interim president. In 2005, VIEIRA was reelected, pledging to pursue economic development and national reconciliation; he was assassinated in 2009. Malam Bacai SANHA was then elected president, but he passed away in 2012 from a long-term illness. A military coup blocked the second round of the election to replace him, but after mediation from the Economic Community of Western African States, a civilian transitional government assumed power. In 2014, Jose Mario VAZ was elected president in a free and fair election, and in 2019, he became the first president in Guinea-Bissau's history to complete a full term. Umaro Sissoco EMBALO was elected president in 2019, but he did not take office until 2020 because of a prolonged challenge to the election results.

GEOGRAPHY

Location: Western Africa, bordering the North Atlantic Ocean, between Guinea and Senegal

Geographic coordinates: 12 00 N, 15 00 W

Map references: Africa

Area: *total:* 36,125 sq km

land: 28,120 sq km
water: 8,005 sq km
comparison ranking: total 137

Area - comparative: slightly less than three times the size of Connecticut

Land boundaries: *total:* 762 km
border countries (2): Guinea 421 km; Senegal 341 km

Coastline: 350 km

Maritime claims: *territorial sea:* 12 nm
exclusive economic zone: 200 nm

Climate: tropical; generally hot and humid; monsoonal-type rainy season (June to November) with southwesterly winds; dry season (December to May) with northeasterly harmattan winds

Terrain: mostly low-lying coastal plain with a deeply indented estuarine coastline rising to savanna in east; numerous off-shore islands including the Arquipelago Dos Bijagos consisting of 18 main islands and many small islets

Elevation: *highest point:* Dongol Ronde 277 m
lowest point: Atlantic Ocean 0 m
mean elevation: 70 m

Natural resources: fish, timber, phosphates, bauxite, clay, granite, limestone, unexploited deposits of petroleum

Land use: *agricultural land:* 30% (2022 est.)
arable land: 14% (2022 est.)
permanent crops: 8.9% (2022 est.)
permanent pasture: 7.1% (2022 est.)
forest: 69.8% (2022 est.)
other: 0.1% (2022 est.)

Irrigated land: 250 sq km (2012)

Major aquifers: Senegalo-Mauritanian Basin

Population distribution: approximately one fifth of the population lives in the capital city of Bissau along the Atlantic coast; the remainder is distributed among the eight mainly rural regions, as shown in this population distribution map

Natural hazards: hot, dry, dusty harmattan haze may reduce visibility during dry season; brush fires

Geography - note: this small country is swampy along its western coast and is low-lying inland

PEOPLE AND SOCIETY

Population: *total:* 2,132,325 (2024 est.)
male: 1,042,910
female: 1,089,415
comparison rankings: total 150; male 151; female 147

Nationality: *noun:* Bissau-Guinean(s)
adjective: Bissau-Guinean

Ethnic groups: Balanta 30%, Fulani 30%, Manjaco 14%, Mandinga 13%, Papel 7%, unspecified smaller ethnic groups 6% (2015 est.)

Languages: Portuguese-based Creole, Portuguese (official; largely used as a second or third language), Pular (a Fula language), Mandingo

Religions: Muslim 46.1%, folk religions 30.6%, Christian 18.9%, other or unaffiliated 4.4% (2020 est.)

Age structure: *0-14 years:* 42.3% (male 453,513/female 448,514)
15-64 years: 54.6% (male 561,868/female 602,280)
65 years and over: 3.1% (2024 est.) (male 27,529/female 38,621)

Dependency ratios: *total dependency ratio:* 83.2 (2024 est.)
youth dependency ratio: 77.5 (2024 est.)
elderly dependency ratio: 5.7 (2024 est.)
potential support ratio: 17.6 (2024 est.)

Median age: *total:* 18.4 years (2024 est.)
male: 17.8 years
female: 18.9 years
comparison ranking: total 221

Population growth rate: 2.54% (2024 est.)
comparison ranking: 18

Birth rate: 36 births/1,000 population (2024 est.)
comparison ranking: 11

Death rate: 7.2 deaths/1,000 population (2024 est.)
comparison ranking: 114

Net migration rate: -3.5 migrant(s)/1,000 population (2024 est.)
comparison ranking: 188

Population distribution: approximately one fifth of the population lives in the capital city of Bissau along the Atlantic coast; the remainder is distributed among the eight mainly rural regions, as shown in this population distribution map

Urbanization: *urban population:* 45.5% of total population (2023)
rate of urbanization: 3.22% annual rate of change (2020-25 est.)

Major urban areas - population: 664,000 BISSAU (capital) (2023)

Sex ratio: *at birth:* 1.03 male(s)/female
0-14 years: 1.01 male(s)/female
15-64 years: 0.93 male(s)/female
65 years and over: 0.71 male(s)/female
total population: 0.96 male(s)/female (2024 est.)

Maternal mortality ratio: 505 deaths/100,000 live births (2023 est.)
comparison ranking: 9

Infant mortality rate: *total:* 46.4 deaths/1,000 live births (2024 est.)
male: 52 deaths/1,000 live births
female: 40.6 deaths/1,000 live births
comparison ranking: total 22

Life expectancy at birth: *total population:* 64.5 years (2024 est.)
male: 62.2 years
female: 66.8 years
comparison ranking: total population 207

Total fertility rate: 4.62 children born/woman (2024 est.)
comparison ranking: 13

Gross reproduction rate: 2.28 (2024 est.)

Drinking water source: *improved: urban:* 73.1% of population (2022 est.)
rural: 52.5% of population (2022 est.)
total: 61.8% of population (2022 est.)
unimproved: urban: 26.9% of population (2022 est.)
rural: 47.5% of population (2022 est.)
total: 38.2% of population (2022 est.)

Health expenditure: 8.2% of GDP (2021)
5.2% of national budget (2022 est.)

Physician density: 0.25 physicians/1,000 population (2022)

Sanitation facility access: *improved: urban:* 72.2% of population (2022 est.)
rural: 23.8% of population (2022 est.)
total: 45.6% of population (2022 est.)
unimproved: urban: 27.8% of population (2022 est.)
rural: 76.2% of population (2022 est.)
total: 54.4% of population (2022 est.)

Obesity - adult prevalence rate: 9.5% (2016)
comparison ranking: 144

Alcohol consumption per capita: *total:* 3.21 liters of pure alcohol (2019 est.)
beer: 0.41 liters of pure alcohol (2019 est.)
wine: 0.98 liters of pure alcohol (2019 est.)
spirits: 0.54 liters of pure alcohol (2019 est.)
other alcohols: 1.28 liters of pure alcohol (2019 est.)
comparison ranking: total 108

Tobacco use: *total:* 6.7% (2025 est.)
male: 13.2% (2025 est.)
female: 0.5% (2025 est.)
comparison ranking: total 152

Children under the age of 5 years underweight: 18.8% (2019)
comparison ranking: 20

Currently married women (ages 15-49): 56.7% (2023 est.)

Child marriage: *women married by age 15:* 8.1% (2019)
women married by age 18: 25.7% (2019)
men married by age 18: 2.2% (2019)

Education expenditure: 2.7% of GDP (2020 est.)
comparison ranking: Education expenditure (% GDP) 167

Literacy: *total population:* 63.9% (2022 est.)
male: 77.3% (2022 est.)
female: 52.2% (2022 est.)

ENVIRONMENT

Environmental issues: deforestation (overharvesting of trees for timber and agricultural purposes); soil erosion; overgrazing; overfishing

International environmental agreements: *party to:* Biodiversity, Climate Change, Climate Change-Kyoto Protocol, Climate Change-Paris Agreement, Comprehensive Nuclear Test Ban, Desertification, Endangered Species, Hazardous Wastes, Law of the Sea, Nuclear Test Ban, Ozone Layer Protection, Ship Pollution, Wetlands, Whaling
signed, but not ratified: none of the selected agreements

Climate: tropical; generally hot and humid; monsoonal-type rainy season (June to November) with southwesterly winds; dry season (December to May) with northeasterly harmattan winds

Urbanization: *urban population:* 45.5% of total population (2023)
rate of urbanization: 3.22% annual rate of change (2020-25 est.)

Carbon dioxide emissions: 366,000 metric tonnes of CO_2 (2023 est.)
from coal and metallurgical coke: 1 metric tonnes of CO_2 (2023 est.)
from petroleum and other liquids: 366,000 metric tonnes of CO_2 (2023 est.)
comparison ranking: total emissions 193

Particulate matter emissions: 42.6 micrograms per cubic meter (2019 est.)

Waste and recycling: *municipal solid waste generated annually:* 289,500 tons (2024 est.)
percent of municipal solid waste recycled: 10.1% (2022 est.)

Total water withdrawal: *municipal:* 34.1 million cubic meters (2022 est.)
industrial: 11.9 million cubic meters (2022 est.)
agricultural: 144 million cubic meters (2022 est.)

Total renewable water resources: 31.4 billion cubic meters (2022 est.)

GOVERNMENT

Country name: *conventional long form:* Republic of Guinea-Bissau
conventional short form: Guinea-Bissau
local long form: Republica da Guine-Bissau
local short form: Guine-Bissau
former: Portuguese Guinea
etymology: the country is partly named after the Guinea region of West Africa that lies along the Gulf of Guinea; the name itself is derived from the Tuareg word *aginaw*, meaning "black people;" Bissau, the name of the capital city, distinguishes the country from neighboring Guinea and is derived from the local Bijuga people

Government type: semi-presidential republic

Capital: *name:* Bissau
geographic coordinates: 11 51 N, 15 35 W
time difference: UTC 0 (5 hours ahead of Washington, DC, during Standard Time)
etymology: the name is derived from the local Bijuga people and is used to distinguish the country from neighboring Guinea

Administrative divisions: 9 regions (*regioes*, singular - *regiao*); Bafata, Biombo, Bissau, Bolama/Bijagos, Cacheu, Gabu, Oio, Quinara, Tombali

Legal system: mixed system of civil law, which incorporated Portuguese law at independence; influenced by Economic Community of West African States (ECOWAS), West African Economic and Monetary Union (UEMOA), African Francophone Public Law, and customary law

Constitution: *history:* promulgated 16 May 1984
amendment process: proposed by the National People's Assembly if supported by at least one third of its members, by the Council of State (a presidential consultant body), or by the government; passage requires approval by at least two-thirds majority vote of the Assembly; constitutional articles on the republican and secular form of government and national sovereignty cannot be amended

International law organization participation: accepts compulsory ICJ jurisdiction; non-party state to the ICCt

Citizenship: *citizenship by birth:* yes
citizenship by descent only: yes
dual citizenship recognized: no
residency requirement for naturalization: 5 years

Suffrage: 18 years of age; universal

Executive branch: *chief of state:* President Umaro Sissoco EMBALO (since 27 February 2020)
head of government: Prime Minister Braima CAMARA (since 7 August 2025)
cabinet: Cabinet nominated by the prime minister, appointed by the president
election/appointment process: president directly elected by absolute-majority popular vote in 2 rounds, if needed, for up to 2 consecutive 5-year terms; prime minister appointed by the president after consultation with party leaders in the National People's Assembly
most recent election date: 24 November 2019, with a runoff on 29 December 2019
election results: *2019:* Umaro Sissoco EMBALO elected president in second round; percent of vote in first round - Domingos Simoes PEREIRA (PAIGC) 40.1%, Umaro Sissoco EMBALO (Madem G15) 27.7%, Nuno Gomez NABIAM (APU-PDGB) 13.2%, Jose Mario VAZ (independent) 12.4%, other 6.6%; percent of vote in second round - Umaro Sissoco EMBALO 53.6%, Domingos Simoes PEREIRA 46.5%
2014: Jose Mario VAZ elected president in second round; percent of vote in first round - Jose Mario VAZ (PAIGC) 41%, Nuno Gomez NABIAM (independent) 25.1%, other 33.9%; percent of vote in second round - Jose Mario VAZ 61.9%, Nuno Gomez NABIAM 38.1% (2019)
expected date of next election: 2025
note: President EMBALO was declared winner of the 2019 runoff presidential election by the electoral commission; in 2020, EMBALO inaugurated himself with only military leadership present, even though the Supreme Court of Justice had yet to rule on an electoral litigation appeal

Legislative branch: *legislature name:* People's National Assembly (Assembleia Nacional Popular)
legislative structure: unicameral
number of seats: 102 (all directly elected)
electoral system: proportional representation
scope of elections: full renewal
term in office: 4 years
most recent election date: 6/4/2023
parties elected and seats per party: Inclusive Alliance Platform/Terra Coalition (54); Movement for Democratic Alternation (MADEM G.15) (29); Party for Social Renewal (PRS) (12); Bissau-Guinean Workers' Party (6); Other (1)
percentage of women in chamber: 9.8%
expected date of next election: November 2025

Judicial branch: *highest court(s):* Supreme Court or Supremo Tribunal de Justica (consists of 9 judges and organized into Civil, Criminal, and Social and Administrative Disputes Chambers)
judge selection and term of office: judges nominated by the Higher Council of the Magistrate, a major government organ responsible for judge appointments, dismissals, and judiciary discipline; judges appointed by the president for life
subordinate courts: Appeals Court; regional (first instance) courts; military court
note: the Supreme Court has both appellate and constitutional jurisdiction

Political parties: African Party for the Independence of Guinea and Cabo Verde or PAIGC
Democratic Convergence Party or PCD
Movement for Democratic Alternation Group of 15 or MADEM-G15
National People's Assembly – Democratic Party of Guinea Bissau or APU-PDGB
New Democracy Party or PND
Party for Social Renewal or PRS
Republican Party for Independence and Development or PRID
Union for Change or UM

Diplomatic representation in the US: *chief of mission:* Ambassador Maria Da Conceição NOBRE CABRAL (since 18 September 2024)
chancery: 918 16th Street, NW (Mezzanine Suite) Washington DC 20006
telephone: [1] (202) 872-4222
FAX: [1] (202) 872-4226

Diplomatic representation from the US: *chief of mission:* Ambassador Michael RAYNOR (since 20 April 2022)
mailing address: 2080 Bissau Place, Washington DC 20521-2080
email address and website: dakarACS@state.gov
https://gw.usmission.gov/

International organization participation: ACP, AfDB, AOSIS, AU, CPLP, ECOWAS, FAO, FZ, G-77, IBRD, ICAO, ICRM, IDA, IDB, IFAD, IFC, IFRCS, ILO, IMF, IMO, Interpol, IOC, IOM, IPU, ITSO, ITU, ITUC (NGOs), MIGA, MINUSMA, NAM, OIC, OIF, OPCW, UN, UNCTAD, UNESCO, UNIDO, UNWTO, UPU, WADB (regional), WAEMU, WCO, WFTU (NGOs), WHO, WIPO, WMO, WTO

Independence: 24 September 1973 (declared); 10 September 1974 (from Portugal)

National holiday: Independence Day, 24 September (1973)

Flag: *description:* two equal horizontal bands of yellow (top) and green, with a vertical red band on the left side; a five-pointed black star is centered in the red band
meaning: yellow stands for the sun, green for hope, red for blood shed during the struggle for independence; the black star stands for African unity
history: uses the colors of the Pan-African movement; the Ghanaian flag heavily influenced the design

National symbol(s): black star

National color(s): red, yellow, green, black

National anthem(s): *title:* "Esta e a Nossa Patria Bem Amada" (This is Our Beloved Country)
lyrics/music: Amilcar Lopes CABRAL/XIAO He
history: adopted 1974; a delegation from Portuguese Guinea visited China in 1963 and heard music by XIAO He; Amilcar Lopes CABRAL, the leader of Guinea-Bissau's independence movement, asked the composer to create a piece that would inspire his people to fight for independence

ECONOMY

Economic overview: extremely poor West African economy; ethnically diverse labor force; increasing government expenditures; slight inflation due to food supply disruptions; major cashew exporter; systemic banking instabilities and corruption; vulnerable to oil price shocks

Real GDP (purchasing power parity): $5.912 billion (2024 est.)
$5.64 billion (2023 est.)
$5.399 billion (2022 est.)
note: data in 2021 dollars
comparison ranking: 177

Real GDP growth rate: 4.8% (2024 est.)
4.5% (2023 est.)
5.6% (2022 est.)
note: annual GDP % growth based on constant local currency
comparison ranking: 50

Real GDP per capita: $2,700 (2024 est.)
$2,600 (2023 est.)
$2,600 (2022 est.)
note: data in 2021 dollars
comparison ranking: 200

GDP (official exchange rate): $2.12 billion (2024 est.)
note: data in current dollars at official exchange rate

Inflation rate (consumer prices): 3.8% (2024 est.)
7.1% (2023 est.)
9.4% (2022 est.)
note: annual % change based on consumer prices
comparison ranking: 120

GDP - composition, by sector of origin: *agriculture:* 36.8% (2024 est.)
industry: 16.6% (2024 est.)
services: 42.1% (2024 est.)
note: figures may not total 100% due to non-allocated consumption not captured in sector-reported data
comparison rankings: agriculture 2; industry 158; services 187

GDP - composition, by end use: *household consumption:* 77% (2024 est.)
government consumption: 17.8% (2024 est.)
investment in fixed capital: 22.8% (2024 est.)
investment in inventories: -1.9% (2024 est.)
exports of goods and services: 12.5% (2024 est.)
imports of goods and services: -28.2% (2024 est.)
note: figures may not total 100% due to rounding or gaps in data collection

Agricultural products: rice, groundnuts, cashews, root vegetables, oil palm fruit, plantains, cassava, coconuts, vegetables, sweet potatoes (2023)
note: top ten agricultural products based on tonnage

Industries: agricultural products processing, beer, soft drinks

Industrial production growth rate: 8% (2024 est.)
note: annual % change in industrial value added based on constant local currency
comparison ranking: 20

Labor force: 845,300 (2024 est.)
note: number of people ages 15 or older who are employed or seeking work
comparison ranking: 149

Unemployment rate: 2.7% (2024 est.)
2.7% (2023 est.)
2.7% (2022 est.)
note: % of labor force seeking employment
comparison ranking: 29

Youth unemployment rate (ages 15-24): *total:* 2.8% (2024 est.)
male: 3.4% (2024 est.)
female: 2% (2024 est.)
note: % of labor force ages 15-24 seeking employment
comparison ranking: total 182

Population below poverty line: 50.5% (2021 est.)
note: % of population with income below national poverty line

Gini Index coefficient - distribution of family income: 33.4 (2021 est.)
note: index (0-100) of income distribution; higher values represent greater inequality
comparison ranking: 96

Household income or consumption by percentage share: *lowest 10%:* 3.4% (2021 est.)
highest 10%: 26.1% (2021 est.)
note: % share of income accruing to lowest and highest 10% of population

Remittances: 9.8% of GDP (2023 est.)
10.3% of GDP (2022 est.)
11% of GDP (2021 est.)
note: personal transfers and compensation between resident and non-resident individuals/households/entities

Budget: *revenues:* $269.794 million (2023 est.)
expenditures: $450.953 million (2023 est.)
note: central government revenues and expenses (excluding grants/extrabudgetary units/social security funds) converted to US dollars at average official exchange rate for year indicated

Taxes and other revenues: 8.8% (of GDP) (2023 est.)
note: central government tax revenue as a % of GDP
comparison ranking: 135

Current account balance: -$160.169 million (2023 est.)
-$146.64 million (2022 est.)
-$14.128 million (2021 est.)
note: balance of payments - net trade and primary/secondary income in current dollars
comparison ranking: 102

Exports: $284.5 million (2023 est.)
$280.065 million (2022 est.)
$334.904 million (2021 est.)
note: balance of payments - exports of goods and services in current dollars
comparison ranking: 198

Exports - partners: India 66%, Chile 9%, Cote d'Ivoire 5%, Ghana 4%, Netherlands 3% (2023)
note: top five export partners based on percentage share of exports

Exports - commodities: coconuts/brazil nuts/cashews, fish, fish oil, processed crustaceans, malt extract (2023)
note: top five export commodities based on value in dollars

Imports: $592.095 million (2023 est.)
$577.899 million (2022 est.)
$518.162 million (2021 est.)
note: balance of payments - imports of goods and services in current dollars
comparison ranking: 197

Imports - partners: Senegal 28%, Portugal 24%, China 11%, Gambia, The 10%, Pakistan 4% (2023)
note: top five import partners based on percentage share of imports

Imports - commodities: refined petroleum, iron bars, rice, plastics, flavored water (2023)
note: top five import commodities based on value in dollars

Debt - external: $896.812 million (2023 est.)
note: present value of external debt in current US dollars
comparison ranking: 108

Exchange rates: Communaute Financiere Africaine francs (XOF) per US dollar -

Exchange rates: 606.345 (2024 est.)
606.57 (2023 est.)
623.76 (2022 est.)
554.531 (2021 est.)
575.586 (2020 est.)

ENERGY

Electricity access: *electrification - total population:* 37.4% (2022 est.)
electrification - urban areas: 61%
electrification - rural areas: 15.8%

Electricity: *installed generating capacity:* 29,000 kW (2023 est.)
consumption: 79.8 million kWh (2023 est.)
transmission/distribution losses: 6 million kWh (2023 est.)
comparison rankings: installed generating capacity 203; consumption 200; transmission/distribution losses 12

Electricity generation sources: *fossil fuels:* 96.5% of total installed capacity (2023 est.)
solar: 3.5% of total installed capacity (2023 est.)

Coal: *imports:* 1 metric tons (2023 est.)

Petroleum: *refined petroleum consumption:* 2,000 bbl/day (2023 est.)

Energy consumption per capita: 2.351 million Btu/person (2023 est.)
comparison ranking: 182

COMMUNICATIONS

Telephones - fixed lines: *total subscriptions:* 0 (2022 est.)
subscriptions per 100 inhabitants: (2022 est.) less than 1
comparison ranking: total subscriptions 220

Telephones - mobile cellular: *total subscriptions:* 2.76 million (2023 est.)
subscriptions per 100 inhabitants: 126 (2022 est.)
comparison ranking: total subscriptions 142

Broadcast media: 1 state-owned TV station, Televisao da Guine-Bissau (TGB) and a second station, Radio e Televisao de Portugal (RTP) Africa, operated by Portuguese public broadcaster (RTP); 1 state-owned radio station, several private radio stations, and some community radio stations; multiple international broadcasters are available (2019)

Internet country code: .gw

Internet users: *percent of population:* 33% (2023 est.)

Broadband - fixed subscriptions: *total:* 7,000 (2023 est.)
subscriptions per 100 inhabitants: (2023 est.) less than 1
comparison ranking: total 189

TRANSPORTATION

Civil aircraft registration country code prefix: J5

Airports: 7 (2025)
comparison ranking: 170

Merchant marine: *total:* 20 (2023)
by type: bulk carrier 3, general cargo 12, other 5
comparison ranking: total 147

Ports: *total ports:* 2 (2024)
large: 0
medium: 0
small: 0
very small: 2

ports with oil terminals: 1
key ports: Bissau, Rio Cacheu

MILITARY AND SECURITY

Military and security forces: People's Revolutionary Armed Force (Forcas Armadas Revolucionarias do Povo or FARP): Army, Navy, Air Force

Ministry of Internal Administration: National Guard (a gendarmerie force), Public Order Police, Border Police, Rapid Intervention Police, Maritime Police (2024)
note: the Public Order Police is responsible for maintaining law and order, while the Judicial Police, under the Ministry of Justice, has primary responsibility for investigating drug trafficking, terrorism, and other transnational crimes

Military expenditures: 1.2% of GDP (2024 est.)
1.2% of GDP (2023 est.)
1.4% of GDP (2022 est.)
1.5% of GDP (2021 est.)
1.5% of GDP (2020 est.)

Military and security service personnel strengths: estimated 4,000 active FARP (2025)

Military equipment inventories and acquisitions: the FARP is outfitted mostly with Soviet-era weapons and equipment, along with a handful of secondhand items from France and Spain (2024)

Military service age and obligation: 18-25 years of age for selective compulsory military service for men and women (Air Force service is voluntary); 16 years of age or younger, with parental consent, for voluntary service (2023)

Military - note: the Armed Forces (FARP) are focused on external security, but also has some internal security duties; the FARP and the paramilitary National Guard have been influential in the country's politics since independence and have attempted several coups; FARP members were suspected of coup plotting as recently as 2021, and it put down an attempted coup in 2022, while the National Guard attempted a coup in December 2023; since the 2000s, the FARP has undergone various attempts at defense and security sector reforms under the auspices of the African Union, the EU, the Economic Community of West Africa (ECOWAS), and the UN (2025)

TRANSNATIONAL ISSUES

Refugees and internally displaced persons: *refugees:* 54 (2024 est.)

GUYANA

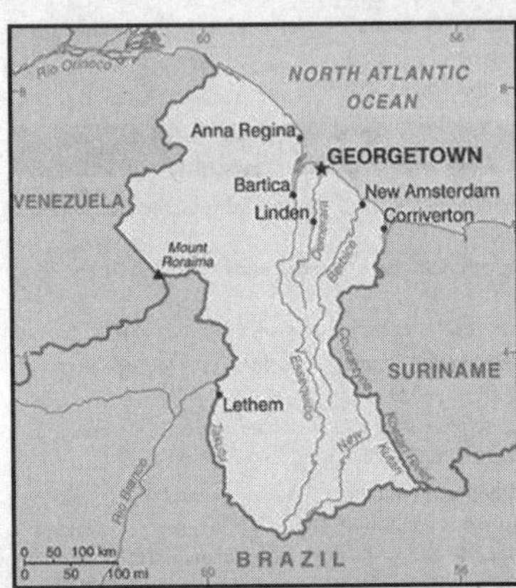

INTRODUCTION

Background: Originally a Dutch colony in the 17th century, by 1815 Guyana had become a British possession. The abolition of slavery led to former slaves settling urban areas and indentured servants being imported from India to work the sugar plantations. The resulting ethnocultural divide has persisted and has led to turbulent politics. Guyana achieved independence from the UK in 1966, and since then primarily socialist-oriented governments have ruled the country.

In 1992, Cheddi JAGAN was elected president in what is considered the country's first free and fair election since independence. After his death five years later, his wife, Janet JAGAN, became president but resigned in 1999 due to poor health. Her successor, Bharrat JAGDEO, was elected in 2001 and again in 2006. Donald RAMOTAR won in 2011, but early elections held in 2015 resulted in the first change in governing party, and David GRANGER took office. After a 2018 no-confidence vote against the GRANGER government, the administration ignored a constitutional requirement to hold elections and remained in place until the 2020 elections, when Irfaan ALI became president.

The discovery of massive offshore oil reserves in 2015 has been Guyana's primary economic and political focus, with many hoping the reserves will transform one of the poorest countries in the region. Guyana is the only English-speaking country in South America and shares cultural and historical bonds with the Anglophone Caribbean.

GEOGRAPHY

Location: Northern South America, bordering the North Atlantic Ocean, between Suriname and Venezuela

Geographic coordinates: 5 00 N, 59 00 W

Map references: South America

Area: *total:* 214,969 sq km
land: 196,849 sq km
water: 18,120 sq km
comparison ranking: total 85

Area - comparative: slightly smaller than Idaho; almost twice the size of Tennessee

Land boundaries: *total:* 2,933 km
border countries (3): Brazil 1,308 km; Suriname 836 km; Venezuela 789 km

Coastline: 459 km

Maritime claims: *territorial sea:* 12 nm
exclusive economic zone: 200 nm
continental shelf: 200 nm or to the outer edge of the continental margin

Climate: tropical; hot, humid, moderated by northeast trade winds; two rainy seasons (May to August, November to January)

Terrain: mostly rolling highlands; low coastal plain; savanna in south

Elevation: *highest point:* Laberintos del Norte on Mount Roraima 2,775 m
lowest point: Atlantic Ocean 0 m
mean elevation: 207 m

Natural resources: bauxite, gold, diamonds, hardwood timber, shrimp, fish

Land use: *agricultural land:* 5.3% (2022 est.)
arable land: 2.1% (2022 est.)
permanent crops: 0.1% (2022 est.)
permanent pasture: 3% (2022 est.)
forest: 93.5% (2022 est.)
other: 1.2% (2022 est.)

Irrigated land: 1,430 sq km (2012)

Major watersheds (area sq km): Atlantic Ocean drainage: Amazon (6,145,186 sq km), Orinoco (953,675 sq km)

Population distribution: population is heavily concentrated in the northeast in and around Georgetown, with notable concentrations along the Berbice River to the east; the remainder of the country is sparsely populated

Natural hazards: flash flood threat during rainy seasons

Geography - note: the third-smallest country in South America after Suriname and Uruguay; contains some of the largest unspoiled rainforests on the continent

PEOPLE AND SOCIETY

Population: *total:* 794,099 (2024 est.)
male: 405,244
female: 388,855
comparison rankings: total 166; male 166; female 166

Nationality: *noun:* Guyanese (singular and plural)
adjective: Guyanese

Ethnic groups: East Indian 39.8%, African descent 29.3%, mixed 19.9%, Indigenous 10.5%, other 0.5% (includes Portuguese, Chinese, White) (2012 est.)

Languages: English (official), Guyanese Creole, Amerindian languages (including Caribbean and Arawak languages), Indian languages (including Caribbean Hindustani, a dialect of Hindi), Chinese (2014 est.)

Religions: Protestant 34.8% (Pentecostal 22.8%, Seventh Day Adventist 5.4%, Anglican 5.2%, Methodist 1.4%), Hindu 24.8%, other Christian 20.8%, Roman Catholic 7.1%, Muslim 6.8%, Jehovah's Witness 1.3%, Rastafarian 0.5%, other 0.9%, none 3.1% (2012 est.)

Age structure: *0-14 years:* 23.5% (male 95,223/female 91,272)
15-64 years: 68.4% (male 281,669/female 261,261)

65 years and over: 8.1% (2024 est.) (male 28,352/ female 36,322)

Dependency ratios: *total dependency ratio:* 46.3 (2024 est.)
youth dependency ratio: 34.3 (2024 est.)
elderly dependency ratio: 11.9 (2024 est.)
potential support ratio: 8.4 (2024 est.)

Median age: *total:* 28.3 years (2024 est.)
male: 28.2 years
female: 28.4 years
comparison ranking: total 150

Population growth rate: 0.32% (2024 est.)
comparison ranking: 164

Birth rate: 16.7 births/1,000 population (2024 est.)
comparison ranking: 95

Death rate: 7 deaths/1,000 population (2024 est.)
comparison ranking: 122

Net migration rate: -6.6 migrant(s)/1,000 population (2024 est.)
comparison ranking: 214

Population distribution: population is heavily concentrated in the northeast in and around Georgetown, with notable concentrations along the Berbice River to the east; the remainder of the country is sparsely populated

Urbanization: *urban population:* 27.2% of total population (2023)
rate of urbanization: 1.01% annual rate of change (2020-25 est.)

Major urban areas - population: 110,000 GEORGETOWN (capital) (2018)

Sex ratio: *at birth:* 1.05 male(s)/female
0-14 years: 1.04 male(s)/female
15-64 years: 1.08 male(s)/female
65 years and over: 0.78 male(s)/female
total population: 1.04 male(s)/female (2024 est.)

Mother's mean age at first birth: 20.8 years (2009 est.)
note: data represents median age at first birth among women 25-29

Maternal mortality ratio: 75 deaths/100,000 live births (2023 est.)
comparison ranking: 76

Infant mortality rate: *total:* 21.1 deaths/1,000 live births (2024 est.)
male: 23.9 deaths/1,000 live births
female: 18.3 deaths/1,000 live births
comparison ranking: total 75

Life expectancy at birth: *total population:* 72.4 years (2024 est.)
male: 70.6 years
female: 74.3 years
comparison ranking: total population 163

Total fertility rate: 2.05 children born/woman (2024 est.)
comparison ranking: 99

Gross reproduction rate: 1 (2024 est.)

Drinking water source: *improved: urban:* 96% of population (2022 est.)
rural: 95.8% of population (2022 est.)
total: 95.9% of population (2022 est.)
unimproved: urban: 4% of population (2022 est.)
rural: 4.2% of population (2022 est.)
total: 4.1% of population (2022 est.)

Health expenditure: 4.9% of GDP (2021)
10.5% of national budget (2022 est.)

Physician density: 1.39 physicians/1,000 population (2020)

Hospital bed density: 2.6 beds/1,000 population (2021 est.)

Sanitation facility access: *improved: urban:* 98.7% of population (2022 est.)
rural: 99.5% of population (2022 est.)
total: 99.3% of population (2022 est.)
unimproved: urban: 1.3% of population (2022 est.)
rural: 0.5% of population (2022 est.)
total: 0.7% of population (2022 est.)

Obesity - adult prevalence rate: 20.2% (2016)
comparison ranking: 102

Alcohol consumption per capita: *total:* 5.11 liters of pure alcohol (2019 est.)
beer: 2.75 liters of pure alcohol (2019 est.)
wine: 0.04 liters of pure alcohol (2019 est.)
spirits: 2.3 liters of pure alcohol (2019 est.)
other alcohols: 0.02 liters of pure alcohol (2019 est.)
comparison ranking: total 83

Tobacco use: *total:* 9.2% (2025 est.)
male: 16.9% (2025 est.)
female: 1.9% (2025 est.)
comparison ranking: total 133

Children under the age of 5 years underweight: 9.4% (2019)
comparison ranking: 54

Currently married women (ages 15-49): 62.6% (2023 est.)

Child marriage: *women married by age 15:* 6.3% (2020)
women married by age 18: 32.3% (2020)
men married by age 18: 11.9% (2020)

Education expenditure: 4.5% of GDP (2018 est.)
16.2% national budget (2018 est.)
comparison ranking: Education expenditure (% GDP) 84

Literacy: *total population:* 85.6% (2020 est.)
male: 84.2% (2020 est.)
female: 86.9% (2020 est.)

ENVIRONMENT

Environmental issues: water pollution from sewage and agricultural/industrial chemicals; deforestation

International environmental agreements: *party to:* Biodiversity, Climate Change, Climate Change-Kyoto Protocol, Climate Change-Paris Agreement, Comprehensive Nuclear Test Ban, Desertification, Endangered Species, Hazardous Wastes, Law of the Sea, Marine Dumping-London Protocol, Ozone Layer Protection, Ship Pollution, Tropical Timber 2006
signed, but not ratified: none of the selected agreements

Climate: tropical; hot, humid, moderated by northeast trade winds; two rainy seasons (May to August, November to January)

Urbanization: *urban population:* 27.2% of total population (2023)
rate of urbanization: 1.01% annual rate of change (2020-25 est.)

Carbon dioxide emissions: 2.639 million metric tonnes of CO2 (2023 est.)
from petroleum and other liquids: 2.635 million metric tonnes of CO2 (2023 est.)
from consumed natural gas: 4,000 metric tonnes of CO2 (2023 est.)
comparison ranking: total emissions 155

Particulate matter emissions: 11.2 micrograms per cubic meter (2019 est.)

Methane emissions: *energy:* 103 kt (2022-2024 est.)
agriculture: 51.9 kt (2019-2021 est.)
waste: 7.7 kt (2019-2021 est.)
other: 2.2 kt (2019-2021 est.)

Waste and recycling: *municipal solid waste generated annually:* 179,300 tons (2024 est.)
percent of municipal solid waste recycled: 23% (2022 est.)

Total water withdrawal: *municipal:* 61.3 million cubic meters (2022 est.)
industrial: 20.4 million cubic meters (2022 est.)
agricultural: 1.363 billion cubic meters (2022 est.)

Total renewable water resources: 271 billion cubic meters (2022 est.)

GOVERNMENT

Country name: *conventional long form:* Cooperative Republic of Guyana
conventional short form: Guyana
former: British Guiana
etymology: the name is derived from Guiana, the original name for the region that included British Guiana, Dutch Guiana, and French Guiana; the name Guiana may be derived from a local term meaning "Land of Water" (referring to the area's multitude of rivers and streams)

Government type: parliamentary republic

Capital: *name:* Georgetown
geographic coordinates: 6 48 N, 58 09 W
time difference: UTC-4 (1 hour ahead of Washington, DC, during Standard Time)
etymology: the British founded the town in 1781 and named it in honor of King GEORGE III (1738-1820)

Administrative divisions: 10 regions; Barima-Waini, Cuyuni-Mazaruni, Demerara-Mahaica, East Berbice-Corentyne, Essequibo Islands-West Demerara, Mahaica-Berbice, Pomeroon-Supenaam, Potaro-Siparuni, Upper Demerara-Berbice, Upper Takutu-Upper Essequibo

Legal system: common law system, based on the English model, with some Roman-Dutch civil law influence

Constitution: *history:* several previous; latest promulgated 6 October 1980
amendment process: proposed by the National Assembly; passage of amendments affecting constitutional articles, such as national sovereignty, government structure and powers, and constitutional amendment procedures, requires approval by the Assembly membership, approval in a referendum, and assent of the president; other amendments only require Assembly approval

International law organization participation: has not submitted an ICJ jurisdiction declaration; accepts ICCt jurisdiction

Citizenship: *citizenship by birth:* yes
citizenship by descent only: yes
dual citizenship recognized: no
residency requirement for naturalization: na

Suffrage: 18 years of age; universal

Executive branch: *chief of state:* President Mohammed Irfaan ALI (since 2 August 2020)
head of government: President Mohammed Irfaan ALI (since 2 August 2020)
cabinet: Cabinet of Ministers appointed by the president, responsible to the National Assembly

election/appointment process: the predesignated candidate of the winning party in the last National Assembly election becomes president for a 5-year term (no term limits); prime minister appointed by the president
most recent election date: 2 March 2020
election results: *2020:* Mohammed Irfaan ALI (PPP/C) designated president by the majority party in the National Assembly
2015: David GRANGER (APNU-AFC) designated president by the majority party in the National Assembly
expected date of next election: 1 September 2025
note: the president is both chief of state and head of government

Legislative branch: *legislature name:* Parliament of the Co-operative Republic of Guyana
legislative structure: unicameral
chamber name: National Assembly
number of seats: 69 (all directly elected)
electoral system: mixed system
scope of elections: full renewal
term in office: 5 years
most recent election date: 9/1/2025
parties elected and seats per party: People's Progressive Party/Civic (PPP/C) (33); A Partnership for National Unity - Alliance for Change (APNU-AFC) (31); Other (1)
percentage of women in chamber: 39.4%
expected date of next election: August 2030

Judicial branch: *highest court(s):* Supreme Court of Judicature (consists of the Court of Appeal with a chief justice and 3 justices, and the High Court with a chief justice and 10 justices organized into 3-or 5-judge panels); Caribbean Court of Justice is the final court of appeal in civil and criminal cases
judge selection and term of office: Court of Appeal and High Court chief justices appointed by the president; other judges of both courts appointed by the Judicial Service Commission, a body appointed by the president; judges appointed for life with retirement at age 65
subordinate courts: Land Court; magistrates' courts

Political parties: A New and United Guyana or ANUG
A Partnership for National Unity or APNU
Alliance for Change or AFC
Justice for All Party
Liberty and Justice Party or LJP
National Independent Party or NIP
People's Progressive Party/Civic or PPP/C
The New Movement or TNM
The United Force or TUF
United Republican Party or URP

Diplomatic representation in the US: *chief of mission:* Ambassador Samuel Archibald HINDS (since 7 July 2021)
chancery: 2490 Tracy Place NW, Washington, DC 20008
telephone: [1] (202) 265-6900
FAX: [1] (202) 232-1297
email address and website: guyanaembassydc@verizon.net
http://www.guyanaembassydc.org/
consulate(s) general: New York

Diplomatic representation from the US: *chief of mission:* Ambassador Nicole THERIOT (since 14 October 2023)
embassy: 100 Young and Duke Streets, Kingston, Georgetown
mailing address: 3170 Georgetown Place, Washington DC 20521-3170
telephone: [592] 225-4900 through 4909
FAX: [592] 225-8497
email address and website: acsgeorge@state.gov
https://gy.usembassy.gov/

International organization participation: ACP, ACS, AOSIS, C, Caricom, CD, CDB, CELAC, FAO, G-77, IADB, IBRD, ICAO, ICCt, ICRM, IDA, IFAD, IFC, IFRCS, ILO, IMF, IMO, Interpol, IOC, IOM, ISO (correspondent), ITU, LAES, MIGA, NAM, OAS, OIC, OPANAL, OPCW, PCA, Petrocaribe, PROSUR, UN, UNASUR, UNCTAD, UNESCO, UNIDO, UPU, WCO, WFTU (NGOs), WHO, WIPO, WMO, WTO

Independence: 26 May 1966 (from the UK)

National holiday: Republic Day, 23 February (1970)

Flag: *description:* green with a red isosceles triangle (based on the left side) on top of a long yellow arrowhead shape that extends to the opposite side of the flag; a narrow black border sits between the red and yellow, and a narrow white border between the yellow and green
meaning: green stands for forest and foliage, yellow for mineral resources and a bright future, white for the rivers, red for zeal and the people's sacrifice, and black for perseverance

National symbol(s): Canje pheasant (hoatzin), jaguar, Victoria Regia water lily

National color(s): red, yellow, green, black, white

National coat of arms: Guyana's coat of arms was adopted in 1966, the year of the country's independence from the United Kingdom; the jaguars signify strength and resilience, with one holding a pickaxe that stands for labor and the other holding stalks of rice and sugarcane for agriculture; two national symbols, the Canje pheasant and the Victorian lily, are on the shield, with the national motto underneath; three wavy blue lines stand for the Essequibo, Demerara, and Berbice rivers, the headdress for the country's ethnic groups, and the diamonds for the mining industry; the helmet is a symbol of past UK rule in Guyana

National anthem(s): *title:* "Dear Land of Guyana, of Rivers and Plains"
lyrics/music: Archibald Leonard LUKERL/Robert Cyril Gladstone POTTER
history: adopted 1966

ECONOMY

Economic overview: small, hydrocarbon-driven South American export economy; major forest coverage being leveraged in carbon credit offsets to encourage preservation; strengthening financial sector; large bauxite and gold resources

Real GDP (purchasing power parity): $58.423 billion (2024 est.)
$40.749 billion (2023 est.)
$30.457 billion (2022 est.)
note: data in 2021 dollars
comparison ranking: 119

Real GDP growth rate: 43.4% (2024 est.)
33.8% (2023 est.)
63.3% (2022 est.)
note: annual GDP % growth based on constant local currency
comparison ranking: 1

Real GDP per capita: $70,300 (2024 est.)
$49,300 (2023 est.)
$37,100 (2022 est.)
note: data in 2021 dollars
comparison ranking: 20

GDP (official exchange rate): $24.836 billion (2024 est.)
note: data in current dollars at official exchange rate

Inflation rate (consumer prices): 2.9% (2024 est.)
2.8% (2023 est.)
6.1% (2022 est.)
note: annual % change based on consumer prices
comparison ranking: 85

GDP - composition, by sector of origin: *agriculture:* 8% (2024 est.)
industry: 74.3% (2024 est.)
services: 15.3% (2024 est.)
note: figures may not total 100% due to non-allocated consumption not captured in sector-reported data
comparison rankings: agriculture 86; industry 1; services 207

Agricultural products: rice, sugarcane, plantains, cassava, papayas, pumpkins/squash, chicken, milk, ginger, eggplants (2023)
note: top ten agricultural products based on tonnage

Industries: bauxite, sugar, rice milling, timber, textiles, gold mining

Industrial production growth rate: 53.3% (2024 est.)
note: annual % change in industrial value added based on constant local currency
comparison ranking: 1

Labor force: 292,200 (2024 est.)
note: number of people ages 15 or older who are employed or seeking work
comparison ranking: 167

Unemployment rate: 10.2% (2024 est.)
12.1% (2023 est.)
12.1% (2022 est.)
note: % of labor force seeking employment
comparison ranking: 148

Youth unemployment rate (ages 15-24): *total:* 22.3% (2024 est.)
male: 17.4% (2024 est.)
female: 28.1% (2024 est.)
note: % of labor force ages 15-24 seeking employment
comparison ranking: total 46

Remittances: 3.2% of GDP (2023 est.)
3.7% of GDP (2022 est.)
6.9% of GDP (2021 est.)
note: personal transfers and compensation between resident and non-resident individuals/households/entities

Budget: *revenues:* $1.333 billion (2019 est.)
expenditures: $1.467 billion (2019 est.)

Current account balance: $2.352 billion (2023 est.)
$4.242 billion (2022 est.)
-$1.36 billion (2021 est.)
note: balance of payments - net trade and primary/secondary income in current dollars
comparison ranking: 42

Exports: $13.739 billion (2023 est.)
$11.517 billion (2022 est.)
$4.594 billion (2021 est.)
note: balance of payments - exports of goods and services in current dollars
comparison ranking: 102

Exports - partners: USA 20%, Trinidad & Tobago 11%, Netherlands 10%, Singapore 10%, Germany 7% (2023)

note: top five export partners based on percentage share of exports

Exports - commodities: crude petroleum, railway cargo containers, gold, ships, rice (2023)
note: top five export commodities based on value in dollars

Imports: $10.956 billion (2023 est.)
$7.033 billion (2022 est.)
$6.588 billion (2021 est.)
note: balance of payments - imports of goods and services in current dollars
comparison ranking: 116

Imports - partners: USA 28%, China 13%, Trinidad & Tobago 11%, Brazil 5%, Bahamas, The 4% (2023)
note: top five import partners based on percentage share of imports

Imports - commodities: refined petroleum, ships, construction vehicles, excavation machinery, cars (2023)
note: top five import commodities based on value in dollars

Reserves of foreign exchange and gold: $1.01 billion (2024 est.)
$895.275 million (2023 est.)
$917.877 million (2022 est.)
note: holdings of gold (year-end prices)/foreign exchange/special drawing rights in current dollars
comparison ranking: 143

Debt - external: $1.805 billion (2023 est.)
note: present value of external debt in current US dollars
comparison ranking: 97

Exchange rates: Guyanese dollars (GYD) per US dollar -

Exchange rates: 208.5 (2024 est.)
208.5 (2023 est.)
208.5 (2022 est.)
208.5 (2021 est.)
208.5 (2020 est.)

ENERGY

Electricity access: *electrification - total population:* 93% (2022 est.)
electrification - urban areas: 98%
electrification - rural areas: 91.6%

Electricity: *installed generating capacity:* 259,000 kW (2023 est.)
consumption: 1.07 billion kWh (2023 est.)
transmission/distribution losses: 268.803 million kWh (2023 est.)
comparison rankings: installed generating capacity 168; consumption 159; transmission/distribution losses 70

Electricity generation sources: *fossil fuels:* 92.9% of total installed capacity (2023 est.)
solar: 1.3% of total installed capacity (2023 est.)
hydroelectricity: 0.3% of total installed capacity (2023 est.)
biomass and waste: 5.4% of total installed capacity (2023 est.)

Petroleum: *total petroleum production:* 391,000 bbl/day (2023 est.)
refined petroleum consumption: 18,000 bbl/day (2023 est.)

Natural gas: *consumption:* 1.991 million cubic meters (2023 est.)
imports: 1.991 million cubic meters (2023 est.)

Energy consumption per capita: 46.045 million Btu/person (2023 est.)
comparison ranking: 97

COMMUNICATIONS

Telephones - fixed lines: *total subscriptions:* 125,000 (2021 est.)
subscriptions per 100 inhabitants: 15 (2022 est.)
comparison ranking: total subscriptions 130

Telephones - mobile cellular: *total subscriptions:* 856,000 (2021 est.)
subscriptions per 100 inhabitants: 106 (2021 est.)
comparison ranking: total subscriptions 168

Broadcast media: government-dominated broadcast media; the National Communications Network (NCN) TV is state-owned; a few private TV stations relay satellite services; the state owns and operates 2 radio stations broadcasting on multiple frequencies; government limits on licensing of new private radio stations has constrained competition

Internet country code: .gy

Internet users: *percent of population:* 82% (2023 est.)

Broadband - fixed subscriptions: *total:* 106,000 (2022 est.)
subscriptions per 100 inhabitants: 13 (2022 est.)
comparison ranking: total 132

TRANSPORTATION

Civil aircraft registration country code prefix: 8R

Airports: 55 (2025)
comparison ranking: 82

Merchant marine: *total:* 80 (2023)
by type: general cargo 45, oil tanker 10, other 25
comparison ranking: total 99

Ports: *total ports:* 3 (2024)
large: 0
medium: 1
small: 0
very small: 2
ports with oil terminals: 3
key ports: Georgetown, Linden, New Amsterdam

MILITARY AND SECURITY

Military and security forces: the Guyana Defense Force (GDF) is a unified force with ground, air, and coast guard components, as well as the Guyana National Reserve (2025)
note: the Guyana Police Force under the Ministry of Home Affairs is responsible for internal security

Military expenditures: 0.9% of GDP (2024 est.)
0.6% of GDP (2023 est.)
0.6% of GDP (2022 est.)
1% of GDP (2021 est.)
1.2% of GDP (2020 est.)

Military and security service personnel strengths: approximately 3,500 active-duty Guyana Defense Forces (2025)

Military equipment inventories and acquisitions: the military has a limited inventory comprised mostly of older or second-hand platforms from a variety of foreign suppliers, including Brazil, China, the former Soviet Union, the UK, and the US (2024)

Military service age and obligation: 18-25 years of age or older for voluntary military service; no conscription (2024)

Military - note: the Guyana Defense Force (GDF) was established in 1965; its primary missions are territorial defense, maritime security, search and rescue, medical evacuation, aviation and engineering support, disaster relief and humanitarian assistance, peace support operations, and community engagement; key areas of concern include illegal fishing, narcotics trafficking, piracy, porous borders, and threats from Venezuela over disputed territory; the GDF participates in both bilateral and multinational exercises and has relationships with Brazil, China, France, the UK, and the US
Guyana joined the Caribbean Regional Security System (RSS) in 2022; RSS signatories (Antigua and Barbuda, Barbados, Dominica, Grenada, Saint Kitts and Nevis, Saint Lucia, and Saint Vincent and the Grenadines) agreed to prepare contingency plans and assist one another, on request, in national emergencies, prevention of smuggling, search and rescue, immigration control, fishery protection, customs and excise control, maritime policing duties, protection of off-shore installations, pollution control, national and other disasters, and threats to national security (2025)

TRANSNATIONAL ISSUES

Refugees and internally displaced persons: *refugees:* 79 (2024 est.)

H

HAITI

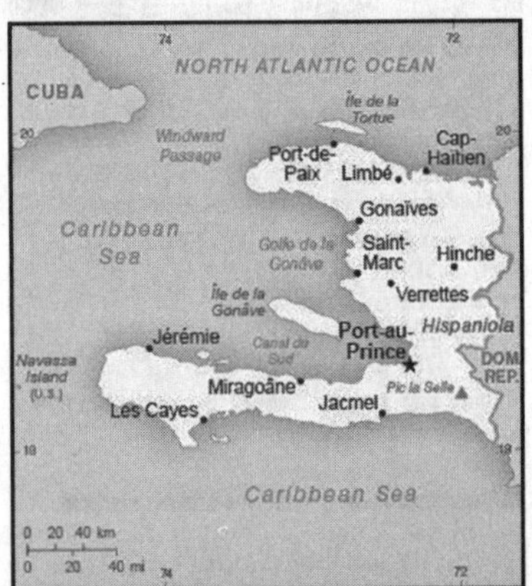

INTRODUCTION

Background: The native Taino – who inhabited the island of Hispaniola when Christopher COLUMBUS first landed in 1492 – were virtually wiped out by Spanish settlers within 25 years. In the early 17th century, the French established a presence on Hispaniola. In 1697, Spain ceded to the French the western third of the island, which later became Haiti. The French colony, based on forestry and sugar-related industries, became one of the wealthiest in the Caribbean but relied heavily on the forced labor of enslaved Africans and environmentally degrading practices. In the late 18th century, Toussaint L'OUVERTURE led a revolution of Haiti's nearly half a million slaves that ended France's rule on the island. After a prolonged struggle, and under the leadership of Jean-Jacques DESSALINES, Haiti became the first country in the world led by former slaves after declaring its independence in 1804, but it was forced to pay an indemnity of 100 million francs (equivalent to $22 billion USD in March 2023) to France for more than a century and was shunned by other countries for nearly 40 years. In 1862, the US officially recognized Haiti, but foreign economic influence and internal political instability induced the US to occupy Haiti from 1915 to 1934.

Francois "Papa Doc" DUVALIER and then his son Jean-Claude "Baby Doc" DUVALIER led repressive and corrupt regimes that ruled Haiti in 1957-1971 and 1971-1986, respectively. Jean-Bertrand ARISTIDE was Haiti's first democratically elected president in 1991 and was elected a second time in 2000, but coups interrupted his first term after only a few months and ended his second term in 2004. President Jovenel MOÏSE was assassinated in 2021, leading the country further into an extra-constitutional governance structure and contributing to the country's growing fragility. The Government of Haiti then installed Ariel HENRY – whom President MOÏSE had nominated shortly before his death – as prime minister.

On 29 February 2024, a significant escalation of gang violence occurred on the 20th anniversary of ARISTIDE's second overthrow, after the announcement that HENRY would not hold elections until August 2025. HENRY's return from an overseas trip was diverted to Puerto Rico when the airport closed due to gang violence. With control of much of the capital, Port-au-Prince, gang leaders called for the ouster of HENRY'S government. By mid-March, Haiti's continued violence, HENRY'S inability to return to the country, and increasing pressure from the international community led HENRY to pledge to resign. On 25 April 2024, HENRY formally submitted his resignation as a nine-member Transitional Presidential Council assumed control, tasked with returning stability to the country and preparing elections. Since January 2023, Haiti has had no sitting elected officials.

The country has long been plagued by natural disasters. In 2010, a major 7.0 magnitude earthquake struck Haiti with an epicenter about 25 km (15 mi) west of the capital, Port-au-Prince. An estimated 300,000 people were killed, and some 1.5 million left homeless. The earthquake was assessed as the worst in this region in 200 years. A 7.2 magnitude earthquake hit Haiti's southern peninsula in 2021, causing well over 2,000 deaths; an estimated 500,000 required emergency humanitarian aid. Haiti is the poorest country in the Western Hemisphere, as well as one of the most unequal in wealth distribution.

GEOGRAPHY

Location: Caribbean, western one-third of the island of Hispaniola, between the Caribbean Sea and the North Atlantic Ocean, west of the Dominican Republic

Geographic coordinates: 19 00 N, 72 25 W

Map references: Central America and the Caribbean

Area: *total:* 27,750 sq km
land: 27,560 sq km
water: 190 sq km
comparison ranking: total 147

Area - comparative: slightly smaller than Maryland

Land boundaries: *total:* 376 km
border countries (1): Dominican Republic 376 km

Coastline: 1,771 km

Maritime claims: *territorial sea:* 12 nm
contiguous zone: 24 nm
exclusive economic zone: 200 nm
continental shelf: to depth of exploitation

Climate: tropical; semiarid where mountains in east cut off trade winds

Terrain: mostly rough and mountainous

Elevation: *highest point:* Pic la Selle 2,674 m
lowest point: Caribbean Sea 0 m
mean elevation: 470 m

Natural resources: bauxite, copper, calcium carbonate, gold, marble, hydropower, arable land

Land use: *agricultural land:* 65.1% (2022 est.)
arable land: 36.5% (2022 est.)
permanent crops: 10.9% (2022 est.)
permanent pasture: 17.8% (2022 est.)
forest: 12.4% (2022 est.)
other: 22.5% (2022 est.)

Irrigated land: 800 sq km (2013)

Population distribution: fairly even distribution; largest concentrations located near coastal areas

Natural hazards: lies in the middle of the hurricane belt and subject to severe storms from June to October; occasional flooding and earthquakes; periodic droughts

Geography - note: shares island of Hispaniola with Dominican Republic (western one-third is Haiti, eastern two-thirds is the Dominican Republic); it is the most mountainous nation in the Caribbean

PEOPLE AND SOCIETY

Population: *total:* 11,753,943 (2024 est.)
male: 5,792,443
female: 5,961,500
comparison rankings: total 83; male 85; female 83

Nationality: *noun:* Haitian(s)
adjective: Haitian

Ethnic groups: Black 95%, mixed and White 5%

Languages: French (official), Creole (official)
major-language sample(s):
The World Factbook, une source indispensable d'informations de base. (French)
The World Factbook, sous endispansab pou enfomasyon debaz. (Haitian Creole)

Religions: Catholic 55%, Protestant 29%, Vodou 2.1%, other 4.6%, none 10% (2018 est.)
note: 50-80% of Haitians incorporate some elements of Vodou culture or practice in addition to another religion, most often Roman Catholicism; Vodou was recognized as an official religion in 2003

Age structure: *0-14 years:* 30.5% (male 1,790,061/female 1,794,210)
15-64 years: 65.3% (male 3,787,782/female 3,887,791)
65 years and over: 4.2% (2024 est.) (male 214,600/female 279,499)

Dependency ratios: *total dependency ratio:* 53.1 (2024 est.)
youth dependency ratio: 46.7 (2024 est.)
elderly dependency ratio: 6.4 (2024 est.)
potential support ratio: 15.5 (2024 est.)

Median age: *total:* 25 years (2024 est.)
male: 24.7 years
female: 25.3 years
comparison ranking: total 173

Population growth rate: 1.23% (2024 est.)
comparison ranking: 77

Birth rate: 21.2 births/1,000 population (2024 est.)
comparison ranking: 60

Death rate: 7.3 deaths/1,000 population (2024 est.)
comparison ranking: 111

Net migration rate: -1.6 migrant(s)/1,000 population (2024 est.)
comparison ranking: 160

Population distribution: fairly even distribution; largest concentrations located near coastal areas

Urbanization: *urban population:* 59.7% of total population (2023)
rate of urbanization: 2.47% annual rate of change (2020-25 est.)

Major urban areas - population: 2.987 million PORT-AU-PRINCE (capital) (2023)

Sex ratio: *at birth:* 1.01 male(s)/female
0-14 years: 1 male(s)/female
15-64 years: 0.97 male(s)/female
65 years and over: 0.77 male(s)/female

total population: 0.97 male(s)/female (2024 est.)

Mother's mean age at first birth: 22.4 years (2016/7 est.)
note: data represents median age at first birth among women 25-49

Maternal mortality ratio: 328 deaths/100,000 live births (2023 est.)
comparison ranking: 24

Infant mortality rate: *total:* 36.8 deaths/1,000 live births (2024 est.)
male: 40.2 deaths/1,000 live births
female: 33.5 deaths/1,000 live births
comparison ranking: total 32

Life expectancy at birth: *total population:* 65.6 years (2024 est.)
male: 63.8 years
female: 67.4 years
comparison ranking: total population 205

Total fertility rate: 2.44 children born/woman (2024 est.)
comparison ranking: 72

Gross reproduction rate: 1.21 (2024 est.)

Drinking water source: *improved: urban:* 84.6% of population (2022 est.)
rural: 42.8% of population (2022 est.)
total: 67.4% of population (2022 est.)
unimproved: urban: 15.4% of population (2022 est.)
rural: 57.2% of population (2022 est.)
total: 32.6% of population (2022 est.)

Health expenditure: 3.5% of GDP (2021)
4.1% of national budget (2022 est.)

Physician density: 0.29 physicians/1,000 population (2022)

Hospital bed density: 4.8 beds/1,000 population (2021 est.)

Sanitation facility access: *improved: urban:* 82.9% of population (2022 est.)
rural: 42.6% of population (2022 est.)
total: 66.3% of population (2022 est.)
unimproved: urban: 17.1% of population (2022 est.)
rural: 57.4% of population (2022 est.)
total: 33.7% of population (2022 est.)

Obesity - adult prevalence rate: 22.7% (2016)
comparison ranking: 72

Alcohol consumption per capita: *total:* 2.85 liters of pure alcohol (2019 est.)
beer: 0.55 liters of pure alcohol (2019 est.)
wine: 0.03 liters of pure alcohol (2019 est.)
spirits: 2.26 liters of pure alcohol (2019 est.)
other alcohols: 0 liters of pure alcohol (2019 est.)
comparison ranking: total 118

Tobacco use: *total:* 7.1% (2025 est.)
male: 12.4% (2025 est.)
female: 2.1% (2025 est.)
comparison ranking: total 150

Children under the age of 5 years underweight: 9.5% (2016/17)
comparison ranking: 53

Currently married women (ages 15-49): 51.4% (2023 est.)

Child marriage: *women married by age 15:* 2.1% (2017)
women married by age 18: 14.9% (2017)
men married by age 18: 1.6% (2017)

Education expenditure: 1.1% of GDP (2023 est.)
13.2% national budget (2025 est.)
comparison ranking: Education expenditure (% GDP) 198

Literacy: *total population:* 68% (2017 est.)
male: 72.9% (2017 est.)
female: 63.9% (2017 est.)

ENVIRONMENT

Environmental issues: deforestation (trees cleared for agriculture and used as fuel); soil erosion; inadequate potable water and lack of sanitation; natural disasters

International environmental agreements: *party to:* Biodiversity, Climate Change, Climate Change-Kyoto Protocol, Climate Change-Paris Agreement, Desertification, Hazardous Wastes, Law of the Sea, Marine Dumping-London Convention, Marine Life Conservation, Ozone Layer Protection
signed, but not ratified: Nuclear Test Ban

Climate: tropical; semiarid where mountains in east cut off trade winds

Urbanization: *urban population:* 59.7% of total population (2023)
rate of urbanization: 2.47% annual rate of change (2020-25 est.)

Carbon dioxide emissions: 2.854 million metric tonnes of CO2 (2023 est.)
from petroleum and other liquids: 2.848 million metric tonnes of CO2 (2023 est.)
from consumed natural gas: 6,000 metric tonnes of CO2 (2023 est.)
comparison ranking: total emissions 151

Particulate matter emissions: 9.8 micrograms per cubic meter (2019 est.)

Waste and recycling: *municipal solid waste generated annually:* 2.31 million tons (2024 est.)
percent of municipal solid waste recycled: 9.1% (2022 est.)

Total water withdrawal: *municipal:* 190 million cubic meters (2022 est.)
industrial: 51 million cubic meters (2022 est.)
agricultural: 1.209 billion cubic meters (2022 est.)

Total renewable water resources: 14.022 billion cubic meters (2022 est.)

GOVERNMENT

Country name: *conventional long form:* Republic of Haiti
conventional short form: Haiti
local long form: République d'Haïti (French)/Repiblik d Ayiti (Haitian Creole)
local short form: Haïti (French)/ Ayiti (Haitian Creole)
etymology: derived from the Arawak name Ayti, meaning "Land of Mountains," that was originally applied to the entire island of Hispaniola

Government type: semi-presidential republic

Capital: *name:* Port-au-Prince
geographic coordinates: 18 32 N, 72 20 W
time difference: UTC-5 (same time as Washington, DC, during Standard Time)
daylight saving time: +1hr, begins second Sunday in March; ends first Sunday in November
etymology: the name means "the port of the prince" and probably came from a ship called The Prince that anchored in the bay in the early 18th century

Administrative divisions: 10 departments *(départements, singular - département)*; Artibonite, Centre, Grand'Anse, Nippes, Nord, Nord-Est, Nord-Ouest, Ouest, Sud, Sud-Est

Legal system: civil law system strongly influenced by Napoleonic Code

Constitution: *history:* many previous; latest adopted 10 March 1987, with substantial revisions in June 2012
amendment process: proposed by the executive branch or by either the Senate or the Chamber of Deputies; consideration of proposed amendments requires support by at least two-thirds majority of both houses; passage requires at least two-thirds majority of the membership present and at least two-thirds majority of the votes cast; approved amendments enter into force after installation of the next president of the republic; constitutional articles on the democratic and republican form of government cannot be amended
note: the constitution is commonly referred to as the "amended 1987 constitution"

International law organization participation: accepts compulsory ICJ jurisdiction; non-party state to the ICCt

Citizenship: *citizenship by birth:* no
citizenship by descent only: at least one parent must be a native-born citizen of Haiti
dual citizenship recognized: yes
residency requirement for naturalization: 5 years

Suffrage: 18 years of age; universal

Executive branch: *chief of state:* President (vacant)
head of government: Prime Minister Alix Didier FILS-AIMÉ (since 10 November 2024)
cabinet: Cabinet chosen by the prime minister in consultation with the president; parliament must ratify the Cabinet and prime minister's governing policy
election/appointment process: president directly elected by absolute-majority popular vote in 2 rounds, if needed, for a 5-year term (eligible for a single non-consecutive term)
most recent election date: 20 November 2016
election results: *2016:* Jovenel MOÏSE elected president in first round; percent of vote - Jovenel MOÏSE (PHTK) 55.6%, Jude CELESTIN (LAPEH) 19.6%, Jean-Charles MOÏSE (PPD) 11%, Maryse NARCISSE (FL) 9%; other 4.8%
2011: Michel MARTELLY elected president in second round; percent of vote in second round - Michel MARTELLY (Peasant's Response) 68%, Mirlande MANIGAT (RDNP) 32%
expected date of next election: elections were delayed in 2022 and 2023 and have not been rescheduled
note: former Prime Minister Ariel HENRY, who had assumed executive responsibilities following the assassination of President MOÏSE on 7 July 2021, resigned on 24 April 2024; a nine-member Presidential Transitional Council, equipped with presidential powers, was sworn in on 25 April 2024 and will remain in place until 7 February 2026

Legislative branch: *legislature name:* National Assembly (Assemblée nationale)
legislative structure: bicameral
note 1: when the two chambers meet collectively, it is known as the National Assembly (or L'Assemblée nationale) and is convened for specific purposes spelled out in the constitution
note 2: as of October 2024, the Senate and Chamber of Deputies were not functional

Legislative branch - lower chamber: *chamber name:* Chamber of Deputies (Chambre des Députés)
number of seats: 119 (all directly elected)
electoral system: plurality/majority
scope of elections: full renewal
term in office: 4 years
most recent election date: 8/9/2015 to 10/25/2015

parties elected and seats per party: Haitian Tet Kale Party (PHTK) (9); Konvansyon Inite Demokratik (KID) (7); Ayiti an aksyon (AAA) (6); Fanmi Lavalas (6); Patriotic Unity Party (Inite Patriyotik) (4); People's Struggle Party (OPL) (7); Other (24)
percentage of women in chamber: 0%
expected date of next election: December 2025

Legislative branch - upper chamber: *chamber name:* Senate (Sénat)
number of seats: 30 (all directly elected)
electoral system: plurality/majority
scope of elections: partial renewal
term in office: 6 years
most recent election date: 11/20/2016 to 1/29/2017
parties elected and seats per party: Haitian Tet Kale Party (PHTK) (9); Truth (Vérité) (3); Konvansyon Inite Demokratik (KID) (2); Bouclier (2); Ayiti an aksyon (AAA) (2); Other (10)
expected date of next election: December 2025

Judicial branch: *highest court(s):* Supreme Court or Cour de cassation (consists of 12 judges)
judge selection and term of office: judges appointed by the president from candidate lists submitted by the Senate of the National Assembly
subordinate courts: Courts of Appeal; Courts of First Instance; magistrate's courts; land, labor, and children's courts
note: the Superior Council of the Judiciary or Conseil Supérieur du Pouvoir Judiciaire is a 9-member body charged with the administration and oversight of the judicial branch of government
note: Haiti is a member of the Caribbean Court of Justice, the Constitutional Court (called for in the 1987 constitution but not yet established), and the High Court of Justice, for trying high government officials (currently not functional)
note: Article 174 of Haiti's constitution states that judges of the Supreme Court are appointed for 10 years, whereas Article 177 states that judges of the Supreme Court are appointed for life

Political parties: Alternative League for Haitian Progress and Emancipation (Ligue Alternative pour le Progrès
et l'Emancipation Haïtienne) or LAPEH
Christian Movement for a New Haiti or MCNH or Mochrenha
Christian National Movement for the Reconstruction of Haiti or UNCRH
Combat of Peasant Workers to Liberate Haiti (Konbit Travaye Peyizan Pou Libere Ayiti) or Kontra Pep La
Convention for Democratic Unity or KID
Cooperative Action to Rebuild Haiti or KONBA
December 16 Platform or Platfom 16 Desanm
Democratic Alliance Party or ALYANS (coalition includes KID and PPRH)
Democratic Centers' National Council or CONACED
Democratic and Popular Sector (Secteur Démocratique et Populaire) or SDP
Democratic Unity Convention (Konvansyon Inite Demokratik) or KID
Dessalinian Patriotic and Popular Movement or MOPOD
Effort and Solidarity to Create an Alternative for the People or ESKAMP
Fanmi Lavalas or FL
Forward (En Avant)
Fusion of Haitian Social Democrats (Fusion Des Sociaux-Démocrates Haïtiens) or FHSD G18 Policy Platform (Plateforme Politique G18)
Haiti in Action (Ayiti An Aksyon Haiti's Action) or AAA
Haitian Tet Kale Party (Parti Haitien Tet Kale) or PHTK
Independent Movement for National Reconciliation or MIRN
Lavni Organization or LAVNI
Lod Demokratik
Love Haiti (Renmen Ayiti) or RA
MTV Ayiti
National Consortium of Haitian Political Parties (Consortium National des Partis Politiques Haitiens) or CNPPH
National Shield Network (Reseau Bouclier National)
Organization of the People's Struggle (Oganizasyon Pep Kap Lite) or OPL
Patriotic Unity (Inite Patriyotik) or Inite
Platform Pitit Desalin (Politik Pitit Dessalines) or PPD
Political Party for Us All or Bridge (Pont) or Pou Nou Tout
Popular Patriotic Dessalinien Movement (Mouvement Patriotique Populaire Dessalinien) or MOPOD
Rally of Progressive National Democrats (Rassemblement des Démocrates Nationaux Progressistes) or RDNP
Respe (Respect)
Women and Families Political Parties (Defile Pati Politik Fanm Ak Fanmi)

Diplomatic representation in the US: *chief of mission:* Ambassador Lionel DELATOUR (since 11 June 2025)
chancery: 2311 Massachusetts Avenue NW, Washington, DC 20008
telephone: [1] (202) 332-4090
FAX: [1] (202) 745-7215
email address and website: amb.washington@diplomatie.ht
https://www.haiti.org/
consulate(s) general: Atlanta, Boston, Chicago, Miami, Orlando (FL), New York

Diplomatic representation from the US: *chief of mission:* Ambassador (vacant); Chargé d'Affaires Henry T. WOOSTER (since 12 June 2025)
embassy: Tabarre 41, Route de Tabarre, Port-au-Prince
mailing address: 3400 Port-au-Prince Place, Washington, DC 20521-3400
telephone: [011] (509) 2229-8000
FAX: [011] (509) 2229-8027
email address and website: acspap@state.gov
https://ht.usembassy. gov/

International organization participation: ACP, ACS, AOSIS, Caricom, CD, CDB, CELAC, FAO, G-77, IADB, IAEA, IBRD, ICAO, ICC (NGOs), ICRM, IDA, IFAD, IFC, IFRCS, ILO, IMF, IMO, Interpol, IOC, IOM, IPU, ITSO, ITU, ITUC (NGOs), LAES, MIGA, NAM, OAS, OIF, OPANAL, OPCW, PCA, Petrocaribe, UN, UNCTAD, UNESCO, UNIDO, Union Latina, UNWTO, UPU, WCO, WFTU (NGOs), WHO, WIPO, WMO, WTO

Independence: 1 January 1804 (from France)

National holiday: Independence Day, 1 January (1804)

Flag: *description:* two equal horizontal bands of blue (top) and red; a centered white rectangle bears the coat of arms, which has a palm tree flanked by flags and two cannons above a scroll with the motto L'UNION FAIT LA FORCE (Union Makes Strength)
meaning: the colors are taken from the French flag and represent the union of ethnic groups

National symbol(s): Hispaniolan trogon (bird), hibiscus flower

National color(s): blue, red

National anthem(s): *title:* "La Dessalinienne" (The Dessalines Song)
lyrics/music: Justin LHERISSON/Nicolas GEFFRARD
history: adopted 1904; named for Jean-Jacques DESSALINES, founder of Haiti

National heritage: *total World Heritage Sites:* 1 (cultural)
selected World Heritage Site locales: National History Park – Citadel, Sans Souci, Ramiers

ECONOMY

Economic overview: small Caribbean island economy and OECS-member state; extreme poverty and inflation; enormous income inequality; ongoing civil unrest due to recent presidential assassination; US preferential market access; very open to foreign direct investment

Real GDP (purchasing power parity): $32.971 billion (2024 est.)
$34.406 billion (2023 est.)
$35.059 billion (2022 est.)
note: data in 2021 dollars
comparison ranking: 145

Real GDP growth rate: -4.2% (2024 est.)
-1.9% (2023 est.)
-1.7% (2022 est.)
note: annual GDP % growth based on constant local currency
comparison ranking: 212

Real GDP per capita: $2,800 (2024 est.)
$3,000 (2023 est.)
$3,000 (2022 est.)
note: data in 2021 dollars
comparison ranking: 198

GDP (official exchange rate): $25.224 billion (2024 est.)
note: data in current dollars at official exchange rate

Inflation rate (consumer prices): 26.9% (2024 est.)
36.8% (2023 est.)
34% (2022 est.)
note: annual % change based on consumer prices
comparison ranking: 194

GDP - composition, by sector of origin: *agriculture:* 15.9% (2024 est.)
industry: 33.4% (2024 est.)
services: 48.3% (2024 est.)
note: figures may not total 100% due to non-allocated consumption not captured in sector-reported data
comparison rankings: agriculture 52; industry 38; services 156

GDP - composition, by end use: *household consumption:* 99.8% (2024 est.)
government consumption: 5.7% (2024 est.)
investment in fixed capital: 9.9% (2024 est.)
investment in inventories: 0% (2024 est.)
exports of goods and services: 3.4% (2024 est.)
imports of goods and services: -18.8% (2024 est.)
note: figures may not total 100% due to rounding or gaps in data collection

Agricultural products: sugarcane, cassava, plantains, bananas, mangoes/guavas, avocados, maize, tropical fruits, rice, vegetables (2023)
note: top ten agricultural products based on tonnage

Industries: textiles, sugar refining, flour milling, cement, light assembly using imported parts

Industrial production growth rate: -4.7% (2024 est.)
note: annual % change in industrial value added based on constant local currency
comparison ranking: 177

Labor force: 5.281 million (2024 est.)
note: number of people ages 15 or older who are employed or seeking work
comparison ranking: 83

Unemployment rate: 15.1% (2024 est.)
14.6% (2023 est.)
14.7% (2022 est.)
note: % of labor force seeking employment
comparison ranking: 173

Youth unemployment rate (ages 15-24): *total:* 37.5% (2024 est.)
male: 30% (2024 est.)
female: 47.1% (2024 est.)
note: % of labor force ages 15-24 seeking employment
comparison ranking: total 10

Remittances: 18.9% of GDP (2023 est.)
18.8% of GDP (2022 est.)
19.1% of GDP (2021 est.)
note: personal transfers and compensation between resident and non-resident individuals/households/entities

Budget: *revenues:* $1.179 billion (2020 est.)
expenditures: $1.527 billion (2020 est.)

Current account balance: -$682.57 million (2023 est.)
-$491.954 million (2022 est.)
$87.656 million (2021 est.)
note: balance of payments - net trade and primary/secondary income in current dollars
comparison ranking: 119

Exports: $1.095 billion (2023 est.)
$1.355 billion (2022 est.)
$1.272 billion (2021 est.)
note: balance of payments - exports of goods and services in current dollars
comparison ranking: 182

Exports - partners: USA 82%, Canada 4%, Mexico 2%, France 2%, India 2% (2023)
note: top five export partners based on percentage share of exports

Exports - commodities: garments, essential oils, scrap iron, industrial acids/oils/alcohols, bedding (2023)
note: top five export commodities based on value in dollars

Imports: $5.303 billion (2023 est.)
$5.451 billion (2022 est.)
$5.048 billion (2021 est.)
note: balance of payments - imports of goods and services in current dollars
comparison ranking: 150

Imports - partners: USA 31%, Dominican Republic 23%, China 14%, Indonesia 4%, India 3% (2023)
note: top five import partners based on percentage share of imports

Imports - commodities: refined petroleum, rice, garments, cotton fabric, plastic products (2023)
note: top five import commodities based on value in dollars

Reserves of foreign exchange and gold: $2.718 billion (2024 est.)
$2.586 billion (2023 est.)
$2.173 billion (2022 est.)
note: holdings of gold (year-end prices)/foreign exchange/special drawing rights in current dollars
comparison ranking: 121

Debt - external: $1.865 billion (2023 est.)
note: present value of external debt in current US dollars
comparison ranking: 96

Exchange rates: gourdes (HTG) per US dollar -

Exchange rates: 131.811 (2024 est.)
141.036 (2023 est.)
115.631 (2022 est.)
89.227 (2021 est.)
93.51 (2020 est.)

ENERGY

Electricity access: *electrification - total population:* 49.3% (2022 est.)
electrification - urban areas: 83%
electrification - rural areas: 1.2% (2019 est.)

Electricity: *installed generating capacity:* 472,000 kW (2023 est.)
consumption: 861 million kWh (2023 est.)
transmission/distribution losses: 152 million kWh (2023 est.)
comparison rankings: installed generating capacity 152; consumption 163; transmission/distribution losses 56

Electricity generation sources: *fossil fuels:* 81.3% of total installed capacity (2023 est.)
solar: 0.4% of total installed capacity (2023 est.)
hydroelectricity: 18.3% of total installed capacity (2023 est.)

Coal: *imports:* 5.7 metric tons (2022 est.)

Petroleum: *refined petroleum consumption:* 19,000 bbl/day (2023 est.)

Natural gas: *consumption:* 3.2 million cubic meters (2023 est.)
imports: 3.2 million cubic meters (2023 est.)

Energy consumption per capita: 3.486 million Btu/person (2023 est.)
comparison ranking: 175

COMMUNICATIONS

Telephones - fixed lines: *total subscriptions:* 6,000 (2021 est.)
subscriptions per 100 inhabitants: (2022 est.) less than 1
comparison ranking: total subscriptions 200

Telephones - mobile cellular: *total subscriptions:* 7.32 million (2021 est.)
subscriptions per 100 inhabitants: 64 (2021 est.)
comparison ranking: total subscriptions 110

Broadcast media: 398 legal broadcasting stations, including about 60 community radio stations; 105 TV stations, including 36 in Port-au-Prince, 41 others in the provinces, and more than 40 radio-television stations; large number of stations operate irregularly or flout regulations; VOA Creole Service broadcasts daily on 30 affiliate stations (2019)

Internet country code: .ht

Internet users: *percent of population:* 39% (2019 est.)

Broadband - fixed subscriptions: *total:* 35,000 (2022 est.)
subscriptions per 100 inhabitants: (2022 est.) less than 1
comparison ranking: total 154

TRANSPORTATION

Civil aircraft registration country code prefix: HH

Airports: 17 (2025)
comparison ranking: 146

Heliports: 2 (2025)
comparison ranking: 124

Merchant marine: *total:* 4 (2023)
by type: general cargo 3, other 1
comparison ranking: total 170

Ports: *total ports:* 5 (2024)
large: 0
medium: 1
small: 0
very small: 4
ports with oil terminals: 1
key ports: Cap Haitien, Jacmel, Miragoane, Petit Goave, Port au Prince

MILITARY AND SECURITY

Military and security forces: *the Haitian Armed Forces (FAdH):* Army

Ministry of Justice and Public Security: Haitian National Police (Police Nationale d'Haïti or PNH) (2025)
note: the PNH is responsible for maintaining public security; it includes police, corrections, fire, emergency response, airport security, port security, and coast guard functions; its units include a presidential guard and a paramilitary rapid-response Motorized Intervention Unit (BIM)

Military and security service personnel strengths: estimates vary; up to 2,000 trained military personnel (the force is planned to eventually have around 5,000 personnel); estimates for the National Police range from a low of 9,000 to a high of about 13,000 (2025)

Military equipment inventories and acquisitions: in recent years, Canada, Taiwan, the US, and the UAE have provide some equipment to the Haitian security forces, including vehicles (2024)

Military service age and obligation: men and women 18-25 may volunteer for the FAdH (2023)

Military - note: Haiti's military was disbanded in 1995 after it participated in multiple coups and was accused of other political interference and human rights violations; the military was reinstated by former President MOISE in 2017 after the UN ended its peacekeeping operation in Haiti; the reconstituted military established an Army command in 2018 and has received some training assistance from Argentina, Colombia, Ecuador, France, and Mexico; the military's stated mission is to assist with natural disaster relief, border security, and combating transnational crime; in 2023, Prime Minister HENRY called upon the military to assist the National Police (PNH) in combating armed gangs, which have overwhelmed the PNH, killed hundreds of Haitians, and seized control of swaths of territory, including much of the capital Port-au-Prince, since the assassination of President MOISE in 2021
in 2023, the UN Security Council approved the deployment of a Kenya-led multinational security support mission (MSS) to help bring gang violence under control; the first contingent of MSS personnel from the Kenya National Police Service arrived in mid-2024; other countries pledging forces included the Bahamas, Bangladesh, Barbados, Benin, Chad, and Jamaica; the mission is slated to have a total of 2,500 personnel (2025)

TERRORISM

Terrorist group(s): Terrorist group(s): Gran Grif; Viv Ansanm
note: details about the history, aims, leadership, organization, areas of operation, tactics, targets, weapons, size, and sources of support of the group(s) appear(s) in Appendix T

TRANSNATIONAL ISSUES

Refugees and internally displaced persons: *refugees:* 5 (2024 est.)
IDPs: 1,041,229 (2024 est.)

Trafficking in persons: *tier rating:* Special Category

Illicit drugs: USG identification: major illicit drug-producing and/or drug-transit country (2025)

HEARD ISLAND AND MCDONALD ISLANDS

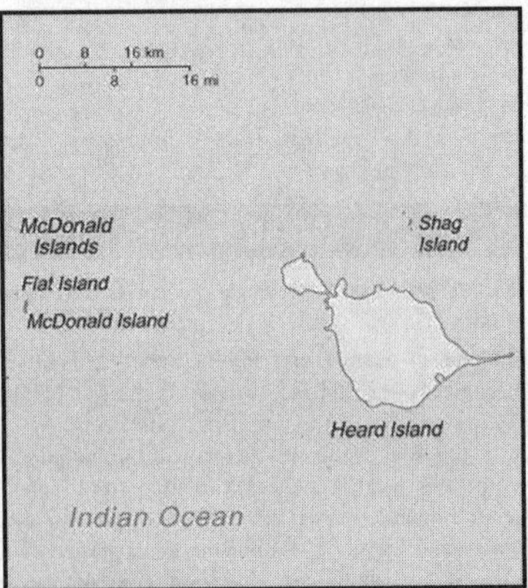

INTRODUCTION

Background: American sailor John HEARD discovered Heard Island in 1853 while fellow American William MCDONALD discovered the McDonald Islands the following year. Starting in 1855, sealers lived on the islands and harvested elephant seal oil; by the time the practice was ended in 1877, most of the islands' seals were killed. The UK formally claimed the islands in 1910, and Australian explorer Douglas MAWSON visited Heard Island in 1929. In 1947, the UK transferred the islands to Australia for its Antarctica research, but Australia closed the research station on Heard Island in 1954 when it opened a new research station on the Antarctic continent. McDonald Island has been an active volcano since it emerged from dormancy in 1992, and the island doubled in size after an eruption in 1996. In 1997, the islands were named a UNESCO World Heritage site. Populated by a large number of bird species, seals, and penguins, the islands are primarily used for research, with limited fishing permitted in the surrounding waters.

GEOGRAPHY

Location: islands in the Indian Ocean, about two-thirds of the way from Madagascar to Antarctica

Geographic coordinates: 53 06 S, 72 31 E

Map references: Antarctic Region

Area: *total:* 412 sq km
land: 412 sq km
water: 0 sq km
comparison ranking: total 202

Area - comparative: slightly more than two times the size of Washington, D.C.

Land boundaries: *total:* 0 km

Coastline: 101.9 km

Maritime claims: *territorial sea:* 12 nm
exclusive fishing zone: 200 nm

Climate: antarctic

Terrain: Heard Island - 80% ice-covered, bleak and mountainous, dominated by a large massif (Big Ben) and an active volcano (Mawson Peak); McDonald Islands - small and rocky

Elevation: *highest point:* Mawson Peak on Big Ben volcano 2,745 m
lowest point: Indian Ocean 0 m

Natural resources: fish

Land use: *agricultural land:* 0% (2011 est.)
other: 100% (2018 est.)

Natural hazards: Mawson Peak, an active volcano, is on Heard Island

Geography - note: Mawson Peak on Heard Island is the highest Australian mountain; at 2,745 m (9,006 ft), Mawson is taller than Mt. Kosciuszko in mainland Australia), and one of only two active volcanoes located in Australian territory; in 1992, McDonald Island, the other active volcano, broke its dormancy and began erupting; it has erupted several times since

PEOPLE AND SOCIETY

Population: *total:* uninhabited
note: limited scientific research and expeditions

ENVIRONMENT

Climate: antarctic

GOVERNMENT

Country name: *conventional long form:* Territory of Heard Island and McDonald Islands
conventional short form: Heard Island and McDonald Islands
abbreviation: HIMI
etymology: named after US Captain John HEARD, who sighted the island on 25 November 1853, and US Captain William McDONALD, who discovered the islands on 4 January 1854

Dependency status: territory of Australia; administered from Canberra by the Department of Agriculture, Water, and the Environment (Australian Antarctic Division)

Legal system: the laws of Australia apply

Diplomatic representation in the US: none (territory of Australia)

Diplomatic representation from the US: *embassy:* none (territory of Australia)

Flag: the flag of Australia is used

National heritage: *total World Heritage Sites:* 1 (natural); note - excerpted from the Australia entry
selected World Heritage Site locales: Heard Island and McDonald Islands

COMMUNICATIONS

Internet country code: .hm

TRANSPORTATION

Heliports: 2 (2025)
comparison ranking: 137

MILITARY AND SECURITY

Military - note: defense is the responsibility of Australia

HOLY SEE (VATICAN CITY)

INTRODUCTION

Background: Popes in their secular role ruled portions of the Italian peninsula for more than a thousand years until the mid-19th century, when the newly established Kingdom of Italy seized many of the Papal States. In 1870, the pope's holdings were further circumscribed when Rome itself was annexed. Disputes between Italy and a series of "prisoner" popes were resolved in 1929 by three Lateran Treaties, which established the independent state of Vatican City and granted Roman Catholicism special status in Italy. In 1984, a concordat between the Holy See and Italy modified some of the earlier treaty provisions, including the primacy of Roman Catholicism as the Italian state religion.

Present concerns of the Holy See include religious freedom, threats against minority Christian communities in Africa and the Middle East, the plight of refugees and migrants, climate change and the environment, conflict and war, nuclear weapons, artificial

intelligence, sexual misconduct by clergy, humanitarian issues, interreligious dialogue and reconciliation, and the application of church doctrine in an era of rapid change and globalization. About 1.3 billion people worldwide profess Catholicism, the world's largest Christian faith.

GEOGRAPHY

Location: Southern Europe, an enclave of Rome (Italy)

Geographic coordinates: 41 54 N, 12 27 E

Map references: Europe

Area: *total:* 0 sq km
land: 0.44 sq km
water: 0 sq km
comparison ranking: total 250

Area - comparative: about 0.7 times the size of the National Mall in Washington, D.C.

Land boundaries: *total:* 3.4 km
border countries (1): Italy 3.4 km

Coastline: 0 km (landlocked)

Maritime claims: none (landlocked)

Climate: temperate; mild, rainy winters (September to May) with hot, dry summers (May to September)

Terrain: urban; low hill

Elevation: *highest point:* Vatican Gardens (Vatican Hill) 78 m
lowest point: Saint Peter's Square 19 m

Natural resources: none

Land use: *agricultural land:* 0% (2022 est.)
forest: 0% (2022 est.)
other: 100% (2022 est.)

Natural hazards: occasional earthquakes

Geography - note: landlocked; an enclave in Rome, Italy; world's smallest state

PEOPLE AND SOCIETY

Population: *total:* 1,000 (2024)
comparison ranking: total 235

Nationality: noun:none
adjective: none

Ethnic groups: Italian, Swiss, Argentinian, and other nationalities from around the world (2017)

Languages: Italian, Latin, French, various other languages
major-language sample(s):
L'Almanacco dei fatti del mondo, l'indispensabile fonte per le informazioni di base. (Italian)

Religions: Roman Catholic

Population growth rate: 0% (2014 est.)
comparison ranking: 194

Urbanization: *urban population:* 100% of total population (2023)
rate of urbanization: 0% annual rate of change (2020-25 est.)

Major urban areas - population: 1,000 VATICAN CITY (capital) (2018)

ENVIRONMENT

Environmental issues: some air pollution from the surrounding city of Rome

International environmental agreements: *party to:* Comprehensive Nuclear Test Ban, Ozone Layer Protection
signed, but not ratified: Air Pollution, Environmental Modification

Climate: temperate; mild, rainy winters (September to May) with hot, dry summers (May to September)

Urbanization: *urban population:* 100% of total population (2023)
rate of urbanization: 0% annual rate of change (2020-25 est.)

GOVERNMENT

Country name: *conventional long form:* The Holy See (Vatican City State)
conventional short form: Holy See (Vatican City)
local long form: La Santa Sede (Stato della Citta del Vaticano)
local short form: Santa Sede (Citta del Vaticano)
etymology: "holy" comes from the Greek word *hera*, meaning "sacred"; "see" comes from the Latin word *sedes*, meaning "seat," and refers to the episcopal chair; the name Vatican derives from the hill Mons Vaticanus on which the Vatican is located and which comes from the Latin *vates* (prophet), referring to the fortune tellers and soothsayers who frequented the area in Roman times

Government type: ecclesiastical elective monarchy; self-described as an "absolute monarchy"

Capital: *name:* Vatican City
geographic coordinates: 41 54 N, 12 27 E
time difference: UTC+1 (6 hours ahead of Washington, DC, during Standard Time)
daylight saving time: +1hr, begins last Sunday in March; ends last Sunday in October
etymology: the name derives from the hill called Mons Vaticanus, on which the Vatican is located and which comes from the Latin *vates* (prophet), referring to the fortune tellers and soothsayers who frequented the area in Roman times

Administrative divisions: none

Legal system: religious system based on canon (religious) law

Constitution: *history:* previous 1929, 2000; latest issued by Pope FRANCIS 13 May 2023, effective 7 June 2023 (Fundamental Law of Vatican City State, the main governing document of the Vatican's civil entities); the Roman Curia is the administrative apparatus – the departments and ministries – used by the pontiff in governing the church
amendment process: although the Fundamental Law of Vatican City State makes no mention of amendments, Article Four (drafting laws), states that this legislative responsibility resides with the Pontifical Commission for Vatican City State; draft legislation is submitted through the Secretariat of State and considered by the pope

International law organization participation: has not submitted an ICJ jurisdiction declaration; non-party state to the ICCt

Citizenship: *citizenship by birth:* no
citizenship by descent only: no
dual citizenship recognized: no
residency requirement for naturalization: not applicable
note: in the Holy See, citizenship is acquired by law, ex iure, or by adminstrative decision; in the first instance, citizenship is a function of holding office within the Holy See as in the case of cardinals resident in Vatican City or diplomats of the Holy See; in the second instance, citizenship may be requested in a limited set of circumstances for those who reside within Vatican City under papal authorization, as a function of their office or service, or as the spouses and children of current citizens; citizenship is lost once an individual no longer permanently resides in Vatican City, normally reverting to the citizenship previously held

Suffrage: election of the pope is limited to cardinals under 80 years old

Executive branch: *chief of state:* Pope LEO XIV (since 8 May 2025)
head of government: President of the Pontifical Commission for the State of Vatican City and President of the Governorate of the Vatican City State Fernando VERGEZ ALZAGA (since 1 October 2021)
cabinet: Pontifical Commission for the State of Vatican City appointed by the pope
election/appointment process: pope elected by the College of Cardinals, usually for life or until voluntary resignation; Secretary of State appointed by the pope
election results: *2025:* Robert PREVOST elected Pope LEO XIV

Legislative branch: *legislature name:* Pontifical Commission for the State of Vatican City (Pontificia Commissione per lo Stato della Citta del Vaticano)
legislative structure: unicameral
number of seats: 7
term in office: 5 years
most recent election date: 22 September 2018
percentage of women in chamber: 0%

Judicial branch: *highest court(s):* Supreme Court or Supreme Tribunal of the Apostolic Signatura (consists of the cardinal prefect, who serves as ex-officio president of the court, and 2 other cardinals of the Prefect Signatura)
judge selection and term of office: cardinal prefect appointed by the pope; the other 2 cardinals of the court appointed by the cardinal prefect on a yearly basis
subordinate courts: Appellate Court of Vatican City; Tribunal of Vatican City
note: the Motu Proprio (papal directive) of Pope PIUS XII established judicial duties on 1 May 1946; most Vatican City criminal matters are handled by the Republic of Italy courts

Political parties: none

Diplomatic representation in the US: *chief of mission:* Apostolic Nuncio Cardinal Christophe PIERRE (since 27 June 2016)
chancery: 3339 Massachusetts Avenue NW, Washington, DC 20008
telephone: [1] (202) 333-7121

FAX: [1] (202) 337-4036
email address and website: nuntiususa@nuntiususa.org http://www.nuntiususa.org/

Diplomatic representation from the US: *chief of mission:* Ambassador Brian Francis BURCH II (since 13 September 2025)
embassy: Via Sallustiana, 49, 00187 Rome
mailing address: 5660 Holy See Place, Washington DC 20521-5660
telephone: [39] (06) 4674-1

FAX: [39] (06) 4674-3411
email address and website: https://va.usembassy.gov/

International organization participation: CE (observer), IAEA, Interpol, IOM, ITSO, ITU, ITUC (NGOs), OAS (observer), OPCW, OSCE, Schengen Convention (de facto member), UN (observer), UNCTAD, UNHCR, UNWTO (observer), UPU, WIPO, WTO (observer)

Independence: 11 February 1929
note: the three treaties signed with Italy on 11 February 1929 acknowledged the full sovereignty of the Holy See and established its territorial extent, but the origin of the Papal States, which over centuries varied considerably in extent, can be traced back to A.D. 754

Flag: *description:* two vertical bands of yellow (left side) and white, with the arms of the Holy See centered in the white band; the arms show the crossed keys of Saint Peter under the three-tiered papal tiara
meaning: yellow stands for the pope's spiritual power, and white for his worldly power

National symbol(s): crossed keys under a papal tiara

National color(s): yellow, white

National anthem(s): *title:* "Hymnus Pontificius" (Pontifical Anthem)
lyrics/music: Raffaello LAVAGNA/Charles-Francois GOUNOD
history: adopted 1949

National heritage: *total World Heritage Sites:* 2 (both cultural)
selected World Heritage Site locales: Historic Center of Rome, the Properties of the Holy See in that City Enjoying Extraterritorial Rights and San Paolo Fuori le Mura; Vatican City

ECONOMY

Economic overview: limited, tourism-based economy; euro user with own minted coins; produces commemorative stamps, coins, and publications to support museums and religious needs; residents pay no direct taxes; "zero deficit" plan to address budget shortfall

Industries: printing; production of coins, medals, postage stamps; mosaics, staff uniforms; worldwide banking and financial activities

Exchange rates: euros (EUR) per US dollar -

Exchange rates: 0.924 (2024 est.)
0.925 (2023 est.)
0.95 (2022 est.)
0.845 (2021 est.)
0.876 (2020 est.)
note: while not an EU member state, the Holy See has a 2000 monetary agreement with Italy and the EU to produce limited euro coinage—but not banknotes—that began enforcement in January 2002

ENERGY

Electricity access: *electrification - total population:* 100% (2021)

COMMUNICATIONS

Broadcast media: the Vatican Television Center (CTV) transmits live broadcasts of the Pope's weekly audiences, as well as his public celebrations; CTV also produces documentaries; Vatican Radio is the official broadcasting service via shortwave, AM, and FM frequencies, as well as satellite and web; Vatican News website partners with Vatican Radio and provides Catholic news from the Vatican (2021)

Internet country code: .va

Internet users: *percent of population:* 87% (2023 est.)

TRANSPORTATION

Heliports: 1 (2025)
comparison ranking: 155

MILITARY AND SECURITY

Military and security forces: the Pontifical Swiss Guard Corps (Corpo della Guardia Svizzera Pontificia) serves as the de facto military force of Vatican City; the Gendarmerie Corps of Vatican City (Corpo della Gendarmeriais) is a police force that helps augment the Pontifical Swiss Guard Corps during the Pope's appearances, as well as providing general security, traffic direction, and investigative duties for the Vatican City State (2025)
note: the Swiss Guard Corps has protected the Pope and his residence since 1506

Military service age and obligation: Pontifical Swiss Guard Corps: 19-30 years of age for voluntary military service; no conscription; must be a single Roman Catholic male with Swiss citizenship who has completed basic training with the Swiss military and can obtain a certificate of good conduct; qualified candidates must apply to serve; the service contract is between 2 and 25 years (2024)

Military - note: defense is the responsibility of Italy

HONDURAS

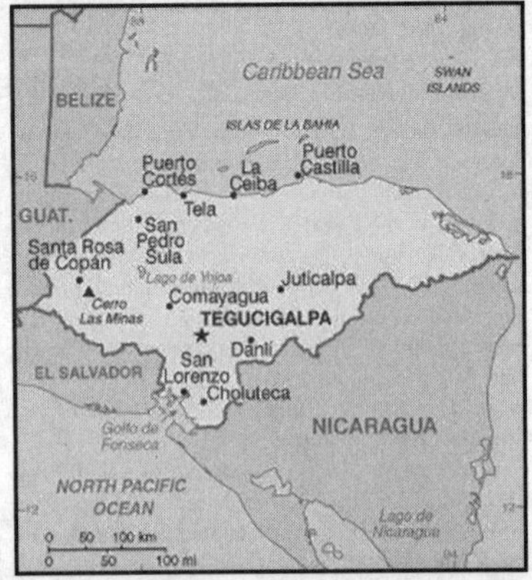

INTRODUCTION

Background: Once part of Spain's vast empire in the New World, Honduras became an independent nation in 1821. After two and a half decades of mostly military rule, a freely elected civilian government came to power in 1982. During the 1980s, Honduras proved a haven for anti-Sandinista contras fighting the Marxist Nicaraguan Government and an ally to Salvadoran Government forces fighting leftist guerrillas. Hurricane Mitch devastated the country in 1998, killing about 5,600 people and causing approximately $2 billion in damage. Since then, the economy has slowly rebounded, despite COVID-19 and severe storm-related setbacks in 2020 and 2021.

GEOGRAPHY

Location: Central America, bordering the Caribbean Sea, between Guatemala and Nicaragua and bordering the Gulf of Fonseca (North Pacific Ocean), between El Salvador and Nicaragua

Geographic coordinates: 15 00 N, 86 30 W

Map references: Central America and the Caribbean

Area: *total:* 112,090 sq km
land: 111,890 sq km
water: 200 sq km
comparison ranking: total 103

Area - comparative: slightly larger than Tennessee

Land boundaries: *total:* 1,575 km
border countries (3): Guatemala 244 km; El Salvador 391 km; Nicaragua 940 km

Coastline: 823 km (Caribbean Sea 669 km; Gulf of Fonseca 163 km)

Maritime claims: *territorial sea:* 12 nm
contiguous zone: 24 nm
exclusive economic zone: 200 nm
continental shelf: natural extension of territory or to 200 nm

Climate: subtropical in lowlands, temperate in mountains

Terrain: mostly mountains in interior, narrow coastal plains

Elevation: *highest point:* Cerro Las Minas 2,870 m
lowest point: Caribbean Sea 0 m
mean elevation: 684 m

Natural resources: timber, gold, silver, copper, lead, zinc, iron ore, antimony, coal, fish, hydropower

Land use: *agricultural land:* 32% (2022 est.)
arable land: 9.1% (2022 est.)
permanent crops: 5.4% (2022 est.)
permanent pasture: 17.5% (2022 est.)
forest: 56.5% (2022 est.)
other: 11.6% (2022 est.)

Irrigated land: 900 sq km (2012)

Major lakes (area sq km): *salt water lake(s):* Laguna de Caratasca - 1,110 sq km

Population distribution: most residents live in the mountainous western half of the country; Honduras is the only Central American nation with an urban population that is distributed between two large centers, the capital of Tegucigalpa and the city of San Pedro Sula; the Rio Ulua valley in the north is the only densely populated lowland area

Natural hazards: frequent, but generally mild, earthquakes; extremely susceptible to damaging hurricanes and floods along the Caribbean coast

Geography - note: has only a short Pacific coast but a long Caribbean shoreline, including the virtually uninhabited eastern Mosquito Coast

PEOPLE AND SOCIETY

Population: *total:* 9,529,188 (2024 est.)
male: 4,591,247
female: 4,937,941
comparison rankings: total 96; male 97; female 96

Nationality: *noun:* Honduran(s)
adjective: Honduran

Ethnic groups: Mestizo (mixed Indigenous and European) 90%, Indigenous 7%, African descent 2%, White 1%

Languages: Spanish (official), Amerindian dialects
major-language sample(s):
La Libreta Informativa del Mundo, la fuente indispensable de información básica. (Spanish)

Religions: Evangelical 55%, Roman Catholic 33.4%, none 10.1%, unspecified 1.5% (2023 est.)

Age structure: *0-14 years:* 28.7% (male 1,378,026/female 1,353,238)
15-64 years: 65.7% (male 2,980,393/female 3,282,159)
65 years and over: 5.6% (2024 est.) (male 232,828/female 302,544)

Dependency ratios: *total dependency ratio:* 52.2 (2024 est.)
youth dependency ratio: 43.6 (2024 est.)
elderly dependency ratio: 8.5 (2024 est.)
potential support ratio: 11.7 (2024 est.)

Median age: *total:* 25.7 years (2024 est.)
male: 24.8 years
female: 26.6 years
comparison ranking: total 168

Population growth rate: 1.29% (2024 est.)
comparison ranking: 74

Birth rate: 19.9 births/1,000 population (2024 est.)
comparison ranking: 68

Death rate: 5.4 deaths/1,000 population (2024 est.)
comparison ranking: 185

Net migration rate: -1.7 migrant(s)/1,000 population (2024 est.)
comparison ranking: 165

Population distribution: most residents live in the mountainous western half of the country; Honduras is the only Central American nation with an urban population that is distributed between two large centers, the capital of Tegucigalpa and the city of San Pedro Sula; the Rio Ulua valley in the north is the only densely populated lowland area

Urbanization: *urban population:* 60.2% of total population (2023)
rate of urbanization: 2.48% annual rate of change (2020-25 est.)

Major urban areas - population: 1.568 million TEGUCIGALPA (capital), 982,000 San Pedro Sula (2023)

Sex ratio: *at birth:* 1.03 male(s)/female
0-14 years: 1.02 male(s)/female
15-64 years: 0.91 male(s)/female
65 years and over: 0.77 male(s)/female
total population: 0.93 male(s)/female (2024 est.)

Mother's mean age at first birth: 20.3 years (2011/12 est.)
note: data represents median age a first birth among women 25-49

Maternal mortality ratio: 47 deaths/100,000 live births (2023 est.)
comparison ranking: 98

Infant mortality rate: *total:* 15.4 deaths/1,000 live births (2024 est.)
male: 17.5 deaths/1,000 live births
female: 13.2 deaths/1,000 live births
comparison ranking: total 90

Life expectancy at birth: *total population:* 73.1 years (2024 est.)
male: 69.6 years
female: 76.8 years
comparison ranking: total population 152

Total fertility rate: 2.33 children born/woman (2024 est.)
comparison ranking: 76

Gross reproduction rate: 1.15 (2024 est.)

Drinking water source: *improved: urban:* 99.2% of population (2022 est.)
rural: 90.8% of population (2022 est.)
total: 95.8% of population (2022 est.)
unimproved: urban: 0.8% of population (2022 est.)
rural: 9.2% of population (2022 est.)
total: 4.2% of population (2022 est.)

Health expenditure: 9.2% of GDP (2021)
14.2% of national budget (2022 est.)

Physician density: 0.49 physicians/1,000 population (2020)

Hospital bed density: 0.7 beds/1,000 population (2021 est.)

Sanitation facility access: *improved: urban:* 96.6% of population (2022 est.)
rural: 88.1% of population (2022 est.)
total: 93.2% of population (2022 est.)
unimproved: urban: 3.4% of population (2022 est.)
rural: 11.9% of population (2022 est.)
total: 6.8% of population (2022 est.)

Obesity - adult prevalence rate: 21.4% (2016)
comparison ranking: 89

Alcohol consumption per capita: *total:* 2.73 liters of pure alcohol (2019 est.)
beer: 1.6 liters of pure alcohol (2019 est.)
wine: 0.04 liters of pure alcohol (2019 est.)
spirits: 1.09 liters of pure alcohol (2019 est.)
other alcohols: 0 liters of pure alcohol (2019 est.)
comparison ranking: total 119

Tobacco use: *total:* 11.9% (2025 est.)
male: 22.2% (2025 est.)
female: 1.6% (2025 est.)
comparison ranking: total 113

Children under the age of 5 years underweight: 7.1% (2019)
comparison ranking: 60

Currently married women (ages 15-49): 53.5% (2023 est.)

Child marriage: *women married by age 15:* 9.2% (2019)
women married by age 18: 34% (2019)
men married by age 18: 10% (2019)

Education expenditure: 4% of GDP (2023 est.)
13.3% national budget (2024 est.)
comparison ranking: Education expenditure (% GDP) 110

Literacy: *total population:* 89% (2019 est.)
male: 88% (2019 est.)
female: 89% (2019 est.)

School life expectancy (primary to tertiary education): *total:* 10 years (2019 est.)
male: 9 years (2019 est.)
female: 10 years (2019 est.)

ENVIRONMENT

Environmental issues: deforestation from logging and agricultural clearing; land degradation and soil erosion from overdevelopment and improper land use practices; mining activities polluting Lago de Yojoa (the country's largest source of fresh water) and other rivers and streams

International environmental agreements: *party to:* Biodiversity, Climate Change, Climate Change-Kyoto Protocol, Climate Change-Paris Agreement, Comprehensive Nuclear Test Ban, Desertification, Endangered Species, Environmental Modification, Hazardous Wastes, Law of the Sea, Marine Dumping-London Convention, Nuclear Test Ban, Ozone Layer Protection, Ship Pollution, Tropical Timber 2006, Wetlands
signed, but not ratified: none of the selected agreements

Climate: subtropical in lowlands, temperate in mountains

Urbanization: *urban population:* 60.2% of total population (2023)
rate of urbanization: 2.48% annual rate of change (2020-25 est.)

Carbon dioxide emissions: 10.534 million metric tonnes of CO2 (2023 est.)
from coal and metallurgical coke: 324,000 metric tonnes of CO2 (2023 est.)
from petroleum and other liquids: 10.21 million metric tonnes of CO2 (2023 est.)
comparison ranking: total emissions 107

Particulate matter emissions: 19.1 micrograms per cubic meter (2019 est.)

Waste and recycling: *municipal solid waste generated annually:* 2.162 million tons (2024 est.)
percent of municipal solid waste recycled: 10.3% (2022 est.)

Total water withdrawal: *municipal:* 315 million cubic meters (2022 est.)
industrial: 114 million cubic meters (2022 est.)
agricultural: 1.178 billion cubic meters (2022 est.)

Total renewable water resources: 92.164 billion cubic meters (2022 est.)

GOVERNMENT

Country name: *conventional long form:* Republic of Honduras
conventional short form: Honduras
local long form: República de Honduras
local short form: Honduras

etymology: the name means "depths" in Spanish and refers to the deep anchorage in the northern Bay of Trujillo

Government type: presidential republic

Capital: *name:* Tegucigalpa
geographic coordinates: 14 06 N, 87 13 W
time difference: UTC-6 (1 hour behind Washington, DC during Standard Time)
etymology: the name is a Nahuatl word meaning "silver mountain," probably referring to nearby silver mines
note: the Honduran constitution states that Tegucigalpa and Comayaguela jointly constitute the capital of Honduras, but virtually all governmental institutions are on the Tegucigalpa side

Administrative divisions: 18 departments (*departamentos,* singular - *departamento);* Atlántida, Choluteca, Colon, Comayagua, Copan, Cortes, El Paraiso, Francisco Morazán, Gracias a Dios, Intibucá, Islas de la Bahia, La Paz, Lempira, Ocotepeque, Olancho, Santa Barbara, Valle, Yoro

Legal system: civil law system

Constitution: *history:* several previous; latest approved 11 January 1982, effective 20 January 1982
amendment process: proposed by the National Congress with at least two-thirds majority vote of the membership; passage requires at least two-thirds majority vote of Congress in its next annual session; constitutional articles, such as the form of government, national sovereignty, the presidential term, and the procedure for amending the constitution, cannot be amended

International law organization participation: accepts compulsory ICJ jurisdiction with reservations; accepts ICCt jurisdiction

Citizenship: *citizenship by birth:* yes
citizenship by descent only: yes
dual citizenship recognized: yes
residency requirement for naturalization: 1 to 3 years

Suffrage: 18 years of age; universal and compulsory

Executive branch: *chief of state:* President Iris Xiomara CASTRO de Zelaya (since 27 January 2022)
head of government: President Iris Xiomara CASTRO de Zelaya (since 27 January 2022)
cabinet: Cabinet appointed by president
election/appointment process: president directly elected by simple-majority popular vote for a 4-year term
most recent election date: 28 November 2021
election results: *2021:* Iris Xiomara CASTRO de Zelaya elected president; percent of vote - Iris Xiomara CASTRO de Zelaya (LIBRE) 51.1%, Nasry Juan ASFURA Zablah (PNH) 36.9%, Yani Benjamin ROSENTHAL Hidalgo (PL) 10%, other 2%
2017: Juan Orlando HERNANDEZ Alvarado reelected president; percent of vote - Juan Orlando HERNANDEZ Alvarado (PNH) 43%, Salvador NASRALLA (Alianza de Oposicion contra la Dictadura) 41.4%, Luis Orlando ZELAYA Medrano (PL) 14.7%, other 0.9%
expected date of next election: 30 November 2025
note: the president is both chief of state and head of government

Legislative branch: *legislature name:* National Congress (Congreso Nacional)
legislative structure: unicameral
number of seats: 128 (all directly elected)
electoral system: proportional representation
scope of elections: full renewal
term in office: 4 years
most recent election date: 11/28/2021
parties elected and seats per party: Liberty and Refoundation Party (LIBRE) (50); National Party (PN) (44); Liberal Party (PL) (22); Salvador de Honduras Party (PSH) (10); Other (2)
percentage of women in chamber: 27.3%
expected date of next election: November 2025

Judicial branch: *highest court(s):* Supreme Court of Justice or Corte Suprema de Justicia (15 principal judges, including the court president, and 6 alternates; court organized into civil, criminal, constitutional, and labor chambers)
judge selection and term of office: court president elected by his peers; judges elected by the National Congress from candidates proposed by the Nominating Board, a diverse 7-member group of judicial officials and other government and non-government officials nominated by each of their organizations; judges elected by Congress for renewable, 7-year terms
subordinate courts: courts of appeal; courts of first instance; justices of the peace
note: the Supreme Court has both judicial and constitutional jurisdiction

Political parties: Anti-Corruption Party or PAC
Christian Democratic Party or DC
Democratic Liberation of Honduras or Liderh
Democratic Unification Party or UD
The Front or El Frente
Honduran Patriotic Alliance or AP
Innovation and Unity Party or PINU
Liberal Party or PL
Liberty and Refoundation Party or LIBRE
National Party of Honduras or PNH
New Route or NR
Opposition Alliance against the Dictatorship or Alianza de Oposicion contra la Dictadura (electoral coalition)
Savior Party of Honduras or PSH
Vamos or Let's Go
We Are All Honduras (Todos Somos Honduras) or TSH

Diplomatic representation in the US: *chief of mission:* Ambassador (vacant); Chargé d'Affaires Leonardo VALENZUELA NEDA (since 10 June 2025)
chancery: 1220 19th Street NW, Suite #320, Washington, DC 20036
telephone: [1] (202) 966-7702
FAX: [1] (202) 966-9751
email address and website: info@wadchn.com
https://hondurasembusa.org/
consulate(s) general: Atlanta, Boston, Charlotte (NC), Chicago, Dallas, Houston, Los Angeles, McAllen (TX), Miami, New Orleans, New York, San Francisco, Seattle

Diplomatic representation from the US: *chief of mission:* Ambassador (vacant); Chargé d'Affaires Colleen Anne HOEY (since 23 June 2025)
embassy: Avenida La Paz, Tegucigalpa M.D.C.
mailing address: 3480 Tegucigalpa Place, Washington DC 20521-3480
telephone: [504] 2236-9320,
FAX: [504] 2236-9037
email address and website: usahonduras@state.gov
https://hn.usembassy.gov/

International organization participation: ACS, BCIE, CACM, CD, CELAC, EITI (candidate country), FAO, G-11, G-77, IADB, IAEA, IBRD, ICAO, ICCt, ICRM, IDA, IFAD, IFC, IFRCS, ILO, IMF, IMO, Interpol, IOC (suspended), IOM, IPU, ISO (subscriber), ITSO, ITU, ITUC (NGOs), LAES, LAIA (observer), MIGA, MINURSO, MINUSTAH, NAM, OAS, OPANAL, OPCW, Pacific Alliance (observer), PCA, Petrocaribe, SICA, UN, UNCTAD, UNHRC, UNESCO, UNIDO, Union Latina, UNWTO, UPU, WCO (suspended), WFTU (NGOs), WHO, WIPO, WMO, WTO

Independence: 15 September 1821 (from Spain)

National holiday: Independence Day, 15 September (1821)

Flag: *description:* three equal horizontal bands of cerulean blue (top), white, and cerulean blue, with five five-pointed cerulean stars arranged in an "X" pattern and centered in the white band
meaning: the stars represent the members of the former Federal Republic of Central America: Costa Rica, El Salvador, Guatemala, Honduras, and Nicaragua; blue stands for the Pacific Ocean and the Caribbean Sea, and white for the land and the people's peace and prosperity
note: similar to the flag of El Salvador, which has a round emblem surrounded by the words REPUBLICA DE EL SALVADOR EN LA AMERICA CENTRAL; also similar to the flag of Nicaragua, which has a triangle with the words REPUBLICA DE NICARAGUA above and AMERICA CENTRAL below

National symbol(s): scarlet macaw, white-tailed deer

National color(s): blue, white

National anthem(s): *title:* "Himno Nacional de Honduras" (National Anthem of Honduras)
lyrics/music: Augusto Constancio COELLO/Carlos HARTLING
history: adopted 1915; the anthem's seven verses chronicle Honduran history; on official occasions, only the chorus and last verse are sung

National heritage: *total World Heritage Sites:* 2 (1 cultural, 1 natural)
selected World Heritage Site locales: Maya Site of Copan (c); Río Plátano Biosphere Reserve (n)

ECONOMY

Economic overview: second-fastest-growing Central American economy; COVID-19 and two hurricanes crippled activity; high poverty and inequality; declining-but-still-high violent crime disruption; systemic corruption; coffee and banana exporter; enormous remittances

Real GDP (purchasing power parity): $71.297 billion (2024 est.)
$68.85 billion (2023 est.)
$66.473 billion (2022 est.)
note: data in 2021 dollars
comparison ranking: 110

Real GDP growth rate: 3.6% (2024 est.)
3.6% (2023 est.)
4.1% (2022 est.)
note: annual GDP % growth based on constant local currency
comparison ranking: 95

Real GDP per capita: $6,600 (2024 est.)
$6,500 (2023 est.)
$6,400 (2022 est.)
note: data in 2021 dollars
comparison ranking: 163

GDP (official exchange rate): $37.094 billion (2024 est.)
note: data in current dollars at official exchange rate

Inflation rate (consumer prices): 4.6% (2024 est.)
6.7% (2023 est.)

9.1% (2022 est.)
note: annual % change based on consumer prices
comparison ranking: 138

GDP - composition, by sector of origin: *agriculture:* 11.2% (2024 est.)
industry: 26.1% (2024 est.)
services: 58.4% (2024 est.)
note: figures may not total 100% due to non-allocated consumption not captured in sector-reported data
comparison rankings: agriculture 67; industry 77; services 99

GDP - composition, by end use: *household consumption:* 86% (2024 est.)
government consumption: 15.5% (2024 est.)
investment in fixed capital: 23.9% (2024 est.)
investment in inventories: -1.4% (2024 est.)
exports of goods and services: 33.5% (2024 est.)
imports of goods and services: -57.6% (2024 est.)
note: figures may not total 100% due to rounding or gaps in data collection

Agricultural products: sugarcane, oil palm fruit, maize, milk, bananas, coffee, cantaloupes/melons, oranges, chicken, beans (2023)
note: top ten agricultural products based on tonnage

Industries: sugar processing, coffee, woven and knit apparel, wood products, cigars

Industrial production growth rate: 0.8% (2024 est.)
note: annual % change in industrial value added based on constant local currency
comparison ranking: 117

Labor force: 4.296 million (2024 est.)
note: number of people ages 15 or older who are employed or seeking work
comparison ranking: 94

Unemployment rate: 6.1% (2024 est.)
6.1% (2023 est.)
8.8% (2022 est.)
note: % of labor force seeking employment
comparison ranking: 115

Youth unemployment rate (ages 15-24): *total:* 10.5% (2024 est.)
male: 7.9% (2024 est.)
female: 15.9% (2024 est.)
note: % of labor force ages 15-24 seeking employment
comparison ranking: total 116

Population below poverty line: 64.1% (2023 est.)
note: % of population with income below national poverty line
Gini Index coefficient - distribution of family income 46.8 (2023 est.)
note: index (0-100) of income distribution; higher values represent greater inequality
comparison ranking: 13

Average household expenditures: *on food:* 31.5% of household expenditures (2023 est.)
on alcohol and tobacco: 4.9% of household expenditures (2023 est.)

Household income or consumption by percentage share: *lowest 10%:* 1.1% (2023 est.)
highest 10%: 33% (2023 est.)
note: % share of income accruing to lowest and highest 10% of population

Remittances: 25.7% of GDP (2024 est.)
26.1% of GDP (2023 est.)
27% of GDP (2022 est.)
note: personal transfers and compensation between resident and non-resident individuals/households/entities

Budget: *revenues:* $5.333 billion (2020 est.)
expenditures: $6.391 billion (2020 est.)
note: central government revenues (excluding grants) and expenditures converted to US dollars at average official exchange rate for year indicated

Taxes and other revenues: 15.1% (of GDP) (2020 est.)
note: central government tax revenue as a % of GDP
comparison ranking: 90

Current account balance: -$1.711 billion (2024 est.)
-$1.368 billion (2023 est.)
-$2.157 billion (2022 est.)
note: balance of payments - net trade and primary/secondary income in current dollars
comparison ranking: 144

Exports: $9.352 billion (2024 est.)
$9.805 billion (2023 est.)
$9.51 billion (2022 est.)
note: balance of payments - exports of goods and services in current dollars
comparison ranking: 120

Exports - partners: USA 49%, Nicaragua 8%, El Salvador 7%, Guatemala 5%, Mexico 5% (2023)
note: top five export partners based on percentage share of exports

Exports - commodities: garments, coffee, insulated wire, palm oil, shellfish (2023)
note: top five export commodities based on value in dollars

Imports: $18.235 billion (2024 est.)
$17.926 billion (2023 est.)
$18.101 billion (2022 est.)
note: balance of payments - imports of goods and services in current dollars
comparison ranking: 103

Imports - partners: USA 36%, China 14%, Guatemala 8%, Mexico 6%, El Salvador 6% (2023)
note: top five import partners based on percentage share of imports

Imports - commodities: refined petroleum, cotton yarn, garments, trucks, packaged medicine (2023)
note: top five import commodities based on value in dollars

Reserves of foreign exchange and gold: $8.036 billion (2024 est.)
$7.543 billion (2023 est.)
$8.41 billion (2022 est.)
note: holdings of gold (year-end prices)/foreign exchange/special drawing rights in current dollars
comparison ranking: 85

Debt - external: $7.785 billion (2023 est.)
note: present value of external debt in current US dollars
comparison ranking: 58

Exchange rates: lempiras (HNL) per US dollar -

Exchange rates: 24.799 (2024 est.)
24.602 (2023 est.)
24.486 (2022 est.)
24.017 (2021 est.)
24.582 (2020 est.)

ENERGY

Electricity access: *electrification - total population:* 94.4% (2022 est.)
electrification - urban areas: 100%
electrification - rural areas: 86.8%

Electricity: *installed generating capacity:* 3.334 million kW (2023 est.)
consumption: 8.303 billion kWh (2023 est.)
exports: 4 million kWh (2023 est.)
imports: 214.601 million kWh (2023 est.)
transmission/distribution losses: 3.617 billion kWh (2023 est.)
comparison rankings: installed generating capacity 106; consumption 114; exports 100; imports 106; transmission/distribution losses 150

Electricity generation sources: *fossil fuels:* 38.4% of total installed capacity (2023 est.)
solar: 8.9% of total installed capacity (2023 est.)
wind: 5.9% of total installed capacity (2023 est.)
hydroelectricity: 33.2% of total installed capacity (2023 est.)
geothermal: 3% of total installed capacity (2023 est.)
biomass and waste: 10.7% of total installed capacity (2023 est.)

Coal: *consumption:* 144,000 metric tons (2023 est.)
imports: 148,000 metric tons (2023 est.)

Petroleum: *total petroleum production:* 20 bbl/day (2023 est.)
refined petroleum consumption: 71,000 bbl/day (2023 est.)

Energy consumption per capita: 16.642 million Btu/person (2023 est.)
comparison ranking: 136

COMMUNICATIONS

Telephones - fixed lines: *total subscriptions:* 444,000 (2023 est.)
subscriptions per 100 inhabitants: 4 (2023 est.)
comparison ranking: total subscriptions 97

Telephones - mobile cellular: *total subscriptions:* 7.92 million (2023 est.)
subscriptions per 100 inhabitants: 76 (2022 est.)
comparison ranking: total subscriptions 103

Broadcast media: multiple privately owned terrestrial TV networks, supplemented by multiple cable TV networks; Radio Honduras is the state-owned radio network; roughly 300 privately owned radio stations (2019)

Internet country code: .hn

Internet users: *percent of population:* 58% (2023 est.)

Broadband - fixed subscriptions: *total:* 476,000 (2023 est.)
subscriptions per 100 inhabitants: 4 (2023 est.)
comparison ranking: total 100

TRANSPORTATION

Civil aircraft registration country code prefix: HR

Airports: 129 (2025)
comparison ranking: 40

Heliports: 6 (2025)
comparison ranking: 95

Railways: *total:* 699 km (2014)
narrow gauge: 164 km (2014) 1.067-m gauge
115 km 1.057-mm gauge
420 km 0.914-mm gauge

Merchant marine: *total:* 489 (2023)
by type: general cargo 233, oil tanker 82, other 174
comparison ranking: total 43

Ports: *total ports:* 8 (2024)
large: 0
medium: 0
small: 1
very small: 7
ports with oil terminals: 3

key ports: Coxen Hole, La Ceiba, Puerto Castilla, Puerto Cortes, Puerto de Hencan, Puerto Este, Tela, Trujillo

MILITARY AND SECURITY

Military and security forces: Honduran Armed Forces (Fuerzas Armadas de Honduras, FFAA): Army (Ejercito), Honduran Naval Force (Fuerza Naval Hondurena, FNH; includes marines), Honduran Air Force (Fuerza Aerea Hondurena, FAH), Honduran Military Police of Public Order (Policía Militar del Orden Público or PMOP) (2025)
note 1: the National Police of Honduras (Policía Nacional de Honduras, PNH) are under the Secretariat of Security and responsible for internal security; some larger cities have police forces that operate independently of the national police and report to municipal authorities
note 2: the PMOP supports the PNH against narcotics trafficking and organized crime; it is subordinate to the Secretariat of Defense/FFAA, but conducts operations sanctioned by civilian security officials as well as by military leaders
note 3: the National Interinstitutional Security Force is an interagency command that coordinates the overlapping responsibilities of the HNP, PMOP, and other security organizations such as the National Intelligence Directorate and the Public Ministry (public prosecutor), but exercises coordination, command, and control responsibilities only during interagency operations involving those forces

Military expenditures: 1.5% of GDP (2024 est.)
1.5% of GDP (2023 est.)
1.4% of GDP (2022 est.)
1.5% of GDP (2021 est.)
1.6% of GDP (2020 est.)

Military and security service personnel strengths: approximately 15,000 active Honduran Armed Forces (2025)

Military equipment inventories and acquisitions: the FFAA's inventory is comprised of a mix of older or secondhand and limited amounts of more equipment from a wide mix of suppliers, including Colombia, Germany, Israel, the Netherlands, South Korea, the UK, and the US (2024)

Military service age and obligation: 18-22 years of age for voluntary military service for men and women; 24-36 month service obligation; no conscription (2024)
note: as of 2023, women made up about 9% of the active duty military

Military - note: the Honduran Armed Forces (FFAA) are responsible for maintaining the country's territory, defending its sovereignty, providing emergency/humanitarian assistance, and supporting the National Police (PNH); the FFAA's primary focus is internal and border security, and since 2011 a considerable portion of it has been deployed to support the PNH in combating narcotics trafficking and organized crime; military support to domestic security included the creation of the Military Police of Public Order (PMOP) in 2013 to provide security in areas controlled by street gangs to combat crime and make arrests; the FFAA, including the PMOP, cooperates with the militaries of El Salvador, Guatemala, and Nicaragua on border security
the FFAA has received military equipment, training, humanitarian, and technical assistance from the US military; the US military maintains a joint service task force co-located with the FFAA at Soto Cano Air Base (2025)

TRANSNATIONAL ISSUES

Refugees and internally displaced persons: *refugees:* 341 (2024 est.)

IDPs: 100,637 (2024 est.)

Illicit drugs: USG identification: major illicit drug-producing and/or drug-transit country
major precursor-chemical producer (2025)

HONG KONG

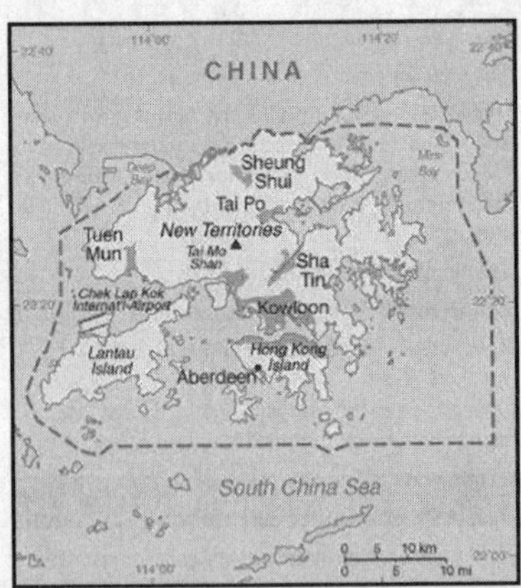

INTRODUCTION

Background: The UK seized Hong Kong in 1841, and China formally ceded it the following year at the end of the First Opium War. The Kowloon Peninsula was added in 1860 at the end of the Second Opium War, and the UK obtained a 99-year lease of the New Territories in 1898. Pursuant to a UK-China agreement in 1984, Hong Kong became the Hong Kong Special Administrative Region (HKSAR) of the People's Republic of China as of 1 July 1997. In this agreement, China promised that, under its "one country, two systems" formula, China's socialist economic and strict political system would not be imposed on Hong Kong and that Hong Kong would enjoy a "high degree of autonomy" in all matters except foreign and defense affairs for the next 50 years.

After the handover, Hong Kong continued to enjoy success as an international financial center. However, growing Chinese political influence and dissatisfaction with the Hong Kong Government in the 2010s became central issues and led to considerable civil unrest, including large-scale pro-democracy demonstrations in 2019 after the HKSAR attempted to revise a local ordinance to allow extraditions to mainland China. In response to the protests, the governments of the HKSAR and China reduced the city's autonomy and placed new restrictions on the rights of Hong Kong residents, moves that were widely criticized as contravening obligations under the Hong Kong Basic Law and the Sino-British Joint Declaration. Democratic lawmakers and political figures were arrested in a widespread crackdown, while others fled abroad. At the same time, dozens of civil society groups and several independent media outlets were closed or disbanded. In 2021, Beijing imposed a more restrictive electoral system, restructuring the Legislative Council (LegCo) and allowing only government-approved candidates to run for office. The changes ensured that virtually all seats in the 2021 LegCo election went to pro-establishment candidates and effectively ended political opposition to Beijing. In 2024, the LegCo passed a new national security law (Article 23 of the Basic Law) further expanding the Hong Kong Government's power to curb dissent.

GEOGRAPHY

Location: Eastern Asia, bordering the South China Sea and China

Geographic coordinates: 22 15 N, 114 10 E

Map references: Southeast Asia

Area: *total:* 1,108 sq km
land: 1,073 sq km
water: 35 sq km
comparison ranking: total 183

Area - comparative: six times the size of Washington, D.C.

Land boundaries: *total:* 33 km
regional borders (1): China 33 km

Coastline: 733 km

Maritime claims: *territorial sea:* 12 nm

Climate: subtropical monsoon; cool and humid in winter, hot and rainy from spring through summer, warm and sunny in fall

Terrain: hilly to mountainous with steep slopes; lowlands in north

Elevation: *highest point:* Tai Mo Shan 958 m
lowest point: South China Sea 0 m

Natural resources: outstanding deepwater harbor, feldspar

Land use: *agricultural land:* 3.8% (2022 est.)
arable land: 1.9% (2022 est.)
permanent crops: 1% (2022 est.)
permanent pasture: 1% (2022 est.)
forest: 0% (2022 est.)
other: 96.2% (2022 est.)

Irrigated land: 10 sq km (2012)

Population distribution: population fairly evenly distributed

Natural hazards: occasional typhoons

Geography - note: consists of a mainland area (the New Territories) and over 200 islands

PEOPLE AND SOCIETY

Population: *total:* 7,297,821 (2024 est.)
male: 3,367,812
female: 3,930,009

comparison rankings: total 106; male 106; female 103
Nationality: *noun:* Chinese/Hong Konger
adjective: Chinese/Hong Kong
Ethnic groups: Chinese 91.6%, Filipino 2.7%, Indonesian 1.9%, other 3.7% (2021 est.)
Languages: Cantonese (official) 85.4%, English (official) 4.5%, Putonghua (official) 2.2%, other Chinese dialects 2.8%, other 2%, persons under 5 or mute 3.2% (2021 est.)
major-language sample(s):

世界概况, 必須擁有的基本資料参考书 (Cantonese)
note: data represent population by usual spoken language
Religions: Buddhist or Taoist 27.9%, Protestant 6.7%, Roman Catholic 5.3%, Muslim 4.2%, Hindu 1.4%, Sikh 0.2%, other or none 54.3% (2016 est.)
note: many people practice Confucianism, regardless of their religion or not having a religious affiliation
Age structure: *0-14 years:* 13.2% (male 505,718/female 459,956)
15-64 years: 64.8% (male 2,123,216/female 2,609,102)
65 years and over: 21.9% (2024 est.) (male 738,878/female 860,951)
Dependency ratios: *total dependency ratio:* 54.2 (2024 est.)
youth dependency ratio: 20.4 (2024 est.)
elderly dependency ratio: 33.8 (2024 est.)
potential support ratio: 3 (2024 est.)
Median age: *total:* 47.2 years (2024 est.)
male: 45.3 years
female: 48.6 years
comparison ranking: total 7
Population growth rate: 0.12% (2024 est.)
comparison ranking: 183
Birth rate: 7.6 births/1,000 population (2024 est.)
comparison ranking: 218
Death rate: 8.1 deaths/1,000 population (2024 est.)
comparison ranking: 89
Net migration rate: 1.6 migrant(s)/1,000 population (2024 est.)
comparison ranking: 54
Population distribution: population fairly evenly distributed
Urbanization: *urban population:* 100% of total population (2023)
rate of urbanization: 0.58% annual rate of change (2020-25 est.)
Major urban areas - population: 7.685 million Hong Kong (2023)
Sex ratio: *at birth:* 1.06 male(s)/female
0-14 years: 1.1 male(s)/female
15-64 years: 0.81 male(s)/female
65 years and over: 0.86 male(s)/female
total population: 0.86 male(s)/female (2024 est.)
Mother's mean age at first birth: 29.8 years (2008 est.)
Infant mortality rate: *total:* 2.5 deaths/1,000 live births (2024 est.)
male: 2.8 deaths/1,000 live births
female: 2.2 deaths/1,000 live births
comparison ranking: total 215
Life expectancy at birth: *total population:* 84 years (2024 est.)
male: 81.3 years
female: 86.8 years
comparison ranking: total population 7
Total fertility rate: 1.24 children born/woman (2024 est.)
comparison ranking: 223
Gross reproduction rate: 0.6 (2024 est.)
Drinking water source: *improved: urban:* 100% of population (2022 est.)
rural: NA
total: 100% of population (2022 est.)
unimproved: urban: 0% of population (2022 est.)
rural: NA
total: 0% of population (2022 est.)
Physician density: 2.04 physicians/1,000 population (2020)
Hospital bed density: 4.9 beds/1,000 population (2020 est.)
Sanitation facility access: *improved: urban:* 96.5% of population (2022 est.)
total: 96.5% of population (2022 est.)
unimproved: urban: 3.5% of population (2022 est.)
total: 3.5% of population (2022 est.)
Currently married women (ages 15-49): 47.7% (2023 est.)
Education expenditure: 3.8% of GDP (2023 est.)
12.7% national budget (2022 est.)
comparison ranking: Education expenditure (% GDP) 120
School life expectancy (primary to tertiary education): *total:* 17 years (2023 est.)
male: 17 years (2023 est.)
female: 17 years (2023 est.)

ENVIRONMENT

Environmental issues: air and water pollution from rapid urbanization; urban waste pollution; industrial pollution
Climate: subtropical monsoon; cool and humid in winter, hot and rainy from spring through summer, warm and sunny in fall
Urbanization: *urban population:* 100% of total population (2023)
rate of urbanization: 0.58% annual rate of change (2020-25 est.)
Carbon dioxide emissions: 58.433 million metric tonnes of CO2 (2023 est.)
from coal and metallurgical coke: 12.935 million metric tonnes of CO2 (2023 est.)
from petroleum and other liquids: 35.453 million metric tonnes of CO2 (2023 est.)
from consumed natural gas: 10.045 million metric tonnes of CO2 (2023 est.)
comparison ranking: total emissions 54
Waste and recycling: *municipal solid waste generated annually:* 5.68 million tons (2024 est.)
percent of municipal solid waste recycled: 34% (2016 est.)

GOVERNMENT

Country name: *conventional long form:* Hong Kong Special Administrative Region
conventional short form: Hong Kong
local long form: Heung Kong Takpit Hangching Ku (Eitel/Dyer-Ball)
local short form: Heung Kong (Eitel/Dyer-Ball)
abbreviation: HK
etymology: probably an imprecise phonetic rendering of the Cantonese name meaning "fragrant harbor"
Government type: presidential limited democracy; a special administrative region of the People's Republic of China
Dependency status: special administrative region of the People's Republic of China
Administrative divisions: none (special administrative region of the People's Republic of China)
Legal system: mixed system of common law based on the English model and Chinese customary law (in matters of family and land tenure); China's imposition of National Security Law incorporates elements of Chinese civil law
Constitution: *history:* several previous (governance documents while under British authority); latest drafted April 1988 to February 1989, approved March 1990, effective 1 July 1997 (Basic Law of the Hong Kong Special Administrative Region of the People's Republic of China serves as the constitution)
amendment process: proposed by the Standing Committee of the National People's Congress (NPC), the People's Republic of China State Council, or the Special Administrative Region of Hong Kong; submittal of proposals to the NPC requires two-thirds majority vote by the Legislative Council of Hong Kong, approval by two thirds of Hong Kong's deputies to the NPC, and approval by the Hong Kong chief executive; final passage requires approval by the NPC
note: since 1990, China's National People's Congress has interpreted specific articles of the Basic Law
Citizenship: see China
Suffrage: 18 years of age in direct elections for 20 of the 90 Legislative Council seats and all of the seats in 18 district councils; universal for permanent residents living in the territory of Hong Kong for the past 7 years
note: in indirect elections, suffrage is limited to about 220,000 members of functional constituencies for the other 70 legislature seats and a 1,500-member election committee for the chief executive drawn from broad sectoral groupings, central government bodies, municipal organizations, and elected Hong Kong officials
Executive branch: *chief of state:* President of China XI Jinping (since 14 March 2013)
head of government: Chief Executive John LEE Ka-chiu (since 1 July 2022)
cabinet: Executive Council or ExCo appointed by the chief executive
election/appointment process: president indirectly elected by National People's Congress for a 5-year term (eligible for a second term); chief executive indirectly elected by the Election Committee and appointed by the PRC Government for a 5-year term (eligible for a second term)
most recent election date: ***president:*** 10 March 2023
chief executive: 8 May 2022
election results: *2022:* John LEE was the only candidate and won with over 99% of the vote by the Election Committee
2017: Carrie LAM elected; Election Committee vote - Carrie LAM (non-partisan) 777, John TSANG (non-partisan) 365, WOO Kwok-hing (non-partisan) 21, 23 ballots rejected (1,186 votes cast)
expected date of next election: ***president:*** March 2028
chief executive: 2027
note: electoral changes that Beijing imposed in March 2021 expanded the Election Committee to 1,500 members
Legislative branch: *legislature name:* Legislative Council or LegCo
legislative structure: unicameral

number of seats: 90
electoral system: 20 members directly elected; 70 members indirectly elected
scope of elections: full
most recent election date: 19 December 2021
parties elected and seats per party: Democratic Alliance for the Betterment and Progress of Hong Kong (DAB) 19, Federation of Hong Kong and Kowloon Labour Unions (HKFTU) 8, Business and Professionals Alliance for Hong Kong (BPA) 7, NPP 5, Liberal (LP) 4, New Territories Association of Societies (NTAS) 4, Hong Kong Federation of Education Workers (HKFEW) 2, Federation of Hong Kong and Kowloon Labour Unions (HKFLU) 2, Civil Force (CF) 2, Roundtable (RT) 1, Professional Power (PP) 1, Kowloon West New Dynamic (KWND) 1, New Prospect for Hong Kong (NPHK) 1, New Century Forum (NCF-1); other/independent 41
expected date of next election: December 2025
note 1: all political candidates are evaluated by the Candidate Eligibility Review Committee (CERC), which was established in April 2022; CERC members are all appointed by the chief executive
note 2: Hong Kong's leading pro-democracy political parties boycotted the 2021 election

Judicial branch: *highest court(s):* Court of Final Appeal (consists of the chief justice, 3 permanent judges, and 20 non-permanent judges)
judge selection and term of office: all judges appointed by the Hong Kong Chief Executive on the recommendation of the Judicial Officers Recommendation Commission, an independent body consisting of the Secretary for Justice, other judges, and judicial and legal professionals; permanent judges serve until normal retirement at age 65, but term can be extended; non-permanent judges appointed for renewable 3-year terms without age limit
subordinate courts: High Court (consists of the Court of Appeal and Court of First Instance); District Courts (includes Family and Land Courts); magistrates' courts; specialized tribunals

Political parties: Business and Professionals Alliance for Hong Kong or BPA
Civil Force or CF
Democratic Alliance for the Betterment and Progress of Hong Kong or DAB
Federation of Hong Kong and Kowloon Labour Unions or HKFLU
Hong Kong Federation of Education Workers or HKFEW
Hong Kong Federation of Trade Unions or HKFTU
Kowloon West New Dynamic or KWND
Liberal Party or LP
New Century Forum or NCF
New People's Party or NPP
New Prospect for Hong Kong or NPHK
New Territories Association of Societies or NTAS
Professional Power or PP
Roundtable or RT
Third Side or TS
note 1: there is no political party ordinance, so there are no registered political parties; politically active groups register as societies or companies
note 2: by the end of 2021, the leading pro-democracy figures in Hong Kong had been effectively removed from the political arena under the provisions of Beijing's 2021 electoral changes or via charges under the 2020 national security law; in addition, dozens of pro-democracy organizations, including political parties, unions, churches, civil rights groups, and media organizations have disbanded or closed; as of 2023, nearly all politically active groups were pro-Beijing

Diplomatic representation in the US: *chief of mission:* none (Special Administrative Region of China)

HKETO offices: New York, San Francisco, Washington DC
note: Hong Kong is a Special Administrative Region of China and does not have a diplomatic presence; the Hong Kong Economic and Trade Office (HKETO) carries out normal liaison activities and communication with the US government and other US entities; the position of the Hong Kong Commissioner to the US Government of the Hong Kong Special Administrative Region is vacant; address: *1520 18th Street NW, Washington, DC 20036; telephone:* [1] (202) 331-8947; FAX: [1] (202) 331-8958; email: *hketo@hketowashington.gov.hk; website:* https://www.hketowashington.gov.hk/

Diplomatic representation from the US: *chief of mission:* Consul General Julie EADEH (since August 2025); note - also accredited to Macau
embassy: 26 Garden Road, Central, Hong Kong
mailing address: 8000 Hong Kong Place, Washington DC 20521-8000
telephone: [852] 2523-9011
FAX: [852] 2845-1598
email address and website: acshk@state.gov
https://hk.usconsulate.gov/

International organization participation: ADB, APEC, BIS, FATF, ICC (national committees), IHO, IMF, IMO (associate), Interpol (subbureau), IOC, ISO (correspondent), ITUC (NGOs), UNWTO (associate), UPU, WCO, WMO, WTO

Independence: none (special administrative region of China)

National holiday: National Day (Anniversary of the Founding of the People's Republic of China), 1 October (1949)
note: 1 July (1997) is celebrated as Hong Kong Special Administrative Region Establishment Day

Flag: *description:* red with a stylized white Bauhinia flower with five petals in the center of the flag; each petal has a tiny five-pointed red star with a fine red line curving toward the center of the flower
meaning: the red color is the same as the Chinese flag and represents the motherland, and the five stars also echo the Chinese flag; the Bauhinia flower was developed in Hong Kong the late 19th century and has come to symbolize the region

National symbol(s): bauhinia flower

National color(s): red, white

National anthem(s): *title:* "Yiyongjun Jinxingqu" (The March of the Volunteers)
lyrics/music: TIAN Han/NIE Er
history: official anthem, as a Special Administrative Region of China

ECONOMY

Economic overview: high-income tourism- and services-based economy; global financial hub; COVID-19 and political protests fueled recent recession; ongoing recovery but lower-skilled unemployment remains high; investing in job-reskilling programs

Real GDP (purchasing power parity): $497.88 billion (2024 est.)
$485.541 billion (2023 est.)
$470.42 billion (2022 est.)
note: data in 2021 dollars
comparison ranking: 50

Real GDP growth rate: 2.5% (2024 est.)
3.2% (2023 est.)
-3.7% (2022 est.)
note: annual GDP % growth based on constant local currency
comparison ranking: 139

Real GDP per capita: $66,200 (2024 est.)
$64,400 (2023 est.)
$64,000 (2022 est.)
note: data in 2021 dollars
comparison ranking: 22

GDP (official exchange rate): $407.107 billion (2024 est.)
note: data in current dollars at official exchange rate

Inflation rate (consumer prices): 1.7% (2024 est.)
2.1% (2023 est.)
1.9% (2022 est.)
note: annual % change based on consumer prices
comparison ranking: 43

GDP - composition, by sector of origin: *agriculture:* 0% (2023 est.)
industry: 6.3% (2023 est.)
services: 91.4% (2023 est.)
note: figures may not total 100% due to non-allocated consumption not captured in sector-reported data
comparison rankings: agriculture 201; industry 201; services 3

GDP - composition, by end use: *household consumption:* 67.4% (2024 est.)
government consumption: 12.8% (2024 est.)
investment in fixed capital: 16.2% (2024 est.)
investment in inventories: -0.5% (2024 est.)
exports of goods and services: 181.7% (2024 est.)
imports of goods and services: -177.7% (2024 est.)
note: figures may not total 100% due to rounding or gaps in data collection

Agricultural products: pork, chicken, spinach, vegetables, pork offal, game meat, beef, fruits, onions, pork fat (2023)
note: top ten agricultural products based on tonnage

Industries: trading and logistics, financial services, professional services, tourism, cultural and creative, clothing and textiles, shipping, electronics, toys, clocks and watches

Industrial production growth rate: 3.4% (2024 est.)
note: annual % change in industrial value added based on constant local currency
comparison ranking: 73

Labor force: 3.836 million (2024 est.)
note: number of people ages 15 or older who are employed or seeking work
comparison ranking: 96

Unemployment rate: 2.8% (2024 est.)
3% (2023 est.)
4.4% (2022 est.)
note: % of labor force seeking employment
comparison ranking: 33

Youth unemployment rate (ages 15-24): *total:* 8.4% (2024 est.)
male: 10.5% (2024 est.)
female: 6.3% (2024 est.)
note: % of labor force ages 15-24 seeking employment
comparison ranking: total 136

Average household expenditures: *on food:* 11.5% of household expenditures (2023 est.)
on alcohol and tobacco: 0.7% of household expenditures (2023 est.)

Remittances: 0.1% of GDP (2024 est.)
0.1% of GDP (2023 est.)
0.1% of GDP (2022 est.)

note: personal transfers and compensation between resident and non-resident individuals/households/entities

Budget: *revenues:* $70.124 billion (2020 est.)
expenditures: $105.849 billion (2020 est.)

Current account balance: $52.475 billion (2024 est.)
$32.338 billion (2023 est.)
$36.525 billion (2022 est.)
note: balance of payments - net trade and primary/secondary income in current dollars
comparison ranking: 11

Exports: $739.915 billion (2024 est.)
$673.738 billion (2023 est.)
$697.583 billion (2022 est.)
note: balance of payments - exports of goods and services in current dollars
comparison ranking: 13

Exports - partners: China 22%, Vietnam 12%, S. Korea 8%, Netherlands 5%, Switzerland 4% (2023)
note: top five export partners based on percentage share of exports

Exports - commodities: gold, integrated circuits, gas turbines, broadcasting equipment, jewelry (2023)
note: top five export commodities based on value in dollars

Imports: $723.397 billion (2024 est.)
$671.492 billion (2023 est.)
$682.881 billion (2022 est.)
note: balance of payments - imports of goods and services in current dollars
comparison ranking: 12

Imports - partners: China 40%, Taiwan 10%, Singapore 7%, Japan 5%, S. Korea 4% (2023)
note: top five import partners based on percentage share of imports

Imports - commodities: integrated circuits, broadcasting equipment, gold, machine parts, jewelry (2023)
note: top five import commodities based on value in dollars

Reserves of foreign exchange and gold: $425.554 billion (2023 est.)
$424.03 billion (2022 est.)
$496.867 billion (2021 est.)
note: holdings of gold (year-end prices)/foreign exchange/special drawing rights in current dollars
comparison ranking: 8

Exchange rates: Hong Kong dollars (HKD) per US dollar -

Exchange rates: 7.804 (2024 est.)
7.83 (2023 est.)
7.831 (2022 est.)
7.773 (2021 est.)
7.757 (2020 est.)

ENERGY

Electricity access: *electrification - total population:* 100% (2022 est.)

Electricity: *installed generating capacity:* 13.3 million kW (2023 est.)
consumption: 45.54 billion kWh (2023 est.)
imports: 11.593 billion kWh (2023 est.)
transmission/distribution losses: 3.684 billion kWh (2023 est.)
comparison rankings: installed generating capacity 57; consumption 56; imports 19; transmission/distribution losses 152

Electricity generation sources: *fossil fuels:* 99.1% of total installed capacity (2023 est.)
solar: 0.5% of total installed capacity (2023 est.)
biomass and waste: 0.4% of total installed capacity (2023 est.)

Coal: *consumption:* 5.567 million metric tons (2023 est.)
exports: 16,000 metric tons (2023 est.)
imports: 5.884 million metric tons (2023 est.)

Petroleum: *total petroleum production:* 96 bbl/day (2023 est.)
refined petroleum consumption: 233,000 bbl/day (2023 est.)

Natural gas: *consumption:* 5.12 billion cubic meters (2023 est.)
imports: 5.12 billion cubic meters (2023 est.)

Energy consumption per capita: 116.811 million Btu/person (2023 est.)
comparison ranking: 36

COMMUNICATIONS

Telephones - fixed lines: *total subscriptions:* 3.487 million (2023 est.)
subscriptions per 100 inhabitants: 47 (2023 est.)
comparison ranking: total subscriptions 35

Telephones - mobile cellular: *total subscriptions:* 23.8 million (2023 est.)
subscriptions per 100 inhabitants: 292 (2022 est.)
comparison ranking: total subscriptions 57

Broadcast media: 34 commercial terrestrial TV networks, each with multiple stations; multi-channel satellite and cable TV systems available; 3 licensed broadcasters, one of which is government-funded, operate about 12 radio stations (2019)

Internet country code: .hk

Internet users: *percent of population:* 96% (2023 est.)

Broadband - fixed subscriptions: *total:* 2.97 million (2023 est.)
subscriptions per 100 inhabitants: 40 (2023 est.)
comparison ranking: total 49

TRANSPORTATION

Civil aircraft registration country code prefix: B-H

Airports: 2 (2025)
comparison ranking: 209

Heliports: 142 (2025)
comparison ranking: 19

Merchant marine: *total:* 2,537 (2023)
by type: bulk carrier 1,047, container ship 560, general cargo 144, oil tanker 394, other 392
comparison ranking: total 10

Ports: *total ports:* 1 (2024)
large: 1
medium: 0
small: 0
very small: 0
ports with oil terminals: 1
key ports: Hong Kong

MILITARY AND SECURITY

Military and security forces: Hong Kong Police Force (specialized units include the Police Counterterrorism Response Unit, the Explosive Ordnance Disposal Bureau, the Special Duties Unit, the Airport Security Unit, and the VIP Protection Unit)
China's People's Liberation Army (PLA) Hong Kong Garrison is responsible for defense duties; the garrison includes elements of the PLA Army, PLA Navy, and PLA Air Force and are under the direct leadership of the Central Military Commission in Beijing and under administrative control of the adjacent Southern Theater Command (2025)

TRANSNATIONAL ISSUES

Refugees and internally displaced persons: *refugees:* 260 (2024 est.)

Trafficking in persons: *tier rating:* Tier 2 Watch List — the government did not demonstrate overall increasing efforts to eliminate trafficking compared with the previous reporting period, therefore Hong Kong remained on Tier 2 Watch List for the second consecutive year; for more details, go to: https:// www.state.gov/reports/2025-trafficking-in-persons-report/hong-kong/

Illicit drugs: USG identification: major precursor-chemical producer (2025)

HUNGARY

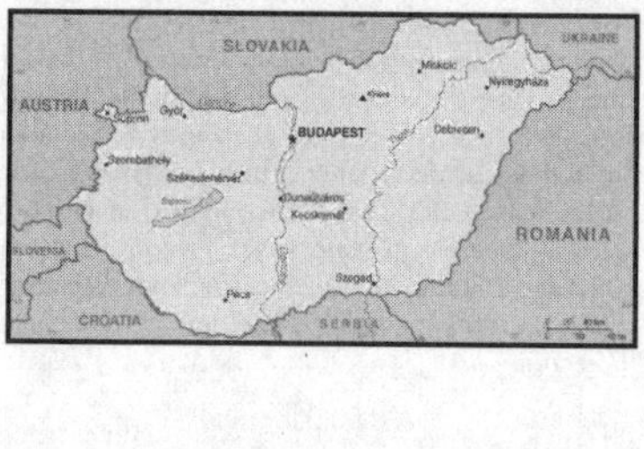

INTRODUCTION

Background: Hungary became a Christian kingdom in A.D. 1000 and for many centuries served as a bulwark against Ottoman Turkish expansion in Europe. The kingdom eventually became part of the Austro-Hungarian Empire, which collapsed during World War I. The country fell under communist rule after World War II. In 1956, Moscow responded to a Hungarian revolt and announcement of its withdrawal from the Warsaw Pact with a massive military intervention. Under the leadership of Janos KADAR in 1968, Hungary began liberalizing its economy, introducing so-called "Goulash Communism." Hungary held its first multiparty elections in 1990 and initiated a free market economy. It joined NATO in 1999 and the EU five years later.

GEOGRAPHY

Location: Central Europe, northwest of Romania
Geographic coordinates: 47 00 N, 20 00 E

Map references: Europe

Area: *total:* 93,028 sq km
land: 89,608 sq km
water: 3,420 sq km
comparison ranking: total 110

Area - comparative: slightly smaller than Virginia; about the same size as Indiana

Land boundaries: *total:* 2,106 km
border countries (7): Austria 321 km; Croatia 348 km; Romania 424 km; Serbia 164 km; Slovakia 627 km; Slovenia 94 km; Ukraine 128 km

Coastline: 0 km (landlocked)

Maritime claims: none (landlocked)

Climate: temperate; cold, cloudy, humid winters; warm summers

Terrain: mostly flat to rolling plains; hills and low mountains on the Slovakian border
Elevation: *highest point:* Kekes 1,014 m
lowest point: Tisza River 78 m
mean elevation: 143 m

Natural resources: bauxite, coal, natural gas, fertile soils, arable land

Land use: *agricultural land:* 55.6% (2022 est.)
arable land: 45.6% (2022 est.)
permanent crops: 1.6% (2022 est.)
permanent pasture: 8.5% (2022 est.)
forest: 22.5% (2022 est.)
other: 21.9% (2022 est.)
Irrigated land: 1,331 sq km (2022)

Major lakes (area sq km): *fresh water lake(s):* Lake Balaton - 590 sq km

Major rivers (by length in km): Duna (Danube) (shared with Germany [s], Austria, Slovakia, Croatia, Serbia, Bulgaria, Ukraine, Moldova, and Romania [m]) - 2,888 km
note: [s] after country name indicates river source; [m] after country name indicates river mouth

Major watersheds (area sq km): Atlantic Ocean drainage: *(Black Sea)* Danube (795,656 sq km)

Population distribution: a fairly even distribution throughout most of the country, with urban areas attracting larger and denser populations

Geography - note: landlocked; strategic location on main land routes between Western Europe and Balkan Peninsula, as well as between Ukraine and the Mediterranean basin; the Duna (Danube) and Tisza Rivers divide the country into three large regions

PEOPLE AND SOCIETY

Population: *total:* 9,855,745 (2024 est.)
male: 4,812,668
female: 5,043,077
comparison rankings: total 95; male 95; female 94

Nationality: *noun:* Hungarian(s)
adjective: Hungarian

Ethnic groups: Hungarian 84.3%, Romani 2.1%, German 1%, other 1.2%, unspecified 13.7% (2022 est.)
note: percentages add up to more than 100% because respondents were able to identify more than one ethnic group; Romani populations are usually underestimated in official statistics and may represent 5–10% of Hungary's population

Languages: Hungarian (official) 98.8%, English 25.3%, German 12.6%, Russian 2.1%, French 1.5%, Romanian 1.4%, other 5.1% (2022 est.)
major-language sample(s):
A World Factbook nélkülözhetetlen forrása az alapvető információknak. (Hungarian)
note: percentages add up to more than 100% because respondents were able to identify more than one spoken language

Religions: Catholic 30.1% (Roman Catholic 27.5%, Greek Catholic 1.7%, other Catholic 0.9%), Calvinist 9.8%, Lutheran 1.8%, other Christian (includes Orthodox) 1.6%, other 0.4%, none 16.1%, no answer 40.1% (2022 est.)

Age structure: *0-14 years:* 14.6% (male 753,955/female 683,943)
15-64 years: 63.9% (male 3,195,761/female 3,104,750)
65 years and over: 21.5% (2024 est.) (male 862,952/female 1,254,384)

Dependency ratios: *total dependency ratio:* 56.4 (2024 est.)
youth dependency ratio: 22.8 (2024 est.)
elderly dependency ratio: 33.6 (2024 est.)
potential support ratio: 3 (2024 est.)

Median age: *total:* 44.8 years (2024 est.)
male: 42.8 years
female: 46.7 years
comparison ranking: total 27

Population growth rate: -0.28% (2024 est.)
comparison ranking: 212

Birth rate: 9.1 births/1,000 population (2024 est.)
comparison ranking: 198

Death rate: 14.5 deaths/1,000 population (2024 est.)
comparison ranking: 6

Net migration rate: 2.5 migrant(s)/1,000 population (2024 est.)
comparison ranking: 44

Population distribution: a fairly even distribution throughout most of the country, with urban areas attracting larger and denser populations

Urbanization: *urban population:* 72.9% of total population (2023)
rate of urbanization: 0.05% annual rate of change (2020-25 est.)
Major urban areas - population: 1.778 million BUDAPEST (capital) (2023)

Sex ratio: *at birth:* 1.06 male(s)/female
0-14 years: 1.1 male(s)/female
15-64 years: 1.03 male(s)/female
65 years and over: 0.69 male(s)/female
total population: 0.95 male(s)/female (2024 est.)

Mother's mean age at first birth: 28.4 years (2020 est.)

Maternal mortality ratio: 12 deaths/100,000 live births (2023 est.)
comparison ranking: 146

Infant mortality rate: *total:* 4.7 deaths/1,000 live births (2024 est.)
male: 5 deaths/1,000 live births
female: 4.3 deaths/1,000 live births
comparison ranking: total 180

Life expectancy at birth: *total population:* 76 years (2024 est.)
male: 72.9 years
female: 79.3 years
comparison ranking: total population 119
Total fertility rate: 1.6 children born/woman (2024 est.)
comparison ranking: 186

Gross reproduction rate: 0.78 (2024 est.)

Drinking water source: *improved: urban:* 100% of population (2022 est.)
rural: 100% of population (2022 est.)
total: 100% of population (2022 est.)
unimproved: urban: 0% of population (2022 est.)
rural: 0% of population (2022 est.)
total: 0% of population (2022 est.)

Health expenditure: 7.4% of GDP (2021)
9.9% of national budget (2022 est.)

Physician density: 3.46 physicians/1,000 population (2022)

Hospital bed density: 6.8 beds/1,000 population (2021 est.)

Sanitation facility access: *improved: urban:* 100% of population (2022 est.)
rural: 100% of population (2022 est.)
total: 100% of population (2022 est.)
unimproved: urban: 0% of population (2022 est.)
rural: 0% of population (2022 est.)
total: 0% of population (2022 est.)

Obesity - adult prevalence rate: 26.4% (2016)
comparison ranking: 42

Alcohol consumption per capita: *total:* 10.79 liters of pure alcohol (2019 est.)
beer: 3.96 liters of pure alcohol (2019 est.)
wine: 3.33 liters of pure alcohol (2019 est.)
spirits: 3.5 liters of pure alcohol (2019 est.)
other alcohols: 0 liters of pure alcohol (2019 est.)
comparison ranking: total 16

Tobacco use: *total:* 28.5% (2025 est.)
male: 33.7% (2025 est.)
female: 23.8% (2025 est.)
comparison ranking: total 28

Currently married women (ages 15-49): 51.4% (2023 est.)

Education expenditure: 5.1% of GDP (2022 est.)
10.4% national budget (2022 est.)
comparison ranking: Education expenditure (% GDP) 60

School life expectancy (primary to tertiary education): *total:* 16 years (2023 est.)
male: 15 years (2023 est.)
female: 16 years (2023 est.)

ENVIRONMENT

Environmental issues: air and soil pollution; water pollution from industry and large-scale agriculture
International environmental agreements: *party to:* Air Pollution, Air Pollution-Heavy Metals, Air Pollution-Multi-effect Protocol, Air Pollution-Nitrogen Oxides, Air Pollution-Persistent Organic Pollutants, Air Pollution-Sulphur 85, Air Pollution-Sulphur 94, Air Pollution-Volatile Organic Compounds, Antarctic Treaty, Biodiversity, Climate Change, Climate Change-Kyoto Protocol, Climate Change-Paris Agreement, Comprehensive Nuclear Test Ban, Desertification, Endangered Species, Environmental Modification, Hazardous Wastes, Law of the Sea, Marine Dumping-London Convention, Nuclear Test Ban, Ozone Layer Protection, Ship Pollution, Tropical Timber 2006, Wetlands, Whaling
signed, but not ratified: Antarctic-Environmental Protection

Climate: temperate; cold, cloudy, humid winters; warm summers

Urbanization: *urban population:* 72.9% of total population (2023)
rate of urbanization: 0.05% annual rate of change (2020-25 est.)

Carbon dioxide emissions: 40.161 million metric tonnes of CO2 (2023 est.)
from coal and metallurgical coke: 3.373 million metric tonnes of CO2 (2023 est.)
from petroleum and other liquids: 20.887 million metric tonnes of CO2 (2023 est.)
from consumed natural gas: 15.901 million metric tonnes of CO2 (2023 est.)
comparison ranking: total emissions 62

Particulate matter emissions: 14.2 micrograms per cubic meter (2019 est.)

Waste and recycling: *municipal solid waste generated annually:* 3.781 million tons (2024 est.)
percent of municipal solid waste recycled: 31% (2022 est.)

Total water withdrawal: *municipal:* 660 million cubic meters (2022)
industrial: 3.758 billion cubic meters (2022)
agricultural: 548.613 million cubic meters (2022)

Total renewable water resources: 104 billion cubic meters (2022 est.)

Geoparks: *total global geoparks and regional networks:* 4 (2024)
global geoparks and regional networks: Bakony-Balaton; Bukk Region; Hungary; Novohrad-Nógrád (includes Slovakia) (2024)

GOVERNMENT

Country name: *conventional long form:* none
conventional short form: Hungary
local long form: none
local short form: Magyarorszag
former: Kingdom of Hungary, Hungarian People's Republic, Hungarian Soviet Republic, Hungarian Republic
etymology: the Byzantine Greeks referred to the tribes that arrived on the steppes of Eastern Europe in the 9th century as the "Oungroi," a name that later became "Hungari," which originally meant an "[alliance of] ten tribes;" the Hungarian name Magyarorszag means "Country of the Magyars," which may be derived from the name of the most prominent of the Hungarian tribes

Government type: parliamentary republic

Capital: *name:* Budapest
geographic coordinates: 47 30 N, 19 05 E
time difference: UTC+1 (6 hours ahead of Washington, DC, during Standard Time)
daylight saving time: +1hr, begins last Sunday in March; ends last Sunday in October
etymology: Buda on the western shore of the Danube and Pest on the eastern shore merged in 1873 to form Budapest; Buda's name may derive from the name of its founder or from a local word meaning "water;" Pest derives from a Slavic word meaning "furnace" or "oven"

Administrative divisions: 19 counties *(megyek*, singular - *megye)*, 25 cities with county rights *(megyei jogu varosok*, singular - *megyei jogu varos)*, and 1 capital city *(fovaros)*
counties: Bacs-Kiskun, Baranya, Bekes, Borsod-Abauj-Zemplen, Csongrad-Csanad, Fejer, Gyor-Moson-Sopron, Hajdu-Bihar, Heves, Jasz-Nagykun-Szolnok, Komarom-Esztergom, Nograd, Pest, Somogy, Szabolcs-Szatmar-Bereg, Tolna, Vas, Veszprem, Zala
cities with county rights: Baja, Bekescsaba, Debrecen, Dunaujvaros, Eger, Erd, Esztergom, Gyor, Hodmezovasarhely, Kaposvar, Kecskemet, Miskolc, Nagykanizsa, Nyiregyhaza, Pecs, Salgotarjan, Sopron, Szeged, Szekesfehervar, Szekszard, Szolnok, Szombathely, Tatabanya, Veszprem, Zalaegerszeg
capital city: Budapest

Legal system: civil system influenced by the German model

Constitution: *history:* previous 1949 (heavily amended in 1989 following the collapse of communism); latest approved 18 April 2011, signed 25 April 2011, effective 1 January 2012
amendment process: proposed by the president of the republic, by the government, by parliamentary committee, or by Parliament members; passage requires two-thirds majority vote of Parliament members and approval by the president

International law organization participation: accepts compulsory ICJ jurisdiction with reservations; accepts ICC jurisdiction

Citizenship: *citizenship by birth:* no
citizenship by descent only: at least one parent must be a citizen of Hungary
dual citizenship recognized: yes
residency requirement for naturalization: 8 years

Suffrage: 18 years of age, 16 if married and marriage is registered in Hungary; universal

Executive branch: *chief of state:* President Tamas SULYOK (since 5 March 2024)
head of government: Prime Minister Viktor ORBAN (since 29 May 2010)
cabinet: Cabinet of Ministers proposed by the prime minister and appointed by the president
election/appointment process: president indirectly elected by the National Assembly with two-thirds majority vote in first round or simple majority vote in second round for a 5-year term (eligible for a second term); prime minister elected by the National Assembly on the recommendation of the president
most recent election date: ***president:*** 26 February 2024
prime minister: 3 April 2022
election results: 2024: Tamas SULYOK elected president; National Assembly vote - 134 to 5
2022: Katalin NOVAK (Fidesz) elected president; National Assembly vote - 137 to 51
expected date of next election: ***president***:spring 2029
prime minister: April or May 2027

Legislative branch: *legislature name:* National Assembly (Országgyülés)
legislative structure: unicameral
chamber name: National Assembly (Orszaggyules)
number of seats: 199 (all directly elected)
electoral system: mixed system
scope of elections: full renewal
term in office: 4 years
most recent election date: 4/3/2022
parties elected and seats per party: Hungarian Civic Union-Christian Democratic People's Party (FIDESZ-KDNP) (135); Democratic Coalition (DK) (15); Movement for a Better Hungary (Jobbik) (10); Hungarian Socialist Party (MSZP) (10); Momentum (10); Other (19)
percentage of women in chamber: 15.2%
expected date of next election: April 2026

Judicial branch: *highest court(s):* Curia or Supreme Judicial Court (consists of the president, vice president, department heads, and has a maximum of 113 judges, and is organized into civil, criminal, and administrative-labor departments; Constitutional Court (consists of 15 judges, including the court president and vice president)
judge selection and term of office: Curia president elected by the National Assembly on the recommendation of the president of the republic; other Curia judges appointed by the president on the recommendation of the National Judicial Council, a separate 15-member administrative body; judge tenure based on interim evaluations until normal retirement at age 62; Constitutional Court judges, including the president of the court, elected by the National Assembly; court vice president elected by the court itself; members serve 12-year terms with mandatory retirement at age 62
subordinate courts: 5 regional courts of appeal; 19 regional or county courts (including Budapest Metropolitan Court); 20 administrative-labor courts; 111 district or local courts

Political parties: Christian Democratic People's Party or KDNP
Democratic Coalition or DK
Dialogue for Hungary or Párbeszéd
Fidesz-Hungarian Civic Alliance or Fidesz
Hungarian Socialist Party or MSZP
Jobbik - Conservatives or Jobbik
LMP-Hungary's Green Party or LMP
Mi Hazank (Our Homeland Movement) or MHM
Momentum Movement or Momentum
Movement for a Better Hungary or Jobbik
National Self-Government of Germans in Hungary or MNOÖ
On the People's Side or A Nép Pártján
Our Homeland Movement or Mi Hazánk
TISZA – Respect and Freedom Party or TISZA

Diplomatic representation in the US: *chief of mission:* Ambassador Szabolcs Ferenc TAKÁCS (since 23 December 2020)
chancery: 1500 Rhode Island Avenue, N.W. Washington, D.C. 20005
telephone: [1] (202) 362-6730
FAX: [1] (202) 966-8135
email address and website: info.was@mfa.gov.hu
https://washington.mfa.gov.hu/eng
consulate(s) general: Chicago, Los Angeles, New York
consulate(s): Houston, Miami

Diplomatic representation from the US: *chief of mission:* Ambassador (vacant); Chargé d'Affaires Robert PALLADINO (since 7 March 2025)
embassy: Szabadsag ter 12, H-1054 Budapest
mailing address: 5270 Budapest Place, US Department of State, Washington, DC 20521-5270
telephone: [36] (1) 475-4400
FAX: [36] (1) 475-4248
email address and website: acs.budapest@state.gov
https://hu.usembassy.gov/

International organization participation: Australia Group, BIS, CD, CE, CEI, CERN, EAPC, EBRD, ECB, EIB, ESA (cooperating state), EU, FAO, G-9, IAEA, IBRD, ICAO, ICC (national committees), ICCt, ICRM, IDA, IEA, IFAD, IFC, IFRCS, ILO, IMF, IMO, IMSO, Interpol, IOC, IOM, IPU, ISO, ITSO, ITU, ITUC (NGOs), MIGA, MINURSO, NATO, NEA, NSG, OAS (observer), OECD, OIF (observer), OPCW, OSCE, PCA, Schengen Convention, SELEC, UN, UNCTAD, UNESCO, UNFICYP, UNHCR, UNIDO, UNIFIL, UNOOSA, UNWTO, UPU, Wassenaar Arrangement, WCO, WFTU (NGOs), WHO, WIPO, WMO, WTO, ZC

Independence: *16 November 1918 (republic proclaimed); notable earlier dates:* 25 December 1000 (crowning of King STEPHEN I, traditional founding date); 30 March 1867 (Austro-Hungarian dual monarchy established)

National holiday: Saint Stephen's Day, 20 August (1083)
note: commemorates the saint's canonization and the transfer of his remains to Buda (now Budapest) in 1083

Flag: *description:* three equal horizontal bands of red (top), white, and green
meaning: folklore attributes virtues to the colors: red for strength, white for faithfulness, and green for hope; alternatively, the red can stand for the blood spilled in defense of the land, white for freedom, and green for pasturelands
history: the flag dates to the national movement of the 18th and 19th centuries and fuses the medieval colors of the Hungarian coat of arms with the revolutionary tricolor of the French flag

National symbol(s): Holy Crown of Hungary (Crown of Saint Stephen)

National color(s): red, white, green

National anthem(s): *title:* "Himnusz" (Hymn)
lyrics/music: Ferenc KOLCSEY/Ferenc ERKEL
history: adopted 1844

National heritage: *total World Heritage Sites:* 8 (7 cultural, 1 natural)
selected World Heritage Site locales: Budapest, including the Banks of the Danube, the Buda Castle Quarter, and Andrássy Avenue (c); Old Village of Hollókő and its Surroundings (c); Caves of Aggtelek Karst and Slovak Karst (n); Millenary Benedictine Abbey of Pannonhalma and its Natural Environment (c); Hortobágy National Park - the Puszta (c); Early Christian Necropolis of Pécs (Sopianae) (c); Fertö / Neusiedlersee Cultural Landscape (c); Tokaj Wine Region Historic Cultural Landscape (c)

ECONOMY

Economic overview: high-income EU and OECD economy; modest recovery from 2024 recession driven by private consumption and moderated inflation; challenges include high fiscal deficits, frozen access to EU funds, and risks from export reliance; implementing tax exemptions, price controls, and mortgage interest caps ahead of 2026 elections

Real GDP (purchasing power parity): $389.207 billion (2024 est.)
$387.223 billion (2023 est.)
$390.513 billion (2022 est.)
note: data in 2021 dollars
comparison ranking: 55

Real GDP growth rate: 0.5% (2024 est.)
-0.8% (2023 est.)
4.3% (2022 est.)
note: annual GDP % growth based on constant local currency
comparison ranking: 188

Real GDP per capita: $40,700 (2024 est.)
$40,400 (2023 est.)
$40,700 (2022 est.)
note: data in 2021 dollars
comparison ranking: 56

GDP (official exchange rate): $222.905 billion (2024 est.)
note: data in current dollars at official exchange rate

Inflation rate (consumer prices): 3.7% (2024 est.)
17.1% (2023 est.)
14.6% (2022 est.)
note: annual % change based on consumer prices
comparison ranking: 118

GDP - composition, by sector of origin: *agriculture:* 2.4% (2024 est.)
industry: 23.9% (2024 est.)
services: 59.7% (2024 est.)
note: figures may not total 100% due to non-allocated consumption not captured in sector-reported data
comparison rankings: agriculture 145; industry 101; services 92

GDP - composition, by end use: *household consumption:* 49.1% (2023 est.)
government consumption: 19.9% (2023 est.)
investment in fixed capital: 25.6% (2023 est.)
investment in inventories: 0.3% (2023 est.)
exports of goods and services: 80.8% (2023 est.)
imports of goods and services: -76.3% (2023 est.)
note: figures may not total 100% due to rounding or gaps in data collection

Agricultural products: maize, wheat, barley, milk, sunflower seeds, sugar beets, rapeseed, apples, pork, grapes (2023)
note: top ten agricultural products based on tonnage

Industries: mining, metallurgy, construction materials, processed foods, textiles, chemicals (especially pharmaceuticals), motor vehicles

Industrial production growth rate: -2.5% (2024 est.)
note: annual % change in industrial value added based on constant local currency
comparison ranking: 165

Labor force: 4.954 million (2024 est.)
note: number of people ages 15 or older who are employed or seeking work
comparison ranking: 87

Unemployment rate: 4.5% (2024 est.)
4.2% (2023 est.)
3.7% (2022 est.)
note: % of labor force seeking employment
comparison ranking: 74

Youth unemployment rate (ages 15-24): *total:* 14.1% (2024 est.)
male: 14.8% (2024 est.)
female: 13.1% (2024 est.)
note: % of labor force ages 15-24 seeking employment
comparison ranking: total 86

Population below poverty line: 12.1% (2021 est.)
note: % of population with income below national poverty line
Gini Index coefficient - distribution of family income 30.2 (2022 est.)
note: index (0-100) of income distribution; higher values represent greater inequality
comparison ranking: 117

Average household expenditures: *on food:* 16.8% of household expenditures (2023 est.)
on alcohol and tobacco: 7% of household expenditures (2023 est.)

Household income or consumption by percentage share: *lowest 10%:* 2.8% (2022 est.)
highest 10%: 24.4% (2022 est.)
note: % share of income accruing to lowest and highest 10% of population

Remittances: 2.3% of GDP (2024 est.)
2.4% of GDP (2023 est.)
2.2% of GDP (2022 est.)
note: personal transfers and compensation between resident and non-resident individuals/households/entities

Budget: *revenues:* $69.793 billion (2022 est.)
expenditures: $80.429 billion (2022 est.)
note: central government revenues (excluding grants) and expenditures converted to US dollars at average official exchange rate for year indicated

Public debt: 75.3% of GDP (2022 est.)
note: central government debt as a % of GDP
comparison ranking: 48

Taxes and other revenues: 23.4% (of GDP) (2022 est.)
note: central government tax revenue as a % of GDP
comparison ranking: 27

Current account balance: $5.074 billion (2024 est.)
$751.071 million (2023 est.)
-$14.699 billion (2022 est.)
note: balance of payments - net trade and primary/secondary income in current dollars
comparison ranking: 36

Exports: $166.503 billion (2024 est.)
$173.034 billion (2023 est.)
$158.98 billion (2022 est.)
note: balance of payments - exports of goods and services in current dollars
comparison ranking: 37

Exports - partners: Germany 25%, Italy 6%, Romania 6%, USA 5%, Slovakia 4% (2023)
note: top five export partners based on percentage share of exports

Exports - commodities: cars, vehicle parts/accessories, electric batteries, packaged medicine, computers (2023)
note: top five export commodities based on value in dollars

Imports: $154.077 billion (2024 est.)
$163.192 billion (2023 est.)
$167.262 billion (2022 est.)
note: balance of payments - imports of goods and services in current dollars
comparison ranking: 39

Imports - partners: Germany 23%, China 7%, Austria 6%, Poland 6%, S. Korea 6% (2023)
note: top five import partners based on percentage share of imports

Imports - commodities: vehicle parts/accessories, natural gas, integrated circuits, broadcasting equipment, industrial acids/oils/alcohols (2023)
note: top five import commodities based on value in dollars

Reserves of foreign exchange and gold: $46.422 billion (2024 est.)
$45.719 billion (2023 est.)
$41.219 billion (2022 est.)
note: holdings of gold (year-end prices)/foreign exchange/special drawing rights in current dollars
comparison ranking: 43

Exchange rates: forints (HUF) per US dollar -

Exchange rates: 365.691 (2024 est.)
353.088 (2023 est.)
372.596 (2022 est.)
303.141 (2021 est.)
307.997 (2020 est.)

ENERGY

Electricity access: *electrification - total population:* 100% (2022 est.)

Electricity: *installed generating capacity:* 14.829 million kW (2023 est.)
consumption: 42.739 billion kWh (2023 est.)
exports: 8.863 billion kWh (2023 est.)

imports: 19.963 billion kWh (2023 est.)
transmission/distribution losses: 2.454 billion kWh (2023 est.)
comparison rankings: installed generating capacity 55; consumption 57; exports 27; imports 11; transmission/distribution losses 133

Electricity generation sources: *fossil fuels:* 28.9% of total installed capacity (2023 est.)
nuclear: 44.2% of total installed capacity (2023 est.)
solar: 19.4% of total installed capacity (2023 est.)
wind: 1.8% of total installed capacity (2023 est.)
hydroelectricity: 0.6% of total installed capacity (2023 est.)
biomass and waste: 4.9% of total installed capacity (2023 est.)

Nuclear energy: Number of operational nuclear reactors: 4 (2025)

Net capacity of operational nuclear reactors: 1.92GW (2025 est.)

Percent of total electricity production: 48.8% (2023 est.)

Coal: *production:* 4.293 million metric tons (2023 est.)
consumption: 4.694 million metric tons (2023 est.)
exports: 115,000 metric tons (2023 est.)
imports: 452,000 metric tons (2023 est.)
proven reserves: 2.633 billion metric tons (2023 est.)

Petroleum: *total petroleum production:* 36,000 bbl/day (2023 est.)
refined petroleum consumption: 179,000 bbl/day (2024 est.)
crude oil estimated reserves: 12.1 million barrels (2021 est.)

Natural gas: *production:* 1.612 billion cubic meters (2023 est.)
consumption: 8.293 billion cubic meters (2023 est.)
imports: 8.216 billion cubic meters (2023 est.)
proven reserves: 3.738 billion cubic meters (2021 est.)

Energy consumption per capita: 96.152 million Btu/person (2023 est.)
comparison ranking: 54

COMMUNICATIONS

Telephones - fixed lines: *total subscriptions:* 2.693 million (2023 est.)
subscriptions per 100 inhabitants: 28 (2023 est.)
comparison ranking: total subscriptions 40

Telephones - mobile cellular: *total subscriptions:* 10.2 million (2023 est.)
subscriptions per 100 inhabitants: 104 (2022 est.)
comparison ranking: total subscriptions 94

Broadcast media: mixed system of state-supported media and private broadcasters; the 5 publicly owned TV channels and the 2 main privately owned TV stations are the major national broadcasters; large number of special-interest channels; highly developed market for satellite and cable TV with about two-thirds of viewers utilizing the services; 4 state-supported radio networks; large number of local stations, including commercial, public service, nonprofit, and community radio stations; digital transition completed in 2013 (2019)

Internet country code: .hu

Internet users: *percent of population:* 92% (2024 est.)

Broadband - fixed subscriptions: *total:* 3.56 million (2023 est.)
subscriptions per 100 inhabitants: 37 (2023 est.)
comparison ranking: total 45

TRANSPORTATION

Civil aircraft registration country code prefix: HA

Airports: 109 (2025)
comparison ranking: 48

Heliports: 15 (2025)
comparison ranking: 60

Railways: *total:* 7,687 km (2020) 3,111 km electrified

Merchant marine: *total:* 1 (2023)
by type: other 1
comparison ranking: total 187

MILITARY AND SECURITY

Military and security forces: Hungarian Defense Forces (HDF or Magyar Honvédség): the HDF is organized as a joint force under a general staff with commands for land, air, cyber, special operations, territorial defense, and support forces (2025)
note: the National Police are under the Ministry of Interior and responsible for maintaining order nationwide; the Ministry of Interior also has the Counterterrorism Center, a special police force responsible for protecting the president and the prime minister and for preventing, uncovering, and detecting terrorist acts

Military expenditures: 2.1% of GDP (2025 est.)
2.1% of GDP (2024 est.)
2.1% of GDP (2023 est.)
1.8% of GDP (2022 est.)
1.7% of GDP (2021 est.)

Military and security service personnel strengths: approximately 22,000 active-duty military personnel (2025)

Military equipment inventories and acquisitions: the HDF has a mix of Soviet-era and more modern, Western equipment from such countries as Germany, France, Sweden, and the US; in 2017, Budapest launched a modernization program aimed at replacing its Soviet-era weaponry with modern systems; Hungary has also placed emphasis on building up its defense industrial capacity (2024)

Military service age and obligation: 18-25 years of age for voluntary military service; no conscription (abolished 2005); 6-month service obligation (2023)
note: as of 2021, women comprised over 20% of Hungary's full-time military personnel

Military deployments: 250 Bosnia-Herzegovina (EUFOR stabilization force); 200 Chad; 365 Kosovo (NATO/KFOR) (2025)

Military - note: the Hungarian Defense Forces (HDF) are responsible for ensuring the defense of the country's sovereignty, territorial integrity, and citizens, and fulfilling Hungary's commitments to the EU and NATO, as well as contributing to other international peacekeeping efforts under the UN; key areas of concern for the HDF the HDF is also responsible for some aspects of domestic security, crisis management, disaster response, and assisting law enforcement forces in border security
Hungary has been a member of NATO since 1999 and considers the collective defense ensured within the Alliance as a cornerstone of the country's security; NATO membership is complemented by Hungary's ties to the EU under its Common Security and Defense Policy; the HDF has participated in multiple NATO-led security missions, including in Afghanistan, Iraq, and Kosovo, as well as EU-led missions in Bosnia and Herzegovina and Mali; it hosts a NATO battlegroup comprised of troops from Croatia, Hungary, Italy, and the US, and NATO's Multinational Division Center, a headquarters capable of commanding a division-sized force (typically 15-20,000 troops) in a crisis; both organizations were established as a result of Russian aggression against Ukraine; Hungary is a member of the Visegrad Group, a regional platform that brings together Czechia, Hungary, Poland, and Slovakia to discuss cultural, defense, and political cooperation (2025)

TERRORISM

Terrorist group(s): Terrorist group(s): Islamic State of Iraq and ash-Sham (ISIS)
note: details about the history, aims, leadership, organization, areas of operation, tactics, targets, weapons, size, and sources of support of the group(s) appear(s) in Appendix T

TRANSNATIONAL ISSUES

Refugees and internally displaced persons: *refugees:* 72,359 (2024 est.)
stateless persons: 101 (2024 est.)

ICELAND

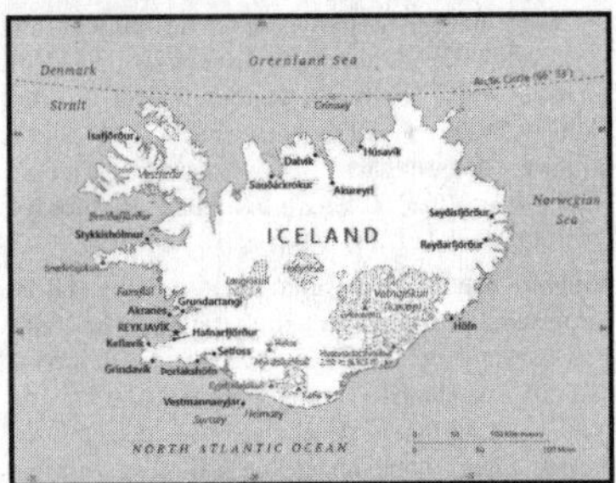

INTRODUCTION

Background: Settled by Norwegian and Celtic (Scottish and Irish) immigrants during the late 9th and 10th centuries A.D., Iceland boasts the world's oldest functioning legislative assembly, the Althingi, which was established in 930. Independent for over 300 years, Iceland was subsequently ruled by Norway and Denmark. Fallout from the Askja volcano of 1875 devastated the Icelandic economy and caused widespread famine. Over the next quarter-century, 20% of the island's population emigrated, mostly to Canada and the US. Denmark granted limited home rule in 1874 and complete independence in 1944. The second half of the 20th century saw substantial economic growth driven primarily by the fishing industry. The economy diversified greatly after the country joined the European Economic Area in 1994, but the global financial crisis hit Iceland especially hard in the years after 2008. The economy is now on an upward trajectory, primarily thanks to a tourism and construction boom. Literacy, longevity, and social cohesion are first-rate by world standards.

GEOGRAPHY

Location: Northern Europe, island between the Greenland Sea and the North Atlantic Ocean, northwest of the United Kingdom

Geographic coordinates: 65 00 N, 18 00 W

Map references: Arctic Region

Area: *total:* 103,000 sq km
land: 100,250 sq km
water: 2,750 sq km
comparison ranking: total 108

Area - comparative: slightly smaller than Pennsylvania; about the same size as Kentucky

Land boundaries: *total:* 0 km

Coastline: 4,970 km

Maritime claims: *territorial sea:* 12 nm
exclusive economic zone: 200 nm
continental shelf: 200 nm or to the edge of the continental margin

Climate: temperate; moderated by North Atlantic Current; mild, windy winters; damp, cool summers

Terrain: mostly plateau interspersed with mountain peaks, icefields; coast deeply indented by bays and fiords

Elevation: *highest point:* Hvannadalshnukur (at Vatnajokull Glacier) 2,110 m
lowest point: Atlantic Ocean 0 m
mean elevation: 557 m

Natural resources: fish, hydropower, geothermal power, diatomite

Land use: *agricultural land:* 18.6% (2022 est.)
arable land: 1.2% (2022 est.)
permanent crops: 0% (2022 est.)
permanent pasture: 17.4% (2022 est.)
forest: 0.5% (2022 est.)
other: 80.9% (2022 est.)

Irrigated land: 0.5 sq km (2022)

Population distribution: Iceland is almost entirely urban, with half of the population located in and around the capital of Reykjavik; smaller clusters are primarily found along the coast in the north and west

Natural hazards: earthquakes and volcanic activity
volcanism: Iceland is situated on top of a hotspot and experiences severe volcanic activity; Eyjafjallajokull (1,666 m) erupted in 2010, sending ash high into the atmosphere and seriously disrupting European air traffic; scientists continue to monitor nearby Katla (1,512 m), which has a high probability of eruption; Grimsvoetn and Hekla are Iceland's most active volcanoes; other historically active volcanoes include Askja, Bardarbunga, Brennisteinsfjoll, Esjufjoll, Hengill, Krafla, Krisuvik, Kverkfjoll, Oraefajokull, Reykjanes, Torfajokull, and Vestmannaeyjar

Geography - note: strategic location between Greenland and Europe; westernmost European country; Reykjavik is the northernmost national capital in the world; more land covered by glaciers than in all of continental Europe

PEOPLE AND SOCIETY

Population: *total:* 364,036 (2024 est.)
male: 182,268
female: 181,768
comparison rankings: total 178; male 178; female 178

Nationality: *noun:* Icelander(s)
adjective: Icelandic

Ethnic groups: Icelandic 78.7%, Polish 5.8%, Danish 1%, Ukrainian 1%, other 13.5% (2024 est.)
note: data represent population by country of birth

Languages: Icelandic, English, Polish, Nordic languages, German

Religions: Evangelical Lutheran Church of Iceland (official) 58.6% Roman Catholic 3.8%, Independent Congregation of Reykjavik 2.6%, Independent Congregation of Hafnarfjordur 1.9%, pagan worship 1.5%, Icelandic Ethical Humanist Association 1.4%, other (includes Zuist and Pentecostal) or unspecified 18.7%, none 7.7% (2024 est.)

Age structure: *0-14 years:* 19.8% (male 36,692/female 35,239)
15-64 years: 63.2% (male 116,210/female 113,810)
65 years and over: 17.1% (2024 est.) (male 29,366/female 32,719)

Dependency ratios: *total dependency ratio:* 58.3 (2024 est.)
youth dependency ratio: 31.3 (2024 est.)
elderly dependency ratio: 27 (2024 est.)
potential support ratio: 3.7 (2024 est.)

Median age: *total:* 38 years (2024 est.)
male: 37.4 years
female: 38.6 years
comparison ranking: total 79

Population growth rate: 0.85% (2024 est.)
comparison ranking: 107

Birth rate: 12.6 births/1,000 population (2024 est.)
comparison ranking: 138

Death rate: 6.6 deaths/1,000 population (2024 est.)
comparison ranking: 132

Net migration rate: 2.5 migrant(s)/1,000 population (2024 est.)
comparison ranking: 45

Population distribution: Iceland is almost entirely urban, with half of the population located in and around the capital of Reykjavik; smaller clusters are primarily found along the coast in the north and west

Urbanization: *urban population:* 94% of total population (2023)
rate of urbanization: 0.74% annual rate of change (2020-25 est.)

Major urban areas - population: 216,000 REYKJAVIK (capital) (2018)

Sex ratio: *at birth:* 1.05 male(s)/female
0-14 years: 1.04 male(s)/female
15-64 years: 1.02 male(s)/female
65 years and over: 0.9 male(s)/female
total population: 1 male(s)/female (2024 est.)

Mother's mean age at first birth: 28.7 years (2020 est.)

Maternal mortality ratio: 3 deaths/100,000 live births (2023 est.)
comparison ranking: 186

Infant mortality rate: *total:* 1.6 deaths/1,000 live births (2024 est.)
male: 1.8 deaths/1,000 live births
female: 1.4 deaths/1,000 live births
comparison ranking: total 225

Life expectancy at birth: *total population:* 84 years (2024 est.)
male: 81.8 years
female: 86.3 years
comparison ranking: total population 8

Total fertility rate: 1.94 children born/woman (2024 est.)
comparison ranking: 113

Gross reproduction rate: 0.95 (2024 est.)

Drinking water source: *improved:* *urban:* 100% of population (2022 est.)
rural: 100% of population (2022 est.)
total: 100% of population (2022 est.)
unimproved: *urban:* 0% of population (2022 est.)
rural: 0% of population (2022 est.)
total: 0% of population (2022 est.)

Health expenditure: 8.6% of GDP (2022)
16.5% of national budget (2022 est.)

Physician density: 4.37 physicians/1,000 population (2023)

Hospital bed density: 2.8 beds/1,000 population (2020 est.)

Sanitation facility access: *improved:* *urban:* 100% of population (2022 est.)
rural: 100% of population (2022 est.)
total: 100% of population (2022 est.)
unimproved: *urban:* 0% of population (2022 est.)
rural: 0% of population (2022 est.)
total: 0% of population (2022 est.)

Obesity - adult prevalence rate: 21.9% (2016)
comparison ranking: 83

Alcohol consumption per capita: *total:* 7.72 liters of pure alcohol (2019 est.)
beer: 4.39 liters of pure alcohol (2019 est.)
wine: 2.11 liters of pure alcohol (2019 est.)
spirits: 1.22 liters of pure alcohol (2019 est.)
other alcohols: 0 liters of pure alcohol (2019 est.)
comparison ranking: total 49

Tobacco use: *total:* 8% (2025 est.)
male: 7.9% (2025 est.)
female: 8% (2025 est.)
comparison ranking: total 143

Currently married women (ages 15-49): 45.1% (2023 est.)

Education expenditure: 6.7% of GDP (2023 est.)
14.8% national budget (2023 est.)
comparison ranking: Education expenditure (% GDP) 19

School life expectancy (primary to tertiary education): *total:* 19 years (2022 est.)
male: 18 years (2022 est.)
female: 20 years (2022 est.)

ENVIRONMENT

Environmental issues: water pollution from fertilizer runoff

International environmental agreements: *party to:* Air Pollution, Air Pollution-Persistent Organic Pollutants, Antarctic Treaty, Biodiversity, Climate Change, Climate Change-Kyoto Protocol, Climate Change-Paris Agreement, Comprehensive Nuclear Test Ban, Desertification, Endangered Species, Hazardous Wastes, Law of the Sea, Marine Dumping-London Convention, Marine Dumping-London Protocol, Nuclear Test Ban, Ozone Layer Protection, Ship Pollution, Wetlands, Whaling
signed, but not ratified: Air Pollution-Heavy Metals, Environmental Modification, Marine Life Conservation

Climate: temperate; moderated by North Atlantic Current; mild, windy winters; damp, cool summers

Urbanization: *urban population:* 94% of total population (2023)
rate of urbanization: 0.74% annual rate of change (2020-25 est.)

Carbon dioxide emissions: 3.101 million metric tonnes of CO2 (2023 est.)
from coal and metallurgical coke: 376,000 metric tonnes of CO2 (2023 est.)
from petroleum and other liquids: 2.725 million metric tonnes of CO2 (2023 est.)
comparison ranking: total emissions 149

Particulate matter emissions: 5.8 micrograms per cubic meter (2019 est.)

Waste and recycling: *municipal solid waste generated annually:* 225,300 tons (2024 est.)
percent of municipal solid waste recycled: 55.5% (2022 est.)

Total water withdrawal: *municipal:* 80 million cubic meters (2022 est.)
industrial: 198 million cubic meters (2022 est.)
agricultural: 300,000 cubic meters (2022 est.)

Total renewable water resources: 170 billion cubic meters (2022 est.)

Geoparks: *total global geoparks and regional networks:* 2
global geoparks and regional networks: Katla; Reykjanes (2023)

GOVERNMENT

Country name: *conventional long form:* none
conventional short form: Iceland
local long form: none
local short form: Island
etymology: Floki VILGERDARSON, an early Norse explorer of the island in the 10th century, applied the name "Land of Ice," from the local words *is* (ice) and *land* (land)

Government type: unitary parliamentary republic

Capital: *name:* Reykjavik
geographic coordinates: 64 09 N, 21 57 W
time difference: UTC 0 (5 hours ahead of Washington, DC, during Standard Time)
etymology: the name means "smoky bay" in Icelandic and refers to the steam from the hot springs in the area

Administrative divisions: 64 municipalities (*sveitarfelog*, singular - *sveitarfelagidh*); Akranes, Akureyri, Arneshreppur, Asahreppur, Blaskogabyggdh, Bolungarvik, Borgarbyggdh, Dalabyggdh, Dalvikurbyggdh, Eyjafjardharsveit, Eyja-og Miklaholtshreppur, Fjallabyggdh, Fjardhabyggdh, Fljotsdalshreppur, Floahreppur, Gardhabaer, Grimsnes-og Grafningshreppur, Grindavikurbaer, Grundarfjardharbaer, Grytubakkahreppur, Hafnarfjordhur, Horgarsveit, Hrunamannahreppur, Hunathing Vestra, Hunabyggdh, Hvalfjardharsveit, Hveragerdhi, Isafjardharbaer, Kaldrananeshreppur, Kjosarhreppur, Kopavogur, Langanesbyggdh, Mosfellsbaer, Mulathing, Myrdalshreppur, Nordhurthing, Rangarthing Eystra, Rangarthing Ytra, Reykholahreppur, Reykjanesbaer, Reykjavik, Seltjarnarnes, Skaftarhreppur, Skagabyggdh, Skagafjordhur, Skeidha-og Gnupverjahreppur, Skorradalshreppur, Snaefellsbaer, Strandabyggdh, Stykkisholmur, Sudhavikurhreppur, Sudhurnesjabaer, Svalbardhsstrandarhreppur, Sveitarfelagidh Arborg, Sveitarfelagidh Hornafjordhur, Sveitarfelagidh Olfus, Sveitarfelagidh Skagastrond, Sveitarfelagidh Vogar, Talknafjardharhreppur, Thingeyjarsveit, Tjorneshreppur, Vestmannaeyjar, Vesturbyggdh, Vopnafjardharhreppur

Legal system: civil law system influenced by the Danish model

Constitution: *history:* several previous; latest ratified 16 June 1944, effective 17 June 1944 (at independence)
amendment process: proposed by the Althingi; passage requires approval by the Althingi and by the next elected Althingi, and confirmation by the president of the republic; proposed amendments to Article 62 of the constitution – that the Evangelical Lutheran Church shall be the state church of Iceland – also require passage by referendum

International law organization participation: has not submitted an ICJ jurisdiction declaration; accepts ICCt jurisdiction

Citizenship: *citizenship by birth:* no
citizenship by descent only: at least one parent must be a citizen of Iceland
dual citizenship recognized: yes
residency requirement for naturalization: 3 to 7 years

Suffrage: 18 years of age; universal

Executive branch: *chief of state:* President Halla TOMASDOTTIR (since 1 August 2024)
head of government: Prime Minister Kristrun FROSTADOTTIR (since 21 December 2024)
cabinet: Cabinet appointed by the president upon the recommendation of the prime minister
election/appointment process: president directly elected by simple-majority popular vote for a 4-year term (no term limits); following legislative elections, the leader of the majority party or majority coalition becomes prime minister
most recent election date: 1 June 2024
election results: *2024:* Halla TOMASDOTTIR elected president; percent of vote - Halla TOMASDOTTIR (independent) 34.1%, Katrin JAKOBSDOTTIR (Left-Green Movement) 25.2%, Halla Hrund LOGADOTTIR (independent) 15.7%, Jon GNARR (Social Democratic Alliance) 10.1%, Baldur PORHALLSSON (independent) 8.4%, other 6.5%
2020: Gudni Thorlacius JOHANNESSON reelected president; percent of vote - Gudni Thorlacius JOHANNESSON (independent) 92.2%, Gudmundur Franklin JONSSON (independent) 7.8%
expected date of next election: June 2028

Legislative branch: *legislature name:* Parliament (Althingi)
legislative structure: unicameral
number of seats: 63 (all directly elected)
electoral system: proportional representation
scope of elections: full renewal
term in office: 4 years
most recent election date: 11/30/2024
parties elected and seats per party: Social Democratic Alliance (S) (15); Independence Party (D) (14); Liberal Reform Party (C) (11); People's Party (F) (10); Center Party (M) (8); Progressive Party (B) (5)
percentage of women in chamber: 46%
expected date of next election: November 2028

Judicial branch: *highest court(s):* Supreme Court or Haestirettur (consists of 7 judges)
judge selection and term of office: judges proposed by Ministry of Interior selection committee and appointed by the president for an indefinite period
subordinate courts: Appellate Court or Landsrettur; 8 district courts; Labor Court

Political parties: Center Party or M
Independence Party or D
Liberal Reform Party or C
People's Party or F
Progressive Party or B
Social Democratic Alliance or S

Diplomatic representation in the US: *chief of mission:* Ambassador Svanhildur Hólm VALSDÓTTIR (since 18 September 2024)
chancery: House of Sweden, 2900 K Street NW, #509, Washington, DC 20007
telephone: [1] (202) 265-6653
FAX: [1] (202) 265-6656
email address and website: washington@mfa.is
https://www.government.is/diplomatic-missions/embassy-of-iceland-in-washington-d.c/

Diplomatic representation from the US: *chief of mission:* Ambassador (vacant); Chargé d'Affaires Erin SAWYER (since January 2025)
embassy: Engjateigur 7, 105 Reykjavik
mailing address: 5640 Reykjavik Place, Washington, D.C. 20521-5640
telephone: [354] 595-2200
FAX: [354] 562-9118
email address and website: ReykjavikConsular@state.gov
https://is.usembassy.gov/

International organization participation: Arctic Council, Australia Group, BIS, CBSS, CD, CE, EAPC, EBRD, EFTA, FAO, FATF, IAEA, IBRD, ICAO, ICC (national committees), ICCt, ICRM, IDA, IFAD, IFC, IFRCS, IHO, ILO, IMF, IMO, IMSO, Interpol, IOC, IOM, IPU, ISO, ITSO, ITU, ITUC (NGOs), MIGA, NATO, NC, NEA, NIB, NSG, OAS (observer), OECD, OPCW, OSCE, PCA, Schengen Convention, UN, UNCTAD, UNESCO, UPU, WCO, WHO, WIPO, WMO, WTO

Independence: 1 December 1918 (became a sovereign state under the Danish Crown); 17 June 1944 (from Denmark; birthday of Jon SIGURDSSON, leader of Iceland's 19th-century independence movement)

National holiday: Independence Day, 17 June (1944)

Flag: *description:* blue with a red cross outlined in white extending to the edges of the flag; the cross is shifted to the left in the style of the Dannebrog (Danish flag)
meaning: red stands for the island's volcanic fires, white for the snow and ice fields, and blue for the ocean

National symbol(s): gyrfalcon

National color(s): blue, white, red

National anthem(s): *title:* "Lofsongur" (Song of Praise)
lyrics/music: Matthias JOCHUMSSON/Sveinbjorn SVEINBJORNSSON
history: adopted 1918

National heritage: *total World Heritage Sites:* 3 (1 cultural, 2 natural)
selected World Heritage Site locales: Thingvellir National Park (c); Surtsey (n); Vatnajökull National Park - Dynamic Nature of Fire and Ice (n)

ECONOMY

Economic overview: high-income North Atlantic island economy; not an EU member but market integration via European Economic Area (EEA); dominant tourism, fishing, and aluminum industries vulnerable to demand swings and disruption from volcanic activity; inflation remains above target rate; barriers to foreign business access and economic diversification

Real GDP (purchasing power parity): $26.561 billion (2024 est.)
$26.424 billion (2023 est.)
$25.012 billion (2022 est.)
note: data in 2021 dollars
comparison ranking: 152

Real GDP growth rate: 0.5% (2024 est.)
5.6% (2023 est.)
9% (2022 est.)
note: annual GDP % growth based on constant local currency
comparison ranking: 189

Real GDP per capita: $65,600 (2024 est.)
$67,200 (2023 est.)
$65,500 (2022 est.)
note: data in 2021 dollars
comparison ranking: 24

GDP (official exchange rate): $33.463 billion (2024 est.)
note: data in current dollars at official exchange rate

Inflation rate (consumer prices): 5.9% (2024 est.)
8.7% (2023 est.)
8.3% (2022 est.)
note: annual % change based on consumer prices
comparison ranking: 153

GDP - composition, by sector of origin: *agriculture:* 4% (2024 est.)
industry: 19.4% (2024 est.)
services: 65.5% (2024 est.)
note: figures may not total 100% due to non-allocated consumption not captured in sector-reported data
comparison rankings: agriculture 119; industry 136; services 54

GDP - composition, by end use: *household consumption:* 49.3% (2023 est.)
government consumption: 25.3% (2023 est.)
investment in fixed capital: 24.8% (2023 est.)
investment in inventories: 0.7% (2023 est.)
exports of goods and services: 43.4% (2023 est.)
imports of goods and services: -43.3% (2023 est.)
note: figures may not total 100% due to rounding or gaps in data collection

Agricultural products: milk, chicken, lamb/mutton, barley, potatoes, pork, beef, eggs, other meats, cucumbers/gherkins (2023)
note: top ten agricultural products based on tonnage

Industries: tourism, fish processing; aluminum smelting; geothermal power, hydropower; medical/pharmaceutical products

Industrial production growth rate: -2.3% (2024 est.)
note: annual % change in industrial value added based on constant local currency
comparison ranking: 161

Labor force: 248,400 (2024 est.)
note: number of people ages 15 or older who are employed or seeking work
comparison ranking: 172

Unemployment rate: 3.2% (2024 est.)
3.6% (2023 est.)
3.8% (2022 est.)
note: % of labor force seeking employment
comparison ranking: 49

Youth unemployment rate (ages 15-24): *total:* 7.6% (2024 est.)
male: 8.3% (2024 est.)
female: 7% (2024 est.)
note: % of labor force ages 15-24 seeking employment
comparison ranking: total 142

Population below poverty line: 8.8% (2017 est.)
note: % of population with income below national poverty line
Gini Index coefficient - distribution of family income 26.6 (2018 est.)
note: index (0-100) of income distribution; higher values represent greater inequality
comparison ranking: 137

Household income or consumption by percentage share: *lowest 10%:* 3.7% (2018 est.)
highest 10%: 21.7% (2018 est.)
note: % share of income accruing to lowest and highest 10% of population

Remittances: 0.7% of GDP (2024 est.)
0.7% of GDP (2023 est.)
0.7% of GDP (2022 est.)
note: personal transfers and compensation between resident and non-resident individuals/households/entities

Budget: *revenues:* $10.023 billion (2023 est.)
expenditures: $10.364 billion (2023 est.)
note: central government revenues (excluding grants) and expenditures converted to US dollars at average official exchange rate for year indicated

Public debt: 80.7% of GDP (2023 est.)
note: central government debt as a % of GDP
comparison ranking: 40

Taxes and other revenues: 23.3% (of GDP) (2023 est.)
note: central government tax revenue as a % of GDP
comparison ranking: 28

Current account balance: -$845.319 million (2024 est.)
$290.603 million (2023 est.)
-$698.165 million (2022 est.)
note: balance of payments - net trade and primary/secondary income in current dollars
comparison ranking: 124

Exports: $13.916 billion (2024 est.)
$13.702 billion (2023 est.)
$13.114 billion (2022 est.)
note: balance of payments - exports of goods and services in current dollars
comparison ranking: 101

Exports - partners: Netherlands 27%, Germany 11%, USA 10%, UK 8%, Norway 6% (2023)
note: top five export partners based on percentage share of exports

Exports - commodities: aluminum, fish, orthopedic appliances, animal meal, iron alloys (2023)
note: top five export commodities based on value in dollars

Imports: $14.298 billion (2024 est.)
$13.63 billion (2023 est.)
$13.237 billion (2022 est.)
note: balance of payments - imports of goods and services in current dollars
comparison ranking: 108

Imports - partners: Norway 11%, China 9%, Germany 9%, Netherlands 8%, USA 7% (2023)
note: top five import partners based on percentage share of imports

Imports - commodities: refined petroleum, cars, carbon-based electronics, aluminum oxide, computers (2023)
note: top five import commodities based on value in dollars

Reserves of foreign exchange and gold: $6.403 billion (2024 est.)
$5.809 billion (2023 est.)
$5.887 billion (2022 est.)
note: holdings of gold (year-end prices)/foreign exchange/special drawing rights in current dollars
comparison ranking: 90

Exchange rates: Icelandic kronur (ISK) per US dollar -

Exchange rates: 137.958 (2024 est.)
137.943 (2023 est.)
135.28 (2022 est.)
126.989 (2021 est.)
135.422 (2020 est.)

ENERGY

Electricity access: *electrification - total population:* 100% (2022 est.)

Electricity: *installed generating capacity:* 3.005 million kW (2023 est.)
consumption: 19.584 billion kWh (2023 est.)
transmission/distribution losses: 543 million kWh (2023 est.)
comparison rankings: installed generating capacity 109; consumption 77; transmission/distribution losses 83

Electricity generation sources: *hydroelectricity:* 70.1% of total installed capacity (2023 est.)
geothermal: 29.9% of total installed capacity (2023 est.)

Coal: *consumption:* 137,000 metric tons (2023 est.)
exports: 81 metric tons (2023 est.)
imports: 106,000 metric tons (2023 est.)

Petroleum: *refined petroleum consumption:* 19,000 bbl/day (2024 est.)

COMMUNICATIONS

Telephones - fixed lines: *total subscriptions:* 82,000 (2023 est.)
subscriptions per 100 inhabitants: 21 (2023 est.)
comparison ranking: total subscriptions 140

Telephones - mobile cellular: *total subscriptions:* 478,000 (2023 est.)
subscriptions per 100 inhabitants: 123 (2022 est.)
comparison ranking: total subscriptions 175

Broadcast media: state-owned public TV broadcaster (RUV) operates 21 TV channels nationally; every household is required to have RUV, which doubles as the emergency broadcast network; 3 privately owned TV stations; 100% of households have multi-channel services though digital and/or fiber-optic connections; RUV operates 3 national and 4 regional radio stations; 1 privately owned radio conglomerate, Syn (4 stations), broadcasts nationwide; over 20 regional radio stations (2019)

Internet country code: .is

Internet users: *percent of population:* 100% (2023 est.)

Broadband - fixed subscriptions: *total:* 145,000 (2023 est.)
subscriptions per 100 inhabitants: 37 (2023 est.)
comparison ranking: total 125

TRANSPORTATION

Civil aircraft registration country code prefix: TF

Airports: 82 (2025)
comparison ranking: 65

Heliports: 1 (2025)
comparison ranking: 158

Merchant marine: *total:* 39 (2023)
by type: general cargo 5, oil tanker 2, other 32
comparison ranking: total 127

Ports: *total ports:* 43 (2024)
large: 0
medium: 2
small: 2
very small: 17
size unknown: 22
ports with oil terminals: 5
key ports: Grundartangi, Reykjavik, Seydhisfjordhur, Vestmannaeyjar

MILITARY AND SECURITY

Military and security forces: no regular military forces; the Icelandic National Police, the regional police forces, and the Icelandic Coast Guard fall under the purview of the Ministry of Justice (2025)
note: the Icelandic Coast Guard is responsible for operational defense tasks in Iceland including but not limited to operation of Keflavik Air Base, special security zones, and the Icelandic air defense system; it also coordinates with NATO in such areas as air surveillance and military defense exercises

Military equipment inventories and acquisitions: the Icelandic Coast Guard's inventory consists of equipment from mostly European suppliers (2024)

Military - note: Iceland was one of the original 12 countries to sign the North Atlantic Treaty (also known as the Washington Treaty) in 1949; Iceland is the only NATO member that has no standing military force; defense of Iceland remains a NATO commitment and NATO maintains an air policing presence in Icelandic airspace; Iceland participates in international peacekeeping missions with the civilian-manned Icelandic Crisis Response Unit (ICRU)
Iceland cooperates with the militaries of other Nordic countries through the Nordic Defense Cooperation (NORDEFCO, established 2009), which consists of Denmark, Finland, Iceland, Norway, and Sweden; areas of cooperation include armaments, education, human resources, training and exercises, and operations
in 1951, Iceland and the US concluded an agreement to make arrangements regarding the defense of Iceland and for the use of facilities in Iceland to that end; the agreement, along with NATO membership, is one of the two pillars of Iceland's security policy; since 2007 Iceland has concluded cooperation agreements with Canada, Denmark, Norway, and the UK which entail dialogue on security and defense issues as well as situational awareness and search and rescue; it also has regular consultations with Germany and France (2025)

TRANSNATIONAL ISSUES

Refugees and internally displaced persons: *refugees:* 8,960 (2024 est.)
IDPs: 3,700 (2024 est.)
stateless persons: 31 (2024 est.)

INDIA

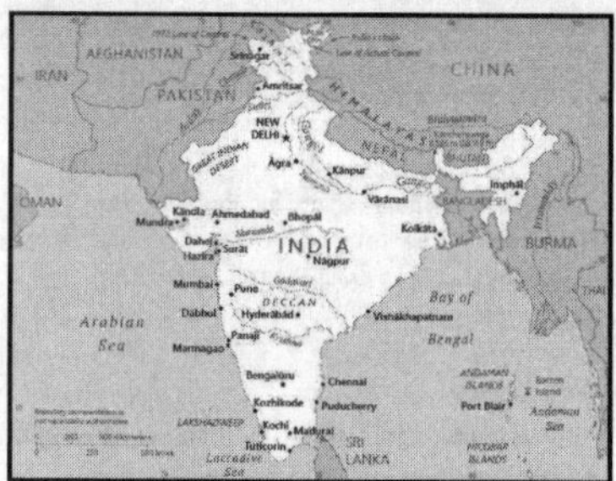

INTRODUCTION

Background: The Indus Valley civilization, one of the world's oldest, flourished during the 3rd and 2nd millennia B.C. and extended into northwestern India. Aryan tribes from the northwest infiltrated the Indian subcontinent about 1500 B.C.; their merger with the earlier Dravidian inhabitants created the classical Indian culture. The Maurya Empire of the 4th and 3rd centuries B.C. – which reached its zenith under ASHOKA – united much of South Asia. The Gupta dynasty (4th to 6th centuries A.D.) ushered in The Golden Age, which saw a flowering of Indian science, art, and culture. Islam spread across the subcontinent over a period of 700 years. In the 10th and 11th centuries, Turks and Afghans invaded India and established the Delhi Sultanate. In the early 16th century, the Emperor BABUR established the Mughal Dynasty, which ruled large sections of India for more than three centuries. European explorers began establishing footholds in India during the 16th century.

By the 19th century, Great Britain had become the dominant political power on the subcontinent, and India was seen as the "Jewel in the Crown" of the British Empire. The British Indian Army played a vital role in both World Wars. Years of nonviolent resistance to British rule, led by Mohandas GANDHI and Jawaharlal NEHRU, eventually resulted in Indian independence in 1947. Large-scale communal violence took place before and after the subcontinent partition into two separate states – India and Pakistan. The neighboring countries have fought three wars since independence, the last of which was in 1971 and resulted in East Pakistan becoming the separate nation of Bangladesh. India's nuclear weapons tests in 1998 emboldened Pakistan to conduct its own tests that same year. In 2008, terrorists originating from Pakistan conducted a series of coordinated attacks in Mumbai, India's financial capital. India's economic growth after economic reforms in 1991, a massive youth population, and a strategic geographic location have contributed to the country's emergence as a regional and global power. However, India still faces pressing problems such as extensive poverty, widespread corruption, and environmental degradation, and its restrictive business climate challenges economic growth expectations.

GEOGRAPHY

Location: Southern Asia, bordering the Arabian Sea and the Bay of Bengal, between Burma and Pakistan

Geographic coordinates: 20 00 N, 77 00 E

Map references: Asia

Area: *total:* 3,287,263 sq km
land: 2,973,193 sq km
water: 314,070 sq km
comparison ranking: total 8

Area - comparative: slightly more than one-third the size of the US

Land boundaries: *total:* 13,888 km
border countries (6): Bangladesh 4,142 km; Bhutan 659 km; Burma 1,468 km; China 2,659 km; Nepal 1,770 km; Pakistan 3,190 km

Coastline: 7,000 km

Maritime claims: *territorial sea:* 12 nm

contiguous zone: 24 nm
exclusive economic zone: 200 nm
continental shelf: 200 nm or to the edge of the continental margin
Climate: varies from tropical monsoon in south to temperate in north
Terrain: upland plain (Deccan Plateau) in south, flat to rolling plain along the Ganges, deserts in west, Himalayas in north
Elevation: *highest point:* Kanchenjunga 8,586 m
lowest point: Indian Ocean 0 m
mean elevation: 160 m
Natural resources: coal (fourth-largest reserves in the world), antimony, iron ore, lead, manganese, mica, bauxite, rare earth elements, titanium ore, chromite, natural gas, diamonds, petroleum, limestone, arable land
Land use: *agricultural land:* 60% (2022 est.)
arable land: 51.9% (2022 est.)
permanent crops: 4.6% (2022 est.)
permanent pasture: 3.5% (2022 est.)
forest: 24.4% (2022 est.)
other: 15.5% (2022 est.)
Irrigated land: 754,562 sq km (2022)
Major lakes (area sq km): *salt water lake(s):* Chilika Lake - 1,170 sq km
Major rivers (by length in km): Brahmaputra (shared with China [s] and Bangladesh [m]) - 3,969 km; Indus (shared with China [s] and Pakistan [m]) - 3,610 km; Ganges river source (shared with Bangladesh [m]) - 2,704 km; Godavari - 1,465 km; Sutlej (shared with China [s] and Pakistan [m]) - 1,372 km; Yamuna - 1,370 km; Narmada - 1,289 km; Chenab river source (shared with Pakistan [m]) - 1,086 km; Ghaghara river mouth (shared with China [s] and Nepal) - 1,080 km
note: [s] after country name indicates river source; [m] after country name indicates river mouth
Major watersheds (area sq km): Indian Ocean drainage: Brahmaputra (651,335 sq km), Ganges (1,016,124 sq km), Indus (1,081,718 sq km), Irrawaddy (413,710 sq km)
Major aquifers: Indus-Ganges-Brahmaputra Basin
Population distribution: a very high population density exists throughout most of the country, with the notable exception of the deserts in the northwest and the mountain fringe in the north; the core of the population is in the north along the banks of the Ganges, with other river valleys and southern coastal areas also having large population concentrations
Natural hazards: droughts; flash floods, as well as widespread and destructive flooding from monsoonal rains; severe thunderstorms; earthquakes
volcanism: Barren Island (354 m) in the Andaman Sea has been active in recent years
Geography - note: dominates South Asian subcontinent; near important Indian Ocean trade routes; Kanchenjunga, third tallest mountain in the world, lies on the border with Nepal

PEOPLE AND SOCIETY

Population: *total:* 1,409,128,296 (2024 est.)
male: 725,784,825
female: 683,343,471
comparison rankings: total 2; male 1; female 2
Nationality: *noun:* Indian(s)
adjective: Indian
Ethnic groups: Indo-Aryan 72%, Dravidian 25%, and other 3% (2000)
Languages: Hindi 43.6%, Bengali 8%, Marathi 6.9%, Telugu 6.7%, Tamil 5.7%, Gujarati 4.6%, Urdu 4.2%, Kannada 3.6%, Odia 3.1%, Malayalam 2.9%, Punjabi 2.7%, Assamese 1.3%, Maithili 1.1%, other 5.6%; English is the subsidiary official language but is the most important one for national, political, and commercial communication (2011 est.)
major-language sample(s):
विश्व फेसबुक, आधारभूत जानकारी का एक अपरिहार्य स्रोत
(Hindi)
note 1: there are 22 other recognized languages – Assamese, Bengali, Bodo, Dogri, Gujarati, Hindi, Kannada, Kashmiri, Konkani, Maithili, Malayalam, Manipuri, Marathi, Nepali, Odia, Punjabi, Sanskrit, Santali, Sindhi, Tamil, Telugu, Urdu
note 2: Hindustani is a popular variant of Hindi/Urdu spoken widely throughout northern India but is not an official language
Religions: Hindu 79.8%, Muslim 14.2%, Christian 2.3%, Sikh 1.7%, other and unspecified 2% (2011 est.)
Age structure: *0-14 years:* 24.5% (male 181,115,052/female 163,647,028)
15-64 years: 68.7% (male 500,568,593/female 467,593,781)
65 years and over: 6.8% (2024 est.) (male 44,101,180/female 52,102,662)
Dependency ratios: *total dependency ratio:* 45.5 (2024 est.)
youth dependency ratio: 35.6 (2024 est.)
elderly dependency ratio: 9.9 (2024 est.)
potential support ratio: 10.1 (2024 est.)
Median age: *total:* 29.8 years (2024 est.)
male: 29.1 years
female: 30.5 years
comparison ranking: total 142
Population growth rate: 0.72% (2024 est.)
comparison ranking: 121
Birth rate: 16.2 births/1,000 population (2024 est.)
comparison ranking: 98
Death rate: 9.1 deaths/1,000 population (2024 est.)
comparison ranking: 56
Net migration rate: 0.1 migrant(s)/1,000 population (2024 est.)
comparison ranking: 77
Population distribution: a very high population density exists throughout most of the country, with the notable exception of the deserts in the northwest and the mountain fringe in the north; the core of the population is in the north along the banks of the Ganges, with other river valleys and southern coastal areas also having large population concentrations
Urbanization: *urban population:* 36.4% of total population (2023)
rate of urbanization: 2.33% annual rate of change (2020-25 est.)
Major urban areas - population: 32.941 million NEW DELHI (capital), 21.297 million Mumbai, 15.333 million Kolkata, 13.608 million Bangalore, 11.776 million Chennai, 10.801 million Hyderabad (2023)
Sex ratio: *at birth:* 1.1 male(s)/female
0-14 years: 1.11 male(s)/female
15-64 years: 1.07 male(s)/female
65 years and over: 0.85 male(s)/female
total population: 1.06 male(s)/female (2024 est.)
Mother's mean age at first birth: 21.2 years (2019/21)
note: data represents median age at first birth among women 25-49
Maternal mortality ratio: 80 deaths/100,000 live births (2023 est.)
comparison ranking: 74
Infant mortality rate: *total:* 30.4 deaths/1,000 live births (2024 est.)
male: 30 deaths/1,000 live births
female: 30.8 deaths/1,000 live births
comparison ranking: total 49
Life expectancy at birth: *total population:* 68.2 years (2024 est.)
male: 66.5 years
female: 70.1 years
comparison ranking: total population 190
Total fertility rate: 2.03 children born/woman (2024 est.)
comparison ranking: 101
Gross reproduction rate: 0.97 (2024 est.)
Drinking water source: *improved: urban:* 95.8% of population (2022 est.)
rural: 91.9% of population (2022 est.)
total: 93.3% of population (2022 est.)
unimproved: urban: 4.2% of population (2022 est.)
rural: 8.1% of population (2022 est.)
total: 6.7% of population (2022 est.)
Health expenditure: 3.3% of GDP (2021)
4.5% of national budget (2022 est.)
Physician density: 0.72 physicians/1,000 population (2020)
Hospital bed density: 1.6 beds/1,000 population (2021 est.)
Sanitation facility access: *improved: urban:* 99.4% of population (2022 est.)
rural: 83% of population (2022 est.)
total: 88.9% of population (2022 est.)
unimproved: urban: 0.6% of population (2022 est.)
rural: 17% of population (2022 est.)
total: 11.1% of population (2022 est.)
Obesity - adult prevalence rate: 3.9% (2016)
comparison ranking: 189
Alcohol consumption per capita: *total:* 3.09 liters of pure alcohol (2019 est.)
beer: 0.23 liters of pure alcohol (2019 est.)
wine: 0 liters of pure alcohol (2019 est.)
spirits: 2.85 liters of pure alcohol (2019 est.)
other alcohols: 0 liters of pure alcohol (2019 est.)
comparison ranking: total 111
Tobacco use: *total:* 21.8% (2025 est.)
male: 34.1% (2025 est.)
female: 8.9% (2025 est.)
comparison ranking: total 55
Children under the age of 5 years underweight: 31.5% (2019/21)
comparison ranking: 4
Currently married women (ages 15-49): 72.6% (2023 est.)
Child marriage: *women married by age 15:* 4.8% (2021)
women married by age 18: 23.3% (2021)
men married by age 18: 2.6% (2021)
Education expenditure: 4.1% of GDP (2022 est.)
14.2% national budget (2022 est.)
comparison ranking: Education expenditure (% GDP) 104
Literacy: *total population:* 82% (2023 est.)
male: 88% (2023 est.)

female: 75% (2023 est.)

School life expectancy (primary to tertiary education): *total:* 13 years (2024 est.)
male: 13 years (2024 est.)
female: 13 years (2024 est.)

ENVIRONMENT

Environmental issues: deforestation; soil erosion; overgrazing; desertification; air pollution from industrial effluents and vehicle emissions; water pollution from raw sewage and agricultural pesticides; tap water not potable; growing population overstraining natural resources; biodiversity loss

International environmental agreements: *party to:* Antarctic-Environmental Protection, Antarctic-Marine Living Resources, Antarctic Treaty, Biodiversity, Climate Change, Climate Change-Kyoto Protocol, Climate Change-Paris Agreement, Desertification, Endangered Species, Environmental Modification, Hazardous Wastes, Law of the Sea, Nuclear Test Ban, Ozone Layer Protection, Ship Pollution, Tropical Timber 2006, Wetlands, Whaling
signed, but not ratified: none of the selected agreements

Climate: varies from tropical monsoon in south to temperate in north

Urbanization: *urban population:* 36.4% of total population (2023)
rate of urbanization: 2.33% annual rate of change (2020-25 est.)

Carbon dioxide emissions: 2.821 billion metric tonnes of CO2 (2023 est.)
from coal and metallurgical coke: 2.054 billion metric tonnes of CO2 (2023 est.)
from petroleum and other liquids: 642.909 million metric tonnes of CO2 (2023 est.)
from consumed natural gas: 124.226 million metric tonnes of CO2 (2023 est.)
comparison ranking: total emissions 3

Particulate matter emissions: 55.6 micrograms per cubic meter (2019 est.)

Methane emissions: *energy:* 8,217.3 kt (2022-2024 est.)
agriculture: 17,971 kt (2019-2021 est.)
waste: 4,773.7 kt (2019-2021 est.)
other: 644.6 kt (2019-2021 est.)

Waste and recycling: *municipal solid waste generated annually:* 189.75 million tons (2024 est.)
percent of municipal solid waste recycled: 17.8% (2022 est.)

Total water withdrawal: *municipal:* 56 billion cubic meters (2022 est.)
industrial: 17 billion cubic meters (2022 est.)
agricultural: 688 billion cubic meters (2022 est.)

Total renewable water resources: 1.911 trillion cubic meters (2022 est.)

GOVERNMENT

Country name: *conventional long form:* Republic of India
conventional short form: India
local long form: Republic of India (English)/ Bharatiya Ganarajya (Hindi)
local short form: India (English)/ Bharat (Hindi)
etymology: the English name derives from the Indus River; the Indian name, Bharat, may derive from the Bharatas tribe mentioned in the Sanskrit Vedas (Hindu religious texts); the name is also associated with Emperor Bharata, the legendary conqueror of India

Government type: federal parliamentary republic

Capital: *name:* New Delhi
geographic coordinates: 28 36 N, 77 12 E
time difference: UTC+5.5 (10.5 hours ahead of Washington, DC, during Standard Time)
etymology: the name is of unknown origin; one theory says it may come from the Hindi word *dehli* (threshold), because of the city's location between the Indus and the Ganges Rivers

Administrative divisions: 28 states and 8 union territories*; Andaman and Nicobar Islands*, Andhra Pradesh, Arunachal Pradesh, Assam, Bihar, Chandigarh*, Chhattisgarh, Dadra and Nagar Haveli and Daman and Diu*, Delhi*, Goa, Gujarat, Haryana, Himachal Pradesh, Jammu and Kashmir*, Jharkhand, Karnataka, Kerala, Ladakh*, Lakshadweep*, Madhya Pradesh, Maharashtra, Manipur, Meghalaya, Mizoram, Nagaland, Odisha, Puducherry*, Punjab, Rajasthan, Sikkim, Tamil Nadu, Telangana, Tripura, Uttar Pradesh, Uttarakhand, West Bengal
note: the official name of Delhi is National Capital Territory of Delhi, even though it is considered a union territory

Legal system: common law system based on the English model; separate personal law codes apply to Muslims, Christians, and Hindus; judicial review of legislative acts

Constitution: *history:* previous 1935 (pre-independence); latest draft completed 4 November 1949, adopted 26 November 1949, effective 26 January 1950
amendment process: proposed by either the Council of States or the House of the People; passage requires majority participation of the total membership in each house and at least two-thirds majority of voting members of each house, followed by assent of the president of India; proposed amendments to the constitutional amendment procedures also must be ratified by at least one half of the India state legislatures before presidential assent

International law organization participation: accepts compulsory ICJ jurisdiction with reservations; non-party state to the ICCt

Citizenship: *citizenship by birth:* no
citizenship by descent only: at least one parent must be a citizen of India
dual citizenship recognized: no
residency requirement for naturalization: 5 years

Suffrage: 18 years of age; universal

Executive branch: *chief of state:* President Droupadi MURMU (since 25 July 2022)
head of government: Prime Minister Narendra MODI (since 26 May 2014)
cabinet: Union Council of Ministers recommended by the prime minister, appointed by the president
election/appointment process: president indirectly elected for a 5-year term (no term limits) by an electoral college consisting of elected members of both houses of Parliament; vice president indirectly elected for a 5-year term (no term limits) by an electoral college consisting of elected members of both houses of Parliament; following legislative elections, the prime minister is elected by Lok Sabha members of the majority party
most recent election date: ***president:*** 18 July 2022
vice president: 5 August 2022
election results: *2022:* Droupadi MURMU elected president; percent of electoral college vote - Droupadi MURMU (BJP) 64%, Yashwant SINHA (AITC) 35.9%; Jagdeep DHANKHAR elected vice president; percent of electoral college vote - Jagdeep DHANKHAR (BJP) 74.4%, Margaret ALVA (INC) 25.6%
2017: Ram Nath KOVIND elected president; percent of electoral college vote - Ram Nath KOVIND (BJP) 65.6%, Meira KUMAR (INC) 34.4%; Venkaiah NAIDU elected vice president; percent of electoral college vote - Venkaiah NAIDU (BJP) 67.9%, Gopal-krishna GANDHI 32.1%
expected date of next election: ***president:*** July 2027
vice president: August 2027

Legislative branch: *legislature name:* Parliament (Sansad)
legislative structure: bicameral
note: in September 2023, both Rajya Sabha and Lok Sabha passed a bill that reserves one third of the House seats for women; implementation could begin for the House election in 2029

Legislative branch - lower chamber: *chamber name:* House of the People (Lok Sabha)
number of seats: 545 (543 directly elected; 2 appointed)
electoral system: plurality/majority
scope of elections: full renewal
term in office: 5 years
most recent election date: 4/19/2024 to 6/1/2024
parties elected and seats per party: Bharatiya Janata Party (BJP) (240); Indian National Congress (INC) (99); Samajwadi Party (SP) (37); All India Trinamool Congress (AITC) (29); Other (138)
percentage of women in chamber: 13.8%
expected date of next election: April 2029

Legislative branch - upper chamber: *chamber name:* Council of States (Rajya Sabha)
number of seats: 245 (233 indirectly elected; 12 appointed)
scope of elections: partial renewal
term in office: 6 years
most recent election date: 1/12/2024 to 6/30/2024
percentage of women in chamber: 16.7%
expected date of next election: January 2026

Judicial branch: *highest court(s):* Supreme Court (consists of 28 judges, including the chief justice)
judge selection and term of office: justices appointed by the president to serve until age 65
subordinate courts: High Courts; District Courts; Labour Court

Political parties: Aam Aadmi Party or AAP
All India Trinamool Congress or AITC
Bahujan Samaj Party or BSP
Bharatiya Janata Party or BJP
Biju Janata Dal or BJD
Communist Party of India-Marxist or CPI(M)
Dravida Munnetra Khazhagam
Indian National Congress or INC
Nationalist Congress Party or NCP
Rashtriya Janata Dal or RJD
Samajwadi Party or SP
Shiromani Akali Dal or SAD
Shiv Sena or SS
Telegana Rashtra Samithi or TRS
Telugu Desam Party or TDP
YSR Congress or YSRCP or YCP

Diplomatic representation in the US: *chief of mission:* Ambassador Vinay Mohan KWATRA (since 18 September 2024)
chancery: 2107 Massachusetts Avenue NW, Washington, DC 20008
telephone: [1] (202) 939-7000
FAX: [1] (202) 265-4351

email address and website: hoc.washington@mea.gov.in
https://www.indianembassyusa.gov.in/
consulate(s) general: Atlanta, Chicago, Houston, New York, San Francisco, Seattle

Diplomatic representation from the US: *chief of mission:* Ambassador (vacant); Chargé d'Affaires Jorgan K. ANDREWS (since January 2025)
embassy: Shantipath, Chanakyapuri, New Delhi - 110021
mailing address: 9000 New Delhi Place, Washington DC 20521-9000
telephone: [91] (11) 2419-8000

FAX: [91] (11) 2419-0017
email address and website: acsnd@state.gov
https://in.usembassy. gov/
consulate(s) general: Chennai (Madras), Hyderabad, Kolkata (Calcutta), Mumbai (Bombay)

International organization participation: ADB, AfDB (nonregional member), Arctic Council (observer), ARF, ASEAN (dialogue partner), BIMSTEC, BIS, BRICS, C, CD, CERN (observer), CICA, CP, EAS, FAO, FATF, G-15, G-20, G-24, G-5, G-77, IAEA, IBRD, ICAO, ICC (national committees), ICRM, IDA, IFAD, IFC, IFRCS, IHO, ILO, IMF, IMO, IMSO, Interpol, IOC, IOM, IPU, ISO, ITSO, ITU, ITUC (NGOs), LAS (observer), MIGA, MINURSO, MONUSCO, NAM, OAS (observer), OECD, OPCW, Pacific Alliance (observer), PCA, PIF (partner), Quad, SAARC, SACEP, SCO (observer), UN, UNCTAD, UNDOF, UNESCO, UNHCR, UNHRC, UNIDO, UNIFIL, UNISFA, UNITAR, UNMISS, UNOCI, UNSOM, UNWTO, UPU, Wassenaar Arrangement, WCO, WFTU (NGOs), WHO, WIPO, WMO, WTO

Independence: 15 August 1947 (from the UK)

National holiday: Republic Day, 26 January (1950)

Flag: *description:* three equal horizontal bands of saffron (top), white, and green, with a blue *chakra* (24-spoked wheel) centered in the white band
meaning: saffron stands for courage, sacrifice, and the spirit of renunciation; white for purity and truth; green for faith and fertility; the chakra symbolizes the wheel of life in movement and death in stagnation
note: similar to the flag of Niger, which has a small orange disk centered in the white band

National symbol(s): the Lion Capital of Ashoka, which depicts four Asiatic lions standing back-to-back and mounted on a circular abacus (official); Bengal tiger and lotus flower (traditional)

National color(s): saffron, white, green

National anthem(s): *title:* "Jana-Gana-Mana" (Thou Art the Ruler of the Minds of All People)
lyrics/music: Rabindranath TAGORE
history: adopted 1950; Rabindranath TAGORE, a Nobel laureate, also wrote Bangladesh's national anthem

National heritage: *total World Heritage Sites:* 43 (35 cultural, 7 natural, 1 mixed)
selected World Heritage Site locales: Taj Mahal (c); Agra Fort (c); Elphanta Caves (c); Hill Forts of Rajasthan (c); Sundarbans National Park (n); Rock Shelters of Bhimbetka (c); Champaner-Pavagadh Archaeological Park (c); Jaipur (c); Mahabodhi Temple Complex at Bodh Gaya (c); Manas Wildlife Sanctuary (n); Nanda Devi and Valley of Flowers National Parks (n); Khangchendzonga National Park (m); Group of Monuments at Mahabalipuram (c); Sun Temple, Konârak (c); Kaziranga National Park (n); Churches and Convents of Goa (c); Great Living Chola Temples (c); Group of Monuments at Pattadakal (c); Buddhist Monuments at Sanchi (c); Humayun's Tomb, Delhi (c); Qutb Minar and its Monuments, Delhi (c); Great Himalayan National Park Conservation Area (n); Rani-ki-Vav (the Queen's Stepwell) at Patan, Gujarat (c); Archaeological Site of Nalanda Mahavihara at Nalanda, Bihar (c); Historic City of Ahmadabad (c); Victorian Gothic and Art Deco Ensembles of Mumbai (c); Jaipur City, Rajasthan (c); Kakatiya Rudreshwara (Ramappa) Temple, Telangana (c); Moidams – the Mound-Burial System of the Ahom Dynasty (c)

ECONOMY

Economic overview: largest South Asian economy; strong, sustained GDP growth led by technology and service sectors, foreign investment, and improved regulatory framework; high poverty rate and income inequality; initiatives on infrastructure development, digitization, manufacturing, and financial access

Real GDP (purchasing power parity): $14.244 trillion (2024 est.)
$13.377 trillion (2023 est.)
$12.251 trillion (2022 est.)
note: data in 2021 dollars
comparison ranking: 3

Real GDP growth rate: 6.5% (2024 est.)
9.2% (2023 est.)
7.6% (2022 est.)
note: annual GDP % growth based on constant local currency
comparison ranking: 20

Real GDP per capita: $9,800 (2024 est.)
$9,300 (2023 est.)
$8,600 (2022 est.)
note: data in 2021 dollars
comparison ranking: 148

GDP (official exchange rate): $3.913 trillion (2024 est.)
note: data in current dollars at official exchange rate

Inflation rate (consumer prices): 5% (2024 est.)
5.6% (2023 est.)
6.7% (2022 est.)
note: annual % change based on consumer prices
comparison ranking: 145

GDP - composition, by sector of origin: *agriculture:* 16.4% (2024 est.)
industry: 24.5% (2024 est.)
services: 49.9% (2024 est.)
note: figures may not total 100% due to non-allocated consumption not captured in sector-reported data
comparison rankings: agriculture 50; industry 94; services 146

GDP - composition, by end use: *household consumption:* 61.5% (2024 est.)
government consumption: 10.1% (2024 est.)
investment in fixed capital: 29.6% (2024 est.)
investment in inventories: 3% (2024 est.)
exports of goods and services: 21.2% (2024 est.)
imports of goods and services: -23.5% (2024 est.)
note: figures may not total 100% due to rounding or gaps in data collection

Agricultural products: sugarcane, rice, milk, wheat, bison milk, potatoes, vegetables, maize, bananas, onions (2023)
note: top ten agricultural products based on tonnage

Industries: textiles, chemicals, food processing, steel, transportation equipment, cement, mining, petroleum, machinery, software, pharmaceuticals

Industrial production growth rate: 5.6% (2024 est.)
note: annual % change in industrial value added based on constant local currency
comparison ranking: 35

Labor force: 607.691 million (2024 est.)
note: number of people ages 15 or older who are employed or seeking work
comparison ranking: 2

Unemployment rate: 4.3% (2024 est.)
4.2% (2023 est.)
4.9% (2022 est.)
note: % of labor force seeking employment
comparison ranking: 70

Youth unemployment rate (ages 15-24): *total:* 16% (2024 est.)
male: 15.5% (2024 est.)
female: 17.6% (2024 est.)
note: % of labor force ages 15-24 seeking employment
comparison ranking: total 74

Gini Index coefficient - distribution of family income: 25.5 (2022 est.)
note: index (0-100) of income distribution; higher values represent greater inequality
comparison ranking: 146

Average household expenditures: *on food:* 29.9% of household expenditures (2023 est.)
on alcohol and tobacco: 2% of household expenditures (2023 est.)

Household income or consumption by percentage share: *lowest 10%:* 4.5% (2022 est.)
highest 10%: 22.1% (2022 est.)
note: % share of income accruing to lowest and highest 10% of population

Remittances: 3.5% of GDP (2024 est.)
3.3% of GDP (2023 est.)
3.3% of GDP (2022 est.)
note: personal transfers and compensation between resident and non-resident individuals/households/entities

Budget: *revenues:* $311.824 billion (2022 est.)
expenditures: $486.598 billion (2022 est.)
note: central government revenues and expenses (excluding grants/extrabudgetary units/social security funds) converted to US dollars at average official exchange rate for year indicated

Public debt: 46.5% of GDP (2018 est.)
note: central government debt as a % of GDP
comparison ranking: 116

Taxes and other revenues: 6.7% (of GDP) (2022 est.)
note: central government tax revenue as a % of GDP
comparison ranking: 144

Current account balance: -$32.428 billion (2024 est.)
-$31.962 billion (2023 est.)
-$79.051 billion (2022 est.)
note: balance of payments - net trade and primary/secondary income in current dollars
comparison ranking: 190

Exports: $822.046 billion (2024 est.)
$773.177 billion (2023 est.)
$767.643 billion (2022 est.)
note: balance of payments - exports of goods and services in current dollars
comparison ranking: 10

Exports - partners: USA 19%, UAE 7%, China 4%, Germany 3%, UK 3% (2023)

note: top five export partners based on percentage share of exports

Exports - commodities: refined petroleum, packaged medicine, diamonds, broadcasting equipment, garments (2023)
note: top five export commodities based on value in dollars

Imports: $923.081 billion (2024 est.)
$859.507 billion (2023 est.)
$902.304 billion (2022 est.)
note: balance of payments - imports of goods and services in current dollars
comparison ranking: 7

Imports - partners: China 19%, Russia 10%, USA 6%, UAE 6%, Saudi Arabia 5% (2023)
note: top five import partners based on percentage share of imports

Imports - commodities: crude petroleum, gold, coal, natural gas, integrated circuits (2023)
note: top five import commodities based on value in dollars

Reserves of foreign exchange and gold: $643.043 billion (2024 est.)
$627.793 billion (2023 est.)
$567.298 billion (2022 est.)
note: holdings of gold (year-end prices)/foreign exchange/special drawing rights in current dollars
comparison ranking: 5

Debt - external: $212.728 billion (2023 est.)
note: present value of external debt in current US dollars
comparison ranking: 4

Exchange rates: Indian rupees (INR) per US dollar -

Exchange rates: 83.669 (2024 est.)
82.599 (2023 est.)
78.604 (2022 est.)
73.918 (2021 est.)
74.1 (2020 est.)

ENERGY

Electricity access: *electrification - total population:* 99.2% (2022 est.)
electrification - urban areas: 100%
electrification - rural areas: 99.3%

Electricity: *installed generating capacity:* 499.136 million kW (2023 est.)
consumption: 1.5 trillion kWh (2023 est.)
exports: 9.529 billion kWh (2023 est.)
imports: 7.843 billion kWh (2023 est.)
transmission/distribution losses: 303.066 billion kWh (2023 est.)
comparison rankings: installed generating capacity 3; consumption 3; exports 24; imports 32; transmission/distribution losses 210

Electricity generation sources: *fossil fuels:* 75.5% of total installed capacity (2023 est.)
nuclear: 2.7% of total installed capacity (2023 est.)
solar: 6.6% of total installed capacity (2023 est.)
wind: 5.1% of total installed capacity (2023 est.)
hydroelectricity: 8.2% of total installed capacity (2023 est.)
biomass and waste: 1.9% of total installed capacity (2023 est.)

Nuclear energy: Number of operational nuclear reactors: 20 (2025)

Number of nuclear reactors under construction: 7 (2025)

Net capacity of operational nuclear reactors: 6.92GW (2025 est.)

Percent of total electricity production: 3.1% (2023 est.)

Coal: *production:* 1.02 billion metric tons (2023 est.)
consumption: 1.262 billion metric tons (2023 est.)
exports: 1.632 million metric tons (2023 est.)
imports: 243.488 million metric tons (2023 est.)
proven reserves: 127.727 billion metric tons (2023 est.)

Petroleum: *total petroleum production:* 822,000 bbl/day (2023 est.)
refined petroleum consumption: 5.271 million bbl/day (2023 est.)
crude oil estimated reserves: 4.605 billion barrels (2021 est.)

Natural gas: *production:* 35.168 billion cubic meters (2023 est.)
consumption: 62.196 billion cubic meters (2023 est.)
exports: 91.921 million cubic meters (2019 est.)
imports: 29.337 billion cubic meters (2023 est.)
proven reserves: 1.381 trillion cubic meters (2021 est.)

Energy consumption per capita: 25.179 million Btu/person (2023 est.)
comparison ranking: 124

COMMUNICATIONS

Telephones - fixed lines: *total subscriptions:* 27.455 million (2022 est.)
subscriptions per 100 inhabitants: 2 (2023 est.)
comparison ranking: total subscriptions 7

Telephones - mobile cellular: *total subscriptions:* 1.14 billion (2022 est.)
subscriptions per 100 inhabitants: 81 (2022 est.)
comparison ranking: total subscriptions 2

Broadcast media: Doordarshan, India's public TV network, has a monopoly on terrestrial broadcasting and operates about 20 national, regional, and local services; a large number of privately owned TV stations are distributed by cable and satellite service providers; cable and satellite TV offer over 850 TV channels; government controls AM radio, with All India Radio operating domestic and external networks; news broadcasts via radio are limited to the All India Radio Network; since 2000, privately owned FM stations have been permitted and have increased rapidly (2020)

Internet country code: .in

Internet users: *percent of population:* 56% (2022 est.)

Broadband - fixed subscriptions: *total:* 39.3 million (2023 est.)
subscriptions per 100 inhabitants: 2 (2022 est.)
comparison ranking: total 5

TRANSPORTATION

Civil aircraft registration country code prefix: VT

Airports: 315 (2025)
comparison ranking: 23

Heliports: 289 (2025)
comparison ranking: 12

Railways: *total:* 65,554 km (2014)
narrow gauge: 1,604 km (2014) 1.000-m gauge
broad gauge: 63,950 km (2014) (39, 329 km electrified)

Merchant marine: *total:* 1,859 (2023)
by type: bulk carrier 66, container ship 22, general cargo 607, oil tanker 144, other 1020
comparison ranking: total 15

Ports: *total ports:* 56 (2024)
large: 4
medium: 4
small: 13
very small: 30
size unknown: 5
ports with oil terminals: 18
key ports: Calcutta, Chennai (Madras), Jawaharlal Nehru Port (Nhava Shiva), Kattupalli Port, Kochi (Cochin), Mumbai (Bombay), New Mangalore, Vishakhapatnam

MILITARY AND SECURITY

Military and security forces: Indian Armed Forces (IAF): Army, Navy, Air Force, Coast Guard

Ministry of Home Affairs: Central Police Organization, Central Armed Police Forces (includes Assam Rifles, Border Security Force, Central Industrial Security Force, Central Reserve Police Force, Indo-Tibetan Border Police, National Security Guards, Sashastra Seema Bal) (2025)
note 1: the Border Security Force (BSF) is responsible for the Indo-Pakistan and Indo- Bangladesh borders; the Sashastra Seema Bal (SSB or Armed Border Force) guards the Indo-Nepal and Indo-Bhutan borders
note 2: the Central Reserve Police Force (CRPF) includes a Rapid Reaction Force (RAF) for riot control and the Commando Battalion for Resolute Action (COBRA) for counter-insurgency operations
note 3: the Assam Rifles are under the administrative control of the Ministry of Home Affairs, while operational control falls under the Ministry of Defense (specifically the Indian Army)

Military expenditures: 2% of GDP (2024 est.)
2.3% of GDP (2023 est.)
2.1% of GDP (2022 est.)
2.2% of GDP (2021 est.)
2.5% of GDP (2020 est.)

Military and security service personnel strengths: information varies; approximately 1.5 million active Indian Armed Forces, including about 1.25 million in the Army (2025)

Military equipment inventories and acquisitions: much of the military's inventory consists of Russian- and Soviet-origin equipment along with a smaller, but growing mix of Western and domestically produced arms; Russia continues to be the leading provider of arms to India, although in recent years India has increased acquisitions from other suppliers, including France, Israel, and the US; India's defense industry is capable of producing a range of air, land, missile, and naval weapons systems for both domestic use and export; it also produces weapons systems under license (2024)

Military service age and obligation: ages vary by service, but generally 16.5-27 years of age for voluntary military service for men and women; no conscription (2023)
note 1: in 2022, the Indian Government began recruiting men aged 17.5-21 annually to serve on 4-year contracts; at the end of their tenure, 25% would be retained for longer terms of service, while the remainder would be forced to leave the military, although some of those leaving would be eligible to serve in the Coast Guard, the Merchant Navy, civilian positions in the Ministry of Defense, and in the paramilitary forces of the Ministry of Home Affairs
note 2: as of 2023, women made up less than 1% of the Army, about 1% of the Air Force, and about 6% of the Navy

note 3: the Indian military accepts citizens of Nepal and Bhutan; descendants of refugees from Tibet who arrived before 1962 and have resided permanently in India; peoples of Indian origin from nations such as Burma, the Democratic Republic of the Congo, Ethiopia, Kenya, Malawi, Pakistan, Sri Lanka, Tanzania, Uganda, and Vietnam with the intention of permanently settling in India; eligible candidates from "friendly foreign nations" may apply to the Armed Forces Medical Services
note 4: the British began to recruit Nepalese citizens (Gurkhas) into the East India Company Army during the Anglo-Nepalese War (1814-1816), and the Gurkhas subsequently were brought into the British Indian Army; following the partition of India in 1947, an agreement between Nepal, India, and Great Britain allowed for the transfer of the 10 regiments from the British Indian Army to the separate British and Indian armies; six regiments of Gurkhas (aka Gorkhas in India) regiments went to the new Indian Army; a seventh regiment was later added

Military deployments: 1,100 Democratic Republic of the Congo (MONUSCO); 200 Golan Heights (UNDOF); 900 Lebanon (UNIFIL); 2,400 South Sudan (UNMISS); 600 Sudan (UNISFA) (2025)
note: India has over 6,000 total military and police personnel deployed on UN missions

Military - note: the Indian military's primary mission is external/territorial defense while secondary missions include regional power projection, UN peacekeeping deployments, humanitarian operations, and support to internal security forces; it participates in multinational exercises and is one of the world's largest contributors to UN peacekeeping operations
the military's chief external focuses are China and Pakistan; the short 1962 Sino-India War left in place one of the World's longest disputed international borders–known as the Line of Actual Control (LAC)–resulting in occasional standoffs between Indian and Chinese security forces, including lethal clashes in 1975 and 2020; naval competition and influence in the Indian Ocean is also an area of interest
India has fought four wars and several skirmishes with Pakistan; three of the wars have been over the disputed region of Jammu and Kashmir, the status of which has been unsettled since the UK's 1947 withdrawal and the partition and independence of India and Pakistan; a fragile cease-fire in Kashmir was reached in 2003, revised in 2018, and reaffirmed in 2021, although the militarized Line of Control which serves as the border remains contested, and India has accused Pakistan of backing armed separatists and terrorist organizations in Jammu and Kashmir where Indian military and security forces have conducted counterinsurgency operations since the 1980s; in the Spring of 2025, India held Pakistan responsible for a terrorist attack in India-controlled Kashmir and retaliated, sparking a brief cross-border conflict involving aircraft, artillery, drone, and missile strikes
the Kashmir dispute also includes the Siachen Glacier, located in the Karakoram Mountain Range, which was seized by India in 1984 with Pakistan attempting to retake the area several times between 1985 and 1995; despite the 2003 cease-fire, both sides continue to maintain a permanent military presence there with outposts at altitudes above 20,000 feet (over 6,000 meters) where most casualties are due to extreme weather and the hazards of operating in the high mountain terrain of the world's highest conflict, including avalanches, exposure, and altitude sickness (2025)

SPACE

Space agency/agencies: Indian Space Research Organization (ISRO; originally established in 1962 as the Indian National Committee for Space Research (INCOSPAR); renamed ISRO in 1969); the ISRO is subordinate to the Department of Space (DOS; established 1972); Defense Space Agency (DSA; established 2019 to command the space assets of the Armed Forces and other defense organizations) (2025)
note: India's first space organization was the Indian National Committee for Space Research (INCOSPAR; established 1962)

Space launch site(s): Satish Dhawan Space Center (aka Sriharikota Range; located in Andhra Pradesh); Vikram Sarabhai Space Center (Kerala) (2025)

Space program overview: has one of the world's largest space programs; designs, builds, launches, operates, and tracks the full spectrum of satellites, including communications, navigation, remote sensing (RS), and scientific/technology; designs, builds, and launches rockets, space/satellite launch vehicles (SLVs), and lunar/interplanetary probes; launches satellites for foreign partners; developing astronaut corps and human flight capabilities (with assistance from Russia, US); researching and developing additional space-related technologies and capabilities; has space-related agreements with more than 50 countries, including China, France, Germany, Japan, Russia, and the US, as well as the European Space Agency; participates in international space projects such as the Square Kilometer Array (SKA) radio telescope; the Department of Space administers two government-controlled space industry corporations; India also has a growing private space sector (2025)
note: further details about the key activities, programs, and milestones of the country's space program, as well as government spending estimates on the space sector, appear in the Space Programs reference guide

TERRORISM

Terrorist group(s): Terrorist group(s): al-Qa'ida; al-Qa'ida in the Indian Subcontinent (AQIS); Harakat ul-Mujahidin; Harakat ul-Jihad-i-Islami (HUJI); Hizbul Mujahideen; Indian Mujahedeen; Islamic State of Iraq and ash-Sham (ISIS) – India (ISI); Jaish-e-Mohammed (JeM); Lashkar-e Tayyiba (LeT); Islamic Revolutionary Guard Corps (IRGC)/Qods Force; The Resistance Front (TRF)
note: details about the history, aims, leadership, organization, areas of operation, tactics, targets, weapons, size, and sources of support of the group(s) appear(s) in Appendix T

TRANSNATIONAL ISSUES

Refugees and internally displaced persons: *refugees:* 250,006 (2024 est.)

IDPs: 642,610 (2024 est.)
stateless persons: 23,262 (2024 est.)

Illicit drugs: USG identification: major illicit drug-producing and/or drug-transit country
major precursor-chemical producer (2025)

INDIAN OCEAN

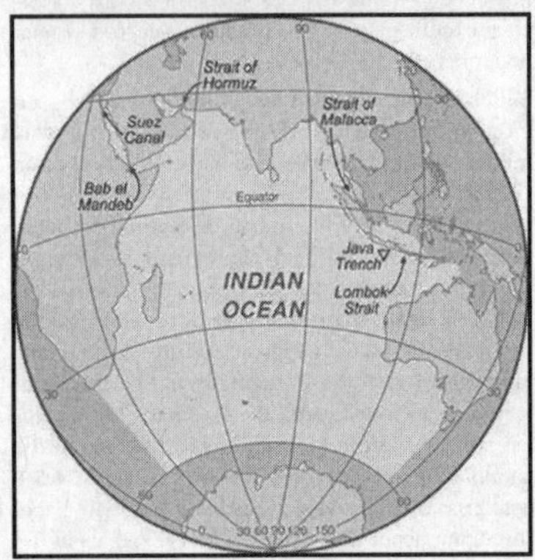

INTRODUCTION

Background: The Indian Ocean is the third largest of the world's five ocean basins (after the Pacific Ocean and Atlantic Ocean, but larger than the Southern Ocean and Arctic Ocean). Four critically important access waterways are the Suez Canal (Egypt), Bab el Mandeb (Djibouti-Yemen), Strait of Hormuz (Iran-Oman), and Strait of Malacca (Indonesia-Malaysia). The International Hydrographic Organization decided in 2000 to delimit a fifth world ocean basin, the Southern Ocean, which removed the portion of the Indian Ocean south of 60 degrees south latitude.

GEOGRAPHY

Location: body of water between Africa, the Southern Ocean, Asia, and Australia

Geographic coordinates: 20 00 S, 80 00 E

Area: *total:* 70.56 million sq km
note: includes Andaman Sea, Arabian Sea, Bay of Bengal, Great Australian Bight, Gulf of Aden, Gulf of Oman, Mozambique Channel, Persian Gulf, Red Sea, Savu Sea, Strait of Malacca, Timor Sea, and other tributary water bodies

Area - comparative: almost seven times the size of the US

Coastline: 66,526 km

Climate: northeast monsoon (December to April), southwest monsoon (June to October); tropical cyclones occur during May/June and October/November in the northern Indian Ocean and January/February in the southern Indian Ocean

Ocean volume: *ocean volume:* 264 million cu km

percent of World Ocean total volume: 19.8%

Major ocean currents: the counterclockwise Indian Ocean Gyre comprised of the southward flowing warm Agulhas and East Madagascar Currents in the west, the eastward flowing South Indian Current in the south, the northward flowing cold West Australian Current in the east, and the westward flowing South Equatorial Current in the north; a distinctive annual reversal of surface currents occurs in the northern Indian Ocean; low atmospheric pressure over southwest Asia from hot, rising, summer air results in the southwest monsoon and southwest-to-northeast winds and clockwise currents, while high pressure over northern Asia from cold, falling, winter air results in the northeast monsoon and northeast-to-southwest winds and counterclockwise currents

Bathymetry: *continental shelf:* the following are examples of features on the continental shelf of the Indian Ocean: Exmouth Plateau
Indus Canyon
The Swatch of No Ground/Ganges Canyon (Bay of Bengal)
Sunda Shelf

continental slope: the following are examples of features on the continental slope of the Indian Ocean: Bengal Fan
Indus Fan

abyssal plains: the following are examples of features on the abyssal plains of the Indian Ocean: Arabian Basin
Crozet Basin
Madagascar Basin
Mid-Indian Basin
Mozambique Basin
Wharton Basin

mid-ocean ridge: the following are examples of mid-ocean ridges on the floor of the Indian Ocean: Central Indian Ridge
Davie Ridge
Southeast Indian Ridge
Southwest Indian Ridge

undersea terrain features: the following are examples of undersea terrain features on the floor of the Indian Ocean: Andaman-Nicobar Ridge
Chagos-Laccadive Ridge
Kerguelen Plateau
Madagascar Plateau
Mascarene Plateau
Mozambique Plateau
Ninetyeast Ridge

ocean trenches: the following are examples of ocean trenches on the floor of the Indian Ocean: Java/Sunda Trench (deepest point in the Indian Ocean)

atolls: the following are examples of atolls in the Indian Ocean: Bassas da India
Chagos Archipelago/Diego Garcia
Europa Island
Juan de Nova Island
Lakshadweep Islands
Maldive Islands
Seychelles

Elevation: *highest point:* sea level
lowest point: Java Trench -7,192 m unnamed deep
mean depth: -3,741 m
ocean zones: the ocean is divided into three zones based on depth and light level; sunlight entering the water may travel about 1,000 m into the oceans under the right conditions, but there is rarely any significant light below 200 m
euphotic zone: the upper 200 m (656 ft) is also called "sunlight" zone; only a small amount of light penetrates beyond this depth
dysphotic zone: between 200 m (656 ft) and 1,000 m (3,280 ft), and also called the twilight zone; the intensity of light rapidly dissipates as depth increases, and photosynthesis is no longer possible
aphotic zone: below 1,000 m (3,280 ft) and also called the midnight zone; sunlight does not penetrate to these depths

Natural resources: oil and gas fields, fish, shrimp, sand and gravel aggregates, placer deposits, polymetallic nodules

Natural hazards: occasional icebergs pose navigational hazard in southern reaches

Geography - note: major chokepoints include Bab el Mandeb, Strait of Hormuz, Strait of Malacca, southern access to the Suez Canal, and the Lombok Strait

ENVIRONMENT

Environmental issues: marine pollution from ocean dumping, improper waste disposal, and oil spills; oil pollution in Arabian Sea, Persian Gulf, and Red Sea; threats to coral reefs; loss of biodiversity; endangered marine species

Climate: northeast monsoon (December to April), southwest monsoon (June to October); tropical cyclones occur during May/June and October/November in the northern Indian Ocean and January/February in the southern Indian Ocean

Marine fisheries: the Indian Ocean fisheries are the third most important in the world, accounting for 15.5%, or 12,220,000 mt of the global catch in 2020; tuna, small pelagic fish, and shrimp are important species in these regions; the Food and Agriculture Organization delineated two fishing regions in the Indian Ocean: Eastern Indian Ocean region (Region 57) is the most important and the fifth-largest-producing region in the world with 8.4%, or 6,590,000 mt, of the global catch in 2020; the region encompasses the waters north of 55° South latitude and east of 80° East longitude, including the Bay of Bengal and Andaman Sea, with the major producers including India (2,362,481 mt), Indonesia (1,940,558 mt), Burma (1,114,777 mt), Bangladesh (877,837 mt), and Sri Lanka (373,369 mt); the principal catches include shad, skipjack tuna, mackerel, shrimp, and sardinellas

Western Indian Ocean region (Region 51) is the world's sixth-largest-producing region with more than 7.1% or 5,630,000 mt of the global catch in 2020; this region encompasses the waters north of 40° South latitude and west of 80° East longitude, including the western Indian Ocean, Arabian Sea, Persian Gulf, and Red Sea, as well as the waters along the east coast of Africa and Madagascar, the south coast of the Arabian Peninsula, and the west coast of India; major producers include India (2,207,125 mt), Oman (580,048 mt), Pakistan (341,730 mt), and Mozambique (274,791 mt); the principal catches include skipjack and yellowfin tuna, mackerel, sardines, shrimp, and cephalopods

Regional fisheries bodies: Indian Ocean Tuna Commission, Commission for the Conservation of Southern Bluefin Tuna, Regional Commission for Fisheries (Persian Gulf/Gulf of Oman), Southeast Asia Fisheries Development Center, Southwest Indian Ocean Fisheries Commission, South Indian Ocean Fisheries Agreement

GOVERNMENT

Country name: *etymology:* named for the country of India, which makes up much of its northern border

INDONESIA

INTRODUCTION

Background: The archipelago was once largely under the control of Buddhist and Hindu rulers. By around the 7th century, a Buddhist kingdom arose on Sumatra and expanded into Java and the Malay Peninsula until it was conquered in the late 13th century by the Hindu Majapahit Empire from Java. Majapahit (1290-1527) united most of modern-day Indonesia and Malaysia. Traders introduced Islam around the 11th century, and the religion gradually expanded over the next 500 years. The Portuguese conquered parts of Indonesia in the 16th century, but the Dutch ousted them (except in East Timor) and began colonizing the islands in the early 17th century. It would be the early 20th century before Dutch colonial rule was established across the entirety of what would become the boundaries of the modern Indonesian state.

Japan occupied the islands from 1942 to 1945. Indonesia declared its independence shortly before Japan's surrender, but it required four years of sometimes brutal fighting, intermittent negotiations, and UN mediation before the Netherlands agreed to transfer sovereignty in 1949. A period of sometimes unruly parliamentary democracy ended in 1957 when President SOEKARNO declared martial law and instituted "Guided Democracy." After an abortive coup in 1965 by alleged communist sympathizers, SOEKARNO was gradually eased from power. From 1967 until 1998, President SUHARTO ruled Indonesia with his "New Order" government. After street protests toppled SUHARTO in 1998, free and fair legislative elections took place in 1999 while the country's first direct presidential election occurred in 2004. Indonesia has since become a robust democracy, holding four direct presidential elections, each considered by international observers to have been largely free and fair.

Indonesia is now the world's third-most-populous democracy and the world's largest Muslim-majority nation. It has had strong economic growth since overcoming the Asian financial crisis of the late 1990s. By the 2020s, it had the largest economy in Southeast Asia, and its economy ranked in the world's top 10 in terms of purchasing power parity. It has also made considerable gains in reducing poverty. Although relations amongst its diverse population–there are more than 300 ethnic groups–have been harmonious in the 2000s, there have been areas of sectarian discontent and violence, as well as instances of religious extremism and terrorism. A political settlement to an armed separatist conflict in Aceh was achieved in 2005, but a separatist group in Papua continued to conduct a low-intensity conflict as of 2024.

GEOGRAPHY

Location: Southeastern Asia, archipelago between the Indian Ocean and the Pacific Ocean

Geographic coordinates: 5 00 S, 120 00 E

Map references: Southeast Asia

Area: *total:* 1,904,569 sq km
land: 1,811,569 sq km
water: 93,000 sq km
comparison ranking: total 16

Area - comparative: slightly less than three times the size of Texas

Land boundaries: *total:* 2,958 km
border countries (3): Malaysia 1,881 km; Papua New Guinea 824 km; Timor-Leste 253 km

Coastline: 54,716 km

Maritime claims: *territorial sea:* 12 nm
exclusive economic zone: 200 nm
note: measured from claimed archipelagic straight baselines

Climate: tropical; hot, humid; more moderate in highlands

Terrain: mostly coastal lowlands; larger islands have interior mountains

Elevation: *highest point:* Puncak Jaya 4,884 m
lowest point: Indian/Pacific Oceans 0 m
mean elevation: 367 m

Natural resources: petroleum, tin, natural gas, nickel, timber, bauxite, copper, fertile soils, coal, gold, silver
note: Indonesia is the World's leading producer of nickel with an output of 1.6 million mt in 2022

Land use: *agricultural land:* 29.8% (2022 est.)
arable land: 9.5% (2022 est.)
permanent crops: 14.5% (2022 est.)
permanent pasture: 5.8% (2022 est.)
forest: 48% (2022 est.)
other: 22.2% (2022 est.)

Irrigated land: 67,220 sq km (2012)

Major lakes (area sq km): *fresh water lake(s):* Danau Toba - 1,150 sq km
note - located in the caldera of a super volcano that erupted more than 70,000 years ago; it is the largest volcanic lake in the World

Major rivers (by length in km): Sepik (shared with Papua New Guinea [s]) - 1,126 km; Fly (shared with Papua New Guinea [s]) - 1,050 km
note: [s] after country name indicates river source; [m] after country name indicates river mouth

Population distribution: major concentration on the island of Java, which is considered one of the most densely populated places on earth; of the outer islands, Sumatra contains some of the most significant clusters, particularly in the south near the Selat Sunda and along the northeastern coast near Medan; the cities of Makasar (Sulawesi), Banjarmasin (Kalimantan) are also heavily populated

Natural hazards: occasional floods; severe droughts; tsunamis; earthquakes; volcanoes; forest fires
volcanism: Indonesia contains the most volcanoes of any country in the world, with over 75 historically active; significant volcanic activity occurs on Java, Sumatra, the Sunda Islands, Halmahera Island, Sulawesi Island, Sangihe Island, and in the Banda Sea; Merapi (2,968 m), Indonesia's most active volcano, has been deemed a Decade Volcano by the International Association of Volcanology and Chemistry of the Earth's Interior, worthy of study due to its explosive history and close proximity to human populations; in 2018, a large explosion and flank collapse destroyed most of the island of Anak Krakatau (Child of Krakatau) and generated a deadly tsunami that left more than 400 dead; other notable historically active volcanoes include Agung, Awu, Karangetang, Krakatau (Krakatoa), Makian, Raung, Sinabung, and Tambora; see note 2 under "Geography - note"

Geography - note: *note 1:* 13,466 islands are in the archipelago, of which 922 are permanently inhabited; Indonesia is the world's largest country composed solely of islands; the country straddles the equator and occupies a strategic location along major sea lanes from the Indian Ocean to the Pacific Ocean
note 2: Indonesia is one of the countries along the Ring of Fire, which is a belt bordering the Pacific Ocean that contains about 75% of the world's volcanoes, up to 90% of the world's earthquakes, and 80% of tsunamis
note 3: despite having the fourth largest population in the world, Indonesia is the most heavily forested region on earth after the Amazon

PEOPLE AND SOCIETY

Population: *total:* 281,562,465 (2024 est.)
male: 140,800,047
female: 140,762,418
comparison rankings: total 4; male 4; female 4

Nationality: *noun:* Indonesian(s)
adjective: Indonesian

Ethnic groups: Javanese 40.1%, Sundanese 15.5%, Malay 3.7%, Batak 3.6%, Madurese 3%, Betawi 2.9%, Minangkabau 2.7%, Buginese 2.7%, Bantenese 2%, Banjarese 1.7%, Balinese 1.7%, Acehnese 1.4%, Dayak 1.4%, Sasak 1.3%, Chinese 1.2%, other 15% (2010 est.)

Languages: Bahasa Indonesia (official, modified form of Malay), English, Dutch, local dialects (of which the most widely spoken is Javanese); note - more than 700 languages are used in Indonesia
major-language sample(s):
Fakta Dunia, sumber informasi dasar yang sangat diperlukan. (Indonesian)

Religions: Muslim 87.4%, Protestant 7.5%, Roman Catholic 3.1%, Hindu 1.7%, other 0.8% (includes Buddhist and Confucian) (2022 est.)

Age structure: *0-14 years:* 23.8% (male 34,247,218/female 32,701,367)
15-64 years: 68.3% (male 96,268,201/female 95,961,293)
65 years and over: 8% (2024 est.) (male 10,284,628/female 12,099,758)

Dependency ratios: *total dependency ratio:* 46.5 (2024 est.)
youth dependency ratio: 34.8 (2024 est.)
elderly dependency ratio: 11.6 (2024 est.)
potential support ratio: 8.6 (2024 est.)

Median age: *total:* 31.5 years (2024 est.)
male: 30.8 years
female: 32.3 years
comparison ranking: total 125

Population growth rate: 0.73% (2024 est.)
comparison ranking: 120

Birth rate: 14.8 births/1,000 population (2024 est.)
comparison ranking: 115

Death rate: 6.8 deaths/1,000 population (2024 est.)
comparison ranking: 128

Net migration rate: -0.7 migrant(s)/1,000 population (2024 est.)
comparison ranking: 132

Population distribution: major concentration on the island of Java, which is considered one of the most densely populated places on earth; of the outer islands, Sumatra contains some of the most significant clusters, particularly in the south near the Selat Sunda and along the northeastern coast near Medan; the cities of Makasar (Sulawesi), Banjarmasin (Kalimantan) are also heavily populated

Urbanization: *urban population:* 58.6% of total population (2023)
rate of urbanization: 1.99% annual rate of change (2020-25 est.)

Major urban areas - population: 11.249 million JAKARTA (capital), 3.729 million Bekasi, 3.044 million Surabaya, 3.041 million Depok, 2.674 million Bandung, 2.514 million Tangerang (2023)

Sex ratio: *at birth:* 1.05 male(s)/female
0-14 years: 1.05 male(s)/female
15-64 years: 1 male(s)/female
65 years and over: 0.85 male(s)/female
total population: 1 male(s)/female (2024 est.)

Mother's mean age at first birth: 22.4 years (2017 est.)
note: data represents median age at first birth among women 25-49

Maternal mortality ratio: 140 deaths/100,000 live births (2023 est.)
comparison ranking: 53

Infant mortality rate: *total:* 18.9 deaths/1,000 live births (2024 est.)
male: 21.3 deaths/1,000 live births
female: 16.4 deaths/1,000 live births
comparison ranking: total 80

Life expectancy at birth: *total population:* 73.6 years (2024 est.)
male: 71.3 years
female: 76 years
comparison ranking: total population 148

Total fertility rate: 1.96 children born/woman (2024 est.)
comparison ranking: 110

Gross reproduction rate: 0.96 (2024 est.)

Drinking water source: *improved: urban:* 98.3% of population (2022 est.)
rural: 88.3% of population (2022 est.)
total: 94.1% of population (2022 est.)
unimproved: urban: 1.7% of population (2022 est.)
rural: 11.7% of population (2022 est.)
total: 5.9% of population (2022 est.)

Health expenditure: 3.7% of GDP (2021)
8% of national budget (2022 est.)

Physician density: 0.52 physicians/1,000 population (2023)

Hospital bed density: 1.4 beds/1,000 population (2021 est.)

Sanitation facility access: *improved: urban:* 97.4% of population (2022 est.)
rural: 91.1% of population (2022 est.)
total: 94.7% of population (2022 est.)
unimproved: urban: 2.6% of population (2022 est.)
rural: 8.9% of population (2022 est.)
total: 5.3% of population (2022 est.)

Obesity - adult prevalence rate: 6.9% (2016)
comparison ranking: 162

Alcohol consumption per capita: *total:* 0.08 liters of pure alcohol (2019 est.)
beer: 0.06 liters of pure alcohol (2019 est.)
wine: 0.01 liters of pure alcohol (2019 est.)
spirits: 0.02 liters of pure alcohol (2019 est.)
other alcohols: 0 liters of pure alcohol (2019 est.)
comparison ranking: total 178

Tobacco use: *total:* 39% (2025 est.)
male: 74.9% (2025 est.)
female: 3.1% (2025 est.)
comparison ranking: total 3

Children under the age of 5 years underweight: 17.7% (2018)
comparison ranking: 24

Currently married women (ages 15-49): 70% (2023 est.)

Child marriage: *women married by age 15:* 2% (2017)
women married by age 18: 16.3% (2017)

Education expenditure: 1.3% of GDP (2023 est.)
13.9% national budget (2022 est.)
comparison ranking: Education expenditure (% GDP) 194

Literacy: *total population:* 96% (2020 est.)
male: 97% (2020 est.)
female: 95% (2020 est.)

School life expectancy (primary to tertiary education): *total:* 13 years (2023 est.)
male: 13 years (2023 est.)
female: 13 years (2023 est.)

People - note: Indonesia is the fourth most populous nation in the World after China, India, and the United States; more than half of the Indonesian population - roughly 150 million people or 55% - live on the island of Java (about the size of California) making it the most crowded island on earth

ENVIRONMENT

Environmental issues: large-scale deforestation (much of it illegal) and related wildfires cause heavy smog; over-exploitation of marine resources; air pollution from vehicle emissions; waste disposal; water pollution from industrial wastes, sewage

International environmental agreements: *party to:* Biodiversity, Climate Change, Climate Change-Kyoto Protocol, Climate Change-Paris Agreement, Comprehensive Nuclear Test Ban, Desertification, Endangered Species, Hazardous Wastes, Law of the Sea, Nuclear Test Ban, Ozone Layer Protection, Ship Pollution, Tropical Timber 2006, Wetlands
signed, but not ratified: Marine Life Conservation

Climate: tropical; hot, humid; more moderate in highlands

Urbanization: *urban population:* 58.6% of total population (2023)
rate of urbanization: 1.99% annual rate of change (2020-25 est.)

Carbon dioxide emissions: 829.655 million metric tonnes of CO_2 (2023 est.)
from coal and metallurgical coke: 527.923 million metric tonnes of CO_2 (2023 est.)
from petroleum and other liquids: 223.352 million metric tonnes of CO_2 (2023 est.)
from consumed natural gas: 78.38 million metric tonnes of CO_2 (2023 est.)
comparison ranking: total emissions 6

Particulate matter emissions: 18.4 micrograms per cubic meter (2019 est.)

Methane emissions: *energy:* 3,621.7 kt (2022-2024 est.)
agriculture: 3,379.3 kt (2019-2021 est.)
waste: 4,200.1 kt (2019-2021 est.)
other: 165.7 kt (2019-2021 est.)

Waste and recycling: *municipal solid waste generated annually:* 65.2 million tons (2024 est.)
percent of municipal solid waste recycled: 15.2% (2022 est.)

Total water withdrawal: *municipal:* 23.8 billion cubic meters (2022 est.)
industrial: 9.135 billion cubic meters (2022 est.)
agricultural: 189.7 billion cubic meters (2022 est.)

Total renewable water resources: 2.019 trillion cubic meters (2022 est.)

Geoparks: *total global geoparks and regional networks:* 12 (2025)
global geoparks and regional networks: Batur; Belitong; Ciletuh - Palabuhanratu; Gunung Sewu; Ijen; Kebumen; Maros Pangkep; Merangin Jambi; Meratus; Raja Ampat; Rinjani-Lombok; Toba Caldera (2025)

GOVERNMENT

Country name: *conventional long form:* Republic of Indonesia
conventional short form: Indonesia
local long form: Republik Indonesia
local short form: Indonesia
former: Netherlands East Indies (Dutch East Indies), Netherlands New Guinea
etymology: the name is an 18th-century construct of two Greek words, "Indos" (India) and "nesoi" (islands), meaning "Indian islands"

Government type: presidential republic

Capital: *name:* Jakarta
geographic coordinates: 6 10 S, 106 49 E
time difference: UTC+7 (12 hours ahead of Washington, DC, during Standard Time)
time zone note: Indonesia has three time zones
etymology: derives from the Sanscrit name Jayakarta, meaning "victory and prosperity;" Prince FATILLAH conquered and renamed the city, formerly known as Sunda Kelapa, in 1527
note: in 2022, the relocation of the country's capital was approved, from Jakarta to a site on the island of Borneo between Samarinda City and the port city of Balikpapan; Nusantara ("archipelago"), the new capital, was in development as of 2024 and is expected to be completed in 2045

Administrative divisions: 35 provinces *(provinsi-provinsi*, singular - *provinsi)*, 1 autonomous province*, 1 special region** *(daerah istimewa)*, and 1 national capital district*** *(daerah khusus ibukota)*; Aceh*, Bali, Banten, Bengkulu, Gorontalo, Jakarta***, Jambi, Jawa Barat (West Java), Jawa Tengah (Central Java), Jawa Timur (East Java), Kalimantan Barat (West Kalimantan), Kalimantan Selatan (South Kalimantan), Kalimantan Tengah (Central Kalimantan), Kalimantan Timur (East Kalimantan), Kalimantan Utara (North Kalimantan), Kepulauan Bangka Belitung (Bangka Belitung Islands), Kepulauan Riau (Riau Islands), Lampung, Maluku, Maluku Utara (North Maluku), Nusa Tenggara Barat (West Nusa Tenggara), Nusa Tenggara Timur (East Nusa Tenggara), Papua, Papua Barat (West Papua), Papua Barat Daya (Southwest Papua), Papua Pegunungan (Papua Highlands), Papua Selatan (South Papua), Papua Tengah (Central Papua), Riau, Sulawesi Barat (West Sulawesi), Sulawesi Selatan (South Sulawesi), Sulawesi Tengah (Central Sulawesi), Sulawesi Tenggara (Southeast Sulawesi), Sulawesi Utara (North Sulawesi), Sumatera Barat (West Sumatra), Sumatera Selatan (South Sumatra), Sumatera Utara (North Sumatra), Yogyakarta**

Legal system: civil law system based on the Roman-Dutch model and influenced by customary law

Constitution: *history:* drafted July to August 1945, effective 18 August 1945, abrogated by 1949 and 1950 constitutions; 1945 constitution restored 5 July 1959
amendment process: proposed by the People's Consultative Assembly, with at least two thirds of its members present; passage requires simple majority vote by the Assembly membership; constitutional articles on the unitary form of the state cannot be amended

International law organization participation: has not submitted an ICJ jurisdiction declaration; non-party state to the ICCt

Citizenship: *citizenship by birth:* no
citizenship by descent only: at least one parent must be a citizen of Indonesia
dual citizenship recognized: no
residency requirement for naturalization: 5 continuous years

Suffrage: 17 years of age; universal; married persons regardless of age

Executive branch: *chief of state:* President PRABOWO Subianto Djojohadikusumo (since 20 October 2024)
head of government: President PRABOWO Subianto Djojohadikusumo (since 20 October 2024)
cabinet: Cabinet appointed by the president

election/appointment process: president and vice president directly elected by absolute-majority popular vote for a 5-year term (eligible for a second term)
most recent election date: 14 February 2024
election results: *2024:* PRABOWO Subianto elected president (assumes office 20 October 2024); percent of vote - PRABOWO Subianto (GERINDRA) 58.6%, Anies Rasyid BASWEDAN (Independent) 24.9%, GANJAR Pranowo (PDI-P) 16.5%
2019: Joko WIDODO reelected president; percent of vote - Joko WIDODO (PDI-P) 55.5%, PRABOWO Subianto Djojohadikusumo (GERINDRA) 44.5%
expected date of next election: 2029
note: the president is both chief of state and head of government

Legislative branch: *legislature name:* House of Representatives (Dewan Perwakilan Rakyat)
legislative structure: unicameral
number of seats: 580 (all directly elected)
electoral system: proportional representation
scope of elections: full renewal
term in office: 5 years
most recent election date: 2/14/2024
parties elected and seats per party: Indonesian Democratic Party - Struggle (PDI-P) (110); Party of Functional Groups (Golkar) (102); Great Indonesia Movement (Gerindra) (86); National Democratic Party (NasDem) (69); National Awakening Party (PKB) (68); Prosperous Justice Party (PKS) (53); National Mandate Party (PAN) (48); Democratic Party (PD) (44)
percentage of women in chamber: 21.9%
expected date of next election: April 2029

Judicial branch: *highest court(s):* Supreme Court or Mahkamah Agung (51 judges divided into 8 chambers); Constitutional Court or Mahkamah Konstitusi (consists of 9 judges)
judge selection and term of office: Supreme Court judges nominated by Judicial Commission, appointed by president with concurrence of parliament; judges serve until retirement at age 65; Constitutional Court judges - 3 nominated by president, 3 by Supreme Court, and 3 by parliament; judges appointed by the president; judges serve until mandatory retirement at age 70
subordinate courts: High Courts of Appeal, district courts, religious courts

Political parties: Democrat Party or PD
Functional Groups Party or GOLKAR
Great Indonesia Movement Party or GERINDRA
Indonesia Democratic Party-Struggle or PDI-P
National Awakening Party or PKB
National Democratic Party or NasDem
National Mandate Party or PAN
Prosperous Justice Party or PKS

Diplomatic representation in the US: *chief of mission:* Ambassador-designate INDROYONO Soesilo; Chargé d'Affaires Nidya KARTIKASARI (since 1 September 2025)
chancery: 2020 Massachusetts Avenue NW, Washington, DC 20036
telephone: [1] (202) 775-5200
FAX: [1] (202) 775-5236
email address and website: washington.kbri@kemlu.go.id
Embassy of The Republic of Indonesia, in Washington D.C., The United States of America (kemlu.go.id)
consulate(s) general: Chicago, Houston, Los Angeles, New York, San Francisco

Diplomatic representation from the US: *chief of mission:* Ambassador (vacant); Chargé d'Affaires Peter M. HAYMOND (since 15 June 2025)
embassy: Jl. Medan Merdeka Selatan No. 3-5, Jakarta 10110
mailing address: 8200 Jakarta Place, Washington DC 20521-8200
telephone: [62] (21) 5083-1000
FAX: [62] (21) 385-7189
email address and website: jakartaacs@state.gov
https://id.usembassy.gov/
consulate(s) general: Surabaya
consulate(s): Medan

International organization participation: ADB, APEC, ARF, ASEAN, BIS, CD, CICA (observer), CP, D-8, EAS, EITI (compliant country), FAO, G-11, G-15, G-20, G-77, IAEA, IBRD, ICAO, ICC (national committees), ICRM, IDA, IDB, IFAD, IFC, IFRCS, IHO, ILO, IMF, IMO, IMSO, Interpol, IOC, IOM (observer), IORA, IPU, ISO, ITSO, ITU, ITUC (NGOs), MIGA, MINURSO, MINUSTAH, MONUSCO, MSG (associate member), NAM, OECD (enhanced engagement), OIC, OPCW, PIF (partner), UN, UNAMID, UNCTAD, UNESCO, UNHRC, UNIDO, UNIFIL, UNISFA, UNMIL, UNOOSA, UNWTO, UPU, WCO, WFTU (NGOs), WHO, WIPO, WMO, WTO

Independence: 17 August 1945 (declared independence from the Netherlands)

National holiday: Independence Day, 17 August (1945)

Flag: *description:* two equal horizontal bands of red (top) and white
meaning: red stands for courage and white for purity
history: the colors derive from the banner of the Majapahit Empire of the 13th-15th centuries
note: similar to the flags of Monaco, which is shorter, and Poland, which is white (top) and red

National symbol(s): garuda (mythical bird)

National color(s): red, white

National anthem(s): *title:* "Indonesia Raya" (Great Indonesia)
lyrics/music: Wage Rudolf SOEPRATMAN
history: adopted 1945

National heritage: *total World Heritage Sites:* 10 (6 cultural, 4 natural)
selected World Heritage Site locales: Borobudur Temple Compounds (c); Komodo National Park (n); Prambanan Temple Compounds (c); Ujung Kulon National Park (n); Sangiran Early Man Site (c); Lorentz National Park (n); Tropical Rainforest Heritage of Sumatra (n); Cultural Landscape of Bali Province (c); Ombilin Coal Mining Heritage of Sawahlunto (c); Cosmological Axis of Yogyakarta and its Historic Landmarks (c)

ECONOMY

Economic overview: one of the fastest growing economies and largest in Southeast Asia; upper middle-income country; human capital and competitiveness phase of its 20-year development plan; COVID-19 reversed poverty reduction trajectory; strengthening financial resilience

Real GDP (purchasing power parity): $4.102 trillion (2024 est.)
$3.906 trillion (2023 est.)
$3.718 trillion (2022 est.)
note: data in 2021 dollars
comparison ranking: 8

Real GDP growth rate: 5% (2024 est.)
5% (2023 est.)
5.3% (2022 est.)
note: annual GDP % growth based on constant local currency
comparison ranking: 43

Real GDP per capita: $14,500 (2024 est.)
$13,900 (2023 est.)
$13,300 (2022 est.)
note: data in 2021 dollars
comparison ranking: 126

GDP (official exchange rate): $1.396 trillion (2024 est.)
note: data in current dollars at official exchange rate

Inflation rate (consumer prices): 3.7% (2023 est.)
4.2% (2022 est.)
1.6% (2021 est.)
note: annual % change based on consumer prices
comparison ranking: 117

GDP - composition, by sector of origin: *agriculture:* 12.6% (2024 est.)
industry: 39.3% (2024 est.)
services: 43.8% (2024 est.)
note: figures may not total 100% due to non-allocated consumption not captured in sector-reported data
comparison rankings: agriculture 63; industry 21; services 180

GDP - composition, by end use: *household consumption:* 55.4% (2024 est.)
government consumption: 7.7% (2024 est.)
investment in fixed capital: 29.1% (2024 est.)
investment in inventories: 2.3% (2024 est.)
exports of goods and services: 22.2% (2024 est.)
imports of goods and services: -20.4% (2024 est.)
note: figures may not total 100% due to rounding or gaps in data collection

Agricultural products: oil palm fruit, rice, sugarcane, maize, coconuts, cassava, bananas, eggs, chicken, mangoes/guavas (2023)
note: top ten agricultural products based on tonnage

Industries: petroleum and natural gas, textiles, automotive, electrical appliances, apparel, footwear, mining, cement, medical instruments and appliances, handicrafts, chemical fertilizers, plywood, rubber, processed food, jewelry, and tourism

Industrial production growth rate: 5.2% (2024 est.)
note: annual % change in industrial value added based on constant local currency
comparison ranking: 42

Labor force: 143.144 million (2024 est.)
note: number of people ages 15 or older who are employed or seeking work
comparison ranking: 4

Unemployment rate: 3.3% (2024 est.)
3.4% (2023 est.)
3.5% (2022 est.)
note: % of labor force seeking employment
comparison ranking: 51

Youth unemployment rate (ages 15-24): *total:* 13.1% (2024 est.)
male: 13.2% (2024 est.)
female: 13% (2024 est.)
note: % of labor force ages 15-24 seeking employment
comparison ranking: total 95

Population below poverty line: 9% (2024 est.)
note: % of population with income below national poverty line
Gini Index coefficient - distribution of family income 34.9 (2024 est.)

note: index (0-100) of income distribution; higher values represent greater inequality
comparison ranking: 77

Average household expenditures: *on food:* 33.5% of household expenditures (2023 est.)
on alcohol and tobacco: 7.3% of household expenditures (2023 est.)

Household income or consumption by percentage share: *lowest 10%:* 3.5% (2024 est.)
highest 10%: 28.8% (2024 est.)
note: % share of income accruing to lowest and highest 10% of population

Remittances: 1.1% of GDP (2024 est.)
1.1% of GDP (2023 est.)
1% of GDP (2022 est.)
note: personal transfers and compensation between resident and non-resident individuals/households/entities

Budget: *revenues:* $182.658 billion (2023 est.)
expenditures: $204.739 billion (2023 est.)
note: central government revenues and expenditures (excluding grants and social security funds) converted to US dollars at average official exchange rate for year indicated

Public debt: 45.34% of GDP (2022 est.)
note: central government debt as a % of GDP
comparison ranking: 119

Taxes and other revenues: 11.6% (of GDP) (2022 est.)
note: central government tax revenue as a % of GDP
comparison ranking: 118

Current account balance: -$8.47 billion (2024 est.)
-$2.042 billion (2023 est.)
$13.215 billion (2022 est.)
note: balance of payments - net trade and primary/secondary income in current dollars
comparison ranking: 181

Exports: $300.868 billion (2024 est.)
$291.287 billion (2023 est.)
$315.746 billion (2022 est.)
note: balance of payments - exports of goods and services in current dollars
comparison ranking: 31

Exports - partners: China 24%, USA 9%, India 8%, Japan 8%, Singapore 5% (2023)
note: top five export partners based on percentage share of exports

Exports - commodities: coal, palm oil, iron alloys, lignite, garments (2023)
note: top five export commodities based on value in dollars

Imports: $279.419 billion (2024 est.)
$262.694 billion (2023 est.)
$273.031 billion (2022 est.)
note: balance of payments - imports of goods and services in current dollars
comparison ranking: 31

Imports - partners: China 29%, Singapore 8%, Japan 7%, USA 5%, Malaysia 5% (2023)
note: top five import partners based on percentage share of imports

Imports - commodities: refined petroleum, crude petroleum, plastics, vehicle parts/accessories, integrated circuits (2023)
note: top five import commodities based on value in dollars

Reserves of foreign exchange and gold: $155.708 billion (2024 est.)
$146.359 billion (2023 est.)
$137.222 billion (2022 est.)
note: holdings of gold (year-end prices)/foreign exchange/special drawing rights in current dollars
comparison ranking: 21

Debt - external: $225.273 billion (2023 est.)
note: present value of external debt in current US dollars
comparison ranking: 3

Exchange rates: Indonesian rupiah (IDR) per US dollar -

Exchange rates: 15,855.448 (2024 est.)
15,236.885 (2023 est.)
14,849.854 (2022 est.)
14,308.144 (2021 est.)
14,582.203 (2020 est.)

ENERGY

Electricity access: *electrification - total population:* 100% (2022 est.)
electrification - urban areas: 100%
electrification - rural areas: 98.2%

Electricity: *installed generating capacity:* 70.826 million kW (2023 est.)
consumption: 356.135 billion kWh (2023 est.)
imports: 828.198 million kWh (2023 est.)
transmission/distribution losses: 27.477 billion kWh (2023 est.)
comparison rankings: installed generating capacity 20; consumption 12; imports 83; transmission/distribution losses 196

Electricity generation sources: *fossil fuels:* 82% of total installed capacity (2023 est.)
solar: 0.2% of total installed capacity (2023 est.)
wind: 0.1% of total installed capacity (2023 est.)
hydroelectricity: 6.4% of total installed capacity (2023 est.)
geothermal: 4.4% of total installed capacity (2023 est.)
biomass and waste: 6.9% of total installed capacity (2023 est.)

Coal: *production:* 783.453 million metric tons (2023 est.)
consumption: 281.159 million metric tons (2023 est.)
exports: 519.23 million metric tons (2023 est.)
imports: 16.935 million metric tons (2023 est.)
proven reserves: 35.055 billion metric tons (2023 est.)

Petroleum: *total petroleum production:* 865,000 bbl/day (2023 est.)
refined petroleum consumption: 1.645 million bbl/day (2023 est.)
crude oil estimated reserves: 2.48 billion barrels (2021 est.)

Natural gas: *production:* 58.691 billion cubic meters (2023 est.)
consumption: 38.378 billion cubic meters (2023 est.)
exports: 20.989 billion cubic meters (2023 est.)
imports: 727.056 million cubic meters (2023 est.)
proven reserves: 1.408 trillion cubic meters (2021 est.)

Energy consumption per capita: 37.39 million Btu/person (2023 est.)
comparison ranking: 104

COMMUNICATIONS

Telephones - fixed lines: *total subscriptions:* 9.16 million (2023 est.)
subscriptions per 100 inhabitants: 3 (2023 est.)
comparison ranking: total subscriptions 19

Telephones - mobile cellular: *total subscriptions:* 352 million (2023 est.)
subscriptions per 100 inhabitants: 115 (2022 est.)
comparison ranking: total subscriptions 4

Broadcast media: mix of about a dozen national TV networks, including 1 public broadcaster and the rest private; more than 100 local TV stations; widespread use of satellite and cable TV systems; public radio broadcaster operates 6 national networks, as well as regional and local stations; more than 700 radio stations, with over 650 privately operated (2019)

Internet country code: .id

Internet users: *percent of population:* 69% (2023 est.)

Broadband - fixed subscriptions: *total:* 13.5 million (2023 est.)
subscriptions per 100 inhabitants: 5 (2023 est.)
comparison ranking: total 19

TRANSPORTATION

Civil aircraft registration country code prefix: PK

Airports: 556 (2025)
comparison ranking: 15

Heliports: 53 (2025)
comparison ranking: 38

Railways: *total:* 8,159 km (2014)
narrow gauge: 8,159 km (2014) 1.067-m gauge (565 km electrified)
note: 4,816 km operational

Merchant marine: *total:* 11,422 (2023)
by type: bulk carrier 160, container ship 219, general cargo 2,347, oil tanker 714, other 7,982
comparison ranking: total 1

Ports: *total ports:* 123 (2024)
large: 3
medium: 6
small: 18
very small: 96
ports with oil terminals: 79
key ports: Belawan, Cilacap, Dumai, Jakarta, Kasim Terminal, Merak Mas Terminal, Palembang, Surabaya, Ujung Pandang

MILITARY AND SECURITY

Military and security forces: Indonesian National Armed Forces (Tentara Nasional Indonesia, TNI): Army (TNI-Angkatan Darat, TNI-AD), Navy (TNI-Angkatan Laut, TNI-AL; includes Marine Corps (Korps Marinir or KorMar)), Air Force (TNI-Angkatan Udara, TNI-AU)
Indonesian National Police (aka The State Police of the Republic of Indonesia or POLRI)

Ministry of Transportation: Indonesia Sea and Coast Guard (Kesatuan Penjagaan Laut dan Pantai Republik Indonesia, KPLP); Coordinating Ministry for Political, Legal, and Security Affairs: Maritime Security Agency of the Republic of Indonesia (Badan Keamanan Laut Republik Indonesia, Bakamla) (2025)
note 1: the National Police are an independent organization reporting directly to the president of Indonesia
note 2: the KPLP ensures the safety of shipping inside the Indonesian Maritime Zone; the Bakamla conducts security and safety patrols in the territorial waters of Indonesia

Military expenditures: 0.8% of GDP (2024 est.)
0.8% of GDP (2023 est.)
0.8% of GDP (2022 est.)

0.8% of GDP (2021 est.)
0.8% of GDP (2020 est.)

Military and security service personnel strengths: approximately 400,000 active Armed Forces, including about 300,000 Army (2025)

Military equipment inventories and acquisitions: the military's inventory is a wide mix of Chinese, Russian, and Western (including US) equipment; in recent years, major suppliers have included China, France, Germany, the Netherlands, South Korea, and the US; the TNI has been engaged in a modernization program for more than a decade; Indonesia has a growing defense industry fueled by technology transfers and cooperation agreements with several countries; in 2019, the Indonesian Government said that growing its domestic defense industry would be a national priority over the following decade (2024)

Military service age and obligation: 18-45 years of age for voluntary military service for men and women, with selective conscription authorized (men, age 18), but not utilized; 24-month service obligation, with reserve obligation to age 45 (officers) (2024)
note: as of 2023, women comprised about 7% of the Indonesian military

Military deployments: 225 (plus about 140 police) Central African Republic (MINUSCA); 1,025 Democratic Republic of the Congo (MONUSCO); 1,225 Lebanon (UNIFIL) (2024)

Military - note: the military is responsible for external defense, combatting separatism, and responding to national emergencies and natural disasters; in certain conditions it may provide operational support to police, such as for counterterrorism operations, maintaining public order, and addressing communal conflicts
key operational priorities include an insurgency on Papua and the security of Indonesia's vast maritime domain; the West Papua Liberation Army, the military wing of the Free Papua Organization, has been fighting a low-level insurgency in Papua since Indonesia annexed the former Dutch colony in the 1960s; maritime issues include piracy, transnational crime, illegal fishing, and incursions by People's Republic of China (PRC) vessels; Indonesia is not a formal claimant in the South China Sea, although some of its waters lie within the PRC's "nine-dash line" maritime claims, resulting in some stand offs in recent years; over the past decade, the Indonesian military has bolstered its presence on and around the strategically located Natuna Islands (2025)

SPACE

Space agency/agencies: Indonesian Space Agency (INASA; formed 2022); National Research and Innovation Agency (BRIN; established 2021); Research Organization for Aeronautics and Space (ORPA; formed 2021) (2025)

Space program overview: space program focused largely on rocket development and the acquisition and operation of satellites; operates satellites; manufactures remote sensing (RS) satellites; has a sounding (research) rocket program geared towards development of an indigenous orbital satellite launch vehicle (SLV) and independent satellite launch capabilities; researching and developing a range of other space-related technologies and capabilities related to satellite payloads, communications, RS, and astronomy; has relations with several foreign space agencies and industries, including those of France, Germany, India, Japan, Russia, South Korea, and the US; national space program includes building up the country's private space sector (2025)
note: further details about the key activities, programs, and milestones of the country's space program, as well as government spending estimates on the space sector, appear in the Space Programs reference guide

TERRORISM

Terrorist group(s): Terrorist group(s): Islamic State of Iraq and ash-Sham (aka Jemaah Anshorut Daulah); Jemaah Islamiyah
note: details about the history, aims, leadership, organization, areas of operation, tactics, targets, weapons, size, and sources of support of the group(s) appear(s) in Appendix T

TRANSNATIONAL ISSUES

Refugees and internally displaced persons: *refugees:* 11,964 (2024 est.)
IDPs: 95,521 (2024 est.)
stateless persons: 2,643 (2024 est.)

IRAN

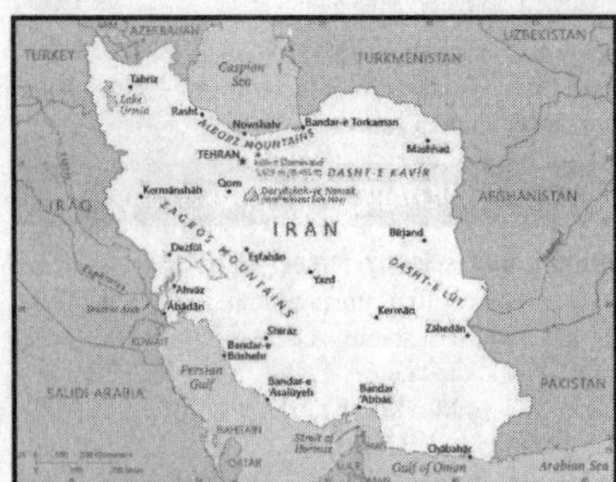

INTRODUCTION

Background: Known as Persia until 1935, Iran became an Islamic republic in 1979 after the ruling monarchy was overthrown and Shah Mohammad Reza PAHLAVI was forced into exile. Conservative clerical forces led by Ayatollah Ruhollah KHOMEINI established a theocratic system of government with ultimate political authority vested in a religious scholar known as the Supreme Leader, who is accountable only to the Assembly of Experts – an elected 88-member body of clerics. US-Iran relations became strained when Iranian students seized the US Embassy in Tehran in November 1979 and held embassy personnel hostage until mid-January 1981. The US cut off diplomatic relations with Iran in April 1980. From 1980 to 1988, Iran fought a bloody, indecisive war with Iraq that eventually expanded into the Persian Gulf and led to clashes between US Navy and Iranian military forces. Iran has been designated a state sponsor of terrorism since 1984.

After the election of reformer Hojjat ol-Eslam Mohammad KHATAMI as president in 1997 and a reformist Majles (legislature) in 2000, a political reform campaign in response to popular dissatisfaction was initiated, but conservative politicians blocked reform measures while increasing repression. Municipal and legislative elections in 2003 and 2004 saw conservatives reestablish control over Iran's elected government institutions, culminating in the 2005 inauguration of hardliner Mahmud AHMADI-NEJAD as president. His reelection in 2009 sparked nationwide protests over allegations of electoral fraud, and the protests persisted until 2011. In 2013, Iranians elected to the presidency centrist cleric Dr. Hasan Fereidun RUHANI, a longtime senior regime member who promised to reform society and foreign policy. In 2019, Tehran's sudden decision to increase the gasoline price sparked nationwide protests, which the regime violently suppressed. Conservatives won the majority in Majles elections in 2020, and hardline cleric Ebrahim RAISI was elected president in 2021, resulting in a conservative monopoly across the regime's elected and unelected institutions.

Iran continues to be subject to a range of international sanctions and export controls because of its involvement in terrorism, weapons proliferation, human rights abuses, and concerns over the nature of its nuclear program. Iran received nuclear-related sanctions relief in exchange for nuclear concessions under the Joint Comprehensive Plan of Action's (JCPOA) Implementation Day beginning in 2016. However, the US reimposed nuclear-related sanctions on Iran after it unilaterally terminated its JCPOA participation in 2018. In October 2023, the EU and the UK also decided to maintain nuclear-proliferation-related measures on Iran, as well as arms and missile embargoes, in response to Iran's non-compliance with its JCPOA commitments.

As president, RAISI has concentrated on deepening Iran's foreign relations with anti-US states – particularly China and Russia – to weather US sanctions and diplomatic pressure, while supporting negotiations to restore a nuclear deal that began in 2021. RAISI contended with nationwide protests that began in September 2022 and persisted for over three months after the death of a Kurdish Iranian woman, Mahsa AMINI, in morality police custody. Young people and women led the protests, and demands focused on regime change.

GEOGRAPHY

Location: Middle East, bordering the Gulf of Oman, the Persian Gulf, and the Caspian Sea, between Iraq and Pakistan

Geographic coordinates: 32 00 N, 53 00 E

Map references: Middle East

Area: *total:* 1,648,195 sq km

land: 1,531,595 sq km
water: 116,600 sq km
comparison ranking: total 19

Area - comparative: almost 2.5 times the size of Texas; slightly smaller than Alaska

Land boundaries: *total:* 5,894 km
border countries (7): Afghanistan 921 km; Armenia 44 km; Azerbaijan 689 km; Iraq 1,599 km; Pakistan 959 km; Turkey 534 km; Turkmenistan 1,148 km

Coastline: 2,440 km
note: Iran also borders the Caspian Sea (740 km)

Maritime claims: *territorial sea:* 12 nm
contiguous zone: 24 nm
exclusive economic zone: bilateral agreements or median lines in the Persian Gulf
continental shelf: natural prolongation

Climate: mostly arid or semiarid, subtropical along Caspian coast

Terrain: rugged, mountainous rim; high, central basin with deserts, mountains; small, discontinuous plains along both coasts

Elevation: *highest point:* Kuh-e Damavand 5,625 m
lowest point: Caspian Sea -28 m
mean elevation: 1,305 m

Natural resources: petroleum, natural gas, coal, chromium, copper, iron ore, lead, manganese, zinc, sulfur

Land use: *agricultural land:* 29% (2022 est.)
arable land: 9.7% (2022 est.)
permanent crops: 1.2% (2022 est.)
permanent pasture: 18.2% (2022 est.)
forest: 6.6% (2022 est.)
other: 64.4% (2022 est.)

Irrigated land: 79,721 sq km (2020)

Major lakes (area sq km): *salt water lake(s):* Caspian Sea (shared with Russia, Azerbaijan, Turkmenistan, and Kazakhstan) - 374,000 sq km; Lake Urmia - 5,200 sq km; Lake Namak - 750 sq km

Major rivers (by length in km): Euphrates (shared with Turkey [s], Syria, and Iraq [m]) - 3,596 km; Tigris (shared with Turkey, Syria, and Iraq [m]) - 1,950 km; Helmand (shared with Afghanistan [s]) - 1,130 km
note: [s] after country name indicates river source; [m] after country name indicates river mouth

Major watersheds (area sq km): Indian Ocean drainage: *(Persian Gulf)* Tigris and Euphrates (918,044 sq km)

Population distribution: population is concentrated in the north, northwest, and west, reflecting the position of the Zagros and Elburz Mountains; the vast, dry areas in the center and eastern parts of the country, around the deserts of the Dasht-e Kavir and Dasht-e Lut, have a much lower population density

Natural hazards: periodic droughts, floods; dust storms, sandstorms; earthquakes

Geography - note: strategic location on the Persian Gulf and Strait of Hormuz

PEOPLE AND SOCIETY

Population: *total:* 88,386,937 (2024 est.)
male: 44,795,539
female: 43,591,398
comparison rankings: total 17; male 17; female 17

Nationality: *noun:* Iranian(s)
adjective: Iranian

Ethnic groups: Persian, Azeri, Kurd, Lur, Baloch, Arab, Turkmen, and Turkic tribes

Languages: Persian Farsi (official), Azeri and other Turkic dialects, Kurdish, Gilaki and Mazandarani, Luri, Balochi, Arabic
major-language sample(s):

ی برای کسب اطلاعات کلی جهان
چکیده نامه جهان، منبعی ضرور

(Persian)

Religions: Muslim (official) 98.5%, Christian 0.7%, Baha'i 0.3%, agnostic 0.3%, other (includes Zoroastrian, Jewish, Hindu) 0.2% (2020 est.)

Age structure: *0-14 years:* 23.3% (male 10,512,797/female 10,040,282)
15-64 years: 69.8% (male 31,413,125/female 30,267,241)
65 years and over: 7% (2024 est.) (male 2,869,617/female 3,283,875)

Dependency ratios: *total dependency ratio:* 43.3 (2024 est.)
youth dependency ratio: 33.3 (2024 est.)
elderly dependency ratio: 10 (2024 est.)
potential support ratio: 10 (2024 est.)

Median age: *total:* 33.8 years (2024 est.)
male: 33.6 years
female: 34.1 years
comparison ranking: total 110

Population growth rate: 0.88% (2024 est.)
comparison ranking: 104

Birth rate: 14.3 births/1,000 population (2024 est.)
comparison ranking: 119

Death rate: 5.3 deaths/1,000 population (2024 est.)
comparison ranking: 187

Net migration rate: -0.3 migrant(s)/1,000 population (2024 est.)
comparison ranking: 113

Population distribution: population is concentrated in the north, northwest, and west, reflecting the position of the Zagros and Elburz Mountains; the vast, dry areas in the center and eastern parts of the country, around the deserts of the Dasht-e Kavir and Dasht-e Lut, have a much lower population density

Urbanization: *urban population:* 77.3% of total population (2023)
rate of urbanization: 1.32% annual rate of change (2020-25 est.)

Major urban areas - population: 9.500 million TEHRAN (capital), 3.368 million Mashhad, 2.258 million Esfahan, 1.721 million Shiraz, 1.661 million Tabriz, 1.594 million Karaj (2023)

Sex ratio: *at birth:* 1.05 male(s)/female
0-14 years: 1.05 male(s)/female
15-64 years: 1.04 male(s)/female
65 years and over: 0.87 male(s)/female
total population: 1.03 male(s)/female (2024 est.)

Maternal mortality ratio: 16 deaths/100,000 live births (2023 est.)
comparison ranking: 134

Infant mortality rate: *total:* 14.3 deaths/1,000 live births (2024 est.)
male: 15.4 deaths/1,000 live births
female: 13.2 deaths/1,000 live births
comparison ranking: total 97

Life expectancy at birth: *total population:* 75.6 years (2024 est.)
male: 74.3 years
female: 77.1 years
comparison ranking: total population 125

Total fertility rate: 1.91 children born/woman (2024 est.)
comparison ranking: 117

Gross reproduction rate: 0.93 (2024 est.)

Drinking water source: *improved:* *urban:* 98.7% of population (2022 est.)
rural: 94.4% of population (2022 est.)
total: 97.7% of population (2022 est.)
unimproved: *urban:* 1.3% of population (2022 est.)
rural: 5.6% of population (2022 est.)
total: 2.3% of population (2022 est.)

Health expenditure: 5.8% of GDP (2021)
19% of national budget (2022 est.)

Physician density: 1.81 physicians/1,000 population (2023)

Hospital bed density: 1.9 beds/1,000 population (2019 est.)

Sanitation facility access: *improved:* *urban:* 100% of population (2022 est.)
rural: 100% of population (2022 est.)
total: 100% of population (2022 est.)
unimproved: *urban:* 0% of population (2022 est.)
rural: 0% of population (2022 est.)
total: 0% of population (2022 est.)

Obesity - adult prevalence rate: 25.8% (2016)
comparison ranking: 47

Alcohol consumption per capita: *total:* 0.02 liters of pure alcohol (2019 est.)
beer: 0 liters of pure alcohol (2019 est.)
wine: 0 liters of pure alcohol (2019 est.)
spirits: 0.02 liters of pure alcohol (2019 est.)
other alcohols: 0 liters of pure alcohol (2019 est.)
comparison ranking: total 181

Tobacco use: *total:* 13.3% (2025 est.)
male: 23.8% (2025 est.)
female: 2.8% (2025 est.)
comparison ranking: total 108

Children under the age of 5 years underweight: 4.3% (2017)
comparison ranking: 69

Currently married women (ages 15-49): 70.3% (2023 est.)

Education expenditure: 2.8% of GDP (2023 est.)
18.8% national budget (2022 est.)
comparison ranking: Education expenditure (% GDP) 162

Literacy: *total population:* 86% (2016 est.)
male: 90% (2016 est.)
female: 81% (2016 est.)

School life expectancy (primary to tertiary education): *total:* 14 years (2020 est.)
male: 14 years (2020 est.)
female: 14 years (2020 est.)

ENVIRONMENT

Environmental issues: air pollution, especially in urban areas, from vehicle emissions, refinery operations, and industrial effluents; deforestation; overgrazing; desertification; oil pollution in the Persian Gulf; wetland losses from drought; soil degradation (salination); inadequate potable water; water pollution from raw sewage and industrial waste

International environmental agreements: *party to:* Biodiversity, Climate Change, Climate Change-Kyoto Protocol, Desertification, Endangered Species, Hazardous Wastes, Marine Dumping-London Convention, Marine Dumping-London Protocol,

Nuclear Test Ban, Ozone Layer Protection, Ship Pollution, Wetlands
signed, but not ratified: Climate Change-Paris Agreement, Comprehensive Nuclear Test Ban, Environmental Modification, Law of the Sea, Marine Life Conservation

Climate: mostly arid or semiarid, subtropical along Caspian coast

Urbanization: *urban population:* 77.3% of total population (2023)
rate of urbanization: 1.32% annual rate of change (2020-25 est.)

Carbon dioxide emissions: 823.364 million metric tonnes of CO2 (2023 est.)
from coal and metallurgical coke: 7.136 million metric tonnes of CO2 (2023 est.)
from petroleum and other liquids: 316.922 million metric tonnes of CO2 (2023 est.)
from consumed natural gas: 499.306 million metric tonnes of CO2 (2023 est.)
comparison ranking: total emissions 7

Particulate matter emissions: 36.4 micrograms per cubic meter (2019 est.)

Methane emissions: *energy:* 6,208.1 kt (2022-2024 est.)
agriculture: 819.7 kt (2019-2021 est.)
waste: 832.7 kt (2019-2021 est.)
other: 37.6 kt (2019-2021 est.)

Waste and recycling: *municipal solid waste generated annually:* 17.885 million tons (2024 est.)
percent of municipal solid waste recycled: 16.8% (2022 est.)

Total water withdrawal: *municipal:* 6.2 billion cubic meters (2022 est.)
industrial: 1.1 billion cubic meters (2022 est.)
agricultural: 86 billion cubic meters (2022 est.)

Total renewable water resources: 137 billion cubic meters (2022 est.)

Geoparks: *total global geoparks and regional networks:* 3
global geoparks and regional networks: Aras; Qeshm Island; Tabas (2023)

GOVERNMENT

Country name: *conventional long form:* Islamic Republic of Iran
conventional short form: Iran
local long form: Jomhuri-ye Eslami-ye Iran
local short form: Iran
former: Persia
etymology: the name derives from the Sanskrit word *arya*, referring to people living in a mountainous land, from the root word *ar-*, or "mountain;" the former name, Persia, was originally "Pars" (or the Arabic-influenced variant "Fars") from the Old Persian *parsi*, meaning "pure"

Government type: theocratic republic

Capital: *name:* Tehran
geographic coordinates: 35 42 N, 51 25 E
time difference: UTC+3.5 (8.5 hours ahead of Washington, DC)
daylight saving time: does not observe daylight savings time
etymology: the name probably means "flat" or "lower," referring to its location in the foothills of the Elburz Mountains

Administrative divisions: 31 provinces (*ostanha*, singular - *ostan*); Alborz, Ardabil, Azarbayjan-e Gharbi (West Azerbaijan), Azarbayjan-e Sharqi (East Azerbaijan), Bushehr, Chahar Mahal va Bakhtiari, Esfahan, Fars, Gilan, Golestan, Hamadan, Hormozgan, Ilam, Kerman, Kermanshah, Khorasan-e Jonubi (South Khorasan), Khorasan-e Razavi (Razavi Khorasan), Khorasan-e Shomali (North Khorasan), Khuzestan, Kohgiluyeh va Bowyer Ahmad, Kordestan, Lorestan, Markazi, Mazandaran, Qazvin, Qom, Semnan, Sistan va Baluchestan, Tehran, Yazd, Zanjan

Legal system: religious system based on secular and Islamic law

Constitution: *history:* previous 1906; latest adopted 24 October 1979, effective 3 December 1979
amendment process: proposed by the supreme leader – after consultation with the Exigency Council – and submitted as an edict to the "Council for Revision of the Constitution," a body consisting of various executive, legislative, judicial, and academic leaders and members; passage requires absolute majority vote in a referendum and approval of the supreme leader; articles including Iran's political system, its religious basis, and its form of government cannot be amended

International law organization participation: has not submitted an ICJ jurisdiction declaration; non-party state to the ICCt

Citizenship: *citizenship by birth:* no
citizenship by descent only: the father must be a citizen of Iran
dual citizenship recognized: no
residency requirement for naturalization: 5 years

Suffrage: 18 years of age; universal

Executive branch: *chief of state:* Supreme Leader Ali Hoseini-KHAMENEI (since 4 June 1989)
head of government: President Masoud PEZESHKIAN (since 30 July 2024)
cabinet: Council of Ministers selected by the president with legislative approval; the supreme leader has some control over appointments to several ministries
election/appointment process: supreme leader appointed for life by Assembly of Experts; president directly elected by absolute-majority popular vote in 2 rounds, if needed, for a 4-year term (eligible for a second term and an additional nonconsecutive term)
most recent election date: 28 June 2024, with runoff held on 5 July 2024
election results: *2024:* first round results - Masoud PEZESHKIAN (independent) 44.4%, Saeed JALILI (Front of Islamic Revolution Stability) 40.4%, Mohammad Baqer QAKIBAF (Progress and Justice Population of Islamic Iran) 14.3%, other 0.9%; second round results - Masoud PEZESHKIAN elected; Masoud PEZESHKIAN 54.8%, Saeed JALILI 45.2%
2021: Ebrahim RAISI elected president; percent of vote - Ebrahim RAISI (independent) 72.4%, Mohsen REZAI (RFII) 13.8%, Abbdolnaser HEMATI (ECP) 9.8%, Amir-Hosein Qazizadeh-HASHEMI (Islamic Law Party) 4%
note: presidential election held early due to the death of President Ebrahim RAISI in a helicopter accident in May 2024

Legislative branch: *legislature name:* Islamic Parliament of Iran (Majles Shoraye Eslami)
legislative structure: unicameral
number of seats: 290 (all directly elected)
electoral system: plurality/majority
scope of elections: full renewal
term in office: 4 years
most recent election date: 3/1/2024 to 5/10/2024
percentage of women in chamber: 4.9%
expected date of next election: February 2028
note: all candidates to the Majles must be approved by the Council of Guardians, a 12-member group of which 6 are appointed by the supreme leader and 6 are jurists nominated by the judiciary and elected by the Majles

Judicial branch: *highest court(s):* Supreme Court (consists of the chief justice and organized into 42 two-bench branches, each with a justice and a judge)
judge selection and term of office: Supreme Court president appointed by the head of the High Judicial Council (HJC), a 5-member body to include the Supreme Court chief justice, the prosecutor general, and 3 clergy, in consultation with judges of the Supreme Court; president appointed for a single, renewable 5-year term; other judges appointed by the HJC; judge tenure NA
subordinate courts: Penal Courts I and II; Islamic Revolutionary Courts; Courts of Peace; Special Clerical Court (functions outside the judicial system and handles cases involving clerics); military courts

Political parties: Combatant Clergy Association (an active political group)
Executives of Construction Party
Front of Islamic Revolutionary Stability
Islamic Coalition Party
Progress and Justice Population of Islamic Iran
Militant Clerics Society (Majma-e Ruhaniyoun-e Mobarez) or MRM
Moderation and Development Party
National Trust Party (Hezb-e E'temad-eMelli) or HEM
Progress and Justice Society
Union of Islamic Iran People's Party (Hezb-e Ettehad-e Iran-e Eslami)

Diplomatic representation in the US: none
note: Iran has an Interests Section in the Pakistani Embassy; address: Iranian Interests Section, Embassy of Pakistan, 1250 23rd Street NW, Washington, DC 20037; telephone: [1] (202) 965-4990; FAX [1] (202) 965-1073; email: *requests@daftar.org; info@daftar-washington.com; website:* https://daftar.org/

Diplomatic representation from the US: *embassy:* none; the US Interests Section is located in the Embassy of Switzerland; US Foreign Interests Section, Embassy of Switzerland, Pasdaran, Shahid Mousavi Street (Golestan 5th), Corner of Paydarfard Street, No. 55, Tehran

International organization participation: BRICS, CICA, CP, D-8, ECO, FAO, G-15, G-24, G-77, IAEA, IBRD, ICAO, ICC (national committees), ICRM, IDA, IDB, IFAD, IFC, IFRCS, IHO, ILO, IMF, IMO, IMSO, Interpol, IOC, IOM, IPU, ISO, ITSO, ITU, MIGA, NAM, OIC, OPCW, OPEC, PCA, SAARC (observer), SCO (observer), UN, UNAMID, UNCTAD, UNESCO, UNHCR, UNIDO, UNITAR, UNOOSA, UNWTO, UPU, WCO, WFTU (NGOs), WHO, WIPO, WMO, WTO (observer)

Independence: *1 April 1979 (Islamic Republic of Iran proclaimed); notable earlier dates:* ca. 550 B.C. (Achaemenid or Persian Empire established); A.D. 1501 (Iran reunified under the Safavid dynasty); 1794 (beginning of Qajar dynasty); 12 December 1925 (modern Iran established under the PAHLAVI dynasty)

National holiday: Republic Day, 1 April (1979)

Flag: *description:* three equal horizontal bands of green (top), white, and red; centered in the white band is the red national emblem, a stylization of the word *Allah* in the shape of a tulip (a symbol of martyrdom); ALLAH AKBAR (God is Great) in white Arabic script is repeated 11 times along the bottom

edge of the green band and 11 times along the top edge of the red band
meaning: green is the color of Islam and also represents growth, white stands for honesty and peace, and red for bravery and martyrdom

National symbol(s): lion

National color(s): green, white, red

National anthem(s): *title:* "Soroud-e Melli-ye Jomhouri-ye Eslami-ye Iran" (National Anthem of the Islamic Republic of Iran)
lyrics/music: multiple authors/Hassan RIAHI
history: adopted 1990
note: a recording of the current Iranian national anthem is unavailable because the US Navy Band does not record anthems for countries from which the US does not anticipate official visits; the US does not have diplomatic relations with Iran

National heritage: *total World Heritage Sites:* 28 (26cultural, 2 natural)
selected World Heritage Site locales: Persepolis (c); Tchogha Zanbil (c); Bam and its Cultural Landscape (c); Golestan Palace (c); Shushtar Historical Hydraulic System (c); Pasargadae (c); Hyrcanian Forests (n); Tabriz Historic Bazaar Complex (c); Meidan Emam, Esfahan (c); Bisotun (c); Takht-e Soleyman (c); Soltaniyeh(c); Bisotun (c); Armenian Monastic Ensembles of Iran(c); Sheikh Safi al-din Khānegāh and Shrine Ensemble in Ardabil (c); The Persian Garden (c); Gonbad-e Qābus (c); Masjed-e Jāmé of Isfahan (c); Shahr-i Sokhta (c); Cultural Landscape of Maymand (c); Susa (c); Lut Desert (n);The Persian Qanat (c); Historic City of Yazd (c); Sassanid Archaeological Landscape of Fars Region (c); Cultural Landscape of Hawraman/Uramanat (c); Trans-Iranian Railway (c); The Persian Caravanserai (c); Hegmataneh (c)

ECONOMY

Economic overview: traditionally state-controlled economy but reforming state-owned financial entities; strong oil/gas, agricultural, and service sectors; recent massive inflation due to exchange rate depreciation, international sanctions, and investor uncertainty; increasing poverty

Real GDP (purchasing power parity): $1.486 trillion (2024 est.)
$1.442 trillion (2023 est.)
$1.373 trillion (2022 est.)
note: data in 2021 dollars
comparison ranking: 23

Real GDP growth rate: 3% (2024 est.)
5% (2023 est.)
3.8% (2022 est.)
note: annual GDP % growth based on constant local currency
comparison ranking: 117

Real GDP per capita: $16,200 (2024 est.)
$15,900 (2023 est.)
$15,300 (2022 est.)
note: data in 2021 dollars
comparison ranking: 120

GDP (official exchange rate): $436.906 billion (2024 est.)
note: data in current dollars at official exchange rate

Inflation rate (consumer prices): 32.5% (2024 est.)
44.6% (2023 est.)
43.5% (2022 est.)
note: annual % change based on consumer prices
comparison ranking: 200

GDP - composition, by sector of origin: *agriculture:* 13% (2024 est.)
industry: 36.4% (2024 est.)
services: 47.9% (2024 est.)
note: figures may not total 100% due to non-allocated consumption not captured in sector-reported data
comparison rankings: agriculture 61; industry 33; services 159

GDP - composition, by end use: *household consumption:* 50.5% (2024 est.)
government consumption: 12.9% (2024 est.)
investment in fixed capital: 26.7% (2024 est.)
investment in inventories: 13.3% (2024 est.)
exports of goods and services: 22.9% (2024 est.)
imports of goods and services: -26.8% (2024 est.)
note: figures may not total 100% due to rounding or gaps in data collection

Agricultural products: wheat, sugarcane, milk, sugar beets, rice, tomatoes, barley, potatoes, oranges, apples (2023)
note: top ten agricultural products based on tonnage

Industries: petroleum, petrochemicals, gas, fertilizer, caustic soda, textiles, cement and other construction materials, food processing (particularly sugar refining and vegetable oil production), ferrous and nonferrous metal fabrication, armaments

Industrial production growth rate: 2.8% (2024 est.)
note: annual % change in industrial value added based on constant local currency
comparison ranking: 87

Labor force: 28.575 million (2024 est.)
note: number of people ages 15 or older who are employed or seeking work
comparison ranking: 24

Unemployment rate: 9.2% (2024 est.)
9.1% (2023 est.)
9.1% (2022 est.)
note: % of labor force seeking employment
comparison ranking: 144

Youth unemployment rate (ages 15-24): *total:* 22.8% (2024 est.)
male: 20% (2024 est.)
female: 35.5% (2024 est.)
note: % of labor force ages 15-24 seeking employment
comparison ranking: total 43

Gini Index coefficient - distribution of family income: 35.9 (2023 est.)
note: index (0-100) of income distribution; higher values represent greater inequality
comparison ranking: 67

Average household expenditures: *on food:* 27.9% of household expenditures (2023 est.)
on alcohol and tobacco: 0.5% of household expenditures (2023 est.)

Household income or consumption by percentage share: *lowest 10%:* 2.8% (2023 est.)
highest 10%: 28.2% (2023 est.)
note: % share of income accruing to lowest and highest 10% of population

Remittances: 0% of GDP (2023 est.)
0% of GDP (2022 est.)
0% of GDP (2021 est.)
note: personal transfers and compensation between resident and non-resident individuals/households/entities

Budget: *revenues:* $60.714 billion (2019 est.)
expenditures: $90.238 billion (2019 est.)

Public debt: 39.5% of GDP (2017 est.)
note: includes publicly guaranteed debt
comparison ranking: 134

Exports: $100.031 billion (2024 est.)
$97.924 billion (2023 est.)
$105.752 billion (2022 est.)
note: GDP expenditure basis - exports of goods and services in current dollars
comparison ranking: 49

Exports - partners: China 35%, Turkey 16%, India 8%, Pakistan 7%, Armenia 5% (2023)
note: top five export partners based on percentage share of exports

Exports - commodities: plastics, iron ore, alcohols, natural gas, refined copper (2023)
note: top five export commodities based on value in dollars

Imports: $117.176 billion (2024 est.)
$113.21 billion (2023 est.)
$97.729 billion (2022 est.)
note: GDP expenditure basis - imports of goods and services in current dollars
comparison ranking: 46

Imports - partners: China 34%, UAE 20%, Turkey 11%, Brazil 8%, Germany 4% (2023)
note: top five import partners based on percentage share of imports

Imports - commodities: broadcasting equipment, vehicle parts/accessories, corn, soybeans, vehicle bodies (2023)
note: top five import commodities based on value in dollars

Debt - external: $6.759 billion (2023 est.)
note: present value of external debt in current US dollars
comparison ranking: 60

Exchange rates: Iranian rials (IRR) per US dollar -

Exchange rates: 42,000 (2023 est.)
42,000 (2022 est.)
42,000 (2021 est.)
42,000 (2020 est.)
42,000 (2019 est.)

ENERGY

Electricity access: *electrification - total population:* 100% (2022 est.)

Electricity: *installed generating capacity:* 86.058 million kW (2023 est.)
consumption: 335.175 billion kWh (2023 est.)
exports: 5.723 billion kWh (2023 est.)
imports: 3.136 billion kWh (2023 est.)
transmission/distribution losses: 37.948 billion kWh (2023 est.)
comparison rankings: installed generating capacity 18; consumption 13; exports 39; imports 58; transmission/distribution losses 201

Electricity generation sources: *fossil fuels:* 94.6% of total installed capacity (2023 est.)
nuclear: 1.6% of total installed capacity (2023 est.)
solar: 0.2% of total installed capacity (2023 est.)
wind: 0.2% of total installed capacity (2023 est.)
hydroelectricity: 3.4% of total installed capacity (2023 est.)

Nuclear energy: Number of operational nuclear reactors: 1 (2025)

Number of nuclear reactors under construction: 1 (2025)

Net capacity of operational nuclear reactors: 0.92GW (2025 est.)

Percent of total electricity production: 1.7% (2023 est.)

Coal: *production:* 2.209 million metric tons (2023 est.)
consumption: 3.032 million metric tons (2023 est.)
exports: 212,000 metric tons (2023 est.)
imports: 1.098 million metric tons (2023 est.)
proven reserves: 1.203 billion metric tons (2023 est.)

Petroleum: *total petroleum production:* 4.112 million bbl/day (2023 est.)
refined petroleum consumption: 2.415 million bbl/day (2023 est.)
crude oil estimated reserves: 208.6 billion barrels (2021 est.)

Natural gas: *production:* 265.088 billion cubic meters (2023 est.)
consumption: 252.353 billion cubic meters (2023 est.)
exports: 14.698 billion cubic meters (2023 est.)
imports: 2.274 billion cubic meters (2023 est.)
proven reserves: 33.987 trillion cubic meters (2021 est.)

Energy consumption per capita: 160.779 million Btu/person (2023 est.)
comparison ranking: 23

COMMUNICATIONS

Telephones - fixed lines: *total subscriptions:* 29.02 million (2023 est.)
subscriptions per 100 inhabitants: 32 (2023 est.)
comparison ranking: total subscriptions 6

Telephones - mobile cellular: *total subscriptions:* 151 million (2023 est.)
subscriptions per 100 inhabitants: 165 (2022 est.)
comparison ranking: total subscriptions 11

Broadcast media: state-run broadcast media with no private, independent broadcasters; Islamic Republic of Iran Broadcasting (IRIB), the state-run TV broadcaster, operates over 60 television channels, over 50 radio stations, and dozens of newspapers and websites; about 20 foreign Persian-language TV stations broadcasting on satellite TV can be seen in Iran; satellite dishes are illegal and sometimes confiscated; most major international broadcasters transmit to Iran (2023)

Internet country code: .ir

Internet users: *percent of population:* 80% (2023 est.)

Broadband - fixed subscriptions: *total:* 10.9 million (2023 est.)
subscriptions per 100 inhabitants: 12 (2023 est.)
comparison ranking: total 23

TRANSPORTATION

Civil aircraft registration country code prefix: EP

Airports: 177 (2025)
comparison ranking: 33

Heliports: 90 (2025)
comparison ranking: 27

Railways: *total:* 8,483.5 km (2014)
standard gauge: 8,389.5 km (2014) 1.435-m gauge (189.5 km electrified)
broad gauge: 94 km (2014) 1.676-m gauge

Merchant marine: *total:* 965 (2023)
by type: bulk carrier 32, container ship 28, general cargo 398, oil tanker 86, other 421
comparison ranking: total 24

Ports: *total ports:* 18 (2024)
large: 0
medium: 4
small: 6
very small: 8
ports with oil terminals: 13
key ports: Abadan, Bandar Abbas, Bushehr, Khorramshahr

MILITARY AND SECURITY

Military and security forces: *the military forces of Iran are divided between the Islamic Republic of Iran Regular Forces (Artesh) and the Islamic Revolutionary Guard Corps (IRGC or Sepah):* Artesh: Ground Forces, Navy (includes marines), Air Force, Air Defense Forces

IRGC: Ground Forces, Navy (includes marines), Aerospace Force (controls strategic missile force), Qods Force (aka Quds Force; special operations), Cyber Electronic Command, Basij Paramilitary Forces

Ministry of Interior: Law Enforcement Command (FARAJA)
Ministry of Intelligence and Security (2025)
note 1: the Artesh primarily focuses on defending Iran's borders and territorial waters from external threats, while the IRGC has a broader mission to defend the Iranian revolution from any foreign or domestic threat
note 2: the Artesh Navy operates Iran's larger warships and operates in the Gulf of Oman, the Caspian Sea, and deep waters in the region and beyond; the IRGC Navy has responsibility for the closer-in waters of the Persian Gulf and Strait of Hormuz
note 3: the Basij is a volunteer paramilitary group, which sometimes acts as an auxiliary law enforcement unit for the IRGC; it is formally known as the Organization for the Mobilization of the Oppressed and also known as the Popular Mobilization Army
note 4: the Ministry of Intelligence and Security and law enforcement forces under the Interior Ministry, which report to the president, and the IRGC, which reports to the supreme leader, share responsibility for law enforcement and maintaining order
note 5: the FARAJA is the uniformed police of Iran; it includes branches for public security, traffic control, anti-narcotics, special forces (riot control, counterterrorism, hostage rescue, etc), intelligence, and criminal investigations; the FARAJA also has responsibility for border security (Border Guard Command)

Military expenditures: 2% of GDP (2024 est.)
2.3% of GDP (2023 est.)
2.5% of GDP (2022 est.)
2.3% of GDP (2021 est.)
2.1% of GDP (2020 est.)

Military and security service personnel strengths: information varies; up to 600,000 total active armed forces personnel; estimated 400,000 Islamic Republic of Iran Regular Forces (350,000 Ground Forces; 18,000 Navy; 40,000 Air Force/Air Defense Forces); up to estimated 190,000 Islamic Revolutionary Guard Corps (100-150,000 Ground Forces; 20,000 Navy; 15,000 Aerospace Force; 5,000 Qods Force); estimated 90,000 active Basij Paramilitary Forces (2025)

Military equipment inventories and acquisitions: the Iranian military's inventory includes a mix of domestically produced and mostly older foreign equipment largely of Chinese, Russian, Soviet, and US origin (US equipment acquired prior to the Islamic Revolution in 1979); it also has some military equipment from North Korea, including midget submarines and ballistic missiles; in recent years, Iran has received some newer equipment from Russia; Iran has a defense industry with the capacity to develop, produce, support, and sustain air, land, missile, and naval weapons programs (2024)

Military service age and obligation: military service is compulsory for all Iranian men 18-19 to approximately age 40; 16 for voluntary military service (may be as low as 15 for the Basij); conscript military service obligation is up to 24 months, depending on the location of service (soldiers serving in places of high security risk and deprived areas serve shorter terms); women exempted from military service (2023)
note: conscripts serve in the Artesh, IRGC, and Law Enforcement, while Navy and Air/Air Defense Force personnel are primarily volunteers

Military deployments: *note:* Iran maintained a military presence in Syria and recruited, trained, and funded thousands of Syrian and foreign fighters to support the ASAD regime during the Syrian civil war (2011-December 2024)

Military - note: the Islamic Revolutionary Guard Corps (IRGC) was formed in May 1979 in the immediate aftermath of Shah Mohammad Reza PAHLAVI's fall, as leftists, nationalists, and Islamists jockeyed for power; while the interim prime minister controlled the government and state institutions, such as the Army, followers of Ayatollah Ruhollah KHOMEINI organized counterweights, including the IRGC, to protect the Islamic revolution; the IRGC's command structure bypassed the elected president and went directly to KHOMEINI; the IRGC played a critical role in helping KHOMEINI consolidate power in the aftermath of the 1979 revolution, and it ensured that KHOMEINI's Islamic revolutionary vision prevailed against domestic challenges from nationalists and leftist factions in the scramble for control after the Shah's departure
the Iran-Iraq War (1980–88) transformed the IRGC into more of a conventional fighting force with its own ground, air, naval, and special forces, plus control over Iran's strategic missile and rocket forces; today, the IRGC is a highly institutionalized and parallel military force to Iran's regular armed forces (Artesh); it is involved in internal security and has influence in the political and economic spheres of Iranian society, as well as Iran's foreign policy; on the economic front, it owns factories and corporations and subsidiaries in banking, infrastructure, housing, airlines, tourism and other sectors; its special operations forces, known as the Qods/Quds Force, specialize in foreign missions and have provided advice, funding, guidance, material support, training, and weapons to militants in countries such as Afghanistan, Iraq, Syria, and Yemen, as well as extremist groups, including HAMAS, Hizballah, Kata'ib Hizballah, and Palestine Islamic Jihad; the Qods Force also conducts intelligence and reconnaissance operations; note - both the IRGC and the Qods Force have been designated as foreign terrorist organizations by the US (see Terrorist Organizations under References)
the Supreme Council for National Security (SCNS) is the senior-most body for formulating Iran's foreign and security policy; it is formally chaired by the president, who also appoints the SCNS secretary; its members include the speaker of the Majles, the head of the judiciary, the chief of the Armed Forces General Staff (chief of defense or CHOD), the commanders of the Artesh (regular forces) and IRGC, and the ministers of defense, foreign affairs, interior,

and intelligence; the SCNS reports to the supreme leader; the supreme leader is the commander-in-chief of the armed forces
the Iranian Armed Forces are divided between the regular forces (Artesh) and the IRGC; the Artesh primarily focuses on defending Iran's borders and territorial waters from external threats, while the IRGC has a broader mission to defend the Iranian revolution from any foreign or domestic threat; in 1989, Iran established the Armed Forces General Staff to coordinate military action across both the Artesh and the IRGC; Iran also has a joint military headquarters, the Khatam ol-Anbia Central Headquarters, to command the Artesh and IRGC in wartime (2024)

SPACE

Space agency/agencies: Iranian Space Agency (ISA; created in 2003); Iran Space Research Center (ISRC; established, 2000); Ministry of Defense and Armed Forces Logistics (MODAFL); Islamic Revolutionary Guard Corps - Aerospace Force (IRGC-ARF) (2024)
note 1: ISA and ISRC are subordinate to the Ministry of Information and Communications Technology; along with the MODAFL, they oversee part of Iran's satellite development programs; they also work with Iranian universities, private industry, and foreign partners to develop satellites
note 2: MODAFL and the IRGC-ARF oversee Iran's satellite/space launch vehicle development program

Space launch site(s): Imam Khomeini Space Center (aka Semnan Space Center; Semnan province); Shahroud Space Center (Semnan Province; IRGC-operated); Chabahar Space Center (Sistan and Baluchistan Province; under development) (2025)

Space program overview: has an ambitious civil and military space program focused on acquiring and operating satellites and developing indigenous satellite/space launch vehicles (SLV); designs, builds, and operates satellites, including communications, remote sensing (RS), and scientific; manufactures and operates SLVs; researching and developing other space-related capabilities and technologies in such areas as telecommunications, RS, navigation, and space situational awareness; UN Security Council and other international sanctions against Iran's weapons of mass destruction program have severely limited Iran's cooperation with foreign space agencies and commercial space industries; in recent years, however, it has cooperated with North Korea and Russia on space issues; Iran has also had relations with regional and international space organizations, such as the Asia-Pacific Space Cooperation Organization and the International Telecommunications Satellite Organization; it was a founding member of the UN Committee on the Peaceful Uses of Outer Space (COPUOS) established in 1958; has a private space industry involved in the development and production of satellites, satellite payloads, and other space technologies (2025)

note: further details about the key activities, programs, and milestones of the country's space program, as well as government spending estimates on the space sector, appear in the Space Programs reference guide

TERRORISM

Terrorist group(s): Terrorist group(s): Islamic Revolutionary Guard Corps (IRGC)/Qods Force; Islamic State of Iraq and ash-Sham (ISIS); Jaysh al Adl (Jundallah); Kurdistan Workers' Party (PKK); al-Qa'ida
note: details about the history, aims, leadership, organization, areas of operation, tactics, targets, weapons, size, and sources of support of the group(s) appear(s) in Appendix T

TRANSNATIONAL ISSUES

Refugees and internally displaced persons: *refugees:* 3,489,257 (2024 est.)

IDPs: 421 (2024 est.)

Trafficking in persons: *tier rating:* Tier 3 — Iran does not fully meet the minimum standards for the elimination of trafficking and is not making significant efforts to do so, therefore, Iran remained on Tier 3; for more details, go to: https://www.state.gov/reports/2025-trafficking-in-persons-report/iran/

IRAQ

INTRODUCTION

Background: Formerly part of the Ottoman Empire, Iraq was occupied by the United Kingdom during World War I and was declared a League of Nations mandate under UK administration in 1920. Iraq attained its independence as a kingdom in 1932. It was proclaimed a republic in 1958 after a coup overthrew the monarchy, but in actuality, a series of strongmen ruled the country until 2003. The last was SADDAM Hussein, from 1979 to 2003. Territorial disputes with Iran led to an inconclusive and costly war from 1980 to 1988. In 1990, Iraq seized Kuwait but was expelled by US-led UN coalition forces during the two-month-long Gulf War of 1991. After Iraq's expulsion, the UN Security Council (UNSC) required Iraq to scrap all weapons of mass destruction and long-range missiles and to allow UN verification inspections. Continued Iraqi noncompliance with UNSC resolutions led to the Second Gulf War in 2003, when US-led forces ousted the SADDAM regime.

In 2005, Iraqis approved a constitution in a national referendum and elected a 275-member Council of Representatives (COR). The COR approved most of the cabinet ministers, marking the transition to Iraq's first constitutional government in nearly a half-century. Iraq's constitution also established the Kurdistan Regional Government (KRG), a semi-autonomous region that administers the governorates of Erbil, Dahuk, and As Sulaymaniyah. Iraq has held four national legislative elections since 2006, most recently in 2021. The COR approved Mohammad Shia' al-SUDANI as prime minister in 2022. Iraq has repeatedly postponed elections for provincial councils – last held in 2013 – and since 2019, the prime minister has had the authority to appoint governors rather than provincial councils.

Between 2014 and 2017, Iraq fought a military campaign against the Islamic State of Iraq and ash-Sham (ISIS) to recapture territory the group seized in 2014. In 2017, then-Prime Minister Haydar al-ABADI publicly declared victory against ISIS, although military operations against the group continue in rural areas. Also in 2017, Baghdad forcefully seized disputed territories across central and northern Iraq from the KRG, after a non-binding Kurdish independence referendum.

GEOGRAPHY

Location: Middle East, bordering the Persian Gulf, between Iran and Kuwait

Geographic coordinates: 33 00 N, 44 00 E

Map references: Middle East

Area: *total:* 438,317 sq km
land: 437,367 sq km
water: 950 sq km
comparison ranking: total 60

Area - comparative: slightly more than three times the size of New York State

Land boundaries: *total:* 3,809 km
border countries (6): Iran 1,599 km; Jordan 179 km; Kuwait 254 km; Saudi Arabia 811 km; Syria 599 km; Turkey 367 km

Coastline: 58 km

Maritime claims: *territorial sea:* 12 nm
continental shelf: not specified

Climate: mostly desert; mild to cool winters with dry, hot, cloudless summers; northern mountainous regions along Iranian and Turkish borders experience cold winters with occasionally heavy snows that melt in early spring, sometimes causing extensive flooding in central and southern Iraq

Terrain: mostly broad plains; reedy marshes along Iranian border in south with large flooded areas; mountains along borders with Iran and Turkey

Elevation: *highest point:* Cheekha Dar (Kurdish for "Black Tent") 3,611 m
lowest point: Persian Gulf 0 m
mean elevation: 312 m

Natural resources: petroleum, natural gas, phosphates, sulfur

Land use: *agricultural land:* 21.8% (2022 est.)
arable land: 11.4% (2022 est.)
permanent crops: 1.1% (2022 est.)
permanent pasture: 9.2% (2022 est.)
forest: 1.9% (2022 est.)
other: 76.3% (2022 est.)

Irrigated land: 35,250 sq km (2012)

Major lakes (area sq km): *fresh water lake(s):* Lake Hammar - 1,940 sq km

Major rivers (by length in km): Euphrates river mouth (shared with Turkey[s], Syria, and Iran) - 3,596 km; Tigris river mouth (shared with Turkey[s], Syria, and Iran) - 1,950 km; the Tigris and Euphrates join to form the Shatt al Arab
note: [s] after country name indicates river source; [m] after country name indicates river mouth

Major watersheds (area sq km): Indian Ocean drainage: *(Persian Gulf)* Tigris and Euphrates (918,044 sq km)

Major aquifers: Arabian Aquifer System

Population distribution: population is concentrated in the north, center, and eastern parts of the country, with many of the larger urban agglomerations found along extensive parts of the Tigris and Euphrates Rivers; much of the western and southern areas are either lightly populated or uninhabited

Natural hazards: dust storms; sandstorms; floods

Geography - note: strategic location on Shatt al Arab waterway and at the head of the Persian Gulf

PEOPLE AND SOCIETY

Population: *total:* 42,083,436 (2024 est.)
male: 21,193,356
female: 20,890,080
comparison rankings: total 35; male 35; female 35

Nationality: *noun:* Iraqi(s)
adjective: Iraqi

Ethnic groups: Arab 75-80%, Kurdish 15-20%, other 5% (includes Turkmen, Yezidi, Shabak, Kaka'i, Bedouin, Romani, Assyrian, Circassian, Sabaean-Mandaean, Persian)
note: data is a 1987 government estimate; no more recent reliable numbers are available

Languages: Arabic (official), Kurdish (official); Turkmen (a Turkish dialect) and Syriac (Neo-Aramaic) are recognized as official languages where native speakers of these languages are present
major-language sample(s):

كتاب حقائق العالم، أحسن مصدر للمعلومات الأساسية
(Arabic)

ڕاستییەکانی جیهان، باشترین سەرچاوەیە بۆ زانیارییە بنەڕەتییەکان
(Kurdish)

Religions: Muslim (official) 95-98% (Shia 61-64%, Sunni 29-34%), Christian 1% (includes Catholic, Orthodox, Protestant, Assyrian Church of the East), other 1-4% (2015 est.)
note: the last census in Iraq was in 1997; while there has been voluntary relocation of many Christian families to northern Iraq, the overall Christian population has decreased at least 50% and perhaps as much as 90% since 2003, according to US Embassy estimates, with many fleeing to Syria, Jordan, and Lebanon

Age structure: *0-14 years:* 34.6% (male 7,447,266/female 7,130,883)
15-64 years: 61.7% (male 13,064,516/female 12,907,702)
65 years and over: 3.6% (2024 est.) (male 681,574/female 851,495)

Dependency ratios: *total dependency ratio:* 62 (2024 est.)
youth dependency ratio: 56.1 (2024 est.)
elderly dependency ratio: 5.9 (2024 est.)
potential support ratio: 16.9 (2024 est.)

Median age: *total:* 22.4 years (2024 est.)
male: 22 years
female: 22.7 years
comparison ranking: total 184

Population growth rate: 1.99% (2024 est.)
comparison ranking: 41

Birth rate: 23.7 births/1,000 population (2024 est.)
comparison ranking: 48

Death rate: 3.9 deaths/1,000 population (2024 est.)
comparison ranking: 217

Net migration rate: 0 migrant(s)/1,000 population (2024 est.)
comparison ranking: 84

Population distribution: population is concentrated in the north, center, and eastern parts of the country, with many of the larger urban agglomerations found along extensive parts of the Tigris and Euphrates Rivers; much of the western and southern areas are either lightly populated or uninhabited

Urbanization: *urban population:* 71.6% of total population (2023)
rate of urbanization: 2.91% annual rate of change (2020-25 est.)

Major urban areas - population: 7.711 million BAGHDAD (capital), 1.792 million Mosul, 1.448 million Basra, 1.075 million Kirkuk, 958,000 Najaf, 897,000 Erbil (2023)

Sex ratio: *at birth:* 1.05 male(s)/female
0-14 years: 1.04 male(s)/female
15-64 years: 1.01 male(s)/female
65 years and over: 0.8 male(s)/female
total population: 1.02 male(s)/female (2024 est.)

Maternal mortality ratio: 66 deaths/100,000 live births (2023 est.)
comparison ranking: 84

Infant mortality rate: *total:* 18.7 deaths/1,000 live births (2024 est.)
male: 20.4 deaths/1,000 live births
female: 17 deaths/1,000 live births
comparison ranking: total 81

Life expectancy at birth: *total population:* 73.7 years (2024 est.)
male: 71.9 years
female: 75.7 years
comparison ranking: total population 146

Total fertility rate: 3.1 children born/woman (2024 est.)
comparison ranking: 47

Gross reproduction rate: 1.51 (2024 est.)

Drinking water source: *improved: urban:* 99.8% of population (2022 est.)
rural: 94.8% of population (2022 est.)
total: 98.4% of population (2022 est.)
unimproved: urban: 0.2% of population (2022 est.)
rural: 5.2% of population (2022 est.)
total: 1.6% of population (2022 est.)

Health expenditure: 5.2% of GDP (2021)
5.8% of national budget (2022 est.)

Physician density: 1.02 physicians/1,000 population (2022)

Hospital bed density: 1.3 beds/1,000 population (2021 est.)

Sanitation facility access: *improved: urban:* 98.8% of population (2022 est.)
rural: 97.6% of population (2022 est.)
total: 98.5% of population (2022 est.)
unimproved: urban: 1.2% of population (2022 est.)
rural: 2.4% of population (2022 est.)
total: 1.5% of population (2022 est.)

Obesity - adult prevalence rate: 30.4% (2016)
comparison ranking: 23

Alcohol consumption per capita: *total:* 0.16 liters of pure alcohol (2019 est.)
beer: 0.11 liters of pure alcohol (2019 est.)
wine: 0 liters of pure alcohol (2019 est.)
spirits: 0.04 liters of pure alcohol (2019 est.)
other alcohols: 0 liters of pure alcohol (2019 est.)
comparison ranking: total 174

Tobacco use: *total:* 18.6% (2025 est.)
male: 36.2% (2025 est.)
female: 1.3% (2025 est.)
comparison ranking: total 79

Children under the age of 5 years underweight: 3.9% (2018)
comparison ranking: 71

Currently married women (ages 15-49): 65.5% (2023 est.)

Child marriage: *women married by age 15:* 7.2% (2018)
women married by age 18: 27.9% (2018)

Education expenditure: 4.7% of GDP (2016)
comparison ranking: Education expenditure (% GDP) 76

Literacy: *total population:* 86% (2017 est.)
male: 91% (2017 est.)
female: 76.3% (2018 est.)

ENVIRONMENT

Environmental issues: habitat loss from wetland draining; inadequate potable water; soil degradation (salination) and erosion; desertification; air, soil, and groundwater pollution from military and industries; water pollution from oil refineries and factory and sewage discharges; soil pollution from fertilizer and chemicals; air pollution in urban areas

International environmental agreements: *party to:* Biodiversity, Climate Change, Climate Change-Kyoto Protocol, Comprehensive Nuclear Test Ban, Desertification, Endangered Species, Hazardous Wastes, Law of the Sea, Nuclear Test Ban, Ozone Layer Protection, Ship Pollution, Wetlands
signed, but not ratified: Climate Change-Paris Agreement, Environmental Modification

Climate: mostly desert; mild to cool winters with dry, hot, cloudless summers; northern mountainous regions along Iranian and Turkish borders experience cold winters with occasionally heavy snows that melt in early spring, sometimes causing extensive flooding in central and southern Iraq

Urbanization: *urban population:* 71.6% of total population (2023)

rate of urbanization: 2.91% annual rate of change (2020-25 est.)

Carbon dioxide emissions: 190.815 million metric tonnes of CO2 (2023 est.)
from coal and metallurgical coke: 7,000 metric tonnes of CO2 (2023 est.)
from petroleum and other liquids: 152.931 million metric tonnes of CO2 (2023 est.)
from consumed natural gas: 37.878 million metric tonnes of CO2 (2023 est.)
comparison ranking: total emissions 32

Particulate matter emissions: 45.4 micrograms per cubic meter (2019 est.)

Methane emissions: *energy:* 2,243 kt (2022-2024 est.)
agriculture: 157 kt (2019-2021 est.)
waste: 325 kt (2019-2021 est.)
other: 2.3 kt (2019-2021 est.)

Waste and recycling: *municipal solid waste generated annually:* 13.14 million tons (2024 est.)
percent of municipal solid waste recycled: 15.4% (2022 est.)

Total water withdrawal: *municipal:* 6.735 billion cubic meters (2022 est.)
industrial: 4.52 billion cubic meters (2022 est.)
agricultural: 31.169 billion cubic meters (2022 est.)

Total renewable water resources: 89.86 billion cubic meters (2022 est.)

GOVERNMENT

Country name: *conventional long form:* Republic of Iraq
conventional short form: Iraq
local long form: Jumhuriyat al-Iraq/Komar-i Eraq
local short form: Al Iraq/Eraq
former: Mesopotamia, Mandatory Iraq, Hashemite Kingdom of Iraq
etymology: the name probably derives from Uruk ("Erech" in Aramaic), the ancient Sumerian and Babylonian city on the Euphrates River

Government type: federal parliamentary republic

Capital: *name:* Baghdad
geographic coordinates: 33 20 N, 44 24 E
time difference: UTC+3 (8 hours ahead of Washington, DC, during Standard Time)
etymology: the origin of the name is unclear; it may mean "gift of God," from the pre-Islamic words *bagh* (god) and *dad* (given)

Administrative divisions: 19 governorates (*muhafazat*, singular - *muhafazah* (Arabic); parezgakan, singular - parezga (Kurdish)); 'Al Anbar; Al Basrah; Al Muthanna; Al Qadisiyah (Ad Diwaniyah); An Najaf; Arbil (Erbil) (Arabic), Halabjah; Hewler (Kurdish); As Sulaymaniyah (Arabic), Slemani (Kurdish); Babil; Baghdad; Dahuk (Arabic), Dihok (Kurdish); Dhi Qar; Diyala; Karbala'; Kirkuk; Maysan; Ninawa; Salah ad Din; Wasit
note: Iraq's Kurdistan Regional Government administers Arbil, Dahuk, and As Sulaymaniyah (as Hewler, Dihok, and Slemani, respectively)

Legal system: mixed system of civil and Islamic law

Constitution: *history:* several previous; latest adopted by referendum 15 October 2005
amendment process: proposed by the president of the republic and the Council of Minsters collectively, or by one fifth of the Council of Representatives members; passage requires at least two-thirds majority vote by the Council of Representatives, approval by referendum, and ratification by the president; passage of amendments to articles on citizen rights and liberties requires two-thirds majority vote of Council of Representatives members after two successive electoral terms, approval in a referendum, and ratification by the president

International law organization participation: has not submitted an ICJ jurisdiction declaration; non-party state to the ICCt

Citizenship: *citizenship by birth:* no
citizenship by descent only: at least one parent must be a citizen of Iraq
dual citizenship recognized: yes
residency requirement for naturalization: 10 years

Suffrage: 18 years of age; universal

Executive branch: *chief of state:* President Latif RASHID (since 13 October 2022)
head of government: Prime Minister Mohammed Shia al-SUDANI (since 27 October 2022)
cabinet: Council of Ministers proposed by the prime minister, approved by Council of Representatives (COR)
election/appointment process: president indirectly elected by COR to serve a 4-year term (eligible for a second term)
most recent election date: 13 October 2022
election results: *2022:* Latif RASHID elected president in second round; COR vote in first round - Latif RASHID (PUK) 157, Barham SALIH (PUK) 99; COR vote in second round - Latif RASHID 167, Barham SALIH 99; Mohammed Shia' al-SUDANI approved as prime minister
2018: Barham SALIH elected president in second round; COR vote in first round - Barham SALIH (PUK) 165, Fuad HUSAYN (KDP) 90; COR vote in second round - Barham SALIH 219, Fuad HUSAYN 22; Adil ABD AL-MAHDI approved as prime minister

Legislative branch: *legislature name:* Council of Representatives of Iraq
legislative structure: unicameral
number of seats: 329 (all directly elected)
electoral system: other systems
scope of elections: full renewal
term in office: 4 years
most recent election date: 10/10/2021
parties elected and seats per party: Sadrist Bloc (73); National Progress Alliance / Taqadum (37); State of Law Coalition (33); Kurdistan Democratic Party (31); Fatah Alliance (17); Kurdistan Alliance (17); Independents (43); Other (78)
percentage of women in chamber: 28.9%
expected date of next election: November 2025
note: seat counts reflect updated numbers following the 12 June 2022 Sadrist Trend withdrawal from government formation; its 73 seats were reallocated to other parties

Judicial branch: *highest court(s):* Federal Supreme Court or FSC (consists of 9 judges); Court of Cassation (consists of a court president, 5 vice presidents, and at least 24 judges)
judge selection and term of office: Federal Supreme Court (FSC) judges nominated by the High Judicial Council (HJC) president, the FSC chief justice, the public prosecutor's office chief, and the head of the Judicial Oversight Commission; FSC members required to retire at age 72; Court of Cassation judges appointed by the HJC and confirmed by the Council of Representatives to serve until retirement, nominally at age 63, but can be extended to age 66
subordinate courts: Courts of Appeal (governorate level); civil courts, including first instance, personal status, labor, and customs; criminal courts including felony, misdemeanor, investigative, major crimes, juvenile, and traffic courts
note: Federal Supreme Court jurisdiction limited to constitutional issues, application of federal laws, ratification of election results for the COR, judicial competency disputes, and disputes between regions or governorates and the central government

Political parties: Al Fatah Alliance
Azm Alliance
Babiliyun Movement
Imtidad
Ishraqat Konun
Kurdistan Democratic Party
National Contract Party
New Generation Movement
Patriotic Union of Kurdistan
Sadrist Bloc
State Forces Alliance
State of Law Coalition
Taqadum
Tasmim Alliance

Diplomatic representation in the US: *chief of mission:* Ambassador Nazar Issa Abdulhadi AL-KHIRULLAH (since 30 June 2023)
chancery: 1801 P Street NW, Washington, DC 20036
telephone: [1] (202) 483-7500
FAX: [1] (202) 462-8815
email address and website: washington@scrdiraq.gov.iq
https://www.iraqiembassy.us/
consulate(s) general: Detroit, Los Angeles

Diplomatic representation from the US: *chief of mission:* Ambassador (vacant); Chargé d'Affaires Ambassador Steven H. FAGIN (since 29 May 2025); note - Ambassador Fagin has served as U.S. Ambassador to the Republic of Yemen since 2022 and will remain accredited as Ambassador there during his time in Baghdad
embassy: Al-Kindi Street, International Zone, Baghdad; note - consulate in Al Basrah closed as of 28 September 2018
mailing address: 6060 Baghdad Place, Washington DC 20521-6060
telephone: 0760-030-3000
email address and website: BaghdadACS@state.gov
https://iq.usembassy.gov/

International organization participation: ABEDA, AFESD, AIIB, AMF, CAEU, CICA, EITI (compliant country), FAO, G-77, IAEA, IBRD, ICAO, ICRM, IDA, IDB, IFAD, IFC, IFRCS, ILO, IMF, IMO, IMSO, Interpol, IOC, IPU, ISO, ITSO, ITU, LAS, MIGA, NAM, OAPEC, OIC, OPCW, OPEC, PCA, UN, UNCTAD, UNESCO, UNIDO, UNWTO, UPU, WCO, WFTU (NGOs), WHO, WIPO, WMO, WTO (observer)

Independence: 3 October 1932 (from League of Nations mandate under British administration)
note: on 28 June 2004, the Coalition Provisional Authority transferred sovereignty to the Iraqi Interim Government

National holiday: Independence Day, 3 October (1932); Republic Day, 14 July (1958)

Flag: *description:* three equal horizontal bands of red (top), white, and black; the Takbir (Arabic phrase meaning "God is great") in green Arabic script is centered in the white band
meaning: the colors come from the Arab Liberation flag and stand for oppression (black) overcome through bloody struggle (red), to be replaced by a bright future (white)

history: the Council of Representatives approved this flag in 2008 as a compromise replacement for the Ba'thist SADDAM-era flag
note: similar to the flags of Syria (two stars but no script), Yemen (plain white band), and Egypt (a golden Eagle of Saladin centered in the white band)

National symbol(s): golden eagle

National color(s): red, white, black

National anthem(s): *title:* "Mawtini" (My Homeland)
lyrics/music: Ibrahim TOUQAN/Mohammad FLAYFEL
history: adopted 2004, after the ouster of SADDAM Husayn; popular Arab folk song that also serves as an unofficial anthem for the Palestinian people

National heritage: *total World Heritage Sites:* 6 (5 cultural, 1 mixed)
selected World Heritage Site locales: Ashur (Qal'at Sherqat) (c); Babylon (c); Erbil Citadel (c); Hatra (c); Samarra Archaeological City (c); The Ahwar (Marshland) of Southern Iraq: Refuge of Biodiversity and the Relict Landscape of the Mesopotamian Cities (m)

ECONOMY

Economic overview: highly oil-dependent Middle Eastern economy; fiscal sustainability subject to fluctuation in oil prices; rising public confidence in economic conditions; import-dependent for most sectors; persistent challenges of corruption, informal markets, banking access, and political fragility

Real GDP (purchasing power parity): $585.887 billion (2024 est.)
$595.082 billion (2023 est.)
$592.017 billion (2022 est.)
note: data in 2021 dollars
comparison ranking: 44

Real GDP growth rate: -1.5% (2024 est.)
0.5% (2023 est.)
8% (2022 est.)
note: annual GDP % growth based on constant local currency
comparison ranking: 204

Real GDP per capita: $12,700 (2024 est.)
$13,200 (2023 est.)
$13,400 (2022 est.)
note: data in 2021 dollars
comparison ranking: 134

GDP (official exchange rate): $279.641 billion (2024 est.)
note: data in current dollars at official exchange rate

Inflation rate (consumer prices): 4.4% (2023 est.)
5% (2022 est.)
6% (2021 est.)
note: annual % change based on consumer prices
comparison ranking: 133

GDP - composition, by sector of origin: *agriculture:* 3.4% (2024 est.)
industry: 51.6% (2024 est.)
services: 45.8% (2024 est.)
note: figures may not total 100% due to non-allocated consumption not captured in sector-reported data
comparison rankings: agriculture 125; industry 7; services 169

GDP - composition, by end use: *household consumption:* 41.2% (2024 est.)
government consumption: 20.3% (2024 est.)
investment in fixed capital: 20.6% (2024 est.)
investment in inventories: 8.8% (2024 est.)
exports of goods and services: 37.5% (2024 est.)
imports of goods and services: -37.2% (2024 est.)
note: figures may not total 100% due to rounding or gaps in data collection

Agricultural products: wheat, dates, maize, tomatoes, rye, grapes, milk, chicken, potatoes, fruits (2023)
note: top ten agricultural products based on tonnage

Industries: petroleum, chemicals, textiles, leather, construction materials, food processing, fertilizer, metal fabrication/processing

Industrial production growth rate: -2.7% (2024 est.)
note: annual % change in industrial value added based on constant local currency
comparison ranking: 168

Labor force: 12.008 million (2024 est.)
note: number of people ages 15 or older who are employed or seeking work
comparison ranking: 49

Unemployment rate: 15.6% (2024 est.)
15.5% (2023 est.)
15.6% (2022 est.)
note: % of labor force seeking employment
comparison ranking: 174

Youth unemployment rate (ages 15-24): *total:* 32.1% (2024 est.)
male: 27.5% (2024 est.)
female: 62.7% (2024 est.)
note: % of labor force ages 15-24 seeking employment
comparison ranking: total 19

Gini Index coefficient - distribution of family income: 29.8 (2023 est.)
note: index (0-100) of income distribution; higher values represent greater inequality
comparison ranking: 122

Average household expenditures: *on food:* 28.7% of household expenditures (2023 est.)
on alcohol and tobacco: 4.3% of household expenditures (2023 est.)

Household income or consumption by percentage share: *lowest 10%:* 3.7% (2023 est.)
highest 10%: 24.2% (2023 est.)
note: % share of income accruing to lowest and highest 10% of population

Remittances: 0.4% of GDP (2023 est.)
0.4% of GDP (2022 est.)
0.4% of GDP (2021 est.)
note: personal transfers and compensation between resident and non-resident individuals/households/entities

Budget: *revenues:* $90.204 billion (2019 est.)
expenditures: $64.512 billion (2019 est.)
note: central government revenues and expenses (excluding grants/extrabudgetary units/social security funds) converted to US dollars at average official exchange rate for year indicated

Public debt: 27.4% of GDP (2018 est.)
note: central government debt as a % of GDP
comparison ranking: 172

Taxes and other revenues: 1.3% (of GDP) (2019 est.)
note: central government tax revenue as a % of GDP
comparison ranking: 151

Current account balance: $28.375 billion (2023 est.)
$58.01 billion (2022 est.)
$24.565 billion (2021 est.)
note: balance of payments - net trade and primary/secondary income in current dollars
comparison ranking: 18

Exports: $107.852 billion (2023 est.)
$127.079 billion (2022 est.)
$78.26 billion (2021 est.)
note: balance of payments - exports of goods and services in current dollars
comparison ranking: 47

Exports - partners: China 33%, India 28%, USA 8%, Greece 5%, UAE 5% (2023)
note: top five export partners based on percentage share of exports

Exports - commodities: crude petroleum, refined petroleum, petroleum coke, gold, natural gas (2023)
note: top five export commodities based on value in dollars

Imports: $81.179 billion (2023 est.)
$69.162 billion (2022 est.)
$50.707 billion (2021 est.)
note: balance of payments - imports of goods and services in current dollars
comparison ranking: 50

Imports - partners: UAE 32%, China 20%, Turkey 18%, India 5%, USA 2% (2023)
note: top five import partners based on percentage share of imports

Imports - commodities: refined petroleum, cars, broadcasting equipment, jewelry, gold (2023)
note: top five import commodities based on value in dollars

Reserves of foreign exchange and gold: $100.691 billion (2024 est.)
$112.233 billion (2023 est.)
$97.009 billion (2022 est.)
note: holdings of gold (year-end prices)/foreign exchange/special drawing rights in current dollars
comparison ranking: 29

Debt - external: $15.58 billion (2023 est.)
note: present value of external debt in current US dollars
comparison ranking: 39

Exchange rates: Iraqi dinars (IQD) per US dollar -

Exchange rates: 1,300 (2024 est.)
1,312.5 (2023 est.)
1,450 (2022 est.)
1,450 (2021 est.)
1,192 (2020 est.)

ENERGY

Electricity access: *electrification - total population:* 100% (2022 est.)

Electricity: *installed generating capacity:* 31.339 million kW (2023 est.)
consumption: 73.521 billion kWh (2023 est.)
imports: 3.134 billion kWh (2023 est.)
transmission/distribution losses: 79.904 billion kWh (2023 est.)
comparison rankings: installed generating capacity 37; consumption 44; imports 59; transmission/distribution losses 206

Electricity generation sources: *fossil fuels:* 98.8% of total installed capacity (2023 est.)
solar: 0.3% of total installed capacity (2023 est.)
hydroelectricity: 0.9% of total installed capacity (2023 est.)

Coal: *imports:* 3,000 metric tons (2023 est.)

Petroleum: *total petroleum production:* 4.448 million bbl/day (2023 est.)
refined petroleum consumption: 1.043 million bbl/day (2023 est.)
crude oil estimated reserves: 145.019 billion barrels (2021 est.)

Natural gas: *production:* 10.537 billion cubic meters (2023 est.)
consumption: 19.308 billion cubic meters (2023 est.)
imports: 8.771 billion cubic meters (2023 est.)
proven reserves: 3.729 trillion cubic meters (2021 est.)

Energy consumption per capita: 64.311 million Btu/person (2023 est.)
comparison ranking: 78

COMMUNICATIONS

Telephones - fixed lines: *total subscriptions:* 1.977 million (2023 est.)
subscriptions per 100 inhabitants: 4 (2023 est.)
comparison ranking: total subscriptions 49

Telephones - mobile cellular: *total subscriptions:* 45.7 million (2023 est.)
subscriptions per 100 inhabitants: 98 (2022 est.)
comparison ranking: total subscriptions 39

Broadcast media: the number of private radio and TV stations has increased rapidly since 2003; state-owned TV and radio stations are operated by the publicly funded Iraqi Media Network; private broadcast media are mostly linked to political, ethnic, or religious groups; satellite TV is available to about 70% of viewers; many broadcasters are based abroad; transmissions of multiple international radio broadcasters are accessible (2019)

Internet country code: .iq

Internet users: *percent of population:* 82% (2023 est.)

Broadband - fixed subscriptions: *total:* 7.77 million (2023 est.)
subscriptions per 100 inhabitants: 17 (2023 est.)
comparison ranking: total 30

TRANSPORTATION

Civil aircraft registration country code prefix: YI

Airports: 73 (2025)
comparison ranking: 72

Heliports: 10 (2025)
comparison ranking: 74

Railways: *total:* 2,272 km (2014)
standard gauge: 2,272 km (2014) 1.435-m gauge

Merchant marine: *total:* 74 (2023)
by type: general cargo 1, oil tanker 6, other 67
comparison ranking: total 103

Ports: *total ports:* 6 (2024)
large: 0
medium: 1
small: 1
very small: 4
ports with oil terminals: 3
key ports: Al Basrah, Al-Basra Oil Terminal, Khawr Al Amaya, Khawr Al Zubair, Umm Qasr

MILITARY AND SECURITY

Military and security forces: Ministry of Defense: Iraqi Army, Iraqi Navy, Iraqi Air Force

Office of the Prime Minister: Iraqi Counterterrorism Service (CTS); Popular Mobilization Committee (PMC)

Ministry of Interior: Federal Police Forces Command, Border Guard Forces Command, Federal Intelligence and Investigations Agency, Emergency Response Division, Facilities Protection Directorate, and Provincial Police; Ministry of Oil: Energy Police Directorate (2025)
note 1: the Iraqi military and associated security forces are collectively known as the Iraqi Security Forces (ISF); the Iraqi Counterterrorism Service (CTS) includes the Iraqi Special Operations Forces (ISOF)
note 2: the PMC includes the Popular Mobilization Forces (PMF), a collection of more than 60 militias of widely varied sizes and political interests; the Iraqi Government funds the PMF and it is mandated by law to act under government control, but many of the militia units take orders from individual government officials and/or associated political parties; some militias have ties to Iran and some have been designated as terrorist organizations by the US
note 3: the federal constitution provides the Kurdistan Regional Government (KRG) the right to maintain its own military and security forces, known as the Kurdish Security Forces (KSF); some forces, such as the Regional Guard Brigades, are unified under the KRG's Ministry of Peshmerga Affairs, but the two main Kurdish political parties, the Kurdistan Democratic Party (KDP) and the Patriotic Union of Kurdistan (PUK), also maintain their own military forces, police, emergency response, and internal security/intelligence services

Military expenditures: 2.5% of GDP (2024 est.)
2.5% of GDP (2023 est.)
1.8% of GDP (2022 est.)
3% of GDP (2021 est.)
3.2% of GDP (2020 est.)

Military and security service personnel strengths: estimated 200,000 active armed forces personnel under the Ministry of Defense (Army, Aviation Command, Air/Air Defense, Navy, Special Forces); approximately 20-25,000 National-Level Security Forces

Ministry of Peshmerga: estimated 150,000 active personnel

Popular Mobilization Forces: estimated 200,000 militia (2025)

Military equipment inventories and acquisitions: the Iraqi military's inventory includes a mix of equipment from a wide variety of sources, including China, several European countries, South Africa, South Korea, Russia, and the US (2024)

Military service age and obligation: 18-40 years of age for voluntary military service; no conscription (2023)
note: service in the armed forces was mandatory in Iraq from 1935 up until 2003; in 2021, the Iraqi cabinet approved a draft law to reinstate compulsory military service and referred the proposed law to the Iraqi parliament; as of 2023, the proposed law had been shelved

Military - note: the Iraqi Security Forces (ISF) are primarily focused on internal and border security; they are actively conducting counterinsurgency and counterterrorism operations against the Islamic State of Iraq and ash-Sham (ISIS) terrorist group, particularly in northern and western Iraq; the operations include securing the border with Syria; the Kurdish Security Forces, as well as are also active in conducting operations against ISIS
two international military task forces operate in Iraq to assist the country's security forces at the request of the Iraqi Government; in 2018, NATO established an advisory, training and capacity-building mission for the Iraqi military known as the NATO Mission Iraq (NMI); in December 2021, the US-led Combined Joint Task Force – Operation Inherent Resolve (CJTF-OIR) transitioned from a combat role to an advise, assist, and enable role (2025)

TERRORISM

Terrorist group(s): Terrorist group(s): Ansar al-Islam; Asa'ib Ahl al-Haq; Islamic Revolutionary Guard Corps (IRGC)/Qods Force; Islamic State of Iraq and ash-Sham (ISIS); Jaysh Rijal al-Tariq al-Naqshabandi; Kata'ib Hizballah; Kurdistan Workers' Party (PKK)
note: details about the history, aims, leadership, organization, areas of operation, tactics, targets, weapons, size, and sources of support of the group(s) appear(s) in Appendix T

TRANSNATIONAL ISSUES

Refugees and internally displaced persons: *refugees:* 335,343 (2024 est.)
IDPs: 1,201,813 (2024 est.)
stateless persons: 233 (2024 est.)

IRELAND

INTRODUCTION

Background: Celtic tribes arrived in Ireland between 600 and 150 B.C. Norse invasions that began in the late 8th century finally ended when King Brian BORU defeated the Danes in 1014. Norman invasions began in the 12th century and set off more than seven centuries of Anglo-Irish struggle marked by fierce rebellions and harsh repressions. The Irish famine of the mid-19th century caused an almost 25-percent decline in the island 's population through starvation, disease, and emigration. The population of the island continued to fall until the 1960s, but over the last 50 years, Ireland 's high birthrate has made it demographically one of the youngest populations in the EU.

The modern Irish state traces its origins to the failed 1916 Easter Monday Uprising that galvanized nationalist sentiment. The ensuing guerrilla war led to independence from the UK in 1921 with the signing of the Anglo-Irish Treaty and the creation of the Irish Free State. The treaty was deeply controversial in Ireland, in part because it helped solidify the country 's partition, with six of the 32 counties remaining in the UK as Northern Ireland. The split between pro-Treaty and anti-Treaty partisans led to the Irish Civil War (1922-23). The traditionally dominant political parties in Ireland, Fine Gael and Fianna Fail, are de facto descendants of the opposing sides of the treaty debate. Ireland declared itself

a republic in 1949 and formally left the British Dominion.

Beginning in the 1960s, deep sectarian divides between the Catholic and Protestant populations and systemic discrimination in Northern Ireland erupted into years of violence known as the Troubles. In 1998, the governments of Ireland and the UK, along with most political parties in Northern Ireland, reached the Belfast/Good Friday Agreement with the support of the US. This agreement helped end the Troubles and initiated a new phase of cooperation between the Irish and British Governments.

Ireland was neutral in World War II and continues its policy of military neutrality. Ireland joined the European Community in 1973 and the euro-zone currency union in 1999. The economic boom years of the Celtic Tiger (1995-2007) saw rapid economic growth that came to an abrupt end in 2008 with the meltdown of the Irish banking system. As a small, open economy, Ireland has excelled at courting foreign direct investment, especially from US multi-nationals, which has helped the economy recover from the financial crisis and insulated it somewhat from the economic shocks of the COVID-19 pandemic.

GEOGRAPHY

Location: Western Europe, occupying five-sixths of the island of Ireland in the North Atlantic Ocean, west of Great Britain

Geographic coordinates: 53 00 N, 8 00 W

Map references: Europe

Area: *total:* 70,273 sq km
land: 68,883 sq km
water: 1,390 sq km
comparison ranking: total 120

Area - comparative: slightly larger than West Virginia

Land boundaries: *total:* 490 km
border countries (1): UK 499 km

Coastline: 1,448 km

Maritime claims: *territorial sea:* 12 nm
exclusive fishing zone: 200 nm

Climate: temperate maritime; modified by North Atlantic Current; mild winters, cool summers; consistently humid; overcast about half the time

Terrain: mostly flat to rolling interior plain surrounded by rugged hills and low mountains; sea cliffs on west coast

Elevation: *highest point:* Carrauntoohil 1,041 m
lowest point: Atlantic Ocean 0 m
mean elevation: 118 m

Natural resources: natural gas, peat, copper, lead, zinc, silver, barite, gypsum, limestone, dolomite

Land use: *agricultural land:* 63.1% (2022 est.)
arable land: 6.5% (2022 est.)
permanent crops: 0% (2022 est.)
permanent pasture: 56.6% (2022 est.)
forest: 11.5% (2022 est.)
other: 25.4% (2022 est.)

Irrigated land: 0 sq km (2022)

Population distribution: population distribution is weighted to the eastern side of the island, with the largest concentration in and around Dublin; populations in the west are small due to mountainous land, poorer soil, and lack of transport routes

Natural hazards: rare extreme weather events

Geography - note: strategic location on major air and sea routes between North America and northern Europe; over 40% of the population resides within 100 km of Dublin

PEOPLE AND SOCIETY

Population: *total:* 5,233,461 (2024 est.)
male: 2,590,542
female: 2,642,919
comparison rankings: total 124; male 124; female 123

Nationality: *noun:* Irishman(men), Irishwoman(women), Irish (collective plural)
adjective: Irish

Ethnic groups: Irish 76.6%, Irish travelers 0.6%, other White 9.9%, Asian 3.3%, Black 1.5%, other (includes Arab, Roma, and persons of mixed backgrounds) 2%, unspecified 2.6% (2022 est.)

Languages: English (official, the language generally used), Irish (Gaelic or Gaeilge) (official, spoken by approximately 37.7% of the population)

Religions: Roman Catholic 69.2% (includes lapsed), Protestant 3.7% (Church of Ireland/England/Anglican/Episcopalian 2.5%, other Protestant 1.2%), Orthodox 2%, other Christian 0.9%, Muslim 1.6%, other 1.4%, agnostic/atheist 0.1%, none 14.5%, unspecified 6.7% (2022 est.)

Age structure: *0-14 years:* 18.6% (male 498,124/female 477,848)
15-64 years: 65.5% (male 1,701,680/female 1,728,041)
65 years and over: 15.8% (2024 est.) (male 390,738/female 437,030)

Dependency ratios: *total dependency ratio:* 52.6 (2024 est.)
youth dependency ratio: 28.5 (2024 est.)
elderly dependency ratio: 24.1 (2024 est.)
potential support ratio: 4.1 (2024 est.)

Median age: *total:* 40.2 years (2024 est.)
male: 39.7 years
female: 40.6 years
comparison ranking: total 60

Population growth rate: 0.93% (2024 est.)
comparison ranking: 100

Birth rate: 11.1 births/1,000 population (2024 est.)
comparison ranking: 163

Death rate: 7.4 deaths/1,000 population (2024 est.)
comparison ranking: 104

Net migration rate: 5.6 migrant(s)/1,000 population (2024 est.)
comparison ranking: 17

Population distribution: population distribution is weighted to the eastern side of the island, with the largest concentration in and around Dublin; populations in the west are small due to mountainous land, poorer soil, and lack of transport routes

Urbanization: *urban population:* 64.5% of total population (2023)
rate of urbanization: 1.15% annual rate of change (2020-25 est.)

Major urban areas - population: 1.270 million DUBLIN (capital) (2023)

Sex ratio: *at birth:* 1.06 male(s)/female
0-14 years: 1.04 male(s)/female
15-64 years: 0.98 male(s)/female
65 years and over: 0.89 male(s)/female
total population: 0.98 male(s)/female (2024 est.)

Mother 's mean age at first birth: 30.9 years (2020 est.)

Maternal mortality ratio: 4 deaths/100,000 live births (2023 est.)
comparison ranking: 174

Infant mortality rate: *total:* 3.3 deaths/1,000 live births (2024 est.)
male: 3.2 deaths/1,000 live births
female: 3.3 deaths/1,000 live births
comparison ranking: total 198

Life expectancy at birth: *total population:* 82 years (2024 est.)
male: 80.3 years
female: 83.9 years
comparison ranking: total population 36

Total fertility rate: 1.72 children born/woman (2024 est.)
comparison ranking: 158

Gross reproduction rate: 0.84 (2024 est.)

Drinking water source: *improved: urban:* 95.4% of population (2022 est.)
rural: 97% of population (2022 est.)
total: 96% of population (2022 est.)
unimproved: urban: 4.6% of population (2022 est.)
rural: 3% of population (2022 est.)
total: 4% of population (2022 est.)

Health expenditure: 6.1% of GDP (2022)
22.3% of national budget (2022 est.)

Physician density: 3.88 physicians/1,000 population (2023)

Hospital bed density: 2.9 beds/1,000 population (2020 est.)

Sanitation facility access: *improved: urban:* 94.8% of population (2022 est.)
rural: 98.2% of population (2022 est.)
total: 96.1% of population (2022 est.)
unimproved: urban: 5.2% of population (2022 est.)
rural: 1.8% of population (2022 est.)
total: 3.9% of population (2022 est.)

Obesity - adult prevalence rate: 25.3% (2016)
comparison ranking: 51

Alcohol consumption per capita: *total:* 10.91 liters of pure alcohol (2019 est.)
beer: 4.92 liters of pure alcohol (2019 est.)
wine: 2.88 liters of pure alcohol (2019 est.)
spirits: 2.29 liters of pure alcohol (2019 est.)
other alcohols: 0.82 liters of pure alcohol (2019 est.)
comparison ranking: total 15

Tobacco use: *total:* 16.8% (2025 est.)
male: 19.2% (2025 est.)
female: 14.4% (2025 est.)
comparison ranking: total 94

Currently married women (ages 15-49): 52.1% (2023 est.)

Education expenditure: 3% of GDP (2021 est.)
12% national budget (2021 est.)
comparison ranking: Education expenditure (% GDP) 152

School life expectancy (primary to tertiary education): *total:* 19 years (2022 est.)
male: 19 years (2022 est.)
female: 20 years (2022 est.)

ENVIRONMENT

Environmental issues: water pollution, especially of lakes, from agricultural runoff; deforestation, including problems with acid rain

International environmental agreements: *party to:* Air Pollution, Air Pollution-Nitrogen Oxides, Air Pollution-Persistent Organic Pollutants, Air Pollution-Sulphur 94, Biodiversity, Climate Change, Climate Change-Kyoto Protocol, Climate Change-Paris Agreement, Comprehensive Nuclear Test Ban, Desertification, Endangered Species, Environmental Modification, Hazardous Wastes, Law of the Sea, Marine Dumping-London Convention, Marine Dumping-London Protocol, Nuclear Test Ban, Ozone Layer Protection, Ship Pollution, Tropical Timber 2006, Wetlands, Whaling
signed, but not ratified: Air Pollution-Heavy Metals, Air Pollution-Multi-effect Protocol, Marine Life Conservation

Climate: temperate maritime; modified by North Atlantic Current; mild winters, cool summers; consistently humid; overcast about half the time

Urbanization: *urban population:* 64.5% of total population (2023)
rate of urbanization: 1.15% annual rate of change (2020-25 est.)

Carbon dioxide emissions: 35.486 million metric tonnes of CO2 (2023 est.)
from coal and metallurgical coke: 3.029 million metric tonnes of CO2 (2023 est.)
from petroleum and other liquids: 22.635 million metric tonnes of CO2 (2023 est.)
from consumed natural gas: 9.822 million metric tonnes of CO2 (2023 est.)
comparison ranking: total emissions 67

Particulate matter emissions: 7.5 micrograms per cubic meter (2019 est.)

Waste and recycling: *municipal solid waste generated annually:* 2.911 million tons (2024 est.)
percent of municipal solid waste recycled: 42.4% (2022 est.)

Total water withdrawal: *municipal:* 1.106 billion cubic meters (2022 est.)
industrial: 531.82 million cubic meters (2022 est.)
agricultural: 39.63 million cubic meters (2022 est.)

Total renewable water resources: 52 billion cubic meters (2022 est.)

Geoparks: *total global geoparks and regional networks:* 3
global geoparks and regional networks: Burren & Cliffs of Moher; Copper Coast; Marble Arch Caves (includes United Kingdom) (2023)

GOVERNMENT

Country name: *conventional long form:* none
conventional short form: Ireland
local long form: none
local short form: Eire
etymology: the Irish name Eire evolved from the Gaelic name Eriu, which is possibly derived from the Old Celtic *iveriu*, meaning "good land; " the English name, Ireland, is a direct translation

Government type: parliamentary republic

Capital: *name:* Dublin
geographic coordinates: 53 19 N, 6 14 W
time difference: UTC 0 (5 hours ahead of Washington, DC, during Standard Time)
daylight saving time: +1hr, begins last Sunday in March; ends last Sunday in October
etymology: derived from the Irish words *dubh* (black or dark) and *linn* (pool), referring to the color of the Liffey River

Administrative divisions: 28 counties and 3 cities*; Carlow, Cavan, Clare, Cork, Cork*, Donegal, Dublin*, Dun Laoghaire-Rathdown, Fingal, Galway, Galway*, Kerry, Kildare, Kilkenny, Laois, Leitrim, Limerick, Longford, Louth, Mayo, Meath, Monaghan, Offaly, Roscommon, Sligo, South Dublin, Tipperary, Waterford, Westmeath, Wexford, Wicklow

Legal system: common law system based on the English model but substantially modified by customary law; Supreme Court reviews legislative acts

Constitution: *history:* previous 1922; latest drafted 14 June 1937, adopted by plebiscite 1 July 1937, effective 29 December 1937
amendment process: proposed as bills by Parliament; passage requires majority vote by both the Senate and House of Representatives, majority vote in a referendum, and presidential signature

International law organization participation: accepts compulsory ICJ jurisdiction with reservations; accepts ICCt jurisdiction

Citizenship: *citizenship by birth:* no, unless a parent of a child born in Ireland has been legally resident in Ireland for at least three of the four years prior to the birth of the child
citizenship by descent only: yes
dual citizenship recognized: yes
residency requirement for naturalization: 4 of the previous 8 years

Suffrage: 18 years of age; universal

Executive branch: *chief of state:* President Michael D. HIGGINS (since 11 November 2011)
head of government: Taoiseach (Prime Minister) Michael MARTIN (since 23 January 2025)
cabinet: Cabinet nominated by the prime minister, appointed by the president, approved by the Dali Eireann (lower house of Parliament)
election/appointment process: president directly elected by majority popular vote for a 7-year term (eligible for a second term); taoiseach (prime minister) nominated by the House of Representatives (Dail Eireann), appointed by the president
most recent election date: 26 October 2018
election results: 2025: Michael MARTIN is elected taoiseach by parliament, 95 votes to 76, and is appointed taoiseach by the president
2024: Simon HARRIS is elected taoiseach by parliament, 88 votes to 69, and is appointed taoiseach by the president
2018: Michael D. HIGGINS reelected president in first round; percent of vote in first round - Michael D. HIGGINS (independent) 55.8%, Peter CASEY (independent) 23.3%, Sean GALLAGHER (independent) 6.4%, Liadh NI RIADA (Sinn Fein) 6.4%, Joan FREEMAN (independent) 6%, Gavin DUFFY (independent) 2.2%
expected date of next election: no later than November 2025

Legislative branch: *legislature name:* Parliament (Oireachtas)
legislative structure: bicameral

Legislative branch - lower chamber: *chamber name:* House of Representatives (Dáil Éireann)
number of seats: 174 (all directly elected)
electoral system: proportional representation
scope of elections: full renewal
term in office: 5 years
most recent election date: 11/29/2024
parties elected and seats per party: Fianna Fáil (48); Sinn Féin (39); Fine Gael (38); Social Democratic Party (11); Labour Party (11); Independents (16); Other (11)
percentage of women in chamber: 25.3%
expected date of next election: November 2029

Legislative branch - upper chamber: *chamber name:* Senate (Seanad Éireann - Senate)
number of seats: 60 (49 indirectly elected; 11 appointed)
scope of elections: full renewal
term in office: 5 years
most recent election date: 1/29/2025 to 1/30/2025
parties elected and seats per party: Fianna Fail (19); Fine Gael (18); Sinn Fein (6); Independents (12); other (5)
percentage of women in chamber: 45%
expected date of next election: January 2030

Judicial branch: *highest court(s):* Supreme Court of Ireland (consists of the chief justice, 9 judges, 2 ex-officio members – the presidents of the High Court and Court of Appeal – and organized in 3-, 5-, or 7-judge panels, depending on the importance or complexity of an issue of law)
judge selection and term of office: judges nominated by the prime minister and Cabinet and appointed by the president; chief justice serves in the position for 7 years; judges can serve until age 70
subordinate courts: High Court, Court of Appeal; circuit and district courts; criminal courts

Political parties: Aontu
Solidarity-People Before Profit or PBP-S
Fianna Fail
Fine Gael
Green Party
Human Dignity Alliance
Independent Ireland
Labor (Labour) Party
100% Redress
Right to Change or RTC
Sinn Fein
Social Democrats
Socialist Party
The Workers ' Party

Diplomatic representation in the US: *chief of mission:* Ambassador Geraldine BYRNE NASON (since 16 September 2022)
chancery: 2234 Massachusetts Avenue NW, Washington, DC 20008
telephone: [1] (202) 462-3939
FAX: [1] (202) 232-5993
email address and website: https://www.ireland.ie/en/usa/washington/
consulate(s) general: Atlanta, Austin (TX), Boston, Chicago, Los Angeles, Miami, New York, San Francisco

Diplomatic representation from the US: *chief of mission:* Ambassador Edward S. WALSH (since 1 July 2025)
embassy: 42 Elgin Road, Ballsbridge, Dublin 4

mailing address: 5290 Dublin Place, Washington DC 20521-5290
telephone: [353] (1) 668-8777

FAX: [353] (1) 688-8056
email address and website: ACSDublin@state.gov https://ie.usembassy.gov/

International organization participation: ADB (nonregional member), Australia Group, BIS, CD, CE, EAPC, EBRD, ECB, EIB, EMU, ESA, EU, FAO, FATF, IAEA, IBRD, ICAO, ICC (national committees), ICCt, ICRM, IDA, IEA, IFAD, IFC, IFRCS, IGAD (partners), IHO, ILO, IMF, IMO, Interpol, IOC, IOM, IPU, ISO, ITSO, ITU, ITUC (NGOs), MIGA, MINURSO, MONUSCO, NEA, NSG, OAS (observer), OECD, OPCW, OSCE, Paris Club, PCA, PFP, UN, UNCTAD, UNDOF, UNESCO, UNHCR, UNIDO, UNIFIL, UNOCI, UNRWA, UNTSO, UPU, Wassenaar Arrangement, WCO, WHO, WIPO, WMO, WTO, ZC

Independence: 6 December 1921 (from the UK); 6 December 1922 (Irish Free State established); 18 April 1949 (Republic of Ireland Act enabled)

National holiday: Saint Patrick 's Day, 17 March
note: marks the traditional death date of Saint Patrick, patron saint of Ireland, during the latter half of the fifth century A.D. (most commonly cited years are c. 461 and c. 493); Saint Patrick 's feast day was celebrated as early as the ninth century, but it only became an official public holiday in 1903

Flag: *description:* three equal vertical bands of green (left side), white, and orange
meaning: the flag colors have no official meaning, but a common interpretation is that the green stands for the Irish nationalist tradition, orange for the Orange tradition (minority supporters of William of Orange), and white for peace or a lasting truce between the green and the orange
note: similar to the flag of Cote d 'Ivoire, which is shorter and has the colors reversed; also similar to the flag of Italy, which is shorter and has red instead of orange

National symbol(s): harp, shamrock (trefoil)

National color(s): blue, green

National coat of arms: the coat of arms features a gold harp on a blue shield and dates back to the 13th century, although it only became official in 1945; the harp, a national symbol that Ireland adopted after gaining independence from the United Kingdom in 1921, represents the country 's history, culture, and national identity

National anthem(s): *title:* "Amhran na bhFiann " (The Soldier 's Song)
lyrics/music: Peadar KEARNEY [English], Liam O RINN [Irish]/Patrick HEENEY and Peadar KEARNEY
history: adopted 1926; the song "Ireland 's Call " is often used as the anthem at athletic events if citizens of Ireland and Northern Ireland are competing as a unified team

National heritage: *total World Heritage Sites:* 2 (both cultural)
selected World Heritage Site locales: Brú na Bóinne - Archaeological Ensemble of the Bend of the Boyne; Sceilg Mhichíl

ECONOMY

Economic overview: high-income, export-oriented EU economy; large multinational business sector contributes to growth and tax revenues but poses volatility risks; high living standards; strong labor market challenged by skill shortages and aging workforce

Real GDP (purchasing power parity): $620.544 billion (2024 est.)
$613.056 billion (2023 est.)
$648.943 billion (2022 est.)
note: data in 2021 dollars
comparison ranking: 42

Real GDP growth rate: 1.2% (2024 est.)
-5.5% (2023 est.)
8.6% (2022 est.)
note: annual GDP % growth based on constant local currency
comparison ranking: 171

Real GDP per capita: $115,300 (2024 est.)
$115,500 (2023 est.)
$124,500 (2022 est.)
note: data in 2021 dollars
comparison ranking: 5

GDP (official exchange rate): $577.389 billion (2024 est.)
note: data in current dollars at official exchange rate

Inflation rate (consumer prices): 2.1% (2024 est.)
6.3% (2023 est.)
7.8% (2022 est.)
note: annual % change based on consumer prices
comparison ranking: 56

GDP - composition, by sector of origin: *agriculture:* 1.1% (2024 est.)
industry: 30.8% (2024 est.)
services: 61.8% (2024 est.)
note: figures may not total 100% due to non-allocated consumption not captured in sector-reported data
comparison rankings: agriculture 174; industry 50; services 78

GDP - composition, by end use: *household consumption:* 26.8% (2023 est.)
government consumption: 12.2% (2023 est.)
investment in fixed capital: 23.2% (2023 est.)
investment in inventories: 3.1% (2023 est.)
exports of goods and services: 135.1% (2023 est.)
imports of goods and services: -102.2% (2023 est.)
note: figures may not total 100% due to rounding or gaps in data collection

Agricultural products: milk, barley, beef, wheat, potatoes, pork, oats, chicken, rapeseed, beans (2023)
note: top ten agricultural products based on tonnage

Industries: pharmaceuticals, chemicals, computer hardware and software, food products, beverages and brewing; medical devices

Industrial production growth rate: -4.9% (2024 est.)
note: annual % change in industrial value added based on constant local currency
comparison ranking: 178

Labor force: 2.857 million (2024 est.)
note: number of people ages 15 or older who are employed or seeking work
comparison ranking: 115

Unemployment rate: 4.4% (2024 est.)
4.3% (2023 est.)
4.6% (2022 est.)
note: % of labor force seeking employment
comparison ranking: 72

Youth unemployment rate (ages 15-24): *total:* 11.1% (2024 est.)
male: 11.2% (2024 est.)
female: 11% (2024 est.)
note: % of labor force ages 15-24 seeking employment
comparison ranking: total 111

Population below poverty line: 14% (2021 est.)
note: % of population with income below national poverty line
Gini Index coefficient - distribution of family income 29.9 (2022 est.)
note: index (0-100) of income distribution; higher values represent greater inequality
comparison ranking: 120

Average household expenditures: *on food:* 8.6% of household expenditures (2023 est.)
on alcohol and tobacco: 4% of household expenditures (2023 est.)

Household income or consumption by percentage share: *lowest 10%:* 3.6% (2022 est.)
highest 10%: 24.5% (2022 est.)
note: % share of income accruing to lowest and highest 10% of population

Remittances: 0.1% of GDP (2023 est.)
0.1% of GDP (2022 est.)
0% of GDP (2021 est.)
note: personal transfers and compensation between resident and non-resident individuals/households/entities

Budget: *revenues:* $118.231 billion (2022 est.)
expenditures: $108.693 billion (2022 est.)
note: central government revenues (excluding grants) and expenditures converted to US dollars at average official exchange rate for year indicated

Public debt: 45.4% of GDP (2022 est.)
note: central government debt as a % of GDP
comparison ranking: 118

Taxes and other revenues: 16.8% (of GDP) (2022 est.)
note: central government tax revenue as a % of GDP
comparison ranking: 78

Current account balance: $44.744 billion (2023 est.)
$48.427 billion (2022 est.)
$65.118 billion (2021 est.)
note: balance of payments - net trade and primary/secondary income in current dollars
comparison ranking: 16

Exports: $761.876 billion (2023 est.)
$763.233 billion (2022 est.)
$722.655 billion (2021 est.)
note: balance of payments - exports of goods and services in current dollars
comparison ranking: 12

Exports - partners: USA 28%, Germany 11%, UK 8%, Belgium 8%, China 7% (2023)
note: top five export partners based on percentage share of exports

Exports - commodities: vaccines, packaged medicine, nitrogen compounds, integrated circuits, hormones (2023)
note: top five export commodities based on value in dollars

Imports: $580.399 billion (2023 est.)
$536.882 billion (2022 est.)
$500.334 billion (2021 est.)
note: balance of payments - imports of goods and services in current dollars
comparison ranking: 16

Imports - partners: UK 20%, USA 17%, France 10%, China 7%, Germany 7% (2023)
note: top five import partners based on percentage share of imports

Imports - commodities: aircraft, nitrogen compounds, vaccines, packaged medicine, integrated circuits (2023)

note: top five import commodities based on value in dollars

Reserves of foreign exchange and gold: $12.698 billion (2024 est.)
$12.905 billion (2023 est.)
$13.039 billion (2022 est.)
note: holdings of gold (year-end prices)/foreign exchange/special drawing rights in current dollars
comparison ranking: 74

Exchange rates: euros (EUR) per US dollar -

Exchange rates: 0.924 (2024 est.)
0.925 (2023 est.)
0.95 (2022 est.)
0.845 (2021 est.)
0.876 (2020 est.)

ENERGY

Electricity access: *electrification - total population:* 100% (2022 est.)

Electricity: *installed generating capacity:* 12.321 million kW (2023 est.)
consumption: 32.282 billion kWh (2023 est.)
exports: 441.615 million kWh (2023 est.)
imports: 3.89 billion kWh (2023 est.)
transmission/distribution losses: 2.489 billion kWh (2023 est.)
comparison rankings: installed generating capacity 62; consumption 67; exports 78; imports 53; transmission/distribution losses 135

Electricity generation sources: *fossil fuels:* 55.7% of total installed capacity (2023 est.)
solar: 1.3% of total installed capacity (2023 est.)
wind: 37% of total installed capacity (2023 est.)
hydroelectricity: 2.3% of total installed capacity (2023 est.)
biomass and waste: 3.7% of total installed capacity (2023 est.)

Coal: *consumption:* 1.341 million metric tons (2023 est.)
exports: 76,000 metric tons (2023 est.)
imports: 1.711 million metric tons (2023 est.)
proven reserves: 40 million metric tons (2023 est.)

Petroleum: *total petroleum production:* 600 bbl/day (2023 est.)
refined petroleum consumption: 159,000 bbl/day (2024 est.)

Natural gas: *production:* 1.165 billion cubic meters (2023 est.)
consumption: 4.919 billion cubic meters (2023 est.)
imports: 3.707 billion cubic meters (2023 est.)
proven reserves: 9.911 billion cubic meters (2021 est.)

Energy consumption per capita: 113.837 million Btu/person (2023 est.)
comparison ranking: 37

COMMUNICATIONS

Telephones - fixed lines: *total subscriptions:* 1.176 million (2023 est.)
subscriptions per 100 inhabitants: 23 (2023 est.)
comparison ranking: total subscriptions 67

Telephones - mobile cellular: *total subscriptions:* 5.76 million (2023 est.)
subscriptions per 100 inhabitants: 113 (2022 est.)
comparison ranking: total subscriptions 123

Broadcast media: publicly owned broadcaster Radio Telefis Eireann (RTE) operates 4 TV stations; commercial TV stations are available; about 75% of households use multi-channel satellite and TV services that provide access to a wide range of stations; RTE operates 4 national radio stations and has launched digital audio broadcasts on several; a number of commercial broadcast stations operate at the national, regional, and local levels (2019)

Internet country code: .ie

Internet users: *percent of population:* 97% (2023 est.)

Broadband - fixed subscriptions: *total:* 1.65 million (2023 est.)
subscriptions per 100 inhabitants: 32 (2023 est.)
comparison ranking: total 67

TRANSPORTATION

Civil aircraft registration country code prefix: EI

Airports: 100 (2025)
comparison ranking: 54

Heliports: 10 (2025)
comparison ranking: 75

Railways: *total:* 1,688 km (2020) 53 km electrified

Merchant marine: *total:* 94 (2023)
by type: bulk carrier 12, general cargo 32, oil tanker 1, other 49
comparison ranking: total 93

Ports: *total ports:* 21 (2024)
large: 1
medium: 3
small: 3
very small: 14
ports with oil terminals: 8
key ports: Cobh, Cork, Dublin, Foynes

MILITARY AND SECURITY

Military and security forces: Irish Defense Forces (Oglaigh na h-Eireannn): Army, Air Corps, Naval Service, Reserve Defense Forces (2025)
note: An Garda Siochana (or Garda) is the national police force and maintains internal security under the auspices of the Department of Justice

Military expenditures: 0.2% of GDP (2024 est.)
0.2% of GDP (2023 est.)
0.3% of GDP (2022 est.)
0.3% of GDP (2021 est.)
0.3% of GDP (2020 est.)

Military and security service personnel strengths: approximately 7,500 active-duty Defense Forces (authorized establishment of 9,500) (2025)

Military equipment inventories and acquisitions: the Irish Defense Forces have a small inventory of imported weapons systems from a variety of mostly European countries, particularly the UK (2024)

Military service age and obligation: 18 years of age for men and women for voluntary military service; 12-year service (5 active, 7 reserves) (2024)
note 1: as of 2024, women made up about 7.5% of the military 's full-time personnel
note 2: the Defense Forces are open to refugees under the Refugee Act of 1996 and nationals of the European Economic Area, which include EU member states, Iceland, Liechtenstein, and Norway

Military deployments: 130 Golan Heights (UNDOF); 325 Lebanon (UNIFIL) (2024)

Military - note: the Irish Defense Forces (IDF) are responsible for external defense, assisting civil authorities upon request, participating in multinational peacekeeping and humanitarian operations, and providing for maritime security; the IDF traces its origins back to the Irish Volunteers, a unit established in 1913 which took part in the 1916 Easter Rising and the Irish War of Independence (1919-1921)
Ireland has a long-standing policy of military neutrality; however, Ireland is a signatory of the EU 's Common Security and Defense Policy and has committed a battalion of troops to the EU 's Rapid Reaction Force; Ireland is not a member of NATO but has a relationship with it going back to 1997, when it deployed personnel in support of the NATO-led peacekeeping operation in Bosnia and Herzegovina; Ireland joined NATO 's Partnership for Peace program in 1999; it has been active in UN peacekeeping operations since the 1950s (2025)

TERRORISM

Terrorist group(s): Terrorist group(s): Continuity Irish Republican Army (CIRA); Real Irish Republican Army (RIRA); Islamic State of Iraq and ash-Sham (ISIS)
note: details about the history, aims, leadership, organization, areas of operation, tactics, targets, weapons, size, and sources of support of the group(s) appear(s) in Appendix T

TRANSNATIONAL ISSUES

Refugees and internally displaced persons: *refugees:* 156,441 (2024 est.)
stateless persons: 48 (2024 est.)

ISLE OF MAN

INTRODUCTION

Background: The Isle of Man was part of the Norwegian Kingdom of the Hebrides until the 13th century, when it was ceded to Scotland. The isle came under English lordship in the 14th century before being purchased by the British Government in 1765. Current concerns include reviving the almost extinct Manx Gaelic language. The Isle of Man is a British Crown dependency, which makes it a self-governing possession of the British Crown that is not part of the UK. The UK Government, however, remains constitutionally responsible for its defense and international representation.

GEOGRAPHY

Location: Western Europe, island in the Irish Sea, between Great Britain and Ireland

Geographic coordinates: 54 15 N, 4 30 W

Map references: Europe

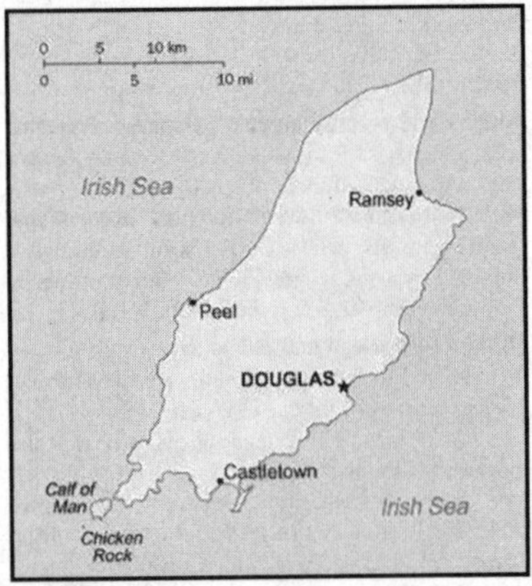

Area: *total:* 572 sq km
land: 572 sq km
water: 0 sq km
comparison ranking: total 193

Area - comparative: slightly more than three times the size of Washington, D.C.

Land boundaries: *total:* 0 km

Coastline: 160 km

Maritime claims: *territorial sea:* 12 nm
exclusive fishing zone: 12 nm

Climate: temperate; cool summers and mild winters; overcast about a third of the time

Terrain: hills in north and south bisected by central valley

Elevation: *highest point:* Snaefell 621 m
lowest point: Irish Sea 0 m

Natural resources: none

Land use: *agricultural land:* 71.4% (2022 est.)
arable land: 42.3% (2022 est.)
permanent crops: 0% (2022 est.)
permanent pasture: 29.1% (2022 est.)
forest: 6.1% (2022 est.)
other: 22.5% (2022 est.)

Irrigated land: 0 sq km (2022)

Population distribution: most people concentrated in cities and large towns; Douglas, in the southeast, is the largest

Natural hazards: occasional high winds and rough seas

Geography - note: one small islet, the Calf of Man, lies to the southwest and is a bird sanctuary

PEOPLE AND SOCIETY

Population: *total:* 92,269 (2024 est.)
male: 46,331
female: 45,938
comparison rankings: total 198; male 198; female 198

Nationality: *noun:* Manxman (men), Manxwoman (women)
adjective: Manx

Ethnic groups: White 94.7%, Asian 3.1%, Mixed 1%, Black 0.6%, other 0.4% (2021 est.)
note: data represent population by nationality

Languages: English, Manx Gaelic (about 2% of the population has some knowledge)

Religions: Christian 54.7%, Muslim 0.5%, Buddhist 0.5%, Hindu 0.4%, Jewish 0.2%, none 43.8% (2021 est.)

Age structure: *0-14 years:* 16% (male 7,701/female 7,100)
15-64 years: 61.9% (male 29,035/female 28,044)
65 years and over: 22.1% (2024 est.) (male 9,595/female 10,794)

Dependency ratios: *total dependency ratio:* 61.7 (2024 est.)
youth dependency ratio: 25.9 (2024 est.)
elderly dependency ratio: 35.7 (2024 est.)
potential support ratio: 2.8 (2024 est.)

Median age: *total:* 44.9 years (2024 est.)
male: 43.7 years
female: 46.1 years
comparison ranking: total 26

Population growth rate: 0.45% (2024 est.)
comparison ranking: 153

Birth rate: 10.4 births/1,000 population (2024 est.)
comparison ranking: 178

Death rate: 10.2 deaths/1,000 population (2024 est.)
comparison ranking: 34

Net migration rate: 4.3 migrant(s)/1,000 population (2024 est.)
comparison ranking: 22

Population distribution: most people concentrated in cities and large towns; Douglas, in the southeast, is the largest

Urbanization: *urban population:* 53.5% of total population (2023)
rate of urbanization: 0.97% annual rate of change (2020-25 est.)

Major urban areas - population: 27,000 DOUGLAS (capital) (2018)

Sex ratio: *at birth:* 1.08 male(s)/female
0-14 years: 1.08 male(s)/female
15-64 years: 1.04 male(s)/female
65 years and over: 0.89 male(s)/female
total population: 1.01 male(s)/female (2024 est.)

Infant mortality rate: *total:* 4.1 deaths/1,000 live births (2024 est.)
male: 4.4 deaths/1,000 live births
female: 3.7 deaths/1,000 live births
comparison ranking: total 186

Life expectancy at birth: *total population:* 82.5 years (2024 est.)
male: 80.7 years
female: 84.4 years
comparison ranking: total population 28

Total fertility rate: 1.88 children born/woman (2024 est.)
comparison ranking: 127

Gross reproduction rate: 0.9 (2024 est.)

Drinking water source: *improved:* total: 99.9% of population (2022 est.)
unimproved: *total:* 0.1% of population (2022 est.)

Sanitation facility access: *improved:* total: 100% of population (2022 est.)
unimproved: *urban:* NA
rural: NA
total: 0% of population (2022 est.) NA

ENVIRONMENT

Environmental issues: air pollution, marine pollution; waste disposal (both household and industrial)

Climate: temperate; cool summers and mild winters; overcast about a third of the time

Urbanization: *urban population:* 53.5% of total population (2023)
rate of urbanization: 0.97% annual rate of change (2020-25 est.)

Waste and recycling: *municipal solid waste generated annually:* 50,600 tons (2024 est.)
percent of municipal solid waste recycled: 50% (2011 est.)

GOVERNMENT

Country name: *conventional long form:* none
conventional short form: Isle of Man
local long form: Ellan Vannin
abbreviation: I.O.M.
etymology: the name "man" may be derived from the Gaelic word for "mountain;" the local name is from the words *ellan*, or "island," and Vannin, a form of the name Mannan

Government type: parliamentary democracy (Tynwald)

Dependency status: British crown dependency

Capital: *name:* Douglas
geographic coordinates: 54 09 N, 4 29 W
time difference: UTC 0 (5 hours ahead of Washington, DC, during Standard Time)
daylight saving time: +1hr, begins last Sunday in March; ends last Sunday in October
etymology: the name comes from the Gaelic name *Dubhghlais*, or "black stream," referring to a nearby river; a second river was called *Fionnghlais*, or "white stream;" both river names were later shortened to Dhoo and Glass, respectively, which coincidentally comprised the elements of the town's name

Administrative divisions: none; no first-order administrative divisions as defined by the US government, but 24 local authorities each hold elections

Legal system: UK laws apply, as well as Manx statutes

Constitution: *history:* development of the Isle of Man constitution dates to at least the 14th century
amendment process: proposed as a bill in the House of Keys, by the "Government," by a "Member of the House," or through petition to the House or Legislative Council; passage normally requires three separate readings and approval of at least 13 House members; following both House and Council agreement, assent is required by the lieutenant governor on behalf of the Crown

Citizenship: see United Kingdom

Suffrage: 16 years of age; universal

Executive branch: *chief of state:* Lord of Mann King CHARLES III (since 8 September 2022); represented by Lieutenant Governor Sir John LORIMER (since 29 September 2021)
head of government: Chief Minister Alfred CANNAN (since 12 October 2021)
cabinet: Council of Ministers appointed by the lieutenant governor
election/appointment process: the monarchy is hereditary; lieutenant governor appointed by the monarch; chief minister indirectly elected by the Tynwald for a 5-year term (eligible for second term)
most recent election date: 23 September 2021
election results: *2021:* Alfred CANNAN (independent) elected chief minister; Tynwald House of Keys vote - 21 of 24
2016: Howard QUAYLE elected chief minister; Tynwald House of Keys vote - 21 of 33
expected date of next election: 2026

Legislative branch: *legislature name:* Tynwald (High Court of Tynwald)
legislative structure: bicameral

note: Legislative Council includes the President of Tynwald, 2 non-voting members (the Lord Bishop of Sodor and Man and the attorney general), and 8 members indirectly elected by the House of Keys

Legislative branch - lower chamber: *chamber name:* House of Keys
number of seats: 24 (directly elected)
electoral system: plurality/majority
scope of elections: full renewal
term in office: 5 years
most recent election date: 9/23/2021
parties elected and seats per party: independent (21); Manx Labour Party (2); Liberal Vannin (1)
percentage of women in chamber: 40%
expected date of next election: September 2026

Legislative branch - upper chamber: *chamber name:* Legislative Council
number of seats: 11 (3 appointed, 8 indirectly elected)
scope of elections: partial renewal
term in office: 4 years
most recent election date: 3/14/2023
percentage of women in chamber: 36.4%
expected date of next election: March 2028

Judicial branch: *highest court(s):* Isle of Man High Court of Justice (consists of 3 permanent judges or "deemsters" and 1 judge of appeal; organized into the Staff of Government Division or Court of Appeal and the Civil Division); the Court of General Gaol Delivery (not formally part of the High Court but is administered as such) deals with serious criminal cases
judge selection and term of office: deemsters appointed by the Lord Chancellor of England on the nomination of the lieutenant governor; deemsters can serve until age 70
subordinate courts: High Court; Court of Summary Gaol Delivery; Summary Courts; Magistrate's Court; specialized courts
note: appeals beyond the Court of Appeal are referred to the Judicial Committee of the Privy Council (in London)

Political parties: Green Party
Liberal Vannin Party or LVP
Manx Labor Party
Mec Vannin (sometimes referred to as the Manx Nationalist Party)
note: most members sit as independents

Diplomatic representation in the US: none (British crown dependency)

Diplomatic representation from the US: *embassy:* none (British crown dependency)

International organization participation: UPU

Independence: none (British Crown dependency)

National holiday: Tynwald Day, 5 July (1417); date Tynwald Day was first recorded

Flag: *description:* red with the Three Legs of Man emblem (triskelion) in the center; the three legs are joined at the thigh and bent at the knee; a two-sided emblem is used to allow the toes to point clockwise on both sides of the flag
history: the flag is based on the coat of arms of the last recognized Norse King of Mann, MAGNUS III (r. 1252-65); the triskelion has its roots in an early Celtic sun symbol

National symbol(s): triskelion (a motif of three legs)

National color(s): red, white

National coat of arms: Queen Elizabeth II of the United Kingdom granted the Isle of Man's coat of arms on July 12, 1996; the triskelion (three conjoined legs) on the shield represents resilience, resourcefulness, and hope; the Latin motto means "Wherever you throw it, it will stand," a reference to the islanders' ability to stand strong; the peregrine falcon represents the two falcons that the Isle of Man has paid to the UK monarch on Coronation Day since 1406, and the raven symbolizes the island's former status as a Viking colony; the crown represents the UK monarch's status as the Lord of Mann, although the island is self-governing

National anthem(s): *title:* "Arrane Ashoonagh dy Vannin" (Isle of Man National Anthem)
lyrics/music: William Henry GILL [English], John J. KNEEN [Manx]/traditional
history: adopted 2003; serves as a local anthem
title: "God Save the King"
lyrics/music: unknown
history: official anthem, as a British Crown dependency; played when the sovereign, members of the royal family, or the lieutenant governor are present

ECONOMY

Economic overview: high-income British island economy; known financial services and tourism industries; taxation incentives for technology and financial firms to operate; historic fishing and agriculture industries are declining; major online gambling and film industry locale

Real GDP growth rate: -4.2% (2022 est.)
3.8% (2021 est.)
-8.8% (2020 est.)
note: annual GDP % growth based on constant local currency
comparison ranking: 211

GDP (official exchange rate): $7.431 billion (2022 est.)
note: data in current dollars at official exchange rate

GDP - composition, by sector of origin: *agriculture:* 0.4% (2022 est.)
industry: 6.9% (2022 est.)
services: 95.1% (2022 est.)
note: figures may not total 100% due to non-allocated consumption not captured in sector-reported data
comparison rankings: agriculture 193; industry 200; services 1

Agricultural products: cereals, vegetables; cattle, sheep, pigs, poultry

Industries: financial services, light manufacturing, tourism

Industrial production growth rate: -29.5% (2022 est.)
note: annual % change in industrial value added based on constant local currency
comparison ranking: 193

Exports - partners: almost entirely United Kingdom (2022)

Exports - commodities: crude petroleum, artwork, vegetables, fruits, whiskies (2022)
note: top five export commodities based on value in dollars

Imports - partners: almost entirely United Kingdom (2022)

Imports - commodities: ships, delivery trucks (2022)

Exchange rates: Manx pounds (IMP) per US dollar -

Exchange rates: 0.782 (2024 est.)
0.805 (2023 est.)
0.811 (2022 est.)
0.727 (2021 est.)
0.78 (2020 est.)

ENERGY

Electricity access: *electrification - total population:* 100% (2022 est.)

COMMUNICATIONS

Broadcast media: national public radio has 3 FM stations and 1 AM station; 2 commercial radio broadcasters; receives radio and TV services via relays from British TV and radio broadcasters

Internet country code: .im

TRANSPORTATION

Civil aircraft registration country code prefix: M

Airports: 4 (2025)
comparison ranking: 181

Heliports: 1 (2025)
comparison ranking: 142

Railways: *total:* 63 km (2008)
narrow gauge: 6 km (2008) 1.076-m gauge (6 km electrified)
57 0.914-mm gauge (29 km electrified) note: primarily summer tourist attractions

Merchant marine: *total:* 269 (2023)
by type: bulk carrier 102, container ship 6, general cargo 27, oil tanker 56, other 78
comparison ranking: total 62

Ports: *total ports:* 2 (2024)
large: 0
medium: 0
small: 2
very small: 0
ports with oil terminals: 1
key ports: Douglas, Ramsey

MILITARY AND SECURITY

Military - note: defense is the responsibility of the UK

ISRAEL

INTRODUCTION

Background: Israel has become a regional economic and military powerhouse, leveraging its prosperous high-tech sector, large defense industry, and concerns about Iran to foster partnerships around the world. The State of Israel was established in 1948. The UN General Assembly proposed in 1947 partitioning the British Mandate for Palestine into an Arab and Jewish state. The Jews accepted the proposal, but the local Arabs and the Arab states rejected the UN plan and launched a war. The Arabs were subsequently defeated

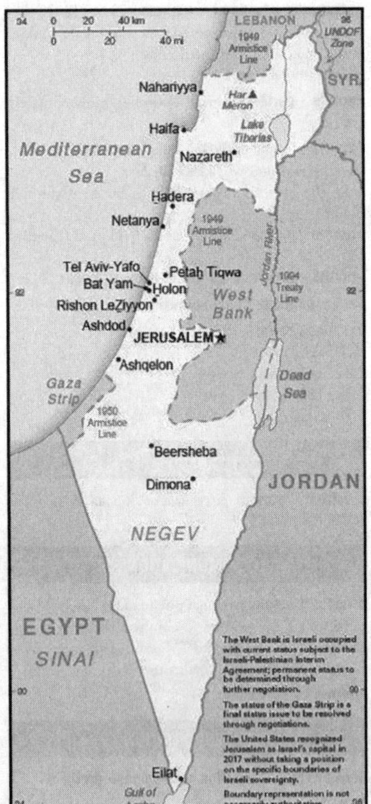

in the 1947-1949 war that followed the UN proposal and the British withdrawal. Israel joined the UN in 1949 and saw rapid population growth, primarily due to Jewish refugee migration from Europe and the Middle East. Israel and its Arab neighbors fought wars in 1956, 1967, and 1973, and Israel signed peace treaties with Egypt in 1979 and Jordan in 1994. Israel took control of the West Bank, the eastern part of Jerusalem, the Gaza Strip, the Sinai Peninsula, and the Golan Heights in the course of the 1967 war. It ceded the Sinai back to Egypt in the 1979-1982 period but has continued to administer the other territories through military authorities. Israel and Palestinian officials signed interim agreements in the 1990s that created a period of Palestinian self-rule in parts of the West Bank and Gaza. Israel withdrew from Gaza in 2005. The most recent formal efforts between Israel and the Palestinian Authority to negotiate final status issues occurred in 2013 and 2014, and the US continues its efforts to advance peace. Israel signed the US-brokered normalization agreements (the Abraham Accords) with Bahrain, the UAE, and Morocco in 2020 and reached an agreement with Sudan in 2021. Immigration to Israel continues, with more than 44,000 estimated new immigrants, mostly Jewish, in the first 11 months of 2023.

Former Prime Minister Benjamin NETANYAHU returned to office in 2022, continuing his dominance of Israel's political landscape at the head of Israel's most rightwing and religious government. NETANYAHU previously served as premier from 1996 to 1999 and from 2009 to 2021, becoming Israel's longest serving prime minister.

On 7 October 2023, HAMAS militants launched a combined unguided rocket and ground terrorist attack from Gaza into southern Israel. The same day Israel's Air Force launched air strikes inside Gaza and initiated a sustained air campaign against HAMAS targets across the Gaza Strip. The following day, NETANYAHU formally declared war on HAMAS, and on 28 October, the Israel Defense Forces launched a large-scale ground assault inside Gaza.

The Israeli economy has undergone a dramatic transformation in the last 30 years, led by cutting-edge high-tech sectors. Offshore gas discoveries in the Mediterranean place Israel at the center of a potential regional natural gas market. In 2022, a US-brokered agreement between Israel and Lebanon established their maritime boundary, allowing Israel to begin production on additional gas fields in the Mediterranean. However, Israel's economic development has been uneven. Structural issues such as low labor-force participation among religious and minority populations, low workforce productivity, high costs for housing and consumer staples, and high income inequality concern both economists and the general population. The current war with Hamas disrupted Israel's solid economic fundamentals, but it is not likely to have long-term structural implications for the economy.

GEOGRAPHY

Location: Middle East, bordering the Mediterranean Sea, between Egypt and Lebanon

Geographic coordinates: 31 30 N, 34 45 E

Map references: Middle East

Area: *total:* 21,937 sq km
land: 21,497 sq km
water: 440 sq km
comparison ranking: total 152

Area - comparative: slightly larger than New Jersey

Land boundaries: *total:* 1,068 km
border countries (6): Egypt 208 km; Gaza Strip 59 km; Jordan 327 km (20 km are within the Dead Sea); Lebanon 81 km; Syria 83 km; West Bank 330 km

Coastline: 273 km

Maritime claims: *territorial sea:* 12 nm
continental shelf: to depth of exploitation

Climate: temperate; hot and dry in southern and eastern desert areas

Terrain: Negev desert in the south; low coastal plain; central mountains; Jordan Rift Valley

Elevation: *highest point:* Mitspe Shlagim 2,224 m; note - this is the highest named point, the actual highest point is an unnamed dome slightly to the west of Mitspe Shlagim at 2,236 m; both points are on the northeastern border of Israel, along the southern end of the Anti-Lebanon mountain range
lowest point: Dead Sea -431 m
mean elevation: 508 m

Natural resources: timber, potash, copper ore, natural gas, phosphate rock, magnesium bromide, clays, sand

Land use: *agricultural land:* 29.5% (2022 est.)
arable land: 17.2% (2022 est.)
permanent crops: 4.7% (2022 est.)
permanent pasture: 7.6% (2022 est.)
forest: 6.5% (2022 est.)
other: 64% (2022 est.)

Irrigated land: 1,927 sq km (2022)

Major lakes (area sq km): *salt water lake(s):* Dead Sea (shared with Jordan and West Bank) - 1,020 sq km
note - endorheic hypersaline lake; 9.6 times saltier than the ocean; lake shore is 431 meters below sea level

Population distribution: population concentrated in and around Tel-Aviv, as well as around the Sea of Galilee; the south remains sparsely populated, with the exception of the shore of the Gulf of Aqaba

Natural hazards: sandstorms may occur during spring and summer; droughts; periodic earthquakes

Geography - note: *note 1:* Lake Tiberias (Sea of Galilee) is an important freshwater source; the Dead Sea is the second saltiest body of water in the world (after Lake Assal in Djibouti)
note 2: the Malham Cave in Mount Sodom is the world's longest salt cave at 10 km (6 mi); Mount Sodom is a hill about 220 m (722 ft) high that is 80% salt, with multiple salt layers covered by a veneer of rock

PEOPLE AND SOCIETY

Population: *total:* 9,402,617 (2024 est.)
male: 4,731,275
female: 4,671,342
note: approximately 236,600 Israeli settlers live in East Jerusalem (2021); following the March 2019 US recognition of the Golan Heights as being part of Israel, *The World Factbook* no longer includes Israeli settler population of the Golan Heights (estimated at 23,400 in 2019) in its overall Israeli settler total
comparison rankings: total 98; male 96; female 97

Nationality: *noun:* Israeli(s)
adjective: Israeli

Ethnic groups: Jewish 73.5% (of which Israel-born 79.7%, Europe/America/Oceania-born 14.3%, Africa-born 3.9%, Asia-born 2.1%), Arab 21.1%, other 5.4% (2022 est.)

Languages: Hebrew (official), Arabic (special status under Israeli law), English (most commonly used foreign language)
major-language sample(s):
העולם, המקור החיוני למידע בסיסי ספר עובדות
(Hebrew)

Religions: Jewish 73.5%, Muslim 18.1%, Christian 1.9%, Druze 1.6%, other 4.9% (2022 est.)

Age structure: *0-14 years:* 27.5% (male 1,320,629/female 1,260,977)
15-64 years: 60.3% (male 2,885,485/female 2,781,777)
65 years and over: 12.3% (2024 est.) (male 525,161/female 628,588)

Dependency ratios: *total dependency ratio:* 65.9 (2024 est.)
youth dependency ratio: 45.6 (2024 est.)
elderly dependency ratio: 20.4 (2024 est.)
potential support ratio: 4.9 (2024 est.)

Median age: *total:* 30.1 years (2024 est.)
male: 29.6 years
female: 30.7 years
comparison ranking: total 140

Population growth rate: 1.58% (2024 est.)
comparison ranking: 59

Birth rate: 19.1 births/1,000 population (2024 est.)
comparison ranking: 74

Death rate: 5.2 deaths/1,000 population (2024 est.)
comparison ranking: 189

Net migration rate: 1.9 migrant(s)/1,000 population (2024 est.)
comparison ranking: 51

Population distribution: population concentrated in and around Tel-Aviv, as well as around the Sea of Galilee; the south remains sparsely populated, with the exception of the shore of the Gulf of Aqaba

Urbanization: *urban population:* 92.9% of total population (2023)
rate of urbanization: 1.51% annual rate of change (2020-25 est.)

Major urban areas - population: 4.421 million Tel Aviv-Yafo, 1.174 million Haifa, 970,000 JERUSALEM (capital) (2023)

Sex ratio: *at birth:* 1.05 male(s)/female
0-14 years: 1.05 male(s)/female
15-64 years: 1.04 male(s)/female
65 years and over: 0.84 male(s)/female
total population: 1.01 male(s)/female (2024 est.)

Mother's mean age at first birth: 27.7 years (2019 est.)

Maternal mortality ratio: 2 deaths/100,000 live births (2023 est.)
comparison ranking: 192

Infant mortality rate: *total:* 2.8 deaths/1,000 live births (2024 est.)
male: 3.3 deaths/1,000 live births
female: 2.3 deaths/1,000 live births
comparison ranking: total 213

Life expectancy at birth: *total population:* 83.1 years (2024 est.)
male: 81.1 years
female: 85.1 years
comparison ranking: total population 16

Total fertility rate: 2.92 children born/woman (2024 est.)
comparison ranking: 50

Gross reproduction rate: 1.42 (2024 est.)

Drinking water source: *improved: urban:* 100% of population (2022 est.)
rural: 100% of population (2022 est.)
total: 100% of population (2022 est.)
unimproved: urban: 0% of population (2022 est.)
rural: 0% of population (2022 est.)
total: 0% of population (2022 est.)

Health expenditure: 7.9% of GDP (2021)
13% of national budget (2022 est.)

Physician density: 3.8 physicians/1,000 population (2023)

Hospital bed density: 3.1 beds/1,000 population (2021 est.)

Sanitation facility access: *improved: urban:* 100% of population (2022 est.)
rural: 99% of population (2022 est.)
total: 99.9% of population (2022 est.)
unimproved: urban: 0% of population (2022 est.)
rural: 1% of population (2022 est.)
total: 0.1% of population (2022 est.)

Obesity - adult prevalence rate: 26.1% (2016)
comparison ranking: 45

Alcohol consumption per capita: *total:* 3.07 liters of pure alcohol (2019 est.)
beer: 1.78 liters of pure alcohol (2019 est.)
wine: 0.08 liters of pure alcohol (2019 est.)
spirits: 1.16 liters of pure alcohol (2019 est.)
other alcohols: 0.04 liters of pure alcohol (2019 est.)
comparison ranking: total 112

Tobacco use: *total:* 18.6% (2025 est.)
male: 24.9% (2025 est.)
female: 12.4% (2025 est.)
comparison ranking: total 78

Currently married women (ages 15-49): 51.7% (2023 est.)

Education expenditure: 6.5% of GDP (2022 est.)
17.5% national budget (2022 est.)
comparison ranking: Education expenditure (% GDP) 23

School life expectancy (primary to tertiary education): *total:* 15 years (2022 est.)
male: 14 years (2022 est.)
female: 16 years (2022 est.)

ENVIRONMENT

Environmental issues: limited arable land and restricted natural freshwater resources; desertification; air pollution from industrial and vehicle emissions; groundwater pollution from industrial and domestic waste, chemical fertilizers, and pesticides

International environmental agreements: *party to:* Biodiversity, Climate Change, Climate Change-Kyoto Protocol, Climate Change-Paris Agreement, Desertification, Endangered Species, Hazardous Wastes, Nuclear Test Ban, Ozone Layer Protection, Ship Pollution, Wetlands, Whaling
signed, but not ratified: Comprehensive Nuclear Test Ban, Marine Life Conservation

Climate: temperate; hot and dry in southern and eastern desert areas

Urbanization: *urban population:* 92.9% of total population (2023)
rate of urbanization: 1.51% annual rate of change (2020-25 est.)

Carbon dioxide emissions: 64.401 million metric tonnes of CO2 (2023 est.)
from coal and metallurgical coke: 11.542 million metric tonnes of CO2 (2023 est.)
from petroleum and other liquids: 28.793 million metric tonnes of CO2 (2023 est.)
from consumed natural gas: 24.066 million metric tonnes of CO2 (2023 est.)
comparison ranking: total emissions 49

Particulate matter emissions: 20.4 micrograms per cubic meter (2019 est.)

Methane emissions: *energy:* 29.2 kt (2022-2024 est.)
agriculture: 40.6 kt (2019-2021 est.)
waste: 272.7 kt (2019-2021 est.)
other: 0.7 kt (2019-2021 est.)

Waste and recycling: *municipal solid waste generated annually:* 5.4 million tons (2024 est.)
percent of municipal solid waste recycled: 30.4% (2022 est.)

Total water withdrawal: *municipal:* 1 billion cubic meters (2022 est.)
industrial: 104.834 million cubic meters (2022 est.)
agricultural: 1.215 billion cubic meters (2022)

Total renewable water resources: 1.78 billion cubic meters (2022 est.)

GOVERNMENT

Country name: *conventional long form:* State of Israel
conventional short form: Israel
local long form: Medinat Yisra'el
local short form: Yisra'el
former: Mandatory Palestine
etymology: named after the ancient Kingdom of Israel; according to Biblical tradition, the Jewish patriarch Jacob received the name Israel (meaning "He who struggles with God") after he wrestled with an angel of the Lord

Government type: parliamentary democracy

Capital: *name:* Jerusalem
geographic coordinates: 31 46 N, 35 14 E
time difference: UTC+2 (7 hours ahead of Washington, DC, during Standard Time)
daylight saving time: +1hr, Friday before the last Sunday in March; ends the last Sunday in October
etymology: the meaning of the ancient name is unclear; the city is called Ursalim or Urusalimmi in Egyptian texts from the 14th century B.C., which may come from the Western Semitic verb *yaru*, meaning "to establish," and the name Shalim, the Canaanite god of dusk; another theory says the root letters s-l-m in the name refer to *shalom*, meaning "peace"
note: the US recognized Jerusalem as Israel's capital in 2017, without taking a position on the specific boundaries of Israeli sovereignty

Administrative divisions: 6 districts (*mehozot*, singular - *mehoz*); Central, Haifa, Jerusalem, Northern, Southern, Tel Aviv

Legal system: mixed system of English common law, British Mandate regulations, and Jewish, Christian, and Muslim religious laws

Constitution: *history:* no formal constitution; some functions of a constitution are filled by the Declaration of Establishment (1948), the Basic Laws, and the Law of Return (as amended)
amendment process: proposed by Government of Israel ministers or by the Knesset; passage requires a majority vote of Knesset members and subject to Supreme Court judicial review

International law organization participation: has not submitted an ICJ jurisdiction declaration; withdrew acceptance of ICCt jurisdiction in 2002

Citizenship: *citizenship by birth:* no
citizenship by descent only: at least one parent must be a citizen of Israel
dual citizenship recognized: yes, but naturalized citizens are not allowed to maintain dual citizenship
residency requirement for naturalization: 3 out of the 5 years preceding the application for naturalization
note: Israeli law (Law of Return, 5 July 1950) provides for the granting of citizenship to any Jew - defined as a person being born to a Jewish mother or having converted to Judaism while renouncing any other religion - who immigrates to and expresses a desire to settle in Israel on the basis of the Right of aliyah; the 1970 amendment of this act extended the right to family members including the spouse of a Jew, any child or grandchild, and the spouses of children and grandchildren

Suffrage: 18 years of age; universal; 17 years of age for municipal elections

Executive branch: *chief of state:* President Isaac HERZOG (since 7 July 2021)
head of government: Prime Minister Benyamin NETANYAHU (since 29 December 2022)
cabinet: Cabinet selected by prime minister and approved by the Knesset
election/appointment process: president indirectly elected by the Knesset for a single 7-year term; following legislative elections, the president, in consultation with party leaders, tasks a Knesset member (usually the member of the largest party) with forming a new government
most recent election date: 2 June 2021

election results: *2021:* Isaac HERZOG elected president; Knesset vote in first round - Isaac HERZOG (independent) 87, Miriam PERETZ (independent) 26, invalid/blank 7
2014: Reuven RIVLIN elected president in second round; Knesset vote - Reuven RIVLIN (Likud) 63, Meir SHEETRIT (The Movement) 53, other/invalid 4
expected date of next election: June 2028

Legislative branch: *legislature name:* Parliament (Knesset)
legislative structure: unicameral
number of seats: 120 (all directly elected)
electoral system: proportional representation
scope of elections: full renewal
term in office: 4 years
most recent election date: 11/1/2022
parties elected and seats per party: Likud (32); Yesh Atid (24); Religious Zionism (14); National Unity (12); Shas (11); United Torah Judaism (Yahadut Hatorah) (7); Yisrael Beiteinu (6); Other (14)
percentage of women in chamber: 24.2%
expected date of next election: October 2026
note 1: a 3.25% vote threshold is required to gain representation
note 2: following the 1 November 2022 election, the Religious Zionism Alliance split into its three constituent parties in the Knesset: Religious Zionism 7 seats, Jewish Power (Otzma Yehudit) 6, and Noam 1

Judicial branch: *highest court(s):* Supreme Court (consists of the president, deputy president, 13 justices, and 2 registrars) and normally sits in panels of 3 justices; in special cases, the panel is expanded with an uneven number of justices
judge selection and term of office: judges selected by the 9-member Judicial Selection Committee, consisting of the Minister of Justice (chair), the president of the Supreme Court, two other Supreme Court justices, 1 other Cabinet minister, 2 Knesset members, and 2 representatives of the Israel Bar Association; judges can serve up to mandatory retirement at age 70
subordinate courts: district and magistrate courts; national and regional labor courts; family and juvenile courts; special and Rabbinical courts

Political parties: Balad
Blue and White
Hadash
Labor Party or HaAvoda
Likud
Meretz
National Unity (alliance includes Blue and White and New Hope)
New Hope
Noam
Otzma Yehudit
Religious Zionist Party
Shas
Ta'al
United Arab List
United Torah Judaism or UTJ (alliance includes Agudat Israel and Degel HaTorah)
Yesh Atid
Yisrael Beiteinu

Diplomatic representation in the US: *chief of mission:* Ambassador Yechiel (Michael) LEITER (since 4 February 2025)
chancery: 3514 International Drive NW, Washington, DC 20008
telephone: [1] (202) 364-5500
FAX: [1] (202) 364-5607
email address and website: consular@washington.mfa.gov.il
https://embassies.gov.il/washington/Pages/default.aspx
consulate(s) general: Atlanta, Boston, Chicago, Houston, Los Angeles, Miami, New York, San Francisco

Diplomatic representation from the US: *chief of mission:* Ambassador Mike HUCKABEE (21 April 2025)
embassy: 14 David Flusser Street, Jerusalem, 9378322
mailing address: 6350 Jerusalem Place, Washington DC 20521-6350
telephone: [972] (2) 630-4000
FAX: [972] (2) 630-4070
email address and website: JerusalemACS@state.gov
https://il.usembassy. gov/
branch office(s): Tel Aviv
note: on 14 May 2018, the US Embassy relocated to Jerusalem from Tel Aviv; on 4 March 2019, Consulate General Jerusalem merged into US Embassy Jerusalem to form a single diplomatic mission

International organization participation: BIS, BSEC (observer), CE (observer), CERN, CICA, EBRD, FAO, IADB, IAEA, IBRD, ICAO, ICC (national committees), ICRM, IDA, IFAD, IFC, IFRCS, ILO, IMF, IMO, IMSO, Interpol, IOC, IOM, IPU, ISO, ITSO, ITU, ITUC (NGOs), MIGA, OAS (observer), OECD, OPCW (signatory), OSCE (partner), Pacific Alliance (observer), Paris Club, PCA, SELEC (observer), UN, UNCTAD, UNESCO, UNHCR, UNIDO, UNWTO, UPU, WCO, WHO, WIPO, WMO, WTO

Independence: 14 May 1948 (following League of Nations mandate under British administration)

National holiday: Independence Day, 14 May (1948)
note: Israel declared independence on 14 May 1948, but the Jewish calendar is lunar, so the holiday can occur in April or May

Flag: *description:* white with a blue hexagram (six-pointed linear star) known as the Magen David (Star of David or Shield of David) centered between two equal horizontal blue bands near the top and bottom edges of the flag
history: the design resembles a traditional Jewish prayer shawl *(tallit)*, which is white with blue stripes; the hexagram as a Jewish symbol dates back to medieval times
note: the Israeli flag proclamation states that the flag colors are sky blue and white, but the exact shade of blue has never been set and can vary

National symbol(s): Star of David (Magen David), menorah (seven-branched lampstand)

National color(s): blue, white

National anthem(s): *title:* "Hatikvah" (The Hope)
lyrics/music: Naftali Herz IMBER/traditional, arranged by Samuel COHEN
history: adopted 2004, unofficial since 1948; used as the anthem of the Zionist movement since 1897; the 1888 arrangement by Samuel COHEN is thought to be based on the Romanian folk song "Carul cu boi" (The Ox-Driven Cart)

National heritage: *total World Heritage Sites:* 9 (all cultural)
selected World Heritage Site locales: Masada; Old City of Acre; White City of Tel-Aviv - the Modern Movement; Biblical Tels - Megiddo, Hazor, Beer Sheba; Incense Route - Desert Cities in the Negev; Bahá'i Holy Places; Sites of Human Evolution at Mount Carmel; Caves of Maresha and Bet-Guvrin; Necropolis of Bet She'arim

ECONOMY

Economic overview: high-income, technology- and industrial-based economy; economic contraction and fiscal deficits resulting from war in Gaza; labor force stabilizing following military reservist mobilization; high-tech industry remains resilient while construction and tourism among hardest-hit sectors

Real GDP (purchasing power parity): $472.177 billion (2024 est.)
$468.095 billion (2023 est.)
$459.698 billion (2022 est.)
note: data in 2021 dollars
comparison ranking: 51

Real GDP growth rate: 0.9% (2024 est.)
1.8% (2023 est.)
6.3% (2022 est.)
note: annual GDP % growth based on constant local currency
comparison ranking: 179

Real GDP per capita: $47,300 (2024 est.)
$47,500 (2023 est.)
$48,100 (2022 est.)
note: data in 2021 dollars
comparison ranking: 44

GDP (official exchange rate): $540.38 billion (2024 est.)
note: data in current dollars at official exchange rate

Inflation rate (consumer prices): 3.1% (2024 est.)
4.2% (2023 est.)
4.4% (2022 est.)
note: annual % change based on consumer prices
comparison ranking: 95

GDP - composition, by sector of origin: *agriculture:* 1.3% (2024 est.)
industry: 17.3% (2024 est.)
services: 72.5% (2024 est.)
note: figures may not total 100% due to non-allocated consumption not captured in sector-reported data
comparison rankings: agriculture 167; industry 153; services 29

GDP - composition, by end use: *household consumption:* 48% (2023 est.)
government consumption: 22.3% (2023 est.)
investment in fixed capital: 24.4% (2023 est.)
investment in inventories: 1.7% (2023 est.)
exports of goods and services: 30.4% (2023 est.)
imports of goods and services: -27.6% (2023 est.)
note: figures may not total 100% due to rounding or gaps in data collection

Agricultural products: milk, chicken, potatoes, tomatoes, tangerines/mandarins, bananas, eggs, avocados, beef, carrots/turnips (2023)
note: top ten agricultural products based on tonnage

Industries: high-technology products (including aviation, communications, computer-aided design and manufactures, medical electronics, fiber optics), wood and paper products, potash and phosphates, food, beverages, and tobacco, caustic soda, cement, pharmaceuticals, construction, metal products, chemical products, plastics, cut diamonds, textiles, footwear

Industrial production growth rate: -4.2% (2024 est.)
note: annual % change in industrial value added based on constant local currency
comparison ranking: 175

Labor force: 4.71 million (2024 est.)

note: number of people ages 15 or older who are employed or seeking work
comparison ranking: 91

Unemployment rate: 3.2% (2024 est.)
3.6% (2023 est.)
3.7% (2022 est.)
note: % of labor force seeking employment
comparison ranking: 50

Youth unemployment rate (ages 15-24): *total:* 6.1% (2024 est.)
male: 6.2% (2024 est.)
female: 6% (2024 est.)
note: % of labor force ages 15-24 seeking employment
comparison ranking: total 156

Gini Index coefficient - distribution of family income: 37.9 (2021 est.)
note: index (0-100) of income distribution; higher values represent greater inequality
comparison ranking: 55

Average household expenditures: *on food:* 15.8% of household expenditures (2023 est.)
on alcohol and tobacco: 2.6% of household expenditures (2023 est.)

Household income or consumption by percentage share: *lowest 10%:* 2% (2021 est.)
highest 10%: 26.6% (2021 est.)
note: % share of income accruing to lowest and highest 10% of population

Remittances: 0.2% of GDP (2024 est.)
0.2% of GDP (2023 est.)
0.2% of GDP (2022 est.)
note: personal transfers and compensation between resident and non-resident individuals/households/entities

Budget: *revenues:* $162.524 billion (2023 est.)
expenditures: $188.905 billion (2023 est.)
note: central government revenues (excluding grants) and expenditures converted to US dollars at average official exchange rate for year indicated

Taxes and other revenues: 22.1% (of GDP) (2023 est.)
note: central government tax revenue as a % of GDP
comparison ranking: 35

Current account balance: $16.713 billion (2024 est.)
$18.604 billion (2023 est.)
$17.104 billion (2022 est.)
note: balance of payments - net trade and primary/secondary income in current dollars
comparison ranking: 22

Exports: $153.248 billion (2024 est.)
$154.638 billion (2023 est.)
$164.407 billion (2022 est.)
note: balance of payments - exports of goods and services in current dollars
comparison ranking: 38

Exports - partners: USA 29%, China 10%, Ireland 6%, Germany 4%, Hong Kong 4% (2023)
note: top five export partners based on percentage share of exports

Exports - commodities: integrated circuits, diamonds, broadcasting equipment, medical instruments, refined petroleum (2023)
note: top five export commodities based on value in dollars

Imports: $140.438 billion (2024 est.)
$140.432 billion (2023 est.)
$153.388 billion (2022 est.)
note: balance of payments - imports of goods and services in current dollars
comparison ranking: 40

Imports - partners: China 17%, USA 12%, Germany 7%, Turkey 6%, Italy 4% (2023)
note: top five import partners based on percentage share of imports

Imports - commodities: cars, diamonds, crude petroleum, broadcasting equipment, garments (2023)
note: top five import commodities based on value in dollars

Reserves of foreign exchange and gold: $214.544 billion (2024 est.)
$204.661 billion (2023 est.)
$194.231 billion (2022 est.)
note: holdings of gold (year-end prices)/foreign exchange/special drawing rights in current dollars
comparison ranking: 19

Exchange rates: new Israeli shekels (ILS) per US dollar -

Exchange rates: 3.7 (2024 est.)
3.667 (2023 est.)
3.36 (2022 est.)
3.23 (2021 est.)
3.442 (2020 est.)

ENERGY

Electricity access: *electrification - total population:* 100% (2022 est.)

Electricity: *installed generating capacity:* 22.612 million kW (2023 est.)
consumption: 63.964 billion kWh (2023 est.)
exports: 6.93 billion kWh (2023 est.)
transmission/distribution losses: 3.51 billion kWh (2023 est.)
comparison rankings: installed generating capacity 46; consumption 46; exports 35; transmission/distribution losses 149

Electricity generation sources: *fossil fuels:* 89.5% of total installed capacity (2023 est.)
solar: 9.4% of total installed capacity (2023 est.)
wind: 1% of total installed capacity (2023 est.)
biomass and waste: 0.1% of total installed capacity (2023 est.)

Coal: *consumption:* 5.297 million metric tons (2023 est.)
exports: 9 metric tons (2022 est.)
imports: 4.887 million metric tons (2023 est.)

Petroleum: *total petroleum production:* 15,000 bbl/day (2023 est.)
refined petroleum consumption: 219,000 bbl/day (2024 est.)
crude oil estimated reserves: 12.73 million barrels (2021 est.)

Natural gas: *production:* 24.186 billion cubic meters (2023 est.)
consumption: 12.608 billion cubic meters (2023 est.)
exports: 11.505 billion cubic meters (2023 est.)
imports: 59.369 million cubic meters (2022 est.)
proven reserves: 176.018 billion cubic meters (2021 est.)

Energy consumption per capita: 112.437 million Btu/person (2023 est.)
comparison ranking: 40

COMMUNICATIONS

Telephones - fixed lines: *total subscriptions:* 2.905 million (2023 est.)
subscriptions per 100 inhabitants: 31 (2023 est.)
comparison ranking: total subscriptions 37

Telephones - mobile cellular: *total subscriptions:* 13.8 million (2022 est.)
subscriptions per 100 inhabitants: 152 (2022 est.)
comparison ranking: total subscriptions 78

Broadcast media: the Israel Broadcasting Corporation (IBC) has 3 channels, two in Hebrew and one in Arabic; multi-channel satellite and cable TV packages provide access to foreign channels; IBC broadcasts on 8 radio networks with multiple repeaters, and Israel Defense Forces Radio broadcasts over multiple stations; about 15 privately owned radio stations (2019)

Internet country code: .il

Internet users: *percent of population:* 87% (2023 est.)

Broadband - fixed subscriptions: *total:* 2.76 million (2023 est.)
subscriptions per 100 inhabitants: 30 (2023 est.)
comparison ranking: total 51

TRANSPORTATION

Civil aircraft registration country code prefix: 4X

Airports: 40 (2025)
comparison ranking: 104

Heliports: 13 (2025)
comparison ranking: 64

Railways: *total:* 1,497 km (2021) (2019)
standard gauge: 1,497 km (2021) 1.435-m gauge

Merchant marine: *total:* 41 (2023)
by type: container ship 4, general cargo 1, oil tanker 4, other 32
comparison ranking: total 123

Ports: *total ports:* 5 (2024)
large: 0
medium: 1
small: 2
very small: 2
ports with oil terminals: 4
key ports: Ashdod, Ashqelon, Elat, Hadera, Haifa

MILITARY AND SECURITY

Military and security forces: Israel Defense Forces (IDF): Ground Forces, Israel Naval Force (IN, includes commandos), Israel Air Force (IAF, includes air defense)

Ministry of National Security: Israeli Police (2025)

Military expenditures: 8% of GDP (2024 est.)
5% of GDP (2023 est.)
4.5% of GDP (2022 est.)
5% of GDP (2021 est.)
5% of GDP (2020 est.)

Military and security service personnel strengths: approximately 170,000 active-duty Defense Forces (130,000 Ground Forces; 10,000 Naval; 30,000 Air Force); more than 400,000 reserves (2025)

Military equipment inventories and acquisitions: the majority of the IDF's inventory is comprised of weapons that are domestically produced or imported from Europe and the uS; the uS has been the leading supplier of arms in recent years; Israel has a broad defense industrial base that can develop, produce, support, and sustain a wide variety of weapons systems for both domestic use and export, particularly armored vehicles, unmanned aerial systems, air defense, and guided missiles (2024)

Military service age and obligation: 18 years of age for compulsory military service; 17 years of age for voluntary military service; Jews and Druze can be conscripted; Christians, Circassians, and Muslims

may volunteer; both sexes are obligated to military service; conscript service obligation is 32 months for enlisted men and about 24 months for enlisted women (varies based on military occupation); officers serve 48 months; Air Force pilots commit to 9 years of service; reserve obligation to age 41-51 (men), age 24 (women) (2024)
note: the IDF recruits foreign Jews and non-Jews with a minimum of one Jewish grandparent, as well as converts to Judaism; each year the IDF brings in about 800-1,000 foreign recruits from around the world

Military - note: the IDF is responsible for external defense but also has some domestic security responsibilities; its primary operational focuses include the threat posed by Iran, instability in Syria, and terrorist organizations, including HAMAS, Hizballah, and Palestine Islamic Jihad; since its creation from armed Jewish militias during the First Arab-Israeli War in 1948-49, the IDF, particularly the Ground Force, has been guided by a requirement to rapidly mobilize and defend the country's territory from numerically superior neighboring countries; the active-duty military is backed up by a large force of trained reserves–approximately 300-400,000 personnel–that can be mobilized rapidly
Israel's primary security partner is the US; consistent with a 10-year (2019-2028) Memorandum of Understanding, the US annually provides over $3 billion in military financing and cooperative military programs, such as missile defense; the US also provides Israel access to US-produced military weapons systems including advanced fighter aircraft; Israel has Major Non-NATO Ally status with the US, a designation under US law that provides foreign partners with certain benefits in the areas of defense trade and security cooperation
the United Nations Disengagement Observer Force (UNDOF) has operated in the Golan between Israel and Syria since 1974 to monitor the ceasefire following the 1973 Arab-Israeli War and supervise the areas of separation between the two countries; UNDOF consists of about 1,300 total personnel (2025)

SPACE

Space agency/agencies: Israel Space Agency (ISA; established 1983 under the Ministry of Science and Technology; origins go back to the creation of a National Committee for Space Research, established 1960); Ministry of Defense Space Department (2025)

Space launch site(s): Palmachim Airbase (Central district) (2025)

Space program overview: has an ambitious space program and one of the most advanced in the region; designs, builds, operates, and launches communications, remote sensing (RS), and scientific satellites; designs, builds, and operates orbital satellite/space launch vehicles (SLVs); researches and develops a range of other space-related capabilities with a focus on lightweight and miniaturized technologies, including robotics and small satellites with high resolution RS imaging and communications capabilities; has relations with a variety of foreign space agencies and space industries, including those of Canada, the European Space Agency (and individual member states, such as France, Germany, and Italy), India, Japan, Mexico, and the US; has a substantial commercial space sector, as well as state-owned enterprises (2025)
note: further details about the key activities, programs, and milestones of the country's space program, as well as government spending estimates on the space sector, appear in the Space Programs reference guide

TERRORISM

Terrorist group(s): Terrorist group(s): Islamic State of Iraq and ash-Sham (ISIS); Popular Front for the Liberation of Palestine (PFLP); Palestinian Islamic Jihad (PIJ); HAMAS
note: details about the history, aims, leadership, organization, areas of operation, tactics, targets, weapons, size, and sources of support of the group(s) appear(s) in Appendix T

TRANSNATIONAL ISSUES

Refugees and internally displaced persons: *refugees:* 27,413 (2024 est.)

IDPs: 68,000 (2024 est.)
stateless persons: 35 (2024 est.)

ITALY

INTRODUCTION

Background: Italy became a nation-state in 1861 when the regional states of the peninsula, along with Sardinia and Sicily, were united under King Victor EMMANUEL II. An era of parliamentary government came to a close in the early 1920s when Benito MUSSOLINI established a Fascist dictatorship. His alliance with Nazi Germany led to Italy's defeat in World War II. A democratic republic replaced the monarchy in 1946, and economic revival followed. Italy is a charter member of NATO, as well as the European Economic Community (EEC) and its successors, the EC and the EU. It has been at the forefront of European economic and political unification, joining the Economic and Monetary Union in 1999. Persistent problems include sluggish economic growth, high youth and female unemployment, organized crime, corruption, and economic disparities between southern Italy and the more prosperous north.

GEOGRAPHY

Location: Southern Europe, a peninsula extending into the central Mediterranean Sea, northeast of Tunisia

Geographic coordinates: 42 50 N, 12 50 E

Map references: Europe

Area: *total:* 301,340 sq km
land: 294,140 sq km
water: 7,200 sq km
note: includes Sardinia and Sicily
comparison ranking: total 73

Area - comparative: almost twice the size of Georgia; slightly larger than Arizona

Land boundaries: *total:* 1,836.4 km
border countries (6): Austria 404 km; France 476 km; Holy See (Vatican City) 3.4 km; San Marino 37 km; Slovenia 218 km; Switzerland 698 km

Coastline: 7,600 km

Maritime claims: *territorial sea:* 12 nm
continental shelf: 200-m depth or to the depth of exploitation

Climate: predominantly Mediterranean; alpine in far north; hot, dry in south

Terrain: mostly rugged and mountainous; some plains, coastal lowlands

Elevation: *highest point:* Mont Blanc (Monte Bianco) de Courmayeur (a secondary peak of Mont Blanc) 4,748 m
lowest point: Mediterranean Sea 0 m
mean elevation: 538 m

Natural resources: coal, antimony, mercury, zinc, potash, marble, barite, asbestos, pumice, fluorspar, feldspar, pyrite (sulfur), natural gas and crude oil reserves, fish, arable land

Land use: *agricultural land:* 44% (2022 est.)
arable land: 24% (2022 est.)
permanent crops: 8.1% (2022 est.)
permanent pasture: 11.9% (2022 est.)
forest: 32.7% (2022 est.)
other: 23.3% (2022 est.)

Irrigated land: 24,460 sq km (2021)

Major watersheds (area sq km): Atlantic Ocean drainage: Rhine-Maas (198,735 sq km), *(Black Sea)* Danube (795,656 sq km), *(Adriatic Sea)* Po (76,997 sq km), *(Mediterranean Sea)* Rhone (100,543 sq km)

Population distribution: a fairly even population distribution exists throughout most of the country, with coastal areas, the Po River Valley, and urban centers (particularly Milan, Rome, and Naples) attracting larger and denser populations

Natural hazards: regional risks include landslides, mudflows, avalanches, earthquakes, volcanic eruptions, flooding; land subsidence in Venice *volcanism:* significant volcanic activity; Etna (3,330 m) is Europe's most active volcano, and its flank eruptions pose a threat to nearby Sicilian villages; Etna, along with the famous Vesuvius, have both been deemed Decade Volcanoes by the International Association of Volcanology and Chemistry of the Earth's Interior, worthy of study due to their explosive history and close proximity to human populations; Stromboli, on its namesake island, has also been continuously active with moderate volcanic activity; other historically active volcanoes include Campi Flegrei, Ischia, Larderello, Pantelleria, Vulcano, and Vulsini

Geography - note: strategic location dominating central Mediterranean, as well as southern sea and air approaches to Western Europe

PEOPLE AND SOCIETY

Population: *total:* 60,964,931 (2024 est.)
male: 29,414,065
female: 31,550,866
comparison rankings: total 24; male 25; female 24

Nationality: *noun:* Italian(s)
adjective: Italian

Ethnic groups: Italian (includes small clusters of German-, French-, and Slovene-Italians in the north, Albanian-Italians, Croat-Italians, and Greek-Italians in the south)

Languages: Italian (official), German (parts of Trentino-Alto Adige region are predominantly German-speaking), French (small French-speaking minority in Valle d'Aosta region), Slovene (Slovene-speaking minority in the Trieste-Gorizia area), Croatian (in Molise)
major-language sample(s):
L'Almanacco dei fatti del mondo, l'indispensabile fonte per le informazioni di base. (Italian)

Religions: Christian 80.8% (overwhelmingly Roman Catholic with very small groups of Jehovah's Witnesses and Protestants), Muslim 4.9%, unaffiliated 13.4%, other 0.9% (2020 est.)

Age structure: *0-14 years:* 11.9% (male 3,699,167/female 3,531,734)
15-64 years: 64.5% (male 19,378,160/female 19,958,137)
65 years and over: 23.6% (2024 est.) (male 6,336,738/female 8,060,995)

Dependency ratios: *total dependency ratio:* 55 (2024 est.)
youth dependency ratio: 18.4 (2024 est.)
elderly dependency ratio: 36.6 (2024 est.)
potential support ratio: 2.7 (2024 est.)

Median age: *total:* 48.4 years (2024 est.)
male: 47.4 years
female: 49.4 years
comparison ranking: total 5

Population growth rate: -0.08% (2024 est.)
comparison ranking: 201

Birth rate: 7.1 births/1,000 population (2024 est.)
comparison ranking: 222

Death rate: 11.2 deaths/1,000 population (2024 est.)
comparison ranking: 22

Net migration rate: 3.4 migrant(s)/1,000 population (2024 est.)
comparison ranking: 33

Population distribution: a fairly even population distribution exists throughout most of the country, with coastal areas, the Po River Valley, and urban centers (particularly Milan, Rome, and Naples) attracting larger and denser populations

Urbanization: *urban population:* 72% of total population (2023)
rate of urbanization: 0.27% annual rate of change (2020-25 est.)

Major urban areas - population: 4.316 million ROME (capital), 3.155 million Milan, 2.179 million Naples, 1.802 million Turin, 913,000 Bergamo, 850,000 Palermo (2023)

Sex ratio: *at birth:* 1.06 male(s)/female
0-14 years: 1.05 male(s)/female
15-64 years: 0.97 male(s)/female
65 years and over: 0.79 male(s)/female
total population: 0.93 male(s)/female (2024 est.)

Mother's mean age at first birth: 31.4 years (2020 est.)

Maternal mortality ratio: 6 deaths/100,000 live births (2023 est.)
comparison ranking: 163

Infant mortality rate: *total:* 3.1 deaths/1,000 live births (2024 est.)
male: 3.2 deaths/1,000 live births
female: 2.9 deaths/1,000 live births
comparison ranking: total 207

Life expectancy at birth: *total population:* 83 years (2024 est.)
male: 80.7 years
female: 85.5 years
comparison ranking: total population 19

Total fertility rate: 1.26 children born/woman (2024 est.)
comparison ranking: 219

Gross reproduction rate: 0.61 (2024 est.)

Drinking water source: *improved:* total: 99.9% of population (2022 est.)
unimproved: total: 0.1% of population (2022 est.)

Health expenditure: 9% of GDP (2022)
11.8% of national budget (2022 est.)

Physician density: 4.19 physicians/1,000 population (2022)

Hospital bed density: 3.2 beds/1,000 population (2020 est.)

Sanitation facility access: *improved: urban:* 100% of population (2022 est.)
rural: 100% of population (2022 est.)
total: 100% of population (2022 est.)
unimproved: urban: 0% of population (2022 est.)
rural: 0% of population (2022 est.)
total: 0% of population (2022 est.)

Obesity - adult prevalence rate: 19.9% (2016)
comparison ranking: 108

Alcohol consumption per capita: *total:* 7.65 liters of pure alcohol (2019 est.)
beer: 1.99 liters of pure alcohol (2019 est.)
wine: 4.83 liters of pure alcohol (2019 est.)
spirits: 0.83 liters of pure alcohol (2019 est.)
other alcohols: 0 liters of pure alcohol (2019 est.)
comparison ranking: total 51

Tobacco use: *total:* 19.8% (2025 est.)
male: 23.2% (2025 est.)
female: 16.6% (2025 est.)
comparison ranking: total 71

Currently married women (ages 15-49): 52.5% (2023 est.)

Education expenditure: 4% of GDP (2022 est.)
7.2% national budget (2022 est.)
comparison ranking: Education expenditure (% GDP) 105

Literacy: *total population:* 99% (2019 est.)
male: 99% (2019 est.)
female: 99% (2019 est.)

School life expectancy (primary to tertiary education): *total:* 17 years (2023 est.)
male: 16 years (2023 est.)
female: 17 years (2023 est.)

ENVIRONMENT

Environmental issues: air pollution from industrial emissions; water pollution from industrial and agricultural effluents, as well as acid rain; inadequate industrial waste treatment and disposal facilities

International environmental agreements: *party to:* Air Pollution, Air Pollution-Nitrogen Oxides, Air Pollution-Persistent Organic Pollutants, Air Pollution-Sulphur 85, Air Pollution-Sulphur 94, Air Pollution-Volatile Organic Compounds, Antarctic-Environmental Protection, Antarctic-Marine Living Resources, Antarctic Seals, Antarctic Treaty, Biodiversity, Climate Change, Climate Change-Kyoto Protocol,
Climate Change-Paris Agreement, Comprehensive Nuclear Test Ban, Desertification, Endangered Species, Environmental Modification, Hazardous Wastes, Law of the Sea, Marine Dumping-London Convention, Marine Dumping-London Protocol, Nuclear Test Ban, Ozone Layer Protection, Ship Pollution, Tropical Timber 2006, Wetlands, Whaling
signed, but not ratified: Air Pollution-Heavy Metals, Air Pollution-Multi-effect Protocol

Climate: predominantly Mediterranean; alpine in far north; hot, dry in south

Urbanization: *urban population:* 72% of total population (2023)
rate of urbanization: 0.27% annual rate of change (2020-25 est.)

Carbon dioxide emissions: 307.442 million metric tonnes of CO2 (2023 est.)
from coal and metallurgical coke: 26.15 million metric tonnes of CO2 (2023 est.)
from petroleum and other liquids: 162.688 million metric tonnes of CO2 (2023 est.)
from consumed natural gas: 118.604 million metric tonnes of CO2 (2023 est.)
comparison ranking: total emissions 19

Particulate matter emissions: 12.3 micrograms per cubic meter (2019 est.)

Methane emissions: *energy:* 276.4 kt (2022-2024 est.)
agriculture: 764.9 kt (2019-2021 est.)
waste: 523.4 kt (2019-2021 est.)
other: 35.3 kt (2019-2021 est.)

Waste and recycling: *municipal solid waste generated annually:* 30.088 million tons (2024 est.)
percent of municipal solid waste recycled: 39.9% (2022 est.)

Total water withdrawal: *municipal:* 9.148 billion cubic meters (2022)
industrial: 7.7 billion cubic meters (2022 est.)
agricultural: 17 billion cubic meters (2022 est.)

Total renewable water resources: 191.3 billion cubic meters (2022 est.)

Geoparks: *total global geoparks and regional networks:* 12 (2025)
global geoparks and regional networks: Adamello-Brenta; Alpi Apuane; Aspromonte; Beigua; Cilento,

Vallo di Diano e Alburni; Madonie; Maiella; MurGEopark; Pollino; Rocca di Cerere; Sesia Val Grande; Tuscan Mining Park (2025)

GOVERNMENT

Country name: *conventional long form:* Italian Republic
conventional short form: Italy
local long form: Repubblica Italiana
local short form: Italia
former: Kingdom of Italy
etymology: derivation is unclear; traditionally said to come from the Vitali, a tribe that settled in what is now Calabria, and whose name is believed to be linked to the Latin word *vitulus*, or "calf;" alternatively, the name may derive from a local ruler known to the Romans as Italus

Government type: parliamentary republic

Capital: *name:* Rome
geographic coordinates: 41 54 N, 12 29 E
time difference: UTC+1 (6 hours ahead of Washington, DC, during Standard Time)
daylight saving time: +1hr, begins last Sunday in March; ends last Sunday in October
etymology: by tradition, named after Romulus, one of the legendary founders of the city, but the name Romulus may instead derive from the city's name; the name Rome may come from an Etruscan name for the Tiber River, which was Roma or Ruma

Administrative divisions: 15 regions (*regioni*, singular - *regione*) and 5 autonomous regions (*regioni autonome*, singular - *regione autonoma*)
regions: Abruzzo, Basilicata, Calabria, Campania, Emilia-Romagna, Lazio (Latium), Liguria, Lombardia, Marche, Molise, Piemonte (Piedmont), Puglia (Apulia), Toscana (Tuscany), Umbria, Veneto
autonomous regions: Friuli Venezia Giulia, Sardegna (Sardinia), Sicilia (Sicily), Trentino-Alto Adige (Trentino-South Tyrol) or Trentino-Suedtirol (German), Valle d'Aosta (Aosta Valley) or Vallée d'Aoste (French)

Legal system: civil law system; Constitutional Court reviews legislation under certain conditions

Constitution: *history:* previous 1848 (originally for the Kingdom of Sardinia and adopted by the Kingdom of Italy in 1861); latest enacted 22 December 1947, adopted 27 December 1947, entered into force 1 January 1948
amendment process: proposed by both houses of Parliament; passage requires two successive debates and approval by absolute majority of each house on the second vote; a referendum is only required when requested by one fifth of the members of either house, by voter petition, or by 5 Regional Councils (elected legislative assemblies of the 15 first-level administrative regions and 5 autonomous regions of Italy); referendum not required if an amendment has been approved by a two-thirds majority in each house in the second vote

International law organization participation: accepts compulsory ICJ jurisdiction with reservations; accepts ICCt jurisdiction

Citizenship: *citizenship by birth:* no
citizenship by descent only: at least one parent must be a citizen of Italy
dual citizenship recognized: yes
residency requirement for naturalization: 4 years for EU nationals, 5 years for refugees and specified exceptions, 10 years for all others

Suffrage: 18 years of age; universal except in senatorial elections, where minimum age is 25

Executive branch: *chief of state:* President Sergio MATTARELLA (since 3 February 2015)
head of government: Prime Minister Giorgia MELONI (since 22 October 2022); the prime minister's official title is President of the Council of Ministers
cabinet: Council of Ministers proposed by the prime minister, who is known officially as the President of the Council of Ministers and locally as the premier; nominated by the president
election/appointment process: president indirectly elected by an electoral college consisting of both houses of Parliament and 58 regional representatives for a 7-year term (no term limits); prime minister appointed by the president, confirmed by parliament
most recent election date: 24-29 January 2022 (eight rounds)
election results: *2022:* Sergio MATTARELLA (independent) reelected president; electoral college vote count in eighth round - 759 out of 1,009 (505 vote threshold)
2015: Sergio MATTARELLA (independent) elected president; electoral college vote count in fourth round - 665 out of 995 (505 vote threshold)
expected date of next election: 2029

Legislative branch: *legislature name:* Parliament (Il Parlamento)
legislative structure: bicameral

Legislative branch - lower chamber: *chamber name:* Chamber of Deputies (Camera dei Deputati)
number of seats: 400 (all directly elected)
electoral system: mixed system
scope of elections: full renewal
term in office: 5 years
most recent election date: 9/25/2022
parties elected and seats per party: Coalition Brothers of Italy (FdI) - Lega - Forza Italia - Us Moderates (Noi moderati, NM) (237); Democratic Party - Democratic and Progressive Italy (PD-IDP) - Greens and Left Alliance (AVS) - +EUROPA" - Civic Commitment (IC) (84); Five Star Movement (M5s) (52); Action - Italia Viva (21); Other (6)
percentage of women in chamber: 32.8%
expected date of next election: September 2027

Legislative branch - upper chamber: *chamber name:* Senate (Senato della Repubblica)
number of seats: 205 (200 directly elected; 5 appointed)
electoral system: mixed system
scope of elections: full renewal
term in office: 5 years
most recent election date: 9/25/2022
parties elected and seats per party: Coalition Brothers of Italy (FdI) - Lega - Forza Italia - Us Moderates (Noi moderati, NM) (115); Democratic Party - Democratic and Progressive Italy (PD-IDP) - Greens and Left Alliance (AVS) - +EUROPA" - Civic Commitment (IC) (44); Five Star Movement (M5s) (28); Other (13)
percentage of women in chamber: 36.3%
expected date of next election: September 2027

Judicial branch: *highest court(s):* Supreme Court of Cassation or Corte Suprema di Cassazione (consists of the first president, deputy president, 54 justices presiding over 6 civil and 7 criminal divisions, and 288 judges; an additional 30 judges of lower courts serve as supporting judges; cases normally heard by 5-judge panels; more complex cases heard by 9-judge panels); Constitutional Court or Corte Costituzionale (consists of the court president and 14 judges)
judge selection and term of office: Supreme Court judges appointed by the High Council of the Judiciary, headed by the president of the republic; judges may serve for life; Constitutional Court judges - 5 appointed by the president, 5 elected by Parliament, 5 elected by select higher courts; judges serve up to 9 years
subordinate courts: various lower civil and criminal courts (primary and secondary tribunals and courts of appeal)

Political parties: Action-Italia Viva
Associative Movement of Italians Abroad or MAIE
Brothers of Italy or FdI
Democratic Party or PD
Five Star Movement or M5S
Forza Italia or FI
Free and Equal (Liberi e Uguali) or LeU
Greens and Left Alliance or AVS
Italexit
League or Lega
More Europe or +EU
Popular Union or PU
South calls North or ScN
South Tyrolean Peoples Party or SVP
other minor parties

Diplomatic representation in the US: *chief of mission:* Ambassador Marco PERONACI (since 5 September 2025)
chancery: 3000 Whitehaven Street NW, Washington, DC 20008
telephone: [1] (202) 612-4400
FAX: [1] (202) 518-2154
email address and website: washington.ambasciata@esteri.it
https://ambwashingtondc.esteri.it/ambasciata_washington/en/
consulate(s) general: Boston, Chicago, Houston, Miami, New York, Los Angeles, Philadelphia, San Francisco
consulate(s): Detroit

Diplomatic representation from the US: *chief of mission:* Ambassador Tilman J. FERTITTA (since 6 May 2025); note - also accredited to San Marino
embassy: via Vittorio Veneto 121, 00187 Roma
mailing address: 9500 Rome Place, Washington DC 20521-9500
telephone: [39] 06-46741
FAX: [39] 06-4674-2244
email address and website: uscitizenrome@state.gov
https://it.usembassy. gov/
consulate(s) general: Florence, Milan, Naples

International organization participation: ADB (nonregional member), AfDB (nonregional member), Arctic Council (observer), Australia Group, BIS, BSEC (observer), CBSS (observer), CD, CDB, CE, CEI, CERN, EAPC, EBRD, ECB, EIB, EITI (implementing country), EMU, ESA, EU, FAO, FATF, G-7, G-8, G-10, G-20, IADB, IAEA, IBRD, ICAO, ICC (national committees), ICCt, ICRM, IDA, IEA, IFAD, IFC, IFRCS, IGAD (partners), IHO, ILO, IMF, IMO, IMSO, Interpol, IOC, IOM, IPU, ISO, ITSO, ITU, ITUC (NGOs), LAIA (observer), MIGA, MINURSO, NATO, NEA, NSG, OAS (observer), OECD, OPCW, OSCE, Pacific Alliance (observer), Paris Club, PCA, PIF (partner), Schengen Convention, SELEC (observer), SICA (observer), UN, UNCTAD, UNESCO, UNHCR, UNIDO, UNIFIL, Union Latina, UNMOGIP, UNOOSA, UNRWA, UNTSO, UNWTO, UPU, Wassenaar Arrangement, WCO, WHO, WIPO, WMO, WTO, ZC

Independence: 17 March 1861
note: the Kingdom of Italy proclaimed on 17 March 1861, but Italy was not fully unified until 1871

National holiday: Republic Day, 2 June (1946)

Flag: *description:* three equal vertical bands of green (left side), white, and red
meaning: colors are those of Milan (red and white) combined with the green uniform color of the Milanese civic guard
history: design inspired by the French flag that Napoleon brought to Italy in 1797
note: similar to the flags of Mexico (longer, darker shades of green and red, and has its coat of arms centered on the white band), Ireland (longer and with orange instead of red), and Cote d'Ivoire (colors reversed)

National symbol(s): five-pointed white star (Stella d'Italia)

National color(s): red, white, green

National coat of arms: this coat of arms has been a symbol of the Italian Republic since May 5, 1948, when Paolo Paschetto's design won a two-year public competition; the olive branch symbolizes national and global peace; the oak branch stands for the strength and the dignity of the Italian people, and the steel cog-wheel for their hard work; the single star represents Italy's solidarity

National anthem(s): *title:* "Il Canto degli Italiani" (The Song of the Italians)
lyrics/music: Goffredo MAMELI/Michele NOVARO
history: adopted 2005; the anthem, originally written in 1847, is also known as "L'Inno di Mameli" (Mameli's Hymn), and "Fratelli d'Italia" (Brothers of Italy)

National heritage: *total World Heritage Sites:* 60 (54 cultural, 6 natural)
selected World Heritage Site locales: Historic Center of Rome (c); Archaeological Areas of Pompeii, Herculaneum, and Torre Annunziata (c); Venice and its Lagoon (c); Historic Center of Florence (c); Piazza del Duomo, Pisa (c); Historic Centre of Naples (c); Portovenere, Cinque Terre, and the Islands (Palmaria, Tino and Tinetto)(c); Mount Etna (n); Cultural landscape of the Benedictine settlements in medieval Italy (c); Church and Dominican Convent of Santa Maria delle Grazie with "The Last Supper" by Leonardo da Vinci (c); City of Vicenza and the Palladian Villas of the Veneto (c); Crespi d'Adda (c); Early Christian Monuments of Ravenna (c); Historic Centre of the City of Pienza (c); Cathedral, Torre Civica and Piazza Grande, Modena (c); Costiera Amalfitana (c); Villa Romana del Casale (c); Archaeological Area and the Patriarchal Basilica of Aquileia (c); Cilento and Vallo di Diano National Park with the Archeological Sites of Paestum and Velia, and the Certosa di Padula (c); Historic Centre of Urbino (c); Villa Adriana (Tivoli) (c); Assisi, the Basilica of San Francesco and Other Franciscan Sites (c); City of Verona (c); Isole Eolie (Aeolian Islands) (n); Etruscan Necropolises of Cerveteri and Tarquinia (c); Val d'Orcia (c); Mantua and Sabbioneta (c); The Dolomites (n); Prehistoric Pile Dwellings around the Alps (c); Medici Villas and Gardens in Tuscany (c); Venetian Works of Defence between the 16th and 17th Centuries: Stato da Terra – Western Stato da Mar (c); Padua's fourteenth-century fresco cycles (c); The Porticoes of Bologna (c); Evaporitic Karst and Caves of Northern Apennines (n); Via Appia: Regina Viarum (c)

ECONOMY

Economic overview: high-income, core EU economy; strong services, manufacturing, and tourism sectors; modest growth supported by net exports, low inflation, and public investments via EU funds; tight labor market with aging workforce and shortages in specialized skills; high public debt levels

Real GDP (purchasing power parity): $3.133 trillion (2024 est.)
$3.11 trillion (2023 est.)
$3.088 trillion (2022 est.)
note: data in 2021 dollars
comparison ranking: 11

Real GDP growth rate: 0.7% (2024 est.)
0.7% (2023 est.)
4.8% (2022 est.)
note: annual GDP % growth based on constant local currency
comparison ranking: 185

Real GDP per capita: $53,100 (2024 est.)
$52,700 (2023 est.)
$52,300 (2022 est.)
note: data in 2021 dollars
comparison ranking: 37

GDP (official exchange rate): $2.373 trillion (2024 est.)
note: data in current dollars at official exchange rate

Inflation rate (consumer prices): 1% (2024 est.)
5.6% (2023 est.)
8.2% (2022 est.)
note: annual % change based on consumer prices
comparison ranking: 23

GDP - composition, by sector of origin: *agriculture:* 2% (2024 est.)
industry: 21.7% (2024 est.)
services: 65.6% (2024 est.)
note: figures may not total 100% due to non-allocated consumption not captured in sector-reported data
comparison rankings: agriculture 151; industry 122; services 52

GDP - composition, by end use: *household consumption:* 58.3% (2023 est.)
government consumption: 17.8% (2023 est.)
investment in fixed capital: 22.5% (2023 est.)
investment in inventories: 0.4% (2023 est.)
exports of goods and services: 33.5% (2023 est.)
imports of goods and services: -32.1% (2023 est.)
note: figures may not total 100% due to rounding or gaps in data collection

Agricultural products: milk, wheat, grapes, tomatoes, maize, olives, apples, oranges, sugar beets, rice (2023)
note: top ten agricultural products based on tonnage

Industries: tourism, machinery, iron and steel, chemicals, food processing, textiles, motor vehicles, clothing, footwear, ceramics

Industrial production growth rate: 0.2% (2024 est.)
note: annual % change in industrial value added based on constant local currency
comparison ranking: 130

Labor force: 25.828 million (2024 est.)
note: number of people ages 15 or older who are employed or seeking work
comparison ranking: 27

Unemployment rate: 6.8% (2024 est.)
7.7% (2023 est.)
8.1% (2022 est.)
note: % of labor force seeking employment
comparison ranking: 123

Youth unemployment rate (ages 15-24): *total:* 21.8% (2024 est.)
male: 19.9% (2024 est.)
female: 24.8% (2024 est.)
note: % of labor force ages 15-24 seeking employment
comparison ranking: total 49

Population below poverty line: 20.1% (2021 est.)
note: % of population with income below national poverty line
Gini Index coefficient - distribution of family income 33.7 (2022 est.)
note: index (0-100) of income distribution; higher values represent greater inequality
comparison ranking: 91

Average household expenditures: *on food:* 14.7% of household expenditures (2023 est.)
on alcohol and tobacco: 3.8% of household expenditures (2023 est.)

Household income or consumption by percentage share: *lowest 10%:* 2.5% (2022 est.)
highest 10%: 25.3% (2022 est.)
note: % share of income accruing to lowest and highest 10% of population

Remittances: 0.5% of GDP (2024 est.)
0.5% of GDP (2023 est.)
0.5% of GDP (2022 est.)
note: personal transfers and compensation between resident and non-resident individuals/households/entities

Budget: *revenues:* $935.038 billion (2023 est.)
expenditures: $1.104 trillion (2023 est.)
note: central government revenues (excluding grants) and expenditures converted to US dollars at average official exchange rate for year indicated

Public debt: 131.8% of GDP (2017 est.)
note: Italy reports its data on public debt according to guidelines set out in the Maastricht Treaty; general government gross debt is defined in the Maastricht Treaty as consolidated general government gross debt at nominal value, outstanding at the end of the year, in the following categories of government liabilities (as defined in ESA95): currency and deposits (AF.2), securities other than shares excluding financial derivatives (AF.3, excluding AF.34), and loans (AF.4); the general government sector comprises central, state, and local government and social security funds
comparison ranking: 8

Taxes and other revenues: 24.8% (of GDP) (2023 est.)
note: central government tax revenue as a % of GDP
comparison ranking: 19

Current account balance: $26.76 billion (2024 est.)
$3.261 billion (2023 est.)
-$36.325 billion (2022 est.)
note: balance of payments - net trade and primary/secondary income in current dollars
comparison ranking: 20

Exports: $778.898 billion (2024 est.)
$774.311 billion (2023 est.)
$737.083 billion (2022 est.)
note: balance of payments - exports of goods and services in current dollars
comparison ranking: 11

Exports - partners: Germany 11%, USA 11%, France 10%, Spain 5%, UK 5% (2023)
note: top five export partners based on percentage share of exports

Exports - commodities: packaged medicine, garments, cars, refined petroleum, vehicle parts/accessories (2023)

note: top five export commodities based on value in dollars

Imports: $717.278 billion (2024 est.)
$739.646 billion (2023 est.)
$775.518 billion (2022 est.)
note: balance of payments - imports of goods and services in current dollars
comparison ranking: 13

Imports - partners: Germany 15%, France 9%, China 8%, Netherlands 6%, Spain 5% (2023)
note: top five import partners based on percentage share of imports

Imports - commodities: natural gas, crude petroleum, cars, packaged medicine, garments (2023)
note: top five import commodities based on value in dollars

Reserves of foreign exchange and gold: $290.547 billion (2024 est.)
$247.396 billion (2023 est.)
$224.581 billion (2022 est.)
note: holdings of gold (year-end prices)/foreign exchange/special drawing rights in current dollars
comparison ranking: 13

Exchange rates: euros (EUR) per US dollar -

Exchange rates: 0.924 (2024 est.)
0.925 (2023 est.)
0.95 (2022 est.)
0.845 (2021 est.)
0.876 (2020 est.)

ENERGY

Electricity access: *electrification - total population:* 100% (2022 est.)

Electricity: *installed generating capacity:* 128.692 million kW (2023 est.)
consumption: 290.664 billion kWh (2023 est.)
exports: 3.32 billion kWh (2023 est.)
imports: 54.572 billion kWh (2023 est.)
transmission/distribution losses: 17.62 billion kWh (2023 est.)
comparison rankings: installed generating capacity 12; consumption 15; exports 45; imports 2; transmission/distribution losses 187

Electricity generation sources: *fossil fuels:* 56% of total installed capacity (2023 est.)
solar: 12% of total installed capacity (2023 est.)
wind: 9.1% of total installed capacity (2023 est.)
hydroelectricity: 14.7% of total installed capacity (2023 est.)
geothermal: 2.1% of total installed capacity (2023 est.)
biomass and waste: 6.2% of total installed capacity (2023 est.)

Nuclear energy: Number of nuclear reactors permanently shut down: 4 (2025)

Coal: *production:* 1.572 million metric tons (2023 est.)
consumption: 12.424 million metric tons (2023 est.)
exports: 304,000 metric tons (2023 est.)
imports: 12.069 million metric tons (2023 est.)
proven reserves: 609.999 million metric tons (2023 est.)

Petroleum: *total petroleum production:* 111,000 bbl/day (2023 est.)
refined petroleum consumption: 1.245 million bbl/day (2024 est.)
crude oil estimated reserves: 497.934 million barrels (2021 est.)

Natural gas: *production:* 2.778 billion cubic meters (2023 est.)
consumption: 61.906 billion cubic meters (2023 est.)
exports: 2.609 billion cubic meters (2023 est.)
imports: 61.851 billion cubic meters (2023 est.)
proven reserves: 45.76 billion cubic meters (2021 est.)

Energy consumption per capita: 96.797 million Btu/person (2023 est.)
comparison ranking: 53

COMMUNICATIONS

Telephones - fixed lines: *total subscriptions:* 20.107 million (2023 est.)
subscriptions per 100 inhabitants: 34 (2023 est.)
comparison ranking: total subscriptions 13

Telephones - mobile cellular: *total subscriptions:* 78.5 million (2023 est.)
subscriptions per 100 inhabitants: 133 (2022 est.)
comparison ranking: total subscriptions 23

Broadcast media: two Italian media giants dominate, with 3 national terrestrial stations; privately owned companies have 3 national terrestrial stations; a large number of private stations, a satellite TV network; 3 AM/FM nationwide radio stations; about 1,300 commercial radio stations

Internet country code: .it

Internet users: *percent of population:* 87% (2023 est.)

Broadband - fixed subscriptions: *total:* 20.1 million (2023 est.)
subscriptions per 100 inhabitants: 34 (2023 est.)
comparison ranking: total 13

TRANSPORTATION

Civil aircraft registration country code prefix: I

Airports: 655 (2025)
comparison ranking: 12

Heliports: 163 (2025)
comparison ranking: 16

Railways: *total:* 18,475 km (2020) 12,936 km electrified
1289.3 0.950-mm gauge (151.3 km electrified)

Merchant marine: *total:* 1,276 (2023)
by type: bulk carrier 17, container ship 6, general cargo 109, oil tanker 95, other 1,049
comparison ranking: total 18

Ports: *total ports:* 123 (2024)
large: 12
medium: 11
small: 71
very small: 28
size unknown: 1
ports with oil terminals: 33
key ports: Brindisi, Civitavecchia, Genova, Gioia Tauro, La Spezia, Livorno, Messina, Napoli, Porto di Lido-Venezia, Siracusa, Taranto, Trieste

MILITARY AND SECURITY

Military and security forces: Italian Armed Forces (Forze Armate Italiane): Army (Esercito Italiano, EI), Navy (Marina Militare Italiana, MMI; includes aviation, marines), Italian Air Force (Aeronautica Militare Italiana, AMI); Carabinieri Corps (Arma dei Carabinieri, CC) (2025)
note 1: the National (or State) Police and Carabinieri (gendarmerie or military police) maintain internal security; the National Police reports to the Ministry of Interior while the Carabinieri reports to the Ministry of Defense but is also under the coordination of the Ministry of Interior; the Carabinieri is primarily a domestic police force organized along military lines, with some overseas responsibilities
note 2: the Financial Guard (Guardia di Finanza) under the Ministry of Economy and Finance is a force with military status and nationwide remit for financial crime investigations, including narcotics trafficking, smuggling, and illegal immigration

Military expenditures: 2% of GDP (2025 est.)
1.5% of GDP (2024 est.)
1.5% of GDP (2023 est.)
1.5% of GDP (2022 est.)
1.5% of GDP (2021 est.)

Military and security service personnel strengths: approximately 170,000 active-duty military personnel; approximately 105,000 Carabinieri (2025)

Military equipment inventories and acquisitions: the military's inventory includes a mix of domestically manufactured, imported, and jointly produced weapons systems, mostly from Europe and the US; in recent years, the US has been the lead supplier of military hardware to Italy; the Italian defense industry is capable of producing equipment across all the military domains with particular strengths in aircraft, armored vehicles, and naval vessels; it also participates in joint development and production of advanced weapons systems with other European countries and the US (2024)

Military service age and obligation: 17-25 years of age for voluntary military service for men and women (some variations on age depending on the military branch); voluntary service is a minimum of 12 months with the option to extend in the Armed Forces or compete for positions in the Military Corps of the Italian Red Cross, the State Police, the Carabinieri, the Guardia di Finanza, the Penitentiary Police, or the National Fire Brigade; recruits can also volunteer for 4 years military service; conscription abolished 2004 (2024)
note: women serve in all military branches; as of 2023, women made up about 8% of the military's full-time personnel

Military deployments: 120 Djibouti; approximately 750 Bulgaria (NATO); approximately 650 Middle East (NATO, European Assistance Mission Iraq); 250 Hungary (NATO; up to 1,500 Kosovo (NATO/KFOR); 250 Latvia (NATO); 1,325 Lebanon (UNIFIL); 200 Libya; 350 Niger; 250 Romania (NATO); 150 Somalia (EUTM) (2024)
note 1: Italy has about 11,500 total air, ground, and naval forces deployed on foreign missions
note 2: since 1960, Italy has committed more than 60,000 troops to UN missions, and it hosts a training center in Vicenza for police personnel destined for peacekeeping missions

Military - note: the Italian military is responsible for Italy's national defense and security and fulfilling the country's commitments to the EU, NATO, the UN, and other multinational military, security, and humanitarian operations; it also has some domestic security duties; key areas of emphasis for Italy's security policy and multinational cooperation are Europe's eastern and southern flanks, including the Mediterranean Sea, East and North Africa, and the Middle East and its adjacent waters
Italy has been an active member of NATO since its founding in 1948, and the Alliance is a cornerstone of Rome's national security strategy; it is one of NATO's leading contributors of military forces and participates in such Alliance missions as Air Policing in the

Baltics, the Enhanced Forward Presence in Eastern Europe, and maritime patrols in the Mediterranean and beyond; it hosts NATO's Joint Force Command in Naples and a NATO Rapid Deployable Corps headquarters in Milan

Italy is also active in European/EU defense cooperation and integration, including hosting the headquarters for the EU's Mediterranean naval operations force in Rome; in addition, Italy has close defense ties with the US and hosts several US military air, army, and naval bases and facilities (2025)

SPACE

Space agency/agencies: Italian Space Agency (L'Agenzia Spaziale Italiana or ASI; established 1988) (2025)

Space launch site(s): the Broglio (aka San Marco, Malindi) Space Center, located near Malindi, Kenya, served from 1967 to 1988 as an Italian and international satellite launch facility; in 2020, Italy concluded a deal with Kenya to conduct rocket launches from the site again in the future; the Italian Space Agency has utilized the site as a satellite ground station since 2004 the Italian Government has designated the Taranto-Grottaglie Airport as a future spaceport and signed framework agreements with commercial space companies that could lead to suborbital and orbital launches from what would be called the Grottaglie Spaceport (2025)

Space program overview: is a key member of the European Space Agency (ESA) and one of its largest contributors; designs, builds, launches, and operates communications, remote sensing (RS), and scientific satellites; designs and manufacturers probes, rockets, and orbital satellite launch vehicles (SLVs); researches, develops, and builds a range of other space-related technologies and participates in a wide array of international programs with astronauts, cargo containers, construction, expertise, modules, scientific experiments, and technology; hosts the ESA Center for Earth Observation; has astronaut cadre in the ESA astronaut corps; outside of the ESA/EU and their individual member states, has cooperated with a variety of foreign space agencies and industries, including those of Argentina, Brazil, Canada, China, Israel, Japan, Kenya, Mexico, Russia, South Korea, Thailand, the UAE, and the US; participates in international space projects such as the International Space Station (ISS); has a considerable commercial space industrial sector encompassing a wide range of capabilities, including manufacturing satellites, satellite payloads, launch vehicles, propulsion systems, cargo containers, and their sub-components (2025)

note: further details about the key activities, programs, and milestones of the country's space program, as well as government spending estimates on the space sector, appear in the Space Programs reference guide

TERRORISM

Terrorist group(s): Terrorist group(s): Islamic State of Iraq and ash-Sham (ISIS)

note: details about the history, aims, leadership, organization, areas of operation, tactics, targets, weapons, size, and sources of support of the group(s) appear(s) in Appendix T

TRANSNATIONAL ISSUES

Refugees and internally displaced persons: *refugees:* 520,127 (2024 est.)

stateless persons: 3,000 (2024 est.)

J

JAMAICA

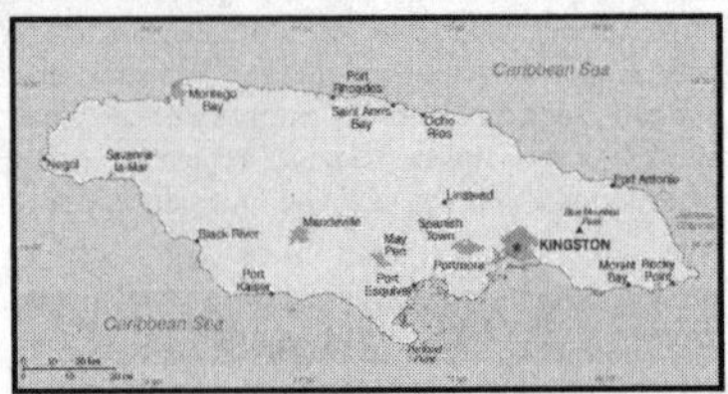

INTRODUCTION

Background: Europeans first saw Jamaica when Christopher COLUMBUS arrived in 1494, and the Spanish settled the island early in the 16th century. The Native Taino, who had inhabited Jamaica for centuries, were gradually exterminated and replaced with African slaves. England seized the island in 1655 and established a plantation economy based on sugar, cocoa, and coffee. The abolition of slavery in 1834 freed a quarter-million slaves, many of whom became small farmers. Jamaica gradually increased its independence from Britain. In 1958, it joined other British Caribbean colonies in forming the Federation of the West Indies. Jamaica withdrew from the Federation in 1961 and gained full independence in 1962. Deteriorating economic conditions during the 1970s led to recurring violence as rival gangs affiliated with the major political parties evolved into powerful organized crime networks involved in international drug smuggling and money laundering. Violent crime, drug trafficking, corruption, and poverty pose significant challenges to the government today. Nonetheless, many rural and resort areas remain relatively safe and contribute substantially to the economy.

GEOGRAPHY

Location: Caribbean, island in the Caribbean Sea, south of Cuba
Geographic coordinates: 18 15 N, 77 30 W

Map references: Central America and the Caribbean

Area: *total:* 10,991 sq km
land: 10,831 sq km
water: 160 sq km
comparison ranking: total 166

Area - comparative: about half the size of New Jersey; slightly smaller than Connecticut

Land boundaries: *total:* 0 km

Coastline: 1,022 km

Maritime claims: *territorial sea:* 12 nm
contiguous zone: 24 nm
exclusive economic zone: 200 nm
continental shelf: 200 nm or to edge of the continental margin
note: measured from claimed archipelagic straight baselines

Climate: tropical; hot, humid; temperate interior
Terrain: mostly mountains, with narrow, discontinuous coastal plain
Elevation: *highest point:* Blue Mountain Peak 2,256 m
lowest point: Caribbean Sea 0 m
mean elevation: 18 m
Natural resources: bauxite, alumina, gypsum, limestone

Land use: *agricultural land:* 38.5% (2022 est.)
arable land: 11.1% (2022 est.)
permanent crops: 6.3% (2022 est.)
permanent pasture: 21.1% (2022 est.)
forest: 55.8% (2022 est.)
other: 5.7% (2022 est.)
Irrigated land: 250 sq km (2012)

Population distribution: population density is high throughout, but increases in and around Kingston, Montego Bay, and Port Esquivel

Natural hazards: hurricanes (especially July to November)

Geography - note: third largest island in the Caribbean (after Cuba and Hispaniola); strategic location between Cayman Trench and Jamaica Channel, the main sea lanes for the Panama Canal

PEOPLE AND SOCIETY

Population: *total:* 2,823,713 (2024 est.)
male: 1,397,495
female: 1,426,218
comparison rankings: total 140; male 141; female 140

Nationality: *noun:* Jamaican(s)
adjective: Jamaican

Ethnic groups: Black 92.1%, mixed 6.1%, East Indian 0.8%, other 0.4%, unspecified 0.7% (2011 est.)
Languages: English, Jamaican patois

Religions: Protestant 64.8% (includes Seventh Day Adventist 12.0%, Pentecostal 11.0%, Other Church of God 9.2%, New Testament Church of God 7.2%, Baptist 6.7%, Church of God in Jamaica 4.8%, Church of God of Prophecy 4.5%, Anglican 2.8%, United Church 2.1%, Methodist 1.6%, Revived 1.4%, Brethren 0.9%, and Moravian 0.7%), Roman Catholic 2.2%, Jehovah's Witness 1.9%, Rastafarian 1.1%, other 6.5%, none 21.3%, unspecified 2.3% (2011 est.)

Age structure: *0-14 years:* 23.8% (male 342,691/female 329,773)
15-64 years: 65.7% (male 914,364/female 941,816)
65 years and over: 10.4% (2024 est.) (male 140,440/female 154,629)

Dependency ratios: *total dependency ratio:* 52.1 (2024 est.)
youth dependency ratio: 36.2 (2024 est.)
elderly dependency ratio: 15.9 (2024 est.)
potential support ratio: 6.3 (2024 est.)

Median age: *total:* 30.9 years (2024 est.)
male: 30.1 years
female: 31.7 years
comparison ranking: total 130

Population growth rate: 0.1% (2024 est.)
comparison ranking: 185

Birth rate: 15.6 births/1,000 population (2024 est.)
comparison ranking: 105

Death rate: 7.5 deaths/1,000 population (2024 est.)
comparison ranking: 100

Net migration rate: -7.1 migrant(s)/1,000 population (2024 est.)
comparison ranking: 217

Population distribution: population density is high throughout, but increases in and around Kingston, Montego Bay, and Port Esquivel

Urbanization: *urban population:* 57.4% of total population (2023)
rate of urbanization: 0.79% annual rate of change (2020-25 est.)
Major urban areas - population: 597,000 KINGSTON (capital) (2023)

Sex ratio: *at birth:* 1.05 male(s)/female
0-14 years: 1.04 male(s)/female
15-64 years: 0.97 male(s)/female
65 years and over: 0.91 male(s)/female
total population: 0.98 male(s)/female (2024 est.)

Mother's mean age at first birth: 21.2 years (2008 est.)
note: data represents median age at first birth among women 25-29
Maternal mortality ratio: 130 deaths/100,000 live births (2023 est.)
comparison ranking: 56
Infant mortality rate: *total:* 10.7 deaths/1,000 live births (2024 est.)
male: 11.9 deaths/1,000 live births
female: 9.4 deaths/1,000 live births
comparison ranking: total 129

Life expectancy at birth: *total population:* 76.3 years (2024 est.)
male: 74.5 years
female: 78.1 years
comparison ranking: total population 111

Total fertility rate: 2.05 children born/woman (2024 est.)
comparison ranking: 98

Gross reproduction rate: 1 (2024 est.)

Drinking water source: *improved:* *urban:* 95.4% of population (2022 est.)
rural: 85.4% of population (2022 est.)
total: 91.1% of population (2022 est.)
unimproved: *urban:* 4.6% of population (2022 est.)
rural: 14.6% of population (2022 est.)
total: 8.9% of population (2022 est.)
Health expenditure: 7.2% of GDP (2021)
19% of national budget (2022 est.)
Physician density: 0.46 physicians/1,000 population (2023)
Hospital bed density: 1.7 beds/1,000 population (2021 est.)
Sanitation facility access: *improved:* *urban:* 98.6% of population (2022 est.)
rural: 99.4% of population (2022 est.)
total: 98.9% of population (2022 est.)
unimproved: *urban:* 1.4% of population (2022 est.)
rural: 0.6% of population (2022 est.)
total: 1.1% of population (2022 est.)
Obesity - adult prevalence rate: 24.7% (2016)
comparison ranking: 55

Alcohol consumption per capita: *total:* 3.46 liters of pure alcohol (2019 est.)
beer: 1.19 liters of pure alcohol (2019 est.)
wine: 0.25 liters of pure alcohol (2019 est.)
spirits: 1.66 liters of pure alcohol (2019 est.)
other alcohols: 0.35 liters of pure alcohol (2019 est.)
comparison ranking: total 104

Tobacco use: *total:* 9% (2025 est.)
male: 15.1% (2025 est.)
female: 3.1% (2025 est.)
comparison ranking: total 135

Children under the age of 5 years underweight: 2.5% (2018/19)
comparison ranking: 88

Currently married women (ages 15-49): 32.7% (2023 est.)

Education expenditure: 5.7% of GDP (2023 est.)
14.5% national budget (2023 est.)
comparison ranking: Education expenditure (% GDP) 36

School life expectancy (primary to tertiary education): *total:* 13 years (2015 est.)
male: 12 years (2015 est.)
female: 14 years (2015 est.)

ENVIRONMENT

Environmental issues: heavy rates of deforestation; coastal waters polluted by industrial waste, sewage, and oil spills; damage to coral reefs; air pollution in Kingston from vehicle emissions; land erosion

International environmental agreements: *party to:* Biodiversity, Climate Change, Climate Change-Kyoto Protocol, Climate Change-Paris Agreement, Comprehensive Nuclear Test Ban, Desertification, Endangered Species, Hazardous Wastes, Law of the Sea, Marine Dumping-London Convention, Marine Life Conservation, Nuclear Test Ban, Ozone Layer Protection, Ship Pollution, Wetlands
signed, but not ratified: none of the selected agreements

Climate: tropical; hot, humid; temperate interior

Urbanization: *urban population:* 57.4% of total population (2023)
rate of urbanization: 0.79% annual rate of change (2020-25 est.)

Carbon dioxide emissions: 7.89 million metric tonnes of CO2 (2023 est.)
from coal and metallurgical coke: 239,000 metric tonnes of CO2 (2023 est.)
from petroleum and other liquids: 6.04 million metric tonnes of CO2 (2023 est.)
from consumed natural gas: 1.611 million metric tonnes of CO2 (2023 est.)
comparison ranking: total emissions 117

Particulate matter emissions: 14.8 micrograms per cubic meter (2019 est.)

Waste and recycling: *municipal solid waste generated annually:* 1.052 million tons (2024 est.)
percent of municipal solid waste recycled: 15% (2022 est.)

Total water withdrawal: *municipal:* 339.867 million cubic meters (2022 est.)
industrial: 43.989 million cubic meters (2022 est.)
agricultural: 78.972 million cubic meters (2022 est.)

Total renewable water resources: 10.823 billion cubic meters (2022 est.)

GOVERNMENT

Country name: *conventional long form:* none
conventional short form: Jamaica
etymology: from the Arawak word *xaymaca*, meaning "Land of Wood and Water" or possibly "Land of Springs"

Government type: parliamentary democracy (Parliament) under a constitutional monarchy; a Commonwealth realm

Capital: *name:* Kingston
geographic coordinates: 18 00 N, 76 48 W
time difference: UTC-5 (same time as Washington, DC, during Standard Time)
etymology: the name is a blend of the words "king's" and "town;" named after the English king at the time of the city's founding in 1692, WILLIAM III

Administrative divisions: 14 parishes; Clarendon, Hanover, Kingston, Manchester, Portland, Saint Andrew, Saint Ann, Saint Catherine, Saint Elizabeth, Saint James, Saint Mary, Saint Thomas, Trelawny, Westmoreland
note: for local government purposes, Kingston and Saint Andrew were amalgamated in 1923 into the present single corporate body known as the Kingston and Saint Andrew Corporation

Legal system: common law system based on the English model

Constitution: *history:* several previous (pre-independence); latest drafted 1961-62, submitted to British Parliament 24 July 1962, entered into force 6 August 1962 (at independence)
amendment process: proposed by Parliament; passage of amendments to "non-entrenched" constitutional sections, such as lowering the voting age, requires majority vote by the Parliament membership; passage of amendments to "entrenched" sections, such as fundamental rights and freedoms, requires two-thirds majority vote of Parliament; passage of amendments to "specially entrenched" sections such as the dissolution of Parliament or the executive authority of the monarch requires two-thirds approval by Parliament and approval in a referendum

International law organization participation: has not submitted an ICJ jurisdiction declaration; non-party state to the ICCt

Citizenship: *citizenship by birth:* yes
citizenship by descent only: yes
dual citizenship recognized: yes
residency requirement for naturalization: 4 out of the previous 5 years

Suffrage: 18 years of age; universal

Executive branch: *chief of state:* King CHARLES III (since 8 September 2022); represented by Governor General Sir Patrick L. ALLEN (since 26 February 2009)
head of government: Prime Minister Andrew HOLNESS (since 3 March 2016)
cabinet: Cabinet appointed by the governor general on the advice of the prime minister
election/appointment process: the monarchy is hereditary; governor general appointed by the monarch on the recommendation of the prime minister; following legislative elections, the governor general appoints the leader of the majority party or majority coalition in the House of Representatives as prime minister

Legislative branch: *legislature name:* Parliament
legislative structure: bicameral

Legislative branch - lower chamber: *chamber name:* House of Representatives
number of seats: 63 (all directly elected)
electoral system: plurality/majority
scope of elections: full renewal
term in office: 5 years
most recent election date: 9/3/2020
parties elected and seats per party: Jamaica Labour Party (JLP) (49); People's National Party (PNP) (14)
percentage of women in chamber: 28.6%
expected date of next election: September 2025

Legislative branch - upper chamber: *chamber name:* Senate
number of seats: 21 (all appointed)
scope of elections: full renewal
term in office: 5 years
most recent election date: 9/15/2020
percentage of women in chamber: 40%
expected date of next election: September 2025

Judicial branch: *highest court(s):* Court of Appeal (consists of president of the court and a minimum of 4 judges); Supreme Court (40 judges organized in specialized divisions)
judge selection and term of office: chief justice of the Supreme Court and president of the Court of Appeal appointed by the governor-general on the advice of the prime minister; other judges of both courts appointed by the governor-general on the advice of the Judicial Service Commission; judges of both courts serve till age 70
subordinate courts: resident magistrate courts, district courts, and petty sessions courts
note: appeals beyond Jamaica's highest courts are referred to the Judicial Committee of the Privy Council (in London) rather than to the Caribbean Court of Justice (the appellate court for member states of the Caribbean Community)

Political parties: Jamaica Labor Party or JLP
Jamaica Progressive Party or JPP
People's National Party or PNP
United Independents' Congress or UIC

Diplomatic representation in the US: *chief of mission:* Ambassador Antony B. ANDERSON (since 24 July 2025)
chancery: 1520 New Hampshire Avenue NW, Washington, DC 20036
telephone: [1] (202) 452-0660

FAX: [1] (202) 452-0036
email address and website: contactus@jamaicaembassy.org
Jamaican Embassy (embassyofjamaica.org)
consulate(s) general: Miami, New York

Diplomatic representation from the US: *chief of mission:* Ambassador (vacant); Chargé d'Affaires Scott RENNER (since 13 August 2025)
embassy: 142 Old Hope Road, Kingston 6
mailing address: 3210 Kingston Place, Washington DC 20521-3210
telephone: (876) 702-6000

FAX: (876) 702-6348
email address and website: KingstonACS@state.gov
https://jm.usembassy.gov/

International organization participation: ACP, ACS, AOSIS, C, Caricom, CDB, CELAC, FAO, G-15, G-77, IADB, IAEA, IBRD, ICAO, ICC (NGOs), ICRM, IDA, IFAD, IFC, IFRCS, IHO, ILO, IMF, IMO, Interpol, IOC, IOM, ISO, ITSO, ITU, LAES, MIGA, NAM, OAS, OPANAL, OPCW, Petrocaribe, UN, UNCTAD, UNESCO, UNIDO, UNITAR, UNWTO, UPU, WCO, WFTU (NGOs), WHO, WIPO, WMO, WTO

Independence: 6 August 1962 (from the UK)

National holiday: Independence Day, 6 August (1962)

Flag: *description:* diagonal yellow cross divides the flag into four triangles, two green (top and bottom) and two black (left and right)
meaning: green stands for hope, vegetation, and agriculture; black for hardships overcome and to be faced; and yellow for sunshine and natural resources

National symbol(s): green-and-black streamertail (bird), guaiacwood (*Guiacum officinale*)

National color(s): green, yellow, black

National anthem(s): *title:* "Jamaica, Land We Love"

lyrics/music: Hugh Braham SHERLOCK/Robert Charles LIGHTBOURNE
history: adopted 1962

National heritage: *total World Heritage Sites:* 1 (mixed)
selected World Heritage Site locales: Blue and John Crow Mountains

ECONOMY

Economic overview: upper-middle-income Caribbean island economy; key agriculture and tourism sectors; high crime, youth unemployment, and poverty; susceptible to natural disasters and global commodity price shocks; progress in reducing public debt and moderating inflation within target range

Real GDP (purchasing power parity): $29.13 billion (2024 est.)
$29.341 billion (2023 est.)
$28.596 billion (2022 est.)
note: data in 2021 dollars
comparison ranking: 148

Real GDP growth rate: -0.7% (2024 est.)
2.6% (2023 est.)
5.2% (2022 est.)
note: annual GDP % growth based on constant local currency
comparison ranking: 198

Real GDP per capita: $10,300 (2024 est.)
$10,300 (2023 est.)
$10,100 (2022 est.)
note: data in 2021 dollars
comparison ranking: 144

GDP (official exchange rate): $19.93 billion (2024 est.)
note: data in current dollars at official exchange rate

Inflation rate (consumer prices): 5.4% (2024 est.)
6.5% (2023 est.)
10.3% (2022 est.)
note: annual % change based on consumer prices
comparison ranking: 148

GDP - composition, by sector of origin: *agriculture:* 9.8% (2024 est.)
industry: 18.3% (2024 est.)
services: 60.3% (2024 est.)
note: figures may not total 100% due to non-allocated consumption not captured in sector-reported data
comparison rankings: agriculture 74; industry 143; services 86

GDP - composition, by end use: *household consumption:* 76.2% (2019 est.)
government consumption: 13.6% (2019 est.)
investment in fixed capital: 24.1% (2019 est.)
investment in inventories: 0.2% (2019 est.)
exports of goods and services: 38% (2019 est.)
imports of goods and services: -52.1% (2019 est.)
note: figures may not total 100% due to rounding or gaps in data collection

Agricultural products: sugarcane, goat milk, yams, chicken, oranges, coconuts, bananas, plantains, pumpkins/squash, pineapples (2023)
note: top ten agricultural products based on tonnage

Industries: agriculture, mining, manufacture, construction, financial and insurance services, tourism, telecommunications

Industrial production growth rate: -1.5% (2024 est.)
note: annual % change in industrial value added based on constant local currency
comparison ranking: 156

Labor force: 1.57 million (2024 est.)
note: number of people ages 15 or older who are employed or seeking work
comparison ranking: 132

Unemployment rate: 4.9% (2024 est.)
4.4% (2023 est.)
4.1% (2022 est.)
note: % of labor force seeking employment
comparison ranking: 87

Youth unemployment rate (ages 15-24): *total:* 14.5% (2024 est.)
male: 12.9% (2024 est.)
female: 16.4% (2024 est.)
note: % of labor force ages 15-24 seeking employment
comparison ranking: total 81

Population below poverty line: 16.7% (2021 est.)
note: % of population with income below national poverty line

Gini Index coefficient - distribution of family income 39.9 (2021 est.)
note: index (0-100) of income distribution; higher values represent greater inequality
comparison ranking: 42

Household income or consumption by percentage share: *lowest 10%:* 2.2% (2021 est.)
highest 10%: 29.6% (2021 est.)
note: % share of income accruing to lowest and highest 10% of population

Remittances: 17.9% of GDP (2024 est.)
18.5% of GDP (2023 est.)
21.6% of GDP (2022 est.)
note: personal transfers and compensation between resident and non-resident individuals/households/entities

Budget: *revenues:* $4.041 billion (2020 est.)
expenditures: $4.466 billion (2020 est.)
note: central government revenues and expenses (excluding grants/extrabudgetary units/social security funds) converted to US dollars at average official exchange rate for year indicated

Public debt: 106.3% of GDP (2020 est.)
note: central government debt as a % of GDP
comparison ranking: 16

Taxes and other revenues: 25.7% (of GDP) (2020 est.)
note: central government tax revenue as a % of GDP
comparison ranking: 15

Current account balance: $678.808 million (2024 est.)
$568.932 million (2023 est.)
-$136.401 million (2022 est.)
note: balance of payments - net trade and primary/secondary income in current dollars
comparison ranking: 62

Exports: $7.124 billion (2024 est.)
$7.275 billion (2023 est.)
$6.424 billion (2022 est.)
note: balance of payments - exports of goods and services in current dollars
comparison ranking: 127

Exports - partners: USA 37%, Russia 7%, Latvia 7%, Iceland 7%, UK 5% (2023)
note: top five export partners based on percentage share of exports

Exports - commodities: aluminum oxide, refined petroleum, natural gas, liquor, processed fruits and nuts (2023)
note: top five export commodities based on value in dollars

Imports: $9.524 billion (2024 est.)
$9.866 billion (2023 est.)
$9.726 billion (2022 est.)
note: balance of payments - imports of goods and services in current dollars
comparison ranking: 124

Imports - partners: USA 39%, China 11%, Brazil 4%, Colombia 4%, Japan 4% (2023)
note: top five import partners based on percentage share of imports

Imports - commodities: refined petroleum, natural gas, cars, crude petroleum, plastic products (2023)
note: top five import commodities based on value in dollars

Reserves of foreign exchange and gold: $4.869 billion (2023 est.)
$4.52 billion (2022 est.)
$4.838 billion (2021 est.)
note: holdings of gold (year-end prices)/foreign exchange/special drawing rights in current dollars
comparison ranking: 103

Debt - external: $9.636 billion (2023 est.)
note: present value of external debt in current US dollars
comparison ranking: 50

Exchange rates: Jamaican dollars (JMD) per US dollar -

Exchange rates: 156.44 (2024 est.)
154.159 (2023 est.)
153.427 (2022 est.)
150.79 (2021 est.)
142.403 (2020 est.)

ENERGY

Electricity access: *electrification - total population:* 100% (2022 est.)

Electricity: *installed generating capacity:* 1.242 million kW (2023 est.)
consumption: 3.301 billion kWh (2023 est.)
transmission/distribution losses: 1.181 billion kWh (2023 est.)
comparison rankings: installed generating capacity 129; consumption 139; transmission/distribution losses 108

Electricity generation sources: *fossil fuels:* 87.1% of total installed capacity (2023 est.)
solar: 2.9% of total installed capacity (2023 est.)
wind: 6.1% of total installed capacity (2023 est.)
hydroelectricity: 2.7% of total installed capacity (2023 est.)
biomass and waste: 1.3% of total installed capacity (2023 est.)

Coal: *consumption:* 106,000 metric tons (2023 est.)
exports: 100 metric tons (2022 est.)
imports: 105,000 metric tons (2023 est.)

Petroleum: *total petroleum production:* 3,000 bbl/day (2023 est.)
refined petroleum consumption: 41,000 bbl/day (2023 est.)

Natural gas: *consumption:* 822.549 million cubic meters (2023 est.)
imports: 822.549 million cubic meters (2023 est.)

Energy consumption per capita: 42.095 million Btu/person (2023 est.)
comparison ranking: 100

COMMUNICATIONS

Telephones - fixed lines: *total subscriptions:* 459,000 (2023 est.)

subscriptions per 100 inhabitants: 16 (2023 est.)
comparison ranking: total subscriptions 95

Telephones - mobile cellular: *total subscriptions:* 3.27 million (2023 est.)
subscriptions per 100 inhabitants: 106 (2022 est.)
comparison ranking: total subscriptions 140

Broadcast media: 3 free-to-air TV stations, subscription cable services, and roughly 30 radio stations (2019)

Internet country code: .jm

Internet users: *percent of population:* 83% (2023 est.)

Broadband - fixed subscriptions: *total:* 448,000 (2023 est.)
subscriptions per 100 inhabitants: 16 (2023 est.)
comparison ranking: total 102

TRANSPORTATION

Civil aircraft registration country code prefix: 6Y

Airports: 20 (2025)
comparison ranking: 138

Heliports: 2 (2025)
comparison ranking: 133

Merchant marine: *total:* 40 (2023)
by type: bulk carrier 1, general cargo 11, oil tanker 1, other 27
comparison ranking: total 125

Ports: *total ports:* 11 (2024)
large: 0
medium: 1
small: 2
very small: 8
ports with oil terminals: 5
key ports: Falmouth, Kingston, Lucea, Montego Bay, Ocho Rios, Port Antonio, Port Esquivel, Port Kaiser, Rio Bueno, Rocky Point, Savannah la Mar

MILITARY AND SECURITY

Military and security forces: Jamaica Defense Force (JDF): Jamaica Regiment (Land Force), Maritime, Air, and Cyber Command (MACC), Support Brigade, Caribbean Military Academy, Jamaica National Reserve (2025)
note: the Jamaica Constabulary Force (JCF) is the country's police force; it has primary responsibility for internal security and has units for community policing, special response, intelligence gathering, and internal affairs; both it and the JDF are under the Ministry of National Security

Military expenditures: 1.4% of GDP (2024 est.)
1.2% of GDP (2023 est.)
1.3% of GDP (2022 est.)
1.4% of GDP (2021 est.)
1.7% of GDP (2020 est.)

Military and security service personnel strengths: approximately 4,000 active Jamaica Defense Forces (2025)

Military equipment inventories and acquisitions: the JDF is lightly armed with a limited inventory featuring equipment mostly from Australia, Canada, Japan, the Netherlands, the UK, and the US (2024)

Military service age and obligation: 18-23 for voluntary military service (17 with parental consent) for men and women; 18-28 for the reserves; no conscription; since 2017, the JDF's standard mode of recruitment is to enroll recruits ages 18-23 through the Jamaica National Service Corps (JNSC), which has a service requirement of 12 months (2025)
note 1: the Jamaica Combined Cadet Force (JCCF), a youth organization under the Ministry of Security, also provides a recruitment pool for the JDF, as well as other government agencies
note 2: as of 2022, women made up about 20% of the JDF's uniformed personnel

Military - note: in addition to its responsibility of defending against external aggression, the Jamaican Defense Force's (JDF) primary missions are border, cyber, internal, and maritime security; other missions include search and rescue, disaster response, humanitarian assistance, and peacekeeping; it has arrest authority and partners with the Jamaica Constabulary Force (JCF), particularly in support of combating crime and violence; both the JDF and JCF are under the Ministry of National Security, which directs policy for the security forces; the JDF participates in bilateral and multinational training exercises, including with the armed forces of Canada, the UK, the US, and other Caribbean nations
while Jamaica had a militia force as early as the 1660s, the JDF was constituted in 1962 from the West India Regiment (WIR), a British colonial regiment which dates back to 1795 (2025)

TRANSNATIONAL ISSUES

Illicit drugs: USG identification: major illicit drug-producing and/or drug-transit country (2025)

JAN MAYEN

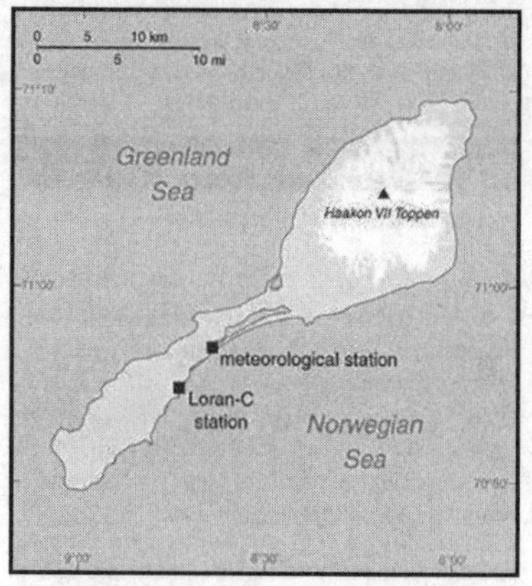

INTRODUCTION

Background: This desolate, mountainous island in the Arctic Ocean was named after a Dutch whaling captain who indisputably discovered it in 1614 (earlier claims are inconclusive). Visited only occasionally by seal hunters and trappers over the centuries, the island came under Norwegian sovereignty in 1929. The long dormant Beerenberg volcano, the northernmost active volcano on earth, resumed activity in 1970, and the most recent eruption occurred in 1985.

GEOGRAPHY

Location: Northern Europe, island between the Greenland Sea and the Norwegian Sea, northeast of Iceland

Geographic coordinates: 71 00 N, 8 00 W

Map references: Arctic Region

Area: *total:* 377 sq km
land: 377 sq km
water: 0 sq km
comparison ranking: total 205

Area - comparative: slightly more than twice the size of Washington, D.C.

Land boundaries: *total:* 0 km
Coastline 124.1 km

Maritime claims: *territorial sea:* 12 nm
contiguous zone: 24 nm
exclusive economic zone: 200 nm
continental shelf: 200-m depth or to the depth of exploitation

Climate: arctic maritime with frequent storms and persistent fog

Terrain: volcanic island, partly covered by glaciers

Elevation: *highest point:* Haakon VII Toppen on Beerenberg 2,277
lowest point: Norwegian/Greenland Seas 0 m
note: Beerenberg volcano has numerous peaks; the highest point on the volcano rim is named Haakon VII Toppen, after Norway's first king following the reestablishment of Norwegian independence in 1905

Natural resources: none

Land use: *agricultural land:* 0% (2011 est.)
other: 100% (2018 est.)

Irrigated land: 0 sq km (2022)

Natural hazards: dominated by the volcano Beerenberg
volcanism: Beerenberg (2,227 m) is Norway's only active volcano; volcanic activity resumed in 1970; the most recent eruption occurred in 1985

Geography - note: *barren volcanic spoon-shaped island with some moss and grass flora; island consists of two parts:* a larger northeast Nord-Jan (the spoon "bowl") and the smaller Sor-Jan (the "handle"), linked by a 2.5 km-wide isthmus (the "stem") with two large lakes, Sorlaguna (South Lagoon) and Nordlaguna (North Lagoon)

PEOPLE AND SOCIETY

Population: *total:* no permanent inhabitants
note: military personnel present on the south side of the island; meteorological stations

ENVIRONMENT

Environmental issues: pollutants transported from southerly latitudes by winds and ocean currents

Climate: arctic maritime with frequent storms and persistent fog

GOVERNMENT

Country name: *conventional long form:* none
conventional short form: Jan Mayen
etymology: named after Dutch Captain Jan Jacobszoon MAY, one of the first explorers to reach the island in 1614

Dependency status: territory of Norway; since 1994, administered from Oslo through the county governor *(fylkesmann)* of Nordland; however, authority has been delegated to a station commander of the Norwegian Defense Communication Service; in 2010, Norway designated the majority of Jan Mayen as a nature reserve

Legal system: the laws of Norway apply

Flag: the flag of Norway is used

COMMUNICATIONS

Broadcast media: a coastal radio station has been remotely operated since 1994

MILITARY AND SECURITY

Military - note: defense is the responsibility of Norway

JAPAN

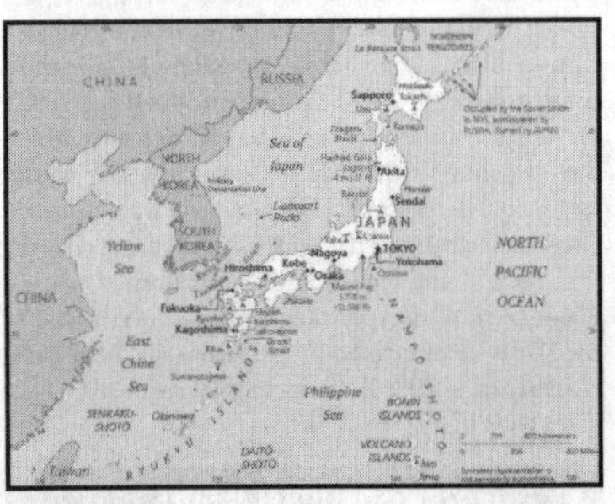

INTRODUCTION

Background: In 1603, after decades of civil warfare, the Tokugawa shogunate (a military-led, dynastic government) ushered in a long period of relative political stability and isolation from foreign influence. For more than two centuries, this policy enabled Japan to enjoy a flowering of its indigenous culture. Japan opened its ports after signing the Treaty of Kanagawa with the US in 1854 and began to intensively modernize and industrialize. During the late 19th and early 20th centuries, Japan became a regional power that was able to defeat the forces of both China and Russia. It occupied Korea, Formosa (Taiwan), and southern Sakhalin Island. In 1931-32, Japan occupied Manchuria, and in 1937, it launched a full-scale invasion of China. Japan attacked US forces at Pearl Harbor, Hawaii, in 1941, triggering America's entry into World War II, and Japan soon occupied much of East and Southeast Asia. After its defeat in World War II, the country recovered to become an economic power and a US ally.

While the emperor retains his throne as a symbol of national unity, elected politicians hold the decisionmaking power. After three decades of unprecedented growth, Japan's economy experienced a major slowdown starting in the 1990s, but the country remains an economic power. In 2011, Japan's strongest-ever earthquake and an accompanying tsunami devastated the northeast part of Honshu, killed thousands, and damaged several nuclear power plants. ABE Shinzo was reelected as prime minister in 2012, and he embarked on ambitious economic and security reforms to improve Japan's economy and bolster the country's international standing. In 2019, ABE became Japan's longest-serving post-war prime minister; he resigned in 2020 and was succeeded by SUGA Yoshihide. KISHIDA Fumio became prime minister in 2021.

GEOGRAPHY

Location: Eastern Asia, island chain between the North Pacific Ocean and the Sea of Japan, east of the Korean Peninsula

Geographic coordinates: 36 00 N, 138 00 E

Map references: Asia

Area: *total:* 377,915 sq km
land: 364,485 sq km
water: 13,430 sq km
note: includes Bonin Islands (Ogasawara-gunto), Daito-shoto, Minami-jima, Okino-tori-shima, Ryukyu Islands (Nansei-shoto), and Volcano Islands (Kazan-retto)
comparison ranking: total 63

Area - comparative: slightly smaller than California

Land boundaries: *total:* 0 km

Coastline: 29,751 km

Maritime claims: *territorial sea:* 12 nm; between 3 nm and 12 nm in the international straits - La Perouse or Soya, Tsugaru, Osumi, and the Korea and Tsushima Straits
contiguous zone: 24 nm
exclusive economic zone: 200 nm

Climate: varies from tropical in south to cool temperate in north

Terrain: mostly rugged and mountainous

Elevation: *highest point:* Mount Fuji 3,776 m
lowest point: Hachiro-gata -4 m
mean elevation: 438 m

Natural resources: negligible mineral resources, fish
note: with virtually no natural energy resources, Japan is almost totally dependent on imported sources of energy

Land use: *agricultural land:* 12.7% (2022 est.)
arable land: 11.2% (2022 est.)
permanent crops: 0.7% (2022 est.)
permanent pasture: 0.9% (2022 est.)
forest: 68.4% (2022 est.)
other: 18.9% (2022 est.)

Irrigated land: 15,730 sq km (2014)

Major lakes (area sq km): *fresh water lake(s):* Biwa-ko 688 sq km

Population distribution: all primary and secondary regions of high population density lie on the coast; one third of the population resides in and around Tokyo on the central plain (Kanto Plain)

Natural hazards: many dormant and some active volcanoes; about 1,500 seismic occurrences (mostly tremors but occasional severe earthquakes) every year; tsunamis; typhoons
volcanism: both Unzen (1,500 m) and Sakura-jima (1,117 m), which lies near the densely populated city of Kagoshima, have been deemed Decade Volcanoes by the International Association of Volcanology and Chemistry of the Earth's Interior, worthy of study due to their explosive history and close proximity to human populations; other notable historically active volcanoes include Asama (Honshu Island's most active volcano), Aso, Bandai, Fuji, Iwo-Jima, Kikai, Kirishima, Komaga-take, Oshima, Suwanosejima, Tokachi, Yake-dake, and Usu; see note 2 under "Geography - note"

Geography - note: *note 1:* strategic location in northeast Asia; composed of four main islands (the "Home Islands") – Hokkaido, Honshu (the largest, most populous, and site of Tokyo, the capital), Shikoku, and Kyushu
note 2: a 2023 Geospatial Information Authority of Japan survey detected 100,000 islands and islets, but only the 14,125 islands with a circumference of at least 100 m (330 ft) were officially counted; about 260 of the islands are inhabited
note 3: Japan annually records the most earthquakes in the world; it is one of the countries along the Ring of Fire, which is a belt bordering the Pacific Ocean that contains about 75% of the world's volcanoes and up to 90% of the world's earthquakes

PEOPLE AND SOCIETY

Population: *total:* 123,201,945 (2024 est.)
male: 59,875,269
female: 63,326,676
comparison rankings: total 11; male 11; female 11

Nationality: *noun:* Japanese (singular and plural)
adjective: Japanese

Ethnic groups: Japanese 97.5%, Chinese 0.6%, Vietnam 0.4%, South Korean 0.3%, other 1.2% (includes Filipino, Brazilian, Nepalese, Indonesian, American, and Taiwanese) (2022 est.)
note: data represent population by nationality; up to 230,000 Brazilians of Japanese origin migrated to Japan in the 1990s to work in industries; some have returned to Brazil

Languages: Japanese
major-language sample(s):
必要不可欠な基本情報の源、ワールド・ファクトブック
(Japanese)

Religions: Shintoism 48.6%, Buddhism 46.4%, Christianity 1.1%, other 4% (2021 est.)

note: total adherents among persons claiming a religious affiliation

Age structure: *0-14 years:* 12.1% (male 7,701,196/female 7,239,389)
15-64 years: 58.4% (male 36,197,840/female 35,777,966)
65 years and over: 29.5% (2024 est.) (male 15,976,233/female 20,309,321)

Dependency ratios: *total dependency ratio:* 71.2 (2024 est.)
youth dependency ratio: 20.8 (2024 est.)
elderly dependency ratio: 50.4 (2024 est.)
potential support ratio: 2 (2024 est.)

Median age: *total:* 49.9 years (2024 est.)
male: 48.3 years
female: 51.3 years
comparison ranking: total 3

Population growth rate: -0.43% (2024 est.)
comparison ranking: 218

Birth rate: 6.9 births/1,000 population (2024 est.)
comparison ranking: 225

Death rate: 11.9 deaths/1,000 population (2024 est.)
comparison ranking: 18

Net migration rate: 0.7 migrant(s)/1,000 population (2024 est.)
comparison ranking: 70

Population distribution: all primary and secondary regions of high population density lie on the coast; one third of the population resides in and around Tokyo on the central plain (Kanto Plain)

Urbanization: *urban population:* 92% of total population (2023)
rate of urbanization: -0.25% annual rate of change (2020-25 est.)

Major urban areas - population: 37.194 million TOKYO (capital), 19.013 million Osaka, 9.569 million Nagoya, 5.490 million Kitakyushu-Fukuoka, 2.937 million Shizuoka-Hamamatsu, 2.666 million Sapporo (2023)

Sex ratio: *at birth:* 1.06 male(s)/female
0-14 years: 1.06 male(s)/female
15-64 years: 1.01 male(s)/female
65 years and over: 0.79 male(s)/female
total population: 0.95 male(s)/female (2024 est.)

Mother's mean age at first birth: 30.7 years (2018 est.)

Maternal mortality ratio: 3 deaths/100,000 live births (2023 est.)
comparison ranking: 183

Infant mortality rate: *total:* 1.9 deaths/1,000 live births (2024 est.)
male: 2 deaths/1,000 live births
female: 1.7 deaths/1,000 live births
comparison ranking: total 222

Life expectancy at birth: *total population:* 85.2 years (2024 est.)
male: 82.3 years
female: 88.2 years
comparison ranking: total population 4

Total fertility rate: 1.4 children born/woman (2024 est.)
comparison ranking: 212

Gross reproduction rate: 0.68 (2024 est.)

Drinking water source: *improved:* total: 99.1% of population (2022 est.)
unimproved: total: 0.9% of population (2022 est.)

Health expenditure: 10.8% of GDP (2021)
23.4% of national budget (2022 est.)

Physician density: 2.65 physicians/1,000 population (2022)

Hospital bed density: 12.7 beds/1,000 population (2020 est.)

Sanitation facility access: *improved:* total: 99.9% of population (2022 est.)
unimproved: total: 0.1% of population (2022 est.)

Obesity - adult prevalence rate: 4.3% (2016)
comparison ranking: 186

Alcohol consumption per capita: *total:* 8.36 liters of pure alcohol (2019 est.)
beer: 1.35 liters of pure alcohol (2019 est.)
wine: 0.29 liters of pure alcohol (2019 est.)
spirits: 1.63 liters of pure alcohol (2019 est.)
other alcohols: 5.09 liters of pure alcohol (2019 est.)
comparison ranking: total 39

Tobacco use: *total:* 15.5% (2025 est.)
male: 24.4% (2025 est.)
female: 7.2% (2025 est.)
comparison ranking: total 101

Currently married women (ages 15-49): 46.8% (2023 est.)

Education expenditure: 3.2% of GDP (2022 est.)
7.5% national budget (2022 est.)
comparison ranking: Education expenditure (% GDP) 142

School life expectancy (primary to tertiary education): *total:* 16 years (2022 est.)
male: 16 years (2022 est.)
female: 16 years (2022 est.)

ENVIRONMENT

Environmental issues: air pollution from power plants results in acid rain; acidification of lakes and reservoirs degrading water quality; waste management issues; ongoing environmental clean-up in small area of Fukushima after nuclear accident in 2011

International environmental agreements: *party to:* Antarctic-Environmental Protection, Antarctic-Marine Living Resources, Antarctic Seals, Antarctic Treaty, Biodiversity, Climate Change, Climate Change-Kyoto Protocol, Climate Change-Paris Agreement, Comprehensive Nuclear Test Ban, Desertification, Endangered Species, Environmental Modification, Hazardous Wastes, Law of the Sea, Marine Dumping-London Convention, Marine Dumping-London Protocol, Nuclear Test Ban, Ozone Layer Protection, Ship Pollution, Tropical Timber 2006, Wetlands
signed, but not ratified: none of the selected agreements

Climate: varies from tropical in south to cool temperate in north

Urbanization: *urban population:* 92% of total population (2023)
rate of urbanization: -0.25% annual rate of change (2020-25 est.)

Carbon dioxide emissions: 960.23 million metric tonnes of CO2 (2023 est.)
from coal and metallurgical coke: 367.144 million metric tonnes of CO2 (2023 est.)
from petroleum and other liquids: 403.042 million metric tonnes of CO2 (2023 est.)
from consumed natural gas: 190.043 million metric tonnes of CO2 (2023 est.)
comparison ranking: total emissions 5

Particulate matter emissions: 10.5 micrograms per cubic meter (2019 est.)

Methane emissions: *energy:* 214.7 kt (2022-2024 est.)
agriculture: 972.8 kt (2019-2021 est.)
waste: 208.2 kt (2019-2021 est.)
other: 22.7 kt (2019-2021 est.)

Waste and recycling: *municipal solid waste generated annually:* 42.72 million tons (2024 est.)
percent of municipal solid waste recycled: 11.5% (2022 est.)

Total water withdrawal: *municipal:* 13.5 billion cubic meters (2022 est.)
industrial: 13 billion cubic meters (2022 est.)
agricultural: 53 billion cubic meters (2022 est.)

Total renewable water resources: 430 billion cubic meters (2022 est.)

Geoparks: *total global geoparks and regional networks:* 10
global geoparks and regional networks: Aso UNESCO; Hakusan Tedorigawa; Itoigawa; Izu Peninsula; Mt. Apoi; Muroto; Oki Islands; San'in Kaigan; Toya - Usu; Unzen (2023)

GOVERNMENT

Country name: *conventional long form:* none
conventional short form: Japan
local long form: Nihon-koku/Nippon-koku
local short form: Nihon/Nippon
etymology: the English word for Japan comes from the Chinese name for the country, Cipangu; both Nihon and Nippon come from the Japanese words *nichi*, or "sun," and *hon*, or "origin," which is frequently translated as "Land of the Rising Sun"

Government type: parliamentary constitutional monarchy

Capital: *name:* Tokyo
geographic coordinates: 35 41 N, 139 45 E
time difference: UTC+9 (14 hours ahead of Washington, DC, during Standard Time)
etymology: originally known as Edo, meaning "estuary" because of its location on a bay; the name was changed to Tokyo, meaning "eastern capital," in 1868, as a contrast to Kyoto, the previous capital to the west

Administrative divisions: 47 prefectures; Aichi, Akita, Aomori, Chiba, Ehime, Fukui, Fukuoka, Fukushima, Gifu, Gunma, Hiroshima, Hokkaido, Hyogo, Ibaraki, Ishikawa, Iwate, Kagawa, Kagoshima, Kanagawa, Kochi, Kumamoto, Kyoto, Mie, Miyagi, Miyazaki, Nagano, Nagasaki, Nara, Niigata, Oita, Okayama, Okinawa, Osaka, Saga, Saitama, Shiga, Shimane, Shizuoka, Tochigi, Tokushima, Tokyo, Tottori, Toyama, Wakayama, Yamagata, Yamaguchi, Yamanashi

Legal system: civil law system based on German model; also reflects Anglo-American influence and Japanese traditions; Supreme Court reviews legislative acts

Constitution: *history:* previous 1890; latest approved 6 October 1946, adopted 3 November 1946, effective 3 May 1947
amendment process: proposed by the Diet; passage requires approval by at least two-thirds majority of both houses of the Diet and approval by majority in a referendum

International law organization participation: accepts compulsory ICJ jurisdiction with reservations; accepts ICCt jurisdiction

Citizenship: *citizenship by birth:* no
citizenship by descent only: at least one parent must be a citizen of Japan
dual citizenship recognized: no
residency requirement for naturalization: 5 years

Suffrage: 18 years of age; universal

Executive branch: *chief of state:* Emperor NARUHITO (since 1 May 2019)
head of government: vacant (since 7 September 2025)
cabinet: Cabinet appointed by the prime minister
election/appointment process: the monarchy is hereditary; the leader of the majority party or majority coalition in the House of Representatives usually becomes prime minister
election results: *2024:* Shigeru ISHIBA (LDP) elected prime minister on 27 September 2024; upper house vote - 143 of 242 votes; lower house vote - 291 of 461 votes
2021: Fumio KISHIDA reelected prime minister on 10 November 2021; upper house vote - Fumio KISHIDA (LDP) 141, Yukio EDANO (CDP) 60; lower house vote - Fumio KISHIDA 297, Yukio EDANO 108
note: Shigeru ISHIBA resigned as prime minister on 7 September 2025; the party vote on the new prime minister is expected in early October 2025

Legislative branch: *legislature name:* National Diet (Kokkai)
legislative structure: bicameral

Legislative branch - lower chamber: *chamber name:* House of Representatives (Shugiin)
number of seats: 465 (all directly elected)
electoral system: mixed system
scope of elections: full renewal
term in office: 4 years
most recent election date: 10/27/2024
parties elected and seats per party: Liberal Democratic Party (LDP) (191); Constitutional Democratic Party of Japan (148); Nippon Ishin (Japan Innovation Party) (38); Democratic Party for the People (28); Komeito (24); Other (36)
percentage of women in chamber: 15.7%
expected date of next election: October 2028

Legislative branch - upper chamber: *chamber name:* House of Councillors (Sangiin)
number of seats: 248 (all directly elected)
electoral system: mixed system
scope of elections: partial renewal
term in office: 6 years
most recent election date: 7/20/2025
parties elected and seats per party: Liberal Democratic Party (LDP) (39); Constitutional Democratic Party of Japan (22); Democratic Party for the People (17); Sanseito (14); Komeito (8); Nippon Ishin (Japan Innovation Party) (7); Independents (8); Other (10)
percentage of women in chamber: 29.4%
expected date of next election: June 2028

Judicial branch: *highest court(s):* Supreme Court or Saiko saibansho (consists of the chief justice and 14 associate justices)
judge selection and term of office: Supreme Court chief justice designated by the Cabinet and appointed by the monarch; associate justices appointed by the Cabinet and confirmed by the monarch; all justices are reviewed in a popular referendum during the first general election of the House of Representatives after each judge's appointment and every 10 years afterward
subordinate courts: 8 High Courts (Koto-saibansho), each with a Family Court (Katei-saiban-sho); 50 District Courts (Chiho saibansho), with 203 additional branches; 438 Summary Courts (Kani saibansho)
note: the Supreme Court has jurisdiction in constitutional issues

Political parties: Conservative Party of Japan or CPJ
Constitutional Democratic Party of Japan or CDP
Democratic Party for the People or DPFP or DPP
Japan Communist Party or JCP
Japan Innovation Party or Nippon Ishin no kai or Ishin
Komeito or Komei
Liberal Democratic Party or LDP
Okinawa Social Mass Party or Okinawa Whirlwind or OW
Party to Protect the People from NHK or NHK
Reiwa Shinsengumi
Sanseito Party
Social Democratic Party or SDP

Diplomatic representation in the US: *chief of mission:* Ambassador YAMADA Shigeo (since 27 February 2024)
chancery: 2520 Massachusetts Avenue NW, Washington, DC 20008
telephone: [1] (202) 238-6700
FAX: [1] (202) 328-2187
email address and website: emb-consulate.dc@ws.mofa.go.jp
https://www.us.emb-japan.go.jp/itprtop_en/index.html
consulate(s) general: Chicago
consulate(s): Anchorage (AK), Atlanta, Boston, Denver (CO), Detroit (MI), Hagatna (Guam), Honolulu, Houston, Los Angeles, Miami, Nashville (TN), New York, Portland (OR), San Francisco, Saipan (Northern Mariana Islands), Seattle (WA)

Diplomatic representation from the US: *chief of mission:* Ambassador George GLASS (since 17 July 2025)
embassy: 1-10-5 Akasaka, Minato-ku, Tokyo 107-8420
mailing address: 9800 Tokyo Place, Washington DC 20521-9800
telephone: [81] (03) 3224-5000
FAX: [81] (03) 3224-5856
email address and website: TokyoACS@state.gov
https://jp.usembassy.gov/
consulate(s) general: Naha (Okinawa), Osaka-Kobe, Sapporo
consulate(s): Fukuoka, Nagoya

International organization participation: ADB, AfDB (nonregional member), APEC, Arctic Council (observer), ARF, ASEAN (dialogue partner), Australia Group, BIS, CD, CE (observer), CERN (observer), CICA (observer), CP, CPLP (associate), EAS, EBRD, EITI (implementing country), FAO, FATF, G-5, G-7, G-8, G-10, G-20, IADB, IAEA, IBRD, ICAO, ICC (national committees), ICCt, ICRM, IDA, IEA, IFAD, IFC, IFRCS, IGAD (partners), IHO, ILO, IMF, IMO, IMSO, Interpol, IOC, IOM, IPU, ISO, ITSO, ITU, ITUC (NGOs), LAIA (observer), MIGA, NEA, NSG, OAS (observer), OECD, OPCW, OSCE (partner), Pacific Alliance (observer), Paris Club, PCA, PIF (partner), Quad, SAARC (observer), SELEC (observer), SICA (observer), UN, UNCTAD, UNESCO, UNHCR, UNHRC, UNIDO, UNMISS, UNOOSA, UNRWA, UNWTO, UPU, Wassenaar Arrangement, WCO, WFTU (NGOs), WHO, WIPO, WMO, WTO, ZC

Independence: 3 May 1947 (current constitution adopted as amendment to Meiji Constitution); notable earlier dates: 11 February 660 B.C. (mythological date of Emperor JIMMU founding the nation); 29 November 1890 (Meiji Constitution provides for constitutional monarchy)

National holiday: Birthday of Emperor NARUHITO, 23 February (1960)
note: celebrates the birthday of the current emperor

Flag: *description:* white with a large red disk that symbolizes the sun without rays, in the center
history: the current flag was adopted in 1854, but a sun flag has been in use in Japan since at least 1184; the sun has long been a national symbol: according to tradition, the sun goddess Amaterasu founded the country in the 7th century B.C.

National symbol(s): red sun disc, chrysanthemum

National color(s): red, white

National coat of arms: the Kikumon is the Japanese emperor's family coat of arms and dates from 1183; the Imperial chrysanthemum emblem ([INSERT IMAGE], *kikunogomon)* is a yellow or orange chrysanthemum with black or red outlines and background; a central disc is surrounded by a front set of 16 petals; a rear set of 16 petals are half-staggered in relation to the front set and are visible at the edges of the flower

National anthem(s): *title:* "Kimigayo" ("His Majesty's Reign)
lyrics/music: unknown/Hiromori HAYASHI
history: adopted 1999; unofficial national anthem since 1883; oldest anthem lyrics in the world, dating to the 10th century or earlier; some oppose the anthem because of its association with militarism and worship of the emperor

National heritage: *total World Heritage Sites:* 26 (21 cultural, 5 natural)
selected World Heritage Site locales: Buddhist Monuments in the Horyu-ji Area (c); Historic Monuments of Ancient Nara (c); Himeji-jo (c); Shiretoko (n); Mozu-Furuichi Kofun Group: Mounded Tombs of Ancient Japan (c); Jomon Prehistoric Sites in Northern Japan (c); Yakushima (n); Historic Monuments of Ancient Kyoto (Kyoto, Uji and Otsu Cities) (c); Hiroshima Peace Memorial (Genbaku Dome) (c); Shirakami-Sanchi (n); Historic Villages of Shirakawa-go and Gokayama (c); Itsukushima Shinto Shrine (c); Historic Monuments of Ancient Nara (c); Shrines and Temples of Nikko (c); Gusuku Sites and Related Properties of the Kingdom of Ryukyu (c); Sacred Sites and Pilgrimage Routes in the Kii Mountain Range (c); Hiraizumi – Temples, Gardens and Archaeological Sites Representing the Buddhist Pure Land (c); Ogasawara Islands (n); Sacred Island of Okinoshima and Associated Sites in the Munakata Region (c); Hidden Christian Sites in the Nagasaki Region (c); Amami-Oshima Island, Tokunoshima Island, Northern part of Okinawa Island, and Iriomote Island (n); Jomon Prehistoric Sites in Northern Japan (c)

ECONOMY

Economic overview: second-largest East Asian economy; trade-oriented and highly diversified; high public debt levels; following years of near-zero interest rates, gradual increases to address inflation and depreciation of yen; strong rebound in tourism; aging population poses challenges to labor force participation

Real GDP (purchasing power parity): $5.715 trillion (2024 est.)
$5.71 trillion (2023 est.)
$5.627 trillion (2022 est.)
note: data in 2021 dollars
comparison ranking: 5

Real GDP growth rate: 0.1% (2024 est.)
1.5% (2023 est.)
0.9% (2022 est.)
note: annual GDP % growth based on constant local currency
comparison ranking: 190

Real GDP per capita: $46,100 (2024 est.)
$45,900 (2023 est.)
$45,000 (2022 est.)
note: data in 2021 dollars
comparison ranking: 47

GDP (official exchange rate): $4.026 trillion (2024 est.)
note: data in current dollars at official exchange rate

Inflation rate (consumer prices): 2.7% (2024 est.)
3.3% (2023 est.)
2.5% (2022 est.)
note: annual % change based on consumer prices
comparison ranking: 77

GDP - composition, by sector of origin: *agriculture:* 0.9% (2023 est.)
industry: 28.6% (2023 est.)
services: 69.8% (2023 est.)
note: figures may not total 100% due to non-allocated consumption not captured in sector-reported data
comparison rankings: agriculture 176; industry 67; services 37

GDP - composition, by end use: *household consumption:* 55.5% (2022 est.)
government consumption: 21.6% (2022 est.)
investment in fixed capital: 26.3% (2022 est.)
investment in inventories: 0.5% (2022 est.)
exports of goods and services: 21.5% (2022 est.)
imports of goods and services: -25.3% (2022 est.)
note: figures may not total 100% due to rounding or gaps in data collection

Agricultural products: rice, milk, sugar beets, vegetables, eggs, chicken, potatoes, onions, cabbages, pork (2023)
note: top ten agricultural products based on tonnage

Industries: motor vehicles, electronic equipment, machine tools, steel and nonferrous metals, ships, chemicals, textiles, processed foods

Industrial production growth rate: 1.4% (2023 est.)
note: annual % change in industrial value added based on constant local currency
comparison ranking: 108

Labor force: 69.382 million (2024 est.)
note: number of people ages 15 or older who are employed or seeking work
comparison ranking: 10

Unemployment rate: 2.6% (2024 est.)
2.6% (2023 est.)
2.6% (2022 est.)
note: % of labor force seeking employment
comparison ranking: 27

Youth unemployment rate (ages 15-24): *total:* 3.9% (2024 est.)
male: 4.2% (2024 est.)
female: 3.7% (2024 est.)
note: % of labor force ages 15-24 seeking employment
comparison ranking: total 170

Gini Index coefficient - distribution of family income: 32.3 (2020 est.)
note: index (0-100) of income distribution; higher values represent greater inequality
comparison ranking: 104

Average household expenditures: *on food:* 15.8% of household expenditures (2023 est.)
on alcohol and tobacco: 2.5% of household expenditures (2023 est.)

Household income or consumption by percentage share: *lowest 10%:* 2.4% (2020 est.)
highest 10%: 23.9% (2020 est.)
note: % share of income accruing to lowest and highest 10% of population

Remittances: 0.1% of GDP (2024 est.)
0.1% of GDP (2023 est.)
0.1% of GDP (2022 est.)
note: personal transfers and compensation between resident and non-resident individuals/households/entities

Budget: *revenues:* $661.986 billion (2022 est.)
expenditures: $897.03 billion (2022 est.)
note: central government revenues and expenditures (excluding grants and social security funds) converted to US dollars at average official exchange rate for year indicated

Public debt: 215.9% of GDP (2022 est.)
note: central government debt as a % of GDP
comparison ranking: 1

Current account balance: $194.257 billion (2024 est.)
$156.592 billion (2023 est.)
$90.21 billion (2022 est.)
note: balance of payments - net trade and primary/secondary income in current dollars
comparison ranking: 3

Exports: $922.447 billion (2024 est.)
$923.488 billion (2023 est.)
$922.813 billion (2022 est.)
note: balance of payments - exports of goods and services in current dollars
comparison ranking: 8

Exports - partners: USA 19%, China 18%, Taiwan 6%, S. Korea 6%, Hong Kong 4% (2023)
note: top five export partners based on percentage share of exports

Exports - commodities: cars, integrated circuits, machinery, vehicle parts/accessories, construction vehicles (2023)
note: top five export commodities based on value in dollars

Imports: $965.047 billion (2024 est.)
$996.364 billion (2023 est.)
$1.081 trillion (2022 est.)
note: balance of payments - imports of goods and services in current dollars
comparison ranking: 6

Imports - partners: China 22%, USA 11%, Australia 8%, UAE 5%, Saudi Arabia 5% (2023)
note: top five import partners based on percentage share of imports

Imports - commodities: crude petroleum, natural gas, coal, integrated circuits, broadcasting equipment (2023)
note: top five import commodities based on value in dollars

Reserves of foreign exchange and gold: $1.231 trillion (2024 est.)
$1.295 trillion (2023 est.)
$1.228 trillion (2022 est.)
note: holdings of gold (year-end prices)/foreign exchange/special drawing rights in current dollars
comparison ranking: 2

Exchange rates: yen (JPY) per US dollar -

Exchange rates: 151.366 (2024 est.)
140.491 (2023 est.)
131.498 (2022 est.)
109.754 (2021 est.)
106.775 (2020 est.)

ENERGY

Electricity access: *electrification - total population:* 100% (2022 est.)

Electricity: *installed generating capacity:* 361.617 million kW (2023 est.)
consumption: 902.769 billion kWh (2023 est.)
transmission/distribution losses: 41.79 billion kWh (2023 est.)
comparison rankings: installed generating capacity 4; consumption 5; transmission/distribution losses 203

Electricity generation sources: *fossil fuels:* 65.8% of total installed capacity (2023 est.)
nuclear: 8.9% of total installed capacity (2023 est.)
solar: 10.3% of total installed capacity (2023 est.)
wind: 1.1% of total installed capacity (2023 est.)
hydroelectricity: 7.1% of total installed capacity (2023 est.)
geothermal: 0.3% of total installed capacity (2023 est.)
biomass and waste: 6.5% of total installed capacity (2023 est.)

Nuclear energy: Number of operational nuclear reactors: 14 (2025)

Number of nuclear reactors under construction: 2 (2025)

Net capacity of operational nuclear reactors: 12.63GW (2025 est.)

Percent of total electricity production: 5.5% (2023 est.)

Number of nuclear reactors permanently shut down: 27 (2025)

Coal: *production:* 27.657 million metric tons (2023 est.)
consumption: 197.612 million metric tons (2023 est.)
exports: 1.615 million metric tons (2023 est.)
imports: 170.874 million metric tons (2023 est.)
proven reserves: 350 million metric tons (2023 est.)

Petroleum: *total petroleum production:* 8,000 bbl/day (2023 est.)
refined petroleum consumption: 3.14 million bbl/day (2024 est.)
crude oil estimated reserves: 44.115 million barrels (2021 est.)

Natural gas: *production:* 2.019 billion cubic meters (2023 est.)
consumption: 88.317 billion cubic meters (2023 est.)
exports: 271.607 million cubic meters (2022 est.)
imports: 85.003 billion cubic meters (2023 est.)
proven reserves: 20.898 billion cubic meters (2021 est.)

Energy consumption per capita: 129.504 million Btu/person (2023 est.)
comparison ranking: 29

COMMUNICATIONS

Telephones - fixed lines: *total subscriptions:* 59.758 million (2023 est.)
subscriptions per 100 inhabitants: 48 (2023 est.)
comparison ranking: total subscriptions 3

Telephones - mobile cellular: *total subscriptions:* 219 million (2023 est.)
subscriptions per 100 inhabitants: 168 (2022 est.)
comparison ranking: total subscriptions 7

Broadcast media: a mix of public and commercial TV and radio stations; 5 national terrestrial TV networks including 1 public broadcaster; large number of radio and TV stations; satellite and cable services provide access to international channels (2023)

Internet country code: .jp

Internet users: *percent of population:* 87% (2023 est.)

Broadband - fixed subscriptions: *total:* 47.9 million (2023 est.)
subscriptions per 100 inhabitants: 39 (2023 est.)
comparison ranking: total 4

TRANSPORTATION

Civil aircraft registration country code prefix: JA

Airports: 280 (2025)
comparison ranking: 24

Heliports: 3,036 (2025)
comparison ranking: 2

Railways: *total:* 27,311 km (2015)
standard gauge: 4,800 km (2015) 1.435-m gauge (4,800 km electrified)
narrow gauge: 124 km (2015) 1.372-m gauge (124 km electrified)
dual gauge: 132 km (2015) 1.435-1.067-m gauge (132 km electrified)
22,207 km 1.067-mm gauge (15,430 km electrified)
48 km 0.762-m gauge (48 km electrified)

Merchant marine: *total:* 5,229 (2023)
by type: bulk carrier 166, container ship 49, general cargo 1,893, oil tanker 666, other 2,455
comparison ranking: total 4

Ports: *total ports:* 163 (2024)
large: 11
medium: 26
small: 54
very small: 71
size unknown: 1
ports with oil terminals: 99
key ports: Kawasaki Ko, Kobe, Mikawa, Nagasaki, Nagoya Ko, Onomichi-Itozaki, Osaka, Tokyo Ko, Wakamatsu Ko, Wakayama-Shimotsu Ko, Yokohama Ko

MILITARY AND SECURITY

Military and security forces: Japan Self-Defense Force (JSDF): Ground Self-Defense Force (Rikujou Jieitai, GSDF; includes aviation), Maritime Self-Defense Force (Kaijou Jieitai, MSDF; includes naval aviation), Air Self-Defense Force (Koukuu Jieitai, ASDF) (2025)
note: the Coast Guard is under the Ministry of Land, Infrastructure, Transport and Tourism; it is barred by law from operating as a military force, but in times of conflict Article 80 of the 1954 Self-Defense Forces Act permits the transfer of control of the coast guard to the Ministry of Defense with Cabinet approval

Military expenditures: 1.4% of GDP (2024 est.)
1.2% of GDP (2023 est.)
1.1% of GDP (2022 est.)
1% of GDP (2021 est.)
1% of GDP (2020 est.)
note: the Japanese Government in 2022 pledged to increase defense expenditures to 2% of GDP in line with NATO standards by March 2028; if the planned increase occurs, Japan would have the world's third largest defense budget

Military and security service personnel strengths: approximately 230-240,000 active Self Defense Forces (145-150,000 Ground; 40-45,000 Maritime; 40-45,000 Air) (2025)

Military equipment inventories and acquisitions: the JSDF is equipped with a mix of imported and domestically produced equipment; Japan has a robust defense industry and is capable of producing a wide range of air, ground, and naval weapons systems; the majority of its weapons imports are from the US and some domestically produced weapons are US-origin and manufactured under license (2024)

Military service age and obligation: 18-32 years of age for voluntary military service for men and women; no conscription (2024)
note: as of 2023, women made up about 9% of the military's full-time personnel

Military deployments: approximately 200 Djibouti (2024)

Military - note: the Japan Self-Defense Force (JSDF) has a range of missions, including territorial defense, monitoring the country's air and maritime spaces, countering piracy and terrorism, and conducting humanitarian operations; the JSDF exercises regularly with the US military and increasingly with other regional countries, including Australia and the Philippines
Japan's alliance with the US is one of the cornerstones of the country's security, as well as a large component of the US security posture in Asia; the US-Japan mutual defense treaty grants the US the right to base US military forces in Japan, including aircraft and ships, in return for US security guarantees; the Japanese Government provides approximately $3 billion on average per year to offset the cost of stationing US forces in Japan; in addition, it pays compensation to localities hosting US troops, rent for bases, and costs for new facilities to support the US presence; Japan also has Major Non-NATO Ally (MNNA) status with the US, a designation under US law that provides foreign partners with certain benefits in the areas of defense trade and security cooperation
Japan was disarmed after its defeat in World War II; shortly after the Korean War began in 1950, US occupation forces in Japan created a 75,000-member lightly armed force called the National Police Reserve; the JSDF was founded in 1954; Article 9 of Japan's 1947 constitution renounced the use of force as a means of settling international disputes; however, Japan has interpreted Article 9 to mean that it can maintain a military for national defense purposes and, since 1991, has allowed the JSDF to participate in noncombat roles overseas in a number of UN peacekeeping missions and in the US-led coalition in Iraq; in 2014-2015, the Japanese Government reinterpreted the constitution as allowing for "collective self-defense," described as the use of force on others' behalf if Japan's security was threatened; in 2022, the government released security policy documents that declared Japan's intention to develop "counterstrike" capabilities, including armed drones and cruise missiles, and outlined plans to increase Japan's security-related expenditures to 2% of GDP (2025)

SPACE

Space agency/agencies: Japan Aerospace Exploration Agency (JAXA; established in 2003) (2025)

Space launch site(s): Tanegashima Space Center/Yoshinobu Launch Complex (Kagoshima), Uchinoura Space Center (Kagoshima), Noshiro Testing Center (Akita) (2025)

Space program overview: has one of the world's largest and most advanced space programs with independent capabilities in all areas of space categories except for autonomous manned space flight; designs, builds, launches, and operates the full spectrum of satellites, including communications, remote sensing (RS), astronomical observation, scientific, and navigational/positional; designs, builds, and independently launches satellite/space launch vehicles (SLVs) and other spacecraft, including interplanetary and Lunar probes, space station modules and space labs, and space transportation systems; has a wide range of research and development programs, including radio waves, robotics, reusable SLVs, solar sails, space-based astronomy, spacecraft components, and space plasma; has an astronaut training program; participates in international space programs, including the International Space Station (ISS) and the Square Kilometer Array radio telescope project, leading the Asia-Pacific Regional Space Agency Forum, and co-leading the Global Earth Observation System of Systems; cooperates with a variety of foreign space agencies and industries, including those of Canada, the European Space Agency (ESA) and its individual member states, India, Russia, the UAE, the US, and a range of other countries and space agencies throughout Africa, Europe, and the Asia-Pacific regions; has a substantial commercial space industry that develops an array of space-related capabilities and technologies, including satellites, satellite payloads and subcomponents, and SLVs; in recent years, the Japanese Government has encouraged and supported the development of space startup companies (2025)
note: further details about the key activities, programs, and milestones of the country's space program, as well as government spending estimates on the space sector, appear in the Space Programs reference guide

TRANSNATIONAL ISSUES

Refugees and internally displaced persons: *refugees:* 60,361 (2024 est.)

IDPs: 29,244 (2024 est.)
stateless persons: 505 (2024 est.)

JERSEY

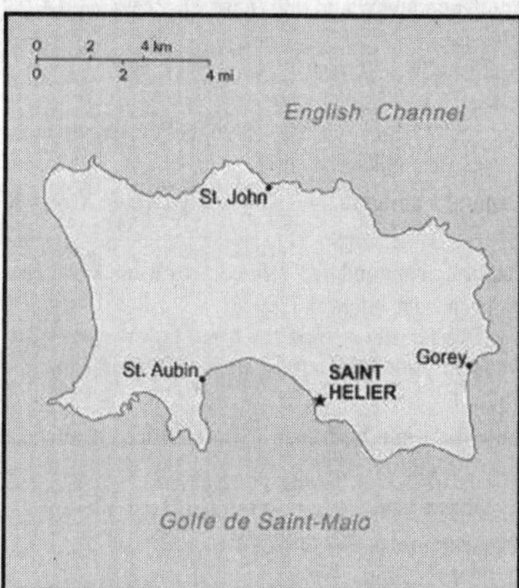

INTRODUCTION

Background: Jersey and the other Channel Islands represent the last remnants of the medieval Duchy of Normandy that held sway in both France and England. These islands were the only British soil that Germany occupied in World War II. The Bailiwick of Jersey is a British Crown dependency, which means that it is not part of the UK but is rather a self-governing possession of the British Crown. However, the UK Government is constitutionally responsible for its defense and international representation.

GEOGRAPHY

Location: Western Europe, island in the English Channel, northwest of France

Geographic coordinates: 49 15 N, 2 10 W

Map references: Europe

Area: *total:* 116 sq km
water: 0 sq km
comparison ranking: total 223

Area - comparative: about two-thirds the size of Washington, D.C.

Land boundaries: *total:* 0 km

Coastline: 70 km

Maritime claims: *territorial sea:* 12 nm
exclusive fishing zone: 12 nm

Climate: temperate; mild winters and cool summers

Terrain: gently rolling plain with low, rugged hills along north coast

Elevation: *highest point:* Les Platons 136 m
lowest point: English Channel 0 m

Natural resources: arable land

Land use: *agricultural land:* 43.3% (2022 est.)
arable land: 18.3% (2022 est.)
permanent crops: 0% (2022 est.)
permanent pasture: 24.9% (2022 est.)
forest: 5.2% (2022 est.)
other: 51.6% (2022 est.)

Irrigated land: NA

Population distribution: fairly even distribution

Natural hazards: very large tidal variation can be hazardous to navigation

Geography - note: largest and southernmost of Channel Islands; about 30% of population concentrated in Saint Helier

PEOPLE AND SOCIETY

Population: *total:* 103,387 (2024 est.)
male: 51,028
female: 52,359
comparison rankings: total 193; male 193; female 193

Nationality: *noun:* Channel Islander(s)
adjective: Channel Islander

Ethnic groups: Jersey 44.4%, British 30.5%, Portuguese/Madeiran 9.4%, Polish 3%, Irish 2.1%, other 10.6% (2021 est.)

Languages: English (official) 94.5%, Portuguese 4.6%, other 0.9% (includes French (official) and Jerriais)
(2001 est.)
note: data represent main spoken language; the traditional language of Jersey is Jerriais or Jersey French (a Norman language), which was spoken by fewer than 3,000 people as of 2001; two thirds of Jerriais speakers are aged 60 and over

Religions: Christian 85.2%, Baha'i 0.3%, Hindu 0.1%, Jewish 0.1%, Muslim 0.1%, atheist 1.1%, agnostic 13.1% (2020 est.)

Age structure: *0-14 years:* 17% (male 9,082/female 8,530)
15-64 years: 64.6% (male 33,840/female 32,989)
65 years and over: 18.3% (2024 est.) (male 8,106/female 10,840)

Dependency ratios: *total dependency ratio:* 54.7 (2024 est.)
youth dependency ratio: 26.4 (2024 est.)
elderly dependency ratio: 28.3 (2024 est.)
potential support ratio: 3.5 (2024 est.)

Median age: *total:* 38.2 years (2024 est.)
male: 37 years
female: 39.7 years
comparison ranking: total 76

Population growth rate: 0.56% (2024 est.)
comparison ranking: 146

Birth rate: 12.2 births/1,000 population (2024 est.)
comparison ranking: 143

Death rate: 7.8 deaths/1,000 population (2024 est.)
comparison ranking: 93

Net migration rate: 1.2 migrant(s)/1,000 population (2024 est.)
comparison ranking: 61

Population distribution: fairly even distribution

Urbanization: *urban population:* 31.2% of total population (2023)
rate of urbanization: 0.68% annual rate of change (2020-25 est.)
note: data include Guernsey and Jersey

Major urban areas - population: 34,000 SAINT HELIER (capital) (2018)

Sex ratio: *at birth:* 1.06 male(s)/female
0-14 years: 1.06 male(s)/female
15-64 years: 1.03 male(s)/female
65 years and over: 0.75 male(s)/female
total population: 0.98 male(s)/female (2024 est.)

Infant mortality rate: *total:* 3.7 deaths/1,000 live births (2024 est.)
male: 4.2 deaths/1,000 live births
female: 3.3 deaths/1,000 live births
comparison ranking: total 192

Life expectancy at birth: *total population:* 83 years (2024 est.)
male: 80.6 years
female: 85.7 years
comparison ranking: total population 17

Total fertility rate: 1.66 children born/woman (2024 est.)
comparison ranking: 170

Gross reproduction rate: 0.81 (2024 est.)

Sanitation facility access: *improved:* total: 98.5% of population

ENVIRONMENT

Environmental issues: habitat and species loss; water pollution; improper solid-waste disposal

Climate: temperate; mild winters and cool summers

Urbanization: *urban population:* 31.2% of total population (2023)
rate of urbanization: 0.68% annual rate of change (2020-25 est.)
note: data include Guernsey and Jersey

Waste and recycling: *municipal solid waste generated annually:* 178,900 tons (2024 est.)
percent of municipal solid waste recycled: 28.4% (2016 est.)
note: data include combined totals for Guernsey and Jersey.

GOVERNMENT

Country name: *conventional long form:* Bailiwick of Jersey
conventional short form: Jersey
former: Norman Isles
etymology: the name is of Old Norse origin, with -*ey* meaning "island;" "Jer(s)" may derive from a person with the Scandinavian name Geirr, meaning "spear"

Government type: parliamentary democracy (Assembly of the States of Jersey)

Dependency status: British crown dependency

Capital: *name:* Saint Helier
geographic coordinates: 49 11 N, 2 06 W
time difference: UTC 0 (5 hours ahead of Washington, DC, during Standard Time)
daylight saving time: +1hr, begins last Sunday in March; ends last Sunday in October
etymology: named after Saint HELIER, the patron saint of Jersey, who was reputedly martyred on the island in A.D. 555

Administrative divisions: none (British crown dependency); no first-order administrative divisions as defined by the US government, but 12 parishes; Grouville, Saint Brelade, Saint Clement, Saint Helier, Saint John, Saint Lawrence, Saint Martin, Saint Mary, Saint Ouen, Saint Peter, Saint Saviour, Trinity

Legal system: the laws of the UK apply, as well as local statutes

Constitution: *history:* unwritten; partly statutes, partly common law and practice
amendment process: proposed by a government minister to the Assembly of the States of Jersey, by an

Assembly member, or by an elected parish head; passage requires several Assembly readings, a majority vote by the Assembly, review by the UK Ministry of Justice, and approval of the British monarch (Royal Assent)

Citizenship: see United Kingdom

Suffrage: 16 years of age; universal

Executive branch: *chief of state:* King CHARLES III (since 8 September 2022); represented by Lieutenant Governor Jerry KYD (since 8 October 2022)
head of government: Chief Minister Lyndon FARNHAM (since 25 January 2024); Bailiff Timothy Le COCQ (since 17 October 2019)
cabinet: Council of Ministers appointed individually by the states
election/appointment process: the monarchy is hereditary; Council of Ministers, including the chief minister, indirectly elected by the Assembly of States; lieutenant governor and bailiff appointed by the monarch

Legislative branch: *legislature name:* Assembly of the States of Jersey
legislative structure: unicameral
number of seats: 54 (49 directly elected, 5 appointed)
term in office: 4 years
most recent election date: 6/22/2022
parties elected and seats per party: BW (35); RJ (10); JLC (2); JA (1); PP (1)
percentage of women in chamber: 42.9%
expected date of next election: 2026
note: 5 non-voting members appointed by the monarch include the bailiff, lieutenant governor, dean of Jersey, attorney general, and the solicitor general

Judicial branch: *highest court(s):* Jersey Court of Appeal (consists of the bailiff, deputy bailiff, and 12 judges); Royal Court (consists of the bailiff, deputy bailiff, 6 commissioners and lay people referred to as jurats, and is organized into Heritage, Family, Probate, and Samedi Divisions); appeals beyond the Court of Appeal are heard by the Judicial Committee of the Privy Council (in London)
judge selection and term of office: Jersey Court of Appeal bailiffs and judges appointed by the Crown upon the advice of the Secretary of State for Justice; bailiffs and judges appointed for "extent of good behavior;" Royal Court bailiffs appointed by the Crown upon the advice of the Secretary of State for Justice; commissioners appointed by the bailiff; jurats appointed by the Electoral College; bailiffs and commissioners appointed for "extent of good behavior;" jurats appointed until retirement at age 72
subordinate courts: Magistrate's Court; Youth Court; Petty Debts Court; Parish Hall Enquiries (a process of preliminary investigation into youth and minor adult offenses to determine need for presentation before a court)

Political parties: Better Way or BW (group of independent candidates)
Jersey Alliance or JA
Jersey Liberal Conservatives or JLC
Progress Party or PP
Reform Jersey or RJ
note: most deputies sit as independents

Diplomatic representation in the US: none (British Crown dependency)

Diplomatic representation from the US: *embassy:* none (British Crown dependency)

International organization participation: UPU

Independence: none (British Crown dependency)

National holiday: Liberation Day, 9 May (1945)

Flag: *description:* white with a diagonal red cross extending to the corners of the flag; a red shield with three lions in yellow is in the upper triangle, with a yellow crown above
history: according to tradition, Jersey ships differentiated themselves from English ships that flew the horizontal cross of St. George by rotating their own cross to the "X" (saltire) configuration; this arrangement resembled the Irish cross of St. Patrick, so the Plantagenet crown and Jersey coat of arms were added

National symbol(s): Jersey cow

National color(s): red, white

National anthem(s): *title:* "Isle de Siez Nous" (Island Home)
lyrics/music: Gerard LE FEUVRE
history: adopted 2008; serves as a local anthem
title: "God Save the King"
lyrics/music: unknown
history: official anthem, as a British Crown dependency

ECONOMY

Economic overview: British territorial island economy; strong offshore banking and finance sectors; low asset taxation; strong tourism sector prior to COVID-19 and Brexit; one of the most expensive places to live; minimal welfare system; historical cider industry

Real GDP (purchasing power parity): $5.569 billion (2016 est.)
$5.514 billion (2015 est.)
$4.98 billion (2014 est.)
note: data are in 2015 dollars
comparison ranking: 181

Real GDP growth rate: 3.7% (2023 est.)
5.3% (2022 est.)
9.9% (2021 est.)
note: annual GDP % growth based on constant local currency; entry includes Jersey and Guernsey
comparison ranking: 91

GDP (official exchange rate): $12.508 billion (2023 est.)
note: data in current dollars at official exchange rate; entry includes Jersey and Guernsey

GDP - composition, by sector of origin: *agriculture:* 0.6% (2023 est.)
industry: 8.2% (2023 est.)
services: 91.2% (2023 est.)
note: figures may not total 100% due to non-allocated consumption not captured in sector-reported data
comparison rankings: agriculture 184; industry 195; services 5

Agricultural products: potatoes, cauliflower, tomatoes; beef, dairy products

Industries: tourism, banking and finance, dairy, electronics

Industrial production growth rate: 1.3% (2023 est.)
note: annual % change in industrial value added based on constant local currency; entry includes Jersey and Guernsey
comparison ranking: 110

Labor force: 82,400 (2024 est.)
note: number of people ages 15 or older who are employed or seeking work;entry includes Jersey and Guernsey
comparison ranking: 184

Unemployment rate: 6.3% (2024 est.)
6.2% (2023 est.)
6.2% (2022 est.)
note: % of labor force seeking employment; entry includes Jersey and Guernsey
comparison ranking: 116

Youth unemployment rate (ages 15-24): *total:* 14.1% (2024 est.)
male: 14.2% (2024 est.)
female: 13.9% (2024 est.)
note: % of labor force ages 15-24 seeking employment
comparison ranking: total 83

Exports - partners: almost entirely United Kingdom (2022)

Exports - commodities: refined petroleum, beverages, ships, jewelry, artwork (2022)
top five export commodities based on value in dollars

Imports - partners: almost entirely United Kingdom (2022)

Imports - commodities: artwork, ships, vegetables, fruits, jewelry (2022)

Exchange rates: Jersey pounds (JEP) per US dollar

Exchange rates: 0.782 (2024 est.)
0.805 (2023 est.)
0.811 (2022 est.)
0.727 (2021 est.)
0.78 (2020 est.)

ENERGY

Electricity access: *electrification - total population:* 100% (2022 est.)
note: includes Guernsey and Jersey

COMMUNICATIONS

Telephones - fixed lines: *total subscriptions:* 48,122 (2021 est.)
subscriptions per 100 inhabitants: 47 (2021 est.)
comparison ranking: total subscriptions 156

Telephones - mobile cellular: *total subscriptions:* 124,083 (2021 est.)
subscriptions per 100 inhabitants: 120 (2021 est.)
comparison ranking: total subscriptions 191

Broadcast media: multiple UK terrestrial TV broadcasts are received via a transmitter in Jersey; satellite packages available; BBC Radio Jersey and 1 other radio station operating

Internet country code: .je

Internet users: *percent of population:* 41% (2012 est.)

Broadband - fixed subscriptions: *total:* 39,699 (2020 est.)
subscriptions per 100 inhabitants: 37 (2020 est.)
comparison ranking: total 150

TRANSPORTATION

Airports: 1 (2025)
comparison ranking: 234

Ports: *total ports:* 1 (2024)
large: 0
medium: 0
small: 1
very small: 0
ports with oil terminals: 1
key ports: Saint Helier Harbour

MILITARY AND SECURITY

Military - note: defense is the responsibility of the UK

JORDAN

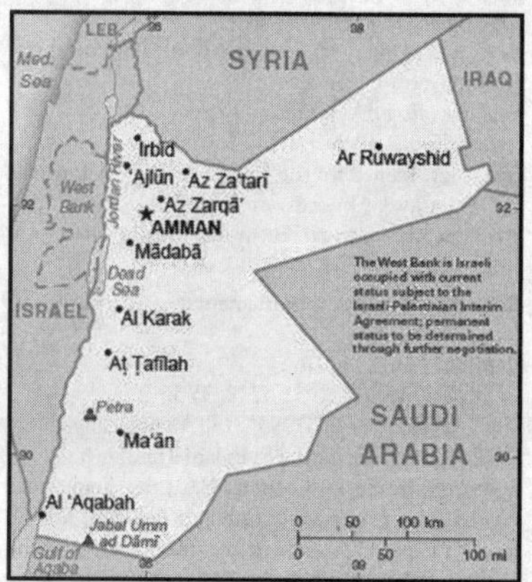

INTRODUCTION

Background: After World War I and the dissolution of the Ottoman Empire, the League of Nations awarded Britain the mandate to govern much of the Middle East. In 1921, Britain demarcated from Palestine a semi-autonomous region of Transjordan and recognized ABDALLAH I from the Hashemite family as the country's first leader. The Hashemites also controlled the Hijaz, or the western coastal area of modern-day Saudi Arabia, until 1925, when IBN SAUD and Wahhabi tribes pushed them out. The country gained its independence in 1946 and thereafter became the Hashemite Kingdom of Jordan.
The country has had four kings. Long-time ruler King HUSSEIN (r. 1953-99) successfully navigated competing pressures from the major powers (US, UK, and Soviet Union), various Arab states, Israel, and Palestinian militants, the latter of which led to a brief civil war in 1970 that is known as "Black September" and ended in King HUSSEIN ousting the militants.
Jordan's borders have changed since it gained independence. In 1948, Jordan took control of the West Bank and East Jerusalem in the first Arab-Israeli War, eventually annexing those territories in 1950 and granting its new Palestinian residents Jordanian citizenship. In 1967, Jordan lost the West Bank and East Jerusalem to Israel in the Six-Day War but retained administrative claims to the West Bank until 1988, when King HUSSEIN permanently relinquished Jordanian claims to the West Bank in favor of the Palestine Liberation Organization (PLO). King HUSSEIN signed a peace treaty with Israel in 1994, after Israel and the PLO signed the Oslo Accords in 1993.

Jordanian kings continue to claim custodianship of the Muslim holy sites in Jerusalem by virtue of their Hashemite heritage as descendants of the Prophet Mohammad and agreements with Israel and Jerusalem-based religious and Palestinian leaders. After Israel captured East Jerusalem in the 1967 War, it authorized the Jordanian-controlled Islamic Trust, or Waqf, to continue administering the Al Haram ash Sharif/Temple Mount holy compound, and the Jordan-Israel peace treaty reaffirmed Jordan's "special role" in administering the Muslim holy shrines in Jerusalem. Jordanian kings claim custodianship of the Christian sites in Jerusalem on the basis of the 7th-century Pact of Omar, when the Muslim leader, after conquering Jerusalem, agreed to permit Christian worship.

King HUSSEIN died in 1999 and was succeeded by his eldest son and current King ABDALLAH II. In 2009, ABDALLAH II designated his son HUSSEIN as the Crown Prince. During his reign, ABDALLAH II has contended with a series of challenges, including the Arab Spring influx of refugees from neighboring states, the COVID-19 pandemic, the effects of the war in Ukraine, a perennially weak economy, and the Israel-HAMAS conflict that began in October 2023.

GEOGRAPHY

Location: Middle East, northwest of Saudi Arabia, between Israel (to the west) and Iraq

Geographic coordinates: 31 00 N, 36 00 E

Map references: Middle East

Area: *total:* 89,342 sq km
land: 88,802 sq km
water: 540 sq km
comparison ranking: total 112

Area - comparative: about three-quarters the size of Pennsylvania; slightly smaller than Indiana

Land boundaries: *total:* 1,744 km
border countries (5): Iraq 179 km; Israel 307 km; Saudi Arabia 731 km; Syria 379 km; West Bank 148 km

Coastline: 26 km

Maritime claims: *territorial sea:* 3 nm

Climate: mostly arid desert; rainy season in west (November to April)

Terrain: mostly arid desert plateau; a great north-south geological rift along the west of the country is the dominant topographical feature and includes the Jordan River Valley, the Dead Sea, and the Jordanian Highlands

Elevation: *highest point:* Jabal Umm ad Dami 1,854 m
lowest point: Dead Sea -431 m
mean elevation: 812 m

Natural resources: phosphates, potash, shale oil

Land use: *agricultural land:* 11.6% (2022 est.)
arable land: 2.3% (2022 est.)
permanent crops: 0.9% (2022 est.)
permanent pasture: 8.4% (2022 est.)
forest: 1.1% (2022 est.)
other: 87.3% (2022 est.)

Irrigated land: 875 sq km (2022)

Major lakes (area sq km): *salt water lake(s):* Dead Sea (shared with Israel and West Bank) - 1,020 sq km note - endorheic hypersaline lake; 9.6 times saltier than the ocean; lake shore is 431 meters below sea level

Major watersheds (area sq km): Indian Ocean drainage: *(Persian Gulf)* Tigris and Euphrates (918,044 sq km)

Major aquifers: Arabian Aquifer System

Population distribution: population heavily concentrated in the west, and particularly the northwest, in and around the capital of Amman; a sizeable but smaller population is located in the southwest along the shore of the Gulf of Aqaba

Natural hazards: droughts; periodic earthquakes; flash floods

Geography - note: strategic location at the head of the Gulf of Aqaba; the Arab country that shares the longest border with Israel and the West Bank; the Dead Sea, the lowest point in Asia and the second saltiest body of water in the world (after Lac Assal in Djibouti), lies on Jordan's western border with Israel and the West Bank; Jordan is almost landlocked but does have a 26 km southwestern coastline with a single port, Al 'Aqabah (Aqaba)

PEOPLE AND SOCIETY

Population: *total:* 11,174,024 (2024 est.)
male: 5,844,979
female: 5,329,045
comparison rankings: total 84; male 84; female 89

Nationality: *noun:* Jordanian(s)
adjective: Jordanian

Ethnic groups: Jordanian 69.3%, Syrian 13.3%, Palestinian 6.7%, Egyptian 6.7%, Iraqi 1.4%, other 2.6% (2015 est.)
note: data represent population by self-identified nationality in national census

Languages: Arabic (official), English (widely understood among upper and middle classes)
major-language sample(s):
يمكن الاستغناء عنه للمعلومات الأساسية
كتاب حقائق العالم، المصدر الذي لا
(Arabic)

Religions: Muslim 97.1% (official; predominantly Sunni), Christian 2.1% (majority Greek Orthodox, but some Greek and Roman Catholics, Syrian Orthodox, Coptic Orthodox, Armenian Orthodox, and Protestant denominations), Buddhist 0.4%, Hindu 0.1%, Jewish <0.1%, folk <0.1%, other <0.1%, unaffiliated <0.1% (2020 est.)

Age structure: *0-14 years:* 30.9% (male 1,771,840/female 1,678,178)
15-64 years: 64.9% (male 3,844,575/female 3,409,164)
65 years and over: 4.2% (2024 est.) (male 228,564/female 241,703)

Dependency ratios: *total dependency ratio:* 54 (2024 est.)
youth dependency ratio: 47.6 (2024 est.)
elderly dependency ratio: 6.5 (2024 est.)
potential support ratio: 15.4 (2024 est.)

Median age: *total:* 25 years (2024 est.)
male: 25.5 years
female: 24.4 years
comparison ranking: total 172

Population growth rate: 0.78% (2024 est.)
comparison ranking: 114

Birth rate: 22.2 births/1,000 population (2024 est.)
comparison ranking: 52

Death rate: 3.5 deaths/1,000 population (2024 est.)
comparison ranking: 222

Net migration rate: -10.9 migrant(s)/1,000 population (2024 est.)
comparison ranking: 223

Population distribution: population heavily concentrated in the west, and particularly the northwest, in and around the capital of Amman; a sizeable but smaller population is located in the southwest along the shore of the Gulf of Aqaba

Urbanization: *urban population:* 92% of total population (2023)
rate of urbanization: 0.98% annual rate of change (2020-25 est.)

Major urban areas - population: 2.232 million AMMAN (capital) (2023)

Sex ratio: *at birth:* 1.06 male(s)/female
0-14 years: 1.06 male(s)/female
15-64 years: 1.13 male(s)/female
65 years and over: 0.95 male(s)/female
total population: 1.1 male(s)/female (2024 est.)

Mother's mean age at first birth: 24.6 years (2017/18 est.)
note: data represents median age at first birth among women 25-49

Maternal mortality ratio: 31 deaths/100,000 live births (2023 est.)
comparison ranking: 116

Infant mortality rate: *total:* 13.2 deaths/1,000 live births (2024 est.)
male: 14.3 deaths/1,000 live births
female: 12.1 deaths/1,000 live births
comparison ranking: total 106

Life expectancy at birth: *total population:* 76.5 years (2024 est.)
male: 75 years
female: 78.1 years
comparison ranking: total population 109

Total fertility rate: 2.87 children born/woman (2024 est.)
comparison ranking: 52

Gross reproduction rate: 1.39 (2024 est.)

Drinking water source: *improved: urban:* 99.1% of population (2022 est.)
rural: 97% of population (2022 est.)
total: 99% of population (2022 est.)
unimproved: urban: 0.9% of population (2022 est.)
rural: 3% of population (2022 est.)
total: 1% of population (2022 est.)

Health expenditure: 7.3% of GDP (2021)
7.6% of national budget (2022 est.)

Physician density: 2.85 physicians/1,000 population (2022)

Hospital bed density: 1.4 beds/1,000 population (2021 est.)

Sanitation facility access: *improved: urban:* 98.9% of population (2022 est.)
rural: 97.9% of population (2022 est.)
total: 98.8% of population (2022 est.)
unimproved: urban: 1.1% of population (2022 est.)
rural: 2.1% of population (2022 est.)
total: 1.2% of population (2022 est.)

Obesity - adult prevalence rate: 35.5% (2016)
comparison ranking: 13

Alcohol consumption per capita: *total:* 0.25 liters of pure alcohol (2019 est.)
beer: 0.06 liters of pure alcohol (2019 est.)
wine: 0 liters of pure alcohol (2019 est.)
spirits: 0.19 liters of pure alcohol (2019 est.)
other alcohols: 0 liters of pure alcohol (2019 est.)
comparison ranking: total 171

Tobacco use: *total:* 37.1% (2025 est.)
male: 58.6% (2025 est.)
female: 13.9% (2025 est.)
comparison ranking: total 5

Children under the age of 5 years underweight: 2.7% (2019)
comparison ranking: 86

Currently married women (ages 15-49): 55.6% (2023 est.)

Child marriage: *women married by age 15:* 1.5% (2018)
women married by age 18: 9.7% (2018)
men married by age 18: 0.1% (2018)

Education expenditure: 3.2% of GDP (2022 est.)
9.7% national budget (2022 est.)
comparison ranking: Education expenditure (% GDP) 143

Literacy: *total population:* 95% (2023 est.)
male: 97% (2023 est.)
female: 92% (2023 est.)

School life expectancy (primary to tertiary education): *total:* 13 years (2023 est.)
male: 13 years (2023 est.)
female: 14 years (2023 est.)

ENVIRONMENT

Environmental issues: limited natural freshwater resources; declining water table; salination; deforestation; overgrazing; soil erosion; desertification; biodiversity and ecosystem damage/loss

International environmental agreements: *party to:* Biodiversity, Climate Change, Climate Change-Kyoto Protocol, Climate Change-Paris Agreement, Comprehensive Nuclear Test Ban, Desertification, Endangered Species, Hazardous Wastes, Law of the Sea, Marine Dumping-London Convention, Nuclear Test Ban, Ozone Layer Protection, Ship Pollution, Wetlands
signed, but not ratified: none of the selected agreements

Climate: mostly arid desert; rainy season in west (November to April)

Urbanization: *urban population:* 92% of total population (2023)
rate of urbanization: 0.98% annual rate of change (2020-25 est.)

Carbon dioxide emissions: 22.434 million metric tonnes of CO2 (2023 est.)
from coal and metallurgical coke: 627,000 metric tonnes of CO2 (2023 est.)
from petroleum and other liquids: 13.264 million metric tonnes of CO2 (2023 est.)
from consumed natural gas: 8.544 million metric tonnes of CO2 (2023 est.)
comparison ranking: total emissions 81

Particulate matter emissions: 26.3 micrograms per cubic meter (2019 est.)

Methane emissions: *energy:* 12.2 kt (2022-2024 est.)
agriculture: 25.4 kt (2019-2021 est.)
waste: 188.2 kt (2019-2021 est.)
other: 0.6 kt (2019-2021 est.)

Waste and recycling: *municipal solid waste generated annually:* 2.53 million tons (2024 est.)
percent of municipal solid waste recycled: 14.6% (2022 est.)

Total water withdrawal: *municipal:* 497.37 million cubic meters (2022 est.)
industrial: 36.88 million cubic meters (2022 est.)
agricultural: 570.61 million cubic meters (2022 est.)

Total renewable water resources: 937 million cubic meters (2022 est.)

GOVERNMENT

Country name: *conventional long form:* Hashemite Kingdom of Jordan
conventional short form: Jordan
local long form: Al Mamlakah al Urduniyah al Hashimiyah
local short form: Al Urdun
former: Transjordan
etymology: named for the Jordan River, which makes up part of Jordan's northwest border; the origin of the river's name is unclear, but it may come from a local word meaning "river"

Government type: parliamentary constitutional monarchy

Capital: *name:* Amman
geographic coordinates: 31 57 N, 35 56 E
time difference: UTC+3 (8 hours ahead of Washington, DC, during Standard Time)
etymology: in the 13th century B.C., the Ammonites named their primary city Rabbath Ammon; *rabbath* meant "capital," so the name translated as "The Capital of [the] Ammon[ites];" over time, the name was shortened to Ammon, and then to Amman

Administrative divisions: 12 governorates (*muhafazat*, singular - *muhafazah*); 'Ajlun, Al 'Aqabah, Al Balqa', Al Karak, Al Mafraq, Al 'Asimah (Amman), At Tafilah, Az Zarqa', Irbid, Jarash, Ma'an, Madaba

Legal system: mixed system developed from Ottoman Empire codes (based on French law), British common law, and Islamic law

Constitution: *history:* previous 1928 (pre-independence); latest initially adopted 28 November 1947, revised and ratified 1 January 1952
amendment process: constitutional amendments require at least a two-thirds majority vote of both the Senate and the House and ratification by the king

International law organization participation: has not submitted an ICJ jurisdiction declaration; accepts ICCt jurisdiction

Citizenship: *citizenship by birth:* no
citizenship by descent only: the father must be a citizen of Jordan
dual citizenship recognized: yes
residency requirement for naturalization: 15 years

Suffrage: 18 years of age; universal

Executive branch: *chief of state:* King ABDALLAH II (since 7 February 1999)
head of government: Prime Minister Jafar HASSAN (since 15 September 2024)
cabinet: Cabinet appointed by the monarch in consultation with the prime minister
election/appointment process: prime minister appointed by the monarch

Legislative branch: *legislature name:* National Assembly (Majlis Al-Umma)
legislative structure: bicameral
Legislative branch - lower chamber
chamber name: House of Representatives (Majlis Al-Nuwaab)
number of seats: 138 (all directly elected)
electoral system: mixed system
scope of elections: full renewal
term in office: 4 years
most recent election date: 9/10/2024
percentage of women in chamber: 19.6%
expected date of next election: September 2028
note: the total number of Chamber of Deputies' seats increased to 138 from 130 for the September 2024 election

Legislative branch - upper chamber: *chamber name:* Senate (Majlis Al-Aayan)
number of seats: 69 (all appointed)
scope of elections: full renewal
term in office: 4 years
most recent election date: 10/24/2024
percentage of women in chamber: 14.5%
expected date of next election: October 2028

Judicial branch: *highest court(s):* Court of Cassation or Supreme Court (consists of 15 members, including the chief justice); Constitutional Court (consists of 9 members)
judge selection and term of office: Supreme Court chief justice appointed by the king; other judges nominated by the Judicial Council, an 11-member judicial policymaking body consisting of high-level judicial officials and judges, and approved by the king; judge tenure not limited; Constitutional Court members appointed by the king for 6-year non-renewable terms with one third of the membership renewed every 2 years
subordinate courts: Courts of Appeal; Great Felonies Court; religious courts; military courts; juvenile courts; Land Settlement Courts; Income Tax Court; Higher Administrative Court; Customs Court; special courts including the State Security Court

Political parties: 'Azem
Blessed Land Party
Building and Labor Coalition
Eradah Party
Growth Party
Islamic Action Front or IAF
Jordanian al-Ansar Party
Jordanian al-Ghad Party
Jordanian Arab Socialist Ba'ath Party or JASBP
Jordanian Civil Democratic Party
Jordanian Communist Party or JCP
Jordanian Equality Party
Jordanian Democratic People's Party or HASD
Jordanian Democratic Popular Unity Party or JDPUP/Wihda
Jordanian Democratic Unionist Party
Jordanian Flame Party
Jordanian Future and Life Party
Jordanian Model Party
Jordanian National Integration Party
Jordanian National Loyalty Party
Jordanian Reform and Renewal Party or Hassad
Jordanian Shura Party
Jordanian Social Democratic Party or JSDP
Justice and Reform Party or JRP
Labor Party
National Charter Party
National Coalition Party
National Constitutional Party
National Current Party or NCP
National Islamic Party
National Union
Nationalist Movement Party or Hsq
New Path Party Progress Party

Diplomatic representation in the US: *chief of mission:* Ambassador Dina Khalil Tawfiq KAWAR (since 27 June 2016)
chancery: 3504 International Drive NW, Washington, DC 20008
telephone: [1] (202) 966-2664
FAX: [1] (202) 966-3110
email address and website: hkjconsular@jordanembassyus.org
http://www.jordanembassyus.org/

Diplomatic representation from the US: *chief of mission:* Ambassador (vacant); Chargé d'Affaires Peter T. SHEA (since 29 June 2025)
embassy: Abdoun, Al-Umawayeen St., Amman
mailing address: 6050 Amman Place, Washington DC 20521-6050
telephone: [962] (6) 590-6000
FAX: [962] (6) 592-0163
email address and website: Amman-ACS@state.gov
https://jo.usembassy.gov/

International organization participation: ABEDA, AFESD, AMF, CAEU, CD, CICA, EBRD, FAO, G-11, G-77, IAEA, IBRD, ICAO, ICC, ICCt, ICRM, IDA, IDB, IFAD, IFC, IFRCS, ILO, IMF, IMO, IMSO, Interpol, IOC, IOM, IPU, ISO, ITSO, ITU, ITUC (NGOs), LAS, MIGA, MINUSTAH, MONUSCO, NAM, NATO (partner), OIC, OPCW, OSCE (partner), PCA, UN, UNAMID, UNCTAD, UNESCO, UNHCR, UNIDO, UNISFA, UNMIL, UNMISS, UNOCI, UNOOSA, UNRWA, UNWTO, UPU, WCO, WFTU (NGOs), WHO, WIPO, WMO, WTO

Independence: 25 May 1946 (from League of Nations mandate under British administration)

National holiday: Independence Day, 25 May (1946)

Flag: *description:* three equal horizontal bands of black (top), white, and green; a red isosceles triangle is on the left side, with a small white seven-pointed star in the center
meaning: black stands for the Abbassid Caliphate, white for the Ummayyad Caliphate, and green for the Fatimid Caliphate; the triangle stands for the Great Arab Revolt of 1916, and the star's points for the seven verses of the opening Sura (Al-Fatiha) of the Quran, as well as faith in One God, humanity, national spirit, humility, social justice, virtue, and aspirations
history: the design is based on the Arab Revolt flag of World War I

National symbol(s): eagle

National color(s): black, white, green, red

National anthem(s): *title:* "As-salam al-malaki al-urdoni" (Long Live the King of Jordan)
lyrics/music: Abdul-Mone'm al-RIFAI'/Abdul-Qader al-TANEER
history: adopted 1946; the shortened version of the anthem is most commonly used; the full version is reserved for special occasions

National heritage: *total World Heritage Sites:* 7 (6 cultural, 1 mixed)
selected World Heritage Site locales: Petra (c); Quseir Amra (c); Um er-Rasas (Kastrom Mefa'a) (c); Wadi Rum Protected Area (m); Baptism Site "Bethany Beyond the Jordan" (Al-Maghtas) (c); As-Salt - The Place of Tolerance and Urban Hospitality (c); Umm Al-Jimal (c)

ECONOMY

Economic overview: upper-middle-income Middle Eastern economy; high debt and unemployment, especially for youth and women; global events triggering trade slump and decreased revenue from tourism; growing manufacturing and agricultural sectors; key US foreign assistance recipient; natural-resource-poor and import-reliant

Real GDP (purchasing power parity): $109.986 billion (2024 est.)
$107.315 billion (2023 est.)
$104.307 billion (2022 est.)
note: data in 2021 dollars
comparison ranking: 94

Real GDP growth rate: 2.5% (2024 est.)
2.9% (2023 est.)
2.6% (2022 est.)
note: annual GDP % growth based on constant local currency
comparison ranking: 135

Real GDP per capita: $9,500 (2024 est.)
$9,400 (2023 est.)
$9,300 (2022 est.)
note: data in 2021 dollars
comparison ranking: 149

GDP (official exchange rate): $53.352 billion (2024 est.)
note: data in current dollars at official exchange rate

Inflation rate (consumer prices): 1.6% (2024 est.)
2.1% (2023 est.)
4.2% (2022 est.)
note: annual % change based on consumer prices
comparison ranking: 39

GDP - composition, by sector of origin: *agriculture:* 5.1% (2024 est.)
industry: 25.1% (2024 est.)
services: 60.4% (2024 est.)
note: figures may not total 100% due to non-allocated consumption not captured in sector-reported data
comparison rankings: agriculture 111; industry 88; services 85

GDP - composition, by end use: *household consumption:* 78.9% (2021 est.)
government consumption: 15.8% (2021 est.)
investment in fixed capital: 22.2% (2021 est.)
investment in inventories: 3% (2021 est.)
exports of goods and services: 30% (2021 est.)
imports of goods and services: -50.4% (2021 est.)
note: figures may not total 100% due to rounding or gaps in data collection

Agricultural products: tomatoes, milk, chicken, potatoes, olives, cucumbers/gherkins, onions, chillies/peppers, peaches/nectarines, sheep milk (2023)
note: top ten agricultural products based on tonnage

Industries: tourism, information technology, clothing, fertilizer, potash, phosphate mining, pharmaceuticals, petroleum refining, cement, inorganic chemicals, light manufacturing

Industrial production growth rate: 3.7% (2024 est.)
note: annual % change in industrial value added based on constant local currency
comparison ranking: 65

Labor force: 3.08 million (2024 est.)
note: number of people ages 15 or older who are employed or seeking work
comparison ranking: 109

Unemployment rate: 18% (2024 est.)
18% (2023 est.)
18.2% (2022 est.)
note: % of labor force seeking employment
comparison ranking: 178

Youth unemployment rate (ages 15-24): *total:* 41.7% (2024 est.)
male: 39.8% (2024 est.)
female: 49.2% (2024 est.)
note: % of labor force ages 15-24 seeking employment
comparison ranking: total 6

Population below poverty line: 15.7% (2018 est.)
note: % of population with income below national poverty line

Average household expenditures: *on food:* 25% of household expenditures (2023 est.)
on alcohol and tobacco: 4.5% of household expenditures (2023 est.)

Remittances: 8.8% of GDP (2023 est.)
10.1% of GDP (2022 est.)
11% of GDP (2021 est.)
note: personal transfers and compensation between resident and non-resident individuals/households/entities

Budget: *revenues:* $13.779 billion (2023 est.)
expenditures: $17.159 billion (2023 est.)
note: central government revenues and expenditures (excluding grants and social security funds) converted to US dollars at average official exchange rate for year indicated

Public debt: 102.8% of GDP (2023 est.)
note: central government debt as a % of GDP
comparison ranking: 19

Taxes and other revenues: 17% (of GDP) (2023 est.)
note: central government tax revenue as a % of GDP
comparison ranking: 76

Current account balance: -$1.91 billion (2023 est.)
-$3.815 billion (2022 est.)
-$3.718 billion (2021 est.)
note: balance of payments - net trade and primary/secondary income in current dollars
comparison ranking: 145

Exports: $22.186 billion (2023 est.)
$20.743 billion (2022 est.)
$13.87 billion (2021 est.)
note: balance of payments - exports of goods and services in current dollars
comparison ranking: 90

Exports - partners: USA 21%, India 13%, Saudi Arabia 11%, China 7%, Iraq 6% (2023)
note: top five export partners based on percentage share of exports

Exports - commodities: fertilizers, garments, phosphates, jewelry, phosphoric acid (2023)
note: top five export commodities based on value in dollars

Imports: $28.922 billion (2023 est.)
$30.019 billion (2022 est.)
$23.321 billion (2021 est.)
note: balance of payments - imports of goods and services in current dollars
comparison ranking: 84

Imports - partners: China 17%, Saudi Arabia 14%, UAE 8%, India 6%, USA 5% (2023)
note: top five import partners based on percentage share of imports

Imports - commodities: cars, refined petroleum, gold, crude petroleum, jewelry (2023)
note: top five import commodities based on value in dollars

Reserves of foreign exchange and gold: $21.939 billion (2024 est.)
$19.069 billion (2023 est.)
$18.198 billion (2022 est.)
note: holdings of gold (year-end prices)/foreign exchange/special drawing rights in current dollars
comparison ranking: 62

Debt - external: $21.058 billion (2023 est.)
note: present value of external debt in current US dollars
comparison ranking: 35

Exchange rates: Jordanian dinars (JOD) per US dollar -

Exchange rates: 0.71 (2024 est.)
0.71 (2023 est.)
0.71 (2022 est.)
0.71 (2021 est.)
0.71 (2020 est.)

ENERGY

Electricity access: *electrification - total population:* 100% (2022 est.)
electrification - urban areas: 100%
electrification - rural areas: 98.9%

Electricity: *installed generating capacity:* 6.891 million kW (2023 est.)
consumption: 20.31 billion kWh (2023 est.)
exports: 162.93 million kWh (2023 est.)
imports: 383.073 million kWh (2023 est.)
transmission/distribution losses: 2.472 billion kWh (2023 est.)
comparison rankings: installed generating capacity 79; consumption 76; exports 88; imports 99; transmission/distribution losses 134

Electricity generation sources: *fossil fuels:* 76.9% of total installed capacity (2023 est.)
solar: 15.3% of total installed capacity (2023 est.)
wind: 7.7% of total installed capacity (2023 est.)
hydroelectricity: 0.1% of total installed capacity (2023 est.)

Coal: *consumption:* 269,000 metric tons (2023 est.)
imports: 110,000 metric tons (2023 est.)

Petroleum: *total petroleum production:* 20 bbl/day (2023 est.)
refined petroleum consumption: 97,000 bbl/day (2023 est.)
crude oil estimated reserves: 1 million barrels (2021 est.)

Natural gas: *production:* 200.004 million cubic meters (2023 est.)
consumption: 5.441 billion cubic meters (2023 est.)
exports: 375.998 million cubic meters (2018 est.)
imports: 4.865 billion cubic meters (2023 est.)
proven reserves: 6.031 billion cubic meters (2021 est.)

Energy consumption per capita: 32.909 million Btu/person (2023 est.)
comparison ranking: 112

COMMUNICATIONS

Telephones - fixed lines: *total subscriptions:* 451,000 (2023 est.)
subscriptions per 100 inhabitants: 4 (2023 est.)
comparison ranking: total subscriptions 96

Telephones - mobile cellular: *total subscriptions:* 7.73 million (2023 est.)
subscriptions per 100 inhabitants: 68 (2022 est.)
comparison ranking: total subscriptions 104

Broadcast media: radio and TV dominated by the government-owned Jordan Radio and Television Corporation (JRTV) that operates a main network, a sports network, a film network, and a satellite channel; first independent TV broadcaster aired in 2007; international satellite TV and Israeli and Syrian TV broadcasts are available; roughly 30 radio stations; transmissions of multiple international radio broadcasters are available

Internet country code: .jo

Internet users: *percent of population:* 93% (2023 est.)

Broadband - fixed subscriptions: *total:* 805,000 (2023 est.)
subscriptions per 100 inhabitants: 7 (2023 est.)
comparison ranking: total 85

TRANSPORTATION

Civil aircraft registration country code prefix: JY

Airports: 18 (2025)
comparison ranking: 143

Heliports: 6 (2025)
comparison ranking: 92

Railways: *total:* 509 km (2020)
narrow gauge: 509 km (2014) 1.050-m gauge

Merchant marine: *total:* 34 (2023)
by type: general cargo 5, other 29
comparison ranking: total 131

Ports: *total ports:* 1 (2024)
large: 0
medium: 0
small: 0
very small: 1
ports with oil terminals: 1
key ports: Al Aqabah

MILITARY AND SECURITY

Military and security forces: Jordanian Armed Forces (JAF; aka Arab Army): Jordanian Army (Jordanian Ground Forces; includes Special Operations Forces, Border Guards, Royal Guard), Jordanian Air Force, Jordanian Navy)

Ministry of Interior: Public Security Directorate (includes national police, the Gendarmerie, and the Civil Defense Directorate) (2025)

Military expenditures: 4.5% of GDP (2024 est.)
4.5% of GDP (2023 est.)
4.8% of GDP (2022 est.)
5% of GDP (2021 est.)
5% of GDP (2020 est.)

Military and security service personnel strengths: approximately 100,000 active-duty Armed Forces (85,000 Army; 14,000 Air Force; 1,000 Navy) (2025)

Military equipment inventories and acquisitions: the JAF inventory is comprised of a wide mix of imported equipment, much of it older or secondhand, from China, Europe, some Gulf States, Russia, and the US (2024)

Military service age and obligation: 17 years of age for voluntary military service for men and women); initial service term is 24 months, with option to reenlist for up to 18 years; conscription was abolished in 1991, but in 2020 Jordan announced the reinstatement of compulsory military service for jobless men aged between 25 and 29 with 12 months of service, made up of 3 months of military training and 9 months of professional and technical training; in 2019, Jordan announced a voluntary 4-month National Military Service program for men and women aged between 18-25 years who have been unemployed for at least 6 months; service would include 1 month for military training with the remaining 3 months dedicated to vocational training in the sectors of construction and tourism (2023)
note: women comprised about 3% of the military as of 2023

Military deployments: Jordan has about 200 police deployed to the MONUSCO mission in the Democratic Republic of the Congo (2024)

Military - note: the Jordanian Armed Forces (JAF) are responsible for territorial defense and border security and have a supporting role for internal security; key areas of concern include regional conflict

and instability and unconventional threats, such as terrorism and weapons smuggling; the JAF participates in both bilateral and multinational exercises, UN peacekeeping missions, and have taken part in regional military operations alongside international forces in Afghanistan, Syria, and Yemen
the US is a key security partner, and Jordan is one of the largest recipients of US military aid in the region; it cooperates with the US on a number of issues, including border security, arms transfers, cybersecurity, and counterterrorism; Jordan has Major Non-NATO Ally status with the US, a designation under US law that provides foreign partners with certain benefits in the areas of defense trade and security cooperation (2025)

TERRORISM

Terrorist group(s): Terrorist group(s): Islamic State of Iraq and ash-Sham (ISIS)

note: details about the history, aims, leadership, organization, areas of operation, tactics, targets, weapons, size, and sources of support of the group(s) appear(s) in Appendix T

TRANSNATIONAL ISSUES

Refugees and internally displaced persons: *refugees:* 675,388 (2024 est.)
stateless persons: 17 (2024 est.)

KAZAKHSTAN

INTRODUCTION

Background: Ethnic Kazakhs derive from a mix of Turkic nomadic tribes that migrated to the region in the 15th century. The Russian Empire conquered the Kazakh steppe in the 18th and 19th centuries, and Kazakhstan became a Soviet Republic in 1925. Forced agricultural collectivization led to repression and starvation, resulting in more than a million deaths in the early 1930s. During the 1950s and 1960s, the agricultural "Virgin Lands " program generated an influx of settlers – mostly ethnic Russians, but also other nationalities – and by the time of Kazakhstan 's independence in 1991, ethnic Kazakhs were a minority. However, non-Muslim ethnic minorities departed Kazakhstan in large numbers from the mid-1990s through the mid-2000s, and a national program has repatriated about a million ethnic Kazakhs (from Uzbekistan, Tajikistan, Mongolia, and the Xinjiang region of China) to Kazakhstan. As a result of this shift, the ethnic Kazakh share of the population now exceeds two-thirds.

Kazakhstan 's economy is the largest in Central Asia, mainly due to the country 's vast natural resources. Current issues include diversifying the economy, attracting foreign direct investment, enhancing Kazakhstan 's economic competitiveness, and strengthening economic relations with neighboring states and foreign powers.

GEOGRAPHY

Location: Central Asia, northwest of China; a small portion west of the Ural (Oral) River in easternmost Europe

Geographic coordinates: 48 00 N, 68 00 E Map references
Asia

Area: *total:* 2,724,900 sq km
land: 2,699,700 sq km
water: 25,200 sq km
comparison ranking: total 10

Area - comparative: slightly less than four times the size of Texas

Land boundaries: *total:* 13,364 km
border countries (5): China 1,765 km; Kyrgyzstan 1,212 km; Russia 7,644 km; Turkmenistan 413 km; Uzbekistan 2,330 km

Coastline: 0 km (landlocked)
note: Kazakhstan borders the Aral Sea, now split into two bodies of water (1,070 km), and the Caspian Sea (1,894 km)

Maritime claims: none (landlocked)

Climate: continental, cold winters and hot summers, arid and semiarid

Terrain: vast flat steppe extending from the Volga in the west to the Altai Mountains in the east and from the plains of western Siberia in the north to oases and deserts of Central Asia in the south

Elevation: *highest point:* Pik Khan-Tengri 7,010 m
note - the northern most 7,000 meter peak in the World
lowest point: Qauyndy Oyysy -132 m
mean elevation: 387 m

Natural resources: major deposits of petroleum, natural gas, coal, iron ore, manganese, chrome ore, nickel, cobalt, copper, molybdenum, lead, zinc, bauxite, gold, uranium

Land use: *agricultural land:* 79.4% (2022 est.)
arable land: 11% (2022 est.)
permanent crops: 0% (2022 est.)
permanent pasture: 68.3% (2022 est.)
forest: 1.3% (2022 est.)
other: 19.3% (2022 est.)

Irrigated land: 17,794 sq km (2022)

Major lakes (area sq km): *fresh water lake(s):* Ozero Balkhash - 22,000 sq km; Ozero Zaysan - 1,800 sq km
salt water lake(s): Caspian Sea (shared with Iran, Azerbaijan, Turkmenistan, and Russia) - 374,000 sq km; Aral Sea (north) - 3,300 sq km; Ozero Alakol - 2,650 sq km; Ozero Teniz 1,590 sq km; Ozero Seletytenzi - 780 sq km; Ozero Sasykkol - 740 sq km

Major rivers (by length in km): Syr Darya river mouth (shared with Kyrgyzstan [s], Uzbekistan, and Tajikistan) - 3,078 km
note: [s] after country name indicates river source; [m] after country name indicates river mouth

Major watersheds (area sq km): Internal (endorheic basin) drainage: Tarim Basin (1,152,448 sq km), Amu Darya (534,739 sq km), Syr Darya (782,617 sq km), Lake Balkash (510,015 sq km)

Population distribution: most of the country displays a low population density, particularly the interior; population clusters appear in urban agglomerations in the far northern and southern portions of the country

Natural hazards: earthquakes in the south; mudslides around Almaty

Geography - note: world 's largest landlocked country and one of only two landlocked countries in the world that extends into two continents (the other is Azerbaijan); Russia leases approximately 6,000 sq km (2,317 sq mi) of territory enclosing the Baikonur Cosmodrome

PEOPLE AND SOCIETY

Population: *total:* 20,260,006 (2024 est.)
male: 9,817,172
female: 10,442,834
comparison rankings: total 64; male 64; female 63

Nationality: *noun:* Kazakhstani(s)
adjective: Kazakhstani

Ethnic groups: Kazakh 71%, Russian 14.9%, Uzbek 3.3%, Ukrainian 1.9%, Uyghurs 1.5%, German 1.1%, Tatar 1.1%, other 4.9%, unspecified 0.3% (2023 est.)

Languages: Kazakh (official, Qazaq) 80.1%, Russian 83.7%, English 35.1% (2021 est.)
major-language sample(s):

Әлемдік деректер кітабы, негізгі ақпараттың таптырмайтын көзі.
(Kazakh)

Книга фактов о мире – незаменимый источник базовой информации.
(Russian)

note: percentages are based on population that understands the spoken language

Religions: Muslim 69.3%, Christian 17.2% (Orthodox 17%, other 0.2%), Buddhism 0.1%, other 0.1%, non-believers 2.3%, unspecified 11% (2021 est.)

Age structure: *0-14 years:* 27.6% (male 2,883,200/ female 2,712,772)
15-64 years: 62.8% (male 6,233,881/female 6,486,019)
65 years and over: 9.6% (2024 est.) (male 700,091/ female 1,244,043)

Dependency ratios: *total dependency ratio:* 59.3 (2024 est.)
youth dependency ratio: 44 (2024 est.)
elderly dependency ratio: 15.3 (2024 est.)
potential support ratio: 6.5 (2024 est.)

Median age: *total:* 31.9 years (2024 est.)
male: 30 years
female: 33.8 years
comparison ranking: total 121

Population growth rate: 0.86% (2024 est.)
comparison ranking: 106

Birth rate: 17.2 births/1,000 population (2024 est.)
comparison ranking: 89

Death rate: 8.1 deaths/1,000 population (2024 est.)
comparison ranking: 84

Net migration rate: -0.4 migrant(s)/1,000 population (2024 est.)
comparison ranking: 117

Population distribution: most of the country displays a low population density, particularly the interior; population clusters appear in urban agglomerations in the far northern and southern portions of the country

Urbanization: *urban population:* 58.2% of total population (2023)
rate of urbanization: 1.19% annual rate of change (2020-25 est.)

Major urban areas - population: 1.987 million Almaty, 1.291 million NUR-SULTAN (capital), 1.155 million Shimkent (2023)

Sex ratio: *at birth:* 1.07 male(s)/female
0-14 years: 1.06 male(s)/female
15-64 years: 0.96 male(s)/female
65 years and over: 0.56 male(s)/female
total population: 0.94 male(s)/female (2024 est.)

Mother 's mean age at first birth: 28.9 years (2019 est.)

Maternal mortality ratio: 10 deaths/100,000 live births (2023 est.)
comparison ranking: 151

Infant mortality rate: *total:* 8 deaths/1,000 live births (2024 est.)

male: 8.9 deaths/1,000 live births
female: 7 deaths/1,000 live births
comparison ranking: total 146

Life expectancy at birth: *total population:* 73.3 years (2024 est.)
male: 69 years
female: 77.9 years
comparison ranking: total population 151

Total fertility rate: 2.58 children born/woman (2024 est.)
comparison ranking: 66

Gross reproduction rate: 1.25 (2024 est.)

Drinking water source: *improved: urban:* 98% of population (2022 est.)
unimproved: urban: 2% of population (2022 est.)

Health expenditure: 3.9% of GDP (2021)
10.6% of national budget (2022 est.)

Physician density: 3.75 physicians/1,000 population (2023)

Hospital bed density: 6.7 beds/1,000 population (2020 est.)

Sanitation facility access: *improved: urban:* 99.9% of population (2022 est.)
rural: 99.9% of population (2022 est.)
total: 99.9% of population (2022 est.)
unimproved: urban: 0.1% of population (2022 est.)
rural: 0.1% of population (2022 est.)
total: 0.1% of population (2022 est.)

Obesity - adult prevalence rate: 21% (2016)
comparison ranking: 94

Alcohol consumption per capita: *total:* 3.73 liters of pure alcohol (2019 est.)
beer: 2.52 liters of pure alcohol (2019 est.)
wine: 0.16 liters of pure alcohol (2019 est.)
spirits: 1.05 liters of pure alcohol (2019 est.)
other alcohols: 0 liters of pure alcohol (2019 est.)
comparison ranking: total 100

Tobacco use: *total:* 20.1% (2025 est.)
male: 35.7% (2025 est.)
female: 6.3% (2025 est.)
comparison ranking: total 68

Children under the age of 5 years underweight: 2% (2015)
comparison ranking: 97

Currently married women (ages 15-49): 61.8% (2023 est.)

Child marriage: *women married by age 15:* 0.2% (2015)
women married by age 18: 7% (2015)

Education expenditure: 4.9% of GDP (2023 est.)
19.9% national budget (2023 est.)
comparison ranking: Education expenditure (% GDP) 68

School life expectancy (primary to tertiary education): *total:* 14 years (2024 est.)
male: 14 years (2024 est.)
female: 14 years (2024 est.)

ENVIRONMENT

Environmental issues: radioactive or toxic chemical sites from former defense industries; severe industrial pollution in some cities; air and soil pollution (including dust storms) from chemical pesticides and natural salts left after two rivers were diverted; soil pollution from overuse of agricultural chemicals; salination from infrastructure and irrigation practices; water pollution; desertification

International environmental agreements: *party to:* Air Pollution, Antarctic Treaty, Biodiversity, Climate Change, Climate Change-Kyoto Protocol, Climate Change-Paris Agreement, Comprehensive Nuclear Test Ban, Desertification, Endangered Species, Environmental Modification, Hazardous Wastes, Ozone Layer Protection, Ship Pollution, Wetlands
signed, but not ratified: none of the selected agreements

Climate: continental, cold winters and hot summers, arid and semiarid

Urbanization: *urban population:* 58.2% of total population (2023)
rate of urbanization: 1.19% annual rate of change (2020-25 est.)

Carbon dioxide emissions: 269.83 million metric tonnes of CO2 (2023 est.)
from coal and metallurgical coke: 175.848 million metric tonnes of CO2 (2023 est.)
from petroleum and other liquids: 50.387 million metric tonnes of CO2 (2023 est.)
from consumed natural gas: 43.596 million metric tonnes of CO2 (2023 est.)
comparison ranking: total emissions 24

Particulate matter emissions: 38.4 micrograms per cubic meter (2019 est.)

Methane emissions: *energy:* 1,903.1 kt (2022-2024 est.)
agriculture: 781.2 kt (2019-2021 est.)
waste: 184.1 kt (2019-2021 est.)
other: 17.7 kt (2019-2021 est.)

Waste and recycling: *municipal solid waste generated annually:* 4.66 million tons (2024 est.)
percent of municipal solid waste recycled: 3.8% (2022 est.)

Total water withdrawal: *municipal:* 4.877 billion cubic meters (2022)
industrial: 5.995 billion cubic meters (2022)
agricultural: 14.264 billion cubic meters (2022)

Total renewable water resources: 108.41 billion cubic meters (2022 est.)

GOVERNMENT

Country name: *conventional long form:* Republic of Kazakhstan
conventional short form: Kazakhstan
local long form: Qazaqstan Respublikasy
local short form: Qazaqstan
former: Kazakh Soviet Socialist Republic
etymology: the name may derive from the Turkic word *kazak*, meaning "nomad; " the Persian suffix *-stan* means "place of " or "country "

Government type: presidential republic

Capital: *name:* Astana
geographic coordinates: 51 10 N, 71 25 E
time difference: UTC+5 (10 hours ahead of Washington, DC, during Standard Time)
time zone note: On 1 March 2024, Kazakhstan moved from using two time zones to one
etymology: the name means "capital city " in Kazakh
note: founded in 1830 as Akmoly, the capital city became Akmolinsk in 1832, Tselinograd in 1961, Akmola (Aqmola) in 1992, Astana in 1998, and Nur-Sultan in 2019; the latest name change back to Astana in 2022 occurred just three and a half years after the city was renamed to honor a former president, who subsequently fell out of favor

Administrative divisions: 17 provinces (*oblystar*, singular - *oblys*) and 4 cities* (*qalalar*, singular - *qala*); Abay (Semey), Almaty (Qonaev), Almaty*, Aqmola (Kokshetau), Aqtobe, Astana*, Atyrau, Batys Qazaqstan [West Kazakhstan] (Oral), Bayqongyr*, Mangghystau (Aqtau), Pavlodar, Qaraghandy, Qostanay, Qyzylorda, Shyghys Qazaqstan [East Kazakhstan] (Oskemen), Shymkent*, Soltustik Qazaqstan [North Kazakhstan] (Petropavl), Turkistan, Ulytau (Zhezqazghan), Zhambyl (Taraz), Zhetisu (Taldyqorghan)
note 1: administrative divisions have the same names as their administrative centers; exceptions show the administrative center name in parentheses
note 2: in 1995, the Kazakh and Russian governments agreed that Russia would lease for 20 years an area of 6,000 sq km (2,317 sq mi) around the Baikonur space launch facilities and the city of Bayqongyr (Baikonur, formerly Leninsk); in 2004, the lease was extended to 2050

Legal system: civil law system influenced by Roman-Germanic law and by the theory and practice of the Russian Federation

Constitution: *history:* previous 1937, 1978 (pre-independence), 1993; latest approved by referendum 30 August 1995, effective 5 September 1995
amendment process: introduced by a referendum initiated by the president of the republic, on the recommendation of Parliament, or by the government; the president has the option of submitting draft amendments to Parliament or directly to a referendum; passage of amendments by Parliament requires four-fifths majority vote of both houses and the signature of the president; passage by referendum requires absolute majority vote by more than one half of the voters in at least two thirds of the oblasts, major cities, and the capital, followed by the signature of the president

International law organization participation: has not submitted an ICJ jurisdiction declaration; non-party state to the ICCt

Citizenship: *citizenship by birth:* no
citizenship by descent only: at least one parent must be a citizen of Kazakhstan
dual citizenship recognized: no
residency requirement for naturalization: 5 years

Suffrage: 18 years of age; universal

Executive branch: *chief of state:* President Kasym-Zhomart TOKAYEV (since 20 March 2019)
head of government: Prime Minister Olzhas BEKTENOV (since 6 February 2024)
cabinet: the president appoints ministers based on the prime minister 's recommendations; the president has veto power over all appointments and independently appoints the ministers of defense, internal affairs, and foreign affairs
election/appointment process: president directly elected by simple-majority popular vote for a single 7-year term (prior to September 2022, the president of Kazakhstan could serve up to two 5-year terms; legislation reduced it to one 7-year term); prime minister and deputy prime ministers appointed by the president, approved by the Mazhilis
most recent election date: 20 November 2022
election results: 2024: Olzhas BEKTENOV elected as prime minister; 69-0 in parliament
2022: Kasym-Zhomart TOKAYEV reelected president; percent of vote - Kassym-Jomart TOKAYEV (Amanat) 81.3%, Zhiguli DAYRABAEV (Auyl) 3.4%, Qaraqat or Karakat ÄBDEN (KÄQŪA) 2.6%, Meyram KAZHYKEN (Amanat) 2.5%, Nurlan AUYESBAYEV (NSDP) 2.2%, Saltanat TURSYNBEKOVA (QA-DJ) 2.1%, other 5.8%

2019: Kasym-Zhomart TOKAYEV elected president; percent of vote - Kasym-Zhomart TOKAYEV (Amanat) 71%, Amirzhan KOSANOV (Ult Tagdyry) 16.2%, Daniya YESPAYEVA (Ak Zhol) 5.1%, other 7.7%
expected date of next election: 2029

Legislative branch: *legislature name:* Parliament (Parlament)
legislative structure: bicameral

Legislative branch - lower chamber: *chamber name:* House of Representatives (Mazhilis)
number of seats: 98 (all directly elected)
electoral system: mixed system
scope of elections: full renewal
term in office: 5 years
most recent election date: 3/19/2023
parties elected and seats per party: Amanat party (62); Auyl party (8); Ak Zhol Democratic Party of Kazakhstan (6); Respublica (6); People 's Party of Kazakhstan (5); Independents (7); Other (4)
percentage of women in chamber: 18.4%
expected date of next election: March 2028

Legislative branch - upper chamber: *chamber name:* Senate
number of seats: 50 (40 indirectly elected; 10 appointed)
scope of elections: partial renewal
term in office: 6 years
most recent election date: 1/14/2023
percentage of women in chamber: 20%
expected date of next election: January 2026

Judicial branch: *highest court(s):* Supreme Court of the Republic (consists of 44 members); Constitutional Council (consists of the chairperson and 6 members)
judge selection and term of office: Supreme Court judges proposed by the president of the republic on recommendation of the Supreme Judicial Council and confirmed by the Senate; judges normally serve until age 65 but can be extended to age 70; Constitutional Council - the president of the republic, the Senate chairperson, and the Mazhilis chairperson each appoints 2 members for a 6-year term; chairperson of the Constitutional Council appointed by the president for a 6-year term
subordinate courts: regional and local courts

Political parties: Ak Zhol Democratic Party or Ak Zhol
Amanat Party (formerly Nur Otan (Radiant Fatherland))
Auyl People 's Democratic Patriotic Party or Auyl Baytak (Boundless) Party
National Social Democratic Party or NSDP
People 's Democratic (Patriotic) Party or Auyl or AHDPP
People 's Party of Kazakhstan or PPK
Respublica

Diplomatic representation in the US: *chief of mission:* Ambassador Yerzhan ASHIKBAYEV (since 7 July 2021)
chancery: 1401 16th Street NW, Washington, DC 20036
telephone: [1] (202) 232-5488
FAX: [1] (202) 232-5845
email address and website: washington@mfa.kz
https://www.gov.kz/memleket/entities/mfa-washington?lang=en
consulate(s) general: New York, San Francisco

Diplomatic representation from the US: *chief of mission:* Ambassador (vacant); Chargé d 'Affaires Deborah ROBINSON (since January 2025)
embassy: Rakhymzhan Koshkarbayev Avenue, No. 3, Astana 010010
mailing address: 2230 Astana Place, Washington DC 20521-2230
telephone: [7] (7172) 70-21-00
FAX: [7] (7172) 54-09-14
email address and website: USAKZ@state.gov
https://kz.usembassy.gov/
consulate(s) general: Almaty

International organization participation: ADB, CICA, CIS, CSTO, EAEU, EAPC, EBRD, ECO, EITI (compliant country), FAO, GCTU, IAEA, IBRD, ICAO, ICC (NGOs), ICRM, IDA, IDB, IFAD, IFC, IFRCS, ILO, IMF, IMO, Interpol, IOC, IOM, IPU, ISO, ITSO, ITU, MIGA, MINURSO, NAM (observer), NSG, OAS (observer), OIC, OPCW, OSCE, PFP, SCO, UN, UNCTAD, UNESCO, UNHRC, UNIDO, UN Security Council (temporary), UNWTO, UPU, WCO, WFTU (NGOs), WHO, WIPO, WMO, WTO, ZC

Independence: 16 December 1991 (from the Soviet Union)

National holiday: Independence Day, 16 December (1991)

Flag: *description:* a gold sun with 32 rays above a soaring golden steppe eagle, both centered on a sky-blue background; the left side displays a national pattern called *koshkar-muiz* (the horns of the ram) in gold
meaning: the blue color has religious significance for the Turkic peoples and symbolizes cultural and ethnic unity, as well as sky and water; the sun stands for wealth and plenitude, with rays shaped like grain; the eagle has appeared on Kazakh tribal flags for centuries and represents freedom, power, and the flight to the future

National symbol(s): golden eagle

National color(s): blue, yellow

National coat of arms: winning design from a competition held in 1992; the design uses the national colors of yellow and blue, with blue standing for the hope for unity, peace, and friendship with all people and gold for a clear future for the country 's population; a *shanyrak* (the upper dome-like portion of a yurt) represents familial well-being, peace, and calmness, with the circular shape standing for life and eternity; the winged horses, or *tulpars*, protect the shanyrak and symbolize bravery, prosperity, and inspiration

National anthem(s): *title:* "Menin Qazaqstanim " (My Kazakhstan)
lyrics/music: Zhumeken NAZHIMEDENOV and Nursultan NAZARBAYEV/Shamshi KALDAYAKOV
history: adopted 2006; President Nursultan NAZARBAYEV played a role in revising the lyrics

National heritage: *total World Heritage Sites:* 6 (3 cultural, 3 natural)
selected World Heritage Site locales: Mausoleum of Khoja Ahmed Yasawi (c); Petroglyphs at Tanbaly (c); Saryarka - Steppe and Lakes of Northern Kazakhstan (n); Silk Roads: the Chang 'an-Tianshan Corridor (c); Western Tien-Shan (n); Cold Winter Deserts of Turan (n)

ECONOMY

Economic overview: oil and gas giant, with growing international investment; domestic economy hit hard by COVID-19 disruptions; reforming civil society and improving business confidence; legacy state controls and Russian influence inhibit growth and autonomy

Real GDP (purchasing power parity): $739.385 billion (2024 est.)
$705.52 billion (2023 est.)
$671.285 billion (2022 est.)
note: data in 2021 dollars
comparison ranking: 39

Real GDP growth rate: 4.8% (2024 est.)
5.1% (2023 est.)
3.2% (2022 est.)
note: annual GDP % growth based on constant local currency
comparison ranking: 51

Real GDP per capita: $35,900 (2024 est.)
$34,700 (2023 est.)
$33,500 (2022 est.)
note: data in 2021 dollars
comparison ranking: 66

GDP (official exchange rate): $288.406 billion (2024 est.)
note: data in current dollars at official exchange rate

Inflation rate (consumer prices): 8.8% (2024 est.)
14.7% (2023 est.)
15% (2022 est.)
note: annual % change based on consumer prices
comparison ranking: 171

GDP - composition, by sector of origin: *agriculture:* 3.9% (2024 est.)
industry: 31.4% (2024 est.)
services: 58.2% (2024 est.)
note: figures may not total 100% due to non-allocated consumption not captured in sector-reported data
comparison rankings: agriculture 120; industry 48; services 102

GDP - composition, by end use: *household consumption:* 51.4% (2023 est.)
government consumption: 11.1% (2023 est.)
investment in fixed capital: 26.5% (2023 est.)
investment in inventories: 3.3% (2023 est.)
exports of goods and services: 34.5% (2023 est.)
imports of goods and services: -27.5% (2023 est.)
note: figures may not total 100% due to rounding or gaps in data collection

Agricultural products: wheat, milk, barley, potatoes, watermelons, cantaloupes/melons, sunflower seeds, maize, onions, tomatoes (2023)
note: top ten agricultural products based on tonnage

Industries: oil, coal, iron ore, manganese, chromite, lead, zinc, copper, titanium, bauxite, gold, silver, phosphates, sulfur, uranium, iron and steel; tractors and other agricultural machinery, electric motors, construction materials

Industrial production growth rate: 6.6% (2024 est.)
note: annual % change in industrial value added based on constant local currency
comparison ranking: 27

Labor force: 10.285 million (2024 est.)
note: number of people ages 15 or older who are employed or seeking work
comparison ranking: 55

Unemployment rate: 4.8% (2024 est.)
4.9% (2023 est.)
4.9% (2022 est.)
note: % of labor force seeking employment
comparison ranking: 84

Youth unemployment rate (ages 15-24): *total:* 3.8% (2024 est.)
male: 3% (2024 est.)
female: 4.8% (2024 est.)
note: % of labor force ages 15-24 seeking employment
comparison ranking: total 173

Population below poverty line: 5.2% (2023 est.)
note: % of population with income below national poverty line
Gini Index coefficient - distribution of family income 29.2 (2021 est.)
note: index (0-100) of income distribution; higher values represent greater inequality
comparison ranking: 128

Average household expenditures: *on food:* 50.4% of household expenditures (2023 est.)
on alcohol and tobacco: 2.2% of household expenditures (2023 est.)

Household income or consumption by percentage share: *lowest 10%:* 4.3% (2021 est.)
highest 10%: 24.8% (2021 est.)
note: % share of income accruing to lowest and highest 10% of population

Remittances: 0.1% of GDP (2024 est.)
0.1% of GDP (2023 est.)
0.2% of GDP (2022 est.)
note: personal transfers and compensation between resident and non-resident individuals/households/entities

Budget: *revenues:* $44.25 billion (2023 est.)
expenditures: $47.247 billion (2023 est.)
note: central government revenues (excluding grants) and expenditures converted to US dollars at average official exchange rate for year indicated

Public debt: 20.9% of GDP (2023 est.)
note: central government debt as a % of GDP
comparison ranking: 178

Taxes and other revenues: 11.9% (of GDP) (2023 est.)
note: central government tax revenue as a % of GDP
comparison ranking: 117

Current account balance: -$3.702 billion (2024 est.)
-$9.448 billion (2023 est.)
$6.436 billion (2022 est.)
note: balance of payments - net trade and primary/secondary income in current dollars
comparison ranking: 162

Exports: $91.908 billion (2024 est.)
$90.926 billion (2023 est.)
$93.822 billion (2022 est.)
note: balance of payments - exports of goods and services in current dollars
comparison ranking: 51

Exports - partners: China 16%, UK 15%, Russia 10%, Turkey 6%, Italy 5% (2023)
note: top five export partners based on percentage share of exports

Exports - commodities: crude petroleum, gold, radioactive chemicals, refined copper, copper ore (2023)
note: top five export commodities based on value in dollars

Imports: $74.246 billion (2024 est.)
$72.723 billion (2023 est.)
$60.439 billion (2022 est.)
note: balance of payments - imports of goods and services in current dollars
comparison ranking: 54

Imports - partners: China 28%, Russia 24%, Gambia, The 4%, Turkey 4%, USA 4% (2023)
note: top five import partners based on percentage share of imports

Imports - commodities: garments, cars, broadcasting equipment, vehicle bodies, packaged medicine (2023)
note: top five import commodities based on value in dollars

Reserves of foreign exchange and gold: $45.808 billion (2024 est.)
$35.965 billion (2023 est.)
$35.076 billion (2022 est.)
note: holdings of gold (year-end prices)/foreign exchange/special drawing rights in current dollars
comparison ranking: 44

Debt - external: $25.765 billion (2023 est.)
note: present value of external debt in current US dollars
comparison ranking: 29

Exchange rates: tenge (KZT) per US dollar -

Exchange rates: 468.962 (2024 est.)
456.165 (2023 est.)
460.165 (2022 est.)
425.908 (2021 est.)
412.953 (2020 est.)

ENERGY

Electricity access: *electrification - total population:* 100% (2022 est.)

Electricity: *installed generating capacity:* 27.624 million kW (2023 est.)
consumption: 106.201 billion kWh (2023 est.)
exports: 2.243 billion kWh (2023 est.)
imports: 3.694 billion kWh (2023 est.)
transmission/distribution losses: 9.439 billion kWh (2023 est.)
comparison rankings: installed generating capacity 40; consumption 34; exports 55; imports 54; transmission/distribution losses 181

Electricity generation sources: *fossil fuels:* 87.7% of total installed capacity (2023 est.)
solar: 1.9% of total installed capacity (2023 est.)
wind: 2.1% of total installed capacity (2023 est.)
hydroelectricity: 8.2% of total installed capacity (2023 est.)

Nuclear energy: Number of nuclear reactors permanently shut down: 1 (2025)

Coal: *production:* 120.279 million metric tons (2023 est.)
consumption: 86.349 million metric tons (2023 est.)
exports: 34.043 million metric tons (2023 est.)
imports: 114,000 metric tons (2023 est.)
proven reserves: 25.605 billion metric tons (2023 est.)

Petroleum: *total petroleum production:* 1.955 million bbl/day (2023 est.)
refined petroleum consumption: 386,000 bbl/day (2023 est.)
crude oil estimated reserves: 30 billion barrels (2021 est.)

Natural gas: *production:* 28.769 billion cubic meters (2023 est.)
consumption: 22.223 billion cubic meters (2023 est.)
exports: 7.071 billion cubic meters (2023 est.)
imports: 408.952 million cubic meters (2023 est.)
proven reserves: 2.407 trillion cubic meters (2021 est.)

Energy consumption per capita: 172.936 million Btu/person (2023 est.)
comparison ranking: 22

COMMUNICATIONS

Telephones - fixed lines: *total subscriptions:* 2.574 million (2023 est.)
subscriptions per 100 inhabitants: 13 (2023 est.)
comparison ranking: total subscriptions 43

Telephones - mobile cellular: *total subscriptions:* 25.8 million (2023 est.)
subscriptions per 100 inhabitants: 130 (2022 est.)
comparison ranking: total subscriptions 53

Broadcast media: the state owns nearly all radio and TV transmission facilities and operates national TV and radio networks; there are 96 TV channels, and 4 state-run radio stations; some former state-owned media outlets have been privatized; households with satellite dishes have access to foreign media; small number of commercial radio stations; all media outlets have to register with the government (2018)

Internet country code: .kz

Internet users: *percent of population:* 93% (2023 est.)

Broadband - fixed subscriptions: *total:* 3.59 million (2023 est.)
subscriptions per 100 inhabitants: 18 (2023 est.)
comparison ranking: total 44

TRANSPORTATION

Civil aircraft registration country code prefix: UP

Airports: 132 (2025)
comparison ranking: 38

Heliports: 32 (2025)
comparison ranking: 45

Railways: *total:* 16,636 km (2021)
broad gauge: 16,636 km (2021) 1.520-m gauge (4,237 km electrified)

Merchant marine: *total:* 122 (2023)
by type: general cargo 3, oil tanker 7, other 112
comparison ranking: total 82

MILITARY AND SECURITY

Military and security forces: Armed Forces of the Republic of Kazakhstan: Land Forces (Army of Kazakhstan), Naval Forces, Air and Air Defense Forces

Ministry of Internal Affairs: National Police, National Guard

Committee for National Security (KNB): Border Guard Service (2025)
note: the National Guard is a gendarmerie type force administered by the Ministry of Internal Affairs, but also serves the Ministry of Defense; it is responsible for fighting crime, maintaining public order, and ensuring public safety; other duties include anti-terrorism operations, guarding prisons, riot control, and territorial defense in time of war

Military expenditures: 0.9% of GDP (2024 est.)
1% of GDP (2023 est.)
0.9% of GDP (2022 est.)
1% of GDP (2021 est.)
1.1% of GDP (2020 est.)

Military and security service personnel strengths: available information varies widely; estimated 50,000

active Armed Forces; estimated 30,000 National Guard (2025)

Military equipment inventories and acquisitions: the Kazakh military 's inventory is comprised of mostly Russian and Soviet-era equipment; in recent years, however, it has sought to diversify to suppliers such as China, France, Israel, South Korea, and Turkey; Kazakhstan has a defense industry capable of assembling or producing such items as naval vessels, combat vehicles, helicopters, and radar systems (2025)

Military service age and obligation: men 18-27 are subject to conscription for 12-24 months; conscripts may be assigned to the Armed Forces, the National Guard, the Border Service, the State Security Service, or the Ministry of Emergency Situations; women may volunteer (2025)
note: as of 2022, more than 10,000 women served in the Armed Forces and the National Guard

Military - note: the military 's principal responsibilities are territorial defense while the National Police, National Guard, Committee for National Security, and Border Service have primary responsibility for internal security, although the military may provide assistance if required; the military also participates in humanitarian and peacekeeping operations, as well as regional exercises; in recent years, Kazakhstan has placed greater emphasis on regional military partnerships and equipment modernization and diversification in order to reduce reliance on Russia, its traditional security partner; other efforts to enhance the country 's security sector have included boosting the capabilities of the National Guard and improving military professionalism
Kazakhstan has been a member of the Collective Security Treaty Organization (CSTO) since 1994 and has obligated troops to CSTO 's rapid reaction force; it also has had a relationship with NATO since 1992 focused on democratic, institutional, and defense reforms (2025)

SPACE

Space agency/agencies: Aerospace Committee of the Kazakh Digital Development, Innovations and Aerospace Industry Ministry (aka National Space Agency of the Republic of Kazakhstan or KazCosmos; established 2007) (2025)

Space launch site(s): Baikonur Cosmodrome/Space Center (Baikonur) (2025)
note 1: Baikonur Cosmodrome is leased and administered by Russia until 2050; the cosmodrome was originally built by the Soviet Union in the mid-1950s and is the site of the World 's first successful satellite launch (Sputnik) in 1957; it is also the largest space launch facility in the World
note 2: in 2018, Kazakhstan and Russia agreed that Kazakhstan would build, maintain, and operate a new space launch facility (Baiterek) at the Baikonur Space Center (estimated to be fully operational in 2027-2028)

Space program overview: space program originated with the former Soviet Union; focused on the acquisition and operation of satellites; builds (with foreign assistance) and operates communications, remote sensing (RS), and scientific satellites; building space infrastructure, such as launch and testing facilities, ground stations, and rocket manufacturing; has an astronaut (cosmonaut) program; has relations with a variety of foreign space agencies and industries, including those of China, France, Germany, India, Israel, Italy, Japan, Russia, Saudi Arabia, Sweden, Thailand, Turkey, Ukraine, UAE, and the UK; participates in international program such as the International Space Station; has state-owned and private companies that assist in the development and building of the country 's space program, including satellites, satellite payloads, and associated capabilities; they also work closely with foreign commercial entities (2025)
note: further details about the key activities, programs, and milestones of the country 's space program, as well as government spending estimates on the space sector, appear in the Space Programs reference guide

TRANSNATIONAL ISSUES

Refugees and internally displaced persons: *refugees:* 66,152 (2024 est.)

IDPs: 0 (2024 est.)

stateless persons: 7,865 (2024 est.)

KENYA

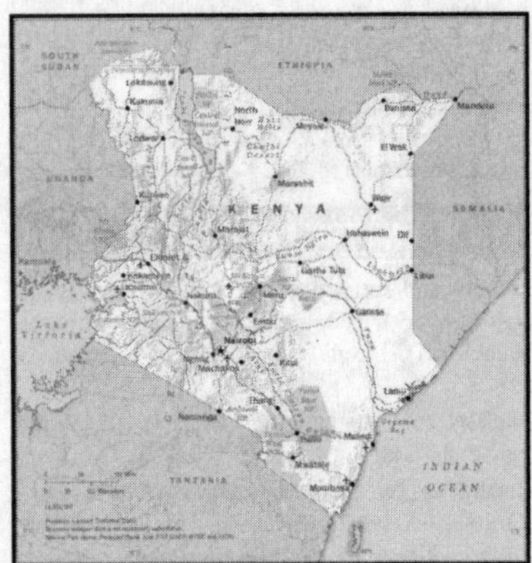

INTRODUCTION

Background: Trade centers such as Mombasa have existed along the Kenyan and Tanzanian coastlines, known as the Land of Zanj, since at least the 2nd century. These centers traded with the outside world, including China, India, Indonesia, the Middle East, North Africa, and Persia. By around the 9th century, the mix of Africans, Arabs, and Persians who lived and traded there became known as Swahili ("people of the coast") with a distinct language (KiSwahili) and culture. The Portuguese arrived in the 1490s and, using Mombasa as a base, sought to monopolize trade in the Indian Ocean. The Portuguese were pushed out in the late 1600s by the combined forces of Oman and Pate, an island off the coast. In 1890, Germany and the UK divided up the region, with the UK taking the north and the Germans the south, including present-day Tanzania, Burundi, and Rwanda. In 1895, the British established the East Africa Protectorate, which in 1920 was converted into a colony, and named Kenya after its highest mountain. Numerous political disputes between the colony and the UK led to the violent Mau Mau Uprising, which began in 1952, and the eventual declaration of independence in 1963.

Jomo KENYATTA, the founding president and an icon of the liberation struggle, led Kenya from independence in 1963 until his death in 1978, when Vice President Daniel Arap MOI took power in a constitutional succession. The country was a de facto one-party state from 1969 until 1982, after which time the ruling Kenya African National Union (KANU) changed the constitution to make itself the sole legal political party. MOI gave in to internal and external pressure for political liberalization in 1991, but the ethnically fractured opposition failed to dislodge KANU from power in elections in 1992 and 1997, which were marred by violence and fraud. MOI stepped down in 2002 after fair and peaceful elections. Mwai KIBAKI, running as the candidate of the multiethnic, united opposition group, the National Rainbow Coalition (NARC), defeated KANU candidate Uhuru KENYATTA, the son of the founding president, and assumed the presidency following a campaign centered on an anticorruption platform.

Opposition candidate Raila ODINGA challenged KIBAKI's reelection in 2007 on the grounds of widespread vote rigging, leading to two months of ethnic violence that caused more than 1,100 deaths and displaced hundreds of thousands. African Union-sponsored mediation resulted in a power-sharing accord that brought ODINGA into the government as prime minister and outlined a reform agenda. In 2010, Kenyans overwhelmingly voted to adopt a new constitution that eliminated the prime minister, introduced additional checks and balances to executive power, and devolved power and resources to 47 newly created counties. Uhuru KENYATTA won the first presidential election under the new constitution in 2013. He won a second and final term in office in 2017 after a contentious repeat election. In 2022, William RUTO won a close presidential election; he assumed the office the following month after the Kenyan Supreme Court upheld the victory.

GEOGRAPHY

Location: Eastern Africa, bordering the Indian Ocean, between Somalia and Tanzania

Geographic coordinates: 1 00 N, 38 00 E

Map references: Africa

Area: *total:* 580,367 sq km
land: 569,140 sq km
water: 11,227 sq km
comparison ranking: total 51

Area - comparative: five times the size of Ohio; slightly more than twice the size of Nevada

Land boundaries: *total:* 3,457 km
border countries (5): Ethiopia 867 km; Somalia 684 km; South Sudan 317 km; Tanzania 775 km; Uganda 814 km

Coastline: 536 km

Maritime claims: *territorial sea:* 12 nm
exclusive economic zone: 200 nm
continental shelf: 200-m depth or to the depth of exploitation

Climate: varies from tropical along coast to arid in interior

Terrain: low plains rise to central highlands bisected by Great Rift Valley; fertile plateau in west

Elevation: *highest point:* Mount Kenya 5,199 m
lowest point: Indian Ocean 0 m
mean elevation: 762 m

Natural resources: limestone, soda ash, salt, gemstones, fluorspar, zinc, diatomite, gypsum, wildlife, hydropower

Land use: *agricultural land:* 49.7% (2022 est.)
arable land: 11.1% (2022 est.)
permanent crops: 1.3% (2022 est.)
permanent pasture: 37.4% (2022 est.)
forest: 6.3% (2022 est.)
other: 43.9% (2022 est.)

Irrigated land: 1,030 sq km (2012)

Major lakes (area sq km): *fresh water lake(s):* Lake Victoria (shared with Tanzania and Uganda) - 62,940 sq km
salt water lake(s): Lake Turkana (shared with Ethiopia) - 6,400 sq km

Major watersheds (area sq km): Atlantic Ocean drainage: ***(Mediterranean Sea)*** Nile (3,254,853 sq km)

Major aquifers: Ogaden-Juba Basin

Population distribution: population heavily concentrated in the west along the shore of Lake Victoria; other areas of high density include the capital of Nairobi, and in the southeast along the Indian Ocean coast, as shown in this population distribution map

Natural hazards: recurring drought; flooding during rainy seasons
volcanism: limited volcanic activity; the Barrier (1,032 m) last erupted in 1921; South Island is the only other historically active volcano

Geography - note: *the Kenyan Highlands comprise one of the most successful agricultural production regions in Africa; glaciers are found on Mount Kenya, Africa's second-highest peak; unique physiography supports abundant and varied wildlife of scientific and economic value; Lake Victoria, the world's largest tropical lake and the second-largest freshwater lake, is shared among three countries: Kenya, Tanzania, and Uganda*

PEOPLE AND SOCIETY

Population: *total:* 58,246,378 (2024 est.)
male: 29,091,800
female: 29,154,578
comparison rankings: total 26; male 26; female 26

Nationality: *noun:* Kenyan(s)
adjective: Kenyan

Ethnic groups: Kikuyu 17.1%, Luhya 14.3%, Kalenjin 13.4%, Luo 10.7%, Kamba 9.8%, Somali 5.8%, Kisii 5.7%, Mijikenda 5.2%, Meru 4.2%, Maasai 2.5%, Turkana 2.1%, non-Kenyan 1%, other 8.2% (2019 est.)

Languages: English (official), Kiswahili (official), numerous indigenous languages
major-language sample(s):
The World Factbook, the indispensable source for basic information. (English)
The World Factbook, Chanzo cha Lazima Kuhusu Habari ya Msingi. (Kiswahili)

Religions: Christian 85.5% (Protestant 33.4%, Catholic 20.6%, Evangelical 20.4%, African Instituted Churches 7%, other Christian 4.1%), Muslim 10.9%, other 1.8%, none 1.6%, don't know/no answer 0.2% (2019 est.)

Age structure: *0-14 years:* 35.8% (male 10,464,384/female 10,366,997)
15-64 years: 60.9% (male 17,731,068/female 17,723,012)
65 years and over: 3.4% (2024 est.) (male 896,348/female 1,064,569)

Dependency ratios: *total dependency ratio:* 65.3 (2024 est.)
youth dependency ratio: 59.8 (2024 est.)
elderly dependency ratio: 5.5 (2024 est.)
potential support ratio: 18.3 (2024 est.)

Median age: *total:* 21.2 years (2024 est.)
male: 21.1 years
female: 21.4 years
comparison ranking: total 196

Population growth rate: 2.06% (2024 est.)
comparison ranking: 38

Birth rate: 25.6 births/1,000 population (2024 est.)
comparison ranking: 44

Death rate: 4.9 deaths/1,000 population (2024 est.)
comparison ranking: 199

Net migration rate: -0.2 migrant(s)/1,000 population (2024 est.)
comparison ranking: 102

Population distribution: population heavily concentrated in the west along the shore of Lake Victoria; other areas of high density include the capital of Nairobi, and in the southeast along the Indian Ocean coast, as shown in this population distribution map

Urbanization: *urban population:* 29.5% of total population (2023)
rate of urbanization: 4.09% annual rate of change (2020-25 est.)

Major urban areas - population: 5.325 million NAIROBI (capital), 1.440 million Mombassa (2023)

Sex ratio: *at birth:* 1.02 male(s)/female
0-14 years: 1.01 male(s)/female
15-64 years: 1 male(s)/female
65 years and over: 0.84 male(s)/female
total population: 1 male(s)/female (2024 est.)

Mother's mean age at first birth: 20.3 years (2014 est.)
note: data represents median age at first birth among women 25-49

Maternal mortality ratio: 379 deaths/100,000 live births (2023 est.)
comparison ranking: 16

Infant mortality rate: *total:* 26.1 deaths/1,000 live births (2024 est.)
male: 29 deaths/1,000 live births
female: 23.1 deaths/1,000 live births
comparison ranking: total 58

Life expectancy at birth: *total population:* 70.4 years (2024 est.)
male: 68.6 years
female: 72.2 years
comparison ranking: total population 176

Total fertility rate: 3.16 children born/woman (2024 est.)
comparison ranking: 45

Gross reproduction rate: 1.56 (2024 est.)

Drinking water source: *improved:* *urban:* 86.4% of population (2022 est.)
rural: 53.3% of population (2022 est.)
total: 62.9% of population (2022 est.)
unimproved: *urban:* 13.6% of population (2022 est.)
rural: 46.7% of population (2022 est.)
total: 37.1% of population (2022 est.)

Health expenditure: 4.5% of GDP (2021)
8.7% of national budget (2022 est.)

Physician density: 0.29 physicians/1,000 population (2023)

Hospital bed density: 1.3 beds/1,000 population (2019 est.)

Sanitation facility access: *improved:* *urban:* 84.7% of population (2022 est.)
rural: 51.1% of population (2022 est.)
total: 60.9% of population (2022 est.)
unimproved: *urban:* 15.3% of population (2022 est.)
rural: 48.9% of population (2022 est.)
total: 39.1% of population (2022 est.)

Obesity - adult prevalence rate: 7.1% (2016)
comparison ranking: 161

Alcohol consumption per capita: *total:* 1.68 liters of pure alcohol (2019 est.)
beer: 0.81 liters of pure alcohol (2019 est.)
wine: 0.04 liters of pure alcohol (2019 est.)
spirits: 0.81 liters of pure alcohol (2019 est.)
other alcohols: 0.03 liters of pure alcohol (2019 est.)
comparison ranking: total 134

Tobacco use: *total:* 8.6% (2025 est.)
male: 15.5% (2025 est.)
female: 1.9% (2025 est.)
comparison ranking: total 136

Children under the age of 5 years underweight: 10.1% (2022)
comparison ranking: 51

Currently married women (ages 15-49): 56.8% (2023 est.)

Child marriage: *women married by age 15:* 2.2% (2022)
women married by age 18: 12.5% (2022)
men married by age 18: 1.8% (2022)

Education expenditure: 4% of GDP (2024 est.)
18.4% national budget (2023 est.)
comparison ranking: Education expenditure (% GDP) 107

ENVIRONMENT

Environmental issues: water pollution from urban and industrial wastes and from use of pesticides and fertilizers; flooding; water-hyacinth infestation in Lake Victoria; deforestation; soil erosion; desertification; poaching

International environmental agreements: *party to:* Biodiversity, Climate Change, Climate Change-Kyoto Protocol, Climate Change-Paris Agreement, Comprehensive Nuclear Test Ban, Desertification, Endangered Species, Hazardous Wastes, Law of the Sea, Marine Dumping-London Convention, Marine Dumping-London Protocol, Marine Life

Conservation, Nuclear Test Ban, Ozone Layer Protection, Ship Pollution, Wetlands, Whaling
signed, but not ratified: none of the selected agreements

Climate: varies from tropical along coast to arid in interior

Urbanization: *urban population:* 29.5% of total population (2023)
rate of urbanization: 4.09% annual rate of change (2020-25 est.)

Carbon dioxide emissions: 19.023 million metric tonnes of CO2 (2023 est.)
from coal and metallurgical coke: 3.316 million metric tonnes of CO2 (2023 est.)
from petroleum and other liquids: 15.707 million metric tonnes of CO2 (2023 est.)
comparison ranking: total emissions 89

Particulate matter emissions: 12.7 micrograms per cubic meter (2019 est.)

Methane emissions: *energy:* 334.4 kt (2022-2024 est.)
agriculture: 1,241 kt (2019-2021 est.)
waste: 127.1 kt (2019-2021 est.)
other: 32.8 kt (2019-2021 est.)

Waste and recycling: *municipal solid waste generated annually:* 5.595 million tons (2024 est.)
percent of municipal solid waste recycled: 19.9% (2022 est.)

Total water withdrawal: *municipal:* 495 million cubic meters (2022 est.)
industrial: 303 million cubic meters (2022 est.)
agricultural: 3.234 billion cubic meters (2022 est.)

Total renewable water resources: 30.7 billion cubic meters (2022 est.)

GOVERNMENT

Country name: *conventional long form:* Republic of Kenya
conventional short form: Kenya
local long form: Republic of Kenya (English)/ Jamhuri ya Kenya (Swahili)
local short form: Kenya
former: British East Africa
etymology: named for Mount Kenya; the mountain's name may derive from the Kikuyu word *kere nyaga*, or "white mountain"

Government type: presidential republic

Capital: *name:* Nairobi
geographic coordinates: 1 17 S, 36 49 E
time difference: UTC+3 (8 hours ahead of Washington, DC, during Standard Time)
etymology: the name derives from the Maasai expression meaning "cool waters," which was used to refer to a local water hole, Enkare Nairobi

Administrative divisions: 47 counties; Baringo, Bomet, Bungoma, Busia, Elgeyo/Marakwet, Embu, Garissa, Homa Bay, Isiolo, Kajiado, Kakamega, Kericho, Kiambu, Kilifi, Kirinyaga, Kisii, Kisumu, Kitui, Kwale, Laikipia, Lamu, Machakos, Makueni, Mandera, Marsabit, Meru, Migori, Mombasa, Murang'a, Nairobi City, Nakuru, Nandi, Narok, Nyamira, Nyandarua, Nyeri, Samburu, Siaya, Taita/ Taveta, Tana River, Tharaka-Nithi, Trans Nzoia, Turkana, Uasin Gishu, Vihiga, Wajir, West Pokot

Legal system: mixed system of English common law, Islamic law, and customary law; Supreme Court reviews laws

Constitution: *history:* current constitution passed by referendum on 4 August 2010
amendment process: amendments can be proposed by either house of Parliament or by petition of at least one million eligible voters; passage of amendments by Parliament requires approval by at least two-thirds majority vote of both houses in each of two readings, approval in a referendum by majority of votes cast by at least 20% of eligible voters in at least one half of Kenya's counties, and approval by the president; passage of amendments introduced by petition requires approval by a majority of county assemblies, approval by majority vote of both houses, and approval by the president

International law organization participation: accepts compulsory ICJ jurisdiction with reservations; accepts ICCt jurisdiction

Citizenship: *citizenship by birth:* no
citizenship by descent only: at least one parent must be a citizen of Kenya
dual citizenship recognized: yes
residency requirement for naturalization: 4 out of the previous 7 years

Suffrage: 18 years of age; universal

Executive branch: *chief of state:* President William RUTO (since 13 September 2022)
head of government: President William RUTO (since 13 September 2022)
cabinet: Cabinet appointed by the president, subject to confirmation by the National Assembly
election/appointment process: president and deputy president directly elected on the same ballot by majority vote nationwide and at least 25% of the votes cast in at least 24 of the 47 counties; failure to meet these thresholds requires a runoff between the top two candidates
most recent election date: 9 August 2022
election results: *2022:* William RUTO elected president in first round; percent of vote - William RUTO (UDA) 50.5%, Raila ODINGA (ODM) 48.9%, other 0.6%
2017: Uhuru KENYATTA reelected president; percent of vote - Uhuru KENYATTA (JP) 98.3%, Raila ODINGA (ODM) 1%, other 0.7%
expected date of next election: 10 August 2027
note: the president is both chief of state and head of government

Legislative branch: *legislature name:* Parliament of Kenya
legislative structure: bicameral

Legislative branch - lower chamber: *chamber name:* National Assembly
number of seats: 350 (all directly elected)
electoral system: plurality/majority
scope of elections: full renewal
term in office: 5 years
most recent election date: 8/9/2022
parties elected and seats per party: United Democratic Alliance (UDA) (145); Orange Democratic Movement (ODM) (86); Jubilee Party (JP) (28); Wiper Democratic Movement-Kenya (WDM-K) (26); Others (19); Other (45)
percentage of women in chamber: 23.4%
expected date of next election: August 2027

Legislative branch - upper chamber: *chamber name:* Senate
number of seats: 68 (all directly elected)
electoral system: plurality/majority
scope of elections: full renewal
term in office: 5 years
most recent election date: 8/9/2022
parties elected and seats per party: Kenya Kwanza Alliance (33); Azimio la Umoja - One Kenya Coalition Party (32); Other (1)
percentage of women in chamber: 31.3%
expected date of next election: August 2027

Judicial branch: *highest court(s):* Supreme Court (consists of chief and deputy chief justices and 5 judges)
judge selection and term of office: chief and deputy chief justices nominated by Judicial Service Commission (JSC) and appointed by the president with approval of the National Assembly; other judges nominated by the JSC and appointed by president; chief justice serves a nonrenewable 10-year term or until age 70, whichever comes first; other judges serve until age 70
subordinate courts: High Court; Court of Appeal; military courts; magistrates' courts; religious courts

Political parties: Azimio La Umoja–One Kenya Coalition Party
Amani National Congress or ANC
Chama Cha Kazi or CCK
Democratic Action Party or DAP-K
Democratic Party or DP
Forum for the Restoration of Democracy–Kenya or FORD-Kenya
Grand Dream Development Party or GDDP
Jubilee Party or JP
Kenya African National Union or KANU
Kenya Kwanza coalition
Kenya Union Party or KUP
Maendeleo Chap Chap Party or MCC
Movement for Democracy and Growth or MDG
National Agenda Party or NAP-K
National Ordinary People Empowerment Union or NOPEU
Orange Democratic Movement or ODM
Pamoja African Alliance or PAAJ
The Service Party or TSP
United Democratic Alliance or UDA
United Democratic Movement or UDM
United Democratic Party or UDP
United Party of Independent Alliance or UPIA
United Progressive Alliance or UPA
Wiper Democratic Movement-Kenya or WDM-K

Diplomatic representation in the US: *chief of mission:* Ambassador David Kipkorir Kiplagat KERICH (since 18 September 2024)
chancery: 2249 R St NW, Washington, DC 20008
telephone: [1] (202) 387-6101
FAX: [1] (202) 462-3829
email address and website: information@kenyaembassydc.org
https://kenyaembassydc.org/#
consulate(s): New York

Diplomatic representation from the US: *chief of mission:* Ambassador (vacant); Chargé d'Affaires Susan M. BURNS (since 25 August 2025)
embassy: P.O. Box 606 Village Market, 00621 Nairobi
mailing address: 8900 Nairobi Place, Washington, DC 20521-8900
telephone: [254] (20) 363-6000
FAX: [254] (20) 363-6157
email address and website: kenya_acs@state.gov
https://ke. usembassy. gov/

International organization participation: ACP, AfDB, ATMIS, AU, C, CD, COMESA, EAC, EADB, FAO, G-15, G-77, IAEA, IBRD, ICAO,

ICCT, ICRM, IDA, IFAD, IFC, IFRCS, IGAD, ILO, IMF, IMO, IMSO, Interpol, IOC, IOM, IPU, ISO, ITSO, ITU, ITUC (NGOs), MIGA, MONUSCO, NAM, OPCW, PCA, UN, UNAMID, UNCTAD, UNESCO, UNHCR, UNIDO, UNIFIL, UNISFA, UNMIL, UNMISS, UNOOSA, UNSOM, UNWTO, UPU, WCO, WHO, WMO, WTO

Independence: 12 December 1963 (from the UK)

National holiday: Jamhuri Day (Independence Day), 12 December (1963)
note: Madaraka Day, 1 June (1963), marks the day Kenya attained internal self-rule

Flag: *description:* three equal horizontal bands of black (top), red, and green; the red band is edged in white; a large Maasai warrior's shield covering crossed spears is at the center
meaning: black stands for the majority population, red for the blood shed in the struggle for freedom, green for natural wealth, and white for peace; the shield and crossed spears symbolize the defense of freedom

National symbol(s): lion

National color(s): black, red, green, white

National coat of arms: *the two lions symbolize protection as they hold a traditional East African shield and spears in defense of freedom and unity; the shield features the national colors:* black for the people, green for agriculture and natural resources, red for the struggle for freedom, and white for unity and peace; on the shield, a rooster greets the new day, and the axe represents both authority and the Kenya Africa National Union (KANU) that led the country to independence; at the base of the shield is Mount Kenya, Africa's second-highest peak; the scroll has the Swahili word *Harambee*, meaning "all for one" or "pulling together"

National anthem(s): *title:* "Ee Mungu Nguvu Yetu" (O God of All Creation)
lyrics/music: Graham HYSLOP, Thomas KALUME, Peter KIBUKOSYA, Washington OmONDI, and George W. SENOGA-ZAKE/traditional, adapted by Graham HYSLOP, Thomas KALUME, Peter KIBUKOSYA, Washington OMONDI, and George W. SENOGA-ZAKE
history: adopted 1963; based on a traditional Kenyan folk song

National heritage: *total World Heritage Sites:* 8(5 cultural, 3 natural)
selected World Heritage Site locales: Lake Turkana National Parks (n); Mount Kenya National Park/ Natural Forest (n); Lamu Old Town (c); Sacred Mijikenda Kaya Forests (c); Fort Jesus, Mombasa (c); Kenya Lake System in the Great Rift Valley (n); Thimlich Ohinga Archaeological Site (c); The Historic Town and Archaeological Site of Gedi (c)

ECONOMY

Economic overview: fast growing, third largest Sub-Saharan economy; strong agriculture sector with emerging services and tourism industries; IMF program to address current account and debt service challenges; business-friendly policies foster infrastructure investment, digital innovation and public-private partnerships; vulnerable to climate change-induced droughts

Real GDP (purchasing power parity): $328.632 billion (2024 est.)
$314.491 billion (2023 est.)
$297.938 billion (2022 est.)
note: data in 2021 dollars
comparison ranking: 59

Real GDP growth rate: 4.5% (2024 est.)
5.6% (2023 est.)
4.9% (2022 est.)
note: annual GDP % growth based on constant local currency
comparison ranking: 54

Real GDP per capita: $5,800 (2024 est.)
$5,700 (2023 est.)
$5,500 (2022 est.)
note: data in 2021 dollars
comparison ranking: 167

GDP (official exchange rate): $124.499 billion (2024 est.)
note: data in current dollars at official exchange rate

Inflation rate (consumer prices): 4.5% (2024 est.)
7.7% (2023 est.)
7.7% (2022 est.)
note: annual % change based on consumer prices
comparison ranking: 135

GDP - composition, by sector of origin: *agriculture:* 21.3% (2024 est.)
industry: 16.1% (2024 est.)
services: 55.9% (2024 est.)
note: figures may not total 100% due to non-allocated consumption not captured in sector-reported data
comparison rankings: agriculture 31; industry 159; services 117

GDP - composition, by end use: *household consumption:* 75.5% (2024 est.)
government consumption: 11.5% (2024 est.)
investment in fixed capital: 17.7% (2024 est.)
investment in inventories: -0.9% (2024 est.)
exports of goods and services: 11.1% (2024 est.)
imports of goods and services: -19.2% (2024 est.)
note: figures may not total 100% due to rounding or gaps in data collection

Agricultural products: sugarcane, milk, maize, bananas, tea, potatoes, cassava, cabbages, camel milk, mangoes/guavas (2023)
note: top ten agricultural products based on tonnage

Industries: agriculture, transportation, services, manufacturing, construction, telecommunications, tourism, retail

Industrial production growth rate: 0.2% (2024 est.)
note: annual % change in industrial value added based on constant local currency
comparison ranking: 129

Labor force: 23.781 million (2024 est.)
note: number of people ages 15 or older who are employed or seeking work
comparison ranking: 29

Unemployment rate: 5.5% (2024 est.)
5.6% (2023 est.)
5.8% (2022 est.)
note: % of labor force seeking employment
comparison ranking: 105

Youth unemployment rate (ages 15-24): *total:* 11.9% (2024 est.)
male: 8.3% (2024 est.)
female: 16% (2024 est.)
note: % of labor force ages 15-24 seeking employment
comparison ranking: total 105

Population below poverty line: 38.6% (2021 est.)
note: % of population with income below national poverty line
Gini Index coefficient - distribution of family income 38.7 (2021 est.)
note: index (0-100) of income distribution; higher values represent greater inequality
comparison ranking: 48

Average household expenditures: *on food:* 42.1% of household expenditures (2023 est.)
on alcohol and tobacco: 3.5% of household expenditures (2023 est.)

Household income or consumption by percentage share: *lowest 10%:* 2.9% (2021 est.)
highest 10%: 31.8% (2021 est.)
note: % share of income accruing to lowest and highest 10% of population

Remittances: 3.9% of GDP (2023 est.)
3.5% of GDP (2022 est.)
3.4% of GDP (2021 est.)
note: personal transfers and compensation between resident and non-resident individuals/households/ entities

Budget: *revenues:* $20.202 billion (2023 est.)
expenditures: $30.924 billion (2023 est.)
note: central government revenues (excluding grants) and expenditures converted to US dollars at average official exchange rate for year indicated

Taxes and other revenues: 14% (of GDP) (2023 est.)
note: central government tax revenue as a % of GDP
comparison ranking: 97

Current account balance: -$4.317 billion (2023 est.)
-$5.889 billion (2022 est.)
-$5.597 billion (2021 est.)
note: balance of payments - net trade and primary/ secondary income in current dollars
comparison ranking: 168

Exports: $12.626 billion (2023 est.)
$13.954 billion (2022 est.)
$11.815 billion (2021 est.)
note: balance of payments - exports of goods and services in current dollars
comparison ranking: 106

Exports - partners: Uganda 10%, USA 10%, UAE 8%, Netherlands 8%, Pakistan 6% (2023)
note: top five export partners based on percentage share of exports

Exports - commodities: tea, cut flowers, garments, gold, tropical fruits (2023)
note: top five export commodities based on value in dollars

Imports: $22.046 billion (2023 est.)
$24.606 billion (2022 est.)
$22.001 billion (2021 est.)
note: balance of payments - imports of goods and services in current dollars
comparison ranking: 93

Imports - partners: China 22%, UAE 14%, India 10%, Saudi Arabia 5%, Malaysia 4% (2023)
note: top five import partners based on percentage share of imports

Imports - commodities: refined petroleum, palm oil, wheat, plastics, garments (2023)
note: top five import commodities based on value in dollars

Reserves of foreign exchange and gold: $10.067 billion (2024 est.)
$7.342 billion (2023 est.)
$7.969 billion (2022 est.)
note: holdings of gold (year-end prices)/foreign exchange/special drawing rights in current dollars
comparison ranking: 76

Debt - external: $31.451 billion (2023 est.)

note: present value of external debt in current US dollars
comparison ranking: 26

Exchange rates: Kenyan shillings (KES) per US dollar -

Exchange rates: 134.822 (2024 est.)
139.846 (2023 est.)
117.866 (2022 est.)
109.638 (2021 est.)
106.451 (2020 est.)

ENERGY

Electricity access: *electrification - total population:* 76% (2022 est.)
electrification - urban areas: 98%
electrification - rural areas: 65.6%

Electricity: *installed generating capacity:* 3.824 million kW (2023 est.)
consumption: 10.002 billion kWh (2023 est.)
exports: 34 million kWh (2023 est.)
imports: 316 million kWh (2023 est.)
transmission/distribution losses: 3.069 billion kWh (2023 est.)
comparison rankings: installed generating capacity 101; consumption 104; exports 93; imports 101; transmission/distribution losses 140

Electricity generation sources: *fossil fuels:* 10.2% of total installed capacity (2023 est.)
solar: 4.5% of total installed capacity (2023 est.)
wind: 15.7% of total installed capacity (2023 est.)
hydroelectricity: 20.9% of total installed capacity (2023 est.)
geothermal: 47.2% of total installed capacity (2023 est.)
biomass and waste: 1.6% of total installed capacity (2023 est.)

Coal: *consumption:* 1.453 million metric tons (2023 est.)
exports: 30 metric tons (2023 est.)
imports: 1.453 million metric tons (2023 est.)

Petroleum: *refined petroleum consumption:* 113,000 bbl/day (2023 est.)

Energy consumption per capita: 5.486 million Btu/person (2023 est.)
comparison ranking: 169

COMMUNICATIONS

Telephones - fixed lines: *total subscriptions:* 68,000 (2023 est.)
subscriptions per 100 inhabitants: (2023 est.) less than 1
comparison ranking: total subscriptions 147

Telephones - mobile cellular: *total subscriptions:* 66.7 million (2023 est.)
subscriptions per 100 inhabitants: 122 (2022 est.)
comparison ranking: total subscriptions 27

Broadcast media: about a half-dozen large, privately owned media companies with TV and radio stations, as well as a state-owned TV broadcaster, provide service nationwide; satellite and cable TV subscription services available; state-owned radio broadcaster operates 2 national radio channels and provides regional and local radio services in multiple languages; many private radio stations broadcast nationally, with over 100 private and non-profit regional stations broadcasting in local languages; TV transmissions of all major international broadcasters available, mostly via paid subscriptions (2019)

Internet country code: .ke

Internet users: *percent of population:* 35% (2023 est.)

Broadband - fixed subscriptions: *total:* 1.32 million (2023 est.)
subscriptions per 100 inhabitants: 2 (2023 est.)
comparison ranking: total 73

TRANSPORTATION

Civil aircraft registration country code prefix: 5Y

Airports: 368 (2025)
comparison ranking: 19

Railways: *total:* 3,819 km (2018)
standard gauge: 485 km (2018) 1.435-m gauge
narrow gauge: 3,334 km (2018) 1.000-m gauge

Merchant marine: *total:* 26 (2023)
by type: oil tanker 4, other 22
comparison ranking: total 138

Ports: *total ports:* 4 (2024)
large: 0
medium: 1
small: 2
very small: 1
ports with oil terminals: 1
key ports: Kilifi, Lamu, Malindi, Mombasa

MILITARY AND SECURITY

Military and security forces: Kenya Defense Forces (KDF): Kenya Army, Kenya Navy, Kenya Air Force

Ministry of Interior: National Police Service, Kenya Coast Guard (2025)
note: the National Police Service maintains internal security and includes a paramilitary General Service Unit and Rapid Deployment Unit, as well as a Border Police Unit

Military expenditures: 1.1% of GDP (2024 est.)
1.1% of GDP (2023 est.)
1.1% of GDP (2022 est.)
1.2% of GDP (2021 est.)
1.2% of GDP (2020 est.)

Military and security service personnel strengths: approximately 25,000 active Kenya Defense Forces (2025)

Military equipment inventories and acquisitions: the KDF's inventory is a mix of older, donated/secondhand, and some modern weapon systems from a variety of sources; major suppliers have included China, France, South Africa, Turkey, the UK, and the US; in late 2023, the Kenyan Government unveiled a five-year spending plan to procure upgraded military equipment, including aerial surveillance drones, tactical vehicles, and air defense systems (2024)

Military service age and obligation: no conscription; 18-26 years of age for voluntary service for men and women (under 18 with parental consent; upper limit 30 years of age for specialists, tradesmen, or women with a diploma; 39 years of age for chaplains/imams); 9-year service obligation (7 years for Kenyan Navy) and subsequent 3-year re-enlistments; applicants must be Kenyan citizens (2024)

Military deployments: 400 Democratic Republic of the Congo (MONUSCO); approximately 1,400 Somalia (African Union Support and Stabilization Mission in Somalia or AUSSOM) (2024)

Military - note: the Kenya Defense Forces (KDF) are responsible for protecting the country's sovereignty and territory and assisting civil authorities in responding to emergency, disaster, or political unrest as requested; the KDF's chief security concerns include regional disputes and instability, maritime crime and piracy, and the threat posed by the Somalia-based al-Shabaab terrorist group, which has conducted attacks inside Kenya; it has conducted operations in neighboring Somalia since 2011 and taken part in numerous regional peacekeeping and security missions; the KDF is a leading member of the Africa Standby Force; it participates in multinational exercises, and has ties to a variety of foreign militaries, including those of France, the UK, and the US
the Kenya Military Forces were created following independence in 1963; the current KDF was established and its composition laid out in the 2010 constitution; it is governed by the Kenya Defense Forces Act of 2012; the Army traces its origins back to the Kings African Rifles (KAR), a British colonial regiment raised from Britain's East Africa possessions from 1902 until independence in the 1960s; the KAR conducted both military and internal security functions within the colonial territories, and served outside the territories during both World Wars (2025)

SPACE

Space agency/agencies: Kenya Space Agency (KSA; established 2017) (2025)
note: KSA's predecessor, the National Space Secretariat, was established in 2009

Space launch site(s): Luigi Broglio Space Center (aka Malindi Space Center, Malindi Station, San Marco Satellite Launching and Tracking Station; Kilifi County; over 20 sounding rockets and nine satellites launched from the site, 1967-1989); in 2020, Kenya concluded a new deal with Italy to conduct rocket launches from the site again in the future (2025)

Space program overview: has a national space strategy focused on acquiring and applying space technologies and applications for agriculture, communications, disaster and resource management, security, urban planning, and weather monitoring; jointly develops and builds nanosatellites with foreign partners; operates satellites; researching and developing satellite payloads and imagery data analysis capabilities; has cooperated on space issues with China, Japan, India, Italy, and the US, as well as a variety African partners; member of the African Space Agency (2025)
note: further details about the key activities, programs, and milestones of the country's space program, as well as government spending estimates on the space sector, appear in the Space Programs reference guide

TERRORISM

Terrorist group(s): Terrorist group(s): al-Shabaab
note: details about the history, aims, leadership, organization, areas of operation, tactics, targets, weapons, size, and sources of support of the group(s) appear(s) in Appendix T

TRANSNATIONAL ISSUES

Refugees and internally displaced persons: *refugees:* 823,904 (2024 est.)

IDPs: 284,886 (2024 est.)
stateless persons: 9,800 (2024 est.)

KIRIBATI

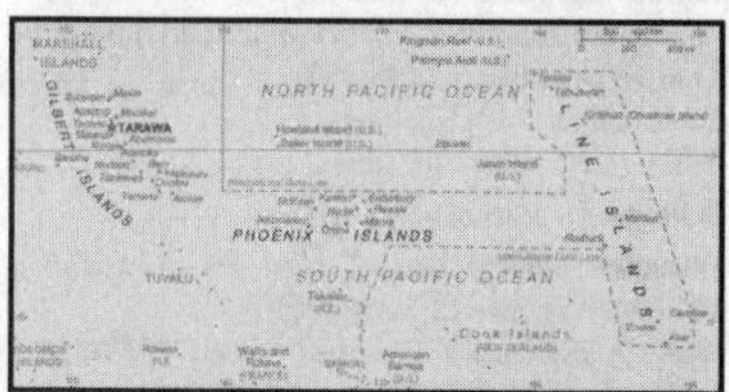

INTRODUCTION

Background: Kiribati is made up of three distinct island groups – the Gilbert Islands, the Line Islands, and the Phoenix Islands. The first Austronesian voyagers arrived in the Gilbert Islands as early as 3000 B.C., but these islands were not widely settled until about A.D. 200 by Micronesians. Around 1300, Samoans and Tongans invaded the southern Gilbert Islands, then known as Tungaru, bringing Polynesian cultural elements with them. Later arrivals of Fijians brought Melanesian elements to the Gilbert Islands, and extensive intermarriage between the Micronesian, Polynesian, and Melanesian people led to the creation of what would become Gilbertese cultural traditions by the time Europeans spotted the islands in the 1600s. The Phoenix Islands and Line Islands were both visited by various Melanesian and Polynesian peoples, but their isolation and lack of natural resources meant that long-term settlements were not possible. Both island groups were uninhabited by the time of European contact.

Kiribati experienced sustained European contact by the 1760s; all three island groups were named and charted by 1826. American whaling ships frequently passed through the islands, and the UK declared a protectorate over the Gilbert and nearby Ellice Islands in 1892, in an attempt to block growing US influence. Phosphate-rich Banaba Island was annexed to the protectorate in 1900. In 1916, the protectorate became a colony, and some Line Islands were added in 1916 and 1919, with the final ones added in 1972. The Phoenix Islands were added to the colony in 1937, and the UK agreed to share jurisdiction of some with the US because of their strategic location for aviation. During World War II, the islands were occupied by Japanese forces but were ejected by US amphibious assaults. The Ellice Islands became its own colony in 1974 and was renamed Tuvalu for "eight standing together" in 1975. The Gilbert Islands became fully self-governing in 1977 and independent in 1979 under the new name of Kiribati, the Gilbertese spelling of Gilberts. The US relinquished all claims to the sparsely inhabited Phoenix and Line Islands in a 1979 treaty of friendship.

In 2012, Kiribati purchased a 22 sq km (8.5 sq mi) plot of land in Fiji for potential eventual resettlement of its population because of climate change, and in 2014 Fijian Prime Minister Voreqe BAINIMARAMA said residents of Kiribati would be welcome to relocate to Fiji if their country is swamped by rising sea levels.

GEOGRAPHY

Location: Oceania, group of 32 coral atolls and one raised coral island in the Pacific Ocean, straddling the Equator; the capital Tarawa is about halfway between Hawaii and Australia

Geographic coordinates: 1 25 N, 173 00 E

Map references: Oceania

Area: *total:* 811 sq km
land: 811 sq km
water: 0 sq km
note: includes three island groups – Gilbert Islands, Line Islands, and Phoenix Islands –dispersed over about 3.5 million sq km (1.35 million sq mi)
comparison ranking: total 186

Area - comparative: four times the size of Washington, D.C.

Land boundaries: *total:* 0 km

Coastline: 1,143 km

Maritime claims: *territorial sea:* 12 nm
exclusive economic zone: 200 nm

Climate: tropical; marine, hot and humid, moderated by trade winds

Terrain: mostly low-lying coral atolls surrounded by extensive reefs

Elevation: *highest point:* unnamed elevation on Banaba 81 m
lowest point: Pacific Ocean 0 m
mean elevation: 2 m

Natural resources: phosphate (production discontinued in 1979), coconuts (copra), fish

Land use: *agricultural land:* 42% (2022 est.)
arable land: 2.5% (2022 est.)
permanent crops: 39.5% (2022 est.)
permanent pasture: 0% (2022 est.)
forest: 1.5% (2022 est.)
other: 56.6% (2022 est.)

Irrigated land: 0 sq km (2022)

Population distribution: consists of three archipelagos spread out over an area roughly the size of India; the eastern Line Islands and central Phoenix Islands are sparsely populated, but the western Gilbert Islands are some of the most densely settled places on earth, with the main island of South Tarawa boasting a population density similar to Tokyo or Hong Kong

Natural hazards: typhoons can occur any time, but usually November to March; occasional tornadoes; low level of some of the islands make them sensitive to changes in sea level

Geography - note: 21 of the 33 islands are inhabited; Banaba (Ocean Island) in Kiribati is one of the three great phosphate rock islands in the Pacific Ocean – the others are Makatea in French Polynesia, and Nauru; Kiribati is the only country in the world to fall into all four hemispheres (northern, southern, eastern, and western)

PEOPLE AND SOCIETY

Population: *total:* 116,545 (2024 est.)
male: 56,364
female: 60,181
comparison rankings: total 189; male 190; female 189

Nationality: *noun:* I-Kiribati (singular and plural)
adjective: Kiribati

Ethnic groups: I-Kiribati 95.78%, I-Kiribati/mixed 3.8%, Tuvaluan 0.2%, other 1.7% (2020 est.)

Languages: Gilbertese, English (official)

Religions: Roman Catholic 58.9%, Kiribati Uniting Church 21.2%, Kiribati Protestant Church 8.4%, Church of Jesus Christ 5.6%, Seventh Day Adventist 2.1%, Baha'i 2.1%, other 1.7% (2020 est.)

Age structure: *0-14 years:* 26.8% (male 15,895/female 15,304)
15-64 years: 67.9% (male 38,046/female 41,059)
65 years and over: 5.4% (2024 est.) (male 2,423/female 3,818)

Dependency ratios: *total dependency ratio:* 47.3 (2024 est.)
youth dependency ratio: 39.4 (2024 est.)
elderly dependency ratio: 7.9 (2024 est.)
potential support ratio: 12.7 (2024 est.)

Median age: *total:* 27.3 years (2024 est.)
male: 26.4 years
female: 28.2 years
comparison ranking: total 160

Population growth rate: 1% (2024 est.)
comparison ranking: 91

Birth rate: 19.7 births/1,000 population (2024 est.)
comparison ranking: 70

Death rate: 6.9 deaths/1,000 population (2024 est.)
comparison ranking: 125

Net migration rate: -2.8 migrant(s)/1,000 population (2024 est.)
comparison ranking: 176

Population distribution: consists of three archipelagos spread out over an area roughly the size of India; the eastern Line Islands and central Phoenix Islands are sparsely populated, but the western Gilbert Islands are some of the most densely settled places on earth, with the main island of South Tarawa boasting a population density similar to Tokyo or Hong Kong

Urbanization: *urban population:* 57.8% of total population (2023)
rate of urbanization: 2.77% annual rate of change (2020-25 est.)

Major urban areas - population: 64,000 TARAWA (capital) (2018)

Sex ratio: *at birth:* 1.05 male(s)/female
0-14 years: 1.04 male(s)/female
15-64 years: 0.93 male(s)/female
65 years and over: 0.63 male(s)/female
total population: 0.94 male(s)/female (2024 est.)

Mother's mean age at first birth: 23.1 years (2009 est.)
note: data represents median age at first birth among women 25-29

Maternal mortality ratio: 80 deaths/100,000 live births (2023 est.)
comparison ranking: 73

Infant mortality rate: *total:* 31.5 deaths/1,000 live births (2024 est.)
male: 33.5 deaths/1,000 live births
female: 29.4 deaths/1,000 live births
comparison ranking: total 45

Life expectancy at birth: *total population:* 68.5 years (2024 est.)
male: 65.9 years
female: 71.3 years
comparison ranking: total population 188

Total fertility rate: 2.15 children born/woman (2024 est.)

comparison ranking: 91

Gross reproduction rate: 1.05 (2024 est.)

Drinking water source: *improved: urban:* 87.9% of population (2022 est.)
rural: 59.5% of population (2022 est.)
total: 75.7% of population (2022 est.)
unimproved: urban: 12.1% of population (2022 est.)
rural: 40.5% of population (2022 est.)
total: 24.3% of population (2022 est.)

Health expenditure: 14.8% of GDP (2021)
9.7% of national budget (2022 est.)

Physician density: 0.2 physicians/1,000 population (2013)

Hospital bed density: 1.9 beds/1,000 population (2016 est.)

Sanitation facility access: *improved: urban:* 72.6% of population (2022 est.)
rural: 48.1% of population (2022 est.)
total: 62.1% of population (2022 est.)
unimproved: urban: 27.4% of population (2022 est.)
rural: 51.9% of population (2022 est.)
total: 37.9% of population (2022 est.)

Obesity - adult prevalence rate: 46% (2016)
comparison ranking: 9

Alcohol consumption per capita: *total:* 0.43 liters of pure alcohol (2019 est.)
beer: 0.26 liters of pure alcohol (2019 est.)
wine: 0 liters of pure alcohol (2019 est.)
spirits: 0.17 liters of pure alcohol (2019 est.)
other alcohols: 0 liters of pure alcohol (2019 est.)
comparison ranking: total 165

Tobacco use: *total:* 35.4% (2025 est.)
male: 48.4% (2025 est.)
female: 23.6% (2025 est.)
comparison ranking: total 9

Children under the age of 5 years underweight: 6.9% (2018/19)
comparison ranking: 61

Currently married women (ages 15-49): 67.6% (2023 est.)

Child marriage: *women married by age 15:* 2.4% (2019)
women married by age 18: 18.4% (2019)
men married by age 18: 8.6% (2019)

Education expenditure: 16.4% of GDP (2023 est.)
13.5% national budget (2023 est.)
comparison ranking: Education expenditure (% GDP) 1

Literacy: *total population:* 98% (2018 est.)
male: 97.3% (2018 est.)
female: 98.6% (2018 est.)

ENVIRONMENT

Environmental issues: heavy pollution in lagoon of south Tarawa atoll due to overcrowding mixed with traditional practices such as lagoon latrines and open-pit dumping; coastal erosion

International environmental agreements: *party to:* Biodiversity, Climate Change, Climate Change-Kyoto Protocol, Climate Change-Paris Agreement, Comprehensive Nuclear Test Ban, Desertification, Hazardous Wastes, Law of the Sea, Marine Dumping-London Convention, Ozone Layer Protection, Ship Pollution, Wetlands, Whaling
signed, but not ratified: none of the selected agreements

Climate: tropical; marine, hot and humid, moderated by trade winds

Urbanization: *urban population:* 57.8% of total population (2023)
rate of urbanization: 2.77% annual rate of change (2020-25 est.)

Carbon dioxide emissions: 81,000 metric tonnes of CO2 (2023 est.)
from petroleum and other liquids: 81,000 metric tonnes of CO2 (2023 est.)
comparison ranking: total emissions 210

Particulate matter emissions: 8 micrograms per cubic meter (2019 est.)

Waste and recycling: *municipal solid waste generated annually:* 35,700 tons (2024 est.)
percent of municipal solid waste recycled: 15.4% (2022 est.)

GOVERNMENT

Country name: *conventional long form:* Republic of Kiribati
conventional short form: Kiribati
local long form: Republic of Kiribati
local short form: Kiribati
former: Gilbert Islands
etymology: the name is the local pronunciation of "Gilbert," the former designation of the islands; originally named after explorer Thomas GILBERT, who mapped many of the islands in 1788
note: pronounced keer-ree-bahss

Government type: presidential republic

Capital: *name:* Tarawa
geographic coordinates: 1 21 N, 173 02 E
time difference: UTC+12 (17 hours ahead of Washington, DC, during Standard Time)
time zone note: Kiribati has three time zones: the Gilbert Islands group at UTC+12, the Phoenix Islands at UTC+13, and the Line Islands at UTC+14
etymology: the name is said to derive from the I-Kiribati words *te* (the) and *rawa* (run), referring to a channel through a nearby reef

Administrative divisions: *3 geographical units:* Gilbert Islands, Line Islands, Phoenix Islands; there are no first-order administrative divisions, but the 6 districts are Banaba, Central Gilberts, Line Islands, Northern Gilberts, Southern Gilberts, Tarawa, with 21 island councils on Abaiang, Abemama, Aranuka, Arorae, Banaba, Beru, Butaritari, Kanton, Kiritimati, Kuria, Maiana, Makin, Marakei, Nikunau, Nonouti, Onotoa, Tabiteuea, Tabuaeran, Tamana, Tarawa, Teraina

Legal system: English common law supplemented by customary law

Constitution: *history:* The Gilbert and Ellice Islands Order in Council 1915, The Gilbert Islands Order in Council 1975 (pre-independence); latest promulgated 12 July 1979 (at independence)
amendment process: proposed by the House of Assembly; passage requires two-thirds majority vote by the Assembly membership; passage of amendments affecting the constitutional section on amendment procedures and parts of the constitutional chapter on citizenship requires deferral of the proposal to the next Assembly meeting where approval is required by at least two-thirds majority vote of the Assembly membership and support of the nominated or elected Banaban member of the Assembly; amendments affecting the protection of fundamental rights and freedoms also requires approval by at least two-thirds majority in a referendum

International law organization participation: has not submitted an ICJ jurisdiction declaration; non-party state to the ICCt

Citizenship: *citizenship by birth:* no
citizenship by descent only: at least one parent must be a native-born citizen of Kiribati
dual citizenship recognized: no
residency requirement for naturalization: 7 years

Suffrage: 18 years of age; universal

Executive branch: *chief of state:* President Taneti MAAMAU (since 11 March 2016)
head of government: President Taneti MAAMAU (since 11 March 2016)
cabinet: Cabinet appointed by the president from among House of Assembly members
election/appointment process: president directly elected for a 4-year term (eligible for 2 additional terms) by simple-majority popular vote, after candidates are nominated from among House of Assembly members; vice president appointed by the president
most recent election date: 25 October 2024
election results: *2024:* Taneti MAAMAU reelected president; percent of vote - Taneti MAAMAU (TKP) 55%, Kaotitaake KOKORIA (independent) 42%, Bautaake BEIA (TKP) 3%
2020: Taneti MAAMAU reelected president; percent of vote - Taneti MAAMAU (TKP) 59.3%, Banuera BERINA (BKM) 40.7%
expected date of next election: 2028
note: the president is both chief of state and head of government

Legislative branch: *legislature name:* House of Assembly (Maneaba Ni Maungatabu)
legislative structure: unicameral
number of seats: 45 (44 directly elected; 1 appointed)
electoral system: plurality/majority
scope of elections: full renewal
term in office: 4 years
most recent election date: 8/14/2024 to 8/19/2024
percentage of women in chamber: 11.1%
expected date of next election: August 2028

Judicial branch: *highest court(s):* High Court (consists of a chief justice and other judges as prescribed by the president)
judge selection and term of office: chief justice appointed by the president on the advice of the cabinet in consultation with the Public Service Commission (PSC); other judges appointed by the president on the advice of the chief justice along with the PSC
subordinate courts: Court of Appeal; magistrates' courts

Political parties: Boutokaan Kiribati Moa Party or BKM
Kiribati Moa Party or KMP
Kamanoan Kiribati Party or KKP
Tobwaan Kiribati Party or TKP

Diplomatic representation in the US: *chief of mission:* Ambassador Teburoro TITO (since 24 January 2018); note - also Permanent Representative to the UN
chancery: 685 Third Avenue, Suite 1109, New York, NY 10017
telephone: [1] (212) 867-3310

FAX: [1] (212) 867-3320
email address and website: Kimission.newyork@mfa.gov.ki

Diplomatic representation from the US: *chief of mission:* Ambassador Marie DAMOUR (since 6 December 2022); note - Ambassador DAMOUR is based in the US Embassy in the Republic of Fiji and is accredited to Kiribati as well as Nauru, Tonga, and Tuvalu

Note: the US does not have an embassy in Kiribati but has announced its intention to open an embassy

International organization participation: ABEDA, ACP, ADB, AOSIS, C, FAO, IBRD, ICAO, ICRM, IDA, IFAD, IFC, IFRCS, ILO, IMF, IMO, IOC, ITU, ITUC (NGOs), OPCW, PIF, Sparteca, SPC, UN, UNCTAD, UNDP, UNESCO, UPU, WHO, WIPO, WMO

Independence: 12 July 1979 (from the UK)

National holiday: Independence Day, 12 July (1979)

Flag: *description:* the upper half is red with a yellow frigatebird flying over a yellow rising sun, and the lower half is blue with three wavy horizontal white stripes to represent the Pacific Ocean
meaning: the white stripes represent the Gilbert, Line, and Phoenix island groups; the 17 rays of the sun represent the 16 Gilbert Islands and Banaba (formerly Ocean Island); the frigatebird symbolizes authority and freedom

National symbol(s): frigatebird

National color(s): red, white, blue, yellow

National anthem(s): *title:* "Teirake kaini Kiribati" (Stand Up, Kiribati)
lyrics/music: Urium Tamuera IOTEBA
history: adopted 1979

National heritage: *total World Heritage Sites:* 1 (natural)
selected World Heritage Site locales: Phoenix Islands Protected Area

ECONOMY

Economic overview: lower-middle income, Pacific island economy; environmentally fragile; sizable remittances; key phosphate mining fund; tourism and fishing industries; public sector-dominated economy; recent withdrawal from Pacific Islands Forum; ongoing constitutional crisis

Real GDP (purchasing power parity): $438.143 million (2024 est.)
$416.221 million (2023 est.)
$405.468 million (2022 est.)
note: data in 2021 dollars
comparison ranking: 210

Real GDP growth rate: 5.3% (2024 est.)
2.7% (2023 est.)
4.6% (2022 est.)
note: annual GDP % growth based on constant local currency
comparison ranking: 33

Real GDP per capita: $3,300 (2024 est.)
$3,100 (2023 est.)
$3,100 (2022 est.)
note: data in 2021 dollars
comparison ranking: 190

GDP (official exchange rate): $307.863 million (2024 est.)
note: data in current dollars at official exchange rate

Inflation rate (consumer prices): 9.3% (2023 est.)
5.3% (2022 est.)
2.1% (2021 est.)
note: annual % change based on consumer prices
comparison ranking: 175

GDP - composition, by sector of origin: *agriculture:* 27.8% (2022 est.)
industry: 9.9% (2022 est.)
services: 65.7% (2022 est.)
comparison rankings: agriculture 15; industry 187; services 51

GDP - composition, by end use: *household consumption:* 101.2% (2022 est.)
government consumption: 61.7% (2022 est.)
investment in fixed capital: 19.1% (2022 est.)
investment in inventories: 1.3% (2022 est.)
exports of goods and services: 7.6% (2022 est.)
imports of goods and services: -100.5% (2022 est.)
note: figures may not total 100% due to rounding or gaps in data collection

Agricultural products: coconuts, bananas, vegetables, taro, tropical fruits, pork, chicken, nuts, eggs, pork offal (2023)
note: top ten agricultural products based on tonnage

Industries: fishing, handicrafts

Industrial production growth rate: -6.2% (2022 est.)
note: annual % change in industrial value added based on constant local currency
comparison ranking: 183

Population below poverty line: 21.9% (2019 est.)
note: % of population with income below national poverty line
Gini Index coefficient - distribution of family income 27.8 (2019 est.)
note: index (0-100) of income distribution; higher values represent greater inequality
comparison ranking: 133

Household income or consumption by percentage share: *lowest 10%:* 4% (2019 est.)
highest 10%: 22.8% (2019 est.)
note: % share of income accruing to lowest and highest 10% of population

Remittances: 4% of GDP (2023 est.)
10.4% of GDP (2022 est.)
4.7% of GDP (2021 est.)
note: personal transfers and compensation between resident and non-resident individuals/households/entities

Budget: *revenues:* $260.557 million (2023 est.)
expenditures: $264.736 million (2023 est.)
note: central government revenues (excluding grants) and expenditures converted to US dollars at average official exchange rate for year indicated

Taxes and other revenues: 17.7% (of GDP) (2023 est.)
note: central government tax revenue as a % of GDP
comparison ranking: 69

Current account balance: -$5.117 million (2023 est.)
-$32.523 million (2022 est.)
$20.251 million (2021 est.)
note: balance of payments - net trade and primary/secondary income in current dollars
comparison ranking: 86

Exports: $17.099 million (2023 est.)
$20.58 million (2022 est.)
$10.754 million (2021 est.)
note: balance of payments - exports of goods and services in current dollars
comparison ranking: 211

Exports - partners: Thailand 85%, Japan 6%, Philippines 3%, UAE 2%, Fiji 1% (2023)
note: top five export partners based on percentage share of exports

Exports - commodities: fish, coconut oil (2023)
note: top export commodities based on value in dollars over $500,000

Imports: $293.624 million (2023 est.)
$272.004 million (2022 est.)
$201.984 million (2021 est.)
note: balance of payments - imports of goods and services in current dollars
comparison ranking: 206

Imports - partners: China 24%, Australia 20%, Fiji 15%, Japan 7%, NZ 6% (2023)
note: top five import partners based on percentage share of imports

Imports - commodities: ships, centrifuges, refined petroleum, rice, raw sugar (2023)
note: top five import commodities based on value in dollars

Exchange rates: Australian dollars (AUD) per US dollar -

Exchange rates: 1.515 (2024 est.)
1.505 (2023 est.)
1.442 (2022 est.)
1.331 (2021 est.)
1.453 (2020 est.)
note: the Australian dollar circulates as legal tender

ENERGY

Electricity access: *electrification - total population:* 94.4% (2022 est.)
electrification - urban areas: 86%
electrification - rural areas: 94.3% (2020 est.)

Electricity: *installed generating capacity:* 12,000 kW (2023 est.)
consumption: 27.388 million kWh (2023 est.)
transmission/distribution losses: 5 million kWh (2023 est.)
comparison rankings: installed generating capacity 207; consumption 207; transmission/distribution losses 9

Electricity generation sources: *fossil fuels:* 81.5% of total installed capacity (2023 est.)
solar: 18.5% of total installed capacity (2023 est.)

Petroleum: *refined petroleum consumption:* 500 bbl/day (2023 est.)

Energy consumption per capita: 8.578 million Btu/person (2023 est.)
comparison ranking: 154

COMMUNICATIONS

Telephones - fixed lines: *total subscriptions:* 0 (2023 est.)
subscriptions per 100 inhabitants: (2023 est.) less than 1
comparison ranking: total subscriptions 223

Telephones - mobile cellular: *total subscriptions:* 70,000 (2023 est.)
subscriptions per 100 inhabitants: 49 (2022 est.)
comparison ranking: total subscriptions 198

Broadcast media: multi-channel TV packages provide access to Australian and US stations; 1 government-operated radio station broadcasts on AM, FM, and shortwave (2017)

Internet country code: .ki

Internet users: *percent of population:* 88% (2023 est.)

Broadband - fixed subscriptions: *total:* 0 (2023 est.)
subscriptions per 100 inhabitants: (2023 est.) less than 1
comparison ranking: total 217

TRANSPORTATION

Civil aircraft registration country code prefix: T3

Airports: 21 (2025)
comparison ranking: 133

Merchant marine: *total:* 74 (2023)
by type: bulk carrier 2, general cargo 24, oil tanker 11, other 37
comparison ranking: total 104

Ports: *total ports:* 3 (2024)
large: 0
medium: 0
small: 0
very small: 3
ports with oil terminals: 0
key ports: Canton Island, English Harbor, Tarawa Atoll

MILITARY AND SECURITY

Military and security forces: Kiribati Police Service (includes Maritime Police) (2025)

Military - note: Australia, NZ, and the US have provided security assistance; Kiribati has a "ship rider" agreement with the US, which allows local maritime law enforcement officers to embark on US Coast Guard (USCG) and US Navy (USN) vessels, including to board and search vessels suspected of violating laws or regulations within Kiribati's designated exclusive economic zone (EEZ) or on the high seas; ship rider agreements also enable USCG personnel and USN vessels with embarked USCG law enforcement personnel to work with host nations to protect critical regional resources (2025)

KOREA, NORTH

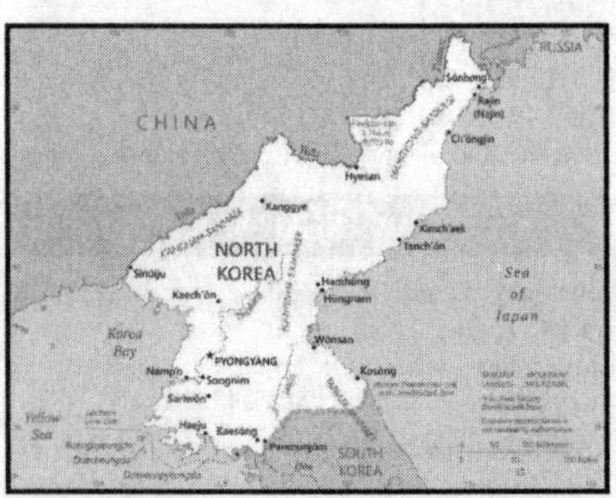

INTRODUCTION

Background: The first recorded kingdom (Choson) on the Korean Peninsula dates from approximately 2300 B.C. Over the subsequent centuries, three main kingdoms – Kogoryo, Paekche, and Silla – were established on the Peninsula. By the 5th century A.D., Kogoryo emerged as the most powerful, with control over much of the Peninsula and part of Manchuria (modern-day northeast China). However, Silla allied with the Chinese to create the first unified Korean state in 688. Following the collapse of Silla in the 9th century, Korea was unified under the Koryo (Goryeo; 918-1392) and the Chosen (Joseon; 1392-1910) dynasties. Korea became the object of intense imperialistic rivalry among the Chinese (its traditional benefactor), Japanese, and Russian empires in the latter half of the 19th and early 20th centuries. After the Sino-Japanese War (1894-95) and the Russo-Japanese War (1904-05), Korea was occupied by Imperial Japan. In 1910, Japan formally annexed the entire peninsula. After World War II, the northern half came under Soviet-sponsored communist control.

In 1948, North Korea (formally known as the Democratic People's Republic of Korea or DPRK) was founded under President KIM Il Sung, who consolidated power and cemented autocratic one-party rule under the Korean Worker's Party (KWP). North Korea failed to conquer UN-backed South Korea (formally the Republic of Korea or ROK) during the Korean War (1950-53), after which a demilitarized zone separated the two Koreas. KIM's authoritarian rule included tight control over North Korean citizens and the demonization of the US as the central threat to North Korea's political and social system. In addition, he molded the country's economic, military, and political policies around the core objective of unifying Korea under Pyongyang's control. North Korea also declared a central ideology of *juche* ("self-reliance") as a check against outside influence, while continuing to rely heavily on China and the Soviet Union for economic support. KIM Il Sung's son, KIM Jong Il, was officially designated as his father's successor in 1980, and he assumed a growing political and managerial role until the elder KIM's death in 1994. Under KIM Jong Il's reign, North Korea continued developing nuclear weapons and ballistic missiles. KIM Jong Un was publicly unveiled as his father's successor in 2010. Following KIM Jong Il's death in 2011, KIM Jong Un quickly assumed power and has since occupied the regime's highest political and military posts.

After the end of Soviet aid in 1991, North Korea faced serious economic setbacks that exacerbated decades of economic mismanagement and resource misallocation. Since the mid-1990s, North Korea has faced chronic food shortages and economic stagnation. In recent years, the North's domestic agricultural production has improved but still falls far short of producing sufficient food for its population. Starting in 2002, North Korea began to tolerate semi-private markets but has made few other efforts to meet its goal of improving the overall standard of living. New economic development plans in the 2010s failed to meet government-mandated goals for key industrial sectors, food production, or overall economic performance. At the onset of the COVID-19 pandemic in 2020, North Korea instituted a nationwide lockdown that severely restricted its economy and international engagement. Since then, KIM has repeatedly expressed concerns with the regime's economic failures and food problems, but in 2021, he vowed to continue "self-reliant" policies and has reinvigorated his pursuit of greater regime control of the economy.

As of 2024, despite slowly renewing cross-border trade with China, North Korea remained one of the world's most isolated countries and one of Asia's poorest. In 2024, Pyongyang announced it was ending all economic cooperation with South Korea. The move followed earlier proclamations that it was scrapping a 2018 military pact with South Korea to de-escalate tensions along their militarized border, abandoning the country's decades-long pursuit of peaceful unification with South Korea, and designating the South as North Korea's "principal enemy."

GEOGRAPHY

Location: Eastern Asia, northern half of the Korean Peninsula bordering the Korea Bay and the Sea of Japan, between China and South Korea

Geographic coordinates: 40 00 N, 127 00 E

Map references: Asia

Area: *total:* 120,538 sq km
land: 120,408 sq km
water: 130 sq km
comparison ranking: total 99

Area - comparative: slightly larger than Virginia; slightly smaller than Mississippi

Land boundaries: *total:* 1,607 km
border countries (3): China 1,352 km; South Korea 237 km; Russia 18 km

Coastline: 2,495 km

Maritime claims: *territorial sea:* 12 nm
exclusive economic zone: 200 nm
note: military boundary line 50 nm in the Sea of Japan and the exclusive economic zone limit in the Yellow Sea where all foreign vessels and aircraft without permission are banned

Climate: temperate, with rainfall concentrated in summer; long, bitter winters

Terrain: mostly hills and mountains separated by deep, narrow valleys; wide coastal plains in west, discontinuous in east

Elevation: *highest point:* Paektu-san 2,744 m
lowest point: Sea of Japan 0 m
mean elevation: 600 m

Natural resources: coal, iron ore, limestone, magnesite, graphite, copper, zinc, lead, precious metals, hydropower

Land use: *agricultural land:* 21.5% (2022 est.)
arable land: 19.1% (2022 est.)
permanent crops: 2.1% (2022 est.)
permanent pasture: 0.4% (2022 est.)
forest: 49.7% (2022 est.)
other: 28.7% (2022 est.)

Irrigated land: 14,600 sq km (2012)

Population distribution: population concentrated in the plains and lowlands; least-populated regions are the mountainous provinces adjacent to the Chinese border; largest concentrations are in the western provinces, particularly the municipal district of Pyongyang, and around Hungnam and Wonsan in the east

Natural hazards: late spring droughts often followed by severe flooding; occasional typhoons during the early fall
volcanism: P'aektu-san (2,744 m) (also known as Baitoushan, Baegdu, or Changbaishan), on the Chinese border, is considered historically active

Geography - note: strategic location bordering China, South Korea, and Russia; mountainous interior is isolated and sparsely populated

PEOPLE AND SOCIETY

Population: *total:* 26,298,666 (2024 est.)
male: 12,828,269
female: 13,470,397
comparison rankings: total 56; male 56; female 54

Nationality: *noun:* Korean(s)
adjective: Korean

Ethnic groups: racially homogeneous; there is a small Chinese community and a few ethnic Japanese

Languages: Korean
major-language sample(s):
월드 팩트북, 필수적인 기본 정보 제공처
(Korean)

Religions: traditionally Buddhist and Confucian, some Christian and syncretic Chondogyo (Religion of the Heavenly Way)
note: autonomous religious activities now almost nonexistent; government-sponsored religious groups exist to provide illusion of religious freedom

Age structure: *0-14 years:* 19.9% (male 2,673,822/female 2,548,775)
15-64 years: 68.9% (male 9,054,771/female 9,066,447)
65 years and over: 11.2% (2024 est.) (male 1,099,676/female 1,855,175)

Dependency ratios: *total dependency ratio:* 45.1 (2024 est.)
youth dependency ratio: 28.8 (2024 est.)
elderly dependency ratio: 16.3 (2024 est.)
potential support ratio: 6.1 (2024 est.)

Median age: *total:* 35.9 years (2024 est.)
male: 34.5 years
female: 37.4 years
comparison ranking: total 94

Population growth rate: 0.4% (2024 est.)
comparison ranking: 158

Birth rate: 13.2 births/1,000 population (2024 est.)
comparison ranking: 130

Death rate: 9.2 deaths/1,000 population (2024 est.)
comparison ranking: 55

Net migration rate: 0 migrant(s)/1,000 population (2024 est.)
comparison ranking: 91

Population distribution: population concentrated in the plains and lowlands; least-populated regions are the mountainous provinces adjacent to the Chinese border; largest concentrations are in the western provinces, particularly the municipal district of Pyongyang, and around Hungnam and Wonsan in the east

Urbanization: *urban population:* 63.2% of total population (2023)
rate of urbanization: 0.85% annual rate of change (2020-25 est.)

Major urban areas - population: 3.158 million PYONGYANG (capital) (2023)

Sex ratio: *at birth:* 1.06 male(s)/female
0-14 years: 1.05 male(s)/female
15-64 years: 1 male(s)/female
65 years and over: 0.59 male(s)/female
total population: 0.95 male(s)/female (2024 est.)

Maternal mortality ratio: 67 deaths/100,000 live births (2023 est.)
comparison ranking: 81

Infant mortality rate: *total:* 15.4 deaths/1,000 live births (2024 est.)
male: 16.9 deaths/1,000 live births
female: 13.8 deaths/1,000 live births
comparison ranking: total 89

Life expectancy at birth: *total population:* 73.5 years (2024 est.)
male: 70.2 years
female: 77 years
comparison ranking: total population 150

Total fertility rate: 1.81 children born/woman (2024 est.)
comparison ranking: 138

Gross reproduction rate: 0.88 (2024 est.)

Drinking water source: *improved: urban:* 96.9% of population (2022 est.)
rural: 88.8% of population (2022 est.)
total: 93.9% of population (2022 est.)
unimproved: urban: 3.1% of population (2022 est.)
rural: 11.2% of population (2022 est.)
total: 6.1% of population (2022 est.)

Physician density: 3.63 physicians/1,000 population (2017)

Sanitation facility access: *improved: urban:* 92.7% of population (2022 est.)
rural: 73.1% of population (2022 est.)
total: 85.4% of population (2022 est.)
unimproved: urban: 7.3% of population (2022 est.)
rural: 26.9% of population (2022 est.)
total: 14.6% of population (2022 est.)

Obesity - adult prevalence rate: 6.8% (2016)
comparison ranking: 163

Alcohol consumption per capita: *total:* 3.61 liters of pure alcohol (2019 est.)
beer: 0.12 liters of pure alcohol (2019 est.)
wine: 0 liters of pure alcohol (2019 est.)
spirits: 3.48 liters of pure alcohol (2019 est.)
other alcohols: 0 liters of pure alcohol (2019 est.)
comparison ranking: total 102

Tobacco use: *total:* 16% (2025 est.)
male: 32.6% (2025 est.)
female: 0% (2025 est.)
comparison ranking: total 98

Children under the age of 5 years underweight: 9.3% (2017)
comparison ranking: 55

Currently married women (ages 15-49): 69.7% (2023 est.)

Child marriage: *women married by age 15:* 0% (2017)
women married by age 18: 0.1% (2017)
men married by age 18: 0% (2017)

Education expenditure: 14.6% national budget (2025 est.)

School life expectancy (primary to tertiary education)
total: 12 years (2018 est.)
male: 12 years (2018 est.)
female: 12 years (2018 est.)

ENVIRONMENT

Environmental issues: water pollution; inadequate potable water; deforestation; soil erosion and degradation

International environmental agreements: *party to:* Antarctic Treaty, Biodiversity, Climate Change, Climate Change-Kyoto Protocol, Climate Change-Paris Agreement, Desertification, Environmental Modification, Hazardous Wastes, Ozone Layer Protection, Ship Pollution, Wetlands
signed, but not ratified: Antarctic-Environmental Protection, Law of the Sea

Climate: temperate, with rainfall concentrated in summer; long, bitter winters

Urbanization: *urban population:* 63.2% of total population (2023)
rate of urbanization: 0.85% annual rate of change (2020-25 est.)

Carbon dioxide emissions: 55.744 million metric tonnes of CO_2 (2023 est.)
from coal and metallurgical coke: 52.985 million metric tonnes of CO_2 (2023 est.)
from petroleum and other liquids: 2.759 million metric tonnes of CO_2 (2023 est.)
comparison ranking: total emissions 56

Particulate matter emissions: 41.8 micrograms per cubic meter (2019 est.)

Total water withdrawal: *municipal:* 902.8 million cubic meters (2022 est.)
industrial: 1.145 billion cubic meters (2022 est.)
agricultural: 6.61 billion cubic meters (2022 est.)

Total renewable water resources: 77.15 billion cubic meters (2022 est.)

Geoparks: *total global geoparks and regional networks:* 1 (2025)
global geoparks and regional networks: Mt Paektu (2025)

GOVERNMENT

Country name: *conventional long form:* Democratic People's Republic of Korea
conventional short form: North Korea
local long form: Choson-minjujuui-inmin-konghwaguk
local short form: Choson
abbreviation: DPRK
etymology: derived from the Chinese name for Goryeo, which was the Korean dynasty that united the peninsula in the 10th century A.D.; the North Korean name "Choson" means "[Land of the] Morning Calm"

Government type: dictatorship, single-party communist state

Capital: *name:* Pyongyang
geographic coordinates: 39 01 N, 125 45 E
time difference: UTC+9 (14 hours ahead of Washington, DC, during Standard Time)
time zone note: on 5 May 2018, North Korea reverted to UTC+9, the same time zone as South Korea
etymology: the name translates as "flat land" in Korean

Administrative divisions: 9 provinces (*do*, singular and plural) and 4 special administration cities (*si*, singular and plural)

provinces: Chagang, Hambuk (North Hamgyong), Hamnam (South Hamgyong), Hwangbuk (North Hwanghae), Hwangnam (South Hwanghae), Kangwon, P'yongbuk (North Pyongan), P'yongnam (South Pyongan), Ryanggang
special administration cities: Kaesong, Nampo, P'yongyang, Rason
note: P'yongyang is considered a directly controlled city; Kaesong, Nampo, and Rason are designated as special cities

Legal system: civil law system based on the Prussian model; influenced by Japanese traditions and Communist legal theory

Constitution: *history:* previous 1948, 1972; latest adopted 1998
amendment process: proposed by the Supreme People's Assembly (SPA); passage requires more than two-thirds majority vote of the total SPA membership

International law organization participation: has not submitted an ICJ jurisdiction declaration; non-party state to the ICCt

Citizenship: *citizenship by birth:* no
citizenship by descent only: at least one parent must be a citizen of North Korea
dual citizenship recognized: no
residency requirement for naturalization: unknown

Suffrage: 17 years of age; universal and compulsory

Executive branch: *chief of state:* State Affairs Commission President KIM Jong Un (since 17 December 2011)
head of government: Supreme People's Assembly President CHOE Ryong Hae (since 11 April 2019)
cabinet: Cabinet or Naegak members appointed by the Supreme People's Assembly, except the Minister of People's Armed Forces
election/appointment process: chief of state and premier indirectly elected by the Supreme People's Assembly
most recent election date: 11 April 2019
election results: *2019:* KIM Jong Un reelected unopposed
expected date of next election: March 2024
note 1: KIM Jong Un's titles include general secretary of the Workers' Party of Korea (KWP), chairman of the KWP Central Military Commission, president of the State Affairs Commission, and supreme commander of the Korean People's Army
note 2: in the North Korean system, KIM Jong Un's role as chief of state is secondary to his role as general secretary of the Korean Workers' Party; chief of state is used to engage with non-communist countries such as the US; North Korea revised its constitution in 2019 to define "the Chairman of the State Affairs Commission" as "the supreme leader who represents the state"; functions as the commander-in-chief and chief executive; the specific titles associated with this office have changed multiple times under KIM's tenure, but KIM Jong Un has been supreme leader since his father's death in 2011
note 3: the head of government functions as the technical head of state and performs related duties, such as receiving ambassadors' credentials

Legislative branch: *legislature name:* Supreme People's Assembly (Choe Go In Min Hoe Ui)
legislative structure: unicameral
number of seats: 687 (all directly elected)
electoral system: plurality/majority
scope of elections: full renewal
term in office: 5 years
most recent election date: 3/10/2019
percentage of women in chamber: 17.6%
expected date of next election: December 2025
note: the SPA functions as a rubberstamp legislature; the Korean Workers' Party selects all candidates

Judicial branch: *highest court(s):* Supreme Court or Central Court (consists of one judge and 2 "People's Assessors" or, for some cases, 3 judges)
judge selection and term of office: judges elected by the Supreme People's Assembly for 5-year terms
subordinate courts: lower provincial courts as determined by the Supreme People's Assembly

Political parties: *major parties:* Korean Workers' Party or KWP (formally known as Workers' Party of Korea)
General Association of Korean Residents in Japan (Chongryon; under KWP control)
minor parties: Chondoist Chongu Party (under KWP control)
Social Democratic Party or KSDP (under KWP control)

Diplomatic representation in the US: none
note: North Korea has a Permanent Mission to the UN in New York

Diplomatic representation from the US: *embassy:* none; the Swedish Embassy in Pyongyang represents the US as consular protecting power

International organization participation: ARF, FAO, G-77, ICAO, ICRM, IFAD, IFRCS, IHO, IMO, IMSO, IOC, IPU, ISO, ITSO, ITU, NAM, UN, UNCTAD, UNESCO, UNIDO, UNWTO, UPU, WFTU (NGOs), WHO, WIPO, WMO

Independence: 15 August 1945 (from Japan)

National holiday: Founding of the Democratic People's Republic of Korea (DPRK), 9 September (1948)

Flag: *description:* three horizontal bands of blue (top), red (triple-width), and blue; the red band is edged in white; on the left side of the red band is a white disk with a red five-pointed star
meaning: the red band stands for revolutionary traditions, the white for purity, strength, and dignity; blue for sovereignty, peace, and friendship; the red star represents socialism

National symbol(s): red star, chollima (winged horse)

National color(s): red, white, blue

National anthem(s): *title:* "Aegukka" (Patriotic Song)
lyrics/music: PAK Se Yong/KIM Won Gyun
history: adopted 1947; North Korea's and South Korea's anthems have the same name and a similar melody, but different lyrics; the North Korean anthem is also known as "Ach'imun pinnara" (Let Morning Shine)

National heritage: *total World Heritage Sites:* 2 (both cultural)
selected World Heritage Site locales: Koguryo Tombs Complex; Historic Monuments and Sites in Kaesong

ECONOMY

Economic overview: one of the last centrally planned economies; hard hit by COVID-19, crop failures, international sanctions, and isolationist policies; declining growth and trade, and heavily reliant on China; poor exchange rate stability; economic data integrity issues

Real GDP (purchasing power parity): $15.416 billion (2023 est.)
$14.959 billion (2022 est.)
$14.982 billion (2021 est.)
note: data in 2015 dollars
comparison ranking: 158

Real GDP per capita: $600 (2023 est.)
$600 (2022 est.)
$600 (2021 est.)
note: data in 2015 dollars
comparison ranking: 217

GDP (official exchange rate): $16.447 billion (2023 est.)
note: data in current dollars at official exchange rate

Agricultural products: maize, vegetables, rice, apples, cabbages, fruits, sweet potatoes, potatoes, beans, soybeans (2023)
note: top ten agricultural products based on tonnage

Industries: military products; machine building, electric power, chemicals; mining (coal, iron ore, limestone, magnesite, graphite, copper, zinc, lead, and precious metals), metallurgy; textiles, food processing; tourism

Labor force: 17.637 million (2024 est.)
note: number of people ages 15 or older who are employed or seeking work
comparison ranking: 38

Unemployment rate: 2.9% (2024 est.)
2.9% (2023 est.)
2.9% (2022 est.)
note: % of labor force seeking employment
comparison ranking: 37

Youth unemployment rate (ages 15-24): *total:* 6.8% (2024 est.)
male: 6.1% (2024 est.)
female: 7.4% (2024 est.)
note: % of labor force ages 15-24 seeking employment
comparison ranking: total 149

Exports - partners: China 74%, Poland 3%, Senegal 3%, Angola 3%, Austria 3% (2023)
note: top five export partners based on percentage share of exports

Exports - commodities: fake hair, iron alloys, tungsten ore, electricity, cars (2023)
note: top five export commodities based on value in dollars

Imports - partners: China 97%, Togo 1%, Peru 1%, Gabon 1%, India 0% (2023)
note: top five import partners based on percentage share of imports

Imports - commodities: processed hair, plastic products, garments, fabric, soybean oil (2023)
note: top five import commodities based on value in dollars

Exchange rates: North Korean won (KPW) per US dollar (average market rate)

Exchange rates: 135 (2017 est.)
130 (2016 est.)
130 (2015 est.)

ENERGY

Electricity access: *electrification - total population:* 54.7% (2022 est.)

Electricity: *installed generating capacity:* 8.357 million kW (2023 est.)
consumption: 22.448 billion kWh (2023 est.)
transmission/distribution losses: 4.101 billion kWh (2023 est.)
comparison rankings: installed generating capacity 71; consumption 73; transmission/distribution losses 154

Electricity generation sources: *fossil fuels:* 36.9% of total installed capacity (2023 est.)
solar: 0.6% of total installed capacity (2023 est.)

hydroelectricity: 62.5% of total installed capacity (2023 est.)

Coal: *production:* 21.928 million metric tons (2023 est.)
consumption: 22.105 million metric tons (2023 est.)
proven reserves: 10.6 billion metric tons (2023 est.)

Petroleum: *refined petroleum consumption:* 18,000 bbl/day (2023 est.)

Energy consumption per capita: 23.83 million Btu/person (2023 est.)
comparison ranking: 126

COMMUNICATIONS

Telephones - fixed lines: *total subscriptions:* 1.18 million (2021 est.)
subscriptions per 100 inhabitants: 4 (2022 est.)
comparison ranking: total subscriptions 66

Telephones - mobile cellular: *total subscriptions:* 6 million (2021 est.)
subscriptions per 100 inhabitants: 23 (2021 est.)
comparison ranking: total subscriptions 120

Broadcast media: no independent media; radios and TVs are pre-tuned to government stations; 4 state-owned TV stations; the Korean Workers' Party owns and operates the Korean Central Broadcasting Station, and the state-run Voice of Korea operates an external broadcast service; the government prohibits listening to and jams foreign broadcasts (2019)

Internet country code: .kp

TRANSPORTATION

Civil aircraft registration country code prefix: P

Airports: 81 (2025)
comparison ranking: 66

Heliports: 8 (2025)
comparison ranking: 82

Railways: *total:* 7,435 km (2014)
standard gauge: 7,435 km (2014) 1.435-m gauge (5,400 km electrified)
note: figures are approximate; some narrow-gauge railway also exists

Merchant marine: *total:* 264 (2023)
by type: bulk carrier 10, container ship 5, general cargo 191, oil tanker 29, other 29
comparison ranking: total 63

Ports: *total ports:* 10 (2024)
large: 0
medium: 0
small: 7
very small: 3
ports with oil terminals: 0
key ports: Ch'ongjin, Haeju Hang, Hungnam, Najin, Nampo, Senbong, Wonsan

MILITARY AND SECURITY

Military and security forces: Korean People's Army (KPA): KPA Ground Forces, KPA Navy, KPA Air Force and Air Defense Forces, KPA Strategic Forces (missile forces), KPA Special Forces (special operations forces); Security Guard Command (aka Bodyguard Command); Military Security Command

Ministry of Social Security (formerly Ministry of Public Security): Border Guard General Bureau, civil security forces; Ministry of State Security: internal security, investigations (2024)
note 1: North Korea employs a systematic and intentional overlap of powers and responsibilities among its multiple internal security organizations to prevent any potential subordinate consolidation of power and assure that each unit provided a check and balance on the other
note 2: Kim Jong Un is the KPA supreme commander, while operational control of the armed forces resides in the General Staff Department (GSD), which reports directly to Kim; the GSD maintains overall control of all military forces and is charged with turning Kim's directives into operational military orders; the Ministry of National Defense (MND) is responsible for administrative control of the military and external relations with foreign militaries
note 3: the Security Guard Command protects the Kim family, other senior leadership figures, and government facilities
note 4: the North also has a large paramilitary/militia force organized into the Worker Peasant Red Guard and Red Youth Guard; these organizations are present at all levels of government (province, county, ward) and are under the control of the Korean Workers' Party in peacetime, but revert to KPA control in crisis or war; they are often mobilized for domestic projects, such as road building and agricultural support

Military expenditures: defense spending is a regime priority; between 2010 and 2020, military expenditures accounted for an estimated 20-30% of North Korea's GDP annually; spending estimates ranged from $7 billion to $11 billion annually; in 2024, North Korea announced that it would spend nearly 16% of state expenditures on defense; North Korea in the 2010s and 2020s has increasingly relied on illicit activities — including cybercrime — to generate revenue for its weapons of mass destruction and ballistic missile programs to evade US and UN sanctions

Military and security service personnel strengths: estimates vary; as many as 1.3 million active-duty Korean People's Army (2025)

Military equipment inventories and acquisitions: the KPA is equipped with older weapon systems originally acquired from the former Soviet Union, Russia, and China, and some domestically produced equipment; North Korea produces a diverse array of military hardware, including small arms, munitions, light armored vehicles, tanks, naval vessels and submarines, and some advanced weapons systems, such as cruise and ballistic missiles; most are copies or upgrades of older foreign supplied equipment (2024)
note: since 2006, the UN Security Council has passed nearly a dozen resolutions sanctioning North Korea for developing nuclear weapons and related activities, starting with Resolution 1718, which condemned the North's first nuclear test and placed sanctions on the supply of heavy weaponry (including tanks, armored combat vehicles, large caliber artillery, combat aircraft, attack helicopters, warships, and missiles and missile launchers), missile technology and material, and select luxury goods; additional resolutions have expanded to include all arms, including small arms and light weapons; the US and other countries have also imposed unilateral sanctions

Military service age and obligation: 17 years of age for compulsory military service for men and women; service obligation varies from 5-13 years; reportedly up to 10 years (7 for women) for those serving in combat units and 13 years (7 for women) for specialized combat units, such as missile forces (2024)
note: the bulk of the KPA is made up of conscripts; as many as 20% of North Korean males between the ages of 16 and 54 are in the military at a given time and possibly up to 30 percent of males between the ages of 18 and 27, not counting the reserves or paramilitary units; women comprise about 20% of the military by some estimates

Military deployments: approximately 10-12,000 Russia (2025)

Military - note: the Korean People's Army (KPA) is one of the World's largest military forces; founded in 1948, the KPA's primary responsibilities are national defense and protection of the Kim regime; it also provides support to domestic economic projects such as agriculture production and infrastructure construction; North Korea views South Korea and the US as its primary external threats and Russia as its closest security partner
in addition to the invasion of South Korea and the subsequent Korean War (1950-53), North Korea from the 1960s to the 1980s launched a number of military and subversive actions against South Korea; including skirmishes along the DMZ, overt attempts to assassinate South Korean leaders, kidnappings, the bombing of an airliner, and a failed effort in 1968 to foment an insurrection and conduct a guerrilla war in the South with more than 100 seaborne commandos; from the 1990s until 2010, the North lost two submarines and a semi-submersible boat attempting to insert infiltrators into the South (1996, 1998) and provoked several engagements in the Northwest Islands area along the disputed Northern Limit Line (NLL), including naval skirmishes between patrol boats in 1999 and 2002, the torpedoing and sinking of a South Korean Navy corvette in 2010, and the bombardment of a South Korean military installation on Yeonpyeong Island, also in 2010; since 2010, further minor incidents continue to occur periodically along the DMZ, where both the KPA and the South Korean military maintain large numbers of troops
North Korea also has a history of provocative regional military actions and posturing that are of major concern to the international community, including: proliferation of military-related items; ballistic and cruise missile development and testing; weapons of mass destruction (WMD) programs including tests of nuclear devices in 2006, 2009, 2013, 2016, and 2017; and large conventional armed forces (2025)

SPACE

Space agency/agencies: National Aerospace Technology Administration (NATA; established 2013; re-named in 2023 from the National Aerospace Development Administration or NADA); State Space Development Bureau; Academy of National Defense Science; Ministry of People's Armed Forces (2025)
note: the predecessor of NATA/NADA was the Korean Committee of Space Technology (KCST), which was established in the 1980s

Space launch site(s): Sohae Satellite Launching Station (aka Tongch'ang-dong Space Launch Center; North Pyongan province); Tonghae Satellite Launching Ground (North Hamgyong province) (2025)

Space program overview: North Korea's leader has emphasized the development of space capabilities, particularly space launch vehicles (SLVs) and remote sensing satellites; manufactures satellites and rockets/SLVs; independently launches rockets/SLVs; SLV program is viewed as closely related to the country's development of intercontinental ballistic missiles; passed a national space law in 2013, which was revised in 2022 to allow for the use of space for

national defense purposes; has cooperated with Iran on space related technologies, and in June 2024, North Korea and Russia signed a mutual defense treaty which stated the two countries would "develop exchanges and joint research in science and technology including space" (2025)
note: further details about the key activities, programs, and milestones of the country's space program, as well as government spending estimates on the space sector, appear in the Space Programs reference guide

TRANSNATIONAL ISSUES

Trafficking in persons: *tier rating:* Tier 3 — the government of North Korea does not fully meet the minimum standards for the elimination of trafficking and is not making significant efforts to do so, therefore, North Korea remained on Tier 3; for more details, go to: https://www.state.gov/reports/2025-trafficking-in-persons-report/north-korea/

KOREA, SOUTH

INTRODUCTION

Background: The first recorded kingdom (Choson) on the Korean Peninsula dates from approximately 2300 B.C. Over the subsequent centuries, three main kingdoms – Kogoryo, Baekche, and Silla – were established on the Peninsula. By the 5th century A.D., Kogoryo emerged as the most powerful, with control over much of the Peninsula and part of Manchuria (modern-day northeast China). However, Silla allied with the Chinese to create the first unified Korean state in 688. Following the collapse of Silla in the 9th century, Korea was unified under the Koryo (Goryeo; 918-1392) and the Chosen (Joseon; 1392-1910) dynasties.

Korea became the object of intense imperialistic rivalry among the Chinese (its traditional benefactor), Japanese, and Russian empires in the latter half of the 19th and early 20th centuries. After the Sino-Japanese War (1894-95) and the Russo-Japanese War (1904-1905), Korea was occupied by Imperial Japan. In 1910, Japan formally annexed the entire Peninsula. Korea regained its independence after Japan's surrender to the US and its allies in 1945. A US-supported democratic government (Republic of Korea, ROK) was set up in the southern half of the Korean Peninsula, while a communist-style government backed by the Soviet Union was installed in the north (North Korea; aka Democratic People's Republic of Korea, DPRK). During the Korean War (1950-53), US troops and UN forces fought alongside ROK soldiers to defend South Korea from a North Korean invasion supported by communist China and the Soviet Union. After the 1953 armistice, the two Koreas were separated by a demilitarized zone.

Syngman RHEE led the country as its first president from 1948 to 1960. PARK Chung-hee took over leadership of the country in a 1961 coup. During his controversial rule (1961-79), South Korea achieved rapid economic growth, with per capita income rising to roughly 17 times the level of North Korea by 1979. PARK was assassinated in 1979, and subsequent years were marked by political turmoil and continued military rule as the country's pro-democracy movement grew. South Korea held its first free presidential election under a revised democratic constitution in 1987, with former South Korean Army general ROH Tae-woo winning a close race. In 1993, KIM Young-sam became the first civilian president of South Korea's new democratic era. President KIM Dae-jung (1998-2003) won the Nobel Peace Prize in 2000 for his contributions to South Korean democracy and his "Sunshine Policy" of engagement with North Korea. President PARK Geun-hye, daughter of former South Korean President PARK Chung-hee, took office in 2013 as South Korea's first female leader. In 2016, the National Assembly passed an impeachment motion against PARK over her alleged involvement in a corruption and influence-peddling scandal, triggering an early presidential election in 2017 won by MOON Jae-in. In 2022, longtime prosecutor and political newcomer YOON Suk Yeol won the presidency by the slimmest margin in South Korean history.

Discord and tensions with North Korea, punctuated by North Korean military provocations, missile launches, and nuclear tests, have permeated inter-Korean relations for years. Relations remained strained, despite a period of respite in 2018-2019 ushered in by North Korea's participation in the 2018 Winter Olympic and Paralympic Games in South Korea and high-level diplomatic meetings, including historic US-North Korea summits. In 2024, Pyongyang announced it was ending all economic cooperation with South Korea, a move that followed earlier proclamations that it was scrapping a 2018 military pact to de-escalate tensions along their militarized border, abandoning the country's decades-long pursuit of peaceful unification with South Korea, and designating the South as North Korea's "principal enemy."

GEOGRAPHY

Location: Eastern Asia, southern half of the Korean Peninsula bordering the Sea of Japan and the Yellow Sea

Geographic coordinates: 37 00 N, 127 30 E

Map references: Asia

Area: *total:* 99,720 sq km
land: 96,920 sq km
water: 2,800 sq km
comparison ranking: total 109

Area - comparative: slightly smaller than Pennsylvania; slightly larger than Indiana

Land boundaries: *total:* 237 km
border countries (1): North Korea 237 km

Coastline: 2,413 km

Maritime claims: *territorial sea:* 12 nm; between 3 nm and 12 nm in the Korea Strait
contiguous zone: 24 nm
exclusive economic zone: 200 nm
continental shelf: not specified

Climate: temperate, with rainfall heavier in summer than winter; cold winters

Terrain: mostly hills and mountains; wide coastal plains in west and south

Elevation: *highest point:* Halla-san 1,950 m
lowest point: Sea of Japan 0 m
mean elevation: 282 m

Natural resources: coal, tungsten, graphite, molybdenum, lead, hydropower potential

Land use: *agricultural land:* 16.2% (2022 est.)
arable land: 13.5% (2022 est.)
permanent crops: 2.1% (2022 est.)
permanent pasture: 0.6% (2022 est.)
forest: 64.2% (2022 est.)
other: 19.6% (2022 est.)

Irrigated land: 7,780 sq km (2012)

Population distribution: the population is primarily concentrated in the lowland areas, where density is high; Gyeonggi Province in the northwest, which surrounds the capital of Seoul and contains the port of Incheon, is the most densely populated province; Gangwon in the northeast is the least populated

Natural hazards: occasional typhoons bring high winds and floods; low-level seismic activity common in southwest
volcanism: Halla (1,950 m) is considered historically active; it has not erupted in many centuries

Geography - note: strategic location on Korea Strait; about 3,000 mostly small and uninhabited islands lie off the western and southern coasts

PEOPLE AND SOCIETY

Population: *total:* 52,081,799 (2024 est.)
male: 26,119,111
female: 25,962,688
comparison rankings: total 28; male 28; female 28

Nationality: *noun:* Korean(s)
adjective: Korean

Ethnic groups: homogeneous

Languages: Korean, English
major-language sample(s):

월드 팩트북, 필수적인 기본 정보 제공처

(Korean)

Religions: Protestant 17%, Buddhist 16%, Catholic 6%, none 60% (2021 est.)

note: many people also carry on at least some Confucian traditions and practices

Age structure: *0-14 years:* 11.3% (male 3,024,508/female 2,873;523)
15-64 years: 69.4% (male 18,653,915/female 17,465,817)
65 years and over: 19.3% (2024 est.) (male 4,440,688/female 5,623,348)

Dependency ratios: *total dependency ratio:* 43.6 (2024 est.)
youth dependency ratio: 15.2 (2024 est.)
elderly dependency ratio: 28.4 (2024 est.)
potential support ratio: 3.5 (2024 est.)

Median age: *total:* 45.5 years (2024 est.)
male: 44 years
female: 47.3 years
comparison ranking: total 15

Population growth rate: 0.21% (2024 est.)
comparison ranking: 175

Birth rate: 7 births/1,000 population (2024 est.)
comparison ranking: 223

Death rate: 7.4 deaths/1,000 population (2024 est.)
comparison ranking: 105

Net migration rate: 2.6 migrant(s)/1,000 population (2024 est.)
comparison ranking: 43

Population distribution: the population is primarily concentrated in the lowland areas, where density is high; Gyeonggi Province in the northwest, which surrounds the capital of Seoul and contains the port of Incheon, is the most densely populated province; Gangwon in the northeast is the least populated

Urbanization: *urban population:* 81.5% of total population (2023)
rate of urbanization: 0.31% annual rate of change (2020-25 est.)

Major urban areas - population: 9.988 million SEOUL (capital), 3.472 million Busan, 2.849 million Incheon, 2.181 million Daegu (Taegu), 1.577 million Daejon (Taejon), 1.529 million Gwangju (Kwangju) (2023)

Sex ratio: *at birth:* 1.05 male(s)/female
0-14 years: 1.05 male(s)/female
15-64 years: 1.07 male(s)/female
65 years and over: 0.79 male(s)/female
total population: 1.01 male(s)/female (2024 est.)

Mother's mean age at first birth: 32.2 years (2019 est.)

Maternal mortality ratio: 4 deaths/100,000 live births (2023 est.)
comparison ranking: 179

Infant mortality rate: *total:* 2.8 deaths/1,000 live births (2024 est.)
male: 3 deaths/1,000 live births
female: 2.6 deaths/1,000 live births
comparison ranking: total 212

Life expectancy at birth: *total population:* 83.4 years (2024 est.)
male: 80.3 years
female: 86.6 years
comparison ranking: total population 15

Total fertility rate: 1.12 children born/woman (2024 est.)
comparison ranking: 226

Gross reproduction rate: 0.55 (2024 est.)

Drinking water source: *improved:* total: 100% of population (2022 est.)
unimproved: total: 0% of population (2022 est.)

Health expenditure: 9.7% of GDP (2022)
14.1% of national budget (2022 est.)

Physician density: 2.61 physicians/1,000 population (2022)

Hospital bed density: 12.8 beds/1,000 population (2021 est.)

Sanitation facility access: *improved:* total: 99.8% of population (2022 est.)
unimproved: total: 0.2% of population (2022 est.)

Obesity - adult prevalence rate: 4.7% (2016)
comparison ranking: 184

Alcohol consumption per capita: *total:* 7.74 liters of pure alcohol (2019 est.)
beer: 1.72 liters of pure alcohol (2019 est.)
wine: 0.15 liters of pure alcohol (2019 est.)
spirits: 0.22 liters of pure alcohol (2019 est.)
other alcohols: 5.66 liters of pure alcohol (2019 est.)
comparison ranking: total 48

Tobacco use: *total:* 17.4% (2025 est.)
male: 29.7% (2025 est.)
female: 5.2% (2025 est.)
comparison ranking: total 88

Children under the age of 5 years underweight: 0.3% (2020)
comparison ranking: 116

Currently married women (ages 15-49): 52.9% (2023 est.)

Education expenditure: 4.9% of GDP (2021 est.)
comparison ranking: Education expenditure (% GDP) 69

Literacy: *total population:* NA
male: NA
female: NA

School life expectancy (primary to tertiary education): *total:* 17 years (2022 est.)
male: 17 years (2022 est.)
female: 16 years (2022 est.)

ENVIRONMENT

Environmental issues: air pollution in large cities; acid rain; water pollution from sewage and industrial effluents; drift-net fishing; solid waste disposal; transboundary air pollution from China

International environmental agreements: *party to:* Antarctic-Environmental Protection, Antarctic-Marine Living Resources, Antarctic Treaty, Biodiversity, Climate Change, Climate Change-Kyoto Protocol, Climate Change-Paris Agreement, Comprehensive Nuclear Test Ban, Desertification, Endangered Species, Environmental Modification, Hazardous Wastes, Law of the Sea, Marine Dumping-London Convention, Marine Dumping-London Protocol, Nuclear Test Ban, Ozone Layer Protection, Ship Pollution, Tropical Timber 2006, Wetlands, Whaling
signed, but not ratified: none of the selected agreements

Climate: temperate, with rainfall heavier in summer than winter; cold winters

Urbanization: *urban population:* 81.5% of total population (2023)
rate of urbanization: 0.31% annual rate of change (2020-25 est.)

Carbon dioxide emissions: 644.231 million metric tonnes of CO2 (2023 est.)
from coal and metallurgical coke: 275.411 million metric tonnes of CO2 (2023 est.)
from petroleum and other liquids: 248.599 million metric tonnes of CO2 (2023 est.)
from consumed natural gas: 120.222 million metric tonnes of CO2 (2023 est.)
comparison ranking: total emissions 9

Particulate matter emissions: 25 micrograms per cubic meter (2019 est.)

Methane emissions: *energy:* 145.7 kt (2022-2024 est.)
agriculture: 500 kt (2019-2021 est.)
waste: 478.6 kt (2019-2021 est.)
other: 27 kt (2019-2021 est.)

Waste and recycling: *municipal solid waste generated annually:* 20.453 million tons (2024 est.)
percent of municipal solid waste recycled: 67.1% (2022 est.)

Total water withdrawal: *municipal:* 6.672 billion cubic meters (2022 est.)
industrial: 4.45 billion cubic meters (2022 est.)
agricultural: 15.96 billion cubic meters (2022 est.)

Total renewable water resources: 69.7 billion cubic meters (2022 est.)

Geoparks: *total global geoparks and regional networks:* 7 (2025)
global geoparks and regional networks: Cheongsong; Danyang; Gyeongbuk Donghaean; Hantangang; Jeju Island; Jeonbuk West Coast; Mudeungsan (2025)

GOVERNMENT

Country name: *conventional long form:* Republic of Korea
conventional short form: South Korea
local long form: Taehan-min'guk
local short form: Han'guk
abbreviation: ROK
etymology: derived from the Chinese name for Goryeo, which was the Korean dynasty that united the peninsula in the 10th century A.D.; the South Korean name "Han'guk" derives from the long form, "Taehan-min'guk," which is itself a derivation from "Daehan-je'guk," which means "the Great Han Empire"

Government type: presidential republic

Capital: *name:* Seoul
geographic coordinates: 37 33 N, 126 59 E
time difference: UTC+9 (14 hours ahead of Washington, DC, during Standard Time)
etymology: the name originates from the Korean word meaning "capital city;" it was the capital of the unified Korea from 1392 to 1910
note: Sejong, located some 120 km (75 mi) south of Seoul, serves as an administrative capital for segments of the South Korean government

Administrative divisions: 9 provinces (*do*, singular and plural), 6 metropolitan cities (*gwangyeoksi*, singular and plural), 1 special city (*teugbyeolsi*), and 1 special self-governing city (*teukbyeoljachisi*)
provinces: Chungcheongbuk-do (North Chungcheong), Chungcheongnam-do (South Chungcheong), Gangwon-do, Gyeongsangbuk-do (North Gyeongsang), Gyeonggi-do, Gyeongsangnam-do (South Gyeongsang), Jeju-do (Jeju), Jeollabuk-do (North Jeolla), Jeollanam-do (South Jeolla)
metropolitan cities: Busan (Pusan), Daegu (Taegu), Daejeon (Taejon), Gwangju (Kwangju), Incheon (Inch'on), Ulsan
special city: Seoul
special self-governing city: Sejong

Legal system: mixed system combining European civil law, Anglo-American law, and Chinese classical thought

Constitution: *history:* several previous; latest passed by National Assembly 12 October 1987, approved in referendum 28 October 1987, effective 25 February 1988
amendment process: proposed by the president or by majority support of the National Assembly membership; passage requires at least two-thirds majority vote by the Assembly membership, approval in a referendum by more than one half of the votes by more than one half of eligible voters, and promulgation by the president

International law organization participation: has not submitted an ICJ jurisdiction declaration; accepts ICCt jurisdiction

Citizenship: *citizenship by birth:* no
citizenship by descent only: at least one parent must be a citizen of South Korea
dual citizenship recognized: no
residency requirement for naturalization: 5 years

Suffrage: 18 years of age; universal

Executive branch: *chief of state:* President LEE Jae-myung (since 4 June 2025)
head of government: Prime Minister KIM Min-seok (since 3 July 2025)
cabinet: State Council appointed by the president on the prime minister's recommendation
election/appointment process: president directly elected by simple-majority popular vote for a single 5-year term; prime minister appointed by president with consent of the National Assembly
most recent election date: 3 June 2025 (special snap election in the wake of the impeachment of former President YOON Suk-yeol)
election results: *2025:* LEE Jae-myung elected president; LEE Jae-myung (DPK) 49.4%, KIM Moon-soo (PPP) 41.2%, LEE Jun-seok (New Reform Party) 8.3%
2022: YOON Suk-yeol elected president; YOON Suk-yeol (PPP) 48.6%, LEE Jae-myung (DPK) 47.8%; other 3.6%
expected date of next election: 2030
note: the president is both chief of state and head of government; the prime minister serves as the principal executive assistant to the president, similar to the role of a vice president

Legislative branch: *legislature name:* National Assembly (Kuk Hoe)
legislative structure: unicameral
number of seats: 300 (all directly elected)
electoral system: mixed system
scope of elections: full renewal
term in office: 4 years
most recent election date: 4/10/2024
parties elected and seats per party: Democratic Party of Korea (161); People Power Party (90); People Future Party (18); Other (31)
percentage of women in chamber: 20.3%
expected date of next election: April 2028

Judicial branch: *highest court(s):* Supreme Court (consists of a chief justice and 13 justices); Constitutional Court (consists of a court head and 8 justices)
judge selection and term of office: Supreme Court chief justice appointed by the president with the consent of the National Assembly; other justices appointed by the president on the recommendation of the chief justice and consent of the National Assembly; position of the chief justice is a 6-year nonrenewable term; other justices serve 6-year renewable terms; Constitutional Court justices appointed - 3 by the president, 3 by the National Assembly, and 3 by the Supreme Court chief justice; court head serves until retirement at age 70, while other justices serve 6-year renewable terms with mandatory retirement at age 65
subordinate courts: High Courts; District Courts; Branch Courts (organized under the District Courts); specialized courts for family and administrative issues

Political parties: Basic Income Party
Democratic Party of Korea or DPK
New Future Party
New Reform Party
Open Democratic Party or ODP
People Power Party or PPP
Progressive Party or Jinbo Party
Rebuilding Korea Party
Social Democratic Party
note: the Democratic Alliance coalition consists of the DPK and the smaller Basic Income, Jinbo, Open Democratic, and Social Democratic parties, as well as two independents; for the 2024 election, the Basic Income Party, the ODP, and the Social Democratic Party formed the New Progressive Alliance

Diplomatic representation in the US: *chief of mission:* Ambassador (vacant); Chargé d'Affaires LEE Joon Ho (since 12 July 2025)
chancery: 2450 Massachusetts Avenue NW, Washington, DC 20008
telephone: [1] (202) 939-5600
FAX: [1] (202) 797-0595
email address and website: generalusa@ mofa.go. kr
https://overseas.mofa.go.kr/us-en/index.do
consulate(s) general: Anchorage (AK), Atlanta, Boston, Chicago, Dallas, Hagatna (Guam), Honolulu, Houston, Los Angeles, New York, San Francisco, Seattle, Philadelphia

Diplomatic representation from the US: *chief of mission:* Ambassador (vacant); Chargé d'Affaires Ambassador Joseph (Joe) YUN (since January 2025)
embassy: 188 Sejong-daero, Jongno-gu, Seoul
mailing address: 9600 Seoul Place, Washington, DC 20521-9600
telephone: [82] (2) 397-4114
FAX: [82] (2) 397-4101
email address and website: seoulinfoACS@state.gov
https://kr. usembassy. gov/
consulate(s): Busan

International organization participation: ADB, AfDB (nonregional member), APEC, Arctic Council (observer), ARF, ASEAN (dialogue partner), Australia Group, BIS, CABEI, CD, CICA, CP, EAS, EBRD, FAO, FATF, G-20, IADB, IAEA, IBRD, ICAO, ICC (national committees), ICCt, ICRM, IDA, IEA, IFAD, IFC, IFRCS, IHO, ILO, IMF, IMO, IMSO, Interpol, IOC, IOM, IPU, ISO, ITSO, ITU, ITUC (NGOs), LAIA (observer), MIGA, MINURSO, MINUSTAH, NEA, NSG, OAS (observer), OECD, OPCW, OSCE (partner), Pacific Alliance (observer), Paris Club (associate), PCA, PIF (partner), SAARC (observer), SICA (observer), UN, UNAMID, UNCTAD, UNESCO, UNHCR, UNHRC, UNIDO, UNIFIL, UNISFA, UNMIL, UNMISS, UNMOGIP, UNOCI, UNOOSA, UNWTO, UPU, Wassenaar Arrangement, WCO, WHO, WIPO, WMO, WTO, ZC

Independence: 15 August 1945 (from Japan)

National holiday: Liberation Day, 15 August (1945)

Flag: *description:* white with a red-and-blue yin-yang symbol in the center; a black trigram (*kwae*) from the ancient I Ching (Book of Changes) is in each corner of the white field
meaning: the flag is called Taegukki; white is a traditional Korean color and represents peace and purity; blue stands for the negative cosmic forces of the yin, and red for the opposite positive forces of the yang; each trigram represents one of the universal elements, which together express the principle of movement and harmony

National symbol(s): taegeuk (yin-yang symbol), Rose of Sharon *(Hibiscus syriacus)*, Siberian tiger

National color(s): red, white, blue, black

National anthem(s): *title:* "Aegukga" (Patriotic Song)
lyrics/music: YUN Ch'i-Ho or AN Ch'ang-Ho/AHN Eaktay
history: adopted 1948, well-known by 1910; North Korea's and South Korea's anthems have the same name and a similar melody, but different lyrics

National heritage: *total World Heritage Sites:* 16 (14 cultural, 2 natural)
selected World Heritage Site locales: Jeju Volcanic Island and Lava Tubes (n); Changdeokgung Palace Complex (c); Jongmyo Shrine (c); Seokguram Grotto and Bulguksa Temple (c); Hwaseong Fortress (c); Gochang, Hwasun, and Ganghwa Dolmen Sites (c); Gyeongju Historic Areas (c); Namhansanseong (c); Baekje Historic Areas (c); Sansa, Buddhist Mountain Monasteries in Korea (c); Royal Tombs of the Joseon Dynasty (c)

ECONOMY

Economic overview: high-income, export- and technology-oriented East Asian economy; manufacturing led by semiconductor and automotive industries; slow growth amid declining construction investment, export risks, and recent political instability; aging workforce; increased restraint in fiscal policy while maintaining industry support initiatives

Real GDP (purchasing power parity): $2.607 trillion (2023 est.)
$2.572 trillion (2022 est.)
$2.507 trillion (2021 est.)
note: data in 2021 dollars
comparison ranking: 14

Real GDP growth rate: 1.4% (2023 est.)
2.6% (2022 est.)
4.3% (2021 est.)
note: annual GDP % growth based on constant local currency
comparison ranking: 166

Real GDP per capita: $50,400 (2023 est.)
$49,800 (2022 est.)
$48,400 (2021 est.)
note: data in 2021 dollars
comparison ranking: 39

GDP (official exchange rate): $1.713 trillion (2023 est.)
note: data in current dollars at official exchange rate

Inflation rate (consumer prices): 2.3% (2024 est.)
3.6% (2023 est.)
5.1% (2022 est.)
note: annual % change based on consumer prices
comparison ranking: 64

GDP - composition, by sector of origin: *agriculture:* 1.6% (2023 est.)
industry: 31.6% (2023 est.)
services: 58.4% (2023 est.)

note: figures may not total 100% due to non-allocated consumption not captured in sector-reported data
comparison rankings: agriculture 161; industry 47; services 98

GDP - composition, by end use: *household consumption:* 48.9% (2023 est.)
government consumption: 18.9% (2023 est.)
investment in fixed capital: 32.2% (2023 est.)
investment in inventories: -0.1% (2023 est.)
exports of goods and services: 44% (2023 est.)
imports of goods and services: -43.9% (2023 est.)
note: figures may not total 100% due to rounding or gaps in data collection

Agricultural products: rice, vegetables, cabbages, milk, onions, pork, chicken, eggs, tangerines/mandarins, potatoes (2023)
note: top ten agricultural products based on tonnage

Industries: electronics, telecommunications, automobile production, chemicals, shipbuilding, steel

Industrial production growth rate: 1.1% (2023 est.)
note: annual % change in industrial value added based on constant local currency
comparison ranking: 113

Labor force: 29.713 million (2024 est.)
note: number of people ages 15 or older who are employed or seeking work
comparison ranking: 23

Unemployment rate: 2.7% (2024 est.)
2.7% (2023 est.)
2.9% (2022 est.)
note: % of labor force seeking employment
comparison ranking: 28

Youth unemployment rate (ages 15-24): *total:* 5.9% (2024 est.)
male: 6% (2024 est.)
female: 5.8% (2024 est.)
note: % of labor force ages 15-24 seeking employment
comparison ranking: total 157

Gini Index coefficient - distribution of family income: 32.9 (2021 est.)
note: index (0-100) of income distribution; higher values represent greater inequality
comparison ranking: 99

Average household expenditures: *on food:* 12.3% of household expenditures (2023 est.)
on alcohol and tobacco: 1.5% of household expenditures (2023 est.)

Household income or consumption by percentage share: *lowest 10%:* 2.9% (2021 est.)
highest 10%: 24.6% (2021 est.)
note: % share of income accruing to lowest and highest 10% of population

Remittances: 0.4% of GDP (2023 est.)
0.5% of GDP (2022 est.)
0.4% of GDP (2021 est.)
note: personal transfers and compensation between resident and non-resident individuals/households/entities

Budget: *revenues:* $513.21 billion (2023 est.)
expenditures: $532.023 billion (2023 est.)
note: central government revenues (excluding grants) and expenditures converted to US dollars at average official exchange rate for year indicated

Public debt: 52.3% of GDP (2023 est.)
note: central government debt as a % of GDP
comparison ranking: 96

Taxes and other revenues: 15.7% (of GDP) (2023 est.)
note: central government tax revenue as a % of GDP
comparison ranking: 86

Current account balance: $99.043 billion (2024 est.)
$32.822 billion (2023 est.)
$25.829 billion (2022 est.)
note: balance of payments - net trade and primary/secondary income in current dollars
comparison ranking: 6

Exports: $835.149 billion (2024 est.)
$769.243 billion (2023 est.)
$825.961 billion (2022 est.)
note: balance of payments - exports of goods and services in current dollars
comparison ranking: 9

Exports - partners: China 25%, USA 18%, Hong Kong 4%, Japan 4%, Taiwan 4% (2023)
note: top five export partners based on percentage share of exports

Exports - commodities: integrated circuits, cars, refined petroleum, plastics, machine parts (2023)
note: top five export commodities based on value in dollars

Imports: $758.724 billion (2024 est.)
$758.41 billion (2023 est.)
$817.594 billion (2022 est.)
note: balance of payments - imports of goods and services in current dollars
comparison ranking: 10

Imports - partners: China 31%, USA 13%, Japan 9%, Germany 5%, Australia 4% (2023)
note: top five import partners based on percentage share of imports

Imports - commodities: integrated circuits, natural gas, crude petroleum, machinery, cars (2023)
note: top five import commodities based on value in dollars

Reserves of foreign exchange and gold: $418.219 billion (2024 est.)
$420.93 billion (2023 est.)
$423.366 billion (2022 est.)
note: holdings of gold (year-end prices)/foreign exchange/special drawing rights in current dollars
comparison ranking: 9

Exchange rates: South Korean won (KRW) per US dollar -

Exchange rates: 1,363.375 (2024 est.)
1,305.662 (2023 est.)
1,291.447 (2022 est.)
1,143.952 (2021 est.)
1,180.266 (2020 est.)

ENERGY

Electricity access: *electrification - total population:* 100% (2022 est.)

Electricity: *installed generating capacity:* 151.139 million kW (2023 est.)
consumption: 575.359 billion kWh (2023 est.)
transmission/distribution losses: 19.688 billion kWh (2023 est.)
comparison rankings: installed generating capacity 10; consumption 7; transmission/distribution losses 189

Electricity generation sources: *fossil fuels:* 61.5% of total installed capacity (2023 est.)
nuclear: 30.3% of total installed capacity (2023 est.)
solar: 5.3% of total installed capacity (2023 est.)
wind: 0.6% of total installed capacity (2023 est.)
hydroelectricity: 0.4% of total installed capacity (2023 est.)
tide and wave: 0.1% of total installed capacity (2023 est.)
biomass and waste: 1.8% of total installed capacity (2023 est.)

Nuclear energy: Number of operational nuclear reactors: 26 (2025)

Number of nuclear reactors under construction: 2 (2025)

Net capacity of operational nuclear reactors: 25.57GW (2025 est.)

Percent of total electricity production: 30.7% (2023 est.)

Number of nuclear reactors permanently shut down: 2 (2025)

Coal: *production:* 16.081 million metric tons (2023 est.)
consumption: 136.817 million metric tons (2023 est.)
exports: 500 metric tons (2023 est.)
imports: 122.845 million metric tons (2023 est.)
proven reserves: 326 million metric tons (2023 est.)

Petroleum: *total petroleum production:* 38,000 bbl/day (2023 est.)
refined petroleum consumption: 2.542 million bbl/day (2024 est.)

Natural gas: *production:* 55.127 million cubic meters (2021 est.)
consumption: 57.314 billion cubic meters (2023 est.)
exports: 93.639 million cubic meters (2022 est.)
imports: 60.025 billion cubic meters (2023 est.)
proven reserves: 7.079 billion cubic meters (2021 est.)

Energy consumption per capita: 234.668 million Btu/person (2023 est.)
comparison ranking: 13

COMMUNICATIONS

Telephones - fixed lines: *total subscriptions:* 22.155 million (2023 est.)
subscriptions per 100 inhabitants: 43 (2023 est.)
comparison ranking: total subscriptions 11

Telephones - mobile cellular: *total subscriptions:* 83.9 million (2023 est.)
subscriptions per 100 inhabitants: 149 (2022 est.)
comparison ranking: total subscriptions 22

Broadcast media: multiple national TV networks, with 2 of the 3 largest networks publicly operated; the largest privately owned network, Seoul Broadcasting Service (SBS), has ties with other commercial TV networks; cable and satellite TV subscription services available; publicly operated radio broadcast networks and many privately owned radio broadcasting networks, each with multiple affiliates, and independent local stations

Internet country code: .kr

Internet users: *percent of population:* 97% (2023 est.)

Broadband - fixed subscriptions: *total:* 24.1 million (2023 est.)
subscriptions per 100 inhabitants: 47 (2023 est.)
comparison ranking: total 11

TRANSPORTATION

Civil aircraft registration country code prefix: HL

Airports: 92 (2025)
comparison ranking: 59

Heliports: 1,280 (2025)
comparison ranking: 4

Railways: *total:* 3,979 km (2016)

standard gauge: 3,979 km (2016) 1.435-m gauge (2,727 km electrified)

Merchant marine: *total:* 2,149 (2023)
by type: bulk carrier 93, container ship 115, general cargo 362, oil tanker 219, other 1,360
comparison ranking: total 12

Ports: *total ports:* 15 (2024)
large: 2
medium: 5
small: 4
very small: 4
ports with oil terminals: 10
key ports: Busan, Gwangyang Hang, Inchon, Masan, Mokpo, Pyeongtaek Hang, Ulsan

MILITARY AND SECURITY

Military and security forces: Armed Forces of the Republic of Korea: Republic of Korea Army (ROKA), Republic of Korea Navy (ROKN, includes Marine Corps, ROKMC), Republic of Korea Air Force (ROKAF)

Ministry of Maritime Affairs and Fisheries: Korea Coast Guard; Ministry of Interior and Safety: Korean National Police Agency (2025)

Military expenditures: 2.3% of GDP (2025 est.)
2.3% of GDP (2024 est.)
2.4% of GDP (2023 est.)
2.4% of GDP (2022 est.)
2.4% of GDP (2021 est.)

Military and security service personnel strengths: approximately 500,000 active Armed Forces (365,000 Army; 70,000 Navy, including about 30,000 Marines; 65,000 Air Force) (2025)

Military equipment inventories and acquisitions: the South Korean military is equipped with a mix of mostly modern domestically produced and imported weapons systems, particularly from the US; South Korea's defense industry produces a wide range of military hardware for both domestic use and export, including armored fighting vehicles, artillery, aircraft, missiles, and naval ships; it also jointly produces equipment with other countries (2024)

Military service age and obligation: 18-35 years of age for compulsory military service for all men; minimum conscript service obligation varies by service - 18 months (Army, Marines, auxiliary police), 20 months (Navy, conscripted firefighters), 21 months (Air Force, social service), 36 months for alternative service; 18-29 years of age for voluntary military service for men and women (2024)
note 1: women, in service since 1950, are able to serve in all branches and as of 2024 more than 15,000 served in the armed forces
note 2: the military brings on over 200,000 conscripts each year

Military deployments: 250 Lebanon (UNIFIL); 275 South Sudan (UNMISS); 170 United Arab Emirates; note - since 2009, South Korea has kept a naval flotilla with approximately 300 personnel in the waters off of the Horn of Africa and the Arabian Peninsula (2024)

Military - note: the South Korean military is responsible for external defense and is primarily focused on the threat from North Korea; it participates in bilateral and multinational exercises and deploys abroad for international missions, including peacekeeping and other security operations
South Korea's primary defense partner is the US, and the 1953 US-South Korea Mutual Defense Treaty is a cornerstone of the country's national security; the Treaty committed the US to provide assistance in the event of an attack and gave the US permission to station land, air, and sea forces in and about the territory of South Korea as determined by mutual agreement; South Korea hosts approximately 28,000 US military troops and regularly conducts bilateral exercises with the US military; South Korea has Major Non-NATO Ally (MNNA) status with the US, a designation under US law that provides foreign partners with certain benefits in the areas of defense trade and security cooperation; the South Korean military has assisted the US in conflicts in Afghanistan (5,000 troops; 2001-2014), Iraq (20,000 troops; 2003-2008), and Vietnam (325,000 troops; 1964-1973)
in 2016, South Korea concluded an agreement with the EU for participation in EU Common Security and Defense Policy (CSDP) missions and operations, such as EU counter-piracy operations off the coast of East Africa; South Korea has had a relationship with NATO since 2005, and in 2022 established a mission to the NATO headquarters to further cooperation; it has participated in NATO-led missions and exercises, including in Afghanistan and the Gulf of Aden (2025)

SPACE

Space agency/agencies: Korea AeroSpace Administration (KASA; established 2024); Korea Aerospace Research Institute (KARI; established 1989 and previously acted as South Korea's space agency) (2025)

Space launch site(s): Naro Space Center (South Jeolla province) (2025)

Space program overview: has an ambitious and growing space program focused on developing satellites, satellite/space launch vehicles (SLVs), and interplanetary probes; has a national space strategy; manufacturers and operates satellites, including those with communications, remote sensing (RS), scientific, and multipurpose capabilities; manufactures and launches SLVs; developing interplanetary space vehicles, including orbital probes and landers; participates in international space programs and has relations with an array of foreign space agencies and industries, including those of Australia, the European Space Agency (ESA) and its member states (particularly France, Germany, Italy, Spain, UK), India, Indonesia, Israel, Japan, Peru, Russia, UAE, and especially the US; has a robust and growing commercial space industry involved in the development of satellites and space launch capabilities (2025)
note: further details about the key activities, programs, and milestones of the country's space program, as well as government spending estimates on the space sector, appear in the Space Programs reference guide

TRANSNATIONAL ISSUES

Refugees and internally displaced persons: *refugees:* 40,084 (2024 est.)
stateless persons: 248 (2024 est.)

Illicit drugs USG identification: major precursor-chemical producer (2025)

KOSOVO

INTRODUCTION

Background: The Ottoman Empire took control of Kosovo in 1389 after defeating Serbian forces. Large numbers of Turks and Albanians moved to the region, and by the end of the 19th century, Albanians had replaced Serbs as the majority ethnic group in Kosovo. Serbia reacquired control of Kosovo during the First Balkan War of 1912, and after World War II, Kosovo became an autonomous province of Serbia in the Socialist Federal Republic of Yugoslavia (SFRY). Increasing Albanian nationalism in the 1980s led to riots and calls for Kosovo's independence, but in 1989, Belgrade – which has in turn served as the capital of Serbia and Yugoslavia – revoked Kosovo's autonomous status. When the SFRY broke up in 1991, Kosovo Albanian leaders organized an independence referendum, and Belgrade's repressive response led to an insurgency. Kosovo remained part of Serbia, which joined with Montenegro to declare a new Federal Republic of Yugoslavia (FRY) in 1992.

In 1998, Belgrade launched a brutal counterinsurgency campaign, with some 800,000 ethnic Albanians expelled from their homes in Kosovo. After international mediation failed, a NATO military operation began in March 1999 and forced Belgrade to withdraw its forces from Kosovo. UN Security Council Resolution 1244 (1999) placed Kosovo under the temporary control of the UN Interim Administration Mission in Kosovo (UNMIK). Negotiations in 2006-07 ended without agreement between Serbia and Kosovo, though the UN issued a comprehensive report that endorsed independence. On 17 February 2008, the Kosovo Assembly declared Kosovo independent.

Serbia continues to reject Kosovo's independence, but the two countries began EU-facilitated discussions in 2013 to normalize relations, which resulted in several agreements. Additional agreements were reached in 2015 and 2023, but implementation remains incomplete. In 2022, Kosovo formally applied for membership in the EU, which is contingent on fulfillment of accession criteria, and the Council of Europe. Kosovo is also seeking UN and NATO memberships.

GEOGRAPHY

Location: Southeastern Europe, between Serbia and Macedonia

Geographic coordinates: 42 35 N, 21 00 E

Map references: Europe

Area: *total:* 10,887 sq km
land: 10,887 sq km
water: 0 sq km
comparison ranking: total 167

Area - comparative: slightly larger than Delaware

Land boundaries: *total:* 714 km
border countries (4): Albania 112 km; North Macedonia 160 km; Montenegro 76 km; Serbia 366 km

Coastline: 0 km (landlocked)

Maritime claims: none (landlocked)

Climate: influenced by continental air masses resulting in relatively cold winters with heavy snowfall and hot, dry summers and autumns; Mediterranean and alpine influences create regional variation; maximum rainfall between October and December

Terrain: flat fluvial basin at an elevation of 400-700 m above sea level surrounded by several high mountain ranges with elevations of 2,000 to 2,500 m

Elevation: *highest point:* Gjeravica/Deravica 2,656 m
lowest point: Drini i Bardhe/Beli Drim (located on the border with Albania) 297 m
mean elevation: 450 m

Natural resources: nickel, lead, zinc, magnesium, lignite, kaolin, chrome, bauxite

Land use: *agricultural land:* 52.8% (2018 est.)
arable land: 27.4% (2018 est.)
permanent crops: 1.9% (2018 est.)
permanent pasture: 23.5% (2018 est.)
forest: 41.7% (2018 est.)
other: 5.5% (2018 est.)

Irrigated land: NA

Major watersheds (area sq km): Atlantic Ocean drainage: ***(Black Sea)*** Danube (795,656 sq km)

Population distribution: population clusters exist throughout the country, with the largest in the east in and around the capital of Pristina

Geography - note: *the 41-km (25-mi) Nerodimka River divides into two branches, each of which flows into a different sea:* the northern branch flows into the Sitnica River, which via the Ibar, Morava, and Danube Rivers ultimately flows into the Black Sea; the southern branch flows via the Lepenac and Vardar Rivers into the Aegean Sea

PEOPLE AND SOCIETY

Population: *total:* 1,977,093 (2024 est.)
male: 1,017,992
female: 959,101
comparison rankings: total 152; male 152; female 152

Nationality: *noun:* Kosovan
adjective: Kosovan
note: Kosovo, a neutral term, is sometimes also used as a noun or adjective as in Kosovo Albanian, Kosovo Serb, Kosovo minority, or Kosovo citizen

Ethnic groups: Albanians 92.9%, Bosniaks 1.6%, Serbs 1.5%, Turk 1.1%, Ashkali 0.9%, Egyptian 0.7%, Gorani 0.6%, Romani 0.5%, other/unspecified 0.2% (2011 est.)
note: these estimates may under-represent Serb, Romani, and some other ethnic minorities because they are based on the 2011 Kosovo national census, which excluded northern Kosovo (a largely Serb-inhabited region) and was partially boycotted by Serb and Romani communities in southern Kosovo

Languages: Albanian (official) 94.5%, Bosnian 1.7%, Serbian (official) 1.6%, Turkish 1.1%, other 0.9% (includes Romani), unspecified 0.1% (2011 est.)
major-language sample(s):
Libri i fakteve boterore, burimi i pazevendesueshem per informacione elementare (Albanian)
Knjiga svetskih činjenica, neophodan izvor osnovnih informacija. (Serbian)
note: these estimates may under-represent Serb, Romani, and other ethnic minority languages because they are based on the 2011 Kosovo national census, which excluded northern Kosovo (a largely Serb-inhabited region) and was partially boycotted by Serb and Romani communities in southern Kosovo

Religions: Muslim 95.6%, Roman Catholic 2.2%, Orthodox 1.5%, other 0.1%, none 0.1%, unspecified 0.6% (2011 est.)
note: these estimates may under-represent Serb, Romani, and some other ethnic minorities because they are based on the 2011 Kosovo national census, which excluded northern Kosovo (a largely Serb-inhabited region) and was partially boycotted by Serb and Romani communities in southern Kosovo

Age structure: *0-14 years:* 22.7% (male 233,010/female 216,304)
15-64 years: 68.9% (male 712,403/female 649,932)
65 years and over: 8.4% (2024 est.) (male 72,579/female 92,865)

Dependency ratios: *total dependency ratio:* 45.1 (2024 est.)
youth dependency ratio: 33 (2024 est.)
elderly dependency ratio: 12.1 (2024 est.)
potential support ratio: 8.2 (2024 est.)

Median age: *total:* 32 years (2024 est.)
male: 31.7 years
female: 32.4 years
comparison ranking: total 119

Population growth rate: 0.68% (2024 est.)
comparison ranking: 130

Birth rate: 14.4 births/1,000 population (2024 est.)
comparison ranking: 117

Death rate: 7.2 deaths/1,000 population (2024 est.)
comparison ranking: 112

Net migration rate: -0.4 migrant(s)/1,000 population (2024 est.)
comparison ranking: 119

Population distribution: population clusters exist throughout the country, with the largest in the east in and around the capital of Pristina

Major urban areas - population: 218,782 PRISTINA (capital) (2020)

Sex ratio: *at birth:* 1.08 male(s)/female
0-14 years: 1.08 male(s)/female
15-64 years: 1.1 male(s)/female
65 years and over: 0.78 male(s)/female
total population: 1.06 male(s)/female (2024 est.)

Infant mortality rate: *total:* 22.9 deaths/1,000 live births (2024 est.)
male: 24.2 deaths/1,000 live births
female: 21.5 deaths/1,000 live births
comparison ranking: total 66

Life expectancy at birth: *total population:* 73.1 years (2024 est.)
male: 71 years
female: 75.5 years
comparison ranking: total population 153

Total fertility rate: 1.87 children born/woman (2024 est.)
comparison ranking: 129

Gross reproduction rate: 0.9 (2024 est.)

Physician density: 0.2 physicians/1,000 population (2015)

ENVIRONMENT

Environmental issues: air pollution from power plants and lignite mines; water scarcity and pollution; land degradation

Climate: influenced by continental air masses resulting in relatively cold winters with heavy snowfall and hot, dry summers and autumns; Mediterranean and alpine influences create regional variation; maximum rainfall between October and December

Carbon dioxide emissions: 7.444 million metric tonnes of CO2 (2023 est.)
from coal and metallurgical coke: 5.005 million metric tonnes of CO2 (2023 est.)
from petroleum and other liquids: 2.439 million metric tonnes of CO2 (2023 est.)
comparison ranking: total emissions 120

Waste and recycling: *municipal solid waste generated annually:* 319,000 tons (2024 est.)

GOVERNMENT

Country name: *conventional long form:* Republic of Kosovo
conventional short form: Kosovo
local long form: Republika e Kosoves (Albanian)/ Republika Kosovo (Serbian)
local short form: Kosove (Albanian)/ Kosovo (Serbian)
etymology: name may derive from the Serbian word *kos*, meaning "blackbird," or from a personal name

Government type: parliamentary republic

Capital: *name:* Pristina (Prishtine, Prishtina)
geographic coordinates: 42 40 N, 21 10 E
time difference: UTC+1 (6 hours ahead of Washington, DC, during Standard Time)
daylight saving time: +1hr, begins last Sunday in March; ends last Sunday in October
etymology: the town takes its name from the river; the origin of the river's name is unclear but could come from a pre-Slavic language

Administrative divisions: 38 municipalities (*komunat*, singular - *komuna* (Albanian); *opstine*, singular - *opstina* (Serbian)); Decan (Decani), Dragash (Dragas), Ferizaj (Urosevac), Fushe Kosove (Kosovo Polje), Gjakove (Dakovica), Gjilan (Gnjilane), Gllogovc (Glogovac), Gracanice (Gracanica), Hani i Elezit (Deneral Jankovic), Istog (Istok), Junik, Kacanik, Kamenice (Kamenica), Kline

(Klina), Kllokot (Klokot), Leposaviq (Leposavic), Lipjan (Lipljan), Malisheve (Malisevo), Mamushe (Mamusa), Mitrovice e Jugut (Juzna Mitrovica) [South Mitrovica], Mitrovice e Veriut (Severna Mitrovica) [North Mitrovica], Novoberde (Novo Brdo), Obiliq (Obilic), Partesh (Partes), Peje (Pec), Podujeve (Podujevo), Prishtine (Pristina), Prizren, Rahovec (Orahovac), Ranillug (Ranilug), Shterpce (Strpce), Shtime (Stimlje), Skenderaj (Srbica), Suhareke (Suva Reka), Viti (Vitina), Vushtrri (Vucitrn), Zubin Potok, Zvecan

Legal system: civil law system

Constitution: *history:* previous 1974, 1990; latest (post-independence) draft finalized 2 April 2008, signed 7 April 2008, ratified 9 April 2008, entered into force 15 June 2008
amendment process: proposed by the government, by the president of the republic, or by one fourth of Assembly deputies; passage requires two-thirds majority vote of the Assembly, including two-thirds majority vote of deputies representing non-majority communities, followed by a favorable Constitutional Court assessment

International law organization participation: has not submitted an ICJ jurisdiction declaration; non-party state to the ICCt

Citizenship: *citizenship by birth:* no
citizenship by descent only: at least one parent must be a citizen of Kosovo
dual citizenship recognized: yes
residency requirement for naturalization: 5 years

Suffrage: 18 years of age; universal

Executive branch: *chief of state:* President Vjosa OSMANI-Sadriu (since 4 April 2021)
head of government: Acting Prime Minister Albin KURTI (since 15 April 2025)
cabinet: Cabinet elected by the Assembly
election/appointment process: president indirectly elected for a 5-year term (eligible for a second term) by at least two-thirds majority vote of the Assembly; if a candidate does not reach this threshold in the first two ballots, the candidate winning a simple majority vote in the third ballot is elected; prime minister indirectly elected by the Assembly
most recent election date: 3-4 April 2021
election results: *2021:* Vjosa OSMANI-Sadriu elected president in third ballot; Assembly vote - Vjosa OSMANI-Sadriu (Guxo!) 71 votes; Albin KURTI (LVV) elected prime minister; Assembly vote - 67 for, 30 against
2017: Ramush HARADINAJ (AAK) elected prime minister; Assembly vote - 61 for, 1 abstention, 0 against (opposition boycott)
2016: Hashim THACI elected president in third ballot; Assembly vote - Hashim THACI (PDK) 71 votes
expected date of next election: 2026
note: Prime Minister Albin KURTI resigned on 15 April 2025; a replacement has not yet been selected

Legislative branch: *legislature name:* Assembly (Kuvendi i Kosoves/Skupstina Kosova)
legislative structure: unicameral
number of seats: 120 (all directly elected)
electoral system: proportional representation
scope of elections: full renewal
term in office: 4 years
most recent election date: 2/14/2021
parties elected and seats per party: Self-Determination Movement (LVV) (58), Democratic Party of Kosovo (PDK) (19), Democratic League of Kosovo (LDK) (15), Serb List (10), Alliance for the Future of Kosovo (AAK) (8), other (10)
percentage of women in chamber: 34%
expected date of next election: 2025
note: 20 seats reserved for ethnic minorities – 10 for Serbs and 10 for other minorities

Judicial branch: *highest court(s):* Supreme Court (consists of the court president and 18 judges and organized into Appeals Panel of the Kosovo Property Agency and Special Chamber); Constitutional Court (consists of the court president, vice president, and 7 judges)
judge selection and term of office: Supreme Court judges nominated by the Kosovo Judicial Council, a 13-member independent body staffed by judges and lay members, and also responsible for overall administration of Kosovo's judicial system; judges appointed by the president of the Republic of Kosovo; judges appointed until mandatory retirement age; Constitutional Court judges nominated by the Kosovo Assembly and appointed by the president of the republic to serve single, 9-year terms
subordinate courts: Court of Appeals (organized into 4 departments: General, Serious Crime, Commercial Matters, and Administrative Matters); Basic Court (located in 7 municipalities, each with several branches)
note: in 2015, the Kosovo Assembly approved a constitutional amendment that established the Kosovo Relocated Specialist Judicial Institution, also referred to as the Kosovo Specialist Chambers or "Special Court"; the court, located at the Hague in the Netherlands, began operating in 2016 and has jurisdiction to try crimes against humanity, war crimes, and other crimes under Kosovo law that occurred in the 1998-2000 period

Political parties: Alliance for the Future of Kosovo or AAK
Ashkali Party for Integration or PAI
Civic Initiative for Freedom, Justice, and Survival
Democratic League of Kosovo or LDK
Democratic Party of Kosovo or PDK
New Democratic Initiative of Kosovo or IRDK
New Democratic Party or NDS
Progressive Movement of Kosovar Roma or LPRK
Romani Initiative
Self-Determination Movement (Lëvizja Vetevendosje or Vetevendosie) or LVV or VV
Serb List or SL
Social Democratic Union or SDU
Turkish Democratic Party of Kosovo or KDTP
Unique Gorani Party or JGP
Vakat Coalition or VAKAT

Diplomatic representation in the US: *chief of mission:* Ambassador Ilir DUGOLLI (since 13 January 2022)
chancery: 3612 Massachusetts Ave NW, Washington, D.C. 20007
telephone: [1] (202) 450-2130
FAX: [1] (202) 735-0609
email address and website: embassy. usa@ rks-gov. net
U.S. Embassies of the Republic of Kosovo (ambasadat.net)
consulate(s) general: New York
consulate(s): Des Moines (IA)

Diplomatic representation from the US: *chief of mission:* Ambassador (vacant); Chargé d'Affaires Anu PRATTIPATI (since January 2025)
embassy: Arberia/Dragodan, Rr. 4 KORRIKU Nr. 25, Pristina
mailing address: 9520 Pristina Place, Washington DC 20521-9520
telephone: [383] 38-59-59-3000
FAX: [383] 38-604-890
email address and website: PristinaACS@state.gov
https://xk.usembassy.gov/

International organization participation: FIFA, IBRD, IDA, IFC, IMF, IOC, ITUC (NGOs), MIGA, OIF (observer)

Independence: 17 February 2008 (from Serbia)

National holiday: Independence Day, 17 February (2008)

Flag: *description:* a dark blue field with a gold-colored silhouette of Kosovo in the center, with six five-pointed white stars in a slight arc over it
meaning: each star represents one of the major ethnic groups of Kosovo: Albanians, Serbs, Turks, Gorani, Roma, and Bosniaks
note: one of two national flags that uses a map as a design element; the flag of Cyprus is the other

National symbol(s): six five-pointed white stars

National color(s): blue, gold, white

National coat of arms: *uses the national colors of blue, gold, and white, and is featured on the country's flag; the golden map symbolizes a rich and peaceful Kosovo, with a blue background that represents the country's aspirations for Euro-Atlantic integration; the six white stars stand for the major ethnic groups in Kosovo:* Albanians, Serbs, Bosniaks, Turks, Roma (including Ashkali and Egyptians), and Gorani

National anthem(s): *title:* "Europe"
lyrics/music: no lyrics/Mendi MENGJIQI
history: adopted 2008; Kosovo chose not to include lyrics in its anthem to avoid offending the country's minority ethnic groups

National heritage: *total World Heritage Sites:* 1 (cultural)
selected World Heritage Site locales: Medieval Monuments in Kosovo

ECONOMY

Economic overview: small-but-growing European economy; non-EU member but unilateral euro user; very high unemployment, especially youth; vulnerable reliance on diaspora tourism services, curtailed by COVID-19 disruptions; unclear public loan portfolio health

Real GDP (purchasing power parity): $25.019 billion (2024 est.)
$23.962 billion (2023 est.)
$23.025 billion (2022 est.)
note: data in 2021 dollars
comparison ranking: 153

Real GDP growth rate: 4.4% (2024 est.)
4.1% (2023 est.)
4.3% (2022 est.)
note: annual GDP % growth based on constant local currency
comparison ranking: 57

Real GDP per capita: $16,400 (2024 est.)
$14,200 (2023 est.)
$13,000 (2022 est.)
note: data in 2021 dollars
comparison ranking: 117

GDP (official exchange rate): $11.149 billion (2024 est.)
note: data in current dollars at official exchange rate

Inflation rate (consumer prices): 1.6% (2024 est.)
4.9% (2023 est.)
11.6% (2022 est.)
note: annual % change based on consumer prices
comparison ranking: 37

GDP - composition, by sector of origin: *agriculture:* 6.9% (2024 est.)
industry: 26.2% (2024 est.)
services: 45.7% (2024 est.)
note: figures may not total 100% due to non-allocated consumption not captured in sector-reported data
comparison rankings: agriculture 93; industry 76; services 170

GDP - composition, by end use: *household consumption:* 84.3% (2024 est.)
government consumption: 12.3% (2024 est.)
investment in fixed capital: 33.8% (2024 est.)
investment in inventories: 0% (2024 est.)
exports of goods and services: 41.9% (2024 est.)
imports of goods and services: -72.3% (2024 est.)
note: figures may not total 100% due to rounding or gaps in data collection

Agricultural products: wheat, corn, berries, potatoes, peppers, fruit; dairy, livestock; fish

Industries: mineral mining, construction materials, base metals, leather, machinery, appliances, foodstuffs and beverages, textiles

Industrial production growth rate: 4% (2024 est.)
note: annual % change in industrial value added based on constant local currency
comparison ranking: 61

Labor force: 500,300 (2017 est.)
note: includes those estimated to be employed in the gray economy
comparison ranking: 159

Population below poverty line: 17.6% (2015 est.)
note: % of population with income below national poverty line
Gini Index coefficient - distribution of family income 49.4 (2021 est.)
note: index (0-100) of income distribution; higher values represent greater inequality
comparison ranking: 11

Household income or consumption by percentage share: *lowest 10%:* 0.4% (2021 est.)
highest 10%: 32.9% (2021 est.)
note: % share of income accruing to lowest and highest 10% of population

Remittances: 17.5% of GDP (2023 est.)
17.2% of GDP (2022 est.)
18% of GDP (2021 est.)
note: personal transfers and compensation between resident and non-resident individuals/households/entities

Budget: *revenues:* $1.951 billion (2020 est.)
expenditures: $2.547 billion (2020 est.)

Current account balance: -$785.09 million (2023 est.)
-$983.283 million (2022 est.)
-$818.351 million (2021 est.)
note: balance of payments - net trade and primary/secondary income in current dollars
comparison ranking: 121

Exports: $4.156 billion (2023 est.)
$3.579 billion (2022 est.)
$3.138 billion (2021 est.)
note: balance of payments - exports of goods and services in current dollars
comparison ranking: 146

Exports - partners: United States 16%, Albania 15%, North Macedonia 12%, Germany 8%, Italy 8% (2021)

Exports - commodities: mattress materials, iron alloys, metal piping, scrap iron, building plastics (2021)
top five export commodities based on value in dollars

Imports: $7.362 billion (2023 est.)
$6.661 billion (2022 est.)
$6.128 billion (2021 est.)
note: balance of payments - imports of goods and services in current dollars
comparison ranking: 136

Imports - partners: Germany 13%, Turkey 13%, China 10%, Serbia 7%, Italy 6% (2021)

Imports - commodities: refined petroleum, cars, iron rods, electricity, cigars, packaged medicines (2021)

Reserves of foreign exchange and gold: $1.31 billion (2024 est.)
$1.245 billion (2023 est.)
$1.248 billion (2022 est.)
note: holdings of gold (year-end prices)/foreign exchange/special drawing rights in current dollars
comparison ranking: 140

Debt - external: $785.739 million (2023 est.)
note: present value of external debt in current US dollars
comparison ranking: 110

Exchange rates: euros (EUR) per US dollar -

Exchange rates: 0.924 (2024 est.)
0.925 (2023 est.)
0.951 (2022 est.)
0.845 (2021 est.)
0.877 (2020 est.)
note: Kosovo, which is neither an EU member state nor a party to a formal EU monetary agreement, uses the euro as its de facto currency

ENERGY

Electricity: *installed generating capacity:* 1.555 million kW (2023 est.)
consumption: 6.571 billion kWh (2023 est.)
exports: 2.442 billion kWh (2023 est.)
imports: 3.449 billion kWh (2023 est.)
transmission/distribution losses: 789.167 million kWh (2023 est.)
comparison rankings: installed generating capacity 126; consumption 121; exports 52; imports 56; transmission/distribution losses 92

Electricity generation sources: *fossil fuels:* 87.3% of total installed capacity (2023 est.)
solar: 0.1% of total installed capacity (2023 est.)
wind: 6.3% of total installed capacity (2023 est.)
hydroelectricity: 6.2% of total installed capacity (2023 est.)

Coal: *production:* 6.924 million metric tons (2023 est.)
consumption: 6.931 million metric tons (2023 est.)
exports: 13,000 metric tons (2023 est.)
imports: 20,000 metric tons (2023 est.)
proven reserves: 1.564 billion metric tons (2023 est.)

Petroleum: *refined petroleum consumption:* 16,000 bbl/day (2023 est.)

Energy consumption per capita: 52.085 million Btu/person (2023 est.)
comparison ranking: 93

COMMUNICATIONS

Telephones - fixed lines: *total subscriptions:* 383,763 (2022 est.)
subscriptions per 100 inhabitants: 7 (2022 est.)
comparison ranking: total subscriptions 102

Telephones - mobile cellular: *total subscriptions:* 1,777,859 (2022 est.)
subscriptions per 100 inhabitants: 98 (2022 est.)
comparison ranking: total subscriptions 155

Internet country code: .xk
note: assigned as a temporary code under UN Security Council resolution 1244/99

Internet users: *percent of population:* 89% (2018 est.)

TRANSPORTATION

Civil aircraft registration country code prefix: Z6

Airports: 2 (2025)
comparison ranking: 196

Heliports: 11 (2025)
comparison ranking: 68

Railways: *total:* 437 km (2020)

MILITARY AND SECURITY

Military and security forces: Kosovo Security Force (KSF; Forca e Sigurisë së Kosovës or FSK): Land Force, National Guard (2025)
note: the Kosovo Police are under the Ministry of Internal Affairs

Military expenditures: 1.5% of GDP (2024 est.)
1.3% of GDP (2023 est.)
1.1% of GDP (2022 est.)
1.1% of GDP (2021 est.)
1% of GDP (2020 est.)

Military and security service personnel strengths: approximately 3,300 Kosovo Security Forces, including about 800 reserves (2024)

Military equipment inventories and acquisitions: the KSF is equipped with small arms and light vehicles and has relied on limited amounts of donated equipment from several countries, particularly Turkey and the US (2025)

Military service age and obligation: any citizen of Kosovo over the age of 18 is eligible to serve in the Kosovo Security Force; upper age for enlisting is 30 for officers, 25 for other ranks, although these may be waived for recruits with key skills considered essential for the KSF (2024)

Military - note: the Kosovo Security Force (KSF) was established in 2009 as a small (1,500 personnel), lightly armed disaster response force; the NATO-led Kosovo Force (KFOR) was charged with assisting in the development of the KSF and bringing it up to standards designated by NATO; the KSF was certified as fully operational by the North Atlantic Council in 2013, indicating the then 2,200-strong KSF was entirely capable of performing the tasks assigned under its mandate, which included non-military security functions that were not appropriate for the police, plus missions such as search and rescue, explosive ordnance disposal, control and clearance of hazardous materials, firefighting, and other humanitarian assistance tasks
in 2019, Kosovo approved legislation that began a process to transition the KSF by 2028 into a professional military (the Kosovo Armed Forces) led by a General Staff and comprised of a Land Force,

a National Guard, a Logistics Command, and a Doctrine and Training Command; it would have a strength of up to 5,000 with about 3,000 reserves; at the same time, the KSF's mission was expanded to include traditional military functions, such as territorial defense and international peacekeeping; the KSF's first international mission was the deployment of a small force to Kuwait in 2021

the NATO-led KFOR has operated in the country as a peace support force since 1999; in addition to assisting in the development of the KSF, KFOR is responsible for providing a safe and secure environment and ensuring freedom of movement for all citizens; as of 2025, it had approximately 4,700 troops from more than 30 countries (2025)

TERRORISM

Terrorist group(s): Terrorist group(s): Islamic State of Iraq and ash-Sham (ISIS)

note: details about the history, aims, leadership, organization, areas of operation, tactics, targets, weapons, size, and sources of support of the group(s) appear(s) in Appendix T

TRANSNATIONAL ISSUES

Refugees and internally displaced persons: IDPs: 15,582 (2024 est.)

KUWAIT

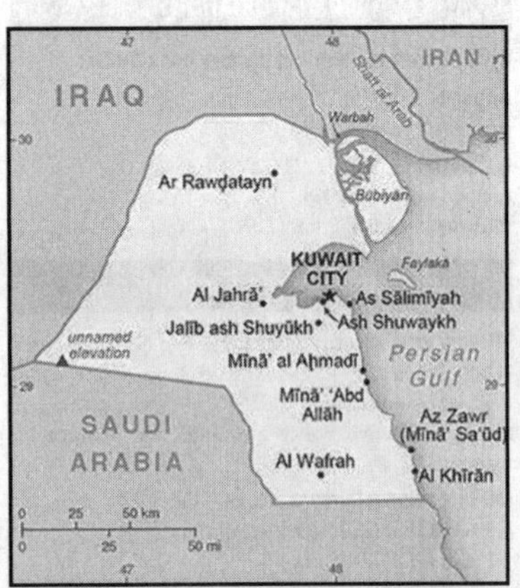

INTRODUCTION

Background: Kuwait has been ruled by the AL-SABAH dynasty since the 18th century. The threat of Ottoman invasion in 1899 prompted Amir Mubarak AL-SABAH to seek protection from Britain, ceding foreign and defense responsibility to Britain until 1961, when the country attained its independence. Iraq attacked and overran Kuwait in 1990. After several weeks of aerial bombardment, a US-led UN coalition began a ground assault in 1991 that liberated Kuwait in four days. In 1992, the Amir reconstituted the parliament that he had dissolved in 1986. Amid the 2010-11 uprisings and protests across the Arab world, stateless Arabs known as Bidoon staged small protests demanding citizenship, jobs, and other benefits available to Kuwaiti nationals. Other demographic groups, notably Islamists and Kuwaitis from tribal backgrounds, soon joined the growing protest movements, which culminated with the resignation of the prime minister amid allegations of corruption. Demonstrations renewed in 2012 in response to a decree amending the electoral law that lessened the voting power of the tribal blocs.

An opposition coalition of Sunni Islamists, tribal populists, and some liberals largely boycotted legislative elections in 2012 and 2013, which ushered in a legislature more amenable to the government's agenda. Faced with the prospect of painful subsidy cuts, oppositionists and independents actively participated in the 2016 election, winning nearly half the seats, but the opposition became increasingly factionalized. Between 2006 and his death in 2020, the Amir dissolved the National Assembly on seven occasions and shuffled the cabinet over a dozen times, usually citing political stagnation and gridlock between the legislature and the government.

The current Amir, who assumed his role in 2020, launched a "National Dialogue" in 2021 meant to resolve political gridlock. As part of this initiative, the Amir pardoned several opposition figures who had been living in exile, and they returned to Kuwait. Legislative challenges remain, and the cabinet has been reshuffled six times since 2020.

GEOGRAPHY

Location: Middle East, bordering the Persian Gulf, between Iraq and Saudi Arabia

Geographic coordinates: 29 30 N, 45 45 E

Map references: Middle East

Area: *total:* 17,818 sq km
land: 17,818 sq km
water: 0 sq km
comparison ranking: total 157

Area - comparative: slightly smaller than New Jersey

Land boundaries: *total:* 475 km
border countries (2): Iraq 254 km; Saudi Arabia 221 km

Coastline: 499 km

Maritime claims: *territorial sea:* 12 nm

Climate: dry desert; intensely hot summers; short, cool winters

Terrain: flat to slightly undulating desert plain

Elevation: *highest point:* 3.6 km W. of Al-Salmi Border Post 300 m
lowest point: Persian Gulf 0 m
mean elevation: 108 m

Natural resources: petroleum, fish, shrimp, natural gas

Land use: *agricultural land:* 8.4% (2022 est.)
arable land: 0.4% (2022 est.)
permanent crops: 0.3% (2022 est.)
permanent pasture: 7.6% (2022 est.)
forest: 0.4% (2022 est.)
other: 91.2% (2022 est.)

Irrigated land: 100 sq km (2015)

Major watersheds (area sq km): Indian Ocean drainage: ***(Persian Gulf)*** Tigris and Euphrates (918,044 sq km)

Major aquifers: Arabian Aquifer System

Population distribution: densest settlement is along the Persian Gulf, particularly in Kuwait City and on Bubiyan Island; significant population threads extend south and west along highways that radiate from the capital, particularly in the southern half of the country

Natural hazards: sudden cloudbursts are common from October to April and bring heavy rain, which can damage roads and houses; sandstorms and dust storms occur throughout the year but are most common between March and August

Geography - note: strategic location at head of Persian Gulf

PEOPLE AND SOCIETY

Population: *total:* 3,138,355 (2024 est.)
male: 1,810,542
female: 1,327,813
comparison rankings: total 136; male 133; female 142

Nationality: *noun:* Kuwaiti(s)
adjective: Kuwaiti

Ethnic groups: Kuwaiti 30.4%, other Arab 27.4%, Asian 40.3%, African 1%, other 0.9% (includes European, North American, South American, and Australian) (2018 est.)

Languages: Arabic (official), English widely spoken
major-language sample(s):
يمكن الاستغناء عنه للمعلومات الأساسية
كتاب حقائق العالم، المصدر الذي لا
(Arabic)

Religions: Muslim (official) 74.6%, Christian 18.2%, other and unspecified 7.2% (2013 est.)
note: data represent the total population; about 72% of the population consists of immigrants

Age structure: *0-14 years:* 23% (male 376,415/female 346,190)
15-64 years: 73.4% (male 1,386,349/female 917,465)
65 years and over: 3.6% (2024 est.) (male 47,778/female 64,158)

Dependency ratios: *total dependency ratio:* 36.2 (2024 est.)
youth dependency ratio: 31.4 (2024 est.)
elderly dependency ratio: 4.9 (2024 est.)
potential support ratio: 20.6 (2024 est.)

Median age: *total:* 30.3 years (2024 est.)
male: 31.1 years
female: 28.9 years
comparison ranking: total 138

Population growth rate: 1.1% (2024 est.)
comparison ranking: 85

Birth rate: 17.5 births/1,000 population (2024 est.)
comparison ranking: 85

Death rate: 2.3 deaths/1,000 population (2024 est.)
comparison ranking: 227

Net migration rate: -4.2 migrant(s)/1,000 population (2024 est.)
comparison ranking: 196

Population distribution: densest settlement is along the Persian Gulf, particularly in Kuwait City and on Bubiyan Island; significant population threads extend south and west along highways that radiate from the capital, particularly in the southern half of the country

Urbanization: *urban population:* 100% of total population (2023)
rate of urbanization: 1.35% annual rate of change (2020-25 est.)
Major urban areas - population: 3.298 million KUWAIT (capital) (2023)
Sex ratio: *at birth:* 1.05 male(s)/female
0-14 years: 1.09 male(s)/female
15-64 years: 1.51 male(s)/female
65 years and over: 0.74 male(s)/female
total population: 1.36 male(s)/female (2024 est.)
Maternal mortality ratio: 8 deaths/100,000 live births (2023 est.)
comparison ranking: 154
Infant mortality rate: *total:* 7.2 deaths/1,000 live births (2024 est.)
male: 7.4 deaths/1,000 live births
female: 6.9 deaths/1,000 live births
comparison ranking: total 155
Life expectancy at birth: *total population:* 79.6 years (2024 est.)
male: 78.1 years
female: 81.1 years
comparison ranking: total population 63
Total fertility rate: 2.21 children born/woman (2024 est.)
comparison ranking: 82
Gross reproduction rate: 1.08 (2024 est.)
Drinking water source: *improved: urban:* 100% of population (2022 est.)
total: 100% of population (2022 est.)
unimproved: urban: 0% of population (2022 est.)
total: 0% of population (2022 est.)
Health expenditure: 5.8% of GDP (2021)
9.4% of national budget (2022 est.)
Physician density: 2.27 physicians/1,000 population (2020)
Hospital bed density: 2.4 beds/1,000 population (2020 est.)
Sanitation facility access: *improved: urban:* 100% of population (2022 est.)
total: 100% of population (2022 est.)
unimproved: urban: 0% of population (2022 est.)
total: 0% of population (2022 est.)
Obesity - adult prevalence rate: 37.9% (2016)
comparison ranking: 11
Alcohol consumption per capita: *total:* 0 liters of pure alcohol (2019 est.)
beer: 0 liters of pure alcohol (2019 est.)
wine: 0 liters of pure alcohol (2019 est.)
spirits: 0 liters of pure alcohol (2019 est.)
other alcohols: 0 liters of pure alcohol (2019 est.)
comparison ranking: total 189
Tobacco use: *total:* 22.4% (2025 est.)
male: 34.9% (2025 est.)
female: 1.9% (2025 est.)
comparison ranking: total 50
Children under the age of 5 years underweight: 2.5% (2020)
comparison ranking: 90
Currently married women (ages 15-49): 59.6% (2023 est.)
Education expenditure: 5% of GDP (2023 est.)
12.6% national budget (2023 est.)
comparison ranking: Education expenditure (% GDP) 66
Literacy: *total population:* 96% (2020 est.)
male: 97% (2020 est.)
female: 95% (2020 est.)
School life expectancy (primary to tertiary education)
total: 15 years (2015 est.)
male: 13 years (2015 est.)
female: 16 years (2015 est.)

ENVIRONMENT

Environmental issues: limited natural freshwater resources; air and water pollution; desertification; loss of biodiversity
International environmental agreements: *party to:* Biodiversity, Climate Change, Climate Change-Kyoto Protocol, Climate Change-Paris Agreement, Comprehensive Nuclear Test Ban, Desertification, Endangered Species, Environmental Modification, Hazardous Wastes, Law of the Sea, Nuclear Test Ban, Ozone Layer Protection, Ship Pollution, Wetlands
signed, but not ratified: Marine Dumping-London Convention
Climate: dry desert; intensely hot summers; short, cool winters
Urbanization: *urban population:* 100% of total population (2023)
rate of urbanization: 1.35% annual rate of change (2020-25 est.)
Carbon dioxide emissions: 100.459 million metric tonnes of CO2 (2023 est.)
from coal and metallurgical coke: 149,000 metric tonnes of CO2 (2023 est.)
from petroleum and other liquids: 48.723 million metric tonnes of CO2 (2023 est.)
from consumed natural gas: 51.587 million metric tonnes of CO2 (2023 est.)
comparison ranking: total emissions 43
Particulate matter emissions: 54.9 micrograms per cubic meter (2019 est.)
Methane emissions: *energy:* 819.9 kt (2022-2024 est.)
agriculture: 7.3 kt (2019-2021 est.)
waste: 256.8 kt (2019-2021 est.)
other: 0.9 kt (2019-2021 est.)
Waste and recycling: *municipal solid waste generated annually:* 1.75 million tons (2024 est.)
percent of municipal solid waste recycled: 15.4% (2022 est.)
Total water withdrawal: *municipal:* 448.3 million cubic meters (2022 est.)
industrial: 23.3 million cubic meters (2022 est.)
agricultural: 778.4 million cubic meters (2022 est.)
Total renewable water resources: 20 million cubic meters (2022 est.)

GOVERNMENT

Country name: *conventional long form:* State of Kuwait
conventional short form: Kuwait
local long form: Dawlat al Kuwayt
local short form: Al Kuwayt
etymology: the name derives from the capital city, which comes from the Arabic ***al-kuwayt,*** itself a diminutive of the Hindustani term ***kut,*** meaning a fortress-like house
Government type: constitutional monarchy (emirate)
Capital: *name:* Kuwait City
geographic coordinates: 29 22 N, 47 58 E
time difference: UTC+3 (8 hours ahead of Washington, DC, during Standard Time)
etymology: the name comes from the Arabic ***al-kuwayt,*** a diminutive of the Hindustani term ***kut,*** meaning a fortress-like house
Administrative divisions: 6 governorates (***muhafazat,*** singular - ***muhafazah***); Al Ahmadi, Al 'Asimah, Al Farwaniyah, Al Jahra', Hawalli, Mubarak al Kabir
Legal system: mixed system consisting of English common law, French civil law, and Islamic sharia law
Constitution: *history:* approved and promulgated 11 November 1962; suspended 1976 to 1981 (4 articles); 1986 to 1991; May to July 1999
amendment process: proposed by the amir or supported by at least one third of the National Assembly; passage requires two-thirds consent of the Assembly membership and promulgation by the amir; constitutional articles on the initiation, approval, and promulgation of general legislation cannot be amended
note: in May 2024, Amir Sheikh MISHAL al-Ahmad al-Sabah dissolved the National Assembly and suspended several articles of the constitution for up to four years
International law organization participation: has not submitted an ICJ jurisdiction declaration; non-party state to the ICCt
Citizenship: *citizenship by birth:* no
citizenship by descent only: at least one parent must be a citizen of Kuwait
dual citizenship recognized: no
residency requirement for naturalization: not specified
Suffrage: 21 years of age and at least 20-year citizenship
Executive branch: *chief of state:* Amir MISHAL al-Ahmad al-Jabir al-Sabah (since 16 December 2023)
head of government: Prime Minister AHMAD ABDULLAH Al-Ahmad al Sabah (since 15 May 2024)
cabinet: Council of Ministers appointed by the prime minister, approved by the amir
election/appointment process: amir chosen from within the ruling family, confirmed by the National Assembly; prime minister appointed by the amir
Legislative branch: *expected date of next election:* April 2028
note: the unicameral National Assembly was dissolved on 10 May 2024 by Emir Sheikh Meshal al-Ahmad AL-SABAH for a period of up to four years; the Emir and cabinet officials have assumed the role of the parliament
Judicial branch: *highest court(s):* Constitutional Court (consists of 5 judges); Supreme Court or Court of Cassation (organized into several circuits, each with 5 judges)
judge selection and term of office: all Kuwaiti judges appointed by the Amir on recommendation of the Supreme Judicial Council, a consultative body comprised of Kuwaiti judges and Ministry of Justice officials
subordinate courts: High Court of Appeal; Court of First Instance; Summary Court
Political parties: none; the government does not recognize any political parties or allow their formation, although no formal law bans political parties
Diplomatic representation in the US: *chief of mission:* Ambassador AL-ZAIN Sabah Naser Saud Al-Sabah (since 19 April 2023)
chancery: 2940 Tilden Street NW, Washington, DC 20008
telephone: [1] (202) 966-0702
FAX: [1] (202) 966-8468
email address and website: info@kuwaitembassy.us
https://www.kuwaitembassy. us/
consulate(s) general: Beverly Hills (CA), New York
Diplomatic representation from the US: *chief of mission:* Ambassador (vacant); Chargé d'Affaires Steven R. BUTLER (since July 2025)
embassy: P.O. Box 77, Safat 13001
mailing address: 6200 Kuwait Place, Washington DC 20521-6200
telephone: [00] (965) 2259-1001

FAX: [00] (965) 2538-0282
email address and website: KuwaitACS@state.gov
https://kw.usembassy.gov/

International organization participation: ABEDA, AfDB (nonregional member), AFESD, AMF, BDEAC, CAEU, CD, FAO, G-77, GCC, IAEA, IBRD, ICAO, ICC (national committees), ICRM, IDA, IDB, IFAD, IFC, IFRCS, IHO, ILO, IMF, IMO, IMSO, Interpol, IOC, IPU, ISO, ITSO, ITU, ITUC (NGOs), LAS, MIGA, NAM, OAPEC, OIC, OPCW, OPEC, Paris Club (associate), PCA, UN, UNCTAD, UNESCO, UNHRC, UNIDO, UNOOSA, UNRWA, UN Security Council (temporary), UNWTO, UPU, WCO, WFTU (NGOs), WHO, WIPO, WMO, WTO

Independence: 19 June 1961 (from the UK)

National holiday: National Day, 25 February (1950)

Flag: *description:* three equal horizontal bands of green (top), white, and red, with a black trapezoid based on the left side
meaning: green stands for fertile fields, white for purity, red for blood on Kuwaiti swords, and black for defeating the enemy
history: colors and design are based on the Arab Revolt flag of World War I

National symbol(s): golden falcon

National color(s): green, white, red, black

National anthem(s): *title:* "Al-Nasheed Al-Watani" (National Anthem)
lyrics/music: Ahmad MUSHARI al-Adwani/Ibrahim Nasir al-SOULA
history: adopted 1978; the anthem is only used on formal occasions

ECONOMY

Economic overview: small, high-income, oil-based Middle East economy; renewable energy proponent; regional finance and investment leader; maintains oldest sovereign wealth fund; emerging space and tourism industries; mid-way through 25-year development program

Real GDP (purchasing power parity): $225.947 billion (2024 est.)
$231.884 billion (2023 est.)
$235.815 billion (2022 est.)
note: data in 2021 dollars
comparison ranking: 72

Real GDP growth rate: -2.6% (2024 est.)
-1.7% (2023 est.)
6.8% (2022 est.)
note: annual GDP % growth based on constant local currency
comparison ranking: 209

Real GDP per capita: $45,400 (2024 est.)
$47,800 (2023 est.)
$51,400 (2022 est.)
note: data in 2021 dollars
comparison ranking: 49

GDP (official exchange rate): $160.227 billion (2024 est.)
note: data in current dollars at official exchange rate

Inflation rate (consumer prices): 2.9% (2024 est.)
3.6% (2023 est.)
4% (2022 est.)
note: annual % change based on consumer prices
comparison ranking: 91

GDP - composition, by sector of origin: *agriculture:* 0.5% (2024 est.)
industry: 57.1% (2024 est.)
services: 55.9% (2024 est.)
note: figures may not total 100% due to non-allocated consumption not captured in sector-reported data
comparison rankings: agriculture 190; industry 5; services 116

GDP - composition, by end use: *household consumption:* 32.6% (2022 est.)
government consumption: 20.7% (2022 est.)
investment in fixed capital: 16.1% (2022 est.)
investment in inventories: 0.8% (2022 est.)
exports of goods and services: 60.4% (2022 est.)
imports of goods and services: -30.5% (2022 est.)
note: figures may not total 100% due to rounding or gaps in data collection

Agricultural products: dates, eggs, milk, tomatoes, chicken, lamb/mutton, cucumbers/gherkins, vegetables, maize, eggplants (2023)
note: top ten agricultural products based on tonnage

Industries: petroleum, petrochemicals, cement, shipbuilding and repair, water desalination, food processing, construction materials

Industrial production growth rate: -5.2% (2024 est.)
note: annual % change in industrial value added based on constant local currency
comparison ranking: 179

Labor force: 3.003 million (2024 est.)
note: number of people ages 15 or older who are employed or seeking work
comparison ranking: 111

Unemployment rate: 2.2% (2024 est.)
2.2% (2023 est.)
2.2% (2022 est.)
note: % of labor force seeking employment
comparison ranking: 18

Youth unemployment rate (ages 15-24): *total:* 15.4% (2024 est.)
male: 9.3% (2024 est.)
female: 28.9% (2024 est.)
note: % of labor force ages 15-24 seeking employment
comparison ranking: total 78

Average household expenditures: *on food:* 19.2% of household expenditures (2023 est.)
on alcohol and tobacco: 0.2% of household expenditures (2023 est.)

Remittances: 0% of GDP (2024 est.)
0% of GDP (2023 est.)
0% of GDP (2022 est.)
note: personal transfers and compensation between resident and non-resident individuals/households/entities

Budget: *revenues:* $44.254 billion (2015 est.)
expenditures: $59.584 billion (2015 est.)
note: central government revenues and expenses (excluding grants and social security funds) converted to US dollars at average official exchange rate for year indicated

Current account balance: $46.703 billion (2024 est.)
$51.396 billion (2023 est.)
$63.078 billion (2022 est.)
note: balance of payments - net trade and primary/secondary income in current dollars
comparison ranking: 14

Exports: $89.71 billion (2024 est.)
$95.476 billion (2023 est.)
$110.923 billion (2022 est.)
note: balance of payments - exports of goods and services in current dollars
comparison ranking: 52

Exports - partners: China 25%, India 13%, Japan 13%, Taiwan 7%, UK 5% (2023)
note: top five export partners based on percentage share of exports

Exports - commodities: crude petroleum, refined petroleum, natural gas, hydrocarbons, plastics (2023)
note: top five export commodities based on value in dollars

Imports: $61.521 billion (2024 est.)
$63.43 billion (2023 est.)
$55.909 billion (2022 est.)
note: balance of payments - imports of goods and services in current dollars
comparison ranking: 60

Imports - partners: China 18%, UAE 10%, USA 9%, Saudi Arabia 6%, Japan 6% (2023)
note: top five import partners based on percentage share of imports

Imports - commodities: cars, natural gas, garments, broadcasting equipment, packaged medicine (2023)
note: top five import commodities based on value in dollars

Reserves of foreign exchange and gold: $50.728 billion (2024 est.)
$52.619 billion (2023 est.)
$52.462 billion (2022 est.)
note: holdings of gold (year-end prices)/foreign exchange/special drawing rights in current dollars
comparison ranking: 42

Exchange rates: Kuwaiti dinars (KD) per US dollar -
Exchange rates: 0.307 (2024 est.)
0.307 (2023 est.)
0.306 (2022 est.)
0.302 (2021 est.)
0.306 (2020 est.)

ENERGY

Electricity access: *electrification - total population:* 100% (2022 est.)

Electricity: *installed generating capacity:* 20.294 million kW (2023 est.)
consumption: 78.047 billion kWh (2023 est.)
transmission/distribution losses: 7.516 billion kWh (2023 est.)
comparison rankings: installed generating capacity 51; consumption 40; transmission/distribution losses 173

Electricity generation sources: *fossil fuels:* 97.8% of total installed capacity (2023 est.)
solar: 0.2% of total installed capacity (2023 est.)
wind: 2% of total installed capacity (2023 est.)

Coal: *consumption:* 60,000 metric tons (2023 est.)
exports: 11 metric tons (2023 est.)
imports: 152,000 metric tons (2023 est.)

Petroleum: *total petroleum production:* 2.91 million bbl/day (2023 est.)
refined petroleum consumption: 430,000 bbl/day (2023 est.)
crude oil estimated reserves: 101.5 billion barrels (2021 est.)

Natural gas: *production:* 19.207 billion cubic meters (2023 est.)
consumption: 26.296 billion cubic meters (2023 est.)
imports: 8.433 billion cubic meters (2023 est.)
proven reserves: 1.784 trillion cubic meters (2021 est.)

Energy consumption per capita: 389.848 million Btu/person (2023 est.)
comparison ranking: 6

COMMUNICATIONS

Telephones - fixed lines: *total subscriptions:* 573,000 (2023 est.)
subscriptions per 100 inhabitants: 12 (2023 est.)
comparison ranking: total subscriptions 88

Telephones - mobile cellular: *total subscriptions:* 8.11 million (2023 est.)
subscriptions per 100 inhabitants: 181 (2022 est.)
comparison ranking: total subscriptions 101

Broadcast media: state-owned TV broadcaster operates 4 networks and a satellite channel; several private TV broadcasters; satellite TV available, and pan-Arab TV stations are especially popular; state-owned Radio Kuwait broadcasts on a number of channels in Arabic and English; first private radio station in 2005; transmissions of at least 2 international radio broadcasters are available (2019)

Internet country code: .kw

Internet users: *percent of population:* 100% (2023 est.)

Broadband - fixed subscriptions: *total:* 49,000 (2023 est.)
subscriptions per 100 inhabitants: 1 (2023 est.)
comparison ranking: total 146

TRANSPORTATION

Civil aircraft registration country code prefix: 9K

Airports: 6 (2025)
comparison ranking: 174

Heliports: 20 (2025)
comparison ranking: 54

Merchant marine: *total:* 176 (2023)
by type: general cargo 15, oil tanker 28, other 133
comparison ranking: total 72

Ports: *total ports:* 6 (2024)
large: 0
medium: 2
small: 1
very small: 3
ports with oil terminals: 4
key ports: Al Kuwayt, Doha Harbor, Mina Abd Allah, Mina Al Ahmadi, Mina Ash Shuaybah, Mina Az Zawr

MILITARY AND SECURITY

Military and security forces: Kuwait Armed Forces (KAF): Kuwait Army (aka Kuwait Land Forces, KLF), Kuwait Navy (aka Kuwait Naval Force), Kuwait Air Force; Kuwait National Guard (KNG)

Ministry of Interior: Kuwait Police, State Security, Kuwait Coast Guard (2025)
note 1: the Emiri Guard Authority and the 25th Commando Brigade are special units within the KAF that exercise independent command authority, although activities such as training and equipment procurement are often coordinated with the other services; the 25th Commando Brigade is Kuwait's leading special forces unit; the Emiri Guard Authority (aka Emiri Guard Brigade) is responsible for protecting Kuwait's heads of state
note 2: the National Guard reports directly to the prime minister and the amir and possesses an independent command structure, equipment inventory, and logistics corps separate from the Ministry of Defense, the regular armed services, and the Ministry of Interior; it is responsible for protecting critical infrastructure and providing support for the Ministries of Interior and Defense as required

Military expenditures: 4.9% of GDP (2024 est.)
4.8% of GDP (2023 est.)
4.5% of GDP (2022 est.)
6.5% of GDP (2021 est.)
6.3% of GDP (2020 est.)

Military and security service personnel strengths: approximately 17,000 active Kuwait Armed Forces; approximately 7,000 National Guard (2025)

Military equipment inventories and acquisitions: the military's inventory consists of weapons from a wide variety of sources, including Western Europe, Russia, and particularly the US (2024)

Military service age and obligation: 18-55 years of age for voluntary military service; Kuwait reintroduced 12-month mandatory service for men aged 18-35 in May 2017 after having suspended conscription in 2001; mandatory service is divided in two phases – 4 months for training and 8 months for military service; women were allowed to volunteer in 2021 (2023)
note: the National Guard is restricted to citizens, but in 2018, the Army began allowing non-Kuwaitis to join on contract or as non-commissioned officers; that same year, it also began allowing stateless people (Bidoon) to join

Military - note: the Kuwaiti Armed Forces (KAF) are responsible for defending Kuwait's sovereignty and territory; Kuwait's security concerns include regional threats from state and non-state actors, maritime security, and terrorism; the KAF participates in bilateral and multilateral exercises, as well as a limited number of multinational security operations such as maritime patrols in the Persian Gulf; it also provided a few fighter aircraft to the Saudi-led coalition intervention in Yemen in 2015; the KAF is part of the Peninsula Shield Forces, a joint military force established by the GCC countries with the aim of maintaining security and stability in the region
Kuwait's key security partner since the 1991 Gulf War has been the US; the US maintains thousands of military personnel as well as logistics and training facilities in Kuwait as part of mutual cooperation agreements signed in 1991 and 2013; the KAF conducts bilateral exercises with the US military and would look to US assistance in the event of an external attack; Kuwait has Major Non-NATO Ally status with the US, a designation under US law that provides foreign partners with certain benefits in the areas of defense trade and security cooperation (2025)

TRANSNATIONAL ISSUES

Refugees and internally displaced persons: *refugees:* 1,271 (2024 est.)
stateless persons: 92,000 (2024 est.)

KYRGYZSTAN

INTRODUCTION

Background: Kyrgyzstan is a Central Asian country of incredible natural beauty and proud nomadic traditions. The Russian Empire annexed most of the territory of present-day Kyrgyzstan in 1876. The Kyrgyz staged a major revolt against the Tsarist Empire in 1916, during which almost one-sixth of the Kyrgyz population was killed. Kyrgyzstan became a Soviet republic in 1926 and achieved independence in 1991 when the USSR dissolved. Nationwide demonstrations in 2005 and 2010 resulted in the ouster of the country's first two presidents, Askar AKAEV and Kurmanbek BAKIEV. Almazbek ATAMBAEV was sworn in as president in 2011. In 2017, ATAMBAEV became the first Kyrgyzstani president to serve a full term and respect constitutional term limits, voluntarily stepping down at the end of his mandate. Former prime minister and ruling Social-Democratic Party of Kyrgyzstan member Sooronbay JEENBEKOV replaced him after winning the 2017 presidential election, which was the most competitive in the country's history despite reported cases of vote buying and abuse of public resources.

In 2020, protests against parliamentary election results spread across Kyrgyzstan, leading to JEENBEKOV's resignation and catapulting previously imprisoned Sadyr JAPAROV to acting president. In 2021, Kyrgyzstanis formally elected JAPAROV as president and approved a referendum to move Kyrgyzstan from a parliamentary to a presidential system. In 2021, Kyrgyzstanis voted in favor of constitutional changes that consolidated power in the presidency. Pro-government parties won a majority in the 2021 legislative elections. Continuing concerns for Kyrgyzstan include the trajectory of democratization, endemic corruption, tense regional relations, vulnerabilities due to climate change, border security vulnerabilities, and potential terrorist threats.

GEOGRAPHY

Location: Central Asia, west of China, south of Kazakhstan

Geographic coordinates: 41 00 N, 75 00 E

Map references: Asia

Area: *total:* 199,951 sq km
land: 191,801 sq km
water: 8,150 sq km
comparison ranking: total 87

Area - comparative: slightly smaller than South Dakota

Land boundaries: *total:* 4,573 km
border countries (4): China 1,063 km; Kazakhstan 1,212 km; Tajikistan 984 km; Uzbekistan 1,314 km

Coastline: 0 km (landlocked)

Maritime claims: none (landlocked)

Climate: dry continental to polar in high Tien Shan Mountains; subtropical in southwest (Fergana Valley); temperate in northern foothill zone

Terrain: peaks of the Tien Shan mountain range and associated valleys and basins encompass the entire country

Elevation: *highest point:* Jengish Chokusu (Pik Pobedy) 7,439 m
lowest point: Kara-Daryya (Karadar'ya) 132 m
mean elevation: 2,988 m

Natural resources: abundant hydropower; gold, rare earth metals; locally exploitable coal, oil, and natural gas; other deposits of nepheline, mercury, bismuth, lead, and zinc

Land use: *agricultural land:* 54% (2022 est.)
arable land: 6.7% (2022 est.)
permanent crops: 0.4% (2022 est.)
permanent pasture: 46.9% (2022 est.)
forest: 7% (2022 est.)
other: 38.9% (2022 est.)

Irrigated land: 10,041 sq km (2022)

Major lakes (area sq km): *salt water lake(s):* Ozero Issyk-Kul 6,240 sq km
note - second largest saline lake after the Caspian Sea; second highest mountain lake after Lake Titicaca; it is an endorheic mountain basin; although surrounded by snow capped mountains it never freezes

Major rivers (by length in km): Syr Darya river source (shared with Tajikistan, Uzbekistan, and Kazakhstan [m]) - 3,078 km
note: [s] after country name indicates river source; [m] after country name indicates river mouth

Major watersheds (area sq km): Internal (endorheic basin) drainage: Tarim Basin (1,152,448 sq km), *(Aral Sea basin)* Amu Darya (534,739 sq km), Syr Darya (782,617 sq km)

Population distribution: the vast majority of Kyrgyzstanis live in rural areas; densest population settlement is to the north in and around the capital, Bishkek, followed by Osh in the west; the least densely populated area is the east, in the Tien Shan mountains

Natural hazards: major flooding during snow melt; prone to earthquakes

Geography - note: landlocked; entirely mountainous, dominated by the Tien Shan range; 94% of the country is 1,000 m above sea level with an average elevation of 2,750 m; many tall peaks, glaciers, and high-altitude lakes

PEOPLE AND SOCIETY

Population: *total:* 6,172,101 (2024 est.)
male: 3,021,318
female: 3,150,783
comparison rankings: total 112; male 113; female 112

Nationality: *noun:* Kyrgyzstani(s)
adjective: Kyrgyzstani

Ethnic groups: Kyrgyz 73.8%, Uzbek 14.8%, Russian 5.1%, Dungan 1.1%, other 5.2% (includes Uyghur, Tajik, Turk, Kazakh, Tatar, Ukrainian, Korean, German) (2021 est.)

Languages: Kyrgyz (state language) 71.4%, Uzbek 14.4%, Russian (official language) 9%, other 5.2% (2009 est.)
major-language sample(s):
Дүйнөлүк фактылар китеби, негизги маалыматтын маанилүү булагы. (Kyrgyz)

Religions: Muslim 90% (majority Sunni), Christian 7% (Russian Orthodox 3%), other 3% (includes Jewish, Buddhist, Baha'i) (2017 est.)

Age structure: *0-14 years:* 29.1% (male 922,086/female 873,245)
15-64 years: 64% (male 1,935,200/female 2,013,733)
65 years and over: 6.9% (2024 est.) (male 164,032/female 263,805)

Dependency ratios: *total dependency ratio:* 56.3 (2024 est.)
youth dependency ratio: 45.5 (2024 est.)
elderly dependency ratio: 10.8 (2024 est.)
potential support ratio: 9.2 (2024 est.)

Median age: *total:* 28.3 years (2024 est.)
male: 26.9 years
female: 29.8 years
comparison ranking: total 151

Population growth rate: 0.79% (2024 est.)
comparison ranking: 111

Birth rate: 18.7 births/1,000 population (2024 est.)
comparison ranking: 76

Death rate: 6 deaths/1,000 population (2024 est.)
comparison ranking: 152

Net migration rate: -4.8 migrant(s)/1,000 population (2024 est.)
comparison ranking: 200

Population distribution: the vast majority of Kyrgyzstanis live in rural areas; densest population settlement is to the north in and around the capital, Bishkek, followed by Osh in the west; the least densely populated area is the east, in the Tien Shan mountains

Urbanization: *urban population:* 37.8% of total population (2023)
rate of urbanization: 2.05% annual rate of change (2020-25 est.)

Major urban areas - population: 1.105 million BISHKEK (capital) (2023)

Sex ratio: *at birth:* 1.07 male(s)/female
0-14 years: 1.06 male(s)/female
15-64 years: 0.96 male(s)/female
65 years and over: 0.62 male(s)/female
total population: 0.96 male(s)/female (2024 est.)

Mother's mean age at first birth: 22.6 years (2019 est.)

Maternal mortality ratio: 42 deaths/100,000 live births (2023 est.)
comparison ranking: 100

Infant mortality rate: *total:* 24.5 deaths/1,000 live births (2024 est.)
male: 28.6 deaths/1,000 live births
female: 20.2 deaths/1,000 live births
comparison ranking: total 61

Life expectancy at birth: *total population:* 72.9 years (2024 est.)
male: 68.9 years
female: 77.2 years
comparison ranking: total population 157

Total fertility rate: 2.45 children born/woman (2024 est.)
comparison ranking: 71

Gross reproduction rate: 1.19 (2024 est.)

Drinking water source: *improved: urban:* 99.2% of population (2022 est.)
rural: 85.8% of population (2022 est.)
total: 90.8% of population (2022 est.)
unimproved: urban: 0.8% of population (2022 est.)
rural: 14.2% of population (2022 est.)
total: 9.2% of population (2022 est.)

Health expenditure: 5.4% of GDP (2021)
7.6% of national budget (2022 est.)

Physician density: 1.85 physicians/1,000 population (2023)

Hospital bed density: 4.2 beds/1,000 population (2021 est.)

Sanitation facility access: *improved: urban:* 100% of population (2022 est.)
rural: 100% of population (2022 est.)
total: 100% of population (2022 est.)
unimproved: urban: 0% of population (2022 est.)
rural: 0% of population (2022 est.)
total: 0% of population (2022 est.)

Obesity - adult prevalence rate: 16.6% (2016)
comparison ranking: 122

Alcohol consumption per capita: *total:* 4.02 liters of pure alcohol (2019 est.)
beer: 0.43 liters of pure alcohol (2019 est.)
wine: 0.23 liters of pure alcohol (2019 est.)
spirits: 3.35 liters of pure alcohol (2019 est.)
other alcohols: 0 liters of pure alcohol (2019 est.)
comparison ranking: total 96

Tobacco use: *total:* 26% (2025 est.)
male: 50.7% (2025 est.)
female: 3.1% (2025 est.)
comparison ranking: total 38

Children under the age of 5 years underweight: 1.8% (2018)
comparison ranking: 102

Currently married women (ages 15-49): 66.2% (2023 est.)

Child marriage: *women married by age 15:* 0.3% (2018)
women married by age 18: 12.9% (2018)

Education expenditure: 6.8% of GDP (2023 est.)
19.8% national budget (2023 est.)
comparison ranking: Education expenditure (% GDP) 17

School life expectancy (primary to tertiary education): *total:* 13 years (2024 est.)
male: 12 years (2024 est.)
female: 13 years (2024 est.)

ENVIRONMENT

Environmental issues: water pollution; increasing soil salinity from irrigation practices; air pollution due to vehicle traffic

International environmental agreements: *party to:* Air Pollution, Biodiversity, Climate Change, Climate Change-Kyoto Protocol, Climate Change-Paris Agreement, Comprehensive Nuclear Test Ban, Desertification, Endangered Species, Environmental Modification, Hazardous Wastes, Ozone Layer Protection, Wetlands
signed, but not ratified: none of the selected agreements

Climate: dry continental to polar in high Tien Shan Mountains; subtropical in southwest (Fergana Valley); temperate in northern foothill zone

Urbanization: *urban population:* 37.8% of total population (2023)
rate of urbanization: 2.05% annual rate of change (2020-25 est.)

Carbon dioxide emissions: 11.389 million metric tonnes of CO2 (2023 est.)
from coal and metallurgical coke: 6.301 million metric tonnes of CO2 (2023 est.)

from petroleum and other liquids: 4.234 million metric tonnes of CO2 (2023 est.)
from consumed natural gas: 854,000 metric tonnes of CO2 (2023 est.)
comparison ranking: total emissions 102

Particulate matter emissions: 40.9 micrograms per cubic meter (2019 est.)

Waste and recycling: *municipal solid waste generated annually:* 1.113 million tons (2024 est.)
percent of municipal solid waste recycled: 14.6% (2022 est.)

Total water withdrawal: *municipal:* 224 million cubic meters (2022 est.)
industrial: 336 million cubic meters (2022 est.)
agricultural: 7.1 billion cubic meters (2022 est.)

Total renewable water resources: 23.618 billion cubic meters (2022 est.)

GOVERNMENT

Country name: *conventional long form:* Kyrgyz Republic
conventional short form: Kyrgyzstan
local long form: Kyrgyz Respublikasy
local short form: Kyrgyzstan
etymology: named for the local Kyrgyz people, with "-stan" coming from the Persian word *ostan*, meaning "country;" the Kyrgyz name may derive from the Turkic root words *kir*, or "steppe," and *gismek*, "to wander;" the name is traditionally said to come from a combination of the Turkic words *kyrg* (forty) and *-is* (hundred), based on a tale about two tribes and the number of their tents

Government type: parliamentary republic

Capital: *name:* Bishkek
geographic coordinates: 42 52 N, 74 36 E
time difference: UTC+6 (11 hours ahead of Washington, DC, during Standard Time)
etymology: the meaning of the name is unknown; the city was founded in 1862 as a Russian settlement on the site of an Uzbek fortress named Bishkek; the Russian version of the name was Pishpek, and the original name only came back into use in 1991

Administrative divisions: 7 provinces (*oblustar*, singular - *oblus*) and 2 cities* (*shaarlar*, singular - *shaar*); Batken Oblusu, Bishkek Shaary*, Chuy Oblusu (Bishkek), Jalal-Abad Oblusu, Naryn Oblusu, Osh Oblusu, Osh Shaary*, Talas Oblusu, Ysyk-Kol Oblusu (Karakol)
note: administrative divisions have the same names as their administrative centers; exceptions show the administrative center name in parentheses

Legal system: civil law system that includes features of French civil law and Russian Federation laws

Constitution: *history:* previous 1993, 2007, 2010; latest approved by referendum in 2021
amendment process: proposed as a draft law by the majority of the Supreme Council membership or by petition of 300,000 voters; passage requires at least two-thirds majority vote of the Council membership in each of at least three readings of the draft two months apart; the draft may be submitted to a referendum if approved by two thirds of the Council membership; adoption requires the signature of the president

International law organization participation: has not submitted an ICJ jurisdiction declaration; non-party state to the ICCt

Citizenship: *citizenship by birth:* no
citizenship by descent only: at least one parent must be a citizen of Kyrgyzstan
dual citizenship recognized: yes, but only if a mutual treaty on dual citizenship is in force
residency requirement for naturalization: 5 years

Suffrage: 18 years of age; universal

Executive branch: *chief of state:* President Sadyr JAPAROV (since 28 January 2021)
head of government: President Adylbek KASYMALIYEV (since 18 December 2024)
cabinet: Cabinet of Ministers appointed by the president
election/appointment process: president directly elected by absolute-majority popular vote in 2 rounds, if needed, for a five-year term (eligible for a second term)
most recent election date: 10 January 2021
election results: *2021:* Sadyr JAPAROV elected president in first round; percent of vote - Sadyr JAPAROV (Mekenchil) 79.2%, Adakhan MADUMAROV (United Kyrgyzstan) 6.8%, other 14%
2017: Sooronbay JEENBEKOV elected president; Sooronbay JEENBEKOV (Social Democratic Party of Kyrgyzstan) 54.7%, Omurbek BABANOV (independent) 33.8%, Adakhan MADUMAROV (United Kyrgyzstan) 6.6%, other 4.9%
expected date of next election: 2027
note: the president is both chief of state and head of government

Legislative branch: *legislature name:* Supreme Council (Jogorku Kenesh)
legislative structure: unicameral
number of seats: 90 (all directly elected)
electoral system: proportional representation
scope of elections: full renewal
term in office: 5 years
most recent election date: 11/28/2021
parties elected and seats per party: Ata-Jurt Kyrgyzstan (Fatherland) (15); Ishenim (Trust) (12); Yntymak (Harmony) (9); Alyans (Alliance) (7); Butun Kyrgyzstan (United) (6); Yiman Nuru (Ray of Faith) (5); Independents (34)
percentage of women in chamber: 22.2%
expected date of next election: November 2026

Judicial branch: *highest court(s):* Supreme Court (consists of 25 judges); Constitutional Chamber of the Supreme Court (consists of the chairperson, deputy chairperson, and 9 judges)
judge selection and term of office: Supreme Court and Constitutional Court judges appointed by the Supreme Council on the recommendation of the president; Supreme Court judges serve for 10 years, Constitutional Court judges serve for 15 years; mandatory retirement at age 70 for judges of both courts
subordinate courts: Higher Court of Arbitration; oblast (provincial) and city courts

Political parties: Afghan's Party
Alliance
Ata-Jurt Kyrgyzstan (Fatherland) or AJK
Cohesion
Ishenim (Trust)
Light of Faith
Mekenchil or the "Patriotic" Political Party
Social Democrats or SDK
United Kyrgyzstan
Yntymak (Unity)

Diplomatic representation in the US: *chief of mission:* Ambassador Aibek MOLDOGAZIEV (since 25 February 2025)
chancery: 2360 Massachusetts Avenue NW, Washington, DC 20008
telephone: [1] (202) 449-9822
FAX: [1] (202) 449-8275
email address and website: kgembassy.usa@mfa.gov.kg
Embassy of the Kyrgyz Republic in the USA and Canada (mfa.gov.kg)

Diplomatic representation from the US: *chief of mission:* Ambassador Lesslie VIGUERIE (since 29 December 2022)
embassy: 171 Prospect Mira, Bishkek 720016
mailing address: 7040 Bishkek Place, Washington DC 20521-7040
telephone: [996] (312) 597-000
FAX: [996] (312) 597-744
email address and website: ConsularBishkek@state.gov
https://kg.usembassy. gov/

International organization participation: ADB, CICA, CIS, CSTO, EAEU, EAPC, EBRD, ECO, EITI (compliant country), FAO, GCTU, IAEA, IBRD, ICAO, ICC (NGOs), ICRM, IDA, IDB, IFAD, IFC, IFRCS, ILO, IMF, Interpol, IOC, IOM, IPU, ISO (correspondent), ITSO, ITU, MIGA, NAM (observer), OIC, OPCW, OSCE, PCA, PFP, SCO, UN, UNAMID, UNCTAD, UNESCO, UNIDO, UNISFA, UNMIL, UNMISS, UNWTO, UPU, WCO, WFTU (NGOs), WHO, WIPO, WMO, WTO

Independence: 31 August 1991 (from the Soviet Union)

National holiday: Independence Day, 31 August (1991)

Flag: *description:* red field with a yellow sun in the center that has 40 rays that run counterclockwise on the front of the flag and clockwise on the reverse; in the center of the sun is a red ring crossed by two sets of three lines in a stylized representation of a *tunduk*, the circular opening at the top of a traditional Kyrgyz yurt
meaning: the sun's rays represent the Kyrgyz tribes; red stands for bravery and valor, and the sun for peace and wealth

National symbol(s): white falcon

National color(s): red, yellow

National anthem(s): *title:* "Kyrgyz Respublikasynyn Mamlekettik Gimni" (National Anthem of the Kyrgyz Republic)
lyrics/music: Djamil SADYKOV and Eshmambet KULUEV/Nasyr DAVLESOV and Kalyi MOLDOBASANOV
history: adopted 1992

National heritage: *total World Heritage Sites:* 3 (2 cultural, 1 natural)
selected World Heritage Site locales: Sulaiman-Too Sacred Mountain (c); Silk Roads: the Chang'an-Tianshan Corridor (c); Western Tien Shan (n)

ECONOMY

Economic overview: landlocked, lower-middle-income Central Asian economy; natural resource rich; growing hydroelectricity and tourism; high remittances; corruption limits investment; COVID-19 and political turmoil hurt GDP, limited public revenues, and increased spending

Real GDP (purchasing power parity): $50.907 billion (2024 est.)
$46.686 billion (2023 est.)
$42.826 billion (2022 est.)
note: data in 2021 dollars
comparison ranking: 128

Real GDP growth rate: 9% (2024 est.)
9% (2023 est.)
9% (2022 est.)
note: annual GDP % growth based on constant local currency
comparison ranking: 6

Real GDP per capita: $7,000 (2024 est.)
$6,600 (2023 est.)
$6,100 (2022 est.)
note: data in 2021 dollars
comparison ranking: 158

GDP (official exchange rate): $17.478 billion (2024 est.)
note: data in current dollars at official exchange rate

Inflation rate (consumer prices): 10.8% (2023 est.)
13.9% (2022 est.)
11.9% (2021 est.)
note: annual % change based on consumer prices
comparison ranking: 181

GDP - composition, by sector of origin: *agriculture:* 8.6% (2024 est.)
industry: 24.7% (2024 est.)
services: 52.1% (2024 est.)
note: figures may not total 100% due to non-allocated consumption not captured in sector-reported data
comparison rankings: agriculture 81; industry 91; services 132

GDP - composition, by end use: *household consumption:* 88.3% (2023 est.)
government consumption: 16% (2023 est.)
investment in fixed capital: 22% (2023 est.)
investment in inventories: 12.5% (2023 est.)
exports of goods and services: 36.9% (2023 est.)
imports of goods and services: -95.5% (2023 est.)
note: figures may not total 100% due to rounding or gaps in data collection

Agricultural products: milk, potatoes, maize, sugar beets, wheat, barley, tomatoes, onions, watermelons, carrots/turnips (2023)
note: top ten agricultural products based on tonnage

Industries: small machinery, textiles, food processing, cement, shoes, lumber, refrigerators, furniture, electric motors, gold, rare earth metals

Industrial production growth rate: 9.4% (2024 est.)
note: annual % change in industrial value added based on constant local currency
comparison ranking: 15

Labor force: 3.197 million (2024 est.)
note: number of people ages 15 or older who are employed or seeking work
comparison ranking: 106

Unemployment rate: 3.3% (2024 est.)
4% (2023 est.)
4.1% (2022 est.)
note: % of labor force seeking employment
comparison ranking: 52

Youth unemployment rate (ages 15-24): *total:* 6.8% (2024 est.)
male: 6.3% (2024 est.)
female: 7.7% (2024 est.)
note: % of labor force ages 15-24 seeking employment
comparison ranking: total 147

Population below poverty line: 33.3% (2021 est.)
note: % of population with income below national poverty line
Gini Index coefficient - distribution of family income 26.4 (2022 est.)
note: index (0-100) of income distribution; higher values represent greater inequality
comparison ranking: 140

Household income or consumption by percentage share: *lowest 10%:* 4.4% (2022 est.)
highest 10%: 22% (2022 est.)
note: % share of income accruing to lowest and highest 10% of population

Remittances: 18.8% of GDP (2023 est.)
26.6% of GDP (2022 est.)
32.6% of GDP (2021 est.)
note: personal transfers and compensation between resident and non-resident individuals/households/entities

Budget: *revenues:* $4.84 billion (2023 est.)
expenditures: $4.452 billion (2023 est.)
note: central government revenues (excluding grants) and expenditures converted to US dollars at average official exchange rate for year indicated

Public debt: 40.5% of GDP (2023 est.)
note: central government debt as a % of GDP
comparison ranking: 130

Taxes and other revenues: 19.6% (of GDP) (2023 est.)
note: central government tax revenue as a % of GDP
comparison ranking: 52

Current account balance: -$5.18 billion (2022 est.)
-$737.696 million (2021 est.)
$374.257 million (2020 est.)
note: balance of payments - net trade and primary/secondary income in current dollars
comparison ranking: 172

Exports: $3.628 billion (2022 est.)
$3.292 billion (2021 est.)
$2.435 billion (2020 est.)
note: balance of payments - exports of goods and services in current dollars
comparison ranking: 150

Exports - partners: Switzerland 30%, Russia 19%, Kazakhstan 14%, UAE 10%, Turkey 8% (2023)
note: top five export partners based on percentage share of exports

Exports - commodities: gold, coal, precious metal ore, refined petroleum, garments (2023)
note: top five export commodities based on value in dollars

Imports: $10.655 billion (2022 est.)
$5.928 billion (2021 est.)
$4.051 billion (2020 est.)
note: balance of payments - imports of goods and services in current dollars
comparison ranking: 118

Imports - partners: China 44%, Russia 12%, Kazakhstan 6%, Turkey 6%, Uzbekistan 4% (2023)
note: top five import partners based on percentage share of imports

Imports - commodities: cars, garments, refined petroleum, fabric, footwear (2023)
note: top five import commodities based on value in dollars

Reserves of foreign exchange and gold: $5.089 billion (2024 est.)
$3.237 billion (2023 est.)
$2.799 billion (2022 est.)
note: holdings of gold (year-end prices)/foreign exchange/special drawing rights in current dollars
comparison ranking: 99

Debt - external: $3.617 billion (2023 est.)
note: present value of external debt in current US dollars
comparison ranking: 81

Exchange rates: soms (KGS) per US dollar -

Exchange rates: 87.15 (2024 est.)
87.856 (2023 est.)
84.116 (2022 est.)
84.641 (2021 est.)
77.346 (2020 est.)

ENERGY

Electricity access: *electrification - total population:* 99.7% (2022 est.)
electrification - urban areas: 100%
electrification - rural areas: 99.6%

Electricity: *installed generating capacity:* 3.944 million kW (2023 est.)
consumption: 14.872 billion kWh (2023 est.)
exports: 428.01 million kWh (2023 est.)
imports: 3.929 billion kWh (2023 est.)
transmission/distribution losses: 2.363 billion kWh (2023 est.)
comparison rankings: installed generating capacity 100; consumption 88; exports 79; imports 52; transmission/distribution losses 130

Electricity generation sources: *fossil fuels:* 14.3% of total installed capacity (2023 est.)
hydroelectricity: 85.7% of total installed capacity (2023 est.)

Coal: *production:* 3.685 million metric tons (2023 est.)
consumption: 4.212 million metric tons (2023 est.)
exports: 1.672 million metric tons (2023 est.)
imports: 1.443 million metric tons (2023 est.)
proven reserves: 28.499 billion metric tons (2023 est.)

Petroleum: *total petroleum production:* 6,000 bbl/day (2023 est.)
refined petroleum consumption: 31,000 bbl/day (2023 est.)
crude oil estimated reserves: 40 million barrels (2021 est.)

Natural gas: *production:* 28.638 million cubic meters (2023 est.)
consumption: 435.336 million cubic meters (2023 est.)
imports: 406.698 million cubic meters (2023 est.)
proven reserves: 5.663 billion cubic meters (2021 est.)

Energy consumption per capita: 27.58 million Btu/person (2023 est.)
comparison ranking: 119

COMMUNICATIONS

Telephones - fixed lines: *total subscriptions:* 185,000 (2023 est.)
subscriptions per 100 inhabitants: 3 (2023 est.)
comparison ranking: total subscriptions 120

Telephones - mobile cellular: *total subscriptions:* 7.68 million (2023 est.)
subscriptions per 100 inhabitants: 130 (2021 est.)
comparison ranking: total subscriptions 105

Broadcast media: state-funded public TV broadcaster NTRK operates Ala-Too 24 news channel and 4 other educational, cultural, and sports channels; ELTR is a state-owned TV station; the switchover to digital TV in 2017 resulted in private TV station growth; approximately 20 TV stations are struggling to increase Kyrgyz-language content to 60% of airtime, as required by law, instead of rebroadcasting programs from Russian channels or airing unlicensed movies and music; several Russian TV stations also broadcast; state-funded radio stations and about 10 significant private radio stations (2023)

Internet country code: .kg

Internet users: *percent of population:* 89% (2023 est.)

Broadband - fixed subscriptions: *total:* 456,000 (2023 est.)
subscriptions per 100 inhabitants: 6 (2023 est.)
comparison ranking: total 101

TRANSPORTATION

Civil aircraft registration country code prefix: EX

Airports: 28 (2025)
comparison ranking: 123

Heliports: 1 (2025)
comparison ranking: 159

Railways: *total:* 424 km (2022)
broad gauge: 424 km (2018) 1.520-m gauge

MILITARY AND SECURITY

Military and security forces: Armed Forces of the Kyrgyz Republic: Land Forces (Kygyz Army), Air Defense Forces (Kyrgyz Air Force), National Guard of the Armed Forces of the Kyrgyz Republic

Ministry of Internal Affairs: Internal Security Service

State Committee for National Security: Border Guard Service (2025)
note: the National Guard's missions include counterterrorism, responding to emergencies, and the protection of government facilities

Military expenditures: 3% of GDP (2024 est.)
3.5% of GDP (2023 est.)
3% of GDP (2022 est.)
2.8% of GDP (2021 est.)
3% of GDP (2020 est.)

Military and security service personnel strengths: limited available information; estimated 10-15,000 active Armed Forces, including the National Guard (2025)

Military equipment inventories and acquisitions: the Kyrgyz military inventory is comprised almost entirely of Russian and Soviet-era weapons and equipment; in recent years, the military has acquired small amounts of material from other suppliers such as Turkey, which provided unmanned aerial vehicles/drones (2024)

Military service age and obligation: 18-27 years of age for compulsory or voluntary service for men in the Armed Forces or Interior Ministry; 12-month service obligation (9 months for university graduates), with optional fee-based 3-year service in the call-up mobilization reserve; women may volunteer at age 19; 16-17 years of age for military cadets, who cannot take part in military operations (2023)

Military - note: the Kyrgyz military's primary responsibility is defense of the country's sovereignty and territory, although it also has some internal security duties; the military also participates in UN and Collective Security Treaty Organization (CSTO) peacekeeping missions, as well as bilateral and multinational exercises; particular issues of concern include border security and terrorism; the military's closest security partner is Russia, which provides training and material assistance, and maintains a presence in the country, including an airbase; the military also conducts training with other regional countries such as India, traditionally with a focus on counterterrorism
Kyrgyzstan has been a member of CSTO since 1994 and contributes troops to CSTO's rapid reaction force; it also started a relationship with NATO in 1992 and joined NATO's Partnership for Peace program in 1994 (2025)

TERRORISM

Terrorist group(s): Terrorist group(s): US-designated foreign terrorist groups such as the Islamic Jihad Union, the Islamic Movement of Uzbekistan, and the Islamic State of Iraq and ash-Sham-Khorasan Province have operated in the area where the Uzbek, Kyrgyz, and Tajik borders converge and ill-defined and porous borders allow for the relatively free movement of people and illicit goods

TRANSNATIONAL ISSUES

Refugees and internally displaced persons: *refugees:* 25,413 (2024 est.)

IDPs: 12 (2024 est.)
stateless persons: 925 (2024 est.)

Trafficking in persons: *tier rating:* Tier 2 Watch List—the government did not demonstrate overall increasing efforts to eliminate trafficking compared with the previous reporting period, therefore Kyrgyzstan remained on Tier 2 Watch List for the second consecutive year; for more details, go to: https://www.state.gov/reports/2025-trafficking-in-persons-report/kyrgyz-republic/

L

LAOS

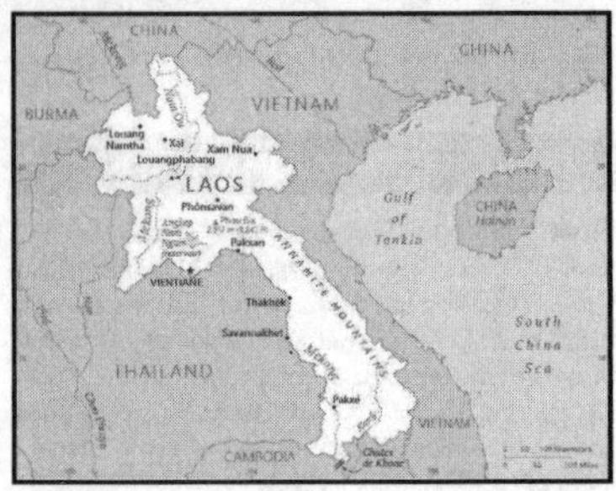

INTRODUCTION

Background: Modern-day Laos has its roots in the ancient Lao kingdom of Lan Xang, established in the 14th century under King FA NGUM. For 300 years, Lan Xang had influence reaching into present-day Cambodia and Thailand, as well as over all of what is now Laos. After centuries of gradual decline, Laos came under the domination of Siam (Thailand) from the late 18th century until the late 19th century, when it became part of French Indochina. The Franco-Siamese Treaty of 1907 defined the current Lao border with Thailand. Following more than 15 years of civil war, the communist Pathet Lao took control of the government in 1975, ending a six-century-old monarchy and instituting a one party–the Lao People's Revolutionary Party–communist state. A gradual, limited return to private enterprise and the liberalization of foreign investment laws began in the late 1980s. Laos became a member of ASEAN in 1997 and the WTO in 2013.

In the 2010s, the country benefited from direct foreign investment, particularly in the natural resource and industry sectors. Construction of a number of large hydropower dams and expanding mining activities have also boosted the economy. Laos has retained its official commitment to communism and maintains close ties with its two communist neighbors, Vietnam and China, both of which continue to exert substantial political and economic influence on the country. China, for example, provided 70% of the funding for a $5.9 billion, 400-km railway line between the Chinese border and the capital Vientiane, which opened for operations in 2021. Laos financed the remaining 30% with loans from China. At the same time, Laos has expanded its economic reliance on the West and other Asian countries, such as Japan, Malaysia, Singapore, Taiwan, and Thailand. Nevertheless, despite steady economic growth for more than a decade, it remains one of Asia's poorest countries.

GEOGRAPHY

Location: Southeastern Asia, northeast of Thailand, west of Vietnam

Geographic coordinates: 18 00 N, 105 00 E

Map references: Southeast Asia

Area: *total:* 236,800 sq km
land: 230,800 sq km
water: 6,000 sq km
comparison ranking: total 84

Area - comparative: about twice the size of Pennsylvania; slightly larger than Utah

Land boundaries: *total:* 5,274 km
border countries (5): Burma 238 km; Cambodia 555 km; China 475 km; Thailand 1,845 km; Vietnam 2,161 km

Coastline: 0 km (landlocked)

Maritime claims: none (landlocked)

Climate: tropical monsoon; rainy season (May to November); dry season (December to April)

Terrain: mostly rugged mountains; some plains and plateaus

Elevation: *highest point:* Phu Bia 2,817 m
lowest point: Mekong River 70 m
mean elevation: 710 m

Natural resources: timber, hydropower, gypsum, tin, gold, gemstones

Land use: *agricultural land:* 9.8% (2022 est.)
arable land: 5.3% (2022 est.)
permanent crops: 1.5% (2022 est.)
permanent pasture: 2.9% (2022 est.)
forest: 71.6% (2022 est.)
other: 18.6% (2022 est.)

Irrigated land: 4,410 sq km (2022)

Major rivers (by length in km): Mènam Khong (Mekong) (shared with China [s], Burma, Thailand, Cambodia, and Vietnam [m]) - 4,350 km
note: [s] after country name indicates river source; [m] after country name indicates river mouth

Major watersheds (area sq km): Pacific Ocean drainage: Mekong (805,604 sq km)

Population distribution: most densely populated area is in and around the capital city of Vientiane; large communities are primarily found along the Mekong River along the southwestern border; overall density is considered one of the lowest in Southeast Asia

Natural hazards: floods, droughts

Geography - note: landlocked; most of the country is mountainous and thickly forested; the Mekong River forms a large part of the western boundary with Thailand

PEOPLE AND SOCIETY

Population: *total:* 7,953,556 (2024 est.)
male: 3,966,320
female: 3,987,236
comparison rankings: total 103; male 103; female 102

Nationality: *noun:* Lao(s) or Laotian(s)
adjective: Lao or Laotian

Ethnic groups: Lao 53.2%, Khmou 11%, Hmong 9.2%, Phouthay 3.4%, Tai 3.1%, Makong 2.5%, Katong 2.2%, Lue 2%, Akha 1.8%, other 11.6% (2015 est.)
note: the Laos Government officially recognizes 49 ethnic groups, but the total number of ethnic groups is estimated to be well over 200

Languages: Lao (official), French, English, various ethnic languages
major-language sample(s):

ແຫລ່ງທີ່ຂາດບໍ່ໄດ້ສໍາລັບຂໍ້ມູນຕົ້ນຕໍ່"

(Lao)

Religions: Buddhist 64.7%, Christian 1.7%, none 31.4%, other/not stated 2.1% (2015 est.)

Age structure: *0-14 years:* 30.1% (male 1,214,429/female 1,181,845)
15-64 years: 65% (male 2,573,668/female 2,599,957)
65 years and over: 4.8% (2024 est.) (male 178,223/female 205,434)

Dependency ratios: *total dependency ratio:* 53.7 (2024 est.)
youth dependency ratio: 46.3 (2024 est.)
elderly dependency ratio: 7.4 (2024 est.)
potential support ratio: 13.5 (2024 est.)

Median age: *total:* 25.4 years (2024 est.)
male: 25 years
female: 25.7 years
comparison ranking: total 170

Population growth rate: 1.26% (2024 est.)
comparison ranking: 75

Birth rate: 19.8 births/1,000 population (2024 est.)
comparison ranking: 69

Death rate: 6.2 deaths/1,000 population (2024 est.)
comparison ranking: 147

Net migration rate: -1 migrant(s)/1,000 population (2024 est.)
comparison ranking: 145

Population distribution: most densely populated area is in and around the capital city of Vientiane; large communities are primarily found along the Mekong River along the southwestern border; overall density is considered one of the lowest in Southeast Asia

Urbanization: *urban population:* 38.2% of total population (2023)
rate of urbanization: 2.99% annual rate of change (2020-25 est.)

Major urban areas - population: 721,000 VIENTIANE (capital) (2023)

Sex ratio: *at birth:* 1.04 male(s)/female
0-14 years: 1.03 male(s)/female
15-64 years: 0.99 male(s)/female
65 years and over: 0.87 male(s)/female
total population: 1 male(s)/female (2024 est.)

Maternal mortality ratio: 112 deaths/100,000 live births (2023 est.)
comparison ranking: 64

Infant mortality rate: *total:* 35.4 deaths/1,000 live births (2024 est.)
male: 39.1 deaths/1,000 live births
female: 31.6 deaths/1,000 live births
comparison ranking: total 38

Life expectancy at birth: *total population:* 69 years (2024 est.)
male: 67.4 years
female: 70.7 years
comparison ranking: total population 183

Total fertility rate: 2.24 children born/woman (2024 est.)
comparison ranking: 81

Gross reproduction rate: 1.1 (2024 est.)

Drinking water source: *improved: urban:* 97.1% of population (2022 est.)
rural: 78.5% of population (2022 est.)
total: 85.5% of population (2022 est.)
unimproved: urban: 2.9% of population (2022 est.)
rural: 21.5% of population (2022 est.)

total: 14.5% of population (2022 est.)

Health expenditure: 2.7% of GDP (2021)
4.3% of national budget (2022 est.)

Physician density: 0.33 physicians/1,000 population (2022)

Hospital bed density: 1.3 beds/1,000 population (2021 est.)

Sanitation facility access: *improved: urban:* 100% of population (2022 est.)
rural: 72% of population (2022 est.)
total: 82.5% of population (2022 est.)
unimproved: urban: 0% of population (2022 est.)
rural: 28% of population (2022 est.)
total: 17.5% of population (2022 est.)

Obesity - adult prevalence rate: 5.3% (2016)
comparison ranking: 179

Alcohol consumption per capita: *total:* 8.15 liters of pure alcohol (2019 est.)
beer: 3.62 liters of pure alcohol (2019 est.)
wine: 0.07 liters of pure alcohol (2019 est.)
spirits: 4.46 liters of pure alcohol (2019 est.)
other alcohols: 0 liters of pure alcohol (2019 est.)
comparison ranking: total 42

Tobacco use: *total:* 24.1% (2025 est.)
male: 41% (2025 est.)
female: 7.2% (2025 est.)
comparison ranking: total 42

Children under the age of 5 years underweight: 21.1% (2017)
comparison ranking: 12

Currently married women (ages 15-49): 60.1% (2023 est.)

Child marriage: *women married by age 15:* 7.1% (2017)
women married by age 18: 32.7% (2017)
men married by age 18: 10.8% (2017)

Education expenditure: 1.2% of GDP (2023 est.)
9.8% national budget (2023 est.)
comparison ranking: Education expenditure (% GDP) 196

Literacy: *total population:* 85% (2015 est.)
male: 90% (2015 est.)
female: 79% (2015 est.)

School life expectancy (primary to tertiary education): *total:* 9 years (2023 est.)
male: 9 years (2023 est.)
female: 9 years (2023 est.)

ENVIRONMENT

Environmental issues: unexploded ordnance; deforestation; soil erosion; loss of biodiversity; water pollution; limited access to potable water

International environmental agreements: *party to:* Biodiversity, Climate Change, Climate Change-Kyoto Protocol, Climate Change-Paris Agreement, Comprehensive Nuclear Test Ban, Desertification, Endangered Species, Environmental Modification, Hazardous Wastes, Law of the Sea, Nuclear Test Ban, Ozone Layer Protection, Wetlands, Whaling
signed, but not ratified: none of the selected agreements

Climate: tropical monsoon; rainy season (May to November); dry season (December to April)

Urbanization: *urban population:* 38.2% of total population (2023)
rate of urbanization: 2.99% annual rate of change (2020-25 est.)

Carbon dioxide emissions: 23.412 million metric tonnes of CO2 (2023 est.)
from coal and metallurgical coke: 19.652 million metric tonnes of CO2 (2023 est.)
from petroleum and other liquids: 3.76 million metric tonnes of CO2 (2023 est.)
comparison ranking: total emissions 80

Particulate matter emissions: 20.5 micrograms per cubic meter (2019 est.)

Waste and recycling: *municipal solid waste generated annually:* 351,900 tons (2024 est.)
percent of municipal solid waste recycled: 15.1% (2022 est.)

Total water withdrawal: *municipal:* 130 million cubic meters (2022 est.)
industrial: 170 million cubic meters (2022 est.)
agricultural: 7.05 billion cubic meters (2022 est.)

Total renewable water resources: 333.5 billion cubic meters (2022 est.)

GOVERNMENT

Country name: *conventional long form:* Lao People's Democratic Republic
conventional short form: Laos
local long form: Sathalanalat Paxathipatai Paxaxon Lao
local short form: Mueang Lao (unofficial)
abbreviation: Lao PDR
etymology: name means "Land of the Lao [people];" it derives from the name of the country's founder, Lao

Government type: communist party-led state

Capital: *name:* Vientiane (Viangchan)
geographic coordinates: 17 58 N, 102 36 E
time difference: UTC+7 (12 hours ahead of Washington, DC, during Standard Time)
etymology: the name Viangchan means "city of sandalwood" in Laotian; the standard spelling reflects French influence

Administrative divisions: 17 provinces (*khoueng*, singular and plural) and 1 prefecture* (*kampheng nakhon*); Attapu, Bokeo, Bolikhamxay, Champasak, Houaphanh, Khammouan, Louangnamtha, Louangphabang (Luang Prabang), Oudomxai, Phongsali, Salavan, Savannakhet, Viangchan (Vientiane)*, Viangchan, Xaignabouli, Xaisomboun, Xekong, Xiangkhouang

Legal system: civil law system similar in form to the French system

Constitution: *history:* previous 1947 (pre-independence); latest promulgated 13-15 August 1991
amendment process: proposed by the National Assembly; passage requires at least two-thirds majority vote of the Assembly membership and promulgation by the president of the republic

International law organization participation: has not submitted an ICJ jurisdiction declaration; non-party state to the ICCt

Citizenship: *citizenship by birth:* no
citizenship by descent only: at least one parent must be a citizen of Laos
dual citizenship recognized: no
residency requirement for naturalization: 10 years

Suffrage: 18 years of age; universal

Executive branch: *chief of state:* President THONGLOUN Sisoulith (since 22 March 2021)
head of government: Prime Minister SONEXAY (also spelled SONXAI) Siphandon (since 30 December 2022)
cabinet: Council of Ministers appointed by the president and approved by the National Assembly
election/appointment process: president and vice president indirectly elected by the National Assembly for a 5-year term (no term limits); prime minister nominated by the president, elected by the National Assembly for a 5-year term
most recent election date: 22 March 2021
election results: *2021:* THONGLOUN Sisoulith (LPRP) elected president; National Assembly vote - 161-1; PHANKHAM Viphavanh (LPRP) elected prime minister; National Assembly vote - 158-3
2016: BOUNNHANG Vorachit (LPRP) elected president; percent of National Assembly vote - NA; THONGLOUN Sisoulith (LPRP) elected prime minister; percent of National Assembly vote - NA
expected date of next election: March 2026

Legislative branch: *legislature name:* National Assembly (Sapha Heng Xat)
legislative structure: unicameral
number of seats: 164 (all directly elected)
electoral system: plurality/majority
scope of elections: full renewal
term in office: 5 years
most recent election date: 2/21/2021
parties elected and seats per party: Lao People's Revolutionary Party (LPRP) (158); Other (6)
percentage of women in chamber: 22%
expected date of next election: February 2026

Judicial branch: *highest court(s):* People's Supreme Court (consists of the court president and organized into criminal, civil, administrative, commercial, family, and juvenile chambers, each with a vice president and several judges)
judge selection and term of office: president of People's Supreme Court appointed by the National Assembly upon the recommendation of the president of the republic for a 5-year term; vice presidents of the People's Supreme Court appointed by the president of the republic upon the recommendation of the National Assembly; appointment of chamber judges NA; tenure of court vice presidents and chamber judges NA
subordinate courts: appellate courts; provincial, municipal, district, and military courts

Political parties: Lao People's Revolutionary Party or LPRP
note: other parties proscribed

Diplomatic representation in the US: *chief of mission:* Ambassador PHOUKHONG Sisoulath (since 5 September 2025)
chancery: 2222 S Street NW, Washington, DC 20008
telephone: [1] (202) 332-6416
FAX: [1] (202) 332-4923
email address and website: embasslao@gmail.com
https://laoembassy.com/

Diplomatic representation from the US: *chief of mission:* Ambassador Heather VARIAVA (since 5 February 2024)
embassy: Ban Somvang Tai, Thadeua Road, Km 9, Hatsayfong District, Vientiane
mailing address: 4350 Vientiane Place, Washington DC 20521-4350
telephone: [856] 21-48-7000
FAX: [856] 21-48-7040
email address and website: CONSLAO@state.gov
https://la.usembassy.gov/

International organization participation: ADB, ARF, ASEAN, CP, EAS, FAO, G-77, IAEA, IBRD, ICAO, ICRM, IDA, IFAD, IFC, IFRCS, ILO, IMF, Interpol,

IOC, IPU, ISO (subscriber), ITU, MIGA, NAM, OIF, OPCW, PCA, UN, UNCTAD, UNESCO, UNIDO, UNWTO, UPU, WCO, WFTU (NGOs), WHO, WIPO, WMO, WTO

Independence: 19 July 1949 (from France); 22 October 1953 (Franco-Lao Treaty recognizes full independence)

National holiday: Republic Day (National Day), 2 December (1975)

Flag: *description:* three horizontal bands of red (top), blue (double-width), and red, with a large white disk centered in the blue band
meaning: red stands for the blood shed for liberation, and blue for the Mekong River and prosperity; the white disk represents the full moon over the Mekong River and the unity of the people under the Lao People's Revolutionary Party, as well as the country's bright future

National symbol(s): elephant

National color(s): red, white, blue

National anthem(s): *title:* "Pheng Xat Lao" (Hymn of the Lao People)
lyrics/music: SISANA Sisane/THONGDY Sounthonevichit
history: music adopted 1945, lyrics adopted 1975; the anthem's lyrics were changed after the communist revolution that overthrew the monarchy in 1975

National heritage: *total World Heritage Sites:* 3 (all cultural)
selected World Heritage Site locales: Town of Luangphrabang; Vat Phou and Associated Ancient Settlements; Megalithic Jar Sites in Xiengkhuang - Plain of Jars

ECONOMY

Economic overview: lower middle-income, socialist Southeast Asian economy; one of the fastest growing economies; declining but still high poverty; natural resource rich; new anticorruption efforts; already high and growing public debt; service sector hit hard by COVID-19

Real GDP (purchasing power parity): $66.905 billion (2024 est.)
$64.173 billion (2023 est.)
$61.856 billion (2022 est.)
note: data in 2021 dollars
comparison ranking: 112

Real GDP growth rate: 4.3% (2024 est.)
3.7% (2023 est.)
2.7% (2022 est.)
note: annual GDP % growth based on constant local currency
comparison ranking: 61

Real GDP per capita: $8,600 (2024 est.)
$8,400 (2023 est.)
$8,200 (2022 est.)
note: data in 2021 dollars
comparison ranking: 151

GDP (official exchange rate): $16.503 billion (2024 est.)
note: data in current dollars at official exchange rate

Inflation rate (consumer prices): 23.1% (2024 est.)
31.2% (2023 est.)
23% (2022 est.)
note: annual % change based on consumer prices
comparison ranking: 193

GDP - composition, by sector of origin: *agriculture:* 16.8% (2024 est.)
industry: 29% (2024 est.)
services: 43.5% (2024 est.)
note: figures may not total 100% due to non-allocated consumption not captured in sector-reported data
comparison rankings: agriculture 47; industry 61; services 181

GDP - composition, by end use: *household consumption:* 65.7% (2016 est.)
government consumption: 14% (2016 est.)
investment in fixed capital: 29% (2016 est.)
investment in inventories: 0% (2016 est.)
exports of goods and services: 33.2% (2016 est.)
imports of goods and services: -41.9% (2016 est.)
note: figures may not total 100% due to rounding or gaps in data collection

Agricultural products: cassava, root vegetables, rice, sugarcane, vegetables, bananas, maize, rubber, coffee, watermelons (2023)
note: top ten agricultural products based on tonnage

Industries: mining (copper, tin, gold, gypsum); timber, electric power, agricultural processing, rubber, construction, garments, cement, tourism

Industrial production growth rate: 3.9% (2024 est.)
note: annual % change in industrial value added based on constant local currency
comparison ranking: 62

Labor force: 3.585 million (2024 est.)
note: number of people ages 15 or older who are employed or seeking work
comparison ranking: 99

Unemployment rate: 1.3% (2024 est.)
1.2% (2023 est.)
1.3% (2022 est.)
note: % of labor force seeking employment
comparison ranking: 8

Youth unemployment rate (ages 15-24): *total:* 2.2% (2024 est.)
male: 2.4% (2024 est.)
female: 2.1% (2024 est.)
note: % of labor force ages 15-24 seeking employment
comparison ranking: total 183

Population below poverty line: 18.3% (2018 est.)
note: % of population with income below national poverty line

Gini Index coefficient - distribution of family income: 38.8 (2018 est.)
note: index (0-100) of income distribution; higher values represent greater inequality
comparison ranking: 46

Average household expenditures: *on food:* 50.5% of household expenditures (2023 est.)
on alcohol and tobacco: 7.8% of household expenditures (2023 est.)

Household income or consumption by percentage share: *lowest 10%:* 3% (2018 est.)
highest 10%: 31.2% (2018 est.)
note: % share of income accruing to lowest and highest 10% of population

Remittances: 1.8% of GDP (2023 est.)
1.5% of GDP (2022 est.)
1.2% of GDP (2021 est.)
note: personal transfers and compensation between resident and non-resident individuals/households/entities

Budget: *revenues:* $2.288 billion (2022 est.)
expenditures: $2.259 billion (2022 est.)
note: central government revenues and expenses (excluding grants/extrabudgetary units/social security funds) converted to US dollars at average official exchange rate for year indicated

Taxes and other revenues: 12.1% (of GDP) (2022 est.)
note: central government tax revenue as a % of GDP
comparison ranking: 115

Current account balance: $404.523 million (2023 est.)
-$458.754 million (2022 est.)
$431.636 million (2021 est.)
note: balance of payments - net trade and primary/secondary income in current dollars
comparison ranking: 67

Exports: $9.698 billion (2023 est.)
$8.604 billion (2022 est.)
$7.82 billion (2021 est.)
note: balance of payments - exports of goods and services in current dollars
comparison ranking: 118

Exports - partners: China 39%, Thailand 34%, Australia 4%, USA 4%, Cambodia 2% (2023)
note: top five export partners based on percentage share of exports

Exports - commodities: electricity, fertilizers, gold, garments, paper (2023)
note: top five export commodities based on value in dollars

Imports: $8.596 billion (2023 est.)
$7.983 billion (2022 est.)
$6.527 billion (2021 est.)
note: balance of payments - imports of goods and services in current dollars
comparison ranking: 128

Imports - partners: Thailand 58%, China 36%, Japan 1%, Singapore 1%, Germany 1% (2023)
note: top five import partners based on percentage share of imports

Imports - commodities: refined petroleum, cars, raw sugar, plastic products, trucks (2023)
note: top five import commodities based on value in dollars

Reserves of foreign exchange and gold: $1.77 billion (2023 est.)
$1.576 billion (2022 est.)
$1.951 billion (2021 est.)
note: holdings of gold (year-end prices)/foreign exchange/special drawing rights in current dollars
comparison ranking: 129

Debt - external: $9.619 billion (2023 est.)
note: present value of external debt in current US dollars
comparison ranking: 51

Exchange rates: kips (LAK) per US dollar -

Exchange rates: 17,688.874 (2023 est.)
14,035.227 (2022 est.)
9,697.916 (2021 est.)
9,045.788 (2020 est.)
8,679.409 (2019 est.)

ENERGY

Electricity access: *electrification - total population:* 100% (2022 est.)

Electricity: *installed generating capacity:* 12.738 million kW (2023 est.)
consumption: 12.803 billion kWh (2023 est.)
exports: 38 billion kWh (2023 est.)
imports: 955.095 million kWh (2023 est.)

transmission/distribution losses: 2.447 billion kWh (2023 est.)
comparison rankings: installed generating capacity 60; consumption 95; exports 4; imports 77; transmission/distribution losses 132

Electricity generation sources: *fossil fuels:* 23.3% of total installed capacity (2023 est.)
solar: 0.2% of total installed capacity (2023 est.)
hydroelectricity: 76.5% of total installed capacity (2023 est.)
biomass and waste: 0.1% of total installed capacity (2023 est.)

Coal: *production:* 16.629 million metric tons (2023 est.)
consumption: 15.944 million metric tons (2023 est.)
exports: 1.065 million metric tons (2023 est.)
imports: 22,000 metric tons (2023 est.)
proven reserves: 62 million metric tons (2023 est.)

Petroleum: *refined petroleum consumption:* 25,000 bbl/day (2023 est.)

Energy consumption per capita: 34.463 million Btu/person (2023 est.)
comparison ranking: 110

COMMUNICATIONS

Telephones - fixed lines: *total subscriptions:* 1.3 million (2021 est.)
subscriptions per 100 inhabitants: 18 (2022 est.)
comparison ranking: total subscriptions 61

Telephones - mobile cellular: *total subscriptions:* 4.82 million (2021 est.)
subscriptions per 100 inhabitants: 65 (2021 est.)
comparison ranking: total subscriptions 127

Broadcast media: 6 TV stations operating out of Vientiane, with half state-operated and half commercial; 17 provincial stations, with nearly all programming relayed via satellite from the state-operated stations in Vientiane; multi-channel satellite and cable TV systems provide access to a wide range of foreign stations; state-controlled radio with state-operated Lao National Radio (LNR) broadcasting on 5 frequencies; transmissions of multiple international broadcasters are accessible

Internet country code: .la

Internet users: *percent of population:* 64% (2023 est.)

Broadband - fixed subscriptions: *total:* 183,000 (2022 est.)
subscriptions per 100 inhabitants: 2 (2022 est.)
comparison ranking: total 123

TRANSPORTATION

Civil aircraft registration country code prefix: RDPL

Airports: 20 (2025)
comparison ranking: 140

Railways: *total:* 422 km (2023)
standard gauge: 422 km (2023) 1.435-m gauge (422 km overhead electrification)

Merchant marine: *total:* 1 (2023)
by type: general cargo 1
comparison ranking: total 184

MILITARY AND SECURITY

Military and security forces: Lao People's Armed Forces (LPAF; aka Lao People's Army): Lao People's Army (LPA, includes Riverine Force), Lao People's Air Force (LPAF); Self-Defense Militia Forces (2025)
note: the Ministry of Public Security maintains internal security and is responsible for law enforcement; it oversees local, traffic, immigration, and security police, village police auxiliaries, and other armed police units

Military expenditures: 0.2% of GDP (2019 est.)
0.2% of GDP (2018 est.)
0.2% of GDP (2017 est.)
0.2% of GDP (2016 est.)
0.2% of GDP (2015 est.)

Military and security service personnel strengths: information limited and varied; estimated 30,000 active Armed Forces; estimated 100,000 Self-Defense Militia Forces (2025)

Military equipment inventories and acquisitions: the LPAF is armed with Chinese, Russian, and Soviet-era equipment and weapons (2024)

Military service age and obligation: 18 years of age for compulsory or voluntary military service; minimum 18-month service obligation (2023)

Military - note: the LPAF's primary missions are border and internal security, including counterinsurgency, counterterrorism, and counter-narcotics operations, as well as protecting the regime; its defense partners include Cambodia, China, Russia, and Vietnam (2025)

TRANSNATIONAL ISSUES

Refugees and internally displaced persons: IDPs: 1,274 (2024 est.)

Trafficking in persons: *tier rating:* Tier 3 — Laos does not fully meet the minimum standards for the elimination of trafficking and is not making significant efforts to do so, therefore, Laos was downgraded to Tier 3; for more details, go to: https://www.state.gov/reports/2025-trafficking-in-persons-report/laos/

Illicit drugs: USG identification: major illicit drug-producing and/or drug-transit country (2025)

LATVIA

INTRODUCTION

Background: Several eastern Baltic tribes merged in medieval times to form the ethnic core of the Latvian people (ca. 8th-12th centuries A.D.). The region subsequently came under the control of Germans, Poles, Swedes, and finally Russians. A Latvian republic emerged following World War I, but the USSR annexed it in 1940 – an action never recognized by the US and many other countries. Latvia reestablished its independence in 1991 after the breakup of the Soviet Union. Although the last Russian troops left in 1994, the status of the Russian minority (some 25% of the population) remains of concern to Moscow. Latvia joined both NATO and the EU in 2004; it joined the euro zone in 2014 and the OECD in 2016.

GEOGRAPHY

Location: Eastern Europe, bordering the Baltic Sea, between Estonia and Lithuania

Geographic coordinates: 57 00 N, 25 00 E

Map references: Europe

Area: *total:* 64,589 sq km
land: 62,249 sq km
water: 2,340 sq km
comparison ranking: total 124

Area - comparative: slightly larger than West Virginia

Land boundaries: *total:* 1,370 km
border countries (4): Belarus 161 km; Estonia 333 km; Lithuania 544 km; Russia 332 km

Coastline: 498 km

Maritime claims: *territorial sea:* 12 nm
exclusive economic zone: limits as agreed to by Estonia, Finland, Latvia, Sweden, and Russia
continental shelf: 200 m depth or to the depth of exploitation

Climate: maritime; wet, moderate winters

Terrain: low plain

Elevation: *highest point:* Gaizina Kalns 312 m
lowest point: Baltic Sea 0 m
mean elevation: 87 m

Natural resources: peat, limestone, dolomite, amber, hydropower, timber, arable land

Land use: *agricultural land:* 31.7% (2022 est.)
arable land: 21.8% (2022 est.)
permanent crops: 0.2% (2022 est.)
permanent pasture: 9.7% (2022 est.)
forest: 54.9% (2022 est.)
other: 13.4% (2022 est.)

Irrigated land: 6 sq km (2016)
note: land in Latvia is often too wet and in need of drainage not irrigation; approximately 16,000 sq km or 85% of agricultural land has been improved by drainage

Population distribution: largest concentration of people is found in and around the port and capital city of Riga; small agglomerations are scattered throughout the country

Natural hazards: large percentage of agricultural fields can become waterlogged and require drainage

Geography - note: most of the country is composed of fertile low-lying plains with some hills in the east

PEOPLE AND SOCIETY

Population: *total:* 1,801,246 (2024 est.)
male: 836,982
female: 964,264
comparison rankings: total 153; male 155; female 151

Nationality: *noun:* Latvian(s)
adjective: Latvian

Ethnic groups: Latvian 62.7%, Russian 24.5%, Belarusian 3.1%, Ukrainian 2.2%, Polish 2%, Lithuanian 1.1%, other 1.8%, unspecified 2.6% (2021 est.)

Languages: Latvian (official) 56.3%, Russian 33.8%, other 0.6% (includes Polish, Ukrainian, and Belarusian), unspecified 9.4% (2011 est.)
major-language sample(s):
World Factbook, neaizstājams avots pamata informāciju. (Latvian)
note: data represent language usually spoken at home

Religions: Lutheran 36.2%, Roman Catholic 19.5%, Orthodox 19.1%, other Christian 1.6%, other 0.1%, unspecified/none 23.5% (2017 est.)

Age structure: *0-14 years:* 14.7% (male 136,482/ female 128,492)
15-64 years: 63% (male 562,754/female 572,850)
65 years and over: 22.2% (2024 est.) (male 137,746/ female 262,922)

Dependency ratios: *total dependency ratio:* 55.6 (2024 est.)
youth dependency ratio: 23.5 (2024 est.)
elderly dependency ratio: 32.1 (2024 est.)
potential support ratio: 3.1 (2024 est.)

Median age: *total:* 45.5 years (2024 est.)
male: 41.6 years
female: 49.2 years
comparison ranking: total 17

Population growth rate: -1.14% (2024 est.)
comparison ranking: 232

Birth rate: 8.3 births/1,000 population (2024 est.)
comparison ranking: 211

Death rate: 14.7 deaths/1,000 population (2024 est.)
comparison ranking: 4

Net migration rate: -4.9 migrant(s)/1,000 population (2024 est.)
comparison ranking: 201

Population distribution: largest concentration of people is found in and around the port and capital city of Riga; small agglomerations are scattered throughout the country

Urbanization: *urban population:* 68.7% of total population (2023)
rate of urbanization: -0.68% annual rate of change (2020-25 est.)

Major urban areas - population: 621,000 RIGA (capital) (2023)

Sex ratio: *at birth:* 1.05 male(s)/female
0-14 years: 1.06 male(s)/female
15-64 years: 0.98 male(s)/female
65 years and over: 0.52 male(s)/female
total population: 0.87 male(s)/female (2024 est.)

Mother's mean age at first birth: 27.3 years (2020 est.)

Maternal mortality ratio: 19 deaths/100,000 live births (2023 est.)
comparison ranking: 123

Infant mortality rate: *total:* 4.7 deaths/1,000 live births (2024 est.)
male: 5.1 deaths/1,000 live births
female: 4.3 deaths/1,000 live births
comparison ranking: total 179

Life expectancy at birth: *total population:* 76.4 years (2024 est.)
male: 72 years
female: 81 years
comparison ranking: total population 110

Total fertility rate: 1.55 children born/woman (2024 est.)
comparison ranking: 192

Gross reproduction rate: 0.76 (2024 est.)

Drinking water source: *improved: urban:* 98.9% of population (2022 est.)
rural: 98.9% of population (2022 est.)
total: 98.9% of population (2022 est.)
unimproved: urban: 1.1% of population (2022 est.)
rural: 1.1% of population (2022 est.)
total: 1.1% of population (2022 est.)

Health expenditure: 9% of GDP (2021)
12.1% of national budget (2022 est.)

Physician density: 3.4 physicians/1,000 population (2022)

Hospital bed density: 5.3 beds/1,000 population (2020 est.)

Obesity - adult prevalence rate: 23.6% (2016)
comparison ranking: 65

Alcohol consumption per capita: *total:* 12.9 liters of pure alcohol (2019 est.)
beer: 4.9 liters of pure alcohol (2019 est.)
wine: 1.7 liters of pure alcohol (2019 est.)
spirits: 5.3 liters of pure alcohol (2019 est.)
other alcohols: 1 liters of pure alcohol (2019 est.)
comparison ranking: total 2

Tobacco use: *total:* 28.8% (2025 est.)
male: 43.5% (2025 est.)
female: 16.4% (2025 est.)
comparison ranking: total 25

Currently married women (ages 15-49): 49.1% (2023 est.)

Education expenditure: 5.4% of GDP (2022 est.)
13.1% national budget (2022 est.)
comparison ranking: Education expenditure (% GDP) 45

School life expectancy (primary to tertiary education): *total:* 16 years (2023 est.)
male: 15 years (2023 est.)
female: 17 years (2023 est.)

ENVIRONMENT

Environmental issues: some soil, water, and air pollution

International environmental agreements: *party to:* Air Pollution, Air Pollution-Heavy Metals, Air Pollution-Multi-effect Protocol, Air Pollution-Persistent Organic Pollutants, Biodiversity, Climate Change, Climate Change-Kyoto Protocol, Climate Change-Paris Agreement, Comprehensive Nuclear Test Ban, Desertification, Endangered Species, Hazardous Wastes, Law of the Sea, Ozone Layer Protection, Ship Pollution, Tropical Timber 2006, Wetlands
signed, but not ratified: none of the selected agreements

Climate: maritime; wet, moderate winters

Urbanization: *urban population:* 68.7% of total population (2023)
rate of urbanization: -0.68% annual rate of change (2020-25 est.)

Carbon dioxide emissions: 6.427 million metric tonnes of CO2 (2023 est.)
from coal and metallurgical coke: 41,000 metric tonnes of CO2 (2023 est.)
from petroleum and other liquids: 4.861 million metric tonnes of CO2 (2023 est.)
from consumed natural gas: 1.526 million metric tonnes of CO2 (2023 est.)
comparison ranking: total emissions 128

Particulate matter emissions: 15.6 micrograms per cubic meter (2019 est.)

Waste and recycling: *municipal solid waste generated annually:* 839,700 tons (2024 est.)
percent of municipal solid waste recycled: 31.3% (2022 est.)

Total water withdrawal: *municipal:* 91.945 million cubic meters (2022)
industrial: 30.291 million cubic meters (2022)
agricultural: 50.098 million cubic meters (2022)

Total renewable water resources: 34.94 billion cubic meters (2022 est.)

GOVERNMENT

Country name: *conventional long form:* Republic of Latvia
conventional short form: Latvia
local long form: Latvijas Republika
local short form: Latvija
former: Latvian Soviet Socialist Republic (while occupied by the USSR)
etymology: the name originates from the Latgalians, one of four eastern Baltic tribes that formed the ethnic core of the Latvian people (ca. 8th-12th centuries A.D.)

Government type: parliamentary republic

Capital: *name:* Riga
geographic coordinates: 56 57 N, 24 06 E
time difference: UTC+2 (7 hours ahead of Washington, DC, during Standard Time)
daylight saving time: +1hr, begins last Sunday in March; ends last Sunday in October
etymology: the name's origin is unclear; it may derive from the Old Lithuanian word *ringa*, meaning "bend" or "curve" and referring to the city's location on the Western Dvina River; alternatively, it may come from the Latvian word *ridzina*, meaning "stream"

Administrative divisions: 36 municipalities (*novadi*, singular - *novads*) and 7 state cities (*valstpilsetu pasvaldibas*, singular - *valstspilsetas pasvaldiba*)
municipalities: Adazi, Aizkraukle, Aluksne, Augsdaugava, Balvi, Bauska, Cesis, Dienvidkurzeme, Dobele, Gulbene, Jekabpils, Jelgava, Kekava, Kraslava, Kuldiga, Limbazi, Livani, Ludza, Madona, Marupe, Ogre, Olaine, Preili, Rezekne, Ropazi, Salaspils, Saldus, Saulkrasti, Sigulda, Smiltene, Talsi, Tukums, Valka, Valmiera, Varaklani, Ventspils
cities: Daugavpils, Jelgava, Jurmala, Liepaja, Rezekne, Riga, Ventspils

Legal system: civil law system with traces of socialist legal traditions and practices

Constitution: *history:* several previous (pre-1991 independence); after independence was restored in 1991,

parts of the 1922 constitution were reintroduced on 4 May 1990 and fully reintroduced on 6 July 1993
amendment process: proposed by two thirds of Parliament members or by petition of one tenth of qualified voters submitted through the president; passage requires at least two-thirds majority vote of Parliament in each of three readings; amendment of constitutional articles, including national sovereignty, language, the parliamentary electoral system, and constitutional amendment procedures, requires passage in a referendum by majority vote of at least one half of the electorate

International law organization participation: has not submitted an ICJ jurisdiction declaration; accepts ICCt jurisdiction

Citizenship: *citizenship by birth:* no
citizenship by descent only: at least one parent must be a citizen of Latvia
dual citizenship recognized: no
residency requirement for naturalization: 5 years

Suffrage: 18 years of age; universal

Executive branch: *chief of state:* President Edgars RINKEVICS (since 8 July 2023)
head of government: Prime Minister Evika SILINA (since 15 September 2023)
cabinet: Cabinet of Ministers nominated by the prime minister, appointed by Parliament
election/appointment process: president indirectly elected by Parliament for a 4-year term (eligible for a second term); prime minister appointed by the president, confirmed by Parliament
most recent election date: 31 May 2023
election results: *2023:* Edgars RINKEVICS elected president in the third round; Parliament vote - Edgars RINKEVICS (Unity Party) 52, Uldis Pīlēns (independent) 25; Evika SILINA confirmed as prime minister 53-39
2019: Egils LEVITS elected president; Parliament vote - Egils LEVITS (independent) 61, Didzis SMITS (KPV LV) 24, Juris JANSONS (independent) 8; Krisjanis KARINS confirmed as prime minister 61-39
expected date of next election: 2027

Legislative branch: *legislature name:* Parliament (Saeima)
legislative structure: unicameral
number of seats: 100 (all directly elected)
electoral system: proportional representation
scope of elections: full renewal
term in office: 4 years
most recent election date: 10/1/2022
parties elected and seats per party: New Unity (VIENOTIBA) (26); Union of Farmers and Greens (ZZS) (16); United List - Latvian Green Party, Latvian Regional Alliance, Liepāja Party (15); National Alliance of All for Latvia!" - "For Fatherland and Freedom / LNNK" (NA) (13); For Stability! (11); Progressives (10); Latvia First (9)
percentage of women in chamber: 31%
expected date of next election: October 2026

Judicial branch: *highest court(s):* Supreme Court (consists of the Senate with 36 judges); Constitutional Court (consists of 7 judges)
judge selection and term of office: Supreme Court judges nominated by chief justice and confirmed by the Saeima; judges serve until age 70, but term can be extended 2 years; Constitutional Court judges - 3 nominated by Saeima members, 2 by Cabinet ministers, and 2 by plenum of Supreme Court; all judges confirmed by Saeima majority vote; Constitutional Court president and vice president serve in their positions for 3 years; all judges serve 10-year terms; mandatory retirement at age 70
subordinate courts: district (city) and regional courts

Political parties: Development/For! or AP!
For Stability or S!
For Latvia's Development LA
Harmony or S
Honor to Serve Riga! or GKR
Latvia First LPV
Latvian Green Party or LZP
National Alliance or NA
New Unity or JV
People, Land, Statehood TZV
Social Democratic Party "Harmony" or S
The Progressives or PRO
Union of Greens and Farmers or ZZS
United List or AS
We for Talsi and Municipality or MTuN

Diplomatic representation in the US: *chief of mission:* Ambassador Elita KUZMA (since 18 September 2024)
chancery: 2306 Massachusetts Avenue NW, Washington, DC 20008
telephone: [1] (202) 328-2840
FAX: [1] (202) 328-2860
email address and website: embassy.usa@mfa.gov.lv
https://www2.mfa.gov.lv/en/usa

Diplomatic representation from the US: *chief of mission:* Ambassador Christopher ROBINSON (since 21 February 2023)
embassy: 1 Samnera Velsa Street (former Remtes), Riga LV-1510
mailing address: 4520 Riga Place, Washington DC 20521-4520
telephone: [371] 6710-7000
FAX: [371] 6710-7050
email address and website: askconsular-riga@state.gov
https://lv.usembassy.gov/

International organization participation: Australia Group, BA, BIS, CBSS, CD, CE, EAPC, EBRD, ECB, EIB, EMU, ESA (cooperating state), EU, FAO, IAEA, IBRD, ICAO, ICC (NGOs), ICCt, ICRM, IDA, IFC, IFRCS, IHO, ILO, IMF, IMO, IMSO, Interpol, IOC, IOM, IPU, ISO (correspondent), ITU, ITUC (NGOs), MIGA, NATO, NIB, NSG, OAS (observer), OIF (observer), OPCW, OSCE, PCA, Schengen Convention, UN, UNCTAD, UNESCO, UNHCR, UNWTO, UPU, Wassenaar Arrangement, WCO, WHO, WIPO, WMO, WTO

Independence: 18 November 1918 (from Soviet Russia); 4 May 1990 (declared from the Soviet Union); 6 September 1991 (recognized by the Soviet Union)

National holiday: Independence Day (Republic of Latvia Proclamation Day), 18 November (1918)
note: 18 November 1918 was the date Latvia established its statehood and independence from Soviet Russia; 4 May 1990 was the date it declared the restoration of statehood and independence from the Soviet Union

Flag: *description:* three horizontal bands of maroon (top), white (half-width), and maroon
history: the flag is one of the older banners in the world – a medieval chronicle mentions Latvian tribes using a red standard with a white stripe around 1280

National symbol(s): white wagtail (bird)

National color(s): maroon, white

National anthem(s): *title:* "Dievs, sveti Latviju!" (God Bless Latvia)
lyrics/music: Karlis BAUMANIS
history: adopted 1920, restored 1990; first performed in 1873 when Latvia was part of Russia; banned during the Soviet occupation from 1940 to 1990

National heritage: *total World Heritage Sites:* 3 (all cultural)
selected World Heritage Site locales: Historic Center of Riga; Struve Geodetic Arc; Old town of Kuldīga

ECONOMY

Economic overview: high-income EU and eurozone member; weak recovery following economic contraction, with slight increase in private consumption and uncertain trade environment; challenges from skilled-labor shortages, capital market access, large informal sector, and green and digital transitions

Real GDP (purchasing power parity): $72.516 billion (2024 est.)
$72.838 billion (2023 est.)
$70.817 billion (2022 est.)
note: data in 2021 dollars
comparison ranking: 109

Real GDP growth rate: -0.4% (2024 est.)
2.9% (2023 est.)
1.8% (2022 est.)
note: annual GDP % growth based on constant local currency
comparison ranking: 196

Real GDP per capita: $38,900 (2024 est.)
$38,800 (2023 est.)
$37,700 (2022 est.)
note: data in 2021 dollars
comparison ranking: 61

GDP (official exchange rate): $43.521 billion (2024 est.)
note: data in current dollars at official exchange rate

Inflation rate (consumer prices): 1.3% (2024 est.)
8.9% (2023 est.)
17.3% (2022 est.)
note: annual % change based on consumer prices
comparison ranking: 32

GDP - composition, by sector of origin: *agriculture:* 4.1% (2024 est.)
industry: 19.9% (2024 est.)
services: 63.1% (2024 est.)
note: figures may not total 100% due to non-allocated consumption not captured in sector-reported data
comparison rankings: agriculture 118; industry 130; services 67

GDP - composition, by end use: *household consumption:* 62.7% (2023 est.)
government consumption: 20.2% (2023 est.)
investment in fixed capital: 24.7% (2023 est.)
investment in inventories: -0.1% (2023 est.)
exports of goods and services: 66.5% (2023 est.)
imports of goods and services: -70.2% (2023 est.)
note: figures may not total 100% due to rounding or gaps in data collection

Agricultural products: wheat, milk, rapeseed, barley, oats, potatoes, rye, beans, peas, chicken (2023)
note: top ten agricultural products based on tonnage

Industries: processed foods, processed wood products, textiles, processed metals, pharmaceuticals, railroad cars, synthetic fibers, electronics

Industrial production growth rate: -4% (2024 est.)
note: annual % change in industrial value added based on constant local currency
comparison ranking: 174

Labor force: 954,900 (2024 est.)
note: number of people ages 15 or older who are employed or seeking work
comparison ranking: 146

Unemployment rate: 6.8% (2024 est.)
6.5% (2023 est.)
6.9% (2022 est.)
note: % of labor force seeking employment
comparison ranking: 122

Youth unemployment rate (ages 15-24): *total:* 12.5% (2024 est.)
male: 13% (2024 est.)
female: 11.9% (2024 est.)
note: % of labor force ages 15-24 seeking employment
comparison ranking: total 98

Population below poverty line: 22.5% (2022 est.)
note: % of population with income below national poverty line

Gini Index coefficient - distribution of family income: 33.7 (2022 est.)
note: index (0-100) of income distribution; higher values represent greater inequality
comparison ranking: 90

Average household expenditures: *on food:* 19.6% of household expenditures (2023 est.)
on alcohol and tobacco: 7.1% of household expenditures (2023 est.)

Household income or consumption by percentage share: *lowest 10%:* 2.6% (2022 est.)
highest 10%: 25.8% (2022 est.)
note: % share of income accruing to lowest and highest 10% of population

Remittances: 3.1% of GDP (2024 est.)
2.9% of GDP (2023 est.)
3.4% of GDP (2022 est.)
note: personal transfers and compensation between resident and non-resident individuals/households/entities

Budget: *revenues:* $14.58 billion (2023 est.)
expenditures: $15.432 billion (2023 est.)
note: central government revenues (excluding grants) and expenditures converted to US dollars at average official exchange rate for year indicated

Public debt: 36.3% of GDP (2017 est.)
note: data cover general government debt, and includes debt instruments issued (or owned) by government entities, including sub-sectors of central government, state government, local government, and social security funds
comparison ranking: 147

Taxes and other revenues: 16.7% (of GDP) (2023 est.)
note: central government tax revenue as a % of GDP
comparison ranking: 81

Current account balance: -$923.266 million (2024 est.)
-$1.663 billion (2023 est.)
-$2.082 billion (2022 est.)
note: balance of payments - net trade and primary/secondary income in current dollars
comparison ranking: 127

Exports: $28.117 billion (2024 est.)
$28.294 billion (2023 est.)
$29.364 billion (2022 est.)
note: balance of payments - exports of goods and services in current dollars
comparison ranking: 86

Exports - partners: Lithuania 19%, Estonia 6%, Russia 6%, Germany 6%, Sweden 5% (2023)
note: top five export partners based on percentage share of exports

Exports - commodities: wood, wheat, broadcasting equipment, packaged medicine, natural gas (2023)
note: top five export commodities based on value in dollars

Imports: $29.234 billion (2024 est.)
$29.875 billion (2023 est.)
$31.206 billion (2022 est.)
note: balance of payments - imports of goods and services in current dollars
comparison ranking: 83

Imports - partners: Lithuania 18%, Germany 11%, Poland 10%, Estonia 8%, Finland 5% (2023)
note: top five import partners based on percentage share of imports

Imports - commodities: refined petroleum, cars, packaged medicine, broadcasting equipment, natural gas (2023)
note: top five import commodities based on value in dollars

Reserves of foreign exchange and gold: $5.141 billion (2024 est.)
$4.957 billion (2023 est.)
$4.46 billion (2022 est.)
note: holdings of gold (year-end prices)/foreign exchange/special drawing rights in current dollars
comparison ranking: 97

Exchange rates: euros (EUR) per US dollar -

Exchange rates: 0.924 (2024 est.)
0.925 (2023 est.)
0.95 (2022 est.)
0.845 (2021 est.)
0.876 (2020 est.)

ENERGY

Electricity access: *electrification - total population:* 100% (2022 est.)

Electricity: *installed generating capacity:* 3.428 million kW (2023 est.)
consumption: 6.822 billion kWh (2023 est.)
exports: 3.271 billion kWh (2023 est.)
imports: 4.075 billion kWh (2023 est.)
transmission/distribution losses: 342.238 million kWh (2023 est.)
comparison rankings: installed generating capacity 105; consumption 120; exports 46; imports 50; transmission/distribution losses 74

Electricity generation sources: *fossil fuels:* 22.4% of total installed capacity (2023 est.)
solar: 3.8% of total installed capacity (2023 est.)
wind: 4.2% of total installed capacity (2023 est.)
hydroelectricity: 59.3% of total installed capacity (2023 est.)
biomass and waste: 10.4% of total installed capacity (2023 est.)

Coal: *consumption:* 20,000 metric tons (2023 est.)
exports: 12,000 metric tons (2023 est.)
imports: 39,000 metric tons (2023 est.)

Petroleum: *total petroleum production:* 2,000 bbl/day (2023 est.)
refined petroleum consumption: 33,000 bbl/day (2024 est.)

Natural gas: *consumption:* 786.523 million cubic meters (2023 est.)
imports: 786.523 million cubic meters (2023 est.)

Energy consumption per capita: 65.908 million Btu/person (2023 est.)
comparison ranking: 76

COMMUNICATIONS

Telephones - fixed lines: *total subscriptions:* 142,000 (2023 est.)
subscriptions per 100 inhabitants: 8 (2023 est.)
comparison ranking: total subscriptions 127

Telephones - mobile cellular: *total subscriptions:* 2.26 million (2023 est.)
subscriptions per 100 inhabitants: 117 (2022 est.)
comparison ranking: total subscriptions 148

Broadcast media: several national and regional commercial TV stations are foreign-owned, 2 national TV stations are publicly owned; system supplemented by privately owned regional and local TV stations; cable and satellite multi-channel TV services with domestic and foreign broadcasts available; publicly owned broadcaster operates 4 radio networks with dozens of stations; dozens of private broadcasters also operate radio stations

Internet country code: .lv

Internet users: *percent of population:* 92% (2023 est.)

Broadband - fixed subscriptions: *total:* 489,000 (2023 est.)
subscriptions per 100 inhabitants: 26 (2023 est.)
comparison ranking: total 98

TRANSPORTATION

Civil aircraft registration country code prefix: YL

Airports: 55 (2025)
comparison ranking: 83

Heliports: 5 (2025)
comparison ranking: 103

Railways: *total:* 2,216 km (2020) 257 km electrified

Merchant marine: *total:* 83 (2023)
by type: container ship 2, general cargo 30, oil tanker 10, other 41
comparison ranking: total 97

Ports: *total ports:* 5 (2024)
large: 1
medium: 2
small: 0
very small: 2
ports with oil terminals: 3
key ports: Lielupe, Liepaja, Riga, Salacgriva, Ventspils

MILITARY AND SECURITY

Military and security forces: National Armed Forces (Nacionalie Brunotie Speki or NBS): Land Forces (Latvijas Sauszemes Speki), Naval Force (Latvijas Juras Speki, includes Coast Guard (Latvijas Kara Flote)), Air Force (Latvijas Gaisa Speki), National Guard (aka Land Guard or Zemessardze)

Ministry of Interior: State Police, State Border Guards, State Security Service (2025)
note: the State Border Guard may become part of the armed forces during an emergency

Military expenditures: 3.7% of GDP (2025 est.)
3.4% of GDP (2024 est.)
3% of GDP (2023 est.)
2.3% of GDP (2022 est.)
2.2% of GDP (2021 est.)

Military and security service personnel strengths: approximately 9,000 active-duty military personnel (2025)

Military equipment inventories and acquisitions: the Latvian military's inventory consists of a mix of European and US weapons and equipment (2024)

Military service age and obligation: 18 years of age for voluntary military service for men and women; 12 months mandatory military service for men 18-27 years of age (2024)
note 1: conscription was reintroduced in 2024
note 2: as of 2024, women comprised about 16.5% of the military's full-time personnel

Military deployments: 135 Kosovo (KFOR/NATO) (2024)

Military - note: the National Armed Forces are responsible for the defense of the country's sovereignty and territory; they also have some domestic security responsibilities, including coast guard functions, search and rescue, humanitarian assistance, and providing support to other internal security services; the Military Police provides protection to the president and other government officials, foreign dignitaries, and key facilities; Latvia's primary external security focus is Russia
in 2004, Latvia joined NATO and the EU, both of which it depends on to play a decisive role in Latvia's security policy; the Latvian military has participated in EU and NATO missions abroad and regularly conducts training and exercises with EU and NATO partner forces; Latvia also hosts NATO partner forces; since 2017, it has hosted a Canadian-led multinational NATO ground force battlegroup as part of the Alliance's Enhanced Forward Presence initiative; in addition, NATO has provided air protection for Latvia since 2004 through its Baltics Air Policing mission
Latvia is a member of the UK-led Joint Expeditionary Force, a pool of high-readiness military forces from 10 Baltic and Scandinavian countries designed to respond to a wide range of contingencies in the North Atlantic, Baltic Sea, and High North regions (2025)

TRANSNATIONAL ISSUES

Refugees and internally displaced persons: *refugees:* 49,483 (2024 est.)
stateless persons: 173,891 (2024 est.)

LEBANON

INTRODUCTION

Background: As a result of its location at the crossroads of three continents, the area that is modern-day Lebanon is rich in cultural and religious diversity. This region was subject to various foreign conquerors for much of its history, including the Romans, Arabs, and Ottomans. Following World War I, France acquired a mandate over the northern portion of the former Ottoman Empire province of Syria. From it the French demarcated the region of Lebanon in 1920, and it gained independence in 1943. Lebanon subsequently experienced periods of political turmoil interspersed with prosperity built on its position as a regional center for finance and trade.

The country's 1975-90 civil war, which resulted in an estimated 120,000 fatalities, was followed by years of social and political instability, and sectarianism remains a key element of Lebanese political life. The Israeli defense forces, which occupied parts of Lebanon during the civil war, did not completely withdraw until 2000. Neighboring Syria influenced Lebanon's foreign and domestic policies while its military occupied Lebanon from 1976 until 2005, but its influence diminished significantly after 2005. Over 1.5 million Syrian refugees fled to Lebanon after the start of the Syrian conflict in 2011. Hizballah – a major Lebanese political party, militia, and US-designated foreign terrorist organization – and Israel continued attacks and counterattacks against each other after Syria's withdrawal and fought a brief war in 2006. After HAMAS attacked Israel on 7 October 2023, the intensity and frequency of these cross-border attacks increased substantially into a cycle of hostilities, mostly limited to the border areas as of January 2024. Lebanon's borders with Syria and Israel remain unresolved. Lebanon's prosperity has significantly diminished since the beginning of the country's economic crisis in 2019, which has crippled its economy, shut down its previously lucrative banking sector, reduced the value of its currency, and caused many Lebanese to emigrate in search of better prospects.

GEOGRAPHY

Location: Middle East, bordering the Mediterranean Sea, between Israel and Syria

Geographic coordinates: 33 50 N, 35 50 E

Map references: Middle East

Area: *total:* 10,400 sq km
land: 10,230 sq km
water: 170 sq km
comparison ranking: total 168

Area - comparative: about one-third the size of Maryland

Land boundaries: *total:* 484 km
border countries (2): Israel 81 km; Syria 403 km

Coastline: 225 km

Maritime claims: *territorial sea:* 12 nm

Climate: Mediterranean; mild to cool, wet winters with hot, dry summers; the Lebanon Mountains experience heavy winter snows

Terrain: narrow coastal plain; El Beqaa (Bekaa Valley) separates Lebanon and Anti-Lebanon Mountains

Elevation: *highest point:* Qornet es Saouda 3,088 m
lowest point: Mediterranean Sea 0 m
mean elevation: 1,250 m

Natural resources: limestone, iron ore, salt, water-surplus state in a water-deficit region, arable land

Land use: *agricultural land:* 66.4% (2022 est.)
arable land: 13.6% (2022 est.)
permanent crops: 13.7% (2022 est.)
permanent pasture: 39.1% (2022 est.)
forest: 14.1% (2022 est.)
other: 19.5% (2022 est.)

Irrigated land: 1,040 sq km (2012)

Population distribution: the majority of people live on or near the Mediterranean coast, particularly in and around the capital of Beirut

Natural hazards: earthquakes; dust storms, sandstorms

Geography - note: smallest country in continental Asia; Nahr el Litani is the only major river in Near East not crossing an international boundary

PEOPLE AND SOCIETY

Population: *total:* 5,364,482 (2024 est.)
male: 2,678,543
female: 2,685,939
comparison rankings: total 122; male 122; female 122

Nationality: *noun:* Lebanese (singular and plural)
adjective: Lebanese

Ethnic groups: Arab 95%, Armenian 4%, other 1%
note: many Christian Lebanese do not identify as Arab but rather as descendants of the ancient Canaanites and prefer to be called Phoenicians

Languages: Arabic (official), French, English, Armenian
major-language sample(s):

يمكن الاستغناء عنه للمعلومات الأساسية

كتاب حقائق العالم، المصدر الذي لا

(Arabic)

The World Factbook, une source indispensable d'informations de base. (French)

Religions: Muslim 67.8% (31.9% Sunni, 31.2% Shia, smaller percentages of Alawites and Ismailis), Christian 32.4% (Maronite Catholics are the largest Christian group), Druze 4.5%, very small numbers of Jews, Baha'is, Buddhists, and Hindus (2020 est.)
note: data represent the religious affiliation of the citizen population (data do not include Lebanon's sizable Syrian and Palestinian refugee populations); 18 religious sects recognized

Age structure: *0-14 years:* 18.9% (male 519,352/ female 495,591)

15-64 years: 71.6% (male 1,939,311/female 1,900,574)
65 years and over: 9.5% (2024 est.) (male 219,880/ female 289,774)

Dependency ratios: *total dependency ratio:* 50.3 (2024 est.)
youth dependency ratio: 39 (2024 est.)
elderly dependency ratio: 11.3 (2024 est.)
potential support ratio: 8.8 (2024 est.)

Median age: *total:* 36.3 years (2024 est.)
male: 35.6 years
female: 36.9 years
comparison ranking: total 90

Population growth rate: 0.61% (2024 est.)
comparison ranking: 137

Birth rate: 12.6 births/1,000 population (2024 est.)
comparison ranking: 139

Death rate: 5.6 deaths/1,000 population (2024 est.)
comparison ranking: 176

Net migration rate: -0.9 migrant(s)/1,000 population (2024 est.)
comparison ranking: 141

Population distribution: the majority of people live on or near the Mediterranean coast, particularly in and around the capital of Beirut

Urbanization: *urban population:* 89.4% of total population (2023)
rate of urbanization: -1.23% annual rate of change (2020-25 est.)

Major urban areas - population: 2.421 million BEIRUT (capital) (2023)

Sex ratio: *at birth:* 1.05 male(s)/female
0-14 years: 1.05 male(s)/female
15-64 years: 1.02 male(s)/female
65 years and over: 0.76 male(s)/female
total population: 1 male(s)/female (2024 est.)

Maternal mortality ratio: 15 deaths/100,000 live births (2023 est.)
comparison ranking: 139

Infant mortality rate: *total:* 6.7 deaths/1,000 live births (2024 est.)
male: 7.3 deaths/1,000 live births
female: 6.2 deaths/1,000 live births
comparison ranking: total 159

Life expectancy at birth: *total population:* 79.2 years (2024 est.)
male: 77.8 years
female: 80.7 years
comparison ranking: total population 67

Total fertility rate: 1.71 children born/woman (2024 est.)
comparison ranking: 159

Gross reproduction rate: 0.83 (2024 est.)

Drinking water source: *improved:* total: 92.6% of population (2022 est.)
unimproved: total: 7.4% of population (2022 est.)

Health expenditure: 10.1% of GDP (2021)
15.5% of national budget (2022 est.)

Physician density: 2.68 physicians/1,000 population (2020)

Hospital bed density: 2.7 beds/1,000 population (2021 est.)

Sanitation facility access: *improved:* total: 100% of population (2022 est.)
unimproved: total: 0% of population (2022 est.)

Obesity - adult prevalence rate: 32% (2016)
comparison ranking: 18

Alcohol consumption per capita: *total:* 1.14 liters of pure alcohol (2019 est.)
beer: 0.38 liters of pure alcohol (2019 est.)
wine: 0.21 liters of pure alcohol (2019 est.)
spirits: 0.53 liters of pure alcohol (2019 est.)
other alcohols: 0.02 liters of pure alcohol (2019 est.)
comparison ranking: total 150

Tobacco use: *total:* 34.1% (2025 est.)
male: 43.8% (2025 est.)
female: 25.4% (2025 est.)
comparison ranking: total 10

Children under the age of 5 years underweight: 3.4% (2021)
comparison ranking: 76

Currently married women (ages 15-49): 51.4% (2023 est.)

Child marriage: *women married by age 15:* 1.4% (2016)
women married by age 18: 6% (2016)

Education expenditure: 2.4% of GDP (2020 est.)
9.9% national budget (2020 est.)
comparison ranking: Education expenditure (% GDP) 175

Literacy: *total population:* 93% (2018 est.)
male: 95% (2018 est.)
female: 90% (2018 est.)

School life expectancy (primary to tertiary education): *total:* 11 years (2023 est.)
male: 12 years
female: 11 years (2014)

ENVIRONMENT

Environmental issues: deforestation; soil deterioration, erosion; desertification; species loss; air pollution in Beirut from vehicular traffic and the burning of industrial wastes; pollution of coastal waters from raw sewage and oil spills; waste-water management

International environmental agreements: *party to:* Biodiversity, Climate Change, Climate Change-Kyoto Protocol, Climate Change-Paris Agreement, Comprehensive Nuclear Test Ban, Desertification, Endangered Species, Hazardous Wastes, Law of the Sea, Nuclear Test Ban, Ozone Layer Protection, Ship Pollution, Wetlands
signed, but not ratified: Environmental Modification, Marine Life Conservation

Climate: Mediterranean; mild to cool, wet winters with hot, dry summers; the Lebanon Mountains experience heavy winter snows

Urbanization: *urban population:* 89.4% of total population (2023)
rate of urbanization: -1.23% annual rate of change (2020-25 est.)

Carbon dioxide emissions: 17.484 million metric tonnes of CO2 (2023 est.)
from coal and metallurgical coke: 375,000 metric tonnes of CO2 (2023 est.)
from petroleum and other liquids: 17.109 million metric tonnes of CO2 (2023 est.)
comparison ranking: total emissions 96

Particulate matter emissions: 23.8 micrograms per cubic meter (2019 est.)

Methane emissions: *energy:* 7.9 kt (2022-2024 est.)
agriculture: 11.8 kt (2019-2021 est.)
waste: 105.3 kt (2019-2021 est.)
other: 0.7 kt (2019-2021 est.)

Waste and recycling: *municipal solid waste generated annually:* 2.04 million tons (2024 est.)
percent of municipal solid waste recycled: 15% (2022 est.)

Total water withdrawal: *municipal:* 240 million cubic meters (2022 est.)
industrial: 900 million cubic meters (2022 est.)
agricultural: 700 million cubic meters (2022 est.)

Total renewable water resources: 4.503 billion cubic meters (2022 est.)

GOVERNMENT

Country name: *conventional long form:* Lebanese Republic
conventional short form: Lebanon
local long form: Al Jumhuriyah al Lubnaniyah
local short form: Lubnan
former: Greater Lebanon
etymology: derives from the Semitic root *lbn*, meaning "white," and probably refers to the country's snow-capped mountains

Government type: parliamentary democratic republic

Capital: *name:* Beirut
geographic coordinates: 33 52 N, 35 30 E
time difference: UTC+2 (7 hours ahead of Washington, DC, during Standard Time)
daylight saving time: +1hr, begins last Sunday in March; ends last Sunday in October
etymology: derived from the Phoenician or Hebrew word *be'erot*, meaning "the wells," which were the only source of water in the region

Administrative divisions: 8 governorates (*mohafazat*, singular - *mohafazah*); Aakkar, Baalbek-Hermel, Beqaa (Bekaa), Beyrouth (Beirut), Liban-Nord (North Lebanon), Liban-Sud (South Lebanon), Mont-Liban (Mount Lebanon), Nabatiye

Legal system: mixed system of civil law based on the French civil code, Ottoman legal tradition, and religious laws covering personal status, marriage, divorce, and other family relations of the Jewish, Islamic, and Christian communities

Constitution: *history:* drafted 15 May 1926, adopted 23 May 1926
amendment process: proposed by the president of the republic and introduced as a government bill to the National Assembly or proposed by at least 10 members of the Assembly and agreed upon by two thirds of its members; if proposed by the National Assembly, review and approval by two-thirds majority of the Cabinet is required; if approved, the proposal is next submitted to the Cabinet for drafting as an amendment; Cabinet approval requires at least two-thirds majority, followed by submission to the National Assembly for discussion and vote; passage requires at least two-thirds majority vote of a required two-thirds quorum of the Assembly membership and promulgation by the president

International law organization participation: has not submitted an ICJ jurisdiction declaration; non-party state to the ICCt

Citizenship: *citizenship by birth:* no
citizenship by descent only: the father must be a citizen of Lebanon
dual citizenship recognized: yes
residency requirement for naturalization: unknown

Suffrage: 21 years of age; authorized for all men and women regardless of religion; excludes persons convicted of felonies and other crimes or those imprisoned; excludes all military and security service personnel regardless of rank

Executive branch: *chief of state:* President Joseph AOUN (since 9 January 2025)
head of government: Prime Minister Nawaf SALAM (since 8 February 2025)
cabinet: Cabinet chosen by the prime minister in consultation with the president and the National Assembly
election/appointment process: president indirectly elected by a qualified majority of two-thirds of Parliament members in the first round and, if needed, a two-thirds quorum of members by simple-majority popular vote for a 6-year term (eligible for non-consecutive terms); prime minister appointed by the president in consultation with the National Assembly
most recent election date: 9 January 2025
election results: *2025:* Joseph AOUN elected president in second round; National Assembly vote - 99 of 128
2016: Michel AWN elected president in second round; National Assembly vote - Michel AWN (FPM) 83; the president elected in its 46th attempt on 31 October 2016
expected date of next election: 2031

Legislative branch: *legislature name:* National Assembly (Majlis Al-Nuwwab)
legislative structure: unicameral
number of seats: 128 (all directly elected)
electoral system: proportional representation
scope of elections: full renewal
term in office: 4 years
most recent election date: 5/15/2022
parties elected and seats per party: Strong Republic (19); Strong Lebanon (18); Development and Liberation (15); Loyalty to the Resistance (15); Independent Deputies (9); Democratic Gathering (8); Independents (20); Other (24)
percentage of women in chamber: 6.3%
expected date of next election: May 2026
note 1: Lebanon's constitution states that the Parliament cannot conduct regular business until it elects a president when the position is vacant
note 2: seats are apportioned evenly between Christians and Muslims

Judicial branch: *highest court(s):* Court of Cassation or Supreme Court (organized into 8 chambers, each with a presiding judge and 2 associate judges); Constitutional Council (consists of 10 members)
judge selection and term of office: Court of Cassation judges appointed by Supreme Judicial Council, a 10-member body headed by the chief justice, and includes other judicial officials; judge tenure NA; Constitutional Council members appointed - 5 by the Council of Ministers and 5 by parliament; members serve 5-year terms
subordinate courts: Courts of Appeal; Courts of First Instance; specialized tribunals, religious courts; military courts

Political parties: Al-Ahbash (Association of Islamic Charitable Projects) or AICP
Amal Movement ("Hope Movement")
Azm Movement
Ba'th Arab Socialist Party of Lebanon
Free Patriotic Movement or FPM
Future Movement Bloc or FM
Hizballah
Islamic Action Front or IAF
Kata'ib Party
Lebanese Democratic Party
Lebanese Forces or LF
Marada Movement
Progressive Socialist Party or PSP
Social Democrat Hunshaqian Party
Syrian Social Nationalist Party or SSNP
Tashnaq or Armenian Revolutionary Federation

Diplomatic representation in the US: *chief of mission:* Ambassador Nada HAMADEH (since 5 September 2025)
chancery: 2560 28th Street NW, Washington, DC 20008
telephone: [1] (202) 939-6300
FAX: [1] (202) 939-6324
email address and website: info@lebanonembassyus.org
http://www.lebanonembassyus.org/
consulate(s) general: Detroit, New York, Los Angeles

Diplomatic representation from the US: *chief of mission:* Ambassador Lisa A. JOHNSON (since 6 February 2025)
embassy: Awkar facing the Municipality
P.O. Box 70-840 Antelias, Beirut
mailing address: 6070 Beirut Place, Washington DC 20521-6070
telephone: [961] (04) 543-600
FAX: [961] (4) 544-019
email address and website: BeirutACS@state.gov
https://lb.usembassy.gov/

International organization participation: ABEDA, AFESD, AMF, CAEU, FAO, G-24, G-77, IAEA, IBRD, ICAO, ICC (national committees), ICRM, IDA, IDB, IFAD, IFC, IFRCS, ILO, IMF, IMO, IMSO, Interpol, IOC, IPU, ISO, ITSO, ITU, LAS, MIGA, NAM, OAS (observer), OIC, OIF, OPCW, PCA, UN, UNCTAD, UNESCO, UNHCR, UNIDO, UNRWA, UNWTO, UPU, WCO, WFTU (NGOs), WHO, WIPO, WMO, WTO (observer)

Independence: 22 November 1943 (from League of Nations mandate under French administration)

National holiday: Independence Day, 22 November (1943)

Flag: *description:* three horizontal bands consisting of red (top), white (middle, double-width), and red (bottom), with a green cedar tree centered on the white band
meaning: red stands for blood shed for liberation, and white for peace, the snow of the mountains, and purity; the green cedar tree is the national symbol and represents eternity, steadiness, happiness, and prosperity

National symbol(s): cedar tree

National color(s): red, white, green

National anthem(s): *title:* "Kulluna lil-watan" (All of Us, For Our Country!)
lyrics/music: Rachid NAKHLE/Wadih SABRA
history: adopted 1927

National heritage: *total World Heritage Sites:* 6 (all cultural)
selected World Heritage Site locales: Anjar; Baalbek; Byblos; Tyre; Ouadi Qadisha (the Holy Valley) and the Forest of the Cedars of God (Horsh Arz el-Rab); Rachid Karami International Fair-Tripoli

ECONOMY

Economic overview: lower middle-income Middle Eastern economy; hyperinflation and sharp poverty increases; banks have ceased lending; economic contraction, destroyed infrastructure, and reduced consumer demand resulting from Israel-Hezbollah conflict

Real GDP (purchasing power parity): $65.415 billion (2023 est.)
$65.917 billion (2022 est.)
$66.329 billion (2021 est.)
note: data in 2021 dollars
comparison ranking: 113

Real GDP growth rate: -0.8% (2023 est.)
-0.6% (2022 est.)
-7% (2021 est.)
note: annual GDP % growth based on constant local currency
comparison ranking: 199

Real GDP per capita: $11,300 (2023 est.)
$11,500 (2022 est.)
$11,600 (2021 est.)
note: data in 2021 dollars
comparison ranking: 139

GDP (official exchange rate): $20.079 billion (2023 est.)
note: data in current dollars at official exchange rate

Inflation rate (consumer prices): 45.2% (2024 est.)
221.3% (2023 est.)
171.2% (2022 est.)
note: annual % change based on consumer prices
comparison ranking: 203

GDP - composition, by sector of origin: *agriculture:* 1% (2023 est.)
industry: 2.1% (2023 est.)
services: 42.4% (2023 est.)
note: figures may not total 100% due to non-allocated consumption not captured in sector-reported data
comparison rankings: agriculture 175; industry 207; services 184

GDP - composition, by end use: *household consumption:* 136% (2023 est.)
government consumption: 5.2% (2023 est.)
investment in fixed capital: 1.9% (2023 est.)
investment in inventories: 0% (2023 est.)
exports of goods and services: 30.6% (2023 est.)
imports of goods and services: -73.7% (2023 est.)
note: figures may not total 100% due to rounding or gaps in data collection

Agricultural products: potatoes, milk, tomatoes, apples, oranges, olives, cucumbers/gherkins, chicken, lemons/limes, wheat (2023)
note: top ten agricultural products based on tonnage

Industries: banking, tourism, real estate and construction, food processing, wine, jewelry, cement, textiles, mineral and chemical products, wood and furniture products, oil refining, metal fabricating

Industrial production growth rate: 0.1% (2023 est.)
note: annual % change in industrial value added based on constant local currency
comparison ranking: 135

Labor force: 1.939 million (2023 est.)
note: number of people ages 15 or older who are employed or seeking work
comparison ranking: 127

Unemployment rate: 11.6% (2023 est.)
11.6% (2022 est.)
12.7% (2021 est.)
note: % of labor force seeking employment
comparison ranking: 160

Youth unemployment rate (ages 15-24): *total:* 23.6% (2023 est.)
male: 24.4% (2023 est.)
female: 21.9% (2023 est.)
note: % of labor force ages 15-24 seeking employment
comparison ranking: total 40

Average household expenditures: *on food:* 37.1% of household expenditures (2023 est.)
on alcohol and tobacco: 0.7% of household expenditures (2023 est.)

Remittances: 33.3% of GDP (2023 est.)
30.7% of GDP (2022 est.)
27.5% of GDP (2021 est.)
note: personal transfers and compensation between resident and non-resident individuals/households/entities

Budget: *revenues:* $12.73 billion (2021 est.)
expenditures: $11.853 billion (2021 est.)
note: central government revenues and expenses (excluding grants/extrabudgetary units/social security funds) converted to US dollars at average official exchange rate for year indicated

Public debt: 146.8% of GDP (2017 est.)
note: data cover central government debt and exclude debt instruments issued (or owned) by government entities other than the treasury; the data include treasury debt held by foreign entities; the data include debt issued by subnational entities, as well as intragovernmental debt; intragovernmental debt consists of treasury borrowings from surpluses in the social funds, such as for retirement, medical care, and unemployment
comparison ranking: 4

Taxes and other revenues: 5.7% (of GDP) (2021 est.)
note: central government tax revenue as a % of GDP
comparison ranking: 148

Current account balance: -$5.643 billion (2023 est.)
-$7.265 billion (2022 est.)
-$4.556 billion (2021 est.)
note: balance of payments - net trade and primary/secondary income in current dollars
comparison ranking: 174

Exports: $11.77 billion (2023 est.)
$12.445 billion (2022 est.)
$9.684 billion (2021 est.)
note: balance of payments - exports of goods and services in current dollars
comparison ranking: 110

Exports - partners: UAE 26%, Egypt 7%, Turkey 5%, Iraq 5%, USA 4% (2023)
note: top five export partners based on percentage share of exports

Exports - commodities: jewelry, cars, diamonds, scrap iron, gold (2023)
note: top five export commodities based on value in dollars

Imports: $23.313 billion (2023 est.)
$24.536 billion (2022 est.)
$17.667 billion (2021 est.)
note: balance of payments - imports of goods and services in current dollars
comparison ranking: 88

Imports - partners: Switzerland 12%, China 11%, Greece 9%, Turkey 8%, Italy 6% (2023)
note: top five import partners based on percentage share of imports

Imports - commodities: refined petroleum, gold, cars, packaged medicine, garments (2023)
note: top five import commodities based on value in dollars

Reserves of foreign exchange and gold: $33.301 billion (2024 est.)
$27.49 billion (2023 est.)
$32.513 billion (2022 est.)
note: holdings of gold (year-end prices)/foreign exchange/special drawing rights in current dollars
comparison ranking: 55

Debt - external: $41.936 billion (2023 est.)
note: present value of external debt in current US dollars
comparison ranking: 20

Exchange rates: Lebanese pounds (LBP) per US dollar -

Exchange rates: 89,500 (2024 est.)
13,875.625 (2023 est.)
1,507.5 (2022 est.)
1,507.5 (2021 est.)
1,507.5 (2020 est.)

ENERGY

Electricity access: *electrification - total population:* 100% (2022 est.)

Electricity: *installed generating capacity:* 5.161 million kW (2023 est.)
consumption: 4.077 billion kWh (2023 est.)
imports: 797 million kWh (2021 est.)
transmission/distribution losses: 436.839 million kWh (2023 est.)
comparison rankings: installed generating capacity 90; consumption 135; imports 85; transmission/distribution losses 78

Electricity generation sources: *fossil fuels:* 52.6% of total installed capacity (2023 est.)
solar: 31% of total installed capacity (2023 est.)
wind: 0.1% of total installed capacity (2023 est.)
hydroelectricity: 15.5% of total installed capacity (2023 est.)
biomass and waste: 0.7% of total installed capacity (2023 est.)

Coal: *consumption:* 166,000 metric tons (2023 est.)
exports: 47 metric tons (2022 est.)
imports: 164,000 metric tons (2023 est.)

Petroleum: *refined petroleum consumption:* 115,000 bbl/day (2023 est.)

Energy consumption per capita: 43.105 million Btu/person (2023 est.)
comparison ranking: 99

COMMUNICATIONS

Telephones - fixed lines: *total subscriptions:* 875,000 (2021 est.)
subscriptions per 100 inhabitants: 16 (2022 est.)
comparison ranking: total subscriptions 71

Telephones - mobile cellular: *total subscriptions:* 4.29 million (2021 est.)
subscriptions per 100 inhabitants: 77 (2021 est.)
comparison ranking: total subscriptions 132

Broadcast media: 7 TV stations, 1 of which is state-owned; more than 30 radio stations, 1 of which is state-owned; satellite and cable TV services available; transmissions of at least 2 international broadcasters are accessible through partner stations (2019)

Internet country code: .lb

Internet users: *percent of population:* 84% (2023 est.)

Broadband - fixed subscriptions: *total:* 419,000 (2022 est.)
subscriptions per 100 inhabitants: 7 (2022 est.)
comparison ranking: total 106

TRANSPORTATION

Civil aircraft registration country code prefix: OD

Airports: 8 (2025)
comparison ranking: 168

Heliports: 27 (2025)
comparison ranking: 49

Railways: *total:* 401 km (2017)
standard gauge: 319 km (2017) 1.435-m gauge
narrow gauge: 82 km (2017) 1.050-m gauge
note: rail system is still unusable due to damage sustained from fighting in the 1980s and in 2006

Merchant marine: *total:* 51 (2023)
by type: bulk carrier 2, container ship 1, general cargo 30, oil tanker 1, other 17
comparison ranking: total 120

Ports: *total ports:* 5 (2024)
large: 1
medium: 1
small: 0
very small: 3
ports with oil terminals: 3
key ports: Bayrut, Sayda, Selaata, Sidon/zahrani Terminal, Tarabulus

MILITARY AND SECURITY

Military and security forces: Lebanese Armed Forces (LAF): Army Command (includes Presidential Guard Brigade, Land Border Regiments), Naval Forces, Air Forces

Ministry of Interior: General Directorate of Internal Security Forces (law enforcement; includes Mobile Gendarmerie), General Directorate for Public Security (border control, some domestic security duties) (2025)
note: the commander of the LAF is also the head of the Army; the LAF patrols external borders, while official border checkpoints are under the authority of Directorate for General Security

Military expenditures: 2.9% of GDP (2022 est.)
3.2% of GDP (2021 est.)
3% of GDP (2020 est.)
4.7% of GDP (2019 est.)
5.1% of GDP (2018 est.)

Military and security service personnel strengths: approximately 70,000 active Lebanese Armed Forces (2025)

Military equipment inventories and acquisitions: the LAF inventory includes a wide mix of mostly older equipment from a diverse array of countries, including the US; the country's economic crisis has limited military procurement efforts (2024)

Military service age and obligation: 17-25 years of age for men and women for voluntary military service; no conscription (2024)
note: women were allowed to volunteer for military service in the 1980s; as of 2023, they comprised about 5% of the active duty military

Military - note: the primary responsibilities of the Lebanese Armed Forces (LAF) are defense against external attack, border security, protecting the country's territorial waters, and assisting with internal security and development projects
the LAF's domestic security responsibilities include countering narcotics trafficking and smuggling, managing protests, conducting search and rescue, and intervening to prevent violence between rival political factions; in recent years, the military has faced a

financial crisis as government debt and national economic difficulties have undercut its ability to train and fully pay and supply personnel; the UN, as well as individual countries such as France, Qatar, and the US have provided financial assistance
the UN Interim Force in Lebanon (UNIFIL) has operated in the southern part of the country since 1978; it has approximately 10,500 personnel assigned and includes a maritime task force; the terrorist group Hizballah maintains thousands of fighters and militia in Lebanon, primarily in the south (see Terrorist Organizations in References) (2025)

TERRORISM

Terrorist group(s): Terrorist group(s): Abdallah Azzam Brigades; al-Aqsa Martyrs Brigade; Asbat al-Ansar; HAMAS; Hizballah; Islamic Revolutionary Guard Corps (IRGC)/Qods Force; Islamic State of Iraq and ash-Sham (ISIS); Palestine Liberation Front (PLF); Popular Front for the Liberation of Palestine (PFLP); PFLP-General Command (PFLP-GC)
note: details about the history, aims, leadership, organization, areas of operation, tactics, targets, weapons, size, and sources of support of the group(s) appear(s) in Appendix T

TRANSNATIONAL ISSUES

Refugees and internally displaced persons: *refugees:* 765,390 (2024 est.)
IDPs: 984,514 (2024 est.)
stateless persons: 40,000 (2024 est.)

LESOTHO

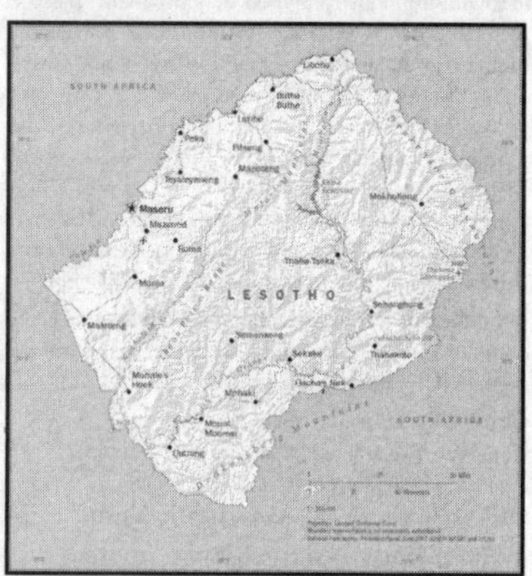

INTRODUCTION

Background: Paramount chief MOSHOESHOE I consolidated what would become Basutoland in the early 19th century and made himself king in 1822. Continuing encroachments by Dutch settlers from the neighboring Orange Free State caused the king to enter into an 1868 agreement with the UK that made Basutoland first a British protectorate and, after 1884, a crown colony. After gaining independence in 1966, the country was renamed the Kingdom of Lesotho. The Basotho National Party ruled the country during its first two decades. King MOSHOESHOE II was exiled in 1990, returned to Lesotho in 1992, was reinstated in 1995, and was then succeeded by his son, King LETSIE III, in 1996. Constitutional government was restored in 1993 after seven years of military rule.

In 1998, violent protests and a military mutiny following a contentious election prompted a brief but bloody intervention by South African and Batswana military forces under the aegis of the Southern African Development Community (SADC). Subsequent constitutional reforms restored relative political stability. Peaceful parliamentary elections were held in 2002, but the National Assembly elections in 2007 were hotly contested, and aggrieved parties disputed how seats were awarded. In 2012, competitive elections saw Prime Minister Motsoahae Thomas THABANE form a coalition government – the first in the country's history – that ousted the 14-year incumbent, Pakalitha MOSISILI, who peacefully transferred power the following month. MOSISILI returned to power in snap elections in 2015 after the collapse of THABANE's coalition government and an alleged attempted military coup. In 2017, THABANE returned to become prime minister but stepped down in 2020 after being implicated in his estranged wife's murder. He was succeeded by Moseketsi MAJORO. In 2022, Ntsokoane Samuel MATEKANE was inaugurated as prime minister and head of a three-party coalition.

GEOGRAPHY

Location: Southern Africa, an enclave of South Africa

Geographic coordinates: 29 30 S, 28 30 E

Map references: Africa

Area: *total:* 30,355 sq km
land: 30,355 sq km
water: 0 sq km
comparison ranking: total 141

Area - comparative: slightly smaller than Maryland

Land boundaries: *total:* 1,106 km
border countries (1): South Africa 1,106 km

Coastline: 0 km (landlocked)

Maritime claims: none (landlocked)

Climate: temperate; cool to cold, dry winters; hot, wet summers

Terrain: mostly highland with plateaus, hills, and mountains

Elevation: *highest point:* Thabana Ntlenyana 3,482 m
lowest point: junction of the Orange and Makhaleng Rivers 1,400 m
mean elevation: 2,161 m

Natural resources: water, agricultural and grazing land, diamonds, sand, clay, building stone

Land use: *agricultural land:* 74.8% (2022 est.)
arable land: 8.8% (2022 est.)
permanent crops: 0.1% (2022 est.)
permanent pasture: 65.9% (2022 est.)
forest: 1.1% (2022 est.)
other: 24.1% (2022 est.)

Irrigated land: 12 sq km (2013)

Major rivers (by length in km): Orange river source (shared with South Africa and Namibia [m]) - 2,092 km
note: [s] after country name indicates river source; [m] after country name indicates river mouth

Major watersheds (area sq km): Atlantic Ocean drainage: Orange (941,351 sq km)

Population distribution: relatively higher population density in the western half of the nation, with the capital of Maseru and the smaller cities of Mafeteng, Teyateyaneng, and Leribe attracting the most people, as shown in this population distribution map

Natural hazards: periodic droughts

Geography - note: landlocked, surrounded by South Africa; mountainous, more than 80% of the country is 1,800 m (5,900 ft) above sea level

PEOPLE AND SOCIETY

Population: *total:* 2,227,548 (2024 est.)
male: 1,101,959
female: 1,125,589
comparison rankings: total 147; male 147; female 146

Nationality: *noun:* Mosotho (singular), Basotho (plural)
adjective: Basotho

Ethnic groups: Sotho 99.7%, other 0.3% (includes Kwena, Nguni (Hlubi and Phuthi), Zulu)

Languages: Sesotho (official), English (official), Phuthi, Xhosa, Zulu

Religions: Protestant 47.8% (Pentecostal 23.1%, Lesotho Evangelical 17.3%, Anglican 7.4%), Roman Catholic 39.3%, other Christian 9.1%, non-Christian 1.4%, none 2.3% (2014 est.)

Age structure: *0-14 years:* 32% (male 358,137/female 353,618)
15-64 years: 62.7% (male 699,197/female 696,626)
65 years and over: 5.4% (2024 est.) (male 44,625/female 75,345)

Dependency ratios: *total dependency ratio:* 59.6 (2024 est.)
youth dependency ratio: 51 (2024 est.)
elderly dependency ratio: 8.6 (2024 est.)
potential support ratio: 11.6 (2024 est.)

Median age: *total:* 23.9 years (2024 est.)
male: 23.4 years
female: 24.3 years
comparison ranking: total 179

Population growth rate: 0.76% (2024 est.)
comparison ranking: 116

Birth rate: 22.9 births/1,000 population (2024 est.)
comparison ranking: 50

Death rate: 10.8 deaths/1,000 population (2024 est.)
comparison ranking: 28

Net migration rate: -4.5 migrant(s)/1,000 population (2024 est.)
comparison ranking: 199

Population distribution: relatively higher population density in the western half of the nation, with the capital of Maseru and the smaller cities of Mafeteng,

Teyateyaneng, and Leribe attracting the most people, as shown in this population distribution map

Urbanization: *urban population:* 30.4% of total population (2023)
rate of urbanization: 2.77% annual rate of change (2020-25 est.)

Major urban areas - population: 202,000 MASERU (capital) (2018)

Sex ratio: *at birth:* 1.03 male(s)/female
0-14 years: 1.01 male(s)/female
15-64 years: 1 male(s)/female
65 years and over: 0.59 male(s)/female
total population: 0.98 male(s)/female (2024 est.)

Mother's mean age at first birth: 20.9 years (2014 est.)
note: data represents median age at first birth among women 25-49

Maternal mortality ratio: 478 deaths/100,000 live births (2023 est.)
comparison ranking: 11

Infant mortality rate: *total:* 45.7 deaths/1,000 live births (2024 est.)
male: 51 deaths/1,000 live births
female: 40.2 deaths/1,000 live births
comparison ranking: total 24

Life expectancy at birth: *total population:* 60.2 years (2024 est.)
male: 58.1 years
female: 62.3 years
comparison ranking: total population 221

Total fertility rate: 2.85 children born/woman (2024 est.)
comparison ranking: 53

Gross reproduction rate: 1.4 (2024 est.)

Drinking water source: *improved: urban:* 93% of population (2022 est.)
rural: 65.9% of population (2022 est.)
total: 74% of population (2022 est.)
unimproved: urban: 7% of population (2022 est.)
rural: 34.1% of population (2022 est.)
total: 26% of population (2022 est.)

Health expenditure: 10.2% of GDP (2021)
13.1% of national budget (2022 est.)

Physician density: 0.24 physicians/1,000 population (2022)

Sanitation facility access: *improved: urban:* 93.6% of population (2022 est.)
rural: 62.4% of population (2022 est.)
total: 71.7% of population (2022 est.)
unimproved: urban: 6.4% of population (2022 est.)
rural: 37.6% of population (2022 est.)
total: 28.3% of population (2022 est.)

Obesity - adult prevalence rate: 16.6% (2016)
comparison ranking: 121

Alcohol consumption per capita: *total:* 3.56 liters of pure alcohol (2019 est.)
beer: 1.98 liters of pure alcohol (2019 est.)
wine: 0.44 liters of pure alcohol (2019 est.)
spirits: 0.31 liters of pure alcohol (2019 est.)
other alcohols: 0.82 liters of pure alcohol (2019 est.)
comparison ranking: total 103

Tobacco use: *total:* 22.8% (2025 est.)
male: 42.4% (2025 est.)
female: 4.1% (2025 est.)
comparison ranking: total 48

Children under the age of 5 years underweight: 10.5% (2018)
comparison ranking: 50

Currently married women (ages 15-49): 53.7% (2023 est.)

Child marriage: *women married by age 15:* 1% (2018)
women married by age 18: 16.4% (2018)
men married by age 18: 1.9% (2018)

Education expenditure: 6.6% of GDP (2024 est.)
10.4% national budget (2024 est.)
comparison ranking: Education expenditure (% GDP) 22

Literacy: *total population:* 86.2% (2018 est.)
male: 80.2% (2018 est.)
female: 91.8% (2018 est.)

School life expectancy (primary to tertiary education): *total:* 11 years (2017 est.)
male: 11 years (2017 est.)
female: 11 years (2017 est.)

ENVIRONMENT

Environmental issues: overgrazing; severe soil erosion; soil exhaustion; desertification; Highlands Water Project controls, stores, and redirects water to South Africa

International environmental agreements: *party to:* Biodiversity, Climate Change, Climate Change-Kyoto Protocol, Climate Change-Paris Agreement, Comprehensive Nuclear Test Ban, Desertification, Endangered Species, Hazardous Wastes, Law of the Sea, Marine Life Conservation, Ozone Layer Protection, Wetlands
signed, but not ratified: none of the selected agreements

Climate: temperate; cool to cold, dry winters; hot, wet summers

Urbanization: *urban population:* 30.4% of total population (2023)
rate of urbanization: 2.77% annual rate of change (2020-25 est.)

Carbon dioxide emissions: 1.148 million metric tonnes of CO2 (2023 est.)
from coal and metallurgical coke: 175,000 metric tonnes of CO2 (2023 est.)
from petroleum and other liquids: 973,000 metric tonnes of CO2 (2023 est.)
comparison ranking: total emissions 171

Particulate matter emissions: 17.4 micrograms per cubic meter (2019 est.)

Waste and recycling: *municipal solid waste generated annually:* 73,500 tons (2024 est.)
percent of municipal solid waste recycled: 11.9% (2022 est.)

Total water withdrawal: *municipal:* 20 million cubic meters (2022 est.)
industrial: 20 million cubic meters (2022 est.)
agricultural: 3.8 million cubic meters (2022 est.)

Total renewable water resources: 3.022 billion cubic meters (2022 est.)

GOVERNMENT

Country name: *conventional long form:* Kingdom of Lesotho
conventional short form: Lesotho
local long form: Kingdom of Lesotho
local short form: Lesotho
former: Basutoland
etymology: the name comes from the Sotho people, whose name means "dark-skinned;" *Le-* is a singular noun prefix; the former name, Basutoland, uses the plural noun prefix, *Ba-*

Government type: parliamentary constitutional monarchy

Capital: *name:* Maseru
geographic coordinates: 29 19 S, 27 29 E
time difference: UTC+2 (7 hours ahead of Washington, DC, during Standard Time)
etymology: the name means "[place of] red sandstones" in the Sesotho language

Administrative divisions: 10 districts; Berea, Butha-Buthe, Leribe, Mafeteng, Maseru, Mohale's Hoek, Mokhotlong, Qacha's Nek, Quthing, Thaba-Tseka

Legal system: mixed system of English common law and Roman-Dutch law; High Court and Court of Appeal review legislative acts

Constitution: *history:* previous 1959, 1967; latest adopted 2 April 1993 (effectively restoring the 1967 version)
amendment process: proposed by Parliament; passage of amendments affecting constitutional provisions, including fundamental rights and freedoms, sovereignty of the kingdom, the office of the king, and powers of Parliament, requires a majority vote by the National Assembly, approval by the Senate, approval in a referendum by a majority of qualified voters, and assent of the king; passage of amendments other than those specified provisions requires at least a two-thirds majority vote in both houses of Parliament

International law organization participation: accepts compulsory ICJ jurisdiction with reservations; accepts ICCt jurisdiction

Citizenship: *citizenship by birth:* yes
citizenship by descent only: yes
dual citizenship recognized: no
residency requirement for naturalization: 5 years

Suffrage: 18 years of age; universal

Executive branch: *chief of state:* King LETSIE III (since 7 February 1996)
head of government: Prime Minister Ntsokoane Samuel MATEKANE (28 October 2022)
cabinet: consists of the prime minister (appointed by the King on the advice of the Council of State), the deputy prime minister, and 18 other ministers; the prime minister is the leader of the majority party or majority coalition in the National Assembly
election/appointment process: the monarchy is hereditary but has no executive or legislative powers under the constitution; under traditional law, the College of Chiefs has the power to depose the monarch, determine next in line of succession, or serve as regent in the event that a successor is not of mature age
note: King LETSIE III previously occupied the throne from November 1990 to February 1995 while his father was in exile

Legislative branch: *legislature name:* Parliament
legislative structure: bicameral

Legislative branch - lower chamber: *chamber name:* National Assembly
number of seats: 122 (all directly elected)
electoral system: mixed system
scope of elections: full renewal
term in office: 5 years
most recent election date: 10/7/2022
parties elected and seats per party: Revolution for Prosperity (RFP) (56); Democratic Congress (DC) (29); All Basotho Convention (ABC) (8); Basotho Action Party (BAP) (6); Other (20)
percentage of women in chamber: 25%
expected date of next election: October 2027

Legislative branch - upper chamber: *chamber name:* Senate

number of seats: 33 (11 appointed)
scope of elections: full renewal
term in office: 5 years
most recent election date: 11/2/2022
percentage of women in chamber: 21.2%
expected date of next election: November 2027

Judicial branch: *highest court(s):* Court of Appeal (consists of the court president, such number of justices of appeal as set by Parliament, and the Chief Justice and the puisne judges of the High Court ex officio); High Court (consists of the chief justice and such number of puisne judges as set by Parliament)
judge selection and term of office: Court of Appeal president and High Court chief justice appointed by the monarch on the advice of the prime minister; puisne judges appointed by the monarch on advice of the Judicial Service Commission, an independent body of judicial officers and officials designated by the monarch; judges of both courts can serve until age 75
subordinate courts: Magistrate Courts; customary or traditional courts; military courts
note: both the Court of Appeal and the High Court have jurisdiction in constitutional issues

Political parties: All Basotho Convention or ABC
Alliance of Democrats or AD
Basotho Action Party or BAP
Basotho National Party or BNP
Democratic Congress or DC
Democratic Party of Lesotho or DPL
Lesotho People's Congress or LPC
Movement of Economic Change or MEC
National Independent Party or NIP
Popular Front for Democracy of PFD
Reformed Congress of Lesotho or RCL

Diplomatic representation in the US: *chief of mission:* Ambassador Tumisang MOSOTHO (since 16 September 2022)
chancery: 2511 Massachusetts Avenue NW, Washington, DC 20008
telephone: [1] (202) 797-5533

FAX: [1] (202) 234-6815
email address and website: lesothoembassy@verizon.net
https://www.gov.ls/

Diplomatic representation from the US: *chief of mission:* Ambassador (vacant); Chargé d'Affaires Thomas HINES (since August 2024)
embassy: 254 Kingsway Avenue, Maseru
mailing address: 2340 Maseru Place, Washington DC 20521-2340
telephone: [266] 22312666

FAX: [266] 22310116
email address and website: USConsularMaseru@state.gov
https://ls.usembassy.gov/

International organization participation: ACP, AfDB, AU, C, CD, FAO, G-77, IAEA, IBRD, ICAO, ICCt, ICRM, IDA, IFAD, IFC, IFRCS, ILO, IMF, Interpol, IOC, IOM, IPU, ISO (correspondent), ITU, MIGA, NAM, OPCW, SACU, SADC, UN, UNCTAD, UNESCO, UNHCR, UNIDO, UNWTO, UPU, WCO, WFTU (NGOs), WHO, WIPO, WMO, WTO

Independence: 4 October 1966 (from the UK)

National holiday: Independence Day, 4 October (1966)

Flag: *description:* three horizontal stripes of blue (top), white, and green; centered on the white stripe is a black *mokorotlo*, a traditional Basotho straw hat and national symbol
meaning: blue stands for rain, white for peace, and green for prosperity
history: the redesigned flag was introduced in 2006 to celebrate 40 years of independence

National symbol(s): mokorotio (Basotho hat)

National color(s): blue, white, green, black

National anthem(s): *title:* "Lesotho fatse la bo ntat'a rona" (Lesotho, Land of Our Fathers)
lyrics/music: Francois COILLARD/Ferdinand-Samuel LAUR
history: adopted 1967; music derives from an 1823 Swiss songbook

National heritage: *total World Heritage Sites:* 1 (mixed)
selected World Heritage Site locales: Maloti-Drakensberg Park

ECONOMY

Economic overview: lower middle-income economy surrounded by South Africa; environmentally fragile and politically unstable; key infrastructure and renewable energy investments; dire poverty; urban job and income losses due to COVID-19; systemic corruption

Real GDP (purchasing power parity): $6.166 billion (2024 est.)
$6 billion (2023 est.)
$5.893 billion (2022 est.)
note: data in 2021 dollars
comparison ranking: 174

Real GDP growth rate: 2.8% (2024 est.)
1.8% (2023 est.)
2.4% (2022 est.)
note: annual GDP % growth based on constant local currency
comparison ranking: 128

Real GDP per capita: $2,600 (2024 est.)
$2,600 (2023 est.)
$2,600 (2022 est.)
note: data in 2021 dollars
comparison ranking: 201

GDP (official exchange rate): $2.272 billion (2024 est.)
note: data in current dollars at official exchange rate

Inflation rate (consumer prices): 6.1% (2024 est.)
6.3% (2023 est.)
8.3% (2022 est.)
note: annual % change based on consumer prices
comparison ranking: 154

GDP - composition, by sector of origin: *agriculture:* 6.5% (2024 est.)
industry: 31% (2024 est.)
services: 48% (2024 est.)
note: figures may not total 100% due to non-allocated consumption not captured in sector-reported data
comparison rankings: agriculture 97; industry 49; services 158

GDP - composition, by end use: *household consumption:* 92.9% (2023 est.)
government consumption: 35.6% (2023 est.)
investment in fixed capital: 28.3% (2023 est.)
investment in inventories: -1.1% (2023 est.)
exports of goods and services: 42.9% (2023 est.)
imports of goods and services: -98.6% (2023 est.)
note: figures may not total 100% due to rounding or gaps in data collection

Agricultural products: milk, potatoes, maize, vegetables, fruits, sorghum, wheat, game meat, beans, wool (2023)
note: top ten agricultural products based on tonnage

Industries: food, beverages, textiles, apparel assembly, handicrafts, construction, tourism

Industrial production growth rate: 2.6% (2024 est.)
note: annual % change in industrial value added based on constant local currency
comparison ranking: 90

Labor force: 884,200 (2024 est.)
note: number of people ages 15 or older who are employed or seeking work
comparison ranking: 148

Unemployment rate: 16.2% (2024 est.)
16.5% (2023 est.)
16.7% (2022 est.)
note: % of labor force seeking employment
comparison ranking: 175

Youth unemployment rate (ages 15-24): *total:* 24.2% (2024 est.)
male: 17.7% (2024 est.)
female: 36.2% (2024 est.)
note: % of labor force ages 15-24 seeking employment
comparison ranking: total 37

Population below poverty line: 49.7% (2017 est.)
note: % of population with income below national poverty line

Gini Index coefficient - distribution of family income: 44.9 (2017 est.)
note: index (0-100) of income distribution; higher values represent greater inequality
comparison ranking: 17

Household income or consumption by percentage share: *lowest 10%:* 1.7% (2017 est.)
highest 10%: 32.9% (2017 est.)
note: % share of income accruing to lowest and highest 10% of population

Remittances: 22% of GDP (2024 est.)
22.9% of GDP (2023 est.)
22.6% of GDP (2022 est.)
note: personal transfers and compensation between resident and non-resident individuals/households/entities

Budget: *revenues:* $1.13 billion (2022 est.)
expenditures: $1.256 billion (2022 est.)
note: central government revenues and expenses (excluding grants/extrabudgetary units/social security funds) converted to US dollars at average official exchange rate for year indicated

Public debt: 3% of GDP (2020 est.)
note: central government debt as a % of GDP
comparison ranking: 198

Taxes and other revenues: 30.4% (of GDP) (2022 est.)
note: central government tax revenue as a % of GDP
comparison ranking: 4

Current account balance: $84.393 million (2024 est.)
-$151.577 million (2023 est.)
-$268.876 million (2022 est.)
note: balance of payments - net trade and primary/secondary income in current dollars
comparison ranking: 77

Exports: $983.027 million (2024 est.)
$885.789 million (2023 est.)
$1.07 billion (2022 est.)
note: balance of payments - exports of goods and services in current dollars
comparison ranking: 183

Exports - partners: South Africa 31%, Belgium 26%, USA 20%, UAE 8%, India 8% (2023)

note: top five export partners based on percentage share of exports

Exports - commodities: diamonds, garments, wool, power equipment, bedding (2023)
note: top five export commodities based on value in dollars

Imports: $2.083 billion (2024 est.)
$2.077 billion (2023 est.)
$2.247 billion (2022 est.)
note: balance of payments - imports of goods and services in current dollars
comparison ranking: 177

Imports - partners: South Africa 78%, China 10%, Taiwan 3%, Japan 1%, India 1% (2023)
note: top five import partners based on percentage share of imports

Imports - commodities: refined petroleum, fabric, trucks, garments, cotton fabric (2023)
note: top five import commodities based on value in dollars

Reserves of foreign exchange and gold: $1.008 billion (2024 est.)
$854.089 million (2023 est.)
$771.278 million (2022 est.)
note: holdings of gold (year-end prices)/foreign exchange/special drawing rights in current dollars
comparison ranking: 144

Debt - external: $928.019 million (2023 est.)
note: present value of external debt in current US dollars
comparison ranking: 104

Exchange rates: maloti (LSL) per US dollar -

Exchange rates: 18.329 (2024 est.)
18.45 (2023 est.)
16.356 (2022 est.)
14.779 (2021 est.)
16.459 (2020 est.)

ENERGY

Electricity access: *electrification - total population:* 50% (2022 est.)
electrification - urban areas: 83.6%
electrification - rural areas: 37.7%

Electricity: *installed generating capacity:* 104,000 kW (2023 est.)
consumption: 833.009 million kWh (2023 est.)
imports: 453.992 million kWh (2023 est.)
transmission/distribution losses: 102.88 million kWh (2023 est.)
comparison rankings: installed generating capacity 186; consumption 164; imports 97; transmission/distribution losses 47

Electricity generation sources: *fossil fuels:* 0.1% of total installed capacity (2023 est.)
solar: 0.3% of total installed capacity (2023 est.)
hydroelectricity: 99.6% of total installed capacity (2023 est.)

Coal: *production:* 57,000 metric tons (2023 est.)
consumption: 81,000 metric tons (2023 est.)
exports: 1 metric tons (2023 est.)
imports: 24,000 metric tons (2023 est.)

Petroleum: *refined petroleum consumption:* 7,000 bbl/day (2023 est.)

Energy consumption per capita: 8.117 million Btu/person (2023 est.)
comparison ranking: 159

COMMUNICATIONS

Telephones - fixed lines: *total subscriptions:* 7,000 (2023 est.)
subscriptions per 100 inhabitants: (2023 est.) less than 1
comparison ranking: total subscriptions 193

Telephones - mobile cellular: *total subscriptions:* 1.6 million (2023 est.)
subscriptions per 100 inhabitants: 68 (2022 est.)
comparison ranking: total subscriptions 157

Broadcast media: 1 state-owned TV station and 2 state-owned radio stations; most private broadcast media transmitters are connected to government radio signal towers; satellite TV subscription service available; transmissions of multiple international broadcasters obtainable (2019)

Internet country code: .ls

Internet users: *percent of population:* 48% (2023 est.)

Broadband - fixed subscriptions: *total:* 9,000 (2023 est.)
subscriptions per 100 inhabitants: (2023 est.) less than 1
comparison ranking: total 186

TRANSPORTATION

Civil aircraft registration country code prefix: 7P

Airports: 34 (2025)
comparison ranking: 114

MILITARY AND SECURITY

Military and security forces: Lesotho Defense Force (LDF) (2025)
note: the Lesotho Mounted Police Service is responsible for internal security and reports to the Minister of Local Government, Chieftainship, Home Affairs and Police

Military expenditures: 1.5% of GDP (2024 est.)
1.6% of GDP (2023 est.)
1.6% of GDP (2022 est.)
1.5% of GDP (2021 est.)
1.6% of GDP (2020 est.)

Military and security service personnel strengths: approximately 2,000 active Defense Forces (2025)

Military equipment inventories and acquisitions: the LDF is lightly armed and has a small inventory of mostly older or second-hand equipment of European, South African, and US origin (2025)

Military service age and obligation: 18-30 years of age for voluntary military service for both men and women (women can serve in combat arms); no conscription (2024)

Military - note: the Lesotho Defense Force (LDF) is responsible for the maintenance of the country's sovereignty and the preservation of internal security; in practice, external security is guaranteed by South Africa; the LDF is a small force that began in 1964 as the Police Mobile Unit (PMU); the PMU was designated as the Lesotho Paramilitary Force in 1980 and became the Royal Lesotho Defense Force in 1986; it was renamed the Lesotho Defense Force in 1993 (2025)

TRANSNATIONAL ISSUES

Refugees and internally displaced persons: *refugees:* 610 (2024 est.)

LIBERIA

INTRODUCTION

Background: With 28 ethnic groups and languages, Liberia is one of the most ethnically diverse countries in the world. For hundreds of years, the Mali and Songhai Empires claimed most of Liberia. Beginning in the 15th century, European traders began establishing outposts along the Liberian coast. Unlike its neighbors, however, Liberia did not fall under European colonial rule. In the early 19th century, the US began sending freed enslaved people and other people of color to Liberia to establish settlements. In 1847, these settlers declared independence from the US, writing their own constitution and establishing Africa's first republic.

Early in Liberia's history, tensions arose between the Americo-Liberian settlers and the indigenous population. In 1980, Samuel DOE, who was from the indigenous population, led a military coup and ushered in a decade of authoritarian rule. In 1989, Charles TAYLOR launched a rebellion that led to a prolonged civil war in which DOE was killed. A period of relative peace in 1997 permitted an election that brought TAYLOR to power. In 2000, fighting resumed. A 2003 peace agreement ended the war and prompted TAYLOR's resignation. He was later convicted by the UN-backed Special Court for Sierra Leone in The Hague for his involvement in Sierra Leone's civil war.

In 2005, Ellen JOHNSON SIRLEAF became president after two years of transitional governments; she was the first female head of state in Africa. In 2011, JOHNSON SIRLEAF won reelection but struggled to rebuild Liberia's economy – particularly after the 2014-15 Ebola epidemic – and to reconcile a nation still recovering from 14 years of fighting.

In 2017, former soccer star George WEAH won the presidential runoff election, marking the first successful transfer of power from one democratically elected government to another since the end of Liberia's civil wars. Like his predecessor, WEAH struggled to improve the country's economy. In 2023, former Vice President Joseph BOAKAI was elected president, edging out WEAH by a thin margin, the first time since 1927 that an incumbent was not re-elected after one term.

GEOGRAPHY

Location: Western Africa, bordering the North Atlantic Ocean, between Cote d'Ivoire and Sierra Leone

Geographic coordinates: 6 30 N, 9 30 W

Map references: Africa

Area: *total:* 111,369 sq km
land: 96,320 sq km
water: 15,049 sq km
comparison ranking: total 104

Area - comparative: slightly larger than Virginia

Land boundaries: *total:* 1,667 km
border countries (3): Guinea 590 km; Cote d'Ivoire 778 km; Sierra Leone 299 km

Coastline: 579 km

Maritime claims: *territorial sea:* 12 nm
contiguous zone: 24 nm
exclusive economic zone: 200 nm
continental shelf: 200 nm

Climate: tropical; hot, humid; dry winters with hot days and cool to cold nights; wet, cloudy summers with frequent heavy showers

Terrain: mostly flat to rolling coastal plains rising to rolling plateau and low mountains in northeast

Elevation: *highest point:* Mount Wuteve 1,447 m
lowest point: Atlantic Ocean 0 m
mean elevation: 243 m

Natural resources: iron ore, timber, diamonds, gold, hydropower

Land use: *agricultural land:* 20% (2022 est.)
arable land: 5.2% (2022 est.)
permanent crops: 2.1% (2022 est.)
permanent pasture: 12.7% (2022 est.)
forest: 78.5% (2022 est.)
other: 1.6% (2022 est.)

Irrigated land: 30 sq km (2012)

Population distribution: more than half of the population lives in urban areas, with approximately one third living within an 80-km (50-mi) radius of Monrovia, as shown in this population distribution map

Natural hazards: dust-laden harmattan winds blow from the Sahara (December to March)

Geography - note: facing the Atlantic Ocean, the coastline is characterized by lagoons, mangrove swamps, and river-deposited sandbars; the inland grassy plateau supports limited agriculture

PEOPLE AND SOCIETY

Population: *total:* 5,437,249 (2024 est.)
male: 2,711,324
female: 2,725,925
comparison rankings: total 121; male 120; female 121

Nationality: *noun:* Liberian(s)
adjective: Liberian

Ethnic groups: Kpelle 20.2%, Bassa 13.6%, Grebo 9.9%, Gio 7.9%, Mano 7.2%, Kru 5.5%, Lorma 4.8%, Krahn 4.5%, Kissi, 4.3%, Mandingo 4.2%, Vai 3.8%, Gola 3.8%, Gbandi 2.9%, Mende 1.7%, Sapo 1%, Belle 0.7%, Dey 0.3%, other Liberian ethnic group 0.4%, other African 3%, non-African 0.2% (2022 est.)

Languages: English 20% (official) and 27 indigenous languages, including Liberian English variants

Religions: Christian 84.9%, Muslim 12%, Traditional 0.5%, other 0.1%, none 2.6% (2022 est.)

Age structure: *0-14 years:* 38.9% (male 1,064,100/female 1,052,556)
15-64 years: 57.9% (male 1,566,263/female 1,579,835)
65 years and over: 3.2% (2024 est.) (male 80,961/female 93,534)

Dependency ratios: *total dependency ratio:* 72.8 (2024 est.)
youth dependency ratio: 67.3 (2024 est.)
elderly dependency ratio: 5.5 (2024 est.)
potential support ratio: 18 (2024 est.)

Median age: *total:* 19.9 years (2024 est.)
male: 19.8 years
female: 20 years
comparison ranking: total 207

Population growth rate: 2.32% (2024 est.)
comparison ranking: 28

Birth rate: 32.4 births/1,000 population (2024 est.)
comparison ranking: 20

Death rate: 8.3 deaths/1,000 population (2024 est.)
comparison ranking: 79

Net migration rate: -0.8 migrant(s)/1,000 population (2024 est.)
comparison ranking: 139

Population distribution: more than half of the population lives in urban areas, with approximately one third living within an 80-km (50-mi) radius of Monrovia, as shown in this population distribution map

Urbanization: *urban population:* 53.6% of total population (2023)
rate of urbanization: 3.41% annual rate of change (2015-20 est.)

Major urban areas - population: 1.678 million MONROVIA (capital) (2023)

Sex ratio: *at birth:* 1.03 male(s)/female
0-14 years: 1.01 male(s)/female
15-64 years: 0.99 male(s)/female
65 years and over: 0.87 male(s)/female
total population: 1 male(s)/female (2024 est.)

Mother's mean age at first birth: 19.1 years (2019/20 est.)
note: data represents median age at first birth among women 25-49

Maternal mortality ratio: 628 deaths/100,000 live births (2023 est.)
comparison ranking: 5

Infant mortality rate: *total:* 55.7 deaths/1,000 live births (2024 est.)
male: 61 deaths/1,000 live births
female: 50.2 deaths/1,000 live births
comparison ranking: total 12

Life expectancy at birth: *total population:* 61.6 years (2024 est.)
male: 59.9 years
female: 63.3 years
comparison ranking: total population 217

Total fertility rate: 3.93 children born/woman (2024 est.)
comparison ranking: 26

Gross reproduction rate: 1.94 (2024 est.)

Drinking water source: *improved: urban:* 84.6% of population (2022 est.)
rural: 65.5% of population (2022 est.)
total: 75.6% of population (2022 est.)
unimproved: urban: 15.4% of population (2022 est.)
rural: 34.5% of population (2022 est.)
total: 24.4% of population (2022 est.)

Health expenditure: 16.6% of GDP (2021)
4.8% of national budget (2022 est.)

Physician density: 0.18 physicians/1,000 population (2022)

Hospital bed density: 1.6 beds/1,000 population (2021 est.)

Sanitation facility access: *improved: urban:* 70.1% of population (2022 est.)
rural: 25.1% of population (2022 est.)
total: 49% of population (2022 est.)
unimproved: urban: 29.9% of population (2022 est.)
rural: 74.9% of population (2022 est.)
total: 51% of population (2022 est.)

Obesity - adult prevalence rate: 9.9% (2016)
comparison ranking: 141

Alcohol consumption per capita: *total:* 3.12 liters of pure alcohol (2019 est.)
beer: 0.38 liters of pure alcohol (2019 est.)
wine: 0.44 liters of pure alcohol (2019 est.)
spirits: 2.28 liters of pure alcohol (2019 est.)
other alcohols: 0.02 liters of pure alcohol (2019 est.)
comparison ranking: total 109

Tobacco use: *total:* 6.4% (2025 est.)
male: 11.5% (2025 est.)
female: 1.5% (2025 est.)
comparison ranking: total 155

Children under the age of 5 years underweight: 10.9% (2019/20)
comparison ranking: 49

Currently married women (ages 15-49): 48.7% (2023 est.)

Child marriage: *women married by age 15:* 5.8% (2020)
women married by age 18: 24.9% (2020)
men married by age 18: 8.4% (2020)

Education expenditure: 2.3% of GDP (2023 est.)
7.4% national budget (2021 est.)
comparison ranking: Education expenditure (% GDP) 178

ENVIRONMENT

Environmental issues: tropical rainforest deforestation; soil erosion; loss of biodiversity; hunting of endangered species for bushmeat; pollution of coastal waters from oil residue and raw sewage; pollution of rivers from industrial run-off; burning and dumping of household waste

International environmental agreements: *party to:* Biodiversity, Climate Change, Climate Change-Kyoto Protocol, Climate Change-Paris Agreement, Comprehensive Nuclear Test Ban, Desertification, Endangered Species, Hazardous Wastes, Law of the Sea, Nuclear Test Ban, Ozone Layer Protection, Ship Pollution, Tropical Timber 2006, Wetlands, Whaling
signed, but not ratified: Environmental Modification, Marine Life Conservation

Climate: tropical; hot, humid; dry winters with hot days and cool to cold nights; wet, cloudy summers with frequent heavy showers

Urbanization: *urban population:* 53.6% of total population (2023)
rate of urbanization: 3.41% annual rate of change (2015-20 est.)

Carbon dioxide emissions: 671,000 metric tonnes of CO2 (2023 est.)
from coal and metallurgical coke: 4 metric tonnes of CO2 (2023 est.)
from petroleum and other liquids: 671,000 metric tonnes of CO2 (2023 est.)
comparison ranking: total emissions 183

Particulate matter emissions: 41.9 micrograms per cubic meter (2019 est.)

Waste and recycling: *municipal solid waste generated annually:* 564,500 tons (2024 est.)
percent of municipal solid waste recycled: 7.9% (2022 est.)

Total water withdrawal: *municipal:* 80.2 million cubic meters (2022 est.)
industrial: 53.4 million cubic meters (2022 est.)
agricultural: 12.3 million cubic meters (2022 est.)

Total renewable water resources: 232 billion cubic meters (2022 est.)

GOVERNMENT

Country name: *conventional long form:* Republic of Liberia
conventional short form: Liberia
etymology: name derives from the Latin word *liber*, meaning "free;" so named because the nation was created as a homeland for liberated African-American slaves

Government type: presidential republic

Capital: *name:* Monrovia
geographic coordinates: 6 18 N, 10 48 W
time difference: UTC 0 (5 hours ahead of Washington, DC, during Standard Time)
etymology: named after James MONROE (1758-1831), the fifth president of the United States and supporter of Liberia's colonization by freed slaves

Administrative divisions: 15 counties; Bomi, Bong, Gbarpolu, Grand Bassa, Grand Cape Mount, Grand Gedeh, Grand Kru, Lofa, Margibi, Maryland, Montserrado, Nimba, River Cess, River Gee, Sinoe

Legal system: mixed system of common law, based on Anglo-American law and customary law

Constitution: *history:* previous 1847 (at independence); latest drafted 19 October 1983, revision adopted by referendum 3 July 1984, effective 6 January 1986
amendment process: proposed by agreement of at least two thirds of both National Assembly houses or by petition of at least 10,000 citizens; passage requires at least two-thirds majority approval of both houses and approval in a referendum by at least two-thirds majority of registered voters

International law organization participation: accepts compulsory ICJ jurisdiction with reservations; accepts ICCt jurisdiction

Citizenship: *citizenship by birth:* no
citizenship by descent only: at least one parent must be a citizen of Liberia
dual citizenship recognized: no
residency requirement for naturalization: 2 years

Suffrage: 18 years of age; universal

Executive branch: *chief of state:* President Joseph BOAKAI (since 22 January 2024)
head of government: President Joseph BOAKAI (since 22 January 2024)
cabinet: Cabinet appointed by the president, confirmed by the Senate
election/appointment process: president directly elected by absolute-majority popular vote in 2 rounds, if needed, for a 6-year term (eligible for a second term)
most recent election date: 10 October 2023, with a runoff on 14 November 2023
election results: *2023:* Joseph BOAKAI elected president in second round; percent of vote in first round - George WEAH (CDC) 43.8%, Joseph BOAKAI (UP) 43.4%, Edward APPLETON (GDM) 2.2%, Lusinee KAMARA (ALCOP) 2%, Alexander B. CUMMINGS, Jr. (CPP) 1.6%, Tiawan Saye GONGLOE (LPP) 1.4%, other 5.6%; percentage of vote in second round - Joseph BOAKAI 50.6%, George WEAH 49.4%
2017: George WEAH elected president in second round; percent of vote in first round - George WEAH (Coalition for Democratic Change) 38.4%, Joseph BOAKAI (UP) 28.8%, Charles BRUMSKINE (LP) 9.6%, Prince JOHNSON (MDR) 8.2%, Alexander B. CUMMINGS (ANC) 7.2%, other 7.8%; percentage of vote in second round - George WEAH 61.5%, Joseph BOAKAI 38.5%
expected date of next election: October 2029
note: the president is both chief of state and head of government

Legislative branch: *legislature name:* Legislature
legislative structure: bicameral

Legislative branch - lower chamber: *chamber name:* House of Representatives
number of seats: 73 (all directly elected)
electoral system: plurality/majority
scope of elections: full renewal
term in office: 6 years
most recent election date: 10/10/2023
parties elected and seats per party: Congress for Democratic Change (CDC) (25); Unity Party (UP) (11); Collaborating Political Parties (CPP) (6); Movement for Democracy and Reconstruction (MDR) (4); Independents (19); Other (8)
percentage of women in chamber: 11%
expected date of next election: October 2029

Legislative branch - upper chamber: *chamber name:* The Liberian Senate
number of seats: 30 (all directly elected)
electoral system: plurality/majority
scope of elections: partial renewal
term in office: 9 years
most recent election date: 10/10/2023
parties elected and seats per party: Congress for Democratic Change (CDC) (6); Unity Party (UP) (1); Movement for Democracy and Reconstruction (MDR) (1); Liberia Restoration Party (LRP) (1); Independents (6)
percentage of women in chamber: 10%
expected date of next election: October 2029

Judicial branch: *highest court(s):* Supreme Court (consists of a chief justice and 4 associate justices)
judge selection and term of office: chief justice and associate justices appointed by the president of Liberia with consent of the Senate; judges can serve until age 70
subordinate courts: judicial circuit courts; special courts, including criminal, civil, labor, traffic; magistrate and traditional or customary courts
note: the Supreme Court has jurisdiction for all constitutional cases

Political parties: All Liberian Party or ALP
Alliance for Peace and Democracy or APD
Alternative National Congress or ANC
Coalition for Democratic Change (includes CDC, NPP, and LPDP)
Collaborating Political Parties or CPP (coalition includes ANC, LP; CPP dissolved in April 2024)
Congress for Democratic Change or CDC
Liberia Destiny Party or LDP
Liberia National Union or LINU
Liberia Transformation Party or LTP
Liberian People Democratic Party or LPDP
Liberian People's Party or LPP
Liberian Restoration Party or LRP
Liberty Party or LP
Movement for Democracy and Reconstruction or MDR
Movement for Economic Empowerment
Movement for Progressive Change or MPC
National Democratic Coalition or NDC
National Democratic Party of Liberia or NDPL
National Patriotic Party or NPP
National Reformist Party or NRP
National Union for Democratic Progress or NUDP
People's Unification Party or PUP
Unity Party or UP
United People's Party
Victory for Change Party or VCP

Diplomatic representation in the US: *chief of mission:* Ambassador Al-Hassan CONTEH (since 24 July 2025)
chancery: 5201 16th Street NW, Washington, DC 20011
telephone: [1] (202) 723-0437
FAX: [1] (202) 723-0436
email address and website: info@liberianembassyus.org
http://www.liberianembassyus.org/
consulate(s) general: New York

Diplomatic representation from the US : *chief of mission:* Ambassador (vacant); Chargé d'Affaires Joseph ZADROZNY (since August 2025)
embassy: 502 Benson Street, Monrovia
mailing address: 8800 Monrovia Place, Washington DC 20521-8800
telephone: [231] 77-677-7000
FAX: [231] 77-677-7370
email address and website: ACSMonrovia@state.gov
https://lr.usembassy.gov/

International organization participation: ACP, AfDB, AU, ECOWAS, EITI (compliant country), FAO, G-77, IAEA, IBRD, ICAO, ICC (NGOs), ICCt, ICRM, IDA, IFAD, IFC, IFRCS, ILO, IMF, IMO, IMSO, Interpol, IOC, IOM, ISO (correspondent), ITU, ITUC (NGOs), MIGA, NAM, OPCW, UN, UNCTAD, UNESCO, UNIDO, UNISFA, UNWTO, UPU, WCO, WFTU (NGOs), WHO, WIPO, WMO, WTO

Independence : 26 July 1847

National holiday: Independence Day, 26 July (1847)

Flag: *description:* 11 equal horizontal stripes of red alternating with white; a five-pointed white star sits on a blue square in the upper-left corner
meaning: the stripes stand for the signatories of the Liberian Declaration of Independence, the blue square for the African mainland, and the star for the freedom granted to ex-slaves; the blue stands for liberty, justice, and fidelity; the white for purity,

cleanliness, and guilelessness; the red for steadfastness, valor, and fervor
note: the design is based on the US flag

National symbol(s): white star

National color(s): red, white, blue

National anthem(s): *title:* "All Hail, Liberia, Hail!"
lyrics/music: Daniel Bashiel WARNER/Olmstead LUCA
history: lyrics adopted 1847, music adopted 1860; the anthem's author later became the third president of Liberia

ECONOMY

Economic overview: low-income West African economy; food scarcity, especially in rural areas; high poverty and inflation; bad recession prior to COVID-19 due to Ebola crisis; growing government debt; longest continuously operated rubber plantation; large informal economy

Real GDP (purchasing power parity): $9.308 billion (2024 est.)
$8.882 billion (2023 est.)
$8.484 billion (2022 est.)
note: data in 2021 dollars
comparison ranking: 166

Real GDP growth rate: 4.8% (2024 est.)
4.7% (2023 est.)
4.8% (2022 est.)
note: annual GDP % growth based on constant local currency
comparison ranking: 52

Real GDP per capita: $1,700 (2024 est.)
$1,600 (2023 est.)
$1,600 (2022 est.)
note: data in 2021 dollars
comparison ranking: 208

GDP (official exchange rate): $4.75 billion (2024 est.)
note: data in current dollars at official exchange rate

Inflation rate (consumer prices): 10.1% (2023 est.)
7.6% (2022 est.)
7.8% (2021 est.)
note: annual % change based on consumer prices
comparison ranking: 178

GDP - composition, by sector of origin: *agriculture:* 33.6% (2024 est.)
industry: 23.3% (2024 est.)
services: 42.1% (2024 est.)
note: figures may not total 100% due to non-allocated consumption not captured in sector-reported data
comparison rankings: agriculture 8; industry 104; services 188

Agricultural products: cassava, sugarcane, rice, oil palm fruit, bananas, rubber, vegetables, plantains, taro, maize (2023)
note: top ten agricultural products based on tonnage

Industries: mining (iron ore and gold), rubber processing, palm oil processing, diamonds

Industrial production growth rate: 6.1% (2024 est.)
note: annual % change in industrial value added based on constant local currency
comparison ranking: 31

Labor force: 2.607 million (2024 est.)
note: number of people ages 15 or older who are employed or seeking work
comparison ranking: 119

Unemployment rate: 2.9% (2024 est.)
3% (2023 est.)
3% (2022 est.)
note: % of labor force seeking employment
comparison ranking: 34

Youth unemployment rate (ages 15-24): *total:* 2.1% (2024 est.)
male: 2.2% (2024 est.)
female: 2% (2024 est.)
note: % of labor force ages 15-24 seeking employment
comparison ranking: total 184

Population below poverty line: 50.9% (2016 est.)
note: % of population with income below national poverty line

Gini Index coefficient - distribution of family income: 35.3 (2016 est.)
note: index (0-100) of income distribution; higher values represent greater inequality
comparison ranking: 73

Household income or consumption by percentage share: *lowest 10%:* 2.9% (2016 est.)
highest 10%: 27.1% (2016 est.)
note: % share of income accruing to lowest and highest 10% of population

Remittances: 18.2% of GDP (2023 est.)
17.2% of GDP (2022 est.)
15.1% of GDP (2021 est.)
note: personal transfers and compensation between resident and non-resident individuals/households/entities

Budget: *revenues:* $5 million (2019 est.)
expenditures: $6 million (2019 est.)

Current account balance: $64.806 million (2022 est.)
-$101.746 million (2021 est.)
-$274.971 million (2020 est.)
note: balance of payments - net trade and primary/secondary income in current dollars
comparison ranking: 80

Exports: $1.22 billion (2022 est.)
$1.041 billion (2021 est.)
$731.658 million (2020 est.)
note: balance of payments - exports of goods and services in current dollars
comparison ranking: 180

Exports - partners: Switzerland 30%, UK 13%, France 8%, Germany 7%, Lebanon 4% (2023)
note: top five export partners based on percentage share of exports

Exports - commodities: gold, ships, iron ore, rubber, refined petroleum (2023)
note: top five export commodities based on value in dollars

Imports: $1.961 billion (2022 est.)
$1.739 billion (2021 est.)
$1.371 billion (2020 est.)
note: balance of payments - imports of goods and services in current dollars
comparison ranking: 178

Imports - partners: China 48%, Japan 21%, Germany 8%, Brazil 3%, Cote d'Ivoire 3% (2023)
note: top five import partners based on percentage share of imports

Imports - commodities: ships, refined petroleum, rice, trucks, centrifuges (2023)
note: top five import commodities based on value in dollars

Reserves of foreign exchange and gold: $599.66 million (2022 est.)
$700.829 million (2021 est.)
$340.966 million (2020 est.)
note: holdings of gold (year-end prices)/foreign exchange/special drawing rights in current dollars
comparison ranking: 154

Debt - external: $1.335 billion (2023 est.)
note: present value of external debt in current US dollars
comparison ranking: 102

Exchange rates: Liberian dollars (LRD) per US dollar -

Exchange rates: 174.956 (2023 est.)
152.934 (2022 est.)
166.154 (2021 est.)
191.518 (2020 est.)
186.43 (2019 est.)

ENERGY

Electricity access: *electrification - total population:* 31.8% (2022 est.)
electrification - urban areas: 53.7%
electrification - rural areas: 14.9%

Electricity: *installed generating capacity:* 199,000 kW (2023 est.)
consumption: 215.96 million kWh (2023 est.)
transmission/distribution losses: 179.222 million kWh (2023 est.)
comparison rankings: installed generating capacity 173; consumption 188; transmission/distribution losses 62

Electricity generation sources: *fossil fuels:* 66.1% of total installed capacity (2023 est.)
solar: 1.3% of total installed capacity (2023 est.)
hydroelectricity: 32.4% of total installed capacity (2023 est.)
biomass and waste: 0.3% of total installed capacity (2023 est.)

Coal: *imports:* 75,000 metric tons (2023 est.)

Petroleum: *refined petroleum consumption:* 5,000 bbl/day (2023 est.)

Energy consumption per capita: 1.822 million Btu/person (2023 est.)
comparison ranking: 186

COMMUNICATIONS

Telephones - fixed lines: *total subscriptions:* 6,000 (2021 est.)
subscriptions per 100 inhabitants: (2022 est.) less than 1
comparison ranking: total subscriptions 199

Telephones - mobile cellular: *total subscriptions:* 1.65 million (2021 est.)
subscriptions per 100 inhabitants: 32 (2021 est.)
comparison ranking: total subscriptions 156

Broadcast media: 8 private and 1 state-owned TV station; satellite TV service available; 1 state-owned radio station; about 20 independent radio stations broadcasting in Monrovia, with about 80 more local stations operating in other areas; transmissions of 4 international broadcasters are available (2019)

Internet country code: .lr

Internet users: *percent of population:* 24% (2023 est.)

Broadband - fixed subscriptions: *total:* 15,000 (2022 est.)
subscriptions per 100 inhabitants: (2022 est.) less than 1
comparison ranking: total 178

TRANSPORTATION

Civil aircraft registration country code prefix: A8

Airports: 19 (2025)
comparison ranking: 141

Railways: *total:* 429 km (2008)
standard gauge: 345 km (2008) 1.435-m gauge
narrow gauge: 84 km (2008) 1.067-m gauge
note: most sections of the railways inoperable due to damage sustained during the civil wars from 1980 to 2003, but many are being rebuilt

Merchant marine: *total:* 4,821 (2023)
by type: bulk carrier 1,895, container ship 1,013, general cargo 170, oil tanker 1,038, other 705
comparison ranking: total 5

Ports: *total ports:* 4 (2024)
large: 0
medium: 0
small: 1
very small: 3
ports with oil terminals: 3
key ports: Buchanan, Cape Palmas, Greenville, Monrovia

MILITARY AND SECURITY

Military and security forces: Armed Forces of Liberia (AFL): Army, Liberian Coast Guard

Ministry of Justice: Liberia National Police, Liberia Drug Enforcement Agency (2025)

Military expenditures: 0.7% of GDP (2024 est.)
1.3% of GDP (2023 est.)
1.3% of GDP (2022 est.)
0.8% of GDP (2021 est.)
0.5% of GDP (2020 est.)

Military and security service personnel strengths: approximately 2,000 active Armed Forces (2025)

Military equipment inventories and acquisitions: the military has a limited inventory; in recent years, it has received small quantities of equipment, including donations, from countries such as China and the US (2024)

Military service age and obligation: 18-35 years of age for men and women for voluntary military service; no conscription (2024)

Military - note: the Armed Forces of Liberia (AFL) are responsible for external defense and some domestic security responsibilities if called upon, such as humanitarian assistance during natural disasters and support to law enforcement; it is a small, lightly equipped force comprised of two combat infantry battalions and supporting units, as well as a few coastal patrol craft for the Coast Guard; the infantry battalions were rebuilt with US assistance in 2007-2008 from the restructured AFL following the end of the second civil war in 2003 when military and police forces were disbanded and approximately 100,000 military, police, and rebel combatants were disarmed
the first militia unit established for defense of the Liberia colony was raised in 1832; the AFL traces its origins to the 1908 establishment of the Liberia Frontier Force, which became the Liberian National Guard in 1965; the AFL was established in 1970 (2025)

TRANSNATIONAL ISSUES

Refugees and internally displaced persons: *refugees:* 1,854 (2024 est.)

Trafficking in persons: *tier rating:* Tier 2 Watch List — the government did not demonstrate overall increasing efforts to eliminate trafficking compared with the previous reporting period, therefore Liberia remained on Tier 2 Watch List for the second consecutive year; for more details, go to: https://www.state.gov/reports/2025-trafficking-in-persons-report/liberia/

LIBYA

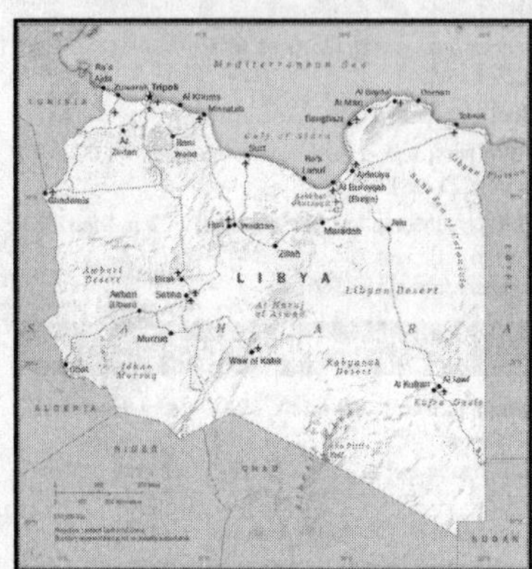

INTRODUCTION

Background: Berbers have inhabited central north Africa since ancient times, but Phoenicians, Greeks, Carthaginians, Persians, Egyptians, Romans, and Vandals have all settled and ruled the region. In the 7th century, Islam spread through the area. In the mid-16th century, Ottoman rule began; the Italians supplanted the Ottoman Turks in the area around Tripoli in 1911 and held it until 1943, when they were defeated in World War II. Libya then came under UN administration and achieved independence in 1951. Col. Muammar al-QADHAFI assumed leadership with a military coup in 1969 and began to espouse a political system that combined socialism and Islam. During the 1970s, QADHAFI used oil revenues to promote his ideology outside Libya, supporting subversive and terrorist activities that included the downing of two airliners – one over Scotland and another in Northern Africa – and a discotheque bombing in Berlin. UN sanctions in 1992 isolated QADHAFI politically and economically; the sanctions were lifted in 2003 when Libya accepted responsibility for the bombings and agreed to claimant compensation. QADHAFI also agreed to end Libya's program to develop weapons of mass destruction, and he made significant strides in normalizing relations with Western nations.

Unrest that began in several Middle Eastern and North African countries in 2010 erupted in Libyan cities in 2011. QADHAFI's brutal crackdown on protesters spawned an eight-month civil war that saw the emergence of a National Transitional Council (NTC), UN authorization of air and naval intervention by the international community, and the toppling of the QADHAFI regime. In 2012, the NTC handed power to an elected parliament, the General National Congress (GNC), which was replaced two years later with the House of Representatives (HoR). In 2015, the UN brokered the Libyan Political Agreement (LPA) among a broad array of political parties and social groups, establishing an interim executive body. However, hardliners continued to oppose and hamper the LPA implementation, leaving Libya with eastern and western-based rival governments. In 2018, the international community supported a recalibrated plan that aimed to break the political deadlock with a National Conference in 2019. These plans, however, were derailed when the eastern-based, self-described Libyan National Army (LNA) launched an offensive to seize Tripoli. The LNA offensive collapsed in 2020, and a subsequent UN-sponsored cease-fire helped formalize the pause in fighting between rival camps.

In 2021, the UN-facilitated Libyan Political Dialogue Forum selected a new prime minister for an interim government – the Government of National Unity (GNU) – and a new presidential council charged with preparing for elections and uniting the country's state institutions. The HoR approved the GNU and its cabinet the same year, providing Libya with its first unified government since 2014, but the parliament then postponed the planned presidential election to an undetermined date in the future. In 2022, the HoR voted to replace GNU interim Prime Minister, Abdul Hamid DUBAYBAH, with another government led by Fathi BASHAGHA. GNU allegations of an illegitimate HoR vote allowed DUBAYBAH to remain in office and rebuff BASHAGHA's attempts to seat his government in Tripoli. In 2023, the HoR voted to replace BASHAGHA with Osma HAMAD. Special Representative of the UN Security-General for Libya, Abdoulaye BATHILY, is leading international efforts to persuade key Libyan political actors to resolve the core issues impeding elections.

GEOGRAPHY

Location: Northern Africa, bordering the Mediterranean Sea, between Egypt, Tunisia, and Algeria

Geographic coordinates: 25 00 N, 17 00 E

Map references: Africa

Area: *total:* 1,759,540 sq km
land: 1,759,540 sq km
water: 0 sq km

comparison ranking: total 18

Area - comparative: about 2.5 times the size of Texas; slightly larger than Alaska

Land boundaries: *total:* 4,339 km
border countries (6): Algeria 989 km; Chad 1,050 km; Egypt 1,115 km; Niger 342 km; Sudan 382 km; Tunisia 461 km

Coastline: 1,770 km

Maritime claims: *territorial sea:* 12 nm
exclusive fishing zone: 62 nm
note: Gulf of Sidra closing line - 32 degrees, 30 minutes north

Climate: Mediterranean along coast; dry, extreme desert interior

Terrain: mostly barren, flat to undulating plains, plateaus, depressions

Elevation: *highest point:* Bikku Bitti 2,267 m
lowest point: Sabkhat Ghuzayyil -47 m
mean elevation: 423 m

Natural resources: petroleum, natural gas, gypsum

Land use: *agricultural land:* 8.7% (2022 est.)
arable land: 1% (2022 est.)
permanent crops: 0.2% (2022 est.)
permanent pasture: 7.6% (2022 est.)
forest: 0.1% (2022 est.)
other: 91.2% (2022 est.)

Irrigated land: 4,700 sq km (2012)

Major watersheds (area sq km): Internal (endorheic basin) drainage: Lake Chad (2,497,738 sq km)

Major aquifers: Nubian Aquifer System, North Western Sahara Aquifer System, Murzuk-Djado Basin

Population distribution: over 90% of the population lives along the Mediterranean coast in and between Tripoli to the west and Al Bayda to the east; the interior remains vastly underpopulated due to the Sahara and its lack of surface water, as shown in this population distribution map

Natural hazards: hot, dry, dust-laden ghibli is a southern wind lasting one to four days in spring and fall; dust storms, sandstorms

Geography - note: *note 1:* more than 90% of the country is desert or semidesert
note 2: the volcano Waw an Namus lies in south central Libya in the middle of the Sahara; the caldera is an oasis – the name means "oasis of mosquitoes" – containing several small lakes that host many species of insects and birds

PEOPLE AND SOCIETY

Population: *total:* 7,361,263 (2024 est.)
male: 3,747,364
female: 3,613,899
note: immigrants make up just over 12% of the total population, according to UN data (2019)
comparison rankings: total 105; male 105; female 105

Nationality: *noun:* Libyan(s)
adjective: Libyan

Ethnic groups: Amazigh and Arab 97%, other 3% (includes Egyptian, Greek, Indian, Italian, Maltese, Pakistani, Tunisian, and Turkish)

Languages: Arabic (official), Italian, English (all widely understood in the major cities); Tamazight (Nafusi, Ghadamis, Suknah, Awjilah, Tamasheq)
major-language sample(s):
يمكن الاستغناء عنه للمعلومات الأساسية
كتاب حقائق العالم، المصدر الذي لا
(Arabic)

Religions: Muslim (official; virtually all Sunni) 96.6%, Christian 2.7%, Buddhist <1%, Hindu <1%, Jewish <1%, folk religion <1%, other <1%, unaffiliated <1% (2020 est.)
note: non-Sunni Muslims include native Ibadhi Muslims (<1% of the population) and foreign Muslims

Age structure: *0-14 years:* 32.3% (male 1,211,087/female 1,165,648)
15-64 years: 63.2% (male 2,385,152/female 2,263,780)
65 years and over: 4.6% (2024 est.) (male 151,125/female 184,471)

Dependency ratios: *total dependency ratio:* 58.3 (2024 est.)
youth dependency ratio: 51.1 (2024 est.)
elderly dependency ratio: 7.2 (2024 est.)
potential support ratio: 13.9 (2024 est.)

Median age: *total:* 26.2 years (2024 est.)
male: 26.3 years
female: 26.2 years
comparison ranking: total 165

Population growth rate: 1.44% (2024 est.)
comparison ranking: 68

Birth rate: 20.3 births/1,000 population (2024 est.)
comparison ranking: 65

Death rate: 3.5 deaths/1,000 population (2024 est.)
comparison ranking: 221

Net migration rate: -2.5 migrant(s)/1,000 population (2024 est.)
comparison ranking: 172

Population distribution: over 90% of the population lives along the Mediterranean coast in and between Tripoli to the west and Al Bayda to the east; the interior remains vastly underpopulated due to the Sahara and its lack of surface water, as shown in this population distribution map

Urbanization: *urban population:* 81.6% of total population (2023)
rate of urbanization: 1.45% annual rate of change (2020-25 est.)

Major urban areas - population: 1.183 million TRIPOLI (capital), 984,000 Misratah, 859,000 Benghazi (2023)

Sex ratio: *at birth:* 1.05 male(s)/female
0-14 years: 1.04 male(s)/female
15-64 years: 1.05 male(s)/female
65 years and over: 0.82 male(s)/female
total population: 1.04 male(s)/female (2024 est.)

Maternal mortality ratio: 59 deaths/100,000 live births (2023 est.)
comparison ranking: 89

Infant mortality rate: *total:* 10.7 deaths/1,000 live births (2024 est.)
male: 12.1 deaths/1,000 live births
female: 9.3 deaths/1,000 live births
comparison ranking: total 128

Life expectancy at birth: *total population:* 77.7 years (2024 est.)
male: 75.5 years
female: 80 years
comparison ranking: total population 87

Total fertility rate: 3 children born/woman (2024 est.)
comparison ranking: 48

Gross reproduction rate: 1.46 (2024 est.)

Drinking water source: *improved:* total: 99.9% of population (2022 est.)
unimproved: total: 0.1% of population (2022 est.)

Health expenditure: 5.1% of national budget (2022 est.)

Physician density: 2.04 physicians/1,000 population (2017)

Hospital bed density: 3.2 beds/1,000 population (2021 est.)

Sanitation facility access: *improved:* total: 99.3% of population (2022 est.)
unimproved: total: 0.7% of population (2022 est.)

Obesity - adult prevalence rate: 32.5% (2016)
comparison ranking: 16

Alcohol consumption per capita: *total:* 0.01 liters of pure alcohol (2019 est.)
beer: 0 liters of pure alcohol (2019 est.)
wine: 0.01 liters of pure alcohol (2019 est.)
spirits: 0 liters of pure alcohol (2019 est.)
other alcohols: 0 liters of pure alcohol (2019 est.)
comparison ranking: total 184

Children under the age of 5 years underweight: 11.7% (2014)
comparison ranking: 44

Currently married women (ages 15-49): 59.2% (2023 est.)

ENVIRONMENT

Environmental issues: desertification; limited natural freshwater resources; water pollution; threats to coastal ecosystem from sewage, oil byproducts, and industrial waste

International environmental agreements: *party to:* Biodiversity, Climate Change, Climate Change-Kyoto Protocol, Comprehensive Nuclear Test Ban, Desertification, Endangered Species, Hazardous Wastes, Marine Dumping-London Convention, Nuclear Test Ban, Ozone Layer Protection, Ship Pollution, Wetlands
signed, but not ratified: Climate Change-Paris Agreement, Law of the Sea

Climate: Mediterranean along coast; dry, extreme desert interior

Urbanization: *urban population:* 81.6% of total population (2023)
rate of urbanization: 1.45% annual rate of change (2020-25 est.)

Carbon dioxide emissions: 46.479 million metric tonnes of CO_2 (2023 est.)
from coal and metallurgical coke: 700 metric tonnes of CO_2 (2023 est.)
from petroleum and other liquids: 29.542 million metric tonnes of CO_2 (2023 est.)
from consumed natural gas: 16.936 million metric tonnes of CO_2 (2023 est.)
comparison ranking: total emissions 59

Particulate matter emissions: 29.8 micrograms per cubic meter (2019 est.)

Methane emissions: *energy:* 1,357.4 kt (2022-2024 est.)
agriculture: 63.4 kt (2019-2021 est.)
waste: 77.3 kt (2019-2021 est.)
other: 3.6 kt (2019-2021 est.)

Waste and recycling: *municipal solid waste generated annually:* 2.148 million tons (2024 est.)

Total water withdrawal: *municipal:* 700 million cubic meters (2022 est.)
industrial: 280 million cubic meters (2022 est.)
agricultural: 4.85 billion cubic meters (2022 est.)

Total renewable water resources: 700 million cubic meters (2022 est.)

GOVERNMENT

Country name: *conventional long form:* State of Libya
conventional short form: Libya
local long form: Dawlat Libiya
local short form: Libiya
etymology: the name probably derives from the Libu, a North African tribe first mentioned in texts from the 13th century B.C.; the ancient Greeks and Romans used the name for the entire North African coast west of Egypt

Government type: in transition

Capital: *name:* Tripoli (Tarabulus)
geographic coordinates: 32 53 N, 13 10 E
time difference: UTC+2 (7 hours ahead of Washington, DC, during Standard Time)
etymology: the name derives from the Greek words *tri* and *polis*, meaning "three cities;" the modern-day city was founded in the 14th century to replace the three ancient cities of Pallantium, Tegea, and Mantineia

Administrative divisions: 22 governorates (*muhafazah*, singular - *muhafazat*); Al Butnan, Al Jabal al Akhdar, Al Jabal al Gharbi, Al Jafarah, Al Jufrah, Al Kufrah, Al Marj, Al Marqab, Al Wahat, An Nuqat al Khams, Az Zawiyah, Banghazi (Benghazi), Darnah, Ghat, Misratah, Murzuq, Nalut, Sabha, Surt, Tarabulus (Tripoli), Wadi al Hayat, Wadi ash Shati

Legal system: Libya's post-revolution system is in flux and driven by state and non-state entities

Constitution: *history:* previous 1951, 1977, 2011 (interim)
note: a draft constitution was approved in 2017, but it is not yet ratified

International law organization participation: has not submitted an ICJ jurisdiction declaration; non-party state to the ICCt

Citizenship: *citizenship by birth:* no
citizenship by descent only: at least one parent or grandparent must be a citizen of Libya
dual citizenship recognized: no
residency requirement for naturalization: varies from 3 to 5 years

Suffrage: 18 years of age, universal

Executive branch: *chief of state:* President, Presidential Council, Mohammed al-MANFI (since 5 February 2021)
head of government: GNU Interim Prime Minister Abd-al-Hamid DUBAYBAH (since 5 February 2021)
election/appointment process: first direct presidential election was not held as planned
most recent election date: scheduled for 24 December 2021 but not held
expected date of next election: no new date has been set for elections

Legislative branch: *legislative structure:* unicameral
chamber name: House of Representatives (Majlis Al-Nuwaab)
number of seats: 200 (all directly elected)
electoral system: other systems
scope of elections: full renewal
most recent election date: 6/25/2014
percentage of women in chamber: 16.5%
expected date of next election: December 2025
note: 32 seats are reserved for women

Judicial branch: *highest court(s):* Libya's judicial system consists of a supreme court, central high courts (in Tripoli, Benghazi, and Sabha), and a series of lower courts

Diplomatic representation in the US: *chief of mission:* Ambassador (vacant); Chargé d'Affaires Fadil S M OMAR (since 17 July 2023)
chancery: 1460 Dahlia Street NW, Washington, DC 20012
telephone: [1] (202) 944-9601
FAX: [1] (202) 944-9606
email address and website: info@embassyoflibyadc.com
https://www.embassyoflibyadc.org/

Diplomatic representation from the US: *chief of mission:* Ambassador (vacant); Chargé d'Affaires Jeremy BERNDT (since 14 October 2023)
embassy: US Embassy Tripoli operations suspended in 2014
mailing address: 8850 Tripoli Place, Washington, DC 20521-8850
telephone: [216] 71-107-000
email address and website: Webmaster_Libya@state.gov
https://ly.usembassy.gov/
note: the US Embassy in Tripoli closed in July 2014 due to Libyan civil unrest; embassy staff and operations currently are located at US Embassy Tunis, Tunisia

International organization participation: ABEDA, AfDB, AFESD, AMF, AMU, AU, BDEAC, CAEU, COMESA, FAO, G-77, IAEA, IBRD, ICAO, ICC (NGOs), ICRM, IDA, IDB, IFAD, IFC, IFRCS, ILO, IMF, IMO, IMSO, Interpol, IOC, IOM, IPU, ISO, ITSO, ITU, LAS, LCBC, MIGA, NAM, OAPEC, OIC, OPCW, OPEC, PCA, UN, UNCTAD, UNESCO, UNHRC, UNIDO, UNSMIL, UNWTO, UPU, WCO, WFTU (NGOs), WHO, WIPO, WMO, WTO (observer)

Independence: 24 December 1951 (from UN trusteeship)

National holiday: Liberation Day, 23 October (2011)

Flag: *description:* three horizontal bands of red (top), black (double-width), and green, with a white crescent and star centered on the black stripe
meaning: the colors represent the three major regions of the country: red stands for Fezzan, black for Cyrenaica, and green for Tripolitania; the crescent and star represent Islam
history: the National Transitional Council reintroduced this flag design from the former Kingdom of Libya (1951-69) in 2011 to replace the all-green banner of the QADHAFI regime

National symbol(s): star and crescent, hawk

National color(s): red, black, green

National anthem(s): *title:* "Libya, Libya, Libya"
lyrics/music: Al Bashir AL AREBI/Mohamad Abdel WAHAB
history: adopted 1951, but replaced in 1969 when QADHAFI came to power; readopted 2011 with some modification to the lyrics; also known as "Ya Beladi" (O My Country)

National heritage: *total World Heritage Sites:* 5 (all cultural)
selected World Heritage Site locales: Archaeological Site of Cyrene; Archaeological Site of Leptis Magna, Archaeological Site of Sabratha; Rock-Art Sites of Tadrart Acacus; Old Town of Ghadamès

ECONOMY

Economic overview: upper middle-income, fossil fuel-based North African economy; 31% economic contraction due to COVID-19 and 2020 oil blockade; reduced government spending; central bank had to devalue currency; public wages are over 60% of expenditures

Real GDP (purchasing power parity): $90.609 billion (2024 est.)
$91.161 billion (2023 est.)
$82.756 billion (2022 est.)
note: data in 2021 dollars
comparison ranking: 101

Real GDP growth rate: -0.6% (2024 est.)
10.2% (2023 est.)
-8.3% (2022 est.)
note: annual GDP % growth based on constant local currency
comparison ranking: 197

Real GDP per capita: $12,300 (2024 est.)
$12,500 (2023 est.)
$11,500 (2022 est.)
note: data in 2021 dollars
comparison ranking: 137

GDP (official exchange rate): $46.636 billion (2024 est.)
note: data in current dollars at official exchange rate

Inflation rate (consumer prices): 2.1% (2024 est.)
2.4% (2023 est.)
4.5% (2022 est.)
note: annual % change based on consumer prices
comparison ranking: 55

GDP - composition, by sector of origin: *agriculture:* 1.7% (2024 est.)
industry: 68.3% (2024 est.)
services: 34.3% (2024 est.)
note: figures may not total 100% due to non-allocated consumption not captured in sector-reported data
comparison rankings: agriculture 160; industry 2; services 203

GDP - composition, by end use: *household consumption:* 32.7% (2024 est.)
government consumption: 36.7% (2024 est.)
investment in fixed capital: 14.8% (2024 est.)
investment in inventories: 0% (2024 est.)
exports of goods and services: 74.8% (2024 est.)
imports of goods and services: -59.1% (2024 est.)
note: figures may not total 100% due to rounding or gaps in data collection

Agricultural products: potatoes, onions, watermelons, tomatoes, dates, olives, milk, chicken, wheat, vegetables (2023)
note: top ten agricultural products based on tonnage

Industries: petroleum, petrochemicals, aluminum, iron and steel, food processing, textiles, handicrafts, cement

Industrial production growth rate: -5.8% (2024 est.)
note: annual % change in industrial value added based on constant local currency
comparison ranking: 182

Labor force: 2.585 million (2024 est.)

note: number of people ages 15 or older who are employed or seeking work
comparison ranking: 120

Unemployment rate: 18.7% (2024 est.)
18.8% (2023 est.)
19.3% (2022 est.)
note: % of labor force seeking employment
comparison ranking: 180

Youth unemployment rate (ages 15-24): *total:* 49.5% (2024 est.)
male: 41.5% (2024 est.)
female: 68.8% (2024 est.)
note: % of labor force ages 15-24 seeking employment
comparison ranking: total 4

Remittances: 0% of GDP (2023 est.)
0% of GDP (2022 est.)
0% of GDP (2021 est.)
note: personal transfers and compensation between resident and non-resident individuals/households/entities

Budget: *revenues:* $28.005 billion (2019 est.)
expenditures: $37.475 billion (2019 est.)

Current account balance: $1.865 billion (2023 est.)
$9.607 billion (2022 est.)
$5.675 billion (2021 est.)
note: balance of payments - net trade and primary/secondary income in current dollars
comparison ranking: 49

Exports: $37.753 billion (2023 est.)
$39.831 billion (2022 est.)
$32.38 billion (2021 est.)
note: balance of payments - exports of goods and services in current dollars
comparison ranking: 75

Exports - partners: Italy 23%, Germany 15%, Spain 9%, France 7%, China 6% (2023)
note: top five export partners based on percentage share of exports

Exports - commodities: crude petroleum, natural gas, refined petroleum, gold, scrap iron (2023)
note: top five export commodities based on value in dollars

Imports: $33.284 billion (2023 est.)
$27.872 billion (2022 est.)
$25.406 billion (2021 est.)
note: balance of payments - imports of goods and services in current dollars
comparison ranking: 78

Imports - partners: China 17%, Turkey 15%, Italy 8%, UAE 8%, Egypt 8% (2023)
note: top five import partners based on percentage share of imports

Imports - commodities: refined petroleum, broadcasting equipment, tobacco, garments, cars (2023)
note: top five import commodities based on value in dollars

Reserves of foreign exchange and gold: $92.894 billion (2024 est.)
$92.427 billion (2023 est.)
$86.683 billion (2022 est.)
note: holdings of gold (year-end prices)/foreign exchange/special drawing rights in current dollars
comparison ranking: 30

Exchange rates: Libyan dinars (LYD) per US dollar -

Exchange rates: 4.832 (2024 est.)
4.813 (2023 est.)
4.813 (2022 est.)
4.514 (2021 est.)
1.389 (2020 est.)

ENERGY

Electricity access: *electrification - total population:* 70% (2022 est.)
electrification - urban areas: 100%

Electricity: *installed generating capacity:* 10.519 million kW (2023 est.)
consumption: 28.826 billion kWh (2023 est.)
imports: 800 million kWh (2023 est.)
transmission/distribution losses: 7.081 billion kWh (2023 est.)
comparison rankings: installed generating capacity 66; consumption 69; imports 84; transmission/distribution losses 171

Electricity generation sources: *fossil fuels:* 100% of total installed capacity (2023 est.)

Coal: *imports:* 4,000 metric tons (2023 est.)

Petroleum: *total petroleum production:* 1.245 million bbl/day (2023 est.)
refined petroleum consumption: 207,000 bbl/day (2023 est.)
crude oil estimated reserves: 48.363 billion barrels (2021 est.)

Natural gas: *production:* 11.16 billion cubic meters (2023 est.)
consumption: 8.633 billion cubic meters (2023 est.)
exports: 2.527 billion cubic meters (2023 est.)
proven reserves: 1.505 trillion cubic meters (2021 est.)

Energy consumption per capita: 100.844 million Btu/person (2023 est.)
comparison ranking: 49

COMMUNICATIONS

Telephones - fixed lines: *total subscriptions:* 1.218 million (2022 est.)
subscriptions per 100 inhabitants: 17 (2022 est.)
comparison ranking: total subscriptions 62

Telephones - mobile cellular: *total subscriptions:* 13.9 million (2022 est.)
subscriptions per 100 inhabitants: 205 (2022 est.)
comparison ranking: total subscriptions 76

Broadcast media: state-funded and private TV stations; some provinces operate local TV stations; pan-Arab satellite TV stations are available; state-funded radio (2019)

Internet country code: .ly

Internet users: *percent of population:* 89% (2023 est.)

Broadband - fixed subscriptions: *total:* 326,000 (2022 est.)
subscriptions per 100 inhabitants: 5 (2022 est.)
comparison ranking: total 115

TRANSPORTATION

Civil aircraft registration country code prefix: 5A

Airports: 75 (2025)
comparison ranking: 68

Merchant marine: *total:* 96 (2023)
by type: general cargo 2, oil tanker 13, other 81
comparison ranking: total 91

Ports: *total ports:* 14 (2024)
large: 0
medium: 2
small: 3
very small: 9
ports with oil terminals: 10
key ports: Al Burayqah, Az Zawiya, Banghazi, Mersa Tobruq, Mina Tarabulus (Tripoli)

MILITARY AND SECURITY

Military and security forces: the Libyan Armed Forces of the Tripoli-based Government of National Unity (GNU) have various ground, air, and naval/coast guard forces, which include a mix of nominally integrated and semi-regular units, tribal armed groups and militias, civilian volunteers, and foreign military contractors; the GNU's armed forces are nominally under the control of the Ministry of Defense; the GNU also has various internal security forces under both the Ministry of Defense and the Ministry of Interior (2025)
note: the self-styled Libyan National Army (LNA; aka Libyan Arab Armed Forces, LAAF) under Khalifa HAFTER also includes various ground, air, and naval/coast guard forces comprised of semi-regular military personnel, militias, other armed groups, and foreign military contractors; some of the armed units nominally under the LNA operate under their own command structures and engage in their own operations

Military expenditures: not available

Military and security service personnel strengths: estimates not available

Military equipment inventories and acquisitions: both the forces aligned with the GNU and the LNA are largely equipped with weapons of Russian or Soviet origin; in recent years, Turkey has the been the primary supplier of arms to the GNU, while the LNA has received quantities from Russia and the United Arab Emirates (2024)
note: Libya is under a UN-imposed arms embargo

Military service age and obligation: not available

Military - note: the western-based forces aligned with the GNU and the eastern-based LNA forces are separated by a fortified line of control just west of the coastal city of Sirte; Turkey has provided support to the GNU forces, including military trainers, ammunition, weapons, and aerial drones; Russia, the United Arab Emirates, and Egypt have been the main supporters of the LNA (2025)

TERRORISM

Terrorist group(s): Terrorist group(s): Ansar al-Sharia groups; Islamic State of Iraq and ash-Sham - Libya (ISIS-L); al-Mulathamun Battalion (al-Mourabitoun); al-Qa'ida in the Islamic Maghreb (AQIM)
note: details about the history, aims, leadership, organization, areas of operation, tactics, targets, weapons, size, and sources of support of the group(s) appear(s) in Appendix T

TRANSNATIONAL ISSUES

Refugees and internally displaced persons: *refugees:* 277,010 (2024 est.)

IDPs: 139,305 (2024 est.)

LIECHTENSTEIN

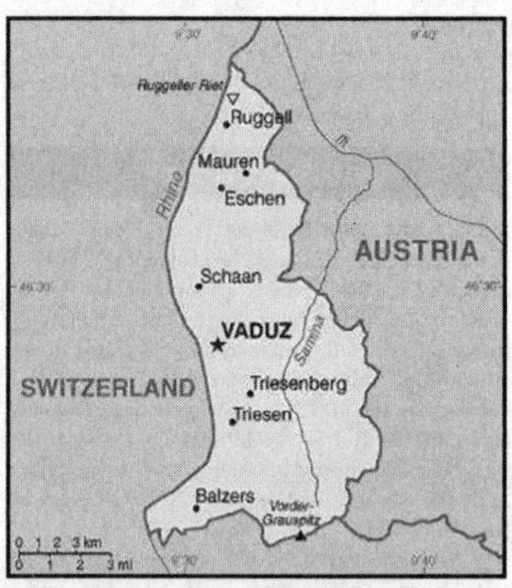

INTRODUCTION

Background: The Principality of Liechtenstein was established within the Holy Roman Empire in 1719. Occupied by both French and Russian troops during the Napoleonic Wars, it became a sovereign state in 1806 and joined the German Confederation in 1815. Liechtenstein became fully independent in 1866 when the Confederation dissolved. Until the end of World War I, it was closely tied to Austria, but the economic devastation caused by that conflict forced Liechtenstein to enter into a customs and monetary union with Switzerland. Since World War II (in which Liechtenstein remained neutral), the country's low taxes have spurred outstanding economic growth. In 2000, shortcomings in banking regulatory oversight resulted in concerns about the use of financial institutions for money laundering. However, Liechtenstein implemented anti-money laundering legislation and a Mutual Legal Assistance Treaty with the US that went into effect in 2003.

GEOGRAPHY

Location: Central Europe, between Austria and Switzerland

Geographic coordinates: 47 16 N, 9 32 E

Map references: Europe

Area: *total:* 160 sq km
land: 160 sq km
water: 0 sq km
comparison ranking: total 219

Area - comparative: about 0.9 times the size of Washington, D.C.

Land boundaries: *total:* 75 km
border countries (2): Austria 34 km; Switzerland 41 km

Coastline: 0 km (doubly landlocked)

Maritime claims: none (landlocked)

Climate: continental; cold, cloudy winters with frequent snow or rain; cool to moderately warm, cloudy, humid summers

Terrain: mostly mountainous (Alps) with Rhine Valley in western third

Elevation: *highest point:* Vorder-Grauspitz 2,599 m
lowest point: Ruggeller Riet 430 m

Natural resources: hydroelectric potential, arable land

Land use: *agricultural land:* 32.3% (2022 est.)
arable land: 10.8% (2022 est.)
permanent crops: 0% (2022 est.)
permanent pasture: 21.5% (2022 est.)
forest: 41.9% (2022 est.)
other: 25.8% (2022 est.)

Irrigated land: 0 sq km (2012)

Major watersheds (area sq km): Atlantic Ocean drainage: Rhine-Maas (198,735 sq km)

Population distribution: most of the population is found in the western half of the country along the Rhine River

Natural hazards: avalanches, landslides

Geography - note: along with Uzbekistan, one of only two doubly landlocked countries in the world; variety of microclimatic variations based on elevation

PEOPLE AND SOCIETY

Population: *total:* 40,272 (2024 est.)
male: 20,072
female: 20,200
comparison rankings: total 212; male 212; female 213

Nationality: *noun:* Liechtensteiner(s)
adjective: Liechtenstein

Ethnic groups: Liechtensteiner 65.6%, Swiss 9.6%, Austrian 5.8%, German 4.5%, Italian 3.1%, other 11.4% (2021 est.)
note: data represent population by nationality

Languages: German 91.5% (official, Alemannic is the main dialect), Italian 1.5%, Turkish 1.3%, Portuguese 1.1%, other 4.6% (2015 est.)
major-language sample(s):
Das World Factbook, die unverzichtbare Quelle für grundlegende Informationen. (German)

Religions: Roman Catholic (official) 73.4%, Protestant Reformed 6.3%, Muslim 5.9%, Christian Orthodox 1.3%, Lutheran 1.2%, other Protestant 0.7%, other Christian 0.3%, other 0.8%, none 7%, unspecified 3.3% (2015 est.)

Age structure: *0-14 years:* 15.3% (male 3,412/female 2,732)
15-64 years: 63.9% (male 12,814/female 12,921)
65 years and over: 20.8% (2024 est.) (male 3,846/female 4,547)

Dependency ratios: *total dependency ratio:* 56.5 (2024 est.)
youth dependency ratio: 23.9 (2024 est.)
elderly dependency ratio: 32.6 (2024 est.)
potential support ratio: 3.1 (2024 est.)

Median age: *total:* 44.2 years (2024 est.)
male: 42.4 years
female: 46.1 years
comparison ranking: total 30

Population growth rate: 0.69% (2024 est.)
comparison ranking: 129

Birth rate: 10.3 births/1,000 population (2024 est.)
comparison ranking: 180

Death rate: 8.2 deaths/1,000 population (2024 est.)
comparison ranking: 81

Net migration rate: 4.7 migrant(s)/1,000 population (2024 est.)
comparison ranking: 20

Population distribution: most of the population is found in the western half of the country along the Rhine River

Urbanization: *urban population:* 14.6% of total population (2023)
rate of urbanization: 1.15% annual rate of change (2020-25 est.)

Major urban areas - population: 5,000 VADUZ (capital) (2018)

Sex ratio: *at birth:* 1.26 male(s)/female
0-14 years: 1.25 male(s)/female
15-64 years: 0.99 male(s)/female
65 years and over: 0.85 male(s)/female
total population: 0.99 male(s)/female (2024 est.)

Mother's mean age at first birth: 31.3 years (2017)

Infant mortality rate: *total:* 3.9 deaths/1,000 live births (2024 est.)
male: 4.3 deaths/1,000 live births
female: 3.5 deaths/1,000 live births
comparison ranking: total 189

Life expectancy at birth: *total population:* 83 years (2024 est.)
male: 80.7 years
female: 85.8 years
comparison ranking: total population 20

Total fertility rate: 1.69 children born/woman (2024 est.)
comparison ranking: 168

Gross reproduction rate: 0.75 (2024 est.)

Drinking water source: *improved:* total: 100% of population (2022 est.)
unimproved: total: 0% of population (2022 est.)

Physician density: 1.3 physicians/1,000 population (2022)

Sanitation facility access: *improved:* total: 100% of population (2022 est.)
unimproved: urban: NA
total: 0% of population (2022 est.)

Currently married women (ages 15-49): 65.2% (2023 est.)

Education expenditure: 2.6% of GDP (2011 est.)
comparison ranking: Education expenditure (% GDP) 169

School life expectancy (primary to tertiary education): *total:* 15 years (2021 est.)
male: 16 years (2021 est.)
female: 14 years (2021 est.)

ENVIRONMENT

Environmental issues: some air pollution generated locally, some carried over from surrounding countries

International environmental agreements: *party to:* Air Pollution, Air Pollution-Heavy Metals, Air Pollution-Nitrogen Oxides, Air Pollution-Persistent Organic Pollutants, Air Pollution-Sulphur 85, Air Pollution-Sulphur 94, Air Pollution-Volatile Organic Compounds, Biodiversity, Climate Change, Climate Change-Kyoto Protocol, Climate Change-Paris

Agreement, Comprehensive Nuclear Test Ban, Desertification, Endangered Species, Hazardous Wastes, Ozone Layer Protection, Wetlands
signed, but not ratified: Air Pollution-Multi-effect Protocol, Law of the Sea

Climate: continental; cold, cloudy winters with frequent snow or rain; cool to moderately warm, cloudy, humid summers

Urbanization: *urban population:* 14.6% of total population (2023)
rate of urbanization: 1.15% annual rate of change (2020-25 est.)

Waste and recycling: *municipal solid waste generated annually:* 32,400 tons (2024 est.)
percent of municipal solid waste recycled: 64.6% (2015 est.)

Total water withdrawal: *municipal:* 10 million cubic meters (2020 est.)

GOVERNMENT

Country name: *conventional long form:* Principality of Liechtenstein
conventional short form: Liechtenstein
local long form: Fuerstentum Liechtenstein
local short form: Liechtenstein
etymology: named after the Liechtenstein family that purchased and united the counties of Schellenburg and Vaduz in 1719; the family name was taken from its Austrian castle of the same name, which in German means "light stone"

Government type: constitutional monarchy

Capital: *name:* Vaduz
geographic coordinates: 47 08 N, 9 31 E
time difference: UTC+1 (6 hours ahead of Washington, DC, during Standard Time)
daylight saving time: +1hr, begins last Sunday in March; ends last Sunday in October
etymology: may be a conflation from the Latin *vallis* (valley) and the Old German *dutsch* (German) to produce *Valdutsch* ("German valley"), which was simplified over time to Vaduz

Administrative divisions: 11 communes (*Gemeinden*, singular - *Gemeinde*); Balzers, Eschen, Gamprin, Mauren, Planken, Ruggell, Schaan, Schellenberg, Triesen, Triesenberg, Vaduz

Legal system: civil law system influenced by Swiss, Austrian, and German law

Constitution: *history:* previous 1862; latest adopted 5 October 1921
amendment process: proposed by Parliament, by the reigning prince (in the form of "Government" proposals), by petition of at least 1,500 qualified voters, or by at least four communes; passage requires unanimous approval of Parliament members in one sitting or three-quarters majority vote in two successive sittings; referendum required only if petitioned by at least 1,500 voters or by at least four communes; passage by referendum requires absolute majority of votes cast

International law organization participation: accepts compulsory ICJ jurisdiction with reservations; accepts ICCt jurisdiction

Citizenship: *citizenship by birth:* no
citizenship by descent only: the father must be a citizen of Liechtenstein; in the case of a child born out of wedlock, the mother must be a citizen
dual citizenship recognized: no
residency requirement for naturalization: 5 years

Suffrage: 18 years of age; universal

Executive branch: *chief of state:* Prince HANS-ADAM II (since 13 November 1989, assumed executive powers on 26 August 1984)
head of government: Prime Minister Brigitte HAAS (since 10 April 2025)
cabinet: Cabinet elected by the Parliament, confirmed by the monarch
election/appointment process: the monarchy is hereditary; following legislative elections, the monarch usually appoints the leader of the majority party in Parliament as the head of government, and also appoints the leader of the largest minority party in Parliament as the deputy head of government if there is a coalition government
note: the prince's successor is his son, Heir Apparent and Regent of Liechtenstein Prince ALOIS; on 15 August 2004, HANS-ADAM II transferred the official duties of the ruling prince to ALOIS, but Prince HANS-ADAM II retains the status of chief of state

Legislative branch: *legislature name:* Diet (Landtag)
legislative structure: unicameral
number of seats: 25 (all directly elected)
electoral system: proportional representation
scope of elections: full renewal
term in office: 4 years
most recent election date: 2/9/2025
parties elected and seats per party: Patriotic Union (VU) (10); Progressive Citizens' Party (FBP) (7); Democrats for Liechtenstein (DpL) (6); Free List (FL) (2)
percentage of women in chamber: 32%
expected date of next election: February 2029

Judicial branch: *highest court(s):* Supreme Court or Supreme Court or Fürstlicher Oberster Gerichtshof (consists of 5 judges and 5 substitutes); Constitutional Court or Staatsgerichtshof (consists of 5 judges, and 5 alternates)
judge selection and term of office: judges of both courts elected by the Landtag and appointed by the monarch; Supreme Court judges serve 4-year renewable terms; Constitutional Court judges appointed for renewable 5-year terms
subordinate courts: Court of Appeal (second instance), Regional Court (first instance), Administrative Court, Tribunal Court, district courts

Political parties: Democrats for Liechtenstein (Demokraten pro Liechtenstein) or DpL
Fatherland Union (Vaterlaendische Union) or VU
Progressive Citizens' Party (Fortschrittliche Buergerpartei) or FBP
The Free List (Die Freie Liste) or FL
The Independents (Die Unabhaengigen) or DU

Diplomatic representation in the US: *chief of mission:* Ambassador Georg SPARBER (since 1 December 2021)
chancery: 2900 K Street NW, Suite 602B, Washington, DC 20007
telephone: [1] (202) 331-0590
FAX: [1] (202) 331-3221
email address and website: washington@llv.li
https://www.liechtensteinusa.org/

Diplomatic representation from the US: *embassy:* the US does not have an embassy in Liechtenstein; the US Ambassador to Switzerland is accredited to Liechtenstein

International organization participation: CD, CE, EBRD, EFTA, IAEA, ICCt, ICRM, IFRCS, Interpol, IOC, IPU, ITSO, ITU, ITUC (NGOs), OAS (observer), OPCW, OSCE, PCA, Schengen Convention, UN, UNCTAD, UPU, WIPO, WTO

Independence: 23 January 1719 (Principality of Liechtenstein established); 12 July 1806 (independence from the Holy Roman Empire); 24 August 1866 (independence from the German Confederation)

National holiday: National Day, 15 August (1940)
note: a National Day was originally established in 1940 to combine celebrations for the Feast of the Assumption (15 August) with those honoring the birthday of former Prince FRANZ JOSEF II (1906-1989) on 16 August; after the prince's death, National Day became the official national holiday in 1990

Flag: *description:* two equal horizontal bands of blue (top) and red, with a gold crown on the left side of the blue band
history: the colors may derive from the blue-and-red livery used in the principality's household in the 18th century; the prince's crown was added in 1937 to distinguish it from Haiti's flag

National symbol(s): princely hat (crown)

National color(s): blue, red

National coat of arms: the six motifs on the coat of arms provide a history of the royal House of Liechtenstein since 1719, when the country was founded; the small shield at the center is the royal family's gold-and-red coat of arms, the gold-crowned eagle signifies the Silesia family, the diamond wreath represents the Kuenringer family, the red-and-silver shield is the Duchy of Troppau, the black eagle comes from the coat of arms of a family that married into the royal line, and the golden hunting horn represents the Duchy of Jägerndorf

National anthem(s): *title:* "Oben am jungen Rhein" (High Above the Young Rhine)
lyrics/music: Jakob Joseph JAUCH/Josef FROMMELT
history: adopted 1850, revised 1963; uses the tune of the United Kingdom's anthem, "God Save the King"

ECONOMY

Economic overview: high-income European economy; Schengen Area participant; key European financial leader; integrated with Swiss economy and franc currency user; one of the highest GDP per capita countries; relies on US and Eurozone markets for exports

Real GDP (purchasing power parity): $7.172 billion (2024 est.)
$7.031 billion (2023 est.)
$6.885 billion (2022 est.)
note: data in 2015 dollars
comparison ranking: 171

Real GDP per capita: $210,600 (2024 est.)
$201,200 (2023 est.)
$187,700 (2022 est.)
note: data in 2015 dollars
comparison ranking: 2

GDP (official exchange rate): $8.395 billion (2024 est.)
note: data in current dollars at official exchange rate

Inflation rate (consumer prices): 2.8% (2022 est.)
0.6% (2021 est.)
-0.7% (2020 est.)
note: annual % change based on consumer prices
comparison ranking: 84

GDP - composition, by sector of origin: *agriculture:* 0.2% (2022 est.)

industry: 40.6% (2022 est.)
services: 55.6% (2022 est.)
note: figures may not total 100% due to non-allocated consumption not captured in sector-reported data
comparison rankings: agriculture 199; industry 18; services 119

Agricultural products: wheat, barley, corn, potatoes; livestock, dairy products

Industries: electronics, metal manufacturing, dental products, ceramics, pharmaceuticals, food products, precision instruments, tourism, optical instruments

Exports: $3.217 billion (2015 est.)
$3.774 billion (2014 est.)
note: trade data exclude trade with Switzerland
comparison ranking: 153

Exports - commodities: small specialty machinery, connectors for audio and video, parts for motor vehicles, dental products, hardware
top five export commodities based on value in dollars

Imports - commodities: agricultural products, raw materials, energy products, machinery, metal goods, textiles, foodstuffs, motor vehicles

Exchange rates: Swiss francs (CHF) per US dollar -

Exchange rates: 0.88 (2024 est.)
0.898 (2023 est.)
0.955 (2022 est.)
0.914 (2021 est.)
0.939 (2020 est.)

ENERGY

Electricity access: *electrification - total population:* 100% (2022 est.)

COMMUNICATIONS

Telephones - fixed lines: *total subscriptions:* 10,000 (2023 est.)
subscriptions per 100 inhabitants: 26 (2023 est.)
comparison ranking: total subscriptions 188

Telephones - mobile cellular: *total subscriptions:* 50,000 (2023 est.)
subscriptions per 100 inhabitants: 126 (2022 est.)
comparison ranking: total subscriptions 207

Broadcast media: relies on foreign terrestrial and satellite broadcasters for most broadcast media services; first Liechtenstein-based TV station established in 2008; Radio Liechtenstein operates multiple radio stations; a Swiss-based broadcaster operates one radio station

Internet country code: .li

Internet users: *percent of population:* 97% (2023 est.)

Broadband - fixed subscriptions: *total:* 20,000 (2023 est.)
subscriptions per 100 inhabitants: 50 (2023 est.)
comparison ranking: total 171

TRANSPORTATION

Civil aircraft registration country code prefix: HB

Heliports: 2 (2025)
comparison ranking: 132

Railways: *total:* 9 km (2018)
standard gauge: 9 km (2018) 1.435-m gauge (electrified)
note: belongs to the Austrian Railway System connecting Austria and Switzerland

Merchant marine: *total:* 17 (2023)
by type: bulk carrier 14, general cargo 1, other 2 (includes Switzerland)
comparison ranking: total 150

MILITARY AND SECURITY

Military and security forces: no regular military forces; National Police of the Principality of Liechtenstein (Landespolizei des Fürstentums Liechtenstein)

TRANSNATIONAL ISSUES

Refugees and internally displaced persons: *refugees:* 875 (2024 est.)

LITHUANIA

INTRODUCTION

Background: Lithuanian lands were united under MINDAUGAS in 1236; over the next century, Lithuania extended its territory through alliances and conquest to include most of present-day Belarus and Ukraine. By the end of the 14th century, Lithuania was the largest state in Europe. An alliance with Poland in 1386 led the two countries into a union through a common ruler. In 1569, Lithuania and Poland formally united into a single dual state, the Polish-Lithuanian Commonwealth. This entity survived until 1795 when surrounding countries partitioned its remnants. Lithuania regained its independence after World War I, but the USSR annexed it in 1940 – an action never recognized by the US and many other countries. In 1990, Lithuania became the first of the Soviet republics to declare its independence, but Moscow did not recognize this proclamation until 1991. The last Russian troops withdrew in 1993. Lithuania subsequently restructured its economy for integration into West European institutions; it joined both NATO and the EU in 2004. In 2015, Lithuania joined the euro zone, and it joined the Organization for Economic Cooperation and Development in 2018.

GEOGRAPHY

Location: Eastern Europe, bordering the Baltic Sea, between Latvia and Russia, west of Belarus

Geographic coordinates: 56 00 N, 24 00 E

Map references: Europe

Area: *total:* 65,300 sq km
land: 62,680 sq km
water: 2,620 sq km
comparison ranking: total 123

Area - comparative: slightly larger than West Virginia

Land boundaries: *total:* 1,545 km
border countries (4): Belarus 640 km; Latvia 544 km; Poland 100 km; Russia (Kaliningrad) 261 km

Coastline: 90 km

Maritime claims: *territorial sea:* 12 nm

Climate: transitional, between maritime and continental; wet, moderate winters and summers

Terrain: lowland, many scattered small lakes, fertile soil

Elevation: *highest point:* Aukstojas 294 m
lowest point: Baltic Sea 0 m
mean elevation: 110 m

Natural resources: peat, arable land, amber

Land use: *agricultural land:* 46.5% (2022 est.)
arable land: 36.6% (2022 est.)
permanent crops: 0.6% (2022 est.)
permanent pasture: 9.3% (2022 est.)
forest: 35.2% (2022 est.)
other: 18.3% (2022 est.)

Irrigated land: 61 sq km (2020)

Major lakes (area sq km): *salt water lake(s):* Curonian Lagoon (shared with Russia) - 1,620 sq km

Population distribution: fairly even population distribution throughout the country, but somewhat greater concentrations in the southern cities of Vilnius and Kaunas, as well as the western port of Klaipeda

Natural hazards: occasional floods, droughts

Geography - note: fertile central plains are separated by hilly uplands that are ancient glacial deposits

PEOPLE AND SOCIETY

Population: *total:* 2,628,186 (2024 est.)
male: 1,214,994
female: 1,413,192
comparison rankings: total 142; male 145; female 141

Nationality: *noun:* Lithuanian(s)
adjective: Lithuanian

Ethnic groups: Lithuanian 84.6%, Polish 6.5%, Russian 5%, Belarusian 1%, other 1.1%, unspecified 1.8% (2021 est.)

Languages: Lithuanian (official) 85.3%, Russian 6.8%, Polish 5.1%, other 1.1%, two mother tongues 1.7% (2021 est.)
major-language sample(s):
Pasaulio enciklopedija – naudingas bendrosios informacijos šaltinis. (Lithuanian)

Religions: Roman Catholic 74.2%, Russian Orthodox 3.7%, Old Believer 0.6%, Evangelical Lutheran 0.6%, Evangelical Reformist 0.2%, other (including Sunni Muslim, Jewish, Greek Catholic, and Karaite) 0.9%, none 6.1%, unspecified 13.7% (2021 est.)

Age structure: *0-14 years:* 15.2% (male 205,154/female 194,386)
15-64 years: 62.6% (male 808,435/female 837,908)
65 years and over: 22.2% (2024 est.) (male 201,405/female 380,898)

Dependency ratios: *total dependency ratio:* 55.9 (2024 est.)
youth dependency ratio: 23.5 (2024 est.)
elderly dependency ratio: 32.3 (2024 est.)
potential support ratio: 3.1 (2024 est.)

Median age: *total:* 45.1 years (2024 est.)
male: 40.9 years
female: 49.2 years
comparison ranking: total 18

Population growth rate: -1.05% (2024 est.)
comparison ranking: 231

Birth rate: 8.9 births/1,000 population (2024 est.)
comparison ranking: 201

Death rate: 15.2 deaths/1,000 population (2024 est.)
comparison ranking: 2

Net migration rate: -4.1 migrant(s)/1,000 population (2024 est.)
comparison ranking: 195

Population distribution: fairly even population distribution throughout the country, but somewhat greater concentrations in the southern cities of Vilnius and Kaunas, as well as the western port of Klaipeda

Urbanization: *urban population:* 68.7% of total population (2023)
rate of urbanization: -0.12% annual rate of change (2020-25 est.)

Major urban areas - population: 541,000 VILNIUS (capital) (2023)

Sex ratio: *at birth:* 1.06 male(s)/female
0-14 years: 1.06 male(s)/female
15-64 years: 0.96 male(s)/female
65 years and over: 0.53 male(s)/female
total population: 0.86 male(s)/female (2024 est.)

Mother's mean age at first birth: 28.2 years (2020 est.)

Maternal mortality ratio: 8 deaths/100,000 live births (2023 est.)
comparison ranking: 153

Infant mortality rate: *total:* 3.6 deaths/1,000 live births (2024 est.)
male: 4 deaths/1,000 live births
female: 3.1 deaths/1,000 live births
comparison ranking: total 193

Life expectancy at birth: *total population:* 76.1 years (2024 est.)
male: 70.8 years
female: 81.7 years
comparison ranking: total population 117

Total fertility rate: 1.62 children born/woman (2024 est.)
comparison ranking: 179

Gross reproduction rate: 0.79 (2024 est.)

Drinking water source: *improved: urban:* 100% of population (2022 est.)
rural: 93.8% of population (2022 est.)
total: 98% of population (2022 est.)
unimproved: urban: 0% of population (2022 est.)
rural: 6.2% of population (2022 est.)
total: 2% of population (2022 est.)

Health expenditure: 7.5% of GDP (2022)
13% of national budget (2022 est.)

Physician density: 6.1 physicians/1,000 population (2023)

Hospital bed density: 6 beds/1,000 population (2020 est.)

Sanitation facility access: *improved: urban:* 99% of population (2022 est.)
rural: 91.9% of population (2022 est.)
total: 96.7% of population (2022 est.)
unimproved: urban: 1% of population (2022 est.)
rural: 8.1% of population (2022 est.)
total: 3.3% of population (2022 est.)

Obesity - adult prevalence rate: 26.3% (2016)
comparison ranking: 43

Alcohol consumption per capita: *total:* 11.93 liters of pure alcohol (2019 est.)
beer: 4.61 liters of pure alcohol (2019 est.)
wine: 0.88 liters of pure alcohol (2019 est.)
spirits: 4.96 liters of pure alcohol (2019 est.)
other alcohols: 1.48 liters of pure alcohol (2019 est.)
comparison ranking: total 4

Tobacco use: *total:* 26.6% (2025 est.)
male: 38% (2025 est.)
female: 16.7% (2025 est.)
comparison ranking: total 34

Children under the age of 5 years underweight: 2.5% (2021)
comparison ranking: 89

Currently married women (ages 15-49): 53.4% (2023 est.)

Child marriage: *women married by age 15:* 0% (2022)
women married by age 18: 0.2% (2022)

Education expenditure: 4.3% of GDP (2021 est.)
12.7% national budget (2021 est.)
comparison ranking: Education expenditure (% GDP) 93

School life expectancy (primary to tertiary education): *total:* 17 years (2022 est.)
male: 16 years (2022 est.)
female: 17 years (2022 est.)

ENVIRONMENT

Environmental issues: water pollution; air pollution; deforestation; groundwater pollution from chemicals and waste; soil degradation and erosion

International environmental agreements: *party to:* Air Pollution, Air Pollution-Heavy Metals, Air Pollution-Multi-effect Protocol, Air Pollution-Nitrogen Oxides, Air Pollution-Persistent Organic Pollutants, Air Pollution-Sulphur 85, Air Pollution-Sulphur 94, Air Pollution-Volatile Organic Compounds, Biodiversity, Climate Change, Climate Change-Kyoto Protocol, Climate Change-Paris Agreement, Comprehensive Nuclear Test Ban, Desertification, Endangered Species, Environmental Modification, Hazardous Wastes, Law of the Sea, Ozone Layer Protection, Ship Pollution, Tropical Timber 2006, Wetlands, Whaling
signed, but not ratified: none of the selected agreements

Climate: transitional, between maritime and continental; wet, moderate winters and summers

Urbanization: *urban population:* 68.7% of total population (2023)
rate of urbanization: -0.12% annual rate of change (2020-25 est.)

Carbon dioxide emissions: 12.877 million metric tonnes of CO2 (2023 est.)
from coal and metallurgical coke: 380,000 metric tonnes of CO2 (2023 est.)
from petroleum and other liquids: 9.61 million metric tonnes of CO2 (2023 est.)
from consumed natural gas: 2.887 million metric tonnes of CO2 (2023 est.)
comparison ranking: total emissions 100

Particulate matter emissions: 11.5 micrograms per cubic meter (2019 est.)

Waste and recycling: *municipal solid waste generated annually:* 1.315 million tons (2024 est.)
percent of municipal solid waste recycled: 34.9% (2022 est.)

Total water withdrawal: *municipal:* 136.78 million cubic meters (2022 est.)
industrial: 87.96 million cubic meters (2022 est.)
agricultural: 58.74 million cubic meters (2022 est.)

Total renewable water resources: 24.5 billion cubic meters (2022 est.)

GOVERNMENT

Country name: *conventional long form:* Republic of Lithuania
conventional short form: Lithuania
local long form: Lietuvos Respublika
local short form: Lietuva
former: Lithuanian Soviet Socialist Republic (while occupied by the USSR)
etymology: meaning of the name is obscure; may be derived from the local words *lietava*, meaning "small river," or *lietus*, meaning "rain" or "land of rain," or the Latin word *litus*, meaning "shore"

Government type: semi-presidential republic

Capital: *name:* Vilnius
geographic coordinates: 54 41 N, 25 19 E
time difference: UTC+2 (7 hours ahead of Washington, DC, during Standard Time)
daylight saving time: +1hr, begins last Sunday in March; ends last Sunday in October
etymology: named after the Vilnia River; the river name is said to derive from the Lithuanian word *vilnis*, meaning "wave"

Administrative divisions: 60 municipalities (*savivaldybe*, singular - *savivaldybe*); Akmene, Alytaus Miestas, Alytus, Anksciai, Birstonas, Birzai, Druskininkai, Elektrenai, Ignalina, Jonava, Joniskis, Jurbarkas, Kaisiadorys, Kalvarija, Kauno Miestas, Kaunas, Kazlu Rudos, Kedainiai, Kelme, Klaipedos Miestas, Klaipeda, Kretinga, Kupiskis, Lazdijai, Marijampole, Mazeikiai, Moletai, Neringa, Pagegiai, Pakruojis, Palangos Miestas, Panevezio Miestas, Panevezys, Pasvalys, Plunge, Prienai, Radviliskis, Raseiniai, Rietavas, Rokiskis, Sakiai, Salcininkai, Siauliu Miestas, Siauliai, Silale, Silute, Sirvintos, Skuodas, Svencionys, Taurage, Telsiai, Trakai, Ukmerge, Utena, Varena, Vilkaviskis, Vilniaus Miestas, Vilnius, Visaginas, Zarasai

Legal system: civil law system; legislative acts can be appealed to the Constitutional Court

Constitution: *history:* several previous; latest adopted by referendum 25 October 1992, entered into force 2 November 1992
amendment process: proposed by at least one fourth of all Parliament members or by petition of at least 300,000 voters; passage requires two-thirds majority vote of Parliament in each of two readings three months apart and a presidential signature;

amendments to constitutional articles on national sovereignty and constitutional amendment procedure also require three-fourths voter approval in a referendum

International law organization participation: accepts compulsory ICJ jurisdiction with reservations; accepts ICCt jurisdiction

Citizenship: *citizenship by birth:* no
citizenship by descent only: at least one parent must be a citizen of Lithuania
dual citizenship recognized: no
residency requirement for naturalization: 10 years

Suffrage: 18 years of age; universal

Executive branch: *chief of state:* President Gitanas NAUSEDA (since 12 July 2019)
head of government: Acting Prime Minister Rimantas SADZIUS (since 4 August 2025)
cabinet: Council of Ministers nominated by the prime minister, appointed by the president, approved by Parliament
election/appointment process: president directly elected by absolute-majority popular vote in 2 rounds, if needed, for a 5-year term (eligible for a second term); prime minister appointed by the president, approved by Parliament
most recent election date: 26 May 2024
election results: *2024:* Gitanas NAUSEDA elected president in second round; percent of vote -Gitanas NAUSEDA (independent) 75.6%, Ingrida SIMONYTE (TS-LKD) 24.4%
2019: Gitanas NAUSEDA elected president in second round; percent of vote - Gitanas NAUSEDA (independent) 66.7%, Ingrida SIMONYTE (independent) 33.3%
expected date of next election: 2029

Legislative branch: *legislature name:* Parliament (Seimas)
legislative structure: unicameral
number of seats: 141 (all directly elected)
electoral system: mixed system
scope of elections: full renewal
term in office: 4 years
most recent election date: 10/13/2024 to 10/27/2024
parties elected and seats per party: Lithuanian Social Democratic Party (LSDP) (52); Homeland Union - Lithuanian Christian Democrats (TS-LKD) (28); Political Party "The Dawn of Nemunas" (PPNA) (20); Union of Democrats "For Lithuania" (DSVL) (14); Liberals Movement of the Republic of Lithuania (LS) (12); Lithuanian Farmers and Greens Union (LVŽS) (8); Other (7)
percentage of women in chamber: 28.4%
expected date of next election: October 2028

Judicial branch: *highest court(s):* Supreme Court (consists of 37 judges); Constitutional Court (consists of 9 judges)
judge selection and term of office: Supreme Court judges nominated by the president and appointed by the Seimas; judges serve 5-year renewable terms; Constitutional Court judges appointed by the Seimas from nominations - 3 each by the president of the republic, the Seimas speaker, and the Supreme Court president; judges serve 9-year, nonrenewable terms; one third of membership reconstituted every 3 years
subordinate courts: Court of Appeals; district and local courts

Political parties: Dawn of Nemunas or NA
Electoral Action of Poles in Lithuania or LLRA–KŠS
Freedom and Justice Party or LT (formerly Lithuanian Freedom Union (Liberals))
Freedom Party or LP
Homeland Union-Lithuanian Christian Democrats or TS-LKD
Labour Party or DP
Lithuanian Center Party or LCP
Lithuanian Christian Democracy Party or LKDP
Lithuanian Farmers and Greens Union or LVZS
Lithuanian Green Party or LZP
Liberals' Movement or LRLS
Lithuanian List or LL
Lithuanian Regions Party or LRP
Social Democratic Party of Lithuania or LSDP
Union of Democrats for Lithuania or DSVL

Diplomatic representation in the US: *chief of mission:* Ambassador Gediminas VARVUOLIS (since 5 September 2025)
chancery: 2622 16th Street NW, Washington, DC 20009
telephone: [1] (202) 234-5860
FAX: [1] (202) 328-0466
email address and website: info@usa.mfa.lt
https://usa.mfa.lt/usa/en/
consulate(s) general: Chicago, Los Angeles, New York

Diplomatic representation from the US: *chief of mission:* Ambassador Kara C. McDONALD (since 26 January 2024)
embassy: Akmenu gatve 6, Vilnius, LT-03106
mailing address: 4510 Vilnius Place, Washington DC 20521-4510
telephone: [370] (5) 266-5500
FAX: [370] (5) 266-5510
email address and website: consec@state.gov
https://lt.usembassy.gov/

International organization participation: Australia Group, BA, BIS, CBSS, CD, CE, EAPC, EBRD, ECB, EIB, EU, FAO, IAEA, IBRD, ICAO, ICC (national committees), ICCt, ICRM, IDA, IFC, IFRCS, ILO, IMF, IMO, Interpol, IOC, IOM, IPU, ISO, ITU, ITUC (NGOs), MIGA, NATO, NIB, NSG, OAS (observer), OECD, OIF (observer), OPCW, OSCE, PCA, Schengen Convention, UN, UNCTAD, UNESCO, UNHRC, UNIDO, UNWTO, UPU, Wassenaar Arrangement, WCO, WHO, WIPO, WMO, WTO

Independence: 16 February 1918 (from Soviet Russia and Germany); 11 March 1990 (declared from the Soviet Union); 6 September 1991 (recognized by the Soviet Union); notable earlier dates: 6 July 1253 (coronation of MINDAUGAS, traditional founding date); 1 July 1569 (Polish-Lithuanian Commonwealth created)

National holiday: Independence Day (or National Day), 16 February (1918)
note: 16 February 1918 was the date Lithuania established its statehood and independence from Soviet Russia and Germany; 11 March 1990 was the date it declared the restoration of statehood and independence from the Soviet Union

Flag: *description:* three equal horizontal bands of yellow (top), green, and red
meaning: yellow stands for golden fields, the sun, light, and goodness; green for the forests, nature, freedom, and hope; red for courage and the blood spilled in defense of the homeland

National symbol(s): mounted knight known as Vytis (the Chaser), white stork

National color(s): yellow, green, red

National anthem(s): *title:* "Tautiska giesme" (The National Song)
lyrics/music: Vincas KUDIRKA
history: adopted 1918, restored 1990; written in 1898 when Lithuania was part of Russia; banned during the Soviet occupation from 1940 to 1990

National heritage: *total World Heritage Sites:* 5 (all cultural)
selected World Heritage Site locales: Vilnius Historic Center; Curonian Spit; Kernavė Archaeological Site; Struve Geodetic Arc; Modernist Kaunas: Architecture of Optimism, 1919-1939

ECONOMY

Economic overview: high-income EU and eurozone member, largest Baltic economy; recovery supported by private consumption and EU fund-driven investments; structural challenges include pension reform, aging workforce, and high energy-import costs

Real GDP (purchasing power parity): $136.227 billion (2024 est.)
$132.552 billion (2023 est.)
$132.099 billion (2022 est.)
note: data in 2021 dollars
comparison ranking: 88

Real GDP growth rate: 2.8% (2024 est.)
0.3% (2023 est.)
2.5% (2022 est.)
note: annual GDP % growth based on constant local currency
comparison ranking: 129

Real GDP per capita: $47,200 (2024 est.)
$46,200 (2023 est.)
$46,700 (2022 est.)
note: data in 2021 dollars
comparison ranking: 45

GDP (official exchange rate): $84.869 billion (2024 est.)
note: data in current dollars at official exchange rate

Inflation rate (consumer prices): 0.7% (2024 est.)
9.1% (2023 est.)
19.7% (2022 est.)
note: annual % change based on consumer prices
comparison ranking: 15

GDP - composition, by sector of origin: *agriculture:* 2.6% (2024 est.)
industry: 23.4% (2024 est.)
services: 63.6% (2024 est.)
note: figures may not total 100% due to non-allocated consumption not captured in sector-reported data
comparison rankings: agriculture 138; industry 103; services 64

GDP - composition, by end use: *household consumption:* 57.3% (2023 est.)
government consumption: 17.3% (2023 est.)
investment in fixed capital: 23.7% (2023 est.)
investment in inventories: -1.8% (2023 est.)
exports of goods and services: 76.5% (2023 est.)
imports of goods and services: -72.6% (2023 est.)
note: figures may not total 100% due to rounding or gaps in data collection

Agricultural products: wheat, milk, sugar beets, rapeseed, barley, potatoes, triticale, oats, beans, peas (2023)
note: top ten agricultural products based on tonnage

Industries: metal-cutting machine tools, electric motors, televisions, refrigerators and freezers, petroleum refining, shipbuilding (small ships), furniture, textiles, food processing, fertilizer, agricultural machinery, optical equipment, lasers, electronic components, computers, amber jewelry, information technology, video game development, app/software development, biotechnology

Industrial production growth rate: 3.2% (2024 est.)
note: annual % change in industrial value added based on constant local currency
comparison ranking: 77

Labor force: 1.548 million (2024 est.)
note: number of people ages 15 or older who are employed or seeking work
comparison ranking: 133

Unemployment rate: 7.6% (2024 est.)
6.9% (2023 est.)
6% (2022 est.)
note: % of labor force seeking employment
comparison ranking: 129

Youth unemployment rate (ages 15-24): *total:* 14.1% (2024 est.)
male: 16.3% (2024 est.)
female: 11.7% (2024 est.)
note: % of labor force ages 15-24 seeking employment
comparison ranking: total 85

Population below poverty line: 20.9% (2021 est.)
note: % of population with income below national poverty line

Gini Index coefficient - distribution of family income: 36.6 (2022 est.)
note: index (0-100) of income distribution; higher values represent greater inequality
comparison ranking: 61

Average household expenditures: *on food:* 19.4% of household expenditures (2023 est.)
on alcohol and tobacco: 5.5% of household expenditures (2023 est.)

Household income or consumption by percentage share: *lowest 10%:* 2.5% (2022 est.)
highest 10%: 28.7% (2022 est.)
note: % share of income accruing to lowest and highest 10% of population

Remittances: 1.2% of GDP (2024 est.)
1.2% of GDP (2023 est.)
1% of GDP (2022 est.)
note: personal transfers and compensation between resident and non-resident individuals/households/entities

Budget: *revenues:* $28.011 billion (2023 est.)
expenditures: $28.68 billion (2023 est.)
note: central government revenues (excluding grants) and expenditures converted to US dollars at average official exchange rate for year indicated

Public debt: 36.9% of GDP (2023 est.)
note: central government debt as a % of GDP
comparison ranking: 144

Taxes and other revenues: 21.4% (of GDP) (2023 est.)
note: central government tax revenue as a % of GDP
comparison ranking: 41

Current account balance: $2.101 billion (2024 est.)
$878.388 million (2023 est.)
-$4.322 billion (2022 est.)
note: balance of payments - net trade and primary/secondary income in current dollars
comparison ranking: 46

Exports: $62.896 billion (2024 est.)
$61.02 billion (2023 est.)
$61.448 billion (2022 est.)
note: balance of payments - exports of goods and services in current dollars
comparison ranking: 59

Exports - partners: Latvia 11%, Poland 8%, Germany 7%, Netherlands 6%, Russia 6% (2023)
note: top five export partners based on percentage share of exports

Exports - commodities: refined petroleum, furniture, plastic products, wheat, cars (2023)
note: top five export commodities based on value in dollars

Imports: $58.491 billion (2024 est.)
$57.899 billion (2023 est.)
$62.916 billion (2022 est.)
note: balance of payments - imports of goods and services in current dollars
comparison ranking: 62

Imports - partners: Germany 13%, Poland 13%, Latvia 8%, USA 7%, Norway 5% (2023)
note: top five import partners based on percentage share of imports

Imports - commodities: crude petroleum, cars, natural gas, packaged medicine, plastic products (2023)
note: top five import commodities based on value in dollars

Reserves of foreign exchange and gold: $7.406 billion (2024 est.)
$6.168 billion (2023 est.)
$5.365 billion (2022 est.)
note: holdings of gold (year-end prices)/foreign exchange/special drawing rights in current dollars
comparison ranking: 86

Exchange rates: euros (EUR) per US dollar -

Exchange rates: 0.924 (2024 est.)
0.925 (2023 est.)
0.95 (2022 est.)
0.845 (2021 est.)
0.876 (2020 est.)

ENERGY

Electricity access: *electrification - total population:* 100% (2022 est.)

Electricity: *installed generating capacity:* 5.426 million kW (2023 est.)
consumption: 10.992 billion kWh (2023 est.)
exports: 3.98 billion kWh (2023 est.)
imports: 10.91 billion kWh (2023 est.)
transmission/distribution losses: 829.9 million kWh (2023 est.)
comparison rankings: installed generating capacity 88; consumption 102; exports 43; imports 22; transmission/distribution losses 93

Electricity generation sources: *fossil fuels:* 16.3% of total installed capacity (2023 est.)
solar: 14.1% of total installed capacity (2023 est.)
wind: 51% of total installed capacity (2023 est.)
hydroelectricity: 4.8% of total installed capacity (2023 est.)
biomass and waste: 13.8% of total installed capacity (2023 est.)

Nuclear energy: Number of nuclear reactors permanently shut down: 2 (2025)

Coal: *consumption:* 166,000 metric tons (2023 est.)
exports: 78,000 metric tons (2023 est.)
imports: 149,000 metric tons (2023 est.)

Petroleum: *total petroleum production:* 4,000 bbl/day (2023 est.)
refined petroleum consumption: 67,000 bbl/day (2024 est.)
crude oil estimated reserves: 12 million barrels (2021 est.)

Natural gas: *consumption:* 1.49 billion cubic meters (2023 est.)
exports: 1.867 billion cubic meters (2023 est.)
imports: 3.282 billion cubic meters (2023 est.)

Energy consumption per capita: 83.7 million Btu/person (2023 est.)
comparison ranking: 62

COMMUNICATIONS

Telephones - fixed lines: *total subscriptions:* 224,000 (2023 est.)
subscriptions per 100 inhabitants: 8 (2023 est.)
comparison ranking: total subscriptions 117

Telephones - mobile cellular: *total subscriptions:* 3.92 million (2023 est.)
subscriptions per 100 inhabitants: 139 (2022 est.)
comparison ranking: total subscriptions 138

Broadcast media: public broadcaster operates 3 channels, with the third channel (satellite) introduced in 2007; various privately owned commercial TV broadcasters operate national and multiple regional channels; many privately owned local TV stations; multi-channel cable and satellite TV services available; publicly owned broadcaster operates 3 radio networks; many privately owned commercial broadcasters, with repeater stations in various regions

Internet country code: .lt

Internet users: *percent of population:* 89% (2023 est.)

Broadband - fixed subscriptions: *total:* 806,000 (2023 est.)
subscriptions per 100 inhabitants: 28 (2023 est.)
comparison ranking: total 84

TRANSPORTATION

Civil aircraft registration country code prefix: LY

Airports: 64 (2025)
comparison ranking: 76

Heliports: 2 (2025)
comparison ranking: 125

Railways: *total:* 1,911 km (2020) 152 km electrified

Merchant marine: *total:* 59 (2023)
by type: container ship 3, general cargo 19, oil tanker 2, other 35
comparison ranking: total 114

Ports: *total ports:* 2 (2024)
large: 0
medium: 1
small: 0
very small: 1
ports with oil terminals: 2
key ports: Butinge Oil Terminal, Klaipeda

MILITARY AND SECURITY

Military and security forces: Lithuanian Armed Forces (Lietuvos Ginkluotosios Pajegos): Lithuanian Land Forces (LLF), Lithuanian Navy, Lithuanian Air Force (LTAF), Lithuanian Special Operations Forces

(LITHSOF); National Defense Volunteer Forces (2025)
note 1: the National Rifleman's Union is a civilian paramilitary organization supported by the Lithuanian Government, which cooperates with the military but is not part of it; however, in a state of war, its armed formations would fall under the Armed Forces
note 2: the Lithuanian Police and State Border Guard Service are under the Ministry of Interior; in wartime, the State Border Guard Service becomes part of the armed forces

Military expenditures: 4% of GDP (2025 est.)
3.1% of GDP (2024 est.)
2.7% of GDP (2023 est.)
2.4% of GDP (2022 est.)
2% of GDP (2021 est.)

Military and security service personnel strengths: approximately 20,000 active-duty military personnel (2025)

Military equipment inventories and acquisitions: the military's inventory is a mix of mostly European and US weapons and equipment (2024)

Military service age and obligation: 19-26 years of age for conscripted military service for men; 9-month service obligation; 18-38 for voluntary service for men and women; 18-60 for the National Defense Volunteer Services (2025)
note 1: in 2015, Lithuania reinstated conscription after having converted to a professional military in 2008; it conscripts up to 4,000 men each year; conscripts are selected using an automated lottery system
note 2: as of 2020, women comprised about 12% of the military's full-time personnel

Military deployments: *note:* contributes about 350-550 troops to the Lithuania, Poland, and Ukraine joint military brigade (LITPOLUKRBRIG), which was established in 2014; the brigade is headquartered in Poland and is comprised of an international staff, three battalions, and specialized units; units affiliated with the multinational brigade remain within the structures of the armed forces of their respective countries until the brigade is activated for participation in an international operation

Military - note: the Lithuanian Armed Forces are responsible for the defense of the country's interests, sovereignty, and territory, fulfilling Lithuania's commitments to NATO and European security, and contributing to UN international peacekeeping efforts; Russia is Lithuania's primary security focus, which has only increased since the Russian seizure of Crimea in 2014 and subsequent full-scale attack on Ukraine in 2022; Lithuania has been a member of NATO since 2004 and is reliant on the Alliance as the country's security guarantor; it is actively engaged in both NATO and EU security, as well as bilaterally with allies such as the other Baltic States, Germany, Poland, the UK, Ukraine, and the US; the Lithuanian military has participated in NATO and EU missions abroad and regularly conducts training and exercises with NATO and EU partner forces; it hosts NATO forces, is a member of the UK-led Joint Expeditionary Force, and contributes troops to a multinational brigade with Poland and Ukraine; Lithuania participated in its first UN peacekeeping mission in 1994
since 2017, Lithuania has hosted a German-led multinational NATO ground force battlegroup as part of the Alliance's Enhanced Forward Presence initiative; NATO has also provided air protection for Lithuania since 2004 through its Baltic Air Policing mission; NATO fighter aircraft are hosted at Lithuania's Šiauliai Air Base (2025)

TRANSNATIONAL ISSUES

Refugees and internally displaced persons: *refugees:* 53,859 (2024 est.)
stateless persons: 2,236 (2024 est.)

LUXEMBOURG

INTRODUCTION

Background: Founded in 963, Luxembourg became a grand duchy in 1815 and a constituent part of the Kingdom of the Netherlands after the Congress of Vienna. When Belgium declared independence from the Netherlands in 1839, Luxembourg lost more than half of its territory to Belgium but gained a larger measure of autonomy within the Kingdom of the Netherlands. Luxembourg gained full independence in 1867 by promising to remain permanently neutral. Overrun by Germany in both world wars, its neutrality ended in 1948 when it entered into the Benelux Customs Union and joined NATO the following year. In 1957, Luxembourg became one of the six founding countries of the EEC (later the EU), and in 1999 it joined the euro currency zone.

GEOGRAPHY

Location: Western Europe, between France and Germany

Geographic coordinates: 49 45 N, 6 10 E

Map references: Europe

Area: *total:* 2,586 sq km
land: 2,586 sq km
water: 0 sq km
comparison ranking: total 178

Area - comparative: slightly smaller than Rhode Island; about half the size of Delaware

Land boundaries: *total:* 327 km
border countries (3): Belgium 130 km; France 69 km; Germany 128 km

Coastline: 0 km (landlocked)

Maritime claims: none (landlocked)

Climate: modified continental with mild winters, cool summers

Terrain: mostly gently rolling uplands with broad, shallow valleys; uplands to slightly mountainous in the north; steep slope down to Moselle flood plain in the southeast

Elevation: *highest point:* Buurgplaatz 559 m
lowest point: Moselle River 133 m
mean elevation: 325 m

Natural resources: iron ore (no longer exploited), arable land

Land use: *agricultural land:* 51.3% (2022 est.)
arable land: 24.1% (2022 est.)
permanent crops: 0.6% (2022 est.)
permanent pasture: 26.7% (2022 est.)
forest: 34.5% (2022 est.)
other: 14.2% (2022 est.)

Irrigated land: 0 sq km (2012)

Major watersheds (area sq km): Atlantic Ocean drainage: Rhine-Maas (198,735 sq km)

Population distribution: most people live in the south, on or near the border with France

Natural hazards: occasional flooding

Geography - note: landlocked

PEOPLE AND SOCIETY

Population: *total:* 671,254 (2024 est.)
male: 338,702
female: 332,552
comparison rankings: total 168; male 168; female 169

Nationality: *noun:* Luxembourger(s)
adjective: Luxembourg

Ethnic groups: Luxembourger 52.9%, Portuguese 14.5%, French 7.6%, Italian 3.7%, Belgian 3%, German 2%, Spanish 1.3%, Romania 1%, other 14% (2022 est.)
note: data represent population by nationality

Languages: Luxembourgish (official administrative, judicial, and national language) 48.9%, Portuguese 15.4%, French (official administrative, judicial, and legislative language) 14.9%, Italian 3.6%, English 3.6%, German (official administrative and judicial language) 2.9%, other 10.8% (2021 est.)

Religions: Christian (predominantly Roman Catholic) 70.6%, Muslim 2.3%, other (includes Buddhist, folk religions, Hindu, Jewish) 0.4%, unaffiliated 26.7% (2020 est.)

Age structure: *0-14 years:* 16.7% (male 57,921/female 54,484)
15-64 years: 67.1% (male 231,214/female 219,497)

65 years and over: 16.1% (2024 est.) (male 49,567/ female 58,571)

Dependency ratios: *total dependency ratio:* 46.6 (2024 est.)
youth dependency ratio: 23.2 (2024 est.)
elderly dependency ratio: 23.4 (2024 est.)
potential support ratio: 4.3 (2024 est.)

Median age: *total:* 39.9 years (2024 est.)
male: 39.4 years
female: 40.4 years
comparison ranking: total 64

Population growth rate: 1.52% (2024 est.)
comparison ranking: 63

Birth rate: 11.6 births/1,000 population (2024 est.)
comparison ranking: 155

Death rate: 7.1 deaths/1,000 population (2024 est.)
comparison ranking: 116

Net migration rate: 10.8 migrant(s)/1,000 population (2024 est.)
comparison ranking: 8

Population distribution: most people live in the south, on or near the border with France

Urbanization: *urban population:* 92.1% of total population (2023)
rate of urbanization: 1.43% annual rate of change (2020-25 est.)

Major urban areas - population: 120,000 LUXEMBOURG (capital) (2018)

Sex ratio: *at birth:* 1.06 male(s)/female
0-14 years: 1.06 male(s)/female
15-64 years: 1.05 male(s)/female
65 years and over: 0.85 male(s)/female
total population: 1.02 male(s)/female (2024 est.)

Mother's mean age at first birth: 31 years (2020 est.)

Maternal mortality ratio: 12 deaths/100,000 live births (2023 est.)
comparison ranking: 145

Infant mortality rate: *total:* 3.2 deaths/1,000 live births (2024 est.)
male: 3.6 deaths/1,000 live births
female: 2.8 deaths/1,000 live births
comparison ranking: total 203

Life expectancy at birth: *total population:* 83.4 years (2024 est.)
male: 80.9 years
female: 85.9 years
comparison ranking: total population 14

Total fertility rate: 1.63 children born/woman (2024 est.)
comparison ranking: 175

Gross reproduction rate: 0.79 (2024 est.)

Drinking water source: *improved: urban:* 100% of population (2022 est.)
rural: 98.6% of population (2022 est.)
total: 99.9% of population (2022 est.)
unimproved: urban: 0% of population (2022 est.)
rural: 1.4% of population (2022 est.)
total: 0.1% of population (2022 est.)

Health expenditure: 5.5% of GDP (2022)
11% of national budget (2022 est.)

Physician density: 2.98 physicians/1,000 population (2017)

Hospital bed density: 4.2 beds/1,000 population (2021 est.)

Sanitation facility access: *improved: urban:* 100% of population (2022 est.)
rural: 99.9% of population (2022 est.)
total: 100% of population (2022 est.)
unimproved: urban: 0% of population (2022 est.)
rural: 0.1% of population (2022 est.)
total: 0% of population (2022 est.)

Obesity - adult prevalence rate: 22.6% (2016)
comparison ranking: 74

Alcohol consumption per capita: *total:* 11 liters of pure alcohol (2019 est.)
beer: 4.04 liters of pure alcohol (2019 est.)
wine: 4.73 liters of pure alcohol (2019 est.)
spirits: 2.14 liters of pure alcohol (2019 est.)
other alcohols: 0 liters of pure alcohol (2019 est.)
comparison ranking: total 11

Tobacco use: *total:* 21% (2025 est.)
male: 22.1% (2025 est.)
female: 19.9% (2025 est.)
comparison ranking: total 61

Currently married women (ages 15-49): 51.4% (2023 est.)

Education expenditure: 4.7% of GDP (2022 est.)
10.7% national budget (2022 est.)
comparison ranking: Education expenditure (% GDP) 77

School life expectancy (primary to tertiary education): *total:* 14 years (2022 est.)
male: 14 years (2022 est.)
female: 15 years (2022 est.)

ENVIRONMENT

Environmental issues: air and water pollution in urban areas; soil pollution of farmland

International environmental agreements: *party to:* Air Pollution, Air Pollution-Heavy Metals, Air Pollution-Multi-effect Protocol, Air Pollution-Nitrogen Oxides, Air Pollution-Persistent Organic Pollutants, Air Pollution-Sulphur 85, Air Pollution-Sulphur 94, Air Pollution-Volatile Organic Compounds, Biodiversity, Climate Change, Climate Change-Kyoto Protocol, Climate Change-Paris Agreement, Comprehensive Nuclear Test Ban, Desertification, Endangered Species, Hazardous Wastes, Law of the Sea, Marine Dumping-London Convention, Marine Dumping-London Protocol, Nuclear Test Ban, Ozone Layer Protection, Ship Pollution, Tropical Timber 2006, Wetlands, Whaling
signed, but not ratified: Environmental Modification

Climate: modified continental with mild winters, cool summers

Urbanization: *urban population:* 92.1% of total population (2023)
rate of urbanization: 1.43% annual rate of change (2020-25 est.)

Carbon dioxide emissions: 8.715 million metric tonnes of CO2 (2023 est.)
from coal and metallurgical coke: 75,000 metric tonnes of CO2 (2023 est.)
from petroleum and other liquids: 7.496 million metric tonnes of CO2 (2023 est.)
from consumed natural gas: 1.144 million metric tonnes of CO2 (2023 est.)
comparison ranking: total emissions 112

Particulate matter emissions: 9.2 micrograms per cubic meter (2019 est.)

Waste and recycling: *municipal solid waste generated annually:* 490,300 tons (2024 est.)
percent of municipal solid waste recycled: 42% (2022 est.)

Total water withdrawal: *municipal:* 43.53 million cubic meters (2022 est.)
industrial: 1.83 million cubic meters (2022 est.)
agricultural: 490,000 cubic meters (2022 est.)

Total renewable water resources: 3.5 billion cubic meters (2022 est.)

Geoparks: *total global geoparks and regional networks:* 1
global geoparks and regional networks: Mëllerdall (2023)

GOVERNMENT

Country name: *conventional long form:* Grand Duchy of Luxembourg
conventional short form: Luxembourg
local long form: Grand Duché de Luxembourg
local short form: Luxembourg
etymology: probably derived from an early Celtic or Germanic form of the name,
Lucilinburhuc, that was thought to mean "little fortress;" the name first referred to the city and was later used for the country

Government type: constitutional monarchy

Capital: *name:* Luxembourg
geographic coordinates: 49 36 N, 6 07 E
time difference: UTC+1 (6 hours ahead of Washington, DC, during Standard Time)
daylight saving time: +1hr, begins last Sunday in March; ends last Sunday in October
etymology: probably derived from an early Celtic or Germanic form of the name, Lucilinburhuc, that was thought to mean "little fortress;" the name first referred to the city and was later used for the country

Administrative divisions: 12 cantons; Capellen, Clervaux, Diekirch, Echternach, Esch-sur-Alzette, Grevenmacher, Luxembourg, Mersch, Redange, Remich, Vianden, Wiltz

Legal system: civil law system

Constitution: *history:* previous 1842 (heavily amended 1848, 1856); latest effective 17 October 1868
amendment process: proposed by the Chamber of Deputies or by the monarch to the Chamber; passage requires at least two-thirds majority vote by the Chamber in two successive readings three months apart; a referendum can be substituted for the second reading if approved by more than a quarter of the Chamber members or by 25,000 valid voters; adoption by referendum requires a majority of all valid voters

International law organization participation: accepts compulsory ICJ jurisdiction; accepts ICCt jurisdiction

Citizenship: *citizenship by birth:* limited to situations where the parents are either unknown, stateless, or when the nationality law of the parents' state of origin does not permit acquisition of citizenship by descent when the birth occurs outside of national territory
citizenship by descent only: at least one parent must be a citizen of Luxembourg
dual citizenship recognized: yes
residency requirement for naturalization: 7 years

Suffrage: 18 years of age; universal and compulsory

Executive branch: *chief of state:* Grand Duke HENRI (since 7 October 2000)

head of government: Prime Minister Luc FRIEDEN (since 17 November 2023)
cabinet: Council of Ministers recommended by the prime minister, appointed by the monarch
election/appointment process: the monarchy is hereditary; following elections to the Chamber of Deputies, monarch usually appoints the leader of the majority party or majority coalition as prime minister; deputy prime minister also appointed by the monarch; prime minister and deputy prime minister are responsible to the Chamber of Deputies

Legislative branch: *legislature name:* Chamber of Deputies (Chambre des députés)
legislative structure: unicameral
number of seats: 60 (all directly elected)
electoral system: proportional representation
scope of elections: full renewal
term in office: 5 years
most recent election date: 10/8/2023
parties elected and seats per party: Christian Social People's Party (CSV) (21); Democratic Party (PD/DP) (14); Socialist Workers' Party (POSL/LSAP) (11); Alternative Democratic Reform Party (ADR) (5); Greens (DEI GRÉNG) (4); Pirate Party (PIRATEN) (3); Other (2)
percentage of women in chamber: 35%
expected date of next election: October 2028
note: a 21-member Council of State is appointed by the Grand Duke on the advice of the prime minister and serves as an advisory body to the Chamber of Deputies

Judicial branch: *highest court(s):* Supreme Court of Justice includes Court of Appeal and Court of Cassation (consists of 27 judges on 9 benches); Constitutional Court (consists of 9 members)
judge selection and term of office: judges of both courts appointed by the monarch for life
subordinate courts: Court of Accounts; district and local tribunals and courts

Political parties: Alternative Democratic Reform Party or ADR
Christian Social People's Party or CSV
Democratic Party or DP
Green Party
Luxembourg Socialist Workers' Party or LSAP
Pirate Party
The Left (dei Lenk/la Gauche)

Diplomatic representation in the US: *chief of mission:* Ambassador Nicole BINTNER-BAKSHIAN (since 15 August 2021)
chancery: 2200 Massachusetts Avenue NW, Washington, DC 20008
telephone: [1] (202) 265-4171
FAX: [1] (202) 328-8270
email address and website: washington.amb@mae.etat.lu
https://washington.mae.lu/en.html
consulate(s) general: New York, San Francisco

Diplomatic representation from the US: *chief of mission:* Ambassador (vacant); Chargé d'Affaires Anthony BAIRD (since 21 July 2025)
embassy: 22 Boulevard Emmanuel Servais, L-2535 Luxembourg City
mailing address: 5380 Luxembourg Place, Washington DC 20521-5380
telephone: [352] 46-01-23-00
FAX: [352] 46-14-01
email address and website: Luxembourgconsular@state.gov
https://lu.usembassy.gov/

International organization participation: ADB (nonregional member), Australia Group, Benelux, BIS, CD, CE, EAPC, EBRD, ECB, EIB, EMU, ESA, EU, FAO, FATF, IAEA, IBRD, ICAO, ICC (national committees), ICCt, ICRM, IDA, IEA, IFAD, IFC, IFRCS, ILO, IMF, IMO, Interpol, IOC, IOM, IPU, ISO, ITSO, ITU, ITUC (NGOs), MIGA, NATO, NEA, NSG, OAS (observer), OECD, OIF, OPCW, OSCE, PCA, Schengen Convention, UN, UNCTAD, UNESCO, UNHCR, UNHRC, UNIDO, UNRWA, UPU, Wassenaar Arrangement, WCO, WHO, WIPO, WMO, WTO, ZC

Independence: 1839 (from the Netherlands)

National holiday: National Day (birthday of Grand Duke HENRI), 23 June
note: this is not the true date of birth for any of the Royals, but the national festivities were shifted in 1962 to allow observance during a more favorable time of year

Flag: *description:* three equal horizontal bands of red (top), white, and light blue
history: the colors are derived from the Grand Duke's coat of arms
note: similar to the flag of the Netherlands, which is shorter and uses a darker blue

National symbol(s): red rampant lion

National color(s): red, white, light blue

National anthem(s): *title:* "Ons Heemecht" (Our Motherland)
lyrics/music: Michel LENTZ/Jean-Antoine ZINNEN
history: adopted 1864
title: "De Wilhelmus" (The William)
lyrics/music: Nikolaus WELTER
history: adopted 1919; royal anthem, for use when members of the grand ducal family enter or exit a ceremony in Luxembourg

National heritage: *total World Heritage Sites:* 1 (cultural)
selected World Heritage Site locales: Luxembourg City Old Quarters and Fortifications

ECONOMY

Economic overview: high-income EU and eurozone economy; global, highly capitalized banking sector; one of highest GDP-per-capita countries; strengthened domestic demand and lower interest rates contributing to economic growth; challenges include pension-system sustainability, labor-market dynamics, and energy price volatility

Real GDP (purchasing power parity): $86.871 billion (2024 est.)
$85.984 billion (2023 est.)
$86.584 billion (2022 est.)
note: data in 2021 dollars
comparison ranking: 102

Real GDP growth rate: 1% (2024 est.)
-0.7% (2023 est.)
-1.1% (2022 est.)
note: annual GDP % growth based on constant local currency
comparison ranking: 176

Real GDP per capita: $128,200 (2024 est.)
$129,000 (2023 est.)
$132,600 (2022 est.)
note: data in 2021 dollars
comparison ranking: 4

GDP (official exchange rate): $93.197 billion (2024 est.)
note: data in current dollars at official exchange rate

Inflation rate (consumer prices): 2.1% (2024 est.)
3.7% (2023 est.)
6.3% (2022 est.)
note: annual % change based on consumer prices
comparison ranking: 53

GDP - composition, by sector of origin: *agriculture:* 0.2% (2024 est.)
industry: 9% (2024 est.)
services: 81.9% (2024 est.)
note: figures may not total 100% due to non-allocated consumption not captured in sector-reported data
comparison rankings: agriculture 200; industry 194; services 10

GDP - composition, by end use: *household consumption:* 31.6% (2023 est.)
government consumption: 18.6% (2023 est.)
investment in fixed capital: 16.1% (2023 est.)
investment in inventories: 1.3% (2023 est.)
exports of goods and services: 217.8% (2023 est.)
imports of goods and services: -186.7% (2023 est.)
note: figures may not total 100% due to rounding or gaps in data collection

Agricultural products: milk, wheat, barley, triticale, potatoes, pork, grapes, beef, rye, rapeseed (2023)
note: top ten agricultural products based on tonnage

Industries: banking and financial services, construction, real estate services, iron, metals, and steel, information technology, telecommunications, cargo transportation and logistics, chemicals, engineering, tires, glass, aluminum, tourism, biotechnology

Industrial production growth rate: -1.1% (2024 est.)
note: annual % change in industrial value added based on constant local currency
comparison ranking: 149

Labor force: 350,000 (2024 est.)
note: number of people ages 15 or older who are employed or seeking work
comparison ranking: 165

Unemployment rate: 6% (2024 est.)
5.2% (2023 est.)
4.6% (2022 est.)
note: % of labor force seeking employment
comparison ranking: 112

Youth unemployment rate (ages 15-24): *total:* 20.2% (2024 est.)
male: 16.9% (2024 est.)
female: 24.2% (2024 est.)
note: % of labor force ages 15-24 seeking employment
comparison ranking: total 55

Population below poverty line: 17.3% (2021 est.)
note: % of population with income below national poverty line

Gini Index coefficient - distribution of family income: 34.1 (2022 est.)
note: index (0-100) of income distribution; higher values represent greater inequality
comparison ranking: 85

Household income or consumption by percentage share: *lowest 10%:* 2.9% (2022 est.)
highest 10%: 25.6% (2022 est.)
note: % share of income accruing to lowest and highest 10% of population

Remittances: 2.6% of GDP (2024 est.)
2.8% of GDP (2023 est.)

2.8% of GDP (2022 est.)
note: personal transfers and compensation between resident and non-resident individuals/households/entities

Budget: *revenues:* $37.951 billion (2023 est.)
expenditures: $38.263 billion (2023 est.)
note: central government revenues (excluding grants) and expenditures converted to US dollars at average official exchange rate for year indicated

Public debt: 23% of GDP (2017 est.)
note: data cover general government debt and include debt instruments issued (or owned) by government entities other than the treasury; the data include treasury debt held by foreign entities; the data include debt issued by subnational entities, as well as intragovernmental debt; intragovernmental debt consists of treasury borrowings from surpluses in the social funds, such as for retirement, medical care, and unemployment; debt instruments for the social funds are not sold at public auctions
comparison ranking: 175

Taxes and other revenues: 27.2% (of GDP) (2023 est.)
note: central government tax revenue as a % of GDP
comparison ranking: 8

Current account balance: $12.877 billion (2024 est.)
$9.861 billion (2023 est.)
$7.509 billion (2022 est.)
note: balance of payments - net trade and primary/secondary income in current dollars
comparison ranking: 24

Exports: $202.203 billion (2024 est.)
$195.294 billion (2023 est.)
$184.53 billion (2022 est.)
note: balance of payments - exports of goods and services in current dollars
comparison ranking: 36

Exports - partners: Germany 18%, France 15%, Belgium 8%, Netherlands 7%, Italy 6% (2023)
note: top five export partners based on percentage share of exports

Exports - commodities: iron blocks, gas turbines, plastic products, rubber tires, plastics (2023)
note: top five export commodities based on value in dollars

Imports: $160.032 billion (2024 est.)
$156.818 billion (2023 est.)
$149.751 billion (2022 est.)
note: balance of payments - imports of goods and services in current dollars
comparison ranking: 37

Imports - partners: Belgium 26%, Germany 23%, France 10%, Netherlands 5%, USA 4% (2023)
note: top five import partners based on percentage share of imports

Imports - commodities: cars, refined petroleum, electricity, plastic products, gas turbines (2023)
note: top five import commodities based on value in dollars

Reserves of foreign exchange and gold: $2.789 billion (2024 est.)
$2.977 billion (2023 est.)
$2.874 billion (2022 est.)
note: holdings of gold (year-end prices)/foreign exchange/special drawing rights in current dollars
comparison ranking: 119

Exchange rates: euros (EUR) per US dollar -

Exchange rates: 0.924 (2024 est.)
0.925 (2023 est.)
0.95 (2022 est.)
0.845 (2021 est.)
0.876 (2020 est.)

ENERGY

Electricity access: *electrification - total population:* 100% (2022 est.)

Electricity: *installed generating capacity:* 2.212 million kW (2023 est.)
consumption: 5.87 billion kWh (2023 est.)
exports: 1.188 billion kWh (2023 est.)
imports: 6.39 billion kWh (2023 est.)
transmission/distribution losses: 141.867 million kWh (2023 est.)
comparison rankings: installed generating capacity 119; consumption 126; exports 67; imports 39; transmission/distribution losses 54

Electricity generation sources: *fossil fuels:* 10.5% of total installed capacity (2023 est.)
solar: 37.2% of total installed capacity (2023 est.)
wind: 55.6% of total installed capacity (2023 est.)
hydroelectricity: -35.8% of total installed capacity (2023 est.) note: Luxembourg has negative net hydroelectric power generation based on losses from use of pumped storage hydropower
biomass and waste: 32.5% of total installed capacity (2023 est.)

Coal: *consumption:* 34,000 metric tons (2023 est.)
exports: 30.2 metric tons (2022 est.)
imports: 34,000 metric tons (2023 est.)

Petroleum: *refined petroleum consumption:* 51,000 bbl/day (2024 est.)

Natural gas: *consumption:* 556.63 million cubic meters (2023 est.)
imports: 552.714 million cubic meters (2023 est.)

Energy consumption per capita: 224.651 million Btu/person (2023 est.)
comparison ranking: 15

COMMUNICATIONS

Telephones - fixed lines: *total subscriptions:* 260,000 (2022 est.)
subscriptions per 100 inhabitants: 40 (2022 est.)
comparison ranking: total subscriptions 111

Telephones - mobile cellular: *total subscriptions:* 961,000 (2023 est.)
subscriptions per 100 inhabitants: 137 (2021 est.)
comparison ranking: total subscriptions 165

Broadcast media: long national tradition of operating radio and TV services for pan-European audiences; home to Europe's largest privately owned broadcast media group, the RTL Group, which operates 46 TV stations and 29 radio stations in Europe; also home to Europe's largest satellite operator, Société Européenne des Satellites (SES); domestically, the RTL Group operates TV and radio networks; other domestic private radio and TV operators and French and German stations available; satellite and cable TV services available

Internet country code: .lu

Internet users: *percent of population:* 99% (2024 est.)

Broadband - fixed subscriptions: *total:* 250,000 (2022 est.)
subscriptions per 100 inhabitants: 38 (2022 est.)
comparison ranking: total 118

TRANSPORTATION

Civil aircraft registration country code prefix: LX

Airports: 3 (2025)
comparison ranking: 193

Heliports: 11 (2025)
comparison ranking: 72

Railways: *total:* 271 km (2020) 262 km electrified

Merchant marine: *total:* 147 (2023)
by type: bulk carrier 3, container ship 1, general cargo 24, oil tanker 4, other 115
comparison ranking: total 76

MILITARY AND SECURITY

Military and security forces: Luxembourg Army (l'Armée Luxembourgeoise) (2025)
note: the Grand Ducal Police maintain internal security and report to the Ministry of Internal Security

Military expenditures: 2% of GDP (2025 est.)
1.2% of GDP (2024 est.)
1.1% of GDP (2023 est.)
0.6% of GDP (2022 est.)
0.5% of GDP (2021 est.)

Military and security service personnel strengths: approximately 900 active military personnel (2025)

Military equipment inventories and acquisitions: the inventory of Luxembourg's Army is a small mix of Western origin equipment (2024)

Military service age and obligation: 18-26 years of age for voluntary military service for men and women; no conscription (abolished 1969) (2025)
note 1: since 2003, the Army has allowed EU citizens 18-24 years of age who have been a resident in the country for at least 36 months to volunteer
note 2: 2024, women made up about 12% of the military's full-time personnel

Military - note: founded in 1881, the Luxembourg Army is responsible for the defense of the country and fulfilling the Grand Duchy's commitments to NATO, European security, and international peacekeeping, as well as providing support to civil authorities in the event of emergencies, such as floods or disease outbreaks; the Army is an active participant in EU, NATO, and UN missions and has contributed small numbers of troops to a number of multinational operations in parts of Africa, Europe, and Asia; it trains and exercises regularly with EU and NATO partners and has contributed to the NATO battlegroup forward deployed in Lithuania since 2017; Luxembourg was one of the original 12 countries to sign the North Atlantic Treaty (also known as the Washington Treaty) establishing NATO in 1949
in 2015, Belgium, the Netherlands, and Luxembourg signed an agreement to conduct joint air policing of their territories; under the agreement, which went into effect in January 2017, the Belgian and Dutch Air Forces trade responsibility for patrolling the skies over the three countries (2025)

SPACE

Space agency/agencies: the Luxembourg Space Agency (LSA; established 2018) (2025)

Space program overview: LSA established largely to develop space policy, encourage and coordinate commercial space ventures, support space education, and to promote the country's space-related capabilities internationally; has a national space strategy; has set up policy and funding initiatives (such as LuxIMPULSE) aimed at encouraging space research, development, innovation, and entrepreneurship and attracting space-based industries; focused on developing commercial satellites and infrastructure (Luxembourg is home to some of the largest commercial satellite companies in the world), as well as other space sector capabilities and technologies, such as autonomous vehicles, robotics, remote sensing (RS), communications, and software; member of the European Space Agency (ESA) since 2005; participates in a variety of ESA programs and cooperates with individual ESA and EU member states; also has relations with other foreign space agencies and industries, including those of Canada, China, Japan, New Zealand, South Korea, the UAE, and the US (2025)

note: further details about the key activities, programs, and milestones of the country's space program, as well as government spending estimates on the space sector, appear in the Space Programs reference guide

TRANSNATIONAL ISSUES

Refugees and internally displaced persons: *refugees:* 14,344 (2024 est.)

stateless persons: 85 (2024 est.)

MACAU

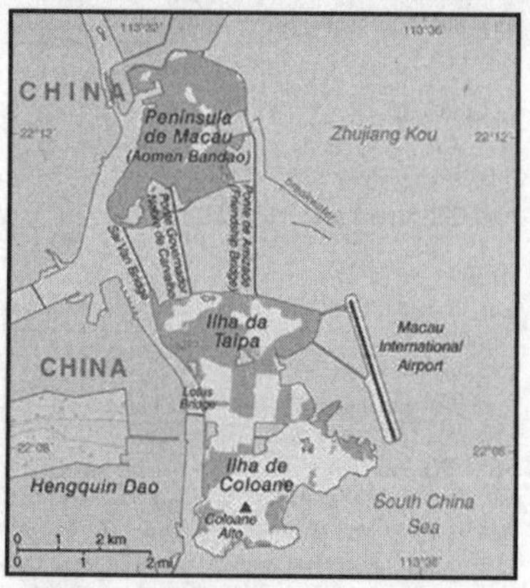

INTRODUCTION

Background: Portuguese ships began arriving in 1513. In the 1550s, Portuguese paying tribute to China settled in Macau, which became the official entrepôt for all international trade with China and Japan and the first European settlement in the Far East. The first governor was appointed in the 17th century, but the Portuguese remained largely under the control of the Chinese. In the 1930s and '40s Macau was declared a neutral territory during the Sino-Japanese War and World War II and became a refuge for both Chinese and Europeans. Portugal officially made Macau an overseas province in 1951.

In April 1987, Portugal and China reached an agreement to return Macau to Chinese rule in 1999, using the Hong Kong Joint Declaration between China and the UK as a model. In this agreement, China promised that, under its "one country, two systems" formula, China's political and economic system would not be imposed on Macau, and that Macau would enjoy a "high degree of autonomy" in all matters except foreign affairs and defense for the next 50 years. However, after China's multi-year crackdown against the pro-democracy movement in nearby Hong Kong, the governments of China and the Macau Special Administrative Region worked to limit Macau's political autonomy by suppressing opposition activity in the 2021 legislative elections.

GEOGRAPHY

Location: Eastern Asia, bordering the South China Sea and China

Geographic coordinates: 22 10 N, 113 33 E

Map references: Southeast Asia

Area: *total:* 28 sq km
land: 28.2 sq km
water: 0 sq km
comparison ranking: total 235

Area - comparative: less than one-sixth the size of Washington, D.C.

Land boundaries: *total:* 3 km
regional borders (1): China 3 km

Coastline: 41 km

Maritime claims: not specified

Climate: subtropical; marine with cool winters, warm summers

Terrain: generally flat

Elevation: *highest point:* Alto Coloane 172 m
lowest point: South China Sea 0 m

Natural resources: NEGL

Land use: *agricultural land:* 0% (2022 est.)
forest: 0% (2022 est.)
other: 100% (2022 est.)

Irrigated land: 0 sq km (2012)

Population distribution: population fairly equally distributed

Natural hazards: typhoons

Geography - note: primarily urban; an area of land reclaimed from the sea measuring 5.2 sq km (2 sq mi) and known as Cotai now connects the islands of Coloane and Taipa; the island area is connected to the mainland peninsula by three bridges

PEOPLE AND SOCIETY

Population: *total:* 644,426 (2024 est.)
male: 304,988
female: 339,438
comparison rankings: total 170; male 170; female 168

Nationality: *noun:* Chinese
adjective: Chinese

Ethnic groups: Chinese 89.4%, Chinese and Portuguese 1%, Portuguese 0.8%, Chinese and non-Portuguese 0.2%, Portuguese and others 0.2%, other 8.5% (2021 est.)

Languages: Cantonese 81%, Mandarin 4.7%, other Chinese dialects 5.4%, English 3.6%, Tagalog 2.9%, Portuguese 0.6%, other 1.8% (2021 est.)
major-language sample(s):
世界概况, 必須擁有的基本資料参考书
(Cantonese)
note: Chinese and Portuguese are official languages; Macanese or Patua, a Portuguese-based Creole, is also spoken

Religions: folk religion 58.9%, Buddhist 17.3%, Christian 7.2%, other 1.2%, none 15.4% (2020 est.)

Age structure: *0-14 years:* 14.4% (male 47,346/ female 45,216)
15-64 years: 69.9% (male 210,059/female 240,577)
65 years and over: 15.7% (2024 est.) (male 47,583/ female 53,645)

Dependency ratios: *total dependency ratio:* 43 (2024 est.)
youth dependency ratio: 20.5 (2024 est.)
elderly dependency ratio: 22.5 (2024 est.)
potential support ratio: 4.5 (2024 est.)

Median age: *total:* 42.5 years (2024 est.)
male: 41.5 years
female: 43.1 years
comparison ranking: total 43

Population growth rate: 0.67% (2024 est.)
comparison ranking: 132

Birth rate: 8.6 births/1,000 population (2024 est.)
comparison ranking: 204

Death rate: 4.9 deaths/1,000 population (2024 est.)
comparison ranking: 197

Net migration rate: 3.1 migrant(s)/1,000 population (2024 est.)
comparison ranking: 35

Population distribution: population fairly equally distributed

Urbanization: *urban population:* 100% of total population (2023)
rate of urbanization: 1.46% annual rate of change (2020-25 est.)

Major urban areas - population: 682,000 Macau (2023)

Sex ratio: *at birth:* 1.05 male(s)/female
0-14 years: 1.05 male(s)/female
15-64 years: 0.87 male(s)/female
65 years and over: 0.89 male(s)/female
total population: 0.9 male(s)/female (2024 est.)

Infant mortality rate: *total:* 4.4 deaths/1,000 live births (2024 est.)
male: 4.5 deaths/1,000 live births
female: 4.3 deaths/1,000 live births
comparison ranking: total 183

Life expectancy at birth: *total population:* 85.3 years (2024 est.)
male: 82.5 years
female: 88.3 years
comparison ranking: total population 3

Total fertility rate: 1.24 children born/woman (2024 est.)
comparison ranking: 222

Gross reproduction rate: 0.6 (2024 est.)

Drinking water source: *improved: urban:* 100% of population

Currently married women (ages 15-49): 53.5% (2023 est.)

Education expenditure: 6.3% of GDP (2020 est.)
comparison ranking: Education expenditure (% GDP) 27

School life expectancy (primary to tertiary education): *total:* 18 years
male: 17 years
female: 19 years (2021)

ENVIRONMENT

Environmental issues: air pollution; coastal water pollution; solid-waste disposal; noise pollution

Climate: subtropical; marine with cool winters, warm summers

Urbanization: *urban population:* 100% of total population (2023)
rate of urbanization: 1.46% annual rate of change (2020-25 est.)

Carbon dioxide emissions: 1.595 million metric tonnes of CO2 (2023 est.)
from coal and metallurgical coke: -1,239 metric tonnes of CO2 (2023 est.)
from petroleum and other liquids: 1.358 million metric tonnes of CO2 (2023 est.)
from consumed natural gas: 238,000 metric tonnes of CO2 (2023 est.)
comparison ranking: total emissions 164

Waste and recycling: *municipal solid waste generated annually:* 377,900 tons (2024 est.)

GOVERNMENT

Country name: *conventional long form:* Macau Special Administrative Region
conventional short form: Macau
official long form: Aomen Tebie Xingzhengqu (Chinese)/ Regiao Administrativa Especial de Macau (Portuguese)
official short form: Aomen (Chinese)/ Macau (Portuguese)
etymology: name derived from the Chinese *ama-gao*, or "Bay of Ama," for Ama, the patron goddess of sailors

Government type: executive-led limited democracy; a special administrative region of the People's Republic of China

Dependency status: special administrative region of the People's Republic of China

Administrative divisions: none (special administrative region of the People's Republic of China)

Legal system: civil law system based on the Portuguese model

Constitution: *history:* previous 1976 (Organic Statute of Macau, under Portuguese authority); latest adopted 31 March 1993, effective 20 December 1999 (Basic Law of the Macau Special Administrative Region of the People's Republic of China serves as Macau's constitution)
amendment process: proposed by the Standing Committee of the National People's Congress (NPC), the People's Republic of China State Council, and the Macau Special Administrative Region; submittal of proposals to the NPC requires two-thirds majority vote by the Legislative Assembly of Macau, approval by two thirds of Macau's deputies to the NPC, and consent of the Macau chief executive; final passage requires approval by the NPC

Citizenship: see China

Suffrage: 18 years of age in direct elections for some legislative positions, universal for permanent residents living in Macau for the past 7 years
note: indirect elections are limited to organizations registered as "corporate voters" and an election committee for the chief executive drawn from broad regional groupings, municipal organizations, central government bodies, and elected Macau officials

Executive branch: *chief of state:* President of China XI Jinping (since 14 March 2013)
head of government: Chief Executive Sam Hou FAI (since 20 December 2024)
cabinet: Executive Council appointed by the chief executive
election/appointment process: president indirectly elected by National People's Congress for a 5-year term (eligible for a second term); chief executive chosen by a 400-member Election Committee for a 5-year term (eligible for a second term)
most recent election date: president: 10 March 2023
chief executive: 13 October 2024
election results: 2024: Sam Hou FAI (unopposed; received 394 out of 400 votes)
2019: HO lat Seng (unopposed; received 392 out of 400 votes)
expected date of next election: president: March 2028
chief executive: 2029

Legislative branch: *legislature name:* Legislative Assembly (Regiao Administrativa Especial de Macau)
legislative structure: unicameral
number of seats: 33 (14 directly elected, 12 indirectly elected, 7 appointed)
electoral system: mixed
scope of elections: full renewal
term in office: 4 years
most recent election date: 9/12/2021
parties elected and seats per party: United Citizens Association of Macau (ACUM) (3); Union for Development (UPD) (2); Macau-Guangdong Union (UGM) (2); Union for Promoting Progress (UPP) (2); Alliance for a Happy Home (ABL) (2); New Hope (NE) (2); Association of Synergy of Macau (PS) (1)
expected date of next election: September 2025

Judicial branch: *highest court(s):* Court of Final Appeal of Macau Special Administrative Region (consists of the court president and 2 associate justices)
judge selection and term of office: justices appointed by the Macau chief executive upon the recommendation of an independent commission of judges, lawyers, and "eminent" persons; judge tenure NA
subordinate courts: Court of Second Instance; Court of First instance; Lower Court; Administrative Court

Political parties: Alliance for a Happy Home or ABL
Association of Synergy of Macau ("Synergy Power" or Poder da Singeria) or PS
Macau-Guangdong Union or UGM
New Hope or NE
Union for Development or UPD
Union for Promoting Progress or UPP or UNIPRO
United Citizens Association of Macau or ACUM
note: there is no political party ordinance, so there are no registered political parties; politically active groups register as societies or companies

Diplomatic representation in the US: none (Special Administrative Region of China)

Diplomatic representation from the US: *embassy:* the US has no offices in Macau; US Consulate General in Hong Kong is accredited to Macau

International organization participation: ICC (national committees), IHO, IMF, IMO (associate), Interpol (subbureau), ISO (correspondent), UNESCO (associate), UNWTO (associate), UPU, WCO, WMO, WTO

Independence: none (special administrative region of China)

National holiday: National Day (anniversary of the Founding of the People's Republic of China), 1 October (1949)
note: 20 December (1999) is celebrated as Macau Special Administrative Region Establishment Day

Flag: *description:* green with a lotus flower above a stylized bridge and water in white, under an arc of five five-pointed gold stars
meaning: the lotus is the national floral emblem, and the three petals represent the country's peninsula and two islands; the five stars echo the Chinese flag

National symbol(s): lotus blossom

National color(s): green, white, yellow

National anthem(s): *title:* "Yiyongjun Jinxingqu" (The March of the Volunteers)
lyrics/music: TIAN Han/NIE Er
history: official anthem, as a Special Administrative Region of China

ECONOMY

Economic overview: high-income, Chinese special administrative region economy; known for apparel exports and gambling tourism; currency pegged to Hong Kong dollar; significant recession due to 2015 Chinese anticorruption campaign; COVID-19 further halved economic activity

Real GDP (purchasing power parity): $77.524 billion (2024 est.)
$71.248 billion (2023 est.)
$40.699 billion (2022 est.)
note: data in 2021 dollars
comparison ranking: 107

Real GDP growth rate: 8.8% (2024 est.)
75.1% (2023 est.)
-19.6% (2022 est.)
note: annual GDP % growth based on constant local currency
comparison ranking: 8

Real GDP per capita: $112,800 (2024 est.)
$105,000 (2023 est.)
$60,100 (2022 est.)
note: data in 2021 dollars
comparison ranking: 6

GDP (official exchange rate): $50.183 billion (2024 est.)
note: data in current dollars at official exchange rate

Inflation rate (consumer prices): 0.5% (2023 est.)
1% (2022 est.)
0% (2021 est.)
note: annual % change based on consumer prices
comparison ranking: 11

GDP - composition, by sector of origin: *industry:* 5.4% (2023 est.)
services: 91.4% (2023 est.)
note: figures may not total 100% due to non-allocated consumption not captured in sector-reported data
comparison rankings: industry 203; services 4

GDP - composition, by end use: *household consumption:* 29% (2024 est.)
government consumption: 12.2% (2024 est.)
investment in fixed capital: 13.8% (2024 est.)
investment in inventories: 0.7% (2024 est.)
exports of goods and services: 89.8% (2024 est.)
imports of goods and services: -45.4% (2024 est.)
note: figures may not total 100% due to rounding or gaps in data collection

Agricultural products: pork, chicken, beef, eggs, pork offal, pork fat, pepper, beef offal, cattle hides, goose meat (2023)
note: top ten agricultural products based on tonnage

Industries: tourism, gambling, clothing, textiles, electronics, footwear, toys

Industrial production growth rate: 6.8% (2023 est.)
note: annual % change in industrial value added based on constant local currency
comparison ranking: 26

Labor force: 382,100 (2024 est.)
note: number of people ages 15 or older who are employed or seeking work
comparison ranking: 164

Unemployment rate: 2.5% (2024 est.)
2.3% (2023 est.)
2.5% (2022 est.)
note: % of labor force seeking employment
comparison ranking: 23

Youth unemployment rate (ages 15-24): *total:* 7.2% (2024 est.)
male: 9.4% (2024 est.)
female: 5.6% (2024 est.)
note: % of labor force ages 15-24 seeking employment
comparison ranking: total 144

Remittances: 0.2% of GDP (2023 est.)
0.4% of GDP (2022 est.)
0.2% of GDP (2021 est.)
note: personal transfers and compensation between resident and non-resident individuals/households/entities

Budget: *revenues:* $12.513 billion (2023 est.)
expenditures: $11.509 billion (2023 est.)
note: central government revenues (excluding grants) and expenditures converted to US dollars at average official exchange rate for year indicated

Taxes and other revenues: 22.8% (of GDP) (2023 est.)
note: central government tax revenue as a % of GDP
comparison ranking: 31

Current account balance: $14.38 billion (2023 est.)
$3.476 billion (2022 est.)
$2.705 billion (2021 est.)
note: balance of payments - net trade and primary/secondary income in current dollars
comparison ranking: 23

Exports: $41.839 billion (2023 est.)
$21.097 billion (2022 est.)
$28.163 billion (2021 est.)
note: balance of payments - exports of goods and services in current dollars
comparison ranking: 71

Exports - partners: Hong Kong 73%, China 6%, USA 6%, Philippines 3%, Singapore 1% (2023)
note: top five export partners based on percentage share of exports

Exports - commodities: jewelry, garments, broadcasting equipment, precious metal watches, video and card games (2023)
note: top five export commodities based on value in dollars

Imports: $23.205 billion (2023 est.)
$20.923 billion (2022 est.)
$23.77 billion (2021 est.)
note: balance of payments - imports of goods and services in current dollars
comparison ranking: 89

Imports - partners: China 36%, Hong Kong 17%, USA 6%, France 6%, Japan 5% (2023)
note: top five import partners based on percentage share of imports

Imports - commodities: jewelry, garments, trunks and cases, broadcasting equipment, electricity (2023)
note: top five import commodities based on value in dollars

Reserves of foreign exchange and gold: $29.392 billion (2024 est.)
$27.771 billion (2023 est.)
$25.971 billion (2022 est.)
note: holdings of gold (year-end prices)/foreign exchange/special drawing rights in current dollars
comparison ranking: 58

Exchange rates: patacas (MOP) per US dollar -

Exchange rates: 8.037 (2024 est.)
8.063 (2023 est.)
8.065 (2022 est.)
8.006 (2021 est.)
7.989 (2020 est.)

ENERGY

Electricity access: *electrification - total population:* 100% (2022 est.)

Electricity: *installed generating capacity:* 427,000 kW (2023 est.)
consumption: 5.659 billion kWh (2023 est.)
imports: 5.327 billion kWh (2023 est.)
transmission/distribution losses: 161.125 million kWh (2023 est.)
comparison rankings: installed generating capacity 155; consumption 128; imports 44; transmission/distribution losses 57

Electricity generation sources: *fossil fuels:* 58.5% of total installed capacity (2023 est.)
biomass and waste: 41.5% of total installed capacity (2023 est.)

Coal: *exports:* 600 metric tons (2023 est.)
imports: 7 metric tons (2023 est.)

Petroleum: *refined petroleum consumption:* 11,000 bbl/day (2023 est.)

Natural gas: *consumption:* 121.747 million cubic meters (2023 est.)
imports: 121.716 million cubic meters (2023 est.)

Energy consumption per capita: 64.641 million Btu/person (2023 est.)
comparison ranking: 77

COMMUNICATIONS

Telephones - fixed lines: *total subscriptions:* 87,000 (2023 est.)
subscriptions per 100 inhabitants: 12 (2023 est.)
comparison ranking: total subscriptions 139

Telephones - mobile cellular: *total subscriptions:* 1.37 million (2023 est.)
subscriptions per 100 inhabitants: 175 (2022 est.)
comparison ranking: total subscriptions 161

Broadcast media: local government dominates broadcast media; 2 TV stations operated by the government, with one broadcasting in Portuguese and the other in Cantonese and Mandarin; 1 cable TV and 4 satellite TV services available; 3 radio stations broadcasting, of which 2 are government-operated (2019)

Internet country code: .mo

Internet users: *percent of population:* 89% (2023 est.)

Broadband - fixed subscriptions: *total:* 212,000 (2023 est.)
subscriptions per 100 inhabitants: 30 (2023 est.)
comparison ranking: total 121

TRANSPORTATION

Civil aircraft registration country code prefix: B-M

Airports: 1 (2025)
comparison ranking: 210

Heliports: 4 (2025)
comparison ranking: 107

Merchant marine: *total:* 5 (2023)
by type: other 5
comparison ranking: total 167

Ports: *total ports:* 1 (2024)
large: 0
medium: 1
small: 0
very small: 0
ports with oil terminals: 1
key ports: Macau

MILITARY AND SECURITY

Military and security forces: Macau Public Security Police Force

Military - note: defense is the responsibility of China; the Chinese People's Liberation Army (PLA) maintains a garrison in Macau

TRANSNATIONAL ISSUES

Trafficking in persons: *tier rating:* Tier 3 — Macau does not fully meet the minimum standards for the elimination of trafficking and is not making significant efforts to do so, therefore, Macau remained on Tier 3; for more details, go to: https://www.state.gov/reports/2025-trafficking-in-persons-report/macau

MADAGASCAR

INTRODUCTION

Background: Madagascar was one of the last major habitable landmasses on earth to be settled by humans. While there is some evidence of human presence on the island in the millennia B.C., large-scale settlement began between A.D. 350 and 550 with settlers from present-day Indonesia. The island attracted Arab and Persian traders as early as the 7th century, and migrants from Africa arrived around A.D. 1000. Madagascar was a pirate stronghold during the late 17th and early 18th centuries and served as a slave trading center into the 19th century. From the 16th to the late 19th century, a native Merina Kingdom dominated much of Madagascar. The French conquered the island in 1896 and made it a colony; independence was regained in 1960.

Free presidential and National Assembly elections were held in 1992-93, ending 17 years of single-party rule. In 1997, in the second presidential race, Didier RATSIRAKA, the leader during the 1970s and 1980s, returned to the presidency. The 2001 presidential election was contested between the followers of RATSIRAKA and Marc RAVALOMANANA, nearly causing half the country to secede. In 2002, the High Constitutional Court announced RAVALOMANANA the winner. He won a second term in 2006 but, following protests in 2009, handed over power to the military, which then conferred the presidency on the mayor of Antananarivo, Andry RAJOELINA, in what amounted to a coup d'etat. After a lengthy mediation process, Madagascar held UN-supported presidential and parliamentary elections in 2013. Former de facto finance minister Hery RAJAONARIMAMPIANINA won in a runoff and was inaugurated in 2014. In 2019, RAJOELINA was declared the winner against RAVALOMANANA. In 2023, RAJOELINA won another term in an election that most of the opposition boycotted,

including RAJAONARIMAMPIANINA and RAVALOMANANA, who claimed it was rigged in favor of RAJOELINA. International observers, however, saw no evidence of systemic fraud, leading the international community to accept the election results.

GEOGRAPHY

Location: Southern Africa, island in the Indian Ocean, east of Mozambique

Geographic coordinates: 20 00 S, 47 00 E

Map references: Africa

Area: *total:* 587,041 sq km
land: 581,540 sq km
water: 5,501 sq km
comparison ranking: total 49

Area - comparative: almost four times the size of Georgia; slightly less than twice the size of Arizona

Land boundaries: *total:* 0 km

Coastline: 4,828 km

Maritime claims: *territorial sea:* 12 nm
contiguous zone: 24 nm
exclusive economic zone: 200 nm
continental shelf: 200 nm or 100 nm from the 2,500-m isobath

Climate: tropical along coast, temperate inland, arid in south

Terrain: narrow coastal plain, high plateau and mountains in center

Elevation: *highest point:* Maromokotro 2,876 m
lowest point: Indian Ocean 0 m
mean elevation: 615 m

Natural resources: graphite, chromite, coal, bauxite, rare earth elements, salt, quartz, tar sands, semiprecious stones, mica, fish, hydropower

Land use: *agricultural land:* 70.3% (2022 est.)
arable land: 5.2% (2022 est.)
permanent crops: 1% (2022 est.)
permanent pasture: 64.1% (2022 est.)
forest: 21.3% (2022 est.)
other: 8.4% (2022 est.)

Irrigated land: 10,860 sq km (2012)

Population distribution: most of population lives on the eastern half of the island; significant clustering is found in the central highlands and eastern coastline, as shown in this population distribution map

Natural hazards: periodic cyclones; drought; and locust infestation
volcanism: Madagascar's volcanoes have not erupted in recorded history

Geography - note: world's fourth-largest island; strategic location along Mozambique Channel; despite Madagascar's close proximity to the African continent, ocean currents isolate the island, resulting in high rates of endemic plant and animal species; approximately 90% of the flora and fauna on the island are found nowhere else

PEOPLE AND SOCIETY

Population: *total:* 29,452,714 (2024 est.)
male: 14,760,501
female: 14,692,213
comparison rankings: total 53; male 53; female 53

Nationality: *noun:* Malagasy (singular and plural)
adjective: Malagasy

Ethnic groups: Malayo-Indonesian (Merina and related Betsileo), Cotiers (mixed African, Malayo-Indonesian, and Arab ancestry - Betsimisaraka, Tsimihety, Antaisaka, Sakalava), French, Indian, Creole, Comoran

Languages: Malagasy (official) 99.9%, French (official) 23.6%, English 8.2%, other 0.6% (2018 est.)
note: shares sum to more than 100% because some respondents gave more than one answer on the census

Religions: Church of Jesus Christ in Madagascar/Malagasy Lutheran Church/Anglican Church 34%, Roman Catholic 32.3%, other Christian 8.1%, traditional/Animist 1.7%, Muslim 1.4%, other 0.6%, none 21.9% (2021 est.)

Age structure: *0-14 years:* 37% (male 5,507,847/female 5,400,551)
15-64 years: 59.1% (male 8,720,012/female 8,673,880)
65 years and over: 3.9% (2024 est.) (male 532,642/female 617,782)

Dependency ratios: *total dependency ratio:* 69.3 (2024 est.)
youth dependency ratio: 62.7 (2024 est.)
elderly dependency ratio: 6.6 (2024 est.)
potential support ratio: 15.1 (2024 est.)

Median age: *total:* 21.3 years (2024 est.)
male: 21.1 years
female: 21.5 years
comparison ranking: total 193

Population growth rate: 2.18% (2024 est.)
comparison ranking: 33

Birth rate: 27.6 births/1,000 population (2024 est.)
comparison ranking: 34

Death rate: 5.8 deaths/1,000 population (2024 est.)
comparison ranking: 163

Net migration rate: 0 migrant(s)/1,000 population (2024 est.)
comparison ranking: 85

Population distribution: most of population lives on the eastern half of the island; significant clustering is found in the central highlands and eastern coastline, as shown in this population distribution map

Urbanization: *urban population:* 40.6% of total population (2023)
rate of urbanization: 4.26% annual rate of change (2020-25 est.)

Major urban areas - population: 3.872 million ANTANANARIVO (capital) (2023)

Sex ratio: *at birth:* 1.03 male(s)/female
0-14 years: 1.02 male(s)/female
15-64 years: 1.01 male(s)/female
65 years and over: 0.86 male(s)/female
total population: 1.01 male(s)/female (2024 est.)

Mother's mean age at first birth: 19.5 years (2021 est.)
note: data represents median age at first birth among women 25-29

Maternal mortality ratio: 445 deaths/100,000 live births (2023 est.)
comparison ranking: 12

Infant mortality rate: *total:* 37.5 deaths/1,000 live births (2024 est.)
male: 40.9 deaths/1,000 live births
female: 34 deaths/1,000 live births
comparison ranking: total 31

Life expectancy at birth: *total population:* 68.8 years (2024 est.)
male: 67.3 years
female: 70.3 years
comparison ranking: total population 186

Total fertility rate: 3.47 children born/woman (2024 est.)
comparison ranking: 35

Gross reproduction rate: 1.71 (2024 est.)

Drinking water source: *improved:* *urban:* 79.8% of population (2022 est.)
rural: 36% of population (2022 est.)
total: 53.5% of population (2022 est.)
unimproved: *urban:* 20.2% of population (2022 est.)
rural: 64% of population (2022 est.)
total: 46.5% of population (2022 est.)

Health expenditure: 3.5% of GDP (2021)
5.7% of national budget (2022 est.)

Physician density: 0.17 physicians/1,000 population (2022)

Sanitation facility access: *improved:* *urban:* 53.9% of population (2022 est.)
rural: 25.2% of population (2022 est.)
total: 36.7% of population (2022 est.)
unimproved: *urban:* 46.1% of population (2022 est.)
rural: 74.8% of population (2022 est.)
total: 63.3% of population (2022 est.)

Obesity - adult prevalence rate: 5.3% (2016)
comparison ranking: 181

Alcohol consumption per capita: *total:* 0.89 liters of pure alcohol (2019 est.)
beer: 0.5 liters of pure alcohol (2019 est.)
wine: 0.07 liters of pure alcohol (2019 est.)
spirits: 0.32 liters of pure alcohol (2019 est.)
other alcohols: 0 liters of pure alcohol (2019 est.)
comparison ranking: total 155

Tobacco use: *total:* 24.1% (2025 est.)
male: 40.2% (2025 est.)
female: 8.2% (2025 est.)
comparison ranking: total 43

Children under the age of 5 years underweight: 22.6% (2021)
comparison ranking: 8

Currently married women (ages 15-49): 60.1% (2023 est.)

Child marriage: *women married by age 15:* 12.7% (2021)
women married by age 18: 38.8% (2021)
men married by age 18: 11.2% (2021)

Education expenditure: 3% of GDP (2023 est.)
18% national budget (2019 est.)
comparison ranking: Education expenditure (% GDP) 154

Literacy: *total population:* 74.7% (2021 est.)
male: 77.9% (2021 est.)
female: 71.8% (2021 est.)

School life expectancy (primary to tertiary education): *total:* 9 years (2019 est.)
male: 9 years (2019 est.)
female: 9 years (2019 est.)

ENVIRONMENT

Environmental issues: erosion and soil degradation from deforestation and overgrazing; desertification; agricultural fires; water pollution from raw sewage and other organic wastes; wildlife preservation

International environmental agreements: *party to:* Biodiversity, Climate Change, Climate Change-Kyoto Protocol, Climate Change-Paris Agreement, Comprehensive Nuclear Test Ban, Desertification, Endangered Species, Hazardous Wastes, Law of the Sea, Marine Dumping-London Protocol, Marine Life Conservation, Nuclear Test Ban, Ozone Layer Protection, Ship Pollution, Tropical Timber 2006, Wetlands
signed, but not ratified: none of the selected agreements

Climate: tropical along coast, temperate inland, arid in south

Urbanization: *urban population:* 40.6% of total population (2023)
rate of urbanization: 4.26% annual rate of change (2020-25 est.)

Carbon dioxide emissions: 3.936 million metric tonnes of CO_2 (2023 est.)
from coal and metallurgical coke: 1.057 million metric tonnes of CO_2 (2023 est.)
from petroleum and other liquids: 2.879 million metric tonnes of CO_2 (2023 est.)
comparison ranking: total emissions 141

Particulate matter emissions: 16.7 micrograms per cubic meter (2019 est.)

Waste and recycling: *municipal solid waste generated annually:* 3.769 million tons (2024 est.)
percent of municipal solid waste recycled: 9.2% (2022 est.)

Total water withdrawal: *municipal:* 395 million cubic meters (2022 est.)
industrial: 161.9 million cubic meters (2022 est.)
agricultural: 13 billion cubic meters (2022 est.)

Total renewable water resources: 337 billion cubic meters (2022 est.)

GOVERNMENT

Country name: *conventional long form:* Republic of Madagascar
conventional short form: Madagascar
local long form: République de Madagascar/ Repoblikan'i Madagasikara
local short form: Madagascar/Madagasikara
former: Malagasy Republic
etymology: a variant of the name was first used by 13th-century Venetian explorer Marco POLO when he confused the island with the Somali port of Mogadishu; the transliteration was later adopted as the official name

Government type: semi-presidential republic

Capital: *name:* Antananarivo
geographic coordinates: 18 55 S, 47 31 E
time difference: UTC+3 (8 hours ahead of Washington, DC, during Standard Time)
etymology: the name means "City of the Thousand," from the Malagasy *an-* (a prefix denoting a place name), *tanana* (town), and *arivo* (thousand); in the 17th century, King ADRIANJAKA named the original fortress after the 1,000 soldiers stationed there

Administrative divisions: 6 provinces (*faritany*); Antananarivo, Antsiranana, Fianarantsoa, Mahajanga, Toamasina, Toliara

Legal system: civil law system based on the old French civil code and customary law in matters of marriage, family, and obligation

Constitution: *history:* previous 1992; latest passed by referendum 17 November 2010, promulgated 11 December 2010
amendment process: proposed by the president of the republic in consultation with the cabinet or supported by a least two thirds of both the Senate and National Assembly membership; passage requires at least three-fourths approval of both the Senate and National Assembly and approval in a referendum; constitutional articles, including the form and powers of government, the sovereignty of the state, and the autonomy of Madagascar's collectivities, cannot be amended

International law organization participation: accepts compulsory ICJ jurisdiction with reservations; accepts ICCt jurisdiction

Citizenship: *citizenship by birth:* no
citizenship by descent only: the father must be a citizen of Madagascar; in the case of a child born out of wedlock, the mother must be a citizen
dual citizenship recognized: no
residency requirement for naturalization: unknown

Suffrage: 18 years of age; universal

Executive branch: *chief of state:* President Michael RANDRIANIRINA (Col.) (since 17 October 2025)
head of government: Prime Minister Herintsalama RAJAONARIVELO (since 22 October 2025)
cabinet: Council of Ministers appointed by the prime minister
election/appointment process: president directly elected by absolute-majority popular vote in 2 rounds, if needed, for a 5-year term (eligible for a second term); prime minister nominated by the National Assembly, appointed by the president
most recent election date: 16 November 2023
election results: *2023:* Andry RAJOELINA reelected president in first round; percent of vote - Andry RAJOELINA (TGV) 59.0%, Siteny Thierry RANDRIANASOLONIAIKO 14.4%, Marc RAVALOMANANA (TIM) 12.1%, other 14.5%
2018: Andry RAJOELINA elected president in second round; percent of vote in first round - Andry RAJOELINA (TGV) 39.2%, Marc RAVALOMANANA (TIM) 35.4%, other 25.4%; percent of vote in second round - Andry RAJOELINA 55.7%, Marc RAVALOMANANA 44.3%
expected date of next election: November 2028

Legislative branch: *legislative structure:* bicameral

Legislative branch - lower chamber: *chamber name:* National Assembly (Antenimierampirenena)
number of seats: 163 (all directly elected)
electoral system: mixed system
scope of elections: full renewal
term in office: 5 years
most recent election date: 5/29/2024
parties elected and seats per party: Isika Rehetra Miaraka Amin'i Andry Rajoelina (IRMAR) (84); Firaisankina (22); Independents (50); Other (7)
percentage of women in chamber: 14.1%
expected date of next election: May 2029

Legislative branch - upper chamber: *chamber name:* Senate (Antenimierandoholona)
number of seats: 18 (12 indirectly elected; 6 appointed)
term in office: 5 years
most recent election date: 12/11/2020
parties elected and seats per party: IRMAR (10); MALAGASY MIARA-MIAINGA (2)
percentage of women in chamber: 11.1%
expected date of next election: December 2025

Judicial branch: *highest court(s):* Supreme Court or Cour Suprême (consists of 11 members; addresses judicial administration issues only); High Constitutional Court or Haute Cour Constitutionnelle (consists of 9 members); High Court of Justice (consists of 11 members; addresses cases brought against the president of Madagascar and senior officials for high treason, grave violations of the Constitution, or breach of duties incompatible with the exercise of the presidential mandate)
judge selection and term of office: Supreme Court heads elected by the president and judiciary officials to serve 3-year, single renewable terms; High Constitutional Court members appointed - 3 each by the president, by both legislative bodies, and by the Council of Magistrates; members serve single, 7-year terms; High Court of Justice members include: first president of the Supreme Court; 2 presidents from the Court of Cassation; 2 presidents from the Court of Appeal; 2 deputies from the National Assembly; 2 senators from the Senate; 2 members from the High Council for the Defense of Democracy and the State of law
subordinate courts: Courts of Appeal; Court of Cassation; Courts of First Instance; military courts; traditional courts (dina); Trade Court

Political parties: Group of Young Malagasy Patriots (Groupe des Jeunes Malgaches Patriotes) or GJMP
I Love Madagascar (Tiako I Madagasikara) or TIM
Isika Rehetra Miaraka amin'i Andry Rajoelina coalition or IRD
Malagasy Aware (Malagasy Tonga Saina) or MTS
Malagasy Tia Tanindrazana or MATITA or ANGADY
Movement for Democracy in Madagascar (Mouvement pour la Démocratie à Madagascar) or MDM
Rally for Democratic Socialism (Rassemblement pour Socialisme Démocratique - Nouveau) or RPSD Vaovao
Young Malagasies Determined (Tanora Malagasy Vonona) or TGV

Diplomatic representation in the US: *chief of mission:* Ambassador Lantosoa RAKOTOMALALA (since 13 January 2025)

chancery: 2374 Massachusetts Avenue NW, Washington, DC 20008
telephone: [1] (202) 265-5525

FAX: [1] (202) 265-3034
email address and website: madagascar.embassy.dc@gmail.com
https://us-madagascar-embassy.org/

Diplomatic representation from the US: *chief of mission:* Ambassador Claire PIERANGELO (since 2 May 2022)
embassy: Lot 207A, Andranoro, Antehiroka, 105 Antananarivo - Madagascar
mailing address: 2040 Antananarivo Place, Washington DC 20521-2040
telephone: [261] 33-44-320-00

FAX: [261] 33-44-320-35
email address and website: antanACS@state.gov
https://mg.usembassy.gov/

International organization participation: ACP, AfDB, AU, CD, COMESA, EITI (candidate country), FAO, G-77, IAEA, IBRD, ICAO, ICC (NGOs), ICCt, ICRM, IDA, IFAD, IFC, IFRCS, ILO, IMF, IMO, InOC, Interpol, IOC, IOM, IPU, ISO (correspondent), ITSO, ITU, ITUC (NGOs), MIGA, NAM, OIF, OPCW, PCA, SADC, UN, UNCTAD, UNESCO, UNHCR, UNIDO, UNWTO, UPU, WCO, WFTU (NGOs), WHO, WIPO, WMO, WTO

Independence: 26 June 1960 (from France)

National holiday: Independence Day, 26 June (1960)

Flag: *description:* two equal horizontal bands of red (top) and green, with a vertical white band on the left side
meaning: red stands for sovereignty, green for hope, and white for purity

National symbol(s): traveller's palm (ravenala), zebu

National color(s): red, green, white

National anthem(s): *title:* "Ry Tanindraza nay malala o" (O Our Beloved Fatherland)
lyrics/music: Pasteur RAHAJASON/Norbert RAHARISOA
history: adopted 1959

National heritage: *total World Heritage Sites:* 3 (1 cultural, 2 natural)
selected World Heritage Site locales: Tsingy de Bemaraha Strict Nature Reserve (n); Ambohimanga Royal Hill (c); Atsinanana Rainforests (n)

ECONOMY

Economic overview: low-income East African island economy; natural resource rich; extreme poverty; return of political stability has helped growth; sharp tax revenue drop due to COVID-19; leading vanilla producer; environmentally fragile

Real GDP (purchasing power parity): $52.968 billion (2024 est.)
$50.833 billion (2023 est.)
$48.782 billion (2022 est.)
note: data in 2021 dollars
comparison ranking: 124

Real GDP growth rate: 4.2% (2024 est.)
4.2% (2023 est.)
4.2% (2022 est.)
note: annual GDP % growth based on constant local currency
comparison ranking: 64

Real GDP per capita: $1,700 (2024 est.)
$1,600 (2023 est.)
$1,600 (2022 est.)
note: data in 2021 dollars
comparison ranking: 209

GDP (official exchange rate): $17.421 billion (2024 est.)
note: data in current dollars at official exchange rate

Inflation rate (consumer prices): 9.9% (2023 est.)
8.2% (2022 est.)
5.8% (2021 est.)
note: annual % change based on consumer prices
comparison ranking: 177

GDP - composition, by sector of origin: *agriculture:* 22.5% (2024 est.)
industry: 22.8% (2024 est.)
services: 46.4% (2024 est.)
note: figures may not total 100% due to non-allocated consumption not captured in sector-reported data
comparison rankings: agriculture 28; industry 110; services 167

GDP - composition, by end use: *household consumption:* 69.8% (2024 est.)
government consumption: 15.3% (2024 est.)
investment in fixed capital: 22.6% (2024 est.)
investment in inventories: 0% (2024 est.)
exports of goods and services: 23.6% (2024 est.)
imports of goods and services: -31.3% (2024 est.)
note: figures may not total 100% due to rounding or gaps in data collection

Agricultural products: rice, sugarcane, cassava, sweet potatoes, milk, bananas, vegetables, mangoes/guavas, maize, potatoes (2023)
note: top ten agricultural products based on tonnage

Industries: meat processing, seafood, soap, beer, leather, sugar, textiles, glassware, cement, automobile assembly plant, paper, petroleum, tourism, mining

Industrial production growth rate: 3.7% (2024 est.)
note: annual % change in industrial value added based on constant local currency
comparison ranking: 66

Labor force: 16.519 million (2024 est.)
note: number of people ages 15 or older who are employed or seeking work
comparison ranking: 40

Unemployment rate: 3.1% (2024 est.)
3.1% (2023 est.)
3.2% (2022 est.)
note: % of labor force seeking employment
comparison ranking: 45

Youth unemployment rate (ages 15-24): *total:* 5.4% (2024 est.)
male: 5.3% (2024 est.)
female: 5.4% (2024 est.)
note: % of labor force ages 15-24 seeking employment
comparison ranking: total 159

Remittances: 2.4% of GDP (2023 est.)
2.5% of GDP (2022 est.)
3.1% of GDP (2021 est.)
note: personal transfers and compensation between resident and non-resident individuals/households/entities

Budget: *revenues:* $2.066 billion (2023 est.)
expenditures: $2.876 billion (2023 est.)
note: central government revenues and expenses (excluding grants/extrabudgetary units/social security funds) converted to US dollars at average official exchange rate for year indicated

Taxes and other revenues: 9.6% (of GDP) (2023 est.)
note: central government tax revenue as a % of GDP
comparison ranking: 132

Current account balance: -$829.376 million (2022 est.)
-$721.953 million (2021 est.)
-$623.653 million (2020 est.)
note: balance of payments - net trade and primary/secondary income in current dollars
comparison ranking: 123

Exports: $4.689 billion (2022 est.)
$3.362 billion (2021 est.)
$2.589 billion (2020 est.)
note: balance of payments - exports of goods and services in current dollars
comparison ranking: 140

Exports - partners: USA 16%, France 15%, Japan 8%, China 6%, S. Korea 6% (2023)
note: top five export partners based on percentage share of exports

Exports - commodities: garments, nickel, vanilla, cloves, gold (2023)
note: top five export commodities based on value in dollars

Imports: $6.041 billion (2022 est.)
$4.769 billion (2021 est.)
$3.718 billion (2020 est.)
note: balance of payments - imports of goods and services in current dollars
comparison ranking: 146

Imports - partners: China 19%, Oman 13%, France 10%, India 8%, South Africa 5% (2023)
note: top five import partners based on percentage share of imports

Imports - commodities: refined petroleum, rice, fabric, cotton fabric, wheat (2023)
note: top five import commodities based on value in dollars

Reserves of foreign exchange and gold: $2.785 billion (2024 est.)
$2.632 billion (2023 est.)
$2.16 billion (2022 est.)
note: holdings of gold (year-end prices)/foreign exchange/special drawing rights in current dollars
comparison ranking: 120

Debt - external: $3.548 billion (2023 est.)
note: present value of external debt in current US dollars
comparison ranking: 83

Exchange rates: Malagasy ariary (MGA) per US dollar -

Exchange rates: 4,525.425 (2024 est.)
4,429.579 (2023 est.)
4,096.116 (2022 est.)
3,829.978 (2021 est.)
3,787.754 (2020 est.)

ENERGY

Electricity access: *electrification - total population:* 36.1% (2022 est.)
electrification - urban areas: 71.6%
electrification - rural areas: 10.9%

Electricity: *installed generating capacity:* 759,000 kW (2023 est.)
consumption: 2.506 billion kWh (2023 est.)
transmission/distribution losses: 139 million kWh (2023 est.)
comparison rankings: installed generating capacity 142; consumption 148; transmission/distribution losses 52

Electricity generation sources: *fossil fuels:* 64.8% of total installed capacity (2023 est.)
solar: 3.2% of total installed capacity (2023 est.)
hydroelectricity: 31.1% of total installed capacity (2023 est.)
biomass and waste: 0.9% of total installed capacity (2023 est.)

Coal: *consumption:* 472,000 metric tons (2023 est.)
imports: 472,000 metric tons (2023 est.)
proven reserves: 150 million metric tons (2023 est.)

Petroleum: *refined petroleum consumption:* 20,000 bbl/day (2023 est.)

Energy consumption per capita: 1.816 million Btu/person (2023 est.)
comparison ranking: 187

COMMUNICATIONS

Telephones - fixed lines: *total subscriptions:* 3,000 (2023 est.)
subscriptions per 100 inhabitants: (2023 est.) less than 1
comparison ranking: total subscriptions 209

Telephones - mobile cellular: *total subscriptions:* 25.4 million (2023 est.)
subscriptions per 100 inhabitants: 70 (2022 est.)
comparison ranking: total subscriptions 55

Broadcast media: state-owned Radio Nationale Malagasy (RNM) and Television Malagasy (TVM) have an extensive national network reach; privately owned radio and TV broadcasters in cities and major towns; state-run radio dominates in rural areas; relays of 2 international broadcasters are available in Antananarivo (2019)

Internet country code: .mg

Internet users: *percent of population:* 20% (2023 est.)

Broadband - fixed subscriptions: *total:* 34,000 (2023 est.)
subscriptions per 100 inhabitants: (2023 est.) less than 1
comparison ranking: total 156

TRANSPORTATION

Civil aircraft registration country code prefix: 5R

Airports: 93 (2025)
comparison ranking: 58

Railways: *total:* 836 km (2018)
narrow gauge: 836 km (2018) 1.000-m gauge

Merchant marine: *total:* 29 (2023)
by type: general cargo 16, oil tanker 2, other 11
comparison ranking: total 135

Ports: *total ports:* 13 (2024)
large: 0
medium: 0
small: 2
very small: 11
ports with oil terminals: 5
key ports: Andoany, Antsiranana, Antsohim Bondrona, Iharana, Mahajanga, Maintirano, Manakara, Mananjary, Maroantsetra, Morondava, Toamasina, Tolanaro, Toliara

MILITARY AND SECURITY

Military and security forces: Madagascar Armed Forces (aka Armed forces of the Republic of Madagascar); Malagasy Army, Naval Forces (or National Navy), Air Force; Malagasy National Gendarmerie (2025)
note: the National Gendarmerie is under the Ministry of Defense but separate from the PAF and is responsible for maintaining law and order in rural areas at the village level, protecting government facilities, and operating a maritime police contingent; the National Police under the Ministry of Security is responsible for maintaining law and order in urban areas

Military expenditures: 0.7% of GDP (2024 est.)
0.7% of GDP (2023 est.)
0.7% of GDP (2022 est.)
0.7% of GDP (2021 est.)
0.7% of GDP (2020 est.)

Military and security service personnel strengths: estimated 13,000 Armed Forces; estimated 10,000 Gendarmerie (2025)

Military equipment inventories and acquisitions: the military's inventory consists mostly of older or secondhand weapons and equipment originating from countries such as France, South Africa, the UAE, the UK, and the former Soviet Union (2024)

Military service age and obligation: 18-25 years of age for men and women; service obligation 18 months; no conscription; women are permitted to serve in all branches (2023)

Military - note: the military's responsibilities include ensuring sovereignty and territorial integrity and protecting Madagascar's maritime domain, particularly against piracy, drug trafficking, and smuggling; it also assists the Gendarmerie with maintaining law and order in rural areas, largely in areas affected by banditry, cattle rustling, and criminal groups; the military has a history of influence in domestic politics and seized control of the government in October 2025; security relationships have included France, India, and Russia; Madagascar's small Navy has traditionally looked to India for assistance with maritime security (2025)

TRANSNATIONAL ISSUES

Refugees and internally displaced persons: *refugees:* 1,256 (2024 est.)

IDPs: 9,868 (2024 est.)

MALAWI

INTRODUCTION

Background: Malawi shares its name with the Chewa word for flames and is linked to the Maravi people from whom the Chewa language originated. The Maravi settled in what is now Malawi around 1400, during one of the later waves of Bantu migration across central and southern Africa. A powerful Maravi kingdom established around 1500 reached its zenith around 1700, when it controlled what is now southern and central Malawi and portions of neighboring Mozambique and Zambia. The kingdom eventually declined because of destabilization from the escalating global trade in enslaved people. In the early 1800s, widespread conflict in southern Africa displaced various ethnic Ngoni groups, some of which moved into Malawi and further undermined the Maravi. Members of the Yao ethnic group – which had long traded with Malawi from Mozambique – introduced Islam and began to settle in Malawi in significant numbers in the mid-1800s, followed by members of the Lomwe ethnic group. British missionary and trading activity increased in the area around Lake Nyasa in the mid-1800s, and in 1891, Britain declared a protectorate called British Central Africa over what is now Malawi. The British renamed the territory Nyasaland in 1907, and it was part of the colonial Federation of Rhodesia and Nyasaland – including present-day Zambia and Zimbabwe – from 1953 to 1963 before gaining independence as Malawi in 1964.

Hastings Kamuzu BANDA served as prime minister at independence and then as president when the country became a republic in 1966. He later instituted one-party rule under his Malawi Congress Party (MCP) and was declared president for life. After three decades of one-party rule, the country held multiparty presidential and parliamentary elections in 1994 under a provisional constitution that came into full effect the following year. Bakili MULUZI of the United Democratic Front party became the first freely elected president of Malawi when he defeated BANDA at the polls in 1994; he won reelection in 1999. President Bingu wa MUTHARIKA was elected in 2004 and reelected to a second term in 2009. He died abruptly in 2012 and was succeeded by Vice President Joyce BANDA. MUTHARIKA's brother, Peter MUTHARIKA, defeated BANDA in the election in 2014. Peter MUTHARIKA was reelected in a disputed election in 2019 that resulted in countrywide protests. The courts ordered a new election, and in 2020, Lazarus CHAKWERA of the MCP was elected president. Population growth, increasing pressure on agricultural lands, corruption, and HIV/AIDS pose major problems for Malawi.

GEOGRAPHY

Location: Southern Africa, east of Zambia, west and north of Mozambique

Geographic coordinates: 13 30 S, 34 00 E

Map references: Africa

Area: *total:* 118,484 sq km
land: 94,080 sq km
water: 24,404 sq km
comparison ranking: total 100

Area - comparative: slightly smaller than Pennsylvania

Land boundaries: *total:* 2,857 km
border countries (3): Mozambique 1,498 km; Tanzania 512 km; Zambia 847 km

Coastline: 0 km (landlocked)

Maritime claims: none (landlocked)

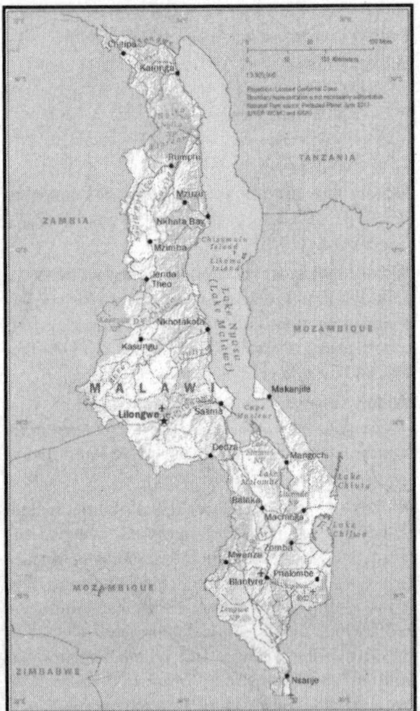

Climate: sub-tropical; rainy season (November to May); dry season (May to November)

Terrain: narrow elongated plateau with rolling plains, rounded hills, some mountains

Elevation: *highest point:* Sapitwa (Mount Mlanje) 3,002 m
lowest point: junction of the Shire River and international boundary with Mozambique 37 m
mean elevation: 779 m

Natural resources: limestone, arable land, hydropower, unexploited deposits of uranium, coal, and bauxite

Land use: *agricultural land:* 64.2% (2022 est.)
arable land: 42.4% (2022 est.)
permanent crops: 2.1% (2022 est.)
permanent pasture: 19.6% (2022 est.)
forest: 22.9% (2022 est.)
other: 12.9% (2022 est.)

Irrigated land: 740 sq km (2012)

Major lakes (area sq km): *fresh water lake(s):* Lake Malawi (shared with Mozambique and Tanzania) - 22,490
salt water lake(s): Lake Chilwa - 1,040 sq km

Major rivers (by length in km): Zambezi (shared with Zambia [s], Angola, Zimbabwe, Namibia, Tanzania, and Mozambique [m]) - 2,740 km
note: [s] after country name indicates river source; [m] after country name indicates river mouth

Major watersheds (area sq km): Atlantic Ocean drainage: Congo (3,730,881 sq km)

Indian Ocean drainage: Zambezi (1,332,412 sq km)

Population distribution: population density is highest south of Lake Nyasa, as shown in this population distribution map

Natural hazards: flooding; droughts; earthquakes

Geography - note: landlocked; Lake Nyasa, about 580 km (360 mi) long, is the country's most prominent physical feature; it contains more fish species than any other lake on earth

PEOPLE AND SOCIETY

Population: *total:* 21,763,309 (2024 est.)
male: 10,674,594
female: 11,088,715
comparison rankings: total 62; male 61; female 62

Nationality: *noun:* Malawian(s)
adjective: Malawian

Ethnic groups: Chewa 34.3%, Lomwe 18.8%, Yao 13.2%, Ngoni 10.4%, Tumbuka 9.2%, Sena 3.8%, Mang'anja 3.2%, Tonga 1.8%, Nyanja 1.8%, Nkhonde 1%, other 2.2%, foreign 0.3% (2018 est.)

Languages: English (official), Chewa (dominant), Lambya, Lomwe, Ngoni, Nkhonde, Nyakyusa, Nyanja, Sena, Tonga, Tumbuka, Yao
note: Chewa and Nyanja are mutually intelligible dialects; Nkhonde and Nyakyusa are mutually intelligible dialects

Religions: Protestant 33.5% (includes Church of Central Africa Presbyterian 14.2%, Seventh Day Adventist/Baptist 9.4%, Pentecostal 7.6%, Anglican 2.3%), Roman Catholic 17.2%, other Christian 26.6%, Muslim 13.8%, traditionalist 1.1%, other 5.6%, none 2.1% (2018 est.)

Age structure: *0-14 years:* 37.7% (male 4,080,567/female 4,132,710)
15-64 years: 58.4% (male 6,217,761/female 6,487,273)
65 years and over: 3.9% (2024 est.) (male 376,266/female 468,732)

Dependency ratios: *total dependency ratio:* 71.3 (2024 est.)
youth dependency ratio: 64.6 (2024 est.)
elderly dependency ratio: 6.7 (2024 est.)
potential support ratio: 15 (2024 est.)

Median age: *total:* 20.3 years (2024 est.)
male: 20 years
female: 20.6 years
comparison ranking: total 204

Population growth rate: 2.22% (2024 est.)
comparison ranking: 31

Birth rate: 26.6 births/1,000 population (2024 est.)
comparison ranking: 40

Death rate: 4.5 deaths/1,000 population (2024 est.)
comparison ranking: 207

Net migration rate: 0 migrant(s)/1,000 population (2024 est.)
comparison ranking: 88

Population distribution: population density is highest south of Lake Nyasa, as shown in this population distribution map

Urbanization: *urban population:* 18.3% of total population (2023)
rate of urbanization: 4.41% annual rate of change (2020-25 est.)

Major urban areas - population: 1.276 million LILONGWE (capital), 1.031 million Blantyre-Limbe (2023)

Sex ratio: *at birth:* 1.01 male(s)/female
0-14 years: 0.99 male(s)/female
15-64 years: 0.96 male(s)/female
65 years and over: 0.8 male(s)/female
total population: 0.96 male(s)/female (2024 est.)

Mother's mean age at first birth: 19.1 years (2015/16 est.)
note: data represents median age at first birth among women 20-49

Maternal mortality ratio: 225 deaths/100,000 live births (2023 est.)
comparison ranking: 37

Infant mortality rate: *total:* 31.9 deaths/1,000 live births (2024 est.)
male: 36.4 deaths/1,000 live births
female: 27.4 deaths/1,000 live births
comparison ranking: total 44

Life expectancy at birth: *total population:* 73 years (2024 est.)
male: 69.9 years
female: 76.1 years
comparison ranking: total population 155

Total fertility rate: 3.19 children born/woman (2024 est.)
comparison ranking: 44

Gross reproduction rate: 1.58 (2024 est.)

Drinking water source: *improved: urban:* 85.9% of population (2022 est.)
rural: 68.8% of population (2022 est.)
total: 71.9% of population (2022 est.)
unimproved: urban: 14.1% of population (2022 est.)
rural: 31.2% of population (2022 est.)
total: 28.1% of population (2022 est.)

Health expenditure: 7.4% of GDP (2021)
3.3% of national budget (2022 est.)

Physician density: 0.05 physicians/1,000 population (2022)

Sanitation facility access: *improved: urban:* 87.1% of population (2022 est.)
rural: 73.4% of population (2022 est.)
total: 75.8% of population (2022 est.)
unimproved: urban: 12.9% of population (2022 est.)
rural: 26.6% of population (2022 est.)
total: 24.2% of population (2022 est.)

Obesity - adult prevalence rate: 5.8% (2016)
comparison ranking: 174

Alcohol consumption per capita: *total:* 2.04 liters of pure alcohol (2019 est.)
beer: 0.08 liters of pure alcohol (2019 est.)
wine: 0 liters of pure alcohol (2019 est.)
spirits: 0.25 liters of pure alcohol (2019 est.)
other alcohols: 1.7 liters of pure alcohol (2019 est.)
comparison ranking: total 129

Tobacco use: *total:* 6.3% (2025 est.)
male: 11.7% (2025 est.)
female: 1.4% (2025 est.)
comparison ranking: total 156

Children under the age of 5 years underweight: 11.7% (2020)
comparison ranking: 43

Currently married women (ages 15-49): 60.7% (2022 est.)

Child marriage: *women married by age 15:* 7.5% (2020)
women married by age 18: 37.7% (2020)
men married by age 18: 7% (2020)

Education expenditure: 3.3% of GDP (2018 est.)
1.2% national budget (2024 est.)
comparison ranking: Education expenditure (% GDP) 135

Literacy: *total population:* 70.2% (2020 est.)
male: 78.6% (2020 est.)
female: 62.7% (2020 est.)

School life expectancy (primary to tertiary education): *total:* 10 years (2021 est.)
male: 10 years (2021 est.)
female: 10 years (2021 est.)

ENVIRONMENT

Environmental issues: deforestation; land degradation; water pollution from agricultural runoff, sewage, industrial wastes; siltation of fish spawning grounds; high temperatures and changing precipitation patterns

International environmental agreements: *party to:* Biodiversity, Climate Change, Climate Change-Kyoto Protocol, Climate Change-Paris Agreement, Comprehensive Nuclear Test Ban, Desertification, Endangered Species, Environmental Modification, Hazardous Wastes, Law of the Sea, Marine Life Conservation, Nuclear Test Ban, Ozone Layer Protection, Ship Pollution, Wetlands
signed, but not ratified: none of the selected agreements

Climate: sub-tropical; rainy season (November to May); dry season (May to November)

Urbanization: *urban population:* 18.3% of total population (2023)
rate of urbanization: 4.41% annual rate of change (2020-25 est.)

Carbon dioxide emissions: 2.265 million metric tonnes of CO2 (2023 est.)
from coal and metallurgical coke: 65,000 metric tonnes of CO2 (2023 est.)
from petroleum and other liquids: 2.2 million metric tonnes of CO2 (2023 est.)
comparison ranking: total emissions 158

Particulate matter emissions: 18.5 micrograms per cubic meter (2019 est.)

Waste and recycling: *municipal solid waste generated annually:* 1.298 million tons (2024 est.)
percent of municipal solid waste recycled: 9.6% (2022 est.)

Total water withdrawal: *municipal:* 143.1 million cubic meters (2022 est.)
industrial: 47.7 million cubic meters (2022 est.)
agricultural: 1.166 billion cubic meters (2022 est.)

Total renewable water resources: 17.28 billion cubic meters (2022 est.)

GOVERNMENT

Country name: *conventional long form:* Republic of Malawi
conventional short form: Malawi
local long form: Dziko la Malawi
local short form: Malawi
former: British Central African Protectorate, Nyasaland Protectorate, Nyasaland
etymology: named for the Maravi people who inhabited the area since the 14th century; the word *maravi* means "flames"

Government type: presidential republic

Capital: *name:* Lilongwe
geographic coordinates: 13 58 S, 33 47 E
time difference: UTC+2 (7 hours ahead of Washington, DC, during Standard Time)
etymology: named after the Lilongwe River that flows through the city; the origin of the river's name is unclear

Administrative divisions: 28 districts; Balaka, Blantyre, Chikwawa, Chiradzulu, Chitipa, Dedza, Dowa, Karonga, Kasungu, Likoma, Lilongwe, Machinga, Mangochi, Mchinji, Mulanje, Mwanza, Mzimba, Neno, Ntcheu, Nkhata Bay, Nkhotakota, Nsanje, Ntchisi, Phalombe, Rumphi, Salima, Thyolo, Zomba

Legal system: mixed system of English common law and customary law; Supreme Court of Appeal reviews legislative acts

Constitution: *history:* previous 1953 (pre-independence), 1964, 1966; latest drafted January to May 1994, approved 16 May 1994, entered into force 18 May 1995
amendment process: proposed by the National Assembly; passage of amendments affecting constitutional articles, including the sovereignty and territory of the state, fundamental constitutional principles, human rights, voting rights, and the judiciary, requires majority approval in a referendum and majority approval by the Assembly; passage of other amendments requires at least two-thirds majority vote of the Assembly

International law organization participation: accepts compulsory ICJ jurisdiction with reservations; accepts ICCt jurisdiction

Citizenship: *citizenship by birth:* no
citizenship by descent only: at least one parent must be a citizen of Malawi
dual citizenship recognized: no
residency requirement for naturalization: 7 years

Suffrage: 18 years of age; universal

Executive branch: *chief of state:* President Peter MUTHARIKA (since 4 October)
head of government: Vice President Jane ANSAH (since 4 October)
cabinet: Cabinet named by the president
election/appointment process: president directly elected by simple-majority popular vote for a 5-year term (eligible for a second term)
most recent election date: September 2030
election results: *2025:* Peter MUTHARIKA elected president; percent of vote- Peter MUTHARIKA (DPP) 56.8%, Lazarus CHAKWERA (MCP) 33.0%, Dalitso KABAMBE (UTM) 3.95, Atupele MULUZI (UDF) 1.92%, Joyce BANDA (PP) 1.61%, other 2.72%
2020: Lazarus CHAKWERA elected president; Lazarus CHAKWERA (MCP) 59.3%, Peter Mutharika (DPP) 39.9%, other 0.8%
expected date of next election: September 2030
note: the president is both chief of state and head of government

Legislative branch: *legislature name:* National Assembly
legislative structure: unicameral
number of seats: 193 (all directly elected)
electoral system: plurality/majority
scope of elections: full renewal
term in office: 5 years
most recent election date: 5/21/2019
parties elected and seats per party: Democratic Progressive Party (DPP) (62); Malawi Congress Party (MCP) (55); United Democratic Front (UDF) (10); Independents (55); Other (10)
percentage of women in chamber: 20.7%
expected date of next election: September 2025

Judicial branch: *highest court(s):* Supreme Court of Appeal (consists of the chief justice and at least 3 judges)
judge selection and term of office: Supreme Court chief justice appointed by the president and confirmed by the National Assembly; other judges appointed by the president on the recommendation of the Judicial Service Commission, which regulates judicial officers; judges serve until age 65
subordinate courts: High Court; magistrate courts; Industrial Relations Court; district and city traditional or local courts

Political parties: Democratic Progressive Party or DPP
Malawi Congress Party or MCP
People's Party or PP
United Democratic Front or UDF
United Transformation Movement or UTM

Diplomatic representation in the US: *chief of mission:* Ambassador Esme Jynet CHOMBO (since 19 April 2022)
chancery: 2408 Massachusetts Avenue NW, Washington, DC 20008
telephone: [1] (202) 451- 0409
email address and website: malawidc@aol.com
Home | Malawi Embassy USA

Diplomatic representation from the US: *chief of mission:* Ambassador (vacant); Chargé d'Affaires Jonathan FISCHER (since 8 August 2025)
embassy: 16 Jomo Kenyatta Road, Lilongwe 3
mailing address: 2280 Lilongwe Place, Washington DC 20521-2280
telephone: [265] (0) 177-3166
FAX: [265] (0) 177-0471
email address and website: LilongweConsular@state.gov
https://mw.usembassy.gov/

International organization participation: ACP, AfDB, AU, C, CD, COMESA, FAO, G-77, IAEA, IBRD, ICAO, ICCt, ICRM, IDA, IFAD, IFC, IFRCS, ILO, IMF, IMO, Interpol, IOC, IOM, IPU, ISO (correspondent), ITSO, ITU, ITUC (NGOs), MIGA, MINURSO, MONUSCO, NAM, OPCW, SADC, UN, UNCTAD, UNESCO, UNHCR, UNHRC, UNIDO, UNISFA, UNOCI, UNWTO, UPU, WCO, WFTU (NGOs), WHO, WIPO, WMO, WTO

Independence: 6 July 1964 (from the UK)

National holiday: Independence Day, 6 July (1964)
note: also called Republic Day since 6 July 1966

Flag: *description:* three equal horizontal bands of black (top), red, and green, with a rising red sun centered on the black band
meaning: black stands for ethnic groups, red for the blood shed in the struggle for freedom, and green for nature; the sun represents the hope of freedom for the continent of Africa

National symbol(s): lion

National color(s): black, red, green

National anthem(s): *title:* "Mulungu dalitsa Malawi" (O God, Bless Our Land of Malawi)
lyrics/music: Michael-Fredrick Paul SAUKA
history: adopted 1964

National heritage: *total World Heritage Sites:* 3 (2 cultural, 1 natural)
selected World Heritage Site locales: Lake Malawi National Park (n); Chongoni Rock-Art Area (c); Mount Mulanje Cultural Landscape (c)

ECONOMY

Economic overview: low-income East African economy; primarily agrarian; investing in human capital; urban poverty increasing due to COVID-19; high public debt; endemic corruption and poor property rights; poor hydroelectric grid; localized pharmaceutical industry

Real GDP (purchasing power parity): $35.425 billion (2024 est.)
$34.789 billion (2023 est.)
$34.143 billion (2022 est.)
note: data in 2021 dollars
comparison ranking: 141

Real GDP growth rate: 1.8% (2024 est.)
1.9% (2023 est.)
0.9% (2022 est.)
note: annual GDP % growth based on constant local currency
comparison ranking: 155

Real GDP per capita: $1,600 (2024 est.)
$1,600 (2023 est.)
$1,700 (2022 est.)
note: data in 2021 dollars
comparison ranking: 210

GDP (official exchange rate): $11.009 billion (2024 est.)
note: data in current dollars at official exchange rate

Inflation rate (consumer prices): 32.2% (2024 est.)
28.8% (2023 est.)
21% (2022 est.)
note: annual % change based on consumer prices
comparison ranking: 199

GDP - composition, by sector of origin: *agriculture:* 32.4% (2024 est.)
industry: 16% (2024 est.)
services: 44.9% (2024 est.)
note: figures may not total 100% due to non-allocated consumption not captured in sector-reported data
comparison rankings: agriculture 11; industry 160; services 175

Agricultural products: sweet potatoes, cassava, maize, sugarcane, mangoes/guavas, potatoes, tomatoes, pigeon peas, pumpkins/squash, plantains (2023)
note: top ten agricultural products based on tonnage

Industries: tobacco, tea, sugar, sawmill products, cement, consumer goods

Industrial production growth rate: 2.1% (2024 est.)
note: annual % change in industrial value added based on constant local currency
comparison ranking: 98

Labor force: 8.602 million (2024 est.)
note: number of people ages 15 or older who are employed or seeking work
comparison ranking: 61

Unemployment rate: 5.1% (2024 est.)
5.1% (2023 est.)
5.1% (2022 est.)
note: % of labor force seeking employment
comparison ranking: 89

Youth unemployment rate (ages 15-24): *total:* 6.8% (2024 est.)
male: 6.4% (2024 est.)
female: 7.1% (2024 est.)
note: % of labor force ages 15-24 seeking employment
comparison ranking: total 146

Population below poverty line: 50.7% (2019 est.)
note: % of population with income below national poverty line

Gini Index coefficient - distribution of family income: 38.5 (2019 est.)
note: index (0-100) of income distribution; higher values represent greater inequality
comparison ranking: 49

Household income or consumption by percentage share: *lowest 10%:* 2.9% (2019 est.)
highest 10%: 31% (2019 est.)
note: % share of income accruing to lowest and highest 10% of population

Remittances: 1.4% of GDP (2023 est.)
2.1% of GDP (2022 est.)
2.6% of GDP (2021 est.)
note: personal transfers and compensation between resident and non-resident individuals/households/entities

Budget: *revenues:* $2.208 billion (2022 est.)
expenditures: $3.523 billion (2022 est.)
note: central government revenues and expenses (excluding grants/extrabudgetary units/social security funds) converted to US dollars at average official exchange rate for year indicated

Public debt: 55.6% of GDP (2022 est.)
note: central government debt as a % of GDP
comparison ranking: 87

Taxes and other revenues: 13.5% (of GDP) (2022 est.)
note: central government tax revenue as a % of GDP
comparison ranking: 103

Current account balance: -$2.276 billion (2023 est.)
-$2.218 billion (2022 est.)
-$1.918 billion (2021 est.)
note: balance of payments - net trade and primary/secondary income in current dollars
comparison ranking: 151

Exports: $1.526 billion (2023 est.)
$1.487 billion (2022 est.)
$1.587 billion (2021 est.)
note: balance of payments - exports of goods and services in current dollars
comparison ranking: 173

Exports - partners: Germany 11%, India 7%, Zimbabwe 6%, South Africa 5%, USA 5% (2023)
note: top five export partners based on percentage share of exports

Exports - commodities: tobacco, tea, dried legumes, soybean meal, raw sugar (2023)
note: top five export commodities based on value in dollars

Imports: $3.995 billion (2023 est.)
$3.834 billion (2022 est.)
$3.768 billion (2021 est.)
note: balance of payments - imports of goods and services in current dollars
comparison ranking: 158

Imports - partners: China 17%, South Africa 16%, UAE 12%, India 7%, Tanzania 7% (2023)
note: top five import partners based on percentage share of imports

Imports - commodities: refined petroleum, fertilizers, plastics, garments, postage stamps/documents (2023)
note: top five import commodities based on value in dollars

Reserves of foreign exchange and gold: $594.498 million (2020 est.)
$846.84 million (2019 est.)
$766.155 million (2018 est.)
note: holdings of gold (year-end prices)/foreign exchange/special drawing rights in current dollars
comparison ranking: 155

Debt - external: $2.269 billion (2023 est.)
note: present value of external debt in current US dollars
comparison ranking: 94

Exchange rates: Malawian kwachas (MWK) per US dollar -
Exchange rates: 1,161.094 (2023 est.)
949.039 (2022 est.)
805.9 (2021 est.)
749.527 (2020 est.)
745.541 (2019 est.)

ENERGY

Electricity access: *electrification - total population:* 14% (2022 est.)
electrification - urban areas: 54%
electrification - rural areas: 5.6%

Electricity: *installed generating capacity:* 731,000 kW (2023 est.)
consumption: 1.585 billion kWh (2023 est.)
exports: 19.938 million kWh (2023 est.)
transmission/distribution losses: 231.785 million kWh (2023 est.)
comparison rankings: installed generating capacity 145; consumption 155; exports 98; transmission/distribution losses 68

Electricity generation sources: *fossil fuels:* 4.2% of total installed capacity (2023 est.)
solar: 0.7% of total installed capacity (2023 est.)
hydroelectricity: 92.2% of total installed capacity (2023 est.)
biomass and waste: 3% of total installed capacity (2023 est.)

Coal: *production:* 3,000 metric tons (2023 est.)
consumption: 22,000 metric tons (2023 est.)
imports: 19,000 metric tons (2023 est.)
proven reserves: 801.999 million metric tons (2023 est.)

Petroleum: *refined petroleum consumption:* 15,000 bbl/day (2023 est.)

Energy consumption per capita: 1.792 million Btu/person (2023 est.)
comparison ranking: 189

COMMUNICATIONS

Telephones - fixed lines: *total subscriptions:* 5,000 (2023 est.)
subscriptions per 100 inhabitants: (2023 est.) less than 1
comparison ranking: total subscriptions 202

Telephones - mobile cellular: *total subscriptions:* 12.9 million (2023 est.)
subscriptions per 100 inhabitants: 60 (2022 est.)
comparison ranking: total subscriptions 80

Broadcast media: radio is the main broadcast medium; privately owned Zodiak radio has the widest national reach, followed by state-run radio; numerous private and community radio stations broadcast in cities and towns; the largest TV network is state-owned, but at least 4 private TV networks broadcast in urban areas; relays of multiple international broadcasters are available (2019)

Internet country code: .mw

Internet users: *percent of population:* 18% (2023 est.)

Broadband - fixed subscriptions: *total:* 17,000 (2023 est.)
subscriptions per 100 inhabitants: (2023 est.) less than 1
comparison ranking: total 176

TRANSPORTATION

Civil aircraft registration country code prefix: 7Q

Airports: 27 (2025)

comparison ranking: 125

Railways: *total:* 767 km (2014)
narrow gauge: 767 km (2014) 1.067-m gauge

MILITARY AND SECURITY

Military and security forces: Malawi Defense Force (MDF): Malawi Army (Land Forces), Malawi Maritime Force (MMF), Malawi Air Force (MAF), Malawi National Service (MNS)

Ministry of Homeland Security: Malawi Police Service (2025)
note: the MDF reports directly to the president as commander in chief

Military expenditures: 0.8% of GDP (2024 est.)
1% of GDP (2023 est.)
0.8% of GDP (2022 est.)
0.9% of GDP (2021 est.)
0.9% of GDP (2020 est.)

Military and security service personnel strengths: estimated 10,000 active Malawi Defense Forces (2025)

Military equipment inventories and acquisitions: the MDF's inventory is a mix of mostly older or secondhand equipment originating from such countries as France, South Africa, and the UK (2024)

Military service age and obligation: 18-30years of age for men and women for voluntary military service; high school equivalent required for enlisted recruits and college equivalent for officer recruits; initial engagement is 7 years for enlisted personnel and 10 years for officers (2023)

Military deployments: 750 Democratic Republic of the Congo (MONUSCO) (2025)

Military - note: the MDF's primary responsibility is external security; it is also tasked as necessary with providing support to civilian authorities during emergencies, supporting the Police Service, protecting national forest reserves, and participating in regional peacekeeping missions, as well as assisting with infrastructure development; key areas of concern include border security, regional conflict, and international terrorism; the MDF participates in exercises with foreign partners and contributes regularly to African Union and UN peace support operations; Malawi contributes regularly to African Union and UN peace support operations
the MDF was established in 1964 from elements of the Kings African Rifles (KAR), a British colonial regiment raised from Great Britain's various possessions in East Africa from 1902 until independence in the 1960s; the KAR conducted both military and internal security functions within the colonial territories, and served outside the territories during the World Wars (2025)

TRANSNATIONAL ISSUES

Refugees and internally displaced persons: *refugees:* 56,659 (2024 est.)

IDPs: 135,728 (2024 est.)

MALAYSIA

INTRODUCTION

Background: Malaysia's location has long made it an important cultural, economic, historical, social, and trade link between the islands of Southeast Asia and the mainland. Through the Strait of Malacca, which separates the Malay Peninsula from the archipelago, flowed maritime trade and with it influences from China, India, the Middle East, and the east coast of Africa. Prior to the 14th century, several powerful maritime empires existed in what is modern-day Malaysia, including the Srivijayan, which controlled much of the southern part of the peninsula between the 7th and 13th centuries, and the Majapahit Empire, which took control over most of the peninsula and the Malay Archipelago between the 13th and 14th centuries. The adoption of Islam between the 13th and 17th centuries also saw the rise of a number of powerful maritime states and sultanates on the Malay Peninsula and the island of Borneo, such as the port city of Malacca (Melaka), which at its height in the 15th century had a navy and hosted thousands of Chinese, Arab, Persian, and Indian merchants.

The Portuguese in the 16th century and the Dutch in the 17th century were the first European colonial powers to establish themselves on the Malay Peninsula and in Southeast Asia. However, it was the British who ultimately secured hegemony across the territory and during the late 18th and 19th centuries established colonies and protectorates in the area that is now Malaysia. Japan occupied these holdings from 1942 to 1945. In 1948, the British-ruled territories on the Malay Peninsula (except Singapore) formed the Federation of Malaya, which became independent in 1957. Malaysia was formed in 1963 when the former British colonies of Singapore, as well as Sabah and Sarawak on the northern coast of Borneo, joined the Federation.

A communist insurgency, confrontations with Indonesia, Philippine claims to Sabah, and Singapore's expulsion in 1965 marred the first several years of the country's independence. During the 22-year term of Prime Minister MAHATHIR Mohamad (1981-2003), Malaysia was successful in diversifying its economy from dependence on exports of raw materials to the development of manufacturing, services, and tourism. Former Prime Minister MAHATHIR and a newly formed coalition of opposition parties defeated Prime Minister Mohamed NAJIB bin Abdul Razak's United Malays National Organization (UMNO) in 2018, ending over 60 years of uninterrupted UMNO rule. From 2018-2022, Malaysia underwent considerable political upheaval, with a succession of coalition governments holding power. Following legislative elections in 2022, ANWAR Ibrahim was appointed prime minister after more than 20 years in opposition. His political coalition, Pakatan Harapan (PH), joined its longtime UNMO rival to form a government, but the two groups have remained deeply divided on many issues.

GEOGRAPHY

Location: Southeastern Asia, peninsula bordering Thailand and northern one-third of the island of Borneo, bordering Indonesia, Brunei, and the South China Sea, south of Vietnam

Geographic coordinates: 2 30 N, 112 30 E

Map references: Southeast Asia

Area: *total:* 329,847 sq km
land: 328,657 sq km
water: 1,190 sq km
comparison ranking: total 68

Area - comparative: slightly larger than New Mexico

Land boundaries: *total:* 2,742 km
border countries (3): Brunei 266 km; Indonesia 1,881 km; Thailand 595 km

Coastline: 4,675 km (Peninsular Malaysia 2,068 km; East Malaysia 2,607 km)

Maritime claims: *territorial sea:* 12 nm
exclusive economic zone: 200 nm
continental shelf: 200-m depth or to the depth of exploitation; specified boundary in the South China Sea

Climate: tropical; annual southwest (April to October) and northeast (October to February) monsoons

Terrain: coastal plains rising to hills and mountains

Elevation: *highest point:* Gunung Kinabalu 4,095 m
lowest point: Indian Ocean 0 m
mean elevation: 419 m

Natural resources: tin, petroleum, timber, copper, iron ore, natural gas, bauxite

Land use: *agricultural land:* 26.1% (2022 est.)
arable land: 2.5% (2022 est.)
permanent crops: 22.7% (2022 est.)
permanent pasture: 0.9% (2022 est.)
forest: 57.9% (2022 est.)
other: 16% (2022 est.)

Irrigated land: 4,420 sq km (2022)

Population distribution: a highly uneven distribution, with over 80% of the population residing on the Malay Peninsula

Natural hazards: flooding; landslides; forest fires

Geography - note: strategic location along Strait of Malacca and southern South China Sea

PEOPLE AND SOCIETY

Population: *total:* 34,564,810 (2024 est.)
male: 17,666,212
female: 16,898,598

comparison rankings: total 45; male 43; female 45

Nationality: *noun:* Malaysian(s)
adjective: Malaysian

Ethnic groups: Bumiputera 63.8% (Malay 52.8% and indigenous peoples, including Orang Asli, Dayak, Anak Negeri, 11%), Chinese 20.6%, Indian 6%, other 0.6%, non-citizens 9% (2023 est.)

Languages: Bahasa Malaysia (official), English, Chinese (Cantonese, Mandarin, Hokkien, Hakka, Hainan, Foochow), Tamil, Telugu, Malayalam, Panjabi, Thai
major-language sample(s):
Buku Fakta Dunia, sumber yang diperlukan untuk maklumat asas. (Bahasa Malaysia)
note: Malaysia has 134 languages (112 indigenous and 22 non-indigenous); in East Malaysia, there are several indigenous languages, and the most widely spoken are Iban and Kadazan

Religions: Muslim (official) 63.5%, Buddhist 18.7%, Christian 9.1%, Hindu 6.1%, other (Confucianism, Taoism, other traditional Chinese religions) 0.9%, none/unspecified 1.8% (2020 est.)

Age structure: *0-14 years:* 22.2% (male 3,947,914/female 3,730,319)
15-64 years: 69.4% (male 12,308,938/female 11,666,947)
65 years and over: 8.4% (2024 est.) (male 1,409,360/female 1,501,332)

Dependency ratios: *total dependency ratio:* 44.2 (2024 est.)
youth dependency ratio: 32 (2024 est.)
elderly dependency ratio: 12.1 (2024 est.)
potential support ratio: 8.2 (2024 est.)

Median age: *total:* 31.8 years (2024 est.)
male: 31.7 years
female: 31.9 years
comparison ranking: total 122

Population growth rate: 0.99% (2024 est.)
comparison ranking: 94

Birth rate: 14.2 births/1,000 population (2024 est.)
comparison ranking: 120

Death rate: 5.8 deaths/1,000 population (2024 est.)
comparison ranking: 166

Net migration rate: 1.5 migrant(s)/1,000 population (2024 est.)
comparison ranking: 57

Population distribution: a highly uneven distribution, with over 80% of the population residing on the Malay Peninsula

Urbanization: *urban population:* 78.7% of total population (2023)
rate of urbanization: 1.87% annual rate of change (2020-25 est.)

Major urban areas - population: 8.622 million KUALA LUMPUR (capital), 1.086 million Johor Bahru, 857,000 Ipoh (2023)

Sex ratio: *at birth:* 1.07 male(s)/female
0-14 years: 1.06 male(s)/female
15-64 years: 1.06 male(s)/female
65 years and over: 0.94 male(s)/female
total population: 1.05 male(s)/female (2024 est.)

Maternal mortality ratio: 26 deaths/100,000 live births (2023 est.)
comparison ranking: 119

Infant mortality rate: *total:* 6.4 deaths/1,000 live births (2024 est.)
male: 6.8 deaths/1,000 live births
female: 6 deaths/1,000 live births
comparison ranking: total 164

Life expectancy at birth: *total population:* 76.6 years (2024 est.)
male: 75 years
female: 78.4 years
comparison ranking: total population 106

Total fertility rate: 1.73 children born/woman (2024 est.)
comparison ranking: 156

Gross reproduction rate: 0.84 (2024 est.)

Drinking water source: *improved: urban:* 99.1% of population (2022 est.)
rural: 90.1% of population (2022 est.)
total: 97.2% of population (2022 est.)
unimproved: urban: 0.9% of population (2022 est.)
rural: 9.9% of population (2022 est.)
total: 2.8% of population (2022 est.)

Health expenditure: 4.4% of GDP (2021)
8% of national budget (2022 est.)

Physician density: 2.34 physicians/1,000 population (2023)

Hospital bed density: 2 beds/1,000 population (2021 est.)

Sanitation facility access: *improved: urban:* 100% of population (2022 est.)
rural: 99.9% of population (2022 est.)
total: 100% of population (2022 est.)
unimproved: urban: 0% of population (2022 est.)
rural: 0.1% of population (2022 est.)
total: 0% of population (2022 est.)

Obesity - adult prevalence rate: 15.6% (2016)
comparison ranking: 125

Alcohol consumption per capita: *total:* 0.64 liters of pure alcohol (2019 est.)
beer: 0.48 liters of pure alcohol (2019 est.)
wine: 0.04 liters of pure alcohol (2019 est.)
spirits: 0.11 liters of pure alcohol (2019 est.)
other alcohols: 0.01 liters of pure alcohol (2019 est.)
comparison ranking: total 158

Tobacco use: *total:* 21.5% (2025 est.)
male: 41.8% (2025 est.)
female: 0.6% (2025 est.)
comparison ranking: total 58

Children under the age of 5 years underweight: 14.1% (2019)
comparison ranking: 36

Currently married women (ages 15-49): 59.3% (2023 est.)

Education expenditure: 3.6% of GDP (2023 est.)
17.1% national budget (2023 est.)
comparison ranking: Education expenditure (% GDP) 129

Literacy: *total population:* 96% (2022 est.)
male: 97% (2022 est.)
female: 95% (2022 est.)

School life expectancy (primary to tertiary education): *total:* 12 years (2023 est.)
male: 11 years (2023 est.)
female: 12 years (2023 est.)

ENVIRONMENT

Environmental issues: air pollution from industrial and vehicular emissions; water pollution from raw sewage; deforestation; smoke/haze from Indonesian forest fires; endangered species; coastal reclamation damaging mangroves and turtle nesting sites

International environmental agreements: *party to:* Antarctic-Environmental Protection, Antarctic Treaty, Biodiversity, Climate Change, Climate Change-Kyoto Protocol, Climate Change-Paris Agreement, Comprehensive Nuclear Test Ban, Desertification, Endangered Species, Hazardous Wastes, Law of the Sea, Marine Life Conservation, Nuclear Test Ban, Ozone Layer Protection, Ship Pollution, Tropical Timber 2006, Wetlands
signed, but not ratified: none of the selected agreements

Climate: tropical; annual southwest (April to October) and northeast (October to February) monsoons

Urbanization: *urban population:* 78.7% of total population (2023)
rate of urbanization: 1.87% annual rate of change (2020-25 est.)

Carbon dioxide emissions: 260.005 million metric tonnes of CO2 (2023 est.)
from coal and metallurgical coke: 76.78 million metric tonnes of CO2 (2023 est.)
from petroleum and other liquids: 90.273 million metric tonnes of CO2 (2023 est.)
from consumed natural gas: 92.951 million metric tonnes of CO2 (2023 est.)
comparison ranking: total emissions 26

Particulate matter emissions: 23.7 micrograms per cubic meter (2019 est.)

Methane emissions: *energy:* 818.9 kt (2022-2024 est.)
agriculture: 182.2 kt (2019-2021 est.)
waste: 847.9 kt (2019-2021 est.)
other: 15.3 kt (2019-2021 est.)

Waste and recycling: *municipal solid waste generated annually:* 12.983 million tons (2024 est.)
percent of municipal solid waste recycled: 22.1% (2022 est.)

Total water withdrawal: *municipal:* 1.342 billion cubic meters (2022 est.)
industrial: 1.641 billion cubic meters (2022 est.)
agricultural: 2.505 billion cubic meters (2022 est.)

Total renewable water resources: 580 billion cubic meters (2022 est.)

Geoparks: *total global geoparks and regional networks:* 2
global geoparks and regional networks: Kinabalu; Langkawi (2023)

GOVERNMENT

Country name: *conventional long form:* none
conventional short form: Malaysia
local long form: none
local short form: Malaysia
former: British Malaya, Malayan Union, Federation of Malaya
etymology: devised in the early 19th century by British geographers; the suffix *-sia* was added to the name of the Malay people to form a classical-style name; the name Malay may come from the Tamil word *malai*, meaning "mountain"

Government type: federal parliamentary constitutional monarchy
note: all Peninsular Malaysian states have hereditary rulers (commonly referred to as sultans) except Melaka (Malacca) and Pulau Pinang (Penang); those two states along with Sabah and Sarawak in East Malaysia have governors appointed by government; powers of state governments are limited by the federal constitution; under terms of federation, Sabah and Sarawak retain certain constitutional

prerogatives (e.g., right to maintain their own immigration controls)

Capital: *name:* Kuala Lumpur
geographic coordinates: 3 10 N, 101 42 E
time difference: UTC+8 (13 hours ahead of Washington, DC, during Standard Time)
etymology: the name means "muddy river junction," referring to the city's location on the confluence of the Kelang and Gombak rivers; it comes from the Malay words *kuala* (river junction or estuary) and *lumpur* (mud)
note: nearby Putrajaya is referred to as a federal government administrative center but not as the capital; the legislature meets in Kuala Lumpur

Administrative divisions: 13 states (*negeri-negeri*, singular - *negeri*); Johor, Kedah, Kelantan, Melaka, Negeri Sembilan, Pahang, Perak, Perlis, Pulau Pinang, Sabah, Sarawak, Selangor, Terengganu; and 1 federal territory (Wilayah Persekutuan) with 3 components, Kuala Lumpur, Labuan, and Putrajaya

Legal system: mixed system of English common law, Islamic law (sharia), and customary law; the Federal Court can review legislative acts at the request of the supreme head of the federation

Constitution: *history:* previous 1948; latest drafted 21 February 1957, effective 27 August 1957
amendment process: proposed as a bill by Parliament; passage requires at least two-thirds majority vote by the Parliament membership in the bill's second and third readings; a number of constitutional sections are excluded from amendment or repeal

International law organization participation: has not submitted an ICJ jurisdiction declaration; non-party state to the ICCt

Citizenship: *citizenship by birth:* no
citizenship by descent only: at least one parent must be a citizen of Malaysia
dual citizenship recognized: no
residency requirement for naturalization: 10 out 12 years preceding application

Suffrage: 18 years of age; universal

Executive branch: *chief of state:* King Sultan IBRAHIM ibni al-Marhum Sultan Iskandar (since 31 January 2024)
head of government: Prime Minister ANWAR Ibrahim (since 24 November 2022)
cabinet: Cabinet appointed by the prime minister from among members of Parliament with the consent of the king
election/appointment process: king elected by and from the hereditary rulers of 9 states for a 5-year term; election is on a rotational basis among rulers of the 9 states; prime minister designated from among members of the House of Representatives; following legislative elections, the leader who has support of the majority of members in the House becomes prime minister
most recent election date: 24 October 2023
expected date of next election: October 2028, with inauguration in January 2029
note: the position of the king is primarily ceremonial, but he is the final arbiter on the appointment of the prime minister

Legislative branch: *legislature name:* Parliament (Parlimen)
legislative structure: bicameral

Legislative branch - lower chamber: *chamber name:* House of Representatives (Dewan Rakyat)
number of seats: 223 (all directly elected)
electoral system: plurality/majority
scope of elections: full renewal
term in office: 5 years
most recent election date: 11/19/2022
parties elected and seats per party: Pakatan Harapan (PH) (76); National Alliance (PN) (52); National Front (BN) (30); Sarawak Parties Alliance (GPS) (23); Pan-Malaysian Islamic Party (PAS) (22); Other (19)
percentage of women in chamber: 13.5%
expected date of next election: November 2027

Legislative branch - upper chamber: *chamber name:* Senate (Dewan Negara)
number of seats: 70 (26 indirectly elected; 44 appointed)
percentage of women in chamber: 16.1%

Judicial branch: *highest court(s):* Federal Court (consists of the chief justice, president of the Court of Appeal, chief justice of the High Court of Malaya, chief judge of the High Court of Sabah and Sarawak, 8 judges, and 1 "additional" judge)
judge selection and term of office: Federal Court justices appointed by the monarch on advice of the prime minister; judges serve until mandatory retirement at age 66 with the possibility of a single 6-month extension
subordinate courts: Court of Appeal; High Court; Sessions Court; Magistrates' Court
note: Malaysia has a dual judicial hierarchy of civil and religious (sharia) courts

Political parties: National Front (Barisan Nasional) or BN: Malaysian Chinese Association (Persatuan Cina Malaysia) or MCA
Malaysian Indian Congress (Kongres India Malaysia) or MIC
United Malays National Organization (Pertubuhan Kebansaan Melayu Bersatu) or UMNO
United Sabah People's Party (Parti Bersatu Rakyat Sabah) or PBRS

Alliance of Hope (Pakatan Harapan) or PH: Democratic Action Party (Parti Tindakan Demokratik) or DAP
National Trust Party (Parti Amanah Negara) or AMANAH
People's Justice Party (Parti Keadilan Rakyat) or PKR
United Progressive Kinabalu Organization (Pertubuhan Kinabalu Progresif Bersatu) or UPKO

National Alliance (Perikatan Nasional) or PN: Malaysian People's Movement Party (Parti Gerakan Rakyat Malaysia) or GERAKAN or PGRM
Malaysian United Indigenous Party (Parti Pribumi Bersatu Malaysia) or PPBM or BERSATU
Pan-Malaysian Islamic Party (Parti Islam Se-Malaysia) or PAS

Sabah People's Alliance (Gabungan Rakya Sabah) or GRS: Homeland Solidarity Party (Parti Solidariti Tanah Airku) or STAR
Love Sabah Party (Parti Cinta Sabah) or PCS
Sabah People's Ideas Party (Parti Gagasan Rakyat Sabah) or GAGASAN or PGRS

Sarawak Parties Alliance (Gabungan Parti Sarawak) or GPS: Progressive Democratic Party (Parti Demokratik Progresif) or PDP
Sarawak People's Party (Parti Rakyat Sarawak) or PRS
Sarawak United People's Party (Parti Rakyat Bersatu Sarawak) or SUPP
United Bumiputera Heritage Party (Parti Pesaka Bumiputera Bersata) or PBB

Homeland Movement/Party (Gerakan Tanah Air) or GTA: Homeland Fighter's Party (Parti Pejuang Tanah Air) or PEJUANG
Perkasa Bumiputera Party of Malaysia (Parti Bumiputera Perkasa Malaysia)
All-Malaysian Jemaah Islamiah Front (Barisan Jemaah Islamiah Se-Malaysia)
National All India Muslim Alliance Party (Parti Perikatan India Muslim Nasional)
others: Malaysian Nation Party (Parti Bangsa Malaysia) or PBM
Heritage Party (Parti Warisan) or WARISAN
Malaysian United Democratic Alliance (Ikatan Demokratik Malaysia) or MUDA
United Sarawak Party (PSB)

Diplomatic representation in the US: *chief of mission:* Ambassador Tan Sri Muhammad SHAHRUL Ikram bin Yaakob (since 24 July 2025)
chancery: 3516 International Court NW, Washington, DC 20008
telephone: [1] (202) 572-9700
FAX: [1] (202) 572-9882
email address and website: mwwashington@kln.gov.my
https://www.kln.gov.my/web/usa_washington/home
consulate(s) general: Los Angeles, New York

Diplomatic representation from the US: *chief of mission:* Ambassador Edgard D. KAGAN (since 20 March 2024)
embassy: 376 Jalan Tun Razak, 50400 Kuala Lumpur
mailing address: 4210 Kuala Lumpur, Washington DC 20521-4210
telephone: [60] (3) 2168-5000
FAX: [60] (3) 2142-2207
email address and website: KLACS@state.gov
https://my.usembassy.gov/

International organization participation: ADB, APEC, ARF, ASEAN, BIS, C, CICA (observer), CP, D-8, EAS, FAO, G-15, G-77, IAEA, IBRD, ICAO, ICC (national committees), ICRM, IDA, IDB, IFAD, IFC, IFRCS, IHO, ILO, IMF, IMO, IMSO, Interpol, IOC, IPU, ISO, ITSO, ITU, ITUC (NGOs), MIGA, MINURSO, MONUSCO, NAM, OIC, OPCW, PCA, PIF (partner), UN, UNAMID, UNCTAD, UNESCO, UNHRC, UNIDO, UNIFIL, UNISFA, UNMIL, UNWTO, UPU, WCO, WFTU (NGOs), WHO, WIPO, WMO, WTO

Independence: 31 August 1957 (from the UK)

National holiday: Independence Day (or Merdeka Day), 31 August (1957) (independence of Malaya); Malaysia Day, 16 September (1963) (formation of Malaysia)

Flag: *description:* 14 equal horizontal stripes of red alternating with white; a dark blue rectangle in the upper-left corner has a yellow crescent and a 14-pointed yellow star
meaning: the flag is often called Jalur Gemilang (Stripes of Glory); the 14 stripes stand for the equal status of the 13 member states and the federal government; the points on the star represent the unity among these entities; the crescent is a traditional symbol of Islam; blue symbolizes the unity of the Malay people, and yellow is the royal color
note: the design is based on the US flag

National symbol(s): tiger, hibiscus

National color(s): gold, black

National anthem(s): *title:* "Negaraku" (My Country)
lyrics/music: collective, led by Tunku ABDUL RAHMAN/Pierre Jean DE BERANGER

history: adopted 1957; full version only performed in the king's presence, the shorter version performed for the queen and lesser officials

National heritage: *total World Heritage Sites:* 6 (4 cultural, 2 natural)
selected World Heritage Site locales: Gunung Mulu National Park (n); Kinabalu Park (n); Melaka and George Town, Historic Cities of the Straits of Melaka (c); Archaeological Heritage of the Lenggong Valley (c); The Archaeological Heritage of Niah National Park's Caves Complex (c); Forest Research Institute Malaysia Forest Park Selangor (c)

ECONOMY

Economic overview: upper middle-income Southeast Asian economy; implementing key anticorruption policies; major electronics, oil, and chemicals exporter; trade sector employs over 40% of jobs; key economic equity initiative; high labor productivity

Real GDP (purchasing power parity): $1.212 trillion (2024 est.)
$1.153 trillion (2023 est.)
$1.113 trillion (2022 est.)
note: data in 2021 dollars
comparison ranking: 30

Real GDP growth rate: 5.1% (2024 est.)
3.6% (2023 est.)
8.9% (2022 est.)
note: annual GDP % growth based on constant local currency
comparison ranking: 36

Real GDP per capita: $34,100 (2024 est.)
$32,800 (2023 est.)
$32,100 (2022 est.)
note: data in 2021 dollars
comparison ranking: 71

GDP (official exchange rate): $421.972 billion (2024 est.)
note: data in current dollars at official exchange rate

Inflation rate (consumer prices): 1.8% (2024 est.)
2.5% (2023 est.)
3.4% (2022 est.)
note: annual % change based on consumer prices
comparison ranking: 46

GDP - composition, by sector of origin: *agriculture:* 8.2% (2024 est.)
industry: 37.1% (2024 est.)
services: 53.6% (2024 est.)
note: figures may not total 100% due to non-allocated consumption not captured in sector-reported data
comparison rankings: agriculture 84; industry 30; services 128

GDP - composition, by end use: *household consumption:* 60.8% (2024 est.)
government consumption: 12% (2024 est.)
investment in fixed capital: 20.6% (2024 est.)
investment in inventories: 1.3% (2024 est.)
exports of goods and services: 71.4% (2024 est.)
imports of goods and services: -66% (2024 est.)
note: figures may not total 100% due to rounding or gaps in data collection

Agricultural products: oil palm fruit, rice, chicken, eggs, tropical fruits, coconuts, vegetables, pineapples, rubber, bananas (2023)
note: top ten agricultural products based on tonnage

Industries: Peninsular Malaysia - rubber and oil palm processing and manufacturing, petroleum and natural gas, light manufacturing, pharmaceuticals, medical technology, electronics and semiconductors, timber processing; Sabah - logging, petroleum and natural gas production; Sarawak - agriculture processing, petroleum and natural gas production, logging

Industrial production growth rate: 4.9% (2024 est.)
note: annual % change in industrial value added based on constant local currency
comparison ranking: 47

Labor force: 18.264 million (2024 est.)
note: number of people ages 15 or older who are employed or seeking work
comparison ranking: 36

Unemployment rate: 3.9% (2024 est.)
3.9% (2023 est.)
4% (2022 est.)
note: % of labor force seeking employment
comparison ranking: 63

Youth unemployment rate (ages 15-24): *total:* 12.3% (2024 est.)
male: 11.3% (2024 est.)
female: 13.8% (2024 est.)
note: % of labor force ages 15-24 seeking employment
comparison ranking: total 100

Population below poverty line: 6.2% (2021 est.)
note: % of population with income below national poverty line

Gini Index coefficient - distribution of family income: 40.7 (2021 est.)
note: index (0-100) of income distribution; higher values represent greater inequality
comparison ranking: 38

Average household expenditures: *on food:* 26.4% of household expenditures (2023 est.)
on alcohol and tobacco: 1.6% of household expenditures (2023 est.)

Household income or consumption by percentage share: *lowest 10%:* 2.3% (2021 est.)
highest 10%: 30.9% (2021 est.)
note: % share of income accruing to lowest and highest 10% of population

Remittances: 0.4% of GDP (2024 est.)
0.4% of GDP (2023 est.)
0.4% of GDP (2022 est.)
note: personal transfers and compensation between resident and non-resident individuals/households/entities

Budget: *revenues:* $69.055 billion (2023 est.)
expenditures: $89.046 billion (2023 est.)
note: central government revenues and expenses (excluding grants/extrabudgetary units/social security funds) converted to US dollars at average official exchange rate for year indicated

Public debt: 64.3% of GDP (2023 est.)
note: central government debt as a % of GDP
comparison ranking: 65

Taxes and other revenues: 12.6% (of GDP) (2023 est.)
note: central government tax revenue as a % of GDP
comparison ranking: 109

Current account balance: $7.15 billion (2024 est.)
$6.257 billion (2023 est.)
$12.738 billion (2022 est.)
note: balance of payments - net trade and primary/secondary income in current dollars
comparison ranking: 28

Exports: $301.789 billion (2024 est.)
$274.1 billion (2023 est.)
$312.88 billion (2022 est.)
note: balance of payments - exports of goods and services in current dollars
comparison ranking: 30

Exports - partners: China 21%, Singapore 12%, USA 12%, Japan 5%, Hong Kong 5% (2023)
note: top five export partners based on percentage share of exports

Exports - commodities: integrated circuits, refined petroleum, crude petroleum, natural gas, palm oil (2023)
note: top five export commodities based on value in dollars

Imports: $279.09 billion (2024 est.)
$253.665 billion (2023 est.)
$283.758 billion (2022 est.)
note: balance of payments - imports of goods and services in current dollars
comparison ranking: 32

Imports - partners: China 24%, Singapore 11%, USA 7%, Japan 5%, Taiwan 5% (2023)
note: top five import partners based on percentage share of imports

Imports - commodities: integrated circuits, refined petroleum, crude petroleum, coal, broadcasting equipment (2023)
note: top five import commodities based on value in dollars

Reserves of foreign exchange and gold: $116.229 billion (2024 est.)
$113.463 billion (2023 est.)
$114.659 billion (2022 est.)
note: holdings of gold (year-end prices)/foreign exchange/special drawing rights in current dollars
comparison ranking: 25

Exchange rates: ringgits (MYR) per US dollar -

Exchange rates: 4.576 (2024 est.)
4.561 (2023 est.)
4.401 (2022 est.)
4.143 (2021 est.)
4.203 (2020 est.)

ENERGY

Electricity access: *electrification - total population:* 100% (2022 est.)

Electricity: *installed generating capacity:* 37.22 million kW (2023 est.)
consumption: 178.653 billion kWh (2023 est.)
exports: 1.2 billion kWh (2023 est.)
imports: 61.678 million kWh (2023 est.)
transmission/distribution losses: 13.188 billion kWh (2023 est.)
comparison rankings: installed generating capacity 34; consumption 24; exports 66; imports 114; transmission/distribution losses 185

Electricity generation sources: *fossil fuels:* 81.9% of total installed capacity (2023 est.)
solar: 1.1% of total installed capacity (2023 est.)
hydroelectricity: 16.3% of total installed capacity (2023 est.)
biomass and waste: 0.6% of total installed capacity (2023 est.)

Coal: *production:* 4.476 million metric tons (2023 est.)
consumption: 35.741 million metric tons (2023 est.)
exports: 462,000 metric tons (2023 est.)
imports: 31.706 million metric tons (2023 est.)
proven reserves: 226 million metric tons (2023 est.)

Petroleum: *total petroleum production:* 582,000 bbl/day (2023 est.)

refined petroleum consumption: 672,000 bbl/day (2023 est.)
crude oil estimated reserves: 3.6 billion barrels (2021 est.)

Natural gas: *production:* 74.32 billion cubic meters (2023 est.)
consumption: 47.112 billion cubic meters (2023 est.)
exports: 37.451 billion cubic meters (2023 est.)
imports: 3.359 billion cubic meters (2023 est.)
proven reserves: 1.189 trillion cubic meters (2021 est.)

Energy consumption per capita: 113.163 million Btu/person (2023 est.)
comparison ranking: 39

COMMUNICATIONS

Telephones - fixed lines: *total subscriptions:* 8.402 million (2023 est.)
subscriptions per 100 inhabitants: 24 (2023 est.)
comparison ranking: total subscriptions 20

Telephones - mobile cellular: *total subscriptions:* 50.1 million (2023 est.)
subscriptions per 100 inhabitants: 141 (2022 est.)
comparison ranking: total subscriptions 37

Broadcast media: state-owned TV broadcaster operates 2 TV networks with relays; the leading private commercial media group operates 4 TV stations with numerous relays; satellite TV subscription service is available; state-owned radio broadcaster operates multiple national networks, as well as regional and local stations; many private commercial radio broadcasters and some subscription satellite radio services are available; about 55 radio stations overall (2019)

Internet country code: .my

Internet users: *percent of population:* 98% (2023 est.)

Broadband - fixed subscriptions: *total:* 4.58 million (2023 est.)
subscriptions per 100 inhabitants: 13 (2023 est.)
comparison ranking: total 37

TRANSPORTATION

Civil aircraft registration country code prefix: 9M

Airports: 100 (2025)
comparison ranking: 55

Heliports: 24 (2025)
comparison ranking: 53

Railways: *total:* 1,851 km (2014)
standard gauge: 59 km (2014) 1.435-m gauge (59 km electrified)
narrow gauge: 1,792 km (2014) 1.000-m gauge (339 km electrified)

Merchant marine: *total:* 1,750 (2023)
by type: bulk carrier 14, container ship 35, general cargo 169, oil tanker 148, other 1,384
comparison ranking: total 16

Ports: *total ports:* 35 (2024)
large: 3
medium: 4
small: 10
very small: 18
ports with oil terminals: 24
key ports: Johor, Kota Kinabalu, Port Dickson, Port Klang, Pulau Pinang, Tanjung Pelepas, Tapis Marine Terminal A

MILITARY AND SECURITY

Military and security forces: Malaysian Armed Forces (Angkatan Tentera Malaysia, ATM): Malaysian Army, Royal Malaysian Navy, Royal Malaysian Air Force

Ministry of Home Affairs: Royal Malaysia Police (RMP or Polis Diraja Malaysia, PDRM), Malaysian Maritime Enforcement Agency (MMEA; aka Malaysian Coast Guard) (2025)
note: the Royal Malaysia Police includes the General Operations Force, a paramilitary force with a variety of roles, including patrolling borders, counterterrorism, maritime security, and counterinsurgency

Military expenditures: 1% of GDP (2024 est.)
0.9% of GDP (2023 est.)
1.1% of GDP (2022 est.)
1% of GDP (2021 est.)
1.1% of GDP (2020 est.)

Military and security service personnel strengths: approximately 110,000 active Malaysian Armed Forces (2025)

Military equipment inventories and acquisitions: the military fields a diverse array of mostly older but growing mix of modern weapons and equipment; its inventory originates from a wide variety of suppliers across Europe, Asia, and the US; Malaysia has a domestic defense industry that has some co-production agreements with countries such as France, Germany, and Turkey in areas including armored vehicles and naval vessels (2024)

Military service age and obligation: 17 years 6 months of age for voluntary military service for men and women (younger with parental consent and proof of age); maximum age of 27 to enlist; mandatory retirement age 60; no conscription (2023)
note: in 2020, the military announced a goal of having 10% of the active force comprised of women

Military deployments: 830 Lebanon (UNIFIL) (2024)

Military - note: the Malaysian military is responsible for defense of the country's national interests, sovereignty, and territorial integrity; it also has some domestic responsibilities, such as responding to natural disasters; key areas of focus for the military include cyber defense, crime and piracy in the Strait of Malacca, and tensions in the South China Sea; the Army has traditionally been the dominant service, but air and maritime security have received increased emphasis in recent years; Malaysia has undertaken efforts to procure more modern aircraft and ships, improve air and maritime surveillance, expand the Navy's support infrastructure (particularly bases/ports) and domestic ship-building capacities, and increase cooperation with regional and international partners such as Australia, Indonesia, the Philippines, Singapore, and the US
Malaysia is a member of the Five Powers Defense Arrangements (FPDA), a series of mutual assistance agreements reached in 1971 embracing Australia, Malaysia, New Zealand, Singapore, and the UK; the FPDA commits the members to consult with one another in the event or threat of an armed attack on any of the members and to mutually decide what measures should be taken, jointly or separately; there is no specific obligation to intervene militarily (2025)

SPACE

Space agency/agencies: Malaysian Space Agency (MYSA; established 2019) (2025)
note: MYSA was established through the merging of the National Space Agency (ANGKASA; established 2002) and the Malaysian Remote Sensing Agency (MRSA; established 1998)

Space launch site(s): has launched feasibility studies for potential space launch sites in Pahang, Sabah, and Sarawak (2025)

Space program overview: has a national space policy and a growing space program focused on the areas of remote sensing (RS), communication, and navigational services to support domestic economic sectors; also seeks to promote a domestic space industry; acquires, manufactures, and operates satellites; conducts research in RS capabilities and space sciences such as astronomy, atmospherics, space environment, and weather; has an astronaut training exchange program with Russia and has relations with a variety of foreign space agencies and industries, including those of the European Space Agency and some of its individual member states, India, Japan, Russia, South Korea, the UK, and the US (2025)
note: further details about the key activities, programs, and milestones of the country's space program, as well as government spending estimates on the space sector, appear in the Space Programs reference guide

TERRORISM

Terrorist group(s): Terrorist group(s): Abu Sayyaf Group, al-Qa'ida, Islamic State of Iraq and ash-Sham (ISIS)
note: details about the history, aims, leadership, organization, areas of operation, tactics, targets, weapons, size, and sources of support of the group(s) appear(s) in Appendix T

TRANSNATIONAL ISSUES

Refugees and internally displaced persons: *refugees:* 191,343 (2024 est.)
stateless persons: 120,857 (2024 est.)

MALDIVES

INTRODUCTION

Background: A sultanate since the 12th century, the Maldives became a British protectorate in 1887 and a republic in 1968, three years after independence. President Maumoon Abdul GAYOOM dominated Maldives' political scene for 30 years, elected to six successive terms by single-party referendums. After political demonstrations in the capital Male in 2003, GAYOOM and his government pledged to embark upon a process of liberalization and democratic reforms, including a more representative political

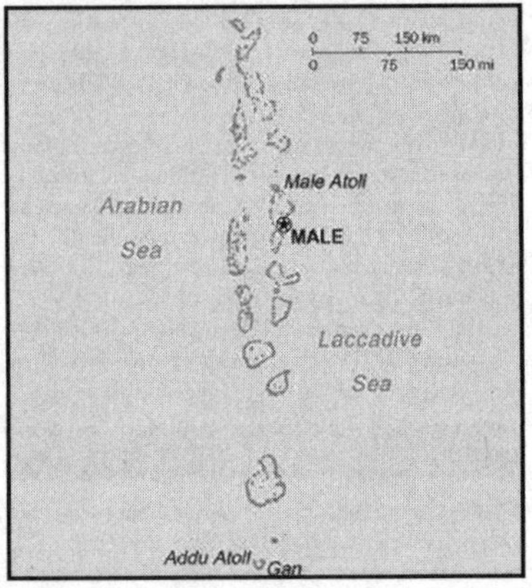

system and expanded political freedoms. Political parties were legalized in 2005.

In 2008, a constituent assembly – termed the "Special Majlis" – finalized a new constitution ratified by GAYOOM. The first-ever presidential elections under a multi-candidate, multi-party system were held later that year. GAYOOM was defeated in a runoff by Mohamed NASHEED, a political activist whom the regime had jailed several years earlier. In 2012, after several weeks of street protests in response to a top judge's arrest, NASHEED resigned the presidency and handed over power to Vice President Mohammed WAHEED Hassan Maniku. A government-appointed Commission of National Inquiry concluded that there was no evidence of a coup, but NASHEED contended that police and military personnel forced him to resign. NASHEED, WAHEED, and Abdulla YAMEEN Abdul Gayoom ran in the 2013 elections with YAMEEN ultimately winning the presidency after three rounds of voting. In 2018, YAMEEN lost his reelection bid to parliamentarian Ibrahim Mohamed SOLIH. YAMEEN was arrested and jailed in 2022 on corruption charges. Maldives' fourth democratic election was held in September 2023. The winner, Male City Mayor Dr. Mohamed MUIZZU, campaigned on a platform of Maldivian sovereignty, vowing to remove Indian military personnel from the country. MUIZZU represents a joint Progressive Pary of Maldives and People's National Congress (PPM/PNC) coalition.

GEOGRAPHY

Location: Southern Asia, group of atolls in the Indian Ocean, south-southwest of India

Geographic coordinates: 3 15 N, 73 00 E

Map references: Asia

Area: *total:* 298 sq km
land: 298 sq km
water: 0 sq km
comparison ranking: total 209

Area - comparative: about 1.7 times the size of Washington, D.C.

Land boundaries: *total:* 0 km

Coastline: 644 km

Maritime claims: *territorial sea:* 12 nm
contiguous zone: 24 nm
exclusive economic zone: 200 nm
note: measured from claimed archipelagic straight baselines

Climate: tropical; hot, humid; dry, northeast monsoon (November to March); rainy, southwest monsoon (June to August)

Terrain: flat coral atolls, with white sandy beaches; sits atop the submarine volcanic Chagos-Laccadive Ridge

Elevation: *highest point:* 8th tee, golf course, Villingi Island 5 m
lowest point: Indian Ocean 0 m
mean elevation: 2 m

Natural resources: fish

Land use: *agricultural land:* 19.7% (2022 est.)
arable land: 13% (2022 est.)
permanent crops: 3.3% (2022 est.)
permanent pasture: 3.3% (2022 est.)
forest: 2.7% (2022 est.)
other: 77.6% (2022 est.)

Irrigated land: 0 sq km (2012)

Population distribution: about a third of the population lives in the centrally located capital city of Male and almost a tenth in southern Addu City; the remainder of the populace is spread over the 200 or so populated islands of the archipelago

Natural hazards: tsunamis; low elevation of islands makes them sensitive to sea level rise

Geography - note: smallest Asian country; archipelago of 1,190 coral islands grouped into 26 atolls (200 inhabited islands, plus 80 islands with tourist resorts); strategic location along major sea lanes in Indian Ocean

PEOPLE AND SOCIETY

Population: *total:* 388,858 (2024 est.)
male: 197,739
female: 191,119
comparison rankings: total 177; male 176; female 177

Nationality: *noun:* Maldivian(s)
adjective: Maldivian

Ethnic groups: homogeneous mixture of Sinhalese, Dravidian, Arab, Australasian, and African resulting from historical changes in regional hegemony over marine trade routes

Languages: Dhivehi (official, closely related to Sinhala, script derived from Arabic), English (spoken by most government officials)

Religions: Sunni Muslim (official)

Age structure: *0-14 years:* 22.4% (male 44,321/female 42,626)
15-64 years: 71.5% (male 143,021/female 135,044)
65 years and over: 6.1% (2024 est.) (male 10,397/female 13,449)

Dependency ratios: *total dependency ratio:* 39.8 (2024 est.)
youth dependency ratio: 31.3 (2024 est.)
elderly dependency ratio: 8.6 (2024 est.)
potential support ratio: 11.7 (2024 est.)

Median age: *total:* 31.9 years (2024 est.)
male: 31.3 years
female: 32.4 years
comparison ranking: total 120

Population growth rate: -0.2% (2024 est.)
comparison ranking: 210

Birth rate: 15.1 births/1,000 population (2024 est.)
comparison ranking: 108

Death rate: 4.3 deaths/1,000 population (2024 est.)
comparison ranking: 210

Net migration rate: -12.8 migrant(s)/1,000 population (2024 est.)
comparison ranking: 225

Population distribution: about a third of the population lives in the centrally located capital city of Male and almost a tenth in southern Addu City; the remainder of the populace is spread over the 200 or so populated islands of the archipelago

Urbanization: *urban population:* 42% of total population (2023)
rate of urbanization: 2.34% annual rate of change (2020-25 est.)

Major urban areas - population: 177,000 MALE (capital) (2018)

Sex ratio: *at birth:* 1.05 male(s)/female
0-14 years: 1.04 male(s)/female
15-64 years: 1.06 male(s)/female
65 years and over: 0.77 male(s)/female
total population: 1.04 male(s)/female (2024 est.)

Mother's mean age at first birth: 23.2 years (2016/17 est.)
note: data represents median age at first birth among women 25-49

Maternal mortality ratio: 32 deaths/100,000 live births (2023 est.)
comparison ranking: 115

Infant mortality rate: *total:* 24.4 deaths/1,000 live births (2024 est.)
male: 27.3 deaths/1,000 live births
female: 21.3 deaths/1,000 live births
comparison ranking: total 62

Life expectancy at birth: *total population:* 77.4 years (2024 est.)
male: 75.1 years
female: 79.9 years
comparison ranking: total population 90

Total fertility rate: 1.7 children born/woman (2024 est.)
comparison ranking: 165

Gross reproduction rate: 0.83 (2024 est.)

Drinking water source: *improved: urban:* 99.1% of population (2022 est.)
rural: 99.9% of population (2022 est.)
total: 99.6% of population (2022 est.)
unimproved: urban: 0.9% of population (2022 est.)
rural: 0.1% of population (2022 est.)
total: 0.4% of population (2022 est.)

Health expenditure: 10% of GDP (2021)
18.2% of national budget (2022 est.)

Physician density: 2.24 physicians/1,000 population (2019)

Hospital bed density: 5 beds/1,000 population (2020 est.)

Sanitation facility access: *improved: urban:* 100% of population (2022 est.)
rural: 100% of population (2022 est.)
total: 100% of population (2022 est.)
unimproved: urban: 0% of population (2022 est.)
rural: 0% of population (2022 est.)
total: 0% of population (2022 est.)

Obesity - adult prevalence rate: 8.6% (2016)
comparison ranking: 149

Alcohol consumption per capita: *total:* 1.38 liters of pure alcohol (2019 est.)
beer: 0.33 liters of pure alcohol (2019 est.)
wine: 0.59 liters of pure alcohol (2019 est.)
spirits: 0.45 liters of pure alcohol (2019 est.)
other alcohols: 0 liters of pure alcohol (2019 est.)

comparison ranking: total 142

Tobacco use: *total:* 28% (2025 est.)
male: 41.5% (2025 est.)
female: 9.2% (2025 est.)
comparison ranking: total 29

Children under the age of 5 years underweight: 14.8% (2016/17)
comparison ranking: 32

Currently married women (ages 15-49): 71.9% (2023 est.)

Child marriage: *women married by age 15:* 0% (2017)
women married by age 18: 2.2% (2017)
men married by age 18: 2.2% (2017)

Education expenditure: 5.2% of GDP (2023 est.)
10.7% national budget (2024 est.)
comparison ranking: Education expenditure (% GDP) 56

Literacy: *total population:* 98.2% (2019 est.)
male: 98.2% (2019 est.)
female: 98.3% (2019 est.)

School life expectancy (primary to tertiary education): *total:* 13 years (2022 est.)
male: 11 years (2022 est.)
female: 15 years (2022 est.)

ENVIRONMENT

Environmental issues: rising sea levels; depletion of freshwater aquifers; inadequate sewage treatment; coral reef bleaching

International environmental agreements: *party to:* Biodiversity, Climate Change, Climate Change-Kyoto Protocol, Climate Change-Paris Agreement, Comprehensive Nuclear Test Ban, Desertification, Endangered Species, Hazardous Wastes, Law of the Sea, Ozone Layer Protection, Ship Pollution
signed, but not ratified: none of the selected agreements

Climate: tropical; hot, humid; dry, northeast monsoon (November to March); rainy, southwest monsoon (June to August)

Urbanization: *urban population:* 42% of total population (2023)
rate of urbanization: 2.34% annual rate of change (2020-25 est.)

Carbon dioxide emissions: 1.908 million metric tonnes of CO2 (2023 est.)
from petroleum and other liquids: 1.908 million metric tonnes of CO2 (2023 est.)
comparison ranking: total emissions 160

Particulate matter emissions: 12.3 micrograms per cubic meter (2019 est.)

Waste and recycling: *municipal solid waste generated annually:* 211,500 tons (2024 est.)
percent of municipal solid waste recycled: 20.9% (2022 est.)

Total water withdrawal: *municipal:* 5.6 million cubic meters (2022 est.)
industrial: 300,000 cubic meters (2022 est.)
agricultural: 268,194 cubic meters (2022 est.)

Total renewable water resources: 30 million cubic meters (2022 est.)

GOVERNMENT

Country name: *conventional long form:* Republic of Maldives
conventional short form: Maldives
local long form: Dhivehi Raajjeyge Jumhooriyyaa
local short form: Dhivehi Raajje
etymology: the origin of the name is obscure but may derive from the Sanskrit word *maladvipa*, meaning "garland of islands;" the local name, Dhivehi Raajje, means "land of the Dhivehi people" in the local language

Government type: presidential republic

Capital: *name:* Malé
geographic coordinates: 4 10 N, 73 30 E
time difference: UTC+5 (10 hours ahead of Washington, DC, during Standard Time)
etymology: the name may come from the Sanskrit word *mala*, or "garland"

Administrative divisions: 21 administrative atolls (*atholhuthah*, singular - *atholhu*); Addu (Addu City), Ariatholhu Dhekunuburi (South Ari Atoll), Ariatholhu Uthuruburi (North Ari Atoll), Faadhippolhu, Felidhuatholhu (Felidhu Atoll), Fuvammulah, Hahdhunmathi, Huvadhuatholhu Dhekunuburi (South Huvadhu Atoll), Huvadhuatholhu Uthuruburi (North Huvadhu Atoll), Kolhumadulu, Maale (Male), Maaleatholhu (Male Atoll), Maalhosmadulu Dhekunuburi (South Maalhosmadulu), Maalhosmadulu Uthuruburi (North Maalhosmadulu), Miladhunmadulu Dhekunuburi (South Miladhunmadulu), Miladhunmadulu Uthuruburi (North Miladhunmadulu), Mulakatholhu (Mulaku Atoll), Nilandheatholhu Dhekunuburi (South Nilandhe Atoll), Nilandheatholhu Uthuruburi (North Nilandhe Atoll), Thiladhunmathee Dhekunuburi (South Thiladhunmathi), Thiladhunmathee Uthuruburi (North Thiladhunmathi)

Legal system: Islamic (sharia) legal system with English common law influences, primarily in commercial matters

Constitution: *history:* many previous; latest ratified 7 August 2008
amendment process: proposed by Parliament; passage requires at least three-quarters majority vote by its membership and the signature of the president of the republic; passage of amendments to constitutional articles on rights and freedoms and the terms of office of Parliament and of the president also requires a majority vote in a referendum

International law organization participation: has not submitted an ICJ jurisdiction declaration; accepts ICCt jurisdiction

Citizenship: *citizenship by birth:* no
citizenship by descent only: at least one parent must be a citizen of Maldives
dual citizenship recognized: yes
residency requirement for naturalization: unknown

Suffrage: 18 years of age; universal

Executive branch: *chief of state:* President Mohamed MUIZZU (since 17 November 2023)
head of government: President Mohamed MUIZZU (since 17 November 2023)
cabinet: Cabinet of Ministers appointed by the president, approved by People's Majlis
election/appointment process: president directly elected by absolute-majority popular vote in 2 rounds, if needed, for a 5-year term (eligible for a second term)
most recent election date: 9 September 2023, with runoff on 30 September 2023
election results: *2023:* Mohamed MUIZZU elected president in the second round; percent of vote in first round - Mohamed MUIZZU (PNC) 46.1%, Ibrahim Mohamed SOLIH (MDP) 39.1%, Ilyas LABEEB (DEMS) 7.1%, other 7.7%; percent of vote in the second round - Mohamed MUIZZU 54%, Ibrahim Mohamed SOLIH 46%
2018: Ibrahim Mohamed SOLIH elected president in first round; Ibrahim Mohamed SOLIH (MDP) 58.3%, Abdulla YAMEEN Abdul Gayoom (PPM) 41.7%
expected date of next election: 2028

Legislative branch: *legislature name:* People's Majlis (Majlis)
legislative structure: unicameral
number of seats: 93 (all directly elected)
electoral system: plurality/majority
scope of elections: full renewal
term in office: 5 years
most recent election date: 4/21/2024
parties elected and seats per party: People's National Congress (PNC) (66); Maldivian Democratic Party (MDP) (12); Independents (11); Other (4)
percentage of women in chamber: 3.2%
expected date of next election: April 2029

Judicial branch: *highest court(s):* Supreme Court (consists of the chief justice and 6 justices)
judge selection and term of office: Supreme Court judges appointed by the president in consultation with the Judicial Service Commission – a 10-member body of selected senior government officials and the public – and on confirmation by voting members of the People's Majlis; judges serve until mandatory retirement at age 70
subordinate courts: High Court; Criminal, Civil, Family, Juvenile, and Drug Courts; Magistrate Courts (on each of the inhabited islands)

Political parties: Adhaalath (Justice) Party or AP
Dhivehi Rayyithunge Party or DRP
Maldives Development Alliance or MDA
Maldivian Democratic Party or MDP
Maldives Third Way Democrats or MTD
People's National Congress or PNC
People's National Front
Republican (Jumhooree) Party or JP

Diplomatic representation in the US: *chief of mission:* Ambassador Abdul GHAFOOR Mohamed (since 15 June 2023)
chancery: 1100 H Street NW, Suite 250, Washington, D.C. 20005
telephone: [1] (202) 516-5458
email address and website: WashingtonInfo@foreign.gov.mv
The Embassy (mdvmission.gov.mv)

Diplomatic representation from the US: *chief of mission:* Ambassador Hugo Yue-Ho YON (since 6 September 2023); note - Ambassador YON is the first resident US ambassador to the Republic of Maldives
embassy: 210 Galle Road, Colombo 03, Sri Lanka; note - as of early November 2023, the US has no consular or diplomatic offices in Maldives; the US Mission to Maldives operates from US Embassy Colombo, Sri Lanka
telephone: [94] (11) 249-8500

FAX: [94] (11) 243-7345
email address and website: Homepage - U.S. Embassy in Maldives

International organization participation: ADB, AOSIS, C, CP, FAO, G-77, IBRD, ICAO, ICC (NGOs), ICCt, IDA, IDB, IFAD, IFC, IFRCS, ILO, IMF, IMO, Interpol, IOC, IOM, IPU, ITU, MIGA, NAM, OIC, OPCW, SAARC, SACEP, UN, UNCTAD, UNESCO, UNIDO, UNWTO, UPU, WCO, WHO, WIPO, WMO, WTO

Independence: 26 July 1965 (from the UK)

National holiday: Independence Day, 26 July (1965)

Flag: *description:* red with a large green rectangle in the center and a vertical white crescent moon centered on the rectangle
meaning: red stands for those who have sacrificed their lives to defend the country, green for peace and prosperity, and the white crescent is a symbol of Islam

National symbol(s): coconut palm, yellowfin tuna

National color(s): red, green, white

National anthem(s): *title:* "Gaumee Salaam" (National Salute)
lyrics/music: Mohamed Jameel DIDI/ Wannakuwattawaduge DON AMARADEVA
history: lyrics adopted 1948, music adopted 1972; the anthem has seven verses, but only the first two are commonly used

ECONOMY

Economic overview: upper middle-income Indian Ocean island economy; major tourism, fishing, and shipping industries; high public debt; systemic corruption; crippled by COVID-19; ongoing deflation; poverty has tripled since pandemic began

Real GDP (purchasing power parity): $12.325 billion (2024 est.)
$11.723 billion (2023 est.)
$11.194 billion (2022 est.)
note: data in 2021 dollars
comparison ranking: 162

Real GDP growth rate: 5.1% (2024 est.)
4.7% (2023 est.)
13.8% (2022 est.)
note: annual GDP % growth based on constant local currency
comparison ranking: 37

Real GDP per capita: $23,400 (2024 est.)
$22,300 (2023 est.)
$21,400 (2022 est.)
note: data in 2021 dollars
comparison ranking: 95

GDP (official exchange rate): $6.975 billion (2024 est.)
note: data in current dollars at official exchange rate

Inflation rate (consumer prices): 1.4% (2024 est.)
2.9% (2023 est.)
2.3% (2022 est.)
note: annual % change based on consumer prices
comparison ranking: 33

GDP - composition, by sector of origin: *agriculture:* 3% (2024 est.)
industry: 9% (2024 est.)
services: 73.8% (2024 est.)
note: figures may not total 100% due to TV monopoly; now 4 state-operated and 7 privately owned sector-reported data
comparison rankings: agriculture 132; industry 193; services 23

GDP - composition, by end use: *household consumption:* 51.4% (2023 est.)
government consumption: 17.1% (2023 est.)
investment in fixed capital: 35% (2023 est.)
investment in inventories: -2% (2023 est.)
exports of goods and services: 74.4% (2023 est.)
imports of goods and services: -75.7% (2023 est.)

Agricultural products: fruits, vegetables, nuts, other meats, papayas, bananas, tomatoes, maize, pulses, chillies/peppers (2023)
note: top ten agricultural products based on tonnage

Industries: tourism, fish processing, shipping, boat building, coconut processing, woven mats, rope, handicrafts, coral and sand mining

Industrial production growth rate: -2.7% (2024 est.)
note: annual % change in industrial value added based on constant local currency
comparison ranking: 167

Labor force: 270,300 (2024 est.)
note: number of people ages 15 or older who are employed or seeking work
comparison ranking: 169

Unemployment rate: 4.7% (2024 est.)
4.3% (2023 est.)
4.5% (2022 est.)
note: % of labor force seeking employment
comparison ranking: 81

Youth unemployment rate (ages 15-24): *total:* 16.1% (2024 est.)
male: 20% (2024 est.)
female: 9.5% (2024 est.)
note: % of labor force ages 15-24 seeking employment
comparison ranking: total 73

Population below poverty line: 5.4% (2019 est.)
note: % of population with income below national poverty line

Gini Index coefficient - distribution of family income: 29.3 (2019 est.)
note: index (0-100) of income distribution; higher values represent greater inequality
comparison ranking: 126

Household income or consumption by percentage share: *lowest 10%:* 3.8% (2019 est.)
highest 10%: 23.3% (2019 est.)
note: % share of income accruing to lowest and highest 10% of population

Remittances: 0.1% of GDP (2024 est.)
0.1% of GDP (2023 est.)
0.1% of GDP (2022 est.)
note: personal transfers and compensation between resident and non-resident individuals/ households/ entities

Budget: *revenues:* $1.407 billion (2021 est.)
expenditures: $1.939 billion (2021 est.)
note: central government revenues and expenses (excluding grants/extrabudgetary units/social security funds) converted to US dollars at average official exchange rate for year indicated

Taxes and other revenues: 19.5% (of GDP) (2021 est.)
note: central government tax revenue as a % of GDP
comparison ranking: 54

Current account balance: -$1.257 billion (2024 est.)
-$1.4 billion (2023 est.)
-$1.042 billion (2022 est.)
note: balance of payments - net trade and primary/ secondary income in current dollars
comparison ranking: 136

Exports: $5.413 billion (2024 est.)
$4.88 billion (2023 est.)
$5.096 billion (2022 est.)
note: balance of payments - exports of goods and services in current dollars
comparison ranking: 138

Exports - partners: Thailand 32%, India 21%, Singapore 9%, UK 7%, Germany 5% (2023)
note: top five export partners based on percentage share of exports

Exports - commodities: fish, aircraft, refined petroleum, scrap iron, natural gas (2023)
note: top five export commodities based on value in dollars

Imports: $5.344 billion (2024 est.)
$4.984 billion (2023 est.)
$4.939 billion (2022 est.)
note: balance of payments - imports of goods and services in current dollars
comparison ranking: 149

Imports - partners: India 15%, UAE 15%, Oman 14%, China 12%, Singapore 8% (2023)
note: top five import partners based on percentage share of imports

Imports - commodities: refined petroleum, plastic products, aircraft, granite, ships (2023)
note: top five import commodities based on value in dollars

Reserves of foreign exchange and gold: $673.886 million (2024 est.)
$590.523 million (2023 est.)
$832.094 million (2022 est.)
note: holdings of gold (year-end prices)/foreign exchange/special drawing rights in current dollars
comparison ranking: 152

Debt - external: $3.113 billion (2023 est.)
note: present value of external debt in current US dollars
comparison ranking: 84

Exchange rates: rufiyaa (MVR) per US dollar -

Exchange rates: 15.389 (2024 est.)
15.387 (2023 est.)
15.387 (2022 est.)
15.373 (2021 est.)
15.381 (2020 est.)

ENERGY

Electricity access: *electrification - total population:* 100% (2022 est.)

Electricity: *installed generating capacity:* 432,000 kW (2023 est.)
consumption: 821.397 million kWh (2023 est.)
transmission/distribution losses: 25.867 million kWh (2023 est.)
comparison rankings: installed generating capacity 153; consumption 166; transmission/distribution losses 29

Electricity generation sources: *fossil fuels:* 93.2% of total installed capacity (2023 est.)
solar: 6.6% of total installed capacity (2023 est.)
wind: 0.2% of total installed capacity (2023 est.)

Coal: *imports:* 8 metric tons (2023 est.)

Petroleum: *refined petroleum consumption:* 13,000 bbl/day (2023 est.)

Energy consumption per capita: 50.886 million Btu/person (2023 est.)
comparison ranking: 94

COMMUNICATIONS

Telephones - fixed lines: *total subscriptions:* 13,000 (2023 est.)
subscriptions per 100 inhabitants: 2 (2023 est.)
comparison ranking: total subscriptions 183

Telephones - mobile cellular: *total subscriptions:* 745,000 (2023 est.)
subscriptions per 100 inhabitants: 137 (2022 est.)
comparison ranking: total subscriptions 171

Broadcast media: formerly a state-owned radio and TV monopoly; now 4 state-operated and 7 privately owned TV stations; 4 state-operated and 7 privately owned radio stations (2019)

Internet country code: .mv

Internet users: *percent of population:* 85% (2023 est.)

Broadband - fixed subscriptions: *total:* 98,000 (2023 est.)
subscriptions per 100 inhabitants: 19 (2023 est.)
comparison ranking: total 135

TRANSPORTATION

Civil aircraft registration country code prefix: 8Q

Airports: 20 (2025)
comparison ranking: 137

Merchant marine: *total:* 82 (2023)
by type: general cargo 30, oil tanker 20, other 32
comparison ranking: total 98

Ports: *total ports:* 1 (2024)
large: 0
medium: 0
small: 0
very small: 1
ports with oil terminals: 1
key ports: Male

MILITARY AND SECURITY

Military and security forces: Maldives National Defense Force (MNDF): Coast Guard, Marine Corps, Air Corps, Fire and Rescue Service

Ministry of Homeland Security and Technology (MOHST): Maldives Police Service (2025)
note: in addition to the MNDF, the Maldives Ministry of Defense controls the Aviation Security Command, which provides security for the civil aviation industry, and the National Counter Terrorism Center

Military expenditures: not available

Military and security service personnel strengths: approximately 3-4,000 active Defense Forces (2025)

Military equipment inventories and acquisitions: the Defense Force has a limited inventory consisting of a mix of mostly secondhand or donated equipment from suppliers such as Germany, India, Japan, Turkey, and the UK (2025)

Military service age and obligation: 18-25 years of age for voluntary service; no conscription (2024)

Military - note: the Maldives National Defense Force (MNDF) is responsible for defending and safeguarding the Maldives' territorial integrity, economic exclusion zone, and people; it is also responsible for disaster relief, and if requested, assisting the Maldives Police Service in maintaining internal security and law and order; maritime security is its largest focus; the Indian Armed Forces have long been the MNDF's most important partner (2025)

TERRORISM

Terrorist group(s): Terrorist group(s): Islamic State of Iraq and ash-Sham (ISIS)
note: details about the history, aims, leadership, organization, areas of operation, tactics, targets, weapons, size, and sources of support of the group(s) appear(s) in Appendix T

TRANSNATIONAL ISSUES

Refugees and internally displaced persons: IDPs: 54 (2023 est.)

Trafficking in persons: *tier rating:* Tier 2 Watch List — the government did not demonstrate overall increasing efforts to eliminate trafficking compared with the previous reporting period, therefore Maldives remained on Tier 2 Watch List for the second consecutive year; for more details, go to: https://www.state.gov/reports/2025-trafficking-in-persons-report/maldives/

MALI

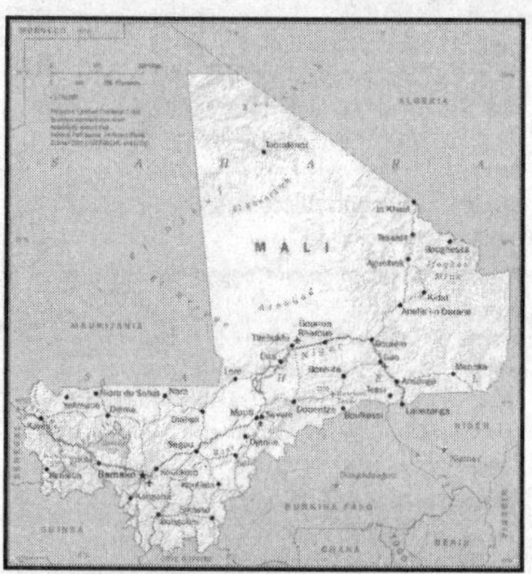

INTRODUCTION

Background: Present-day Mali is named after the Mali Empire that ruled the region between the 13th and 16th centuries. At its peak in the 14th century, it was the largest and wealthiest empire in West Africa and controlled an area about twice the size of modern-day France. Primarily a trading empire, Mali derived its wealth from gold and maintained several goldfields and trade routes in the Sahel. The empire also influenced West African culture through the spread of its language, laws, and customs, but by the 16th century, it had fragmented into mostly small chiefdoms. The Songhai Empire, previously a Mali dependency centered in Timbuktu, gained prominence in the 15th and 16th centuries. Under Songhai rule, Timbuktu became a large commercial center, well-known for its scholarship and religious teaching. Timbuktu remains a center of culture in West Africa today. In the late 16th century, the Songhai Empire fell to Moroccan invaders and disintegrated into independent sultanates and kingdoms.

France, expanding from Senegal, seized control of the area in the 1890s and incorporated it into French West Africa as French Sudan. In 1960, French Sudan gained independence from France and became the Mali Federation. When Senegal withdrew after only a few months, the remaining area was renamed the Republic of Mali. Mali saw 31 years of dictatorship until 1991, when a military coup led by Amadou Toumani TOURE ousted the government, established a new constitution, and instituted a multiparty democracy. Alpha Oumar KONARE won Mali's first two democratic presidential elections in 1992 and 1997. In keeping with Mali's two-term constitutional limit, he stepped down in 2002 and was succeeded by Amadou Toumani TOURE, who won a second term in 2007.

In 2012, rising ethnic tensions and an influx of fighters – some linked to Al-Qa'ida – from Libya led to a rebellion and military coup. Following the coup, rebels expelled the military from the country's three northern regions, allowing terrorist organizations to develop strongholds in the area. With a 2013 French-led military intervention, the Malian government managed to retake most of the north. However, the government's grasp in the region remains weak with local militias, terrorists, and insurgent groups competing for control. In 2015, the Malian Government and northern rebels signed an internationally mediated peace accord. Despite a 2017 target for implementation of the agreement, the signatories have made little progress. Terrorist groups were left out of the peace process, and terrorist attacks remain common.

Ibrahim Boubacar KEITA won the Malian presidential elections in 2013 and 2018. Aside from security and logistic shortfalls, international observers deemed these elections credible. Terrorism, banditry, ethnic-based violence, and extra-judicial military killings plagued the country during KEITA's second term. In 2020, the military arrested KEITA, his prime minister, and other senior members of the government and established a military junta called the National Committee for the Salvation of the People (CNSP). The junta then established a transition government and appointed Bah N'DAW, a retired army officer and former defense minister, as interim president and Colonel Assimi GOITA, the coup leader and chairman of the CNSP, as interim vice president. The transition government's charter allowed it to rule for up to 18 months before calling a general election.

In 2021, GOITA led a military takeover, arresting the interim president after a Cabinet shake-up removed GOITA's key allies. GOITA was sworn in as transition president, and Choguel Kokalla MAIGA was sworn in as prime minister. In 2022, the Economic Community of West African States (ECOWAS) imposed sanctions on the transition government, and member states closed their borders with Mali after the transition government presented a five-year extension to the electoral calendar. The transition government and ECOWAS agreed to a new two-year timeline, which would have included presidential elections in February 2024, but the transition government postponed the elections indefinitely in September 2023 and withdrew from ECOWAS in January 2024.

GEOGRAPHY

Location: interior Western Africa, southwest of Algeria, north of Guinea, Cote d'Ivoire, and Burkina Faso, west of Niger

Geographic coordinates: 17 00 N, 4 00 W

Map references: Africa

Area: *total:* 1,240,192 sq km
land: 1,220,190 sq km
water: 20,002 sq km
comparison ranking: total 25

Area - comparative: slightly less than twice the size of Texas

Land boundaries: *total:* 7,908 km
border countries (6): Algeria 1,359 km; Burkina Faso 1,325 km; Cote d'Ivoire 599 km; Guinea 1,062 km; Mauritania 2,236 km; Niger 838 km, Senegal 489 km

Coastline: 0 km (landlocked)

Maritime claims: none (landlocked)

Climate: subtropical to arid; hot and dry (February to June); rainy, humid, and mild (June to November); cool and dry (November to February)

Terrain: mostly flat to rolling northern plains covered by sand; savanna in south, rugged hills in northeast

Elevation: *highest point:* Hombori Tondo 1,155 m
lowest point: Senegal River 23 m
mean elevation: 343 m

Natural resources: gold, phosphates, kaolin, salt, limestone, uranium, gypsum, granite, hydropower
note: bauxite, iron ore, manganese, tin, and copper deposits are known but not exploited

Land use: *agricultural land:* 35.5% (2022 est.)
arable land: 6.8% (2022 est.)
permanent crops: 0.2% (2022 est.)
permanent pasture: 28.4% (2022 est.)
forest: 10.9% (2022 est.)
other: 53.6% (2022 est.)

Irrigated land: 3,780 sq km (2012)

Major lakes (area sq km): *fresh water lake(s):* Lac Faguibine - 590 sq km
note - the Niger River is the only source of water for the lake; in recent years the lake is dry

Major rivers (by length in km): Niger (shared with Guinea [s], Niger, and Nigeria [m]) - 4,200 km; Senegal (shared with Guinea [s], Senegal, and Mauritania [m]) - 1,641 km
note: [s] after country name indicates river source; [m] after country name indicates river mouth

Major watersheds (area sq km): Atlantic Ocean drainage: Niger (2,261,741 sq km), Senegal (456,397 sq km), Volta (410,991 sq km)

Major aquifers: Lullemeden-Irhazer Basin, Taodeni-Tanezrouft Basin

Population distribution: the overwhelming majority of the population lives in the southern half of the country, with greater density along the border with Burkina Faso, as shown in this population distribution map

Natural hazards: hot, dust-laden harmattan haze common during dry seasons; recurring droughts; occasional Niger River flooding

Geography - note: *landlocked; divided into three natural zones:* the southern, cultivated Sudanese; the central, semiarid Sahelian; and the northern, arid Saharan

PEOPLE AND SOCIETY

Population: *total:* 21,990,607 (2024 est.)
male: 10,688,755
female: 11,301,852
comparison rankings: total 60; male 60; female 61

Nationality: *noun:* Malian(s)
adjective: Malian

Ethnic groups: Bambara 33.3%, Fulani (Peuhl) 13.3%, Sarakole/Soninke/Marka 9.8%, Senufo/Manianka 9.6%, Malinke 8.8%, Dogon 8.7%, Sonrai 5.9%, Bobo 2.1%, Tuareg/Bella 1.7%, other Malian 6%, from members of Economic Community of West Africa 0.4%, other 0.3% (2018 est.)

Languages: Bambara (official), French 17.2%, Peuhl/Foulfoulbe/Fulani 9.4%, Dogon 7.2%, Maraka/Soninke 6.4%, Malinke 5.6%, Sonrhai/Djerma 5.6%, Minianka 4.3%, Tamacheq 3.5%, Senoufo 2.6%, Bobo 2.1%, other 6.3%, unspecified 0.7% (2009 est.)
note: Mali has 13 national languages in addition to its official language

Religions: Muslim 93.9%, Christian 2.8%, animist 0.7%, none 2.5% (2018 est.)

Age structure: *0-14 years:* 46.8% (male 5,175,714/female 5,114,128)
15-64 years: 50.1% (male 5,178,742/female 5,842,456)
65 years and over: 3.1% (2024 est.) (male 334,299/female 345,268)

Dependency ratios: *total dependency ratio:* 99.5 (2024 est.)
youth dependency ratio: 93.4 (2024 est.)
elderly dependency ratio: 6.2 (2024 est.)
potential support ratio: 16.2 (2024 est.)

Median age: *total:* 16.4 years (2024 est.)
male: 15.7 years
female: 17.1 years
comparison ranking: total 226

Population growth rate: 2.9% (2024 est.)
comparison ranking: 9

Birth rate: 40 births/1,000 population (2024 est.)
comparison ranking: 4

Death rate: 8.1 deaths/1,000 population (2024 est.)
comparison ranking: 86

Net migration rate: -2.9 migrant(s)/1,000 population (2024 est.)
comparison ranking: 177

Population distribution: the overwhelming majority of the population lives in the southern half of the country, with greater density along the border with Burkina Faso, as shown in this population distribution map

Urbanization: *urban population:* 46.2% of total population (2023)
rate of urbanization: 4.57% annual rate of change (2020-25 est.)

Major urban areas - population: 2.929 million BAMAKO (capital) (2023)

Sex ratio: *at birth:* 1.03 male(s)/female
0-14 years: 1.01 male(s)/female
15-64 years: 0.89 male(s)/female
65 years and over: 0.97 male(s)/female
total population: 0.95 male(s)/female (2024 est.)

Mother's mean age at first birth: 19.2 years (2018 est.)
note: data represents median age at first birth among women 20-49

Maternal mortality ratio: 367 deaths/100,000 live births (2023 est.)
comparison ranking: 17

Infant mortality rate: *total:* 57.4 deaths/1,000 live births (2024 est.)
male: 62.6 deaths/1,000 live births
female: 52 deaths/1,000 live births
comparison ranking: total 10

Life expectancy at birth: *total population:* 63.2 years (2024 est.)
male: 60.9 years
female: 65.6 years
comparison ranking: total population 211

Total fertility rate: 5.35 children born/woman (2024 est.)
comparison ranking: 4

Gross reproduction rate: 2.64 (2024 est.)

Drinking water source: *improved: urban:* 94.7% of population (2022 est.)
rural: 74.4% of population (2022 est.)
total: 83.6% of population (2022 est.)
unimproved: urban: 5.3% of population (2022 est.)
rural: 25.6% of population (2022 est.)
total: 16.4% of population (2022 est.)

Health expenditure: 4.5% of GDP (2021)
5.7% of national budget (2022 est.)

Physician density: 0.19 physicians/1,000 population (2023)

Hospital bed density: 0.2 beds/1,000 population (2018 est.)

Sanitation facility access: *improved: urban:* 88.6% of population (2022 est.)
rural: 49.3% of population (2022 est.)
total: 67.2% of population (2022 est.)
unimproved: urban: 11.4% of population (2022 est.)
rural: 50.7% of population (2022 est.)
total: 32.8% of population (2022 est.)

Obesity - adult prevalence rate: 8.6% (2016)
comparison ranking: 150

Alcohol consumption per capita: *total:* 0.6 liters of pure alcohol (2019 est.)
beer: 0.09 liters of pure alcohol (2019 est.)
wine: 0 liters of pure alcohol (2019 est.)
spirits: 0.02 liters of pure alcohol (2019 est.)
other alcohols: 0.49 liters of pure alcohol (2019 est.)
comparison ranking: total 159

Tobacco use: *total:* 6.9% (2025 est.)
male: 13.1% (2025 est.)
female: 0.6% (2025 est.)
comparison ranking: total 151

Children under the age of 5 years underweight: 18.5% (2022)
comparison ranking: 22

Currently married women (ages 15-49): 77.9% (2023 est.)

Child marriage: *women married by age 15:* 15.9% (2018)
women married by age 18: 53.7% (2018)
men married by age 18: 2.1% (2018)

Education expenditure: 4.2% of GDP (2023 est.)
17.8% national budget (2024 est.)
comparison ranking: Education expenditure (% GDP) 99

Literacy: *total population:* 35% (2018 est.)
male: 46% (2018 est.)
female: 26% (2018 est.)

School life expectancy (primary to tertiary education): *total:* 7 years (2017 est.)
male: 8 years (2017 est.)
female: 6 years (2017 est.)

ENVIRONMENT

Environmental issues: deforestation; soil erosion; desertification; loss of pasture land; inadequate supplies of potable water

International environmental agreements: *party to:* Biodiversity, Climate Change, Climate Change-Kyoto Protocol, Climate Change-Paris Agreement, Comprehensive Nuclear Test Ban, Desertification, Endangered Species, Hazardous Wastes, Law of the Sea, Ozone Layer Protection, Tropical Timber 2006, Wetlands, Whaling
signed, but not ratified: Nuclear Test Ban

Climate: subtropical to arid; hot and dry (February to June); rainy, humid, and mild (June to November); cool and dry (November to February)

Urbanization: *urban population:* 46.2% of total population (2023)
rate of urbanization: 4.57% annual rate of change (2020-25 est.)

Carbon dioxide emissions: 6.858 million metric tonnes of CO_2 (2023 est.)
from coal and metallurgical coke: 83 metric tonnes of CO_2 (2023 est.)
from petroleum and other liquids: 6.858 million metric tonnes of CO_2 (2023 est.)
comparison ranking: total emissions 125

Particulate matter emissions: 48.5 micrograms per cubic meter (2019 est.)

Waste and recycling: *municipal solid waste generated annually:* 1.937 million tons (2024 est.)
percent of municipal solid waste recycled: 10.4% (2022 est.)

Total water withdrawal: *municipal:* 107 million cubic meters (2022 est.)
industrial: 4 million cubic meters (2022 est.)
agricultural: 5.075 billion cubic meters (2022 est.)

Total renewable water resources: 120 billion cubic meters (2022 est.)

GOVERNMENT

Country name: *conventional long form:* Republic of Mali
conventional short form: Mali
local long form: République de Mali
local short form: Mali
former: French Sudan, Sudanese Republic, Mali Federation
etymology: name derives from the Mali Empire of the 13th to 16th centuries A.D.; the Mali name may come from a local ethnic group, the Malinke, whose name is derived from the words *ma*, meaning "mother," and *dink*, meaning "child" – a reference to the matrilinear descent of Malinke families

Government type: semi-presidential republic

Capital: *name:* Bamako
geographic coordinates: 12 39 N, 8 00 W
time difference: UTC 0 (5 hours ahead of Washington, DC, during Standard Time)
etymology: the origin of the name is unclear, but it comes from the Bambara language and can refer either to a crocodile or to a person's name

Administrative divisions: 19 regions (*régions*, singular - *région*), 1 district*; Bamako*, Bandiagara, Bougouni, Dioila, Douentza, Gao, Kayes, Kidal, Kita, Koulikoro, Koutiala, Menaka, Mopti, Nara, Nioro, San, Segou, Sikasso, Taoudenni, Tombouctou (Timbuktu)

Legal system: civil law system based on the French civil law model and influenced by customary law; Constitutional Court reviews legislative acts

Constitution: *history:* several previous; latest drafted 13 October 2022 and submitted to Transition President Assimi GOITA; final draft completed 1 March 2023; approved by referendum 18 June 2023; validated by Constitutional Court 22 July 2023

International law organization participation: has not submitted an ICJ jurisdiction declaration; accepts ICCt jurisdiction

Citizenship: *citizenship by birth:* no
citizenship by descent only: at least one parent must be a citizen of Mali
dual citizenship recognized: yes
residency requirement for naturalization: 5 years

Suffrage: 18 years of age; universal

Executive branch: *chief of state:* Transition President Assimi GOITA (since 7 June 2021)
head of government: Transition Prime Minister Abdoulaye MAIGA (since 22 November 2024)
cabinet: Council of Ministers appointed by the prime minister
election/appointment process: president directly elected by absolute-majority popular vote in 2 rounds, if needed, for a 5-year term (eligible for a second term); prime minister appointed by the president
most recent election date: 29 July 2018, with runoff on 12 August 2018
election results: *2018:* Ibrahim Boubacar KEITA reelected president in second round; percent of vote in first round - Ibrahim Boubacar KEITA (RPM) 41.7%, Soumaila CISSE (URD) 17.8%, other 40.5%; percent of vote in second round - Ibrahim Boubacar KEITA 67.2%, Soumaila CISSE 32.8%
2013: Ibrahim Boubacar KEITA elected president in second round; percent of vote in first round - Ibrahim Boubacar KEITA (RPM) 39.8%, Soumaila CISSE (URD) 19.7%, other 40.5%; percent of vote in second round - Ibrahim Boubacar KEITA (RPM) 77.6%, Soumaila CISSE (URD) 22.4%
note: in 2022, the transition government adopted a charter allowing transition authorities to rule for up to 5 years, but the military junta pushed through a referendum in 2023 that created the potential for transition President GOITA to maintain his hold on power indefinitely

Legislative branch: *legislature name:* Transitional National Council (Conseil national de transition)
legislative structure: unicameral
chamber name: Transitional National Council (Conseil national de transition)
number of seats: 147 (all appointed)
electoral system: plurality/majority
scope of elections: full renewal
most recent election date: 12/5/2020
percentage of women in chamber: 30.1%
expected date of next election: December 2030
note 1: the National Assembly was dissolved on 18 August 2020 after a military coup; the transitional government created a Transitional National Council (CNT) that acts as the transitional government's legislative body; a new constitution was ratified in July 2023 that expanded the military junta's powers, and no plans for legislative elections have been announced
note 2: coup leaders appointed a president and vice president; the president then apportioned CNT seats to various groups and political parties

Judicial branch: *highest court(s):* Supreme Court or Cour Suprême (consists of 19 judges organized into judicial, administrative, and accounting sections); Constitutional Court (consists of 9 judges)
judge selection and term of office: Supreme Court judges appointed by the Ministry of Justice to serve 5-year terms; Constitutional Court judges selected - 3 each by the president, the National Assembly, and the Supreme Council of the Magistracy; members serve single renewable 7-year terms
subordinate courts: Court of Appeal; High Court of Justice (jurisdiction limited to cases of high treason or criminal offenses by the president or ministers while in office); administrative courts (first instance and appeal); commercial courts; magistrate courts; labor courts; juvenile courts; special court of state security

Political parties: African Solidarity for Democracy and Independence or SADI
Alliance for Democracy and Progress or ADP-Maliba
Alliance for Democracy in Mali-Pan-African Party for Liberty, Solidarity, and Justice or ADEMA-PASJ
Alliance for the Solidarity of Mali-Convergence of Patriotic Forces or ASMA-CFP
Convergence for the Development of Mali or CODEM
Democratic Alliance for Peace or ADP-Maliba
Movement for Mali or MPM
Party for National Renewal (also Rebirth or Renaissance or PARENA)
Rally for Mali or RPM
Social Democratic Convention or CDS
Union for Democracy and Development or UDD
Union for Republic and Democracy or URD
Yéléma
note 1: only parties with 2 or more seats in the last National Assembly parliamentary elections (30 March and 19 April 2020) included
note 2: the National Assembly was dissolved on 18 August 2020 following a military coup and replaced with a National Transition Council; currently 121 members, party affiliations unknown

Diplomatic representation in the US: *chief of mission:* Ambassador Sékou BERTHE (since 16 September 2022)
chancery: 2130 R Street NW, Washington, DC 20008
telephone: [1] (202) 332-2249
FAX: [1] (202) 332-6603
email address and website: administration@maliembassy.us
https://www.maliembassy.us/

Diplomatic representation from the US: *chief of mission:* Ambassador Rachna KORHONEN (since 16 March 2023)
embassy: ACI 2000, Rue 243, (located off the Roi Bin Fahad Aziz Bridge west of the Bamako central district), Porte 297, Bamako
mailing address: 2050 Bamako Place, Washington DC 20521-2050
telephone: [223] 20-70-23-00
FAX: [223] 20-70-24-79
email address and website: ACSBamako@state.gov
https://ml.usembassy.gov/

International organization participation: ACP, AfDB, AU (suspended), CD, EITI (compliant country), FAO, FZ, G-77, IAEA, IBRD, ICAO, ICCt, ICRM, IDA, IDB, IFAD, IFC, IFRCS, ILO, IMF,

Interpol, IOC, IOM, IPU, ISO, ITSO, ITU, ITUC (NGOs), MIGA, MINUSCA, MONUSCO, NAM, OIC, OPCW, UN, UNCTAD, UNDP, UNESCO, UNFPA, UNHCR, UNIDO, UNOPS, UN Women, UNWTO, UPU, WADB (regional), WAEMU, World Bank Group, WCO, WFTU (NGOs), WHO, WIPO, WMO, WTO

Independence: 22 September 1960 (from France)

National holiday: Independence Day, 22 September (1960)

Flag: *description:* three equal vertical bands of green (left side), yellow, and red
history: uses the colors of the Pan-African movement
note: the colors from left to right are the same as those of neighboring Senegal (which has an additional green central star) and the reverse of the flag of neighboring Guinea

National symbol(s): Great Mosque of Djenne

National color(s): green, yellow, red

National anthem(s): *title:* "Le Mali" (Mali)
lyrics/music: Seydou Badian KOUYATE/Banzoumana SISSOKO
history: adopted 1962

National heritage: *total World Heritage Sites:* 4 (3 cultural, 1 mixed)
selected World Heritage Site locales: Old Towns of Djenné (c); Timbuktu (c); Cliff of Bandiagara (Land of the Dogons) (m); Tomb of Askia (c)

ECONOMY

Economic overview: low-income Saharan economy; recession due to COVID-19 and political instability; extreme poverty; environmentally fragile; high public debt; agricultural and gold exporter; terrorism and warfare are common

Real GDP (purchasing power parity): $71.253 billion (2024 est.)
$67.857 billion (2023 est.)
$64.8 billion (2022 est.)
note: data in 2021 dollars
comparison ranking: 111

Real GDP growth rate: 5% (2024 est.)
4.7% (2023 est.)
3.5% (2022 est.)
note: annual GDP % growth based on constant local currency
comparison ranking: 40

Real GDP per capita: $2,900 (2024 est.)
$2,900 (2023 est.)
$2,800 (2022 est.)
note: data in 2021 dollars
comparison ranking: 197

GDP (official exchange rate): $26.588 billion (2024 est.)
note: data in current dollars at official exchange rate

Inflation rate (consumer prices): 3.2% (2024 est.)
2.1% (2023 est.)
9.6% (2022 est.)
note: annual % change based on consumer prices
comparison ranking: 102

GDP - composition, by sector of origin: *agriculture:* 33.4% (2024 est.)
industry: 22.7% (2024 est.)
services: 36.7% (2024 est.)
note: figures may not total 100% due to non-allocated consumption not captured in sector-reported data
comparison rankings: agriculture 9; industry 112; services 200

GDP - composition, by end use: *household consumption:* 71.9% (2024 est.)
government consumption: 13.1% (2024 est.)
investment in fixed capital: 21.6% (2024 est.)
investment in inventories: -0.7% (2024 est.)
exports of goods and services: 22.5% (2024 est.)
imports of goods and services: -28.4% (2024 est.)
note: figures may not total 100% due to rounding or gaps in data collection

Agricultural products: maize, rice, millet, sorghum, onions, okra, sugarcane, cotton, mangoes/guavas, sweet potatoes (2023)
note: top ten agricultural products based on tonnage

Industries: food processing; construction; phosphate and gold mining

Industrial production growth rate: -2.4% (2024 est.)
note: annual % change in industrial value added based on constant local currency
comparison ranking: 162

Labor force: 9.126 million (2024 est.)
note: number of people ages 15 or older who are employed or seeking work
comparison ranking: 59

Unemployment rate: 3.1% (2024 est.)
3% (2023 est.)
2.4% (2022 est.)
note: % of labor force seeking employment
comparison ranking: 41

Youth unemployment rate (ages 15-24): *total:* 4% (2024 est.)
male: 4% (2024 est.)
female: 3.9% (2024 est.)
note: % of labor force ages 15-24 seeking employment
comparison ranking: total 169

Population below poverty line: 44.6% (2021 est.)
note: % of population with income below national poverty line

Gini Index coefficient - distribution of family income: 35.7 (2021 est.)
note: index (0-100) of income distribution; higher values represent greater inequality
comparison ranking: 70

Household income or consumption by percentage share: *lowest 10%:* 3.2% (2021 est.)
highest 10%: 28.3% (2021 est.)
note: % share of income accruing to lowest and highest 10% of population

Remittances: 4.2% of GDP (2023 est.)
4.9% of GDP (2022 est.)
4.9% of GDP (2021 est.)
note: personal transfers and compensation between resident and non-resident individuals/households/entities

Budget: *revenues:* $2.841 billion (2020 est.)
expenditures: $3.563 billion (2020 est.)
note: central government revenues and expenses (excluding grants/extrabudgetary units/social security funds) converted to US dollars at average official exchange rate for year indicated

Taxes and other revenues: 12% (of GDP) (2020 est.)
note: central government tax revenue as a % of GDP
comparison ranking: 116

Current account balance: -$1.61 billion (2023 est.)
-$1.475 billion (2022 est.)
-$1.469 billion (2021 est.)
note: balance of payments - net trade and primary/secondary income in current dollars
comparison ranking: 141

Exports: $6.13 billion (2023 est.)
$5.855 billion (2022 est.)
$5.381 billion (2021 est.)
note: balance of payments - exports of goods and services in current dollars
comparison ranking: 132

Exports - partners: UAE 73%, Switzerland 15%, Australia 5%, China 1%, Uganda 1% (2023)
note: top five export partners based on percentage share of exports

Exports - commodities: gold, cotton, oil seeds, fertilizers, gum resins (2023)
note: top five export commodities based on value in dollars

Imports: $8.066 billion (2023 est.)
$7.942 billion (2022 est.)
$7.596 billion (2021 est.)
note: balance of payments - imports of goods and services in current dollars
comparison ranking: 133

Imports - partners: Cote d'Ivoire 25%, Senegal 19%, China 12%, France 5%, Burkina Faso 4% (2023)
note: top five import partners based on percentage share of imports

Imports - commodities: refined petroleum, broadcasting equipment, cement, cotton fabric, plastic products (2023)
note: top five import commodities based on value in dollars

Debt - external: $4.085 billion (2023 est.)
note: present value of external debt in current US dollars
comparison ranking: 75

Exchange rates: Communaute Financiere Africaine francs (XOF) per US dollar -

Exchange rates: 606.345 (2024 est.)
606.57 (2023 est.)
623.76 (2022 est.)
554.531 (2021 est.)
575.586 (2020 est.)

ENERGY

Electricity access: *electrification - total population:* 53% (2022 est.)
electrification - urban areas: 99.7%
electrification - rural areas: 18.3%

Electricity: *installed generating capacity:* 1.222 million kW (2023 est.)
consumption: 4.261 billion kWh (2023 est.)
exports: 661.63 million kWh (2023 est.)
imports: 880 million kWh (2023 est.)
transmission/distribution losses: 320.616 million kWh (2023 est.)
comparison rankings: installed generating capacity 130; consumption 133; exports 73; imports 80; transmission/distribution losses 72

Electricity generation sources: *fossil fuels:* 57.3% of total installed capacity (2023 est.)
solar: 3.5% of total installed capacity (2023 est.)
hydroelectricity: 37.6% of total installed capacity (2023 est.)
biomass and waste: 1.6% of total installed capacity (2023 est.)

Coal: *imports:* 36 metric tons (2023 est.)

Petroleum: *refined petroleum consumption:* 46,000 bbl/day (2023 est.)

Energy consumption per capita: 4.307 million Btu/person (2023 est.)
comparison ranking: 172

COMMUNICATIONS

Telephones - fixed lines: *total subscriptions:* 307,000 (2022 est.)
subscriptions per 100 inhabitants: 1 (2022 est.)
comparison ranking: total subscriptions 107

Telephones - mobile cellular: *total subscriptions:* 25.9 million (2022 est.)
subscriptions per 100 inhabitants: 114 (2022 est.)
comparison ranking: total subscriptions 52

Broadcast media: national public TV broadcaster; 2 privately owned companies provide subscription services to foreign multi-channel TV packages; national public radio broadcaster supplemented by a large number of privately owned and community broadcast stations; transmissions of multiple international broadcasters are available (2019)

Internet country code: .ml

Internet users: *percent of population:* 35% (2023 est.)

Broadband - fixed subscriptions: *total:* 179,000 (2022 est.)
subscriptions per 100 inhabitants: 1 (2022 est.)
comparison ranking: total 124

TRANSPORTATION

Civil aircraft registration country code prefix: TZ, TT

Airports: 30 (2025)
comparison ranking: 121

Heliports: 4 (2025)
comparison ranking: 106

Railways: *total:* 593 km (2014)
narrow gauge: 593 km (2014) 1.000-m gauge

MILITARY AND SECURITY

Military and security forces: Malian Armed Forces (Forces Armées Maliennes or FAMa): Army (l'Armée de Terre), Air Force (l'Armée de l'Air); National Guard (la Garde Nationale du Mali); National Gendarmerie of Mali (Gendarmerie Nationale du Mali) (2025)
note 1: the Gendarmerie and the National Guard are under the authority of the Ministry of Defense and Veterans Affairs (Ministere De La Defense Et Des Anciens Combattants, MDAC), but operational control is shared with the Ministry of Internal Security and Civil Protection which also controls the National Police; the National Police has responsibility for law enforcement and maintenance of order in urban areas and supports the FAMa in internal military operations
note 2: the Gendarmerie's primary mission is internal security and public order; its duties also include territorial defense, humanitarian operations, intelligence gathering, and protecting private property, mainly in rural areas; it also has a specialized border security unit
note 3: the National Guard is a military force responsible for providing security to government facilities and institutions, prison service, public order, humanitarian operations, some border security, and intelligence gathering; its forces include a camel corps for patrolling the deserts and borders of northern Mali
note 4: there are also pro-government militias operating in Mali, such as the Imghad Tuareg Self-Defense Group and Allies (GATIA); the leader of GATIA is also a general in the national army

Military expenditures: 4.3% of GDP (2024 est.)
4% of GDP (2023 est.)
3.5% of GDP (2022 est.)
3.4% of GDP (2021 est.)
3.4% of GDP (2020 est.)

Military and security service personnel strengths: information varies; estimated 35-40,000 active FAMa, Gendarmerie, and National Guard (2025)

Military equipment inventories and acquisitions: the FAMa's inventory includes mostly Soviet-era weapons and equipment along with smaller quantities of secondhand and some more modern material from a variety of other countries, including China, Czechia, France, Russia, Turkey, and the UAE (2025)

Military service age and obligation: 18 years of age for men and women for selective compulsory and voluntary military service; 24-month compulsory service obligation (2023)

Military deployments: *note 1:* in 2024, Mali, Burkina Faso, and Niger announced they were forming joint force of 5,000 troops to combat extremist groups in the Sahel
note 2: until announcing its withdrawal in May of 2022, Mali was part of a five-nation anti-jihadist task force known as the G5 Sahel Group, set up in 2014 with Burkina Faso, Chad, Mauritania, and Niger; Mali had committed 1,100 troops and 200 gendarmes to the force

Military - note: the FAMa is responsible for the defense of the country's sovereignty and territory, but also has some domestic security duties, including the maintenance of public order and support to law enforcement; it also participates in socio-economic development projects; the military has traditionally played a large role in Mali's politics; prior to the coup in August 2020 and military takeover in May 2021, it had intervened in the political arena at least five times since the country gained independence in 1960 (1968, 1976, 1978, 1991, 2012)
the FAMa and other security forces are actively engaged in combat operations against several insurgent/terrorist groups affiliated with al-Qa'ida and the Islamic State of Iraq and ash-Sham (ISIS), as well as other armed rebel organizations, communal militias, and criminal bands spread across the central, northern, and southern regions of the country; a large portion of the country–up to 50% by some estimates–is outside of government control
the FAMa and the remainder of the security forces collapsed in 2012 during the fighting against Tuareg rebels and Islamic militants and were rebuilt beginning in 2013 with external assistance from the EU and the UN; the UN Multidimensional Integrated Stabilization Mission in Mali (MINUSMA) and the EU Training Mission in Mali (EUTM) ended their missions in 2023 and 2024, respectively; France intervened militarily in Mali in 2013 to assist with regaining the northern half of the country from rebel and Islamic militant groups; French troops withdrew in 2022; since 2021, Mali has increased security ties with Russia, which has provided equipment, training, and other forms of military support (2025)

TERRORISM

Terrorist group(s): Terrorist group(s): Ansar al-Dine; Islamic State of Iraq and ash-Sham in the Greater Sahara (ISIS-GS); Jama'at Nusrat al-Islam wal-Muslimin (JNIM); al-Mulathamun Battalion (al-Mourabitoun)
note: details about the history, aims, leadership, organization, areas of operation, tactics, targets, weapons, size, and sources of support of the group(s) appear(s) in Appendix T

TRANSNATIONAL ISSUES

Refugees and internally displaced persons: *refugees:* 135,827 (2024 est.)

IDPs: 378,363 (2024 est.)

MALTA

INTRODUCTION

Background: With a civilization that dates back thousands of years, Malta boasts some of the oldest megalithic sites in the world. Situated in the center of the Mediterranean, Malta's islands have long served as a strategic military asset, with the islands at various times falling under the control of the Phoenicians, Carthaginians, Greeks, Romans, Byzantines, Moors, Normans, Sicilians, Spanish, Knights of St. John, and French. Most recently a British colony (since 1814), Malta gained its independence in 1964 and declared itself a republic 10 years later. While under British rule, the island staunchly supported the UK through both world wars. Since the mid-1980s, the island has transformed itself into a freight transshipment point, a financial center, and a tourist destination, as its key industries moved toward more service-oriented activities. Malta became an EU member in 2004 and joined the eurozone in 2008.

GEOGRAPHY

Location: Southern Europe, islands in the Mediterranean Sea, south of Sicily (Italy)

Geographic coordinates: 35 50 N, 14 35 E

Map references: Europe

Area: *total:* 316 sq km
land: 316 sq km
water: 0 sq km
comparison ranking: total 208

Area - comparative: slightly less than twice the size of Washington, D.C.

Land boundaries: *total:* 0 km

Coastline: 196.8 km (excludes 56 km for the island of Gozo)

Maritime claims: *territorial sea:* 12 nm
contiguous zone: 24 nm

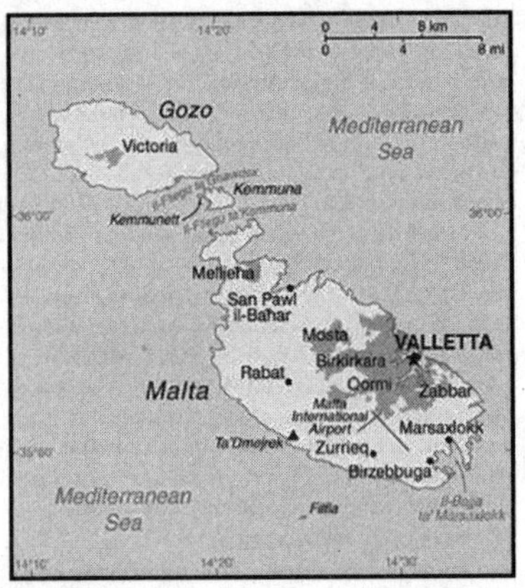

continental shelf: 200-m depth or to the depth of exploitation
exclusive fishing zone: 25 nm

Climate: Mediterranean; mild, rainy winters; hot, dry summers

Terrain: mostly low, rocky, flat to dissected plains; many coastal cliffs

Elevation: *highest point*: Ta'Dmejrek on Dingli Cliffs 253 m
lowest point: Mediterranean Sea 0 m

Natural resources: limestone, salt, arable land

Land use: *agricultural land*: 27.3% (2022 est.)
arable land: 24.4% (2022 est.)
permanent crops: 3% (2022 est.)
permanent pasture: 0% (2022 est.)
forest: 1.4% (2022 est.)
other: 71.2% (2022 est.)

Irrigated land: 39 sq km (2022)

Population distribution: most of the population lives on the eastern half of Malta, the largest of the three inhabited islands

Natural hazards: occasional droughts

Geography - note: the country is an archipelago, with only the three largest islands (Malta, Ghawdex or Gozo, and Kemmuna or Comino) inhabited; numerous bays provide good harbors

PEOPLE AND SOCIETY

Population: *total*: 469,730 (2024 est.)
male: 237,023
female: 232,707
comparison rankings: total 174; male 174; female 174

Nationality: *noun*: Maltese (singular and plural)
adjective: Maltese

Ethnic groups: Maltese (descendants of ancient Carthaginians and Phoenicians with strong elements of Italian and other Mediterranean stock)

Languages: Maltese (official) 90.1%, English (official) 6%, multilingual 3%, other 0.9% (2005 est.)

Religions: Roman Catholic (official) more than 90% (2006 est.)

Age structure: *0-14 years*: 14.5% (male 35,034/female 33,181)
15-64 years: 62.4% (male 151,836/female 141,248)
65 years and over: 23.1% (2024 est.) (male 50,153/female 58,278)

Dependency ratios: *total dependency ratio*: 53.7 (2024 est.)
youth dependency ratio: 21.4 (2024 est.)
elderly dependency ratio: 32.4 (2024 est.)
potential support ratio: 3.1 (2024 est.)

Median age: *total*: 43.5 years (2024 est.)
male: 42.4 years
female: 44.7 years
comparison ranking: total 35

Population growth rate: 0.51% (2024 est.)
comparison ranking: 150

Birth rate: 9.4 births/1,000 population (2024 est.)
comparison ranking: 193

Death rate: 8.8 deaths/1,000 population (2024 est.)
comparison ranking: 67

Net migration rate: 4.4 migrant(s)/1,000 population (2024 est.)
comparison ranking: 21

Population distribution: most of the population lives on the eastern half of Malta, the largest of the three inhabited islands

Urbanization: *urban population*: 94.9% of total population (2023)
rate of urbanization: 0.28% annual rate of change (2020-25 est.)

Major urban areas - population: 213,000 VALLETTA (capital) (2018)

Sex ratio: *at birth*: 1.04 male(s)/female
0-14 years: 1.06 male(s)/female
15-64 years: 1.07 male(s)/female
65 years and over: 0.86 male(s)/female
total population: 1.02 male(s)/female (2024 est.)

Mother's mean age at first birth: 29.3 years (2020 est.)
note: data refers to the average of the different childbearing ages of first-order births

Maternal mortality ratio: 8 deaths/100,000 live births (2023 est.)
comparison ranking: 157

Infant mortality rate: *total*: 4.4 deaths/1,000 live births (2024 est.)
male: 4.3 deaths/1,000 live births
female: 4.5 deaths/1,000 live births
comparison ranking: total 182

Life expectancy at birth: *total population*: 83.6 years (2024 est.)
male: 81.5 years
female: 85.8 years
comparison ranking: total population 12

Total fertility rate: 1.51 children born/woman (2024 est.)
comparison ranking: 201

Gross reproduction rate: 0.74 (2024 est.)

Drinking water source: *improved*: *urban*: 100% of population (2022 est.)
rural: 100% of population (2022 est.)
total: 100% of population (2022 est.)
unimproved: *urban*: 0% of population (2022 est.)
rural: 0% of population (2022 est.)
total: 0% of population (2022 est.)

Health expenditure: 10.6% of GDP (2021)
16.2% of national budget (2022 est.)

Physician density: 7.86 physicians/1,000 population (2022)

Hospital bed density: 4.4 beds/1,000 population (2020 est.)

Sanitation facility access: *improved*: *urban*: 100% of population (2022 est.)
rural: 100% of population (2022 est.)
total: 100% of population (2022 est.)
unimproved: *urban*: 0% of population (2022 est.)
rural: 0% of population (2022 est.)
total: 0% of population (2022 est.)

Obesity - adult prevalence rate: 28.9% (2016)
comparison ranking: 29

Alcohol consumption per capita: *total*: 8.07 liters of pure alcohol (2019 est.)
beer: 2.8 liters of pure alcohol (2019 est.)
wine: 2.34 liters of pure alcohol (2019 est.)
spirits: 2.51 liters of pure alcohol (2019 est.)
other alcohols: 0.42 liters of pure alcohol (2019 est.)
comparison ranking: total 43

Tobacco use: *total*: 22.1% (2025 est.)
male: 23.9% (2025 est.)
female: 20.2% (2025 est.)
comparison ranking: total 51

Currently married women (ages 15-49): 63.2% (2023 est.)

Education expenditure: 4.8% of GDP (2022 est.)
12.7% national budget (2022 est.)
comparison ranking: Education expenditure (% GDP) 70

School life expectancy (primary to tertiary education): *total*: 16 years (2023 est.)
male: 15 years (2023 est.)
female: 17 years (2023 est.)

ENVIRONMENT

Environmental issues: limited natural freshwater resources; deforestation; wildlife preservation

International environmental agreements: *party to*: Air Pollution, Biodiversity, Climate Change, Climate Change-Kyoto Protocol, Climate Change-Paris Agreement, Comprehensive Nuclear Test Ban, Desertification, Endangered Species, Hazardous Wastes, Law of the Sea, Marine Dumping-London Convention, Nuclear Test Ban, Ozone Layer Protection, Ship Pollution, Tropical Timber 2006, Wetlands
signed, but not ratified: none of the selected agreements

Climate: Mediterranean; mild, rainy winters; hot, dry summers

Urbanization: *urban population*: 94.9% of total population (2023)
rate of urbanization: 0.28% annual rate of change (2020-25 est.)

Carbon dioxide emissions: 8.965 million metric tonnes of CO2 (2023 est.)
from petroleum and other liquids: 8.113 million metric tonnes of CO2 (2023 est.)
from consumed natural gas: 852,000 metric tonnes of CO2 (2023 est.)
comparison ranking: total emissions 111

Particulate matter emissions: 13.1 micrograms per cubic meter (2019 est.)

Waste and recycling: *municipal solid waste generated annually*: 348,800 tons (2024 est.)
percent of municipal solid waste recycled: 10.5% (2022 est.)

Total water withdrawal: *municipal*: 39.497 million cubic meters (2022)
industrial: 1 million cubic meters (2022)
agricultural: 21.358 million cubic meters (2022)

Total renewable water resources: 50.5 million cubic meters (2022 est.)

GOVERNMENT

Country name: *conventional long form:* Republic of Malta
conventional short form: Malta
local long form: Repubblika ta' Malta
local short form: Malta
etymology: the origin is unclear; the name may come from the ancient term *mel*, meaning "high " and probably referring to the island's rocks; the ancient Greeks called the island "Melite, " possibly from the Greek word *meli*, meaning "honey " and referring to the island's honey production

Government type: parliamentary republic

Capital: *name:* Valletta
geographic coordinates: 35 53 N, 14 30 E
time difference: UTC+1 (6 hours ahead of Washington, DC, during Standard Time)
daylight saving time: +1hr, begins last Sunday in March; ends last Sunday in October
etymology: named in honor of Jean Parizot de la VALETTE, the Grand Master of the Order of Saint John (crusader knights), who founded the city in 1566

Administrative divisions: 68 localities (*Il-lokalita*); Attard, Balzan, Birgu, Birkirkara, Birzebbuga, Bormla, Dingli, Fgura, Floriana, Fontana, Ghajnsielem, Gharb, Gharghur, Ghasri, Ghaxaq, Gudja, Gzira, Hamrun, Iklin, Imdina, Imgarr, Imqabba, Imsida, Imtarfa, Isla, Kalkara, Kercem, Kirkop, Lija, Luqa, Marsa, Marsaskala, Marsaxlokk, Mellieha, Mosta, Munxar, Nadur, Naxxar, Paola, Pembroke, Pieta, Qala, Qormi, Qrendi, Rabat, Rabat (Ghawdex), Safi, San Giljan/Saint Julian, San Gwann/Saint John, San Lawrenz/Saint Lawrence, Sannat, San Pawl il-Bahar/ Saint Paul's Bay, Santa Lucija/Saint Lucia, Santa Venera/Saint Venera, Siggiewi, Sliema, Swieqi, Tarxien, Ta' Xbiex, Valletta, Xaghra, Xewkija, Xghajra, Zabbar, Zebbug, Zebbug (Ghawdex), Zejtun, Zurrieq

Legal system: mixed system of English common law and civil law based on the Roman and Napoleonic civil codes; subject to European Union law

Constitution: *history:* many previous; latest adopted 21 September 1964
amendment process: proposals (Acts of Parliament) require at least two-thirds majority vote by the House of Representatives; passage of Acts requires majority vote by referendum, followed by final majority vote by the House and assent of the president of the republic

International law organization participation: accepts compulsory ICJ jurisdiction with reservations; accepts ICCt jurisdiction

Citizenship: *citizenship by birth:* no
citizenship by descent only: at least one parent must be a citizen of Malta
dual citizenship recognized: no
residency requirement for naturalization: 5 years

Suffrage: 18 years of age (16 in local council elections); universal

Executive branch: *chief of state:* President Myriam Spiteri DEBONO (since 4 April 2024)
head of government: Prime Minister Robert ABELA (since 13 January 2020)
cabinet: Cabinet appointed by the president on the advice of the prime minister
election/appointment process: president indirectly elected by the House of Representatives for a single 5-year term; following legislative elections, the president usually appoints the leader of the majority party or majority coalition as prime minister for a 5-year term; deputy prime minister appointed by the president on the advice of the prime minister
most recent election date: 27 March 2024
election results: *2024:* Myriam Spiteri DEBONO (PL) elected president; House of Representatives vote - unanimous
2019: George VELLA (PL) elected president; House of Representatives vote - unanimous
expected date of next election: by March 2029

Legislative branch: *legislature name:* House of Representatives (Il-Kamra Tad-Deputati)
legislative structure: unicameral
number of seats: 65 (all directly elected)
electoral system: proportional representation
scope of elections: full renewal
term in office: 5 years
most recent election date: 3/26/2022
parties elected and seats per party: Labour Party (LP) (44); Nationalist Party (PN) (35)
percentage of women in chamber: 29.1%
expected date of next election: March 2027

Judicial branch: *highest court(s):* Court of Appeal (consists of either 1 or 3 judges); Constitutional Court (consists of 3 judges); Court of Criminal Appeal (consists of either 1 or 3 judges)
judge selection and term of office: Court of Appeal and Constitutional Court judges appointed by the president, usually on the advice of the prime minister; judges of both courts serve until age 65
subordinate courts: Civil Court (divided into the General Jurisdiction Section, Family Section, and Voluntary Section); Criminal Court; Court of Magistrates; Gozo Courts (for the islands of Gozo and Comino)

Political parties: AD+PD or ADPD (formed from the merger of Democratic Alternative or AD and Democratic Party (Partit Demokratiku) or PD)
Labor Party (Partit Laburista) or PL
Nationalist Party (Partit Nazzjonalista) or PN

Diplomatic representation in the US: *chief of mission:* Ambassador Godfrey C. XUEREB (since 19 April 2023)
chancery: 2017 Connecticut Avenue NW, Washington, DC 20008
telephone: [1] (771) 213-4050
FAX: [1] (202) 530-9753
email address and website: maltaembassy.washington@gov.mt
The Embassy (gov.mt)

Diplomatic representation from the US: *chief of mission:* Ambassador (vacant); Chargé d'Affaires Ken TOKO (since 20 January 2025)
embassy: Ta' Qali National Park, Attard, ATD 4000
mailing address: 5800 Valletta Place, Washington DC 20521-5800
telephone: [356] 2561-4000
email address and website: ACSMalta@state.gov
https://mt.usembassy.gov/

International organization participation: Australia Group, C, CD, CE, EAPG, EBRD, ECB, EIB, EMU, EU, FAO, IAEA, IBRD, ICAO, ICC (NGOs), ICCt, ICRM, IDA, IFAD, IFC, IFRCS, ILO, IMF, IMO, IMSO, Interpol, IOC, IOM, IPU, ISO, ITSO, ITU, ITUC (NGOs), MIGA, NATO (partner), NSG, OAS (observer), OPCW, OSCE, PCA, PFP, Schengen Convention, UN, UNCTAD, UNESCO, UNIDO, Union Latina (observer), UNWTO, UPU, Wassenaar Arrangement, WCO, WHO, WIPO, WMO, WTO

Independence: 21 September 1964 (from the UK)

National holiday: Independence Day, 21 September (1964); Republic Day, 13 December (1974)

Flag: *description:* two equal vertical bands of white (left side) and red; in the upper-left corner is the George Cross, edged in red
history: according to legend, the colors come from the red-and-white checkered banner of Count Roger of Sicily, who removed a bicolored corner and granted it to Malta in 1091, but the colors more likely come from the Knights of Saint John, who ruled Malta from 1530 to 1798; in 1942, Britain's King George VI awarded the George Cross to the islanders for their exceptional bravery and gallantry in World War II, and the George Cross bordered in red was added to the flag after independence in 1964

National symbol(s): Maltese eight-pointed cross

National color(s): red, white

National anthem(s): *title:* "L-Innu Malti " (The Hymn of Malta)
lyrics/music: Dun Karm PSAILA/Robert SAMMUT
history: adopted 1945; written in the form of a prayer to bind together the political parties and the country

National heritage: *total World Heritage Sites:* 3 (all cultural)
selected World Heritage Site locales: City of Valletta; Ħal Saflieni Hypogeum; Megalithic Temples of Malta

ECONOMY

Economic overview: high-income, EU-member European economy; diversified portfolio; euro user; dependent on food and energy imports; strong tourism, trade, and manufacturing sectors; high North African immigration; large welfare system; educated workforce

Real GDP (purchasing power parity): $34.731 billion (2024 est.)
$32.774 billion (2023 est.)
$30.689 billion (2022 est.)
note: data in 2021 dollars
comparison ranking: 142

Real GDP growth rate: 6% (2024 est.)
6.8% (2023 est.)
4.3% (2022 est.)
note: annual GDP % growth based on constant local currency
comparison ranking: 22

Real GDP per capita: $60,500 (2024 est.)
$59,300 (2023 est.)
$57,800 (2022 est.)
note: data in 2021 dollars
comparison ranking: 30

GDP (official exchange rate): $24.322 billion (2024 est.)
note: data in current dollars at official exchange rate

Inflation rate (consumer prices): 1.7% (2024 est.)
5.1% (2023 est.)
6.2% (2022 est.)
note: annual % change based on consumer prices
comparison ranking: 40

GDP - composition, by sector of origin: *agriculture:* 0.2% (2024 est.)
industry: 11.4% (2024 est.)
services: 80.8% (2024 est.)

note: figures may not total 100% due to non-allocated consumption not captured in sector-reported data
comparison rankings: agriculture 198; industry 178; services 11

GDP - composition, by end use: *household consumption:* 46.6% (2024 est.)
government consumption: 17.2% (2024 est.)
investment in fixed capital: 17.9% (2024 est.)
investment in inventories: 0.9% (2024 est.)
exports of goods and services: 123.5% (2024 est.)
imports of goods and services: -106.1% (2024 est.)
note: figures may not total 100% due to rounding or gaps in data collection

Agricultural products: milk, tomatoes, onions, potatoes, chicken, cauliflower/broccoli, cabbages, pork, pumpkins/squash, watermelons (2023)
note: top ten agricultural products based on tonnage

Industries: tourism, electronics, ship building and repair, construction, food and beverages, pharmaceuticals, footwear, clothing, tobacco, aviation services, financial services, information technology services

Industrial production growth rate: 5.6% (2024 est.)
note: annual % change in industrial value added based on constant local currency
comparison ranking: 38

Labor force: 318,200 (2024 est.)
note: number of people ages 15 or older who are employed or seeking work
comparison ranking: 166

Unemployment rate: 2.8% (2024 est.)
3.2% (2023 est.)
3% (2022 est.)
note: % of labor force seeking employment
comparison ranking: 30

Youth unemployment rate (ages 15-24): *total:* 7.8% (2024 est.)
male: 9.6% (2024 est.)
female: 5.7% (2024 est.)
note: % of labor force ages 15-24 seeking employment
comparison ranking: total 140

Population below poverty line: 16.7% (2021 est.)
note: % of population with income below national poverty line

Gini Index coefficient - distribution of family income: 34.6 (2022 est.)
note: index (0-100) of income distribution; higher values represent greater inequality
comparison ranking: 79

Household income or consumption by percentage share: *lowest 10%:* 2.7% (2022 est.)
highest 10%: 27.7% (2022 est.)
note: % share of income accruing to lowest and highest 10% of population

Remittances: 0.1% of GDP (2024 est.)
0.1% of GDP (2023 est.)
0.1% of GDP (2022 est.)
note: personal transfers and compensation between resident and non-resident individuals/households/entities

Budget: *revenues:* $6.95 billion (2023 est.)
expenditures: $7.966 billion (2023 est.)
note: central government revenues (excluding grants) and expenditures converted to US dollars at average official exchange rate for year indicated

Public debt: 50.7% of GDP (2017 est.)
note: Malta reports public debt at nominal value outstanding at the end of the year, according to guidelines set out in the Maastricht Treaty for general government gross debt; the data include the following categories of government liabilities (as defined in ESA95): currency and deposits (AF.2), securities other than shares excluding financial derivatives (AF.3, excluding AF.34), and loans (AF.4); general government comprises the central, state, and local governments, and social security funds
comparison ranking: 99

Taxes and other revenues: 21.9% (of GDP) (2023 est.)
note: central government tax revenue as a % of GDP
comparison ranking: 36

Current account balance: $1.383 billion (2024 est.)
$1.425 billion (2023 est.)
-$167.611 million (2022 est.)
note: balance of payments - net trade and primary/secondary income in current dollars
comparison ranking: 55

Exports: $29.245 billion (2024 est.)
$26.647 billion (2023 est.)
$23.566 billion (2022 est.)
note: balance of payments - exports of goods and services in current dollars
comparison ranking: 84

Exports - partners: Nigeria 28%, Germany 10%, China 6%, Singapore 5%, Hong Kong 4% (2023)
note: top five export partners based on percentage share of exports

Exports - commodities: refined petroleum, integrated circuits, packaged medicine, ships, postage stamps/documents (2023)
note: top five export commodities based on value in dollars

Imports: $24.505 billion (2024 est.)
$22.637 billion (2023 est.)
$21.406 billion (2022 est.)
note: balance of payments - imports of goods and services in current dollars
comparison ranking: 87

Imports - partners: Italy 18%, China 10%, Germany 8%, France 7%, Turkey 7% (2023)
note: top five import partners based on percentage share of imports

Imports - commodities: ships, refined petroleum, integrated circuits, aircraft, packaged medicine (2023)
note: top five import commodities based on value in dollars

Reserves of foreign exchange and gold: $1.418 billion (2024 est.)
$1.223 billion (2023 est.)
$1.199 billion (2022 est.)
note: holdings of gold (year-end prices)/foreign exchange/special drawing rights in current dollars
comparison ranking: 137

Exchange rates: euros (EUR) per US dollar -

Exchange rates: 0.924 (2024 est.)
0.925 (2023 est.)
0.95 (2022 est.)
0.845 (2021 est.)
0.876 (2020 est.)

ENERGY

Electricity access: *electrification - total population:* 100% (2022 est.)

Electricity: *installed generating capacity:* 829,000 kW (2023 est.)
consumption: 2.766 billion kWh (2023 est.)
exports: 28 million kWh (2023 est.)
imports: 648 million kWh (2023 est.)
transmission/distribution losses: 199.086 million kWh (2023 est.)
comparison rankings: installed generating capacity 138; consumption 145; exports 96; imports 88; transmission/distribution losses 65

Electricity generation sources: *fossil fuels:* 86.4% of total installed capacity (2023 est.)
solar: 13.2% of total installed capacity (2023 est.)
biomass and waste: 0.4% of total installed capacity (2023 est.)

Coal: *consumption:* 8.4 metric tons (2021 est.)
imports: 3.9 metric tons (2022 est.)

Petroleum: *refined petroleum consumption:* 50,000 bbl/day (2023 est.)

Natural gas: *consumption:* 444.715 million cubic meters (2023 est.)
imports: 444.715 million cubic meters (2023 est.)

Energy consumption per capita: 234.698 million Btu/person (2023 est.)
comparison ranking: 12

COMMUNICATIONS

Telephones - fixed lines: *total subscriptions:* 259,000 (2023 est.)
subscriptions per 100 inhabitants: 49 (2023 est.)
comparison ranking: total subscriptions 112

Telephones - mobile cellular: *total subscriptions:* 749,000 (2023 est.)
subscriptions per 100 inhabitants: 132 (2022 est.)
comparison ranking: total subscriptions 170

Broadcast media: 2 publicly owned TV stations, Television Malta and an educational channel; several privately owned national television stations, 2 of which are owned by political parties; Italian and British broadcast programs are available; multi-channel cable and satellite TV services are available; publicly owned radio broadcaster operates 3 stations; roughly 20 commercial radio stations (2019)

Internet country code: .mt

Internet users: *percent of population:* 92% (2023 est.)

Broadband - fixed subscriptions: *total:* 236,000 (2023 est.)
subscriptions per 100 inhabitants: 44 (2023 est.)
comparison ranking: total 119

TRANSPORTATION

Civil aircraft registration country code prefix: 9H

Airports: 1 (2025)
comparison ranking: 220

Heliports: 2 (2025)
comparison ranking: 139

Merchant marine: *total:* 1,957 (2023)
by type: bulk carrier 490, container ship 348, general cargo 152, oil tanker 354, other 613
comparison ranking: total 14

Ports: *total ports:* 2 (2024)
large: 0
medium: 1
small: 1
very small: 0
ports with oil terminals: 0
key ports: Marsaxlokk, Valletta Harbors

MILITARY AND SECURITY

Military and security forces: *the Armed Forces of Malta (AFM):* Land Component (combat, combat support, and combat service support divided into three regiments), Maritime Squadron, Air Wing; Volunteer Reserve Force (2025)
note: the Malta Police Force maintains internal security; both the Police and the AFM report to the Ministry of Home Affairs, National Security, and Law Enforcement

Military expenditures: 0.5% of GDP (2024 est.)
0.5% of GDP (2023 est.)
0.7% of GDP (2022 est.)
0.5% of GDP (2021 est.)
0.6% of GDP (2020 est.)

Military and security service personnel strengths: approximately 2,000 active Armed Forces of Malta (2025)

Military equipment inventories and acquisitions: the military has a small inventory that consists of equipment from a mix of European countries, particularly Italy, and the US (2024)

Military service age and obligation: 18-30 years of age for men and women for voluntary military service; no conscription (2024)

Military - note: the Armed Forces of Malta (AFM) are responsible for external security but also have some domestic security responsibilities; the AFM's primary roles include maintaining the country's sovereignty and territorial integrity, monitoring and policing its territorial waters, participating in overseas peacekeeping and stability operations, and providing search and rescue and explosive ordnance disposal capabilities; secondary missions include assisting civil authorities during emergencies, supporting the police and other security services, and providing ceremonial and other public support duties Malta maintains a security policy of neutrality but contributes to EU, Organization for the Security and Cooperation (OSCE), and UN military missions and joined NATO's Partnership for Peace program in 1995 (suspended in 1996, but reactivated in 2008); it also participates in various bilateral and multinational military exercises; Malta cooperates closely with Italy on defense matters; in 1973, Italy established a military mission in Malta to provide advice, training, and search and rescue assistance (2025)

TRANSNATIONAL ISSUES

Refugees and internally displaced persons: *refugees:* 9,284 (2024 est.)
stateless persons: 171 (2024 est.)

MARSHALL ISLANDS

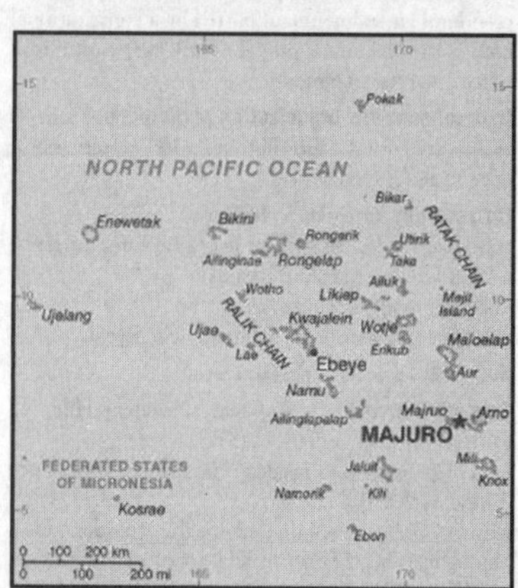

INTRODUCTION

Background: Humans arrived in the Marshall Islands in the first millennium B.C. and gradually created permanent settlements on the various atolls. The early inhabitants were skilled navigators who frequently traveled between atolls using stick charts to map the islands. Society became organized under two paramount chiefs, one each for the Ratak (Sunrise) Chain and the Ralik (Sunset) Chain. Spain formally claimed the islands in 1592. Germany established a supply station on Jaluit Atoll and bought the islands from Spain in 1884, although paramount chiefs continued to rule.

Japan seized the Marshall Islands in 1914 and was granted a League of Nations Mandate to administer the islands in 1920. The US captured the islands in heavy fighting during World War II, and the islands came under US administration as part of the Trust Territory of the Pacific Islands (TTPI) in 1947. Between 1946 and 1958, the US resettled populations from Bikini and Enewetak Atolls and conducted 67 nuclear tests; people from Ailinginae, Rongelap, and Utrik Atolls were also evacuated because of nuclear fallout, and Bikini and Rongelap remain largely uninhabited. In 1979, the Marshall Islands drafted a constitution separate from the rest of the TTPI and declared independence under President Amata KABUA, a paramount chief. In 2000, Kessai NOTE became the first commoner elected president. In 2016, Hilda HEINE was the first woman elected president.

GEOGRAPHY

Location: Oceania, consists of 29 atolls and five isolated islands in the North Pacific Ocean, about halfway between Hawaii and Australia; the atolls and islands are situated in two, almost-parallel island chains - the Ratak (Sunrise) group and the Ralik (Sunset) group; the total number of islands and islets is about 1,225; 22 of the atolls and four of the islands are uninhabited

Geographic coordinates: 9 00 N, 168 00 E

Map references: Oceania

Area: *total:* 181 sq km
land: 181 sq km
water: 0 sq km
note: the archipelago includes 11,673 sq km (4,507 sq mi) of lagoon and encompasses the atolls of Bikini, Enewetak, Kwajalein, Majuro, Rongelap, and Utirik
comparison ranking: total 217

Area - comparative: about the size of Washington, D.C.

Land boundaries: *total:* 0 km

Coastline: 370.4 km

Maritime claims: *territorial sea:* 12 nm
contiguous zone: 24 nm
exclusive economic zone: 200 nm

Climate: tropical; hot and humid; wet season May to November; islands border typhoon belt

Terrain: low coral limestone and sand islands

Elevation: *highest point:* East-central Airik Island, Maloelap Atoll 14 m
lowest point: Pacific Ocean 0 m
mean elevation: 2 m

Natural resources: coconut products, marine products, deep seabed minerals

Land use: *agricultural land:* 38.9% (2022 est.)
arable land: 2.8% (2022 est.)
permanent crops: 36.1% (2022 est.)
permanent pasture: 0% (2022 est.)
forest: 52.2% (2022 est.)
other: 8.9% (2022 est.)

Irrigated land: 0 sq km (2022)

Population distribution: most people live in urban clusters on many of the country's islands; more than two thirds of the population lives on the atolls of Majuro and Ebeye

Natural hazards: infrequent typhoons

Geography - note: Kwajalein atoll surrounds the world's largest lagoon; the island city of Ebeye is the second largest settlement in the Marshall Islands, after the capital of Majuro, and one of the most densely populated locations in the Pacific

PEOPLE AND SOCIETY

Population: *total:* 82,011 (2024 est.)
male: 41,581
female: 40,430
comparison rankings: total 200; male 200; female 200

Nationality: *noun:* Marshallese (singular and plural)
adjective: Marshallese

Ethnic groups: Marshallese 95.6%, Filipino 1.1%, other 3.3% (2021 est.)

Languages: Marshallese (official) 98.2%, other languages 1.8% (1999)
major-language sample(s):
Bok eo an Lalin kin Melele ko Rejimwe ej jikin ebōk melele ko raurōk. (Marshallese)
note: English (official), widely spoken as a second language

Religions: Protestant 79.3% (United Church of Christ 47.9%, Assembly of God 14.1%, Full Gospel 5%, Bukot Nan Jesus 3%, Salvation Army 2.3%, Reformed Congressional Church 2.2%, Seventh Day Adventist 1.7%, New Beginning Church 1.4%, other Protestant 1.6%), Roman Catholic 9.3%, Church of Jesus Christ 5.7%, Jehovah's Witness 1.3%, other 3.3%, none 1.1% (2021 est.)

Age structure: *0-14 years:* 30% (male 12,538/female 12,072)
15-64 years: 64.3% (male 26,750/female 25,944)
65 years and over: 5.7% (2024 est.) (male 2,293/female 2,414)

Dependency ratios: *total dependency ratio:* 55.6 (2024 est.)
youth dependency ratio: 46.7 (2024 est.)
elderly dependency ratio: 8.9 (2024 est.)
potential support ratio: 11.2 (2024 est.)

Median age: *total:* 25.5 years (2024 est.)
male: 25.4 years
female: 25.6 years
comparison ranking: total 169

Population growth rate: 1.26% (2024 est.)
comparison ranking: 76

Birth rate: 21.2 births/1,000 population (2024 est.)
comparison ranking: 61

Death rate: 4.3 deaths/1,000 population (2024 est.)
comparison ranking: 211

Net migration rate: -4.3 migrant(s)/1,000 population (2024 est.)
comparison ranking: 197

Population distribution: most people live in urban clusters on many of the country's islands; more than two thirds of the population lives on the atolls of Majuro and Ebeye

Urbanization: *urban population:* 78.9% of total population (2023)
rate of urbanization: 0.61% annual rate of change (2020-25 est.)

Major urban areas - population: 31,000 MAJURO (capital) (2018)

Sex ratio: *at birth:* 1.05 male(s)/female
0-14 years: 1.04 male(s)/female
15-64 years: 1.03 male(s)/female
65 years and over: 0.95 male(s)/female
total population: 1.03 male(s)/female (2024 est.)

Maternal mortality ratio: 155 deaths/100,000 live births (2023 est.)
comparison ranking: 49

Infant mortality rate: *total:* 20.6 deaths/1,000 live births (2024 est.)
male: 24 deaths/1,000 live births
female: 17.1 deaths/1,000 live births
comparison ranking: total 77

Life expectancy at birth: *total population:* 75.2 years (2024 est.)
male: 73 years
female: 77.5 years
comparison ranking: total population 130

Total fertility rate: 2.67 children born/woman (2024 est.)
comparison ranking: 61

Gross reproduction rate: 1.3 (2024 est.)

Drinking water source: *improved: urban:* 84.5% of population (2022 est.)
rural: 87.2% of population (2022 est.)
total: 85.1% of population (2022 est.)
unimproved: urban: 15.5% of population (2022 est.)
rural: 12.8% of population (2022 est.)
total: 14.9% of population (2022 est.)

Health expenditure: 12.5% of GDP (2021)
6.7% of national budget (2022 est.)

Physician density: 0.47 physicians/1,000 population (2012)

Sanitation facility access: *improved: urban:* 92.8% of population (2022 est.)
rural: 70.4% of population (2022 est.)
total: 88% of population (2022 est.)
unimproved: urban: 7.2% of population (2022 est.)
rural: 29.6% of population (2022 est.)
total: 12% of population (2022 est.)

Obesity - adult prevalence rate: 52.9% (2016)
comparison ranking: 4

Tobacco use: *total:* 30.9% (2025 est.)
male: 52.9% (2025 est.)
female: 8.5% (2025 est.)
comparison ranking: total 18

Children under the age of 5 years underweight: 11.9% (2017)
comparison ranking: 41

Currently married women (ages 15-49): 68.3% (2022 est.)

Education expenditure: 7.5% of GDP (2022 est.)
11.3% national budget (2022 est.)
comparison ranking: Education expenditure (% GDP) 13

School life expectancy (primary to tertiary education): *total:* 14 years (2022 est.)
male: 14 years (2022 est.)
female: 15 years (2022 est.)

ENVIRONMENT

Environmental issues: inadequate potable water; pollution of Majuro lagoon from household waste and discharges from fishing vessels; sea-level rise

International environmental agreements: *party to:* Biodiversity, Climate Change, Climate Change-Kyoto Protocol, Climate Change-Paris Agreement, Comprehensive Nuclear Test Ban, Desertification, Hazardous Wastes, Law of the Sea, Marine Dumping-London Protocol, Ozone Layer Protection, Ship Pollution, Wetlands, Whaling
signed, but not ratified: none of the selected agreements

Climate: tropical; hot and humid; wet season May to November; islands border typhoon belt

Urbanization: *urban population:* 78.9% of total population (2023)
rate of urbanization: 0.61% annual rate of change (2020-25 est.)

Carbon dioxide emissions: 293,700 metric tonnes of CO2 (2017 est.)
comparison ranking: total emissions 199

Particulate matter emissions: 7.2 micrograms per cubic meter (2019 est.)

Waste and recycling: *municipal solid waste generated annually:* 8,600 tons (2024 est.)
percent of municipal solid waste recycled: 39.7% (2022 est.)

GOVERNMENT

Country name: *conventional long form:* Republic of the Marshall Islands
conventional short form: Marshall Islands
local long form: Republic of the Marshall Islands
local short form: Marshall Islands
former: Trust Territory of the Pacific Islands, Marshall Islands District
abbreviation: RMI
etymology: named after British Captain John MARSHALL, who charted many of the islands in 1788

Government type: mixed presidential-parliamentary system in free association with the US

Capital: *name:* Majuro
geographic coordinates: 7 06 N, 171 23 E
time difference: UTC+12 (17 hours ahead of Washington, DC, during Standard Time)
etymology: Majuro means "two openings" or "two eyes" and refers to the two major passages through the atoll into the Majuro lagoon
note: the capital is an atoll of 64 islands; governmental buildings are housed on three fused islands on the eastern side of the atoll: Djarrit, Uliga, and Delap

Administrative divisions: 24 municipalities; Ailinglaplap, Ailuk, Arno, Aur, Bikini & Kili, Ebon, Enewetak & Ujelang, Jabat, Jaluit, Kwajalein, Lae, Lib, Likiep, Majuro, Maloelap, Mejit, Mili, Namorik, Namu, Rongelap, Ujae, Utrik, Wotho, Wotje

Legal system: mixed system of US and English common law, customary law, and local statutes

Constitution: *history:* effective 1 May 1979
amendment process: proposed by the National Parliament or by a constitutional convention; passage by Parliament requires at least two-thirds majority vote of the total membership in each of two readings and approval by a majority of votes in a referendum; amendments submitted by a constitutional convention require approval of at least two thirds of votes in a referendum

International law organization participation: accepts compulsory ICJ jurisdiction with reservations; accepts ICCt jurisdiction

Citizenship: *citizenship by birth:* no
citizenship by descent only: at least one parent must be a citizen of the Marshall Islands
dual citizenship recognized: no
residency requirement for naturalization: 5 years

Suffrage: 18 years of age; universal

Executive branch: *chief of state:* President Hilda C. HEINE (since 3 January 2023)
head of government: President Hilda C. HEINE (since 3 January 2023)
cabinet: Cabinet nominated by the president from among members of the Nitijela, appointed by Nitijela speaker
election/appointment process: president indirectly elected by the Nitijela from among its members for a 4-year term (no term limits)
most recent election date: 2 January 2023
election results: *2023:* Hilda C. HEINE elected president; National Parliament vote - Hilda C. HEINE (independent) 17, David KABUA (independent) 16
2020: David KABUA elected president; National Parliament vote - David KABUA (independent) 20, Hilda C. HEINE (independent) 12
expected date of next election: 2027
note: the president is both chief of state and head of government

Legislative branch: *legislature name:* Parliament (Nitijela)
legislative structure: unicameral
number of seats: 33 (all directly elected)
electoral system: plurality/majority
scope of elections: full renewal
term in office: 4 years
most recent election date: 11/20/2023
percentage of women in chamber: 12.1%
expected date of next election: November 2027
note: the Council of Iroij is a 12-member consultative group of tribal leaders that advises the Presidential

Cabinet and reviews legislation affecting customary law or any traditional practice

Judicial branch: *highest court(s):* Supreme Court (consists of the chief justice and 2 associate justices)
judge selection and term of office: judges appointed by the Cabinet on the recommendation of the Judicial Service Commission (consists of the chief justice of the High Court, the attorney general and a private citizen selected by the Cabinet) and upon approval of the Nitijela; the current chief justice, appointed in 2013, serves for 10 years; Marshallese citizens appointed as justices serve until retirement at age 72
subordinate courts: High Court; District Courts; Traditional Rights Court; Community Courts

Political parties: traditionally there have been no formally organized political parties; what has existed more closely resembles factions or interest groups because they do not have party headquarters, formal platforms, or party structures

Diplomatic representation in the US: *chief of mission:* Ambassador Charles Rudolph PAUL (since 27 February 2024)
chancery: 2433 Massachusetts Avenue NW, Washington, DC 20008
telephone: [1] (202) 234-5414
FAX: [1] (202) 232-3236
email address and website: info@rmiembassyus.org
consulate(s) general: Honolulu, Springdale (AR)

Diplomatic representation from the US: *chief of mission:* Ambassador Laura M. STONE (since 12 July 2024)
embassy: Mejen Weto, Ocean Side, Majuro
mailing address: 4380 Majuro Place, Washington DC 20521-4380
telephone: [692] 247-4011
FAX: [692] 247-4012
email address and website: MAJConsular@state.gov
https://mh.usembassy.gov/

International organization participation: ACP, ADB, AOSIS, FAO, G-77, IAEA, IBRD, ICAO, ICCt, IDA, IFAD, IFC, ILO, IMF, IMO, IMSO, Interpol, IOC, IOM, ITU, OPCW, PIF, Sparteca, SPC, UN, UNCTAD, UNESCO, UNHRC, WHO

Independence: 21 October 1986 (from the US-administered UN trusteeship)

National holiday: Constitution Day, 1 May (1979)

Flag: *description:* blue with an orange stripe and a white stripe radiating from the lower-left corner to the upper-right corner; a white star with four large rays and 20 small rays appears on the left side above the two stripes
meaning: blue stands for the Pacific Ocean, orange for the Ralik Chain (or sunset and courage), and white for the Ratak Chain (or sunrise and peace); the star symbolizes the Christian cross, with a small ray for each electoral district and a larger ray for the principal cultural centers of Majuro, Jaluit, Wotje, and Ebeye; the diagonal stripes can also be interpreted as representing the equator, with the star showing the archipelago's position

National symbol(s): a 24-rayed star

National color(s): blue, white, orange

National anthem(s): *title:* "Forever Marshall Islands"
lyrics/music: Amata KABUA
history: adopted 1981; words and music written by the first president of the Marshall Islands

National heritage: *total World Heritage Sites:* 1 (cultural)
selected World Heritage Site locales: Bikini Atoll Nuclear Test Site

ECONOMY

Economic overview: upper middle-income Pacific island economy; US aid reliance; large public sector; coconut oil production as diesel fuel substitute; growing offshore banking locale; fishing rights seller; import-dependent

Real GDP (purchasing power parity): $270.809 million (2024 est.)
$263.507 million (2023 est.)
$274.3 million (2022 est.)
note: data in 2021 dollars
comparison ranking: 215

Real GDP growth rate: 2.8% (2024 est.)
-3.9% (2023 est.)
-1.1% (2022 est.)
note: annual GDP % growth based on constant local currency
comparison ranking: 126

Real GDP per capita: $7,200 (2024 est.)
$6,800 (2023 est.)
$6,800 (2022 est.)
note: data in 2021 dollars
comparison ranking: 155

GDP (official exchange rate): $280.358 million (2024 est.)
note: data in current dollars at official exchange rate

Inflation rate (consumer prices): 6.2% (2022 est.)
2.6% (2021 est.)
-0.7% (2020 est.)
note: annual % change based on consumer prices
comparison ranking: 157

GDP - composition, by sector of origin: *agriculture:* 19.5% (2023 est.)
industry: 11.1% (2023 est.)
services: 70.5% (2023 est.)
note: figures may not total 100% due to non-allocated consumption not captured in sector-reported data
comparison rankings: agriculture 35; industry 181; services 32

GDP - composition, by end use: *household consumption:* 70.7% (2023 est.)
government consumption: 53.5% (2023 est.)
investment in fixed capital: 20.2% (2023 est.)
investment in inventories: -0.5% (2023 est.)
exports of goods and services: 38.9% (2023 est.)
imports of goods and services: -71.2% (2023 est.)
note: figures may not total 100% due to rounding or gaps in data collection

Agricultural products: coconuts (2023)
note: top ten agricultural products based on tonnage

Industries: copra, tuna processing, tourism, craft items (from seashells, wood, and pearls)

Industrial production growth rate: -2.8% (2023 est.)
note: annual % change in industrial value added based on constant local currency
comparison ranking: 170

Population below poverty line: 7.2% (2019 est.)
note: % of population with income below national poverty line

Gini Index coefficient - distribution of family income: 35.5 (2019 est.)
note: index (0-100) of income distribution; higher values represent greater inequality
comparison ranking: 71

Household income or consumption by percentage share: *lowest 10%:* 2.8% (2019 est.)
highest 10%: 27.5% (2019 est.)
note: % share of income accruing to lowest and highest 10% of population

Remittances: 13.3% of GDP (2023 est.)
13.6% of GDP (2022 est.)
13.3% of GDP (2021 est.)
note: personal transfers and compensation between resident and non-resident individuals/ households/ entities

Budget: *revenues:* $171.267 million (2020 est.)
expenditures: $159.095 million (2020 est.)
note: central government revenues and expenses (excluding grants/extrabudgetary units/social security funds) converted to US dollars at average official exchange rate for year indicated

Public debt: 41.6% of GDP (2019 est.)
note: central government debt as a % of GDP
comparison ranking: 128

Taxes and other revenues: 17.2% (of GDP) (2020 est.)
note: central government tax revenue as a % of GDP
comparison ranking: 75

Current account balance: $76.263 million (2021 est.)
$90.281 million (2020 est.)
$86.133 million (2019 est.)
note: balance of payments - net trade and primary/ secondary income in current dollars
comparison ranking: 78

Exports: $130.016 million (2021 est.)
$88.042 million (2020 est.)
$91.394 million (2019 est.)
note: balance of payments - exports of goods and services in current dollars
comparison ranking: 205

Exports - partners: UK 16%, Germany 13%, Denmark 10%, Ghana 9%, Cyprus 9% (2023)
note: top five export partners based on percentage share of exports

Exports - commodities: ships, refined petroleum, fish, natural gas, stone processing machines (2023)
note: top five export commodities based on value in dollars

Imports: $206.025 million (2021 est.)
$132.845 million (2020 est.)
$129.682 million (2019 est.)
note: balance of payments - imports of goods and services in current dollars
comparison ranking: 209

Imports - partners: China 47%, Japan 15%, Germany 5%, Brazil 4%, Cyprus 4% (2023)
note: top five import partners based on percentage share of imports

Imports - commodities: ships, refined petroleum, additive manufacturing machines, iron structures, crude petroleum (2023)
note: top five import commodities based on value in dollars

Exchange rates: the US dollar is used

ENERGY

Electricity access: *electrification - total population:* 100% (2022 est.)
electrification - urban areas: 96.1%
electrification - rural areas: 100%

COMMUNICATIONS

Telephones - fixed lines: *total subscriptions:* 2,000 (2014 est.)
subscriptions per 100 inhabitants: 5 (2022 est.)
comparison ranking: total subscriptions 212

Telephones - mobile cellular: *total subscriptions:* 16,000 (2021 est.)
subscriptions per 100 inhabitants: 38 (2021 est.)
comparison ranking: total subscriptions 218

Broadcast media: no TV broadcast station; a cable network is available on Majuro with programming via videotape replay and satellite relays; 4 radio broadcast stations; US Armed Forces Radio and Television Service (AFRTS) provides satellite radio and TV service to Kwajalein Atoll (2019)

Internet country code: .mh

Internet users: *percent of population:* 66% (2023 est.)

Broadband - fixed subscriptions: *total:* 1,000 (2022 est.)
subscriptions per 100 inhabitants: 2 (2022 est.)
comparison ranking: total 210

TRANSPORTATION

Civil aircraft registration country code prefix: V7

Airports: 33 (2025)
comparison ranking: 116

Merchant marine: *total:* 4,180 (2023)
by type: bulk carrier 1,939, container ship 277, general cargo 66, oil tanker 1039, other 859
comparison ranking: total 6

Ports: *total ports:* 3 (2024)
large: 0
medium: 0
small: 0
very small: 3
ports with oil terminals: 2
key ports: Enitwetak Island, Kwajalein, Majuro Atoll

MILITARY AND SECURITY

Military and security forces: no regular military forces; Marshall Islands Police Department (includes a Sea Patrol Division) (2025)

Military - note: defense is the responsibility of the US; in 1982, the Marshall Islands signed a Compact of Free Association (COFA) with the US, which granted the Marshall Islands financial assistance and access to many US domestic programs in exchange for exclusive US military access and defense responsibilities; the COFA entered into force in 1986; the Marshall Islands hosts a US Army missile test site
the Marshall Islands has a "shiprider" agreement with the US, which allows local maritime law enforcement officers to embark on US Coast Guard (USCG) and US Navy (USN) vessels, including to board and search vessels suspected of violating laws or regulations within its designated exclusive economic zone (EEZ) or on the high seas; "shiprider" agreements also enable USCG personnel and USN vessels with embarked USCG law enforcement personnel to work with host nations to protect critical regional resources (2025)

TRANSNATIONAL ISSUES

Refugees and internally displaced persons: IDPs: 35 (2024 est.)

MAURITANIA

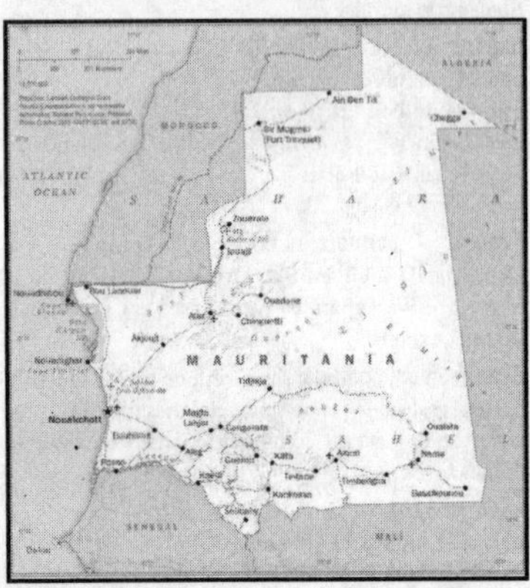

INTRODUCTION

Background: The Amazigh and Bafour people were among the earliest settlers in what is now Mauritania and among the first in recorded history to convert from a nomadic to agricultural lifestyle. These groups account for roughly one third of Mauritania's ethnic makeup. The remainder of Mauritania's ethnic groups derive from Sub-Saharan ethnic groups originating mainly from the Senegal River Valley, including descendants of former enslaved peoples. These three groups are organized according to a strict caste system with deep ethnic divides that impact access to resources and power dynamics.

A former French colony, Mauritania achieved independence from France in 1960. Mauritania initially began as a single-party, authoritarian regime and experienced 49 years of dictatorships, flawed elections, failed attempts at democracy, and military coups. Ould Abdel AZIZ led the last coup in 2008, was elected president in 2009, and was reelected in 2014. Mohamed Ould Cheikh GHAZOUANI was elected president in 2019, and his inauguration marked the first peaceful transition of power from one democratically elected president to another, solidifying the country's status as an emerging democracy. International observers recognized the elections as relatively free and fair. GHAZOUANI is seeking re-election in June 2024 for a second, and final, five-year term.

The country is working to address vestigial practices of slavery and its hereditary impacts. Mauritania officially abolished slavery in 1981, but the practice was not criminalized until 2007. Between 2005 and 2011, Al-Qaeda in the Islamic Maghreb (AQIM) launched a series of attacks killing western tourists and aid workers, attacking diplomatic and government facilities, and ambushing Mauritanian soldiers and gendarmes. Although Mauritania has not seen an attack since 2011, AQIM and similar groups remain active in the Sahel region.

GEOGRAPHY

Location: Western Africa, bordering the North Atlantic Ocean, between Senegal and Western Sahara

Geographic coordinates: 20 00 N, 12 00 W

Map references: Africa

Area: *total:* 1,030,700 sq km
land: 1,030,700 sq km
water: 0 sq km
comparison ranking: total 30

Area - comparative: slightly larger than three times the size of New Mexico; about six times the size of Florida

Land boundaries: *total:* 5,002 km
border countries (4): Algeria 460 km; Mali 2,236 km; Morocco 1,564 km; Senegal 742 km

Coastline: 754 km

Maritime claims: *territorial sea:* 12 nm
contiguous zone: 24 nm
exclusive economic zone: 200 nm
continental shelf: 200 nm or to the edge of the continental margin

Climate: desert; constantly hot, dry, dusty

Terrain: mostly barren, flat plains of the Sahara; some central hills

Elevation: *highest point:* Kediet Ijill 915 m
lowest point: Sebkhet Te-n-Dghamcha -5 m
mean elevation: 276 m

Natural resources: iron ore, gypsum, copper, phosphate, diamonds, gold, oil, fish

Land use: *agricultural land:* 38.5% (2022 est.)
arable land: 0.4% (2022 est.)
permanent crops: 0% (2022 est.)
permanent pasture: 38.1% (2022 est.)
forest: 0.3% (2022 est.)
other: 61.2% (2022 est.)

Irrigated land: 450 sq km (2012)

Major rivers (by length in km): Senegal river mouth (shared with Guinea [s], Senegal and Mali) - 1,641 km
note: [s] after country name indicates river source; [m] after country name indicates river mouth

Major watersheds (area sq km): Atlantic Ocean drainage: Niger (2,261,741 sq km), Senegal (456,397 sq km)

Major aquifers: Senegalo-Mauritanian Basin, Taodeni-Tanzerouft Basin

Population distribution: vast areas of the country, particularly in the central, northern, and eastern areas, are desert and lack sizeable population clusters; half the population lives in or around the coastal capital of Nouakchott; smaller clusters are found near the southern border with Mali and Senegal, as shown in this population distribution map

Natural hazards: hot, dry, dust/sand-laden sirocco wind primarily in March and April; periodic droughts

Geography - note: Mauritania is considered part of both North Africa's Maghreb region and West Africa's Sahel region; most of the population is concentrated in the cities of Nouakchott and Nouadhibou and along the Senegal River in the southern part of the country

PEOPLE AND SOCIETY

Population: *total:* 4,328,040 (2024 est.)
male: 2,083,690
female: 2,244,350
comparison rankings: total 128; male 129; female 127

Nationality: *noun:* Mauritanian(s)
adjective: Mauritanian

Ethnic groups: Black Moors (Haratines - Arabic-speaking descendants of African origin who are or were enslaved by White Moors) 40%, White Moors (of Arab-Amazigh descent, known as Beydane) 30%, Sub-Saharan Mauritanians (non-Arabic speaking, largely resident in or originating from the Senegal River Valley, including Halpulaar, Fulani, Soninke, Wolof, and Bambara ethnic groups) 30%

Languages: Arabic (official and national), Pular, Soninke, Wolof (all national languages), French
major-language sample(s):
يمكن الاستغناء عنه للمعلومات الأساسية
كتاب حقائق العالم، المصدر الذي لا
(Arabic)
note: the spoken Arabic in Mauritania differs considerably from Modern Standard Arabic; the Mauritanian dialect, which incorporates many Tamazight words, is referred to as Hassaniya

Religions: Muslim (official) 100%

Age structure: *0-14 years:* 35.7% (male 776,035/female 770,132)
15-64 years: 59.9% (male 1,227,347/female 1,363,938)
65 years and over: 4.4% (2024 est.) (male 80,308/female 110,280)

Dependency ratios: *total dependency ratio:* 85.4 (2024 est.)
youth dependency ratio: 78.5 (2024 est.)
elderly dependency ratio: 6.9 (2024 est.)
potential support ratio: 14.5 (2024 est.)

Median age: *total:* 22.1 years (2024 est.)
male: 21.1 years
female: 23.1 years
comparison ranking: total 185

Population growth rate: 1.92% (2024 est.)
comparison ranking: 43

Birth rate: 27.2 births/1,000 population (2024 est.)
comparison ranking: 37

Death rate: 7.2 deaths/1,000 population (2024 est.)
comparison ranking: 115

Net migration rate: -0.7 migrant(s)/1,000 population (2024 est.)
comparison ranking: 133

Population distribution: vast areas of the country, particularly in the central, northern, and eastern areas, are desert and lack sizeable population clusters; half the population lives in or around the coastal capital of Nouakchott; smaller clusters are found near the southern border with Mali and Senegal, as shown in this population distribution map

Urbanization: *urban population:* 57.7% of total population (2023)
rate of urbanization: 3.84% annual rate of change (2020-25 est.)

Major urban areas - population: 1.492 million NOUAKCHOTT (capital) (2023)

Sex ratio: *at birth:* 1.03 male(s)/female
0-14 years: 1.01 male(s)/female
15-64 years: 0.9 male(s)/female
65 years and over: 0.73 male(s)/female
total population: 0.93 male(s)/female (2024 est.)

Mother's mean age at first birth: 21.8 years (2019/21)
note: data represents median age at first birth among women 25-49

Maternal mortality ratio: 381 deaths/100,000 live births (2023 est.)
comparison ranking: 15

Infant mortality rate: *total:* 48.9 deaths/1,000 live births (2024 est.)
male: 54.8 deaths/1,000 live births
female: 42.9 deaths/1,000 live births
comparison ranking: total 19

Life expectancy at birth: *total population:* 65.9 years (2024 est.)
male: 63.4 years
female: 68.5 years
comparison ranking: total population 204

Total fertility rate: 3.4 children born/woman (2024 est.)
comparison ranking: 38

Gross reproduction rate: 1.68 (2024 est.)

Drinking water source: *improved: urban:* 94.6% of population (2022 est.)
rural: 55.6% of population (2022 est.)
total: 77.8% of population (2022 est.)
unimproved: urban: 5.4% of population (2022 est.)
rural: 44.4% of population (2022 est.)
total: 22.2% of population (2022 est.)

Health expenditure: 4.1% of GDP (2021)
6.3% of national budget (2022 est.)

Physician density: 0.26 physicians/1,000 population (2022)

Sanitation facility access: *improved: urban:* 89.4% of population (2022 est.)
rural: 33.9% of population (2022 est.)
total: 65.5% of population (2022 est.)
unimproved: urban: 10.6% of population (2022 est.)
rural: 66.1% of population (2022 est.)
total: 34.5% of population (2022 est.)

Obesity - adult prevalence rate: 12.7% (2016)
comparison ranking: 132

Alcohol consumption per capita: *total:* 0 liters of pure alcohol (2019 est.)
beer: 0 liters of pure alcohol (2019 est.)
wine: 0 liters of pure alcohol (2019 est.)
spirits: 0 liters of pure alcohol (2019 est.)
other alcohols: 0 liters of pure alcohol (2019 est.)
comparison ranking: total 186

Tobacco use: *total:* 8.3% (2025 est.)
male: 15.5% (2025 est.)
female: 1.7% (2025 est.)
comparison ranking: total 140

Children under the age of 5 years underweight: 22.4% (2022)
comparison ranking: 10

Currently married women (ages 15-49): 66% (2023 est.)

Child marriage: *women married by age 15:* 15.5% (2021)
women married by age 18: 36.6% (2021)
men married by age 18: 1.2% (2021)

Education expenditure: 4.8% of GDP (2023 est.)
10.2% national budget (2024 est.)
comparison ranking: Education expenditure (% GDP) 72

Literacy: *total population:* 59.5% (2020 est.)
male: 70.1% (2020 est.)
female: 51.8% (2020 est.)

School life expectancy (primary to tertiary education): *total:* 8 years (2020 est.)
male: 8 years (2020 est.)
female: 8 years (2020 est.)

ENVIRONMENT

Environmental issues: desertification caused in part by overgrazing, deforestation, and drought-aggravated soil erosion; limited natural freshwater resources; locust infestation

International environmental agreements: *party to:* Biodiversity, Climate Change, Climate Change-Kyoto Protocol, Climate Change-Paris Agreement, Comprehensive Nuclear Test Ban, Desertification, Endangered Species, Hazardous Wastes, Law of the Sea, Nuclear Test Ban, Ozone Layer Protection, Ship Pollution, Wetlands, Whaling
signed, but not ratified: none of the selected agreements

Climate: desert; constantly hot, dry, dusty

Urbanization: *urban population:* 57.7% of total population (2023)
rate of urbanization: 3.84% annual rate of change (2020-25 est.)

Carbon dioxide emissions: 4.86 million metric tonnes of CO2 (2023 est.)
from petroleum and other liquids: 4.86 million metric tonnes of CO2 (2023 est.)
comparison ranking: total emissions 138

Particulate matter emissions: 35.1 micrograms per cubic meter (2019 est.)

Waste and recycling: *municipal solid waste generated annually:* 454,000 tons (2024 est.)
percent of municipal solid waste recycled: 10% (2022 est.)

Total water withdrawal: *municipal:* 95.4 million cubic meters (2022 est.)
industrial: 31.8 million cubic meters (2022 est.)
agricultural: 1.223 billion cubic meters (2022 est.)

Total renewable water resources: 11.4 billion cubic meters (2022 est.)

GOVERNMENT

Country name: *conventional long form:* Islamic Republic of Mauritania
conventional short form: Mauritania
local long form: Al Jumhuriyah al Islamiyah al Muritaniyah
local short form: Muritaniyah
etymology: named for the ancient kingdom of Mauretania (3rd century B.C. to 1st century A.D.); its name derives from the Mauri (Moors) of northwest Africa

Government type: presidential republic

Capital: *name:* Nouakchott
geographic coordinates: 18 04 N, 15 58 W
time difference: UTC 0 (5 hours ahead of Washington, DC, during Standard Time)
etymology: the meaning of the name is unclear; it may derive from the Berber *nawakshut,* meaning

"place of the winds;" other variants could translate as "the place where water appears in a new well," "the land where shells abound," "a place with pasture," "a windy place," or "without ears" (the last referring to a local chieftain who could have been the place's namesake)

Administrative divisions: 15 regions (*wilayas*, singular - *wilaya*); Adrar, Assaba, Brakna, Dakhlet Nouadhibou, Gorgol, Guidimaka, Hodh ech Chargui, Hodh El Gharbi, Inchiri, Nouakchott Nord, Nouakchott Ouest, Nouakchott Sud, Tagant, Tiris Zemmour, Trarza

Legal system: mixed system of Islamic and French civil law

Constitution: *history:* previous 1964; latest adopted 12 July 1991
amendment process: proposed by the president of the republic or by Parliament; consideration of amendments by Parliament requires approval of at least one third of the membership; a referendum is held only if the amendment is approved by two-thirds majority vote; passage by referendum requires simple majority vote by eligible voters; passage of amendments proposed by the president can bypass a referendum if approved by at least three-fifths majority vote by Parliament

International law organization participation: has not submitted an ICJ jurisdiction declaration; non-party state to the ICCt

Citizenship: *citizenship by birth:* no
citizenship by descent only: at least one parent must be a citizen of Mauritania
dual citizenship recognized: no
residency requirement for naturalization: 5 years

Suffrage: 18 years of age; universal

Executive branch: *chief of state:* President Mohamed Ould Cheikh el GHAZOUANI (since 1 August 2019)
head of government: Prime Minister Moctar Ould DIAY (since 2 August 2024)
cabinet: Council of Ministers nominees suggested by the prime minister, appointed by the president
election/appointment process: president directly elected by absolute-majority popular vote in 2 rounds, if needed, for a 5-year term (eligible for a second term); prime minister appointed by the president
most recent election date: 29 June 2024
election results: *2024:* Mohamed Ould Cheikh el GHAZOUANI reelected president in first round; percent of vote - Mohamed Ould Cheikh el GHAZOUANI (UPR) 56.1%, Biram Dah Ould ABEID (independent) 22.1%, Hamadi Sidi el MOKHTAR independent) 12.8%, other 9.0%
2019: Mohamed Ould Cheikh el GHAZOUANI elected president in first round; percent of vote - Mohamed Ould Cheikh el GHAZOUANI (UPR) 52%, Biram Dah Ould ABEID (independent) 18.6%, Sidi Mohamed Ould BOUBACAR (independent) 17.9%, other 11.5%
expected date of next election: June 2029

Legislative branch: *legislature name:* Parliament (Barlamane)
legislative structure: unicameral
chamber name: National Assembly (Al Jamiya-Al-Wataniya)
number of seats: 176 (all directly elected)
electoral system: mixed system
scope of elections: full renewal
term in office: 5 years
most recent election date: 5/13/2023 to 5/27/2023
percentage of women in chamber: 23.3%
expected date of next election: May 2028
note: the early parliamentary elections in 2023 were the first to be held under President Mohamed Ould Cheikh El GHAZOUANI, elected in 2019 in the first peaceful transition of power; the elections followed the agreement between the government and parties in September 2022 to renew the Independent National Electoral Commission (CENI) and hold the elections in the first semester of 2023 for climatic and logistical reasons

Judicial branch: *highest court(s):* Supreme Court or Cour Suprême (subdivided into 7 chambers: 2 civil, 2 labor, 1 commercial, 1 administrative, and 1 criminal, each with a chamber president and 2 councilors); Constitutional Council (consists of 9 members); High Court of Justice (consists of 9 members)
judge selection and term of office: Supreme Court president appointed by the president of the republic to serve a 5-year renewable term; Constitutional Council members appointed - 3 by the president of the republic, 2 by the president of the National Assembly, 1 by the prime minister, 1 by the leader of the democratic opposition, 1 by the largest opposition party in the National Assembly, and 1 by the second largest party in the National Assembly; members serve single, 9-year terms with one-third of membership renewed every 3 years; High Court of Justice members appointed by Parliament - 6 by the ruling Coalition of Majority Parties and 3 by opposition parties
subordinate courts: Courts of Appeal; courts of first instance, or wilya courts, are established in the regions' headquarters and include commercial and labor courts, criminal courts, Moughataa (district) Courts, and informal/customary courts

Political parties: Alliance for Justice and Democracy/ Movement for Renewal or AJD/MR
El Insaf or Equity Party
El Islah or Reform Party
El Karama or Dignity Party
El Vadila or Virtue Party
Mauritanian Party of Union and Change or HATEM
National Democratic Alliance or AND
National Rally for Reform and Development or RNRD or TAWASSOUL
Nida El-Watan
Party for Conciliation and Prosperity or HIWAR
Party of the Mauritanian Masses or Hakam
Republican Front for Unity and Democracy or FRUD
Sawab Party
Union for Democracy and Progress or UDP
Union of Planning and Construction or UPC

Diplomatic representation in the US: *chief of mission:* Ambassador Cissé Mint Cheikh Ould BOIDE (since 15 September 2021)
chancery: 2129 Leroy Place NW, Washington, DC 20008
telephone: [1] (202) 232-5700
FAX: [1] (202) 319-2623
email address and website: ambarimwashington@diplomatie.gov.mr
mauritaniaembassyus.org – Mauritania Embassy washington

Diplomatic representation from the US: *chief of mission:* Ambassador (vacant); John T. ICE Chargé d'Affaires (since July 2024)
embassy: Nouadhibou Road, Avenue Al Quds, NOT PRTZ, Nouakchott
mailing address: 2430 Nouakchott Place, Washington DC 20521-2430
telephone: [222] 4525-2660
FAX: [222] 4525-1592
email address and website: consularnkc@state.gov
https://mr.usembassy.gov/

International organization participation: ABEDA, ACP, AfDB, AFESD, AIIB, AMF, AMU, AU, CAEU, EITI (compliant country), FAO, G-77, IAEA, IBRD, ICAO, ICC (NGOs), ICRM, IDA, IDB, IFAD, IFC, IFRCS, IHO (pending member), ILO, IMF, IMO, Interpol, IOC, IOM, IPU, ISO (correspondent), ITSO, ITU, ITUC (NGOs), LAS, MIGA, NAM, OIC, OIF, OPCW, UN, UNCTAD, UNESCO, UNHRC, UNIDO, UNWTO, UPU, WCO, WHO, WIPO, WMO, WTO

Independence: 28 November 1960 (from France)

National holiday: Independence Day, 28 November (1960)

Flag: *description:* green with red stripes along the top and bottom edges; on the green field, a five-pointed yellow star is centered over a yellow, upward-pointing crescent moon
meaning: the crescent, star, and color green are traditional symbols of Islam; green also represents hope for a bright future; yellow stands for the sands of the Sahara, and red for blood shed in the fight for independence

National symbol(s): five-pointed star between the horns of a horizontal crescent moon

National color(s): green, yellow

National anthem(s): *title:* "National Anthem of Mauritania"
lyrics/music: unknown/Rageh DAOUD
history: adopted 2017
"Bilāda l-ʾubāti l-hudāti l-kirām" (Land of the Proud, Guided by Noblemen): National heritage: *total World Heritage Sites:* 2 (1 cultural, 1 natural)
selected World Heritage Site locales: Ancient Ksour (Fortified Villages) of Ouadane, Chinguetti, Tichitt, and Oualata (c); Banc d'Arguin National Park (n)

ECONOMY

Economic overview: lower middle-income West African economy; primarily agrarian; rising urbanization; poor property rights; systemic corruption; endemic social and workforce tensions; wide-scale terrorism; foreign over-fishing; environmentally fragile

Real GDP (purchasing power parity): $33.069 billion (2024 est.)
$31.434 billion (2023 est.)
$29.514 billion (2022 est.)
note: data in 2021 dollars
comparison ranking: 144

Real GDP growth rate: 5.2% (2024 est.)
6.5% (2023 est.)
6.8% (2022 est.)
note: annual GDP % growth based on constant local currency
comparison ranking: 35

Real GDP per capita: $6,400 (2024 est.)
$6,300 (2023 est.)
$6,100 (2022 est.)
note: data in 2021 dollars
comparison ranking: 164

GDP (official exchange rate): $10.767 billion (2024 est.)
note: data in current dollars at official exchange rate

Inflation rate (consumer prices): 2.5% (2024 est.)

5% (2023 est.)
9.5% (2022 est.)
note: annual % change based on consumer prices
comparison ranking: 71

GDP - composition, by sector of origin: *agriculture:* 18.6% (2024 est.)
industry: 30.6% (2024 est.)
services: 43.2% (2024 est.)
note: figures may not total 100% due to non-allocated consumption not captured in sector-reported data
comparison rankings: agriculture 36; industry 53; services 182

GDP - composition, by end use: *household consumption:* 55.3% (2023 est.)
government consumption: 17.2% (2023 est.)
investment in fixed capital: 23.5% (2023 est.)
investment in inventories: 18.9% (2023 est.)
exports of goods and services: 38.3% (2023 est.)
imports of goods and services: -53.2% (2023 est.)
note: figures may not total 100% due to rounding or gaps in data collection

Agricultural products: rice, milk, goat milk, sorghum, sheep milk, lamb/mutton, beef, camel meat, camel milk, dates (2023)
note: top ten agricultural products based on tonnage

Industries: fish processing, oil production, mining (iron ore, gold, copper)
note: gypsum deposits have never been exploited

Industrial production growth rate: 2.8% (2024 est.)
note: annual % change in industrial value added based on constant local currency
comparison ranking: 84

Labor force: 1.21 million (2024 est.)
note: number of people ages 15 or older who are employed or seeking work
comparison ranking: 141

Unemployment rate: 10.4% (2024 est.)
10.5% (2023 est.)
10.6% (2022 est.)
note: % of labor force seeking employment
comparison ranking: 151

Youth unemployment rate (ages 15-24): *total:* 23.2% (2024 est.)
male: 19.9% (2024 est.)
female: 30.1% (2024 est.)
note: % of labor force ages 15-24 seeking employment
comparison ranking: total 41

Population below poverty line: 31.8% (2019 est.)
note: % of population with income below national poverty line

Gini Index coefficient - distribution of family income: 32 (2019 est.)
note: index (0-100) of income distribution; higher values represent greater inequality
comparison ranking: 108

Household income or consumption by percentage share: *lowest 10%:* 3.1% (2019 est.)
highest 10%: 24.6% (2019 est.)
note: % share of income accruing to lowest and highest 10% of population

Remittances: 1.6% of GDP (2023 est.)
1.1% of GDP (2022 est.)
0.1% of GDP (2021 est.)
note: personal transfers and compensation between resident and non-resident individuals/households/entities

Budget: *revenues:* $1.617 billion (2019 est.)
expenditures: $1.407 billion (2019 est.)

Current account balance: -$966.506 million (2023 est.)
-$1.424 billion (2022 est.)
-$807.862 million (2021 est.)
note: balance of payments - net trade and primary/secondary income in current dollars
comparison ranking: 128

Exports: $3.955 billion (2023 est.)
$4.132 billion (2022 est.)
$3.18 billion (2021 est.)
note: balance of payments - exports of goods and services in current dollars
comparison ranking: 147

Exports - partners: China 25%, Switzerland 14%, Canada 12%, UAE 9%, Spain 7% (2023)
note: top five export partners based on percentage share of exports

Exports - commodities: gold, iron ore, fish, processed crustaceans, copper ore (2023)
note: top five export commodities based on value in dollars

Imports: $5.271 billion (2023 est.)
$5.77 billion (2022 est.)
$4.312 billion (2021 est.)
note: balance of payments - imports of goods and services in current dollars
comparison ranking: 151

Imports - partners: China 19%, UAE 14%, Morocco 6%, Spain 6%, France 5% (2023)
note: top five import partners based on percentage share of imports

Imports - commodities: refined petroleum, raw sugar, palm oil, wheat, soybean oil (2023)
note: top five import commodities based on value in dollars

Reserves of foreign exchange and gold: $2.039 billion (2021 est.)
$1.493 billion (2020 est.)
$1.029 billion (2019 est.)
note: holdings of gold (year-end prices)/foreign exchange/special drawing rights in current dollars
comparison ranking: 126

Debt - external: $3.072 billion (2023 est.)
note: present value of external debt in current US dollars
comparison ranking: 85

Exchange rates: ouguiyas (MRO) per US dollar -
Exchange rates: 36.489 (2023 est.)
36.935 (2022 est.)
36.063 (2021 est.)
37.189 (2020 est.)
36.691 (2019 est.)

ENERGY

Electricity access: *electrification - total population:* 49% (2022 est.)
electrification - urban areas: 91.6%

Electricity: *installed generating capacity:* 812,000 kW (2023 est.)
consumption: 1.7 billion kWh (2023 est.)
imports: 378 million kWh (2023 est.)
transmission/distribution losses: 320 million kWh (2023 est.)
comparison rankings: installed generating capacity 139; consumption 153; imports 100; transmission/distribution losses 71

Electricity generation sources: *fossil fuels:* 72.4% of total installed capacity (2023 est.)
solar: 8.5% of total installed capacity (2023 est.)
wind: 6.3% of total installed capacity (2023 est.)
hydroelectricity: 12.8% of total installed capacity (2023 est.)

Coal: *imports:* 1 metric tons (2023 est.)

Petroleum: *refined petroleum consumption:* 32,000 bbl/day (2023 est.)
crude oil estimated reserves: 20 million barrels (2021 est.)

Natural gas: *proven reserves:* 28.317 billion cubic meters (2021 est.)

Energy consumption per capita: 14.135 million Btu/person (2023 est.)
comparison ranking: 141

COMMUNICATIONS

Telephones - fixed lines: *total subscriptions:* 48,000 (2022 est.)
subscriptions per 100 inhabitants: 1 (2022 est.)
comparison ranking: total subscriptions 157

Telephones - mobile cellular: *total subscriptions:* 5.36 million (2022 est.)
subscriptions per 100 inhabitants: 113 (2022 est.)
comparison ranking: total subscriptions 124

Broadcast media: 12 TV stations, 6 state-owned and 6 private; 19 radio broadcasters, including 15 state-owned and 4 (Radio Nouakchott Libre, Radio Tenwir, Radio Kobeni and Mauritanid) private; of the 15 government stations, 4 broadcast from Nouakchott (Radio Mauritanie, Radio Jeunesse, Radio Koran and Mauritanid) and the other 12 broadcast from each of the 12 regions outside Nouakchott (2022)

Internet country code: .mr

Internet users: *percent of population:* 37% (2023 est.)

Broadband - fixed subscriptions: *total:* 14,000 (2022 est.)
subscriptions per 100 inhabitants: (2022 est.) less than 1
comparison ranking: total 181

TRANSPORTATION

Civil aircraft registration country code prefix: 5T

Airports: 25 (2025)
comparison ranking: 130

Heliports: 3 (2025)
comparison ranking: 119

Railways: *total:* 728 km (2014)
standard gauge: 728 km (2014) 1.435-m gauge

Merchant marine: *total:* 11 (2023)
by type: general cargo 2, other 9
comparison ranking: total 158

Ports: *total ports:* 2 (2024)
large: 0
medium: 1
small: 1
very small: 0
ports with oil terminals: 2
key ports: Nouadhibou, Nouakchott

MILITARY AND SECURITY

Military and security forces: Mauritanian Armed Forces (aka Armée Nationale Mauritanienne): National Army, National Navy, Air Force; Gendarmerie

Ministry of Interior and Decentralization: National Police, National Guard (2025)

note 1: the National Police are responsible for enforcing the law and maintaining order in urban areas, while the paramilitary Gendarmerie is responsible for maintaining civil order around metropolitan areas and providing law enforcement services in rural areas; like the Mauritanian Armed Forces, the Gendarmerie is under the Ministry of Defense, but also supports the ministries of Interior and Justice
note 2: the National Guard performs a limited police function in keeping with its peacetime role of providing security at government facilities, to include prisons; regional authorities may call upon the National Guard to restore civil order during riots and other large-scale disturbances; the National Guard includes the nomadic Camel Corps or Nomad Group, also known as the Méhariste

Military expenditures: 2.4% of GDP (2024 est.)
2.5% of GDP (2023 est.)
2.5% of GDP (2022 est.)
2.4% of GDP (2021 est.)
2.5% of GDP (2020 est.)

Military and security service personnel strengths: estimated 17,000 active Mauritanian Armed Forces; estimated 3,000 Gendarmerie (2025)

Military equipment inventories and acquisitions: the military's inventory is limited and made up largely of older French and Soviet-era equipment; in recent years, Mauritania has received some secondhand and new military equipment, including unmanned aircraft (drones), from several suppliers, including China and the UAE (2024)

Military service age and obligation: 18 is the legal minimum age for voluntary military service; has a compulsory two-year military service law, but the law has reportedly never been applied (2023)

Military deployments: 450 (plus about 325 police) Central African Republic (MINUSCA) (2024)

Military - note: founded in 1960, the Mauritanian military is responsible for territorial defense and internal security; it also assists in economic development projects, humanitarian missions, and disaster response; border and maritime security, regional stability, and the threat of terrorist groups operating in the Sahel, particularly Mali, are key areas of focus; Mauritania has received security assistance from the EU, France, NATO, and the US (2025)

TERRORISM

Terrorist group(s): Terrorist group(s): Al-Qa'ida in the Islamic Maghreb (AQIM)

TRANSNATIONAL ISSUES

Refugees and internally displaced persons: *refugees:* 162,277 (2024 est.)

MAURITIUS

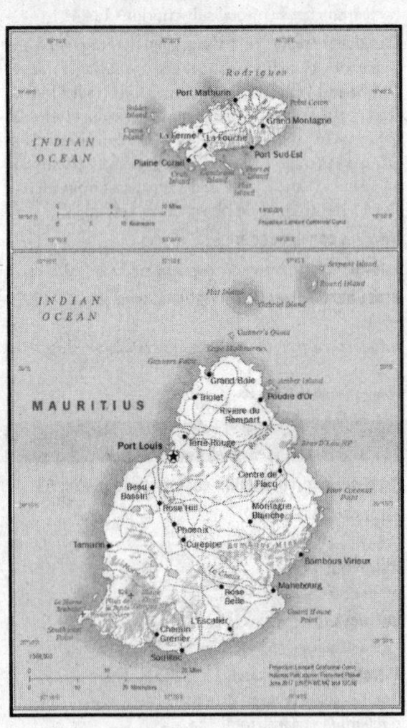

INTRODUCTION

Background: Although known to Arab and European sailors since at least the early 1500s, the island of Mauritius was uninhabited until 1638 when the Dutch established a settlement named in honor of Prince Maurits van NASSAU. Their presence led to the rapid disappearance of the flightless dodo bird that has since become one of the most well-known examples of extinction in modern times. The Dutch abandoned their financially distressed settlement in 1710, although a number of formerly enslaved people remained. In 1722, the French established what would become a highly profitable settlement focused on sugar cane plantations that were reliant on the labor of enslaved people brought to Mauritius from other parts of Africa. In the 1790s, the island had a brief period of autonomous rule when plantation owners rejected French control because of laws ending slavery that were temporarily in effect during the French Revolution. Britain captured the island in 1810 as part of the Napoleonic Wars but kept most of the French administrative structure, which remains to this day in the form of the country's legal codes and widespread use of the French Creole language. The abolition of slavery in 1835 – later than most other British colonies – led to increased reliance on contracted laborers from the Indian subcontinent to work on plantations. Today their descendants form the majority of the population. Mauritius remained a strategically important British naval base and later an air station, and it played a role during World War II in anti-submarine and convoy operations, as well as in the collection of signals intelligence.

Mauritius gained independence from the UK in 1968 as a Parliamentary Republic and has remained a stable democracy with regular free elections and a positive human rights record. The country also attracted considerable foreign investment and now has one of Africa's highest per capita incomes. Mauritius' often-fractious coalition politics has been dominated by two prominent families, each of which has had father-son pairs who have been prime minister over multiple, often nonconsecutive, terms. Seewoosagur RAMGOOLAM (1968-76) was Mauritius' first prime minister, and he was succeeded by Anerood JUGNAUTH (1982-95, 2000-03, 2014-17); his son Navin RAMGOOLAM (1995-2000, 2005-14); and Paul Raymond BERENGER (2003-05), the only non-Hindu prime minister of post-independence Mauritius. In 2017, Pravind JUGNAUTH became prime minister after his father stepped down short of completing his term, and he was elected in his own right in 2019.

Mauritius claims the French island of Tromelin and the British Chagos Archipelago (British Indian Ocean Territory). Since 2017, Mauritius has secured favorable UN General Assembly resolutions and an International Court of Justice advisory opinion relating to its sovereignty dispute with the UK.

GEOGRAPHY

Location: Southern Africa, island in the Indian Ocean, about 800 km (500 mi) east of Madagascar

Geographic coordinates: 20 17 S, 57 33 E

Map references: Africa

Area: *total:* 2,040 sq km
land: 2,030 sq km
water: 10 sq km
note: includes Agalega Islands, Cargados Carajos Shoals (Saint Brandon), and Rodrigues
comparison ranking: total 180

Area - comparative: almost 11 times the size of Washington, D.C.

Land boundaries: *total:* 0 km

Coastline: 177 km

Maritime claims: *territorial sea:* 12 nm
exclusive economic zone: 200 nm
continental shelf: 200 nm or to the edge of the continental margin
note: measured from claimed archipelagic straight baselines

Climate: tropical, modified by southeast trade winds; warm, dry winter (May to November); hot, wet, humid summer (November to May)

Terrain: small coastal plain rising to discontinuous mountains encircling central plateau

Elevation: *highest point:* Mont Piton 828 m
lowest point: Indian Ocean 0 m

Natural resources: arable land, fish

Land use: *agricultural land:* 43.1% (2022 est.)
arable land: 37.6% (2022 est.)
permanent crops: 2% (2022 est.)
permanent pasture: 3.5% (2022 est.)
forest: 19.5% (2022 est.)
other: 37.5% (2022 est.)

Irrigated land: 143 sq km (2022)

Population distribution: population density is one of the highest in the world; urban clusters are found throughout the main island, with a greater density in and around Port Luis; the population on Rodrigues Island is fairly evenly spread, with a slightly denser cluster on the north coast, as shown in this population distribution map

Natural hazards: cyclones (November to April); almost completely surrounded by reefs that may pose maritime hazards

Geography - note: the main island, from which the country derives its name, is of volcanic origin and is almost entirely surrounded by coral reefs; former home of the extinct dodo, a large flightless bird related to pigeons

PEOPLE AND SOCIETY

Population: *total:* 1,310,504 (2024 est.)
male: 639,270
female: 671,234
comparison rankings: total 159; male 159; female 156

Nationality: *noun:* Mauritian(s)
adjective: Mauritian

Ethnic groups: Indo-Mauritian (compose approximately two thirds of the total population), Creole, Sino-Mauritian, Franco-Mauritian
note: Mauritius has not had a question on ethnicity on its national census since 1972

Languages: Creole 86.5%, Bhojpuri 5.3%, French 4.1%, two languages 1.4%, other 2.6% (includes English, one of the two official languages of the National Assembly, which is spoken by less than 1% of the population), unspecified 0.1% (2011 est.)

Religions: Hindu 48.5%, Roman Catholic 26.3%, Muslim 17.3%, other Christian 6.4%, other 0.6%, none 0.7%, unspecified 0.1% (2011 est.)

Age structure: *0-14 years:* 15.1% (male 100,973/female 96,711)
15-64 years: 71% (male 462,833/female 467,509)
65 years and over: 13.9% (2024 est.) (male 75,464/female 107,014)

Dependency ratios: *total dependency ratio:* 40.9 (2024 est.)
youth dependency ratio: 21.2 (2024 est.)
elderly dependency ratio: 19.6 (2024 est.)
potential support ratio: 5.1 (2024 est.)

Median age: *total:* 39.6 years (2024 est.)
male: 38.1 years
female: 41 years
comparison ranking: total 66

Population growth rate: 0.07% (2024 est.)
comparison ranking: 189

Birth rate: 9.8 births/1,000 population (2024 est.)
comparison ranking: 191

Death rate: 9 deaths/1,000 population (2024 est.)
comparison ranking: 59

Net migration rate: 0 migrant(s)/1,000 population (2024 est.)
comparison ranking: 78

Population distribution: population density is one of the highest in the world; urban clusters are found throughout the main island, with a greater density in and around Port Luis; the population on Rodrigues Island is fairly evenly spread, with a slightly denser cluster on the north coast, as shown in this population distribution map

Urbanization: *urban population:* 40.9% of total population (2023)
rate of urbanization: 0.28% annual rate of change (2020-25 est.)

Major urban areas - population: 149,000 PORT LOUIS (capital) (2018)

Sex ratio: *at birth:* 1.07 male(s)/female
0-14 years: 1.04 male(s)/female
15-64 years: 0.99 male(s)/female
65 years and over: 0.71 male(s)/female
total population: 0.95 male(s)/female (2024 est.)

Maternal mortality ratio: 66 deaths/100,000 live births (2023 est.)
comparison ranking: 85

Infant mortality rate: *total:* 11.6 deaths/1,000 live births (2024 est.)
male: 13.1 deaths/1,000 live births
female: 10 deaths/1,000 live births
comparison ranking: total 116

Life expectancy at birth: *total population:* 75.4 years (2024 est.)
male: 72.6 years
female: 78.4 years
comparison ranking: total population 127

Total fertility rate: 1.36 children born/woman (2024 est.)
comparison ranking: 215

Gross reproduction rate: 0.66 (2024 est.)

Drinking water source: *improved: urban:* 100% of population (2022 est.)
rural: 100% of population (2022 est.)
total: 100% of population (2022 est.)
unimproved: urban: 0% of population (2022 est.)
rural: 0% of population (2022 est.)
total: 0% of population (2022 est.)

Health expenditure: 6.4% of GDP (2021)
9.4% of national budget (2022 est.)

Physician density: 1.44 physicians/1,000 population (2022)

Hospital bed density: 3.7 beds/1,000 population (2021 est.)

Sanitation facility access: *improved: urban:* 99.7% of population (2022 est.)
unimproved: urban: 0.3% of population (2022 est.)

Obesity - adult prevalence rate: 10.8% (2016)
comparison ranking: 137

Alcohol consumption per capita: *total:* 3.39 liters of pure alcohol (2019 est.)
beer: 1.94 liters of pure alcohol (2019 est.)
wine: 0.23 liters of pure alcohol (2019 est.)
spirits: 0.88 liters of pure alcohol (2019 est.)
other alcohols: 0.03 liters of pure alcohol (2019 est.)
comparison ranking: total 106

Tobacco use: *total:* 19.6% (2025 est.)
male: 37.4% (2025 est.)
female: 2.6% (2025 est.)
comparison ranking: total 73

Currently married women (ages 15-49): 62% (2023 est.)

Education expenditure: 3.3% of GDP (2024 est.)
12.8% national budget (2023 est.)
comparison ranking: Education expenditure (% GDP) 136

Literacy: *total population:* 93% (2016 est.)
male: 95% (2016 est.)
female: 91% (2016 est.)

School life expectancy (primary to tertiary education): *total:* 14 years (2020 est.)
male: 14 years (2020 est.)
female: 15 years (2020 est.)

ENVIRONMENT

Environmental issues: water pollution, degradation of coral reefs; soil erosion; wildlife preservation; solid-waste disposal

International environmental agreements: *party to:* Antarctic-Marine Living Resources, Biodiversity, Climate Change, Climate Change-Kyoto Protocol, Climate Change-Paris Agreement, Desertification, Endangered Species, Environmental Modification, Hazardous Wastes, Law of the Sea, Marine Life Conservation, Nuclear Test Ban, Ozone Layer Protection, Ship Pollution, Wetlands
signed, but not ratified: none of the selected agreements

Climate: tropical, modified by southeast trade winds; warm, dry winter (May to November); hot, wet, humid summer (November to May)

Urbanization: *urban population:* 40.9% of total population (2023)
rate of urbanization: 0.28% annual rate of change (2020-25 est.)

Carbon dioxide emissions: 5.551 million metric tonnes of CO_2 (2023 est.)
from coal and metallurgical coke: 1.495 million metric tonnes of CO_2 (2023 est.)
from petroleum and other liquids: 4.056 million metric tonnes of CO_2 (2023 est.)
comparison ranking: total emissions 134

Particulate matter emissions: 10.5 micrograms per cubic meter (2019 est.)

Waste and recycling: *municipal solid waste generated annually:* 438,000 tons (2024 est.)
percent of municipal solid waste recycled: 15.9% (2022 est.)

Total water withdrawal: *municipal:* 320 million cubic meters (2022)
industrial: 10 million cubic meters (2022)
agricultural: 303 million cubic meters (2022)

Total renewable water resources: 2.751 billion cubic meters (2022 est.)

GOVERNMENT

Country name: *conventional long form:* Republic of Mauritius
conventional short form: Mauritius
local long form: Republic of Mauritius
local short form: Mauritius
etymology: named after Prince Maurice VAN NASSAU, stadtholder (governor) of the Dutch Republic, in 1598
note: pronounced mahr-ish-us

Government type: parliamentary republic

Capital: *name:* Port Louis
geographic coordinates: 20 09 S, 57 29 E
time difference: UTC+4 (9 hours ahead of Washington, DC, during Standard Time)
etymology: named after LOUIS XV, who was king of France in 1736 when the port became the administrative center of Mauritius

Administrative divisions: 9 districts and 3 dependencies*; Agalega Islands*, Black River, Cargados Carajos Shoals*, Flacq, Grand Port, Moka, Pamplemousses, Plaines Wilhems, Port Louis, Riviere du Rempart, Rodrigues*, Savanne

Legal system: civil system based on French civil law with some elements of English common law

Constitution: *history:* several previous; latest adopted 12 March 1968
amendment process: proposed by the National Assembly; passage of amendments affecting constitutional articles, including the sovereignty of the state, fundamental rights and freedoms, citizenship, or the branches of government, requires approval in a referendum by at least three-fourths majority of voters followed by a unanimous vote by the Assembly; passage of other amendments requires only two-thirds majority vote by the Assembly

International law organization participation: accepts compulsory ICJ jurisdiction with reservations; accepts ICCt jurisdiction

Citizenship: *citizenship by birth:* yes
citizenship by descent only: yes
dual citizenship recognized: yes
residency requirement for naturalization: 5 out of the previous 7 years including the last 12 months

Suffrage: 18 years of age; universal

Executive branch: *chief of state:* President Dharam GOKHOOL (since 7 December 2024)
head of government: Prime Minister Navin RAMGOOLAM (since 13 November 2024)
cabinet: Cabinet of Ministers (Council of Ministers) appointed by the president on the recommendation of the prime minister
election/appointment process: president and vice president indirectly elected by the National Assembly for 5-year renewable terms; the president appoints the prime minister and deputy prime minister who have the majority support in the National Assembly
most recent election date: 7 November 2019
election results: *2019:* Prithvirajsing ROOPUN (MSM) elected president by the National Assembly - unanimous vote
2015: Ameenah GURIB-FAKIM (independent) elected president by the National Assembly - unanimous vote
expected date of next election: 2024

Legislative branch: *legislature name:* National Assembly - Assemblée nationale
legislative structure: unicameral
chamber name: National Assembly
number of seats: 67 (62 directly elected; 4 appointed)
electoral system: plurality/majority
scope of elections: full renewal
term in office: 5 years
most recent election date: 11/10/2024
parties elected and seats per party: Alliance Du Changement (Alliance for Change, AdC) (60); Other (2)
percentage of women in chamber: 17.9%
expected date of next election: October 2029

Judicial branch: *highest court(s):* Supreme Court of Mauritius (consists of the chief justice, a senior puisne judge, and 24 puisne judges)
judge selection and term of office: chief justice appointed by the president after consultation with the prime minister; senior puisne judge appointed by the president with the advice of the chief justice; other puisne judges appointed by the president with the advice of the Judicial and Legal Commission, a 4-member body of judicial officials including the chief justice; all judges serve until retirement at age 67
subordinate courts: lower regional courts known as District Courts, Court of Civil Appeal; Court of Criminal Appeal; Public Bodies Appeal Tribunal
note: the Judicial Committee of the Privy Council (in London) serves as the final court of appeal

Political parties: Alliance Morisien (Mauritian Alliance)
Jean-Claude Barbier Movement (Mouvement Jean-Claude Barbier) or MJCB
Mauritian Militant Movement (Mouvement Militant Mauricien) or MMM
Mauritian Social Democratic Party (Parti Mauricien Social Democrate) or PMSD
Mauritius Labor Party (Parti Travailliste) or PTR or MLP
Militant Platform (Plateforme Militante) or PM
Militant Socialist Movement (Mouvement Socialist Mauricien) or MSM
Muvman Liberater or ML
National Alliance
Patriotic Movement (Mouvement Patriotique) or MAG
Rodrigues Peoples Organization (Organisation du Peuple Rodriguais) or OPR

Diplomatic representation in the US: *chief of mission:* Ambassador (vacant); Chargé d'Affaires Gajjaluxmi MOOTOOSAMY (since 5 June 2025)
chancery: 1709 N Street NW, Washington, DC 20036
telephone: [1] (202) 244-1491
FAX: [1] (202) 966-0983
email address and website: mauritius.embassy@verizon.net
https://mauritius-washington.govmu.org/Pages/index.aspx

Diplomatic representation from the US: *chief of mission:* Ambassador Henry V. JARDINE (since 22 February 2023); note - also accredited to Seychelles
embassy: 4th Floor, Rogers House, John Kennedy Avenue, Port Louis
mailing address: 2450 Port Louis Place, Washington, DC 20521-2450
telephone: [230] 202-4400
FAX: [230] 208-9534
email address and website: PTLConsular@state.gov
https://mu.usembassy.gov/

International organization participation: ACP, AfDB, AOSIS, AU, CD, COMESA, CPLP (associate), FAO, G-77, IAEA, IBRD, ICAO, ICC (NGOs), ICCt, ICRM, IDA, IFAD, IFC, IFRCS, IHO, ILO, IMF, IMO, IMSO, InOC, Interpol, IOC, IOM, IPU, ISO, ITSO, ITU, ITUC (NGOs), MIGA, NAM, OIF, OPCW, PCA, SAARC (observer), SADC, UN, UNCTAD, UNESCO, UNIDO, UNWTO, UPU, WCO, WFTU (NGOs), WHO, WIPO, WMO, WTO

Independence: 12 March 1968 (from the UK)

National holiday: Independence and Republic Day, 12 March (1968, 1992)
note: became independent and a republic on the same date in 1968 and 1992, respectively

Flag: *description:* four equal horizontal bands of red (top), blue, yellow, and green
meaning: red stands for self-determination and independence; blue for the Indian Ocean; yellow for the new light of independence, golden sunshine, or the bright future; and green for agriculture or the island's lush vegetation
note: Mauritius has the only national flag with four horizontal color bands

National symbol(s): dodo bird, earring tree flower (*Trochetia boutoniana*)

National color(s): red, blue, yellow, green

National anthem(s): *title:* "Motherland"
lyrics/music: Jean Georges PROSPER/Philippe GENTIL
history: adopted 1968

National heritage: *total World Heritage Sites:* 2 (both cultural)
selected World Heritage Site locales: Aapravasi Ghat; Le Morne Cultural Landscape

ECONOMY

Economic overview: upper middle-income Indian Ocean island economy; diversified portfolio; investing in maritime security; strong tourism sector decimated by COVID-19; expanding in information and financial services; environmentally fragile

Real GDP (purchasing power parity): $34.406 billion (2024 est.)
$32.864 billion (2023 est.)
$31.296 billion (2022 est.)
note: data in 2021 dollars
comparison ranking: 143

Real GDP growth rate: 4.7% (2024 est.)
5% (2023 est.)
8.7% (2022 est.)
note: annual GDP % growth based on constant local currency
comparison ranking: 53

Real GDP per capita: $27,300 (2024 est.)
$26,100 (2023 est.)
$24,800 (2022 est.)
note: data in 2021 dollars
comparison ranking: 85

GDP (official exchange rate): $14.953 billion (2024 est.)
note: data in current dollars at official exchange rate

Inflation rate (consumer prices): 3.6% (2024 est.)
7.1% (2023 est.)
10.8% (2022 est.)
note: annual % change based on consumer prices
comparison ranking: 115

GDP - composition, by sector of origin: *agriculture:* 4.3% (2024 est.)
industry: 17.8% (2024 est.)
services: 64.4% (2024 est.)
note: figures may not total 100% due to non-allocated consumption not captured in sector-reported data
comparison rankings: agriculture 116; industry 145; services 61

GDP - composition, by end use: *household consumption:* 68.6% (2024 est.)
government consumption: 14.7% (2024 est.)
investment in fixed capital: 21% (2024 est.)
investment in inventories: 0.2% (2024 est.)
exports of goods and services: 46.2% (2024 est.)
imports of goods and services: -57.8% (2024 est.)
note: figures may not total 100% due to rounding or gaps in data collection

Agricultural products: sugarcane, chicken, pumpkins/squash, tomatoes, eggs, potatoes, cabbages, bananas, onions, cucumbers/gherkins (2023)
note: top ten agricultural products based on tonnage

Industries: food processing (largely sugar milling), textiles, clothing, mining, chemicals, metal products, transport equipment, nonelectrical machinery, tourism

Industrial production growth rate: 4.7% (2024 est.)
note: annual % change in industrial value added based on constant local currency
comparison ranking: 51

Labor force: 594,900 (2024 est.)
note: number of people ages 15 or older who are employed or seeking work
comparison ranking: 158

Unemployment rate: 5.5% (2024 est.)
5.6% (2023 est.)
6.4% (2022 est.)
note: % of labor force seeking employment
comparison ranking: 103

Youth unemployment rate (ages 15-24): *total:* 16.6% (2024 est.)
male: 15.3% (2024 est.)
female: 18.4% (2024 est.)
note: % of labor force ages 15-24 seeking employment
comparison ranking: total 71

Population below poverty line: 10.3% (2017 est.)
note: % of population with income below national poverty line

Gini Index coefficient - distribution of family income: 36.8 (2017 est.)
note: index (0-100) of income distribution; higher values represent greater inequality
comparison ranking: 60

Household income or consumption by percentage share: *lowest 10%:* 2.9% (2017 est.)
highest 10%: 29.9% (2017 est.)
note: % share of income accruing to lowest and highest 10% of population

Remittances: 2.2% of GDP (2023 est.)
2.1% of GDP (2022 est.)
2.4% of GDP (2021 est.)
note: personal transfers and compensation between resident and non-resident individuals/households/entities

Budget: *revenues:* $3.801 billion (2024 est.)
expenditures: $5.042 billion (2024 est.)
note: central government revenues (excluding grants) and expenditures converted to US dollars at average official exchange rate for year indicated

Public debt: 58% of GDP (2019 est.)
note: central government debt as a % of GDP
comparison ranking: 82

Taxes and other revenues: 20.5% (of GDP) (2023 est.)
note: central government tax revenue as a % of GDP
comparison ranking: 49

Current account balance: -$647.743 million (2023 est.)
-$1.437 billion (2022 est.)
-$1.497 billion (2021 est.)
note: balance of payments - net trade and primary/secondary income in current dollars
comparison ranking: 115

Exports: $6.381 billion (2023 est.)
$6.138 billion (2022 est.)
$4.213 billion (2021 est.)
note: balance of payments - exports of goods and services in current dollars
comparison ranking: 131

Exports - partners: USA 11%, France 11%, Zimbabwe 10%, South Africa 7%, Zambia 7% (2023)
note: top five export partners based on percentage share of exports

Exports - commodities: fish, garments, raw sugar, fertilizers, diamonds (2023)
note: top five export commodities based on value in dollars

Imports: $8.027 billion (2023 est.)
$8.052 billion (2022 est.)
$6.057 billion (2021 est.)
note: balance of payments - imports of goods and services in current dollars
comparison ranking: 134

Imports - partners: China 15%, UAE 11%, India 10%, South Africa 9%, France 6% (2023)
note: top five import partners based on percentage share of imports

Imports - commodities: refined petroleum, cars, fish, coal, packaged medicine (2023)
note: top five import commodities based on value in dollars

Reserves of foreign exchange and gold: $8.506 billion (2024 est.)
$7.248 billion (2023 est.)
$7.793 billion (2022 est.)
note: holdings of gold (year-end prices)/foreign exchange/special drawing rights in current dollars
comparison ranking: 84

Debt - external: $3.632 billion (2023 est.)
note: present value of external debt in current US dollars
comparison ranking: 80

Exchange rates: Mauritian rupees (MUR) per US dollar -

Exchange rates: 46.415 (2024 est.)
45.267 (2023 est.)
44.183 (2022 est.)
41.692 (2021 est.)
39.347 (2020 est.)

ENERGY

Electricity access: *electrification - total population:* 100% (2022 est.)
electrification - urban areas: 99%
electrification - rural areas: 100%

Electricity: *installed generating capacity:* 955,000 kW (2023 est.)
consumption: 3.084 billion kWh (2023 est.)
transmission/distribution losses: 179.996 million kWh (2023 est.)
comparison rankings: installed generating capacity 135; consumption 142; transmission/distribution losses 63

Electricity generation sources: *fossil fuels:* 82.4% of total installed capacity (2023 est.)
solar: 4.6% of total installed capacity (2023 est.)
wind: 0.3% of total installed capacity (2023 est.)
hydroelectricity: 2.9% of total installed capacity (2023 est.)
biomass and waste: 9.9% of total installed capacity (2023 est.)

Coal: *consumption:* 651,000 metric tons (2023 est.)
imports: 610,000 metric tons (2023 est.)

Petroleum: *refined petroleum consumption:* 28,000 bbl/day (2023 est.)

Energy consumption per capita: 60.188 million Btu/person (2023 est.)
comparison ranking: 83

COMMUNICATIONS

Telephones - fixed lines: *total subscriptions:* 464,000 (2023 est.)
subscriptions per 100 inhabitants: 36 (2023 est.)
comparison ranking: total subscriptions 94

Telephones - mobile cellular: *total subscriptions:* 2.1 million (2023 est.)
subscriptions per 100 inhabitants: 161 (2022 est.)
comparison ranking: total subscriptions 149

Broadcast media: the Mauritius Broadcasting Corporation (MBC) is the national public TV and radio broadcaster, with programming in French, English, Hindi, Creole, and Chinese; MBC provides 17 television channels in Mauritius; 9 FM radio stations and 2 AM radio stations (2022)

Internet country code: .mu

Internet users: *percent of population:* 80% (2023 est.)

Broadband - fixed subscriptions: *total:* 343,000 (2023 est.)
subscriptions per 100 inhabitants: 27 (2023 est.)
comparison ranking: total 113

TRANSPORTATION

Civil aircraft registration country code prefix: 3B

Airports: 5 (2025)
comparison ranking: 177

Heliports: 1 (2025)
comparison ranking: 163

Merchant marine: *total:* 32 (2023)
by type: general cargo 1, oil tanker 4, other 27
comparison ranking: total 132

Ports: *total ports:* 2 (2024)
large: 0
medium: 0
small: 1
very small: 1
ports with oil terminals: 1
key ports: Port Louis, Port Mathurin

MILITARY AND SECURITY

Military and security forces: no regular military forces; the Mauritius Police Force (MPF) under the Ministry of Defense is responsible for the country's security; it includes a paramilitary unit known as the Special Mobile Force, which includes some motorized infantry and light armored units; the MPF also has a Police Helicopter Squadron, a Special Support Unit (riot police), and the National Coast Guard (2025)

Military equipment inventories and acquisitions: the MPF's inventory is comprised of mostly secondhand equipment from Western European countries and India (2024)

Military - note: key security priorities for the Maritius Police Force (MPF) include combating narcotics trafficking, ensuring public order, fighting cybercrime, improving maritime security, and responding to natural disasters; the MPF's primary security partner is India, which provides training and other support to the National Coast Guard, while Indian naval vessels often patrol the country's waters; the MPF has also received assistance and training from France, the UK, and the US
the Special Mobile Force was created in 1960 following the withdrawal of the British garrison (2025)

TRANSNATIONAL ISSUES

Refugees and internally displaced persons: *refugees:* 82 (2024 est.)

IDPs: 39 (2024 est.)

MEXICO

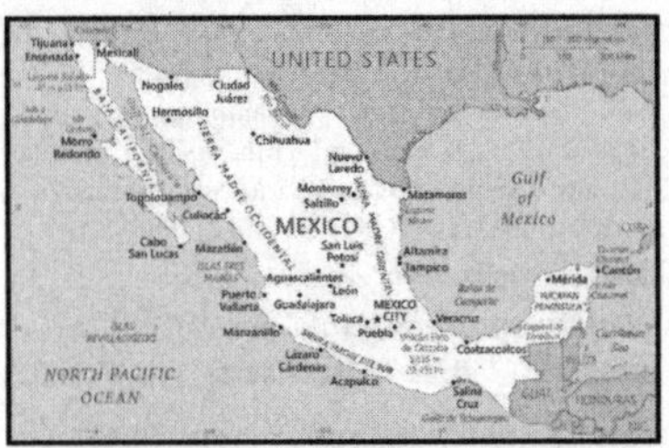

INTRODUCTION

Background: Mexico was the site of several advanced Amerindian civilizations – including the Olmec, Toltec, Teotihuacan, Zapotec, Maya, and Aztec – until Spain conquered and colonized the area in the early 16th century. Administered as the Viceroyalty of New Spain for three centuries, it achieved independence early in the 19th century. Elections held in 2000 marked the first time since Mexican Revolution in 1910 that an opposition candidate – Vicente FOX of the National Action Party (PAN) – defeated the party in government, the Institutional Revolutionary Party (PRI). He was succeeded in 2006 by another PAN candidate Felipe CALDERON, but Enrique PEÑA NIETO regained the presidency for the PRI in 2012. Left-leaning anti-establishment politician and former mayor of Mexico City (2000-05) Andrés Manuel LÓPEZ OBRADOR, from the National Regeneration Movement (MORENA), became president in 2018.

The US-Mexico-Canada Agreement (USMCA, or T-MEC by its Spanish acronym) entered into force in 2020 and replaced its predecessor, the North American Free Trade Agreement (NAFTA). Mexico amended its constitution in 2019 to facilitate the implementation of the labor components of USMCA.

Mexico is currently the US's second-largest goods trading partner, after Canada. Ongoing economic and social concerns include low real wages, high underemployment, inequitable income distribution, and few advancement opportunities, particularly for the largely indigenous population in the impoverished southern states. Since 2007, Mexico's powerful transnational criminal organizations have engaged in a struggle to control criminal markets, resulting in tens of thousands of drug-related homicides and forced disappearances.

GEOGRAPHY

Location: North America, bordering the Caribbean Sea and the Gulf of America, between Belize and the United States and bordering the North Pacific Ocean, between Guatemala and the United States

Geographic coordinates: 23 00 N, 102 00 W

Map references: North America

Area: *total:* 1,964,375 sq km
land: 1,943,945 sq km
water: 20,430 sq km
comparison ranking: total 15

Area - comparative: slightly less than three times the size of Texas

Land boundaries: *total:* 4,389 km
border countries (3): Belize 276 km; Guatemala 958 km; US 3,155 km

Coastline: 9,330 km

Maritime claims: *territorial sea:* 12 nm
contiguous zone: 24 nm
exclusive economic zone: 200 nm
continental shelf: 200 nm or to the edge of the continental margin

Climate: varies from tropical to desert

Terrain: high, rugged mountains; low coastal plains; high plateaus; desert

Elevation: *highest point:* Volcan Pico de Orizaba 5,636 m
lowest point: Laguna Salada -10 m
mean elevation: 1,111 m

Natural resources: petroleum, silver, antimony, copper, gold, lead, zinc, natural gas, timber

Land use: *agricultural land:* 49.4% (2022 est.)
arable land: 9.8% (2022 est.)
permanent crops: 1.5% (2022 est.)
permanent pasture: 38.1% (2022 est.)
forest: 33.7% (2022 est.)
other: 16.9% (2022 est.)

Irrigated land: 59,910 sq km (2022)

Major lakes (area sq km): *fresh water lake(s):* Laguna de Chapala - 1,140 sq km
salt water lake(s): Laguna de Terminos - 1,550 sq km

Major rivers (by length in km): Rio Grande river mouth (shared with US [s]) - 3,057 km; Colorado river mouth (shared with US [s]) - 2,333 km
note: [s] after country name indicates river source; [m] after country name indicates river mouth

Major watersheds (area sq km): Atlantic Ocean drainage: *(Gulf of America)* Rio Grande/Bravo (607,965 sq km)

Pacific Ocean drainage: *(Gulf of California)* Colorado (703,148 sq km)

Major aquifers: Atlantic and Gulf Coastal Plains Aquifer

Population distribution: most of the population is found in the middle of the country between the states of Jalisco and Veracruz; approximately a quarter of the population lives in and around Mexico City

Natural hazards: tsunamis along the Pacific coast; volcanoes and destructive earthquakes in the center and south; hurricanes on the Pacific, Gulf of America, and Caribbean coasts
volcanism: volcanic activity in the central-southern part of the country; the volcanoes in Baja California are mostly dormant; Colima (3,850 m) is Mexico's most active volcano and is responsible for periodic evacuations of nearby villagers; it has been deemed a Decade Volcano by the International Association of Volcanology and Chemistry of the Earth's Interior, worthy of study due to its explosive history and close proximity to human populations; Popocatepetl (5,426 m) poses a threat to Mexico City; other historically active volcanoes include Barcena, Ceboruco, El Chichon, Michoacan-Guanajuato, Pico de Orizaba, San Martin, Socorro, and Tacana; see note 2 under "Geography - note"

Geography - note: *note 1:* strategic location on southern border of the US; Mexico is one of the countries along the Ring of Fire, which is a belt bordering the Pacific Ocean that contains about 75% of the world's volcanoes and up to 90% of the world's earthquakes
note 2: the Sac Actun cave system at 348 km (216 mi) is the longest underwater cave in the world and the second longest cave worldwide, after Mammoth Cave in the United States (see "Geography - note" under United States)
note 3: the prominent Yucatán Peninsula that divides the Gulf of America from the Caribbean Sea is shared by Mexico, Guatemala, and Belize; on the northern coast of Yucatan near the town of Chicxulub lie the remnants of a massive asteroid or comet crater about 150 km (93 mi) in diameter and extending into the Gulf of America; the impact is believed to have initiated a worldwide climate disruption that caused a mass extinction of 75% of the earth's plant and animal species, including the non-avian dinosaurs

PEOPLE AND SOCIETY

Population: *total:* 130,739,927 (2024 est.)
male: 63,899,138
female: 66,840,789
comparison rankings: total 10; male 10; female 10

Nationality: *noun:* Mexican(s)
adjective: Mexican

Ethnic groups: Mestizo (Indigenous-Spanish) 62%, predominantly Indigenous 21%, Indigenous 7%, other 10% (mostly European) (2012 est.)
note: Mexico does not collect census data on ethnicity

Languages: Spanish only 93.8%, Spanish and indigenous languages (including Mayan, Nahuatl, and others) 5.4%, indigenous only 0.6%, unspecified 0.2% (2020 est.)
major-language sample(s):
La Libreta Informativa del Mundo, la fuente indispensable de información básica. (Spanish)

Religions: Roman Catholic 78%, Protestant/evangelical Christian 11.2%, other 0.002%, unaffiliated (includes atheism) 10.6% (2020 est.)

Age structure: *0-14 years:* 23.3% (male 15,647,805/ female 14,754,004)
15-64 years: 68.6% (male 43,651,105/female 45,983,174)
65 years and over: 8.2% (2024 est.) (male 4,600,228/ female 6,103,611)

Dependency ratios: *total dependency ratio:* 45.9 (2024 est.)
youth dependency ratio: 33.9 (2024 est.)
elderly dependency ratio: 11.9 (2024 est.)
potential support ratio: 8.4 (2024 est.)

Median age: *total:* 30.8 years (2024 est.)
male: 28.8 years
female: 32.7 years
comparison ranking: total 132

Population growth rate: 0.72% (2024 est.)
comparison ranking: 122

Birth rate: 14.3 births/1,000 population (2024 est.)
comparison ranking: 118

Death rate: 6.5 deaths/1,000 population (2024 est.)
comparison ranking: 134

Net migration rate: -0.7 migrant(s)/1,000 population (2024 est.)

comparison ranking: 131

Population distribution: most of the population is found in the middle of the country between the states of Jalisco and Veracruz; approximately a quarter of the population lives in and around Mexico City

Urbanization: *urban population:* 81.6% of total population (2023)
rate of urbanization: 1.4% annual rate of change (2020-25 est.)

Major urban areas - population: 22.281 million MEXICO CITY (capital), 5.420 million Guadalajara, 5.117 million Monterrey, 3.345 million Puebla, 2.626 million Toluca de Lerdo, 2.260 million Tijuana (2023)

Sex ratio: *at birth:* 1.05 male(s)/female
0-14 years: 1.06 male(s)/female
15-64 years: 0.95 male(s)/female
65 years and over: 0.75 male(s)/female
total population: 0.96 male(s)/female (2024 est.)

Mother's mean age at first birth: 21.3 years (2008 est.)

Maternal mortality ratio: 42 deaths/100,000 live births (2023 est.)
comparison ranking: 101

Infant mortality rate: *total:* 12.1 deaths/1,000 live births (2024 est.)
male: 13.4 deaths/1,000 live births
female: 10.9 deaths/1,000 live births
comparison ranking: total 109

Life expectancy at birth: *total population:* 74.6 years (2024 est.)
male: 71.6 years
female: 77.7 years
comparison ranking: total population 140

Total fertility rate: 1.79 children born/woman (2024 est.)
comparison ranking: 142

Gross reproduction rate: 0.88 (2024 est.)

Drinking water source: *improved: urban:* 100% of population (2022 est.)
rural: 98.4% of population (2022 est.)
total: 99.7% of population (2022 est.)
unimproved: urban: 0% of population (2022 est.)
rural: 1.6% of population (2022 est.)
total: 0.3% of population (2022 est.)

Health expenditure: 6.1% of GDP (2021)
10.4% of national budget (2022 est.)

Physician density: 2.59 physicians/1,000 population (2022)

Hospital bed density: 1 beds/1,000 population (2021 est.)

Sanitation facility access: *improved: urban:* 100% of population (2022 est.)
rural: 98.2% of population (2022 est.)
total: 99.7% of population (2022 est.)
unimproved: urban: 0% of population (2022 est.)
rural: 1.8% of population (2022 est.)
total: 0.3% of population (2022 est.)

Obesity - adult prevalence rate: 28.9% (2016)
comparison ranking: 28

Alcohol consumption per capita: *total:* 4.25 liters of pure alcohol (2019 est.)
beer: 3.72 liters of pure alcohol (2019 est.)
wine: 0.19 liters of pure alcohol (2019 est.)
spirits: 0.19 liters of pure alcohol (2019 est.)
other alcohols: 0.15 liters of pure alcohol (2019 est.)
comparison ranking: total 91

Tobacco use: *total:* 13.8% (2025 est.)
male: 21.8% (2025 est.)
female: 6.3% (2025 est.)
comparison ranking: total 107

Children under the age of 5 years underweight: 4.2% (2021)
comparison ranking: 70

Currently married women (ages 15-49): 56.6% (2023 est.)

Child marriage: *women married by age 15:* 3.6% (2018)
women married by age 18: 20.7% (2018)

Education expenditure: 4.2% of GDP (2021 est.)
15.9% national budget (2021 est.)
comparison ranking: Education expenditure (% GDP) 97

Literacy: *total population:* 95% (2020 est.)
male: 96% (2020 est.)
female: 94% (2020 est.)

School life expectancy (primary to tertiary education): *total:* 15 years (2022 est.)
male: 14 years (2022 est.)
female: 15 years (2022 est.)

ENVIRONMENT

Environmental issues: scarcity of hazardous waste disposal facilities; natural freshwater resources scarce and polluted in north, inaccessible and poor quality in center and extreme southeast; urban river pollution from raw sewage and industrial effluents; deforestation; widespread erosion; desertification; serious air and water pollution in urban areas; land subsidence in Valley of Mexico caused by groundwater depletion
note: the government considers the lack of clean water and deforestation as national security issues

International environmental agreements: *party to:* Biodiversity, Climate Change, Climate Change-Kyoto Protocol, Climate Change-Paris Agreement, Comprehensive Nuclear Test Ban, Desertification, Endangered Species, Hazardous Wastes, Law of the Sea, Marine Dumping-London Convention, Marine Dumping-London Protocol, Marine Life Conservation, Nuclear Test Ban, Ozone Layer Protection, Ship Pollution, Tropical Timber 2006, Wetlands, Whaling
signed, but not ratified: none of the selected agreements

Climate: varies from tropical to desert

Urbanization: *urban population:* 81.6% of total population (2023)
rate of urbanization: 1.4% annual rate of change (2020-25 est.)

Carbon dioxide emissions: 441.049 million metric tonnes of CO2 (2023 est.)
from coal and metallurgical coke: 32.087 million metric tonnes of CO2 (2023 est.)
from petroleum and other liquids: 228.279 million metric tonnes of CO2 (2023 est.)
from consumed natural gas: 180.684 million metric tonnes of CO2 (2023 est.)
comparison ranking: total emissions 13

Particulate matter emissions: 17.8 micrograms per cubic meter (2019 est.)

Methane emissions: *energy:* 1,389 kt (2022-2024 est.)
agriculture: 2,372.1 kt (2019-2021 est.)
waste: 1,832.6 kt (2019-2021 est.)
other: 49.8 kt (2019-2021 est.)

Waste and recycling: *municipal solid waste generated annually:* 53.1 million tons (2024 est.)
percent of municipal solid waste recycled: 9.6% (2022 est.)

Total water withdrawal: *municipal:* 13.33 billion cubic meters (2022)
industrial: 7.953 billion cubic meters (2022)
agricultural: 68.523 billion cubic meters (2022)

Total renewable water resources: 461.888 billion cubic meters (2022 est.)

Geoparks: *total global geoparks and regional networks:* 2
global geoparks and regional networks: Comarca Minera, Hidalgo; Mixteca Alta, Oaxaca (2023)

GOVERNMENT

Country name: *conventional long form:* United Mexican States
conventional short form: Mexico
local long form: Estados Unidos Mexicanos
local short form: Mexico
former: Mexican Republic, Mexican Empire
etymology: name may derive from one of the Nahuatl (Aztec) names for the capital city, Metztlixihtlico, which probably meant "the center of the moon;" alternatively, it may come from Mexica, the original name of the Aztec people

Government type: federal presidential republic

Capital: *name:* Mexico City (Ciudad de Mexico)
geographic coordinates: 19 26 N, 99 08 W
time difference: UTC-6 (1 hour behind Washington, DC, during Standard Time)
daylight saving time: DST was permanently removed in October 2022
time zone note: Mexico has four time zones
etymology: name may derive from one of the Nahuatl (Aztec) names for the capital city, Metztlixihtlico, which probably meant "the center of the moon;" alternatively, it may come from Mexica, the original name of the Aztec people

Administrative divisions: 32 states (*estados*, singular - *estado*); Aguascalientes, Baja California, Baja California Sur, Campeche, Chiapas, Chihuahua, Coahuila, Colima, Cuidad de Mexico, Durango, Guanajuato, Guerrero, Hidalgo, Jalisco, Mexico, Michoacán, Morelos, Nayarit, Nuevo Leon, Oaxaca, Puebla, Queretaro, Quintana Roo, San Luis Potosi, Sinaloa, Sonora, Tabasco, Tamaulipas, Tlaxcala, Veracruz, Yucatan, Zacatecas

Legal system: civil law system with US constitutional law influence; judicial review of legislative acts

Constitution: *history:* several previous; latest approved 5 February 1917
amendment process: proposed by the Congress of the Union; passage requires approval by at least two thirds of the members present and approval by a majority of the state legislatures

International law organization participation: accepts compulsory ICJ jurisdiction with reservations; accepts ICCt jurisdiction

Citizenship: *citizenship by birth:* yes
citizenship by descent only: yes
dual citizenship recognized: not specified
residency requirement for naturalization: 5 years

Suffrage: 18 years of age; universal and compulsory

Executive branch: *chief of state:* President Claudia SHEINBAUM Pardo (since 1 October 2024)
head of government: President Claudia SHEINBAUM Pardo (since 1 October 2024)

cabinet: Cabinet appointed by the president
election/appointment process: president directly elected by simple-majority popular vote for a single 6-year term
most recent election date: 2 June 2024
election results: *2024:* Claudia SHEINBAUM Pardo elected president; percent of vote - Claudia SHEINBAUM Pardo (MORENA) 59.4%, Xóchitl GÁLVEZ Ruiz (PAN) 27.9%, Jorge Álvarez MÁYNEZ (MC) 10.4%, other 2.3%
2018: Andrés Manuel LÓPEZ OBRADOR elected president; percent of vote - Andrés Manuel LÓPEZ OBRADOR (MORENA) 53.2%, Ricardo ANAYA Cortés (PAN) 22.3%, José Antonio MEADE Kuribreña (PRI) 16.4%, Jaime RODRÍGUEZ Calderón (independent) 5.2%, other 2.9%
2012: Enrique PEÑA NIETO elected president; percent of vote - Enrique PEÑA NIETO (PRI) 38.2%, Andrés Manuel LÓPEZ OBRADOR (PRD) 31.6%, Josefina Eugenia VÁZQUEZ Mota (PAN) 25.4%, other 4.8%
expected date of next election: 2030
note: the president is both chief of state and head of government

Legislative branch: *legislature name:* Congress of the Union (Congreso de la Unión)
legislative structure: bicameral
note: as of the 2018 election, senators will be eligible for a second term and deputies up to 4 consecutive terms

Legislative branch - lower chamber: *chamber name:* Chamber of Deputies (Cámara de Diputados)
number of seats: 500 (all directly elected)
electoral system: mixed system
scope of elections: full renewal
term in office: 3 years
most recent election date: 6/2/2024
parties elected and seats per party: National Regeneration Movement (MORENA) (236); Ecologist Green Party of Mexico (PVEM) (77); National Action Party (PAN) (72); Labour Party (PT) (51); Institutional Revolutionary Party (PRI) (35); Citizens' Movement (MC) (27); Other (2)
percentage of women in chamber: 50.2%
expected date of next election: June 2027

Legislative branch - upper chamber: *chamber name:* Senate (Cámara de Senadores)
number of seats: 128 (all directly elected)
electoral system: mixed system
scope of elections: full renewal
term in office: 6 years
most recent election date: 6/2/2024
parties elected and seats per party: National Regeneration Movement (MORENA) (60); National Action Party (PAN) (22); Institutional Revolutionary Party (PRI) (16); Ecologist Green Party of Mexico (PVEM) (14); Labour Party (PT) (9); Other (7)
percentage of women in chamber: 50%
expected date of next election: June 2030

Judicial branch: *highest court(s):* Supreme Court of Justice or Suprema Corte de Justicia de la Nación (consists of the chief justice and 11 justices and organized into civil, criminal, administrative, and labor panels) and the Electoral Tribunal of the Federal Judiciary (organized into the superior court, with 7 judges including the court president, and 5 regional courts, each with 3 judges)
judge selection and term of office: Supreme Court justices nominated by the president of the republic and approved by two-thirds vote of the members present in the Senate; justices serve 15-year terms; Electoral Tribunal superior and regional court judges nominated by the Supreme Court and elected by two-thirds vote of members present in the Senate; superior court president elected from among its members to hold office for a 4-year term; other judges of the superior and regional courts serve staggered, 9-year terms
subordinate courts: federal level includes circuit, collegiate, and unitary courts; state and district level courts
note: in April 2021, the Mexican congress passed a judicial reform which changed 7 articles of the constitution and preceded a new Organic Law on the Judicial Branch of the Federation

Political parties: Citizen's Movement (Movimiento Ciudadano) or MC
Institutional Revolutionary Party (Partido Revolucionario Institucional) or PRI
Labor Party (Partido del Trabajo) or PT
Mexican Green Ecological Party (Partido Verde Ecologista de México) or PVEM
Movement for National Regeneration (Movimiento Regeneración Nacional) or MORENA
National Action Party (Partido Acción Nacional) or PAN
Party of the Democratic Revolution (Partido de la Revolución Democrática) or PRD

Diplomatic representation in the US: *chief of mission:* Ambassador Esteban MOCTEZUMA Barragán (since 20 April 2021)
chancery: 1911 Pennsylvania Avenue NW, Washington, DC 20006
telephone: [1] (202) 728-1600
FAX: [1] (202) 728-1698
email address and website: mexembusa@sre.gob.mx
https://embamex.sre.gob.mx/eua/index.php/en/
consulate(s) general: Atlanta (GA), Austin (TX), Boston (MA), Chicago (IL), Dallas (TX), Denver (GA), El Paso (TX), Houston (TX), Laredo (TX), Miami (FL), New York (NY), Nogales (AZ), Phoenix (AZ), Raleigh (NC), Sacramento (CA), San Antonio (TX), San Diego (CA), San Francisco (CA), San Jose (CA), San Juan (Puerto Rico)
consulate(s): Albuquerque (NM), Boise (ID), Brownsville (TX), Calexico (CA), Del Rio (TX), Detroit (MI), Douglas (AZ), Eagle Pass (TX), Fresno (CA), Indianapolis (IN), Kansas City (MO), Las Vegas (NV), Little Rock (AR), Los Angeles (CA), McAllen (TX), Milwaukee (WI), New Orleans (LA), Oklahoma City (OK), Omaha (NE), Orlando (FL), Oxnard (CA), Philadelphia (PA), Portland (OR), Presidio (TX), Salt Lake City (UT), San Bernardino (CA), Santa Ana (CA), Seattle (WA), St. Paul (MN), Tucson (AZ), Yuma (AZ)

Diplomatic representation from the US: *chief of mission:* Ambassador Ronald D. JOHNSON (since 19 May 2025)
embassy: Paseo de la Reforma 305, Colonia Cuauhtémoc, 06500 Mexico, CDMX
mailing address: 8700 Mexico City Place, Washington DC 20521-8700
telephone: (011) [52]-55-5080-2000
FAX: (011) 52-55-5080-2005
email address and website: ACSMexicoCity@state.gov
https://mx.usembassy.gov/
consulate(s) general: Ciudad Juárez, Guadalajara, Hermosillo, Matamoros, Mérida, Monterrey, Nogales, Nuevo Laredo, Tijuana

International organization participation: ACS, APEC, Australia Group, BCIE, BIS, CABEI, CAN (observer), Caricom (observer), CD, CDB, CE (observer), CELAC, CSN (observer), EBRD, FAO, FATF, G-3, G-15, G-20, G-24, G-5, IADB, IAEA, IBRD, ICAO, ICC (national committees), ICCt, ICRM, IDA, IFAD, IFC, IFRCS, IHO, ILO, IMF, IMO, IMSO, Interpol, IOC, IOM, IPU, ISO, ITSO, ITU, ITUC (NGOs), LAES, LAIA, MIGA, NAFTA, NAM (observer), NEA, NSG, OAS, OECD, OPANAL, OPCW, Pacific Alliance, Paris Club (associate), PCA, SICA (observer), UN, UNASUR (observer), UNCTAD, UNESCO, UNHCR, UNIDO, Union Latina (observer), UNOOSA, UNWTO, UPU, USMCA, Wassenaar Arrangement, WCO, WFTU (NGOs), WHO, WIPO, WMO, WTO

Independence: 16 September 1810 (declared independence from Spain); 27 September 1821 (recognized by Spain)

National holiday: Independence Day, 16 September (1810)

Flag: *description:* three equal vertical bands of green (left side), white, and red; Mexico's coat of arms (an eagle with a snake in its beak, perched on a cactus) is centered in the white band
meaning: green stands for hope, joy, and love; white for peace and honesty; red for hardiness, bravery, strength, and valor

National symbol(s): golden eagle, dahlia

National color(s): green, white, red

National anthem(s): *title:* "Himno Nacional Mexicano" (National Anthem of Mexico)
lyrics/music: Francisco Gonzalez BOCANEGRA/ Jaime Nuno ROCA
history: adopted 1943

National heritage: *total World Heritage Sites:* 36 (28 cultural, 6 natural, 2 mixed)
selected World Heritage Site locales: Historic Mexico City (c); Earliest 16th-Century Monasteries on the Slopes of Popocatepetl (c); Teotihuacan (c); Whale Sanctuary of El Vizcaino (n); Monarch Butterfly Biosphere Reserve (n); Tehuacán-Cuicatlán Valley (m); Historic Puebla (c); El Tajin (c); Historic Tlacotalpan (c); Historic Oaxaca and Monte Albán (c); Palenque (c); Chichen-Itza (c); Uxmal (c); Wixárika Route through Sacred Sites to Wirikuta (Tatehuarí Huajuyé) (c)

ECONOMY

Economic overview: upper-middle-income economy; highly integrated with US via trade and nearshore manufacturing; weak domestic demand, fiscal consolidation, and trade uncertainty contributing to sluggish growth; low unemployment; challenges from income inequality, corruption, and cartel-based violence

Real GDP (purchasing power parity): $2.883 trillion (2024 est.)
$2.842 trillion (2023 est.)
$2.751 trillion (2022 est.)
note: data in 2021 dollars
comparison ranking: 13

Real GDP growth rate: 1.5% (2024 est.)
3.3% (2023 est.)
3.7% (2022 est.)
note: annual GDP % growth based on constant local currency
comparison ranking: 162

Real GDP per capita: $22,000 (2024 est.)
$21,900 (2023 est.)

$21,400 (2022 est.)
note: data in 2021 dollars
comparison ranking: 98

GDP (official exchange rate): $1.853 trillion (2024 est.)
note: data in current dollars at official exchange rate

Inflation rate (consumer prices): 4.7% (2024 est.)
5.5% (2023 est.)
7.9% (2022 est.)
note: annual % change based on consumer prices
comparison ranking: 142

GDP - composition, by sector of origin: *agriculture:* 3.8% (2024 est.)
industry: 31.6% (2024 est.)
services: 58.2% (2024 est.)
note: figures may not total 100% due to non-allocated consumption not captured in sector-reported data
comparison rankings: agriculture 122; industry 46; services 103

GDP - composition, by end use: *household consumption:* 70.3% (2024 est.)
government consumption: 11.2% (2024 est.)
investment in fixed capital: 24.2% (2024 est.)
investment in inventories: 0% (2024 est.)
exports of goods and services: 36.8% (2024 est.)
imports of goods and services: -37.9% (2024 est.)
note: figures may not total 100% due to rounding or gaps in data collection

Agricultural products: sugarcane, maize, milk, oranges, sorghum, tomatoes, chicken, chillies/peppers, wheat, lemons/limes (2023)
note: top ten agricultural products based on tonnage

Industries: food and beverages, tobacco, chemicals, iron and steel, petroleum, mining, textiles, clothing, motor vehicles, consumer durables, tourism

Industrial production growth rate: 0.2% (2024 est.)
note: annual % change in industrial value added based on constant local currency
comparison ranking: 131

Labor force: 60.959 million (2024 est.)
note: number of people ages 15 or older who are employed or seeking work
comparison ranking: 11

Unemployment rate: 2.8% (2024 est.)
2.8% (2023 est.)
3.3% (2022 est.)
note: % of labor force seeking employment
comparison ranking: 31

Youth unemployment rate (ages 15-24): *total:* 5.5% (2024 est.)
male: 5.2% (2024 est.)
female: 6.1% (2024 est.)
note: % of labor force ages 15-24 seeking employment
comparison ranking: total 158

Population below poverty line: 36.3% (2022 est.)
note: % of population with income below national poverty line

Gini Index coefficient - distribution of family income: 43.5 (2022 est.)
note: index (0-100) of income distribution; higher values represent greater inequality
comparison ranking: 25

Average household expenditures: *on food:* 25.7% of household expenditures (2023 est.)
on alcohol and tobacco: 2.3% of household expenditures (2023 est.)

Household income or consumption by percentage share: *lowest 10%:* 2.1% (2022 est.)
highest 10%: 34.4% (2022 est.)
note: % share of income accruing to lowest and highest 10% of population

Remittances: 3.7% of GDP (2024 est.)
3.7% of GDP (2023 est.)
4.2% of GDP (2022 est.)
note: personal transfers and compensation between resident and non-resident individuals/households/entities

Budget: *revenues:* $342.571 billion (2023 est.)
expenditures: $417.843 billion (2023 est.)
note: central government revenues (excluding grants) and expenditures converted to US dollars at average official exchange rate for year indicated

Public debt: 45.1% of GDP (2023 est.)
note: central government debt as a % of GDP
comparison ranking: 121

Taxes and other revenues: 14.2% (of GDP) (2023 est.)
note: central government tax revenue as a % of GDP
comparison ranking: 95

Current account balance: -$5.986 billion (2024 est.)
-$5.611 billion (2023 est.)
-$17.701 billion (2022 est.)
note: balance of payments - net trade and primary/secondary income in current dollars
comparison ranking: 178

Exports: $680.798 billion (2024 est.)
$649.729 billion (2023 est.)
$630.347 billion (2022 est.)
note: balance of payments - exports of goods and services in current dollars
comparison ranking: 15

Exports - partners: USA 76%, Canada 5%, China 2%, Germany 2%, Spain 1% (2023)
note: top five export partners based on percentage share of exports

Exports - commodities: cars, vehicle parts/accessories, crude petroleum, trucks, computers (2023)
note: top five export commodities based on value in dollars

Imports: $697.067 billion (2024 est.)
$674.695 billion (2023 est.)
$672.914 billion (2022 est.)
note: balance of payments - imports of goods and services in current dollars
comparison ranking: 14

Imports - partners: USA 46%, China 20%, Germany 4%, Japan 3%, S. Korea 3% (2023)
note: top five import partners based on percentage share of imports

Imports - commodities: vehicle parts/accessories, refined petroleum, integrated circuits, broadcasting equipment, cars (2023)
note: top five import commodities based on value in dollars

Reserves of foreign exchange and gold: $232.035 billion (2024 est.)
$214.317 billion (2023 est.)
$201.119 billion (2022 est.)
note: holdings of gold (year-end prices)/foreign exchange/special drawing rights in current dollars
comparison ranking: 17

Debt - external: $306.308 billion (2023 est.)
note: present value of external debt in current US dollars
comparison ranking: 2

Exchange rates: Mexican pesos (MXN) per US dollar -
Exchange rates: 18.305 (2024 est.)
17.759 (2023 est.)
20.127 (2022 est.)
20.272 (2021 est.)
21.486 (2020 est.)

ENERGY

Electricity access: *electrification - total population:* 100% (2022 est.)
electrification - urban areas: 99.8%
electrification - rural areas: 100%

Electricity: *installed generating capacity:* 105.586 million kW (2023 est.)
consumption: 332.042 billion kWh (2023 est.)
exports: 1.97 billion kWh (2023 est.)
imports: 4.863 billion kWh (2023 est.)
transmission/distribution losses: 45.47 billion kWh (2023 est.)
comparison rankings: installed generating capacity 17; consumption 14; exports 61; imports 47; transmission/distribution losses 204

Electricity generation sources: *fossil fuels:* 79.6% of total installed capacity (2023 est.)
nuclear: 3.2% of total installed capacity (2023 est.)
solar: 4.2% of total installed capacity (2023 est.)
wind: 5.7% of total installed capacity (2023 est.)
hydroelectricity: 5.2% of total installed capacity (2023 est.)
geothermal: 1.1% of total installed capacity (2023 est.)
biomass and waste: 1% of total installed capacity (2023 est.)

Nuclear energy: Number of operational nuclear reactors: 2 (2025)

Net capacity of operational nuclear reactors: 1.55GW (2025 est.)

Percent of total electricity production: 4.9% (2023 est.)

Coal: *production:* 6.296 million metric tons (2023 est.)
consumption: 15.132 million metric tons (2023 est.)
exports: 4,000 metric tons (2023 est.)
imports: 8.809 million metric tons (2023 est.)
proven reserves: 1.16 billion metric tons (2023 est.)

Petroleum: *total petroleum production:* 2.101 million bbl/day (2023 est.)
refined petroleum consumption: 1.741 million bbl/day (2024 est.)
crude oil estimated reserves: 5.786 billion barrels (2021 est.)

Natural gas: *production:* 33.118 billion cubic meters (2023 est.)
consumption: 97.118 billion cubic meters (2023 est.)
exports: 27.92 million cubic meters (2023 est.)
imports: 64.289 billion cubic meters (2023 est.)
proven reserves: 180.322 billion cubic meters (2021 est.)

Energy consumption per capita: 57.539 million Btu/person (2023 est.)
comparison ranking: 86

COMMUNICATIONS

Telephones - fixed lines: *total subscriptions:* 25.637 million (2023 est.)
subscriptions per 100 inhabitants: 20 (2023 est.)
comparison ranking: total subscriptions 9

Telephones - mobile cellular: *total subscriptions:* 140 million (2023 est.)

subscriptions per 100 inhabitants: 100 (2022 est.)
comparison ranking: total subscriptions 12

Broadcast media: telecom reform in 2013 ended a quasi-monopoly; now 885 TV stations and 1,841 radio stations, most privately owned; foreign satellite and cable operators are available; completed transition to digital in 2016 (2022)

Internet country code: .mx

Internet users: *percent of population:* 81% (2023 est.)

Broadband - fixed subscriptions: *total:* 26.6 million (2023 est.)
subscriptions per 100 inhabitants: 21 (2023 est.)
comparison ranking: total 10

TRANSPORTATION

Civil aircraft registration country code prefix: XA

Airports: 1,580 (2025)
comparison ranking: 4

Heliports: 488 (2025)
comparison ranking: 7

Railways: *total:* 23,389 km (2017)
standard gauge: 23,389 km (2017) 1.435-m gauge (27 km electrified)

Merchant marine: *total:* 674 (2023)
by type: bulk carrier 4, general cargo 11, oil tanker 32, other 627
comparison ranking: total 34

Ports: *total ports:* 35 (2024)
large: 0
medium: 7
small: 10
very small: 14
size unknown: 4
ports with oil terminals: 21
key ports: Acapulco, Ensenada, Manzanillo, Mazatlan, Tampico, Tuxpan, Veracruz

MILITARY AND SECURITY

Military and security forces: *the Mexican Armed Forces (Fuerzas Armadas de México) are divided between the Secretariat of National Defense and the Secretariat of the Navy:* Secretariat of National Defense (Secretaria de Defensa Nacional, SEDENA): Army (Ejercito), Mexican Air Force (Fuerza Aerea Mexicana, FAM), National Guard (Guardia Nacional); Secretariat of the Navy (Secretaria de Marina, SEMAR): Mexican Navy (Armada de Mexico (ARM), includes Naval Air Force (FAN), Mexican Naval Infantry Corps (Cuerpo de Infanteria de Marina, Mexmar or CIM))

Secretariat of Security and Civilian Protection/SEDENA: National Guard (2025)
note: the National Guard was formed in 2019 of personnel from the former Federal Police (disbanded in December 2019) and military police units of the Army and Navy

Military expenditures: 0.9% of GDP (2024 est.)
0.7% of GDP (2023 est.)
0.7% of GDP (2022 est.)
0.7% of GDP (2021 est.)
0.6% of GDP (2020 est.)

Military and security service personnel strengths: information varies; approximately 260,000 active-duty Armed Forces; approximately 110,000 National Guard personnel (2025)

Military equipment inventories and acquisitions: the Mexican military inventory includes a mix of domestically produced and imported weapons and equipment from a variety of mostly Western suppliers, particularly the US; a considerable portion of its inventory, such as ships and fighter aircraft, are older, secondhand items from the US; over the past decade, the Mexican military has made efforts to acquire more modern equipment; Mexico's defense industry produces some naval vessels and light armored vehicles, as well as small arms and other miscellaneous equipment (2023)

Military service age and obligation: *18 years of age (16 with parental consent) for voluntary enlistment for men and women; 18 years of age for compulsory military service for men (selection for service determined by lottery); conscript service obligation is 12 months; those selected serve on Saturdays in a Batallón del Servicio Militar Nacional (National Military Service Battalion) composed entirely of 12-month Servicio Militar Nacional (SMN) conscripts; conscripts remain in reserve status until the age of 40; cadets enrolled in military schools from the age of 15 are considered members of the armed forces; National Guard:* single men and women 18-30 years of age may volunteer (2024)
note: as of 2023, women comprised about 10% of the active-duty Army, Air Force, and Navy, and about 14% of the National Guard

Military - note: the Mexican military is responsible for defending the independence, integrity, and sovereignty of Mexico, as well as providing for internal security, disaster response, humanitarian assistance, and socio-economic development; internal security duties are a key focus, particularly combating narcotics trafficking and organized crime groups, as well as border control and immigration enforcement; the constitution was amended in 2019 to grant the president the authority to use the armed forces to protect internal and national security, and courts have upheld the legality of the armed forces' role in law enforcement activities in support of civilian authorities through 2028; the military also provides security for strategic facilities, such as oil production infrastructure, and administers most of the country's land and sea ports and customs services, plus a state-owned development bank; in addition, President LÓPEZ OBRADOR placed the military in charge of a growing number of infrastructure projects, such as building and operating a new airport for Mexico City and sections of a train line in the country's southeast (2025)

SPACE

Space agency/agencies: Mexican Space Agency (Agencia Espacial Mexicana or AEM; established 2010 and began operating in 2013) (2025)

Space program overview: has a national space policy with a focus on expanding Mexico's commercial space sector, including developing specialists, technologies, and infrastructure, and acquiring satellites; manufactures and operates communications and scientific satellites; conducts research in a range of space-related capabilities and technologies, including satellite payloads, telecommunications, remote sensing, robotics, Earth and weather sciences, astronomy, and astrophysics; has relations with a variety of foreign space agencies and commercial space industries, including those of Argentina, Brazil, Chile, the European Space Agency (ESA) and its member states (particularly France, Germany, and the UK), India, Japan, Peru, Russia, Ukraine, and the US; led effort to establish the Latin American and Caribbean Space Agency (ALCE) and hosts its headquarters (2025)
note: further details about the key activities, programs, and milestones of the country's space program, as well as government spending estimates on the space sector, appear in the Space Programs reference guide

TERRORISM

Terrorist group(s): Terrorist group(s): Gulf Cartel (CDG); Jalisco Cartel New Generation (CJNG); La Mara Salvatruche (MS-13); Northeast Cartel (CDN); The New Family Michoacana (LNFM); Sinaloa Cartel; United Cartels (CU)
note: details about the history, aims, leadership, organization, areas of operation, tactics, targets, weapons, size, and sources of support of the group(s) appear(s) in Appendix T

TRANSNATIONAL ISSUES

Refugees and internally displaced persons: *refugees:* 417,546 (2024 est.)
IDPs: 390,250 (2024 est.)
stateless persons: 13 (2024 est.)

Illicit drugs: USG identification: major illicit drug-producing and/or drug-transit country
major precursor-chemical producer (2025)

MICRONESIA, FEDERATED STATES OF

INTRODUCTION

Background: Each of the four states that compose the Federated States of Micronesia (FSM) – Chuuk, Kosrae, Pohnpei, and Yap – has its own unique history and cultural traditions. The first humans arrived in what is now the FSM in the second millennium B.C. In the 800s A.D., construction of the artificial islets at the Nan Madol complex in Pohnpei began, with the main architecture being built around 1200. At its height, Nan Madol united the approximately 25,000 people of Pohnpei under the Saudeleur Dynasty. By 1250, Kosrae was united in a kingdom centered in Leluh. Yap's society became strictly hierarchical, with chiefs receiving tributes from islands up to 1,100 km (700 mi) away. Widespread human settlement in Chuuk began in the 1300s, and the different islands in the Chuuk Lagoon were frequently at war with one another.

Portuguese and Spanish explorers visited a few of the islands in the 1500s, and Spain began exerting nominal, but not day-to-day, control over some

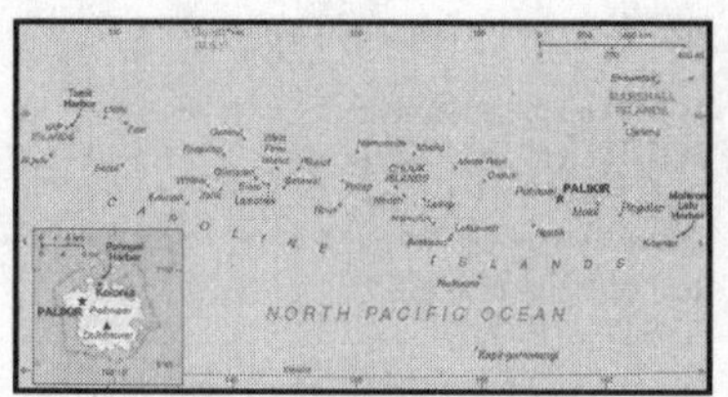

of the islands – which they named the Caroline Islands – in the 1600s. In 1899, Spain sold all of the FSM to Germany. Japan seized the islands in 1914 and was granted a League of Nations mandate to administer them in 1920. During WWII, Japan built military bases across most of the islands and headquartered their Pacific naval operations in Chuuk. The US bombed Chuuk in 1944 but largely bypassed the other islands in its leapfrog campaign across the Pacific.

In 1947, the FSM came under US administration as part of the Trust Territory of the Pacific Islands, which comprised six districts: Chuuk, the Marshall Islands, the Northern Mariana Islands, Palau, Pohnpei, and Yap; Kosrae was separated from Pohnpei into a separate district in 1977. In 1979, Chuuk, Kosrae, Pohnpei, and Yap ratified the FSM Constitution and declared independence while the other three districts opted to pursue separate political status. There are significant inter-island rivalries stemming from their different histories and cultures. Chuuk, the most populous but poorest state, has pushed for secession, but an independence referendum has been repeatedly postponed.

GEOGRAPHY

Location: Oceania, island group in the North Pacific Ocean, about three-quarters of the way from Hawaii to Indonesia

Geographic coordinates: 6 55 N, 158 15 E

Map references: Oceania

Area: *total:* 702 sq km
land: 702 sq km
water: 0 sq km (fresh water only)
note: includes Pohnpei (Ponape), Chuuk (Truk) Islands, Yap Islands, and Kosrae (Kosaie)
comparison ranking: total 191

Area - comparative: four times the size of Washington, D.C. (land area only)

Land boundaries: *total:* 0 km

Coastline: 6,112 km

Maritime claims: *territorial sea:* 12 nm
exclusive economic zone: 200 nm

Climate: tropical; heavy year-round rainfall, especially in the eastern islands; located on southern edge of the typhoon belt with occasionally severe damage

Terrain: islands vary geologically from high mountainous islands to low, coral atolls; volcanic outcroppings on Pohnpei, Kosrae, and Chuuk

Elevation: *highest point:* Nanlaud on Pohnpei 782 m
lowest point: Pacific Ocean 0 m

Natural resources: timber, marine products, deep-seabed minerals, phosphate

Land use: *agricultural land:* 7.1% (2022 est.)
arable land: 2.9% (2022 est.)
permanent crops: 0% (2022 est.)
permanent pasture: 4.3% (2022 est.)
forest: 92.1% (2022 est.)
other: 0.8% (2022 est.)

Irrigated land: 0 sq km (2022)

Population distribution: the majority of the population lives in the coastal areas of the high islands; the mountainous interior is largely uninhabited; less than half of the population lives in urban areas

Natural hazards: typhoons (June to December)

Geography - note: composed of four major island groups totaling 607 islands

PEOPLE AND SOCIETY

Population: *total:* 99,603 (2024 est.)
male: 48,708
female: 50,895
comparison rankings: total 196; male 196; female 195

Nationality: *noun:* Micronesian(s)
adjective: Micronesian; Chuukese, Kosraen(s), Pohnpeian(s), Yapese

Ethnic groups: Chuukese/Mortlockese 49.3%, Pohnpeian 29.8%, Kosraean 6.3%, Yapese 5.7%, Yap outer islanders 5.1%, Polynesian 1.6%, Asian 1.4%, other 0.8% (2010 est.)

Languages: English (official and common language), Chuukese, Kosrean, Pohnpeian, Yapese, Ulithian, Woleaian, Nukuoro, Kapingamarangi

Religions: Roman Catholic 54.7%, Protestant 41.1% (includes Congregational 38.5%, Baptist 1.1%, Seventh Day Adventist 0.8%, Assembly of God 0.7%), Church of Jesus Christ 1.5%, other 1.9%, none 0.7%, unspecified 0.1% (2010 est.)

Age structure: *0-14 years:* 27% (male 13,673/female 13,239)
15-64 years: 67.3% (male 32,527/female 34,487)
65 years and over: 5.7% (2024 est.) (male 2,508/female 3,169)

Dependency ratios: *total dependency ratio:* 48.6 (2024 est.)
youth dependency ratio: 40.2 (2024 est.)
elderly dependency ratio: 8.5 (2024 est.)
potential support ratio: 11.8 (2024 est.)

Median age: *total:* 28.2 years (2024 est.)
male: 27.3 years
female: 29.1 years
comparison ranking: total 152

Population growth rate: -0.73% (2024 est.)
comparison ranking: 227

Birth rate: 17.8 births/1,000 population (2024 est.)
comparison ranking: 80

Death rate: 4.2 deaths/1,000 population (2024 est.)
comparison ranking: 213

Net migration rate: -21 migrant(s)/1,000 population (2024 est.)
comparison ranking: 228

Population distribution: the majority of the population lives in the coastal areas of the high islands; the mountainous interior is largely uninhabited; less than half of the population lives in urban areas

Urbanization: *urban population:* 23.4% of total population (2023)
rate of urbanization: 1.52% annual rate of change (2020-25 est.)

Major urban areas - population: 7,000 PALIKIR (capital) (2018)

Sex ratio: *at birth:* 1.05 male(s)/female
0-14 years: 1.03 male(s)/female
15-64 years: 0.94 male(s)/female
65 years and over: 0.79 male(s)/female
total population: 0.96 male(s)/female (2024 est.)

Maternal mortality ratio: 129 deaths/100,000 live births (2023 est.)
comparison ranking: 57

Infant mortality rate: *total:* 20.9 deaths/1,000 live births (2024 est.)
male: 23.8 deaths/1,000 live births
female: 17.8 deaths/1,000 live births
comparison ranking: total 76

Life expectancy at birth: *total population:* 75 years (2024 est.)
male: 72.9 years
female: 77.2 years
comparison ranking: total population 133

Total fertility rate: 2.19 children born/woman (2024 est.)
comparison ranking: 86

Gross reproduction rate: 1.07 (2024 est.)

Health expenditure: 11% of GDP (2021)
1.9% of national budget (2022 est.)

Physician density: 0.97 physicians/1,000 population (2020)

Sanitation facility access: *improved:* total: 88.3% of population

Obesity - adult prevalence rate: 45.8% (2016)
comparison ranking: 10

Alcohol consumption per capita: *total:* 1.59 liters of pure alcohol (2019 est.)
beer: 0.92 liters of pure alcohol (2019 est.)
wine: 0.13 liters of pure alcohol (2019 est.)
spirits: 0.52 liters of pure alcohol (2019 est.)
other alcohols: 0.01 liters of pure alcohol (2019 est.)
comparison ranking: total 138

Currently married women (ages 15-49): 51.7% (2023 est.)

Education expenditure: 11.6% of GDP (2020 est.)
18.6% national budget (2020 est.)
comparison ranking: Education expenditure (% GDP) 3

ENVIRONMENT

Environmental issues: overfishing; sea-level rise; water and toxic pollution from mining; solid waste disposal

International environmental agreements: *party to:* Biodiversity, Climate Change, Climate Change-Kyoto Protocol, Climate Change-Paris Agreement, Comprehensive Nuclear Test Ban, Desertification, Hazardous Wastes, Law of the Sea, Ozone Layer Protection
signed, but not ratified: none of the selected agreements

Climate: tropical; heavy year-round rainfall, especially in the eastern islands; located on southern edge of the typhoon belt with occasionally severe damage

Urbanization: *urban population:* 23.4% of total population (2023)
rate of urbanization: 1.52% annual rate of change (2020-25 est.)

Carbon dioxide emissions: 121,000 metric tonnes of CO2 (2023 est.)
from petroleum and other liquids: 121,000 metric tonnes of CO2 (2023 est.)
comparison ranking: total emissions 207

Particulate matter emissions: 8.1 micrograms per cubic meter (2019 est.)

Waste and recycling: *municipal solid waste generated annually:* 26,000 tons (2024 est.)

percent of municipal solid waste recycled: 15.2% (2022 est.)

GOVERNMENT

Country name: *conventional long form:* Federated States of Micronesia
conventional short form: none
local long form: Federated States of Micronesia
local short form: none
former: New Philippines; Caroline Islands; Trust Territory of the Pacific Islands, Ponape, Truk, and Yap Districts
abbreviation: FSM
etymology: the name is a 19th-century construct of two Greek words, *mikros* (small) and *nesoi* (islands), and refers to its thousands of small islands in the western Pacific Ocean

Government type: federal republic in free association with the US

Capital: *name:* Palikir
geographic coordinates: 6 55 N, 158 09 E
time difference: UTC+11 (16 hours ahead of Washington, DC, during Standard Time)
time zone note: Micronesia has two time zones
note: Palikir became the new capital of the country in 1989, three years after independence; Kolonia, the former capital, remains the site for many foreign embassies; it also serves as the Pohnpei state capital

Administrative divisions: 4 states; Chuuk (Truk), Kosrae (Kosaie), Pohnpei (Ponape), Yap

Legal system: mixed system of common and customary law

Constitution: *history:* drafted June 1975, ratified 1 October 1978, entered into force 10 May 1979
amendment process: proposed by Congress, by a constitutional convention, or by public petition; passage requires approval by at least three-fourths majority vote in at least three fourths of the states
note: at least every ten years, voters are asked as part of a general or special election whether to hold a constitution convention; a majority of affirmative votes is required to proceed

International law organization participation: has not submitted an ICJ jurisdiction declaration; non-party state to the ICCt

Citizenship: *citizenship by birth:* no
citizenship by descent only: at least one parent must be a citizen of FSM
dual citizenship recognized: no
residency requirement for naturalization: 5 years

Suffrage: 18 years of age; universal

Executive branch: *chief of state:* President Wesley W. SIMINA (since 12 May 2023)
head of government: President Wesley W. SIMINA (since 12 May 2023)
cabinet: Cabinet includes the vice president and the heads of the 8 executive departments
election/appointment process: president and vice president indirectly elected by Congress from among the 4 'at large' senators for a 4-year term (eligible for a second term)
most recent election date: 12 May 2023
expected date of next election: 2027
note: the president is both chief of state and head of government

Legislative branch: *legislature name:* Congress
legislative structure: unicameral
number of seats: 14 (all directly elected)
electoral system: plurality/majority
scope of elections: partial renewal
term in office: 2 years
most recent election date: 3/4/2025
percentage of women in chamber: 21.4%
expected date of next election: March 2027

Judicial branch: *highest court(s):* Federated States of Micronesia Supreme Court (consists of the chief justice and not more than 5 associate justices and organized into appellate and criminal divisions)
judge selection and term of office: justices appointed by the FSM president with the approval of two-thirds of Congress; justices appointed for life
subordinate courts: the highest state-level courts are: Chuuk Supreme Court; Korsae State Court; Pohnpei State Court; Yap State Court

Political parties: no formal parties

Diplomatic representation in the US: *chief of mission:* Ambassador Jackson T. SORAM (since 27 February 2024)
chancery: 1725 N Street NW, Washington, DC 20036
telephone: [1] (202) 223-4383
FAX: [1] (202) 223-4391
email address and website: dcmission@fsmembassy.fm
https://fsmembassy.fm/
consulate(s) general: Honolulu, Portland (OR), Tamuning (Guam)

Diplomatic representation from the US: *chief of mission:* Ambassador Jennifer JOHNSON (since 13 September 2023)
embassy: 1286 US Embassy Place, Kolonia, Pohnpei, FM 96941
mailing address: 4120 Kolonia Place, Washington, D.C. 20521-4120
telephone: [691] 320-2187
FAX: [691] 320-2186
email address and website: koloniaacs@state.gov
https://fm.usembassy.gov/

International organization participation: ACP, ADB, AOSIS, FAO, G-77, IBRD, ICAO, ICRM, IDA, IFC, IFRCS, IMF, IOC, IOM, IPU, ITSO, ITU, MIGA, OPCW, PIF, Sparteca, SPC, UN, UNCTAD, UNESCO, WHO, WMO

Independence: 3 November 1986 (from the US-administered UN trusteeship)

National holiday: Constitution Day, 10 May (1979)

Flag: *description:* light blue with four five-pointed white stars centered and arranged in a diamond pattern
meaning: blue stands for the Pacific Ocean, and the stars for the four island groups of Chuuk, Kosrae, Pohnpei, and Yap

National symbol(s): four five-pointed white stars on a light blue field, hibiscus flower

National color(s): light blue, white

National anthem(s): *title:* "Patriots of Micronesia"
lyrics/music: unknown
history: adopted 1991

National heritage: *total World Heritage Sites:* 1 (cultural)
selected World Heritage Site locales: Nan Madol: Ceremonial Center of Eastern Micronesia

ECONOMY

Economic overview: lower middle-income Pacific island economy; US aid reliance, sunsetting in 2024; low entrepreneurship; mostly fishing and farming; US dollar user; no patent laws; tourism remains underdeveloped; significant corruption

Real GDP (purchasing power parity): $432.679 million (2024 est.)
$429.59 million (2023 est.)
$427.529 million (2022 est.)
note: data in 2021 dollars
comparison ranking: 211

Real GDP growth rate: 0.7% (2024 est.)
0.5% (2023 est.)
-2.9% (2022 est.)
note: annual GDP % growth based on constant local currency
comparison ranking: 186

Real GDP per capita: $3,800 (2024 est.)
$3,800 (2023 est.)
$3,800 (2022 est.)
note: data in 2021 dollars
comparison ranking: 183

GDP (official exchange rate): $471.425 million (2024 est.)
note: data in current dollars at official exchange rate

Inflation rate (consumer prices): 5.4% (2022 est.)
3.2% (2021 est.)
0.6% (2020 est.)
note: annual % change based on consumer prices
comparison ranking: 147

GDP - composition, by sector of origin: *agriculture:* 23.3% (2023 est.)
industry: 5% (2023 est.)
services: 69.2% (2023 est.)
note: figures may not total 100% due to non-allocated consumption not captured in sector-reported data
comparison rankings: agriculture 26; industry 204; services 39

Agricultural products: coconuts, cassava, vegetables, sweet potatoes, bananas, pork, plantains, fruits, beef, eggs (2023)
note: top ten agricultural products based on tonnage

Industries: tourism, construction; specialized aquaculture, craft items (shell and wood)

Industrial production growth rate: 0.8% (2023 est.)
note: annual % change in industrial value added based on constant local currency
comparison ranking: 118

Remittances: 5.3% of GDP (2023 est.)
5.6% of GDP (2022 est.)
6% of GDP (2021 est.)
note: personal transfers and compensation between resident and non-resident individuals/households/entities

Budget: *revenues:* $137.795 million (2020 est.)
expenditures: $111.963 million (2020 est.)
note: central government revenues and expenses (excluding grants/extrabudgetary units/social security funds) converted to US dollars at average official exchange rate for year indicated

Public debt: 27.8% of GDP (2020 est.)
note: central government debt as a % of GDP
comparison ranking: 169

Taxes and other revenues: 7% (of GDP) (2020 est.)
note: central government tax revenue as a % of GDP
comparison ranking: 143

Current account balance: $12 million (2017 est.)
$11 million (2016 est.)
$22.408 million (2014 est.)
note: balance of payments - net trade and primary/secondary income in current dollars
comparison ranking: 82

Exports: $129.5 million (2024 est.)
$125.789 million (2023 est.)

$90.466 million (2022 est.)
note: GDP expenditure basis - exports of goods and services in current dollars
comparison ranking: 206

Exports - partners: Thailand 64%, China 16%, Philippines 11%, Japan 5%, Ecuador 1% (2023)
note: top five export partners based on percentage share of exports

Exports - commodities: fish, diamonds, garments (2023)
note: top export commodities based on value in dollars over $500,000

Imports: $325.9 million (2024 est.)
$310.669 million (2023 est.)
$274.334 million (2022 est.)
note: GDP expenditure basis - imports of goods and services in current dollars
comparison ranking: 205

Imports - partners: USA 35%, China 20%, Japan 13%, Taiwan 6%, Philippines 4% (2023)
note: top five import partners based on percentage share of imports

Imports - commodities: poultry, fish, plastic products, cars, prepared meat (2023)
note: top five import commodities based on value in dollars

Reserves of foreign exchange and gold: $497.434 million (2021 est.)
$451.913 million (2020 est.)
$397.158 million (2019 est.)
note: holdings of gold (year-end prices)/foreign exchange/special drawing rights in current dollars
comparison ranking: 159

Exchange rates: the US dollar is used

ENERGY

Electricity access: *electrification - total population:* 85.3% (2022 est.)
electrification - urban areas: 98.6%
electrification - rural areas: 79.4%

Petroleum: *refined petroleum consumption:* 800 bbl/day (2023 est.)

COMMUNICATIONS

Telephones - fixed lines: *total subscriptions:* 7,000 (2021 est.)
subscriptions per 100 inhabitants: 6 (2022 est.)
comparison ranking: total subscriptions 196

Telephones - mobile cellular: *total subscriptions:* 22,000 (2021 est.)
subscriptions per 100 inhabitants: 19 (2021 est.)
comparison ranking: total subscriptions 215

Broadcast media: no TV broadcast stations; each state has a multi-channel cable service with TV transmissions carrying roughly 95% imported programming and 5% local programming; about half a dozen radio stations (2009)

Internet country code: .fm

Internet users: *percent of population:* 41% (2022 est.)

Broadband - fixed subscriptions: *total:* 7,000 (2022 est.)
subscriptions per 100 inhabitants: 6 (2022 est.)
comparison ranking: total 188

TRANSPORTATION

Civil aircraft registration country code prefix: V6

Airports: 7 (2025)
comparison ranking: 169

Merchant marine: *total:* 38 (2023)
by type: general cargo 17, oil tanker 4, other 17
comparison ranking: total 128

Ports: *total ports:* 4 (2024)
large: 0
medium: 0
small: 1
very small: 3
ports with oil terminals: 3
key ports: Colonia, Lele Harbor, Moen, Pohnpei Harbor

MILITARY AND SECURITY

Military and security forces: no military forces; Federated States of Micronesia National Police (includes a maritime wing) (2025)

Military - note: defense is the responsibility of the US; in 1982, the FSM signed a Compact of Free Association (COFA) with the US, which granted the FSM financial assistance and access to many US domestic programs in exchange for exclusive US military access and defense responsibilities; the COFA entered into force in 1986; Micronesians can serve in the US armed forces
the FSM has a "shiprider" agreement with the US, which allows local maritime law enforcement officers to embark on US Coast Guard (USCG) and US Navy (USN) vessels, including to board and search vessels suspected of violating laws or regulations within the FSM's designated exclusive economic zone (EEZ) or on the high seas; "shiprider" agreements also enable USCG personnel and USN vessels with embarked USCG law enforcement personnel to work with host nations to protect critical regional resources (2025)

MOLDOVA

INTRODUCTION

Background: A large portion of present-day Moldovan territory became a province of the Russian Empire in 1812 and then unified with Romania in 1918 in the aftermath of World War I. This territory was then incorporated into the Soviet Union at the close of World War II. Although Moldova has been independent from the Soviet Union since 1991, Russian forces have remained on Moldovan territory east of the Nistru River in the breakaway region of Transnistria.

Years of Communist Party rule in Moldova from 2001 to 2009 ultimately ended with election-related violent protests and a rerun of parliamentary elections in 2009. A series of pro-Europe ruling coalitions governed Moldova from 2010 to 2019, but pro-Russia candidate Igor DODON won the presidency in 2016, and his Socialist Party of the Republic of Moldova won a plurality in the legislative election in 2019. Pro-EU reformist candidate Maia SANDU defeated DODON in his reelection bid in 2020, and SANDU's Party of Action and Solidarity won a parliamentary majority in an early legislative election in 2021. Prime Minister Natalia GAVRILITA and her cabinet took office in 2021. In early 2023, Moldova's parliament confirmed a new cabinet led by Prime Minister Dorin RECEAN, which retained the majority of the former ministers.

GEOGRAPHY

Location: Eastern Europe, northeast of Romania

Geographic coordinates: 47 00 N, 29 00 E

Map references: Europe

Area: *total:* 33,851 sq km
land: 32,891 sq km
water: 960 sq km
comparison ranking: total 139

Area - comparative: slightly larger than Maryland

Land boundaries: *total:* 1,885 km
border countries (2): Romania 683 km; Ukraine 1202 km

Coastline: 0 km (landlocked)

Maritime claims: none (landlocked)

Climate: moderate winters, warm summers

Terrain: rolling steppe, gradual slope south to Black Sea

Elevation: *highest point:* Dealul Balanesti 430 m
lowest point: Dniester (Nistru) 2 m
mean elevation: 139 m

Natural resources: lignite, phosphorites, gypsum, limestone, arable land

Land use: *agricultural land:* 69.3% (2022 est.)
arable land: 52.4% (2022 est.)
permanent crops: 6.7% (2022 est.)
permanent pasture: 10.2% (2022 est.)
forest: 11.8% (2022 est.)
other: 18.9% (2022 est.)

Irrigated land: 2,150 sq km (2022)

Major rivers (by length in km): Dunărea (Danube) (shared with Germany [s], Austria, Slovakia, Hungary, Croatia, Serbia, Bulgaria, Ukraine, and

Romania [m]) - 2,888 km; Nistru (Dniester) (shared with Ukraine [s/m]) - 1,411 km
note: [s] after country name indicates river source; [m] after country name indicates river mouth

Major watersheds (area sq km): Atlantic Ocean drainage: *(Black Sea)* Danube (795,656 sq km)

Population distribution: pockets of agglomeration exist throughout the country, with the largest in the center of the country around the capital of Chisinau, followed by Tiraspol and Balti

Natural hazards: landslides

Geography - note: landlocked; has many types of sedimentary rocks and minerals, including sand, gravel, gypsum, and limestone

PEOPLE AND SOCIETY

Population: *total:* 3,599,528 (2024 est.)
male: 1,698,249
female: 1,901,279
comparison rankings: total 132; male 134; female 131

Nationality: *noun:* Moldovan(s)
adjective: Moldovan

Ethnic groups: Moldovan 75.1%, Romanian 7%, Ukrainian 6.6%, Gagauz 4.6%, Russian 4.1%, Bulgarian 1.9%, other 0.8% (2014 est.)

Languages: Moldovan/Romanian 80.2% (official) (56.7% Moldovan; 23.5% Romanian), Russian 9.7%, Gagauz 4.2% (a Turkish language), Ukrainian 3.9%, Bulgarian 1.5%, Romani 0.3%, other 0.2% (2014)
major-language sample(s):
Cartea informativa a lumii, sursa indispensabila pentru informatii de baza. (Moldovan/Romanian)
note: data represent mother tongue; as of March 2023, "Romanian" replaced "Moldovan" as the name of Moldova's official language

Religions: Orthodox 90.1%, other Christian 2.6%, other 0.1%, agnostic <0.1%, atheist 0.2%, unspecified 6.9% (2014 est.)

Age structure: *0-14 years:* 14.8% (male 266,493/ female 266,166)
15-64 years: 70.2% (male 1,225,535/female 1,300,640)
65 years and over: 15% (2024 est.) (male 206,221/ female 334,473)

Dependency ratios: *total dependency ratio:* 42.5 (2024 est.)
youth dependency ratio: 21.1 (2024 est.)
elderly dependency ratio: 21.4 (2024 est.)
potential support ratio: 4.7 (2024 est.)

Median age: *total:* 39.9 years (2024 est.)
male: 38.6 years
female: 41.3 years
comparison ranking: total 63

Population growth rate: -0.58% (2024 est.)
comparison ranking: 224

Birth rate: 8.4 births/1,000 population (2024 est.)
comparison ranking: 208

Death rate: 14.2 deaths/1,000 population (2024 est.)
comparison ranking: 8

Net migration rate: 0 migrant(s)/1,000 population (2024 est.)
comparison ranking: 81

Population distribution: pockets of agglomeration exist throughout the country, with the largest in the center of the country around the capital of Chisinau, followed by Tiraspol and Balti

Urbanization: *urban population:* 43.4% of total population (2023)
rate of urbanization: 0.09% annual rate of change (2020-25 est.)

Major urban areas - population: 488,000 CHISINAU (capital) (2023)

Sex ratio: *at birth:* 1.07 male(s)/female
0-14 years: 1 male(s)/female
15-64 years: 0.94 male(s)/female
65 years and over: 0.62 male(s)/female
total population: 0.89 male(s)/female (2024 est.)

Mother's mean age at first birth: 25.2 years (2019 est.)

Maternal mortality ratio: 19 deaths/100,000 live births (2023 est.)
comparison ranking: 124

Infant mortality rate: *total:* 13.8 deaths/1,000 live births (2024 est.)
male: 16 deaths/1,000 live births
female: 11.5 deaths/1,000 live births
comparison ranking: total 102

Life expectancy at birth: *total population:* 70.1 years (2024 est.)
male: 66.1 years
female: 74.4 years
comparison ranking: total population 179

Total fertility rate: 1.26 children born/woman (2024 est.)
comparison ranking: 221

Gross reproduction rate: 0.61 (2024 est.)

Drinking water source: *improved: urban:* 97.7% of population (2022 est.)
rural: 87.7% of population (2022 est.)
total: 92% of population (2022 est.)
unimproved: urban: 2.3% of population (2022 est.)
rural: 12.3% of population (2022 est.)
total: 8% of population (2022 est.)

Health expenditure: 7.8% of GDP (2021)
12.3% of national budget (2022 est.)

Physician density: 4.02 physicians/1,000 population (2023)

Hospital bed density: 5.7 beds/1,000 population (2021 est.)

Sanitation facility access: *improved: urban:* 98.7% of population (2022 est.)
rural: 82.9% of population (2022 est.)
total: 89.7% of population (2022 est.)
unimproved: urban: 1.3% of population (2022 est.)
rural: 17.1% of population (2022 est.)
total: 10.3% of population (2022 est.)

Obesity - adult prevalence rate: 18.9% (2016)
comparison ranking: 113

Alcohol consumption per capita: *total:* 7.45 liters of pure alcohol (2019 est.)
beer: 1.53 liters of pure alcohol (2019 est.)
wine: 3.57 liters of pure alcohol (2019 est.)
spirits: 2.25 liters of pure alcohol (2019 est.)
other alcohols: 0.1 liters of pure alcohol (2019 est.)
comparison ranking: total 54

Tobacco use: *total:* 28.7% (2025 est.)
male: 54.2% (2025 est.)
female: 6.4% (2025 est.)
comparison ranking: total 26

Currently married women (ages 15-49): 67% (2023 est.)

Education expenditure: 6.6% of GDP (2023 est.)
15.9% national budget (2023 est.)
comparison ranking: Education expenditure (% GDP) 21

School life expectancy (primary to tertiary education): *total:* 15 years (2023 est.)
male: 15 years (2023 est.)
female: 15 years (2023 est.)

ENVIRONMENT

Environmental issues: soil and water pollution from heavy use of agricultural chemicals; extensive soil erosion and declining soil fertility from farming methods

International environmental agreements: *party to:* Air Pollution, Air Pollution-Heavy Metals, Air Pollution-Persistent Organic Pollutants, Biodiversity, Climate Change, Climate Change-Kyoto Protocol, Climate Change-Paris Agreement, Comprehensive Nuclear Test Ban, Desertification, Endangered Species, Hazardous Wastes, Law of the Sea, Ozone Layer Protection, Ship Pollution, Wetlands
signed, but not ratified: Air Pollution-Multi-effect Protocol

Climate: moderate winters, warm summers

Urbanization: *urban population:* 43.4% of total population (2023)
rate of urbanization: 0.09% annual rate of change (2020-25 est.)

Carbon dioxide emissions: 7.093 million metric tonnes of CO2 (2023 est.)
from coal and metallurgical coke: 219,000 metric tonnes of CO2 (2023 est.)
from petroleum and other liquids: 3.087 million metric tonnes of CO2 (2023 est.)
from consumed natural gas: 3.786 million metric tonnes of CO2 (2023 est.)
comparison ranking: total emissions 123

Particulate matter emissions: 12.3 micrograms per cubic meter (2019 est.)

Waste and recycling: *municipal solid waste generated annually:* 3.981 million tons (2024 est.)
percent of municipal solid waste recycled: 36.9% (2022 est.)

Total water withdrawal: *municipal:* 160 million cubic meters (2022 est.)
industrial: 583 million cubic meters (2022 est.)
agricultural: 55 million cubic meters (2022 est.)

Total renewable water resources: 12.27 billion cubic meters (2022 est.)

GOVERNMENT

Country name: *conventional long form:* Republic of Moldova
conventional short form: Moldova
local long form: Republica Moldova
local short form: Moldova
former: Moldavian Soviet Socialist Republic, Moldovan Soviet Socialist Republic
etymology: named for the Moldova River in neighboring eastern Romania; the river's name probably comes from the Indoeuropean root word *mel*, meaning "dark" or "black"

Government type: parliamentary republic

Capital: *name:* Chisinau in Romanian (Kishinev in Russian)
geographic coordinates: 47 00 N, 28 51 E
time difference: UTC+2 (7 hours ahead of Washington, DC, during Standard Time)

daylight saving time: +1hr, begins last Sunday in March; ends last Sunday in October
etymology: origin unclear but may derive from the Old Moldovan word *kishineu* ("spring" or "artesian well")
note: pronounced KEE-shee-now (KIH-shi-nyov)

Administrative divisions: 32 districts (*raioane*, singular - *raion*), 3 municipalities (*municipii*, singular - *municipiul*), 1 autonomous territorial unit (*unitatea teritoriala autonoma*), and 1 territorial unit (*unitatea teritoriala*)
districts: Anenii Noi, Basarabeasca, Briceni, Cahul, Cantemir, Calarasi, Causeni, Cimislia, Criuleni, Donduseni, Drochia, Dubasari, Edinet, Falesti, Floresti, Glodeni, Hincesti, Ialoveni, Leova, Nisporeni, Ocnita, Orhei, Rezina, Riscani, Singerei, Soldanesti, Soroca, Stefan Voda, Straseni, Taraclia, Telenesti, Ungheni
municipalities: Balti, Bender, Chisinau
autonomous territorial unit: Gagauzia
territorial unit: Stinga Nistrului (Transnistria)

Legal system: civil law system with Germanic law influences; Constitutional Court reviews legislative acts

Constitution: *history:* previous 1978; latest adopted 29 July 1994, effective 27 August 1994
amendment process: proposed by voter petition (at least 200,000 eligible voters), by at least one third of Parliament members, or by the government; passage requires two-thirds majority vote of Parliament within one year of initial proposal; revisions to constitutional articles on sovereignty, independence, and neutrality require majority vote by referendum; articles on fundamental rights and freedoms cannot be amended

International law organization participation: has not submitted an ICJ jurisdiction declaration; accepts ICCt jurisdiction

Citizenship: *citizenship by birth:* no
citizenship by descent only: at least one parent must be a citizen of Moldova
dual citizenship recognized: no
residency requirement for naturalization: 10 years

Suffrage: 18 years of age; universal

Executive branch: *chief of state:* President Maia SANDU (since 24 December 2020)
head of government: Prime Minister Dorin RECEAN (since 16 February 2023)
cabinet: Cabinet proposed by the prime minister-designate, nominated by the president, approved through a vote of confidence in Parliament
election/appointment process: president directly elected for a 4-year term (eligible for a second term); prime minister designated by the president in consultation with Parliament; within 15 days from designation, the prime minister-designate must request a vote of confidence for his/her proposed work program from the Parliament
most recent election date: 3 November 2024
election results: *2024:* In the second round of presidential elections, incumbent Maia SANDU (PAS) wins 55.4% of the vote, Alexandr STOIANOGLO (PSRM) 44.6; turnout is 54.3%
2020: Maia SANDU elected president in second round; percent of vote in second round - Maia SANDU (PAS) 57.7%, Igor DODON (PSRM) 42.3%
2016: Igor DODON elected president in second round; percent of vote - Igor DODON (PSRM) 52.1%, Maia SANDU (PAS) 47.9%
expected date of next election: 2028

Legislative branch: *legislature name:* Parliament (Parlament)
legislative structure: unicameral
number of seats: 101 (all directly elected)
electoral system: proportional representation
scope of elections: full renewal
term in office: 4 years
most recent election date: 7/11/2021
parties elected and seats per party: Action and Solidarity Party (PAS) (63); Electoral Bloc of Communists and Socialists (BECS) (32); Şor Party (PPŞ) (6)
percentage of women in chamber: 40%
expected date of next election: September 2025

Judicial branch: *highest court(s):* Supreme Court of Justice (consists of the chief judge, 3 deputy-chief judges, 45 judges, and 7 assistant judges); Constitutional Court (consists of the court president and 6 judges)
judge selection and term of office: Supreme Court of Justice judges appointed by the president on the recommendation of the Superior Council of Magistracy, an 11-member body of judicial officials; all judges serve 4-year renewable terms; Constitutional Court judges appointed 2 each by Parliament, the president, and the Higher Council of Magistracy for 6- year terms; court president elected by other court judges for a 3-year term
subordinate courts: Courts of Appeal; Court of Business Audit; municipal courts
note: the Constitutional Court is autonomous; it interprets the Constitution and reviews the constitutionality of parliamentary laws and decisions, decrees of the president, and acts of the government

Political parties: Bloc of Communists and Socialists or BCS
Party of Action and Solidarity or PAS

Diplomatic representation in the US: *chief of mission:* Ambassador Vladislav KULMINSKI (since 5 September 2025)
chancery: 2101 S Street NW, Washington, DC 20008
telephone: [1] (202) 667-1130
FAX: [1] (202) 667-2624
email address and website: washington@mfa.gov.md
https://sua.mfa.gov.md/en

Diplomatic representation from the US: *chief of mission:* Ambassador (vacant); Chargé d'Affaires Nick PIETROWICZ (since 2025)
embassy: 103 Mateevici Street, Chisinau MD-2009
mailing address: 7080 Chisinau Place, Washington DC 20521-7080
telephone: [373] (22) 408-300
FAX: [373] (22) 233-044
email address and website: ChisinauACS@state.gov
https://md.usembassy.gov/

International organization participation: BSEC, CD, CE, CEI, CIS, EAEU (observer), EAPC, EBRD, FAO, GCTU, GUAM, IAEA, IBRD, ICAO, ICC (NGOs), ICCt, ICRM, IDA, IFAD, IFC, IFRCS, ILO, IMF, IMO, Interpol, IOC, IOM, IPU, ISO (correspondent), ITU, ITUC (NGOs), MIGA, OIF, OPCW, OSCE, PFP, SELEC, UN, UNCTAD, UNESCO, UNHCR, UNIDO, Union Latina, UNMIL, UNMISS, UNOCI, UNWTO, UPU, WCO, WHO, WIPO, WMO, WTO
note: Moldova is an EU candidate country whose satisfactory completion of accession criteria is required before being granted full EU membership

Independence: 27 August 1991 (from the Soviet Union)

National holiday: Independence Day, 27 August (1991)

Flag: *description:* three equal vertical bands of Prussian blue (left side), chrome yellow, and vermilion red; the Moldavan coat of arms in the center is a dark gold Roman eagle outlined in black, with a red beak and talons; the eagle carries a yellow cross in its beak, a green olive branch in its right talons, and a yellow scepter in its left talons; on the eagle's breast is a red-and-blue shield divided horizontally, with a stylized aurochs head, star, rose, and crescent in black and outlined yellow; the reverse of the flag displays a mirror image of the coat of arms
history: replaced the communist flag in 1990; the coat of arms is based on traditional designs
note 1: colors are based on the Romanian flag, but Moldova's blue band is lighter
note 2: one of three national flags that differ on each side – the others are Paraguay and Saudi Arabia

National symbol(s): aurochs (type of wild cattle)

National color(s): blue, yellow, red

National anthem(s): *title:* "Limba noastra" (Our Tongue)
lyrics/music: Alexei MATEEVICI/Alexandru CRISTEA
history: adopted 1994; originally a 12-verse poem, but only stanzas 1, 2, 5, 9, and 12 are included in the anthem

National heritage: *total World Heritage Sites:* 1 (cultural)
selected World Heritage Site locales: Struve Geodetic Arc

ECONOMY

Economic overview: upper middle-income Eastern European economy; sustained growth reversed by COVID-19; significant remittances; Russian energy and regional dependence; agricultural exporter; declining workforce due to emigration and low fertility

Real GDP (purchasing power parity): $39.342 billion (2024 est.)
$39.301 billion (2023 est.)
$38.835 billion (2022 est.)
note: data in 2021 dollars
comparison ranking: 138

Real GDP growth rate: 0.1% (2024 est.)
1.2% (2023 est.)
-4.6% (2022 est.)
note: annual GDP % growth based on constant local currency
comparison ranking: 191

Real GDP per capita: $16,500 (2024 est.)
$16,000 (2023 est.)
$15,400 (2022 est.)
note: data in 2021 dollars
comparison ranking: 116

GDP (official exchange rate): $18.2 billion (2024 est.)
note: data in current dollars at official exchange rate

Inflation rate (consumer prices): 4.7% (2024 est.)
13.4% (2023 est.)
28.7% (2022 est.)
note: annual % change based on consumer prices
comparison ranking: 140

GDP - composition, by sector of origin: *agriculture:* 7.1% (2024 est.)
industry: 16.8% (2024 est.)
services: 62.3% (2024 est.)

note: figures may not total 100% due to non-allocated consumption not captured in sector-reported data
comparison rankings: agriculture 92; industry 156; services 74

GDP - composition, by end use: *household consumption:* 86.8% (2024 est.)
government consumption: 17.9% (2024 est.)
investment in fixed capital: 20% (2024 est.)
investment in inventories: 1.1% (2024 est.)
exports of goods and services: 31.4% (2024 est.)
imports of goods and services: -57.3% (2024 est.)
note: figures may not total 100% due to rounding or gaps in data collection

Agricultural products: wheat, maize, sunflower seeds, grapes, apples, sugar beets, barley, milk, rapeseed, potatoes (2023)
note: top ten agricultural products based on tonnage

Industries: sugar processing, vegetable oil, food processing, agricultural machinery; foundry equipment, refrigerators and freezers, washing machines; hosiery, shoes, textiles

Industrial production growth rate: 3.3% (2024 est.)
note: annual % change in industrial value added based on constant local currency
comparison ranking: 74

Labor force: 1.358 million (2024 est.)
note: number of people ages 15 or older who are employed or seeking work
comparison ranking: 139

Unemployment rate: 1.5% (2024 est.)
1.6% (2023 est.)
0.9% (2022 est.)
note: % of labor force seeking employment
comparison ranking: 10

Youth unemployment rate (ages 15-24): *total:* 3.3% (2024 est.)
male: 3.4% (2024 est.)
female: 3.3% (2024 est.)
note: % of labor force ages 15-24 seeking employment
comparison ranking: total 178

Population below poverty line: 31.1% (2022 est.)
note: % of population with income below national poverty line

Gini Index coefficient - distribution of family income: 25.9 (2022 est.)
note: index (0-100) of income distribution; higher values represent greater inequality
comparison ranking: 142

Household income or consumption by percentage share: *lowest 10%:* 4.5% (2022 est.)
highest 10%: 22.5% (2022 est.)
note: % share of income accruing to lowest and highest 10% of population

Remittances: 10.5% of GDP (2024 est.)
12% of GDP (2023 est.)
14% of GDP (2022 est.)
note: personal transfers and compensation between resident and non-resident individuals/ households/ entities

Budget: *revenues:* $5.197 billion (2023 est.)
expenditures: $6.037 billion (2023 est.)
note: central government revenues (excluding grants) and expenditures converted to US dollars at average official exchange rate for year indicated

Public debt: 34.3% of GDP (2023 est.)
note: central government debt as a % of GDP
comparison ranking: 155

Taxes and other revenues: 18.6% (of GDP) (2023 est.)
note: central government tax revenue as a % of GDP
comparison ranking: 59

Current account balance: -$2.917 billion (2024 est.)
-$1.893 billion (2023 est.)
-$2.482 billion (2022 est.)
note: balance of payments - net trade and primary/ secondary income in current dollars
comparison ranking: 158

Exports: $5.717 billion (2024 est.)
$5.866 billion (2023 est.)
$5.981 billion (2022 est.)
note: balance of payments - exports of goods and services in current dollars
comparison ranking: 137

Exports - partners: Romania 31%, Ukraine 13%, Italy 6%, Germany 6%, Czechia 4% (2023)
note: top five export partners based on percentage share of exports

Exports - commodities: insulated wire, garments, refined petroleum, seed oils, wheat (2023)
note: top five export commodities based on value in dollars

Imports: $10.418 billion (2024 est.)
$9.84 billion (2023 est.)
$10.265 billion (2022 est.)
note: balance of payments - imports of goods and services in current dollars
comparison ranking: 120

Imports - partners: Romania 16%, Ukraine 13%, China 11%, Turkey 8%, Germany 7% (2023)
note: top five import partners based on percentage share of imports

Imports - commodities: refined petroleum, natural gas, cars, packaged medicine, plastic products (2023)
note: top five import commodities based on value in dollars

Reserves of foreign exchange and gold: $5.484 billion (2024 est.)
$5.453 billion (2023 est.)
$4.474 billion (2022 est.)
note: holdings of gold (year-end prices)/foreign exchange/special drawing rights in current dollars
comparison ranking: 95

Debt - external: $2.637 billion (2023 est.)
note: present value of external debt in current US dollars
comparison ranking: 90

Exchange rates: Moldovan lei (MDL) per US dollar -
Exchange rates: 17.792 (2024 est.)
18.164 (2023 est.)
18.897 (2022 est.)
17.68 (2021 est.)
17.322 (2020 est.)

ENERGY

Electricity access: *electrification - total population:* 100% (2022 est.)

Electricity: *installed generating capacity:* 779,000 kW (2023 est.)
consumption: 5.674 billion kWh (2023 est.)
exports: 94 million kWh (2023 est.)
imports: 1.264 billion kWh (2023 est.)
transmission/distribution losses: 550.069 million kWh (2023 est.)
comparison rankings: installed generating capacity 141; consumption 127; exports 90; imports 73; transmission/distribution losses 84

Electricity generation sources: *fossil fuels:* 88% of total installed capacity (2023 est.)
solar: 1.7% of total installed capacity (2023 est.)
wind: 3.8% of total installed capacity (2023 est.)
hydroelectricity: 6.3% of total installed capacity (2023 est.)
biomass and waste: 0.2% of total installed capacity (2023 est.)

Coal: *consumption:* 90,000 metric tons (2023 est.)
imports: 86,000 metric tons (2023 est.)

Petroleum: *refined petroleum consumption:* 22,000 bbl/ day (2023 est.)

Natural gas: *production:* 10,000 cubic meters (2021 est.)
consumption: 2.223 billion cubic meters (2023 est.)
imports: 2.223 billion cubic meters (2023 est.)

Energy consumption per capita: 35.686 million Btu/ person (2023 est.)
comparison ranking: 108

COMMUNICATIONS

Telephones - fixed lines: *total subscriptions:* 847,000 (2023 est.)
subscriptions per 100 inhabitants: 28 (2023 est.)
comparison ranking: total subscriptions 74

Telephones - mobile cellular: *total subscriptions:* 4.01 million (2023 est.)
subscriptions per 100 inhabitants: 127 (2022 est.)
comparison ranking: total subscriptions 136

Broadcast media: state-owned national radio-TV broadcaster operates 1 TV and 1 radio station; total of nearly 70 terrestrial TV channels and about 50 radio stations; Russian and Romanian channels are available (2019)

Internet country code: .md

Internet users: *percent of population:* 80% (2023 est.)

Broadband - fixed subscriptions: *total:* 841,000 (2023 est.)
subscriptions per 100 inhabitants: 27 (2023 est.)
comparison ranking: total 82

TRANSPORTATION

Civil aircraft registration country code prefix: ER

Airports: 10 (2025)
comparison ranking: 160

Heliports: 1 (2025)
comparison ranking: 165

Railways: *total:* 1,171 km (2014)
standard gauge: 14 km (2014) 1.435-m gauge
broad gauge: 1,157 km (2014) 1.520-m gauge

Merchant marine: *total:* 75 (2023)
by type: bulk carrier 1, container ship 1, general cargo 44, oil tanker 7, other 22
comparison ranking: total 102

MILITARY AND SECURITY

Military and security forces: Armed Forces of the Republic of Moldova (Forţele Armate ale Republicii Moldova): National Army (comprised of Land Forces, Air Force)

Ministry of Internal Affairs: General Inspectorate of Police (GPI), Border Police Department, Carabinieri Troops Department (2025)
note: the Carabinieri is a quasi-militarized gendarmerie responsible for protecting public buildings, maintaining public order, and other national security

functions; the GPI is the primary law enforcement body, responsible for internal security, public order, traffic, and criminal investigations

Military expenditures: 0.6% of GDP (2024 est.)
0.6% of GDP (2023 est.)
0.4% of GDP (2022 est.)
0.4% of GDP (2021 est.)
0.4% of GDP (2020 est.)

Military and security service personnel strengths: approximately 6,500 Moldovan Armed Forces (2025)

Military equipment inventories and acquisitions: the military's inventory is limited and almost entirely comprised of Soviet-era equipment; in recent years, it has received donated equipment from Western European nations and the US (2024)

Military service age and obligation: 18-27 years of age for compulsory or voluntary military service; male registration required at age 16; 12-month service obligation (2024)
note: as of 2024, women made up about 23% of the military's full-time personnel

Military - note: the National Army is responsible for defense against external aggression, suppressing illegal military violence along the state border or inside the country, and supporting other internal security forces in maintaining public order if necessary; its primary focuses are Transnistrian separatist forces and their Russian backers; the 1992 war between Moldovan forces and the Transnistrian separatists backed by Russian troops ended with a cease-fire; the separatists maintain several armed paramilitary combat units, plus other security forces and reserves; Russia maintains approximately 1,500 troops in the breakaway region, including some Transnistrian locals who serve as Russian troops; some of those troops are under the authority of a peacekeeping force known as a Joint Control Commission that also includes Moldovan and separatist personnel, while the remainder of the Russian contingent guard a depot of Soviet-era ammunition and train separatist forces
Moldova is constitutionally neutral but has maintained a relationship with NATO since 1992 and since 2022 has enhanced bilateral security cooperation with some NATO members; it has contributed small numbers of troops to NATO's Kosovo Force (KFOR) since 2014, and a civilian NATO liaison office was established in Moldova in 2017 at the request of the Moldovan Government to promote practical cooperation and facilitate support; in 2024, Moldova signed a security and defense partnership agreement with the EU; it maintains close security relations with Romania, a member of the EU and NATO (2025)

TRANSNATIONAL ISSUES

Refugees and internally displaced persons: *refugees:* 136,845 (2024 est.)
IDPs: 6 (2024 est.)
stateless persons: 3,164 (2024 est.)

MONACO

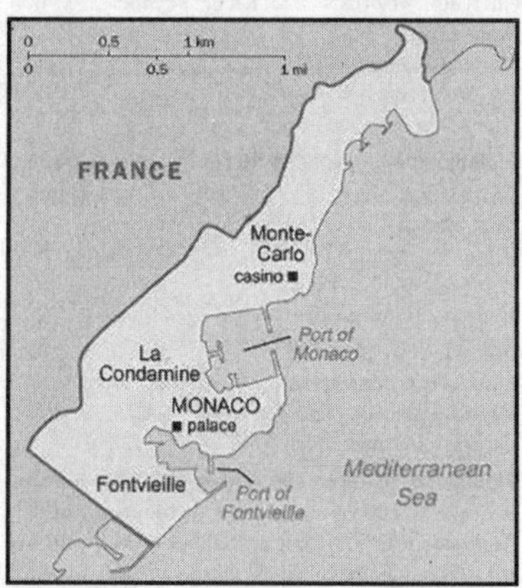

INTRODUCTION

Background: The Genoese built a fortress on the site of present-day Monaco in 1215. The current ruling GRIMALDI family first seized control in 1297 but was not able to permanently secure its holding until 1419. Economic development was spurred in the late 19th century with a railroad linkup to France and the opening of a casino. Since then, the principality's mild climate, coastal Mediterranean scenery, and gambling facilities have made Monaco world-famous as a tourist and recreation center.

GEOGRAPHY

Location: Western Europe, bordering the Mediterranean Sea on the southern coast of France, near the border with Italy

Geographic coordinates: 43 44 N, 7 24 E

Map references: Europe

Area: *total:* 2 sq km
land: 2 sq km
water: 0 sq km
comparison ranking: total 249

Area - comparative: about three times the size of the National Mall in Washington, D.C.

Land boundaries: *total:* 6 km
border countries (1): France 6 km

Coastline: 4.1 km

Maritime claims: *territorial sea:* 12 nm
exclusive economic zone: 12 nm

Climate: Mediterranean with mild, wet winters and hot, dry summers

Terrain: hilly, rugged, rocky

Elevation: *highest point:* Chemin des Revoires on Mont Agel 162 m
lowest point: Mediterranean Sea 0 m

Natural resources: none

Land use: *agricultural land:* 0% (2022 est.)
arable land: 0% (2018 est.)
permanent crops: 1% (2018 est.)
permanent pasture: 0% (2018 est.)
forest: 0% (2022 est.)
other: 100% (2022 est.)

Irrigated land: 0 sq km (2022)

Population distribution: the second most densely populated country in the world (after Macau); its entire population lives on 2 sq km (0.8 sq mi)

Natural hazards: none

Geography - note: second-smallest independent state in the world (after the Holy See); smallest country with a coastline; almost entirely urban

PEOPLE AND SOCIETY

Population: *total:* 31,813 (2024 est.)
male: 15,366
female: 16,447
comparison rankings: total 216; male 216; female 216

Nationality: *noun:* Monegasque(s) or Monacan(s)
adjective: Monegasque or Monacan

Ethnic groups: Monegasque 32.1%, French 19.9%, Italian 15.3%, British 5%, Belgian 2.3%, Swiss 2%, German 1.9%, Russian 1.8%, American 1.1%, Dutch 1.1%, Moroccan 1%, other 16.6% (2016 est.)
note: data represent population by country of birth

Languages: French (official), English, Italian, Monegasque
major-language sample(s):
The World Factbook, une source indispensable d'informations de base. (French)

Religions: Roman Catholic 90% (official), other 10%

Age structure: *0-14 years:* 9.1% (male 1,485/female 1,408)
15-64 years: 53.8% (male 8,620/female 8,490)
65 years and over: 37.1% (2024 est.) (male 5,261/female 6,549)

Dependency ratios: *total dependency ratio:* 85.9 (2024 est.)
youth dependency ratio: 16.9 (2024 est.)
elderly dependency ratio: 69 (2024 est.)
potential support ratio: 1.4 (2024 est.)

Median age: *total:* 56.9 years (2024 est.)
male: 55 years
female: 58.4 years
comparison ranking: total 1

Population growth rate: 0.71% (2024 est.)
comparison ranking: 124

Birth rate: 6.5 births/1,000 population (2024 est.)
comparison ranking: 226

Death rate: 11.1 deaths/1,000 population (2024 est.)
comparison ranking: 25

Net migration rate: 11.7 migrant(s)/1,000 population (2024 est.)
comparison ranking: 7

Population distribution: the second most densely populated country in the world (after Macau); its entire population lives on 2 sq km (0.8 sq mi)

Urbanization: *urban population:* 100% of total population (2023)
rate of urbanization: 0.5% annual rate of change (2020-25 est.)

Major urban areas - population: 39,000 MONACO (capital) (2018)

Sex ratio: *at birth:* 1.04 male(s)/female
0-14 years: 1.05 male(s)/female
15-64 years: 1.02 male(s)/female
65 years and over: 0.8 male(s)/female
total population: 0.93 male(s)/female (2024 est.)

Maternal mortality ratio: 5 deaths/100,000 live births (2023 est.)
comparison ranking: 173

Infant mortality rate: *total:* 1.7 deaths/1,000 live births (2024 est.)
male: 2 deaths/1,000 live births
female: 1.4 deaths/1,000 live births
comparison ranking: total 224

Life expectancy at birth: *total population:* 89.8 years (2024 est.)
male: 86 years
female: 93.7 years
comparison ranking: total population 1

Total fertility rate: 1.54 children born/woman (2024 est.)
comparison ranking: 196

Gross reproduction rate: 0.76 (2024 est.)

Drinking water source: *improved: urban:* 100% of population (2022 est.)
total: 100% of population (2022 est.)
unimproved: urban: 0% of population (2022 est.)
total: 0% of population (2022 est.)

Health expenditure: 3.7% of GDP (2021)
12% of national budget (2022 est.)

Physician density: 8.61 physicians/1,000 population (2020)

Sanitation facility access: *improved: urban:* 100% of population (2022 est.)
total: 100% of population (2022 est.)
unimproved: urban: 0% of population (2022 est.)
total: 0% of population (2022 est.)

Education expenditure: 1.2% of GDP (2022 est.)
7.7% national budget (2023 est.)
comparison ranking: Education expenditure (% GDP) 197

School life expectancy (primary to tertiary education): *total:* 21 years (2024 est.)
male: 20 years (2024 est.)
female: 22 years (2024 est.)

ENVIRONMENT

International environmental agreements: *party to:* Air Pollution, Air Pollution-Heavy Metals, Air Pollution-Sulphur 94, Air Pollution-Volatile Organic Compounds, Antarctic-Environmental Protection, Antarctic Treaty, Biodiversity, Climate Change, Climate Change-Kyoto Protocol, Climate Change-Paris Agreement, Comprehensive Nuclear Test Ban, Desertification, Endangered Species, Hazardous Wastes, Law of the Sea, Marine Dumping-London Convention, Ozone Layer Protection, Ship Pollution, Wetlands, Whaling
signed, but not ratified: none of the selected agreements

Climate: Mediterranean with mild, wet winters and hot, dry summers

Urbanization: *urban population:* 100% of total population (2023)
rate of urbanization: 0.5% annual rate of change (2020-25 est.)

Particulate matter emissions: 9.2 micrograms per cubic meter (2019 est.)

Waste and recycling: *municipal solid waste generated annually:* 46,000 tons (2024 est.)
percent of municipal solid waste recycled: 5.4% (2012 est.)

Total water withdrawal: *municipal:* 10 million cubic meters (2020 est.)
industrial: 0 cubic meters (2017 est.)
agricultural: 0 cubic meters (2017 est.)

GOVERNMENT

Country name: *conventional long form:* Principality of Monaco
conventional short form: Monaco
local long form: Principauté de Monaco
local short form: Monaco
etymology: founded as a Greek colony in the 6th century B.C., the name's origin is unclear; it could derive from the Greek term *monoikos* (solitary), the Ligurian word *monegu* (rock), or the Basque word *muno* (mountain)

Government type: constitutional monarchy

Capital: *name:* Monaco
geographic coordinates: 43 44 N, 7 25 E
time difference: UTC+1 (6 hours ahead of Washington, DC, during Standard Time)
daylight saving time: +1hr, begins last Sunday in March; ends last Sunday in October
etymology: founded as a Greek colony in the 6th century B.C., the name's origin is unclear; it could derive from the Greek term *monoikos* (solitary), the Ligurian word *monegu* (rock), or the Basque word *muno* (mountain)

Administrative divisions: none; no first-order administrative divisions as defined by the US government, but 4 quarters (*quartiers*, singular - *quartier*); Fontvieille, La Condamine, Monaco-Ville, Monte-Carlo
note: Moneghetti, part of La Condamine, is sometimes called the fifth quarter of Monaco

Legal system: civil law system influenced by French legal tradition

Constitution: *history:* previous 1911 (suspended 1959); latest adopted 17 December 1962
amendment process: proposed by joint agreement of the chief of state (the prince) and the National Council; passage requires two-thirds majority vote of National Council members

International law organization participation: has not submitted an ICJ jurisdiction declaration; non-party state to the ICCt

Citizenship: *citizenship by birth:* no
citizenship by descent only: the father must be a citizen of Monaco; in the case of a child born out of wedlock, the mother must be a citizen and father unknown
dual citizenship recognized: no
residency requirement for naturalization: 10 years

Suffrage: 18 years of age; universal

Executive branch: *chief of state:* Prince ALBERT II (since 6 April 2005)
head of government: Minister of State Christophe MIRMAND (since 21 July 2025)
cabinet: Council of Government under the authority of the monarch
election/appointment process: the monarchy is hereditary; minister of state appointed by the monarch from a list of three French national candidates presented by the French Government

Legislative branch: *legislature name:* National Council (Conseil national)
legislative structure: unicameral
number of seats: 24 (all directly elected)
electoral system: proportional representation
scope of elections: full renewal
term in office: 5 years
most recent election date: 2/5/2023
parties elected and seats per party: Monegasque National Union - l'Union (24)
percentage of women in chamber: 45.8%
expected date of next election: February 2028

Judicial branch: *highest court(s):* Supreme Court (consists of 5 permanent members and 2 substitutes)
judge selection and term of office: Supreme Court members appointed by the monarch upon the proposals of the National Council, State Council, Crown Council, Court of Appeal, and Trial Court
subordinate courts: Court of Appeal; Civil Court of First Instance

Political parties: Monegasque National Union (includes Horizon Monaco, Primo!, Union Monegasque)
Horizon Monaco
Priorite Monaco or Primo!
Union Monegasque

Diplomatic representation in the US: *chief of mission:* Ambassador Maguy MACCARIO DOYLE (since 3 December 2013)
chancery: 888 17th Street NW, Suite 500, Washington, DC 20006
telephone: [1] (202) 234-1530
FAX: [1] (202) 244-7656
email address and website: info@monacodc.org
https://monacodc.org/index.html
consulate(s) general: New York

Diplomatic representation from the US: *embassy:* US does not have an embassy in Monaco; the US Ambassador to France is accredited to Monaco; the US Consul General in Marseille (France), under the authority of the US Ambassador to France, handles diplomatic and consular matters concerning Monaco; +(33)(1) 43-12-22-22, enter zero "0" after the automated greeting; US Embassy Paris, 2 Avenue Gabriel, 75008 Paris, France

International organization participation: CD, CE, FAO, IAEA, ICAO, ICC (national committees), ICRM, IFRCS, IHO, IMO, IMSO, Interpol, IOC, IPU, ITSO, ITU, OAS (observer), OIF, OPCW, OSCE, Schengen Convention (de facto member), UN, UNCTAD, UNESCO, UNIDO, Union Latina, UNWTO, UPU, WHO, WIPO, WMO

Independence: 1419 (beginning of permanent rule by the House of GRIMALDI)

National holiday: National Day (Saint Rainier's Day), 19 November (1857)

Flag: *description:* two equal horizontal bands of red (top) and white
history: uses the colors of the ruling House of Grimaldi; colors have been in use since 1339, making it one of the world's oldest national flags
note: similar to the flags of Indonesia (longer) and Poland (colors reversed)

National symbol(s): red and white lozenges (diamond shapes)

National color(s): red, white

National anthem(s): *title:* "A Marcia de Muneghu" (The March of Monaco)
lyrics/music: Louis NOTARI/Charles ALBRECHT
history: music adopted 1867, lyrics adopted 1931; only the Monegasque lyrics are official; the French version is known as "Hymne Monegasque" (Monegasque Anthem); the words are usually only sung on official occasions

ECONOMY

Economic overview: high-income European economy; non-EU euro user; considered a tax haven; tourism and banking are largest sectors; negatively impacted by COVID-19; major oceanographic museum; among most expensive real estate; major state-owned enterprises

Real GDP (purchasing power parity): $8.924 billion (2024 est.)
$8.749 billion (2023 est.)
$8.329 billion (2022 est.)
note: data in 2015 dollars
comparison ranking: 167

Real GDP growth rate: 5% (2023 est.)
11% (2022 est.)
22.2% (2021 est.)
note: annual GDP % growth based on constant local currency
comparison ranking: 39

Real GDP per capita: $270,100 (2024 est.)
$256,600 (2023 est.)
$226,100 (2022 est.)
note: data in 2015 dollars
comparison ranking: 1

GDP (official exchange rate): $10.434 billion (2024 est.)
note: data in current dollars at official exchange rate

Inflation rate (consumer prices): 5.9% (2022 est.)
2.1% (2021 est.)
0.5% (2020 est.)
note: annual % change based on consumer prices
comparison ranking: 152

GDP - composition, by sector of origin: *industry:* 11.5% (2023 est.)
services: 88.5% (2023 est.)
note: figures may not total 100% due to non-allocated consumption not captured in sector-reported data
comparison rankings: industry 177; services 8

Agricultural products: none

Industries: banking, insurance, tourism, construction, small-scale industrial and consumer products

Exports - partners: Italy, Switzerland, Germany, Belgium, Spain
(2021)

Exports - commodities: jewelry, perfumes, watches, packaged medicines, cars (2021)
top five export commodities based on value in dollars

Imports - partners: Italy, Switzerland, United Kingdom, Germany, China (2021)

Imports - commodities: jewelry, cars and vehicle parts, recreational boats, plastic products, artwork (2021)

Exchange rates: euros (EUR) per US dollar -

Exchange rates: 0.924 (2024 est.)
0.925 (2023 est.)
0.95 (2022 est.)
0.845 (2021 est.)
0.876 (2020 est.)
note: while not an EU member state, Monaco, due to its preexisting monetary and banking agreements with France, has a 1998 monetary agreement with the EU to produce limited euro coinage—but not banknotes—that began enforcement in January 2002 and superseded by a new EU agreement in 2012

ENERGY

Electricity access: *electrification - total population:* 100% (2022 est.)

COMMUNICATIONS

Telephones - fixed lines: *total subscriptions:* 43,000 (2023 est.)
subscriptions per 100 inhabitants: 111 (2023 est.)
comparison ranking: total subscriptions 159

Telephones - mobile cellular: *total subscriptions:* 41,000 (2023 est.)
subscriptions per 100 inhabitants: 107 (2022 est.)
comparison ranking: total subscriptions 208

Broadcast media: TV Monte-Carlo operates a TV network; cable TV available; Radio Monte-Carlo has extensive radio networks in France and Italy, with French-language broadcasts to France beginning in the 1960s and Italian-language broadcasts to Italy beginning in the 1970s; other radio stations include Riviera Radio and Radio Monaco

Internet country code: .mc

Internet users: *percent of population:* 99% (2023 est.)

Broadband - fixed subscriptions: *total:* 22,000 (2023 est.)
subscriptions per 100 inhabitants: 56 (2023 est.)
comparison ranking: total 168

TRANSPORTATION

Civil aircraft registration country code prefix: 3A

Heliports: 3 (2025)
comparison ranking: 117

Railways: *note:* Monaco has a single railway station but does not operate its own train service; the French operator SNCF operates rail services in Monaco

Merchant marine: *total:* 1
comparison ranking: total 185

Ports: *total ports:* 1 (2024)
large: 0
medium: 0
small: 0
very small: 1
ports with oil terminals: 0
key ports: Monaco

MILITARY AND SECURITY

Military and security forces: no regular military forces; Prince's Company of Carabiniers (Compagnie des Carabiniers du Prince, Police Department (Direction de la Sûreté Publique), Fire and Emergency Service (Corps des Sapeurs-pompiers de Monaco) (2025)
note: the primary responsibility for the Compagnie des Carabiniers du Prince is guarding the palace; the Police maintain public order

Military service age and obligation: the Compagnie des Carabiniers du Prince is staffed by French nationals (2024)

Military - note: by treaty, France is responsible for defending the independence and sovereignty of Monaco

TRANSNATIONAL ISSUES

Refugees and internally displaced persons: *refugees:* 17 (2024 est.)

MONGOLIA

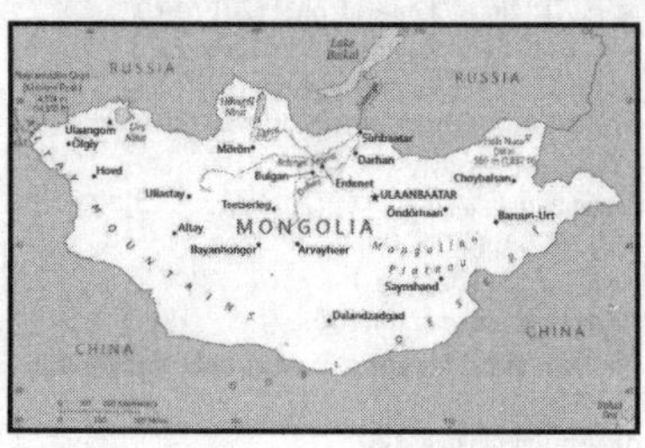

INTRODUCTION

Background: The peoples of Mongolia have a long history under a number of nomadic empires dating back to the Xiongnu in the 4th century B.C., and the name Mongol goes back to at least the 11th century A.D. The most famous Mongol, TEMÜÜJIN (aka Genghis Khan), emerged as the ruler of all Mongols in the early 1200s. By the time of his death in 1227, he had created through conquest a Mongol Empire that extended across much of Eurasia. His descendants, including ÖGÖDEI and KHUBILAI (aka Kublai Khan), continued to conquer Eastern Europe, the Middle East, and the rest of China, where KHUBILAI established the Yuan Dynasty in the 1270s. The Mongols attempted to invade Japan and Java before their empire broke apart in the 14th century. In the 17th century, Mongolia fell under the rule of the Manchus of the Chinese Qing Dynasty. After Manchu rule collapsed in 1911, Mongolia declared independence, finally winning it in 1921 with help from the Soviet Union. Mongolia became a socialist state (the Mongolian People's Republic) in 1924. Until the collapse of the Soviet Union in 1989,

Mongolia was a Soviet satellite state and relied heavily on economic, military, and political assistance from Moscow. The period was also marked by purges, political repression, economic stagnation, and tensions with China.

Mongolia peacefully transitioned to an independent democracy in 1990. In 1992, it adopted a new constitution and established a free-market economy. Since the country's transition, it has conducted a series of successful presidential and legislative elections. Throughout the period, the ex-communist Mongolian People's Revolutionary Party – which took the name Mongolian People's Party (MPP) in 2010 – has competed for political power with the Democratic Party and several other smaller parties. For most of its democratic history, Mongolia has had a divided government, with the presidency and the parliamentary majority held by different parties but that changed in 2021, when the MPP won the presidency after having secured a supermajority in parliament in 2020. Mongolia's June 2021 presidential election delivered a decisive victory for MPP candidate Ukhnaagiin KHURELSUKH.

Mongolia maintains close cultural, political, and military ties with Russia, while China is its largest economic partner. Mongolia's foreign relations are focused on preserving its autonomy by balancing relations with China and Russia, as well as its other major partners, Japan, South Korea, and the US.

GEOGRAPHY

Location: Northern Asia, between China and Russia

Geographic coordinates: 46 00 N, 105 00 E

Map references: Asia

Area: *total:* 1,564,116 sq km
land: 1,553,556 sq km
water: 10,560 sq km
comparison ranking: total 20

Area - comparative: slightly smaller than Alaska; more than twice the size of Texas

Land boundaries: *total:* 8,082 km
border countries (2): China 4,630 km; Russia 3,452 km

Coastline: 0 km (landlocked)

Maritime claims: none (landlocked)

Climate: desert; continental (large daily and seasonal temperature ranges)

Terrain: vast semidesert and desert plains, grassy steppe, mountains in west and southwest; Gobi Desert in south-central

Elevation: *highest point:* Nayramadlin Orgil (Khuiten Peak) 4,374 m
lowest point: Hoh Nuur 560 m
mean elevation: 1,528 m

Natural resources: oil, coal, copper, molybdenum, tungsten, phosphates, tin, nickel, zinc, fluorspar, gold, silver, iron

Land use: *agricultural land:* 71.9% (2022 est.)
arable land: 0.7% (2022 est.)
permanent crops: 0% (2022 est.)
permanent pasture: 71.2% (2022 est.)
forest: 9.1% (2022 est.)
other: 19% (2022 est.)

Irrigated land: 796 sq km (2022)

Major lakes (area sq km): *fresh water lake(s):* Hovsgol Nuur - 2,620 sq km; Har Us Nuur - 1,760 sq km;
salt water lake(s): Uvs Nuur - 3,350 sq km; Hyargas Nuur - 1,360 sq km

Major rivers (by length in km): Amur (shared with China [s] and Russia [m]) - 4,444 km
note: [s] after country name indicates river source; [m] after country name indicates river mouth

Population distribution: population sparsely distributed throughout the country; the capital of Ulaanbaatar and the northern city of Darhan support the highest population densities

Natural hazards: dust storms; grassland and forest fires; drought; "zud," which is harsh winter conditions

Geography - note: landlocked; strategic location between China and Russia

PEOPLE AND SOCIETY

Population: *total:* 3,281,676 (2024 est.)
male: 1,595,596
female: 1,686,080
comparison rankings: total 134; male 137; female 134

Nationality: *noun:* Mongolian(s)
adjective: Mongolian

Ethnic groups: Khalkh 83.8%, Kazak 3.8%, Durvud 2.6%, Bayad 2%, Buriad 1.4%, Zakhchin 1.2%, Dariganga 1.1%, other 4.1% (2020 est.)

Languages: Mongolian 90% (official, Khalkha dialect is predominant), Turkic, Russian (1999)
major-language sample(s):

major-language sample(s): Дэлхийн баримтат ном, үндсэн мэдээллийн зайлшгүй эх сурвалж. (Mongolian)

Religions: Buddhist 51.7%, Muslim 3.2%, Shamanist 2.5%, Christian 1.3%, other 0.7%, none 40.6% (2020 est.)

Age structure: *0-14 years:* 25.7% (male 429,867/female 412,943)
15-64 years: 68.4% (male 1,087,487/female 1,156,547)
65 years and over: 5.9% (2024 est.) (male 78,242/female 116,590)

Dependency ratios: *total dependency ratio:* 59.1 (2024 est.)
youth dependency ratio: 50.2 (2024 est.)
elderly dependency ratio: 8.9 (2024 est.)
potential support ratio: 11.2 (2024 est.)

Median age: *total:* 31.5 years (2024 est.)
male: 30.1 years
female: 32.8 years
comparison ranking: total 126

Population growth rate: 0.78% (2024 est.)
comparison ranking: 113

Birth rate: 14.9 births/1,000 population (2024 est.)
comparison ranking: 109

Death rate: 6.4 deaths/1,000 population (2024 est.)
comparison ranking: 144

Net migration rate: -0.8 migrant(s)/1,000 population (2024 est.)
comparison ranking: 138

Population distribution: population sparsely distributed throughout the country; the capital of Ulaanbaatar and the northern city of Darhan support the highest population densities

Urbanization: *urban population:* 69.1% of total population (2023)
rate of urbanization: 1.4% annual rate of change (2020-25 est.)

Major urban areas - population: 1.673 million ULAANBAATAR (capital) (2023)

Sex ratio: *at birth:* 1.05 male(s)/female
0-14 years: 1.04 male(s)/female
15-64 years: 0.94 male(s)/female
65 years and over: 0.67 male(s)/female
total population: 0.95 male(s)/female (2024 est.)

Mother's mean age at first birth: 20.5 years (2008 est.)
note: data represents median age at first birth among women 20-24

Maternal mortality ratio: 41 deaths/100,000 live births (2023 est.)
comparison ranking: 103

Infant mortality rate: *total:* 19.4 deaths/1,000 live births (2024 est.)
male: 22.4 deaths/1,000 live births
female: 16.2 deaths/1,000 live births
comparison ranking: total 78

Life expectancy at birth: *total population:* 71.9 years (2024 est.)
male: 67.8 years
female: 76.3 years
comparison ranking: total population 168

Total fertility rate: 1.87 children born/woman (2024 est.)
comparison ranking: 128

Gross reproduction rate: 0.91 (2024 est.)

Drinking water source: *improved: urban:* 94.2% of population (2022 est.)
rural: 59.7% of population (2022 est.)
total: 83.5% of population (2022 est.)
unimproved: urban: 5.8% of population (2022 est.)
rural: 40.3% of population (2022 est.)
total: 16.5% of population (2022 est.)

Health expenditure: 6.9% of GDP (2021)
9.2% of national budget (2022 est.)

Physician density: 4.13 physicians/1,000 population (2022)

Hospital bed density: 10.6 beds/1,000 population (2021 est.)

Sanitation facility access: *improved: urban:* 97.8% of population (2022 est.)
rural: 78.7% of population (2022 est.)
total: 91.9% of population (2022 est.)
unimproved: urban: 2.2% of population (2022 est.)
rural: 21.3% of population (2022 est.)
total: 8.1% of population (2022 est.)

Obesity - adult prevalence rate: 20.6% (2016)
comparison ranking: 97

Alcohol consumption per capita: *total:* 5.46 liters of pure alcohol (2019 est.)
beer: 2.18 liters of pure alcohol (2019 est.)
wine: 1.46 liters of pure alcohol (2019 est.)
spirits: 1.82 liters of pure alcohol (2019 est.)
other alcohols: 0 liters of pure alcohol (2019 est.)
comparison ranking: total 80

Tobacco use: *total:* 28.9% (2025 est.)
male: 51.9% (2025 est.)
female: 7.2% (2025 est.)
comparison ranking: total 23

Children under the age of 5 years underweight: 1.8% (2018)
comparison ranking: 100

Currently married women (ages 15-49): 58.9% (2023 est.)

Child marriage: *women married by age 15:* 0.9% (2018)
women married by age 18: 12% (2018)
men married by age 18: 2.1% (2018)

Education expenditure: 3.7% of GDP (2023 est.)
10% national budget (2021 est.)
comparison ranking: Education expenditure (% GDP) 123

Literacy: *total population:* 98.7% (2022 est.)
male: 98.5% (2022 est.)
female: 98.9% (2022 est.)

School life expectancy (primary to tertiary education): *total:* 14 years (2023 est.)
male: 13 years (2023 est.)
female: 14 years (2023 est.)

ENVIRONMENT

Environmental issues: limited natural freshwater resources in some areas; air pollution from coal-burning power plants and lax regulations in Ulaanbaatar; soil erosion from deforestation and overgrazing; water pollution; desertification; effects from mining

International environmental agreements: *party to:* Antarctic Treaty, Biodiversity, Climate Change, Climate Change-Kyoto Protocol, Climate Change-Paris Agreement, Comprehensive Nuclear Test Ban, Desertification, Endangered Species, Environmental Modification, Hazardous Wastes, Law of the Sea, Nuclear Test Ban, Ozone Layer Protection, Ship Pollution, Wetlands, Whaling
signed, but not ratified: none of the selected agreements

Climate: desert; continental (large daily and seasonal temperature ranges)

Urbanization: *urban population:* 69.1% of total population (2023)
rate of urbanization: 1.4% annual rate of change (2020-25 est.)

Carbon dioxide emissions: 19.203 million metric tonnes of CO2 (2023 est.)
from coal and metallurgical coke: 13.489 million metric tonnes of CO2 (2023 est.)
from petroleum and other liquids: 5.714 million metric tonnes of CO2 (2023 est.)
comparison ranking: total emissions 87

Particulate matter emissions: 41.3 micrograms per cubic meter (2019 est.)

Methane emissions: *energy:* 532.2 kt (2022-2024 est.)
agriculture: 525.2 kt (2019-2021 est.)
waste: 14.2 kt (2019-2021 est.)
other: 2.9 kt (2019-2021 est.)

Waste and recycling: *municipal solid waste generated annually:* 2.9 million tons (2024 est.)
percent of municipal solid waste recycled: 13% (2022 est.)

Total water withdrawal: *municipal:* 45.3 million cubic meters (2022 est.)
industrial: 166.2 million cubic meters (2022 est.)
agricultural: 250.9 million cubic meters (2022 est.)

Total renewable water resources: 34.8 billion cubic meters (2022 est.)

GOVERNMENT

Country name: *conventional long form:* none
conventional short form: Mongolia
local long form: none
local short form: Mongol Uls
former: Outer Mongolia, Mongolian People's Republic
etymology: name comes from the Mongol people, whose name derives from the Mongol root word *mengu* or *mongu*, meaning "brave" or "unconquered;" the Mongolian name Mongol Uls translates as "Mongol State"

Government type: semi-presidential republic

Capital: *name:* Ulaanbaatar
geographic coordinates: 47 55 N, 106 55 E
time difference: UTC+8 (13 hours ahead of Washington, DC, during Standard Time)
daylight saving time: +1hr, begins last Saturday in March; ends last Saturday in September
time zone note: Mongolia has two time zones - Ulaanbaatar Time (8 hours in advance of UTC) and Hovd Time (7 hours in advance of UTC)
etymology: the name means "red hero" in Mongolian and honors national hero Damdin SUKHBAATAR, leader of the partisan army that, with Soviet help, liberated Mongolia from Chinese occupation in the early 1920s

Administrative divisions: 21 provinces (*aymguud*, singular - *aymag*) and 1 municipality* (*hot*); Arhangay, Bayanhongor, Bayan-Olgiy, Bulgan, Darhan-Uul, Dornod, Dornogovi, Dundgovi, Dzavhan (Zavkhan), Govi-Altay, Govisumber, Hentiy, Hovd, Hovsgol, Omnogovi, Orhon, Ovorhangay, Selenge, Suhbaatar, Tov, Ulaanbaatar*, Uvs

Legal system: civil law system influenced by Soviet and Romano-Germanic systems; constitution ambiguous on judicial review of legislative acts

Constitution: *history:* several previous; latest adopted 13 January 1992, effective 12 February 1992
amendment process: proposed by the State Great Hural, by the president of the republic, by the government, or by petition submitted to the State Great Hural by the Constitutional Court; conducting referenda on proposed amendments requires at least two-thirds majority vote of the State Great Hural; passage of amendments by the State Great Hural requires at least three-quarters majority vote; passage by referendum requires majority participation of qualified voters and a majority of votes

International law organization participation: has not submitted an ICJ jurisdiction declaration; accepts ICCt jurisdiction

Citizenship: *citizenship by birth:* no
citizenship by descent only: both parents must be citizens of Mongolia; one parent if born within Mongolia
dual citizenship recognized: no
residency requirement for naturalization: 5 years

Suffrage: 18 years of age; universal

Executive branch: *chief of state:* President Ukhnaagiin KHURELSUKH (since 25 June 2021)
head of government: Prime Minister Gombojavyn ZANDANSHATAR (since 13 June 2025)
cabinet: Cabinet directly appointed by the prime minister
election/appointment process: presidential candidates nominated by political parties represented in the State Great Hural and directly elected by simple-majority popular vote for one 6-year term; following legislative elections, the State Great Hural usually elects the leader of the majority party or majority coalition as prime minister
most recent election date: 9 June 2021
election results: *2021:* Ukhnaagiin KHURELSUKH elected president in first round; percent of vote - Ukhnaagiin KHURELSUKH (MPP) 68%, Dangaasuren ENKHBAT (RPEC) 20.1%, Sodnomzundui ERDENE (DP) 6%
2017: Khaltmaa BATTULGA elected president in second round; percent of vote in first round - Khaltmaa BATTULGA (DP) 38.1%, Miyegombo ENKHBOLD (MPP) 30.3%, Sainkhuu GANBAATAR (MPRP) 30.2%, invalid 1.4%; percent of vote in second round - Khaltmaa BATTULGA 55.2%, Miyegombo ENKHBOLD 44.8%
expected date of next election: 2027

Legislative branch: *legislature name:* State Great Hural (Ulsiin Ih Hural)
legislative structure: unicameral
number of seats: 126 (all directly elected)
electoral system: mixed system
scope of elections: full renewal
term in office: 4 years
most recent election date: 6/28/2024
parties elected and seats per party: Mongolian People's Party (MPP) (68); Democratic Party (DP) (42); HUN Party (8); Other (8)
percentage of women in chamber: 25.4%
expected date of next election: June 2028

Judicial branch: *highest court(s):* Supreme Court (consists of the Chief Justice and 24 judges organized into civil, criminal, and administrative chambers); Constitutional Court or Tsets (consists of the chairman and 8 members)
judge selection and term of office: Supreme Court chief justice and judges appointed by the president on recommendation of the General Council of Courts – a 14-member body of judges and judicial officials – to the State Great Hural; appointment is for life; chairman of the Constitutional Court elected from among its members; members appointed from nominations by the State Great Hural - 3 each by the president, the State Great Hural, and the Supreme Court; appointment is 6 years; chairmanship limited to a single renewable 3-year term
subordinate courts: aimag (provincial) and capital city appellate courts; soum, inter-soum, and district courts; Administrative Cases Courts

Political parties: Democratic Party or DP
Mongolian People's Party or MPP
National Coalition (consists of Mongolian Green Party or MGP and the Mongolian National Democratic Party or MNDP)
National Labor Party or HUN
Civil Will-Green Party or CWGP

Diplomatic representation in the US: *chief of mission:* Ambassador BATBAYAR Ulziidelger (since 1 December 2021)
chancery: 2833 M Street NW, Washington, DC 20007
telephone: [1] (202) 333-7117
FAX: [1] (202) 298-9227
email address and website: washington@mfa.gov.mn
http://mongolianembassy.us/
consulate(s) general: New York, San Francisco

Diplomatic representation from the US: *chief of mission:* Ambassador Richard L. BUANGAN (since November 2022)
embassy: Denver Street #3, 11th Micro-District, Ulaanbaatar 14190
mailing address: 4410 Ulaanbaatar Place, Washington DC 20521-4410
telephone: [976] 7007-6001

FAX: [976] 7007-6174
email address and website: UlaanbaatarACS@state.gov
https://mn.usembassy.gov/

International organization participation: ADB, ARF, CD, CICA, CP, EBRD, EITI (compliant country), FAO, G-77, IAEA, IBRD, ICAO, ICC (NGOs), ICCt, ICRM, IDA, IFAD, IFC, IFRCS, ILO, IMF, IMO, IMSO, Interpol, IOC, IOM, IPU, ISO, ITSO, ITU, ITUC, MIGA, MINURSO, MONUSCO, NAM, OPCW, OSCE, SCO (observer), UN, UNAMID, UNCTAD, UNESCO, UNIDO, UNISFA, UNMISS, UNWTO, UPU, WCO, WHO, WIPO, WMO, WTO

Independence: 29 December 1911 (independence declared from China; in actuality, autonomy attained); 11 July 1921 (from China)

National holiday: Naadam (games) holiday, 11-15 July; Constitution Day, 26 November (1924)
note: the first holiday commemorates independence from China in the 1921 Revolution, and the second marks the date that the Mongolian People's Republic was created under a new constitution

Flag: *description:* three equal vertical bands of red (left side), blue, and red; centered on the left-side red band is the national emblem in yellow, the *soyombo*, which is an abstract representation of fire, sun, moon, earth, water, and the yin-yang symbol
meaning: blue stands for the sky, and red for progress and prosperity

National symbol(s): Soyombo character (from the Soyombo writing system)

National color(s): red, blue, yellow

National anthem(s): *title:* "Mongol ulsyn toriin duulal" (National Anthem of Mongolia)
lyrics/music: Tsendiin DAMDINSUREN/Bilegiin DAMDINSUREN and Luvsanjamts MURJORJ
history: music adopted 1950, lyrics adopted 2006; lyrics altered on numerous occasions

National heritage: *total World Heritage Sites:* 6 (4 cultural, 2 natural)
selected World Heritage Site locales: Uvs Nuur Basin (n); Orkhon Valley Cultural Landscape (c); Petroglyphic Complexes of the Mongolian Altai (c); Great Burkhan Khaldun Mountain and surrounding sacred landscape (c); Landscapes of Dauria (n); Deer Stone Monuments and Related Bronze Age Sites (c)

ECONOMY

Economic overview: lower middle-income East Asian economy; large human capital improvements over last 3 decades; agricultural and natural resource rich; export and consumption-led growth; high inflation due to supply bottlenecks and increased food and energy prices; currency depreciation

Real GDP (purchasing power parity): $59.221 billion (2024 est.)
$56.474 billion (2023 est.)
$52.572 billion (2022 est.)
note: data in 2021 dollars
comparison ranking: 118

Real GDP growth rate: 4.9% (2024 est.)
7.4% (2023 est.)
5% (2022 est.)
note: annual GDP % growth based on constant local currency
comparison ranking: 47

Real GDP per capita: $16,800 (2024 est.)
$16,200 (2023 est.)
$15,300 (2022 est.)
note: data in 2021 dollars
comparison ranking: 115

GDP (official exchange rate): $23.586 billion (2024 est.)
note: data in current dollars at official exchange rate

Inflation rate (consumer prices): 6.8% (2024 est.)
10.3% (2023 est.)
15.1% (2022 est.)
note: annual % change based on consumer prices
comparison ranking: 163

GDP - composition, by sector of origin: *agriculture:* 7.4% (2024 est.)
industry: 38.1% (2024 est.)
services: 44.2% (2024 est.)
note: figures may not total 100% due to non-allocated consumption not captured in sector-reported data
comparison rankings: agriculture 89; industry 23; services 178

GDP - composition, by end use: *household consumption:* 49.8% (2024 est.)
government consumption: 16.3% (2024 est.)
investment in fixed capital: 26.8% (2024 est.)
investment in inventories: 7.8% (2024 est.)
exports of goods and services: 69.1% (2024 est.)
imports of goods and services: -69.8% (2024 est.)
note: figures may not total 100% due to rounding or gaps in data collection

Agricultural products: milk, wheat, lamb/mutton, potatoes, beef, carrots/turnips, goat milk, goat meat, bison milk, horse meat (2023)
note: top ten agricultural products based on tonnage

Industries: construction and construction materials; mining (coal, copper, molybdenum, fluorspar, tin, tungsten, gold); oil; food and beverages; processing of animal products, cashmere and natural fiber manufacturing

Industrial production growth rate: 6.5% (2024 est.)
note: annual % change in industrial value added based on constant local currency
comparison ranking: 28

Labor force: 1.449 million (2024 est.)
note: number of people ages 15 or older who are employed or seeking work
comparison ranking: 135

Unemployment rate: 5.5% (2024 est.)
5.6% (2023 est.)
6.3% (2022 est.)
note: % of labor force seeking employment
comparison ranking: 101

Youth unemployment rate (ages 15-24): *total:* 13.8% (2024 est.)
male: 15.9% (2024 est.)
female: 10.8% (2024 est.)
note: % of labor force ages 15-24 seeking employment
comparison ranking: total 92

Population below poverty line: 27.1% (2022 est.)
note: % of population with income below national poverty line

Gini Index coefficient - distribution of family income: 31.4 (2022 est.)
note: index (0-100) of income distribution; higher values represent greater inequality
comparison ranking: 111

Household income or consumption by percentage share: *lowest 10%:* 3.4% (2022 est.)
highest 10%: 24.6% (2022 est.)
note: % share of income accruing to lowest and highest 10% of population

Remittances: 2.2% of GDP (2023 est.)
2.3% of GDP (2022 est.)
3.1% of GDP (2021 est.)
note: personal transfers and compensation between resident and non-resident individuals/households/entities

Budget: *revenues:* $4.721 billion (2021 est.)
expenditures: $5.623 billion (2021 est.)
note: central government revenues (excluding grants) and expenditures converted to US dollars at average official exchange rate for year indicated

Public debt: 67.6% of GDP (2021 est.)
note: central government debt as a % of GDP
comparison ranking: 61

Taxes and other revenues: 16.9% (of GDP) (2021 est.)
note: central government tax revenue as a % of GDP
comparison ranking: 77

Current account balance: $121.266 million (2023 est.)
-$2.303 billion (2022 est.)
-$2.108 billion (2021 est.)
note: balance of payments - net trade and primary/secondary income in current dollars
comparison ranking: 74

Exports: $15.501 billion (2023 est.)
$10.989 billion (2022 est.)
$8.95 billion (2021 est.)
note: balance of payments - exports of goods and services in current dollars
comparison ranking: 99

Exports - partners: China 92%, Switzerland 6%, Italy 1%, Thailand 0%, Japan 0% (2023)
note: top five export partners based on percentage share of exports

Exports - commodities: coal, copper ore, gold, iron ore, crude petroleum (2023)
note: top five export commodities based on value in dollars

Imports: $13.545 billion (2023 est.)
$12.112 billion (2022 est.)
$9.256 billion (2021 est.)
note: balance of payments - imports of goods and services in current dollars
comparison ranking: 110

Imports - partners: China 57%, Japan 13%, Germany 3%, Singapore 3%, USA 3% (2023)
note: top five import partners based on percentage share of imports

Imports - commodities: cars, trucks, trailers, tractors, construction vehicles (2023)
note: top five import commodities based on value in dollars

Reserves of foreign exchange and gold: $5.508 billion (2024 est.)
$4.916 billion (2023 est.)
$3.398 billion (2022 est.)
note: holdings of gold (year-end prices)/foreign exchange/special drawing rights in current dollars
comparison ranking: 94

Debt - external: $8.379 billion (2023 est.)
note: present value of external debt in current US dollars
comparison ranking: 54

Exchange rates: togrog/tugriks (MNT) per US dollar -

Exchange rates: 3,389.982 (2024 est.)
3,465.737 (2023 est.)
3,140.678 (2022 est.)
2,849.289 (2021 est.)
2,813.29 (2020 est.)

ENERGY

Electricity access: *electrification - total population:* 100% (2022 est.)

Electricity: *installed generating capacity:* 1.51 million kW (2023 est.)
consumption: 8.997 billion kWh (2023 est.)
exports: 24 million kWh (2023 est.)
imports: 2.224 billion kWh (2023 est.)
transmission/distribution losses: 1.113 billion kWh (2023 est.)
comparison rankings: installed generating capacity 127; consumption 110; exports 97; imports 66; transmission/distribution losses 103

Electricity generation sources: *fossil fuels:* 90.4% of total installed capacity (2023 est.)
solar: 2.4% of total installed capacity (2023 est.)
wind: 6.4% of total installed capacity (2023 est.)
hydroelectricity: 0.8% of total installed capacity (2023 est.)

Coal: *production:* 64.824 million metric tons (2023 est.)
consumption: 8.941 million metric tons (2023 est.)
exports: 55.884 million metric tons (2023 est.)
imports: 900 metric tons (2023 est.)
proven reserves: 2.52 billion metric tons (2023 est.)

Petroleum: *total petroleum production:* 15,000 bbl/day (2023 est.)
refined petroleum consumption: 39,000 bbl/day (2023 est.)

Energy consumption per capita: 67.132 million Btu/person (2023 est.)
comparison ranking: 73

COMMUNICATIONS

Telephones - fixed lines: *total subscriptions:* 524,000 (2023 est.)
subscriptions per 100 inhabitants: 15 (2023 est.)
comparison ranking: total subscriptions 91

Telephones - mobile cellular: *total subscriptions:* 4.84 million (2023 est.)
subscriptions per 100 inhabitants: 142 (2022 est.)
comparison ranking: total subscriptions 125

Broadcast media: state-run radio and TV provider is now a public-service provider; also available are 68 radio and 160 TV stations, including multi-channel satellite and cable TV providers; transmissions of multiple international broadcasters are available (2019)

Internet country code: .mn

Internet users: *percent of population:* 83% (2023 est.)

Broadband - fixed subscriptions: *total:* 499,000 (2023 est.)
subscriptions per 100 inhabitants: 15 (2023 est.)
comparison ranking: total 97

TRANSPORTATION

Civil aircraft registration country code prefix: JU

Airports: 37 (2025)
comparison ranking: 110

Railways: *total:* 1,815 km (2017)
broad gauge: 1,815 km (2017) 1.520-m gauge
note: national operator Ulaanbaatar Railway is jointly owned by the Mongolian Government and by the Russian State Railway

Merchant marine: *total:* 318 (2023)
by type: bulk carrier 8, container ship 8, general cargo 151, oil tanker 58, other 93
comparison ranking: total 55

MILITARY AND SECURITY

Military and security forces: Mongolian Armed Forces (MAF): Land Force, Air Force, Cyber Security Forces, Special Forces, Construction-Engineering Forces (2025)
note: the National Police Agency and the General Authority for Border Protection, which operate under the Ministry of Justice and Home Affairs, are primarily responsible for internal security; they are assisted by the General Intelligence Agency under the prime minister

Military expenditures: 0.7% of GDP (2024 est.)
0.6% of GDP (2023 est.)
0.6% of GDP (2022 est.)
0.8% of GDP (2021 est.)
0.8% of GDP (2020 est.)

Military and security service personnel strengths: information varies; estimated 10-20,000 active Mongolian Armed Forces (2025)

Military equipment inventories and acquisitions: the MAF's inventory is comprised largely of Soviet-era and Russian equipment (2024)

Military service age and obligation: 18-25 years of age for compulsory and voluntary military service (can enter military schools at age 17); 12-month conscript service obligation for men can be extended 3 months under special circumstances; conscription service can be exchanged for a 24-month stint in the civil service or a cash payment determined by the Mongolian Government; after conscription, soldiers can contract into military service for 2 or 4 years; volunteer military service for men and women is 24 months, which can be extended for another two years up to the age of 31 (2024)

Military deployments: 850 South Sudan (UNMISS) (2025)
note: since 2002, Mongolia has deployed more than 20,000 peacekeepers and observers to UN operations in more than a dozen countries

Military - note: the Mongolian Armed Forces (MAF) are responsible for ensuring the country's independence, security, and territorial integrity, as well as supporting Mongolia's developmental goals and diplomacy; it has a range of missions, including counterterrorism, international peacekeeping duties, and assisting the internal security forces in providing emergency aid and disaster relief; Mongolia hosts an annual international peacekeeping exercise known as "Khaan Quest"; it has no formal military alliances, but has defense ties and conducts training exercises with several regional countries and others, such as China, India, Russia, and the US
Mongolia actively cooperates with NATO on issues such as counterterrorism, nonproliferation, and cybersecurity through an Individual Partnership and Cooperation Program; it supported the NATO-led Kosovo Force from 2005-2007 and contributed troops to the NATO-led missions in Afghanistan from 2009-2021; Mongolia also is an observer in the Shanghai Cooperation Organization (2025)

TRANSNATIONAL ISSUES

Refugees and internally displaced persons: *refugees:* 26 (2024 est.)

IDPs: 22 (2024 est.)
stateless persons: 17 (2024 est.)

MONTENEGRO

INTRODUCTION

Background: The use of the name Crna Gora or Black Mountain (Montenegro) began in the 13th century in reference to a highland region in the Serbian province of Zeta. Under Ottoman control beginning in 1496, Montenegro was a semi-autonomous theocracy ruled by a series of bishop princes until 1852, when it became a secular principality. Montenegro fought a series of wars with the Ottomans and eventually won recognition as an independent sovereign principality at the Congress of Berlin in 1878. In 1918, the country was absorbed by the Kingdom of Serbs, Croats, and Slovenes, which became the Kingdom of Yugoslavia in 1929. At the end of World War II, Montenegro joined the Socialist Federal Republic of Yugoslavia (SFRY). When the SFRY dissolved in 1992, Montenegro and Serbia created the Federal Republic of Yugoslavia (FRY), which shifted in 2003 to a looser State Union of Serbia and Montenegro. Montenegro voted to restore its independence on 3 June 2006. Montenegro became an official EU candidate in 2010 and joined NATO in 2017.

GEOGRAPHY

Location: Southeastern Europe, between the Adriatic Sea and Serbia

Geographic coordinates: 42 30 N, 19 18 E

Map references: Europe

Area: *total:* 13,812 sq km
land: 13,452 sq km
water: 360 sq km
comparison ranking: total 161

Area - comparative: slightly smaller than Connecticut; slightly larger than twice the size of Delaware

Land boundaries: *total:* 680 km
border countries (5): Albania 186 km; Bosnia and Herzegovina 242 km; Croatia 19 km; Kosovo 76 km; Serbia 157 km

Coastline: 293.5 km

Maritime claims: *territorial sea:* 12 nm
continental shelf: defined by treaty

Climate: Mediterranean climate, hot dry summers and autumns and relatively cold winters with heavy snowfalls inland

Terrain: highly indented coastline with narrow coastal plain backed by rugged high limestone mountains and plateaus

Elevation: *highest point:* Zia Kolata 2,534 m
lowest point: Adriatic Sea 0 m
mean elevation: 1,086 m

Natural resources: bauxite, hydroelectricity

Land use: *agricultural land:* 18.8% (2022 est.)
arable land: 0.7% (2022 est.)
permanent crops: 0.4% (2022 est.)
permanent pasture: 17.8% (2022 est.)
forest: 61.5% (2022 est.)
other: 19.7% (2022 est.)

Irrigated land: 24 sq km (2012)

Major lakes (area sq km): *fresh water lake(s):* Lake Scutari (shared with Albania) - 400 sq km note - largest lake in the Balkans

Major watersheds (area sq km): Atlantic Ocean drainage: *(Black Sea)* Danube (795,656 sq km)

Population distribution: highest population density is concentrated in the south and southwest; the extreme eastern border is the least populated area

Natural hazards: destructive earthquakes

Geography - note: strategic location along the Adriatic coast

PEOPLE AND SOCIETY

Population: *total:* 599,849 (2024 est.)
male: 294,482
female: 305,367
comparison rankings: total 172; male 172; female 172

Nationality: *noun:* Montenegrin(s)
adjective: Montenegrin

Ethnic groups: Montenegrin 45%, Serbian 28.7%, Bosniak 8.7%, Albanian 4.9%, Muslim 3.3%, Romani 1%, Croat 1%, other 2.6%, unspecified 4.9% (2011 est.)

Languages: Serbian 42.9%, Montenegrin (official) 37%, Bosnian 5.3%, Albanian 5.3%, Serbo-Croat 2%, other 3.5%, unspecified 4% (2011 est.)
major-language sample(s):
Knjiga svetskih činjenica, neophodan izvor osnovnih informacija. (Serbian)
Knjiga svjetskih činjenica, neophodan izvor osnovnih informacija. (Montenegrin/Bosnian)

Religions: Orthodox 72.1%, Muslim 19.1%, Catholic 3.4%, atheist 1.2%, other 1.5%, unspecified 2.6% (2011 est.)

Age structure: *0-14 years:* 17.7% (male 54,608/female 51,594)
15-64 years: 64.4% (male 192,631/female 193,515)
65 years and over: 17.9% (2024 est.) (male 47,243/female 60,258)

Dependency ratios: *total dependency ratio:* 55.3 (2024 est.)
youth dependency ratio: 27.5 (2024 est.)
elderly dependency ratio: 27.8 (2024 est.)
potential support ratio: 3.6 (2024 est.)

Median age: *total:* 41.1 years (2024 est.)
male: 39.5 years
female: 42.5 years
comparison ranking: total 54

Population growth rate: -0.44% (2024 est.)
comparison ranking: 219

Birth rate: 10.9 births/1,000 population (2024 est.)
comparison ranking: 165

Death rate: 10.3 deaths/1,000 population (2024 est.)
comparison ranking: 31

Net migration rate: -5 migrant(s)/1,000 population (2024 est.)
comparison ranking: 203

Population distribution: highest population density is concentrated in the south and southwest; the extreme eastern border is the least populated area

Urbanization: *urban population:* 68.5% of total population (2023)
rate of urbanization: 0.45% annual rate of change (2020-25 est.)

Major urban areas - population: 177,000 PODGORICA (capital) (2018)

Sex ratio: *at birth:* 1.04 male(s)/female
0-14 years: 1.06 male(s)/female
15-64 years: 1 male(s)/female
65 years and over: 0.78 male(s)/female
total population: 0.96 male(s)/female (2024 est.)

Mother's mean age at first birth: 26.3 years (2010 est.)

Maternal mortality ratio: 6 deaths/100,000 live births (2023 est.)
comparison ranking: 165

Infant mortality rate: *total:* 3.2 deaths/1,000 live births (2024 est.)
male: 2.7 deaths/1,000 live births
female: 3.7 deaths/1,000 live births
comparison ranking: total 202

Life expectancy at birth: *total population:* 78.2 years (2024 est.)
male: 75.8 years
female: 80.7 years
comparison ranking: total population 82

Total fertility rate: 1.8 children born/woman (2024 est.)
comparison ranking: 141

Gross reproduction rate: 0.89 (2024 est.)

Drinking water source: *improved: urban:* 99.2% of population (2022 est.)
rural: 98.2% of population (2022 est.)
total: 98.9% of population (2022 est.)
unimproved: urban: 0.8% of population (2022 est.)
rural: 1.8% of population (2022 est.)
total: 1.1% of population (2022 est.)

Health expenditure: 10.6% of GDP (2021)
16.3% of national budget (2022 est.)

Physician density: 2.78 physicians/1,000 population (2023)

Hospital bed density: 3.8 beds/1,000 population (2020 est.)

Sanitation facility access: *improved: urban:* 100% of population (2022 est.)
rural: 93.9% of population (2022 est.)
total: 98.1% of population (2022 est.)
unimproved: urban: 0% of population (2022 est.)
rural: 6.1% of population (2022 est.)
total: 1.9% of population (2022 est.)

Obesity - adult prevalence rate: 23.3% (2016)
comparison ranking: 66

Alcohol consumption per capita: *total:* 9.91 liters of pure alcohol (2019 est.)
beer: 3.83 liters of pure alcohol (2019 est.)
wine: 2.68 liters of pure alcohol (2019 est.)
spirits: 3.22 liters of pure alcohol (2019 est.)
other alcohols: 0.16 liters of pure alcohol (2019 est.)
comparison ranking: total 23

Tobacco use: *total:* 31.6% (2025 est.)
male: 29.9% (2025 est.)
female: 33.1% (2025 est.)
comparison ranking: total 17

Children under the age of 5 years underweight: 3.7% (2018/19)
comparison ranking: 73

Currently married women (ages 15-49): 57.1% (2023 est.)

Child marriage: *women married by age 15:* 1.9% (2018)
women married by age 18: 5.8% (2018)
men married by age 18: 3.2% (2018)

Literacy: *total population:* 98.5% (2018 est.)
male: 99.1% (2018 est.)
female: 97.9% (2018 est.)

School life expectancy (primary to tertiary education): *total:* 16 years (2023 est.)
male: 15 years (2023 est.)
female: 16 years (2023 est.)

ENVIRONMENT

Environmental issues: pollution of coastal waters from sewage outlets; serious air pollution in some cities from lignite power plants and household use of coal and wood for heating

International environmental agreements: *party to:* Air Pollution, Air Pollution-Heavy Metals, Air Pollution-Persistent Organic Pollutants, Biodiversity, Climate Change, Climate Change-Kyoto Protocol, Climate Change-Paris Agreement, Comprehensive Nuclear Test Ban, Desertification, Endangered Species, Hazardous Wastes, Law of the Sea, Marine Dumping-London Convention, Marine Life Conservation, Nuclear Test Ban, Ozone Layer Protection, Ship Pollution, Wetlands
signed, but not ratified: none of the selected agreements

Climate: Mediterranean climate, hot dry summers and autumns and relatively cold winters with heavy snowfalls inland

Urbanization: *urban population:* 68.5% of total population (2023)
rate of urbanization: 0.45% annual rate of change (2020-25 est.)

Carbon dioxide emissions: 2.808 million metric tonnes of CO2 (2023 est.)

from coal and metallurgical coke: 1.543 million metric tonnes of CO_2 (2023 est.)
from petroleum and other liquids: 1.265 million metric tonnes of CO_2 (2023 est.)
comparison ranking: total emissions 152

Particulate matter emissions: 17.9 micrograms per cubic meter (2019 est.)

Waste and recycling: *municipal solid waste generated annually:* 329,800 tons (2024 est.)
percent of municipal solid waste recycled: 6.4% (2022 est.)

Total water withdrawal: *municipal:* 121.32 million cubic meters (2022 est.)
industrial: 2.079 billion cubic meters (2022 est.)
agricultural: 6.76 million cubic meters (2022 est.)

GOVERNMENT

Country name: *conventional long form:* none
conventional short form: Montenegro
local long form: none
local short form: Crna Gora
former: People's Republic of Montenegro, Socialist Republic of Montenegro, Republic of Montenegro
etymology: the name in Italian means "dark mountain" and is a translation of the Serbo-Croatian name Crna Gora; both refer to the dark coniferous forests in the mountainous region

Government type: parliamentary republic

Capital: *name:* Podgorica
geographic coordinates: 42 26 N, 19 16 E
time difference: UTC+1 (6 hours ahead of Washington, DC, during Standard Time)
daylight saving time: +1 hr, begins last Sunday in March; ends last Sunday in October
etymology: the Slavic name translates as "under the mountain," from *pod* (under) and *gora* (mountain)
note: Cetinje retains the status of "Old Royal Capital"

Administrative divisions: 25 municipalities (*opstine*, singular - *opstina*); Andrijevica, Bar, Berane, Bijelo Polje, Budva, Cetinje, Danilovgrad, Gusinje, Herceg Novi, Kolasin, Kotor, Mojkovac, Niksic, Petnjica, Plav, Pljevlja, Pluzine, Podgorica, Rozaje, Savnik, Tivat, Tuzi, Ulcinj, Zabljak, Zeta

Legal system: civil law

Constitution: *history:* several previous; latest adopted 22 October 2007
amendment process: proposed by the president of Montenegro, by the government, or by at least 25 members of the Assembly; passage of draft proposals requires two-thirds majority vote of the Assembly, followed by a public hearing; passage of draft amendments requires two-thirds majority vote of the Assembly; changes to certain constitutional articles, such as sovereignty, state symbols, citizenship, and constitutional change procedures, require three-fifths majority vote in a referendum

International law organization participation: has not submitted an ICJ jurisdiction declaration; accepts ICCt jurisdiction

Citizenship: *citizenship by birth:* no
citizenship by descent only: at least one parent must be a citizen of Montenegro
dual citizenship recognized: no
residency requirement for naturalization: 10 years

Suffrage: 18 years of age; universal

Executive branch: *chief of state:* President Jakov MILATOVIC (since 20 May 2023)
head of government: Prime Minister Milojko SPAJIC (since 31 October 2023)
cabinet: ministers serve as the cabinet
election/appointment process: president directly elected by absolute-majority popular vote in 2 rounds, if needed, for a 5-year term (eligible for a second term); prime minister nominated by the president, approved by the Assembly
most recent election date: 19 March 2023, with a runoff on 2 April 2023
election results: *2023:* Jakov MILATOVIC elected president in second round; percent of vote in first round - Milo DUKANOVIC (DPS) 35.4%, Jakov MILATOVIC (Europe Now!) 28.9%, Andrija MANDIC (DF) 19.3%, Aleksa BECIC (DCG) 11.1%, other 5.3%; percent of vote in second round - Jakov MILATOVIC 58.9%, Milo DUKANOVIC 41.1%
2018: Milo DJUKANOVIC elected president in first round; percent of vote - Milo DJUKANOVIC (DPS) 53.9%, Mladen BOJANIC (independent) 33.4%, Draginja VUKSANOVIC (SDP) 8.2%, Marko MILACIC (PRAVA) 2.8%, other 1.7%
expected date of next election: 2028

Legislative branch: *legislature name:* Parliament (Skupstina)
legislative structure: unicameral
number of seats: 81 (all directly elected)
electoral system: proportional representation
scope of elections: full renewal
term in office: 4 years
most recent election date: 6/11/2023
parties elected and seats per party: Europe now! (Evropa sad) (24); Together! For the future that belongs to you (DPS – SD – DUA – LP - UDSh) (21); For the future of Montenegro (New Serb Democracy; Democratic People's Party of Montenegro, Labour Party) (13); Bravery counts! (HRABRO se broji!) (11); It's clear! (Jasno je!) – Bosniak Party (6); Other (6)
percentage of women in chamber: 27.2%
expected date of next election: June 2027

Judicial branch: *highest court(s):* Supreme Court or Vrhovni Sud (consists of the court president, deputy president, and 15 judges); Constitutional Court or Ustavni Sud (consists of the court president and 7 judges)
judge selection and term of office: Supreme Court president proposed by general session of the Supreme Court and elected by the Judicial Council, a 9-member body consisting of judges, lawyers designated by the Assembly, and the minister of judicial affairs; Supreme Court president elected for a single renewable, 5-year term; other judges elected by the Judicial Council for life; Constitutional Court judges - 2 proposed by the president of Montenegro and 5 by the Assembly, and elected by the Assembly; court president elected from among the court members; court president elected for a 3-year term, other judges serve 9-year terms
subordinate courts: Administrative Courts; Appellate Court; Commercial Courts; High Courts; basic courts

Political parties: Albanian Alliance (electoral coalition includes FORCA, PD, DSCG)
Albanian Alternative or AA
Albanian Democratic League or LDSH
Albanian Forum (electoral coalition includes AA, LDSH, UDSH)
Aleksa and Dritan - Count Bravely! (electoral coalition includes Democrats, URA)
Bosniak Party or BS
Civic Movement United Reform Action or United Reform Action or URA
Croatian Civic Initiative or HGI
Democratic Alliance or DEMOS
Democratic League in Montenegro or DSCG
Democratic Montenegro or Democrats
Democratic Party of Socialists or DPS
Democratic People's Party or DNP
Democratic Union of Albanians or UDSH
Europe Now!
For the Future of Montenegro or ZBCG (coalition includes NSD, DNP, RP)
Liberal Party or LP
New Democratic Power or FORCA
New Serb Democracy or NSD or NOVA
Social Democrats or SD
Socialist People's Party or SNP
Together! (electoral coalition includes DPS, SD, LP, UDSH)
United Montenegro or UCG (split from DEMOS)
Workers' Party or RP

Diplomatic representation in the US: *chief of mission:* Ambassador Jovan MIRKOVIĆ (since 18 September 2024)
chancery: 1610 New Hampshire Avenue NW, Washington, DC, 20009
telephone: [1] (202) 234-6108
FAX: [1] (202) 234-6109
email address and website: usa@mfa.gov.me
United States of America - Embassies and consulates of Montenegro and visa regimes for foreign citizens (www.gov.me)
consulate(s) general: New York

Diplomatic representation from the US: *chief of mission:* Ambassador Judy Rising REINKE (since 20 December 2018)
embassy: Dzona Dzeksona 2, 81000 Podgorica
mailing address: 5570 Podgorica Place, Washington DC 20521-5570
telephone: [382] (0) 20-410-500
FAX: [382] (0) 20-241-358
email address and website: PodgoricaACS@state.gov
https://me.usembassy.gov/

International organization participation: CE, CEI, EAPC, EBRD, FAO, IAEA, IBRD, ICAO, ICC (NGOs), ICCt, ICRM, IDA, IFC, IFRCS, IHO, ILO, IMF, IMO, IMSO, Interpol, IOC, IOM, IPU, ISO (correspondent), ITSO, ITU, ITUC (NGOs), MIGA, NATO, OAS (observer), OIF (observer), OPCW, OSCE, PCA, PFP, SELEC, UN, UNCTAD, UNESCO, UNHCR, UNHRC, UNIDO, UNWTO, UPU, WCO, WHO, WIPO, WMO, WTO
note: Montenegro is an EU candidate country whose satisfactory completion of accession criteria is required before being granted full EU membership

Independence: *3 June 2006 (from the State Union of Serbia and Montenegro); notable earlier dates:* 13 March 1852 (Principality of Montenegro established); 13 July 1878 (Congress of Berlin recognizes Montenegrin independence); 28 August 1910 (Kingdom of Montenegro established)

National holiday: Statehood Day, 13 July (1878, 1941)
note: the holiday celebrates the day in 1878 when the Berlin Congress recognized Montenegro as an independent state, as well as the day in 1941 when the Montenegrins staged an uprising against its occupiers

Flag: *description:* a red field bordered with a narrow golden-yellow stripe; the Montenegrin coat of arms in the center is a double-headed golden eagle, with a

crown above; the eagle holds a golden scepter in its right claw and a blue orb in its left; the eagle's breast shield shows a golden lion on a green field in front of a blue sky
meaning: the eagle symbolizes the unity of church and state; the lion is a symbol of episcopal authority, a reference to the three-and-a-half centuries when Montenegro was ruled as a theocracy

National symbol(s): double-headed eagle

National color(s): red, gold

National anthem(s): *title:* "Oj, svijetla majska zoro" (Oh, Bright Dawn of May)
lyrics/music: Sekula DRLJEVIC/unknown, arranged by Zarko MIKOVIC
history: adopted 2004; music based on a Montenegrin folk song

National heritage: *total World Heritage Sites:* 4 (3 cultural, 1 natural)
selected World Heritage Site locales: Natural and Culturo-Historical Region of Kotor (c); Durmitor National Park (n); Stećci Medieval Tombstones Graveyards (c); Fortified City of Kotor Venetian Defense Works (c)

ECONOMY

Economic overview: upper-middle-income, small Balkan economy; uses euro as de facto currency; reduced growth due to slowdown in tourism and industrial production; new impetus for EU accession under Europe Now government; energy price cap and declining food and services prices easing inflation rate

Real GDP (purchasing power parity): $17.375 billion (2024 est.)
$16.862 billion (2023 est.)
$15.857 billion (2022 est.)
note: data in 2021 dollars
comparison ranking: 157

Real GDP growth rate: 3% (2024 est.)
6.3% (2023 est.)
6.4% (2022 est.)
note: annual GDP % growth based on constant local currency
comparison ranking: 116

Real GDP per capita: $27,900 (2024 est.)
$27,000 (2023 est.)
$25,400 (2022 est.)
note: data in 2021 dollars
comparison ranking: 83

GDP (official exchange rate): $8.07 billion (2024 est.)
note: data in current dollars at official exchange rate

Inflation rate (consumer prices): 3.3% (2024 est.)
8.6% (2023 est.)
13% (2022 est.)
note: annual % change based on consumer prices
comparison ranking: 105

GDP - composition, by sector of origin: *agriculture:* 5.2% (2024 est.)
industry: 11.6% (2024 est.)
services: 62.1% (2024 est.)
note: figures may not total 100% due to non-allocated consumption not captured in sector-reported data
comparison rankings: agriculture 110; industry 176; services 76

GDP - composition, by end use: *household consumption:* 76.3% (2024 est.)
government consumption: 17.9% (2024 est.)
investment in fixed capital: 20.2% (2024 est.)
investment in inventories: 8.3% (2024 est.)
exports of goods and services: 44.9% (2024 est.)
imports of goods and services: -67.5% (2024 est.)
note: figures may not total 100% due to rounding or gaps in data collection

Agricultural products: milk, potatoes, watermelons, grapes, sheep milk, cabbages, oranges, eggs, goat milk, figs (2023)
note: top ten agricultural products based on tonnage

Industries: steelmaking, aluminum, agricultural processing, consumer goods, tourism

Industrial production growth rate: -1.7% (2024 est.)
note: annual % change in industrial value added based on constant local currency
comparison ranking: 158

Labor force: 245,300 (2024 est.)
note: number of people ages 15 or older who are employed or seeking work
comparison ranking: 173

Unemployment rate: 14.1% (2024 est.)
14.7% (2023 est.)
14.9% (2022 est.)
note: % of labor force seeking employment
comparison ranking: 171

Youth unemployment rate (ages 15-24): *total:* 25.9% (2024 est.)
male: 27.5% (2024 est.)
female: 23.6% (2024 est.)
note: % of labor force ages 15-24 seeking employment
comparison ranking: total 32

Population below poverty line: 20.3% (2021 est.)
note: % of population with income below national poverty line

Gini Index coefficient - distribution of family income: 34.3 (2021 est.)
note: index (0-100) of income distribution; higher values represent greater inequality
comparison ranking: 82

Average household expenditures: *on food:* 24.8% of household expenditures (2022 est.)
on alcohol and tobacco: 5.6% of household expenditures (2022 est.)

Household income or consumption by percentage share: *lowest 10%:* 2.1% (2021 est.)
highest 10%: 24.7% (2021 est.)
note: % share of income accruing to lowest and highest 10% of population

Remittances: 10.6% of GDP (2024 est.)
10.7% of GDP (2023 est.)
13.3% of GDP (2022 est.)
note: personal transfers and compensation between resident and non-resident individuals/households/entities

Budget: *revenues:* $1.463 billion (2015 est.)
expenditures: $1.491 billion (2015 est.)
note: central government revenues and expenses (excluding grants/extrabudgetary units/social security funds) converted to US dollars at average official exchange rate for year indicated

Public debt: 67.2% of GDP (2017 est.)
note: data cover general government debt, and includes debt instruments issued (or owned) by government entities other than the treasury; the data include treasury debt held by foreign entities; the data include debt issued by subnational entities, as well as intragovernmental debt; intragovernmental debt consists of treasury borrowings from surpluses in the social funds, such as for retirement, medical care, and unemployment; debt instruments for the social funds are not sold at public auctions
comparison ranking: 62

Current account balance: -$1.406 billion (2024 est.)
-$851.525 million (2023 est.)
-$817.858 million (2022 est.)
note: balance of payments - net trade and primary/secondary income in current dollars
comparison ranking: 138

Exports: $3.629 billion (2024 est.)
$3.769 billion (2023 est.)
$3.177 billion (2022 est.)
note: balance of payments - exports of goods and services in current dollars
comparison ranking: 149

Exports - partners: Italy 38%, Serbia 13%, Spain 6%, Slovenia 5%, Bosnia & Herzegovina 4% (2023)
note: top five export partners based on percentage share of exports

Exports - commodities: electricity, aluminum, copper ore, aluminum ore, packaged medicine (2023)
note: top five export commodities based on value in dollars

Imports: $5.478 billion (2024 est.)
$5.167 billion (2023 est.)
$4.614 billion (2022 est.)
note: balance of payments - imports of goods and services in current dollars
comparison ranking: 148

Imports - partners: Serbia 21%, China 10%, Germany 8%, Croatia 6%, Italy 6% (2023)
note: top five import partners based on percentage share of imports

Imports - commodities: refined petroleum, cars, electricity, packaged medicine, aluminum (2023)
note: top five import commodities based on value in dollars

Reserves of foreign exchange and gold: $1.741 billion (2024 est.)
$1.574 billion (2023 est.)
$2.041 billion (2022 est.)
note: holdings of gold (year-end prices)/foreign exchange/special drawing rights in current dollars
comparison ranking: 130

Debt - external: $3.643 billion (2023 est.)
note: present value of external debt in current US dollars
comparison ranking: 79

Exchange rates: euros (EUR) per US dollar -

Exchange rates: 0.924 (2024 est.)
0.925 (2023 est.)
0.951 (2022 est.)
0.845 (2021 est.)
0.877 (2020 est.)
note: Montenegro, which is neither an EU member state nor a party to a formal EU monetary agreement, uses the euro as its de facto currency

ENERGY

Electricity access: *electrification - total population:* 100% (2022 est.)

Electricity: *installed generating capacity:* 1.082 million kW (2023 est.)
consumption: 2.719 billion kWh (2023 est.)
exports: 6.288 billion kWh (2023 est.)
imports: 5.421 billion kWh (2023 est.)
transmission/distribution losses: 601.023 million kWh (2023 est.)

comparison rankings: installed generating capacity 133; consumption 146; exports 36; imports 42; transmission/distribution losses 85

Electricity generation sources: *fossil fuels:* 39.1% of total installed capacity (2023 est.)
solar: 0.4% of total installed capacity (2023 est.)
wind: 7.5% of total installed capacity (2023 est.)
hydroelectricity: 53% of total installed capacity (2023 est.)

Coal: *production:* 1.862 million metric tons (2023 est.)
consumption: 1.658 million metric tons (2023 est.)
exports: 205,000 metric tons (2023 est.)
imports: 2.8 metric tons (2022 est.)
proven reserves: 337 million metric tons (2023 est.)

Petroleum: *refined petroleum consumption:* 9,000 bbl/day (2023 est.)

Energy consumption per capita: 63.407 million Btu/person (2023 est.)
comparison ranking: 80

COMMUNICATIONS

Telephones - fixed lines: *total subscriptions:* 190,000 (2023 est.)
subscriptions per 100 inhabitants: 30 (2023 est.)
comparison ranking: total subscriptions 119

Telephones - mobile cellular: *total subscriptions:* 1.31 million (2023 est.)
subscriptions per 100 inhabitants: 203 (2022 est.)
comparison ranking: total subscriptions 162

Broadcast media: state-funded national radio and TV broadcaster operates 2 terrestrial TV networks, 1 satellite TV channel, and 2 radio networks; 4 local public TV stations and 14 private TV stations; 14 local public radio stations, 35 private radio stations, and several online media (2019)

Internet country code: .me

Internet users: *percent of population:* 90% (2023 est.)

Broadband - fixed subscriptions: *total:* 203,000 (2023 est.)
subscriptions per 100 inhabitants: 32 (2023 est.)
comparison ranking: total 122

TRANSPORTATION

Civil aircraft registration country code prefix: 4O

Airports: 5 (2025)
comparison ranking: 178

Heliports: 1 (2025)
comparison ranking: 162

Railways: *total:* 250 km (2017)
standard gauge: 250 km (2017) 1.435-m gauge (224 km electrified)

Merchant marine: *total:* 18 (2023)
by type: bulk carrier 4, other 14
comparison ranking: total 148

Ports: *total ports:* 4 (2024)
large: 0
medium: 0
small: 1
very small: 3
ports with oil terminals: 1
key ports: Bar, Kotor, Risan, Tivat

MILITARY AND SECURITY

Military and security forces: Army of Montenegro (Vojska Crne Gore or VCG): Ground Forces, Air Force, Navy

Ministry of Interior: Police Directorate of Montenegro (2025)

Military expenditures: 2% of GDP (2025 est.)
1.7% of GDP (2024 est.)
1.5% of GDP (2023 est.)
1.4% of GDP (2022 est.)
1.6% of GDP (2021 est.)

Military and security service personnel strengths: approximately 2,000 active-duty military personnel (2025)

Military equipment inventories and acquisitions: the military's inventory is small and consists largely of Soviet-era equipment inherited from the former Yugoslavia military, along with a limited but growing mix of imported Western systems (2024)

Military service age and obligation: 18 is the legal minimum age for voluntary military service; conscription abolished in 2006 (2024)
note: as of 2024, women made up over 11% of the military's full-time personnel

Military - note: the Army of Montenegro is responsible for the defense of Montenegro's sovereignty and territorial integrity, cooperating in international and multinational security, and assisting civil authorities during emergencies such as natural disasters; since Montenegro joined NATO in 2017, another focus has been integrating into the Alliance, including adapting NATO standards for planning and professionalization, structural reforms, and modernization by replacing its Soviet-era equipment; the Army trains and exercises with NATO partners and actively supports NATO missions and operations, committing small numbers of troops in Afghanistan, Kosovo, and NATO's Enhanced Forward Presence mission in Eastern Europe; a few personnel have also been deployed on EU- and UN-led operations (2025)

TRANSNATIONAL ISSUES

Refugees and internally displaced persons: *refugees:* 18,820 (2024 est.)
stateless persons: 423 (2024 est.)

MONTSERRAT

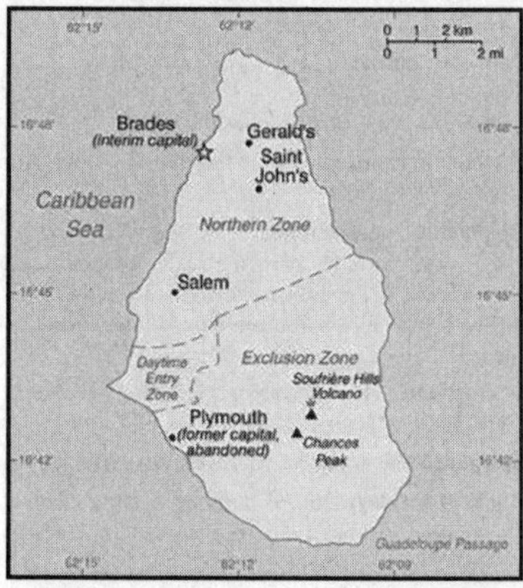

INTRODUCTION

Background: English and Irish colonists from St. Kitts first settled on Montserrat in 1632; the first African slaves arrived three decades later. The British and French fought for possession of the island for most of the 18th century, but it finally was confirmed as a British possession in 1783. The island's sugar plantation economy was converted to small farm landholdings in the mid-19th century. The Soufriere Hills Volcano erupted in 1995, devastating much of the island; two thirds of the population fled abroad. Montserrat has endured volcanic activity since, with the last eruption occurring in 2013.

GEOGRAPHY

Location: Caribbean, island in the Caribbean Sea, southeast of Puerto Rico

Geographic coordinates: 16 45 N, 62 12 W

Map references: Central America and the Caribbean

Area: *total:* 102 sq km
land: 102 sq km
water: 0 sq km
comparison ranking: total 224

Area - comparative: about 0.6 times the size of Washington, D.C.

Land boundaries: *total:* 0 km

Coastline: 40 km

Maritime claims: *territorial sea:* 12 nm
exclusive fishing zone: 200 nm

Climate: tropical; little daily or seasonal temperature variation

Terrain: volcanic island, mostly mountainous, with small coastal lowland

Elevation: *highest point:* Soufriere Hills volcano pre-eruption height was 915 m; current lava dome is subject to periodic build up and collapse; estimated dome height was 1,050 m in 2015
lowest point: Caribbean Sea 0 m

Natural resources: NEGL

Land use: *agricultural land:* 30% (2022 est.)
arable land: 20% (2022 est.)
permanent crops: 0% (2022 est.)
permanent pasture: 10% (2022 est.)
forest: 25% (2022 est.)
other: 45% (2022 est.)

Irrigated land: 0 sq km (2022)

Population distribution: only the northern half of the island is populated; the southern portion is uninhabitable due to volcanic activity

Natural hazards: volcanic eruptions; severe hurricanes (June to November)

volcanism: Soufrière Hills volcano (915 m) has erupted continuously since 1995; a massive eruption in 1997 destroyed most of the capital, Plymouth, and made about half of the island uninhabitable; the island of Montserrat is part of the volcanic island arc of the Lesser Antilles that extends from Saba in the north to Grenada in the south

Geography - note: the island is entirely volcanic in origin and composed of three major volcanic centers of differing ages

PEOPLE AND SOCIETY

Population: *total:* 5,468 (2024 est.)
male: 2,728
female: 2,740
comparison rankings: total 226; male 226; female 226

Nationality: *noun:* Montserratian(s)
adjective: Montserratian

Ethnic groups: African/Black 86.2%, mixed 4.8%, Hispanic/Spanish 3%, Caucasian/White 2.7%, East Indian/Indian 1.6%, other 1.8% (2018 est.)

Languages: English

Religions: Protestant 71.4% (includes Anglican 17.7%, Pentecostal/Full Gospel 16.1%, Seventh Day Adventist 15%, Methodist 13.9%, Church of God 6.7%, other Protestant 2%), Roman Catholic 11.4%, Rastafarian 1.4%, Hindu 1.2%, Jehovah's Witness 1%, Muslim 0.4%, other/not stated 5.1%, none 7.9% (2018 est.)

Age structure: *0-14 years:* 15.8% (male 446/female 420)
15-64 years: 76.1% (male 2,062/female 2,101)
65 years and over: 8% (2024 est.) (male 220/female 219)

Dependency ratios: *total dependency ratio:* 31.3 (2024 est.)
youth dependency ratio: 20.8 (2024 est.)
elderly dependency ratio: 10.5 (2024 est.)
potential support ratio: 9.5 (2024 est.)

Median age: *total:* 36.8 years (2024 est.)
male: 35.4 years
female: 37.8 years
comparison ranking: total 87

Population growth rate: 0.59% (2024 est.)
comparison ranking: 141

Birth rate: 11.9 births/1,000 population (2024 est.)
comparison ranking: 149

Death rate: 6 deaths/1,000 population (2024 est.)
comparison ranking: 156

Net migration rate: 0 migrant(s)/1,000 population (2024 est.)
comparison ranking: 83

Population distribution: only the northern half of the island is populated; the southern portion is uninhabitable due to volcanic activity

Urbanization: *urban population:* 9.3% of total population (2023)
rate of urbanization: 0.94% annual rate of change (2020-25 est.)

Sex ratio: *at birth:* 1.03 male(s)/female
0-14 years: 1.06 male(s)/female
15-64 years: 0.98 male(s)/female
65 years and over: 1 male(s)/female
total population: 1 male(s)/female (2024 est.)

Infant mortality rate: *total:* 9.7 deaths/1,000 live births (2024 est.)
male: 8 deaths/1,000 live births
female: 11.6 deaths/1,000 live births
comparison ranking: total 134

Life expectancy at birth: *total population:* 76.1 years (2024 est.)
male: 76.9 years
female: 75.3 years
comparison ranking: total population 116

Total fertility rate: 1.33 children born/woman (2024 est.)
comparison ranking: 216

Gross reproduction rate: 0.63 (2024 est.)

Drinking water source: *improved:* total: 98.1% of population (2022 est.)
unimproved: total: 1.9% of population (2022 est.)

Sanitation facility access: *improved:* total: 99.6% of population (2022 est.)
unimproved: total: 0.4% of population (2022 est.)

Currently married women (ages 15-49): 35.8% (2023 est.)

Education expenditure: 7.2% of GDP (2023 est.)
7.7% national budget (2024 est.)
comparison ranking: Education expenditure (% GDP) 15

ENVIRONMENT

Environmental issues: land erosion on slopes that have been cleared for cultivation

Climate: tropical; little daily or seasonal temperature variation

Urbanization: *urban population:* 9.3% of total population (2023)
rate of urbanization: 0.94% annual rate of change (2020-25 est.)

Carbon dioxide emissions: 24,000 metric tonnes of CO2 (2023 est.)
from petroleum and other liquids: 24,000 metric tonnes of CO2 (2023 est.)
comparison ranking: total emissions 213

GOVERNMENT

Country name: *conventional long form:* none
conventional short form: Montserrat
etymology: explorer Christopher COLUMBUS named the island in 1493 after the Benedictine abbey Santa Maria de Montserrat, near Barcelona, Spain

Government type: parliamentary democracy; self-governing overseas territory of the UK

Dependency status: overseas territory of the UK

Capital: *name:* Plymouth
geographic coordinates: 16 42 N, 62 13 W
time difference: UTC-4 (1 hour ahead of Washington, DC, during Standard Time)
etymology: now entirely deserted because of volcanic activity, the city was named after Plymouth, England
note: Plymouth was abandoned in 1997 because of volcanic activity; interim government buildings have been built at Brades Estate, the de facto capital, at the northwest end of Montserrat

Administrative divisions: 3 parishes; Saint Anthony, Saint Georges, Saint Peter

Legal system: English common law

Constitution: *history:* previous 1960; latest put into force 20 October 2010 (The Montserrat Constitution Order 2010)

Citizenship: see United Kingdom

Suffrage: 18 years of age; universal

Executive branch: *chief of state:* King CHARLES III (since 8 September 2022); represented by Governor Sarah TUCKER (since 6 April 2023)
head of government: Premier Easton TAYLOR-FARRELL (since 19 November 2019)
cabinet: Executive Council consists of the governor, the premier, 3 other ministers, the attorney general, and the finance secretary
election/appointment process: the monarchy is hereditary; governor appointed by the monarch; following legislative elections, the leader of the majority party usually becomes premier

Legislative branch: *legislature name:* Legislative Assembly
legislative structure: unicameral
number of seats: 12 (directly elected)
electoral system: plurality/majority
scope of elections: full renewal
term in office: 5 years
most recent election date: 11/18/2019
parties elected and seats per party: MCAP (5); PDM (3); independent (1)
percentage of women in chamber: 33.3%
expected date of next election: 2024
note: the Assembly elects the speaker from the outside for a 5-year term; the Assembly includes 2 ex-officio members, the attorney general and the financial secretary

Judicial branch: *highest court(s):* the Eastern Caribbean Supreme Court (ECSC) is the superior court of the Organization of Eastern Caribbean States; the ECSC is headquartered on St. Lucia and consists of the Court of Appeal – headed by the chief justice and 4 judges – and the High Court with 18 judges; the Court of Appeal travels to member states on a schedule to hear appeals from the High Court and subordinate courts; Montserrat is a member of the Caribbean Court of Justice
judge selection and term of office: chief justice of Eastern Caribbean Supreme Court appointed by the British monarch; other justices and judges appointed by the Judicial and Legal Services Commission, and independent body of judicial officials; Court of Appeal justices appointed for life with mandatory retirement at age 65; High Court judges appointed for life with mandatory retirement at age 62
subordinate courts: magistrate's court

Political parties: Movement for Change and Prosperity or MCAP
People's Democratic Movement or PDM

Diplomatic representation in the US: none (overseas territory of the UK)

Diplomatic representation from the US: *embassy:* none (overseas territory of the UK); alternate contact is the US Embassy in Barbados [1] (246) 227-4000; US Embassy Bridgetown, Wildey Business Park, St. Michael BB 14006, Barbados, WI

International organization participation: Caricom, CDB, Interpol (subbureau), OECS, UPU

Independence: none (overseas territory of the UK)

National holiday: Official birthday of King Charles III, usually celebrated the second Saturday in June (1948)

Flag: *description:* blue with the UK flag in the upper-left quadrant and the Montserratian coat of arms centered in the right half of the flag; the arms show a woman in a green dress standing beside a yellow harp and embracing a large, dark-brown cross with her right arm *meaning:* the woman is Erin, the female personification of Ireland, the harp is an Irish symbol, and the cross represents the Christian faith; blue stands for awareness, trustworthiness, determination, and righteousness

National coat of arms: Montserrat's coat of arms dates back to 1909 and reflects the country's Irish settlers, who first arrived in 1632; the woman in the green dress is Erin, the personification of Ireland, and she holds Ireland's symbol, a gold harp; the cross represents Christianity, Monserrat's predominant religion

National anthem(s): *title:* "Motherland"
lyrics/music: Howard FERGUS/George IRISH
history: adopted 2013; used as a local anthem and for sporting events and local ceremonies
title: "God Save the King"
lyrics/music: unknown
history: official anthem, as a UK territory

ECONOMY

Economic overview: formerly high-income economy; volcanic activity destroyed much of original infrastructure and economy; new capital and port is being developed; key geothermal and solar power generation; key music recording operations

Real GDP (purchasing power parity): $89.254 million (2024 est.)
$86.875 million (2023 est.)
$80.972 million (2022 est.)
note: data in 2015 dollars
comparison ranking: 218

Real GDP per capita: $19,300 (2024 est.)
$18,200 (2023 est.)
$16,200 (2022 est.)
note: data in 2015 dollars
comparison ranking: 105

GDP (official exchange rate): $84.537 million (2024 est.)
note: data in current dollars at official exchange rate

Inflation rate (consumer prices): 4% (2022 est.)
1.7% (2021 est.)
-1.9% (2020 est.)
note: annual % change based on consumer prices
comparison ranking: 125

GDP - composition, by end use: *household consumption:* 90.8% (2017 est.)
government consumption: 50.4% (2017 est.)
investment in fixed capital: 17.9% (2017 est.)
investment in inventories: -0.1% (2017 est.)
exports of goods and services: 29.5% (2017 est.)
imports of goods and services: -88.6% (2017 est.)

Agricultural products: cabbages, carrots, cucumbers, tomatoes, onions, peppers; livestock products

Industries: tourism, rum, textiles, electronic appliances

Budget: *revenues:* $55.651 million (2014 est.)
expenditures: $43.652 million (2014 est.)
note: central government revenues and expenses (excluding grants/extrabudgetary units/social security funds) converted to US dollars at average official exchange rate for year indicated

Exports - partners: USA 25%, Antigua & Barbuda 13%, Guyana 13%, Egypt 12%, France 10% (2023)
note: top five export partners based on percentage share of exports

Exports - commodities: gravel and crushed stone, sand (2023)
note: top export commodities based on value in dollars over $500,000

Imports: $15.3 million (2021 est.)
$39.44 million (2017 est.)
$36.1 million (2016 est.)
comparison ranking: 212

Imports - partners: USA 62%, Antigua & Barbuda 6%, UK 5%, Belgium 4%, Trinidad & Tobago 3% (2023)
note: top five import partners based on percentage share of imports

Imports - commodities: refined petroleum, electric generating sets, cars, stone processing machines, x-ray equipment (2023)
note: top five import commodities based on value in dollars

Exchange rates: East Caribbean dollars (XCD) per US dollar -

Exchange rates: 2.7 (2024 est.)
2.7 (2023 est.)
2.7 (2022 est.)
2.7 (2021 est.)
2.7 (2020 est.)

ENERGY

Electricity access: *electrification - total population:* 100% (2020)

Electricity: *installed generating capacity:* 6,000 kW (2023 est.)
consumption: 15.968 million kWh (2023 est.)
transmission/distribution losses: 370,000 kWh (2023 est.)
comparison rankings: installed generating capacity 209; consumption 209; transmission/distribution losses 1

Electricity generation sources: *fossil fuels:* 87.8% of total installed capacity (2023 est.)
solar: 12.2% of total installed capacity (2023 est.)

Petroleum: *refined petroleum consumption:* 200 bbl/day (2023 est.)

COMMUNICATIONS

Telephones - fixed lines: *total subscriptions:* 3,000 (2020 est.)
subscriptions per 100 inhabitants: 67 (2020 est.)
comparison ranking: total subscriptions 210

Telephones - mobile cellular: *total subscriptions:* 5,000 (2020 est.)
subscriptions per 100 inhabitants: 110 (2020 est.)
comparison ranking: total subscriptions 222

Broadcast media: Radio Montserrat, a public radio broadcaster, transmits on 1 station and has a repeater transmission to a second station; repeater transmissions from the GEM Radio Network of Trinidad and Tobago provide another 2 radio stations; cable and satellite TV available (2007)

Internet country code: .ms

Internet users: *percent of population:* 54.6% (2011 est.)

Broadband - fixed subscriptions: *total:* 2,700 (2018 est.)
subscriptions per 100 inhabitants: 55 (2018 est.)
comparison ranking: total 201

TRANSPORTATION

Civil aircraft registration country code prefix: VP-M

Airports: 1 (2025)
comparison ranking: 218

MILITARY AND SECURITY

Military and security forces: no regular military forces; Royal Montserrat Defense Force (ceremonial, civil defense duties), Montserrat Police Force (2025)

Military - note: defense is the responsibility of the UK

MOROCCO

INTRODUCTION

Background: In 788, about a century after the Arab conquest of North Africa, a series of Muslim dynasties began to rule in Morocco. In the 16th century, the Sa'adi monarchy, particularly under Ahmad al-MANSUR (1578-1603), repelled foreign invaders and inaugurated a golden age. The Alaouite Dynasty, to which the current Moroccan royal family belongs, dates from the 17th century. In 1860, Spain occupied northern Morocco and ushered in a half-century of trade rivalry among European powers that saw Morocco's sovereignty steadily erode; in 1912, the French imposed a protectorate over the country. A protracted independence struggle with France ended successfully in 1956. The internationalized city of Tangier and most Spanish possessions were turned over to the new country that same year. Sultan MOHAMMED V, the current monarch's grandfather, organized the new state as a constitutional monarchy and in 1957 assumed the title of king.

Since Spain's 1976 withdrawal from Western Sahara, Morocco has extended its de facto administrative control to roughly 75% of this territory; however, the UN does not recognize Morocco as the administering power for Western Sahara. The UN since 1991 has monitored a cease-fire, which broke down in late 2020, between Morocco and the Polisario Front – an organization advocating the territory's independence – and restarted negotiations over the status of the territory in 2018. In 2020, the US recognized Morocco's sovereignty over all of Western Sahara.

In 2011, King MOHAMMED VI responded to the spread of pro-democracy protests in the North Africa region by implementing a reform program that included a new constitution, passed by popular referendum, under which some new powers were extended to parliament and the prime minister, but ultimate authority remains in the hands of the monarch. Later that year, the Justice and Development Party (PJD) – a moderate Islamist democratic party – won

the largest number of seats in parliamentary elections, becoming the first Islamist party to lead the Moroccan Government. In 2015, Morocco held its first direct elections for regional councils, which was one of the reforms included in the 2011 constitution. The PJD again won the largest number of seats in nationwide parliamentary elections in 2016, but it lost its plurality to the probusiness National Rally of Independents (RNI) in 2021. In 2020, Morocco signed a normalization agreement with Israel, similar to those that Bahrain, the United Arab Emirates, and Sudan had concluded with Israel earlier that year.

GEOGRAPHY

Location: Northern Africa, bordering the North Atlantic Ocean and the Mediterranean Sea, between Algeria and Mauritania

Geographic coordinates: 28 30 N, 10 00 W

Map references: Africa

Area: *total:* 716,550 sq km
land: 716,300 sq km
water: 250 sq km
comparison ranking: total 41

Area - comparative: slightly larger than twice the size of California

Land boundaries: *total:* 3,523.5 km
border countries (3): Algeria 1,941 km; Mauritania 1,564 km; Spain (Ceuta) 8 km and Spain (Melilla) 10.5 km
note: an additional 75-meter border segment exists between Morocco and the Spanish exclave of Penon de Velez de la Gomera

Coastline: 2,945 km

Maritime claims: *territorial sea:* 12 nm
contiguous zone: 24 nm
exclusive economic zone: 200 nm
continental shelf: 200-m depth or to the depth of exploitation

Climate: Mediterranean in the north, becoming more extreme in the interior; in the south, hot, dry desert; rain is rare; cold offshore air currents produce fog and heavy dew
note: data does not include former Western Sahara

Terrain: mountainous northern coast (Rif Mountains) and interior (Atlas Mountains) bordered by large plateaus with intermontane valleys, and fertile coastal plains; the south is mostly low, flat desert with large areas of rocky or sandy surfaces

Elevation: *highest point:* Jebel Toubkal 4,165 m
lowest point: Sebkha Tah -59 m
mean elevation: 909 m

Natural resources: phosphates, iron ore, manganese, lead, zinc, fish, salt

Land use: *agricultural land:* 67.9% (2022 est.)
arable land: 16.8% (2022 est.)
permanent crops: 4% (2022 est.)
permanent pasture: 47.1% (2022 est.)
forest: 12.9% (2022 est.)
other: 19.2% (2022 est.)
note: does not include the area of the former Western Sahara, which is almost exclusively desert

Irrigated land: 17,645 sq km (2019)

Major rivers (by length in km): Draa - 1,100 km

Population distribution: the highest population density is found along the Atlantic and Mediterranean coasts; a number of densely populated agglomerations are scattered through the Atlas Mountains, as shown in this population distribution map

Natural hazards: in the north, the mountains are geologically unstable and subject to earthquakes; periodic droughts; windstorms; flash floods; landslides; in the south, a hot, dry, dust/sand-laden sirocco wind can occur during winter and spring; widespread harmattan haze exists 60% of time, often severely restricting visibility

Geography - note: strategic location along Strait of Gibraltar; the only African nation to have both Atlantic and Mediterranean coastlines; the waters off the Atlantic coast are particularly rich fishing areas

PEOPLE AND SOCIETY

Population: *total:* 37,387,585 (2024 est.)
male: 18,664,263
female: 18,723,322
comparison rankings: total 39; male 39; female 40

Nationality: *noun:* Moroccan(s)
adjective: Moroccan

Ethnic groups: Arab-Amazigh 99%, other 1%
note: does not include data from the former Western Sahara

Languages: Arabic (official), Tamazight languages (Tamazight (official), Tachelhit, Tarifit), French (often the language of business, government, and diplomacy)
major-language sample(s):
احسن مصدر متاع المعلومات الأساسية
كتاب ديال لحقائق متاع العالم،
(Arabic)
note: the proportion of Tamazight speakers is disputed

Religions: Muslim 99% (official; virtually all Sunni, <0.1% Shia), other 1% (includes Christian, Jewish, and Baha'i); note - Jewish about 3,000-3,500 (2020 est.)
note: does not include data from the former Western Sahara

Age structure: *0-14 years:* 25.7% (male 4,898,154/female 4,701,786)
15-64 years: 65.9% (male 12,236,752/female 12,410,567)
65 years and over: 8.4% (2024 est.) (male 1,529,357/female 1,610,969)

Dependency ratios: *total dependency ratio:* 51.7 (2024 est.)
youth dependency ratio: 38.9 (2024 est.)
elderly dependency ratio: 12.7 (2024 est.)
potential support ratio: 7.8 (2024 est.)

Median age: *total:* 30.6 years (2024 est.)
male: 30.1 years
female: 31 years
comparison ranking: total 135

Population growth rate: 0.84% (2024 est.)
comparison ranking: 108

Birth rate: 16.8 births/1,000 population (2024 est.)
comparison ranking: 92

Death rate: 6.6 deaths/1,000 population (2024 est.)
comparison ranking: 131

Net migration rate: -1.7 migrant(s)/1,000 population (2024 est.)
comparison ranking: 163

Population distribution: the highest population density is found along the Atlantic and Mediterranean coasts; a number of densely populated agglomerations are scattered through the Atlas Mountains, as shown in this population distribution map

Urbanization: *urban population:* 65.1% of total population (2023)
rate of urbanization: 1.88% annual rate of change (2020-25 est.)
note: data does not include former Western Sahara

Major urban areas - population: 3.893 million Casablanca, 1.959 million RABAT (capital), 1.290 million Fes, 1.314 million Tangier, 1.050 million Marrakech, 979,000 Agadir (2023)

Sex ratio: *at birth:* 1.05 male(s)/female
0-14 years: 1.04 male(s)/female
15-64 years: 0.99 male(s)/female
65 years and over: 0.95 male(s)/female
total population: 1 male(s)/female (2024 est.)

Maternal mortality ratio: 70 deaths/100,000 live births (2023 est.)
comparison ranking: 79

Infant mortality rate: *total:* 18.3 deaths/1,000 live births (2024 est.)
male: 20.4 deaths/1,000 live births
female: 16 deaths/1,000 live births
comparison ranking: total 84

Life expectancy at birth: *total population:* 74.2 years (2024 est.)
male: 72.5 years
female: 76 years
comparison ranking: total population 145

Total fertility rate: 2.25 children born/woman (2024 est.)
comparison ranking: 80

Gross reproduction rate: 1.1 (2024 est.)

Drinking water source: *improved: urban:* 98.8% of population (2022 est.)
rural: 65.6% of population (2022 est.)
total: 87% of population (2022 est.)
unimproved: urban: 1.2% of population (2022 est.)
rural: 34.4% of population (2022 est.)
total: 13% of population (2022 est.)

Health expenditure: 5.7% of GDP (2021)
6.8% of national budget (2022 est.)

Physician density: 0.74 physicians/1,000 population (2021)

Hospital bed density: 0.7 beds/1,000 population (2020 est.)
note: does not include data from the former Western Sahara

Sanitation facility access: *improved: urban:* 98.2% of population (2022 est.)

rural: 72.4% of population (2022 est.)
total: 89.1% of population (2022 est.)
unimproved: urban: 1.8% of population (2022 est.)
rural: 27.6% of population (2022 est.)
total: 10.9% of population (2022 est.)

Obesity - adult prevalence rate: 26.1% (2016)
note: does not include data from the former Western Sahara
comparison ranking: 44

Alcohol consumption per capita: *total:* 0.51 liters of pure alcohol (2019 est.)
beer: 0.18 liters of pure alcohol (2019 est.)
wine: 0.24 liters of pure alcohol (2019 est.)
spirits: 0.09 liters of pure alcohol (2019 est.)
other alcohols: 0 liters of pure alcohol (2019 est.)
comparison ranking: total 163

Tobacco use: *total:* 12.3% (2025 est.)
male: 23.7% (2025 est.)
female: 0.9% (2025 est.)
comparison ranking: total 111

Children under the age of 5 years underweight: 2.8% (2019/20)
comparison ranking: 84

Currently married women (ages 15-49): 58.8% (2023 est.)

Child marriage: *women married by age 15:* 0.5% (2018)
women married by age 18: 13.7% (2018)

Education expenditure: 6% of GDP (2023 est.)
23.3% national budget (2024 est.)
comparison ranking: Education expenditure (% GDP) 32

School life expectancy (primary to tertiary education): *total:* 15 years (2023 est.)
male: 15 years (2023 est.)
female: 15 years (2023 est.)

ENVIRONMENT

Environmental issues: *in the north:* land degradation and desertification, with soil erosion from farming, overgrazing, and vegetation removal; water and soil pollution from industrial-waste dumping; in the south: desertification; overgrazing; sparse water
note: data does not include former Western Sahara

International environmental agreements: *party to:* Biodiversity, Climate Change, Climate Change-Kyoto Protocol, Climate Change-Paris Agreement, Comprehensive Nuclear Test Ban, Desertification, Endangered Species, Hazardous Wastes, Law of the Sea, Marine Dumping-London Convention, Marine Dumping-London Protocol, Nuclear Test Ban, Ozone Layer Protection, Ship Pollution, Wetlands, Whaling
signed, but not ratified: Environmental Modification

Climate: Mediterranean in the north, becoming more extreme in the interior; in the south, hot, dry desert; rain is rare; cold offshore air currents produce fog and heavy dew
note: data does not include former Western Sahara
note: does not include the area of the former Western Sahara, which is almost exclusively desert

Urbanization: *urban population:* 65.1% of total population (2023)
rate of urbanization: 1.88% annual rate of change (2020-25 est.)
note: data does not include former Western Sahara

Carbon dioxide emissions: 64.173 million metric tonnes of CO2 (2023 est.)
from coal and metallurgical coke: 23.024 million metric tonnes of CO2 (2023 est.)
from petroleum and other liquids: 39.329 million metric tonnes of CO2 (2023 est.)
from consumed natural gas: 1.82 million metric tonnes of CO2 (2023 est.)
comparison ranking: total emissions 50

Particulate matter emissions: 13.2 micrograms per cubic meter (2019 est.)

Methane emissions: *energy:* 36.6 kt (2022-2024 est.)
agriculture: 283.7 kt (2019-2021 est.)
waste: 377.5 kt (2019-2021 est.)
other: 4.5 kt (2019-2021 est.)

Waste and recycling: *municipal solid waste generated annually:* 6.852 million tons (2024 est.)
percent of municipal solid waste recycled: 25.4% (2022 est.)
note: data does not include former Western Sahara

Total water withdrawal: *municipal:* 1.063 billion cubic meters (2022 est.)
industrial: 212 million cubic meters (2022 est.)
agricultural: 9.156 billion cubic meters (2022 est.)
note: data does not include former Western Sahara

Total renewable water resources: 29 billion cubic meters (2022 est.)
note: data does not include former Western Sahara

Geoparks: *total global geoparks and regional networks:* 1
global geoparks and regional networks: M'Goun (2023)

GOVERNMENT

Country name: *conventional long form:* Kingdom of Morocco
conventional short form: Morocco
local long form: Al Mamlakah al Maghribiyah
local short form: Al Maghrib
former: French Protectorate in Morocco, Spanish Protectorate in Morocco, Ifni, Spanish Sahara, Western Sahara
etymology: the English name of Morocco derives from, respectively, the Spanish and Portuguese names Marruecos and Marrocos, which stem from Marrakesh, the Latin name for the former capital of ancient Morocco; the Arabic name, Al Maghrib, translates as "The West"

Government type: parliamentary constitutional monarchy

Capital: *name:* Rabat
geographic coordinates: 34 01 N, 6 49 W
time difference: UTC+1 (6 hours ahead of Washington, DC, during Standard Time)
etymology: derives from the Arabic name Ribat el-Fath, from the words *ribat* (fortified monastery) and *fath* (conquest); the third Almohad sultan, Abu Yusuf Yaqub al-Manşur, gave the name to a fort on the site in the 12th century

Administrative divisions: 12 regions; Beni Mellal-Khenifra, Casablanca-Settat, Dakhla-Oued Ed-Dahab, Draa-Tafilalet, Fes-Meknes, Guelmim-Oued Noun, Laayoune-Sakia El Hamra, Marrakech-Safi, Oriental, Rabat-Sale-Kenitra, Souss-Massa, Tanger-Tetouan-Al Hoceima
note: effective 10 December 2020, the US government recognizes Morocco's sovereignty over the territory of former Western Sahara

Legal system: mixed system of civil law based on French civil law and Islamic (sharia) law; Constitutional Court reviews legislative acts

Constitution: *history:* several previous; latest drafted 17 June 2011, approved by referendum 1 July 2011
amendment process: proposed by the king, by the prime minister, or by members in either chamber of Parliament; passage requires at least two-thirds majority vote by both chambers and approval in a referendum; the king can opt to submit self-initiated proposals directly to a referendum

International law organization participation: has not submitted an ICJ jurisdiction declaration; non-party state to the ICCt

Citizenship: *citizenship by birth:* no
citizenship by descent only: the father must be a citizen of Morocco; if the father is unknown or stateless, the mother must be a citizen
dual citizenship recognized: yes
residency requirement for naturalization: 5 years

Suffrage: 18 years of age; universal

Executive branch: *chief of state:* King MOHAMMED VI (since 30 July 1999)
head of government: Prime Minister Aziz AKHANNOUCH (since 7 October 2021)
cabinet: Council of Ministers chosen by the prime minister in consultation with Parliament and appointed by the monarch; the monarch chooses the ministers of Interior, Foreign Affairs, Islamic Affairs, and National Defense Administration
election/appointment process: the monarchy is hereditary; monarch appoints the prime minister from the majority party following legislative elections

Legislative branch: *legislature name:* Parliament (Barlaman)
legislative structure: bicameral

Legislative branch - lower chamber: *chamber name:* House of Representatives (Majliss-annouwab)
number of seats: 395 (all directly elected)
electoral system: proportional representation
scope of elections: full renewal
term in office: 5 years
most recent election date: 9/8/2021
parties elected and seats per party: National Rally of Independents (RNI) (102); Authenticity and Modernity Party (PAM) (87); Istiqlal Party (PI) (81); Socialist Union of Popular Forces (USFP) (34); Popular Movement (MP) (28); Progress and Socialism Party (PPS) (22); Other (41)
percentage of women in chamber: 24.3%
expected date of next election: September 2026

Legislative branch - upper chamber: *chamber name:* House of Councillors (Majlis al-Mustacharin)
number of seats: 120 (all indirectly elected)
scope of elections: full renewal
term in office: 6 years
most recent election date: 10/5/2021
percentage of women in chamber: 11.7%
expected date of next election: October 2027

Judicial branch: *highest court(s):* Supreme Court or Court of Cassation (consists of 5-judge panels organized into civil, family matters, commercial, administrative, social, and criminal sections); Constitutional Court (consists of 12 members)
judge selection and term of office: Supreme Court judges appointed by the Superior Council of Judicial Power, a 20-member body presided over by the monarch, which includes the Supreme Court president, the prosecutor general, representatives of the appeals and first instance courts (among them 1 woman magistrate), the president of the National Council for Human Rights (CNDH), and 5 "notable persons" appointed by the monarch; judges appointed for life; Constitutional Court members - 6 designated by the monarch and 6 elected by Parliament; court

president appointed by the monarch from among the court members; members serve 9-year nonrenewable terms
subordinate courts: courts of appeal; High Court of Justice; administrative and commercial courts; regional and Sadad courts (for religious, civil and administrative, and penal adjudication); first instance courts

Political parties: Action Party or PA
Amal (hope) Party
An-Nahj Ad-Dimocrati or An-Nahj or Democratic Way
Authenticity and Modernity Party or PAM
Constitutional Union Party or UC
Democratic and Social Movement or MDS
Democratic Forces Front or FFD
Environment and Sustainable Development Party or PEDD
Federation of the Democratic Left or FGD
Green Left Party or PGV
Istiqlal (Independence) Party or PI
Moroccan Liberal Party or PML
Moroccan Union for Democracy or UMD
National Democratic Party
National Rally of Independents or RNI
Neo-Democrats Party
Party of Development Reform or PRD
Party of Justice and Development or PJD
Party of Liberty and Social Justice or PLJS
Party of Progress and Socialism or PPS
Popular Movement or MP
Renaissance and Virtue Party or PRV
Renaissance Party
Renewal and Equity Party or PRE
Shoura (consultation) and Istiqlal Party
Socialist Union of Popular Forces or USFP
Unified Socialist Party or GSU
Unity and Democracy Party

Diplomatic representation in the US: *chief of mission:* Ambassador Youssef AMRANI (since 27 February 2024)
chancery: 3508 International Drive NW, Washington, DC 20008
telephone: [1] (202) 462-7979
FAX: [1] (202) 265-0161
email address and website: washingtonembmorocco@maec.gov.ma
Embassy of the Kingdom of Morocco in the United States (diplomatie.ma)
consulate(s) general: New York

Diplomatic representation from the US: *chief of mission:* Ambassador (vacant); Chargé d'Affaires Ben ZIFF (since 28 August 2025)
embassy: Km 5.7 Avenue Mohammed VI, Souissi, Rabat 10170
mailing address: 9400 Rabat Place, Washington DC 20521-9400
telephone: [212] 0537-637-200
FAX: [212] 0537-637-201
email address and website: https://ma.usembassy.gov/
consulate(s) general: Casablanca

International organization participation: ABEDA, AfDB, AFESD, AIIB, AMF, AMU, AU, CAEU, CD, EBRD, FAO, G-11, G-77, IAEA, IBRD, ICAO, ICC (national committees), ICRM, IDA, IDB, IFAD, IFC, IFRCS, IHO, ILO, IMF, IMO, IMSO, Interpol, IOC, IOM, IPU, ISO, ITSO, ITU, ITUC (NGOs), LAS, MIGA, MONUSCO, NAM, OAS (observer), OIC, OIF, OPCW, OSCE (partner), Pacific Alliance (observer), Paris Club (associate), PCA, SICA (observer), UN, UNCTAD, UNESCO, UNHCR, UNIDO, UNOCI, UNOOSA, UNSC (temporary), UNWTO, UPU, WCO, WHO, WIPO, WMO, WTO

Independence: 2 March 1956 (from France)

National holiday: Throne Day (accession of King MOHAMMED VI to the throne), 30 July (1999)

Flag: *description:* red with a green pentacle (five-pointed linear star) known as Sulayman's (Solomon's) seal in the center of the flag
meaning: red and green are traditional colors in Arab flags, although the use of red is more commonly associated with the Arab states of the Persian Gulf; the pentacle represents the five pillars of Islam and the association between God and the nation
history: the design dates to 1912

National symbol(s): pentacle symbol, lion

National color(s): red, green

National anthem(s): *title:* "Hymne Cherifien" (Hymn of the Sharif)
lyrics/music: Ali Squalli HOUSSAINI/Leo MORGAN
history: music adopted 1956, lyrics adopted 1970

National heritage: *total World Heritage Sites:* 9 (all cultural)
selected World Heritage Site locales: Medina of Fez; Medina of Marrakesh; Ksar of Ait-Ben-Haddou; Historic City of Meknes; Archaeological Site of Volubilis; Medina of Tétouan (formerly known as Titawin); Medina of Essaouira (formerly Mogador); Portuguese City of Mazagan (El Jadida); Historic and Modern Rabat

ECONOMY

Economic overview: lower middle-income North African economy; ongoing recovery from recent drought and earthquake; rebounding via tourism, manufacturing, and raw materials processing; significant trade and investment with EU; reform programs include fiscal rebalancing, state enterprise governance and private sector investments

Real GDP (purchasing power parity): $350.594 billion (2024 est.)
$339.603 billion (2023 est.)
$328.425 billion (2022 est.)
note: data in 2021 dollars
comparison ranking: 58

Real GDP growth rate: 3.2% (2024 est.)
3.4% (2023 est.)
1.5% (2022 est.)
note: annual GDP % growth based on constant local currency
comparison ranking: 110

Real GDP per capita: $9,100 (2024 est.)
$8,900 (2023 est.)
$8,700 (2022 est.)
note: data in 2021 dollars
comparison ranking: 150

GDP (official exchange rate): $154.431 billion (2024 est.)
note: data in current dollars at official exchange rate

Inflation rate (consumer prices): 1% (2024 est.)
6.1% (2023 est.)
6.7% (2022 est.)
note: annual % change based on consumer prices
comparison ranking: 20

GDP - composition, by sector of origin: *agriculture:* 10.1% (2024 est.)
industry: 24.1% (2024 est.)
services: 54.1% (2024 est.)
note: figures may not total 100% due to non-allocated consumption not captured in sector-reported data
comparison rankings: agriculture 72; industry 97; services 125

GDP - composition, by end use: *household consumption:* 61.3% (2024 est.)
government consumption: 18% (2024 est.)
investment in fixed capital: 26.1% (2024 est.)
investment in inventories: 3.8% (2024 est.)
exports of goods and services: 43.3% (2024 est.)
imports of goods and services: -52.5% (2024 est.)
note: figures may not total 100% due to rounding or gaps in data collection

Agricultural products: wheat, milk, potatoes, sugar beets, tomatoes, barley, olives, apples, tangerines/mandarins, onions (2023)
note: top ten agricultural products based on tonnage

Industries: automotive parts, phosphate mining and processing, aerospace, food processing, leather goods, textiles, construction, energy, tourism

Industrial production growth rate: 5% (2024 est.)
note: annual % change in industrial value added based on constant local currency
comparison ranking: 45

Labor force: 12.475 million (2024 est.)
note: number of people ages 15 or older who are employed or seeking work
comparison ranking: 48

Unemployment rate: 9% (2024 est.)
9.1% (2023 est.)
9.5% (2022 est.)
note: % of labor force seeking employment
comparison ranking: 142

Youth unemployment rate (ages 15-24): *total:* 22.1% (2024 est.)
male: 22% (2024 est.)
female: 22.4% (2024 est.)
note: % of labor force ages 15-24 seeking employment
comparison ranking: total 48

Population below poverty line: 3.9% (2022 est.)
note: % of population with income below national poverty line

Average household expenditures: *on food:* 34.5% of household expenditures (2023 est.)
on alcohol and tobacco: 2.1% of household expenditures (2023 est.)

Remittances: 8.1% of GDP (2023 est.)
8.5% of GDP (2022 est.)
7.7% of GDP (2021 est.)
note: personal transfers and compensation between resident and non-resident individuals/households/entities

Budget: *revenues:* $38.458 billion (2023 est.)
expenditures: $44.819 billion (2023 est.)
note: central government revenues and expenses (excluding grants/extrabudgetary units/social security funds) converted to US dollars at average official exchange rate for year indicated

Taxes and other revenues: 21% (of GDP) (2023 est.)
note: central government tax revenue as a % of GDP
comparison ranking: 44

Current account balance: -$891.222 million (2023 est.)
-$4.8 billion (2022 est.)
-$3.349 billion (2021 est.)
note: balance of payments - net trade and primary/secondary income in current dollars
comparison ranking: 126

Exports: $61.746 billion (2023 est.)
$58.575 billion (2022 est.)
$47.09 billion (2021 est.)
note: balance of payments - exports of goods and services in current dollars
comparison ranking: 62

Exports - partners: Spain 20%, France 17%, Germany 6%, UK 5%, Italy 4% (2023)
note: top five export partners based on percentage share of exports

Exports - commodities: fertilizers, cars, garments, insulated wire, tomatoes (2023)
note: top five export commodities based on value in dollars

Imports: $73.759 billion (2023 est.)
$73.81 billion (2022 est.)
$60.215 billion (2021 est.)
note: balance of payments - imports of goods and services in current dollars
comparison ranking: 55

Imports - partners: Spain 16%, China 11%, France 10%, USA 9%, Turkey 5% (2023)
note: top five import partners based on percentage share of imports

Imports - commodities: refined petroleum, cars, vehicle parts/accessories, natural gas, coal (2023)
note: top five import commodities based on value in dollars

Reserves of foreign exchange and gold: $37.134 billion (2024 est.)
$36.328 billion (2023 est.)
$32.314 billion (2022 est.)
note: holdings of gold (year-end prices)/foreign exchange/special drawing rights in current dollars
comparison ranking: 53

Debt - external: $42.262 billion (2023 est.)
note: present value of external debt in current US dollars
comparison ranking: 18

Exchange rates: Moroccan dirhams (MAD) per US dollar -

Exchange rates: 9.942 (2024 est.)
10.131 (2023 est.)
10.161 (2022 est.)
8.988 (2021 est.)
9.497 (2020 est.)

ENERGY

Electricity access: *electrification - total population:* 100% (2022 est.)

Electricity: *installed generating capacity:* 14.615 million kW (2023 est.)
consumption: 36.379 billion kWh (2023 est.)
exports: 462 million kWh (2023 est.)
imports: 2.311 billion kWh (2023 est.)
transmission/distribution losses: 7.781 billion kWh (2023 est.)
comparison rankings: installed generating capacity 56; consumption 61; exports 77; imports 64; transmission/distribution losses 174

Electricity generation sources: *fossil fuels:* 78.6% of total installed capacity (2023 est.)
solar: 5% of total installed capacity (2023 est.)
wind: 15.5% of total installed capacity (2023 est.)
hydroelectricity: 0.9% of total installed capacity (2023 est.)
biomass and waste: 0.1% of total installed capacity (2023 est.)

Coal: *consumption:* 10.304 million metric tons (2023 est.)
exports: 25 metric tons (2023 est.)
imports: 10.344 million metric tons (2023 est.)
proven reserves: 96 million metric tons (2023 est.)

Petroleum: *total petroleum production:* 25 bbl/day (2023 est.)
refined petroleum consumption: 296,000 bbl/day (2023 est.)
crude oil estimated reserves: 684,000 barrels (2021 est.)

Natural gas: *production:* 55.473 million cubic meters (2023 est.)
consumption: 912.277 million cubic meters (2023 est.)
imports: 861.38 million cubic meters (2023 est.)
proven reserves: 1.444 billion cubic meters (2021 est.)

Energy consumption per capita: 23.52 million Btu/person (2023 est.)
comparison ranking: 127

COMMUNICATIONS

Telephones - fixed lines: *total subscriptions:* 2.874 million (2023 est.)
subscriptions per 100 inhabitants: 8 (2023 est.)
comparison ranking: total subscriptions 38

Telephones - mobile cellular: *total subscriptions:* 55.9 million (2023 est.)
subscriptions per 100 inhabitants: 137 (2021 est.)
comparison ranking: total subscriptions 31

Broadcast media: 2 TV broadcast networks with state-run Radio-Television Marocaine (RTM) operating one network and the state partially owning the other; foreign TV is available via satellite dish; 3 radio broadcast networks, with RTM operating one; the state-owned network includes 10 regional radio channels in addition to its national service (2019)

Internet country code: .ma

Internet users: *percent of population:* 91% (2023 est.)

Broadband - fixed subscriptions: *total:* 2.42 million (2022 est.)
subscriptions per 100 inhabitants: 6 (2022 est.)
comparison ranking: total 57

TRANSPORTATION

Civil aircraft registration country code prefix: CN

Airports: 48 (2025)
comparison ranking: 91

Heliports: 17 (2025)
comparison ranking: 57

Railways: *total:* 2,067 km (2014)
standard gauge: 2,067 km (2014) 1.435-m gauge (1,022 km electrified)

Merchant marine: *total:* 94 (2023)
by type: container ship 6, general cargo 5, oil tanker 2, other 81
comparison ranking: total 94

Ports: *total ports:* 12 (2024)
large: 3
medium: 1
small: 3
very small: 5
ports with oil terminals: 2
key ports: Agadir, Casablanca, Tanger, Tangier-Mediterranean

MILITARY AND SECURITY

Military and security forces: Royal Moroccan Armed Forces (FAR): Royal Moroccan Army (includes the Moroccan Royal Guard), Royal Moroccan Navy (includes Coast Guard, marines), Royal Moroccan Air Force, Moroccan Royal Guard, Royal Moroccan Gendarmerie

Ministry of Interior: General Directorate for National Security (DGSN; aka National Police), Auxiliary Forces (2025)
note 1: the Royal Guard is officially part of the Army, but is under the direct operational control of the Royal Military Household of His Majesty the King; it provides for the security and safety of the King and royal family; it was established in the 11th century and is considered one of the world's oldest active units still in military service
note 2: the DGSN manages internal law enforcement in cities; the Gendarmerie is responsible for law enforcement in rural regions and on national highways and has a counterterrorism role; the Auxiliary Forces provide support to the Gendarmerie and DGSN

Military expenditures: 4% of GDP (2024 est.)
4% of GDP (2023 est.)
4.5% of GDP (2022 est.)
4.5% of GDP (2021 est.)
4.5% of GDP (2020 est.)

Military and security service personnel strengths: estimated 220,000 active Armed Forces (175,000 Army; 10,000 Navy; 15,000 Air Force, 20,000 Gendarmerie) (2025)

Military equipment inventories and acquisitions: the Moroccan military's inventory is comprised of mostly older French and US equipment, although in recent years it has embarked on a modernization program and received quantities of more modern equipment from a variety of countries, particularly France, Spain, and the US (2024)

Military service age and obligation: 19-25 years of age for 12-month compulsory and voluntary military service for men and women (conscription abolished 2006 and reintroduced in 2019) (2023)

Military deployments: 770 Central African Republic (MINUSCA); 930 Democratic Republic of the Congo (MONUSCO) (2024)

Military - note: the Royal Armed Forces (FAR) are responsible for protecting Morocco's national interests, sovereignty, and territorial integrity; key areas of concern for the FAR include international terrorism, maritime security, and regional challenges such as the Polisario Front in Western Sahara and Algeria; the Polisario Front (Popular Front for the Liberation of Saguia el Hamra and Rio de Oro), an organization that seeks the independence of Western Sahara, disputes Morocco's claim of sovereignty over the territory; Moroccan and Polisario forces fought intermittently from 1975, when Spain relinquished colonial authority over the territory, until a 1991 cease-fire and the establishment of a UN peacekeeping mission; the Polisario withdrew from the cease-fire in November 2020, and since then there have been reports of low-intensity hostilities between Morocco and the Polisario Front across the 2,500-kilometer-long berm built in 1987 that separates the two sides; Algeria is seen as a regional rival and has openly backed the Polisario Front

the FAR participates in international peacekeeping operations, as well as both bilateral and multinational training exercises; it has relations with a variety of partners including the militaries of France, Qatar, Saudi Arabia, Spain, and the US, as well as NATO, the Arab League, and the African Union; Morocco has Major Non-NATO Ally (MNNA) status with the US, a designation under US law that provides foreign partners with certain benefits in the areas of defense trade and security cooperation
the FAR was created in May 1956; Moroccans were recruited for service in the Spahi and Tirailleur regiments of the French Army during the period of the French protectorate (1912-1956), and Moroccans fought under the French Army during both World Wars, as well as the First Indochina War (1946-1954); the Spanish Army recruited Moroccans from the Spanish Protectorate during both the Rif War (1921-26) and the Spanish Civil War (1936-39)
the UN Mission for the Referendum in Western Sahara (MINURSO) was established by Security Council resolution 690 in April 1991 in accordance with settlement proposals accepted in August 1988 by Morocco and the Polisario Front; MINURSO was unable to carry out all the original settlement proposals, but continues to monitor the cease-fire and reduce the threat of mines and unexploded ordnance, and has provided logistic support to the Office of the UN High Commissioner for Refugees (UNHCR) (2025)

TERRORISM

Terrorist group(s): Terrorist group(s): Islamic State of Iraq and ash-Sham (ISIS)
note: details about the history, aims, leadership, organization, areas of operation, tactics, targets, weapons, size, and sources of support of the group(s) appear(s) in Appendix T

TRANSNATIONAL ISSUES

Refugees and internally displaced persons: *refugees:* 18,848 (2024 est.)

IDPs: 256 (2024 est.)

MOZAMBIQUE

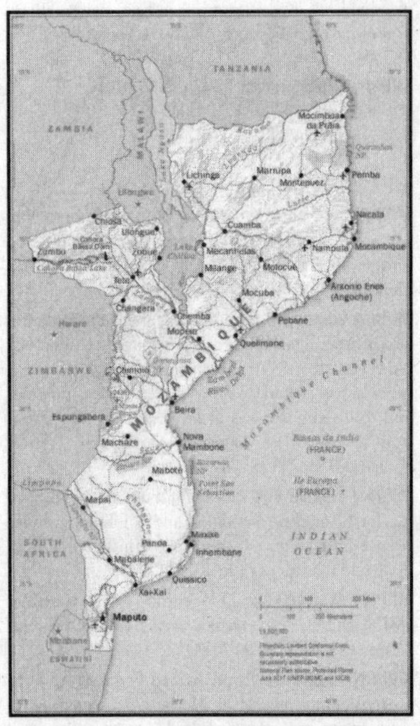

INTRODUCTION

Background: In the first half of the second millennium A.D., northern Mozambican port towns were frequented by traders from Somalia, Ethiopia, Egypt, Arabia, Persia, and India. The Portuguese were able to wrest much of the coastal trade from Arab Muslims in the centuries after 1500, and they set up their own colonies. Portugal did not relinquish Mozambique until 1975. Large-scale emigration, economic dependence on South Africa, a severe drought, and a prolonged civil war hindered the country's development until the mid-1990s.

The ruling Front for the Liberation of Mozambique (FRELIMO) party formally abandoned Marxism in 1989, and a new constitution the following year provided for multiparty elections and a free-market economy. A UN-negotiated peace agreement between FRELIMO and rebel Mozambique National Resistance (RENAMO) forces ended the fighting in 1992. In 2004, Mozambique underwent a delicate transition as Joaquim CHISSANO stepped down after 18 years in office. His elected successor, Armando GUEBUZA, served two terms and then passed executive power to Filipe NYUSI in 2015. RENAMO's residual armed forces intermittently engaged in a low-level insurgency after 2012, but a 2016 cease-fire eventually led to the two sides signing a comprehensive peace deal in 2019.

Since 2017, violent extremists – who an official ISIS media outlet recognized as ISIS's network in Mozambique for the first time in 2019 – have been conducting attacks against civilians and security services in the northern province of Cabo Delgado. In 2021, Rwanda and the Southern African Development Community deployed forces to support Mozambique's efforts to counter the extremist group.

GEOGRAPHY

Location: Southeastern Africa, bordering the Mozambique Channel, between South Africa and Tanzania

Geographic coordinates: 18 15 S, 35 00 E

Map references: Africa

Area: *total:* 799,380 sq km
land: 786,380 sq km
water: 13,000 sq km
comparison ranking: total 36

Area - comparative: slightly more than five times the size of Georgia; slightly less than twice the size of California

Land boundaries: *total:* 4,783 km
border countries (6): Malawi 1498 km; South Africa 496 km; Eswatini 108 km; Tanzania 840 km; Zambia 439 km; Zimbabwe 1,402 km

Coastline: 2,470 km

Maritime claims: *territorial sea:* 12 nm
exclusive economic zone: 200 nm

Climate: tropical to subtropical

Terrain: mostly coastal lowlands, uplands in center, high plateaus in northwest, mountains in west

Elevation: *highest point:* Monte Binga 2,436 m
lowest point: Indian Ocean 0 m
mean elevation: 345 m

Natural resources: coal, titanium, natural gas, hydropower, tantalum, graphite

Land use: *agricultural land:* 52.7% (2022 est.)
arable land: 7.2% (2022 est.)
permanent crops: 0.4% (2022 est.)
permanent pasture: 45.1% (2022 est.)
forest: 46.1% (2022 est.)
other: 1.2% (2022 est.)

Irrigated land: 1,180 sq km (2012)

Major lakes (area sq km): *fresh water lake(s):* Lake Malawi (shared with Malawi and Tanzania) - 22,490

Major rivers (by length in km): Rio Zambeze (Zambezi) river mouth (shared with Zambia [s]), Angola, Namibia, Botswana, and Zimbabwe) - 2,740 km; Rio Limpopo river mouth (shared with South Africa [s], Botswana, and Zimbabwe) - 1,800 km
note: [s] after country name indicates river source; [m] after country name indicates river mouth

Major watersheds (area sq km): Indian Ocean drainage: Zambezi (1,332,412 sq km)

Population distribution: three large population clusters are found along the southern coast between Maputo and Inhambane, in the central area between Beira and Chimoio along the Zambezi River, and in and around the northern cities of Nampula, Cidade de Nacala, and Pemba; the northwest and southwest are the least populated areas, as shown in this population distribution map

Natural hazards: severe droughts; devastating cyclones and floods in central and southern provinces

Geography - note: the Zambezi River flows through the north-central and most fertile part of the country

PEOPLE AND SOCIETY

Population: *total:* 33,350,954 (2024 est.)
male: 16,449,734
female: 16,901,220
comparison rankings: total 46; male 46; female 44

Nationality: *noun:* Mozambican(s)
adjective: Mozambican

Ethnic groups: African 99% (Makhuwa, Tsonga, Lomwe, Sena, and others), Mestizo 0.8%, other (includes European, Indian, Pakistani, Chinese) 0.2% (2017 est.)

Languages: Makhuwa 26.1%, Portuguese (official) 16.6%, Tsonga 8.6%, Nyanja 8.1, Sena 7.1%, Lomwe 7.1%, Chuwabo 4.7%, Ndau 3.8%, Tswa 3.8%, other Mozambican languages 11.8%, other 0.5%, unspecified 1.8% (2017 est.)

Religions: Roman Catholic 27.2%, Muslim 18.9%, Zionist Christian 15.6%, Evangelical/Pentecostal 15.3%, Anglican 1.7%, other 4.8%, none 13.9%, unspecified 2.5% (2017 est.)

Age structure: *0-14 years:* 44.7% (male 7,548,247/ female 7,350,012)
15-64 years: 52.4% (male 8,428,457/female 9,061,065)
65 years and over: 2.9% (2024 est.) (male 473,030/ female 490,143)

Dependency ratios: *total dependency ratio:* 90.7 (2024 est.)
youth dependency ratio: 85.2 (2024 est.)
elderly dependency ratio: 5.5 (2024 est.)
potential support ratio: 18.2 (2024 est.)

Median age: *total:* 17.3 years (2024 est.)
male: 16.7 years
female: 17.9 years
comparison ranking: total 222

Population growth rate: 2.54% (2024 est.)
comparison ranking: 17

Birth rate: 36.5 births/1,000 population (2024 est.)
comparison ranking: 9

Death rate: 9.6 deaths/1,000 population (2024 est.)
comparison ranking: 40

Net migration rate: -1.5 migrant(s)/1,000 population (2024 est.)
comparison ranking: 158

Population distribution: three large population clusters are found along the southern coast between Maputo and Inhambane, in the central area between Beira and Chimoio along the Zambezi River, and in and around the northern cities of Nampula, Cidade de Nacala, and Pemba; the northwest and southwest are the least populated areas, as shown in this population distribution map

Urbanization: *urban population:* 38.8% of total population (2023)
rate of urbanization: 4.24% annual rate of change (2020-25 est.)

Major urban areas - population: 1.852 million Matola, 1.163 million MAPUTO (capital), 969,000 Nampula (2023)

Sex ratio: *at birth:* 1.03 male(s)/female
0-14 years: 1.03 male(s)/female
15-64 years: 0.93 male(s)/female
65 years and over: 0.97 male(s)/female
total population: 0.97 male(s)/female (2024 est.)

Mother's mean age at first birth: 19.2 years (2011 est.)
note: data represents median age at first birth among women 20-49

Maternal mortality ratio: 82 deaths/100,000 live births (2023 est.)
comparison ranking: 72

Infant mortality rate: *total:* 58.2 deaths/1,000 live births (2024 est.)
male: 60.1 deaths/1,000 live births
female: 56.2 deaths/1,000 live births
comparison ranking: total 9

Life expectancy at birth: *total population:* 58.3 years (2024 est.)
male: 57.1 years
female: 59.6 years
comparison ranking: total population 224

Total fertility rate: 4.66 children born/woman (2024 est.)
comparison ranking: 12

Gross reproduction rate: 2.29 (2024 est.)

Drinking water source: *improved: urban:* 87.3% of population (2022 est.)
rural: 48.3% of population (2022 est.)
total: 63.2% of population (2022 est.)
unimproved: urban: 12.7% of population (2022 est.)
rural: 51.7% of population (2022 est.)
total: 36.8% of population (2022 est.)

Health expenditure: 9.1% of GDP (2021)
8% of national budget (2022 est.)

Physician density: 0.18 physicians/1,000 population (2022)

Hospital bed density: 0.7 beds/1,000 population (2021 est.)

Sanitation facility access: *improved: urban:* 71.8% of population (2022 est.)
rural: 24.3% of population (2022 est.)
total: 42.4% of population (2022 est.)
unimproved: urban: 28.2% of population (2022 est.)
rural: 75.7% of population (2022 est.)
total: 57.6% of population (2022 est.)

Obesity - adult prevalence rate: 7.2% (2016)
comparison ranking: 160

Alcohol consumption per capita: *total:* 1.46 liters of pure alcohol (2019 est.)
beer: 1.03 liters of pure alcohol (2019 est.)
wine: 0.22 liters of pure alcohol (2019 est.)
spirits: 0.21 liters of pure alcohol (2019 est.)
other alcohols: 0 liters of pure alcohol (2019 est.)
comparison ranking: total 140

Tobacco use: *total:* 14.3% (2020 est.)
male: 23% (2020 est.)
female: 5.6% (2020 est.)
comparison ranking: total 105

Children under the age of 5 years underweight: 14.8% (2019/20)
comparison ranking: 33

Currently married women (ages 15-49): 63.7% (2023 est.)

Child marriage: *women married by age 15:* 16.8% (2015)
women married by age 18: 52.9% (2015)
men married by age 18: 9.7% (2015)

Education expenditure: 6% of GDP (2022 est.)
18.8% national budget (2021 est.)
comparison ranking: Education expenditure (% GDP) 30

Literacy: *total population:* 60% (2020 est.)
male: 72% (2020 est.)
female: 49% (2020 est.)

School life expectancy (primary to tertiary education): *total:* 10 years (2017 est.)
male: 11 years (2017 est.)
female: 10 years (2017 est.)

ENVIRONMENT

Environmental issues: increased population migration to urban and coastal areas; desertification; soil erosion; deforestation; water pollution from artisanal mining; pollution of surface and coastal waters; wildlife preservation (elephant poaching for ivory)

International environmental agreements: *party to:* Biodiversity, Climate Change, Climate Change-Kyoto Protocol, Climate Change-Paris Agreement, Comprehensive Nuclear Test Ban, Desertification, Endangered Species, Hazardous Wastes, Law of the Sea, Ozone Layer Protection, Ship Pollution, Tropical Timber 2006, Wetlands
signed, but not ratified: none of the selected agreements

Climate: tropical to subtropical

Urbanization: *urban population:* 38.8% of total population (2023)
rate of urbanization: 4.24% annual rate of change (2020-25 est.)

Carbon dioxide emissions: 9.549 million metric tonnes of CO2 (2023 est.)
from coal and metallurgical coke: -68,287 metric tonnes of CO2 (2023 est.)
from petroleum and other liquids: 6.244 million metric tonnes of CO2 (2023 est.)
from consumed natural gas: 3.373 million metric tonnes of CO2 (2023 est.)
comparison ranking: total emissions 110

Particulate matter emissions: 17.5 micrograms per cubic meter (2019 est.)

Methane emissions: *energy:* 320.1 kt (2022-2024 est.)
agriculture: 169.5 kt (2019-2021 est.)
waste: 117.5 kt (2019-2021 est.)
other: 101.2 kt (2019-2021 est.)

Waste and recycling: *municipal solid waste generated annually:* 2.5 million tons (2024 est.)
percent of municipal solid waste recycled: 5.2% (2022 est.)

Total water withdrawal: *municipal:* 372 million cubic meters (2022 est.)
industrial: 25 million cubic meters (2022 est.)
agricultural: 1.076 billion cubic meters (2022 est.)

Total renewable water resources: 217.1 billion cubic meters (2022 est.)

GOVERNMENT

Country name: *conventional long form:* Republic of Mozambique
conventional short form: Mozambique
local long form: Republica de Mocambique
local short form: Mocambique
former: Portuguese East Africa, People's Republic of Mozambique
etymology: named for an offshore island; the island was named after Mussa bin BIQUE (or Mussa Ibn MALIK), an influential Arab slave trader who set himself up as sultan on the island in the 15th century

Government type: presidential republic

Capital: *name:* Maputo
geographic coordinates: 25 57 S, 32 35 E
time difference: UTC+2 (7 hours ahead of Washington, DC, during Standard Time)
etymology: named after the Maputo River, which drains into Maputo Bay south of the city; the river is said to be named after the son of Muagobe, a local chief in the 18th century

Administrative divisions: 10 provinces (*provincias*, singular - *provincia*), 1 city (*cidade*)*; Cabo Delgado, Gaza, Inhambane, Manica, Maputo, Cidade de Maputo*, Nampula, Niassa, Sofala, Tete, Zambezia

Legal system: mixed system of Portuguese civil law and customary law

Constitution: *history:* previous 1975, 1990; latest adopted 16 November 2004, effective 21 December 2004
amendment process: proposed by the president of the republic or supported by at least one third of the Assembly of the Republic membership; passage of amendments affecting constitutional provisions, including the independence and sovereignty of the

state, the republican form of government, basic rights and freedoms, and universal suffrage, requires at least a two-thirds majority vote by the Assembly and approval in a referendum; referenda not required for passage of other amendments

International law organization participation: has not submitted an ICJ jurisdiction declaration; non-party state to the ICCt

Citizenship: *citizenship by birth:* no
citizenship by descent only: at least one parent must be a citizen of Mozambique
dual citizenship recognized: no
residency requirement for naturalization: 5 years

Suffrage: 18 years of age; universal

Executive branch: *chief of state:* President Daniel Francisco CHAPO (since 15 January 2025)
head of government: Prime Minister Maria Benvinda Delfina LEVI (since 17 January 2025)
cabinet: Cabinet appointed by the president
election/appointment process: president elected directly by absolute-majority popular vote in 2 rounds, if needed, for a 5-year term (eligible for 2 consecutive terms); election last held on 9 October 2024 (next to be held by October 2029); prime minister appointed by the president
most recent election date: 9 October 2024
election results: 2024: Daniel CHAPO elected president in first round; percent of vote - Daniel CHAPO (FRELIMO) 65.2%, Venâncio MONDLANE (PODEMOS) 24.2%, Ossufo MOMADE (RENAMO) 6.6%

Legislative branch: *legislature name:* Assembly of the Republic (Assembleia da Republica)
legislative structure: unicameral
number of seats: 250 (all directly elected)
electoral system: proportional representation
scope of elections: full renewal
term in office: 5 years
most recent election date: 10/9/2024
parties elected and seats per party: Mozambique Liberation Front (FRELIMO) (171); Optimist Party for the Development of Mozambique (PODEMOS) (43); Mozambican National Resistance (RENAMO) (28); Other (8)
percentage of women in chamber: 39.2%
expected date of next election: October 2029

Judicial branch: *highest court(s):* Supreme Court (consists of the court president, vice president, and 5 judges); Constitutional Council (consists of 7 judges)
judge selection and term of office: Supreme Court president appointed by the president of the republic; vice president appointed by the president in consultation with the Higher Council of the Judiciary (CSMJ) and ratified by the Assembly of the Republic; other judges elected by the Assembly; judges serve 5-year renewable terms; Constitutional Council judges appointed - 1 by the president, 5 by the Assembly, and 1 by the CSMJ; judges serve 5-year nonrenewable terms
subordinate courts: Administrative Court (capital city only); provincial courts or Tribunais Judicias de Provincia; District Courts or Tribunais Judicias de Districto; customs courts; maritime courts; courts marshal; labor courts; community courts

Political parties: Democratic Movement of Mozambique (Movimento Democratico de Mocambique) or MDM Liberation Front of Mozambique (Frente de Liberatacao de Mocambique) or FRELIMO Mozambican National Resistance (Resistencia Nacional Mocambicana) or RENAMO

Diplomatic representation in the US: *chief of mission:* Ambassador Alfredo Fabião NUVUNGA (since 19 April 2023)
chancery: 1525 New Hampshire Avenue NW, Washington, DC 20036
telephone: [1] (202) 293-7147
FAX: [1] (202) 835-0245
email address and website: washington.dc@embamoc.gov.mz
https://usa.embamoc.gov.mz/

Diplomatic representation from the US: *chief of mission:* Ambassador (vacant); Chargé d'Affaires Abigail L. DRESSEL (since 11 August 2025)
embassy: Avenida Marginal 5467, Maputo
mailing address: 2330 Maputo Place, Washington DC 20521-2330
telephone: [258] (84) 095-8000
email address and website: MaputaConsular@state.gov
https://mz.usembassy.gov/

International organization participation: ACP, AfDB, AU, C, CD, CPLP, EITI (compliant country), FAO, G-77, IAEA, IBRD, ICAO, ICC (NGOs), ICRM, IDA, IDB, IFAD, IFC, IFRCS, IHO, ILO, IMF, IMO, IMSO, Interpol, IOC, IOM, IPU, ISO (correspondent), ITSO, ITU, ITUC (NGOs), MIGA, NAM, OIC, OIF (observer), OPCW, SADC, UN, UNCDF, UNCTAD, UNDP, UNDSS, UNECA, UNEP, UNESCO, UNFPA, UNHCR, UNIDO, UNODC, UNOPS, UNV, UNWTO, Union Latina, UPU, WCO, WFP, WFTU (NGOs), WHO, WIPO, WMO, WTO

Independence: 25 June 1975 (from Portugal)

National holiday: Independence Day, 25 June (1975)

Flag: *description:* three equal horizontal bands of green (top), black, and yellow, with a red isosceles triangle based on the left side; the black band is edged in white; centered in the triangle is a five-pointed yellow star with a crossed black-and-white rifle and hoe, on top of an open white book
meaning: green stands for the riches of the land, white for peace, black for the African continent, yellow for the country's minerals, and red for the fight for independence; the rifle stands for defense and vigilance, the hoe for agriculture, the open book for the importance of education, and the star for Marxism and internationalism
note: one of two national flags featuring a firearm; the other is Guatemala

National symbol(s): rifle, hoe, and book

National color(s): green, black, yellow, white, red

National anthem(s): *title:* "Pátria Amada" (Lovely Fatherland)
lyrics/music: Salomão J. MANHICA/unkown
history: adopted 2002; the new anthem reflects the new multi-party political system

National heritage: *total World Heritage Sites:* 1 (cultural)
selected World Heritage Site locales: Island of Mozambique

ECONOMY

Economic overview: low-income East African economy; subsistence farming dominates labor force; return to growth led by agriculture and extractive industries; Islamist insurgency threatens natural gas projects in north; ongoing foreign debt restructuring and resolution under IMF Highly Indebted Poor Countries (HIPC) initiative

Real GDP (purchasing power parity): $51.786 billion (2024 est.)
$50.844 billion (2023 est.)
$48.222 billion (2022 est.)
note: data in 2021 dollars
comparison ranking: 126

Real GDP growth rate: 1.9% (2024 est.)
5.4% (2023 est.)
4.4% (2022 est.)
note: annual GDP % growth based on constant local currency
comparison ranking: 151

Real GDP per capita: $1,500 (2024 est.)
$1,500 (2023 est.)
$1,500 (2022 est.)
note: data in 2021 dollars
comparison ranking: 211

GDP (official exchange rate): $22.417 billion (2024 est.)
note: data in current dollars at official exchange rate

Inflation rate (consumer prices): 4.1% (2024 est.)
7.1% (2023 est.)
10.3% (2022 est.)
note: annual % change based on consumer prices
comparison ranking: 126

GDP - composition, by sector of origin: *agriculture:* 26.3% (2024 est.)
industry: 24.6% (2024 est.)
services: 38.4% (2024 est.)
note: figures may not total 100% due to non-allocated consumption not captured in sector-reported data
comparison rankings: agriculture 16; industry 93; services 196

GDP - composition, by end use: *household consumption:* 69% (2024 est.)
government consumption: 17.1% (2024 est.)
investment in fixed capital: 24.1% (2024 est.)
investment in inventories: 0% (2024 est.)
exports of goods and services: 42.7% (2024 est.)
imports of goods and services: -52.9% (2024 est.)
note: figures may not total 100% due to rounding or gaps in data collection

Agricultural products: cassava, maize, sugarcane, tomatoes, beans, potatoes, sweet potatoes, bananas, coconuts, onions (2023)
note: top ten agricultural products based on tonnage

Industries: aluminum, petroleum products, chemicals (fertilizer, soap, paints), textiles, cement, glass, asbestos, tobacco, food, beverages

Industrial production growth rate: 2.9% (2024 est.)
note: annual % change in industrial value added based on constant local currency
comparison ranking: 81

Labor force: 15.173 million (2024 est.)
note: number of people ages 15 or older who are employed or seeking work
comparison ranking: 42

Unemployment rate: 3.6% (2024 est.)
3.6% (2023 est.)
3.6% (2022 est.)
note: % of labor force seeking employment
comparison ranking: 59

Youth unemployment rate (ages 15-24): *total:* 7.4% (2024 est.)
male: 7.5% (2024 est.)
female: 7.2% (2024 est.)
note: % of labor force ages 15-24 seeking employment
comparison ranking: total 143

Population below poverty line: 62.8% (2019 est.)

note: % of population with income below national poverty line

Gini Index coefficient - distribution of family income: 50.3 (2019 est.)
note: index (0-100) of income distribution; higher values represent greater inequality
comparison ranking: 9

Household income or consumption by percentage share: *lowest 10%:* 1.7% (2019 est.)
highest 10%: 41.1% (2019 est.)
note: % share of income accruing to lowest and highest 10% of population

Remittances: 1.2% of GDP (2024 est.)
1.2% of GDP (2023 est.)
0.9% of GDP (2022 est.)
note: personal transfers and compensation between resident and non-resident individuals/households/entities

Budget: *revenues:* $6.243 billion (2024 est.)
expenditures: $7.223 billion (2024 est.)
note: central government revenues and expenses (excluding grants/extrabudgetary units/social security funds) converted to US dollars at average official exchange rate for year indicated

Public debt: 76.6% of GDP (2022 est.)
note: central government debt as a % of GDP
comparison ranking: 43

Taxes and other revenues: 22.7% (of GDP) (2022 est.)
note: central government tax revenue as a % of GDP
comparison ranking: 33

Current account balance: -$2.498 billion (2024 est.)
-$2.207 billion (2023 est.)
-$6.367 billion (2022 est.)
note: balance of payments - net trade and primary/secondary income in current dollars
comparison ranking: 155

Exports: $9.358 billion (2024 est.)
$9.405 billion (2023 est.)
$9.409 billion (2022 est.)
note: balance of payments - exports of goods and services in current dollars
comparison ranking: 119

Exports - partners: India 18%, China 13%, South Africa 9%, UAE 6%, Thailand 4% (2023)
note: top five export partners based on percentage share of exports

Exports - commodities: coal, natural gas, aluminum, gold, precious stones (2023)
note: top five export commodities based on value in dollars

Imports: $10.488 billion (2024 est.)
$11.18 billion (2023 est.)
$15.932 billion (2022 est.)
note: balance of payments - imports of goods and services in current dollars
comparison ranking: 119

Imports - partners: South Africa 34%, China 14%, India 13%, UAE 6%, Singapore 3% (2023)
note: top five import partners based on percentage share of imports

Imports - commodities: refined petroleum, chromium ore, iron alloys, iron ore, palm oil (2023)
note: top five import commodities based on value in dollars

Reserves of foreign exchange and gold: $3.843 billion (2024 est.)
$3.637 billion (2023 est.)
$2.939 billion (2022 est.)
note: holdings of gold (year-end prices)/foreign exchange/special drawing rights in current dollars
comparison ranking: 107

Debt - external: $8.274 billion (2023 est.)
note: present value of external debt in current US dollars
comparison ranking: 55

Exchange rates: meticais (MZM) per US dollar -

Exchange rates: 63.905 (2024 est.)
63.886 (2023 est.)
63.851 (2022 est.)
65.465 (2021 est.)
69.465 (2020 est.)

ENERGY

Electricity access: *electrification - total population:* 33.2% (2022 est.)
electrification - urban areas: 79.4%
electrification - rural areas: 5%

Electricity: *installed generating capacity:* 2.86 million kW (2023 est.)
consumption: 12.983 billion kWh (2023 est.)
exports: 11.483 billion kWh (2023 est.)
imports: 8.287 billion kWh (2023 est.)
transmission/distribution losses: 3.38 billion kWh (2023 est.)
comparison rankings: installed generating capacity 110; consumption 92; exports 21; imports 30; transmission/distribution losses 147

Electricity generation sources: *fossil fuels:* 16.3% of total installed capacity (2023 est.)
solar: 0.4% of total installed capacity (2023 est.)
hydroelectricity: 82.7% of total installed capacity (2023 est.)
biomass and waste: 0.6% of total installed capacity (2023 est.)

Coal: *production:* 10.583 million metric tons (2023 est.)
consumption: 13,000 metric tons (2023 est.)
exports: 10.658 million metric tons (2023 est.)
imports: 900 metric tons (2023 est.)
proven reserves: 1.792 billion metric tons (2023 est.)

Petroleum: *refined petroleum consumption:* 42,000 bbl/day (2023 est.)

Natural gas: *production:* 8.873 billion cubic meters (2023 est.)
consumption: 1.625 billion cubic meters (2023 est.)
exports: 7.09 billion cubic meters (2023 est.)
proven reserves: 2.832 trillion cubic meters (2021 est.)

Energy consumption per capita: 5.789 million Btu/person (2023 est.)
comparison ranking: 167

COMMUNICATIONS

Telephones - fixed lines: *total subscriptions:* 29,000 (2022 est.)
subscriptions per 100 inhabitants: (2022 est.) less than 1
comparison ranking: total subscriptions 168

Telephones - mobile cellular: *total subscriptions:* 15 million (2022 est.)
subscriptions per 100 inhabitants: 42 (2022 est.)
comparison ranking: total subscriptions 73

Broadcast media: 1 state-run TV station supplemented by a private TV station; Portuguese state TV's African service, RTP Africa, and Brazilian-owned TV Miramar are available; state-run radio provides nearly 100% territorial coverage and broadcasts in multiple languages; a number of privately owned and community-operated stations; transmissions of multiple international broadcasters are available (2019)

Internet country code: .mz

Internet users: *percent of population:* 20% (2023 est.)

Broadband - fixed subscriptions: *total:* 65,000 (2022 est.)
subscriptions per 100 inhabitants: (2022 est.) less than 1
comparison ranking: total 142

TRANSPORTATION

Civil aircraft registration country code prefix: C9

Airports: 92 (2025)
comparison ranking: 60

Railways: *total:* 4,787 km (2014)
narrow gauge: 4,787 km (2014) 1.067-m gauge

Merchant marine: *total:* 36 (2023)
by type: general cargo 9, other 27
comparison ranking: total 130

Ports: *total ports:* 11 (2024)
large: 0
medium: 2
small: 5
very small: 4
ports with oil terminals: 3
key ports: Beira, Chinde, Inhambane, Maputo, Mocambique, Pebane, Porto Belo

MILITARY AND SECURITY

Military and security forces: Armed Forces for the Defense of Mozambique (Forcas Armadas de Defesa de Mocambique, FADM): Army, Mozambique Navy, Mozambique Air Force

Ministry of Interior: Mozambique National Police (PRM; includes the Rapid Intervention Unit, UIR), the National Criminal Investigation Service (SERNIC), Border Security Force; other security forces include the Presidential Guard and the Force for the Protection of High-Level Individuals (2025)
note 1: the FADM and other security forces are referred to collectively as the Mozambican Defense and Security Forces (FDS)
note 2: the PRM, SERNIC, and the UIR are responsible for law enforcement and internal security; the Border Security Force is responsible for protecting the country's international borders and for carrying out police duties within 24 miles of borders
note 3: in 2023, the Mozambique Government legalized local militias that have been assisting security forces operating in Cabo Delgado against Islamic militants since 2020; this Local Force is comprised of ex-combatants and other civilians and receives training, uniforms, weapons, and logistical support from the FADM

Military expenditures: 2% of GDP (2024 est.)
1.5% of GDP (2023 est.)
1.3% of GDP (2022 est.)
1.2% of GDP (2021 est.)
1.1% of GDP (2020 est.)

Military and security service personnel strengths: estimated 12,000 active FADM (2025)

Military equipment inventories and acquisitions: the FADM's inventory consists primarily of Russian and Soviet-era equipment, although in recent years it has received some more modern equipment from a variety of countries, mostly as aid/donations (2024)

Military service age and obligation: registration for military service is mandatory for all men and women at 18 years of age; 18-35 years of age for selective compulsory military service; 18 years of age for voluntary service for men and women; 60-month service obligation (2025)

Military - note: the FADM is responsible for external security, cooperating with police on internal security, and responding to natural disasters and other emergencies; the primary focus of the FADM is countering an insurgency in the northern province of Cabo Delgado by militants affiliated with the Islamic State of Iraq and ash-Sham terrorist group (ISIS-Mozambique; known locally as Ahl al-Sunna wal-Jama'a); since 2017, the conflict has claimed an estimated 6,000 lives and displaced an estimated one million persons; at Mozambique's request, Rwanda and several southern African countries under the Southern Africa Development Community (SADC) deployed forces to Mozambique to combat the insurgency in 2021; the SADC forces departed in 2024; as of 2025, Rwanda continued to provide approximately 3,000 military and police personnel to assist Mozambican Defense and Security Forces, along with several hundred Tanzanian troops; the EU has also provided training assistance (2025)

TERRORISM

Terrorist group(s): Terrorist group(s): Islamic State of Iraq and ash-Sham - Mozambique (ISIS-M)
note: details about the history, aims, leadership, organization, areas of operation, tactics, targets, weapons, size, and sources of support of the group(s) appear(s) in Appendix T

TRANSNATIONAL ISSUES

Refugees and internally displaced persons: *refugees:* 24,250 (2024 est.)

IDPs: 718,154 (2024 est.)

NAMIBIA

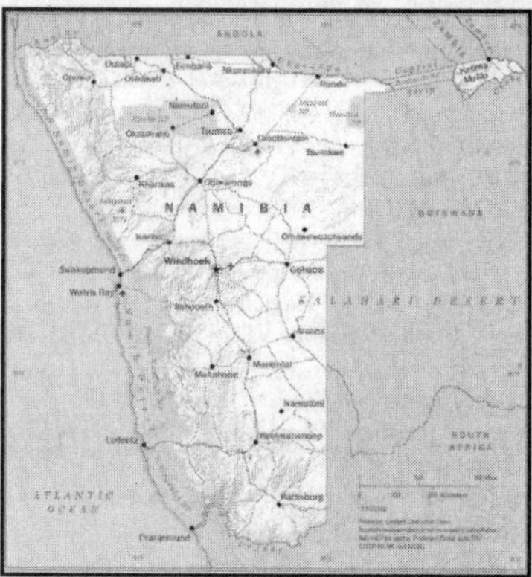

INTRODUCTION

Background: Various ethnic groups occupied southwestern Africa prior to Germany establishing a colony over most of the territory in 1884. South Africa occupied the colony, then known as German South West Africa, in 1915 during World War I and administered it as a mandate until after World War II, when it annexed the territory. In 1966, the Marxist South-West Africa People's Organization (SWAPO) guerrilla group launched a war of independence for the area that became Namibia, but it was not until 1988 that South Africa agreed to end its administration in accordance with a UN peace plan for the entire region. Namibia gained independence in 1990, and SWAPO has governed it since, although the party has dropped much of its Marxist ideology. President Hage GEINGOB was elected in 2014 in a landslide victory, replacing Hifikepunye POHAMBA, who stepped down after serving two terms. SWAPO retained its parliamentary super majority in the 2014 elections. In 2019 elections, GEINGOB was reelected but by a substantially reduced majority, and SWAPO narrowly lost its super majority in parliament.

GEOGRAPHY

Location: Southern Africa, bordering the South Atlantic Ocean, between Angola and South Africa

Geographic coordinates: 22 00 S, 17 00 E

Map references: Africa

Area: *total:* 824,292 sq km
land: 823,290 sq km
water: 1,002 sq km
comparison ranking: total 35

Area - comparative: almost seven times the size of Pennsylvania; slightly more than half the size of Alaska

Land boundaries: *total:* 4,220 km
border countries (4): Angola 1,427 km; Botswana 1,544 km; South Africa 1,005 km; Zambia 244 km

Coastline: 1,572 km

Maritime claims: *territorial sea:* 12 nm
contiguous zone: 24 nm
exclusive economic zone: 200 nm

Climate: desert; hot, dry; rainfall sparse and erratic

Terrain: mostly high plateau; Namib Desert along coast; Kalahari Desert in east

Elevation: *highest point:* Konigstein on Brandberg 2,573 m
lowest point: Atlantic Ocean 0 m
mean elevation: 1,141 m

Natural resources: diamonds, copper, uranium, gold, silver, lead, tin, lithium, cadmium, tungsten, zinc, salt, hydropower, fish
note: suspected deposits of oil, coal, and iron ore

Land use: *agricultural land:* 47.1% (2022 est.)
arable land: 1% (2022 est.)
permanent crops: 0% (2022 est.)
permanent pasture: 46.2% (2022 est.)
forest: 7.9% (2022 est.)
other: 45% (2022 est.)

Irrigated land: 80 sq km (2012)

Major rivers (by length in km): Zambezi (shared with Zambia [s]), Angola, Botswana, Zimbabwe, and Mozambique [m]) - 2,740 km; Orange river mouth (shared with Lesotho [s], and South Africa) - 2,092 km; Okavango (shared with Angola [s], and Botswana [m]) - 1,600 km
note: [s] after country name indicates river source; [m] after country name indicates river mouth

Major watersheds (area sq km): Atlantic Ocean drainage: Orange (941,351 sq km)

Indian Ocean drainage: Zambezi (1,332,412 sq km)

Internal (endorheic basin) drainage: Okavango Basin (863,866 sq km)

Major aquifers: Lower Kalahari-Stampriet Basin, Upper Kalahari-Cuvelai-Upper Zambezi Basin

Population distribution: population density is very low, with the largest clusters found in the extreme north-central area along the border with Angola, as shown in this population distribution map

Natural hazards: prolonged periods of drought

Geography - note: the Namib Desert, after which the country is named, is considered to be the oldest desert in the world; some 14% of the land is protected, including virtually the entire Namib Desert coastal strip

PEOPLE AND SOCIETY

Population: *total:* 2,803,660 (2024 est.)
male: 1,377,286
female: 1,426,374
comparison rankings: total 141; male 142; female 139

Nationality: *noun:* Namibian(s)
adjective: Namibian

Ethnic groups: Ovambo 50%, Kavangos 9%, Herero 7%, Damara 7%, mixed European and African ancestry 6.5%, European 6%, Nama 5%, Caprivian 4%, San 3%, Baster 2%, Tswana 0.5%

Languages: Oshiwambo languages 49.7%, Nama/Damara 11%, Kavango languages 10.4%, Afrikaans 9.4%, Herero languages 9.2%, Zambezi languages 4.9%, English (official) 2.3%, other African languages 1.5%, other European languages 0.7%, other 1% (2016 est.)
note: Namibia has 13 recognized national languages, including 10 indigenous African languages and 3 European languages

Religions: Christian 97.5%, other 0.6% (includes Muslim, Baha'i, Jewish, Buddhist), unaffiliated 1.9% (2020 est.)

Age structure: *0-14 years:* 34.1% (male 482,790/female 473,306)
15-64 years: 62% (male 846,810/female 890,099)
65 years and over: 3.9% (2024 est.) (male 47,686/female 62,969)

Dependency ratios: *total dependency ratio:* 61.4 (2024 est.)
youth dependency ratio: 55 (2024 est.)
elderly dependency ratio: 6.4 (2024 est.)
potential support ratio: 15.7 (2024 est.)

Median age: *total:* 22.8 years (2024 est.)
male: 22.1 years
female: 23.5 years
comparison ranking: total 182

Population growth rate: 1.72% (2024 est.)
comparison ranking: 54

Birth rate: 24.3 births/1,000 population (2024 est.)
comparison ranking: 47

Death rate: 7.1 deaths/1,000 population (2024 est.)
comparison ranking: 117

Net migration rate: 0 migrant(s)/1,000 population (2024 est.)
comparison ranking: 87

Population distribution: population density is very low, with the largest clusters found in the extreme north-central area along the border with Angola, as shown in this population distribution map

Urbanization: *urban population:* 54.9% of total population (2023)
rate of urbanization: 3.64% annual rate of change (2020-25 est.)

Major urban areas - population: 477,000 WINDHOEK (capital) (2023)

Sex ratio: *at birth:* 1.03 male(s)/female
0-14 years: 1.02 male(s)/female
15-64 years: 0.95 male(s)/female
65 years and over: 0.76 male(s)/female
total population: 0.97 male(s)/female (2024 est.)

Mother's mean age at first birth: 21.6 years (2013 est.)
note: data represents median age at first birth among women 25-49

Maternal mortality ratio: 139 deaths/100,000 live births (2023 est.)
comparison ranking: 54

Infant mortality rate: *total:* 27.9 deaths/1,000 live births (2024 est.)
male: 31 deaths/1,000 live births
female: 24.7 deaths/1,000 live births
comparison ranking: total 55

Life expectancy at birth: *total population:* 65.9 years (2024 est.)
male: 64.2 years
female: 67.6 years
comparison ranking: total population 203

Total fertility rate: 2.89 children born/woman (2024 est.)
comparison ranking: 51

Gross reproduction rate: 1.43 (2024 est.)

Drinking water source: *improved:* *urban:* 96.2% of population (2022 est.)

rural: 73.8% of population (2022 est.)
total: 85.9% of population (2022 est.)
unimproved: urban: 3.8% of population (2022 est.)
rural: 26.2% of population (2022 est.)
total: 14.1% of population (2022 est.)

Health expenditure: 9.4% of GDP (2021)
11.7% of national budget (2022 est.)

Physician density: 0.55 physicians/1,000 population (2022)

Sanitation facility access: *improved: urban:* 70.6% of population (2022 est.)
rural: 23.6% of population (2022 est.)
total: 49% of population (2022 est.)
unimproved: urban: 29.4% of population (2022 est.)
rural: 76.4% of population (2022 est.)
total: 51% of population (2022 est.)

Obesity - adult prevalence rate: 17.2% (2016)
comparison ranking: 119

Alcohol consumption per capita: *total:* 2.38 liters of pure alcohol (2019 est.)
beer: 1.37 liters of pure alcohol (2019 est.)
wine: 0.16 liters of pure alcohol (2019 est.)
spirits: 0.53 liters of pure alcohol (2019 est.)
other alcohols: 0.32 liters of pure alcohol (2019 est.)
comparison ranking: total 126

Tobacco use: *total:* 11.8% (2025 est.)
male: 20.5% (2025 est.)
female: 3.9% (2025 est.)
comparison ranking: total 114

Currently married women (ages 15-49): 33.3% (2023 est.)

Education expenditure: 9.4% of GDP (2022 est.)
24.7% national budget (2022 est.)
comparison ranking: Education expenditure (% GDP) 6

ENVIRONMENT

Environmental issues: depletion and degradation of water and aquatic resources; desertification; land degradation; loss of biodiversity; wildlife poaching

International environmental agreements: *party to:* Antarctic-Marine Living Resources, Biodiversity, Climate Change, Climate Change-Kyoto Protocol, Climate Change-Paris Agreement, Comprehensive Nuclear Test Ban, Desertification, Endangered Species, Hazardous Wastes, Law of the Sea, Ozone Layer Protection, Ship Pollution, Wetlands
signed, but not ratified: none of the selected agreements

Climate: desert; hot, dry; rainfall sparse and erratic

Urbanization: *urban population:* 54.9% of total population (2023)
rate of urbanization: 3.64% annual rate of change (2020-25 est.)

Carbon dioxide emissions: 3.46 million metric tonnes of CO2 (2023 est.)
from coal and metallurgical coke: 48,000 metric tonnes of CO2 (2023 est.)
from petroleum and other liquids: 3.412 million metric tonnes of CO2 (2023 est.)
comparison ranking: total emissions 145

Particulate matter emissions: 11.8 micrograms per cubic meter (2019 est.)

Methane emissions: *energy:* 2.1 kt (2022-2024 est.)
agriculture: 193.6 kt (2019-2021 est.)
waste: 13.7 kt (2019-2021 est.)
other: 0.9 kt (2019-2021 est.)

Waste and recycling: *municipal solid waste generated annually:* 256,700 tons (2024 est.)
percent of municipal solid waste recycled: 19.6% (2022 est.)

Total water withdrawal: *municipal:* 61.568 million cubic meters (2022 est.)
industrial: 18.61 million cubic meters (2022 est.)
agricultural: 201 million cubic meters (2022 est.)

Total renewable water resources: 39.91 billion cubic meters (2022 est.)

GOVERNMENT

Country name: *conventional long form:* Republic of Namibia
conventional short form: Namibia
local long form: Republic of Namibia
local short form: Namibia
former: German South-West Africa (Deutsch-Suedwestafrika), South-West Africa
etymology: named for the coastal Namib Desert; the word *namib* comes from the local Nama language and means "an area where there is nothing"

Government type: presidential republic

Capital: *name:* Windhoek
geographic coordinates: 22 34 S, 17 05 E
time difference: UTC+2 (7 hours ahead of Washington, DC, during Standard Time)
etymology: the name is an Afrikaans word meaning "windy corner;" a local Khoikhoin chief first used the name in the 19th century and may have derived it from the name of his childhood South African village of Winterhoek

Administrative divisions: 14 regions; Erongo, Hardap, //Karas, Kavango East, Kavango West, Khomas, Kunene, Ohangwena, Omaheke, Omusati, Oshana, Oshikoto, Otjozondjupa, Zambezi
note: the Karas region was renamed //Karas in 2013 to include the alveolar lateral click of the Khoekhoegowab language

Legal system: mixed system of uncodified civil law based on Roman-Dutch law and customary law

Constitution: *history:* adopted 9 February 1990, entered into force 21 March 1990
amendment process: passage requires majority vote of the National Assembly membership and of the National Council of Parliament and assent of the president of the republic; if the National Council fails to pass an amendment, the president can call for a referendum; passage by referendum requires two-thirds majority of votes cast; amendments that detract from or repeal constitutional articles on fundamental rights and freedoms cannot be amended, and the requisite majorities needed by Parliament to amend the constitution cannot be changed

International law organization participation: has not submitted an ICJ jurisdiction declaration; accepts ICCt jurisdiction

Citizenship: *citizenship by birth:* no
citizenship by descent only: at least one parent must be a citizen of Namibia
dual citizenship recognized: no
residency requirement for naturalization: 5 years

Suffrage: 18 years of age; universal

Executive branch: *chief of state:* President Netumbo Nandi-NDAITWAH (since 21 March 2025)
head of government: President Netumbo Nandi-NDAITWAH (since 21 March 2025)
cabinet: Cabinet appointed by the president from among members of the National Assembly
election/appointment process: president directly elected by absolute-majority popular vote in 2 rounds, if needed, for a 5-year term (eligible for a second term)
most recent election date: 27 November 2024
election results: *2024:* Netumbo Nandi-NDAITWAH elected president in the first round; percent of vote - Netumbo Nandi-NDAITWAH (SWAPO) 57%, Panduleni ITULA (IPC) 26%, McHenry VENAANI (PDM) 5.10%, Bernadus SWARTBOOI (LPM) 4.72%, Job AMUPANDA (AR) 1.80%, Hendrik GAOBEAB (UDF) 1.16%; other 3.31%
2019: Hage GEINGOB reelected president in the first round; percent of vote - Hage GEINGOB (SWAPO) 56.3%, Panduleni ITULA (independent) 29.4%, McHenry VENAANI (PDM) 5.3%, other.9%
expected date of next election: November 2029
note: the president is both chief of state and head of government

Legislative branch: *legislature name:* Parliament
legislative structure: bicameral

Legislative branch - lower chamber: *chamber name:* National Assembly
number of seats: 104 (96 directly elected; 8 appointed)
electoral system: proportional representation
scope of elections: full renewal
term in office: 5 years
most recent election date: 11/27/2024 to 11/30/2024
parties elected and seats per party: SWAPO Party (51); Independent Patriots of Change (IPC) (20); Affirmative Repositioning (AR) (6); Landless People's Movement (LPM) (5); Popular Democratic Movement (PDM) (5); Other (9)
percentage of women in chamber: 40.6%
expected date of next election: November 2029

Legislative branch - upper chamber: *chamber name:* National Council
number of seats: 42 (all indirectly elected)
electoral system: proportional representation
term in office: 5 years
most recent election date: 12/15/2020
percentage of women in chamber: 14.3%
expected date of next election: December 2025
note: the Council primarily reviews legislation passed and referred by the National Assembly

Judicial branch: *highest court(s):* Supreme Court (consists of the chief justice and at least 3 judges in quorum sessions)
judge selection and term of office: judges appointed by the president of Namibia on the recommendation of the Judicial Service Commission; judges serve until age 65, but terms can be extended by the president until age 70
subordinate courts: High Court; Electoral Court, Labor Court; regional and district magistrates' courts; community courts

Political parties: All People's Party or APP
Christian Democratic Voice or CDV
Landless People's Movement or LPM
National Unity Democratic Organization or NUDO
Namibian Economic Freedom Fighters or NEFF
Popular Democratic Movement or PDM (formerly Democratic Turnhalle Alliance or DTA)
Rally for Democracy and Progress or RDP
Republican Party or RP
South West Africa National Union or SWANU
South West Africa People's Organization or SWAPO
United Democratic Front or UDF
United People's Movement or UPM

Diplomatic representation in the US: *chief of mission:* Ambassador Margareth Natalie MENSAH-WILLIAMS (since 18 January 2021)
chancery: 1605 New Hampshire Avenue NW, Washington, DC 20009
telephone: [1] (202) 986-0540
FAX: [1] (202) 986-0443
email address and website: info@namibiaembassyusa.org
https://namibiaembassyusa.org/

Diplomatic representation from the US: *chief of mission:* Ambassador (vacant); Chargé d'Affaires Brandon HUDSPETH (since 1 January 2025)
embassy: 38 Metje Street, Klein Windhoek, Windhoek
mailing address: 2540 Windhoek Place, Washington DC 20521-2540
telephone: [264] (61) 202-5000
FAX: [264] (61) 202-5219
email address and website: ConsularWindhoek@state.gov
https://na.usembassy.gov/

International organization participation: ACP, AfDB, AU, C, CD, CPLP (associate observer), FAO, G-77, IAEA, IBRD, ICAO, ICCt, ICRM, IDA, IFAD, IFC, IFRCS, ILO, IMF, IMO, Interpol, IOC, IOM, IPU, ISO, ITSO, ITU, ITUC (NGOs), MIGA, NAM, OPCW, SACU, SADC, UN, UNAMID, UNCTAD, UNESCO, UNHCR, UNHRC, UNIDO, UNISFA, UNMIL, UNMISS, UNOCI, UNWTO, UPU, WCO, WHO, WIPO, WMO, WTO

Independence: 21 March 1990 (from South African mandate)

National holiday: Independence Day, 21 March (1990)

Flag: *description:* a wide red stripe edged with narrow white stripes divides the flag diagonally from lower-left corner to upper-right corner; the upper triangle is blue and has a golden-yellow, 12-ray sunburst, and the lower triangle is green
meaning: red stands for the heroism of the people and their determination to build a future of equal opportunity; white stands for peace, unity, tranquility, and harmony; blue stands for the sky and the Atlantic Ocean, the sun for power and existence, and green for vegetation and agricultural resources

National symbol(s): oryx (antelope)

National color(s): blue, red, green, white, yellow

National anthem(s): *title:* "Namibia, Land of the Brave"
lyrics/music: Axali DOESEB
history: adopted 1991

National heritage: *total World Heritage Sites:* 2 (1 cultural, 1 natural)
selected World Heritage Site locales: Twyfelfontein or /Ui-//aes (c); Namib Sand Sea (n)

ECONOMY

Economic overview: upper middle-income, export-driven Sub-Saharan economy; natural resource rich; Walvis Bay port expansion for trade; high potential for renewable power generation and energy independence; major nature-based tourist locale; natural resource rich; shortage of skilled labor

Real GDP (purchasing power parity): $31.154 billion (2024 est.)
$30.039 billion (2023 est.)
$28.761 billion (2022 est.)
note: data in 2021 dollars
comparison ranking: 146

Real GDP growth rate: 3.7% (2024 est.)
4.4% (2023 est.)
5.4% (2022 est.)
note: annual GDP % growth based on constant local currency
comparison ranking: 85

Real GDP per capita: $10,300 (2024 est.)
$10,100 (2023 est.)
$10,000 (2022 est.)
note: data in 2021 dollars
comparison ranking: 145

GDP (official exchange rate): $13.372 billion (2024 est.)
note: data in current dollars at official exchange rate

Inflation rate (consumer prices): 4.2% (2024 est.)
5.9% (2023 est.)
6.1% (2022 est.)
note: annual % change based on consumer prices
comparison ranking: 127

GDP - composition, by sector of origin: *agriculture:* 7.3% (2024 est.)
industry: 28.9% (2024 est.)
services: 54.5% (2024 est.)
note: figures may not total 100% due to non-allocated consumption not captured in sector-reported data
comparison rankings: agriculture 90; industry 62; services 124

GDP - composition, by end use: *household consumption:* 79.3% (2024 est.)
government consumption: 21.5% (2024 est.)
investment in fixed capital: 23.7% (2024 est.)
investment in inventories: 1.9% (2024 est.)
exports of goods and services: 41.6% (2024 est.)
imports of goods and services: -68% (2024 est.)
note: figures may not total 100% due to rounding or gaps in data collection

Agricultural products: *root vegetables, milk, maize, beef, grapes, onions, wheat, fruits, pulses, vegetables (2023) note:* top ten agricultural products based on tonnage

Industries: mining, tourism, fishing, agriculture

Industrial production growth rate: 1% (2024 est.)
note: annual % change in industrial value added based on constant local currency
comparison ranking: 115

Labor force: 1.131 million (2024 est.)
note: number of people ages 15 or older who are employed or seeking work
comparison ranking: 144

Unemployment rate: 19.2% (2024 est.)
19.4% (2023 est.)
19.7% (2022 est.)
note: % of labor force seeking employment
comparison ranking: 182

Youth unemployment rate (ages 15-24): *total:* 37.3% (2024 est.)
male: 36.7% (2024 est.)
female: 38% (2024 est.)
note: % of labor force ages 15-24 seeking employment
comparison ranking: total 11

Population below poverty line: 17.4% (2015 est.)
note: % of population with income below national poverty line
Gini Index coefficient - distribution of family income 59.1 (2015 est.)
note: index (0-100) of income distribution; higher values represent greater inequality
comparison ranking: 1

Household income or consumption by percentage share: *lowest 10%:* 1% (2015 est.)
highest 10%: 47.2% (2015 est.)
note: % share of income accruing to lowest and highest 10% of population

Remittances: 1.1% of GDP (2024 est.)
1% of GDP (2023 est.)
0.7% of GDP (2022 est.)
note: personal transfers and compensation between resident and non-resident individuals/households/entities

Budget: *revenues:* $4.415 billion (2023 est.)
expenditures: $4.779 billion (2023 est.)
note: central government revenues (excluding grants) and expenditures converted to US dollars at average official exchange rate for year indicated

Public debt: 4.64% of GDP (2019 est.)
note: central government debt as a % of GDP
comparison ranking: 196

Taxes and other revenues: 33% (of GDP) (2023 est.)
note: central government tax revenue as a % of GDP
comparison ranking: 2

Current account balance: -$2.055 billion (2024 est.)
-$1.893 billion (2023 est.)
-$1.605 billion (2022 est.)
note: balance of payments - net trade and primary/secondary income in current dollars
comparison ranking: 150

Exports: $5.887 billion (2024 est.)
$5.729 billion (2023 est.)
$5.361 billion (2022 est.)
note: balance of payments - exports of goods and services in current dollars
comparison ranking: 135

Exports - partners: South Africa 27%, China 12%, Botswana 8%, Belgium 7%, France 5% (2023)
note: top five export partners based on percentage share of exports

Exports - commodities: gold, diamonds, radioactive chemicals, fish, refined petroleum (2023)
note: top five export commodities based on value in dollars

Imports: $9.199 billion (2024 est.)
$8.443 billion (2023 est.)
$7.43 billion (2022 est.)
note: balance of payments - imports of goods and services in current dollars
comparison ranking: 125

Imports - partners: South Africa 36%, China 9%, India 7%, UAE 4%, USA 3% (2023)
note: top five import partners based on percentage share of imports

Imports - commodities: refined petroleum, copper ore, ships, electricity, trucks (2023)
note: top five import commodities based on value in dollars

Reserves of foreign exchange and gold: $3.356 billion (2024 est.)
$2.956 billion (2023 est.)
$2.803 billion (2022 est.)
note: holdings of gold (year-end prices)/foreign exchange/special drawing rights in current dollars
comparison ranking: 114

Exchange rates: Namibian dollars (NAD) per US dollar -

Exchange rates: 18.329 (2024 est.)
18.446 (2023 est.)
16.356 (2022 est.)
14.779 (2021 est.)

16.463 (2020 est.)

ENERGY

Electricity access: *electrification - total population:* 56.2% (2022 est.)
electrification - urban areas: 74.8%
electrification - rural areas: 33.2%

Electricity: *installed generating capacity:* 646,000 kW (2023 est.)
consumption: 3.891 billion kWh (2023 est.)
exports: 169 million kWh (2023 est.)
imports: 2.917 billion kWh (2023 est.)
transmission/distribution losses: 747.409 million kWh (2023 est.)
comparison rankings: installed generating capacity 146; consumption 136; exports 87; imports 61; transmission/distribution losses 89

Electricity generation sources: *fossil fuels:* 1.9% of total installed capacity (2023 est.)
solar: 26.9% of total installed capacity (2023 est.)
wind: 1.2% of total installed capacity (2023 est.)
hydroelectricity: 70% of total installed capacity (2023 est.)

Coal: *consumption:* 24,000 metric tons (2023 est.)
exports: 900 metric tons (2023 est.)
imports: 26,000 metric tons (2023 est.)
proven reserves: 350 million metric tons (2023 est.)

Petroleum: *refined petroleum consumption:* 23,000 bbl/day (2023 est.)

Natural gas: *proven reserves:* 62.297 billion cubic meters (2021 est.)

Energy consumption per capita: 21.734 million Btu/person (2023 est.)
comparison ranking: 131

COMMUNICATIONS

Telephones - fixed lines: *total subscriptions:* 81,000 (2023 est.)
subscriptions per 100 inhabitants: 3 (2023 est.)
comparison ranking: total subscriptions 143

Telephones - mobile cellular: *total subscriptions:* 2.6 million (2023 est.)
subscriptions per 100 inhabitants: 113 (2022 est.)
comparison ranking: total subscriptions 146

Broadcast media: 1 private and 1 state-run TV station; satellite and cable TV service available; state-run radio broadcasts in multiple languages; about a dozen private radio stations; transmissions of multiple international broadcasters available

Internet country code: .na

Internet users: *percent of population:* 64% (2023 est.)

Broadband - fixed subscriptions: *total:* 104,000 (2023 est.)
subscriptions per 100 inhabitants: 4 (2023 est.)
comparison ranking: total 133

TRANSPORTATION

Civil aircraft registration country code prefix: V5

Airports: 259 (2025)
comparison ranking: 26

Heliports: 1 (2025)
comparison ranking: 152

Railways: *total:* 2,628 km (2014)
narrow gauge: 2,628 km (2014) 1.067-m gauge

Merchant marine: *total:* 15 (2023)
by type: general cargo 1, other 14
comparison ranking: total 152

Ports: *total ports:* 2 (2024)
large: 0
medium: 0
small: 2
very small: 0
ports with oil terminals: 2
key ports: Luderitz Bay, Walvis Bay

MILITARY AND SECURITY

Military and security forces: Namibian Defense Force (NDF): Namibian Army, Namibian Navy, Namibian Air Force (2025)
note: the Namibian Police Force is under the Ministry of Home Affairs, Immigration, Safety, and Security; it has a paramilitary Special Field Force responsible for protecting borders and government installations

Military expenditures: 2.8% of GDP (2024 est.)
2.8% of GDP (2023 est.)
3% of GDP (2022 est.)
3% of GDP (2021 est.)
3.4% of GDP (2020 est.)

Military and security service personnel strengths: estimated 12,000 active Namibian Defense Forces (2025)

Military equipment inventories and acquisitions: the NDF's inventory consists of a mix of Soviet-era and some more modern systems from a variety of countries, including Brazil, China, Germany, India, and South Africa; most of the Navy's vessels and the Air Force's fighter aircraft were acquired from China; Namibia has a small defense industry that produces items such as armored personnel carriers (2024)

Military service age and obligation: 18-25 years of age for men and women for voluntary military service; no conscription (2024)
note: as of 2022, women comprised about 23% of the active-duty military

Military - note: the NDF's primary responsibility is defending Namibia's territorial integrity and national interests; other responsibilities include support to civil authorities and participating in peace and stability missions under the African Union, Southern African Development Community, and the UN; Namibia has bilateral defense ties with several countries, including Botswana, India, South Africa, Tanzania, and Zambia
the NDF was created in 1990, largely from demobilized former members of the People's Liberation Army of Namibia (PLAN) and the South West Africa Territorial Force (SWATF); the PLAN was the armed wing of the South West Africa People's Organization (SWAPO), while SWATF was an auxiliary of the South African Defense Force and comprised the armed forces of the former South West Africa, 1977-1989; from 1990-1995, the British military assisted with the forming and training the NDF (2025)

TRANSNATIONAL ISSUES

Refugees and internally displaced persons: *refugees:* 6,575 (2024 est.)

IDPs: 1,399 (2024 est.)
stateless persons: 14,796 (2024 est.)

NAURU

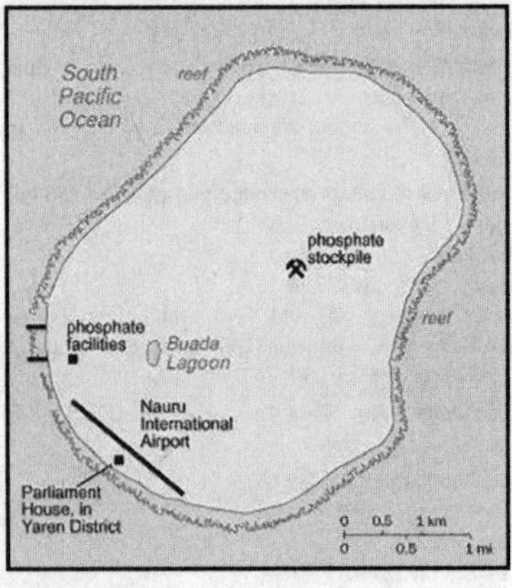

INTRODUCTION

Background: By 1000 B.C., Micronesian and Polynesian settlers inhabited Nauru, and the island was divided among 12 clans. Nauru developed in relative isolation because ocean currents made landfall on the island difficult. As a result, the Nauruan language does not clearly resemble any other in the Pacific region. In 1798, a British mariner was the first European to spot the island and by 1830, European whalers used Nauru as a supply stop, trading firearms for food. A civil war in 1878 reduced the population by more than a third. Germany forcibly annexed Nauru in 1888 by holding the 12 chiefs under house arrest until they consented to the annexation. Phosphate was discovered in 1900 and was heavily mined, although Nauru and Nauruans earned about one tenth of one percent of the profits from the phosphate deposits.

Australian forces captured Nauru from Germany during World War I, and in 1919, it was placed under a joint Australian-British-New Zealand mandate with Australian administration. Japan occupied Nauru during World War II and used its residents as forced labor elsewhere in the Pacific while destroying much of the infrastructure on the island. After the war, Nauru became a UN trust territory under Australian administration. In 1962, recognizing the phosphate stocks would eventually be depleted, Australian Prime Minister Robert MENZIES offered to resettle all Nauruans on Curtis Island in Queensland, but Nauruans rejected that plan and opted for independence, which was achieved in 1968. In 1970, Nauru purchased the phosphate mining assets, and income from the mines made Nauruans among the richest people in the world. However, a series of unwise investments led to near bankruptcy by 2000. Widespread phosphate mining officially ceased in 2006.

As its economy faltered, Nauru briefly tried to rebrand itself as an offshore banking haven, an initiative that ended in 2005, and the country made a successful bid for Russian humanitarian aid in 2008. In 2001, Australia set up the Nauru Regional Processing Center (NRPC), an offshore refugee detention facility, paying Nauru per person at the center. The NRPC closed in 2008 but reopened in 2012. The number of refugees steadily declined after 2014, and in 2020, the remaining people were moved to Brisbane, Australia, effectively shuttering the NRPC. However, in 2023, Australia agreed to continue funding NRPC for two years and restarted settling asylees in the center in mid-2023. The center remains the Government of Nauru's largest source of income.

GEOGRAPHY

Location: Oceania, island in the South Pacific Ocean, south of the Marshall Islands

Geographic coordinates: 0 32 S, 166 55 E

Map references: Oceania

Area: *total:* 21 sq km
land: 21 sq km
water: 0 sq km
comparison ranking: total 238

Area - comparative: about 0.1 times the size of Washington, D.C.

Land boundaries: *total:* 0 km

Coastline: 30 km

Maritime claims: *territorial sea:* 12 nm
contiguous zone: 24 nm
exclusive economic zone: 200 nm

Climate: tropical with a monsoonal pattern; rainy season (November to February)

Terrain: sandy beach rises to fertile ring around raised coral reefs with phosphate plateau in center

Elevation: *highest point:* Command Ridge 70 m
lowest point: Pacific Ocean 0 m

Natural resources: phosphates, fish

Land use: *agricultural land:* 20% (2022 est.)
arable land: 0% (2022 est.)
permanent crops: 20% (2022 est.)
permanent pasture: 0% (2022 est.)
forest: 0% (2022 est.)
other: 80% (2022 est.)

Irrigated land: 0 sq km (2022)

Population distribution: most people live in the fertile coastal areas, especially along the southwest coast

Natural hazards: periodic droughts

Geography - note: Nauru is the third-smallest country in the world behind the Holy See (Vatican City) and Monaco; it is the smallest country in the Pacific Ocean, the smallest country outside Europe, the world's smallest island country, and the world's smallest independent republic; situated just 53 km south of the equator, Nauru is one of the three great phosphate rock islands in the Pacific Ocean – the others are Banaba (Ocean Island) in Kiribati and Makatea in French Polynesia

PEOPLE AND SOCIETY

Population: *total:* 9,892 (2024 est.)
male: 4,856
female: 5,036
comparison rankings: total 222; male 222; female 222

Nationality: *noun:* Nauruan(s)
adjective: Nauruan

Ethnic groups: Nauruan 94.6%, I-Kiribati 2.2%, Fijian 1.3%, other 1.9% (2021 est.)

Languages: Nauruan 93% (official, a distinct Pacific Island language), English 2% (widely understood, spoken, and used for most government and commercial purposes), other 5% (includes Gilbertese 2% and Chinese 2%) (2011 est.)
note: data represent main language spoken at home; Nauruan is spoken by 95% of the population, English by 66%, and other languages by 12%

Religions: Protestant 60.4% (Nauruan Congregational 34.7%, Assemblies of God 11.6%, Pacific Light House 6.3%, Nauru Independent 3.6%, Baptist 1.5, Seventh Day Adventist 1.3%, other Protestant 1.4%), Roman Catholic 33.9%, other 4.2%, none 1.3%, no answer 0.3% (2021 est.)

Age structure: *0-14 years:* 29.6% (male 1,493/female 1,433)
15-64 years: 66% (male 3,220/female 3,309)
65 years and over: 4.4% (2024 est.) (male 143/female 294)

Dependency ratios: *total dependency ratio:* 51.5 (2024 est.)
youth dependency ratio: 44.8 (2024 est.)
elderly dependency ratio: 6.7 (2024 est.)
potential support ratio: 14.9 (2024 est.)

Median age: *total:* 27.8 years (2024 est.)
male: 27.3 years
female: 28.4 years
comparison ranking: total 156

Population growth rate: 0.39% (2024 est.)
comparison ranking: 161

Birth rate: 20.2 births/1,000 population (2024 est.)
comparison ranking: 66

Death rate: 6.5 deaths/1,000 population (2024 est.)
comparison ranking: 138

Net migration rate: -9.8 migrant(s)/1,000 population (2024 est.)
comparison ranking: 222

Population distribution: most people live in the fertile coastal areas, especially along the southwest coast

Urbanization: *urban population:* 100% of total population (2023)
rate of urbanization: 0.18% annual rate of change (2020-25 est.)

Sex ratio: *at birth:* 1.04 male(s)/female
0-14 years: 1.04 male(s)/female
15-64 years: 0.97 male(s)/female
65 years and over: 0.49 male(s)/female
total population: 0.96 male(s)/female (2024 est.)

Maternal mortality ratio: 273 deaths/100,000 live births (2023 est.)
comparison ranking: 27

Infant mortality rate: *total:* 7.6 deaths/1,000 live births (2024 est.)
male: 9.8 deaths/1,000 live births
female: 5.3 deaths/1,000 live births
comparison ranking: total 151

Life expectancy at birth: *total population:* 68.6 years (2024 est.)
male: 65 years
female: 72.3 years
comparison ranking: total population 187

Total fertility rate: 2.55 children born/woman (2024 est.)
comparison ranking: 68

Gross reproduction rate: 1.25 (2024 est.)

Drinking water source: *improved:* total: 100% of population
unimproved: urban: 0% of population
total: 0% of population (2020 est.)

Health expenditure: 13.1% of GDP (2021)
11.8% of national budget (2022 est.)

Physician density: 1.27 physicians/1,000 population (2015)

Obesity - adult prevalence rate: 61% (2016)
comparison ranking: 1

Alcohol consumption per capita: *total:* 2.44 liters of pure alcohol (2019 est.)
beer: 0.54 liters of pure alcohol (2019 est.)
wine: 0.09 liters of pure alcohol (2019 est.)
spirits: 1.81 liters of pure alcohol (2019 est.)
other alcohols: 0 liters of pure alcohol (2019 est.)
comparison ranking: total 125

Tobacco use: *total:* 47.7% (2025 est.)
male: 49.3% (2025 est.)
female: 46.1% (2025 est.)
comparison ranking: total 1

Currently married women (ages 15-49): 59.6% (2023 est.)

Education expenditure: 5.6% of GDP (2023 est.) NA
9.6% national budget (2018 est.)
comparison ranking: Education expenditure (% GDP) 39

Literacy: *total population:* 96.6% (2023 est.)
male: 93.4% (2023 est.)
female: 99.7% (2023 est.)

ENVIRONMENT

Environmental issues: limited natural freshwater resources; effects of intensive phosphate mining that left the central 90% of Nauru a wasteland; air and water pollution from cadmium residue, phosphate dust, and other contaminants; rising sea levels

International environmental agreements: *party to:* Biodiversity, Climate Change, Climate Change-Kyoto Protocol, Climate Change-Paris Agreement, Comprehensive Nuclear Test Ban, Desertification, Hazardous Wastes, Law of the Sea, Marine Dumping-London Convention, Ozone Layer Protection, Whaling
signed, but not ratified: none of the selected agreements

Climate: tropical with a monsoonal pattern; rainy season (November to February)

Urbanization: *urban population:* 100% of total population (2023)
rate of urbanization: 0.18% annual rate of change (2020-25 est.)

Carbon dioxide emissions: 86,000 metric tonnes of CO2 (2023 est.)
from petroleum and other liquids: 86,000 metric tonnes of CO2 (2023 est.)
comparison ranking: total emissions 209

Particulate matter emissions: 7.4 micrograms per cubic meter (2019 est.)

Waste and recycling: *municipal solid waste generated annually:* 6,200 tons (2024 est.)

Total renewable water resources: 10 million cubic meters (2022 est.)

GOVERNMENT

Country name: *conventional long form:* Republic of Nauru

conventional short form: Nauru
local long form: Republic of Nauru
local short form: Nauru
former: Pleasant Island
etymology: the island name may derive from the Nauruan word "anaoero" meaning "I go to the beach"; the former name, Pleasant Island, came from British navigator John Frean, who visited in 1798

Government type: parliamentary republic

Capital: *name:* no official capital; government offices in the Yaren District
time difference: UTC+12 (17 hours ahead of Washington, DC, during Standard Time)

Administrative divisions: 14 districts; Aiwo, Anabar, Anetan, Anibare, Baitsi, Boe, Buada, Denigomodu, Ewa, Ijuw, Meneng, Nibok, Uaboe, Yaren

Legal system: mixed system of common law based on the English model and customary law

Constitution: *history:* effective 29 January 1968
amendment process: proposed by Parliament; passage requires two-thirds majority vote of Parliament; amendments to constitutional articles, such as the republican form of government, protection of fundamental rights and freedoms, the structure and authorities of the executive and legislative branches, also require two-thirds majority of votes in a referendum

International law organization participation: has not submitted an ICJ jurisdiction declaration; accepts ICCt jurisdiction

Suffrage: 20 years of age; universal and compulsory

Executive branch: *chief of state:* President David ADEANG (since 30 October 2023)
head of government: President David ADEANG (since 30 October 2023)
cabinet: Cabinet appointed by the president from among members of Parliament
election/appointment process: president indirectly elected by Parliament for 3-year term (eligible for a second term)
most recent election date: 14 October 2025
election results: *2025:* David ADEAGN elected president (unopposed)
2023: David ADEAGN elected president over Delvin THOMA, 10-8
expected date of next election: 2028
note: the president is both chief of state and head of government

Legislative branch: *legislature name:* Parliament
legislative structure: unicameral
number of seats: 19 (all directly elected)
electoral system: plurality/majority
term in office: 3 years
most recent election date: 10/11/2025
percentage of women in chamber: 10.5%
expected date of next election: September 2028

Judicial branch: *highest court(s):* Supreme Court (consists of the chief justice and several justices)
judge selection and term of office: judges appointed by the president to serve until age 65
subordinate courts: District Court, Family Court
note: in 2017, the Nauruan Government revoked the 1976 High Court Appeals Act, which had allowed appeals beyond the Nauruan Supreme Court, and in 2018, the government formed its own appeals court

Political parties: Nauru does not have formal political parties; alliances within the government are often formed based on extended family ties

Diplomatic representation in the US: *chief of mission:* Ambassador Lara Erab DANIEL (since 13 January 2025); note - also Permanent Representative to the UN
chancery: 801 2nd Avenue, Third Floor, New York, NY 10017
telephone: [1] (212) 937-0074
FAX: [1] (212) 937-0079
email address and website: nauru@onecommonwealth.org
https://www.un.int/nauru/

Diplomatic representation from the US: *embassy:* the US does not have an embassy in Nauru; the US Ambassador to Fiji is accredited to Nauru

International organization participation: ACP, ADB, AOSIS, C, FAO, G-77, ICAO, ICCt, IFAD, Interpol, IOC, IOM, ITU, OPCW, PIF, Sparteca, SPC, UN, UNCTAD, UNESCO, UPU, WHO, WMO

Independence: 31 January 1968 (from the Australia-, NZ-, and UK-administered UN trusteeship)

National holiday: Independence Day, 31 January (1968)

Flag: *description:* blue with a narrow horizontal gold stripe across the center and a large white 12- pointed star below the stripe on the left side
meaning: blue stands for the Pacific Ocean; the star indicates the country's location in relation to the equator (the gold stripe), and the 12 points stand for the original tribes of Nauru; the star's white color represents phosphate, the basis of the island's wealth

National symbol(s): frigatebird, calophyllum flower

National color(s): blue, yellow, white

National anthem(s): *title:* "Nauru Bwiema" (Nauru, Our Homeland)
lyrics/music: Margaret HENDRIE/Laurence Henry HICKS
history: adopted 1968

ECONOMY

Economic overview: upper-middle-income Pacific island country; phosphate resource exhaustion made island interior uninhabitable; licenses fishing rights; houses Australia's Regional Processing Centre; former tax haven; largely dependent on foreign subsidies

Real GDP (purchasing power parity): $150.581 million (2024 est.)
$147.976 million (2023 est.)
$147.026 million (2022 est.)
note: data in 2021 dollars
comparison ranking: 217

Real GDP growth rate: 1.8% (2024 est.)
0.6% (2023 est.)
3% (2022 est.)
note: annual GDP % growth based on constant local currency
comparison ranking: 154

Real GDP per capita: $12,600 (2024 est.)
$12,500 (2023 est.)
$12,500 (2022 est.)
note: data in 2021 dollars
comparison ranking: 135

GDP (official exchange rate): $160.351 million (2024 est.)
note: data in current dollars at official exchange rate

Inflation rate (consumer prices): 2.6% (2022 est.)
2.4% (2021 est.)
1.8% (2020 est.)
note: annual % change based on consumer prices
comparison ranking: 72

Agricultural products: coconuts, tropical fruits, pork, eggs, pork offal, pork fat, chicken, papayas, vegetables, cabbages (2023)
note: top ten agricultural products based on tonnage

Industries: phosphate mining, offshore banking, coconut products

Remittances: 0.6% of GDP (2023 est.)
0.6% of GDP (2022 est.)
0.7% of GDP (2021 est.)
note: personal transfers and compensation between resident and non-resident individuals/households/entities

Budget: *revenues:* $199.74 million (2020 est.)
expenditures: $157.86 million (2020 est.)
note: central government revenues (excluding grants) and expenditures converted to US dollars at average official exchange rate for year indicated

Taxes and other revenues: 44.4% (of GDP) (2020 est.)
note: central government tax revenue as a % of GDP
comparison ranking: 1

Current account balance: $1.923 million (2023 est.)
$2.966 million (2022 est.)
$6.597 million (2021 est.)
note: balance of payments - net trade and primary/secondary income in current dollars
comparison ranking: 85

Exports: $64.931 million (2023 est.)
$78.383 million (2022 est.)
$54.403 million (2021 est.)
note: balance of payments - exports of goods and services in current dollars
comparison ranking: 209

Exports - partners: Thailand 78%, Philippines 11%, NZ 5%, Japan 1%, Canada 1% (2023)
note: top five export partners based on percentage share of exports

Exports - commodities: fish, phosphates (2023)
note: top export commodities based on value in dollars over $500,000

Imports: $150.193 million (2023 est.)
$165.371 million (2022 est.)
$141.185 million (2021 est.)
note: balance of payments - imports of goods and services in current dollars
comparison ranking: 210

Imports - partners: Australia 50%, Japan 11%, Fiji 9%, Senegal 9%, China 9% (2023)
note: top five import partners based on percentage share of imports

Imports - commodities: ships, titanium ore, refined petroleum, plastic products, other foods (2023)
note: top five import commodities based on value in dollars

Exchange rates: Australian dollars (AUD) per US dollar -

Exchange rates: 1.515 (2024 est.)
1.505 (2023 est.)
1.442 (2022 est.)
1.331 (2021 est.)
1.453 (2020 est.)

ENERGY

Electricity access: *electrification - total population:* 100% (2022 est.)

Electricity: *installed generating capacity:* 19,000 kW (2023 est.)
consumption: 37.893 million kWh (2023 est.)

transmission/distribution losses: 3.922 million kWh (2023 est.)
comparison rankings: installed generating capacity 205; consumption 205; transmission/distribution losses 8

Electricity generation sources: *fossil fuels:* 88% of total installed capacity (2023 est.)
solar: 12% of total installed capacity (2023 est.)

Petroleum: *refined petroleum consumption:* 500 bbl/day (2023 est.)

COMMUNICATIONS

Telephones - fixed lines: *total subscriptions:* 0 (2019 est.) 0
subscriptions per 100 inhabitants: (2022 est.) less than 1
comparison ranking: total subscriptions 224

Telephones - mobile cellular: *total subscriptions:* 10,000 (2021 est.)
subscriptions per 100 inhabitants: 80 (2021 est.)
comparison ranking: total subscriptions 219

Broadcast media: 1 state-owned TV station broadcasting programs from New Zealand; 1 state-owned radio station, broadcasting on AM and FM, uses Australian and British programs (2019)

Internet country code: .nr

Internet users: *percent of population:* 82% (2020 est.)

Broadband - fixed subscriptions: *total:* 1,000 (2022 est.)
subscriptions per 100 inhabitants: 10 (2022 est.)
comparison ranking: total 207

TRANSPORTATION

Civil aircraft registration country code prefix: C2

Airports: 1 (2025)
comparison ranking: 227

Merchant marine: *total:* 6 (2023)
by type: other 6
comparison ranking: total 164

Ports: *total ports:* 1 (2024)
large: 0
medium: 0
small: 0
very small: 1
ports with oil terminals: 1
key ports: Nauru

MILITARY AND SECURITY

Military and security forces: no regular military forces; Nauru Police Force (2025)

Military - note: under the terms of a security deal signed in December 2024, Australia and Nauru agreed to "deepen and expand security cooperation" and "consult and consider" in the event of threats; Nauru pledged to seek Australia's agreement before it signed any bilateral accords on maritime security, defense, and policing, and would receive Australian financial assistance in support of Nauru's police and security needs
Nauru has a "shiprider" agreement with the US, which allows local maritime law enforcement officers to embark on US Coast Guard (USCG) and US Navy (USN) vessels, including to board and search vessels suspected of violating laws or regulations within Nauru's designated exclusive economic zone (EEZ) or on the high seas; "shiprider" agreements also enable USCG personnel and USN vessels with embarked USCG law enforcement personnel to work with host nations to protect critical regional resources (2025)

TRANSNATIONAL ISSUES

Refugees and internally displaced persons: *refugees:* 95 (2024 est.)

NAVASSA ISLAND

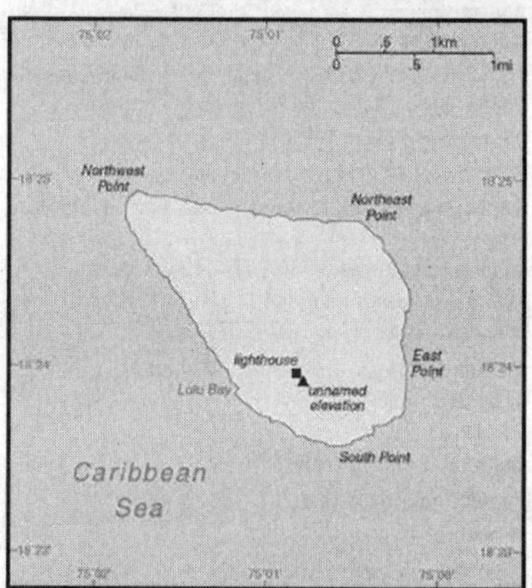

INTRODUCTION

Background: The US claimed uninhabited Navassa Island in 1857 for its guano. Mining took place between 1865 and 1898. The lighthouse, built in 1917, was shut down in 1996, and administration of Navassa Island was transferred from the US Coast Guard to the Department of the Interior, Office of Insular Affairs. A 1998 scientific expedition to the island described it as a "unique preserve of Caribbean biodiversity." The following year it became a National Wildlife Refuge, and annual scientific expeditions have continued.

GEOGRAPHY

Location: Caribbean, island in the Caribbean Sea, 30 nm west of Tiburon Peninsula of Haiti

Geographic coordinates: 18 25 N, 75 02 W

Map references: Central America and the Caribbean

Area: *total:* 5 sq km
land: 5.4 sq km
water: 0 sq km
comparison ranking: total 246

Area - comparative: about nine times the size of the National Mall in Washington, D.C.

Land boundaries: *total:* 0 km

Coastline: 8 km

Maritime claims: *territorial sea:* 12 nm
exclusive economic zone: 200 nm

Climate: marine, tropical

Terrain: raised flat to undulating coral and limestone plateau; ringed by vertical white cliffs (9 to 15 m high)

Elevation: *highest point:* 200 m NNW of lighthouse 85 m
lowest point: Caribbean Sea 0 m

Natural resources: guano (mining discontinued in 1898)

Land use: *other:* 100% (2018 est.)

Natural hazards: hurricanes

Geography - note: strategic location 160 km south of the US Naval Base at Guantanamo Bay, Cuba; mostly exposed rock with numerous solution holes (limestone sinkholes) but with enough grassland to support goat herds; dense stands of fig trees, scattered cactus

PEOPLE AND SOCIETY

Population: *total:* uninhabited

ENVIRONMENT

Environmental issues: some coral bleaching

Climate: marine, tropical

GOVERNMENT

Country name: *conventional long form:* none
conventional short form: Navassa Island
etymology: the flat island was named "Navaza" by sailors with the Christopher COLUMBUS expedition in 1504; the name derives from the Spanish word *nava*, meaning "flat land or level ground"

Dependency status: unorganized, unincorporated territory of the US; administered by the Fish and Wildlife Service, US Department of the Interior, from the Caribbean Islands National Wildlife Refuge in Boqueron, Puerto Rico; Haiti has claimed the island since the 19th century

Legal system: the laws of the US apply

Diplomatic representation from the US: *embassy:* none (territory of the US)

Flag: the flag of the US is used

MILITARY AND SECURITY

Military - note: defense is the responsibility of the US

NEPAL

INTRODUCTION

Background: During the late 18th and early 19th centuries, the principality of Gorkha united many of the other principalities and states of the sub-Himalayan region into a Nepali Kingdom. Nepal retained its independence after the Anglo-Nepalese War of 1814-16, and the subsequent peace treaty laid the foundations for two centuries of amicable relations between Britain and Nepal. In 1951, the Nepali monarch ended the century-old system of hereditary rule and instituted a cabinet system that brought political parties into the government. That arrangement lasted until 1960, when political parties were again banned, but it was reinstated in 1990 with the establishment of a multiparty democracy within the framework of a constitutional monarchy.

A Maoist-led insurgency broke out in 1996. During the ensuing 10-year civil war between Maoist and government forces, the monarchy dissolved the cabinet and parliament. In 2001, Crown Prince DIPENDRA first massacred the royal family and then shot himself. His brother GYANENDRA became king, and the monarchy reassumed absolute power the next year. A peace accord in 2006 led to the promulgation of an interim constitution in 2007. After a nationwide Constituent Assembly (CA) election in 2008, the newly formed CA declared Nepal a federal democratic republic, abolished the monarchy, and elected the country's first president.

When the CA failed to draft a Supreme Court-mandated constitution, then-Prime Minister Baburam BHATTARAI dissolved the CA. An interim government held elections in 2013, in which the Nepali Congress (NC) won the largest share of seats. In 2014, NC formed a coalition government with the second-place Communist Party of Nepal-Unified Marxist-Leninist (UML). Nepal's new constitution came into effect in 2015, at which point the CA became the Parliament and Khagda Prasad Sharma OLI the first post-constitution prime minister (2015-16). He resigned ahead of a no-confidence motion, and Parliament elected Communist Party of Nepal-Maoist (CPN-M) leader Pushpa Kamal DAHAL as prime minister.

The parties headed by OLI and DAHAL ran in coalition and swept the parliamentary elections in 2017, and OLI was sworn in as prime minister in 2018. OLI's efforts to dissolve parliament and hold elections were declared unconstitutional in 2021, and the opposition-supported NC leader Sher Bahadur DEUBA was named prime minister. The NC won a majority of seats in the parliamentary elections in 2022, but DAHAL then broke with the ruling coalition and partnered with OLI and the CPN-UML to become prime minister. DAHAL's first cabinet lasted about two months, until OLI withdrew his support over disagreements about ministerial assignments. In early 2023, DAHAL survived a vote of confidence and formed a coalition with the NC to remain prime minister.

GEOGRAPHY

Location: Southern Asia, between China and India

Geographic coordinates: 28 00 N, 84 00 E

Map references: Asia

Area: *total:* 147,181 sq km
land: 143,351 sq km
water: 3,830 sq km
comparison ranking: total 95

Area - comparative: slightly larger than New York State

Land boundaries: *total:* 3,159 km
border countries (2): China 1,389 km; India 1,770 km

Coastline: 0 km (landlocked)

Maritime claims: none (landlocked)

Climate: varies from cool summers and severe winters in north to subtropical summers and mild winters in south

Terrain: Tarai or flat river plain of the Ganges in south; central hill region with rugged Himalayas in north

Elevation: *highest point:* Mount Everest (highest peak in Asia and highest point on earth above sea level) 8,849 m
lowest point: Kanchan Kalan 70 m
mean elevation: 2,565 m

Natural resources: quartz, water, timber, hydropower, scenic beauty, small deposits of lignite, copper, cobalt, iron ore

Land use: *agricultural land:* 26.1% (2022 est.)
arable land: 12.6% (2022 est.)
permanent crops: 1% (2022 est.)
permanent pasture: 12.5% (2022 est.)
forest: 41.6% (2022 est.)
other: 32.3% (2022 est.)

Irrigated land: 12,090 sq km (2022)

Major watersheds (area sq km): Indian Ocean drainage: Brahmaputra (651,335 sq km), Ganges (1,016,124 sq km), Indus (1,081,718 sq km)

Major aquifers: Indus-Ganges-Brahmaputra Basin

Population distribution: most of the population is divided nearly equally between a concentration in the southern-most plains of the Tarai region and the central hilly region; overall density is low

Natural hazards: severe thunderstorms; flooding; landslides; drought and famine depending on the timing, intensity, and duration of the summer monsoons

Geography - note: landlocked; strategic location between China and India; contains eight of world's 10 highest peaks, including Mount Everest and Kanchenjunga – the world's tallest and third-tallest mountains – on the borders with China and India, respectively

PEOPLE AND SOCIETY

Population: *total:* 31,122,387 (2024 est.)
male: 15,240,643
female: 15,881,744
comparison rankings: total 50; male 51; female 48

Nationality: *noun:* Nepali (singular and plural)
adjective: Nepali

Ethnic groups: Chhettri 16.5%, Brahman-Hill 11.3%, Magar 6.9%, Tharu 6.2%, Tamang 5.6%, Bishwokarma 5%, Musalman 4.9%, Newar 4.6%, Yadav 4.2%, Rai 2.2%, Pariyar 1.9%, Gurung 1.9%, Thakuri 1.7%, Mijar 1.6%, Teli 1.5%, Yakthung/Limbu 1.4%, Chamar/Harijan/Ram 1.4%, Koiri/Kushwaha 1.2%, other 20% (2021 est.)
note: 141 caste/ethnic groups were reported in the 2021 national census

Languages: Nepali (official) 44.9%, Maithali 11.1%, Bhojpuri 6.2%, Tharu 5.9%, Tamang 4.9%, Bajjika 3.9%, Avadhi 3%, Nepalbhasha (Newari) 3%, Magar Dhut 2.8%, Doteli 1.7%, Urdu 1.4%, Yakthung/Limbu 1.2%, Gurung 1.1%, other 8.9% (2021 est.)
major-language sample(s):
विश्व तथ्य पुस्तक,आधारभूत जानकारीको लागि अपरिहार्य स्रोत
(Nepali)
note: 123 languages reported as mother tongue in 2021 national census; many in government and business also speak English

Religions: Hindu 81.2%, Buddhist 8.2%, Muslim 5.1%, Kirat 3.2%, Christian 1.8%, other 0.5% (2021 est.)

Age structure: *0-14 years:* 25.8% (male 4,125,244/female 3,909,135)
15-64 years: 67.8% (male 10,153,682/female 10,957,011)
65 years and over: 6.4% (2024 est.) (male 961,717/female 1,015,598)

Dependency ratios: *total dependency ratio:* 47.4 (2024 est.)
youth dependency ratio: 38.1 (2024 est.)
elderly dependency ratio: 9.4 (2024 est.)
potential support ratio: 10.7 (2024 est.)

Median age: *total:* 27.6 years (2024 est.)
male: 26.5 years
female: 28.6 years
comparison ranking: total 157

Population growth rate: 0.7% (2024 est.)
comparison ranking: 128

Birth rate: 17 births/1,000 population (2024 est.)
comparison ranking: 91

Death rate: 5.6 deaths/1,000 population (2024 est.)
comparison ranking: 178

Net migration rate: -4.4 migrant(s)/1,000 population (2024 est.)
comparison ranking: 198

Population distribution: most of the population is divided nearly equally between a concentration in the southern-most plains of the Tarai region and the central hilly region; overall density is low

Urbanization: *urban population:* 21.9% of total population (2023)
rate of urbanization: 3.09% annual rate of change (2020-25 est.)

Major urban areas - population: 1.571 million KATHMANDU (capital) (2023)

Sex ratio: *at birth:* 1.06 male(s)/female
0-14 years: 1.06 male(s)/female

15-64 years: 0.93 male(s)/female
65 years and over: 0.95 male(s)/female
total population: 0.96 male(s)/female (2024 est.)

Mother's mean age at first birth: 20.4 years (2016 est.)
note: data represents median age at first birth among women 25-49

Maternal mortality ratio: 142 deaths/100,000 live births (2023 est.)
comparison ranking: 52

Infant mortality rate: *total:* 24 deaths/1,000 live births (2024 est.)
male: 25.2 deaths/1,000 live births
female: 22.7 deaths/1,000 live births
comparison ranking: total 64

Life expectancy at birth: *total population:* 73 years (2024 est.)
male: 72.2 years
female: 73.7 years
comparison ranking: total population 154

Total fertility rate: 1.85 children born/woman (2024 est.)
comparison ranking: 132

Gross reproduction rate: 0.9 (2024 est.)

Drinking water source: *improved: urban:* 90% of population (2022 est.)
rural: 91.6% of population (2022 est.)
total: 91.2% of population (2022 est.)
unimproved: urban: 10% of population (2022 est.)
rural: 8.4% of population (2022 est.)
total: 8.8% of population (2022 est.)

Health expenditure: 5.4% of GDP (2021)
8% of national budget (2022 est.)

Physician density: 1.01 physicians/1,000 population (2023)

Hospital bed density: 0.4 beds/1,000 population (2021 est.)

Sanitation facility access: *improved: urban:* 96.1% of population (2022 est.)
rural: 89.2% of population (2022 est.)
total: 90.7% of population (2022 est.)
unimproved: urban: 3.9% of population (2022 est.)
rural: 10.8% of population (2022 est.)
total: 9.3% of population (2022 est.)

Obesity - adult prevalence rate: 4.1% (2016)
comparison ranking: 187

Alcohol consumption per capita: *total:* 0.36 liters of pure alcohol (2019 est.)
beer: 0.22 liters of pure alcohol (2019 est.)
wine: 0 liters of pure alcohol (2019 est.)
spirits: 0.13 liters of pure alcohol (2019 est.)
other alcohols: 0 liters of pure alcohol (2019 est.)
comparison ranking: total 167

Tobacco use: *total:* 22.9% (2025 est.)
male: 40.3% (2025 est.)
female: 7.6% (2025 est.)
comparison ranking: total 47

Children under the age of 5 years underweight: 18.7% (2022)
comparison ranking: 21

Currently married women (ages 15-49): 74.6% (2023 est.)

Child marriage: *women married by age 15:* 5.8% (2022)
women married by age 18: 34.9% (2022)
men married by age 18: 7% (2022)

Education expenditure: 4% of GDP (2023 est.)
12.8% national budget (2021 est.)
comparison ranking: Education expenditure (% GDP) 109

Literacy: *total population:* 68.7% (2019 est.)
male: 79.7% (2019 est.)
female: 59.4% (2019 est.)

School life expectancy (primary to tertiary education): *total:* 14 years (2023 est.)
male: 14 years (2023 est.)
female: 14 years (2023 est.)

ENVIRONMENT

Environmental issues: deforestation (overuse of wood for fuel and lack of alternatives); forest degradation; soil erosion; contaminated water from human and animal wastes, agricultural runoff, and industrial effluents; unmanaged solid waste; wildlife conservation; air pollution from vehicular emissions

International environmental agreements: *party to:* Biodiversity, Climate Change, Climate Change-Kyoto Protocol, Climate Change-Paris Agreement, Desertification, Endangered Species, Hazardous Wastes, Law of the Sea, Nuclear Test Ban, Ozone Layer Protection, Wetlands
signed, but not ratified: Comprehensive Nuclear Test Ban, Marine Life Conservation

Climate: varies from cool summers and severe winters in north to subtropical summers and mild winters in south

Urbanization: *urban population:* 21.9% of total population (2023)
rate of urbanization: 3.09% annual rate of change (2020-25 est.)

Carbon dioxide emissions: 11.357 million metric tonnes of CO2 (2023 est.)
from coal and metallurgical coke: 2.025 million metric tonnes of CO2 (2023 est.)
from petroleum and other liquids: 9.332 million metric tonnes of CO2 (2023 est.)
comparison ranking: total emissions 103

Particulate matter emissions: 36.9 micrograms per cubic meter (2019 est.)

Waste and recycling: *municipal solid waste generated annually:* 1.769 million tons (2024 est.)
percent of municipal solid waste recycled: 4.6% (2022 est.)

Total water withdrawal: *municipal:* 147.6 million cubic meters (2022 est.)
industrial: 29.5 million cubic meters (2022 est.)
agricultural: 9.32 billion cubic meters (2022 est.)

Total renewable water resources: 210.2 billion cubic meters (2022 est.)

GOVERNMENT

Country name: *conventional long form:* none
conventional short form: Nepal
local long form: none
local short form: Nepal
etymology: the name probably comes from the Sanskrit term *nepala*, from the words for "fly down" and "house," which would refer to the villages at the base of the mountains

Government type: federal parliamentary republic

Capital: *name:* Kathmandu
geographic coordinates: 27 43 N, 85 19 E
time difference: UTC+5.75 (10.75 hours ahead of Washington, DC, during Standard Time)
etymology: the name comes from the Nepalese words *kath* (wooden) and *mandu* (temple), referring to the local temples that are often still built from wood

Administrative divisions: 7 provinces (*pradesh*, singular - *pradesh*); Bagmati, Gandaki, Karnali, Koshi, Lumbini, Madhesh, Sudurpashchim

Legal system: English common law and Hindu legal concepts

Constitution: *history:* several previous; latest approved by the Second Constituent Assembly 16 September 2015, signed by the president and effective 20 September 2015
amendment process: proposed as a bill by either house of the Federal Parliament; bills affecting a state border or powers delegated to a state must be submitted to the affected state assembly; passage of such bills requires a majority vote of that state assembly membership; bills not requiring state assembly consent require at least two-thirds majority vote by the membership of both houses of the Federal Parliament; parts of the constitution on the sovereignty, territorial integrity, independence, and sovereignty vested in the people cannot be amended

International law organization participation: has not submitted an ICJ jurisdiction declaration; non-party state to the ICCt

Citizenship: *citizenship by birth:* yes
citizenship by descent only: yes
dual citizenship recognized: no
residency requirement for naturalization: 15 years

Suffrage: 18 years of age; universal

Executive branch: *chief of state:* President Ram Chandra POUDEL (since 13 March 2023)
head of government: Prime Minister Sushila KARKI; note - KARKI was sworn in as interim prime minister on 12 September 2025 after Khadga Prasad Sharma OLI resigned on 9 September following violent protests; KARKI will serve until elections are held in March 2026
cabinet: Council of Ministers appointed by the prime minister; cabinet positions shared among Nepali Congress, Communist Party of Nepal-Maoist Centre, and various coalition partners
election/appointment process: president indirectly elected by an electoral college of the Federal Parliament and the state assemblies for a 5-year term (eligible for a second term)
most recent election date: 9 March 2023
election results: 2023: Ram Chandra POUDEL elected president; electoral college vote - Ram Chandra POUDEL (NC) 33,802, Subash Chandra NEMBANG (CPN-UML) 15,518
2018: Bidhya Devi BHANDARI reelected president; electoral vote - Bidhya Devi BHANDARI (CPN-UML) 39,275, Kumari Laxmi RAI (NC) 11,730
expected date of next election: 5 March 2026

Legislative branch: *legislature name:* Federal Parliament (Sanghiya Sansad)
legislative structure: bicameral
note: violent student-led protests in early September 2025 led to the resignation of the Prime Minister; the President dissolved Parliament on 12 September 2015 following the swearing in of an interim prime minister and set elections for 5 March 2026; the major political parties have demanded reinstatement of the Parliament

Legislative branch - lower chamber: *chamber name:* House of Representatives (Pratinidhi Sabha)
number of seats: 275 (all directly elected)
electoral system: mixed system

scope of elections: full renewal
term in office: 5 years
most recent election date: 11/19/2013
parties elected and seats per party: Nepali Congress (NC) (89); Communist Party of Nepal (Unified Marxist-Leninist, UML) (78); Communist Party of Nepal-Maoist Centre (CPN-MC) (32); Rastriya Swatantra Party (20); Rastriya Prajatantra Party Nepal (RPP) (14); People's Socialist Party, Nepal (12); Communist Party of Nepal (Unified Socialist) (10); Janamat Party (6); Democratic Socialist Party, Nepal (4); People's Freedom Party (3); Nepal Workers Peasants Party (1); Rastriya Janamorcha (1); Independents (5)
percentage of women in chamber: 33.5%
expected date of next election: 5 March 2026; note - Parliament was dissolved by the President on 12 September following violent protests, the resignation of the Prime Minister, and the appointment of an interim prime minister with new elections set for March 2026

Legislative branch - upper chamber: *chamber name:* National Assembly (Rastriya Sabha)
number of seats: 59 (56 indirectly elected; 3 appointed)
scope of elections: partial renewal
term in office: 6 years
most recent election date: 1/25/2024
percentage of women in chamber: 37.3%
expected date of next election: January 2026

Judicial branch: *highest court(s):* Supreme Court (consists of the chief justice and up to 20 judges)
judge selection and term of office: Supreme Court chief justice appointed by the president on the recommendation of the Constitutional Council, a 5-member, high-level advisory body headed by the prime minister; other judges appointed by the president on the recommendation of the Judicial Council, a 5-member advisory body headed by the chief justice; the chief justice serves a 6-year term; judges serve until age 65
subordinate courts: High Court; district courts

Political parties: Communist Party of Nepal (Maoist Centre) or CPN-MC
Communist Party of Nepal (Unified Marxist-Leninist) or CPN-UML
Communist Party of Nepal (Unified Socialist) or CPN-US
Janamat Party
Janata Samajbaadi Party or JSP
Loktantrik Samajwadi Party or LSP
Naya Shakti Party, Nepal
Nepali Congress or NC
Nepal Mazdoor Kisan Party (Nepal Workers' and Peasants' Party) or NWPP
Rastriya Janamorcha (National People's Front)
Rastriya Prajatantra Party (National Democratic Party) or RPP
Rastriya Swatantra Party or RSP

Diplomatic representation in the US: *chief of mission:* Ambassador Lok Darshan REGMI (since 11 June 2025)
chancery: 2730 34th Place NW, Washington, DC 20007
telephone: [1] (202) 667-4550
FAX: [1] (202) 667-5534
email address and website: info@nepalembassyusa.org
https://us.nepalembassy.gov.np/
consulate(s) general: New York

Diplomatic representation from the US: *chief of mission:* Ambassador Dean R. THOMPSON (since October 2022)
embassy: Maharajgunj, Kathmandu
mailing address: 6190 Kathmandu Place, Washington DC 20521-6190
telephone: [977] (1) 423-4000
FAX: [977] (1) 400-7272
email address and website: usembktm@state.gov
https://np.usembassy.gov/

International organization participation: ADB, BIMSTEC, CD, CP, FAO, G-77, IAEA, IBRD, ICAO, ICC (NGOs), ICRM, IDA, IFAD, IFC, IFRCS, ILO, IMF, IMO, Interpol, IOC, IOM, IPU, ISO, ITSO, ITU, ITUC (NGOs), MIGA, MINURSO, MINUSTAH, MONUSCO, NAM, OPCW, SAARC, SACEP, UN, UNAMID, UNCTAD, UNDOF, UNESCO, UNIDO, UNIFIL, UNISFA, UNMIL, UNMISS, UNOCI, UNSOM, UNTSO, UNWTO, UPU, WCO, WFTU (NGOs), WHO, WIPO, WMO, WTO

Independence: 1768 (unified by Prithvi Narayan SHAH)

National holiday: Constitution Day, 20 September (2015)
note: replaces the previous Republic Day on 28 May as the official national day in Nepal; the Gregorian date fluctuates based on Nepal's Hindu calendar

Flag: *description:* crimson red with a blue border, in the shape of two overlapping right triangles; the smaller upper triangle has a stylized white moon, and the larger lower triangle has a 12-pointed white sun
meaning: red stands for the rhododendron (the national flower) and victory and bravery, and the blue border for peace and harmony; the two triangles are a combination of two pennants that originally symbolized the Himalaya Mountains, but today they refer to Hinduism and Buddhism, the country's two main religions; the moon stands for the serenity of the people, as well as Himalayan shade and cool weather, and the sun for the heat and higher temperatures in the rest of the country
note: Nepal is the only country with a flag that is not rectangular or square

National symbol(s): rhododendron blossom

National color(s): red

National anthem(s): *title:* "Sayaun Thunga Phool Ka" (Hundreds of Flowers)
lyrics/music: Pradeep Kumar RAI/Ambar GURUNG
history: adopted 2007

National heritage: *total World Heritage Sites:* 4 (2 cultural, 2 natural)
selected World Heritage Site locales: Kathmandu Valley (c); Sagarmatha National Park (n); Chitwan National Park (n); Lumbini, Buddha Birthplace (c)

ECONOMY

Economic overview: low-income South Asian economy; post-conflict fiscal federalism increasing stability; COVID-19 hurt trade and tourism; widening current account deficits; environmentally fragile economy from earthquakes; growing Chinese relations and investments

Real GDP (purchasing power parity): $149.643 billion (2024 est.)
$144.352 billion (2023 est.)
$141.546 billion (2022 est.)
note: data in 2021 dollars
comparison ranking: 83

Real GDP growth rate: 3.7% (2024 est.)
2% (2023 est.)
5.6% (2022 est.)
note: annual GDP % growth based on constant local currency
comparison ranking: 92

Real GDP per capita: $5,000 (2024 est.)
$4,900 (2023 est.)
$4,800 (2022 est.)
note: data in 2021 dollars
comparison ranking: 173

GDP (official exchange rate): $42.914 billion (2024 est.)
note: data in current dollars at official exchange rate

Inflation rate (consumer prices): 7.1% (2023 est.)
7.7% (2022 est.)
4.1% (2021 est.)
note: annual % change based on consumer prices
comparison ranking: 164

GDP - composition, by sector of origin: *agriculture:* 21.9% (2024 est.)
industry: 11.4% (2024 est.)
services: 55.2% (2024 est.)
note: figures may not total 100% due to non-allocated consumption not captured in sector-reported data
comparison rankings: agriculture 30; industry 180; services 120

GDP - composition, by end use: *household consumption:* 86.3% (2024 est.)
government consumption: 7.4% (2024 est.)
investment in fixed capital: 24.3% (2024 est.)
investment in inventories: 6.1% (2024 est.)
exports of goods and services: 7.6% (2024 est.)
imports of goods and services: -32.9% (2024 est.)
note: figures may not total 100% due to rounding or gaps in data collection

Agricultural products: rice, vegetables, potatoes, sugarcane, maize, wheat, bison milk, milk, mangoes/guavas, bananas (2023)
note: top ten agricultural products based on tonnage

Industries: tourism, carpets, textiles, small rice, jute, sugar, oilseed mills, cigarettes, cement and brick production

Industrial production growth rate: 0.1% (2024 est.)
note: annual % change in industrial value added based on constant local currency
comparison ranking: 134

Labor force: 8.435 million (2024 est.)
note: number of people ages 15 or older who are employed or seeking work
comparison ranking: 63

Unemployment rate: 10.8% (2024 est.)
10.7% (2023 est.)
10.9% (2022 est.)
note: % of labor force seeking employment
comparison ranking: 153

Youth unemployment rate (ages 15-24): *total:* 20.8% (2024 est.)
male: 19.3% (2024 est.)
female: 23.6% (2024 est.)
note: % of labor force ages 15-24 seeking employment
comparison ranking: total 54

Population below poverty line: 20.3% (2022 est.)
note: % of population with income below national poverty line
Gini Index coefficient - distribution of family income 30 (2022 est.)
note: index (0-100) of income distribution; higher values represent greater inequality
comparison ranking: 118

Household income or consumption by percentage share: *lowest 10%:* 3.7% (2022 est.)

highest 10%: 24.2% (2022 est.)
note: % share of income accruing to lowest and highest 10% of population

Remittances: 33.1% of GDP (2024 est.)
25.3% of GDP (2023 est.)
22% of GDP (2022 est.)
note: personal transfers and compensation between resident and non-resident individuals/households/entities

Budget: *revenues:* $7.625 billion (2021 est.)
expenditures: $9.1 billion (2021 est.)
note: central government revenues (excluding grants) and expenditures converted to US dollars at average official exchange rate for year indicated

Public debt: 39.9% of GDP (2021 est.)
note: central government debt as a % of GDP
comparison ranking: 133

Taxes and other revenues: 17.5% (of GDP) (2021 est.)
note: central government tax revenue as a % of GDP
comparison ranking: 72

Current account balance: $1.954 billion (2024 est.)
$146.66 million (2023 est.)
-$3.088 billion (2022 est.)
note: balance of payments - net trade and primary/secondary income in current dollars
comparison ranking: 47

Exports: $3.744 billion (2024 est.)
$2.258 billion (2023 est.)
$2.106 billion (2022 est.)
note: balance of payments - exports of goods and services in current dollars
comparison ranking: 148

Exports - partners: India 67%, USA 12%, Germany 3%, China 2%, UK 2% (2023)
note: top five export partners based on percentage share of exports

Exports - commodities: knotted carpets, garments, flat-rolled iron, synthetic fibers, palm oil (2023)
note: top five export commodities based on value in dollars

Imports: $17.777 billion (2024 est.)
$13.877 billion (2023 est.)
$15.227 billion (2022 est.)
note: balance of payments - imports of goods and services in current dollars
comparison ranking: 104

Imports - partners: India 71%, China 17%, UAE 3%, Singapore 2%, Germany 1% (2023)
note: top five import partners based on percentage share of imports

Imports - commodities: refined petroleum, natural gas, garments, iron reductions, broadcasting equipment (2023)
note: top five import commodities based on value in dollars

Reserves of foreign exchange and gold: $12.456 billion (2023 est.)
$9.319 billion (2022 est.)
$9.639 billion (2021 est.)
note: holdings of gold (year-end prices)/foreign exchange/special drawing rights in current dollars
comparison ranking: 75

Debt - external: $5.719 billion (2023 est.)
note: present value of external debt in current US dollars
comparison ranking: 68

Exchange rates: Nepalese rupees (NPR) per US dollar -

Exchange rates: 133.727 (2024 est.)
132.115 (2023 est.)
125.199 (2022 est.)
118.134 (2021 est.)
118.345 (2020 est.)

ENERGY

Electricity access: *electrification - total population:* 91.3% (2022 est.)
electrification - urban areas: 97.7%
electrification - rural areas: 93.7%

Electricity: *installed generating capacity:* 2.853 million kW (2023 est.)
consumption: 9.806 billion kWh (2023 est.)
exports: 1.1 billion kWh (2023 est.)
imports: 1.846 billion kWh (2023 est.)
transmission/distribution losses: 1.638 billion kWh (2023 est.)
comparison rankings: installed generating capacity 112; consumption 107; exports 69; imports 69; transmission/distribution losses 115

Electricity generation sources: *solar:* 1% of total installed capacity (2023 est.)
wind: 0.1% of total installed capacity (2023 est.)
hydroelectricity: 99% of total installed capacity (2023 est.)

Coal: *production:* 9,000 metric tons (2023 est.)
consumption: 1.091 million metric tons (2023 est.)
exports: 100 metric tons (2023 est.)
imports: 1.076 million metric tons (2023 est.)
proven reserves: 8 million metric tons (2023 est.)

Petroleum: *refined petroleum consumption:* 71,000 bbl/day (2023 est.)

Energy consumption per capita: 6.604 million Btu/person (2023 est.)
comparison ranking: 164

COMMUNICATIONS

Telephones - fixed lines: *total subscriptions:* 726,000 (2021 est.)
subscriptions per 100 inhabitants: 2 (2022 est.)
comparison ranking: total subscriptions 80

Telephones - mobile cellular: *total subscriptions:* 38.2 million (2021 est.)
subscriptions per 100 inhabitants: 127 (2021 est.)
comparison ranking: total subscriptions 42

Broadcast media: state operates 3 TV stations, as well as national and regional radio stations; 117 television channels are licensed, 71 of which are cable TV, 3 are distributed through Direct-To-Home (DTH) system, and 4 are digital terrestrial; 736 FM radio stations are licensed, and at least 314 of those are community stations (2019)

Internet country code: .np

Internet users: *percent of population:* 56% (2023 est.)

Broadband - fixed subscriptions: *total:* 1.44 million (2022 est.)
subscriptions per 100 inhabitants: 5 (2022 est.)
comparison ranking: total 71

TRANSPORTATION

Civil aircraft registration country code prefix: 9N

Airports: 51 (2025)
comparison ranking: 87

Heliports: 14 (2025)
comparison ranking: 61

Railways: *total:* 59 km (2018)
narrow gauge: 59 km (2018) 0.762-m gauge

MILITARY AND SECURITY

Military and security forces: Nepalese Armed Forces (Ministry of Defense): Nepali Army (includes Air Wing)

Ministry of Home Affairs: Nepal Police, Nepal Armed Police Force (APF) (2025)
note: the Nepal Police are responsible for enforcing law and order across the country; the Armed Police Force is responsible for combating terrorism, providing security during riots and public disturbances, assisting in natural disasters, and protecting vital infrastructure, public officials, and the borders; it also conducts counterinsurgency and counterterrorism operations and would assist the Army in the event of an external invasion

Military expenditures: 1% of GDP (2024 est.)
1% of GDP (2023 est.)
1.1% of GDP (2022 est.)
1.3% of GDP (2021 est.)
1.3% of GDP (2020 est.)

Military and security service personnel strengths: approximately 95,000 active Armed Forces (2025)

Military equipment inventories and acquisitions: the Army's inventory includes a mix of mostly older equipment largely of British, Chinese, Indian, Russian, and South African origin; in recent years, Nepal has received limited amounts of newer hardware from several countries, including China, Indonesia, Italy, and Russia (2023)

Military service age and obligation: 18 years of age for voluntary military service for men and women; no conscription (2023)
note: as of 2023, about 7,000 women served in the Nepalese Armed Forces

Military deployments: 1240 Central African Republic (MINUSCA); 1,150 Democratic Republic of the Congo (MONUSCO); 400 Golan Heights (UNDOF); 875 Lebanon (UNIFIL); 225 Liberia (UNSMIL); 100 South Sudan/Sudan (UNISFA); 1,725 (plus about 220 police) South Sudan (UNMISS); note - Nepal has over 6,000 total personnel deployed on 15 UN missions (2024)

Military - note: the Nepali Army is responsible for territorial defense, fulfilling Nepal's commitments to UN peacekeeping, and some domestic duties such as disaster relief/humanitarian assistance, social services, and nature conservation efforts; during the 10-year civil war that ended in 2006, it conducted counterinsurgency operations against Maoist guerrillas; the Army has a long history of supporting UN missions, having sent its first UN observers to Lebanon in 1958 and its first troop contingent to Egypt in 1974; as of 2025, 150,000 Nepali military personnel have deployed on over 40 UN missions; Nepal's key security partners are China, India, and the US
the British began to recruit Nepalese citizens (Gurkhas) into the East India Company Army during the Anglo-Nepalese War (1814-1816); the Gurkhas subsequently were brought into the British Indian Army and by 1914, there were 10 Gurkha regiments, collectively known as the Gurkha Brigade; following the partition of India in 1947, an agreement between Nepal, India, and Great Britain allowed for the transfer of the 10 regiments from the British Indian Army to the separate British and Indian armies; four regiments were transferred to the British Army, where they have since served continuously as the Brigade

of Gurkhas; six Gurkha (aka Gorkha in India) regiments went to the new Indian Army; a seventh regiment was later added; Gurkhas are also recruited into the Singaporean Police and a special guard in the Sultanate of Brunei known as the Gurkha Reserve Unit (2025)

TERRORISM

Terrorist group(s): Terrorist group(s): Indian Mujahedeen

note: details about the history, aims, leadership, organization, areas of operation, tactics, targets, weapons, size, and sources of support of the group(s) appear(s) in Appendix T

TRANSNATIONAL ISSUES

Refugees and internally displaced persons: *refugees:* 19,874 (2024 est.)

IDPs: 18,671 (2024 est.)

stateless persons: 467 (2024 est.)

Trafficking in persons: *tier rating:* Tier 2 Watch List — the government did not demonstrate overall increasing efforts to eliminate trafficking compared with the previous reporting period, therefore Nepal remained on Tier 2 Watch List for the second consecutive year; for more details, go to: https://www.state.gov/reports/2025-trafficking-in-persons-report/nepal/

NETHERLANDS

INTRODUCTION

Background: The Dutch United Provinces declared their independence from Spain in 1581; during the 17th century, they became a leading seafaring and commercial power, with settlements and colonies around the world. After 18 years of French domination, the Netherlands regained its independence in 1813. In 1830, Belgium seceded and formed a separate kingdom. The Netherlands remained neutral in World War I but suffered German invasion and occupation in World War II. A modern, industrialized nation, the Netherlands is also a large exporter of agricultural products. The country was a founding member of NATO and the EEC (now the EU) and participated in the introduction of the euro in 1999. In 2010, the former Netherlands Antilles was dissolved and the three smallest islands – Bonaire, Sint Eustatius, and Saba – became special municipalities in the Netherlands administrative structure. The larger islands of Sint Maarten and Curacao joined the Netherlands and Aruba as constituent countries forming the Kingdom of the Netherlands.

In 2018, the Sint Eustatius island council (governing body) was dissolved and replaced by a government commissioner to restore the integrity of public administration. According to the Dutch Government, the intervention will be as "short as possible and as long as needed."

GEOGRAPHY

Location: Western Europe, bordering the North Sea, between Belgium and Germany

Geographic coordinates: 52 31 N, 5 46 E

Map references: Europe

Area: *total:* 41,543 sq km
land: 33,893 sq km
water: 7,650 sq km
comparison ranking: total 134

Area - comparative: slightly less than twice the size of New Jersey

Land boundaries: *total:* 1,053 km
border countries (2): Belgium 478 km; Germany 575 km

Coastline: 451 km

Maritime claims: *territorial sea:* 12 nm
contiguous zone: 24 nm
exclusive fishing zone: 200 nm

Climate: temperate; marine; cool summers and mild winters

Terrain: mostly coastal lowland and reclaimed land (polders); some hills in southeast

Elevation: *highest point:* Mount Scenery (on the island of Saba in the Caribbean, now considered an integral part of the Netherlands following the dissolution of the Netherlands Antilles) 862 m
lowest point: Zuidplaspolder -7 m
mean elevation: 30 m
note: the highest point on continental Netherlands is Vaalserberg at 322 m

Natural resources: natural gas, petroleum, peat, limestone, salt, sand and gravel, arable land

Land use: *agricultural land:* 53.6% (2022 est.)
arable land: 29.8% (2022 est.)
permanent crops: 1.1% (2022 est.)
permanent pasture: 22.7% (2022 est.)
forest: 11% (2022 est.)
other: 35.4% (2022 est.)

Irrigated land: 2,969 sq km (2019)

Major rivers (by length in km): Rijn (Rhine) river mouth (shared with Switzerland [s], Germany, and France) - 1,233 km
note: [s] after country name indicates river source; [m] after country name indicates river mouth

Major watersheds (area sq km): Atlantic Ocean drainage: Rhine-Maas (198,735 sq km)

Population distribution: an area known as the Randstad, anchored by the cities of Amsterdam, Rotterdam, the Hague, and Utrecht, is the most densely populated region; the north tends to be less dense, but sizeable communities can be found throughout the entire country

Natural hazards: flooding

volcanism: Mount Scenery (887 m), located on the island of Saba in the Caribbean, last erupted in 1640; Round Hill (601 m), a dormant volcano also known as "The Quill," is located on the island of St. Eustatius in the Caribbean; these islands are at the northern end of the volcanic island arc of the Lesser Antilles that extends south to Grenada

Geography - note: located at mouths of three major European rivers (Rhine (Rijn), Meuse (Maas), and Scheldt (Schelde)); about a quarter of the country lies below sea level and only about half of the land exceeds one meter above sea level

PEOPLE AND SOCIETY

Population: *total:* 17,772,378 (2024 est.)
male: 8,844,100
female: 8,928,278
comparison rankings: total 71; male 70; female 71

Nationality: *noun:* Dutchman(men), Dutchwoman(women)
adjective: Dutch

Ethnic groups: Dutch 75.4%, EU (excluding Dutch) 6.4%, Turkish 2.4%, Moroccan 2.4%, Surinamese 2.1%, Indonesian 2%, other 9.3% (2021 est.)

Languages: Dutch (official), Frisian (official in Fryslan province)
major-language sample(s):
Het Wereld Feitenboek, een onmisbare bron van informatie. (Dutch)
note: Frisian, Low Saxon, Limburgish, Romani, and Yiddish have protected status; Dutch is the official language of the three special municipalities of the Caribbean Netherlands; English is a recognized regional language on Sint Eustatius and Saba; Papiamento is a recognized regional language on Bonaire

Religions: Roman Catholic 20.1%, Protestant 14.8% (includes Dutch Reformed, Protestant Church of The Netherlands, Calvinist), Muslim 5%, other 5.9% (includes Hindu, Buddhist, Jewish), none 54.1% (2019 est.)

Age structure: *0-14 years:* 15.2% (male 1,384,142/female 1,312,455)
15-64 years: 64.1% (male 5,750,034/female 5,640,691)
65 years and over: 20.7% (2024 est.) (male 1,709,924/female 1,975,132)

Dependency ratios: *total dependency ratio:* 56 (2024 est.)
youth dependency ratio: 23.7 (2024 est.)
elderly dependency ratio: 32.4 (2024 est.)
potential support ratio: 3.1 (2024 est.)

Median age: *total:* 42.2 years (2024 est.)
male: 40.9 years
female: 43.5 years
comparison ranking: total 44

Population growth rate: 0.39% (2024 est.)
comparison ranking: 160

Birth rate: 10.6 births/1,000 population (2024 est.)
comparison ranking: 175

Death rate: 9.7 deaths/1,000 population (2024 est.)
comparison ranking: 38

Net migration rate: 3 migrant(s)/1,000 population (2024 est.)
comparison ranking: 37

Population distribution: an area known as the Randstad, anchored by the cities of Amsterdam, Rotterdam, the Hague, and Utrecht, is the most densely populated region; the north tends to be less dense, but sizeable communities can be found throughout the entire country

Urbanization: *urban population:* 93.2% of total population (2023)
rate of urbanization: 0.59% annual rate of change (2020-25 est.)

Major urban areas - population: 1.174 million AMSTERDAM (capital), 1.018 million Rotterdam (2023)

Sex ratio: *at birth:* 1.05 male(s)/female
0-14 years: 1.05 male(s)/female
15-64 years: 1.02 male(s)/female
65 years and over: 0.87 male(s)/female
total population: 0.99 male(s)/female (2024 est.)

Mother's mean age at first birth: 30.2 years (2020 est.)

Maternal mortality ratio: 4 deaths/100,000 live births (2023 est.)
comparison ranking: 176

Infant mortality rate: *total:* 3.6 deaths/1,000 live births (2024 est.)
male: 3.9 deaths/1,000 live births
female: 3.3 deaths/1,000 live births
comparison ranking: total 194

Life expectancy at birth: *total population:* 81.9 years (2024 est.)
male: 80.3 years
female: 83.5 years
comparison ranking: total population 39

Total fertility rate: 1.61 children born/woman (2024 est.)
comparison ranking: 180

Gross reproduction rate: 0.78 (2024 est.)

Drinking water source: *improved: urban:* 100% of population (2022 est.)
rural: 100% of population (2022 est.)
total: 100% of population (2022 est.)
unimproved: urban: 0% of population (2022 est.)
rural: 0% of population (2022 est.)
total: 0% of population (2022 est.)

Health expenditure: 11.3% of GDP (2021)
15.9% of national budget (2022 est.)

Physician density: 3.88 physicians/1,000 population (2022)

Hospital bed density: 2.9 beds/1,000 population (2020 est.)

Sanitation facility access: *improved: urban:* 100% of population (2022 est.)
rural: 100% of population (2022 est.)
total: 100% of population (2022 est.)
unimproved: urban: 0% of population (2022 est.)
rural: 0% of population (2022 est.)
total: 0% of population (2022 est.)

Obesity - adult prevalence rate: 20.4% (2016)
comparison ranking: 99

Alcohol consumption per capita: *total:* 8.23 liters of pure alcohol (2019 est.)
beer: 3.95 liters of pure alcohol (2019 est.)
wine: 2.92 liters of pure alcohol (2019 est.)
spirits: 1.36 liters of pure alcohol (2019 est.)
other alcohols: 0 liters of pure alcohol (2019 est.)
comparison ranking: total 40

Tobacco use: *total:* 18.7% (2025 est.)
male: 21% (2025 est.)
female: 16.4% (2025 est.)
comparison ranking: total 77

Currently married women (ages 15-49): 53.7% (2023 est.)

Education expenditure: 5.1% of GDP (2022 est.)
11.6% national budget (2022 est.)
comparison ranking: Education expenditure (% GDP) 58

School life expectancy (primary to tertiary education): *total:* 19 years (2021 est.)
male: 18 years (2021 est.)
female: 19 years (2021 est.)

ENVIRONMENT

Environmental issues: water pollution, including industrial and agricultural chemicals in rivers; air pollution from vehicles and refining activities

International environmental agreements: *party to:* Air Pollution, Air Pollution-Heavy Metals, Air Pollution-Multi-effect Protocol, Air Pollution-Nitrogen Oxides, Air Pollution-Persistent Organic Pollutants, Air Pollution-Sulphur 85, Air Pollution-Sulphur 94, Air Pollution-Volatile Organic Compounds, Antarctic- Environmental Protection, Antarctic-Marine Living Resources, Antarctic Treaty, Biodiversity, Climate Change, Climate Change-Kyoto Protocol, Climate Change-Paris Agreement, Comprehensive Nuclear Test Ban, Desertification, Endangered Species, Environmental Modification, Hazardous Wastes, Law of the Sea, Marine Dumping-London Convention, Marine Dumping-London Protocol, Marine Life Conservation, Nuclear Test Ban, Ozone Layer Protection, Ship Pollution, Tropical Timber 2006, Wetlands, Whaling
signed, but not ratified: none of the selected agreements

Climate: temperate; marine; cool summers and mild winters

Urbanization: *urban population:* 93.2% of total population (2023)
rate of urbanization: 0.59% annual rate of change (2020-25 est.)

Carbon dioxide emissions: 188.191 million metric tonnes of CO2 (2023 est.)
from coal and metallurgical coke: 23.701 million metric tonnes of CO2 (2023 est.)
from petroleum and other liquids: 112.037 million metric tonnes of CO2 (2023 est.)
from consumed natural gas: 52.454 million metric tonnes of CO2 (2023 est.)
comparison ranking: total emissions 33

Particulate matter emissions: 10 micrograms per cubic meter (2019 est.)

Methane emissions: *energy:* 63.1 kt (2022-2024 est.)
agriculture: 449 kt (2019-2021 est.)
waste: 123.3 kt (2019-2021 est.)
other: 17.4 kt (2019-2021 est.)

Waste and recycling: *municipal solid waste generated annually:* 8.805 million tons (2024 est.)
percent of municipal solid waste recycled: 28.3% (2022 est.)

Total water withdrawal: *municipal:* 2.185 billion cubic meters (2022)
industrial: 5.784 billion cubic meters (2022)
agricultural: 265.086 million cubic meters (2022)

Total renewable water resources: 91 billion cubic meters (2022 est.)

Geoparks: *total global geoparks and regional networks:* 2 (2024)
global geoparks and regional networks: De Hondsrug; Schelde Delta (includes Belgium) (2024)

GOVERNMENT

Country name: *conventional long form:* Kingdom of the Netherlands
conventional short form: Netherlands
local long form: Koninkrijk der Nederlanden
local short form: Nederland
abbreviation: NL
etymology: the English name is derived from the country's Dutch name, which means "the lowlands" and describes the geographic area; only about half the Netherlands is more than 1 meter (3.3 ft) above sea level

Government type: parliamentary constitutional monarchy; part of the Kingdom of the Netherlands

Capital: *name:* Amsterdam
geographic coordinates: 52 21 N, 4 55 E
time difference: UTC+1 (6 hours ahead of Washington, DC, during Standard Time)
daylight saving time: +1hr, begins last Sunday in March; ends last Sunday in October
time zone note: time descriptions apply to the continental Netherlands only, for the constituent countries in the Caribbean, the time difference is UTC-4
etymology: the name is derived from the Dutch name of the local river, the Amstel, and the Dutch word *dam*, which has the same meaning in English; the river name is said to derive from the Germanic words *ama* (current) and *stelle* (place)
note: The Hague is the seat of government

Administrative divisions: 12 provinces (*provincies*, singular - *provincie*), 3 public entities* (*openbare lichamen*, singular - *openbaar lichaam* (Dutch); *entidatnan publiko*, singular - *entidat publiko* (Papiamento)); Bonaire*, Drenthe, Flevoland, Fryslan (Friesland), Gelderland, Groningen, Limburg, Noord- Brabant (North Brabant), Noord-Holland (North Holland), Overijssel, Saba*, Sint Eustatius*, Utrecht, Zeeland (Zealand), Zuid-Holland (South Holland)
note 1: the Netherlands is one of four constituent countries of the Kingdom of the Netherlands; the other three, Aruba, Curacao, and Sint Maarten, are Caribbean islands; all four are considered equal partners, but the Netherlands makes up about 98% of the Kingdom's total land area and population and administers most of the Kingdom's affairs
note 2: although Bonaire, Saba, and Sint Eustatius are officially incorporated into the country of the Netherlands under the broad designation of "public entities," Dutch government sources often call them "special municipalities;" Bonaire, Saba, and Sint Eustatius are collectively referred to as the Caribbean Netherlands

Legal system: civil law system based on the French system; constitution does not permit judicial review of acts of the States General

Constitution: *history:* many previous to adoption of the "Basic Law of the Kingdom of the Netherlands" on 24 August 1815; revised 8 times, the latest in 1983
amendment process: proposed as an Act of Parliament by or on behalf of the king or by the Second Chamber of the States General; the Second Chamber is dissolved after its first reading of the Act; passage requires a second reading by both the First Chamber and the newly elected Second Chamber, followed by at least two-thirds majority vote of both chambers, and ratification by the king

International law organization participation: accepts compulsory ICJ jurisdiction with reservations; accepts ICCt jurisdiction

Citizenship: *citizenship by birth:* no
citizenship by descent only: at least one parent must be a citizen of the Netherlands
dual citizenship recognized: no
residency requirement for naturalization: 5 years

Suffrage: 18 years of age; universal

Executive branch: *chief of state:* King WILLEM-ALEXANDER (since 30 April 2013)
head of government: Caretaker Prime Minister Dick SCHOOF (since 3 June 2025)
cabinet: Council of Ministers appointed by the monarch
election/appointment process: the monarchy is hereditary; following Second Chamber elections, the monarch usually appoints the leader of the majority party or majority coalition as prime minister; deputy prime ministers are also appointed by the monarch
note: Prime Minister Dick SCHOOF resigned on 3 June 2025 after a party withdrew from his governing coalition, but he will continue in a caretaker capacity until new elections are held, probably in the fall of 2025

Legislative branch: *legislature name:* States General (Staten-Generaal)
legislative structure: bicameral
Legislative branch - lower chamber
chamber name: House of Representatives (Tweede Kamer der Staten-Generaal)
number of seats: 150 (all directly elected)
electoral system: proportional representation
scope of elections: full renewal
term in office: 4 years
most recent election date: 11/22/2023
parties elected and seats per party: Party for Freedom (PVV) (37); Labour Party (PvdA) (25); People's Party for Freedom and Democracy (VVD) (24); New Social Contract (NSC) (20); Democrats 66 (D66) (9); Other (35)
percentage of women in chamber: 39.3%
expected date of next election: October 2025

Legislative branch - upper chamber: *chamber name:* Senate (Eerste Kamer der Staten-Generaal)
number of seats: 75 (all indirectly elected)
scope of elections: full renewal
term in office: 4 years
most recent election date: 5/30/2023
percentage of women in chamber: 40%
expected date of next election: May 2027

Judicial branch: *highest court(s):* Supreme Court or Hoge Raad (consists of 41 judges: the president, 6 vice presidents, 31 justices, and 3 justices in exceptional service); the court is divided into criminal, civil, tax, and ombuds chambers
judge selection and term of office: justices appointed by the monarch from a list provided by the House of Representatives of the States General; justices appointed for life or until mandatory retirement at age 70
subordinate courts: courts of appeal; district courts, each with up to 5 subdistrict courts; Netherlands Commercial Court

Political parties: Christian Democratic Appeal or CDA
Christian Union or CU
Correct Answer 2021 or JA21
Democrats 66 or D66
Denk
Farmer-Citizen Movement or BBB
50Plus
Forum for Democracy or FvD
Green Left (GroenLinks) or GL
Labor Party or PvdA
New Social Contract or NSC
Party for Freedom or PVV
Party for the Animals or PvdD
People's Party for Freedom and Democracy or VVD
Reformed Political Party or SGP
Socialist Party or SP
Together or BIJ1
Volt Netherlands or Volt

Diplomatic representation in the US: *chief of mission:* Ambassador Birgitta TAZELAAR (since 15 September 2023)
chancery: 4200 Linnean Avenue NW, Washington, DC 20008
telephone: [1] (202) 244-5300
FAX: [1] (202) 362-3430
email address and website: was@minbuza.nl
https://www.netherlandsworldwide.nl/countries/united-states/about-us/embassy-in-washington-dc
consulate(s) general: Atlanta, Chicago, Miami, New York, San Francisco

Diplomatic representation from the US: *chief of mission:* Ambassador (vacant); Chargé d'Affaires Marcus MICHELI (since January 2025)
embassy: John Adams Park 1, 2244 BZ Wassenaar
mailing address: 5780 Amsterdam Place, Washington DC 20521-5780
telephone: [31] (70) 310-2209
FAX: [31] (70) 310-2207
email address and website: AmsterdamUSC@state.gov
https://nl.usembassy.gov/
consulate(s) general: Amsterdam

International organization participation: ADB (nonregional member), AfDB (nonregional member), Arctic Council (observer), Australia Group, Benelux, BIS, CBSS (observer), CD, CE, CERN, EAPC, EBRD, ECB, EIB, EITI (implementing country), EMU, ESA, EU, FAO, FATF, G-10, IADB, IAEA, IBRD, ICAO, ICC (national committees), ICCt, ICRM, IDA, IEA, IFAD, IFC, IFRCS, IGAD (partners), IHO, ILO, IMF, IMO, IMSO, Interpol, IOC, IOM, IPU, ISO, ITSO, ITU, ITUC (NGOs), MIGA, NATO, NEA, NSG, OAS (observer), OECD, OPCW, OSCE, Pacific Alliance (observer), Paris Club, PCA, Schengen Convention, SELEC (observer), UN, UNCTAD, UNESCO, UNHCR, UNHRC, UNIDO, UNMISS, UNOOSA, UNRWA, UN Security Council (temporary), UNTSO, UNWTO, UPU, Wassenaar Arrangement, WCO, WHO, WIPO, WMO, WTO, ZC

Independence: 26 July 1581
note: the northern provinces of the Low Countries formally declared their independence with an Act of Abjuration in 1581, but, it was not until 30 January 1648 and the Peace of Westphalia that Spain recognized this independence

National holiday: King's Day (birthday of King WILLEM-ALEXANDER), 27 April (1967)
note: observed on the ruling monarch's birthday; celebrated on 26 April if 27 April is a Sunday

Flag: *description:* three equal horizontal bands of bright red (top), white, and cobalt blue
history: the colors come from WILLIAM I, Prince of Orange; originally the upper band was orange, but the dye would turn red over time, so red was eventually made the permanent color
note: similar to the flag of Luxembourg, which uses a lighter blue and is wider

National symbol(s): lion, daisy

National color(s): orange

National anthem(s): *title:* "Het Wilhelmus" (The William)
lyrics/music: Philips VAN MARNIX van Sint Aldegonde (presumed)/unknown
history: adopted 1932, in use since the 17th century

National heritage: *total World Heritage Sites:* 13 (12 cultural, 1 natural)
selected World Heritage Site locales: Schokland and Surroundings (c); Dutch Water Defense Lines (c); Van Nellefabriek (c); Mill Network at Kinderdijk-Elshout (c); Droogmakerij de Beemster (Beemster Polder) (c); Rietveld Schröderhuis (Rietveld Schröder House) (c); Wadden Sea (n); Seventeenth Century Canal Ring Area of Amsterdam inside the Singelgracht (c); Colonies of Benevolence (c); Frontiers of the Roman Empire - The Lower German Limes (c)
note: includes one site in Curacao

ECONOMY

Economic overview: high-income, core EU- and eurozone-member economy; strong services, logistics, and tech sectors; strongly trade-oriented with heightened risks from global tensions; declining inflation aided by easing energy prices and wage growth; rising but manageable deficits and public debt; strong ratings for innovation, competitiveness, and business climate

Real GDP (purchasing power parity): $1.276 trillion (2024 est.)
$1.263 trillion (2023 est.)
$1.263 trillion (2022 est.)
note: data in 2021 dollars
comparison ranking: 28

Real GDP growth rate: 1% (2024 est.)
0.1% (2023 est.)
5% (2022 est.)
note: annual GDP % growth based on constant local currency
comparison ranking: 175

Real GDP per capita: $70,900 (2024 est.)
$70,700 (2023 est.)
$71,300 (2022 est.)
note: data in 2021 dollars
comparison ranking: 17

GDP (official exchange rate): $1.228 trillion (2024 est.)
note: data in current dollars at official exchange rate

Inflation rate (consumer prices): 3.3% (2024 est.)

3.8% (2023 est.)
10% (2022 est.)
note: annual % change based on consumer prices
comparison ranking: 107

GDP - composition, by sector of origin: *agriculture:* 1.7% (2024 est.)
industry: 17.9% (2024 est.)
services: 70.3% (2024 est.)
note: figures may not total 100% due to non-allocated consumption not captured in sector-reported data
comparison rankings: agriculture 158; industry 144; services 34

GDP - composition, by end use: *household consumption:* 42.1% (2023 est.)
government consumption: 24.5% (2023 est.)
investment in fixed capital: 20.1% (2023 est.)
investment in inventories: -0.1% (2023 est.)
exports of goods and services: 88.5% (2023 est.)
imports of goods and services: -77.4% (2023 est.)
note: figures may not total 100% due to rounding or gaps in data collection

Agricultural products: milk, sugar beets, potatoes, onions, pork, wheat, chicken, tomatoes, carrots/turnips, beef (2023)
note: top ten agricultural products based on tonnage

Industries: agroindustries, metal and engineering products, electrical machinery and equipment, chemicals, petroleum, construction, microelectronics, fishing

Industrial production growth rate: -1.5% (2024 est.)
note: annual % change in industrial value added based on constant local currency
comparison ranking: 155

Labor force: 10.315 million (2024 est.)
note: number of people ages 15 or older who are employed or seeking work
comparison ranking: 54

Unemployment rate: 3.6% (2024 est.)
3.6% (2023 est.)
3.6% (2022 est.)
note: % of labor force seeking employment
comparison ranking: 60

Youth unemployment rate (ages 15-24): *total:* 8.2% (2024 est.)
male: 8.4% (2024 est.)
female: 7.9% (2024 est.)
note: % of labor force ages 15-24 seeking employment
comparison ranking: total 137

Population below poverty line: 14.5% (2021 est.)
note: % of population with income below national poverty line
Gini Index coefficient - distribution of family income 25.7 (2021 est.)
note: index (0-100) of income distribution; higher values represent greater inequality
comparison ranking: 144

Average household expenditures: *on food:* 11.7% of household expenditures (2023 est.)
on alcohol and tobacco: 3% of household expenditures (2023 est.)

Household income or consumption by percentage share: *lowest 10%:* 3.6% (2021 est.)
highest 10%: 21.4% (2021 est.)
note: % share of income accruing to lowest and highest 10% of population

Remittances: 0.4% of GDP (2024 est.)
0.4% of GDP (2023 est.)
0.4% of GDP (2022 est.)
note: personal transfers and compensation between resident and non-resident individuals/households/entities

Budget: *revenues:* $451.11 billion (2023 est.)
expenditures: $455.334 billion (2023 est.)
note: central government revenues (excluding grants) and expenditures converted to US dollars at average official exchange rate for year indicated

Public debt: 56.5% of GDP (2017 est.)
note: data cover general government debt and include debt instruments issued (or owned) by government entities other than the treasury; the data include treasury debt held by foreign entities; the data include debt issued by subnational entities, as well as intragovernmental debt; intragovernmental debt consists of treasury borrowings from surpluses in the social funds, such as for retirement, medical care, and unemployment, debt instruments for the social funds are not sold at public auctions
comparison ranking: 85

Taxes and other revenues: 24.8% (of GDP) (2023 est.)
note: central government tax revenue as a % of GDP
comparison ranking: 18

Current account balance: $121.825 billion (2024 est.)
$113.676 billion (2023 est.)
$69.676 billion (2022 est.)
note: balance of payments - net trade and primary/secondary income in current dollars
comparison ranking: 4

Exports: $1.032 trillion (2024 est.)
$1.022 trillion (2023 est.)
$1.007 trillion (2022 est.)
note: balance of payments - exports of goods and services in current dollars
comparison ranking: 6

Exports - partners: Germany 16%, Belgium 15%, France 11%, Italy 6%, USA 6% (2023)
note: top five export partners based on percentage share of exports

Exports - commodities: refined petroleum, vaccines, machinery, crude petroleum, broadcasting equipment (2023)
note: top five export commodities based on value in dollars

Imports: $884.154 billion (2024 est.)
$893.132 billion (2023 est.)
$915.294 billion (2022 est.)
note: balance of payments - imports of goods and services in current dollars
comparison ranking: 8

Imports - partners: Germany 16%, Belgium 10%, China 10%, USA 10%, UK 5% (2023)
note: top five import partners based on percentage share of imports

Imports - commodities: crude petroleum, refined petroleum, broadcasting equipment, cars, natural gas (2023)
note: top five import commodities based on value in dollars

Reserves of foreign exchange and gold: $79.129 billion (2024 est.)
$69.83 billion (2023 est.)
$63.353 billion (2022 est.)
note: holdings of gold (year-end prices)/foreign exchange/special drawing rights in current dollars
comparison ranking: 35

Exchange rates: euros (EUR) per US dollar -

Exchange rates: 0.924 (2024 est.)
0.925 (2023 est.)
0.95 (2022 est.)
0.845 (2021 est.)
0.876 (2020 est.)

ENERGY

Electricity access: *electrification - total population:* 100% (2022 est.)

Electricity: *installed generating capacity:* 59.982 million kW (2023 est.)
consumption: 108.141 billion kWh (2023 est.)
exports: 25.206 billion kWh (2023 est.)
imports: 19.547 billion kWh (2023 est.)
transmission/distribution losses: 4.936 billion kWh (2023 est.)
comparison rankings: installed generating capacity 25; consumption 32; exports 9; imports 13; transmission/distribution losses 162

Electricity generation sources: *fossil fuels:* 46.8% of total installed capacity (2023 est.)
nuclear: 3.2% of total installed capacity (2023 est.)
solar: 17.2% of total installed capacity (2023 est.)
wind: 24.6% of total installed capacity (2023 est.)
hydroelectricity: 0.1% of total installed capacity (2023 est.)
biomass and waste: 8.2% of total installed capacity (2023 est.)

Nuclear energy: Number of operational nuclear reactors: 1 (2025)

Net capacity of operational nuclear reactors: 0.48GW (2025 est.)

Percent of total electricity production: 3.2% (2023 est.)

Number of nuclear reactors permanently shut down: 1 (2025)

Coal: *production:* 1.761 million metric tons (2023 est.)
consumption: 12.796 million metric tons (2023 est.)
exports: 13.586 million metric tons (2023 est.)
imports: 24.663 million metric tons (2023 est.)
proven reserves: 3.247 billion metric tons (2023 est.)

Petroleum: *total petroleum production:* 70,000 bbl/day (2023 est.)
refined petroleum consumption: 840,000 bbl/day (2024 est.)
crude oil estimated reserves: 137.747 million barrels (2021 est.)

Natural gas: *production:* 11.788 billion cubic meters (2023 est.)
consumption: 31.288 billion cubic meters (2023 est.)
exports: 45.129 billion cubic meters (2023 est.)
imports: 66.783 billion cubic meters (2023 est.)
proven reserves: 132.608 billion cubic meters (2021 est.)

Energy consumption per capita: 185.536 million Btu/person (2023 est.)
comparison ranking: 20

COMMUNICATIONS

Telephones - fixed lines: *total subscriptions:* 4.262 million (2023 est.)
subscriptions per 100 inhabitants: 24 (2023 est.)
comparison ranking: total subscriptions 31

Telephones - mobile cellular: *total subscriptions:* 21.2 million (2023 est.)
subscriptions per 100 inhabitants: 118 (2022 est.)

comparison ranking: total subscriptions 61

Broadcast media: more than 90% of households are connected to cable or satellite TV systems with a wide range of domestic and foreign channels; public service broadcast system includes multiple broadcasters, 3 with a national reach and the remainder in regional and local markets; 2 nationwide commercial TV companies, each with 3 or more stations, and many commercial TV stations in regional and local markets; nearly 600 radio stations with a mix of public and private stations

Internet country code: .nl

Internet users: *percent of population:* 97% (2023 est.)

Broadband - fixed subscriptions: *total:* 7.83 million (2023 est.)
subscriptions per 100 inhabitants: 43 (2023 est.)
comparison ranking: total 29

TRANSPORTATION

Civil aircraft registration country code prefix: PH

Airports: 44 (2025)
note: Includes 3 airports in Bonaire, Sint Eustatius and Saba
comparison ranking: 97

Heliports: 194 (2025)
comparison ranking: 15

Railways: *total:* 3,055 km (2020) 2,310 km electrified

Merchant marine: *total:* 1,187 (2023)
by type: bulk carrier 11, container ship 36, general cargo 521, oil tanker 27, other 592
comparison ranking: total 21

Ports: *total ports:* 18 (2024)
large: 2
medium: 4
small: 5
very small: 7
ports with oil terminals: 12
key ports: Amsterdam, Dordrecht, Europoort, Rotterdam, Terneuzen, Vlissingen

MILITARY AND SECURITY

Military and security forces: Netherlands (Dutch) Armed Forces (Nederlandse Krijgsmacht): Royal Netherlands Army, Royal Netherlands Navy (includes Marine Corps), Royal Netherlands Air Force, Royal Netherlands Marechaussee (Military Constabulary) (2025)
note 1: the Netherlands Coast Guard and the Dutch Caribbean Coast Guard are civilian in nature but managed by the Royal Netherlands Navy
note 2: the core missions of the Royal Netherlands Marechaussee are border security, security and surveillance, and international and military police tasks; it has 21 brigades based in eight Dutch provinces, plus Curaçao in the Caribbean, a special missions security brigade, and separate security platoons to guard and protect domestic sites that are most likely to be the targets of attacks, such as government buildings
note 3: the Netherlands (or National) Police maintain internal security and report to the Ministry of Justice and Security, which oversees law enforcement organizations, as do the justice ministries in Aruba, Curacao, and Sint Maarten

Military expenditures: 2.5% of GDP (2025 est.)
2% of GDP (2024 est.)
1.6% of GDP (2023 est.)
1.4% of GDP (2022 est.)
1.3% of GDP (2021 est.)

Military and security service personnel strengths: approximately 43,000 active-duty professional military personnel (2025)

Military equipment inventories and acquisitions: the military's inventory consists of a mix of domestically produced and modern European- and US-sourced equipment; the Netherlands has an advanced domestic defense industry that focuses on armored vehicles, naval ships, and air defense systems; it also participates with the US and other European countries on joint development and production of advanced weapons systems (2025)

Military service age and obligation: 17 years of age for voluntary service for men and women; the military is an all-volunteer force; conscription remains in place, but the requirement to show up for compulsory military service was suspended in 1997; must be a citizen of the Netherlands (2024)
note: in 2023, women made up about 14% of the military's full-time personnel

Military deployments: 350 Lithuania (NATO); 150 Romania (NATO); approximately 800 deployed to Dutch territories in the Caribbean (2025)
note: the Netherlands contributes naval assets to support freedom of the sea missions in such places as the Red Sea and the Strait of Hormuz; it also assists with monitoring the airspace of the eastern flank of NATO territory by means of fighter aircraft and provides some ground personnel to a variety of other NATO, UN, and EU security missions

Military - note: the Dutch military is charged with the three core tasks of defending the country's national territory and that of its allies, enforcing the national and international rule of law, and providing assistance during disasters and other crises; it also has some domestic security duties, including in the Dutch Caribbean territories; the military operates globally but rarely carries out its operations independently, focusing instead on working through NATO and bilaterally with regional partners; it has particularly close ties with Belgium, Denmark, Germany, and the UK, including some combined military units and staffs
the Netherlands has been a member of NATO since its founding in 1949, and the Dutch military is involved in NATO missions and operations with air, ground, and naval forces, including air policing missions over the Benelux countries and Eastern Europe, NATO's Enhanced Forward Presence initiative in the Baltic States and Eastern Europe, and several NATO naval flotillas, as well as standby units for NATO's rapid response force; the military has previously deployed forces to NATO-led operations in Afghanistan, Iraq, and Kosovo and also contributes to EU- and UN-led missions; Royal Netherlands Marechaussee detachments have been included in international police units deployed by NATO (2025)

SPACE

Space agency/agencies: Netherlands Space Office (NSO; established 2009) (2025)

Space program overview: has a national space program focused on the development of advanced space technologies and services based on satellite data; builds and operates a range of satellites, including communications and remote sensing (RS); researches and develops technologies related to astrophysics, telecommunications, RS, propulsion systems, atmospheric measuring instruments (such as spectrometers), planetary/exoplanetary research, and robotics; founding member of the European Space Agency (ESA) and active in the EU space community; hosts the ESA's main research and technology center; participates in the construction of European satellite launch vehicles and a range of other European space programs, such as Copernicus Earth observation and the Galileo global navigation satellite system; participates in international space programs, including the International Space Station and the Square Kilometer Array Project; also works with other foreign space agencies and industries, including those of Japan and the the US; has a robust commercial space sector tied in to the larger European space economy (2025)
note: further details about the key activities, programs, and milestones of the country's space program, as well as government spending estimates on the space sector, appear in the Space Programs reference guide

TERRORISM

Terrorist group(s): Terrorist group(s): Islamic State of Iraq and ash-Sham (ISIS)
note: details about the history, aims, leadership, organization, areas of operation, tactics, targets, weapons, size, and sources of support of the group(s) appear(s) in Appendix T

TRANSNATIONAL ISSUES

Refugees and internally displaced persons: *refugees:* 310,239 (2024 est.)
stateless persons: 4,428 (2024 est.)

Illicit drugs: USG identification: major precursor-chemical producer (2025)

NEW CALEDONIA

INTRODUCTION

Background: The first humans settled in New Caledonia around 1600 B.C. The Lapita were skilled navigators, and evidence of their pottery around the Pacific has served as a guide for understanding human expansion in the region. Successive waves of migrants from other islands in Melanesia intermarried with the Lapita, giving rise to the Kanak ethnic group considered indigenous to New Caledonia. British explorer James COOK was the first European to visit New Caledonia in 1774, giving it the Latin name for Scotland. Missionaries first landed in New Caledonia in 1840. In 1853, France annexed New Caledonia to preclude any British attempt to claim

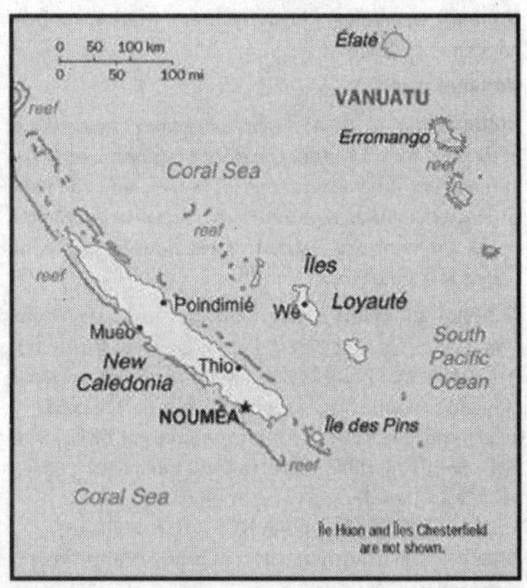

the island. France declared it a penal colony in 1864 and sent more than 20,000 prisoners to New Caledonia in the ensuing three decades.

Nickel was discovered in 1864, and French prisoners were directed to mine it. France brought in indentured servants and enslaved labor from elsewhere in Southeast Asia to work the mines, blocking Kanaks from accessing the most profitable part of the local economy. In 1878, High Chief ATAI led a rebellion against French rule. The Kanaks were relegated to reservations, leading to periodic smaller uprisings and culminating in a large revolt in 1917 that colonial authorities brutally suppressed. During World War II, New Caledonia became an important base for Allied troops, and the US moved its South Pacific headquarters to the island in 1942. Following the war, France made New Caledonia an overseas territory and granted French citizenship to all inhabitants in 1953, thereby permitting the Kanaks to move off the reservations.

The Kanak nationalist movement began in the 1950s, but most voters chose to remain a territory in an independence referendum in 1958. The European population of New Caledonia boomed in the 1970s with a renewed focus on nickel mining, reigniting Kanak nationalism. Key Kanak leaders were assassinated in the early 1980s, leading to escalating violence and dozens of fatalities. The Matignon Accords of 1988 provided for a 10-year transition period. The Noumea Accord of 1998 transferred increasing governing responsibility from France to New Caledonia over a 20-year period and provided for three independence referenda. In the first held in 2018, voters rejected independence by 57% to 43%; in the second held in 2020, voters rejected independence 53% to 47%. In the third referendum held in 2021, voters rejected independence 96% to 4%; however, a boycott by key Kanak groups spurred challenges about the legitimacy of the vote. Pro-independence parties subsequently won a majority in the New Caledonian Government for the first time. France and New Caledonia officials remain in talks about the status of the territory.

GEOGRAPHY

Location: Oceania, islands in the South Pacific Ocean, east of Australia

Geographic coordinates: 21 30 S, 165 30 E

Map references: Oceania

Area: *total:* 18,575 sq km
land: 18,275 sq km
water: 300 sq km
comparison ranking: total 155

Area - comparative: slightly smaller than New Jersey

Land boundaries: *total:* 0 km

Coastline: 2,254 km

Maritime claims: *territorial sea:* 12 nm
exclusive economic zone: 200 nm

Climate: tropical; modified by southeast trade winds; hot, humid

Terrain: coastal plains with interior mountains

Elevation: *highest point:* Mont Panie 1,628 m
lowest point: Pacific Ocean 0 m

Natural resources: nickel, chrome, iron, cobalt, manganese, silver, gold, lead, copper

Land use: *agricultural land:* 10.1% (2022 est.)
arable land: 0.3% (2022 est.)
permanent crops: 0.2% (2022 est.)
permanent pasture: 9.5% (2022 est.)
forest: 45.8% (2022 est.)
other: 44.1% (2022 est.)

Irrigated land: 100 sq km (2012)

Population distribution: most of the populace lives in the southern part of the main island, in and around the capital of Noumea

Natural hazards: cyclones, most frequent from November to March
volcanism: Matthew and Hunter Islands are historically active

Geography - note: consists of the main island of New Caledonia (one of the largest in the Pacific Ocean), the archipelago of Iles Loyauté, and numerous small, sparsely populated islands and atolls

PEOPLE AND SOCIETY

Population: *total:* 304,167 (2024 est.)
male: 151,389
female: 152,778
comparison rankings: total 180; male 181; female 181

Nationality: *noun:* New Caledonian(s)
adjective: New Caledonian

Ethnic groups: Kanak 39.1%, European 27.1%, Wallisian, Futunian 8.2%, Tahitian 2.1%, Indonesian 1.4%, Ni-Vanuatu 1%, Vietnamese 0.9%, other 17.7%, unspecified 2.5% (2014 est.)

Languages: French (official), 33 Melanesian-Polynesian dialects
major-language sample(s):
The World Factbook, une source indispensable d'informations de base. (French)

Religions: Christian 85.2%, Muslim 2.8%, other 1.6%, unaffiliated 10.4% (2020 est.)

Age structure: *0-14 years:* 20.7% (male 32,238/female 30,858)
15-64 years: 68.4% (male 104,825/female 103,349)
65 years and over: 10.8% (2024 est.) (male 14,326/female 18,571)

Dependency ratios: *total dependency ratio:* 46.1 (2024 est.)
youth dependency ratio: 30.3 (2024 est.)
elderly dependency ratio: 15.8 (2024 est.)
potential support ratio: 6.3 (2024 est.)

Median age: *total:* 34.3 years (2024 est.)
male: 33.5 years
female: 35.1 years
comparison ranking: total 103

Population growth rate: 1.14% (2024 est.)
comparison ranking: 80

Birth rate: 13.8 births/1,000 population (2024 est.)
comparison ranking: 123

Death rate: 6 deaths/1,000 population (2024 est.)
comparison ranking: 157

Net migration rate: 3.6 migrant(s)/1,000 population (2024 est.)
comparison ranking: 30

Population distribution: most of the populace lives in the southern part of the main island, in and around the capital of Noumea

Urbanization: *urban population:* 72.7% of total population (2023)
rate of urbanization: 1.72% annual rate of change (2020-25 est.)

Major urban areas - population: 198,000 NOUMEA (capital) (2018)

Sex ratio: *at birth:* 1.05 male(s)/female
0-14 years: 1.04 male(s)/female
15-64 years: 1.01 male(s)/female
65 years and over: 0.77 male(s)/female
total population: 0.99 male(s)/female (2024 est.)

Infant mortality rate: *total:* 4.8 deaths/1,000 live births (2024 est.)
male: 5.8 deaths/1,000 live births
female: 3.9 deaths/1,000 live births
comparison ranking: total 178

Life expectancy at birth: *total population:* 79.3 years (2024 est.)
male: 75.4 years
female: 83.3 years
comparison ranking: total population 65

Total fertility rate: 1.83 children born/woman (2024 est.)
comparison ranking: 135

Gross reproduction rate: 0.89 (2024 est.)

Drinking water source: *improved:* total: 99.5% of population (2022 est.)
unimproved: total: 0.5% of population (2022 est.)

Physician density: 0.24 physicians/1,000 population (2018)

Sanitation facility access: *improved:* total: 100% of population (2022 est.)
unimproved: total: 0% of population (2022 est.)

Currently married women (ages 15-49): 22.5% (2023 est.)

ENVIRONMENT

Environmental issues: preservation of coral reefs; prevention of invasive species; limiting erosion caused by nickel mining and forest fires

Climate: tropical; modified by southeast trade winds; hot, humid

Urbanization: *urban population:* 72.7% of total population (2023)
rate of urbanization: 1.72% annual rate of change (2020-25 est.)

Carbon dioxide emissions: 4.887 million metric tonnes of CO2 (2023 est.)
from coal and metallurgical coke: 2.312 million metric tonnes of CO2 (2023 est.)
from petroleum and other liquids: 2.575 million metric tonnes of CO2 (2023 est.)
comparison ranking: total emissions 137

Waste and recycling: *municipal solid waste generated annually:* 108,200 tons (2024 est.)

GOVERNMENT

Country name: *conventional long form:* Territory of New Caledonia and Dependencies
conventional short form: New Caledonia
local long form: Territoire des Nouvelle-Calédonie et dépendances
local short form: Nouvelle-Calédonie
etymology: the name came from British explorer Captain James COOK in 1774 and uses the Latin name for Scotland, Caledonia

Government type: parliamentary democracy (Territorial Congress); an overseas collectivity of France

Dependency status: special collectivity of France
note: independence referenda took place in 2018, 2020, and 2021, with a majority voting in each case to reject independence in favor of the status quo

Capital: *name:* Noumea
geographic coordinates: 22 16 S, 166 27 E
time difference: UTC+11 (16 hours ahead of Washington, DC, during Standard Time)
etymology: established in 1854 as Port-de-France, the settlement was renamed Noumea in 1866 to avoid confusion with Fort-de-France in Martinique; the name Noumea may come from the local name of the peninsula the city was founded on

Administrative divisions: 3 provinces; Province Iles (Islands Province), Province Nord (North Province), and Province Sud (South Province)

Legal system: civil law system based on French civil law

Constitution: *history:* 4 October 1958 (French Constitution with changes as reflected in the Noumea Accord of 5 May 1998)
amendment process: French constitution amendment procedures apply

Citizenship: see France

Suffrage: 18 years of age; universal

Executive branch: *chief of state:* President Emmanuel MACRON (since 14 May 2017); represented by High Commissioner Jacques BILLANT (since 3 May 2025)
head of government: President of the Government Alcide PONGA (since 8 January 2025)
cabinet: Cabinet elected from and by the Territorial Congress
election/appointment process: French president directly elected by absolute-majority popular vote in 2 rounds, if needed, for a 5-year term (eligible for a second term); high commissioner appointed by the French president on the advice of the French Ministry of Interior; president of New Caledonia elected by Territorial Congress for a 5-year term (no term limits)
most recent election date: 8 July 2021
election results: *2025:* Alcide PONGA (The Republicans) elected president by Territorial Congress with 6 of 11 votes
2021: Louis MAPOU (PALIKA) elected president by Territorial Congress with 6 of 11 votes
expected date of next election: 2026

Legislative branch: *legislature name:* Territorial Congress (Congrès du Territoire)
legislative structure: unicameral
number of seats: 54 (indirectly elected)
electoral system: proportional representation
scope of elections: full renewal
term in office: 5 years
most recent election date: 5/12/2019
parties elected and seats per party: Future With Confidence 18, UNI 9, UC 9, CE 7, FLNKS 6, Oceanic Awakening 3, PT 1, LKS 1 (Anti-Independence 28, Pro-Independence 26)
expected date of next election: December 2025
note 1: the Customary Senate is the assembly of the various traditional councils of the Kanaks, the indigenous population; it rules on laws affecting Kanaks
note 2: New Caledonia indirectly elects 2 members to the French Senate and directly elects 2 members to the French National Assembly (see France entry for electoral details)

Judicial branch: *highest court(s):* Court of Appeal or Cour d'Appel; organized into civil, commercial, social, and pre-trial investigation chambers; court bench normally includes the court president and 2 counselors); Administrative Court (number of judges NA)
judge selection and term of office: judge appointment and tenure based on France's judicial system
subordinate courts: Courts of First Instance include: civil, juvenile, commercial, labor, police, criminal, assizes, and also a pre-trial investigation chamber; Joint Commerce Tribunal; administrative courts
note: final appeals beyond the Court of Appeal are referred to the Court of Cassation or Cour de Cassation (in Paris); final appeals beyond the Administrative Court are referred to the Administrative Court of Appeal (in Paris)

Political parties: Caledonia Together or CE
Caledonian Union or UC
Future With Confidence or AEC
Kanak Socialist Front for National Liberation or FLNKS (alliance includes PALIKA, UNI, UC, and UPM)
Labor Party or PT
National Union for Independence or UNI
Oceanian Awakening
Party of Kanak Liberation or PALIKA
Socialist Kanak Liberation or LKS
The Republicans (formerly The Rally or UMP)

Diplomatic representation in the US: none (overseas territory of France)

Diplomatic representation from the US: *embassy:* none (overseas territory of France)

International organization participation: ITUC (NGOs), PIF, SPC, UPU, WFTU (NGOs), WMO

Independence: none (overseas collectivity of France)
note: in three independence referenda, on 4 November 2018, 4 October 2020, and 12 December 2021, the majority voted to reject independence in favor of maintaining the status quo

National holiday: Fête de la Fédération, 14 July (1790)
note 1: the local holiday is New Caledonia Day, 24 September (1853)
note 2: often incorrectly referred to as Bastille Day, France's national celebration commemorates the storming of the Bastille prison on 14 July 1789 and the establishment of a constitutional monarchy; other names for the holiday are *la Fête nationale* (National Holiday) and *le Quatorze Juillet* (14th of July)

Flag: *description:* the country has two official flags with equal status, the flag of France and the Kanak (ethnic Melanesian) flag; the latter consists of three equal horizontal bands of blue (top), red, and green; a large yellow disk shifted slightly to the left side is edged in black and displays a black *fleche faîtière* symbol, a native rooftop adornment

National symbol(s): flèche faîtière (native rooftop adornment), kagu bird

National color(s): grey, red

National coat of arms: *the emblem features two symbols of the local Kanak people:* the flèche faîtière, which is a common rooftop adornment on houses, and the nautilus shell, which represents the sea; the third part of the emblem is a stylized representation of a New Caledonia pine tree

National anthem(s): *title:* "Soyons unis, devenons frères" (Let Us Be United, Let Us Become Brothers)
lyrics/music: Chorale Melodia (a local choir), Edouard "Gulaan" Wamedjo (Nengone)/Chorale Melodia
history: adopted 2010; contains a mixture of lyrics in both French and Nengone (a local language)
title: "La Marseillaise" (The Song of Marseille)
lyrics/music: Claude-Joseph ROUGET de Lisle
history: official anthem, as a self-governing French territory

National heritage: *total World Heritage Sites:* 1 (natural); note - excerpted from the France entry
selected World Heritage Site locales: Lagoons of New Caledonia

ECONOMY

Economic overview: upper-middle-income French Pacific territorial economy; enormous nickel reserves; ongoing French independence negotiations; large Chinese nickel exporter; luxury eco-tourism destination; large French aid recipient; high cost-of-living; lingering wealth disparities

Real GDP (purchasing power parity): $8.469 billion (2024 est.)
$8.642 billion (2023 est.)
$8.678 billion (2022 est.)
note: data in 2015 dollars
comparison ranking: 168

Real GDP growth rate: 3.5% (2022 est.)
-2.1% (2021 est.)
-2.4% (2020 est.)
note: annual GDP % growth based on constant local currency
comparison ranking: 96

Real GDP per capita: $34,600 (2024 est.)
$35,000 (2023 est.)
$33,500 (2022 est.)
note: data in 2015 dollars
comparison ranking: 69

GDP (official exchange rate): $10.129 billion (2024 est.)
note: data in current dollars at official exchange rate

Inflation rate (consumer prices): 3.7% (2022 est.)
0.6% (2021 est.)
-0.5% (2020 est.)
note: annual % change based on consumer prices
comparison ranking: 119

GDP - composition, by sector of origin: *agriculture:* 1.8% (2019 est.)
industry: 22.3% (2019 est.)
services: 65.2% (2019 est.)
note: figures may not total 100% due to non-allocated consumption not captured in sector-reported data
comparison rankings: agriculture 156; industry 117; services 58

GDP - composition, by end use: *household consumption:* 65.6% (2017 est.)
government consumption: 23.5% (2017 est.)
investment in fixed capital: 27.9% (2017 est.)

investment in inventories: -0.1% (2017 est.)
exports of goods and services: 21% (2017 est.)
imports of goods and services: -37.9% (2017 est.)
note: figures may not total 100% due to rounding or gaps in data collection

Agricultural products: coconuts, vegetables, fruits, pork, beef, maize, eggs, bananas, yams, oranges (2023)
note: top ten agricultural products based on tonnage

Industries: nickel mining and smelting

Labor force: 130,800 (2024 est.)
note: number of people ages 15 or older who are employed or seeking work
comparison ranking: 179

Unemployment rate: 11.2% (2024 est.)
11% (2023 est.)
10.8% (2022 est.)
note: % of labor force seeking employment
comparison ranking: 155

Youth unemployment rate (ages 15-24): *total:* 32.7% (2024 est.)
male: 30.2% (2024 est.)
female: 35.7% (2024 est.)
note: % of labor force ages 15-24 seeking employment
comparison ranking: total 17

Remittances: 6.5% of GDP (2022 est.)
6.2% of GDP (2021 est.)
6.6% of GDP (2020 est.)
note: personal transfers and compensation between resident and non-resident individuals/households/entities

Budget: *revenues:* $1.995 billion (2015 est.)
expenditures: $1.993 billion (2015 est.)

Current account balance: -$654.237 million (2016 est.)
-$1.119 billion (2015 est.)
-$1.3 billion (2014 est.)
note: balance of payments - net trade and primary/secondary income in current dollars
comparison ranking: 116

Exports: $1.92 billion (2021 est.)
$1.8 billion (2020 est.)
$1.79 billion (2019 est.)
note: balance of payments - exports of goods and services in current dollars
comparison ranking: 166

Exports - partners: China 75%, Japan 9%, Taiwan 3%, India 3%, France 2% (2023)
note: top five export partners based on percentage share of exports

Exports - commodities: iron alloys, nickel, nickel ore, processed crustaceans, shellfish (2023)
note: top five export commodities based on value in dollars

Imports: $2.26 billion (2021 est.)
$2.1 billion (2020 est.)
$2.48 billion (2019 est.)
note: balance of payments - imports of goods and services in current dollars
comparison ranking: 174

Imports - partners: France 36%, Singapore 16%, Australia 15%, China 6%, NZ 3% (2023)
note: top five import partners based on percentage share of imports

Imports - commodities: refined petroleum, coal, cars, aircraft, packaged medicine (2023)
note: top five import commodities based on value in dollars

Exchange rates: Comptoirs Francais du Pacifique francs (XPF) per US dollar -

Exchange rates: 110.306 (2024 est.)
110.347 (2023 est.)
113.474 (2022 est.)
100.88 (2021 est.)
104.711 (2020 est.)

ENERGY

Electricity access: *electrification - total population:* 100% (2022 est.)

Electricity: *installed generating capacity:* 1.174 million kW (2023 est.)
consumption: 3.02 billion kWh (2023 est.)
transmission/distribution losses: 66.3 million kWh (2023 est.)
comparison rankings: installed generating capacity 131; consumption 143; transmission/distribution losses 41

Electricity generation sources: *fossil fuels:* 73.8% of total installed capacity (2023 est.)
solar: 7.3% of total installed capacity (2023 est.)
wind: 1.4% of total installed capacity (2023 est.)
hydroelectricity: 17.5% of total installed capacity (2023 est.)

Coal: *consumption:* 1.026 million metric tons (2023 est.)
imports: 1.001 million metric tons (2023 est.)
proven reserves: 2 million metric tons (2023 est.)

Petroleum: *refined petroleum consumption:* 17,000 bbl/day (2023 est.)

COMMUNICATIONS

Telephones - fixed lines: *total subscriptions:* 46,000 (2021 est.)
subscriptions per 100 inhabitants: 16 (2022 est.)
comparison ranking: total subscriptions 158

Telephones - mobile cellular: *total subscriptions:* 260,000 (2021 est.)
subscriptions per 100 inhabitants: 90 (2021 est.)
comparison ranking: total subscriptions 181

Broadcast media: the publicly owned French Overseas Network (RFO), which operates in France's overseas departments and territories, broadcasts over the RFO Nouvelle-Calédonie TV and radio stations; a small number of privately owned radio stations also broadcast

Internet country code: .nc

Internet users: *percent of population:* 82% (2017 est.)

Broadband - fixed subscriptions: *total:* 56,000 (2022 est.)
subscriptions per 100 inhabitants: 19 (2022 est.)
comparison ranking: total 145

TRANSPORTATION

Airports: 21 (2025)
comparison ranking: 134

Heliports: 2 (2025)
comparison ranking: 130

Merchant marine: *total:* 23 (2023)
by type: general cargo 5, oil tanker 1, other 17
comparison ranking: total 146

Ports: *total ports:* 3 (2024)
large: 0
medium: 0
small: 1
very small: 2
ports with oil terminals: 1
key ports: Baie de Kouaoua, Baie Ugue, Noumea

MILITARY AND SECURITY

Military and security forces: no regular military forces; Territorial Directorate of the National Police of New Caledonia (DTPN), Gendarmerie of New Caledonia (2025)

Military - note: defense is the responsibility of France, which bases land, air, and naval forces on New Caledonia (Forces Armées de la Nouvelle-Calédonie, FANC)

NEW ZEALAND

INTRODUCTION

Background: Polynesians settled New Zealand between the late 1200s and the mid-1300s. They called the land Aotearoa, which legend holds is the name of the canoe that Kupe, the first Polynesian in New Zealand, used to sail to the country; the name Aotearoa is now in widespread use as the local Maori name for the country. By the 1500s, competition for land and resources led to intermittent fighting between different Maori tribes as large game became extinct. Dutch explorer Abel TASMAN was the first European to see the islands in 1642 but left after an encounter with local Maori. British sea captain James COOK arrived in 1769, followed by whalers, sealers, and traders. The UK only nominally claimed New Zealand and included it as part of New South Wales in Australia. Concerns about increasing lawlessness led the UK to appoint its first British Resident in New Zealand in 1832, although the position had few legal powers. In 1835, some Maori tribes from the North Island declared independence. Fearing an impending French settlement and takeover, the majority of Maori chiefs signed the Treaty of Waitangi with the British in 1840. Land tenure issues stemming from the treaty are still being actively negotiated in New Zealand.

The UK declared New Zealand a separate colony in 1841 and granted limited self-government in 1852. Different traditions of authority and land use led to a series of wars between Europeans and various Maori tribes from the 1840s to the 1870s. Along with disease, these conflicts halved the Maori population. In the 1890s, New Zealand initially expressed interest in joining independence talks with Australia but ultimately opted against it and changed its status to an independent dominion in 1907. New Zealand provided more than 100,000 troops during each

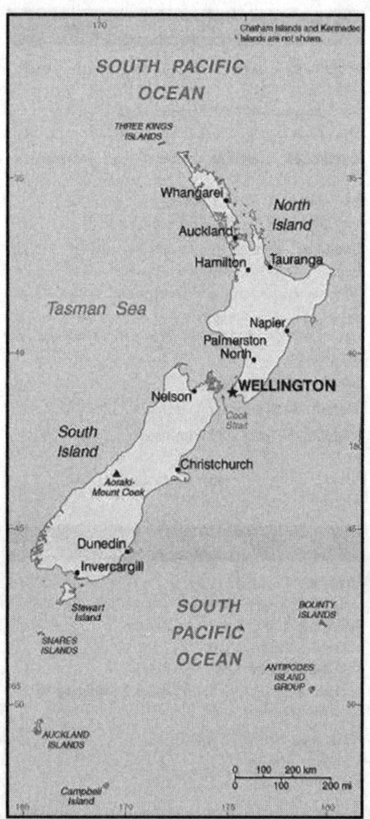

World War, many of whom fought as part of the Australia and New Zealand Army Corps (ANZAC). New Zealand reaffirmed its independence in 1947 and signed the Australia, New Zealand, and US (ANZUS) Treaty in 1951.

Beginning in 1984, New Zealand began to adopt nuclear-free policies, contributing to a dispute with the US over naval ship visits that led the US to suspend its defense obligations to New Zealand in 1986, but bilateral relations and military ties have been revitalized since the 2010s with new security agreements. A key challenge for Auckland that has emerged over the past decade is balancing concerns over China's growing influence in the Pacific region with its role as New Zealand's largest export destination. New Zealand has close ties with Australia based to a large extent on the two nations' common origins as British colonies and their shared military history.

GEOGRAPHY

Location: Oceania, islands in the South Pacific Ocean, southeast of Australia

Geographic coordinates: 41 00 S, 174 00 E

Map references: Oceania

Area: *total:* 268,838 sq km
land: 264,537 sq km
water: 4,301 sq km
note: includes Antipodes Islands, Auckland Islands, Bounty Islands, Campbell Island, Chatham Islands, and Kermadec Islands
comparison ranking: total 77

Area - comparative: almost twice the size of North Carolina; about the size of Colorado

Land boundaries: *total:* 0 km

Coastline: 15,134 km

Maritime claims: *territorial sea:* 12 nm
contiguous zone: 24 nm
exclusive economic zone: 200 nm
continental shelf: 200 nm or to the edge of the continental margin

Climate: temperate with sharp regional contrasts

Terrain: predominately mountainous with large coastal plains

Elevation: *highest point:* Aoraki/Mount Cook 3,724 m; note - the mountain's height was 3,764 m until 14 December 1991 when it lost about 10 m in an avalanche of rock and ice; erosion of the ice cap since then has brought the height down another 30 m
lowest point: Pacific Ocean 0 m
mean elevation: 388 m

Natural resources: natural gas, iron ore, sand, coal, timber, hydropower, gold, limestone

Land use: *agricultural land:* 37% (2022 est.)
arable land: 2% (2022 est.)
permanent crops: 0.3% (2022 est.)
permanent pasture: 34.7% (2022 est.)
forest: 37.7% (2022 est.)
other: 25.3% (2022 est.)

Irrigated land: 7,000 sq km (2014)

Major lakes (area sq km): *fresh water lake(s):* Lake Taupo - 610 sq km

Population distribution: over three quarters of New Zealanders, including the Maori, live on the North Island, primarily in urban areas

Natural hazards: earthquakes are common, though usually not severe; volcanic activity
volcanism: significant volcanism on North Island; Ruapehu (2,797 m) has a history of large eruptions in the past century; Taranaki has the potential to produce dangerous avalanches and lahars; other historically active volcanoes include Okataina, Raoul Island, Tongariro, and White Island; see note 2 under "Geography - note"

Geography - note: *note 1:* consists of two main islands and a number of smaller islands; South Island, the larger main island, is the 12th-largest island in the world and is divided along its length by the Southern Alps; North Island is the 14th-largest island in the world and is not as mountainous, but it is marked by volcanism
note 2: New Zealand lies along the Ring of Fire, which is a belt bordering the Pacific Ocean that contains about 75% of the world's volcanoes and up to 90% of the world's earthquakes
note 3: almost 90% of the population lives in cities and over three-quarters on North Island; Wellington is the southernmost national capital in the world

PEOPLE AND SOCIETY

Population: *total:* 5,161,211 (2024 est.)
male: 2,584,607
female: 2,576,604
comparison rankings: total 125; male 125; female 125

Nationality: *noun:* New Zealander(s)
adjective: New Zealand

Ethnic groups: European 64.1%, Maori 16.5%, Chinese 4.9%, Indian 4.7%, Samoan 3.9%, Tongan 1.8%, Cook Islands Maori 1.7%, English 1.5%, Filipino 1.5%, New Zealander 1%, other 13.7% (2018 est.)
note: based on the 2018 census of the usually resident population; percentages add up to more than 100% because respondents were able to identify more than one ethnic group

Languages: English (de facto official) 95.4%, Maori (de jure official) 4%, Samoan 2.2%, Northern Chinese 2%, Hindi 1.5%, French 1.2%, Yue 1.1%, New Zealand Sign Language (de jure official) 0.5%, other or not stated 17.2% (2018 est.)
note: shares sum to 124.1% due to multiple responses on the 2018 census

Religions: Christian 37.3% (Catholic 10.1%, Anglican 6.8%, Presbyterian and Congregational 5.2%, Pentecostal 1.8%, Methodist 1.6%, Church of Jesus Christ 1.2%, other 10.7%), Hindu 2.7%, Maori 1.3%, Muslim, 1.3%, Buddhist 1.1%, other religion 1.6% (includes Judaism, Spiritualism and New Age religions, Baha'i, Asian religions other than Buddhism), no religion 48.6%, objected to answering 6.7% (2018 est.)
note: based on the 2018 census of the usually resident population; percentages add up to more than 100% because respondents were able to identify more than one religion

Age structure: *0-14 years:* 19% (male 503,120/female 475,490)
15-64 years: 64.2% (male 1,674,407/female 1,638,276)
65 years and over: 16.9% (2024 est.) (male 407,080/female 462,838)

Dependency ratios: *total dependency ratio:* 55.8 (2024 est.)
youth dependency ratio: 29.5 (2024 est.)
elderly dependency ratio: 26.3 (2024 est.)
potential support ratio: 3.8 (2024 est.)

Median age: *total:* 37.9 years (2024 est.)
male: 37.2 years
female: 38.6 years
comparison ranking: total 80

Population growth rate: 0.95% (2024 est.)
comparison ranking: 96

Birth rate: 12.6 births/1,000 population (2024 est.)
comparison ranking: 137

Death rate: 6.9 deaths/1,000 population (2024 est.)
comparison ranking: 126

Net migration rate: 3.8 migrant(s)/1,000 population (2024 est.)
comparison ranking: 29

Population distribution: over three quarters of New Zealanders, including the Maori, live on the North Island, primarily in urban areas

Urbanization: *urban population:* 87% of total population (2023)
rate of urbanization: 0.92% annual rate of change (2020-25 est.)

Major urban areas - population: 1.673 million Auckland, 422,000 WELLINGTON (capital) (2023)

Sex ratio: *at birth:* 1.05 male(s)/female
0-14 years: 1.06 male(s)/female
15-64 years: 1.02 male(s)/female
65 years and over: 0.88 male(s)/female
total population: 1 male(s)/female (2024 est.)

Mother's mean age at first birth: 27.8 years

Maternal mortality ratio: 7 deaths/100,000 live births (2023 est.)
comparison ranking: 161

Infant mortality rate: *total:* 3.3 deaths/1,000 live births (2024 est.)

male: 3.5 deaths/1,000 live births
female: 3.1 deaths/1,000 live births
comparison ranking: total 199

Life expectancy at birth: *total population:* 82.9 years (2024 est.)
male: 81.2 years
female: 84.8 years
comparison ranking: total population 23

Total fertility rate: 1.85 children born/woman (2024 est.)
comparison ranking: 131

Gross reproduction rate: 0.9 (2024 est.)

Drinking water source: *improved: urban:* 100% of population (2022 est.)
rural: 100% of population (2022 est.)
total: 100% of population (2022 est.)
unimproved: urban: 0% of population (2022 est.)
rural: 0% of population (2022 est.)
total: 0% of population (2022 est.)

Health expenditure: 10% of GDP (2021)
19.8% of national budget (2022 est.)

Physician density: 3.61 physicians/1,000 population (2022)

Hospital bed density: 2.7 beds/1,000 population (2021 est.)

Sanitation facility access: *improved: urban:* 100% of population (2022 est.)
rural: 100% of population (2022 est.)
total: 100% of population (2022 est.)
unimproved: urban: 0% of population (2022 est.)
rural: 0% of population (2022 est.)
total: 0% of population (2022 est.)

Obesity - adult prevalence rate: 30.8% (2016)
comparison ranking: 22

Alcohol consumption per capita: *total:* 9.17 liters of pure alcohol (2019 est.)
beer: 3.41 liters of pure alcohol (2019 est.)
wine: 2.88 liters of pure alcohol (2019 est.)
spirits: 1.62 liters of pure alcohol (2019 est.)
other alcohols: 1.26 liters of pure alcohol (2019 est.)
comparison ranking: total 32

Tobacco use: *total:* 10% (2025 est.)
male: 11.2% (2025 est.)
female: 8.9% (2025 est.)
comparison ranking: total 127

Currently married women (ages 15-49): 57.6% (2023 est.)

Education expenditure: 5.2% of GDP (2022 est.)
13.1% national budget (2022 est.)
comparison ranking: Education expenditure (% GDP) 54

School life expectancy (primary to tertiary education): *total:* 19 years (2023 est.)
male: 19 years (2023 est.)
female: 20 years (2023 est.)

ENVIRONMENT

Environmental issues: water quality and availability; rapid urbanization; deforestation; soil erosion and degradation; native flora and fauna hard-hit by invasive species

International environmental agreements: *party to:* Antarctic-Environmental Protection, Antarctic-Marine Living Resources, Antarctic Treaty, Biodiversity, Climate Change, Climate Change-Kyoto Protocol, Climate Change-Paris Agreement, Comprehensive Nuclear Test Ban, Desertification, Endangered Species, Environmental Modification, Hazardous Wastes, Law of the Sea, Marine Dumping-London Convention, Marine Dumping-London Protocol, Nuclear Test Ban, Ozone Layer Protection, Ship Pollution, Tropical Timber 2006, Wetlands, Whaling
signed, but not ratified: Antarctic Seals, Marine Life Conservation

Climate: temperate with sharp regional contrasts

Urbanization: *urban population:* 87% of total population (2023)
rate of urbanization: 0.92% annual rate of change (2020-25 est.)

Carbon dioxide emissions: 33.506 million metric tonnes of CO2 (2023 est.)
from coal and metallurgical coke: 4.24 million metric tonnes of CO2 (2023 est.)
from petroleum and other liquids: 21.836 million metric tonnes of CO2 (2023 est.)
from consumed natural gas: 7.43 million metric tonnes of CO2 (2023 est.)
comparison ranking: total emissions 70

Particulate matter emissions: 8.7 micrograms per cubic meter (2019 est.)

Methane emissions: *energy:* 95.4 kt (2022-2024 est.)
agriculture: 1,105.6 kt (2019-2021 est.)
waste: 158.8 kt (2019-2021 est.)
other: 6.2 kt (2019-2021 est.)

Waste and recycling: *municipal solid waste generated annually:* 3.405 million tons (2024 est.)
percent of municipal solid waste recycled: 22% (2022 est.)

Total water withdrawal: *municipal:* 547 million cubic meters (2022)
industrial: 1.184 billion cubic meters (2022 est.)
agricultural: 3.207 billion cubic meters (2022 est.)

Total renewable water resources: 327 billion cubic meters (2022)

GOVERNMENT

Country name: *conventional long form:* none
conventional short form: New Zealand
former: Nieuw Zeeland
abbreviation: NZ
etymology: the name is an anglicized form of the Dutch name Nieuw Zeeland, or "New Sea Land," which was first used in 1643 in honor of the Dutch province of Zeeland

Government type: parliamentary democracy under a constitutional monarchy; a Commonwealth realm

Capital: *name:* Wellington
geographic coordinates: 41 18 S, 174 47 E
time difference: UTC+12 (17 hours ahead of Washington, DC, during Standard Time)
daylight saving time: +1hr, begins last Sunday in September; ends first Sunday in April
time zone note: New Zealand has two time zones: New Zealand standard time (UTC+12) and Chatham Islands time (45 minutes in advance of New Zealand standard time; UTC+12:45)
etymology: named in 1840 after Arthur WELLESLEY, the first Duke of Wellington, who was famous for his victory at Waterloo in 1815 and was a benefactor of the New Zealand Company that settled North Island

Administrative divisions: 16 regions and 1 territory*; Auckland, Bay of Plenty, Canterbury, Chatham Islands*, Gisborne, Hawke's Bay, Manawatu-Wanganui, Marlborough, Nelson, Northland, Otago, Southland, Taranaki, Tasman, Waikato, Wellington, West Coast

Dependent areas: Tokelau (1)

Legal system: common law system, based on English model, with special legislation and land courts for the Maori

Constitution: *history:* New Zealand has no single constitution document; the Constitution Act 1986, effective 1 January 1987, includes only part of the uncodified constitution; others include a collection of statutes or "acts of Parliament," the Treaty of Waitangi, Orders in Council, letters patent, court decisions, and unwritten conventions
amendment process: proposed as bill by Parliament or by referendum called either by the government or by citizens; passage of a bill as an act normally requires two separate readings with committee reviews in between to make changes and corrections, a third reading approved by the House of Representatives membership or by the majority of votes in a referendum, and assent of the governor-general; passage of amendments to reserved constitutional provisions affecting the term of Parliament, electoral districts, and voting restrictions requires approval by 75% of the House membership or the majority of votes in a referendum

International law organization participation: accepts compulsory ICJ jurisdiction with reservations; accepts ICCt jurisdiction

Citizenship: *citizenship by birth:* no
citizenship by descent only: at least one parent must be a citizen of New Zealand
dual citizenship recognized: yes
residency requirement for naturalization: 3 years

Suffrage: 18 years of age; universal

Executive branch: *chief of state:* King CHARLES III (since 8 September 2022); represented by Governor-General Dame Cindy KIRO (since 21 October 2021)
head of government: Prime Minister Christopher LUXON (since 27 November 2023)
cabinet: Executive Council appointed by the governor-general on the recommendation of the prime minister
election/appointment process: the monarchy is hereditary; governor-general appointed by the monarch on the advice of the prime minister; following legislative elections, the governorgeneral appoints the leader of the majority party or majority coalition as prime minister; deputy prime minister also appointed by the governor-general

Legislative branch: *legislature name:* House of Representatives
legislative structure: unicameral
number of seats: 120 (all directly elected)
electoral system: mixed system
scope of elections: full renewal
term in office: 3 years
most recent election date: 10/14/2023
parties elected and seats per party: National Party (49); Labour Party (34); Green Party (15); ACT New Zealand (11); New Zealand First (8); Other (6)
percentage of women in chamber: 45.1%
expected date of next election: September 2026

Judicial branch: *highest court(s):* Supreme Court (consists of 5 justices, including the chief justice)
judge selection and term of office: justices appointed by the governor-general upon the recommendation of the attorney-general; justices appointed until compulsory retirement at age 70
subordinate courts: Court of Appeal; High Court; tribunals and authorities; district courts; specialized

courts for issues related to employment, environment, family, Maori lands, youth, military; tribunals

Political parties: ACT New Zealand
Green Party
New Zealand First Party or NZ First
New Zealand Labor Party
New Zealand National Party
Te Pāti Māori

Diplomatic representation in the US: *chief of mission:* Ambassador Rosemary BANKS (since 17 June 2024)
chancery: 37 Observatory Circle NW, Washington, DC 20008
telephone: [1] (202) 328-4800

FAX: [1] (202) 667-5277
email address and website: wshinfo@mfat.govt.nz
https://www.mfat.govt.nz/en/countries-and-regions/americas/united-states-of-america/
consulate(s) general: Honolulu, Los Angeles, New York

Diplomatic representation from the US: *chief of mission:* Ambassador (vacant); Chargé d'Affaires David GEHRENBECK (since January 2025); note - also accredited to Samoa
embassy: 29 Fitzherbert Terrace, Thorndon, Wellington 6011
mailing address: 4370 Auckland Place, Washington DC 20521-4370
telephone: [64] (4) 462-6000

FAX: [64] (4) 499-0490
email address and website: AucklandACS@state.gov
https://nz.usembassy.gov/
consulate(s) general: Auckland

International organization participation: ADB, ANZUS, APEC, ARF, ASEAN (dialogue partner), Australia Group, BIS, C, CD, CP, EAS, EBRD, FAO, FATF, IAEA, IBRD, ICAO, ICC (national committees), ICCt, ICRM, IDA, IEA, IFAD, IFC, IFRCS, IHO, ILO, IMF, IMO, IMSO, Interpol, IOC, IOM, IPU, ISO, ITSO, ITU, ITUC (NGOs), MIGA, NSG, OECD, OPCW, Pacific Alliance (observer), Paris Club (associate), PCA, PIF, SICA (observer), Sparteca, SPC, UN, UNCTAD, UNESCO, UNHCR, UNIDO, UNMISS, UNTSO, UPU, Wassenaar Arrangement, WCO, WFTU (NGOs), WHO, WIPO, WMO, WTO

Independence: 26 September 1907 (from the UK)

National holiday: Waitangi Day, 6 February (1840); Anzac Day, 25 April (1915)
note: the Treaty of Waitangi established British sovereignty over New Zealand, and the second holiday commemorates the landing of the Australian and New Zealand Army Corps in Gallipoli, Turkey, during World War I

Flag: *description:* blue with the UK flag in the upper-left quadrant, with four five-pointed red stars edged in white centered in the right half of the flag
meaning: the stars represent the Southern Cross constellation

National symbol(s): Southern Cross constellation (four five-pointed stars), kiwi (bird), silver fern

National color(s): black, white, red (ochre)

National coat of arms: the first quarter of the shield shows four stars that represent the Southern Cross constellation and three ships that symbolize New Zealand's sea trade; in the second quarter, a fleece represents the sheep farming industry; the wheat sheaf in the third quarter represents the agricultural industry; the crossed hammers in the fourth quarter represent mining; the Maori chieftain holds a *taiaha* (a Maori war weapon) and a European woman holds the New Zealand flag; St. Edward's crown, shown above the shield, symbolizes the British monarch

National anthem(s): *title:* "God Defend New Zealand"
"Aotearoa" (Maori)
lyrics/music: Thomas BRACKEN [English], Thomas Henry SMITH [Maori]/John Joseph WOODS
history: adopted 1940 as the national song, adopted 1977 as one of two official national anthems
title: "God Save the King"
lyrics/music: unknown
history: royal anthem and one of two official national anthems; usually played only when a member of the royal family or a representative is present or when allegiance to the crown is demonstrated
note: New Zealand is one of only two countries that has two national anthems of equal status (Denmark is the other)

National heritage: *total World Heritage Sites:* 3 (2 natural, 1 mixed)
selected World Heritage Site locales: Te Wahipounamu – South West New Zealand (n); Tongariro National Park (m); New Zealand Sub-Antarctic Islands (n)

ECONOMY

Economic overview: high-income, globally integrated Pacific island economy; strong agriculture, manufacturing, and tourism sectors; reliant on Chinese market for exports; recovery trajectory following deep post-pandemic recession; challenges of fiscal deficits, below-average productivity, cost of living, and drop in net migration

Real GDP (purchasing power parity): $257.117 billion (2024 est.)
$257.443 billion (2023 est.)
$253.903 billion (2022 est.)
note: data in 2021 dollars
comparison ranking: 67

Real GDP growth rate: -0.1% (2024 est.)
1.4% (2023 est.)
3.5% (2022 est.)
note: annual GDP % growth based on constant local currency
comparison ranking: 192

Real GDP per capita: $48,200 (2024 est.)
$49,100 (2023 est.)
$49,600 (2022 est.)
note: data in 2021 dollars
comparison ranking: 42

GDP (official exchange rate): $260.236 billion (2024 est.)
note: data in current dollars at official exchange rate

Inflation rate (consumer prices): 2.9% (2024 est.)
5.7% (2023 est.)
7.2% (2022 est.)
note: annual % change based on consumer prices
comparison ranking: 90

GDP - composition, by sector of origin: *agriculture:* 4.6% (2022 est.)
industry: 19.6% (2022 est.)
services: 67.4% (2022 est.)
note: figures may not total 100% due to non-allocated consumption not captured in sector-reported data
comparison rankings: agriculture 113; industry 134; services 45

GDP - composition, by end use: *household consumption:* 57.5% (2022 est.)
government consumption: 20.9% (2022 est.)
investment in fixed capital: 25.4% (2022 est.)
investment in inventories: 0.9% (2022 est.)
exports of goods and services: 24% (2022 est.)
imports of goods and services: -29.4% (2022 est.)
note: figures may not total 100% due to rounding or gaps in data collection

Agricultural products: milk, beef, kiwifruit, apples, grapes, lamb/mutton, potatoes, wheat, barley, chicken (2023)
note: top ten agricultural products based on tonnage

Industries: agriculture, forestry, fishing, logs and wood articles, manufacturing, mining, construction, financial services, real estate services, tourism

Industrial production growth rate: -1% (2023 est.)
note: annual % change in industrial value added based on constant local currency
comparison ranking: 147

Labor force: 3.124 million (2024 est.)
note: number of people ages 15 or older who are employed or seeking work
comparison ranking: 108

Unemployment rate: 4.9% (2024 est.)
3.8% (2023 est.)
3.3% (2022 est.)
note: % of labor force seeking employment
comparison ranking: 85

Youth unemployment rate (ages 15-24): *total:* 14.3% (2024 est.)
male: 14.6% (2024 est.)
female: 14% (2024 est.)
note: % of labor force ages 15-24 seeking employment
comparison ranking: total 82

Average household expenditures: *on food:* 12.8% of household expenditures (2023 est.)
on alcohol and tobacco: 4.7% of household expenditures (2023 est.)

Remittances: 0.3% of GDP (2023 est.)
0.2% of GDP (2022 est.)
0.3% of GDP (2021 est.)
note: personal transfers and compensation between resident and non-resident individuals/households/entities

Budget: *revenues:* $83.167 billion (2022 est.)
expenditures: $91.782 billion (2022 est.)
note: central government revenues (excluding grants) and expenditures converted to US dollars at average official exchange rate for year indicated

Public debt: 54% of GDP (2022 est.)
note: central government debt as a % of GDP
comparison ranking: 90

Taxes and other revenues: 29.6% (of GDP) (2022 est.)
note: central government tax revenue as a % of GDP
comparison ranking: 5

Current account balance: -$15.978 billion (2024 est.)
-$17.065 billion (2023 est.)
-$21.627 billion (2022 est.)
note: balance of payments - net trade and primary/secondary income in current dollars
comparison ranking: 186

Exports: $61.799 billion (2024 est.)
$59.029 billion (2023 est.)
$57.485 billion (2022 est.)
note: balance of payments - exports of goods and services in current dollars
comparison ranking: 61

Exports - partners: China 28%, USA 12%, Australia 12%, Japan 6%, S. Korea 3% (2023)

note: top five export partners based on percentage share of exports

Exports - commodities: milk, wood, beef, butter, sheep and goat meat (2023)
note: top five export commodities based on value in dollars

Imports: $67.998 billion (2024 est.)
$68.412 billion (2023 est.)
$71.35 billion (2022 est.)
note: balance of payments - imports of goods and services in current dollars
comparison ranking: 57

Imports - partners: China 20%, Australia 11%, USA 9%, S. Korea 7%, Japan 7% (2023)
note: top five import partners based on percentage share of imports

Imports - commodities: refined petroleum, cars, gas turbines, broadcasting equipment, trucks (2023)
note: top five import commodities based on value in dollars

Reserves of foreign exchange and gold: $22.065 billion (2024 est.)
$15.487 billion (2023 est.)
$14.4 billion (2022 est.)
note: holdings of gold (year-end prices)/foreign exchange/special drawing rights in current dollars
comparison ranking: 61

Exchange rates: New Zealand dollars (NZD) per US dollar -

Exchange rates: 1.652 (2024 est.)
1.628 (2023 est.)
1.577 (2022 est.)
1.414 (2021 est.)
1.542 (2020 est.)

ENERGY

Electricity access: *electrification - total population:* 100% (2022 est.)

Electricity: *installed generating capacity:* 10.643 million kW (2023 est.)
consumption: 40.794 billion kWh (2023 est.)
transmission/distribution losses: 3.058 billion kWh (2023 est.)
comparison rankings: installed generating capacity 65; consumption 58; transmission/distribution losses 139

Electricity generation sources: *fossil fuels:* 12.4% of total installed capacity (2023 est.)
solar: 0.8% of total installed capacity (2023 est.)
wind: 8% of total installed capacity (2023 est.)
hydroelectricity: 59.7% of total installed capacity (2023 est.)
geothermal: 17.6% of total installed capacity (2023 est.)
biomass and waste: 1.5% of total installed capacity (2023 est.)

Coal: *production:* 3.011 million metric tons (2023 est.)
consumption: 2.696 million metric tons (2023 est.)
exports: 906,000 metric tons (2023 est.)
imports: 283,000 metric tons (2023 est.)
proven reserves: 6.75 billion metric tons (2023 est.)

Petroleum: *total petroleum production:* 12,000 bbl/day (2023 est.)
refined petroleum consumption: 154,000 bbl/day (2024 est.)
crude oil estimated reserves: 40.993 million barrels (2021 est.)

Natural gas: *production:* 3.97 billion cubic meters (2023 est.)
consumption: 3.891 billion cubic meters (2023 est.)
proven reserves: 31.149 billion cubic meters (2021 est.)

Energy consumption per capita: 121.647 million Btu/person (2023 est.)
comparison ranking: 33

COMMUNICATIONS

Telephones - fixed lines: *total subscriptions:* 660,000 (2023 est.)
subscriptions per 100 inhabitants: 13 (2023 est.)
comparison ranking: total subscriptions 82

Telephones - mobile cellular: *total subscriptions:* 6.56 million (2023 est.)
subscriptions per 100 inhabitants: 115 (2022 est.)
comparison ranking: total subscriptions 116

Broadcast media: state-owned Television New Zealand operates multiple TV networks; state-owned Radio New Zealand operates 3 radio networks and an external shortwave radio service to the South Pacific region; a small number of national commercial TV and radio stations and many regional commercial TV and radio stations are available; cable and satellite TV systems are available (2019)

Internet country code: .nz

Internet users: *percent of population:* 96% (2023 est.)

Broadband - fixed subscriptions: *total:* 1.93 million (2023 est.)
subscriptions per 100 inhabitants: 37 (2023 est.)
comparison ranking: total 63

TRANSPORTATION

Civil aircraft registration country code prefix: ZK

Airports: 206 (2025)
comparison ranking: 29

Heliports: 62 (2025)
comparison ranking: 32

Railways: *total:* 4,128 km (2018)
narrow gauge: 4,128 km (2018) 1.067-m gauge (506 km electrified)

Merchant marine: *total:* 117 (2023)
by type: container ship 2, general cargo 12, oil tanker 3, other 100
comparison ranking: total 84

Ports: *total ports:* 22 (2024)
large: 2
medium: 1
small: 10
very small: 9
ports with oil terminals: 14
key ports: Auckland, Bluff Harbor, Gisborne, Manukau Harbor, Napier, Nelson, New Plymouth, Otago Harbor, Picton, Tauranga, Timaru, Wellington, Whangarei

MILITARY AND SECURITY

Military and security forces: New Zealand Defense Force (NZDF): New Zealand Army, Royal New Zealand Navy, Royal New Zealand Air Force (2025)
note: the New Zealand Police, under the Minister of Police, is the primary law enforcement body agency of New Zealand and responsible for internal security

Military expenditures: 1.2% of GDP (2024 est.)
1.3% of GDP (2023 est.)
1.3% of GDP (2022 est.)
1.3% of GDP (2021 est.)
1.5% of GDP (2020 est.)

Military and security service personnel strengths: approximately 8,800 active (Regular Force) New Zealand Defense Forces (4,300 Army; 2,100 Navy; 2,400 Air Force) (2025)
note: the total NZDF complement is about 15,300 including the Regular Force, Reserves, and civilians

Military equipment inventories and acquisitions: the NZDF's inventory is comprised of domestically produced and Western-supplied weapons and equipment, including from Australia, Canada, the US, and the UK (2025)

Military service age and obligation: 17 years of age for voluntary military service for men and women; soldiers cannot be deployed until the age of 18; no conscription (2025)
note: New Zealand opened up all military occupations to women in 2000; as of 2024, women accounted for about 20% of Regular Force personnel

Military deployments: small numbers of NZ military personnel are deployed on a variety of international missions in Africa, Antarctica, the Asia-Pacific region, and the Middle East (2025)

Military - note: the NZDF is responsible for protecting New Zealand's sovereignty, promoting its interests, safeguarding peace and security, and conducting peacekeeping, humanitarian, and other international missions
New Zealand is a member of the Five Powers Defense Arrangements (FPDA), a series of mutual assistance agreements reached in 1971 embracing Australia, Malaysia, New Zealand, Singapore, and the UK; the FPDA commits the members to consult with one another in the event or threat of an armed attack on any of the members and to mutually decide what measures should be taken, jointly or separately; there is no specific obligation to intervene militarily
New Zealand has been part of the Australia, New Zealand, and US Security (ANZUS) Treaty since 1951; however, the US suspended its ANZUS security obligations to New Zealand in 1986 after Auckland implemented a policy barring nuclear-armed and nuclear-powered warships from its ports; the US and New Zealand signed the Wellington Declaration in 2010, which reaffirmed close ties between the two countries, and in 2012 signed the Washington Declaration, which provided a framework for future security cooperation and defense dialogues; in 2016, a US naval ship conducted the first bilateral warship visit to New Zealand since the 1980s; New Zealand has Major Non-NATO Ally (MNNA) status with the US, a designation under US law that provides foreign partners with certain benefits in the areas of defense trade and security cooperation (2025)

SPACE

Space agency/agencies: New Zealand Space Agency (NZSA; established 2016 under the Ministry of Business, Innovation, and Employment) (2025)

Space launch site(s): Mahia Peninsula Launch Complex (Hawke's Bay) (2025)

Space program overview: national space program focused largely on the development of a commercial space sector, particularly in the field of satellites and satellite/space launch vehicles (SLV); manufactures and launches commercial satellites and SLVs; researches and develops a range of other space-related technologies, including propulsion systems; participates in international space programs and partners with a range of foreign space agencies and industries, including those of Australia, Canada, the EU and its

member states, the European Space Agency (ESA) and its member states, South Africa, and the US; has a growing commercial space sector (2025)
note: further details about the key activities, programs, and milestones of the country's space program, as well as government spending estimates on the space sector, appear in the Space Programs reference guide

TERRORISM

Terrorist group(s): Terrorist group(s): Islamic State of Iraq and ash-Sham (ISIS)
note: details about the history, aims, leadership, organization, areas of operation, tactics, targets, weapons, size, and sources of support of the group(s) appear(s) in Appendix T

TRANSNATIONAL ISSUES

Refugees and internally displaced persons: *refugees:* 5,622 (2024 est.)

IDPs: 26 (2024 est.)
stateless persons: 29 (2024 est.)

NICARAGUA

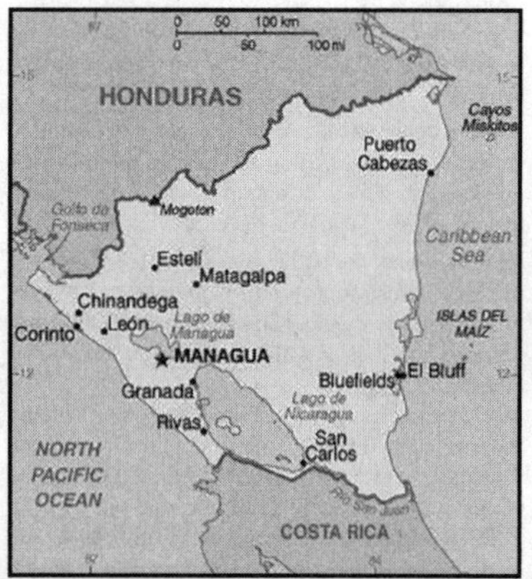

INTRODUCTION

Background: The Pacific coast of Nicaragua was settled as a Spanish colony in the early 16th century. Independence from Spain was declared in 1821, and the country became an independent republic in 1838. Britain occupied the Caribbean Coast in the first half of the 19th century, but gradually ceded control of the region in subsequent decades. By 1978, violent opposition to governmental manipulation and corruption resulted in a short-lived civil war that brought a civil-military coalition to power in 1979, spearheaded by Marxist Sandinista guerrillas led by Daniel ORTEGA Saavedra. Nicaraguan aid to leftist rebels in El Salvador prompted the US to sponsor anti-Sandinista Contra guerrillas through much of the 1980s.

After losing free and fair elections in 1990, 1996, and 2001, ORTEGA was elected president in 2006, 2011, 2016, and most recently in 2021. Municipal, regional, and national-level elections since 2008 have been marred by widespread irregularities. Democratic institutions have lost their independence under the ORTEGA regime as the president has assumed full control over all branches of government, as well as cracking down on a nationwide prodemocracy protest movement in 2018 and shuttering over 3,300 civil society organizations between 2018 and 2024. In the lead-up to the 2021 presidential election, authorities arrested over 40 individuals linked to the opposition, including presidential candidates, private sector leaders, NGO workers, human rights defenders, and journalists. Only five lesser-known presidential candidates from mostly small parties allied to ORTEGA's Sandinistas were allowed to run against ORTEGA. He then awarded the Sandinistas control of all 153 of Nicaraguan municipalities in the 2022 municipal elections, consolidating one-party rule.

GEOGRAPHY

Location: Central America, bordering both the Caribbean Sea and the North Pacific Ocean, between Costa Rica and Honduras

Geographic coordinates: 13 00 N, 85 00 W

Map references: Central America and the Caribbean

Area: *total:* 130,370 sq km
land: 119,990 sq km
water: 10,380 sq km
comparison ranking: total 98

Area - comparative: slightly larger than Pennsylvania; slightly smaller than New York State

Land boundaries: *total:* 1,253 km
border countries (2): Costa Rica 313 km; Honduras 940 km

Coastline: 910 km

Maritime claims: *territorial sea:* 12 nm
contiguous zone: 24 nm
continental shelf: natural prolongation

Climate: tropical in lowlands, cooler in highlands

Terrain: extensive Atlantic coastal plains rising to central interior mountains; narrow Pacific coastal plain interrupted by volcanoes

Elevation: *highest point:* Mogoton 2,085 m
lowest point: Pacific Ocean 0 m
mean elevation: 298 m

Natural resources: gold, silver, copper, tungsten, lead, zinc, timber, fish

Land use: *agricultural land:* 42.3% (2022 est.)
arable land: 12.5% (2022 est.)
permanent crops: 2.5% (2022 est.)
permanent pasture: 27.4% (2022 est.)
forest: 26.7% (2022 est.)
other: 31% (2022 est.)

Irrigated land: 1,990 sq km (2012)

Major lakes (area sq km): *fresh water lake(s):* Lago de Nicaragua - 8,150 sq km; Lago de Managua - 1,040 sq km

Population distribution: the overwhelming majority of the population resides in the western half of the country, with much of the urban growth centered in the capital city of Managua; coastal areas also show large population clusters

Natural hazards: destructive earthquakes; volcanoes; landslides; extremely susceptible to hurricanes
volcanism: significant volcanic activity; Cerro Negro (728 m) is one of Nicaragua's most active volcanoes; its lava flows and ash have been known to cause significant damage to farmland and buildings; other historically active volcanoes include Concepcion, Cosiguina, Las Pilas, Masaya, Momotombo, San Cristobal, and Telica

Geography - note: largest country in Central America; contains the largest freshwater body in Central America, Lago de Nicaragua

PEOPLE AND SOCIETY

Population: *total:* 6,676,948 (2024 est.)
male: 3,273,900
female: 3,403,048
comparison rankings: total 108; male 108; female 109

Nationality: *noun:* Nicaraguan(s)
adjective: Nicaraguan

Ethnic groups: Mestizo (mixed Indigenous and White) 69%, White 17%, Black 9%, Indigenous 5%

Languages: Spanish (official) 99.5%, Indigenous 0.3%, Portuguese 0.1%, other 0.1% (2020 est.)
major-language sample(s):
La Libreta Informativa del Mundo, la fuente indispensable de información básica. (Spanish)
note: English and indigenous languages found on the Caribbean coast

Religions: Roman Catholic 44.9%, Protestant 38.7% (Evangelical 38.2, Adventist 0.5%), other 1.2%, (includes Jehovah's Witness and Church of Jesus Christ), believer but not belonging to a church 1%, agnostic or atheist 0.4%, none 13.7%, unspecified 0.2% (2020 est.)

Age structure: *0-14 years:* 25.1% (male 855,256/female 818,714)
15-64 years: 68.9% (male 2,240,297/female 2,360,244)
65 years and over: 6% (2024 est.) (male 178,347/female 224,090)

Dependency ratios: *total dependency ratio:* 45.1 (2024 est.)
youth dependency ratio: 36.4 (2024 est.)
elderly dependency ratio: 8.7 (2024 est.)
potential support ratio: 11.4 (2024 est.)

Median age: *total:* 29 years (2024 est.)
male: 28.1 years
female: 29.9 years
comparison ranking: total 147

Population growth rate: 0.95% (2024 est.)
comparison ranking: 97

Birth rate: 16.4 births/1,000 population (2024 est.)
comparison ranking: 97

Death rate: 5.1 deaths/1,000 population (2024 est.)
comparison ranking: 191

Net migration rate: -1.8 migrant(s)/1,000 population (2024 est.)
comparison ranking: 166

Population distribution: the overwhelming majority of the population resides in the western half of the country, with much of the urban growth centered in the capital city of Managua; coastal areas also show large population clusters

Urbanization: *urban population:* 59.8% of total population (2023)
rate of urbanization: 1.45% annual rate of change (2020-25 est.)

Major urban areas - population: 1.095 million MANAGUA (capital) (2023)

Sex ratio: *at birth:* 1.05 male(s)/female
0-14 years: 1.04 male(s)/female
15-64 years: 0.95 male(s)/female
65 years and over: 0.8 male(s)/female
total population: 0.96 male(s)/female (2024 est.)

Mother's mean age at first birth: 19.2 years (2011/12 est.)
note: data represents median age at first birth among women 25-29

Maternal mortality ratio: 60 deaths/100,000 live births (2023 est.)
comparison ranking: 87

Infant mortality rate: *total:* 14.4 deaths/1,000 live births (2024 est.)
male: 15.9 deaths/1,000 live births
female: 12.8 deaths/1,000 live births
comparison ranking: total 96

Life expectancy at birth: *total population:* 74.7 years (2024 est.)
male: 73.2 years
female: 76.4 years
comparison ranking: total population 139

Total fertility rate: 1.83 children born/woman (2024 est.)
comparison ranking: 134

Gross reproduction rate: 0.89 (2024 est.)

Health expenditure: 9.7% of GDP (2021)
17.8% of national budget (2022 est.)

Physician density: 0.68 physicians/1,000 population (2018)

Hospital bed density: 0.9 beds/1,000 population (2021 est.)

Sanitation facility access: *unimproved:* rural: 33.5% of population

Obesity - adult prevalence rate: 23.7% (2016)
comparison ranking: 63

Alcohol consumption per capita: *total:* 3.69 liters of pure alcohol (2019 est.)
beer: 1.57 liters of pure alcohol (2019 est.)
wine: 0.02 liters of pure alcohol (2019 est.)
spirits: 2.1 liters of pure alcohol (2019 est.)
other alcohols: 0 liters of pure alcohol (2019 est.)
comparison ranking: total 101

Currently married women (ages 15-49): 56% (2023 est.)

Education expenditure: 2.9% of GDP (2023 est.)
17.7% national budget (2023 est.)
comparison ranking: Education expenditure (% GDP) 157

School life expectancy (primary to tertiary education): *total:* 12 years (2023 est.)
male: 12 years (2023 est.)
female: 12 years (2023 est.)

ENVIRONMENT

Environmental issues: deforestation; soil erosion; water pollution; drought

International environmental agreements: *party to:* Biodiversity, Climate Change, Climate Change-Kyoto Protocol, Climate Change-Paris Agreement, Comprehensive Nuclear Test Ban, Desertification, Endangered Species, Environmental Modification, Hazardous Wastes, Law of the Sea, Nuclear Test Ban, Ozone Layer Protection, Ship Pollution, Wetlands, Whaling
signed, but not ratified: none of the selected agreements

Climate: tropical in lowlands, cooler in highlands

Urbanization: *urban population:* 59.8% of total population (2023)
rate of urbanization: 1.45% annual rate of change (2020-25 est.)

Carbon dioxide emissions: 3.806 million metric tonnes of CO2 (2023 est.)
from coal and metallurgical coke: 2 metric tonnes of CO2 (2023 est.)
from petroleum and other liquids: 3.806 million metric tonnes of CO2 (2023 est.)
comparison ranking: total emissions 144

Particulate matter emissions: 16.3 micrograms per cubic meter (2019 est.)

Waste and recycling: *municipal solid waste generated annually:* 1.529 million tons (2024 est.)
percent of municipal solid waste recycled: 15% (2022 est.)

Total water withdrawal: *municipal:* 190 million cubic meters (2022 est.)
industrial: 620,000 cubic meters (2022 est.)
agricultural: 1.084 billion cubic meters (2022 est.)

Total renewable water resources: 164.52 billion cubic meters (2022 est.)

Geoparks: *total global geoparks and regional networks:* 1
global geoparks and regional networks: Rio Coco (2023)

GOVERNMENT

Country name: *conventional long form:* Republic of Nicaragua
conventional short form: Nicaragua
local long form: República de Nicaragua
local short form: Nicaragua
etymology: 16th-century Spanish explorer Gil GONZALEZ Davila is said to have combined the name of a local chieftain, Nicarao, with the Spanish word *agua* (water), referring to the two large lakes in the west of the country (Lake Managua and Lake Nicaragua)

Government type: presidential republic

Capital: *name:* Managua
geographic coordinates: 12 08 N, 86 15 W
time difference: UTC-6 (1 hour behind Washington, DC, during Standard Time)
etymology: the name comes from Lake Managua, whose name is composed of the Guaraní words *ama* (rain) and *nagua* (spirit) and refers to a local deity

Administrative divisions: 15 departments *(departamentos*, singular - *departamento)* and 2 autonomous regions* *(regiones autonomistas*, singular - *region autonoma)*; Boaco, Carazo, Chinandega, Chontales, Costa Caribe Norte*, Costa Caribe Sur*, Esteli, Granada, Jinotega, Leon, Madriz, Managua, Masaya, Matagalpa, Nueva Segovia, Rio San Juan, Rivas

Legal system: civil law system; Supreme Court may review administrative acts

Constitution: *history:* several previous; latest adopted 19 November 1986, effective 9 January 1987
amendment process: proposed by the president of the republic or assent of at least half of the National Assembly membership; passage requires approval by 60% of the membership of the next elected Assembly and promulgation by the president of the republic

International law organization participation: accepts compulsory ICJ jurisdiction with reservations; non-party state to the ICCt

Citizenship: *citizenship by birth:* yes
citizenship by descent only: yes
dual citizenship recognized: no, except in cases where bilateral agreements exist
residency requirement for naturalization: 4 years

Suffrage: 16 years of age; universal

Executive branch: *chief of state:* President Jose Daniel ORTEGA Saavedra (since 10 January 2007)
head of government: President Jose Daniel ORTEGA Saavedra (since 10 January 2007)
cabinet: Council of Ministers appointed by the president
election/appointment process: president and vice president directly elected on the same ballot by qualified plurality vote for a 6-year term (no term limits)
most recent election date: 7 November 2021
election results: *2021:* Jose Daniel ORTEGA Saavedra reelected president for a fourth consecutive term; percent of vote - Jose Daniel ORTEGA Saavedra (FSLN) 75.9%, Walter ESPINOZA (PLC) 14.3%, Guillermo OSORNO (CCN) 3.3%, Marcelo MONTIEL (ALN) 3.1%, other 3.4%
2016: Jose Daniel ORTEGA Saavedra reelected president for a third consecutive term; percent of vote - Jose Daniel ORTEGA Saavedra (FSLN) 72.4%, Maximino RODRIGUEZ (PLC) 15%, Jose del Carmen ALVARADO (PLI) 4.5%, Saturnino CERRATO Hodgson (ALN) 4.3%, other 3.7%
expected date of next election: 1 November 2026
note: the president is both chief of state and head of government

Legislative branch: *legislature name:* National Assembly (Asamblea Nacional)
legislative structure: unicameral
number of seats: 91 (all directly elected)
electoral system: proportional representation
scope of elections: full renewal
term in office: 5 years
most recent election date: 11/7/2021
parties elected and seats per party: Sandinista National Liberation Front (FSLN) (75); Liberal and Constitutionalist Party (PLC) (9); Other (6)
percentage of women in chamber: 54.9%
expected date of next election: November 2026

Judicial branch: *highest court(s):* Supreme Court or Corte Suprema de Justicia (consists of 16 judges organized into administrative, civil, criminal, and constitutional chambers)
judge selection and term of office: Supreme Court judges elected by the National Assembly to serve 5-year staggered terms
subordinate courts: Appeals Court; first instance civil, criminal, and labor courts; military courts are independent of the Supreme Court

Political parties: Alliance for the Republic or APRE
Alternative for Change or AC (operates in a political alliance with the FSLN)
Autonomous Liberal Party or PAL
Caribbean Unity Movement or PAMUC
Christian Unity Party or PUC (operates in a political alliance with the FSLN)
Independent Liberal Party or PLI
Liberal Constitutionalist Party or PLC

Moskitia Indigenous Progressive Movement or MOSKITIA PAWANKA (operates in a political alliance with the FSLN)
Multiethnic Indigenous Party or PIM (operates in a political alliance with the FSLN)
Nationalist Liberal Party or PLN (operates in a political alliance with the FSLN)
Nicaraguan Liberal Alliance or ALN
Nicaraguan Party of the Christian Path or CCN
Nicaraguan Resistance Party or PRN (operates in a political alliance with the FSLN)
Sandinista National Liberation Front or FSLN
Sons of Mother Earth or YATAMA
The New Sons of Mother Earth Movement or MYATAMARAN (operates in a political alliance with the FSLN)

Diplomatic representation in the US: *chief of mission:* Ambassador (vacant); Chargé d'Affaires Sammia Alicia HODGSON MCKENZIE (since 3 June 2025)
chancery: 1627 New Hampshire Avenue NW, Washington, DC 20009
telephone: [1] (202) 939-6570
FAX: [1] (202) 939-6545
email address and website: mperalta@cancilleria.gob.ni United States of America | ConsuladoDeNicaragua.com
consulate(s) general: Houston, Los Angeles, Miami, New York, San Francisco

Diplomatic representation from the US: *chief of mission:* Ambassador (vacant); Chargé d'Affaires Kevin Michael O'REILLY (since 28 June 2023)
embassy: Kilometer 5.5 Carretera Sur, Managua
mailing address: 3240 Managua Place, Washington DC 20521-3240
telephone: [505] 2252-7100,
FAX: [505] 2252-7250
email address and website: ACS.Managua@state.gov https://ni.usembassy.gov/

International organization participation: ACS, BCIE, CACM, CD, CELAC, FAO, G-77, IADB, IAEA, IBRD, ICAO, ICRM, IDA, IFAD, IFC, IFRCS, ILO, IMF, IMO, Interpol, IOC, IOM, IPU, ISO (correspondent), ITSO, ITU, ITUC (NGOs), LAES, LAIA (observer), MIGA, NAM, OAS, OPANAL, OPCW, PCA, Petrocaribe, SICA, UN, UNCTAD, UNESCO, UNHCR, UNIDO, Union Latina, UNOOSA, UNWTO, UPU, WCO, WHO, WIPO, WMO, WTO

Independence: 15 September 1821 (from Spain)

National holiday: Independence Day, 15 September (1821)

Flag: *description:* three equal horizontal bands of blue (top), white, and blue, with the national coat of arms centered in the white band; the coat of arms has a triangle with the words REPUBLICA DE NICARAGUA in an arc over it and AMERICA CENTRAL in an arc underneath
meaning: blue stands for the Pacific Ocean and the Caribbean Sea, and white for the land between the two bodies of water
history: the banner is based on the former blue-white-blue flag of the Federal Republic of Central America
note: similar to the flag of El Salvador, which has a round emblem; also similar to the flag of Honduras, which has five blue stars in an "X" pattern centered on the white band

National symbol(s): turquoise-browed motmot (bird)

National color(s): blue, white

National anthem(s): *title:* "Salve a ti, Nicaragua" (Hail to Thee, Nicaragua)
lyrics/music: Salomon Ibarra MAYORGA/traditional, arranged by Luis Abraham DELGADILLO
history: music was approved in 1918 and the lyrics in 1939

National heritage: *total World Heritage Sites:* 2 (both cultural)
selected World Heritage Site locales: Ruins of León Viejo; León Cathedral

ECONOMY

Economic overview: low-income Central American economy; until 2018, nearly 20 years of sustained GDP growth; recent struggles due to COVID-19, political instability, and hurricanes; significant remittances; increasing poverty and food scarcity since 2005; sanctions limit investment

Real GDP (purchasing power parity): $52.989 billion (2024 est.)
$51.153 billion (2023 est.)
$48.985 billion (2022 est.)
note: data in 2021 dollars
comparison ranking: 123

Real GDP growth rate: 3.6% (2024 est.)
4.4% (2023 est.)
3.6% (2022 est.)
note: annual GDP % growth based on constant local currency
comparison ranking: 94

Real GDP per capita: $7,700 (2024 est.)
$7,500 (2023 est.)
$7,300 (2022 est.)
note: data in 2021 dollars
comparison ranking: 153

GDP (official exchange rate): $19.694 billion (2024 est.)
note: data in current dollars at official exchange rate

Inflation rate (consumer prices): 4.6% (2024 est.)
8.4% (2023 est.)
10.5% (2022 est.)
note: annual % change based on consumer prices
comparison ranking: 139

GDP - composition, by sector of origin: *agriculture:* 14.4% (2024 est.)
industry: 27.6% (2024 est.)
services: 46.8% (2024 est.)
note: figures may not total 100% due to non-allocated consumption not captured in sector-reported data
comparison rankings: agriculture 57; industry 70; services 164

GDP - composition, by end use: *household consumption:* 80.6% (2024 est.)
government consumption: 12.3% (2024 est.)
investment in fixed capital: 22.9% (2024 est.)
investment in inventories: 1.8% (2024 est.)
exports of goods and services: 40.5% (2024 est.)
imports of goods and services: -58.1% (2024 est.)
note: figures may not total 100% due to rounding or gaps in data collection

Agricultural products: sugarcane, milk, rice, oil palm fruit, maize, plantains, cassava, groundnuts, beans, chicken (2023)
note: top ten agricultural products based on tonnage

Industries: food processing, chemicals, machinery and metal products, knit and woven apparel, petroleum refining and distribution, beverages, footwear, wood, electric wire harness manufacturing, mining

Industrial production growth rate: 3.6% (2024 est.)
note: annual % change in industrial value added based on constant local currency
comparison ranking: 68

Labor force: 3.225 million (2024 est.)
note: number of people ages 15 or older who are employed or seeking work
comparison ranking: 104

Unemployment rate: 4.6% (2024 est.)
4.8% (2023 est.)
5% (2022 est.)
note: % of labor force seeking employment
comparison ranking: 77

Youth unemployment rate (ages 15-24): *total:* 9% (2024 est.)
male: 7.8% (2024 est.)
female: 12% (2024 est.)
note: % of labor force ages 15-24 seeking employment
comparison ranking: total 130

Population below poverty line: 24.9% (2016 est.)
note: % of population with income below national poverty line

Remittances: 26.6% of GDP (2024 est.)
26.2% of GDP (2023 est.)
20.6% of GDP (2022 est.)
note: personal transfers and compensation between resident and non-resident individuals/households/entities

Budget: *revenues:* $3.856 billion (2023 est.)
expenditures: $3.382 billion (2023 est.)
note: central government revenues and expenses (excluding grants/extrabudgetary units/social security funds) converted to US dollars at average official exchange rate for year indicated

Public debt: 33.3% of GDP (2017 est.)
note: official data; data cover general government debt and include debt instruments issued (or owned) by Government entities other than the treasury; the data include treasury debt held by foreign entities, as well as intragovernmental debt; intragovernmental debt consists of treasury borrowings from surpluses in the social funds, such as retirement, medical care, and unemployment, debt instruments for the social funds are not sold at public auctions; Nicaragua rebased its GDP figures in 2012, which reduced the figures for debt as a percentage of GDP
comparison ranking: 158

Taxes and other revenues: 19.9% (of GDP) (2023 est.)
note: central government tax revenue as a % of GDP
comparison ranking: 51

Current account balance: $817.618 million (2024 est.)
$1.465 billion (2023 est.)
-$459.6 million (2022 est.)
note: balance of payments - net trade and primary/secondary income in current dollars
comparison ranking: 60

Exports: $8.135 billion (2024 est.)
$8.248 billion (2023 est.)
$7.87 billion (2022 est.)
note: balance of payments - exports of goods and services in current dollars
comparison ranking: 124

Exports - partners: USA 51%, Mexico 12%, El Salvador 6%, Canada 6%, Switzerland 4% (2023)
note: top five export partners based on percentage share of exports

Exports - commodities: garments, gold, insulated wire, coffee, beef (2023)
note: top five export commodities based on value in dollars

Imports: $11.437 billion (2024 est.)
$10.519 billion (2023 est.)
$10.213 billion (2022 est.)
note: balance of payments - imports of goods and services in current dollars
comparison ranking: 115

Imports - partners: USA 24%, China 13%, Mexico 9%, Honduras 9%, Guatemala 8% (2023)
note: top five import partners based on percentage share of imports

Imports - commodities: garments, refined petroleum, crude petroleum, plastic products, fabric (2023)
note: top five import commodities based on value in dollars

Reserves of foreign exchange and gold: $6.105 billion (2024 est.)
$5.447 billion (2023 est.)
$4.404 billion (2022 est.)
note: holdings of gold (year-end prices)/foreign exchange/special drawing rights in current dollars
comparison ranking: 91

Debt - external: $6.753 billion (2023 est.)
note: present value of external debt in current US dollars
comparison ranking: 61

Exchange rates: cordobas (NIO) per US dollar -

Exchange rates: 36.624 (2024 est.)
36.441 (2023 est.)
35.874 (2022 est.)
35.171 (2021 est.)
34.342 (2020 est.)

ENERGY

Electricity access: *electrification - total population:* 86.5% (2022 est.)
electrification - urban areas: 100%
electrification - rural areas: 66.3%

Electricity: *installed generating capacity:* 1.849 million kW (2023 est.)
consumption: 4.654 billion kWh (2023 est.)
imports: 1.125 billion kWh (2023 est.)
transmission/distribution losses: 839 million kWh (2023 est.)
comparison rankings: installed generating capacity 121; consumption 131; imports 75; transmission/distribution losses 94

Electricity generation sources: *fossil fuels:* 35.5% of total installed capacity (2023 est.)
solar: 0.6% of total installed capacity (2023 est.)
wind: 12.9% of total installed capacity (2023 est.)
hydroelectricity: 14.9% of total installed capacity (2023 est.)
geothermal: 15.7% of total installed capacity (2023 est.)
biomass and waste: 20.4% of total installed capacity (2023 est.)

Coal: *imports:* 22 metric tons (2023 est.)

Petroleum: *total petroleum production:* 200 bbl/day (2023 est.)
refined petroleum consumption: 28,000 bbl/day (2023 est.)

Energy consumption per capita: 10.66 million Btu/person (2023 est.)
comparison ranking: 148

COMMUNICATIONS

Telephones - fixed lines: *total subscriptions:* 234,000 (2023 est.)
subscriptions per 100 inhabitants: 3 (2023 est.)
comparison ranking: total subscriptions 116

Telephones - mobile cellular: *total subscriptions:* 7.22 million (2023 est.)
subscriptions per 100 inhabitants: 97 (2021 est.)
comparison ranking: total subscriptions 111

Broadcast media: multiple terrestrial TV stations, supplemented by cable TV in most urban areas; nearly all are state-owned or affiliated; more than 300 radio stations, both state-affiliated and privately owned (2019)

Internet country code: .ni

Internet users: *percent of population:* 58% (2023 est.)

Broadband - fixed subscriptions: *total:* 371,000 (2023 est.)
subscriptions per 100 inhabitants: 5 (2023 est.)
comparison ranking: total 109

TRANSPORTATION

Civil aircraft registration country code prefix: YN

Airports: 39 (2025)
comparison ranking: 105

Merchant marine: *total:* 5 (2023)
by type: general cargo 1, oil tanker 1, other 3
comparison ranking: total 168

Ports: *total ports:* 5 (2024)
large: 0
medium: 0
small: 2
very small: 3
ports with oil terminals: 4
key ports: Bluefields, Corinto, El Bluff, Puerto Cabezas, Puerto Sandino

MILITARY AND SECURITY

Military and security forces: Armed Forces of Nicaragua (formal name is Army of Nicaragua or Ejercito de Nicaragua, EN): Land Force; Naval Force; Air Force (2025)
note: both the military and the Nicaraguan National Police (Policía Nacional de Nicaragua or PNN) report directly to the president; Parapolice, which are non-uniformed, armed, and masked units with marginal tactical training and loose hierarchical organization, act in coordination with government security forces and report to the National Police; they have been used to suppress anti-government protesters

Military expenditures: 0.5% of GDP (2024 est.)
0.6% of GDP (2023 est.)
0.6% of GDP (2022 est.)
0.6% of GDP (2021 est.)
0.6% of GDP (2020 est.)

Military and security service personnel strengths: approximately 12,000 active Armed Forces (2025)

Military equipment inventories and acquisitions: the military's air and ground force inventories include mostly secondhand Russian or Soviet-era equipment; its naval force has a miscellaneous mix of patrol boats from several foreign suppliers, as well as some commercial vessels converted into gunboats domestically (2024)
note: in 2024, the US imposed restrictions on the import and export of US origin defense articles and defense services destined for or originating in Nicaragua

Military service age and obligation: 18-30 years of age for voluntary military service; no conscription; tour of duty 18-36 months (2024)

Military - note: the military is responsible for defending Nicaragua's independence, sovereignty, and territory; it also has some domestic security responsibilities, including border security, assisting the police, protecting natural resources, and providing disaster relief and humanitarian assistance; Nicaragua has defense ties with Cuba, Venezuela, and Russia; Russia has provided training support and equipment; in 2025, Nicaragua signed an agreement of "mutual protection" with Russia
the modern Army of Nicaragua was created in 1979 as the Sandinista Popular Army (1979-1984); prior to 1979, the military was known as the National Guard, which was organized and trained by the US in the 1920s and 1930s; the first commander of the National Guard, Anastasio SOMOZA GARCIA, seized power in 1937 and ran the country as a military dictator until his assassination in 1956; his sons ran the country either directly or through figureheads until the Sandinistas came to power in 1979; the defeated National Guard was disbanded by the Sandinistas (2025)

SPACE

Space agency/agencies: National Secretariat for Extraterrestrial Space Affairs, The Moon and Other Celestial Bodies (Secretaría Nacional para Asuntos del Espacio Ultraterrestre, la Luna y otros Cuerpos Celestes, established 2021; operates under the military's control) (2025)

Space program overview: stated mission of the space agency is to promote the development of space activities with the aim of broadening the country's capacities in the fields of education, industry, science, and technology; has cooperated with China and Russia; is a signatory of the convention establishing the Latin American and Caribbean Space Agency (ALCE) (2025)
note: further details about the key activities, programs, and milestones of the country's space program, as well as government spending estimates on the space sector, appear in the Space Programs reference guide

TRANSNATIONAL ISSUES

Refugees and internally displaced persons: IDPs: 89 (2024 est.)

Trafficking in persons: *tier rating:* Tier 3 — Nicaragua does not fully meet the minimum standards for the elimination of trafficking and is not making significant efforts to do so, therefore, Nicaragua remained on Tier 3; for more details, go to: https://www.state.gov/reports/2025-trafficking-in-persons-report/nicaragua/

Illicit drugs: USG identification: major illicit drug-producing and/or drug-transit country (2025)

NIGER

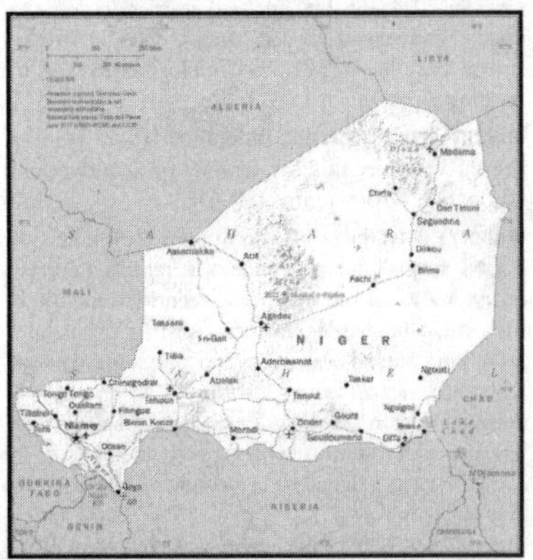

INTRODUCTION

Background: Nomadic peoples from the Saharan north and agriculturalists from the south settled present-day Niger. The Taureg kingdom of Takedda was one of the largest kingdoms in the north and played a prominent role in regional trade in the 14th century. In the south, the primary ethnic groups were the Songhai-Zarma in the west, the Hausa in the center, and the Kanuri in the east. When European colonizers arrived in the 19th century, the region was an assemblage of disparate local kingdoms.

In the late 19th century, the British and French agreed to partition the middle regions of the Niger River, and France began its conquest of what would become the colony of Niger. France experienced determined local resistance – particularly during the Tuareg uprising (1916-1917) – but established a colonial administration in 1922.

After achieving independence from France in 1960, Niger experienced single-party or military rule until 1991, when political pressure forced General Ali SAIBOU to allow multiparty elections. Political infighting and democratic backsliding led to coups in 1996 and 1999. In 1999, military officers restored democratic rule and held elections that brought Mamadou TANDJA to power. TANDJA was reelected in 2004 and spearheaded a 2009 constitutional amendment allowing him to extend his presidential term. In 2010, military officers led another coup that deposed TANDJA. ISSOUFOU Mahamadou was elected in 2011 and reelected in 2016. In 2021, BAZOUM Mohamed won the presidential election, marking Niger's first transition from one democratically elected president to another. Nonetheless, a military junta led by General Abdourahamane TIANI once again seized power in July 2023, detaining President BAZOUM and announcing the creation of a National Council for the Safeguarding of the Homeland (CNSP).

Niger is one of the poorest countries in the world with minimal government services and insufficient funds to develop its resource base. It is ranked fourth to last in the world on the UN Development Program's Human Development Index of 2023/2024. The largely agrarian and subsistence-based economy is frequently disrupted by extended droughts common to the Sahel region of Africa. The Nigerien Government continues its attempts to diversify the economy through increased oil production and mining projects. In addition, Niger is facing increased security concerns on its borders from various external threats including insecurity in Libya, spillover from the conflict and terrorism in Mali, and violent extremism in northeastern Nigeria.

GEOGRAPHY

Location: Western Africa, southeast of Algeria

Geographic coordinates: 16 00 N, 8 00 E

Map references: Africa

Area: *total:* 1.267 million sq km
land: 1,266,700 sq km
water: 300 sq km
comparison ranking: total 23

Area - comparative: slightly less than twice the size of Texas

Land boundaries: *total:* 5,834 km
border countries (7): Algeria 951 km; Benin 277 km; Burkina Faso 622 km; Chad 1,196 km; Libya 342 km; Mali 838 km; Nigeria 1,608 km

Coastline: 0 km (landlocked)

Maritime claims: none (landlocked)

Climate: desert; mostly hot, dry, dusty; tropical in extreme south

Terrain: predominately desert plains and sand dunes; flat to rolling plains in south; hills in north

Elevation: *highest point:* Idoukal-n-Taghes 2,022 m
lowest point: Niger River 200 m
mean elevation: 474 m

Natural resources: uranium, coal, iron ore, tin, phosphates, gold, molybdenum, gypsum, salt, petroleum

Land use: *agricultural land:* 36.8% (2022 est.)
arable land: 14% (2022 est.)
permanent crops: 0.1% (2022 est.)
permanent pasture: 22.7% (2022 est.)
forest: 0.8% (2022 est.)
other: 62.4% (2022 est.)

Irrigated land: 2,881 sq km (2022)

Major lakes (area sq km): *fresh water lake(s):* Lake Chad (endorheic lake shared with Chad, Nigeria, and Cameroon) - 10,360-25,900 sq km
note - area varies by season and year to year

Major rivers (by length in km): Niger (shared with Guinea [s], Mali, Benin, and Nigeria [m]) - 4,200 km
note: [s] after country name indicates river source; [m] after country name indicates river mouth

Major watersheds (area sq km): Atlantic Ocean drainage: Niger (2,261,741 sq km)

Internal (endorheic basin) drainage: Lake Chad (2,497,738 sq km)

Major aquifers: Lake Chad Basin, Lullemeden-Irhazer Basin, Murzuk-Djado Basin

Population distribution: majority of the populace is located in the southernmost extreme of the country along the border with Nigeria and Benin, as shown in this population distribution map

Natural hazards: recurring droughts

Geography - note: landlocked; one of the hottest countries in the world; northern four-fifths is desert, southern one-fifth is savanna that is suitable for livestock and limited agriculture

PEOPLE AND SOCIETY

Population: *total:* 26,342,784 (2024 est.)
male: 13,056,203
female: 13,286,581
comparison rankings: total 55; male 55; female 56

Nationality: *noun:* Nigerien(s)
adjective: Nigerien

Ethnic groups: Hausa 53.1%, Zarma/Songhai 21.2%, Tuareg 11%, Fulani (Peuhl) 6.5%, Kanuri 5.9%, Gurma 0.8%, Arab 0.4%, Tubu 0.4%, other/unavailable 0.9% (2006 est.)

Languages: Hausa, Zarma, French (official), Fufulde, Tamashek, Kanuri, Gurmancema, Tagdal
note: represents the most-spoken languages; Niger has 10 national languages: Arabic, Buduma, Fulfuldé, Guimancema, Hausa, Kanuri, Sonay-Zarma, Tamajaq, Tassawaq, and Tubu

Religions: Muslim 95.5%, ethnic religionist 4.1%, Christian 0.3%, agnostics and other 0.1% (2020 est.)

Age structure: *0-14 years:* 49.5% (male 6,567,460/female 6,463,877)
15-64 years: 47.8% (male 6,146,355/female 6,451,574)
65 years and over: 2.7% (2024 est.) (male 342,388/female 371,130)

Dependency ratios: *total dependency ratio:* 109.1 (2024 est.)
youth dependency ratio: 103.4 (2024 est.)
elderly dependency ratio: 5.7 (2024 est.)
potential support ratio: 17.7 (2024 est.)

Median age: *total:* 15.2 years (2024 est.)
male: 14.9 years
female: 15.6 years
comparison ranking: total 229

Population growth rate: 3.66% (2024 est.)
comparison ranking: 2

Birth rate: 46.6 births/1,000 population (2024 est.)
comparison ranking: 1

Death rate: 9.5 deaths/1,000 population (2024 est.)
comparison ranking: 44

Net migration rate: -0.6 migrant(s)/1,000 population (2024 est.)
comparison ranking: 125

Population distribution: majority of the populace is located in the southernmost extreme of the country along the border with Nigeria and Benin, as shown in this population distribution map

Urbanization: *urban population:* 17.1% of total population (2023)
rate of urbanization: 4.72% annual rate of change (2020-25 est.)

Major urban areas - population: 1.437 million NIAMEY (capital) (2023)

Sex ratio: *at birth:* 1.03 male(s)/female
0-14 years: 1.02 male(s)/female
15-64 years: 0.95 male(s)/female
65 years and over: 0.92 male(s)/female
total population: 0.98 male(s)/female (2024 est.)

Mother's mean age at first birth: 18.5 years (2012 est.)

note: data represents median age at first birth among women 20-49

Maternal mortality ratio: 350 deaths/100,000 live births (2023 est.)
comparison ranking: 22

Infant mortality rate: *total:* 64.3 deaths/1,000 live births (2024 est.)
male: 69.2 deaths/1,000 live births
female: 59.2 deaths/1,000 live births
comparison ranking: total 6

Life expectancy at birth: *total population:* 60.9 years (2024 est.)
male: 59.3 years
female: 62.5 years
comparison ranking: total population 218

Total fertility rate: 6.64 children born/woman (2024 est.)
comparison ranking: 1

Gross reproduction rate: 3.27 (2024 est.)

Drinking water source: *improved: urban:* 88.3% of population (2022 est.)
rural: 40.9% of population (2022 est.)
total: 48.9% of population (2022 est.)
unimproved: urban: 11.7% of population (2022 est.)
rural: 59.1% of population (2022 est.)
total: 51.1% of population (2022 est.)

Health expenditure: 5.8% of GDP (2021)
7.1% of national budget (2022 est.)

Physician density: 0.04 physicians/1,000 population (2023)

Hospital bed density: 0.3 beds/1,000 population (2020 est.)

Sanitation facility access: *improved: urban:* 81.9% of population (2022 est.)
rural: 15.2% of population (2022 est.)
total: 26.4% of population (2022 est.)
unimproved: urban: 18.1% of population (2022 est.)
rural: 84.8% of population (2022 est.)
total: 73.6% of population (2022 est.)

Obesity - adult prevalence rate: 5.5% (2016)
comparison ranking: 176

Alcohol consumption per capita: *total:* 0.11 liters of pure alcohol (2019 est.)
beer: 0.04 liters of pure alcohol (2019 est.)
wine: 0.01 liters of pure alcohol (2019 est.)
spirits: 0.06 liters of pure alcohol (2019 est.)
other alcohols: 0 liters of pure alcohol (2019 est.)
comparison ranking: total 177

Tobacco use: *total:* 7.5% (2025 est.)
male: 13.7% (2025 est.)
female: 1.2% (2025 est.)
comparison ranking: total 147

Children under the age of 5 years underweight: 34.6% (2022)
comparison ranking: 1

Currently married women (ages 15-49): 80.3% (2023 est.)

Education expenditure: 4.1% of GDP (2023 est.)
12.8% national budget (2023 est.)
comparison ranking: Education expenditure (% GDP) 100

Literacy: *total population:* 35.6% (2022 est.)
male: 47.9% (2022 est.)
female: 25.7% (2022 est.)

School life expectancy (primary to tertiary education): *total:* 6 years (2017 est.)
male: 7 years (2017 est.)
female: 6 years (2017 est.)

ENVIRONMENT

Environmental issues: overgrazing; soil erosion; deforestation; desertification; contaminated water; inadequate potable water; wildlife populations (such as elephant, hippopotamus, giraffe, and lion) threatened by poaching and habitat destruction

International environmental agreements: *party to:* Biodiversity, Climate Change, Climate Change-Kyoto Protocol, Climate Change-Paris Agreement, Comprehensive Nuclear Test Ban, Desertification, Endangered Species, Environmental Modification, Hazardous Wastes, Law of the Sea, Nuclear Test Ban, Ozone Layer Protection, Wetlands
signed, but not ratified: none of the selected agreements

Climate: desert; mostly hot, dry, dusty; tropical in extreme south

Urbanization: *urban population:* 17.1% of total population (2023)
rate of urbanization: 4.72% annual rate of change (2020-25 est.)

Carbon dioxide emissions: 3.132 million metric tonnes of CO2 (2023 est.)
from coal and metallurgical coke: 622,000 metric tonnes of CO2 (2023 est.)
from petroleum and other liquids: 2.457 million metric tonnes of CO2 (2023 est.)
from consumed natural gas: 52,000 metric tonnes of CO2 (2023 est.)
comparison ranking: total emissions 148

Particulate matter emissions: 59.5 micrograms per cubic meter (2019 est.)

Methane emissions: *energy:* 137.8 kt (2022-2024 est.)
agriculture: 713.8 kt (2019-2021 est.)
waste: 128.2 kt (2019-2021 est.)
other: 11.1 kt (2019-2021 est.)

Waste and recycling: *municipal solid waste generated annually:* 1.866 million tons (2024 est.)
percent of municipal solid waste recycled: 20.3% (2022 est.)

Total water withdrawal: *municipal:* 193.247 million cubic meters (2022 est.)
industrial: 38.654 million cubic meters (2022 est.)
agricultural: 2.351 billion cubic meters (2022 est.)

Total renewable water resources: 34,050,000,000 cubic meters (2022 est.)

GOVERNMENT

Country name: *conventional long form:* Republic of Niger
conventional short form: Niger
local long form: République du Niger
local short form: Niger
etymology: named for the Niger River that passes through the southwest of the country; the name of the river probably comes from the local Tuareg name, *egereou n-igereouen* (big rivers)
note: pronounced nee-ZHAIR

Government type: formerly, semi-presidential republic

Note: on 26 July 2023, the National Council for the Safeguard of the Homeland, a military junta which took control of Niger's government, dissolved all government institutions, and rules by decree

Capital: *name:* Niamey
geographic coordinates: 13 31 N, 2 07 E
time difference: UTC+1 (6 hours ahead of Washington, DC, during Standard Time)
etymology: the origin of the name is unclear; one of many stories says that an African chief told his seven slaves "*Wa niammane*," meaning "stay here," and the name was later shortened to its present form

Administrative divisions: 7 regions (*régions*, singular - *région*) and 1 capital district* (*communauté urbaine*); Agadez, Diffa, Dosso, Maradi, Niamey*, Tahoua, Tillaberi, Zinder

Legal system: *note:* following the 26 July 2023 military coup, the National Council for the Safeguard of the Homeland assumed control of all government institutions and rules by decree; formerly, mixed system of civil law, based on French civil law, Islamic law, and customary law

Constitution: *history:* several previous; passed by referendum 31 October 2010, entered into force 25 November 2010
amendment process: formerly proposed by the president of the republic or the National Assembly; consideration of amendments requires at least three-fourths majority vote by the Assembly; passage requires at least four-fifths majority vote; if disapproved, the proposed amendment is dropped or submitted to a referendum; constitutional articles on the form of government, the multiparty system, the separation of state and religion, disqualification of Assembly members, amendment procedures, and amnesty of participants in the 2010 coup cannot be amended
note: on 26 July 2023, the National Council for the Safeguard of the Homeland, a military junta which took control of Niger's government, dissolved the country's constitution

International law organization participation: has not submitted an ICJ jurisdiction declaration; accepts ICCt jurisdiction

Citizenship: *citizenship by birth:* no
citizenship by descent only: at least one parent must be a citizen of Niger
dual citizenship recognized: yes
residency requirement for naturalization: unknown

Suffrage: 18 years of age; universal

Executive branch: *chief of state:* President of the National Council for the Safeguard of the Homeland (CNSP) General Abdourahame TIANI (since 28 July 2023)
head of government: CNSP Prime Minister Ali Mahaman Lamine ZEINE (since 9 August 2023)
cabinet: Cabinet appointed by the CNSP
election/appointment process: the CNSP rules by decree; previously, the president was directly elected by absolute-majority popular vote in 2 rounds, if needed, for a 5-year term (eligible for a second term); prime minister was appointed by the president, authorized by the National Assembly
most recent election date: 27 December 2020, with a runoff held on 21 February 2021
election results: *2020/2021:* Mohamed BAZOUM elected president in second round; percent of vote in first round - Mohamed BAZOUM (PNDS-Tarrayya) 39.3%, Mahamane OUSMANE (MODEN/FA Lumana Africa) 17%, Seini OUMAROU (MNSD-Nassara) 9%, Albade ABOUDA (MPR-Jamhuriya) 7.1%, other 27.6%; percent of vote in second round - Mohamed BAZOUM 55.7%, Mahamane OUSMANE 44.3%
2016: ISSOUFOU Mahamadou reelected president in second round; percent of vote in first round

- ISSOUFOU Mahamadou (PNDS-Tarrayya) 48.6%, Hama AMADOU (MODEN/FA Lumana Africa) 17.8%, Seini OUMAROU (MNSD-Nassara) 11.3%, other 22.3%; percent of vote in second round - ISSOUFOU Mahamadou 92%, Hama AMADOU 8%
expected date of next election: 2025
note: deposed president BAZOUM has been under house arrest since a military coup on 26 July 2023

Legislative branch: *legislature name:* Advisory Council for the Refoundation (Conseil consultatif de la refondation)
legislative structure: unicameral
number of seats: 194 (all appointed)
electoral system: mixed system
scope of elections: full renewal
most recent election date: 5/1/2025
percentage of women in chamber: 19.6%

Note: on 26 July 2023, the National Council for the Safeguard of the Homeland, a military junta which took control of Niger's government, dissolved the National Assembly; a commission recommended to the junta in February 2025 a minimum of a five-year transition to democratic rule

Judicial branch: *highest court(s):* High Court of Justice (consists of 7 members); Supreme Court (membership NA); Constitutional Court (consists of 7 judges)
judge selection and term of office: High Judicial Court members selected from among the legislature and judiciary to 5-year terms; Constitutional Court judges nominated/elected - 1 by the president of the Republic, 1 by the president of the National Assembly, 2 by peer judges, 2 by peer lawyers, 1 law professor by peers, and 1 from within Nigerien society; all appointed by the president; judges serve 6-year nonrenewable terms with one-third of membership renewed every 2 years
subordinate courts: Court of Cassation; Council of State; Court of Finances; various specialized tribunals and customary courts

Political parties: Alliance for Democracy and the Republic
Alliance for Democratic Renewal or ARD-Adaltchi-Mutuntchi
Alliance of Movements for the Emergence of Niger or AMEN AMIN
Congress for the Republic or CPR-Inganci
Democratic Alternation for Equity in Niger
Democratic and Republican Renewal-RDR-Tchanji
Democratic Movement for the Emergence of Niger Falala
Democratic Patriots' Rally or RPD Bazara
National Movement for the Development of Society-Nassara or MNSD-Nassara
Nigerien Alliance for Democracy and Progress-Zaman Lahiya or ANDP-Zaman Lahiya
Nigerien Democratic Movement for an African Federation or MODEN/FA Lumana
Nigerien Party for Democracy and Socialism or PNDS-Tarrayya
Nigerien Patriotic Movement or MPN-Kishin Kassa
Nigerien Rally for Democracy and Peace
Patriotic Movement for the Republic or MPR-Jamhuriya
Peace, Justice, Progress–Generation Doubara
Rally for Democracy and Progress-Jama'a or RDP-Jama'a
Rally for Peace and Progress or RPP Farilla
Social Democratic Rally or RSD-Gaskiyya
Social Democratic Party or PSD-Bassira
note: after the 26 July 2023 military coup, the National Council for the Safeguard of the Homeland dissolved the National Assembly and prohibited all political party activity

Diplomatic representation in the US: *chief of mission:* Ambassador (vacant); Chargé d'Affaires Hassane IDI (since 3 August 2023)
chancery: 2204 R Street NW, Washington, DC 20008
telephone: [1] (202) 483-4224
FAX: [1] (202) 483-3169
email address and website: communication@embassy-ofniger.org
http://www.embassyofniger.org/

Diplomatic representation from the US: *chief of mission:* Ambassador Kathleen FITZGIBBON (since 2 December 2023)
embassy: BP 11201, Niamey
mailing address: 2420 Niamey Place, Washington DC 20521-2420
telephone: [227] 20-72-26-61
FAX: [227] 20-73-55-60
email address and website: consulateniamey@state.gov
https://ne.usembassy.gov/

International organization participation: ACP, AfDB, AU (suspended), CD, EITI (compliant country), Entente, FAO, FZ, G-77, IAEA, IBRD, ICAO, ICCt, ICRM, IDA, IDB, IFAD, IFC, IFRCS, ILO, IMF, Interpol, IOC, IOM, IPU, ISO (correspondent), ITSO, ITU, ITUC (NGOs), LCBC, MIGA, MINUSCA, MNJTF, MONUSCO, NAM, OIC, OIF, OPCW, UN, UNCTAD, UNESCO, UNIDO, UNOOSA, UNWTO, UPU, WADB (regional), WAEMU, WCO, WFTU (NGOs), WHO, WIPO, WMO, WTO

Independence: 3 August 1960 (from France)

National holiday: Republic Day, 18 December (1958)
note: commemorates the founding of the Republic of Niger, which predated independence from France in 1960

Flag: *description:* three equal horizontal bands of orange (top), white, and green, with an orange disk centered on the white band
meaning: orange stands for the northern Sahara regions, white for purity and innocence, and green for hope and the fertile and productive southern and western areas, as well as the Niger River; the orange disc represents the sun and the people's sacrifices
note: similar to the flag of India, which has a blue spoked wheel centered on the white band

National symbol(s): zebu

National color(s): orange, white, green

National anthem(s): *title:* "L'Honneur de la Patrie" (The Honor of the Fatherland)
lyrics/music: a government-appointed committee wrote both the lyrics and the music
history: adopted 2023; replaced previous national anthem, "La Nigérienne" (The Nigerien), that was adopted in 1961

National heritage: *total World Heritage Sites:* 3 (1 cultural, 2 natural)
selected World Heritage Site locales: Air and Ténéré Natural Reserves (n); W-Arly-Pendjari Complex (n); Historic Agadez (c)

ECONOMY

Economic overview: low-income Sahel economy; major instability and humanitarian crises limit economic activity; COVID-19 eliminated recent antipoverty gains; economy rebounding since December 2020 Nigerian border reopening and new investments; uranium resource rich

Real GDP (purchasing power parity): $47.921 billion (2024 est.)
$44.199 billion (2023 est.)
$43.474 billion (2022 est.)
note: data in 2021 dollars
comparison ranking: 132

Real GDP growth rate: 8.4% (2024 est.)
1.7% (2023 est.)
11.9% (2022 est.)
note: annual GDP % growth based on constant local currency
comparison ranking: 10

Real GDP per capita: $1,800 (2024 est.)
$1,700 (2023 est.)
$1,700 (2022 est.)
note: data in 2021 dollars
comparison ranking: 207

GDP (official exchange rate): $19.538 billion (2024 est.)
note: data in current dollars at official exchange rate

Inflation rate (consumer prices): 9.1% (2024 est.)
3.7% (2023 est.)
4.2% (2022 est.)
note: annual % change based on consumer prices
comparison ranking: 174

GDP - composition, by sector of origin: *agriculture:* 33.8% (2024 est.)
industry: 17.8% (2024 est.)
services: 45.4% (2024 est.)
note: figures may not total 100% due to non-allocated consumption not captured in sector-reported data
comparison rankings: agriculture 6; industry 147; services 172

GDP - composition, by end use: *household consumption:* 59.2% (2024 est.)
government consumption: 11.8% (2024 est.)
investment in fixed capital: 18.7% (2024 est.)
investment in inventories: 0% (2024 est.)
exports of goods and services: 31.2% (2024 est.)
imports of goods and services: -20.8% (2024 est.)
note: figures may not total 100% due to rounding or gaps in data collection

Agricultural products: millet, cowpeas, sorghum, onions, milk, sugarcane, cabbages, cassava, groundnuts, tomatoes (2023)
note: top ten agricultural products based on tonnage

Industries: uranium mining, petroleum, cement, brick, soap, textiles, food processing, chemicals, slaughterhouses

Industrial production growth rate: 12.1% (2024 est.)
note: annual % change in industrial value added based on constant local currency
comparison ranking: 4

Labor force: 10.486 million (2024 est.)
note: number of people ages 15 or older who are employed or seeking work
comparison ranking: 53

Unemployment rate: 0.4% (2024 est.)
0.5% (2023 est.)
0.5% (2022 est.)
note: % of labor force seeking employment
comparison ranking: 3

Youth unemployment rate (ages 15-24): *total:* 0.3% (2024 est.)
male: 0.4% (2024 est.)
female: 0.2% (2024 est.)

note: % of labor force ages 15-24 seeking employment
comparison ranking: total 189

Population below poverty line: 45.5% (2021 est.)
note: % of population with income below national poverty line

Gini Index coefficient - distribution of family income: 32.9 (2021 est.)
note: index (0-100) of income distribution; higher values represent greater inequality
comparison ranking: 98

Household income or consumption by percentage share: *lowest 10%:* 3.8% (2021 est.)
highest 10%: 27.8% (2021 est.)
note: % share of income accruing to lowest and highest 10% of population

Remittances: 3.7% of GDP (2023 est.)
4.7% of GDP (2022 est.)
2.4% of GDP (2021 est.)
note: personal transfers and compensation between resident and non-resident individuals/households/entities

Budget: *revenues:* $2.325 billion (2019 est.)
expenditures: $2.785 billion (2019 est.)

Current account balance: -$2.333 billion (2023 est.)
-$2.5 billion (2022 est.)
-$2.099 billion (2021 est.)
note: balance of payments - net trade and primary/secondary income in current dollars
comparison ranking: 152

Exports: $1.223 billion (2023 est.)
$1.376 billion (2022 est.)
$1.487 billion (2021 est.)
note: balance of payments - exports of goods and services in current dollars
comparison ranking: 179

Exports - partners: UAE 31%, France 23%, China 18%, India 6%, Sweden 5% (2023)
note: top five export partners based on percentage share of exports

Exports - commodities: gold, oil seeds, uranium and thorium ore, radioactive chemicals, refined petroleum (2023)
note: top five export commodities based on value in dollars

Imports: $3.808 billion (2023 est.)
$4.194 billion (2022 est.)
$4.027 billion (2021 est.)
note: balance of payments - imports of goods and services in current dollars
comparison ranking: 159

Imports - partners: China 26%, France 15%, India 12%, Nigeria 7%, UAE 6% (2023)
note: top five import partners based on percentage share of imports

Imports - commodities: rice, aircraft parts, iron structures, refined petroleum, centrifuges (2023)
note: top five import commodities based on value in dollars

Debt - external: $3.793 billion (2023 est.)
note: present value of external debt in current US dollars
comparison ranking: 76

Exchange rates: Communaute Financiere Africaine francs (XOF) per US dollar -

Exchange rates: 606.345 (2024 est.)
606.57 (2023 est.)
623.76 (2022 est.)
554.531 (2021 est.)
575.586 (2020 est.)

ENERGY

Electricity access: *electrification - total population:* 19.5% (2022 est.)
electrification - urban areas: 66.1%
electrification - rural areas: 7.7%

Electricity: *installed generating capacity:* 377,000 kW (2023 est.)
consumption: 1.645 billion kWh (2023 est.)
imports: 1.213 billion kWh (2023 est.)
transmission/distribution losses: 372.245 million kWh (2023 est.)
comparison rankings: installed generating capacity 156; consumption 154; imports 74; transmission/distribution losses 75

Electricity generation sources: *fossil fuels:* 97% of total installed capacity (2023 est.)
solar: 3% of total installed capacity (2023 est.)

Coal: *production:* 427,000 metric tons (2023 est.)
consumption: 426,000 metric tons (2023 est.)
imports: 400 metric tons (2023 est.)
proven reserves: 90 million metric tons (2023 est.)

Petroleum: *total petroleum production:* 13,000 bbl/day (2023 est.)
refined petroleum consumption: 18,000 bbl/day (2023 est.)
crude oil estimated reserves: 150 million barrels (2021 est.)

Natural gas: *production:* 26.805 million cubic meters (2023 est.)
consumption: 26.872 million cubic meters (2023 est.)

Energy consumption per capita: 1.772 million Btu/person (2023 est.)
comparison ranking: 190

COMMUNICATIONS

Telephones - fixed lines: *total subscriptions:* 58,000 (2021 est.)
subscriptions per 100 inhabitants: (2022 est.) less than 1
comparison ranking: total subscriptions 152

Telephones - mobile cellular: *total subscriptions:* 14.2 million (2021 est.)
subscriptions per 100 inhabitants: 56 (2021 est.)
comparison ranking: total subscriptions 75

Broadcast media: state-run TV station; 3 private TV stations provide a mix of local and foreign programming; state-run radio has the only radio station with national coverage; about 30 private local radio stations; as many as 100 community radio stations; transmissions of multiple international broadcasters are available

Internet country code: .ne

Internet users: *percent of population:* 23% (2023 est.)

Broadband - fixed subscriptions: *total:* 14,000 (2022 est.)
subscriptions per 100 inhabitants: (2022 est.) less than 1
comparison ranking: total 180

TRANSPORTATION

Civil aircraft registration country code prefix: 5U

Airports: 26 (2025)
comparison ranking: 127

MILITARY AND SECURITY

Military and security forces: Nigerien Armed Forces (Forces Armees Nigeriennes, FAN): Army, Nigerien Air Force, Niger Gendarmerie (GN)

Ministry of Interior, Public Safety and Decentralization: Niger National Guard (GNN), National Police (2025)
note 1: the Gendarmerie (GN) and the National Guard (GNN) are paramilitary forces; the GN has primary responsibility for rural security while the GNN is responsible for domestic security and the protection of high-level officials and government buildings
note 2: the National Police includes the Directorate of Territorial Surveillance, which is charged with border management

Military expenditures: 2.2% of GDP (2024 est.)
2% of GDP (2023 est.)
1.7% of GDP (2022 est.)
1.8% of GDP (2021 est.)
2% of GDP (2020 est.)

Military and security service personnel strengths: estimated 35-40,000 active Nigerien Armed Forces, including Gendarmerie; estimated 5-10,000 National Guard (2025)
note: in 2020, the Nigerien Government announced it intended to increase the size of the FAN to 50,000 by 2025 and 100,000 by 2030

Military equipment inventories and acquisitions: the FAN has a wide mix of mostly older, typically Soviet-era, or donated/secondhand weapons and equipment, along with small quantities of more modern items such as unmanned aerial vehicles/drones and air defense systems; suppliers have included China, Egypt, France, Italy, Russia, Turkey, and the US (2024)

Military service age and obligation: 18 is the legal minimum age for selective compulsory or voluntary military service for unmarried men and women; 24-month service term (2023)

Military deployments: *note:* in 2024, Mali, Burkina Faso, and Niger announced they were forming a joint force of 5,000 troops to combat extremist groups in the Sahel

Military - note: the military of Niger is responsible for territorial defense, but most of its focus is on internal and border security operations; the Islamic State of Iraq and ash-Sham in the Greater Sahara (ISIS-GS) and the al-Qaida affiliate Jama'at Nusrat al-Islam wal-Muslimin (JNIM) terrorist groups are active in western Niger and in adjacent strongholds in Burkina Faso and Mali, while the Nigeria-based Boko Haram and ISIS-West Africa groups threaten southeast Niger; parts of Niger also face spillover from communal, criminal, and vigilante violence in neighboring Nigeria; since the 2023 coup, some former ethnic separatist rebels have taken up arms in support of deposed President BAZOUM
the military has played a significant role in Niger's domestic politics since its establishment in 1960-61; prior to seizing control of the government in 2023, it attempted coups in 1974, 1996, 1999, 2010, and 2021, and ruled the country for much of the period before 1999 (2025)

TERRORISM

Terrorist group(s): Terrorist group(s): Boko Haram; Islamic State of Iraq and ash-Sham in the Greater

Sahara (ISIS-GS); Islamic State of Iraq and ash-Sham – West Africa (ISIS-WA); Jama'at Nusrat al-Islam wal-Muslimin (JNIM); al-Mulathamun Battalion (al-Mourabitoun)
note: details about the history, aims, leadership, organization, areas of operation, tactics, targets, weapons, size, and sources of support of the group(s) appear(s) in Appendix T

TRANSNATIONAL ISSUES

Refugees and internally displaced persons: *refugees:* 421,795 (2024 est.)
IDPs: 891,565 (2024 est.)
Trafficking in persons: *tier rating:* Tier 2 Watch List — the government did not demonstrate overall increasing efforts to eliminate trafficking compared with the previous reporting period, therefore Niger remained on Tier 2 Watch List for the second consecutive year; for more details, go to: https://www.state.gov/reports/2025-trafficking-in-persons-report/niger/

NIGERIA

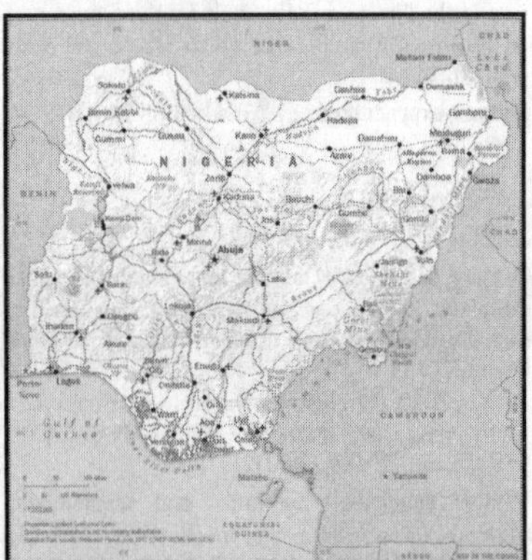

INTRODUCTION

Background: In ancient and pre-colonial times, the area of present-day Nigeria was occupied by a variety of ethnic groups with different languages and traditions. These included large Islamic kingdoms such as Borno, Kano, and the Sokoto Caliphate dominating the north, the Benin and Oyo Empires that controlled much of modern western Nigeria, and more decentralized political entities and city states in the south and southeast. In 1914, the British amalgamated their separately administered northern and southern territories into a Colony and Protectorate of Nigeria.

Nigeria achieved independence from Britain in 1960 and transitioned to a federal republic with three constituent states in 1963 under President Nnamdi AZIKIWE. This structure served to enflame regional and ethnic tension, contributing to a bloody coup led by predominately southeastern military officers in 1966 and a countercoup later that year masterminded by northern officers. In the aftermath of this tension, the governor of Nigeria's Eastern Region, centered on the southeast, declared the region independent as the Republic of Biafra. The ensuring civil war (1967-1970), resulted in more than a million deaths, many from starvation. While the war forged a stronger Nigerian state and national identity, it contributed to long-lasting mistrust of the southeast's predominantly Igbo population. Wartime military leader Yakubu GOWON ruled until a bloodless coup by frustrated junior officers in 1975. This generation of officers, including Olusegun OBASANJO, Ibrahim BABANGIDA, and Muhammadu BUHARI, who would all later serve as president, continue to exert significant influence in Nigeria to the present day.

Military rule predominated until the first durable transition to civilian government and adoption of a new constitution in 1999. The elections of 2007 marked the first civilian-to-civilian transfer of power in the country's history. National and state elections in 2011 and 2015 were generally regarded as credible. The 2015 election was also heralded for the fact that the then-umbrella opposition party, the All Progressives Congress, defeated the long-ruling (since 1999) People's Democratic Party and assumed the presidency, marking the first peaceful transfer of power from one party to another. Presidential and legislative elections in 2019 and 2023 were deemed broadly free and fair despite voting irregularities, intimidation, and violence. The government of Africa's most populous nation continues to face the daunting task of institutionalizing democracy and reforming a petroleum-based economy whose revenues have been squandered through decades of corruption and mismanagement. In addition, Nigeria faces increasing violence from Islamic terrorism, largely in the northeast, large scale criminal banditry, secessionist violence in the southeast, and competition over land and resources nationwide.

GEOGRAPHY

Location: Western Africa, bordering the Gulf of Guinea, between Benin and Cameroon
Geographic coordinates: 10 00 N, 8 00 E
Map references: Africa
Area: *total:* 923,768 sq km
land: 910,768 sq km
water: 13,000 sq km
comparison ranking: total 33
Area - comparative: about six times the size of Georgia; slightly more than twice the size of California
Land boundaries: *total:* 4,477 km
border countries (4): Benin 809 km; Cameroon 1,975 km; Chad 85 km; Niger 1,608 km
Coastline: 853 km
Maritime claims: *territorial sea:* 12 nm
exclusive economic zone: 200 nm
continental shelf: 200-m depth or to the depth of exploitation
Climate: varies; equatorial in south, tropical in center, arid in north
Terrain: southern lowlands merge into central hills and plateaus; mountains in southeast, plains in north
Elevation: *highest point:* Chappal Waddi 2,419 m
lowest point: Atlantic Ocean 0 m
mean elevation: 380 m
Natural resources: natural gas, petroleum, tin, iron ore, coal, limestone, niobium, lead, zinc, arable land
Land use: *agricultural land:* 75.8% (2022 est.)
arable land: 40% (2022 est.)
permanent crops: 8.4% (2022 est.)
permanent pasture: 27.3% (2022 est.)
forest: 23.1% (2022 est.)
other: 1.1% (2022 est.)
Irrigated land: 2,188 sq km (2017)
Major lakes (area sq km): *fresh water lake(s):* Lake Chad (endorheic lake shared with Niger, Chad, and Cameroon) - 10,360-25,900 sq km
note - area varies by season and year to year
Major rivers (by length in km): Niger river mouth (shared with Guinea [s], Mali, Benin, and Niger) - 4,200 km
note: [s] after country name indicates river source; [m] after country name indicates river mouth
Major watersheds (area sq km): Atlantic Ocean drainage: Niger (2,261,741 sq km)
Internal (endorheic basin) drainage: Lake Chad (2,497,738 sq km)
Major aquifers: Lake Chad Basin, Lullemeden-Irhazer Aquifer System
Population distribution: largest population of any African nation; significant population clusters are scattered throughout the country, with the highest density areas being in the south and southwest, as shown in this population distribution map
Natural hazards: periodic droughts; flooding
Geography - note: the Niger River enters the country in the northwest and flows southward through tropical rainforests and swamps to its delta in the Gulf of Guinea

PEOPLE AND SOCIETY

Population: *total:* 236,747,130 (2024 est.)
male: 119,514,449
female: 117,232,681
comparison rankings: total 6; male 6; female 6
Nationality: *noun:* Nigerian(s)
adjective: Nigerian
Ethnic groups: Hausa 30%, Yoruba 15.5%, Igbo (Ibo) 15.2%, Fulani 6%, Tiv 2.4%, Kanuri/Beriberi 2.4%, Ibibio 1.8%, Ijaw/Izon 1.8%, other 24.9% (2018 est.)
note: Nigeria, Africa's most populous country, is composed of more than 250 ethnic groups
Languages: English (official), Hausa, Yoruba, Igbo (Ibo), Fulani, over 500 additional indigenous languages
Religions: Muslim 53.5%, Roman Catholic 10.6%, other Christian 35.3%, other 0.6% (2018 est.)
Age structure: *0-14 years:* 40.4% (male 48,856,606/female 46,770,810)
15-64 years: 56.2% (male 66,897,900/female 66,187,584)

65 years and over: 3.4% (2024 est.) (male 3,759,943/female 4,274,287)

Dependency ratios: *total dependency ratio:* 77.9 (2024 est.)
youth dependency ratio: 71.9 (2024 est.)
elderly dependency ratio: 6 (2024 est.)
potential support ratio: 16.6 (2024 est.)

Median age: *total:* 19.3 years (2024 est.)
male: 19.1 years
female: 19.6 years
comparison ranking: total 211

Population growth rate: 2.52% (2024 est.)
comparison ranking: 19

Birth rate: 33.8 births/1,000 population (2024 est.)
comparison ranking: 17

Death rate: 8.4 deaths/1,000 population (2024 est.)
comparison ranking: 75

Net migration rate: -0.2 migrant(s)/1,000 population (2024 est.)
comparison ranking: 110

Population distribution: largest population of any African nation; significant population clusters are scattered throughout the country, with the highest density areas being in the south and southwest, as shown in this population distribution map

Urbanization: *urban population:* 54.3% of total population (2023)
rate of urbanization: 3.92% annual rate of change (2020-25 est.)

Major urban areas - population: 15.946 million Lagos, 4.348 million Kano, 3.875 million Ibadan, 3.840 million ABUJA (capital), 3.480 million Port Harcourt, 1.905 million Benin City (2023)

Sex ratio: *at birth:* 1.06 male(s)/female
0-14 years: 1.04 male(s)/female
15-64 years: 1.01 male(s)/female
65 years and over: 0.88 male(s)/female
total population: 1.02 male(s)/female (2024 est.)

Mother's mean age at first birth: 20.4 years (2018 est.)
note: data represents median age at first birth among women 25-49

Maternal mortality ratio: 993 deaths/100,000 live births (2023 est.)
comparison ranking: 1

Infant mortality rate: *total:* 53.7 deaths/1,000 live births (2024 est.)
male: 58.9 deaths/1,000 live births
female: 48.2 deaths/1,000 live births
comparison ranking: total 15

Life expectancy at birth: *total population:* 62.2 years (2024 est.)
male: 60.4 years
female: 64.2 years
comparison ranking: total population 216

Total fertility rate: 4.52 children born/woman (2024 est.)
comparison ranking: 14

Gross reproduction rate: 2.19 (2024 est.)

Drinking water source: *improved: urban:* 93.7% of population (2022 est.)
rural: 63.5% of population (2022 est.)
total: 79.6% of population (2022 est.)
unimproved: urban: 6.3% of population (2022 est.)
rural: 36.5% of population (2022 est.)
total: 20.4% of population (2022 est.)

Health expenditure: 4.1% of GDP (2021)
4.3% of national budget (2022 est.)

Physician density: 0.38 physicians/1,000 population (2023)

Sanitation facility access: *improved: urban:* 81.9% of population (2022 est.)
rural: 41.1% of population (2022 est.)
total: 62.9% of population (2022 est.)
unimproved: urban: 18.1% of population (2022 est.)
rural: 58.9% of population (2022 est.)
total: 37.1% of population (2022 est.)

Obesity - adult prevalence rate: 8.9% (2016)
comparison ranking: 145

Alcohol consumption per capita: *total:* 4.49 liters of pure alcohol (2019 est.)
beer: 0.73 liters of pure alcohol (2019 est.)
wine: 0.09 liters of pure alcohol (2019 est.)
spirits: 0.4 liters of pure alcohol (2019 est.)
other alcohols: 3.27 liters of pure alcohol (2019 est.)
comparison ranking: total 88

Tobacco use: *total:* 2.6% (2025 est.)
male: 4.8% (2025 est.)
female: 0.3% (2025 est.)
comparison ranking: total 168

Children under the age of 5 years underweight: 18.4% (2019/20)
comparison ranking: 23

Currently married women (ages 15-49): 66.2% (2023 est.)

Child marriage: *women married by age 15:* 12.3% (2021)
women married by age 18: 30.3% (2021)
men married by age 18: 1.6% (2021)
note: due to prolonged insecurity concerns, some parts of states, including Borno state, were not sampled

Education expenditure: 0.3% of GDP (2022 est.)
4.3% national budget (2022 est.)
comparison ranking: Education expenditure (% GDP) 201

Literacy: *total population:* 63.2% (2021 est.)
male: 73.7% (2021 est.)
female: 53.3% (2021 est.)

ENVIRONMENT

Environmental issues: urban air and water pollution; rapid deforestation; soil degradation; loss of arable land; water, air, and soil pollution from oil spills

International environmental agreements: *party to:* Biodiversity, Climate Change, Climate Change-Kyoto Protocol, Climate Change-Paris Agreement, Comprehensive Nuclear Test Ban, Desertification, Endangered Species, Hazardous Wastes, Law of the Sea, Marine Dumping-London Convention, Marine Dumping-London Protocol, Marine Life Conservation, Nuclear Test Ban, Ozone Layer Protection, Ship Pollution, Wetlands
signed, but not ratified: Tropical Timber 2006

Climate: varies; equatorial in south, tropical in center, arid in north

Urbanization: *urban population:* 54.3% of total population (2023)
rate of urbanization: 3.92% annual rate of change (2020-25 est.)

Carbon dioxide emissions: 114.397 million metric tonnes of CO2 (2023 est.)
from coal and metallurgical coke: 2.962 million metric tonnes of CO2 (2023 est.)
from petroleum and other liquids: 72.425 million metric tonnes of CO2 (2023 est.)
from consumed natural gas: 39.01 million metric tonnes of CO2 (2023 est.)
comparison ranking: total emissions 38

Particulate matter emissions: 56 micrograms per cubic meter (2019 est.)

Methane emissions: *energy:* 2,794.3 kt (2022-2024 est.)
agriculture: 1,991.9 kt (2019-2021 est.)
waste: 729.4 kt (2019-2021 est.)
other: 362.7 kt (2019-2021 est.)

Waste and recycling: *municipal solid waste generated annually:* 27.615 million tons (2024 est.)
percent of municipal solid waste recycled: 4.7% (2022 est.)

Total water withdrawal: *municipal:* 5 billion cubic meters (2022 est.)
industrial: 1.965 billion cubic meters (2022 est.)
agricultural: 5.51 billion cubic meters (2022 est.)

Total renewable water resources: 286.2 billion cubic meters (2022 est.)

GOVERNMENT

Country name: *conventional long form:* Federal Republic of Nigeria
conventional short form: Nigeria
etymology: named for the Niger River that flows through the west of the country to the Atlantic Ocean; the name of the river probably comes from the local Tuareg name, *egereou nigereouen* (big rivers)

Government type: federal presidential republic

Capital: *name:* Abuja
geographic coordinates: 9 05 N, 7 32 E
time difference: UTC+1 (6 hours ahead of Washington, DC, during Standard Time)
etymology: the newly built city of Abuja replaced Lagos as the capital city in 1991; Abuja takes its name from a nearby town, now renamed Suleja, that was named after Abu JA ("Abu the Red") in 1828

Administrative divisions: 36 states and 1 territory*; Abia, Adamawa, Akwa Ibom, Anambra, Bauchi, Bayelsa, Benue, Borno, Cross River, Delta, Ebonyi, Edo, Ekiti, Enugu, Federal Capital Territory*, Gombe, Imo, Jigawa, Kaduna, Kano, Katsina, Kebbi, Kogi, Kwara, Lagos, Nasarawa, Niger, Ogun, Ondo, Osun, Oyo, Plateau, Rivers, Sokoto, Taraba, Yobe, Zamfara

Legal system: mixed system of English common law, Islamic law (in 12 northern states), and traditional law

Constitution: *history:* several previous; latest adopted 5 May 1999, effective 29 May 1999
amendment process: proposed by the National Assembly; passage requires at least two-thirds majority vote of both houses and approval by the Houses of Assembly of at least two thirds of the states; amendments to constitutional articles on the creation of a new state, fundamental constitutional rights, or constitution-amending procedures requires at least four-fifths majority vote by both houses of the National Assembly and approval by the Houses of Assembly in at least two thirds of the states; passage of amendments limited to the creation of a new state require at least two-thirds majority vote by the proposing National Assembly house and approval by the Houses of Assembly in two thirds of the states

International law organization participation: accepts compulsory ICJ jurisdiction with reservations; accepts ICCt jurisdiction

Citizenship: *citizenship by birth:* no

citizenship by descent only: at least one parent must be a citizen of Nigeria
dual citizenship recognized: yes
residency requirement for naturalization: 15 years

Suffrage: 18 years of age; universal

Executive branch: *chief of state:* President Bola Ahmed Adekunle TINUBU (since 29 May 2023)
head of government: President Bola Ahmed Adekunle TINUBU (since 29 May 2023)
cabinet: Federal Executive Council appointed by the president but constitutionally required to include at least one member from each of the 36 states
election/appointment process: president directly elected by qualified-majority popular vote with at least 25% of the votes cast in 24 of Nigeria's 36 states; president elected for a 4-year term (eligible for a second term)
most recent election date: 25 February 2023
election results: *2023:* Bola Ahmed Adekunle TINUBU elected president; percent of vote - Bola Ahmed Adekunle TINUBU (APC) 36.6%, Atiku ABUBAKAR (PDP) 29.1%, Peter OBI (LP) 25.4%, Rabiu KWANKWASO (NNPP) 6.4%, other 2.5%
2019: Muhammadu BUHARI elected president; percent of vote - Muhammadu BUHARI (APC) 53%, Atiku ABUBAKAR (PDP) 39%, other 8%
expected date of next election: 27 February 2027
note: the president is chief of state, head of government, and commander-in-chief of the armed forces

Legislative branch: *legislature name:* National Assembly
legislative structure: bicameral

Legislative branch - lower chamber: *chamber name:* House of Representatives
number of seats: 360 (all directly elected)
electoral system: plurality/majority
scope of elections: full renewal
term in office: 4 years
most recent election date: 2/25/2023
parties elected and seats per party: All Progressives Congress (APC) (180); People's Democratic Party (PDP) (116); Labour Party (LP) (35); New Nigeria Peoples Party (NNPP) (19); Other (10)
percentage of women in chamber: 3.9%
expected date of next election: February 2027

Legislative branch - upper chamber: *chamber name:* Senate
number of seats: 109 (all directly elected)
electoral system: plurality/majority
scope of elections: full renewal
term in office: 4 years
most recent election date: 2/25/2023
parties elected and seats per party: All Progressives Congress (APC) (59); People's Democratic Party (PDP) (36); Labour Party (LP) (8); Other (6)
percentage of women in chamber: 2.8%
expected date of next election: February 2027

Judicial branch: *highest court(s):* Supreme Court (consists of the chief justice and 15 justices)
judge selection and term of office: judges appointed by the president upon the recommendation of the National Judicial Council, a 23-member independent body of federal and state judicial officials; judge appointments confirmed by the Senate; judges serve until age 70
subordinate courts: Court of Appeal; Federal High Court; High Court of the Federal Capital Territory; Sharia Court of Appeal of the Federal Capital Territory; Customary Court of Appeal of the Federal Capital Territory; state court system similar in structure to federal system

Political parties: Accord Party or ACC
Africa Democratic Congress or ADC
All Progressives Congress or APC
All Progressives Grand Alliance or APGA
Labor Party or LP
New Nigeria People's Party or NNPP
Peoples Democratic Party or PDP
Young Progressive Party or YPP

Diplomatic representation in the US: *chief of mission:* Ambassador (vacant); Chargé d'Affaires Samson Sunday ITEGBOJE (since 22 October 2024)
chancery: 3519 International Court NW, Washington, DC 20008
telephone: [1] (202) 800-7201 (ext. 100)
FAX: [1] (202) 362-6541
email address and website: info@nigeriaembassyusa.org
https://www.nigeriaembassyusa.org/
consulate(s) general: Atlanta, New York

Diplomatic representation from the US: *chief of mission:* Ambassador Richard MILLS, Jr. (since 25 July 2024)
embassy: Plot 1075 Diplomatic Drive, Central District Area, Abuja
mailing address: 8320 Abuja Place, Washington DC 20521-8320
telephone: [234] (9) 461-4000
FAX: [234] (9) 461-4036
email address and website: AbujaACS@state.gov
https://ng.usembassy.gov/
consulate(s) general: Lagos

International organization participation: ACP, AfDB, ATMIS, AU, C, CD, D-8, ECOWAS, EITI (compliant country), FAO, G-15, G-24, G-77, IAEA, IBRD, ICAO, ICC (national committees), ICCt, ICRM, IDA, IDB, IFAD, IFC, IFRCS, IHO, ILO, IMF, IMO, IMSO, Interpol, IOC, IOM, IPU, ISO, ITSO, ITU, ITUC (NGOs), LCBC, MIGA, MINURSO, MNJTF, MONUSCO, NAM, OAS (observer), OIC, OPCW, OPEC, PCA, UN, UNAMID, UNCTAD, UNESCO, UNHCR, UNIDO, UNIFIL, UNISFA, UNITAR, UNMIL, UNMISS, UNOCI, UNOOSA, UNWTO, UPU, WCO, WFTU (NGOs), WHO, WIPO, WMO, WTO

Independence: 1 October 1960 (from the UK)

National holiday: Independence Day (National Day), 1 October (1960)

Flag: *description:* three equal vertical bands of green (left side), white, and green
meaning: green stands for the country's forests and natural resources, and white for peace and unity

National symbol(s): eagle

National color(s): green, white

National anthem(s): *title:* "Nigeria, We Hail Thee"
lyrics/music: Lillie Jean WILLIAMS/Frances BERDA
history: adopted 2024
note: Parliament voted in 2024 to revert to the former national anthem used from 1960 to 1978

National heritage: *total World Heritage Sites:* 2 (both cultural)
selected World Heritage Site locales: Sukur Cultural Landscape; Osun-Osogbo Sacred Grove

ECONOMY

Economic overview: largest African market economy; enormous but mostly lower middle income labor force; major oil exporter; key telecommunications and finance industries; susceptible to energy prices; regional leader in critical infrastructure; primarily agrarian employment

Real GDP (purchasing power parity): $1.318 trillion (2024 est.)
$1.275 trillion (2023 est.)
$1.239 trillion (2022 est.)
note: data in 2021 dollars
comparison ranking: 27

Real GDP growth rate: 3.4% (2024 est.)
2.9% (2023 est.)
3.3% (2022 est.)
note: annual GDP % growth based on constant local currency
comparison ranking: 102

Real GDP per capita: $5,700 (2024 est.)
$5,600 (2023 est.)
$5,600 (2022 est.)
note: data in 2021 dollars
comparison ranking: 169

GDP (official exchange rate): $187.76 billion (2024 est.)
note: data in current dollars at official exchange rate

Inflation rate (consumer prices): 33.2% (2024 est.)
24.7% (2023 est.)
18.8% (2022 est.)
note: annual % change based on consumer prices
comparison ranking: 201

GDP - composition, by sector of origin: *agriculture:* 20.4% (2024 est.)
industry: 29.6% (2024 est.)
services: 47% (2024 est.)
note: figures may not total 100% due to non-allocated consumption not captured in sector-reported data
comparison rankings: agriculture 34; industry 58; services 163

Agricultural products: cassava, yams, maize, oil palm fruit, rice, taro, bananas, vegetables, sorghum, groundnuts (2023)
note: top ten agricultural products based on tonnage

Industries: crude oil, coal, tin, columbite; rubber products, wood; hides and skins, textiles, cement and other construction materials, food products, footwear, chemicals, fertilizer, printing, ceramics, steel

Industrial production growth rate: 2.4% (2024 est.)
note: annual % change in industrial value added based on constant local currency
comparison ranking: 93

Labor force: 113.35 million (2024 est.)
note: number of people ages 15 or older who are employed or seeking work
comparison ranking: 5

Unemployment rate: 3% (2024 est.)
3.1% (2023 est.)
3.9% (2022 est.)
note: % of labor force seeking employment
comparison ranking: 40

Youth unemployment rate (ages 15-24): *total:* 5.1% (2024 est.)
male: 3.7% (2024 est.)
female: 6.5% (2024 est.)
note: % of labor force ages 15-24 seeking employment
comparison ranking: total 164

Population below poverty line: 40.1% (2018 est.)
note: % of population with income below national poverty line
Gini Index coefficient - distribution of family income 35.1 (2018 est.)
note: index (0-100) of income distribution; higher values represent greater inequality
comparison ranking: 76

Average household expenditures: *on food:* 59.3% of household expenditures (2023 est.)

on alcohol and tobacco: 0.9% of household expenditures (2023 est.)

Household income or consumption by percentage share: *lowest 10%:* 2.9% (2018 est.)
highest 10%: 26.7% (2018 est.)
note: % share of income accruing to lowest and highest 10% of population

Remittances: 11.3% of GDP (2024 est.)
5.4% of GDP (2023 est.)
4.2% of GDP (2022 est.)
note: personal transfers and compensation between resident and non-resident individuals/households/entities

Budget: *revenues:* $37.298 billion (2019 est.)
expenditures: $59.868 billion (2019 est.)

Current account balance: $17.215 billion (2024 est.)
$6.423 billion (2023 est.)
$1.019 billion (2022 est.)
note: balance of payments - net trade and primary/secondary income in current dollars
comparison ranking: 21

Exports: $57.536 billion (2024 est.)
$60.261 billion (2023 est.)
$69.091 billion (2022 est.)
note: balance of payments - exports of goods and services in current dollars
comparison ranking: 65

Exports - partners: USA 10%, Spain 9%, France 8%, Netherlands 7%, India 6% (2023)
note: top five export partners based on percentage share of exports

Exports - commodities: crude petroleum, natural gas, gold, fertilizers, cocoa beans (2023)
note: top five export commodities based on value in dollars

Imports: $57.73 billion (2024 est.)
$65.423 billion (2023 est.)
$77.049 billion (2022 est.)
note: balance of payments - imports of goods and services in current dollars
comparison ranking: 63

Imports - partners: China 26%, Singapore 14%, Belgium 8%, India 6%, USA 4% (2023)
note: top five import partners based on percentage share of imports

Imports - commodities: refined petroleum, tanks and armored vehicles, wheat, plastics, cars (2023)
note: top five import commodities based on value in dollars

Reserves of foreign exchange and gold: $38.612 billion (2024 est.)
$32.035 billion (2023 est.)
$35.564 billion (2022 est.)
note: holdings of gold (year-end prices)/foreign exchange/special drawing rights in current dollars
comparison ranking: 52

Debt - external: $45.009 billion (2023 est.)
note: present value of external debt in current US dollars
comparison ranking: 17

Exchange rates: nairas (NGN) per US dollar -

Exchange rates: 1,478.965 (2024 est.)
645.194 (2023 est.)
425.979 (2022 est.)
401.152 (2021 est.)
358.811 (2020 est.)

ENERGY

Electricity access: *electrification - total population:* 60.5% (2022 est.)
electrification - urban areas: 89%
electrification - rural areas: 27%

Electricity: *installed generating capacity:* 4.094 million kW (2023 est.)
consumption: 34.135 billion kWh (2023 est.)
exports: 2.4 billion kWh (2023 est.)
transmission/distribution losses: 5.974 billion kWh (2023 est.)
comparison rankings: installed generating capacity 98; consumption 66; exports 53; transmission/distribution losses 168

Electricity generation sources: *fossil fuels:* 77.1% of total installed capacity (2023 est.)
solar: 0.2% of total installed capacity (2023 est.)
hydroelectricity: 22.5% of total installed capacity (2023 est.)
biomass and waste: 0.1% of total installed capacity (2023 est.)

Coal: *production:* 1.322 million metric tons (2023 est.)
consumption: 1.326 million metric tons (2023 est.)
exports: 17 metric tons (2023 est.)
imports: 600 metric tons (2023 est.)
proven reserves: 2.144 billion metric tons (2023 est.)

Petroleum: *total petroleum production:* 1.514 million bbl/day (2023 est.)
refined petroleum consumption: 527,000 bbl/day (2023 est.)
crude oil estimated reserves: 36.89 billion barrels (2021 est.)

Natural gas: *production:* 38.248 billion cubic meters (2023 est.)
consumption: 19.885 billion cubic meters (2023 est.)
exports: 16.324 billion cubic meters (2023 est.)
proven reserves: 5.761 trillion cubic meters (2021 est.)

Energy consumption per capita: 7.993 million Btu/person (2023 est.)
comparison ranking: 160

COMMUNICATIONS

Telephones - fixed lines: *total subscriptions:* 112,000 (2023 est.)
subscriptions per 100 inhabitants: (2023 est.) less than 1
comparison ranking: total subscriptions 134

Telephones - mobile cellular: *total subscriptions:* 224 million (2023 est.)
subscriptions per 100 inhabitants: 102 (2022 est.)
comparison ranking: total subscriptions 6

Broadcast media: nearly 70 federal government-controlled national and regional TV stations; all 36 states operate TV stations; several private TV stations; cable and satellite TV subscription services are available; network of federal government-controlled national, regional, and state radio stations; roughly 40 state government-owned radio stations; about 20 private radio stations; transmissions of international broadcasters are available; transition to digital completed in three states in 2018 (2019)

Internet country code: .ng

Internet users: *percent of population:* 39% (2023 est.)

Broadband - fixed subscriptions: *total:* 117,000 (2023 est.)
subscriptions per 100 inhabitants: (2023 est.) less than 1
comparison ranking: total 129

TRANSPORTATION

Civil aircraft registration country code prefix: 5N

Airports: 50 (2025)
comparison ranking: 88

Heliports: 15 (2025)
comparison ranking: 59

Railways: *total:* 3,798 km (2014)
standard gauge: 293 km (2014) 1.435-m gauge
narrow gauge: 3,505 km (2014) 1.067-m gauge
note: as of the end of 2018, there were only six operational locomotives in Nigeria primarily used for passenger service; the majority of the rail lines are in a severe state of disrepair and need to be replaced

Merchant marine: *total:* 928 (2023)
by type: general cargo 23, oil tanker 128, other 777
comparison ranking: total 25

Ports: *total ports:* 28 (2024)
large: 2
medium: 1
small: 1
very small: 24
ports with oil terminals: 23
key ports: Antan Oil Terminal, Bonny, Lagos, Pennington Oil Terminal

MILITARY AND SECURITY

Military and security forces: Armed Forces of Nigeria (AFN): Nigerian Army, Nigerian Navy (includes Coast Guard), Nigerian Air Force

Ministry of Interior: Nigeria Security and Civil Defense Corps (NSCDC); Ministry of Police Affairs: Nigeria Police Force (NPF) (2025)
note 1: the NSCDC is a paramilitary agency commissioned to assist the military in the management of threats to internal security, including attacks and natural disasters
note 2: some states have created local security forces in response to increased violence, insecurity, and criminality that have exceeded the response capacity of federal government security forces, but official security forces remained the constitutional prerogative of the federal government; in 2023, the federal government began deploying thousands of "agro rangers" across 19 states and the Federal Capital Territory to help safeguard farmland and mediate conflicts, especially in areas hit by farmer-herder clashes

Military expenditures: 0.7% of GDP (2024)
0.7% of GDP (2023 est.)
0.6% of GDP (2022 est.)
0.7% of GDP (2021 est.)
0.6% of GDP (2020 est.)

Military and security service personnel strengths: information varies; estimated 140,000 active Armed Forces (2025)

Military equipment inventories and acquisitions: the military's inventory consists of a wide variety of imported weapons systems of Chinese, European, Middle Eastern, Russian (including Soviet-era), and US origin; the military is undergoing a modernization program, and in recent years has received equipment from a range of suppliers, including Brazil, China, France, Italy, Russia, South Korea, Turkey, and the US; Nigeria is also developing a defense-industry capacity, including small arms, armored personnel vehicles, and small-scale naval production (2025)

Military service age and obligation: 18-26 years of age for voluntary military service for men and women; no conscription (2023)

Military deployments: 190 Sudan/South Sudan (UNISFA) (2024)

note: Nigeria has committed an Army combat brigade (approximately 3,000 troops) to the Multinational Joint Task Force (MNJTF), a regional counter-terrorism force comprised of troops from Benin, Cameroon, Chad, and Niger; MNJTF conducts operations against Boko Haram and other terrorist groups operating in the general area of the Lake Chad Basin and along Nigeria's northeast border; national MNJTF troop contingents are deployed within their own country territories, although cross-border operations are conducted periodically

Military - note: the Nigerian military is responsible for defending against external aggression, maintaining the country's territorial integrity, securing national borders, participating in international peacekeeping and other security missions, suppressing insurrection, and aiding civil authorities in restoring order, as well as other duties such as providing humanitarian assistance; its primary concerns are internal and maritime security; in the northeast part of the country, the military is conducting operations against the Boko Haram (BH) and Islamic State of Iraq and ash-Sham in West Africa (ISIS-WA) terrorist groups, where it has deployed as many as 70,000 troops at times and terrorist-related violence has killed an estimated 35-40,000 people, mostly civilians, since 2009; in the northwest, the military faces threats from criminal gangs–locally referred to as bandits–and violence associated with long-standing farmer-herder conflicts, as well as BH and ISIS-WA terrorists; the military also continues to protect the oil industry in the Niger Delta region against militants and criminal activity and since 2021, has deployed troops alongside other security forces to quell renewed agitation in the state of Biafra; maritime security concerns include piracy and the protection of natural resources in the Gulf of Guinea

the Nigerian military traces its origins to the Nigeria Regiment of the West African Frontier Force (WAFF), a multi-regiment force formed by the British colonial office in 1900 to garrison Great Britain's West African colonies; the WAFF (the honorary title "Royal" was added later) served in both World Wars; in 1956, the Nigeria Regiment of the Royal WAFF was renamed the Nigerian Military Forces (NMF) and in 1958, the colonial government of Nigeria took over control of the NMF from the British War Office; the Nigerian Armed Forces were established following independence in 1960 (2025)

SPACE

Space agency/agencies: National Space Research and Development Agency (NARSDA; established 1999); Defense Space Administration (DSA; established 2014) (2025)

note: NARSDA originated from the National Centre for Remote Sensing, the National Committee on Space Applications (both established in 1987), and the Directorate of Science (established 1993)

Space program overview: has a national space program with a focus on acquiring satellites for agricultural, environmental, meteorology, mining and disaster monitoring, socio-economic development, and security purposes; designs, builds (mostly with foreign assistance), and operates satellites; processes overhead imagery data for analysis and sharing; developing additional capabilities in satellite and satellite payload production, including remote sensing (RS) technologies; has a sounding rocket program for researching rockets and rocket propulsion systems with goal of launching domestically produced satellites into space from a Nigerian spaceport by 2030; has relations and/or cooperation agreements with a variety of foreign space agencies and industries, including those of Algeria, Bangladesh, Belarus, China, Ghana, India, Japan, Kenya, Mongolia, South Africa, Thailand, Turkey, the UK, the US, and Vietnam; has a government-owned satellite company and a small commercial aerospace sector (2025)

note: further details about the key activities, programs, and milestones of the country's space program, as well as government spending estimates on the space sector, appear in the Space Programs reference guide

TERRORISM

Terrorist group(s): Terrorist group(s): Boko Haram; Islamic State of Iraq and ash-Sham – West Africa; Jama'atu Ansarul Muslimina Fi Biladis-Sudan (Ansaru)

note: details about the history, aims, leadership, organization, areas of operation, tactics, targets, weapons, size, and sources of support of the group(s) appear(s) in Appendix T

TRANSNATIONAL ISSUES

Refugees and internally displaced persons: *refugees:* 127,131 (2024 est.)

IDPs: 3,709,022 (2024 est.)

Illicit drugs: USG identification: major precursor-chemical producer (2025)

NIUE

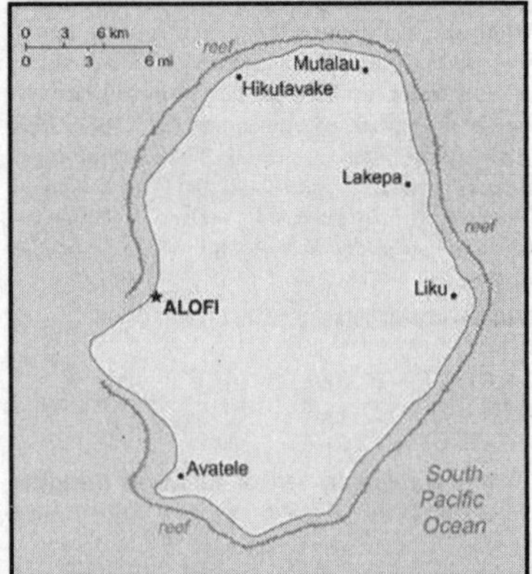

INTRODUCTION

Background: Voyagers from Samoa first settled on Niue around A.D. 900, and a second main group of settlers came from Tonga around 1500. With only one reliable source of fresh water, conflict was high on the island. Samoan and Tongan customs heavily influenced Niuean culture, including the formation of an islandwide elected kingship system in the early 1700s. In 1774, British explorer James COOK landed on the island and named it Savage Island because of the Niueans' hostility. Missionaries arrived in 1830 but were also largely unsuccessful at staying on the island until 1846, when a Niuean trained as a Samoan missionary returned to the island and provided a space from which the missionaries could work. In addition to converting the population, the missionaries worked to stop the violent conflicts and helped establish the first parliament in 1849.

Great Britain established a protectorate over Niue in 1900. The following year, Niue was annexed to New Zealand and included as part of the Cook Islands. Niue's remoteness and cultural and linguistic differences with the Cook Islands led New Zealand to separate Niue into its own administration in 1904. The island became internally self-governing in 1974; it is an independent member of international organizations but is in free association with New Zealand, which is responsible for defense and foreign affairs. In September 2023, the US recognized Niue as a sovereign and independent state.

GEOGRAPHY

Location: Oceania, island in the South Pacific Ocean, east of Tonga

Geographic coordinates: 19 02 S, 169 52 W

Map references: Oceania

Area: *total:* 260 sq km
land: 260 sq km
water: 0 sq km
comparison ranking: total 212

Area - comparative: 1.5 times the size of Washington, D.C.

Land boundaries: *total:* 0 km

Coastline: 64 km

Maritime claims: *territorial sea:* 12 nm
exclusive economic zone: 200 nm

Climate: tropical; modified by southeast trade winds

Terrain: steep limestone cliffs along coast, central plateau

Elevation: *highest point:* unnamed elevation 1.4 km east of Hikutavake 80 m
lowest point: Pacific Ocean 0 m

Natural resources: arable land, fish

Land use: *agricultural land:* 18.5% (2022 est.)
arable land: 3.8% (2022 est.)
permanent crops: 10.8% (2022 est.)
permanent pasture: 3.8% (2022 est.)
forest: 72.7% (2022 est.)
other: 8.9% (2022 est.)

Irrigated land: 0 sq km (2022)

Population distribution: population distributed around the peripheral coastal areas of the island

Natural hazards: tropical cyclones

Geography - note: one of world's largest coral islands; the only major break in the surrounding coral reef occurs in the central western part of the coast

PEOPLE AND SOCIETY

Population: *total:* 1,815 (2024 est.)
male: 877 (2024 est.)
female: 938 (2024 est.)
comparison rankings: total 232; male 232; female 231

Nationality: *noun:* Niuean(s)
adjective: Niuean

Ethnic groups: Niuean 65.4%, part-Niuean 14%, non-Niuean 20.6% (2017 est.)
note: data represent the resident population

Languages: Niuean 46% (official, a Polynesian language closely related to Tongan and Samoan), Niuean and English 32%, English (official) 11%, Niuean and others 5%, other 6% (2011 est.)

Religions: Ekalesia Niue (Congregational Christian Church of Niue - a Protestant church founded by missionaries from the London Missionary Society) 61.7%, Church of Jesus Christ 8.7%, Roman Catholic 8.4%, Jehovah's Witness 2.7%, Seventh Day Adventist 1.4%, other 8.2%, none 8.9% (2017 est.)

Dependency ratios: *total dependency ratio:* 64.6 (2024)
youth dependency ratio: 38.2 (2024)
elderly dependency ratio: 26.4 (2024)
potential support ratio: 3.8 (2024)

Population growth rate: -0.03% (2021 est.)
comparison ranking: 198

Population distribution: population distributed around the peripheral coastal areas of the island

Urbanization: *urban population:* 48.2% of total population (2023)
rate of urbanization: 1.43% annual rate of change (2020-25 est.)

Major urban areas - population: 1,000 ALOFI (capital) (2018)

Life expectancy at birth: *male:* 71.8 years (2016)
female: 75.7 years (2016 est.)

Drinking water source: *improved:* total: 97% of population (2022 est.)
unimproved: total: 3% of population (2022 est.)

Health expenditure: 7.8% of GDP (2020)
6.9% of national budget (2022 est.)

Sanitation facility access: *improved:* total: 97.4% of population (2022 est.)
unimproved: total: 2.6% of population (2022 est.)

Obesity - adult prevalence rate: 50% (2016)
comparison ranking: 6

Alcohol consumption per capita: *total:* 8.5 liters of pure alcohol (2019 est.)
beer: 4.28 liters of pure alcohol (2019 est.)
wine: 1.89 liters of pure alcohol (2019 est.)
spirits: 2.33 liters of pure alcohol (2019 est.)
other alcohols: 0 liters of pure alcohol (2019 est.)
comparison ranking: total 38

Education expenditure: 5.6% national budget (2025 est.)

ENVIRONMENT

Environmental issues: increasing attention to conservationist practices to counter loss of soil fertility from traditional slash-and-burn agriculture

International environmental agreements: *party to:* Biodiversity, Climate Change, Climate Change-Kyoto Protocol, Climate Change-Paris Agreement, Comprehensive Nuclear Test Ban, Desertification, Law of the Sea, Ozone Layer Protection, Ship Pollution
signed, but not ratified: none of the selected agreements

Climate: tropical; modified by southeast trade winds

Urbanization: *urban population:* 48.2% of total population (2023)
rate of urbanization: 1.43% annual rate of change (2020-25 est.)

Carbon dioxide emissions: 9,000 metric tonnes of CO2 (2023 est.)
from petroleum and other liquids: 9,000 metric tonnes of CO2 (2023 est.)
comparison ranking: total emissions 216

Particulate matter emissions: 6.7 micrograms per cubic meter (2019 est.)

GOVERNMENT

Country name: *conventional long form:* none
conventional short form: Niue
former: Savage Island
etymology: the origin of the name is obscure; in Niuean, the word translates as "behold the coconut;" the former name, Savage Island, was the result of an acrimonious meeting in 1774 between English explorer Captain James COOK and local people
note: pronunciation falls between nyu-way and new-way, but not like new-wee

Government type: parliamentary democracy

Dependency status: self-governing in free association with New Zealand since 1974; Niue is fully responsible for internal affairs; under the Niue Constitution Act of 1974, New Zealand provides necessary economic and administrative assistance to Niue, as well as assistance with foreign affairs, defense, and security if requested

Capital: *name:* Alofi
geographic coordinates: 19 01 S, 169 55 W
time difference: UTC-11 (6 hours behind Washington, DC, during Standard Time)
etymology: a traditional name for an area of the island; became the name for the newly declared capital in the 20th century

Administrative divisions: none; no first-order administrative divisions as defined by the US government, but 14 villages are considered second-order

Legal system: English common law

Constitution: *history:* several previous (New Zealand colonial statutes); latest 19 October 1974 (Niue Constitution Act 1974)
amendment process: proposed by the Assembly; passage requires at least two-thirds majority vote of the Assembly membership in each of three readings and approval by at least two-thirds majority votes in a referendum; passage of amendments to a number of sections, including Niue's self-governing status, British nationality and New Zealand citizenship, external affairs and defense, economic and administrative assistance by New Zealand, and amendment procedures, requires at least two-thirds majority vote by the Assembly and at least two thirds of votes in a referendum

Suffrage: 18 years of age; universal

Executive branch: *chief of state:* King CHARLES III (since 8 September 2022); represented by Governor-General of New Zealand Cindy KIRO (since 21 October 2021); the UK and New Zealand are represented by New Zealand High Commissioner Mark GIBBS (since 5 March 2024)
head of government: Prime Minister Dalton TAGELAGI; also referred to as premier (since 10 June 2020)
cabinet: Cabinet chosen by the prime minister
election/appointment process: the monarchy is hereditary; prime minister indirectly elected by the Legislative Assembly for a 3-year term
most recent election date: 8 May 2023
election results: Dalton TAGELAGI reelected prime minister; Legislative Assembly vote - Dalton TAGELAGI (independent) 16, O'Love JACOBSEN (independent) 4
expected date of next election: 2026

Legislative branch: *legislature name:* Niue Assembly (Fono Ekepule)
legislative structure: unicameral
number of seats: 20
electoral system: plurality/majority
scope of elections: full renewal
term in office: 3 years
most recent election date: 29 April 2023
parties elected and seats per party: independents (20)
percentage of women in chamber: 15%
expected date of next election: April 2026

Judicial branch: *highest court(s):* Court of Appeal (consists of the chief justice and up to 3 judges)
judge selection and term of office: Niue chief justice appointed by the governor general on the advice of the Cabinet and tendered by the premier; other judges appointed by the governor general on the advice of the Cabinet and tendered by the chief justice and the minister of justice; judges serve until age 68
subordinate courts: High Court
note: the Judicial Committee of the Privy Council (in London) is the final appeal court beyond the Niue Court of Appeal

Political parties: none

Diplomatic representation in the US: none (self-governing territory in free association with New Zealand)

Diplomatic representation from the US: *embassy:* none (self-governing territory in free association with New Zealand)
note: on 25 September 2023, the US officially established diplomatic relations with Niue

International organization participation: ACP, AOSIS, FAO, IFAD, OPCW, PIF, Sparteca, SPC, UNESCO, UPU, WHO, WIPO, WMO

Independence: 19 October 1974 (Niue became a self-governing state in free association with New Zealand)

National holiday: Waitangi Day (Treaty of Waitangi established British sovereignty over New Zealand), 6 February (1840)

Flag: *description:* yellow with the UK flag in the upper-left quadrant; the UK flag has five yellow five-pointed stars, with a large star on a blue disk in the center and smaller stars on each arm of the red cross *meaning:* the large star represents Niue, and the smaller stars symbolize links with New Zealand; yellow stands for sunshine, as well as the warmth and friendship between Niue and New Zealand

National symbol(s): yellow five-pointed star

National color(s): yellow

National anthem(s): *title:* "Ko e Iki he Lagi" (The Lord in Heaven)
lyrics/music: unknown/unknown, prepared by Sioeli FUSIKATA
history: adopted 1974
title: "God Save the King"
lyrics/music: unknown
history: in use since 1745

ECONOMY

Economic overview: upper-middle-income self-governing New Zealand territorial economy; environmentally fragile; massive emigration; post-pandemic tourism rebound; postage stamps, small-scale agricultural processing, and subsistence farming; most recent Asian Development Bank member

Real GDP (purchasing power parity): $18.7 million (2021 est.)
$19.9 million (2020 est.)
$20.9 million (2019 est.)
comparison ranking: 220

Real GDP per capita: $11,100 (2021 est.)
$11,800 (2020 est.)
$12,400 (2019 est.)
note: data are in 2009 dollars
comparison ranking: 140

Agricultural products: coconuts, taro, fruits, sweet potatoes, tropical fruits, yams, vegetables, lemons/limes, bananas, pork (2023)
note: top ten agricultural products based on tonnage

Industries: handicrafts, food processing

Exports - partners: USA 54%, Germany 8%, Canada 5%, UK 5%, Guatemala 4% (2023)
note: top five export partners based on percentage share of exports

Exports - commodities: abrasive powder, coin (2023)
note: top export commodities based on value in dollars over $500,000

Imports - partners: NZ 87%, Fiji 6%, UAE 2%, Slovakia 1%, Australia 1% (2023)
note: top five import partners based on percentage share of imports

Imports - commodities: refined petroleum, plastic products, machine parts, construction vehicles, cars (2023)
note: top five import commodities based on value in dollars

Exchange rates: New Zealand dollars (NZD) per US dollar -

Exchange rates: 1.652 (2024 est.)
1.628 (2023 est.)
1.577 (2022 est.)
1.414 (2021 est.)
1.542 (2020 est.)

ENERGY

Electricity: *installed generating capacity:* 3,000 kW (2023 est.)
consumption: 3 million kWh (2023 est.)
transmission/distribution losses: 400,000 kWh (2023 est.)
comparison rankings: installed generating capacity 211; consumption 211; transmission/distribution losses 2

Electricity generation sources: *fossil fuels:* 100% of total installed capacity (2023 est.)

Petroleum: *refined petroleum consumption:* 61 bbl/day (2023 est.)

COMMUNICATIONS

Telephones - fixed lines: *total subscriptions:* 1,000 (2021 est.)
subscriptions per 100 inhabitants: 52 (2021 est.)
comparison ranking: total subscriptions 218

Broadcast media: 1 state-owned TV station, with many of the programs supplied by Television New Zealand; 1 state-owned radio station broadcasting in AM and FM (2019)

Internet country code: .nu

Internet users: *percent of population:* 80% (2024 est.)

TRANSPORTATION

Airports: 1 (2025)
comparison ranking: 224

Merchant marine: *total:* 70 (2023)
by type: bulk carrier 5, container ship 2, general cargo 29, oil tanker 4, other 30
comparison ranking: total 109

Ports: *total ports:* 1 (2024)
large: 0
medium: 0
small: 0
very small: 1
ports with oil terminals: 0
key ports: Alofi

MILITARY AND SECURITY

Military and security forces: no regular indigenous military forces; Niue Police Department

Military - note: under the Niue Constitution Act of 1974, New Zealand provides assistance with foreign affairs, defense, and security if requested by the Niue government

NORFOLK ISLAND

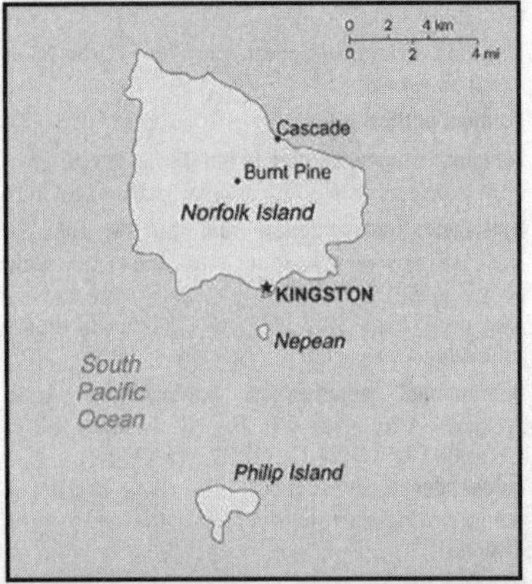

INTRODUCTION

Background: Polynesians lived on Norfolk Island between 1200 and 1500, but the remote island was uninhabited by the time British explorer James COOK landed on the island in 1774. Two British attempts at establishing the island as a penal colony (1788-1814 and 1825-55) were ultimately abandoned.

In 1856, almost 200 Pitcairn Islanders – descendants of the *Bounty* mutineers and their Tahitian companions – were relocated to Norfolk Island because of overcrowding on the Pitcairn Islands. Some returned to the Pitcairn Islands over the next few years, but most settled permanently on Norfolk Island and recreated their previous land tenure and governance structures. Norfolk Island retained a great degree of local control until 1897, when it became a dependency of New South Wales. During World War II, Norfolk Island was an airbase and an important refueling stop in the South Pacific. In 1976, an Australian judge recommended Norfolk Island be incorporated fully into Australia, which Norfolk Islanders rejected. After an appeal to the UN, Australia granted limited self-government to Norfolk Island in 1979.

With growing financial troubles during the 2000s, Australia abolished the Norfolk Island Legislative Assembly in 2015, reduced Norfolk Island's autonomy in 2016, and suspended the local council in 2020. Most services are provided by a mix of the Australian Capital Territory and the states of New South Wales and Queensland. These moves were unpopular on Norfolk Island, which has sought to have its self-government restored and as of 2024, the Australian Government was working with Norfolk Island to establish a new local governing body.

GEOGRAPHY

Location: Oceania, island in the South Pacific Ocean, east of Australia

Geographic coordinates: 29 02 S, 167 57 E

Map references: Oceania

Area: *total:* 36 sq km
land: 36 sq km
water: 0 sq km
comparison ranking: total 233

Area - comparative: about 0.2 times the size of Washington, D.C.

Land boundaries: *total:* 0 km

Coastline: 32 km

Maritime claims: *territorial sea:* 12 nm
contiguous zone: 24 nm
exclusive fishing zone: 200 nm

Climate: subtropical; mild, little seasonal temperature variation

Terrain: volcanic island with mostly rolling plains

Elevation: *highest point:* Mount Bates 319 m
lowest point: Pacific Ocean 0 m

Natural resources: fish

Land use: *agricultural land:* 25% (2022 est.)
arable land: 0% (2022 est.)
permanent crops: 0% (2022 est.)
permanent pasture: 25% (2022 est.)
forest: 12.3% (2022 est.)
other: 62.8% (2022 est.)

Irrigated land: 0 sq km (2022)

Population distribution: population concentrated around the capital of Kingston

Natural hazards: tropical cyclones (especially May to July)

Geography - note: most of the 32-km (20-mi) coastline consists of almost inaccessible cliffs, but the land slopes down to the sea in one small southern area on Sydney Bay, where the capital of Kingston is located

PEOPLE AND SOCIETY

Population: *total:* 1,739 (2021)
male: 823
female: 916
comparison rankings: total 233; male 233; female 232

Nationality: *noun:* Norfolk Islander(s)
adjective: Norfolk Islander(s)

Ethnic groups: Australian 22.8%, English 22.4%, Pitcairn Islander 20%, Scottish 6%, Irish 5.2% (2011 est.)
note: respondents were able to identify up to two ancestries; percentages represent a proportion of all responses from people in Norfolk Island, including those who did not identify an ancestry; only top responses are shown

Languages: English (official) 44.9%, Norfolk (official, a mixture of 18th century English and ancient Tahitian) 40.3%, Fijian 1.8%, other 6.8%, unspecified 6.2% (2016 est.)
note: data represent language spoken at home

Religions: Protestant 46.8% (Anglican 29.2%, Uniting Church in Australia 9.8%, Presbyterian 2.9%, Seventh Day Adventist 2.7%, other 2.2%), Roman Catholic 12.6%, other Christian 2.9%, other 1.4%, none 26.7%, unspecified 9.5% (2016 est.)

Population growth rate: 0.01% (2014 est.)
comparison ranking: 192

Population distribution: population concentrated around the capital of Kingston

ENVIRONMENT

Environmental issues: inadequate solid-waste management; most freshwater obtained through rainwater catchment; preservation of unique ecosystem

Climate: subtropical; mild, little seasonal temperature variation

GOVERNMENT

Country name: *conventional long form:* Territory of Norfolk Island
conventional short form: Norfolk Island
etymology: named by British explorer Captain James COOK after Edward HOWARD, the ninth Duke of Norfolk, in 1774

Government type: administered as an overseas territory of Australia
note: the Norfolk Island Regional Council, which began operations 1 July 2016, is responsible for planning and managing a variety of public services, including those funded by the Government of Australia

Dependency status: administered as a territory of Australia; administered by the Australian Government through the Department of Infrastructure, Transport, Cities, & Regional Development

Capital: *name:* Kingston
geographic coordinates: 29 03 S, 167 58 E
time difference: UTC+11 (16 hours ahead of Washington, DC, during Standard Time)
daylight saving time: +1hr, begins first Sunday in October; ends first Sunday in April
etymology: the name blends the words "king's" and "town;" the English king at the time of the town's settlement in the late 18th century was GEORGE III

Administrative divisions: none (territory of Australia)

Legal system: *history:* previous 1913, 1957; latest effective 7 August 1979

Citizenship: see Australia

Suffrage: 18 years of age; universal

Executive branch: *chief of state:* King CHARLES III (since 8 September 2022); represented by Governor General of the Commonwealth of Australia General Sam MOSTYN (since 1 July 2024)
head of government: Administrator George PLANT (since 1 June 2023)
election/appointment process: the monarchy is hereditary; governor general appointed by the monarch; administrator appointed by the governor general of Australia for a 2-year term and represents the monarch and Australia

Legislative branch: *legislature name:* Norfolk Island Regional Council
legislative structure: unicameral
number of seats: 5 (directly elected)
electoral system: plurality/majority
scope of elections: full renewal
term in office: 4 years
most recent election date: 5/28/2016
parties elected and seats per party: independent (5)
percentage of women in chamber: 20%
expected date of next election: March 2021 (postponed)

Judicial branch: *highest court(s):* Supreme Court of Norfolk Island (consists of the chief justice and several justices)
judge selection and term of office: justices appointed by the governor general of Australia from among justices of the Federal Court of Australia; justices serve until mandatory retirement at age 70
subordinate courts: Petty Court of Sessions; specialized courts, including a Coroner's Court and the Employment Tribunal
note: appeals beyond the Supreme Court of Norfolk Island are heard by the Federal Court and the High Court of Australia

Political parties: Norfolk Island Labor Party
Norfolk Liberals

Diplomatic representation in the US: none (territory of Australia)

Diplomatic representation from the US: *embassy:* none (territory of Australia)

International organization participation: UPU

Independence: none (territory of Australia)

National holiday: Bounty Day (commemorates the arrival of Pitcairn Islanders), 8 June (1856)

Flag: *description:* three vertical bands of green (left side), white, and green, with a large green Norfolk Island pine tree centered on the white band
meaning: green stands for the island's rich vegetation, and the native pine tree is an island symbol
note: resembles Canada's flag in its use of only two colors and depiction of a symbol based on a native tree in the central white band; also resembles Nigeria's green-and-white tri-band flag

National symbol(s): Norfolk Island pine

National coat of arms: Norfolk Island is part of the Commonwealth of Australia, and in 1980, Queen Elizabeth II granted it a separate coat of arms (pictured); in the center is the island's symbol, the Norfolk Island Pine, with Britain's lion and Australia's kangaroo supporting the shield; the island's motto, "Inasmuch," comes from a verse in the Bible's Gospel of Matthew

National anthem(s): *title:* "Come Ye Blessed"
lyrics/music: New Testament/John Prindle SCOTT
history: the local anthem, whose lyrics come from the Bible's Book of Matthew (25:34-36, 40), is also known as "The Pitcairn Anthem;"
title: "God Save the King"
lyrics/music: unknown
history: royal anthem, as an Australian overseas territory

ECONOMY

Economic overview: high-income Australian territorial economy; key tourism and re-exportation industries; small labor force and declining participation creating more part-time jobs; former tax haven; increasing medical cannabis exporter; little transportation infrastructure

Agricultural products: Norfolk Island pine seed, Kentia palm seed, cereals, vegetables, fruit; cattle, poultry

Industries: tourism, light industry, ready mixed concrete

Exports - partners: USA 31%, Belgium 9%, Philippines 7%, Israel 6%, Singapore 6% (2023)
note: top five export partners based on percentage share of exports

Exports - commodities: pine seeds, lumber, cars and vehicle parts, soybeans, lactose syrup (2021)
top five export commodities based on value in dollars

Imports - partners: Australia 52%, Fiji 13%, NZ 12%, Saudi Arabia 12%, Malaysia 5% (2023)
note: top five import partners based on percentage share of imports

Imports - commodities: refined petroleum, plastics, electrical lighting/signalling equipment, cars, machinery (2023)

Exchange rates: Australian dollars (AUD) per US dollar -

Exchange rates: 1.515 (2024 est.)
1.505 (2023 est.)
1.442 (2022 est.)
1.331 (2021 est.)
1.453 (2020 est.)

COMMUNICATIONS

Broadcast media: 1 local radio station; broadcasts of several Australian radio and TV stations available via satellite (2009)

Internet country code: .nf

Internet users: *percent of population:* 46.1% (2021 est.)

TRANSPORTATION

Airports: 1 (2025)
comparison ranking: 216

Ports: *total ports:* 1 (2024)
large: 0
medium: 0
small: 0
very small: 1
ports with oil terminals: 1
key ports: Kingston

MILITARY AND SECURITY

Military - note: defense is the responsibility of Australia

NORTH MACEDONIA

INTRODUCTION

Background: North Macedonia gained its independence peacefully from Yugoslavia in 1991 under the name of "Macedonia." Greece objected to the new country's name, insisting it implied territorial pretensions to the northern Greek province of Macedonia, and democratic backsliding for several years stalled North Macedonia's movement toward Euro-Atlantic integration. Immediately after Macedonia declared independence, Greece sought to block its efforts to gain UN membership if the name "Macedonia" was used. The country was eventually admitted to the UN in 1993 as "The former Yugoslav Republic of Macedonia," and at the same time it agreed to UN-sponsored negotiations on the name dispute. In 1995, Greece lifted a 20-month trade embargo and the two countries agreed to normalize relations, but the issue of the name remained unresolved amid ongoing negotiations. As an interim measure, the US and over 130 other nations recognized Macedonia by its constitutional name, Republic of Macedonia.

Ethnic Albanian grievances over perceived political and economic inequities escalated into an armed conflict in 2001 that eventually led to the internationally brokered Ohrid Framework Agreement, which ended the fighting and established guidelines for constitutional amendments and new laws that enhanced the rights of minorities. In 2018, the government adopted a new law on languages, which elevated the Albanian language to an official language at the national level and kept the Macedonian language as the sole official language in international relations, but ties between ethnic Macedonians and ethnic Albanians remain complicated.

In 2018, Macedonia and Greece signed the Prespa Agreement whereby Macedonia agreed to change its name to North Macedonia, and the agreement went in to force on 12 February 2019. North Macedonia joined NATO in 2020 after amending its constitution as agreed and opened EU accession talks in 2022 after a two-year veto by Bulgaria over identity, language, and historical disputes. The 2014 legislative and presidential election triggered a political crisis that lasted almost three years and escalated in 2015 when the opposition party began releasing wiretapped material revealing alleged widespread government corruption and abuse. The country still faces challenges, including fully implementing reforms to overcome years of democratic backsliding, stimulating economic growth and development, and fighting organized crime and corruption.

GEOGRAPHY

Location: Southeastern Europe, north of Greece

Geographic coordinates: 41 50 N, 22 00 E

Map references: Europe

Area: *total:* 25,713 sq km
land: 25,433 sq km
water: 280 sq km
comparison ranking: total 149

Area - comparative: slightly larger than Vermont; almost four times the size of Delaware

Land boundaries: *total:* 838 km
border countries (5): Albania 181 km; Bulgaria 162 km; Greece 234 km; Kosovo 160 km; Serbia 101 km

Coastline: 0 km (landlocked)

Maritime claims: none (landlocked)

Climate: warm, dry summers and autumns; relatively cold winters with heavy snowfall

Terrain: mountainous with deep basins and valleys; three large lakes, each divided by a frontier line; country bisected by the Vardar River

Elevation: *highest point:* Golem Korab (Maja e Korabit) 2,764 m
lowest point: Vardar River 50 m
mean elevation: 741 m

Natural resources: low-grade iron ore, copper, lead, zinc, chromite, manganese, nickel, tungsten, gold, silver, asbestos, gypsum, timber, arable land

Land use: *agricultural land:* 49.8% (2022 est.)
arable land: 16.5% (2022 est.)
permanent crops: 1.6% (2022 est.)
permanent pasture: 31.8% (2022 est.)
forest: 39.7% (2022 est.)
other: 10.4% (2022 est.)

Irrigated land: 844 sq km (2016)

Major watersheds (area sq km): Atlantic Ocean drainage: ***(Black Sea)*** Danube (795,656 sq km)

Population distribution: a fairly even distribution throughout most of the country, with urban areas attracting larger and denser populations

Natural hazards: high seismic risks

Geography - note: landlocked; major transportation corridor from Western and Central Europe to Aegean Sea and Southern Europe to Western Europe

PEOPLE AND SOCIETY

Population: *total:* 2,135,622 (2024 est.)
male: 1,064,727
female: 1,070,895
comparison rankings: total 149; male 149; female 148

Nationality: *noun:* Macedonian(s)
adjective: Macedonian

Ethnic groups: Macedonian 58.4%, Albanian 24.3%, Turkish 3.9%, Romani 2.5%, Serb 1.3%, other 2.3%, no ethnic affiliation data available 7.2% (2021 est.)
note: data represent total resident population; Romani populations are usually underestimated in official statistics and may represent 6.5–13% of North Macedonia's population

Languages: Macedonian (official) 61.4%, Albanian (official) 24.3%, Turkish 3.4%, Romani 1.7%, other (includes Aromanian (Vlach) and Bosnian) 2%, unspecified 7.2% (2021 est.)
major-language sample(s):
Книга на Светски Факти, неопходен извор на основни информации. (Macedonian)
note: data represent mother tongue; minority languages are co-official with Macedonian in municipalities where at least 20% of the population are speakers, with Albanian co-official in Tetovo, Brvenica, Vrapciste, and other municipalities, Turkish in Centar Zupa and Plasnica, Romani in Suto Orizari, Aromanian in Krusevo, Serbian in Cucer Sandevo

Religions: Macedonian Orthodox 46.1%, Muslim 32.2%, other Christian 13.8%, other and non-believers 0.5%, unspecified 7.4% (2021 est.)

Age structure: *0-14 years:* 16% (male 176,423/female 164,945)
15-64 years: 68.4% (male 740,649/female 719,627)
65 years and over: 15.6% (2024 est.) (male 147,655/female 186,323)

Dependency ratios: *total dependency ratio:* 46.2 (2024 est.)
youth dependency ratio: 23.4 (2024 est.)
elderly dependency ratio: 22.9 (2024 est.)
potential support ratio: 4.4 (2024 est.)

Median age: *total:* 40.5 years (2024 est.)
male: 39.4 years

female: 41.6 years
comparison ranking: total 59

Population growth rate: 0.1% (2024 est.)
comparison ranking: 187

Birth rate: 10.2 births/1,000 population (2024 est.)
comparison ranking: 181

Death rate: 9.6 deaths/1,000 population (2024 est.)
comparison ranking: 43

Net migration rate: 0.4 migrant(s)/1,000 population (2024 est.)
comparison ranking: 72

Population distribution: a fairly even distribution throughout most of the country, with urban areas attracting larger and denser populations

Urbanization: *urban population:* 59.5% of total population (2023)
rate of urbanization: 0.61% annual rate of change (2020-25 est.)

Major urban areas - population: 611,000 SKOPJE (capital) (2023)

Sex ratio: *at birth:* 1.07 male(s)/female
0-14 years: 1.07 male(s)/female
15-64 years: 1.03 male(s)/female
65 years and over: 0.79 male(s)/female
total population: 0.99 male(s)/female (2024 est.)

Mother's mean age at first birth: 26.9 years (2020 est.)

Maternal mortality ratio: 3 deaths/100,000 live births (2023 est.)
comparison ranking: 185

Infant mortality rate: *total:* 7 deaths/1,000 live births (2024 est.)
male: 7.9 deaths/1,000 live births
female: 6 deaths/1,000 live births
comparison ranking: total 156

Life expectancy at birth: *total population:* 77.3 years (2024 est.)
male: 75.3 years
female: 79.6 years
comparison ranking: total population 92

Total fertility rate: 1.53 children born/woman (2024 est.)
comparison ranking: 198

Gross reproduction rate: 0.74 (2024 est.)

Drinking water source: *improved: urban:* 98.1% of population (2022 est.)
rural: 97.4% of population (2022 est.)
total: 97.8% of population (2022 est.)
unimproved: urban: 1.9% of population (2022 est.)
rural: 2.6% of population (2022 est.)
total: 2.2% of population (2022 est.)

Health expenditure: 8.5% of GDP (2021)
12.4% of national budget (2022 est.)

Physician density: 2.94 physicians/1,000 population (2022)

Hospital bed density: 4.2 beds/1,000 population (2020 est.)

Sanitation facility access: *improved: urban:* 100% of population (2022 est.)
rural: 98.6% of population (2022 est.)
total: 99.4% of population (2022 est.)
unimproved: urban: 0% of population (2022 est.)
rural: 1.4% of population (2022 est.)
total: 0.6% of population (2022 est.)

Obesity - adult prevalence rate: 22.4% (2016)
comparison ranking: 77

Alcohol consumption per capita: *total:* 3.9 liters of pure alcohol (2019 est.)
beer: 1.93 liters of pure alcohol (2019 est.)
wine: 1.03 liters of pure alcohol (2019 est.)
spirits: 0.9 liters of pure alcohol (2019 est.)
other alcohols: 0.03 liters of pure alcohol (2019 est.)
comparison ranking: total 97

Children under the age of 5 years underweight: 0.9% (2018/19)
comparison ranking: 110

Currently married women (ages 15-49): 66.5% (2023 est.)

Child marriage: *women married by age 15:* 0.3% (2019)
women married by age 18: 7.5% (2019)

Literacy: *female:* 97.8% (2018 est.)

School life expectancy (primary to tertiary education): *total:* 15 years (2022 est.)
male: 14 years (2022 est.)
female: 15 years (2022 est.)

ENVIRONMENT

Environmental issues: air pollution from metallurgical plants, smoke from wood-burning stoves, and vehicle emissions

International environmental agreements: *party to:* Air Pollution, Air Pollution-Heavy Metals, Air Pollution-Multi-effect Protocol, Air Pollution-Nitrogen Oxides, Air Pollution-Persistent Organic Pollutants, Air Pollution-Sulphur 85, Air Pollution-Sulphur 94, Air Pollution-Volatile Organic Compounds, Biodiversity, Climate Change, Climate Change-Kyoto Protocol, Climate Change-Paris Agreement, Comprehensive Nuclear Test Ban, Desertification, Endangered Species, Hazardous Wastes, Law of the Sea, Ozone Layer Protection, Wetlands
signed, but not ratified: none of the selected agreements

Climate: warm, dry summers and autumns; relatively cold winters with heavy snowfall

Urbanization: *urban population:* 59.5% of total population (2023)
rate of urbanization: 0.61% annual rate of change (2020-25 est.)

Carbon dioxide emissions: 7.369 million metric tonnes of CO2 (2023 est.)
from coal and metallurgical coke: 3.014 million metric tonnes of CO2 (2023 est.)
from petroleum and other liquids: 3.682 million metric tonnes of CO2 (2023 est.)
from consumed natural gas: 673,000 metric tonnes of CO2 (2023 est.)
comparison ranking: total emissions 121

Particulate matter emissions: 28.7 micrograms per cubic meter (2019 est.)

Waste and recycling: *municipal solid waste generated annually:* 627,000 tons (2024 est.)
percent of municipal solid waste recycled: 4.9% (2022 est.)

Total water withdrawal: *municipal:* 305.4 million cubic meters (2022 est.)
industrial: 31.54 million cubic meters (2022 est.)
agricultural: 139 million cubic meters (2022 est.)

Total renewable water resources: 6.4 billion cubic meters (2022 est.)

GOVERNMENT

Country name: *conventional long form:* Republic of North Macedonia
conventional short form: North Macedonia
local long form: Republika Severna Makedonija
local short form: Severna Makedonija
former: Democratic Federal Macedonia, People's Republic of Macedonia, Socialist Republic of Macedonia, Republic of Macedonia
etymology: the name derives from the ancient kingdom of Macedon (7th to 2nd centuries B.C.), whose name origin is unclear; it may derive from the mythological Macedon, the son of the Greek god Zeus; alternatively, it may come from the Greek word *makednos*, meaning "tail," or the Illyrian word *maketia*, meaning "cattle"

Government type: parliamentary republic

Capital: *name:* Skopje
geographic coordinates: 42 00 N, 21 26 E
time difference: UTC+1 (6 hours ahead of Washington, DC, during Standard Time)
daylight saving time: +1hr, begins last Sunday in March; ends last Sunday in October
etymology: the name is of Illyrian or Macedonian origin, and the meaning is unclear; derives from Scupi, its name during the Roman era

Administrative divisions: 80 municipalities (*opstini*, singular - *opstina*) and 1 city* (*grad*); Aracinovo, Berovo, Bitola, Bogdanci, Bogovinje, Bosilovo, Brvenica, Caska, Centar Zupa, Cesinovo-Oblesevo, Cucer Sandevo, Debar, Debarca, Delcevo, Demir Hisar, Demir Kapija, Dojran, Dolneni, Gevgelija, Gostivar, Gradsko, Ilinden, Jegunovce, Karbinci, Kavadarci, Kicevo, Kocani, Konce, Kratovo, Kriva Palanka, Krivogastani, Krusevo, Kumanovo, Lipkovo, Lozovo, Makedonska Kamenica, Makedonski Brod, Mavrovo i Rostuse, Mogila, Negotino, Novaci, Novo Selo, Ohrid, Pehcevo, Petrovec, Plasnica, Prilep, Probistip, Radovis, Rankovce, Resen, Rosoman, Skopje*, Sopiste, Staro Nagoricane, Stip, Struga, Strumica, Studenicani, Sveti Nikole, Tearce, Tetovo, Valandovo, Vasilevo, Veles, Vevcani, Vinica, Vrapciste, Zelenikovo, Zelino, Zrnovci
*the Greater Skopje area is composed of 10 municipalities: Aerodrom, Butel, Centar, Chair, Gazi Baba, Gjorce Petrov, Karposh, Kisela Voda, Saraj, and Shuto Orizari

Legal system: civil law system; judicial review of legislative acts

Constitution: *history:* several previous (since 1944); latest adopted 17 November 1991, effective 20 November 1991
amendment process: proposed by the president of the republic, by the government, by at least 30 members of the Assembly, or by petition of at least 150,000 citizens; final approval requires a two-thirds majority vote by the Assembly

International law organization participation: has not submitted an ICJ jurisdiction declaration; accepts ICCt jurisdiction

Citizenship: *citizenship by birth:* no
citizenship by descent only: at least one parent must be a citizen of North Macedonia
dual citizenship recognized: no
residency requirement for naturalization: 8 years

Suffrage: 18 years of age; universal

Executive branch: *chief of state:* President Gordana SILJANOVSKA-DAVKOVA (since 12 May 2024)

head of government: Prime Minister Hristijan MICKOSKI (since 23 June 2024)
cabinet: Council of Ministers elected by the Assembly by simple majority vote
election/appointment process: president directly elected using a modified 2-round system; a candidate can only be elected in the first round with an absolute majority from all registered voters; in the second round, voter turnout must be at least 40% for the result to be valid; president elected for a 5-year term (eligible for a second term); following legislative elections, the Assembly usually elects the leader of the majority party or majority coalition as prime minister
most recent election date: 24 April and 8 May 2024
election results: 2024: Hristijan MICKOSKI elected prime minister; Assembly vote - 77 for, 22 against
2024: Gordana SILJANOVSKA-DAVKOVA elected president in the second round; percent of vote - Gordana SILJANOVSKA-DAVKOVA (VMRO-DPMNE) 69%, Stevo PENDAROVSKI (SDSM) 31%
2024: Talat XHAFERI elected caretaker prime minister; Assembly vote - 65 for (opposition boycott)
2022: Dimitar KOVACEVSKI elected prime minister; Assembly vote - NA
expected date of next election: 2029

Legislative branch: *legislature name:* Assembly of the Republic (Sobranie)
legislative structure: unicameral
number of seats: 123 (all directly elected)
electoral system: mixed system
scope of elections: full renewal
term in office: 4 years
most recent election date: 5/8/2024
parties elected and seats per party: Coalition "Your Macedonia" (led by VMRO-DPMNE) (58); Coalition "European Front" (led by the Democratic Union for Integration – DUI) (18); Coalition "For a European Future" (led by the Social Democratic Union of Macedonia – SDSM) (18); Coalition VLEN (14); ZNAM (Movement "I know": For our Macedonia) (6); The Left (Levica) (6)
percentage of women in chamber: 39.2%
expected date of next election: May 2028

Judicial branch: *highest court(s):* Supreme Court (consists of 22 judges); Constitutional Court (consists of 9 judges)
judge selection and term of office: Supreme Court judges nominated by the Judicial Council, a 7-member body of legal professionals, and appointed by the Assembly; judge tenure NA; Constitutional Court judges appointed by the Assembly for nonrenewable, 9-year terms
subordinate courts: Courts of Appeal; Basic Courts

Political parties: Alliance for Albanians or AfA or ASH
Alternative (Alternativa) or AAA
Besa Movement or BESA
Citizen Option for Macedonia or GROM
Democratic Alliance or DS
Democratic Movement or LD
Democratic Party of Albanians or PDSH
Democratic Party of Serbs or DPSM
Democratic Renewal of Macedonia or DOM
Democratic Union for Integration or BDI
European Democratic Party or PDE
Internal Macedonian Revolutionary Organization - Democratic Party for Macedonian National Unity or VMRO-DPMNE
Internal Macedonian Revolutionary Organization - People's Party or VMRO-NP
Liberal Democratic Party or LDP
New Social-Democratic Party or NSDP
Social Democratic Union of Macedonia or SDSM
Socialist Party of Macedonia or SPM
Srpska Stranka in Macedonia or SSM
The Left (Levica)
The People Movement or LP
Turkish Democratic Party or TDP
Turkish Movement Party or THP
We Can! (coalition includes SDSM/BESA/VMRO-NP, DPT, LDP)

Diplomatic representation in the US: *chief of mission:* Ambassador Zoran POPOV (since 16 September 2022)
chancery: 2129 Wyoming Avenue NW, Washington, DC 20008
telephone: [1] (202) 667-0501
FAX: [1] (202) 667-2104
email address and website: washington@mfa.gov.mk United States (mfa.gov.mk)
consulate(s) general: Chicago, Detroit, New York

Diplomatic representation from the US: *chief of mission:* Ambassador Angela AGGELER (since 8 November 2022)
embassy: Str. Samoilova, Nr. 21, 1000 Skopje
mailing address: 7120 Skopje Place, Washington, DC 20521-7120
telephone: [389] (2) 310-2000
FAX: [389] (2) 310-2499
email address and website: SkopjeACS@state.gov https://mk.usembassy.gov/

International organization participation: BIS, CD, CE, CEI, EAPC, EBRD, EU (candidate country), FAO, IAEA, IBRD, ICAO, ICC (NGOs), ICCt, ICRM, IDA, IFAD, IFC, IFRCS, ILO, IMF, IMO, Interpol, IOC, IOM, IPU, ISO, ITU, ITUC (NGOs), MIGA, NATO, OAS (observer), OIF, OPCW, OSCE, PCA, PFP, SELEC, UN, UNCTAD, UNESCO, UNHCR, UNIDO, UNIFIL, UNWTO, UPU, WCO, WHO, WIPO, WMO, WTO
note: North Macedonia is an EU candidate country whose satisfactory completion of accession criteria is required before being granted full EU membership

Independence: 8 September 1991 (referendum endorsed independence from Yugoslavia)

National holiday: Independence Day, 8 September (1991), also known as National Day

Flag: *description:* a red field with a yellow sun (the Sun of Liberty) in the center, with eight broadening rays extending to the edges
meaning: the red and yellow colors have long been associated with Macedonia

National symbol(s): eight-rayed sun

National color(s): red, yellow

National anthem(s): *title:* "Denes nad Makedonija" (Today Over Macedonia)
lyrics/music: Vlado MALESKI/Todor SKALOVSKI
history: written in 1943 and adopted in 1991, the song previously served as the anthem of the Socialist Republic of Macedonia, when it was part of Yugoslavia

National heritage: *total World Heritage Sites:* 2 (both natural)
selected World Heritage Site locales: Natural and Cultural Heritage of the Ohrid Region; Ancient and Primeval Beech Forests of the Carpathians

ECONOMY

Economic overview: upper-middle-income European economy; GDP growth driven by private consumption, public infrastructure investments, and wage growth; stalled progress on EU accession; public debt rising due to high pensions, wages, and interest payments; structural challenges of emigration, low productivity growth, and governance

Real GDP (purchasing power parity): $43.844 billion (2024 est.)
$42.668 billion (2023 est.)
$41.801 billion (2022 est.)
note: data in 2021 dollars
comparison ranking: 136

Real GDP growth rate: 2.8% (2024 est.)
2.1% (2023 est.)
2.8% (2022 est.)
note: annual GDP % growth based on constant local currency
comparison ranking: 122

Real GDP per capita: $24,500 (2024 est.)
$23,300 (2023 est.)
$22,800 (2022 est.)
note: data in 2021 dollars
comparison ranking: 90

GDP (official exchange rate): $16.685 billion (2024 est.)
note: data in current dollars at official exchange rate

Inflation rate (consumer prices): 3.5% (2024 est.)
9.4% (2023 est.)
14.2% (2022 est.)
note: annual % change based on consumer prices
comparison ranking: 112

GDP - composition, by sector of origin: *agriculture:* 6% (2024 est.)
industry: 22.7% (2024 est.)
services: 59.2% (2024 est.)
note: figures may not total 100% due to non-allocated consumption not captured in sector-reported data
comparison rankings: agriculture 101; industry 111; services 95

GDP - composition, by end use: *household consumption:* 67.9% (2024 est.)
government consumption: 16.8% (2024 est.)
investment in fixed capital: 28.4% (2024 est.)
investment in inventories: 0% (2024 est.)
exports of goods and services: 62.7% (2024 est.)
imports of goods and services: -75.8% (2024 est.)
note: figures may not total 100% due to rounding or gaps in data collection

Agricultural products: chillies/peppers, milk, wheat, potatoes, grapes, barley, cabbages, maize, watermelons, tomatoes (2023)
note: top ten agricultural products based on tonnage

Industries: food processing, beverages, textiles, chemicals, iron, steel, cement, energy, pharmaceuticals, automotive parts

Industrial production growth rate: 1.8% (2024 est.)
note: annual % change in industrial value added based on constant local currency
comparison ranking: 103

Labor force: 779,200 (2024 est.)
note: number of people ages 15 or older who are employed or seeking work
comparison ranking: 152

Unemployment rate: 13.5% (2024 est.)
13.2% (2023 est.)
14.5% (2022 est.)
note: % of labor force seeking employment
comparison ranking: 170

Youth unemployment rate (ages 15-24): *total:* 30.3% (2024 est.)

male: 29.2% (2024 est.)
female: 32.3% (2024 est.)
note: % of labor force ages 15-24 seeking employment
comparison ranking: total 21

Population below poverty line: 21.8% (2019 est.)
note: % of population with income below national poverty line
Gini Index coefficient - distribution of family income 33.5 (2019 est.)
note: index (0-100) of income distribution; higher values represent greater inequality
comparison ranking: 93

Average household expenditures: *on food:* 30.6% of household expenditures (2023 est.)
on alcohol and tobacco: 4.8% of household expenditures (2023 est.)

Household income or consumption by percentage share: *lowest 10%:* 1.9% (2019 est.)
highest 10%: 22.9% (2019 est.)
note: % share of income accruing to lowest and highest 10% of population

Remittances: 2.7% of GDP (2024 est.)
2.9% of GDP (2023 est.)
3.3% of GDP (2022 est.)
note: personal transfers and compensation between resident and non-resident individuals/households/entities

Budget: *revenues:* $4.787 billion (2023 est.)
expenditures: $5.514 billion (2023 est.)
note: central government revenues (excluding grants) and expenditures converted to US dollars at average official exchange rate for year indicated

Public debt: 39.3% of GDP (2017 est.)
note: official data from Ministry of Finance; data cover central government debt; this data excludes debt instruments issued (or owned) by government entities other than the treasury; includes treasury debt held by foreign entitites; excludes debt issued by sub-national entities; there are no debt instruments sold for social funds
comparison ranking: 135

Taxes and other revenues: 17.9% (of GDP) (2023 est.)
note: central government tax revenue as a % of GDP
comparison ranking: 66

Current account balance: -$374.385 million (2024 est.)
$56.573 million (2023 est.)
-$868.965 million (2022 est.)
note: balance of payments - net trade and primary/secondary income in current dollars
comparison ranking: 107

Exports: $10.445 billion (2024 est.)
$10.691 billion (2023 est.)
$10.123 billion (2022 est.)
note: balance of payments - exports of goods and services in current dollars
comparison ranking: 116

Exports - partners: Germany 39%, Serbia 8%, Bulgaria 6%, Greece 5%, Czechia 3% (2023)
note: top five export partners based on percentage share of exports

Exports - commodities: reaction and catalytic products, insulated wire, electricity, garments, seats (2023)
note: top five export commodities based on value in dollars

Imports: $12.644 billion (2024 est.)
$12.748 billion (2023 est.)
$13.009 billion (2022 est.)
note: balance of payments - imports of goods and services in current dollars
comparison ranking: 112

Imports - partners: UK 12%, Germany 10%, Greece 9%, China 9%, Serbia 8% (2023)
note: top five import partners based on percentage share of imports

Imports - commodities: platinum, refined petroleum, laboratory ceramic ware, cars, natural gas (2023)
note: top five import commodities based on value in dollars

Reserves of foreign exchange and gold: $5.252 billion (2024 est.)
$5.015 billion (2023 est.)
$4.12 billion (2022 est.)
note: holdings of gold (year-end prices)/foreign exchange/special drawing rights in current dollars
comparison ranking: 96

Debt - external: $5.637 billion (2023 est.)
note: present value of external debt in current US dollars
comparison ranking: 69

Exchange rates: Macedonian denars (MKD) per US dollar -

Exchange rates: 56.873 (2024 est.)
56.947 (2023 est.)
58.574 (2022 est.)
52.102 (2021 est.)
54.144 (2020 est.)

ENERGY

Electricity access: *electrification - total population:* 100% (2022 est.)

Electricity: *installed generating capacity:* 2.467 million kW (2023 est.)
consumption: 5.896 billion kWh (2023 est.)
exports: 7.081 billion kWh (2023 est.)
imports: 7.232 billion kWh (2023 est.)
transmission/distribution losses: 993.662 million kWh (2023 est.)
comparison rankings: installed generating capacity 115; consumption 125; exports 34; imports 35; transmission/distribution losses 99

Electricity generation sources: *fossil fuels:* 68.2% of total installed capacity (2023 est.)
solar: 4.6% of total installed capacity (2023 est.)
wind: 2.3% of total installed capacity (2023 est.)
hydroelectricity: 24% of total installed capacity (2023 est.)
biomass and waste: 0.8% of total installed capacity (2023 est.)

Coal: *production:* 4 million metric tons (2023 est.)
consumption: 5.344 million metric tons (2023 est.)
exports: 58,000 metric tons (2023 est.)
imports: 41,000 metric tons (2023 est.)
proven reserves: 332 million metric tons (2023 est.)

Petroleum: *refined petroleum consumption:* 24,000 bbl/day (2023 est.)

Natural gas: *consumption:* 348.078 million cubic meters (2023 est.)
imports: 347.981 million cubic meters (2023 est.)

Energy consumption per capita: 56.104 million Btu/person (2023 est.)
comparison ranking: 87

COMMUNICATIONS

Telephones - fixed lines: *total subscriptions:* 439,000 (2022 est.)
subscriptions per 100 inhabitants: 24 (2022 est.)
comparison ranking: total subscriptions 98

Telephones - mobile cellular: *total subscriptions:* 1.92 million (2023 est.)
subscriptions per 100 inhabitants: 98 (2022 est.)
comparison ranking: total subscriptions 152

Broadcast media: public TV broadcaster Macedonian Radio and Television operates 5 national terrestrial TV channels and 2 satellite TV channels; 11 regional TV stations broadcast nationally; 29 regional and local broadcasters; a large number of cable operators offer domestic and international programming; the public radio broadcaster operates 3 stations; 4 privately owned national radio stations and 60 regional and local operators (2023)

Internet country code: .mk

Internet users: *percent of population:* 87% (2023 est.)

Broadband - fixed subscriptions: *total:* 515,000 (2022 est.)
subscriptions per 100 inhabitants: 28 (2022 est.)
comparison ranking: total 95

TRANSPORTATION

Civil aircraft registration country code prefix: Z3

Airports: 13 (2025)
comparison ranking: 152

Heliports: 13 (2025)
comparison ranking: 65

Railways: *total:* 699 km (2020) 313 km electrified

MILITARY AND SECURITY

Military and security forces: Army of the Republic of North Macedonia (ARSM or ARNM): joint force with air, ground, reserve, special operations, and support forces (2025)
note: the Police of Macedonia maintain internal security, including migration and border enforcement, and report to the Ministry of the Interior

Military expenditures: 2% of GDP (2025 est.)
1.9% of GDP (2024 est.)
1.7% of GDP (2023 est.)
1.6% of GDP (2022 est.)
1.5% of GDP (2021 est.)

Military and security service personnel strengths: approximately 6,000 active military personnel (2025)

Military equipment inventories and acquisitions: the military's inventory is a mix of Soviet-era and increasing amounts of modern equipment from countries such as Turkey, the UK, and the US, with more on order (2024)

Military service age and obligation: 18 years of age for voluntary military service; conscription abolished in 2007 (2024)
note: as of 2024, women made up about 10% of the military's full-time personnel

Military - note: the Army of the Republic of North Macedonia (ARSM) is responsible for the defense of the country's territory and independence, fulfilling North Macedonia's commitments to NATO and European security, and contributing to EU, NATO, and UN peace and security missions; the ARSM has participated in multinational missions and operations in Afghanistan (NATO), Bosnia and Herzegovina (EU), Eastern Europe (NATO), Iraq (NATO), Kosovo (NATO), and Lebanon (UN); a key area of focus over the past decade has been improving capabilities and bringing the largely Soviet-era-equipped ARSM up to NATO standards; it has increased its participation in NATO training exercises since becoming the 30th member of the Alliance in 2020 and currently has small numbers of combat troops deployed to Bulgaria and Romania as part of NATO's Enhance Forward Presence mission implemented because of Russian military aggression against Ukraine (2025)

TERRORISM

Terrorist group(s): Terrorist group(s): Islamic State of Iraq and ash-Sham (ISIS)
note: details about the history, aims, leadership, organization, areas of operation, tactics, targets, weapons, size, and sources of support of the group(s) appear(s) in Appendix T

TRANSNATIONAL ISSUES

Refugees and internally displaced persons: *refugees:* 20,937 (2024 est.)
stateless persons: 159 (2024 est.)

NORTHERN MARIANA ISLANDS

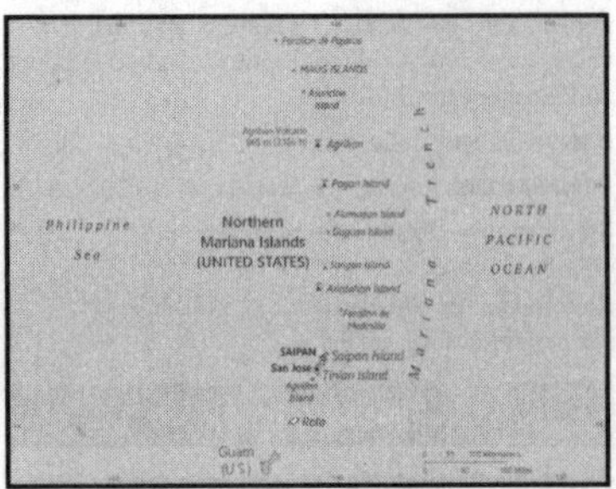

INTRODUCTION

Background: Austronesian people settled the Northern Mariana Islands around 1500 B.C. These people became the indigenous Chamorro and were influenced by later migrations, including Micronesians in the first century A.D. and island Southeast Asians around 900. Spanish explorer Ferdinand MAGELLAN sailed through the Mariana Islands in 1521, and Spain claimed them in 1565. Spain formally colonized the Mariana Islands in 1668 and administered the archipelago from Guam. Spain's brutal repression of the Chamorro, along with new diseases and intermittent warfare, reduced the indigenous population by about 90% in the 1700s. With a similar dynamic occurring on Guam, Spain forced the Chamorro from the Northern Mariana Islands to resettle there. By the time they returned, many other Micronesians, including Chuukese and Yapese, had already settled on their islands.

In 1898, Spain ceded Guam to the US after the Spanish-American War but sold the Northern Mariana Islands to Germany under the German-Spanish Treaty of 1899. Germany administered the territory from German New Guinea but took a hands-off approach to day-to-day life. Following World War I, Japan administered the islands under a League of Nations mandate. Japan focused on sugar production and brought in thousands of Japanese laborers, who quickly outnumbered the Chamorro on the islands. During World War II, Japan invaded Guam from the Northern Mariana Islands and used Marianan Chamorro as translators with Guamanian Chamorro, creating friction between the two Chamorro communities that continues to this day. The US captured the Northern Mariana Islands in 1944 after the Battle of Saipan and later administered them as part of the Trust Territory of the Pacific Islands (TTPI).

On four occasions in the 1950s and 1960s, voters opted for integration with Guam, which Guam rejected in 1969. In 1978, the Northern Mariana Islands was granted self-governance separate from the rest of the TTPI, and in 1986, islanders were granted US citizenship, with the territory coming under US sovereignty as the Commonwealth of the Northern Mariana Islands (CNMI). In 2009, the CNMI became the final US territory to elect a nonvoting delegate to the US Congress.

GEOGRAPHY

Location: Oceania, islands in the North Pacific Ocean, about three-quarters of the way from Hawaii to the Philippines

Geographic coordinates: 15 12 N, 145 45 E

Map references: Oceania

Area: *total:* 464 sq km
land: 464 sq km
water: 0 sq km
note: consists of 14 islands including Saipan, Rota, and Tinian
comparison ranking: total 196

Area - comparative: 2.5 times the size of Washington, D.C.

Land boundaries: *total:* 0 km

Coastline: 1,482 km

Maritime claims: *territorial sea:* 12 nm
exclusive economic zone: 200 nm

Climate: tropical marine; moderated by northeast trade winds, little seasonal temperature variation; dry season December to June, rainy season July to October

Terrain: the southern islands in this north-south trending archipelago are limestone, with fringing coral reefs; the northern islands are volcanic, with active volcanoes on several islands

Elevation: *highest point:* Agrihan Volcano 965 m
lowest point: Pacific Ocean 0 m

Natural resources: arable land, fish

Land use: *agricultural land:* 1.2% (2022 est.)
arable land: 0.2% (2022 est.)
permanent crops: 0.2% (2022 est.)
permanent pasture: 0.8% (2022 est.)
forest: 53% (2022 est.)
other: 45.9% (2022 est.)

Irrigated land: 1 sq km (2012)

Population distribution: approximately 90% of the population lives on the island of Saipan

Natural hazards: active volcanoes on Pagan and Agrihan; typhoons (especially August to November)

Geography - note: strategic location in the North Pacific Ocean

PEOPLE AND SOCIETY

Population: *total:* 51,118 (2024 est.)
male: 27,044
female: 24,074
comparison rankings: total 209; male 209; female 209

Nationality: *noun:* NA (US citizens)
adjective: NA

Ethnic groups: Asian 50% (includes Filipino 35.3%, Chinese 6.8%, Korean 4.2%, and other Asian 3.7%), Native Hawaiian or other Pacific Islander 34.9% (includes Chamorro 23.9%, Carolinian 4.6%, and other Native Hawaiian or Pacific Islander 6.4%), other 2.5%, two or more ethnicities or races 12.7% (2010 est.)

Languages: Philippine languages 32.8%, Chamorro (official) 24.1%, English (official) 17%, other Pacific island languages 10.1% (includes Carolinian (official), Chinese 6.8%, other Asian languages 7.3%, other 1.9% (2010 est.)

Religions: Christian (Roman Catholic majority, although traditional beliefs and taboos may still be found)

Age structure: *0-14 years:* 22.1% (male 6,066/female 5,231)
15-64 years: 67.7% (male 18,206/female 16,377)
65 years and over: 10.2% (2024 est.) (male 2,772/female 2,466)

Dependency ratios: *total dependency ratio:* 47.8 (2024 est.)
youth dependency ratio: 32.7 (2024 est.)
elderly dependency ratio: 15.1 (2024 est.)
potential support ratio: 6.6 (2024 est.)

Median age: *total:* 32.4 years (2024 est.)
male: 31.8 years
female: 33.2 years
comparison ranking: total 116

Population growth rate: -0.34% (2024 est.)
comparison ranking: 214

Birth rate: 15.7 births/1,000 population (2024 est.)
comparison ranking: 104

Death rate: 5.7 deaths/1,000 population (2024 est.)
comparison ranking: 172

Net migration rate: -13.4 migrant(s)/1,000 population (2024 est.)
comparison ranking: 226

Population distribution: approximately 90% of the population lives on the island of Saipan

Urbanization: *urban population:* 92.1% of total population (2023)
rate of urbanization: 0.36% annual rate of change (2020-25 est.)

Major urban areas - population: 51,000 SAIPAN (capital) (2018)

Sex ratio: *at birth:* 1.17 male(s)/female
0-14 years: 1.16 male(s)/female
15-64 years: 1.11 male(s)/female
65 years and over: 1.12 male(s)/female
total population: 1.12 male(s)/female (2024 est.)

Infant mortality rate: *total:* 11.9 deaths/1,000 live births (2024 est.)
male: 14.4 deaths/1,000 live births
female: 9 deaths/1,000 live births
comparison ranking: total 110

Life expectancy at birth: *total population:* 77.1 years (2024 est.)
male: 75 years
female: 79.5 years
comparison ranking: total population 98

Total fertility rate: 2.56 children born/woman (2024 est.)
comparison ranking: 67

Gross reproduction rate: 1.18 (2024 est.)

Drinking water source: *improved:* total: 100% of population (2022 est.)
unimproved: total: 0% of population (2022 est.)

Sanitation facility access: *improved:* total: 99.4% of population (2022 est.)
unimproved: total: 0.6% of population (2022 est.)

ENVIRONMENT

Environmental issues: contamination of groundwater on Saipan; clean-up of landfill; protection of endangered species

Climate: tropical marine; moderated by northeast trade winds, little seasonal temperature variation; dry season December to June, rainy season July to October

Urbanization: *urban population:* 92.1% of total population (2023)
rate of urbanization: 0.36% annual rate of change (2020-25 est.)

Waste and recycling: *municipal solid waste generated annually:* 32,800 tons (2024 est.)
percent of municipal solid waste recycled: 36% (2016 est.)

GOVERNMENT

Country name: *conventional long form:* Commonwealth of the Northern Mariana Islands
conventional short form: Northern Mariana Islands
former: Trust Territory of the Pacific Islands, Mariana Islands District
abbreviation: CNMI
etymology: Spain named the islands in 1667 in honor of the Spanish Queen, MARIANA of Austria

Government type: a commonwealth in political union with and under the sovereignty of the US; republican form of government with separate executive, legislative, and judicial branches

Dependency status: commonwealth in political union with and under the sovereignty of the US; federal funds administered by the US Department of the Interior, Office of Insular Affairs

Capital: *name:* Saipan
geographic coordinates: 15 12 N, 145 45 E
time difference: UTC+10 (15 hours ahead of Washington, DC, during Standard Time)
etymology: the origin of the name is unclear; it probably comes from a local word meaning "deserted" or "uninhabited," but stories vary on how it came to be used

Administrative divisions: *none (commonwealth in political union with the US); no first-order administrative divisions as defined by the US government, but 4 municipalities are considered second-order:* Northern Islands, Rota, Saipan, Tinian

Legal system: the laws of the US apply, except for customs and some aspects of taxation

Constitution: *history:* partially effective 9 January 1978 (Constitution of the Commonwealth of the Northern Mariana Islands); fully effective 4 November 1986 (Covenant Agreement)
amendment process: proposed by constitutional convention, by public petition, or by the Legislature; ratification of proposed amendments requires approval by voters at the next general election or special election; amendments proposed by constitutional convention or by petition become effective if approved by a majority of voters and at least two-thirds majority of voters in each of two senatorial districts; amendments proposed by the Legislature are effective if approved by majority vote

Citizenship: see United States

Suffrage: 18 years of age; universal
note: inhabitants are US citizens but do not vote in US presidential elections

Executive branch: *chief of state:* President Donald J. TRUMP (since 20 January 2025)
head of government: Governor David M. APATANG (since 24 July 2025)
cabinet: Sworn in by CNMI Chief Justice Alexandro Castro on Thursday, 24 July 2025
election/appointment process: president and vice president indirectly elected on the same ballot by an Electoral College of electors chosen from each state; president and vice president serve a 4-year term (eligible for a second term); under the US Constitution, residents of the Northern Mariana Islands do not vote in elections for US president and vice president; however, they may vote in Democratic and Republican party presidential primary elections; governor directly elected by absolute majority vote in 2 rounds, if needed
most recent election date: 8 November 2022, with a runoff held on 25 November 2022
election results: *2022:* Arnold PALACIOS elected governor in second round; percent of vote in first round - Ralph TORRES (Republican) 38.8%; Arnold PALACIOS (independent) 32.2%, Tina SABLAN (Democrat) 28%; percent of vote in second round - Arnold PALACIOS 54%, Ralph TORRES 46%; David APATANG (independent) elected lieutenant governor
2018: Ralph TORRES elected governor; percent of vote - Ralph TORRES (Republican) 62.2%, Juan BABAUTA (independent) 37.8%; Arnold PALACIOS elected lieutenant governor
expected date of next election: 2026

Legislative branch: *note:* the Northern Mariana Islands delegate to the US House of Representatives can vote when serving on a committee and when the House meets as the "Committee of the Whole House," but not when legislation is submitted for a "full floor" House vote

Judicial branch: *highest court(s):* Supreme Court of the Commonwealth of the Northern Mariana Islands (CNMI) (consists of the chief justice and 2 associate justices); US Federal District Court (consists of 1 judge)
judge selection and term of office: CNMI Supreme Court judges appointed by the governor and confirmed by the CNMI Senate; judges appointed for 8-year terms and another term if directly elected in a popular election; US Federal District Court judges appointed by the US president and confirmed by the US Senate; judges appointed for renewable 10-year terms
subordinate courts: Superior Court
note: US Federal District Court jurisdiction limited to US federal laws; appeals beyond the CNMI Supreme Court are referred to the US Supreme Court

Political parties: Democratic Party
Republican Party

Diplomatic representation from the US: *embassy:* none (commonwealth in political union with the US)

International organization participation: PIF (observer), SPC, UPU

Independence: none (commonwealth in political union with the US)

National holiday: Commonwealth Day, 8 January (1978)

Flag: *description:* blue with a five-pointed white star on a gray latte stone (a traditional foundation stone) in the center, surrounded by a *mwáár* or head lei (wreath)
meaning: blue stands for the Pacific Ocean, the star for the Commonwealth, and the latte stone and mwáár for Marianas culture; the mwáár is made from four kinds of flowers: flores mayo *(Plumeria)*, ylang-ylang or langilang *(Cananga odorata)*, angagha or peacock flower *(Caesalpinia pulcherrima)*, and teibwo or Pacific basil *(Ocimum tenuiflorum)*

National symbol(s): latte stone

National color(s): blue, white

National anthem(s): *title:* "Gi Talo Gi Halom Tasi" (In the Middle of the Sea)
"Satil Matawal Pacifico" (Carolinian)
lyrics/music: Jose S. PANGELINAN [Chamoru], David PETER [Carolinian]/Wilhelm GANZHOM
history: adopted 1996
title: "The Star-Spangled Banner"
lyrics/music: Francis Scott KEY/John Stafford SMITH
history: official anthem, as a US commonwealth

ECONOMY

Economic overview: US Pacific island commonwealth economy; growing Chinese and Korean tourist destination; hit hard by 2018 typhoon; dependent on energy imports; exempt from some US labor and immigration laws; longstanding garment production

Real GDP (purchasing power parity): $1.242 billion (2016 est.)
$933 million (2015 est.)
$845 million (2014 est.)
note: GDP estimate includes US subsidy; data are in 2013 dollars
comparison ranking: 205

Real GDP growth rate: 16.6% (2022 est.)
5% (2021 est.)
-29.1% (2020 est.)
note: annual GDP % growth based on constant local currency
comparison ranking: 2

GDP (official exchange rate): $1.096 billion (2022 est.)
note: data in current dollars at official exchange rate
Agricultural products: vegetables and melons, fruits and nuts; ornamental plants; livestock, poultry, eggs; fish and aquaculture products
Industries: tourism, banking, construction, fishing, handicrafts, other services
Budget: *revenues:* $389.6 million (2016 est.)
expenditures: $344 million (2015 est.)
Exports: $244 million (2022 est.)
$55 million (2021 est.)
$128 million (2020 est.)
note: GDP expenditure basis - exports of goods and services in current dollars
comparison ranking: 200
Exports - partners: Sweden 21%, Singapore 20%, Hong Kong 12%, UK 8%, India 7% (2023)
note: top five export partners based on percentage share of exports
Exports - commodities: scrap iron, refined petroleum, scrap copper, hydraulic engines, integrated circuits (2021)
top five export commodities based on value in dollars
Imports: $777 million (2022 est.)
$666 million (2021 est.)
$556 million (2020 est.)
note: GDP expenditure basis - imports of goods and services in current dollars
comparison ranking: 193
Imports - partners: Singapore 63%, Japan 12%, Hong Kong 8%, Taiwan 4%, Philippines 3% (2023)
note: top five import partners based on percentage share of imports
Imports - commodities: refined petroleum, cars, jewelry, trunks and cases, flavored water (2023)
Exchange rates: the US dollar is used

ENERGY

Electricity access: *electrification - total population:* 100% (2022 est.)

COMMUNICATIONS

Telephones - fixed lines: *total subscriptions:* 20,000 (2021 est.)
subscriptions per 100 inhabitants: 42 (2022 est.)
comparison ranking: total subscriptions 172
Telephones - mobile cellular: *total subscriptions:* 20,474 (2004 est.)
subscriptions per 100 inhabitants: 28 (2004)
comparison ranking: total subscriptions 216
Broadcast media: 1 TV station on Saipan; multi-channel cable TV services are available on Saipan; 9 licensed radio stations (2009)
Internet country code: .mp
Internet users: *percent of population:* 25.1% (2021 est.)

TRANSPORTATION

Airports: 4 (2025)
comparison ranking: 183
Heliports: 7 (2025)
comparison ranking: 89
Ports: *total ports:* 3 (2024)
large: 0
medium: 0
small: 1
very small: 2
ports with oil terminals: 1
key ports: Rota, Saipan, Tinian

MILITARY AND SECURITY

Military - note: defense is the responsibility of the US

NORWAY

INTRODUCTION

Background: Two centuries of Viking raids into Europe tapered off after King Olav TRYGGVASON adopted Christianity in 994; conversion of the Norwegian kingdom occurred over the next several decades. In 1397, Norway was absorbed into a union with Denmark that lasted more than four centuries. In 1814, Norwegians resisted the cession of their country to Sweden and adopted a new constitution. Sweden then invaded Norway but agreed to let Norway keep its constitution in return for accepting the union under a Swedish king. Rising nationalism throughout the 19th century led to a 1905 referendum granting Norway independence. Norway remained neutral in World War I and proclaimed its neutrality at the outset of World War II, but Nazi Germany nonetheless occupied the country for five years (1940-45). In 1949, Norway abandoned neutrality and became a member of NATO. Discovery of oil and gas in adjacent waters in the late 1960s boosted Norway's economic fortunes. In referenda held in 1972 and 1994, Norway rejected joining the EU. Key domestic issues include immigration and integration of ethnic minorities, maintaining the country's extensive social safety net with an aging population, and preserving economic competitiveness.

GEOGRAPHY

Location: Northern Europe, bordering the North Sea and the North Atlantic Ocean, west of Sweden
Geographic coordinates: 62 00 N, 10 00 E
Map references: Europe
Area: *total:* 323,802 sq km
land: 304,282 sq km
water: 19,520 sq km
comparison ranking: total 69
Area - comparative: slightly larger than twice the size of Georgia; slightly larger than New Mexico
Land boundaries: *total:* 2,566 km
border countries (3): Finland 709 km; Sweden 1,666 km; Russia 191 km
Coastline: 25,148 km
note: includes the mainland at 2,650 km, as well as long fjords, numerous small islands, and minor indentations at 22,498 km; length of island coastlines is 58,133 km
Maritime claims: *territorial sea:* 12 nm
contiguous zone: 10 nm
exclusive economic zone: 200 nm
continental shelf: 200 nm
Climate: temperate along coast, modified by North Atlantic Current; colder interior with increased precipitation and colder summers; rainy year-round on west coast
Terrain: glaciated; mostly high plateaus and rugged mountains broken by fertile valleys; small, scattered plains; coastline deeply indented by fjords; arctic tundra in north
Elevation: *highest point:* Galdhopiggen 2,469 m
lowest point: Norwegian Sea 0 m
mean elevation: 460 m
Natural resources: petroleum, natural gas, iron ore, copper, lead, zinc, titanium, pyrites, nickel, fish, timber, hydropower
Land use: *agricultural land:* 2.7% (2022 est.)
arable land: 2.2% (2022 est.)
permanent crops: 0% (2022 est.)
permanent pasture: 0.5% (2022 est.)
forest: 33.5% (2022 est.)
other: 63.8% (2022 est.)
Irrigated land: 337 sq km (2016)

Population distribution: most people live in the south; population clusters are found along the North Sea coast in the southwest and Skaggerak in the southeast; the interior areas of the north remain sparsely populated

Natural hazards: rockslides, avalanches

volcanism: Beerenberg (2,227 m) on Jan Mayen Island in the Norwegian Sea is the country's only active volcano

Geography - note: about two-thirds mountains; some 50,000 islands off its much-indented coastline; strategic location adjacent to sea lanes and air routes in North Atlantic; one of the most rugged and longest coastlines in the world

PEOPLE AND SOCIETY

Population: *total:* 5,509,733 (2024 est.)
male: 2,780,972
female: 2,728,761
comparison rankings: total 120; male 118; female 120

Nationality: *noun:* Norwegian(s)
adjective: Norwegian

Ethnic groups: Norwegian 81.5% (includes about 60,000 Sami), other European 8.9%, other 9.6% (2021 est.)

Languages: Bokmal Norwegian (official), Nynorsk Norwegian (official), small Sami- and Finnish-speaking minorities
major-language sample(s):
Verdens Faktabok, den essensielle kilden for grunnleggende informasjon. (Norwegian)
note: Sami has three dialects (Lule, North Sami, and South Sami) and is an official language in nine municipalities in the northernmost counties of Finnmark, Nordland, and Troms

Religions: Church of Norway (Evangelical Lutheran - official) 67.5%, Muslim 3.1%, Roman Catholic 3.1%, other Christian 3.8%, other 2.6%, unspecified 19.9% (2021 est.)

Age structure: *0-14 years:* 16.3% (male 461,979/female 438,243)
15-64 years: 64.5% (male 1,820,692/female 1,734,818)
65 years and over: 19.1% (2024 est.) (male 498,301/female 555,700)

Dependency ratios: *total dependency ratio:* 55 (2024 est.)
youth dependency ratio: 25.3 (2024 est.)
elderly dependency ratio: 29.6 (2024 est.)
potential support ratio: 3.4 (2024 est.)
note: data include Svalbard and Jan Mayen Islands

Median age: *total:* 40.8 years (2024 est.)
male: 40.1 years
female: 41.5 years
comparison ranking: total 57

Population growth rate: 0.59% (2024 est.)
comparison ranking: 142

Birth rate: 10.4 births/1,000 population (2024 est.)
comparison ranking: 179

Death rate: 8.4 deaths/1,000 population (2024 est.)
comparison ranking: 74

Net migration rate: 3.9 migrant(s)/1,000 population (2024 est.)
comparison ranking: 28

Population distribution: most people live in the south; population clusters are found along the North Sea coast in the southwest and Skaggerak in the southeast; the interior areas of the north remain sparsely populated

Urbanization: *urban population:* 84% of total population (2023)
rate of urbanization: 1.32% annual rate of change (2020-25 est.)
note: data include Svalbard and Jan Mayen Islands

Major urban areas - population: 1.086 million OSLO (capital) (2023)

Sex ratio: *at birth:* 1.05 male(s)/female
0-14 years: 1.05 male(s)/female
15-64 years: 1.05 male(s)/female
65 years and over: 0.9 male(s)/female
total population: 1.02 male(s)/female (2024 est.)

Mother's mean age at first birth
29.8 years (2020 est.)
note: data is calculated based on actual age at first births

Maternal mortality ratio: 1 deaths/100,000 live births (2023 est.)
comparison ranking: 195

Infant mortality rate: *total:* 1.8 deaths/1,000 live births (2024 est.)
male: 2.1 deaths/1,000 live births
female: 1.5 deaths/1,000 live births
comparison ranking: total 223

Life expectancy at birth: *total population:* 82.9 years (2024 est.)
male: 81.3 years
female: 84.6 years
comparison ranking: total population 22

Total fertility rate: 1.57 children born/woman (2024 est.)
comparison ranking: 191

Gross reproduction rate: 0.77 (2024 est.)

Drinking water source: *improved: urban:* 100% of population (2022 est.)
rural: 100% of population (2022 est.)
total: 100% of population (2022 est.)
unimproved: urban: 0% of population (2022 est.)
rural: 0% of population (2022 est.)
total: 0% of population (2022 est.)

Health expenditure: 8.1% of GDP (2022)
17.8% of national budget (2022 est.)

Physician density: 4.98 physicians/1,000 population (2023)

Hospital bed density: 3.4 beds/1,000 population (2020 est.)

Sanitation facility access: *improved: urban:* 100% of population (2022 est.)
rural: 100% of population (2022 est.)
total: 100% of population (2022 est.)
unimproved: urban: 0% of population (2022 est.)
rural: 0% of population (2022 est.)
total: 0% of population (2022 est.)

Obesity - adult prevalence rate: 23.1% (2016)
comparison ranking: 67

Alcohol consumption per capita: *total:* 6.05 liters of pure alcohol (2019 est.)
beer: 2.63 liters of pure alcohol (2019 est.)
wine: 2.23 liters of pure alcohol (2019 est.)
spirits: 1 liters of pure alcohol (2019 est.)
other alcohols: 0.19 liters of pure alcohol (2019 est.)
comparison ranking: total 70

Tobacco use: *total:* 12% (2025 est.)
male: 12.6% (2025 est.)
female: 11.3% (2025 est.)
comparison ranking: total 112

Currently married women (ages 15-49): 50.2% (2023 est.)

Child marriage: *women married by age 15:* 0% (2022)
women married by age 18: 0% (2022)

Education expenditure: 4% of GDP (2022 est.)
10.1% national budget (2022 est.)
comparison ranking: Education expenditure (% GDP) 111

School life expectancy (primary to tertiary education): *total:* 19 years (2023 est.)
male: 18 years (2023 est.)
female: 20 years (2023 est.)

ENVIRONMENT

Environmental issues: water pollution; acid rain damaging forests and affecting lakes and fish stocks; air pollution from vehicle emissions

International environmental agreements: *party to:* Air Pollution, Air Pollution-Heavy Metals, Air Pollution-Multi-effect Protocol, Air Pollution-Nitrogen Oxides, Air Pollution-Persistent Organic Pollutants, Air Pollution-Sulphur 85, Air Pollution-Sulphur 94, Air Pollution-Volatile Organic Compounds, Antarctic- Environmental Protection, Antarctic-Marine Living Resources, Antarctic Seals, Antarctic Treaty, Biodiversity, Climate Change, Climate Change-Kyoto Protocol, Climate Change-Paris Agreement, Comprehensive Nuclear Test Ban, Desertification, Endangered Species, Environmental Modification, Hazardous Wastes, Law of the Sea, Marine Dumping-London Convention, Marine Dumping-London Protocol, Nuclear Test Ban, Ozone Layer Protection, Ship Pollution, Tropical Timber 2006, Wetlands, Whaling
signed, but not ratified: none of the selected agreements

Climate: temperate along coast, modified by North Atlantic Current; colder interior with increased precipitation and colder summers; rainy year-round on west coast

Urbanization: *urban population:* 84% of total population (2023)
rate of urbanization: 1.32% annual rate of change (2020-25 est.)
note: data include Svalbard and Jan Mayen Islands

Carbon dioxide emissions: 38.535 million metric tonnes of CO_2 (2023 est.)
from coal and metallurgical coke: 2.929 million metric tonnes of CO_2 (2023 est.)
from petroleum and other liquids: 25.576 million metric tonnes of CO_2 (2023 est.)
from consumed natural gas: 10.029 million metric tonnes of CO_2 (2023 est.)
comparison ranking: total emissions 64

Particulate matter emissions: 7 micrograms per cubic meter (2019 est.)

Methane emissions: *energy:* 31 kt (2022-2024 est.)
agriculture: 99.8 kt (2019-2021 est.)
waste: 33 kt (2019-2021 est.)
other: 6.2 kt (2019-2021 est.)

Waste and recycling: *municipal solid waste generated annually:* 4.15 million tons (2024 est.)
percent of municipal solid waste recycled: 35.3% (2022 est.)

Total water withdrawal: *municipal:* 773.41 million cubic meters (2022 est.)
industrial: 1.071 billion cubic meters (2022 est.)
agricultural: 844.9 million cubic meters (2022 est.)

Total renewable water resources: 393 billion cubic meters (2022 est.)

Geoparks: *total global geoparks and regional networks:* 5 (2025)
global geoparks and regional networks: Gea Norvegica; Fjord Coast; Magma; Sunnhordland; Trollfjell (2025)

GOVERNMENT

Country name: *conventional long form:* Kingdom of Norway
conventional short form: Norway
local long form: Kongeriket Norge
local short form: Norge
etymology: derives from the Old Norse words *norre* and *vegr*, meaning "northern way," and refers to the long coastline of western Norway

Government type: parliamentary constitutional monarchy

Capital: *name:* Oslo
geographic coordinates: 59 55 N, 10 45 E
time difference: UTC+1 (6 hours ahead of Washington, DC, during Standard Time)
daylight saving time: +1hr, begins last Sunday in March; ends last Sunday in October
etymology: the name may derive from the Old Norwegian word os, meaning "estuary" and referring to the city's location on a fjord; alternatively, the name may come from As, a Scandinavian god, and Lo, a nearby river

Administrative divisions: 12 counties *(fylker,* singular - *fylke);* Agder, Innlandet, More og Romsdal, Nordland, Oslo, Rogaland, Romsdal, Troms og Finnmark, Trondelag, Vestfold og Telemark, Vestland, Viken (2024)

Dependent areas: Bouvet Island, Jan Mayen, Svalbard (3)

Legal system: mixed system of civil, common, and customary law; Supreme Court can advise on legislative acts

Constitution: *history:* drafted spring 1814, adopted 16 May 1814, signed by Constituent Assembly 17 May 1814
amendment process: proposals submitted by members of Parliament or by the government within the first three years of Parliament's four-year term; passage requires two-thirds majority vote of a two-thirds quorum in the next elected Parliament

International law organization participation: accepts compulsory ICJ jurisdiction with reservations; accepts ICCt jurisdiction

Citizenship: *citizenship by birth:* no
citizenship by descent only: at least one parent must be a citizen of Norway
dual citizenship recognized: yes
residency requirement for naturalization: 7 years

Suffrage: 18 years of age; universal

Executive branch: *chief of state:* King HARALD V (since 17 January 1991)
head of government: Prime Minister Jonas Gahr STORE (since 14 October 2021)
cabinet: Council of State appointed by the monarch, approved by Parliament
election/appointment process: the monarchy is hereditary; following legislative elections, the monarch usually appoints the leader of the majority party or majority coalition as prime minister, with the approval of Parliament

Legislative branch: *legislature name:* Parliament (Stortinget)
legislative structure: unicameral
number of seats: 169 (all directly elected)
electoral system: proportional representation
scope of elections: full renewal
term in office: 4 years
most recent election date: 9/13/2021
parties elected and seats per party: Labour Party (48); Conservative Party (36); Center Party (28); Progress Party (21); Socialist Left Party (13); Other (23)
percentage of women in chamber: 44.4%
expected date of next election: September 2025

Judicial branch: *highest court(s):* Supreme Court or Hoyesterett (consists of the chief justice and 18 associate justices)
judge selection and term of office: justices appointed by the monarch (King in Council) on the recommendation of the Judicial Appointments Board; justices can serve until mandatory retirement at age 70
subordinate courts: Courts of Appeal or Lagmennsrett; regional and district courts; Conciliation Boards; ordinary and special courts
note: in addition to professionally trained judges, elected lay judges sit on the bench with professional judges in the Courts of Appeal and district courts

Political parties: Center Party or Sp
Christian Democratic Party or KrF
Conservative Party or H
Green Party or MDG
Labor Party or Ap
Liberal Party or V
Patient Focus or PF
Progress Party or FrP
Red Party or R
Socialist Left Party or SV

Diplomatic representation in the US: *chief of mission:* Ambassador Anniken Scharning HUITFELDT (since 18 September 2024)
chancery: 2720 34th Street NW, Washington, DC 20008
telephone: [1] (202) 333-6000
FAX: [1] (202) 469-3990
email address and website: emb.washington@mfa.no
https://www.norway.no/en/usa/
consulate(s) general: New York, San Francisco

Diplomatic representation from the US: *chief of mission:* Ambassador (vacant); Chargé d'Affaires Eric MEYER (since August 2024)
embassy: Morgedalsvegen 36, 0378 Oslo
mailing address: 5460 Oslo Place, Washington DC 20521-5460
telephone: [47] 21-30-85-40
FAX: [47] 22-56-27-51
email address and website: OsloACS@state.gov
https://no.usembassy.gov/

International organization participation: ADB (nonregional member), AfDB (nonregional member), Arctic Council, Australia Group, BIS, CBSS, CD, CE, CERN, EAPC, EBRD, EFTA, EITI (implementing country), ESA, FAO, FATF, IADB, IAEA, IBRD, ICAO, ICC (national committees), ICCt, ICRM, IDA, IEA, IFAD, IFC, IFRCS, IGAD (partners), IHO, ILO, IMF, IMO, IMSO, Interpol, IOC, IOM, IPU, ISO, ITSO, ITU, ITUC (NGOs), MIGA, NATO, NC, NEA, NIB, NSG, OAS (observer), OECD, OPCW, OSCE, Paris Club, PCA, Schengen Convention, UN, UNCTAD, UNESCO, UNHCR, UNIDO, UNITAR, UNMISS, UNOOSA, UNRWA, UNTSO, UNWTO, UPU, Wassenaar Arrangement, WCO, WHO, WIPO, WMO, WTO, ZC

Independence: 7 June 1905 (union with Sweden declared dissolved); 26 October 1905 (Sweden agreed to the repeal of the union); notable earlier dates: ca. 872 (traditional unification of Norwegian kingdoms by HARALD Fairhair); 1397 (Kalmar Union of Denmark, Norway, and Sweden); 1524 (Denmark-Norway); 17 May 1814 (Norwegian constitution adopted); 4 November 1814 (Sweden-Norway union confirmed)

National holiday: Constitution Day, 17 May (1814)

Flag: *description:* red with a blue cross outlined in white that extends to the edges of the flag; the the cross is shifted to the left side in the style of the Dannebrog (Danish flag)
meaning: the colors represent Norway's past political unions with Denmark (red and white) and Sweden (blue)

National symbol(s): lion

National color(s): red, white, blue

National anthem(s): *title:* "Ja, vi elsker dette landet" (Yes, We Love This Country)
lyrics/music: Bjornstjerne BJORNSON/Rikard NORDRAAK
history: in use since 1864, but never officially adopted
title: "Kongesangen" (Song of the King)
lyrics/music: Gustav JENSEN
history: royal anthem; uses the tune of "God Save the King," the United Kingdom's anthem
note: since 2011, the patriotic song "Mitt lille land" has been called a new national anthem and is sometimes performed at patriotic events, but it is not used as often as "Ja, vi elsker dette landet"

National heritage: *total World Heritage Sites:* 8 (7 cultural, 1 natural)
selected World Heritage Site locales: Bryggen (c); Urnes Stave Church (c); Røros Mining Town and the Circumference (c); Rock Art of Alta (c); Vegaøyan – The Vega Archipelago (c); Struve Geodetic Arc (c); West Norwegian Fjords – Geirangerfjord and Nærøyfjord (n); Rjukan-Notodden Industrial Heritage Site (c)

ECONOMY

Economic overview: high-income, non-EU economy with trade links via European Economic Area (EEA); key role in European energy security as leader in oil, gas, and electricity exports; major fishing, forestry, and oil(?) extraction industries; oil sovereign fund supports generous welfare system; low unemployment; inflation moderating but remains above target level

Real GDP (purchasing power parity): $507.68 billion (2024 est.)
$497.236 billion (2023 est.)
$496.877 billion (2022 est.)
note: data in 2021 dollars
comparison ranking: 49

Real GDP growth rate: 2.1% (2024 est.)
0.1% (2023 est.)
3.2% (2022 est.)
note: annual GDP % growth based on constant local currency
comparison ranking: 144

Real GDP per capita: $91,100 (2024 est.)
$90,100 (2023 est.)
$91,100 (2022 est.)
note: data in 2021 dollars
comparison ranking: 9

GDP (official exchange rate): $483.727 billion (2024 est.)
note: data in current dollars at official exchange rate

Inflation rate (consumer prices): 3.1% (2024 est.)
5.5% (2023 est.)
5.8% (2022 est.)
note: annual % change based on consumer prices
comparison ranking: 98

GDP - composition, by sector of origin: *agriculture:* 2% (2024 est.)
industry: 37% (2024 est.)
services: 51.8% (2024 est.)
note: figures may not total 100% due to non-allocated consumption not captured in sector-reported data
comparison rankings: agriculture 150; industry 31; services 136

GDP - composition, by end use: *household consumption:* 37.7% (2023 est.)
government consumption: 22% (2023 est.)
investment in fixed capital: 21.7% (2023 est.)
investment in inventories: 2.6% (2023 est.)
exports of goods and services: 47.9% (2023 est.)
imports of goods and services: -32.5% (2023 est.)
note: figures may not total 100% due to rounding or gaps in data collection

Agricultural products: milk, barley, potatoes, oats, wheat, pork, chicken, beef, eggs, carrots/turnips (2023)
note: top ten agricultural products based on tonnage

Industries: petroleum and gas, shipping, fishing, aquaculture, food processing, shipbuilding, pulp and paper products, metals, chemicals, timber, mining, textiles

Industrial production growth rate: 2.4% (2024 est.)
note: annual % change in industrial value added based on constant local currency
comparison ranking: 91

Labor force: 3.042 million (2024 est.)
note: number of people ages 15 or older who are employed or seeking work
comparison ranking: 110

Unemployment rate: 4% (2024 est.)
3.6% (2023 est.)
3.3% (2022 est.)
note: % of labor force seeking employment
comparison ranking: 64

Youth unemployment rate (ages 15-24): *total:* 11.6% (2024 est.)
male: 12.3% (2024 est.)
female: 10.8% (2024 est.)
note: % of labor force ages 15-24 seeking employment
comparison ranking: total 109

Population below poverty line: 12.2% (2021 est.)
note: % of population with income below national poverty line
Gini Index coefficient - distribution of family income 26.9 (2022 est.)
note: index (0-100) of income distribution; higher values represent greater inequality
comparison ranking: 136

Average household expenditures: *on food:* 11.7% of household expenditures (2023 est.)
on alcohol and tobacco: 3.9% of household expenditures (2023 est.)

Household income or consumption by percentage share: *lowest 10%:* 3.5% (2022 est.)
highest 10%: 22% (2022 est.)
note: % share of income accruing to lowest and highest 10% of population

Remittances: 0.1% of GDP (2024 est.)
0.1% of GDP (2023 est.)
0.1% of GDP (2022 est.)
note: personal transfers and compensation between resident and non-resident individuals/households/entities

Budget: *revenues:* $261.945 billion (2023 est.)
expenditures: $178.156 billion (2023 est.)
note: central government revenues (excluding grants) and expenditures converted to US dollars at average official exchange rate for year indicated

Public debt: 36.5% of GDP (2017 est.)
note: data cover general government debt and include debt instruments issued (or owned) by government entities other than the treasury; the data exclude treasury debt held by foreign entities; the data exclude debt issued by subnational entities, as well as intragovernmental debt; intragovernmental debt consists of treasury borrowings from surpluses in the social funds, such as for retirement, medical care, and unemployment; debt instruments for the social funds are not sold at public auctions
comparison ranking: 146

Taxes and other revenues: 27.1% (of GDP) (2023 est.)
note: central government tax revenue as a % of GDP
comparison ranking: 9

Current account balance: $82.511 billion (2024 est.)
$84.104 billion (2023 est.)
$170.714 billion (2022 est.)
note: balance of payments - net trade and primary/secondary income in current dollars
comparison ranking: 8

Exports: $229.205 billion (2024 est.)
$230.882 billion (2023 est.)
$323.875 billion (2022 est.)
note: balance of payments - exports of goods and services in current dollars
comparison ranking: 35

Exports - partners: Germany 18%, UK 17%, Sweden 9%, Denmark 7%, Netherlands 6% (2023)
note: top five export partners based on percentage share of exports

Exports - commodities: natural gas, crude petroleum, fish, refined petroleum, aluminum (2023)
note: top five export commodities based on value in dollars

Imports: $162.467 billion (2024 est.)
$156.11 billion (2023 est.)
$160.649 billion (2022 est.)
note: balance of payments - imports of goods and services in current dollars
comparison ranking: 35

Imports - partners: Sweden 11%, Germany 11%, China 11%, USA 7%, Netherlands 5% (2023)
note: top five import partners based on percentage share of imports

Imports - commodities: cars, refined petroleum, ships, nickel, garments (2023)
note: top five import commodities based on value in dollars

Reserves of foreign exchange and gold: $81.242 billion (2024 est.)
$80.459 billion (2023 est.)
$72.077 billion (2022 est.)
note: holdings of gold (year-end prices)/foreign exchange/special drawing rights in current dollars
comparison ranking: 33

Exchange rates: Norwegian kroner (NOK) per US dollar -

Exchange rates: 10.746 (2024 est.)
10.563 (2023 est.)
9.614 (2022 est.)
8.59 (2021 est.)
9.416 (2020 est.)

ENERGY

Electricity access: *electrification - total population:* 100% (2022 est.)

Electricity: *installed generating capacity:* 41.1 million kW (2023 est.)
consumption: 127.335 billion kWh (2023 est.)
exports: 30.978 billion kWh (2023 est.)
imports: 13.232 billion kWh (2023 est.)
transmission/distribution losses: 7.025 billion kWh (2023 est.)
comparison rankings: installed generating capacity 32; consumption 29; exports 7; imports 18; transmission/distribution losses 170

Electricity generation sources: *fossil fuels:* 1.2% of total installed capacity (2023 est.)
solar: 0.2% of total installed capacity (2023 est.)
wind: 9.2% of total installed capacity (2023 est.)
hydroelectricity: 89.1% of total installed capacity (2023 est.)
biomass and waste: 0.2% of total installed capacity (2023 est.)

Coal: *production:* 120,000 metric tons (2023 est.)
consumption: 1.096 million metric tons (2023 est.)
exports: 60,000 metric tons (2023 est.)
imports: 1.042 million metric tons (2023 est.)
proven reserves: 2 million metric tons (2023 est.)

Petroleum: *total petroleum production:* 2.02 million bbl/day (2023 est.)
refined petroleum consumption: 229,000 bbl/day (2024 est.)
crude oil estimated reserves: 8.122 billion barrels (2021 est.)

Natural gas: *production:* 121.637 billion cubic meters (2023 est.)
consumption: 5.082 billion cubic meters (2023 est.)
exports: 117.597 billion cubic meters (2023 est.)
imports: 104.744 million cubic meters (2023 est.)
proven reserves: 1.544 trillion cubic meters (2021 est.)

Energy consumption per capita: 206.961 million Btu/person (2023 est.)
comparison ranking: 17

COMMUNICATIONS

Telephones - fixed lines: *total subscriptions:* 145,000 (2022 est.)
subscriptions per 100 inhabitants: 3 (2022 est.)
comparison ranking: total subscriptions 126

Telephones - mobile cellular: *total subscriptions:* 6.09 million (2022 est.)
subscriptions per 100 inhabitants: 111 (2022 est.)
comparison ranking: total subscriptions 119

Broadcast media: state-owned public radio and TV broadcaster operates 3 nationwide TV stations, 3 nationwide radio stations, and 16 regional radio stations; roughly a dozen privately owned TV stations broadcast nationally, and another 25 locally; nearly 75% of households have access to multichannel cable or satellite TV; 2 privately owned radio stations broadcast nationwide, with another 240 local stations; Norway was the first country to phase out FM radio in favor of Digital Audio Broadcasting (DAB) (2019)

Internet country code: .no

Internet users: *percent of population:* 99% (2023 est.)

Broadband - fixed subscriptions: *total:* 2.49 million (2022 est.)
subscriptions per 100 inhabitants: 46 (2022 est.)
comparison ranking: total 55

TRANSPORTATION

Civil aircraft registration country code prefix: LN

Airports: 146 (2025)
comparison ranking: 36

Heliports: 113 (2025)
comparison ranking: 23

Railways: *total:* 3,848 km (2020) 2,482 km electrified

Merchant marine: *total:* 1,720 (2022)
by type: bulk carrier 109, container ship 1, general cargo 274, oil tanker 95, other 1,241
comparison ranking: total 17

Ports: *total ports:* 141 (2024)
large: 1
medium: 10
small: 34
very small: 90
size unknown: 6
ports with oil terminals: 54
key ports: Bergen, Drammen, Hammerfest, Harstad, Horten, Karsto, Mongstad, Oslo, Stavanger, Tromso, Trondheim

MILITARY AND SECURITY

Military and security forces: Norwegian Armed Forces (Forsvaret or "the Defense"): Norwegian Army (Haeren), Royal Norwegian Navy (Kongelige Norske Sjoeforsvaret; includes Coastal Rangers and Coast Guard (Kystvakt)), Royal Norwegian Air Force (Kongelige Norske Luftforsvaret), Home Guard (Heimevernet, HV) (2025)
note: the Norwegian Police Service is under the Ministry of Justice and Public Security

Military expenditures: 3.4% of GDP (2025 est.)
2.3% of GDP (2024 est.)
1.8% of GDP (2023 est.)
1.5% of GDP (2022 est.)
1.7% of GDP (2021 est.)

Military and security service personnel strengths: approximately 27,000 active military personnel; approximately 40,000 Home Guard (2025)

Military equipment inventories and acquisitions: the military's inventory includes a mix of modern, imported Western European and US, as well as domestically produced weapons systems and equipment; in 2024, the Norwegian Government announced a new long-term defense plan which would double defense spending by the mid-2030s with priorities placed in such areas as the acquisition of air defenses and naval capabilities; Norway has a defense industry with a focus in niche capabilities and participates in joint development and production of weapons systems with other European countries (2025)

Military service age and obligation: 19-35 years of age for selective compulsory military service for men and women; 17 years of age for male volunteers; 18 years of age for women volunteers; 12-19 month service obligation; conscripts first serve 12 months between the ages of 19 and 28, and then up to 4-5 refresher training periods until age 35, 44, 55, or 60 depending on rank and function (2024)
note 1: Norway has had compulsory military service since 1907; individuals conscripted each year are selected from a larger cohort who are evaluated through online assessments and physical tests
note 2: Norway was the first NATO country to allow women to serve in all combat arms branches of the military (1985); it also has an all-female special operations unit known as Jegertroppen (The Hunter Troop), which was established in 2014; as of 2023, women comprised about 20% of the military's full-time personnel
note 3: beginning in 1995, the military began offering Icelandic citizens the opportunity to apply for admission to officer schools in Norway with an associated education and service contract under special reasons and based on recommendations from Icelandic authorities; as early as 1996, Norway and Iceland entered into a cooperation agreement on the voluntary participation of Icelandic personnel in Norwegian force contributions in foreign operations

Military deployments: around 100 Lithuania (NATO); Norway also deploys air and naval assets in support of other NATO operations (2025)

Military - note: the Norwegian Armed Forces (Forsvaret) are responsible for protecting Norway and its allies, including monitoring Norway's airspace, digital, land, and maritime areas, maintaining the country's borders and sovereignty, contributing to NATO and UN missions, and providing support to civil society, such as assisting the police, search and rescue, and maritime counterterrorism efforts; the military's territorial and sovereignty defense missions are complicated by Norway's vast sea areas, numerous islands, long and winding fjords, and difficult and mountainous terrain; a key area of emphasis is its far northern border with Russia
Norway is one of the original members of NATO, and the Alliance is a key component of Norway's defense policy; the Forsvaret participates in NATO exercises, missions, and operations, including air policing of NATO territory, NATO's Enhanced Forward Presence mission in the Baltic States and Eastern Europe, and standing naval missions, as well as operations in non-NATO areas, such as the Middle East
the Forsvaret also cooperates closely with the militaries of other Nordic countries through the Nordic Defense Cooperation (NORDEFCO; established 2009), which consists of Denmark, Finland, Iceland, Norway, and Sweden; Norway contributes to the UK-led Joint Expeditionary Force, a pool of high-readiness military forces from 10 Baltic and Scandinavian countries designed to respond to a wide range of contingencies in the High North, North Atlantic, and Baltic Sea regions; Norway has close military ties with the US, including rotational US military deployments and an agreement allowing for mutual defense activities and US military forces to access some Norwegian facilities
the Forsvaret's origins go back to the leidangen, defense forces which were established along the coastline in the 10th century to protect the Norwegian coast (2025)

SPACE

Space agency/agencies: the Norwegian Space Agency (NOSA, aka Norsk Romsenter; established 1987) (2025)

Space launch site(s): Andøya Space Center (Andøya Island; note - first operational spaceport in continental Europe) (2025)

Space program overview: has a broad and active space program coordinated with the European Space Agency (ESA) and the EU; jointly designs and builds satellites with foreign partners, including communications, remote sensing (RS), scientific, and navigational/positional; operates satellites; develops and launches sounding rockets; researches and produces a range of other space-related technologies, including satellite/space launch vehicle (SLV) and space station components, telescopes, and robotics; conducts solar and telecommunications research; participates in international space programs, such as the International Space Station; hosts training for Mars landing missions on the island of Svalbard; active member of the ESA and cooperates with a variety of foreign space agencies and industries, including those of Canada, ESA/EU member states, Japan, Russia, and the US; has an active and advanced space industry that cooperates with both the NOSA and foreign space programs and produces a variety of space-related products, from terminals for satellite communications and technologies for RS satellites to sensors for gamma radiation in deep space (2025)
note: further details about the key activities, programs, and milestones of the country's space program, as well as government spending estimates on the space sector, appear in the Space Programs reference guide

TRANSNATIONAL ISSUES

Refugees and internally displaced persons: *refugees:* 129,894 (2024 est.)
stateless persons: 1,621 (2024 est.)

OMAN

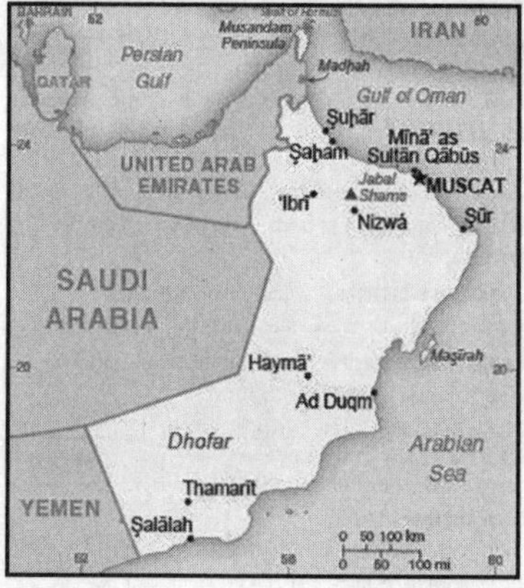

INTRODUCTION

Background: The inhabitants of the area of present-day Oman have long prospered from Indian Ocean trade. In the late 18th century, the nascent sultanate in Muscat signed the first in a series of friendship treaties with Britain. Over time, Oman's dependence on British political and military advisors increased, although the sultanate never became a British colony. In 1970, QABOOS bin Said Al Said overthrew his father and ruled as sultan for the next five decades. His extensive modernization program opened the country to the outside world. He prioritized strategic ties to the UK and US, and his moderate, independent foreign policy allowed Oman to maintain good relations with its neighbors and avoid external entanglements.

In 2011, the popular uprisings that swept the Middle East and North Africa inspired demonstrations in Oman that called for more jobs and economic benefits and an end to corruption. In response, QABOOS implemented economic and political reforms such as granting Oman's legislative body more power and authorizing direct elections for its lower house. Additionally, the sultan increased unemployment benefits and issued a royal directive mandating a national public- and private-sector job creation plan. As part of the government's efforts to decentralize authority and allow greater citizen participation in local governance, Oman successfully conducted its first municipal council elections in 2012. QABOOS, Oman's longest reigning monarch, died in 2020. His cousin, HAYTHAM bin Tariq Al Said, former Minister of Heritage and Culture, was sworn in as Oman's new sultan the same day.

GEOGRAPHY

Location: Middle East, bordering the Arabian Sea, Gulf of Oman, and Persian Gulf, between Yemen and the UAE

Geographic coordinates: 21 00 N, 57 00 E

Map references: Middle East

Area: *total:* 309,500 sq km
land: 309,500 sq km
water: 0 sq km
comparison ranking: total 72

Area - comparative: twice the size of Georgia

Land boundaries: *total:* 1,561 km
border countries (3): Saudi Arabia 658 km; UAE 609 km; Yemen 294 km

Coastline: 2,092 km

Maritime claims: *territorial sea:* 12 nm
contiguous zone: 24 nm
exclusive economic zone: 200 nm

Climate: dry desert; hot, humid along coast; hot, dry interior; strong southwest summer monsoon (May to September) in far south

Terrain: central desert plain, rugged mountains in north and south

Elevation: *highest point:* Jabal Shams 3,004 m
lowest point: Arabian Sea 0 m
mean elevation: 310 m

Natural resources: petroleum, copper, asbestos, some marble, limestone, chromium, gypsum, natural gas

Land use: *agricultural land:* 4.7% (2022 est.)
arable land: 0.3% (2022 est.)
permanent crops: 0.1% (2022 est.)
permanent pasture: 4.4% (2022 est.)
forest: 0% (2022 est.)
other: 95.3% (2022 est.)

Irrigated land: 1,162 sq km (2022)

Major aquifers: Arabian Aquifer System

Population distribution: the vast majority of the population is located in and around the Al Hagar Mountains in the north; another smaller cluster is found around the city of Salalah in the far south; most of the country remains sparsely populated

Natural hazards: summer winds often raise large sandstorms and dust storms in interior; periodic droughts

Geography - note: consists of Oman proper and two northern exclaves, Musandam and Al Madhah; the former is a peninsula that occupies a strategic location adjacent to the Strait of Hormuz

PEOPLE AND SOCIETY

Population: *total:* 3,901,992 (2024 est.)
male: 2,096,126
female: 1,805,866
comparison rankings: total 130; male 128; female 132

Nationality: *noun:* Omani(s)
adjective: Omani

Ethnic groups: Arab, Baluchi, South Asian (Indian, Pakistani, Sri Lankan, Bangladeshi), African

Languages: Arabic (official), English, Baluchi, Swahili, Urdu, Indian dialects
major-language sample(s):
يمكن الاستغناء عنه للمعلومات الأساسية
كتاب حقائق العالم، المصدر الذي لا
(Arabic)

Religions: Muslim 85.9%, Christian 6.4%, Hindu 5.7%, other and unaffiliated 2% (2020 est.)
note: Omani citizens represent approximately 56.4% of the population and are overwhelming Muslim (Ibadhi and Sunni sects each constitute about 45% and Shia about 5%); Christians, Hindus, and Buddhists account for roughly 5% of Omani citizens

Age structure: *0-14 years:* 29.8% (male 594,909/female 566,682)
15-64 years: 66.2% (male 1,428,141/female 1,155,438)
65 years and over: 4% (2024 est.) (male 73,076/female 83,746)

Dependency ratios: *total dependency ratio:* 51 (2024 est.)
youth dependency ratio: 45 (2024 est.)
elderly dependency ratio: 6.1 (2024 est.)
potential support ratio: 16.5 (2024 est.)

Median age: *total:* 27.3 years (2024 est.)
male: 28.1 years
female: 26.3 years
comparison ranking: total 159

Population growth rate: 1.75% (2024 est.)
comparison ranking: 52

Birth rate: 21.1 births/1,000 population (2024 est.)
comparison ranking: 62

Death rate: 3.2 deaths/1,000 population (2024 est.)
comparison ranking: 224

Net migration rate: -0.5 migrant(s)/1,000 population (2024 est.)
comparison ranking: 121

Population distribution: the vast majority of the population is located in and around the Al Hagar Mountains in the north; another smaller cluster is found around the city of Salalah in the far south; most of the country remains sparsely populated

Urbanization: *urban population:* 88.4% of total population (2023)
rate of urbanization: 2.32% annual rate of change (2020-25 est.)

Major urban areas - population: 1.650 million MUSCAT (capital) (2023)

Sex ratio: *at birth:* 1.05 male(s)/female
0-14 years: 1.05 male(s)/female
15-64 years: 1.24 male(s)/female
65 years and over: 0.87 male(s)/female
total population: 1.16 male(s)/female (2024 est.)

Maternal mortality ratio: 13 deaths/100,000 live births (2023 est.)
comparison ranking: 142

Infant mortality rate: *total:* 13.9 deaths/1,000 live births (2024 est.)
male: 15.1 deaths/1,000 live births
female: 12.6 deaths/1,000 live births
comparison ranking: total 100

Life expectancy at birth: *total population:* 77.4 years (2024 est.)
male: 75.5 years
female: 79.4 years
comparison ranking: total population 91

Total fertility rate: 2.64 children born/woman (2024 est.)
comparison ranking: 64

Gross reproduction rate: 1.29 (2024 est.)

Drinking water source: *improved: urban:* 94.7% of population (2022 est.)
rural: 76.3% of population (2022 est.)
total: 92.4% of population (2022 est.)
unimproved: urban: 5.3% of population (2022 est.)
rural: 23.7% of population (2022 est.)
total: 7.6% of population (2022 est.)

Health expenditure: 4.4% of GDP (2021)
8.3% of national budget (2022 est.)
Physician density: 1.99 physicians/1,000 population (2022)
Hospital bed density: 1.2 beds/1,000 population (2020 est.)
Sanitation facility access: *improved: urban:* 100% of population (2022 est.)
rural: 100% of population (2022 est.)
total: 100% of population (2022 est.)
unimproved: urban: 0% of population (2022 est.)
rural: 0% of population (2022 est.)
total: 0% of population (2022 est.)
Obesity - adult prevalence rate: 27% (2016)
comparison ranking: 39
Alcohol consumption per capita: *total:* 0.47 liters of pure alcohol (2019 est.)
beer: 0.17 liters of pure alcohol (2019 est.)
wine: 0.02 liters of pure alcohol (2019 est.)
spirits: 0.29 liters of pure alcohol (2019 est.)
other alcohols: 0 liters of pure alcohol (2019 est.)
comparison ranking: total 164
Tobacco use: *total:* 11.6% (2025 est.)
male: 17.9% (2025 est.)
female: 0.4% (2025 est.)
comparison ranking: total 117
Children under the age of 5 years underweight: 11.2% (2016/17)
comparison ranking: 47
Currently married women (ages 15-49): 56.4% (2023 est.)
Education expenditure: 4.2% of GDP (2022 est.)
14.2% national budget (2022 est.)
comparison ranking: Education expenditure (% GDP) 96
Literacy: *total population:* 97% (2022 est.)
male: 99% (2022 est.)
female: 95% (2022 est.)
School life expectancy (primary to tertiary education): *total:* 13 years (2021 est.)
male: 13 years (2021 est.)
female: 14 years (2021 est.)

ENVIRONMENT

Environmental issues: limited natural freshwater resources; high levels of soil and water salinity in the coastal plains; beach pollution from oil spills; industrial effluents in the water table and aquifers; desertification due to high winds driving desert sand into arable lands
International environmental agreements: *party to:* Biodiversity, Climate Change, Climate Change-Kyoto Protocol, Climate Change-Paris Agreement, Comprehensive Nuclear Test Ban, Desertification, Endangered Species, Hazardous Wastes, Law of the Sea, Marine Dumping-London Convention, Ozone Layer Protection, Ship Pollution, Wetlands, Whaling
signed, but not ratified: none of the selected agreements
Climate: dry desert; hot, humid along coast; hot, dry interior; strong southwest summer monsoon (May to September) in far south
Urbanization: *urban population:* 88.4% of total population (2023)
rate of urbanization: 2.32% annual rate of change (2020-25 est.)
Carbon dioxide emissions: 84.073 million metric tonnes of CO_2 (2023 est.)
from coal and metallurgical coke: 661,000 metric tonnes of CO_2 (2023 est.)
from petroleum and other liquids: 28.611 million metric tonnes of CO_2 (2023 est.)
from consumed natural gas: 54.8 million metric tonnes of CO_2 (2023 est.)
comparison ranking: total emissions 45
Particulate matter emissions: 34.9 micrograms per cubic meter (2019 est.)
Methane emissions: *energy:* 673.6 kt (2022-2024 est.)
agriculture: 36.8 kt (2019-2021 est.)
waste: 62.4 kt (2019-2021 est.)
other: 9.9 kt (2019-2021 est.)
Waste and recycling: *municipal solid waste generated annually:* 3.308 million tons (2024 est.)
percent of municipal solid waste recycled: 13.9% (2022 est.)
Total water withdrawal: *municipal:* 130 million cubic meters (2022 est.)
industrial: 238 million cubic meters (2022 est.)
agricultural: 1.547 billion cubic meters (2022 est.)
Total renewable water resources: 1.4 billion cubic meters (2022 est.)

GOVERNMENT

Country name: *conventional long form:* Sultanate of Oman
conventional short form: Oman
local long form: Saltanat Uman
local short form: Uman
former: Sultanate of Muscat and Oman
etymology: the origin of the name is uncertain, but it may date back at least 2,000 years, with an "Omana" mentioned by Pliny the Elder (1st century A.D.) and an "Omanon" by Ptolemy (2nd century A.D.); it is said to derive from Oman ben Ibrahim al Khalil (Oman ben Kahtan), who founded the state
Government type: absolute monarchy
Capital: *name:* Muscat
geographic coordinates: 23 37 N, 58 35 E
time difference: UTC+4 (9 hours ahead of Washington, DC, during Standard Time)
etymology: the name derives from the Arabic name for the city, Masqat, which is said to mean "hidden" and refers to the range of hills that isolate the port city from the rest of the country
Administrative divisions: 11 governorates (*muhafazat*, singular - *muhafaza*); Ad Dakhiliyah, Al Buraymi, Al Wusta, Az Zahirah, Janub al Batinah (Al Batinah South), Janub ash Sharqiyah (Ash Sharqiyah South), Masqat (Muscat), Musandam, Shamal al Batinah (Al Batinah North), Shamal ash Sharqiyah (Ash Sharqiyah North), Zufar (Dhofar)
Legal system: mixed system of Anglo-Saxon law and Islamic law
Constitution: *history:* promulgated by royal decree 6 November 1996 (the Basic Law of the Sultanate of Oman serves as the constitution); amended by royal decree in 2011
amendment process: promulgated by the sultan or proposed by the Council of Oman and drafted by a technical committee as stipulated by royal decree and then promulgated through royal decree
International law organization participation: has not submitted an ICJ jurisdiction declaration; non-party state to the ICCt
Citizenship: *citizenship by birth:* no
citizenship by descent only: the father must be a citizen of Oman
dual citizenship recognized: no
residency requirement for naturalization: unknown
Suffrage: 21 years of age; universal
note: members of the military and security forces by law cannot vote
Executive branch: *chief of state:* Sultan and Prime Minister HAITHAM bin Tarik Al Said (since 11 January 2020)
head of government: Sultan and Prime Minister HAITHAM bin Tarik Al Said (since 11 January 2020)
cabinet: Cabinet appointed by the monarch
note: the monarch is both chief of state and head of government
Legislative branch: *legislature name:* Majles
legislative structure: bicameral
Legislative branch - lower chamber: *chamber name:* Shura Council (Majles A'Shura)
number of seats: 90 (all directly elected)
electoral system: other systems
scope of elections: full renewal
term in office: 4 years
most recent election date: 10/29/2023
percentage of women in chamber: 0%
expected date of next election: October 2027
Legislative branch - upper chamber: *chamber name:* State Council (Majles Addawla)
number of seats: 87 (all appointed)
scope of elections: full renewal
term in office: 4 years
most recent election date: 11/1/2023
percentage of women in chamber: 20.9%
expected date of next election: November 2027
Judicial branch: *highest court(s):* Supreme Court (consists of 5 judges)
judge selection and term of office: judges nominated by the 9-member Supreme Judicial Council (chaired by the monarch) and appointed by the monarch; judges appointed for life
subordinate courts: Courts of Appeal; Administrative Court; Courts of First Instance; sharia courts; magistrates' courts; military courts
Political parties: *note:* organized political parties are banned in Oman, and loyalties tend to form around tribal affiliations
Diplomatic representation in the US: *chief of mission:* Ambassador Talal Sulaiman AL-RAHBI (since 24 July 2025)
chancery: 2535 Belmont Road, NW, Washington, DC 20008
telephone: [1] (202) 387-1980
FAX: [1] (202) 745-4933
email address and website: washington@fm.gov.om
Embassy of the Sultanate of Oman, Washington, USA - FM.gov.om
Diplomatic representation from the US: *chief of mission:* Ambassador Ana ESCROGIMA (since 4 December 2023)
embassy: P.C. 115, Madinat Al Sultan Qaboos, Muscat
mailing address: 6220 Muscat Place, Washington DC 20521
telephone: [968] 2464-3400
FAX: [968] 2464-3740
email address and website: ConsularMuscat@state.gov
https://om.usembassy.gov/
International organization participation: ABEDA, AFESD, AMF, CAEU, FAO, G-77, GCC, IAEA, IBRD, ICAO, ICC (NGOs), IDA, IDB, IFAD, IFC, IHO, ILO, IMF, IMO, IMSO, Interpol, IOC, IPU, ISO, ITSO, ITU, LAS, MIGA, NAM, OIC, OPCW,

UN, UNCTAD, UNESCO, UNIDO, UNWTO, UPU, WCO, WFTU (NGOs), WHO, WIPO, WMO, WTO

Independence: 1650 (expulsion of the Portuguese)

National holiday: National Day, 18 November
note: celebrates Oman's independence from Portugal in 1650 and the birthday of Sultan QABOOS bin Said al Said, who reigned from 1970 to 2020

Flag: *description:* three equal horizontal bands of white (top), red, and green, with a vertical red band on the left side; the national emblem (a *khanjar* dagger in its sheath on top of crossed swords in scabbards) in white is centered near the top of the vertical band
meaning: white stands for peace and prosperity, red for battles against foreign invaders, and green for the Jebel al Akhdar (Green Mountains) and fertility

National symbol(s): khanjar dagger on top of two crossed swords

National color(s): red, white, green

National anthem(s): *title:* "Nashid as-Salaam as-Sultani" (The Sultan's Anthem)
lyrics/music: Rashid bin Uzayyiz al KHUSAIDI/ James Frederick MILLS, arranged by Bernard EBBINGHAUS
history: adopted 1932; new lyrics written after QABOOS bin Said al Said came to power in 1970; first performed by the band of the HMS Hawkins as a salute to the Sultan during a 1932 visit to Muscat; the ship's bandmaster did the arrangement

National heritage: *total World Heritage Sites:* 5 (all cultural)
selected World Heritage Site locales: Bahla Fort; Archaeological Sites of Bat; Land of Frankincense; Aflaj Irrigation Systems of Oman; Ancient Qalhat

ECONOMY

Economic overview: high-income, oil-based economy; large welfare system; growing government debt; citizenship-based labor force growth policy; US free trade agreement; diversifying portfolio; high female labor force participation

Real GDP (purchasing power parity): $193.591 billion (2024 est.)
$190.403 billion (2023 est.)
$188.169 billion (2022 est.)
note: data in 2021 dollars
comparison ranking: 77

Real GDP growth rate: 1.7% (2024 est.)
1.2% (2023 est.)
8% (2022 est.)
note: annual GDP % growth based on constant local currency
comparison ranking: 157

Real GDP per capita: $36,700 (2024 est.)
$37,700 (2023 est.)
$39,800 (2022 est.)
note: data in 2021 dollars
comparison ranking: 63

GDP (official exchange rate): $106.943 billion (2024 est.)
note: data in current dollars at official exchange rate

Inflation rate (consumer prices): 1% (2023 est.)
2.5% (2022 est.)
1.7% (2021 est.)
note: annual % change based on consumer prices
comparison ranking: 22

GDP - composition, by sector of origin: *agriculture:* 2.6% (2024 est.)
industry: 54.2% (2024 est.)
services: 46.5% (2024 est.)
note: figures may not total 100% due to non-allocated consumption not captured in sector-reported data
comparison rankings: agriculture 140; industry 6; services 165

GDP - composition, by end use: *household consumption:* 37.8% (2023 est.)
government consumption: 19.1% (2023 est.)
investment in fixed capital: 24.3% (2023 est.)
investment in inventories: 2.4% (2023 est.)
exports of goods and services: 61.1% (2023 est.)
imports of goods and services: -44.8% (2023 est.)
note: figures may not total 100% due to rounding or gaps in data collection

Agricultural products: vegetables, dates, milk, tomatoes, sorghum, chillies/peppers, goat milk, cucumbers/gherkins, cantaloupes/melons, cabbages (2023)
note: top ten agricultural products based on tonnage

Industries: crude oil production and refining, natural and liquefied natural gas production; construction, cement, copper, steel, chemicals, optic fiber

Industrial production growth rate: 0.2% (2024 est.)
note: annual % change in industrial value added based on constant local currency
comparison ranking: 132

Labor force: 2.696 million (2024 est.)
note: number of people ages 15 or older who are employed or seeking work
comparison ranking: 118

Unemployment rate: 3.2% (2024 est.)
3.2% (2023 est.)
3.3% (2022 est.)
note: % of labor force seeking employment
comparison ranking: 47

Youth unemployment rate (ages 15-24): *total:* 13.9% (2024 est.)
male: 11% (2024 est.)
female: 30.9% (2024 est.)
note: % of labor force ages 15-24 seeking employment
comparison ranking: total 89

Average household expenditures: *on food:* 18.7% of household expenditures (2023 est.)
on alcohol and tobacco: 0.1% of household expenditures (2023 est.)

Remittances: 0% of GDP (2023 est.)
0% of GDP (2022 est.)
0% of GDP (2021 est.)
note: personal transfers and compensation between resident and non-resident individuals/households/entities

Budget: *revenues:* $29.334 billion (2018 est.)
expenditures: $35.984 billion (2018 est.)

Public debt: 46.9% of GDP (2017 est.)
note: excludes indebtedness of state-owned enterprises
comparison ranking: 114

Current account balance: $2.638 billion (2023 est.)
$4.362 billion (2022 est.)
-$4.836 billion (2021 est.)
note: balance of payments - net trade and primary/secondary income in current dollars
comparison ranking: 41

Exports: $64.749 billion (2023 est.)
$69.483 billion (2022 est.)
$46.572 billion (2021 est.)
note: balance of payments - exports of goods and services in current dollars
comparison ranking: 58

Exports - partners: China 43%, India 6%, Saudi Arabia 5%, UAE 5%, South Africa 4% (2023)
note: top five export partners based on percentage share of exports

Exports - commodities: crude petroleum, refined petroleum, natural gas, semi-finished iron, fertilizers (2023)
note: top five export commodities based on value in dollars

Imports: $47.412 billion (2023 est.)
$46.682 billion (2022 est.)
$37.216 billion (2021 est.)
note: balance of payments - imports of goods and services in current dollars
comparison ranking: 70

Imports - partners: UAE 25%, Saudi Arabia 12%, India 8%, China 7%, Qatar 5% (2023)
note: top five import partners based on percentage share of imports

Imports - commodities: refined petroleum, cars, crude petroleum, iron ore, iron pipes (2023)
note: top five import commodities based on value in dollars

Reserves of foreign exchange and gold: $18.287 billion (2024 est.)
$17.455 billion (2023 est.)
$17.606 billion (2022 est.)
note: holdings of gold (year-end prices)/foreign exchange/special drawing rights in current dollars
comparison ranking: 65

Exchange rates: Omani rials (OMR) per US dollar -
Exchange rates: 0.384 (2024 est.)
0.384 (2023 est.)
0.384 (2022 est.)
0.384 (2021 est.)
0.384 (2020 est.)

ENERGY

Electricity access: *electrification - total population:* 100% (2022 est.)

Electricity: *installed generating capacity:* 11.589 million kW (2023 est.)
consumption: 40.738 billion kWh (2023 est.)
transmission/distribution losses: 4.267 billion kWh (2023 est.)
comparison rankings: installed generating capacity 63; consumption 59; transmission/distribution losses 157

Electricity generation sources: *fossil fuels:* 96% of total installed capacity (2023 est.)
solar: 3.8% of total installed capacity (2023 est.)
wind: 0.3% of total installed capacity (2023 est.)

Coal: *consumption:* 82,000 metric tons (2023 est.)
exports: 70,000 metric tons (2023 est.)
imports: 323,000 metric tons (2023 est.)

Petroleum: *total petroleum production:* 1.056 million bbl/day (2023 est.)
refined petroleum consumption: 218,000 bbl/day (2023 est.)
crude oil estimated reserves: 5.373 billion barrels (2021 est.)

Natural gas: *production:* 41.726 billion cubic meters (2023 est.)
consumption: 28.646 billion cubic meters (2023 est.)
exports: 15.536 billion cubic meters (2023 est.)
imports: 1.924 billion cubic meters (2023 est.)

proven reserves: 651.287 billion cubic meters (2021 est.)

Energy consumption per capita: 296.586 million Btu/person (2023 est.)
comparison ranking: 9

COMMUNICATIONS

Telephones - fixed lines: *total subscriptions:* 579,000 (2023 est.)
subscriptions per 100 inhabitants: 11 (2023 est.)
comparison ranking: total subscriptions 87

Telephones - mobile cellular: *total subscriptions:* 6.98 million (2023 est.)
subscriptions per 100 inhabitants: 135 (2021 est.)
comparison ranking: total subscriptions 115

Broadcast media: 1 state-run TV broadcaster; TV stations transmitting from Saudi Arabia, the UAE, Iran, and Yemen available via satellite TV; state-run radio operates multiple stations; first private radio station began operating in 2007, and several additional stations now operating (2019)

Internet country code: .om

Internet users: *percent of population:* 95% (2024 est.)

Broadband - fixed subscriptions: *total:* 562,000 (2023 est.)
subscriptions per 100 inhabitants: 11 (2023 est.)
comparison ranking: total 92

TRANSPORTATION

Civil aircraft registration country code prefix: A4O

Airports: 37 (2025)
comparison ranking: 109

Heliports: 20 (2025)
comparison ranking: 55

Merchant marine: *total:* 57 (2023)
by type: general cargo 11, other 46
comparison ranking: total 117

Ports: *total ports:* 7 (2024)
large: 0
medium: 1
small: 4
very small: 2
ports with oil terminals: 6
key ports: Duqm, Khawr Khasab, Mina Al Fahl, Mina Raysut, Sohar

MILITARY AND SECURITY

Military and security forces: Sultan's Armed Forces (SAF): Royal Army of Oman (RAO), Royal Navy of Oman (RNO), Royal Air Force of Oman (RAFO), Royal Guard of Oman (RGO), Sultan's Special Forces

Royal Oman Police (ROP): Civil Defense, Immigration, Infrastructure Security Police, Coast Guard Police, Special Security Police, Special Task Force (2024)
note: in addition to its policing duties, the ROP conducts many administrative functions similar to the responsibilities of a Ministry of Interior in other countries

Military expenditures: 6% of GDP (2024 est.)
5.5% of GDP (2023 est.)
5.5% of GDP (2022 est.)
8% of GDP (2021 est.)
11% of GDP (2020 est.)

Military and security service personnel strengths: approximately 40,000 active Sultan's Armed Forces (25,000 Army, 5,000 Navy; 5,000 Air Force; 5,000 Royal Guard) (2025)

Military equipment inventories and acquisitions: the SAF's inventory includes a mix of older and some more modern weapons systems from a variety of suppliers, particularly the UK and the US; other suppliers have included China, EU countries, South Africa, and Turkey (2024)

Military service age and obligation: 18 for voluntary military service for men and women (women have been allowed to serve since 2011); no conscription (2023)

Military - note: the Sultan's Armed Forces (SAF) are responsible for defending the country, ensuring internal security, and protecting the monarchy; it trains with foreign partners such as the Gulf Cooperation Council (GCC) countries, the UK, and the US; the SAF has a security relationship with the British military going back to the 18th century; today, the SAF and the British maintain a joint training base in Oman, and the British military uses the facilities at Al Duqm Port; in 2019, the US obtained access to the port, expanding on previous military cooperation agreements in 2014, 2010, and 1980; Oman also allows other nations to use some of its maritime facilities, including China; the SAF is part of the Peninsula Shield Forces, a joint military force established by the GCC countries with the aim of maintaining security and stability in the region
Oman's naval forces conduct maritime security operations along the country's long coastline, including patrolling, ensuring freedom of navigation in the key naval chokepoint of the Strait of Hormuz, and countering piracy and smuggling; Oman participates in the US-led, multinational Combined Maritime Forces (CMF), which operates multinational task forces conducting maritime security in regional waters (2025)

TERRORISM

Terrorist group(s): Terrorist group(s): Islamic State of Iraq and ash-Sham (ISIS)
note: details about the history, aims, leadership, organization, areas of operation, tactics, targets, weapons, size, and sources of support of the group(s) appear(s) in Appendix T

TRANSNATIONAL ISSUES

Refugees and internally displaced persons: *refugees:* 714 (2024 est.)

P

PACIFIC OCEAN

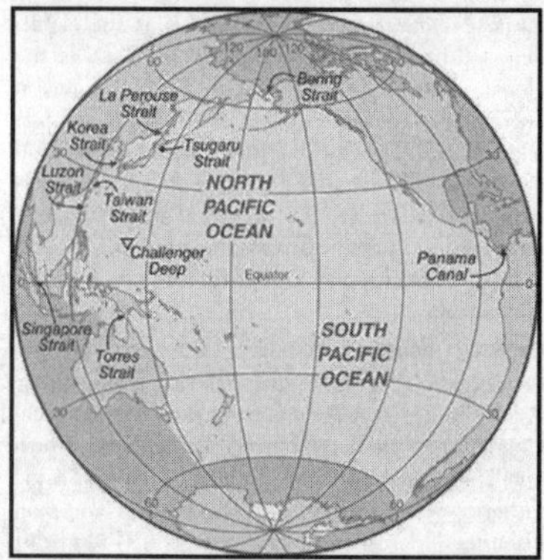

INTRODUCTION

Background: The Pacific Ocean is the largest of the world's five ocean basins (followed by the Atlantic Ocean, Indian Ocean, Southern Ocean, and Arctic Ocean). Strategically important access waterways include the La Perouse, Tsugaru, Tsushima, Taiwan, Singapore, and Torres Straits. The International Hydrographic Organization decision in 2000 to delimit a fifth world ocean basin, the Southern Ocean, removed the portion of the Pacific Ocean south of 60 degrees south. For convenience and because of its immense size, the Pacific Ocean is often divided at the Equator and designated as the North Pacific Ocean and the South Pacific Ocean.

GEOGRAPHY

Location: body of water between the Southern Ocean, Asia, Australia, and the Western Hemisphere

Geographic coordinates: 0 00 N, 160 00 W

Area: *total:* 168.723 million sq km
note: includes Arafura Sea, Bali Sea, Banda Sea, Bering Sea, Bering Strait, Celebes Sea, Coral Sea, East China Sea, Flores Sea, Gulf of Alaska, Gulf of Thailand, Gulf of Tonkin, Java Sea, Philippine Sea, Sea of Japan, Sea of Okhotsk, Solomon Sea, South China Sea, Sulu Sea, Tasman Sea, and other tributary water bodies

Area - comparative: about 15 times the size of the US; covers about 28% of the global surface; almost equal to the total land area of the world

Coastline: 135,663 km

Climate: planetary air pressure systems and resultant wind patterns exhibit remarkable uniformity in the south and east; trade winds and westerly winds are well-developed patterns, modified by seasonal fluctuations; tropical cyclones (hurricanes) may form south of Mexico from June to October and affect Mexico and Central America; continental influences cause climatic uniformity to be much less pronounced in the eastern and western regions at the same latitude in the North Pacific Ocean; the western Pacific is monsoonal - a rainy season occurs during the summer months, when moisture-laden winds blow from the ocean over the land, and a dry season during the winter months, when dry winds blow from the Asian landmass back to the ocean; tropical cyclones (typhoons) may strike southeast and east Asia from May to December

Ocean volume: *ocean volume:* 669.88 million cu km
percent of World Ocean total volume: 50.1%

Major ocean currents: the clockwise North Pacific Gyre formed by the warm northward flowing Kuroshio Current in the west, the eastward flowing North Pacific Current in the north, the southward flowing cold California Current in the east, and the westward flowing North Equatorial Current in the south; the counterclockwise South Pacific Gyre composed of the southward flowing warm East Australian Current in the west, the eastward flowing South Pacific Current in the south, the northward flowing cold Peru (Humbolt) Current in the east, and the westward flowing South Equatorial Current in the north

Bathymetry: *continental shelf:* the following are examples of features on the continental shelf of the Pacific Ocean: Arafura Shelf
Sahul Shelf
Sunda Shelf
Taiwan Banks
continental slope: the following are examples of features on the continental slope of the Pacific Ocean: Pribilof Canyon
Zhemchug Canyon (deepest submarine canyon)
abyssal plains: the following are examples of features on the abyssal plains of the Pacific
Ocean: Aleutian Basin
Central Pacific Basin
Northeast Pacific Basin
Northwest Pacific Basin
Philippine Basin
Southwest Pacific Basin
Tasman Basin
mid-ocean ridge: the following are examples of mid-ocean ridges on the floor of the Pacific
Ocean: East Pacific Rise
Pacific-Antarctic Ridge
undersea terrain features: the following are examples of undersea terrain features on the floor of the Pacific Ocean: Caroline Seamounts
East Mariana Ridge
Emperor Seamount Chain
Hawaiian Ridge
Lord Howe Seamount Chain
Louisville Ridge
Kapingamarangi (Ontong-Java) Rise (largest submarine plateau)
Macclesfield Bank
Marshall Seamounts
Magellan Seamounts
Mid-Pacific Seamounts
Reed Tablemount
Shatsky Rise (third-largest submarine plateau)
Tonga-Kermadec Ridge
ocean trenches: the following are examples of ocean trenches on the floor of the Pacific Ocean: Aleutian Trench
Chile Trench
Izu-Ogasawara Trench
Japan Trench
Kermadec Trench
Kuril-Kamchatka Trench
Manus Trench
Mariana Trench (deepest ocean trench)
Middle America Trench
Nansei-Shoto Trench
Palau Trench
Philippine Trench
Peru-Chile Trench
South New Hebrides Trench
Tonga Trench
Yap Trench
atolls: the following are examples of atolls in the Pacific Ocean, and because they are also countries or territories, they have entries in The World Factbook with additional information: Federated States of Micronesia
French Polynesia
Kiribati
Marshall Islands
Midway Island
Tonga
Tuvalu
Vanuatu
Wake Island

Elevation: *highest point:* sea level
lowest point: Challenger Deep in the Mariana Trench -10,924 m
mean depth: -4,080 m
ocean zones: the ocean is divided into three zones based on depth and light level; sunlight entering the water may travel about 1,000 m into the oceans under the right conditions, but there is rarely any significant light below 200 m
euphotic zone: the upper 200 m (656 ft) is also called "sunlight" zone; only a small amount of light penetrates beyond this depth
dysphotic zone: between 200 m (656 ft) and 1,000 m (3,280 ft), and also called the twilight zone; the intensity of light rapidly dissipates as depth increases, and photosynthesis is no longer possible
aphotic zone: below 1,000 m (3,280 ft) and also called the midnight zone; sunlight does not penetrate to these depths
note: the Pacific Ocean is the deepest ocean basin

Natural resources: oil and gas fields, polymetallic nodules, sand and gravel aggregates, placer deposits, fish

Natural hazards: surrounded by a zone of violent volcanic and earthquake activity sometimes referred to as the "Pacific Ring of Fire"; up to 90% of the world's earthquakes and some 75% of the world's volcanoes occur within the Ring of Fire; 80% of tsunamis, caused by volcanic or seismic events, occur within the "Pacific Ring of Fire"; subject to tropical cyclones (typhoons) in southeast and east Asia from May to December (most frequent from July to October); tropical cyclones (hurricanes) may form south of Mexico and strike Central America and Mexico from June to October (most common in August and September); cyclical El Niño/La Niña phenomenon occurs in the equatorial Pacific, influencing weather in the Western Hemisphere and the western Pacific; ships subject to superstructure icing in extreme north from October to May; persistent fog in the northern Pacific can be a maritime hazard from June to December

Geography - note: the major chokepoints are the Bering Strait, Panama Canal, Luzon Strait, and the Singapore Strait; the equator divides the Pacific

Ocean into the North Pacific Ocean and the South Pacific Ocean; dotted with low coral islands and rugged volcanic islands in the southwestern Pacific Ocean; much of the Pacific Ocean's rim lies along the Ring of Fire, which is a belt that contains about 75% of the world's volcanoes and up to 90% of the world's earthquakes; the Pacific Ocean is the deepest ocean basin, averaging 4,000 m (13,123 ft) in depth

ENVIRONMENT

Environmental issues: pollution from sources such as sewage, nutrient runoff from agriculture, plastic pollution, and toxic waste; habitat destruction; overfishing; sea level-rise and ocean acidification; endangered marine species include the dugong, sea lion, sea otter, seals, turtles, and whales; oil pollution in Philippine Sea and South China Sea

Climate: planetary air pressure systems and resultant wind patterns exhibit remarkable uniformity in the south and east; trade winds and westerly winds are well-developed patterns, modified by seasonal fluctuations; tropical cyclones (hurricanes) may form south of Mexico from June to October and affect Mexico and Central America; continental influences cause climatic uniformity to be much less pronounced in the eastern and western regions at the same latitude in the North Pacific Ocean; the western Pacific is monsoonal - a rainy season occurs during the summer months, when moisture-laden winds blow from the ocean over the land, and a dry season during the winter months, when dry winds blow from the Asian landmass back to the ocean; tropical cyclones (typhoons) may strike southeast and east Asia from May to December

Marine fisheries: *the Pacific Ocean fisheries are the most important in the world, accounting for 58.1%, or 45,800,000 mt, of the global marine capture in 2020; of the six regions delineated by the Food and Agriculture Organization in the Pacific Ocean, the following are the most important: Northwest Pacific* region (Region 61) is the world's most important fishery, producing 24.3% of the global catch or 19,150,000 mt in 2020; it encompasses the waters north of 20° north latitude and west of 175° west longitude, with the major producers including China (29,080726 mt), Japan (3,417,871 mt), South Korea (1,403,892 mt), and Taiwan (487,739 mt); the principal catches include Alaska pollock, Japanese anchovy, chub mackerel, and scads

Western Central Pacific region (Region 71) is the world's second most important fishing region producing 16.8%, or 13,260,000 mt, of the global catch in 2020; tuna is the most important species in this region; the region includes the waters between 20° North and 25° South latitude and west of 175° West longitude with the major producers including Indonesia (6,907,932 mt), Vietnam (4,571,497 mt), Philippines (2,416,879 mt), Thailand (1,509,574 mt), and Malaysia (692,553 mt); the principal catches include skipjack and yellowfin tuna, sardinellas, and cephalopods

Southeast Pacific region (Region 87) is the third largest fishery in the world, producing 10.7%, or 8,400,000 mt, of the global catch in 2020; this region includes the nutrient-rich waters off the west coast of South America between 5° North and 60° South latitude and east of 120° West longitude, with the major producers including Peru (4,888,730 mt), Chile (3,298,795 mt), and Ecuador (1,186,249 mt); the principal catches include Peruvian anchovy (68.5% of the catch), jumbo flying squid, and Chilean jack mackerel

Pacific Northeast region (Region 67) is the eighth largest fishery in the world, producing 3.6% of the global catch or 2,860,000 mt in 2020; this region encompasses the waters north of 40° North latitude and east of 175° West longitude, including the Gulf of Alaska and Bering Sea, with the major producers including the US (3,009,568 mt), Canada (276,677 mt), and Russia (6,908 mt); the principal catches include Alaska pollock, Pacific cod, and North Pacific hake

Regional fisheries bodies: Commission for the Conservation of Southern Bluefin Tuna, Inter-American Tropical Tuna Commission, International Council for the Exploration of the Seas, North Pacific Anadromous Fish Commission, North Pacific Fisheries Commission, South Pacific Regional Fisheries Management Organization, Southeast Asian Fisheries Development Center, Western and Central Pacific Fisheries Commission

GOVERNMENT

Country name: *etymology:* named by Portuguese explorer Ferdinand MAGELLAN while circumnavigating the world in 1520; he called it "Mar Pacifico," which means "peaceful sea" in both Portuguese and Spanish, because he encountered no storms during the crossing

PAKISTAN

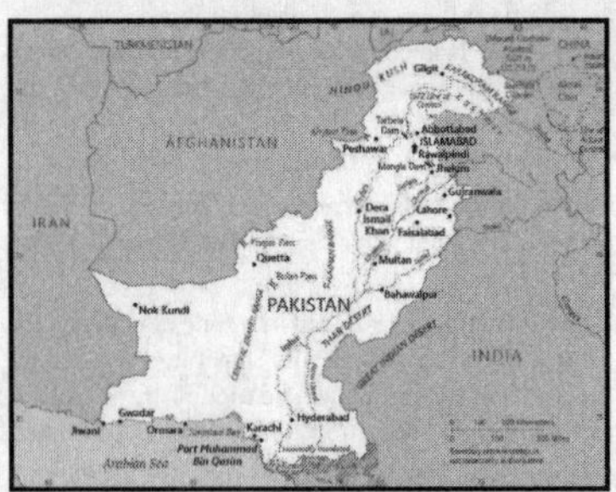

INTRODUCTION

Background: The Indus Valley civilization, one of the oldest in the world and dating back at least 5,000 years, spread over much of modern-day Pakistan. During the second millennium B.C., remnants of this culture fused with the migrating Indo-Aryan peoples. The area underwent successive invasions in subsequent centuries from the Persians, Greeks, Scythians, Arabs (who brought Islam), Afghans, and Turks. The Mughal Empire flourished in the 16th and 17th centuries; the British came to dominate the region in the 18th century. The partition in 1947 of British India into the Muslim state of Pakistan (with West and East sections) and largely Hindu India created lasting tension between the two countries. They have fought two wars and a limited conflict – in 1947-48, 1965, and 1999 respectively – over the Kashmir territory, a dispute that continues to this day. A third war in 1971 – in which India assisted an indigenous movement reacting to Bengali marginalization in Pakistani politics – resulted in East Pakistan becoming the separate nation of Bangladesh.

In response to Indian nuclear weapons testing, Pakistan conducted its own tests in 1998. Pakistan has been engaged in a decades-long armed conflict with militant groups, including the Tehreek-e-Taliban Pakistan (TTP) and other militant networks that target government institutions and civilians.

GEOGRAPHY

Location: Southern Asia, bordering the Arabian Sea, between India on the east and Iran and Afghanistan on the west and China in the north

Geographic coordinates: 30 00 N, 70 00 E

Map references: Asia

Area: *total:* 796,095 sq km
land: 770,875 sq km
water: 25,220 sq km
comparison ranking: total 37

Area - comparative: slightly more than five times the size of Georgia; slightly less than twice the size of California

Land boundaries: *total:* 7,257 km
border countries (4): Afghanistan 2,670 km; China 438 km; India 3,190 km; Iran 959 km

Coastline: 1,046 km

Maritime claims: *territorial sea:* 12 nm
contiguous zone: 24 nm
exclusive economic zone: 200 nm
continental shelf: 200 nm or to the edge of the continental margin

Climate: mostly hot, dry desert; temperate in northwest; arctic in north

Terrain: *divided into three major geographic areas:* the northern highlands, the Indus River plain in the center and east, and the Balochistan Plateau in the south and west

Elevation: *highest point:* K2 (Mt. Godwin-Austen) 8,611 m
lowest point: Arabian Sea 0 m
mean elevation: 900 m

Natural resources: arable land, extensive natural gas reserves, limited petroleum, poor quality coal, iron ore, copper, salt, limestone

Land use: *agricultural land:* 46.6% (2022 est.)
arable land: 39.2% (2022 est.)
permanent crops: 0.9% (2022 est.)
permanent pasture: 6.5% (2022 est.)
forest: 4.7% (2022 est.)
other: 48.6% (2022 est.)

Irrigated land: 194,200 sq km (2022)

Major rivers (by length in km): Indus river mouth (shared with China [s] and India) - 3,610 km; Sutlej river mouth (shared with China [s] and India) - 1,372 km; Chenab river mouth (shared with India [s]) - 1,086 km
note: [s] after country name indicates river source; [m] after country name indicates river mouth

Major watersheds (area sq km): Indian Ocean drainage: Indus (1,081,718 sq km)

Internal (endorheic basin) drainage: Tarim Basin (1,152,448 sq km), *(Aral Sea basin)* Amu Darya (534,739 sq km)

Major aquifers: Indus Basin

Population distribution: the Indus River and its tributaries attract most of the settlement, with Punjab province the most densely populated

Natural hazards: frequent earthquakes, occasionally severe especially in north and west; flooding along the Indus after heavy rains (July and August)

Geography - note: controls Khyber Pass and Bolan Pass, traditional invasion routes between Central Asia and India

PEOPLE AND SOCIETY

Population: *total:* 252,363,571 (2024 est.)
male: 128,387,797
female: 123,975,774
comparison rankings: total 5; male 5; female 5

Nationality: *noun:* Pakistani(s)
adjective: Pakistani

Ethnic groups: Punjabi 44.7%, Pashtun (Pathan) 15.4%, Sindhi 14.1%, Saraiki 8.4%, Muhajirs 7.6%, Baloch 3.6%, other 6.3%

Languages: Punjabi 38.8%, Pashto (alternate name, Pashtu) 18.2%, Sindhi 14.6%, Saraiki (a Punjabi variant) 12.2%, Urdu 7.1%, Balochi 3%, Hindko 2.4%, Brahui 1.2%, other 2.4%
major-language sample(s):
دنیا کا قاموس، ایک لازمی زریہ بنیادی معلومات کا
(Urdu)
note: data represent population by mother tongue; English (official; lingua franca of Pakistani elite and most government ministries)

Religions: Islam (official) 96.5% (Sunni 85-90%, Shia 10-15%), other (includes Christian and Hindu) 3.5% (2020 est.)

Age structure: *0-14 years:* 34.4% (male 44,330,669/female 42,529,007)
15-64 years: 60.7% (male 78,321,834/female 74,833,003)
65 years and over: 4.9% (2024 est.) (male 5,735,294/female 6,613,764)

Dependency ratios: *total dependency ratio:* 64.8 (2024 est.)
youth dependency ratio: 56.7 (2024 est.)
elderly dependency ratio: 8.1 (2024 est.)
potential support ratio: 12.4 (2024 est.)

Median age: *total:* 22.9 years (2024 est.)
male: 22.8 years
female: 23 years
comparison ranking: total 180

Population growth rate: 1.86% (2024 est.)
comparison ranking: 46

Birth rate: 25.5 births/1,000 population (2024 est.)
comparison ranking: 45

Death rate: 5.9 deaths/1,000 population (2024 est.)
comparison ranking: 159

Net migration rate: -1.1 migrant(s)/1,000 population (2024 est.)
comparison ranking: 148

Population distribution: the Indus River and its tributaries attract most of the settlement, with Punjab province the most densely populated

Urbanization: *urban population:* 38% of total population (2023)
rate of urbanization: 2.1% annual rate of change (2020-25 est.)

Major urban areas - population: 17.236 million Karachi, 13.979 million Lahore, 3.711 million Faisalabad, 2.415 million Gujranwala, 2.412 million Peshawar, 1.232 million ISLAMABAD (capital) (2023)

Sex ratio: *at birth:* 1.05 male(s)/female
0-14 years: 1.04 male(s)/female
15-64 years: 1.05 male(s)/female
65 years and over: 0.87 male(s)/female
total population: 1.04 male(s)/female (2024 est.)

Mother's mean age at first birth: 22.8 years (2017/18 est.)
note: data represents median age at first birth among women 25-49

Maternal mortality ratio: 155 deaths/100,000 live births (2023 est.)
comparison ranking: 48

Infant mortality rate: *total:* 51.5 deaths/1,000 live births (2024 est.)
male: 56 deaths/1,000 live births
female: 46.8 deaths/1,000 live births
comparison ranking: total 18

Life expectancy at birth: *total population:* 70.3 years (2024 est.)
male: 68.2 years
female: 72.5 years
comparison ranking: total population 178

Total fertility rate: 3.32 children born/woman (2024 est.)
comparison ranking: 40

Gross reproduction rate: 1.62 (2024 est.)

Drinking water source: *improved: urban:* 92.9% of population (2022 est.)
rural: 89.3% of population (2022 est.)
total: 90.6% of population (2022 est.)
unimproved: urban: 7.1% of population (2022 est.)
rural: 10.7% of population (2022 est.)
total: 9.4% of population (2022 est.)

Health expenditure: 2.9% of GDP (2021)
5.6% of national budget (2022 est.)

Physician density: 1.16 physicians/1,000 population (2021)

Hospital bed density: 0.5 beds/1,000 population (2019 est.)

Sanitation facility access: *improved: urban:* 90.5% of population (2022 est.)
rural: 76.1% of population (2022 est.)
total: 81.5% of population (2022 est.)
unimproved: urban: 9.5% of population (2022 est.)
rural: 23.9% of population (2022 est.)
total: 18.5% of population (2022 est.)

Obesity - adult prevalence rate: 8.6% (2016)
comparison ranking: 148

Alcohol consumption per capita: *total:* 0.04 liters of pure alcohol (2019 est.)
beer: 0 liters of pure alcohol (2019 est.)
wine: 0 liters of pure alcohol (2019 est.)
spirits: 0.04 liters of pure alcohol (2019 est.)
other alcohols: 0 liters of pure alcohol (2019 est.)
comparison ranking: total 180

Tobacco use: *total:* 15.5% (2025 est.)
male: 25.7% (2025 est.)
female: 5.4% (2025 est.)
comparison ranking: total 100

Children under the age of 5 years underweight: 23.1% (2018)
comparison ranking: 7

Currently married women (ages 15-49): 63.5% (2023 est.)

Child marriage: *women married by age 15:* 3.6% (2018)
women married by age 18: 18.3% (2018)
men married by age 18: 4.7% (2018)

Education expenditure: 1.9% of GDP (2023 est.)
8.3% national budget (2023 est.)
comparison ranking: Education expenditure (% GDP) 186

Literacy: *total population:* 58.9% (2021 est.)
male: 69.1% (2021 est.)
female: 48.5% (2021 est.)

School life expectancy (primary to tertiary education): *total:* 8 years (2022 est.)
male: 8 years (2022 est.)
female: 7 years (2022 est.)

ENVIRONMENT

Environmental issues: water pollution from raw sewage, industrial wastes, and agricultural runoff; limited natural freshwater resources; most of the population does not have access to potable water; deforestation; soil erosion; desertification; air pollution and noise pollution in urban areas

International environmental agreements: *party to:* Antarctic-Environmental Protection, Antarctic-Marine Living Resources, Antarctic Treaty, Biodiversity, Climate Change, Climate Change-Kyoto Protocol, Climate Change-Paris Agreement, Desertification, Endangered Species, Environmental Modification, Hazardous Wastes, Law of the Sea, Marine Dumping-London Convention, Nuclear Test Ban, Ozone Layer Protection, Ship Pollution, Wetlands
signed, but not ratified: Marine Life Conservation

Climate: mostly hot, dry desert; temperate in northwest; arctic in north

Urbanization: *urban population:* 38% of total population (2023)
rate of urbanization: 2.1% annual rate of change (2020-25 est.)

Carbon dioxide emissions: 212.655 million metric tonnes of CO2 (2023 est.)
from coal and metallurgical coke: 59.937 million metric tonnes of CO2 (2023 est.)
from petroleum and other liquids: 93.713 million metric tonnes of CO2 (2023 est.)
from consumed natural gas: 59.006 million metric tonnes of CO2 (2023 est.)
comparison ranking: total emissions 30

Particulate matter emissions: 50.1 micrograms per cubic meter (2019 est.)

Methane emissions: *energy:* 1,625.2 kt (2022-2024 est.)
agriculture: 5,381.3 kt (2019-2021 est.)
waste: 700.4 kt (2019-2021 est.)
other: 128.7 kt (2019-2021 est.)

Waste and recycling: *municipal solid waste generated annually:* 30.76 million tons (2024 est.)
percent of municipal solid waste recycled: 13.8% (2022 est.)

Total water withdrawal: *municipal:* 9.65 billion cubic meters (2022 est.)
industrial: 1.4 billion cubic meters (2022 est.)
agricultural: 172.4 billion cubic meters (2022 est.)

Total renewable water resources: 246.8 billion cubic meters (2022 est.)

GOVERNMENT

Country name: *conventional long form:* Islamic Republic of Pakistan
conventional short form: Pakistan
local long form: Jamhuryat Islami Pakistan
local short form: Pakistan
former: West Pakistan
etymology: the name is said to have been proposed in the early 1930s by Muslim students at Cambridge University, created from the initials of Punjab, Afghanistan, and Kashmir; the word *pak* also means "pure" in Persian or Pashto, and the Persian suffix *-stan* means "place of" or "country," so Pakistan literally means "Land of the Pure"

Government type: federal parliamentary republic

Capital: *name:* Islamabad
geographic coordinates: 33 41 N, 73 03 E
time difference: UTC+5 (10 hours ahead of Washington, DC, during Standard Time)
etymology: the name means "city of Islam" and derives from the Arabic *islam*, referring to the Islamic faith, and the Persian suffix *-abad*, meaning "inhabited place" or "city"

Administrative divisions: 4 provinces, 2 Pakistan-administered areas*, and 1 capital territory**; Azad Kashmir*, Balochistan, Gilgit-Baltistan*, Islamabad Capital Territory**, Khyber Pakhtunkhwa, Punjab, Sindh

Legal system: common law system with Islamic law influence

Constitution: *history:* several previous; latest endorsed 12 April 1973, passed 19 April 1973, entered into force 14 August 1973 (suspended and restored several times)
amendment process: proposed by the Senate or by the National Assembly; passage requires at least two-thirds majority vote of both houses

International law organization participation: accepts compulsory ICJ jurisdiction with reservations; non-party state to the ICCt

Citizenship: *citizenship by birth:* yes
citizenship by descent only: at least one parent must be a citizen of Pakistan
dual citizenship recognized: yes, but limited to select countries
residency requirement for naturalization: 4 out of the previous 7 years and including the 12 months preceding application

Suffrage: 18 years of age; universal
note: women and non-Muslims have joint electorates and reserved parliamentary seats

Executive branch: *chief of state:* President Asif Ali ZARDARI (since 10 March 2024)
head of government: Prime Minister Muhammad Shehbaz SHARIF (since 3 March 2024)
cabinet: Cabinet appointed by the president on the advice of the prime minister
election/appointment process: president indirectly elected for a 5-year term (limited to 2 consecutive terms) by the Electoral College, which consists of members of the Senate, National Assembly, and provincial assemblies; prime minister elected for a 5-year term by the National Assembly
most recent election date: 9 March 2024
election results: *2024:* Asif Ali ZARDARI elected president; National Assembly vote - Asif Ali ZARDARI (PPP) 411 votes, Mehmood Khan ACHAKZALI (PMAP) 181 votes; Shehbaz SHARIF elected prime minister; National Assembly vote - Shehbaz SHARIF (PML-N) 201, Omar AYUB (PTI) 92
2018: Arif ALVI elected president; Electoral College vote - Arif ALVI (PTI) 352, Fazl-ur-REHMAN (MMA) 184, Aitzaz AHSAN (PPP) 124; Imran KHAN elected prime minister; National Assembly vote - Imran KHAN (PTI) 176, Shehbaz SHARIF (PML-N) 96
expected date of next election: 2029

Legislative branch: *legislature name:* Parliament (Majlis-E-Shoora)
legislative structure: bicameral
note: in May 2018, the Parliament of Pakistan and the Khyber Pakhtunkhwa Assembly passed a constitutional amendment to merge the Federally Administrated Tribal Areas and Provincially Administered Tribal Areas with the province of Khyber Pakhtunkhwa; the amendment reduces the Senate from 104 to 96 members - 4 in the 2024 election and 4 in the 2027 election

Legislative branch - lower chamber: *chamber name:* National Assembly
number of seats: 336 (all directly elected)
electoral system: plurality/majority
scope of elections: full renewal
term in office: 5 years
most recent election date: 2/8/2024
parties elected and seats per party: Pakistan Muslim League-Nawaz (PML-N) (75); Pakistan People's Party Parliamentarians (PPPP) (54); Muttahida Quami Movement Pakistan (MQMP) (17); Independents (101); Other (16)
percentage of women in chamber: 17%
expected date of next election: February 2029

Legislative branch - upper chamber: *chamber name:* Senate
number of seats: 96 (all indirectly elected)
scope of elections: partial renewal
term in office: 6 years
most recent election date: 4/2/2024
percentage of women in chamber: 18.8%
expected date of next election: March 2027
note: in 2018, the Parliament of Pakistan and the Khyber Pakhtunkhwa Assembly passed a constitutional amendment to merge the Federally Administrated Tribal Areas and Provincially Administered Tribal Areas with the province of Khyber Pakhtunkhwa; the amendment reduces the Senate from 104 to 96 members – by 4 in the 2024 election and another 4 in the 2027 election

Judicial branch: *highest court(s):* Supreme Court of Pakistan (consists of the chief justice and 16 judges)
judge selection and term of office: justices nominated by an 8-member parliamentary committee on the recommendation of the Judicial Commission, a 9-member body of judges and other judicial professionals, and appointed by the president; justices can serve until age 65
subordinate courts: High Courts; Federal Shariat Court; provincial and district civil and criminal courts; specialized courts for issues, such as taxation, banking, and customs

Political parties: Awami National Party or ANP
Awami Muslim League or AML
Balochistan Awami Party or BAP
Balochistan National Party-Awami or BNP-A
Balochistan National Party-Mengal or BNP-M
Grand Democratic Alliance or GDA (alliance of several parties)
Hazara Democratic Party or HDP
Istehkam-e-Pakistan Party
Jamaat-e-Islami or JI
Jamhoori Wattan Party or JWP
Jamiat Ulema-e-Islam-Fazl or JUI-F
Majlis Wahdat-e-Muslimeen Pakistan or MWM
Muttahida Majlis-e-Amal or MMA (alliance of several parties)
Muttahida Qaumi Movement-Pakistan or MQM-P
National Party or NP
Pakistan Muslim League or PML-Z
Pakistan Muslim League-Functional or PML-F
Pakistan Muslim League-Nawaz or PML-N
Pakistan Muslim League-Quaid-e-Azam or PML-Q
Pakistan Peoples Party or PPP
Pakistan Rah-e-Haq Party or PRHP
Pakistan Tehrik-e Insaaf or PTI (Pakistan Movement for Justice)
Pashtoonkhwa Milli Awami Party or PMAP or PKMAP
Tehreek-e-Labbaik Pakistan or TLP

Diplomatic representation in the US: *chief of mission:* Ambassador Rizwan Saeed SHEIKH (since 18 September 2024)
chancery: 3517 International Court NW, Washington, DC 20008
telephone: [1] (202) 243-6500
FAX: [1] (202) 686-1534
email address and website: consularsection@embassyofpakistanusa.org
https://embassyofpakistanusa.org/
consulate(s) general: Chicago, Houston, Los Angeles, New York

Diplomatic representation from the US: *chief of mission:* Ambassador (vacant); Chargé d'Affaires Natalie A. BAKER (since January 2025)
embassy: Diplomatic Enclave, Ramna 5, Islamabad
mailing address: 8100 Islamabad Place, Washington, DC 20521-8100
telephone: [92] 051-201-4000
FAX: [92] 51-2338071
email address and website: ACSIslamabad@state.gov
https://pk.usembassy.gov/
consulate(s) general: Karachi, Lahore, Peshawar

International organization participation: ADB, AIIB, ARF, ASEAN (sectoral dialogue partner), C, CERN (associate member), CICA, CP, D-8, ECO, FAO, G-11, G-24, G-77, IAEA, IBRD, ICAO, ICC (national committees), ICRM, IDA, IDB, IFAD, IFC, IFRCS, IHO, ILO, IMF, IMO, IMSO, Interpol, IOC, IOM, IPU, ISO, ITSO, ITU, ITUC (NGOs), MIGA, MINURCAT, MINURSO, MINUSCA, MONUSCO, NAM, OAS (observer), OIC, OPCW, PCA, SAARC, SACEP, SCO, UN, UNAMID, UNCTAD, UNESCO, UNFICYP, UNHCR, UNIDO, UNISFA, UNISFA, UNMISS, UNOOSA, UNSOS, UNWTO, UPU, WCO, WFTU (NGOs), WHO, WIPO, WMO, WTO

Independence: 14 August 1947 (from British India)

National holiday: Pakistan Day, 23 March, also referred to as Pakistan Resolution Day (1940) or Republic Day (1956)
note: commemorates the adoption of the Lahore Resolution on 23 March 1940, which called for the creation of independent Muslim states, and also the adoption of Pakistan's first constitution on 23 March 1956, during the transition to the Islamic Republic of Pakistan

Flag: *description:* green with a vertical white band on the left side; a large white crescent and star are centered in the green field
meaning: the crescent, star, and color green are all traditional Islamic symbols; the white band symbolizes the role of religious minorities

National symbol(s): five-pointed star between the horns of a waxing crescent moon, jasmine

National color(s): green, white

National anthem(s): *title:* "Qaumi Tarana" (National Anthem)
lyrics/music: Abu-Al-Asar Hafeez JULLANDHURI/ Ahmed Ghulamali CHAGLA
history: adopted 1954; also known as "Pak sarzamin shad bad" (Blessed Be the Sacred Land)

National heritage: *total World Heritage Sites:* 6 (all cultural)
selected World Heritage Site locales: Archaeological Ruins at Moenjodaro; Buddhist Ruins of Takht-i-Bahi; Taxila; Fort and Shalamar Gardens in Lahore; Historical Monuments at Makli, Thatta; Rohtas Fort

ECONOMY

Economic overview: lower middle-income South Asian economy; extremely high debt; endemic corruption; regional disputes with India and Afghanistan hinder investment; falling inflation, IMF relief programs, and strong agricultural output slowly contributing to economic recovery

Real GDP (purchasing power parity): $1.39 trillion (2024 est.)
$1.346 trillion (2023 est.)
$1.347 trillion (2022 est.)
note: data in 2021 dollars
comparison ranking: 26

Real GDP growth rate: 3.2% (2024 est.)
0% (2023 est.)
4.8% (2022 est.)
note: annual GDP % growth based on constant local currency
comparison ranking: 113

Real GDP per capita: $5,500 (2024 est.)
$5,400 (2023 est.)
$5,500 (2022 est.)
note: data in 2021 dollars
comparison ranking: 171

GDP (official exchange rate): $373.072 billion (2024 est.)
note: data in current dollars at official exchange rate

Inflation rate (consumer prices): 12.6% (2024 est.)
30.8% (2023 est.)
19.9% (2022 est.)
note: annual % change based on consumer prices
comparison ranking: 186

GDP - composition, by sector of origin: *agriculture:* 23.5% (2024 est.)
industry: 20% (2024 est.)
services: 50.5% (2024 est.)
note: figures may not total 100% due to non-allocated consumption not captured in sector-reported data
comparison rankings: agriculture 24; industry 129; services 143

GDP - composition, by end use: *household consumption:* 85.2% (2024 est.)
government consumption: 8.5% (2024 est.)
investment in fixed capital: 11.2% (2024 est.)
investment in inventories: 1.7% (2024 est.)
exports of goods and services: 10.4% (2024 est.)
imports of goods and services: -17.1% (2024 est.)
note: figures may not total 100% due to rounding or gaps in data collection

Agricultural products: sugarcane, bison milk, wheat, milk, rice, maize, potatoes, cotton, mangoes/guavas, chicken (2023)
note: top ten agricultural products based on tonnage

Industries: textiles and apparel, food processing, pharmaceuticals, surgical instruments, construction materials, paper products, fertilizer, shrimp

Industrial production growth rate: -1.7% (2024 est.)
note: annual % change in industrial value added based on constant local currency
comparison ranking: 157

Labor force: 83.644 million (2024 est.)
note: number of people ages 15 or older who are employed or seeking work
comparison ranking: 7

Unemployment rate: 5.5% (2024 est.)
5.5% (2023 est.)
5.5% (2022 est.)
note: % of labor force seeking employment
comparison ranking: 97

Youth unemployment rate (ages 15-24): *total:* 9.9% (2024 est.)
male: 9.8% (2024 est.)
female: 10.1% (2024 est.)
note: % of labor force ages 15-24 seeking employment
comparison ranking: total 121

Population below poverty line: 21.9% (2018 est.)
note: % of population with income below national poverty line

Gini Index coefficient - distribution of family income: 29.6 (2018 est.)
note: index (0-100) of income distribution; higher values represent greater inequality
comparison ranking: 123

Average household expenditures: *on food:* 37.8% of household expenditures (2023 est.)
on alcohol and tobacco: 1.3% of household expenditures (2023 est.)

Household income or consumption by percentage share: *lowest 10%:* 4.2% (2018 est.)
highest 10%: 25.5% (2018 est.)
note: % share of income accruing to lowest and highest 10% of population

Remittances: 9.4% of GDP (2024 est.)
7.9% of GDP (2023 est.)
8% of GDP (2022 est.)
note: personal transfers and compensation between resident and non-resident individuals/households/entities

Budget: *revenues:* $40.774 billion (2015 est.)
expenditures: $49.558 billion (2015 est.)
note: central government revenues and expenses (excluding grants/extrabudgetary units/social security funds) converted to US dollars at average official exchange rate for year indicated

Current account balance: $699.22 million (2024 est.)
-$1.039 billion (2023 est.)
-$12.216 billion (2022 est.)
note: balance of payments - net trade and primary/secondary income in current dollars
comparison ranking: 61

Exports: $40.219 billion (2024 est.)
$36.215 billion (2023 est.)
$38.967 billion (2022 est.)
note: balance of payments - exports of goods and services in current dollars
comparison ranking: 73

Exports - partners: USA 14%, UAE 10%, China 9%, Germany 7%, UK 6% (2023)
note: top five export partners based on percentage share of exports

Exports - commodities: garments, fabric, refined petroleum, rice, cotton fabric (2023)
note: top five export commodities based on value in dollars

Imports: $66.844 billion (2024 est.)
$58.069 billion (2023 est.)
$76.594 billion (2022 est.)
note: balance of payments - imports of goods and services in current dollars
comparison ranking: 59

Imports - partners: China 25%, Qatar 11%, UAE 9%, Saudi Arabia 8%, Indonesia 6% (2023)
note: top five import partners based on percentage share of imports

Imports - commodities: natural gas, refined petroleum, crude petroleum, palm oil, plastics (2023)
note: top five import commodities based on value in dollars

Reserves of foreign exchange and gold: $18.408 billion (2024 est.)
$13.73 billion (2023 est.)
$9.927 billion (2022 est.)
note: holdings of gold (year-end prices)/foreign exchange/special drawing rights in current dollars
comparison ranking: 64

Debt - external: $89.148 billion (2023 est.)
note: present value of external debt in current US dollars
comparison ranking: 12

Exchange rates: Pakistani rupees (PKR) per US dollar -

Exchange rates: 278.581 (2024 est.)
280.356 (2023 est.)
204.867 (2022 est.)
162.906 (2021 est.)
161.838 (2020 est.)

ENERGY

Electricity access: *electrification - total population:* 95% (2022 est.)
electrification - urban areas: 100%
electrification - rural areas: 93%

Electricity: *installed generating capacity:* 43.512 million kW (2023 est.)
consumption: 145.357 billion kWh (2023 est.)
imports: 481.25 million kWh (2023 est.)
transmission/distribution losses: 25.811 billion kWh (2023 est.)
comparison rankings: installed generating capacity 31; consumption 28; imports 93; transmission/distribution losses 193

Electricity generation sources: *fossil fuels:* 60.4% of total installed capacity (2023 est.)
nuclear: 14.1% of total installed capacity (2023 est.)
solar: 0.7% of total installed capacity (2023 est.)

wind: 3.7% of total installed capacity (2023 est.)
hydroelectricity: 19.9% of total installed capacity (2023 est.)
biomass and waste: 1.1% of total installed capacity (2023 est.)

Nuclear energy: Number of operational nuclear reactors: 6 (2025)

Number of nuclear reactors under construction: 1 (2025)

Net capacity of operational nuclear reactors: 3.26GW (2025 est.)

Percent of total electricity production: 17.4% (2023 est.)

Number of nuclear reactors permanently shut down: 1 (2025)

Coal: *production:* 13.765 million metric tons (2023 est.)
consumption: 30.191 million metric tons (2023 est.)
exports: 900 metric tons (2023 est.)
imports: 16.185 million metric tons (2023 est.)
proven reserves: 2.857 billion metric tons (2023 est.)

Petroleum: *total petroleum production:* 91,000 bbl/day (2023 est.)
refined petroleum consumption: 645,000 bbl/day (2023 est.)
crude oil estimated reserves: 540 million barrels (2021 est.)

Natural gas: *production:* 27.476 billion cubic meters (2023 est.)
consumption: 36.323 billion cubic meters (2023 est.)
imports: 8.847 billion cubic meters (2023 est.)
proven reserves: 592.219 billion cubic meters (2021 est.)

Energy consumption per capita: 14.076 million Btu/person (2023 est.)
comparison ranking: 142

COMMUNICATIONS

Telephones - fixed lines: *total subscriptions:* 2.573 million (2023 est.)
subscriptions per 100 inhabitants: 1 (2023 est.)
comparison ranking: total subscriptions 44

Telephones - mobile cellular: *total subscriptions:* 189 million (2023 est.)
subscriptions per 100 inhabitants: 82 (2022 est.)
comparison ranking: total subscriptions 10

Broadcast media: 120 satellite TV stations; 42 media companies/channels; state-run Pakistan Television Corporation (PTV) is the largest TV network, serves over 85 percent of the population with 9 TV channels; over 100 private cable and satellite channels; state-owned Pakistan Broadcasting Corporation (PBC or Radio Pakistan) has the largest radio audience, particularly in rural areas, with AM/SW/FM stations covering most of the country (2022)

Internet country code: .pk

Internet users: *percent of population:* 27% (2023 est.)

Broadband - fixed subscriptions: *total:* 3.36 million (2023 est.)
subscriptions per 100 inhabitants: 1 (2023 est.)
comparison ranking: total 47

TRANSPORTATION

Civil aircraft registration country code prefix: AP

Airports: 117 (2025)
comparison ranking: 45

Heliports: 48 (2025)
comparison ranking: 41

Railways: *total:* 11,881 km (2021)
narrow gauge: 389 km (2021) 1.000-m gauge
broad gauge: 11,492 km (2021) 1.676-m gauge (286 km electrified)

Merchant marine: *total:* 60 (2023)
by type: bulk carrier 5, oil tanker 9, other 46
comparison ranking: total 113

Ports: *total ports:* 3 (2024)
large: 0
medium: 2
small: 1
very small: 0
ports with oil terminals: 2
key ports: Gwadar, Karachi, Muhamamad Bin Qasim

MILITARY AND SECURITY

Military and security forces: Pakistan Armed Forces: Pakistan Army (includes National Guard), Pakistan Navy (includes Pakistan Marines, Pakistan Maritime Security Agency), Pakistan Air Force

Ministry of Interior: Frontier Constabulary, Frontier Corps, National Police, Pakistan Coast Guard, Punjab (Pakistan) Rangers, Sindh (Pakistan) Rangers (2025)
note: the National Guard is a paramilitary force and one of the Army's reserve forces; other Army reserves include the Pakistan Army Reserve, the Frontier Corps, and the Pakistan Rangers

Military expenditures: 2.5% of GDP (2024 est.)
3% of GDP (2023 est.)
4% of GDP (2022 est.)
4% of GDP (2021 est.)
4% of GDP (2020 est.)

Military and security service personnel strengths: information varies; approximately 650,000 active Armed Forces (550,000 Army; 30,000 Navy; 70,000 Air Force) (2025)

Military equipment inventories and acquisitions: the military's inventory is a broad mix of mostly imported and some domestically produced weapons and equipment; most of its imported weapons are from China; other suppliers include France, Russia, Turkey, Ukraine, the UK, and the US; Pakistan also has a large domestic defense industry, which produces or co-produces such items as armored vehicles, aircraft, missiles, naval vessels (2024)

Military service age and obligation: 16 (or 17 depending on service) to 23 years of age for voluntary military service; soldiers cannot be deployed for combat until age 18; women serve in all three armed forces; reserve obligation to age 45 for enlisted men, age 50 for officers (2023)

Military deployments: 1,300 Central African Republic (MINUSCA); 290 South Sudan (UNMISS); 590 Sudan (UNISFA) (2024)

Military - note: the Pakistan military is responsible for external defense but also has a domestic security role; its chief external focus is India; the military is the lead security agency in many areas of the former Federally Administered Tribal Areas (FATA) and has for decades conducted operations against various internal militant groups; it is also one of the longest serving and largest contributors to UN peacekeeping missions; China is its closest security partner
the military operates largely independently and without effective civilian oversight; it has ruled the country for more than 30 years since independence in 1947 and continues to play a significant role in Pakistan's political arena; it also has a large stake in the country's economic sector and is involved in a diverse array of commercial activities, including banking, construction of public projects, employment services, energy and power generation, fertilizer, food, housing, real estate, and security services
Pakistan has fought four wars and several skirmishes with India; three of the wars have been over the disputed region of Jammu and Kashmir, the status of which has been unsettled since the UK's 1947 withdrawal and the partition and independence of India and Pakistan; a fragile cease-fire was reached in 2003, revised in 2018, and reaffirmed in 2021, although the militarized Line of Control which serves as the border remains contested, and India has accused Pakistan of backing armed separatists and terrorist organizations in the territory New Delhi controls; in the Spring of 2025, Indian held Pakistan responsible for a terrorist attack in India-controlled Kashmir and retaliated, sparking a brief cross-border conflict involving aircraft, artillery, drone, and missile strikes
the Kashmir dispute also includes the Siachen Glacier, located in the Karakoram Mountain Range, which was seized by India in 1984 with Pakistan attempting to retake the area several times between 1985 and 1995; despite the 2003 cease-fire, both sides continue to maintain a permanent military presence there with outposts at altitudes above 20,000 feet (over 6,000 meters) where most casualties are due to extreme weather and the hazards of operating in the high mountain terrain of the world's highest conflict, including avalanches, exposure, and altitude sickness (2025)

SPACE

Space agency/agencies: Pakistan Space & Upper Atmosphere Research Commission (SUPARCO; established 1961) (2025)

Space launch site(s): none; missile test sites at Somiani (Balochistan) and Tilla Jogian (Punjab) (2025)

Space program overview: space program dates back to the early 1960s but funding shortfalls and shifts in priority toward ballistic missile development in the 1980s and 1990s hampered the program's development; more recently, the program has regained attention and become more ambitious, particularly in acquiring satellites and reaching agreements with other space powers for additional capabilities; manufactures and operates satellites; researching and developing other space-related capabilities and technologies, such as satellite payloads and probably satellite/space launch vehicles (SLVs); also conducts research in such areas as astronomy, astrophysics, environmental monitoring, and space sciences; has relations or cooperation agreements on space with China, Russia, and Turkey (cooperated with the UK and US prior to the 1990s) (2024)
note: further details about the key activities, programs, and milestones of the country's space program, as well as government spending estimates on the space sector, appear in the Space Programs reference guide

TERRORISM

Terrorist group(s): Terrorist group(s): al-Qa'ida; al-Qa'ida in the Indian Subcontinent (AQIS); Haqqani Network (HQN); Harakat ul-Jihad-i-Islami (HUJI); Harakat ul-Mujahidin; Hizbul Mujahideen;

Indian Mujahedeen; Islamic State of Iraq and ash-Sham-Khorasan (ISIS-K); Islamic State of Iraq and ash-Sham – India (ISI); Islamic State of ash-Sham – Pakistan (ISP); Islamic Movement of Uzbekistan (IMU); Jaish-e-Mohammed (JeM); Jaysh al Adl (Jundallah); Lashkar i Jhangvi (LJ); Lashkar-e Tayyiba (LeT); The Resistance Front (TRF); Tehrik-e-Taliban Pakistan (TTP)
note 1: details about the history, aims, leadership, organization, areas of operation, tactics, targets, weapons, size, and sources of support of the group(s) appear(s) in Appendix T
note 2: the Balochistan Liberation Army (BLA), an armed separatist group that targets security forces and civilians, has been active in Pakistan since the 2000s, mainly in ethnic Baloch areas of the country; in 2019, the US designated BLA as Specially Designated Global Terrorists

TRANSNATIONAL ISSUES

Refugees and internally displaced persons: *refugees:* 1,759,332 (2024 est.)
IDPs: 224,813 (2024 est.)
stateless persons: 60 (2024 est.)

Illicit drugs: USG identification: major illicit drug-producing and/or drug-transit country
major precursor-chemical producer (2025)

PALAU

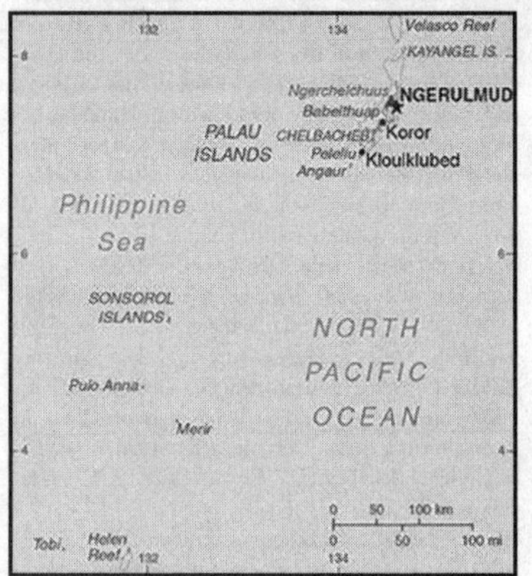

INTRODUCTION

Background: Humans arrived in the Palauan archipelago from Southeast Asia around 1000 B.C. and developed a complex, highly organized matrilineal society where high-ranking women picked the chiefs. The islands were the westernmost part of the widely scattered Pacific islands north of New Guinea that Spanish explorers named the Caroline Islands in the 17th century. The 18th and 19th centuries saw occasional visits of whalers and traders as Spain gained some influence in the islands and administered it from the Philippines. Spain sold Palau to Germany in 1899 after losing the Philippines in the Spanish-American War.

Japan seized Palau in 1914, was granted a League of Nations mandate to administer the islands in 1920, and made Koror the capital of its South Seas Mandate in 1922. By the outbreak of World War II, there were four times as many Japanese living in Koror as Palauans. In 1944, the US invasion of the island of Peleliu was one of the bloodiest island fights of the Pacific War. After the war, Palau became part of the US-administered Trust Territory of the Pacific Islands.

Palau voted against joining the Federated States of Micronesia in 1978 and adopted its own constitution in 1981, which stated that Palau was a nuclear-free country. In 1982, Palau signed a Compact of Free Association (COFA) with the US, which granted Palau financial assistance and access to many US domestic programs in exchange for exclusive US military access and defense responsibilities. However, many Palauans saw the COFA as incompatible with the Palauan Constitution because of the US military's nuclear arsenal, and seven referenda failed to achieve ratification. Following a constitutional amendment and eighth referendum in 1993, the COFA was ratified and entered into force in 1994 when the islands gained their independence. Its funding was renewed in 2010.

Palau has been on the frontlines of combatting climate change and protecting marine resources. In 2011, Palau banned commercial shark fishing and created the world's first shark sanctuary. In 2017, Palau began stamping the Palau Pledge into passports, reminding visitors to act in ecologically and culturally responsible ways. In 2020, Palau banned coral reef-toxic sunscreens and expanded its fishing prohibition to include 80% of its exclusive economic zone.

GEOGRAPHY

Location: Oceania, group of islands in the North Pacific Ocean, southeast of the Philippines

Geographic coordinates: 7 30 N, 134 30 E

Map references: Oceania

Area: *total:* 459 sq km
land: 459 sq km
water: 0 sq km
comparison ranking: total 197

Area - comparative: slightly more than 2.5 times the size of Washington, D.C.

Land boundaries: *total:* 0 km

Coastline: 1,519 km

Maritime claims: *territorial sea:* 12 nm
contiguous zone: 24 nm
exclusive economic zone: 200 nm
continental shelf: 200 nm

Climate: tropical; hot and humid; wet season May to November

Terrain: varying topography from the high, mountainous main island of Babelthuap to low, coral islands usually fringed by large barrier reefs

Elevation: *highest point:* Mount Ngerchelchuus 242 m
lowest point: Pacific Ocean 0 m

Natural resources: forests, minerals (especially gold), marine products, deep-seabed minerals

Land use: *agricultural land:* 9.3% (2022 est.)
arable land: 0.7% (2022 est.)
permanent crops: 4.3% (2022 est.)
permanent pasture: 4.3% (2022 est.)
forest: 90.4% (2022 est.)
other: 0.3% (2022 est.)

Irrigated land: 0 sq km (2022)

Population distribution: most of the population is located on the southern end of the main island of Babelthuap

Natural hazards: typhoons (June to December)

Geography - note: westernmost archipelago in the Caroline chain, consists of six island groups totaling more than 300 islands; includes world-famous Rock Islands

PEOPLE AND SOCIETY

Population: *total:* 21,864 (2024 est.)
male: 11,235
female: 10,629
comparison rankings: total 218; male 218; female 218

Nationality: *noun:* Palauan(s)
adjective: Palauan

Ethnic groups: Palauan (Micronesian with Malayan and Melanesian admixtures) 70.6%, Carolinian 1.2%, Asian 26.5%, other 1.7% (2020 est.)

Languages: Palauan (official on most islands) 65.2%, other Micronesian 1.9%, English (official) 19.1%, Filipino 9.9%, Chinese 1.2%, other 2.8% (2015 est.)
note: Sonsoralese is official in Sonsoral; Tobian is official in Tobi; Angaur and Japanese are official in Angaur

Religions: Roman Catholic 46.9%, Protestant 30.9% (Evangelical 24.6%, Seventh Day Adventist 5%, other Protestant 1.4%), Modekngei 5.1% (indigenous to Palau), Muslim 4.9%, other 12.3% (2020 est.)

Age structure: *0-14 years:* 17.5% (male 1,976/female 1,849)
15-64 years: 71.3% (male 8,647/female 6,935)
65 years and over: 11.2% (2024 est.) (male 612/female 1,845)

Dependency ratios: *total dependency ratio:* 40.3 (2024 est.)
youth dependency ratio: 24.5 (2024 est.)
elderly dependency ratio: 15.8 (2024 est.)
potential support ratio: 6.3 (2024 est.)

Median age: *total:* 35.3 years (2024 est.)
male: 34.1 years
female: 37.4 years
comparison ranking: total 99

Population growth rate: 0.38% (2024 est.)
comparison ranking: 162

Birth rate: 11.6 births/1,000 population (2024 est.)
comparison ranking: 157

Death rate: 8.4 deaths/1,000 population (2024 est.)
comparison ranking: 77

Net migration rate: 0.7 migrant(s)/1,000 population (2024 est.)
comparison ranking: 71

Population distribution: most of the population is located on the southern end of the main island of Babelthuap

Urbanization: *urban population:* 82.4% of total population (2023)
rate of urbanization: 1.59% annual rate of change (2020-25 est.)

Major urban areas - population: 277 NGERULMUD (capital) (2018)

Sex ratio: *at birth:* 1.06 male(s)/female
0-14 years: 1.07 male(s)/female
15-64 years: 1.25 male(s)/female
65 years and over: 0.33 male(s)/female
total population: 1.06 male(s)/female (2024 est.)

Maternal mortality ratio: 89 deaths/100,000 live births (2023 est.)
comparison ranking: 68

Infant mortality rate: *total:* 10.8 deaths/1,000 live births (2024 est.)
male: 12.7 deaths/1,000 live births
female: 8.8 deaths/1,000 live births
comparison ranking: total 126

Life expectancy at birth: *total population:* 75.2 years (2024 est.)
male: 72 years
female: 78.5 years
comparison ranking: total population 131

Total fertility rate: 1.7 children born/woman (2024 est.)
comparison ranking: 166

Gross reproduction rate: 0.83 (2024 est.)

Drinking water source: *improved: urban:* 99.6% of population (2022 est.)
rural: 99.4% of population (2022 est.)
total: 99.6% of population (2022 est.)
unimproved: urban: 0.4% of population (2022 est.)
rural: 0.6% of population (2022 est.)
total: 0.4% of population (2022 est.)

Health expenditure: 16.4% of GDP (2021)
9.5% of national budget (2022 est.)

Physician density: 1.81 physicians/1,000 population (2023)

Sanitation facility access: *improved: urban:* 99.1% of population (2022 est.)
rural: 98.4% of population (2022 est.)
total: 99% of population (2022 est.)
unimproved: urban: 0.9% of population (2022 est.)
rural: 1.6% of population (2022 est.)
total: 1% of population (2022 est.)

Obesity - adult prevalence rate: 55.3% (2016)
comparison ranking: 3

Tobacco use: *total:* 16.3% (2025 est.)
male: 25.2% (2025 est.)
female: 6.8% (2025 est.)
comparison ranking: total 96

Currently married women (ages 15-49): 45.6% (2023 est.)

Education expenditure: 3.5% of GDP (2023 est.)
9.8% national budget (2023 est.)
comparison ranking: Education expenditure (% GDP) 131

Literacy: *total population:* 97% (2015 est.)
male: 97% (2015 est.)
female: 96% (2015 est.)

School life expectancy (primary to tertiary education): *total:* 15 years (2023 est.)
male: 14 years (2023 est.)
female: 16 years (2023 est.)

ENVIRONMENT

Environmental issues: inadequate facilities for disposal of solid waste; threats to the marine ecosystem from sand and coral dredging, illegal fishing practices, and overfishing; rising sea level; coral bleaching; drought

International environmental agreements: *party to:* Biodiversity, Climate Change, Climate Change-Kyoto Protocol, Climate Change-Paris Agreement, Comprehensive Nuclear Test Ban, Desertification, Endangered Species, Hazardous Wastes, Law of the Sea, Ozone Layer Protection, Ship Pollution, Wetlands, Whaling
signed, but not ratified: none of the selected agreements

Climate: tropical; hot and humid; wet season May to November

Urbanization: *urban population:* 82.4% of total population (2023)
rate of urbanization: 1.59% annual rate of change (2020-25 est.)

Particulate matter emissions: 7.9 micrograms per cubic meter (2019 est.)

Waste and recycling: *municipal solid waste generated annually:* 9,400 tons (2024 est.)

GOVERNMENT

Country name: *conventional long form:* Republic of Palau
conventional short form: Palau
local long form: Beluu er a Belau
local short form: Belau
former: Trust Territory of the Pacific Islands, Palau District
etymology: from the Palauan name for the islands, Belau, which likely derives from the Palauan word *beluu*, meaning "village"

Government type: presidential republic in free association with the US

Capital: *name:* Ngerulmud
geographic coordinates: 7 30 N, 134 37 E
time difference: UTC+9 (14 hours ahead of Washington, DC, during Standard Time)
etymology: the name comes from a Palauan term meaning "place of fermented angelfish;" the site of the capital was the traditional location for women to gather and offer fermented angelfish to the gods

Administrative divisions: 16 states; Aimeliik, Airai, Angaur, Hatohobei, Kayangel, Koror, Melekeok, Ngaraard, Ngarchelong, Ngardmau, Ngatpang, Ngchesar, Ngeremlengui, Ngiwal, Peleliu, Sonsorol

Legal system: mixed system of civil, common, and customary law

Constitution: *history:* ratified 9 July 1980, effective 1 January 1981
amendment process: proposed by a constitutional convention (held at least once every 15 years with voter approval), by public petition of at least 25% of eligible voters, or by a resolution adopted by at least three fourths of National Congress members; passage requires approval by a majority of votes in at least three fourths of the states in the next regular general election

International law organization participation: has not submitted an ICJ jurisdiction declaration; non-party state to the ICCt

Citizenship: *citizenship by birth:* no
citizenship by descent only: at least one parent must be a citizen of Palau
dual citizenship recognized: no
residency requirement for naturalization: note - no procedure for naturalization

Suffrage: 18 years of age; universal

Executive branch: *chief of state:* President Surangel WHIPPS, Jr. (since 21 January 2021)
head of government: President Surangel WHIPPS, Jr. (since 21 January 2021)
cabinet: Cabinet appointed by the president with the advice and consent of the Senate; also includes the vice president; the Council of Chiefs consists of chiefs from each of the states who advise the president on issues concerning traditional laws, customs, and their relationship to the constitution and laws
election/appointment process: president and vice president directly elected on separate ballots by absolute-majority popular vote in 2 rounds, if needed, for a 4-year term (eligible for a second term)
most recent election date: 5 November 2024
election results: 2024: Surangel WHIPPS, Jr. elected president in second round; percent of vote - Surangel WHIPPS, Jr. (independent) 57.7%, Tommy REMENGESAU (independent) 42.1%, other 0.2%
2020: Surangel WHIPPS, Jr. elected president in second round; percent of vote - Surangel WHIPPS, Jr. (independent) 56.7%, Raynold OILUCH (independent) 43.3%
expected date of next election: November 2028
note: the president is both chief of state and head of government

Legislative branch: *legislature name:* National Congress (Olbiil Era Kelulau)
legislative structure: bicameral

Legislative branch - lower chamber: *chamber name:* House of Delegates
number of seats: 16 (all directly elected)
electoral system: plurality/majority
scope of elections: full renewal
term in office: 4 years
most recent election date: 11/5/2024
percentage of women in chamber: 25%
expected date of next election: November 2028

Legislative branch - upper chamber: *chamber name:* Senate
number of seats: 15 (all directly elected)
electoral system: plurality/majority
scope of elections: full renewal
term in office: 4 years
most recent election date: 11/5/2024
percentage of women in chamber: 13.3%
expected date of next election: November 2028

Judicial branch: *highest court(s):* Supreme Court (consists of the chief justice and 3 associate justices organized into appellate trial divisions; the Supreme Court organization also includes the Common Pleas and Land Courts)
judge selection and term of office: justices nominated by a 7-member independent body consisting of judges, presidential appointees, and lawyers and appointed by the president; judges can serve until mandatory retirement at age 65
subordinate courts: National Court and other inferior courts

Political parties: none

Diplomatic representation in the US: *chief of mission:* Ambassador Hersey KYOTA (since 12 November 1997)
chancery: 1701 Pennsylvania Avenue NW, Suite 200, Washington, DC 20006
telephone: [1] (202) 349-8598
FAX: [1] (202) 452-6281
email address and website: info@palauembassy.org
https://www.palauembassy.org/
consulate(s): Tamuning (Guam)

Diplomatic representation from the US: *chief of mission:* Ambassador Joel EHRENDREICH (since 29 September 2023)
embassy: Omsangel/Beklelachieb, Airai 96940
mailing address: 4260 Koror Place, Washington, DC 20521-4260
telephone: [680] 587-2920
FAX: [680] 587-2911
email address and website: ConsularKoror@state.gov
https://pw.usembassy.gov/

International organization participation: ACP, ADB, AOSIS, FAO, IAEA, IBRD, ICAO, ICRM, IDA, IFC, IFRCS, ILO, IMF, IMO, IMSO, IOC, IPU, MIGA, OPCW, PIF, Sparteca, SPC, UN, UNAMID, UNCTAD, UNESCO, WHO, WIPO

Independence: 1 October 1994 (from the US-administered UN trusteeship)

National holiday: Constitution Day, 9 July (1981); Independence Day, 1 October (1994)

Flag: *description:* light blue with a large yellow disk to the left side
meaning: blue stands for the ocean, and the disk for the moon, which is considered a symbol of peace, love, and tranquility

National symbol(s): bai (native meeting house)

National color(s): blue, yellow

National anthem(s): *title:* "Belau rekid" (Our Palau)
lyrics/music: multiple/Ymesei O. EZEKIEL
history: adopted 1980

National heritage: *total World Heritage Sites:* 1 (mixed)
selected World Heritage Site locales: Rock Islands Southern Lagoon

ECONOMY

Economic overview: high-income Pacific island economy; environmentally fragile; subsistence agriculture and fishing industries; US aid reliance; rebounding post-pandemic tourism industry and services sector; very high living standard and low unemployment

Real GDP (purchasing power parity): $280.025 million (2023 est.)
$274.866 million (2022 est.)
$278.538 million (2021 est.)
note: data in 2021 dollars
comparison ranking: 214

Real GDP growth rate: 1.9% (2023 est.)
-1.3% (2022 est.)
-13.8% (2021 est.)
note: annual GDP % growth based on constant local currency
comparison ranking: 150

Real GDP per capita: $15,800 (2023 est.)
$15,500 (2022 est.)
$15,700 (2021 est.)
note: data in 2021 dollars
comparison ranking: 121

GDP (official exchange rate): $281.849 million (2023 est.)
note: data in current dollars at official exchange rate

Inflation rate (consumer prices): 2.2% (2024 est.)
12.8% (2023 est.)
12.4% (2022 est.)
note: annual % change based on consumer prices
comparison ranking: 60

GDP - composition, by sector of origin: *agriculture:* 3% (2023 est.)
industry: 9.9% (2023 est.)
services: 76.7% (2023 est.)
note: figures may not total 100% due to non-allocated consumption not captured in sector-reported data
comparison rankings: agriculture 131; industry 186; services 17

GDP - composition, by end use: *household consumption:* 77.8% (2022 est.)
government consumption: 36.3% (2022 est.)
investment in fixed capital: 36.6% (2022 est.)
investment in inventories: 1.8% (2022 est.)
exports of goods and services: 13.5% (2022 est.)
imports of goods and services: -74.3% (2022 est.)
note: figures may not total 100% due to rounding or gaps in data collection

Agricultural products: coconuts, cassava (manioc, tapioca), sweet potatoes; fish, pigs, chickens, eggs, bananas, papaya, breadfruit, calamansi, soursop, Polynesian chestnuts, Polynesian almonds, mangoes, taro, guava, beans, cucumbers, squash/pumpkins (various), eggplant, green onions, kangkong (watercress), cabbages (various), radishes, betel nuts, melons, peppers, noni, okra

Industries: tourism, fishing, subsistence agriculture

Industrial production growth rate: -19.5% (2023 est.)
note: annual % change in industrial value added based on constant local currency
comparison ranking: 191

Remittances: 0.7% of GDP (2023 est.)
0.8% of GDP (2022 est.)
0.8% of GDP (2021 est.)
note: personal transfers and compensation between resident and non-resident individuals/households/entities

Budget: *revenues:* $127.757 million (2020 est.)
expenditures: $152.398 million (2020 est.)
note: central government revenues and expenses (excluding grants/extrabudgetary units/social security funds) converted to US dollars at average official exchange rate for year indicated

Public debt: 85.2% of GDP (2019 est.)
note: central government debt as a % of GDP
comparison ranking: 32

Taxes and other revenues: 18.1% (of GDP) (2020 est.)
note: central government tax revenue as a % of GDP
comparison ranking: 64

Current account balance: -$135.428 million (2022 est.)
-$115.739 million (2021 est.)
-$115.61 million (2020 est.)
note: balance of payments - net trade and primary/secondary income in current dollars
comparison ranking: 98

Exports: $24.48 million (2022 est.)
$10.566 million (2021 est.)
$52.897 million (2020 est.)
note: balance of payments - exports of goods and services in current dollars
comparison ranking: 210

Exports - partners: India 41%, Turkey 26%, Taiwan 10%, USA 9%, Japan 5% (2023)
note: top five export partners based on percentage share of exports

Exports - commodities: ships, refined petroleum (2023)
note: top export commodities based on value in dollars over $500,000

Imports: $216.681 million (2022 est.)
$169.938 million (2021 est.)
$207.224 million (2020 est.)
note: balance of payments - imports of goods and services in current dollars
comparison ranking: 208

Imports - partners: Italy 32%, China 25%, USA 11%, Turkey 10%, Japan 6% (2023)
note: top five import partners based on percentage share of imports

Imports - commodities: ships, refined petroleum, additive manufacturing machines, cars, plastic products (2023)
note: top five import commodities based on value in dollars

Exchange rates: the US dollar is used

ENERGY

Electricity access: *electrification - total population:* 100% (2022 est.)
electrification - urban areas: 99.9%
electrification - rural areas: 100%

COMMUNICATIONS

Telephones - fixed lines: *total subscriptions:* 8,000 (2023 est.)
subscriptions per 100 inhabitants: 45 (2023 est.)
comparison ranking: total subscriptions 191

Telephones - mobile cellular: *total subscriptions:* 24,000 (2023 est.)
subscriptions per 100 inhabitants: 133 (2022 est.)
comparison ranking: total subscriptions 214

Broadcast media: no broadcast TV stations; a cable TV network covers the major islands and provides access to 4 local cable stations, rebroadcasts (on a delayed basis) of a number of US stations, as well as access to a number of real-time satellite TV channels; about a half dozen radio stations (1 government-owned) (2019)

Internet country code: .pw

Internet users: *percent of population:* 27% (2004 est.)

Broadband - fixed subscriptions: *total:* 1,000 (2023 est.)
subscriptions per 100 inhabitants: 7 (2023 est.)
comparison ranking: total 204

TRANSPORTATION

Civil aircraft registration country code prefix: T8

Airports: 3 (2025)
comparison ranking: 188

Merchant marine: *total:* 427 (2023)
by type: bulk carrier 49, container ship 8, general cargo 200, oil tanker 52, other 118
comparison ranking: total 47

Ports: *total ports:* 1 (2024)
large: 0
medium: 0

small: 0
very small: 1
ports with oil terminals: 1
key ports: Malakal Harbor

MILITARY AND SECURITY

Military and security forces: no regular military forces; the Bureau of Public Safety (Ministry of Justice) has divisions for police functions and maritime security (2025)

Military - note: under the Compact of Free Association between Palau and the US, the US is responsible for the defense of Palau and the US military is granted access to the islands; the COFA also allows citizens of Palau to serve in the US armed forces

Palau has a "shiprider" agreement with the US, which allows local maritime law enforcement officers to embark on US Coast Guard (USCG) and US Navy (USN) vessels, including to board and search vessels suspected of violating laws or regulations within Palau's designated exclusive economic zone (EEZ) or on the high seas; "shiprider" agreements also enable USCG personnel and USN vessels with embarked USCG law enforcement personnel to work with host nations to protect critical regional resources (2025)

TRANSNATIONAL ISSUES

Refugees and internally displaced persons: *refugees:* 5 (2024 est.)

PANAMA

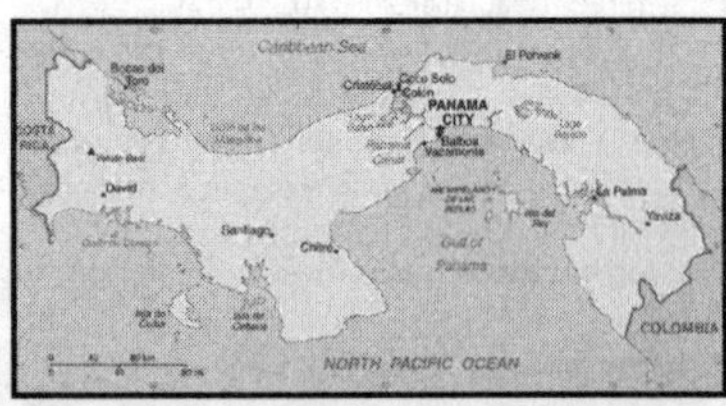

INTRODUCTION

Background: Explored and settled by the Spanish in the 16th century, Panama broke with Spain in 1821 and joined a union of Colombia, Ecuador, and Venezuela that was named the Republic of Gran Colombia. When the union dissolved in 1830, Panama remained part of Colombia. With US backing, Panama seceded from Colombia in 1903 and promptly signed a treaty with the US allowing for the construction of a canal and US sovereignty over a strip of land known as the Panama Canal Zone on either side of the structure. The US Army Corps of Engineers built the Panama Canal between 1904 and 1914. In 1977, an agreement was signed for the complete transfer of the Canal from the US to Panama by the end of the century. Certain portions of the Zone and increasing responsibility over the Canal were turned over in the subsequent decades. With US help, Panamanian dictator Manuel NORIEGA was deposed in 1989. The entire Panama Canal, the area supporting the Canal, and remaining US military bases were transferred to Panama by the end of 1999. An ambitious expansion project to more than double the Canal's capacity by allowing for more Canal transits and larger ships was carried out between 2007 and 2016.

GEOGRAPHY

Location: Central America, bordering both the Caribbean Sea and the North Pacific Ocean, between Colombia and Costa Rica

Geographic coordinates: 9 00 N, 80 00 W

Map references: Central America and the Caribbean

Area: *total:* 75,420 sq km
land: 74,340 sq km
water: 1,080 sq km
comparison ranking: total 118

Area - comparative: slightly smaller than South Carolina

Land boundaries: *total:* 687 km
border countries (2): Colombia 339 km; Costa Rica 348 km

Coastline: 2,490 km

Maritime claims: *territorial sea:* 12 nm
contiguous zone: 24 nm
exclusive economic zone: 200 nm or edge of continental margin

Climate: tropical maritime; hot, humid, cloudy; prolonged rainy season (May to January), short dry season (January to May)

Terrain: interior mostly steep, rugged mountains with dissected, upland plains; coastal plains with rolling hills

Elevation: *highest point:* Volcan Baru 3,475 m
lowest point: Pacific Ocean 0 m
mean elevation: 360 m

Natural resources: copper, mahogany forests, shrimp, hydropower

Land use: *agricultural land:* 29.4% (2022 est.)
arable land: 7.6% (2022 est.)
permanent crops: 1.4% (2022 est.)
permanent pasture: 20.3% (2022 est.)
forest: 56.5% (2022 est.)
other: 14.1% (2022 est.)

Irrigated land: 394 sq km (2022)

Major lakes (area sq km): *salt water lake(s):* Laguna de Chiriqui - 900 sq km

Population distribution: population is concentrated towards the center of the country, particularly around the Canal, but a sizeable segment of the populace also lives in the far west around David; the eastern third of the country is sparsely inhabited

Natural hazards: occasional severe storms and forest fires in the Darien area

Geography - note: strategic location on eastern end of isthmus forming land bridge that connects North and South America; controls the Panama Canal, which links the North Atlantic Ocean with the North Pacific Ocean via the Caribbean Sea

PEOPLE AND SOCIETY

Population: *total:* 4,470,241 (2024 est.)
male: 2,251,257
female: 2,218,984
comparison rankings: total 127; male 127; female 128

Nationality: *noun:* Panamanian(s)
adjective: Panamanian

Ethnic groups: Mestizo (mixed Indigenous and White) 65%, Indigenous 12.3% (Ngabe 7.6%, Kuna 2.4%, Embera 0.9%, Bugle 0.8%, other 0.4%, unspecified 0.2%), Black or African descent 9.2%, Mulatto 6.8%, White 6.7% (2010 est.)

Languages: Spanish (official), Indigenous languages (including Ngabere (Guaymi), Buglere, Kuna, Embera, Wounaan, Naso (Teribe), and Bri Bri), Panamanian English Creole (a mixture of English and Spanish with elements of Ngabere, also known as Guari Guari and Colon Creole), English, Chinese (Yue and Hakka), Arabic, French Creole, other (Yiddish, Hebrew, Korean, Japanese)
major-language sample(s):
La Libreta Informativa del Mundo, la fuente indispensable de información básica. (Spanish)

Religions: Evangelical 55%, Roman Catholic 33.4%, none 10.1%, unspecified 1.5% (2023 est.)

Age structure: *0-14 years:* 25% (male 574,336/female 544,180)
15-64 years: 64.8% (male 1,465,907/female 1,433,023)
65 years and over: 10.1% (2024 est.) (male 211,014/female 241,781)

Dependency ratios: *total dependency ratio:* 54.2 (2024 est.)
youth dependency ratio: 38.6 (2024 est.)
elderly dependency ratio: 15.6 (2024 est.)
potential support ratio: 6.4 (2024 est.)

Median age: *total:* 31.5 years (2024 est.)
male: 31 years
female: 31.9 years
comparison ranking: total 127

Population growth rate: 1.48% (2024 est.)
comparison ranking: 66

Birth rate: 17.4 births/1,000 population (2024 est.)
comparison ranking: 86

Death rate: 5.7 deaths/1,000 population (2024 est.)
comparison ranking: 170

Net migration rate: 3 migrant(s)/1,000 population (2024 est.)
comparison ranking: 36

Population distribution: population is concentrated towards the center of the country, particularly around the Canal, but a sizeable segment of the populace also lives in the far west around David; the eastern third of the country is sparsely inhabited

Urbanization: *urban population:* 69.5% of total population (2023)
rate of urbanization: 1.92% annual rate of change (2020-25 est.)

Major urban areas - population: 1.977 million PANAMA CITY (capital) (2023)

Sex ratio: *at birth:* 1.06 male(s)/female

0-14 years: 1.06 male(s)/female
15-64 years: 1.02 male(s)/female
65 years and over: 0.87 male(s)/female
total population: 1.02 male(s)/female (2024 est.)

Maternal mortality ratio: 37 deaths/100,000 live births (2023 est.)
comparison ranking: 106

Infant mortality rate: *total:* 14.2 deaths/1,000 live births (2024 est.)
male: 15.4 deaths/1,000 live births
female: 12.9 deaths/1,000 live births
comparison ranking: total 98

Life expectancy at birth: *total population:* 79.2 years (2024 est.)
male: 76.4 years
female: 82.2 years
comparison ranking: total population 66

Total fertility rate: 2.35 children born/woman (2024 est.)
comparison ranking: 74

Gross reproduction rate: 1.14 (2024 est.)

Drinking water source: *improved: urban:* 98.5% of population (2022 est.)
rural: 86.1% of population (2022 est.)
total: 94.7% of population (2022 est.)
unimproved: urban: 1.5% of population (2022 est.)
rural: 13.9% of population (2022 est.)
total: 5.3% of population (2022 est.)

Health expenditure: 9.7% of GDP (2021)
22.2% of national budget (2022 est.)

Physician density: 1.63 physicians/1,000 population (2022)

Hospital bed density: 1.9 beds/1,000 population (2020 est.)

Sanitation facility access: *improved: urban:* 96.1% of population (2022 est.)
rural: 70.1% of population (2022 est.)
total: 88% of population (2022 est.)
unimproved: urban: 3.9% of population (2022 est.)
rural: 29.9% of population (2022 est.)
total: 12% of population (2022 est.)

Obesity - adult prevalence rate: 22.7% (2016)
comparison ranking: 73

Alcohol consumption per capita: *total:* 6.54 liters of pure alcohol (2019 est.)
beer: 5.29 liters of pure alcohol (2019 est.)
wine: 0.02 liters of pure alcohol (2019 est.)
spirits: 1.2 liters of pure alcohol (2019 est.)
other alcohols: 0.02 liters of pure alcohol (2019 est.)
comparison ranking: total 63

Tobacco use: *total:* 4.5% (2025 est.)
male: 7.4% (2025 est.)
female: 1.7% (2025 est.)
comparison ranking: total 166

Children under the age of 5 years underweight: 2.9% (2019)
comparison ranking: 83

Currently married women (ages 15-49): 58.6% (2023 est.)

Education expenditure: 3.9% of GDP (2023 est.)
11.9% national budget (2023 est.)
comparison ranking: Education expenditure (% GDP) 112

Literacy: *total population:* 96% (2019 est.)
male: 96% (2019 est.)
female: 95% (2019 est.)

School life expectancy (primary to tertiary education): *total:* 13 years (2016 est.)
male: 12 years (2016 est.)
female: 14 years (2016 est.)

ENVIRONMENT

Environmental issues: water pollution from agricultural runoff; deforestation of tropical rainforest; land degradation and soil erosion in Panama Canal; air pollution in urban areas; effects of mining

International environmental agreements: *party to:* Antarctic-Marine Living Resources, Biodiversity, Climate Change, Climate Change-Kyoto Protocol, Climate Change-Paris Agreement, Comprehensive Nuclear Test Ban, Desertification, Endangered Species, Environmental Modification, Hazardous Wastes, Law of the Sea, Marine Dumping-London Convention, Nuclear Test Ban, Ozone Layer Protection, Ship Pollution, Tropical Timber 2006, Wetlands, Whaling
signed, but not ratified: Marine Life Conservation

Climate: tropical maritime; hot, humid, cloudy; prolonged rainy season (May to January), short dry season (January to May)

Urbanization: *urban population:* 69.5% of total population (2023)
rate of urbanization: 1.92% annual rate of change (2020-25 est.)

Carbon dioxide emissions: 23.458 million metric tonnes of CO2 (2023 est.)
from coal and metallurgical coke: 1.969 million metric tonnes of CO2 (2023 est.)
from petroleum and other liquids: 20.389 million metric tonnes of CO2 (2023 est.)
from consumed natural gas: 1.101 million metric tonnes of CO2 (2023 est.)
comparison ranking: total emissions 79

Particulate matter emissions: 11.9 micrograms per cubic meter (2019 est.)

Waste and recycling: *municipal solid waste generated annually:* 1.472 million tons (2024 est.)
percent of municipal solid waste recycled: 14.2% (2022 est.)

Total water withdrawal: *municipal:* 759.1 million cubic meters (2022 est.)
industrial: 6.2 million cubic meters (2022 est.)
agricultural: 446.1 million cubic meters (2022 est.)

Total renewable water resources: 139.304 billion cubic meters (2022 est.)

GOVERNMENT

Country name: *conventional long form:* Republic of Panama
conventional short form: Panama
local long form: República de Panama
local short form: Panama
etymology: origin is unclear; may come from a Guarani word meaning "place of many fish"

Government type: presidential republic

Capital: *name:* Panama City
geographic coordinates: 8 58 N, 79 32 W
time difference: UTC-5 (same time as Washington, DC, during Standard Time)
etymology: origin is unclear; may come from a Guaraní word meaning "place of many fish"

Administrative divisions: 10 provinces (*provincias*, singular - *provincia*) and 4 indigenous regions* (*comarcas*); Bocas del Toro, Chiriqui, Cocle, Colon, Darien, Embera-Wounaan*, Guna Yala*, Herrera, Los Santos, Naso Tjer Di*, Ngabe-Bugle*, Panama, Panama Oeste, Veraguas

Legal system: civil law system; Supreme Court of Justice reviews legislative acts

Constitution: *history:* several previous; latest effective 11 October 1972
amendment process: proposed by the National Assembly, by the Cabinet, or by the Supreme Court of Justice; passage requires approval by one of two procedures: 1) absolute majority vote of the Assembly membership in each of three readings and by absolute majority vote of the next elected Assembly in a single reading without textual modifications; 2) absolute majority vote of the Assembly membership in each of three readings, followed by absolute majority vote of the next elected Assembly in each of three readings with textual modifications, and approval in a referendum

International law organization participation: accepts compulsory ICJ jurisdiction with reservations; accepts ICCt jurisdiction

Citizenship: *citizenship by birth:* yes
citizenship by descent only: yes
dual citizenship recognized: no
residency requirement for naturalization: 5 years

Suffrage: 18 years of age; universal

Executive branch: *chief of state:* President José Raúl MULINO Quintero (since 1 July 2024)
head of government: President José Raúl MULINO Quintero (since 1 July 2024)
cabinet: Cabinet appointed by the president
election/appointment process: president and vice president directly elected on the same ballot by simple-majority popular vote for a 5-year term; president eligible for a single non-consecutive term)
most recent election date: 5 May 2024
election results: 2024: José Raúl MULINO Quintero elected president; percent of vote - José Raúl MULINO Quintero (RM) 34.2%, Ricardo Alberto LOMBANA González (MOCA) 24.6%, Martín Erasto TORRIJOS Espino (PP) 16%, Alberto ROUX Moses (CD) 11.4%, Zulay RODRÍGUEZ Lu (independent) 6.6%, José Gabriel CARRIZO Jaén (PRD) 5.9%, other 1.3%
2019: Laurentino "Nito" CORTIZO Cohen elected president; percent of vote - Laurentino CORTIZO Cohen (PRD) 33.3%, Romulo ROUX (CD) 31%, Ricardo LOMBANA (independent) 18.8%, Jose BLANDON (Panameñista Party) 10.8%, Ana Matilde GOMEZ Ruiloba (independent) 4.8%, other 1.3%
expected date of next election: May 2029
note: the president is both chief of state and head of government

Legislative branch: *legislature name:* National Assembly (Asamblea Nacional)
legislative structure: unicameral
number of seats: 71 (all directly elected)
electoral system: mixed system
scope of elections: full renewal
term in office: 5 years
most recent election date: 5/5/2024
parties elected and seats per party: Realizing Goals (RM) (14); Democratic Revolutionary Party (PRD) (13); Democratic Change (CD) (8); Panamenista Party (8); Independents (20); Other (8)
percentage of women in chamber: 21.7%
expected date of next election: May 2029

Judicial branch: *highest court(s):* Supreme Court of Justice or Corte Suprema de Justicia (consists of 9 magistrates and 9 alternates and divided into

civil, criminal, administrative, and general business chambers)
judge selection and term of office: magistrates appointed by the president for staggered 10-year terms
subordinate courts: appellate courts or Tribunal Superior; Labor Supreme Courts; Court of Audit; circuit courts or Tribunal Circuital (2 each in 9 of the 10 provinces); municipal courts; electoral, family, maritime, and adolescent courts

Political parties: Alliance Party or PA
Alternative Independent Socialist Party or PAIS
Another Way Movement or MOCA
Democratic Change or CD
Democratic Revolutionary Party or PRD
Nationalist Republican Liberal Movement or MOLIRENA
Panameñista Party (formerly the Arnulfista Party)
Popular Party or PP (formerly Christian Democratic Party or PDC)
Realizing Goals Party or RM

Diplomatic representation in the US: *chief of mission:* Ambassador José Miguel ALEMÁN HEALY (since 18 September 2024)
chancery: 2862 McGill Terrace NW, Washington, DC 20008
telephone: [1] (202) 483-1407
FAX: [1] (202) 483-8413
email address and website: info@embassyofpanama.org
https://www.embassyofpanama.org/
consulate(s) general: Houston, Los Angeles, Miami, New Orleans, New York, Philadelphia, Tampa

Diplomatic representation from the US: *chief of mission:* Ambassador Kevin Marino CABRERA (since 5 May 2025)
embassy: Building 783, Demetrio Basilio Lakas Avenue, Clayton
mailing address: 9100 Panama City PL, Washington, DC 20521-9100
telephone: [507] 317-5000
FAX: [507] 317-5568
email address and website: Panama-ACS@state.gov
https://pa.usembassy.gov/

International organization participation: ACS, BCIE, CAN (observer), CD, CELAC, FAO, G-77, IADB, IAEA, IBRD, ICAO, ICC (national committees), ICCt, ICRM, IDA, IFAD, IFC, IFRCS, ILO, IMF, IMO, IMSO, Interpol, IOC, IOM, IPU, ISO, ITSO, ITU, ITUC (NGOs), LAES, LAIA, MIGA, NAM, OAS, OPANAL, OPCW, Pacific Alliance (observer), PCA, SICA, UN, UNASUR (observer), UNCTAD, UNESCO, UNIDO, Union Latina, UNOOSA, UNWTO, UPU, WCO, WFTU (NGOs), WHO, WIPO, WMO, WTO

Independence: 3 November 1903 (from Colombia); 28 November 1821 (from Spain)

National holiday: Independence Day (Separation Day), 3 November (1903)

Flag: *description:* divided into four equal rectangles; one of the top quadrants is white (left side) with a five-pointed blue star in the center, and the other is plain red; one of the bottom quadrants is plain blue (left side), and the other is white with a five-pointed red star in the center
meaning: blue and red stand for the main political parties, and white for peace between them; the blue star stands for the civic virtues of purity and honesty, and the red star for authority and law

National symbol(s): harpy eagle

National color(s): blue, white, red

National anthem(s): *title:* "Himno Istmeno" (Isthmus Hymn)
lyrics/music: Jeronimo DE LA OSSA/Santos A. JORGE
history: adopted 1925

National heritage: *total World Heritage Sites:* 6 (3 cultural, 3 natural)
selected World Heritage Site locales: Caribbean Fortifications (c); Darien National Park (n); Talamanca Range-La Amistad National Park (n); Panamá Viejo and Historic District of Panamá (c); Coiba National Park (n); The Colonial Transisthmian Route of Panamá (c)

ECONOMY

Economic overview: upper middle-income Central American economy; increasing Chinese trade; US dollar user; canal expansion fueling broader infrastructure investment; services sector dominates economy; historic money-laundering and illegal drug hub

Real GDP (purchasing power parity): $164.484 billion (2024 est.)
$159.908 billion (2023 est.)
$148.891 billion (2022 est.)
note: data in 2021 dollars
comparison ranking: 80

Real GDP growth rate: 2.9% (2024 est.)
7.4% (2023 est.)
10.8% (2022 est.)
note: annual GDP % growth based on constant local currency
comparison ranking: 120

Real GDP per capita: $36,400 (2024 est.)
$35,900 (2023 est.)
$33,800 (2022 est.)
note: data in 2021 dollars
comparison ranking: 64

GDP (official exchange rate): $86.26 billion (2024 est.)
note: data in current dollars at official exchange rate

Inflation rate (consumer prices): 0.7% (2024 est.)
1.5% (2023 est.)
2.9% (2022 est.)
note: annual % change based on consumer prices
comparison ranking: 14

GDP - composition, by sector of origin: *agriculture:* 2.6% (2024 est.)
industry: 26.3% (2024 est.)
services: 68.8% (2024 est.)
note: figures may not total 100% due to non-allocated consumption not captured in sector-reported data
comparison rankings: agriculture 136; industry 75; services 42

GDP - composition, by end use: *household consumption:* 46.7% (2023 est.)
government consumption: 12.2% (2023 est.)
investment in fixed capital: 32.3% (2023 est.)
investment in inventories: 5.4% (2023 est.)
exports of goods and services: 46.5% (2023 est.)
imports of goods and services: -43.1% (2023 est.)
note: figures may not total 100% due to rounding or gaps in data collection

Agricultural products: sugarcane, rice, bananas, oranges, oil palm fruit, chicken, plantains, maize, milk, pineapples (2023)
note: top ten agricultural products based on tonnage

Industries: construction, brewing, cement and other construction materials, sugar milling

Industrial production growth rate: -2.6% (2024 est.)
note: annual % change in industrial value added based on constant local currency
comparison ranking: 166

Labor force: 2.206 million (2024 est.)
note: number of people ages 15 or older who are employed or seeking work
comparison ranking: 124

Unemployment rate: 6.6% (2024 est.)
6.6% (2023 est.)
8.1% (2022 est.)
note: % of labor force seeking employment
comparison ranking: 121

Youth unemployment rate (ages 15-24): *total:* 16.8% (2024 est.)
male: 13.4% (2024 est.)
female: 22.1% (2024 est.)
note: % of labor force ages 15-24 seeking employment
comparison ranking: total 66

Population below poverty line: 21.8% (2021 est.)
note: % of population with income below national poverty line

Gini Index coefficient - distribution of family income: 48.9 (2023 est.)
note: index (0-100) of income distribution; higher values represent greater inequality
comparison ranking: 12

Average household expenditures: *on food:* 15.4% of household expenditures (2023 est.)
on alcohol and tobacco: 1.6% of household expenditures (2023 est.)

Household income or consumption by percentage share: *lowest 10%:* 1.2% (2023 est.)
highest 10%: 36.9% (2023 est.)
note: % share of income accruing to lowest and highest 10% of population

Remittances: 0.6% of GDP (2024 est.)
0.6% of GDP (2023 est.)
0.7% of GDP (2022 est.)
note: personal transfers and compensation between resident and non-resident individuals/households/entities

Budget: *revenues:* $7.57 billion (2021 est.)
expenditures: $12.046 billion (2021 est.)
note: central government revenues and expenses (excluding grants/extrabudgetary units/social security funds) converted to US dollars at average official exchange rate for year indicated

Taxes and other revenues: 7.5% (of GDP) (2021 est.)
note: central government tax revenue as a % of GDP
comparison ranking: 140

Current account balance: $1.672 billion (2024 est.)
-$2.581 billion (2023 est.)
$28.769 million (2022 est.)
note: balance of payments - net trade and primary/secondary income in current dollars
comparison ranking: 52

Exports: $37.376 billion (2024 est.)
$37.905 billion (2023 est.)
$35.717 billion (2022 est.)
note: balance of payments - exports of goods and services in current dollars
comparison ranking: 76

Exports - partners: China 25%, Japan 10%, USA 6%, Thailand 5%, Costa Rica 5% (2023)
note: top five export partners based on percentage share of exports

Exports - commodities: copper ore, ships, refined petroleum, bananas, fish (2023)

note: top five export commodities based on value in dollars

Imports: $30.887 billion (2024 est.)
$35.927 billion (2023 est.)
$32.646 billion (2022 est.)
note: balance of payments - imports of goods and services in current dollars
comparison ranking: 81

Imports - partners: USA 15%, Colombia 13%, China 13%, Ecuador 13%, Japan 11% (2023)
note: top five import partners based on percentage share of imports

Imports - commodities: crude petroleum, ships, refined petroleum, nitrogen compounds, cars (2023)
note: top five import commodities based on value in dollars

Reserves of foreign exchange and gold: $6.856 billion (2024 est.)
$6.757 billion (2023 est.)
$6.876 billion (2022 est.)
note: holdings of gold (year-end prices)/foreign exchange/special drawing rights in current dollars
comparison ranking: 88

Exchange rates: balboas (PAB) per US dollar -

Exchange rates: 1 (2024 est.)
1 (2023 est.)
1 (2022 est.)
1 (2021 est.)
1 (2020 est.)

ENERGY

Electricity access: *electrification - total population:* 95% (2022 est.)
electrification - urban areas: 99%
electrification - rural areas: 100%

Electricity: *installed generating capacity:* 4.485 million kW (2023 est.)
consumption: 11.777 billion kWh (2023 est.)
exports: 404.9 million kWh (2023 est.)
imports: 234 million kWh (2023 est.)
transmission/distribution losses: 924.16 million kWh (2023 est.)
comparison rankings: installed generating capacity 95; consumption 101; exports 80; imports 104; transmission/distribution losses 95

Electricity generation sources: *fossil fuels:* 38.2% of total installed capacity (2023 est.)
solar: 6.8% of total installed capacity (2023 est.)
wind: 6.9% of total installed capacity (2023 est.)
hydroelectricity: 47.8% of total installed capacity (2023 est.)
biomass and waste: 0.3% of total installed capacity (2023 est.)

Coal: *consumption:* 863,000 metric tons (2023 est.)
imports: 863,000 metric tons (2023 est.)

Petroleum: *refined petroleum consumption:* 131,000 bbl/day (2023 est.)

Natural gas: *consumption:* 564.786 million cubic meters (2023 est.)
imports: 564.786 million cubic meters (2023 est.)

Energy consumption per capita: 78.01 million Btu/person (2023 est.)
comparison ranking: 67

COMMUNICATIONS

Telephones - fixed lines: *total subscriptions:* 811,000 (2023 est.)
subscriptions per 100 inhabitants: 18 (2023 est.)
comparison ranking: total subscriptions 75

Telephones - mobile cellular: *total subscriptions:* 6.98 million (2023 est.)
subscriptions per 100 inhabitants: 156 (2022 est.)
comparison ranking: total subscriptions 114

Broadcast media: multiple privately owned TV networks and a government-owned educational TV station; multichannel cable and satellite TV subscription services are available; more than 100 commercial radio stations (2019)

Internet country code: .pa

Internet users: *percent of population:* 78% (2023 est.)

Broadband - fixed subscriptions: *total:* 809,000 (2023 est.)
subscriptions per 100 inhabitants: 18 (2023 est.)
comparison ranking: total 83

TRANSPORTATION

Civil aircraft registration country code prefix: HP

Airports: 77 (2025)
comparison ranking: 67

Heliports: 1 (2025)
comparison ranking: 157

Railways: *total:* 77 km (2014)
standard gauge: 77 km (2014) 1.435-m gauge

Merchant marine: *total:* 8,174 (2023)
by type: bulk carrier 2732, container ship 671, general cargo 1,428, oil tanker 866, other 2,477
comparison ranking: total 3

Ports: *total ports:* 12 (2024)
large: 0
medium: 3
small: 3
very small: 5
size unknown: 1
ports with oil terminals: 5
key ports: Bahia de las Minas, Balboa, Pedregal, Puerto Armuelles, Puerto Colon, Puerto Cristobal

MILITARY AND SECURITY

Military and security forces: *no regular military forces; Ministry of Public Security:* National Police (Policía Nacional, PN), National Aeronaval Service (Servicio Nacional Aeronaval, SENAN), National Border Service (Servicio Nacional de Fronteras, SENAFRONT) (2025)
note 1: collectively, the security forces are known as the Panamanian Public Forces
note 2: the PNP includes a special forces directorate with counterterrorism and counternarcotics units; SENAFRONT has four regionally based border security brigades, plus a specialized brigade comprised of special forces, counternarcotics, maritime, and rapid reaction units

Military expenditures: 1.1% of GDP (2024 est.)
1.1% of GDP (2023 est.)
1.2% of GDP (2022 est.)
1.3% of GDP (2021 est.)
1.4% of GDP (2020 est.)

Military and security service personnel strengths: approximately 30,000 Ministry of Public Security personnel (2025)

Military - note: the Panamanian Public Forces focus on law enforcement, border control, and maritime security; the National Police are responsible for internal law enforcement and public order, while the National Border Service (SENAFRONT) handles border security; the Aeronaval Service is responsible for carrying out air and naval operations that include some internal security responsibilities; key areas of focus are countering narcotics trafficking and securing the border, particularly along the frontier with Colombia where SENAFRONT maintains a significant presence
Panama created a paramilitary National Guard (Guardia Nacional de Panamá) in the 1950s from the former National Police (established 1904); the National Guard subsequently evolved into more of a military force with some police responsibilities; it seized power in a coup in 1968 and military officers ran the country until 1989; in 1983, the National Guard was renamed the Panama Defense Force (PDF); the PDF was disbanded after the 1989 US invasion and the current national police forces were formed in 1990; the armed forces were officially abolished under the 1994 Constitution (2025)

TERRORISM

Terrorist group(s): Terrorist group(s): Tren de Aragua (TdA)
note: details about the history, aims, leadership, organization, areas of operation, tactics, targets, weapons, size, and sources of support of the group(s) appear(s) in Appendix T

TRANSNATIONAL ISSUES

Refugees and internally displaced persons: *refugees:* 10,801 (2024 est.)
stateless persons: 928 (2024 est.)

Illicit drugs: USG identification: major illicit drug-producing and/or drug-transit country (2025)

PAPUA NEW GUINEA

INTRODUCTION

Background: Papua New Guinea (PNG) occupies the eastern half of the island of New Guinea; the western half is part of Indonesia. PNG was first settled between 50,000 and 60,000 years ago. Its harsh geography of mountains, jungles, and numerous river valleys kept many of the arriving groups isolated, giving rise to PNG's ethnic and linguistic diversity. Around 500 B.C., Austronesian voyagers settled along the coast. Spanish and Portuguese explorers periodically visited the island starting in the 1500s, but none made it into the country's interior. American and British whaling ships frequented the islands off the coast of New Guinea in the mid-1800s. In 1884,

Germany declared a protectorate – and eventually a colony – over the northern part of what would become PNG and named it German New Guinea; days later the UK followed suit on the southern part and nearby islands and called it Papua. Most of their focus was on the coastal regions, leaving the highlands largely unexplored.

The UK put its colony under Australian administration in 1902 and formalized the act in 1906. At the outbreak of World War I, Australia occupied German New Guinea and continued to rule it after the war as a League of Nations Mandate. The discovery of gold along the Bulolo River in the 1920s led prospectors to venture into the highlands, where they found about 1 million people living in isolated communities. The New Guinea campaign of World War II lasted from January 1942 to the Japanese surrender in August 1945. After the war, Australia combined the two territories and administered PNG as a UN trusteeship. In 1975, PNG gained independence and became a member of the Commonwealth.

Between 1988-1997, a secessionist movement on the island province of Bougainville, located off the eastern PNG coast, fought the PNG Government, resulting in 15,000-20,000 deaths. In 1997, the PNG Government and Bougainville leaders reached a cease-fire and subsequently signed a peace agreement in 2001. The Autonomous Bougainville Government was formally established in 2005. Bougainvilleans voted in favor of independence in a 2019 non-binding referendum. The Bougainville and PNG governments are in the process of negotiating a roadmap for independence, which requires approval by the PNG parliament.

GEOGRAPHY

Location: Oceania, group of islands including the eastern half of the island of New Guinea between the Coral Sea and the South Pacific Ocean, east of Indonesia

Geographic coordinates: 6 00 S, 147 00 E

Map references: Oceania

Area: *total:* 462,840 sq km
land: 452,860 sq km
water: 9,980 sq km
comparison ranking: total 57

Area - comparative: slightly larger than California

Land boundaries: *total:* 824 km
border countries (1): Indonesia 824 km

Coastline: 5,152 km

Maritime claims: *territorial sea:* 12 nm
continental shelf: 200-m depth or to the depth of exploitation
exclusive fishing zone: 200 nm
note: measured from claimed archipelagic baselines

Climate: tropical; northwest monsoon (December to March), southeast monsoon (May to October); slight seasonal temperature variation

Terrain: mostly mountains with coastal lowlands and rolling foothills

Elevation: *highest point:* Mount Wilhelm 4,509 m
lowest point: Pacific Ocean 0 m
mean elevation: 667 m

Natural resources: gold, copper, silver, natural gas, timber, oil, fisheries

Land use: *agricultural land:* 3.1% (2022 est.)
arable land: 0.7% (2022 est.)
permanent crops: 2% (2022 est.)
permanent pasture: 0.4% (2022 est.)
forest: 79% (2022 est.)
other: 17.9% (2022 est.)

Irrigated land: 0 sq km (2022)

Major rivers (by length in km): Sepik river source and mouth (shared with Indonesia) - 1,126 km; Fly river source and mouth (shared with Indonesia) - 1,050 km

Population distribution: population concentrated in the highlands and eastern coastal areas on the island of New Guinea; predominantly a rural distribution with only about one fifth of the population residing in urban areas

Natural hazards: active volcanism; frequent and sometimes severe earthquakes; mud slides; tsunamis
volcanism: severe volcanic activity; Ulawun (2,334 m), one of Papua New Guinea's potentially most dangerous volcanoes, has been deemed a Decade Volcano by the International Association of Volcanology and Chemistry of the Earth's Interior, worthy of study due to its explosive history and close proximity to human populations; Rabaul (688 m) destroyed the city of Rabaul in 1937 and 1994; Lamington erupted in 1951, killing 3,000 people; Manam's 2004 eruption forced the island's abandonment; other historically active volcanoes include Bam, Bagana, Garbuna, Karkar, Langila, Lolobau, Long Island, Pago, St. Andrew Strait, Victory, and Waiowa; see note 2 under "Geography - note"

Geography - note: *note 1:* shares island of New Guinea with Indonesia; highlands that trend from east to west break up New Guinea into diverse ecoregions; one of world's largest swamps lies along the southwest coast
note 2: Papua New Guinea is one of the countries along the Ring of Fire, which is a belt bordering the Pacific Ocean that contains about 75% of the world's volcanoes and up to 90% of the world's earthquakes

PEOPLE AND SOCIETY

Population: *total:* 10,046,233 (2024 est.)
male: 5,092,262
female: 4,953,971
comparison rankings: total 93; male 93; female 95

Nationality: *noun:* Papua New Guinean(s)
adjective: Papua New Guinean

Ethnic groups: Melanesian, Papuan, Negrito, Micronesian, Polynesian

Languages: Tok Pisin (official), English (official), Hiri Motu (official), some 839 living indigenous languages are spoken (about 12% of the world's total)
note: Tok Pisin, a creole language, is widely used and understood; English is spoken by 1%-2%; Hiri Motu is spoken by less than 2%

Religions: Protestant 64.3% (Evangelical Lutheran 18.4%, Seventh Day Adventist 12.9%, Pentecostal 10.4%, United Church 10.3%, Evangelical Alliance 5.9%, Anglican 3.2%, Baptist 2.8%, Salvation Army 0.4%), Roman Catholic 26%, other Christian 5.3%, non-Christian 1.4%, unspecified 3.1% (2011 est.)
note: data represent only the citizen population; roughly 0.3% of the population are non-citizens, consisting of Christian 52% (predominantly Roman Catholic), other 10.7%, none 37.3%

Age structure: *0-14 years:* 37.1% (male 1,902,272/female 1,825,471)
15-64 years: 58.9% (male 2,991,479/female 2,923,410)
65 years and over: 4% (2024 est.) (male 198,511/female 205,090)

Dependency ratios: *total dependency ratio:* 69.8 (2024 est.)
youth dependency ratio: 63 (2024 est.)
elderly dependency ratio: 6.8 (2024 est.)
potential support ratio: 14.7 (2024 est.)

Median age: *total:* 21.7 years (2024 est.)
male: 21.6 years
female: 21.9 years
comparison ranking: total 190

Population growth rate: 2.26% (2024 est.)
comparison ranking: 30

Birth rate: 28.1 births/1,000 population (2024 est.)
comparison ranking: 31

Death rate: 5.4 deaths/1,000 population (2024 est.)
comparison ranking: 186

Net migration rate: 0 migrant(s)/1,000 population (2024 est.)
comparison ranking: 94

Population distribution: population concentrated in the highlands and eastern coastal areas on the island of New Guinea; predominantly a rural distribution with only about one fifth of the population residing in urban areas

Urbanization: *urban population:* 13.7% of total population (2023)
rate of urbanization: 2.91% annual rate of change (2020-25 est.)

Major urban areas - population: 410,000 PORT MORESBY (capital) (2023)

Sex ratio: *at birth:* 1.05 male(s)/female
0-14 years: 1.04 male(s)/female
15-64 years: 1.02 male(s)/female
65 years and over: 0.97 male(s)/female
total population: 1.03 male(s)/female (2024 est.)

Mother's mean age at first birth: 21.9 years (2016/18)
note: data represents median age a first birth among women 25-49

Maternal mortality ratio: 189 deaths/100,000 live births (2023 est.)
comparison ranking: 40

Infant mortality rate: *total:* 32 deaths/1,000 live births (2024 est.)
male: 35.3 deaths/1,000 live births
female: 28.6 deaths/1,000 live births
comparison ranking: total 43

Life expectancy at birth: *total population:* 70.1 years (2024 est.)
male: 68.3 years
female: 71.9 years
comparison ranking: total population 181

Total fertility rate: 3.79 children born/woman (2024 est.)
comparison ranking: 28

Gross reproduction rate: 1.85 (2024 est.)

Drinking water source: *improved: urban:* 86.9% of population (2022 est.)
rural: 44.5% of population (2022 est.)
total: 50.2% of population (2022 est.)
unimproved: urban: 13.1% of population (2022 est.)
rural: 55.5% of population (2022 est.)
total: 49.8% of population (2022 est.)

Health expenditure: 2.3% of GDP (2021)
7% of national budget (2022 est.)

Physician density: 0.06 physicians/1,000 population (2023)

Hospital bed density: 0.2 beds/1,000 population (2019 est.)

Sanitation facility access: *improved: urban:* 57.8% of population (2022 est.)
rural: 18.2% of population (2022 est.)
total: 23.6% of population (2022 est.)
unimproved: urban: 42.2% of population (2022 est.)
rural: 81.8% of population (2022 est.)
total: 76.4% of population (2022 est.)

Obesity - adult prevalence rate: 21.3% (2016)
comparison ranking: 90

Alcohol consumption per capita: *total:* 1.26 liters of pure alcohol (2019 est.)
beer: 0.6 liters of pure alcohol (2019 est.)
wine: 0.06 liters of pure alcohol (2019 est.)
spirits: 0.6 liters of pure alcohol (2019 est.)
other alcohols: 0 liters of pure alcohol (2019 est.)
comparison ranking: total 144

Tobacco use: *total:* 38.9% (2025 est.)
male: 53.4% (2025 est.)
female: 23.8% (2025 est.)
comparison ranking: total 4

Currently married women (ages 15-49): 65.5% (2023 est.)

Child marriage: *women married by age 15:* 8% (2018)
women married by age 18: 27.3% (2018)
men married by age 18: 3.7% (2018)

Education expenditure: 1.4% of GDP (2021 est.)
3.9% national budget (2021 est.)
comparison ranking: Education expenditure (% GDP) 193

Literacy: *total population:* 70.1% (2017 est.)
male: 78.4% (2017 est.)
female: 61.6% (2017 est.)

People - note: the indigenous population of Papua New Guinea (PNG) is one of the most heterogeneous in the world; PNG has several thousand separate communities, most with only a few hundred people; divided by language, customs, and tradition, some of these communities have engaged in low-scale tribal conflict with their neighbors for millennia; the advent of modern weapons and modern migrants into urban areas has greatly magnified the impact of this lawlessness

ENVIRONMENT

Environmental issues: rainforest loss as a result of commercial demand for tropical timber; soil erosion, water-quality degradation, and loss of habitat from logging; effects of large-scale mining projects (discharge of heavy metals, cyanide, and acids into rivers); severe drought; land degradation from poor farming practices; poor fishing practices; coastal pollution due to runoff and oil spills

International environmental agreements: *party to:* Antarctic Treaty, Biodiversity, Climate Change, Climate Change-Kyoto Protocol, Climate Change-Paris Agreement, Desertification, Endangered Species, Environmental Modification, Hazardous Wastes, Law of the Sea, Marine Dumping-London Convention, Nuclear Test Ban, Ozone Layer Protection, Ship Pollution, Tropical Timber 2006, Wetlands
signed, but not ratified: Comprehensive Nuclear Test Ban

Climate: tropical; northwest monsoon (December to March), southeast monsoon (May to October); slight seasonal temperature variation

Urbanization: *urban population:* 13.7% of total population (2023)
rate of urbanization: 2.91% annual rate of change (2020-25 est.)

Carbon dioxide emissions: 5.798 million metric tonnes of CO2 (2023 est.)
from coal and metallurgical coke: 1,000 metric tonnes of CO2 (2023 est.)
from petroleum and other liquids: 4.467 million metric tonnes of CO2 (2023 est.)
from consumed natural gas: 1.33 million metric tonnes of CO2 (2023 est.)
comparison ranking: total emissions 133

Particulate matter emissions: 8.8 micrograms per cubic meter (2019 est.)

Waste and recycling: *municipal solid waste generated annually:* 1 million tons (2024 est.)
percent of municipal solid waste recycled: 6.3% (2022 est.)

Total water withdrawal: *municipal:* 223.5 million cubic meters (2022 est.)
industrial: 167.6 million cubic meters (2022 est.)
agricultural: 1 million cubic meters (2022 est.)

Total renewable water resources: 801 billion cubic meters (2022 est.)

GOVERNMENT

Country name: *conventional long form:* Independent State of Papua New Guinea
conventional short form: Papua New Guinea
local short form: Papuaniugini
former: German New Guinea, British New Guinea, Territory of Papua and New Guinea
abbreviation: PNG
etymology: the name derives from the Malay word *pua-pua*, describing the tightly curled hair of the Papuan people; Spanish explorer Ynigo ORTIZ de RETEZ applied the term "Nueva Guinea" to the island in 1545 because he thought the locals resembled the peoples of the Guinea coast of Africa

Government type: parliamentary democracy under a constitutional monarchy; a Commonwealth realm

Capital: *name:* Port Moresby
geographic coordinates: 9 27 S, 147 11 E
time difference: UTC+10 (15 hours ahead of Washington, DC, during Standard Time)
time zone note: Papua New Guinea has two time zones, including Bougainville (UTC+11)
etymology: named in 1873 by Captain John MORESBY in honor of his father, British Admiral Sir Fairfax MORESBY (1786-1877)

Administrative divisions: 20 provinces, 1 autonomous region*, and 1 district**; Bougainville*, Central, Chimbu, Eastern Highlands, East New Britain, East Sepik, Enga, Gulf, Hela, Jiwaka, Madang, Manus, Milne Bay, Morobe, National Capital**, New Ireland, Northern, Southern Highlands, Western, Western Highlands, West New Britain, West Sepik

Legal system: mixed system of English common law and customary law

Constitution: *history:* adopted 15 August 1975, effective at independence 16 September 1975
amendment process: proposed by the National Parliament; passage has prescribed majority vote requirements depending on the constitutional sections being amended – absolute majority, two-thirds majority, or three-fourths majority

International law organization participation: has not submitted an ICJ jurisdiction declaration; non-party state to the ICCt

Citizenship: *citizenship by birth:* no
citizenship by descent only: at least one parent must be a citizen of Papua New Guinea
dual citizenship recognized: no
residency requirement for naturalization: 8 years

Suffrage: 18 years of age; universal

Executive branch: *chief of state:* King CHARLES III (since 8 September 2022); represented by Governor General Grand Chief Sir Bob DADAE (since 28 February 2017)
head of government: Prime Minister James MARAPE (since 30 May 2019)
cabinet: National Executive Council appointed by the governor general on the recommendation of the prime minister
election/appointment process: the monarchy is hereditary; governor general nominated by the National Parliament and appointed by the chief of state; following legislative elections, the governor general usually appoints the leader of the majority party or majority coalition as prime minister, pending a National Parliament vote
election results: James MARAPE reelected prime minister; National Parliament vote - 105 out of 118

Legislative branch: *legislature name:* National Parliament
legislative structure: unicameral
number of seats: 118 (all directly elected)
electoral system: plurality/majority
scope of elections: full renewal
term in office: 5 years
most recent election date: 7/4/2022 to 7/22/2022
parties elected and seats per party: Papua & Niugini Union Pati (PANGU) (39); People's National Congress Party (PNC) (15); United Resource Party (URP) (11); Others (40); Independents (10)
percentage of women in chamber: 2.7%
expected date of next election: July 2027

Judicial branch: *highest court(s):* Supreme Court (consists of the chief justice, deputy chief justice, 35 justices, and 5 acting justices); National Courts (consists of 13 courts located in the provincial capitals, with a total of 19 resident judges)
judge selection and term of office: Supreme Court chief justice appointed by the governor general on advice of the National Executive Council (cabinet) after consultation with the National Justice Administration minister; deputy chief justice and

other justices appointed by the Judicial and Legal Services Commission, a 5-member body that includes the Supreme Court chief and deputy chief justices, the chief ombudsman, and a member of the National Parliament; full-time citizen judges appointed for 10-year renewable terms; non-citizen judges initially appointed for 3-year renewable terms and after first renewal can serve until age 70; appointment and tenure of National Court resident judges NA
subordinate courts: district, village, and juvenile courts, military courts, taxation courts, coronial courts, mining warden courts, land courts, traffic courts, committal courts, grade five courts

Political parties: Destiny Party
Liberal Party
Melanesian Alliance Party or MAP
Melanesian Liberal Party or MLP
National Alliance Party or NAP
Our Development Party or ODP
Papua and Niugini Union Party or PANGU PATI
Papua New Guinea Greens Party
Papua New Guinea National Party
Papua New Guinea Party or PNGP
People's First Party or PFP
People's Movement for Change or PMC
People's National Congress Party or PNC
People's National Party
People's Party or PP
People's Progress Party or PPP
People's Reform Party or PRP
Social Democratic Party or SDP
Triumph Heritage Empowerment Party or THE
United Labor Party or ULP
United Resources Party or URP

Diplomatic representation in the US: *chief of mission:* Ambassador Arnold Karibone AMET (since 5 September 2025)
chancery: 1825 K Street NW, Suite 1010, Washington, DC 20006
telephone: [1] (202) 745-3680

FAX: [1] (202) 745-3679
email address and website: info@pngembassy.org
http://www.pngembassy.org/

Diplomatic representation from the US: *chief of mission:* Ambassador Ann Marie YASTISHOCK (since 22 February 2024); note - also accredited to the Solomon Islands and Vanuatu
embassy: Harbour City Road, Konedobu, Port Moresby, NCD, Papua New Guinea
mailing address: 4240 Port Moresby Pl, Washington DC 20521-4240
telephone: [675] 308-9100
email address and website: ConsularPortMoresby@state.gov
https://pg.usembassy.gov/

International organization participation: ACP, ADB, AOSIS, APEC, ARF, ASEAN (observer), C, CD, CP, EITI (candidate country), FAO, G-77, IAEA, IBRD, ICAO, ICRM, IDA, IFAD, IFC, IFRCS, IHO, ILO, IMF, IMO, Interpol, IOC, IOM, IPU, ISO (correspondent), ITSO, ITU, MIGA, NAM, OPCW, PIF, Sparteca, SPC, UN, UNCTAD, UNESCO, UNIDO, UNMISS, UNWTO, UPU, WCO, WFTU (NGOs), WHO, WIPO, WMO, WTO

Independence: 16 September 1975 (from the Australia-administered UN trusteeship)

National holiday: Independence Day, 16 September (1975)

Flag: *description:* divided diagonally from upper-left corner; the upper triangle is red and has a soaring yellow bird of paradise in the center; the lower triangle is black with five five-pointed white stars of the Southern Cross constellation
meaning: red, black, and yellow are the country's traditional colors; the bird of paradise is an emblem of regional tribal culture and represents the emergence of Papua New Guinea as a nation; the Southern Cross symbolizes the country's connection with Australia and several other countries in the South Pacific

National symbol(s): bird of paradise

National color(s): red, black

National coat of arms: Papua New Guinea's coat of arms was adopted on July 1, 1971, and features the country's national symbol, the Raggiana bird-of-paradise; the bird stands for the nation's freedom and rich natural environment; the traditional spear under the bird represents the country's ethnic groups and the protection of its heritage, and the Kundu drum, which is used in ceremonies, represents local artistic traditions and communication

National anthem(s): *title:* "O Arise, All You Sons"
lyrics/music: Thomas SHACKLADY
history: adopted 1975

National heritage: *total World Heritage Sites:* 1 (cultural)
selected World Heritage Site locales: Kuk Early Agricultural Site

ECONOMY

Economic overview: lower-middle-income Pacific island economy; primarily informal agrarian sector; natural-resource-rich and key exporter of liquified natural gas; collapse in betel nut prices, tighter monetary policy, and improved foreign-exchange availability contributing to declining inflation; challenges include lack of progress in infrastructure, agricultural reform, and corruption

Real GDP (purchasing power parity): $45.487 billion (2024 est.)
$43.697 billion (2023 est.)
$42.093 billion (2022 est.)
note: data in 2021 dollars
comparison ranking: 135

Real GDP growth rate: 4.1% (2024 est.)
3.8% (2023 est.)
5.7% (2022 est.)
note: annual GDP % growth based on constant local currency
comparison ranking: 69

Real GDP per capita: $4,300 (2024 est.)
$4,200 (2023 est.)
$4,100 (2022 est.)
note: data in 2021 dollars
comparison ranking: 178

GDP (official exchange rate): $32.538 billion (2024 est.)
note: data in current dollars at official exchange rate

Inflation rate (consumer prices): 0.6% (2024 est.)
2.3% (2023 est.)
5.3% (2022 est.)
note: annual % change based on consumer prices
comparison ranking: 13

GDP - composition, by sector of origin: *agriculture:* 17.2% (2024 est.)
industry: 37.2% (2024 est.)
services: 41.5% (2024 est.)
note: figures may not total 100% due to non-allocated consumption not captured in sector-reported data
comparison rankings: agriculture 44; industry 29; services 190

GDP - composition, by end use: *household consumption:* 43.7% (2017 est.)
government consumption: 19.7% (2017 est.)
investment in fixed capital: 10% (2017 est.)
investment in inventories: 0.4% (2017 est.)
exports of goods and services: 49.3% (2017 est.)
imports of goods and services: -22.3% (2017 est.)

Agricultural products: oil palm fruit, coconuts, bananas, fruits, sweet potatoes, game meat, yams, root vegetables, vegetables, sugarcane (2023)
note: top ten agricultural products based on tonnage

Industries: oil and gas; mining (gold, copper, and nickel); palm oil processing; plywood and wood chip production; copra crushing; construction; tourism; fishing; livestock (pork, poultry, cattle) and dairy farming; spice products (turmeric, vanilla, ginger, cardamom, chili, pepper, citronella, and nutmeg)

Industrial production growth rate: 3.6% (2024 est.)
note: annual % change in industrial value added based on constant local currency
comparison ranking: 67

Labor force: 3.66 million (2024 est.)
note: number of people ages 15 or older who are employed or seeking work
comparison ranking: 98

Unemployment rate: 2.8% (2024 est.)
2.7% (2023 est.)
2.7% (2022 est.)
note: % of labor force seeking employment
comparison ranking: 32

Youth unemployment rate (ages 15-24): *total:* 3.8% (2024 est.)
male: 4.6% (2024 est.)
female: 3% (2024 est.)
note: % of labor force ages 15-24 seeking employment
comparison ranking: total 174

Remittances: 0% of GDP (2023 est.)
0% of GDP (2022 est.)
0% of GDP (2021 est.)
note: personal transfers and compensation between resident and non-resident individuals/households/entities

Budget: *revenues:* $5.518 billion (2023 est.)
expenditures: $6.856 billion (2023 est.)
note: central government revenues and expenses (excluding grants/extrabudgetary units/social security funds) converted to US dollars at average official exchange rate for year indicated

Public debt: 52.4% of GDP (2023 est.)
note: central government debt as a % of GDP
comparison ranking: 95

Taxes and other revenues: 15.9% (of GDP) (2023 est.)
note: central government tax revenue as a % of GDP
comparison ranking: 84

Current account balance: $4.183 billion (2023 est.)
$4.567 billion (2022 est.)
$3.284 billion (2021 est.)
note: balance of payments - net trade and primary/secondary income in current dollars
comparison ranking: 38

Exports: $12.93 billion (2023 est.)

$14.862 billion (2022 est.)
$11.032 billion (2021 est.)
note: balance of payments - exports of goods and services in current dollars
comparison ranking: 105

Exports - partners: China 28%, Japan 25%, Australia 17%, Taiwan 8%, India 4% (2023)
note: top five export partners based on percentage share of exports

Exports - commodities: natural gas, gold, copper ore, palm oil, nickel (2023)
note: top five export commodities based on value in dollars

Imports: $7.192 billion (2023 est.)
$8.568 billion (2022 est.)
$6.43 billion (2021 est.)
note: balance of payments - imports of goods and services in current dollars
comparison ranking: 138

Imports - partners: Australia 27%, China 24%, Singapore 15%, Malaysia 9%, Japan 4% (2023)
note: top five import partners based on percentage share of imports

Imports - commodities: refined petroleum, trucks, rice, plastic products, excavation machinery (2023)
note: top five import commodities based on value in dollars

Reserves of foreign exchange and gold: $3.901 billion (2023 est.)
$3.983 billion (2022 est.)
$3.24 billion (2021 est.)
note: holdings of gold (year-end prices)/foreign exchange/special drawing rights in current dollars
comparison ranking: 106

Debt - external: $7.011 billion (2023 est.)
note: present value of external debt in current US dollars
comparison ranking: 59

Exchange rates: kina (PGK) per US dollar -

Exchange rates: 3.59 (2023 est.)
3.519 (2022 est.)
3.509 (2021 est.)
3.46 (2020 est.)
3.388 (2019 est.)

ENERGY

Electricity access: *electrification - total population:* 19% (2022 est.)
electrification - urban areas: 65.1%
electrification - rural areas: 14.2%

Electricity: *installed generating capacity:* 1.148 million kW (2023 est.)
consumption: 4.399 billion kWh (2023 est.)
transmission/distribution losses: 328.234 million kWh (2023 est.)
comparison rankings: installed generating capacity 132; consumption 132; transmission/distribution losses 73

Electricity generation sources: *fossil fuels:* 76.4% of total installed capacity (2023 est.)
solar: 0.1% of total installed capacity (2023 est.)
hydroelectricity: 21.2% of total installed capacity (2023 est.)
geothermal: 2% of total installed capacity (2023 est.)
biomass and waste: 0.3% of total installed capacity (2023 est.)

Coal: *imports:* 2,000 metric tons (2023 est.)

Petroleum: *total petroleum production:* 32,000 bbl/day (2023 est.)
refined petroleum consumption: 30,000 bbl/day (2023 est.)
crude oil estimated reserves: 159.656 million barrels (2021 est.)

Natural gas: *production:* 11.57 billion cubic meters (2023 est.)
consumption: 677.736 million cubic meters (2023 est.)
exports: 10.892 billion cubic meters (2023 est.)
proven reserves: 183.125 billion cubic meters (2021 est.)

Energy consumption per capita: 8.781 million Btu/person (2023 est.)
comparison ranking: 153

COMMUNICATIONS

Telephones - fixed lines: *total subscriptions:* 166,000 (2021 est.)
subscriptions per 100 inhabitants: 2 (2022 est.)
comparison ranking: total subscriptions 123

Telephones - mobile cellular: *total subscriptions:* 4.82 million (2021 est.)
subscriptions per 100 inhabitants: 48 (2021 est.)
comparison ranking: total subscriptions 126

Broadcast media: 5 *TV stations:* 1 commercial (TV Wan), 2 state-run (National Broadcasting Corporation and EMTV); 1 digital free-to-view network, and 1 satellite network (Click TV or PNGTV); the state-run NBC operates 3 radio networks with multiple repeaters and about 20 provincial stations; several commercial radio stations with multiple transmission points as well as several community stations; transmissions of several international broadcasters are accessible (2023)

Internet country code: .pg

Internet users: *percent of population:* 24% (2023 est.)

Broadband - fixed subscriptions: *total:* 22,000 (2022 est.)
subscriptions per 100 inhabitants: (2022 est.) less than 1
comparison ranking: total 170

TRANSPORTATION

Civil aircraft registration country code prefix: P2

Airports: 569 (2025)
comparison ranking: 14

Heliports: 3 (2025)
comparison ranking: 115

Merchant marine: *total:* 205 (2023)
by type: container ship 6, general cargo 89, oil tanker 4, other 106
comparison ranking: total 65

Ports: *total ports:* 22 (2024)
large: 0
medium: 0
small: 6
very small: 16
ports with oil terminals: 8
key ports: Kavieng Harbor, Kieta, Port Moresby, Rabaul, Vanimo, Wewak Harbor

MILITARY AND SECURITY

Military and security forces: Papua New Guinea Defense Force (PNGDF): Land, Air, Maritime elements

Ministry of Internal Security: Royal Papua New Guinea Constabulary (RPNGC) (2025)

Military expenditures: 0.3% of GDP (2024 est.)
0.3% of GDP (2023 est.)
0.3% of GDP (2022 est.)
0.4% of GDP (2021 est.)
0.4% of GDP (2020 est.)

Military and security service personnel strengths: estimated 4,000 active PNGDF (2025)

Military equipment inventories and acquisitions: the PNGDF is lightly armed; the Land Force has no heavy weapons while the Air and the Maritime forces have a handful of light aircraft and small patrol boats provided by Australia (2024)

Military service age and obligation: 18-27 (30 for officers) for voluntary military service for men and women; no conscription (2025)

Military - note: the Papua New Guinea Defense Force (PNGDF) is tasked with defense of the country and its territories against external attack, as well as internal security and socio-economic development duties; following some inter-tribal violence in Wapenamanda in 2024, the PNGDF was given arrest powers
since 2023, Papua New Guinea has signed bilateral defense cooperation agreements with Australia, Indonesia, the UK, and the US; the 2023 defense cooperation agreement with the US allowed the US military to develop and operate out of bases in PNG with the PNG Government's approval; PNG has also military relations with France and New Zealand and has discussed a security cooperation agreement with China
the PNGDF was established in 1973, and its primary combat unit, the Royal Pacific Islands Regiment (RPIR), is descended from Australian Army infantry battalions comprised of native soldiers and led by Australian officers and non-commissioned officers formed during World War II to help fight the Japanese; the RPIR was disbanded after the war, but reestablished in 1951 as part of the Australian Army where it continued to serve until PNG gained its independence in 1975, when it became part of the PNGDF (2025)

TRANSNATIONAL ISSUES

Refugees and internally displaced persons: *refugees:* 10,983 (2024 est.)

IDPs: 107,985 (2024 est.)

Trafficking in persons: *tier rating:* Tier 3 — Papua New Guinea does not fully meet the minimum standards for the elimination of trafficking and is not making significant efforts to do so; therefore, Papua New Guinea remained on Tier 3; for more details, go to: https://www.state.gov/reports/2025-trafficking-in-persons-report/papua-new-guinea/

PARACEL ISLANDS

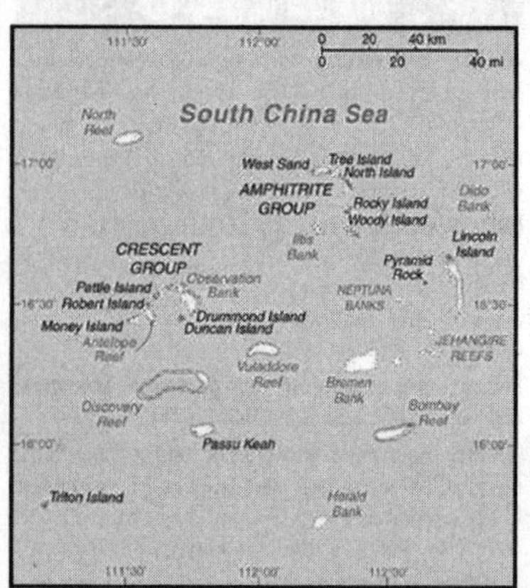

INTRODUCTION

Background: The Paracel Islands are surrounded by productive fishing grounds and potential oil and gas reserves. In 1932, French Indochina annexed the islands and set up a weather station on Pattle Island. China has occupied all the Paracel Islands since 1974, when its troops seized a South Vietnamese garrison occupying the western islands. China has built a military installation on Woody Island with an airfield and artificial harbor, and it has scattered garrisons on some of the other islands. Taiwan and Vietnam also claim the Paracel Islands.

GEOGRAPHY

Location: Southeastern Asia, group of small islands and reefs in the South China Sea, about one-third of the way from central Vietnam to the northern Philippines

Geographic coordinates: 16 30 N, 112 00 E

Map references: Southeast Asia

Area: *total:* 8 sq km ca.
land: 7.75 sq km ca.
water: 0 sq km
comparison ranking: total 241

Area - comparative: land area is about 13 times the size of the National Mall in Washington, D.C.

Land boundaries: *total:* 0 km

Coastline: 518 km

Climate: tropical

Terrain: mostly low and flat

Elevation: *highest point:* unnamed location on Rocky Island 14 m
lowest point: South China Sea 0 m

Natural resources: none

Land use: *other:* 100% (2018 est.)

Irrigated land: 0 sq km (2022)

Population distribution: a population of over 1,000 Chinese resides on Woody Island, the largest of the Paracels; there are scattered Chinese garrisons on some other islands

Natural hazards: typhoons

Geography - note: composed of 130 small coral islands and reefs divided into the northeast Amphitrite Group and the western Crescent Group

PEOPLE AND SOCIETY

Population: *total:* 2,230 (2024 est.)
comparison ranking: total 231

Population growth rate: 0.75% (2021 est.)
comparison ranking: 118

Net migration rate: -0.66 migrant(s)/1,000 population (2021 est.)
comparison ranking: 130

Population distribution: a population of over 1,000 Chinese resides on Woody Island, the largest of the Paracels; there are scattered Chinese garrisons on some other islands

ENVIRONMENT

Environmental issues: harm to reef systems from China's use of dredged sand and coral to build artificial islands; damage to ecosystem from human activities, including military operations, infrastructure construction, and tourism

Climate: tropical

GOVERNMENT

Country name: *conventional long form:* none
conventional short form: Paracel Islands

TRANSPORTATION

Airports: 2 (2025)
comparison ranking: 201

Heliports: 7 (2025)
comparison ranking: 91

MILITARY AND SECURITY

Military - note: occupied by China, which is assessed to maintain 20 outposts or bases in the Paracels (Antelope, Bombay, and North reefs; Drummond, Duncan, Lincoln, Middle, Money, North, Pattle, Quanfu, Robert, South, Tree, Triton, Woody, and Yagong islands; South Sand and West Sand; Observation Bank); Woody Island is the main military base and includes an airstrip with fighter aircraft hangers, naval facilities, surveillance radars, and defenses such as surface-to-air missiles and anti-ship cruise missiles; combat aircraft have deployed to the island (2025)

PARAGUAY

INTRODUCTION

Background: Several Indigenous groups, principally belonging to the Guarani language family, inhabited the area of modern Paraguay before the arrival of the Spanish in the early 16th century, when the territory was incorporated into the Viceroyalty of Peru. Paraguay achieved its independence from Spain in 1811 with the help of neighboring states. In the aftermath of independence, a series of military dictators ruled the country until 1870. During the disastrous War of the Triple Alliance (1864-70) – fought against Argentina, Brazil, and Uruguay – Paraguay lost two thirds of its adult males and much of its territory. The country stagnated economically for the next half-century and experienced a tumultuous series of political regimes. Following the Chaco War of 1932-35 with Bolivia, Paraguay gained a large part of the Chaco lowland region. The 35-year military dictatorship of Alfredo STROESSNER ended in 1989, and Paraguay has held relatively free and regular presidential elections since the country's return to democracy.

GEOGRAPHY

Location: Central South America, northeast of Argentina, southwest of Brazil

Geographic coordinates: 23 00 S, 58 00 W

Map references: South America

Area: *total:* 406,752 sq km
land: 397,302 sq km
water: 9,450 sq km
comparison ranking: total 61

Area - comparative: about three times the size of New York State; slightly smaller than California

Land boundaries: *total:* 4,655 km

border countries (3): Argentina 2,531 km; Bolivia 753 km; Brazil 1,371 km

Coastline: 0 km (landlocked)

Maritime claims: none (landlocked)

Climate: subtropical to temperate; substantial rainfall in the eastern portions, becoming semiarid in the far west

Terrain: grassy plains and wooded hills east of Rio Paraguay; Gran Chaco region west of Rio Paraguay mostly low, marshy plain near the river, and dry forest and thorny scrub elsewhere

Elevation: *highest point:* Cerro Pero 842 m
lowest point: junction of Río Paraguay and Río Paraná 46 m
mean elevation: 178 m

Natural resources: hydropower, timber, iron ore, manganese, limestone

Land use: *agricultural land:* 42% (2022 est.)
arable land: 11.5% (2022 est.)
permanent crops: 0.2% (2022 est.)
permanent pasture: 30.3% (2022 est.)
forest: 39.3% (2022 est.)
other: 18.8% (2022 est.)

Irrigated land: 1,362 sq km (2012)

Major rivers (by length in km): Río de la Plata/Paraná (shared with Brazil [s], Argentina, and Uruguay [m]) - 4,880 km;
Paraguay river mouth (shared with Brazil [s] and Argentina) - 2,549 km
note: [s] after country name indicates river source; [m] after country name indicates river mouth

Major watersheds (area sq km): Atlantic Ocean drainage: Paraná (2,582,704 sq km)

Major aquifers: Guarani Aquifer System

Population distribution: most of the population resides in the eastern half of the country; to the west lies the Gran Chaco (a semi-arid lowland plain), which accounts for 60% of the land territory, but only 2% of the overall population

Natural hazards: local flooding in southeast (early September to June); poorly drained plains may become boggy (early October to June)

Geography - note: landlocked; lies between Argentina, Bolivia, and Brazil; population concentrated in eastern and southern part of country

PEOPLE AND SOCIETY

Population: *total:* 7,522,549 (2024 est.)
male: 3,769,376
female: 3,753,173
comparison rankings: total 104; male 104; female 104

Nationality: *noun:* Paraguayan(s)
adjective: Paraguayan

Ethnic groups: Mestizo (mixed Spanish and Indigenous ancestry) 95%, other 5%

Languages: Spanish (official) and Guarani (official) 46.3%, only Guarani 34%, only Spanish 15.2%, other (includes Portuguese, German, other Indigenous languages) 4.1%, no response 0.4% (2012 est.)
major-language sample(s):
La Libreta Informativa del Mundo, la fuente indispensable de información básica. (Spanish)
note: data represent predominant household language

Religions: Roman Catholic 80.4%, Protestant 7% (Evangelical (non-specific) 6.7%, Evangelical Pentecostal <0.1%, Adventist <0.1%, Protestant (non-specific) <0.1%), Believer (not belonging to the church) 5.7%, other 0.6%, agnostic <0.1%, none 0.2%, unspecified 6.2% (2023 est.)

Age structure: *0-14 years:* 22.2% (male 850,191/female 821,237)
15-64 years: 68.4% (male 2,582,021/female 2,561,962)
65 years and over: 9.4% (2024 est.) (male 337,164/female 369,974)

Dependency ratios: *total dependency ratio:* 46.2 (2024 est.)
youth dependency ratio: 32.5 (2024 est.)
elderly dependency ratio: 13.7 (2024 est.)
potential support ratio: 7.3 (2024 est.)

Median age: *total:* 31.8 years (2024 est.)
male: 31.6 years
female: 32 years
comparison ranking: total 123

Population growth rate: 1.09% (2024 est.)
comparison ranking: 86

Birth rate: 15.9 births/1,000 population (2024 est.)
comparison ranking: 100

Death rate: 4.9 deaths/1,000 population (2024 est.)
comparison ranking: 196

Net migration rate: -0.1 migrant(s)/1,000 population (2024 est.)
comparison ranking: 95

Population distribution: most of the population resides in the eastern half of the country; to the west lies the Gran Chaco (a semi-arid lowland plain), which accounts for 60% of the land territory, but only 2% of the overall population

Urbanization: *urban population:* 63.1% of total population (2023)
rate of urbanization: 1.64% annual rate of change (2020-25 est.)

Major urban areas - population: 3.511 million ASUNCION (capital) (2023)

Sex ratio: *at birth:* 1.05 male(s)/female
0-14 years: 1.04 male(s)/female
15-64 years: 1.01 male(s)/female
65 years and over: 0.91 male(s)/female
total population: 1 male(s)/female (2024 est.)

Mother's mean age at first birth: 22.9 years (2008 est.)
note: data represents median age at first birth among women 25-29

Maternal mortality ratio: 58 deaths/100,000 live births (2023 est.)
comparison ranking: 90

Infant mortality rate: *total:* 22 deaths/1,000 live births (2024 est.)
male: 26.1 deaths/1,000 live births
female: 17.7 deaths/1,000 live births
comparison ranking: total 70

Life expectancy at birth: *total population:* 78.8 years (2024 est.)
male: 76.2 years
female: 81.6 years
comparison ranking: total population 73

Total fertility rate: 1.88 children born/woman (2024 est.)
comparison ranking: 126

Gross reproduction rate: 0.92 (2024 est.)

Drinking water source: *improved: urban:* 99.9% of population (2022 est.)
rural: 99.1% of population (2022 est.)
total: 99.6% of population (2022 est.)
unimproved: urban: 0.1% of population (2022 est.)
rural: 0.9% of population (2022 est.)
total: 0.4% of population (2022 est.)

Health expenditure: 8% of GDP (2021)
17.4% of national budget (2022 est.)

Physician density: 3.89 physicians/1,000 population (2022)

Hospital bed density: 1 beds/1,000 population (2020 est.)

Sanitation facility access: *improved: urban:* 100% of population (2022 est.)
rural: 94.9% of population (2022 est.)
total: 98.1% of population (2022 est.)
unimproved: urban: 0% of population (2022 est.)
rural: 5.1% of population (2022 est.)
total: 1.9% of population (2022 est.)

Obesity - adult prevalence rate: 20.3% (2016)
comparison ranking: 100

Alcohol consumption per capita: *total:* 5.47 liters of pure alcohol (2019 est.)
beer: 3.27 liters of pure alcohol (2019 est.)
wine: 0.59 liters of pure alcohol (2019 est.)
spirits: 1.59 liters of pure alcohol (2019 est.)
other alcohols: 0.03 liters of pure alcohol (2019 est.)
comparison ranking: total 79

Tobacco use: *total:* 9.3% (2025 est.)
male: 15.5% (2025 est.)
female: 3.3% (2025 est.)
comparison ranking: total 132

Children under the age of 5 years underweight: 1.3% (2016)
comparison ranking: 107

Currently married women (ages 15-49): 59.4% (2023 est.)

Child marriage: *women married by age 15:* 3.6% (2016)
women married by age 18: 21.6% (2016)

Education expenditure: 3.4% of GDP (2023 est.)
22% national budget (2023 est.)
comparison ranking: Education expenditure (% GDP) 134

Literacy: *total population:* 95% (2020 est.)
male: 95% (2020 est.)
female: 94% (2020 est.)

ENVIRONMENT

Environmental issues: deforestation; water pollution; toxic dumping in rivers and streams; loss of wetlands; inadequate means for waste disposal in urban areas

International environmental agreements: *party to:* Biodiversity, Climate Change, Climate Change-Kyoto Protocol, Climate Change-Paris Agreement, Comprehensive Nuclear Test Ban, Desertification, Endangered Species, Hazardous Wastes, Law of the Sea, Ozone Layer Protection, Wetlands
signed, but not ratified: Nuclear Test Ban, Tropical Timber 2006

Climate: subtropical to temperate; substantial rainfall in the eastern portions, becoming semiarid in the far west

Urbanization: *urban population:* 63.1% of total population (2023)
rate of urbanization: 1.64% annual rate of change (2020-25 est.)

Carbon dioxide emissions: 7.509 million metric tonnes of CO2 (2023 est.)
from coal and metallurgical coke: 2,000 metric tonnes of CO2 (2023 est.)

from petroleum and other liquids: 7.507 million metric tonnes of CO2 (2023 est.)
comparison ranking: total emissions 119

Particulate matter emissions: 12.5 micrograms per cubic meter (2019 est.)

Methane emissions: *energy:* 37.3 kt (2022-2024 est.)
agriculture: 813 kt (2019-2021 est.)
waste: 101.2 kt (2019-2021 est.)
other: 10 kt (2019-2021 est.)

Waste and recycling: *municipal solid waste generated annually:* 1.819 million tons (2024 est.)
percent of municipal solid waste recycled: 18.1% (2022 est.)

Total water withdrawal: *municipal:* 362 million cubic meters (2022 est.)
industrial: 154 million cubic meters (2022 est.)
agricultural: 1.897 billion cubic meters (2022 est.)

Total renewable water resources: 387.77 billion cubic meters (2022 est.)

GOVERNMENT

Country name: *conventional long form:* Republic of Paraguay
conventional short form: Paraguay
local long form: República del Paraguay
local short form: Paraguay
etymology: derives from the river of the same name; the river's name may come from the Guarani words *para* (water or river) and *guay* (born)

Government type: presidential republic

Capital: *name:* Asunción
geographic coordinates: 25 16 S, 57 40 W
time difference: UTC-3 (2 hour ahead of Washington, DC, during Standard Time)
etymology: the name means "assumption" in Spanish; the Spanish founded the city on August 15, 1537, the Catholic feast day for the Assumption of the Virgin Mary

Administrative divisions: 17 departments (*departamentos*, singular - *departamento*) and 1 capital city*; Alto Paraguay, Alto Parana, Amambay, Asuncion*, Boquerón, Caaguazú, Caazapá, Canindeyú, Central, Concepcion, Cordillera, Guairá, Itapúa, Misiones, Ñeembucú, Paraguarí, Presidente Hayes, San Pedro

Legal system: civil law system with influences from Argentine, Spanish, Roman, and French civil law models; Supreme Court of Justice reviews legislative acts

Constitution: *history:* several previous; latest approved and promulgated 20 June 1992
amendment process: proposed at the initiative of at least one quarter of either chamber of the National Congress, by the president of the republic, or by petition of at least 30,000 voters; passage requires a two-thirds majority vote by both chambers and approval in a referendum

International law organization participation: accepts compulsory ICJ jurisdiction; accepts ICCt jurisdiction

Citizenship: *citizenship by birth:* yes
citizenship by descent only: at least one parent must be a native-born citizen of Paraguay
dual citizenship recognized: yes
residency requirement for naturalization: 3 years

Suffrage: 18 years of age; universal and compulsory until the age of 75

Executive branch: *chief of state:* President Santiago PEÑA Palacios (since 15 August 2023)
head of government: President Santiago PEÑA Palacios (since 15 August 2023)
cabinet: Council of Ministers appointed by the president
election/appointment process: president and vice president directly elected on the same ballot by simple-majority popular vote for a single 5-year term
most recent election date: 30 April 2023
election results: *2023:* Santiago PEÑA Palacios elected president; percent of vote - Santiago PEÑA Palacios (ANR) 43.9%, Efraín ALEGRE (PLRA) 28.3%, Paraguayo "Payo" CUBAS Colomés (PCN) 23.6%, other 4.2%
2018: Mario ABDO BENÍTEZ elected president; percent of vote - Mario ABDO BENÍTEZ (ANR) 49%, Efraín ALEGRE (PLRA) 45.1%, other 5.9%
expected date of next election: April 2028
note: the president is both chief of state and head of government

Legislative branch: *legislature name:* Congress (Congreso)
legislative structure: bicameral

Legislative branch - lower chamber: *chamber name:* Chamber of Deputies (Cámara de Diputados)
number of seats: 80 (all directly elected)
electoral system: proportional representation
scope of elections: full renewal
term in office: 5 years
most recent election date: 4/30/2023
parties elected and seats per party: National Republican Association/Colorado Party (ANR) (48); Authentic Radical Liberal Party (PLRA) - Alliances (23); National Crusade Party (CN) (4); Other (5)
percentage of women in chamber: 23.8%
expected date of next election: April 2028

Legislative branch - upper chamber: *chamber name:* Senate (Cámara de Senadores)
number of seats: 45 (all directly elected)
electoral system: proportional representation
scope of elections: full renewal
term in office: 5 years
most recent election date: 4/30/2023
parties elected and seats per party: National Republican Association/Colorado Party (ANR) (23); Authentic Radical Liberal Party (PLRA) - Alliances (12); National Crusade Party (CN) (5); Other (5)
percentage of women in chamber: 22.2%
expected date of next election: April 2028

Judicial branch: *highest court(s):* Supreme Court of Justice or Corte Suprema de Justicia (consists of 9 justices divided 3 each into the Constitutional Court, Civil and Commercial Chamber, and Criminal Division)
judge selection and term of office: justices proposed by the Council of Magistrates or Consejo de la Magistratura, a 6-member independent body, and appointed by the Chamber of Senators with presidential concurrence; judges can serve until mandatory retirement at age 75
subordinate courts: appellate courts; first instance courts; minor courts, including justices of the peace

Political parties: Asociacion Nacional Republicana (National Republican Association) - Colorado Party or ANR
Avanza Pais coalition or AP
Frente Guasu (Broad Front coalition) or FG
GANAR Alliance (Great Renewed National Alliance) (alliance between PLRA and Guasú Front)
Movimiento Hagamos or MH
Movimiento Union Nacional de Ciudadanos Eticos (National Union of Ethical Citizens) or UNACE
Partido Cruzada Nacional (National Crusade Party) or PCN; note - formerly Movimiento Cruzada Nacional
Partido del Movimiento al Socialismo or P-MAS
Partido Democratica Progresista (Progressive Democratic Party) or PDP
Partido Encuentro Nacional or PEN
Partido Liberal Radical Autentico (Authentic Radical Liberal Party) or PLRA
Partido Pais Solidario or PPS
Partido Popular Tekojoja or PPT
Patria Querida (Beloved Fatherland Party) or PPQ

Diplomatic representation in the US: *chief of mission:* Ambassador Gustavo Alfredo LEITE Gusinky (since 5 September 2025)
chancery: 2209 Massachusetts Avenue, NW, Washington DC 20008
telephone: [1] (202) 483-6960
FAX: [1] (202) 234-4508
email address and website: gabineteembaparusa@mre.gov.py

Embajada de la República del Paraguay ante los Estados Unidos de América:: The Embassy (mre.gov.py)
consulate(s) general: Los Angeles, Miami, New York

Diplomatic representation from the US: *chief of mission:* Ambassador (vacant); Chargé d'Affaires Robert ALTER (since July 2025)
embassy: 1776 Mariscal Lopez Avenue, Asuncion
mailing address: 3020 Asuncion Place, Washington DC 20521-3020
telephone: [595] (21) 248-3000
FAX: [595] (21) 213-728
email address and website: ParaguayACS@state.gov
https://py.usembassy.gov/

International organization participation: CAN (associate), CD, CELAC, FAO, G-11, G-77, IADB, IAEA, IBRD, ICAO, ICC (national committees), ICCt, ICRM, IDA, IFAD, IFC, IFRCS, ILO, IMF, IMO, Interpol, IOC, IOM, IPU, ISO (correspondent), ITSO, ITU, ITUC (NGOs), LAES, LAIA, Mercosur, MIGA, MINURSO, MINUSTAH, MONUSCO, NAM (observer), OAS, OPANAL, OPCW, Pacific Alliance (observer), PCA, PROSUR, UN, UNASUR, UNCTAD, UNESCO, UNFICYP, UNHRC, UNIDO, Union Latina, UNISFA, UNMIL, UNMISS, UNOCI, UNWTO, UPU, WCO, WHO, WIPO, WMO, WTO

Independence: 14-15 May 1811 (from Spain)
note: the uprising against Spanish authorities took place during the night of 14-15 May 1811, so both days are celebrated in Paraguay

National holiday: Independence Day, 14-15 May (1811) (observed 15 May); 14 May is celebrated as Flag Day

Flag: *description:* three equal horizontal bands of red (top), white, and blue, with an emblem centered on the white band; the emblem on one side of the flag is the national coat of arms, which has a five-pointed yellow star in a green wreath with the words REPUBLICA DEL PARAGUAY around it, all inside two circles; the other side of the flag has a circular treasury seal (a yellow lion below a red Cap of Liberty and the words PAZ Y JUSTICIA)
meaning: red stands for bravery and patriotism, white for integrity and peace, and blue for liberty and generosity
note 1: resembles the flag of the Netherlands, which does not have a central emblem

note 2: one of three national flags that differ on each side – the others are Moldova and Saudi Arabia

National symbol(s): lion

National color(s): red, white, blue

National anthem(s): *title:* "Paraguayos, Republica o muerte!" (Paraguayans, the Republic or Death!)
lyrics/music: Francisco Esteban ACUNA de Figueroa/ Remberto GIMENEZ
history: adopted 1846 (lyrics) and 1934 (music)

National heritage: *total World Heritage Sites:* 1 (cultural)
selected World Heritage Site locales: Jesuit Missions of La Santísima Trinidad de Paraná and Jesús de Tavarangue

ECONOMY

Economic overview: upper middle-income South American economy; COVID-19 hit while still recovering from 2019 Argentina-driven recession; global hydroelectricity leader; major corruption and money-laundering locale; highly agrarian economy; significant income inequality

Real GDP (purchasing power parity): $112.919 billion (2024 est.)
$108.316 billion (2023 est.)
$103.159 billion (2022 est.)
note: data in 2021 dollars
comparison ranking: 92

Real GDP growth rate: 4.2% (2024 est.)
5% (2023 est.)
0.2% (2022 est.)
note: annual GDP % growth based on constant local currency
comparison ranking: 67

Real GDP per capita: $16,300 (2024 est.)
$15,800 (2023 est.)
$15,300 (2022 est.)
note: data in 2021 dollars
comparison ranking: 118

GDP (official exchange rate): $44.458 billion (2024 est.)
note: data in current dollars at official exchange rate

Inflation rate (consumer prices): 3.8% (2024 est.)
4.6% (2023 est.)
9.8% (2022 est.)
note: annual % change based on consumer prices
comparison ranking: 122

GDP - composition, by sector of origin: *agriculture:* 10.7% (2024 est.)
industry: 32.5% (2024 est.)
services: 48.7% (2024 est.)
note: figures may not total 100% due to non-allocated consumption not captured in sector-reported data
comparison rankings: agriculture 70; industry 41; services 155

GDP - composition, by end use: *household consumption:* 67% (2024 est.)
government consumption: 12.6% (2024 est.)
investment in fixed capital: 21% (2024 est.)
investment in inventories: 1.8% (2024 est.)
exports of goods and services: 37.2% (2024 est.)
imports of goods and services: -39.6% (2024 est.)
note: figures may not total 100% due to rounding or gaps in data collection

Agricultural products: soybeans, sugarcane, maize, cassava, wheat, rice, milk, beef, oranges, bananas (2023)
note: top ten agricultural products based on tonnage

Industries: sugar processing, cement, textiles, beverages, wood products, steel, base metals, electric power

Industrial production growth rate: 2.2% (2024 est.)
note: annual % change in industrial value added based on constant local currency
comparison ranking: 95

Labor force: 3.502 million (2024 est.)
note: number of people ages 15 or older who are employed or seeking work
comparison ranking: 100

Unemployment rate: 6.1% (2024 est.)
5.8% (2023 est.)
6.8% (2022 est.)
note: % of labor force seeking employment
comparison ranking: 114

Youth unemployment rate (ages 15-24): *total:* 14.1% (2024 est.)
male: 11% (2024 est.)
female: 18.8% (2024 est.)
note: % of labor force ages 15-24 seeking employment
comparison ranking: total 84

Population below poverty line: 24.7% (2022 est.)
note: % of population with income below national poverty line

Gini Index coefficient - distribution of family income: 44.4 (2023 est.)
note: index (0-100) of income distribution; higher values represent greater inequality
comparison ranking: 21

Average household expenditures: *on food:* 29.3% of household expenditures (2023 est.)
on alcohol and tobacco: 4.2% of household expenditures (2023 est.)

Household income or consumption by percentage share: *lowest 10%:* 1.8% (2023 est.)
highest 10%: 34.4% (2023 est.)
note: % share of income accruing to lowest and highest 10% of population

Remittances: 2% of GDP (2024 est.)
1.7% of GDP (2023 est.)
1.4% of GDP (2022 est.)
note: personal transfers and compensation between resident and non-resident individuals/households/ entities

Budget: *revenues:* $7.751 billion (2023 est.)
expenditures: $9.397 billion (2023 est.)
note: central government revenues (excluding grants) and expenditures converted to US dollars at average official exchange rate for year indicated

Taxes and other revenues: 10.1% (of GDP) (2023 est.)
note: central government tax revenue as a % of GDP
comparison ranking: 128

Current account balance: -$1.666 billion (2024 est.)
-$176.597 million (2023 est.)
-$2.948 billion (2022 est.)
note: balance of payments - net trade and primary/ secondary income in current dollars
comparison ranking: 143

Exports: $17.395 billion (2024 est.)
$18.581 billion (2023 est.)
$14.971 billion (2022 est.)
note: balance of payments - exports of goods and services in current dollars
comparison ranking: 95

Exports - partners: Argentina 33%, Brazil 25%, Chile 10%, USA 2%, Uruguay 2% (2023)
note: top five export partners based on percentage share of exports

Exports - commodities: soybeans, beef, electricity, corn, soybean meal (2023)
note: top five export commodities based on value in dollars

Imports: $18.377 billion (2024 est.)
$17.848 billion (2023 est.)
$17.088 billion (2022 est.)
note: balance of payments - imports of goods and services in current dollars
comparison ranking: 101

Imports - partners: China 33%, Brazil 24%, USA 8%, Argentina 7%, Germany 2% (2023)
note: top five import partners based on percentage share of imports

Imports - commodities: broadcasting equipment, refined petroleum, fertilizers, cars, pesticides (2023)
note: top five import commodities based on value in dollars

Reserves of foreign exchange and gold: $9.886 billion (2023 est.)
$9.519 billion (2022 est.)
$9.661 billion (2021 est.)
note: holdings of gold (year-end prices)/foreign exchange/special drawing rights in current dollars
comparison ranking: 77

Debt - external: $13.783 billion (2023 est.)
note: present value of external debt in current US dollars
comparison ranking: 43

Exchange rates: guarani (PYG) per US dollar -

Exchange rates: 7,560.248 (2024 est.)
7,288.872 (2023 est.)
6,982.752 (2022 est.)
6,774.163 (2021 est.)
6,771.097 (2020 est.)

ENERGY

Electricity access: *electrification - total population:* 100% (2022 est.)

Electricity: *installed generating capacity:* 8.928 million kW (2023 est.)
consumption: 14.835 billion kWh (2023 est.)
exports: 24.202 billion kWh (2023 est.)
transmission/distribution losses: 5.209 billion kWh (2023 est.)
comparison rankings: installed generating capacity 68; consumption 89; exports 10; transmission/distribution losses 165

Electricity generation sources: *hydroelectricity:* 99.4% of total installed capacity (2023 est.)
biomass and waste: 0.5% of total installed capacity (2023 est.)

Coal: *consumption:* 700 metric tons (2023 est.)
exports: 10 metric tons (2023 est.)
imports: 100 metric tons (2023 est.)

Petroleum: *total petroleum production:* 2,000 bbl/day (2023 est.)
refined petroleum consumption: 52,000 bbl/day (2023 est.)

Energy consumption per capita: 25.733 million Btu/ person (2023 est.)
comparison ranking: 122

COMMUNICATIONS

Telephones - fixed lines: *total subscriptions:* 206,000 (2023 est.)
subscriptions per 100 inhabitants: 3 (2023 est.)

comparison ranking: total subscriptions 118

Telephones - mobile cellular: *total subscriptions:* 8.67 million (2023 est.)
subscriptions per 100 inhabitants: 128 (2022 est.)
comparison ranking: total subscriptions 97

Broadcast media: 6 privately owned TV stations; about 75 commercial and community radio stations; 1 state-owned radio network (2019)

Internet country code: .py

Internet users: *percent of population:* 78% (2023 est.)

Broadband - fixed subscriptions: *total:* 878,000 (2023 est.)
subscriptions per 100 inhabitants: 13 (2023 est.)
comparison ranking: total 81

TRANSPORTATION

Civil aircraft registration country code prefix: ZP

Airports: 83 (2025)
comparison ranking: 63

Heliports: 29 (2025)
comparison ranking: 46

Railways: *total:* 30 km (2014)
standard gauge: 30 km (2014) 1.435-m gauge

Merchant marine: *total:* 108 (2023)
by type: container ship 2, general cargo 22, oil tanker 5, other 79
comparison ranking: total 87

Ports: *total ports:* 1 (2024)
large: 0
medium: 0
small: 0
very small: 1
ports with oil terminals: 0
key ports: Puerto de Asuncion

MILITARY AND SECURITY

Military and security forces: Armed Forces of Paraguay (Fuerzas Armadas de Paraguay; aka Armed Forces of the Nation or Fuerzas Armadas de la Nación): Paraguayan Army (Ejército Paraguayo), Paraguayan Navy (Armada Paraguaya; includes marines), Paraguayan Air Force (Fuerza Aérea Paraguaya)

Ministry of Internal Affairs: National Police of Paraguay (Policía Nacional del Paraguay, PNP) (2025)

Military expenditures: 0.8% of GDP (2024 est.)
0.8% of GDP (2023 est.)
0.8% of GDP (2022 est.)
1% of GDP (2021 est.)
1% of GDP (2020 est.)

Military and security service personnel strengths: approximately 15,000 active-duty Armed Forces (2025)

Military equipment inventories and acquisitions: the military's inventory is comprised of mostly older or obsolescent equipment from a variety of foreign suppliers, particularly Brazil and the US; in recent years, the military has received small quantities of more modern equipment, such as light attack aircraft and secondhand helicopters (2025)

Military service age and obligation: 18 years of age for compulsory (men) and voluntary (men and women) military service; conscript service obligation is 12 months for Army, 24 months for Navy; conscripts also serve in the National Police (2024)
note: as of 2021, women made up about 6% of the active military

Military - note: the Paraguayan military is responsible for external defense and has a role in domestic security duties; it provides support for natural disasters and cooperates with the National Police and other internal security organizations in combating the Paraguayan People's Army (Ejército del Pueblo Paraguayo or EPP) and transnational criminal organizations, largely narcotics traffickers; the EPP is a small, domestic criminal/guerrilla group operating in the rural northern part of the country along the border with Brazil; the activities of the EPP and its offshoots—Marsical López's Army (EML) and the Armed Peasant Association (ACA)—have consisted largely of isolated attacks on remote police and army posts, or against ranchers and peasants accused of aiding Paraguayan security forces
the Paraguayan military has deployed small numbers of troops on UN peacekeeping missions and cooperates with neighboring countries, such as Argentina and Brazil, on security issues, particularly organized crime and narco-trafficking in what is known as the Tri-Border Area; Paraguay has not fought a war against a neighboring country since the Chaco War with Bolivia in the 1930s (2025)

SPACE

Space agency/agencies: Space Agency of Paraguay (Agencia Especial del Paraguay, AEP; established 2014) (2025)

Space program overview: has a small, recently established space program focused on the acquisition of satellites, satellite data, and the technologies and capabilities to manufacture satellites, as well as promoting in-country expertise building and space industry; a priority is acquiring remote sensing capabilities to support socio-economic develop, including resource mapping, weather, and crop monitoring; has built a cube satellite with foreign assistance; operates satellites; cooperates with foreign space agencies and industries, including those of India, Japan, Taiwan, the US, and member states of the Latin American and Caribbean Space Agency (2025)
note: further details about the key activities, programs, and milestones of the country's space program, as well as government spending estimates on the space sector, appear in the Space Programs reference guide

TERRORISM

Terrorist group(s): Terrorist group(s): Hizballah
note: details about the history, aims, leadership, organization, areas of operation, tactics, targets, weapons, size, and sources of support of the group(s) appear(s) in Appendix T

TRANSNATIONAL ISSUES

Refugees and internally displaced persons: *refugees:* 7,649 (2024 est.)

IDPs: 141 (2024 est.)
stateless persons: 5 (2024 est.)

PERU

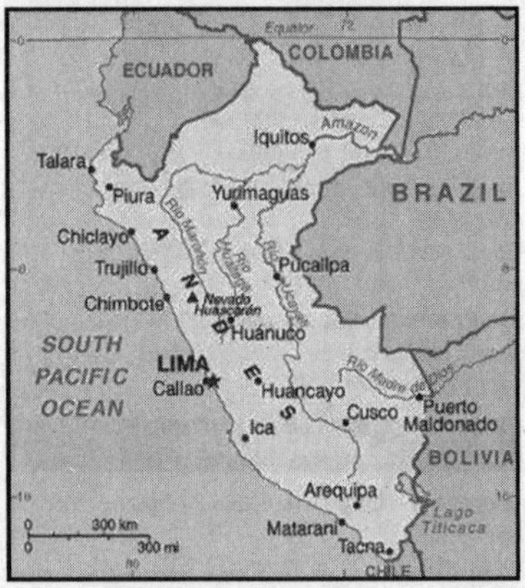

INTRODUCTION

Background: Ancient Peru was the seat of several prominent Andean civilizations, most notably that of the Incas whose empire was captured by Spanish conquistadors in 1533. Peru declared its independence in 1821, and remaining Spanish forces were defeated in 1824. After a dozen years of military rule, Peru returned to democratic leadership in 1980 but experienced economic problems and the growth of a violent insurgency. President Alberto FUJIMORI's election in 1990 ushered in a decade that saw a dramatic turnaround in the economy and significant progress in curtailing guerrilla activity. Nevertheless, an economic slump and the president's increasing reliance on authoritarian measures in the late 1990s generated mounting dissatisfaction with his regime, which led to his resignation in 2000.

A caretaker government oversaw a new election in 2001 that installed Alejandro TOLEDO Manrique as the new head of government - Peru's first democratically elected president of indigenous ethnicity. The presidential election of 2006 saw the return of Alan GARCIA Perez who, after a disappointing presidential term from 1985 to 1990, presided over a robust economic rebound. Former army officer Ollanta HUMALA Tasso was elected president in 2011 and carried on the market-oriented economic policies of the three preceding administrations. Pedro Pablo KUCZYNSKI Godard won a very narrow runoff in the 2016 presidential election. Facing impeachment after evidence surfaced of his involvement in a vote-buying scandal, KUCZYNSKI offered his resignation in 2018, and First Vice President Martin Alberto VIZCARRA Cornejo was sworn in as president. In 2019, VIZCARRA invoked his constitutional authority to dissolve Peru's Congress after months of battling with the body over anti-corruption reforms. New congressional elections in 2020 resulted in an opposition-led legislature. The Congress impeached VIZCARRA for a second time and removed him from office after accusations of corruption and mishandling of the COVID-19 pandemic. Because of vacancies in the vice-presidential positions, the President of the Peruvian Congress, Manuel MERINO, became the next president. His ascension to office was not well received, and large protests forced his resignation later in 2020. Francisco SAGASTI assumed the position of President of Peru after being appointed President of the Congress the previous day. Jose Pedro CASTILLO Terrones won presidential election in 2021 but was impeached and ousted the following year; his vice president, Dina BOLUARTE, assumed the presidency by constitutional succession in 2022.

GEOGRAPHY

Location: Western South America, bordering the South Pacific Ocean, between Chile and Ecuador

Geographic coordinates: 10 00 S, 76 00 W

Map references: South America

Area: *total:* 1,285,216 sq km
land: 1,279,996 sq km
water: 5,220 sq km
comparison ranking: total 21

Area - comparative: almost twice the size of Texas; slightly smaller than Alaska

Land boundaries: *total:* 7,062 km
border countries (5): Bolivia 1,212 km; Brazil 2,659 km; Chile 168 km; Colombia 1,494 km; Ecuador 1,529 km

Coastline: 2,414 km

Maritime claims: *territorial sea:* 200 nm; note: the US does not recognize this claim
exclusive economic zone: 200 nm
continental shelf: 200 nm

Climate: varies from tropical in east to dry desert in west; temperate to frigid in Andes

Terrain: western coastal plain (costa), high and rugged Andes in center (sierra), eastern lowland jungle of Amazon Basin (selva)

Elevation: *highest point:* Nevado Huascaran 6,746 m
lowest point: Pacific Ocean 0 m
mean elevation: 1,555 m

Natural resources: copper, silver, gold, petroleum, timber, fish, iron ore, coal, phosphate, potash, hydropower, natural gas

Land use: *agricultural land:* 19.1% (2022 est.)
arable land: 3.1% (2022 est.)
permanent crops: 1.8% (2022 est.)
permanent pasture: 14.2% (2022 est.)
forest: 56.2% (2022 est.)
other: 24.7% (2022 est.)

Irrigated land: 25,800 sq km (2012)

Major lakes (area sq km): *fresh water lake(s):* Lago Titicaca (shared with Bolivia) - 8,030 sq km

Major rivers (by length in km): Amazon river source (shared with Brazil [m]) - 6,400 km
note: [s] after country name indicates river source; [m] after country name indicates river mouth

Major watersheds (area sq km): Atlantic Ocean drainage: Amazon (6,145,186 sq km)

Major aquifers: Amazon Basin

Population distribution: approximately one third of the population resides along the desert coastal belt in the west, with a strong focus on the capital city of Lima; the Andean highlands, or sierra, contain roughly half of the population; the eastern slopes of the Andes and adjoining rainforest are sparsely populated

Natural hazards: earthquakes, tsunamis, flooding, landslides, mild volcanic activity
volcanism: volcanic activity in the Andes Mountains; Ubinas (5,672 m) is the country's most active volcano; other historically active volcanoes include El Misti, Huaynaputina, Sabancaya, and Yucamane; see note 2 under "Geography - note"

Geography - note: *note 1:* shares control of Lago Titicaca, world's highest navigable lake, with Bolivia; a remote slope of Nevado Mismi, a 5,316-m (17,441-ft) peak, is the ultimate source of the Amazon River
note 2: Peru is one of the countries along the Ring of Fire, which is a belt bordering the Pacific Ocean that contains about 75% of the world's volcanoes and up to 90% of the world's earthquakes
note 3: on 19 February 1600, Mount Huaynaputina in the southern Peruvian Andes erupted in the largest volcanic explosion in South America in historical times; intermittent eruptions lasted until 5 March 1600 and pumped an estimated 16 to 32 million metric tons of particulates into the atmosphere, reducing the amount of sunlight reaching the earth's surface and affecting weather worldwide; over the next two-and-a-half years, millions died around the globe in famines from bitterly cold winters, cool summers, and the loss of crops and animals

PEOPLE AND SOCIETY

Population: *total:* 32,600,249 (2024 est.)
male: 15,952,556
female: 16,647,693
comparison rankings: total 47; male 48; female 46

Nationality: *noun:* Peruvian(s)
adjective: Peruvian

Ethnic groups: Mestizo (mixed Indigenous and White) 60.2%, Indigenous 25.8%, White 5.9%, African descent 3.6%, other (includes Chinese and Japanese descent) 1.2%, unspecified 3.3% (2017 est.)

Languages: Spanish (official) 82.9%, Quechua (official) 13.6%, Aymara (official) 1.6%, Ashaninka 0.3%, other native languages (includes many minor Amazonian languages) 0.8%, other 0.2%, none 0.1%, unspecified 0.7% (2017 est.)
major-language sample(s):
La Libreta Informativa del Mundo, la fuente indispensable de información básica. (Spanish)

Religions: Catholic 76%, Evangelical Christian 15.7%, no religion 5.1%, other religions 3.2% (2023 est.)

Age structure: *0-14 years:* 25.8% (male 4,293,229/female 4,119,269)
15-64 years: 66.2% (male 10,546,502/female 11,041,106)
65 years and over: 8% (2024 est.) (male 1,112,825/female 1,487,318)

Dependency ratios: *total dependency ratio:* 51 (2024 est.)
youth dependency ratio: 39 (2024 est.)
elderly dependency ratio: 12 (2024 est.)
potential support ratio: 8.3 (2024 est.)

Median age: *total:* 30.2 years (2024 est.)
male: 29.1 years
female: 31.3 years
comparison ranking: total 139

Population growth rate: 0.48% (2024 est.)
comparison ranking: 151

Birth rate: 16.7 births/1,000 population (2024 est.)
comparison ranking: 96

Death rate: 10.9 deaths/1,000 population (2024 est.)
comparison ranking: 26

Net migration rate: -1 migrant(s)/1,000 population (2024 est.)
comparison ranking: 146

Population distribution: approximately one third of the population resides along the desert coastal belt in the west, with a strong focus on the capital city of Lima; the Andean highlands, or sierra, contain roughly half of the population; the eastern slopes of the Andes and adjoining rainforest are sparsely populated

Urbanization: *urban population:* 78.9% of total population (2023)
rate of urbanization: 1.33% annual rate of change (2020-25 est.)

Major urban areas - population: 11.204 million LIMA (capital), 959,000 Arequipa, 904,000 Trujillo (2023)

Sex ratio: *at birth:* 1.05 male(s)/female
0-14 years: 1.04 male(s)/female
15-64 years: 0.96 male(s)/female
65 years and over: 0.75 male(s)/female
total population: 0.96 male(s)/female (2024 est.)

Mother's mean age at first birth: 21.9 years (2013 est.)
note: data represents median age at first birth among women 25-49

Maternal mortality ratio: 51 deaths/100,000 live births (2023 est.)
comparison ranking: 94

Infant mortality rate: *total:* 10.8 deaths/1,000 live births (2024 est.)
male: 11.9 deaths/1,000 live births
female: 9.7 deaths/1,000 live births
comparison ranking: total 125

Life expectancy at birth: *total population:* 68.9 years (2024 est.)
male: 65.4 years
female: 72.7 years
comparison ranking: total population 185

Total fertility rate: 2.15 children born/woman (2024 est.)
comparison ranking: 90

Gross reproduction rate: 1.05 (2024 est.)

Drinking water source: *improved: urban:* 97.5% of population (2022 est.)
rural: 84.9% of population (2022 est.)
total: 94.8% of population (2022 est.)
unimproved: urban: 2.5% of population (2022 est.)
rural: 15.1% of population (2022 est.)
total: 5.2% of population (2022 est.)

Health expenditure: 6.2% of GDP (2021)
16.7% of national budget (2022 est.)

Physician density: 1.69 physicians/1,000 population (2023)

Hospital bed density: 1.6 beds/1,000 population (2021 est.)

Sanitation facility access: *improved: urban:* 94.1% of population (2022 est.)
rural: 65.9% of population (2022 est.)

total: 88.1% of population (2022 est.)
unimproved: *urban*: 5.9% of population (2022 est.)
rural: 34.1% of population (2022 est.)
total: 11.9% of population (2022 est.)

Obesity - adult prevalence rate: 19.7% (2016)
comparison ranking: 110

Alcohol consumption per capita: *total*: 5.74 liters of pure alcohol (2019 est.)
beer: 3.01 liters of pure alcohol (2019 est.)
wine: 0.46 liters of pure alcohol (2019 est.)
spirits: 2.26 liters of pure alcohol (2019 est.)
other alcohols: 0.01 liters of pure alcohol (2019 est.)
comparison ranking: total 76

Tobacco use: *total*: 5.7% (2025 est.)
male: 9.5% (2025 est.)
female: 2.1% (2025 est.)
comparison ranking: total 158

Children under the age of 5 years underweight: 2.1% (2021)
comparison ranking: 95

Currently married women (ages 15-49): 51.2% (2023 est.)

Child marriage: *women married by age 15*: 2% (2020)
women married by age 18: 14.1% (2020)

Education expenditure: 4.2% of GDP (2023 est.)
19.2% national budget (2025 est.)
comparison ranking: Education expenditure (% GDP) 98

Literacy: *total population*: 94% (2020 est.)
male: 97% (2020 est.)
female: 92% (2020 est.)

School life expectancy (primary to tertiary education): *total*: 15 years (2017 est.)
male: 15 years (2017 est.)
female: 15 years (2017 est.)

ENVIRONMENT

Environmental issues: deforestation (some the result of illegal logging); overgrazing leading to soil erosion; desertification; air pollution in Lima; pollution of rivers and coastal waters from municipal and mining wastes; overfishing

International environmental agreements: *party to*: Antarctic-Environmental Protection, Antarctic-Marine Living Resources, Antarctic Treaty, Biodiversity, Climate Change, Climate Change-Kyoto Protocol, Climate Change-Paris Agreement, Desertification, Endangered Species, Hazardous Wastes, Marine Dumping-London Convention, Marine Dumping-London Protocol, Nuclear Test Ban, Ozone Layer Protection, Ship Pollution, Tropical Timber 2006, Wetlands, Whaling
signed, but not ratified: none of the selected agreements

Climate: varies from tropical in east to dry desert in west; temperate to frigid in Andes

Urbanization: *urban population*: 78.9% of total population (2023)
rate of urbanization: 1.33% annual rate of change (2020-25 est.)

Carbon dioxide emissions: 58.903 million metric tonnes of CO2 (2023 est.)
from coal and metallurgical coke: 2.177 million metric tonnes of CO2 (2023 est.)
from petroleum and other liquids: 34.863 million metric tonnes of CO2 (2023 est.)
from consumed natural gas: 21.863 million metric tonnes of CO2 (2023 est.)
comparison ranking: total emissions 53

Particulate matter emissions: 31.7 micrograms per cubic meter (2019 est.)

Methane emissions: *energy*: 233.6 kt (2022-2024 est.)
agriculture: 623.5 kt (2019-2021 est.)
waste: 317 kt (2019-2021 est.)
other: 51.9 kt (2019-2021 est.)

Waste and recycling: *municipal solid waste generated annually*: 8.357 million tons (2024 est.)
percent of municipal solid waste recycled: 9.2% (2022 est.)

Total water withdrawal: *municipal*: 3.141 billion cubic meters (2022)
industrial: 1.666 billion cubic meters (2022)
agricultural: 21.112 billion cubic meters (2022)

Total renewable water resources: 1.88 trillion cubic meters (2022 est.)

Geoparks: *total global geoparks and regional networks*: 1
global geoparks and regional networks: Colca y Volcanes de Andagua (2023)

GOVERNMENT

Country name: *conventional long form*: Republic of Peru
conventional short form: Peru
local long form: República del Perú
local short form: Perú
etymology: the name may derive from the Guarani word biru, meaning "river"

Government type: presidential republic

Capital: *name*: Lima
geographic coordinates: 12 03 S, 77 03 W
time difference: UTC-5 (same time as Washington, DC, during Standard Time)
etymology: the name is an early Spanish mispronunciation of the Quechua name *Rimak*, referring to a god and deriving from the word *rima* (to speak); Quechua priests used to speak to worshippers from inside statues of their gods

Administrative divisions: 24 departments (*departamentos*, singular - *departamento*), 1 province* (*provincia*), and 1 constitutional province** (*provincia constitucional*); Amazonas, Ancash, Apurimac, Arequipa, Ayacucho, Cajamarca, Callao**, Cusco, Huancavelica, Huánuco, Ica, Junín, La Libertad, Lambayeque, Lima, Lima*, Loreto, Madre de Dios, Moquegua, Pasco, Piura, Puno, San Martin, Tacna, Tumbes, Ucayali

Legal system: civil law system

Constitution: *history*: several previous; latest promulgated 29 December 1993, enacted 31 December 1993
amendment process: proposed by Congress, by the president of the republic with the approval of the Council of Ministers or by petition of at least 0.3% of voters; passage requires absolute majority approval by the Congress membership, followed by approval in a referendum; a referendum is not required if Congress approves the amendment by greater than two-thirds majority vote in each of two successive sessions

International law organization participation: accepts compulsory ICJ jurisdiction with reservations; accepts ICCt jurisdiction

Citizenship: *citizenship by birth*: yes
citizenship by descent only: yes
dual citizenship recognized: yes
residency requirement for naturalization: 2 years

Suffrage: 18 years of age; universal and compulsory until the age of 70

Executive branch: *chief of state*: President José Enrique JERÍ Oré (since 10 October 2025)
head of government: President José Enrique JERÍ Oré (since 10 October 2025)
cabinet: Council of Ministers appointed by the president
election/appointment process: president directly elected by absolute-majority popular vote in 2 rounds, if needed, for a 5-year term (eligible for nonconsecutive terms)
most recent election date: 11 April 2021, with a runoff on 6 June 2021
election results: *2021*: Jose Pedro CASTILLO Terrones elected president in second round; percent of vote in first round - Jose Pedro CASTILLO Terrones (PL) 18.9%, Keiko Sofia FUJIMORI Higuchi (FP) 13.4%, Rafael LOPEZ ALIAGA Cazorla (RP) 11.8%, Hernando DE SOTO Polar (Social Integration Party) 11.6%, Yonhy LESCANO Ancieta (AP) 9.1%, Veronika MENDOZA Frisch (JP) 7.9%, Cesar ACUNA Peralta (APP) 6%, George FORSYTH Sommer (VN) 5.7%, Daniel Belizario URRESTI Elera (PP) 5.6%, other 10%; percent of vote second round - Jose Pedro CASTILLO Terrones 50.1%, Keiko Sofia FUJIMORI Higuchi 49.9%
2016: Pedro Pablo KUCZYNSKI Godard elected president in second round; percent of vote in first round - Keiko FUJIMORI Higuchi (FP) 39.9%, Pedro Pablo KUCZYNSKI Godard (PPK) 21.1%, Veronika MENDOZA (FA) 18.7%, Alfredo BARNECHEA (AP) 7%, Alan GARCIA (APRA) 5.8%, other 7.5%; percent of vote in second round - Pedro Pablo KUCZYNSKI Godard 50.1%, Keiko FUJIMORI Higuchi 49.9%
expected date of next election: 12 April 2026
note 1: First Vice President Dina Ercilia BOLUARTE Zegarra assumed the office of the president on 7 December 2022 after President Jose Pedro CASTILLO Terrones was impeached and arrested; on 10 October 2025, the president of the Congress, José Enrique JERÍ Oré, was sworn in as the new president after Congress overwhelmingly voted to remove BOLUARTE from office
note 2: Prime Minister Ernesto ÁLVAREZ (since 14 October 2025) does not exercise executive power; this power rests with the president
note 3: the president is both chief of state and head of government

Legislative branch: *legislature name*: Congress of the Republic (Congreso de la República)
legislative structure: unicameral
number of seats: 130 (all directly elected)
electoral system: proportional representation
scope of elections: full renewal
term in office: 5 years
most recent election date: 4/11/2021
parties elected and seats per party: Free Peru (PL) (37); Popular Force (FP) (24); Popular Action (AP) (16); Alliance for Progress (APP) (15); Go on Country - Social Integration Party (AvP) (10); Popular Renewal (RP) (9); We Are Peru" (SP) - Purple Party (PM) (9); Other (10)
percentage of women in chamber: 41.5%
expected date of next election: April 2026

Judicial branch: *highest court(s)*: Supreme Court (consists of 16 judges and divided into civil, criminal, and constitutional-social sectors)
judge selection and term of office: justices proposed by the National Board of Justice (a 7-member independent body), nominated by the president, and confirmed by the Congress; justices can serve until mandatory retirement at age 70

subordinate courts: Court of Constitutional Guarantees; Superior Courts or Cortes Superiores; specialized civil, criminal, and mixed courts; 2 types of peace courts in which professional judges and selected members of the local communities preside

Political parties: Advance the Nation (Avanza País) or AvP
Alliance for Progress (Alianza para el Progreso) or APP
Broad Front (Frente Amplio) or FA
Free Peru (Perú Libre) or PL
Front for Hope (Frente Esperanza)
Magisterial Block of National Concentration (Bloque Magisterial de Concertación Nacional) or BMCN
National Victory (Victoria Nacional) or VN
Peru Bicentennial (Perú Bicentenario) or PB
Popular Action (Acción Popular) or AP
Popular Force (Fuerza Popular) or FP
Popular Renewal (Renovación Popular) or RP
Purple Party (Partido Morado)
Social Integration Party (Avanza País - Partido de Integración Social)
Together For Perú (Juntos por el Peru) or JP
We Are Peru (Somos Perú) of SP
We Can Peru (Podemos Perú) or PP

Diplomatic representation in the US: *chief of mission:* Ambassador Alfredo Santiago Carlos FERRERO DIEZ CANSECO (since 27 February 2024)
chancery: 1700 Massachusetts Avenue NW, Washington, DC 20036
telephone: [1] (202) 833-9860
FAX: [1] (202) 659-8124
email address and website: Webadmin@embassyofperu.us
Embassy of Peru in the United States - E-United States - Platform of the Peruvian State (www.gob.pe)
consulate(s) general: Atlanta, Boston, Chicago, Dallas, Denver, Hartford (CT), Houston, Los Angeles, Miami, New York, Paterson (NJ), San Francisco

Diplomatic representation from the US: *chief of mission:* Ambassador (vacant); Chargé d'Affaires Joan PERKINS (since 18 April 2025)
embassy: Avenida La Encalada, Cuadra 17 s/n, Surco, Lima 33
mailing address: 3230 Lima Place, Washington DC 20521-3230
telephone: [51] (1) 618-2000
FAX: [51] (1) 618-2724
email address and website: lima_webmaster@state.gov
https://pe.usembassy.gov/

International organization participation: AIIB, APEC, BIS, CAN, CD, CELAC, EITI (compliant country), FAO, G-24, G-77, IADB, IAEA, IBRD, ICAO, ICC (NGOs), ICCt, ICRM, IDA, IFAD, IFC, IFRCS, IHO, ILO, IMF, IMO, IMSO, Interpol, IOC, IOM, IPU, ISO, ITSO, ITU, ITUC (NGOs), LAES, LAIA, Mercosur (associate), MIGA, MINUSTAH, MONUSCO, NAM, OAS, OPANAL, OPCW, Pacific Alliance, PCA, PROSUR, SICA (observer), UN, UNAMID, UNASUR, UNCTAD, UNESCO, UNHCR, UNIDO, Union Latina, UNISFA, UNMISS, UNOCI, UNOOSA, UN Security Council (temporary), UNWTO, UPU, WCO, WFTU (NGOs), WHO, WIPO, WMO, WTO

Independence: 28 July 1821 (from Spain)

National holiday: Independence Day, 28-29 July (1821)

Flag: *description:* three equal vertical bands of red (left side), white, and red, with the coat of arms centered on the white band; the coat of arms has a shield with a vicuna, a cinchona tree, and a yellow cornucopia spilling out coins
meaning: the vicuna represents fauna, the cinchona tree is the source of quinine, and the cornucopia symbolizes mineral wealth; red stands for blood shed for independence, and white for peace

National symbol(s): vicuna (a camelid related to the llama)

National color(s): red, white

National anthem(s): *title:* "Himno Nacional del Peru" (National Anthem of Peru)
lyrics/music: Jose DE LA TORRE Ugarte/Jose Bernardo ALZEDO
history: adopted 1821

National heritage: *total World Heritage Sites:* 13 (9 cultural, 2 natural, 2 mixed)
selected World Heritage Site locales: Cuzco (c); Machu Picchu (m); Chavin (c); Historic Lima (c); Huascarán National Park (n); Chan Chan (c); Manú National Park (n); Lines and Geoglyphs of Nazca (c); Rio Abiseo National Park (m); Historic Arequipa (c); Sacred City of Caral-Supe (c); Qhapaq Ñan/ Andean Road System (c)

ECONOMY

Economic overview: upper-middle-income South American economy; strong post-COVID rebound tempered by political uncertainty and climate risks; exports driven by mineral extraction and agriculture; large informal sector and uneven access to public services; stable fiscal position and financial sector

Real GDP (purchasing power parity): $535.911 billion (2024 est.)
$518.771 billion (2023 est.)
$520.872 billion (2022 est.)
note: data in 2021 dollars
comparison ranking: 47

Real GDP growth rate: 3.3% (2024 est.)
-0.4% (2023 est.)
2.8% (2022 est.)
note: annual GDP % growth based on constant local currency
comparison ranking: 107

Real GDP per capita: $15,700 (2024 est.)
$15,300 (2023 est.)
$15,600 (2022 est.)
note: data in 2021 dollars
comparison ranking: 122

GDP (official exchange rate): $289.222 billion (2024 est.)
note: data in current dollars at official exchange rate

Inflation rate (consumer prices): 2% (2024 est.)
6.5% (2023 est.)
8.3% (2022 est.)
note: annual % change based on consumer prices
comparison ranking: 48

GDP - composition, by sector of origin: *agriculture:* 6.1% (2024 est.)
industry: 32.2% (2024 est.)
services: 52.7% (2024 est.)
note: figures may not total 100% due to non-allocated consumption not captured in sector-reported data
comparison rankings: agriculture 100; industry 42; services 131

GDP - composition, by end use: *household consumption:* 61.6% (2024 est.)
government consumption: 13.4% (2024 est.)
investment in fixed capital: 20.8% (2024 est.)
investment in inventories: -1.4% (2024 est.)
exports of goods and services: 28.5% (2024 est.)
imports of goods and services: -22.9% (2024 est.)
note: figures may not total 100% due to rounding or gaps in data collection

Agricultural products: sugarcane, potatoes, rice, bananas, milk, maize, chicken, oil palm fruit, cassava, grapes (2023)
note: top ten agricultural products based on tonnage

Industries: mining and refining of minerals; steel, metal fabrication; petroleum extraction and refining, natural gas and natural gas liquefaction; fishing and fish processing, cement, glass, textiles, clothing, food processing, beer, soft drinks, rubber, machinery, electrical machinery, chemicals, furniture

Industrial production growth rate: 3.1% (2024 est.)
note: annual % change in industrial value added based on constant local currency
comparison ranking: 79

Labor force: 18.918 million (2024 est.)
note: number of people ages 15 or older who are employed or seeking work
comparison ranking: 35

Unemployment rate: 4.9% (2024 est.)
4.9% (2023 est.)
3.9% (2022 est.)
note: % of labor force seeking employment
comparison ranking: 86

Youth unemployment rate (ages 15-24): *total:* 8.8% (2024 est.)
male: 7.9% (2024 est.)
female: 9.8% (2024 est.)
note: % of labor force ages 15-24 seeking employment
comparison ranking: total 132

Population below poverty line: 27.5% (2022 est.)
note: % of population with income below national poverty line

Gini Index coefficient - distribution of family income: 40.7 (2023 est.)
note: index (0-100) of income distribution; higher values represent greater inequality
comparison ranking: 39

Average household expenditures: *on food:* 26.9% of household expenditures (2023 est.)
on alcohol and tobacco: 2.5% of household expenditures (2023 est.)

Household income or consumption by percentage share: *lowest 10%:* 2% (2023 est.)
highest 10%: 30.6% (2023 est.)
note: % share of income accruing to lowest and highest 10% of population

Remittances: 1.7% of GDP (2023 est.)
1.5% of GDP (2022 est.)
1.6% of GDP (2021 est.)
note: personal transfers and compensation between resident and non-resident individuals/households/ entities

Budget: *revenues:* $48.003 billion (2021 est.)
expenditures: $55.34 billion (2021 est.)
note: central government revenues (excluding grants) and expenditures converted to US dollars at average official exchange rate for year indicated

Public debt: 35.2% of GDP (2021 est.)
note: central government debt as a % of GDP
comparison ranking: 153

Taxes and other revenues: 15.9% (of GDP) (2021 est.)

note: central government tax revenue as a % of GDP
comparison ranking: 85

Current account balance: $6.39 billion (2024 est.)
$881.934 million (2023 est.)
-$9.972 billion (2022 est.)
note: balance of payments - net trade and primary/secondary income in current dollars
comparison ranking: 31

Exports: $83.325 billion (2024 est.)
$72.97 billion (2023 est.)
$71.39 billion (2022 est.)
note: balance of payments - exports of goods and services in current dollars
comparison ranking: 54

Exports - partners: China 34%, USA 14%, Canada 5%, India 4%, Switzerland 4% (2023)
note: top five export partners based on percentage share of exports

Exports - commodities: copper ore, gold, refined copper, refined petroleum, grapes (2023)
note: top five export commodities based on value in dollars

Imports: $67.16 billion (2024 est.)
$63.776 billion (2023 est.)
$69.936 billion (2022 est.)
note: balance of payments - imports of goods and services in current dollars
comparison ranking: 58

Imports - partners: China 26%, USA 21%, Brazil 7%, Argentina 5%, Mexico 3% (2023)
note: top five import partners based on percentage share of imports

Imports - commodities: refined petroleum, crude petroleum, cars, trucks, broadcasting equipment (2023)
note: top five import commodities based on value in dollars

Reserves of foreign exchange and gold: $79.246 billion (2024 est.)
$71.394 billion (2023 est.)
$72.328 billion (2022 est.)
note: holdings of gold (year-end prices)/foreign exchange/special drawing rights in current dollars
comparison ranking: 34

Debt - external: $38.102 billion (2023 est.)
note: present value of external debt in current US dollars
comparison ranking: 22

Exchange rates: nuevo sol (PEN) per US dollar -

Exchange rates: 3.744 (2023 est.)
3.835 (2022 est.)
3.881 (2021 est.)
3.495 (2020 est.)
3.337 (2019 est.)

ENERGY

Electricity access: *electrification - total population:* 96.2% (2022 est.)
electrification - urban areas: 99%
electrification - rural areas: 85.1%

Electricity: *installed generating capacity:* 16.164 million kW (2023 est.)
consumption: 53.3 billion kWh (2023 est.)
imports: 47.696 million kWh (2023 est.)
transmission/distribution losses: 6.638 billion kWh (2023 est.)
comparison rankings: installed generating capacity 54; consumption 51; imports 118; transmission/distribution losses 169

Electricity generation sources: *fossil fuels:* 44.8% of total installed capacity (2023 est.)
solar: 1.4% of total installed capacity (2023 est.)
wind: 3.2% of total installed capacity (2023 est.)
hydroelectricity: 49.6% of total installed capacity (2023 est.)
biomass and waste: 1% of total installed capacity (2023 est.)

Coal: *production:* 1.382 million metric tons (2023 est.)
consumption: 973,000 metric tons (2023 est.)
exports: 1.261 million metric tons (2023 est.)
imports: 446,000 metric tons (2023 est.)
proven reserves: 1.567 billion metric tons (2023 est.)

Petroleum: *total petroleum production:* 118,000 bbl/day (2023 est.)
refined petroleum consumption: 255,000 bbl/day (2023 est.)
crude oil estimated reserves: 858.89 million barrels (2021 est.)

Natural gas: *production:* 14.647 billion cubic meters (2023 est.)
consumption: 9.675 billion cubic meters (2023 est.)
exports: 4.883 billion cubic meters (2023 est.)
proven reserves: 300.159 billion cubic meters (2021 est.)

Energy consumption per capita: 30.923 million Btu/person (2023 est.)
comparison ranking: 114

COMMUNICATIONS

Telephones - fixed lines: *total subscriptions:* 1.504 million (2023 est.)
subscriptions per 100 inhabitants: 4 (2023 est.)
comparison ranking: total subscriptions 57

Telephones - mobile cellular: *total subscriptions:* 41.3 million (2023 est.)
subscriptions per 100 inhabitants: 122 (2022 est.)
comparison ranking: total subscriptions 41

Broadcast media: 10 major TV networks of which only one, Television Nacional de Peru, is state owned; multi-channel cable TV services are available; in excess of 5,000 radio stations including a substantial number of local-language stations (2021)

Internet country code: .pe

Internet users: *percent of population:* 80% (2023 est.)

Broadband - fixed subscriptions: *total:* 3.53 million (2023 est.)
subscriptions per 100 inhabitants: 10 (2023 est.)
comparison ranking: total 46

TRANSPORTATION

Civil aircraft registration country code prefix: OB

Airports: 174 (2025)
comparison ranking: 34

Heliports: 7 (2025)
comparison ranking: 87

Railways: *total:* 1,854.4 km (2017)
standard gauge: 1,730.4 km (2014) 1.435-m gauge (34 km electrified)
narrow gauge: 124 km (2014) 0.914-m gauge

Merchant marine: *total:* 111 (2023)
by type: general cargo 1, oil tanker 9, other 101
comparison ranking: total 85

Ports: *total ports:* 20 (2024)
large: 0
medium: 1
small: 3
very small: 16
ports with oil terminals: 16
key ports: Bahia de Matarani, Iquitos, Puerto del Callao, Talara

MILITARY AND SECURITY

Military and security forces: Armed Forces of Peru (Fuerzas Armadas del Perú or FAP): Peruvian Army (Ejercito del Peru), Peruvian Navy (Marina de Guerra del Peru, MGP, includes naval infantry and General Directorate of Captaincies and Coast Guards, DICAPI), Air Force of Peru (Fuerza Aerea del Peru, FAP)

Ministry of the Interior: Peruvian National Police (Policía Nacional del Perú, PNP) (2025)

Military expenditures: 0.8% of GDP (2024 est.)
1% of GDP (2023 est.)
1.1% of GDP (2022 est.)
1.1% of GDP (2021 est.)
1.2% of GDP (2020 est.)

Military and security service personnel strengths: information varies; approximately 85,000 active-duty Armed Forces (50,000 Army; 25,000 Navy; 10,000 Air Force); approximately 75,000 National Police (2025)

Military equipment inventories and acquisitions: the military has a broad mix of mostly older but some more modern equipment from a range of suppliers, including Brazil, China, France, Germany, Italy, Russia and the former Soviet Union, South Korea, and the US; some deliveries have been secondhand weapons systems; Peru has a small defense industry, including a shipyard that builds and upgrades naval vessels; it also has defense industrial cooperation agreements with several countries, including Russia, South Korea, Spain, and the US (2024)

Military service age and obligation: 18-30 years of age for voluntary military service (12 months) (2024)
note: as of 2024, women made up about 11% of the active-duty military

Military deployments: 225 Central African Republic (MINUSCA) (2024)

Military - note: the Peruvian Armed Forces (FAP) are responsible for external defense in addition to some domestic security responsibilities in designated emergency areas and in exceptional circumstances; key areas of focus include counterinsurgency, counter-narcotics, cyber defense, disaster relief, and maritime security operations; the FAP supported the police during anti-government protests in early 2023; it has contributed to UN missions since 1958 and has ties to regional militaries, particularly Colombia, as well as those of numerous other countries such as China, Russia, Spain, and the US; the FAP's last external conflict was a brief border war with Ecuador in 1995 the Special Command of the Valley of the Apurimac, Ene, and Mantaro rivers (CE-VRAEM) is responsible for combating the remnants of the Shining Path terrorist group (aka Sendero Luminoso) and includes several thousand air, ground, naval, police, and special forces personnel; the FAP also provides aircraft, vehicles, and logistical support to the command (2025)

SPACE

Space agency/agencies: National Aerospace Research and Development Commission (Comisión Nacional de Investigación y Desarrollo Aeroespacia, CONIDA; established 1974) (2025)
Space launch site(s) in 2024, Peru and the US signed an agreement to construct a spaceport in the Talara Desert in the Piura region

Space program overview: has a small space program focused on acquiring satellites, applying space applications such as data satellite imagery, and building small rockets; has built a small science/technology satellite; operates satellites and processes satellite imagery data; builds and launches sounding rockets with goal of developing a satellite/space launch vehicle (SLV); researching, developing, and acquiring technologies for manufacturing satellites and satellite payloads with a focus on remote sensing (RS) capabilities; member of Latin American and Caribbean Space Agency (ALCE) since its formation in 2021; cooperates with a variety of foreign space agencies and industries, including those of Brazil, China, the European Space Agency and individual member states (particularly France and Germany), India, Russia, South Korea, Thailand, and the US, as well as other signatories of the ALCE (2025)
note: further details about the key activities, programs, and milestones of the country's space program, as well as government spending estimates on the space sector, appear in the Space Programs reference guide

TERRORISM

Terrorist group(s): Terrorist group(s): Shining Path (Sendero Luminoso); Tren de Aragua (TdA)
note: details about the history, aims, leadership, organization, areas of operation, tactics, targets, weapons, size, and sources of support of the group(s) appear(s) in Appendix T

TRANSNATIONAL ISSUES

Refugees and internally displaced persons: *refugees:* 546,699 (2024 est.)

IDPs: 83,441 (2024 est.)
stateless persons: 32 (2024 est.)

Illicit drugs: USG identification: major illicit drug-producing and/or drug-transit country
major precursor-chemical producer (2025)

PHILIPPINES

INTRODUCTION

Background: The Philippine Islands became a Spanish colony during the 16th century; they were ceded to the US in 1898 following the Spanish-American War. Led by Emilio AGUINALDO, the Filipinos conducted an insurgency against US rule from 1899-1902, although some fighting continued in outlying islands as late as 1913. In 1935, the Philippines became a self-governing commonwealth. Manuel QUEZON was elected president and was tasked with preparing the country for independence after a 10-year transition. The islands fell under Japanese occupation during World War II, and US forces and Filipinos fought together during 1944-45 to regain control. On 4 July 1946 the Republic of the Philippines attained its independence.

Twenty-one years of authoritarian rule under Ferdinand MARCOS ended in 1986, when a "people power" movement in Manila ("EDSA 1") forced him into exile and installed Corazon AQUINO as president. Several coup attempts hampered her presidency, and progress on political stability and economic development faltered until Fidel RAMOS was elected president in 1992. The US closed its last military bases on the islands the same year. Joseph ESTRADA was elected president in 1998. His vice-president, Gloria MACAPAGAL-ARROYO, succeded him in 2001 after ESTRADA's stormy impeachment trial on corruption charges broke down and another "people power" movement ("EDSA 2") demanded his resignation. MACAPAGAL-ARROYO was elected president in 2004. Corruption allegations marred her presidency, but the Philippine economy was one of the few to avoid contraction after the 2008 global financial crisis. Benigno AQUINO III was elected as president in 2010, followed by Rodrigo DUTERTE in 2016. During his term, DUTERTE pursued a controversial drug war that garnered international criticism for alleged human rights abuses. Ferdinand MARCOS, Jr. was elected president in 2022 with the largest popular vote in a presidential election since his father's ouster.

For decades, the country has been challenged by armed ethnic separatists, communist rebels, and Islamic terrorist groups, particularly in the southern islands and remote areas of Luzon.

GEOGRAPHY

Location: Southeastern Asia, archipelago between the Philippine Sea and the South China Sea, east of Vietnam

Geographic coordinates: 13 00 N, 122 00 E

Map references: Southeast Asia

Area: *total:* 300,000 sq km
land: 298,170 sq km
water: 1,830 sq km
comparison ranking: total 74

Area - comparative: slightly less than twice the size of Georgia; slightly larger than Arizona

Land boundaries: *total:* 0 km

Coastline: 36,289 km

Maritime claims: *territorial sea:* irregular polygon extending up to 100 nm from coastline as defined by 1898 treaty; since late 1970s has also claimed polygonal-shaped area in South China Sea as wide as 285 nm
exclusive economic zone: 200 nm
continental shelf: to the depth of exploitation

Climate: tropical marine; northeast monsoon (November to April); southwest monsoon (May to October)

Terrain: mostly mountains with narrow to extensive coastal lowlands

Elevation: *highest point:* Mount Apo 2,954 m
lowest point: Philippine Sea 0 m
mean elevation: 442 m

Natural resources: timber, petroleum, nickel, cobalt, silver, gold, salt, copper

Land use: *agricultural land:* 42.5% (2022 est.)
arable land: 18.7% (2022 est.)
permanent crops: 18.8% (2022 est.)
permanent pasture: 5% (2022 est.)
forest: 24.3% (2022 est.)
other: 33.1% (2022 est.)

Irrigated land: 16,270 sq km (2012)

Major lakes (area sq km): *salt water lake(s):* Laguna de Bay - 890 sq km

Population distribution: population concentrated in areas with good farmland; highest concentrations are northwest and south-central Luzon, the southeastern extension of Luzon, and the islands of the Visayan Sea, particularly Cebu and Negros; Manila is home to one eighth of the national population

Natural hazards: astride typhoon belt, usually affected by several cyclonic storms each year; landslides; active volcanoes; destructive earthquakes; tsunamis
volcanism: significant volcanic activity; Taal (311 m) has been deemed a Decade Volcano by the International Association of Volcanology and Chemistry of the Earth's Interior, worthy of study due to its explosive history and close proximity to human populations; Mayon (2,462 m), the country's most active volcano, erupted in 2009 and forced over 33,000 to be evacuated; other historically active volcanoes include Biliran, Babuyan Claro, Bulusan, Camiguin, Camiguin de Babuyanes, Didicas, Iraya, Jolo, Kanlaon, Makaturing, Musuan, Parker, Pinatubo, and Ragang; see note 2 under "Geography - note"

Geography - note: *note 1:* for decades, the Philippine archipelago was reported as having 7,107 islands; in 2016, the national mapping authority reported that hundreds of new islands had been discovered and increased the number of islands to 7,641, though not all of the new islands have been verified
note 2: the Philippines is one of the countries along the Ring of Fire, which is a belt bordering the Pacific Ocean that contains about 75% of the world's volcanoes and up to 90% of the world's earthquakes
note 3: the Philippines sits on the Pacific typhoon belt, and an average of 9 typhoons make landfall on the islands each year, with about 5 being destructive; the country is the most exposed in the world to tropical storms

PEOPLE AND SOCIETY

Population: *total:* 118,277,063 (2024 est.)
male: 59,227,092
female: 59,049,971
comparison rankings: total 13; male 12; female 13

Nationality: *noun:* Filipino(s)
adjective: Philippine

Ethnic groups: Tagalog 26%, Bisaya/Binisaya 14.3%, Ilocano 8%, Cebuano 8%, Illonggo 7.9%, Bikol/Bicol 6.5%, Waray 3.8%, Kapampangan 3%, Maguindanao 1.9%, Pangasinan 1.9%, other local ethnicities 18.5%, foreign ethnicities 0.2% (2020 est.)

Languages: Tagalog 39.9%, Bisaya/Binisaya 16%, Hiligaynon/Ilonggo 7.3%, Ilocano 7.1%, Cebuano 6.5%, Bikol/Bicol 3.9%, Waray 2.6%, Kapampangan 2.4%, Maguindanao 1.4%, Pangasinan/Panggalato 1.3%, other languages/dialects 11.2%, unspecified 0.4% (2020 est.)
major-language sample(s):
Ang World Factbook, ang mapagkukunan ng kailangang impormasyon. (Tagalog)
note: data represent percentage of households; unspecified Filipino (based on Tagalog) and English are official languagesTaga; eight major dialects - Tagalog, Cebuano, Ilocano, Hiligaynon or Ilonggo, Bicol, Waray, Pampango, and Pangasinan

Religions: Roman Catholic 78.8%, Muslim 6.4%, Iglesia ni Cristo 2.6%, other Christian 3.9%, other 8.2%, none/unspecified <0.1 (2020 est.)

Age structure: *0-14 years:* 30.2% (male 18,234,279/female 17,462,803)
15-64 years: 64.3% (male 38,381,583/female 37,613,294)
65 years and over: 5.6% (2024 est.) (male 2,611,230/female 3,973,874)

Dependency ratios: *total dependency ratio:* 55.6 (2024 est.)
youth dependency ratio: 47 (2024 est.)
elderly dependency ratio: 8.7 (2024 est.)
potential support ratio: 11.5 (2024 est.)

Median age: *total:* 25.7 years (2024 est.)
male: 25.1 years
female: 26.3 years
comparison ranking: total 167

Population growth rate: 1.56% (2024 est.)
comparison ranking: 60

Birth rate: 22.1 births/1,000 population (2024 est.)
comparison ranking: 53

Death rate: 6.2 deaths/1,000 population (2024 est.)
comparison ranking: 146

Net migration rate: -0.2 migrant(s)/1,000 population (2024 est.)
comparison ranking: 109

Population distribution: population concentrated in areas with good farmland; highest concentrations are northwest and south-central Luzon, the southeastern extension of Luzon, and the islands of the Visayan Sea, particularly Cebu and Negros; Manila is home to one eighth of the national population

Urbanization: *urban population:* 48.3% of total population (2023)
rate of urbanization: 2.04% annual rate of change (2020-25 est.)

Major urban areas - population: 14.667 million MANILA (capital), 1.949 million Davao, 1.025 million Cebu City, 931,000 Zamboanga, 960,000 Antipolo, 803,000 Cagayan de Oro City, 803,000 Dasmarinas (2023)

Sex ratio: *at birth:* 1.05 male(s)/female
0-14 years: 1.04 male(s)/female
15-64 years: 1.02 male(s)/female
65 years and over: 0.66 male(s)/female
total population: 1 male(s)/female (2024 est.)

Mother's mean age at first birth: 23.6 years (2022 est.)
note: data represents median age at first birth among women 25-49

Maternal mortality ratio: 84 deaths/100,000 live births (2023 est.)
comparison ranking: 70

Infant mortality rate: *total:* 22 deaths/1,000 live births (2024 est.)
male: 24.4 deaths/1,000 live births
female: 19.6 deaths/1,000 live births
comparison ranking: total 69

Life expectancy at birth: *total population:* 70.8 years (2024 est.)
male: 67.3 years
female: 74.5 years
comparison ranking: total population 170

Total fertility rate: 2.75 children born/woman (2024 est.)
comparison ranking: 58

Gross reproduction rate: 1.34 (2024 est.)

Drinking water source: *improved: urban:* 97.8% of population (2022 est.)
rural: 92.2% of population (2022 est.)
total: 94.9% of population (2022 est.)
unimproved: urban: 2.2% of population (2022 est.)
rural: 7.8% of population (2022 est.)
total: 5.1% of population (2022 est.)

Health expenditure: 5.1% of GDP (2022)
9% of national budget (2022 est.)

Physician density: 0.79 physicians/1,000 population (2021)

Hospital bed density: 1 beds/1,000 population (2021 est.)

Sanitation facility access: *improved: urban:* 96.5% of population (2022 est.)
rural: 92.7% of population (2022 est.)
total: 94.5% of population (2022 est.)
unimproved: urban: 3.5% of population (2022 est.)
rural: 7.3% of population (2022 est.)
total: 5.5% of population (2022 est.)

Obesity - adult prevalence rate: 6.4% (2016)
comparison ranking: 167

Alcohol consumption per capita: *total:* 4.85 liters of pure alcohol (2019 est.)
beer: 1.47 liters of pure alcohol (2019 est.)
wine: 0.03 liters of pure alcohol (2019 est.)
spirits: 3.34 liters of pure alcohol (2019 est.)
other alcohols: 0.01 liters of pure alcohol (2019 est.)
comparison ranking: total 84

Tobacco use: *total:* 19.2% (2025 est.)
male: 34.4% (2025 est.)
female: 3.7% (2025 est.)
comparison ranking: total 75

Children under the age of 5 years underweight: 19.1% (2015)
comparison ranking: 15

Currently married women (ages 15-49): 59.3% (2023 est.)

Child marriage: *women married by age 15:* 1.5% (2022)
women married by age 18: 9.4% (2022)

Education expenditure: 3.6% of GDP (2023 est.)
16.7% national budget (2023 est.)
comparison ranking: Education expenditure (% GDP) 126

Literacy: *total population:* 98% (2020 est.)
male: 98% (2020 est.)
female: 97% (2022 est.)

School life expectancy (primary to tertiary education): *total:* 12 years (2021 est.)
male: 12 years (2021 est.)
female: 13 years (2021 est.)

People - note: one of only two predominantly Christian nations in Southeast Asia, the other being Timor-Leste

ENVIRONMENT

Environmental issues: deforestation, especially in watershed areas; illegal mining and logging; soil erosion; air and water pollution in major urban centers; coral reef degradation; increasing pollution of coastal mangrove swamps; coastal erosion; dynamite fishing; wildlife extinction

International environmental agreements: *party to:* Biodiversity, Climate Change, Climate Change-Kyoto Protocol, Climate Change-Paris Agreement, Comprehensive Nuclear Test Ban, Desertification, Endangered Species, Hazardous Wastes, Law of the Sea, Marine Dumping-London Convention, Marine Dumping-London Protocol, Nuclear Test Ban, Ozone Layer Protection, Ship Pollution, Tropical Timber 2006, Wetlands
signed, but not ratified: none of the selected agreements

Climate: tropical marine; northeast monsoon (November to April); southwest monsoon (May to October)

Urbanization: *urban population:* 48.3% of total population (2023)

rate of urbanization: 2.04% annual rate of change (2020-25 est.)

Carbon dioxide emissions: 156.228 million metric tonnes of CO2 (2023 est.)
from coal and metallurgical coke: 88.581 million metric tonnes of CO2 (2023 est.)
from petroleum and other liquids: 61.597 million metric tonnes of CO2 (2023 est.)
from consumed natural gas: 6.05 million metric tonnes of CO2 (2023 est.)
comparison ranking: total emissions 35

Particulate matter emissions: 25.4 micrograms per cubic meter (2019 est.)

Methane emissions: *energy:* 230.7 kt (2022-2024 est.)
agriculture: 1,662.2 kt (2019-2021 est.)
waste: 452.7 kt (2019-2021 est.)
other: 39.1 kt (2019-2021 est.)

Waste and recycling: *municipal solid waste generated annually:* 14.632 million tons (2024 est.)
percent of municipal solid waste recycled: 49.9% (2022 est.)

Total water withdrawal: *municipal:* 9.498 billion cubic meters (2022)
industrial: 13.602 billion cubic meters (2022)
agricultural: 67.937 billion cubic meters (2022)

Total renewable water resources: 479 billion cubic meters (2022 est.)

Geoparks: *total global geoparks and regional networks:* 1
global geoparks and regional networks: Bohol Island (2023)

GOVERNMENT

Country name: *conventional long form:* Republic of the Philippines
conventional short form: Philippines
local long form: Republika ng Pilipinas
local short form: Pilipinas
etymology: named in honor of King PHILLIP II of Spain by Spanish explorer Ruy LOPEZ de VILLALOBOS, who visited the islands in 1543

Government type: presidential republic

Capital: *name:* Manila
geographic coordinates: 14 36 N, 120 58 E
time difference: UTC+8 (13 hours ahead of Washington, DC, during Standard Time)
etymology: derives from the Tagalog word *may*, meaning "there is," and *nila*, the local name for a shrub in the indigo family

Administrative divisions: 81 provinces and 38 chartered cities
provinces: Abra, Agusan del Norte, Agusan del Sur, Aklan, Albay, Antique, Apayao, Aurora, Basilan, Bataan, Batanes, Batangas, Biliran, Benguet, Bohol, Bukidnon, Bulacan, Cagayan, Camarines Norte, Camarines Sur, Camiguin, Capiz, Catanduanes, Cavite, Cebu, Cotabato, Davao del Norte, Davao del Sur, Davao de Oro, Davao Occidental, Davao Oriental, Dinagat Islands, Eastern Samar, Guimaras, Ifugao, Ilocos Norte, Ilocos Sur, Iloilo, Isabela, Kalinga, Laguna, Lanao del Norte, Lanao del Sur, La Union, Leyte, Maguindanao, Marinduque, Masbate, Mindoro Occidental, Mindoro Oriental, Misamis Occidental, Misamis Oriental, Mountain, Negros Occidental, Negros Oriental, Northern Samar, Nueva Ecija, Nueva Vizcaya, Palawan, Pampanga, Pangasinan, Quezon, Quirino, Rizal, Romblon, Samar, Sarangani, Siquijor, Sorsogon, South Cotabato, Southern Leyte, Sultan Kudarat, Sulu, Surigao del Norte, Surigao del Sur, Tarlac, Tawi-Tawi, Zambales, Zamboanga del Norte, Zamboanga del Sur, Zamboanga Sibugay
chartered cities: Angeles, Bacolod, Baguio, Butuan, Cagayan de Oro, Caloocan, Cebu, Cotabato, Dagupan, Davao, General Santos, Iligan, Iloilo, Lapu-Lapu, Las Pinas, Lucena, Makati, Malabon, Mandaluyong, Mandaue, Manila, Marikina, Muntinlupa, Naga, Navotas, Olongapo, Ormoc, Paranaque, Pasay, Pasig, Puerto Princesa, Quezon, San Juan, Santiago, Tacloban, Taguig, Valenzuela, Zamboanga

Legal system: mixed system of civil, common, Islamic (sharia), and customary law

Constitution: *history:* several previous; latest ratified 2 February 1987, effective 11 February 1987
amendment process: proposed by Congress if supported by three fourths of the membership, by a constitutional convention called by Congress, or by public petition; passage by either of the three proposal methods requires a majority vote in a national referendum

International law organization participation: accepts compulsory ICJ jurisdiction with reservations; withdrew from the ICCt in March 2019

Citizenship: *citizenship by birth:* no
citizenship by descent only: at least one parent must be a citizen of the Philippines
dual citizenship recognized: no
residency requirement for naturalization: 10 years

Suffrage: 18 years of age; universal

Executive branch: *chief of state:* President Ferdinand "BongBong" MARCOS, Jr. (since 30 June 2022)
head of government: President Ferdinand "BongBong" MARCOS, Jr. (since 30 June 2022)
cabinet: Cabinet appointed by the president with the consent of the Commission of Appointments, an independent body of 25 Congressional members that includes the Senate president (ex officio chairman) and is appointed by the president
election/appointment process: president and vice president directly elected on separate ballots by simple-majority popular vote for a single 6-year term
most recent election date: 9 May 2022
election results: *2022:* Ferdinand MARCOS, Jr. elected president; percent of vote - Ferdinand MARCOS, Jr. (PFP) 58.7%, Leni ROBREDO (independent) 27.9%, Manny PACQUIAO (PROMDI) 6.8%, other 6.6%; Sara DUTERTE-Carpio elected vice president; percent of vote Sara DUTERTE-Carpio (Lakas-CMD) 61.5%, Francis PANGILINAN (LP) 17.8%, Tito SOTTO 15.8%, other 4.9%
2016: Rodrigo DUTERTE elected president; percent of vote - Rodrigo DUTERTE (PDP-Laban) 39%, Manuel "Mar" ROXAS (LP) 23.5%, Grace POE (independent) 21.4%, Jejomar BINAY (UNA) 12.7%, Miriam Defensor SANTIAGO (PRP) 3.4%; Leni ROBREDO elected vice president; percent of vote Leni ROBREDO (LP) 35.1%, Ferdinand MARCOS, Jr. (independent) 34.5%, Alan CAYETANO 14.4%, Francis ESCUDERO (independent) 12%, other 4%
expected date of next election: 9 May 2028
note: the president is both chief of state and head of government

Legislative branch: *legislature name:* Congress (Kongreso)
legislative structure: bicameral

Legislative branch - lower chamber: *chamber name:* House of Representatives (Kapulungan Ng Mga Kinatawan)
number of seats: 317 (all directly elected)
electoral system: mixed system
scope of elections: full renewal
term in office: 3 years
most recent election date: 5/12/2025
percentage of women in chamber: 28.3%
expected date of next election: May 2028

Legislative branch - upper chamber: *chamber name:* Senate (Senado)
number of seats: 24 (all directly elected)
electoral system: plurality/majority
scope of elections: partial renewal
term in office: 6 years
most recent election date: 5/12/2025
parties elected and seats per party: Nationalist People's Coalition (NPC) (2); Nacionalista Party (NP) (3); Partido Demokratiko Pilipino-Laban (PDP-Laban) (2); Lakas- CMD party (1); Katipunan ng Nagkakaisang Pilipino (KANP) (1); Liberal Party (1); Independents (2)
percentage of women in chamber: 20.8%
expected date of next election: May 2028

Judicial branch: *highest court(s):* Supreme Court (consists of a chief justice and 14 associate justices)
judge selection and term of office: justices are appointed by the president on the recommendation of the Judicial and Bar Council, a constitutionally created, 6-member body that recommends Supreme Court nominees; justices serve until age 70
subordinate courts: Court of Appeals; Sandiganbayan (special court for corruption cases of government officials); Court of Tax Appeals; regional, metropolitan, and municipal trial courts; sharia courts

Political parties: Democratic Action (Aksyon Demokratiko)
Alliance for Change (Hugpong ng Pagbabago or HNP)
Lakas ng EDSA-Christian Muslim Democrats or Lakas-CMD
Liberal Party or LP
Nacionalista Party or NP
Nationalist People's Coalition or NPC
National Unity Party or NUP
Partido Demokratiko Pilipino-Lakas ng Bayan or PDP-Laban
Partido Federal ng Pilipinas or PFP
Progressive Movement for the Devolution of Initiatives or PROMDI

Diplomatic representation in the US: *chief of mission:* Ambassador Jose Manuel del Gallego ROMUALDEZ (since 29 November 2017)
chancery: 1600 Massachusetts Avenue NW, Washington, DC 20036
telephone: [1] (202) 467-9300
FAX: [1] (202) 328-7614
email address and website: info@phembassy-us.org
The Embassy of the Republic of the Philippines in Washington D.C. (philippineembassy-dc.org)
consulate(s) general: Chicago, Honolulu, Houston, Los Angeles, New York, San Francisco, Tamuning (Guam)

Diplomatic representation from the US: *chief of mission:* Ambassador MaryKay Loss CARLSON (since 22 July 2022)
embassy: 1201 Roxas Boulevard, Manila 1000
mailing address: 8600 Manila Place, Washington DC 20521-8600

telephone: [63] (2) 5301-2000
FAX: [63] (2) 5301-2017
email address and website: acsinfomanila@state.gov https://ph.usembassy.gov/

International organization participation: ADB, APEC, ARF, ASEAN, BIS, CD, CICA (observer), CP, EAS, FAO, G-24, G-77, IAEA, IBRD, ICAO, ICRM, IDA, IFAD, IFC, IFRCS, IHO, ILO, IMF, IMO, IMSO, Interpol, IOC, IOM, IPU, ISO, ITSO, ITU, ITUC (NGOs), MIGA, MINUSTAH, NAM, OAS (observer), OPCW, PCA, PIF (partner), UN, UNCTAD, UNESCO, UNHCR, UNIDO, Union Latina, UNMIL, UNMOGIP, UNOCI, UNOOSA, UNWTO, UPU, WCO, WFTU (NGOs), WHO, WIPO, WMO, WTO

Independence: 4 July 1946 (from the US)

National holiday: Independence Day, 12 June (1898)
note: 12 June 1898 was the date of independence from Spain; 4 July 1946 was the date of independence from the US

Flag: *description:* two equal horizontal bands of blue (top) and red; a white equilateral triangle is based on the left side; the center of the triangle has a yellow sun with eight rays, each split into smaller rays; the triangle's corners each have a small five-pointed yellow star
meaning: blue stands for peace and justice, red for courage, and the triangle for equality; the rays represent the first eight provinces that sought independence from Spain, and the stars represent the country's three parts: Luzon, Visayas, and Mindanao
history: the design dates to 1897
note: in wartime, the flag is flown upside-down with the red band at the top

National symbol(s): three stars and sun, Philippine eagle

National color(s): red, white, blue, yellow

National coat of arms: the coat of arms was adopted on 3 July 1946; the three gold stars represent the major island groups of Luzon, the Visayas, and Mindanao; the rays of the sun represent the provinces of the Philippines; the American eagle and lion of Spain represent the nation's colonial past

National anthem(s): *title:* "Lupang Hinirang" (Chosen Land)
lyrics/music: collectively/Julian FELIPE
history: music adopted 1898 and lyrics adopted 1956; only sung in Tagalog

National heritage: *total World Heritage Sites:* 6 (3 cultural, 3 natural)
selected World Heritage Site locales: Baroque Churches of the Philippines (c); Tubbataha Reefs Natural Park (n); Rice Terraces of the Philippine Cordilleras (c); Historic Vigan (c); Puerto-Princesa Subterranean River National Park (n); Mount Hamiguitan Range Wildlife Sanctuary (n)

ECONOMY

Economic overview: growing Southeast Asian economy; commercial rebound led by transportation, construction and financial services; electronics exports recovering from sector slowdown; significant remittances; interest rate rises following heightened inflation; uncertainties due to increased regional tensions with China

Real GDP (purchasing power parity): $1.202 trillion (2024 est.)
$1.137 trillion (2023 est.)
$1.078 trillion (2022 est.)
note: data in 2021 dollars
comparison ranking: 31

Real GDP growth rate: 5.7% (2024 est.)
5.5% (2023 est.)
7.6% (2022 est.)
note: annual GDP % growth based on constant local currency
comparison ranking: 28

Real GDP per capita: $10,400 (2024 est.)
$9,900 (2023 est.)
$9,500 (2022 est.)
note: data in 2021 dollars
comparison ranking: 143

GDP (official exchange rate): $461.618 billion (2024 est.)
note: data in current dollars at official exchange rate

Inflation rate (consumer prices): 3.2% (2024 est.)
6% (2023 est.)
5.8% (2022 est.)
note: annual % change based on consumer prices
comparison ranking: 100

GDP - composition, by sector of origin: *agriculture:* 9.1% (2024 est.)
industry: 27.7% (2024 est.)
services: 63.2% (2024 est.)
note: figures may not total 100% due to non-allocated consumption not captured in sector-reported data
comparison rankings: agriculture 79; industry 69; services 66

GDP - composition, by end use: *household consumption:* 76.1% (2024 est.)
government consumption: 14.5% (2024 est.)
investment in fixed capital: 23.6% (2024 est.)
investment in inventories: 0.1% (2024 est.)
exports of goods and services: 25.8% (2024 est.)
imports of goods and services: -40.1% (2024 est.)
note: figures may not total 100% due to rounding or gaps in data collection

Agricultural products: sugarcane, rice, coconuts, maize, bananas, vegetables, tropical fruits, plantains, pineapples, cassava (2023)
note: top ten agricultural products based on tonnage

Industries: semiconductors and electronics assembly, business process outsourcing, food and beverage manufacturing, construction, electric/gas/water supply, chemical products, radio/television/communications equipment and apparatus, petroleum and fuel, textile and garments, non-metallic minerals, basic metal industries, transport equipment

Industrial production growth rate: 5.6% (2024 est.)
note: annual % change in industrial value added based on constant local currency
comparison ranking: 37

Labor force: 50.979 million (2024 est.)
note: number of people ages 15 or older who are employed or seeking work
comparison ranking: 14

Unemployment rate: 2.2% (2024 est.)
2.3% (2023 est.)
2.6% (2022 est.)
note: % of labor force seeking employment
comparison ranking: 19

Youth unemployment rate (ages 15-24): *total:* 6.6% (2024 est.)
male: 5.6% (2024 est.)
female: 8.3% (2024 est.)
note: % of labor force ages 15-24 seeking employment
comparison ranking: total 152

Population below poverty line: 15.5% (2023 est.)
note: % of population with income below national poverty line

Gini Index coefficient - distribution of family income: 39.3 (2023 est.)
note: index (0-100) of income distribution; higher values represent greater inequality
comparison ranking: 44

Average household expenditures: *on food:* 37.3% of household expenditures (2023 est.)
on alcohol and tobacco: 1.9% of household expenditures (2023 est.)

Household income or consumption by percentage share: *lowest 10%:* 2.9% (2023 est.)
highest 10%: 31.6% (2023 est.)
note: % share of income accruing to lowest and highest 10% of population

Remittances: 8.7% of GDP (2024 est.)
8.9% of GDP (2023 est.)
9.4% of GDP (2022 est.)
note: personal transfers and compensation between resident and non-resident individuals/households/entities

Budget: *revenues:* $65.069 billion (2022 est.)
expenditures: $93.871 billion (2022 est.)
note: central government revenues and expenditures (excluding grants and social security funds) converted to US dollars at average official exchange rate for year indicated

Public debt: 39.9% of GDP (2017 est.)
note: central government debt as a % of GDP
comparison ranking: 132

Taxes and other revenues: 14.1% (of GDP) (2023 est.)
note: central government tax revenue as a % of GDP
comparison ranking: 96

Current account balance: -$17.514 billion (2024 est.)
-$12.387 billion (2023 est.)
-$18.261 billion (2022 est.)
note: balance of payments - net trade and primary/secondary income in current dollars
comparison ranking: 188

Exports: $106.99 billion (2024 est.)
$103.588 billion (2023 est.)
$98.832 billion (2022 est.)
note: balance of payments - exports of goods and services in current dollars
comparison ranking: 48

Exports - partners: China 19%, USA 13%, Hong Kong 12%, Japan 11%, Germany 5% (2023)
note: top five export partners based on percentage share of exports

Exports - commodities: integrated circuits, machine parts, gold, insulated wire, semiconductors (2023)
note: top five export commodities based on value in dollars

Imports: $161.154 billion (2024 est.)
$151.441 billion (2023 est.)
$152.638 billion (2022 est.)
note: balance of payments - imports of goods and services in current dollars
comparison ranking: 36

Imports - partners: China 25%, Indonesia 8%, Japan 8%, S. Korea 6%, USA 6% (2023)
note: top five import partners based on percentage share of imports

Imports - commodities: integrated circuits, refined petroleum, cars, crude petroleum, coal (2023)
note: top five import commodities based on value in dollars

Reserves of foreign exchange and gold: $106.195 billion (2024 est.)
$103.742 billion (2023 est.)
$96.04 billion (2022 est.)
note: holdings of gold (year-end prices)/foreign exchange/special drawing rights in current dollars
comparison ranking: 28

Debt - external: $63.241 billion (2023 est.)
note: present value of external debt in current US dollars
comparison ranking: 14

Exchange rates: Philippine pesos (PHP) per US dollar -

Exchange rates: 57.291 (2024 est.)
55.63 (2023 est.)
54.478 (2022 est.)
49.255 (2021 est.)
49.624 (2020 est.)

ENERGY

Electricity access: *electrification - total population:* 94.8% (2022 est.)
electrification - urban areas: 98%
electrification - rural areas: 91.1%

Electricity: *installed generating capacity:* 29.174 million kW (2023 est.)
consumption: 100.824 billion kWh (2023 est.)
transmission/distribution losses: 10.693 billion kWh (2023 est.)
comparison rankings: installed generating capacity 38; consumption 35; transmission/distribution losses 183

Electricity generation sources: *fossil fuels:* 77.9% of total installed capacity (2023 est.)
solar: 1.6% of total installed capacity (2023 est.)
wind: 0.9% of total installed capacity (2023 est.)
hydroelectricity: 9% of total installed capacity (2023 est.)
geothermal: 9.3% of total installed capacity (2023 est.)
biomass and waste: 1.2% of total installed capacity (2023 est.)

Coal: *production:* 14.457 million metric tons (2023 est.)
consumption: 42.859 million metric tons (2023 est.)
exports: 8.151 million metric tons (2023 est.)
imports: 36.542 million metric tons (2023 est.)
proven reserves: 361 million metric tons (2023 est.)

Petroleum: *total petroleum production:* 10,000 bbl/day (2023 est.)
refined petroleum consumption: 457,000 bbl/day (2023 est.)
crude oil estimated reserves: 138.5 million barrels (2021 est.)

Natural gas: *production:* 2.325 billion cubic meters (2023 est.)
consumption: 3.12 billion cubic meters (2023 est.)
imports: 794.289 million cubic meters (2023 est.)
proven reserves: 98.543 billion cubic meters (2021 est.)

Energy consumption per capita: 17.654 million Btu/person (2023 est.)
comparison ranking: 134

COMMUNICATIONS

Telephones - fixed lines: *total subscriptions:* 4.627 million (2023 est.)
subscriptions per 100 inhabitants: 4 (2023 est.)
comparison ranking: total subscriptions 30

Telephones - mobile cellular: *total subscriptions:* 135 million (2023 est.)
subscriptions per 100 inhabitants: 144 (2022 est.)
comparison ranking: total subscriptions 13

Broadcast media: multiple national private TV and radio networks; multi-channel satellite and cable TV systems available; more than 400 TV stations; about 1,500 cable TV providers with more than 2 million subscribers; over 1,400 radio stations; was scheduled to move to digital by the end of 2023 (2019)

Internet country code: .ph

Internet users: *percent of population:* 84% (2023 est.)

Broadband - fixed subscriptions: *total:* 7.51 million (2023 est.)
subscriptions per 100 inhabitants: 7 (2023 est.)
comparison ranking: total 31

TRANSPORTATION

Civil aircraft registration country code prefix: RP

Airports: 256 (2025)
comparison ranking: 27

Heliports: 416 (2025)
comparison ranking: 9

Railways: *total:* 77 km (2017)
standard gauge: 49 km (2017) 1.435-m gauge
narrow gauge: 28 km (2017) 1.067-m gauge

Merchant marine: *total:* 2,203 (2023)
by type: bulk carrier 52, container ship 43, general cargo 955, oil tanker 207, other 946
comparison ranking: total 11

Ports: *total ports:* 70 (2024)
large: 2
medium: 4
small: 8
very small: 56
ports with oil terminals: 22
key ports: Batangas City, Cagayan de Oro, Cebu, Manila, San Fernando Harbor, Subic Bay

MILITARY AND SECURITY

Military and security forces: Armed Forces of the Philippines (AFP): Army, Navy (includes Marine Corps), Air Force

Department of Transportation: Philippine Coast Guard (PCG); Department of the Interior: Philippine National Police Force (PNP) (2025)
note 1: the PCG is an armed and uniformed service that would be attached to the AFP during a conflict
note 2: the Philippine Government also arms and supports civilian militias; the AFP controls the Civilian Armed Force Geographical Units, while the Civilian Volunteer Organizations fall under PNP command

Military expenditures: 1.7% of GDP (2024 est.)
1.5% of GDP (2023 est.)
1.4% of GDP (2022 est.)
1.2% of GDP (2021 est.)
1.1% of GDP (2020 est.)

Military and security service personnel strengths: approximately 145,000 active Armed Forces (105,000 Army; 25,000 Navy, including about 8,000 Marine Corps; 15,000 Air Force) (2025)

Military equipment inventories and acquisitions: the AFP is equipped with a wide mix of imported weapons systems; in recent years, it has received equipment from more than a dozen countries, including Israel, South Korea, and the US (2024)

Military service age and obligation: some small variations in age based on the branch, but generally 18-27 years of age for voluntary military service for men and women; no conscription (2025)
note: as of 2023, women made up about 8% of the active military; women have attended the Philippine Military Academy and trained as combat soldiers since 1993

Military - note: the Armed Forces of the Philippines (AFP) are responsible for territorial defense and assisting with internal security; much of the AFP's operational focus is on internal security alongside the Philippines National Police, particularly in the south, where several separatist insurgent, terrorist, and criminal groups operate and a considerable portion of the AFP is typically deployed; additional combat operations are conducted against the Communist People's Party/New People's Army, which is active mostly on Luzon, as well as the Visayas and areas of Mindanao; prior to a peace deal in 2014, the AFP fought a decades-long conflict against the Moro Islamic Liberation Front (MILF), a separatist organization based mostly on the island of Mindanao, which had up to 40,000 fighters under arms
maritime security is also a priority; the AFP's naval forces conduct naval interdiction missions in support of security operations on the southern islands, including joint maritime patrols with Indonesia and Malaysia; rising tensions with China over disputed waters and land features in the South China Sea since 2012 have spurred the AFP to place more emphasis on blue-water naval capabilities, including acquiring larger warships such as guided missile frigates, corvettes, offshore patrol vessels, and landing platform dock (LPD) amphibious assault ships
the Philippine military was formally organized during the American colonial period as the Philippine Army; they were established by the National Defense Act of 1935 and comprised of both Filipinos and Americans; the US and Philippines agreed to a mutual defense treaty in 1951; based on agreements signed in 2014 and 2023, the Philippine Government allows the rotational presence of US military forces, aircraft, and ships at up to nine bases in the Philippines; also in 2023, the US agreed to assist in modernizing Philippine defense capabilities, deepen interoperability, enhance bilateral planning and information-sharing, and combat transnational and nonconventional threats (2025)

SPACE

Space agency/agencies: Philippine Space Agency (PhilSA; established 2019) (2025)

Space program overview: has a small but ambitious space program focused on acquiring satellites and related technologies, largely for the areas of climate studies, national security, and risk management; also prioritizing development of the country's space expertise and industry; manufactures and operates satellites (mostly micro- and nano-sized), including remote sensing and scientific/experimental; has relations with a variety of foreign space agencies and industries, including those of China, the European Space Agency and some of its member states, India, Japan, Russia, and the US (2025)
note: further details about the key activities, programs, and milestones of the country's space program, as well as government spending estimates on the space sector, appear in the Space Programs reference guide

TERRORISM

Terrorist group(s): Terrorist group(s): Abu Sayyaf Group; Communist Party of the Philippines/New People's Army (CPP/NPA); Islamic State of Iraq and ash-Sham – East Asia (ISIS-EA) in the Philippines
note 1: ISIS-EA factions include Daulah Islamiya-Lanao (aka Maute Group), Daulah Islamiya-Maguindanao, Daulah Islamiya-Socsargen, ISIS-aligned elements of the Abu Sayyaf Group (ASG), ISIS-aligned elements of the Bangsamoro Islamic Freedom Fighters (BIFF), and rogue elements of the Moro Islamic Liberation Front (MILF)
note 2: details about the history, aims, leadership, organization, areas of operation, tactics, targets, weapons, size, and sources of support of the group(s) appear(s) in Appendix T

TRANSNATIONAL ISSUES

Refugees and internally displaced persons: *refugees:* 2,342 (2024 est.)

IDPs: 1,158,643 (2024 est.)
stateless persons: 30 (2024 est.)

PITCAIRN ISLANDS

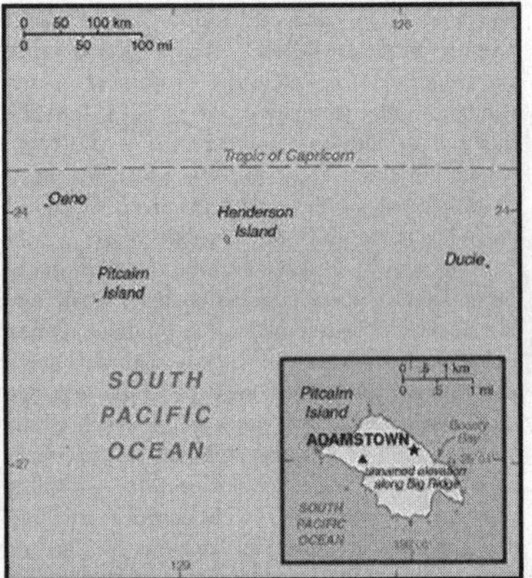

INTRODUCTION

Background: Polynesians were the first settlers on the four tiny islands that are now called the Pitcairn Islands, but all four were uninhabited by the time Europeans discovered them in 1606. Pitcairn Island – the only one now inhabited – was rediscovered by a British explorer in 1767. In 1789, Fletcher CHRISTIAN led a mutiny on the HMS Bounty, and after several months of searching for Pitcairn Island, he landed on it with eight other mutineers and their Tahitian companions. They lived in isolation and evaded detection by English authorities until 1808, when only one man, 10 women, and 23 children remained. In 1831, with the population of 87 proving too big for the island, the British attempted to move all the islanders to Tahiti, but they were soon returned to Pitcairn Island. The island became an official British colony in 1838, and in 1856, the British again determined that the population of 193 was too high and relocated all the residents to Norfolk Island. Several families returned in 1858 and 1864, bringing the island's population to 43, and almost all of the island's current population are descendants of these returnees.

The UK annexed the nearby uninhabited islands of Henderson, Oeno, and Ducie in 1902 and incorporated them into the Pitcairn Islands colony in 1938. The population peaked at 233 in 1937 as outmigration, primarily to New Zealand, has since thinned the population. Only two children were born between 1986 and 2012, and in 2005, a couple became the first outsiders to obtain citizenship in more than a century. Since 2013, the Pitcairn Islands has tried to attract new migrants but has had no applicants because it requires prospective migrants to front significant sums of money and prohibits employment during a two-year trial period, at which point the local council can deny long-term resident status.

GEOGRAPHY

Location: Oceania, islands in the South Pacific Ocean, about midway between Peru and New Zealand

Geographic coordinates: 25 04 S, 130 06 W

Map references: Oceania

Area: *total:* 47 sq km
land: 47 sq km
water: 0 sq km
comparison ranking: total 232

Area - comparative: about three-tenths the size of Washington, D.C.

Land boundaries: *total:* 0 km

Coastline: 51 km

Maritime claims: *territorial sea:* 12 nm
exclusive economic zone: 200 nm

Climate: tropical; hot and humid; modified by southeast trade winds; rainy season (November to March)

Terrain: rugged volcanic formation; rocky coastline with cliffs

Elevation: *highest point:* Palwala Valley Point on Big Ridge 347 m
lowest point: Pacific Ocean 0 m

Natural resources: miro trees (used for handicrafts), fish
note: manganese, iron, copper, gold, silver, and zinc have been discovered offshore

Land use: *agricultural land:* 0% (2022 est.)
forest: 74.5% (2022 est.)
other: 25.5% (2022 est.)

Irrigated land: 0 sq km (2022)

Population distribution: a handful of inhabitants, most residing near the village of Adamstown

Natural hazards: occasional tropical cyclones (especially November to March), but generally only heavy tropical storms; landslides

Geography - note: Britain's most isolated dependency; only the larger island of Pitcairn is inhabited, but it has no port or natural harbor; supplies must be transported by longboat from larger ships stationed offshore

PEOPLE AND SOCIETY

Population: *total:* 50 (2025 est.)
comparison ranking: total 237

Nationality: *noun:* Pitcairn Islander(s)
adjective: Pitcairn Islander

Ethnic groups: descendants of the Bounty mutineers and their Tahitian wives

Languages: English (official), Pitkern (mixture of an 18th century English dialect and a Tahitian dialect)

Religions: Seventh Day Adventist 100%

Population growth rate: 0% (2014 est.)
comparison ranking: 195

Population distribution: a handful of inhabitants, most residing near the village of Adamstown

ENVIRONMENT

Environmental issues: deforestation (only a small portion of the original forest remains because of burning and clearing for settlement)

Climate: tropical; hot and humid; modified by southeast trade winds; rainy season (November to March)

GOVERNMENT

Country name: *conventional long form:* Pitcairn, Henderson, Ducie, and Oeno Islands
conventional short form: Pitcairn Islands
etymology: named after English midshipman Robert PITCAIRN, who first sighted the island in 1767

Government type: parliamentary democracy

Dependency status: overseas territory of the UK

Capital: *name:* Adamstown
geographic coordinates: 25 04 S, 130 05 W
time difference: UTC-9 (4 hours behind Washington, DC, during Standard Time)
etymology: named after John ADAMS (1767–1829), the last survivor of the Bounty mutineers who settled on Pitcairn Island in 1790

Administrative divisions: none (overseas territory of the UK)

Legal system: local island by-laws

Constitution: *history:* several previous; latest drafted 10 February 2010, presented 17 February 2010, effective 4 March 2010

Citizenship: see United Kingdom

Suffrage: 18 years of age; universal with three years of residency

Executive branch: *chief of state:* King CHARLES III (since 8 September 2022); represented by UK High Commissioner to New Zealand and Governor (nonresident) of the Pitcairn Islands Iona THOMAS (since 9 August 2022)
head of government: Mayor and Chairman of the Island Council Shawn CHRISTIAN (since 5 November 2025)

cabinet: none
election/appointment process: the monarchy is hereditary; governor and commissioner appointed by the monarch; island mayor directly elected by majority popular vote for a 3-year term
most recent election date: 5 November 2025
election results: Shawn CHRISTIAN elected mayor and chairman of the Island Council
expected date of next election: November 2028

Legislative branch: *legislature name:* Island Council
legislative structure: unicameral
number of seats: 10 (directly elected and appointed)
electoral system: plurality/majority
scope of elections: full renewal
term in office: 2 years *note:* the councilors and the deputy mayor serve 2-year terms, the mayor serves a 3-year term, and the administrator is appointed by the governor for an indefinite term
most recent election date: 6 November 2019
parties elected and seats per party: independent (5)
percentage of women in chamber: 60%
expected date of next election: N/A
note: the Council includes 5 councilors, the mayor, and the deputy mayor (who are elected by popular vote) and 3 ex officio non-voting members – the administrator, who serves as both the head of government and the representative of the governor of Pitcairn Islands, the governor, and the deputy governor

Judicial branch: *highest court(s):* Pitcairn Court of Appeal (consists of the court president, 2 judges, and the Supreme Court chief justice, an ex-officio member); Pitcairn Supreme Court (consists of the chief justice and 2 judges)
judge selection and term of office: all judges of both courts appointed by the governor of the Pitcairn Islands on the instructions of the British monarch through the Secretary of State; all judges can serve until retirement, normally at age 75
subordinate courts: Magistrate's Court
note: appeals beyond the Pitcairn Court of Appeal are referred to the Judicial Committee of the Privy Council (in London)

Political parties: none

Diplomatic representation in the US: none (overseas territory of the UK)

Diplomatic representation from the US: *embassy:* none (overseas territory of the UK)

International organization participation: SPC, UPU

Independence: none (overseas territory of the UK)

National holiday: Official birthday of King Charles III, usually celebrated the second Saturday in June (1948); Discovery Day (Pitcairn Day), 2 July (1767)

Flag: *description:* blue with the UK flag in the upper-left quadrant and the Pitcairn Islander coat of arms centered on the right half of the flag; the green field features a yellow anchor with a Bible over it (both were on the *HMS Bounty*); a Pitcairn Island wheelbarrow is on the crest, with a flowering twig of miro (a local plant)
meaning: the green, yellow, and blue of the shield represents the island rising from the ocean

National anthem(s): *title:* "We From Pitcairn Island"
lyrics/music: unknown/Frederick M. LEHMAN
history: serves as a local anthem
title: "God Save the King"
lyrics/music: unknown
history: official anthem, as a UK overseas territory

ECONOMY

Economic overview: small South Pacific British island territorial economy; exports primarily postage stamps, handicraft goods, honey, and tinctures; extremely limited infrastructure; dependent upon UK and EU aid; recent border reopening post-COVID-19

Agricultural products: honey; wide variety of fruits and vegetables; goats, chickens; fish

Industries: postage stamps, handicrafts, beekeeping, honey

Exports - partners: UK 21%, Canada 19%, Tanzania 12%, Colombia 11%, Spain 8% (2023)
note: top five export partners based on percentage share of exports

Exports - commodities: fertilizers, sulfur, refined petroleum, excavation machinery, ethylene polymers (2022)
note: top five export commodities based on value in dollars

Imports - partners: USA 59%, NZ 37%, Italy 2%, UAE 1%, Brazil 1% (2023)
note: top five import partners based on percentage share of imports

Imports - commodities: construction vehicles, refined petroleum, beef, computers, other foods (2023)
note: top five import commodities based on value in dollars

Exchange rates: New Zealand dollars (NZD) per US dollar -

Exchange rates: 1.652 (2024 est.)
1.628 (2023 est.)
1.577 (2022 est.)
1.414 (2021 est.)
1.542 (2020 est.)

COMMUNICATIONS

Broadcast media: satellite TV from Fiji-based Sky Pacific offering a wide range of international channels

Internet country code: .pn

Internet users: *percent of population:* 96.2% (2021 est.)

MILITARY AND SECURITY

Military - note: defense is the responsibility of the UK

POLAND

INTRODUCTION

Background: Poland's history as a state began near the middle of the 10th century. By the mid-16th century, the Polish-Lithuanian Commonwealth ruled a vast tract of land in Central and Eastern Europe. During the 18th century, internal disorder weakened the nation, and in a series of agreements between 1772 and 1795, Russia, Prussia, and Austria partitioned Poland among themselves. Poland regained its independence in 1918 only to be overrun by Germany and the Soviet Union in World War II. It became a Soviet satellite state following the war. Labor turmoil in 1980 led to the formation of the independent trade union Solidarity that over time became a political force with over 10 million members. Free elections in 1989 and 1990 won Solidarity control of the parliament and the presidency, bringing the communist era to a close. A "shock therapy" program during the early 1990s enabled the country to transform its economy into one of the most robust in Central Europe. Poland joined NATO in 1999 and the EU in 2004.

GEOGRAPHY

Location: Central Europe, east of Germany

Geographic coordinates: 52 00 N, 20 00 E

Map references: Europe

Area: *total:* 312,685 sq km
land: 304,255 sq km
water: 8,430 sq km
comparison ranking: total 71

Area - comparative: about twice the size of Georgia; slightly smaller than New Mexico

Land boundaries: *total:* 2,865 km
border countries (6): Belarus 375 km; Czechia 699 km; Germany 467 km; Lithuania 100 km, Russia (Kaliningrad Oblast) 209 km; Slovakia 517 km; Ukraine 498 km

Coastline: 440 km

Maritime claims: *territorial sea:* 12 nm
exclusive economic zone: defined by international treaties

Climate: temperate with cold, cloudy, moderately severe winters with frequent precipitation; mild summers with frequent showers and thundershowers

Terrain: mostly flat plain; mountains along southern border

Elevation: *highest point:* Rysy 2,499 m
lowest point: near Raczki Elblaskie -2 m
mean elevation: 173 m

Natural resources: coal, sulfur, copper, natural gas, silver, lead, salt, amber, arable land

Land use: *agricultural land:* 46.3% (2022 est.)
arable land: 36.5% (2022 est.)
permanent crops: 1.2% (2022 est.)
permanent pasture: 8.6% (2022 est.)
forest: 31.1% (2022 est.)
other: 22.6% (2022 est.)

Irrigated land: 1,327 sq km (2016)

Major lakes (area sq km): *salt water lake(s):* Zalew Szczecinski/Stettiner Haff (shared with Germany) - 900 sq km

Major rivers (by length in km): Wisla (Vistula) river source and mouth (shared with Belarus and Ukraine) - 1,213 km
note: longest river in Poland

Major watersheds (area sq km): Atlantic Ocean drainage: *(Black Sea)* Danube (795,656 sq km)

Population distribution: population concentrated in the southern area around Krakow and the central area around Warsaw and Lodz, with an extension to the northern coastal city of Gdansk

Natural hazards: flooding

Geography - note: historically an area of conflict because of flat terrain and the lack of natural barriers on the North European Plain

PEOPLE AND SOCIETY

Population: *total:* 38,746,310 (2024 est.)
male: 18,441,415
female: 20,304,895
comparison rankings: total 38; male 40; female 36

Nationality: *noun:* Pole(s)
adjective: Polish

Ethnic groups: Polish 96.9%, Silesian 1.1%, German 0.2%, Ukrainian 0.1%, other and unspecified 1.7% (2011 est.)
note: represents ethnicity declared first

Languages: Polish (official) 98.2%, Silesian 1.4%, other 1.1%, unspecified 1.2% (2011 est.)
major-language sample(s):
Księga Faktów Świata, niezbędne źródło podstawowych informacji. (Polish)
note 1: shares of languages sum to more than 100% because some respondents gave more than one answer on the census; data represent language spoken at home
note 2: Poland also recognizes Kashub as a regional language; Czech, Hebrew, Yiddish, Belarusian, Lithuanian, German, Armenian, Russian, Slovak, and Ukrainian as national minority languages; and Karaim, Lemko, Romani (Polska Roma and Bergitka Roma), and Tatar as ethnic minority languages

Religions: Roman Catholic 70.7%, refused to answer 20.9%, no religion 6.9%; less than 1 percent: Orthodox, Jehovah Witness, Evangelic of Augsburg, Greek Catholic, Pentecostal, other Protestant, not stated, old Catholic Mariavite Church, other Christians, Islam, Buddhist, Polish Catholic Church, other, Baptist Union of Poland, Pagan, Seventh Day Adventist, Hindu, other Catholic (2021 est.)

Age structure: *0-14 years:* 14.2% (male 2,830,048/ female 2,676,300)
15-64 years: 65.9% (male 12,513,402/female 13,036,977)
65 years and over: 19.8% (2024 est.) (male 3,097,965/ female 4,591,618)

Dependency ratios: *total dependency ratio:* 51.6 (2024 est.)
youth dependency ratio: 21.6 (2024 est.)
elderly dependency ratio: 30.1 (2024 est.)
potential support ratio: 3.3 (2024 est.)

Median age: *total:* 42.9 years (2024 est.)
male: 41.5 years
female: 44.3 years
comparison ranking: total 38

Population growth rate: -1% (2024 est.)
comparison ranking: 230

Birth rate: 8.4 births/1,000 population (2024 est.)
comparison ranking: 207

Death rate: 12.2 deaths/1,000 population (2024 est.)
comparison ranking: 14

Net migration rate: -6.2 migrant(s)/1,000 population (2024 est.)
comparison ranking: 210

Population distribution: population concentrated in the southern area around Krakow and the central area around Warsaw and Lodz, with an extension to the northern coastal city of Gdansk

Urbanization: *urban population:* 60.2% of total population (2023)
rate of urbanization: -0.16% annual rate of change (2020-25 est.)

Major urban areas - population: 1.798 million WARSAW (capital), 769,000 Krakow (2023)

Sex ratio: *at birth:* 1.06 male(s)/female
0-14 years: 1.06 male(s)/female
15-64 years: 0.96 male(s)/female
65 years and over: 0.67 male(s)/female
total population: 0.91 male(s)/female (2024 est.)

Mother's mean age at first birth: 27.9 years (2020 est.)

Maternal mortality ratio: 2 deaths/100,000 live births (2023 est.)
comparison ranking: 193

Infant mortality rate: *total:* 4.9 deaths/1,000 live births (2024 est.)
male: 5.3 deaths/1,000 live births
female: 4.4 deaths/1,000 live births
comparison ranking: total 177

Life expectancy at birth: *total population:* 76.7 years (2024 est.)
male: 72.8 years
female: 80.9 years
comparison ranking: total population 101

Total fertility rate: 1.32 children born/woman (2024 est.)
comparison ranking: 217

Gross reproduction rate: 0.64 (2024 est.)

Drinking water source: *improved: urban:* 95.8% of population (2022 est.)
rural: 82.2% of population (2022 est.)
total: 90.4% of population (2022 est.)
unimproved: urban: 4.2% of population (2022 est.)
rural: 17.8% of population (2022 est.)
total: 9.6% of population (2022 est.)

Health expenditure: 6.7% of GDP (2022)
10.7% of national budget (2022 est.)

Physician density: 4.03 physicians/1,000 population (2023)

Hospital bed density: 6.1 beds/1,000 population (2020 est.)

Sanitation facility access: *improved: urban:* 100% of population (2022 est.)
rural: 100% of population (2022 est.)
total: 100% of population (2022 est.)
unimproved: urban: 0% of population (2022 est.)
rural: 0% of population (2022 est.)
total: 0% of population (2022 est.)

Obesity - adult prevalence rate: 23.1% (2016)
comparison ranking: 68

Alcohol consumption per capita: *total:* 10.96 liters of pure alcohol (2019 est.)
beer: 5.72 liters of pure alcohol (2019 est.)
wine: 0.88 liters of pure alcohol (2019 est.)
spirits: 4.36 liters of pure alcohol (2019 est.)
other alcohols: 0 liters of pure alcohol (2019 est.)
comparison ranking: total 13

Tobacco use: *total:* 21.6% (2025 est.)
male: 25.6% (2025 est.)
female: 17.8% (2025 est.)
comparison ranking: total 56

Currently married women (ages 15-49): 56.6% (2023 est.)

Education expenditure: 4.6% of GDP (2022 est.)
10.5% national budget (2022 est.)
comparison ranking: Education expenditure (% GDP) 80

School life expectancy (primary to tertiary education): *total:* 17 years (2023 est.)
male: 16 years (2023 est.)
female: 18 years (2023 est.)

ENVIRONMENT

Environmental issues: air pollution (despite environmental policy improvements) because of coal-burning in homes and power plants; acid rain leading to forest damage; water pollution from industrial and municipal sources; disposal of hazardous wastes

International environmental agreements: *party to:* Air Pollution, Air Pollution-Nitrogen Oxides, Air Pollution-Sulphur 94, Antarctic-Environmental Protection, Antarctic- Marine Living Resources, Antarctic Seals, Antarctic Treaty, Biodiversity, Climate Change, Climate Change-Kyoto Protocol, Climate Change-Paris Agreement, Comprehensive Nuclear Test Ban, Desertification, Endangered Species, Environmental Modification, Hazardous Wastes, Law of the Sea, Marine Dumping-London Convention, Nuclear Test Ban, Ozone Layer Protection, Ship Pollution, Tropical Timber 2006, Wetlands, Whaling
signed, but not ratified: Air Pollution-Heavy Metals, Air Pollution-Multi-effect Protocol, Air Pollution-Persistent Organic Pollutants

Climate: temperate with cold, cloudy, moderately severe winters with frequent precipitation; mild summers with frequent showers and thundershowers

Urbanization: *urban population:* 60.2% of total population (2023)
rate of urbanization: -0.16% annual rate of change (2020-25 est.)

Carbon dioxide emissions: 264.031 million metric tonnes of CO2 (2023 est.)
from coal and metallurgical coke: 132.101 million metric tonnes of CO2 (2023 est.)
from petroleum and other liquids: 95.095 million metric tonnes of CO2 (2023 est.)
from consumed natural gas: 36.835 million metric tonnes of CO2 (2023 est.)
comparison ranking: total emissions 25

Particulate matter emissions: 18.8 micrograms per cubic meter (2019 est.)

Methane emissions: *energy:* 954.2 kt (2022-2024 est.)
agriculture: 595.9 kt (2019-2021 est.)
waste: 292 kt (2019-2021 est.)
other: 36.3 kt (2019-2021 est.)

Waste and recycling: *municipal solid waste generated annually:* 12.758 million tons (2024 est.)
percent of municipal solid waste recycled: 38.3% (2022 est.)

Total water withdrawal: *municipal:* 2.113 billion cubic meters (2022)
industrial: 6.44 billion cubic meters (2022)
agricultural: 1.28 billion cubic meters (2022 est.)

Total renewable water resources: 60.5 billion cubic meters (2022 est.)

Geoparks: *total global geoparks and regional networks:* 3 (2024)
global geoparks and regional networks: Land of Extinct Volcanoes; Muskauer Faltenboge / Łuk Mużakowa (includes Germany); Holy Cross Mountains (2024)

GOVERNMENT

Country name: *conventional long form:* Republic of Poland
conventional short form: Poland
local long form: Rzeczpospolita Polska
local short form: Polska
former: Polish People's Republic
etymology: the name probably comes from the Slavic word *pole* (field or plain), indicating the flat nature of the country

Government type: parliamentary republic

Capital: *name:* Warsaw
geographic coordinates: 52 15 N, 21 00 E
time difference: UTC+1 (6 hours ahead of Washington, DC, during Standard Time)
daylight saving time: +1hr, begins last Sunday in March; ends last Sunday in October
etymology: the origin of the name is unknown; Warszawa was the name of a fishing village, and several legends link the city's founding to a man named Wars or Warsz

Administrative divisions: 16 provinces or voivodships (*wojewodztwa*, singular - *wojewodztwo*); Dolnoslaskie (Lower Silesia), Kujawsko-Pomorskie (Kuyavia-Pomerania), Lodzkie (Lodz), Lubelskie (Lublin), Lubuskie (Lubusz), Malopolskie (Lesser Poland), Mazowieckie (Masovia), Opolskie (Opole), Podkarpackie (Subcarpathia), Podlaskie, Pomorskie (Pomerania), Slaskie (Silesia), Swietokrzyskie (Holy Cross), Warminsko-Mazurskie (Warmia-Masuria), Wielkopolskie (Greater Poland), Zachodniopomorskie (West Pomerania)

Legal system: civil law system; judicial review of legislative, administrative, and other governmental acts; constitutional law rulings of the Constitutional Tribunal are final

Constitution: *history:* several previous; latest adopted 2 April 1997, approved by referendum 25 May 1997, effective 17 October 1997
amendment process: proposed by at least one fifth of Sejm deputies, by the Senate, or by the president of the republic; passage requires at least two-thirds majority vote in the Sejm and absolute majority vote in the Senate; amendments to articles relating to sovereignty, personal freedoms, and constitutional amendment procedures also require passage by majority vote in a referendum

International law organization participation: accepts compulsory ICJ jurisdiction with reservations; accepts ICCt jurisdiction

Citizenship: *citizenship by birth:* no
citizenship by descent only: both parents must be citizens of Poland
dual citizenship recognized: no
residency requirement for naturalization: 5 years

Suffrage: 18 years of age; universal

Executive branch: *chief of state:* President Karol NAWROCKI (since 6 August 2025)
head of government: Prime Minister Donald TUSK (since 11 December 2023)
cabinet: Council of Ministers proposed by the prime minister, appointed by the president, and approved by the Sejm
election/appointment process: president directly elected by absolute-majority popular vote in 2 rounds, if needed, for a 5-year term (eligible for a second term); prime minister, deputy prime ministers, and Council of Ministers appointed by the president and confirmed by the Sejm; all presidential candidates resign their party affiliation
most recent election date: 18 May 2025, with the second round on 1 June 2025
election results: *2025:* Karol NAWROCKI elected president in second round; percent of vote - Karol NAWROCKI (PiS) 50.9%, Rafal TRZASKOWSKI (KO) 49.1%; NAWROCKI takes office 6 August 2025
2025: First round Rafal TRZASKOWSKI (KO) 31.4%, Karol NAWROCKI 29.5% (PiS), Slawomir MENTZEN 14.8%, Grzegorz BRAUN 6.3%, and Szymon HOLOWNIA 5.0%; second round to be held on 1 June 2025;
2020: Andrzej DUDA reelected president in second round; percent of vote - Andrzej DUDA (independent) 51%, Rafal TRZASKOWSKI (KO) 49%
2015: Andrzej DUDA elected president in second round; percent of vote - Andrzej DUDA (independent) 51.5%, Bronislaw KOMOROWSKI (independent) 48.5%
expected date of next election: July 2030

Legislative branch: *legislative structure:* bicameral
note: the designation "National Assembly" (or Zgromadzenie Narodowe) is only used on those rare occasions when the two houses meet jointly

Legislative branch - lower chamber: *chamber name:* Sejm
number of seats: 460 (all directly elected)
electoral system: proportional representation
scope of elections: full renewal
term in office: 4 years
most recent election date: 10/15/2023
parties elected and seats per party: Law and Justice (PiS) (194); Civic Coalition (KO) (157); The Third Way (65); The New Left (Nowa Lewica) (26); Other (18)
percentage of women in chamber: 31.3%
expected date of next election: October 2027

Legislative branch - upper chamber: *chamber name:* Senate (Senat)
number of seats: 100 (all directly elected)
electoral system: plurality/majority
scope of elections: full renewal
term in office: 4 years
most recent election date: 10/15/2023
parties elected and seats per party: Civic Coalition (KO) (41); Law and Justice (PiS) (34); The Third Way (11); The New Left (Nowa Lewica) (9); Independents (5)
percentage of women in chamber: 19%
expected date of next election: October 2027

Judicial branch: *highest court(s):* Supreme Court or Sad Najwyzszy (consists of the first president of the Supreme Court and 120 justices organized in criminal, civil, labor and social insurance, and extraordinary appeals and public affairs and disciplinary chambers); Constitutional Tribunal (consists of 15 judges, including the court president and vice president)
judge selection and term of office: president of the Supreme Court nominated by the General Assembly of the Supreme Court and selected by the president of Poland; other judges nominated by the 25-member National Judicial Council and appointed by the president of Poland; judges serve until retirement, usually at age 65, but tenure can be extended; Constitutional Tribunal judges chosen by the Sejm for single 9-year terms
subordinate courts: administrative courts; military courts; local, regional and appellate courts subdivided into military, civil, criminal, labor, and family courts

Political parties: AGROunion or AU
Center for Poland or CdP
Civic Platform or PO
Confederation of the Polish Crown or KKP
Kukiz' 15 or K'15
Labor Union or UP
Law and Justice or PiS
Left Together or LR
Modern or.N
National Movement or NN
New Hope or RN
New Left or NL
Poland 2050 or PL2050
Polish Initiative or iPL
Polish People's Party or PSL
Polish Socialist Party or PPS
Renewal of the Republic of Poland or ON RP
Sovereign Poland or SP
The Greens or Zieloni
Union of European Democrats or UED
Yes! For Poland or T!DPL

Diplomatic representation in the US: *chief of mission:* Ambassador (vacant); Chargé d'Affaires Bogdan Adam KLICH (since 21 November 2024)
chancery: 2640 16th Street NW, Washington, DC 20009
telephone: [1] (202) 499-1700
FAX: [1] (202) 328-2152
email address and website: washington.amb.sekretariat@msz.gov.pl
https://www.gov.pl/web/usa-en/embassy-washington
consulate(s) general: Chicago, Houston, Los Angeles, New York

Diplomatic representation from the US: *chief of mission:* Ambassador (vacant); Chargé d'Affaires Stephanie HOLMES (since August 2025)
embassy: Aleje Ujazdowskie 29/31, 00-540 Warsaw
mailing address: 5010 Warsaw Place, Washington, DC 20521-5010
telephone: [48] (22) 504-2000
FAX: [48] (22) 504-2088
email address and website: acswarsaw@state.gov
https://pl.usembassy.gov/
consulate(s) general: Krakow

International organization participation: Arctic Council (observer), Australia Group, BIS, BSEC (observer), CBSS, CD, CE, CEI, CERN, EAPC, EBRD, ECB, EIB, ESA, EU, FAO, IAEA, IBRD, ICAO, ICC (national committees), ICCt, ICRM, IDA, IEA, IFC, IFRCS, IHO, ILO, IMF, IMO,

IMSO, Interpol, IOC, IOM, IPU, ISO, ITSO, ITU, ITUC (NGOs), MIGA, MONUSCO, NATO, NEA, NSG, OAS (observer), OECD, OIF (observer), OPCW, OSCE, PCA, Schengen Convention, UN, UNCTAD, UNESCO, UNHCR, UNHRC, UNIDO, UNMIL, UNMISS, UNOCI, UN Security Council (temporary), UNWTO, UPU, Wassenaar Arrangement, WCO, WFTU (NGOs), WHO, WIPO, WMO, WTO, ZC

Independence: *11 November 1918 (republic proclaimed)*; *notable earlier dates:* 14 April 966 (adoption of Christianity, traditional founding date), 1 July 1569 (Polish-Lithuanian Commonwealth created)

National holiday: Constitution Day, 3 May (1791)

Flag: *description:* two equal horizontal bands of white (top) and red
meaning: colors derive from the Polish emblem, a white eagle on a red field
note: similar to the flags of Indonesia and Monaco, which are red (top) and white

National symbol(s): white crowned eagle

National color(s): white, red

National anthem(s): *title:* "Mazurek Dabrowskiego" (Dabrowski's Mazurka)
lyrics/music: Jozef WYBICKI/traditional
history: adopted 1927;

National heritage: *total World Heritage Sites:* 17 (15 cultural, 2 natural)
selected World Heritage Site locales: Historic Krakow (c); Historic Warsaw (c); Medieval Torun (c); Wooden Tserkvas of the Carpathian Region (c); Castle of the Teutonic Order in Malbork (c); Wieliczka and Bochnia Royal Salt Mines (c); Auschwitz Birkenau Concentration Camp (c); Ancient and Primeval Beech Forests of the Carpathians (n); Białowieza Forest (n); Old City of Zamość (c)

ECONOMY

Economic overview: high-income, diversified, EU-member economy; significant growth in GDP, trade, and investment since joining EU in 2004; private consumption and EU-funded public investments driving GDP growth; increased social spending, flooding recovery costs, and defense spending have added to public debt

Real GDP (purchasing power parity): $1.649 trillion (2024 est.)
$1.602 trillion (2023 est.)
$1.598 trillion (2022 est.)
note: data in 2021 dollars
comparison ranking: 20

Real GDP growth rate: 2.9% (2024 est.)
0.2% (2023 est.)
5.3% (2022 est.)
note: annual GDP % growth based on constant local currency
comparison ranking: 121

Real GDP per capita: $45,100 (2024 est.)
$43,700 (2023 est.)
$43,400 (2022 est.)
note: data in 2021 dollars
comparison ranking: 50

GDP (official exchange rate): $914.696 billion (2024 est.)
note: data in current dollars at official exchange rate

Inflation rate (consumer prices): 3.8% (2024 est.)
11.5% (2023 est.)
14.4% (2022 est.)
note: annual % change based on consumer prices
comparison ranking: 121

GDP - composition, by sector of origin: *agriculture:* 2.6% (2024 est.)
industry: 26.4% (2024 est.)
services: 59.9% (2024 est.)
note: figures may not total 100% due to non-allocated consumption not captured in sector-reported data
comparison rankings: agriculture 137; industry 74; services 88

GDP - composition, by end use: *household consumption:* 57.6% (2024 est.)
government consumption: 20.8% (2024 est.)
investment in fixed capital: 16.9% (2024 est.)
investment in inventories: 0.8% (2024 est.)
exports of goods and services: 52.3% (2024 est.)
imports of goods and services: -48.3% (2024 est.)
note: figures may not total 100% due to rounding or gaps in data collection

Agricultural products: sugar beets, milk, wheat, maize, potatoes, triticale, apples, rapeseed, barley, rye (2023)
note: top ten agricultural products based on tonnage

Industries: machine building, iron and steel, coal mining, chemicals, shipbuilding, food processing, glass, beverages, textiles

Industrial production growth rate: -0.6% (2023 est.)
note: annual % change in industrial value added based on constant local currency
comparison ranking: 144

Labor force: 18.245 million (2024 est.)
note: number of people ages 15 or older who are employed or seeking work
comparison ranking: 37

Unemployment rate: 2.5% (2024 est.)
2.8% (2023 est.)
2.9% (2022 est.)
note: % of labor force seeking employment
comparison ranking: 22

Youth unemployment rate (ages 15-24): *total:* 9.9% (2024 est.)
male: 10.1% (2024 est.)
female: 9.6% (2024 est.)
note: % of labor force ages 15-24 seeking employment
comparison ranking: total 120

Population below poverty line: 12.2% (2023 est.)
note: % of population with income below national poverty line

Gini Index coefficient - distribution of family income: 28.9 (2022 est.)
note: index (0-100) of income distribution; higher values represent greater inequality
comparison ranking: 129

Average household expenditures: *on food:* 18.6% of household expenditures (2023 est.)
on alcohol and tobacco: 6.2% of household expenditures (2023 est.)

Household income or consumption by percentage share: *lowest 10%:* 3.3% (2022 est.)
highest 10%: 23.1% (2022 est.)
note: % share of income accruing to lowest and highest 10% of population

Remittances: 0.9% of GDP (2024 est.)
1.1% of GDP (2023 est.)
1.1% of GDP (2022 est.)
note: personal transfers and compensation between resident and non-resident individuals/households/entities

Budget: *revenues:* $291.603 billion (2023 est.)
expenditures: $328.497 billion (2023 est.)
note: central government revenues (excluding grants) and expenditures converted to US dollars at average official exchange rate for year indicated

Public debt: 50.6% of GDP (2017 est.)
note: data cover general government debt and include debt instruments issued (or owned) by government entities other than the treasury; the data include treasury debt held by foreign entities, the data include subnational entities, as well as intragovernmental debt; intragovernmental debt consists of treasury borrowings from surpluses in the social funds, such as for retirement, medical care, and unemployment; debt instruments for the social funds are not sold at public auctions
comparison ranking: 101

Taxes and other revenues: 18% (of GDP) (2023 est.)
note: central government tax revenue as a % of GDP
comparison ranking: 65

Current account balance: $1.789 billion (2024 est.)
$14.535 billion (2023 est.)
-$15.822 billion (2022 est.)
note: balance of payments - net trade and primary/secondary income in current dollars
comparison ranking: 50

Exports: $478.579 billion (2024 est.)
$471.571 billion (2023 est.)
$436.388 billion (2022 est.)
note: balance of payments - exports of goods and services in current dollars
comparison ranking: 20

Exports - partners: Germany 25%, UK 6%, Czechia 6%, France 6%, Italy 5% (2023)
note: top five export partners based on percentage share of exports

Exports - commodities: vehicle parts/accessories, electric batteries, plastic products, cars, seats (2023)
note: top five export commodities based on value in dollars

Imports: $441.945 billion (2024 est.)
$423.797 billion (2023 est.)
$421.765 billion (2022 est.)
note: balance of payments - imports of goods and services in current dollars
comparison ranking: 20

Imports - partners: Germany 22%, China 12%, Italy 5%, Netherlands 4%, USA 4% (2023)
note: top five import partners based on percentage share of imports

Imports - commodities: crude petroleum, cars, garments, vehicle parts/accessories, plastic products (2023)
note: top five import commodities based on value in dollars

Reserves of foreign exchange and gold: $223.115 billion (2024 est.)
$193.783 billion (2023 est.)
$166.664 billion (2022 est.)
note: holdings of gold (year-end prices)/foreign exchange/special drawing rights in current dollars
comparison ranking: 18

Exchange rates: zlotych (PLN) per US dollar -

Exchange rates: 3.981 (2024 est.)
4.204 (2023 est.)
4.458 (2022 est.)
3.862 (2021 est.)
3.9 (2020 est.)

ENERGY

Electricity access: *electrification - total population:* 100% (2022 est.)

Electricity: *installed generating capacity:* 64.806 million kW (2023 est.)
consumption: 159.639 billion kWh (2023 est.)
exports: 11.403 billion kWh (2023 est.)
imports: 15.14 billion kWh (2023 est.)
transmission/distribution losses: 8.549 billion kWh (2023 est.)
comparison rankings: installed generating capacity 22; consumption 26; exports 22; imports 15; transmission/distribution losses 178

Electricity generation sources: *fossil fuels:* 72.7% of total installed capacity (2023 est.)
solar: 6.9% of total installed capacity (2023 est.)
wind: 14.4% of total installed capacity (2023 est.)
hydroelectricity: 1.1% of total installed capacity (2023 est.)
biomass and waste: 4.9% of total installed capacity (2023 est.)

Coal: *production:* 96.72 million metric tons (2023 est.)
consumption: 99.932 million metric tons (2023 est.)
exports: 10.805 million metric tons (2023 est.)
imports: 10.041 million metric tons (2023 est.)
proven reserves: 27.758 billion metric tons (2023 est.)

Petroleum: *total petroleum production:* 24,000 bbl/day (2023 est.)
refined petroleum consumption: 743,000 bbl/day (2024 est.)
crude oil estimated reserves: 113 million barrels (2021 est.)

Natural gas: *production:* 5.345 billion cubic meters (2023 est.)
consumption: 20.602 billion cubic meters (2023 est.)
exports: 747.124 million cubic meters (2023 est.)
imports: 15.111 billion cubic meters (2023 est.)
proven reserves: 91.492 billion cubic meters (2021 est.)

Energy consumption per capita: 103.651 million Btu/person (2023 est.)
comparison ranking: 46

COMMUNICATIONS

Telephones - fixed lines: *total subscriptions:* 4.987 million (2023 est.)
subscriptions per 100 inhabitants: 13 (2023 est.)
comparison ranking: total subscriptions 28

Telephones - mobile cellular: *total subscriptions:* 52.4 million (2023 est.)
subscriptions per 100 inhabitants: 132 (2022 est.)
comparison ranking: total subscriptions 34

Broadcast media: state-run public TV operates 2 national channels supplemented by 16 regional and several niche channels; privately owned entities operate several national TV networks and some special interest channels; many privately owned local channels; roughly half of all households are linked to satellite or cable TV systems with access to foreign TV; state-run public radio operates 5 national networks and 17 regional stations; 2 privately owned national radio networks, several commercial stations, and many privately owned local radio stations (2019)

Internet country code: .pl

Internet users: *percent of population:* 86% (2023 est.)

Broadband - fixed subscriptions: *total:* 10.1 million (2023 est.)
subscriptions per 100 inhabitants: 26 (2023 est.)
comparison ranking: total 25

TRANSPORTATION

Civil aircraft registration country code prefix: SP

Airports: 318 (2025)
comparison ranking: 21

Heliports: 16 (2025)
comparison ranking: 58

Railways: *total:* 19,461 km (2020) 11,946 km electrified

Merchant marine: *total:* 152 (2023)
by type: general cargo 6, oil tanker 6, other 140
comparison ranking: total 75

Ports: *total ports:* 10 (2024)
large: 2
medium: 2
small: 4
very small: 2
ports with oil terminals: 5
key ports: Gdansk, Gdynia, Port Polnochny, Szczecin

MILITARY AND SECURITY

Military and security forces: Polish Armed Forces (Polskie Siły Zbrojne): Land Forces (Wojska Ladowe), Navy (Marynarka Wojenna), Air Force (Sily Powietrzne), Special Forces (Wojska Specjalne), Territorial Defense Forces (Wojska Obrony Terytorialnej), Cyberspace Defense Forces (Wojska Obrony Cyberprzestrzeni)

Ministry of Interior and Administration: Polish National Police (Policja); Border Guard (Straż Graniczna or SG) (2025)

Military expenditures: 4.5% of GDP (2025 est.)
3.8% of GDP (2024 est.)
3.3% of GDP (2023 est.)
2.2% of GDP (2022 est.)
2.2% of GDP (2021 est.)

Military and security service personnel strengths: approximately 235,000 active military personnel (2025)
note: a new national defense law in 2022 set a goal to double the size of Poland's armed forces to 300,000 personnel, including 250,000 professional soldiers and 50,000 territorials

Military equipment inventories and acquisitions: the military's inventory consists of a mix of some Soviet-era and a growing amount of more modern, NATO-compatible weapons systems; in recent years, the leading suppliers of armaments have included several European countries, South Korea, and the US; Poland has a domestic defense sector that produces or provides upgrades to a wide variety of weapons systems, particularly ground systems such as tanks and other armored vehicles; it also cooperates with the European and US defense sectors (2024)
note: in late 2018, Poland announced a 7-year (through 2026) approximately $50 billion defense modernization plan that would include such items as 5th generation combat aircraft, unmanned aerial vehicles, rocket artillery, helicopters, submarines, frigates, and improved cyber security; in 2022-2023, it signed large military weapons contracts with South Korea, the UK, and the US

Military service age and obligation: 18 years of age for voluntary military service for men and women; no conscription; professional soldiers serve on a permanent basis (for an unspecified period of time) or on a contract basis (for a specified period of time); initial contract period is 24 months (2025)
note 1: as of 2024, women made up about 16.5% of the military's full-time personnel
note 2: in 2022, Poland announced a new 12-month voluntary military service program with recruits going through a one-month basic training period with a military unit, followed by 11 months of specialized training; upon completion of service, the volunteers would be allowed to join the Territorial Defense Forces or the active reserve, and have priority to join the professional army and be given preference for employment in the public sector; the program is part of an effort to increase the size of the Polish military

Military deployments: 210 Kosovo (NATO/KFOR); up to 180 Latvia (NATO); 190 Lebanon (UNIFIL); approximately 230 Romania (NATO) (2024)
note 1: Poland has obligated about 2,500 troops to the Lithuania, Poland, and Ukraine joint military brigade (LITPOLUKRBRIG), which was established in 2014; the brigade is headquartered in Poland and is comprised of an international staff, three battalions, and specialized units; units affiliated with the multinational brigade remain within the structures of the armed forces of their respective countries until the brigade is activated for participation in an international operation

Military - note: the Polish Armed Forces are responsible for defense of the country's sovereignty and territory, deterring potential threats, and fulfilling Poland's commitments to NATO, EU, and European security; Poland's geographic location on NATO's eastern flank and its history of foreign invasion underpin the Polish military's focus on territorial and border defense; in peacetime, the Armed Forces provide support to the Border Guard; other security concerns include hybrid threats from Russia and Belarus, such as cyberattacks, sabotage, and weaponized migration; since the 2010s, Poland has taken steps to enhance the security of its borders with Russia and Belarus
since 2014, Poland has hosted several NATO military formations designed to enhance the defense of Poland and NATO's eastern flank, including a US-led multinational NATO ground force battlegroup as part of the Alliance's Enhanced Forward Presence initiative, NATO fighter detachments at Malbork Air Base, a NATO-led divisional headquarters (Multinational Division Northeast), which coordinates training and preparation activities of its respective subordinate battlegroups in Poland and Lithuania, and a corps-level NATO field headquarters (Multinational Corps Northeast); Poland also has increased the the US military presence in the country; Poland participates in a variety of EU and NATO military deployments in Africa, the Baltic States, Southern Europe, and the Middle East; Poland also provided support to the NATO mission in Afghanistan (2025)

SPACE

Space agency/agencies: Polish Space Agency (POLSA; established 2014; operational in 2015) (2025)

Space program overview: space program is integrated within the framework of the European Space Agency (ESA); builds satellites, including nano/cube remote sensing (RS) and educational/scientific/technology satellites; researches and develops communications,

RS, navigational, and other scientific applications for satellite payloads; creating infrastructure for receiving, storing, processing and distributing data from meteorological and environmental satellites; researches and develops other space-related technologies, including sensors and robotic probes for interplanetary landers, and launcher systems; participates in ESA/EU and other international space programs; cooperates with a variety of foreign space agencies and industries, including those of Brazil, Canada, China, ESA/EU member states (particularly France, Germany, Italy), India, Japan, Mexico, Russia, Ukraine, UK, and the US; has a growing commercial space sector with more than 300 active enterprises (2025)

note: further details about the key activities, programs, and milestones of the country's space program, as well as government spending estimates on the space sector, appear in the Space Programs reference guide

TERRORISM

Terrorist group(s): Terrorist group(s): Islamic State of Iraq and ash-Sham (ISIS)

note: details about the history, aims, leadership, organization, areas of operation, tactics, targets, weapons, size, and sources of support of the group(s) appear(s) in Appendix T

TRANSNATIONAL ISSUES

Refugees and internally displaced persons: *refugees:* 1,019,863 (2024 est.)

stateless persons: 1,486 (2024 est.)

Illicit drugs: USG identification: major precursor-chemical producer (2025)

PORTUGAL

INTRODUCTION

Background: A global maritime power during the 15th and 16th centuries, Portugal lost much of its wealth and status with the destruction of Lisbon in a 1755 earthquake, occupation during the Napoleonic Wars, and the independence of Brazil, its wealthiest colony, in 1822. A revolution deposed the monarchy in 1910, and for most of the next six decades, repressive governments ran the country. In 1974, a left-wing military coup ushered in broad democratic reforms. The following year, Portugal granted independence to all its African colonies. Portugal is a founding member of NATO and entered the EC (now the EU) in 1986.

GEOGRAPHY

Location: Southwestern Europe, bordering the North Atlantic Ocean, west of Spain

Geographic coordinates: 39 30 N, 8 00 W

Map references: Europe

Area: *total:* 92,090 sq km
land: 91,470 sq km
water: 620 sq km
note: includes Azores and Madeira Islands
comparison ranking: total 111

Area - comparative: slightly smaller than Virginia

Land boundaries: *total:* 1,224 km
border countries (1): Spain 1,224 km

Coastline: 1,793 km

Maritime claims: *territorial sea:* 12 nm
contiguous zone: 24 nm
exclusive economic zone: 200 nm
continental shelf: 200-m depth or to the depth of exploitation

Climate: maritime temperate; cool and rainy in north, warmer and drier in south

Terrain: *the west-flowing Tagus River divides the country:* the north is mountainous toward the interior, while the south is characterized by rolling plains

Elevation: *highest point:* Ponta do Pico (Pico or Pico Alto) on Ilha do Pico in the Azores 2,351 m
lowest point: Atlantic Ocean 0 m
mean elevation: 372 m

Natural resources: fish, forests (cork), iron ore, copper, zinc, tin, tungsten, silver, gold, uranium, marble, clay, gypsum, salt, arable land, hydropower

Land use: *agricultural land:* 42.8% (2022 est.)
arable land: 10.2% (2022 est.)
permanent crops: 9.5% (2022 est.)
permanent pasture: 23.1% (2022 est.)
forest: 36.2% (2022 est.)
other: 21.1% (2022 est.)

Irrigated land: 5,662 sq km (2019)

Population distribution: concentrations are primarily along or near the Atlantic coast; both Lisbon and the second largest city, Porto, are coastal cities

Natural hazards: Azores subject to severe earthquakes
volcanism: limited volcanic activity in the Azores Islands; Fayal or Faial (1,043 m) last erupted in 1958; most volcanoes have not erupted in centuries; historically active volcanoes include Agua de Pau, Furnas, Pico, Picos Volcanic System, San Jorge, Sete Cidades, and Terceira

Geography - note: Azores and Madeira Islands occupy strategic locations along western sea approaches to Strait of Gibraltar; they are two of the four North Atlantic archipelagos that make up Macaronesia; the others are the Canary Islands (Spain) and Cabo Verde

PEOPLE AND SOCIETY

Population: *total:* 10,207,177 (2024 est.)
male: 4,835,763
female: 5,371,414
comparison rankings: total 92; male 94; female 86

Nationality: *noun:* Portuguese (singular and plural)
adjective: Portuguese

Ethnic groups: Portuguese 95%; citizens from Portugal's former colonies in Africa, Asia (Han Chinese), and South America (Brazilian) and other foreign born 5%

Languages: Portuguese (official), Mirandese (official, but locally used)

Religions: Roman Catholic 79.7%, Protestant 2.2%, other Christian 2.5%, other non-Christian, 1.1%, none 14.5% (2021 est.)
note: data represent population 15 years of age and older

Age structure: *0-14 years:* 12.7% (male 662,419/ female 631,284)
15-64 years: 65% (male 3,264,766/female 3,371,087)
65 years and over: 22.3% (2024 est.) (male 908,578/ female 1,369,043)

Dependency ratios: *total dependency ratio:* 53.8 (2024 est.)
youth dependency ratio: 19.5 (2024 est.)
elderly dependency ratio: 34.3 (2024 est.)
potential support ratio: 2.9 (2024 est.)

Median age: *total:* 46.4 years (2024 est.)
male: 44.3 years
female: 48.3 years
comparison ranking: total 11

Population growth rate: -0.14% (2024 est.)
comparison ranking: 207

Birth rate: 8 births/1,000 population (2024 est.)
comparison ranking: 214

Death rate: 10.9 deaths/1,000 population (2024 est.)
comparison ranking: 27

Net migration rate: 1.5 migrant(s)/1,000 population (2024 est.)
comparison ranking: 56

Population distribution: concentrations are primarily along or near the Atlantic coast; both Lisbon and the second largest city, Porto, are coastal cities

Urbanization: *urban population:* 67.9% of total population (2023)
rate of urbanization: 0.44% annual rate of change (2020-25 est.)

Major urban areas - population: 3.001 million LISBON (capital), 1.325 million Porto (2023)

Sex ratio: *at birth:* 1.05 male(s)/female
0-14 years: 1.05 male(s)/female
15-64 years: 0.97 male(s)/female
65 years and over: 0.66 male(s)/female
total population: 0.9 male(s)/female (2024 est.)

Mother's mean age at first birth: 29.9 years (2020 est.)

Maternal mortality ratio: 15 deaths/100,000 live births (2023 est.)
comparison ranking: 137

Infant mortality rate: *total:* 2.4 deaths/1,000 live births (2024 est.)
male: 2.8 deaths/1,000 live births
female: 2.1 deaths/1,000 live births
comparison ranking: total 216

Life expectancy at birth: *total population:* 81.9 years (2024 est.)
male: 78.8 years
female: 85.2 years
comparison ranking: total population 37

Total fertility rate: 1.45 children born/woman (2024 est.)
comparison ranking: 207

Gross reproduction rate: 0.71 (2024 est.)

Drinking water source: *improved: urban:* 99.9% of population (2022 est.)
rural: 97.9% of population (2022 est.)
total: 99.3% of population (2022 est.)
unimproved: urban: 0.1% of population (2022 est.)
rural: 2.1% of population (2022 est.)
total: 0.7% of population (2022 est.)

Health expenditure: 10.6% of GDP (2022)
14.8% of national budget (2022 est.)

Physician density: 5.85 physicians/1,000 population (2022)

Hospital bed density: 3.5 beds/1,000 population (2020 est.)

Sanitation facility access: *improved: urban:* 100% of population (2022 est.)
rural: 100% of population (2022 est.)
total: 100% of population (2022 est.)
unimproved: urban: 0% of population (2022 est.)
rural: 0% of population (2022 est.)
total: 0% of population (2022 est.)

Obesity - adult prevalence rate: 20.8% (2016)
comparison ranking: 95

Alcohol consumption per capita: *total:* 10.37 liters of pure alcohol (2019 est.)
beer: 2.62 liters of pure alcohol (2019 est.)
wine: 6.04 liters of pure alcohol (2019 est.)
spirits: 1.34 liters of pure alcohol (2019 est.)
other alcohols: 0.37 liters of pure alcohol (2019 est.)
comparison ranking: total 20

Tobacco use: *total:* 20.7% (2025 est.)
male: 26.1% (2025 est.)
female: 15.9% (2025 est.)
comparison ranking: total 63

Children under the age of 5 years underweight: 0.4% (2015/16)
comparison ranking: 114

Currently married women (ages 15-49): 52.6% (2023 est.)

Education expenditure: 4.3% of GDP (2022 est.)
9.8% national budget (2022 est.)
comparison ranking: Education expenditure (% GDP) 90

School life expectancy (primary to tertiary education): *total:* 18 years (2022 est.)
male: 17 years (2022 est.)
female: 18 years (2022 est.)

ENVIRONMENT

Environmental issues: soil erosion; air pollution from industrial and vehicle emissions; water pollution, especially in urban centers and coastal areas

International environmental agreements: *party to:* Air Pollution, Air Pollution-Heavy Metals, Air Pollution-Multi-effect Protocol, Antarctic-Environmental Protection, Antarctic Treaty, Biodiversity, Climate Change, Climate Change-Kyoto Protocol, Climate Change-Paris Agreement, Comprehensive Nuclear Test Ban, Desertification, Endangered Species, Hazardous Wastes, Law of the Sea, Marine Dumping-London Convention, Marine Life Conservation, Ozone Layer Protection, Ship Pollution, Tropical Timber 2006, Wetlands, Whaling
signed, but not ratified: Air Pollution-Persistent Organic Pollutants, Air Pollution-Volatile Organic Compounds, Environmental Modification, Nuclear Test Ban

Climate: maritime temperate; cool and rainy in north, warmer and drier in south

Urbanization: *urban population:* 67.9% of total population (2023)
rate of urbanization: 0.44% annual rate of change (2020-25 est.)

Carbon dioxide emissions: 38.272 million metric tonnes of CO_2 (2023 est.)
from coal and metallurgical coke: 20,000 metric tonnes of CO_2 (2023 est.)
from petroleum and other liquids: 29.525 million metric tonnes of CO_2 (2023 est.)
from consumed natural gas: 8.727 million metric tonnes of CO_2 (2023 est.)
comparison ranking: total emissions 66

Particulate matter emissions: 7.6 micrograms per cubic meter (2019 est.)

Waste and recycling: *municipal solid waste generated annually:* 5.268 million tons (2024 est.)
percent of municipal solid waste recycled: 23.5% (2022 est.)

Total water withdrawal: *municipal:* 920.03 million cubic meters (2022 est.)
industrial: 1.83 billion cubic meters (2022 est.)
agricultural: 3.419 billion cubic meters (2022 est.)

Total renewable water resources: 77.4 billion cubic meters (2022 est.)

Geoparks: *total global geoparks and regional networks:* 6 (2024)
global geoparks and regional networks: Açores; Arouca; Estrela; Naturtejo da Meseta Meridional; Oeste; Terras de Cavaleiros (2024)

GOVERNMENT

Country name: *conventional long form:* Portuguese Republic
conventional short form: Portugal
local long form: Republica Portuguesa
local short form: Portugal
etymology: name derives from the Roman designation "Portus Cale," meaning "Port of Cale;" Cale was located in present-day northern Portugal, and its name is said to come from the Latin word *calere* (to be warm) because the harbor never iced over

Government type: semi-presidential republic

Capital: *name:* Lisbon
geographic coordinates: 38 43 N, 9 08 W
time difference: UTC 0 (5 hours ahead of Washington, DC, during Standard Time)
daylight saving time: +1hr, begins last Sunday in March; ends last Sunday in October
time zone note: Portugal has two time zones, including the Azores (UTC-1)
etymology: the origin of the name is unclear; some trace it back to the legendary Greek hero Ulysses; others claim a derivation from the Phoenician *alis-ubbo*, or "joyful bay"

Administrative divisions: 18 districts (*distritos*, singular - *distrito*) and 2 autonomous regions* (*regioes autonomas*, singular - *regiao autonoma*); Aveiro, Acores (Azores)*, Beja, Braga, Braganca, Castelo Branco, Coimbra, Evora, Faro, Guarda, Leiria, Lisboa (Lisbon), Madeira*, Portalegre, Porto, Santarem, Setubal, Viana do Castelo, Vila Real, Viseu

Legal system: civil law system; Constitutional Court reviews legislative acts

Constitution: *history:* several previous; latest adopted 2 April 1976, effective 25 April 1976
amendment process: proposed by the Assembly of the Republic; adoption requires two-thirds majority vote of Assembly members

International law organization participation: accepts compulsory ICJ jurisdiction with reservations; accepts ICCt jurisdiction

Citizenship: *citizenship by birth:* no
citizenship by descent only: at least one parent must be a citizen of Portugal
dual citizenship recognized: yes
residency requirement for naturalization: 10 years; 6 years if from a Portuguese-speaking country

Suffrage: 18 years of age; universal

Executive branch: *chief of state:* President Marcelo REBELO DE SOUSA (since 9 March 2016)
head of government: Prime Minister Antonio Luis MONTENEGRO (since 2 April 2024)
cabinet: Council of Ministers appointed by the president on the recommendation of the prime minister
election/appointment process: president directly elected by absolute-majority popular vote in 2 rounds, if needed, for a 5-year term (eligible for a second term); following legislative elections, the president usually appoints the leader of the majority party or majority coalition as prime minister
most recent election date: 24 January 2021
election results: *2021:* Marcelo REBELO DE SOUSA reelected president in the first round; percent of vote - Marcelo REBELO DE SOUSA (PSD) 60.7%, Ana GOMES (ran as an independent but is a member of PS) 13%, Andre VENTURA (CH) 11.9%, João FERREIRA (PCP-PEV) 4.3%, other 10.1%
2016: Marcelo REBELO DE SOUSA elected president in the first round; percent of vote - Marcelo REBELO DE SOUSA (PSD) 52%, António SAMPAIO DA NOVOA (independent) 22.9%, Marisa MATIAS (BE) 10.1%, Maria DE BELEM ROSEIRA (PS) 4.2%, other 10.8%
expected date of next election: January 2026
note: there is also a Council of State that acts as a consultative body to the president

Legislative branch: *legislature name:* Assembly of the Republic (Assembleia da Republica)
legislative structure: unicameral
number of seats: 230 (all directly elected)
electoral system: proportional representation
scope of elections: full renewal
term in office: 4 years
most recent election date: 5/18/2025
parties elected and seats per party: Social Democratic Party (PPD/PSD) - Democratic and Social Centre - People's Party (CDS-PP) (88); Chega (CH) (60); Socialist Party (PS) (58); Other (24)
percentage of women in chamber: 35.7%
expected date of next election: September 2029

Judicial branch: *highest court(s):* Supreme Court or Supremo Tribunal de Justica (consists of 12 justices);

Constitutional Court or Tribunal Constitucional (consists of 13 judges)
judge selection and term of office: Supreme Court justices nominated by the president and appointed by the Assembly of the Republic; judges can serve for life; Constitutional Court judges - 10 elected by the Assembly and 3 elected by the other Constitutional Court judges; judges elected for 6-year nonrenewable terms
subordinate courts: Supreme Administrative Court (Supremo Tribunal Administrativo); Audit Court (Tribunal de Contas); appellate, district, and municipal courts

Political parties: Democratic Alliance or AD (2024 electoral alliance in the Azores, includes PSD, CDS-PP, PPM)
Democratic and Social Center/People's Party (Partido do Centro Democratico Social-Partido Popular) or CDS-PP
Ecologist Party "The Greens" or "Os Verdes" (Partido Ecologista-Os Verdes) or PEV
Enough (Chega)
Liberal Initiative (Iniciativa Liberal) or IL
LIVRE or L
People-Animals-Nature Party (Pessoas-Animais-Natureza) or PAN
People's Monarchist Party or PPM
Portuguese Communist Party (Partido Comunista Portugues) or PCP
Social Democratic Party (Partido Social Democrata) or PSD (formerly the Partido Popular Democratico or PPD)
Socialist Party (Partido Socialista) or PS
The Left Bloc (Bloco de Esquerda) or BE or O Bloco
Unitary Democratic Coalition (Coligacao Democratica Unitaria) or CDU (includes PCP and PEV) (2024)

Diplomatic representation in the US: *chief of mission:* Ambassador Francisco Antonio DUARTE LOPES (since 7 June 2022)
chancery: 2012 Massachusetts Avenue NW, Washington, DC 20036
telephone: [1] (202) 350-5400
FAX: [1] (202) 462-3726
email address and website: info.washington@mne.pt
https://washingtondc.embaixadaportugal.mne.gov.pt/en/
consulate(s) general: Boston, Newark (NJ), New York, San Francisco
consulate(s): New Bedford (MA), Providence (RI)

Diplomatic representation from the US: *chief of mission:* Ambassador John Joseph ARRIGO (since 30 September 2025)
embassy: Avenida das Forcas Armadas, 1600-081 Lisboa
mailing address: 5320 Lisbon Place, Washington DC 20521-5320
telephone: [351] (21) 727-3300
FAX: [351] (21) 726-9109
email address and website: conslisbon@state.gov
https://pt.usembassy.gov/
consulate(s): Ponta Delgada (Azores)

International organization participation: ADB (nonregional member), AfDB (nonregional member), Australia Group, BIS, CD, CE, CERN, CPLP, EAPC, EBRD, ECB, EIB, EMU, ESA, EU, FAO, FATF, IADB, IAEA, IBRD, ICAO, ICC (national committees), ICCt, ICRM, IDA, IEA, IFAD, IFC, IFRCS, IHO, ILO, IMF, IMO, IMSO, Interpol, IOC, IOM, IPU, ISO, ITSO, ITU, ITUC (NGOs), LAIA (observer), MIGA, NATO, NEA, NSG, OAS (observer), OECD, OPCW, OSCE, Pacific Alliance (observer), Paris Club (associate), PCA, Schengen Convention, SELEC (observer), UN, UNCTAD, UNESCO, UNHCR, UNIDO, Union Latina, UNOOSA, UNWTO, UPU, Wassenaar Arrangement, WCO, WFTU (NGOs), WHO, WIPO, WMO, WTO, ZC

Independence: 1143 (Kingdom of Portugal recognized); 1 December 1640 (independence reestablished after 60 years of Spanish rule); 5 October 1910 (republic proclaimed)

National holiday: Portugal Day (Dia de Portugal), 10 June (1580)
note: also called Camoes Day, the day that revered national poet Luis DE CAMOES (1524-80) died

Flag: *description:* two vertical bands of green (left side, two-fifths) and red (three-fifths), with the national coat of arms (armillary sphere and national shield) centered on the dividing line
meaning: explanations for the color meanings are ambiguous, but a popular interpretation says that green symbolizes hope and red the blood of those defending the nation

National symbol(s): armillary sphere (a spherical astrolabe for modeling objects in the sky)

National color(s): red, green

National anthem(s): *title:* "A Portugesa" (The Song of the Portuguese)
lyrics/music: Henrique LOPES DE MENDOCA/ Alfredo KEIL
history: adopted 1911; originally written to protest the Portuguese monarchy's acquiescence to the 1890 British ultimatum forcing Portugal to give up areas of Africa

National heritage: *total World Heritage Sites:* 17 (16 cultural, 1 natural)
selected World Heritage Site locales: Historic Évora (c); Central Zone of the Town of Angra do Heroismo in the Azores (c); Cultural Landscape of Sintra (c); Laurisilva of Madeira (n); Historic Guimarães (c); Monastery of the Hieronymites and Tower of Belém in Lisbon (c); Convent of Christ in Tomar (c); Prehistoric Rock Art Sites in the Côa Valley and Siega Verde (c); University of Coimbra – Alta and Sofia (c); Sanctuary of Bom Jesus do Monte in Braga (c)

ECONOMY

Economic overview: high-income EU and eurozone economy; strong services sector led by tourism and banking; tight labor market; growth driven by private consumption, trade surplus, and public investment from EU funds; declining public debt

Real GDP (purchasing power parity): $448.226 billion (2024 est.)
$439.745 billion (2023 est.)
$428.547 billion (2022 est.)
note: data in 2021 dollars
comparison ranking: 52

Real GDP growth rate: 1.9% (2024 est.)
2.6% (2023 est.)
7% (2022 est.)
note: annual GDP % growth based on constant local currency
comparison ranking: 152

Real GDP per capita: $41,900 (2024 est.)
$41,600 (2023 est.)
$41,100 (2022 est.)
note: data in 2021 dollars
comparison ranking: 53

GDP (official exchange rate): $308.683 billion (2024 est.)
note: data in current dollars at official exchange rate

Inflation rate (consumer prices): 2.4% (2024 est.)
4.3% (2023 est.)
7.8% (2022 est.)
note: annual % change based on consumer prices
comparison ranking: 70

GDP - composition, by sector of origin: *agriculture:* 2% (2024 est.)
industry: 18.4% (2024 est.)
services: 66.4% (2024 est.)
note: figures may not total 100% due to non-allocated consumption not captured in sector-reported data
comparison rankings: agriculture 149; industry 141; services 46

GDP - composition, by end use: *household consumption:* 62% (2023 est.)
government consumption: 16.8% (2023 est.)
investment in fixed capital: 20.1% (2023 est.)
investment in inventories: 0.4% (2023 est.)
exports of goods and services: 47.5% (2023 est.)
imports of goods and services: -46.4% (2023 est.)
note: figures may not total 100% due to rounding or gaps in data collection

Agricultural products: milk, tomatoes, olives, grapes, maize, pork, potatoes, chicken, apples, oranges (2023)
note: top ten agricultural products based on tonnage

Industries: textiles, clothing, footwear, wood and cork, paper and pulp, chemicals, fuels and lubricants, automobiles and auto parts, base metals, minerals, porcelain and ceramics, glassware, technology, telecommunications; dairy products, wine, other foodstuffs; ship construction and refurbishment; tourism, plastics, financial services, optics

Industrial production growth rate: 1.2% (2024 est.)
note: annual % change in industrial value added based on constant local currency
comparison ranking: 111

Labor force: 5.464 million (2024 est.)
note: number of people ages 15 or older who are employed or seeking work
comparison ranking: 80

Unemployment rate: 6.4% (2024 est.)
6.6% (2023 est.)
6.1% (2022 est.)
note: % of labor force seeking employment
comparison ranking: 118

Youth unemployment rate (ages 15-24): *total:* 21.2% (2024 est.)
male: 21.6% (2024 est.)
female: 20.7% (2024 est.)
note: % of labor force ages 15-24 seeking employment
comparison ranking: total 51

Population below poverty line: 16.4% (2021 est.)
note: % of population with income below national poverty line

Gini Index coefficient - distribution of family income: 36.3 (2022 est.)
note: index (0-100) of income distribution; higher values represent greater inequality
comparison ranking: 64

Average household expenditures: *on food:* 17.3% of household expenditures (2023 est.)
on alcohol and tobacco: 3.1% of household expenditures (2023 est.)

Household income or consumption by percentage share: *lowest 10%:* 2.5% (2022 est.)
highest 10%: 28.8% (2022 est.)
note: % share of income accruing to lowest and highest 10% of population

Remittances: 0.6% of GDP (2024 est.)
0.6% of GDP (2023 est.)
0.6% of GDP (2022 est.)
note: personal transfers and compensation between resident and non-resident individuals/households/entities

Budget: *revenues:* $112.802 billion (2023 est.)
expenditures: $109.044 billion (2023 est.)
note: central government revenues (excluding grants) and expenditures converted to US dollars at average official exchange rate for year indicated

Public debt: 125.7% of GDP (2017 est.)
note: data cover general government debt and include debt instruments issued (or owned) by government entities other than the treasury; the data include treasury debt held by foreign entities; the data include debt issued by subnational entities, as well as intragovernmental debt; intragovernmental debt consists of treasury borrowings from surpluses in the social funds, such as for retirement, medical care, and unemployment; debt instruments for the social funds are not sold at public auctions
comparison ranking: 11

Taxes and other revenues: 22.8% (of GDP) (2023 est.)
note: central government tax revenue as a % of GDP
comparison ranking: 30

Current account balance: $6.708 billion (2024 est.)
$1.624 billion (2023 est.)
-$5.356 billion (2022 est.)
note: balance of payments - net trade and primary/secondary income in current dollars
comparison ranking: 30

Exports: $144.237 billion (2024 est.)
$137.934 billion (2023 est.)
$126.953 billion (2022 est.)
note: balance of payments - exports of goods and services in current dollars
comparison ranking: 39

Exports - partners: Spain 21%, France 11%, Germany 10%, USA 8%, UK 5% (2023)
note: top five export partners based on percentage share of exports

Exports - commodities: cars, garments, vehicle parts/accessories, unpackaged medicine, refined petroleum (2023)
note: top five export commodities based on value in dollars

Imports: $136.976 billion (2024 est.)
$133.617 billion (2023 est.)
$132.193 billion (2022 est.)
note: balance of payments - imports of goods and services in current dollars
comparison ranking: 41

Imports - partners: Spain 33%, Germany 11%, France 7%, Netherlands 5%, China 5% (2023)
note: top five import partners based on percentage share of imports

Imports - commodities: cars, crude petroleum, vehicle parts/accessories, refined petroleum, garments (2023)
note: top five import commodities based on value in dollars

Reserves of foreign exchange and gold: $42.434 billion (2024 est.)
$35.243 billion (2023 est.)
$32.232 billion (2022 est.)
note: holdings of gold (year-end prices)/foreign exchange/special drawing rights in current dollars
comparison ranking: 49

Exchange rates: euros (EUR) per US dollar -

Exchange rates: 0.924 (2024 est.)
0.925 (2023 est.)
0.95 (2022 est.)
0.845 (2021 est.)
0.876 (2020 est.)

ENERGY

Electricity access: *electrification - total population:* 100% (2022 est.)

Electricity: *installed generating capacity:* 25.409 million kW (2023 est.)
consumption: 50.317 billion kWh (2023 est.)
exports: 3.422 billion kWh (2023 est.)
imports: 13.656 billion kWh (2023 est.)
transmission/distribution losses: 5.129 billion kWh (2023 est.)
comparison rankings: installed generating capacity 43; consumption 53; exports 44; imports 16; transmission/distribution losses 164

Electricity generation sources: *fossil fuels:* 25.7% of total installed capacity (2023 est.)
solar: 12.6% of total installed capacity (2023 est.)
wind: 29% of total installed capacity (2023 est.)
hydroelectricity: 24.7% of total installed capacity (2023 est.)
geothermal: 0.4% of total installed capacity (2023 est.)
biomass and waste: 7.6% of total installed capacity (2023 est.)

Coal: *consumption:* 7,000 metric tons (2023 est.)
exports: 1 metric tons (2023 est.)
imports: 6,000 metric tons (2023 est.)
proven reserves: 3 million metric tons (2023 est.)

Petroleum: *total petroleum production:* 8,000 bbl/day (2023 est.)
refined petroleum consumption: 204,000 bbl/day (2024 est.)

Natural gas: *consumption:* 4.325 billion cubic meters (2023 est.)
imports: 4.251 billion cubic meters (2023 est.)

Energy consumption per capita: 73.285 million Btu/person (2023 est.)
comparison ranking: 69

COMMUNICATIONS

Telephones - fixed lines: *total subscriptions:* 5.505 million (2023 est.)
subscriptions per 100 inhabitants: 53 (2023 est.)
comparison ranking: total subscriptions 27

Telephones - mobile cellular: *total subscriptions:* 12.8 million (2023 est.)
subscriptions per 100 inhabitants: 125 (2022 est.)
comparison ranking: total subscriptions 82

Broadcast media: Radio e Televisao de Portugal, the publicly owned TV broadcaster, operates 4 domestic channels and external service channels to Africa; roughly 40 domestic TV stations; widespread access to international broadcasters, with more than half of households connected to multi-channel cable or satellite TV systems; publicly owned radio operates 3 national networks and provides regional and external services; several privately owned national radio stations and about 300 regional and local commercial radio stations

Internet country code: .pt

Internet users: *percent of population:* 86% (2023 est.)

Broadband - fixed subscriptions: *total:* 4.6 million (2023 est.)
subscriptions per 100 inhabitants: 44 (2023 est.)
comparison ranking: total 36

TRANSPORTATION

Civil aircraft registration country code prefix: CR, CS

Airports: 128 (2025)
comparison ranking: 41

Heliports: 65 (2025)
comparison ranking: 31

Railways: *total:* 2,526 km (2020) 1,696 km electrified

Merchant marine: *total:* 888 (2023)
by type: bulk carrier 110, container ship 299, general cargo 191, oil tanker 29, other 259
comparison ranking: total 27

Ports: *total ports:* 18 (2024)
large: 3
medium: 2
small: 4
very small: 9
ports with oil terminals: 5
key ports: Aveiro, Funchal, Lagos, Lisboa, Sines

MILITARY AND SECURITY

Military and security forces: Portuguese Armed Forces (Forças Armadas Portuguesa): Portuguese Army (Exercito Portuguesa), Portuguese Navy (Marinha Portuguesa; includes Marine Corps, aka Corpo de Fuzileiros or Corps of Fusiliers), Portuguese Air Force (Forca Aerea Portuguesa, FAP)

Ministry of Internal Administration: Public Security Police (Polícia de Segurança Pública, PSP), National Republican Guard (Guarda Nacional Republicana, GNR) (2025)
note: the PSP has jurisdiction in cities while the GNR has jurisdiction in rural areas; the GNR is a national gendarmerie force comprised of military personnel with law enforcement, internal security, civil defense, disaster response, and coast guard duties; it is responsible to both the Ministry of Internal Administration and to the Ministry of National Defense; it is not part of the Armed Forces, but may be placed under its operational command in the event of a national emergency

Military expenditures: 2% of GDP (2025 est.)
1.6% of GDP (2024 est.)
1.3% of GDP (2023 est.)
1.4% of GDP (2022 est.)
1.5% of GDP (2021 est.)

Military and security service personnel strengths: approximately 25,000 active-duty military personnel (2025)

Military equipment inventories and acquisitions: the military's inventory includes mostly European- and US-origin weapons systems along with a smaller mix of domestically produced equipment; in recent years, leading foreign suppliers have included Germany and the US; Portugal's defense industry is noted for its shipbuilding (2024)

note: in 2023, Portugal announced a modernization program that included the acquisition of land, naval, air, cyber security, and space capabilities, as well as emerging disruptive technologies

Military service age and obligation: 18-30 years of age for voluntary or contract military service; no compulsory military service (abolished 2004) but conscription possible if insufficient volunteers available; women serve in the armed forces but are prohibited from serving in some combatant specialties; contract service lasts for an initial period of 2-6 years, and can be extended to a maximum of 20 years of service; initial voluntary military service lasts 12 months; reserve obligation to age 35 (2023)
note: as of 2023, women made up about 14% of the military's full-time personnel

Military deployments: the Portuguese Armed Forces have more than 1,100 military personnel deployed around the world engaged in missions supporting the EU, NATO, the UN, and partner nations; key deployments include 225 troops in the Central African Republic (MINUSCA), approximately 200 in Lithuania (NATO), and approximately 150 in Romania (NATO); it also participates in NATO air policing and maritime patrolling operations (2024)

Military - note: the Portuguese military is responsible for external defense, humanitarian operations, and fulfilling Portugal's commitments to European and international security; maritime security has long been a key component of the military's portfolio, and Portugal has one of the world's oldest navies

Portugal was one of the original signers of the North Atlantic Treaty (also known as the Washington Treaty) in 1949 establishing NATO, and the Alliance forms a key pillar of Portugal's defense policy; Portugal is also a signatory of the EU's Common Security and Defense Policy, and it regularly participates in a variety of EU and NATO, as well as UN deployments around the world; the military's largest commitments include air, ground, and naval forces under NATO-led missions and standing task forces in the Baltics, Eastern Europe, and the Mediterranean Sea; the military also participates in exercises with NATO partners (2025)

SPACE

Space agency/agencies: Portuguese Space Agency (Agência Espacial Portuguesa; aka Portugal Space; established 2019) (2025)

Space launch site(s): in August 2025, Portugal granted a license to a commercial consortium to build and operate a space launch center on the island of Santa Maria in the Azores; the first orbital launches are expected in 2027 (2025)

Space program overview: national space program is integrated within the framework of the European Space Agency (ESA); builds and operates satellites; researches and develops a range of space-related technologies with an emphasis on small/micro/nano satellites for remote sensing (RS), navigational, science/technology, and telecommunications, as well as satellite launch services; in addition to the ESA/EU and their member states, cooperates with the space agencies and industries of a variety of countries, including those of Algeria, Angola, Brazil, China, India, Japan, Morocco, South Korea, and the US; also cooperates with international organizations and projects as the Europe South Observatory (ESO) and the Square Kilometer Array (SKA) Observatory project; one of the objectives of the country's national space strategy (Portugal Space 2030) is to increase the annual outcome of commercial space related activities in the country to about $500 million by 2030 (2025)
note: further details about the key activities, programs, and milestones of the country's space program, as well as government spending estimates on the space sector, appear in the Space Programs reference guide

TERRORISM

Terrorist group(s): Terrorist group(s): Islamic State of Iraq and ash-Sham (ISIS)
note: details about the history, aims, leadership, organization, areas of operation, tactics, targets, weapons, size, and sources of support of the group(s) appear(s) in Appendix T

TRANSNATIONAL ISSUES

Refugees and internally displaced persons: *refugees:* 71,166 (2024 est.)

IDPs: 21 (2024 est.)
stateless persons: 31 (2024 est.)

PUERTO RICO

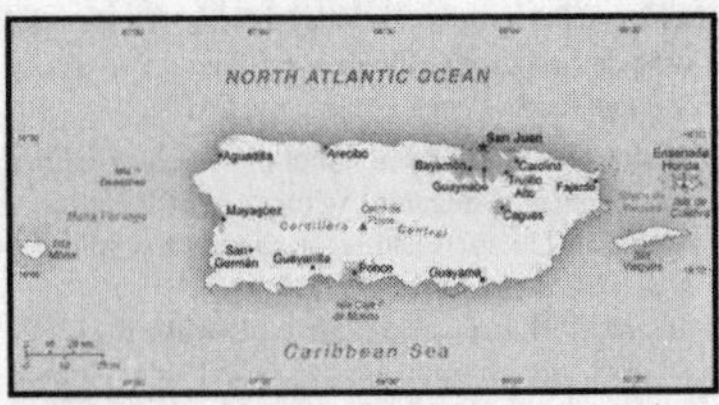

INTRODUCTION

Background: Populated for centuries by aboriginal peoples, Puerto Rico was claimed by the Spanish Crown in 1493 after Christopher COLUMBUS' second voyage to the Americas. In 1898, after 400 years of colonial rule that saw the indigenous population nearly exterminated and African slave labor introduced, Puerto Rico was ceded to the US as a result of the Spanish-American War. Puerto Ricans were granted US citizenship in 1917. Popularly elected governors have served since 1948. In 1952, a constitution was enacted that provided for internal self-government. In plebiscites held in 1967, 1993, and 1998, voters chose not to alter the existing political status with the US, but the results of a 2012 vote left open the possibility of American statehood. A referendum held in late 2020 showed a narrow preference for statehood.

Economic recession on the island has led to a net population loss since about 2005, as large numbers of residents moved to the US mainland. In 2017, Hurricane Maria was the worst storm to hit the island in eight decades, and damage was estimated in the tens of billions of dollars.

GEOGRAPHY

Location: Caribbean, island between the Caribbean Sea and the North Atlantic Ocean, east of the Dominican Republic

Geographic coordinates: 18 15 N, 66 30 W

Map references: Central America and the Caribbean

Area: *total:* 9,104 sq km
land: 8,959 sq km
water: 145 sq km
comparison ranking: total 170

Area - comparative: slightly less than three times the size of Rhode Island

Land boundaries: *total:* 0 km

Coastline: 501 km

Maritime claims: *territorial sea:* 12 nm
exclusive economic zone: 200 nm

Climate: tropical marine, mild; little seasonal temperature variation

Terrain: mostly mountains with coastal plain in north; precipitous mountains to the sea on west coast; sandy beaches along most coastal areas

Elevation: *highest point:* Cerro de Punta 1,338 m
lowest point: Caribbean Sea 0 m
mean elevation: 261 m

Natural resources: some copper and nickel; potential for onshore and offshore oil

Land use: *agricultural land:* 19% (2022 est.)
arable land: 5.7% (2022 est.)
permanent crops: 1.8% (2022 est.)
permanent pasture: 11.6% (2022 est.)
forest: 56.1% (2022 est.)
other: 24.9% (2022 est.)

Irrigated land: 220 sq km (2012)

Population distribution: population clusters tend to be found along the coast, with the largest of these in and around San Juan; an exception is a sizeable population located in the interior of the island immediately south of the capital around Caguas; most of the interior, particularly in the western half of the island, is dominated by the Cordillera Central mountains, where population density is low

Natural hazards: periodic droughts; hurricanes

Geography - note: important location along the Mona Passage, a key shipping lane to the Panama Canal; San Juan is one of the biggest and best natural harbors in the Caribbean; many small rivers and high central mountains ensure land is well-watered; south coast relatively dry; fertile coastal plain belt in north

PEOPLE AND SOCIETY

Population: *total:* 3,019,450 (2024 est.)
male: 1,418,753
female: 1,600,697
comparison rankings: total 138; male 140; female 135

Nationality: *noun:* Puerto Rican(s) (US citizens)
adjective: Puerto Rican

Ethnic groups: White 75.8%, Black/African American 12.4%, other 8.5% (includes American Indian, Alaskan Native, Native Hawaiian, other Pacific Islander, and others), mixed 3.3% (2010 est.)
note: 99% of the population is Latino

Languages: Spanish, English
major-language sample(s):
La Libreta Informativa del Mundo, la fuente indispensable de información básica. (Spanish)

Religions: Roman Catholic 56%, Protestant 33% (largely Pentecostal), other 2%, atheist 1%, none 7% (2014 est.)

Age structure: *0-14 years:* 12.5% (male 191,649/female 184,597)
15-64 years: 62.6% (male 904,406/female 986,778)
65 years and over: 24.9% (2024 est.) (male 322,698/female 429,322)

Dependency ratios: *total dependency ratio:* 59.7 (2024 est.)
youth dependency ratio: 19.9 (2024 est.)
elderly dependency ratio: 39.8 (2024 est.)
potential support ratio: 2.5 (2024 est.)

Median age: *total:* 46.1 years (2024 est.)
male: 44.2 years
female: 47.8 years
comparison ranking: total 13

Population growth rate: -1.2% (2024 est.)
comparison ranking: 233

Birth rate: 7.8 births/1,000 population (2024 est.)
comparison ranking: 217

Death rate: 10.2 deaths/1,000 population (2024 est.)
comparison ranking: 33

Net migration rate: -9.6 migrant(s)/1,000 population (2024 est.)
comparison ranking: 221

Population distribution: population clusters tend to be found along the coast, with the largest of these in and around San Juan; an exception is a sizeable population located in the interior of the island immediately south of the capital around Caguas; most of the interior, particularly in the western half of the island, is dominated by the Cordillera Central mountains, where population density is low

Urbanization: *urban population:* 93.6% of total population (2023)
rate of urbanization: -0.12% annual rate of change (2020-25 est.)

Major urban areas - population: 2.440 million SAN JUAN (capital) (2023)

Sex ratio: *at birth:* 1.06 male(s)/female
0-14 years: 1.04 male(s)/female
15-64 years: 0.92 male(s)/female
65 years and over: 0.75 male(s)/female
total population: 0.89 male(s)/female (2024 est.)

Maternal mortality ratio: 11 deaths/100,000 live births (2023 est.)
comparison ranking: 149

Infant mortality rate: *total:* 5.8 deaths/1,000 live births (2024 est.)
male: 6.4 deaths/1,000 live births
female: 5.2 deaths/1,000 live births
comparison ranking: total 170

Life expectancy at birth: *total population:* 82.1 years (2024 est.)
male: 78.9 years
female: 85.5 years
comparison ranking: total population 34

Total fertility rate: 1.26 children born/woman (2024 est.)
comparison ranking: 220

Gross reproduction rate: 0.61 (2024 est.)

Drinking water source: *improved:* total: 100% of population (2022 est.)
unimproved: total: 0% of population (2022 est.)

Physician density: 3.06 physicians/1,000 population (2018)

Sanitation facility access: *improved:* total: 100% of population (2022 est.)
unimproved: total: 0% of population (2022 est.)

Currently married women (ages 15-49): 37.4% (2023 est.)

Education expenditure: 3.6% of GDP (2021 est.)
comparison ranking: Education expenditure (% GDP) 127

Literacy: *total population:* 92% (2017 est.)
male: 92% (2017 est.)
female: 92% (2017 est.)

School life expectancy (primary to tertiary education): *total:* 17 years (2023 est.)
male: 16 years (2023 est.)
female: 18 years (2023 est.)

ENVIRONMENT

Environmental issues: soil erosion; occasional droughts cause water shortages; industrial pollution

Climate: tropical marine, mild; little seasonal temperature variation

Urbanization: *urban population:* 93.6% of total population (2023)
rate of urbanization: -0.12% annual rate of change (2020-25 est.)

Carbon dioxide emissions: 18.833 million metric tonnes of CO2 (2023 est.)
from coal and metallurgical coke: 2.49 million metric tonnes of CO2 (2023 est.)
from petroleum and other liquids: 11.801 million metric tonnes of CO2 (2023 est.)
from consumed natural gas: 4.542 million metric tonnes of CO2 (2023 est.)
comparison ranking: total emissions 90

Waste and recycling: *municipal solid waste generated annually:* 4.171 million tons (2024 est.)

Total water withdrawal: *municipal:* 796 million cubic meters (2022 est.)
industrial: 2.365 billion cubic meters (2022 est.)
agricultural: 113.5 million cubic meters (2022 est.)

Total renewable water resources: 7.1 billion cubic meters (2022)

GOVERNMENT

Country name: *conventional long form:* Commonwealth of Puerto Rico
conventional short form: Puerto Rico
abbreviation: PR
etymology: Christopher COLUMBUS originally named the island San Juan Bautista (Saint John the Baptist) and the capital city and main port Cuidad de Puerto Rico (Rich Port City); over time, the names were shortened and transposed

Government type: unincorporated organized territory of the US with local self-government; republican form of territorial government with separate executive, legislative, and judicial branches; note - reference Puerto Rican Federal Relations Act, 2 March 1917, as amended by Public Law 600, 3 July 1950

Dependency status: unincorporated organized territory of the US with commonwealth status; policy relations between Puerto Rico and the US conducted under the jurisdiction of the Office of the President

Capital: *name:* San Juan
geographic coordinates: 18 28 N, 66 07 W
time difference: UTC-4 (1 hour ahead of Washington, DC, during Standard Time)
etymology: Spanish explorer Juan PONCE de Leon named the city in 1511 both for himself and for his name saint, Saint John

Administrative divisions: *none (territory of the US); no first-order administrative divisions as defined by the US government, but 78 municipalities (municipios, singular - municipio) are considered second-order:* Adjuntas, Aguada, Aguadilla, Aguas Buenas, Aibonito, Anasco, Arecibo, Arroyo, Barceloneta, Barranquitas, Bayamon, Cabo Rojo, Caguas, Camuy, Canovanas, Carolina, Catano, Cayey, Ceiba, Ciales, Cidra, Coamo, Comerio, Corozal, Culebra, Dorado, Fajardo, Florida, Guanica, Guayama, Guayanilla, Guaynabo, Gurabo, Hatillo, Hormigueros, Humacao, Isabela, Jayuya, Juana Diaz, Juncos, Lajas, Lares, Las Marias, Las Piedras, Loiza, Luquillo, Manati, Maricao, Maunabo, Mayaguez, Moca, Morovis, Naguabo, Naranjito, Orocovis, Patillas, Penuelas, Ponce, Quebradillas, Rincon, Rio Grande, Sabana Grande, Salinas, San German, San Juan, San Lorenzo, San Sebastian, Santa Isabel, Toa Alta, Toa Baja, Trujillo Alto, Utuado, Vega Alta, Vega Baja, Vieques, Villalba, Yabucoa, Yauco

Legal system: civil law system based on the Spanish civil code, within the framework of the US federal system

Constitution: *history:* previous 1900 (Organic Act, or Foraker Act); latest ratified by referendum 3 March 1952, approved 3 July 1952, effective 25 July 1952
amendment process: proposed by a concurrent resolution of at least two-thirds majority by the total Legislative Assembly membership; approval requires at least two-thirds majority vote by the membership of both houses and approval by a majority of voters in a special referendum; if passed by at least three-fourths Assembly vote, the referendum can be held concurrently with the next general election; constitutional articles such as the republican form of government or the bill of rights cannot be amended

Citizenship: see United States

Suffrage: 18 years of age; universal
note: residents are US citizens but do not vote in US presidential elections

Executive branch: *chief of state:* President Donald J. TRUMP (since 20 January 2025)
head of government: Governor Jenniffer GONZÁLEZ-COLÓN (since 2 January 2025)
cabinet: Cabinet appointed by governor with the consent of the Legislative Assembly
election/appointment process: president and vice president indirectly elected on the same ballot by an Electoral College of electors chosen from each state; president and vice president serve a 4-year term (eligible for a second term); under the US Constitution, residents of Puerto Rico do not vote in elections for US president and vice president, but they can vote in Democratic and Republican party presidential primary elections; governor directly elected by

simple-majority popular vote for a 4-year term (no term limits)
most recent election date: 5 November 2024
election results: *2024:* Jenniffer GONZÁLEZ-COLÓN elected governor; percent of vote - Jenniffer GONZÁLEZ-COLÓN (PNP) 39.4%, Juan DALMAU Ramírez (PIP) 32.7%, Jesús Manuel ORTIZ (PPD) 21.1%, Javier JIMÉNEZ (PD) 6.7%, other 0.1%
2020: Pedro PIERLUISI elected governor; percent of vote - Pedro PIERLUISI (PNP) 32.9%, Carlos DELGADO (PPD) 31.6%, Alexandra LUGARO (independent) 14.2%, Juan DALMAU (PIP) 13.7%, other 7.6%
expected date of next election: 7 November 2028

Legislative branch: *legislature name:* Legislative Assembly (Asamblea Legislativa)
legislative structure: bicameral
term in office: 4 years
note: Puerto Rico directly elects 1 member by simple majority vote to serve a 4-year term as a commissioner to the US House of Representatives; the commissioner can vote when serving on a committee and when the House meets as the Committee of the Whole House but not when legislation is submitted for a 'full floor' House vote; election of commissioner last held on 6 November 2018 (next to be held in November 2022)

Legislative branch - lower chamber: *chamber name:* House of Representatives (Camara de Representantes)
number of seats: 51 (directly elected)
electoral system: plurality/majority
scope of elections: full renewal
term in office: 4 years
most recent election date: 11/3/2020
parties elected and seats per party: PPD (26); PNP (21); MVC (2); PIP (1); PD (1)
percentage of women in chamber: 19.6%
expected date of next election: November 2024

Legislative branch - upper chamber: *chamber name:* Senate (Senado)
number of seats: 30 (directly elected)
electoral system: plurality/majority
scope of elections: full renewal
term in office: 4 years
most recent election date: 11/3/2020
parties elected and seats per party: PPD (12); NP (10); MVC (2); PD (1); PIP (1); independent (1)
percentage of women in chamber: 48.1%
expected date of next election: November 2024

Judicial branch: *highest court(s):* Supreme Court (consists of the chief justice and 8 associate justices)
judge selection and term of office: justices appointed by the governor and confirmed by majority Senate vote; judges serve until compulsory retirement at age 70
subordinate courts: Court of Appeals; First Instance Court comprised of superior and municipal courts

Political parties: Citizens' Victory Movement (Movimiento Victoria Ciudadana) or MVC
Democratic Party of Puerto Rico
New Progressive Party or PNP (pro-US statehood)
Popular Democratic Party or PPD (pro-commonwealth)
Project Dignity (Projecto Dignidad) or PD
Puerto Rican Independence Party or PIP (pro-independence)
Republican Party of Puerto Rico

Diplomatic representation in the US: none (territory of the US)

Diplomatic representation from the US: *embassy:* none (territory of the US with commonwealth status)

International organization participation: AOSIS (observer), Caricom (observer), Interpol (subbureau), IOC, UNWTO (associate), UPU, WFTU (NGOs)

Independence: none (territory of the US with commonwealth status)

National holiday: US Independence Day, 4 July (1776); Puerto Rico Constitution Day, 25 July (1952)

Flag: *description:* five equal horizontal bands of red alternating with white; a blue isosceles triangle based on the left side has a large five-pointed white star in the center
meaning: the star stands for the country; the three sides of the triangle stand for the executive, legislative, and judicial branches of the government; blue stands for the sky and the coastal waters, red for the blood shed by warriors, and white for liberty, victory, and peace
note: design initially influenced by the US flag, but similar to the Cuban flag, with the colors of the bands and triangle reversed

National symbol(s): Puerto Rican spindalis (bird), coqui (frog)

National color(s): red, white, blue

National anthem(s): *title:* "La Borinquena" (The Puerto Rican)
lyrics/music: Manuel Fernandez JUNCOS/Felix Astol ARTES
history: music adopted 1952, lyrics adopted 1977; the local anthem's name refers to the local name for the island, Borinquen; the music was originally composed as a dance in 1867 and gained popularity in the early 20th century
title: "The Star-Spangled Banner"
lyrics/music: Francis Scott KEY/John Stafford SMITH
history: official anthem, as a US commonwealth

National heritage: *total World Heritage Sites:* 1 (cultural); note - excerpted from the US entry
selected World Heritage Site locales: La Fortaleza and San Juan National Historic Site

ECONOMY

Economic overview: US Caribbean island territorial economy; hit hard by COVID-19 and hurricanes; declining labor force and job growth after a decade of continuous recession; capital-based industry and tourism; high poverty; energy import-dependent

Real GDP (purchasing power parity): $141.344 billion (2024 est.)
$136.926 billion (2023 est.)
$136.247 billion (2022 est.)
note: data in 2021 dollars
comparison ranking: 86

Real GDP growth rate: 3.2% (2024 est.)
0.5% (2023 est.)
3% (2022 est.)
note: annual GDP % growth based on constant local currency
comparison ranking: 112

Real GDP per capita: $44,100 (2024 est.)
$42,700 (2023 est.)
$42,300 (2022 est.)
note: data in 2021 dollars
comparison ranking: 51

GDP (official exchange rate): $125.842 billion (2024 est.)
note: data in current dollars at official exchange rate

Inflation rate (consumer prices): 4.3% (2022 est.)
2.4% (2021 est.)
-0.5% (2020 est.)
note: annual % change based on consumer prices
comparison ranking: 131

GDP - composition, by sector of origin: *agriculture:* 0.7% (2024 est.)
industry: 48% (2024 est.)
services: 51.5% (2024 est.)
note: figures may not total 100% due to non-allocated consumption not captured in sector-reported data
comparison rankings: agriculture 183; industry 9; services 139

GDP - composition, by end use: *household consumption:* 76% (2024 est.)
government consumption: 8.2% (2024 est.)
investment in fixed capital: 14.6% (2024 est.)
investment in inventories: 0.2% (2024 est.)
exports of goods and services: 51.9% (2024 est.)
imports of goods and services: -42.8% (2024 est.)
note: figures may not total 100% due to rounding or gaps in data collection

Agricultural products: milk, plantains, bananas, tomatoes, chicken, oranges, mangoes/guavas, pineapples, eggs, pumpkins/squash (2023)
note: top ten agricultural products based on tonnage

Industries: pharmaceuticals, electronics, apparel, food products, tourism

Labor force: 1.152 million (2024 est.)
note: number of people ages 15 or older who are employed or seeking work
comparison ranking: 143

Unemployment rate: 5.5% (2024 est.)
5.8% (2023 est.)
6% (2022 est.)
note: % of labor force seeking employment
comparison ranking: 98

Youth unemployment rate (ages 15-24): *total:* 12.5% (2024 est.)
male: 14% (2024 est.)
female: 9.8% (2024 est.)
note: % of labor force ages 15-24 seeking employment
comparison ranking: total 97

Budget: *revenues:* $9.268 billion (2017 est.)
expenditures: $9.974 billion (2017 est.)

Exports: $65.368 billion (2024 est.)
$63.563 billion (2023 est.)
$59.712 billion (2022 est.)
note: GDP expenditure basis - exports of goods and services in current dollars
comparison ranking: 57

Exports - partners: Italy 15%, Netherlands 15%, Belgium 9%, Japan 8%, Germany 8%, Austria 8%, Spain 7%, China 5% (2019)

Exports - commodities: packaged medicines, medical cultures/vaccines, hormones, orthopedic and medical appliances, sulfur compounds (2019)
top five export commodities based on value in dollars

Imports: $53.898 billion (2024 est.)
$56.889 billion (2023 est.)
$52.15 billion (2022 est.)
note: GDP expenditure basis - imports of goods and services in current dollars
comparison ranking: 65

Imports - partners: Ireland 38%, Singapore 9%, Switzerland 8%, South Korea 5% (2019)

Imports - commodities: nitrogen compounds, sulfur compounds, refined petroleum, medical cultures/vaccines, cars (2019)

Exchange rates: the US dollar is used

ENERGY

Electricity access: *electrification - total population:* 100% (2022 est.)

Electricity: *installed generating capacity:* 6.898 million kW (2023 est.)
consumption: 18.669 billion kWh (2023 est.)
transmission/distribution losses: 1.224 billion kWh (2023 est.)
comparison rankings: installed generating capacity 78; consumption 80; transmission/distribution losses 109

Electricity generation sources: *fossil fuels:* 94.6% of total installed capacity (2023 est.)
solar: 4.3% of total installed capacity (2023 est.)
wind: 0.8% of total installed capacity (2023 est.)
hydroelectricity: 0.2% of total installed capacity (2023 est.)
biomass and waste: 0.1% of total installed capacity (2023 est.)

Coal: *consumption:* 1.124 million metric tons (2023 est.)
exports: 500 metric tons (2023 est.)
imports: 1.124 million metric tons (2023 est.)

Petroleum: *refined petroleum consumption:* 80,000 bbl/day (2023 est.)

Natural gas: *consumption:* 2.315 billion cubic meters (2023 est.)
exports: 15.627 million cubic meters (2023 est.)
imports: 2.331 billion cubic meters (2023 est.)

Energy consumption per capita: 86.286 million Btu/person (2023 est.)
comparison ranking: 60

COMMUNICATIONS

Telephones - fixed lines: *total subscriptions:* 758,000 (2023 est.)
subscriptions per 100 inhabitants: 23 (2023 est.)
comparison ranking: total subscriptions 77

Telephones - mobile cellular: *total subscriptions:* 4.04 million (2023 est.)
subscriptions per 100 inhabitants: 120 (2022 est.)
comparison ranking: total subscriptions 135

Broadcast media: more than 30 TV stations; cable TV subscription services are available; roughly 125 radio stations

Internet country code: .pr

Internet users: *percent of population:* 87% (2022 est.)

Broadband - fixed subscriptions: *total:* 751,000 (2023 est.)
subscriptions per 100 inhabitants: 23 (2023 est.)
comparison ranking: total 86

TRANSPORTATION

Airports: 20 (2025)
comparison ranking: 136

Heliports: 40 (2025)
comparison ranking: 43

Ports: *total ports:* 14 (2024)
large: 0
medium: 3
small: 4
very small: 7
ports with oil terminals: 7
key ports: Arroyo, Ensenada Honda, Mayaguez, Playa de Guanica, Playa de Guayanilla, Playa de Ponce, San Juan

MILITARY AND SECURITY

Military and security forces: Puerto Rico Police; Puerto Rico (US) National Guard (Guardia Nacional de Puerto Rico or GNPR) (2025)
note: the GNPR was created by order of the US Congress in June 1919; the organization traces its lineage and history to Spanish militias created in 1511 and is one of the oldest organizations in the US National Guard system

Military - note: defense is the responsibility of the US

TRANSNATIONAL ISSUES

Refugees and internally displaced persons: IDPs: 146 (2024 est.)

QATAR

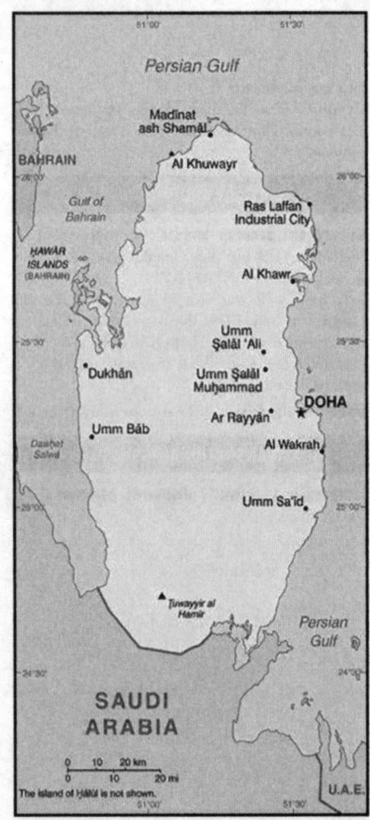

INTRODUCTION

Background: Ruled by the Al Thani family since the mid-1800s, Qatar within the last 60 years transformed itself from a poor British protectorate noted mainly for pearling into an independent state with significant hydrocarbon revenues. Former Amir HAMAD bin Khalifa Al Thani, who overthrew his father in a bloodless coup in 1995, ushered in wide-sweeping political and media reforms, unprecedented economic investment, and a growing Qatari regional leadership role, in part through the creation of the pan-Arab satellite news network Al-Jazeera and Qatar's mediation of some regional conflicts. In the 2000s, Qatar resolved its longstanding border disputes with both Bahrain and Saudi Arabia, and by 2007, Doha had attained the highest per capita income in the world. Qatar did not experience domestic unrest or violence like that seen in other Near Eastern and North African countries in 2011, due in part to its immense wealth and patronage network. In mid-2013, HAMAD peacefully abdicated, transferring power to his son, the current Amir TAMIM bin Hamad. TAMIM is popular with the Qatari public for his role in shepherding the country through an economic embargo from some other regional countries, for his efforts to improve the country's healthcare and education systems, and for his expansion of the country's infrastructure in anticipation of hosting international sporting events. Qatar became the first country in the Arab world to host the FIFA Men's World Cup in 2022.

Following the outbreak of regional unrest in 2011, Doha prided itself on its support for many popular revolutions, particularly in Libya and Syria. This stance was to the detriment of Qatar's relations with Bahrain, Egypt, Saudi Arabia, and the United Arab Emirates (UAE), which temporarily recalled their respective ambassadors from Doha in 2014. TAMIM later oversaw a warming of Qatar's relations with Bahrain, Egypt, Saudi Arabia, and the UAE in November 2014 following Kuwaiti mediation and signing of the Riyadh Agreement. This reconciliation, however, was short-lived. In 2017, Bahrain, Egypt, Saudi Arabia, and the UAE (the "Quartet") cut diplomatic and economic ties with Qatar in response to alleged violations of the agreement, among other complaints. They restored ties in 2021 after signing a declaration at the Gulf Cooperation Council Summit in Al Ula, Saudi Arabia. In 2022, the United States designated Qatar as a major non-NATO ally.

GEOGRAPHY

Location: Middle East, peninsula bordering the Persian Gulf and Saudi Arabia

Geographic coordinates: 25 30 N, 51 15 E

Map references: Middle East

Area: *total:* 11,586 sq km
land: 11,586 sq km
water: 0 sq km
comparison ranking: total 164

Area - comparative: almost twice the size of Delaware; slightly smaller than Connecticut

Land boundaries: *total:* 87 km
border countries (1): Saudi Arabia 87 km

Coastline: 563 km

Maritime claims: *territorial sea:* 12 nm
contiguous zone: 24 nm
exclusive economic zone: as determined by bilateral agreements or the median line

Climate: arid; mild, pleasant winters; very hot, humid summers

Terrain: mostly flat and barren desert

Elevation: *highest point:* Tuwayyir al Hamir 103 m
lowest point: Persian Gulf 0 m
mean elevation: 28 m

Natural resources: petroleum, fish, natural gas

Land use: *agricultural land:* 6.4% (2022 est.)
arable land: 1.8% (2022 est.)
permanent crops: 0.3% (2022 est.)
permanent pasture: 4.4% (2022 est.)
forest: 0% (2022 est.)
other: 93.6% (2022 est.)

Irrigated land: 130 sq km (2022)

Major aquifers: Arabian Aquifer System

Population distribution: most of the population is clustered in or around the capital of Doha on the eastern side of the peninsula

Natural hazards: haze, dust storms, sandstorms common

Geography - note: the peninsula occupies a strategic location in the central Persian Gulf near major petroleum deposits

PEOPLE AND SOCIETY

Population: *total:* 2,552,088 (2024 est.)
male: 1,961,135
female: 590,953
comparison rankings: total 143; male 131; female 161

Nationality: *noun:* Qatari(s)
adjective: Qatari

Ethnic groups: non-Qatari 88.4%, Qatari 11.6% (2015 est.)

Languages: Arabic (official), English commonly used as a second language
major-language sample(s):
كتاب حقائق العالم، المصدر الذي لا يمكن الاستغناء عنه للمعلومات الأساسية (Arabic)

Religions: Muslim 65.2%, Christian 13.7%, Hindu 15.9%, Buddhist 3.8%, folk religion <0.1%, Jewish <0.1%, other <1%, unaffiliated <1% (2020 est.)

Age structure: *0-14 years:* 13.1% (male 168,844/female 165,905)
15-64 years: 85.4% (male 1,767,294/female 411,977)
65 years and over: 1.5% (2024 est.) (male 24,997/female 13,071)

Dependency ratios: *total dependency ratio:* 17.1 (2024 est.)
youth dependency ratio: 15.4 (2024 est.)
elderly dependency ratio: 1.7 (2024 est.)
potential support ratio: 57.2 (2024 est.)

Median age: *total:* 34.3 years (2024 est.)
male: 35.7 years
female: 28.1 years
comparison ranking: total 105

Population growth rate: 0.71% (2024 est.)
comparison ranking: 126

Birth rate: 9.2 births/1,000 population (2024 est.)
comparison ranking: 197

Death rate: 1.4 deaths/1,000 population (2024 est.)
comparison ranking: 229

Net migration rate: -0.7 migrant(s)/1,000 population (2024 est.)
comparison ranking: 135

Population distribution: most of the population is clustered in or around the capital of Doha on the eastern side of the peninsula

Urbanization: *urban population:* 99.4% of total population (2023)
rate of urbanization: 1.66% annual rate of change (2020-25 est.)

Major urban areas - population: 798,000 Ar-Rayyan, 658,000 DOHA (capital) (2023)

Sex ratio: *at birth:* 1.02 male(s)/female
0-14 years: 1.02 male(s)/female
15-64 years: 4.29 male(s)/female
65 years and over: 1.91 male(s)/female
total population: 3.32 male(s)/female (2024 est.)

Maternal mortality ratio: 4 deaths/100,000 live births (2023 est.)
comparison ranking: 175

Infant mortality rate: *total:* 6.4 deaths/1,000 live births (2024 est.)

male: 7 deaths/1,000 live births
female: 5.8 deaths/1,000 live births
comparison ranking: total 163

Life expectancy at birth: *total population:* 80.3 years (2024 est.)
male: 78.2 years
female: 82.4 years
comparison ranking: total population 53

Total fertility rate: 1.9 children born/woman (2024 est.)
comparison ranking: 120

Gross reproduction rate: 0.94 (2024 est.)

Drinking water source: *improved:* total: 100% of population (2022 est.)
unimproved: total: 0% of population (2022 est.)

Health expenditure: 2.9% of GDP (2021)
7.4% of national budget (2022 est.)

Physician density: 3.02 physicians/1,000 population (2023)

Hospital bed density: 1.1 beds/1,000 population (2019 est.)

Sanitation facility access: *improved:* total: 99.9% of population (2022 est.)
unimproved: total: 0.1% of population (2022 est.)

Obesity - adult prevalence rate: 35.1% (2016)
comparison ranking: 15

Alcohol consumption per capita: *total:* 0.96 liters of pure alcohol (2019 est.)
beer: 0.29 liters of pure alcohol (2019 est.)
wine: 0.07 liters of pure alcohol (2019 est.)
spirits: 0.59 liters of pure alcohol (2019 est.)
other alcohols: 0.01 liters of pure alcohol (2019 est.)
comparison ranking: total 151

Tobacco use: *total:* 19.2% (2025 est.)
male: 24.6% (2025 est.)
female: 2.3% (2025 est.)
comparison ranking: total 74

Currently married women (ages 15-49): 65.8% (2023 est.)

Education expenditure: 3.2% of GDP (2020 est.)
9.3% national budget (2020 est.)
comparison ranking: Education expenditure (% GDP) 140

School life expectancy (primary to tertiary education): *total:* 13 years (2022 est.)
male: 12 years (2022 est.)
female: 15 years (2022 est.)

ENVIRONMENT

Environmental issues: air, land, and water pollution; limited natural freshwater resources; limited conservation of oil and wildlife

International environmental agreements: *party to:* Biodiversity, Climate Change, Climate Change-Kyoto Protocol, Comprehensive Nuclear Test Ban, Desertification, Endangered Species, Hazardous Wastes, Law of the Sea, Ozone Layer Protection, Ship Pollution
signed, but not ratified: none of the selected agreements

Climate: arid; mild, pleasant winters; very hot, humid summers

Urbanization: *urban population:* 99.4% of total population (2023)
rate of urbanization: 1.66% annual rate of change (2020-25 est.)

Carbon dioxide emissions: 127.783 million metric tonnes of CO2 (2023 est.)
from coal and metallurgical coke: 10,000 metric tonnes of CO2 (2023 est.)
from petroleum and other liquids: 27.781 million metric tonnes of CO2 (2023 est.)
from consumed natural gas: 99.991 million metric tonnes of CO2 (2023 est.)
comparison ranking: total emissions 36

Particulate matter emissions: 59 micrograms per cubic meter (2019 est.)

Methane emissions: *energy:* 1,040.8 kt (2022-2024 est.)
agriculture: 9.5 kt (2019-2021 est.)
waste: 64.7 kt (2019-2021 est.)
other: 5.5 kt (2019-2021 est.)

Waste and recycling: *municipal solid waste generated annually:* 1.001 million tons (2024 est.)
percent of municipal solid waste recycled: 6% (2022 est.)

Total water withdrawal: *municipal:* 582.862 million cubic meters (2022)
industrial: 40.18 million cubic meters (2022)
agricultural: 311.156 million cubic meters (2022)

Total renewable water resources: 58 million cubic meters (2022 est.)

GOVERNMENT

Country name: *conventional long form:* State of Qatar
conventional short form: Qatar
local long form: Dawlat Qatar
local short form: Qatar
etymology: the name may derive from the Arabic word *katran*, meaning "tar" or "resin" in reference to the area's oil and natural gas reserves
note: closest approximation of the native pronunciation is GAT-tar or COT-tar

Government type: absolute monarchy

Capital: *name:* Doha
geographic coordinates: 25 17 N, 51 32 E
time difference: UTC+3 (8 hours ahead of Washington, DC, during Standard Time)
etymology: the name is derived from the Arabic *ad-dawha*, meaning "the big tree," and probably referred to a large tree at the site of the original fishing village

Administrative divisions: 8 municipalities (*baladiyat*, singular - *baladiyah*); Ad Dawhah, Al Khawr wa adh Dhakhirah, Al Wakrah, Ar Rayyan, Ash Shamal, Ash Shihaniyah, Az Za'ayin, Umm Salal

Legal system: mixed system of civil law and Islamic (sharia) law (in family and personal matters)

Constitution: *history:* previous 1972 (provisional); latest drafted 2 July 2002, approved by referendum 29 April 2003, endorsed 8 June 2004, effective 9 June 2005
amendment process: proposed by the Amir or by one third of Advisory Council members; passage requires two-thirds majority vote of Advisory Council members and approval and promulgation by the emir; articles pertaining to the rule of state and its inheritance, functions of the emir, and citizen rights and liberties cannot be amended

International law organization participation: has not submitted an ICJ jurisdiction declaration; non-party state to the ICCt

Citizenship: *citizenship by birth:* no
citizenship by descent only: the father must be a citizen of Qatar
dual citizenship recognized: no
residency requirement for naturalization: 20 years; 15 years if an Arab national

Suffrage: 18 years of age; universal

Executive branch: *chief of state:* Amir TAMIM bin Hamad Al Thani (since 25 June 2013)
head of government: Prime Minister and Foreign Minister MUHAMMAD bin Abd al-Rahman Al Thani (since 7 March 2023)
cabinet: Council of Ministers appointed by the amir
election/appointment process: the monarchy is hereditary; prime minister appointed by the amir

Legislative branch: *legislature name:* Shura Council (Majlis Al-Shura)
legislative structure: unicameral
number of seats: 45 (30 directly elected; 15 appointed)
electoral system: plurality/majority
scope of elections: full renewal
term in office: 4 years
most recent election date: 10/2/2021
percentage of women in chamber: 4.4%
expected date of next election: September 2025

Judicial branch: *highest court(s):* Supreme Court or Court of Cassation (consists of the court president and several judges); Supreme Constitutional Court (consists of the chief justice and 6 members)
judge selection and term of office: Supreme Court judges nominated by the Supreme Judiciary Council, a 9-member independent body consisting of judiciary heads appointed by the amir; judges appointed for 3-year renewable terms; Supreme Constitutional Court members nominated by the Supreme Judiciary Council and appointed by the monarch; term of appointment NA
subordinate courts: Courts of Appeal; Administrative Court; Courts of First Instance; sharia courts; Courts of Justice; Qatar International Court and Dispute Resolution Center, established in 2009, provides dispute resolution services for institutions and bodies in Qatar, as well as internationally

Political parties: political parties are banned

Diplomatic representation in the US: *chief of mission:* Ambassador Meshal bin Hamad AL THANI (since 24 April 2017)
chancery: 2555 M Street NW, Washington, DC 20037
telephone: [1] (202) 274-1600
FAX: [1] (202) 237-0682
email address and website: info.dc@mofa.gov.qa
https://washington.embassy.qa/en/home
consulate(s) general: Houston, Los Angeles, New York

Diplomatic representation from the US: *chief of mission:* Ambassador (vacant); Chargé d'Affaires Stefanie ALTMAN-WINANS (since June 2025)
embassy: 22 February Street, Al Luqta District, P.O. Box 2399, Doha
mailing address: 6130 Doha Place, Washington DC 20521-6130
telephone: [974] 4496-6000
FAX: [974] 4488-4298
email address and website: PasDoha@state.gov
https://qa.usembassy.gov/

International organization participation: ABEDA, AFESD, AMF, CAEU, CD, CICA (observer), EITI (implementing country), FAO, G-77, GCC, IAEA, IBRD, ICAO, ICC (national committees), ICRM, IDA, IDB, IFAD, IFC, IFRCS, IHO, ILO, IMF, IMO, IMSO, Interpol, IOC, IOM (observer), IPU, ISO, ITSO, ITU, LAS, MIGA, NAM, OAPEC, OAS (observer), OIC, OIF, OPCW, OPEC, PCA, UN, UNCTAD, UNESCO, UNHRC, UNIDO, UNIFIL,

UNWTO, UPU, WCO, WHO, WIPO, WMO, WTO

Independence: 3 September 1971 (from the UK)

National holiday: National Day, 18 December (1878), anniversary of Al Thani family accession to the throne; Independence Day, 3 September (1971)

Flag: *description:* maroon with a broad, serrated white band on the left side
meaning: maroon stands for the blood shed in Qatari wars, and white for peace; the nine-pointed serrated edge is a reference to Qatar's status as the ninth member of the "reconciled emirates" after the Qatari-British treaty of 1916 – the other eight members are Bahrain and the seven that make up the UAE

National symbol(s): a white serrated band with nine white points on top of a maroon field

National color(s): maroon, white

National anthem(s): *title:* "Al-Salam Al-Amiri" (Peace be to the Emir)
lyrics/music: Sheikh MUBARAK bin Saif al-Thani/ Abdul Aziz Nasser OBAIDAN
history: adopted 1996

National heritage: *total World Heritage Sites:* 1 (cultural)
selected World Heritage Site locales: Al Zubarah Archaeological Site

ECONOMY

Economic overview: high-income, oil-and-gas-based Middle Eastern economy; implementing "National Vision 2030" government strategy for economic development, diversification, and favorable business conditions to boost investment and employment; expansion of LNG sector expected to boost growth; Islamic finance leader

Real GDP (purchasing power parity): $317.064 billion (2024 est.)
$308.522 billion (2023 est.)
$304.903 billion (2022 est.)
note: data in 2021 dollars
comparison ranking: 60

Real GDP growth rate: 2.8% (2024 est.)
1.2% (2023 est.)
4.2% (2022 est.)
note: annual GDP % growth based on constant local currency
comparison ranking: 123

Real GDP per capita: $110,900 (2024 est.)
$116,200 (2023 est.)
$114,700 (2022 est.)
note: data in 2021 dollars
comparison ranking: 7

GDP (official exchange rate): $217.983 billion (2024 est.)
note: data in current dollars at official exchange rate

Inflation rate (consumer prices): 1.3% (2024 est.)
3% (2023 est.)
5% (2022 est.)
note: annual % change based on consumer prices
comparison ranking: 31

GDP - composition, by sector of origin: *agriculture:* 0.3% (2024 est.)
industry: 58.5% (2024 est.)
services: 45.9% (2024 est.)
note: figures may not total 100% due to non-allocated consumption not captured in sector-reported data
comparison rankings: agriculture 196; industry 4; services 168

GDP - composition, by end use: *household consumption:* 19.5% (2022 est.)
government consumption: 12.9% (2022 est.)
investment in fixed capital: 30.6% (2022 est.)
investment in inventories: 0% (2022 est.)
exports of goods and services: 68.6% (2022 est.)
imports of goods and services: -31.6% (2022 est.)
note: figures may not total 100% due to rounding or gaps in data collection

Agricultural products: dates, chicken, tomatoes, camel milk, vegetables, cucumbers/gherkins, pumpkins/squash, eggs, sheep milk, eggplants (2023)
note: top ten agricultural products based on tonnage

Industries: liquefied natural gas, crude oil production and refining, ammonia, fertilizer, petrochemicals, steel reinforcing bars, cement, commercial ship repair

Industrial production growth rate: 1.6% (2024 est.)
note: annual % change in industrial value added based on constant local currency
comparison ranking: 107

Labor force: 2.123 million (2024 est.)
note: number of people ages 15 or older who are employed or seeking work
comparison ranking: 125

Unemployment rate: 0.2% (2024 est.)
0.2% (2023 est.)
0.2% (2022 est.)
note: % of labor force seeking employment
comparison ranking: 1

Youth unemployment rate (ages 15-24): *total:* 0.4% (2024 est.)
male: 0.1% (2024 est.)
female: 1.2% (2024 est.)
note: % of labor force ages 15-24 seeking employment
comparison ranking: total 188

Gini Index coefficient - distribution of family income: 35.1 (2017 est.)
note: index (0-100) of income distribution; higher values represent greater inequality
comparison ranking: 74

Average household expenditures: *on food:* 14.6% of household expenditures (2023 est.)
on alcohol and tobacco: 0.3% of household expenditures (2023 est.)

Household income or consumption by percentage share: *lowest 10%:* 2.6% (2017 est.)
highest 10%: 25.8% (2017 est.)
note: % share of income accruing to lowest and highest 10% of population

Remittances: 0.7% of GDP (2024 est.)
0.7% of GDP (2023 est.)
0.4% of GDP (2022 est.)
note: personal transfers and compensation between resident and non-resident individuals/households/ entities

Budget: *revenues:* $65.922 billion (2019 est.)
expenditures: $57.258 billion (2019 est.)

Current account balance: $38.117 billion (2024 est.)
$36.453 billion (2023 est.)
$63.118 billion (2022 est.)
note: balance of payments - net trade and primary/ secondary income in current dollars
comparison ranking: 17

Exports: $125.216 billion (2024 est.)
$128.709 billion (2023 est.)
$161.693 billion (2022 est.)
note: balance of payments - exports of goods and services in current dollars
comparison ranking: 42

Exports - partners: China 18%, India 11%, S. Korea 10%, Japan 7%, Pakistan 6% (2023)
note: top five export partners based on percentage share of exports

Exports - commodities: natural gas, crude petroleum, refined petroleum, plastics, fertilizers (2023)
note: top five export commodities based on value in dollars

Imports: $69.692 billion (2024 est.)
$72.174 billion (2023 est.)
$74.52 billion (2022 est.)
note: balance of payments - imports of goods and services in current dollars
comparison ranking: 56

Imports - partners: USA 12%, China 12%, UAE 9%, UK 7%, India 5% (2023)
note: top five import partners based on percentage share of imports

Imports - commodities: gas turbines, cars, aircraft, iron pipes, ships (2023)
note: top five import commodities based on value in dollars

Reserves of foreign exchange and gold: $53.987 billion (2024 est.)
$51.539 billion (2023 est.)
$47.389 billion (2022 est.)
note: holdings of gold (year-end prices)/foreign exchange/special drawing rights in current dollars
comparison ranking: 41

Exchange rates: Qatari rials (QAR) per US dollar -

Exchange rates: 3.64 (2024 est.)
3.64 (2023 est.)
3.64 (2022 est.)
3.64 (2021 est.)
3.64 (2020 est.)

ENERGY

Electricity access: *electrification - total population:* 100% (2022 est.)

Electricity: *installed generating capacity:* 11.4 million kW (2023 est.)
consumption: 51.965 billion kWh (2023 est.)
transmission/distribution losses: 3.177 billion kWh (2023 est.)
comparison rankings: installed generating capacity 64; consumption 52; transmission/distribution losses 144

Electricity generation sources: *fossil fuels:* 99.7% of total installed capacity (2023 est.)
biomass and waste: 0.2% of total installed capacity (2023 est.)

Coal: *exports:* 300 metric tons (2023 est.)
imports: 4,000 metric tons (2023 est.)

Petroleum: *total petroleum production:* 1.818 million bbl/day (2023 est.)
refined petroleum consumption: 268,000 bbl/day (2023 est.)
crude oil estimated reserves: 25.244 billion barrels (2021 est.)

Natural gas: *production:* 171.805 billion cubic meters (2023 est.)
consumption: 48.034 billion cubic meters (2023 est.)
exports: 124.747 billion cubic meters (2023 est.)
proven reserves: 23.861 trillion cubic meters (2021 est.)

Energy consumption per capita: 814.308 million Btu/ person (2023 est.)
comparison ranking: 1

COMMUNICATIONS

Telephones - fixed lines: *total subscriptions:* 526,000 (2023 est.)
subscriptions per 100 inhabitants: 18 (2023 est.)
comparison ranking: total subscriptions 90

Telephones - mobile cellular: *total subscriptions:* 4.7 million (2023 est.)
subscriptions per 100 inhabitants: 174 (2022 est.)
comparison ranking: total subscriptions 129

Broadcast media: state-controlled TV and radio licensing and access to local media markets; home of satellite TV channel Al-Jazeera, which was originally state-owned but is now independent; local radio includes state, private, and international broadcasters on FM frequencies; satellite TV available (2019)

Internet country code: .qa

Internet users: *percent of population:* 100% (2023 est.)

Broadband - fixed subscriptions: *total:* 347,000 (2023 est.)
subscriptions per 100 inhabitants: 12 (2023 est.)
comparison ranking: total 112

TRANSPORTATION

Civil aircraft registration country code prefix: A7

Airports: 8 (2025)
comparison ranking: 166

Heliports: 12 (2025)
comparison ranking: 66

Merchant marine: *total:* 123 (2023)
by type: bulk carrier 5, container ship 4, general cargo 4, oil tanker 2, other 108
comparison ranking: total 80

Ports: *total ports:* 6 (2024)
large: 0
medium: 1
small: 2
very small: 3
ports with oil terminals: 5
key ports: Al Rayyan Terminal, Al Shaheen Terminal, Doha, Jazirat Halul, Ras Laffan, Umm Said

MILITARY AND SECURITY

Military and security forces: Qatar Armed Forces (QAF): Qatari Amiri Land Force (QALF, includes Emiri Guard), Qatari Amiri Navy (QAN, includes Coast Guard), Qatari Amiri Air Force (QAAF)

Ministry of Interior: General Directorate of Public Security, General Directorate of Coasts and Border Security, Internal Security Force (ISF or Lekhwiya) (2025)

Military expenditures: 5% of GDP (2023 est.)
5% of GDP (2022 est.)
4% of GDP (2021 est.)
4% of GDP (2020 est.)
3.4% of GDP (2019 est.)

Military and security service personnel strengths: approximately 15,000 active-duty Qatar Armed Forces (2025)

Military equipment inventories and acquisitions: the Qatari military's inventory includes a broad mix of older and modern weapons systems, mostly from the US and Europe; in the 2010s, Qatar embarked on a military expansion and modernization program with large air, ground, and naval equipment purchases; in recent years, major suppliers have included France, Germany, Italy, the UK, and the US; Qatar is one of the world's largest arms importers (2024)

Military service age and obligation: conscription for men aged 18-35 introduced in 2013; compulsory service times range from 4-12 months, depending on educational and professional circumstances; since 2018, women have been permitted to serve as volunteers in the armed forces, including as uniformed officers and pilots (2023)
note: the military incorporates about 2,000 conscripts annually and recruits foreign contract soldiers to overcome manpower limitations

Military - note: Qatar's military is responsible for territorial defense and maritime security; the military is in the midst of a large equipment acquisition program designed to enhance its capabilities and Qatar's regional standing; Qatar has military ties with a variety of countries, including France, the UK, the US, Turkey, and member countries of the Gulf Cooperation Council (GCC); it hosts the regional headquarters for the US Central Command (CENTCOM; established 1983) and several thousand US military forces at various military facilities, including the Al Udeid Air Base; Qatar has Major Non-NATO Ally status with the US, a designation under US law that provides foreign partners with certain benefits in the areas of defense trade and security cooperation; Qatar also hosts Turkish military forces at two bases established in 2014 and 2019; the Qatari military is part of the Peninsula Shield Forces, a joint military force established by the GCC countries with the aim of maintaining security and stability in the region (2025)

TRANSNATIONAL ISSUES

Refugees and internally displaced persons: *refugees:* 349 (2024 est.)
stateless persons: 1,200 (2024 est.)

R

ROMANIA

INTRODUCTION

Background: The principalities of Wallachia and Moldavia – for centuries under the control of the Turkish Ottoman Empire – secured their autonomy through the Treaty of Paris in 1856. They were de facto linked in 1859 and formally united in 1862 under the new name of Romania. The country joined the Allied Powers in World War I and subsequently acquired new territories – most notably Transylvania – that more than doubled its size. In 1940, Romania allied with the Axis powers and participated in the 1941 German invasion of the USSR. Three years later, overrun by the Soviets, Romania signed an armistice. The post-war Soviet occupation led to the formation of a communist "people's republic" in 1947 and the abdication of the king. The decades-long rule of dictator Nicolae CEAUSESCU, who took power in 1965, and his Securitate police state became increasingly oppressive and draconian through the 1980s. CEAUSESCU was overthrown and executed in late 1989. Former communists dominated the government until 1996 when they were swept from power. Romania joined NATO in 2004, the EU in 2007, and the Schengen Area for air and sea travel in 2024.

GEOGRAPHY

Location: Southeastern Europe, bordering the Black Sea, between Bulgaria and Ukraine

Geographic coordinates: 46 00 N, 25 00 E

Map references: Europe

Area: *total:* 238,391 sq km
land: 229,891 sq km
water: 8,500 sq km
comparison ranking: total 83

Area - comparative: twice the size of Pennsylvania; slightly smaller than Oregon

Land boundaries: *total:* 2,844 km
border countries (5): Bulgaria 605 km; Hungary 424 km; Moldova 683 km; Serbia 531 km; Ukraine 601 km

Coastline: 225 km

Maritime claims: *territorial sea:* 12 nm
contiguous zone: 24 nm
exclusive economic zone: 200 nm
continental shelf: 200-m depth or to the depth of exploitation

Climate: temperate; cold, cloudy winters with frequent snow and fog; sunny summers with frequent showers and thunderstorms

Terrain: central Transylvanian Basin is separated from the Moldavian Plateau on the east by the Eastern Carpathian Mountains and separated from the Walachian Plain on the south by the Transylvanian Alps

Elevation: *highest point:* Moldoveanu 2,544 m
lowest point: Black Sea 0 m
mean elevation: 414 m

Natural resources: petroleum (reserves declining), timber, natural gas, coal, iron ore, salt, arable land, hydropower

Land use: *agricultural land:* 55.1% (2022 est.)
arable land: 35.7% (2022 est.)
permanent crops: 1.7% (2022 est.)
permanent pasture: 17.7% (2022 est.)
forest: 30.1% (2022 est.)
other: 14.8% (2022 est.)

Irrigated land: 5,280 sq km (2022)

Major rivers (by length in km): Dunărea (Danube) river mouth (shared with Germany [s], Austria, Slovakia, Hungary, Croatia, Serbia, Bulgaria, Moldova, and Ukraine) - 2,888 km
note: [s] after country name indicates river source; [m] after country name indicates river mouth

Major watersheds (area sq km): Atlantic Ocean drainage: *(Black Sea)* Danube (795,656 sq km)

Population distribution: urbanization is not particularly high, and the population distribution is fairly even throughout most of the country, with urban areas attracting larger and denser populations

Natural hazards: earthquakes, most severe in south and southwest; geologic structure and climate promote landslides

Geography - note: controls the most easily traversable land route between the Balkans, Moldova, and Ukraine; the Carpathian Mountains dominate the center of the country, and the Danube River forms much of the southern boundary with Serbia and Bulgaria

PEOPLE AND SOCIETY

Population: *total:* 18,148,155 (2024 est.)
male: 8,747,795
female: 9,400,360
comparison rankings: total 70; male 71; female 68

Nationality: *noun:* Romanian(s)
adjective: Romanian

Ethnic groups: Romanian 89.3%, Hungarian 6%, Romani 3.4%, Ukrainian 0.3%, German 0.1%, other 0.9% (2021 est.)
note: data represent individuals who declared an ethnic group in the 2021 national census; 13% did not respond; Romani populations are usually underestimated in official statistics and may represent 5–11% of Romania's population

Languages: Romanian (official) 91.6%, Hungarian 6.3%, Romani 1.2%, other 0.7% (2021 est.)
major-language sample(s):
Cartea informativa a lumii, sursa indispensabila pentru informatii de baza. (Romanian)
note: data represent individuals who declared a maternal language in the 2021 national census; 13.1% did not respond

Religions: Romanian Orthodox 85.3%, Roman Catholic 4.5%, Reformed 3%, Pentecostal 2.5%, other 4.7% (2021 est.)
note: data represent individuals who declared a religion in the 2021 national census; 13.9% did not respond

Age structure: *0-14 years:* 15.4% (male 1,441,359/female 1,362,304)
15-64 years: 62% (male 5,618,366/female 5,632,718)
65 years and over: 22.6% (2024 est.) (male 1,688,070/female 2,405,338)

Dependency ratios: *total dependency ratio:* 61.3 (2024 est.)
youth dependency ratio: 24.9 (2024 est.)
elderly dependency ratio: 36.4 (2024 est.)
potential support ratio: 2.7 (2024 est.)

Median age: *total:* 45.5 years (2024 est.)
male: 44 years
female: 46.9 years
comparison ranking: total 16

Population growth rate: -0.94% (2024 est.)
comparison ranking: 229

Birth rate: 8.5 births/1,000 population (2024 est.)
comparison ranking: 206

Death rate: 14.6 deaths/1,000 population (2024 est.)
comparison ranking: 5

Net migration rate: -3.3 migrant(s)/1,000 population (2024 est.)
comparison ranking: 187

Population distribution: urbanization is not particularly high, and the population distribution is fairly even throughout most of the country, with urban areas attracting larger and denser populations

Urbanization: *urban population:* 54.7% of total population (2023)
rate of urbanization: -0.15% annual rate of change (2020-25 est.)

Major urban areas - population: 1.776 million BUCHAREST (capital) (2023)

Sex ratio: *at birth:* 1.06 male(s)/female
0-14 years: 1.06 male(s)/female
15-64 years: 1 male(s)/female
65 years and over: 0.7 male(s)/female
total population: 0.93 male(s)/female (2024 est.)

Mother's mean age at first birth: 27.1 years (2020 est.)

Maternal mortality ratio: 12 deaths/100,000 live births (2023 est.)
comparison ranking: 144

Infant mortality rate: *total:* 5.5 deaths/1,000 live births (2024 est.)
male: 5.8 deaths/1,000 live births
female: 5.2 deaths/1,000 live births
comparison ranking: total 172

Life expectancy at birth: *total population:* 76.9 years (2024 est.)

male: 73.4 years
female: 80.5 years
comparison ranking: total population 99

Total fertility rate: 1.63 children born/woman (2024 est.)
comparison ranking: 176

Gross reproduction rate: 0.79 (2024 est.)

Drinking water source: *improved: urban:* 100% of population (2022 est.)
rural: 100% of population (2022 est.)
total: 100% of population (2022 est.)
unimproved: urban: 0% of population (2022 est.)
rural: 0% of population (2022 est.)
total: 0% of population (2022 est.)

Health expenditure: 6.5% of GDP (2021)
11.2% of national budget (2022 est.)

Physician density: 3.63 physicians/1,000 population (2022)

Hospital bed density: 7.1 beds/1,000 population (2020 est.)

Sanitation facility access: *improved: urban:* 97.5% of population (2022 est.)
rural: 77.9% of population (2022 est.)
total: 88.5% of population (2022 est.)
unimproved: urban: 2.5% of population (2022 est.)
rural: 22.1% of population (2022 est.)
total: 11.5% of population (2022 est.)

Obesity - adult prevalence rate: 22.5% (2016)
comparison ranking: 76

Alcohol consumption per capita: *total:* 10.96 liters of pure alcohol (2019 est.)
beer: 5.33 liters of pure alcohol (2019 est.)
wine: 3.38 liters of pure alcohol (2019 est.)
spirits: 2.25 liters of pure alcohol (2019 est.)
other alcohols: 0 liters of pure alcohol (2019 est.)
comparison ranking: total 14

Tobacco use: *total:* 26.7% (2025 est.)
male: 36.2% (2025 est.)
female: 17.9% (2025 est.)
comparison ranking: total 33

Currently married women (ages 15-49): 54.8% (2023)

Child marriage: *women married by age 15:* 0.5% (2021)
women married by age 18: 6.9% (2021)

Education expenditure: 3.3% of GDP (2021 est.)
8.1% national budget (2021 est.)
comparison ranking: Education expenditure (% GDP) 137

Literacy: *total population:* 99% (2021 est.)
male: 99% (2021 est.)
female: 99% (2021 est.)

School life expectancy (primary to tertiary education): *total:* 14 years (2023 est.)
male: 13 years (2023 est.)
female: 14 years (2023 est.)

ENVIRONMENT

Environmental issues: soil erosion, degradation, and desertification; water pollution; air pollution in south from industrial effluents; contamination of Danube delta wetlands

International environmental agreements: *party to:* Air Pollution, Air Pollution-Heavy Metals, Air Pollution-Multi-effect Protocol, Air Pollution-Persistent Organic Pollutants, Antarctic-Environmental Protection, Antarctic Treaty, Biodiversity, Climate Change, Climate Change-Kyoto Protocol, Climate Change-Paris Agreement, Comprehensive Nuclear Test Ban, Desertification, Endangered Species, Environmental Modification, Hazardous Wastes, Law of the Sea, Nuclear Test Ban, Ozone Layer Protection, Ship Pollution, Tropical Timber 2006, Wetlands, Whaling
signed, but not ratified: none of the selected agreements

Climate: temperate; cold, cloudy winters with frequent snow and fog; sunny summers with frequent showers and thunderstorms

Urbanization: *urban population:* 54.7% of total population (2023)
rate of urbanization: -0.15% annual rate of change (2020-25 est.)

Carbon dioxide emissions: 61.416 million metric tonnes of CO2 (2023 est.)
from coal and metallurgical coke: 13.07 million metric tonnes of CO2 (2023 est.)
from petroleum and other liquids: 30.902 million metric tonnes of CO2 (2023 est.)
from consumed natural gas: 17.444 million metric tonnes of CO2 (2023 est.)
comparison ranking: total emissions 52

Particulate matter emissions: 14.6 micrograms per cubic meter (2019 est.)

Methane emissions: *energy:* 325.6 kt (2022-2024 est.)
agriculture: 355.4 kt (2019-2021 est.)
waste: 247.7 kt (2019-2021 est.)
other: 11.8 kt (2019-2021 est.)

Waste and recycling: *municipal solid waste generated annually:* 5.42 million tons (2024 est.)
percent of municipal solid waste recycled: 13% (2022 est.)

Total water withdrawal: *municipal:* 1.256 billion cubic meters (2022)
industrial: 3.94 billion cubic meters (2022)
agricultural: 2.955 billion cubic meters (2022)

Total renewable water resources: 212.01 billion cubic meters (2022 est.)

Geoparks: *total global geoparks and regional networks:* 2
global geoparks and regional networks: Buzău; Haţeg (2023)

GOVERNMENT

Country name: *conventional long form:* none
conventional short form: Romania
local long form: none
local short form: Romania
former: Kingdom of Romania, Romanian People's Republic, Socialist Republic of Romania
etymology: the name derives from the Latin *Romani*, meaning "people from Rome;" the area was an outpost of the Roman Empire in the 2nd century A.D., and the current name was adopted when Moldavia and Wallachia merged in 1861

Government type: semi-presidential republic

Capital: *name:* Bucharest
geographic coordinates: 44 26 N, 26 06 E
time difference: UTC+2 (7 hours ahead of Washington, DC, during Standard Time)
daylight saving time: +1hr, begins last Sunday in March; ends last Sunday in October
etymology: the name is said to come from a shepherd named Bucur who is reputed to have founded the town in 1457, but a settlement probably already existed on the site; the name may come from the personal name of an early landowner

Administrative divisions: 41 counties (*judete*, singular - *judet*) and 1 municipality* (*municipiu*); Alba, Arad, Arges, Bacau, Bihor, Bistrita-Nasaud, Botosani, Braila, Brasov, Bucuresti (Bucharest)*, Buzau, Calarasi, Caras-Severin, Cluj, Constanta, Covasna, Dambovita, Dolj, Galati, Gorj, Giurgiu, Harghita, Hunedoara, Ialomita, Iasi, Ilfov, Maramures, Mehedinti, Mures, Neamt, Olt, Prahova, Salaj, Satu Mare, Sibiu, Suceava, Teleorman, Timis, Tulcea, Vaslui, Valcea, Vrancea

Legal system: civil law system

Constitution: *history:* several previous; latest adopted 21 November 1991, approved by referendum and effective 8 December 1991
amendment process: initiated by the president of Romania through a proposal by the government, by at least one fourth of deputies or senators in Parliament, or by petition of eligible voters representing at least half of Romania's counties; passage requires at least two-thirds majority vote by both chambers or – if mediation is required - by three-fourths majority vote in a joint session, followed by approval in a referendum; articles, including those on national sovereignty, form of government, political pluralism, and fundamental rights and freedoms cannot be amended

International law organization participation: accepts compulsory ICJ jurisdiction with reservations; accepts ICCt jurisdiction

Citizenship: *citizenship by birth:* no
citizenship by descent only: at least one parent must be a citizen of Romania
dual citizenship recognized: yes
residency requirement for naturalization: 5 years

Suffrage: 18 years of age; universal

Executive branch: *chief of state:* President Nicuşor DAN (since 26 May 2025)
head of government: Prime Minister Ilie BOLOJAN (since 23 June 2005)
cabinet: Council of Ministers appointed by the prime minister
election/appointment process: president directly elected by absolute-majority popular vote in 2 rounds, if needed, for a 5-year term (eligible for a second term); prime minister appointed by the president with consent of Parliament
most recent election date: 18 May 2025
election results: *2025:* Nicuşor DAN elected president in runoff; percent of vote - Nicuşor DAN (unaffiliated) 53.6%, George SIMION (AUR) 46.4%
2019: Klaus IOHANNIS reelected president in second round; percent of vote - Klaus IOHANNIS (PNL) 66.1%, Viorica DĂNCILA (PSD) 33.9%
expected date of next election: 2030
note: the prime ministerial position will be rotated in 2027 from BOLOJAN to another coalition party member as part of a power-sharing agreement

Legislative branch: *legislature name:* Parliament of Romania (Parlamentul României)
legislative structure: bicameral

Legislative branch - lower chamber: *chamber name:* Chamber of Deputies (Camera Deputatilor)
number of seats: 331 (all directly elected)
electoral system: proportional representation
scope of elections: full renewal
term in office: 4 years
most recent election date: 12/1/2024
parties elected and seats per party: Social Democratic Party (PSD) (86); Alliance for the Union of Romanians (AUR) (63); National Liberal Party

(PNL) (49); Save Romania Union (USR) (40); S.O.S. Romania (28); Party of Young People (POT) (24); Democratic Union of Hungarians in Romania (UDMR) (22)
percentage of women in chamber: 22.4%
expected date of next election: November 2028

Legislative branch - upper chamber: *chamber name:* Senate (Senatul)
number of seats: 136 (all directly elected)
electoral system: proportional representation
scope of elections: full renewal
term in office: 4 years
most recent election date: 12/1/2024
parties elected and seats per party: Social Democratic Party (PSD) (36); Alliance for the Union of Romanians (AUR) (28); National Liberal Party (PNL) (22); Save Romania Union (USR) (19); S.O.S. Romania (12); Democratic Union of Hungarians in Romania (UDMR) (10); Party of Young People (POT) (7)
percentage of women in chamber: 20.9%
expected date of next election: November 2028

Judicial branch: *highest court(s):* High Court of Cassation and Justice (consists of 111 judges organized into civil, penal, commercial, contentious administrative and fiscal business, and joint sections); Supreme Constitutional Court (consists of 9 members)
judge selection and term of office: High Court of Cassation and Justice judges appointed by the president upon nomination by the Superior Council of Magistracy, a 19-member body of judges, prosecutors, and law specialists; judges appointed for 6-year renewable terms; Constitutional Court members - 6 elected by Parliament and 3 appointed by the president; members serve 9-year, nonrenewable terms
subordinate courts: Courts of Appeal; regional tribunals; first instance courts; military and arbitration courts

Political parties: Alliance for the Fatherland or APP
Alliance for the Unity of Romanians or AUR
Christian-Democratic National Peasants' Party or PNT-CD
Civic Hungarian Party
Democratic Union of Hungarians in Romania or UDMR
Ecologist Party of Romania or PER
Force of the Right or FD
Greater Romania Party or PRM
Green Party
National Liberal Party or PNL
Popular Movement Party or PMP
PRO Romania or PRO
Romanian Nationhood Party or PNR
Save Romania Union Party or USR
Social Democratic Party or PSD
Social Liberal Humanist Party or PUSL (formerly Humanist Power Party (Social-Liberal) or PPU-SL)
S.O.S. Romania
The Right Alternative or AD
United Romania Party or PRU
We are Renewing the European Project in Romania or REPER

Diplomatic representation in the US: *chief of mission:* Ambassador Dan-Andrei MURARU (since 15 September 2021)
chancery: 1607 23rd Street NW, Washington, DC 20008
telephone: [1] (202) 332-4829
FAX: [1] (202) 232-4748
email address and website: washington@mae.ro
https://washington.mae.ro/en
consulate(s) general: Chicago, Los Angeles, Miami, New York

Diplomatic representation from the US: *chief of mission:* Ambassador (vacant); Chargé d'Affaires Michael L. DICKERSON (since 20 May 2025)
embassy: 4-6, Dr. Liviu Librescu Blvd., District 1, Bucharest, 015118
mailing address: 5260 Bucharest Place, Washington, DC 20521-5260
telephone: [40] (21) 200-3300
FAX: [40] (21) 200-3442
email address and website: ACSBucharest@state.gov
https://ro.usembassy.gov/

International organization participation: Australia Group, BIS, BSEC, CBSS (observer), CD, CE, CEI, EAPC, EBRD, ECB, EIB, ESA, EU, FAO, G-9, IAEA, IBRD, ICAO, ICC (national committees), ICCt, ICRM, IDA, IFAD, IFC, IFRCS, IHO, ILO, IMF, IMO, IMSO, Interpol, IOC, IOM, IPU, ISO, ITSO, ITU, ITUC (NGOs), LAIA (observer), MIGA, MONUSCO, NATO, NSG, OAS (observer), OIF, OPCW, OSCE, PCA, SELEC, UN, UNCTAD, UNESCO, UNHCR, UNIDO, Union Latina, UNMIL, UNMISS, UNOCI, UNWTO, UPU, Wassenaar Arrangement, WCO, WFTU (NGOs), WHO, WIPO, WMO, WTO, ZC

Independence: 9 May 1877 (independence proclaimed from the Ottoman Empire; 13 July 1878 (independence recognized by the Treaty of Berlin); 26 March 1881 (kingdom proclaimed); 30 December 1947 (republic proclaimed)

National holiday: Unification Day (unification of Romania and Transylvania), 1 December (1918)

Flag: *description:* three equal vertical bands of blue (left side), yellow, and red
meaning: the colors come from the principalities of Walachia (red and yellow) and Moldavia (red and blue), which united in 1862 to form Romania
history: modeled on the French flag; the national coat of arms that used to be centered on the yellow band has been removed
note: similar to the flag of Chad, which has a darker blue band; also resembles the flags of Andorra and Moldova

National symbol(s): golden eagle

National color(s): blue, yellow, red

National anthem(s): *title:* "Desteapta-te romane!" (Wake up, Romanian!)
lyrics/music: Andrei MURESIANU/Anton PANN
history: adopted 1990; the anthem was written during the 1848 Revolution

National heritage: *total World Heritage Sites:* 11 (9 cultural, 2 natural)
selected World Heritage Site locales: Danube Delta (n); Churches of Moldavia (c); Monastery of Horezu (c); Villages with Fortified Churches in Transylvania (c); Dacian Fortresses of the Orastie Mountains (c); Historic Center of Sighişoara (c); Wooden Churches of Maramureş (c); Ancient and Primeval Beech Forests of the Carpathians and Other Regions of Europe (n); Roşia Montană Mining Landscape (c); Brâncuşi Monumental Ensemble of Târgu Jiu (c); Frontiers of the Roman Empire – Dacia (c)

ECONOMY

Economic overview: high-income, EU-member economy; euro membership delayed over macroeconomic indicators; persistent inflation, but consumption and EU-funded investments driving recovery; skilled labor shortage; high public debt and budget deficit; challenges include fiscal sustainability and political instability

Real GDP (purchasing power parity): $774.376 billion (2024 est.)
$768.126 billion (2023 est.)
$750.091 billion (2022 est.)
note: data in 2021 dollars
comparison ranking: 35

Real GDP growth rate: 0.8% (2024 est.)
2.4% (2023 est.)
4% (2022 est.)
note: annual GDP % growth based on constant local currency
comparison ranking: 183

Real GDP per capita: $40,600 (2024 est.)
$40,300 (2023 est.)
$39,400 (2022 est.)
note: data in 2021 dollars
comparison ranking: 57

GDP (official exchange rate): $382.768 billion (2024 est.)
note: data in current dollars at official exchange rate

Inflation rate (consumer prices): 5.7% (2024 est.)
10.4% (2023 est.)
13.8% (2022 est.)
note: annual % change based on consumer prices
comparison ranking: 149

GDP - composition, by sector of origin: *agriculture:* 3.3% (2024 est.)
industry: 25% (2024 est.)
services: 62.5% (2024 est.)
note: figures may not total 100% due to non-allocated consumption not captured in sector-reported data
comparison rankings: agriculture 128; industry 89; services 72

GDP - composition, by end use: *household consumption:* 63.5% (2024 est.)
government consumption: 18.3% (2024 est.)
investment in fixed capital: 25.7% (2024 est.)
investment in inventories: -1.4% (2024 est.)
exports of goods and services: 35.6% (2024 est.)
imports of goods and services: -41.7% (2024 est.)
note: figures may not total 100% due to rounding or gaps in data collection

Agricultural products: wheat, maize, milk, sunflower seeds, barley, rapeseed, potatoes, grapes, plums, apples (2023)
note: top ten agricultural products based on tonnage

Industries: electric machinery and equipment, auto assembly, textiles and footwear, light machinery, metallurgy, chemicals, food processing, petroleum refining, mining, timber, construction materials

Industrial production growth rate: -0.9% (2024 est.)
note: annual % change in industrial value added based on constant local currency
comparison ranking: 145

Labor force: 8.263 million (2024 est.)
note: number of people ages 15 or older who are employed or seeking work
comparison ranking: 64

Unemployment rate: 5.4% (2024 est.)
5.6% (2023 est.)
5.7% (2022 est.)
note: % of labor force seeking employment
comparison ranking: 96

Youth unemployment rate (ages 15-24): *total:* 21.3% (2024 est.)

male: 21.1% (2024 est.)
female: 21.8% (2024 est.)
note: % of labor force ages 15-24 seeking employment
comparison ranking: total 50

Population below poverty line: 21.1% (2022 est.)
note: % of population with income below national poverty line

Gini Index coefficient - distribution of family income: 32.3 (2022 est.)
note: index (0-100) of income distribution; higher values represent greater inequality
comparison ranking: 103

Average household expenditures: *on food:* 25.1% of household expenditures (2023 est.)
on alcohol and tobacco: 6.1% of household expenditures (2023 est.)

Household income or consumption by percentage share: *lowest 10%:* 1.9% (2022 est.)
highest 10%: 22.6% (2022 est.)
note: % share of income accruing to lowest and highest 10% of population

Remittances: 2.5% of GDP (2024 est.)
2.8% of GDP (2023 est.)
3% of GDP (2022 est.)
note: personal transfers and compensation between resident and non-resident individuals/households/entities

Budget: *revenues:* $93.691 billion (2022 est.)
expenditures: $112.799 billion (2022 est.)
note: central government revenues (excluding grants) and expenditures converted to US dollars at average official exchange rate for year indicated

Public debt: 50.9% of GDP (2022 est.)
note: central government debt as a % of GDP
comparison ranking: 98

Taxes and other revenues: 16.2% (of GDP) (2022 est.)
note: central government tax revenue as a % of GDP
comparison ranking: 82

Current account balance: -$31.988 billion (2024 est.)
-$24.461 billion (2023 est.)
-$27.326 billion (2022 est.)
note: balance of payments - net trade and primary/secondary income in current dollars
comparison ranking: 189

Exports: $136.253 billion (2024 est.)
$136.488 billion (2023 est.)
$129.286 billion (2022 est.)
note: balance of payments - exports of goods and services in current dollars
comparison ranking: 40

Exports - partners: Germany 19%, Italy 10%, France 6%, UK 5%, Hungary 4% (2023)
note: top five export partners based on percentage share of exports

Exports - commodities: cars, vehicle parts/accessories, insulated wire, garments, wheat (2023)
note: top five export commodities based on value in dollars

Imports: $159.575 billion (2024 est.)
$153.427 billion (2023 est.)
$149.209 billion (2022 est.)
note: balance of payments - imports of goods and services in current dollars
comparison ranking: 38

Imports - partners: Germany 19%, Italy 8%, Hungary 6%, Poland 6%, China 6% (2023)
note: top five import partners based on percentage share of imports

Imports - commodities: vehicle parts/accessories, packaged medicine, cars, crude petroleum, plastic products (2023)
note: top five import commodities based on value in dollars

Reserves of foreign exchange and gold: $73.391 billion (2024 est.)
$73 billion (2023 est.)
$55.81 billion (2022 est.)
note: holdings of gold (year-end prices)/foreign exchange/special drawing rights in current dollars
comparison ranking: 36

Exchange rates: lei (RON) per US dollar -

Exchange rates: 4.598 (2024 est.)
4.574 (2023 est.)
4.688 (2022 est.)
4.16 (2021 est.)
4.244 (2020 est.)

ENERGY

Electricity access: *electrification - total population:* 100% (2022 est.)

Electricity: *installed generating capacity:* 19.748 million kW (2023 est.)
consumption: 48.73 billion kWh (2023 est.)
exports: 13.106 billion kWh (2023 est.)
imports: 10.088 billion kWh (2023 est.)
transmission/distribution losses: 5.817 billion kWh (2023 est.)
comparison rankings: installed generating capacity 52; consumption 54; exports 19; imports 25; transmission/distribution losses 167

Electricity generation sources: *fossil fuels:* 32.2% of total installed capacity (2023 est.)
nuclear: 18% of total installed capacity (2023 est.)
solar: 3.9% of total installed capacity (2023 est.)
wind: 13% of total installed capacity (2023 est.)
hydroelectricity: 32.5% of total installed capacity (2023 est.)
biomass and waste: 0.4% of total installed capacity (2023 est.)

Nuclear energy: Number of operational nuclear reactors: 2 (2025)

Net capacity of operational nuclear reactors: 1.3GW (2025 est.)

Percent of total electricity production: 18.9% (2023 est.)

Coal: *production:* 14.752 million metric tons (2023 est.)
consumption: 15.533 million metric tons (2023 est.)
exports: 290,000 metric tons (2023 est.)
imports: 736,000 metric tons (2023 est.)
proven reserves: 291 million metric tons (2023 est.)

Petroleum: *total petroleum production:* 67,000 bbl/day (2023 est.)
refined petroleum consumption: 220,000 bbl/day (2023 est.)
crude oil estimated reserves: 600 million barrels (2021 est.)

Natural gas: *production:* 9.632 billion cubic meters (2023 est.)
consumption: 9.395 billion cubic meters (2023 est.)
exports: 2.231 billion cubic meters (2023 est.)
imports: 2.793 billion cubic meters (2023 est.)
proven reserves: 105.48 billion cubic meters (2021 est.)

Energy consumption per capita: 59.377 million Btu/person (2023 est.)
comparison ranking: 84

COMMUNICATIONS

Telephones - fixed lines: *total subscriptions:* 1.96 million (2023 est.)
subscriptions per 100 inhabitants: 10 (2023 est.)
comparison ranking: total subscriptions 50

Telephones - mobile cellular: *total subscriptions:* 23.2 million (2022 est.)
subscriptions per 100 inhabitants: 118 (2022 est.)
comparison ranking: total subscriptions 58

Broadcast media: a mixture of public and private TV stations; 7 public (2 national, 5 regional) and 187 private TV stations using terrestrial broadcasting, plus 11 public and 86 private TV stations using satellite broadcasting; state-owned public radio broadcaster operates 4 national networks, as well as regional and local stations; 502 private radio stations using terrestrial broadcasting, and 26 using satellite broadcasting

Internet country code: .ro

Internet users: *percent of population:* 89% (2023 est.)

Broadband - fixed subscriptions: *total:* 6.63 million (2023 est.)
subscriptions per 100 inhabitants: 35 (2023 est.)
comparison ranking: total 32

TRANSPORTATION

Civil aircraft registration country code prefix: YR

Airports: 103 (2025)
comparison ranking: 52

Heliports: 24 (2025)
comparison ranking: 52

Railways: *total:* 10,628 km (2020) 4,030 km electrified

Merchant marine: *total:* 127 (2023)
by type: general cargo 9, oil tanker 7, other 111
comparison ranking: total 79

Ports: *total ports:* 11 (2024)
large: 0
medium: 2
small: 1
very small: 8
ports with oil terminals: 4
key ports: Basarabi, Braila, Cernavoda, Constanta, Danube-Black Sea Canal, Galati, Mangalia, Medgidia, Midia, Sulina, Tulcea

MILITARY AND SECURITY

Military and security forces: Romanian Armed Forces (Forțele Armate Române or Armata Română): Romanian Land Forces, Romanian Naval Forces, Romanian Air Force

Ministry of Internal Affairs: Romanian Police, Romanian Gendarmerie, Romanian Border Police (2025)

Military expenditures: 2.3% of GDP (2025 est.)
2.2% of GDP (2024 est.)
1.6% of GDP (2023 est.)
1.8% of GDP (2022 est.)
1.9% of GDP (2021 est.)

Military and security service personnel strengths: approximately 70,000 active Armed Forces (2025)

Military equipment inventories and acquisitions: the military's inventory includes a considerable amount of Soviet-era and older domestically produced weapons systems, although in recent years Romania has launched an effort to acquire more modern and NATO-standard equipment from European countries and the US, including aircraft and armored vehicles (2025)

Military service age and obligation: 18 years of age for voluntary service for men and women; all military inductees contract for an initial 5-year term of service, with subsequent successive 3-year terms until age 36; conscription ended in 2006 (2023)

Military deployments: up to 120 Poland (NATO); Romania also has small numbers of military personnel deployed on other international missions under the EU, NATO, and UN (2024)

Military - note: the Romanian Armed Forces are responsible for territorial defense, fulfilling the country's commitments to European security, and contributing to multinational peacekeeping operations; the military has a variety of concerns, including Russian aggression against Ukraine, Russia's activities in the Black Sea and in Moldova, cyber attacks, hybrid threats, and terrorism; a key focus for the military is equipment modernization

Romania joined NATO in 2004, and its membership forms a key pillar of the country's defense policy; it hosts a NATO multinational divisional headquarters (Multinational Division Southeast) and a French-led ground force battlegroup as part of NATO's Enhanced Forward Presence initiative in the southeastern part of the Alliance, which came about in response to Russia's 2022 invasion of Ukraine; NATO allies have also sent detachments of fighters to augment the Romanian Air Force since 2014 because of aggressive Russian activity in the Black Sea region; the Romanian military trains with NATO and its member states and has participated in NATO- and EU-led multinational missions in Bosnia and Herzegovina, Kosovo, and Poland; it also participates in UN peacekeeping missions (2024)

SPACE

Space agency/agencies: Romanian Space Agency (Agentia Spatiala Romania, ROSA; established 1991) (2025)

Space program overview: space program is integrated into the European Space Agency (ESA), which it first started cooperating with in 1992 and formally joined in 2011; program is involved in the development and production of a wide range of capabilities and technologies, including satellites, satellite/ space launch vehicles (SLVs), remote sensing, human space flight, navigation, telecommunications, and other space-related applications; in addition to the ESA/ EU and their member states (particularly Bulgaria, France, Germany, Hungary, Italy), it cooperates with a variety of other space agencies and commercial space entities, including those of Azerbaijan, China, Japan, Russia, and the US; also participates in international programs; has an active space industry sector with over 50 entities involved in space-related activities (2025)

note: further details about the key activities, programs, and milestones of the country's space program, as well as government spending estimates on the space sector, appear in the Space Programs reference guide

TERRORISM

Terrorist group(s): Terrorist group(s): Islamic State of Iraq and ash-Sham (ISIS)

note: details about the history, aims, leadership, organization, areas of operation, tactics, targets, weapons, size, and sources of support of the group(s) appear(s) in Appendix T

TRANSNATIONAL ISSUES

Refugees and internally displaced persons: *refugees:* 184,991 (2024 est.)

stateless persons: 297 (2024 est.)

RUSSIA

INTRODUCTION

Background: Founded in the 12th century, the Principality of Muscovy emerged from over 200 years of Mongol domination (13th-15th centuries) and gradually conquered and absorbed surrounding principalities. In the early 17th century, a new ROMANOV dynasty continued this policy of expansion across Siberia to the Pacific. Under PETER I (1682-1725), hegemony was extended to the Baltic Sea and the country was renamed the Russian Empire. During the 19th century, more territorial acquisitions were made in Europe and Asia. Defeat in the Russo-Japanese War of 1904-05 contributed to the Revolution of 1905, which resulted in the formation of a parliament and other reforms. Devastating defeats and food shortages in World War I led to widespread rioting in the major cities of the Russian Empire and to the overthrow of the ROMANOV Dynasty in 1917. The communists under Vladimir LENIN seized power soon after and formed the Union of Soviet Socialist Republics (USSR).

The brutal rule of Iosif STALIN (1928-53) strengthened communist control and Russian dominance of the Soviet Union at a cost of tens of millions of lives. After defeating Germany in World War II as part of an alliance with the US (1939-1945), the USSR expanded its territory and influence in Eastern Europe and emerged as a global power. The USSR was the principal US adversary during the Cold War (1947-1991). The Soviet economy and society stagnated in the decades following Stalin's rule, until General Secretary Mikhail GORBACHEV (1985-91) introduced glasnost (openness) and perestroika (restructuring) in an attempt to modernize communism. His initiatives inadvertently released political and economic forces that by December 1991 led to the dissolution of the USSR into Russia and 14 other independent states. In response to the ensuing turmoil during President Boris YELTSIN's term (1991-99), Russia shifted toward a centralized authoritarian state under President Vladimir PUTIN (2000-2008, 2012-present) in which the regime seeks to legitimize its rule through managed elections, populist appeals, a foreign policy focused on enhancing the country's geopolitical influence, and commodity-based economic growth.

In 2014, Russia purported to annex Ukraine's Crimean Peninsula and occupied large portions of two eastern Ukrainian oblasts. In sporadic fighting over the next eight years, more than 14,000 civilians were killed or wounded as a result of the Russian invasion in eastern Ukraine. On 24 February 2022, Russia escalated its conflict with Ukraine by invading the country on several fronts in what has become the largest conventional military attack on a sovereign state in Europe since World War II. The invasion received near-universal international condemnation, and many countries imposed sanctions on Russia and supplied humanitarian and military aid to Ukraine. In September 2022, Russia unilaterally declared its annexation of four Ukrainian oblasts – Donetsk, Kherson, Luhansk, and Zaporizhzhia – even though none were fully under Russian control. The annexations remain unrecognized by the international community.

GEOGRAPHY

Location: North Asia bordering the Arctic Ocean, extending from Eastern Europe (the portion west of the Urals) to the North Pacific Ocean

Geographic coordinates: 60 00 N, 100 00 E

Map references: Asia

Area: *total:* 17,098,242 sq km

land: 16,377,742 sq km

water: 720,500 sq km

comparison ranking: total 1

Area - comparative: approximately 1.8 times the size of the US

Land boundaries: *total:* 22,407 km

border countries (14): Azerbaijan 338 km; Belarus 1,312 km; China (southeast) 4,133 km and China (south) 46 km; Estonia 324 km; Finland 1,309 km; Georgia 894 km; Kazakhstan 7,644 km; North Korea 18 km; Latvia 332 km; Lithuania (Kaliningrad Oblast) 261 km; Mongolia 3,452 km; Norway 191 km; Poland (Kaliningrad Oblast) 209 km; Ukraine 1,944 km

Coastline: 37,653 km

Maritime claims: *territorial sea:* 12 nm

contiguous zone: 24 nm

exclusive economic zone: 200 nm

continental shelf: 200-m depth or to the depth of exploitation

Climate: ranges from steppes in the south through humid continental in much of European Russia; subarctic in Siberia to tundra climate in the polar north; winters vary from cool along Black Sea coast to frigid in Siberia; summers vary from warm in the steppes to cool along Arctic coast

Terrain: broad plain with low hills west of Urals; vast coniferous forest and tundra in Siberia; uplands and mountains along southern border regions

Elevation: *highest point:* Gora El'brus (highest point in Europe) 5,642 m
lowest point: Caspian Sea -28 m
mean elevation: 600 m

Natural resources: wide natural-resource base including major deposits of oil, natural gas, coal, and many strategic minerals, bauxite, reserves of rare earth elements, timber
note: formidable obstacles of climate, terrain, and distance hinder exploitation of natural resources

Land use: *agricultural land:* 13.2% (2022 est.)
arable land: 7.4% (2022 est.)
permanent crops: 0.1% (2022 est.)
permanent pasture: 5.6% (2022 est.)
forest: 49.8% (2022 est.)
other: 37.1% (2022 est.)

Irrigated land: 43,000 sq km (2012)

Major lakes (area sq km): *fresh water lake(s):* Lake Baikal - 31,500 sq km; Lake Ladoga - 18,130 sq km; Lake Onega - 9,720 sq km; Lake Khanka (shared with China) - 5,010 sq km; Lake Peipus - 4,300 sq km (shared with Estonia); Ozero Vygozero - 1,250 sq km; Ozero Beloye - 1,120 sq km
salt water lake(s): Caspian Sea (shared with Iran, Azerbaijan, Turkmenistan, and Kazakhstan) - 374,000 sq km; Ozero Malyye Chany - 2,500 sq km; Curonian Lagoon (shared with Lithuania) - 1,620 sq km
note - the Caspian Sea is the World's largest lake

Major rivers (by length in km): Yenisey-Angara - 5,539 km; Ob-Irtysh - 5,410 km; Amur river mouth (shared with China [s] and Mongolia) - 4,444 km; Lena - 4,400 km; Volga - 3,645 km; Kolyma - 2,513 km; Ural river source (shared with Kazakhstan [m]) - 2,428 km; Dnepr (Dnieper) river source (shared with Belarus and Ukraine [m]) - 2,287 km; Don - 1,870 km; Pechora - 1,809 km
note: [s] after country name indicates river source; [m] after country name indicates river mouth

Major watersheds (area sq km): Arctic Ocean drainage: Kolyma (679,934 sq km), Lena (2,306,743 sq km), Ob (2,972,493 sq km), Pechora (289,532 sq km), Yenisei (2,554,388 sq km)

Atlantic Ocean drainage: *(Black Sea)* Don (458,694 sq km), Dnieper (533,966 sq km)

Pacific Ocean drainage: Amur (1,929,955 sq km)

Internal (endorheic basin) drainage: *(Caspian Sea basin)* Volga (1,410,951 sq km)

Major aquifers: Angara-Lena Basin, Pechora Basin, North Caucasus Basin, East European Aquifer System, West Siberian Basin, Tunguss Basin, Yakut Basin

Population distribution: population is heavily concentrated in the westernmost fifth of the country, extending from the Baltic Sea south to the Caspian Sea, and eastward parallel to the Kazakh border; elsewhere, sizeable population pockets are isolated and generally found in the south

Natural hazards: permafrost over much of Siberia is a major impediment to development; volcanic activity in the Kuril Islands; volcanoes and earthquakes on the Kamchatka Peninsula; spring floods and summer/autumn forest fires in Siberia and parts of European Russia
volcanism: Kamchatka Peninsula is home to 29 historically active volcanoes, with dozens more in the Kuril Islands; Kliuchevskoi (4,835 m) is Kamchatka's most active volcano; Avachinsky and Koryaksky volcanoes, which pose a threat to the city of Petropavlovsk-Kamchatsky, have been deemed Decade Volcanoes by the International Association of Volcanology and Chemistry of the Earth's Interior, worthy of study due to their explosive history and close proximity to human populations; other notable historically active volcanoes include Bezymianny, Chikurachki, Ebeko, Gorely, Grozny, Karymsky, Ketoi, Kronotsky, Ksudach, Medvezhia, Mutnovsky, Sarychev Peak, Shiveluch, Tiatia, Tolbachik, and Zheltovsky; see note 2 under "Geography - note"

Geography - note: *note 1:* largest country in the world in terms of area; despite its size, much of the country lacks the soil and climate (either too cold or too dry) for agriculture
note 2: Russia's far east, particularly the Kamchatka Peninsula, lies along the Ring of Fire, which is a belt bordering the Pacific Ocean that contains about 75% of the world's volcanoes and up to 90% of the world's earthquakes
note 3: Mount El'brus is Europe's tallest peak; Lake Baikal, the deepest lake in the world, is estimated to hold one fifth of the world's fresh surface water
note 4: Kaliningrad oblast is an exclave annexed from Germany after World War II; its capital city of Kaliningrad – formerly Koenigsberg – is the only Baltic port in Russia that remains ice-free in the winter

PEOPLE AND SOCIETY

Population: *total:* 140,820,810 (2024 est.)
male: 65,496,805
female: 75,324,005
comparison rankings: total 9; male 9; female 9

Nationality: *noun:* Russian(s)
adjective: Russian

Ethnic groups: Russian 77.7%, Tatar 3.7%, Ukrainian 1.4%, Bashkir 1.1%, Chuvash 1%, Chechen 1%, other 10.2%, unspecified 3.9% (2010 est.)
note: nearly 200 national and/or ethnic groups are represented in Russia's 2010 census

Languages: Russian (official) 85.7%, Tatar 3.2%, Chechen 1%, other 10.1% (2010 est.)
major-language sample(s):
Книга фактов о мире – незаменимый источник базовой информации. (Russian)
note: data represent native language spoken

Religions: Russian Orthodox 15-20%, Muslim 10-15%, other Christian 2% (2006 est.)
note: estimates are of practicing worshipers; Russia has large populations of non-practicing believers and non-believers, a legacy of over seven decades of official atheism under Soviet rule; Russia officially recognizes Orthodox Christianity, Islam, Judaism, and Buddhism as the country's traditional religions

Age structure: *0-14 years:* 16.5% (male 11,956,284/female 11,313,829)
15-64 years: 65.7% (male 45,007,073/female 47,518,221)
65 years and over: 17.8% (2024 est.) (male 8,533,448/female 16,491,955)

Dependency ratios: *total dependency ratio:* 52.2 (2024 est.)
youth dependency ratio: 25.2 (2024 est.)
elderly dependency ratio: 27 (2024 est.)
potential support ratio: 3.7 (2024 est.)

Median age: *total:* 41.9 years (2024 est.)
male: 39.4 years
female: 44.5 years
comparison ranking: total 48

Population growth rate: -0.49% (2024 est.)
comparison ranking: 221

Birth rate: 8.4 births/1,000 population (2024 est.)
comparison ranking: 209

Death rate: 14 deaths/1,000 population (2024 est.)
comparison ranking: 9

Net migration rate: 0.8 migrant(s)/1,000 population (2024 est.)
comparison ranking: 68

Population distribution: population is heavily concentrated in the westernmost fifth of the country, extending from the Baltic Sea south to the Caspian Sea, and eastward parallel to the Kazakh border; elsewhere, sizeable population pockets are isolated and generally found in the south

Urbanization: *urban population:* 75.3% of total population (2023)
rate of urbanization: 0.11% annual rate of change (2020-25 est.)

Major urban areas - population: 12.680 million MOSCOW (capital), 5.561 million Saint Petersburg, 1.695 million Novosibirsk, 1.528 million Yekaterinburg, 1.292 million Kazan, 1.251 million Nizhniy Novgorod (2023)

Sex ratio: *at birth:* 1.06 male(s)/female
0-14 years: 1.06 male(s)/female
15-64 years: 0.95 male(s)/female
65 years and over: 0.52 male(s)/female
total population: 0.87 male(s)/female (2024 est.)

Mother's mean age at first birth: 25.2 years (2013 est.)

Maternal mortality ratio: 9 deaths/100,000 live births (2023 est.)
comparison ranking: 152

Infant mortality rate: *total:* 6.5 deaths/1,000 live births (2024 est.)
male: 7.2 deaths/1,000 live births
female: 5.8 deaths/1,000 live births
comparison ranking: total 162

Life expectancy at birth: *total population:* 72.3 years (2024 est.)
male: 67.4 years
female: 77.4 years
comparison ranking: total population 164

Total fertility rate: 1.52 children born/woman (2024 est.)
comparison ranking: 199

Gross reproduction rate: 0.74 (2024 est.)

Drinking water source: *improved: urban:* 98.9% of population (2022 est.)
rural: 91.5% of population (2022 est.)
total: 97.1% of population (2022 est.)
unimproved: urban: 1.1% of population (2022 est.)
rural: 8.5% of population (2022 est.)
total: 2.9% of population (2022 est.)

Health expenditure: 7.4% of GDP (2021)
13.8% of national budget (2022 est.)

Physician density: 5.11 physicians/1,000 population (2022)

Hospital bed density: 7 beds/1,000 population (2021 est.)

Sanitation facility access: *improved: urban:* 95.4% of population (2022 est.)
rural: 71.4% of population (2022 est.)

total: 89.4% of population (2022 est.)
unimproved: urban: 4.6% of population (2022 est.)
rural: 28.6% of population (2022 est.)
total: 10.6% of population (2022 est.)

Obesity - adult prevalence rate: 23.1% (2016)
comparison ranking: 70

Alcohol consumption per capita: *total:* 7.29 liters of pure alcohol (2019 est.)
beer: 3.04 liters of pure alcohol (2019 est.)
wine: 0.97 liters of pure alcohol (2019 est.)
spirits: 3.16 liters of pure alcohol (2019 est.)
other alcohols: 0.12 liters of pure alcohol (2019 est.)
comparison ranking: total 56

Tobacco use: *total:* 26.5% (2025 est.)
male: 40.2% (2025 est.)
female: 15.1% (2025 est.)
comparison ranking: total 35

Currently married women (ages 15-49): 53.1% (2023 est.)

Child marriage: *women married by age 15:* 0.3% (2017)
women married by age 18: 6.2% (2017)

Education expenditure: 4.1% of GDP (2022 est.)
8.9% national budget (2020 est.)
comparison ranking: Education expenditure (% GDP) 103

School life expectancy (primary to tertiary education): *total:* 15 years (2023 est.)
male: 15 years (2023 est.)
female: 15 years (2023 est.)

ENVIRONMENT

Environmental issues: air pollution from heavy industry, coal-fired electric plants, and transportation in major cities; industrial, municipal, and agricultural pollution of inland waterways and seacoasts; deforestation; soil erosion; soil contamination from agricultural chemicals; nuclear waste disposal; scattered areas of radioactive contamination; groundwater contamination from toxic waste; urban solid-waste management; abandoned stocks of pesticides

International environmental agreements: *party to:* Air Pollution, Air Pollution-Nitrogen Oxides, Air Pollution-Sulphur 85, Antarctic-Environmental Protection, Antarctic-Marine Living Resources, Antarctic Seals, Antarctic Treaty, Biodiversity, Climate Change, Climate Change-Kyoto Protocol, Climate Change-Paris Agreement, Comprehensive Nuclear Test Ban, Desertification, Endangered Species, Environmental Modification, Hazardous Wastes, Law of the Sea, Marine Dumping-London Convention, Nuclear Test Ban, Ozone Layer Protection, Ship Pollution, Wetlands, Whaling
signed, but not ratified: Air Pollution-Sulfur 94

Climate: ranges from steppes in the south through humid continental in much of European Russia; subarctic in Siberia to tundra climate in the polar north; winters vary from cool along Black Sea coast to frigid in Siberia; summers vary from warm in the steppes to cool along Arctic coast

Urbanization: *urban population:* 75.3% of total population (2023)
rate of urbanization: 0.11% annual rate of change (2020-25 est.)

Carbon dioxide emissions: 1.844 billion metric tonnes of CO2 (2023 est.)
from coal and metallurgical coke: 479.311 million metric tonnes of CO2 (2023 est.)
from petroleum and other liquids: 453.103 million metric tonnes of CO2 (2023 est.)
from consumed natural gas: 912.076 million metric tonnes of CO2 (2023 est.)
comparison ranking: total emissions 4

Particulate matter emissions: 9.1 micrograms per cubic meter (2019 est.)

Methane emissions: *energy:* 13,815.3 kt (2022-2024 est.)
agriculture: 1,972.6 kt (2019-2021 est.)
waste: 4,069.8 kt (2019-2021 est.)
other: 363.2 kt (2019-2021 est.)

Waste and recycling: *municipal solid waste generated annually:* 60 million tons (2024 est.)
percent of municipal solid waste recycled: 5.3% (2022 est.)

Total water withdrawal: *municipal:* 17.15 billion cubic meters (2022 est.)
industrial: 29.03 billion cubic meters (2022 est.)
agricultural: 18.64 billion cubic meters (2022 est.)

Total renewable water resources: 4.53 trillion cubic meters (2022 est.)

Geoparks: *total global geoparks and regional networks:* 1
global geoparks and regional networks: Yangan-Tau (2023)

GOVERNMENT

Country name: *conventional long form:* Russian Federation
conventional short form: Russia
local long form: Rossiyskaya Federatsiya
local short form: Rossiya
former: Russian Empire, Russian Soviet Federative Socialist Republic
etymology: Russian lands were referred to as Muscovy until PETER I declared the Empire of All Russias in 1721; the new name aimed at identifying the new Russia with European political tradition; "Rus" was the Old Finnish name given to Varangians (eastern Vikings) who entered the area in the 9th century

Government type: semi-presidential federation

Capital: *name:* Moscow
geographic coordinates: 55 45 N, 37 36 E
time difference: UTC+3 (8 hours ahead of Washington, DC, during Standard Time)
daylight saving time: does not observe daylight savings time (DST)
time zone note: Russia has 11 time zones, the largest number of contiguous time zones of any country in the world; in 2014, two time zones were added and DST dropped
etymology: named after the Moskva River; the origin of the river's name is unclear

Administrative divisions: 46 provinces (*oblasti*, singular - *oblast*), 21 republics (*respubliki*, singular - *respublika*), 4 autonomous districts (*avtonomnyye okrugi*, singular - *avtonomnyy okrug*), 9 federal subjects (*kraya*, singular - *kray*), 2 federal cities (*goroda*, singular - *gorod*), and 1 autonomous province (*avtonomnaya oblast'*)
oblasts: Amur (Blagoveshchensk), Arkhangelsk, Astrakhan, Belgorod, Bryansk, Chelyabinsk, Irkutsk, Ivanovo, Kaliningrad, Kaluga, Kemerovo, Kirov, Kostroma, Kurgan, Kursk, Leningrad (Gatchina), Lipetsk, Magadan, Moscow, Murmansk, Nizhniy Novgorod, Novgorod, Novosibirsk, Omsk, Orenburg, Orel, Penza, Pskov, Rostov, Ryazan, Sakhalin (Yuzhno-Sakhalinsk), Samara, Saratov, Smolensk, Sverdlovsk (Yekaterinburg), Tambov, Tomsk, Tula, Tver, Tyumen, Ulyanovsk, Vladimir, Volgograd, Vologda, Voronezh, Yaroslavl
republics: Adygeya (Maykop), Altay (Gorno-Altaysk), Bashkortostan (Ufa), Buryatiya (Ulan-Ude), Chechnya (Groznyy), Chuvashiya (Cheboksary), Dagestan (Makhachkala), Ingushetiya (Magas), Kabardino-Balkariya (Nal'chik), Kalmykiya (Elista), Karachayevo-Cherkesiya (Cherkessk), Kareliya (Petrozavodsk), Khakasiya (Abakan), Komi (Syktyvkar), Mariy-El (Yoshkar-Ola), Mordoviya (Saransk), North Ossetia (Vladikavkaz), Sakha [Yakutiya] (Yakutsk), Tatarstan (Kazan), Tyva (Kyzyl), Udmurtiya (Izhevsk)
autonomous districts: Chukotka (Anadyr'), Khanty-Mansi-Yugra (Khanty-Mansiysk), Nenets (Nar'yan-Mar), Yamalo-Nenets (Salekhard)
federal subjects: Altay (Barnaul), Kamchatka (Petropavlovsk-Kamchatskiy), Khabarovsk, Krasnodar, Krasnoyarsk, Perm, Primorskiy [Maritime] (Vladivostok), Stavropol, Zabaykalsk [Transbaikal] (Chita)
federal cities: Moscow [Moskva], Saint Petersburg [Sankt-Peterburg]
autonomous province: Yevreyskaya [Jewish] (Birobidzhan)
note 1: administrative divisions have the same names as their administrative centers; exceptions show the administrative center name in parentheses
note 2: the United States does not recognize Russia's annexation or renaming of Ukraine's Autonomous Republic of Crimea and the municipality of Sevastopol; it similarly does not recognize the annexation of the Ukrainian oblasts Donetsk, Luhansk, Zaporizhzhia, and Kherson

Legal system: civil law system; judicial review of legislative acts

Constitution: *history:* several previous (during Russian Empire and Soviet era); latest drafted 12 July 1993, adopted by referendum 12 December 1993, effective 25 December 1993
amendment process: proposed by the president of the Russian Federation, by either house of the Federal Assembly, by the government of the Russian Federation, or by legislative (representative) bodies of the Federation's constituent entities; proposals to amend the government's constitutional system, human and civil rights and freedoms, and procedures for amending or drafting a new constitution require formation of a Constitutional Assembly; passage of such amendments requires two-thirds majority vote of its total membership; passage in a referendum requires participation of an absolute majority of eligible voters and an absolute majority of valid votes; approval of proposed amendments to the government structure, authorities, and procedures requires approval by the legislative bodies of at least two thirds of the Russian Federation's constituent entities

International law organization participation: has not submitted an ICJ jurisdiction declaration; non-party state to the ICCt

Citizenship: *citizenship by birth:* no
citizenship by descent only: at least one parent must be a citizen of Russia
dual citizenship recognized: yes
residency requirement for naturalization: 3-5 years

Suffrage: 18 years of age; universal

Executive branch: *chief of state:* President Vladimir Vladimirovich PUTIN (since 7 May 2012)
head of government: Premier Mikhail Vladimirovich MISHUSTIN (since 16 January 2020)

cabinet: the government is composed of the premier, his deputies, and ministers, all appointed by the president; the premier is also confirmed by the Duma
election/appointment process: president directly elected by absolute-majority popular vote in 2 rounds, if needed, for a 6-year term (eligible for a second consecutive term)
most recent election date: 15-17 March 2024
election results: 2024: Vladimir PUTIN reelected president; percent of vote - Vladimir PUTIN (independent) 88.5%, Nikolay KHARITONOV (Communist Party) 4.4%, Vladislav DAVANKOV (New People party) 3.9%, Leonid SLUTSKY (Liberal Democrats) 3.2%
2018: Vladimir PUTIN reelected president; percent of vote - Vladimir PUTIN (independent) 77.5%, Pavel GRUDININ (CPRF) 11.9%, Vladimir ZHIRINOVSKIY (LDPR) 5.7%, other 4.9%; Mikhail MISHUSTIN (independent) approved as premier by Duma; vote - 383 to 0
expected date of next election: 2030
note: a Presidential Administration provides staff and policy support to the president, drafts presidential decrees, and coordinates policy among government agencies; a Security Council also reports directly to the president

Legislative branch: *legislature name:* Federal Assembly (Federalnoye Sobraniye)
legislative structure: bicameral
note 1: the State Duma now includes 3 representatives from the "Republic of Crimea," while the Federation Council includes 2 each from the "Republic of Crimea" and the "Federal City of Sevastopol," both regions that Russia occupied and attempted to annex from Ukraine and that the US does not recognize as part of Russia

Legislative branch - lower chamber: *chamber name:* State Duma (Gossoudarstvennaya Duma)
number of seats: 450 (all directly elected)
electoral system: mixed system
scope of elections: full renewal
term in office: 5 years
most recent election date: 9/19/2021
parties elected and seats per party: United Russia (326); Communist Party (KPRF) (57); A Just Russia (28); Liberal Democratic Party of Russia (LDPR) (23); Other (16)
percentage of women in chamber: 16.4%
expected date of next election: September 2026

Legislative branch - upper chamber: *chamber name:* Council of the Federation (Soviet Federatsii)
number of seats: 170 (all appointed)
percentage of women in chamber: 18.5%

Judicial branch: *highest court(s):* Supreme Court of the Russian Federation (consists of 170 members organized into the Judicial Panel for Civil Affairs, the Judicial Panel for Criminal Affairs, and the Military Panel); Constitutional Court (consists of 11 members, including the chairperson and deputy)
judge selection and term of office: all members of Russia's 3 highest courts nominated by the president and appointed by the Federation Council (the upper house of the legislature); members of all 3 courts appointed for life
subordinate courts: regional (kray) and provincial (oblast) courts; Moscow and St. Petersburg city courts; autonomous province and district courts (the 21 Russian republics have court systems specified by their own constitutions)

Political parties: A Just Russia or SRZP
Civic Platform or GP
Communist Party of the Russian Federation or KPRF
Liberal Democratic Party of Russia or LDPR
New People or NL
Party of Growth or PR
Rodina
United Russia or ER

Diplomatic representation in the US: *chief of mission:* Ambassador Alexander Nikitich DARCHIEV (since 11 June 2025)
chancery: 2650 Wisconsin Avenue NW, Washington, DC 20007
telephone: [1] (202) 298-5700
FAX: [1] (202) 298-5735
email address and website: rusembusa@mid.ru
https://washington.mid.ru/en/
consulate(s) general: Houston, New York

Diplomatic representation from the US: *chief of mission:* Ambassador (vacant); Chargé d'Affaires J. Douglas DYKHOUSE (since June 2025)
embassy: 55,75566° N, 37,58028° E
mailing address: 5430 Moscow Place, Washington DC 20521-5430
telephone: [7] (495) 728-5000
FAX: [7] (495) 728-5090
email address and website: MoscowACS@state.gov
https://ru.usembassy.gov/
consulate(s) general: Vladivostok (suspended status), Yekaterinburg (suspended status)

International organization participation: APEC, Arctic Council, ARF, ASEAN (dialogue partner), BIS, BRICS, BSEC, CBSS, CD, CE, CERN (observer), CICA, CIS, CSTO, EAEC, EAEU, EAPC, EAS, EBRD, FAO, FATF, G-20, GCTU, IAEA, IBRD, ICAO, ICC (national committees), ICRM, IDA, IFAD, IFC, IFRCS, IHO, ILO, IMF, IMO, IMSO, Interpol, IOC, IOM (observer), IPU, ISO, ITSO, ITU, ITUC (NGOs), LAIA (observer), MIGA, MINURSO, MONUSCO, NEA, NSG, OAS (observer), OIC (observer), OPCW, OSCE, Paris Club, PCA, PFP, SCO, UN, UNCTAD, UNESCO, UNHCR, UNIDO, UNISFA, UNMIL, UNMISS, UNOCI, UN Security Council (permanent), UNTSO, UNWTO, UPU, Wassenaar Arrangement, WCO, WFTU (NGOs), WHO, WIPO, WMO, WTO, ZC

Independence: *25 December 1991 (from the Soviet Union; Russian SFSR renamed Russian Federation); notable earlier dates:* 1157 (Principality of Vladimir-Suzdal created); 16 January 1547 (Tsardom of Muscovy established); 22 October 1721 (Russian Empire proclaimed); 30 December 1922 (Soviet Union established)

National holiday: Russia Day, 12 June (1990)
note: commemorates the Declaration of State Sovereignty of the Russian Soviet Federative Socialist Republic (RSFSR)

Flag: *description:* three equal horizontal bands of white (top), blue, and red
meaning: colors may have been based on the Dutch flag, but no official meaning is assigned
history: created when Russia built its first naval vessels, and was used mostly as a naval flag until the 19th century
note: inspired several other Slavic countries to adopt horizontal tricolors of the same colors in different arrangements

National symbol(s): bear, double-headed eagle

National color(s): white, blue, red

National coat of arms: the current coat of arms of Russia was adopted by presidential decree on 30 November 1993; the double-headed eagle was adopted as a Russian symbol in 1472 when Ivan III married Sophia Palaiologina, niece of the last Byzantine emperor in Constantinople – the eagle was her family's emblem

National anthem(s): *title:* "Gosudarstvenny Gimn Rossiyskoy Federatsii" (National Anthem of the Russian Federation)
lyrics/music: Sergey Vladimirovich MIKHALKOV/ Aleksandr Vasilyevich ALEKSANDROV
history: adopted 2000; Russia adopted the tune of the Soviet Union's anthem (composed in 1939), as well as new lyrics; MIKHALKOV, who wrote the new lyrics, also authored the Soviet lyrics in 1943

National heritage: *total World Heritage Sites:* 33 (22 cultural, 11 natural)
selected World Heritage Site locales: Historic Centre of Saint Petersburg and Related Groups of Monuments (c); Kizhi Pogost (c); Kremlin and Red Square, Moscow (c); Historic Monuments of Novgorod and Surroundings (c); White Monuments of Vladimir and Suzdal (c); Architectural Ensemble of the Trinity Sergius Lavra in Sergiev Posad (c); Church of the Ascension, Kolomenskoye (c); Lake Baikal (n); Volcanoes of Kamchatka (n); Ensemble of the Ferapontov Monastery (c); Historic and Architectural Complex of the Kazan Kremlin (c); Citadel, Ancient City and Fortress Buildings of Derbent (c); Uvs Nuur Basin (n); Ensemble of the Novodevichy Convent (c); Natural System of Wrangel Island Reserve (n); Historical Centre of the City of Yaroslavl (c); Lena Pillars Nature Park (n); Bolgar Historical and Archaeological Complex (c); Assumption Cathedral and Monastery of the town-island of Sviyazhsk (c); Churches of the Pskov School of Architecture (c); Petroglyphs of Lake Onega and the White Sea (c); Rock Paintings of Shulgan-Tash Cave (c)

ECONOMY

Economic overview: natural resource-rich Eurasian economy; leading energy exporter to Europe and Asia; decreased oil export reliance; endemic corruption, Ukrainian invasion, and lack of green infrastructure limit investment and have led to sanctions

Real GDP (purchasing power parity): $6.089 trillion (2024 est.)
$5.835 trillion (2023 est.)
$5.607 trillion (2022 est.)
note: data in 2021 dollars
comparison ranking: 4

Real GDP growth rate: 4.3% (2024 est.)
4.1% (2023 est.)
-1.4% (2022 est.)
note: annual GDP % growth based on constant local currency
comparison ranking: 62

Real GDP per capita: $41,700 (2024 est.)
$39,900 (2023 est.)
$38,200 (2022 est.)
note: data in 2021 dollars
comparison ranking: 54

GDP (official exchange rate): $2.174 trillion (2024 est.)
note: data in current dollars at official exchange rate

Inflation rate (consumer prices): 6.7% (2021 est.)
3.4% (2020 est.)
4.5% (2019 est.)
note: annual % change based on consumer prices
comparison ranking: 161

GDP - composition, by sector of origin: *agriculture:* 2.7% (2024 est.)
industry: 30.7% (2024 est.)
services: 57.5% (2024 est.)
note: figures may not total 100% due to non-allocated consumption not captured in sector-reported data
comparison rankings: agriculture 134; industry 51; services 108

GDP - composition, by end use: *household consumption:* 49.4% (2024 est.)
government consumption: 18.6% (2024 est.)
investment in fixed capital: 22.1% (2024 est.)
investment in inventories: 4.2% (2024 est.)
exports of goods and services: 21.9% (2024 est.)
imports of goods and services: -17.6% (2024 est.)
note: figures may not total 100% due to rounding or gaps in data collection

Agricultural products: wheat, sugar beets, milk, barley, potatoes, sunflower seeds, maize, soybeans, chicken, pork (2023)
note: top ten agricultural products based on tonnage

Industries: complete range of mining and extractive industries producing coal, oil, gas, chemicals, and metals; all forms of machine building from rolling mills to high-performance aircraft and space vehicles; defense industries (including radar, missile production, advanced electronic components), shipbuilding; road and rail transportation equipment; communications equipment; agricultural machinery, tractors, and construction equipment; electric power generating and transmitting equipment; medical and scientific instruments; consumer durables, textiles, foodstuffs, handicrafts

Industrial production growth rate: 4.1% (2024 est.)
note: annual % change in industrial value added based on constant local currency
comparison ranking: 58

Labor force: 72.517 million (2024 est.)
note: number of people ages 15 or older who are employed or seeking work
comparison ranking: 9

Unemployment rate: 2.6% (2024 est.)
3.1% (2023 est.)
3.9% (2022 est.)
note: % of labor force seeking employment
comparison ranking: 24

Youth unemployment rate (ages 15-24): *total:* 9.3% (2024 est.)
male: 8.8% (2024 est.)
female: 9.8% (2024 est.)
note: % of labor force ages 15-24 seeking employment
comparison ranking: total 129

Population below poverty line: 12.1% (2020 est.)
note: % of population with income below national poverty line

Gini Index coefficient - distribution of family income: 35.1 (2021 est.)
note: index (0-100) of income distribution; higher values represent greater inequality
comparison ranking: 75

Average household expenditures: *on food:* 25.3% of household expenditures (2023 est.)
on alcohol and tobacco: 5.9% of household expenditures (2023 est.)

Household income or consumption by percentage share: *lowest 10%:* 2.7% (2021 est.)
highest 10%: 26.6% (2021 est.)
note: % share of income accruing to lowest and highest 10% of population

Remittances: 0.1% of GDP (2024 est.)
0.1% of GDP (2023 est.)
0.1% of GDP (2022 est.)
note: personal transfers and compensation between resident and non-resident individuals/households/entities

Budget: *revenues:* $704.613 billion (2023 est.)
expenditures: $635.809 billion (2023 est.)
note: central government revenues (excluding grants) and expenditures converted to US dollars at average official exchange rate for year indicated

Public debt: 18.5% of GDP (2023 est.)
note: central government debt as a % of GDP
comparison ranking: 186

Taxes and other revenues: 12.1% (of GDP) (2023 est.)
note: central government tax revenue as a % of GDP
comparison ranking: 114

Current account balance: $62.287 billion (2024 est.)
$49.439 billion (2023 est.)
$237.735 billion (2022 est.)
note: balance of payments - net trade and primary/secondary income in current dollars
comparison ranking: 9

Exports: $475.277 billion (2024 est.)
$465.22 billion (2023 est.)
$640.878 billion (2022 est.)
note: balance of payments - exports of goods and services in current dollars
comparison ranking: 21

Exports - partners: China 33%, India 17%, Turkey 8%, Kazakhstan 4%, Brazil 3% (2023)
note: top five export partners based on percentage share of exports

Exports - commodities: crude petroleum, refined petroleum, natural gas, coal, fertilizers (2023)
note: top five export commodities based on value in dollars

Imports: $381.45 billion (2024 est.)
$379.659 billion (2023 est.)
$347.384 billion (2022 est.)
note: balance of payments - imports of goods and services in current dollars
comparison ranking: 23

Imports - partners: China 53%, Turkey 5%, Germany 5%, Kazakhstan 5%, Italy 2% (2023)
note: top five import partners based on percentage share of imports

Imports - commodities: cars, packaged medicine, broadcasting equipment, garments, plastic products (2023)
note: top five import commodities based on value in dollars

Reserves of foreign exchange and gold: $597.217 billion (2023 est.)
$581.71 billion (2022 est.)
$632.242 billion (2021 est.)
note: holdings of gold (year-end prices)/foreign exchange/special drawing rights in current dollars
comparison ranking: 6

Debt - external: $135.301 billion (2022 est.)
note: present value of external debt in current US dollars
comparison ranking: 7

Exchange rates: Russian rubles (RUB) per US dollar -

Exchange rates: 85.162 (2023 est.)
68.485 (2022 est.)
73.654 (2021 est.)
72.105 (2020 est.)
64.738 (2019 est.)

ENERGY

Electricity access: *electrification - total population:* 100% (2022 est.)
electrification - urban areas: 99.1%
electrification - rural areas: 100%

Electricity: *installed generating capacity:* 301.926 million kW (2023 est.)
consumption: 1.011 trillion kWh (2023 est.)
exports: 18.66 billion kWh (2023 est.)
imports: 2.852 billion kWh (2023 est.)
transmission/distribution losses: 97.301 billion kWh (2023 est.)
comparison rankings: installed generating capacity 5; consumption 4; exports 15; imports 62; transmission/distribution losses 207

Electricity generation sources: *fossil fuels:* 61.8% of total installed capacity (2023 est.)
nuclear: 19.3% of total installed capacity (2023 est.)
solar: 0.2% of total installed capacity (2023 est.)
wind: 0.7% of total installed capacity (2023 est.)
hydroelectricity: 17.6% of total installed capacity (2023 est.)
biomass and waste: 0.3% of total installed capacity (2023 est.)

Nuclear energy: Number of operational nuclear reactors: 36 (2025)

Number of nuclear reactors under construction: 4 (2025)

Net capacity of operational nuclear reactors: 26.8GW (2025 est.)

Percent of total electricity production: 18.4% (2023 est.)

Number of nuclear reactors permanently shut down: 11 (2025)

Coal: *production:* 531.13 million metric tons (2023 est.)
consumption: 290.763 million metric tons (2023 est.)
exports: 211.944 million metric tons (2023 est.)
imports: 20.765 million metric tons (2023 est.)
proven reserves: 162.166 billion metric tons (2023 est.)

Petroleum: *total petroleum production:* 10.879 million bbl/day (2023 est.)
refined petroleum consumption: 3.863 million bbl/day (2023 est.)
crude oil estimated reserves: 80 billion barrels (2021 est.)

Natural gas: *production:* 613.447 billion cubic meters (2023 est.)
consumption: 474.448 billion cubic meters (2023 est.)
exports: 124.479 billion cubic meters (2023 est.)
imports: 5.724 billion cubic meters (2023 est.)
proven reserves: 47.805 trillion cubic meters (2021 est.)

Energy consumption per capita: 224.858 million Btu/person (2023 est.)
comparison ranking: 14

COMMUNICATIONS

Telephones - fixed lines: *total subscriptions:* 20,816,300 (2023 est.)
subscriptions per 100 inhabitants: 15 (2022 est.)
comparison ranking: total subscriptions 12

Telephones - mobile cellular: *total subscriptions:* 245 million (2022 est.)
subscriptions per 100 inhabitants: 169 (2021 est.)
comparison ranking: total subscriptions 5

Broadcast media: *13 national TV stations:* the federal government owns 1 and controls a second, state-owned Gazprom controls 2, state-affiliated Bank Rossiya controls 2, Moscow city administration runs 1, the Russian Orthodox Church owns 1, and the Russian military owns 1; around 3,300 national, regional, and local TV stations, with over two-thirds completely or partially state-controlled; satellite TV available; 2 state-run national radio networks, with a third majority-owned by Gazprom; around 2,400 public and commercial radio stations

Internet country code: .ru

Internet users: *percent of population:* 92% (2023 est.)

Broadband - fixed subscriptions: *total:* 35.9 million (2022 est.)
subscriptions per 100 inhabitants: 25 (2022 est.)
comparison ranking: total 7

TRANSPORTATION

Civil aircraft registration country code prefix: RA

Airports: 905 (2025)
comparison ranking: 8

Heliports: 494 (2025)
comparison ranking: 6

Railways: *total:* 85,494 km (2019)
narrow gauge: 957 km

Merchant marine: *total:* 2,910 (2023)
by type: bulk carrier 15, container ship 20, general cargo 976, oil tanker 387, other 1,512
comparison ranking: total 9

Ports: *total ports:* 67 (2024)
large: 4
medium: 5
small: 19
very small: 38
size unknown: 1
ports with oil terminals: 32
key ports: Arkhangels'k, De Kastri, Dudinka, Kaliningrad, Murmansk, Novorossiysk, Sankt-Peterburg, Vladivostok, Vyborg

MILITARY AND SECURITY

Military and security forces: Armed Forces of the Russian Federation: Ground Forces (SV), Aerospace Forces (VKS), Navy (VMF); separate or independent troop branches include the Airborne Forces (VDV), Missile Troops of Strategic Purpose (RVSN; commonly to as Strategic Rocket Forces), Special Operations Forces, and Unmanned Systems Forces
Federal National Guard Troops Service of the Russian Federation (FSVNG, National Guard, Russian Guard, or Rosgvardiya)

Federal Security Services (FSB): Federal Border Guard Service (includes land and maritime forces) (2025)
note 1: the Unmanned Systems Forces were established in 2025
note 2: the National Guard was created in 2016 as an independent agency for internal/regime security, combating terrorism and narcotics trafficking, protecting important state facilities and government personnel, and supporting border security; it also works closely with the Armed Forces; forces under the National Guard include the Special Purpose Mobile Units (OMON), Special Rapid Response Detachment (SOBR), and Interior Troops (VV)
note 3: the Ministry of Internal Affairs, Federal Security Service, Investigative Committee, Office of the Prosecutor General, and National Guard are responsible for law enforcement; the Federal Security Service is responsible for state security, counterintelligence, and counterterrorism, as well as for fighting organized crime and corruption; the Ministry of Internal Affairs includes the national police force

Military expenditures: 7% of GDP (2024 est.)
5% of GDP (2023 est.)
4.5% of GDP (2022 est.)
4% of GDP (2021 est.)
4% of GDP (2020 est.)

Military and security service personnel strengths: estimated 1.1-1.2 million active Armed Forces; estimated 350,000 Federal National Guard Troops (2025)
note: in September 2024, President PUTIN ordered the Russian military to increase in size to 1.5 million personnel

Military equipment inventories and acquisitions: the Russian Federation's military and paramilitary services are equipped with domestically produced weapons systems, although in recent years Russia has imported considerable amounts of military hardware from external suppliers such as Iran and North Korea; the Russian defense industry is capable of designing, developing, and producing a full range of advanced air, land, missile, and naval systems; Russia is the world's second largest exporter of military hardware (2024)

Military service age and obligation: 18-30 years of age for compulsory service for men; 18-40 for voluntary/contractual service; women and non-Russian citizens (18-30) may volunteer; 12-month service obligation (Russia offers the option of serving on a 24-month contract instead of completing a 12-month conscription period) (2024)
note 1: in 2022, Russia's parliament approved a law removing the upper age limit for contractual service in the military; also in 2022, President Vladimir PUTIN signed a decree allowing dual-national Russians and those with permanent residency status in foreign countries to be drafted into the army for military service
note 2: historically, the Russian military has taken in about 260,000 conscripts each year in two semi-annual drafts (Spring and Fall)
note 3: prior to the full-scale invasion of Ukraine in 2022, approximately 40-45,000 women served in the Russian Armed Forces
note 4: since 2015, foreigners 18-30 with a good command of Russian have been allowed to join the military on five-year contracts and become eligible for Russian citizenship after serving three years; in October 2022, the Interior Ministry opened up recruitment centers for foreigners to sign a one-year service contract with the armed forces, other troops, or military formations participating in the invasion of Ukraine with the promise of simplifying the process of obtaining Russian citizenship

Military deployments: estimated 600,000 in Ukraine; more than 20,000 additional military personnel deployed in former Soviet states and elsewhere, including Armenia, Belarus, Georgia, Kyrgyzstan, Libya, Moldova, Syria, sub-Saharan Africa, and Tajikistan (2025)
note: Russia is also assessed to have thousands of paramilitary security personnel and private military contractors deployed in Africa, including in Burkina Faso, Central African Republic, Libya, Mali, Niger, and Sudan

Military - note: the Russian military is responsible for protecting the country's sovereignty and territorial integrity, providing maritime security, and supporting Moscow's national security objectives, including projecting influence and power abroad and deterring perceived external threats; its missions include air, land, maritime, strategic missile, and expeditionary operations; it is also active in the areas of cyber warfare, electronic warfare, and space; the Russian military's focus is its ongoing war on Ukraine and the perceived threat from NATO and the US
in February 2022, Russia launched a full-scale military invasion of Ukraine, beginning what is the largest war in Europe since World War II ended in 1945; Russian military forces occupied Ukraine's province of Crimea in 2014, and Moscow subsequently backed separatist forces in the Donbas region of Ukraine with arms, equipment, and training, as well as Russian military troops, although Moscow denied their presence prior to 2022
Russia intervened in the Syrian civil war at the request of the Syrian Government from September 2015 until the collapse of the ASAD regime in December 2024; it was Moscow's first overseas military expeditionary operation since the Soviet era; Russian assistance included air support, arms and equipment, intelligence, military advisors, private military contractors, special operations forces, and training; Russia seized the Georgian regions of Abkhazia and South Ossetia by force in 2008 (2025)

SPACE

Space agency/agencies: State Space Corporation of the Russian Federation (Roscosmos; established 2015); Russian Space Forces (Kosmicheskie voyska Rossii, KV; under the Russian Aerospace Forces) (2025)
note 1: Russia's space strategy is defined jointly by Roscosmos and the Ministry of Defense
note 2: Roscosmos was established from a merger of the Federal Space Agency and the state-owned United Rocket and Space Corporation; it began as the Russian Space Agency (RSA or RKA) in 1992 and restructured in 1999 and 2004 as the Russian Aviation and Space Agency and then the Federal Space Agency

Space launch site(s): Baikonur Cosmodrome (Kazakhstan); Vostochny Cosmodrome (Amur Oblast); Plesetsk Cosmodrome (Arkhangel'sk Oblast) (2025)
note 1: the Baikonur cosmodrome and the surrounding area are leased and administered by Russia until 2050 for approximately $115 million/year; the cosmodrome was originally built by the Soviet Union in the mid-1950s and is the site of the World's first successful satellite launch (Sputnik) in 1957; it is also the largest space launch facility in the World, comprising 15 launch pads for space launch vehicles, four launch pads for testing intercontinental ballistic missiles, more than 10 assembly and test facilities, and other infrastructure
note 2: in 2018, Kazakhstan and Russia agreed that Kazakhstan would build, maintain, and operate a new space launch facility (Baiterek) at the Baikonur space center (estimated to be ready for operations in 2025)

Space program overview: has one of the world's largest space programs and is active across all areas of the space sector; builds, launches, and operates rockets/

space launch vehicles (SLVs), satellites, space stations, interplanetary probes, and manned, robotic, and re-usable spacecraft; has astronaut (cosmonaut) training program and conducts human space flight; researching and developing a broad range of other space-related technologies; participates in international space programs such as the International Space Station (ISS); prior to Russia's 2022 full-scale invasion of Ukraine, Russia had relations with dozens of foreign space agencies and commercial entities, including those of China, the European Space Agency (ESA), India, Japan, and the US; Roscosmos and its public subsidiaries comprise the majority of the Russian space industry; Roscosmos has eight operating areas, including manned space flights, launch systems, unmanned spacecraft, rocket propulsion, military missiles, space avionics, special military space systems, and flight control systems; private companies are also involved in a range of space systems, including satellites, telecommunications, remote-sensing, and geo-spatial services (2024)
note: further details about the key activities, programs, and milestones of the country's space program, as well as government spending estimates on the space sector, appear in the Space Programs reference guide

TERRORISM

Terrorist group(s): Terrorist group(s): Islamic State of Iraq and ash-Sham (ISIS)
note: details about the history, aims, leadership, organization, areas of operation, tactics, targets, weapons, size, and sources of support of the group(s) appear(s) in Appendix T

TRANSNATIONAL ISSUES

Refugees and internally displaced persons: *refugees:* 11,440 (2024 est.)

IDPs: 172,783 (2024 est.)
stateless persons: 90,185 (2024 est.)

Trafficking in persons: *tier rating:* Tier 3 — Russia does not fully meet the minimum standards for the elimination of trafficking and is not making significant efforts to do so, therefore, Russia remained on Tier 3; for more details, go to: https://www.state.gov/reports/2025-trafficking-in-persons-report/russia/

RWANDA

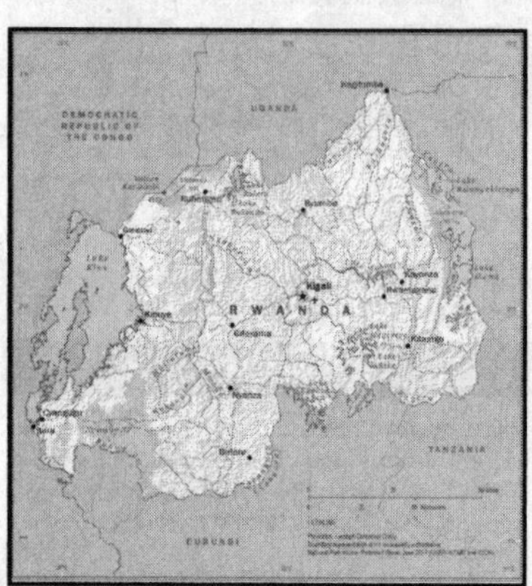

INTRODUCTION

Background: Rwanda – a small and centralized country dominated by rugged hills and fertile volcanic soil – has exerted disproportionate influence over the African Great Lakes region for centuries. A Rwandan kingdom increasingly dominated the region from the mid-18th century onward, with the Tutsi monarchs gradually extending the power of the royal court into peripheral areas and expanding their borders through military conquest. While the current ethnic labels Hutu and Tutsi predate colonial rule, their flexibility and importance have varied significantly over time and often manifested more as a hierarchical class distinction than an ethnic or cultural distinction. The majority Hutu and minority Tutsi have long shared a common language and culture, and intermarriage was frequent.

The Rwandan royal court centered on the Tutsi king (*mwami*), who relied on an extensive network of political, cultural, and economic relationships. Social categories became more rigid during the reign of RWABUGIRI (1860-1895), who focused on aggressive expansion and solidifying Rwanda's bureaucratic structures. German colonial conquest began in the late 1890s, but the territory was ceded to Belgian forces in 1916 during World War I. Both European nations quickly realized the benefits of ruling through the already centralized Rwandan Tutsi kingdom. Colonial rule reinforced existing trends toward autocratic and exclusionary rule, leading to the elimination of traditional positions of authority for Hutus. Belgian administrators significantly increased requirements for communal labor and instituted harsh taxes, which fed the population's frustration. Changing political attitudes in Belgium contributed to colonial and Catholic officials shifting their support from Tutsi to Hutu leaders in the years leading up to independence.

Simmering resentment of minority rule exploded in 1959, three years before independence from Belgium, when Hutus overthrew the Tutsi king. Thousands of Tutsis were killed over the next several years, and some 150,000 were driven into exile in neighboring countries. Army Chief of Staff Juvenal HABYARIMANA seized power in a coup in 1973 and ruled Rwanda as a single-party state for two decades. HABYARIMANA increasingly discriminated against Tutsis, and extremist Hutu factions gained prominence after multiple parties were introduced in the early 1990s. The children of Tutsi exiles later formed a rebel group, the Rwandan Patriotic Front (RPF) and began a civil war in 1990. The civil war exacerbated ethnic tensions and culminated in the shooting down of HABYARIMANA's private jet in 1994. The event sparked a state-orchestrated genocide in which Rwandans killed more than 800,000 of their fellow citizens, including approximately three-quarters of the Tutsi population. The genocide ended later the same year when the predominantly Tutsi RPF, operating out of Uganda and northern Rwanda, defeated the national army and Hutu militias and established an RPF-led government of national unity. Rwanda held its first local elections in 1999 and its first post-genocide presidential and legislative elections in 2003, formalizing President Paul KAGAME's de facto role as head of government. KAGAME was formally elected in 2010, and again in 2017 after changing the constitution to allow him to run for a third term.

GEOGRAPHY

Location: Central Africa, east of the Democratic Republic of the Congo, north of Burundi

Geographic coordinates: 2 00 S, 30 00 E

Map references: Africa

Area: *total:* 26,338 sq km
land: 24,668 sq km
water: 1,670 sq km
comparison ranking: total 148

Area - comparative: slightly smaller than Maryland

Land boundaries: *total:* 930 km
border countries (4): Burundi 315 km; Democratic Republic of the Congo 221 km; Tanzania 222 km; Uganda 172 km

Coastline: 0 km (landlocked)

Maritime claims: none (landlocked)

Climate: temperate; two rainy seasons (February to April, November to January); mild in mountains with frost and snow possible

Terrain: mostly grassy uplands and hills; relief is mountainous with altitude declining from west to east

Elevation: *highest point:* Volcan Karisimbi 4,519 m
lowest point: Rusizi River 950 m
mean elevation: 1,598 m

Natural resources: gold, cassiterite (tin ore), wolframite (tungsten ore), methane, hydropower, arable land

Land use: *agricultural land:* 81.3% (2022 est.)
arable land: 51.4% (2022 est.)
permanent crops: 14.2% (2022 est.)
permanent pasture: 15.6% (2022 est.)
forest: 11.3% (2022 est.)
other: 7.5% (2022 est.)

Irrigated land: 96 sq km (2012)

Major lakes (area sq km): *fresh water lake(s):* Lake Kivu (shared with Democratic Republic of Congo) - 2,220 sq km

Major rivers (by length in km): Nile river source (shared with Tanzania, Uganda, South Sudan, Sudan, and Egypt [m]) - 6,650 km
note: [s] after country name indicates river source; [m] after country name indicates river mouth

Major watersheds (area sq km): Atlantic Ocean drainage: Congo (3,730,881 sq km), *(Mediterranean Sea)* Nile (3,254,853 sq km)

Population distribution: one of Africa's most densely populated countries; large concentrations tend to be in the central regions and along the shore of Lake

Kivu in the west, as shown in this population distribution map

Natural hazards: periodic droughts; the volcanic Virunga Mountains are in the northwest along the border with Democratic Republic of the Congo
volcanism: Visoke (3,711 m), on the border with the Democratic Republic of the Congo, is the country's only historically active volcano

Geography - note: landlocked; most of the country is intensively cultivated and rugged, with the population predominantly rural

PEOPLE AND SOCIETY

Population: *total:* 13,623,302 (2024 est.)
male: 6,684,655
female: 6,938,647
comparison rankings: total 76; male 78; female 76

Nationality: *noun:* Rwandan(s)
adjective: Rwandan

Ethnic groups: Hutu, Tutsi, Twa

Languages: Kinyarwanda (official, universal Bantu vernacular) 93.2%, French (official) <0.1%, English (official) <0.1%, Swahili/Kiswahili (official, used in commercial centers) <0.1%, more than one language, other 6.3%, unspecified 0.3% (2002 est.)
major-language sample(s):
Inkoranya nzimbuzi y'isi, isoko fatizo y'amakuru y'ibanze. (Kinyarwanda)

Religions: Christian 95.9% (Protestant 57.7% [includes Adventist 12.6%], Roman Catholic 38.2%), Muslim 2.1%, other 1% (includes traditional, Jehovah's Witness), none 1.1% (2019-20 est.)

Age structure: *0-14 years:* 37.2% (male 2,561,884/female 2,508,218)
15-64 years: 59.7% (male 3,954,608/female 4,179,844)
65 years and over: 3.1% (2024 est.) (male 168,163/female 250,585)

Dependency ratios: *total dependency ratio:* 67.5 (2024 est.)
youth dependency ratio: 62.3 (2024 est.)
elderly dependency ratio: 5.1 (2024 est.)
potential support ratio: 19.4 (2024 est.)

Median age: *total:* 20.8 years (2024 est.)
male: 20.1 years
female: 21.5 years
comparison ranking: total 198

Population growth rate: 1.62% (2024 est.)
comparison ranking: 58

Birth rate: 25 births/1,000 population (2024 est.)
comparison ranking: 46

Death rate: 5.7 deaths/1,000 population (2024 est.)
comparison ranking: 169

Net migration rate: -3.1 migrant(s)/1,000 population (2024 est.)
comparison ranking: 182

Population distribution: one of Africa's most densely populated countries; large concentrations tend to be in the central regions and along the shore of Lake Kivu in the west, as shown in this population distribution map

Urbanization: *urban population:* 17.9% of total population (2023)
rate of urbanization: 3.07% annual rate of change (2020-25 est.)

Major urban areas - population: 1.248 million KIGALI (capital) (2023)

Sex ratio: *at birth:* 1.03 male(s)/female
0-14 years: 1.02 male(s)/female
15-64 years: 0.95 male(s)/female
65 years and over: 0.67 male(s)/female
total population: 0.96 male(s)/female (2024 est.)

Mother's mean age at first birth: 23 years (2019/20 est.)
note: data represents median age at first birth among women 25-49

Maternal mortality ratio: 229 deaths/100,000 live births (2023 est.)
comparison ranking: 35

Infant mortality rate: *total:* 24.9 deaths/1,000 live births (2024 est.)
male: 27.3 deaths/1,000 live births
female: 22.5 deaths/1,000 live births
comparison ranking: total 60

Life expectancy at birth: *total population:* 66.6 years (2024 est.)
male: 64.6 years
female: 68.6 years
comparison ranking: total population 200

Total fertility rate: 3.14 children born/woman (2024 est.)
comparison ranking: 46

Gross reproduction rate: 1.54 (2024 est.)

Drinking water source: *improved: urban:* 88.1% of population (2022 est.)
rural: 60.1% of population (2022 est.)
total: 65.1% of population (2022 est.)
unimproved: urban: 11.9% of population (2022 est.)
rural: 39.9% of population (2022 est.)
total: 34.9% of population (2022 est.)

Health expenditure: 7.3% of GDP (2021)
9.5% of national budget (2022 est.)

Physician density: 0.09 physicians/1,000 population (2022)

Hospital bed density: 0.7 beds/1,000 population (2020 est.)

Sanitation facility access: *improved: urban:* 91.4% of population (2022 est.)
rural: 87% of population (2022 est.)
total: 87.8% of population (2022 est.)
unimproved: urban: 8.6% of population (2022 est.)
rural: 13% of population (2022 est.)
total: 12.2% of population (2022 est.)

Obesity - adult prevalence rate: 5.8% (2016)
comparison ranking: 172

Alcohol consumption per capita: *total:* 6.35 liters of pure alcohol (2019 est.)
beer: 0.23 liters of pure alcohol (2019 est.)
wine: 0.03 liters of pure alcohol (2019 est.)
spirits: 0.09 liters of pure alcohol (2019 est.)
other alcohols: 6 liters of pure alcohol (2019 est.)
comparison ranking: total 65

Tobacco use: *total:* 11.4% (2025 est.)
male: 17% (2025 est.)
female: 6.3% (2025 est.)
comparison ranking: total 120

Children under the age of 5 years underweight: 7.7% (2019/20)
comparison ranking: 56

Currently married women (ages 15-49): 50.4% (2023 est.)

Child marriage: *women married by age 15:* 0.3% (2020)
women married by age 18: 5.5% (2020)
men married by age 18: 0.4% (2020)

Education expenditure: 4.7% of GDP (2024 est.)
13.9% national budget (2025 est.)
comparison ranking: Education expenditure (% GDP) 78

Literacy: *total population:* 79% (2022 est.)
male: 81% (2022 est.)
female: 77% (2022 est.)

School life expectancy (primary to tertiary education): *total:* 13 years (2023 est.)
male: 13 years (2023 est.)
female: 13 years (2023 est.)

ENVIRONMENT

Environmental issues: deforestation; overgrazing; land degradation; soil erosion; a decline in soil fertility (soil exhaustion); wetland degradation and loss of biodiversity; widespread poaching

International environmental agreements: *party to:* Biodiversity, Climate Change, Climate Change-Kyoto Protocol, Comprehensive Nuclear Test Ban, Desertification, Endangered Species, Hazardous Wastes, Nuclear Test Ban, Ozone Layer Protection, Wetlands
signed, but not ratified: Law of the Sea

Climate: temperate; two rainy seasons (February to April, November to January); mild in mountains with frost and snow possible

Urbanization: *urban population:* 17.9% of total population (2023)
rate of urbanization: 3.07% annual rate of change (2020-25 est.)

Carbon dioxide emissions: 1.645 million metric tonnes of CO2 (2023 est.)
from coal and metallurgical coke: 226,000 metric tonnes of CO2 (2023 est.)
from petroleum and other liquids: 1.295 million metric tonnes of CO2 (2023 est.)
from consumed natural gas: 124,000 metric tonnes of CO2 (2023 est.)
comparison ranking: total emissions 163

Particulate matter emissions: 35.7 micrograms per cubic meter (2019 est.)

Waste and recycling: *municipal solid waste generated annually:* 4.385 million tons (2024 est.)
percent of municipal solid waste recycled: 11.5% (2022 est.)

Total water withdrawal: *municipal:* 230 million cubic meters (2022 est.)
industrial: 10 million cubic meters (2022 est.)
agricultural: 361 million cubic meters (2022 est.)

Total renewable water resources: 13.3 billion cubic meters (2022 est.)

GOVERNMENT

Country name: *conventional long form:* Republic of Rwanda
conventional short form: Rwanda
local long form: Republika y'u Rwanda
local short form: Rwanda
former: Kingdom of Rwanda, Ruanda, German East Africa
etymology: the country is named for a local people, but the meaning of their own name is obscure

Government type: presidential republic

Capital: *name:* Kigali
geographic coordinates: 1 57 S, 30 03 E

time difference: UTC+2 (7 hours ahead of Washington, DC, during Standard Time)
etymology: the city takes its name from nearby Mount Kigali; the name is composed of the Bantu prefix *ki-* and the Rwandan word *gali*, meaning "broad," which is probably meant to describe the terrain

Administrative divisions: 4 provinces (*provinces*, singular - *province* (French); *intara* for singular and plural (Kinyarwanda)) and 1 city* (*ville* (French); *umujyi* (Kinyarwanda)); Est (Eastern), Kigali*, Nord (Northern), Ouest (Western), Sud (Southern)

Legal system: mixed system of civil law, based on German and Belgian models, and customary law; Supreme Court reviews legislative acts

Constitution: *history:* several previous; latest adopted by referendum 26 May 2003, effective 4 June 2003
amendment process: proposed by the president of the republic (with Council of Ministers approval) or by two-thirds majority vote of both houses of Parliament; passage requires at least three-quarters majority vote in both houses; changes to constitutional articles on national sovereignty, the presidential term, the form and system of government, and political pluralism also require approval in a referendum

International law organization participation: has not submitted an ICJ jurisdiction declaration; non-party state to the ICCt

Citizenship: *citizenship by birth:* no
citizenship by descent only: the father must be a citizen of Rwanda; if the father is stateless or unknown, the mother must be a citizen
dual citizenship recognized: no
residency requirement for naturalization: 10 years

Suffrage: 18 years of age; universal

Executive branch: *chief of state:* President Paul KAGAME (since 22 April 2000)
head of government: Prime Minister Justin NSENGIYUMVA (since 23 July 2025)
cabinet: Council of Ministers appointed by the president
election/appointment process: president directly elected by simple-majority popular vote for a 5-year term (eligible for a second term); prime minister appointed by the president
most recent election date: 4 August 2017
election results: *2024:* Paul KAGAME reelected president; Paul KAGAME (RPF) 99.2%, Frank HABINEZA (DGPR) 0.5%, Philippe MPAYIMANA (independent) 0.3%
2017: Paul KAGAME reelected president; Paul KAGAME (RPF) 98.8%, Philippe MPAYIMANA (independent), other 1.2%
expected date of next election: 15 July 2029
note: a constitutional amendment in 2016 reduced the presidential term from 7 to 5 years but included an exception that allowed President KAGAME to serve another 7-year term in 2017, potentially followed by two additional 5-year terms

Legislative branch: *legislature name:* Parlement (Parliament)
legislative structure: bicameral

Legislative branch - lower chamber: *chamber name:* Chamber of Deputies (Chambre des Députés)
number of seats: 80 (53 directly elected; 27 indirectly elected)
electoral system: proportional representation
scope of elections: full renewal
term in office: 5 years
most recent election date: 7/15/2024 to 7/16/2024
parties elected and seats per party: Rwandan Patriotic Front (FPR) and its allies (37); Liberal Party (PL) (5); Social Democratic Party (PSD) (5); Other (6)
percentage of women in chamber: 63.8%
expected date of next election: July 2029
note: 24 women are selected for seats by special-interest groups, and 3 members are selected by youth and disability organizations

Legislative branch - upper chamber: *chamber name:* Senate (Sénat)
number of seats: 26 (18 indirectly elected; 8 appointed)
scope of elections: full renewal
term in office: 5 years
most recent election date: 9/16/2024 to 9/17/2024
percentage of women in chamber: 53.8%
expected date of next election: September 2029

Judicial branch: *highest court(s):* Supreme Court (consists of the chief and deputy chief justices and 5 judges; normally organized into 3-judge panels); High Court (consists of the court president, vice president, and a minimum of 24 judges and organized into 5 chambers)
judge selection and term of office: Supreme Court judges nominated by the president after consultation with the Cabinet and the Superior Council of the Judiciary (SCJ), a 27-member body of judges, other judicial officials, and legal professionals, and approved by the Senate; chief and deputy chief justices appointed for 8-year nonrenewable terms; tenure of judges NA; High Court president and vice president appointed by the president of the republic upon approval by the Senate; judges appointed by the Supreme Court chief justice upon approval of the SCJ; judge tenure NA
subordinate courts: High Court of the Republic; commercial courts including the High Commercial Court; intermediate courts; primary courts; and military specialized courts

Political parties: Democratic Green Party of Rwanda or DGPR
Liberal Party or PL
Party for Progress and Concord or PPC
Rwandan Patriotic Front or RPF
Rwandan Patriotic Front Coalition (includes RPF, PPC, PSP, UDPR, PDI, PSR, PDC)
Social Democratic Party or PSD
Social Party Imberakuri or PS-Imberakuri

Diplomatic representation in the US: *chief of mission:* Ambassador Mathilde MUKANTABANA (since 18 July 2013)
chancery: 1714 New Hampshire Avenue NW, Washington, DC 20009
telephone: [1] (202) 232-2882
FAX: [1] (202) 232-4544
email address and website: info@rwandaembassy.org
https://rwandaembassy.org/

Diplomatic representation from the US: *chief of mission:* Ambassador Eric KNEEDLER (since 3 October 2023)
embassy: 2657 Avenue de la Gendarmerie (Kaciyiru), P. O. Box 28 Kigali
mailing address: 2210 Kigali Place, Washington DC 20521-2210
telephone: [250] 252 596-400
FAX: [250] 252 580-325
email address and website: consularkigali@state.gov
https://rw.usembassy.gov/

International organization participation: ACP, AfDB, AU, CEPGL, COMESA, EAC, EADB, FAO, G-77, IAEA, IBRD, ICAO, ICRM, IDA, IFAD, IFC, IFRCS, ILO, IMF, Interpol, IOC, IOM, IPU, ISO, ITSO, ITU, ITUC (NGOs), MIGA, MINUSMA, NAM, OIF, OPCW, PCA, UN, UNCTAD, UNESCO, UNHCR, UNIDO, UNISFA, UNMISS, UNOOSA, UNWTO, UPU, WCO, WHO, WIPO, WMO, WTO

Independence: 1 July 1962 (from Belgium-administered UN trusteeship)

National holiday: Independence Day, 1 July (1962)

Flag: *description:* three horizontal bands of sky blue (top, double-width), yellow, and green, with a golden sun with 24 rays on the right end of the blue band
meaning: blue stands for happiness and peace, yellow for economic development and mineral wealth, and green for hope for prosperity and natural resources; the sun symbolizes unity and enlightenment

National symbol(s): traditional woven basket with peaked lid

National color(s): blue, yellow, green

National anthem(s): *title:* "Rwanda nziza" (Rwanda, Our Beautiful Country)
lyrics/music: Faustin MURIGO/Jean-Bosco HASHAKAIMANA
history: adopted 2001

National heritage: *total World Heritage Sites:* 2 (1 cultural, 1 natural)
selected World Heritage Site locales: Memorial sites of the Genocide: Nyamata, Murambi, Gisozi and Bisesero (c); Nyungwe National Park (n)

ECONOMY

Economic overview: fast-growing Sub-Saharan economy; major public investments; trade and tourism hit hard by COVID-19; increasing poverty after 2 decades of declines; Ugandan competition for regional influence; major coffee exporter; contested GDP figures

Real GDP (purchasing power parity): $46.543 billion (2024 est.)
$42.743 billion (2023 est.)
$39.485 billion (2022 est.)
note: data in 2021 dollars
comparison ranking: 133

Real GDP growth rate: 8.9% (2024 est.)
8.2% (2023 est.)
8.2% (2022 est.)
note: annual GDP % growth based on constant local currency
comparison ranking: 7

Real GDP per capita: $3,300 (2024 est.)
$3,100 (2023 est.)
$2,900 (2022 est.)
note: data in 2021 dollars
comparison ranking: 191

GDP (official exchange rate): $14.252 billion (2024 est.)
note: data in current dollars at official exchange rate

Inflation rate (consumer prices): 1.8% (2024 est.)
19.8% (2023 est.)
17.7% (2022 est.)
note: annual % change based on consumer prices
comparison ranking: 45

GDP - composition, by sector of origin: *agriculture:* 24.6% (2024 est.)
industry: 21% (2024 est.)
services: 47.6% (2024 est.)
note: figures may not total 100% due to non-allocated consumption not captured in sector-reported data

comparison rankings: agriculture 21; industry 126; services 160

GDP - composition, by end use: *household consumption:* 64.9% (2024 est.)
government consumption: 17.1% (2024 est.)
investment in fixed capital: 29.1% (2024 est.)
investment in inventories: -3.2% (2024 est.)
exports of goods and services: 30.8% (2024 est.)
imports of goods and services: -39.1% (2024 est.)
note: figures may not total 100% due to rounding or gaps in data collection

Agricultural products: bananas, cassava, sweet potatoes, plantains, potatoes, maize, beans, pumpkins/squash, taro, sorghum (2023)
note: top ten agricultural products based on tonnage

Industries: cement, agricultural products, small-scale beverages, soap, furniture, shoes, plastic goods, textiles, cigarettes

Industrial production growth rate: 10% (2024 est.)
note: annual % change in industrial value added based on constant local currency
comparison ranking: 9

Labor force: 5.671 million (2024 est.)
note: number of people ages 15 or older who are employed or seeking work
comparison ranking: 78

Unemployment rate: 12% (2024 est.)
12.4% (2023 est.)
15.1% (2022 est.)
note: % of labor force seeking employment
comparison ranking: 164

Youth unemployment rate (ages 15-24): *total:* 17.5% (2024 est.)
male: 15.8% (2024 est.)
female: 19.4% (2024 est.)
note: % of labor force ages 15-24 seeking employment
comparison ranking: total 65

Population below poverty line: 38.2% (2016 est.)
note: % of population with income below national poverty line

Gini Index coefficient - distribution of family income: 43.7 (2016 est.)
note: index (0-100) of income distribution; higher values represent greater inequality
comparison ranking: 24

Household income or consumption by percentage share: *lowest 10%:* 2.4% (2016 est.)
highest 10%: 35.6% (2016 est.)
note: % share of income accruing to lowest and highest 10% of population

Remittances: 3.6% of GDP (2023 est.)
3.6% of GDP (2022 est.)
3.5% of GDP (2021 est.)
note: personal transfers and compensation between resident and non-resident individuals/households/entities

Budget: *revenues:* $3.41 billion (2023 est.)
expenditures: $3.996 billion (2023 est.)
note: central government revenues (excluding grants) and expenditures converted to US dollars at average official exchange rate for year indicated

Taxes and other revenues: 13.5% (of GDP) (2023 est.)
note: central government tax revenue as a % of GDP
comparison ranking: 102

Current account balance: -$1.654 billion (2023 est.)
-$1.246 billion (2022 est.)
-$1.209 billion (2021 est.)
note: balance of payments - net trade and primary/secondary income in current dollars
comparison ranking: 142

Exports: $3.509 billion (2023 est.)
$2.993 billion (2022 est.)
$2.11 billion (2021 est.)
note: balance of payments - exports of goods and services in current dollars
comparison ranking: 152

Exports - partners: UAE 66%, China 10%, USA 3%, Kenya 3%, Thailand 2% (2023)
note: top five export partners based on percentage share of exports

Exports - commodities: gold, rare earth ores, coffee, tea, tin ores (2023)
note: top five export commodities based on value in dollars

Imports: $5.783 billion (2023 est.)
$4.978 billion (2022 est.)
$3.856 billion (2021 est.)
note: balance of payments - imports of goods and services in current dollars
comparison ranking: 147

Imports - partners: China 19%, Kenya 14%, Uganda 13%, Tanzania 9%, UAE 7% (2023)
note: top five import partners based on percentage share of imports

Imports - commodities: broadcasting equipment, fish, corn, packaged medicine, plastic products (2023)
note: top five import commodities based on value in dollars

Reserves of foreign exchange and gold: $2.406 billion (2024 est.)
$1.834 billion (2023 est.)
$1.726 billion (2022 est.)
note: holdings of gold (year-end prices)/foreign exchange/special drawing rights in current dollars
comparison ranking: 123

Debt - external: $5.531 billion (2023 est.)
note: present value of external debt in current US dollars
comparison ranking: 70

Exchange rates: Rwandan francs (RWF) per US dollar -

Exchange rates: 1,318.128 (2024 est.)
1,160.099 (2023 est.)
1,030.308 (2022 est.)
988.625 (2021 est.)
943.278 (2020 est.)

ENERGY

Electricity access: *electrification - total population:* 50.6% (2022 est.)
electrification - urban areas: 98%
electrification - rural areas: 38.2%

Electricity: *installed generating capacity:* 294,000 kW (2023 est.)
consumption: 876.401 million kWh (2023 est.)
exports: 8.674 million kWh (2023 est.)
imports: 32 million kWh (2023 est.)
transmission/distribution losses: 197.606 million kWh (2023 est.)
comparison rankings: installed generating capacity 165; consumption 162; exports 99; imports 119; transmission/distribution losses 64

Electricity generation sources: *fossil fuels:* 43.6% of total installed capacity (2023 est.)
solar: 3.4% of total installed capacity (2023 est.)
hydroelectricity: 52.8% of total installed capacity (2023 est.)
biomass and waste: 0.2% of total installed capacity (2023 est.)

Coal: *consumption:* 123,000 metric tons (2023 est.)
imports: 89,000 metric tons (2023 est.)

Petroleum: *refined petroleum consumption:* 9,000 bbl/day (2023 est.)

Natural gas: *production:* 63.666 million cubic meters (2023 est.)
consumption: 63.696 million cubic meters (2023 est.)
proven reserves: 56.634 billion cubic meters (2021 est.)

Energy consumption per capita: 1.808 million Btu/person (2023 est.)
comparison ranking: 188

COMMUNICATIONS

Telephones - fixed lines: *total subscriptions:* 8,000 (2023 est.)
subscriptions per 100 inhabitants: (2023 est.) less than 1
comparison ranking: total subscriptions 190

Telephones - mobile cellular: *total subscriptions:* 12.8 million (2023 est.)
subscriptions per 100 inhabitants: 80 (2022 est.)
comparison ranking: total subscriptions 81

Broadcast media: 13 TV stations; 35 radio stations, including international broadcasters; government owns most popular TV and radio stations; regional satellite-based TV available

Internet country code: .rw

Internet users: *percent of population:* 34% (2023 est.)

Broadband - fixed subscriptions: *total:* 62,000 (2023 est.)
subscriptions per 100 inhabitants: (2023 est.) less than 1
comparison ranking: total 143

TRANSPORTATION

Civil aircraft registration country code prefix: 9XR

Airports: 8 (2025)
comparison ranking: 165

MILITARY AND SECURITY

Military and security forces: Rwanda Defense Force (RDF; Ingabo z'u Rwanda): Rwanda Army (Rwanda Land Force), Rwanda Air Force (Force Aerienne Rwandaise, FAR), Rwanda Reserve Force, Special Units

Ministry of Internal Security: Rwanda National Police (2025)

Military expenditures: 1.3% of GDP (2024 est.)
1.3% of GDP (2023 est.)
1.4% of GDP (2022 est.)
1.4% of GDP (2021 est.)
1.3% of GDP (2020 est.)

Military and security service personnel strengths: approximately 30-35,000 active Rwanda Defense Forces (2025)

Military equipment inventories and acquisitions: the RDF's inventory includes a mix of older and some modern equipment from suppliers such as China, France, Israel, Russia and the former Soviet Union, South Africa, and Turkey (2024)

Military service age and obligation: 18 years of age for men and women for voluntary military service; no conscription; Rwandan citizenship is required; enlistment is either as contract (5-years, renewable twice) or career professional (2024)
note: as of 2022, women comprised approximately 6% of the Rwanda Defense Force

Military deployments: approximately 3,200 Central African Republic (about 2,200 under MINUSCA, plus some 700 police; approximately 1,000 under a bi-lateral agreement); estimated 3-4,000 Democratic Republic of the Congo; estimated 3,000 Mozambique (bilateral agreement to assist with combating an insurgency; includes both military and police forces); 2,600 (plus about 450 police) South Sudan (UNMISS) (2025)

Military - note: the principle responsibilities of the Rwanda Defense Force (RDF) are ensuring territorial integrity and national sovereignty and preventing infiltrations of illegal armed groups from neighboring countries, particularly the Democratic Republic of the Congo (DRC); since 2021, Rwanda has deployed RDF troops to the border region with the DRC to combat the rebel Democratic Forces for the Liberation of Rwanda (FDLR), which it has accused the DRC of backing; Rwanda has been accused by the DRC, the UN, and the US of deploying RDF troops in the DRC and providing material support to the March 23 Movement (M23, aka Congolese Revolutionary Army) rebel group; the RDF also participates in UN and regional military operations, as well as multinational exercises; it has deployed several thousand RDF troops and police personnel to Mozambique to assist in combating an insurgency since 2021; Rwanda has mutual defense treaties with Kenya and Uganda
the Rwandan Armed Forces (FAR) were established following independence in 1962; after the 1990-1994 civil war and genocide, the victorious Tutsi-dominated Rwandan Patriotic Front's military wing, the Rwandan Patriotic Army (RPA), became the country's military force; the RPA participated in the First (1996-1997) and Second (1998-2003) Congolese Wars; the RPA was renamed the Rwanda Defense Force (RDF) in 2003, by which time it had assumed a more national character with the inclusion of many former Hutu officers as well as newly recruited soldiers (2025)

SPACE

Space agency/agencies: Rwanda Space Agency (L'Agence Spatiale Rwandaise; RSA; established 2020 and approved by legislature in 2021) (2025)

Space program overview: has a small program focused on developing and utilizing space technologies, such as satellite communications and imagery for connectivity, disaster management, security purposes, and socioeconomic development; seeks to establish itself as an African hub for satellite development; operates communications and remote sensing (RS) satellites; the RSA is responsible for regulating and coordinating the country's space activities and encouraging commercial and industrial development; has established ties with the space agencies or industries of several countries, including France, Israel, Japan, Poland, the UAE, and the US, as well as those of the African Space Agency (2025)
note: further details about the key activities, programs, and milestones of the country's space program, as well as government spending estimates on the space sector, appear in the Space Programs reference guide

TRANSNATIONAL ISSUES

Refugees and internally displaced persons: *refugees:* 128,561 (2024 est.)

IDPs: 21,948 (2024 est.)
stateless persons: 14,500 (2024 est.)

Trafficking in persons: *tier rating:* Tier 2 Watch List — the government did not demonstrate overall increasing efforts to eliminate trafficking compared with the previous reporting period, therefore Rwanda remained on Tier 2 Watch List for the second consecutive year; for more details, go to: https://www.state.gov/reports/2025-trafficking-in-persons-report/rwanda

S

SAINT BARTHELEMY

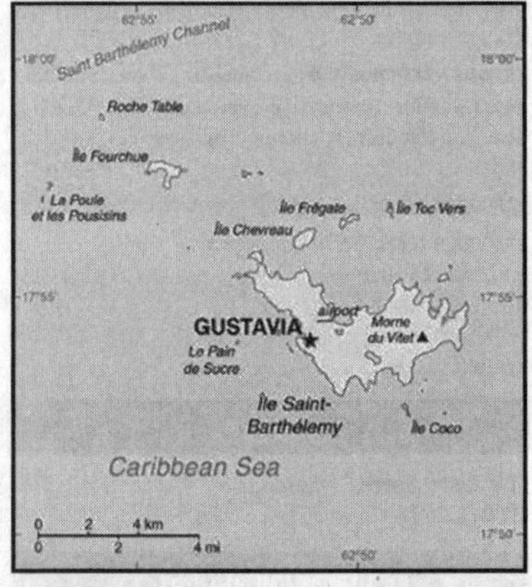

INTRODUCTION

Background: In 1493, Christopher COLUMBUS named Saint Barthelemy for his brother Bartolomeo, but the island was first settled by the French in 1648. In 1784, France sold the island to Sweden, which renamed the largest town Gustavia after the Swedish King GUSTAV III and made it a free port; the island prospered as a trade and supply center during the colonial wars of the 18th century. France repurchased the island in 1877 and took control the following year, placing it under the administration of Guadeloupe. Saint Barthelemy retained its free port status along with various Swedish appellations such as Swedish street and town names, and the three-crown symbol on the coat of arms. In 2003, the islanders voted to secede from Guadeloupe, and in 2007, the island became a French overseas collectivity. In 2012, it became an overseas territory of the EU, allowing it to exert local control over the permanent and temporary immigration of foreign workers, including non-French European citizens. Hurricane Irma hit the island in 2017 and caused extensive damage.

GEOGRAPHY

Location: Caribbean, island between the Caribbean Sea and the North Atlantic Ocean; located in the Leeward Islands (northern) group; Saint Barthelemy lies east of the US Virgin Islands

Geographic coordinates: 17 90 N, 62 85 W

Map references: Central America and the Caribbean

Area: *total:* 25 sq km
land: 25 sq km
water: negligible
comparison ranking: total 237

Area - comparative: less than one-eighth the size of Washington, D.C.

Land boundaries: *total:* 0 km

Climate: tropical, with practically no variation in temperature; has two seasons (dry and humid)

Terrain: hilly, almost completely surrounded by shallow-water reefs, with plentiful beaches

Elevation: *highest point:* Morne du Vitet 286 m
lowest point: Caribbean Sea 0 m

Natural resources: few natural resources; beaches foster tourism

Land use: *agricultural land:* 0% (2022 est.)
forest: 8.5% (2022 est.)
other: 91.5% (2022 est.)

Population distribution: most of the populace is concentrated in and around the capital of Gustavia, but scattered settlements exist around the island's periphery

Geography - note: a 1,200-hectare (3,000-acre) marine nature reserve, the Reserve Naturelle, is made up of five zones around the island that form a network to protect the island's coral reefs, seagrass, and endangered marine species

PEOPLE AND SOCIETY

Population: *total:* 7,086 (2024 est.)
male: 3,737
female: 3,349
comparison rankings: total 225; male 225; female 225

Ethnic groups: French, Portuguese, Caribbean, Afro-Caribbean

Languages: French (primary), English
major-language sample(s):
The World Factbook, une source indispensable d'informations de base. (French)

Religions: Roman Catholic, Protestant, Jehovah's Witnesses

Age structure: *0-14 years:* 13.9% (male 506/female 479)
15-64 years: 63.1% (male 2,413/female 2,057)
65 years and over: 23% (2024 est.) (male 818/female 813)

Dependency ratios: *total dependency ratio:* 58.5 (2024 est.)
youth dependency ratio: 22 (2024 est.)
elderly dependency ratio: 36.5 (2024 est.)
potential support ratio: 2.7 (2024 est.)

Median age: *total:* 47.4 years (2024 est.)
male: 47 years
female: 47.8 years
comparison ranking: total 6

Population growth rate: -0.11% (2024 est.)
comparison ranking: 204

Birth rate: 9.3 births/1,000 population (2024 est.)
comparison ranking: 195

Death rate: 9.5 deaths/1,000 population (2024 est.)
comparison ranking: 47

Net migration rate: -1 migrant(s)/1,000 population (2024 est.)
comparison ranking: 144

Population distribution: most of the populace is concentrated in and around the capital of Gustavia, but scattered settlements exist around the island's periphery

Sex ratio: *at birth:* 1.06 male(s)/female
0-14 years: 1.06 male(s)/female
15-64 years: 1.17 male(s)/female
65 years and over: 1.01 male(s)/female
total population: 1.12 male(s)/female (2024 est.)

Infant mortality rate: *total:* 6.5 deaths/1,000 live births (2024 est.)
male: 7.6 deaths/1,000 live births
female: 5.3 deaths/1,000 live births
comparison ranking: total 161

Life expectancy at birth: *total population:* 81 years (2024 est.)
male: 78 years
female: 84.2 years
comparison ranking: total population 47

Total fertility rate: 1.64 children born/woman (2024 est.)
comparison ranking: 173

Gross reproduction rate: 0.79 (2024 est.)

Drinking water source: *improved: urban:* 100% of population (2022 est.)
total: 100% of population (2022 est.)
unimproved: urban: 0% of population (2022 est.)
total: 0% of population (2022 est.)

Sanitation facility access: *improved: urban:* 100% of population (2022 est.)
total: 100% of population (2022 est.)
unimproved: urban: 0% of population (2022 est.)
total: 0% of population (2022 est.)

ENVIRONMENT

Environmental issues: land-based pollution; urbanization; limited freshwater resources; overfishing

Climate: tropical, with practically no variation in temperature; has two seasons (dry and humid)

GOVERNMENT

Country name: *conventional long form:* Overseas Collectivity of Saint Barthelemy
conventional short form: Saint Barthelemy
local long form: Collectivité d'outre mer de Saint-Barthélemy
local short form: Saint-Barthélemy
abbreviation: Saint-Barth (French)/ St. Barts or St. Barths (English)
etymology: explorer Christopher COLUMBUS named the island in honor of his brother Bartolomeo in 1493

Government type: parliamentary democracy (Territorial Council); overseas collectivity of France

Dependency status: overseas collectivity of France

Capital: *name:* Gustavia
geographic coordinates: 17 53 N, 62 51 W
time difference: UTC-4 (1 hour ahead of Washington, DC, during Standard Time)
etymology: named in honor of King GUSTAV III of Sweden, who was ruler when Sweden bought the island from France in 1784; the name was retained when the island was sold back to France in 1878

Legal system: French civil law

Constitution: *history:* 4 October 1958 (French Constitution)
amendment process: amendment procedures of France's constitution apply

Citizenship: see France

Suffrage: 18 years of age, universal

Executive branch: *chief of state:* President Emmanuel MACRON (since 14 May 2017), represented by Prefect Cyrille LE VELY (since 15 January 2025)
head of government: President of Territorial Council Xavier LEDEE (since 3 April 2022)

cabinet: Executive Council elected by the Territorial Council; there is also an advisory, economic, social, and cultural council
election/appointment process: French president directly elected by absolute-majority popular vote in 2 rounds, if needed, for a 5-year term (eligible for a second term); prefect appointed by the French president on the advice of French Ministry of Interior; president of Territorial Council indirectly elected by its members for a 5-year term
most recent election date: 27 March 2022
election results: 2022: Xavier LEDEE (Saint Barth United) elected president; Territorial Council vote - 13 votes for, 6 blank votes
2017: Bruno MAGRAS (Saint Barth First!) elected president; Territorial Council vote - 14 out of 19 votes
expected date of next election: 2027

Legislative branch: *legislature name:* Territorial Council
legislative structure: unicameral
number of seats: 19 (directly elected)
electoral system: mixed
scope of elections: full renewal
term in office: 5 years
most recent election date: 3/27/2022
parties elected and seats per party: Saint Barth Action-Équilibre and Unis pour Saint Barthelemy (13); SBA (6)
expected date of next election: 2027
note: 1 senator is indirectly elected to the French Senate by an electoral college for a 6-year term, and 1 deputy (shared with Saint Martin) is directly elected to the French National Assembly for a five-year term

Political parties: All for Saint Barth (Tous pour Saint-Barth)
Saint Barth Action Equilibre
Saint Barth First! (Saint-Barth d'Abord!) or SBA (affiliated with France's Republican party, Les Republicans)
Saint Barth United (Unis pour Saint-Barthelemy)

Diplomatic representation in the US: none (overseas collectivity of France)

Diplomatic representation from the US: *embassy:* none (overseas collectivity of France)

International organization participation: ACS (associate), UPU

Independence: none (overseas collectivity of France)

National holiday: Fête de la Fédération, 14 July (1790)
note 1: local holiday is St. Barthelemy Day, 24 August (1572)
note 2: often incorrectly referred to as Bastille Day, France's national celebration commemorates the storming of the Bastille prison on 14 July 1789 and the establishment of a constitutional monarchy; other names for the holiday are *la Fête nationale* (National Holiday) and *le Quatorze Juillet* (14th of July)

Flag: the flag of France is used

National symbol(s): pelican

National anthem(s): *title:* "L'Hymne à St. Barthelemy" (Hymn to St. Barthelemy)
lyrics/music: Isabelle Massart DERAVIN/Michael VALENTI
history: local anthem in use since 1999
title: "La Marseillaise"
lyrics/music: Claude-Joseph ROUGET de Lisle
history: official anthem, as a French collectivity

ECONOMY

Economic overview: high-income French Caribbean territorial economy; duty-free luxury commerce and tourism industries; import-dependent for food, water, energy, and manufacturing; large Brazilian and Portuguese labor supply; environmentally fragile

Exports - partners: Spain 57%, Switzerland 24%, France 6%, Ireland 5%, Canada 2% (2023)
note: top five export partners based on percentage share of exports

Exports - commodities: refined copper, jewelry (2023)
note: top export commodities based on value in dollars over $500,000

Imports - partners: Switzerland 50%, Portugal 14%, Brazil 6%, Japan 5%, Ireland 5% (2023)
note: top five import partners based on percentage share of imports

Imports - commodities: precious metal watches, base metal watches, jewelry, cars, garments (2023)
note: top five import commodities based on value in dollars

Exchange rates: euros (EUR) per US dollar -

Exchange rates: 0.924 (2024 est.)
0.925 (2023 est.)
0.95 (2022 est.)
0.845 (2021 est.)
0.876 (2020 est.)

ENERGY

Electricity access: *electrification - total population:* 100% (2021)

COMMUNICATIONS

Broadcast media: 2 local TV broadcasters; 5 FM radio channels (2021)

Internet country code: .bl
note:.gp, the Internet country code for Guadeloupe, and.fr, the Internet country code for France, are also used

Internet users: *percent of population:* 71.3% (2022 est.)

TRANSPORTATION

Airports: 1 (2025)
comparison ranking: 213

MILITARY AND SECURITY

Military - note: defense is the responsibility of France

SAINT HELENA, ASCENSION, AND TRISTAN DA CUNHA

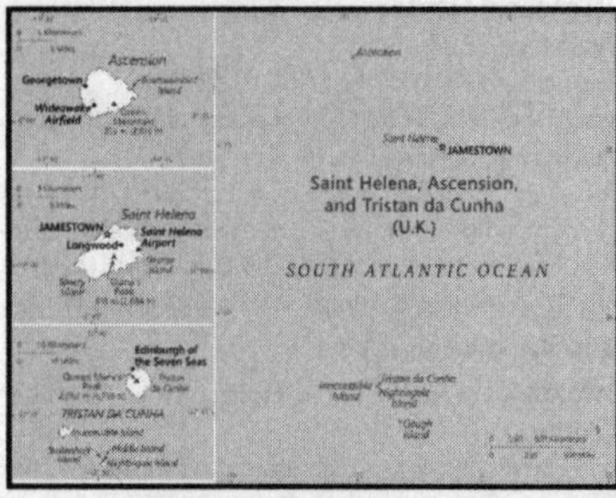

INTRODUCTION

Background: Saint Helena is a British Overseas Territory off the coast of Africa in the South Atlantic Ocean, and it consists of Saint Helena, Ascension Island, and the island group of Tristan da Cunha.

Saint Helena: The island was uninhabited when the Portuguese first discovered it in 1502, and the British garrisoned troops on Saint Helena during the 17th century. It acquired fame as the place of Napoleon BONAPARTE's exile from 1815 until his death in 1821, but its importance as a port of call declined after the opening of the Suez Canal in 1869. During the Anglo-Boer War in South Africa, several thousand Boer prisoners were confined on the island between 1900 and 1903.

Saint Helena is one of the most remote populated places in the world. The British Government committed to building an airport on Saint Helena in 2005. After more than a decade of delays and construction, a commercial air service to South Africa via Namibia was inaugurated in 2017. The weekly service to Saint Helena from Johannesburg via Windhoek in Namibia takes just over six hours (including the refueling stop in Windhoek) and replaces the mail ship that had made a five-day journey to the island every three weeks.

Ascension Island: This barren and uninhabited island was discovered and named by the Portuguese in 1503. The British garrisoned the island in 1815 to prevent a rescue of NAPOLEON from Saint Helena. It served as a provisioning station for the Royal Navy's West Africa Squadron on anti-slavery patrol. The island remained under Admiralty control until 1922, when it became a dependency of Saint Helena. During World War II, the UK permitted the US to construct an airfield on Ascension in support of transatlantic flights to Africa and anti-submarine operations in the South Atlantic. In the 1960s, the island became an important space tracking station for the US. In 1982, Ascension was an essential staging area for British forces during the Falklands War. It remains a critical refueling point in the air-bridge from the UK to the South Atlantic.

The island hosts one of four dedicated ground antennas that assist in the operation of the Global Positioning System (GPS) navigation system – the others are on Diego Garcia (British Indian Ocean Territory), Kwajalein (Marshall Islands), and at

Cape Canaveral, Florida (US). NASA and the US Air Force also operate a Meter-Class Autonomous Telescope (MCAT) on Ascension as part of the deep space surveillance system for tracking orbital debris, which can be a hazard to spacecraft and astronauts.

Tristan da Cunha: The island group consists of Tristan da Cunha, Nightingale, Inaccessible, and Gough Islands. Tristan da Cunha, named after its Portuguese discoverer (1506), was garrisoned by the British in 1816 to prevent any attempt to rescue NAPOLEON from Saint Helena. Gough and Inaccessible Islands have been designated World Heritage Sites. South Africa leases a site for a meteorological station on Gough Island.

GEOGRAPHY

Location: islands in the South Atlantic Ocean, about midway between South America and Africa; Ascension Island lies 1,300 km (800 mi) northwest of Saint Helena; Tristan da Cunha lies 4,300 km (2,700 mi) southwest of Saint Helena

Geographic coordinates: Saint Helena: 15 57 S, 5 42 W

Ascension Island: 7 57 S, 14 22 W

Tristan da Cunha island group: 37 15 S, 12 30 W

Map references: Africa

Area: *total:* 394 sq km
land: 122 sq km Saint Helena Island
water: 0 sq km
88 sq km Ascension Island, 184 sq km Tristan da Cunha island group (includes Tristan (98 sq km), Inaccessible, Nightingale, and Gough islands)
comparison ranking: total 203

Area - comparative: slightly more than twice the size of Washington, D.C.

Land boundaries: *total:* 0 km

Coastline: Saint Helena: 60 km

Ascension Island: NA

Tristan da Cunha (island only): 34 km

Maritime claims: *territorial sea:* 12 nm
exclusive fishing zone: 200 nm

Climate: Saint Helena: tropical marine; mild, tempered by trade winds

Ascension Island: tropical marine; mild, semi-arid

Tristan da Cunha: temperate marine; mild, tempered by trade winds (tends to be cooler than Saint Helena)

Terrain: the islands of this group are of volcanic origin associated with the Atlantic Mid-Ocean Ridge

Saint Helena: rugged, volcanic; small scattered plateaus and plains

Ascension: surface covered by lava flows and cinder cones of 44 dormant volcanoes; terrain rises to the east

Tristan da Cunha: sheer cliffs line the coastline of the nearly circular island; the flanks of the central volcanic peak are deeply dissected; narrow coastal plain lies between The Peak and the coastal cliffs

Elevation: *highest point:* Queen Mary's Peak on Tristan da Cunha 2,060 m; Green Mountain on Ascension Island 859 m; Diana's Peak on Saint Helena Island 818 m
lowest point: Atlantic Ocean 0 m

Natural resources: fish, lobster

Land use: *agricultural land:* 30.8% (2022 est.)
arable land: 10.3% (2022 est.)
permanent crops: 0% (2022 est.)
permanent pasture: 20.5% (2022 est.)
forest: 5.1% (2022 est.)
other: 64.1% (2022 est.)

Irrigated land: 0 sq km (2022)

Population distribution: *Saint Helena:* population is concentrated in and around the capital of Jamestown in the northwest, with another significant cluster in the interior Longwood area

Ascension: most of the population lives in and around Georgetown

Tristan da Cunha: most of the nearly 300 inhabitants live in the northern coastal town of Edinburgh of the Seven Seas

Natural hazards: active volcanism
volcanism: the volcanoes of Tristan da Cunha (2,060 m) and Nightingale Island (365 m) are active

Geography - note: Saint Helena harbors at least 40 species of plants unknown elsewhere in the world; Ascension is a breeding ground for sea turtles and sooty terns; Queen Mary's Peak on Tristan da Cunha is the highest island mountain in the South Atlantic and a prominent landmark on the sea lanes around southern Africa

PEOPLE AND SOCIETY

Population: *total:* 7,943 (2024 est.)
male: 3,978
female: 3,965
comparison rankings: total 223; male 224; female 223

Nationality: *noun:* Saint Helenian(s)
adjective: Saint Helenian
note: referred to locally as "Saints"

Ethnic groups: St. Helena 82.1%, UK 7.6%, South Africa 3.6%, Ascension 2.8%, other 3.9% (2021 est.)
note: data represent population of Saint Helena by country of birth

Languages: English

Religions: Anglican 63.2%, unspecified 11.4%, no religion 9%, Jehovah's Witness 3.8%, Baptist 2.3%, Salvation Army 2%, Roman Catholic 2.2%, Seventh Day Adventist 1.9%, New Apostolic 1.6%, other Christian 1.4%, other 1.1% (2021 est.)
note: data represent Saint Helena only Age structure
0-14 years: 14.3% (male 579/female 556)
15-64 years: 66.5% (male 2,626/female 2,655)
65 years and over: 19.2% (2024 est.) (male 773/ female 754)

Dependency ratios: *total dependency ratio:* 50.4 (2024 est.)
youth dependency ratio: 21.5 (2024 est.)
elderly dependency ratio: 28.9 (2024 est.)
potential support ratio: 3.5 (2024 est.)

Median age: *total:* 45.1 years (2024 est.)
male: 44.8 years
female: 45.4 years
comparison ranking: total 21

Population growth rate: 0.1% (2024 est.)
comparison ranking: 186

Birth rate: 9.3 births/1,000 population (2024 est.)
comparison ranking: 196

Death rate: 8.3 deaths/1,000 population (2024 est.)
comparison ranking: 80

Net migration rate: 0 migrant(s)/1,000 population (2024 est.)
comparison ranking: 90

Population distribution: *Saint Helena:* population is concentrated in and around the capital of Jamestown in the northwest, with another significant cluster in the interior Longwood area

Ascension: most of the population lives in and around Georgetown

Tristan da Cunha: most of the nearly 300 inhabitants live in the northern coastal town of Edinburgh of the Seven Seas

Urbanization: *urban population:* 40.7% of total population (2023)
rate of urbanization: 0.98% annual rate of change (2020-25 est.)

Major urban areas - population: 1,000 JAMESTOWN (capital) (2018)

Sex ratio: *at birth:* 1.06 male(s)/female
0-14 years: 1.04 male(s)/female
15-64 years: 0.99 male(s)/female
65 years and over: 1.03 male(s)/female
total population: 1 male(s)/female (2024 est.)

Infant mortality rate: *total:* 18.1 deaths/1,000 live births (2024 est.)
male: 21.7 deaths/1,000 live births
female: 14.2 deaths/1,000 live births
comparison ranking: total 86

Life expectancy at birth: *total population:* 80.9 years (2024 est.)
male: 78.1 years
female: 83.9 years
comparison ranking: total population 50

Total fertility rate: 1.61 children born/woman (2024 est.)
comparison ranking: 181

Gross reproduction rate: 0.78 (2024 est.)

Drinking water source: *improved:* total: 99.1% of population (2022 est.)
unimproved: total: 0.9% of population (2022 est.)

Sanitation facility access: *improved:* total: 100% of population (2022 est.)
unimproved: total: 0% of population (2022 est.)

ENVIRONMENT

Environmental issues: development threatens wildlife on Saint Helena

Climate: Saint Helena: tropical marine; mild, tempered by trade winds

Ascension Island: tropical marine; mild, semi-arid

Tristan da Cunha: temperate marine; mild, tempered by trade winds (tends to be cooler than Saint Helena)

Urbanization: *urban population:* 40.7% of total population (2023)
rate of urbanization: 0.98% annual rate of change (2020-25 est.)

Carbon dioxide emissions: 12,000 metric tonnes of CO_2 (2023 est.)
from petroleum and other liquids: 12,000 metric tonnes of CO_2 (2023 est.)
comparison ranking: total emissions 215

GOVERNMENT

Country name: *conventional long form:* Saint Helena, Ascension, and Tristan da Cunha
conventional short form: none
etymology: on the feast day of Saint Helena in 1502, Spanish navigator Joao da NOVA (sailing for Portugal) sighted and named the island that now bears the saint's name; da NOVA originally named Ascension "Conception Island" in honor of

the Virgin Mary, but Portuguese navigator Afonso de ALBUQUERQUE later found the island on the feast day of the Ascension in 1508 and renamed it; Portuguese explorer Tristao da CUNHA sighted the third island in 1506 and named it after himself (the name was later anglicized)

Government type: parliamentary democracy

Dependency status: overseas territory of the UK

Capital: *name:* Jamestown
geographic coordinates: 15 56 S, 5 43 W
time difference: UTC 0 (5 hours ahead of Washington, DC, during Standard Time)
etymology: founded in 1659 and named after James, Duke of York, who would become King JAMES II of England

Administrative divisions: 3 administrative areas; Ascension, Saint Helena, Tristan da Cunha

Legal system: English common law and local statutes

Constitution: *history:* several previous; latest effective 1 September 2009 (St. Helena, Ascension and Tristan da Cunha Constitution Order 2009)

Citizenship: see United Kingdom

Suffrage: 18 years of age

Executive branch: *chief of state:* King CHARLES III (since 8 September 2022)
head of government: Governor Nigel PHILLIPS (since 13 August 2022)
cabinet: Executive Council consists of the governor, 3 ex-officio officers, and 5 elected members of the Legislative Council
election/appointment process: none; the monarchy is hereditary; governor appointed by the monarch
note: the constitution order provides for an administrator for Ascension and Tristan da Cunha, appointed by the governor

Legislative branch: *note:* the Constitution Order provides for separate Island Councils for both Ascension and Tristan da Cunha

Judicial branch: *highest court(s):* Court of Appeal (consists of the court president and 2 justices); Supreme Court (consists of the chief justice and judges)
judge selection and term of office: Court of Appeal and Supreme Court justices appointed by the governor acting upon the instructions from a secretary of state acting on behalf of the British monarch; justices of both courts serve until retirement at age 70, but terms can be extended
subordinate courts: Magistrates' Court; Small Claims Court; Juvenile Court
note: appeals beyond the Court of Appeal are heard by the Judicial Committee of the Privy Council (in London)

Political parties: none

Diplomatic representation in the US: none (overseas territory of the UK)

Diplomatic representation from the US: *embassy:* none (overseas territory of the UK)

International organization participation: UPU

Independence: none (overseas territory of the UK)

National holiday: Official birthday of King Charles III, celebrated in April or June as designated by the governor (1948)

Flag: *description:* blue with the UK flag in the upper-left quadrant and the Saint Helenian shield centered on the right half of the flag; the upper third of the shield depicts a white plover on a yellow field; under the bird is a rocky coastline and a three-masted sailing ship with sails furled and flying an English flag
history: the flag has been in use since 1984, when it was commissioned to mark the 150th anniversary of Saint Helena becoming a Crown Colony
note: the French flag flies at Longwood House (Napoleon's former residence) and Napoleon's (now-empty) tomb on the island, because the French Government has owned the properties since 1858

National symbol(s): Saint Helena plover (wire bird)

National coat of arms: the coat of arms of Saint Helena was officially granted on January 30, 1984; the national bird, the Saint Helena plover *(Charadrius sanctaehelenae)*, is at the top of the shield; the lower part of the shield shows a three-masted sailing ship with the mountainous island to the left; below the shield is a scroll with the motto "Loyal and unshakable;" the crest shows an image of Saint Helena, holding a cross and a flower

National anthem(s): *title:* "My St. Helena Island"
lyrics/music: Dave MITCHELL
history: in use since 1975
title: "God Save the King"
lyrics/music: unknown
history: official anthem, as a UK overseas territory

ECONOMY

Economic overview: upper middle-income, British Atlantic Ocean territorial economy; native (but pegged to British pound) currency user on 2 of 3 islands; significant UK financial support; unique land/farming commune structure; military-related economic activity; sport fishing locale

Agricultural products: coffee, corn, potatoes, vegetables; fish, lobster; livestock; timber

Industries: construction, crafts (furniture, lacework, fancy woodwork), fishing, collectible postage stamps

Exports - partners: Singapore 33%, USA 16%, Japan 10%, Turkey 10%, Senegal 8% (2023)
note: top five export partners based on percentage share of exports

Exports - commodities: fish, shellfish, natural gas, trucks, construction vehicles (2023)
note: top five export commodities based on value in dollars

Imports - partners: UK 34%, Greece 26%, Spain 16%, South Africa 15%, Namibia 2% (2023)
note: top five import partners based on percentage share of imports

Imports - commodities: refined petroleum, baked goods, plastic products, vehicle parts/accessories, air pumps (2023)
note: top five import commodities based on value in dollars

Exchange rates: Saint Helena pounds (SHP) per US dollar -

Exchange rates: 0.805 (2023 est.)
0.811 (2022 est.)
0.727 (2021 est.)
0.78 (2020 est.)
0.783 (2019 est.)

ENERGY

Electricity access: *electrification - total population:* 100% (2021)

Electricity: *installed generating capacity:* 5,000 kW (2023 est.)
consumption: 6.962 million kWh (2023 est.)
transmission/distribution losses: 1.5 million kWh (2023 est.)
comparison rankings: installed generating capacity 210; consumption 210; transmission/distribution losses 4

Electricity generation sources: *fossil fuels:* 100% of total installed capacity (2023 est.)

Coal: *imports:* 70 metric tons (2022 est.)

Petroleum: *refined petroleum consumption:* 85 bbl/day (2023 est.)

COMMUNICATIONS

Telephones - fixed lines: *total subscriptions:* 4,000 (2021 est.)
subscriptions per 100 inhabitants: 74 (2021 est.)
comparison ranking: total subscriptions 205

Telephones - mobile cellular: *total subscriptions:* 4,000 (2021 est.)
subscriptions per 100 inhabitants: 74 (2021 est.)
comparison ranking: total subscriptions 223

Broadcast media: *Saint Helena:* no local TV station; 2 local radio stations, one of which is relayed to Ascension Island; satellite TV stations rebroadcast terrestrially

Ascension Island: no local TV station; 1 local radio station and receives relays of broadcasts from radio station on Saint Helena; broadcasts from the British Forces Broadcasting Service (BFBS) available, as well as US military TV

Tristan da Cunha: 1 local radio station and receives BFBS TV and radio broadcasts

Internet country code: .sh
note: Ascension Island assigned.ac

Internet users: *percent of population:* 37.6% (2021 est.)

Broadband - fixed subscriptions: *total:* 1,000 (2018 est.)
subscriptions per 100 inhabitants: 17 (2020 est.)
comparison ranking: total 208

TRANSPORTATION

Civil aircraft registration country code prefix: VQ-H

Airports: 2 (2025)
comparison ranking: 195

Heliports: 2 (2025)
comparison ranking: 122

Ports: *total ports:* 4 (2024)
large: 1
medium: 1
small: 1
very small: 1
ports with oil terminals: 2
key ports: Edinburgh of the Seven Seas, Georgetown, Jamestown, North Point

Transportation - note
the new airport on Saint Helena opened for limited operations in 2016, and the first commercial flight took place in 2017; the military airport on Ascension Island is closed to civilian traffic; there is no air connection to Tristan da Cunha and very limited sea connections

MILITARY AND SECURITY

Military - note: defense is the responsibility of the UK

SAINT KITTS AND NEVIS

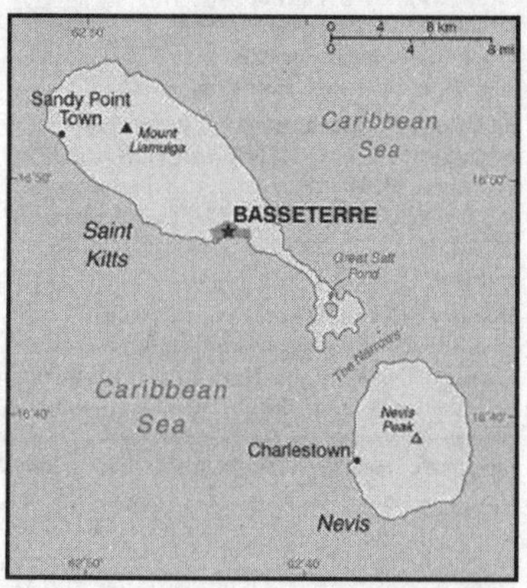

INTRODUCTION

Background: Carib Indians occupied the islands of the West Indies for hundreds of years before the British and French began settlement in 1623. During the 17th century, Saint Kitts became the premier base for British and French expansion into the Caribbean. The French ceded the territory to the UK in 1713. At the turn of the 18th century, Saint Kitts was the richest British Crown Colony per capita in the Caribbean, a result of the sugar trade. Although small in size and separated by only 3 km (2 mi) of water, Saint Kitts and Nevis were viewed and governed as different states until the late-19th century, when the British forcibly unified them along with the island of Anguilla. In 1967, the island territory of Saint Christopher-Nevis-Anguilla became an associated state of the UK with full internal autonomy. The island of Anguilla rebelled and was allowed to secede in 1971. The remaining islands achieved independence in 1983 as Saint Kitts and Nevis. In 1998, a referendum on Nevis to separate from Saint Kitts fell short of the necessary two-thirds majority.

GEOGRAPHY

Location: Caribbean, islands in the Caribbean Sea, about one-third of the way from Puerto Rico to Trinidad and Tobago

Geographic coordinates: 17 20 N, 62 45 W

Map references: Central America and the Caribbean

Area: *total:* 261 sq km (Saint Kitts 168 sq km; Nevis 93 sq km)
land: 261 sq km
water: 0 sq km
comparison ranking: total 211

Area - comparative: 1.5 times the size of Washington, D.C.

Land boundaries: *total:* 0 km

Coastline: 135 km

Maritime claims: *territorial sea:* 12 nm
contiguous zone: 24 nm
exclusive economic zone: 200 nm
continental shelf: 200 nm or to the edge of the continental margin

Climate: tropical, tempered by constant sea breezes; little seasonal temperature variation; rainy season (May to November)

Terrain: volcanic with mountainous interiors

Elevation: *highest point:* Mount Liamuiga 1,156 m
lowest point: Caribbean Sea 0 m

Natural resources: arable land

Land use: *agricultural land:* 23.1% (2022 est.)
arable land: 19.2% (2022 est.)
permanent crops: 0.4% (2022 est.)
permanent pasture: 3.5% (2022 est.)
forest: 42.3% (2022 est.)
other: 34.6% (2022 est.)

Irrigated land: 8 sq km (2012)

Population distribution: population clusters are found in the small towns located on the periphery of both islands

Natural hazards: hurricanes (July to October)
volcanism: Mount Liamuiga (1,156 m) on Saint Kitts and Nevis Peak (985 m) on Nevis are part of the volcanic-island arc of the Lesser Antilles, which extends from Saba in the north to Grenada in the south

Geography - note: smallest country in the Western Hemisphere in terms of both area and population; the two volcanic islands are separated by a 3-km-wide (9-mi-wide) channel called The Narrows; on the southern tip of baseball-bat-shaped Saint Kitts lies the Great Salt Pond; Nevis Peak sits in the center of its ball-shaped namesake island

PEOPLE AND SOCIETY

Population: *total:* 55,133 (2024 est.)
male: 27,599
female: 27,534
comparison rankings: total 207; male 207; female 207

Nationality: *noun:* Kittitian(s), Nevisian(s)
adjective: Kittitian, Nevisian

Ethnic groups: African descent 92.5%, mixed 3%, White 2.1%, East Indian 1.5%, other 0.6%, unspecified 0.3% (2001 est.)

Languages: English (official)

Religions: Protestant 75.6% (includes Anglican 16.6%, Methodist 15.8%, Pentecostal 10.8%, Church of God 7.4%, Baptist 5.4%, Seventh Day Adventist 5.4%, Wesleyan Holiness 5.3%, Moravian 4.8%, Evangelical 2.1%, Brethren 1.7%, Presbyterian 0.3%), Roman Catholic 5.9%, Hindu 1.8%, Jehovah's Witness 1.4%, Rastafarian 1.3%, other 5%, none 8.8%, unspecified 0.1% (2011 est.)

Age structure: *0-14 years:* 19.2% (male 5,314/female 5,277)
15-64 years: 68.1% (male 18,944/female 18,575)
65 years and over: 12.7% (2024 est.) (male 3,341/female 3,682)

Dependency ratios: *total dependency ratio:* 46.9 (2024 est.)
youth dependency ratio: 28.2 (2024 est.)
elderly dependency ratio: 18.7 (2024 est.)
potential support ratio: 5.3 (2024 est.)

Median age: *total:* 38.6 years (2024 est.)
male: 38.8 years
female: 38.3 years
comparison ranking: total 72

Population growth rate: 0.56% (2024 est.)
comparison ranking: 147

Birth rate: 11.8 births/1,000 population (2024 est.)
comparison ranking: 153

Death rate: 7.4 deaths/1,000 population (2024 est.)
comparison ranking: 106

Net migration rate: 1.1 migrant(s)/1,000 population (2024 est.)
comparison ranking: 64

Population distribution: population clusters are found in the small towns located on the periphery of both islands

Urbanization: *urban population:* 31.1% of total population (2023)
rate of urbanization: 1.06% annual rate of change (2020-25 est.)

Major urban areas - population: 14,000 BASSETERRE (capital) (2018)

Sex ratio: *at birth:* 1.02 male(s)/female
0-14 years: 1.01 male(s)/female
15-64 years: 1.02 male(s)/female
65 years and over: 0.91 male(s)/female
total population: 1 male(s)/female (2024 est.)

Maternal mortality ratio: 74 deaths/100,000 live births (2023 est.)
comparison ranking: 78

Infant mortality rate: *total:* 8 deaths/1,000 live births (2024 est.)
male: 5.5 deaths/1,000 live births
female: 10.6 deaths/1,000 live births
comparison ranking: total 147

Life expectancy at birth: *total population:* 77.6 years (2024 est.)
male: 75.2 years
female: 80.1 years
comparison ranking: total population 89

Total fertility rate: 1.76 children born/woman (2024 est.)
comparison ranking: 146

Gross reproduction rate: 0.87 (2024 est.)

Health expenditure: 6.2% of GDP (2021)
5.9% of national budget (2022 est.)

Physician density: 3.09 physicians/1,000 population (2018)

Hospital bed density: 4.3 beds/1,000 population (2021 est.)

Obesity - adult prevalence rate: 22.9% (2016)
comparison ranking: 71

Alcohol consumption per capita: *total:* 8.84 liters of pure alcohol (2019 est.)
beer: 3.73 liters of pure alcohol (2019 est.)
wine: 1.02 liters of pure alcohol (2019 est.)
spirits: 3.89 liters of pure alcohol (2019 est.)
other alcohols: 0.21 liters of pure alcohol (2019 est.)
comparison ranking: total 36

Currently married women (ages 15-49): 57.2% (2023 est.)

Education expenditure: 3.5% of GDP (2023 est.)
11% national budget (2025 est.)
comparison ranking: Education expenditure (% GDP) 130

School life expectancy (primary to tertiary education): *total:* 19 years (2015 est.)

male: 18 years (2015 est.)
female: 20 years (2015 est.)

ENVIRONMENT

Environmental issues: deforestation; soil erosion and silting affects marine life on coral reefs; water pollution from uncontrolled dumping of sewage

International environmental agreements: *party to:* Biodiversity, Climate Change, Climate Change-Kyoto Protocol, Climate Change-Paris Agreement, Comprehensive Nuclear Test Ban, Desertification, Endangered Species, Hazardous Wastes, Law of the Sea, Marine Dumping-London Protocol, Ozone Layer Protection, Ship Pollution, Whaling
signed, but not ratified: none of the selected agreements

Climate: tropical, tempered by constant sea breezes; little seasonal temperature variation; rainy season (May to November)

Urbanization: *urban population:* 31.1% of total population (2023)
rate of urbanization: 1.06% annual rate of change (2020-25 est.)

Carbon dioxide emissions: 269,000 metric tonnes of CO2 (2023 est.)
from petroleum and other liquids: 269,000 metric tonnes of CO2 (2023 est.)
comparison ranking: total emissions 201

Particulate matter emissions: 8 micrograms per cubic meter (2019 est.)

Waste and recycling: *municipal solid waste generated annually:* 32,900 tons (2024 est.)

Total water withdrawal: *municipal:* 15.4 million cubic meters (2022 est.)
industrial: 0 cubic meters (2022 est.)
agricultural: 200,000 cubic meters (2022 est.)

Total renewable water resources: 24 million cubic meters (2022 est.)

GOVERNMENT

Country name: *conventional long form:* Federation of Saint Kitts and Nevis
conventional short form: Saint Kitts and Nevis
former: Federation of Saint Christopher and Nevis
etymology: explorer Christopher COLUMBUS visited the islands in 1493 and named one for his own patron saint; a common nickname for Christopher during the following centuries was Kit or Kitt, and Saint Kitts is still referred to as Saint Christopher; the name of Nevis is said to derive from the original Spanish name "Las Nieves" (The Snows) and refers to its cloud-topped mountain
note: Nevis is pronounced NEE-vis

Government type: federal parliamentary democracy under a constitutional monarchy; a Commonwealth realm

Capital: *name:* Basseterre
geographic coordinates: 17 18 N, 62 43 W
time difference: UTC-4 (1 hour ahead of Washington, DC, during Standard Time)
etymology: the French name translates as "low land" in English; the reference is probably to the city's location in a valley

Administrative divisions: 14 parishes; Christ Church Nichola Town, Saint Anne Sandy Point, Saint George Basseterre, Saint George Gingerland, Saint James Windward, Saint John Capesterre, Saint John Figtree, Saint Mary Cayon, Saint Paul Capesterre, Saint Paul Charlestown, Saint Peter Basseterre, Saint Thomas Lowland, Saint Thomas Middle Island, Trinity Palmetto Point

Legal system: English common law

Constitution: *history:* several previous (pre-independence); latest presented 22 June 1983, effective 23 June 1983
amendment process: proposed by the National Assembly; passage requires approval by at least two-thirds majority vote of the total Assembly membership and assent of the governor general; amendments to constitutional provisions such as the sovereignty of the federation, fundamental rights and freedoms, the judiciary, and the Nevis Island Assembly also require approval in a referendum by at least two thirds of the votes cast in Saint Kitts and in Nevis

International law organization participation: has not submitted an ICJ jurisdiction declaration; accepts ICCt jurisdiction

Citizenship: *citizenship by birth:* yes
citizenship by descent only: yes
dual citizenship recognized: yes
residency requirement for naturalization: 14 years

Suffrage: 18 years of age; universal

Executive branch: *chief of state:* King CHARLES III (since 8 September 2022); represented by Governor General Marcella LIBURD (since 1 February 2023)
head of government: Prime Minister Dr. Terrance DREW (since 6 August 2022)
cabinet: Cabinet appointed by governor general in consultation with prime minister
election/appointment process: the monarchy is hereditary; governor general appointed by the monarch; following legislative elections, the governor general usually appoints the leader of the majority party or majority coalition as prime minister; deputy prime minister also appointed by governor general

Legislative branch: *legislature name:* National Assembly
legislative structure: unicameral
number of seats: 16 (11 directly elected; 4 appointed)
electoral system: plurality/majority
scope of elections: full renewal
term in office: 5 years
most recent election date: 8/5/2022
parties elected and seats per party: St. Kitts-Nevis Labour Party (SKNLP) (6); Concerned Citizens' Movement (CCM) (3); Peoples Labour Party (PLP) (1); People's Action Movement (PAM) (1)
percentage of women in chamber: 31.3%
expected date of next election: October 2027

Judicial branch: *highest court(s):* the Eastern Caribbean Supreme Court (ECSC) is the superior court of the Organization of Eastern Caribbean States; the ECSC is headquartered on St. Lucia and consists of the Court of Appeal – headed by the chief justice and 4 judges – and the High Court with 18 judges; the Court of Appeal travels to member states on a schedule to hear appeals from the High Court and subordinate courts; member of the Caribbean Court of Justice
judge selection and term of office: chief justice of Eastern Caribbean Supreme Court appointed by the British monarch; other justices and judges appointed by the Judicial and Legal Services Commission, an independent body of judicial officials; Court of Appeal justices appointed for life with mandatory retirement at age 65; High Court judges appointed for life with mandatory retirement at age 62
subordinate courts: magistrates' courts

Political parties: Concerned Citizens Movement or CCM
Nevis Reformation Party or NRP
People's Action Movement or PAM
People's Labour Party or PLP
Saint Kitts and Nevis Labor Party or SKNLP

Diplomatic representation in the US: *chief of mission:* Ambassador Jacinth HENRY-MARTIN (since 15 September 2023)
chancery: 1203 19th St. NW, 5th Floor, Washington, DC 20036
telephone: [1] (202) 686-2636
FAX: [1] (202) 686-5740
email address and website: stkittsnevis@embskn.com
Embassy of St.Kitts and Nevis to the USA – and Permanent Mission to the OAS (embassydc.gov.kn)
consulate(s) general: Los Angeles, New York

Diplomatic representation from the US: *embassy:* the US does not have an embassy in Saint Kitts and Nevis; the US Ambassador to Barbados is accredited to Saint Kitts and Nevis

International organization participation: ACP, ACS, AOSIS, C, Caricom, CDB, CELAC, FAO, G-77, IBRD, ICAO, ICCt, ICRM, IDA, IFAD, IFC, IFRCS, ILO, IMF, IMO, Interpol, IOC, ITU, MIGA, OAS, OECS, OPANAL, OPCW, Petrocaribe, UN, UNCTAD, UNESCO, UNIDO, UPU, WHO, WIPO, WTO

Independence: 19 September 1983 (from the UK)

National holiday: Independence Day, 19 September (1983)

Flag: *description:* divided diagonally from the lower left side by a broad black band with two five-pointed white stars; the black band is edged in yellow; the upper triangle is green, and the lower is red
meaning: green stands for the island's fertility, red for the struggles of the people from slavery, yellow for year-round sunshine, and black for the people's African heritage; the white stars stand for the islands of Saint Kitts and Nevis but can also express hope and liberty, or independence and optimism

National symbol(s): brown pelican, royal poinciana (flamboyant) tree

National color(s): green, yellow, red, black, white
National coat of arms
the coat of arms of Saint Kitts and Nevis features a Carib who represents the original inhabitants of the islands, and a fleur-de-lis and rose that represent the French and English who arrived in the 1620; the shield also features the poinciana (the national flower) and a traditional boat; three hands hold the torch, which represents the quest for freedom: the hand of an African, a European, and a person of mixed ethnicity; pelicans (the national bird) support the shield, with a sugarcane plant and a coconut tree that symbolize the land

National anthem(s): *title:* "O Land of Beauty!"
lyrics/music: Kenrick Anderson GEORGES
history: adopted 1983
title: "God Save the King"
lyrics/music: unknown
history: in use since 1745

National heritage: *total World Heritage Sites:* 1 (cultural)
selected World Heritage Site locales: Brimstone Hill Fortress National Park

ECONOMY

Economic overview: high-income, tourism-based Caribbean OECS economy; better debt balancing; CARICOM and ECCU member; growing offshore financial and telecommunications hub; environmentally fragile; unique citizenship-driven growth model

Real GDP (purchasing power parity): $1.465 billion (2024 est.)
$1.448 billion (2023 est.)
$1.388 billion (2022 est.)
note: data in 2021 dollars
comparison ranking: 203

Real GDP growth rate: 1.2% (2024 est.)
4.3% (2023 est.)
10.3% (2022 est.)
note: annual GDP % growth based on constant local currency
comparison ranking: 172

Real GDP per capita: $31,300 (2024 est.)
$31,000 (2023 est.)
$29,700 (2022 est.)
note: data in 2021 dollars
comparison ranking: 76

GDP (official exchange rate): $1.067 billion (2024 est.)
note: data in current dollars at official exchange rate

Inflation rate (consumer prices): 3.6% (2023 est.)
2.7% (2022 est.)
1.2% (2021 est.)
note: annual % change based on consumer prices
comparison ranking: 114

GDP - composition, by sector of origin: *agriculture:* 1.3% (2024 est.)
industry: 21.1% (2024 est.)
services: 65.5% (2024 est.)
note: figures may not total 100% due to non-allocated consumption not captured in sector-reported data
comparison rankings: agriculture 166; industry 125; services 53

Agricultural products: coconuts, tropical fruits, root vegetables, vegetables, eggs, pulses, sweet potatoes, watermelons, cucumbers/gherkins, tomatoes (2023)
note: top ten agricultural products based on tonnage

Industries: tourism, cotton, salt, copra, clothing, footwear, beverages

Industrial production growth rate: -2.7% (2024 est.)
note: annual % change in industrial value added based on constant local currency
comparison ranking: 169

Remittances: 3.4% of GDP (2024 est.)
3.5% of GDP (2023 est.)
3.8% of GDP (2022 est.)
note: personal transfers and compensation between resident and non-resident individuals/households/entities

Budget: *revenues:* $262 million (2020 est.)
expenditures: $281.889 million (2020 est.)
note: central government revenues and expenses (excluding grants/extrabudgetary units/social security funds) converted to US dollars at average official exchange rate for year indicated

Public debt: 62.9% of GDP (2017 est.)
note: central government debt as a % of GDP
comparison ranking: 70

Taxes and other revenues: 15% (of GDP) (2020 est.)
note: central government tax revenue as a % of GDP
comparison ranking: 92

Current account balance: -$169.221 million (2024 est.)
-$122.386 million (2023 est.)
-$111.685 million (2022 est.)
note: balance of payments - net trade and primary/secondary income in current dollars
comparison ranking: 103

Exports: $504.391 million (2024 est.)
$579.568 million (2023 est.)
$542.983 million (2022 est.)
note: balance of payments - exports of goods and services in current dollars
comparison ranking: 191

Exports - partners: Malta 49%, USA 21%, Turkey 7%, St. Vincent & the Grenadines 5%, Guyana 3% (2023)
note: top five export partners based on percentage share of exports

Exports - commodities: ships, measuring instruments, beer, electrical transformers, electrical control boards (2023)
note: top five export commodities based on value in dollars

Imports: $642.934 million (2024 est.)
$669.168 million (2023 est.)
$606.856 million (2022 est.)
note: balance of payments - imports of goods and services in current dollars
comparison ranking: 195

Imports - partners: USA 50%, Italy 11%, China 8%, Japan 2%, UK 2% (2023)
note: top five import partners based on percentage share of imports

Imports - commodities: refined petroleum, ships, cars, jewelry, poultry (2023)
note: top five import commodities based on value in dollars

Reserves of foreign exchange and gold: $294.748 million (2024 est.)
$286.075 million (2023 est.)
$293.98 million (2022 est.)
note: holdings of gold (year-end prices)/foreign exchange/special drawing rights in current dollars
comparison ranking: 171

Exchange rates: East Caribbean dollars (XCD) per US dollar -

Exchange rates: 2.7 (2024 est.)
2.7 (2023 est.)
2.7 (2022 est.)
2.7 (2021 est.)
2.7 (2020 est.)

ENERGY

Electricity access: *electrification - total population:* 100% (2022 est.)

Electricity: *installed generating capacity:* 72,000 kW (2023 est.)
consumption: 182.455 million kWh (2023 est.)
transmission/distribution losses: 39.522 million kWh (2023 est.)
comparison rankings: installed generating capacity 189; consumption 190; transmission/distribution losses 32

Electricity generation sources: *fossil fuels:* 95% of total installed capacity (2023 est.)
solar: 2.3% of total installed capacity (2023 est.)
wind: 2.7% of total installed capacity (2023 est.)

Petroleum: *refined petroleum consumption:* 2,000 bbl/day (2023 est.)

Energy consumption per capita: 81.454 million Btu/person (2023 est.)
comparison ranking: 63

COMMUNICATIONS

Telephones - fixed lines: *total subscriptions:* 16,000 (2022 est.)
subscriptions per 100 inhabitants: 33 (2022 est.)
comparison ranking: total subscriptions 180

Telephones - mobile cellular: *total subscriptions:* 56,000 (2023 est.)
subscriptions per 100 inhabitants: 119 (2021 est.)
comparison ranking: total subscriptions 206

Broadcast media: national state-operated TV network that broadcasts on 2 channels; cable subscription available for local and international channels; national state-operated radio network; mix of state-owned and privately owned broadcasters with about 15 radio stations (2019)

Internet country code: .kn

Internet users: *percent of population:* 76% (2022 est.)

Broadband - fixed subscriptions: *total:* 22,000 (2022 est.)
subscriptions per 100 inhabitants: 47 (2022 est.)
comparison ranking: total 169

TRANSPORTATION

Civil aircraft registration country code prefix: V4

Airports: 2 (2025)
comparison ranking: 205

Heliports: 1 (2025)
comparison ranking: 150

Railways: *total:* 50 km (2008)
narrow gauge: 50 km (2008) 0.762-m gauge on Saint Kitts for tourists

Merchant marine: *total:* 341 (2023)
by type: bulk carrier 22, container ship 16, general cargo 85, oil tanker 59, other 159
comparison ranking: total 53

Ports: *total ports:* 2 (2024)
large: 0
medium: 0
small: 0
very small: 2
ports with oil terminals: 2
key ports: Basseterre, Charlestown

MILITARY AND SECURITY

Military and security forces: St. Kitts and Nevis Defense Force (SKNDF); Regular Force, Coast Guard Force (SKNDF Coast Guard), Reserve Force, Cadet Force

Ministry of National Security: the Royal St. Christopher and Nevis Police Force (2025)

Military and security service personnel strengths: estimated 200 active Defense Forces (2024)

Military equipment inventories and acquisitions: the SKNDF is lightly armed with equipment from Belgium, the UK, and the US (2024)

Military service age and obligation: 18 years of age for voluntary military service for men and women (under 18 with written parental permission); no conscription (2025)

Military - note: SKNDF's missions include protecting the country's territorial integrity, assisting the police in combating the illegal narcotic trade and other crimes, and providing humanitarian and disaster relief assistance; the force also has a regional role through the Caribbean Regional Security System (RSS); St. Kitts joined the RSS in 1984; RSS signatories (Antigua and Barbuda, Barbados, Dominica, Grenada, Guyana, Saint Lucia, and Saint Vincent and the Grenadines) agreed to prepare contingency plans and assist one another, on request, in national emergencies, prevention of smuggling, search and rescue, immigration control, fishery protection, customs and excise control, maritime policing duties, protection of off-shore installations, pollution control, national and other disasters, and threats to national security (2025)

TRANSNATIONAL ISSUES

Refugees and internally displaced persons: *refugees:* 5 (2024 est.)

SAINT LUCIA

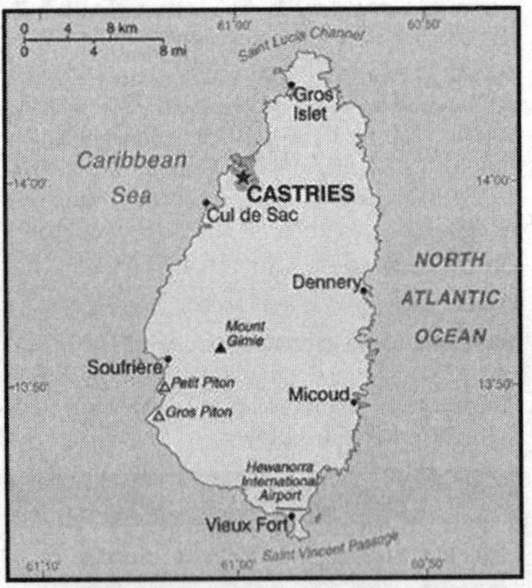

INTRODUCTION

Background: England and France contested Saint Lucia – with its fine natural harbor at Castries and burgeoning sugar industry – throughout the 17th and early 18th centuries, with possession changing 14 times; it was finally ceded to the UK in 1814 and became part of the British Windward Islands colony. Even after the abolition of slavery on its plantations in 1834, Saint Lucia remained an agricultural island, dedicated to producing tropical commodity crops. In the mid-20th century, Saint Lucia joined the West Indies Federation (1958–1962) and in 1967 became one of the six members of the West Indies Associated States, with internal selfgovernment. In 1979, Saint Lucia gained full independence.

GEOGRAPHY

Location: Caribbean, island between the Caribbean Sea and North Atlantic Ocean, north of Trinidad and Tobago

Geographic coordinates: 13 53 N, 60 58 W

Map references: Central America and the Caribbean

Area: *total:* 616 sq km
land: 606 sq km
water: 10 sq km
comparison ranking: total 192

Area - comparative: 3.5 times the size of Washington, D.C.

Land boundaries: *total:* 0 km

Coastline: 158 km

Maritime claims: *territorial sea:* 12 nm
contiguous zone: 24 nm
exclusive economic zone: 200 nm
continental shelf: 200 nm or to the edge of the continental margin

Climate: tropical, moderated by northeast trade winds; dry season January to April, rainy season May to August

Terrain: volcanic and mountainous with broad, fertile valleys

Elevation: *highest point:* Mount Gimie 948 m
lowest point: Caribbean Sea 0 m

Natural resources: forests, sandy beaches, minerals (pumice), mineral springs, geothermal potential

Land use: *agricultural land:* 16.3% (2022 est.)
arable land: 4.4% (2022 est.)
permanent crops: 11.3% (2022 est.)
permanent pasture: 0.6% (2022 est.)
forest: 34% (2022 est.)
other: 49.7% (2022 est.)

Irrigated land: 30 sq km (2012)

Population distribution: most of the population is found on the periphery of the island, with a larger concentration in the north around the capital of Castries

Natural hazards: hurricanes
volcanism: Mount Gimie (948 m), also known as Qualibou, is a caldera on the west of the island; the iconic twin pyramidal peaks of Gros Piton (771 m) and Petit Piton (743 m) are lava-dome remnants associated with the Soufrière volcano; there have been no historical magmatic eruptions, but a minor steam eruption in 1766 spread a thin layer of ash over a wide area; Saint Lucia is part of the volcanic-island arc of the Lesser Antilles that extends from Saba in the north to Grenada in the south

Geography - note: the twin Pitons (Gros Piton and Petit Piton), striking cone-shaped peaks south of Soufrière, are one of the scenic natural highlights of the Caribbean

PEOPLE AND SOCIETY

Population: *total:* 168,038 (2024 est.)
male: 81,517
female: 86,521
comparison rankings: total 186; male 186; female 185

Nationality: *noun:* Saint Lucian(s)
adjective: Saint Lucian

Ethnic groups: Black/African descent 85.3%, mixed 10.9%, East Indian 2.2%, other 1.6%, unspecified 0.1% (2010 est.)

Languages: English (official), Saint Lucian Creole

Religions: Roman Catholic 61.5%, Protestant 25.5% (includes Seventh Day Adventist 10.4%, Pentecostal 8.9%, Baptist 2.2%, Anglican 1.6%, Church of God 1.5%, other Protestant 0.9%), other Christian 3.4% (includes Evangelical 2.3% and Jehovah's Witness 1.1%), Rastafarian 1.9%, other 0.4%, none 5.9%, unspecified 1.4% (2010 est.)

Age structure: *0-14 years:* 17.9% (male 15,505/ female 14,607)
15-64 years: 66.7% (male 54,260/female 57,747)
65 years and over: 15.4% (2024 est.) (male 11,752/ female 14,167)

Dependency ratios: *total dependency ratio:* 50 (2024 est.)
youth dependency ratio: 26.9 (2024 est.)
elderly dependency ratio: 23.1 (2024 est.)
potential support ratio: 4.3 (2024 est.)

Median age: *total:* 39.7 years (2024 est.)
male: 38.4 years
female: 40.9 years
comparison ranking: total 65

Population growth rate: 0.26% (2024 est.)
comparison ranking: 171

Birth rate: 11.4 births/1,000 population (2024 est.)
comparison ranking: 159

Death rate: 8.3 deaths/1,000 population (2024 est.)
comparison ranking: 78

Net migration rate: -0.6 migrant(s)/1,000 population (2024 est.)
comparison ranking: 128

Population distribution: most of the population is found on the periphery of the island, with a larger concentration in the north around the capital of Castries

Urbanization: *urban population:* 19.2% of total population (2023)
rate of urbanization: 0.98% annual rate of change (2020-25 est.)

Major urban areas - population: 22,000 CASTRIES (capital) (2018)

Sex ratio: *at birth:* 1.06 male(s)/female
0-14 years: 1.06 male(s)/female
15-64 years: 0.94 male(s)/female
65 years and over: 0.83 male(s)/female
total population: 0.94 male(s)/female (2024 est.)

Maternal mortality ratio: 44 deaths/100,000 live births (2023 est.)
comparison ranking: 99

Infant mortality rate: *total:* 11.5 deaths/1,000 live births (2024 est.)
male: 10.8 deaths/1,000 live births
female: 12.2 deaths/1,000 live births
comparison ranking: total 118

Life expectancy at birth: *total population:* 79.4 years (2024 est.)
male: 76.7 years
female: 82.3 years
comparison ranking: total population 64

Total fertility rate: 1.71 children born/woman (2024 est.)
comparison ranking: 161

Gross reproduction rate: 0.83 (2024 est.)

Drinking water source: *improved: urban:* 97.2% of population (2022 est.)
rural: 96.8% of population (2022 est.)
total: 96.9% of population (2022 est.)
unimproved: urban: 2.8% of population (2022 est.)
rural: 3.2% of population (2022 est.)
total: 3.1% of population (2022 est.)

Health expenditure: 6.2% of GDP (2021)
9% of national budget (2022 est.)

Physician density: 4.23 physicians/1,000 population (2020)

Hospital bed density: 2 beds/1,000 population (2021 est.)

Sanitation facility access: *improved: urban:* 97.6% of population (2022 est.)
rural: 92.9% of population (2022 est.)
total: 93.8% of population (2022 est.)
unimproved: urban: 2.4% of population (2022 est.)
rural: 7.1% of population (2022 est.)
total: 6.2% of population (2022 est.)

Obesity - adult prevalence rate: 19.7% (2016)
comparison ranking: 111

Alcohol consumption per capita: *total:* 9.3 liters of pure alcohol (2019 est.)
beer: 3.21 liters of pure alcohol (2019 est.)
wine: 0.4 liters of pure alcohol (2019 est.)
spirits: 5.1 liters of pure alcohol (2019 est.)
other alcohols: 0.6 liters of pure alcohol (2019 est.)
comparison ranking: total 31

Tobacco use: *total:* 13.1% (2025 est.)
male: 24.1% (2025 est.)
female: 2.6% (2025 est.)
comparison ranking: total 109

Currently married women (ages 15-49): 53.6% (2023 est.)

Education expenditure: 2.7% of GDP (2023 est.)
11.8% national budget (2023 est.)
comparison ranking: Education expenditure (% GDP) 166

School life expectancy (primary to tertiary education): *total:* 13 years (2023 est.)
male: 12 years (2023 est.)
female: 13 years (2023 est.)

ENVIRONMENT

Environmental issues: deforestation; soil erosion, particularly in the northern region

International environmental agreements: *party to:* Biodiversity, Climate Change, Climate Change-Kyoto Protocol, Climate Change-Paris Agreement, Comprehensive Nuclear Test Ban, Desertification, Endangered Species, Environmental Modification, Hazardous Wastes, Law of the Sea, Marine Dumping-London Convention, Ozone Layer Protection, Ship Pollution, Wetlands, Whaling
signed, but not ratified: none of the selected agreements

Climate: tropical, moderated by northeast trade winds; dry season January to April, rainy season May to August

Urbanization: *urban population:* 19.2% of total population (2023)
rate of urbanization: 0.98% annual rate of change (2020-25 est.)

Carbon dioxide emissions: 605,000 metric tonnes of CO2 (2023 est.)
from petroleum and other liquids: 605,000 metric tonnes of CO2 (2023 est.)
comparison ranking: total emissions 186

Particulate matter emissions: 8.9 micrograms per cubic meter (2019 est.)

Waste and recycling: *municipal solid waste generated annually:* 77,600 tons (2024 est.)
percent of municipal solid waste recycled: 13.3% (2022 est.)

Total water withdrawal: *municipal:* 12.5 million cubic meters (2022 est.)
industrial: 0 cubic meters (2022 est.)
agricultural: 30.4 million cubic meters (2022 est.)

Total renewable water resources: 300 million cubic meters (2022 est.)

GOVERNMENT

Country name: *conventional long form:* none
conventional short form: Saint Lucia
etymology: believed to be named after Saint LUCY (Sainte ALOUSIE) of Syracuse by French sailors who were shipwrecked on the island on 13 December 1502, the saint's feast day
note: pronounced saynt-LOO-shuh

Government type: parliamentary democracy under a constitutional monarchy; a Commonwealth realm

Capital: *name:* Castries
geographic coordinates: 14 00 N, 61 00 W
time difference: UTC-4 (1 hour ahead of Washington, DC, during Standard Time)
etymology: in 1785, the village of Carenage was renamed Castries, after Charles Eugene Gabriel de La Croix de CASTRIES, who was then the French Minister of the Navy and Colonies

Administrative divisions: 10 districts; Anse-la-Raye, Canaries, Castries, Choiseul, Dennery, Gros-Islet, Laborie, Micoud, Soufrière, Vieux-Fort

Legal system: English common law

Constitution: *history:* previous 1958, 1960 (pre-independence); latest presented 20 December 1978, effective 22 February 1979
amendment process: proposed by Parliament; passage requires at least two-thirds majority vote by the House of Assembly membership in the final reading and assent of the governor general; passage of amendments to various constitutional sections, such as those on fundamental rights and freedoms, government finances, the judiciary, and procedures for amending the constitution, require at least three-quarters majority vote by the House and assent of the governor general; passage of amendments approved by the House but rejected by the Senate require a majority of votes cast in a referendum

International law organization participation: has not submitted an ICJ jurisdiction declaration; accepts ICCt jurisdiction

Citizenship: *citizenship by birth:* yes
citizenship by descent only: at least one parent must be a citizen of Saint Lucia
dual citizenship recognized: yes
residency requirement for naturalization: 8 years

Suffrage: 18 years of age; universal

Executive branch: *chief of state:* King CHARLES III (since 8 September 2022); represented by Acting Governor General Errol CHARLES (since 11 November 2021)
head of government: Prime Minister Philip J. PIERRE (since 28 July 2021)
cabinet: Cabinet appointed by the governor general on the advice of the prime minister
election/appointment process: the monarchy is hereditary; governor general appointed by the monarch; following legislative elections, the governor general usually appoints the leader of the majority party or majority coalition as prime minister; deputy prime minister also appointed by governor general

Legislative branch: *legislature name:* Houses of Parliament
legislative structure: bicameral

Legislative branch - lower chamber: *chamber name:* House of Assembly
number of seats: 18 (all directly elected)
electoral system: plurality/majority
scope of elections: full renewal
term in office: 5 years
most recent election date: 7/26/2021
parties elected and seats per party: Saint Lucia Labour Party (SLP) (13); United Workers Party (UWP) (2); Independents (2)
percentage of women in chamber: 10.5%
expected date of next election: July 2026

Legislative branch - upper chamber: *chamber name:* Senate
number of seats: 11 (all appointed)
scope of elections: full renewal
term in office: 5 years
most recent election date: 8/17/2021
percentage of women in chamber: 54.5%
expected date of next election: August 2026

Judicial branch: *highest court(s):* the Eastern Caribbean Supreme Court (ECSC) is the superior court of the Organization of Eastern Caribbean States; the ECSC is headquartered on St. Lucia and consists of the Court of Appeal – headed by the chief justice and 4 judges – and the High Court with 18 judges; the Court of Appeal travels to member states on a schedule to hear appeals from the High Court and subordinate courts; member of the Caribbean Court of Justice
judge selection and term of office: chief justice of Eastern Caribbean Supreme Court appointed by the British monarch; other justices and judges appointed by the Judicial and Legal Services Commission, an independent body of judicial officials; Court of Appeal justices appointed for life with mandatory retirement at age 65; High Court judges appointed for life with mandatory retirement at age 62
subordinate courts: magistrate's court

Political parties: Saint Lucia Labor Party or SLP
United Workers Party or UWP

Diplomatic representation in the US: *chief of mission:* Ambassador Elizabeth DARIUS-CLARKE (since 7 June 2022)
chancery: 1629 K Street NW, Suite 1250, Washington, DC 20006
telephone: [1] (202) 364-6792
FAX: [1] (202) 364-6723
email address and website: embassydc@gosl.gov.lc
https://www.embassyofstlucia.org/
consulate(s) general: Miami, New York

Diplomatic representation from the US: *embassy:* the US does not have an embassy in Saint Lucia; the US Ambassador to Barbados is accredited to Saint Lucia

International organization participation: ACP, ACS, AOSIS, C, Caricom, CD, CDB, CELAC, FAO, G-77, IBRD, ICAO, ICCt, ICRM, IDA, IFAD, IFC,

IFRCS, ILO, IMF, IMO, Interpol, IOC, ISO, ITU, ITUC (NGOs), MIGA, NAM, OAS, OECS, OIF, OPANAL, OPCW, Petrocaribe, UN, UNCTAD, UNESCO, UNIDO, UPU, WCO, WFTU (NGOs), WHO, WIPO, WMO, WTO

Independence: 22 February 1979 (from the UK)

National holiday: Independence Day, 22 February (1979)

Flag: *description:* cerulean blue with a gold isosceles triangle below a black arrowhead; the upper edges of the arrowhead have a white border
meaning: blue stands for the sky and sea, gold for sunshine and prosperity, and white and black for the ethnic composition of the island; the triangles represent Gros Piton and Petit Piton, the cone-shaped volcanic plugs that are a symbol of the island

National symbol(s): twin pitons (volcanic peaks), Saint Lucia parrot

National color(s): cerulean blue, gold, black, white

National anthem(s): *title:* "Sons and Daughters of St. Lucia"
lyrics/music: Charles JESSE/Leton Felix THOMAS
history: adopted 1967
title: "God Save the King"
lyrics/music: unknown
history: in use since 1745

National heritage: *total World Heritage Sites:* 1 (natural)
selected World Heritage Site locales: Pitons Management Area

ECONOMY

Economic overview: upper middle-income, tourism-based Caribbean island economy; environmentally fragile; energy import-dependent; major banana producer; well-educated labor force; key infrastructure, IT, and communications investments

Real GDP (purchasing power parity): $4.359 billion (2024 est.)
$4.196 billion (2023 est.)
$4.105 billion (2022 est.)
note: data in 2021 dollars
comparison ranking: 186

Real GDP growth rate: 3.9% (2024 est.)
2.2% (2023 est.)
20.4% (2022 est.)
note: annual GDP % growth based on constant local currency
comparison ranking: 80

Real GDP per capita: $24,300 (2024 est.)
$23,400 (2023 est.)
$23,000 (2022 est.)
note: data in 2021 dollars
comparison ranking: 91

GDP (official exchange rate): $2.549 billion (2024 est.)
note: data in current dollars at official exchange rate

Inflation rate (consumer prices): -0.1% (2024 est.)
4.1% (2023 est.)
6.4% (2022 est.)
note: annual % change based on consumer prices
comparison ranking: 6

GDP - composition, by sector of origin: *agriculture:* 1.1% (2024 est.)
industry: 9.8% (2024 est.)
services: 75.9% (2024 est.)
note: figures may not total 100% due to non-allocated consumption not captured in sector-reported data
comparison rankings: agriculture 172; industry 188; services 19

GDP - composition, by end use: *household consumption:* 66.1% (2017 est.)
government consumption: 11.2% (2017 est.)
investment in fixed capital: 16.9% (2017 est.)
investment in inventories: 0.1% (2017 est.)
exports of goods and services: 62.7% (2017 est.)
imports of goods and services: -56.9% (2017 est.)

Agricultural products: coconuts, bananas, tropical fruits, fruits, root vegetables, plantains, vegetables, cassava, chicken, milk (2023)
note: top ten agricultural products based on tonnage

Industries: tourism; clothing, assembly of electronic components, beverages, corrugated cardboard boxes, lime processing, coconut processing

Industrial production growth rate: 5.6% (2024 est.)
note: annual % change in industrial value added based on constant local currency
comparison ranking: 36

Labor force: 102,400 (2024 est.)
note: number of people ages 15 or older who are employed or seeking work
comparison ranking: 182

Unemployment rate: 11% (2024 est.)
11.1% (2023 est.)
16% (2022 est.)
note: % of labor force seeking employment
comparison ranking: 154

Youth unemployment rate (ages 15-24): *total:* 29% (2024 est.)
male: 31.4% (2024 est.)
female: 26.3% (2024 est.)
note: % of labor force ages 15-24 seeking employment
comparison ranking: total 24

Population below poverty line: 25% (2015 est.)
note: % of population with income below national poverty line

Gini Index coefficient - distribution of family income 51.2 (2016 est.)
note: index (0-100) of income distribution; higher values represent greater inequality
comparison ranking: 8

Household income or consumption by percentage share: *lowest 10%:* 2.1% (2015 est.)
highest 10%: 34.1% (2015 est.)
note: % share of income accruing to lowest and highest 10% of population

Remittances: 2.5% of GDP (2024 est.)
2.6% of GDP (2023 est.)
2.6% of GDP (2022 est.)
note: personal transfers and compensation between resident and non-resident individuals/households/entities

Budget: *revenues:* $414.77 million (2017 est.)
expenditures: $351.956 million (2017 est.)
note: central government revenues and expenses (excluding grants/extrabudgetary units/social security funds) converted to US dollars at average official exchange rate for year indicated

Taxes and other revenues: 18.2% (of GDP) (2017 est.)
note: central government tax revenue as a % of GDP
comparison ranking: 63

Current account balance: -$64.121 million (2024 est.)
-$38.069 million (2023 est.)
-$83.442 million (2022 est.)
note: balance of payments - net trade and primary/secondary income in current dollars
comparison ranking: 91

Exports: $1.6 billion (2024 est.)
$1.419 billion (2023 est.)
$1.29 billion (2022 est.)
note: balance of payments - exports of goods and services in current dollars
comparison ranking: 171

Exports - partners: Guyana 20%, Suriname 15%, USA 11%, Barbados 8%, Dominica 7% (2023)
note: top five export partners based on percentage share of exports

Exports - commodities: refined petroleum, gravel and crushed stone, beer, liquor, paper containers (2023)
note: top five export commodities based on value in dollars

Imports: $1.446 billion (2024 est.)
$1.292 billion (2023 est.)
$1.2 billion (2022 est.)
note: balance of payments - imports of goods and services in current dollars
comparison ranking: 186

Imports - partners: USA 59%, Guyana 8%, Brazil 7%, China 5%, UK 3% (2023)
note: top five import partners based on percentage share of imports

Imports - commodities: refined petroleum, crude petroleum, cars, poultry, plastic products (2023)
note: top five import commodities based on value in dollars

Reserves of foreign exchange and gold: $406.064 million (2024 est.)
$424.324 million (2023 est.)
$389.083 million (2022 est.)
note: holdings of gold (year-end prices)/foreign exchange/special drawing rights in current dollars
comparison ranking: 165

Debt - external: $901.317 million (2023 est.)
note: present value of external debt in current US dollars
comparison ranking: 107

Exchange rates: East Caribbean dollars (XCD) per US dollar -

Exchange rates: 2.7 (2024 est.)
2.7 (2023 est.)
2.7 (2022 est.)
2.7 (2021 est.)
2.7 (2020 est.)

ENERGY

Electricity access: *electrification - total population:* 100% (2022 est.)

Electricity: *installed generating capacity:* 93,000 kW (2023 est.)
consumption: 365.178 million kWh (2023 est.)
transmission/distribution losses: 31.038 million kWh (2023 est.)
comparison rankings: installed generating capacity 188; consumption 183; transmission/distribution losses 30

Electricity generation sources: *fossil fuels:* 98% of total installed capacity (2023 est.)
solar: 2% of total installed capacity (2023 est.)

Petroleum: *refined petroleum consumption:* 4,000 bbl/day (2023 est.)

Energy consumption per capita: 47.522 million Btu/person (2023 est.)

comparison ranking: 96

COMMUNICATIONS

Telephones - fixed lines: *total subscriptions:* 31,000 (2022 est.)
subscriptions per 100 inhabitants: 17 (2022 est.)
comparison ranking: total subscriptions 166

Telephones - mobile cellular: *total subscriptions:* 176,000 (2022 est.)
subscriptions per 100 inhabitants: 96 (2021 est.)
comparison ranking: total subscriptions 184

Broadcast media: 3 privately owned TV stations; 1 public TV station on a cable network; multi-channel cable TV service available; mix of state-owned and privately owned radio broadcasters with about 25 stations, including repeater transmission stations (2019)

Internet country code: .lc

Internet users: *percent of population:* 74% (2022 est.)

Broadband - fixed subscriptions: *total:* 24,000 (2022 est.)
subscriptions per 100 inhabitants: 14 (2022 est.)
comparison ranking: total 164

TRANSPORTATION

Civil aircraft registration country code prefix: J6

Airports: 2 (2025)
comparison ranking: 204

Ports: *total ports:* 3 (2024)
large: 0
medium: 0
small: 2
very small: 1
ports with oil terminals: 2
key ports: Castries, Grand Cul de Sac Bay, Vieux Fort

MILITARY AND SECURITY

Military and security forces: *no regular military forces; Ministry of Home Affairs, Justice, and National Security:* Royal Saint Lucia Police Force (RSLPF) (2024)

Military - note: Saint Lucia has been a member of the Caribbean Regional Security System (RSS) since its creation in 1982; RSS signatories (Antigua and Barbuda, Barbados, Dominica, Grenada, Guyana, Saint Kitts, and Saint Vincent and the Grenadines) agreed to prepare contingency plans and assist one another, on request, in national emergencies, prevention of smuggling, search and rescue, immigration control, fishery protection, customs and excise control, maritime policing duties, protection of off-shore installations, pollution control, national and other disasters, and threats to national security (2025)

TRANSNATIONAL ISSUES

Refugees and internally displaced persons: *refugees:* 5 (2024 est.)

Trafficking in persons: *tier rating:* Tier 2 Watch List — the government did not demonstrate overall increasing efforts to eliminate trafficking compared with the previous reporting period, therefore Saint Lucia was downgraded to Tier 2 Watch List; for more details, go to: https://www.state.gov/reports/2025- trafficking-in-persons-report/saint-lucia/

SAINT MARTIN

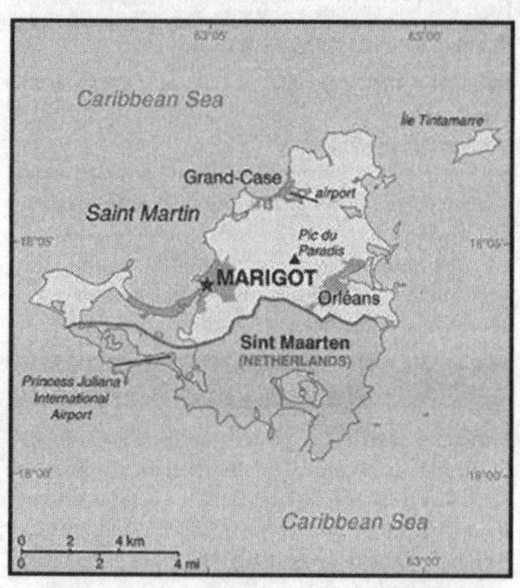

INTRODUCTION

Background: Christopher COLUMBUS claimed Saint Martin for Spain in 1493, naming it after the feast day of St. Martin of Tours, but it was the Dutch who occupied the island in 1631 to exploit its salt deposits. The Spanish retook Saint Martin in 1633, but the Dutch continued to assert their claims. The Spanish finally relinquished the island to the French and Dutch, who divided it between themselves in 1648. The border frequently fluctuated over the next 200 years because of friction between the two countries, with the French eventually holding the greater portion of the island (about 61%).

The cultivation of sugarcane introduced African slavery to the island in the late 18th century; the practice was not abolished until 1848. The island became a free port in 1939, and the tourism industry was dramatically expanded during the 1970s and 1980s. In 2003, the populace of Saint Martin voted to secede from Guadeloupe, and in 2007, the northern portion of the island became a French overseas collectivity. In 2010, the southern Dutch portion of the island became the independent nation of Sint Maarten within the Kingdom of the Netherlands. In 2017, Hurricane Irma passed over the island of Saint Martin, causing extensive damage to roads, communications, electrical power, and housing; the UN estimated that 90% of the buildings were damaged or destroyed.

GEOGRAPHY

Location: Caribbean, located in the Leeward Islands (northern) group; French part of the island of Saint Martin in the Caribbean Sea; Saint Martin lies east of the US Virgin Islands

Geographic coordinates: 18 05 N, 63 57 W

Map references: Central America and the Caribbean

Area: *total:* 50 sq km
land: 50 sq km
water: negligible
comparison ranking: total 230

Area - comparative: more than one-third the size of Washington, D.C.

Land boundaries: *total:* 16 km
border countries (1): Sint Maarten 16 km

Coastline: 58.9 km (for entire island)

Climate: temperature averages 27-29 degrees Celsius all year long; low humidity, gentle trade winds, brief, intense rain showers; hurricane season stretches from July to November

Elevation: *highest point:* Pic du Paradis 424 m
lowest point: Caribbean Sea 0 m

Natural resources: salt

Land use: *agricultural land:* 0% (2022 est.)
forest: 24.8% (2022 est.)
other: 75.2% (2022 est.)

Population distribution: most of the population is found along the coast, with the largest concentration around the capital of Marigot, as well as Orleans and Grand-Case

Natural hazards: subject to hurricanes from July to Novembe

Geography - note: *note 1:* the southern border is shared with Sint Maarten, which is part of the Kingdom of the Netherlands; together, these two entities make up the smallest landmass in the world that is shared by two self-governing states
note 2: Simpson Bay Lagoon (aka Simson Bay Lagoon or The Great Pond) is one of the largest inland lagoons in the West Indies; the border between the French and Dutch halves of the island runs across the center of the lagoon, which is shared by both of the island's entities

PEOPLE AND SOCIETY

Population: *total:* 32,996 (2024 est.)
male: 15,791
female: 17,205
comparison rankings: total 215; male 215; female 215

Ethnic groups: Creole (Mulatto), Black, Guadeloupe Mestizo (French-East Asian), White, East Indian, other

Languages: French (official), Dutch, English, Guadeloupian Creole, Haitian Creole, Italian, Martiniquan Creole, Papiamento (dialect of Netherlands Antilles), Spanish
major-language sample(s):
The World Factbook, une source indispensable d'informations de base. (French)

Religions: Roman Catholic, Jehovah's Witness, Protestant, Hindu

Age structure: *0-14 years:* 24.7% (male 4,039/female 4,100)
15-64 years: 64.5% (male 10,216/female 11,068)
65 years and over: 10.8% (2024 est.) (male 1,536/female 2,037)

Dependency ratios: *total dependency ratio:* 55 (2024 est.) N
youth dependency ratio: 38.2 (2024 est.)
elderly dependency ratio: 16.8 (2024 est.)
potential support ratio: 6 (2024 est.)

Median age: *total:* 34.2 years (2024 est.)
male: 33.4 years
female: 34.9 years
comparison ranking: total 106

Population growth rate: 0.3% (2024 est.)
comparison ranking: 166

Birth rate: 13.9 births/1,000 population (2024 est.)
comparison ranking: 121

Death rate: 4.8 deaths/1,000 population (2024 est.)
comparison ranking: 202

Net migration rate: -6.2 migrant(s)/1,000 population (2024 est.)
comparison ranking: 211

Population distribution: most of the population is found along the coast, with the largest concentration around the capital of Marigot, as well as Orleans and Grand-Case

Sex ratio: *at birth:* 1.04 male(s)/female
0-14 years: 0.99 male(s)/female
15-64 years: 0.92 male(s)/female
65 years and over: 0.75 male(s)/female
total population: 0.92 male(s)/female (2024 est.)

Infant mortality rate: *total:* 6.5 deaths/1,000 live births (2024 est.)
male: 7.6 deaths/1,000 live births
female: 5.3 deaths/1,000 live births
comparison ranking: total 160

Life expectancy at birth: *total population:* 81 years (2024 est.)
male: 78 years
female: 84.2 years
comparison ranking: total population 46

Total fertility rate: 1.8 children born/woman (2024 est.)
comparison ranking: 140

Gross reproduction rate: 0.88 (2024 est.)

Drinking water source: *improved:* total: 100% of population
unimproved: urban: 0% of population

Sanitation facility access: *improved: urban:* 100% of population (2022 est.)
total: 100% of population (2022 est.)
unimproved: urban: 0% of population (2022 est.)
total: 0% of population (2022 est.)

Education expenditure: 3.9% of GDP (2023 est.) NA 23% national budget (2023 est.)
comparison ranking: Education expenditure (% GDP) 117

ENVIRONMENT

Environmental issues: waste management; salinity intrusions; limited freshwater resources; over-exploitation of marine resources (reef fisheries, coral, and shell); water pollution and damage to coral reefs from boats

Climate: temperature averages 27-29 degrees Celsius all year long; low humidity, gentle trade winds, brief, intense rain showers; hurricane season stretches from July to November

Waste and recycling: *municipal solid waste generated annually:* 15,500 tons (2024 est.)

GOVERNMENT

Country name: *conventional long form:* Overseas Collectivity of Saint Martin
conventional short form: Saint Martin
local long form: Collectivité d'outre mer de Saint-Martin
local short form: Saint-Martin
etymology: explorer Christopher COLUMBUS named the island after Saint MARTIN of Tours during a visit on 11 November 1493, the saint's feast day

Government type: parliamentary democracy (Territorial Council); overseas collectivity of France

Dependency status: overseas collectivity of France
note: the only French overseas collectivity that is part of the EU

Capital: *name:* Marigot
geographic coordinates: 18 04 N, 63 05 W
time difference: UTC-4 (1 hour ahead of Washington, DC, during Standard Time)
etymology: the name is taken from the French word *marigot*, meaning "backwater" or "swampy area;" it probably comes from the original fishing village's location next to a water-logged area on a lagoon

Legal system: French civil law

Constitution: *history:* 4 October 1958 (French Constitution)
amendment process: amendment procedures of France's constitution apply

Citizenship: see France

Suffrage: 18 years of age, universal

Executive branch: *chief of state:* President Emmanuel MACRON (since 14 May 2017); represented by Prefect Cyrille LE VELY (since 10 February 2025)
head of government: President of Territorial Council Louis MUSSINGTON (since 3 April 2022)
cabinet: Executive Council, as well as an advisory economic, social, and cultural council
election/appointment process: French president directly elected by absolute-majority popular vote in 2 rounds, if needed, for a 5-year term (eligible for a second term); prefect appointed by French president on the advice of French Ministry of Interior; president of Territorial Council elected by its members for a 5-year term
most recent election date: 3 April 2022
election results: *2022:* Louis MUSSINGTON (RSM) elected president; Territorial Council vote - unanimous
2017: Daniel Gibbs (UD) elected president; Territorial Council vote - 18 of 23 votes
expected date of next election: 2027

Legislative branch: *legislature name:* Territorial Council
legislative structure: unicameral
number of seats: 23 (directly elected)
electoral system: plurality/majority
scope of elections: full renewal
term in office: 5 years
most recent election date: 3/27/2022
parties elected and seats per party: RSM and Alternative (16); UD (5); HOPE, Saint Martin with You, and Future Saint Martin (2)
percentage of women in chamber: 43.5%
expected date of next election: March 2027
note: 1 senator is indirectly elected to the French Senate by an electoral college for a 6-year term, and 1 deputy (shared with Saint Barthelemy) is directly elected to the French National Assembly for a 5-year term

Political parties: Alternative
Future Saint Martin (Avenir Saint Martin)
Generation Hope or HOPE
Rassemblement Saint-Martinois or RSM (formerly Movement for Justice and Prosperity or MJP)
Saint Martin with You
Union for Democracy or UD

Diplomatic representation in the US: none (overseas collectivity of France)

Diplomatic representation from the US: *embassy:* none (overseas collectivity of France)

International organization participation: ACS (associate), UPU

Independence: none (overseas collectivity of France)

National holiday: Fête de la Fédération, 14 July (1790)
note 1: local holiday is Schoelcher Day (Slavery Abolition Day) 12 July (1848), as well as St. Martin's Day, 11 November (1985); the latter holiday celebrated on both halves of the island
note 2: often incorrectly referred to as Bastille Day, France's national celebration commemorates the storming of the Bastille prison on 14 July 1789 and the establishment of a constitutional monarchy; other names for the holiday are *la Fête nationale* (National Holiday) and *le Quatorze Juillet* (14th of July)

Flag: the flag of France is used

National symbol(s): brown pelican

National anthem(s): *title:* "O Sweet Saint Martin's Land"
lyrics/music: Gerard KEMPS
history: the song, written in 1958, is used as an unofficial anthem for the entire island (both French and Dutch sides)
title: "La Marseillaise" (The Song of Marseille)
lyrics/music: Claude-Joseph ROUGET de Lisle
history: official anthem, as a French collectivity

ECONOMY

Economic overview: high-income French Caribbean territorial economy; extremely reliant on tourism, with severe COVID-19 impacts; near-total destruction from Hurricane Irma in 2017; some offshore banking; import-dependent; duty-free commerce; yachting destination

Real GDP growth rate: 4.9% (2021 est.)
-12.5% (2020 est.)
6.5% (2019 est.)
note: annual GDP % growth based on constant local currency
comparison ranking: 49

GDP (official exchange rate): $649.206 million (2021 est.)
note: data in current dollars at official exchange rate

Industries: tourism, light industry and manufacturing, heavy industry

Exports - partners: United States 35%, Netherlands 26%, Antigua and Barbuda 21%, France 10% (2019)

Exports - commodities: gold, special use vessels, furniture, scrap aluminum, rum (2019)
top five export commodities based on value in dollars

Imports - partners: United States 76%, Netherlands 7%, France 7% (2019)

Imports - commodities: jewelry, diamonds, pearls, recreational boats, cars (2019)

Exchange rates: euros (EUR) per US dollar -

Exchange rates: 0.924 (2024 est.)
0.925 (2023 est.)
0.95 (2022 est.)
0.845 (2021 est.)
0.876 (2020 est.)

ENERGY

Electricity access: *electrification - total population:* 100% (2022 est.)

COMMUNICATIONS

Telephones - mobile cellular: *total subscriptions:* 68,840 (2012 est.)
subscriptions per 100 inhabitants: 196 (2012 est.)
comparison ranking: total subscriptions 199

Broadcast media: 1 local TV station; access to about 20 radio stations, including RFO Guadeloupe radio broadcasts via repeater

Internet country code: .mf
note:.gp, the Internet country code for Guadeloupe, and.fr, the Internet country code for France, are also used

Internet users: *percent of population:* 48.5% (2022 est.)

TRANSPORTATION

Airports: 1 (2025)
comparison ranking: 231

MILITARY AND SECURITY

Military and security forces: *no regular military forces; Ministry of Justice:* Police Force of Sint Maaten (Korps Politie Sint Marteen, KPSM) (2025)

Military - note: defense is the responsibility of France

TRANSNATIONAL ISSUES

Refugees and internally displaced persons: *refugees:* 156 (2024 est.)

SAINT PIERRE AND MIQUELON

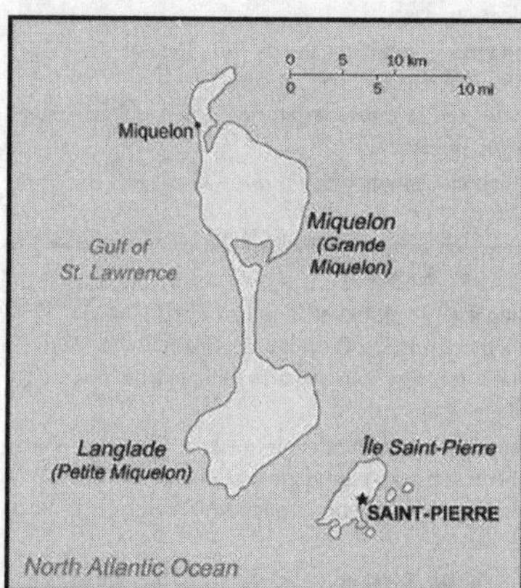

INTRODUCTION

Background: First settled by the French in the early 17th century, Saint Pierre and Miquelon are the sole remaining vestige of France's once vast North American possessions. They attained the status of an overseas collectivity in 2003.

GEOGRAPHY

Location: Northern North America, islands in the North Atlantic Ocean, south of Newfoundland (Canada)

Geographic coordinates: 46 50 N, 56 20 W

Map references: North America

Area: *total:* 242 sq km
land: 242 sq km
water: 0 sq km
note: includes eight small islands in the Saint Pierre and the Miquelon groups
comparison ranking: total 214

Area - comparative: 1.5 times the size of Washington, D.C.

Land boundaries: *total:* 0 km

Coastline: 120 km

Maritime claims: *territorial sea:* 12 nm
exclusive economic zone: 200 nm

Climate: cold and wet, with considerable mist and fog; spring and autumn are often windy

Terrain: mostly barren rock

Elevation: *highest point:* Morne de la Grande Montagne 240 m
lowest point: Atlantic Ocean 0 m

Natural resources: fish, deepwater ports

Land use: *agricultural land:* 8.7% (2022 est.)
arable land: 8.7% (2022 est.)
permanent crops: 0% (2022 est.)
permanent pasture: 0% (2022 est.)
forest: 5.1% (2022 est.)
other: 86.2% (2022 est.)

Irrigated land: 0 sq km (2022)

Population distribution: most of the population is found on Saint Pierre Island; a small settlement is located on the north end of Miquelon Island

Natural hazards: persistent fog throughout the year can be a maritime hazard

Geography - note: vegetation scanty; the islands are part of the northern Appalachians, along with Newfoundland

PEOPLE AND SOCIETY

Population: *total:* 5,132 (2024 est.)
male: 2,476
female: 2,656
comparison rankings: total 227; male 227; female 227

Nationality: *noun:* Frenchman(men), Frenchwoman(women)
adjective: French

Ethnic groups: Basques and Bretons (French fishermen)

Languages: French (official)
major-language sample(s):
The World Factbook, une source indispensable d'informations de base. (French)

Religions: Roman Catholic 99%, other 1%

Age structure: *0-14 years:* 13.1% (male 346/female 328)
15-64 years: 61.6% (male 1,559/female 1,600)
65 years and over: 25.3% (2024 est.) (male 571/female 728)

Dependency ratios: *total dependency ratio:* 62.5 (2024 est.)
youth dependency ratio: 21.3 (2024 est.)
elderly dependency ratio: 41.1 (2024 est.)
potential support ratio: 2.4 (2024 est.)

Median age: *total:* 51.2 years (2024 est.)
male: 50.5 years
female: 51.9 years
comparison ranking: total 2

Population growth rate: -1.21% (2024 est.)
comparison ranking: 234

Birth rate: 6.4 births/1,000 population (2024 est.)
comparison ranking: 227

Death rate: 11.7 deaths/1,000 population (2024 est.)
comparison ranking: 20

Net migration rate: -6.8 migrant(s)/1,000 population (2024 est.)
comparison ranking: 215

Population distribution: most of the population is found on Saint Pierre Island; a small settlement is located on the north end of Miquelon Island

Urbanization: *urban population:* 90.1% of total population (2023)
rate of urbanization: 0.75% annual rate of change (2020-25 est.)

Major urban areas - population: 6,000 SAINT-PIERRE (capital) (2018)

Sex ratio: *at birth:* 1.06 male(s)/female
0-14 years: 1.05 male(s)/female
15-64 years: 0.97 male(s)/female
65 years and over: 0.78 male(s)/female
total population: 0.93 male(s)/female (2024 est.)

Infant mortality rate: *total:* 7.8 deaths/1,000 live births (2024 est.)
male: 9.6 deaths/1,000 live births
female: 5.8 deaths/1,000 live births
comparison ranking: total 148

Life expectancy at birth: *total population:* 81.8 years (2024 est.)
male: 79.5 years
female: 84.3 years
comparison ranking: total population 41

Total fertility rate: 1.6 children born/woman (2024 est.)
comparison ranking: 183

Gross reproduction rate: 0.78 (2024 est.)

Sanitation facility access: *improved:* total: 99.9% of population (2022 est.)
unimproved: total: 0.1% of population (2022 est.)

Currently married women (ages 15-49): 64.1% (2023 est.)

ENVIRONMENT

Environmental issues: overfishing

Climate: cold and wet, with considerable mist and fog; spring and autumn are often windy

Urbanization: *urban population:* 90.1% of total population (2023)
rate of urbanization: 0.75% annual rate of change (2020-25 est.)

Carbon dioxide emissions: 57,000 metric tonnes of CO2 (2023 est.)
from petroleum and other liquids: 57,000 metric tonnes of CO2 (2023 est.)
comparison ranking: total emissions 211

GOVERNMENT

Country name: *conventional long form:* Territorial Collectivity of Saint Pierre and Miquelon
conventional short form: Saint Pierre and Miquelon
local long form: Département de Saint-Pierre et Miquelon
local short form: Saint-Pierre et Miquelon
etymology: Saint-Pierre and Miquelon is reputed to be named after two navigators, one called Peter and one called Michael (in a nickname form) or Mikelon, a Basque name

Government type: parliamentary democracy (Territorial Council); overseas collectivity of France

Dependency status: overseas collectivity of France

Capital: *name:* Saint-Pierre
geographic coordinates: 46 46 N, 56 11 W
time difference: UTC-3 (2 hours ahead of Washington, DC, during Standard Time)
daylight saving time: +1hr, begins second Sunday in March; ends first Sunday in November
etymology: may be named after Saint Peter, the patron saint of fisherman; alternatively, the name may come from one of the two navigators for whom the island as a whole is named

Administrative divisions: *none (territorial overseas collectivity of France); no first-order administrative divisions as defined by the US government, but 2 communes are considered second-order:* Saint Pierre, Miquelon

Legal system: French civil law

Constitution: *history:* 4 October 1958 (French Constitution)
amendment process: amendment procedures of France's constitution apply

Citizenship: see France

Suffrage: 18 years of age; universal

Executive branch: *chief of state:* President Emmanuel MACRON (since 14 May 2017); represented by Prefect Bruno ANDRE (since September 2023)
head of government: President of Territorial Council Bernard BRIAND (since 13 October 2020)
cabinet: Le Cabinet du Préfet
election/appointment process: French president directly elected by absolute-majority popular vote in 2 rounds, if needed, for a 5-year term (eligible for a second term); prefect appointed by French president on the advice of French Ministry of Interior; Territorial Council president elected by Territorial Council councilors by absolute majority vote; term NA
most recent election date: 13 October 2020
election results: *2020:* Bernard BRIAND elected President of Territorial Council; Territorial Council vote - 17 for, 2 abstentions
2017: Stephane LENORMAND elected President of Territorial Council vote - NA

Legislative branch: *legislature name:* Territorial Council (Conseil Territorial)
legislative structure: unicameral
number of seats: 19 (directly elected)
electoral system: plurality/majority
scope of elections: full renewal
term in office: 6 years
most recent election date: 3/27/2022
parties elected and seats per party: AD (15); Focus on the Future (4)
expected date of next election: March 2028
note: 1 senator is indirectly elected to the French Senate by an electoral college for a 6-year term, and 1 deputy is directly elected to the French National Assembly for a 5-year term

Judicial branch: *highest court(s):* Superior Tribunal of Appeals or Tribunal Supérieur d'Appel (composition NA)
judge selection and term of office: judge selection and tenure NA

Political parties: Archipelago Tomorrow (Archipel Domain) or AD (affiliated with The Republicans)
Focus on the Future (Cap sur l'Avenir) (affiliated with Left Radical Party)
Together to Build (Ensemble pour Construire)

Diplomatic representation in the US: none (overseas territory of France)

Diplomatic representation from the US: *embassy:* none (territorial overseas collectivity of France)

International organization participation: UPU, WFTU (NGOs)

Independence: none (overseas collectivity collectivity of France; has been under French control since 1763)

National holiday: Fête de la Fédération, 14 July (1790)
note: often incorrectly referred to as Bastille Day, France's national celebration commemorates the storming of the Bastille prison on 14 July 1789 and the establishment of a constitutional monarchy; other names for the holiday are *la Fête nationale* (National Holiday) and *le Quatorze Juillet* (14th of July)

Flag: *description:* a yellow three-masted sailing ship facing the left side rides on a blue background with wavy white lines; a black-over-white wavy line divides the ship from the white wavy lines; on the left side, a vertical band is divided into three heraldic arms: the top (called *ikkurina*) is red with a green diagonal cross extending to the corners and overlaid with a white cross, the middle is white with an ermine pattern, and the bottom is red with two yellow lions outlined in black
meaning: the arms represent settlers from the Basque Country (top), Brittany, and Normandy in France; blue symbolizes the Atlantic Ocean, and the ship represents explorer Jacques Cartier's ship when he visited the islands in 1536
note: the flag of France used for official occasions

National symbol(s): 16th-century sailing ship

National anthem(s): *title:* "La Marseillaise" (The Song of Marseille)
lyrics/music: Claude-Joseph ROUGET de Lisle
history: official anthem, as a French collectivity

ECONOMY

Economic overview: high-income, French North American territorial economy; primarily fishing exports; substantial French Government support; highly seasonal labor force; euro user; increasing tourism and aquaculture investments

Real GDP (purchasing power parity): $261.3 million (2015 est.)
note: supplemented by annual payments from France of about $60 million
comparison ranking: 216

GDP (official exchange rate): $261.3 million (2015 est.)

Agricultural products: vegetables; poultry, cattle, sheep, pigs; fish

Industries: fish processing and supply base for fishing fleets; tourism

Exports - partners: Canada 78%, Ireland 5%, France 5%, Djibouti 4%, UK 2% (2023)
note: top five export partners based on percentage share of exports

Exports - commodities: processed crustaceans, shellfish (2023)
note: top export commodities based on value in dollars over $500,000

Imports - partners: France 57%, Canada 37%, Netherlands 3%, Belgium 2%, Spain 0% (2023)
note: top five import partners based on percentage share of imports

Imports - commodities: refined petroleum, packaged medicine, cars, plastic products, other foods (2023)
note: top five import commodities based on value in dollars

Exchange rates: euros (EUR) per US dollar -

Exchange rates: 0.924 (2024 est.)
0.925 (2023 est.)
0.95 (2022 est.)
0.845 (2021 est.)
0.876 (2020 est.)

ENERGY

Electricity: *installed generating capacity:* 26,000 kW (2023 est.)
consumption: 48.714 million kWh (2023 est.)
transmission/distribution losses: 2 million kWh (2023 est.)
comparison rankings: installed generating capacity 204; consumption 203; transmission/distribution losses 5

Electricity generation sources: *fossil fuels:* 100% of total installed capacity (2023 est.)

Petroleum: *refined petroleum consumption:* 400 bbl/day (2023 est.)

COMMUNICATIONS

Telephones - fixed lines: *total subscriptions:* 4,800 (2015 est.)
subscriptions per 100 inhabitants: 76 (2015 est.)
comparison ranking: total subscriptions 204

Broadcast media: 8 TV stations, all part of the French Overseas Network, and local cable provided by SPM Telecom; 3 of 4 radio stations are part of the French Overseas Network (2021)

Internet country code: .pm

Internet users: *percent of population:* 88.7% (2022 est.)

TRANSPORTATION

Airports: 2 (2025)
comparison ranking: 202

Ports: *total ports:* 2 (2024)
large: 0
medium: 0
small: 1
very small: 0
size unknown: 1
ports with oil terminals: 1
key ports: Miquelon, St. Pierre

MILITARY AND SECURITY

Military - note: defense is the responsibility of France

SAINT VINCENT AND THE GRENADINES

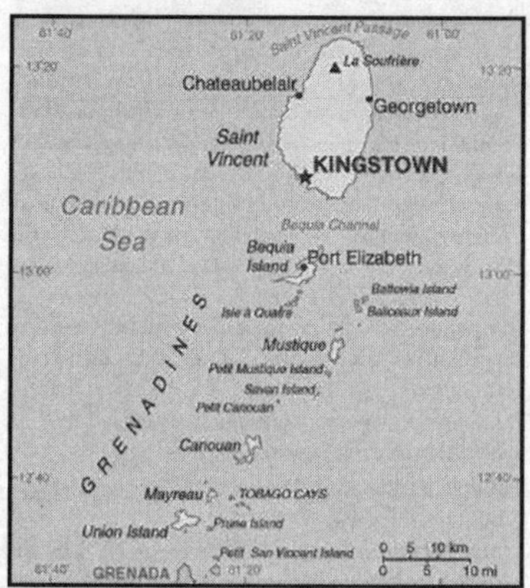

INTRODUCTION

Background: Resistance from native Caribs prevented colonization on Saint Vincent until 1719. France and England disputed the island for most of the 18th century, but it was ceded to England in 1783. The British prized Saint Vincent because of its fertile soil, which allowed for thriving slave-run plantations of sugar, coffee, indigo, tobacco, cotton, and cocoa. In 1834, the British abolished slavery. Immigration of indentured servants eased the ensuing labor shortage, as did subsequent immigrant waves from Portugal and East India. Conditions remained harsh for both former slaves and immigrant agricultural workers, however, as depressed world sugar prices kept the economy stagnant until the early 1900s. The economy then went into a period of decline, with many landowners abandoning their estates and leaving the land to be cultivated by liberated slaves.

Between 1960 and 1962, Saint Vincent and the Grenadines was a separate administrative unit of the Federation of the West Indies. Autonomy was granted in 1969 and independence in 1979. In 2021, the eruption of the La Soufrière volcano in the north of Saint Vincent destroyed much of Saint Vincent's most productive agricultural lands. Unlike most of its tourism- dependent neighbors, the Vincentian economy is primarily agricultural.

GEOGRAPHY

Location: Caribbean, islands between the Caribbean Sea and North Atlantic Ocean, north of Trinidad and Tobago

Geographic coordinates: 13 15 N, 61 12 W

Map references: Central America and the Caribbean

Area: *total:* 389 sq km (Saint Vincent 344 sq km)
land: 389 sq km
water: 0 sq km
comparison ranking: total 204

Area - comparative: twice the size of Washington, D.C.

Land boundaries: *total:* 0 km

Coastline: 84 km

Maritime claims: *territorial sea:* 12 nm
contiguous zone: 24 nm
exclusive economic zone: 200 nm
continental shelf: 200 nm

Climate: tropical; little seasonal temperature variation; rainy season (May to November)

Terrain: volcanic, mountainous

Elevation: *highest point:* La Soufriere 1,234 m
lowest point: Caribbean Sea 0 m

Natural resources: hydropower, arable land

Land use: *agricultural land:* 17.9% (2022 est.)
arable land: 5.1% (2022 est.)
permanent crops: 7.7% (2022 est.)
permanent pasture: 5.1% (2022 est.)
forest: 73.2% (2022 est.)
other: 8.9% (2022 est.)

Irrigated land: 10 sq km (2012)

Population distribution: most of the population is concentrated in and around the capital of Kingstown

Natural hazards: hurricanes; La Soufrière volcano on the island of Saint Vincent is a constant threat
volcanism: La Soufrière (1,234 m) last erupted in 1979; the island of Saint Vincent is part of the volcanic-island arc of the Lesser Antilles that extends from Saba in the north to Grenada in the south

Geography - note: the administration of the islands of the Grenadines group is divided between Saint Vincent and the Grenadines and Grenada; Saint Vincent and the Grenadines is composed of 32 islands and cays

PEOPLE AND SOCIETY

Population: *total:* 100,647 (2024 est.)
male: 51,249
female: 49,398
comparison rankings: total 195; male 192; female 196

Nationality: *noun:* Saint Vincentian(s) or Vincentian(s)
adjective: Saint Vincentian or Vincentian

Ethnic groups: African descent 71.2%, mixed 23%, Indigenous 3%, East Indian/Indian 1.1%, European 1.5%, other 0.2% (2012 est.)

Languages: English, Vincentian Creole English, French patois

Religions: Protestant 75% (Pentecostal 27.6%, Anglican 13.9%, Seventh Day Adventist 11.6%, Baptist 8.9%, Methodist 8.7%, Evangelical 3.8%, Salvation Army 0.3%, Presbyterian/Congregational 0.3%), Roman Catholic 6.3%, Rastafarian 1.1%, Jehovah's Witness 0.8%, other 4.7%, none 7.5%, unspecified 4.7% (2012 est.)

Age structure: *0-14 years:* 18.8% (male 9,527/female 9,353)
15-64 years: 68.2% (male 35,401/female 33,288)
65 years and over: 13% (2024 est.) (male 6,321/female 6,757)

Dependency ratios: *total dependency ratio:* 46.5 (2024 est.)
youth dependency ratio: 27.5 (2024 est.)
elderly dependency ratio: 19 (2024 est.)
potential support ratio: 5.3 (2024 est.)

Median age: *total:* 37.6 years (2024 est.)
male: 37.7 years
female: 37.4 years
comparison ranking: total 82

Population growth rate: -0.15% (2024 est.)
comparison ranking: 208

Birth rate: 11.9 births/1,000 population (2024 est.)
comparison ranking: 150

Death rate: 7.7 deaths/1,000 population (2024 est.)
comparison ranking: 96

Net migration rate: -5.8 migrant(s)/1,000 population (2024 est.)
comparison ranking: 208

Population distribution: most of the population is concentrated in and around the capital of Kingstown

Urbanization: *urban population:* 54.3% of total population (2023)
rate of urbanization: 0.94% annual rate of change (2020-25 est.)

Major urban areas - population: 27,000 KINGSTOWN (capital) (2018)

Sex ratio: *at birth:* 1.03 male(s)/female
0-14 years: 1.02 male(s)/female
15-64 years: 1.06 male(s)/female
65 years and over: 0.94 male(s)/female
total population: 1.04 male(s)/female (2024 est.)

Maternal mortality ratio: 56 deaths/100,000 live births (2023 est.)
comparison ranking: 91

Infant mortality rate: *total:* 12.3 deaths/1,000 live births (2024 est.)
male: 13.9 deaths/1,000 live births
female: 10.7 deaths/1,000 live births
comparison ranking: total 108

Life expectancy at birth: *total population:* 77.2 years (2024 est.)
male: 75.2 years
female: 79.3 years
comparison ranking: total population 96

Total fertility rate: 1.74 children born/woman (2024 est.)
comparison ranking: 152

Gross reproduction rate: 0.85 (2024 est.)

Health expenditure: 5.4% of GDP (2021)
8.6% of national budget (2022 est.)

Physician density: 0.66 physicians/1,000 population (2012)

Hospital bed density: 4.2 beds/1,000 population (2021 est.)

Sanitation facility access: *improved:* total: 90.2% of population

Obesity - adult prevalence rate: 23.7% (2016)
comparison ranking: 64

Alcohol consumption per capita: *total:* 7.48 liters of pure alcohol (2019 est.)
beer: 2.52 liters of pure alcohol (2019 est.)
wine: 0.24 liters of pure alcohol (2019 est.)
spirits: 4.48 liters of pure alcohol (2019 est.)
other alcohols: 0.23 liters of pure alcohol (2019 est.)
comparison ranking: total 52

Currently married women (ages 15-49): 53.3% (2023 est.)

Education expenditure: 6.5% of GDP (2023 est.)
12.6% national budget (2024 est.)
comparison ranking: Education expenditure (% GDP) 24

School life expectancy (primary to tertiary education): *total:* 15 years (2015 est.)
male: 14 years (2015 est.)
female: 15 years (2015 est.)

ENVIRONMENT

Environmental issues: pollution of coastal waters and shorelines from boats; poor land-use planning; deforestation; watershed management; squatter settlement control

International environmental agreements: *party to:* Biodiversity, Climate Change, Climate Change-Kyoto Protocol, Climate Change-Paris Agreement, Comprehensive Nuclear Test Ban, Desertification, Endangered Species, Environmental Modification, Hazardous Wastes, Law of the Sea, Marine Dumping-London Convention, Ozone Layer Protection, Ship Pollution, Whaling
signed, but not ratified: none of the selected agreements

Climate: tropical; little seasonal temperature variation; rainy season (May to November)

Urbanization: *urban population:* 54.3% of total population (2023)
rate of urbanization: 0.94% annual rate of change (2020-25 est.)

Carbon dioxide emissions: 268,000 metric tonnes of CO_2 (2023 est.)
from coal and metallurgical coke: 19,000 metric tonnes of CO_2 (2023 est.)
from petroleum and other liquids: 249,000 metric tonnes of CO_2 (2023 est.)
comparison ranking: total emissions 202

Particulate matter emissions: 9.5 micrograms per cubic meter (2019 est.)

Waste and recycling: *municipal solid waste generated annually:* 31,600 tons (2024 est.)
percent of municipal solid waste recycled: 13.3% (2022 est.)

Total water withdrawal: *municipal:* 8.5 million cubic meters (2022 est.)
industrial: 2,000 cubic meters (2022 est.)
agricultural: 0 cubic meters (2022 est.)

Total renewable water resources: 100 million cubic meters (2022 est.)

GOVERNMENT

Country name: *conventional long form:* none
conventional short form: Saint Vincent and the Grenadines
etymology: explorer Christopher COLUMBUS named the island after Saint VINCENT of Saragossa because 22 January 1498, the day of discovery, was the saint's feast day

Government type: parliamentary democracy under a constitutional monarchy; a Commonwealth realm

Capital: *name:* Kingstown
geographic coordinates: 13 08 N, 61 13 W
time difference: UTC-4 (1 hour ahead of Washington, DC, during Standard Time)

Administrative divisions: 6 parishes; Charlotte, Grenadines, Saint Andrew, Saint David, Saint George, Saint Patrick

Legal system: English common law

Constitution: *history:* previous 1969, 1975; latest drafted 26 July 1979, effective 27 October 1979 (The Saint Vincent Constitution Order 1979)
amendment process: proposed by the House of Assembly; passage requires at least two-thirds majority vote of the Assembly membership and assent of the governor general; passage of amendments to constitutional sections on fundamental rights and freedoms, citizen protections, various government functions and authorities, and constitutional amendment procedures requires approval by the Assembly membership, approval in a referendum of at least two thirds of the votes cast, and assent of the governor general

International law organization participation: has not submitted an ICJ jurisdiction declaration; accepts ICCt jurisdiction

Citizenship: *citizenship by birth:* yes
citizenship by descent only: at least one parent must be a citizen of Saint Vincent and the Grenadines
dual citizenship recognized: yes
residency requirement for naturalization: 7 years

Suffrage: 18 years of age; universal

Executive branch: *chief of state:* King CHARLES III (since 8 September 2022); represented by Governor General Susan DOUGAN (since 1 August 2019)
head of government: Prime Minister Ralph Everard GONSALVES (since 29 March 2001)
cabinet: Cabinet appointed by the governor general on the advice of the prime minister
election/appointment process: the monarchy is hereditary; governor general appointed by the monarch; following legislative elections, the governor general usually appoints the leader of the majority party or majority coalition as prime minister; deputy prime minister also appointed by governor general on the advice of the prime minister

Legislative branch: *legislature name:* House of Assembly
legislative structure: unicameral
number of seats: 22 (15 directly elected; 6 appointed)
electoral system: plurality/majority
scope of elections: full renewal
term in office: 5 years
most recent election date: 11/5/2020
parties elected and seats per party: United Labour Party (ULP) (9); New Democratic Party (NDP) (6)
percentage of women in chamber: 21.7%
expected date of next election: November 2025

Judicial branch: *highest court(s):* the Eastern Caribbean Supreme Court (ECSC) is the superior court of the Organization of Eastern Caribbean States; the ECSC is headquartered on St. Lucia and consists of the Court of Appeal – headed by the chief justice and 4 judges – and the High Court with 18 judges; the Court of Appeal travels to member states on a schedule to hear appeals from the High Court and subordinate courts; Saint Vincent and the Grenadines is a member of the Caribbean Court of Justice
judge selection and term of office: chief justice of Eastern Caribbean Supreme Court appointed by the British monarch; other justices and judges appointed by the Judicial and Legal Services Commission, an independent body of judicial officials; Court of Appeal justices appointed for life with mandatory retirement at age 65; High Court judges appointed for life with mandatory retirement at age 62
subordinate courts: magistrates' courts

Political parties: New Democratic Party or NDP
SVG Green Party or SVGP
Unity Labor Party or ULP (formed in 1994 by the coalition of Saint Vincent Labor Party or SVLP and the Movement for National Unity or MNU)

Diplomatic representation in the US: *chief of mission:* Ambassador Lou-Anne Gaylene GILCHRIST (since 18 January 2017)
chancery: 1627 K Street, NW, Suite 704, Washington, DC 20006
telephone: [1] (202) 364-6730
FAX: [1] (202) 364-6736
email address and website: mail@embsvg.com
http://wa.embassy.gov.vc/washington/
consulate(s) general: New York

Diplomatic representation from the US: *embassy:* the US does not have an embassy in Saint Vincent and the Grenadines; the US Ambassador to Barbados is accredited to Saint Vincent and the Grenadines

International organization participation: ACP, ACS, AOSIS, C, Caricom, CDB, CELAC, FAO, G-77, IBRD, ICAO, ICCt, ICRM, IDA, IFAD, IFRCS, ILO, IMF, IMO, Interpol, IOC, IOM, ISO (subscriber), ITU, MIGA, NAM, OAS, OECS, OPANAL, OPCW, Petrocaribe, UN, UNCTAD, UNESCO, UNIDO, UPU, WFTU (NGOs), WHO, WIPO, WTO

Independence: 27 October 1979 (from the UK)

National holiday: Independence Day, 27 October (1979)

Flag: *description:* three vertical bands of blue (left side), gold (double-width), and green; the gold band has three green diamonds arranged in a "V" pattern that stands for "Vincent"
meaning: the diamonds represent the islands as "the Gems of the Antilles" and are set slightly lowered in the gold band to reflect the country's position in the Antilles; blue stands for the tropical sky and sea, yellow for the sand, and green for vegetation

National symbol(s): Saint Vincent parrot

National color(s): blue, gold, green

National anthem(s): *title:* "St. Vincent! Land So Beautiful!"
lyrics/music: Phyllis Joyce MCCLEAN PUNNETT/ Joel Bertram MIGUEL
history: adopted 1969
title: "God Save the King"
lyrics/music: unknown
history: in use since 1745

ECONOMY

Economic overview: upper middle-income Caribbean island economy; key agriculture and tourism sectors; environmentally fragile; diversifying economy across services, science and knowledge, and creative industries; CARICOM member and US Caribbean Basin Initiative beneficiary

Real GDP (purchasing power parity): $1.883 billion (2024 est.)
$1.809 billion (2023 est.)
$1.718 billion (2022 est.)
note: data in 2021 dollars
comparison ranking: 199

Real GDP growth rate: 4.1% (2024 est.)
5.3% (2023 est.)
3.1% (2022 est.)
note: annual GDP % growth based on constant local currency
comparison ranking: 70

Real GDP per capita: $18,700 (2024 est.)
$17,900 (2023 est.)
$16,800 (2022 est.)
note: data in 2021 dollars
comparison ranking: 109

GDP (official exchange rate): $1.157 billion (2024 est.)
note: data in current dollars at official exchange rate

Inflation rate (consumer prices): 3.6% (2024 est.)
4.6% (2023 est.)
5.7% (2022 est.)
note: annual % change based on consumer prices
comparison ranking: 113

GDP - composition, by sector of origin: *agriculture:* 3.5% (2024 est.)
industry: 15.4% (2024 est.)
services: 66.4% (2024 est.)
note: figures may not total 100% due to non-allocated consumption not captured in sector-reported data
comparison rankings: agriculture 124; industry 161; services 47

Agricultural products: bananas, root vegetables, plantains, spices, coconuts, fruits, apples, vegetables, mangoes/ guavas, sweet potatoes (2023)
note: top ten agricultural products based on tonnage

Industries: tourism; food processing, cement, furniture, clothing, starch

Industrial production growth rate: 7.3% (2024 est.)
note: annual % change in industrial value added based on constant local currency
comparison ranking: 21

Labor force: 52,100 (2024 est.)
note: number of people ages 15 or older who are employed or seeking work
comparison ranking: 187

Unemployment rate: 18.1% (2024 est.)
18.6% (2023 est.)
19.5% (2022 est.)
note: % of labor force seeking employment
comparison ranking: 179

Youth unemployment rate (ages 15-24): *total:* 41.4% (2024 est.)
male: 41.4% (2024 est.)
female: 41.4% (2024 est.)
note: % of labor force ages 15-24 seeking employment
comparison ranking: total 7

Remittances: 8.2% of GDP (2024 est.)
8.5% of GDP (2023 est.)
9% of GDP (2022 est.)
note: personal transfers and compensation between resident and non-resident individuals/ households/ entities

Budget: *revenues:* $226.404 million (2017 est.)
expenditures: $208.744 million (2017 est.)
note: central government revenues and expenses (excluding grants/extrabudgetary units/ social security funds) converted to US dollars at average official exchange rate for year indicated

Taxes and other revenues: 23.8% (of GDP) (2017 est.)
note: central government tax revenue as a % of GDP
comparison ranking: 24

Current account balance: -$156.589 million (2024 est.)
-$180.43 million (2023 est.)
-$199.727 million (2022 est.)
note: balance of payments - net trade and primary/ secondary income in current dollars
comparison ranking: 100

Exports: $425.182 million (2024 est.)
$345.098 million (2023 est.)
$278.292 million (2022 est.)
note: balance of payments - exports of goods and services in current dollars
comparison ranking: 193

Exports - partners: Croatia 16%, Barbados 14%, USA 10%, St. Lucia 10%, St. Kitts & Nevis 8% (2023)
note: top five export partners based on percentage share of exports

Exports - commodities: ships, wheat flours, animal food, shellfish, construction vehicles (2023)
note: top five export commodities based on value in dollars

Imports: $641.179 million (2024 est.)
$588.865 million (2023 est.)
$540.833 million (2022 est.)
note: balance of payments - imports of goods and services in current dollars
comparison ranking: 196

Imports - partners: USA 37%, Italy 7%, Trinidad & Tobago 7%, China 6%, UK 6% (2023)
note: top five import partners based on percentage share of imports

Imports - commodities: ships, refined petroleum, wheat, coal, poultry (2023)
note: top five import commodities based on value in dollars

Reserves of foreign exchange and gold: $316.824 million (2024 est.)
$280.564 million (2023 est.)
$320.193 million (2022 est.)
note: holdings of gold (year-end prices)/foreign exchange/special drawing rights in current dollars
comparison ranking: 170

Debt - external: $456.971 million (2023 est.)
note: present value of external debt in current US dollars
comparison ranking: 114

Exchange rates: East Caribbean dollars (XCD) per US dollar -

Exchange rates: 2.7 (2024 est.)
2.7 (2023 est.)
2.7 (2022 est.)
2.7 (2021 est.)
2.7 (2020 est.)

ENERGY

Electricity access: *electrification - total population:* 100% (2022 est.)

Electricity: *installed generating capacity:* 55,000 kW (2023 est.)
consumption: 140.316 million kWh (2023 est.)
transmission/distribution losses: 10.868 million kWh (2023 est.)
comparison rankings: installed generating capacity 193; consumption 195; transmission/distribution losses 19

Electricity generation sources: *fossil fuels:* 86.1% of total installed capacity (2023 est.)
solar: 1.3% of total installed capacity (2023 est.)
hydroelectricity: 12.6% of total installed capacity (2023 est.)

Coal: *exports:* 8 metric tons (2023 est.)
imports: 8,000 metric tons (2023 est.)

Petroleum: *refined petroleum consumption:* 2,000 bbl/ day (2023 est.)

Energy consumption per capita: 37.253 million Btu/ person (2023 est.)
comparison ranking: 105

COMMUNICATIONS

Telephones - fixed lines: *total subscriptions:* 10,000 (2023 est.)
subscriptions per 100 inhabitants: 10 (2023 est.)
comparison ranking: total subscriptions 186

Telephones - mobile cellular: *total subscriptions:* 103,000 (2023 est.)
subscriptions per 100 inhabitants: 100 (2022 est.)
comparison ranking: total subscriptions 193

Broadcast media: St. Vincent and the Grenadines Broadcasting Corporation operates 1 TV station and 5 repeater stations that provide near total coverage to the multi-island state; multi-channel cable TV service available; a partially government-funded national radio service broadcasts on 1 station and has 2 repeater stations; about a dozen privately owned radio stations and repeater stations

Internet country code: .vc

Internet users: *percent of population:* 76% (2023 est.)

Broadband - fixed subscriptions: *total:* 31,000 (2023 est.)
subscriptions per 100 inhabitants: 30 (2023 est.)
comparison ranking: total 160

TRANSPORTATION

Civil aircraft registration country code prefix: J8

Airports: 5 (2025)
comparison ranking: 176

Merchant marine: *total:* 830 (2023)
by type: bulk carrier 30, container ship 18, general cargo 137, oil tanker 16, other 629

comparison ranking: total 30

Ports: *total ports:* 1 (2024)
large: 0
medium: 0
small: 1
very small: 0
ports with oil terminals: 1
key ports: Kingstown

MILITARY AND SECURITY

Military and security forces: *no regular military forces; Ministry of National Security:* Royal Saint Vincent and the Grenadines Police Force (RSVPF) (2025)

Military - note: the country has been a member of the Caribbean Regional Security System (RSS) since its creation in 1982; RSS signatories (Antigua and Barbuda, Barbados, Dominica, Grenada, Guyana, Saint Kitts and Nevis, and Saint Lucia) agreed to prepare contingency plans and assist one another, on request, in national emergencies, prevention of smuggling, search and rescue, immigration control, fishery protection, customs and excise control, maritime policing duties, protection of off-shore installations, pollution control, national and other disasters, and threats to national security (2025)

SAMOA

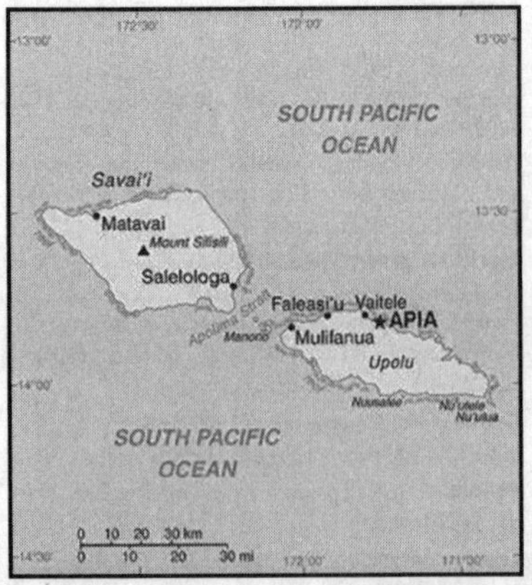

INTRODUCTION

Background: The first Austronesian settlers arrived in Samoa around 1000 B.C., and early Samoans traded and intermarried with Fijian and Tongan nobility. The fa'amatai system of titles and nobility developed, which dominates Samoan politics to this day; all but two seats in the legislature are reserved for matai, or heads of families. A Dutch explorer was the first European to spot the islands in 1722. Christian missionaries arrived in the 1830s and were followed by an influx of American and European settlers and influence. By the 1880s, Germany, the UK, and the US had trading posts and claimed parts of the kingdom. In 1886, an eight-year civil war broke out, with rival matai factions fighting over royal succession and the three foreign powers providing support to the factions. Germany, the UK, and the US all sent warships to Apia in 1889 and came close to conflict, but a cyclone damaged or destroyed the ships of all three navies.

At the end of the civil war in 1894, Malietoa LAUPEPA was installed as king, but upon his death in 1898, a second civil war over succession broke out. When the war ended in 1899, the Western powers abolished the monarchy, giving the western Samoan islands to Germany and the eastern Samoan islands to the US. The UK abandoned claims in Samoa and received former German territory in the Solomon Islands.

New Zealand occupied Samoa during World War I but was accused of negligence and opposed by many Samoans, particularly an organized political movement called the Mau ("Strongly Held View") that advocated for independence. During the 1918-1919 influenza pandemic, about 20% of the population died. In 1929, New Zealand police shot into a crowd of peaceful Mau protestors, killing 11, in an event known as Black Sunday. In 1962, Samoa became the first Polynesian nation to reestablish its independence as Western Samoa but dropped the "Western" from its name in 1997. The Human Rights Protection Party dominated politics from 1982 until Prime Minister FIAME Naomi Mata'afa's Fa'atuatua i le Atua Samoa ua Tasi (FAST) party gained a majority in elections in 2021.

GEOGRAPHY

Location: Oceania, group of islands in the South Pacific Ocean, about halfway between Hawaii and New Zealand

Geographic coordinates: 13 35 S, 172 20 W

Map references: Oceania

Area: *total:* 2,831 sq km
land: 2,821 sq km
water: 10 sq km
comparison ranking: total 177

Area - comparative: slightly smaller than Rhode Island

Land boundaries: *total:* 0 km

Coastline: 403 km

Maritime claims: *territorial sea:* 12 nm
contiguous zone: 24 nm
exclusive economic zone: 200 nm

Climate: tropical; rainy season (November to April), dry season (May to October)

Terrain: two main islands (Savaii, Upolu) and several smaller islands and uninhabited islets; narrow coastal plain with volcanic, rugged mountains in interior

Elevation: *highest point:* Mount Silisili 1,857 m
lowest point: Pacific Ocean 0 m

Natural resources: hardwood forests, fish, hydropower

Land use: *agricultural land:* 17.8% (2022 est.)
arable land: 4.1% (2022 est.)
permanent crops: 11.4% (2022 est.)
permanent pasture: 2.3% (2022 est.)
forest: 57.8% (2022 est.)
other: 24.4% (2022 est.)

Irrigated land: 0 sq km (2022)

Population distribution: about three quarters of the population lives on the island of Upolu

Natural hazards: occasional cyclones; active volcanism
volcanism: Savai'I Island (1,858 m) is historically active

Geography - note: occupies an almost central position within Polynesia

PEOPLE AND SOCIETY

Population: *total:* 208,853 (2024 est.)
male: 105,920
female: 102,933
comparison rankings: total 184; male 184; female 184

Nationality: *noun:* Samoan(s)
adjective: Samoan

Ethnic groups: Samoan 96%, Samoan/New Zealander 2%, other 1.9% (2011 est.)
note: data represent the population by country of citizenship

Languages: Samoan (Polynesian) (official) 91.1%, Samoan/English 6.7%, English (official) 0.5%, other 0.2%, unspecified 1.6% (2006 est.)

Religions: Protestant 54.9% (Congregationalist 29%, Methodist 12.4%, Assembly of God 6.8%, Seventh Day Adventist 4.4%, other Protestant 2.3%), Roman Catholic 18.8%, Church of Jesus Christ 16.9%, Worship Centre 2.8%, other Christian 3.6%, other 2.9% (includes Baha'i, Muslim), none 0.2% (2016 est.)

Age structure: *0-14 years:* 26.9% (male 28,952/female 27,173)
15-64 years: 65.9% (male 70,225/female 67,427)
65 years and over: 7.2% (2024 est.) (male 6,743/female 8,333)

Dependency ratios: *total dependency ratio:* 51.7 (2024 est.)
youth dependency ratio: 40.8 (2024 est.)
elderly dependency ratio: 11 (2024 est.)
potential support ratio: 9.1 (2024 est.)

Median age: *total:* 27.4 years (2024 est.)
male: 27 years
female: 27.8 years
comparison ranking: total 158

Population growth rate: 0.65% (2024 est.)
comparison ranking: 134

Birth rate: 18.8 births/1,000 population (2024 est.)
comparison ranking: 75

Death rate: 5.4 deaths/1,000 population (2024 est.)
comparison ranking: 184

Net migration rate: -6.9 migrant(s)/1,000 population (2024 est.)
comparison ranking: 216

Population distribution: about three quarters of the population lives on the island of Upolu

Urbanization: *urban population:* 17.5% of total population (2023)
rate of urbanization: -0.03% annual rate of change (2020-25 est.)

Major urban areas - population: 36,000 APIA (capital) (2018)

Sex ratio: *at birth:* 1.05 male(s)/female

0-14 years: 1.07 male(s)/female
15-64 years: 1.04 male(s)/female
65 years and over: 0.81 male(s)/female
total population: 1.03 male(s)/female (2024 est.)

Maternal mortality ratio: 101 deaths/100,000 live births (2023 est.)
comparison ranking: 65

Infant mortality rate: *total:* 17.3 deaths/1,000 live births (2024 est.)
male: 20.9 deaths/1,000 live births
female: 13.6 deaths/1,000 live births
comparison ranking: total 87

Life expectancy at birth: *total population:* 75.7 years (2024 est.)
male: 72.8 years
female: 78.7 years
comparison ranking: total population 124

Total fertility rate: 2.33 children born/woman (2024 est.)
comparison ranking: 77

Gross reproduction rate: 1.14 (2024 est.)

Drinking water source: *improved: urban:* 100% of population (2022 est.)
rural: 98.8% of population (2022 est.)
total: 99% of population (2022 est.)
unimproved: urban: 0% of population (2022 est.)
rural: 1.2% of population (2022 est.)
total: 1% of population (2022 est.)

Health expenditure: 6.8% of GDP (2021)
15.2% of national budget (2022 est.)

Physician density: 0.56 physicians/1,000 population (2021)

Sanitation facility access: *improved: urban:* 99.7% of population (2022 est.)
rural: 98.9% of population (2022 est.)
total: 99% of population (2022 est.)
unimproved: urban: 0.3% of population (2022 est.)
rural: 1.1% of population (2022 est.)
total: 1% of population (2022 est.)

Obesity - adult prevalence rate: 47.3% (2016)
comparison ranking: 8

Alcohol consumption per capita: *total:* 2.18 liters of pure alcohol (2019 est.)
beer: 2.01 liters of pure alcohol (2019 est.)
wine: 0 liters of pure alcohol (2019 est.)
spirits: 0.17 liters of pure alcohol (2019 est.)
other alcohols: 0 liters of pure alcohol (2019 est.)
comparison ranking: total 127

Tobacco use: *total:* 20.5% (2025 est.)
male: 28.6% (2025 est.)
female: 12.3% (2025 est.)
comparison ranking: total 65

Children under the age of 5 years underweight: 3.4% (2019)
comparison ranking: 75

Currently married women (ages 15-49): 61.7% (2023 est.)

Child marriage: *women married by age 15:* 0.9% (2020)
women married by age 18: 7.4% (2020)
men married by age 18: 2% (2020)

Education expenditure: 5.5% of GDP (2024 est.)
12.9% national budget (2024 est.)
comparison ranking: Education expenditure (% GDP) 42

Literacy: *total population:* 98% (2019 est.)
male: 98.3% (2019 est.)
female: 97.7% (2019 est.)

ENVIRONMENT

Environmental issues: soil erosion; deforestation; invasive species; overfishing

International environmental agreements: *party to:* Biodiversity, Climate Change, Climate Change-Kyoto Protocol, Climate Change-Paris Agreement, Comprehensive Nuclear Test Ban, Desertification, Endangered Species, Hazardous Wastes, Law of the Sea, Nuclear Test Ban, Ozone Layer Protection, Ship Pollution, Wetlands
signed, but not ratified: none of the selected agreements

Climate: tropical; rainy season (November to April), dry season (May to October)

Urbanization: *urban population:* 17.5% of total population (2023)
rate of urbanization: -0.03% annual rate of change (2020-25 est.)

Carbon dioxide emissions: 335,000 metric tonnes of CO_2 (2023 est.)
from petroleum and other liquids: 335,000 metric tonnes of CO_2 (2023 est.)
comparison ranking: total emissions 195

Particulate matter emissions: 7.8 micrograms per cubic meter (2019 est.)

Waste and recycling: *municipal solid waste generated annually:* 27,400 tons (2024 est.)
percent of municipal solid waste recycled: 57.6% (2022 est.)

GOVERNMENT

Country name: *conventional long form:* Independent State of Samoa
conventional short form: Samoa
local long form: Malo Sa'oloto Tuto'atasi o Samoa
local short form: Samoa
former: Western Samoa
etymology: the name's meaning and origin are unclear; some assert that it can mean "place of the moa bird" of Polynesian mythology, or it could be a local chieftain's name

Government type: parliamentary republic

Capital: *name:* Apia
geographic coordinates: 13 49 S, 171 46 W
time difference: UTC+13 (18 hours ahead of Washington, DC, during Standard Time)

Administrative divisions: 11 districts; A'ana, Aiga-i-le-Tai, Atua, Fa'asaleleaga, Gaga'emauga, Gagaifomauga, Palauli, Satupa'itea, Tuamasaga, Va'a-o-Fonoti, Vaisigano

Legal system: mixed system of English common law and customary law; judicial review of legislative acts involving fundamental citizen rights

Constitution: *history:* several previous (pre-independence); latest 1 January 1962
amendment process: proposed as an act by the Legislative Assembly; passage requires at least two-thirds majority vote by the Assembly membership in the third reading, provided at least 90 days have elapsed since the second reading, and assent of the chief of state; passage of amendments affecting constitutional articles on customary land or constitutional amendment procedures also requires at least two-thirds majority approval in a referendum

International law organization participation: has not submitted an ICJ jurisdiction declaration; accepts ICCt jurisdiction

Citizenship: *citizenship by birth:* no
citizenship by descent only: at least one parent must be a citizen of Samoa
dual citizenship recognized: no
residency requirement for naturalization: 5 years

Suffrage: 21 years of age; universal

Executive branch: *chief of state:* TUIMALEALI'IFANO Va'aletoa Sualauvi II (since 21 July 2017)
head of government: Prime Minister La'auli Leuatea SCHMIDT (since 16 September 2025)
cabinet: Cabinet appointed by the chief of state on the advice of the prime minister
election/appointment process: chief of state indirectly elected by the Legislative Assembly to serve a 5-year term (2-term limit); following legislative elections, the chief of state usually appoints the leader of the majority party as prime minister, with the approval of the Legislative Assembly
most recent election date: 23 August 2022
election results: TUIMALEALI'IFANO Va'aletoa Sualauvi II (independent) unanimously reelected by the Legislative Assembly
expected date of next election: 2026

Legislative branch: *legislature name:* Legislative Assembly (Fono)
legislative structure: unicameral
number of seats: 51 (all directly elected)
electoral system: plurality/majority
scope of elections: full renewal
term in office: 5 years
most recent election date: 8/29/2025
parties elected and seats per party: Faatuatua ile Atua Samoa ua Tasi (FAST) (32); Human Rights Protection Party (HRPP) (22)
percentage of women in chamber: 13%
expected date of next election: August 2030

Judicial branch: *highest court(s):* Court of Appeal (consists of the chief justice and 2 Supreme Court judges and meets once or twice a year); Supreme Court (consists of the chief justice and several judges)
judge selection and term of office: chief justice appointed by the chief of state on the advice of the prime minister; other Supreme Court judges appointed by the Judicial Service Commission, a 3-member body chaired by the chief justice and includes the attorney general and an appointee of the Minister of Justice; judges normally serve until retirement at age 68
subordinate courts: District Court; Magistrates' Courts; Land and Titles Courts; village chief councils

Political parties: Fa'atuatua i le Atua Samoa ua Tasi or FAST
Human Rights Protection Party or HRPP
Tautua Samoa Party or TSP

Diplomatic representation in the US: *chief of mission:* Ambassador Pa'olelei LUTERU (since 7 July 2021); note - also Permanent Representative to the UN
chancery: 685 Third Avenue, 44th Street, 11th Floor, Suite 1102, New York, NY 10017
telephone: [1] (212) 599-6196

FAX: [1] (212) 599-0797
email address and website: samoa@samoanymission.ws
About | Samoa Permanent Mission to the United Nations
consulate(s) general: Pago Pago (American Samoa)

Diplomatic representation from the US: *chief of mission:* the US Ambassador to New Zealand is accredited to Samoa
embassy: 5th Floor, Accident Corporation Building, Matafele Apia

mailing address: 4400 Apia Place, Washington DC 20521-4400
telephone: [685] 21-436
FAX: [685] 22-030
email address and website: ApiaConsular@state.gov https://ws.usembassy.gov/

International organization participation: ACP, ADB, AOSIS, C, FAO, G-77, IBRD, ICAO, ICCt, ICRM, IDA, IFAD, IFC, IFRCS, ILO, IMF, IMO, Interpol, IOC, IPU, ITU, ITUC (NGOs), MIGA, OPCW, PIF, Sparteca, SPC, UN, UNCTAD, UNESCO, UNIDO, UPU, WCO, WHO, WIPO, WMO, WTO

Independence: 1 January 1962 (from New Zealand-administered UN trusteeship)

National holiday: Independence Day Celebration, 1 June (1962)
note: 1 January 1962 is the date of independence from the New Zealand-administered UN trusteeship, but it is observed in June

Flag: *description:* red with a blue rectangle in the upper-left quadrant; on the rectangle are five five-pointed white stars that represent the Southern Cross constellation
meaning: red stands for courage, blue for freedom, and white for purity
note: similar to the flag of Taiwan

National symbol(s): Southern Cross constellation (five five-pointed stars)

National color(s): red, white, blue

National anthem(s): *title:* «O le Fu'a o le Sa'olotoga o Samoa" (The Banner of Freedom)
lyrics/music: Sauni Liga KURESA
history: adopted 1962; also known as "Samoa Tula'i" (Samoa Arise)

ECONOMY

Economic overview: ower middle-income Pacific island economy; enormous fishing and agriculture industries; significant remittances; growing offshore financial hub; recently hosted Pacific Games to drive tourism and infrastructure growth

Real GDP (purchasing power parity): $1.503 billion (2024 est.)
$1.374 billion (2023 est.)
$1.258 billion (2022 est.)
note: data in 2021 dollars
comparison ranking: 202

Real GDP growth rate: 9.4% (2024 est.)
9.2% (2023 est.)
-5.3% (2022 est.)
note: annual GDP % growth based on constant local currency
comparison ranking: 5

Real GDP per capita: $6,900 (2024 est.)
$6,300 (2023 est.)
$5,800 (2022 est.)
note: data in 2021 dollars
comparison ranking: 160

GDP (official exchange rate): $1.068 billion (2024 est.)
note: data in current dollars at official exchange rate

Inflation rate (consumer prices): 2.2% (2024 est.)
7.9% (2023 est.)
11% (2022 est.)
note: annual % change based on consumer prices
comparison ranking: 58

GDP - composition, by sector of origin: *agriculture:* 11% (2024 est.)
industry: 10.9% (2024 est.)
services: 72.5% (2024 est.)
note: figures may not total 100% due to non-allocated consumption not captured in sector-reported data
comparison rankings: agriculture 69; industry 182; services 28

GDP - composition, by end use: *household consumption:* 80.8% (2024 est.)
government consumption: 18.2% (2024 est.)
investment in fixed capital: 30.5% (2024 est.)
investment in inventories: 2.3% (2024 est.)
exports of goods and services: 29.3% (2024 est.)
imports of goods and services: -53.8% (2024 est.)
note: figures may not total 100% due to rounding or gaps in data collection

Agricultural products: coconuts, bananas, taro, tropical fruits, pineapples, mangoes/guavas, papayas, root vegetables, milk, avocados (2023)
note: top ten agricultural products based on tonnage

Industries: food processing, building materials, auto parts

Industrial production growth rate: 4.2% (2024 est.)
note: annual % change in industrial value added based on constant local currency
comparison ranking: 57

Labor force: 57,200 (2024 est.)
note: number of people ages 15 or older who are employed or seeking work
comparison ranking: 186

Unemployment rate: 4.6% (2024 est.)
5% (2023 est.)
5.1% (2022 est.)
note: % of labor force seeking employment
comparison ranking: 79

Youth unemployment rate (ages 15-24): *total:* 11.9% (2024 est.)
male: 7.4% (2024 est.)
female: 20.9% (2024 est.)
note: % of labor force ages 15-24 seeking employment
comparison ranking: total 104

Population below poverty line: 21.9% (2018 est.)
note: % of population with income below national poverty line

Remittances: 26.4% of GDP (2024 est.)
28.2% of GDP (2023 est.)
33.6% of GDP (2022 est.)
note: personal transfers and compensation between resident and non-resident individuals/households/entities

Budget: *revenues:* $371.764 million (2023 est.)
expenditures: $326.052 million (2023 est.)
note: central government revenues (excluding grants) and expenditures converted to US dollars at average official exchange rate for year indicated

Taxes and other revenues: 26.7% (of GDP) (2023 est.)
note: central government tax revenue as a % of GDP
comparison ranking: 10

Current account balance: $64.616 million (2024 est.)
$40.177 million (2023 est.)
-$74.039 million (2022 est.)
note: balance of payments - net trade and primary/secondary income in current dollars
comparison ranking: 81

Exports: $369.73 million (2024 est.)
$346.187 million (2023 est.)
$175.377 million (2022 est.)
note: balance of payments - exports of goods and services in current dollars
comparison ranking: 197

Exports - partners: India 26%, NZ 14%, USA 12%, American Samoa 10%, Australia 9% (2023)
note: top five export partners based on percentage share of exports

Exports - commodities: refined petroleum, integrated circuits, coconut oil, fish, insulated wire (2023)
note: top five export commodities based on value in dollars

Imports: $575.749 million (2024 est.)
$560.776 million (2023 est.)
$512.021 million (2022 est.)
note: balance of payments - imports of goods and services in current dollars
comparison ranking: 199

Imports - partners: NZ 20%, Singapore 19%, China 17%, Australia 10%, Fiji 9% (2023)
note: top five import partners based on percentage share of imports

Imports - commodities: refined petroleum, poultry, cars, plastic products, milk (2023)
note: top five import commodities based on value in dollars

Reserves of foreign exchange and gold: $507.74 million (2024 est.)
$447.09 million (2023 est.)
$321.163 million (2022 est.)
note: holdings of gold (year-end prices)/foreign exchange/special drawing rights in current dollars
comparison ranking: 157

Debt - external: $269.974 million (2023 est.)
note: present value of external debt in current US dollars
comparison ranking: 118

Exchange rates: tala (SAT) per US dollar -

Exchange rates: 2.754 (2024 est.)
2.738 (2023 est.)
2.689 (2022 est.)
2.556 (2021 est.)
2.665 (2020 est.)

ENERGY

Electricity access: *electrification - total population:* 98.3% (2022 est.)
electrification - urban areas: 100%
electrification - rural areas: 97.9%

Electricity: *installed generating capacity:* 54,000 kW (2023 est.)
consumption: 141.846 million kWh (2023 est.)
transmission/distribution losses: 17.284 million kWh (2023 est.)
comparison rankings: installed generating capacity 194; consumption 194; transmission/distribution losses 23

Electricity generation sources: *fossil fuels:* 59.7% of total installed capacity (2023 est.)
solar: 15.1% of total installed capacity (2023 est.)
wind: 0.1% of total installed capacity (2023 est.)
hydroelectricity: 18.9% of total installed capacity (2023 est.)
biomass and waste: 6.3% of total installed capacity (2023 est.)

Petroleum: *refined petroleum consumption:* 2,000 bbl/day (2023 est.)

Energy consumption per capita: 23.476 million Btu/person (2023 est.)
comparison ranking: 128

COMMUNICATIONS

Telephones - fixed lines: *total subscriptions:* 5,000 (2022 est.)
subscriptions per 100 inhabitants: 2 (2022 est.)
comparison ranking: total subscriptions 201

Telephones - mobile cellular: *total subscriptions:* 134,000 (2022 est.)
subscriptions per 100 inhabitants: 60 (2022 est.)
comparison ranking: total subscriptions 189

Broadcast media: state-owned TV station privatized in 2008; 4 privately owned TV stations; about a half-dozen privately owned radio stations and one state-owned; TV and radio broadcasts of several stations from American Samoa are available (2019)

Internet country code: .ws

Internet users: *percent of population:* 58% (2023 est.)

Broadband - fixed subscriptions: *total:* 2,000 (2022 est.)
subscriptions per 100 inhabitants: 1 (2022 est.)
comparison ranking: total 203

TRANSPORTATION

Civil aircraft registration country code prefix: 5W

Airports: 4 (2025)
comparison ranking: 179

Merchant marine: *total:* 13 (2023)
by type: general cargo 3, oil tanker 1, other 9
comparison ranking: total 155

Ports: *total ports:* 1 (2024)
large: 0
medium: 0
small: 0
very small: 1
ports with oil terminals: 1
key ports: Apia

MILITARY AND SECURITY

Military and security forces: no regular military forces; Samoa Police Service (includes a maritime unit) (2025)

Military - note: informal defense ties exist with New Zealand, which pledged to afford assistance to Samoa in the conduct of its international relations under the 1962 Treaty of Friendship; New Zealand naval vessels patrol Samoan waters
Samoa has a "shiprider" agreement with the US, which allows local maritime law enforcement officers to embark on US Coast Guard (USCG) and US Navy (USN) vessels, including to board and search vessels suspected of violating laws or regulations within Somoa's designated exclusive economic zone (EEZ) or on the high seas; "shiprider" agreements also enable USCG personnel and USN vessels with embarked USCG law enforcement personnel to work with host nations to protect critical regional resources (2025)

SAN MARINO

INTRODUCTION

Background: Geographically the third-smallest state in Europe (after the Holy See and Monaco), San Marino also claims to be the world's oldest republic. According to tradition, it was founded by a Christian stonemason named MARINUS in A.D. 301. San Marino's foreign policy is aligned with that of the EU, although it is not a member. San Marino is negotiating an Association Agreement that is expected to allow participation in the EU's internal market and cooperation in other policy areas by late 2024. Social and political trends in the republic track closely with those of its larger neighbor, Italy.

GEOGRAPHY

Location: Southern Europe, an enclave in central Italy

Geographic coordinates: 43 46 N, 12 25 E

Map references: Europe

Area: *total:* 61 sq km
land: 61 sq km
water: 0 sq km
comparison ranking: total 227

Area - comparative: about one-third the size of Washington, D.C.

Land boundaries: *total:* 37 km
border countries (1): Italy 37 km

Coastline: 0 km (landlocked)

Maritime claims: none (landlocked)

Climate: Mediterranean; mild to cool winters; warm, sunny summers

Terrain: rugged mountains

Elevation: *highest point:* Monte Titano 739 m
lowest point: Torrente Ausa 55 m

Natural resources: building stone

Land use: *agricultural land:* 38.3% (2022 est.)
arable land: 33.1% (2022 est.)
permanent crops: 5.3% (2022 est.)
permanent pasture: 0% (2022 est.)
forest: 16.7% (2022 est.)
other: 45% (2022 est.)

Irrigated land: 0 sq km (2022)

Natural hazards: occasional earthquakes

Geography - note: landlocked; an enclave of (completely surrounded by) Italy; smallest independent state in Europe after the Holy See and Monaco; dominated by the Apennine Mountains

PEOPLE AND SOCIETY

Population: *total:* 35,095 (2024 est.)
male: 16,944
female: 18,151
comparison rankings: total 214; male 214; female 214

Nationality: *noun:* Sammarinese (singular and plural)
adjective: Sammarinese

Ethnic groups: Sammarinese, Italian

Languages: Italian
major-language sample(s):
L'Almanacco dei fatti del mondo, l'indispensabile fonte per le informazioni di base. (Italian)

Religions: Roman Catholic

Age structure: *0-14 years:* 14.2% (male 2,614/female 2,387)
15-64 years: 64.3% (male 10,916/female 11,648)
65 years and over: 21.5% (2024 est.) (male 3,414/female 4,116)

Dependency ratios: *total dependency ratio:* 55.5 (2024 est.)
youth dependency ratio: 22.2 (2024 est.)
elderly dependency ratio: 33.4 (2024 est.)
potential support ratio: 3 (2024 est.)

Median age: *total:* 46.1 years (2024 est.)
male: 44.5 years
female: 47.4 years
comparison ranking: total 14

Population growth rate: 0.57% (2024 est.)
comparison ranking: 144

Birth rate: 9 births/1,000 population (2024 est.)
comparison ranking: 199

Death rate: 8.9 deaths/1,000 population (2024 est.)
comparison ranking: 63

Net migration rate: 5.6 migrant(s)/1,000 population (2024 est.)
comparison ranking: 18

Urbanization: *urban population:* 97.8% of total population (2023)
rate of urbanization: 0.41% annual rate of change (2020-25 est.)

Major urban areas - population: 4,000 SAN MARINO (2018)

Sex ratio: *at birth:* 1.09 male(s)/female
0-14 years: 1.1 male(s)/female
15-64 years: 0.94 male(s)/female
65 years and over: 0.83 male(s)/female
total population: 0.93 male(s)/female (2024 est.)

Mother's mean age at first birth: 31.9 years (2019)

Maternal mortality ratio: 8 deaths/100,000 live births (2023 est.)
comparison ranking: 158

Infant mortality rate: *total:* 6.2 deaths/1,000 live births (2024 est.)
male: 7.4 deaths/1,000 live births

female: 5 deaths/1,000 live births
comparison ranking: total 168

Life expectancy at birth: *total population:* 84.2 years (2024 est.)
male: 81.7 years
female: 87 years
comparison ranking: total population 6

Total fertility rate: 1.54 children born/woman (2024 est.)
comparison ranking: 195

Gross reproduction rate: 0.74 (2024 est.)

Drinking water source: *improved:* total: 100% of population (2022 est.)
unimproved: total: 0% of population (2022 est.)

Health expenditure: 8% of GDP (2021)
29.5% of national budget (2022 est.)

Physician density: 4.63 physicians/1,000 population (2023)

Sanitation facility access: *improved:* total: 100% of population (2022 est.)
unimproved: total: 0% of population (2022 est.)

Currently married women (ages 15-49): 47.7% (2023 est.)

Education expenditure: 3.4% of GDP (2022 est.)
7.5% national budget (2022 est.)
comparison ranking: Education expenditure (% GDP) 132

Literacy: *total population:* 100% (2022 est.)
male: 100% (2022 est.)
female: 100% (2022 est.)

School life expectancy (primary to tertiary education): *total:* 16 years (2015 est.)
male: 15 years (2015 est.)
female: 16 years (2015 est.)

ENVIRONMENT

Environmental issues: air pollution; urbanization decreasing rural farmlands; water shortage

International environmental agreements: *party to:* Biodiversity, Climate Change, Climate Change-Kyoto Protocol, Climate Change-Paris Agreement, Comprehensive Nuclear Test Ban, Desertification, Endangered Species, Nuclear Test Ban, Ozone Layer Protection, Whaling
signed, but not ratified: Air Pollution

Climate: Mediterranean; mild to cool winters; warm, sunny summers

Urbanization: *urban population:* 97.8% of total population (2023)
rate of urbanization: 0.41% annual rate of change (2020-25 est.)

Particulate matter emissions: 9.8 micrograms per cubic meter (2019 est.)

Waste and recycling: *municipal solid waste generated annually:* 17,200 tons (2024 est.)
percent of municipal solid waste recycled: 45.1% (2016 est.)

GOVERNMENT

Country name: *conventional long form:* Republic of San Marino
conventional short form: San Marino
local long form: Repubblica di San Marino
local short form: San Marino
etymology: named after Saint MARINUS, who founded a monastic settlement on Monte Titano in the early 4th century

Government type: parliamentary republic

Capital: *name:* San Marino (city)
geographic coordinates: 43 56 N, 12 25 E
time difference: UTC+1 (6 hours ahead of Washington, DC, during Standard Time)
daylight saving time: +1hr, begins last Sunday in March; ends last Sunday in October
etymology: named after Saint MARINUS, who founded a monastic settlement on Monte Titano in the early 4th century

Administrative divisions: 9 municipalities *(castelli, singular - castello)*; Acquaviva, Borgo Maggiore, Chiesanuova, Domagnano, Faetano, Fiorentino, Montegiardino, San Marino Citta, Serravalle

Legal system: civil law system with Italian civil law influences

Constitution: *history:* San Marino's principal legislative instruments consist of old customs *(antiche consuetudini)*, the Statutory Laws of San Marino (Leges Statutae Sancti Marini), old statutes *(antichi statute)* from the1600s, Brief Notes on the Constitutional Order and Institutional Organs of the Republic of San Marino (Brevi Cenni sull'Ordinamento Costituzionale e gli Organi Istituzionali della Repubblica di San Marino) and successive legislation, chief among them is the Declaration of the Rights of Citizens and Fundamental Principles of the San Marino Legal Order (Dichiarazione dei Diritti dei Cittadini e dei Principi Fondamentali dell'Ordinamento Sammarinese), approved 8 July 1974
amendment process: proposed by the Great and General Council; passage requires two-thirds majority Council vote; Council passage by absolute majority vote also requires passage in a referendum

International law organization participation: has not submitted an ICJ jurisdiction declaration; accepts ICCt jurisdiction

Citizenship: *citizenship by birth:* no
citizenship by descent only: at least one parent must be a citizen of San Marino
dual citizenship recognized: no
residency requirement for naturalization: 30 years

Suffrage: 18 years of age; universal

Executive branch: *chief of state:* co-chiefs of state Captains Regent Denise BRONZETTI and Italo RIGHI (for the period 1 April 2025 - 30 September 2025)
head of government: Secretary of State for Foreign and Political Affairs Luca BECCARI (since 8 January 2020)
cabinet: Congress of State elected by the Grand and General Council
election/appointment process: co-chiefs of state (captains regent) indirectly elected by the Grand and General Council for a single 6-month term; Secretary of State for Foreign and Political Affairs indirectly elected by the Grand and General Council for a single 5-year term
most recent election date: ***co-chiefs of state:*** 1 April 2025
secretary of state: 28 December 2019
election results: *2025:* Denise BRONZETTI (Reformist Alliance) and Italo RIGHI (Christian Democrat) elected captains regent: percent of Grand and General Council vote - NA
2024: Francesca CIVERCHIA (PDCS) and Dalibor RICCARDI (Free San Marino) elected captains regent; percent of Grand and General Council vote - NA
2019: Luca BECCARI (PDCS) elected Secretary of State for Foreign and Political Affairs; percent of Grand and General Council vote - NA
expected date of next election: ***co-chiefs of state:*** September 2025
note: the captains regent preside over meetings of the Grand and General Council and its cabinet (Congress of State), which has seven other members who are selected by the Grand and General Council; assisting the captains regent are seven secretaries of state; the secretary of state for Foreign Affairs has some prime ministerial roles

Legislative branch: *legislature name:* Great and General Council (Consiglio grande e generale)
legislative structure: unicameral
number of seats: 60 (all directly elected)
electoral system: proportional representation
scope of elections: full renewal
term in office: 5 years
most recent election date: 6/9/2024
parties elected and seats per party: Christian Democratic Party of San Marino (PDCS) (22); Free (Libera) – Socialist Party (PS) (10); Future Republic (RF) (8); Party of Socialists and Democrats (PSD) (8); Tomorrow - Motus Liberi (5); Reformist Alliance (AR) (4); R.E.T.E. Citizens' Movement (3)
percentage of women in chamber: 35%
expected date of next election: June 2029

Judicial branch: *highest court(s):* Council of Twelve or Consiglio dei XII (consists of 12 members)
judge selection and term of office: judges elected by the Grand and General Council from among its own to serve 5-year terms
subordinate courts: first instance and first appeal criminal, administrative, and civil courts; Court for the Trust and Trustee Relations; justices of the peace or conciliatory judges
note: the College of Guarantors for the Constitutionality and General Norms functions as San Marino's constitutional court

Political parties: Domani - Modus Liberi or DML
Free San Marino (Libera San Marino) or Libera
Future Republic or RF
Party of Socialists and Democrats or PSD
Reformist Alliance or AR
RETE Movement
Sammarinese Christian Democratic Party or PDCS
Socialist Party or PS
Tomorrow in Movement coalition (includes RETE Movement, DML)

Diplomatic representation in the US: *chief of mission:* Ambassador Damiano BELEFFI (since 21 July 2017); note - also Permanent Representative to the UN
chancery: 327 E 50th Street, New York, NY 10022
telephone: [1] (212) 751-1234

FAX: [1] (212) 751-1436
email address and website: sanmarinoun@gmail.com
Republic of San Marino Permanent Mission to the United Nations

Diplomatic representation from the US: *embassy:* the United States does not have an Embassy in San Marino; the US Ambassador to Italy is accredited to San Marino, and the US Consulate General in Florence maintains day-to-day ties

International organization participation: CE, FAO, IAEA, IBRD, ICAO, ICC (NGOs), ICCt, ICRM, IDA, IFRCS, ILO, IMF, IMO, Interpol, IOC, IOM (observer), IPU, ITU, ITUC (NGOs), LAIA (observer), OPCW, OSCE, Schengen Convention (de facto member), UN, UNCTAD, UNESCO, Union Latina, UNWTO, UPU, WHO, WIPO

Independence: 3 September 301 (traditional founding date)

National holiday: Founding of the Republic (or Feast of Saint Marinus), 3 September (A.D. 301)

Flag: *description:* two equal horizontal bands of white (top) and light blue, with the national coat of arms in the center; the main colors come from the shield on the coat of arms, which features three white towers on mountain peaks on a blue field; a wreath and a crown are around the shield, above a scroll with the word LIBERTAS (Liberty)
meaning: the towers represent the Guaita, Cesta, and Montale castles on Mount Titano; white and blue are said to stand for peace and liberty

National symbol(s): three peaks, each displaying a tower

National color(s): white, blue

National anthem(s): *title:* "Inno Nazionale della Repubblica" (National Anthem of the Republic)
lyrics/music: no lyrics/Federico CONSOLO
history: adopted 1894; the music for the anthem, which has no lyrics, is based on a 10th-century chorale piece

National heritage: *total World Heritage Sites:* 1 (cultural)
selected World Heritage Site locales: San Marino Historic Center and Mount Titano

ECONOMY

Economic overview: high-income, non-EU European economy; surrounded by Italy, which is the dominant importer and exporter; open border to EU and a euro user; strong financial sector; high foreign investments; low taxation; increasingly high and risky debt

Real GDP (purchasing power parity): $2.393 billion (2022 est.)
$2.218 billion (2021 est.)
$1.947 billion (2020 est.)
note: data in 2021 dollars
comparison ranking: 195

Real GDP growth rate: 7.9% (2022 est.)
13.9% (2021 est.)
-6.6% (2020 est.)
note: annual GDP % growth based on constant local currency
comparison ranking: 12

Real GDP per capita: $70,900 (2022 est.)
$64,700 (2021 est.)
$56,000 (2020 est.)
note: data in 2021 dollars
comparison ranking: 16

GDP (official exchange rate): $1.832 billion (2022 est.)
note: data in current dollars at official exchange rate

Inflation rate (consumer prices): 1.2% (2024 est.)
5.9% (2023 est.)
5.3% (2022 est.)
note: annual % change based on consumer prices
comparison ranking: 29

GDP - composition, by sector of origin: *agriculture:* 0% (2022 est.)
industry: 37.6% (2022 est.)
services: 55.1% (2022 est.)
note: figures may not total 100% due to non-allocated consumption not captured in sector-reported data
comparison rankings: agriculture 202; industry 27; services 121

GDP - composition, by end use: *household consumption:* 35.5% (2022 est.)
government consumption: 17.1% (2022 est.)
investment in fixed capital: 17.8% (2022 est.)
investment in inventories: 5.2% (2022 est.)
exports of goods and services: 197.4% (2022 est.)
imports of goods and services: -173% (2022 est.)
note: figures may not total 100% due to rounding or gaps in data collection

Agricultural products: wheat, grapes, corn, olives; cattle, pigs, horses, beef, cheese, hides

Industries: tourism, banking, textiles, electronics, ceramics, cement, wine

Industrial production growth rate: 10.7% (2022 est.)
note: annual % change in industrial value added based on constant local currency
comparison ranking: 7

Remittances: 1.2% of GDP (2022 est.)
1.1% of GDP (2021 est.)
1.1% of GDP (2020 est.)
note: personal transfers and compensation between resident and non-resident individuals/households/entities

Budget: *revenues:* $841.03 million (2023 est.)
expenditures: $816.886 million (2023 est.)
note: central government revenues (excluding grants) and expenditures converted to US dollars at average official exchange rate for year indicated

Public debt: 103.2% of GDP (2022 est.)
note: central government debt as a % of GDP
comparison ranking: 17

Taxes and other revenues: 17.8% (of GDP) (2022 est.)
note: central government tax revenue as a % of GDP
comparison ranking: 67

Current account balance: $284.256 million (2022 est.)
$100.118 million (2021 est.)
$42.98 million (2020 est.)
note: balance of payments - net trade and primary/secondary income in current dollars
comparison ranking: 68

Exports: $3.616 billion (2022 est.)
$3.23 billion (2021 est.)
$2.439 billion (2020 est.)
note: balance of payments - exports of goods and services in current dollars
comparison ranking: 151

Exports - partners: Germany 12%, Austria 10%, USA 9%, Romania 8%, Brazil 7% (2023)
note: top five export partners based on percentage share of exports

Exports - commodities: washing and bottling machines, other foods, packaged medicine, woodworking machines, aircraft (2023)
note: top five export commodities based on value in dollars

Imports: $3.169 billion (2022 est.)
$2.94 billion (2021 est.)
$2.232 billion (2020 est.)
note: balance of payments - imports of goods and services in current dollars
comparison ranking: 164

Imports - partners: Germany 24%, Italy 13%, Netherlands 9%, Spain 9%, Poland 8% (2023)
note: top five import partners based on percentage share of imports

Imports - commodities: garments, cars, electricity, animal food, footwear (2023)
note: top five import commodities based on value in dollars

Reserves of foreign exchange and gold: $836.088 million (2023 est.)
$716.066 million (2022 est.)
$954.383 million (2021 est.)
note: holdings of gold (year-end prices)/foreign exchange/special drawing rights in current dollars
comparison ranking: 146

Exchange rates: euros (EUR) per US dollar -

Exchange rates: 0.924 (2024 est.)
0.925 (2023 est.)
0.951 (2022 est.)
0.845 (2021 est.)
0.877 (2020 est.)
note: while not an EU member state, San Marino, due to its preexisting monetary and banking agreements with Italy, has a 2000 monetary agreement with the EU to produce limited euro coinage—but not banknotes—that began enforcement in January 2002 and was superseded by a new EU agreement in 2012

ENERGY

Electricity access: *electrification - total population:* 100% (2022 est.)

COMMUNICATIONS

Telephones - fixed lines: *total subscriptions:* 16,000 (2022 est.)
subscriptions per 100 inhabitants: 47 (2022 est.)
comparison ranking: total subscriptions 179

Telephones - mobile cellular: *total subscriptions:* 41,000 (2022 est.)
subscriptions per 100 inhabitants: 122 (2022 est.)
comparison ranking: total subscriptions 209

Broadcast media: state-owned public broadcaster operates 1 TV station and 3 radio stations; receives radio and TV broadcasts from Italy (2019)

Internet country code: .sm

Internet users: *percent of population:* 87% (2023 est.)

Broadband - fixed subscriptions: *total:* 12,000 (2022 est.)
subscriptions per 100 inhabitants: 36 (2022 est.)
comparison ranking: total 182

TRANSPORTATION

Civil aircraft registration country code prefix: T7

Airports: 1 (2025)
comparison ranking: 215

MILITARY AND SECURITY

Military and security forces: San Marino Military Corps (Corpi Militari Sammarinesi; aka Sammarinese Armed Forces or Forze Armate Sammarinesi): Fortress Guard Command (or Guard of the Rock), Uniformed Company of the Militias, Guard of the Great and General Council, Corps of the Gendarmerie

Ministry of Internal Affairs: Civil Police Corps (2025)

Military service age and obligation: 18 is the legal minimum age for voluntary military service; no conscription; government has the authority to call up all San Marino citizens from 16-60 years of age to serve in the military (2024)

Military - note: defense is the responsibility of Italy

SAO TOME AND PRINCIPE

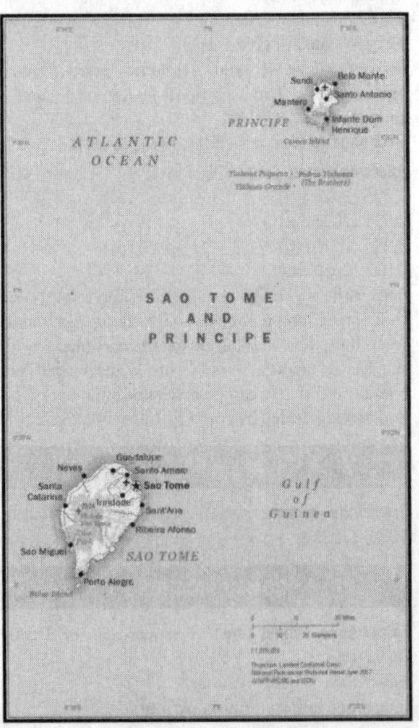

INTRODUCTION

Background: Portugal discovered and colonized the uninhabited Sao Tome and Principe islands in the late 15th century, setting up a sugar-based economy that gave way to coffee and cocoa in the 19th century – all grown with African slave labor, a form of which lingered into the 20th century. While independence was achieved in 1975, democratic reforms were not instituted until the late 1980s.

The country held its first free elections in 1991, but frequent internal wrangling among the various political parties precipitated repeated changes in leadership and failed, non-violent coup attempts in 1995, 1998, 2003, and 2009. In 2012, three opposition parties combined in a no-confidence vote to bring down the majority government of former Prime Minister Patrice TROVOADA, but legislative elections returned him to the office two years later. President Evaristo CARVALHO, of the same political party as TROVOADA, was elected in 2016, marking a rare instance in which the same party held the positions of president and prime minister. TROVOADA resigned in 2018 and was replaced by Jorge BOM JESUS. Carlos Vila NOVA was elected president in 2021. TROVOADA began his fourth stint as prime minister in 2022, after his party's victory in legislative elections.

GEOGRAPHY

Location: Central Africa, islands in the Gulf of Guinea, just north of the Equator, west of Gabon

Geographic coordinates: 1 00 N, 7 00 E

Map references: Africa

Area: *total:* 964 sq km
land: 964 sq km
water: 0 sq km
comparison ranking: total 184

Area - comparative: more than five times the size of Washington, D.C.

Land boundaries: *total:* 0 km

Coastline: 209 km

Maritime claims: *territorial sea:* 12 nm
exclusive economic zone: 200 nm
note: measured from claimed archipelagic baselines

Climate: tropical; hot, humid; one rainy season (October to May)

Terrain: volcanic, mountainous

Elevation: *highest point:* Pico de Sao Tome 2,024 m
lowest point: Atlantic Ocean 0 m

Natural resources: fish, hydropower

Land use: *agricultural land:* 44.8% (2022 est.)
arable land: 4.2% (2022 est.)
permanent crops: 39.6% (2022 est.)
permanent pasture: 1% (2022 est.)
forest: 52.8% (2022 est.)
other: 2.4% (2022 est.)

Irrigated land: 100 sq km (2012)

Population distribution: Sao Tome, the capital city, has roughly a quarter of the nation's population; Santo Antonio is the largest town on Principe; the northern areas of both islands have the highest population densities, as shown in this population distribution map

Natural hazards: flooding

Geography - note: the second-smallest African country (after the Seychelles); the two main islands form part of a chain of extinct volcanoes, and both are mountainous

PEOPLE AND SOCIETY

Population: *total:* 223,561 (2024 est.)
male: 111,553
female: 112,008
comparison rankings: total 183; male 183; female 183

Nationality: *noun:* Sao Tomean(s)
adjective: Sao Tomean

Ethnic groups: Mestico, Angolares (descendants of Angolan slaves), Forros (descendants of freed slaves), Servicais (contract laborers from Angola, Mozambique, and Cabo Verde), Tongas (children of servicais born on the islands), Europeans (primarily Portuguese), Asians (mostly Chinese)

Languages: Portuguese 98.4% (official), Forro 36.2%, Cabo Verdian 8.5%, French 6.8%, Angolar 6.6%, English 4.9%, Lunguie 1%, other (including sign language) 2.4%; other Portuguese-based Creoles are also spoken (2012 est.)
note: shares of language sum to more than 100% because some respondents gave more than one answer on the census

Religions: Catholic 55.7%, Adventist 4.1%, Assembly of God 3.4%, New Apostolic 2.9%, Mana 2.3%, Universal Kingdom of God 2%, Jehovah's Witness 1.2%, other 6.2%, none 21.2%, unspecified 1% (2012 est.)

Age structure: *0-14 years:* 36.4% (male 41,337/ female 40,106)
15-64 years: 60.3% (male 67,101/female 67,775)
65 years and over: 3.2% (2024 est.) (male 3,115/ female 4,127)

Dependency ratios: *total dependency ratio:* 65.8 (2024 est.)
youth dependency ratio: 60.4 (2024 est.)
elderly dependency ratio: 5.4 (2024 est.)
potential support ratio: 18.6 (2024 est.)

Median age: *total:* 20.8 years (2024 est.)
male: 20.4 years
female: 21.2 years
comparison ranking: total 197

Population growth rate: 1.42% (2024 est.)
comparison ranking: 70

Birth rate: 26.7 births/1,000 population (2024 est.)
comparison ranking: 39

Death rate: 6 deaths/1,000 population (2024 est.)
comparison ranking: 155

Net migration rate: -6.5 migrant(s)/1,000 population (2024 est.)
comparison ranking: 213

Population distribution: Sao Tome, the capital city, has roughly a quarter of the nation's population; Santo Antonio is the largest town on Principe; the northern areas of both islands have the highest population densities, as shown in this population distribution map

Urbanization: *urban population:* 76.4% of total population (2023)
rate of urbanization: 2.96% annual rate of change (2020-25 est.)

Major urban areas - population: 80,000 SAO TOME (capital) (2018)

Sex ratio: *at birth:* 1.03 male(s)/female
0-14 years: 1.03 male(s)/female
15-64 years: 0.99 male(s)/female
65 years and over: 0.75 male(s)/female
total population: 1 male(s)/female (2024 est.)

Mother's mean age at first birth: 19.4 years (2008/09 est.)
note: data represents median age at first birth among women 25-29

Maternal mortality ratio: 75 deaths/100,000 live births (2023 est.)
comparison ranking: 77

Infant mortality rate: *total:* 42.6 deaths/1,000 live births (2024 est.)
male: 46.1 deaths/1,000 live births
female: 39 deaths/1,000 live births
comparison ranking: total 27

Life expectancy at birth: *total population:* 67.7 years (2024 est.)
male: 66 years
female: 69.4 years
comparison ranking: total population 195

Total fertility rate: 3.31 children born/woman (2024 est.)
comparison ranking: 41

Gross reproduction rate: 1.63 (2024 est.)

Drinking water source: *improved: urban:* 79.3% of population (2022 est.)
rural: 71.1% of population (2022 est.)
total: 77.3% of population (2022 est.)
unimproved: urban: 20.7% of population (2022 est.)
rural: 28.9% of population (2022 est.)

total: 22.7% of population (2022 est.)

Health expenditure: 7.8% of GDP (2021)
14.9% of national budget (2022 est.)

Physician density: 0.46 physicians/1,000 population (2022)

Hospital bed density: 2.9 beds/1,000 population (2019 est.)

Sanitation facility access: *improved: urban:* 56.8% of population (2022 est.)
rural: 43.2% of population (2022 est.)
total: 53.5% of population (2022 est.)
unimproved: urban: 43.2% of population (2022 est.)
rural: 56.8% of population (2022 est.)
total: 46.5% of population (2022 est.)

Obesity - adult prevalence rate: 12.4% (2016)
comparison ranking: 133

Alcohol consumption per capita: *total:* 4.23 liters of pure alcohol (2019 est.)
beer: 0.42 liters of pure alcohol (2019 est.)
wine: 3.58 liters of pure alcohol (2019 est.)
spirits: 0.23 liters of pure alcohol (2019 est.)
other alcohols: 0 liters of pure alcohol (2019 est.)
comparison ranking: total 92

Tobacco use: *total:* 7.3% (2025 est.)
male: 13.1% (2025 est.)
female: 1.7% (2025 est.)
comparison ranking: total 149

Children under the age of 5 years underweight: 5.4% (2019)
comparison ranking: 64

Currently married women (ages 15-49): 51.9% (2023 est.)

Child marriage: *women married by age 15:* 5.4% (2019)
women married by age 18: 28% (2019)
men married by age 18: 3.1% (2019)

Education expenditure: 5% of GDP (2023 est.)
18.1% national budget (2024 est.)
comparison ranking: Education expenditure (% GDP) 65

Literacy: *total population:* 87.4% (2019 est.)
male: 92.5% (2019 est.)
female: 82.8% (2019 est.)

School life expectancy (primary to tertiary education): *total:* 13 years (2021 est.)
male: 13 years (2021 est.)
female: 13 years (2021 est.)

ENVIRONMENT

Environmental issues: deforestation and illegal logging; soil erosion and exhaustion; inadequate sewage treatment in cities; biodiversity

International environmental agreements: *party to:* Biodiversity, Climate Change, Climate Change-Kyoto Protocol, Climate Change-Paris Agreement, Desertification, Endangered Species, Environmental Modification, Hazardous Wastes, Law of the Sea, Ozone Layer Protection, Ship Pollution, Wetlands, Whaling
signed, but not ratified: Comprehensive Nuclear Test Ban

Climate: tropical; hot, humid; one rainy season (October to May)

Urbanization: *urban population:* 76.4% of total population (2023)
rate of urbanization: 2.96% annual rate of change (2020-25 est.)

Carbon dioxide emissions: 146,000 metric tonnes of CO2 (2023 est.)
from petroleum and other liquids: 146,000 metric tonnes of CO2 (2023 est.)
comparison ranking: total emissions 206

Particulate matter emissions: 29 micrograms per cubic meter (2019 est.)

Waste and recycling: *municipal solid waste generated annually:* 25,600 tons (2024 est.)
percent of municipal solid waste recycled: 16.9% (2022 est.)

Total water withdrawal: *municipal:* 14.7 million cubic meters (2022 est.)
industrial: 600,000 cubic meters (2022 est.)
agricultural: 25.6 million cubic meters (2022 est.)

Total renewable water resources: 2.18 billion cubic meters (2022)

GOVERNMENT

Country name: *conventional long form:* Democratic Republic of Sao Tome and Principe
conventional short form: Sao Tome and Principe
local long form: Republica Democratica de Sao Tome e Principe
local short form: Sao Tome e Principe
etymology: Sao Tome was named after Saint THOMAS the Apostle by the Portuguese who discovered the island on 21 December 1470 (or 1471), the saint's feast day; Principe is a shortening of the original Portuguese name of "Ilha do Principe" (Isle of the Prince), referring to Prince ALPHONSO of Portugal

Government type: semi-presidential republic

Capital: *name:* Sao Tome
geographic coordinates: 0 20 N, 6 44 E
time difference: UTC 0 (5 hours ahead of Washington, DC, during Standard Time)
etymology: named after Saint THOMAS the Apostle by the Portuguese, who discovered the island on 21 December 1470 (or 1471), the saint's feast day

Administrative divisions: 6 districts (*distritos*, singular - *distrito*), 1 autonomous region* (*regiao autonoma*); Agua Grande, Cantagalo, Caue, Lemba, Lobata, Me-Zochi, Principe*

Legal system: mixed system of civil law based on the Portuguese model and customary law

Constitution: *history:* approved 5 November 1975
amendment process: proposed by the National Assembly; passage requires two-thirds majority vote by the Assembly; the Assembly can propose to the president of the republic that an amendment be submitted to a referendum

International law organization participation: has not submitted an ICJ jurisdiction declaration; non-party state to the ICCt

Citizenship: *citizenship by birth:* no
citizenship by descent only: at least one parent must be a citizen of Sao Tome and Principe
dual citizenship recognized: no
residency requirement for naturalization: 5 years

Suffrage: 18 years of age; universal

Executive branch: *chief of state:* President Carlos Manuel VILA NOVA (since 2 October 2021)
head of government: Prime Minister Américo d'Oliveira DOS RAMOS (since 12 January 2025)
cabinet: Council of Ministers proposed by the prime minister, appointed by the president
election/appointment process: president directly elected by absolute-majority popular vote in 2 rounds, if needed, for a 5-year term (eligible for a second term); prime minister chosen by the National Assembly and approved by the president
most recent election date: 18 July 2021, with a runoff on 5 September 2021
election results: *2021:* Carlos Manuel VILA NOVA elected president in the second round; percent of vote in the first round - Carlos Manuel VILA NOVA (IDA) 39.5%; Guilherme POSSER DA COSTA (MLSTP-PSD) 20.8%; Delfim NEVES (PCD-GR) 16.9%; Abel BOM JESUS (independent) 3.6%; Maria DAS NEVES (independent) 3.3%; other 15.9%; percent of the vote in second round - Carlos Manuel VILA NOVA 57.5%, Guilherme POSSER DA COSTA 42.5%
2016: Evaristo CARVALHO elected president; percent of vote - Evaristo CARVALHO (ADI) 49.8%, Manuel Pinto DA COSTA (independent) 24.8%, Maria DAS NEVES (MLSTP-PSD) 24.1%
expected date of next election: 2026

Legislative branch: *legislature name:* National Assembly (Assembleia Nacional)
legislative structure: unicameral
number of seats: 55 (all directly elected)
electoral system: proportional representation
scope of elections: full renewal
term in office: 4 years
most recent election date: 9/25/2022
parties elected and seats per party: Independent Democratic Alliance (ADI) (30); Sao Tome and Principe Liberation Movement/Social Democratic Party (MLSTP - PSD) (18); Movement of Independent Citizens - Socialist Party (MÇI - PS) - National Unity Party (PUN) (5); Other (2)
percentage of women in chamber: 14.5%
expected date of next election: September 2026

Judicial branch: *highest court(s):* Supreme Court or Supremo Tribunal Justica (consists of 5 judges); Constitutional Court or Tribunal Constitucional (consists of 5 judges, 3 of whom are from the Supreme Court)
judge selection and term of office: Supreme Court judges appointed by the National Assembly; judge tenure NA; Constitutional Court judges nominated by the president and elected by the National Assembly for 5-year terms
subordinate courts: Court of First Instance; Audit Court

Political parties: BASTA Movement
Independent Democratic Action or ADI
Movement for the Liberation of Sao Tome and Principe-Social Democratic Party or MLSTP-PSD
Movement of Independent Citizens of São Tomé and Príncipe - Socialist Party or MCI-PS
National Unity Party or PUN

Diplomatic representation in the US: *chief of mission:* Ambassador (vacant)
chancery: 122 East 42nd Street, Suite 1604 New York, NY 101168
telephone: [1] (212) 317-0533

FAX: [1] (212) 317-0580
email address and website: stp1@attglobal.net
Sao Tome and Principe Permanent Mission to the United Nations

Diplomatic representation from the US: *embassy:* the US does not have an embassy in Sao Tome and Principe; the US Ambassador to Angola is accredited to Sao Tome and Principe *mailing address:* 2290 Sao Tome Place, Washington DC 20521-2290

International organization participation: ACP, AfDB, AOSIS, AU, CD, CEMAC, CPLP, EITI (candidate country), FAO, G-77, IBRD, ICAO, ICRM, IDA, IFAD, IFC, IFRCS, ILO, IMF, IMO, Interpol, IOC, IOM (observer), IPU, ITU, ITUC (NGOs), MIGA, NAM, OIF, OPCW, PCA, UN, UNCTAD, UNESCO, UNIDO, Union Latina, UNWTO, UPU, WCO, WHO, WIPO, WMO, WTO (observer)

Independence: 12 July 1975 (from Portugal)

National holiday: Independence Day, 12 July (1975)

Flag: *description:* three horizontal bands of green (top), yellow (double-width), and green with two five-pointed black stars in the center of the yellow band and a red isosceles triangle based on the left side
meaning: green stands for the country's rich vegetation, red for the struggle for independence, and yellow for cocoa, one of the country's main agricultural products; the two stars symbolize the main islands
history: uses the colors of the Pan-African movement

National symbol(s): palm tree

National color(s): green, yellow, red, black

National anthem(s): *title:* "Independencia total" (Total Independence)
lyrics/music: Alda Neves DA GRACA do Espirito Santo/Manuel dos Santos Barreto de Sousa e ALMEIDA
history: adopted 1975

ECONOMY

Economic overview: lower middle-income Central African island economy; falling cocoa production due to drought and mismanagement; joint oil venture with Nigeria; government owns 90% of land; high debt, partly from fuel subsidies; tourism gutted by COVID-19

Real GDP (purchasing power parity): $1.291 billion (2024 est.)
$1.279 billion (2023 est.)
$1.275 billion (2022 est.)
note: data in 2021 dollars
comparison ranking: 204

Real GDP growth rate: 0.9% (2024 est.)
0.4% (2023 est.)
0.2% (2022 est.)
note: annual GDP % growth based on constant local currency
comparison ranking: 182

Real GDP per capita: $5,500 (2024 est.)
$5,500 (2023 est.)
$5,600 (2022 est.)
note: data in 2021 dollars
comparison ranking: 170

GDP (official exchange rate): $764.274 million (2024 est.)
note: data in current dollars at official exchange rate

Inflation rate (consumer prices): 14.4% (2024 est.)
21.3% (2023 est.)
18% (2022 est.)
note: annual % change based on consumer prices
comparison ranking: 187

GDP - composition, by sector of origin: *agriculture:* 12.8% (2024 est.)
industry: 2.9% (2024 est.)
services: 76.6% (2024 est.)
note: figures may not total 100% due to non-allocated consumption not captured in sector-reported data
comparison rankings: agriculture 62; industry 206; services 18

GDP - composition, by end use: *household consumption:* 81.4% (2017 est.)
government consumption: 17.6% (2017 est.)
investment in fixed capital: 33.4% (2017 est.)
investment in inventories: 0% (2017 est.)
exports of goods and services: 7.9% (2017 est.)
imports of goods and services: -40.4% (2017 est.)

Agricultural products: plantains, oil palm fruit, taro, bananas, fruits, cocoa beans, yams, coconuts, cassava, vegetables (2023)
note: top ten agricultural products based on tonnage

Industries: light construction, textiles, soap, beer, fish processing, timber

Industrial production growth rate: 3.2% (2024 est.)
note: annual % change in industrial value added based on constant local currency
comparison ranking: 78

Labor force: 34,500 (2024 est.)
note: number of people ages 15 or older who are employed or seeking work
comparison ranking: 190

Unemployment rate: 9.2% (2024 est.)
9.1% (2023 est.)
9% (2022 est.)
note: % of labor force seeking employment
comparison ranking: 145

Youth unemployment rate (ages 15-24): *total:* 8.6% (2024 est.)
male: 8% (2024 est.)
female: 9.2% (2024 est.)
note: % of labor force ages 15-24 seeking employment
comparison ranking: total 133

Population below poverty line: 55.5% (2017 est.)
note: % of population with income below national poverty line
Gini Index coefficient - distribution of family income 40.7 (2017 est.)
note: index (0-100) of income distribution; higher values represent greater inequality
comparison ranking: 37

Household income or consumption by percentage share: *lowest 10%:* 2.6% (2017 est.)
highest 10%: 32.8% (2017 est.)
note: % share of income accruing to lowest and highest 10% of population

Remittances: 1.5% of GDP (2023 est.)
1.9% of GDP (2022 est.)
2% of GDP (2021 est.)
note: personal transfers and compensation between resident and non-resident individuals/ households/ entities

Budget: *revenues:* $128.767 million (2022 est.)
expenditures: $165.95 million (2022 est.)
note: central government revenues and expenses (excluding grants/extrabudgetary units/ social security funds) converted to US dollars at average official exchange rate for year indicated

Current account balance: -$79.437 million (2022 est.)
-$95.248 million (2021 est.)
-$59.595 million (2020 est.)
note: balance of payments - net trade and primary/ secondary income in current dollars
comparison ranking: 94

Exports: $96.977 million (2022 est.)
$75.256 million (2021 est.)
$49.337 million (2020 est.)
note: balance of payments - exports of goods and services in current dollars
comparison ranking: 208

Exports - partners: Pakistan 54%, Germany 11%, Netherlands 7%, France 5%, UAE 3% (2023)
note: top five export partners based on percentage share of exports

Exports - commodities: crude petroleum, cocoa beans, vehicle parts/accessories, palm oil, aircraft parts (2023)
note: top five export commodities based on value in dollars

Imports: $219.322 million (2022 est.)
$201.145 million (2021 est.)
$160.097 million (2020 est.)
note: balance of payments - imports of goods and services in current dollars
comparison ranking: 207

Imports - partners: Portugal 35%, Angola 13%, Gabon 11%, Japan 8%, China 6% (2023)
note: top five import partners based on percentage share of imports

Imports - commodities: ships, refined petroleum, rice, electric generating sets, cars (2023)
note: top five import commodities based on value in dollars

Reserves of foreign exchange and gold: $46.247 million (2023 est.)
$64.476 million (2022 est.)
$75.017 million (2021 est.)
note: holdings of gold (year-end prices)/foreign exchange/special drawing rights in current dollars
comparison ranking: 178

Debt - external: $327.248 million (2023 est.)
note: present value of external debt in current US dollars
comparison ranking: 115

Exchange rates: dobras (STD) per US dollar -

Exchange rates: 22.658 (2023 est.)
23.29 (2022 est.)
20.71 (2021 est.)
21.507 (2020 est.)
21.885 (2019 est.)

ENERGY

Electricity access: *electrification - total population:* 78% (2022 est.)
electrification - urban areas: 80%
electrification - rural areas: 73.7%

Electricity: *installed generating capacity:* 29,000 kW (2023 est.)
consumption: 47.05 million kWh (2023 est.)
transmission/distribution losses: 40.95 million kWh (2023 est.)
comparison rankings: installed generating capacity 202; consumption 204; transmission/distribution losses 34

Electricity generation sources: *fossil fuels:* 93.2% of total installed capacity (2023 est.)
hydroelectricity: 6.8% of total installed capacity (2023 est.)

Petroleum: *refined petroleum consumption:* 1,000 bbl/day (2023 est.)

Energy consumption per capita: 8.875 million Btu/person (2023 est.)
comparison ranking: 152

COMMUNICATIONS

Telephones - fixed lines: *total subscriptions:* 2,000 (2023 est.)
subscriptions per 100 inhabitants: 1 (2023 est.)
comparison ranking: total subscriptions 216

Telephones - mobile cellular: *total subscriptions:* 152,000 (2023 est.)
subscriptions per 100 inhabitants: 87 (2022 est.)
comparison ranking: total subscriptions 187

Broadcast media: 1 state-owned TV station; 2 state-owned radio stations; 7 independent local radio stations; transmissions of multiple international broadcasters are available

Internet country code: .st

Internet users: *percent of population:* 62% (2023 est.)

Broadband - fixed subscriptions: *total:* 6,000 (2023 est.)
subscriptions per 100 inhabitants: 3 (2023 est.)
comparison ranking: total 192

TRANSPORTATION

Civil aircraft registration country code prefix: S9

Airports: 2 (2025)
comparison ranking: 199

Merchant marine: *total:* 25 (2023)
by type: general cargo 15, oil tanker 4, other 6
comparison ranking: total 141

Ports: *total ports:* 2 (2024)
large: 0
medium: 0
small: 0
very small: 2
ports with oil terminals: 0
key ports: Santo Antonio, Sao Tome

MILITARY AND SECURITY

Military and security forces: Armed Forces of Sao Tome and Principe (Forcas Armadas de Sao Tome e Principe, FASTP): Army, Coast Guard of Sao Tome e Principe (Guarda Costeira de Sao Tome e Principe, GCSTP), Presidential Guard, National Guard (2024)
note: the Army and Coast Guard are responsible for external security while the public security police and judicial police maintain internal security; both the public security police and the military report to the Ministry of Defense and Internal Affairs; the judicial police report to the Ministry of Justice, Public Administration, and Human Rights

Military and security service personnel strengths: approximately 500 active Armed Forces (2023)

Military equipment inventories and acquisitions: the FASTP is lightly armed and has a small inventory of mostly older weapons and equipment (2023)

Military service age and obligation: 18 is the legal minimum age for compulsory military service (reportedly not enforced); 17 is the legal minimum age for voluntary service (2023)

Military - note: the FASTP is one of the smallest militaries in Africa and consists of only a few companies of ground troops and some small patrol boats
in November 2022, the FASTP's headquarters was attacked shortly after the prime minister's inauguration in what São Tomé authorities described as an attempted coup; in 2024, the governments of Russia and São Tomé and Principe signed a military cooperation agreement, which included training, materiel and logistics support, and information sharing (2024)

SAUDI ARABIA

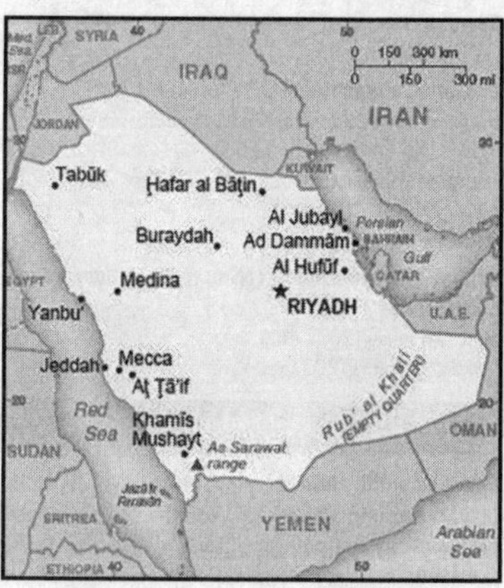

INTRODUCTION

Background: Saudi Arabia is the birthplace of Islam and home to Islam's two holiest shrines in Mecca and Medina. The king's official title is the Custodian of the Two Holy Mosques. ABD AL-AZIZ bin Abd al-Rahman AL SAUD (Ibn Saud) founded the modern Saudi state in 1932 after a 30-year campaign to unify most of the Arabian Peninsula. One of his male descendants rules the country today, as required by the country's 1992 Basic Law. After Iraq invaded Kuwait in 1990, Saudi Arabia took in the Kuwaiti royal family and 400,000 refugees, while allowing Western and Arab troops to deploy on its soil and liberate Kuwait the following year. Major terrorist attacks in 2003 spurred a strong ongoing campaign against domestic terrorism and extremism. US troops returned to the Kingdom in 2019 after attacks on Saudi oil infrastructure.

From 2005 to 2015, King ABDALLAH bin Abd al-Aziz Al Saud incrementally modernized the Kingdom through a series of social and economic initiatives that included expanding employment and social opportunities for women, attracting foreign investment, increasing the private sector's role in the economy, and discouraging the hiring of foreign workers. Saudi Arabia saw some protests during the 2011 Arab Spring but not the level of bloodshed seen in protests elsewhere in the region; Riyadh took a cautious but firm approach, arresting and quickly releasing some protesters and using its state-sponsored clerics to counter political and Islamist activism. The government held its first-ever elections in 2005 and 2011, when Saudis voted for municipal councilors. King ABDALLAH's reforms accelerated under King SALMAN bin Abd al-Aziz, who ascended to the throne in 2015 and lifted the Kingdom's ban on women driving, implemented education reforms, funded green initiatives, and allowed cinemas to operate for the first time in decades. In 2015, women were allowed to vote and stand as candidates for the first time in municipal elections, with 19 women winning seats. King SALMAN initially named his nephew, MUHAMMAD BIN NAYIF bin Abd al-Aziz Al Saud, as the Crown Prince, but a palace coup in 2017 resulted in King SALMAN's son, Deputy Crown Prince MUHAMMAD BIN SALMAN bin Abd al-Aziz Al Saud, taking over as Crown Prince. King SALMAN appointed MUHAMMAD BIN SALMAN as prime minister in 2022.

In 2015, Saudi Arabia led a coalition of 10 countries in a military campaign to restore Yemen's legitimate government, which had been ousted by Houthi forces. The war in Yemen has drawn international criticism for civilian casualties and its effect on the country's dire humanitarian situation. The same year, MUHAMMAD BIN SALMAN announced that Saudi Arabia would lead a multi-nation Islamic Coalition to fight terrorism, and in 2017, Saudi Arabia inaugurated the Global Center for Combatting Extremist Ideology (also known as "Etidal").

The country remains a leading producer of oil and natural gas and holds about 17% of the world's proven oil reserves as of 2020. The government continues to pursue economic reform and diversification – particularly since Saudi Arabia's accession to the WTO in 2005 – and promotes foreign investment in the Kingdom. In 2016, the Saudi Government announced broad socio-economic reforms known as Vision 2030. Low global oil prices in 2015 and 2016 significantly lowered Saudi Arabia's governmental revenue, prompting cuts to subsidies on water, electricity, and gasoline; reduced government-employee compensation; and new land taxes. In coordination with OPEC and some key non-OPEC countries, Saudi Arabia agreed to cut oil output in 2017 to regulate supply and help boost global prices. In 2020, this agreement collapsed, and Saudi Arabia launched a price war by flooding the market with low-priced oil before returning to the negotiating table to agree to a major output cut that helped buoy prices.

GEOGRAPHY

Location: Middle East, bordering the Persian Gulf and the Red Sea, north of Yemen

Geographic coordinates: 25 00 N, 45 00 E

Map references: Middle East

Area: *total:* 2,149,690 sq km
land: 2,149,690 sq km
water: 0 sq km
comparison ranking: total 14

Area - comparative: slightly more than one-fifth the size of the US

Land boundaries: *total:* 4,272 km

border countries (7): Iraq 811 km; Jordan 731 km; Kuwait 221 km; Oman 658 km; Qatar 87 km; UAE 457 km; Yemen 1,307 km

Coastline: 2,640 km

Maritime claims: *territorial sea:* 12 nm
contiguous zone: 18 nm
continental shelf: not specified

Climate: harsh, dry desert with great temperature extremes

Terrain: mostly sandy desert

Elevation: *highest point:* As Sarawat range, 3,000 m
lowest point: Persian Gulf 0 m
mean elevation: 665 m

Natural resources: petroleum, natural gas, iron ore, gold, copper

Land use: *agricultural land:* 80.8% (2022 est.)
arable land: 1.6% (2022 est.)
permanent crops: 0.1% (2022 est.)
permanent pasture: 79.1% (2022 est.)
forest: 0.5% (2022 est.)
other: 18.8% (2022 est.)

Irrigated land: 7,575 sq km (2022)

Major watersheds (area sq km): Indian Ocean drainage: *(Persian Gulf)* Tigris and Euphrates (918,044 sq km)

Major aquifers: Arabian Aquifer System

Population distribution: historically a population that was mostly nomadic or semi-nomadic, the Saudi population has become more settled since oil was discovered in the 1930s; most of the country's population is now concentrated in a wide area across the middle of the peninsula, from Ad Dammam in the east through Riyadh in the interior to Mecca-Medina in the west near the Red Sea

Natural hazards: frequent sand and dust storms
volcanism: little activity in the past few centuries, despite many volcanic formations; volcanoes include Harrat Rahat, Harrat Khaybar, Harrat Lunayyir, and Jabal Yar

Geography - note: Saudi Arabia is the largest country in the world without a river; extensive coastlines on the Persian Gulf and Red Sea allow for considerable shipping (especially of crude oil) through the Persian Gulf and Suez Canal

PEOPLE AND SOCIETY

Population: *total:* 36,544,431 (2024 est.)
male: 20,700,838
female: 15,843,593
comparison rankings: total 41; male 36; female 49

Nationality: *noun:* Saudi(s)
adjective: Saudi or Saudi Arabian

Ethnic groups: Arab 90%, Afro-Asian 10%

Languages: Arabic (official)
major-language sample(s):
كتاب حقائق العالم، المصدر الذي لا يمكن الاستغناء عنه للمعلومات الأساسية
(Arabic)

Religions: Muslim (official; citizens are 85-90% Sunni and 10-12% Shia), other (includes Eastern Orthodox, Protestant, Roman Catholic, Jewish, Hindu, Buddhist, and Sikh) (2020 est.)
note: despite having a large expatriate community of various faiths (more than 30% of the population), most forms of public religious expression inconsistent with the government-sanctioned interpretation of Sunni Islam are restricted; non-Muslims are not allowed to have Saudi citizenship and non-Muslim places of worship are not permitted (2013)

Age structure: *0-14 years:* 22.9% (male 4,266,720/ female 4,097,270)
15-64 years: 72.7% (male 15,577,133/female 10,994,061)
65 years and over: 4.4% (2024 est.) (male 856,985/ female 752,262)

Dependency ratios: *total dependency ratio:* 37.5 (2024 est.)
youth dependency ratio: 31.5 (2024 est.)
elderly dependency ratio: 6.1 (2024 est.)
potential support ratio: 16.5 (2024 est.)

Median age: *total:* 32.4 years (2024 est.)
male: 34.6 years
female: 29.3 years
comparison ranking: total 115

Population growth rate: 1.68% (2024 est.)
comparison ranking: 55

Birth rate: 13.6 births/1,000 population (2024 est.)
comparison ranking: 125

Death rate: 3.5 deaths/1,000 population (2024 est.)
comparison ranking: 220

Net migration rate: 6.7 migrant(s)/1,000 population (2024 est.)
comparison ranking: 12

Population distribution: historically a population that was mostly nomadic or semi-nomadic, the Saudi population has become more settled since oil was discovered in the 1930s; most of the country's population is now concentrated in a wide area across the middle of the peninsula, from Ad Dammam in the east through Riyadh in the interior to Mecca-Medina in the west near the Red Sea

Urbanization: *urban population:* 85% of total population (2023)
rate of urbanization: 1.69% annual rate of change (2020-25 est.)

Major urban areas - population: 7.682 million RIYADH (capital), 4.863 million Jeddah, 2.150 million Mecca, 1.573 million Medina, 1.329 million Ad Dammam, 872,000 million Hufuf-Mubarraz (2023)

Sex ratio: *at birth:* 1.05 male(s)/female
0-14 years: 1.04 male(s)/female
15-64 years: 1.42 male(s)/female
65 years and over: 1.14 male(s)/female
total population: 1.31 male(s)/female (2024 est.)

Maternal mortality ratio: 7 deaths/100,000 live births (2023 est.)
comparison ranking: 162

Infant mortality rate: *total:* 11.7 deaths/1,000 live births (2024 est.)
male: 12.8 deaths/1,000 live births
female: 10.5 deaths/1,000 live births
comparison ranking: total 113

Life expectancy at birth: *total population:* 77.2 years (2024 est.)
male: 75.6 years
female: 78.8 years
comparison ranking: total population 97

Total fertility rate: 1.87 children born/woman (2024 est.)
comparison ranking: 130

Gross reproduction rate: 0.91 (2024 est.)

Drinking water source: *improved:* *urban:* 98.4% of population (2022 est.)
rural: 100% of population (2022 est.)
total: 98.6% of population (2022 est.)
unimproved: *urban:* 1.6% of population (2022 est.)
rural: 0% of population (2022 est.)
total: 1.4% of population (2022 est.)

Health expenditure: 6% of GDP (2021)
12.8% of national budget (2022 est.)

Physician density: 3.41 physicians/1,000 population (2023)

Hospital bed density: 2.2 beds/1,000 population (2021 est.)

Sanitation facility access: *improved:* *urban:* 99.7% of population (2022 est.)
rural: 99.7% of population (2022 est.)
total: 99.7% of population (2022 est.)
unimproved: *urban:* 0.3% of population (2022 est.)
rural: 0.3% of population (2022 est.)
total: 0.3% of population (2022 est.)

Obesity - adult prevalence rate: 35.4% (2016)
comparison ranking: 14

Alcohol consumption per capita: *total:* 0 liters of pure alcohol (2019 est.)
beer: 0 liters of pure alcohol (2019 est.)
wine: 0 liters of pure alcohol (2019 est.)
spirits: 0 liters of pure alcohol (2019 est.)
other alcohols: 0 liters of pure alcohol (2019 est.)
comparison ranking: total 185

Tobacco use: *total:* 17.6% (2025 est.)
male: 28.3% (2025 est.)
female: 2% (2025 est.)
comparison ranking: total 87

Children under the age of 5 years underweight: 3.5% (2020)
comparison ranking: 74

Currently married women (ages 15-49): 63.2% (2023 est.)

Education expenditure: 5.1% of GDP (2023 est.)
comparison ranking: Education expenditure (% GDP) 62

Literacy: *total population:* 98% (2020 est.)
male: 99% (2020 est.)
female: 96% (2020 est.)

School life expectancy (primary to tertiary education): *total:* 17 years (2022 est.)
male: 16 years (2022 est.)
female: 18 years (2022 est.)

ENVIRONMENT

Environmental issues: desertification; depletion of underground water resources; limited freshwater resources; coastal pollution from oil spills; air pollution; waste management

International environmental agreements: *party to:* Biodiversity, Climate Change, Climate Change-Kyoto Protocol, Climate Change-Paris Agreement, Desertification, Endangered Species, Hazardous Wastes, Law of the Sea, Marine Dumping-London Protocol, Ozone Layer Protection, Ship Pollution
signed, but not ratified: none of the selected agreements

Climate: harsh, dry desert with great temperature extremes

Urbanization: *urban population:* 85% of total population (2023)
rate of urbanization: 1.69% annual rate of change (2020-25 est.)

Carbon dioxide emissions: 656.511 million metric tonnes of CO2 (2023 est.)
from coal and metallurgical coke: 384,000 metric tonnes of CO2 (2023 est.)
from petroleum and other liquids: 418.326 million metric tonnes of CO2 (2023 est.)

from consumed natural gas: 237.801 million metric tonnes of CO2 (2023 est.)
comparison ranking: total emissions 8

Particulate matter emissions: 60.7 micrograms per cubic meter (2019 est.)

Methane emissions: *energy:* 1,743.8 kt (2022-2024 est.)
agriculture: 162.9 kt (2019-2021 est.)
waste: 927.6 kt (2019-2021 est.)
other: 28.3 kt (2019-2021 est.)

Waste and recycling: *municipal solid waste generated annually:* 16.126 million tons (2024 est.)
percent of municipal solid waste recycled: 18.8% (2022 est.)

Total water withdrawal: *municipal:* 3.392 billion cubic meters (2022 est.)
industrial: 1.4 billion cubic meters (2022 est.)
agricultural: 21.2 billion cubic meters (2022 est.)

Total renewable water resources: 2.4 billion cubic meters (2022 est.)

Geoparks: *total global geoparks and regional networks:* 2 (2025)
global geoparks and regional networks: North Riyadh; Salma (2025)

GOVERNMENT

Country name: *conventional long form:* Kingdom of Saudi Arabia
conventional short form: Saudi Arabia
local long form: Al Mamlakah al Arabiyah as Suudiyah
local short form: Al Arabiyah as Suudiyah
etymology: named after the ruling dynasty of the country, the House of Saud; the name Arabia can be traced back at least as far as the ancient Romans, who referred to the peninsula as "Arabia Felix" (Arabia the Fortunate)

Government type: absolute monarchy

Capital: *name:* Riyadh
geographic coordinates: 24 39 N, 46 42 E
time difference: UTC+3 (8 hours ahead of Washington, DC, during Standard Time)
etymology: the name derives from the Arabic word *riyadh*, meaning "gardens;" the city was built around a small oasis

Administrative divisions: 13 regions (*manatiq*, singular - *mintaqah*); Al Bahah, Al Hudud ash Shamaliyah (Northern Border), Al Jawf, Al Madinah al Munawwarah (Medina), Al Qasim, Ar Riyad (Riyadh), Ash Sharqiyah (Eastern), 'Asir, Ha'il, Jazan, Makkah al Mukarramah (Mecca), Najran, Tabuk

Legal system: Islamic (sharia) system with some elements of Egyptian, French, and customary law; commercial disputes handled by special committees

Constitution: *history:* 1 March 1992 – Basic Law of Government, issued by royal decree, serves as the constitutional framework and is based on the Qur'an and the life and traditions of the Prophet Muhammad
amendment process: proposed by the king directly or proposed to the king by the Consultative Assembly or by the Council of Ministers; passage by the king through royal decree

International law organization participation: has not submitted an ICJ jurisdiction declaration; non-party state to the ICCt

Citizenship: *citizenship by birth:* no
citizenship by descent only: the father must be a citizen of Saudi Arabia; a child born out of wedlock in Saudi Arabia to a Saudi mother and unknown father
dual citizenship recognized: no
residency requirement for naturalization: 5 years

Suffrage: 18 years of age; universal for municipal elections

Executive branch: *chief of state:* King SALMAN bin Abd al-Aziz Al Saud (since 23 January 2015)
head of government: Crown Prince and Prime Minister MUHAMMAD BIN SALMAN bin Abd al-Aziz Al Saud (since 27 September 2022)
cabinet: Council of Ministers appointed by the monarch every 4 years and includes many royal family members
election/appointment process: none; the monarchy is hereditary; an Allegiance Council created by royal decree in 2006 established a committee of Saudi princes who have a voice in selecting future Saudi kings

Legislative branch: *legislature name:* Shura Council (Majlis Ash-Shura)
legislative structure: unicameral
number of seats: 151 (all appointed)
scope of elections: full renewal
term in office: 4 years
most recent election date: 9/2/2024
percentage of women in chamber: 19.9%
expected date of next election: August 2028

Judicial branch: *highest court(s):* High Court (consists of the court chief; organized into circuits with 3-judge panels, except for the criminal circuit, which has a 5-judge panel for cases involving major punishments)
judge selection and term of office: High Court chief and chiefs of the High Court Circuits appointed by royal decree on the recommendation of the Supreme Judiciary Council, a 10- member body of high-level judges and other judicial heads; new judges and assistant judges serve 1- and 2-year probations, respectively, before permanent assignment
subordinate courts: Court of Appeals; Specialized Criminal Court, first-degree courts composed of general, criminal, personal status, and commercial courts; Labor Court; a hierarchy of administrative courts

Political parties: none

Diplomatic representation in the US: *chief of mission:* Ambassador Reema Bint Bandar Bin Sultan AL SAUD (since 8 July 2019)
chancery: 601 New Hampshire Avenue NW, Washington, DC 20037
telephone: [1] (202) 342-3800
FAX: [1] (202) 295-3625
email address and website: saudisusemb@mofa.gov.sa
https://www.saudiembassy.net/
consulate(s) general: Houston, Los Angeles, New York

Diplomatic representation from the US: *chief of mission:* Ambassador (vacant); Chargé d'Affaires Alison DILWORTH (since January 2025)
embassy: Riyadh 11564
mailing address: 6300 Riyadh Place, Washington DC 20521-6300
telephone: [966] (11) 835-4000
FAX: [966] (11) 488-7360
email address and website: RiyadhACS@state.gov
https://sa.usembassy.gov/
consulate(s) general: Dhahran, Jeddah

International organization participation: ABEDA, AfDB (nonregional member), AFESD, AMF, BIS, BRICS, CAEU, CP, FAO, G-20, G-77, GCC, IAEA, IBRD, ICAO, ICC (national committees), ICRM, IDA, IDB, IFAD, IFC, IFRCS, IHO, ILO, IMF, IMO, IMSO, Interpol, IOC, IOM (observer), IPU, ISO, ITSO, ITU, LAS, MIGA, NAM, OAPEC, OAS (observer), OIC, OPCW, OPEC, PCA, UN, UNCTAD, UNESCO, UNIDO, UNOOSA, UNRWA, UNWTO, UPU, WCO, WFTU (NGOs), WHO, WIPO, WMO, WTO

Independence: 23 September 1932 (unification of the kingdom)

National holiday: Saudi National Day (Unification of the Kingdom), 23 September (1932)

Flag: *description:* green (traditional Islamic color) with the Shahada, or Muslim creed, in large white Arabic script that translates as, "There is no god but God; Muhammad is the messenger of God;" the text is above a white horizontal saber pointing to the left
history: design dates to the early 20th century and is closely associated with the Al Saud family that established the kingdom in 1932; the flag has different sides so that the text reads correctly from right to left and the saber points in the same direction on both sides
note 1: the only national flag that has an inscription as its primary design
note 2: one of three national flags that differ on each side – the others are Moldova and Paraguay

National symbol(s): palm tree over two crossed swords

National color(s): green, white

National anthem(s): *title:* "Aash Al Maleek" (Long Live Our Beloved King)
lyrics/music: Ibrahim KHAFAJI/Abdul Rahman al-KHATEEB
history: music adopted 1947, lyrics adopted 1984

National heritage: *total World Heritage Sites:* 7 (7 cultural, 1 natural)
selected World Heritage Site locales: Hegra Archaeological Site (al-Hijr / [INSERT IMAGE] in Ṣāliḥ) (c); At-Turaif District in ad-Dir'iyah (c); Historic Jeddah, the Gate to Makkah (c); Rock Art in the Hail Region of Saudi Arabia (c); Al-Ahsa Oasis, an Evolving Cultural Landscape (c); Ḥimā Cultural Area (c); 'Uruq Bani Ma'arid (n);The Cultural Landscape of Al-Faw Archaeological Area (c)

ECONOMY

Economic overview: high-income, oil-based Middle Eastern economy; OPEC founding member; Vision 2030 strategy prioritizing economic diversification, increased private sector involvement, and projects funded by sovereign wealth fund and foreign investment; young labor force; falling but significant poverty rate despite lack of official statistics

Real GDP (purchasing power parity): $2.213 trillion (2024 est.)
$2.173 trillion (2023 est.)
$2.161 trillion (2022 est.)
note: data in 2021 dollars
comparison ranking: 17

Real GDP growth rate: 1.8% (2024 est.)
0.5% (2023 est.)
12% (2022 est.)
note: annual GDP % growth based on constant local currency
comparison ranking: 153

Real GDP per capita: $62,700 (2024 est.)
$64,500 (2023 est.)
$67,200 (2022 est.)
note: data in 2021 dollars
comparison ranking: 29

GDP (official exchange rate): $1.238 trillion (2024 est.)
note: data in current dollars at official exchange rate

Inflation rate (consumer prices): 1.7% (2024 est.)
2.3% (2023 est.)
2.5% (2022 est.)
note: annual % change based on consumer prices
comparison ranking: 41

GDP - composition, by sector of origin: *agriculture:* 2.5% (2024 est.)
industry: 44.8% (2024 est.)
services: 47.2% (2024 est.)
note: figures may not total 100% due to non-allocated consumption not captured in sector-reported data
comparison rankings: agriculture 144; industry 13; services 162

GDP - composition, by end use: *household consumption:* 45% (2024 est.)
government consumption: 21.4% (2024 est.)
investment in fixed capital: 28.7% (2024 est.)
investment in inventories: 1.4% (2024 est.)
exports of goods and services: 29.2% (2024 est.)
imports of goods and services: -25.6% (2024 est.)
note: figures may not total 100% due to rounding or gaps in data collection

Agricultural products: milk, dates, chicken, wheat, tomatoes, watermelons, potatoes, olives, eggs, onions (2023)
note: top ten agricultural products based on tonnage

Industries: crude oil production, petroleum refining, basic petrochemicals, ammonia, industrial gases, sodium hydroxide (caustic soda), cement, fertilizer, plastics, metals, commercial ship repair, commercial aircraft repair, construction

Industrial production growth rate: -1.3% (2024 est.)
note: annual % change in industrial value added based on constant local currency
comparison ranking: 153

Labor force: 17.168 million (2024 est.)
note: number of people ages 15 or older who are employed or seeking work
comparison ranking: 39

Unemployment rate: 3.9% (2024 est.)
4.1% (2023 est.)
5.6% (2022 est.)
note: % of labor force seeking employment
comparison ranking: 61

Youth unemployment rate (ages 15-24): *total:* 13.8% (2024 est.)
male: 9.8% (2024 est.)
female: 23.8% (2024 est.)
note: % of labor force ages 15-24 seeking employment
comparison ranking: total 91

Average household expenditures: *on food:* 20.5% of household expenditures (2023 est.)
on alcohol and tobacco: 0.7% of household expenditures (2023 est.)

Remittances: 0% of GDP (2024 est.)
0% of GDP (2023 est.)
0% of GDP (2022 est.)
note: personal transfers and compensation between resident and non-resident individuals/households/entities

Budget: *revenues:* $378.413 billion (2023 est.)
expenditures: $388.489 billion (2023 est.)
note: central government revenues (excluding grants) and expenditures converted to US dollars at average official exchange rate for year indicated

Taxes and other revenues: 7.8% (of GDP) (2023 est.)
note: central government tax revenue as a % of GDP
comparison ranking: 137

Current account balance: -$5.685 billion (2024 est.)
$35.133 billion (2023 est.)
$150.353 billion (2022 est.)
note: balance of payments - net trade and primary/secondary income in current dollars
comparison ranking: 176

Exports: $360.897 billion (2024 est.)
$368.731 billion (2023 est.)
$445.881 billion (2022 est.)
note: balance of payments - exports of goods and services in current dollars
comparison ranking: 28

Exports - partners: China 21%, India 12%, Japan 12%, USA 6%, UAE 4% (2023)
note: top five export partners based on percentage share of exports

Exports - commodities: crude petroleum, refined petroleum, plastics, alcohols, ships (2023)
note: top five export commodities based on value in dollars

Imports: $317.012 billion (2024 est.)
$289.91 billion (2023 est.)
$258.371 billion (2022 est.)
note: balance of payments - imports of goods and services in current dollars
comparison ranking: 28

Imports - partners: China 21%, UAE 8%, USA 7%, India 6%, Germany 5% (2023)
note: top five import partners based on percentage share of imports

Imports - commodities: cars, refined petroleum, gold, broadcasting equipment, packaged medicine (2023)
note: top five import commodities based on value in dollars

Reserves of foreign exchange and gold: $463.87 billion (2024 est.)
$457.949 billion (2023 est.)
$478.232 billion (2022 est.)
note: holdings of gold (year-end prices)/foreign exchange/special drawing rights in current dollars
comparison ranking: 7

Exchange rates: Saudi riyals (SAR) per US dollar -

Exchange rates: 3.75 (2024 est.)
3.75 (2023 est.)
3.75 (2022 est.)
3.75 (2021 est.)
3.75 (2020 est.)

ENERGY

Electricity access: *electrification - total population:* 100% (2022 est.)

Electricity: *installed generating capacity:* 119.62 million kW (2023 est.)
consumption: 383.512 billion kWh (2023 est.)
exports: 352 million kWh (2023 est.)
imports: 308 million kWh (2023 est.)
transmission/distribution losses: 38.23 billion kWh (2023 est.)
comparison rankings: installed generating capacity 13; consumption 11; exports 84; imports 102; transmission/distribution losses 202

Electricity generation sources: *fossil fuels:* 99.3% of total installed capacity (2023 est.)
solar: 0.3% of total installed capacity (2023 est.)
wind: 0.4% of total installed capacity (2023 est.)

Coal: *consumption:* 66,000 metric tons (2023 est.)
exports: 500 metric tons (2023 est.)
imports: 223,000 metric tons (2023 est.)

Petroleum: *total petroleum production:* 11.174 million bbl/day (2023 est.)
refined petroleum consumption: 3.524 million bbl/day (2023 est.)
crude oil estimated reserves: 258.6 billion barrels (2021 est.)

Natural gas: *production:* 121.219 billion cubic meters (2023 est.)
consumption: 121.219 billion cubic meters (2023 est.)
proven reserves: 9.423 trillion cubic meters (2021 est.)

Energy consumption per capita: 349.692 million Btu/person (2023 est.)
comparison ranking: 7

COMMUNICATIONS

Telephones - fixed lines: *total subscriptions:* 6.788 million (2023 est.)
subscriptions per 100 inhabitants: 20 (2023 est.)
comparison ranking: total subscriptions 23

Telephones - mobile cellular: *total subscriptions:* 52.5 million (2023 est.)
subscriptions per 100 inhabitants: 132 (2022 est.)
comparison ranking: total subscriptions 33

Broadcast media: state-controlled broadcast media; state-run TV operates 4 networks; major market for pan- Arab satellite TV broadcasters; state-run radio with several networks; multiple international broadcasters available

Internet country code: .sa

Internet users: *percent of population:* 100% (2023 est.)

Broadband - fixed subscriptions: *total:* 14.5 million (2023 est.)
subscriptions per 100 inhabitants: 44 (2023 est.)
comparison ranking: total 17

TRANSPORTATION

Civil aircraft registration country code prefix: HZ

Airports: 90 (2025)
comparison ranking: 61

Heliports: 69 (2025)
comparison ranking: 29

Railways: *total:* 5,410 km (2016)
standard gauge: 5,410 km (2016) 1.435-m gauge (with branch lines and sidings)

Merchant marine: *total:* 433 (2023)
by type: bulk carrier 9, container ship 1, general cargo 20, oil tanker 55, other 348
comparison ranking: total 46

Ports: *total ports:* 16 (2024)
large: 0
medium: 1
small: 7
very small: 8
ports with oil terminals: 10
key ports: Dammam, Duba, Jiddah, Jizan, Ju Aymah Oil Terminal, Ras Tannurah, Ras Al Khafji, Ras Al Mishab

MILITARY AND SECURITY

Military and security forces: *the Saudi Arabian Armed Forces (SAAF) are divided into two ministries:* Ministry of Defense: Royal Saudi Land Forces, Royal Saudi Naval Forces (includes marines, special forces, naval aviation), Royal Saudi Air Force, Royal Saudi Air Defense Forces, Royal Saudi Strategic Missiles Force;

Ministry of the National Guard: Saudi Arabian National Guard (SANG)

Other security forces include: Ministry of Interior: Facilities Security Forces, Public Security Forces (police), General Directorate of Border Guard

State Security Presidency (SSP): General Directorate of Investigation (Mabahith), Special Security Forces, Special Emergency Forces (2025)

note 1: the regular armed forces under the Ministry of Defense are responsible for external defense, although they can be called for domestic security duties if needed

note 2: the SANG (also known as the White Army) is a land force comprised off tribal elements loyal to the House of Saud; it is responsible for internal security, protecting the royal family, guarding against military coups, defending strategic facilities and resources, and providing security for the cities of Mecca and Medina; it may also assist the regular armed forces in combat operations

note 3: the SAAF includes the Saudi Royal Guard Command, a unit which provides security and protection to the ruling family and other dignitaries

Military expenditures: 7.1% of GDP (2024 est.)
7% of GDP (2023 est.)
6.5% of GDP (2022 est.)
7% of GDP (2021 est.)
8% of GDP (2020 est.)

Military and security service personnel strengths: approximately 250,000 active Saudi Armed Forces, including 125,000 under the Ministry of Defense and 125,000 in the National Guard (2025)

Military equipment inventories and acquisitions: the inventory of the Saudi military forces, including the SANG, includes a mix of mostly modern weapons and equipment from Europe and the US; the US has been the largest supplier; major European suppliers have included France, Spain, and the UK; Saudi Arabia is one of the world's largest importers of arms (2024)

note: the Saudi Navy is in the midst of a multi-year and multi-billion-dollar expansion and modernization program to purchase new frigates, corvettes, and other naval craft from such suppliers as Spain and the US

Military service age and obligation: men (17-40) and women (21-40) may volunteer for military service; no conscription (2023)

note: in 2021, women were allowed to serve in the Army, Air Defense, Navy, Strategic Missile Force, medical services, and internal security forces up to the rank of non-commissioned officer

Military deployments: continues to maintain a military presence in Yemen; has also established and supports several local militias, including the National Shield Forces in Aden and the Amajid Brigade in Abyan (2023)

Military - note: Saudi Arabia's security concerns include border security, cyberattacks, instability and Houthi (Ansarallah) rebels in Yemen, international terrorism, maritime security, and regional rivals such as Iran and Turkey

Saudi Arabia has close security ties with the US; the SAAF conducts bilateral exercises with the US military and hosts US forces; the US has participated in a cooperative program to equip and train the SANG since 1973, and much of the equipment for both the regular forces and the SANG has been acquired from the US; Saudi Arabia also has defense relationships with China, France, India, Pakistan, the UK, and fellow Gulf Cooperation Council (GCC) members; it is a member of the Peninsula Shield Forces, a joint military force established by the GCC countries with the aim of maintaining security and stability in the region; the force was established in 1982, and its leadership is based in Saudi Arabia

in 2015, Saudi Arabia led a military intervention into Yemen by a coalition of Arab states in support of the Republic of Yemen Government against the separatist Houthis (Ansarallah); Saudi forces from both the Ministry of Defense and the SANG participated in combat operations in Yemen; Saudi Arabia also raised and equipped paramilitary/militia security forces in Yemen–based largely on tribal or regional affiliation–to deploy along the Saudi- Yemen border (2025)

SPACE

Space agency/agencies: Saudi Space Agency (SSA; elevated to agency level from previous Saudi Space Commission or SSC, which was established in 2018); King Abdulaziz City for Science and Technology (KACST; established 1977) (2024)

Space program overview: has a national space strategy and an ambitious space program; manufactures and operates communications, remote sensing (RS), and scientific satellites; develops a range of satellite subsystems and payload technologies; SSA's missions include accelerating economic diversification, enhancing research and development, and raising private sector participation in the global space industry; is the main founder and financier of the Arab Satellite Communications Organization (Arabsat; launched in 1976; headquartered in Riyadh, Saudi Arabia and the primary satellite communications service provider the Arab world); cooperates with the space agencies and industries of a wide range of countries, including those of Belarus, China, Egypt, the European Space Agency and its member states (particularly France, Germany, Greece, and Hungary), India, Kazakhstan, Morocco, Russia, South Africa, South Korea, Ukraine, the UAE, the UK, and the US; member of the Arab Space Cooperation Group (2024)

note: further details about the key activities, programs, and milestones of the country's space program, as well as government spending estimates on the space sector, appear in the Space Programs reference guide

TERRORISM

Terrorist group(s): Terrorist group(s): Islamic State of Iraq and ash-Sham (ISIS); al-Qa'ida

note: details about the history, aims, leadership, organization, areas of operation, tactics, targets, weapons, size, and sources of support of the group(s) appear(s) in Appendix T

TRANSNATIONAL ISSUES

Refugees and internally displaced persons: *refugees:* 4,355 (2024 est.)
stateless persons: 70,000 (2024 est.)

SENEGAL

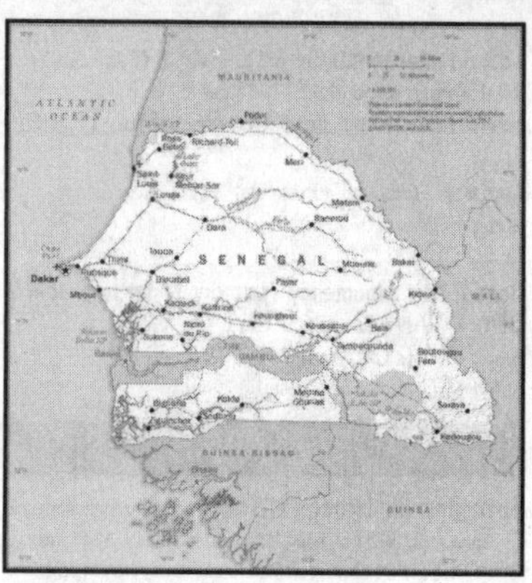

INTRODUCTION

Background: Senegal is one of the few countries in the world with evidence of continuous human life from the Paleolithic period to present. Between the 14th and 16th centuries, the Jolof Empire ruled most of Senegal. Starting in the 15th century, Portugal, the Netherlands, France, and Great Britain traded along the Senegalese coast. Senegal's location on the western tip of Africa made it a favorable base for the European slave trade. European powers used the Senegalese island of Goree as a base to purchase slaves from the warring chiefdoms on the mainland, and at the height of the slave trade in Senegal, over one-third of the Senegalese population was enslaved. In 1815, France abolished slavery and began expanding inland. During the second half of the 19th century, France took possession of Senegal as a French colony. In 1959, the French colonies of Senegal and French Sudan were merged and granted independence in 1960 as the Mali Federation. The union broke up after only a few months. In 1982, Senegal joined with The Gambia to form the nominal confederation of Senegambia. The envisaged integration of the two countries was never implemented, and the union dissolved in 1989.

Since the 1980s, the Movement of Democratic Forces in the Casamance – a separatist movement based in southern Senegal – has led a low-level insurgency. Several attempts at reaching a comprehensive peace agreement have failed. Since 2012, despite sporadic incidents of violence, an unofficial ceasefire has remained largely in effect. Senegal is one of the most stable democracies in Africa and has a long history of participating in international peacekeeping and regional mediation. The Socialist Party of Senegal ruled for 40 years until Abdoulaye WADE was elected president in 2000 and re-elected in 2007.

WADE amended Senegal's constitution over a dozen times to increase executive power and weaken the opposition. In 2012, WADE's decision to run for a third presidential term sparked public backlash that led to his loss to current President Macky SALL. A 2016 constitutional referendum limited future presidents to two consecutive five-year terms. President Bassirou Diomaye FAYE took office in April 2024.

GEOGRAPHY

Location: Western Africa, bordering the North Atlantic Ocean, between Guinea-Bissau and Mauritania

Geographic coordinates: 14 00 N, 14 00 W

Map references: Africa

Area: *total:* 196,722 sq km
land: 192,530 sq km
water: 4,192 sq km
comparison ranking: total 88

Area - comparative: slightly smaller than South Dakota; slightly larger than twice the size of Indiana

Land boundaries: *total:* 2,684 km
border countries (5): The Gambia 749 km; Guinea 363 km; Guinea-Bissau 341 km; Mali 489 km; Mauritania 742 km

Coastline: 531 km

Maritime claims: *territorial sea:* 12 nm
contiguous zone: 24 nm
exclusive economic zone: 200 nm
continental shelf: 200 nm or to the edge of the continental margin

Climate: tropical; hot, humid; rainy season (May to November) has strong southeast winds; dry season (December to April) dominated by hot, dry, harmattan wind

Terrain: generally low, rolling, plains rising to foothills in southeast

Elevation: *highest point:* unnamed elevation 2.8 km southeast of Nepen Diaka 648 m
lowest point: Atlantic Ocean 0 m
mean elevation: 69 m

Natural resources: fish, phosphates, iron ore

Land use: *agricultural land:* 49.4% (2022 est.)
arable land: 19.9% (2022 est.)
permanent crops: 0.4% (2022 est.)
permanent pasture: 29.1% (2022 est.)
forest: 41.5% (2022 est.)
other: 9.1% (2022 est.)

Irrigated land: 1,200 sq km (2012)

Major rivers (by length in km): Senegal (shared with Guinea [s], Mali, and Mauritania [m]) - 1,641 km; Gambie (Gambia) (shared with Guinea [s] and The Gambia [m]) - 1,094 km
note: [s] after country name indicates river source; [m] after country name indicates river mouth

Major watersheds (area sq km): Atlantic Ocean drainage: Senegal (456,397 sq km)

Major aquifers: Senegalo-Mauritanian Basin

Population distribution: the population is concentrated in the west, with Dakar anchoring a well-defined core area; approximately 70% of the population is rural, as shown in this population distribution map

Natural hazards: lowlands seasonally flooded; periodic droughts

Geography - note: westernmost country on the African continent; The Gambia is almost an enclave within Senegal

PEOPLE AND SOCIETY

Population: *total:* 18,847,519 (2024 est.)
male: 9,283,314
female: 9,564,205
comparison rankings: total 66; male 66; female 66

Nationality: *noun:* Senegalese (singular and plural)
adjective: Senegalese

Ethnic groups: Wolof 39.7%, Pulaar 27.5%, Sereer 16%, Mandinka 4.9%, Jola 4.2%, Soninke 2.4%, other 5.4% (includes Europeans and persons of Lebanese descent) (2019 est.)

Languages: French (official), Wolof, Pulaar, Jola, Mandinka, Serer, Soninke

Religions: Muslim 97.2% (most adhere to one of the four main Sufi brotherhoods), Christian 2.7% (mostly Roman Catholic) (2019 est.)

Age structure: *0-14 years:* 40.7% (male 3,907,986/female 3,760,594)
15-64 years: 55.9% (male 5,098,038/female 5,437,195)
65 years and over: 3.4% (2024 est.) (male 277,290/female 366,416)

Dependency ratios: *total dependency ratio:* 78.9 (2024 est.)
youth dependency ratio: 72.8 (2024 est.)
elderly dependency ratio: 6.1 (2024 est.)
potential support ratio: 16.4 (2024 est.)

Median age: *total:* 19.2 years (2024 est.)
male: 18.4 years
female: 20 years
comparison ranking: total 213

Population growth rate: 2.46% (2024 est.)
comparison ranking: 20

Birth rate: 30.2 births/1,000 population (2024 est.)
comparison ranking: 25

Death rate: 4.9 deaths/1,000 population (2024 est.)
comparison ranking: 198

Net migration rate: -0.7 migrant(s)/1,000 population (2024 est.)
comparison ranking: 134

Population distribution: the population is concentrated in the west, with Dakar anchoring a well-defined core area; approximately 70% of the population is rural, as shown in this population distribution map

Urbanization: *urban population:* 49.6% of total population (2023)
rate of urbanization: 3.59% annual rate of change (2020-25 est.)

Major urban areas - population: 3.340 million DAKAR (capital) (2023)

Sex ratio: *at birth:* 1.05 male(s)/female
0-14 years: 1.04 male(s)/female
15-64 years: 0.94 male(s)/female
65 years and over: 0.76 male(s)/female
total population: 0.97 male(s)/female (2024 est.)

Mother's mean age at first birth: 21.9 years (2019 est.)
note: data represents median age at first birth among women 25-49

Maternal mortality ratio: 237 deaths/100,000 live births (2023 est.)
comparison ranking: 32

Infant mortality rate: *total:* 31.1 deaths/1,000 live births (2024 est.)
male: 34.4 deaths/1,000 live births
female: 27.6 deaths/1,000 live births
comparison ranking: total 47

Life expectancy at birth: *total population:* 70.6 years (2024 est.)
male: 68.8 years
female: 72.4 years
comparison ranking: total population 172

Total fertility rate: 4.06 children born/woman (2024 est.)
comparison ranking: 22

Gross reproduction rate: 1.98 (2024 est.)

Drinking water source: *improved: urban:* 95.9% of population (2022 est.)
rural: 77% of population (2022 est.)
total: 86.2% of population (2022 est.)
unimproved: urban: 4.1% of population (2022 est.)
rural: 23% of population (2022 est.)
total: 13.8% of population (2022 est.)

Health expenditure: 4.4% of GDP (2021)
3.4% of national budget (2022 est.)

Physician density: 0.11 physicians/1,000 population (2023)

Hospital bed density: 0.7 beds/1,000 population (2019 est.)

Sanitation facility access: *improved: urban:* 95.3% of population (2022 est.)
rural: 60.1% of population (2022 est.)
total: 77.4% of population (2022 est.)
unimproved: urban: 4.7% of population (2022 est.)
rural: 39.9% of population (2022 est.)
total: 22.6% of population (2022 est.)

Obesity - adult prevalence rate: 8.8% (2016)
comparison ranking: 146

Alcohol consumption per capita: *total:* 0.25 liters of pure alcohol (2019 est.)
beer: 0.21 liters of pure alcohol (2019 est.)
wine: 0.02 liters of pure alcohol (2019 est.)
spirits: 0.02 liters of pure alcohol (2019 est.)
other alcohols: 0 liters of pure alcohol (2019 est.)
comparison ranking: total 170

Tobacco use: *total:* 5.4% (2025 est.)
male: 10.5% (2025 est.)
female: 0.5% (2025 est.)
comparison ranking: total 159

Children under the age of 5 years underweight: 14.4% (2019)
comparison ranking: 35

Currently married women (ages 15-49): 65.3% (2023 est.)

Child marriage: *women married by age 15:* 8.8% (2019)
women married by age 18: 30.5% (2019)
men married by age 18: 0.7% (2019)

Education expenditure: 6.2% of GDP (2023 est.)
20.9% national budget (2025 est.)
comparison ranking: Education expenditure (% GDP) 28

Literacy: *total population:* 50.4% (2023 est.)
male: 61.5% (2023 est.)
female: 41.5% (2023 est.)

School life expectancy (primary to tertiary education): *total:* 9 years (2023 est.)
male: 8 years (2023 est.)
female: 10 years (2023 est.)

ENVIRONMENT

Environmental issues: deforestation; overgrazing; soil erosion; desertification; droughts; seasonal flooding; overfishing; weak environmental laws; poaching

International environmental agreements: *party to:* Biodiversity, Climate Change, Climate Change-Kyoto Protocol, Climate Change-Paris Agreement, Comprehensive Nuclear Test Ban, Desertification, Endangered Species, Hazardous Wastes, Law of the Sea, Marine Life Conservation, Nuclear Test Ban, Ozone Layer Protection, Ship Pollution, Wetlands, Whaling
signed, but not ratified: none of the selected agreements
Climate: tropical; hot, humid; rainy season (May to November) has strong southeast winds; dry season (December to April) dominated by hot, dry, harmattan wind

Urbanization: *urban population:* 49.6% of total population (2023)
rate of urbanization: 3.59% annual rate of change (2020-25 est.)

Carbon dioxide emissions: 10.373 million metric tonnes of CO2 (2023 est.)
from coal and metallurgical coke: 456,000 metric tonnes of CO2 (2023 est.)
from petroleum and other liquids: 9.859 million metric tonnes of CO2 (2023 est.)
from consumed natural gas: 58,000 metric tonnes of CO2 (2023 est.)
comparison ranking: total emissions 108

Particulate matter emissions: 42.2 micrograms per cubic meter (2019 est.)

Methane emissions: *energy:* 37 kt (2022-2024 est.)
agriculture: 258.5 kt (2019-2021 est.)
waste: 89.6 kt (2019-2021 est.)
other: 4.5 kt (2019-2021 est.)

Waste and recycling: *municipal solid waste generated annually:* 2.454 million tons (2024 est.)
percent of municipal solid waste recycled: 11.9% (2022 est.)

Total water withdrawal: *municipal:* 261 million cubic meters (2022 est.)
industrial: 1.416 million cubic meters (2022 est.)
agricultural: 2.759 billion cubic meters (2022 est.)
Total renewable water resources: 38.97 billion cubic meters (2022 est.)

GOVERNMENT

Country name: *conventional long form:* Republic of Senegal
conventional short form: Senegal
local long form: République du Sénégal
local short form: Sénégal
former: Senegambia (along with The Gambia), Mali Federation
etymology: named for the Senegal River that forms the northern border of the country; the river's name may derive from "Azenegue," the Portuguese name for the Berber Zenaga people who lived north of the river, or it could come from a local word meaning "navigable"

Government type: presidential republic

Capital: *name:* Dakar
geographic coordinates: 14 44 N, 17 38 W
time difference: UTC 0 (5 hours ahead of Washington, D.C., during Standard Time)
etymology: the name comes from the Wolof word *n'dakar,* meaning "tamarind tree"
Administrative divisions: 14 regions (*régions,* singular - *région*); Dakar, Diourbel, Fatick, Kaffrine, Kaolack, Kéedougou, Kolda, Louga, Matam, Saint-Louis, Sedhiou, Tambacounda, Thies, Ziguinchor

Legal system: civil law system based on French law; Constitutional Council reviews legislative acts
Constitution: *history:* previous 1959 (pre-independence), 1963; latest adopted by referendum 7 January 2001, promulgated 22 January 2001
amendment process: proposed by the president of the republic or by the National Assembly; passage requires Assembly approval and approval in a referendum; the president can bypass a referendum and submit an amendment directly to the Assembly, which requires at least three-fifths majority vote; the republican form of government is not amendable

International law organization participation: accepts compulsory ICJ jurisdiction with reservations; accepts ICCt jurisdiction
Citizenship: *citizenship by birth:* no
citizenship by descent only: at least one parent must be a citizen of Senegal
dual citizenship recognized: no, but Senegalese citizens do not automatically lose their citizenship if they acquire citizenship in another state
residency requirement for naturalization: 5 years

Suffrage: 18 years of age; universal

Executive branch: *chief of state:* President Bassirou Diomaye FAYE (since 2 April 2024)
head of government: Prime Minister Ousmane SONKO (since 2 April 2024)
cabinet: Council of Ministers appointed by the president
election/appointment process: president directly elected by absolute-majority popular vote in 2 rounds, if needed, for a single, renewable 5-year term
most recent election date: 24 March 2024
election results: *2024:* Bassirou Diomaye FAYE elected president in first round; percent of vote - Bassirou Diomaye FAYE (PASTEF) 54%, Amadou BA (APR) 36%, other 10%
2019: Macky SALL reelected president in first round; percent of vote - Macky SALL (APR) 58.3%, Idrissa SECK (Rewmi) 20.5%, Ousmane SONKO (PASTEF) 15.7%, other 5.5%
expected date of next election: March 2029

Legislative branch: *legislature name:* National Assembly (Assemblée nationale)
legislative structure: unicameral
number of seats: 165 (all directly elected)
electoral system: mixed system
scope of elections: full renewal
term in office: 5 years
most recent election date: 11/17/2024
parties elected and seats per party: Pastef Party (130); Coalition Takku Wallu Sénégal (16); Other (19)
percentage of women in chamber: 41.2%
expected date of next election: November 2029

Judicial branch: *highest court(s):* Supreme Court or Cour Suprême (consists of the court president and 12 judges and organized into civil and commercial, criminal, administrative, and social chambers); Constitutional Council or Conseil Constitutionnel (consists of 7 members, including the court president, vice president, and 5 judges)
judge selection and term of office: Supreme Court judges appointed by the president of the republic upon recommendation of the Superior Council of the Magistrates, a body chaired by the president and minister of justice; judge tenure varies, with mandatory retirement either at 65 or 68 years; Constitutional Council members are appointed, 5 by the president and 2 by the National Assembly speaker; judges serve 6-year terms, with renewal of 2 members every 2 years
subordinate courts: High Court of Justice (for crimes of high treason by the president); Courts of Appeal; Court of Auditors; assize courts; regional and district courts; Labor Court

Political parties: Alliance for Citizenship and Work or ACT
Alliance for the Republic-Yakaar or APR
Alliance of Forces of Progress or AFP
AND (National Alliance for Democracy)
And-Jef/African Party for Democracy and Socialism or AJ/PADS
ARC (Alternative for the next generation of citizens)
Awalé
Benno Bokk Yakaar or BBY (United in Hope); coalition includes AFP, APR, BGC, LD-MPT, PIT, PS, and UNP
Bokk Gis Gis coalition
Citizen Movement for National Reform or MCRN-Bes Du Nakk
Coalition Mimi 2024
Dare the Future movement
Democratic League-Labor Party Movement or LD-MPT
Democratic Renaissance Congress
Front for Socialism and Democracy/Benno Jubel or FSD/BJ
Gainde Centrist Bloc or BCG
General Alliance for the Interests of the Republic or AGIR
Grand Party or GP
Gueum sa Bopp (Believe in yourself)
Independence and Labor Party or PIT
Jotna Coalition
Liberate the People (Yewwi Askan Wi) or YAW
Madicke 2019 coalition
National Union for the People or UNP
Only Senegal Movement
Party for Truth and Development or PVD
Party of Unity and Rally or PUR
Patriotic Convergence Kaddu Askan Wi or CP-Kaddu Askan Wi
PRP (Republican party for Progress)
Rewmi Party
Save Senegal (Wallu Senegal Grand Coalition) or WS; coalition includes PDS, Jotna Coalition, Democratic Renaissance Congress
Senegalese Democratic Party or PDS
Socialist Party or PS
Tekki Movement
Réewum Ngor (Republic of Values)
Servants (Les Serviteurs)

Diplomatic representation in the US: *chief of mission:* Ambassador Abdoul Wahab HAIDARA (since 24 July 2025)
chancery: 2215 M ST NW, Washington, D.C. 20037
telephone: [1] (202) 234-0540
FAX: [1] (202) 629-2961
email address and website: contact@ambasenegal-us.org
http://www.ambasenegal-us.org/index.php
consulate(s) general: New York

Diplomatic representation from the US: *chief of mission:* Ambassador Michael RAYNOR (since 10 March 2022); note - also accredited to Guinea-Bissau
embassy: Route des Almadies, Dakar
mailing address: 2130 Dakar Place, Washington D.C. 20521-2130
telephone: [221] 33-879-4000
email address and website: DakarACS@state.gov
https://sn.usembassy.gov/

International organization participation: ACP, AfDB, AU, CD, CPLP (associate), ECOWAS, EITI (candidate country), FAO, FZ, G-15, G-77, IAEA, IBRD, ICAO, ICC (national committees), ICCt, ICRM, IDA, IDB, IFAD, IFC, IFRCS, ILO, IMF, IMO, IMSO, Interpol, IOC, IOM, IPU, ISO, ITSO, ITU, ITUC (NGOs), MIGA, MONUSCO, NAM, OIC, OIF, OPCW, PCA, UN, UNAMID, UNCTAD, UNESCO, UNHCR, UNIDO, UNMIL, UNMISS, UNOCI, UNOOSA, UNWTO, UPU, WADB (regional), WAEMU, WCO, WFTU (NGOs), WHO, WIPO, WMO, WTO

Independence: 4 April 1960 (from France); 20 August 1960 (full independence after federation with Mali is dissolved)

National holiday: Independence Day, 4 April (1960)

Flag: *description:* three equal vertical bands of green (left side), yellow, and red, with a small five-pointed green star centered on the yellow band; green stands for Islam, progress, and hope, yellow for natural wealth and progress, and red for sacrifice and determination; the star represents unity and hope
history: uses the colors of the Pan-African movement
note: the colors from left to right are the same as Mali's flag and the reverse of Guinea's flag

National symbol(s): lion

National color(s): green, yellow, red

National anthem(s): *title:* "Pincez tous vos koras, frappez les balafons" (Pluck Your Koras, Strike the Balafons)
lyrics/music: Leopold Sedar SENGHOR/Herbert PEPPER
history: adopted 1960; lyrics written by Leopold Sedar SENGHOR, Senegal's first president; the anthem sometimes played incorporating the koras (harp-like stringed instruments) and balafons (types of xylophones) mentioned in the title

National heritage: *total World Heritage Sites:* 7 (5 cultural, 2 natural)
selected World Heritage Site locales: Island of Gorée (c); Niokolo-Koba National Park (n); Djoudj National Bird Sanctuary (n); Island of Saint-Louis (c); Stone Circles of Senegambia (c); Saloum Delta (c); Bassari Country: Bassari, Fula, and Bedik Cultural Landscapes (c)

ECONOMY

Economic overview: lower middle-income, services-driven West African economy; key mining, construction, agriculture, and fishing industries; tourism and exports hit hard by COVID-19; large informal economy; developing offshore oil and gas fields; systemic corruption

Real GDP (purchasing power parity): $83.183 billion (2024 est.)
$77.82 billion (2023 est.)
$74.642 billion (2022 est.)
note: data in 2021 dollars
comparison ranking: 103

Real GDP growth rate: 6.9% (2024 est.)
4.3% (2023 est.)
3.9% (2022 est.)
note: annual GDP % growth based on constant local currency
comparison ranking: 17

Real GDP per capita: $4,500 (2024 est.)
$4,300 (2023 est.)
$4,200 (2022 est.)
note: data in 2021 dollars
comparison ranking: 177

GDP (official exchange rate): $32.267 billion (2024 est.)
note: data in current dollars at official exchange rate

Inflation rate (consumer prices): 0.8% (2024 est.)
5.9% (2023 est.)
9.7% (2022 est.)
note: annual % change based on consumer prices
comparison ranking: 16

GDP - composition, by sector of origin: *agriculture:* 15.5% (2024 est.)
industry: 25.4% (2024 est.)
services: 49.1% (2024 est.)
note: figures may not total 100% due to non-allocated consumption not captured in sector-reported data
comparison rankings: agriculture 55; industry 85; services 150

GDP - composition, by end use: *household consumption:* 65.8% (2024 est.)
government consumption: 16.4% (2024 est.)
investment in fixed capital: 32.1% (2024 est.)
investment in inventories: 0.8% (2024 est.)
exports of goods and services: 28.1% (2024 est.)
imports of goods and services: -43.1% (2024 est.)
note: figures may not total 100% due to rounding or gaps in data collection

Agricultural products: rice, groundnuts, watermelons, millet, cassava, sugarcane, maize, sorghum, onions, milk (2023)
note: top ten agricultural products based on tonnage

Industries: agricultural and fish processing, phosphate mining, fertilizer production, petroleum refining, zircon, and gold mining, construction materials, ship construction and repair

Industrial production growth rate: 20% (2024 est.)
note: annual % change in industrial value added based on constant local currency
comparison ranking: 2

Labor force: 5.763 million (2024 est.)
note: number of people ages 15 or older who are employed or seeking work
comparison ranking: 76

Unemployment rate: 3% (2024 est.)
2.8% (2023 est.)
2.9% (2022 est.)
note: % of labor force seeking employment
comparison ranking: 38

Youth unemployment rate (ages 15-24): *total:* 4.1% (2024 est.)
male: 3.2% (2024 est.)
female: 6.3% (2024 est.)
note: % of labor force ages 15-24 seeking employment
comparison ranking: total 168

Gini Index coefficient - distribution of family income: 36.2 (2021 est.)
note: index (0-100) of income distribution; higher values represent greater inequality
comparison ranking: 65

Household income or consumption by percentage share: *lowest 10%:* 3% (2021 est.)
highest 10%: 28.8% (2021 est.)
note: % share of income accruing to lowest and highest 10% of population

Remittances: 10.6% of GDP (2023 est.)
10.5% of GDP (2022 est.)
11.3% of GDP (2021 est.)
note: personal transfers and compensation between resident and non-resident individuals/households/entities

Budget: *revenues:* $7.749 billion (2023 est.)
expenditures: $9.267 billion (2023 est.)
note: central government revenues (excluding grants) and expenditures converted to US dollars at average official exchange rate for year indicated

Taxes and other revenues: 19.5% (of GDP) (2023 est.)
note: central government tax revenue as a % of GDP
comparison ranking: 55

Current account balance: -$6.072 billion (2023 est.)
-$5.542 billion (2022 est.)
-$3.327 billion (2021 est.)
note: balance of payments - net trade and primary/secondary income in current dollars
comparison ranking: 179

Exports: $7.001 billion (2023 est.)
$7.418 billion (2022 est.)
$6.78 billion (2021 est.)
note: balance of payments - exports of goods and services in current dollars
comparison ranking: 128

Exports - partners: Mali 21%, India 12%, Switzerland 11%, China 5%, UAE 4% (2023)
note: top five export partners based on percentage share of exports

Exports - commodities: gold, refined petroleum, phosphoric acid, fish, cement (2023)
note: top five export commodities based on value in dollars

Imports: $14.916 billion (2023 est.)
$14.698 billion (2022 est.)
$12.278 billion (2021 est.)
note: balance of payments - imports of goods and services in current dollars
comparison ranking: 107

Imports - partners: China 19%, France 9%, Nigeria 7%, India 7%, Russia 5% (2023)
note: top five import partners based on percentage share of imports

Imports - commodities: refined petroleum, crude petroleum, rice, garments, wheat (2023)
note: top five import commodities based on value in dollars

Debt - external: $14.985 billion (2023 est.)
note: present value of external debt in current US dollars
comparison ranking: 41

Exchange rates: Communaute Financiere Africaine francs (XOF) per US dollar -

Exchange rates: 606.345 (2024 est.)
606.57 (2023 est.)
623.76 (2022 est.)
554.531 (2021 est.)
575.586 (2020 est.)

ENERGY

Electricity access: *electrification - total population:* 67.9% (2022 est.)
electrification - urban areas: 96.6%
electrification - rural areas: 43.4%

Electricity: *installed generating capacity:* 1.772 million kW (2023 est.)
consumption: 7.547 billion kWh (2023 est.)
imports: 486 million kWh (2023 est.)
transmission/distribution losses: 983 million kWh (2023 est.)
comparison rankings: installed generating capacity 125; consumption 115; imports 92; transmission/distribution losses 96

Electricity generation sources: *fossil fuels:* 78.3% of total installed capacity (2023 est.)
solar: 7.4% of total installed capacity (2023 est.)
wind: 9.1% of total installed capacity (2023 est.)
hydroelectricity: 3.9% of total installed capacity (2023 est.)
biomass and waste: 1.4% of total installed capacity (2023 est.)

Coal: *consumption:* 138,000 metric tons (2023 est.)
exports: 21 metric tons (2023 est.)
imports: 181,000 metric tons (2023 est.)

Petroleum: *total petroleum production:* 9,000 bbl/day (2023 est.)
refined petroleum consumption: 65,000 bbl/day (2023 est.)

Natural gas: *production:* 34.646 million cubic meters (2023 est.)
consumption: 34.604 million cubic meters (2023 est.)

Energy consumption per capita: 8.303 million Btu/person (2023 est.)
comparison ranking: 157

COMMUNICATIONS

Telephones - fixed lines: *total subscriptions:* 399,000 (2023 est.)
subscriptions per 100 inhabitants: 2 (2023 est.)
comparison ranking: total subscriptions 99

Telephones - mobile cellular: *total subscriptions:* 22.4 million (2023 est.)
subscriptions per 100 inhabitants: 120 (2022 est.)
comparison ranking: total subscriptions 60

Broadcast media: over 25 private TV stations; state-run Radiodiffusion Télévision Sénégalaise (RTS) broadcasts from five cities; wide range of independent TV available via satellite; hundreds of radio stations; transmissions of several international broadcasters are accessible on FM in Dakar

Internet country code: .sn

Internet users: *percent of population:* 61% (2023 est.)

Broadband - fixed subscriptions: *total:* 357,000 (2023 est.)
subscriptions per 100 inhabitants: 2 (2023 est.)
comparison ranking: total 111

TRANSPORTATION

Civil aircraft registration country code prefix: 6V

Airports: 20 (2025)
comparison ranking: 135

Railways: *total:* 906 km (2017) (713 km operational in 2017)
narrow gauge: 906 km (2017) 1.000-m gauge

Merchant marine: *total:* 36 (2023)
by type: general cargo 5, oil tanker 1, other 30
comparison ranking: total 129

Ports: *total ports:* 6 (2024)
large: 0
medium: 1
small: 1
very small: 4
ports with oil terminals: 4
key ports: Dakar, Karabane, Lyndiane, M'bao Oil Terminal, Rufisque, St. Louis

MILITARY AND SECURITY

Military and security forces: Senegalese Armed Forces (les Forces Armées Sénégalaises, FAS): Army (l'Armée de Terre, AT), Senegalese National Navy (Marine Séenéegalaise, MNS), Senegalese Air Force (l'Arméee de l'Air du Séenéegal, AAS), National Gendarmerie

Ministry of Interior: National Police (2025)
note: the National Police operates in major cities, while the Gendarmerie under the FAS primarily operates outside urban areas; both services have specialized anti-terrorism units, and the Gendarmerie has both Territorial and Mobile components

Military expenditures: 1.6% of GDP (2024 est.)
1.5% of GDP (2023 est.)
1.6% of GDP (2022 est.)
1.7% of GDP (2021 est.)
1.5% of GDP (2020 est.)

Military and security service personnel strengths: approximately 25,000 active Armed Forces personnel, including the Gendarmerie (2025)

Military equipment inventories and acquisitions: the military's inventory includes a mix of older, second-hand, and more modern equipment from a variety of countries, including France, South Africa, and Russia/former Soviet Union; in recent years, the military has undertaken a modernization program and has received newer equipment from more than 10 countries, including France and the US (2024)

Military service age and obligation: 19 years of age for voluntary military service for men and women (18 years of age for cadets); 24-month service commitment (2024)

Military deployments: 200 Central African Republic (MINUSCA; plus about 525 police); 800 (ECOWAS Military Intervention in The Gambia–ECOMIG); 500 (ECOWAS Stabilization Support Mission in Guinea-Bissau–EESMGB); 450 police Democratic Republic of the Congo (MONUSCO) (2024)

Military - note: the Senegalese military is responsible for both territorial defense and internal security; it also assists the civilian government in such areas as preventive healthcare, infrastructure development, environmental protection, and disaster response; key areas of focus for the military include a low-level insurgency in the country's south, maritime security, and securing the border against smuggling and Sahel-based Islamist insurgent groups affiliated with al- Qa'ida and the Islamic State; the military participates in foreign peacekeeping deployments and multinational exercises; its closest security partner is France, which has long maintained a military presence in Senegal
Senegalese security forces have been engaged in a low-level counterinsurgency campaign in the southern Casamance region against factions of the separatist Movement of Democratic Forces of the Casamance (MDFC) since 1982; the conflict is one of longest running low-level insurgencies in the World, having claimed more than 5,000 lives while leaving another 60,000 displaced; in recent years, nearly all of the MDFC factions have agreed to cease hostilities (2025)

SPACE

Space agency/agencies: Senegalese Space Study Agency (Agence Sénégalaise d'Etudes Spatiales or ASES; launched in 2023 under the Ministry of Higher Education, Research, and Innovation) (2025)

Space program overview: small, nascent program focused on earth observation capabilities, largely for climate resilience, environmental management, research, and socio-economic development; conducts research in such fields as astronomy and planetary sciences; has cooperated with the European Space Agency, and the space agencies of China, France, Turkey, and the US (2025)

TERRORISM

Terrorist group(s): Terrorist group(s): Jama'at Nusrat al-Islam wal-Muslimin (JNIM)

TRANSNATIONAL ISSUES

Refugees and internally displaced persons: *refugees:* 13,064 (2024 est.)

IDPs: 5,922 (2024 est.)

SERBIA

INTRODUCTION

Background: In 1918, the Croats, Serbs, and Slovenes formed a kingdom known after 1929 as Yugoslavia. The monarchy remained in power until 1945, when the communist Partisans headed by Josip Broz (aka TITO) took control of the newly created Socialist Federal Republic of Yugoslavia (SFRY). After TITO died in 1980, communism in Yugoslavia gradually gave way to resurgent nationalism. In 1989, Slobodan MILOSEVIC became president of the Republic of Serbia, and his calls for Serbian domination led to the violent breakup of Yugoslavia along ethnic lines. In 1991, Croatia, Slovenia, and Macedonia declared independence, followed by Bosnia in 1992. The remaining republics of Serbia and Montenegro declared a new Federal Republic of Yugoslavia (FRY) in 1992, and MILOSEVIC led military campaigns to unite ethnic Serbs in neighboring republics into a "Greater Serbia." These actions ultimately failed, and international intervention led to the signing of the Dayton Accords in 1995.

In 1998, an ethnic Albanian insurgency in the formerly autonomous Serbian province of Kosovo resulted in a brutal Serbian counterinsurgency campaign. Serbia rejected a proposed international settlement, and NATO responded with a bombing campaign that forced Serbian forces to withdraw from Kosovo in June 1999. In 2003, the FRY became the State Union of Serbia and Montenegro, a loose federation of the two republics. In 2006, Montenegro seceded and declared itself an independent nation.

In 2008, Kosovo also declared independence – an action Serbia still refuses to recognize. In 2013, Serbia and Kosovo signed the first agreement of principles governing the normalization of relations between the two countries. Additional agreements were reached in 2015 and 2023, but implementation remains incomplete. Serbia has been an official candidate for EU membership since 2012, and President Aleksandar VUCIC has promoted the ambitious goal of Serbia joining the EU by 2025.

GEOGRAPHY

Location: Southeastern Europe, between Macedonia and Hungary

Geographic coordinates: 44 00 N, 21 00 E

Map references: Europe

Area: *total:* 77,474 sq km
land: 77,474 sq km
water: 0 sq km
comparison ranking: total 117

Area - comparative: slightly smaller than South Carolina

Land boundaries: *total:* 2,322 km
border countries (8): Bosnia and Herzegovina 345 km; Bulgaria 344 km; Croatia 314 km; Hungary 164 km; Kosovo 366 km; North Macedonia 101 km; Montenegro 157 km; Romania 531 km

Coastline: 0 km (landlocked)

Maritime claims: none (landlocked)

Climate: in the north, continental climate (cold winters and hot, humid summers with well-distributed rainfall); in other parts, continental and Mediterranean climate (relatively cold winters with heavy snowfall and hot, dry summers and autumns)

Terrain: extremely varied; to the north, rich fertile plains; to the east, limestone ranges and basins; to the southeast, ancient mountains and hills

Elevation: *highest point:* Midzor 2,169 m
lowest point: Danube and Timok Rivers 35 m
mean elevation: 442 m

Natural resources: oil, gas, coal, iron ore, copper, zinc, antimony, chromite, gold, silver, magnesium, pyrite, limestone, marble, salt, arable land

Land use: *agricultural land:* 41.3% (2022 est.)
arable land: 30.9% (2022 est.)
permanent crops: 2.5% (2022 est.)
permanent pasture: 7.9% (2022 est.)
forest: 32.4% (2022 est.)
other: 26.4% (2022 est.)

Irrigated land: 550 sq km (2022)

Major rivers (by length in km): Dunav (Danube) (shared with Germany [s], Austria, Slovakia, Hungary, Croatia, Bulgaria, Ukraine, Moldova, and Romania [m]) - 2,888 km
note: [s] after country name indicates river source; [m] after country name indicates river mouth

Major watersheds (area sq km): Atlantic Ocean drainage: ***(Black Sea)*** Danube (795,656 sq km)

Population distribution: a fairly even distribution throughout most of the country, with urban areas attracting larger and denser populations

Natural hazards: destructive earthquakes

Geography - note: landlocked; controls one of the major land routes from Western Europe to Turkey and the Near East

PEOPLE AND SOCIETY

Population: *total:* 6,652,212 (2024 est.)
male: 3,242,751
female: 3,409,461
comparison rankings: total 109; male 109; female 108

Nationality: *noun:* Serb(s)
adjective: Serbian

Ethnic groups: Serb 83.3%, Hungarian 3.5%, Romani 2.1%, Bosniak 2%, other 5.7%, undeclared or unknown 3.4% (2011 est.)
note: most ethnic Albanians boycotted the 2011 census; Romani populations are usually underestimated in official statistics and may represent 5–11% of Serbia's population

Languages: Serbian (official) 88.1%, Hungarian 3.4%, Bosnian 1.9%, Romani 1.4%, other 3.4%, undeclared or unknown 1.8% (2011 est.)
major-language sample(s):
Knjiga svetskih činjenica, neophodan izvor osnovnih informacija. (Serbian)
note: Serbian, Hungarian, Slovak, Romanian, Croatian, and Ruthenian (Rusyn) are official in the Autonomous Province of Vojvodina; most ethnic Albanians boycotted the 2011 census

Religions: Orthodox 84.6%, Catholic 5%, Muslim 3.1%, Protestant 1%, atheist 1.1%, other 0.8% (includes agnostics, other Christians, Eastern, Jewish), undeclared or unknown 4.5% (2011 est.)
note: most ethnic Albanians boycotted the 2011 census

Age structure: *0-14 years:* 14.4% (male 492,963/female 463,995)
15-64 years: 65.6% (male 2,198,591/female 2,168,113)
65 years and over: 20% (2024 est.) (male 551,197/female 777,353)

Dependency ratios: *total dependency ratio:* 52.3 (2024 est.)
youth dependency ratio: 21.9 (2024 est.)
elderly dependency ratio: 30.4 (2024 est.)
potential support ratio: 3.3 (2024 est.)

Median age: *total:* 43.9 years (2024 est.)
male: 42.4 years
female: 45.4 years
comparison ranking: total 33

Population growth rate: -0.61% (2024 est.)
comparison ranking: 225

Birth rate: 8.8 births/1,000 population (2024 est.)
comparison ranking: 202

Death rate: 14.9 deaths/1,000 population (2024 est.)
comparison ranking: 3

Net migration rate: 0 migrant(s)/1,000 population (2024 est.)
comparison ranking: 82

Population distribution: a fairly even distribution throughout most of the country, with urban areas attracting larger and denser populations

Urbanization: *urban population:* 57.1% of total population (2023)
rate of urbanization: 0.04% annual rate of change (2020-25 est.)
note: data include Kosovo

Major urban areas - population: 1.408 million BELGRADE (capital) (2023)

Sex ratio: *at birth:* 1.06 male(s)/female
0-14 years: 1.06 male(s)/female
15-64 years: 1.01 male(s)/female
65 years and over: 0.71 male(s)/female
total population: 0.95 male(s)/female (2024 est.)

Mother's mean age at first birth: 28.2 years (2020 est.)
note: data does not cover Kosovo or Metohija

Maternal mortality ratio: 11 deaths/100,000 live births (2023 est.)
comparison ranking: 148

Infant mortality rate: *total:* 4.5 deaths/1,000 live births (2024 est.)
male: 5.1 deaths/1,000 live births
female: 3.9 deaths/1,000 live births
comparison ranking: total 181

Life expectancy at birth: *total population:* 75.3 years (2024 est.)
male: 72.7 years
female: 78.1 years
comparison ranking: total population 128

Total fertility rate: 1.46 children born/woman (2024 est.)
comparison ranking: 205

Gross reproduction rate: 0.71 (2024 est.)

Drinking water source: *improved: urban:* 95.4% of population (2022 est.)
rural: 96.1% of population (2022 est.)
total: 95.7% of population (2022 est.)
unimproved: urban: 4.6% of population (2022 est.)
rural: 3.9% of population (2022 est.)
total: 4.3% of population (2022 est.)

Health expenditure: 10% of GDP (2021)
13.7% of national budget (2022 est.)

Physician density: 3.1 physicians/1,000 population (2022)

Hospital bed density: 5.4 beds/1,000 population (2020 est.)

Sanitation facility access: *improved: urban:* 99.7% of population (2022 est.)
rural: 95.6% of population (2022 est.)
total: 97.9% of population (2022 est.)
unimproved: urban: 0.3% of population (2022 est.)
rural: 4.4% of population (2022 est.)
total: 2.1% of population (2022 est.)

Obesity - adult prevalence rate: 21.5% (2016)
comparison ranking: 88

Alcohol consumption per capita: *total:* 7.45 liters of pure alcohol (2019 est.)
beer: 3.24 liters of pure alcohol (2019 est.)
wine: 1.62 liters of pure alcohol (2019 est.)
spirits: 2.37 liters of pure alcohol (2019 est.)
other alcohols: 0.22 liters of pure alcohol (2019 est.)
comparison ranking: total 55

Tobacco use: *total:* 36% (2025 est.)
male: 37.8% (2025 est.)
female: 34.5% (2025 est.)
comparison ranking: total 8

Children under the age of 5 years underweight: 1% (2019)
comparison ranking: 108

Currently married women (ages 15-49): 60.8% (2023 est.)

Child marriage: *women married by age 15:* 1.2% (2019)
women married by age 18: 5.5% (2019)

Education expenditure: 3.2% of GDP (2022 est.)
7.4% national budget (2022 est.)
comparison ranking: Education expenditure (% GDP) 139

Literacy: *total population:* 99% (2019 est.)
male: 100% (2019 est.)
female: 99% (2019 est.)

School life expectancy (primary to tertiary education): *total:* 15 years (2022 est.)
male: 14 years (2022 est.)
female: 16 years (2022 est.)

ENVIRONMENT

Environmental issues: air pollution around Belgrade and other industrial cities; water pollution from industrial wastes in rivers; inadequate management of domestic, industrial, and hazardous waste

International environmental agreements: *party to:* Air Pollution, Air Pollution-Heavy Metals, Air Pollution-Persistent Organic Pollutants, Biodiversity, Climate Change, Climate Change-Kyoto Protocol, Climate Change-Paris Agreement, Comprehensive Nuclear Test Ban, Desertification, Endangered Species, Hazardous Wastes, Law of the Sea, Marine Dumping-London Convention, Marine Life Conservation, Nuclear Test Ban, Ozone Layer Protection, Ship Pollution, Wetlands
signed, but not ratified: none of the selected agreements

Climate: in the north, continental climate (cold winters and hot, humid summers with well-distributed rainfall); in other parts, continental and Mediterranean climate (relatively cold winters with heavy snowfall and hot, dry summers and autumns)

Urbanization: *urban population:* 57.1% of total population (2023)
rate of urbanization: 0.04% annual rate of change (2020-25 est.)
note: data include Kosovo

Carbon dioxide emissions: 44.782 million metric tonnes of CO_2 (2023 est.)
from coal and metallurgical coke: 27.743 million metric tonnes of CO_2 (2023 est.)
from petroleum and other liquids: 11.665 million metric tonnes of CO_2 (2023 est.)
from consumed natural gas: 5.374 million metric tonnes of CO_2 (2023 est.)
comparison ranking: total emissions 60

Particulate matter emissions: 21.7 micrograms per cubic meter (2019 est.)

Waste and recycling: *municipal solid waste generated annually:* 2.347 million tons (2024 est.)
percent of municipal solid waste recycled: 1% (2022 est.)

Total water withdrawal: *municipal:* 702 million cubic meters (2022)
industrial: 3.967 billion cubic meters (2022)
agricultural: 422 million cubic meters (2022)

Total renewable water resources: 162.2 billion cubic meters (2022 est.)
note: data includes Kosovo

Geoparks: *total global geoparks and regional networks:* 1
global geoparks and regional networks: Djerdap (2023)

GOVERNMENT

Country name: *conventional long form:* Republic of Serbia
conventional short form: Serbia
local long form: Republika Srbija
local short form: Srbija
former: People's Republic of Serbia, Socialist Republic of Serbia
etymology: the country takes its name from the Serb people; the origin of their name is unclear but may derive from the Caucasian root word *ser*, meaning "man"

Government type: parliamentary republic

Capital: *name:* Belgrade (Beograd)
geographic coordinates: 44 50 N, 20 30 E
time difference: UTC+1 (6 hours ahead of Washington, DC, during Standard Time)
daylight saving time: +1hr, begins last Sunday in March; ends last Sunday in October
etymology: the name comes from the Serbian words *beo* (white) and *grad* (city); it probably referred to the white stone of the city fortress

Administrative divisions: 117 municipalities *(opstine*, singular - *opstina)* and 28 cities *(gradovi*, singular - *grad)*
municipalities: Ada*, Aleksandrovac, Aleksinac, Alibunar*, Apatin*, Arandelovac, Arilje, Babusnica, Bac*, Backa Palanka*, Backa Topola*, Backi Petrovac*, Bajina Basta, Batocina, Becej*, Bela Crkva*, Bela Palanka, Beocin*, Blace, Bogatic, Bojnik, Boljevac, Bosilegrad, Brus, Bujanovac, Cajetina, Cicevac, Coka*, Crna Trava, Cuprija, Despotovac, Dimitrov, Doljevac, Gadzin Han, Golubac, Gornji Milanovac, Indija*, Irig*, Ivanjica, Kanjiza*, Kladovo, Knic, Knjazevac, Koceljeva, Kosjeric, Kovacica*, Kovin*, Krupanj, Kucevo, Kula*, Kursumlija, Lajkovac, Lapovo, Lebane, Ljig, Ljubovija, Lucani, Majdanpek, Mali Idos*, Mali Zvornik, Malo Crnice, Medveda, Merosina, Mionica, Negotin, Nova Crnja*, Nova Varos, Novi Becej*, Novi Knezevac*, Odzaci*, Opovo*, Osecina, Paracin, Pecinci*, Petrovac na Mlavi, Plandiste*, Pozega, Presevo, Priboj, Prijepolje, Raca, Raska, Razanj, Rekovac, Ruma*, Secanj*, Senta*, Sid*, Sjenica, Smederevska Palanka, Sokobanja, Srbobran*, Sremski Karlovci*, Stara Pazova*, Surdulica, Svilajnac, Svrljig, Temerin*, Titel*, Topola, Trgoviste, Trstenik, Tutin, Ub, Varvarin, Velika Plana, Veliko Gradiste, Vladicin Han, Vladimirci, Vlasotince, Vrbas*, Vrnjacka Banja, Zabalj*, Zabari, Zagubica, Zitiste*, Zitorada
cities: Beograd (Belgrade), Bor, Cacak, Jagodina, Kikinda*, Kragujevac, Kraljevo, Krusevac, Leskovac, Loznica, Nis, Novi Pazar, Novi Sad*, Pancevo*, Pirot, Pozarevac, Prokuplje, Sabac, Smederevo, Sombor*, Sremska Mitrovica*, Subotica*, Uzice, Valjevo, Vranje, Vrsac*, Zajecar, Zrenjanin*
note: the northern 37 municipalities and 8 cities – about 28% of Serbia's area – compose the Autonomous Province of Vojvodina and are indicated with an asterisk

Legal system: civil law system

Constitution: *history:* many previous; latest adopted 30 September 2006, approved by referendum 28-29 October 2006, effective 8 November 2006
amendment process: proposed by at least one third of deputies in the National Assembly, by the president of the republic, by the government, or by petition of at least 150,000 voters; passage of proposals and draft amendments each requires at least two-thirds majority vote in the Assembly; amendments to constitutional articles including the preamble, constitutional principles, and human and minority rights and freedoms also require passage by simple majority vote in a referendum

International law organization participation: has not submitted an ICJ jurisdiction declaration; accepts ICCt jurisdiction

Citizenship: *citizenship by birth:* no
citizenship by descent only: at least one parent must be a citizen of Serbia
dual citizenship recognized: yes
residency requirement for naturalization: 3 years

Suffrage: 18 years of age, 16 if employed; universal

Executive branch: *chief of state:* President Aleksandar VUCIC (since 31 May 2017)
head of government: Prime Minister Djuro MACUT (since 16 April 2025)
cabinet: Cabinet elected by the National Assembly
election/appointment process: president directly elected by absolute-majority popular vote in 2 rounds, if needed, for a 5-year term (eligible for a second term); prime minister elected by the National Assembly
most recent election date: 17 December 2023
election results: *2022:* Aleksandar VUCIC reelected in first round; percent of vote - Aleksandar VUCIC (SNS) 60%, Zdravko PONOS (US) 18.9%, Milos JOVANOVIC (NADA) 6.1%, Bosko OBRADOVIC (Dveri-POKS) 4.5%, Milica DJURDJEVIC STAMENKOVSKI (SSZ) 4.3%, other 6.2%
2017: Aleksandar VUCIC elected president in first round; percent of vote - Aleksandar VUCIC (SNS) 55.1%, Sasa JANKOVIC (independent) 16.4%, Luka MAKSIMOVIC (independent) 9.4%, Vuk JEREMIC (independent) 5.7%, Vojislav SESELJ (SRS) 4.5%, other 7.3%, invalid/blank 1.6%; Prime Minister Ana BRNABıC reelected by the National Assembly on 5 October 2020; National Assembly vote - NA
expected date of next election: 2028

Legislative branch: *legislature name:* National Assembly (Narodna skupstina)
legislative structure: unicameral
number of seats: 250 (all directly elected)
electoral system: proportional representation
scope of elections: full renewal
term in office: 4 years
most recent election date: 12/17/2023
parties elected and seats per party: Aleksandar Vucic – Serbia Must Not Stop (129); Serbia Against Violence (65); Ivica Dacic - Prime Minister of Serbia (18); Dr Miloš Jovanović - Hope for Serbia (13); We – Voice of the People, Prof. Dr. Branimir Nestorovic (13); Other (12)
percentage of women in chamber: 37.2%
expected date of next election: December 2027

Judicial branch: *highest court(s):* Supreme Court of Cassation (consists of 36 judges, including the court president); Constitutional Court (consists of 15 judges, including the court president and vice president)

judge selection and term of office: Supreme Court justices proposed by the High Judicial Council (HJC), an 11-member independent body consisting of 8 judges elected by the National Assembly and 3 ex-officio members; justices appointed by the National Assembly; Constitutional Court judges elected - 5 each by the National Assembly, the president, and the Supreme Court of Cassation; initial appointment of Supreme Court judges by the HJC is 3 years and beyond that period tenure is permanent; Constitutional Court judges elected for 9-year terms
subordinate courts: basic courts, higher courts, appellate courts; courts of special jurisdiction include the Administrative Court, commercial courts, and misdemeanor courts

Political parties: Alliance of Vojvodina Hungarians or SVM or VMSZ
Democratic Alliance of Croats in Vojvodina or DSHV
Democratic Party or DS
Ecological Uprising or EU
Green - Left Front or ZLF
Greens of Serbia or ZS
Justice and Reconciliation Party or SPP (formerly Bosniak Democratic Union of Sandzak or BDZS)
Movement for Reversal or PZP
Movement for the Restoration of the Kingdom of Serbia or POKS
Movement of Free Citizens or PSG Movement of Socialists or PS
National Democratic Alternative or NADA (electoral coalition includes NDSS and POKS)
New Communist Party of Yugoslavia or NKPJ
New Democratic Party of Serbia or NDSS or New DSS (formerly Democratic Party of Serbia or DSS)
New Face of Serbia or NLS
Party of Democratic Action of the Sandzak or SDAS
Party of Freedom and Justice or SSP
Party of United Pensioners, Farmers, and Proletarians of Serbia – Solidarity and Justice or PUPS - Solidarity and Justice (formerly Party of United Pensioners of Serbia or PUPS)
People's Movement of Serbia or NPS
People's Movement of Serbs from Kosovo and Metohija or Fatherland
People's Peasant Party or NSS
Political Battle of the Albanians Continues
Russian Party or RS
Serbia Against Violence or SPN (electoral coalition includes DS, SSP, ZLF, Zajedno, NPS, PSG, EU, PZP, USS Sloga, NLS, Fatherland)
Serbia Must Not Stop (electoral coalitions includes SNS, SDPS, PUPS, PSS, SNP, SPO, PS, NSS, USS)
Serbian People's Party or SNP
Serbian Progressive Party or SNS
Serbian Renewal Movement or SPO
Social Democratic Party of Serbia or SDPS
Socialist Party of Serbia or SPS
Strength of Serbia or PSS
Together or ZAJEDNO
United Peasant Party or USS
United Serbia or JS
United Trade Unions of Serbia "Sloga" or USS Sloga
We - The Voice from the People or MI-GIN

Diplomatic representation in the US: *chief of mission:* Ambassador Dragan ŠUTANOVAC (since 24 July 2025)
chancery: 1333 16th Street, NW Washington, D.C. 20036
telephone: [1] (202) 507-8654
FAX: [1] (202) 332-3933
email address and website: info@serbiaembusa.org
http://www.washington.mfa.gov.rs/
consulate(s) general: Chicago, New York

Diplomatic representation from the US: *chief of mission:* Ambassador (vacant); Chargé d'Affaires Alexander TITOLO (since January 2025)
embassy: 92 Bulevar kneza Aleksandra Karadjordjevica, 11040 Belgrade
mailing address: 5070 Belgrade Place, Washington, DC 20521-5070
telephone: [381] (11) 706-4000
FAX: [381] (11) 706-4481
email address and website: belgradeacs@state.gov
https://rs.usembassy. gov/

International organization participation: BIS, BSEC, CD, CE, CEI, EAPC, EBRD, EU (candidate country), FAO, G-9, IAEA, IBRD, ICAO, ICC (national committees), ICCt, ICRM, IDA, IFC, IFRCS, IHO, ILO, IMF, IMO, IMSO, Interpol, IOC, IOM, IPU, ISO, ITSO, ITU, ITUC (NGOs), MIGA, MONUSCO, NAM (observer), NSG, OAS (observer), OIF (observer), OPCW, OSCE, PCA, PFP, SELEC, UN, UNCTAD, UNESCO, UNFICYP, UNHCR, UNIDO, UNIFIL, UNMIL, UNOCI, UNTSO, UNWTO, UPU, WCO, WHO, WIPO, WMO, WTO (observer)
note: Serbia is an EU candidate country and must complete accession criteria before being granted full membership

Independence: 5 *June 2006 (from the State Union of Serbia and Montenegro); notable earlier dates:* 1217 (Serbian Kingdom established); 16 April 1346 (Serbian Empire established); 13 July 1878 (Congress of Berlin recognizes Serbian independence); 1 December 1918 (Kingdom of Serbs, Croats, and Slovenes established, later known as Yugoslavia)

National holiday: Statehood Day, 15 February (1835), the day the first constitution of the country was adopted

Flag: *description:* three equal horizontal stripes of red (top), blue, and white; the national coat of arms is shifted to the left side; the principal field of the coat of arms displays a two-headed white eagle on a red shield; a smaller red shield on the eagle is divided into four quarters by a white cross; a royal crown is on top of the coat of arms
meaning: red, blue, and white are the pan-Slav colors that represent freedom and revolutionary ideals; the eagle on a red shield represents the government; the smaller shield represents the country; the meaning and origin of the curved white symbols in each quarter are not clear
note: the pan-Slav colors were inspired by Russia's flag

National symbol(s): white double-headed eagle

National color(s): red, blue, white

National anthem(s): *title:* "Boze pravde" (God of Justice)
lyrics/music: Jovan DORDEVIC/Davorin JENKO
history: adopted 1904; song originally written as part of a play in 1872, and the Serbian people have used it as an anthem in the 20th and 21st centuries

National heritage: *total World Heritage Sites:* 4 (all cultural)
selected World Heritage Site locales: Stari Ras and Sopocani; Studenica Monastery; Gamzigrad-Romuliana, Palace of Galerius; Stecci Medieval Tombstone Graveyards

ECONOMY

Economic overview: upper middle-income Balkan economy; current EU accession candidate; hit by COVID-19; pursuing green growth development; manageable public debt; new anticorruption efforts; falling unemployment; historic Russian relations; energy import-dependent

Real GDP (purchasing power parity): $177.093 billion (2024 est.)
$170.482 billion (2023 est.)
$164.166 billion (2022 est.)
note: data in 2021 dollars
comparison ranking: 78

Real GDP growth rate: 3.9% (2024 est.)
3.8% (2023 est.)
2.6% (2022 est.)
note: annual GDP % growth based on constant local currency
comparison ranking: 79

Real GDP per capita: $26,900 (2024 est.)
$25,700 (2023 est.)
$24,600 (2022 est.)
note: data in 2021 dollars
comparison ranking: 87

GDP (official exchange rate): $89.084 billion (2024 est.)
note: data in current dollars at official exchange rate

Inflation rate (consumer prices): 4.7% (2024 est.)
12.4% (2023 est.)
12% (2022 est.)
note: annual % change based on consumer prices
comparison ranking: 141

GDP - composition, by sector of origin: *agriculture:* 3.1% (2024 est.)
industry: 23.3% (2024 est.)
services: 58.5% (2024 est.)
note: figures may not total 100% due to non-allocated consumption not captured in sector-reported data
comparison rankings: agriculture 129; industry 105; services 97

GDP - composition, by end use: *household consumption:* 62.7% (2024 est.)
government consumption: 17.8% (2024 est.)
investment in fixed capital: 23.6% (2024 est.)
investment in inventories: 2% (2024 est.)
exports of goods and services: 52.7% (2024 est.)
imports of goods and services: -58.8% (2024 est.)
note: figures may not total 100% due to rounding or gaps in data collection

Agricultural products: maize, wheat, sugar beets, milk, sunflower seeds, soybeans, potatoes, barley, apples, plums (2023)
note: top ten agricultural products based on tonnage

Industries: automobiles, base metals, furniture, food processing, machinery, chemicals, sugar, tires, clothes, pharmaceuticals

Industrial production growth rate: 2.9% (2024 est.)
note: annual % change in industrial value added based on constant local currency
comparison ranking: 82

Labor force: 3.23 million (2024 est.)
note: number of people ages 15 or older who are employed or seeking work
comparison ranking: 103

Unemployment rate: 7.4% (2024 est.)
8.3% (2023 est.)
8.5% (2022 est.)

note: % of labor force seeking employment
comparison ranking: 128

Youth unemployment rate (ages 15-24): *total:* 22.7% (2024 est.)
male: 21.8% (2024 est.)
female: 24.1% (2024 est.)
note: % of labor force ages 15-24 seeking employment
comparison ranking: total 44

Population below poverty line: 20% (2021 est.)
note: % of population with income below national poverty line
Gini Index coefficient - distribution of family income 32.8 (2022 est.)
note: index (0-100) of income distribution; higher values represent greater inequality
comparison ranking: 100

Average household expenditures: *on food:* 24.1% of household expenditures (2023 est.)
on alcohol and tobacco: 7.8% of household expenditures (2023 est.)

Household income or consumption by percentage share: *lowest 10%:* 2.4% (2022 est.)
highest 10%: 24.7% (2022 est.)
note: % share of income accruing to lowest and highest 10% of population

Remittances: 7.1% of GDP (2023 est.)
8.5% of GDP (2022 est.)
6.9% of GDP (2021 est.)
note: personal transfers and compensation between resident and non-resident individuals/households/entities

Budget: *revenues:* $26.077 billion (2022 est.)
expenditures: $28.12 billion (2022 est.)
note: central government revenues (excluding grants) and expenditures converted to US dollars at average official exchange rate for year indicated

Taxes and other revenues: 23.9% (of GDP) (2022 est.)
note: central government tax revenue as a % of GDP
comparison ranking: 22

Current account balance: -$1.947 billion (2023 est.)
-$4.457 billion (2022 est.)
-$2.654 billion (2021 est.)
note: balance of payments - net trade and primary/secondary income in current dollars
comparison ranking: 147

Exports: $44.352 billion (2023 est.)
$39.905 billion (2022 est.)
$34.035 billion (2021 est.)
note: balance of payments - exports of goods and services in current dollars
comparison ranking: 70

Exports - partners: Germany 15%, Hungary 7%, Bosnia & Herzegovina 5%, Italy 5%, Romania 5% (2023)
note: top five export partners based on percentage share of exports

Exports - commodities: insulated wire, electricity, copper ore, plastic products, electric motors (2023)
note: top five export commodities based on value in dollars

Imports: $48.158 billion (2023 est.)
$47.395 billion (2022 est.)
$39.476 billion (2021 est.)
note: balance of payments - imports of goods and services in current dollars
comparison ranking: 69

Imports - partners: Germany 12%, China 10%, Italy 7%, Turkey 5%, Hungary 5% (2023)
note: top five import partners based on percentage share of imports

Imports - commodities: crude petroleum, natural gas, packaged medicine, plastic products, cars (2023)
note: top five import commodities based on value in dollars

Reserves of foreign exchange and gold: $30.484 billion (2024 est.)
$27.569 billion (2023 est.)
$20.68 billion (2022 est.)
note: holdings of gold (year-end prices)/foreign exchange/special drawing rights in current dollars
comparison ranking: 56

Debt - external: $21.726 billion (2023 est.)
note: present value of external debt in current US dollars
comparison ranking: 32

Exchange rates: Serbian dinars (RSD) per US dollar -

Exchange rates: 108.208 (2024 est.)
108.403 (2023 est.)
111.662 (2022 est.)
99.396 (2021 est.)
103.163 (2020 est.)

ENERGY

Electricity access: *electrification - total population:* 100% (2022 est.)

Electricity: *installed generating capacity:* 8.202 million kW (2023 est.)
consumption: 34.413 billion kWh (2023 est.)
exports: 7.351 billion kWh (2023 est.)
imports: 5.395 billion kWh (2023 est.)
transmission/distribution losses: 4.881 billion kWh (2023 est.)
comparison rankings: installed generating capacity 72; consumption 64; exports 31; imports 43; transmission/distribution losses 161

Electricity generation sources: *fossil fuels:* 65.1% of total installed capacity (2023 est.)
solar: 1% of total installed capacity (2023 est.)
wind: 2.6% of total installed capacity (2023 est.)
hydroelectricity: 30.7% of total installed capacity (2023 est.)
biomass and waste: 0.6% of total installed capacity (2023 est.)

Coal: *production:* 33.219 million metric tons (2023 est.)
consumption: 37.828 million metric tons (2023 est.)
exports: 16,000 metric tons (2023 est.)
imports: 4.542 million metric tons (2023 est.)
proven reserves: 7.112 billion metric tons (2023 est.)

Petroleum: *total petroleum production:* 13,000 bbl/day (2023 est.)
refined petroleum consumption: 88,000 bbl/day (2023 est.)
crude oil estimated reserves: 77.5 million barrels (2021 est.)

Natural gas: *production:* 336.605 million cubic meters (2023 est.)
consumption: 2.886 billion cubic meters (2023 est.)
imports: 2.471 billion cubic meters (2023 est.)
proven reserves: 48.139 billion cubic meters (2021 est.)

Energy consumption per capita: 91.884 million Btu/person (2023 est.)
comparison ranking: 57

COMMUNICATIONS

Telephones - fixed lines: *total subscriptions:* 2.485 million (2023 est.)
subscriptions per 100 inhabitants: 37 (2023 est.)
comparison ranking: total subscriptions 45

Telephones - mobile cellular: *total subscriptions:* 8.53 million (2023 est.)
subscriptions per 100 inhabitants: 124 (2021 est.)
comparison ranking: total subscriptions 99

Internet country code: .rs

Internet users: *percent of population:* 85% (2023 est.)

Broadband - fixed subscriptions: *total:* 2.08 million (2023 est.)
subscriptions per 100 inhabitants: 31 (2023 est.)
comparison ranking: total 60

TRANSPORTATION

Civil aircraft registration country code prefix: YU

Airports: 46 (2025)
comparison ranking: 93

Heliports: 11 (2025)
comparison ranking: 70

Railways: *total:* 3,333 km (2020) 1,274 km electrified

MILITARY AND SECURITY

Military and security forces: Serbian Armed Forces (Vojska Srbije, VS): Army (aka Land Forces; includes Riverine Component, consisting of a naval flotilla on the Danube), Air and Air Defense Forces, Serbian Guard

Serbian Ministry of Internal Affairs: Police Directorate (2025)
note: the Serbian Guard is a brigade-sized unit that is directly subordinate to the Serbian Armed Forces Chief of General Staff; its duties include safeguarding key defense facilities and rendering military honors to top foreign, state, and military officials

Military expenditures: 2.5% of GDP (2024 est.)
2.4% of GDP (2023 est.)
2.2% of GDP (2022 est.)
2.2% of GDP (2021 est.)
2% of GDP (2020 est.)

Military and security service personnel strengths: approximately 25,000 active-duty Armed Forces (15,000 Land Forces; 5,000 Air/Air Defense; 5,000 other, including Serbian Guard) (2025)

Military equipment inventories and acquisitions: the military's inventory consists of a mix of domestically produced, Russian/Soviet-era, and Yugoslav equipment and weapons systems; in recent years, it has purchased some weapons systems from China, such as anti-aircraft missiles and armed aerial drones (2024)

Military service age and obligation: 18 years of age for voluntary military service for men and women; conscription abolished in 2011 (2025)
note: as of 2024, women made up about 11% of the military's full-time personnel

Military deployments: 180 Lebanon (UNIFIL) (2025)

Military - note: the Serbian military is responsible for defense and deterrence against external threats, supporting international peacekeeping operations, and providing support to civil authorities for internal security; specific areas of concerns for the military include ethnic and religious extremism, separatism, and deepening international recognition of Kosovo; Serbia has cooperated with NATO since 2006, when it joined the Partnership for Peace program, and the military trains with NATO countries, particularly other Balkan states; Serbia has participated in EU peacekeeping missions, as well as missions under the Organization for Security and Cooperation in Europe and the UN; it traditionally has maintained close security ties with Russia and has a growing security relationship with China the modern Serbian military was established in 2006 but traces its origins back through World War II, World War I, the Balkan Wars of 1912-1913, and the Bulgarian-Serb War of 1885 to the First (1804-1813) and Second (1815-1817) Uprisings against the Ottoman Empire (2025)

TRANSNATIONAL ISSUES

Refugees and internally displaced persons: *refugees:* 36,270 (2024 est.)

IDPs: 194,171 (2024 est.)
stateless persons: 1,715 (2024 est.)

SEYCHELLES

INTRODUCTION

Background: Seychelles was uninhabited before Europeans discovered the islands early in the 16th century. After a lengthy struggle, France eventually ceded control of the islands to Great Britain in 1814. During colonial rule, a plantation-based economy developed that relied on imported labor, primarily from European colonies in Africa. Seychelles gained independence in 1976 through negotiations with Great Britain. In 1977, Prime Minister France-Albert RENE launched a coup against the country's first president, and Seychelles became a socialist one-party state until adopting a new constitution and holding elections in 1993. RENE continued to lead Seychelles through two election cycles until he stepped down in 2004. Vice President James Alix MICHEL took over the presidency and in 2006 was elected to a new five-year term; he was reelected in 2011 and again in 2015. In 2016, James MICHEL resigned and handed over the presidency to his vice-president, Danny FAURE. In 2020, Wavel RAMKALAWAN was elected president, the first time an opposition candidate has won the presidency.

GEOGRAPHY

Location: archipelago in the Indian Ocean, northeast of Madagascar

Geographic coordinates: 4 35 S, 55 40 E

Map references: Africa

Area: *total:* 455 sq km
land: 455 sq km
water: 0 sq km
comparison ranking: total 198

Area - comparative: 2.5 times the size of Washington, D.C.

Land boundaries: *total:* 0 km

Coastline: 491 km

Maritime claims: *territorial sea:* 12 nm
contiguous zone: 24 nm
exclusive economic zone: 200 nm
continental shelf: 200 nm or to the edge of the continental margin

Climate: tropical marine; humid; cooler season during southeast monsoon (late May to September); warmer season during northwest monsoon (March to May)

Terrain: Mahe Group is volcanic with a narrow coastal strip and rocky, hilly interior; others are relatively flat coral atolls, or elevated reefs; sits atop the submarine Mascarene Plateau

Elevation: *highest point:* Morne Seychellois 905 m
lowest point: Indian Ocean 0 m

Natural resources: fish, coconuts (copra), cinnamon trees

Land use: *agricultural land:* 3.4% (2022 est.)
arable land: 0.3% (2022 est.)
permanent crops: 3% (2022 est.)
permanent pasture: 0% (2022 est.)
forest: 73.3% (2022 est.)
other: 23.4% (2022 est.)

Irrigated land: 3 sq km (2012)

Population distribution: more than three quarters of the population lives on the main island of Mahe; Praslin is home to less than 10%, and a smaller percentage is on La Digue and the outer islands, as shown in this population distribution map

Natural hazards: lies outside the cyclone belt, so severe storms are rare; occasional short droughts

Geography - note: the smallest African country in terms of both area and population; the constitution of the Republic of Seychelles lists 155 islands, including 42 granitic and 113 coralline; the largest island by far is Mahe, which is home to about 90% of the population and is the site of the capital city of Victoria

PEOPLE AND SOCIETY

Population: *total:* 98,187 (2024 est.)
male: 50,973
female: 47,214
comparison rankings: total 197; male 194; female 197

Nationality: *noun:* Seychellois (singular and plural)
adjective: Seychellois

Ethnic groups: predominantly Creole (mainly of East African and Malagasy heritage); also French, Indian, Chinese, and Arab populations

Languages: Seychellois Creole (official) 89.1%, English (official) 5.1%, French (official) 0.7%, other 3.8%, unspecified 1.4% (2010 est.)

Religions: Roman Catholic 76.2%, Protestant 10.5% (Anglican 6.1%, Pentecostal Assembly 1.5%, Seventh Day Adventist 1.2%, other Protestant 1.7%), other Christian 2.4%, Hindu 2.4%, Muslim 1.6%, other non-Christian 1.1%, unspecified 4.8%, none 0.9% (2010 est.)

Age structure: *0-14 years:* 17.7% (male 8,912/female 8,439)
15-64 years: 72.4% (male 37,841/female 33,210)
65 years and over: 10% (2024 est.) (male 4,220/female 5,565)

Dependency ratios: *total dependency ratio:* 38.2 (2024 est.)
youth dependency ratio: 24.4 (2024 est.)
elderly dependency ratio: 13.8 (2024 est.)
potential support ratio: 7.3 (2024 est.)

Median age: *total:* 38.7 years (2024 est.)
male: 38.2 years
female: 39.4 years
comparison ranking: total 71

Population growth rate: 0.56% (2024 est.)
comparison ranking: 145

Birth rate: 11.8 births/1,000 population (2024 est.)
comparison ranking: 152

Death rate: 7 deaths/1,000 population (2024 est.)
comparison ranking: 121

Net migration rate: 0.8 migrant(s)/1,000 population (2024 est.)
comparison ranking: 69

Population distribution: more than three quarters of the population lives on the main island of Mahe; Praslin is home to less than 10%, and a smaller percentage is on La Digue and the outer islands, as shown in this population distribution map

Urbanization: *urban population:* 58.8% of total population (2023)
rate of urbanization: 0.99% annual rate of change (2020-25 est.)

Major urban areas - population: 28,000 VICTORIA (capital) (2018)

Sex ratio: *at birth:* 1.03 male(s)/female
0-14 years: 1.06 male(s)/female
15-64 years: 1.14 male(s)/female
65 years and over: 0.76 male(s)/female
total population: 1.08 male(s)/female (2024 est.)

Maternal mortality ratio: 42 deaths/100,000 live births (2023 est.)
comparison ranking: 102

Infant mortality rate: *total:* 10.2 deaths/1,000 live births (2024 est.)
male: 12.8 deaths/1,000 live births
female: 7.4 deaths/1,000 live births
comparison ranking: total 131

Life expectancy at birth: *total population:* 76.6 years (2024 est.)
male: 72.2 years
female: 81.1 years
comparison ranking: total population 105

Total fertility rate: 1.81 children born/woman (2024 est.)
comparison ranking: 139

Gross reproduction rate: 0.89 (2024 est.)

Drinking water source: *improved:* total: 96.4% of population (2022 est.)
unimproved: total: 3.6% of population (2022 est.)

Health expenditure: 5.3% of GDP (2021)
10.2% of national budget (2022 est.)

Physician density: 2.25 physicians/1,000 population (2019)

Hospital bed density: 3.2 beds/1,000 population (2020 est.)

Sanitation facility access: *improved:* total: 100% of population (2022 est.)
unimproved: total: 0% of population (2022 est.)

Obesity - adult prevalence rate: 14% (2016)
comparison ranking: 130

Alcohol consumption per capita: *total:* 9.48 liters of pure alcohol (2019 est.)
beer: 4.11 liters of pure alcohol (2019 est.)
wine: 0.49 liters of pure alcohol (2019 est.)
spirits: 4.62 liters of pure alcohol (2019 est.)
other alcohols: 0.25 liters of pure alcohol (2019 est.)
comparison ranking: total 28

Tobacco use: *total:* 20.5% (2025 est.)
male: 34.2% (2025 est.)
female: 5.2% (2025 est.)
comparison ranking: total 64

Currently married women (ages 15-49): 45% (2023 est.)

Education expenditure: 4.5% of GDP (2023 est.)
13.1% national budget (2024 est.)
comparison ranking: Education expenditure (% GDP) 83

School life expectancy (primary to tertiary education): *total:* 13 years (2023 est.)
male: 13 years (2023 est.)
female: 15 years (2023 est.)

ENVIRONMENT

Environmental issues: limited freshwater resources; water pollution; biodiversity

International environmental agreements: *party to:* Biodiversity, Climate Change, Climate Change-Kyoto Protocol, Climate Change-Paris Agreement, Comprehensive Nuclear Test Ban, Desertification, Endangered Species, Hazardous Wastes, Law of the Sea, Marine Dumping-London Convention, Nuclear Test Ban, Ozone Layer Protection, Ship Pollution, Wetlands
signed, but not ratified: none of the selected agreements

Climate: tropical marine; humid; cooler season during southeast monsoon (late May to September); warmer season during northwest monsoon (March to May)

Urbanization: *urban population:* 58.8% of total population (2023)
rate of urbanization: 0.99% annual rate of change (2020-25 est.)

Carbon dioxide emissions: 893,000 metric tonnes of CO2 (2023 est.)
from coal and metallurgical coke: 92 metric tonnes of CO2 (2023 est.)
from petroleum and other liquids: 893,000 metric tonnes of CO2 (2023 est.)
comparison ranking: total emissions 173

Particulate matter emissions: 17.4 micrograms per cubic meter (2019 est.)

Waste and recycling: *municipal solid waste generated annually:* 48,000 tons (2024 est.)
percent of municipal solid waste recycled: 24.4% (2022 est.)

Total water withdrawal: *municipal:* 9 million cubic meters (2022 est.)
industrial: 3.8 million cubic meters (2022 est.)
agricultural: 900,000 cubic meters (2022 est.)

GOVERNMENT

Country name: *conventional long form:* Republic of Seychelles
conventional short form: Seychelles
local long form: Republic of Seychelles
local short form: Seychelles
etymology: named by French Captain Corneille Nicholas MORPHEY after Jean Moreau de SÉCHELLES, the finance minister of France, in 1756; the British changed the spelling of the name in 1815 when they acquired the islands

Government type: presidential republic

Capital: *name:* Victoria
geographic coordinates: 4 37 S, 55 27 E
time difference: UTC+4 (9 hours ahead of Washington, DC, during Standard Time)
etymology: the British named the town Port Victoria in 1841 after Queen VICTORIA; the name was later shortened

Administrative divisions: 27 administrative districts; Anse aux Pins, Anse Boileau, Anse Etoile, Anse Royale, Au Cap, Baie Lazare, Baie Sainte Anne, Beau Vallon, Bel Air, Bel Ombre, Cascade, Glacis, Grand Anse Mahe, Grand Anse Praslin, Ile Persévérance I, Ile Persévérance II, La Digue, La Rivière Anglaise, Les Mamelles, Mont Buxton, Mont Fleuri, Plaisance, Pointe Larue, Port Glaud, Roche Caiman, Saint Louis, Takamaka

Legal system: mixed system of English common law, French civil law, and customary law

Constitution: *history:* previous 1970, 1979; latest drafted May 1993, approved by referendum 18 June 1993, effective 23 June 1993
amendment process: proposed by the National Assembly; passage requires at least two- thirds majority vote by the National Assembly; passage of amendments affecting the country's sovereignty, symbols and languages, the supremacy of the constitution, fundamental rights and freedoms, amendment procedures, and dissolution of the Assembly also requires approval by at least 60% of voters in a referendum

International law organization participation: has not submitted an ICJ jurisdiction declaration; accepts ICCt jurisdiction

Citizenship: *citizenship by birth:* no
citizenship by descent only: at least one parent must be a citizen of the Seychelles
dual citizenship recognized: no
residency requirement for naturalization: 5 years

Suffrage: 18 years of age; universal

Executive branch: *chief of state:* President Patrick HERMINIE (since 26 October 2025)
head of government: President Patrick HERMINIE (since 26 October 2025)
cabinet: Council of Ministers appointed by the president
election/appointment process: president directly elected by absolute-majority popular vote in 2 rounds, if needed, for a 5-year term (eligible for a second term)
most recent election date: 22-24 October 2020
election results: *2020:* Wavel RAMKALAWAN elected president; Wavel RAMKALAWAN (LDS) 54.9%, Danny FAURE (US) 43.5%, other 1.6%
2015: President James Alix MICHEL reelected president in second round; percent of vote in first round - James Alix MICHEL (PL) 47.8%, Wavel RAMKALAWAN (SNP) 35.3%, other 16.9%; percent of vote in second round - James Alix MICHEL 50.2%, Wavel RAMKALAWAN 49.8%
expected date of next election: 2025
note: the president is both chief of state and head of government

Legislative branch: *legislature name:* National Assembly
legislative structure: unicameral
number of seats: 35 (all directly elected)
electoral system: mixed system
scope of elections: full renewal
term in office: 5 years
most recent election date: 10/22/2020 to 10/24/2020
parties elected and seats per party: Seychelles Democratic Alliance (Linyon Demokratik Seselwa, LDS) (25); United Seychelles (US) (10)
percentage of women in chamber: 28.6%
expected date of next election: September 2025

Judicial branch: *highest court(s):* Seychelles Court of Appeal (consists of the court president and 4 justices);
Supreme Court of Seychelles (consists of the chief justice and 9 puisne judges);
Constitutional Court (consists of 3 Supreme Court judges)
judge selection and term of office: all judges appointed by the president of the republic upon the recommendation of the Constitutional Appointments Authority, a 3-member body, with 1 member appointed by the president of the republic, 1 by the opposition leader in the National Assembly, and 1 by the other 2 appointees; judges serve until retirement at age 70
subordinate courts: Magistrates' Courts of Seychelles; Family Tribunal for issues such as domestic violence, child custody, and maintenance; Employment Tribunal for labor-related disputes

Political parties: Seychelles Party for Social Justice and Democracy or SPSJD

Seychellois Democratic Alliance or LDS (Linyon Demokratik Seselwa/Union Démocratique Seychelloise)
Seychelles National Party or SNP
United Seychelles or US

Diplomatic representation in the US: *chief of mission:* Ambassador-designate Vivianne FOCK TAVE (since August 2025); note - also Permanent Representative to the UN-designate
chancery: 685 Third Avenue, Suite 1107, 11th Floor, New York, NY 10017
telephone: [1] (212) 972-1785

FAX: [1] (212) 972-1786
email address and website: seychellesmission@sycun.org
Foreign Affairs Department Republic of Seychelles » United States of America (mfa.gov.sc)

Diplomatic representation from the US: *chief of mission:* Ambassador Henry V. JARDINE (since 22 February 2023) and Chargé d'Affaires Adham LOUTFI (since 6 October 2023); note - Ambassador JARDINE is posted in Mauritius and is accredited to Seychelles, and Chargé d'Affaires LOUTFI is posted in Victoria, Seychelles
embassy: 2nd Floor, Oliaji Trade Center, Victoria Mahe, Seychelles; note - US Embassy in Seychelles reopened on 1 June 2023 after having been closed in 1996
telephone: [248] 422 5256

International organization participation: ACP, AfDB, AOSIS, AU, C, CD, COMESA, EITI (candidate country), FAO, G-77, IAEA, IBRD, ICAO, ICC (NGOs), ICCt, ICRM, IDA, IFAD, IFC, IFRCS, ILO, IMF, IMO, InOC, Interpol, IOC, IOM, IPU, ISO (correspondent), ITU, MIGA, NAM, OIF, OPCW, SADC, UN, UNCTAD, UNESCO, UNIDO, UNWTO, UPU, WCO, WHO, WIPO, WMO, WTO

Independence: 29 June 1976 (from the UK)

National holiday: Constitution Day, 18 June (1993); Independence Day (National Day), 29 June (1976)

Flag: *description:* five expanding bands of blue, yellow, red, white, and green, radiating from the bottom left corner
meaning: the bands symbolize a dynamic new country moving into the future; blue stands for the sky and sea, yellow for the sun giving light and life, red for the people's determination to work for the future in unity and love, white for social justice and harmony, and green for the land and natural environment

National symbol(s): coco de mer (sea coconut)

National color(s): blue, yellow, red, white, green

National anthem(s): *title:* "Koste Seselwa" (Seychellois Unite)
lyrics/music: David Francois Marc ANDRE and George Charles Robert PAYET
history: adopted 1996

National heritage: *total World Heritage Sites:* 2 (both natural)
selected World Heritage Site locales: Aldabra Atoll; Vallée de Mai Nature Reserve

ECONOMY

Economic overview: high-income Indian Ocean island economy; rapidly growing tourism sector; major tuna exporter; offshore financial hub; environmentally fragile and investing in ocean rise mitigation; recently discovered offshore oil potential; successful anticorruption efforts

Real GDP (purchasing power parity): $3.549 billion (2024 est.)
$3.43 billion (2023 est.)
$3.354 billion (2022 est.)
note: data in 2021 dollars
comparison ranking: 191

Real GDP growth rate: 3.5% (2024 est.)
2.3% (2023 est.)
12.7% (2022 est.)
note: annual GDP % growth based on constant local currency
comparison ranking: 98

Real GDP per capita: $29,200 (2024 est.)
$28,600 (2023 est.)
$28,000 (2022 est.)
note: data in 2021 dollars
comparison ranking: 81

GDP (official exchange rate): $2.167 billion (2024 est.)
note: data in current dollars at official exchange rate

Inflation rate (consumer prices): 0.3% (2024 est.)
-1% (2023 est.)
2.6% (2022 est.)
note: annual % change based on consumer prices
comparison ranking: 9

GDP - composition, by sector of origin: *agriculture:* 2.5% (2024 est.)
industry: 12.3% (2024 est.)
services: 65.8% (2024 est.)
note: figures may not total 100% due to non-allocated consumption not captured in sector- reported data
comparison rankings: agriculture 143; industry 173; services 50

GDP - composition, by end use: *household consumption:* 74.6% (2024 est.)
government consumption: 26.3% (2024 est.)
investment in fixed capital: 17.2% (2024 est.)
investment in inventories: 0% (2024 est.)
exports of goods and services: 85.2% (2024 est.)
imports of goods and services: -103.2% (2024 est.)
note: figures may not total 100% due to rounding or gaps in data collection

Agricultural products: coconuts, vegetables, bananas, eggs, chicken, pork, fruits, tomatoes, tropical fruits, cassava (2023)
note: top ten agricultural products based on tonnage

Industries: fishing, tourism, beverages

Industrial production growth rate: -6.4% (2024 est.)
note: annual % change in industrial value added based on constant local currency comparison ranking: 184

Population below poverty line: 25.3% (2018 est.)
note: % of population with income below national poverty line

Gini Index coefficient - distribution of family income: 32.1 (2018 est.)
note: index (0-100) of income distribution; higher values represent greater inequality comparison ranking: 107

Household income or consumption by percentage share: *lowest 10%:* 2.6% (2018 est.)
highest 10%: 23.9% (2018 est.)
note: % share of income accruing to lowest and highest 10% of population

Remittances: 0.5% of GDP (2023 est.)
0.5% of GDP (2022 est.)
0.6% of GDP (2021 est.)
note: personal transfers and compensation between resident and non-resident individuals/households/entities

Budget: *revenues:* $695.973 million (2023 est.)
expenditures: $728.171 million (2023 est.)
note: central government revenues and expenditures (excluding grants and social security funds) converted to US dollars at average official exchange rate for year indicated

Public debt: 63.6% of GDP (2017 est.)
note: central government debt as a % of GDP
comparison ranking: 69

Taxes and other revenues: 26.18% (of GDP) (2020 est.)
note: central government tax revenue as a % of GDP
comparison ranking: 12

Current account balance: -$155.194 million (2023 est.)
-$141.648 million (2022 est.)
-$160.168 million (2021 est.)
note: balance of payments - net trade and primary/secondary income in current dollars comparison ranking: 99

Exports: $2.375 billion (2023 est.)
$2.247 billion (2022 est.)
$1.751 billion (2021 est.)
note: balance of payments - exports of goods and services in current dollars
comparison ranking: 161

Exports - partners: France 20%, Mauritius 12%, UK 9%, Japan 8%, Italy 8% (2023)
note: top five export partners based on percentage share of exports

Exports - commodities: fish, scrap iron, animal meal, broadcasting equipment, ships (2023)
note: top five export commodities based on value in dollars

Imports: $2.437 billion (2023 est.)
$2.298 billion (2022 est.)
$1.821 billion (2021 est.)
note: balance of payments - imports of goods and services in current dollars
comparison ranking: 169

Imports - partners: UAE 32%, Spain 10%, France 6%, South Africa 6%, India 6% (2023)
note: top five import partners based on percentage share of imports

Imports - commodities: refined petroleum, fish, ships, cars, plastic products (2023)
note: top five import commodities based on value in dollars

Reserves of foreign exchange and gold: $773.678 million (2024 est.)
$682.794 million (2023 est.)
$638.961 million (2022 est.)
note: holdings of gold (year-end prices)/foreign exchange/special drawing rights in current dollars
comparison ranking: 148

Exchange rates: Seychelles rupees (SCR) per US dollar -

Exchange rates: 14.53 (2024 est.)
14.018 (2023 est.)
14.273 (2022 est.)
16.921 (2021 est.)
17.617 (2020 est.)

ENERGY

Electricity access: *electrification - total population:* 100% (2022 est.)

Electricity: *installed generating capacity:* 156,000 kW (2023 est.)
consumption: 581.227 million kWh (2023 est.)

transmission/distribution losses: 44.034 million kWh (2023 est.)
comparison rankings: installed generating capacity 181; consumption 173; transmission/distribution losses 37

Electricity generation sources: *fossil fuels:* 86.4% of total installed capacity (2023 est.)
solar: 12.7% of total installed capacity (2023 est.)
wind: 1% of total installed capacity (2023 est.)

Coal: *imports:* 500 metric tons (2023 est.)

Petroleum: *refined petroleum consumption:* 6,000 bbl/day (2023 est.)

Energy consumption per capita: 98.847 million Btu/person (2023 est.)
comparison ranking: 51

COMMUNICATIONS

Telephones - fixed lines: *total subscriptions:* 18,000 (2023 est.)
subscriptions per 100 inhabitants: 14 (2023 est.)
comparison ranking: total subscriptions 175

Telephones - mobile cellular: *total subscriptions:* 165,000 (2023 est.)
subscriptions per 100 inhabitants: 192 (2022 est.)
comparison ranking: total subscriptions 186

Broadcast media: state-run national broadcaster Seychelles Broadcasting Corporation (SBC) has the only terrestrial TV station, which also airs broadcasts from international services; privately owned Internet Protocol Television (IPTV) channel; multi-channel cable and satellite TV available through 2 providers; SBC operates 1 AM and 1 FM radio station; 2 privately operated radio stations; transmissions of 2 international broadcasters available in Victoria (2019)

Internet country code: .sc

Internet users: *percent of population:* 87% (2023 est.)

Broadband - fixed subscriptions: *total:* 39,000 (2023 est.)
subscriptions per 100 inhabitants: 31 (2023 est.)
comparison ranking: total 151

TRANSPORTATION

Civil aircraft registration country code prefix: S7

Airports: 16 (2025)
comparison ranking: 149

Heliports: 6 (2025)
comparison ranking: 94

Merchant marine: *total:* 30 (2023)
by type: general cargo 6, oil tanker 6, other 18
comparison ranking: total 134

Ports: *total ports:* 1 (2024)
large: 0
medium: 0
small: 0
very small: 1
ports with oil terminals: 1
key ports: Victoria

MILITARY AND SECURITY

Military and security forces: Seychelles People's Defense Forces (SPDF; aka Seychelles Defense Forces, SDF): Army (includes infantry, special forces, and a presidential security unit), Coast Guard, and Air Force

Ministry of Internal Affairs: Seychelles Police Force (2025)

Military expenditures: 1.5% of GDP (2024 est.)
1.6% of GDP (2023 est.)
1.4% of GDP (2022 est.)
1.5% of GDP (2021 est.)
1.6% of GDP (2020 est.)

Military and security service personnel strengths: approximately 500 active Defense Forces (2025)

Military equipment inventories and acquisitions: the SDF's inventory primarily consists of Soviet-era equipment delivered in the 1970s and 1980s; in recent years, the SDF has received limited amounts of more modern equipment, mostly donations of patrol boats and aircraft, from several suppliers, including Bahrain, China, India, and the UAE (2024)

Military service age and obligation: 18-28 (18-25 for officers) years of age for voluntary military service for men and women; 6- year initial commitment; no conscription (2023)

Military - note: formed in 1977, the SDF is one of the World's smallest militaries; its primary responsibility is maritime security, including countering illegal fishing, piracy, and drug smuggling; it was given police powers in 2022; the Seychelles maintains close security ties with India, which has provided support to the SDF's maritime security operations (2025)

SIERRA LEONE

INTRODUCTION

Background: Continuously populated for at least 2,500 years, the area now known as Sierra Leone is covered with dense jungle that allowed the region to remain relatively protected from invading West African empires. Traders introduced Sierra Leone to Islam, which occupies a central role in Sierra Leonean culture and history. In the 17th century, the British set up a trading post near present-day Freetown. The trade originally involved timber and ivory but later expanded to enslaved people. In 1787, after the American Revolution, Sierra Leone became a destination for Black British loyalists from the new United States. When Britain abolished the slave trade in 1807, British ships delivered thousands of liberated Africans to Sierra Leone. During the 19th century, the colony gradually expanded inland.

In 1961, Sierra Leone became independent of the UK. Sierra Leone held free and fair elections in 1962 and 1967, but Siaka STEVENS – Sierra Leone's second prime minister – quickly reverted to authoritarian tendencies, outlawing most political parties and ruling from 1967 to 1985. In 1991, Sierra Leonean soldiers launched a civil war against STEVENS' ruling party. The war caused tens of thousands of deaths and displaced more than 2 million people (about one third of the population). In 1998, a Nigerian-led West African coalition military force intervened, installing Tejan KABBAH – who was originally elected in 1996 – as prime minister. In 2002, KABBAH officially announced the end of the war. Since 1998, Sierra Leone has conducted democratic elections dominated by the two main political parties, the Sierra Leone People's Party (SLPP) and the All People's Congress (APC) party. In 2018, Julius Maada BIO of the Sierra Leone People's Party won the presidential election that saw a high voter turnout despite some allegations of voter intimidation. BIO won again in June 2023, although irregularities were noted that called into question the integrity of the results. In October 2023, the Government of Sierra Leone and the main opposition party, the All People's Congress, signed the Agreement for National Unity to boost cooperation between political parties and begin the process of reforming the country's electoral system.

GEOGRAPHY

Location: Western Africa, bordering the North Atlantic Ocean, between Guinea and Liberia

Geographic coordinates: 8 30 N, 11 30 W

Map references: Africa

Area: *total:* 71,740 sq km
land: 71,620 sq km
water: 120 sq km
comparison ranking: total 119

Area - comparative: slightly smaller than South Carolina

Land boundaries: *total:* 1,093 km
border countries (2): Guinea 794 km; Liberia 299 km

Coastline: 402 km

Maritime claims: *territorial sea:* 12 nm
contiguous zone: 24 nm
exclusive economic zone: 200 nm
continental shelf: 200 nm

Climate: tropical; hot, humid; summer rainy season (May to December); winter dry season (December to April)

Terrain: coastal belt of mangrove swamps, wooded hill country, upland plateau, mountains in east

Elevation: *highest point:* Loma Mansa (Bintimani) 1,948 m
lowest point: Atlantic Ocean 0 m
mean elevation: 279 m

Natural resources: diamonds, titanium ore, bauxite, iron ore, gold, chromite

Land use: *agricultural land:* 54.7% (2022 est.)
arable land: 21.9% (2022 est.)
permanent crops: 2.3% (2022 est.)
permanent pasture: 30.5% (2022 est.)
forest: 34.6% (2022 est.)
other: 10.7% (2022 est.)

Irrigated land: 300 sq km (2012)

Major watersheds (area sq km): Atlantic Ocean drainage: Niger (2,261,741 sq km)

Population distribution: population clusters are found in the lower elevations of the south and west; the northern third of the country is less populated, as shown on this population distribution map

Natural hazards: dry, sand-laden harmattan winds blow from the Sahara (December to February); sandstorms, dust storms

Geography - note: rainfall along the coast can reach 495 cm (195 in) a year, making it one of the wettest places along coastal western Africa

PEOPLE AND SOCIETY

Population: *total:* 9,121,049 (2024 est.)
male: 4,515,726
female: 4,605,323
comparison rankings: total 99; male 98; female 98

Nationality: *noun:* Sierra Leonean(s)
adjective: Sierra Leonean

Ethnic groups: Temne 35.4%, Mende 30.8%, Limba 8.8%, Kono 4.3%, Korankoh 4%, Fullah 3.8%, Mandingo
2.8%, Loko 2%, Sherbro 1.9%, Creole 1.2% (descendants of freed Jamaican slaves who were settled in the Freetown area in the late-18th century; also known as Krio), other 5% (2019 est.)

Languages: English (official, regular use limited to literate minority), Mende (principal vernacular in the south), Temne (principal vernacular in the north), Krio (English-based Creole, spoken by the descendants of freed Jamaican slaves; a first language for 10% of the population but understood by 95%)

Religions: Muslim 77.1%, Christian 22.9% (2019 est.)

Age structure: *0-14 years:* 40.1% (male 1,843,606/ female 1,812,304)
15-64 years: 57.4% (male 2,557,715/female 2,675,418)
65 years and over: 2.5% (2024 est.) (male 114,405/ female 117,601)

Dependency ratios: *total dependency ratio:* 74.3 (2024 est.)
youth dependency ratio: 69.9 (2024 est.)
elderly dependency ratio: 4.4 (2024 est.)
potential support ratio: 22.6 (2024 est.)

Median age: *total:* 19.4 years (2024 est.)
male: 19 years
female: 19.9 years
comparison ranking: total 210

Population growth rate: 2.32% (2024 est.)
comparison ranking: 29

Birth rate: 30.8 births/1,000 population (2024 est.)
comparison ranking: 24

Death rate: 9 deaths/1,000 population (2024 est.)
comparison ranking: 58

Net migration rate: 1.4 migrant(s)/1,000 population (2024 est.)
comparison ranking: 60

Population distribution: population clusters are found in the lower elevations of the south and west; the northern third of the country is less populated, as shown on this population distribution map

Urbanization: *urban population:* 44.3% of total population (2023)
rate of urbanization: 3.02% annual rate of change (2020-25 est.)

Major urban areas - population: 1.309 million FREETOWN (capital) (2023)

Sex ratio: *at birth:* 1.03 male(s)/female
0-14 years: 1.02 male(s)/female
15-64 years: 0.96 male(s)/female
65 years and over: 0.97 male(s)/female
total population: 0.98 male(s)/female (2024 est.)

Mother's mean age at first birth: 19.6 years (2019 est.)
note: data represents median age at first birth among women 20-49

Maternal mortality ratio: 354 deaths/100,000 live births (2023 est.)
comparison ranking: 21

Infant mortality rate: *total:* 71.2 deaths/1,000 live births (2024 est.)
male: 76 deaths/1,000 live births
female: 66.2 deaths/1,000 live births
comparison ranking: total 5

Life expectancy at birth: *total population:* 59.4 years (2024 est.)
male: 57.8 years
female: 61 years
comparison ranking: total population 223

Total fertility rate: 3.61 children born/woman (2024 est.)
comparison ranking: 30

Gross reproduction rate: 1.78 (2024 est.)

Drinking water source: *improved: urban:* 79.8% of population (2022 est.)
rural: 54.1% of population (2022 est.)
total: 65.3% of population (2022 est.)
unimproved: urban: 20.2% of population (2022 est.)
rural: 45.9% of population (2022 est.)
total: 34.7% of population (2022 est.)

Health expenditure: 8.6% of GDP (2021)
5.2% of national budget (2022 est.)

Physician density: 0.13 physicians/1,000 population (2022)

Sanitation facility access: *improved: urban:* 81.9% of population (2022 est.)
rural: 37.9% of population (2022 est.)
total: 57.2% of population (2022 est.)
unimproved: urban: 18.1% of population (2022 est.)
rural: 62.1% of population (2022 est.)
total: 42.8% of population (2022 est.)

Obesity - adult prevalence rate: 8.7% (2016)
comparison ranking: 147

Alcohol consumption per capita: *total:* 3.22 liters of pure alcohol (2019 est.)
beer: 0.17 liters of pure alcohol (2019 est.)
wine: 0.01 liters of pure alcohol (2019 est.)
spirits: 0.15 liters of pure alcohol (2019 est.)
other alcohols: 2.9 liters of pure alcohol (2019 est.)
comparison ranking: total 107

Tobacco use: *total:* 9.8% (2025 est.)
male: 14.8% (2025 est.)
female: 4.9% (2025 est.)
comparison ranking: total 129

Children under the age of 5 years underweight: 12% (2021)
comparison ranking: 40

Currently married women (ages 15-49): 58.9% (2023 est.)

Child marriage: *women married by age 15:* 8.6% (2019)
women married by age 18: 29.6% (2019)
men married by age 18: 4.1% (2019)

Education expenditure: 8.5% of GDP (2022 est.)
29.4% national budget (2022 est.)
comparison ranking: Education expenditure (% GDP) 7

Literacy: *total population:* 43.6% (2019 est.)
male: 54.6% (2019 est.)
female: 33.9% (2019 est.)

ENVIRONMENT

Environmental issues: overharvesting of timber, expansion of cattle grazing, and slash-and-burn agriculture resulting in deforestation, soil exhaustion, and flooding; loss of biodiversity; air pollution; water pollution; overfishing

International environmental agreements: *party to:* Biodiversity, Climate Change, Climate Change-Kyoto Protocol, Climate Change- Paris Agreement, Comprehensive Nuclear Test Ban, Desertification, Endangered Species, Hazardous Wastes, Law of the Sea, Marine Dumping-London Convention, Marine Dumping- London Protocol, Marine Life Conservation, Nuclear Test Ban, Ozone Layer Protection, Ship Pollution, Wetlands
signed, but not ratified: Environmental Modification

Climate: tropical; hot, humid; summer rainy season (May to December); winter dry season (December to April)

Urbanization: *urban population:* 44.3% of total population (2023)
rate of urbanization: 3.02% annual rate of change (2020-25 est.)

Carbon dioxide emissions: 1.342 million metric tonnes of CO_2 (2023 est.)
from petroleum and other liquids: 1.342 million metric tonnes of CO_2 (2023 est.)
comparison ranking: total emissions 167

Particulate matter emissions: 45.4 micrograms per cubic meter (2019 est.)

Waste and recycling: *municipal solid waste generated annually:* 610,200 tons (2024 est.)
percent of municipal solid waste recycled: 9.7% (2022 est.)

Total water withdrawal: *municipal:* 111 million cubic meters (2022 est.)
industrial: 55.5 million cubic meters (2022 est.)
agricultural: 45.7 million cubic meters (2022 est.)

Total renewable water resources: 160 billion cubic meters (2022 est.)

GOVERNMENT

Country name: *conventional long form:* Republic of Sierra Leone

conventional short form: Sierra Leone
local long form: Republic of Sierra Leone
local short form: Sierra Leone
etymology: Portuguese explorer Pedro de SINTRA is usually credited with naming the country "Serra da Leao" (Lion Mountains) in 1462, but Venetian explorer Alvise CA' DA MOSTO recorded the name as "Serre-Lionne" in 1457, referring to the rumbling of thunder over the mountains

Government type: presidential republic

Capital: *name:* Freetown
geographic coordinates: 8 29 N, 13 14 W
time difference: UTC 0 (5 hours ahead of Washington, DC, during Standard Time)
etymology: the name described the original settlement in 1781, which served as a haven for free-born and freed African Americans

Administrative divisions: 4 provinces and 1 area*; Eastern, Northern, North Western, Southern, Western*

Legal system: mixed system of English common law and customary law

Constitution: *history:* several previous; latest effective 1 October 1991
amendment process: proposed by Parliament; passage of amendments requires at least two-thirds majority vote of Parliament in two successive readings and assent of the president of the republic; passage of amendments affecting fundamental rights and freedoms and many other constitutional sections also requires approval in a referendum with participation of at least one half of qualified voters and at least two thirds of votes cast

International law organization participation: has not submitted an ICJ jurisdiction declaration; accepts ICCt jurisdiction

Citizenship: *citizenship by birth:* no
citizenship by descent only: at least one parent or grandparent must be a citizen of Sierra Leone
dual citizenship recognized: yes
residency requirement for naturalization: 5 years

Suffrage: 18 years of age; universal

Executive branch: *chief of state:* President Julius Maada BIO (since 27 June 2023)
head of government: President Julius Maada BIO (since 27 June 2023)
cabinet: Ministers of State appointed by the president, approved by Parliament; the cabinet is responsible to the president
election/appointment process: president directly elected by 55% in the first round or absolute-majority popular vote in 2 rounds, if needed, for a 5-year term (eligible for a second term)
most recent election date: 24 June 2023
election results: *2023:* Julius Maada BIO reelected president in first round; percent of vote - Julius Maada BIO (SLPP) 56.2%, Samura KAMARA (APC) 41.2%, other 2.6%
2018: Julius Maada BIO elected president in second round; percent of vote - Julius Maada BIO (SLPP) 51.8%, Samura KAMARA (APC) 48.2%
expected date of next election: June 2028
note: the president is chief of state, head of government, and minister of defense

Legislative branch: *legislature name:* Parliament
legislative structure: unicameral
number of seats: 149 (135 directly elected; 14 indirectly elected)
electoral system: proportional representation
scope of elections: full renewal
term in office: 5 years
most recent election date: 6/24/2023
parties elected and seats per party: Sierra Leone People's Party (SLPP) (81); All People's Congress (APC) (54)
percentage of women in chamber: 29.5%
expected date of next election: June 2028
note: 14 seats are reserved for "paramount chiefs," who are indirectly elected to represent the 14 provincial districts

Judicial branch: *highest court(s):* Superior Court of Judicature (consists of the Supreme Court at the top, with the chief justice and 4 other judges, the Court of Appeal with the chief justice and 7 other judges, and the High Court of Justice with the chief justice and 9 other judges)
judge selection and term of office: Supreme Court chief justice and other judges of the Judicature appointed by the president on the advice of the Judicial and Legal Service Commission, a 7-member independent body of judges, presidential appointees, and the Commission chairman, and are subject to approval by Parliament; all Judicature judges serve until retirement at age 65
subordinate courts: magistrates' courts; District Appeals Court; local courts

Political parties: All People's Congress or APC
Sierra Leone People's Party or SLPP

Diplomatic representation in the US: *chief of mission:* Ambassador Amara Sheikh Mohammed SOWA (since 24 July 2025)
chancery: 1701 19th Street NW, Washington, DC 20009-1605
telephone: [1] (202) 939-9261
FAX: [1] (202) 483-1793
email address and website: info@embassyofsierraleone.net
https://embassyofsierraleone.net/

Diplomatic representation from the US: *chief of mission:* Ambassador Bryan David HUNT (since 8 September 2023)
embassy: Southridge-Hill Station, Freetown
mailing address: 2160 Freetown Place, Washington DC 20521-2160
telephone: [232] 99 105 000
email address and website: consularfreetown@state.gov
https://sl.usembassy.gov/

International organization participation: ACP, AfDB, ATMIS, AU, C, ECOWAS, EITI (compliant country), FAO, G-77, IAEA, IBRD, ICAO, ICCt, ICRM, IDA, IDB, IFAD, IFC, IFRCS, IHO (pending member), ILO, IMF, IMO, Interpol, IOC, IOM, IPU, ISO (correspondent), ITU, ITUC (NGOs), MIGA, NAM, OIC, OPCW, UN, UNAMID, UNCTAD, UNESCO, UNIDO, UNIFIL, UNISFA, UNOOSA, UNSOM, UNWTO, UPU, WCO, WFTU (NGOs), WHO, WIPO, WMO, WTO

Independence: 27 April 1961 (from the UK)

National holiday: Independence Day, 27 April (1961)

Flag: *description:* three equal horizontal bands of light green (top), white, and light blue
meaning: green stands for agriculture, mountains, and natural resources; white for unity and justice; and blue for the sea and the natural harbor in Freetown

National symbol(s): lion

National color(s): green, white, blue

National anthem(s): *title:* "High We Exalt Thee, Realm of the Free"
lyrics/music: Clifford Nelson FYLE/John Joseph AKA
history: adopted 1961

National heritage: *total World Heritage Sites:* 1 (natural)
selected World Heritage Site locales: Gola-Tiwai Complex (n)

ECONOMY

Economic overview: low-income West African economy; primarily subsistent agriculture; key iron and diamond mining activities suspended; slow recovery from 1990s civil war; systemic corruption; high-risk debt; high youth unemployment; natural resource rich

Real GDP (purchasing power parity): $26.728 billion (2024 est.)
$25.7 billion (2023 est.)
$24.312 billion (2022 est.)
note: data in 2021 dollars
comparison ranking: 151

Real GDP growth rate: 4% (2024 est.)
5.7% (2023 est.)
5.3% (2022 est.)
note: annual GDP % growth based on constant local currency
comparison ranking: 75

Real GDP per capita: $3,100 (2024 est.)
$3,000 (2023 est.)
$2,900 (2022 est.)
note: data in 2021 dollars
comparison ranking: 193

GDP (official exchange rate): $7.548 billion (2024 est.)
note: data in current dollars at official exchange rate

Inflation rate (consumer prices): 28.6% (2024 est.)
47.6% (2023 est.)
27.2% (2022 est.)
note: annual % change based on consumer prices
comparison ranking: 197

GDP - composition, by sector of origin: *agriculture:* 25.4% (2024 est.)
industry: 27.3% (2024 est.)
services: 44.8% (2024 est.)
note: figures may not total 100% due to non-allocated consumption not captured in sector- reported data
comparison rankings: agriculture 17; industry 72; services 177

GDP - composition, by end use: *household consumption:* 87.6% (2024 est.)
government consumption: 5.5% (2024 est.)
investment in fixed capital: 29.5% (2024 est.)
investment in inventories: 0% (2024 est.)
exports of goods and services: 20.9% (2024 est.)
imports of goods and services: -43.5% (2024 est.)
note: figures may not total 100% due to rounding or gaps in data collection

Agricultural products: cassava, rice, oil palm fruit, vegetables, sweet potatoes, milk, citrus fruits, fruits, groundnuts, sugarcane (2023)
note: top ten agricultural products based on tonnage

Industries: diamond mining; iron ore, rutile and bauxite mining; small-scale manufacturing (beverages, textiles, footwear)

Industrial production growth rate: 4.7% (2024 est.)

note: annual % change in industrial value added based on constant local currency
comparison ranking: 49

Labor force: 2.863 million (2024 est.)
note: number of people ages 15 or older who are employed or seeking work
comparison ranking: 114

Unemployment rate: 3.2% (2024 est.)
3.2% (2023 est.)
3.2% (2022 est.)
note: % of labor force seeking employment
comparison ranking: 48

Youth unemployment rate (ages 15-24): *total:* 3.6% (2024 est.)
male: 4.8% (2024 est.)
female: 2.5% (2024 est.)
note: % of labor force ages 15-24 seeking employment
comparison ranking: total 175

Population below poverty line: 56.8% (2018 est.)
note: % of population with income below national poverty line

Gini Index coefficient - distribution of family income: 35.7 (2018 est.)
note: index (0-100) of income distribution; higher values represent greater inequality
comparison ranking: 68

Household income or consumption by percentage share: *lowest 10%:* 3.4% (2018 est.)
highest 10%: 29.4% (2018 est.)
note: % share of income accruing to lowest and highest 10% of population

Remittances: 4.6% of GDP (2023 est.)
4.1% of GDP (2022 est.)
2.6% of GDP (2021 est.)
note: personal transfers and compensation between resident and non-resident individuals/households/entities

Budget: *revenues:* $740 million (2019 est.)
expenditures: $867 million (2019 est.)

Current account balance: -$606.358 million (2023 est.)
-$452.094 million (2022 est.)
-$522.815 million (2021 est.)
note: balance of payments - net trade and primary/secondary income in current dollars
comparison ranking: 111

Exports: $1.382 billion (2023 est.)
$1.202 billion (2022 est.)
$928.689 million (2021 est.)
note: balance of payments - exports of goods and services in current dollars
comparison ranking: 176

Exports - partners: China 67%, India 6%, Belgium 5%, Netherlands 4%, Ireland 3% (2023)
note: top five export partners based on percentage share of exports

Exports - commodities: iron ore, titanium ore, diamonds, aluminum ore, cocoa beans (2023)
note: top five export commodities based on value in dollars

Imports: $2.264 billion (2023 est.)
$2.074 billion (2022 est.)
$1.91 billion (2021 est.)
note: balance of payments - imports of goods and services in current dollars
comparison ranking: 173

Imports - partners: China 32%, India 15%, UAE 5%, USA 5%, Turkey 5% (2023)
note: top five import partners based on percentage share of imports

Imports - commodities: rice, plastic products, packaged medicine, cement, cars (2023)
note: top five import commodities based on value in dollars

Reserves of foreign exchange and gold: $495.699 million (2023 est.)
$624.496 million (2022 est.)
$945.908 million (2021 est.)
note: holdings of gold (year-end prices)/foreign exchange/special drawing rights in current dollars
comparison ranking: 160

Debt - external: $1.451 billion (2023 est.)
note: present value of external debt in current US dollars
comparison ranking: 99

Exchange rates: leones (SLL) per US dollar -

Exchange rates: 21.305 (2023 est.)
14.048 (2022 est.)
10.439 (2021 est.)
9.83 (2020 est.)
9.01 (2019 est.)

ENERGY

Electricity access: *electrification - total population:* 29.4% (2022 est.)
electrification - urban areas: 55.3%
electrification - rural areas: 5%

Electricity: *installed generating capacity:* 149,000 kW (2023 est.)
consumption: 131.321 million kWh (2023 est.)
transmission/distribution losses: 81.921 million kWh (2023 est.)
comparison rankings: installed generating capacity 182; consumption 197; transmission/distribution losses 42

Electricity generation sources: *fossil fuels:* 3.4% of total installed capacity (2023 est.)
solar: 9.8% of total installed capacity (2023 est.)
hydroelectricity: 84.4% of total installed capacity (2023 est.)
biomass and waste: 2.3% of total installed capacity (2023 est.)

Petroleum: *refined petroleum consumption:* 9,000 bbl/day (2023 est.)

Energy consumption per capita: 2.301 million Btu/person (2023 est.)
comparison ranking: 183

COMMUNICATIONS

Telephones - fixed lines: *total subscriptions:* 0 (2021 est.)
subscriptions per 100 inhabitants: (2022 est.) less than 1
comparison ranking: total subscriptions 222

Telephones - mobile cellular: *total subscriptions:* 8.23 million (2021 est.)
subscriptions per 100 inhabitants: 98 (2021 est.)
comparison ranking: total subscriptions 100

Broadcast media: 1 state-owned TV station; 3 private TV stations; 1 pay-TV service; 1 state-owned national radio station; about 24 private radio stations; transmissions of several international broadcasters available (2019)

Internet country code: .sl

Internet users: *percent of population:* 21% (2023 est.)

Broadband - fixed subscriptions: *total:* 0 (2021 est.)
subscriptions per 100 inhabitants: (2021 est.) less than 1
comparison ranking: total 216

TRANSPORTATION

Civil aircraft registration country code prefix: 9L

Airports: 8 (2025)
comparison ranking: 167

Heliports: 3 (2025)
comparison ranking: 120

Merchant marine: *total:* 584 (2023)
by type: bulk carrier 33, container ship 8, general cargo 320, oil tanker 97, other 126
comparison ranking: total 39

Ports: *total ports:* 3 (2024)
large: 0
medium: 0
small: 1
very small: 2
ports with oil terminals: 2
key ports: Bonthe, Freetown, Pepel

MILITARY AND SECURITY

Military and security forces: Republic of Sierra Leone Armed Forces (RSLAF): organized as a Joint Force Command with land, air, and maritime components

Ministry of Internal Affairs: Sierra Leone Police (2025)

Military expenditures: 0.5% of GDP (2024 est.)
0.6% of GDP (2023 est.)
0.6% of GDP (2022 est.)
0.3% of GDP (2021 est.)
0.3% of GDP (2020 est.)

Military and security service personnel strengths: estimated 10,000 active Armed Forces (2025)

Military equipment inventories and acquisitions: the RSLAF has a small inventory that includes a mix of Soviet-origin and other older foreign-supplied equipment; in recent years, it has received limited amounts of newer equipment, mostly as donations, such as patrol boats from China and South Korea (2024)

Military service age and obligation: 18-25 for voluntary military service for men and women; no conscription (2025)

Military - note: the RSLAF's primary responsibilities are securing the country's borders and territorial waters, supporting civil authorities during internal emergencies, and participating in peacekeeping missions; since the end of the civil war in 2002, it has received assistance from several foreign militaries, including those of Canada, China, France, the UK, and the US
the RSLAF's origins lie in the Sierra Leone Battalion of the Royal West African Frontier Force (RWAFF), a multi-regiment force formed by the British colonial office in 1900 to garrison the West African colonies of Gold Coast (Ghana), Nigeria (Lagos and the protectorates of Northern and Southern Nigeria), Sierra Leone, and The Gambia; the RWAFF fought in both World Wars (2025)

SINGAPORE

INTRODUCTION

Background: A Malay trading port known as Temasek existed on the island of Singapore by the 14th century. The settlement changed hands several times in the ensuing centuries and was eventually burned in the 17th century, falling into obscurity. In 1819, the British founded modern Singapore as a trading colony on the same site and granted it full internal self-government for all matters except defense and foreign affairs in 1959. Singapore joined the Malaysian Federation in 1963 but was ousted two years later and became independent. Singapore subsequently became one of the world's most prosperous countries, with strong international trading links and per capita GDP among the highest globally. The People's Action Party has won every general election in Singapore since the end of the British colonial era, aided by its success in delivering consistent economic growth, as well as the city-state's fragmented opposition and electoral procedures that strongly favor the ruling party.

GEOGRAPHY

Location: Southeastern Asia, islands between Malaysia and Indonesia

Geographic coordinates: 1 22 N, 103 48 E

Map references: Southeast Asia

Area: *total:* 719 sq km
land: 709.2 sq km
water: 10 sq km
comparison ranking: total 190

Area - comparative: slightly more than 3.5 times the size of Washington, D.C.

Land boundaries: *total:* 0 km

Coastline: 193 km

Maritime claims: *territorial sea:* 3 nm
exclusive fishing zone: within and beyond territorial sea, as defined in treaties and practice

Climate: tropical; hot, humid, rainy; two distinct monsoon seasons - northeastern monsoon (December to March) and southwestern monsoon (June to September); inter-monsoon - frequent afternoon and early evening thunderstorms

Terrain: lowlying, gently undulating central plateau

Elevation: *highest point:* Bukit Timah 166 m
lowest point: Singapore Strait 0 m

Natural resources: fish, deepwater ports

Land use: *agricultural land:* 0.9% (2022 est.)
arable land: 0.8% (2022 est.)
permanent crops: 0.1% (2022 est.)
permanent pasture: 0% (2022 est.)
forest: 21.2% (2022 est.)
other: 77.9% (2022 est.)

Irrigated land: 0 sq km (2022)

Population distribution: most of the urbanization is along the southern coast, with relatively dense population clusters found in the central areas

Natural hazards: flash floods

Geography - note: focal point for Southeast Asian sea routes; consists of about 60 islands, the largest of which by far is Pulau Ujong; land reclamation has removed many former islands and created a number of new ones

PEOPLE AND SOCIETY

Population: *total:* 6,028,459 (2024 est.)
male: 3,013,630
female: 3,014,829
comparison rankings: total 114; male 114; female 114

Nationality: *noun:* Singaporean(s)
adjective: Singapore

Ethnic groups: Chinese 74.2%, Malay 13.7%, Indian 8.9%, other 3.2% (2021 est.)
note: data represent population by self-identification; the population is divided into four categories: Chinese, Malay (includes indigenous Malays and Indonesians), Indian (includes Indian, Pakistani, Bangladeshi, or Sri Lankan), and other ethnic groups (includes Eurasians, Caucasians, Japanese, Filipino, Vietnamese)

Languages: English (official) 48.3%, Mandarin (official) 29.9%, other Chinese dialects (includes Hokkien, Cantonese, Teochew, Hakka) 8.7%, Malay (official) 9.2%, Tamil (official) 2.5%, other 1.4% (2020 est.)
major-language sample(s):
The World Factbook, the indispensable source for basic information. (English)
世界概況 – 不可缺少的基本消息來源 (Mandarin)
note: data represent language most frequently spoken at home

Religions: Buddhist 31.1%, Christian 18.9%, Muslim 15.6%, Taoist 8.8%, Hindu 5%, other 0.6%, none 20% (2020 est.)

Age structure: *0-14 years:* 14.6% (male 455,536/female 424,969)
15-64 years: 71.1% (male 2,157,441/female 2,126,799)
65 years and over: 14.3% (2024 est.) (male 400,653/female 463,061)

Dependency ratios: *total dependency ratio:* 40.7 (2024 est.)
youth dependency ratio: 20.6 (2024 est.)
elderly dependency ratio: 20.2 (2024 est.)
potential support ratio: 5 (2024 est.)

Median age: *total:* 39.4 years (2024 est.)
male: 38 years
female: 40.6 years
comparison ranking: total 68

Population growth rate: 0.87% (2024 est.)
comparison ranking: 105

Birth rate: 8.8 births/1,000 population (2024 est.)
comparison ranking: 203

Death rate: 4.3 deaths/1,000 population (2024 est.)
comparison ranking: 209

Net migration rate: 4.2 migrant(s)/1,000 population (2024 est.)
comparison ranking: 24

Population distribution: most of the urbanization is along the southern coast, with relatively dense population clusters found in the central areas

Urbanization: *urban population:* 100% of total population (2023)
rate of urbanization: 0.74% annual rate of change (2020-25 est.)

Major urban areas - population: 6.081 million SINGAPORE (capital) (2023)

Sex ratio: *at birth:* 1.05 male(s)/female
0-14 years: 1.07 male(s)/female
15-64 years: 1.01 male(s)/female
65 years and over: 0.87 male(s)/female
total population: 1 male(s)/female (2024 est.)

Mother's mean age at first birth: 30.5 years (2015 est.)
note: data represents median age

Maternal mortality ratio: 6 deaths/100,000 live births (2023 est.)
comparison ranking: 166

Infant mortality rate: *total:* 1.5 deaths/1,000 live births (2024 est.)
male: 1.7 deaths/1,000 live births
female: 1.4 deaths/1,000 live births
comparison ranking: total 226

Life expectancy at birth: *total population:* 86.7 years (2024 est.)
male: 84 years
female: 89.5 years
comparison ranking: total population 2

Total fertility rate: 1.17 children born/woman (2024 est.)
comparison ranking: 225

Gross reproduction rate: 0.57 (2024 est.)

Drinking water source: *improved: urban:* 100% of population (2022 est.)
total: 100% of population (2022 est.)
unimproved: urban: 0% of population (2022 est.)
total: 0% of population (2022 est.)

Health expenditure: 5.6% of GDP (2021)
18.1% of national budget (2022 est.)

Physician density: 2.83 physicians/1,000 population (2022)

Hospital bed density: 2.6 beds/1,000 population (2021 est.)

Sanitation facility access: *improved: urban:* 100% of population (2022 est.)
total: 100% of population (2022 est.)
unimproved: urban: 0% of population (2022 est.)
total: 0% of population (2022 est.)

Obesity - adult prevalence rate: 6.1% (2016)

comparison ranking: 170

Alcohol consumption per capita: *total:* 1.81 liters of pure alcohol (2019 est.)
beer: 1.26 liters of pure alcohol (2019 est.)
wine: 0.27 liters of pure alcohol (2019 est.)
spirits: 0.24 liters of pure alcohol (2019 est.)
other alcohols: 0.04 liters of pure alcohol (2019 est.)
comparison ranking: total 132

Tobacco use: *total:* 16.2% (2025 est.)
male: 27.6% (2025 est.)
female: 3.8% (2025 est.)
comparison ranking: total 97

Currently married women (ages 15-49): 54.3% (2023 est.)

Child marriage: *women married by age 15:* 0% (2023)
women married by age 18: 0.1% (2023)

Education expenditure: 2.2% of GDP (2024 est.)
10.8% national budget (2023 est.)
comparison ranking: Education expenditure (% GDP) 181

Literacy: *total population:* 98% (2021 est.)
male: 99% (2021 est.)
female: 96% (2021 est.)

School life expectancy (primary to tertiary education): *total:* 17 years (2022 est.)
male: 17 years (2022 est.)
female: 17 years (2022 est.)

ENVIRONMENT

Environmental issues: water pollution; industrial pollution; limited freshwater resources; waste disposal problems from limited land availability; air pollution; deforestation; seasonal smoke/haze from forest fires in Indonesia

International environmental agreements: *party to:* Biodiversity, Climate Change, Climate Change-Kyoto Protocol, Climate Change-Paris Agreement, Comprehensive Nuclear Test Ban, Desertification, Endangered Species, Hazardous Wastes, Law of the Sea, Nuclear Test Ban, Ozone Layer Protection, Ship Pollution
signed, but not ratified: none of the selected agreements

Climate: tropical; hot, humid, rainy; two distinct monsoon seasons - northeastern monsoon (December to March) and southwestern monsoon (June to September); inter-monsoon - frequent afternoon and early evening thunderstorms

Urbanization: *urban population:* 100% of total population (2023)
rate of urbanization: 0.74% annual rate of change (2020-25 est.)

Carbon dioxide emissions: 238.962 million metric tonnes of CO2 (2023 est.)
from coal and metallurgical coke: 2.338 million metric tonnes of CO2 (2023 est.)
from petroleum and other liquids: 210.859 million metric tonnes of CO2 (2023 est.)
from consumed natural gas: 25.765 million metric tonnes of CO2 (2023 est.)
comparison ranking: total emissions 28

Particulate matter emissions: 10 micrograms per cubic meter (2019 est.)

Waste and recycling: *municipal solid waste generated annually:* 1.87 million tons (2024 est.)
percent of municipal solid waste recycled: 51.7% (2022 est.)

Total water withdrawal: *municipal:* 198.207 million cubic meters (2022)
industrial: 162.624 million cubic meters (2022)
agricultural: 0 cubic meters (2022)

Total renewable water resources: 600 million cubic meters (2022)

GOVERNMENT

Country name: *conventional long form:* Republic of Singapore
conventional short form: Singapore
local long form: Republic of Singapore
local short form: Singapore
etymology: name derives from the Sanskrit words *simha* (lion) and *pur* (city); according to Malayan folklore, an Indian prince visited Singapore in the 7th century and mistook the first animal he saw for a lion, which is not native to the country

Government type: parliamentary republic

Capital: *name:* Singapore
geographic coordinates: 1 17 N, 103 51 E
time difference: UTC+8 (13 hours ahead of Washington, DC, during Standard Time)
etymology: name derives from the Sanskrit words *simha* (lion) and *pur* (city); according to Malayan folklore, an Indian prince visited Singapore in the 7th century and mistook the first animal he saw for a lion, which is not native to the country

Administrative divisions: *no first-order administrative divisions; five community development councils:* Central Singapore Development Council, North East Development Council, North West Development Council, South East Development Council, South West Development Council (2019)

Legal system: English common law

Constitution: *history:* several previous; latest adopted 22 December 1965
amendment process: proposed by Parliament; passage requires two-thirds majority vote in the second and third readings by the elected Parliament membership and assent of the president of the republic; passage of amendments affecting sovereignty or control of the Police Force or the Armed Forces requires at least two-thirds majority vote in a referendum

International law organization participation: has not submitted an ICJ jurisdiction declaration; non-party state to the ICCt

Citizenship: *citizenship by birth:* no
citizenship by descent only: at least one parent must be a citizen of Singapore
dual citizenship recognized: no
residency requirement for naturalization: 10 years

Suffrage: 21 years of age; universal and compulsory

Executive branch: *chief of state:* President THARMAN Shanmugaratnam (since 14 September 2023)
head of government: Prime Minister Lawrence WONG (since 15 May 2024)
cabinet: Cabinet appointed by the president on the advice of the prime minister; responsible to Parliament
election/appointment process: president directly elected by simple-majority popular vote for a 6-year term (no term limits); following legislative elections, the president appoints the leader of the majority party or majority coalition as prime minister; deputy prime ministers also appointed by the president
most recent election date: 1 September 2023
election results: 2023: THARMAN Shanmugaratnam elected president; percent of vote - THARMAN Shanmugaratnam (independent) 70.4%, NG Kok Song (independent) 15.7%, TAN Kin Lian (independent) 13.9%
2017: HALIMAH Yacob declared president on 13 September 2017, being the only eligible candidate
expected date of next election: 2029

Legislative branch: *legislature name:* Parliament
legislative structure: unicameral
number of seats: 108 (97 directly elected; 9 appointed)
electoral system: plurality/majority
scope of elections: full renewal
term in office: 5 years
most recent election date: 5/3/2025
percentage of women in chamber: 32.3%
expected date of next election: May 2030

Judicial branch: *highest court(s):* Supreme Court (number of judges varies but includes judicial commissioners, judges of appeal, and international judges); the court is organized into an upper-tier Appeal Court and a lower-tier High Court
judge selection and term of office: judges appointed by the president from candidates recommended by the prime minister after consultation with the chief justice; judges usually serve until retirement at age 65, but terms can be extended
subordinate courts: district, magistrates', juvenile, family, community, and coroners' courts; small claims tribunals; employment claims tribunals

Political parties: People's Action Party or PAP
Progress Singapore Party or PSP
Workers' Party or WP
note: the PAP has won every general election since the end of the British colonial era in 1959

Diplomatic representation in the US: *chief of mission:* Ambassador LUI Tuck Yew (since 30 June 2023)
chancery: 3501 International Place NW, Washington, DC 20008
telephone: [1] (202) 537-3100
FAX: [1] (202) 537-0876
email address and website: singemb_was@mfa.sg
https://www.mfa.gov.sg/washington/
consulate(s) general: San Francisco
consulate(s): New York

Diplomatic representation from the US: *chief of mission:* Ambassador (vacant); Chargé d'Affaires Graham MAYER (since August 2025)
embassy: 27 Napier Road, Singapore 258508
mailing address: 4280 Singapore Place, Washington DC 20521-4280
telephone: [65] 6476-9100
FAX: [65] 6476-9340
email address and website: singaporeusembassy@state.gov
https://sg.usembassy.gov/

International organization participation: ADB, AOSIS, APEC, Arctic Council (observer), ARF, ASEAN, BIS, C, CP, EAS, FAO, FATF, G-77, IAEA, IBRD, ICAO, ICC (national committees), ICCt, ICRM, IDA, IFC, IFRCS, IHO, ILO, IMF, IMO, IMSO, Interpol, IOC, IPU, ISO, ITSO, ITU, ITUC (NGOs), MIGA, NAM, OPCW, Pacific Alliance (observer), PCA, UN, UNCTAD, UNESCO, UNHCR, UPU, WCO, WHO, WIPO, WMO, WTO

Independence: 9 August 1965 (from Malaysian Federation)

National holiday: National Day, 9 August (1965)

Flag: *description:* two equal horizontal bands of red (top) and white; a vertical white crescent is on the left side of the red band, with a circle of five five-pointed white stars to the right of the crescent *meaning:* red stands for brotherhood and equality, and white for purity and virtue; the waxing crescent moon symbolizes a young nation on the ascendancy; the stars represent the national ideals of democracy, peace, progress, justice, and equality

National symbol(s): lion, merlion (mythical half-lion, half-fish creature), orchid

National color(s): red, white

National anthem(s): *title:* "Majulah Singapura" (Onward, Singapore)
lyrics/music: Zubir SAID
history: adopted 1959; the anthem is sung only in Malay; first four lines of the melody are used as a presidential salute

National heritage: *total World Heritage Sites:* 1 (cultural)
selected World Heritage Site locales: Singapore Botanic Gardens

ECONOMY

Economic overview: high-income, service-based economy; global financial hub; business-friendly policies and open to investment and trade; inflation easing but persistent in services; public investments in education, healthcare, and infrastructure; strong human capital development challenged by aging population

Real GDP (purchasing power parity): $800.304 billion (2024 est.)
$766.662 billion (2023 est.)
$752.948 billion (2022 est.)
note: data in 2021 dollars
comparison ranking: 34

Real GDP growth rate: 4.4% (2024 est.)
1.8% (2023 est.)
4.1% (2022 est.)
note: annual GDP % growth based on constant local currency
comparison ranking: 58

Real GDP per capita: $132,600 (2024 est.)
$129,600 (2023 est.)
$133,600 (2022 est.)
note: data in 2021 dollars
comparison ranking: 3

GDP (official exchange rate): $547.387 billion (2024 est.)
note: data in current dollars at official exchange rate

Inflation rate (consumer prices): 2.4% (2024 est.)
4.8% (2023 est.)
6.1% (2022 est.)
note: annual % change based on consumer prices
comparison ranking: 67

GDP - composition, by sector of origin: *agriculture:* 0% (2024 est.)
industry: 21.4% (2024 est.)
services: 73% (2024 est.)
note: figures may not total 100% due to non-allocated consumption not captured in sector-reported data
comparison rankings: agriculture 204; industry 123; services 25

GDP - composition, by end use: *household consumption:* 31.5% (2024 est.)
government consumption: 10.6% (2024 est.)
investment in fixed capital: 21.9% (2024 est.)
investment in inventories: 0.3% (2024 est.)
exports of goods and services: 178.8% (2024 est.)
imports of goods and services: -143.6% (2024 est.)
note: figures may not total 100% due to rounding or gaps in data collection

Agricultural products: chicken, eggs, vegetables, pork, duck, spinach, lettuce, pork offal, cabbages, pork fat (2023)
note: top ten agricultural products based on tonnage

Industries: electronics, chemicals, financial services, oil drilling equipment, petroleum refining, biomedical products, scientific instruments, telecommunication equipment, processed food and beverages, ship repair, offshore platform construction, entrepot trade

Industrial production growth rate: 4.2% (2024 est.)
note: annual % change in industrial value added based on constant local currency
comparison ranking: 56

Labor force: 3.722 million (2024 est.)
note: number of people ages 15 or older who are employed or seeking work
comparison ranking: 97

Unemployment rate: 3.2% (2024 est.)
3.5% (2023 est.)
3.6% (2022 est.)
note: % of labor force seeking employment
comparison ranking: 46

Youth unemployment rate (ages 15-24): *total:* 7.8% (2024 est.)
male: 5.6% (2024 est.)
female: 10.8% (2024 est.)
note: % of labor force ages 15-24 seeking employment
comparison ranking: total 141

Gini Index coefficient - distribution of family income: 45.8 (2016)
comparison ranking: 14

Average household expenditures: *on food:* 7% of household expenditures (2023 est.)
on alcohol and tobacco: 1.7% of household expenditures (2023 est.)

Remittances: 0% of GDP (2023 est.)
0% of GDP (2022 est.)
0% of GDP (2021 est.)
note: personal transfers and compensation between resident and non-resident individuals/households/entities

Budget: *revenues:* $80.836 billion (2022 est.)
expenditures: $73.144 billion (2022 est.)
note: central government revenues (excluding grants) and expenditures converted to US dollars at average official exchange rate for year indicated

Public debt: 175.6% of GDP (2023 est.)
note: central government debt as a % of GDP
comparison ranking: 3

Taxes and other revenues: 13.9% (of GDP) (2023 est.)
note: central government tax revenue as a % of GDP
comparison ranking: 99

Current account balance: $96.015 billion (2024 est.)
$89.403 billion (2023 est.)
$93.771 billion (2022 est.)
note: balance of payments - net trade and primary/secondary income in current dollars
comparison ranking: 7

Exports: $978.597 billion (2024 est.)
$917.683 billion (2023 est.)
$947.355 billion (2022 est.)
note: balance of payments - exports of goods and services in current dollars
comparison ranking: 7

Exports - partners: Hong Kong 13%, China 11%, USA 10%, Malaysia 9%, S. Korea 6% (2023)
note: top five export partners based on percentage share of exports

Exports - commodities: integrated circuits, refined petroleum, machinery, vaccines, gold (2023)
note: top five export commodities based on value in dollars

Imports: $786.02 billion (2024 est.)
$728.5 billion (2023 est.)
$744.364 billion (2022 est.)
note: balance of payments - imports of goods and services in current dollars
comparison ranking: 9

Imports - partners: China 15%, Malaysia 11%, Taiwan 11%, USA 10%, S. Korea 6% (2023)
note: top five import partners based on percentage share of imports

Imports - commodities: integrated circuits, refined petroleum, crude petroleum, gold, gas turbines (2023)
note: top five import commodities based on value in dollars

Reserves of foreign exchange and gold: $383.946 billion (2024 est.)
$359.835 billion (2023 est.)
$296.629 billion (2022 est.)
note: holdings of gold (year-end prices)/foreign exchange/special drawing rights in current dollars
comparison ranking: 10

Exchange rates: Singapore dollars (SGD) per US dollar -

Exchange rates: 1.336 (2024 est.)
1.343 (2023 est.)
1.379 (2022 est.)
1.343 (2021 est.)
1.38 (2020 est.)

ENERGY

Electricity access: *electrification - total population:* 100% (2022 est.)

Electricity: *installed generating capacity:* 13.134 million kW (2023 est.)
consumption: 56.672 billion kWh (2023 est.)
transmission/distribution losses: 169.447 million kWh (2023 est.)
comparison rankings: installed generating capacity 58; consumption 48; transmission/distribution losses 60

Electricity generation sources: *fossil fuels:* 94.8% of total installed capacity (2023 est.)
solar: 2% of total installed capacity (2023 est.)
biomass and waste: 3.1% of total installed capacity (2023 est.)

Coal: *consumption:* 1.153 million metric tons (2023 est.)
exports: 97 metric tons (2023 est.)
imports: 1.326 million metric tons (2023 est.)

Petroleum: *refined petroleum consumption:* 1.514 million bbl/day (2023 est.)

Natural gas: *consumption:* 13.134 billion cubic meters (2023 est.)
exports: 399.452 million cubic meters (2023 est.)
imports: 13.973 billion cubic meters (2023 est.)

Energy consumption per capita: 643.259 million Btu/person (2023 est.)
comparison ranking: 2

COMMUNICATIONS

Telephones - fixed lines: *total subscriptions:* 1.912 million (2023 est.)
subscriptions per 100 inhabitants: 33 (2023 est.)
comparison ranking: total subscriptions 52

Telephones - mobile cellular: *total subscriptions:* 9.65 million (2023 est.)
subscriptions per 100 inhabitants: 156 (2022 est.)
comparison ranking: total subscriptions 95

Broadcast media: state-controlled broadcast media; 6 domestic TV stations operated by state-owned MediaCorp; broadcasts from Malaysian and Indonesian stations available; satellite dishes banned; multi-channel cable TV services available; 19 domestic radio stations, including 11 for MediaCorp, 5 for state-linked Singapore Press Holdings, 2 for Singapore Armed Forces Reservists Association, and 1 for BBC Radio; Malaysian and Indonesian radio stations available (2019)

Internet country code: .sg

Internet users: *percent of population:* 94% (2023 est.)

Broadband - fixed subscriptions: *total:* 1.57 million (2023 est.)
subscriptions per 100 inhabitants: 27 (2023 est.)
comparison ranking: total 69

TRANSPORTATION

Civil aircraft registration country code prefix: 9V

Airports: 9 (2025)
comparison ranking: 164

Heliports: 1 (2025)
comparison ranking: 164

Merchant marine: *total:* 3,202 (2023)
by type: bulk carrier 591, container ship 604, general cargo 107, oil tanker 600, other 1,300
comparison ranking: total 8

Ports: *total ports:* 5 (2024)
large: 2
medium: 1
small: 1
very small: 1
ports with oil terminals: 3
key ports: Jurong Island, Keppel - (East Singapore), Pulau Bukom, Pulau Sebarok

MILITARY AND SECURITY

Military and security forces: Singapore Armed Forces (SAF; aka Singapore Defense Force): Singapore Army, Republic of Singapore Navy, Republic of Singapore Air Force (includes air defense), Digital and Intelligence Service

Ministry of Home Affairs: Singapore Police Force (SPF; includes Police Coast Guard and the Gurkha Contingent) (2025)
note 1: the Gurkha Contingent of the Singapore Police Force (GCSPF) is a paramilitary unit for riot control and acts as a rapid reaction force
note 2: the Navy includes the multi-agency standing Maritime Security Task Force (MSTF), which assists the Police Coast Guard in conducting maritime security operations

Military expenditures: 3% of GDP (2024 est.)
3% of GDP (2023 est.)
3% of GDP (2022 est.)
3% of GDP (2021 est.)
3% of GDP (2020 est.)

Military and security service personnel strengths: information varies; approximately 55,000 active-duty Armed Forces (40,000 Army; 7,000 Navy; 8,000 Air Force) (2025)
note: the Army is comprised mostly of conscripts and reservists with a small core of professional soldiers, while the Air Force and Navy are staffed mainly by professional personnel

Military equipment inventories and acquisitions: the SAF has a diverse and largely modern mix of domestically produced and imported Western weapons systems; in recent years, France, Germany, and the US have been among the top suppliers of arms; Singapore has the most developed arms industry in Southeast Asia and is also its largest importer of weapons (2024)

Military service age and obligation: 18-21 years of age for compulsory military service for men; 16.5 years of age for voluntary enlistment (with parental consent); 24-month conscript service obligation, with a reserve obligation to age 40 (enlisted) or age 50 (officers); women are not conscripted, but they are allowed to volunteer for all services and branches, including combat arms (2025)
note 1: all male Singaporean citizens and permanent residents, unless exempted, are required to enter National Service (NS) upon attaining the age of 18; most NS conscripts serve in the Armed Forces, but some go into the Police Force or Civil Defense Force; conscripts comprise over half of the defense establishment
note 2: as of 2022, women made up about 8% of the regular force
note 3: the Singapore Armed Forces (SAF) also has a uniformed volunteer auxiliary branch known as the Volunteer Corps (SAFVC); the SAFVC allows citizens and residents not subject to the National Service obligation, including Singaporean women, first generation permanent residents, and naturalized citizens, to contribute towards Singapore's defense; the volunteers must be 18-45 and physically fit
note 4: members of the Gurkha Contingent (GC) of the Singapore Police Force are mostly recruited from a small number of hill tribes in Nepal; the GC was formed in 1949 originally from selected ex-British Army Gurkhas

Military deployments: maintains permanent training detachments of military personnel in Australia, France, and the US (2025)

Military - note: the SAF's primary responsibility is external defense, particularly maritime security, but it also trains for certain domestic security operations, including joint deterrence patrols with police in instances of heightened terrorism alerts; the Army includes a "people's defense force," which is a divisional headquarters responsible for homeland security and counterterrorism; the SAF regularly participates in bilateral and multilateral training exercises
Singapore is a member of the Five Powers Defense Arrangements (FPDA), a series of mutual assistance agreements reached in 1971 embracing Australia, Malaysia, New Zealand, Singapore, and the UK; the FPDA commits the members to consult with one another in the event or threat of an armed attack on any of the members and to mutually decide what measures should be taken, jointly or separately; there is no specific obligation to intervene militarily; Singapore also has close security ties with the US, including granting the US military access, basing, and overflight privileges
the SAF's roots go back to 1854 when the Singapore Volunteer Rifle Corps was formed under colonial rule; the first battalion of regular soldiers, the First Singapore Infantry Regiment, was organized in 1957; the modern SAF was established in 1965 (2025)

TRANSNATIONAL ISSUES

Refugees and internally displaced persons: *stateless persons:* 1,109 (2024 est.)

SINT MAARTEN

INTRODUCTION

Background: Christopher COLUMBUS claimed Saint Martin for Spain in 1493, naming it after the feast day of St. Martin of Tours, but it was the Dutch who occupied the island in 1631 to exploit its salt deposits. The Spanish retook Saint Martin in 1633, but the Dutch continued to assert their claims. The Spanish finally relinquished the island to the French and Dutch, who divided it between themselves in 1648. The border frequently fluctuated over the next 200 years because of friction between the two countries, with the Dutch eventually holding the smaller portion of the island (about 39%) and adopting the Dutch spelling of the island's name for their territory.

The establishment of cotton, tobacco, and sugar plantations dramatically expanded African slavery on the island in the 18th and 19th centuries; the practice was not abolished in the Dutch half until 1863. The island's economy declined until 1939 when it became a free port; the tourism industry was dramatically expanded beginning in the 1950s. In 1954, Sint Maarten and several other Dutch Caribbean possessions became part of the Kingdom of the Netherlands as the Netherlands Antilles. In a 2000 referendum, the citizens of Sint Maarten voted to become a self-governing country within the Kingdom of the Netherlands, effective in 2010. In 2017, Hurricane Irma hit Saint Martin/Sint Maarten, causing extensive damage to roads, communications, electrical power, and housing; the UN estimated that 90% of the buildings were damaged or destroyed.

GEOGRAPHY

Location: Caribbean, located in the Leeward Islands (northern) group; Dutch part of the island of Saint Martin in the Caribbean Sea; Sint Maarten lies east of the US Virgin Islands

Geographic coordinates: 18 4 N, 63 4 W

Map references: Central America and the Caribbean

Area: *total:* 34 sq km
land: 34 sq km
water: 0 sq km

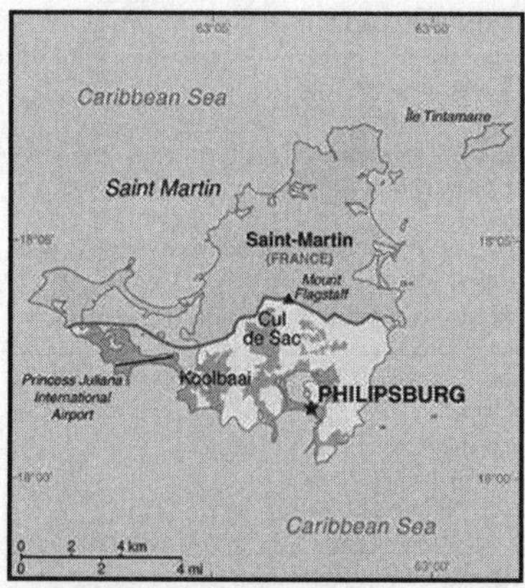

note: Dutch part of the island of Saint Martin
comparison ranking: total 234

Area - comparative: one-fifth the size of Washington, D.C.

Land boundaries: *total:* 16 km
border countries (1): Saint Martin (France) 16 km

Coastline: 58.9 km (for entire island)

Maritime claims: *territorial sea:* 12 nm
exclusive economic zone: 200 nm

Climate: tropical marine climate, ameliorated by northeast trade winds, results in moderate temperatures; average rainfall of 150 cm/year; hurricane season stretches from July to November

Terrain: low, hilly terrain, volcanic origin

Elevation: *highest point:* 250 m SW of Mount Flagstaff summit, 383 m
lowest point: Caribbean Sea 0 m

Natural resources: fish, salt

Land use: *agricultural land:* 0% (2022 est.)
forest: 10.9% (2022 est.)
other: 89.1% (2022 est.)

Population distribution: the most populous areas are Lower Prince's Quarter (north of Philipsburg) and Cul de Sac

Natural hazards: subject to hurricanes from July to November

Geography - note: *note 1:* the northern border is shared with the French overseas collectivity of Saint Martin; together, these two entities make up the smallest landmass in the world that is shared by two self-governing states
note 2: Simpson Bay Lagoon (aka, Simson Bay Lagoon or The Great Pond) is one of the largest inland lagoons in the West Indies; the border between the French and Dutch halves of the island of Saint Martin runs across the center of the lagoon, which is shared

PEOPLE AND SOCIETY

Population: *total:* 46,215 (2024 est.)
male: 22,817
female: 23,398
comparison rankings: total 210; male 210; female 210

Ethnic groups: Saint Maarten 29.9%, Dominican Republic 10.2%, Haiti 7.8%, Jamaica 6.6%, Saint Martin 5.9%, Guyana 5%, Dominica 4.4%, Curacao 4.1%, Aruba 3.4%, Saint Kitts and Nevis 2.8%, India 2.6%, Netherlands 2.2%, US 1.6%, Suriname 1.4%, Saint Lucia 1.3%, Anguilla 1.1%, other 8%, unspecified 1.7% (2011 est.)
note: data represent population by country of birth

Languages: English (official) 67.5%, Spanish 12.9%, Creole 8.2%, Dutch (official) 4.2%, Papiamento (a Spanish-Portuguese-Dutch-English dialect) 2.2%, French 1.5%, other 3.5% (2001 est.)

Religions: Protestant 41.9% (Pentecostal 14.7%, Methodist 10.0%, Seventh Day Adventist 6.6%, Baptist 4.7%, Anglican 3.1%, other Protestant 2.8%), Roman Catholic 33.1%, Hindu 5.2%, Christian 4.1%, Jehovah's Witness 1.7%, Evangelical 1.4%, Muslim/Jewish 1.1%, other 1.3% (includes Buddhist, Sikh, Rastafarian), none 7.9%, no response 2.4% (2011 est.)

Age structure: *0-14 years:* 18.4% (male 4,409/female 4,114)
15-64 years: 66.3% (male 15,158/female 15,496)
65 years and over: 15.2% (2024 est.) (male 3,250/female 3,788)

Dependency ratios: *total dependency ratio:* 50.8 (2024 est.)
youth dependency ratio: 27.8 (2024 est.)
elderly dependency ratio: 23 (2024 est.)
potential support ratio: 4.4 (2024 est.)

Median age: *total:* 41 years (2024 est.)
male: 39 years
female: 42.8 years
comparison ranking: total 55

Population growth rate: 1.15% (2024 est.)
comparison ranking: 79

Birth rate: 12.2 births/1,000 population (2024 est.)
comparison ranking: 144

Death rate: 6.4 deaths/1,000 population (2024 est.)
comparison ranking: 141

Net migration rate: 5.7 migrant(s)/1,000 population (2024 est.)
comparison ranking: 16

Population distribution: the most populous areas are Lower Prince's Quarter (north of Philipsburg) and Cul de Sac

Urbanization: *urban population:* 100% of total population (2023)
rate of urbanization: 1.16% annual rate of change (2020-25 est. est.)

Major urban areas - population: 1,327 PHILIPSBURG (capital) (2011)

Sex ratio: *at birth:* 1.05 male(s)/female
0-14 years: 1.07 male(s)/female
15-64 years: 0.98 male(s)/female
65 years and over: 0.86 male(s)/female
total population: 0.98 male(s)/female (2024 est.)

Infant mortality rate: *total:* 7.6 deaths/1,000 live births (2024 est.)
male: 8.4 deaths/1,000 live births
female: 6.8 deaths/1,000 live births
comparison ranking: total 150

Life expectancy at birth: *total population:* 79.7 years (2024 est.)
male: 77.4 years
female: 82.2 years
comparison ranking: total population 62

Total fertility rate: 1.97 children born/woman (2024 est.)
comparison ranking: 107

Gross reproduction rate: 0.96 (2024 est.)

ENVIRONMENT

Environmental issues: scarcity of potable water; inadequate solid waste management; pollution from construction, chemical runoff, and sewage

Climate: tropical marine climate, ameliorated by northeast trade winds, results in moderate temperatures; average rainfall of 150 cm/year; hurricane season stretches from July to November

GOVERNMENT

Country name: *conventional long form:* Country of Sint Maarten
conventional short form: Sint Maarten
local long form: Land Sint Maarten (Dutch)/Country of Sint Maarten (English)
local short form: Sint Maarten (Dutch and English)
former: Netherlands Antilles; Curacao and Dependencies
etymology: explorer Christopher COLUMBUS named the island in 1493 after Saint MARTIN of Tours because he visited on 11 November, the saint's feast day

Government type: parliamentary democracy under a constitutional monarchy

Dependency status: part of the Kingdom of the Netherlands; full autonomy in internal affairs granted in 2010; Dutch government responsible for defense and foreign affairs

Capital: *name:* Philipsburg
geographic coordinates: 18 1 N, 63 2 W
time difference: UTC-4 (1 hour ahead of Washington, DC, during Standard Time)
etymology: founded and named in 1763 by John PHILIPS, a Scottish captain in the Dutch navy

Administrative divisions: none (part of the Kingdom of the Netherlands)
note: Sint Maarten is one of four constituent countries of the Kingdom of the Netherlands; the other three are the Netherlands, Aruba, and Curacao

Legal system: based on Dutch civil law system with some English common law influence

Constitution: *history:* previous 1947, 1955; latest adopted 21 July 2010, entered into force 10 October 2010 (regulates governance of Sint Maarten but is subordinate to the Charter for the Kingdom of the Netherlands)
amendment process: proposals initiated by the Government or by Parliament; passage requires at least a two-thirds majority of the Parliament membership; passage of amendments relating to fundamental rights, authorities of the governor and of Parliament must include the "views" of the Kingdom of the Netherlands Government prior to ratification by Parliament

Citizenship: see the Netherlands

Suffrage: 18 years of age; universal

Executive branch: *chief of state:* King WILLEM-ALEXANDER of the Netherlands (since 30 April 2013); represented by Governor Ajamu G. BALY (since 10 October 2022)
head of government: Prime Minister Luc MERCELINA (since 3 May 2024)
cabinet: Cabinet nominated by the prime minister and appointed by the governor
election/appointment process: the monarch is hereditary; governor appointed by the monarch for a 6-year term; following legislative elections, the Parliament

usually elects the leader of the majority party as prime minister

Legislative branch: *legislature name:* Parliament of Sint Maarten
legislative structure: unicameral
number of seats: 15 (directly elected)
electoral system: proportional representation
scope of elections: full renewal
term in office: 4 years
most recent election date: 1/11/2024
parties elected and seats per party: NA (4); UPP (3); URSM (2); DP (2); PFP (2); NOW (2)
percentage of women in chamber: 46.7%
expected date of next election: 2028

Judicial branch: *highest court(s):* Joint Court of Justice of Aruba, Curacao, Sint Maarten, and of Bonaire, Sint Eustatius and Saba or "Joint Court of Justice" (consists of the presiding judge, other members, and their substitutes); final appeals heard by the Supreme Court in The Hague, Netherlands
judge selection and term of office: Joint Court judges appointed by the monarch serve for life
subordinate courts: Courts in First Instance

Political parties: Democratic Party or DP
National Alliance or NA
National Opportunity Wealth or NOW
Party for Progress or PFP
Sint Maarten Christian Party or SMCP
Unified Resilient St Maarten Movement or URSM
United People's Party or UPP
United Sint Maarten Party or US Party

Diplomatic representation in the US: none (represented by the Kingdom of the Netherlands)

Diplomatic representation from the US: *embassy:* the US does not have an embassy in Sint Maarten; the Consul General to Curacao is accredited to Sint Maarten

International organization participation: Caricom (observer), ILO, Interpol, UNESCO (associate), UPU, WMO

Independence: none (part of the Kingdom of the Netherlands)

National holiday: King's Day (birthday of King WILLEM-ALEXANDER), 27 April (1967)
note: observed on the ruling monarch's birthday; celebrated on 26 April if 27 April is a Sunday; local holiday is Sint Maarten's Day, 11 November (1985), and is celebrated on both halves of the island

Flag: *description:* two equal horizontal bands of red (top) and blue, with a white isosceles triangle based on the left side; the national coat of arms is in the center of the triangle, with an orangebordered blue shield that displays the white courthouse in Philipsburg, as well as yellow sage (the national flower) in the upper left and the silhouette of a Dutch-French friendship monument in the upper right; over the shield is a yellow rising sun and a brown pelican in flight; a yellow scroll below the shield has the motto SEMPER PROGREDIENS (Always Progressing)
note: the flag resembles Philippines' flag, but with the red and blue bands reversed; the three main colors are the same as the Dutch flag

National symbol(s): brown pelican, yellow sage (flower)

National color(s): red, white, blue

National anthem(s): *title:* "O Sweet Saint Martin's Land"
lyrics/music: Gerard KEMPS
history: the song, written in 1958, is used as a local anthem for the entire island (both French and Dutch sides)
title: "Het Wilhelmus" (The William)
lyrics/music: Philips VAN MARNIX van Sint Aldegonde (presumed)/unknown
history: adopted 1932

ECONOMY

Economic overview: high-income, tourism-based Dutch autonomous constituent economy; severe hurricane-and COVID-19-related economic recessions; multilateral trust fund helping offset economic downturn; no property taxation; re-exporter to Saint Martin

Real GDP (purchasing power parity): $1.986 billion (2024 est.)
$1.919 billion (2023 est.)
$1.849 billion (2022 est.)
note: data in 2021 dollars
comparison ranking: 198

Real GDP growth rate: 3.5% (2024 est.)
3.8% (2023 est.)
9.8% (2022 est.)
note: annual GDP % growth based on constant local currency
comparison ranking: 97

Real GDP per capita: $45,800 (2024 est.)
$44,900 (2023 est.)
$43,900 (2022 est.)
note: data in 2021 dollars
comparison ranking: 48

GDP (official exchange rate): $1.735 billion (2024 est.)
note: data in current dollars at official exchange rate

Inflation rate (consumer prices): 2.2% (2017 est.)
0.1% (2016 est.)
0.3% (2015 est.)
note: annual % change based on consumer prices
comparison ranking: 63

GDP - composition, by sector of origin: *industry:* 6% (2021 est.)
services: 89.3% (2021 est.)
note: figures may not total 100% due to non-allocated consumption not captured in sector-reported data
comparison rankings: industry 202; services 7

Agricultural products: sugar

Industries: tourism, light industry

Industrial production growth rate: 0.5% (2021 est.)
note: annual % change in industrial value added based on constant local currency
comparison ranking: 123

Remittances: 3% of GDP (2023 est.)
3.2% of GDP (2022 est.)
3.4% of GDP (2021 est.)
note: personal transfers and compensation between resident and non-resident individuals/households/entities

Current account balance: -$116.693 million (2023 est.)
-$56.984 million (2022 est.)
-$311.463 million (2021 est.)
note: balance of payments - net trade and primary/secondary income in current dollars
comparison ranking: 95

Exports: $1.504 billion (2023 est.)
$1.375 billion (2022 est.)
$790.938 million (2021 est.)
note: balance of payments - exports of goods and services in current dollars
comparison ranking: 174

Exports - partners: Antigua & Barbuda 28%, USA 16%, France 12%, Netherlands 8%, Morocco 7% (2023)
note: top five export partners based on percentage share of exports

Exports - commodities: scrap iron, ships, jewelry, flavored water, liquor (2023)
note: top five export commodities based on value in dollars

Imports: $1.489 billion (2023 est.)
$1.32 billion (2022 est.)
$1.003 billion (2021 est.)
note: balance of payments - imports of goods and services in current dollars
comparison ranking: 184

Imports - partners: USA 82%, Netherlands 7%, France 4%, Brazil 1%, Switzerland 1% (2023)
note: top five import partners based on percentage share of imports

Imports - commodities: jewelry, refined petroleum, ships, pearl products, diamonds (2023)
note: top five import commodities based on value in dollars

Exchange rates: Netherlands Antillean guilders (ANG) per US dollar -

Exchange rates: 1.79 (2024 est.)
1.79 (2023 est.)
1.79 (2022 est.)
1.79 (2021 est.)
1.79 (2020 est.)

ENERGY

Electricity access: *electrification - total population:* 100% (2022 est.)

COMMUNICATIONS

Telephones - mobile cellular: *total subscriptions:* 68,840 (2012 est.)
subscriptions per 100 inhabitants: 196 (2012 est.)
comparison ranking: total subscriptions 200

Internet country code: .sx

Internet users: *percent of population:* 89.5% (2022)

TRANSPORTATION

Airports: 1 (2025)
comparison ranking: 233

Ports: *total ports:* 2 (2024)
large: 0
medium: 0
small: 2
very small: 0
ports with oil terminals: 1
key ports: Coles Bay Oil Terminal, Philipsburg

MILITARY AND SECURITY

Military and security forces: no regular military forces; Police Force of Sint Maarten (KPSM) (2025)
note: the KPSM is supported by the Royal Netherlands Marechaussee (Gendarmerie), the Dutch Caribbean Police Force (Korps Politie Caribisch Nederland, KPCN), and the Dutch

Caribbean Coast Guard (DCCG or Kustwacht Caribisch Gebied (KWCARIB))

Military - note: defense is the responsibility of the Kingdom of the Netherlands

TRANSNATIONAL ISSUES

Trafficking in persons: *tier rating:* Tier 3 — Sint Maarten does not fully meet the minimum standards for the elimination of trafficking and is not making significant efforts to do so, therefore, Sint Maarten remained on Tier 3; for more details, go to: https://www.state.gov/reports/2025-trafficking-in-persons-report/sint-maarten/

SLOVAKIA

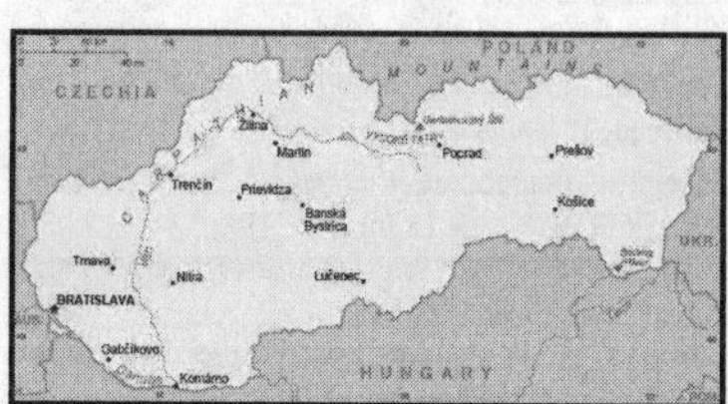

INTRODUCTION

Background: Slovakia traces its roots to the 9th century state of Great Moravia. The Slovaks then became part of the Hungarian Kingdom, where they remained for the next 1,000 years. After the formation of the dual Austro-Hungarian monarchy in 1867, language and education policies favoring the use of Hungarian (known as "Magyarization") led to a public backlash that boosted Slovak nationalism and strengthened Slovak cultural ties with the closely related Czechs, who fell administratively under the Austrian half of the empire. When the Austro-Hungarian Empire dissolved at the end of World War I, the Slovaks joined the Czechs to form Czechoslovakia. During the interwar period, Slovak nationalist leaders pushed for autonomy within Czechoslovakia, and in 1939, in the wake of Germany's annexation of the Sudetenland, the newly established Slovak Republic became a German client state for the remainder of World War II.

After World War II, Czechoslovakia was reconstituted and came under communist rule within Soviet-dominated Eastern Europe. In 1968, Warsaw Pact troops invaded and ended the efforts of Czechoslovakia's leaders to liberalize communist rule and create "socialism with a human face," ushering in a period of repression known as "normalization." The peaceful Velvet Revolution swept the Communist Party from power at the end of 1989 and inaugurated a return to democratic rule and a market economy. On 1 January 1993, Czechoslovakia underwent a nonviolent "velvet divorce" into its two national components, Slovakia and the Czech Republic. Slovakia joined both NATO and the EU in 2004 and the euro zone in 2009.

GEOGRAPHY

Location: Central Europe, south of Poland

Geographic coordinates: 48 40 N, 19 30 E

Map references: Europe

Area: *total:* 49,035 sq km
land: 48,105 sq km
water: 930 sq km
comparison ranking: total 130

Area - comparative: about 1.5 times the size of Maryland; about twice the size of New Hampshire

Land boundaries: *total:* 1,587 km
border countries (5): Austria 105 km; Czechia 241 km; Hungary 627 km; Poland 517 km; Ukraine 97 km

Coastline: 0 km (landlocked)

Maritime claims: none (landlocked)

Climate: temperate; cool summers; cold, cloudy, humid winters

Terrain: rugged mountains in the central and northern part and lowlands in the south

Elevation: *highest point:* Gerlachovsky Stit 2,655 m
lowest point: Bodrok River 94 m
mean elevation: 458 m

Natural resources: lignite, small amounts of iron ore, copper and manganese ore; salt; arable land

Land use: *agricultural land:* 38.8% (2022 est.)
arable land: 27.9% (2022 est.)
permanent crops: 0.4% (2022 est.)
permanent pasture: 10.6% (2022 est.)
forest: 40.1% (2022 est.)
other: 21.1% (2022 est.)

Irrigated land: 259 sq km (2022)

Major rivers (by length in km): Dunaj (Danube) (shared with Germany [s], Austria, Hungary, Croatia, Serbia, Bulgaria, Ukraine, Moldova, and Romania [m]) - 2,888 km
note – [s] after country name indicates river source; [m] after country name indicates river mouth

Major watersheds (area sq km): Atlantic Ocean drainage: *(Black Sea)* Danube (795,656 sq km)

Population distribution: a fairly even distribution throughout most of the country; slightly larger concentration in the west in proximity to the Czech border

Natural hazards: flooding

Geography - note: landlocked; most of the country is rugged and mountainous; the Tatra Mountains in the north are interspersed with many scenic lakes and valleys

PEOPLE AND SOCIETY

Population: *total:* 5,563,649 (2024 est.)
male: 2,684,747
female: 2,878,902
comparison rankings: total 119; male 121; female 117

Nationality: *noun:* Slovak(s)
adjective: Slovak

Ethnic groups: Slovak 83.8%, Hungarian 7.8%, Romani 1.2%, other 1.8% (includes Czech, Ruthenian, Ukrainian, Russian, German, Polish), unspecified 5.4% (2021 est.)
note: data represent population by nationality; Romani populations are usually underestimated in official statistics and may represent 7–11% of Slovakia's population

Languages: Slovak (official) 81.8%, Hungarian 8.5%, Roma 1.8%, other 2.2%, unspecified 5.7% (2021 est.)
major-language sample(s):
Svetova Kniha Faktov, nenahraditelny zdroj zakladnej informacie. (Slovak)

Religions: Roman Catholic 55.8%, Evangelical Church of the Augsburg Confession 5.3%, Greek Catholic 4%, Reformed Christian 1.6%, other 3%, none 23.8%, unspecified 6.5% (2021 est.)

Age structure: *0-14 years:* 15.3% (male 444,033/female 408,902)
15-64 years: 66.5% (male 1,834,359/female 1,867,158)
65 years and over: 18.1% (2024 est.) (male 406,355/female 602,842)

Dependency ratios: *total dependency ratio:* 50.3 (2024 est.)
youth dependency ratio: 23 (2024 est.)
elderly dependency ratio: 27.3 (2024 est.)
potential support ratio: 3.7 (2024 est.)

Median age: *total:* 42.8 years (2024 est.)
male: 41.3 years
female: 44.4 years
comparison ranking: total 39

Population growth rate: -0.08% (2024 est.)
comparison ranking: 202

Birth rate: 10 births/1,000 population (2024 est.)
comparison ranking: 187

Death rate: 11.2 deaths/1,000 population (2024 est.)
comparison ranking: 24

Net migration rate: 0.4 migrant(s)/1,000 population (2024 est.)
comparison ranking: 73

Population distribution: a fairly even distribution throughout most of the country; slightly larger concentration in the west in proximity to the Czech border

Urbanization: *urban population:* 54% of total population (2023)
rate of urbanization: 0.17% annual rate of change (2020-25 est.)

Major urban areas - population: 441,000 BRATISLAVA (capital) (2023)

Sex ratio: *at birth:* 1.07 male(s)/female
0-14 years: 1.09 male(s)/female
15-64 years: 0.98 male(s)/female
65 years and over: 0.67 male(s)/female
total population: 0.93 male(s)/female (2024 est.)

Mother's mean age at first birth: 27.2 years (2020 est.)

Maternal mortality ratio: 4 deaths/100,000 live births (2023 est.)
comparison ranking: 181

Infant mortality rate: *total:* 5.1 deaths/1,000 live births (2024 est.)

male: 5.7 deaths/1,000 live births
female: 4.5 deaths/1,000 live births
comparison ranking: total 174

Life expectancy at birth: *total population:* 77.2 years (2024 est.)
male: 73.7 years
female: 81 years
comparison ranking: total population 94

Total fertility rate: 1.6 children born/woman (2024 est.)
comparison ranking: 184

Gross reproduction rate: 0.77 (2024 est.)

Drinking water source: *improved: urban:* 99.6% of population (2022 est.)
rural: 100% of population (2022 est.)
total: 99.8% of population (2022 est.)
unimproved: urban: 0.4% of population (2022 est.)
rural: 0% of population (2022 est.)
total: 0.2% of population (2022 est.)

Health expenditure: 7.8% of GDP (2021)
14.6% of national budget (2022 est.)

Physician density: 3.7 physicians/1,000 population (2022)

Hospital bed density: 5.7 beds/1,000 population (2020 est.)

Sanitation facility access improved: *urban:* 99.9% of population (2022 est.)
rural: 100% of population (2022 est.)
total: 100% of population (2022 est.)
unimproved: urban: 0.1% of population (2022 est.)
rural: 0% of population (2022 est.)
total: 0% of population (2022 est.)

Obesity - adult prevalence rate: 20.5% (2016)
comparison ranking: 98

Alcohol consumption per capita: *total:* 10.3 liters of pure alcohol (2019 est.)
beer: 4.14 liters of pure alcohol (2019 est.)
wine: 2.01 liters of pure alcohol (2019 est.)
spirits: 4.14 liters of pure alcohol (2019 est.)
other alcohols: 0 liters of pure alcohol (2019 est.)
comparison ranking: total 21

Tobacco use: *total:* 30.3% (2025 est.)
male: 34.5% (2025 est.)
female: 26.3% (2025 est.)
comparison ranking: total 20

Currently married women (ages 15-49): 47.9% (2023 est.)

Education expenditure: 4.5% of GDP (2022 est.)
10.7% national budget (2022 est.)
comparison ranking: Education expenditure (% GDP) 82

School life expectancy (primary to tertiary education): *total:* 15 years (2023 est.)
male: 15 years (2023 est.)
female: 16 years (2023 est.)

ENVIRONMENT

Environmental issues: air pollution and acid rain; land erosion from agricultural and mining practices; water pollution

International environmental agreements: *party to:* Air Pollution, Air Pollution-Heavy Metals, Air Pollution-Multi-effect Protocol, Air Pollution-Nitrogen Oxides, Air Pollution-Persistent Organic Pollutants, Air Pollution-Sulphur 85, Air Pollution-Sulphur 94, Air Pollution-Volatile Organic Compounds, Antarctic Treaty, Biodiversity, Climate Change, Climate Change-Kyoto Protocol, Climate Change-Paris Agreement, Comprehensive Nuclear Test Ban, Desertification, Endangered Species, Environmental Modification, Hazardous Wastes, Law of the Sea, Nuclear Test Ban, Ozone Layer Protection, Ship Pollution, Tropical Timber 2006, Wetlands, Whaling
signed, but not ratified: Antarctic-Environmental Protection

Climate: temperate; cool summers; cold, cloudy, humid winters

Urbanization: *urban population:* 54% of total population (2023)
rate of urbanization: 0.17% annual rate of change (2020-25 est.)

Carbon dioxide emissions: 30.087 million metric tonnes of CO2 (2023 est.)
from coal and metallurgical coke: 9.607 million metric tonnes of CO2 (2023 est.)
from petroleum and other liquids: 12.112 million metric tonnes of CO2 (2023 est.)
from consumed natural gas: 8.368 million metric tonnes of CO2 (2023 est.)
comparison ranking: total emissions 73

Particulate matter emissions: 16.6 micrograms per cubic meter (2019 est.)

Waste and recycling: *municipal solid waste generated annually:* 2.296 million tons (2024 est.)
percent of municipal solid waste recycled: 13.2% (2022 est.)

Total water withdrawal: *municipal:* 306.21 million cubic meters (2022)
industrial: 224.562 million cubic meters (2022)
agricultural: 32.851 million cubic meters (2022)

Total renewable water resources: 50.1 billion cubic meters (2022 est.)

Geoparks: *total global geoparks and regional networks:* 1
global geoparks and regional networks: Novohrad-Nógrád (includes Hungary) (2023)

GOVERNMENT

Country name: *conventional long form:* Slovak Republic
conventional short form: Slovakia
local long form: Slovenska republika
local short form: Slovensko
etymology: the country takes its name from the local Slav ethnic group; the origin of the group's name is unclear, although early forms were used in Medieval Latin (Sclavus) and Byzantine Greek (Sklabos)

Government type: parliamentary republic

Capital: *name:* Bratislava
geographic coordinates: 48 09 N, 17 07 E
time difference: UTC+1 (6 hours ahead of Washington, DC, during Standard Time)
daylight saving time: +1hr, begins last Sunday in March; ends last Sunday in October
etymology: the meaning is unclear but has medieval Slavic origins; the name was adopted in 1919 after Czechoslovakia gained its independence, replacing the name Prešporok

Administrative divisions: 8 regions (*kraje*, singular - *kraj*); Banska Bystrica, Bratislava, Kosice, Nitra, Presov, Trencin, Trnava, Zilina

Legal system: civil law system based on Austro-Hungarian codes

Constitution: *history:* several previous (pre-independence); latest passed by the National Council 1 September 1992, signed 3 September 1992, effective 1 October 1992
amendment process: proposed by the National Council; passage requires at least three-fifths majority vote of Council members

International law organization participation: accepts compulsory ICJ jurisdiction with reservations; accepts ICCt jurisdiction

Citizenship: *citizenship by birth:* no
citizenship by descent only: at least one parent must be a citizen of Slovakia
dual citizenship recognized: no
residency requirement for naturalization: 5 years

Suffrage: 18 years of age; universal

Executive branch: *chief of state:* President Peter PELLEGRINI (since 15 June 2024)
head of government: Prime Minister Robert FICO (since 25 October 2023)
cabinet: Cabinet appointed by the president on the recommendation of the prime minister
election/appointment process: president directly elected by absolute-majority popular vote in 2 rounds, if needed, for a 5-year term (eligible for a second term); following National Council elections, the president designates a prime minister candidate, usually the leader of the party or coalition that wins the most votes, who must win a vote of confidence in the National Council
most recent election date: 23 March 2024, with a runoff on 6 April 2024
election results: *2024:* Peter PELLEGRINI elected president in the second round; percent of vote in second round Peter PELLEGRINI 53.1%; Ivan KORCOK 46.9%; percent of vote in first round - Ivan KORCOK (independent) 42.5%; Peter PELLEGRINI (Hlas-SD) 37%; Stefan HARABIN (independent) 11.7%, other 8.8%;
2019: Zuzana CAPUTOVA elected president in second round; percent of vote - Zuzana CAPUTOVA (PS) 58.4%, Maros SEFCOVIC (independent) 41.6%
expected date of next election: 2029

Legislative branch: *legislature name:* National Council (Narodna rada Slovenskej republiky)
legislative structure: unicameral
chamber name: National Council (Národná rada)
number of seats: 150 (all directly elected)
electoral system: proportional representation
scope of elections: full renewal
term in office: 4 years
most recent election date: 9/30/2023
parties elected and seats per party: Smer - Social Democracy (Smer-SD) (42); Progressive Slovakia (PS) (32); Hlas ("Voice") - SD (27); Coalition OĽaNO and Friends, 'For the People' and 'Christian Union' (16); Christian Democratic Movement (KDH) (12); Freedom and Solidarity (SaS) (11); Slovak National Party (SNS) (10)
percentage of women in chamber: 23.3%
expected date of next election: September 2027

Judicial branch: *highest court(s):* Supreme Court of the Slovak Republic (consists of the court president, vice president, and approximately 80 judges organized into criminal, civil, commercial, and administrative divisions with 3- and 5-judge panels); Constitutional Court of the Slovak Republic (consists of 13 judges organized into 3-judge panels)
judge selection and term of office: Supreme Court judge candidates nominated by the Judicial Council of the Slovak Republic, an 18-member self-governing body that includes the Supreme Court chief justice and

presidential, governmental, parliamentary, and judiciary appointees; judges appointed by the president serve for life, subject to removal by the president at age 65; Constitutional Court judges nominated by the National Council of the Republic and appointed by the president; judges serve 12-year terms
subordinate courts: regional and district civil courts; Special Criminal Court; Higher Military Court; military district courts; Court of Audit

Political parties: Alliance-Szovetseg or A-S
Christian Union or KÚ
Civic Conservative Party or OKS
Democrats
Direction-Social Democracy or Smer-SSD
For the People or Za Ludi
Freedom and Solidarity or SaS
Life National Party or Život–NS (formerly Christian Democracy - Life and Prosperity - Alliance for Slovkia)
New Majority or NOVA
Ordinary People and Independent Personalities - New Majority or OLaNO-NOVA
People's Party Our Slovakia or LSNS
Progressive Slovakia or PS
Republic
Slovak National Party or SNS
Voice - Social Democracy or Hlas-SD
We Are Family or Sme-Rodina (formerly Party of Citizens of Slovakia)

Diplomatic representation in the US: *chief of mission:* Ambassador Radovan JAVORČÍK (since 18 January 2021)
chancery: 3523 International Court NW, Washington, DC 20008
telephone: [1] (202) 237-1054
FAX: [1] (202) 237-6438
email address and website: emb.washington@mzv.sk
https://www.mzv.sk/web/washington-en
consulate(s) general: New York

Diplomatic representation from the US: *chief of mission:* Ambassador Gautam A. RANA (since 28 September 2022)
embassy: P.O. Box 309, 814 99 Bratislava
mailing address: 5840 Bratislava Place, Washington DC 20521-5840
telephone: [421] (2) 5443-3338
FAX: [421] (2) 5441-8861
email address and website: consulbratislava@state.gov
https://sk.usembassy.gov/

International organization participation: Australia Group, BIS, BSEC (observer), CBSS (observer), CD, CE, CEI, CERN, EAPC, EBRD, ECB, EIB, EMU, EU, FAO, IAEA, IBRD, ICAO, ICC (national committees), ICRM, IDA, IEA, IFC, IFRCS, ILO, IMF, IMO, IMSO, Interpol, IOC, IOM, IPU, ISO, ITU, ITUC (NGOs), MIGA, NATO, NEA, NSG, OAS (observer), OECD, OIF (observer), OPCW, OSCE, PCA, Schengen Convention, SELEC (observer), UN, UNCTAD, UNESCO, UNFICYP, UNIDO, UNTSO, UNWTO, UPU, Wassenaar Arrangement, WCO, WFTU (NGOs), WHO, WIPO, WMO, WTO, ZC

Independence: 1 January 1993 (Czechoslovakia split into the Czech Republic and Slovakia)

National holiday: Constitution Day, 1 September (1992)

Flag: *description:* three equal horizontal bands of white (top), blue, and red; the national coat of arms (a red shield bordered in white, with a white double-barred cross of St. Cyril and St. Methodius on top of three blue hills) is centered over the bands but offset to the left
meaning: white, blue, and red are the pan-Slav colors
note: the pan-Slav colors were inspired by Russia's flag

National symbol(s): double-barred cross (Cross of St. Cyril and St. Methodius) over three peaks

National color(s): white, blue, red

National anthem(s): *title:* "Nad Tatrou sa blyska" (Storm Over the Tatras)
lyrics/music: Janko MATUSKA/traditional
history: adopted 1993; music based on an 1843 Slovak folk song "Kopala studienku" (She Was Digging a Well)

National heritage: *total World Heritage Sites:* 8 (6 cultural, 2 natural)
selected World Heritage Site locales: Historic Town of Banská Štiavnica (c); Levoča, Spišský Hrad, and the Associated Cultural Monuments (c); Vlkolínec (c); Caves of Aggtelek Karst and Slovak Karst (n); Bardejov Town (c); Ancient and Primeval Beech Forests of the Carpathians (n); Wooden Churches of the Slovak Carpathians (c); Frontiers of the Roman Empire - The Danube Limes (Western Segment) (c)

ECONOMY

Economic overview: high-income EU and eurozone economy; manufacturing and exports led by automotive sector; growth supported by private consumption and public investment from EU funds, tempered by trade risks;
increased taxes and withdrawal of energy subsidies contributing to rising but manageable inflation; strong labor demand and influx of foreign labor offsets aging workforce

Real GDP (purchasing power parity): $218.762 billion (2024 est.)
$214.343 billion (2023 est.)
$209.794 billion (2022 est.)
note: data in 2021 dollars
comparison ranking: 75

Real GDP growth rate: 2.1% (2024 est.)
2.2% (2023 est.)
0.4% (2022 est.)
note: annual GDP % growth based on constant local currency
comparison ranking: 147

Real GDP per capita: $40,300 (2024 est.)
$39,500 (2023 est.)
$38,600 (2022 est.)
note: data in 2021 dollars
comparison ranking: 60

GDP (official exchange rate): $141.776 billion (2024 est.)
note: data in current dollars at official exchange rate

Inflation rate (consumer prices): 2.8% (2024 est.)
10.5% (2023 est.)
12.8% (2022 est.)
note: annual % change based on consumer prices
comparison ranking: 80

GDP - composition, by sector of origin: *agriculture:* 2% (2024 est.)
industry: 28.5% (2024 est.)
services: 60% (2024 est.)
note: figures may not total 100% due to non-allocated consumption not captured in sector-reported data
comparison rankings: agriculture 152; industry 68; services 87

GDP - composition, by end use: *household consumption:* 58.4% (2023 est.)
government consumption: 20% (2023 est.)
investment in fixed capital: 21.1% (2023 est.)
investment in inventories: -1.3% (2023 est.)
exports of goods and services: 91.3% (2023 est.)
imports of goods and services: -89.8% (2023 est.)
note: figures may not total 100% due to rounding or gaps in data collection

Agricultural products: wheat, sugar beets, maize, milk, barley, rapeseed, sunflower seeds, potatoes, soybeans, pork (2023)
note: top ten agricultural products based on tonnage

Industries: automobiles; metal and metal products; electricity, gas, coke, oil, nuclear fuel; chemicals, synthetic fibers, wood and paper products; machinery; earthenware and ceramics; textiles; electrical and optical apparatus; rubber products; food and beverages; pharmaceutical

Industrial production growth rate: 0.3% (2024 est.)
note: annual % change in industrial value added based on constant local currency
comparison ranking: 127

Labor force: 2.779 million (2024 est.)
note: number of people ages 15 or older who are employed or seeking work
comparison ranking: 117

Unemployment rate: 5.3% (2024 est.)
5.9% (2023 est.)
6.2% (2022 est.)
note: % of labor force seeking employment
comparison ranking: 95

Youth unemployment rate (ages 15-24): *total:* 18.2% (2024 est.)
male: 20.1% (2024 est.)
female: 15% (2024 est.)
note: % of labor force ages 15-24 seeking employment
comparison ranking: total 62

Population below poverty line: 13.7% (2021 est.)
note: % of population with income below national poverty line

Gini Index coefficient - distribution of family income: 24.1 (2022 est.)
note: index (0-100) of income distribution; higher values represent greater inequality
comparison ranking: 149

Average household expenditures: *on food:* 19.4% of household expenditures (2023 est.)
on alcohol and tobacco: 4.9% of household expenditures (2023 est.)

Household income or consumption by percentage share: *lowest 10%:* 2.8% (2022 est.)
highest 10%: 18.2% (2022 est.)
note: % share of income accruing to lowest and highest 10% of population

Remittances: 1.9% of GDP (2024 est.)
2% of GDP (2023 est.)
2% of GDP (2022 est.)
note: personal transfers and compensation between resident and non-resident individuals/households/entities

Budget: *revenues:* $43.882 billion (2022 est.)
expenditures: $46.056 billion (2022 est.)
note: central government revenues (excluding grants) and expenses converted to US dollars at average official exchange rate for year indicated

Public debt: 64.3% of GDP (2022 est.)
note: central government debt as a % of GDP
comparison ranking: 66

Taxes and other revenues: 19.4% (of GDP) (2022 est.)
note: central government tax revenue as a % of GDP
comparison ranking: 56

Current account balance: -$3.895 billion (2024 est.)
-$1.169 billion (2023 est.)
-$11.126 billion (2022 est.)
note: balance of payments - net trade and primary/secondary income in current dollars
comparison ranking: 166

Exports: $120.355 billion (2024 est.)
$122.04 billion (2023 est.)
$114.519 billion (2022 est.)
note: balance of payments - exports of goods and services in current dollars
comparison ranking: 44

Exports - partners: Germany 20%, Czechia 10%, Hungary 7%, USA 6%, Poland 6% (2023)
note: top five export partners based on percentage share of exports

Exports - commodities: cars, vehicle parts/accessories, video displays, broadcasting equipment, refined petroleum (2023)
note: top five export commodities based on value in dollars

Imports: $120.29 billion (2024 est.)
$119.739 billion (2023 est.)
$121.473 billion (2022 est.)
note: balance of payments - imports of goods and services in current dollars
comparison ranking: 44

Imports - partners: Germany 16%, Czechia 14%, Poland 8%, China 7%, Hungary 6% (2023)
note: top five import partners based on percentage share of imports

Imports - commodities: vehicle parts/accessories, broadcasting equipment, cars, plastic products, insulated wire (2023)
note: top five import commodities based on value in dollars

Reserves of foreign exchange and gold: $14.452 billion (2024 est.)
$11.288 billion (2023 est.)
$10.28 billion (2022 est.)
note: holdings of gold (year-end prices)/foreign exchange/special drawing rights in current dollars
comparison ranking: 69

Exchange rates: euros (EUR) per US dollar -

Exchange rates: 0.924 (2024 est.)
0.925 (2023 est.)
0.95 (2022 est.)
0.845 (2021 est.)
0.876 (2020 est.)

ENERGY

Electricity access: *electrification - total population:* 100% (2022 est.)

Electricity: *installed generating capacity:* 8.138 million kW (2023 est.)
consumption: 24.18 billion kWh (2023 est.)
exports: 14.078 billion kWh (2023 est.)
imports: 10.671 billion kWh (2023 est.)
transmission/distribution losses: 1.233 billion kWh (2023 est.)
comparison rankings: installed generating capacity 73; consumption 70; exports 18; imports 24; transmission/distribution losses 110

Electricity generation sources: *fossil fuels:* 14.4% of total installed capacity (2023 est.)
nuclear: 63.7% of total installed capacity (2023 est.)
solar: 2.1% of total installed capacity (2023 est.)
hydroelectricity: 13.9% of total installed capacity (2023 est.)
biomass and waste: 5.9% of total installed capacity (2023 est.)

Nuclear energy: Number of operational nuclear reactors: 5 (2025)

Number of nuclear reactors under construction: 1 (2025)

Net capacity of operational nuclear reactors: 2.3GW (2025 est.)

Percent of total electricity production: 61.3% (2023 est.)

Number of nuclear reactors permanently shut down: 3 (2025)

Coal: *production:* 2.315 million metric tons (2023 est.)
consumption: 6.066 million metric tons (2023 est.)
exports: 13,000 metric tons (2023 est.)
imports: 3.658 million metric tons (2023 est.)
proven reserves: 19 million metric tons (2023 est.)

Petroleum: *total petroleum production:* 7,000 bbl/day (2023 est.)
refined petroleum consumption: 90,000 bbl/day (2024 est.)
crude oil estimated reserves: 9 million barrels (2021 est.)

Natural gas: *production:* 46.585 million cubic meters (2023 est.)
consumption: 4.277 billion cubic meters (2023 est.)
imports: 4.56 billion cubic meters (2023 est.)
proven reserves: 14.158 billion cubic meters (2021 est.)

Energy consumption per capita: 127.582 million Btu/person (2023 est.)
comparison ranking: 30

COMMUNICATIONS

Telephones - fixed lines: *total subscriptions:* 505,000 (2023 est.)
subscriptions per 100 inhabitants: 9 (2023 est.)
comparison ranking: total subscriptions 92

Telephones - mobile cellular: *total subscriptions:* 7.63 million (2023 est.)
subscriptions per 100 inhabitants: 132 (2022 est.)
comparison ranking: total subscriptions 107

Broadcast media: state-owned public broadcaster, Radio and Television of Slovakia (RTVS), has 2 national TV stations; roughly 50 privately owned national, regional, and local TV stations; about 40% of households connected to multi-channel cable or satellite TV; multiple RTVS national and regional radio networks; 32 privately owned radio stations

Internet country code: .sk

Internet users: *percent of population:* 90% (2024 est.)

Broadband - fixed subscriptions: *total:* 1.83 million (2023 est.)
subscriptions per 100 inhabitants: 33 (2023 est.)
comparison ranking: total 64

TRANSPORTATION

Civil aircraft registration country code prefix: OM

Airports: 116 (2025)
comparison ranking: 47

Heliports: 2 (2025)
comparison ranking: 131

Railways: *total:* 3,627 km (2020) 1,585 km electrified

MILITARY AND SECURITY

Military and security forces: Armed Forces of the Slovak Republic (Ozbrojene Sily Slovenskej Republiky): Ground Forces (Slovenské Pozemné Sily), Air Forces (Slovenské Vzdušné Sily), Special Operations Forces (Sily Pre Speciálne Operácie)

Ministry of Interior: Slovak Police Force (SPF or Policajný Zbor) (2025)
note: the SPF has sole responsibility for internal and border security

Military expenditures: 2% of GDP (2025 est.)
2% of GDP (2024 est.)
1.8% of GDP (2023 est.)
1.8% of GDP (2022 est.)
1.7% of GDP (2021 est.)

Military and security service personnel strengths: approximately 17,000 active-duty military personnel (2025)

Military equipment inventories and acquisitions: the military's inventory consists mostly of Soviet-era platforms; in recent years it has imported limited quantities of more modern, NATO-compatible equipment, particularly from Italy and the US (2024)

Military service age and obligation: 18-30 years of age for voluntary military service for men and women; conscription in peacetime suspended in 2004 (2023)
note: as of 2021, women made up nearly 13% of the military's full-time personnel

Military deployments: 240 Cyprus (UNFICYP); up to 150 Latvia (NATO) (2024)

Military - note: the Slovak military is responsible for external defense and fulfilling Slovakia's commitments to European and international security; Slovakia has been a member of both the EU and NATO since 2004; a key focus of the Slovak military is fulfilling the country's security responsibilities to NATO, including modernizing and acquiring NATO-compatible equipment, participating in training exercises, and providing forces for security missions such as NATO's Enhanced Forward Presence in the Baltic States; since 2022, Slovakia has hosted a multinational NATO ground force battlegroup as part of the NATO effort to boost the defenses of Eastern Europe since the Russian invasion of Ukraine; Slovakia also contributes to EU and UN peacekeeping missions
the Slovak Air Force has only a handful of fighter aircraft and is assisted by NATO's air policing mission over Slovakia, which includes fighter aircraft from Czechia and Poland; in 2022, Slovakia signed a defense agreement with the US that allows the US to use two Slovak military air bases (2025)

TRANSNATIONAL ISSUES

Refugees and internally displaced persons: *refugees:* 144,349 (2024 est.)
stateless persons: 65 (2024 est.)

SLOVENIA

INTRODUCTION

Background: The Slovene lands were part of the Austro-Hungarian Empire until the latter's dissolution at the end of World War I. In 1918, Slovenia became part of the Kingdom of Serbs, Croats, and Slovenes, which was renamed Yugoslavia in 1929. After World War II, Slovenia joined Bosnia and Herzegovina, Croatia, Macedonia, Montenegro, and Serbia as one of the constituent republics in the new Socialist Federal Republic of Yugoslavia (SFRY). In 1990, Slovenia held its first multiparty elections, as well as a referendum on independence. Serbia responded with an economic blockade and military action, but after a short 10-day war, Slovenia declared independence in 1991. Slovenia acceded to both NATO and the EU in the spring of 2004; it joined the euro zone and the Schengen Area in 2007.

GEOGRAPHY

Location: south Central Europe, Julian Alps between Austria and Croatia

Geographic coordinates: 46 07 N, 14 49 E

Map references: Europe

Area: *total:* 20,273 sq km
land: 20,151 sq km
water: 122 sq km
comparison ranking: total 154

Area - comparative: slightly smaller than New Jersey

Land boundaries: *total:* 1,211 km
border countries (4): Austria 299 km; Croatia 600 km; Hungary 94 km; Italy 218 km

Coastline: 46.6 km

Maritime claims: *territorial sea:* 12 nm

Climate: Mediterranean climate on the coast, continental climate with mild to hot summers and cold winters in the plateaus and valleys to the east

Terrain: a short southwestern coastal strip of Karst topography on the Adriatic; an alpine mountain region lies adjacent to Italy and Austria in the north; mixed mountains and valleys with numerous rivers to the east

Elevation: *highest point:* Triglav 2,864 m
lowest point: Adriatic Sea 0 m
mean elevation: 492 m

Natural resources: lignite, lead, zinc, building stone, hydropower, forests

Land use: *agricultural land:* 30.3% (2022 est.)
arable land: 8.9% (2022 est.)
permanent crops: 2.7% (2022 est.)
permanent pasture: 18.8% (2022 est.)
forest: 61.3% (2022 est.)
other: 8.4% (2022 est.)

Irrigated land: 50 sq km (2022)

Major watersheds (area sq km): Atlantic Ocean drainage: *(Black Sea)* Danube (795,656 sq km)

Population distribution: a fairly even distribution throughout most of the country, with urban areas attracting larger and denser populations; pockets in the mountainous northwest are less dense

Natural hazards: flooding; earthquakes

Geography - note: despite its small size, this eastern Alpine country controls some of Europe's major transit routes

PEOPLE AND SOCIETY

Population: *total:* 2,097,893 (2024 est.)
male: 1,051,044
female: 1,046,849
comparison rankings: total 151; male 150; female 150

Nationality: *noun:* Slovene(s)
adjective: Slovenian

Ethnic groups: Slovene 83.1%, Serb 2%, Croat 1.8%, Bosniak 1.1%, other or unspecified 12% (2002 est.)

Languages: Slovene (official) 87.7%, Croatian 2.8%, Serbo-Croatian 1.8%, Bosnian 1.6%, Serbian 1.6%, Hungarian 0.4% (official, only in municipalities where Hungarian nationals reside), Italian 0.2% (official, only in municipalities where Italian nationals reside), other or unspecified 3.9% (2002 est.)
major-language sample(s):
Svetovni informativni zvezek - neobhoden vir osnovnih informacij. (Slovene)

Religions: Catholic 69%, Orthodox 4%, Muslim 3%, Christian 1%, other 3%, atheist 14%, non-believer/agnostic 4%, refused to answer 2% (2019 est.)

Age structure: *0-14 years:* 14.3% (male 153,852/female 146,628)
15-64 years: 62.5% (male 683,573/female 627,788)
65 years and over: 23.2% (2024 est.) (male 213,619/female 272,433)

Dependency ratios: *total dependency ratio:* 58.5 (2024 est.)
youth dependency ratio: 22.8 (2024 est.)
elderly dependency ratio: 35.7 (2024 est.)
potential support ratio: 2.8 (2024 est.)

Median age: *total:* 46.3 years (2024 est.)
male: 45 years
female: 47.9 years
comparison ranking: total 12

Population growth rate: -0.1% (2024 est.)
comparison ranking: 203

Birth rate: 8 births/1,000 population (2024 est.)
comparison ranking: 215

Death rate: 10.5 deaths/1,000 population (2024 est.)
comparison ranking: 29

Net migration rate: 1.5 migrant(s)/1,000 population (2024 est.)
comparison ranking: 58

Population distribution: a fairly even distribution throughout most of the country, with urban areas attracting larger and denser populations; pockets in the mountainous northwest are less dense

Urbanization: *urban population:* 56.1% of total population (2023)
rate of urbanization: 0.54% annual rate of change (2020-25 est.)

Major urban areas - population: 286,000 LJUBLJANA (capital) (2018)

Sex ratio: *at birth:* 1.04 male(s)/female
0-14 years: 1.05 male(s)/female
15-64 years: 1.09 male(s)/female
65 years and over: 0.78 male(s)/female
total population: 1 male(s)/female (2024 est.)

Mother's mean age at first birth: 29 years (2020 est.)

Maternal mortality ratio: 3 deaths/100,000 live births (2023 est.)
comparison ranking: 190

Infant mortality rate: *total:* 1.5 deaths/1,000 live births (2024 est.)
male: 1.6 deaths/1,000 live births
female: 1.4 deaths/1,000 live births
comparison ranking: total 227

Life expectancy at birth: *total population:* 82.2 years (2024 est.)
male: 79.4 years
female: 85.2 years
comparison ranking: total population 32

Total fertility rate: 1.6 children born/woman (2024 est.)
comparison ranking: 185

Gross reproduction rate: 0.79 (2024 est.)

Drinking water source: *improved:* total: 99.5% of population (2022 est.)
unimproved: total: 0.5% of population (2022 est.)

Health expenditure: 8.8% of GDP (2022)
15% of national budget (2022 est.)

Physician density: 3.37 physicians/1,000 population (2022)

Hospital bed density: 4.2 beds/1,000 population (2020 est.)

Sanitation facility access: *improved:* total: 99.2% of population (2022 est.)
unimproved: total: 0.8% of population (2022 est.)

Obesity - adult prevalence rate: 20.2% (2016)
comparison ranking: 104

Alcohol consumption per capita: *total:* 11.05 liters of pure alcohol (2019 est.)
beer: 4.54 liters of pure alcohol (2019 est.)
wine: 5.26 liters of pure alcohol (2019 est.)
spirits: 1.26 liters of pure alcohol (2019 est.)
other alcohols: 0 liters of pure alcohol (2019 est.)
comparison ranking: total 10

Tobacco use: *total:* 17.3% (2025 est.)
male: 19.3% (2025 est.)
female: 15.3% (2025 est.)
comparison ranking: total 90

Currently married women (ages 15-49): 46.4% (2023 est.)

Education expenditure: 5.7% of GDP (2022 est.)
12% national budget (2022 est.)
comparison ranking: Education expenditure (% GDP) 35

School life expectancy (primary to tertiary education): *total:* 17 years (2023 est.)
male: 17 years (2023 est.)
female: 18 years (2023 est.)

ENVIRONMENT

Environmental issues: air pollution from road traffic, domestic heating (wood burning), power generation, and industry; water pollution; biodiversity protection

International environmental agreements: *party to:* Air Pollution, Air Pollution-Heavy Metals, Air Pollution-Multi-effect Protocol, Air Pollution-Nitrogen Oxides, Air Pollution-Persistent Organic Pollutants, Air Pollution-Sulphur 94, Antarctic Treaty, Biodiversity, Climate Change, Climate Change-Kyoto Protocol, Climate Change-Paris Agreement, Comprehensive Nuclear Test Ban, Desertification, Endangered Species, Environmental Modification, Hazardous Wastes, Law of the Sea, Marine Dumping-London Convention, Marine Dumping-London Protocol, Nuclear Test Ban, Ozone Layer Protection, Ship Pollution, Tropical Timber 2006, Wetlands, Whaling
signed, but not ratified: none of the selected agreements

Climate: Mediterranean climate on the coast, continental climate with mild to hot summers and cold winters in the plateaus and valleys to the east

Urbanization: *urban population:* 56.1% of total population (2023)
rate of urbanization: 0.54% annual rate of change (2020-25 est.)

Carbon dioxide emissions: 10.772 million metric tonnes of CO2 (2023 est.)
from coal and metallurgical coke: 2.706 million metric tonnes of CO2 (2023 est.)
from petroleum and other liquids: 6.521 million metric tonnes of CO2 (2023 est.)
from consumed natural gas: 1.545 million metric tonnes of CO2 (2023 est.)
comparison ranking: total emissions 105

Particulate matter emissions: 14.1 micrograms per cubic meter (2019 est.)

Methane emissions: *energy:* 8.5 kt (2022-2024 est.)
agriculture: 46.5 kt (2019-2021 est.)
waste: 15.6 kt (2019-2021 est.)
other: 1.9 kt (2019-2021 est.)

Waste and recycling: *municipal solid waste generated annually:* 1.052 million tons (2024 est.)
percent of municipal solid waste recycled: 24.8% (2022 est.)

Total water withdrawal: *municipal:* 179 million cubic meters (2022)
industrial: 645 million cubic meters (2022)
agricultural: 3.4 million cubic meters (2022)

Total renewable water resources: 31.87 billion cubic meters (2022 est.)

Geoparks: *total global geoparks and regional networks:* 2
global geoparks and regional networks: Idrija; Karawanken / Karavanke (includes Austria) (2023)

GOVERNMENT

Country name: *conventional long form:* Republic of Slovenia
conventional short form: Slovenia
local long form: Republika Slovenija
local short form: Slovenija
former: People's Republic of Slovenia, Socialist Republic of Slovenia
etymology: the country's name means "Land of the Slavs" in Slovene; the origin of the Slav name is unclear, although early forms were used in Medieval Latin (Sclavus) and Byzantine Greek (Sklabos)

Government type: parliamentary republic

Capital: *name:* Ljubljana
geographic coordinates: 46 03 N, 14 31 E
time difference: UTC+1 (6 hours ahead of Washington, DC, during Standard Time)
daylight saving time: +1hr, begins last Sunday in March; ends last Sunday in October
etymology: by tradition, the name is related to the Slovene word *ljubljena*, meaning "beloved," but the origin is probably pre-Slavic and remains obscure

Administrative divisions: 200 municipalities (*obcine*, singular - *obcina*) and 12 urban municipalities (*mestne obcine*, singular - *mestna obcina*)
municipalities: Ajdovscina, Ankaran, Apace, Beltinci, Benedikt, Bistrica ob Sotli, Bled, Bloke, Bohinj, Borovnica, Bovec, Braslovce, Brda, Brezice, Brezovica, Cankova, Cerklje na Gorenjskem, Cerknica, Cerkno, Cerkvenjak, Cirkulane, Crensovci, Crna na Koroskem, Crnomelj, Destrnik, Divaca, Dobje, Dobrepolje, Dobrna, Dobrova-Polhov Gradec, Dobrovnik/Dobronak, Dolenjske Toplice, Dol pri Ljubljani, Domzale, Dornava, Dravograd, Duplek, Gorenja Vas-Poljane, Gorisnica, Gorje, Gornja Radgona, Gornji Grad, Gornji Petrovci, Grad, Grosuplje, Hajdina, Hoce-Slivnica, Hodos, Horjul, Hrastnik, Hrpelje-Kozina, Idrija, Ig, Ilirska Bistrica, Ivancna Gorica, Izola/Isola, Jesenice, Jezersko, Jursinci, Kamnik, Kanal ob Soci, Kidricevo, Kobarid, Kobilje, Kocevje, Komen, Komenda, Kosanjevica na Krki, Kostel, Kozje, Kranjska Gora, Krizevci, Kungota, Kuzma, Lasko, Lenart, Lendava/Lendva, Litija, Ljubno, Ljutomer, Log-Dragomer, Logatec, Loska Dolina, Loski Potok, Lovrenc na Pohorju, Luce, Lukovica, Majsperk, Makole, Markovci, Medvode, Menges, Metlika, Mezica, Miklavz na Dravskem Polju, Miren-Kostanjevica, Mirna, Mirna Pec, Mislinja, Mokronog-Trebelno, Moravce, Moravske Toplice, Mozirje, Muta, Naklo, Nazarje, Odranci, Oplotnica, Ormoz, Osilnica, Pesnica, Piran/Pirano, Pivka, Podcetrtek, Podlehnik, Podvelka, Poljcane, Polzela, Postojna, Prebold, Preddvor, Prevalje, Puconci, Race-Fram, Radece, Radenci, Radlje ob Dravi, Radovljica, Ravne na Koroskem, Razkrizje, Recica ob Savinji, Rence-Vogrsko, Ribnica, Ribnica na Pohorju, Rogaska Slatina, Rogasovci, Rogatec, Ruse, Salovci, Selnica ob Dravi, Semic, Sempeter-Vrtojba, Sencur, Sentilj, Sentjernej, Sentjur, Sentrupert, Sevnica, Sezana, Skocjan, Skofja Loka, Skofljica, Slovenska Bistrica, Slovenske Konjice, Smarje pri Jelsah, Smarjeske Toplice, Smartno ob Paki, Smartno pri Litiji, Sodrazica, Solcava, Sostanj, Sredisce ob Dravi, Starse, Store, Straza, Sveta Ana, Sveta Trojica v Slovenskih Goricah, Sveti Andraz v Slovenskih Goricah, Sveti Jurij ob Scavnici, Sveti Jurij v Slovenskih Goricah, Sveti Tomaz, Tabor, Tisina, Tolmin, Trbovlje, Trebnje, Trnovska Vas, Trzic, Trzin, Turnisce, Velika Polana, Velike Lasce, Verzej, Videm, Vipava, Vitanje, Vodice, Vojnik, Vransko, Vrhnika, Vuzenica, Zagorje ob Savi, Zalec, Zavrc, Zelezniki, Zetale, Ziri, Zirovnica, Zrece, Zuzemberk
urban municipalities: Celje, Koper, Kranj, Krsko, Ljubljana, Maribor, Murska Sobota, Nova Gorica, Novo Mesto, Ptuj, Slovenj Gradec, Velenje

Legal system: civil law system

Constitution: *history:* previous 1974 (pre-independence); latest passed by Parliament 23 December 1991
amendment process: proposed by at least 20 National Assembly members, by the government, or by petition of at least 30,000 voters; passage requires at least two-thirds majority vote by the Assembly; referendum required if agreed upon by at least 30 Assembly members; passage in a referendum requires participation of a majority of eligible voters and a simple majority of votes cast

International law organization participation: has not submitted an ICJ jurisdiction declaration; accepts ICCt jurisdiction

Citizenship: *citizenship by birth:* no
citizenship by descent only: at least one parent must be a citizen of Slovenia; both parents if the child is born outside of Slovenia
dual citizenship recognized: yes, for select cases
residency requirement for naturalization: 10 years, the last 5 of which have been continuous

Suffrage: 18 years of age; universal

Executive branch: *chief of state:* President Natasa PIRC MUSAR (since 23 December 2022)
head of government: Prime Minister Robert GOLOB (since 1 June 2022)
cabinet: Council of Ministers nominated by the prime minister, elected by the National Assembly
election/appointment process: president directly elected by absolute-majority popular vote in 2 rounds, if needed, for a 5-year term (eligible for a second consecutive term); following National Assembly elections, the president usually nominates the leader of the majority party or majority coalition as prime minister, and the National Assembly elects the nominee
most recent election date: 23 October 2022, with a runoff on 13 November 2022
election results: *2022:* Natasa PIRC MUSAR elected president in second round: percent of vote in first round - Anze LOGAR (SDS) 34%, Natasa PIRC MUSAR (independent) 26.9%, Milan BRGLEZ (SD) 15.5%, Vladimir PREBILIC (independent) 10.6%, Sabina SENCAR (Resni.ca) 5.9%, Janez CIGLER KRALJ (NSi) 4.4%, other 2.7%; percent of vote in second round - Natasa PIRC MUSAR 53.9%, Anze LOGAR 46.1%; Robert GOLOB (GS) elected prime minister on 25 May 2022, National Assembly vote - 54-30
2017: Borut PAHOR reelected president in second round; percent of vote in first round - Borut PAHOR (independent) 47.1%, Marjan SAREC (Marjan Sarec List) 25%, Romana TOMC (SDS) 13.7%, Ljudmila NOVAK (NSi) 7.2%, other 7%; percent of vote in second round - Borut PAHOR 52.9%, Marjan SAREC 47.1%
expected date of next election: 2027

Legislative branch: *legislative structure:* bicameral

Legislative branch - lower chamber: *chamber name:* National Assembly (Drzavni Zbor)
number of seats: 90 (all directly elected)
electoral system: proportional representation
scope of elections: full renewal
term in office: 4 years
most recent election date: 4/24/2022
parties elected and seats per party: Freedom Movement (SVOBODA) (41); Slovenian Democratic Party

(SDS) (27); New Slovenia - Christian Democrats (NSi) (8); Social Democrats (SD) (7); Left (LEVICA) (5); Other (2)
percentage of women in chamber: 35.6%
expected date of next election: April 2026

Legislative branch - upper chamber: *chamber name:* National Council (Drzavni Svet)
number of seats: 40 (all indirectly elected)
scope of elections: full renewal
term in office: 5 years
most recent election date: 11/23/2022 to 11/24/2022
percentage of women in chamber: 17.5%
expected date of next election: November 2027
note: the National Council is primarily an advisory body with limited legislative powers

Judicial branch: *highest court(s):* Supreme Court (consists of the court president and 37 judges organized into civil, criminal, commercial, labor and social security, administrative, and registry departments); Constitutional Court (consists of the court president, vice president, and 7 judges)
judge selection and term of office: Supreme Court president and vice president appointed by the National Assembly on the proposal of the Minister of Justice, based on the opinions of the Judicial Council, an 11-member independent body elected by the National Assembly from proposals submitted by the president, attorneys, law universities, and sitting judges; other Supreme Court judges elected by the National Assembly from candidates proposed by the Judicial Council; Supreme Court judges serve for life; Constitutional Court judges appointed by the National Assembly from nominations by the president of the republic; Constitutional Court president selected from among its own membership for a 3-year term; other judges elected for single 9-year terms
subordinate courts: county, district, regional, and high courts; specialized labor-related and social courts; Court of Audit; Administrative Court

Political parties: Democratic Party of Pensioners of Slovenia or DeSUS
Freedom Movement or GS (formerly Greens Actions Party or Z.DEJ)
List of Marjan Sarec or LMS
New Slovenia - Christian Democrats or NSi
Party of Alenka Bratusek or SAB (formerly Alliance of Social Liberal Democrats or ZSD and before that Alliance of Alenka Bratusek or ZaAB)
Resni.ca
Slovenian Democratic Party or SDS (formerly the Social Democratic Party of Slovenia or SDSS)
Slovenian National Party or SNS
Social Democrats or SD
The Left or Levica (successor to United Left or ZL)

Diplomatic representation in the US: *chief of mission:* Ambassador Iztok MIROŠIČ (since 15 September 2023)
chancery: 2410 California Street NW, Washington, DC 20008
telephone: [1] (202) 386-6611
FAX: [1] (202) 386-6633
email address and website: sloembassy.washington@gov.si
http://www.washington.embassy.si/
consulate(s) general: Cleveland (OH)

Diplomatic representation from the US: *chief of mission:* Ambassador (vacant); Chargé d'Affaires Brian GREANEY (since August 2025)
embassy: Presernova 31, 1000 Ljubljana
mailing address: 7140 Ljubljana Place, Washington, DC 20521-7140
telephone: [386] (1) 200-5500
FAX: [386] (1) 200-5555
email address and website: LjubljanaACS@state.gov
https://si.usembassy.gov/

International organization participation: Australia Group, BIS, CD, CE, CEI, EAPC, EBRD, ECB, EIB, EMU, ESA (cooperating state), EU, FAO, IADB, IAEA, IBRD, ICAO, ICC (national committees), ICCt, ICRM, IDA, IFC, IFRCS, IHO, ILO, IMF, IMO, Interpol, IOC, IOM, IPU, ISO, ITU, MIGA, NATO, NEA, NSG, OAS (observer), OECD, OIF (observer), OPCW, OSCE, PCA, Schengen Convention, SELEC, UN, UNCTAD, UNESCO, UNHCR, UNIDO, UNIFIL, UNTSO, UNWTO, UPU, Wassenaar Arrangement, WCO, WHO, WIPO, WMO, WTO, ZC

Independence: 25 June 1991 (from Yugoslavia)

National holiday: Independence Day/Statehood Day, 25 June (1991)

Flag: *description:* three equal horizontal bands of white (top), blue, and red; the Slovenian seal (a shield with Triglav, the country's highest peak, in white on a blue background) is at the center, with two wavy blue lines under it; three six-pointed stars in an inverted triangle appear on the upper-left
meaning: the wavy lines represent seas and rivers; the colors come from the medieval coat of arms of the Duchy of Carniola; the stars come from the coat of arms of the Counts of Celje (a Slovene dynastic house)

National symbol(s): Mount Triglav

National color(s): white, blue, red

National anthem(s): *title:* "Zdravljica" (A Toast)
lyrics/music: France PRESEREN/Stanko PREMRL
history: adopted in 1989; originally written in 1848; only the seventh verse of the poem is used as the anthem

National heritage: *total World Heritage Sites:* 5 (3 cultural, 2 natural)
selected World Heritage Site locales: Škocjan Caves (n); Ancient and Primeval Beech Forests of the Carpathians and Other Regions of Europe (n); Prehistoric Pile Dwellings around the Alps (c); Heritage of Mercury: Almadén and Idrija (c); The works of Jože Plečnik in Ljubljana (c)

ECONOMY

Economic overview: high-income EU and eurozone economy; high per-capita income and low inequality; key exports in automotive and pharmaceuticals; tight labor market with low unemployment; growth supported by private consumption and public investment, with risks from tight labor market and trade conditions; narrowing fiscal deficit and declining public debt

Real GDP (purchasing power parity): $103.118 billion (2024 est.)
$101.503 billion (2023 est.)
$99.403 billion (2022 est.)
note: data in 2021 dollars
comparison ranking: 96

Real GDP growth rate: 1.6% (2024 est.)
2.1% (2023 est.)
2.7% (2022 est.)
note: annual GDP % growth based on constant local currency
comparison ranking: 160

Real GDP per capita: $48,500 (2024 est.)
$47,900 (2023 est.)
$47,100 (2022 est.)
note: data in 2021 dollars
comparison ranking: 40

GDP (official exchange rate): $72.485 billion (2024 est.)
note: data in current dollars at official exchange rate

Inflation rate (consumer prices): 2% (2024 est.)
7.4% (2023 est.)
8.8% (2022 est.)
note: annual % change based on consumer prices
comparison ranking: 50

GDP - composition, by sector of origin: *agriculture:* 1.5% (2024 est.)
industry: 28.8% (2024 est.)
services: 58.2% (2024 est.)
note: figures may not total 100% due to non-allocated consumption not captured in sector-reported data
comparison rankings: agriculture 164; industry 64; services 104

GDP - composition, by end use: *household consumption:* 52.3% (2023 est.)
government consumption: 19.2% (2023 est.)
investment in fixed capital: 21.3% (2023 est.)
investment in inventories: 0.9% (2023 est.)
exports of goods and services: 83.3% (2023 est.)
imports of goods and services: -76.8% (2023 est.)
note: figures may not total 100% due to rounding or gaps in data collection

Agricultural products: milk, maize, wheat, barley, grapes, chicken, potatoes, beef, apples, pork (2023)
note: top ten agricultural products based on tonnage

Industries: ferrous metallurgy and aluminum products, lead and zinc smelting; electronics (including military electronics), trucks, automobiles, electric power equipment, wood products, textiles, chemicals, machine tools

Industrial production growth rate: 1.8% (2024 est.)
note: annual % change in industrial value added based on constant local currency
comparison ranking: 105

Labor force: 1.058 million (2024 est.)
note: number of people ages 15 or older who are employed or seeking work
comparison ranking: 145

Unemployment rate: 3.4% (2024 est.)
3.7% (2023 est.)
4.1% (2022 est.)
note: % of labor force seeking employment
comparison ranking: 56

Youth unemployment rate (ages 15-24): *total:* 9.4% (2024 est.)
male: 10.6% (2024 est.)
female: 7.9% (2024 est.)
note: % of labor force ages 15-24 seeking employment
comparison ranking: total 126

Population below poverty line: 12.7% (2022 est.)
note: % of population with income below national poverty line

Gini Index coefficient - distribution of family income: 24.3 (2022 est.)
note: index (0-100) of income distribution; higher values represent greater inequality
comparison ranking: 148

Average household expenditures: *on food:* 13.9% of household expenditures (2023 est.)
on alcohol and tobacco: 4.5% of household expenditures (2023 est.)

Household income or consumption by percentage share: *lowest 10%:* 4.2% (2022 est.)
highest 10%: 20.7% (2022 est.)
note: % share of income accruing to lowest and highest 10% of population

Remittances: 1.2% of GDP (2024 est.)
1.3% of GDP (2023 est.)
1.3% of GDP (2022 est.)
note: personal transfers and compensation between resident and non-resident individuals/households/entities

Budget: *revenues:* $28.874 billion (2023 est.)
expenditures: $30.714 billion (2023 est.)
note: central government revenues (excluding grants) and expenditures converted to US dollars at average official exchange rate for year indicated

Public debt: 73.6% of GDP (2017 est.)
note: defined by the EU's Maastricht Treaty as consolidated general government gross debt at nominal value, outstanding at the end of the year in the following categories of government liabilities: currency and deposits, securities other than shares excluding financial derivatives, and loans; general government sector comprises the central, state, local government, and social security funds
comparison ranking: 50

Taxes and other revenues: 20.3% (of GDP) (2023 est.)
note: central government tax revenue as a % of GDP
comparison ranking: 50

Current account balance: $3.231 billion (2024 est.)
$3.093 billion (2023 est.)
-$617.374 million (2022 est.)
note: balance of payments - net trade and primary/secondary income in current dollars
comparison ranking: 40

Exports: $59.159 billion (2024 est.)
$57.66 billion (2023 est.)
$56.51 billion (2022 est.)
note: balance of payments - exports of goods and services in current dollars
comparison ranking: 64

Exports - partners: Switzerland 22%, Germany 12%, Italy 10%, Croatia 8%, Austria 6% (2023)
note: top five export partners based on percentage share of exports

Exports - commodities: packaged medicine, cars, refined petroleum, vehicle parts/accessories, plastic products (2023)
note: top five export commodities based on value in dollars

Imports: $54.583 billion (2024 est.)
$53.309 billion (2023 est.)
$55.158 billion (2022 est.)
note: balance of payments - imports of goods and services in current dollars
comparison ranking: 64

Imports - partners: Switzerland 17%, China 15%, Germany 11%, Italy 9%, Austria 6% (2023)
note: top five import partners based on percentage share of imports

Imports - commodities: nitrogen compounds, packaged medicine, refined petroleum, cars, vaccines (2023)
note: top five import commodities based on value in dollars

Reserves of foreign exchange and gold: $2.832 billion (2024 est.)
$2.37 billion (2023 est.)
$2.268 billion (2022 est.)
note: holdings of gold (year-end prices)/foreign exchange/special drawing rights in current dollars
comparison ranking: 118

Exchange rates: euros (EUR) per US dollar -

Exchange rates: 0.924 (2024 est.)
0.925 (2023 est.)
0.95 (2022 est.)
0.845 (2021 est.)
0.876 (2020 est.)

ENERGY

Electricity access: *electrification - total population:* 100% (2022 est.)

Electricity: *installed generating capacity:* 4.739 million kW (2023 est.)
consumption: 12.953 billion kWh (2023 est.)
exports: 10.62 billion kWh (2023 est.)
imports: 9.114 billion kWh (2023 est.)
transmission/distribution losses: 774.138 million kWh (2023 est.)
comparison rankings: installed generating capacity 92; consumption 93; exports 23; imports 29; transmission/distribution losses 91

Electricity generation sources: *fossil fuels:* 24.6% of total installed capacity (2023 est.)
nuclear: 35.2% of total installed capacity (2023 est.)
solar: 6.7% of total installed capacity (2023 est.)
hydroelectricity: 31.5% of total installed capacity (2023 est.)
biomass and waste: 2% of total installed capacity (2023 est.)

Nuclear energy: Number of operational nuclear reactors: 1 (2025)

Net capacity of operational nuclear reactors: 0.7GW (2025 est.)

Percent of total electricity production: 36.8% (2023 est.)

Coal: *production:* 2.44 million metric tons (2023 est.)
consumption: 2.309 million metric tons (2023 est.)
exports: 2,000 metric tons (2023 est.)
imports: 866,000 metric tons (2023 est.)
proven reserves: 95 million metric tons (2023 est.)

Petroleum: *total petroleum production:* 4 bbl/day (2021 est.)
refined petroleum consumption: 44,000 bbl/day (2024 est.)

Natural gas: *production:* 4.014 million cubic meters (2023 est.)
consumption: 811.395 million cubic meters (2023 est.)
exports: 11.387 million cubic meters (2018 est.)
imports: 810.948 million cubic meters (2023 est.)

Energy consumption per capita: 104.502 million Btu/person (2023 est.)
comparison ranking: 44

COMMUNICATIONS

Telephones - fixed lines: *total subscriptions:* 647,000 (2023 est.)
subscriptions per 100 inhabitants: 30 (2023 est.)
comparison ranking: total subscriptions 83

Telephones - mobile cellular: *total subscriptions:* 2.73 million (2023 est.)
subscriptions per 100 inhabitants: 126 (2022 est.)
comparison ranking: total subscriptions 143

Broadcast media: public TV broadcaster, Radiotelevizija Slovenija (RTV), operates a system of national and regional TV stations; 35 commercial TV stations; about 60% of households connected to multi-channel cable TV; public radio broadcaster with 3 national and 4 regional stations; more than 75 regional and local commercial and non-commercial radio stations

Internet country code: .si

Internet users: *percent of population:* 90% (2023 est.)

Broadband - fixed subscriptions: *total:* 683,000 (2023 est.)
subscriptions per 100 inhabitants: 32 (2023 est.)
comparison ranking: total 87

TRANSPORTATION

Civil aircraft registration country code prefix: S5

Airports: 42 (2025)
comparison ranking: 102

Heliports: 4 (2025)
comparison ranking: 105

Railways: *total:* 1,207 km (2020) 609 km electrified

Merchant marine: *total:* 8 (2023)
by type: other 8
comparison ranking: total 163

Ports: *total ports:* 2 (2024)
large: 0
medium: 0
small: 1
very small: 1
ports with oil terminals: 0
key ports: Koper, Piran

MILITARY AND SECURITY

Military and security forces: Slovenian Armed Forces (Slovenska Vojska, SV): structured as a combined force with air, land, maritime, and special operations components

Ministry of Interior: National Police (2025)

Military expenditures: 2% of GDP (2025 est.)
1.4% of GDP (2024 est.)
1.3% of GDP (2023 est.)
1.3% of GDP (2022 est.)
1.2% of GDP (2021 est.)

Military and security service personnel strengths: approximately 6,000 active military personnel (2025)

Military equipment inventories and acquisitions: the military's inventory is a mix of Soviet-era and smaller quantities of more modern, mostly Western equipment; in recent years, Slovenia has begun a modernization program and imported growing amounts of NATO-standard European and US equipment (2024)

Military service age and obligation: 18-30 years of age for voluntary military service for men and women; must be a citizen of the Republic of Slovenia; recruits sign up for 3-, 5-, or 10-year service contracts; conscription abolished in 2003 (2023)
note: as of 2023, women comprised about 16% of the military's full-time personnel

Military deployments: 100 Kosovo (NATO); 100 Slovakia (NATO) (2024)
note: in response to Russia's 2022 invasion of Ukraine, some NATO countries, including Slovenia, have sent additional troops and equipment to the battlegroups deployed in NATO territory in eastern Europe

Military - note: the Slovenian Armed Forces (Slovenska Vojska or SV) are responsible for the defense of the country's sovereignty and territory, deterring external threats, and contributing to European security and other international peacekeeping missions; the SV is also active in civil-military cooperation, such as the maintenance of local infrastructure; Slovenia has been a member of the EU and NATO since 2004, and one of the SV's key missions is fulfilling the country's commitments to NATO, including equipment modernization, participating in training exercises, and contributing to NATO operations; the SV provides troops to NATO's efforts to enhance its presence in the Baltics (Latvia) and Eastern Europe (Slovakia); it has also participated in other international security missions with small numbers of personnel in such places as Africa, southern Europe, the Mediterranean Sea, and the Middle East; NATO allies Hungary and Italy provide air policing for Slovenia
the SV was formally established in 1993 as a reorganization of the Slovenia Defense Force; the Defense Force, along with the Slovenian police, comprised the majority of the forces that engaged with the Yugoslav People's Army during the 10-Day War after Slovenia declared its independence in 1991 (2025)

TRANSNATIONAL ISSUES

Refugees and internally displaced persons: *refugees:* 13,369 (2024 est.)

IDPs: 10 (2023 est.)

stateless persons: 10 (2024 est.)

SOLOMON ISLANDS

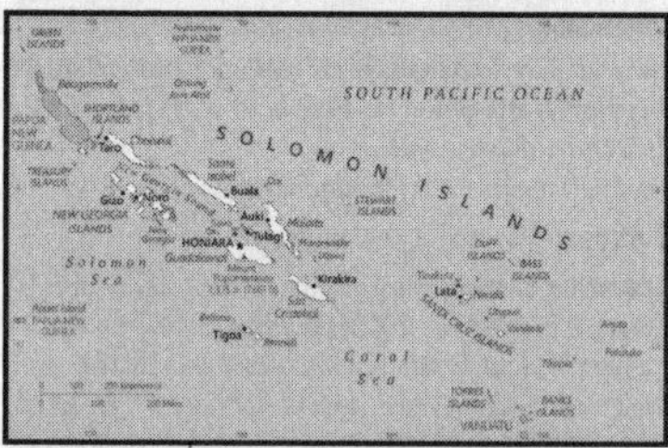

INTRODUCTION

Background: Settlers from Papua arrived on the Solomon Islands around 30,000 years ago. About 6,000 years ago, Austronesian settlers came to the islands, and the two groups mixed extensively. Despite significant inter-island trade, no attempts were made to unite the islands into a single political entity. In 1568, a Spanish explorer became the first European to spot the islands. After a failed Spanish attempt at creating a permanent European settlement in the late 1500s, the Solomon Islands remained free of European contact until a British explorer arrived in 1767. European explorers and US and British whaling ships regularly visited the islands into the 1800s.

Germany declared a protectorate over the northern Solomon Islands in 1885, and the UK established a protectorate over the southern islands in 1893. In 1899, Germany transferred its islands to the UK in exchange for the UK relinquishing all claims in Samoa. In 1942, Japan invaded the islands, and the Guadalcanal Campaign (August 1942-February 1943) proved a turning point in the Pacific theater of WWII. The fighting destroyed large parts of the Solomon Islands, and a nationalist movement emerged near the end of the war. By 1960, the British allowed some local autonomy. The islands were granted self-government in 1976 and independence two years later under Prime Minister Sir Peter KENILOREA.

In 1999, longstanding tensions between ethnic Guale in Honiara and ethnic Malaitans in Honiara's suburbs erupted in civil war, leading thousands of Malaitans to take refuge in Honiara and prompting Guale to flee the city. In 2000, newly elected Prime Minister Manasseh SOGAVARE focused on peace agreements and distributing resources equally among groups, but his actions bankrupted the government in 2001 and led to his ouster. In 2003, the Solomon Islands requested international assistance to reestablish law and order; the Australian-led Regional Assistance Mission to the Solomon Islands, which ended in 2017, improved the security situation. In 2006, however, riots broke out in Honiara, and the city's Chinatown was burned amid allegations that the prime minister took money from China. SOGAVARE was reelected prime minister for a fourth time in 2019. When a small group of protestors, mostly from the island of Malaita, approached parliament to lodge a petition calling for SOGAVARE's removal and more development in Malaita in 2021, police fired tear gas into the crowd which sparked rioting and looting in Honiara.

GEOGRAPHY

Location: Oceania, group of islands in the South Pacific Ocean, east of Papua New Guinea

Geographic coordinates: 8 00 S, 159 00 E

Map references: Oceania

Area: *total:* 28,896 sq km
land: 27,986 sq km
water: 910 sq km
comparison ranking: total 143

Area - comparative: slightly smaller than Maryland

Land boundaries: *total:* 0 km

Coastline: 5,313 km

Maritime claims: *territorial sea:* 12 nm
exclusive economic zone: 200 nm
continental shelf: 200 nm
note: measured from claimed archipelagic baselines

Climate: tropical monsoon; few temperature and weather extremes

Terrain: mostly rugged mountains with some low coral atolls

Elevation: *highest point:* Mount Popomanaseu 2,335 m
lowest point: Pacific Ocean 0 m

Natural resources: fish, forests, gold, bauxite, phosphates, lead, zinc, nickel

Land use: *agricultural land:* 4.3% (2022 est.)
arable land: 0.8% (2022 est.)
permanent crops: 3.2% (2022 est.)
permanent pasture: 0.3% (2022 est.)
forest: 90.1% (2022 est.)
other: 5.6% (2022 est.)

Irrigated land: 0 sq km (2022)

Population distribution: most of the population lives along the coastal regions; about one in five live in urban areas, and of these about two thirds reside in Honiara, the largest town and chief port

Natural hazards: tropical cyclones, but rarely destructive; geologically active region with frequent earthquakes, tremors, and volcanic activity; tsunamis
volcanism: Tinakula (851 m) has frequent eruption activity, and an eruption of Savo (485 m) could affect the capital Honiara on nearby Guadalcanal

Geography - note: strategic location on sea routes between the South Pacific Ocean, the Solomon Sea, and the Coral Sea; Rennell Island, the southernmost in the Solomon Islands chain, is one of the world's largest raised coral atolls; the island's Lake Tegano, formerly a lagoon on the atoll, is the largest lake in the insular Pacific (15,500 hectares; 38,300 acres)

PEOPLE AND SOCIETY

Population: *total:* 726,799 (2024 est.)
male: 370,970
female: 355,829
comparison rankings: total 167; male 167; female 167

Nationality: *noun:* Solomon Islander(s)
adjective: Solomon Islander

Ethnic groups: Melanesian 95.3%, Polynesian 3.1%, Micronesian 1.2%, other 0.3% (2009 est.)

Languages: Melanesian pidgin (lingua franca in much of the country), English (official but spoken by only 1%-2% of the population), 120 indigenous languages

Religions: Protestant 73.4% (Church of Melanesia 31.9%, South Sea Evangelical 17.1%, Seventh Day Adventist 11.7%, United Church 10.1%, Christian Fellowship Church 2.5%), Roman Catholic 19.6%, other Christian 2.9%, other 4%, unspecified 0.1% (2009 est.)

Age structure: *0-14 years:* 30.6% (male 114,246/female 108,020)
15-64 years: 64.2% (male 238,708/female 227,636)
65 years and over: 5.3% (2024 est.) (male 18,016/female 20,173)

Dependency ratios: *total dependency ratio:* 55.9 (2024 est.)
youth dependency ratio: 47.7 (2024 est.)
elderly dependency ratio: 8.2 (2024 est.)
potential support ratio: 12.2 (2024 est.)

Median age: *total:* 25.2 years (2024 est.)
male: 25 years
female: 25.4 years
comparison ranking: total 171

Population growth rate: 1.65% (2024 est.)
comparison ranking: 57

Birth rate: 22 births/1,000 population (2024 est.)

comparison ranking: 54

Death rate: 3.9 deaths/1,000 population (2024 est.)
comparison ranking: 216

Net migration rate: -1.5 migrant(s)/1,000 population (2024 est.)
comparison ranking: 157

Population distribution: most of the population lives along the coastal regions; about one in five live in urban areas, and of these about two thirds reside in Honiara, the largest town and chief port

Urbanization: *urban population:* 26% of total population (2023)
rate of urbanization: 3.57% annual rate of change (2020-25 est.)

Major urban areas - population: 82,000 HONIARA (capital) (2018)

Sex ratio: *at birth:* 1.05 male(s)/female
0-14 years: 1.06 male(s)/female
15-64 years: 1.05 male(s)/female
65 years and over: 0.89 male(s)/female
total population: 1.04 male(s)/female (2024 est.)

Mother's mean age at first birth: 22.6 years (2015 est.)
note: data represents median age at first birth among women 25-29

Maternal mortality ratio: 123 deaths/100,000 live births (2023 est.)
comparison ranking: 59

Infant mortality rate: *total:* 19.1 deaths/1,000 live births (2024 est.)
male: 22.7 deaths/1,000 live births
female: 15.2 deaths/1,000 live births
comparison ranking: total 79

Life expectancy at birth: *total population:* 77.2 years (2024 est.)
male: 74.6 years
female: 80 years
comparison ranking: total population 95

Total fertility rate: 2.77 children born/woman (2024 est.)
comparison ranking: 56

Gross reproduction rate: 1.35 (2024 est.)

Drinking water source: *improved:* rural: 59.4% of population (2022 est.)
total: 73.1% of population
unimproved: rural: 40.6% of population (2022 est.)

Health expenditure: 4.8% of GDP (2021)
9.7% of national budget (2022 est.)

Physician density: 0.24 physicians/1,000 population (2023)

Sanitation facility access: *improved:* rural: 22.6% of population (2022 est.)
unimproved: rural: 77.4% of population (2022 est.)
total: 59.4% of population

Obesity - adult prevalence rate: 22.5% (2016)
comparison ranking: 75

Alcohol consumption per capita: *total:* 1.19 liters of pure alcohol (2019 est.)
beer: 1.1 liters of pure alcohol (2019 est.)
wine: 0.06 liters of pure alcohol (2019 est.)
spirits: 0.02 liters of pure alcohol (2019 est.)
other alcohols: 0 liters of pure alcohol (2019 est.)
comparison ranking: total 146

Tobacco use: *total:* 36.8% (2025 est.)
male: 54.5% (2025 est.)
female: 18.8% (2025 est.)
comparison ranking: total 6

Children under the age of 5 years underweight: 16.2% (2015)
comparison ranking: 30

Currently married women (ages 15-49): 64.1% (2023 est.)

Child marriage: *women married by age 15:* 5.6% (2015)
women married by age 18: 21.3% (2015)
men married by age 18: 4.4% (2015)

Education expenditure: 8.3% of GDP (2023 est.)
25.9% national budget (2023 est.)
comparison ranking: Education expenditure (% GDP) 9

ENVIRONMENT

Environmental issues: deforestation; soil erosion; damage to coral reefs

International environmental agreements: *party to:* Biodiversity, Climate Change, Climate Change-Kyoto Protocol, Climate Change-Paris Agreement, Desertification, Endangered Species, Environmental Modification, Law of the Sea, Marine Dumping-London Convention, Marine Life Conservation, Ozone Layer Protection, Ship Pollution, Whaling
signed, but not ratified: Comprehensive Nuclear Test Ban

Climate: tropical monsoon; few temperature and weather extremes

Urbanization: *urban population:* 26% of total population (2023)
rate of urbanization: 3.57% annual rate of change (2020-25 est.)

Carbon dioxide emissions: 318,000 metric tonnes of CO_2 (2023 est.)
from petroleum and other liquids: 318,000 metric tonnes of CO_2 (2023 est.)
comparison ranking: total emissions 196

Particulate matter emissions: 8.8 micrograms per cubic meter (2019 est.)

Waste and recycling: *municipal solid waste generated annually:* 180,000 tons (2024 est.)
percent of municipal solid waste recycled: 6.1% (2022 est.)

Total renewable water resources: 44.7 billion cubic meters (2022 est.)

GOVERNMENT

Country name: *conventional long form:* none
conventional short form: Solomon Islands
local long form: none
local short form: Solomon Islands
former: British Solomon Islands
etymology: Spanish explorer Alvaro de MENDANA named the isles in 1568 after the wealthy biblical King SOLOMON in the mistaken belief that the islands contained great riches

Government type: parliamentary democracy under a constitutional monarchy; a Commonwealth realm

Capital: *name:* Honiara
geographic coordinates: 9 26 S, 159 57 E
time difference: UTC+11 (16 hours ahead of Washington, DC, during Standard Time)
etymology: the name derives from the local term *nagho ni ara*, meaning "place of the east wind" or "facing the trade winds"

Administrative divisions: 9 provinces and 1 city*; Central, Choiseul, Guadalcanal, Honiara*, Isabel, Makira and Ulawa, Malaita, Rennell and Bellona, Temotu, Western

Legal system: mixed system of English common law and customary law

Constitution: *history:* adopted 31 May 1978, effective 7 July 1978
amendment process: proposed by the National Parliament; passage of constitutional sections, including those on fundamental rights and freedoms, the legal system, Parliament, alteration of the constitution and the ombudsman, requires three-fourths majority vote by Parliament and assent of the governor general; passage of other amendments requires two-thirds majority vote and assent of the governor general

International law organization participation: has not submitted an ICJ jurisdiction declaration; non-party state to the ICCt

Citizenship: *citizenship by birth:* no
citizenship by descent only: at least one parent must be a citizen of the Solomon Islands
dual citizenship recognized: no
residency requirement for naturalization: 7 years

Suffrage: 21 years of age; universal

Executive branch: *chief of state:* King CHARLES III (since 8 September 2022); represented by Governor General David Tiva KAPU (since 7 July 2024)
head of government: Prime Minister Jeremiah MANELE (since 2 May 2024)
cabinet: Cabinet appointed by the governor general on the advice of the prime minister
election/appointment process: the monarchy is hereditary; governor general appointed by the monarch on the advice of the National Parliament for up to 5 years (eligible for a second term); following legislative elections, the National Parliament usually elects the leader of the majority party or majority coalition as prime minister; deputy prime minister appointed by the governor general on the advice of the prime minister

Legislative branch: *legislature name:* National Parliament
legislative structure: unicameral
number of seats: 50 (all directly elected)
electoral system: plurality/majority
scope of elections: full renewal
term in office: 4 years
most recent election date: 4/17/2024
parties elected and seats per party: Ownership Unity and Responsibility (OUR Party) (15); Solomon Islands Democratic Party (SIDP) (11); Solomon Islands United Party (UP) (6); Solomon Islands People First Party (SIPFP) (3); Independents (11); Other (4)
percentage of women in chamber: 6%
expected date of next election: April 2028

Judicial branch: *highest court(s):* Court of Appeal (consists of the court president and ex officio members including the High Court chief justice and puisne judges); High Court (consists of the chief justice and puisne judges)
judge selection and term of office: Court of Appeal and High Court president, chief justices, and puisne judges appointed by the governor general on recommendation of the Judicial and Legal Service Commission, chaired by the chief justice and includes 5 members, mostly judicial officials and legal professionals; all judges serve until retirement at age 60
subordinate courts: Magistrates' Courts; Customary Land Appeal Court; local courts

Political parties: Democratic Alliance Party or DAP
Kadere Party of Solomon Islands or KAD
Ownership, Unity, and Responsibility Party (OUR Party)
People First Party or PFP
Solomon Islands Democratic Party or SIDP
Solomon Islands Party for Rural Advancement or SIPRA
Solomon Islands United Party or SIUP
United for Change Party or U4C
Coalition for Accountability Reform and Empowerment (CARE) (includes DAP, SIDP, and U4C)
note: the Solomon Islands political party system is characterized by fluid coalitions

Diplomatic representation in the US: *chief of mission:* Ambassador Jane Mugafalu Kabui WAETARA (since 16 September 2022); note - also Permanent Representative to the UN
chancery: 685 Third Avenue, 11th Floor, Suite 1102, New York, NY 10017
telephone: [1] (212) 599-6192
FAX: [1] (212) 661-8925
email address and website: simun@solomons.com

Diplomatic representation from the US: *chief of mission:* Ambassador Ann Marie YASTISHOCK (since 14 March 2024); note - also accredited to the Papua New Guinea and Vanuatu, based in Port Moresby, Papua New Guinea
embassy: BJS Building
Commonwealth Avenue
Honiara, Solomon Islands
telephone: [677] 23426
FAX: [677] 27429
email address and website: EmbassyHoniara@state.gov
https://pg.usembassy.gov/

International organization participation: ACP, ADB, AOSIS, C, EITI (candidate country), ESCAP, FAO, G-77, IBRD, ICAO, ICRM, IDA, IFAD, IFC, IFRCS, ILO, IMF, IMO, IOC, ITU, MIGA, OPCW, PIF, Sparteca, SPC, UN, UNCTAD, UNESCO, UPU, WFTU, WHO, WMO, WTO

Independence: 7 July 1978 (from the UK)

National holiday: Independence Day, 7 July (1978)

Flag: *description:* divided diagonally by a yellow stripe from the lower-left corner; the upper triangle (left side) is blue with five five-pointed white stars in an "X" pattern; the lower triangle is green
meaning: blue stands for the ocean, green for the land, and yellow for sunshine; the five stars stand for the main island groups

National color(s): blue, yellow, green, white

National anthem(s): *title:* "God Save Our Solomon Islands"
lyrics/music: Panapasa BALEKANA and Matila BALEKANA/Panapasa BALEKANA
history: adopted 1978
title: "God Save the King"
lyrics/music: unknown
history: in use since 1745

National heritage: *total World Heritage Sites:* 1 (natural)
selected World Heritage Site locales: East Rennell

ECONOMY

Economic overview: lower middle-income Pacific island economy; natural resource rich but environmentally fragile; key agrarian sector; growing Chinese economic relationship; infrastructure damage due to social unrest; metal mining operations

Real GDP (purchasing power parity): $2.07 billion (2024 est.)
$2.019 billion (2023 est.)
$1.967 billion (2022 est.)
note: data in 2021 dollars
comparison ranking: 197

Real GDP growth rate: 2.5% (2024 est.)
2.7% (2023 est.)
2.4% (2022 est.)
note: annual GDP % growth based on constant local currency
comparison ranking: 136

Real GDP per capita: $2,500 (2024 est.)
$2,500 (2023 est.)
$2,500 (2022 est.)
note: data in 2021 dollars
comparison ranking: 203

GDP (official exchange rate): $1.761 billion (2024 est.)
note: data in current dollars at official exchange rate

Inflation rate (consumer prices): 5.9% (2023 est.)
5.5% (2022 est.)
-0.1% (2021 est.)
note: annual % change based on consumer prices
comparison ranking: 151

GDP - composition, by sector of origin: *agriculture:* 33.8% (2022 est.)
industry: 18.7% (2022 est.)
services: 47.3% (2022 est.)
note: figures may not total 100% due to non-allocated consumption not captured in sector-reported data
comparison rankings: agriculture 7; industry 140; services 161

GDP - composition, by end use: *household consumption:* 61.7% (2022 est.)
government consumption: 29.2% (2022 est.)
investment in fixed capital: 24.4% (2022 est.)
investment in inventories: -1% (2022 est.)
exports of goods and services: 26.3% (2022 est.)
imports of goods and services: -51.7% (2022 est.)
note: figures may not total 100% due to rounding or gaps in data collection

Agricultural products: oil palm fruit, coconuts, sweet potatoes, yams, taro, fruits, pulses, vegetables, cocoa beans, cassava (2023)
note: top ten agricultural products based on tonnage

Industries: fish (tuna), mining, timber

Industrial production growth rate: 4.7% (2022 est.)
note: annual % change in industrial value added based on constant local currency
comparison ranking: 50

Labor force: 435,600 (2024 est.)
note: number of people ages 15 or older who are employed or seeking work
comparison ranking: 160

Unemployment rate: 1.5% (2024 est.)
1.5% (2023 est.)
1.5% (2022 est.)
note: % of labor force seeking employment
comparison ranking: 9

Youth unemployment rate (ages 15-24): *total:* 3% (2024 est.)
male: 2.6% (2024 est.)
female: 3.4% (2024 est.)
note: % of labor force ages 15-24 seeking employment
comparison ranking: total 181

Remittances: 5.4% of GDP (2024 est.)
5.1% of GDP (2023 est.)
5.2% of GDP (2022 est.)
note: personal transfers and compensation between resident and non-resident individuals/ households/ entities

Budget: *revenues:* $436.174 million (2022 est.)
expenditures: $482.24 million (2022 est.)
note: central government revenues and expenses (excluding grants/extrabudgetary units/ social security funds) converted to US dollars at average official exchange rate for year indicated

Public debt: 15.4% of GDP (2022 est.)
note: central government debt as a % of GDP
comparison ranking: 189

Taxes and other revenues: 20.7% (of GDP) (2022 est.)
note: central government tax revenue as a % of GDP
comparison ranking: 46

Current account balance: -$66.231 million (2024 est.)
-$178.197 million (2023 est.)
-$218.534 million (2022 est.)
note: balance of payments - net trade and primary/ secondary income in current dollars
comparison ranking: 92

Exports: $642.877 million (2024 est.)
$546.025 million (2023 est.)
$411.359 million (2022 est.)
note: balance of payments - exports of goods and services in current dollars
comparison ranking: 188

Exports - partners: China 56%, Australia 11%, Italy 10%, Spain 5%, Netherlands 4% (2023)
note: top five export partners based on percentage share of exports

Exports - commodities: wood, fish, gold, precious metal ore, palm oil (2023)
note: top five export commodities based on value in dollars

Imports: $857.128 million (2024 est.)
$883.611 million (2023 est.)
$764.641 million (2022 est.)
note: balance of payments - imports of goods and services in current dollars
comparison ranking: 192

Imports - partners: China 42%, Singapore 13%, Australia 13%, Taiwan 5%, Malaysia 5% (2023)
note: top five import partners based on percentage share of imports

Imports - commodities: refined petroleum, plastic products, fish, broadcasting equipment, iron structures (2023)
note: top five import commodities based on value in dollars

Reserves of foreign exchange and gold: $688.22 million (2023 est.)
$661.604 million (2022 est.)
$694.515 million (2021 est.)
note: holdings of gold (year-end prices)/foreign exchange/special drawing rights in current dollars
comparison ranking: 151

Debt - external: $184.191 million (2023 est.)
note: present value of external debt in current US dollars
comparison ranking: 121

Exchange rates: Solomon Islands dollars (SBD) per US dollar -

Exchange rates: 8.455 (2024 est.)
8.376 (2023 est.)

8.156 (2022 est.)
8.03 (2021 est.)
8.213 (2020 est.)

ENERGY

Electricity access: *electrification - total population:* 76% (2022 est.)
electrification - urban areas: 79%
electrification - rural areas: 75.4%

Electricity: *installed generating capacity:* 37,000 kW (2023 est.)
consumption: 91.031 million kWh (2023 est.)
transmission/distribution losses: 19.969 million kWh (2023 est.)
comparison rankings: installed generating capacity 199; consumption 199; transmission/distribution losses 25

Electricity generation sources: *fossil fuels:* 90.1% of total installed capacity (2023 est.)
solar: 5.4% of total installed capacity (2023 est.)
hydroelectricity: 0.9% of total installed capacity (2023 est.)
biomass and waste: 3.6% of total installed capacity (2023 est.)

Petroleum: *refined petroleum consumption:* 2,000 bbl/day (2023 est.)

Energy consumption per capita: 5.655 million Btu/person (2023 est.)
comparison ranking: 168

COMMUNICATIONS

Telephones - fixed lines: *total subscriptions:* 7,000 (2021 est.)
subscriptions per 100 inhabitants: 1 (2022 est.) less than 1
comparison ranking: total subscriptions 194

Telephones - mobile cellular: *total subscriptions:* 474,000 (2021 est.)
subscriptions per 100 inhabitants: 67 (2021 est.)
comparison ranking: total subscriptions 176

Broadcast media: multi-channel pay-TV is available; Solomon Islands Broadcasting Corporation (SIBC) operates 2 national radio stations and 2 provincial stations; 2 local commercial radio stations; Radio Australia is available via satellite (2019)

Internet country code: .sb

Internet users: *percent of population:* 43% (2023 est.)

Broadband - fixed subscriptions: *total:* 1,000 (2022 est.)
subscriptions per 100 inhabitants: (2022 est.) less than 1
comparison ranking: total 209

TRANSPORTATION

Civil aircraft registration country code prefix: H4

Airports: 36 (2025)
comparison ranking: 111

Heliports: 2 (2025)
comparison ranking: 135

Merchant marine: *total:* 25 (2023)
by type: general cargo 8, oil tanker 1, other 16
comparison ranking: total 142

Ports: *total ports:* 6 (2024)
large: 0
medium: 0
small: 2
very small: 4
ports with oil terminals: 1
key ports: Gizo Harbor, Honiara, Port Noro, Ringgi Cove, Tulaghi, Yandina

MILITARY AND SECURITY

Military and security forces: Ministry of Police, National Security and Correctional Services (MPNSCS): the Royal Solomon Islands Police Force (RSIPF) (2025)

Military - note: in 2017, the Solomon Islands and Australia signed a security treaty allowing Australian police, defense, and associated civilian personnel to deploy rapidly to Solomon Islands should the need arise and where both countries consent; the treaty was activated for the first time in November 2021 following civil unrest in Honiara; Australia was the first country Solomon Islands called upon for support, and from November 2021, Australia deployed police and defense personnel to work alongside partners from Fiji, Papua New Guinea, and New Zealand to restore law and order in Honiara
in 2022, the Solomon Islands Government has also signed a police and security agreement with China (2025)

TRANSNATIONAL ISSUES

Refugees and internally displaced persons: IDPs: 1,638 (2023 est.)

Trafficking in persons: *tier rating:* Tier 2 Watch List — Solomon Islands does not fully meet the minimum standards for the elimination of trafficking, but the government has devoted sufficient resources to a written plan that, if implemented, would constitute significant efforts to meet the minimum standards; therefore, Solomon Islands was granted a waiver per the Trafficking Victims Protection Act from an otherwise required downgrade to Tier 3 and remained on Tier 2 Watch List for the third consecutive year; for more details, go to: https://www.state.gov/reports/2025-trafficking-in-persons-report/solomon-islands/

SOMALIA

INTRODUCTION

Background: Between A.D. 800 and 1100, immigrant Muslim Arabs and Persians set up coastal trading posts along the Gulf of Aden and the Indian Ocean, solidifying present-day Somalia's close trading relationship with the Arab Peninsula. In the late 19th century, Britain, France, and Italy established colonies in the Somali Peninsula that lasted until 1960, when British Somaliland gained independence and joined with Italian Somaliland to form the Republic of Somalia.

The country functioned as a parliamentary democracy until 1969, when General Mohamed SIAD Barre took control in a coup, beginning a 22-year socialist dictatorship. In an effort to centralize power, SIAD called for the eradication of the clan, the key cultural and social organizing principle in Somali society. Resistance to SIAD's socialist leadership, which was causing a rapid deterioration of the country, prompted allied clan militias to overthrow SIAD in 1991, resulting in state collapse. Subsequent fighting between rival clans for resources and territory overwhelmed the country, causing a manmade famine and prompting international intervention. Beginning in 1993, the UN spearheaded an international humanitarian mission, but the international community largely withdrew by 1995 after an incident that became known as Black Hawk Down, in which two US military helicopters were shot down in Mogadishu. The fighting and subsequent siege and rescue resulted in 21 deaths and 82 wounded among the international forces.

International peace conferences in the 2000s resulted in a number of transitional governments that operated outside Somalia. Left largely to themselves, Somalis in the country established alternative governance structures; some areas formed their own administrations, such as Somaliland and Puntland, while others developed localized institutions. Many local populations turned to sharia courts, an Islamic judicial system that implements religious law. Several of these courts came together in 2006 to form the Islamic Courts Union (ICU). The ICU established order in many areas of central and southern Somalia, including Mogadishu, but was forced out when Ethiopia intervened militarily in 2006 on behalf of the Somali Transitional Federal Government (TFG). As the TFG settled in the capital, the ICU fled to rural areas or left Somalia altogether, but the organization reemerged less than a year later as the Islamic insurgent and terrorist movement al-Shabaab, which is still active today.

In 2007, the African Union (AU) established a peacekeeping force, took over security responsibility for the country, and gave the TFG space to develop Somalia's new government. By 2012, Somali powerbrokers agreed on a provisional constitution with a loose federal structure and established a central government in Mogadishu called the Somali Federal Government (SFG). Since then, the country has seen several interim regional administrations and three presidential elections, but significant governance and security problems remain because al-Shabaab still controls large portions of the country.

GEOGRAPHY

Location: Eastern Africa, bordering the Gulf of Aden and the Indian Ocean, east of Ethiopia

Geographic coordinates: 10 00 N, 49 00 E

Map references: Africa

Area: *total:* 637,657 sq km
land: 627,337 sq km

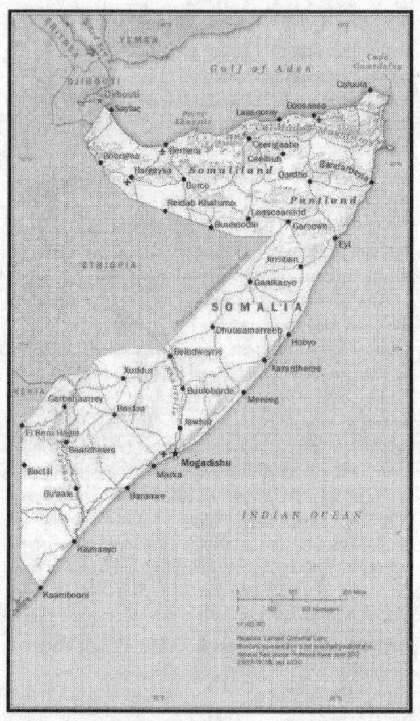

water: 10,320 sq km
comparison ranking: total 46

Area - comparative: almost five times the size of Alabama; slightly smaller than Texas

Land boundaries: *total:* 2,385 km
border countries (3): Djibouti 61 km; Ethiopia 1,640 km; Kenya 684 km

Coastline: 3,025 km

Maritime claims: *territorial sea:* 200 nm; note: the US does not recognize this claim
exclusive economic zone: 200 nm

Climate: principally desert; northeast monsoon (December to February), moderate temperatures in north and hot in south; southwest monsoon (May to October), torrid in the north and hot in the south, irregular rainfall, hot and humid periods (tangambili) between monsoons

Terrain: mostly flat to undulating plateau rising to hills in north

Elevation: *highest point:* Mount Shimbiris 2,460 m
lowest point: Indian Ocean 0 m
mean elevation: 410 m

Natural resources: uranium and largely unexploited reserves of iron ore, tin, gypsum, bauxite, copper, salt, natural gas, likely oil reserves

Land use: *agricultural land:* 70.3% (2022 est.)
arable land: 1.8% (2022 est.)
permanent crops: 0% (2022 est.)
permanent pasture: 68.5% (2022 est.)
forest: 9.3% (2022 est.)
other: 20.4% (2022 est.)

Irrigated land: 2,000 sq km (2012)

Major aquifers: Ogaden-Juba Basin

Population distribution: distribution varies greatly throughout the country; least densely populated areas are in the northeast and central regions, as well as areas along the Kenyan border; most populated areas are in and around the cities of Mogadishu, Marka, Boorama, Hargeysa, and Baidoa, as shown on this population distribution map

Natural hazards: recurring droughts; frequent dust storms over eastern plains in summer; floods during rainy season

Geography - note: strategic location on Horn of Africa along southern approaches to Bab el Mandeb and route through Red Sea and Suez Canal

PEOPLE AND SOCIETY

Population: *total:* 13,017,273 (2024 est.)
male: 6,546,312
female: 6,470,961
comparison rankings: total 78; male 79; female 78

Nationality: *noun:* Somali(s)
adjective: Somali

Ethnic groups: predominantly Somali with lesser numbers of Arabs, Bantus, and others

Languages: Somali (official), Arabic (official), Italian, English
major-language sample(s):
Buugga Xaqiiqda Aduunka, waa laga maarmaanka macluumaadka assasiga. (Somali)

Religions: Muslim 99.9% (Sunni Muslim 98.1%, Shia Muslim 1.2%, Islamic schismatic 0.6%), ethnic religionist 0.1% (2020 est.)

Age structure: *0-14 years:* 41.4% (male 2,689,086/ female 2,694,372)
15-64 years: 55.8% (male 3,699,721/female 3,568,163)
65 years and over: 2.8% (2024 est.) (male 157,505/ female 208,426)

Dependency ratios: *total dependency ratio:* 100.9 (2024 est.)
youth dependency ratio: 97.6 (2024 est.)
elderly dependency ratio: 3.2 (2024 est.)
potential support ratio: 30.8 (2024 est.)

Median age: *total:* 19.1 years (2024 est.)
male: 19.3 years
female: 18.9 years
comparison ranking: total 215

Population growth rate: 2.55% (2024 est.)
comparison ranking: 15

Birth rate: 37.4 births/1,000 population (2024 est.)
comparison ranking: 8

Death rate: 11.2 deaths/1,000 population (2024 est.)
comparison ranking: 23

Net migration rate: -0.7 migrant(s)/1,000 population (2024 est.)
comparison ranking: 136

Population distribution: distribution varies greatly throughout the country; least densely populated areas are in the northeast and central regions, as well as areas along the Kenyan border; most populated areas are in and around the cities of Mogadishu, Marka, Boorama, Hargeysa, and Baidoa, as shown on this population distribution map

Urbanization: *urban population:* 47.9% of total population (2023)
rate of urbanization: 4.2% annual rate of change (2020-25 est.)

Major urban areas - population: 2.610 million MOGADISHU (capital), 1.127 million Hargeysa (2023)

Sex ratio: *at birth:* 1.03 male(s)/female
0-14 years: 1 male(s)/female
15-64 years: 1.04 male(s)/female
65 years and over: 0.76 male(s)/female
total population: 1.01 male(s)/female (2024 est.)

Maternal mortality ratio: 563 deaths/100,000 live births (2023 est.)
comparison ranking: 6

Infant mortality rate: *total:* 83.6 deaths/1,000 live births (2024 est.)
male: 93.2 deaths/1,000 live births
female: 73.7 deaths/1,000 live births
comparison ranking: total 2

Life expectancy at birth: *total population:* 56.5 years (2024 est.)
male: 54.1 years
female: 59 years
comparison ranking: total population 225

Total fertility rate: 5.12 children born/woman (2024 est.)
comparison ranking: 8

Gross reproduction rate: 2.52 (2024 est.)

Drinking water source: *improved: urban:* 80.1% of population (2022 est.)
rural: 38.6% of population (2022 est.)
total: 58.3% of population (2022 est.)
unimproved: urban: 19.9% of population (2022 est.)
rural: 61.4% of population (2022 est.)
total: 41.7% of population (2022 est.)

Health expenditure: 2.5% of national budget (2022 est.)

Physician density: 0.05 physicians/1,000 population (2014)

Hospital bed density: 0.9 beds/1,000 population (2019 est.)

Sanitation facility access: *improved: urban:* 82.9% of population (2022 est.)
rural: 34.8% of population (2022 est.)
total: 57.6% of population (2022 est.)
unimproved: urban: 17.1% of population (2022 est.)
rural: 65.2% of population (2022 est.)
total: 42.4% of population (2022 est.)

Obesity - adult prevalence rate: 8.3% (2016)
comparison ranking: 153

Alcohol consumption per capita: *total:* 0 liters of pure alcohol (2019 est.)
beer: 0 liters of pure alcohol (2019 est.)
wine: 0 liters of pure alcohol (2019 est.)
spirits: 0 liters of pure alcohol (2019 est.)
other alcohols: 0 liters of pure alcohol (2019 est.)
comparison ranking: total 188

Currently married women (ages 15-49): 62.9% (2023 est.)

Education expenditure: 0.3% of GDP (2019 est.)
4.2% national budget (2019 est.)
comparison ranking: Education expenditure (% GDP) 200

Literacy: *total population:* 54% (2022 est.)
male: 65% (2022 est.)
female: 44% (2022 est.)

ENVIRONMENT

Environmental issues: water scarcity; contaminated water; improper waste disposal; deforestation; land degradation; overgrazing; soil erosion; desertification

International environmental agreements: *party to:* Biodiversity, Climate Change, Climate Change-Kyoto Protocol, Climate Change-Paris Agreement, Desertification, Endangered Species, Hazardous Wastes, Law of the Sea, Ozone Layer Protection *signed, but not ratified:* Nuclear Test Ban

Climate: principally desert; northeast monsoon (December to February), moderate temperatures in north and hot in south; southwest monsoon (May to October), torrid in the north and hot in the south, irregular rainfall, hot and humid periods (tangambili) between monsoons

Urbanization: *urban population:* 47.9% of total population (2023)
rate of urbanization: 4.2% annual rate of change (2020-25 est.)

Carbon dioxide emissions: 838,000 metric tonnes of CO2 (2023 est.)
from coal and metallurgical coke: 10 metric tonnes of CO2 (2023 est.)
from petroleum and other liquids: 838,000 metric tonnes of CO2 (2023 est.)
comparison ranking: total emissions 175

Particulate matter emissions: 14.3 micrograms per cubic meter (2019 est.)

Waste and recycling: *municipal solid waste generated annually:* 2.326 million tons (2024 est.)

Total water withdrawal: *municipal:* 15 million cubic meters (2022 est.)
industrial: 2 million cubic meters (2022 est.)
agricultural: 3.281 billion cubic meters (2022 est.)

Total renewable water resources: 14.7 billion cubic meters (2022 est.)

GOVERNMENT

Country name: *conventional long form:* Federal Republic of Somalia
conventional short form: Somalia
local long form: Jamhuuriyadda Federaalka Soomaaliya (Somali)/Jumhuriyat as Sumal al Fidiraliyah (Arabic)
local short form: Soomaaliya (Somali)/As Sumal (Arabic)
former: British Somaliland, Italian Somaliland, Somali Republic, Somali Democratic Republic
etymology: the name means "Land of the Somali," a local ethnic group; the origin of the group's name is unclear but may come from 1) a Cushitic word meaning "dark," 2) the local phrase *soo mal*, meaning "go and milk" (referring to offering guests milk), 3) the name of a local chief, or 4) the Arabic *zamla*, meaning "cattle"

Government type: federal parliamentary republic

Capital: *name:* Mogadishu
geographic coordinates: 2 04 N, 45 20 E
time difference: UTC+3 (8 hours ahead of Washington, DC, during Standard Time)
etymology: the name is probably derived from the Arabic word *mukaddas*, meaning "holy"

Administrative divisions: 18 regions (*gobollo*, singular - *gobol*); Awdal, Bakool, Banaadir, Bari, Bay, Galguduud, Gedo, Hiiraan, Jubbada Dhexe (Middle Jubba), Jubbada Hoose (Lower Jubba), Mudug, Nugaal, Sanaag, Shabeellaha Dhexe (Middle Shabeelle), Shabeellaha Hoose (Lower Shabeelle), Sool, Togdheer, Woqooyi Galbeed

Legal system: mixed system of civil law, Islamic (sharia) law, and customary law (referred to as Xeer)

Constitution: *history:* previous 1961, 1979; latest drafted 12 June 2012, adopted 1 August 2012
amendment process: proposed by the federal government, by members of the state governments, the Federal Parliament, or by public petition; proposals require review by a joint committee of Parliament with inclusion of public comments and state legislatures' comments; passage requires at least two-thirds majority vote in both houses of Parliament and approval by a majority of votes cast in a referendum; constitutional clauses on Islamic principles, the federal system, human rights and freedoms, powers and authorities of the government branches, and inclusion of women in national institutions cannot be amended

International law organization participation: accepts compulsory ICJ jurisdiction with reservations; non-party state to the ICCt

Citizenship: *citizenship by birth:* no
citizenship by descent only: the father must be a citizen of Somalia
dual citizenship recognized: no
residency requirement for naturalization: 7 years

Suffrage: 18 years of age; universal suffrage starting with 24 June 2024 local elections

Executive branch: *chief of state:* President HASSAN SHEIKH Mohamud (since 23 May 2022)
head of government: Prime Minister Hamza Abdi BARRE (since 25 June 2022)
cabinet: Cabinet appointed by the prime minister, approved by the House of the People
election/appointment process: president indirectly elected by the Federal Parliament by two-thirds majority vote in 2 rounds, if needed, for a single 4-year term; prime minister appointed by the president, approved by the House of the People
most recent election date: 15 May 2022
election results: *2022:* HASSAN SHEIKH Mohamud elected president in third round - Federal Parliament percent of vote in first round - Said ABDULLAHI DENI (Kaah) 20.2%, Mohamed ABDULLAHI Mohamed "Farmaajo" (TPP) 18.3%, HASSAN SHEIKH Mohamud (PDP) 16.2%, Hassan Ali KHAYRE (independent) 14.6%, other 30.7%; Federal Parliament percent of vote in second round - HASSAN SHEIKH Mohamud 34.1%, Mohamed ABDULLAHI Mohamed "Farmaajo" 25.7%, Said ABDULLAHI DENI 21%, Hassan Ali KHAYRE 19.2%; Federal Parliament percent of vote in third round - HASSAN SHEIKH Mohamud 66%, Mohamed ABDULLAHI Mohamed "Farmaajo" 34%
2017: Mohamed ABDULLAHI Mohamed "Farmaajo" elected president in second round; Federal Parliament number of votes in first round - HASSAN SHEIKH Mohamud (PDP) 88, Mohamed ABDULLAHI Mohamed "Farmaajo" (TPP) 72, Sheikh SHARIF Sheikh Ahmed (ARS) 49, other 37; Federal Parliament number of votes in second round - Mohamed ABDULLAHI Mohamed "Farmaajo" 184, HASSAN SHEIKH Mohamud 97, Sheikh SHARIF Sheikh Ahmed 45
expected date of next election: 2026

Legislative branch: *legislature name:* Federal Parliament
legislative structure: bicameral
note: despite the formation of political parties in 2020, the 2021 parliamentary elections maintained a primarily clan-based system of appointments; seats in the legislature were apportioned to Somali member states and not by party representation

Legislative branch - lower chamber: *chamber name:* House of the People (Golaha Shacabka)
number of seats: 275 (all indirectly elected)
scope of elections: full renewal
term in office: 5 years
most recent election date: 11/1/2021 to 5/5/2022
percentage of women in chamber: 19%
expected date of next election: October 2026

Legislative branch - upper chamber: *chamber name:* Upper House (Aqalka Sare)
number of seats: 54 (all indirectly elected)
scope of elections: full renewal
term in office: 5 years
most recent election date: 7/27/2021 to 11/13/2021
percentage of women in chamber: 25.9%
expected date of next election: July 2026

Judicial branch: *highest court(s):* the provisional constitution stipulates the establishment of the Constitutional Court (consists of 5 judges, including the chief judge and deputy chief judge)
judge selection and term of office: judges appointed by the president on proposal of the Judicial Service Commission, a 9-member judicial and administrative body; judge tenure NA
subordinate courts: federal courts; federal member state-level courts; military courts; sharia courts
note: under the terms of the 2004 Transitional National Charter, a Supreme Court based in Mogadishu and the Appeal Court were established, but most regions have reverted to local forms of conflict resolution, whether secular, Somali customary law, or Islamic law

Political parties: Cosmopolitan Democratic Party
Green Party
Himilo Qaran Party
Ilays Party
Justice and Reconciliation Party
National Progressive Party
Peace and Unity Party
Qaransoor Party
Qiimo Qaran Party
Security and Justice Party
Social Justice Party
Somali Labour Party
Somali Republic Party
Somali Social Unity Party or SSUP
Union for Peace and Development Party or PDP
Wadajir Party
note: in 2017 an independent electoral commission (the NIEC) was inaugurated with a mandate to oversee the process of registration of political parties in the country; as of 2021, the NIEC had registered a total of 110 parties

Diplomatic representation in the US: *chief of mission:* Ambassador DAHIR Hassan Abdi (since 18 September 2024)
chancery: 1609 22nd Street NW, Washington, DC 20008
telephone: [1] (202) 853-9164
email address and website: washingtonembassy@mfa.gov.so
https://usa.mfa.gov.so/

Diplomatic representation from the US: *chief of mission:* Ambassador Richard H. RILEY (since 20 June 2024)
embassy: Mogadishu, (reopened October 2019 on the grounds of the Mogadishu Airport)
mailing address: P.O. Box 606 Village Market 00621 Nairobi, Kenya
telephone: [254] 20 363-6451
email address and website: SomaliaPublicAffairs@state.gov
https://so.usembassy.gov/

International organization participation: ACP, AfDB, AFESD, AMF, AU, CAEU (candidate), EAC, FAO, G-77, IBRD, ICAO, ICRM, IDA, IDB, IFAD, IFC, IFRCS, IGAD, ILO, IMF, IMO, Interpol, IOC, IOM, IPU, ITSO, ITU, LAS, NAM, OIC, OPCW, OPCW (signatory), UN, UNCTAD, UNESCO, UNHCR, UNHRC, UNIDO, UPU, WFTU (NGOs), WHO, WIPO, WMO

Independence: 1 July 1960 (from a merger of British Somaliland, which became independent from the UK on 26 June 1960, and Italian Somaliland, which became independent from the Italian-administered UN trusteeship on 1 July 1960 to form the Somali Republic)

National holiday: Foundation of the Somali Republic, 1 July (1960); note - 26 June (1960) in Somaliland

Flag: *description:* light blue with a large white five-pointed star in the center
meaning: the blue field was originally influenced by the UN flag but today is said to represent the sky and the Indian Ocean; the five points of the star represent the regions in the horn of Africa where Somali people live: the former British Somaliland and Italian Somaliland (which together make up Somalia), Djibouti, Ogaden (Ethiopia), and the Northeast Province (Kenya)

National symbol(s): leopard

National color(s): blue, white

National anthem(s): *title:* "Qolobaa Calankeed" (Every Nation Has Its Own Flag)
lyrics/music: Abdullahi QARSHE
history: adopted 2012
"Qolobaa Calankeed" (Every Nation Has its own Flag): Government - note: regional and local governing bodies continue to exist and control various areas of the country, including the self-declared Republic of Somaliland in northwestern Somalia

ECONOMY

Economic overview: low-income African Horn economy; 30 years of war and instability crippled economic potential; high remittances for basic survival; new fiscal federalism approach; cleared some unsustainable debt; environmentally fragile; digitally driven urbanization efforts

Real GDP (purchasing power parity): $26.77 billion (2024 est.)
$25.747 billion (2023 est.)
$24.706 billion (2022 est.)
note: data in 2021 dollars
comparison ranking: 150

Real GDP growth rate: 4% (2024 est.)
4.2% (2023 est.)
2.7% (2022 est.)
note: annual GDP % growth based on constant local currency
comparison ranking: 72

Real GDP per capita: $1,400 (2024 est.)
$1,400 (2023 est.)
$1,400 (2022 est.)
note: data in 2021 dollars
comparison ranking: 213

GDP (official exchange rate): $12.109 billion (2024 est.)
note: data in current dollars at official exchange rate

Inflation rate (consumer prices): 6.8% (2022 est.)
4.6% (2021 est.)
4.3% (2020 est.)
note: annual % change based on consumer prices
comparison ranking: 162

GDP - composition, by end use: *household consumption:* 124% (2024 est.)
government consumption: 7.6% (2024 est.)
investment in fixed capital: 22.7% (2024 est.)
investment in inventories: 0% (2024 est.)
exports of goods and services: 20% (2024 est.)
imports of goods and services: -74.3% (2024 est.)
note: figures may not total 100% due to rounding or gaps in data collection

Agricultural products: camel milk, milk, goat milk, sheep milk, sugarcane, fruits, sorghum, cassava, vegetables, maize (2023)
note: top ten agricultural products based on tonnage

Industries: light industries, including sugar refining, textiles, wireless communication

Labor force: 3.439 million (2024 est.)
note: number of people ages 15 or older who are employed or seeking work
comparison ranking: 101

Unemployment rate: 18.9% (2024 est.)
19% (2023 est.)
19.1% (2022 est.)
note: % of labor force seeking employment
comparison ranking: 181

Youth unemployment rate (ages 15-24): *total:* 33.9% (2024 est.)
male: 32.1% (2024 est.)
female: 37% (2024 est.)
note: % of labor force ages 15-24 seeking employment
comparison ranking: total 16

Population below poverty line: 54.4% (2022 est.)
note: % of population with income below national poverty line

Remittances: 15.8% of GDP (2023 est.)
17% of GDP (2022 est.)
18.3% of GDP (2021 est.)
note: personal transfers and compensation between resident and non-resident individuals/households/entities

Taxes and other revenues: 0% (of GDP) (2023 est.)
note: central government tax revenue as a % of GDP
comparison ranking: 153

Exports: $2.424 billion (2024 est.)
$2.164 billion (2023 est.)
$1.804 billion (2022 est.)
note: GDP expenditure basis - exports of goods and services in current dollars
comparison ranking: 159

Exports - partners: UAE 35%, Saudi Arabia 27%, Oman 18%, Djibouti 8%, India 3% (2023)
note: top five export partners based on percentage share of exports

Exports - commodities: sheep and goats, gold, postage stamps/documents, other animals, cattle (2023)
note: top five export commodities based on value in dollars

Imports: $9.002 billion (2024 est.)
$8.002 billion (2023 est.)
$7.456 billion (2022 est.)
note: GDP expenditure basis - imports of goods and services in current dollars
comparison ranking: 127

Imports - partners: UAE 29%, China 19%, India 15%, Turkey 8%, Oman 5% (2023)
note: top five import partners based on percentage share of imports

Imports - commodities: raw sugar, tobacco, broadcasting equipment, rice, milk (2023)
note: top five import commodities based on value in dollars

Debt - external: $2.563 billion (2023 est.)
note: present value of external debt in current US dollars
comparison ranking: 91

Exchange rates: Somali shillings (SOS) per US dollar -

Exchange rates: 23,097.987 (2017 est.)
23,061.784 (2016 est.)
22,254.236 (2015 est.)
20,230.929 (2014 est.)
19,283.8 (2013 est.)

ENERGY

Electricity access: *electrification - total population:* 48.9% (2022 est.)
electrification - urban areas: 76.7%
electrification - rural areas: 30.6%

Electricity: *installed generating capacity:* 156,000 kW (2023 est.)
consumption: 396.792 million kWh (2023 est.)
transmission/distribution losses: 15.408 million kWh (2023 est.)
comparison rankings: installed generating capacity 180; consumption 181; transmission/distribution losses 22

Electricity generation sources: *fossil fuels:* 82.5% of total installed capacity (2023 est.)
solar: 16% of total installed capacity (2023 est.)
wind: 1.5% of total installed capacity (2023 est.)

Coal: *imports:* 4 metric tons (2023 est.)

Petroleum: *refined petroleum consumption:* 6,000 bbl/day (2023 est.)

Natural gas: *proven reserves:* 5.663 billion cubic meters (2021 est.)

Energy consumption per capita: 649,000 Btu/person (2023 est.)
comparison ranking: 195

COMMUNICATIONS

Telephones - fixed lines: *total subscriptions:* 91,000 (2022 est.)
subscriptions per 100 inhabitants: 1 (2022 est.) less than 1
comparison ranking: total subscriptions 136

Telephones - mobile cellular: *total subscriptions:* 8.84 million (2022 est.)
subscriptions per 100 inhabitants: 50 (2022 est.)
comparison ranking: total subscriptions 96

Broadcast media: 2 private TV stations rebroadcast Al-Jazeera and CNN; 1 state-operated TV station and 1 private TV station; state-operated Radio Mogadishu; 1 SW and roughly 10 private FM radio stations in Mogadishu; several radio stations in central and southern regions; transmissions of at least 2 international broadcasters available (2019)

Internet country code: .so

Internet users: *percent of population:* 28% (2022 est.)

Broadband - fixed subscriptions: *total:* 119,000 (2022 est.)
subscriptions per 100 inhabitants: 1 (2022 est.)
comparison ranking: total 128

TRANSPORTATION

Civil aircraft registration country code prefix: 6O

Airports: 40 (2025)
comparison ranking: 103

Merchant marine: *total:* 4 (2023)

by type: general cargo 1, other 3
comparison ranking: total 172

Ports: *total ports:* 6 (2024)
large: 1
medium: 0
small: 2
very small: 3
ports with oil terminals: 2
key ports: Baraawe, Berbera, Boosaaso, Kismaayo, Marka, Muqdisho

MILITARY AND SECURITY

Military and security forces: Somali Armed Forces (SAF; aka Somali Defense Force): Somali National Army (SNA; aka Land Forces), Somali Navy, Somali Air Force

Ministry of Internal Security: Somali National Police (SNP, includes Coast Guard, commando unit) (2025)
note 1: Somalia has numerous militia and regional/state forces operating throughout the country; the militia include clan- and warlord-based militias, as well as some that are externally sponsored; regional forces include semi-official paramilitary and special police forces ("darwish")
note 2: Somaliland and Puntland have separate military, security, and paramilitary forces

Military expenditures: 6% of GDP (2021 est.)
6% of GDP (2020 est.)
5.6% of GDP (2019 est.)
6% of GDP (2018 est.)
5.9% of GDP (2017 est.)

Military and security service personnel strengths: estimated 20,000 active Somali Armed Forces (2025)
note: tens of thousands of militia forces are also active in Somalia

Military equipment inventories and acquisitions: the SNA's inventory is a mix of older, secondhand, and donated equipment from a variety of suppliers, including Italy, Russia, South Africa, Turkey, the UK, and the US (2024)

Military service age and obligation: 18 is the legal minimum age for voluntary military service for men and women; conscription of men aged 18-40 and women aged 18-30 is authorized, but not currently utilized (2023)

Military - note: the primary responsibility of the Somali National Army (SNA) is combating the al-Shabaab terrorist group, which controls large portions of central and southern Somalia and continues to conduct attacks targeting both military and civilian sites, including military bases, government institutions, and civilian gatherings; the SNA is supported by the National Police, regional/state security forces, and allied militias, as well as international forces; some African Union (AU) countries have provided military assistance to the SNA since 2007 under the AU Mission in Somalia (AMISOM, 2007-2022), the AU Transition Mission in Somalia (ATMIS, 2022-2024), and the AU Support and Stabilization Mission in Somalia (AUSSOM, January 2025-present); Turkey and the US have also provided direct military support to SNA operations, primarily air strikes
Turkey and the US have formed and trained SNA units, including the US-backed Danab ("Lightning") Brigade and the Turkish-trained Gorgor ("Eagle") brigades; SNA soldiers have also received training from Egypt, Eritrea, Ethiopia, the EU, Uganda, the UAE, and the UK (2025)

TERRORISM

Terrorist group(s): Terrorist group(s): al-Shabaab; Islamic State of Iraq and ash-Sham – Somalia
note: details about the history, aims, leadership, organization, areas of operation, tactics, targets, weapons, size, and sources of support of the group(s) appear(s) in Appendix T

TRANSNATIONAL ISSUES

Refugees and internally displaced persons: *refugees:* 41,763 (2024 est.)

IDPs: 3,869,345 (2024 est.)

SOUTH AFRICA

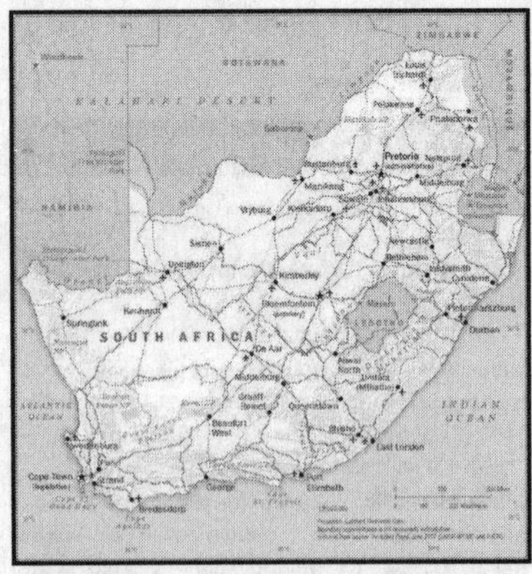

INTRODUCTION

Background: Some of the earliest human remains in the fossil record were found in South Africa. By about A.D. 500, Bantu-speaking groups began settling into what is now northeastern South Africa, displacing Khoisan-speaking groups to the southwest. Dutch traders landed at the southern tip of present-day South Africa in 1652 and established a stopover point on the spice route between the Netherlands and the Far East, founding the city of Cape Town. After the British seized the Cape of Good Hope area in 1806, many settlers of Dutch descent – known then as "Boers," or farmers, but later called Afrikaners – trekked north to found their own republics, Transvaal and Orange Free State. In the 1820s, several decades of wars began as the Zulus expanded their territory, moving out of what is today southeastern South Africa and clashing with other indigenous peoples and the growing European settlements. The discovery of diamonds (1867) and gold (1886) spurred mass immigration, predominantly from Europe.

The Zulu kingdom's territory was incorporated into the British Empire after the Anglo-Zulu War in 1879, and the Afrikaner republics were incorporated after their defeat in the Second South African War (1899-1902). Beginning in 1910, the British and the Afrikaners ruled together under the Union of South Africa, which left the British Commonwealth to become a fully self-governing republic in 1961 after a Whites-only referendum. In 1948, the National Party was voted into power and instituted a policy of apartheid – billed as "separate development" of the races – which favored the White minority and suppressed the Black majority and other non-White groups. The African National Congress (ANC) led the resistance to apartheid, and many top ANC leaders such as Nelson MANDELA spent decades in South Africa's prisons. Internal protests and insurgency, as well as boycotts from some Western nations and institutions, led to the regime's eventual willingness to unban the ANC and negotiate a peaceful transition to majority rule.

The first multi-racial elections in 1994 ushered in majority rule under an ANC-led government. South Africa has since struggled to address apartheid-era imbalances in wealth, housing, education, and health care under successive administrations. President Cyril RAMAPHOSA, who was reelected as the ANC leader in 2022, has made some progress in reigning in corruption.

GEOGRAPHY

Location: Southern Africa, at the southern tip of the continent of Africa

Geographic coordinates: 29 00 S, 24 00 E

Map references: Africa

Area: *total:* 1,219,090 sq km
land: 1,214,470 sq km
water: 4,620 sq km
note: includes Prince Edward Islands (Marion Island and Prince Edward Island)
comparison ranking: total 26

Area - comparative: slightly less than twice the size of Texas

Land boundaries: *total:* 5,244 km
border countries (6): Botswana 1,969 km; Lesotho 1,106 km; Mozambique 496 km; Namibia 1,005 km; Eswatini 438 km; Zimbabwe 230 km

Coastline: 2,798 km

Maritime claims: *territorial sea:* 12 nm
contiguous zone: 24 nm
exclusive economic zone: 200 nm
continental shelf: 200 nm or to edge of the continental margin

Climate: mostly semiarid; subtropical along east coast; sunny days, cool nights

Terrain: vast interior plateau rimmed by rugged hills and narrow coastal plain

Elevation: *highest point:* Ntheledi (Mafadi) 3,450 m
lowest point: Atlantic/Indian Oceans 0 m
mean elevation: 1,034 m

Natural resources: gold, chromium, antimony, coal, iron ore, manganese, nickel, phosphates, tin, rare earth elements, uranium, gem diamonds, platinum, copper, vanadium, salt, natural gas
note: South Africa was the World's leading chromite ore producer in 2022 with an output of 18,000 mt

Land use: *agricultural land:* 79.4% (2022 est.)
arable land: 9.9% (2022 est.)
permanent crops: 0.3% (2022 est.)
permanent pasture: 69.2% (2022 est.)
forest: 14% (2022 est.)
other: 6.6% (2022 est.)

Irrigated land: 16,700 sq km (2012)

Major rivers (by length in km): Orange (shared with Lesotho [s], and Namibia [m]) - 2,092 km; Limpoporivier (Limpopo) river source (shared with Botswana, Zimbabwe, and Mozambique [m]) - 1,800 km; Vaal [s] - 1,210 km
note: [s] after country name indicates river source; [m] after country name indicates river mouth

Major watersheds (area sq km): Atlantic Ocean drainage: Orange (941,351 sq km)

Major aquifers: Karoo Basin, Lower Kalahari-Stampriet Basin

Population distribution: the population is concentrated along the southern and southeastern coast, and inland around Pretoria; the eastern half of the country is more densely populated than the west, as shown in this population distribution map

Natural hazards: prolonged droughts
volcanism: the volcano that formed Marion Island in the Prince Edward Islands is South Africa's only active volcano

Geography - note: *note 1:* South Africa completely surrounds Lesotho and almost completely surrounds Eswatini
note 2: sometimes mistaken for the southernmost point of Africa, the Cape of Good Hope is more accurately described as the southwestern-most point of the African continent; Cape Agulhas, the meeting point of the Atlantic and Indian Oceans, is the southernmost point of the African continent

PEOPLE AND SOCIETY

Population: *total:* 60,442,647 (2024 est.)
male: 29,664,388
female: 30,778,259
comparison rankings: total 25; male 24; female 25

Nationality: *noun:* South African(s)
adjective: South African

Ethnic groups: Black African 80.9%, Colored 8.8%, White 7.8%, Indian/Asian 2.6% (2021 est.)
note: Colored is a term used in South Africa, including on the national census, for persons of mixed race ancestry who developed a distinct cultural identity over several hundred years

Languages: isiZulu or Zulu (official) 25.3%, isiXhosa or Xhosa (official) 14.8%, Afrikaans (official) 12.2%, Sepedi or Pedi (official) 10.1%, Setswana or Tswana (official) 9.1%, English (official) 8.1%, Sesotho or Sotho (official) 7.9%, Xitsonga or Tsonga (official) 3.6%, siSwati or Swati (official) 2.8%, Tshivenda or Venda (official) 2.5%, isiNdebele or Ndebele (official) 1.6%, other (includes South African sign language (official) and Khoi or Khoisan or Khoe languages) 2% (2018 est.)
major-language sample(s):
Die Wereld Feite Boek, n' onontbeerlike bron vir basiese informasie. (Afrikaans)
note: data represent language spoken most often at home

Religions: Christian 86%, ancestral, tribal, animist, or other traditional African religions 5.4%, Muslim 1.9%, other 1.5%, nothing in particular 5.2% (2015 est.)

Age structure: *0-14 years:* 27.2% (male 8,227,690/ female 8,194,392)
15-64 years: 65.3% (male 19,524,873/female 19,947,839)
65 years and over: 7.5% (2024 est.) (male 1,911,825/ female 2,636,028)

Dependency ratios: *total dependency ratio:* 53.1 (2024 est.)
youth dependency ratio: 41.6 (2024 est.)
elderly dependency ratio: 11.5 (2024 est.)
potential support ratio: 8.7 (2024 est.)

Median age: *total:* 30.4 years (2024 est.)
male: 30.1 years
female: 30.6 years
comparison ranking: total 136

Population growth rate: 1.07% (2024 est.)
comparison ranking: 90

Birth rate: 17.7 births/1,000 population (2024 est.)
comparison ranking: 82

Death rate: 6.9 deaths/1,000 population (2024 est.)
comparison ranking: 124

Net migration rate: -0.2 migrant(s)/1,000 population (2024 est.)
comparison ranking: 104

Population distribution: the population is concentrated along the southern and southeastern coast, and inland around Pretoria; the eastern half of the country is more densely populated than the west, as shown in this population distribution map

Urbanization: *urban population:* 68.8% of total population (2023)
rate of urbanization: 1.72% annual rate of change (2020-25 est.)

Major urban areas - population: 10.316 million Johannesburg (includes Ekurhuleni), 4.890 million Cape Town (legislative capital), 3.228 million Durban, 2.818 million PRETORIA (administrative capital), 1.296 million Port Elizabeth, 934,000 West Rand (2023)

Sex ratio: *at birth:* 1.02 male(s)/female
0-14 years: 1 male(s)/female
15-64 years: 0.98 male(s)/female
65 years and over: 0.73 male(s)/female
total population: 0.96 male(s)/female (2024 est.)

Maternal mortality ratio: 118 deaths/100,000 live births (2023 est.)
comparison ranking: 60

Infant mortality rate: *total:* 21.9 deaths/1,000 live births (2024 est.)
male: 23.9 deaths/1,000 live births
female: 20 deaths/1,000 live births
comparison ranking: total 71

Life expectancy at birth: *total population:* 71.9 years (2024 est.)
male: 70.3 years
female: 73.5 years
comparison ranking: total population 166

Total fertility rate: 2.27 children born/woman (2024 est.)
comparison ranking: 78

Gross reproduction rate: 1.12 (2024 est.)

Drinking water source: *improved: urban:* 99.1% of population (2022 est.)
rural: 84.5% of population (2022 est.)
total: 94.5% of population (2022 est.)
unimproved: urban: 0.9% of population (2022 est.)
rural: 15.5% of population (2022 est.)
total: 5.5% of population (2022 est.)

Health expenditure: 8.3% of GDP (2021)
16.9% of national budget (2022 est.)

Physician density: 0.79 physicians/1,000 population (2022)

Sanitation facility access: *improved: urban:* 95.9% of population (2022 est.)
rural: 81.7% of population (2022 est.)
total: 91.4% of population (2022 est.)
unimproved: urban: 4.1% of population (2022 est.)
rural: 18.3% of population (2022 est.)
total: 8.6% of population (2022 est.)

Obesity - adult prevalence rate: 28.3% (2016)
comparison ranking: 30

Alcohol consumption per capita: *total:* 7.21 liters of pure alcohol (2019 est.)
beer: 3.99 liters of pure alcohol (2019 est.)
wine: 1.21 liters of pure alcohol (2019 est.)
spirits: 1.31 liters of pure alcohol (2019 est.)
other alcohols: 0.7 liters of pure alcohol (2019 est.)
comparison ranking: total 58

Tobacco use: *total:* 20.1% (2025 est.)
male: 35.3% (2025 est.)
female: 6% (2025 est.)
comparison ranking: total 69

Children under the age of 5 years underweight: 4.9% (2017)
comparison ranking: 66

Currently married women (ages 15-49): 36.9% (2023 est.)

Child marriage: *women married by age 15:* 0.9% (2016)
women married by age 18: 3.6% (2016)
men married by age 18: 0.6% (2016)

Education expenditure: 6.7% of GDP (2024 est.)
18.6% national budget (2022 est.)
comparison ranking: Education expenditure (% GDP) 18

Literacy: *total population:* 90% (2021 est.)
male: 91% (2021 est.)
female: 89% (2021 est.)

School life expectancy (primary to tertiary education): *total:* 14 years (2022 est.)
male: 14 years (2022 est.)
female: 14 years (2022 est.)

ENVIRONMENT

Environmental issues: limited freshwater resources due to lack of major rivers or lakes; pollution of rivers from agricultural runoff and urban waste; air pollution resulting in acid rain; deforestation; soil erosion;

land degradation; desertification; solid waste pollution; significant floral extinctions

International environmental agreements: *party to:* Antarctic-Environmental Protection, Antarctic-Marine Living Resources, Antarctic Seals, Antarctic Treaty, Biodiversity, Climate Change, Climate Change-Kyoto Protocol, Climate Change-Paris Agreement, Comprehensive Nuclear Test Ban, Desertification, Endangered Species, Hazardous Wastes, Law of the Sea, Marine Dumping-London Convention, Marine Dumping-London Protocol, Marine Life Conservation, Nuclear Test Ban, Ozone Layer Protection, Ship Pollution, Wetlands, Whaling
signed, but not ratified: none of the selected agreements

Climate: mostly semiarid; subtropical along east coast; sunny days, cool nights

Urbanization: *urban population:* 68.8% of total population (2023)
rate of urbanization: 1.72% annual rate of change (2020-25 est.)

Carbon dioxide emissions: 446.704 million metric tonnes of CO2 (2023 est.)
from coal and metallurgical coke: 365.269 million metric tonnes of CO2 (2023 est.)
from petroleum and other liquids: 73.913 million metric tonnes of CO2 (2023 est.)
from consumed natural gas: 7.522 million metric tonnes of CO2 (2023 est.)
comparison ranking: total emissions 12

Particulate matter emissions: 17 micrograms per cubic meter (2019 est.)

Methane emissions: *energy:* 1,489.2 kt (2022-2024 est.)
agriculture: 754.2 kt (2019-2021 est.)
waste: 770.2 kt (2019-2021 est.)
other: 32.1 kt (2019-2021 est.)

Waste and recycling: *municipal solid waste generated annually:* 18.457 million tons (2024 est.)
percent of municipal solid waste recycled: 28.2% (2022 est.)

Total water withdrawal: *municipal:* 3.476 billion cubic meters (2022)
industrial: 4.616 billion cubic meters (2022)
agricultural: 11.839 billion cubic meters (2022)

Total renewable water resources: 51.35 billion cubic meters (2022 est.)

GOVERNMENT

Country name: *conventional long form:* Republic of South Africa
conventional short form: South Africa
former: Union of South Africa
abbreviation: RSA
etymology: self-descriptive name from the country's location on the continent; "Africa" is derived from the Roman designation of the area corresponding to present-day Tunisia "Africa terra," which meant "Land of the Afri" (the tribe resident in that area), but which eventually came to mean the entire continent

Government type: parliamentary republic

Capital: *name:* Pretoria (administrative capital); Cape Town (legislative capital); Bloemfontein (judicial capital)
geographic coordinates: 25 42 S, 28 13 E
time difference: UTC+2 (7 hours ahead of Washington, DC, during Standard Time)
etymology: Pretoria was named in honor of Boer statesman Andries PRETORIUS in 1855; Cape Town's name refers to its location on the Cape of Good Hope; Bloemfontein was named after the farm on which it was built in 1846, whose name combined the Dutch words *bloem* (flower) and *fontein* (fountain)

Administrative divisions: 9 provinces; Eastern Cape, Free State, Gauteng, KwaZulu-Natal, Limpopo, Mpumalanga, Northern Cape, North West, Western Cape

Legal system: mixed system of Roman-Dutch civil law, English common law, and customary law

Constitution: *history:* several previous; latest drafted 8 May 1996, approved by the Constitutional Court 4 December 1996, effective 4 February 1997
amendment process: proposed by the National Assembly of Parliament; passage of amendments affecting constitutional sections on human rights and freedoms, non-racism and non-sexism, supremacy of the constitution, suffrage, the multi-party system of democratic government, and amendment procedures requires at least 75% majority vote of the Assembly, approval by at least six of the nine provinces represented in the National Council of Provinces, and assent of the president of the republic; passage of amendments affecting the Bill of Rights, and those related to provincial boundaries, powers, and authorities requires at least two-thirds majority vote of the Assembly, approval by at least six of the nine provinces represented in the National Council, and assent of the president

International law organization participation: has not submitted an ICJ jurisdiction declaration; accepts ICCt jurisdiction

Citizenship: *citizenship by birth:* no
citizenship by descent only: at least one parent must be a citizen of South Africa
dual citizenship recognized: yes, but requires prior permission of the government
residency requirement for naturalization: 5 year

Suffrage: 18 years of age; universal

Executive branch: *chief of state:* President Matamela Cyril RAMAPHOSA (since 19 June 2024)
head of government: President Matamela Cyril RAMAPHOSA (since 19 June 2024)
cabinet: Cabinet appointed by the president
election/appointment process: president indirectly elected by the National Assembly for a 5-year term (eligible for a second term)
most recent election date: 29 May 2024
election results: *2024:* Matamela Cyril RAMAPHOSA (ANC) elected president by the National Assembly unopposed
2019: Matamela Cyril RAMAPHOSA (ANC) elected president by the National Assembly unopposed
expected date of next election: May 2029
note: the president is both chief of state and head of government

Legislative branch: *legislature name:* Parliament
legislative structure: bicameral

Legislative branch - lower chamber: *chamber name:* National Assembly
number of seats: 400 (all directly elected)
electoral system: proportional representation
scope of elections: full renewal
term in office: 5 years
most recent election date: 5/29/2024
percentage of women in chamber: 45%
expected date of next election: May 2029

Legislative branch - upper chamber: *chamber name:* National Council of Provinces
number of seats: 90 (all appointed)
scope of elections: full renewal
term in office: 5 years
most recent election date: 6/15/2024
percentage of women in chamber: 44.4%
expected date of next election: June 2029
note: the Council has special powers to protect regional interests, including safeguarding cultural and linguistic traditions among ethnic minorities

Judicial branch: *highest court(s):* Supreme Court of Appeals (consists of the court president, deputy president, and 21 judges); Constitutional Court (consists of the chief and deputy chief justices and 9 judges)
judge selection and term of office: Supreme Court of Appeals president and vice president appointed by the national president after consultation with the Judicial Services Commission (JSC), a 23-member body chaired by the chief justice; other Supreme Court judges appointed by the national president on the advice of the JSC and hold office until discharged from active service by an Act of Parliament; Constitutional Court chief and deputy chief justices appointed by the president of South Africa after consultation with the JSC and with heads of the National Assembly; other Constitutional Court judges appointed by the national president after consultation with the chief justice and leaders of the National Assembly; Constitutional Court judges serve 12-year nonrenewable terms or until age 70
subordinate courts: High Courts; Magistrates' Courts; labor courts; land claims courts

Political parties: African Christian Democratic Party or ACDP
African Independent Congress or AIC
African National Congress or ANC
African People's Convention or APC
Agang SA
Congress of the People or COPE
Democratic Alliance or DA
Economic Freedom Fighters or EFF
Freedom Front Plus or FF+
GOOD
Inkatha Freedom Party or IFP
National Freedom Party or NFP
Pan-Africanist Congress of Azania or PAC
United Christian Democratic Party or UCDP
United Democratic Movement or UDM

Diplomatic representation in the US: *chief of mission:* Ambassador (vacant); Chargé d'Affaires Ismail ESAU (since 17 March 2025)
chancery: 3051 Massachusetts Avenue NW, Washington, DC 20008
telephone: [1] (240) 937-5760
FAX: [1] (202) 265-1607
email address and website: Info.saembassyDC@dirco.gov.za
https://www.saembassy.org/
consulate(s) general: Los Angeles, New York

Diplomatic representation from the US: *chief of mission:* Ambassador (vacant); Chargé d'Affaires Marc DILLARD (since October 2025)
embassy: 877 Pretorius Street, Arcadia, Pretoria
mailing address: 9300 Pretoria Place, Washington DC 20521-9300

telephone: [27] (12) 431-4000
FAX: [27] (12) 342-2299
email address and website: ACSJohannesburg@state.gov
https://za.usembassy.gov/
consulate(s) general: Cape Town, Durban, Johannesburg

International organization participation: ACP, AfDB, AIIB, AU, BIS, BRICS, C, CD, FAO, FATF, G-20, G-24, G-5, G-77, IAEA, IBRD, ICAO, ICC (national committees), ICCt, ICRM, IDA, IFAD, IFC, IFRCS, IHO, ILO, IMF, IMO, IMSO, Interpol, IOC, IOM, IPU, ISO, ITSO, ITU, ITUC (NGOs), MIGA, MONUSCO, NAM, NSG, OECD (enhanced engagement), OPCW, Paris Club (associate), PCA, SACU, SADC, UN, UNAMID, UNCTAD, UNESCO, UNHCR, UNIDO, UNISFA, UNITAR, UNOOSA, UNWTO, UPU, Wassenaar Arrangement, WCO, WFTU (NGOs), WHO, WIPO, WMO, WTO, ZC

Independence: *31 May 1910 (Union of South Africa formed from four British colonies:* Cape Colony, Natal, Transvaal, and Orange Free State); 22 August 1934 (Status of the Union Act); 31 May 1961 (republic declared); 27 April 1994 (majority rule)

National holiday: Freedom Day, 27 April (1994)

Flag: *description:* two equal-width horizontal bands of red (top) and blue separated by a central green band that splits into a horizontal Y; a black isosceles triangle is in the Y, with narrow yellow bands around it; the red and blue bands are bordered by narrow white stripes
meaning: the colors have no official meaning, but the Y stands for "the convergence of diverse elements within South African society, taking the road ahead in unity"
note: South Africa has one of two national flags that display six colors as part of the primary design – the other is South Sudan's

National symbol(s): springbok (antelope), king protea flower

National color(s): red, green, blue, yellow, black, white

National anthem(s): *title:* "National Anthem of South Africa"
lyrics/music: Enoch SONTONGA and Cornelius Jacob LANGENHOVEN/Enoch SONTONGA and Marthinus LOURENS de Villiers
history: adopted 1997; a combination of "N'kosi Sikelel' iAfrica" (God Bless Africa) and "Die Stem van Suid Afrika" (The Call of South Africa), which were respectively the anthems of the non-white and white communities under apartheid; official lyrics contain a mixture of Xhosa, Zulu, Sesotho, Afrikaans, and English (the five most widely spoken of South Africa's 11 official languages)

National heritage: *total World Heritage Sites:* 12 (7 cultural, 4 natural, 1 mixed)
selected World Heritage Site locales: Fossil Hominid Sites of South Africa (c); iSimangaliso Wetland Park (n); Robben Island (c); Maloti-Drakensberg Park (m); Mapungubwe Cultural Landscape (c); Cape Floral Region Protected Areas (n); Vredefort Dome (n); Richtersveld Cultural and Botanical Landscape (c); Khomani Cultural Landscape (c); Barberton Makhonjwa Mountains (n); Human Rights, Liberation and Reconciliation: Nelson Mandela Legacy Sites (c); The Emergence of Modern Human Behaviour: The Pleistocene Occupation Sites of South Africa (c)

ECONOMY

Economic overview: upper-middle-income, largest southern African economy; Government of National Unity facing slow growth, fiscal gaps, and structural challenges; high income inequality, unemployment, and poverty; reforms to address electricity generation, transport, and logistics; leading producer and exporter of critical minerals

Real GDP (purchasing power parity): $870.42 billion (2024 est.)
$865.402 billion (2023 est.)
$859.399 billion (2022 est.)
note: data in 2021 dollars
comparison ranking: 33

Real GDP growth rate: 0.6% (2024 est.)
0.7% (2023 est.)
1.9% (2022 est.)
note: annual GDP % growth based on constant local currency
comparison ranking: 187

Real GDP per capita: $13,600 (2024 est.)
$13,700 (2023 est.)
$13,800 (2022 est.)
note: data in 2021 dollars
comparison ranking: 131

GDP (official exchange rate): $400.261 billion (2024 est.)
note: data in current dollars at official exchange rate

Inflation rate (consumer prices): 4.4% (2024 est.)
6.1% (2023 est.)
7% (2022 est.)
note: annual % change based on consumer prices
comparison ranking: 134

GDP - composition, by sector of origin: *agriculture:* 2.9% (2024 est.)
industry: 24.4% (2024 est.)
services: 62.7% (2024 est.)
note: figures may not total 100% due to non-allocated consumption not captured in sector-reported data
comparison rankings: agriculture 133; industry 95; services 70

GDP - composition, by end use: *household consumption:* 64.8% (2024 est.)
government consumption: 19.2% (2024 est.)
investment in fixed capital: 14.5% (2024 est.)
investment in inventories: -0.6% (2024 est.)
exports of goods and services: 31.8% (2024 est.)
imports of goods and services: -29.9% (2024 est.)
note: figures may not total 100% due to rounding or gaps in data collection

Agricultural products: sugarcane, maize, milk, soybeans, potatoes, wheat, grapes, chicken, oranges, apples (2023)
note: top ten agricultural products based on tonnage

Industries: mining (world's largest producer of platinum, gold, chromium), automobile assembly, metalworking, machinery, textiles, iron and steel, chemicals, fertilizer, foodstuffs, commercial ship repair

Industrial production growth rate: -0.4% (2024 est.)
note: annual % change in industrial value added based on constant local currency
comparison ranking: 141

Labor force: 27.766 million (2024 est.)
note: number of people ages 15 or older who are employed or seeking work
comparison ranking: 25

Unemployment rate: 33.2% (2024 est.)
32.1% (2023 est.)
33.3% (2022 est.)
note: % of labor force seeking employment
comparison ranking: 189

Youth unemployment rate (ages 15-24): *total:* 60.9% (2024 est.)
male: 57.1% (2024 est.)
female: 65.5% (2024 est.)
note: % of labor force ages 15-24 seeking employment
comparison ranking: total 2

Average household expenditures: *on food:* 16.1% of household expenditures (2023 est.)
on alcohol and tobacco: 4.1% of household expenditures (2023 est.)

Remittances: 0.2% of GDP (2024 est.)
0.2% of GDP (2023 est.)
0.2% of GDP (2022 est.)
note: personal transfers and compensation between resident and non-resident individuals/households/entities

Budget: *revenues:* $123.263 billion (2022 est.)
expenditures: $137.593 billion (2022 est.)
note: central government revenues (excluding grants) and expenditures converted to US dollars at average official exchange rate for year indicated

Public debt: 76.2% of GDP (2022 est.)
note: central government debt as a % of GDP
comparison ranking: 44

Taxes and other revenues: 26% (of GDP) (2022 est.)
note: central government tax revenue as a % of GDP
comparison ranking: 13

Current account balance: -$2.384 billion (2024 est.)
-$6.143 billion (2023 est.)
-$1.878 billion (2022 est.)
note: balance of payments - net trade and primary/secondary income in current dollars
comparison ranking: 153

Exports: $127.629 billion (2024 est.)
$124.671 billion (2023 est.)
$136.01 billion (2022 est.)
note: balance of payments - exports of goods and services in current dollars
comparison ranking: 41

Exports - partners: China 19%, USA 8%, Germany 7%, India 7%, UK 6% (2023)
note: top five export partners based on percentage share of exports

Exports - commodities: gold, platinum, coal, cars, iron ore (2023)
note: top five export commodities based on value in dollars

Imports: $119.59 billion (2024 est.)
$123.454 billion (2023 est.)
$127.669 billion (2022 est.)
note: balance of payments - imports of goods and services in current dollars
comparison ranking: 45

Imports - partners: China 21%, India 7%, USA 7%, Germany 6%, UAE 4% (2023)
note: top five import partners based on percentage share of imports

Imports - commodities: refined petroleum, crude petroleum, gold, cars, broadcasting equipment (2023)
note: top five import commodities based on value in dollars

Reserves of foreign exchange and gold: $65.435 billion (2024 est.)
$62.492 billion (2023 est.)
$60.553 billion (2022 est.)
note: holdings of gold (year-end prices)/foreign exchange/special drawing rights in current dollars
comparison ranking: 37

Debt - external: $93.879 billion (2023 est.)
note: present value of external debt in current US dollars
comparison ranking: 10

Exchange rates: rand (ZAR) per US dollar -

Exchange rates: 18.329 (2024 est.)
18.45 (2023 est.)
16.356 (2022 est.)
14.779 (2021 est.)
16.459 (2020 est.)

ENERGY

Electricity access: *electrification - total population:* 86.5% (2022 est.)
electrification - urban areas: 87.1%
electrification - rural areas: 93.4%

Electricity: *installed generating capacity:* 65.989 million kW (2023 est.)
consumption: 194.978 billion kWh (2023 est.)
exports: 12.629 billion kWh (2023 est.)
imports: 10.837 billion kWh (2023 est.)
transmission/distribution losses: 22.838 billion kWh (2023 est.)
comparison rankings: installed generating capacity 21; consumption 23; exports 20; imports 23; transmission/distribution losses 190

Electricity generation sources: *fossil fuels:* 87.3% of total installed capacity (2023 est.)
nuclear: 3.7% of total installed capacity (2023 est.)
solar: 2.9% of total installed capacity (2023 est.)
wind: 5.3% of total installed capacity (2023 est.)
hydroelectricity: 0.7% of total installed capacity (2023 est.)
biomass and waste: 0.2% of total installed capacity (2023 est.)

Nuclear energy: Number of operational nuclear reactors: 2 (2025)

Net capacity of operational nuclear reactors: 1.85GW (2025 est.)

Percent of total electricity production: 4.4% (2023 est.)

Coal: *production:* 239.712 million metric tons (2023 est.)
consumption: 176.095 million metric tons (2023 est.)
exports: 66.918 million metric tons (2023 est.)
imports: 3.301 million metric tons (2023 est.)
proven reserves: 9.893 billion metric tons (2023 est.)

Petroleum: *total petroleum production:* 88,000 bbl/day (2023 est.)
refined petroleum consumption: 609,000 bbl/day (2023 est.)
crude oil estimated reserves: 15 million barrels (2021 est.)

Natural gas: *production:* 66.094 million cubic meters (2023 est.)
consumption: 3.834 billion cubic meters (2023 est.)
imports: 3.768 billion cubic meters (2023 est.)

Energy consumption per capita: 86.197 million Btu/person (2023 est.)
comparison ranking: 61

COMMUNICATIONS

Telephones - fixed lines: *total subscriptions:* 1.353 million (2023 est.)
subscriptions per 100 inhabitants: 2 (2023 est.)
comparison ranking: total subscriptions 60

Telephones - mobile cellular: *total subscriptions:* 108 million (2023 est.)
subscriptions per 100 inhabitants: 167 (2022 est.)
comparison ranking: total subscriptions 16

Broadcast media: the South African Broadcasting Corporation (SABC) operates 6 free-to-air TV stations; 1 private TV station; multiple subscription TV services with mix of local and international channels; mix of public and private radio stations at the national, regional, and local levels; state-owned SABC radio network has 18 stations, including one for each of the 11 official languages, 4 community stations, and 3 commercial stations; over 100 community stations with rural coverage

Internet country code: .za

Internet users: *percent of population:* 76% (2023 est.)

Broadband - fixed subscriptions: *total:* 2.15 million (2023 est.)
subscriptions per 100 inhabitants: 3 (2023 est.)
comparison ranking: total 58

TRANSPORTATION

Civil aircraft registration country code prefix: ZS

Airports: 573 (2025)
comparison ranking: 13

Heliports: 49 (2025)
comparison ranking: 40

Railways: *total:* 30,400 km (2021)
standard gauge: 80 km (2021) 1.435-m gauge (80 km electrified)
narrow gauge: 19,756 km (2014) 1.065-m gauge (8,271 km electrified)

Merchant marine: *total:* 110 (2023)
by type: bulk carrier 3, general cargo 1, oil tanker 7, other 99
comparison ranking: total 86

Ports: *total ports:* 8 (2024)
large: 2
medium: 4
small: 1
very small: 1
ports with oil terminals: 7
key ports: Cape Town, Durban, Mossel Bay, Port Elizabeth, Richards Bay, Saldanha Bay

MILITARY AND SECURITY

Military and security forces: South African National Defense Force (SANDF): South African Army (includes Reserve Force), South African Navy (SAN), South African Air Force (SAAF), South African Military Health Services

Ministry of Police: South African Police Service (SAPS) (2025)

Military expenditures: 0.7% of GDP (2024 est.)
0.7% of GDP (2023 est.)
0.8% of GDP (2022 est.)
0.9% of GDP (2021 est.)
1.1% of GDP (2020 est.)

Military and security service personnel strengths: approximately 65-70,000 active-duty National Defense Forces (2025)

Military equipment inventories and acquisitions: the SANDF's inventory consists of a mix of domestically produced and foreign-supplied equipment; South Africa's domestic defense industry produced most of the Army's major weapons systems (some were jointly produced with foreign companies), while the Air Force and Navy inventories include a mix of aging European-, Israeli-, and US-origin weapons and equipment; South Africa has one of Africa's leading defense industries (2024)

Military service age and obligation: 18-22 (18-26 for college graduates) years of age for voluntary military service for men and women; 2-year service obligation (2023)
note: in 2023, women comprised nearly 30% of the military

Military deployments: approximately 1,100 Democratic Republic of the Congo (MONUSCO) (2025)

Military - note: the South African National Defense Force's (SANDF) primary responsibilities include territorial and maritime defense, supporting the Police Service, protecting key infrastructure, responding to disasters, and participating in international peacekeeping missions; border security and maintaining a rapid reaction capability for regional security missions and disaster response are priorities; in recent years, it has been deployed internally to assist the Police with quelling unrest and assisting with border security; the SANDF also regularly participates in African and UN peacekeeping missions and is a member of the Southern Africa Development Community (SADC) Standby Force; in 2021, South AFrica sent about 1,500 SANDF troops to Mozambique as part of a multinational SADC force to help combat an insurgency
the SANDF was created in 1994 to replace the South African Defense Force (SADF); the SANDF was opened to all South Africans who met military requirements, while the SADF was a mostly white force (only whites were subject to conscription) with non-whites only allowed to join in a voluntary capacity; the SANDF also absorbed members of the various anti-apartheid opposition groups, including the African National Congress, the Pan Africanist Congress, and the Inkatha Freedom Party, as well as the security forces of the formerly independent Bantustan homelands (2025)

SPACE

Space agency/agencies: South African National Space Agency (SANSA; established 2010) (2025)

Space launch site(s): Arniston launch facility (Western Cape) used to support space launch vehicle and ballistic missile program (1980s-1990s); it is now a weapons testing facility called the Denel Overberg Test Range (2024)

Space program overview: space program is one of the most advanced in Africa; key areas of emphasis include Earth observation/remote sensing (RS), space weather monitoring, space scientific research, space engineering, and space operations (tracking, telemetry, etc); produces and operates satellites; has a sounding rocket program for carrying experimental payloads for research purposes; cooperates with a variety of foreign space agencies and industries,

including those of China, France, India, Russia, and the US; member of the African Space Agency; participates in international programs such as the Square Kilometer Array (SKA) Project, an effort to build the world's largest radio telescope by 2030; has a substantial number of state- and privately-owned aerospace companies, as well as academic and research institutions involved in space-related activities (2025)
note: further details about the key activities, programs, and milestones of the country's space program, as well as government spending estimates on the space sector, appear in the Space Programs reference guide

TERRORISM

Terrorist group(s): Terrorist group(s): Islamic State of Iraq and ash-Sham (ISIS)
note: details about the history, aims, leadership, organization, areas of operation, tactics, targets, weapons, size, and sources of support of the group(s) appear(s) in Appendix T

TRANSNATIONAL ISSUES

Refugees and internally displaced persons: *refugees:* 171,484 (2024 est.)

IDPs: 7,385 (2024 est.)

Trafficking in persons: *tier rating:* Tier 2 Watch List — the government did not demonstrate overall increasing efforts to eliminate trafficking compared with the previous reporting period, therefore South Africa was downgraded to Tier 2 Watch List; for more details, go to: https://www.state.gov/reports/2025-trafficking-in-persons-report/south-africa/

Illicit drugs: USG identification: major precursor-chemical producer (2025)

SOUTH GEORGIA AND SOUTH SANDWICH ISLANDS

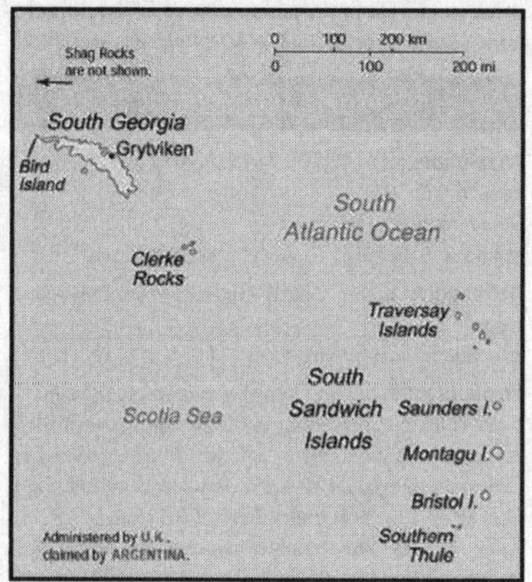

INTRODUCTION

Background: South Georgia and the South Sandwich Islands lie approximately 1,000 km east of the Falkland Islands and have been under British administration since 1908 – except for a brief period in 1982 when Argentina occupied them. Grytviken, on South Georgia, was a 19th- and early 20th-century whaling station. Famed explorer Ernest SHACKLETON stopped there in 1914 en route to his ill-fated attempt to cross Antarctica on foot. He returned some 20 months later with a few companions in a small boat and arranged a successful rescue for the rest of his crew, which was stranded off the Antarctic Peninsula. He died in 1922 on a subsequent expedition and is buried in Grytviken. Today, the station houses scientists from the British Antarctic Survey. Recognizing the importance of preserving the marine stocks in adjacent waters, the UK extended the exclusive fishing zone in 1993, from 12 nm to 200 nm around each island.

GEOGRAPHY

Location: Southern South America, islands in the South Atlantic Ocean, east of the tip of South America

Geographic coordinates: 54 30 S, 37 00 W

Map references: Antarctic Region

Area: *total:* 3,903 sq km
land: 3,903 sq km
water: 0 sq km
note: includes Shag Rocks, Black Rock, Clerke Rocks, South Georgia Island, Bird Island, and the South Sandwich Islands, which consist of 11 islands
comparison ranking: total 176

Area - comparative: slightly larger than Rhode Island

Land boundaries: *total:* 0 km

Coastline: NA

Maritime claims: *territorial sea:* 12 nm
exclusive fishing zone: 200 nm

Climate: variable, with mostly westerly winds throughout the year interspersed with periods of calm; nearly all precipitation falls as snow

Terrain: most of the islands are rugged and mountainous rising steeply from the sea; South Georgia is largely barren with steep, glacier-covered mountains; the South Sandwich Islands are of volcanic origin with some active volcanoes

Elevation: *highest point:* Mount Paget (South Georgia) 2,934 m
lowest point: Atlantic Ocean 0 m

Natural resources: fish

Land use: *other:* 100% (2018 est.)

Irrigated land: 0 sq km (2022)

Natural hazards: the South Sandwich Islands have prevailing weather conditions that generally make them difficult to approach by ship; they are also subject to active volcanism

Geography - note: the north coast of South Georgia has several large bays, which provide good anchorage

PEOPLE AND SOCIETY

Population: *total:* no permanent inhabitants

ENVIRONMENT

Environmental issues: damage to native wildlife from imported animals

Climate: variable, with mostly westerly winds throughout the year interspersed with periods of calm; nearly all precipitation falls as snow

GOVERNMENT

Country name: *conventional long form:* South Georgia and the South Sandwich Islands
conventional short form: South Georgia and South Sandwich Islands
abbreviation: SGSSI
etymology: Captain James COOK originally named it "the Isle of Georgia" in 1775 in honor of British King GEORGE III; the word "South" was later added to distinguish these islands from the other Sandwich Islands, now known as the Hawaiian Islands

Dependency status: overseas territory of the UK, also claimed by Argentina; administered from the Falkland Islands by a commissioner, who is concurrently governor of the Falkland Islands, representing the British monarch

Legal system: the laws of the UK apply

Diplomatic representation in the US: none (administered by the UK, claimed by Argentina)

Diplomatic representation from the US: none (administered by the UK, claimed by Argentina)

International organization participation: UPU

Flag: *description:* blue with the UK flag in the upper-left quadrant; the islands' coat of arms is centered on the right half of the flag and has a green shield with a golden lion holding a torch; a fur seal is to the left of the shield and a Macaroni penguin to the right; a reindeer appears above the crest, and below the shield on a scroll is the motto LEO TERRAM PROPRIAM PROTEGAT (Let the Lion Protect its Own Land)
meaning: the lion represents the UK and discovery; the seal, penguin, and reindeer are native to the islands

TRANSPORTATION

Heliports: 1 (2025)
comparison ranking: 149

Ports: *total ports:* 3 (2024)
large: 0
medium: 0
small: 0
very small: 3
ports with oil terminals: 1
key ports: Grytviken, Prince Olav Harbor, Stromness Harbor

MILITARY AND SECURITY

Military - note: defense is the responsibility of the UK

SOUTH SUDAN

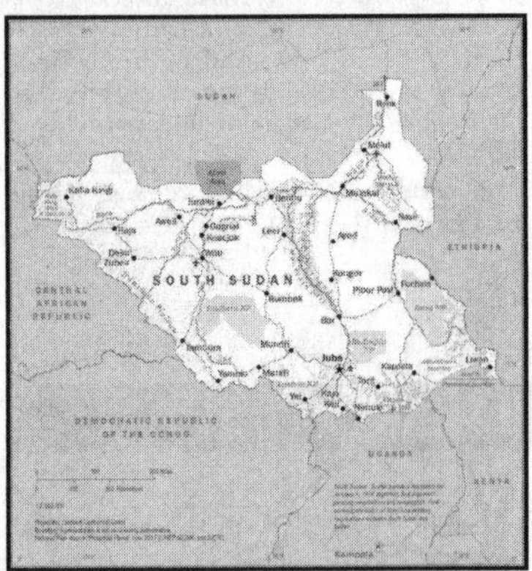

INTRODUCTION

Background: South Sudan, which gained independence from Sudan in 2011, is the world's newest country. Home to a diverse array of mainly Nilotic ethnolinguistic groups that settled in the territory in the 15th through 19th centuries, South Sudanese society is heavily dependent on seasonal migration and seasonal fluctuations in precipitation. Modern-day South Sudan was conquered first by Egypt and later ruled jointly by Egyptian-British colonial administrators in the late 19th century. Christian missionaries helped spread the English language and Christianity in the area, leading to significant cultural differences with the northern part of Sudan, where Arabic and Islam are dominant. When Sudan gained its independence in 1956, the southern region received assurances that it would participate fully in the political system. However, the Arab government in Khartoum reneged on its promises, prompting two periods of civil war (1955-1972 and 1983-2005) in which as many as 2.5 million people died – mostly civilians – due largely to starvation and drought. The second Sudanese civil war was one of the deadliest since WWII and left southern Sudanese society devastated. Peace talks resulted in a US-backed Comprehensive Peace Agreement in 2005, which granted the South six years of autonomy followed by a referendum on final status. The result of this referendum, held in 2011, was a vote of 98% in favor of secession.

Since independence, South Sudan has struggled to form a viable governing system and has been plagued by widespread corruption, political conflict, and communal violence. In 2013, conflict erupted between forces loyal to President Salva KIIR, a Dinka, and forces loyal to Vice President Riek MACHAR, a Nuer. The conflict quickly spread through the country along ethnic lines, killing tens of thousands and creating a humanitarian crisis with millions of South Sudanese displaced. KIIR and MACHAR signed a peace agreement in 2015 that created a Transitional Government of National Unity the next year. However, renewed fighting broke out in Juba between KIIR and MACHAR's forces, plunging the country back into conflict and drawing in additional armed opposition groups. A "revitalized" peace agreement was signed in 2018, mostly ending the fighting and laying the groundwork for a unified national army, a transitional government, and elections. The transitional government was formed in 2020, when MACHAR returned to Juba as first vice president. Since 2020, implementation of the peace agreement has been stalled amid wrangling over power-sharing, which has contributed to an uptick in communal violence and the country's worst food crisis since independence, with 7 of 11 million South Sudanese citizens in need of humanitarian assistance. The transitional period was extended an additional two years in 2022, pushing elections to late 2024.

GEOGRAPHY

Location: East-Central Africa; south of Sudan, north of Uganda and Kenya, west of Ethiopia

Geographic coordinates: 8 00 N, 30 00 E

Map references: Africa

Area: *total:* 644,329 sq km
land: NA
water: NA
comparison ranking: total 44

Area - comparative: more than four times the size of Georgia; slightly smaller than Texas

Land boundaries: *total:* 6,018 km
border countries (6): Central African Republic 1,055 km; Democratic Republic of the Congo 714 km; Ethiopia 1,299 km; Kenya 317 km; Sudan 2,158 km; Uganda 475 km
note: South Sudan-Sudan boundary represents 1 January 1956 alignment; final alignment pending negotiations and demarcation; final sovereignty status of Abyei Area pending negotiations between South Sudan and Sudan

Coastline: 0 km (landlocked)

Maritime claims: none (landlocked)

Climate: hot with seasonal rainfall influenced by the annual shift of the Inter-Tropical Convergence Zone; rainfall heaviest in upland areas of the south and diminishes to the north

Terrain: plains in the north and center rise to southern highlands along the border with Uganda and Kenya; the White Nile, flowing north out of the uplands of Central Africa, is the major geographic feature of the country; The Sudd (a name derived from floating vegetation that hinders navigation) is a large swampy area of more than 100,000 sq km fed by the waters of the White Nile that dominates the center of the country

Elevation: *highest point:* Kinyeti 3,187 m
lowest point: White Nile 381 m

Natural resources: hydropower, fertile agricultural land, gold, diamonds, petroleum, hardwoods, limestone, iron ore, copper, chromium ore, zinc, tungsten, mica, silver

Land use: *agricultural land:* 44.7% (2022 est.)
arable land: 3.8% (2022 est.)
permanent crops: 0.1% (2022 est.)
permanent pasture: 40.8% (2022 est.)
forest: 11.3% (2022 est.)
other: 44% (2022 est.)

Irrigated land: 1,000 sq km (2012)

Major rivers (by length in km): Nile (shared with Rwanda [s], Tanzania, Uganda, Sudan, and Egypt [m]) - 6,650 km
note: [s] after country name indicates river source; [m] after country name indicates river mouth

Major watersheds (area sq km): Atlantic Ocean drainage: Congo (3,730,881 sq km), *(Mediterranean Sea)* Nile (3,254,853 sq km)

Population distribution: clusters found in urban areas, particularly in the western interior and around the White Nile, as shown in this population distribution map

Geography - note: landlocked; The Sudd is a vast swamp in the north central region of South Sudan, formed by the White Nile; its size is variable but can reach some 15% of the country's total area during the rainy season; it is one of the world's largest wetlands

PEOPLE AND SOCIETY

Population: *total:* 12,703,714 (2024 est.)
male: 6,476,341
female: 6,227,373
comparison rankings: total 79; male 80; female 79

Nationality: *noun:* South Sudanese (singular and plural)
adjective: South Sudanese

Ethnic groups: Dinka (Jieng) approximately 35-40%, Nuer (Naath) approximately 15%, Shilluk (Chollo), Azande, Bari, Kakwa, Kuku, Murle, Mandari, Didinga, Ndogo, Bviri, Lndi, Anuak, Bongo, Lango, Dungotona, Acholi, Baka, Fertit (2011 est.)
note: Figures are estimations due to population changes during South Sudan's civil war and the lack of updated demographic studies

Languages: English (official), Arabic (includes Juba and Sudanese variants), ethnic languages include Dinka, Nuer, Bari, Zande, Shilluk
major-language sample(s):
كتاب حقائق العالم، المصدر الذي لا يمكن الاستغناء عنه للمعلومات الأساسية (Arabic)

Religions: Christian 60.5%, folk religion 32.9%, Muslim 6.2%, other <1%, unaffiliated <1% (2020 est.)

Age structure: *0-14 years:* 42.1% (male 2,725,520/female 2,619,035)
15-64 years: 55.3% (male 3,568,064/female 3,458,804)
65 years and over: 2.6% (2024 est.) (male 182,757/female 149,534)

Dependency ratios: *total dependency ratio:* 80.8 (2024 est.)
youth dependency ratio: 76.1 (2024 est.)
elderly dependency ratio: 4.7 (2024 est.)
potential support ratio: 21.1 (2024 est.)

Median age: *total:* 18.7 years (2024 est.)
male: 18.7 years
female: 18.7 years
comparison ranking: total 217

Population growth rate: 4.65% (2024 est.)
comparison ranking: 1

Birth rate: 36.4 births/1,000 population (2024 est.)
comparison ranking: 10

Death rate: 8.9 deaths/1,000 population (2024 est.)

comparison ranking: 65

Net migration rate: 19.1 migrant(s)/1,000 population (2024 est.)
comparison ranking: 2

Population distribution: clusters found in urban areas, particularly in the western interior and around the White Nile, as shown in this population distribution map

Urbanization: *urban population:* 21.2% of total population (2023)
rate of urbanization: 4.12% annual rate of change (2020-25 est.)

Major urban areas - population: 459,000 JUBA (capital) (2023)

Sex ratio: *at birth:* 1.05 male(s)/female
0-14 years: 1.04 male(s)/female
15-64 years: 1.03 male(s)/female
65 years and over: 1.22 male(s)/female
total population: 1.04 male(s)/female (2024 est.)

Maternal mortality ratio: 692 deaths/100,000 live births (2023 est.)
comparison ranking: 3

Infant mortality rate: *total:* 60.1 deaths/1,000 live births (2024 est.)
male: 65.8 deaths/1,000 live births
female: 54.1 deaths/1,000 live births
comparison ranking: total 8

Life expectancy at birth: *total population:* 60.3 years (2024 est.)
male: 58.4 years
female: 62.2 years
comparison ranking: total population 220

Total fertility rate: 5.09 children born/woman (2024 est.)
comparison ranking: 9

Gross reproduction rate: 2.48 (2024 est.)

Drinking water source: *improved: urban:* 70% of population (2022 est.)
rural: 33.6% of population (2022 est.)
total: 41.2% of population (2022 est.)
unimproved: urban: 30% of population (2022 est.)
rural: 66.4% of population (2022 est.)
total: 58.8% of population (2022 est.)

Health expenditure: 5.9% of GDP (2021)
2.1% of national budget (2022 est.)

Physician density: 0.04 physicians/1,000 population (2022)

Sanitation facility access: *improved: urban:* 60.6% of population (2022 est.)
rural: 15.5% of population (2022 est.)
total: 24.9% of population (2022 est.)
unimproved: urban: 39.4% of population (2022 est.)
rural: 84.5% of population (2022 est.)
total: 75.1% of population (2022 est.)

Obesity - adult prevalence rate: 6.6% (2014)
comparison ranking: 166

Currently married women (ages 15-49): 72% (2023 est.)

Education expenditure: 1.6% of GDP (2016 est.)
8.1% national budget (2023 est.)
comparison ranking: Education expenditure (% GDP) 191

ENVIRONMENT

Environmental issues: water pollution; inadequate supplies of potable water; wildlife conservation and loss of biodiversity; deforestation; soil erosion; desertification; drought

International environmental agreements: *party to:* Biodiversity, Climate Change, Climate Change-Paris Agreement, Desertification, Ozone Layer Protection, Wetlands
signed, but not ratified: none of the selected agreements

Climate: hot with seasonal rainfall influenced by the annual shift of the Inter-Tropical Convergence Zone; rainfall heaviest in upland areas of the south and diminishes to the north

Urbanization: *urban population:* 21.2% of total population (2023)
rate of urbanization: 4.12% annual rate of change (2020-25 est.)

Carbon dioxide emissions: 1.725 million metric tonnes of CO2 (2023 est.)
from petroleum and other liquids: 1.725 million metric tonnes of CO2 (2023 est.)
comparison ranking: total emissions 162

Particulate matter emissions: 20.6 micrograms per cubic meter (2019 est.)

Methane emissions: *energy:* 59.4 kt (2022-2024 est.)
agriculture: 696 kt (2019-2021 est.)
waste: 120.2 kt (2019-2021 est.)
other: 12.7 kt (2019-2021 est.)

Waste and recycling: *municipal solid waste generated annually:* 2.681 million tons (2024 est.)

Total water withdrawal: *municipal:* 193 million cubic meters (2022 est.)
industrial: 225 million cubic meters (2022 est.)
agricultural: 240 million cubic meters (2022 est.)

Total renewable water resources: 49.5 billion cubic meters (2022 est.)

GOVERNMENT

Country name: *conventional long form:* Republic of South Sudan
conventional short form: South Sudan
etymology: self-descriptive name from the country's geographic position within Sudan prior to independence; the name Sudan derives from the Arabic *balad-as-sudan*, meaning "Land of the Black [peoples]"

Government type: presidential republic

Capital: *name:* Juba
geographic coordinates: 04 51 N, 31 37 E
time difference: UTC+2 (8 hours ahead of Washington, DC, during Standard Time)
etymology: the name comes from the name of a small Bari village that was located near the present-day city

Administrative divisions: 10 states; Central Equatoria, Eastern Equatoria, Jonglei, Lakes, Northern Bahr el Ghazal, Unity, Upper Nile, Warrap, Western Bahr el Ghazal, Western Equatoria
note: in 2015, 28 new states were created, and 4 additional states in 2017; after the 2020 peace agreement, the country was again reorganized into the 10 original states, plus 2 administrative areas, Pibor and Ruweng, and 1 special administrative status area, Abyei (which is disputed between South Sudan and Sudan)

Constitution: *history:* previous 2005 (pre-independence); latest signed 7 July 2011, effective 9 July 2011 (Transitional Constitution of the Republic of South Sudan, 2011)
amendment process: proposed by the National Legislature or by the president of the republic; passage requires submission of the proposal to the Legislature at least one month prior to consideration, approval by at least two-thirds majority vote in both houses of the Legislature, and assent of the president

Citizenship: *citizenship by birth:* no
citizenship by descent only: at least one parent must be a citizen of South Sudan
dual citizenship recognized: yes
residency requirement for naturalization: 10 years

Suffrage: 18 years of age; universal

Executive branch: *chief of state:* President Salva KIIR Mayardit (since 9 July 2011)
head of government: President Salva KIIR Mayardit (since 9 July 2011)
cabinet: National Council of Ministers appointed by the president, approved by the Transitional National Legislative Assembly
election/appointment process: president directly elected by simple-majority popular vote for a 4-year term (eligible for a second term)
most recent election date: 11-15 April 2010
election results: 2010: Salva KIIR Mayardit elected leader of then-Southern Sudan; percent of vote - Salva KIIR Mayardit (SPLM) 93%, Lam AKOL (SPLM-DC) 7%
expected date of next election: scheduled for 2015 but has been postponed multiple times, currently to be held in December 2026
note: the president is both chief of state and head of government

Legislative branch: *legislature name:* Législature nationale (National Legislature)
legislative structure: bicameral

Legislative branch - lower chamber: *chamber name:* Transitional National Legislative Assembly (Al-Majlis Al-Tachirii)
number of seats: 550 (all appointed)
scope of elections: full renewal
most recent election date: 5/10/2021
percentage of women in chamber: 32.4%
expected date of next election: December 2026

Legislative branch - upper chamber: *chamber name:* Council of States (Al-Watani)
number of seats: 100 (all appointed)
scope of elections: full renewal
most recent election date: 8/2/2021
percentage of women in chamber: 32.1%
expected date of next election: December 2026

Judicial branch: *highest court(s):* Supreme Court of South Sudan (consists of a chief justice, deputy chief justice, and 5 additional justices); the 2011 Transitional Constitution of South Sudan calls for 9, rather than 5 additional justices
judge selection and term of office: the 2011 Transitional Constitution of South Sudan calls for the establishment of a Judicial Service Council to recommend prospective justices to the president, and for the justices' tenures to be set by the National Legislature
subordinate courts: national level - Courts of Appeal; High Courts; County Courts; state level - High Courts; County Courts; customary courts; other specialized courts and tribunals
note: in mid-2022, the Government of South Sudan inaugurated an ad-hoc judiciary committee, a 12-member body led by two eminent jurists, that is charged with reviewing relevant laws, advising on judicial reform, and restructuring the judiciary

Political parties: Democratic Change or DC
Democratic Forum or DF
Labour Party or LPSS
South Sudan Opposition Alliance or SSOA
Sudan African National Union or SANU
Sudan People's Liberation Movement or SPLM
Sudan People's Liberation Movement-In Opposition or SPLM-IO

United Democratic Salvation Front or UDSF
United South Sudan African Party or USSAP
United South Sudan Party or USSP

Diplomatic representation in the US: *chief of mission:* Ambassador Santino Fardol Watod DICKEN (since 18 September 2024)
chancery: 1015 31st Street NW, Suite 300, Washington, DC 20007
telephone: [1] (202) 600-2238

FAX: [1] (202) 644-9910
email address and website: info.ssdembassy@gmail.com
https://www.ssembassydc.org/

Diplomatic representation from the US: *chief of mission:* Ambassador Michael J. ADLER (since 24 August 2022)
embassy: Kololo Road adjacent to the EU's compound, Juba
mailing address: 4420 Juba Place, Washington DC 20521-4420
telephone: [211] 912-105-188
email address and website: ACSJuba@state.gov
https://ss.usembassy.gov/

International organization participation: AU, EAC, FAO, G-77, IBRD, ICAO, IDA, IFAD, IFC, IFRCS, IGAD, ILO, IMF, Interpol, IOM, IPU, ITU, MIGA, UN, UNCTAD, UNESCO, UPU, WCO, WHO, WMO

Independence: 9 July 2011 (from Sudan)

National holiday: Independence Day, 9 July (2011)

Flag: *description:* three equal horizontal bands of black (top), red, and green; the red band is edged in white; a five-pointed gold star is in the middle of a blue isosceles triangle based on the left side
meaning: black stands for the people, red for the blood shed in the struggle for freedom, green for the land, and blue for the Nile; the gold star represents the unity of the country's states
note 1: similar to the flag of Kenya
note 2: South Sudan has one of two national flags that display six colors as part of the primary design – the other is South Africa's

National symbol(s): African fish eagle

National color(s): red, green, blue, yellow, black, white

National anthem(s): *title:* "South Sudan Oyee!" (South Sudan, Hooray!)
lyrics/music: collective/Mido SAMUEL and Juba University students
history: adopted 2011; anthem selected in a national contest

ECONOMY

Economic overview: low-income, oil-based Sahelian economy; extreme poverty and food insecurity; COVID-19 and ongoing violence threaten socioeconomic potential; environmentally fragile; ongoing land and property rights issues; natural resource rich but lacks infrastructure

Real GDP (purchasing power parity): $6.752 billion (2023 est.)
$6.585 billion (2022 est.)
$6.945 billion (2021 est.)
note: data in 2015 dollars
comparison ranking: 173

Real GDP growth rate: -5.2% (2017 est.)
-13.9% (2016 est.)
-10.8% (2015 est.)
note: annual GDP % growth based on constant local currency
comparison ranking: 213

Real GDP per capita: $400 (2023 est.)
$400 (2022 est.)
$400 (2021 est.)
note: data in 2015 dollars
comparison ranking: 218

GDP (official exchange rate): $4.629 billion (2023 est.)
note: data in current dollars at official exchange rate

Inflation rate (consumer prices): 91.4% (2024 est.)
2.4% (2023 est.)
-6.7% (2022 est.)
note: annual % change based on consumer prices
comparison ranking: 209

GDP - composition, by sector of origin: *agriculture:* 10.4% (2015 est.)
industry: 33.1% (2015 est.)
services: 56.6% (2015 est.)
note: figures may not total 100% due to non-allocated consumption not captured in sector-reported data
comparison rankings: agriculture 71; industry 39; services 113

Agricultural products: milk, cassava, sorghum, goat milk, vegetables, fruits, groundnuts, sesame seeds, beef, maize (2023)
note: top ten agricultural products based on tonnage

Industrial production growth rate: -36.8% (2015 est.)
note: annual % change in industrial value added based on constant local currency
comparison ranking: 196

Labor force: 5.091 million (2023 est.)
note: number of people ages 15 or older who are employed or seeking work
comparison ranking: 85

Unemployment rate: 12.5% (2023 est.)
12.6% (2022 est.)
14.1% (2021 est.)
note: % of labor force seeking employment
comparison ranking: 166

Youth unemployment rate (ages 15-24): *total:* 18.5% (2023 est.)
male: 19.4% (2023 est.)
female: 17.6% (2023 est.)
note: % of labor force ages 15-24 seeking employment
comparison ranking: total 60

Population below poverty line: 82.3% (2016 est.)
note: % of population with income below national poverty line

Gini Index coefficient - distribution of family income: 44 (2016 est.)
note: index (0-100) of income distribution; higher values represent greater inequality
comparison ranking: 22

Household income or consumption by percentage share: *lowest 10%:* 1.8% (2016 est.)
highest 10%: 33% (2016 est.)
note: % share of income accruing to lowest and highest 10% of population

Remittances: 9.5% of GDP (2015 est.)
0% of GDP (2014 est.)
0% of GDP (2013 est.)
note: personal transfers and compensation between resident and non-resident individuals/households/entities

Budget: *revenues:* $2.513 billion (2023 est.)
expenditures: $1.984 billion (2023 est.)
note: central government revenues and expenses (excluding grants/extrabudgetary units/social security funds) converted to US dollars at average official exchange rate for year indicated

Current account balance: $577.9 million (2023 est.)
-$596.748 million (2022 est.)
-$6.55 million (2021 est.)
note: balance of payments - net trade and primary/secondary income in current dollars comparison ranking: 64

Exports: $4.499 billion (2023 est.)
$5.811 billion (2022 est.)
$4.652 billion (2021 est.)
note: balance of payments - exports of goods and services in current dollars
comparison ranking: 144

Exports - partners: China 51%, Singapore 29%, UAE 10%, Germany 4%, Uganda 3% (2023)
note: top five export partners based on percentage share of exports

Exports - commodities: crude petroleum, refined petroleum, forage crops, gold, scrap iron (2023)
note: top five export commodities based on value in dollars

Imports: $4.443 billion (2023 est.)
$6.402 billion (2022 est.)
$4.037 billion (2021 est.)
note: balance of payments - imports of goods and services in current dollars
comparison ranking: 155

Imports - partners: Uganda 33%, UAE 26%, Kenya 14%, China 10%, USA 3% (2023)
note: top five import partners based on percentage share of imports

Imports - commodities: garments, cement, other foods, iron bars, cereal flours (2023)
note: top five import commodities based on value in dollars

Reserves of foreign exchange and gold: $72.881 million (2023 est.)
$94.914 million (2022 est.)
$341.932 million (2021 est.)
note: holdings of gold (year-end prices)/foreign exchange/special drawing rights in current dollars
comparison ranking: 177

Exchange rates: South Sudanese pounds (SSP) per US dollar -

Exchange rates: 2,163.104 (2024 est.)
930.331 (2023 est.)
534.511 (2022 est.)
306.355 (2021 est.)
165.907 (2020 est.)

ENERGY

Electricity access: *electrification - total population:* 8.4% (2022 est.)
electrification - urban areas: 15%
electrification - rural areas: 1.7%

Electricity: *installed generating capacity:* 136,000 kW (2023 est.)
consumption: 566.034 million kWh (2023 est.)
transmission/distribution losses: 23.966 million kWh (2023 est.)
comparison rankings: installed generating capacity 184; consumption 174; transmission/distribution losses 27

Electricity generation sources: *fossil fuels:* 93.2% of total installed capacity (2023 est.)
solar: 6.8% of total installed capacity (2023 est.)

Coal: *imports:* 100 metric tons (2022 est.)

Petroleum: *total petroleum production:* 146,000 bbl/day (2023 est.)
refined petroleum consumption: 11,000 bbl/day (2023 est.)
crude oil estimated reserves: 3.75 billion barrels (2021 est.)

Energy consumption per capita: 2.092 million Btu/person (2023 est.)
comparison ranking: 185

COMMUNICATIONS

Telephones - fixed lines: *total subscriptions:* 0 (2023 est.)
subscriptions per 100 inhabitants: (2023 est.) less than 1
comparison ranking: total subscriptions 225

Telephones - mobile cellular: *total subscriptions:* 6.17 million (2023 est.)
subscriptions per 100 inhabitants: 30 (2022 est.)
comparison ranking: total subscriptions 118

Broadcast media: 1 state-controlled TV channel and radio station; several community and commercial FM stations, mostly sponsored by outside aid donors; some foreign radio broadcasts available (2019)

Internet country code: .ss

Internet users: *percent of population:* 9% (2022 est.)

Broadband - fixed subscriptions: *total:* 0 (2023 est.)
subscriptions per 100 inhabitants: (2023 est.) less than 1
comparison ranking: total 215

TRANSPORTATION

Civil aircraft registration country code prefix: Z8

Airports: 89 (2025)
comparison ranking: 62

Heliports: 2 (2025)
comparison ranking: 129

Railways: *total:* 248 km (2018)
note: a narrow gauge, single-track railroad between Babonosa (Sudan) and Wau, the only existing rail system, was repaired in 2010 with $250 million in UN funds, but is not currently operational

MILITARY AND SECURITY

Military and security forces: South Sudan People's Defense Force (SSPDF): Land Forces (includes Presidential Guard), Air Forces, Marine (Riverine) Forces, Reserve Forces; National (or Necessary) Unified Forces (NUF)

Ministry of Interior: South Sudan National Police Service (SSNPS) (2025)
note 1: the NUF are being formed by retraining rebel and pro-government militia fighters into military, police, and other government security forces; the first operational NUF deployed in November 2023
note 2: numerous irregular forces operate in the country with official knowledge, including militias operated by the National Security Service (an internal security force under the Ministry of National Security) and proxy forces

Military expenditures: 2% of GDP (2024 est.)
2% of GDP (2023 est.)
2% of GDP (2022 est.)
2% of GDP (2021 est.)
2% of GDP (2020 est.)

Military and security service personnel strengths: information varies; estimated 150-200,000 active Defense Forces (2025)
note: some active SSPDF personnel may be militia; the National/Necessary Unified Forces (NUF) were expected to have up to 80,000 personnel when training and integration is completed; the first batch of approximately 20,000 NUF personnel completed training in late 2022

Military equipment inventories and acquisitions: the SSPDF inventory is comprised primarily of Soviet-era equipment; South Sudan has been under a UN arms embargo since 2018 (2024)

Military service age and obligation: 18 is the legal minimum age for compulsory (men) and voluntary (men and women) military service; 12-24 months service (2023)

Military - note: the South Sudan People's Defense Forces (SSPDF) are largely focused on border and internal security; areas of concern include disputed national borders, conflict spillover from neighboring Sudan, banditry, and armed rebel groups and militias that continue to operate in the country since the civil war ended in 2020
the SSPDF, formerly the Sudan People's Liberation Army (SPLA), was founded as a guerrilla movement against the Sudanese Government in 1983 and participated in the Second Sudanese Civil War (1983-2005); the Juba Declaration that followed the Comprehensive Peace Agreement of 2005 unified the SPLA and the South Sudan Defense Forces (SSDF), the second-largest rebel militia remaining from the civil war, under the SPLA name; in 2017, the SPLA was renamed the South Sudan Defense Forces (SSDF) and in September 2018 was renamed again as the SSPDF
the UN Mission in South Sudan (UNMISS) has operated in the country since 2011 with the objectives of consolidating peace and security and helping establish conditions for the successful economic and political development of South Sudan; UNMISS has about 18,000 personnel assigned; the UN Interim Security Force for Abyei (UNISFA) has operated in the disputed Abyei region along the border between Sudan and South Sudan since 2011; its mission includes ensuring security, protecting civilians, strengthening the capacity of the Abyei Police Service, de-mining, monitoring/verifying the redeployment of armed forces from the area, and facilitating the flow of humanitarian aid; UNISFA has approximately 3,800 personnel assigned (2025)

TRANSNATIONAL ISSUES

Refugees and internally displaced persons: *refugees:* 517,471 (2024 est.)

IDPs: 1,359,795 (2024 est.)
stateless persons: 18,000 (2024 est.)

Trafficking in persons: *tier rating:* Tier 3 — South Sudan does not fully meet the minimum standards for the elimination of trafficking and is not making significant efforts to do so, therefore, South Sudan remained on Tier 3; for more details, go to: https://www.state.gov/reports/2025-trafficking-in-persons-report/south-sudan/

SOUTHERN OCEAN

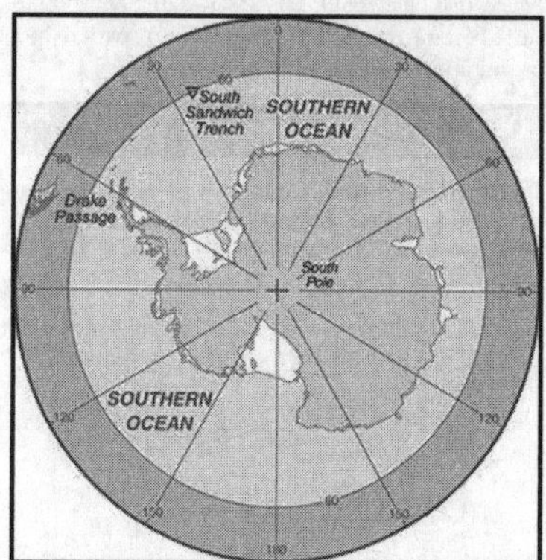

INTRODUCTION

Background: A large body of recent oceanographic research has shown that the Antarctic Circumpolar Current (ACC), an ocean current that flows from west to east around Antarctica, plays a crucial role in global ocean circulation. The region where the cold waters of the ACC meet and mingle with the warmer waters of the north defines a distinct border – the Antarctic Convergence – which fluctuates with the seasons but encompasses a discrete body of water and a unique ecologic region. The Convergence concentrates nutrients, which promotes marine plant life, which in turn allows for a greater abundance of animal life. In 2000, the International Hydrographic Organization delimited the waters within the Convergence as a fifth world ocean basin – the Southern Ocean – by combining the southern portions of the Atlantic Ocean, Indian Ocean, and Pacific Ocean. The Southern Ocean extends from the coast of Antarctica north to 60 degrees south latitude, which coincides with the Antarctic Treaty region and which approximates the extent of the Antarctic Convergence. As such, the Southern Ocean is now the fourth largest of the world's five ocean basins (after the Pacific Ocean, Atlantic Ocean, and Indian Ocean). It should be noted that inclusion of the Southern Ocean does not imply US Government recognition of this feature as one of the world's primary ocean basins.

GEOGRAPHY

Location: body of water between 60 degrees south latitude and Antarctica

Geographic coordinates: 60 00 S, 90 00 E (nominally), but the Southern Ocean has the unique distinction of being a large circumpolar body of water totally encircling the continent of Antarctica; this ring of water lies between 60 degrees south latitude and the coast of Antarctica and encompasses 360 degrees of longitude

Map references: Antarctic Region

Area: *total:* 21.96 million sq km
note: includes Amundsen Sea, Bellingshausen Sea, part of the Drake Passage, Ross Sea, a small part of the Scotia Sea, Weddell Sea, and other tributary water bodies

Area - comparative: slightly more than twice the size of the US

Coastline: 17,968 km

Climate: sea temperatures vary from about 10 degrees Celsius to -2 degrees Celsius; cyclonic storms travel eastward around the continent and frequently are intense because of the temperature contrast between ice and open ocean; the ocean area from about latitude 40 south to the Antarctic Circle has the strongest average winds found anywhere on Earth; in winter the ocean freezes outward to 65 degrees south latitude in the Pacific sector and 55 degrees south latitude in the Atlantic sector, lowering surface temperatures well below 0 degrees Celsius; at some coastal points intense persistent drainage winds from the interior keep the shoreline ice-free throughout the winter

Ocean volume: *ocean volume:* 71.8 million cu km
percent of World Ocean total volume: 5.4%

Major ocean currents: the cold, clockwise-flowing Antarctic Circumpolar Current (West Wind Drift; 21,000 km long) moves perpetually eastward around the continent and is the world's largest and strongest ocean current, transporting 130 million cubic meters of water per second - 100 times the flow of all the world's rivers; it is also the only current that flows all the way around the planet and connects the Atlantic, Pacific, and Indian Ocean basins; the cold Antarctic Coastal Current (East Wind Drift) is the southernmost current in the world, flowing westward and parallel to the Antarctic coastline

Bathymetry: *continental shelf:* the following are examples of features on the continental shelf of the Southern Ocean: Astrid Ridge
Belgrano Bank
Gunnerus Ridge
Hayes Bank
Iselin Bank
continental slope: the following are examples of features on the continental slope of the Southern Ocean: Amery Basin
Filchner Trough
Hillary Canyon
Pobeda Canyon
abyssal plains: the following are examples of features on the abyssal plains of the Southern Ocean: Amundsen (Abyssal) Plain
Enderby (Abyssal) Plain
South Indian/Australian-Antarctic Basin
Southeast Pacific/Bellinghausen Basin
Weddell (Abyssal) Plain
mid-ocean ridge: the following are examples of mid-ocean ridges on the floor of the Southern Ocean: Pacific-Antarctic Ridge
undersea terrain features: the following are examples of undersea terrain features on the floor of the Southern Ocean: Akopov Seamounts
De Gerlache Seamounts
Endurance Ridge
Marie Byrd Seamount
Maud Rise
Scott Seamounts
ocean trenches: the following are examples of ocean trenches on the floor of the Southern Ocean: South Sandwich Trench (the deepest location in the Southern Ocean)
atolls: none, due to the extremely cold water

Elevation: *highest point:* sea level
lowest point: southern end of the South Sandwich Trench -7,434 m unnamed deep
mean depth: -3,270 m
ocean zones: the ocean is divided into three zones based on depth and light level; sunlight entering the water may travel about 1,000 m into the oceans under the right conditions, but there is rarely any significant light below 200 m
euphotic zone: the upper 200 m (656 ft) is also called "sunlight" zone; only a small amount of light penetrates beyond this depth
dysphotic zone: between 200 m (656 ft) and 1,000 m (3,280 ft), and also called the twilight zone; the intensity of light rapidly dissipates as depth increases, and photosynthesis is no longer possible
aphotic zone: below 1,000 m (3,280 ft) and also called the midnight zone; sunlight does not penetrate to these depths

Natural resources: probable large oil and gas fields on the continental margin; manganese nodules, possible placer deposits, sand and gravel, fresh water as icebergs; krill, fish

Natural hazards: huge icebergs with drafts up to several hundred meters; smaller bergs and iceberg fragments; sea ice (generally 0.5 to 1 m thick) with sometimes dynamic short-term variations and with large annual and interannual variations; deep continental shelf floored by glacial deposits varying widely over short distances; high winds and large waves much of the year; ship icing, especially May-October; most of region is remote from sources of search and rescue

Geography - note: the major chokepoint is the Drake Passage between South America and Antarctica; the Polar Front (Antarctic Convergence) is the best natural definition of the northern extent of the Southern Ocean; it is a distinct region at the middle of the Antarctic Circumpolar Current that separates the cold polar surface waters to the south from the warmer waters to the north; the Front and the Current extend entirely around Antarctica, reaching south of 60 degrees south near New Zealand and near 48 degrees south in the far South Atlantic, coinciding with the path of the maximum westerly winds

ENVIRONMENT

Environmental issues: natural and man-made changes to the ocean's physical, chemical, and biological systems

International environmental agreements: the Southern Ocean is subject to all international agreements regarding the world's oceans; in addition, it is subject to these agreements specific to the Antarctic region: International Whaling Commission (prohibits commercial whaling south of 40 degrees south [south of 60 degrees south between 50 degrees and 130 degrees west]); Convention on the Conservation of Antarctic Seals (limits sealing); Convention on the Conservation of Antarctic Marine Living Resources (regulates fishing)
note: mineral exploitation except for scientific research is banned by the Environmental Protocol to the Antarctic Treaty; additionally, many nations (including the US) prohibit mineral resource exploration and exploitation south of the fluctuating Polar Front (Antarctic Convergence), which is in the middle of the Antarctic Circumpolar Current and serves as the dividing line between the cold polar surface waters to the south and the warmer waters to the north

Climate: sea temperatures vary from about 10 degrees Celsius to -2 degrees Celsius; cyclonic storms travel eastward around the continent and frequently are intense because of the temperature contrast between ice and open ocean; the ocean area from about latitude 40 south to the Antarctic Circle has the strongest average winds found anywhere on Earth; in winter the ocean freezes outward to 65 degrees south latitude in the Pacific sector and 55 degrees south latitude in the Atlantic sector, lowering surface temperatures well below 0 degrees Celsius; at some coastal points intense persistent drainage winds from the interior keep the shoreline ice-free throughout the winter

Marine fisheries: the Southern Ocean fishery is relatively small with a total catch of 388,901 mt in 2021; the Food and Agriculture Organization has delineated three regions in the Southern Ocean (Regions 48, 58, 88) that generally encompass the waters south of 40° to 60° South latitude; the most important producers in these regions include Norway (241,408 mt), China (47,605 mt), and South Korea (39,487 mt); Antarctic krill made up 95.5% of the total catch in 2021, while other important species include Patagonian and Antarctic toothfish

Regional fisheries bodies: Commission for the Conservation of Antarctic Marine Living Resources

GOVERNMENT

Country name: *etymology:* the International Hydrographic Organization (IHO) has not formally adopted the definition of the Southern Ocean as the waters south of 60 degrees south; the definition, however, was circulated in a draft edition of the IHO's *Names and Limits of Oceans and Seas* in 2002 and has since become the de facto name for many nations and organizations, including the CIA

TRANSPORTATION

Transportation - note: Drake Passage offers alternative to transit through the Panama Canal

SPAIN

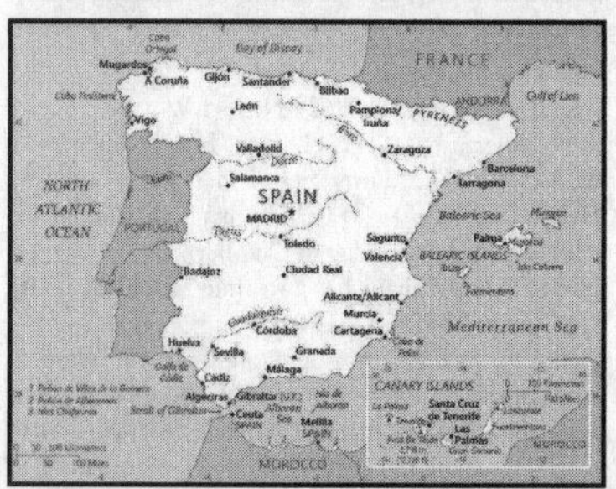

INTRODUCTION

Background: Spain's powerful world empire of the 16th and 17th centuries ultimately yielded command of the seas to England. Spain remained neutral during both World Wars but suffered through a devastating civil war (1936-39) resulting in a dictatorship. A peaceful transition to democracy after the death of dictator Francisco FRANCO in 1975 and rapid economic modernization after Spain joined the EU in 1986 gave Spain a dynamic and rapidly growing economy. After a severe recession in the wake of the global financial crisis in 2008, Spain has posted solid years of GDP growth above the EU average. Unemployment has fallen but remains high, especially among youth. Spain is the eurozone's fourth-largest economy. The country has faced increased domestic turmoil in recent years due to the independence movement in its restive Catalonia region.

GEOGRAPHY

Location: Southwestern Europe, bordering the Mediterranean Sea, North Atlantic Ocean, Bay of Biscay, and Pyrenees Mountains; southwest of France

Geographic coordinates: 40 00 N, 4 00 W

Map references: Europe

Area: *total:* 505,370 sq km
land: 498,980 sq km
water: 6,390 sq km
note: includes two autonomous cities (Ceuta and Melilla), 17 autonomous communities (including Balearic Islands and Canary Islands), and three small Spanish possessions off the coast of Morocco – Islas Chafarinas, Penon de Alhucemas, and Penon de Velez de la Gomera
comparison ranking: total 54

Area - comparative: almost five times the size of Kentucky; slightly more than twice the size of Oregon

Land boundaries: *total:* 1,952.7 km
border countries (5): Andorra 63 km; France 646 km; Gibraltar 1.2 km; Portugal 1,224 km; Morocco (Ceuta) 8 km and Morocco (Melilla) 10.5 km
note: an additional 75-meter border segment exists between Morocco and the Spanish exclave of Penon de Velez de la Gomera

Coastline: 4,964 km

Maritime claims: *territorial sea:* 12 nm
contiguous zone: 24 nm
exclusive economic zone: 200 nm (applies only to the Atlantic Ocean)

Climate: temperate; clear, hot summers in interior, more moderate and cloudy along coast; cloudy, cold winters in interior, partly cloudy and cool along coast

Terrain: large, flat to dissected plateau surrounded by rugged hills; Pyrenees Mountains in north

Elevation: *highest point:* Pico de Teide (Tenerife) on Canary Islands 3,718 m
lowest point: Atlantic Ocean 0 m
mean elevation: 660 m

Natural resources: coal, lignite, iron ore, copper, lead, zinc, uranium, tungsten, mercury, pyrites, magnesite, fluorspar, gypsum, sepiolite, kaolin, potash, hydropower, arable land

Irrigated land: 38,012 sq km (2022)

Major rivers (by length in km): Tagus river source (shared with Portugal [m]) - 1,006 km
note: [s] after country name indicates river source; [m] after country name indicates river mouth

Population distribution: with the notable exception of Madrid, Sevilla, and Zaragoza, the largest urban agglomerations are found along the Mediterranean and Atlantic coasts; numerous smaller cities are spread throughout the interior; very dense settlement around the capital of Madrid, as well as the port city of Barcelona

Natural hazards: periodic droughts, occasional flooding
volcanism: volcanic activity in the Canary Islands, located off Africa's northwest coast; Teide (3,715 m) has been deemed a Decade Volcano by the International Association of Volcanology and Chemistry of the Earth's Interior, worthy of study due to its explosive history and close proximity to human populations; La Palma (2,426 m) is the most active of the Canary Islands volcanoes; Lanzarote is the only other historically active volcano

Geography - note: strategic location along approaches to Strait of Gibraltar; Spain controls a number of territories in northern Morocco, including the enclaves of Ceuta and Melilla and the islands of Penon de Velez de la Gomera, Penon de Alhucemas, and Islas Chafarinas; Spain's Canary Islands are one of four North Atlantic archipelagos that make up Macaronesia; the others are the Azores (Portugal), Madeira (Portugal), and Cabo Verde

PEOPLE AND SOCIETY

Population: *total:* 47,280,433 (2024 est.)
male: 23,069,327
female: 24,211,106
comparison rankings: total 32; male 34; female 32

Nationality: *noun:* Spaniard(s)
adjective: Spanish

Ethnic groups: Spanish 84.8%, Moroccan 1.7%, Romanian 1.2%, other 12.3% (2021 est.)
note: data represent population by country of birth

Languages: Castilian Spanish (official) 74%, Catalan (official in Catalonia, the Balearic Islands, and the Valencian Community) 17%, Galician (official in Galicia) 7%, Basque (official in the Basque Country and Navarre) 2%, Aranese (official in part of Catalonia) <5,000 speakers
major-language sample(s):
La Libreta Informativa del Mundo, la fuente indispensable de información básica. (Spanish)
note: Aragonese, Aranese Asturian, Calo, and Valencian are also recognized as regional languages

Religions: Roman Catholic 58.2%, atheist 16.2%, agnostic 10.8%, other 2.7%, non-believer 10.5%, unspecified 1.7% (2021 est.)

Age structure: *0-14 years:* 13% (male 3,147,019/female 3,012,821)
15-64 years: 66.1% (male 15,662,492/female 15,585,138)
65 years and over: 20.9% (2024 est.) (male 4,259,816/female 5,613,147)

Dependency ratios: *total dependency ratio:* 51.3 (2024 est.)
youth dependency ratio: 19.7 (2024 est.)
elderly dependency ratio: 31.6 (2024 est.)
potential support ratio: 3.2 (2024 est.)

Median age: *total:* 46.8 years (2024 est.)
male: 45.7 years
female: 47.8 years
comparison ranking: total 8

Population growth rate: 0.12% (2024 est.)
comparison ranking: 182

Birth rate: 7.1 births/1,000 population (2024 est.)
comparison ranking: 221

Death rate: 10 deaths/1,000 population (2024 est.)
comparison ranking: 36

Net migration rate: 4.1 migrant(s)/1,000 population (2024 est.)
comparison ranking: 25

Population distribution: with the notable exception of Madrid, Sevilla, and Zaragoza, the largest urban agglomerations are found along the Mediterranean and Atlantic coasts; numerous smaller cities are spread throughout the interior; very dense settlement around the capital of Madrid, as well as the port city of Barcelona

Urbanization: *urban population:* 81.6% of total population (2023)
rate of urbanization: 0.24% annual rate of change (2020-25 est.)
note: data include Canary Islands, Ceuta, and Melilla

Major urban areas - population: 6.751 million MADRID (capital), 5.687 million Barcelona, 838,000 Valencia (2023)

Sex ratio: *at birth:* 1.05 male(s)/female
0-14 years: 1.04 male(s)/female
15-64 years: 1 male(s)/female
65 years and over: 0.76 male(s)/female
total population: 0.95 male(s)/female (2024 est.)

Mother's mean age at first birth: 31.2 years (2020 est.)

Maternal mortality ratio: 3 deaths/100,000 live births (2023 est.)
comparison ranking: 184

Infant mortality rate: *total:* 2.4 deaths/1,000 live births (2024 est.)
male: 2.7 deaths/1,000 live births
female: 2.1 deaths/1,000 live births

comparison ranking: total 217

Life expectancy at birth: *total population:* 83 years (2024 est.)
male: 80.3 years
female: 85.8 years
comparison ranking: total population 18

Total fertility rate: 1.3 children born/woman (2024 est.)
comparison ranking: 218

Gross reproduction rate: 0.64 (2024 est.)

Drinking water source: *improved: urban:* 99.9% of population (2022 est.)
rural: 100% of population (2022 est.)
total: 99.9% of population (2022 est.)
unimproved: urban: 0.1% of population (2022 est.)
rural: 0% of population (2022 est.)
total: 0.1% of population (2022 est.)

Health expenditure: 10.7% of GDP (2021)
15.2% of national budget (2022 est.)

Physician density: 4.29 physicians/1,000 population (2022)

Hospital bed density: 2.9 beds/1,000 population (2021 est.)

Sanitation facility access: *improved: urban:* 100% of population (2022 est.)
rural: 100% of population (2022 est.)
total: 100% of population (2022 est.)
unimproved: urban: 0% of population (2022 est.)
rural: 0% of population (2022 est.)
total: 0% of population (2022 est.)

Obesity - adult prevalence rate: 23.8% (2016)
comparison ranking: 62

Alcohol consumption per capita: *total:* 10.72 liters of pure alcohol (2019 est.)
beer: 4.67 liters of pure alcohol (2019 est.)
wine: 3.52 liters of pure alcohol (2019 est.)
spirits: 2.34 liters of pure alcohol (2019 est.)
other alcohols: 0.19 liters of pure alcohol (2019 est.)
comparison ranking: total 17

Tobacco use: *total:* 23.9% (2025 est.)
male: 25.8% (2025 est.)
female: 22% (2025 est.)
comparison ranking: total 45

Currently married women (ages 15-49): 50.1% (2023 est.)

Education expenditure: 4.3% of GDP (2022 est.)
9.2% national budget (2022 est.)
comparison ranking: Education expenditure (% GDP) 91

Literacy: *total population:* 100% (2021 est.)
male: 100% (2021 est.)
female: 100% (2021 est.)

School life expectancy (primary to tertiary education): *total:* 18 years (2023 est.)
male: 17 years (2023 est.)
female: 18 years (2023 est.)

ENVIRONMENT

Environmental issues: pollution of the Mediterranean Sea from raw sewage and effluents from oil and gas production; drought; air pollution; deforestation; desertification

International environmental agreements: *party to:* Air Pollution, Air Pollution-Heavy Metals, Air Pollution-Multi-effect Protocol, Air Pollution-Nitrogen Oxides, Air Pollution-Persistent Organic Pollutants, Air Pollution-Sulphur 94, Air Pollution-Volatile Organic Compounds, Antarctic-Environmental Protection, Antarctic-Marine Living Resources, Antarctic Treaty, Biodiversity, Climate Change, Climate Change-Kyoto Protocol, Climate Change-Paris Agreement, Comprehensive Nuclear Test Ban, Desertification, Endangered Species, Environmental Modification, Hazardous Wastes, Law of the Sea, Marine Dumping-London Convention, Marine Dumping-London Protocol, Marine Life Conservation, Nuclear Test Ban, Ozone Layer Protection, Ship Pollution, Tropical Timber 2006, Wetlands, Whaling
signed, but not ratified: none of the selected agreements

Climate: temperate; clear, hot summers in interior, more moderate and cloudy along coast; cloudy, cold winters in interior, partly cloudy and cool along coast

Land use: *agricultural land:* 53.4% (2022 est.)
arable land: 23.4% (2022 est.)
permanent crops: 10.2% (2022 est.)
permanent pasture: 19.8% (2022 est.)
forest: 37.2% (2022 est.)
other: 9.5% (2022 est.)

Urbanization: *urban population:* 81.6% of total population (2023)
rate of urbanization: 0.24% annual rate of change (2020-25 est.)
note: data include Canary Islands, Ceuta, and Melilla

Carbon dioxide emissions: 254.823 million metric tonnes of CO_2 (2023 est.)
from coal and metallurgical coke: 13.39 million metric tonnes of CO_2 (2023 est.)
from petroleum and other liquids: 182.327 million metric tonnes of CO_2 (2023 est.)
from consumed natural gas: 59.105 million metric tonnes of CO_2 (2023 est.)
comparison ranking: total emissions 27

Particulate matter emissions: 8.3 micrograms per cubic meter (2019 est.)

Waste and recycling: *municipal solid waste generated annually:* 22.409 million tons (2024 est.)
percent of municipal solid waste recycled: 27.7% (2022 est.)

Total water withdrawal: *municipal:* 4.56 billion cubic meters (2022 est.)
industrial: 5.5 billion cubic meters (2022 est.)
agricultural: 18.96 billion cubic meters (2022 est.)

Total renewable water resources: 111.5 billion cubic meters (2022 est.)

Geoparks: *total global geoparks and regional networks:* 18 (2025)
global geoparks and regional networks: Basque Coast UNESCO; Cabo de Gata-Níjar; Cabo Ortegal; Calatrava Volcanoes. Ciudad Real; Central Catalonia; Costa Quebrada; Courel Mountains; El Hierro; Granada; Lanzarote and Chinijo Islands; Las Loras; Maestrazgo; Molina-Alto; Origens; Sierra Norte de Sevilla; Sierras Subbéticas; Sobrarbe-Pirineos: Villuercas Ibores Jara (2025)

GOVERNMENT

Country name: *conventional long form:* Kingdom of Spain
conventional short form: Spain
local long form: Reino de España
local short form: España
etymology: derivation of the name España is uncertain; the Basque words *ezpain* or *espan* ("edge," as in a river bank) are possible sources, or the Punic word *span*, meaning "rabbit;" some academics tie it to the god Hesperus from Greco-Roman mythology

Government type: parliamentary constitutional monarchy

Capital: *name:* Madrid
geographic coordinates: 40 24 N, 3 41 W
time difference: UTC+1 (6 hours ahead of Washington, DC, during Standard Time)
daylight saving time: +1hr, begins last Sunday in March; ends last Sunday in October
time zone note: Spain has two time zones, including the Canary Islands (UTC 0)
etymology: the meaning and origin of the name is unclear; the city grew from a small Moorish fort that was called Majerit in the first recorded mention in A.D. 932; some trace the modern-day name back to the Roman era, with the Latin word *materia* (materials) as a possible source

Administrative divisions: 17 autonomous communities (*comunidades autonomas*, singular - *comunidad autonoma*) and 2 autonomous cities* (*ciudades autonomas*, singular - *ciudad autonoma*); Andalucia; Aragon; Asturias; Canarias (Canary Islands); Cantabria; Castilla-La Mancha; Castilla-Leon; Cataluña (Castilian), Catalunya (Catalan), Catalonha (Aranese) [Catalonia]; Ceuta*; Comunidad Valenciana (Castilian), Comunitat Valenciana (Valencian) [Valencian Community]; Extremadura; Galicia; Illes Baleares (Balearic Islands); La Rioja; Madrid; Melilla*; Murcia; Navarra (Castilian), Nafarroa (Basque) [Navarre]; Pais Vasco (Castilian), Euskadi (Basque)
[Basque Country]
note: Spain administers the autonomous cities of Ceuta and Melilla and the three small islands of Islas Chafarinas, Penon de Alhucemas, and Penon de Velez de la Gomera, which are all located along the coast of Morocco; they are collectively referred to as Places of Sovereignty (Plazas de Soberania)

Legal system: civil law system with regional variations

Constitution: *history:* several previous; latest approved by the General Courts 31 October 1978, passed by referendum 6 December 1978, signed by the king 27 December 1978, effective 29 December 1978
amendment process: proposed by the government, by the General Courts (the Congress or the Senate), or by the self-governing communities submitted through the government; passage requires three-fifths majority vote by both houses and passage by referendum if requested by one tenth of the members of either house; proposals disapproved by both houses are submitted to a joint committee, which submits an agreed upon text for another vote; passage requires two-thirds majority vote in Congress and simple majority vote in the Senate

International law organization participation: accepts compulsory ICJ jurisdiction with reservations; accepts ICCt jurisdiction

Citizenship: *citizenship by birth:* no
citizenship by descent only: at least one parent must be a citizen of Spain
dual citizenship recognized: only with select Latin American countries
residency requirement for naturalization: 10 years for persons with no ties to Spain

Suffrage: 18 years of age; universal

Executive branch: *chief of state:* King FELIPE VI (since 19 June 2014)
head of government: President of the Government of Spain (prime minister-equivalent) Pedro SANCHEZ PEREZ-CASTEJON (since 2 June 2018)
cabinet: Council of Ministers designated by the president
election/appointment process: the monarchy is hereditary; following legislative elections, the monarch usually proposes as president the leader of the majority party or coalition, who is then indirectly elected by the Congress of Deputies; vice president and Council of Ministers appointed by the president
most recent election date: 23 July 2023
election results: Congress of Deputies vote - 179 to 171 (16 November 2023)
expected date of next election: 31 July 2027
note: there is also a Council of State that is the supreme consultative organ of the government, but its recommendations are non-binding

Legislative branch: *legislature name:* The Cortes (Las Cortes Generales)
legislative structure: bicameral

Legislative branch - lower chamber: *chamber name:* Congress of Deputies (Congreso de los Diputados)
number of seats: 350 (all directly elected)
electoral system: proportional representation
scope of elections: full renewal
term in office: 4 years
most recent election date: 7/23/2023
parties elected and seats per party: People's Party (PP) (136); Spanish Socialist Workers' Party (PSOE) (122); Vox (33); SUMAR (31); Other (28)
percentage of women in chamber: 44.3%
expected date of next election: July 2027

Legislative branch - upper chamber: *chamber name:* Senate (Senado)
number of seats: 265 (208 directly elected; 57 indirectly elected)
electoral system: mixed system
scope of elections: full renewal
term in office: 4 years
most recent election date: 7/23/2023
parties elected and seats per party: People's Party (PP) (120); Spanish Socialist Workers' Party (PSOE) (72); Other (16)
percentage of women in chamber: 42.5%
expected date of next election: July 2027

Judicial branch: *highest court(s):* Supreme Court or Tribunal Supremo (consists of the court president and organized into the Civil Room, with a president and 9 judges; the Penal Room, with a president and 14 judges; the Administrative Room, with a president and 32 judges; the Social Room, with a president and 12 judges; and the Military Room, with a president and 7 judges); Constitutional Court or Tribunal Constitucional de Espana (consists of 12 judges)
judge selection and term of office: Supreme Court judges appointed by the monarch from candidates proposed by the General Council of the Judiciary Power, a 20-member governing board chaired by the monarch; judges can serve until age 70; Constitutional Court judges nominated by the National Assembly, executive branch, and the General Council of the Judiciary, and appointed by the monarch for 9-year terms
subordinate courts: National High Court; High Courts of Justice (in each of the autonomous communities); provincial courts; courts of first instance

Political parties: Asturias Forum or FAC
Basque Country Unite (Euskal Herria Bildu) or EH Bildu (coalition of 4 Basque pro-independence parties)
Basque Nationalist Party or PNV or EAJ
Canarian Coalition or CC (coalition of 5 parties)
Ciudadanos Party (Citizens Party) or Cs
Compromis - Compromise Coalition
Navarrese People's Union or UPN
Together for Catalonia or Junts
People's Party or PP
Republican Left of Catalonia or ERC
Spanish Socialist Workers Party or PSOE
Teruel Existe or TE
Unidas (Unite) or Sumar (electoral coalition formed in March 2022) (formerly Unidas Podemos or UP)
Vox or VOX

Diplomatic representation in the US: *chief of mission:* Ambassador Ángeles MORENO Bau (since 27 February 2024)
chancery: 2375 Pennsylvania Avenue NW, Washington, DC 20037
telephone: [1] (202) 452-0100
FAX: [1] (202) 833-5670
email address and website: emb.washington@maec.es
https://www.exteriores.gob.es/Embajadas/washington/en/Paginas/index.aspx
consulate(s) general: Boston, Chicago, Houston, Los Angeles, Miami, New York, San Francisco, San Juan (Puerto Rico)

Diplomatic representation from the US: *chief of mission:* Ambassador (vacant); Chargé d'Affaires Rian Harker HARRIS (since 15 July 2024); note - also accredited to Andorra
embassy: Calle de Serrano, 75, 28006 Madrid
mailing address: 8500 Madrid Place, Washington DC 20521-8500
telephone: [34] (91) 587-2200
FAX: [34] (91) 587-2303
email address and website: askACS@state.gov
https://es.usembassy.gov/
consulate(s) general: Barcelona

International organization participation: ADB (nonregional member), AfDB (nonregional member), Arctic Council (observer), Australia Group, BCIE, BIS, CABEI, CAN (observer), CBSS (observer), CD, CE, CERN, EAPC, EBRD, ECB, EIB, EITI (implementing country), EMU, ESA, EU, FAO, FATF, IADB, IAEA, IBRD, ICAO, ICC (national committees), ICCt, ICRM, IDA, IEA, IFAD, IFC, IFRCS, IHO, ILO, IMF, IMO, IMSO, Interpol, IOC, IOM, IPU, ISO, ITSO, ITU, ITUC (NGOs), LAIA (observer), MIGA, NATO, NEA, NSG, OAS (observer), OECD, OPCW, OSCE, Pacific Alliance (observer), Paris Club, PCA, PIF (partner), Schengen Convention, SELEC (observer), SICA (observer), UN, UNCTAD, UNESCO, UNHCR, UNIDO, UNIFIL, Union Latina, UNOCI, UNOOSA, UNRWA, UNWTO, UPU, Wassenaar Arrangement, WCO, WHO, WIPO, WMO, WTO, ZC

Independence: 1492
note: the Iberian peninsula was home to a variety of independent kingdoms prior to the Muslim occupation that began in the early 8th century A.D. and lasted nearly seven centuries; the small Christian redoubts of the north began the reconquest almost immediately, culminating in the seizure of Granada in 1492; this completed the unification of several kingdoms and is traditionally considered the forging of present-day Spain

National holiday: National Day (Hispanic Day), 12 October (1492)
note: commemorates the arrival of explorer Christopher COLUMBUS in the Americas

Flag: *description:* three horizontal bands of red (top), yellow (double-width), and red, with the national coat of arms on the left side of the yellow band; the coat of arms shows the emblems of the area's former kingdoms (clockwise from upper left: Castile, Leon, Navarre, and Aragon), which also used red and yellow as their colors; the stylized pomegranate at the bottom of the shield represents Granada; the two columns represent the Pillars of Hercules, which are promontories (Gibraltar and Ceuta) on the Strait of Gibraltar; a red scroll bears the imperial motto of "Plus Ultra" (further beyond), referring to Spanish lands outside Europe

National symbol(s): Pillars of Hercules

National color(s): red, yellow

National anthem(s): *title:* "Himno Nacional Espanol" (National Anthem of Spain)
lyrics/music: no lyrics/unknown
history: adopted 1942;officially in use between 1770 and 1931, restored in 1939; the Spanish anthem was the first to be officially adopted; it first appeared in a 1761 military bugle-call book and was replaced by "Himno de Riego" in the years between 1931 and 1939; the long version of the anthem is used for the king, and the short version is used for the prince, prime minister, and occasions such as sporting events

National heritage: *total World Heritage Sites:* 50 (44 cultural, 4 natural, 2 mixed)
selected World Heritage Site locales: Cave of Altamira and Paleolithic Cave Art of Northern Spain (c); Works of Antoni Gaudí (c); Santiago de Compostela (Old Town) (c); Historic City of Toledo (c); Archaeological Ensemble of Mérida (c); Tower of Hercules (c); Doñana National Park (n); Pyrénées - Mont Perdu (m); Alhambra, Generalife, and Albayzín in Granada (c); Old City of Salamanca (c); Teide National Park (n); Historic Walled Town of Cuenca (c); Old Town of Segovia and its Aqueduct (c); Historic Cordoba (c); Royal Site of Saint Lorenzo de El Escorial (c); Cathedral, Alcázar, and Archivo de Indias in Seville

ECONOMY

Economic overview: high-income, core-EU and eurozone economy; strong growth driven by public consumption, tourism, and other service exports; tight labor market despite high structural unemployment; efforts to narrow persistent fiscal deficits through tax and spending measures; high but declining unemployment supported by job growth and immigration

Real GDP (purchasing power parity): $2.361 trillion (2024 est.)
$2.289 trillion (2023 est.)
$2.229 trillion (2022 est.)
note: data in 2021 dollars
comparison ranking: 15

Real GDP growth rate: 3.2% (2024 est.)
2.7% (2023 est.)
6.2% (2022 est.)
note: annual GDP % growth based on constant local currency

comparison ranking: 111

Real GDP per capita: $48,400 (2024 est.)
$47,300 (2023 est.)
$46,600 (2022 est.)
note: data in 2021 dollars
comparison ranking: 41

GDP (official exchange rate): $1.723 trillion (2024 est.)
note: data in current dollars at official exchange rate

Inflation rate (consumer prices): 2.8% (2024 est.)
3.5% (2023 est.)
8.4% (2022 est.)
note: annual % change based on consumer prices
comparison ranking: 81

GDP - composition, by sector of origin: *agriculture:* 2.5% (2024 est.)
industry: 19.5% (2024 est.)
services: 69.1% (2024 est.)
note: figures may not total 100% due to non-allocated consumption not captured in sector-reported data
comparison rankings: agriculture 141; industry 135; services 40

GDP - composition, by end use: *household consumption:* 54.3% (2023 est.)
government consumption: 19.5% (2023 est.)
investment in fixed capital: 19.7% (2023 est.)
investment in inventories: 1.3% (2023 est.)
exports of goods and services: 38.1% (2023 est.)
imports of goods and services: -34.1% (2023 est.)
note: figures may not total 100% due to rounding or gaps in data collection

Agricultural products: milk, olives, pork, grapes, wheat, tomatoes, barley, sugar beets, maize, oranges (2023)
note: top ten agricultural products based on tonnage

Industries: textiles and apparel (including footwear), food and beverages, metals and metal manufactures, chemicals, shipbuilding, automobiles, machine tools, tourism, clay and refractory products, footwear, pharmaceuticals, medical equipment

Industrial production growth rate: 2.6% (2024 est.)
note: annual % change in industrial value added based on constant local currency
comparison ranking: 89

Labor force: 24.386 million (2024 est.)
note: number of people ages 15 or older who are employed or seeking work
comparison ranking: 28

Unemployment rate: 11.4% (2024 est.)
12.2% (2023 est.)
13% (2022 est.)
note: % of labor force seeking employment
comparison ranking: 156

Youth unemployment rate (ages 15-24): *total:* 27% (2024 est.)
male: 26.4% (2024 est.)
female: 27.7% (2024 est.)
note: % of labor force ages 15-24 seeking employment
comparison ranking: total 29

Population below poverty line: 20.2% (2022 est.)
note: % of population with income below national poverty line

Gini Index coefficient - distribution of family income: 33.6 (2022 est.)
note: index (0-100) of income distribution; higher values represent greater inequality comparison ranking: 92

Average household expenditures: *on food:* 12.9% of household expenditures (2023 est.)
on alcohol and tobacco: 4% of household expenditures (2023 est.)

Household income or consumption by percentage share: *lowest 10%:* 2.3% (2022 est.)
highest 10%: 24.8% (2022 est.)
note: % share of income accruing to lowest and highest 10% of population

Remittances: 0.4% of GDP (2024 est.)
0.3% of GDP (2023 est.)
0.3% of GDP (2022 est.)
note: personal transfers and compensation between resident and non-resident individuals/households/entities

Budget: *revenues:* $512.57 billion (2023 est.)
expenditures: $549.772 billion (2023 est.)
note: central government revenues (excluding grants) and expenditures converted to US dollars at average official exchange rate for year indicated

Public debt: 107.3% of GDP (2023 est.)
note: central government debt as a % of GDP
comparison ranking: 15

Taxes and other revenues: 15% (of GDP) (2023 est.)
note: central government tax revenue as a % of GDP
comparison ranking: 91

Current account balance: $52.182 billion (2024 est.)
$43.012 billion (2023 est.)
$4.482 billion (2022 est.)
note: balance of payments - net trade and primary/secondary income in current dollars comparison ranking: 12

Exports: $642.358 billion (2024 est.)
$616.648 billion (2023 est.)
$573.598 billion (2022 est.)
note: balance of payments - exports of goods and services in current dollars
comparison ranking: 17

Exports - partners: France 15%, Germany 10%, Portugal 9%, Italy 9%, UK 6% (2023)
note: top five export partners based on percentage share of exports

Exports - commodities: cars, packaged medicine, refined petroleum, vehicle parts/accessories, garments (2023)
note: top five export commodities based on value in dollars

Imports: $568.502 billion (2024 est.)
$552.948 billion (2023 est.)
$561.448 billion (2022 est.)
note: balance of payments - imports of goods and services in current dollars
comparison ranking: 17

Imports - partners: Germany 11%, China 10%, France 10%, Italy 7%, USA 7% (2023)
note: top five import partners based on percentage share of imports

Imports - commodities: crude petroleum, cars, garments, vehicle parts/accessories, natural gas (2023)
note: top five import commodities based on value in dollars

Reserves of foreign exchange and gold: $107.774 billion (2024 est.)
$103.089 billion (2023 est.)
$92.905 billion (2022 est.)
note: holdings of gold (year-end prices)/foreign exchange/special drawing rights in current dollars
comparison ranking: 27

Exchange rates: euros (EUR) per US dollar -

Exchange rates: 0.924 (2024 est.)
0.925 (2023 est.)
0.95 (2022 est.)
0.845 (2021 est.)
0.876 (2020 est.)

ENERGY

Electricity access: *electrification - total population:* 100% (2022 est.)

Electricity: *installed generating capacity:* 130.366 million kW (2023 est.)
consumption: 227.187 billion kWh (2023 est.)
exports: 25.279 billion kWh (2023 est.)
imports: 11.315 billion kWh (2023 est.)
transmission/distribution losses: 24.532 billion kWh (2023 est.)
comparison rankings: installed generating capacity 11; consumption 21; exports 8; imports 21; transmission/distribution losses 191

Electricity generation sources: *fossil fuels:* 28% of total installed capacity (2023 est.)
nuclear: 20.4% of total installed capacity (2023 est.)
solar: 17.3% of total installed capacity (2023 est.)
wind: 23.6% of total installed capacity (2023 est.)
hydroelectricity: 8.5% of total installed capacity (2023 est.)
biomass and waste: 2.2% of total installed capacity (2023 est.)

Nuclear energy: Number of operational nuclear reactors: 7 (2025)

Net capacity of operational nuclear reactors: 7.12GW (2025 est.)

Percent of total electricity production: 20.3% (2023 est.)

Number of nuclear reactors permanently shut down: 3 (2025)

Coal: *production:* 1.28 million metric tons (2023 est.)
consumption: 7.388 million metric tons (2023 est.)
exports: 1.629 million metric tons (2023 est.)
imports: 9.798 million metric tons (2023 est.)
proven reserves: 1.187 billion metric tons (2023 est.)

Petroleum: *total petroleum production:* 47,000 bbl/day (2023 est.)
refined petroleum consumption: 1.325 million bbl/day (2024 est.)
crude oil estimated reserves: 150 million barrels (2021 est.)

Natural gas: *production:* 34.124 million cubic meters (2023 est.)
consumption: 29.041 billion cubic meters (2023 est.)
exports: 6.576 billion cubic meters (2023 est.)
imports: 35.252 billion cubic meters (2023 est.)
proven reserves: 2.549 billion cubic meters (2021 est.)

Energy consumption per capita: 101.12 million Btu/person (2023 est.)
comparison ranking: 48

COMMUNICATIONS

Telephones - fixed lines: *total subscriptions:* 18.431 million (2023 est.)
subscriptions per 100 inhabitants: 38 (2023 est.)
comparison ranking: total subscriptions 14

Telephones - mobile cellular: *total subscriptions:* 61.2 million (2023 est.)
subscriptions per 100 inhabitants: 124 (2022 est.)
comparison ranking: total subscriptions 30

Broadcast media: mix of publicly operated and privately owned TV and radio stations; hundreds of TV channels available, including national, regional, local, public, and international channels; satellite and cable TV available; multiple national radio networks, large number of regional radio networks, and larger number of local radio stations (2019)

Internet country code: .es

Internet users: *percent of population:* 95% (2023 est.)

Broadband - fixed subscriptions: *total:* 18.2 million (2023 est.)
subscriptions per 100 inhabitants: 38 (2023 est.)
comparison ranking: total 15

TRANSPORTATION

Civil aircraft registration country code prefix: EC

Airports: 365 (2025)
comparison ranking: 20

Heliports: 162 (2025)
comparison ranking: 17

Railways: *total:* 15,489 km (2020) 9,953 km electrified

Merchant marine: *total:* 503 (2023)
by type: bulk carrier 1, general cargo 33, oil tanker 24, other 445
comparison ranking: total 42

Ports: *total ports:* 52 (2024)
large: 3
medium: 14
small: 9
very small: 24
size unknown: 2
ports with oil terminals: 13
key ports: Alicante, Barcelona, Cadiz, Ceuta, Ferrol, Huelva, Las Palmas, Malaga, Palma de Mallorca, Puerto de Bilbao, Puerto de Pasajes, Santa Cruz de Tenerife, Santander, Sevilla, Tarragona, Valencia, Vigo

MILITARY AND SECURITY

Military and security forces: Spanish Armed Forces (Fuerzas Armadas de España): Army (Ejército de Tierra), Spanish Navy (Armada Espanola; includes Marine Corps), Air and Space Force (Ejército del Aire y del Espacio), Emergency Response Unit (Unidad Militar de Emergencias); Civil Guard (Guardia Civil)

Ministry of the Interior: Spanish National Police (Cuerpo Nacional de Policía, CNP) (2025)
note 1: the Civil Guard is a military force with police duties (including coast guard) under both the Ministry of Defense and the Ministry of the Interior; it also responds to the needs of the Ministry of Finance; the CNP and the Civil Guard maintain internal security as well as migration and border enforcement under the authority of the Ministry of the Interior; the regional police under the authority of the Catalan and the Basque Country regional governments and municipal police throughout the country also support domestic security
note 2: the Emergency Response Unit was established in 2006 as a separate branch of service for responding to natural disasters and providing disaster relief both domestically and abroad; it has personnel from all the other military services
note 3: the Royal Guard is an independent joint-service regiment of the military dedicated to the protection of the King and members of the royal family

Military expenditures: 2% of GDP (2025 est.)
1.4% of GDP (2024 est.)
1.2% of GDP (2023 est.)
1.1% of GDP (2022 est.)
1% of GDP (2021 est.)

Military and security service personnel strengths: approximately 120,000 active-duty military personnel; approximately 80,000 Guardia Civil (2025)

Military equipment inventories and acquisitions: the military's inventory is comprised of weapons and equipment that were produced domestically, co-produced with or imported from other EU countries, or purchased from the US; in recent years, leading suppliers have included France, Germany, and the US; Spain's defense industry manufactures land, air, and sea weapons systems and is integrated within the European defense-industrial sector (2024)

Military service age and obligation: 18 years of age for voluntary military service for men and women; 24-36 month initial obligation; women allowed to serve in all branches, including combat units; no conscription (abolished 2001), but the Spanish Government retains the right to mobilize citizens 19-25 years of age in a national emergency; 18-58 for the voluntary reserves (2024)
note 1: as of 2024, women comprised about 13% of the military's full-time personnel
note 2: the military recruits foreign nationals with residency in Spain from countries of its former empire, including Argentina, Costa Rica, Bolivia, Colombia, Chile, Cuba, Dominican Republic, Ecuador, El Salvador, Equatorial Guinea, Guatemala, Honduras, Mexico, Nicaragua, Panama, Paraguay, Peru, Uruguay, and Venezuela

Military deployments: Spain has up to 3,000 military personnel deployed on 17 missions supporting the EU, NATO, and the UN on four continents, as well as naval missions in the Mediterranean and the seas off the Horn of Africa; its largest deployments are up to 700 troops in Lebanon (UNIFIL) and about 1,700 personnel in Eastern Europe supporting NATO missions in Latvia, Romania, and Slovakia (2024)

Military - note: the Spanish military has a wide range of responsibilities, including protecting the country's national interests, sovereignty, and territory, providing support during natural disasters, and fulfilling Spain's responsibilities to European and international security; it maintains garrisons in the Balearic Islands, the Canary Islands, Ceuta, and Melilla, conducts operations worldwide, and participates in a variety of EU-, NATO-, and UN-led missions; Spain joined NATO in 1982 and is fully integrated into the NATO structure; it routinely conducts exercises with NATO (and EU) partners, and hosts one of NATO's two combined air operations centers
the Spanish military has a rich history going back to the 13th century; the Army has an infantry regiment, formed in the 13th century, that is considered the oldest still active military unit in the Western world; the Marine Corps, which traces its roots back to 1537, is the oldest naval infantry force in the World; Spain created a Spanish Legion for foreigners in 1920, but early on the Legion was primarily filled by native Spaniards due to difficulties in recruiting foreigners, and most of its foreign members were from the Republic of Cuba; it was modeled after the French Foreign Legion and its purpose was to provide a corps of professional troops to fight in Spain's colonial campaigns in North Africa; in more recent years, it has been used in NATO peacekeeping deployments; today's Legion includes a mix of native Spaniards and foreigners with Spanish residency (2025)

SPACE

Space agency/agencies: Spanish Space Agency (AEE; became operational in 2023); Center for the Development of Industrial Technology (CDTI) (2025)
note 1: the CDTI coordinates the activities of the commercial space sector
note 2: prior to the establishment of the AEE, the National Institute of Aerospace Technology (Instituto Nacional de Técnica Aeroespacial or INTA, established 1942), a public research organization that depends on the Ministry of Defense, acted as Spain's space agency

Space launch site(s): El Arenosillo Test Center/Range (Andalusia) (2025)

Space program overview: space program is integrated into the European Space Agency (ESA) and dates back to the 1940s; manufactures and operates communications, remote sensing (RS), and scientific/technology satellites; has developed sounding rockets; conducts research and development in a broad range of space-related capabilities, including astrobiology, astronomy, imaging/RS, materials, meteorology, optics, propulsion, robotics, satellites (particularly micro- and nano-satellites), satellite systems and subsystems, satellite/space launch vehicles (SLVs), and space sciences; participates in ESA, EU, and other international programs; hosts the European Space Astronomy Center (ESOC) and the ESA's Space Surveillance and Tracking Data Centre (ESAC); cooperates with foreign space agencies and industries, including those of ESA and EU member states and the US; has a considerable commercial space industry, which is involved in a wide range of space-related research, development, and production, including satellites and SLVs (2025)
note: further details about the key activities, programs, and milestones of the country's space program, as well as government spending estimates on the space sector, appear in the Space Programs reference guide

TERRORISM

Terrorist group(s): Terrorist group(s): Islamic State of Iraq and ash-Sham (ISIS); al-Qa'ida
note: details about the history, aims, leadership, organization, areas of operation, tactics, targets, weapons, size, and sources of support of the group(s) appear(s) in Appendix T

TRANSNATIONAL ISSUES

Refugees and internally displaced persons: *refugees:* 693,298 (2024 est.)

IDPs: 3,960 (2024 est.)
stateless persons: 10,164 (2024 est.)

SPRATLY ISLANDS

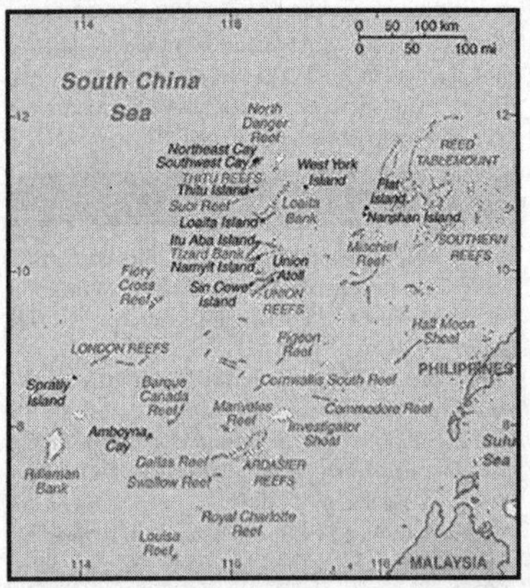

INTRODUCTION

Background: The Spratly Islands consist of more than 100 small islands or reefs surrounded by rich fishing grounds – and potentially by gas and oil deposits. China, Taiwan, and Vietnam all claim the islands in their entirety, while portions are claimed by Malaysia and the Philippines. Around 70 disputed islets and reefs in the Spratly Islands are occupied by China, Malaysia, the Philippines, Taiwan, and Vietnam. Since 1985, Brunei has claimed a continental shelf that overlaps a southern reef but has not made any formal claim to the reef. Brunei claims an exclusive economic zone over this area.

GEOGRAPHY

Location: Southeastern Asia, group of reefs and islands in the South China Sea, about two-thirds of the way from southern Vietnam to the southern Philippines

Geographic coordinates: 8 38 N, 111 55 E

Map references: Southeast Asia

Area: *total:* 5 sq km less than
land: 5 sq km less than
water: 0 sq km
note: includes over 100 islets, coral reefs, and sea mounts scattered over an area of nearly 410,000 sq km (158,000 sq mi) in the central South China Sea
comparison ranking: total 247

Area - comparative: land area is about seven times the size of the National Mall in Washington, D.C.

Land boundaries: *total:* 0 km

Coastline: 926 km

Climate: tropical

Terrain: small, flat islands, islets, cays, and reefs

Elevation: *highest point:* unnamed location on Southwest Cay 6 m
lowest point: South China Sea 0 m

Natural resources: fish, guano, undetermined oil and natural gas potential

Land use: *other:* 100% (2018 est.)

Natural hazards: typhoons; numerous reefs and shoals pose a serious maritime hazard

Geography - note: strategically located near several primary shipping lanes in the central South China Sea; includes numerous small islands, atolls, shoals, and coral reefs

PEOPLE AND SOCIETY

Population: *total:* no permanent inhabitants
note: scattered garrisons are occupied by military personnel of several claimant states

ENVIRONMENT

Environmental issues: harm to reefs from China's use of dredged sand and coral to build artificial islands; illegal fishing practices

Climate: Tropical

GOVERNMENT

Country name: *conventional long form:* none
conventional short form: Spratly Islands
etymology: named after British whaling captain Richard SPRATLY, who sighted the islands in 1843

MILITARY AND SECURITY

Military - note: around 70 disputed islets and reefs in the Spratly Islands are occupied by China, Malaysia, the Philippines, Taiwan, and Vietnam

China: occupies seven outposts (Fiery Cross, Mischief, Subi, Cuarteron, Gavin, Hughes, and Johnson reefs); the outposts on Fiery Cross, Mischief, and Subi include air bases with helipads and aircraft hangers, naval port facilities, surveillance radars, air defense and anti-ship missile sites, and other military infrastructure such as communications, barracks, maintenance facilities, and ammunition and fuel bunkers

Malaysia: occupies five outposts in the southern portion of the archipelago, closest to the Malaysian state of Sabah (Ardasier Reef, Eric Reef, Mariveles Reef, Shallow Reef, and Investigator Shoal); all the outposts have helicopter landing pads, while Shallow Reef also has an airstrip

Philippines: occupies nine features (Commodore Reef, Second Thomas Shoal, Flat Island, Loaita Cay, Loaita Island, Nanshan Island, Northeast Cay, Thitu Island, and West York Island); Thitu Island has an airstrip and a coast guard station

Taiwan: maintains a coast guard outpost with an airstrip on Itu Aba Island

Vietnam: occupies about 50 outposts, plus some 14 platforms known as "economic, scientific, and technological service stations" (Dịch vụ-Khoa) that sit on underwater banks to the southeast that Vietnam does not consider part of the disputed island chain, although China and Taiwan disagree; Spratly Islands outposts are on Alison Reef, Amboyna Cay, Barque Canada Reef, Central Reef, Collins Reef, Cornwallis South Reef, Discovery Great Reef, East Reef, Grierson Reef, Ladd Reef, Landsdowne Reef, Namyit Island, Pearson Reef, Petley Reef, Sand Cay, Sin Cowe Island, South Reef, Southwest Cay, Spratly Island, Tennent Reef, West Reef; the underwater banks with stations include Vanguard, Rifleman, Prince of Wales, Prince Consort, Grainger, and Alexandra; in recent years, Vietnam has continued to make improvements to its outposts, including defensive positions and infrastructure (2025)

SRI LANKA

INTRODUCTION

Background: The first Sinhalese arrived in Sri Lanka late in the 6th century B.C., probably from northern India. Buddhism was introduced circa 250 B.C., and the first kingdoms developed at the cities of Anuradhapura (from about 200 B.C. to about A.D. 1000) and Polonnaruwa (from about A.D. 1070 to 1200). In the 14th century, a South Indian dynasty established a Tamil kingdom in northern Sri Lanka. The Portuguese controlled the coastal areas of the island in the 16th century, followed by the Dutch in the 17th century. The island was ceded to the British in 1796, became a crown colony in 1802, and was formally united under British rule by 1815. As Ceylon, it became independent in 1948; the name was changed to Sri Lanka in 1972. Prevailing tensions between the Sinhalese majority and Tamil separatists erupted into war in 1983. Fighting between the government and Liberation Tigers of Tamil Eelam (LTTE) continued for over a quarter-century. Although Norway brokered peace negotiations that led to a cease-fire in 2002, the fighting slowly resumed and was again in full force by 2006. The government defeated the LTTE in 2009.

During the post-conflict years under then-President Mahinda RAJAPAKSA, the government initiated infrastructure development projects, many of which were financed by loans from China. His regime faced allegations of human rights violations and a shrinking democratic space for civil society. In 2015, a new coalition government headed by President Maithripala SIRISENA of the Sri Lanka Freedom Party and Prime Minister Ranil WICKREMESINGHE of the United National Party came to power with pledges to advance economic, political, and judicial reforms. However, implementation of these reforms was uneven. In 2019, Gotabaya RAJAPAKSA won the presidential election and appointed his brother Mahinda prime minister. Civil society raised concerns about the RAJAPAKSA administration's commitment to

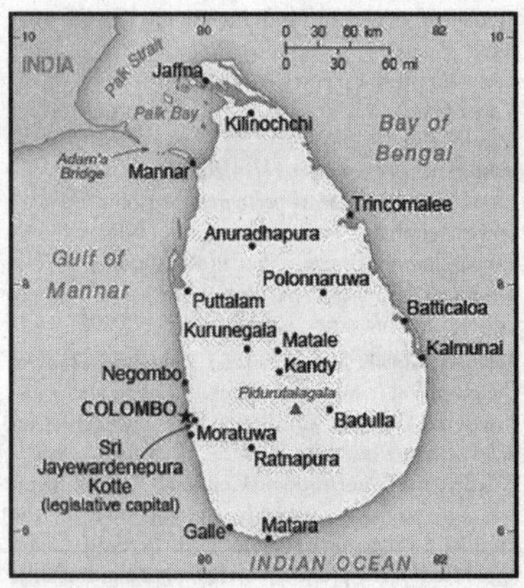

pursuing justice, human rights, and accountability reforms, as well as the risks to foreign creditors that Sri Lanka faced given its ongoing economic crisis. A combination of factors including the COVID-19 pandemic; severe shortages of food, medicine, and fuel; and power outages triggered increasingly violent protests in Columbo beginning in 2022. In response, WICKREMESINGHE – who had already served as prime minister five times – was named to replace the prime minister, but he became president within a few months when Gotabaya RAJAPAKSA fled the country.

GEOGRAPHY

Location: Southern Asia, island in the Indian Ocean, south of India

Geographic coordinates: 7 00 N, 81 00 E

Map references: Asia

Area: *total:* 65,610 sq km
land: 64,630 sq km
water: 980 sq km
comparison ranking: total 122

Area - comparative: slightly larger than West Virginia

Land boundaries: *total:* 0 km

Coastline: 1,340 km

Maritime claims: *territorial sea:* 12 nm
contiguous zone: 24 nm
exclusive economic zone: 200 nm
continental shelf: 200 nm or to the edge of the continental margin

Climate: tropical monsoon; northeast monsoon (December to March); southwest monsoon (June to October)

Terrain: mostly low, flat to rolling plain; mountains in south-central interior

Elevation: *highest point:* Pidurutalagala 2,524 m
lowest point: Indian Ocean 0 m
mean elevation: 228 m

Natural resources: limestone, graphite, mineral sands, gems, phosphates, clay, hydropower, arable land

Land use: *agricultural land:* 45.5% (2022 est.)
arable land: 22.2% (2022 est.)
permanent crops: 16.2% (2022 est.)
permanent pasture: 7.1% (2022 est.)
forest: 34.1% (2022 est.)
other: 20.5% (2022 est.)

Irrigated land: 5,700 sq km (2012)

Population distribution: the population is primarily concentrated within a broad wet zone in the southwest, urban centers along the eastern coast, and on the Jaffna Peninsula in the north

Natural hazards: occasional cyclones and tornadoes

Geography - note: strategic location near major Indian Ocean sea lanes; Adam's Bridge is a chain of limestone shoals between the southeastern coast of India and the northwestern coast of Sri Lanka; geological evidence suggests that this 50-km (31-mi) bridge once connected India and Sri Lanka; ancient records seem to indicate that a foot passage was possible between the two land masses until the 15th century, when the land bridge broke up in a cyclone

PEOPLE AND SOCIETY

Population: *total:* 21,982,608 (2024 est.)
male: 10,642,043
female: 11,340,565
comparison rankings: total 61; male 62; female 60

Nationality: *noun:* Sri Lankan(s)
adjective: Sri Lankan

Ethnic groups: Sinhalese 74.9%, Sri Lankan Tamil 11.2%, Sri Lankan Moors 9.2%, Indian Tamil 4.2%, other 0.5% (2012 est.)

Languages: Sinhala (official) 87%, Tamil (official) 28.5%, English 23.8% (2012 est.)
note: data represent main languages spoken by the population aged 10 years and older; shares sum to more than 100% because some respondents gave more than one answer on the census; English is commonly used in government and is referred to as the "link language" in the constitution

Religions: Buddhist (official) 70.2%, Hindu 12.6%, Muslim 9.7%, Roman Catholic 6.1%, other Christian 1.3%, other 0.05% (2012 est.)

Age structure: *0-14 years:* 22.6% (male 2,537,918/female 2,423,615)
15-64 years: 65% (male 6,954,869/female 7,336,897)
65 years and over: 12.4% (2024 est.) (male 1,149,256/female 1,580,053)

Dependency ratios: *total dependency ratio:* 53.8 (2024 est.)
youth dependency ratio: 34.7 (2024 est.)
elderly dependency ratio: 19.1 (2024 est.)
potential support ratio: 5.2 (2024 est.)

Median age: *total:* 34.1 years (2024 est.)
male: 32.2 years
female: 35.8 years
comparison ranking: total 107

Population growth rate: 0.39% (2024 est.)
comparison ranking: 159

Birth rate: 14.5 births/1,000 population (2024 est.)
comparison ranking: 116

Death rate: 7.5 deaths/1,000 population (2024 est.)
comparison ranking: 101

Net migration rate: -3 migrant(s)/1,000 population (2024 est.)
comparison ranking: 179

Population distribution: the population is primarily concentrated within a broad wet zone in the southwest, urban centers along the eastern coast, and on the Jaffna Peninsula in the north

Urbanization: *urban population:* 19.2% of total population (2023)
rate of urbanization: 1.22% annual rate of change (2020-25 est.)

Major urban areas - population: 103,000 Sri Jayewardenepura Kotte (legislative capital) (2018), 633,000 COLOMBO (capital) (2023)

Sex ratio: *at birth:* 1.05 male(s)/female
0-14 years: 1.05 male(s)/female
15-64 years: 0.95 male(s)/female
65 years and over: 0.73 male(s)/female
total population: 0.94 male(s)/female (2024 est.)

Mother's mean age at first birth: 25.6 years (2016 est.)
note: data represents median age at first birth among women 30-34

Maternal mortality ratio: 18 deaths/100,000 live births (2023 est.)
comparison ranking: 126

Infant mortality rate: *total:* 6.8 deaths/1,000 live births (2024 est.)
male: 7.5 deaths/1,000 live births
female: 6.1 deaths/1,000 live births
comparison ranking: total 157

Life expectancy at birth: *total population:* 76.8 years (2024 est.)
male: 73.7 years
female: 79.9 years
comparison ranking: total population 100

Total fertility rate: 2.13 children born/woman (2024 est.)
comparison ranking: 93

Gross reproduction rate: 1.04 (2024 est.)

Drinking water source: *improved: urban:* 98.1% of population (2022 est.)
rural: 87.2% of population (2022 est.)
total: 89.3% of population (2022 est.)
unimproved: urban: 1.9% of population (2022 est.)
rural: 12.8% of population (2022 est.)
total: 10.7% of population (2022 est.)

Health expenditure: 4.1% of GDP (2021)
9.5% of national budget (2022 est.)

Physician density: 1.14 physicians/1,000 population (2023)

Hospital bed density: 4 beds/1,000 population (2020 est.)

Sanitation facility access: *improved: urban:* 97.9% of population (2022 est.)
rural: 99.2% of population (2022 est.)
total: 99% of population (2022 est.)
unimproved: urban: 2.1% of population (2022 est.)
rural: 0.8% of population (2022 est.)
total: 1% of population (2022 est.)

Obesity - adult prevalence rate: 5.2% (2016)
comparison ranking: 182

Alcohol consumption per capita: *total:* 2.58 liters of pure alcohol (2019 est.)
beer: 0.22 liters of pure alcohol (2019 est.)
wine: 0.01 liters of pure alcohol (2019 est.)
spirits: 2.32 liters of pure alcohol (2019 est.)
other alcohols: 0.03 liters of pure alcohol (2019 est.)
comparison ranking: total 122

Tobacco use: *total:* 18.2% (2025 est.)
male: 36.3% (2025 est.)
female: 2% (2025 est.)
comparison ranking: total 82

Children under the age of 5 years underweight: 20.5% (2016)
comparison ranking: 14

Currently married women (ages 15-49): 65.1% (2023 est.)

Child marriage: *women married by age 15:* 0.9% (2016)
women married by age 18: 9.8% (2016)

Education expenditure: 1.8% of GDP (2023 est.)
7.2% national budget (2024 est.)
comparison ranking: Education expenditure (% GDP) 188

Literacy: *total population:* 93% (2023 est.)
male: 93% (2023 est.)
female: 92% (2023 est.)

School life expectancy (primary to tertiary education): *total:* 13 years (2023 est.)
male: 12 years (2023 est.)
female: 14 years (2023 est.)

ENVIRONMENT

Environmental issues: deforestation; soil erosion; poaching; effects of urbanization; coastal degradation from mining activities and pollution; coral reef destruction; freshwater resources polluted by industrial wastes and sewage runoff; waste disposal; air pollution in Colombo

International environmental agreements: *party to:* Biodiversity, Climate Change, Climate Change-Kyoto Protocol, Climate Change-Paris Agreement, Desertification, Endangered Species, Environmental Modification, Hazardous Wastes, Law of the Sea, Nuclear Test Ban, Ozone Layer Protection, Ship Pollution, Wetlands
signed, but not ratified: Comprehensive Nuclear Test Ban, Marine Life Conservation

Climate: tropical monsoon; northeast monsoon (December to March); southwest monsoon (June to October)

Urbanization: *urban population:* 19.2% of total population (2023)
rate of urbanization: 1.22% annual rate of change (2020-25 est.)

Carbon dioxide emissions: 19.153 million metric tonnes of CO2 (2023 est.)
from coal and metallurgical coke: 5.15 million metric tonnes of CO2 (2023 est.)
from petroleum and other liquids: 14.003 million metric tonnes of CO2 (2023 est.)
comparison ranking: total emissions 88

Particulate matter emissions: 24.8 micrograms per cubic meter (2019 est.)

Waste and recycling: *municipal solid waste generated annually:* 2.632 million tons (2024 est.)
percent of municipal solid waste recycled: 24.5% (2022 est.)

Total water withdrawal: *municipal:* 805 million cubic meters (2022 est.)
industrial: 831 million cubic meters (2022 est.)
agricultural: 11.31 billion cubic meters (2022 est.)

Total renewable water resources: 52.8 billion cubic meters (2022 est.)

GOVERNMENT

Country name: *conventional long form:* Democratic Socialist Republic of Sri Lanka
conventional short form: Sri Lanka: *local long form:* Shri Lanka Prajatantrika Samajavadi Janarajaya (Sinhala)/Ilankai Jananayaka Choshalichak Kutiyarachu (Tamil)
local short form: Shri Lanka (Sinhala)/Ilankai (Tamil)
former: Serendib, Ceylon
etymology: the name is composed of the Sanskrit words *shri* (happiness or holiness) and *lanka* (island); the former name Serendib was an Arabic derivation of the Sanskrit word *simhaladvipa*, or "island of the place of lions;" the former name Ceylon came from the Sanskrit *simha*, or "lion"

Government type: presidential republic

Capital: *name:* Colombo (commercial capital); Sri Jayewardenepura Kotte (legislative capital)
geographic coordinates: 6 55 N, 79 50 E
time difference: UTC+5.5 (10.5 hours ahead of Washington, DC, during Standard Time)
etymology: the origin of Colombo's name is unclear; it may derive from the Sinhalese words *kola* (leaves) and *amba* (mango), referring to local mango trees, or from the name Kelantotta, referring to a ferry that crossed the Kelani River; the name was corrupted to Kolambu by Arab traders, and 16th-century Portuguese settlers then called it Colombo, possibly referring to explorer Christopher COLUMBUS; the legislative capital's name, Sri Jayewardenepura Kotte, is composed of the Sanskrit honorific *sri*, the name of Sri Lankan President J.R.
JAYEWARDENE, and the Hindi word *pura* (town)

Administrative divisions: 9 provinces; Central, Eastern, North Central, Northern, North Western, Sabaragamuwa, Southern, Uva, Western

Legal system: mixed system of Roman-Dutch civil law, English common law, Jaffna Tamil customary law, and Muslim personal law

Constitution: *history:* several previous; latest adopted 16 August 1978, certified 31 August 1978
amendment process: proposed by Parliament; passage requires at least two-thirds majority vote of its total membership, certification by the president of the republic or the Parliament speaker, and in some cases approval in a referendum by absolute majority of valid votes

International law organization participation: has not submitted an ICJ jurisdiction declaration; non-party state to the ICCt

Citizenship: *citizenship by birth:* no
citizenship by descent only: at least one parent must be a citizen of Sri Lanka
dual citizenship recognized: no, except in cases where the government rules it is to the benefit of Sri Lanka
residency requirement for naturalization: 7 years

Suffrage: 18 years of age; universal

Executive branch: *chief of state:* President Anura Kumara DISSANAYAKE (since 23 September 2024)
head of government: Prime Minister Harini AMARASURIYA (since 24 September 2024)
cabinet: Cabinet appointed by the president in consultation with the prime minister
election/appointment process: president directly elected by preferential majority popular vote for a 5-year term (eligible for a second term); prime minister appointed by the president
most recent election date: 21 September 2024
election results: *2024:* Anura Kumara DISSANAYAKE elected president; percent of vote after reallocation - Anura Kumara DISSANAYAKE (JVP) 55.9%, Sajith PREMADASA (SJB) 44.1%
2022: Ranil WICKREMESINGHE elected president by Parliament on 20 July 2022; Parliament vote - WICKREMESINGHE (UNP) 134, Dullas ALAHAPPERUMA (SLPP) 82
expected date of next election: 2029

Legislative branch: *legislature name:* Parliament
legislative structure: unicameral
number of seats: 225 (196 directly elected; 29 indirectly elected)
electoral system: proportional representation
scope of elections: full renewal
term in office: 5 years
most recent election date: 11/14/2024
parties elected and seats per party: National People's Power (Jathika Jana Balawegaya, NPP) (159); Samagi Jana Balawegaya (SJB) (40); Other (26)
percentage of women in chamber: 9.8%
expected date of next election: November 2029

Judicial branch: *highest court(s):* Supreme Court of the Republic (consists of the chief justice and 9 justices); has exclusive jurisdiction to review legislation
judge selection and term of office: chief justice nominated by the Constitutional Council (CC), a 9-member high-level advisory body, and appointed by the president; other justices nominated by the CC and appointed by the president on the advice of the chief justice; all justices can serve until age 65
subordinate courts: Court of Appeals; High Courts; Magistrates' Courts; municipal and primary courts

Political parties: Crusaders for Democracy or CFD
Eelam People's Democratic Party or EPDP
Eelam People's Revolutionary Liberation Front or EPRLF
Illankai Tamil Arasu Kachchi or ITAK
Janatha Vimukthi Peramuna or JVP
Jathika Hela Urumaya or JHU
National People's Power or NPP (also known as Jathika Jana Balawegaya or JJB)
People's Liberation Organisation of Tamil Eelam or PLOTE
Samagi Jana Balawegaya or SJB
Sri Lanka Freedom Party or SLFP
Sri Lanka Muslim Congress or SLMC
Sri Lanka People's Freedom Alliance or SLPFA (includes SLPFP, SLPP, and several smaller parties)
Sri Lanka Podujana Peramuna (Sri Lanka's People's Front) or SLPP
Tamil Eelam Liberation Organization or TELO
Tamil National Alliance or TNA (includes ITAK, PLOTE, TELO)
Tamil National People's Front or TNPF
Tamil People's National Alliance or TPNA
United National Front for Good Governance or UNFGG (coalition includes JHU, UNP)
United National Party or UNP

Diplomatic representation in the US: *chief of mission:* Ambassador Mahinda SAMARASINGHE (since 13 January 2022)
chancery: 3025 Whitehaven Street NW, Washington, DC 20008
telephone: [1] (202) 483-4025
FAX: [1] 202-232-2329
email address and website: slemb.washington@mfa.gov.lk
https://slembassyusa.org/
consulate(s) general: Los Angeles
consulate(s): New York

Diplomatic representation from the US: *chief of mission:* Ambassador Julie J. CHUNG (since 17 February 2022)
embassy: 210 Galle Road, Colombo 03
mailing address: 6100 Colombo Place, Washington DC 20521-6100
telephone: [94] (11) 249-8500
FAX: [94] (11) 243-7345
email address and website: colomboacs@state.gov
https://lk.usembassy.gov/

International organization participation: ABEDA, ADB, ARF, BIMSTEC, C, CD, CICA (observer), CP, FAO, G-11, G-15, G-24, G-77, IAEA, IBRD, ICAO, ICC (national committees), ICRM, IDA, IFAD, IFC, IFRCS, IHO, ILO, IMF, IMO, IMSO, Interpol, IOC, IOM, IPU, ISO, ITSO, ITU, ITUC (NGOs), MIGA, MINURSO, MINUSTAH, MONUSCO, NAM, OAS (observer), OPCW, PCA, SAARC, SACEP, SCO (dialogue member), UN, UNCTAD, UNESCO, UNIDO, UNIFIL, UNISFA, UNMISS, UNWTO, UPU, WCO, WFTU (NGOs), WHO, WIPO, WMO, WTO

Independence: 4 February 1948 (from the UK)

National holiday: Independence Day (National Day), 4 February (1948)

Flag: *description:* yellow with two panels; the smaller panel on the left has two equal vertical bands of green (left side) and orange; the larger panel has a yellow lion holding a sword on a maroon field, with a yellow bo leaf in each corner
meaning: the sword stands for national sovereignty; the lion for Sinhalese ethnicity, the strength of the nation, and bravery; the four bo leaves for Buddhism and the four virtues of kindness, friendliness, happiness, and equanimity; orange stands for Tamils, green for Moors, and maroon for the Sinhalese majority; yellow represents other ethnic groups
note: the banner is sometimes referred to as the Lion Flag

National symbol(s): lion, water lily

National color(s): maroon, yellow

National anthem(s): *title:* "Sri Lanka Matha" (Mother Sri Lanka)
lyrics/music: Ananda SAMARKONE (Sinhala),M. NALLATHAMBY (Tamil)/Ananda SAMARKONE
history: adopted 1951

National heritage: *total World Heritage Sites:* 8 (6 cultural, 2 natural)
selected World Heritage Site locales: Ancient City of Polonnaruwa (c); Ancient City of Sigiriya (c); Sacred City of Anuradhapura (c); Old Town of Galle and its Fortifications (c); Sacred City of Kandy (c); Sinharaja Forest Reserve (n); Rangiri Dambulla Cave Temple (c); Central Highlands of Sri Lanka (n)

ECONOMY

Economic overview: economic contraction in 2022-23 marked by increased poverty and significant inflation; IMF two-year debt relief program following 2022 sovereign default; structural challenges from non-diversified economy and rigid labor laws; heavy dependence on tourism receipts and remittances

Real GDP (purchasing power parity): $301.407 billion (2024 est.)
$287.031 billion (2023 est.)
$293.878 billion (2022 est.)
note: data in 2021 dollars
comparison ranking: 62

Real GDP growth rate: 5% (2024 est.)
-2.3% (2023 est.)
-7.3% (2022 est.)
note: annual GDP % growth based on constant local currency
comparison ranking: 41

Real GDP per capita: $13,800 (2024 est.)
$13,000 (2023 est.)
$13,200 (2022 est.)
note: data in 2021 dollars
comparison ranking: 130

GDP (official exchange rate): $98.963 billion (2024 est.)
note: data in current dollars at official exchange rate

Inflation rate (consumer prices): -0.4% (2024 est.)
16.5% (2023 est.)
49.7% (2022 est.)
note: annual % change based on consumer prices
comparison ranking: 5

GDP - composition, by sector of origin: *agriculture:* 8.3% (2024 est.)
industry: 25.5% (2024 est.)
services: 57.5% (2024 est.)
note: figures may not total 100% due to non-allocated consumption not captured in sector-reported data
comparison rankings: agriculture 83; industry 82; services 107

GDP - composition, by end use: *household consumption:* 68.7% (2024 est.)
government consumption: 7% (2024 est.)
investment in fixed capital: 18.8% (2024 est.)
investment in inventories: 8.2% (2024 est.)
exports of goods and services: 19.9% (2024 est.)
imports of goods and services: -22.5% (2024 est.)
note: figures may not total 100% due to rounding or gaps in data collection

Agricultural products: rice, coconuts, tea, sugarcane, plantains, milk, fiber crops, cassava, chicken, pumpkins/squash (2023)
note: top ten agricultural products based on tonnage

Industries: processing of rubber, tea, coconuts, tobacco and other agricultural commodities; tourism; clothing and textiles; mining

Industrial production growth rate: 11% (2024 est.)
note: annual % change in industrial value added based on constant local currency
comparison ranking: 6

Labor force: 8.499 million (2024 est.)
note: number of people ages 15 or older who are employed or seeking work
comparison ranking: 62

Unemployment rate: 5% (2024 est.)
6% (2023 est.)
4.6% (2022 est.)
note: % of labor force seeking employment
comparison ranking: 88

Youth unemployment rate (ages 15-24): *total:* 22.3% (2024 est.)
male: 18.4% (2024 est.)
female: 29.6% (2024 est.)
note: % of labor force ages 15-24 seeking employment
comparison ranking: total 45

Population below poverty line: 14.3% (2019 est.)
note: % of population with income below national poverty line

Gini Index coefficient - distribution of family income: 37.7 (2019 est.)
note: index (0-100) of income distribution; higher values represent greater inequality
comparison ranking: 56

Average household expenditures: *on food:* 27.1% of household expenditures (2023 est.)
on alcohol and tobacco: 3.4% of household expenditures (2023 est.)

Household income or consumption by percentage share: *lowest 10%:* 3.1% (2019 est.)
highest 10%: 30.8% (2019 est.)
note: % share of income accruing to lowest and highest 10% of population

Remittances: 7.2% of GDP (2023 est.)
5.2% of GDP (2022 est.)
6.2% of GDP (2021 est.)
note: personal transfers and compensation between resident and non-resident individuals/households/entities

Budget: *revenues:* $9.387 billion (2023 est.)
expenditures: $17.144 billion (2023 est.)
note: central government revenues and expenses (excluding grants/extrabudgetary units/social security funds) converted to US dollars at average official exchange rate for year indicated

Public debt: 79.1% of GDP (2017 est.)
note: central government debt as a % of GDP
comparison ranking: 41

Taxes and other revenues: 9.9% (of GDP) (2023 est.)
note: central government tax revenue as a % of GDP
comparison ranking: 130

Current account balance: $1.559 billion (2023 est.)
-$1.448 billion (2022 est.)
-$3.284 billion (2021 est.)
note: balance of payments - net trade and primary/secondary income in current dollars
comparison ranking: 53

Exports: $17.327 billion (2023 est.)
$16.169 billion (2022 est.)
$14.974 billion (2021 est.)
note: balance of payments - exports of goods and services in current dollars
comparison ranking: 96

Exports - partners: USA 22%, India 7%, Germany 7%, UK 7%, Italy 5% (2023)
note: top five export partners based on percentage share of exports

Exports - commodities: garments, tea, precious stones, used rubber tires, rubber products (2023)
note: top five export commodities based on value in dollars

Imports: $18.823 billion (2023 est.)
$19.244 billion (2022 est.)
$21.526 billion (2021 est.)
note: balance of payments - imports of goods and services in current dollars
comparison ranking: 99

Imports - partners: India 21%, China 19%, UAE 10%, Singapore 5%, Malaysia 4% (2023)
note: top five import partners based on percentage share of imports

Imports - commodities: refined petroleum, fabric, crude petroleum, packaged medicine, cotton fabric (2023)
note: top five import commodities based on value in dollars

Reserves of foreign exchange and gold: $6.094 billion (2024 est.)
$4.405 billion (2023 est.)
$1.896 billion (2022 est.)
note: holdings of gold (year-end prices)/foreign exchange/special drawing rights in current dollars
comparison ranking: 92

Debt - external: $42.198 billion (2023 est.)
note: present value of external debt in current US dollars
comparison ranking: 19

Exchange rates: Sri Lankan rupees (LKR) per US dollar -

Exchange rates: 327.507 (2023 est.)
322.633 (2022 est.)
198.764 (2021 est.)
185.593 (2020 est.)

178.745 (2019 est.)

ENERGY

Electricity access: *electrification - total population:* 100% (2022 est.)

Electricity: *installed generating capacity:* 5.326 million kW (2023 est.)
consumption: 15.763 billion kWh (2023 est.)
transmission/distribution losses: 1.457 billion kWh (2023 est.)
comparison rankings: installed generating capacity 89; consumption 85; transmission/distribution losses 114

Electricity generation sources: *fossil fuels:* 49.4% of total installed capacity (2023 est.)
solar: 4.6% of total installed capacity (2023 est.)
wind: 4.6% of total installed capacity (2023 est.)
hydroelectricity: 40.7% of total installed capacity (2023 est.)
biomass and waste: 0.7% of total installed capacity (2023 est.)

Coal: *consumption:* 2.323 million metric tons (2023 est.)
imports: 2.238 million metric tons (2023 est.)

Petroleum: *refined petroleum consumption:* 100,000 bbl/day (2023 est.)

Energy consumption per capita: 12.372 million Btu/person (2023 est.)
comparison ranking: 145

COMMUNICATIONS

Telephones - fixed lines: *total subscriptions:* 1.707 million (2023 est.)
subscriptions per 100 inhabitants: 7 (2023 est.)
comparison ranking: total subscriptions 54

Telephones - mobile cellular: *total subscriptions:* 30 million (2023 est.)
subscriptions per 100 inhabitants: 143 (2022 est.)
comparison ranking: total subscriptions 47

Broadcast media: government operates 5 TV channels and 19 radio channels; multi-channel satellite and cable TV subscription services available; 25 private TV stations and about 43 radio stations; 6 non-profit TV stations and 4 radio stations

Internet country code: .lk

Internet users: *percent of population:* 51% (2023 est.)

Broadband - fixed subscriptions: *total:* 2.01 million (2023 est.)
subscriptions per 100 inhabitants: 9 (2023 est.)
comparison ranking: total 61

TRANSPORTATION

Civil aircraft registration country code prefix: 4R

Airports: 18 (2025)
comparison ranking: 144

Heliports: 1 (2025)
comparison ranking: 147

Railways: *total:* 1,562 km (2016)
broad gauge: 1,562 km (2016) 1.676-m gauge

Merchant marine: *total:* 96 (2023)
by type: bulk carrier 5, general cargo 15, oil tanker 11, other 65
comparison ranking: total 92

Ports: *total ports:* 6 (2024)
large: 0
medium: 2
small: 1
very small: 1
size unknown: 2
ports with oil terminals: 2
key ports: Batticaloa Roads, Colombo, Galle Harbor, Hambantota, Kankesanturai, Trincomalee Harbor

MILITARY AND SECURITY

Military and security forces: Sri Lanka Armed Forces: Sri Lanka Army (includes National Guard and the Volunteer Force), Sri Lanka Navy (includes Marine Corps), Sri Lanka Air Force, Sri Lanka Coast Guard; Civil Security Department (Home Guard)

Ministry of Public Security: Sri Lanka Police (2025)
note: the Civil Security Department, also known as the Civil Defense Force, is an auxiliary force administered by the Ministry of Defense

Military expenditures: 1.5% of GDP (2024 est.)
1.6% of GDP (2023 est.)
1.7% of GDP (2022 est.)
1.9% of GDP (2021 est.)
2% of GDP (2020 est.)

Military and security service personnel strengths: estimated 210,000 active Armed Forces (140,000 Army; 25,000 Air Force; 45,000 Navy) (2025)
note: the Sri Lankan military has been downsizing for several years; in 2025, the Sri Lankan Government announced its intent to decrease the size of the Army to 100,000, the Air Force to 18,000, and the Navy to 40,000 by 2030

Military equipment inventories and acquisitions: the military's inventory consists mostly of Chinese- and Russian-origin equipment with a smaller mix of material from countries such as India and the US, including donations; defense acquisitions have been limited over the past decade (2024)

Military service age and obligation: 18-22 years of age for voluntary military service for men and women; no conscription (2023)

Military deployments: 110 Central African Republic (MINUSCA); 125 Lebanon (UNIFIL); 240 Mali (MINUSMA) (2024)

Military - note: the military of Sri Lanka is responsible for external defense, maritime security, and maintaining internal security; it has sent small numbers of personnel on UN peacekeeping missions; from 1983 to 2009, the military fought against the Liberation Tigers of Tamil Eelam (LTTE), a conflict that involved both guerrilla and conventional warfare, as well as acts of terrorism and human rights abuses, and cost the military nearly 30,000 killed; since the end of the war, a large portion of the Army reportedly remains deployed in the majority Tamil-populated northern and eastern provinces; the military over the past decade also has increased its role in a range of commercial sectors including agriculture, hotels, leisure, and restaurants
Sri Lanka traditionally has had close security ties to India; the Sri Lankan and Indian militaries conduct exercises together, and India trains approximately 1,000 Sri Lankan soldiers per year; in recent years, Sri Lanka has increased military ties with China, including acquiring military equipment, hosting naval port calls, and sending personnel to China for training (2025)

TERRORISM

Terrorist group(s): Terrorist group(s): Islamic State of Iraq and ash-Sham (ISIS); Liberation Tigers of Tamil Eelam (LTTE)
note: details about the history, aims, leadership, organization, areas of operation, tactics, targets, weapons, size, and sources of support of the group(s) appear(s) in Appendix T

TRANSNATIONAL ISSUES

Refugees and internally displaced persons: *refugees:* 500 (2024 est.)

IDPs: 5,549 (2024 est.)
stateless persons: 229 (2024 est.)

SUDAN

INTRODUCTION

Background: Long referred to as Nubia, modern-day Sudan was the site of the Kingdom of Kerma (ca. 2500-1500 B.C.) until it was absorbed into the New Kingdom of Egypt. By the 11th century B.C., the Kingdom of Kush gained independence from Egypt; it lasted in various forms until the middle of the 4th century A.D. After the fall of Kush, the Nubians formed three Christian kingdoms of Nobatia, Makuria, and Alodia, with the latter two enduring until around 1500. Between the 14th and 15th centuries, Arab nomads settled much of Sudan, leading to extensive Islamization between the 16th and 19th centuries. Following Egyptian occupation early in the 19th century, an agreement in 1899 set up a joint British-Egyptian government in Sudan, but it was effectively a British colony.

Military regimes favoring Islamic-oriented governments have dominated national politics since Sudan gained independence from Anglo-Egyptian co-rule in 1956. During most of the second half of the 20th century, Sudan was embroiled in two prolonged civil wars rooted in northern domination of the largely non-Muslim, non-Arab southern portion of the country. The first civil war ended in 1972, but another broke out in 1983. Peace talks gained momentum in 2002-04, and the final North/South Comprehensive Peace Agreement in 2005 granted the southern rebels autonomy for six years, followed by a referendum on independence for Southern Sudan. South Sudan became independent in 2011, but Sudan and South Sudan have yet to fully

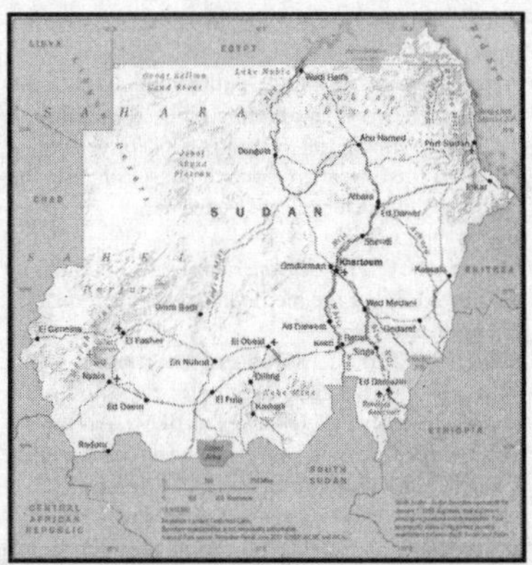

implement security and economic agreements to normalize relations between the two countries. Sudan has also faced conflict in Darfur, Southern Kordofan, and Blue Nile starting in 2003.

In 2019, after months of nationwide protests, the 30-year reign of President Omar Hassan Ahmad al-BASHIR ended when the military forced him out. Economist and former international civil servant Abdalla HAMDOUK al-Kinani was selected to serve as the prime minister of a transitional government as the country prepared for elections in 2022. In late 2021, however, the Sudanese military ousted

HAMDOUK and his government and replaced civilian members of the Sovereign Council (Sudan's collective Head of State) with individuals selected by the military. HAMDOUK was briefly reinstated but resigned in January 2022. General Abd-al-Fatah al-BURHAN Abd-al-Rahman, the Chair of Sudan's Sovereign Council and Commander-in-Chief of the Sudanese Armed Forces, currently serves as de facto head of state and government. He presides over a Sovereign Council consisting of military leaders, former armed opposition group representatives, and military-appointed civilians. A cabinet of acting ministers handles day-to-day administration.

GEOGRAPHY

Location: north-eastern Africa, bordering the Red Sea, between Egypt and Eritrea

Geographic coordinates: 15 00 N, 30 00 E

Map references: Africa

Area: *total:* 1,861,484 sq km
land: 1,731,671 sq km
water: 129,813 sq km
comparison ranking: total 17

Area - comparative: slightly less than one-fifth the size of the US

Land boundaries: *total:* 6,819 km
border countries (7): Central African Republic 174 km; Chad 1,403 km; Egypt 1,276 km; Eritrea 682 km; Ethiopia 744 km; Libya 382 km; South Sudan 2,158 km
note: Sudan-South Sudan boundary represents 1 January 1956 alignment; final alignment pending negotiations and demarcation; final sovereignty status of Abyei region pending negotiations between Sudan and South Sudan

Coastline: 853 km

Maritime claims: *territorial sea:* 12 nm
contiguous zone: 18 nm
continental shelf: 200-m depth or to the depth of exploitation

Climate: hot and dry; arid desert; rainy season varies by region (April to November)

Terrain: generally flat, featureless plain; desert dominates the north

Elevation: *highest point:* Jabal Marrah 3,042 m
lowest point: Red Sea 0 m
mean elevation: 568 m

Natural resources: petroleum; small reserves of iron ore, copper, chromium ore, zinc, tungsten, mica, silver, gold; hydropower

Land use: *agricultural land:* 60.3% (2022 est.)
arable land: 11.2% (2022 est.)
permanent crops: 0.1% (2022 est.)
permanent pasture: 49% (2022 est.)
forest: 9.6% (2022 est.)
other: 30% (2022 est.)

Irrigated land: 15,504 sq km (2019)

Major rivers (by length in km): An Nīl (Nile) (shared with Rwanda [s], Tanzania, Uganda, South Sudan, and Egypt [m]) - 6,650 km; Blue Nile river mouth (shared with Ethiopia [s]) - 1,600 km
note: [s] after country name indicates river source; [m] after country name indicates river mouth

Major watersheds (area sq km): Atlantic Ocean drainage: *(Mediterranean Sea)* Nile (3,254,853 sq km)

Internal (endorheic basin) drainage: Lake Chad (2,497,738 sq km)

Major aquifers: Nubian Aquifer System, Sudd Basin (Umm Ruwaba Aquifer)

Population distribution: with the exception of a ribbon of settlement that corresponds to the banks of the Nile, northern Sudan is sparsely populated; sizeable areas of population are found around Khartoum, southeast between the Blue and White Nile Rivers, and throughout South Darfur, as shown on this population distribution map

Natural hazards: dust storms and periodic persistent droughts

Geography - note: the Nile is Sudan's primary water source; its major tributaries, the White Nile and the Blue Nile, meet at Khartoum to form the River Nile, which flows northward through Egypt to the Mediterranean Sea

PEOPLE AND SOCIETY

Population: *total:* 50,467,278 (2024 est.)
male: 25,335,092
female: 25,132,186
comparison rankings: total 29; male 29; female 31

Nationality: *noun:* Sudanese (singular and plural)
adjective: Sudanese

Ethnic groups: Sudanese Arab (approximately 70%), Fur, Beja, Nuba, Ingessana, Uduk, Fallata, Masalit, Dajo, Gimir, Tunjur, Berti; there are over 500 ethnic groups

Languages: Arabic (official), English (official), Nubian, Ta Bedawie, Fur
major-language sample(s):
كتاب حقائق العالم، المصدر الذي لا يمكن الاستغناء عنه للمعلومات الأساسية
(Arabic)

Religions: Sunni Muslim, small Christian minority

Age structure: *0-14 years:* 40.1% (male 10,278,453/female 9,949,343)
15-64 years: 56.7% (male 14,211,514/female 14,390,486)
65 years and over: 3.2% (2024 est.) (male 845,125/female 792,357)

Dependency ratios: *total dependency ratio:* 76.4 (2024 est.)
youth dependency ratio: 70.7 (2024 est.)
elderly dependency ratio: 5.7 (2024 est.)
potential support ratio: 17.5 (2024 est.)

Median age: *total:* 19.3 years (2024 est.)
male: 19 years
female: 19.6 years
comparison ranking: total 212

Population growth rate: 2.55% (2024 est.)
comparison ranking: 16

Birth rate: 33.1 births/1,000 population (2024 est.)
comparison ranking: 18

Death rate: 6.1 deaths/1,000 population (2024 est.)
comparison ranking: 148

Net migration rate: -1.6 migrant(s)/1,000 population (2024 est.)
comparison ranking: 159

Population distribution: with the exception of a ribbon of settlement that corresponds to the banks of the Nile, northern Sudan is sparsely populated; sizeable areas of population are found around Khartoum, southeast between the Blue and White Nile Rivers, and throughout South Darfur, as shown on this population distribution map

Urbanization: *urban population:* 36.3% of total population (2023)
rate of urbanization: 3.43% annual rate of change (2020-25 est.)

Major urban areas - population: 6.344 million KHARTOUM (capital), 1.057 million Nyala (2023)

Sex ratio: *at birth:* 1.05 male(s)/female
0-14 years: 1.03 male(s)/female
15-64 years: 0.99 male(s)/female
65 years and over: 1.07 male(s)/female
total population: 1.01 male(s)/female (2024 est.)

Maternal mortality ratio: 256 deaths/100,000 live births (2023 est.)
comparison ranking: 29

Infant mortality rate: *total:* 40.6 deaths/1,000 live births (2024 est.)
male: 46 deaths/1,000 live births
female: 34.8 deaths/1,000 live births
comparison ranking: total 28

Life expectancy at birth: *total population:* 67.8 years (2024 est.)
male: 65.5 years
female: 70.2 years
comparison ranking: total population 194

Total fertility rate: 4.47 children born/woman (2024 est.)
comparison ranking: 15

Gross reproduction rate: 2.18 (2024 est.)

Drinking water source: *improved: urban:* 74.2% of population (2022 est.)
rural: 59.7% of population (2022 est.)
total: 64.9% of population (2022 est.)
unimproved: urban: 25.8% of population (2022 est.)
rural: 40.3% of population (2022 est.)
total: 35.1% of population (2022 est.)

Health expenditure: 2.8% of GDP (2021)
6.7% of national budget (2022 est.)

Physician density: 0.25 physicians/1,000 population (2017)

Hospital bed density: 0.7 beds/1,000 population (2020 est.)

Obesity - adult prevalence rate: 6.6% (2014)
comparison ranking: 165

Alcohol consumption per capita: *total:* 1.93 liters of pure alcohol (2019 est.)
beer: 0 liters of pure alcohol (2019 est.)
wine: 0 liters of pure alcohol (2019 est.)
spirits: 0.29 liters of pure alcohol (2019 est.)
other alcohols: 1.63 liters of pure alcohol (2019 est.)
comparison ranking: total 131

Children under the age of 5 years underweight: 33% (2014)
comparison ranking: 2

Currently married women (ages 15-49): 61.4% (2023 est.)

School life expectancy (primary to tertiary education): *total:* 7 years (2015 est.)
male: 7 years (2015 est.)
female: 7 years (2015 est.)

ENVIRONMENT

Environmental issues: water pollution; inadequate supplies of potable water; water scarcity and drought; overhunting; soil erosion; desertification; deforestation; loss of biodiversity

International environmental agreements: *party to:* Biodiversity, Climate Change, Climate Change-Kyoto Protocol, Climate Change-Paris Agreement, Comprehensive Nuclear Test Ban, Desertification, Endangered Species, Hazardous Wastes, Law of the Sea, Nuclear Test Ban, Ozone Layer Protection, Wetlands
signed, but not ratified: none of the selected agreements

Climate: hot and dry; arid desert; rainy season varies by region (April to November)

Urbanization: *urban population:* 36.3% of total population (2023)
rate of urbanization: 3.43% annual rate of change (2020-25 est.)

Carbon dioxide emissions: 18.242 million metric tonnes of CO_2 (2023 est.)
from coal and metallurgical coke: 300 metric tonnes of CO_2 (2023 est.)
from petroleum and other liquids: 18.242 million metric tonnes of CO_2 (2023 est.)
comparison ranking: total emissions 94

Particulate matter emissions: 24.4 micrograms per cubic meter (2019 est.)

Methane emissions: *energy:* 218.5 kt (2022-2024 est.)
agriculture: 1,509.6 kt (2019-2021 est.)
waste: 198.7 kt (2019-2021 est.)
other: 38.8 kt (2019-2021 est.)

Waste and recycling: *municipal solid waste generated annually:* 2.831 million tons (2024 est.)
percent of municipal solid waste recycled: 8.9% (2022 est.)

Total water withdrawal: *municipal:* 950 million cubic meters (2022 est.)
industrial: 75 million cubic meters (2022 est.)
agricultural: 25.91 billion cubic meters (2022 est.)

Total renewable water resources: 37.8 billion cubic meters (2022 est.)

GOVERNMENT

Country name: *conventional long form:* Republic of the Sudan
conventional short form: Sudan
local long form: Jumhuriyat as-Sudan
local short form: As-Sudan
former: Anglo-Egyptian Sudan, Democratic Republic of the Sudan
etymology: the name derives from the Arabic *balad-as-sudan*, meaning "Land of the Black [peoples]"

Government type: presidential republic

Capital: *name:* Khartoum
geographic coordinates: 15 36 N, 32 32 E
time difference: UTC+3 (8 hours ahead of Washington, DC, during Standard Time)
etymology: the name derives from the Arabic words *ras* (head or end) and *al-khurtum* (elephant's trunk), referring to the narrow strip of land between the Blue and White Niles where the city is located

Administrative divisions: 18 states (*wilayat*, singular - *wilayah*); Blue Nile, Central Darfur, East Darfur, Gedaref, Gezira, Kassala, Khartoum, North Darfur, North Kordofan, Northern, Red Sea, River Nile, Sennar, South Darfur, South Kordofan, West Darfur, West Kordofan, White Nile
note: the peace agreement signed in 2020 included a provision to establish a system of governance to restructure the country's current 18 states into regions

Legal system: mixed system of Islamic law and English common law

Constitution: *history:* previous 1973, 1998, 2005 (interim constitution, which was suspended in April 2019); latest initial draft completed by Transitional Military Council in May 2019; revised draft known as the "Draft Constitutional Charter for the 2019 Transitional Period," or "2019 Constitutional Declaration" was signed by the Council and opposition coalition on 4 August 2019
note: amended 2020 to incorporate the Juba Agreement for Peace in Sudan; the military suspended several provisions of the Constitutional Declaration in October 2021

International law organization participation: accepts compulsory ICJ jurisdiction with reservations; withdrew acceptance of ICCt jurisdiction in 2008

Citizenship: *citizenship by birth:* no
citizenship by descent only: the father must be a citizen of Sudan
dual citizenship recognized: no
residency requirement for naturalization: 10 years

Suffrage: 17 years of age; universal

Executive branch: *chief of state:* Sovereign Council Chair and Commander-in-Chief of the Sudanese Armed Forces General Abd-al-Fattah al-BURHAN Abd-al-Rahman (since 11 November 2021)
head of government: Sovereign Council Chair and Commander-in-Chief of the Sudanese Armed Forces General Abd-al-Fattah al-BURHAN Abd-al-Rahman (since 11 November 2021)
cabinet: the military forced most members of the Council of Ministers out of office in 2021; a handful of ministers appointed by former armed opposition groups were allowed to retain their posts; at present, most of the members of the Council are appointed senior civil servants serving in an acting-minister capacity
election/appointment process: military members of the Sovereign Council are selected by the leadership of the security forces; representatives of former armed groups to the Sovereign Council are selected by the signatories of the Juba Peace Agreement
election results: NA
expected date of next election: supposed to be held in 2022 or 2023, but the methodology for elections has still not been defined
note 1: the 2019 Constitutional Declaration established a collective chief of state of the "Sovereign Council," which was chaired by al-BURHAN; on 25 October 2021, al-BURHAN dissolved the Sovereign Council but reinstated it on 11 November 2021, replacing its civilian members (previously selected by the umbrella civilian coalition the Forces for Freedom and Change) with civilians of the military's choosing, but then relieved the newly appointed civilian members of their duties on 6 July 2022
note 2: Sovereign Council currently consists of 5 generals

Legislative branch: *note:* the Parliament of Sudan was dissolved after a coup in April 2019; the August 2019 Constitutional Declaration established Sudan's transitional government; a Transitional Legislative Council (TLC) was to have served as the national legislature during the transitional period until elections could be held, but the TLC has not been created

Judicial branch: *highest court(s):* National Supreme Court (consists of 70 judges organized into panels of 3 judges and includes 4 circuits that operate outside the capital); a Constitutional Court was required in the 2019 Constitutional Declaration, but it has yet to be implemented
judge selection and term of office: National Supreme Court and Constitutional Court judges selected by the Supreme Judicial Council
subordinate courts: Court of Appeal; other national courts; public courts; district, town, and rural courts

Political parties: Democratic Unionist Party
Democratic Unionist Party or DUP
Federal Umma Party
Muslim Brotherhood or MB
National Congress Party or NCP
National Umma Party or NUP
Popular Congress Party or PCP
Reform Movement Now
Sudan National Front
Sudanese Communist Party or SCP
Sudanese Congress Party or SCoP
Umma Party for Reform and Development
Unionist Movement Party or UMP
note: in November 2019, the transitional government banned the National Congress Party

Diplomatic representation in the US: *chief of mission:* Ambassador Mohamed Abdalla IDRIS (since 16 September 2022)
chancery: 2210 Massachusetts Avenue NW, Washington, DC 20008
telephone: [1] (202) 338-8565

FAX: [1] (202) 667-2406
email address and website: consular@sudanembassy.org
https://www.sudanembassy.org/

Diplomatic representation from the US: *chief of mission:* Ambassador (vacant); Chargé d'Affaires Colleen Crenwelge (since May 2024)
embassy: P.O. Box 699, Kilo 10, Soba, Khartoum

mailing address: 2200 Khartoum Place, Washington DC 20521-2200
telephone: [249] 187-0-22000
email address and website: ACSKhartoum@state.gov https://sd.usembassy.gov/
note: the U.S. Embassy in Khartoum suspended operations (to include visa, passport, and other routine consular services) on 22 April 2023

International organization participation: ABEDA, ACP, AfDB, AFESD, AMF, AU (suspended), CAEU, COMESA, FAO, G-77, IAEA, IBRD, ICAO, ICC (NGOs), ICRM, IDA, IDB, IFAD, IFC, IFRCS, IGAD, ILO, IMF, IMO, Interpol, IOC, IOM, IPU, ISO, ITSO, ITU, LAS, MIGA, NAM, OIC, OPCW, PCA, UN, UNCTAD, UNESCO, UNHCR, UNHRC, UNIDO, UNOOSA, UNWTO, UPU, WCO, WFTU (NGOs), WHO, WIPO, WMO, WTO (observer)

Independence: 1 January 1956 (from Egypt and the UK)

National holiday: Independence Day, 1 January (1956)

Flag: *description:* three equal horizontal bands of red (top), white, and black, with a green isosceles triangle based on the left side
meaning: red stands for the struggle for freedom; white for peace, light, and love, black for the people; green for Islam, agriculture, and prosperity
history: colors and design are based on the Arab Revolt flag of World War I

National symbol(s): secretary bird

National color(s): red, white, black, green

National anthem(s): *title:* "Nahnu Djundulla Djundulwatan" (We Are the Army of God and of Our Land)
lyrics/music: Sayed Ahmad Muhammad SALIH/ Ahmad MURJAN
history: adopted 1956; originally served as the anthem of the Sudanese military

National heritage: *total World Heritage Sites:* 3 (2 cultural, 1 natural)
selected World Heritage Site locales: Gebel Barkal and the Sites of the Napatan Region (c); Archaeological Sites of the Island of Meroe (c); Sanganeb Marine National Park and Dungonab Bay – Mukkawar Island Marine National Park (n)

ECONOMY

Economic overview: low-income Sahel economy devastated by ongoing civil war; major impacts on rural income, basic commodity prices, industrial production, agricultural supply chain, communications and commerce; hyperinflation and currency depreciation worsening food access and humanitarian conditions

Real GDP (purchasing power parity): $94.42 billion (2024 est.)
$109.147 billion (2023 est.)
$154.672 billion (2022 est.)
note: data in 2021 dollars
comparison ranking: 98

Real GDP growth rate: -13.5% (2024 est.)
-29.4% (2023 est.)
-1% (2022 est.)
note: annual GDP % growth based on constant local currency
comparison ranking: 214

Real GDP per capita: $1,900 (2024 est.)
$2,200 (2023 est.)
$3,100 (2022 est.)
note: data in 2021 dollars
comparison ranking: 206

GDP (official exchange rate): $49.91 billion (2024 est.)
note: data in current dollars at official exchange rate

Inflation rate (consumer prices): 138.8% (2022 est.)
359.1% (2021 est.)
163.3% (2020 est.)
note: annual % change based on consumer prices
comparison ranking: 212

GDP - composition, by sector of origin: *agriculture:* 22.1% (2024 est.)
industry: 23% (2024 est.)
services: 54.9% (2024 est.)
note: figures may not total 100% due to non-allocated consumption not captured in sector-reported data
comparison rankings: agriculture 29; industry 109; services 123

GDP - composition, by end use: *household consumption:* 80.7% (2024 est.)
government consumption: 16.5% (2024 est.)
investment in fixed capital: 2.9% (2024 est.)
investment in inventories: 0% (2024 est.)
exports of goods and services: 1.2% (2024 est.)
imports of goods and services: -1.3% (2024 est.)
note: figures may not total 100% due to rounding or gaps in data collection

Agricultural products: sugarcane, sorghum, milk, onions, groundnuts, sesame seeds, goat milk, bananas, mangoes/ guavas, millet (2023)
note: top ten agricultural products based on tonnage

Industries: oil, cotton ginning, textiles, cement, edible oils, sugar, soap distilling, shoes, petroleum refining, pharmaceuticals, armaments, automobile/light truck assembly, milling

Industrial production growth rate: -13.1% (2024 est.)
note: annual % change in industrial value added based on constant local currency
comparison ranking: 188

Labor force: 10.949 million (2022 est.)
note: number of people ages 15 or older who are employed or seeking work
comparison ranking: 52

Unemployment rate: 11.45% (2023 est.)
7.6% (2022 est.)
11.1% (2021 est.)
note: % of labor force seeking employment
comparison ranking: 157

Youth unemployment rate (ages 15-24): *total:* 12% (2022 est.)
male: 11.8% (2022 est.)
female: 13.1% (2022 est.)
note: % of labor force ages 15-24 seeking employment
comparison ranking: total 103

Remittances: 2.5% of GDP (2023 est.)
2.9% of GDP (2022 est.)
3.3% of GDP (2021 est.)
note: personal transfers and compensation between resident and non-resident individuals/ households/ entities

Budget: *revenues:* $9.045 billion (2015 est.)
expenditures: $9.103 billion (2015 est.)
note: central government revenues and expenses (excluding grants/extrabudgetary units/ social security funds) converted to US dollars at average official exchange rate for year indicated

Taxes and other revenues: 7.4% (of GDP) (2016 est.)
note: central government tax revenue as a % of GDP
comparison ranking: 141

Current account balance: -$4.443 billion (2022 est.)
-$2.62 billion (2021 est.)
-$5.841 billion (2020 est.)
note: balance of payments - net trade and primary/ secondary income in current dollars
comparison ranking: 169

Exports: $5.908 billion (2022 est.)
$6.664 billion (2021 est.)
$5.065 billion (2020 est.)
note: balance of payments - exports of goods and services in current dollars
comparison ranking: 134

Exports - partners: UAE 21%, China 17%, Saudi Arabia 16%, Malaysia 9%, Egypt 8% (2023)
note: top five export partners based on percentage share of exports

Exports - commodities: crude petroleum, gold, oil seeds, sheep and goats, ground nuts (2023)
note: top five export commodities based on value in dollars

Imports: $11.575 billion (2022 est.)
$10.271 billion (2021 est.)
$10.52 billion (2020 est.)
note: balance of payments - imports of goods and services in current dollars
comparison ranking: 114

Imports - partners: China 21%, India 19%, Egypt 16%, UAE 14%, Saudi Arabia 7% (2023)
note: top five import partners based on percentage share of imports

Imports - commodities: raw sugar, wheat flours, refined petroleum, garments, packaged medicine (2023)
note: top five import commodities based on value in dollars

Reserves of foreign exchange and gold: $177.934 million (2017 est.)
$168.284 million (2016 est.)
$173.516 million (2015 est.)
note: holdings of gold (year-end prices)/foreign exchange/special drawing rights in current dollars
comparison ranking: 174

Debt - external: $21.65 billion (2023 est.)
note: present value of external debt in current US dollars
comparison ranking: 33

Exchange rates: Sudanese pounds (SDG) per US dollar -

Exchange rates: 546.759 (2022 est.)
370.791 (2021 est.)
53.996 (2020 est.)
45.767 (2019 est.)
24.329 (2018 est.)

ENERGY

Electricity access: *electrification - total population:* 63.2% (2022 est.)
electrification - urban areas: 84%
electrification - rural areas: 49.4%

Electricity: *installed generating capacity:* 3.815 million kW (2023 est.)

consumption: 13.983 billion kWh (2023 est.)
imports: 882 million kWh (2023 est.)
transmission/distribution losses: 3.646 billion kWh (2023 est.)
comparison rankings: installed generating capacity 102; consumption 91; imports 79; transmission/distribution losses 151

Electricity generation sources: *fossil fuels:* 29.9% of total installed capacity (2023 est.)
solar: 0.8% of total installed capacity (2023 est.)
hydroelectricity: 68.7% of total installed capacity (2023 est.)
biomass and waste: 0.6% of total installed capacity (2023 est.)

Coal: *exports:* 15 metric tons (2023 est.)
imports: 200 metric tons (2023 est.)

Petroleum: *total petroleum production:* 68,000 bbl/day (2023 est.)
refined petroleum consumption: 129,000 bbl/day (2023 est.)
crude oil estimated reserves: 1.25 billion barrels (2021 est.)

Natural gas: *proven reserves:* 84.951 billion cubic meters (2021 est.)

Energy consumption per capita: 6.145 million Btu/person (2023 est.)
comparison ranking: 166

COMMUNICATIONS

Telephones - fixed lines: *total subscriptions:* 156,000 (2022 est.)
subscriptions per 100 inhabitants: (2022 est.) less than 1
comparison ranking: total subscriptions 125

Telephones - mobile cellular: *total subscriptions:* 34.7 million (2022 est.)
subscriptions per 100 inhabitants: 74 (2022 est.)
comparison ranking: total subscriptions 45

Broadcast media: state-owned broadcasters that self-censor but are somewhat independent (2022)

Internet country code: .sd

Internet users: *percent of population:* 26% (2020 est.)

Broadband - fixed subscriptions: *total:* 30,000 (2022 est.)
subscriptions per 100 inhabitants: (2022 est.) less than 1
comparison ranking: total 161

TRANSPORTATION

Civil aircraft registration country code prefix: ST

Airports: 45 (2025)
comparison ranking: 94

Heliports: 8 (2025)
comparison ranking: 83

Railways: *total:* 7,251 km (2014)
narrow gauge: 5,851 km (2014) 1.067-m gauge
1,400 km 0.600-m gauge for cotton plantations

Merchant marine: *total:* 14 (2023)
by type: other 14
comparison ranking: total 153

Ports: *total ports:* 4 (2024)
large: 0
medium: 2
small: 2
very small: 0
ports with oil terminals: 3
key ports: Al Khair Oil Terminal, Beshayer Oil Terminal, Port Sudan, Sawakin Harbor

MILITARY AND SECURITY

Military and security forces: Sudanese Armed Forces (SAF): Ground Force (Sudanese Army), Sudanese Navy, Sudanese Air Force; Rapid Support Forces (RSF); Border Guards

Ministry of Interior: Sudan Police Forces (SPF), Central Reserve Police (CRP) (2025)
note 1: the RSF is a semi-autonomous paramilitary force formed in 2013 to fight armed rebel groups in Sudan, with Mohammed Hamdan DAGALO (aka Hemeti) as its commander; it was initially placed under the National Intelligence and Security Service, then came under the direct command of former president Omar al-BASHIR, who boosted the RSF as his own personal security force; as a result, the RSF was better funded and equipped than the regular armed forces; the RSF has since recruited from all parts of Sudan beyond its original Darfuri Arab groups but remains under the personal patronage and control of DAGALO
note 2: the Central Reserve Police (aka Abu Tira) is a combat-trained paramilitary force
note 3: the October 2020 peace agreement provided for the establishment of a Joint Security Keeping Forces (JSKF) tasked with securing the Darfur region in the place of the UN African Union Hybrid Operation in Darfur (UNAMID), a joint African Union-UN peacekeeping force that operated in the war-torn region from 2007-December 2020; the force was intended to include the SAF, RSF, police, intelligence, and representatives from armed groups involved in peace negotiations; while the first 2,000 members of the JSKF completed training in September 2022, the status of the force since the start of the civil war is not available
note 4: there are also numerous armed militias operating in Sudan

Military expenditures: 1% of GDP (2021 est.)
1% of GDP (2020 est.)
2.4% of GDP (2019 est.)
2% of GDP (2018 est.)
3.6% of GDP (2017 est.)
note: many defense expenditures are probably off-budget

Military and security service personnel strengths: *prior to the outbreak of fighting between the SAF and the RSF in 2023, size estimates for Sudan's armed forces varied widely:* up to 200,000 SAF; up to 100,000 RSF; up to 80,000 Central Reserve Police (2023)

Military equipment inventories and acquisitions: the SAF's inventory includes a mix of mostly Chinese, Russian, Soviet-era, and domestically produced weapons systems; Sudan has one of the largest defense industries in Africa, which includes state-owned companies with military involvement; it has mostly manufactured weapons systems under license from China, Russia, Turkey, and Ukraine (2024)
note 1: Sudan has been under a UN Security Council approved arms embargo since 2005 as a result of violence in Darfur; in September 2024, the embargo was extended for another year
note 2: the RSF traditionally has been a lightly armed paramilitary force but over the years is reported to have acquired some heavier weapons and equipment such as armored vehicles, artillery, and anti-aircraft guns; it has captured some SAF arms and equipment during the ongoing conflict; since the start of the conflict, both the RSF and the SAF are reported to have received additional weaponry from various foreign suppliers

Military service age and obligation: 18-33 years of age for compulsory or voluntary military service for men and women; 12-24 month service obligation (2023)
note: implementation of conscription is reportedly uneven

Military - note: the primary responsibilities of the Sudanese Armed Forces (SAF) are border control, external defense, and internal security; SAF operations have traditionally been supported by militia and paramilitary forces, particularly the Rapid Support Forces (RSF); in the Spring of 2023, fighting broke out between the SAF and the RSF, particularly around the capital Khartoum and in the western region of Darfur, amid disputes over an internationally-backed plan for a transition towards civilian rule; fighting subsequently spread and continued into 2025 with reports of atrocities, ethnic cleansing, food insecurity, heavy civilian casualties, and millions of internally displaced persons; each side is supported by allied militias and both reportedly have received foreign support
the Sudanese military has been a dominant force in the ruling of the country since its independence in 1956; in addition, the military has a large role in the country's economy, reportedly controlling over 200 commercial companies, including businesses involved in gold mining, rubber production, agriculture, and meat exports
the UN Interim Security Force for Abyei (UNISFA) has operated in the disputed Abyei region along the border between Sudan and South Sudan since 2011; UNISFA's mission includes ensuring security, protecting civilians, strengthening the capacity of the Abyei Police Service, de-mining, monitoring/verifying the redeployment of armed forces from the area, and facilitating the flow of humanitarian aid; as of 2025, UNISFA had approximately 3,800 personnel assigned (2025)

TERRORISM

Terrorist group(s): Terrorist group(s): Islamic State of Iraq and ash-Sham (ISIS); al-Qa'ida; Harakat Sawa'd Misr
note: details about the history, aims, leadership, organization, areas of operation, tactics, targets, weapons, size, and sources of support of the group(s) appear(s) in Appendix T

TRANSNATIONAL ISSUES

Refugees and internally displaced persons: *refugees:* 837,988 (2024 est.)

IDPs: 11,559,970 (2024 est.)

Trafficking in persons: *tier rating:* Tier 3 — Sudan does not fully meet the minimum standards for the elimination of trafficking and is not making significant efforts to do so; therefore, Sudan remained on Tier 3; for more details, go to: https://www.state.gov/reports/2025-trafficking-in-persons-report/sudan

SURINAME

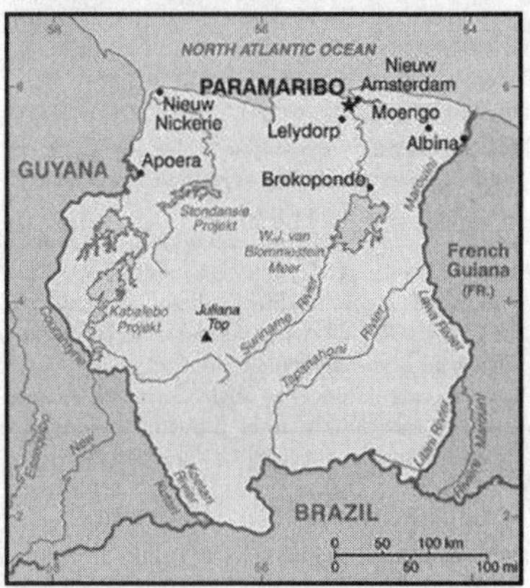

INTRODUCTION

Background: The Spaniards first explored Suriname in the 16th century, and the English then settled it in the mid-17th century. Suriname became a Dutch colony in 1667. With the abolition of African slavery in 1863, workers were brought in from India and Java. The Netherlands granted the colony independence in 1975. Five years later, the civilian government was replaced by a military regime that soon declared Suriname a socialist republic. It continued to exert control through a succession of nominally civilian administrations until 1987, when international pressure finally forced a democratic election. In 1990, the military overthrew the civilian leadership, but a democratically elected government – a four-party coalition – returned to power in 1991. The coalition expanded to eight parties in 2005 and ruled until 2010, when voters returned former military leader Desire BOUTERSE and his opposition coalition to power. President BOUTERSE ran unopposed in 2015 and was reelected. Opposition parties campaigned hard against BOUTERSE in the run-up to the 2020 elections, and a multi-party coalition led by Chandrikapersad SANTOKHI's VHP and Ronnie Brunswijk's ABOP was installed.

GEOGRAPHY

Location: Northern South America, bordering the North Atlantic Ocean, between French Guiana and Guyana

Geographic coordinates: 4 00 N, 56 00 W

Map references: South America

Area: *total:* 163,820 sq km
land: 156,000 sq km
water: 7,820 sq km
comparison ranking: total 92

Area - comparative: slightly larger than Georgia

Land boundaries: *total:* 1,907 km
border countries (3): Brazil 515 km; French Guiana 556 km; Guyana 836 km

Coastline: 386 km

Maritime claims: *territorial sea:* 12 nm
exclusive economic zone: 200 nm

Climate: tropical; moderated by trade winds

Terrain: mostly rolling hills; narrow coastal plain with swamps

Elevation: *highest point:* Juliana Top 1,230 m
lowest point: unnamed location in the coastal plain -2 m
mean elevation: 246 m

Natural resources: timber, hydropower, fish, kaolin, shrimp, bauxite, gold, and small amounts of nickel, copper, platinum, iron ore

Land use: *agricultural land:* 0.4% (2022 est.)
arable land: 0.3% (2022 est.)
permanent crops: 0% (2022 est.)
permanent pasture: 0.1% (2022 est.)
forest: 94.5% (2022 est.)
other: 5% (2022 est.)

Irrigated land: 600 sq km (2020)

Major watersheds (area sq km): Atlantic Ocean drainage: Amazon (6,145,186 sq km)

Population distribution: population is concentrated along the northern coastal strip; the remainder of the country is sparsely populated

Natural hazards: flooding

Geography - note: smallest independent country on the South American continent; mostly tropical rainforest; great diversity of flora and fauna; relatively small population, mostly along the coast

PEOPLE AND SOCIETY

Population: *total:* 646,758 (2024 est.)
male: 320,352
female: 326,406
comparison rankings: total 169; male 169; female 170

Nationality: *noun:* Surinamer(s)
adjective: Surinamese

Ethnic groups: Hindustani (also known locally as "East Indians"; their ancestors emigrated from northern India in the latter part of the 19th century) 27.4%, Maroon (their African ancestors were brought to the country in the 17th and 18th centuries as slaves and escaped to the interior) 21.7%, Creole (mixed White and Black) 15.7%, Javanese 13.7%, mixed 13.4%, other 7.6%, unspecified 0.6% (2012 est.)

Languages: Dutch (official), English (widely spoken), Sranang Tongo (Surinamese, sometimes called Taki-Taki, is the native language of Creoles and much of the younger population), Caribbean Hindustani (a dialect of Hindi), Javanese
major-language sample(s):
Het Wereld Feitenboek, een omnisbare bron van informatie. (Dutch)

Religions: Protestant 23.6% (includes Evangelical 11.2%, Moravian 11.2%, Reformed 0.7%, Lutheran 0.5%), Hindu 22.3%, Roman Catholic 21.6%, Muslim 13.8%, other Christian 3.2%, Winti 1.8%, Jehovah's Witness 1.2%, other 1.7%, none 7.5%, unspecified 3.2% (2012 est.)

Age structure: *0-14 years:* 22.5% (male 73,864/female 71,573)
15-64 years: 70% (male 226,417/female 226,235)
65 years and over: 7.5% (2024 est.) (male 20,071/female 28,598)

Dependency ratios: *total dependency ratio:* 42.9 (2024 est.)
youth dependency ratio: 32.1 (2024 est.)
elderly dependency ratio: 10.8 (2024 est.)
potential support ratio: 9.3 (2024 est.)

Median age: *total:* 32 years (2024 est.)
male: 31 years
female: 32.9 years
comparison ranking: total 118

Population growth rate: 1.07% (2024 est.)
comparison ranking: 89

Birth rate: 14.9 births/1,000 population (2024 est.)
comparison ranking: 110

Death rate: 6.7 deaths/1,000 population (2024 est.)
comparison ranking: 129

Net migration rate: 2.5 migrant(s)/1,000 population (2024 est.)
comparison ranking: 46

Population distribution: population is concentrated along the northern coastal strip; the remainder of the country is sparsely populated

Urbanization: *urban population:* 66.4% of total population (2023)
rate of urbanization: 0.88% annual rate of change (2020-25 est.)

Major urban areas - population: 239,000 PARAMARIBO (capital) (2018)

Sex ratio: *at birth:* 1.07 male(s)/female
0-14 years: 1.03 male(s)/female
15-64 years: 1 male(s)/female
65 years and over: 0.7 male(s)/female
total population: 0.98 male(s)/female (2024 est.)

Maternal mortality ratio: 84 deaths/100,000 live births (2023 est.)
comparison ranking: 71

Infant mortality rate: *total:* 29.6 deaths/1,000 live births (2024 est.)
male: 37.6 deaths/1,000 live births
female: 21 deaths/1,000 live births
comparison ranking: total 50

Life expectancy at birth: *total population:* 72.7 years (2024 est.)
male: 69 years
female: 76.7 years
comparison ranking: total population 159

Total fertility rate: 1.89 children born/woman (2024 est.)
comparison ranking: 122

Gross reproduction rate: 0.91 (2024 est.)

Drinking water source: *improved: urban:* 98.7% of population (2022 est.)
rural: 96.6% of population (2022 est.)
total: 98% of population (2022 est.)
unimproved: urban: 1.3% of population (2022 est.)
rural: 3.4% of population (2022 est.)
total: 2% of population (2022 est.)

Health expenditure: 5.7% of GDP (2021)
13.1% of national budget (2022 est.)

Physician density: 1.36 physicians/1,000 population (2023)

Hospital bed density: 2.9 beds/1,000 population (2020 est.)

Sanitation facility access: *improved: urban:* 98.5% of population (2022 est.)
rural: 91.2% of population (2022 est.)
total: 96.1% of population (2022 est.)
unimproved: urban: 1.5% of population (2022 est.)
rural: 8.8% of population (2022 est.)
total: 3.9% of population (2022 est.)

Obesity - adult prevalence rate: 26.4% (2016)
comparison ranking: 41

Alcohol consumption per capita: *total:* 6.6 liters of pure alcohol (2019 est.)
beer: 3.4 liters of pure alcohol (2019 est.)
wine: 0.14 liters of pure alcohol (2019 est.)
spirits: 2.87 liters of pure alcohol (2019 est.)
other alcohols: 0.18 liters of pure alcohol (2019 est.)
comparison ranking: total 62

Children under the age of 5 years underweight: 6.7% (2018)
comparison ranking: 62

Currently married women (ages 15-49): 52.1% (2023 est.)

Child marriage: *women married by age 15:* 8.8% (2018)
women married by age 18: 36% (2018)
men married by age 18: 19.6% (2018)

Education expenditure: 2.9% of GDP (2023 est.)
8.6% national budget (2024 est.)
comparison ranking: Education expenditure (% GDP) 156

School life expectancy (primary to tertiary education): *total:* 11 years (2021 est.)
male: 10 years (2021 est.)
female: 11 years (2021 est.)

ENVIRONMENT

Environmental issues: deforestation; pollution of inland waterways from small-scale mining activities

International environmental agreements: *party to:* Biodiversity, Climate Change, Climate Change-Kyoto Protocol, Climate Change-Paris Agreement, Comprehensive Nuclear Test Ban, Desertification, Endangered Species, Hazardous Wastes, Law of the Sea, Marine Dumping-London Convention, Marine Dumping-London Protocol, Nuclear Test Ban, Ozone Layer Protection, Ship Pollution, Tropical Timber 2006, Wetlands, Whaling
signed, but not ratified: none of the selected agreements

Climate: tropical; moderated by trade winds

Urbanization: *urban population:* 66.4% of total population (2023)
rate of urbanization: 0.88% annual rate of change (2020-25 est.)

Carbon dioxide emissions: 2.521 million metric tonnes of CO2 (2023 est.)
from petroleum and other liquids: 2.507 million metric tonnes of CO2 (2023 est.)
from consumed natural gas: 14,000 metric tonnes of CO2 (2023 est.)
comparison ranking: total emissions 156

Particulate matter emissions: 12.2 micrograms per cubic meter (2019 est.)

Waste and recycling: *municipal solid waste generated annually:* 78,600 tons (2024 est.)
percent of municipal solid waste recycled: 16.9% (2022 est.)

Total water withdrawal: *municipal:* 49.3 million cubic meters (2022 est.)
industrial: 135.5 million cubic meters (2022 est.)
agricultural: 431.1 million cubic meters (2022 est.)

Total renewable water resources: 99 billion cubic meters (2022 est.)

GOVERNMENT

Country name: *conventional long form:* Republic of Suriname
conventional short form: Suriname
local long form: Republiek Suriname
local short form: Suriname
former: Netherlands Guiana, Dutch Guiana
etymology: name may derive from the Surinen people who inhabited the area at the time of European contact

Government type: presidential republic

Capital: *name:* Paramaribo
geographic coordinates: 5 50 N, 55 10 W
time difference: UTC-3 (2 hours ahead of Washington, DC, during Standard Time)
etymology: the name comes from the Guaraní words *para* (water or river) and *maribo* (inhabitants)

Administrative divisions: 10 districts (*distrikten*, singular - *distrikt*); Brokopondo, Commewijne, Coronie, Marowijne, Nickerie, Para, Paramaribo, Saramacca, Sipaliwini, Wanica

Legal system: civil law system influenced by Dutch civil law

Constitution: *history:* previous 1975; latest ratified 30 September 1987, effective 30 October 1987
amendment process: proposed by the National Assembly; passage requires at least two-thirds majority vote of the total membership

International law organization participation: accepts compulsory ICJ jurisdiction with reservations; accepts ICCt jurisdiction

Citizenship: *citizenship by birth:* no
citizenship by descent only: at least one parent must be a citizen of Suriname
dual citizenship recognized: no
residency requirement for naturalization: 5 years

Suffrage: 18 years of age; universal

Executive branch: *chief of state:* President Jennifer GEERLINGS-SIMONS (since 16 July 2025)
head of government: President Jennifer GEERLINGS-SIMONS (since 16 July 2025)
cabinet: Cabinet of Ministers appointed by the president
election/appointment process: president and vice president indirectly elected by the National Assembly; president and vice president serve a 5-year term (no term limits)
most recent election date: 6 July 2025
election results: *2025:* Jennifer GEERLINGS-SIMONS elected president unopposed; National Assembly vote - NA
2020: Chandrikapersad "Chan" SANTOKHI elected president unopposed; National Assembly vote - NA
2015: Desire Delano BOUTERSE reelected president unopposed; National Assembly vote - NA
expected date of next election: 2030
note: the president is both chief of state and head of government

Legislative branch: *legislature name:* National Assembly (Nationale Assembleе)
legislative structure: unicameral
number of seats: 51 (all directly elected)
electoral system: proportional representation
scope of elections: full renewal
term in office: 5 years
most recent election date: 5/25/2025
parties elected and seats per party: National Democratic Party (NDP) (18); Progressive Reform Party (VHP) (17); National Party of Suriname (NPS) (6); General Liberation and Development Party (ABOP) (6); Other (4)
percentage of women in chamber: 31.4%
expected date of next election: May 2030

Judicial branch: *highest court(s):* High Court of Justice of Suriname (consists of the court president, vice president, and 4 judges)
judge selection and term of office: court judges appointed by the national president in consultation with the National Assembly, the State Advisory Council, and the Order of Private Attorneys; judges serve for life
subordinate courts: cantonal courts
note: appeals beyond the High Court are referred to the Caribbean Court of Justice; human rights violations can be appealed to the Inter-American Commission on Human Rights with judgments issued by the Inter-American Court on Human Rights

Political parties: Brotherhood and Unity in Politics or BEP
Democratic Alternative '91 or DA91
General Liberation and Development Party or ABOP
National Democratic Party or NDP
National Party of Suriname or NPS
Party for Democracy and Development in Unity or DOE
Party for National Unity and Solidarity or KTPI
People's Alliance (Pertjajah Luhur) or PL
Progressive Workers' and Farmers' Union or PALU
Progressive Reform Party or VHP
Reform and Renewal Movement or HVB
Surinamese Labor Party or SPA

Diplomatic representation in the US: *chief of mission:* Ambassador Jan Marten Willem SCHALKWIJK (since 19 April 2022)
chancery: 4301 Connecticut Avenue NW, Suite 400, Washington, DC 20008
telephone: [1] (202) 629-4302
FAX: [1] (202) 629-4769
email address and website: amb.vs@gov.sr
https://surinameembassy.org/index.html
consulate(s) general: Miami

Diplomatic representation from the US: *chief of mission:* Ambassador Robert J. FAUCHER (since 31 January 2023)
embassy: 165 Kristalstraat, Paramaribo
mailing address: 3390 Paramaribo Place, Washington DC 20521-3390
telephone: [597] 556-700
FAX: [597] 551-524
email address and website: caparamar@state.gov
https://sr.usembassy.gov/

International organization participation: ACP, ACS, AOSIS, Caricom, CD, CDB, CELAC, FAO, G-77, IADB, IBRD, ICAO, ICCt, ICRM, IDA, IDB, IFAD, IFC, IFRCS, IHO, ILO, IMF, IMO, Interpol, IOC, IOM, IPU, ISO (correspondent), ITU, ITUC (NGOs), LAES, MIGA, NAM, OAS, OIC, OPANAL, OPCW, PCA, Petrocaribe, UN, UNASUR, UNCTAD, UNESCO, UNIDO, UPU, WHO, WIPO, WMO, WTO

Independence: 25 November 1975 (from the Netherlands)

National holiday: Independence Day, 25 November (1975)

Flag: *description:* five horizontal bands of green (top, double-width), white, red (quadruple-width), white,

and green (double-width); a five-pointed yellow star is centered on the red band
meaning: red stands for progress and love, green for hope and fertility, and white for peace, justice, and freedom; the star represents the unity of ethnic groups

National symbol(s): royal palm, faya lobi (flower)

National color(s): green, white, red, yellow

National anthem(s): *title:* "God zij met ons Suriname!" (God Be With Our Suriname)
lyrics/music: Cornelis Atses HOEKSTRA and Henry DE ZIEL/Johannes Corstianus DE PUY
history: adopted 1959; originally adapted from a Sunday-school song written in 1893; contains lyrics in both Dutch and Sranang Tongo

National heritage: *total World Heritage Sites:* 3 (2 cultural, 1 natural)
selected World Heritage Site locales: Central Suriname Nature Reserve (n); Historic Inner City of Paramaribo (c); Jodensavanne Archaeological Site: Jodensavanne Settlement and Cassipora Creek Cemetery (c)

ECONOMY

Economic overview: upper middle-income South American economy; new floating currency regime; key aluminum goods, gold, and hydrocarbon exporter; new IMF plan for economic recovery and fiscal sustainability; controversial hardwood industry

Real GDP (purchasing power parity): $12.316 billion (2024 est.)
$11.976 billion (2023 est.)
$11.68 billion (2022 est.)
note: data in 2021 dollars
comparison ranking: 163

Real GDP growth rate: 2.8% (2024 est.)
2.5% (2023 est.)
2.4% (2022 est.)
note: annual GDP % growth based on constant local currency
comparison ranking: 125

Real GDP per capita: $19,400 (2024 est.)
$19,000 (2023 est.)
$18,700 (2022 est.)
note: data in 2021 dollars
comparison ranking: 104

GDP (official exchange rate): $4.714 billion (2024 est.)
note: data in current dollars at official exchange rate

Inflation rate (consumer prices): 16.2% (2024 est.)
51.6% (2023 est.)
52.4% (2022 est.)
note: annual % change based on consumer prices
comparison ranking: 189

GDP - composition, by sector of origin: *agriculture:* 7.5% (2023 est.)
industry: 39.9% (2023 est.)
services: 48.3% (2023 est.)
note: figures may not total 100% due to non-allocated consumption not captured in sector-reported data
comparison rankings: agriculture 88; industry 20; services 157

Agricultural products: rice, sugarcane, oranges, vegetables, chicken, cassava, plantains, pineapples, eggs, citrus fruits (2023)
note: top ten agricultural products based on tonnage

Industries: gold mining, oil, lumber, food processing, fishing

Industrial production growth rate: 2.1% (2023 est.)
note: annual % change in industrial value added based on constant local currency
comparison ranking: 97

Labor force: 255,500 (2024 est.)
note: number of people ages 15 or older who are employed or seeking work
comparison ranking: 171

Unemployment rate: 7.4% (2024 est.)
7.7% (2023 est.)
8.2% (2022 est.)
note: % of labor force seeking employment
comparison ranking: 126

Youth unemployment rate (ages 15-24): *total:* 24.2% (2024 est.)
male: 16.9% (2024 est.)
female: 35.9% (2024 est.)
note: % of labor force ages 15-24 seeking employment
comparison ranking: total 36

Gini Index coefficient - distribution of family income: 39.2 (2022 est.)
note: index (0-100) of income distribution; higher values represent greater inequality
comparison ranking: 45

Household income or consumption by percentage share: *lowest 10%:* 2.2% (2022 est.)
highest 10%: 30.1% (2022 est.)
note: % share of income accruing to lowest and highest 10% of population

Remittances: 3.4% of GDP (2024 est.)
4.3% of GDP (2023 est.)
3.9% of GDP (2022 est.)
note: personal transfers and compensation between resident and non-resident individuals/households/entities

Budget: *revenues:* $863 million (2019 est.)
expenditures: $1.648 billion (2019 est.)

Current account balance: $9.306 million (2024 est.)
$148.118 million (2023 est.)
$76.321 million (2022 est.)
note: balance of payments - net trade and primary/secondary income in current dollars
comparison ranking: 83

Exports: $2.793 billion (2024 est.)
$2.533 billion (2023 est.)
$2.6 billion (2022 est.)
note: balance of payments - exports of goods and services in current dollars
comparison ranking: 158

Exports - partners: Switzerland 49%, UAE 28%, Guyana 5%, USA 4%, France 3% (2023)
note: top five export partners based on percentage share of exports

Exports - commodities: gold, fish, refined petroleum, wood, tobacco (2023)
note: top five export commodities based on value in dollars

Imports: $2.571 billion (2024 est.)
$2.203 billion (2023 est.)
$2.342 billion (2022 est.)
note: balance of payments - imports of goods and services in current dollars
comparison ranking: 167

Imports - partners: USA 22%, China 12%, Netherlands 11%, Trinidad & Tobago 9%, Guyana 8% (2023)
note: top five import partners based on percentage share of imports

Imports - commodities: refined petroleum, ships, excavation machinery, trucks, tobacco (2023)
note: top five import commodities based on value in dollars

Reserves of foreign exchange and gold: $1.632 billion (2024 est.)
$1.346 billion (2023 est.)
$1.195 billion (2022 est.)
note: holdings of gold (year-end prices)/foreign exchange/special drawing rights in current dollars
comparison ranking: 131

Debt - external: $2.645 billion (2023 est.)
note: present value of external debt in current US dollars
comparison ranking: 89

Exchange rates: Surinamese dollars (SRD) per US dollar -

Exchange rates: 33.181 (2024 est.)
36.776 (2023 est.)
24.709 (2022 est.)
18.239 (2021 est.)
9.31 (2020 est.)

ENERGY

Electricity access: *electrification - total population:* 99% (2022 est.)
electrification - urban areas: 100%
electrification - rural areas: 98%

Electricity: *installed generating capacity:* 537,000 kW (2023 est.)
consumption: 1.896 billion kWh (2023 est.)
transmission/distribution losses: 245.206 million kWh (2023 est.)
comparison rankings: installed generating capacity 149; consumption 150; transmission/distribution losses 69

Electricity generation sources: *fossil fuels:* 57.1% of total installed capacity (2023 est.)
solar: 0.6% of total installed capacity (2023 est.)
hydroelectricity: 42% of total installed capacity (2023 est.)
biomass and waste: 0.3% of total installed capacity (2023 est.)

Coal: *imports:* 2 metric tons (2023 est.)

Petroleum: *total petroleum production:* 14,000 bbl/day (2023 est.)
refined petroleum consumption: 17,000 bbl/day (2023 est.)
crude oil estimated reserves: 89 million barrels (2021 est.)

Natural gas: *production:* 7.173 million cubic meters (2023 est.)
consumption: 6.967 million cubic meters (2023 est.)

Energy consumption per capita: 60.896 million Btu/person (2023 est.)
comparison ranking: 82

COMMUNICATIONS

Telephones - fixed lines: *total subscriptions:* 129,000 (2023 est.)
subscriptions per 100 inhabitants: 20 (2023 est.)
comparison ranking: total subscriptions 129

Telephones - mobile cellular: *total subscriptions:* 989,000 (2023 est.)
subscriptions per 100 inhabitants: 150 (2022 est.)
comparison ranking: total subscriptions 164

Broadcast media: 2 state-owned TV stations; 1 state-owned radio station; multiple private radio and TV stations (2019)

Internet country code: .sr

Internet users: *percent of population:* 78% (2023 est.)

Broadband - fixed subscriptions: *total:* 125,000 (2022 est.)
subscriptions per 100 inhabitants: 20 (2022 est.)
comparison ranking: total 127

TRANSPORTATION

Civil aircraft registration country code prefix: PZ

Airports: 55 (2025)
comparison ranking: 84

Heliports: 1 (2025)
comparison ranking: 148

Merchant marine: *total:* 13 (2023)
by type: general cargo 5, oil tanker 3, other 5
comparison ranking: total 154

Ports: *total ports:* 4 (2024)
large: 0
medium: 0
small: 1
very small: 3
ports with oil terminals: 3
key ports: Moengo, Nieuw Nickerie, Paramaribo, Paranam

MILITARY AND SECURITY

Military and security forces: Suriname National Army (Nationaal Leger or NL); Army (Landmacht), Navy (Marine); Air Force (Luchtmacht), Military Police (Korps Militaire Politie)

Ministry of Justice and Police: Suriname Police Force (Korps Politie Suriname or KPS) (2025)

Military expenditures: 1.2% of GDP (2019 est.)
1.1% of GDP (2018 est.)
1.1% of GDP (2017 est.)
1.2% of GDP (2016 est.)
1.4% of GDP (2015 est.)

Military and security service personnel strengths: approximately 2,000 National Army (2025)

Military equipment inventories and acquisitions: the Suriname Army has a limited inventory comprised of a mix of older weapons and equipment, largely originating from such suppliers as Brazil, the Netherlands, and India; France also provides material assistance (2024)

Military service age and obligation: 18 is the legal minimum age for voluntary military service for men and women; no conscription (2024)

Military - note: the National Leger is responsible for defending the sovereignty and territorial integrity of Suriname against foreign aggression; other special tasks include border control and supporting domestic security as required; the military police, for example, have direct responsibility for immigration control at the country's ports of entry, and the military assists the police in combating crime, particularly narco-trafficking, including joint military and police patrols, as well as joint special security teams; in addition, the military provides aid and assistance during times of natural emergencies and participates in socio-economic development projects (2025)

TRANSNATIONAL ISSUES

Refugees and internally displaced persons: *refugees:* 3,241 (2024 est.)

SVALBARD

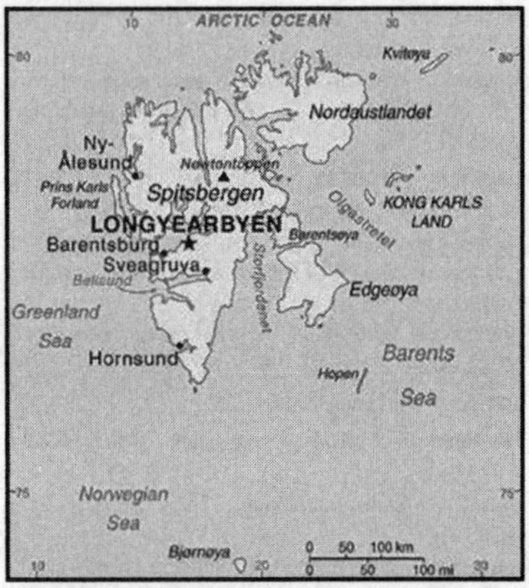

INTRODUCTION

Background: Norse explorers may have first discovered the Svalbard archipelago in the 12th century. The islands served as an international whaling base during the 17th and 18th centuries. Norway's sovereignty was internationally recognized by treaty in 1920, and five years later Norway officially took over the territory. Coal mining started in the 20th century, and a Norwegian company and a Russian company are still in operation today. Travel between the settlements is accomplished with snowmobiles, aircraft, and boats.

GEOGRAPHY

Location: Northern Europe, islands between the Arctic Ocean, Barents Sea, Greenland Sea, and Norwegian Sea, north of Norway

Geographic coordinates: 78 00 N, 20 00 E

Map references: Arctic Region

Area: *total:* 62,045 sq km
land: 62,045 sq km
water: 0 sq km
note: includes Spitsbergen and Bjornoya (Bear Island)
comparison ranking: total 125

Area - comparative: slightly smaller than West Virginia

Land boundaries: *total:* 0 km

Coastline: 3,587 km

Maritime claims: *territorial sea:* 12 nm
contiguous zone: 24 nm
continental shelf: extends to depth of exploitation
exclusive fishing zone: 200 nm

Climate: arctic, tempered by warm North Atlantic Current; cool summers, cold winters; North Atlantic Current flows along west and north coasts of Spitsbergen, keeping water open and navigable most of the year

Terrain: rugged mountains; much of the upland areas are ice covered; west coast clear of ice about half the year; fjords along west and north coasts

Elevation: *highest point:* Newtontoppen 1,717 m
lowest point: Arctic Ocean 0 m

Natural resources: coal, iron ore, copper, zinc, phosphate, wildlife, fish

Land use: *agricultural land:* 0% (2018 est.)
other: 100% (2018 est.)

Population distribution: the small population is primarily concentrated on the island of Spitsbergen in a handful of settlements on the south side of the Isfjorden, with Longyearbyen being the largest

Natural hazards: ice floes often block the entrance to Bellsund (a transit point for coal export) on the west coast and occasionally make parts of the northeastern coast inaccessible to maritime traffic

Geography - note: northernmost part of the Kingdom of Norway; consists of nine main islands; glaciers and snowfields cover 60% of the total area

PEOPLE AND SOCIETY

Population: *total:* 2,556 (2025 est.)
male: 1,353
female: 1,203
comparison rankings: total 229; male 229; female 230

Ethnic groups: Norwegian 61.1%, foreign population 38.9% (consists primarily of Russians, Thais, Swedes, Filipinos, and Ukrainians) (2021 est.)
note: foreigners account for almost one third of the population of the Norwegian settlements, Longyearbyen and Ny-Alesund (where the majority of Svalbard's resident population lives), as of mid-2021

Languages: Norwegian, Russian
major-language sample(s):
Verdens Faktabok, den essensielle kilden for grunnleggende informasjon. (Norwegian)

Population growth rate: -0.03% (2019 est.)
comparison ranking: 199

Net migration rate: -5.57 migrant(s)/1,000 population (2021 est.)
comparison ranking: 207

Population distribution: the small population is primarily concentrated on the island of Spitsbergen in a handful of settlements on the south side of the Isfjorden, with Longyearbyen being the largest

ENVIRONMENT

Climate: arctic, tempered by warm North Atlantic Current; cool summers, cold winters; North Atlantic Current flows along west and north coasts of Spitsbergen, keeping water open and navigable most of the year

GOVERNMENT

Country name: *conventional long form:* none
conventional short form: Svalbard (sometimes referred to as Spitsbergen, the largest island in the archipelago)
etymology: the archipelago was traditionally known as Spitsbergen, a Dutch name meaning "jagged peaks," but Norway renamed it Svalbard in the 1920s when it assumed sovereignty of the islands, from the Norwegian *sval* (cold) and *bard* (shore); the Norwegian name may have been used during the Norse era for other locations

Government type: non-self-governing territory of Norway

Dependency status: territory of Norway; administered by the Polar Department of the Ministry of Justice, through a governor (*sysselmann*) residing in Longyearbyen, Spitsbergen; by treaty (9 February 1920), sovereignty was awarded to Norway

Capital: *name:* Longyearbyen
geographic coordinates: 78 13 N, 15 38 E
time difference: UTC+1 (6 hours ahead of Washington, DC, during Standard Time)
daylight saving time: +1hr, begins last Sunday in March; ends last Sunday in October
etymology: the name in Norwegian means Longyear Town; the site was established by and named after John Munro LONGYEAR, whose Arctic Coal Company began mining operations there in 1906

Legal system: laws of Norway that explicitly apply to Svalbard, including the Svalbard Act, the Svalbard Environmental Protection Act, and certain regulations; the Spitsbergen Treaty and the Svalbard Treaty grant certain rights to citizens and corporations of signatory nations

Citizenship: see Norway

Executive branch: *chief of state:* King HARALD V of Norway (since 17 January 1991)
head of government: Governor Lars FAUSE (since 24 June 2021)
election/appointment process: none; the monarchy is hereditary; governor and assistant governor responsible to the Polar Department of the Ministry of Justice

Legislative branch: *note:* the Council acts much like a Norwegian municipality, with responsibility for infrastructure and utilities (including power, land-use and community planning, education, and child welfare); however, the state provides healthcare services

Judicial branch: *highest court(s):* Svalbard is subordinate to Norway's Nord-Troms District Court and Halogaland Court of Appeal, both located in Tromso

Political parties: Conservative
Labor
Liberal
Progress
Socialist Left

International organization participation: none

Independence: none (territory of Norway)

Flag: the flag of Norway is used

National anthem(s): *title:* "Ja, vi elsker dette landet" (Yes, We Love This Country)
lyrics/music: Bjornstjerne BJORNSON/Rikard NORDRAAK
history: official anthem, as a Norwegian territory

ECONOMY

Economic overview: high-income Norwegian island economy; major coal mining, tourism, and research sectors; recently established northernmost brewery; key whaling and fishing base; home to the Global Seed Vault

Exchange rates: Norwegian kroner (NOK) per US dollar -

Exchange rates: 10.746 (2024 est.)
10.563 (2023 est.)
9.614 (2022 est.)
8.59 (2021 est.)
9.416 (2020 est.)

COMMUNICATIONS

Broadcast media: Norwegian Broadcasting Corporation (NRK) provides TV transmission to Svalbard via satellite; access to 3 NRK radio stations and 2 TV stations

Internet country code: .sj

TRANSPORTATION

Ports: *total ports:* 3 (2024)
large: 0
medium: 0
small: 0
very small: 3
ports with oil terminals: 0
key ports: Barentsburg, Longyearbyen, Ny Alesund

MILITARY AND SECURITY

Military and security forces: no regular military forces

Military - note: Svalbard is a territory of Norway, demilitarized by treaty on 9 February 1920; Norwegian military activity is limited to fisheries surveillance by the Norwegian Coast Guard (2025)

SWEDEN

INTRODUCTION

Background: A military power during the 17th century, Sweden maintained a policy of military non-alignment until it applied to join NATO in 2022. Sweden has not participated in any war for two centuries. Stockholm preserved an armed neutrality in both World Wars. Since then, Sweden has pursued a successful economic formula consisting of a capitalist system intermixed with substantial welfare elements. Sweden joined the EU in 1995, but the public rejected the introduction of the euro in a 2003 referendum. The share of Sweden's population born abroad increased from 11.3% in 2000 to 20% in 2022.

GEOGRAPHY

Location: Northern Europe, bordering the Baltic Sea, Gulf of Bothnia, Kattegat, and Skagerrak, between Finland and Norway

Geographic coordinates: 62 00 N, 15 00 E

Map references: Europe

Area: *total:* 450,295 sq km
land: 410,335 sq km
water: 39,960 sq km
comparison ranking: total 58

Area - comparative: almost three times the size of Georgia; slightly larger than California

Land boundaries: *total:* 2,211 km
border countries (2): Finland 545 km; Norway 1,666 km

Coastline: 3,218 km

Maritime claims: *territorial sea:* 12 nm (adjustments made to return a portion of straits to high seas)
exclusive economic zone: agreed boundaries or midlines
continental shelf: 200-m depth or to the depth of exploitation

Climate: temperate in south with cold, cloudy winters and cool, partly cloudy summers; subarctic in north

Terrain: mostly flat or gently rolling lowlands; mountains in west

Elevation: *highest point:* Kebnekaise South 2,100 m
lowest point: reclaimed bay of Lake Hammarsjon, near Kristianstad -2.4 m
mean elevation: 320 m

Natural resources: iron ore, copper, lead, zinc, gold, silver, tungsten, uranium, arsenic, feldspar, timber, hydropower

Land use: *agricultural land:* 7.4% (2022 est.)
arable land: 6.2% (2022 est.)
permanent crops: 0% (2022 est.)
permanent pasture: 1.1% (2022 est.)
forest: 68.7% (2022 est.)
other: 23.9% (2022 est.)

Irrigated land: 510 sq km (2016)

Major lakes (area sq km): *fresh water lake(s):* Vanern - 5,580 sq km; Vattern - 1,910 sq km; Malaren - 1,140 sq km

Population distribution: most of the population lives in the south where the climate is milder and there is better connectivity to mainland Europe; population clusters are found along the Baltic coast in the east; the interior areas of the north remain sparsely populated

Natural hazards: ice floes in the surrounding waters, especially in the Gulf of Bothnia, can interfere with maritime traffic

Geography - note: strategic location along Danish Straits linking Baltic and North Seas; Sweden has almost 100,000 lakes, the largest of which, Vanern, is the third-largest in Europe

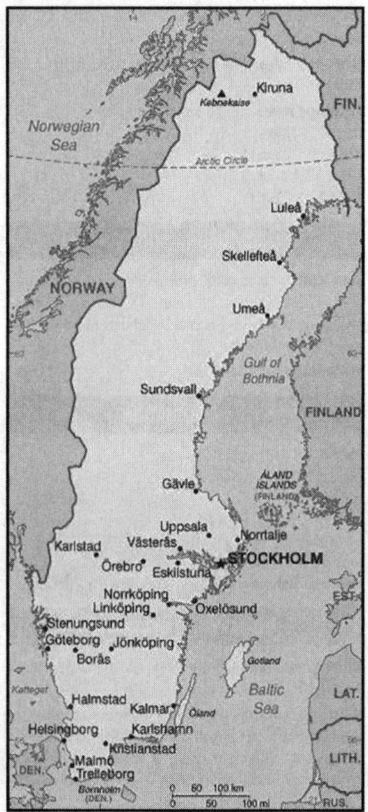

PEOPLE AND SOCIETY

Population: *total:* 10,589,835 (2024 est.)
male: 5,332,701
female: 5,257,134
comparison rankings: total 89; male 89; female 91

Nationality: *noun:* Swede(s)
adjective: Swedish

Ethnic groups: Swedish 79.6%, Syrian 1.9%, Iraqi 1.4%, Finnish 1.3%, other 15.8%
(2022 est.)
note: data represent the population by country of birth; the indigenous Sami people are estimated to number between 20,000 and 40,000

Languages: Swedish (official)
major-language sample(s):
The World Factbook, den obestridliga källan för grundläggande information. (Swedish)
note: Finnish, Sami, Romani, Yiddish, and Meankieli are official minority languages

Religions: Church of Sweden (Lutheran) 53.9%, other (includes Roman Catholic, Orthodox, Baptist, Muslim, Jewish, and Buddhist) 8.9%, none or unspecified 37.2% (2021 est.)
note: estimates reflect registered members of faith communities eligible for state funding (not all religions are state-funded and not all people who identify with a particular religion are registered members) and the Church of Sweden

Age structure: *0-14 years:* 17.1% (male 934,668/ female 880,310)
15-64 years: 62.1% (male 3,365,754/female 3,208,248)
65 years and over: 20.8% (2024 est.) (male 1,032,279/ female 1,168,576)

Dependency ratios: *total dependency ratio:* 61.1 (2024 est.)
youth dependency ratio: 27.6 (2024 est.)
elderly dependency ratio: 33.5 (2024 est.)
potential support ratio: 3 (2024 est.)

Median age: *total:* 41.1 years (2024 est.)
male: 40.1 years
female: 42.1 years
comparison ranking: total 52

Population growth rate: 0.51% (2024 est.)
comparison ranking: 149

Birth rate: 10.7 births/1,000 population (2024 est.)
comparison ranking: 173

Death rate: 9.6 deaths/1,000 population (2024 est.)
comparison ranking: 39

Net migration rate: 4 migrant(s)/1,000 population (2024 est.)
comparison ranking: 26

Population distribution: most of the population lives in the south where the climate is milder and there is better connectivity to mainland Europe; population clusters are found along the Baltic coast in the east; the interior areas of the north remain sparsely populated

Urbanization: *urban population:* 88.7% of total population (2023)
rate of urbanization: 0.89% annual rate of change (2020-25 est.)

Major urban areas - population: 1.700 million STOCKHOLM (capital) (2023)

Sex ratio: *at birth:* 1.06 male(s)/female
0-14 years: 1.06 male(s)/female
15-64 years: 1.05 male(s)/female
65 years and over: 0.88 male(s)/female
total population: 1.01 male(s)/female (2024 est.)

Mother's mean age at first birth: 29.7 years (2020 est.)

Maternal mortality ratio: 4 deaths/100,000 live births (2023 est.)
comparison ranking: 180

Infant mortality rate: *total:* 2.3 deaths/1,000 live births (2024 est.)
male: 2.5 deaths/1,000 live births
female: 2 deaths/1,000 live births
comparison ranking: total 218

Life expectancy at birth: *total population:* 82.9 years (2024 est.)
male: 81.2 years
female: 84.7 years
comparison ranking: total population 21

Total fertility rate: 1.67 children born/woman (2024 est.)
comparison ranking: 169

Gross reproduction rate: 0.8 (2024 est.)

Drinking water source: *improved:* *urban:* 99.8% of population (2022 est.)
rural: 99.6% of population (2022 est.)
total: 99.7% of population (2022 est.)
unimproved: *urban:* 0.2% of population (2022 est.)
rural: 0.4% of population (2022 est.)
total: 0.3% of population (2022 est.)

Health expenditure: 10.7% of GDP (2022)
19% of national budget (2022 est.)

Physician density: 4.41 physicians/1,000 population (2021)

Hospital bed density: 2 beds/1,000 population (2020 est.)

Sanitation facility access: *improved:* *urban:* 99.6% of population (2022 est.)
rural: 99.5% of population (2022 est.)
total: 99.6% of population (2022 est.)
unimproved: *urban:* 0.4% of population (2022 est.)
rural: 0.5% of population (2022 est.)
total: 0.4% of population (2022 est.)

Obesity - adult prevalence rate: 20.6% (2016)
comparison ranking: 96

Alcohol consumption per capita: *total:* 7.1 liters of pure alcohol (2019 est.)
beer: 2.6 liters of pure alcohol (2019 est.)
wine: 3.4 liters of pure alcohol (2019 est.)
spirits: 1 liters of pure alcohol (2019 est.)
other alcohols: 0.1 liters of pure alcohol (2019 est.)
comparison ranking: total 59

Tobacco use: *total:* 19.9% (2025 est.)
male: 25.8% (2025 est.)
female: 13.9% (2025 est.)
comparison ranking: total 70

Currently married women (ages 15-49): 53.4% (2023 est.)

Education expenditure: 7.1% of GDP (2022 est.)
14.6% national budget (2022 est.)
comparison ranking: Education expenditure (% GDP) 16

School life expectancy (primary to tertiary education): *total:* 19 years (2023 est.)
male: 17 years (2023 est.)
female: 20 years (2023 est.)

ENVIRONMENT

Environmental issues: marine pollution (Baltic Sea and North Sea); acid rain damage to soil and lakes; air pollution; poor timber-harvesting practices

International environmental agreements: *party to:* Air Pollution, Air Pollution-Heavy Metals, Air Pollution-Multi-effect Protocol, Air Pollution-Nitrogen Oxides, Air Pollution-Persistent Organic Pollutants, Air Pollution-Sulphur 85, Air Pollution-Sulphur 94, Air Pollution-Volatile Organic Compounds, Antarctic-Environmental Protection, Antarctic-Marine Living Resources, Antarctic Treaty, Biodiversity, Climate Change, Climate Change-Kyoto Protocol, Climate Change-Paris Agreement, Comprehensive Nuclear Test Ban, Desertification, Endangered Species, Environmental Modification, Hazardous Wastes, Law of the Sea, Marine Dumping-London Convention, Marine Dumping-London Protocol, Nuclear Test Ban, Ozone Layer Protection, Ship Pollution, Tropical Timber 2006, Wetlands, Whaling
signed, but not ratified: none of the selected agreements

Climate: temperate in south with cold, cloudy winters and cool, partly cloudy summers; subarctic in north

Urbanization: *urban population:* 88.7% of total population (2023)

rate of urbanization: 0.89% annual rate of change (2020-25 est.)

Carbon dioxide emissions: 43.96 million metric tonnes of CO2 (2023 est.)
from coal and metallurgical coke: 5.324 million metric tonnes of CO2 (2023 est.)
from petroleum and other liquids: 36.768 million metric tonnes of CO2 (2023 est.)
from consumed natural gas: 1.868 million metric tonnes of CO2 (2023 est.)
comparison ranking: total emissions 61

Particulate matter emissions: 6 micrograms per cubic meter (2019 est.)

Methane emissions: *energy:* 39.6 kt (2022-2024 est.)
agriculture: 127.8 kt (2019-2021 est.)
waste: 112.7 kt (2019-2021 est.)
other: 9.8 kt (2019-2021 est.)

Waste and recycling: *municipal solid waste generated annually:* 4.618 million tons (2024 est.)
percent of municipal solid waste recycled: 39.7% (2022 est.)

Total water withdrawal: *municipal:* 699 million cubic meters (2022 est.)
industrial: 1.267 billion cubic meters (2022 est.)
agricultural: 102 million cubic meters (2022 est.)

Total renewable water resources: 174 billion cubic meters (2022 est.)

Geoparks: *total global geoparks and regional networks:* 1
global geoparks and regional networks: Platåbergens (2023)

GOVERNMENT

Country name: *conventional long form:* Kingdom of Sweden
conventional short form: Sweden
local long form: Konungariket Sverige
local short form: Sverige
etymology: name derives from the North Germanic Svea tribe that inhabited central Sweden; the tribe's name probably comes from the Old German word *sweba*, meaning "independent;" the local form of the country's name, Sverige, means "kingdom of the Svea"

Government type: parliamentary constitutional monarchy

Capital: *name:* Stockholm
geographic coordinates: 59 20 N, 18 03 E
time difference: UTC+1 (6 hours ahead of Washington, DC, during Standard Time)
daylight saving time: +1hr, begins last Sunday in March; ends last Sunday in October
etymology: the name of the city probably comes from the Swedish words *stak* (bay) or *stock* (stake or pole) and *holm* (island); it was built in the mid-13th century on the site of a fishing village, so the name may refer to building over earlier foundations

Administrative divisions: 21 counties (*lan*, singular and plural); Blekinge, Dalarna, Gavleborg, Gotland, Halland, Jamtland, Jonkoping, Kalmar, Kronoberg, Norrbotten, Orebro, Ostergotland, Skane, Sodermanland, Stockholm, Uppsala, Varmland, Vasterbotten, Vasternorrland, Vastmanland, Vastra Gotaland

Legal system: civil law system influenced by Roman-Germanic law and customary law

Constitution: *history:* Sweden has four fundamental laws which together make up the Constitution: The Instrument of Government (several previous; latest 1974); The Act of Succession (enacted 1810; changed in 1937 and 1980); The Freedom of the Press Act (many previous; latest in 1949); The Fundamental Law on Freedom of Expression (adopted 1991)
amendment process: proposed by Parliament; passage requires simple majority vote in two consecutive parliamentary terms with an intervening general election; passage also requires approval by simple majority vote in a referendum if Parliament approves a motion for a referendum by one third of its members; the results of such a referendum are only binding if a majority vote against the proposal

International law organization participation: accepts compulsory ICJ jurisdiction with reservations; accepts ICCt jurisdiction

Citizenship: *citizenship by birth:* no
citizenship by descent only: the father must be a citizen of Sweden; in the case of a child born out of wedlock, the mother must be a citizen of Sweden and the father unknown
dual citizenship recognized: no, unless the other citizenship was acquired involuntarily
residency requirement for naturalization: 5 years

Suffrage: 18 years of age; universal

Executive branch: *chief of state:* King CARL XVI GUSTAF (since 15 September 1973)
head of government: Prime Minister Ulf KRISTERSSON (since 18 October 2022)
cabinet: Cabinet appointed by the prime minister
election/appointment process: the monarchy is hereditary; following legislative elections, the leader of the majority party or majority coalition usually becomes the prime minister

Legislative branch: *legislature name:* Parliament (Riksdagen)
legislative structure: unicameral
number of seats: 349 (all directly elected)
electoral system: proportional representation
scope of elections: full renewal
term in office: 4 years
most recent election date: 9/11/2022
parties elected and seats per party: Social Democratic Party (SAP) (107); Sweden Democrats (SD) (73); Moderate Party (M) (68); Left Party (VP) (24); Centre Party (CP) (24); Christian Democrats (KD) (19); Green Party (Mpg) (18); Other (16)
percentage of women in chamber: 45%
expected date of next election: September 2026

Judicial branch: *highest court(s):* Supreme Court of Sweden (consists of 16 justices, including the court chairman); Supreme Administrative Court (consists of 18 justices, including the court president)
judge selection and term of office: Supreme Court and Supreme Administrative Court justices nominated by the Judges Proposal Board, a 9-member nominating body consisting of high-level judges, prosecutors, and members of Parliament; justices appointed by the government; after a probationary period, justices' appointments are permanent
subordinate courts: first instance, appellate, general, and administrative courts; specialized courts that handle cases such as land and environment, immigration, labor, markets, and patents

Political parties: Center Party (Centerpartiet) or C
Christian Democrats (Kristdemokraterna) or KD
Green Party (Miljopartiet de Grona) or MP
Left Party (Vansterpartiet) or V
Moderate Party (Moderaterna) or M
Sweden Democrats (Sverigedemokraterna) or SD
Swedish Social Democratic Party (Socialdemokraterna) or S/SAP
The Liberals (Liberalerna) or L

Diplomatic representation in the US: *chief of mission:* Ambassador Urban AHLIN (since 15 September 2023)
chancery: 2900 K Street NW, Washington, DC 20007
telephone: [1] (202) 467-2600
FAX: [1] (202) 467-2699
email address and website: ambassaden.washington@gov.se
https://www.swedenabroad.se/en/embassies/usa-washington/
consulate(s) general: New York, San Francisco

Diplomatic representation from the US: *chief of mission:* Ambassador (vacant); Chargé d'Affaires Viraj LeBAILLY (since August 2025)
embassy: Dag Hammarskjolds Vag 31, SE-115 89 Stockholm
mailing address: 5750 Stockholm Place, Washington, DC 20521-5750
telephone: [46] (08) 783-53-00
FAX: [46] (08) 661-19-64
email address and website: STKACSinfo@state.gov
https://se.usembassy.gov/

International organization participation: ADB (nonregional member), AfDB (nonregional member), Arctic Council, Australia Group, BIS, CBSS, CD, CE, CERN, EAPC, EBRD, ECB, EIB, EITI (implementing country), EMU, ESA, EU, FAO, FATF, G-9, G-10, IADB, IAEA, IBRD, ICAO, ICC (national committees), ICCt, ICRM, IDA, IEA, IFAD, IFC, IFRCS, IGAD (partners), IHO, ILO, IMF, IMO, IMSO, Interpol, IOC, IOM, IPU, ISO, ITSO, ITU, ITUC (NGOs), MIGA, MONUSCO, NATO, NC, NEA, NIB, NSG, OAS (observer), OECD, OPCW, OSCE, Paris Club, PCA, PFP, Schengen Convention, UN, UNCTAD, UNESCO, UNHCR, UNIDO, UNMISS, UNMOGIP, UNOOSA, UNRWA, UN Security Council (temporary), UNSOM, UNTSO, UPU, Wassenaar Arrangement, WCO, WFTU (NGOs), WHO, WIPO, WMO, WTO, ZC

Independence: 6 June 1523 (Gustav VASA elected king of Sweden, marking the abolishment of the Kalmar Union of Denmark, Norway, and Sweden)

National holiday: National Day, 6 June (1983)
note: celebrated as Swedish Flag Day from 1916 to 1982

Flag: *description:* blue with a golden yellow cross extending to the edges of the flag; the cross is shifted to the left side in the style of the Dannebrog (Danish flag)
meaning: the colors come from the Swedish coat of arms

National symbol(s): three crowns, lion

National color(s): blue, yellow

National anthem(s): *title:* "Du Gamla, Du Fria" (Thou Ancient, Thou Free)
lyrics/music: Richard DYBECK/traditional
history: in use since 1893; also known as "Sang till Norden" (Song of the North); based on a Swedish folk tune; has never been officially adopted
title: "Kungssangen" (Royal Song)
lyrics/music: Carl Wilhelm August Strandberg/Otto Lindblad

history: adopted 1844 as the royal anthem, but also used as the national anthem until 1893; only the first verse is sung if the monarch is present

National heritage: *total World Heritage Sites:* 15 (13 cultural, 1 natural, 1 mixed)
selected World Heritage Site locales: Royal Domain of Drottningholm (c); Laponian Area (m); High Coast/ Kvarken Archipelago (n); Birka and Hovgården (c); Hanseatic Town of Visby (c); Church Town of Gammelstad, Luleå (c); Naval Port of Karlskrona (c); Rock Carvings in Tanum (c); Engelsberg Ironworks (c); Mining Area of the Great Copper Mountain in Falun (c)

ECONOMY

Economic overview: high-income, largest Nordic economy; EU member but does not use the euro; export-oriented, led by automotive, electronics, machinery, and pharmaceuticals; highly ranked for competitiveness, R&D investments and governance; recovery, with falling inflation and real wage growth balanced by risks from trade uncertainty

Real GDP (purchasing power parity): $668.628 billion (2024 est.)
$662.18 billion (2023 est.)
$662.937 billion (2022 est.)
note: data in 2021 dollars
comparison ranking: 41

Real GDP growth rate: 1% (2024 est.)
-0.1% (2023 est.)
1.5% (2022 est.)
note: annual GDP % growth based on constant local currency
comparison ranking: 177

Real GDP per capita: $63,300 (2024 est.)
$62,800 (2023 est.)
$63,200 (2022 est.)
note: data in 2021 dollars
comparison ranking: 25

GDP (official exchange rate): $610.118 billion (2024 est.)
note: data in current dollars at official exchange rate

Inflation rate (consumer prices): 2.8% (2024 est.)
8.5% (2023 est.)
8.4% (2022 est.)
note: annual % change based on consumer prices
comparison ranking: 82

GDP - composition, by sector of origin: *agriculture:* 1.1% (2024 est.)
industry: 22.6% (2024 est.)
services: 65.9% (2024 est.)
note: figures may not total 100% due to non-allocated consumption not captured in sector-reported data
comparison rankings: agriculture 173; industry 113; services 49

GDP - composition, by end use: *household consumption:* 43.7% (2023 est.)
government consumption: 26% (2023 est.)
investment in fixed capital: 25% (2023 est.)
investment in inventories: -0.1% (2023 est.)
exports of goods and services: 55.4% (2023 est.)
imports of goods and services: -51.4% (2023 est.)
note: figures may not total 100% due to rounding or gaps in data collection

Agricultural products: milk, wheat, sugar beets, barley, potatoes, oats, rapeseed, pork, chicken, beef (2023)
note: top ten agricultural products based on tonnage

Industries: iron and steel, precision equipment (bearings, radio and telephone parts, armaments), wood pulp and paper products, processed foods, motor vehicles

Industrial production growth rate: 0.3% (2024 est.)
note: annual % change in industrial value added based on constant local currency
comparison ranking: 126

Labor force: 5.699 million (2024 est.)
note: number of people ages 15 or older who are employed or seeking work
comparison ranking: 77

Unemployment rate: 8.6% (2024 est.)
7.7% (2023 est.)
7.4% (2022 est.)
note: % of labor force seeking employment
comparison ranking: 141

Youth unemployment rate (ages 15-24): *total:* 23.8% (2024 est.)
male: 24.3% (2024 est.)
female: 23.2% (2024 est.)
note: % of labor force ages 15-24 seeking employment
comparison ranking: total 38

Population below poverty line: 16.1% (2022 est.)
note: % of population with income below national poverty line

Gini Index coefficient - distribution of family income: 31.6 (2022 est.)
note: index (0-100) of income distribution; higher values represent greater inequality
comparison ranking: 109

Average household expenditures: *on food:* 13% of household expenditures (2023 est.)
on alcohol and tobacco: 3.1% of household expenditures (2023 est.)

Household income or consumption by percentage share: *lowest 10%:* 2.5% (2022 est.)
highest 10%: 24.7% (2022 est.)
note: % share of income accruing to lowest and highest 10% of population

Remittances: 0.8% of GDP (2024 est.)
0.7% of GDP (2023 est.)
0.6% of GDP (2022 est.)
note: personal transfers and compensation between resident and non-resident individuals/households/ entities

Budget: *revenues:* $195.468 billion (2022 est.)
expenditures: $191.095 billion (2022 est.)
note: central government revenues (excluding grants) and expenditures converted to US dollars at average official exchange rate for year indicated

Public debt: 36.9% of GDP (2022 est.)
note: central government debt as a % of GDP
comparison ranking: 143

Taxes and other revenues: 27.6% (of GDP) (2022 est.)
note: central government tax revenue as a % of GDP
comparison ranking: 6

Current account balance: $45.274 billion (2024 est.)
$40.819 billion (2023 est.)
$27.404 billion (2022 est.)
note: balance of payments - net trade and primary/ secondary income in current dollars
comparison ranking: 15

Exports: $338.852 billion (2024 est.)
$329.332 billion (2023 est.)
$318.203 billion (2022 est.)
note: balance of payments - exports of goods and services in current dollars
comparison ranking: 29

Exports - partners: Germany 10%, USA 10%, Denmark 8%, Norway 6%, Netherlands 5% (2023)
note: top five export partners based on percentage share of exports

Exports - commodities: cars, refined petroleum, packaged medicine, paper, vehicle parts/accessories (2023)
note: top five export commodities based on value in dollars

Imports: $309.526 billion (2024 est.)
$304.194 billion (2023 est.)
$304.101 billion (2022 est.)
note: balance of payments - imports of goods and services in current dollars
comparison ranking: 29

Imports - partners: Germany 17%, Netherlands 10%, Norway 9%, Denmark 6%, China 6% (2023)
note: top five import partners based on percentage share of imports

Imports - commodities: cars, crude petroleum, refined petroleum, vehicle parts/accessories, garments (2023)
note: top five import commodities based on value in dollars

Reserves of foreign exchange and gold: $62.569 billion (2024 est.)
$60.863 billion (2023 est.)
$64.289 billion (2022 est.)
note: holdings of gold (year-end prices)/foreign exchange/special drawing rights in current dollars
comparison ranking: 38

Exchange rates: Swedish kronor (SEK) per US dollar -

Exchange rates: 10.568 (2024 est.)
10.61 (2023 est.)
10.114 (2022 est.)
8.577 (2021 est.)
9.21 (2020 est.)

ENERGY

Electricity access: *electrification - total population:* 100% (2022 est.)

Electricity: *installed generating capacity:* 55.307 million kW (2023 est.)
consumption: 125.273 billion kWh (2023 est.)
exports: 36.151 billion kWh (2023 est.)
imports: 7.335 billion kWh (2023 est.)
transmission/distribution losses: 9.109 billion kWh (2023 est.)
comparison rankings: installed generating capacity 28; consumption 30; exports 5; imports 34; transmission/ distribution losses 179

Electricity generation sources: *fossil fuels:* 0.5% of total installed capacity (2023 est.)
nuclear: 28.6% of total installed capacity (2023 est.)
solar: 1.9% of total installed capacity (2023 est.)
wind: 21% of total installed capacity (2023 est.)
hydroelectricity: 40.2% of total installed capacity (2023 est.)
biomass and waste: 7.8% of total installed capacity (2023 est.)

Nuclear energy: Number of operational nuclear reactors: 6 (2025)

Net capacity of operational nuclear reactors: 7.01GW (2025 est.)

Percent of total electricity production: 28.6% (2023 est.)

Number of nuclear reactors permanently shut down: 7 (2025)

Coal: *production:* 1.042 million metric tons (2023 est.)
consumption: 3.17 million metric tons (2023 est.)
exports: 23,000 metric tons (2023 est.)
imports: 2.078 million metric tons (2023 est.)
proven reserves: 5 million metric tons (2023 est.)

Petroleum: *total petroleum production:* 11,000 bbl/day (2023 est.)
refined petroleum consumption: 270,000 bbl/day (2024 est.)

Natural gas: *consumption:* 896.109 million cubic meters (2023 est.)
exports: 10.625 million cubic meters (2023 est.)
imports: 897.487 million cubic meters (2023 est.)

Energy consumption per capita: 142.102 million Btu/person (2023 est.)
comparison ranking: 27

COMMUNICATIONS

Telephones - fixed lines: *total subscriptions:* 898,000 (2023 est.)
subscriptions per 100 inhabitants: 9 (2023 est.)
comparison ranking: total subscriptions 69

Telephones - mobile cellular: *total subscriptions:* 14.8 million (2023 est.)
subscriptions per 100 inhabitants: 125 (2022 est.)
comparison ranking: total subscriptions 74

Broadcast media: publicly owned TV broadcaster has 2 terrestrial networks plus regional stations; multiple privately owned TV broadcasters operating nationally, regionally, and locally; about 50 local TV stations; widespread access to pan-Nordic and international broadcasters through multi-channel cable and satellite TV; publicly owned radio broadcaster has 3 national stations and a network of 25 regional channels; roughly 100 privately owned local radio stations, with some consolidating into near-national networks; an estimated 900 community and neighborhood radio stations broadcast intermittently

Internet country code: .se

Internet users: *percent of population:* 96% (2023 est.)

Broadband - fixed subscriptions: *total:* 4.3 million (2023 est.)
subscriptions per 100 inhabitants: 41 (2023 est.)
comparison ranking: total 41

TRANSPORTATION

Civil aircraft registration country code prefix: SE

Airports: 206 (2025)
comparison ranking: 30

Heliports: 11 (2025)
comparison ranking: 71

Railways: *total:* 10,910 km (2020) 8,184 km electrified
narrow gauge: 65 km

Merchant marine: *total:* 361 (2023)
by type: general cargo 44, oil tanker 18, other 299
comparison ranking: total 52

Ports: *total ports:* 92 (2024)
large: 3
medium: 10
small: 30
very small: 49
ports with oil terminals: 49
key ports: Falkenberg, Goteborg, Helsingborg, Karlsborg, Karlshamn, Lulea, Malmo, Norrkoping, Stockholm, Sundsvall, Uddevalla, Varberg, Vasteras

MILITARY AND SECURITY

Military and security forces: Swedish Armed Forces (Försvarsmakten): Army, Navy, Air Force, Home Guard (202)

Military expenditures: 2.5% of GDP (2025 est.)
2.3% of GDP (2024 est.)
1.7% of GDP (2023 est.)
1.5% of GDP (2022 est.)
1.4% of GDP (2021 est.)

Military and security service personnel strengths: approximately 25,000 active military personnel; approximately 21,000 Home Guard (2025)
note 1: SAF personnel are divided into continuously serving (full-time) and temporary service troops (part-timers who serve periodically and have another main employer or attend school); additional personnel have signed service agreements with the SAF and mostly serve in the Home Guard
note 2: in 2021, Sweden announced plans that increase the total size of the armed forces to about 100,000 personnel by 2030

Military equipment inventories and acquisitions: the SAF's inventory is comprised of domestically produced and imported Western weapons systems, including from Finland, Germany, and the US; Sweden has a defense industry that produces a range of air, land, and naval systems, including armored vehicles, combat aircraft, and submarines; it also produces weapons systems jointly with other countries (2024)

Military service age and obligation: *18-47 years of age for voluntary military service for men and women; service obligation:* 7-15 months (Army), 7-15 months (Navy), 8-12 months (Air Force); after completing initial service, soldiers have a reserve commitment until age 47; compulsory military service, abolished in 2010, was reinstated in January 2018; conscription is selective, includes both men and women (age 18), and requires 6-15 months of service (2024)
note 1: Sweden conscripts about 5,500 men and women each year; it plans to increase this number to 8,000 by 2025; conscientious objectors in Sweden have the right to apply for alternative service (called vapenfri tjänst); after completing alternative service, the conscript then belongs to the civilian reserve
note 2: as of 2024, women made nearly 25% of the military's personnel

Military deployments: approximately 600 Latvia (NATO) (2025)

Military - note: the Swedish military is responsible for deterrence and the defense of the country and its territories against armed attack, supporting Sweden's national security interests, providing societal support, such as humanitarian aid, and contributing to international peacekeeping and peacemaking operations; the military has a relatively small active duty force that is designed to be rapidly mobilized in a crisis with a trained reserve and a Home Guard

Sweden maintained a policy of military non-alignment for over 200 years before applying for NATO membership in May 2022 following Russia's full-scale invasion of Ukraine; it became a NATO member in March 2024; prior to membership, Stockholm joined NATO's Partnership for Peace program in 1994 and contributed to NATO-led missions, including those in Afghanistan, Iraq, and Kosovo; the military cooperates closely with the forces of other Nordic countries through the Nordic Defense Cooperation (NORDEFCO; established 2009), which consists of Denmark, Finland, Iceland, Norway, and Sweden; Sweden is a signatory of the EU's Common Security and Defense Policy (CSDP) and contributes to CSDP missions and operations, including EU battlegroups; it also participates in UN-led missions; Sweden has close bilateral security relations with some individual NATO member states, particularly Finland, Germany, Norway, the UK, and the US (2025)

SPACE

Space agency/agencies: Swedish National Space Agency (SNSA; established 1972; known until 2018 as the Swedish National Space Board) (2025)

Space launch site(s): Esrange Space Center (Kiruna) (2025)

Space program overview: member of the European Space Agency (ESA) and program is integrated within its framework; aims to have one of Europe's leading space programs; produces and operates satellites; builds and launches sounding rockets; involved in the research, development, production, and operations of a wide variety of other space-related areas and capabilities, including astronomy, atmospheric monitoring, geographic information systems, infrared imaging, meteorology, propulsion systems, remote sensing, satellite subsystems, spacecraft systems and structures, space physics, scientific research, stratospheric balloons, and telecommunications; conducts extensive bilateral and multilateral international cooperation, in particular through the ESA and EU and their member states, as well as with the US; participates in such programs as Europe's Copernicus Earth observation and the Galileo global navigation satellite system, France's Pleiades project for sharing satellite imagery, and the international Square Kilometer Array Project; has a robust commercial space industry, including state-owned enterprises (2025)
note: further details about the key activities, programs, and milestones of the country's space program, as well as government spending estimates on the space sector, appear in the Space Programs reference guide

TERRORISM

Terrorist group(s): Terrorist group(s): Islamic State of Iraq and ash-Sham (ISIS)
note: details about the history, aims, leadership, organization, areas of operation, tactics, targets, weapons, size, and sources of support of the group(s) appear(s) in Appendix T

TRANSNATIONAL ISSUES

Refugees and internally displaced persons: *refugees:* 168,519 (2024 est.)
stateless persons: 6,835 (2024 est.)

SWITZERLAND

INTRODUCTION

Background: The Swiss Confederation was founded in 1291 as a defensive alliance among three cantons. In succeeding years, other localities joined the original three. The Swiss Confederation secured its independence from the Holy Roman Empire in 1499. A constitution of 1848, which was modified in 1874 to allow voters to introduce referenda on proposed laws, replaced the confederation with a centralized federal government. The major European powers have long honored Switzerland's sovereignty and neutrality, and the country was not involved in either World War. The political and economic integration of Europe over the past half-century, as well as Switzerland's role in many UN and international organizations, has strengthened Switzerland's ties with its neighbors. However, the country did not officially become a UN member until 2002. Switzerland remains active in many UN and international organizations but retains a strong commitment to neutrality.

GEOGRAPHY

Location: Central Europe, east of France, north of Italy

Geographic coordinates: 47 00 N, 8 00 E

Map references: Europe

Area: *total:* 41,277 sq km
land: 39,997 sq km
water: 1,280 sq km
comparison ranking: total 135

Area - comparative: slightly less than twice the size of New Jersey

Land boundaries: *total:* 1,770 km
border countries (5): Austria 158 km; France 525 km; Italy 698 km; Liechtenstein 41 km; Germany 348 km

Coastline: 0 km (landlocked)

Maritime claims: none (landlocked)

Climate: temperate, but varies with altitude; cold, cloudy, rainy/snowy winters; cool to warm, cloudy, humid summers with occasional showers

Terrain: mostly mountains (Alps in south, Jura in northwest) with a central plateau of rolling hills, plains, and large lakes

Elevation: *highest point:* Dufourspitze on Monte Rosa 4,634 m
lowest point: Lake Maggiore 195 m
mean elevation: 1,350 m

Natural resources: hydropower potential, timber, salt

Land use: *agricultural land:* 37.9% (2022 est.)
arable land: 10% (2022 est.)
permanent crops: 0.6% (2022 est.)
permanent pasture: 27.2% (2022 est.)
forest: 32.3% (2022 est.)
other: 29.8% (2022 est.)

Irrigated land: 494 sq km (2020)

Major lakes (area sq km): *fresh water lake(s):* Lake Constance (shared with Germany and Austria) - 540 sq km; Lake Geneva (shared with France) - 580 sq km

Major rivers (by length in km): Rhein (Rhine) river source (shared with Germany, France, and Netherlands [m]) - 1,233 km
note: [s] after country name indicates river source; [m] after country name indicates river mouth

Major watersheds (area sq km): Atlantic Ocean drainage: Rhine-Maas (198,735 sq km), *(Black Sea)* Danube (795,656 sq km), *(Adriatic Sea)* Po (76,997 sq km), *(Mediterranean Sea)* Rhone (100,543 sq km)

Population distribution: population distribution corresponds to elevation, with the northern and western areas far more heavily populated; the higher Alps of the south limit settlement

Natural hazards: avalanches, landslides; flash floods

Geography - note: landlocked; crossroads of northern and southern Europe; along with southeastern France, northern Italy, and southwestern Austria, has the highest elevations in the Alps

PEOPLE AND SOCIETY

Population: *total:* 8,860,574 (2024 est.)
male: 4,403,105
female: 4,457,469
comparison rankings: total 102; male 100; female 101

Nationality: *noun:* Swiss (singular and plural)
adjective: Swiss

Ethnic groups: Swiss 69.2%, German 4.2%, Italian 3.2%, Portuguese 2.5%, French 2.1%, Kosovan 1.1%, Turkish 1%, other 16.7% (2020 est.)
note: data represent permanent and non-permanent resident population by country of birth

Languages: German (or Swiss German) (official) 62.1%, French (official) 22.8%, Italian (official) 8%, English 5.7%, Portuguese 3.5%, Albanian 3.3%, Serbo-Croatian 2.3%, Spanish 2.3%, Romansh (official) 0.5%, other 7.9% (2019 est.)
major-language sample(s):
Das World Factbook, die unverzichtbare Quelle für grundlegende Informationen. (German)
The World Factbook, une source indispensable d'informations de base. (French)
L'Almanacco dei fatti del mondo, l'indispensabile fonte per le informazioni di base. (Italian)
note: shares sum to more than 100% because respondents could indicate more than one main language

Religions: Roman Catholic 34.4%, Protestant 22.5%, other Christian 5.7%, Muslim 5.4%, other 1.5%, none 29.4%, unspecified 1.1% (2020 est.)

Age structure: *0-14 years:* 15.1% (male 685,221/female 650,802)
15-64 years: 64.6% (male 2,887,767/female 2,834,842)
65 years and over: 20.3% (2024 est.) (male 830,117/female 971,825)

Dependency ratios: *total dependency ratio:* 54.8 (2024 est.)
youth dependency ratio: 23.3 (2024 est.)
elderly dependency ratio: 31.5 (2024 est.)
potential support ratio: 3.2 (2024 est.)

Median age: *total:* 44.2 years (2024 est.)
male: 43.5 years
female: 44.9 years
comparison ranking: total 32

Population growth rate: 0.75% (2024 est.)
comparison ranking: 117

Birth rate: 10.1 births/1,000 population (2024 est.)
comparison ranking: 185

Death rate: 8.5 deaths/1,000 population (2024 est.)
comparison ranking: 73

Net migration rate: 5.9 migrant(s)/1,000 population (2024 est.)
comparison ranking: 14

Population distribution: population distribution corresponds to elevation, with the northern and western areas far more heavily populated; the higher Alps of the south limit settlement

Urbanization: *urban population:* 74.2% of total population (2023)
rate of urbanization: 0.79% annual rate of change (2020-25 est.)

Major urban areas - population: 1.432 million Zurich, 441,000 BERN (capital) (2023)

Sex ratio: *at birth:* 1.05 male(s)/female
0-14 years: 1.05 male(s)/female
15-64 years: 1.02 male(s)/female
65 years and over: 0.85 male(s)/female
total population: 0.99 male(s)/female (2024 est.)

Mother's mean age at first birth: 31.1 years (2020 est.)

Maternal mortality ratio: 5 deaths/100,000 live births (2023 est.)
comparison ranking: 172

Infant mortality rate: *total:* 3 deaths/1,000 live births (2024 est.)
male: 3.4 deaths/1,000 live births
female: 2.5 deaths/1,000 live births
comparison ranking: total 209

Life expectancy at birth: *total population:* 83.9 years (2024 est.)
male: 82 years
female: 85.8 years
comparison ranking: total population 9

Total fertility rate: 1.59 children born/woman (2024 est.)
comparison ranking: 187

Gross reproduction rate: 0.77 (2024 est.)

Drinking water source: *improved: urban:* 100% of population (2022 est.)
rural: 100% of population (2022 est.)
total: 100% of population (2022 est.)
unimproved: urban: 0% of population (2022 est.)
rural: 0% of population (2022 est.)
total: 0% of population (2022 est.)

Health expenditure: 11.8% of GDP (2021)
12.4% of national budget (2022 est.)

Physician density: 4.48 physicians/1,000 population (2022)

Hospital bed density: 4.4 beds/1,000 population (2021 est.)

Sanitation facility access: *improved: urban:* 100% of population (2022 est.)
rural: 100% of population (2022 est.)
total: 100% of population (2022 est.)
unimproved: urban: 0% of population (2022 est.)
rural: 0% of population (2022 est.)
total: 0% of population (2022 est.)

Obesity - adult prevalence rate: 19.5% (2016)
comparison ranking: 112

Alcohol consumption per capita: *total:* 9.41 liters of pure alcohol (2019 est.)
beer: 3.17 liters of pure alcohol (2019 est.)
wine: 4.35 liters of pure alcohol (2019 est.)
spirits: 1.76 liters of pure alcohol (2019 est.)
other alcohols: 0.12 liters of pure alcohol (2019 est.)
comparison ranking: total 30

Tobacco use: *total:* 22.8% (2025 est.)
male: 25.5% (2025 est.)
female: 20.1% (2025 est.)
comparison ranking: total 49

Currently married women (ages 15-49): 57.5% (2023 est.)

Education expenditure: 5.1% of GDP (2023 est.)
15.9% national budget (2023 est.)
comparison ranking: Education expenditure (% GDP) 57

School life expectancy (primary to tertiary education): *total:* 17 years (2023 est.)
male: 17 years (2023 est.)
female: 17 years (2023 est.)

ENVIRONMENT

Environmental issues: air pollution from vehicle emissions; water pollution from agricultural fertilizers; soil pollution from chemical contaminants; soil erosion; loss of biodiversity

International environmental agreements: *party to:* Air Pollution, Air Pollution-Heavy Metals, Air Pollution-Multi-effect Protocol, Air Pollution-Nitrogen Oxides, Air Pollution-Persistent Organic Pollutants, Air Pollution-Sulphur 85, Air Pollution-Sulphur 94, Air Pollution-Volatile Organic Compounds, Antarctic-Environmental Protection, Antarctic Treaty, Biodiversity, Climate Change, Climate Change-Kyoto Protocol, Climate Change-Paris Agreement, Comprehensive Nuclear Test Ban, Desertification, Endangered Species, Environmental Modification, Hazardous Wastes, Law of the Sea, Marine Dumping-London Convention, Marine Dumping-London Protocol, Marine Life Conservation, Nuclear Test Ban, Ozone Layer Protection, Ship Pollution, Tropical Timber 2006, Wetlands, Whaling
signed, but not ratified: none of the selected agreements

Climate: temperate, but varies with altitude; cold, cloudy, rainy/snowy winters; cool to warm, cloudy, humid summers with occasional showers

Urbanization: *urban population:* 74.2% of total population (2023)
rate of urbanization: 0.79% annual rate of change (2020-25 est.)

Carbon dioxide emissions: 33.306 million metric tonnes of CO2 (2023 est.)
from coal and metallurgical coke: 195,000 metric tonnes of CO2 (2023 est.)
from petroleum and other liquids: 27.528 million metric tonnes of CO2 (2023 est.)
from consumed natural gas: 5.583 million metric tonnes of CO2 (2023 est.)
comparison ranking: total emissions 72

Particulate matter emissions: 9 micrograms per cubic meter (2019 est.)

Waste and recycling: *municipal solid waste generated annually:* 6.08 million tons (2024 est.)
percent of municipal solid waste recycled: 30.1% (2022 est.)

Total water withdrawal: *municipal:* 930 million cubic meters (2022)
industrial: 642.7 million cubic meters (2022 est.)
agricultural: 160.1 million cubic meters (2022 est.)

Total renewable water resources: 53.5 billion cubic meters (2022 est.)

GOVERNMENT

Country name: *conventional long form:* Swiss Confederation
conventional short form: Switzerland
local long form: Schweizerische Eidgenossenschaft (German)/Confederation Suisse (French)/Confederazione Svizzera (Italian)/Confederaziun Svizra (Romansh)
local short form: Schweiz (German)/Suisse (French)/Svizzera (Italian)/Svizra (Romansh)
abbreviation: CH
etymology: name derives from the canton of Schwyz, one of the founding cantons of the Swiss Confederacy formed in the late 13th century

Government type: federal republic (formally a confederation)

Capital: *name:* Bern
geographic coordinates: 46 55 N, 7 28 E
time difference: UTC+1 (6 hours ahead of Washington, DC, during Standard Time)
daylight saving time: +1hr, begins last Sunday in March; ends last Sunday in October
etymology: the origin of the name is uncertain; it is sometimes associated with the German word *Baer* (bear), but a more likely origin is an Indo-European root word *ber*, meaning "marshy place"

Administrative divisions: 26 cantons (*cantons*, singular - *canton* in French; *cantoni*, singular - *cantone* in Italian; *Kantone*, singular - *Kanton* in German); Aargau, Appenzell Ausserrhoden, Appenzell Innerrhoden, Basel-Landschaft, Basel-Stadt, Berne/Bern, Fribourg/Freiburg, Genève (Geneva), Glarus, Graubuenden/Grigioni/Grischun, Jura, Luzern (Lucerne), Neuchatel, Nidwalden, Obwalden, Sankt Gallen, Schaffhausen, Schwyz, Solothurn, Thurgau, Ticino, Uri, Valais/Wallis, Vaud, Zug, Zuerich
note 1: the names listed above are in the canton's official language(s), with conventional names in parentheses
note 2: 6 of the cantons – Appenzell Ausserrhoden, Appenzell Innerrhoden, Basel-Landschaft, Basel-Stadt, Nidwalden, Obwalden – are referred to as half cantons because they elect only one member (instead of two) to the Council of States, and in popular referendums where a majority of popular votes and cantonal votes are required, these 6 cantons have a half vote

Legal system: civil law system; judicial review of legislative acts, except federal decrees of a general obligatory character

Constitution: *history:* previous 1848, 1874; latest adopted by referendum 18 April 1999, effective 1 January 2000
amendment process: proposed by the two houses of the Federal Assembly or by petition of at least one hundred thousand voters (called the "federal popular initiative"); passage of proposals requires majority vote in a referendum; following drafting of an amendment by the Assembly, its passage requires approval by majority vote in a referendum and approval by the majority of cantons

International law organization participation: accepts compulsory ICJ jurisdiction with reservations; accepts ICCt jurisdiction

Citizenship: *citizenship by birth:* no
citizenship by descent only: at least one parent must be a citizen of Switzerland
dual citizenship recognized: yes
residency requirement for naturalization: 12 years including at least 3 of the last 5 years prior to application

Suffrage: 18 years of age; universal

Executive branch: *chief of state:* President of the Swiss Confederation Karin KELLER-SUTTER (since 1 January 2025)
head of government: President of the Swiss Confederation Karin KELLER-SUTTER (since 1 January 2025)
cabinet: Federal Council or Bundesrat (in German), Conseil Federal (in French), Consiglio Federale (in Italian) indirectly elected by the Federal Assembly for a 4-year term
election/appointment process: president and vice president elected by the Federal Assembly from among members of the Federal Council for a 1-year, non-consecutive term
most recent election date: 11 December 2024
election results: *2024:* Karin KELLER-SUTTER elected president for 2025; Federal Assembly vote - Karin KELLER-SUTTER (FDP.The Liberals) 168 of 203; Guy PARLEMIN (SVP) elected vice president for 2025; Federal Assembly vote - 196 of 219
2023: Viola AMHERD elected president for 2024; Federal Assembly vote - Viola AMHERD (The Center) 158 of 204; Karin KELLER-SUTTER (FDP. The Liberals) elected vice president for 2024; Federal Assembly vote - 138 of 196
2022: Alain BERSET elected president for 2023; Federal Assembly vote - Alain BERSET (SP) 140 OF 181; Viola AMHERD elected vice president; Federal assembly vote - 207 of 223
expected date of next election: December 2025
note: the Federal Council, composed of 7 federal councilors, constitutes the federal government of Switzerland; council members rotate the 1-year term of federal president

Legislative branch: *legislature name:* Federal Assembly (Bundesversammlung - Assemblée fédérale - Assemblea federale)
legislative structure: bicameral

Legislative branch - lower chamber: *chamber name:* National Council (Nationalrat - Conseil national - Consiglio nazionale)
number of seats: 200 (all directly elected)
electoral system: proportional representation
scope of elections: full renewal
term in office: 4 years
most recent election date: 10/22/2023
parties elected and seats per party: Swiss People's Party (SVP/UDC) (62); Socialist Party (SP/PS) (41); Centre Party (29); FDP/The Liberals (FDP/PLR) (28); Green Party (GPS/PES) (23); Liberal Green Party (GLP/PVL) (10); Other (7)
percentage of women in chamber: 39%
expected date of next election: October 2027

Legislative branch - upper chamber: *chamber name:* Council of States (Ständerat - Conseil des Etats - Consiglio degli Stati)
number of seats: 46 (all directly elected)
electoral system: other systems
scope of elections: full renewal
term in office: 4 years
most recent election date: 10/22/2023
parties elected and seats per party: Centre Party (15); FDP/The Liberals (FDP/PLR) (11); Socialist Party (SP/PS) (9); Swiss People's Party (SVP/UDC) (6); Green Party (GPS/PES) (3); Other (2)
percentage of women in chamber: 33.3%
expected date of next election: October 2027

Judicial branch: *highest court(s):* Federal Supreme Court (consists of 38 justices and 19 deputy justices organized into 7 divisions)
judge selection and term of office: judges elected by the Federal Assembly for 6-year terms; judges are affiliated with political parties and are elected according to linguistic and regional criteria in approximate proportion to party representation in the Federal Assembly
subordinate courts: Federal Criminal Court (established in 2004); Federal Administrative Court (established in 2007)
note: each of Switzerland's 26 cantons has its own courts

Political parties: The Center (Die Mitte, Alleanza del Centro, Le Centre, Allianza dal Center) (merger of the Christian Democratic People's Party and the Conservative Democratic Party)
Evangelical Peoples' Party or EVP/PEV
Federal Democrats or EDU
Geneva Citizens Movement or MCR/MCG
Green Liberal Party (Gruenliberale Partei or GLP, Parti vert liberale or PVL, Partito Verde-Liberale or PVL, Partida Verde Liberale or PVL)
Green Party (Gruene Partei der Schweiz or Gruene, Parti Ecologiste Suisse or Les Verts, Partito Ecologista Svizzero or I Verdi, Partida Ecologica Svizra or La Verda)
The Liberals or FDP.The Liberals (FDP.Die Liberalen, PLR.Les Liberaux-Radicaux, PLR.I Liberali, Ils Liberals)
Social Democratic Party (Sozialdemokratische Partei der Schweiz or SP, Parti Socialiste Suisse or PSS, Partito Socialista Svizzero or PSS, Partida Socialdemocratica de la Svizra or PSS)
Swiss People's Party (Schweizerische Volkspartei or SVP, Union Democratique du Centre or UDC, Unione Democratica di Centro or UDC, Uniun Democratica dal Center or UDC)

Diplomatic representation in the US: *chief of mission:* Ambassador Ralph HECKNER (since 18 September 2024)
chancery: 2900 Cathedral Ave NW, Washington, DC 20008
telephone: [1] (202) 745-7900
FAX: [1] (202) 387-2564
email address and website: washington@eda.admin.ch https://www.eda.admin.ch/washington
consulate(s) general: Atlanta, Chicago, New York, San Francisco
consulate(s): Boston

Diplomatic representation from the US: *chief of mission:* Ambassador (vacant); Chargé d'Affaires Bradford BELL (since January 2025) note - also accredited to Liechtenstein
embassy: Sulgeneckstrasse 19, CH-3007 Bern
mailing address: 5110 Bern Place, Washington DC 20521-5110
telephone: [41] (031) 357-70-11
FAX: [41] (031) 357-73-20
email address and website: https://ch.usembassy.gov/

International organization participation: ADB (nonregional member), AfDB (nonregional member), Australia Group, BIS, CD, CE, CERN, EAPC, EBRD, EFTA, EITI (implementing country), ESA, FAO, FATF, G-10, IADB, IAEA, IBRD, ICAO, ICC (national committees), ICCt, ICRM, IDA, IEA, IFAD, IFC, IFRCS, IGAD (partners), ILO, IMF, IMO, IMSO, Interpol, IOC, IOM, IPU, ISO, ITSO, ITU, ITUC (NGOs), LAIA (observer), MIGA, MONUSCO, NEA, NSG, OAS (observer), OECD, OIF, OPCW, OSCE, Pacific Alliance (observer), Paris Club, PCA, PFP, Schengen Convention, UN, UNCTAD, UNESCO, UNHCR, UNIDO, UNITAR, UNMISS, UNMOGIP, UNOOSA, UNRWA, UNTSO, UNWTO, UPU, Wassenaar Arrangement, WCO, WHO, WIPO, WMO, WTO, ZC

Independence: 1 August 1291 (founding of the Swiss Confederation)

National holiday: Founding of the Swiss Confederation in 1291
note: celebrated as Swiss National Day since 1 August 1891

Flag: *description:* red square with an equal-armed white cross in the center that does not extend to the edges of the flag
history: the origin of the flag is unclear, but a white cross was used to identify Swiss Confederation troops at the Battle of Laupen (1339)
note: in 1863, the newly formed International Red Cross chose the inverse of the Swiss flag – a red cross on a white field – as its symbol

National symbol(s): Swiss cross (white cross on red field)

National color(s): red, white

National anthem(s): *title:* the Swiss anthem has four names: "Schweizerpsalm" [German] "Cantique Suisse" [French] "Salmo svizzero," [Italian] "Psalm svizzer" [Romansch] (Swiss Psalm)
lyrics/music: Leonhard WIDMER [German], Charles CHATELANAT [French], Camillo VALSANGIACOMO [Italian], and Flurin CAMATHIAS [Romansch]/Alberik ZWYSSIG
history: adopted 1981; all four of the versions (German, French, Italian, Romansch) are considered official

National heritage: *total World Heritage Sites:* 13 (9 cultural, 4 natural)
selected World Heritage Site locales: Old City of Berne (c); Swiss Alps Jungfrau-Aletsch (n); Monte San Giorgio (n); Abbey of St Gall (c); Three Castles, Defensive Wall, and Ramparts of the Market-Town of Bellinzona (c); Rhaetian Railway in the Albula/Bernina Landscapes (c); La Chaux-de-Fonds/Le Locle, Watchmaking Town Planning (c); Prehistoric Pile Dwellings around the Alps (c); Benedictine Convent of St John at Müstair (c); Lavaux, Vineyard Terraces (c)

ECONOMY

Economic overview: high-income, non-EU European economy; top ten in GDP per capita; renowned banking and financial hub; low unemployment and inflation; slowed GDP growth post-pandemic; highly skilled but aging workforce; key pharmaceutical and precision manufacturing exporter; leader in innovation and competitiveness indices

Real GDP (purchasing power parity): $741.035 billion (2024 est.)
$731.508 billion (2023 est.)
$726.544 billion (2022 est.)
note: data in 2021 dollars
comparison ranking: 38

Real GDP growth rate: 1.3% (2024 est.)
0.7% (2023 est.)
3% (2022 est.)
note: annual GDP % growth based on constant local currency
comparison ranking: 168

Real GDP per capita: $82,000 (2024 est.)
$82,300 (2023 est.)
$82,800 (2022 est.)
note: data in 2021 dollars
comparison ranking: 10

GDP (official exchange rate): $936.564 billion (2024 est.)
note: data in current dollars at official exchange rate

Inflation rate (consumer prices): 1.1% (2024 est.)
2.1% (2023 est.)
2.8% (2022 est.)
note: annual % change based on consumer prices
comparison ranking: 26

GDP - composition, by sector of origin: *agriculture:* 0.6% (2024 est.)
industry: 24.7% (2024 est.)
services: 72% (2024 est.)
note: figures may not total 100% due to non-allocated consumption not captured in sector-reported data
comparison rankings: agriculture 186; industry 92; services 31

GDP - composition, by end use: *household consumption:* 51.1% (2023 est.)
government consumption: 11.3% (2023 est.)
investment in fixed capital: 25.8% (2023 est.)
investment in inventories: 0.2% (2023 est.)
exports of goods and services: 73.3% (2023 est.)
imports of goods and services: -62% (2023 est.)
note: figures may not total 100% due to rounding or gaps in data collection

Agricultural products: milk, sugar beets, wheat, potatoes, pork, apples, barley, beef, maize, grapes (2023)
note: top ten agricultural products based on tonnage

Industries: machinery, chemicals, watches, textiles, precision instruments, tourism, banking, insurance, pharmaceuticals

Industrial production growth rate: 1.7% (2024 est.)
note: annual % change in industrial value added based on constant local currency
comparison ranking: 106

Labor force: 5.153 million (2024 est.)
note: number of people ages 15 or older who are employed or seeking work
comparison ranking: 84

Unemployment rate: 4.2% (2024 est.)
4.1% (2023 est.)
4.2% (2022 est.)
note: % of labor force seeking employment
comparison ranking: 66

Youth unemployment rate (ages 15-24): *total:* 7.9% (2024 est.)
male: 8.3% (2024 est.)
female: 7.5% (2024 est.)
note: % of labor force ages 15-24 seeking employment

comparison ranking: total 139

Population below poverty line: 15.8% (2021 est.)
note: % of population with income below national poverty line

Gini Index coefficient - distribution of family income: 33.8 (2021 est.)
note: index (0-100) of income distribution; higher values represent greater inequality
comparison ranking: 88

Average household expenditures: *on food:* 9% of household expenditures (2023 est.)
on alcohol and tobacco: 3.5% of household expenditures (2023 est.)

Household income or consumption by percentage share: *lowest 10%:* 3% (2021 est.)
highest 10%: 26.6% (2021 est.)
note: % share of income accruing to lowest and highest 10% of population

Remittances: 0.4% of GDP (2024 est.)
0.4% of GDP (2023 est.)
0.4% of GDP (2022 est.)
note: personal transfers and compensation between resident and non-resident individuals/households/entities

Budget: *revenues:* $153.795 billion (2023 est.)
expenditures: $152.488 billion (2023 est.)
note: central government revenues (excluding grants) and expenditures converted to US dollars at average official exchange rate for year indicated

Public debt: 19.9% of GDP (2023 est.)
note: central government debt as a % of GDP
comparison ranking: 180

Taxes and other revenues: 9% (of GDP) (2023 est.)
note: central government tax revenue as a % of GDP
comparison ranking: 134

Current account balance: $47.162 billion (2024 est.)
$47.455 billion (2023 est.)
$72.325 billion (2022 est.)
note: balance of payments - net trade and primary/secondary income in current dollars
comparison ranking: 13

Exports: $675.059 billion (2024 est.)
$654.175 billion (2023 est.)
$628.737 billion (2022 est.)
note: balance of payments - exports of goods and services in current dollars
comparison ranking: 16

Exports - partners: Germany 14%, China 12%, USA 11%, Italy 5%, Turkey 5% (2023)
note: top five export partners based on percentage share of exports

Exports - commodities: gold, packaged medicine, vaccines, nitrogen compounds, base metal watches (2023)
note: top five export commodities based on value in dollars

Imports: $582.554 billion (2024 est.)
$556.351 billion (2023 est.)
$518.002 billion (2022 est.)
note: balance of payments - imports of goods and services in current dollars
comparison ranking: 15

Imports - partners: Germany 17%, USA 9%, Italy 8%, France 6%, China 5% (2023)
note: top five import partners based on percentage share of imports

Imports - commodities: gold, packaged medicine, vaccines, cars, jewelry (2023)
note: top five import commodities based on value in dollars

Reserves of foreign exchange and gold: $909.366 billion (2024 est.)
$863.892 billion (2023 est.)
$923.628 billion (2022 est.)
note: holdings of gold (year-end prices)/foreign exchange/special drawing rights in current dollars
comparison ranking: 4

Exchange rates: Swiss francs (CHF) per US dollar -

Exchange rates: 0.88 (2024 est.)
0.898 (2023 est.)
0.955 (2022 est.)
0.914 (2021 est.)
0.939 (2020 est.)

ENERGY

Electricity access: *electrification - total population:* 100% (2022 est.)

Electricity: *installed generating capacity:* 26.502 million kW (2023 est.)
consumption: 55.643 billion kWh (2023 est.)
exports: 33.856 billion kWh (2023 est.)
imports: 27.462 billion kWh (2023 est.)
transmission/distribution losses: 4.81 billion kWh (2023 est.)
comparison rankings: installed generating capacity 42; consumption 50; exports 6; imports 6; transmission/distribution losses 160

Electricity generation sources: *fossil fuels:* 0.6% of total installed capacity (2023 est.)
nuclear: 34.9% of total installed capacity (2023 est.)
solar: 6.6% of total installed capacity (2023 est.)
wind: 0.3% of total installed capacity (2023 est.)
hydroelectricity: 53% of total installed capacity (2023 est.)
biomass and waste: 4.7% of total installed capacity (2023 est.)

Nuclear energy: Number of operational nuclear reactors: 4 (2025)

Net capacity of operational nuclear reactors: 2.97GW (2025 est.)

Percent of total electricity production: 32.4% (2023 est.)

Number of nuclear reactors permanently shut down: 2 (2025)

Coal: *consumption:* 126,000 metric tons (2023 est.)
exports: 300 metric tons (2023 est.)
imports: 156,000 metric tons (2023 est.)

Petroleum: *total petroleum production:* 300 bbl/day (2023 est.)
refined petroleum consumption: 194,000 bbl/day (2024 est.)

Natural gas: *consumption:* 2.915 billion cubic meters (2023 est.)
imports: 2.869 billion cubic meters (2023 est.)

Energy consumption per capita: 99.578 million Btu/person (2023 est.)
comparison ranking: 50

COMMUNICATIONS

Telephones - fixed lines: *total subscriptions:* 3.003 million (2023 est.)
subscriptions per 100 inhabitants: 34 (2023 est.)
comparison ranking: total subscriptions 36

Telephones - mobile cellular: *total subscriptions:* 10.9 million (2023 est.)
subscriptions per 100 inhabitants: 120 (2022 est.)
comparison ranking: total subscriptions 92

Broadcast media: publicly owned Swiss Broadcasting Corporation (SRG/SSR) has 8 national TV networks, 3 broadcasting in German, 3 in French, and 2 in Italian; private commercial TV stations broadcast regionally and locally; German, Italian, and French TV broadcasts widely available via multi-channel cable and satellite TV; SRG/SSR has 17 radio stations (2019)

Internet country code: .ch

Internet users: *percent of population:* 97% (2023 est.)

Broadband - fixed subscriptions: *total:* 4.33 million (2023 est.)
subscriptions per 100 inhabitants: 49 (2023 est.)
comparison ranking: total 40

TRANSPORTATION

Civil aircraft registration country code prefix: HB

Airports: 66 (2025)
comparison ranking: 74

Heliports: 52 (2025)
comparison ranking: 39

Railways: *total:* 5,296 km (2020) 5,296 km electrified; Switzerland remains the only country with a fully electrified network

Merchant marine: *total:* 17 (2023)
by type: bulk carrier 14, general cargo 1, other 2 (includes Liechtenstein)
comparison ranking: total 149

MILITARY AND SECURITY

Military and security forces: Swiss Armed Forces (aka Swiss Army or Schweizer Armee); Army (aka Land Forces), Swiss Air Force (2025)
note: the federal police maintain internal security and report to the Federal Department of Justice and Police

Military expenditures: 0.7% of GDP (2024 est.)
0.7% of GDP (2023 est.)
0.7% of GDP (2022 est.)
0.7% of GDP (2021 est.)
0.7% of GDP (2020 est.)

Military and security service personnel strengths: approximately 145,000 Swiss Armed Forces (2024)
note: the strength figures include professional cadre (approximately 20,000 personnel), people awaiting or participating in mandatory annual training, and people who have already completed their training service obligation

Military equipment inventories and acquisitions: the military's inventory includes a mix of domestically produced and imported European and US weapons systems; the Swiss defense industry produces a range of military land vehicles (2024)

Military service age and obligation: 18-30 years of age for compulsory military service for men; 18 years of age for voluntary military service for men and women; every Swiss male has to serve at least 245 days in the armed forces; conscripts receive 18 weeks of mandatory training, followed by six 19-day intermittent recalls for training during the next 10 years (2024)
note: conscientious objectors can choose 390 days of community service instead of military service; as of 2023, women comprised about 1% of the active Swiss military

Military deployments: 175 Kosovo (NATO/KFOR) (2024)

Military - note: the Swiss military is responsible for territorial defense, limited support to international disaster response and peacekeeping, and providing support to civil authorities when their resources are not sufficient to ward off threats to internal security or provide sufficient relief during disasters; Switzerland has long maintained a policy of military neutrality but does periodically participate in EU, NATO, Organization for Security and Cooperation in Europe (OSCE), and UN military and peacekeeping operations; however, Swiss units will only participate in operations under the mandate of the UN or OSCE; Switzerland joined NATO's Partnership for Peace program in 1996; it has contributed to the NATO-led force in Kosovo (KFOR) since 1999 (2025)

TERRORISM

Terrorist group(s): Terrorist group(s): Islamic State of Iraq and ash-Sham (ISIS)

note: details about the history, aims, leadership, organization, areas of operation, tactics, targets, weapons, size, and sources of support of the group(s) appear(s) in Appendix T

TRANSNATIONAL ISSUES

Refugees and internally displaced persons: *refugees:* 213,177 (2024 est.)

IDPs: 97 (2024 est.)

stateless persons: 1,267 (2024 est.)

SYRIA

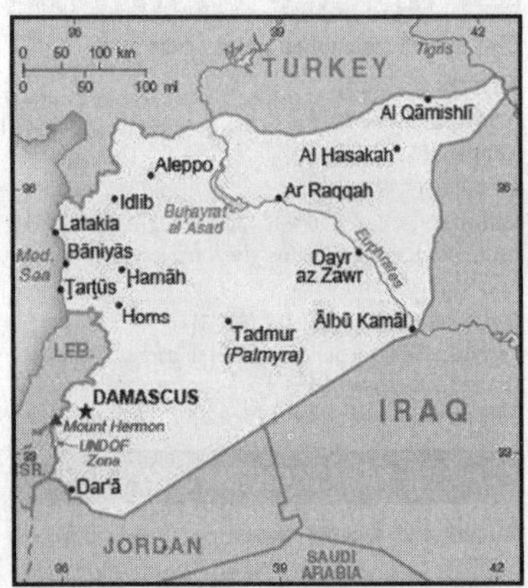

INTRODUCTION

Background: After World War I, France acquired a mandate over the northern portion of the former Ottoman Empire province of Syria. The French administered the area until granting it independence in 1946. The new country lacked political stability and experienced a series of military coups. Syria united with Egypt in 1958 to form the United Arab Republic. In 1961, the two entities separated, and the Syrian Arab Republic was reestablished. In the 1967 Arab-Israeli War, Syria lost control of the Golan Heights region to Israel. During the 1990s, Syria and Israel held occasional, albeit unsuccessful, peace talks over its return. In 1970, Hafiz al-ASAD, a member of the socialist Ba'ath Party and the minority Alawi sect, seized power in a bloodless coup and brought political stability to the country. Following the death of al-ASAD, his son, Bashar al-ASAD, was approved as president by popular referendum in 2000. Syrian troops that were stationed in Lebanon since 1976 in an ostensible peacekeeping role were withdrawn in 2005. During the 2006 conflict between Israel and Hizballah, Syria placed its military forces on alert but did not intervene directly on behalf of its ally Hizballah. In 2007, Bashar al-ASAD's second term as president was again approved in a referendum.

In the wake of major uprisings elsewhere in the region, antigovernment protests broke out in the southern province of Dar'a in 2011. Protesters called for the legalization of political parties, the removal of corrupt local officials, and the repeal of the restrictive Emergency Law allowing arrests without charge. Demonstrations and violent unrest spread across Syria, and the government responded with concessions, but also with military force and detentions that led to extended clashes and eventually civil war. International pressure on the Syrian Government intensified after 2011, as the Arab League, the EU, Turkey, and the US expanded economic sanctions against the ASAD regime and those entities that supported it. In 2012, more than 130 countries recognized the Syrian National Coalition as the sole legitimate representative of the Syrian people. In 2015, Russia launched a military intervention on behalf of the ASAD regime, and domestic and foreign-government-aligned forces recaptured swaths of territory from opposition forces. With foreign support, the regime continued to periodically regain opposition-held territory until 2020, when Turkish firepower halted a regime advance and forced a stalemate between regime and opposition forces. The government lacks territorial control over much of the northeastern part of the country, which the predominantly Kurdish Syrian Democratic Forces (SDF) hold, and a smaller area dominated by Turkey.

Since 2016, Turkey has conducted three large-scale military operations to capture territory along Syria's northern border. Some opposition forces organized under the Turkish-backed Syrian National Army and Turkish forces have maintained control of northwestern Syria along the Turkish border with the Afrin area of Aleppo Province since 2018. The violent extremist organization Hay'at Tahrir al-Sham (formerly the Nusrah Front) emerged in 2017 as the predominant opposition force in Idlib Province, and still dominates an area also hosting Turkish forces. Negotiations have failed to produce a resolution to the conflict, and the UN estimated in 2022 that at least 306,000 people have died during the civil war. Approximately 6.7 million Syrians were internally displaced as of 2022, and 14.6 million people were in need of humanitarian assistance across the country. An additional 5.6 million Syrians were registered refugees in Turkey, Jordan, Iraq, Egypt, and North Africa. The conflict in Syria remains one of the two largest displacement crises worldwide (the other is the full-scale invasion of Ukraine).

On 8 December 2024, Syrian Islamist rebels captured the capital city of Damascus and overthrew President Bashar al-ASAD. The former president and his family fled to Moscow, where they were granted political asylum. The al-ASAD regime had ruled Syria for over 50 years.

GEOGRAPHY

Location: Middle East, bordering the Mediterranean Sea, between Lebanon and Turkey

Geographic coordinates: 35 00 N, 38 00 E

Map references: Middle East

Area: *total:* 187,437 sq km
land: 185,887 sq km
water: 1,550 sq km
note: includes 1,295 sq km of Israeli-occupied territory
comparison ranking: total 89

Area - comparative: slightly more than 1.5 times the size of Pennsylvania

Land boundaries: *total:* 2,363 km
border countries (5): Iraq 599 km; Israel 83 km; Jordan 379 km; Lebanon 403 km; Turkey 899 km

Coastline: 193 km

Maritime claims: *territorial sea:* 12 nm
contiguous zone: 24 nm

Climate: mostly desert; hot, dry, sunny summers (June to August) and mild, rainy winters (December to February) along coast; cold weather with snow or sleet periodically in Damascus

Terrain: primarily semiarid and desert plateau; narrow coastal plain; mountains in west

Elevation: *highest point:* Mount Hermon (Jabal a-Shayk) 2,814 m
lowest point: Yarmuk River -66 m
mean elevation: 514 m

Natural resources: petroleum, phosphates, chrome and manganese ores, asphalt, iron ore, rock salt, marble, gypsum, hydropower

Land use: *agricultural land:* 73.5% (2022 est.)
arable land: 23.8% (2022 est.)
permanent crops: 5.6% (2022 est.)
permanent pasture: 44.1% (2022 est.)
forest: 2.8% (2022 est.)
other: 23.7% (2022 est.)

Irrigated land: 9,820 sq km (2022)

Major rivers (by length in km): Euphrates (shared with Turkey [s], Iran, and Iraq [m]) - 3,596 km; Tigris (shared with Turkey, Iran, and Iraq [m]) - 1,950 km
note: [s] after country name indicates river source; [m] after country name indicates river mouth

Major watersheds (area sq km): Indian Ocean drainage: *(Persian Gulf)* Tigris and Euphrates (918,044 sq km)

Population distribution: significant population density along the Mediterranean coast; larger concentrations found in the major cities of Damascus, Aleppo (the country's largest city), and Hims (Homs); more than half of the population lives in the coastal plain, the province of Halab, and the Euphrates River valley
note: the recent civil war has altered the population distribution

Natural hazards: dust storms, sandstorms
volcanism: Syria's two historically active volcanoes, Es Safa and an unnamed volcano near the Turkish border, have not erupted in centuries

Geography - note: the capital of Damascus is located at an oasis fed by the Barada River and is thought to be one of the world's oldest continuously inhabited cities; there are Israeli settlements and civilian land-use sites in the Israeli-controlled Golan Heights (2017)

PEOPLE AND SOCIETY

Population: *total:* 23,865,423 (2024 est.)
male: 11,981,578
female: 11,883,845
comparison rankings: total 57; male 57; female 58

Nationality: *noun:* Syrian(s)
adjective: Syrian

Ethnic groups: Arab ~50%, Alawite ~15%, Kurd ~10%, Levantine ~10%, other ~15% (includes Druze, Ismaili, Imami, Nusairi, Assyrian, Turkoman, Armenian)

Languages: Arabic (official), Kurdish, Armenian, Aramaic, Circassian, French, English
major-language sample(s):
كتاب حقائق العالم، المصدر الذي لا يمكن الاستغناء عنه للمعلومات الأساسية
(Arabic)
ڕاستییەکانی جیهان، باشترین سەرچاوەیە بۆ زانیارییە بنەڕەتییەکان
(Kurdish)
The World Factbook, the indispensable source for basic information.

Religions: Muslim 87% (official; includes Sunni 74% and Alawi, Ismaili, and Shia 13%), Christian 10% (includes Orthodox, Uniate, and Nestorian), Druze 3%
note: the Christian population may be considerably smaller as a result of Christians fleeing the country during the ongoing civil war

Age structure: *0-14 years:* 33% (male 4,037,493/female 3,828,777)
15-64 years: 62.8% (male 7,475,355/female 7,522,797)
65 years and over: 4.2% (2024 est.) (male 468,730/female 532,271)

Dependency ratios: *total dependency ratio:* 59.1 (2024 est.)
youth dependency ratio: 52.4 (2024 est.)
elderly dependency ratio: 6.7 (2024 est.)
potential support ratio: 15 (2024 est.)

Median age: *total:* 24.1 years (2024 est.)
male: 23.6 years
female: 24.7 years
comparison ranking: total 178

Population growth rate: 1.67% (2024 est.)
comparison ranking: 56

Birth rate: 21.7 births/1,000 population (2024 est.)
comparison ranking: 57

Death rate: 4 deaths/1,000 population (2024 est.)
comparison ranking: 214

Net migration rate: -1.1 migrant(s)/1,000 population (2024 est.)
comparison ranking: 147

Population distribution: significant population density along the Mediterranean coast; larger concentrations found in the major cities of Damascus, Aleppo (the country's largest city), and Hims (Homs); more than half of the population lives in the coastal plain, the province of Halab, and the Euphrates River valley
note: the recent civil war has altered the population distribution

Urbanization: *urban population:* 57.4% of total population (2023)
rate of urbanization: 5.38% annual rate of change (2020-25 est.)

Major urban areas - population: 2.585 million DAMASCUS (capital), 2.203 million Aleppo, 1.443 million Hims (Homs), 996,000 Hamah (2023)

Sex ratio: *at birth:* 1.06 male(s)/female
0-14 years: 1.05 male(s)/female
15-64 years: 0.99 male(s)/female
65 years and over: 0.88 male(s)/female
total population: 1.01 male(s)/female (2024 est.)

Maternal mortality ratio: 20 deaths/100,000 live births (2023 est.)
comparison ranking: 122

Infant mortality rate: *total:* 15.1 deaths/1,000 live births (2024 est.)
male: 16.6 deaths/1,000 live births
female: 13.5 deaths/1,000 live births
comparison ranking: total 92

Life expectancy at birth: *total population:* 74.8 years (2024 est.)
male: 73.4 years
female: 76.4 years
comparison ranking: total population 137

Total fertility rate: 2.69 children born/woman (2024 est.)
comparison ranking: 60

Gross reproduction rate: 1.31 (2024 est.)

Drinking water source: *improved: urban:* 95.6% of population (2022 est.)
rural: 92.1% of population (2022 est.)
total: 94.1% of population (2022 est.)
unimproved: urban: 4.4% of population (2022 est.)
rural: 7.9% of population (2022 est.)
total: 5.9% of population (2022 est.)

Health expenditure: 7.8% of national budget (2022 est.)

Physician density: 1.52 physicians/1,000 population (2021)

Hospital bed density: 1.4 beds/1,000 population (2021 est.)

Sanitation facility access: *improved: urban:* 99.8% of population (2022 est.)
rural: 99.3% of population (2022 est.)
total: 99.6% of population (2022 est.)
unimproved: urban: 0.2% of population (2022 est.)
rural: 0.7% of population (2022 est.)
total: 0.4% of population (2022 est.)

Obesity - adult prevalence rate: 27.8% (2016)
comparison ranking: 35

Alcohol consumption per capita: *total:* 0.13 liters of pure alcohol (2019 est.)
beer: 0.02 liters of pure alcohol (2019 est.)
wine: 0 liters of pure alcohol (2019 est.)
spirits: 0.11 liters of pure alcohol (2019 est.)
other alcohols: 0 liters of pure alcohol (2019 est.)
comparison ranking: total 176

Currently married women (ages 15-49): 52.6% (2023 est.)

Literacy: *total population:* 94% (2021 est.)
male: 97% (2021 est.)
female: 92% (2021 est.)

ENVIRONMENT

Environmental issues: deforestation; overgrazing; soil erosion; desertification; depletion of water resources; water pollution from raw sewage and petroleum refining wastes; inadequate potable water

International environmental agreements: *party to:* Biodiversity, Climate Change, Climate Change-Kyoto Protocol, Climate Change-Paris Agreement, Desertification, Endangered Species, Hazardous Wastes, Marine Dumping-London Convention, Nuclear Test Ban, Ozone Layer Protection, Ship Pollution, Wetlands
signed, but not ratified: Environmental Modification

Climate: mostly desert; hot, dry, sunny summers (June to August) and mild, rainy winters (December to February) along coast; cold weather with snow or sleet periodically in Damascus

Urbanization: *urban population:* 57.4% of total population (2023)
rate of urbanization: 5.38% annual rate of change (2020-25 est.)

Carbon dioxide emissions: 20.243 million metric tonnes of CO2 (2023 est.)
from coal and metallurgical coke: 33,000 metric tonnes of CO2 (2023 est.)
from petroleum and other liquids: 14.79 million metric tonnes of CO2 (2023 est.)
from consumed natural gas: 5.42 million metric tonnes of CO2 (2023 est.)
comparison ranking: total emissions 84

Particulate matter emissions: 25.3 micrograms per cubic meter (2019 est.)

Methane emissions: *energy:* 519.8 kt (2022-2024 est.)
agriculture: 144.7 kt (2019-2021 est.)
waste: 138 kt (2019-2021 est.)
other: 1.3 kt (2019-2021 est.)

Waste and recycling: *municipal solid waste generated annually:* 4.5 million tons (2024 est.)
percent of municipal solid waste recycled: 2.5% (2010 est.)

Total water withdrawal: *municipal:* 1.475 billion cubic meters (2022 est.)
industrial: 615.4 million cubic meters (2022 est.)
agricultural: 14.67 billion cubic meters (2022 est.)

Total renewable water resources: 16.802 billion cubic meters (2022 est.)

GOVERNMENT

Country name: *conventional long form:* Syrian Arab Republic
conventional short form: Syria
local long form: Al Jumhuriyah al Arabiyah as Suriyah
local short form: Suriyah
former: United Arab Republic (with Egypt)
etymology: the source of the name is uncertain; the name appears as "Suri" in Babylonian cuneiform writings dating from about 4000 B.C.

Government type: presidential republic; highly authoritarian regime

Capital: *name:* Damascus
geographic coordinates: 33 30 N, 36 18 E
time difference: UTC+3 (8 hours ahead of Washington, DC, during Standard Time)
etymology: the city has an ancient, pre-Semitic name of unknown origin

Administrative divisions: 14 provinces (*muhafazat*, singular - *muhafazah*); Al Hasakah, Al Ladhiqiyah (Latakia), Al Qunaytirah, Ar Raqqah, As Suwayda', Dar'a, Dayr az Zawr, Dimashq (Damascus), Halab (Aleppo), Hamah, Hims (Homs), Idlib, Rif Dimashq (Damascus Countryside), Tartus

Legal system: mixed system of civil and Islamic (sharia) law (for family courts)

Constitution: *history:* Syria's 2012 constitution was rescinded by the Hayat Tahrir al-Sham-led government in January 2025; in March 2025, interim authorities announced a transitional constitution to remain in effect for up to five years

International law organization participation: has not submitted an ICJ jurisdiction declaration; non-party state to the ICC

Citizenship: *citizenship by birth:* no
citizenship by descent only: the father must be a citizen of Syria; if the father is unknown or stateless, the mother must be a citizen of Syria
dual citizenship recognized: yes
residency requirement for naturalization: 10 years

Suffrage: 18 years of age; universal

Executive branch: *chief of state:* vacant; former President Bashar al-ASAD was overthrown by Islamist rebels on 8 December 2024; ASAD and his family flew to Moscow where they were granted political asylum
head of government: Prime Minister Muhammad al-BASHIR (since 8 December 2024) cabinet: Council of Ministers appointed by the president
election/appointment process: president directly elected by simple-majority popular vote for a 7-year term (eligible for a second term); the president appoints the vice president and prime minister
most recent election date: 26 May 2021
election results: *2021:* Bashar al-ASAD elected president; percent of vote - Bashar al-ASAD (Ba'th Party) 95.2%, Mahmoud Ahmad MAREI (Democratic Arab Socialist Union) 3.3%, other 1.5%
2014: Bashar al-ASAD elected president; percent of vote - Bashar al-ASAD (Ba'th Party) 88.7%, Hassan al-NOURI (independent) 4.3%, Maher HAJJER (independent) 3.2%, other/invalid 3.8%
expected date of next election: 2028

Legislative branch: *legislature name:* People's Assembly (Majlis Al-Chaab)
legislative structure: unicameral
number of seats: 250 (all directly elected)
electoral system: plurality/majority
scope of elections: full renewal
term in office: 4 years
most recent election date: 7/15/2024
percentage of women in chamber: 9.6%
expected date of next election: September 2025

Judicial branch: *highest court(s):* Court of Cassation (organized into civil, criminal, religious, and military divisions, each with 3 judges); Supreme Constitutional Court (consists of 7 members)
judge selection and term of office: Court of Cassation judges appointed by the Supreme Judicial Council (SJC), a judicial management body headed by the minister of justice with 7 members, including the national president; judge tenure NA; Supreme Constitutional Court judges nominated by the president and appointed by the SJC; judges serve 4-year renewable terms
subordinate courts: courts of first instance; magistrates' courts; religious and military courts; Economic Security Court; Counterterrorism Court

Political parties: *legal parties/alliances:* Arab Socialist Ba'ath Party
Arab Socialist (Ba'ath) Party – Syrian Regional
Arab Socialist Ba'ath Party – Syrian Regional Branch, Socialist Unionist Democratic Party
Arab Socialist Union of Syria or ASU
Democratic Arab Socialist Union
National Progressive Front or NPF
Socialist Unionist Democratic Party
Socialist Unionist Party
Syrian Communist Party (two branches)
Syrian Social Nationalist Party or SSNP
Unionist Socialist Party
major political organizations: Kurdish Democratic Union Party or PYD
Kurdish National Council or KNC
Syriac Union Party
Syrian Democratic Council or SDC
Syrian Democratic Party
Syrian Opposition Coalition
de facto governance entities: Democratic Autonomous Administration of Northeast Syria or DAANES
Syrian Interim Government or SIG
Syrian Salvation Government or SSG

Diplomatic representation in the US: none
note: operations at the embassy were suspended on 18 March 2014

Diplomatic representation from the US: *chief of mission:* Ambassador (vacant); note - on 6 February 2012, the US suspended operations at its embassy in Damascus; Czechia serves as a protecting power for US interests in Syria
mailing address: 6110 Damascus Place, Washington DC 20521-6110
email address and website: USIS_damascus@embassy.mzv.cz
https://sy.usembassy.gov/

International organization participation: ABEDA, AFESD, AMF, CAEU, FAO, G-24, G-77, IAEA, IBRD, ICAO, ICC (national committees), ICRM, ICSID, IDA, IDB, IFAD, IFC, IFRCS, IHO, ILO, IMF, IMO, Interpol, IOC, IPU, ISO, ITSO, ITU, LAS, MIGA, NAM, OAPEC, OIC, OPCW, UN, UNCTAD, UNESCO, UNIDO, UNRWA, UNWTO, UPU, WBG, WCO, WFTU (NGOs), WHO, WIPO, WMO, WTO (observer)

Independence: 17 April 1946 (from League of Nations mandate under French administration)

National holiday: Independence Day (Evacuation Day), 17 April (1946)
note: celebrates the last French troops departing and the proclamation of full independence

Flag: *description:* three equal horizontal bands of green (top), white, and black; three five-pointed red stars in a horizontal line, centered on the white band
meaning: the design is the same as a previous Syrian national flag (in use 1932-58 and 1961-63), but it is still unclear if the elements will retain the same meanings; the bands formerly represented Syria's past rulers: white (Umayyad Caliphate), black (Abbasid Caliphate), and green (Rashidun Caliphate); the first star represented Damascus, Aleppo, and Deir ez-Zor, the three administrative subdivisions in Syria in the 1930s; the second star stood for Jabal Druze (the Mountain of the Druze), and the third star for the Alawite Mountains
history: in 2011, opponents to the Asad regime adopted the flag; in 2025, it became the new national flag, replacing the two-star design

National symbol(s): northern bald ibis

National color(s): red, white, black, green

National anthem(s): *title:* "Humāt ad-Diyār (Guardians of the Homeland)
lyrics/music: Khalil Mardam BEY/Mohammad Salim FLAYFEL and Ahmad Salim FLAYFEL
history: adopted 1936, restored 1961; the country had a different anthem between 1958 and 1961, when Syria was part of the United Arab Republic

National heritage: *total World Heritage Sites:* 6 (all cultural)
selected World Heritage Site locales: Ancient City of Damascus; Ancient City of Bosra; Site of Palmyra; Ancient City of Aleppo; Crac des Chevaliers and Qal'at Salah El-Din; Ancient Villages of Northern Syria

ECONOMY

Economic overview: low-income Middle Eastern economy; prior infrastructure and economy devastated by 11-year civil war; ongoing US sanctions; sporadic trans-migration during conflict; currently being supported by World Bank trust fund; ongoing hyperinflation

Real GDP (purchasing power parity): $98.858 billion (2023 est.)
$100.066 billion (2022 est.)
$99.338 billion (2021 est.)
note: data in 2021 dollars
comparison ranking: 97

Real GDP growth rate: -1.2% (2023 est.)
0.7% (2022 est.)
1.9% (2021 est.)
note: annual GDP % growth based on constant local currency
comparison ranking: 201

Real GDP per capita: $4,200 (2023 est.)
$4,500 (2022 est.)
$4,600 (2021 est.)
note: data in 2021 dollars
comparison ranking: 179

GDP (official exchange rate): $19.993 billion (2023 est.)
note: data in current dollars at official exchange rate

Inflation rate (consumer prices): 94.1% (2022 est.)
98.3% (2021 est.)
114.2% (2020 est.)
note: annual % change based on consumer prices
comparison ranking: 210

GDP - composition, by sector of origin: *agriculture:* 43.1% (2022 est.)
industry: 12% (2022 est.)
services: 44.9% (2022 est.)
note: figures may not total 100% due to non-allocated consumption not captured in sector-reported data
comparison rankings: agriculture 1; industry 174; services 176

GDP - composition, by end use: *household consumption:* 114.8% (2022 est.)
government consumption: 2.7% (2022 est.)
investment in fixed capital: 4.5% (2022 est.)
exports of goods and services: 6.8% (2022 est.)
imports of goods and services: -28.8% (2022 est.)

note: figures may not total 100% due to rounding or gaps in data collection

Agricultural products: wheat, barley, milk, sheep milk, tomatoes, olives, potatoes, maize, oranges, grapes (2023)
note: top ten agricultural products based on tonnage

Industries: petroleum, textiles, food processing, beverages, tobacco, phosphate rock mining, cement, oil seeds crushing, automobile assembly

Industrial production growth rate: -13.4% (2022 est.)
note: annual % change in industrial value added based on constant local currency
comparison ranking: 189

Labor force: 6.617 million (2024 est.)
note: number of people ages 15 or older who are employed or seeking work
comparison ranking: 70

Unemployment rate: 13% (2024 est.)
13.2% (2023 est.)
13.3% (2022 est.)
note: % of labor force seeking employment
comparison ranking: 167

Youth unemployment rate (ages 15-24): *total:* 31.5% (2024 est.)
male: 27.8% (2024 est.)
female: 47.9% (2024 est.)
note: % of labor force ages 15-24 seeking employment
comparison ranking: total 20

Gini Index coefficient - distribution of family income: 26.6 (2022 est.)
note: index (0-100) of income distribution; higher values represent greater inequality
comparison ranking: 138

Household income or consumption by percentage share: *lowest 10%:* 3.8% (2022 est.)
highest 10%: 21.1% (2022 est.)
note: % share of income accruing to lowest and highest 10% of population

Remittances: 0% of GDP (2023 est.)
0% of GDP (2022 est.)
0% of GDP (2021 est.)
note: personal transfers and compensation between resident and non-resident individuals/households/entities

Budget: *revenues:* $1.162 billion (2017 est.)
expenditures: $3.211 billion (2017 est.)
note: government projections for FY2016

Exports: $1.609 billion (2022 est.)
$2.227 billion (2021 est.)
$1.649 billion (2020 est.)
note: GDP expenditure basis - exports of goods and services in current dollars
comparison ranking: 170

Exports - partners: Turkey 29%, Saudi Arabia 16%, Lebanon 10%, India 10%, UAE 5% (2023)
note: top five export partners based on percentage share of exports

Exports - commodities: olive oil, phosphates, spice seeds, cotton, tomatoes (2023)
note: top five export commodities based on value in dollars

Imports: $6.803 billion (2022 est.)
$6.56 billion (2021 est.)
$3.751 billion (2020 est.)
note: GDP expenditure basis - imports of goods and services in current dollars
comparison ranking: 143

Imports - partners: Turkey 49%, UAE 11%, China 8%, Egypt 7%, Lebanon 3% (2023)
note: top five import partners based on percentage share of imports

Imports - commodities: tobacco, plastics, wheat flours, plastic products, seed oils (2023)
note: top five import commodities based on value in dollars

Debt - external: $4.573 billion (2023 est.)
note: present value of external debt in current US dollars
comparison ranking: 74

Exchange rates: Syrian pounds (SYP) per US dollar -
Exchange rates: 2,505.747 (2022 est.)
1,256 (2021 est.)
877.945 (2020 est.)
436.5 (2019 est.)
436.5 (2018 est.)

ENERGY

Electricity access: *electrification - total population:* 89% (2022 est.)
electrification - urban areas: 100%
electrification - rural areas: 75%

Electricity: *installed generating capacity:* 9.636 million kW (2023 est.)
consumption: 15.522 billion kWh (2023 est.)
exports: 358.723 million kWh (2023 est.)
transmission/distribution losses: 4.214 billion kWh (2023 est.)
comparison rankings: installed generating capacity 67; consumption 86; exports 83; transmission/distribution losses 156

Electricity generation sources: *fossil fuels:* 95.6% of total installed capacity (2023 est.)
solar: 0.5% of total installed capacity (2023 est.)
hydroelectricity: 3.8% of total installed capacity (2023 est.)
biomass and waste: 0.2% of total installed capacity (2023 est.)

Coal: *consumption:* 15,000 metric tons (2023 est.)
imports: 15,000 metric tons (2023 est.)

Petroleum: *total petroleum production:* 65,000 bbl/day (2023 est.)
refined petroleum consumption: 102,000 bbl/day (2023 est.)
crude oil estimated reserves: 2.5 billion barrels (2021 est.)

Natural gas: *production:* 2.763 billion cubic meters (2023 est.)
consumption: 2.763 billion cubic meters (2023 est.)
proven reserves: 240.693 billion cubic meters (2021 est.)

Energy consumption per capita: 13.569 million Btu/person (2023 est.)
comparison ranking: 143

COMMUNICATIONS

Telephones - fixed lines: *total subscriptions:* 2.816 million (2023 est.)
subscriptions per 100 inhabitants: 12 (2023 est.)
comparison ranking: total subscriptions 39

Telephones - mobile cellular: *total subscriptions:* 15.1 million (2023 est.)
subscriptions per 100 inhabitants: 80 (2021 est.)
comparison ranking: total subscriptions 71

Broadcast media: state-run TV has 2 networks and 5 satellite channels; roughly two-thirds of homes have a satellite dish with access to foreign TV; 3 state-run radio channels; first private radio station launched in 2005; private radio broadcasters prohibited from transmitting news or political content (2018)

Internet country code: .sy

Internet users: *percent of population:* 35% (2019 est.)

Broadband - fixed subscriptions: *total:* 1.62 million (2023 est.)
subscriptions per 100 inhabitants: 7 (2023 est.)
comparison ranking: total 68

TRANSPORTATION

Civil aircraft registration country code prefix: YK

Airports: 42 (2025)
comparison ranking: 99

Heliports: 13 (2025)
comparison ranking: 63

Railways: *total:* 2,052 km (2014)
standard gauge: 1,801 km (2014) 1.435-m gauge
narrow gauge: 251 km (2014) 1.050-m gauge

Merchant marine: *total:* 24 (2023)
by type: bulk carrier 1, container ship 1, general cargo 8, oil tanker 1, other 13
comparison ranking: total 144

Ports: *total ports:* 3 (2024)
large: 1
medium: 1
small: 1
very small: 0
ports with oil terminals: 3
key ports: Al Ladhiqiyah, Baniyas, Tartus

MILITARY AND SECURITY

Military and security forces: the interim government authorities in Syria have established a Ministry of Defense and are attempting to unify the dozens of armed factions operating in Syria under a single, state-linked army; it has also established a Ministry of Interior to manage police and other security forces (2025)

Military expenditures: 6.5% of GDP (2019 est.)
6.7% of GDP (2018 est.)
6.8% of GDP (2017 est.)
6.9% of GDP (2016 est.)
7.2% of GDP (2015 est.)

Military and security service personnel strengths: not available

Military equipment inventories and acquisitions: prior to the fall of the ASAD regime in December 2024, the SAF was inventory was comprised mostly of Russian and Soviet-era weapons and equipment (2024)

Military service age and obligation: prior to the fall of the ASAD regime in December 2024, men 18-42 were obligated to perform military service; compulsory service obligation was up to 30 months; women were not conscripted but could volunteer to serve, including in combat arms (2024)

Military - note: as of September 2025, the government did not exercise control over all of Syria; areas of the northeast were under the control of ethnic Kurdish-led forces and areas south of the capital Damascus were controlled by members of the Druze

religious minority; Turkish forces remained in parts of the north, while Israeli forces had moved into formerly demilitarized areas between Syria and Israel and into some Syrian territory near the frontier
the UN Disengagement Observer Force (UNDOF) has operated in the Golan between Israel and Syria since 1974 to monitor the ceasefire following the 1973 Arab-Israeli War and supervise the areas of separation between the two countries; UNDOF has about 1,300 personnel (2025)

SPACE

Space agency/agencies: Syrian Space Agency (created in 2014); status is unclear since the fall of the ASAD Government (2025)

Space program overview: status unclear; has been handicapped by the impact of the civil war, including the loss of students and scientists who fled the country; had previously focused on satellite development and related space technologies, as well as scientific research; has relations with the space agency and space industries of Russia (2024)
note: further details about the key activities, programs, and milestones of the country's space program, as well as government spending estimates on the space sector, appear in the Space Programs reference guide

TERRORISM

Terrorist group(s): Terrorist group(s): Abdallah Azzam Brigades; Ansar al-Islam; Asa'ib Ahl Al-Haq; Hizballah; Hurras al-Din; Islamic Jihad Union; Islamic Revolutionary Guard Corps (IRGC)/Qods Force; Islamic State of Iraq and ash-Sham (ISIS); Kata'ib Hizballah; Kurdistan Workers' Party (PKK); al-Qa'ida; Palestine Liberation Front (PLF); Popular Front for the Liberation of Palestine (PFLP); PFLP-General Command (PLFP-GC)
note: details about the history, aims, leadership, organization, areas of operation, tactics, targets, weapons, size, and sources of support of the group(s) appear(s) in Appendix T

TRANSNATIONAL ISSUES

Refugees and internally displaced persons: *refugees:* 16,402 (2024 est.)

IDPs: 7,408,809 (2024 est.)
stateless persons: 160,000 (2024 est.)

Trafficking in persons: *tier rating:* Tier 3 — Syria does not fully meet the minimum standards for the elimination of trafficking and is not making significant efforts to do so, therefore, Syria remained on Tier 3; for more details, go to: https://www.state.gov/reports/2025-trafficking-in-persons-report/syria/

TAIWAN

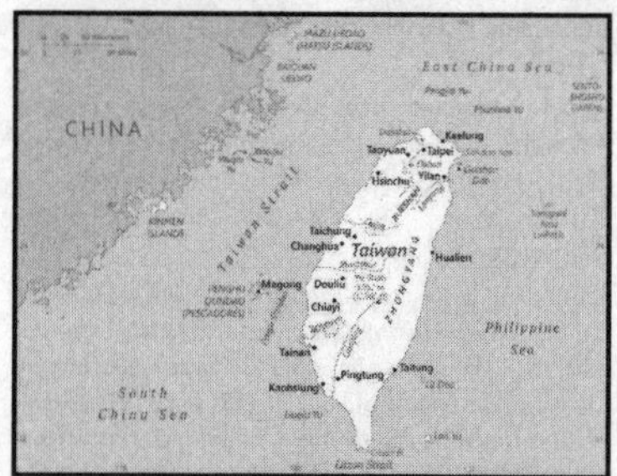

INTRODUCTION

Background: First inhabited by Austronesian people, Taiwan became home to Han immigrants beginning in the late Ming Dynasty (17th century). In 1895, military defeat forced China's Qing Dynasty to cede Taiwan to Japan, which then governed Taiwan for 50 years. Taiwan came under Chinese Nationalist (Kuomintang, KMT) control after World War II. With the communist victory in the Chinese civil war in 1949, the Nationalist-controlled Republic of China government and 2 million Nationalists fled to Taiwan and continued to claim to be the legitimate government for mainland China and Taiwan, based on a 1947 constitution drawn up for all of China. Until 1987, however, the Nationalist Government ruled Taiwan under a civil war martial law declaration dating to 1948. Beginning in the 1970s, Nationalist authorities gradually began to incorporate the native population into the governing structure beyond the local level.

The democratization process expanded rapidly in the 1980s, leading to the then-illegal founding of the Democratic Progressive Party (DPP), Taiwan's first opposition party, in 1986 and the lifting of martial law the following year. Taiwan held legislative elections in 1992, the first in over 40 years, and its first direct presidential election in 1996. In the 2000 presidential elections, Taiwan underwent its first peaceful transfer of power with the KMT loss to the DPP and afterwards experienced two additional democratic transfers of power in 2008 and 2016. Throughout this period, the island prospered and turned into one of East Asia's economic "Tigers," becoming a major investor in mainland China after 2000 as cross-Strait ties matured. The dominant political issues continue to be economic reform and growth, as well as management of sensitive relations between Taiwan and China.

GEOGRAPHY

Location: Eastern Asia, islands bordering the East China Sea, Philippine Sea, South China Sea, and Taiwan Strait, north of the Philippines, off the southeastern coast of China

Geographic coordinates: 23 30 N, 121 00 E

Map references: Southeast Asia

Area: *total:* 35,980 sq km
land: 32,260 sq km
water: 3,720 sq km
note: includes the Pescadores, Matsu, and Kinmen islands
comparison ranking: total 138

Area - comparative: slightly smaller than Maryland and Delaware combined

Land boundaries: *total:* 0 km

Coastline: 1,566.3 km

Maritime claims: *territorial sea:* 12 nm
exclusive economic zone: 200 nm

Climate: tropical; marine; rainy season during southwest monsoon (June to August); persistent and extensive cloudiness all year

Terrain: eastern two-thirds mostly rugged mountains; flat to gently rolling plains in west

Elevation: *highest point:* Yu Shan 3,952 m
lowest point: South China Sea 0 m
mean elevation: 1,150 m

Natural resources: small deposits of coal, natural gas, limestone, marble, asbestos, arable land

Land use: *agricultural land:* 22% (2022 est.)
arable land: 16.7% (2022 est.)
permanent crops: 5.4% (2022 est.)
permanent pasture: 0% (2022 est.)
forest: 0% (2022 est.)
other: 78% (2022 est.)

Irrigated land: 3,820 sq km (2012)

Population distribution: distribution exhibits a peripheral coastal settlement pattern, with the largest populations on the north and west coasts

Natural hazards: earthquakes; typhoons
volcanism: Kueishantao Island (401 m), east of Taiwan, is the only historically active volcano, but it has not erupted in centuries

Geography - note: strategic location adjacent to both the Taiwan Strait and the Luzon Strait

PEOPLE AND SOCIETY

Population: *total:* 23,595,274 (2024 est.)
male: 11,606,491
female: 11,988,783
comparison rankings: total 58; male 58; female 57

Nationality: *noun:* Taiwan (singular and plural)
adjective: Taiwan (or Taiwanese)
note: example - he or she is from Taiwan; they are from Taiwan

Ethnic groups: Han Chinese (including Holo, who compose approximately 70% of Taiwan's population, Hakka, and other groups originating in mainland China) more than 95%, indigenous Malayo-Polynesian peoples 2.3%
note 1: there are 16 officially recognized indigenous groups: Amis, Atayal, Bunun, Hla'alua, Kanakaravu, Kavalan, Paiwan, Puyuma, Rukai, Saisiyat, Sakizaya, Seediq, Thao, Truku, Tsou, and Yami; Amis, Paiwan, and Atayal are the largest and account for roughly 70% of the indigenous population
note 2: although not definitive, the majority of current genetic, archeological, and linguistic data support the theory that Taiwan is the ultimate source for the spread of humans across the Pacific to Polynesia; the expansion (ca. 3000 B.C. to A.D. 1200) took place via the Philippines and eastern Indonesia and reached Fiji and Tonga by about 900 B.C.; from there voyagers spread across the rest of the Pacific islands over the next two millennia

Languages: Mandarin (official), Min Nan, Hakka dialects, approximately 16 indigenous languages
major-language sample(s):
世界概況 – 不可缺少的基本消息來源 (Mandarin)

Religions: Buddhist 35.3%, Taoist 33.2%, Christian 3.9%, folk religion (includes Confucian) approximately 10%, none or unspecified 18.2% (2005 est.)

Age structure: *0-14 years:* 12.1% (male 1,472,059/female 1,391,031)
15-64 years: 69% (male 8,132,356/female 8,155,582)
65 years and over: 18.8% (2024 est.) (male 2,002,076/female 2,442,170)

Dependency ratios: *total dependency ratio:* 44.9 (2024 est.)
youth dependency ratio: 17.6 (2024 est.)
elderly dependency ratio: 27.3 (2024 est.)
potential support ratio: 3.7 (2024 est.)

Median age: *total:* 44.6 years (2024 est.)
male: 43.6 years
female: 45.5 years
comparison ranking: total 29

Population growth rate: 0.03% (2024 est.)
comparison ranking: 191

Birth rate: 7.3 births/1,000 population (2024 est.)
comparison ranking: 220

Death rate: 8.1 deaths/1,000 population (2024 est.)
comparison ranking: 88

Net migration rate: 1.1 migrant(s)/1,000 population (2024 est.)
comparison ranking: 66

Population distribution: distribution exhibits a peripheral coastal settlement pattern, with the largest populations on the north and west coasts

Urbanization: *urban population:* 80.1% of total population (2023)
rate of urbanization: 0.65% annual rate of change (2020-25 est.)

Major urban areas - population: 4.504 million New Taipei City, 2.754 million TAIPEI (capital), 2.319 million Taoyuan, 1.553 million Kaohsiung, 1.369 million Taichung, 863,000 Tainan (2023)

Sex ratio: *at birth:* 1.06 male(s)/female
0-14 years: 1.06 male(s)/female
15-64 years: 1 male(s)/female
65 years and over: 0.82 male(s)/female
total population: 0.97 male(s)/female (2024 est.)

Infant mortality rate: *total:* 3.8 deaths/1,000 live births (2024 est.)
male: 4.2 deaths/1,000 live births
female: 3.5 deaths/1,000 live births
comparison ranking: total 191

Life expectancy at birth: *total population:* 81.6 years (2024 est.)
male: 78.6 years
female: 84.7 years
comparison ranking: total population 43

Total fertility rate: 1.11 children born/woman (2024 est.)
comparison ranking: 227

Gross reproduction rate: 0.54 (2024 est.)

Currently married women (ages 15-49): 51% (2023 est.)

ENVIRONMENT

Environmental issues: air pollution; water pollution from industrial emissions, raw sewage; contamination of drinking water supplies; trade in endangered species; low-level radioactive waste disposal

Climate: tropical; marine; rainy season during southwest monsoon (June to August); persistent and extensive cloudiness all year

Urbanization: *urban population:* 80.1% of total population (2023)
rate of urbanization: 0.65% annual rate of change (2020-25 est.)

Carbon dioxide emissions: 289.109 million metric tonnes of CO2 (2023 est.)
from coal and metallurgical coke: 140.734 million metric tonnes of CO2 (2023 est.)
from petroleum and other liquids: 92.014 million metric tonnes of CO2 (2023 est.)
from consumed natural gas: 56.361 million metric tonnes of CO2 (2023 est.)
comparison ranking: total emissions 22

Waste and recycling: *municipal solid waste generated annually:* 7.336 million tons (2015 est.)
percent of municipal solid waste recycled: 13.8% (2022 est.)

Total renewable water resources: 67 cubic meters (2011)

GOVERNMENT

Country name: *conventional long form:* none
conventional short form: Taiwan
local long form: none
local short form: Taiwan
former: Formosa
etymology: the name may derive from the Chinese words *tai* (terrace) and *wan* (bay), referring to the island's terrain; in 1590, the Portuguese named it Formosa, meaning "beautiful"

Government type: semi-presidential republic

Capital: *name:* Taipei
geographic coordinates: 25 02 N, 121 31 E
time difference: UTC+8 (13 hours ahead of Washington, DC, during Standard Time)
etymology: the name means "Northern Taiwan," from the Chinese words *tai* (a short form of Taiwan) and *bei* (north), reflecting the city's position in the far north of the island

Administrative divisions: includes main island of Taiwan, plus smaller islands nearby and off coast of China's Fujian Province; Taiwan is divided into 13 counties (*xian*, singular and plural), 3 cities (*shi*, singular and plural), and 6 special municipalities directly under the jurisdiction of the Executive Yuan
counties: Changhua, Chiayi, Hsinchu, Hualien, Kinmen, Lienchiang, Miaoli, Nantou, Penghu, Pingtung, Taitung, Yilan, Yunlin
cities: Chiayi, Hsinchu, Keelung
special municipalities: Kaohsiung (city), New Taipei (city), Taichung (city), Tainan (city), Taipei (city), Taoyuan (city)
note: Taiwan uses a variety of romanization systems; a modified Wade-Giles system still dominates, but the city of Taipei has adopted a Pinyin romanization for street and place names; other local authorities use different romanization systems

Legal system: civil law system

Constitution: *history:* previous 1912, 1931; latest adopted 25 December 1946, promulgated 1 January 1947, effective 25 December 1947
amendment process: proposed by at least one fourth of the Legislative Yuan membership; passage requires approval by at least three-fourths majority vote of at least three fourths of the Legislative Yuan membership and approval in a referendum by more than half of eligible voters

International law organization participation: has not submitted an ICJ jurisdiction declaration; non-party state to the ICCt

Citizenship: *citizenship by birth:* no
citizenship by descent only: at least one parent must be a citizen of Taiwan
dual citizenship recognized: yes, except that citizens of Taiwan are not recognized as dual citizens of the People's Republic of China
residency requirement for naturalization: 5 years

Suffrage: 20 years of age; universal

Executive branch: *chief of state:* President LAI Ching-te (since 20 May 2024)
head of government: Premier CHO Jung-tai (President of the Executive Yuan) (since 20 May 2024)
cabinet: Executive Yuan; ministers appointed by president on recommendation of premier
election/appointment process: president and vice president directly elected on the same ballot by simple-majority popular vote for a 4-year term (eligible for a second term); premier appointed by the president; vice premiers appointed by the president on the recommendation of the premier
most recent election date: 13 January 2024
election results: 2024:LAI Ching-te elected president; percent of vote - LAI Ching-te (DPP) 40.1%, HOU Yu-ih (KMT) 33.5%, KO Wen-je (TPP) 26.5%)
2020: TSAI Ing-wen reelected president; percent of vote - TSAI Ing-wen (DPP) 57.1%, HAN Kuo-yu (KMT) 38.6%, James SOONG (PFP) 4.3%
expected date of next election: 2028

Legislative branch: *legislature name:* Legislative Yuan
legislative structure: unicameral
number of seats: 113 (directly elected)
electoral system: plurality/majority
scope of elections: full renewal
term in office: 4 years
most recent election date: 13 January 2024
parties elected and seats per party: Kuomintang (KMT) 52, Democratic Progressive Party (DPP) 51, Taiwan People's Party (TPP) 8, independent 2
percentage of women in chamber: 41.6%
expected date of next election: January 2028

Judicial branch: *highest court(s):* Supreme Court (consists of the court president, vice president, and approximately 100 judges organized into civil and criminal panels, each with a chief justice and 4 associate justices); Constitutional Court (consists of the court president, vice president, and 13 justices)
judge selection and term of office: Supreme Court justices appointed for life by the president; Constitutional Court justices appointed by the president, with approval of the Legislative Yuan, for 8-year terms, with half the membership renewed every 4 years
subordinate courts: high courts; district courts; hierarchy of administrative courts

Political parties: Democratic Progressive Party or DPP
Kuomintang or KMT (Nationalist Party)
Taiwan People's Party or TPP
note: the DPP and the KMT are the two major political parties; more than 30 parties garnered votes in the 2024 election

Diplomatic representation in the US: *chief of mission:* none

Taipei Economic and Cultural Offices (branch offices): Atlanta, Boston, Chicago, Denver (CO), Hagatna (Guam), Honolulu, Houston, Los Angeles, Miami, New York, San Francisco, Seattle, Washington DC

Note: *commercial and cultural relations with its citizens in the US are maintained through an unofficial instrumentality, the Taipei Economic and Cultural Representative Office in the United States (TECRO), a private nonprofit corporation that performs citizen and consular services similar to those at diplomatic posts, represented by Ambassador Alexander YUI (since 11 December 2023);* *office:* 4201 Wisconsin Avenue NW, Washington, DC 20016; telephone: [1] (202) 895-1800; fax: [1] (202) 363-0999

Diplomatic representation from the US: *chief of mission:* the US does not have an embassy in Taiwan; commercial and cultural relations with the people of Taiwan are maintained through an unofficial instrumentality, the American Institute in Taiwan (AIT), a private nonprofit corporation that performs citizen and consular services similar to those at diplomatic posts; it is managed by Director Raymond F. GREENE (since 8 July 2024)
mailing address: 4170 AIT Taipei Place, Washington DC 20521-4170
telephone: [886] 2-2162-2000
FAX: [886] 2-2162-2251
email address and website: TaipeiACS@state.gov
https://www.ait.org.tw/
branch office(s): American Institute in Taiwan
No. 100, Jinhu Road,
Neihu District 11461, Taipei City
other offices: Kaohsiung (Branch Office)

International organization participation: ADB (Chinese Taipei), APEC (Chinese Taipei), BCIE, CABEI, IOC, ITUC (NGOs), SICA (observer), WTO (Chinese Taipei)
note: separate customs territory of Taiwan, Penghu, Kinmen, and Matsu

National holiday: Republic Day (National Day), 10 October (1911)
note: celebrates the anniversary of the Chinese Revolution, also known as Double Ten (10-10) Day

Flag: *description:* red field with a dark blue rectangle in the upper-left corner, bearing a white sun with 12 triangular rays
meaning: blue stands for liberty, justice, and democracy; red for fraternity, sacrifice, and nationalism; white for equality, frankness, and the people's livelihood; the 12 rays represent the months of the year and the traditional Chinese hours (each ray equals two hours)
history: the blue-and-white design of the canton (symbolizing the sun of progress) dates to 1895
note: similar to the flag of Samoa

National symbol(s): white sun with 12 rays on a blue field

National color(s): blue, white, red

National anthem(s): *title:* "Zhonghua Minguo guoge" (National Anthem of the Republic of China)
lyrics/music: HU Han-min, TAI Chi-t'ao, and LIAO Chung-k'ai/CHENG Mao-yun

history: adopted 1937; also the song of the Kuomintang Party; informally known as "San Min Chu I" or "San Min Zhu Yi" (Three Principles of the People); the anthem is banned from performance in mainland China, Hong Kong, and Macau

ECONOMY

Economic overview: high-income East Asian economy; most technologically advanced computer microchip manufacturing; increasing Chinese interference threatens market capabilities; minimum wages rising; longstanding regional socioeconomic inequality

Real GDP (purchasing power parity): $1.743 trillion (2023 est.)
$1.664 trillion (2022 est.)
$1.512 trillion (2021 est.)
comparison ranking: 19

Real GDP growth rate: 1.28% (2023 est.)
2.59% (2022 est.)
6.62% (2021 est.)
note: annual GDP % growth based on constant local currency
comparison ranking: 169

Real GDP per capita: $32,300 (2023 est.)
$32,600 (2022 est.)
$32,900 (2021 est.)
note: data are in current dollars
comparison ranking: 73

GDP (official exchange rate): $611.391 billion (2023 est.)
note: data in current dollars at official exchange rate

Inflation rate (consumer prices): 2.2% (2024 est.)
2.5% (2023 est.)
2.9% (2022 est.)
note: annual % change based on consumer prices
comparison ranking: 59

GDP - composition, by end use: *household consumption:* 48.3% (2023 est.)
government consumption: 13.3% (2023 est.)
investment in fixed capital: 23.7% (2023 est.)
investment in inventories: -0.6% (2023 est.)
exports of goods and services: 64% (2023 est.)
imports of goods and services: -49.1% (2023 est.)

Agricultural products: rice, vegetables, pork, chicken, cabbages, milk, sugarcane, tropical fruits, pineapples, eggs (2023)
note: top ten agricultural products based on tonnage

Industries: electronics, communications and information technology products, petroleum refining, chemicals, textiles, iron and steel, machinery, cement, food processing, vehicles, consumer products, pharmaceuticals

Unemployment rate: 3.4% (2024 est.)
3.5% (2023 est.)
3.7% (2022 est.)
note: % of labor force seeking employment
comparison ranking: 54

Gini Index coefficient - distribution of family income: 33.9 (2023 est.)
note: index (0-100) of income distribution; higher values represent greater inequality
comparison ranking: 87

Average household expenditures: *on food:* 13.8% of household expenditures (2023 est.)
on alcohol and tobacco: 2.5% of household expenditures (2023 est.)

Budget: *revenues:* $94.943 billion (2019 est.)
expenditures: $105.833 billion (2019 est.)

Public debt: 35.7% of GDP (2017 est.)
note: data for central government
comparison ranking: 150

Current account balance: $105.076 billion (2023 est.)
$101.032 billion (2022 est.)
$118.298 billion (2021 est.)
note: balance of payments - net trade and primary/secondary income in current dollars
comparison ranking: 5

Exports: $432.432 billion (2023 est.)
$479.415 billion (2022 est.)
$446.371 billion (2021 est.)
note: figures complied according to the General Trade System - exports of goods and services in current dollars
comparison ranking: 22

Exports - partners: China 20%, USA 17%, Hong Kong 13%, Singapore 9%, Japan 7% (2023)
note: top five export partners based on percentage share of exports

Exports - commodities: integrated circuits, machine parts, broadcasting equipment, computers, plastics (2023)
note: top five export commodities based on value in dollars

Imports: $351.441 billion (2023 est.)
$428.083 billion (2022 est.)
$381.958 billion (2021 est.)
note: figures complied according to the General Trade System - imports of goods and services in current dollars
comparison ranking: 26

Imports - partners: China 21%, Japan 13%, USA 11%, S. Korea 9%, Australia 5% (2023)
note: top five import partners based on percentage share of imports

Imports - commodities: integrated circuits, crude petroleum, machinery, natural gas, coal (2023)
note: top five import commodities based on value in dollars

Exchange rates: New Taiwan dollars (TWD) per US dollar -

Exchange rates: 32.108 (2024 est.)
31.15 (2023 est.)
29.777 (2022 est.)
28.022 (2021 est.)
28.211 (2020 est.)

ENERGY

Electricity: *installed generating capacity:* 64.535 million kW (2023 est.)
consumption: 270.648 billion kWh (2023 est.)
transmission/distribution losses: 7.907 billion kWh (2023 est.)
comparison rankings: installed generating capacity 23; consumption 18; transmission/distribution losses 175

Electricity generation sources: *fossil fuels:* 84.2% of total installed capacity (2023 est.)
nuclear: 6.4% of total installed capacity (2023 est.)
solar: 4.6% of total installed capacity (2023 est.)
wind: 2.2% of total installed capacity (2023 est.)
hydroelectricity: 1.2% of total installed capacity (2023 est.)
biomass and waste: 1.3% of total installed capacity (2023 est.)

Nuclear energy: Number of operational nuclear reactors: 1 (2025)

Net capacity of operational nuclear reactors: 0.94GW (2025 est.)

Percent of total electricity production: 6.9% (2023 est.)

Number of nuclear reactors permanently shut down: 5 (2025)

Coal: *production:* 5.212 million metric tons (2023 est.)
consumption: 64.609 million metric tons (2023 est.)
exports: 47,000 metric tons (2023 est.)
imports: 58.15 million metric tons (2023 est.)
proven reserves: 1 million metric tons (2023 est.)

Petroleum: *total petroleum production:* 800 bbl/day (2023 est.)
refined petroleum consumption: 954,000 bbl/day (2023 est.)
crude oil estimated reserves: 2.38 million barrels (2021 est.)

Natural gas: *production:* 60.761 million cubic meters (2023 est.)
consumption: 27.222 billion cubic meters (2023 est.)
imports: 26.997 billion cubic meters (2023 est.)
proven reserves: 6.23 billion cubic meters (2021 est.)

Energy consumption per capita: 206.102 million Btu/person (2023 est.)
comparison ranking: 18

COMMUNICATIONS

Telephones - fixed lines: *total subscriptions:* 10 million (2023 est.)
subscriptions per 100 inhabitants: 43 (2023 est.)
comparison ranking: total subscriptions 17

Telephones - mobile cellular: *total subscriptions:* 30 million (2023 est.)
subscriptions per 100 inhabitants: 128 (2023 est.)
comparison ranking: total subscriptions 48

Broadcast media: 5 national TV networks with about 22 stations; over 300 satellite TV channels available; about half of households use multi-channel cable TV; almost all subscribe to digital cable TV; national and regional radio networks with about 171 radio stations (2023)

Internet country code: .tw

Internet users: *percent of population:* 90% (2021 est.)

Broadband - fixed subscriptions: *total:* 5,831,470 (2019 est.)
subscriptions per 100 inhabitants: 25 (2019 est.)
comparison ranking: total 33

TRANSPORTATION

Civil aircraft registration country code prefix: B

Airports: 57 (2025)
comparison ranking: 80

Heliports: 56 (2025)
comparison ranking: 36

Railways: *total:* 1,613.1 km (2018)
standard gauge: 345 km (2018) 1.435-m gauge (345 km electrified)
narrow gauge: 1,118.1 km (2018) 1.067-m gauge (793.9 km electrified)
150 0.762-m gauge note: the 0.762-gauge track belongs to three entities: the Forestry Bureau, Taiwan Cement, and TaiPower

Merchant marine: *total:* 465 (2023)

by type: bulk carrier 29, container ship 53, general cargo 58, oil tanker 35, other 290
comparison ranking: total 44

Ports: *total ports:* 8 (2024)
large: 1
medium: 3
small: 2
very small: 2
ports with oil terminals: 8
key ports: Chi-Lung, Hua-Lien Kang, Kao-Hsiung, Su-Ao

MILITARY AND SECURITY

Military and security forces: Taiwan Armed Forces: Army, Navy (includes Marine Corps), Air Force

Ocean Affairs Council: Coast Guard Administration (CGA)

Ministry of Interior: National Police (2025)
note: the CGA is a law enforcement organization with homeland security functions during peacetime and national defense missions during wartime

Military expenditures: 2.4% of GDP (2024 est.)
2.5% of GDP (2023 est.)
2.1% of GDP (2022 est.)
2.1% of GDP (2021 est.)
2.1% of GDP (2020 est.)

Military and security service personnel strengths: approximately 180,000 active-duty Armed Forces (95,000 Army; 45,000 Navy, including approximately 10,000 marines; 40,000 Air Force) (2025)
note: the military is comprised of both volunteers and conscripts; the conscripts serve 4-month tours, or 12 months for those born in 2005 and after; as of mid-2024, there were reportedly about 153,000 volunteer personnel serving in Taiwan's armed forces; in 2025, the military is expected to conscript about 75,000 men; Taiwan aims to maintain a military of about 215,000 plus reservists; Taiwan trains about 120,000 reservists annually, but in 2022 announced intentions to increase that figure to 260,000

Military equipment inventories and acquisitions: the Taiwan military's inventory is a mix of domestically produced items and equipment acquired from the US, either as secondhand or direct acquisitions; Taiwan's domestic defense industry produces weapons systems such as aircraft, armored vehicles, missiles, and naval platforms (2024)

Military service age and obligation: men 18-36 years of age may volunteer or must complete 12 months of compulsory military service; civil service can be substituted for military service in some cases; women may enlist but are restricted to noncombat roles in most cases (2024)
note 1: in January 2024, Taiwan extended compulsory service from 4 to 12 months for men born in 2005 and thereafter
note 2: as of 2023, women made up about 15% of the active-duty military

Military - note: the military's primary responsibility is external security, including the defense of the country's sovereignty and territory, and the protection of Taiwan's air space, maritime claims, and sea lines of communication; its main focus is the challenge posed by the People's Republic of China
the US Taiwan Relations Act of April 1979 states that the US shall provide Taiwan with arms of a defensive character and shall maintain the capacity of the US to resist any resort to force or other forms of coercion that would jeopardize the security, or social or economic system, of the people of Taiwan (2025)

SPACE

Space agency/agencies: Taiwan Space Agency (TASA; renamed and reorganized in 2023 from the former National Space Program Organization or NSPO, which was established in 1991) (2025)

Space launch site(s): sounding rockets launched from Jui Peng Air Base (Pingtung); has announced intentions to build a future national space port on the southeast coast (Pingtung) (2025)

Space program overview: has had a formal national space development program since the early 1990s with a focus on the acquisition of satellites and the development of independent space capabilities, such as rocket manufacturing and satellite launch services; manufactures and operates satellites; manufactures and tests sounding rockets; researching and developing other space technologies, including remote sensing, telecommunications, small satellites, satellite payloads and ground station components, spacecraft components, navigational control, and rocket propulsion systems; has bi-lateral relations with the space programs of France, India, Japan, Paraguay, Poland, the UK, and the US; has a commercial space industry that provides components and expertise for TASA and is independently developing satellites and a small satellite launch vehicle; the government passed a space promotion act in 2021 encouraging private investment in the space industry (2025)
note: further details about the key activities, programs, and milestones of the country's space program, as well as government spending estimates on the space sector, appear in the Space Programs reference guide

TRANSNATIONAL ISSUES

Refugees and internally displaced persons: IDPs: 380 (2024 est.)

Illicit drugs: USG identification: major precursor-chemical producer (2025)

TAJIKISTAN

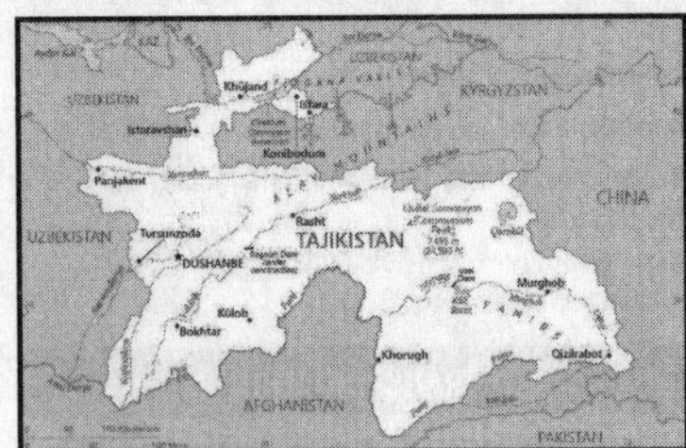

INTRODUCTION

Background: The Tajik people came under Russian imperial rule in the 1860s and 1870s, but Russia's hold on Central Asia weakened following the Revolution of 1917. At that time, bands of indigenous guerrillas (known as "basmachi") fiercely contested Bolshevik control of the area, which was not fully reestablished until 1925. Tajikistan was first established as an autonomous Soviet Socialist Republic within the Uzbek Soviet Socialist Republic in 1924, but in 1929 the Soviet Union made Tajikistan as a separate republic and transferred to it much of present-day Sughd Province. Ethnic Uzbeks form a substantial minority in Tajikistan, and ethnic Tajiks an even larger minority in Uzbekistan. Tajikistan became independent in 1991 after the breakup of the Soviet Union, and the country experienced a civil war among political, regional, and religious factions from 1992 to 1997.

Despite Tajikistan's general elections for both the presidency (once every seven years) and legislature (once every five years), observers note an electoral system rife with irregularities and abuse, and results that are neither free nor fair. President Emomali RAHMON, who came to power in 1992 during the civil war and was first elected president in 1994, used an attack planned by a disaffected deputy defense minister in 2015 to ban the last major opposition party in Tajikistan. RAHMON further strengthened his position by having himself declared "Founder of Peace and National Unity, Leader of the Nation," with limitless terms and lifelong immunity through constitutional amendments ratified in a referendum. The referendum also lowered the minimum age required to run for president from 35 to 30, which made RAHMON's first-born son Rustam EMOMALI, the mayor of the capital city of Dushanbe, eligible to run for president in 2020. RAHMON orchestrated EMOMALI's selection in 2020 as chairman of the Majlisi Milli (the upper chamber of Tajikistan's parliament), positioning EMOMALI as next in line of succession for the presidency. RAHMON opted to run in the presidential election later that year and received 91% of the vote.

The country remains the poorest of the former Soviet republics. Tajikistan became a member of the WTO in 2013, but its economy continues to face major challenges, including dependence on remittances from Tajikistani migrant laborers in Russia and Kazakhstan, pervasive corruption, the opiate trade, and destabilizing violence emanating from neighboring Afghanistan. Tajikistan has endured several domestic security incidents since 2010, including armed conflict between government forces and local strongmen in the Rasht Valley and between government forces and informal leaders in Gorno-Badakhshan Autonomous Oblast. Tajikistan suffered its first ISIS-claimed attack in 2018, when assailants attacked a group of Western bicyclists, killing four. Friction between forces on the border between Tajikistan and the Kyrgyz Republic flared up in 2021, culminating in fatal clashes between border forces in 2021 and 2022.

GEOGRAPHY

Location: Central Asia, west of China, south of Kyrgyzstan

Geographic coordinates: 39 00 N, 71 00 E

Map references: Asia

Area: *total:* 144,100 sq km
land: 141,510 sq km
water: 2,590 sq km
comparison ranking: total 96

Area - comparative: slightly smaller than Wisconsin

Land boundaries: *total:* 4,130 km
border countries (4): Afghanistan 1,357 km; China 477 km; Kyrgyzstan 984 km; Uzbekistan 1,312 km

Coastline: 0 km (landlocked)

Maritime claims: none (landlocked)

Climate: mid-latitude continental, hot summers, mild winters; semiarid to polar in Pamir Mountains

Terrain: mountainous region dominated by the Alay Mountains in the north and the Pamirs in the southeast; western Fergana Valley in north, Kofirnihon and Vakhsh Valleys in southwest

Elevation: *highest point:* Qullai Somoniyon 7,495 m
lowest point: Syr Darya (Sirdaryo) 300 m
mean elevation: 3,186 m

Natural resources: hydropower, some petroleum, uranium, mercury, brown coal, lead, zinc, antimony, tungsten, silver, gold

Land use: *agricultural land:* 28.1% (2022 est.)
arable land: 6% (2022 est.)
permanent crops: 1.7% (2022 est.)
permanent pasture: 20.3% (2022 est.)
forest: 3.1% (2022 est.)
other: 68.9% (2022 est.)

Irrigated land: 5,681 sq km (2022)

Major rivers (by length in km): Syr Darya (shared with Kyrgyzstan [s], Uzbekistan, and Kazakhstan [m]) - 3,078 km; Amu Darya river source (shared with Turkmenistan, Afghanistan, and Uzbekistan [m]) - 2,620 km
note: [s] after country name indicates river source; [m] after country name indicates river mouth

Major watersheds (area sq km): Internal (endorheic basin) drainage: Tarim Basin (1,152,448 sq km), *(Aral Sea Basin)* Amu Darya (534,739 sq km), Syr Darya (782,617 sq km)

Population distribution: the population is concentrated at lower elevations, with perhaps as many as 90% living in valleys; overall density increases from east to west

Natural hazards: earthquakes; floods

Geography - note: landlocked; highest point, Qullai Ismoili Somoni (formerly Communism Peak), was the tallest mountain in the former USSR

PEOPLE AND SOCIETY

Population: *total:* 10,394,063 (2024 est.)
male: 5,221,818
female: 5,172,245
comparison rankings: total 91; male 91; female 92

Nationality: *noun:* Tajikistani(s)
adjective: Tajikistani

Ethnic groups: Tajik 84.3% (includes Pamiri and Yagnobi), Uzbek 13.8%, other 2% (includes Kyrgyz, Russian, Turkmen, Tatar, Arab) (2014 est.)

Languages: Tajik (official) 84.4%, Uzbek 11.9%, Kyrgyz 0.8%, Russian 0.5%, other 2.4% (2010 est.)
major-language sample(s):
Китоби Фактҳои Ҷаҳонӣ, манбаи бебадали маълумоти асосӣ (Tajik)
note: Russian widely used in government and business

Religions: Muslim 98% (Sunni 95%, Shia 3%) other 2% (2014 est.)

Age structure: *0-14 years:* 36.9% (male 1,953,472/ female 1,877,192)
15-64 years: 59.3% (male 3,086,964/female 3,071,642)
65 years and over: 3.9% (2024 est.) (male 181,382/ female 223,411)

Dependency ratios: *total dependency ratio:* 68.8 (2024 est.)
youth dependency ratio: 62.2 (2024 est.)
elderly dependency ratio: 6.6 (2024 est.)
potential support ratio: 15.2 (2024 est.)

Median age: *total:* 22.8 years (2024 est.)
male: 22.3 years
female: 23.2 years
comparison ranking: total 181

Population growth rate: 1.92% (2024 est.)
comparison ranking: 42

Birth rate: 25.8 births/1,000 population (2024 est.)
comparison ranking: 42

Death rate: 4.7 deaths/1,000 population (2024 est.)
comparison ranking: 205

Net migration rate: -2 migrant(s)/1,000 population (2024 est.)
comparison ranking: 167

Population distribution: the population is concentrated at lower elevations, with perhaps as many as 90% living in valleys; overall density increases from east to west

Urbanization: *urban population:* 28.2% of total population (2023)
rate of urbanization: 2.73% annual rate of change (2020-25 est.)

Major urban areas - population: 987,000 DUSHANBE (capital) (2023)

Sex ratio: *at birth:* 1.05 male(s)/female
0-14 years: 1.04 male(s)/female
15-64 years: 1 male(s)/female
65 years and over: 0.81 male(s)/female
total population: 1.01 male(s)/female (2024 est.)
Mother's mean age at first birth
23.2 years (2017 est.)

Maternal mortality ratio: 14 deaths/100,000 live births (2023 est.)
comparison ranking: 141

Infant mortality rate: *total:* 21.7 deaths/1,000 live births (2024 est.)
male: 24.3 deaths/1,000 live births
female: 18.9 deaths/1,000 live births
comparison ranking: total 73

Life expectancy at birth: *total population:* 71.9 years (2024 est.)
male: 70.1 years
female: 73.8 years
comparison ranking: total population 167

Total fertility rate: 3.56 children born/woman (2024 est.)
comparison ranking: 31

Gross reproduction rate: 1.73 (2024 est.)

Drinking water source: *improved: urban:* 95.6% of population (2022 est.)
rural: 76.6% of population (2022 est.)
total: 81.9% of population (2022 est.)
unimproved: urban: 4.4% of population (2022 est.)
rural: 23.4% of population (2022 est.)
total: 18.1% of population (2022 est.)

Health expenditure: 8% of GDP (2021)
6.4% of national budget (2022 est.)

Physician density: 1.87 physicians/1,000 population (2023)

Hospital bed density: 4.3 beds/1,000 population (2021 est.)

Sanitation facility access: *improved: urban:* 98.9% of population (2022 est.)
rural: 99.6% of population (2022 est.)
total: 99.4% of population (2022 est.)
unimproved: urban: 1.1% of population (2022 est.)
rural: 0.4% of population (2022 est.)
total: 0.6% of population (2022 est.)

Obesity - adult prevalence rate: 14.2% (2016)
comparison ranking: 128

Alcohol consumption per capita: *total:* 0.85 liters of pure alcohol (2019 est.)
beer: 0.38 liters of pure alcohol (2019 est.)
wine: 0.01 liters of pure alcohol (2019 est.)
spirits: 0.45 liters of pure alcohol (2019 est.)
other alcohols: 0 liters of pure alcohol (2019 est.)
comparison ranking: total 156

Children under the age of 5 years underweight: 7.6% (2017)
comparison ranking: 58

Currently married women (ages 15-49): 72% (2023 est.)

Child marriage: *women married by age 15:* 0.1% (2017)
women married by age 18: 8.7% (2017)

Education expenditure: 5.4% of GDP (2023 est.)
19.7% national budget (2023 est.)
comparison ranking: Education expenditure (% GDP) 48

Literacy: *female:* 94.6% (2017 est.)

School life expectancy (primary to tertiary education): *total:* 12 years (2024 est.)
male: 12 years (2024 est.)
female: 11 years (2024 est.)

ENVIRONMENT

Environmental issues: air pollution from motor vehicles and industry; water pollution from agricultural runoff and untreated industrial waste and sewage; poor management of water resources; soil erosion; increasing levels of soil salinity

International environmental agreements: *party to:* Biodiversity, Climate Change, Climate Change-Kyoto Protocol, Climate Change-Paris Agreement, Comprehensive Nuclear Test Ban, Desertification, Endangered Species, Environmental Modification, Hazardous Wastes, Ozone Layer Protection, Ship Pollution, Wetlands
signed, but not ratified: none of the selected agreements

Climate: mid-latitude continental, hot summers, mild winters; semiarid to polar in Pamir Mountains

Urbanization: *urban population:* 28.2% of total population (2023)
rate of urbanization: 2.73% annual rate of change (2020-25 est.)

Carbon dioxide emissions: 8.616 million metric tonnes of CO2 (2023 est.)

from coal and metallurgical coke: 4.676 million metric tonnes of CO2 (2023 est.)
from petroleum and other liquids: 3.855 million metric tonnes of CO2 (2023 est.)
from consumed natural gas: 86,000 metric tonnes of CO2 (2023 est.)
comparison ranking: total emissions 114

Particulate matter emissions: 53.8 micrograms per cubic meter (2019 est.)

Waste and recycling: *municipal solid waste generated annually:* 1.787 million tons (2024 est.)
percent of municipal solid waste recycled: 13.9% (2022 est.)

Total water withdrawal: *municipal:* 912 million cubic meters (2022 est.)
industrial: 1.61 billion cubic meters (2022 est.)
agricultural: 7.378 billion cubic meters (2022 est.)

Total renewable water resources: 21.91 billion cubic meters (2022 est.)

GOVERNMENT

Country name: *conventional long form:* Republic of Tajikistan
conventional short form: Tajikistan
local long form: Jumhurii Tojikiston
local short form: Tojikiston
former: Tajik Soviet Socialist Republic
etymology: the Persian suffix *-ostan* means "land," so the country name means "Land of the Tajik [people];" the name Tajik comes from the Sanskrit *tajika*, a name originally used to distinguish Arabs from Turks and derived from the Tay, an Arab people

Government type: presidential republic

Capital: *name:* Dushanbe
geographic coordinates: 38 33 N, 68 46 E
time difference: UTC+5 (10 hours ahead of Washington, DC, during Standard Time)
etymology: the name means Monday in Persian; today's city was originally at the crossroads where a large bazaar was held on Mondays, or the second day (*du*) after Saturday (*shambe*)

Administrative divisions: 2 provinces (*viloyatho*, singular - *viloyat*), 1 autonomous province* (*viloyati mukhtor*), 1 capital region** (*viloyati poytakht*), and 1 area referred to as Districts Under Republic Administration***; Dushanbe**, Khatlon (Bokhtar), Kuhistoni Badakhshon [Gorno-Badakhshan]* (Khorugh), Nohiyahoi Tobei Jumhuri***, Sughd (Khujand)
note: the administrative center name follows in parentheses

Legal system: civil law system

Constitution: *history:* several previous; latest adopted 6 November 1994
amendment process: proposed by the president of the republic or by at least one third of the total membership of both houses of the Supreme Assembly; adoption of any amendment requires a referendum, which includes approval of the president or approval by at least two-thirds majority of the Assembly of Representatives; passage in a referendum requires participation of an absolute majority of eligible voters and an absolute majority of votes; constitutional articles, including Tajikistan's form of government, its territory, and its democratic nature, cannot be amended

International law organization participation: has not submitted an ICJ jurisdiction declaration; accepts ICCt jurisdiction

Citizenship: *citizenship by birth:* no
citizenship by descent only: at least one parent must be a citizen of Tajikistan
dual citizenship recognized: no
residency requirement for naturalization: 5 years or 3 years of continuous residence prior to application

Suffrage: 18 years of age; universal

Executive branch: *chief of state:* President Emomali RAHMON (since 16 November 1994; head of state and Supreme Assembly Chairman since 20 November 1992)
head of government: Prime Minister Qohir RASULZODA (since 23 November 2013)
cabinet: Council of Ministers appointed by the president, approved by the Supreme Assembly
election/appointment process: president directly elected by simple-majority popular vote for a 7-year term (two-term limit), but as the "Leader of the Nation," president has no term limit; prime minister appointed by the president
most recent election date: 11 October 2020
election results: *2020:* Emomali RAHMON reelected president; percent of vote - Emomali RAHMON (PDPT) 92.1%, Rustam LATIFZODA (APT) 3.1%, other 4.8%
2013: Emomali RAHMON reelected president; percent of vote - Emomali RAHMON (PDPT) 84%, Ismoil TALBAKOV CPT) 5%, other 11%
expected date of next election: 2027

Legislative branch: *legislature name:* Supreme Council (Majlisi Oli)
legislative structure: bicameral

Legislative branch - lower chamber: *chamber name:* House of Representatives (Majlisi namoyandogon)
number of seats: 63 (all directly elected)
electoral system: mixed system
scope of elections: full renewal
term in office: 5 years
most recent election date: 3/2/2025
parties elected and seats per party: People's Democratic Party of Tajikistan (PDPT) (49); Agrarian Party of Tajikistan (APT) (7); Party of Economic Reforms of Tajikistan (PERT) (5); Other (2)
percentage of women in chamber: 28.6%
expected date of next election: March 2030

Legislative branch - upper chamber: *chamber name:* National Assembly (Majlisi milli)
number of seats: 33 (25 indirectly elected; 8 appointed)
scope of elections: full renewal
term in office: 5 years
most recent election date: 3/28/2025
percentage of women in chamber: 30.3%
expected date of next election: March 2030

Judicial branch: *highest court(s):* Supreme Court (consists of the chairman, deputy chairmen, and 34 judges organized into civil, family, criminal, administrative offense, and military chambers); Constitutional Court (consists of the court chairman, deputy chairman, and 5 judges); High Economic Court (consists of 16 judicial positions)
judge selection and term of office: Supreme Court, Constitutional Court, and High Economic Court judges nominated by the president and approved by the National Assembly; judges of all 3 courts appointed for 10-year renewable terms with no term limits, but the last appointment must occur before the age of 65
subordinate courts: regional and district courts; Dushanbe City Court; viloyat (province-level) courts; Court of Gorno-Badakhshan Autonomous Region

Political parties: Agrarian Party of Tajikistan or APT
Communist Party of Tajikistan or CPT
Democratic Party of Tajikistan or DPT
Party of Economic Reform of Tajikistan or PERT
People's Democratic Party of Tajikistan or PDPT
Social Democratic Party of Tajikistan or SDPT
Socialist Party of Tajikistan or SPT

Diplomatic representation in the US: *chief of mission:* Ambassador-designate Zavqi ZAVQIZODA (since November 2021)
chancery: 1005 New Hampshire Avenue NW, Washington, DC 20037
telephone: [1] (202) 223-6090

FAX: [1] (202) 223-6091
email address and website: tajemus@mfa.tj
https://mfa.tj/en/washington

Diplomatic representation from the US: *chief of mission:* Ambassador Manuel P. MICALLER Jr. (since 9 March 2023)
embassy: 109-A Ismoili Somoni Avenue (Zarafshon district), Dushanbe 734019
mailing address: 7090 Dushanbe Place, Washington DC 20521-7090
telephone: [992] (37) 229-20-00

FAX: [992] (37) 229-20-50
email address and website: DushanbeConsular@state.gov
https://tj.usembassy.gov/

International organization participation: ADB, CICA, CIS, CSTO, EAEC, EAPC, EBRD, ECO, EITI (candidate country), FAO, G-77, GCTU, IAEA, IBRD, ICAO, ICC (NGOs), ICCt, ICRM, IDA, IDB, IFAD, IFC, IFRCS, ILO, IMF, Interpol, IOC, IOM, IPU, ISO (correspondent), ITSO, ITU, MIGA, NAM (observer), OIC, OPCW, OSCE, PFP, SCO, UN, UNCTAD, UNESCO, UNIDO, UNISFA, UNWTO, UPU, WCO, WFTU (NGOs), WHO, WIPO, WMO, WTO

Independence: 9 September 1991 (from the Soviet Union)

National holiday: Independence Day (or National Day), 9 September (1991)

Flag: *description:* three horizontal stripes of red (top), a wider stripe of white, and green; a gold crown under seven five-pointed gold stars is in the center of the white stripe
meaning: red stands for the sun, victory, and the unity of the nation; white for purity, cotton, and mountain snows; green for Islam and nature's bounty; the crown symbolizes the Tajik people; the stars represent the number seven, which is considered a symbol of perfection and the embodiment of happiness

National symbol(s): arc of seven five-pointed stars over a crown, Marco Polo sheep

National color(s): red, white, green

National anthem(s): *title:* "Surudi milli" (National Anthem)
lyrics/music: Gulnazar KELDI/Sulaimon YUDAKOV
history: adopted 1994; after the fall of the Soviet Union, Tajikistan kept the music of its Soviet-era anthem, but adopted new lyrics

National heritage: *total World Heritage Sites:* 5 (3 cultural, 2 natural)
selected World Heritage Site locales: Proto-urban Site of Sarazm (c); Tajik National Park (Mountains of the Pamirs) (n); Silk Roads: Zarafshan-Karakum Corridor (c); Tugay forests of the Tigrovaya Balka

Nature Reserve (n); Cultural Heritage Sites of Ancient Khuttal (c)

ECONOMY

Economic overview: lower middle-income Central Asian economy; key gold, cotton, and aluminum exporter; declining poverty; sustained high growth; very limited private sector; substantial illicit drug trade; significant remittances; environmentally fragile

Real GDP (purchasing power parity): $50.37 billion (2024 est.)
$46.467 billion (2023 est.)
$42.905 billion (2022 est.)
note: data in 2021 dollars
comparison ranking: 129

Real GDP growth rate: 8.4% (2024 est.)
8.3% (2023 est.)
8% (2022 est.)
note: annual GDP % growth based on constant local currency
comparison ranking: 9

Real GDP per capita: $4,800 (2024 est.)
$4,500 (2023 est.)
$4,200 (2022 est.)
note: data in 2021 dollars
comparison ranking: 176

GDP (official exchange rate): $14.205 billion (2024 est.)
note: data in current dollars at official exchange rate

Inflation rate (consumer prices): 7.7% (2019 est.)
3.9% (2018 est.)
7.3% (2017 est.)
note: annual % change based on consumer prices
comparison ranking: 167

GDP - composition, by sector of origin: *agriculture:* 22.9% (2023 est.)
industry: 33.6% (2023 est.)
services: 34.7% (2023 est.)
note: figures may not total 100% due to non-allocated consumption not captured in sector-reported data
comparison rankings: agriculture 27; industry 37; services 202

GDP - composition, by end use: *household consumption:* 89.6% (2023 est.)
government consumption: 10.7% (2023 est.)
investment in fixed capital: 28.3% (2023 est.)
investment in inventories: 3.4% (2023 est.)
exports of goods and services: 17.2% (2023 est.)
imports of goods and services: -48.4% (2023 est.)
note: figures may not total 100% due to rounding or gaps in data collection

Agricultural products: potatoes, milk, wheat, watermelons, onions, tomatoes, carrots/turnips, cotton, vegetables, grapes (2023)
note: top ten agricultural products based on tonnage

Industries: aluminum, cement, coal, gold, silver, antimony, textile, vegetable oil

Industrial production growth rate: 9.9% (2023 est.)
note: annual % change in industrial value added based on constant local currency
comparison ranking: 10

Labor force: 2.78 million (2024 est.)
note: number of people ages 15 or older who are employed or seeking work
comparison ranking: 116

Unemployment rate: 11.7% (2024 est.)
11.6% (2023 est.)
11.7% (2022 est.)
note: % of labor force seeking employment
comparison ranking: 161

Youth unemployment rate (ages 15-24): *total:* 27.1% (2024 est.)
male: 30% (2024 est.)
female: 23.3% (2024 est.)
note: % of labor force ages 15-24 seeking employment
comparison ranking: total 28

Population below poverty line: 20.4% (2023 est.)
note: % of population with income below national poverty line

Gini Index coefficient - distribution of family income: 34 (2015 est.)
note: index (0-100) of income distribution; higher values represent greater inequality
comparison ranking: 86

Household income or consumption by percentage share: *lowest 10%:* 3% (2015 est.)
highest 10%: 26.4% (2015 est.)
note: % share of income accruing to lowest and highest 10% of population

Remittances: 47.9% of GDP (2024 est.)
37.8% of GDP (2023 est.)
49.9% of GDP (2022 est.)
note: personal transfers and compensation between resident and non-resident individuals/households/entities

Budget: *revenues:* $2.911 billion (2023 est.)
expenditures: $3.036 billion (2023 est.)
note: central government revenues (excluding grants) and expenditures converted to US dollars at average official exchange rate for year indicated

Taxes and other revenues: 10.8% (of GDP) (2023 est.)
note: central government tax revenue as a % of GDP
comparison ranking: 125

Current account balance: $887.016 million (2024 est.)
$584.022 million (2023 est.)
$1.635 billion (2022 est.)
note: balance of payments - net trade and primary/secondary income in current dollars
comparison ranking: 59

Exports: $1.618 billion (2024 est.)
$2.105 billion (2023 est.)
$1.753 billion (2022 est.)
note: balance of payments - exports of goods and services in current dollars
comparison ranking: 169

Exports - partners: Switzerland 31%, Kazakhstan 18%, China 17%, Uzbekistan 10%, Turkey 8% (2023)
note: top five export partners based on percentage share of exports

Exports - commodities: gold, precious metal ore, aluminum, lead ore, antimony (2023)
note: top five export commodities based on value in dollars

Imports: $6.907 billion (2024 est.)
$5.931 billion (2023 est.)
$5.261 billion (2022 est.)
note: balance of payments - imports of goods and services in current dollars
comparison ranking: 141

Imports - partners: China 57%, Kazakhstan 13%, Uzbekistan 8%, Turkey 6%, UAE 4% (2023)
note: top five import partners based on percentage share of imports

Imports - commodities: garments, footwear, cars, wheat, vehicle parts/accessories (2023)
note: top five import commodities based on value in dollars

Reserves of foreign exchange and gold: $3.304 billion (2023 est.)
$3.847 billion (2022 est.)
$2.499 billion (2021 est.)
note: holdings of gold (year-end prices)/foreign exchange/special drawing rights in current dollars
comparison ranking: 116

Debt - external: $3.024 billion (2023 est.)
note: present value of external debt in current US dollars
comparison ranking: 86

Exchange rates: Tajikistani somoni (TJS) per US dollar -

Exchange rates: 10.799 (2024 est.)
10.845 (2023 est.)
11.031 (2022 est.)
11.309 (2021 est.)
10.322 (2020 est.)

ENERGY

Electricity access: *electrification - total population:* 100% (2022 est.)
electrification - urban areas: 99%
electrification - rural areas: 100%

Electricity: *installed generating capacity:* 6.481 million kW (2023 est.)
consumption: 15.275 billion kWh (2023 est.)
exports: 3.101 billion kWh (2023 est.)
imports: 714.025 million kWh (2023 est.)
transmission/distribution losses: 3.94 billion kWh (2023 est.)
comparison rankings: installed generating capacity 83; consumption 87; exports 49; imports 87; transmission/distribution losses 153

Electricity generation sources: *fossil fuels:* 7.4% of total installed capacity (2023 est.)
hydroelectricity: 92.6% of total installed capacity (2023 est.)

Coal: *production:* 2.394 million metric tons (2023 est.)
consumption: 2.297 million metric tons (2023 est.)
exports: 475,000 metric tons (2023 est.)
imports: 147,000 metric tons (2023 est.)
proven reserves: 4.075 billion metric tons (2023 est.)

Petroleum: *total petroleum production:* 300 bbl/day (2023 est.)
refined petroleum consumption: 31,000 bbl/day (2023 est.)
crude oil estimated reserves: 12 million barrels (2021 est.)

Natural gas: *production:* 18.476 million cubic meters (2023 est.)
consumption: 43.767 million cubic meters (2023 est.)
imports: 24.196 million cubic meters (2023 est.)
proven reserves: 5.663 billion cubic meters (2021 est.)

Energy consumption per capita: 16.192 million Btu/person (2023 est.)
comparison ranking: 137

COMMUNICATIONS

Telephones - fixed lines: *total subscriptions:* 502,000 (2021 est.)
subscriptions per 100 inhabitants: 5 (2022 est.)
comparison ranking: total subscriptions 93

Telephones - mobile cellular: *total subscriptions:* 11.6 million (2021 est.)
subscriptions per 100 inhabitants: 119 (2021 est.)
comparison ranking: total subscriptions 87

Broadcast media: state-run broadcaster has 9 national TV and 10 radio stations, and 4 regional stations; 31 independent TV and 20 independent radio stations broadcast locally and regionally; Russian and other foreign stations available via cable and satellite (2016)

Internet country code: .tj

Internet users: *percent of population:* 57% (2023 est.)

Broadband - fixed subscriptions: *total:* 6,000 (2022 est.)
subscriptions per 100 inhabitants: (2022 est.) less than 1
comparison ranking: total 191

TRANSPORTATION

Civil aircraft registration country code prefix: EY

Airports: 19 (2025)
comparison ranking: 142

Heliports: 1 (2025)
comparison ranking: 143

Railways: *total:* 680 km (2014)
broad gauge: 680 km (2014) 1.520-m gauge

MILITARY AND SECURITY

Military and security forces: Armed Forces of the Republic of Tajikistan: Ground Forces, Mobile Forces, Air and Air Defense Forces

Tajik National Guard (TNG); Ministry of Internal Affairs: Internal Troops of Tajikistan; State Committee on National Security: Border Troops (aka Border Service) (2025)
note 1: the Mobile Forces are the airborne, air assault, mountain, and rapid reaction troops of the Armed Forces
note 2: the Tajik National Guard, formerly the Presidential Guard, is a paramilitary force under direct authority of the President; it is tasked with ensuring public safety and security, similar to the tasks of the Internal Troops; it also has ceremonial duties

Military expenditures: 1.8% of GDP (2024 est.)
2% of GDP (2023 est.)
1.9% of GDP (2022 est.)
1.2% of GDP (2021 est.)
1.1% of GDP (2020 est.)

Military and security service personnel strengths: estimated 10,000 active Armed Forces; estimated 5-10,000 active paramilitary National Guard, Border Service, and Internal Troops personnel (2025)

Military equipment inventories and acquisitions: the military's inventory is comprised mostly of older Russian and Soviet-era weapons and equipment; it also has smaller amounts of items from suppliers such as China, Turkey, and the US; in 2022, Tajikistan opened a plant to produce an Iranian-designed unmanned aerial vehicle under license (2024)

Military service age and obligation: 18-27 years of age for compulsory (men only) or voluntary (men and women) military service; 24-month conscript service obligation or 12 months for those with a higher education (2024)
note: in August 2021, the Tajik Government removed an exemption for university graduates but began allowing men to pay a fee in order to avoid conscription, although there is a cap on the number of individuals who can take advantage of this exemption

Military - note: the military's primary concerns are terrorism, border security, territorial defense, and regional security, particularly in neighboring Afghanistan; Russia is traditionally Tajikistan's most important security partner and thousands of Russian troops are stationed in the country, primarily at the 201st military base, which is leased until at least 2042; Russia and Tajikistan have a joint air defense system and they conduct periodic joint exercises; Tajikistan has been a member of the Russian-led Collective Security Treaty Organization (CSTO) since 1994 and contributes troops to CSTO's rapid reaction force; Tajikistan also cooperates on security matters with China, including joint military training
Tajikistan is the only former Soviet republic that did not form its armed forces from old Soviet Army units following the collapse of the USSR in 1991; rather, Russia retained command of the Soviet units there while the Tajik government raised a military from scratch; the first ground forces were officially created in 1993 from groups that fought for the government during the Tajik Civil War (2025)

TERRORISM

Terrorist group(s)

Terrorist group(s): Islamic State of Iraq and ash-Sham (ISIS)
note 1: US-designated foreign terrorist groups such as the Islamic Jihad Union, the Islamic Movement of Uzbekistan, and the Islamic State of Iraq and ash-Sham-Khorasan Province have operated in the area where the Uzbek, Kyrgyz, and Tajik borders converge and ill-defined and porous borders allow for the relatively free movement of people and illicit goods
note 2: details about the history, aims, leadership, organization, areas of operation, tactics, targets, weapons, size, and sources of support of the group(s) appear(s) in Appendix T

TRANSNATIONAL ISSUES

Refugees and internally displaced persons: *refugees:* 15,191 (2024 est.)

IDPs: 238 (2024 est.)
stateless persons: 4,466 (2024 est.)

TANZANIA

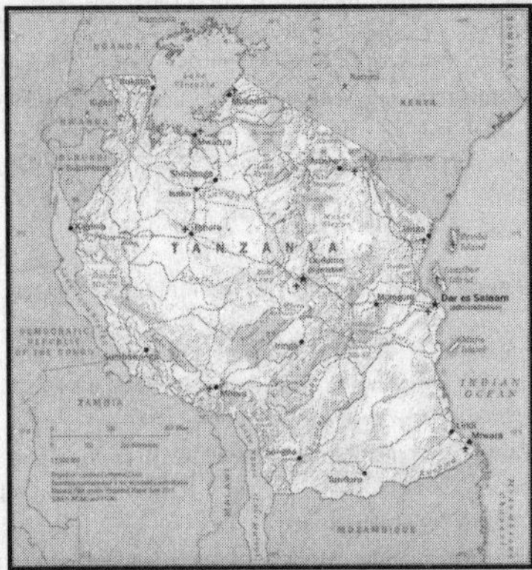

INTRODUCTION

Background: Tanzania contains some of Africa's most iconic national parks and famous paleoanthropological sites, and its diverse cultural heritage reflects the multiple ethnolinguistic groups that live in the country. Its long history of integration into trade networks spanning the Indian Ocean and the African interior led to the development of Swahili as a common language in much of east Africa and the introduction of Islam into the region. A number of independent coastal and island trading posts in what is now Tanzania came under Portuguese control after 1498 when they began to take control of much of the coast and Indian Ocean trade. By 1700, the Sultanate of Oman had become the dominant power in the region after ousting the Portuguese, who were also facing a series of local uprisings. During the next hundred years, Zanzibar – an archipelago off the coast that is now part of Tanzania – became a hub of Indian Ocean trade, with Arab and Indian traders establishing and consolidating trade routes with communities in mainland Tanzania that contributed to the expansion of the slave trade. Zanzibar briefly became the capital of the Sultanate of Oman before it split into separate Omani and Zanzibar Sultanates in 1856. Beginning in the mid-1800s, European explorers, traders, and Christian missionaries became more active in the region. The Germans eventually established control over mainland Tanzania – which they called Tanganyika – and the British established control over Zanzibar. Tanganyika came under British administration after the German defeat in World War I.

Tanganyika gained independence from Great Britain in 1961, and Zanzibar followed in 1963 as a constitutional monarchy. In Tanganyika, Julius NYERERE, a charismatic and idealistic socialist, established a one-party political system that centralized power and encouraged national self-reliance and rural development. In 1964, a popular uprising overthrew the Sultan in Zanzibar and either killed or expelled many of the Arabs and Indians who had dominated the isles for more than 200 years. Later that year, Tanganyika and Zanzibar combined to form the United Republic of Tanzania, but Zanzibar retained considerable autonomy. Their two ruling parties combined to form the Chama Cha Mapinduzi (CCM) party in 1977, which has since won every presidential election. Tanzania held its first multiparty elections in 1995, but CCM candidates have continued to dominate politics. The ruling party has claimed victory in four contentious elections since 1995, despite international observers' claims of voting irregularities. In 2001, 35 people died in Zanzibar when soldiers fired on protestors. John MAGUFULI won the 2015 and 2020 presidential elections, and the CCM won over two-thirds of the seats in Parliament in both elections. MAGUFULI died in 2021 while in office and was succeeded by his vice president, Samia Suluhu HASSAN.

GEOGRAPHY

Location: Eastern Africa, bordering the Indian Ocean, between Kenya and Mozambique

Geographic coordinates: 6 00 S, 35 00 E

Map references: Africa

Area: *total:* 947,300 sq km
land: 885,800 sq km
water: 61,500 sq km
note: includes the islands of Mafia, Pemba, and Zanzibar
comparison ranking: total 32

Area - comparative: more than six times the size of Georgia; slightly larger than twice the size of California

Land boundaries: *total:* 4,161 km
border countries (8): Burundi 589 km; Democratic Republic of the Congo 479 km; Kenya 775 km; Malawi 512 km; Mozambique 840 km; Rwanda 222 km; Uganda 391 km; Zambia 353 km

Coastline: 1,424 km

Maritime claims: *territorial sea:* 12 nm
exclusive economic zone: 200 nm

Climate: varies from tropical along coast to temperate in highlands

Terrain: plains along coast; central plateau; highlands in north, south

Elevation: *highest point:* Kilimanjaro (highest point in Africa) 5,895 m
lowest point: Indian Ocean 0 m
mean elevation: 1,018 m

Natural resources: hydropower, tin, phosphates, iron ore, coal, diamonds, gemstones (including tanzanite, found only in Tanzania), gold, natural gas, nickel

Land use: *agricultural land:* 44.6% (2022 est.)
arable land: 15.2% (2022 est.)
permanent crops: 2.3% (2022 est.)
permanent pasture: 27.1% (2022 est.)
forest: 50.6% (2022 est.)
other: 4.8% (2022 est.)

Irrigated land: 1,840 sq km (2012)

Major lakes (area sq km): *fresh water lake(s):* Lake Victoria (shared with Uganda and Kenya) - 62,940 sq km; Lake Tanganyika (shared with Democratic Republic of Congo, Burundi, and Zambia) - 32,000 sq km; Lake Malawi (shared with Mozambique and Malawi) - 22,490
salt water lake(s): Lake Rukwa - 5,760 sq km

Major rivers (by length in km): Nile (shared with Rwanda [s], Uganda, South Sudan, Sudan, and Egypt [m]) - 6,650 km
note: [s] after country name indicates river source; [m] after country name indicates river mouth

Major watersheds (area sq km): Atlantic Ocean drainage: Congo (3,730,881 sq km), *(Mediterranean Sea)* Nile (3,254,853 sq km)

Indian Ocean drainage: Zambezi (1,332,412 sq km)

Population distribution: the largest and most populous East African country; population distribution is extremely uneven, but greater population clusters occur in the northern half of country and along the east coast, as shown in this population distribution map

Natural hazards: flooding on the central plateau during the rainy season; drought
volcanism: limited volcanic activity; Ol Doinyo Lengai (2,962 m) has emitted lava in recent years; other historically active volcanoes include Kieyo and Meru

Geography - note: Kilimanjaro is the highest point in Africa and one of only three mountain ranges on the continent that has glaciers (the others are Mount Kenya in Kenya and the Ruwenzori Mountains on the Uganda-Democratic Republic of the Congo border); Tanzania is bordered by three of the largest lakes on the continent: Lake Victoria (the world's second-largest freshwater lake) in the north, Lake Tanganyika (the world's second-deepest) in the west, and Lake Nyasa (Lake Malawi) in the southwest

PEOPLE AND SOCIETY

Population: *total:* 67,462,121 (2024 est.)
male: 33,691,904
female: 33,770,217
comparison rankings: total 23; male 22; female 23

Nationality: *noun:* Tanzanian(s)
adjective: Tanzanian

Ethnic groups: mainland - African 99% (of which 95% are Bantu consisting of more than 130 tribes), other 1% (consisting of Asian, European, and Arab); Zanzibar - Arab, African, mixed Arab and African

Languages: Kiswahili or Swahili (official), Kiunguja (name for Swahili in Zanzibar), English (official, primary language of commerce, administration, and higher education), Arabic, many local languages
major-language sample(s):
The World Factbook, Chanzo cha Lazima Kuhusu Habari ya Msingi. (Kiswahili)

Religions: Christian 63.1%, Muslim 34.1%, folk religion 1.1%, Buddhist <1%, Hindu <1%, Jewish <1%, other <1%, unspecified 1.6% (2020 est.)
note: Zanzibar is almost entirely Muslim

Age structure: *0-14 years:* 41.2% (male 14,039,292/female 13,740,439)
15-64 years: 55.4% (male 18,677,388/female 18,708,390)
65 years and over: 3.4% (2024 est.) (male 975,224/female 1,321,388)

Dependency ratios: *total dependency ratio:* 82.5 (2024 est.)
youth dependency ratio: 76.8 (2024 est.)
elderly dependency ratio: 5.7 (2024 est.)
potential support ratio: 17.5 (2024 est.)

Median age: *total:* 19.1 years (2024 est.)
male: 18.8 years
female: 19.4 years
comparison ranking: total 214

Population growth rate: 2.72% (2024 est.)
comparison ranking: 13

Birth rate: 32.5 births/1,000 population (2024 est.)
comparison ranking: 19

Death rate: 5 deaths/1,000 population (2024 est.)
comparison ranking: 193

Net migration rate: -0.4 migrant(s)/1,000 population (2024 est.)
comparison ranking: 120

Population distribution: the largest and most populous East African country; population distribution is extremely uneven, but greater population clusters occur in the northern half of country and along the east coast, as shown in this population distribution map

Urbanization: *urban population:* 37.4% of total population (2023)
rate of urbanization: 4.89% annual rate of change (2020-25 est.)

Major urban areas - population: 262,000 Dodoma (legislative capital) (2018), 7.776 million DAR ES SALAAM (administrative capital), 1.311 million Mwanza, 800,000 Zanzibar (2023)

Sex ratio: *at birth:* 1.03 male(s)/female
0-14 years: 1.02 male(s)/female
15-64 years: 1 male(s)/female
65 years and over: 0.74 male(s)/female
total population: 1 male(s)/female (2024 est.)

Mother's mean age at first birth: 19.9 years (2022 est.)
note: data represents median age at first birth among women 15-49

Maternal mortality ratio: 276 deaths/100,000 live births (2023 est.)
comparison ranking: 26

Infant mortality rate: *total:* 29.6 deaths/1,000 live births (2024 est.)
male: 32.3 deaths/1,000 live births
female: 26.9 deaths/1,000 live births
comparison ranking: total 51

Life expectancy at birth: *total population:* 70.8 years (2024 est.)
male: 69 years
female: 72.6 years
comparison ranking: total population 171

Total fertility rate: 4.27 children born/woman (2024 est.)
comparison ranking: 19

Gross reproduction rate: 2.1 (2024 est.)

Drinking water source: *improved: urban:* 81.1% of population (2022 est.)
rural: 49% of population (2022 est.)
total: 60.8% of population (2022 est.)
unimproved: urban: 18.9% of population (2022 est.)
rural: 51% of population (2022 est.)
total: 39.2% of population (2022 est.)

Health expenditure: 3.4% of GDP (2021)
5.1% of national budget (2022 est.)

Physician density: 0.13 physicians/1,000 population (2022)

Hospital bed density: 0.6 beds/1,000 population (2020 est.)

Sanitation facility access: *improved: urban:* 89.6% of population (2022 est.)
rural: 27.2% of population (2022 est.)
total: 50.1% of population (2022 est.)
unimproved: urban: 10.4% of population (2022 est.)
rural: 72.8% of population (2022 est.)
total: 49.9% of population (2022 est.)

Obesity - adult prevalence rate: 8.4% (2016)
comparison ranking: 152

Alcohol consumption per capita: *total:* 7.81 liters of pure alcohol (2019 est.)
beer: 0.74 liters of pure alcohol (2019 est.)
wine: 0.09 liters of pure alcohol (2019 est.)
spirits: 0.38 liters of pure alcohol (2019 est.)
other alcohols: 6.6 liters of pure alcohol (2019 est.)
comparison ranking: total 46

Tobacco use: *total:* 6.5% (2025 est.)
male: 11.3% (2025 est.)
female: 2% (2025 est.)
comparison ranking: total 153

Children under the age of 5 years underweight: 12.1% (2022)
comparison ranking: 39

Currently married women (ages 15-49): 59.5% (2023 est.)

Child marriage: *women married by age 15:* 5.2% (2022)
women married by age 18: 29.1% (2022)
men married by age 18: 3.5% (2022)

Education expenditure: 3.2% of GDP (2024 est.)
13.4% national budget (2024 est.)
comparison ranking: Education expenditure (% GDP) 141

Literacy: *total population:* 78% (2015 est.)
male: 83% (2015 est.)
female: 73% (2015 est.)

School life expectancy (primary to tertiary education): *total:* 9 years (2021 est.)
male: 9 years (2021 est.)
female: 9 years (2021 est.)

ENVIRONMENT

Environmental issues: water pollution; improper management of liquid waste; indoor air pollution from burning wood or charcoal for cooking and heating; soil degradation; deforestation; desertification; coral reef destruction; illegal hunting and animal trade, especially ivory; loss of biodiversity; solid waste disposal

International environmental agreements: *party to:* Biodiversity, Climate Change, Climate Change-Kyoto Protocol, Climate Change- Paris Agreement, Comprehensive Nuclear Test Ban, Desertification, Endangered Species, Hazardous Wastes, Law of the Sea, Marine Dumping-London Convention, Nuclear Test Ban, Ozone Layer Protection, Ship Pollution, Wetlands, Whaling
signed, but not ratified: none of the selected agreements

Climate: varies from tropical along coast to temperate in highlands

Urbanization: *urban population:* 37.4% of total population (2023)
rate of urbanization: 4.89% annual rate of change (2020-25 est.)

Carbon dioxide emissions: 17.707 million metric tonnes of CO2 (2023 est.)
from coal and metallurgical coke: 1.687 million metric tonnes of CO2 (2023 est.)
from petroleum and other liquids: 12.066 million metric tonnes of CO2 (2023 est.)
from consumed natural gas: 3.954 million metric tonnes of CO2 (2023 est.)
comparison ranking: total emissions 95

Particulate matter emissions: 14.5 micrograms per cubic meter (2019 est.)

Methane emissions: *energy:* 568.3 kt (2022-2024 est.)
agriculture: 1,176.8 kt (2019-2021 est.)
waste: 168.3 kt (2019-2021 est.)
other: 1,226.8 kt (2019-2021 est.)

Waste and recycling: *municipal solid waste generated annually:* 9.277 million tons (2024 est.)
percent of municipal solid waste recycled: 12.3% (2022 est.)

Total water withdrawal: *municipal:* 527 million cubic meters (2022 est.)
industrial: 25 million cubic meters (2022 est.)
agricultural: 4.632 billion cubic meters (2022 est.)

Total renewable water resources: 96.27 billion cubic meters (2022 est.)

Geoparks: *total global geoparks and regional networks:* 1
global geoparks and regional networks: Ngorongoro Lengai (2023)

GOVERNMENT

Country name: *conventional long form:* United Republic of Tanzania
conventional short form: Tanzania
local long form: Jamhuri ya Muungano wa Tanzania
local short form: Tanzania
former: German East Africa, Trust Territory of Tanganyika, Republic of Tanganyika, People's Republic of Zanzibar, United Republic of Tanganyika and Zanzibar
etymology: the country's name is a combination of the first letters of Tanganyika and Zanzibar, the two states that merged to form Tanzania in 1964

Government type: presidential republic

Capital: *name:* Dodoma
geographic coordinates: 6 48 S, 39 17 E
time difference: UTC+3 (8 hours ahead of Washington, DC, during Standard Time)
etymology: the name comes from the name of a nearby mountain; the origin of the mountain's name is unclear

Administrative divisions: 31 regions; Arusha, Dar es Salaam, Dodoma, Geita, Iringa, Kagera, Kaskazini Pemba (Pemba North), Kaskazini Unguja (Zanzibar North), Katavi, Kigoma, Kilimanjaro, Kusini Pemba (Pemba South), Kusini Unguja (Zanzibar Central/South), Lindi, Manyara, Mara, Mbeya, Mjini Magharibi (Zanzibar Urban/West), Morogoro, Mtwara, Mwanza, Njombe, Pwani (Coast), Rukwa, Ruvuma, Shinyanga, Simiyu, Singida, Songwe, Tabora, Tanga

Legal system: English common law; judicial review of legislative acts limited to matters of interpretation

Constitution: *history:* several previous; latest adopted 25 April 1977
amendment process: proposed by the National Assembly; passage of amendments to constitutional articles including those on sovereignty of the United Republic, the authorities and powers of the government, the president, the Assembly, and the High Court requires two-thirds majority vote of the mainland Assembly membership and of the Zanzibar House of Representatives membership; House of Representatives approval of other amendments is not required

International law organization participation: has not submitted an ICJ jurisdiction declaration; accepts ICCt jurisdiction

Citizenship: *citizenship by birth:* no
citizenship by descent only: at least one parent must be a citizen of Tanzania; if a child is born abroad, the father must be a citizen of Tanzania
dual citizenship recognized: no
residency requirement for naturalization: 5 years

Suffrage: 18 years of age; universal

Executive branch: *chief of state:* President Samia Suluhu HASSAN (since 19 March 2021)
head of government: President Samia Suluhu HASSAN (since 19 March 2021)
cabinet: Cabinet appointed by the president from among members of the National Assembly
election/appointment process: president and vice president directly elected on the same ballot by simple majority popular vote for a 5-year term (eligible for a second term); prime minister appointed by the president
most recent election date: 28 October 2020
election results: *2020:* John MAGUFULI reelected president; percent of vote - John MAGUFULI (CCM) 84.4%, Tundu LISSU (CHADEMA) 13%, other 2.6%
2015: John MAGUFULI elected president; percent of vote - John MAGUFULI (CCM) 58.5%, Edward LOWASSA (CHADEMA) 40%, other 1.5%
expected date of next election: October 2025
note 1: Zanzibar elects a president as head of government for internal matters; election held on 28 October 2020; Hussein MWINYI (CCM) 76.3%, Maalim Seif SHARIF (ACT-Wazalendo) 19.9%, other 3.8%
note 2: the president is both chief of state and head of government
note 3: after the death of President John MAGUFULI in March 2021, Vice President Samia Suluhu HASSAN assumed the presidency

Legislative branch: *legislature name:* National Assembly (Bunge)
legislative structure: unicameral
number of seats: 393 (264 directly elected; 118 indirectly elected; 10 appointed)
electoral system: plurality/majority
scope of elections: full renewal
term in office: 5 years
most recent election date: 10/28/2020
parties elected and seats per party: Revolutionary Party of Tanzania (CCM) (350); Chadema (Party for Democracy and Development) (20); Other (7)
percentage of women in chamber: 37.8%
expected date of next election: October 2025

Judicial branch: *highest court(s):* Court of Appeal of the United Republic of Tanzania (consists of the chief justice and 14 justices); High Court of the United Republic for Mainland Tanzania (consists of the principal judge and 30 judges organized into commercial, land, and labor courts); High Court of Zanzibar (consists of the chief justice and 10 justices)
judge selection and term of office: Court of Appeal and High Court justices appointed by the national president after consultation with the Judicial Service Commission for Tanzania, a judicial body of high-level judges and 2 members appointed by the national president; Court of Appeal and High Court judges serve until mandatory retirement at age 60, but terms can be extended; High Court of Zanzibar judges appointed by the national president after consultation with the Judicial Commission of Zanzibar; judges can serve until mandatory retirement at age 65

subordinate courts: Resident Magistrates Courts; Kadhi courts (for Islamic family matters); district and primary courts

Political parties: Alliance for Change and Transparency (Wazalendo) or ACT-Wazalendo
Civic United Front (Chama Cha Wananchi) or CUF
Party of Democracy and Development (Chama Cha Demokrasia na Maendeleo) or CHADEMA
Revolutionary Party of Tanzania (Chama Cha Mapinduzi) or CCM

Diplomatic representation in the US: *chief of mission:* Ambassador Elsie Sia KANZA (since 1 December 2021)
chancery: 1232 22nd Street NW, Washington, DC 20037
telephone: [1] (202) 884-1080
FAX: [1] (202) 797-7408
email address and website: ubalozi@tanzaniaembassy-us.org
https://us.tzembassy.go.tz/

Diplomatic representation from the US: *chief of mission:* Ambassador (vacant); Chargé d'Affaires Andrew LENTZ (since January 2025)
embassy: 686 Old Bagamoyo Road, Msasani, P.O. Box 9123, Dar es Salaam
mailing address: 2140 Dar es Salaam Place, Washington, DC 20521-2140
telephone: [255] (22) 229-4000
FAX: [255] (22) 229-4721
email address and website: DRSACS@state.gov
https://tz.usembassy.gov/

International organization participation: ACP, AfDB, AU, C, CD, EAC, EADB, EITI, FAO, G-77, IAEA, IBRD, ICAO, ICC (NGOs), ICCt, ICRM, IDA, IFAD, IFC, IFRCS, ILO, IMF, IMO, IMSO, Interpol, IOC, IOM, IPU, ISO, ITSO, ITU, ITUC (NGOs), MIGA, MONUSCO, NAM, OPCW, SADC, UN, UNAMID, UNCTAD, UNESCO, UNHCR, UNIDO, UNIFIL, UNISFA, UNMISS, UNWTO, UPU, WCO, WFTU (NGOs), WHO, WIPO, WMO, WTO

Independence: *26 April 1964 (Tanganyika united with Zanzibar to form the United Republic of Tanganyika and Zanzibar); 29 October 1964 (renamed United Republic of Tanzania); notable earlier dates:* 9 December 1961 (Tanganyika became independent from UK-administered UN trusteeship); 10 December 1963 (Zanzibar became independent from UK)

National holiday: Union Day (Tanganyika and Zanzibar), 26 April (1964)

Flag: *description:* divided diagonally by a yellow-edged black band, from the lower left corner to the upper right corner; the upper triangle (left side) is green, and the lower is blue
meaning: colors come from the flags of Tanganyika and Zanzibar; green stands for natural vegetation, gold for rich mineral deposits, black for the Swahili people, and blue for lakes and rivers, as well as the Indian Ocean

National symbol(s): Uhuru (freedom) torch, giraffe

National color(s): green, yellow, blue, black

National anthem(s): *title:* "Mungu ibariki Afrika" (God Bless Africa)
lyrics/music: collective/Enoch Mankayi SONTONGA
history: adopted 1961; the anthem, which is also a popular African popular song in Africa, shares the melody of Zambia's anthem and is part of South Africa's anthem

National heritage: *total World Heritage Sites:* 7 (3 cultural, 3 natural, 1 mixed)
selected World Heritage Site locales: Ngorongoro Conservation Area (m); Ruins of Kilwa Kisiwani and Songo Mnara (c); Serengeti National Park (n); Selous Game Reserve (n); Kilimanjaro National Park (n); Stone Town of Zanzibar (c); Kondoa Rock-Art Sites (c)

ECONOMY

Economic overview: emerging lower middle-income East African economy; resource-rich and growing tourism; strong post-pandemic recovery from hospitality, electricity, mining, and transit sectors; declining poverty; stable inflation; gender-based violence economic and labor force disruptions

Real GDP (purchasing power parity): $246.706 billion (2024 est.)
$233.786 billion (2023 est.)
$222.506 billion (2022 est.)
note: data in 2021 dollars
comparison ranking: 69

Real GDP growth rate: 5.5% (2024 est.)
5.1% (2023 est.)
4.6% (2022 est.)
note: annual GDP % growth based on constant local currency
comparison ranking: 32

Real GDP per capita: $3,700 (2024 est.)
$3,600 (2023 est.)
$3,500 (2022 est.)
note: data in 2021 dollars
comparison ranking: 187

GDP (official exchange rate): $78.78 billion (2024 est.)
note: data in current dollars at official exchange rate

Inflation rate (consumer prices): 3.1% (2024 est.)
3.8% (2023 est.)
4.4% (2022 est.)
note: annual % change based on consumer prices
comparison ranking: 99

GDP - composition, by sector of origin: *agriculture:* 23.4% (2024 est.)
industry: 28.7% (2024 est.)
services: 28.4% (2024 est.)
note: figures may not total 100% due to non-allocated consumption not captured in sector-reported data
comparison rankings: agriculture 25; industry 66; services 206

GDP - composition, by end use: *household consumption:* 52.9% (2024 est.)
government consumption: 9.2% (2024 est.)
investment in fixed capital: 41.4% (2024 est.)
investment in inventories: -1.6% (2024 est.)
exports of goods and services: 19.8% (2024 est.)
imports of goods and services: -21.7% (2024 est.)
note: figures may not total 100% due to rounding or gaps in data collection

Agricultural products: maize, cassava, sweet potatoes, bananas, milk, sugarcane, rice, vegetables, beans, sunflower seeds (2023)
note: top ten agricultural products based on tonnage

Industries: agricultural processing (sugar, beer, cigarettes, sisal twine); mining (diamonds, gold, and iron), salt, soda ash; cement, oil refining, shoes, apparel, wood products, fertilizer

Industrial production growth rate: 5.2% (2024 est.)
note: annual % change in industrial value added based on constant local currency
comparison ranking: 41

Labor force: 32.983 million (2024 est.)
note: number of people ages 15 or older who are employed or seeking work
comparison ranking: 21

Unemployment rate: 2.6% (2024 est.)
2.6% (2023 est.)
2.6% (2022 est.)
note: % of labor force seeking employment
comparison ranking: 26

Youth unemployment rate (ages 15-24): *total:* 3.3% (2024 est.)
male: 2.6% (2024 est.)
female: 4.2% (2024 est.)
note: % of labor force ages 15-24 seeking employment
comparison ranking: total 180

Population below poverty line: 26.4% (2018 est.)
note: % of population with income below national poverty line

Gini Index coefficient - distribution of family income: 40.5 (2018 est.)
note: index (0-100) of income distribution; higher values represent greater inequality
comparison ranking: 40

Average household expenditures: *on food:* 26.2% of household expenditures (2023 est.)
on alcohol and tobacco: 1.3% of household expenditures (2023 est.)

Household income or consumption by percentage share: *lowest 10%:* 2.9% (2018 est.)
highest 10%: 33.1% (2018 est.)
note: % share of income accruing to lowest and highest 10% of population

Remittances: 1% of GDP (2023 est.)
0.9% of GDP (2022 est.)
0.8% of GDP (2021 est.)
note: personal transfers and compensation between resident and non-resident individuals/households/entities

Budget: *revenues:* $11.716 billion (2024 est.)
expenditures: $13.583 billion (2024 est.)
note: central government revenues and expenses (excluding grants/extrabudgetary units/social security funds) converted to US dollars at average official exchange rate for year indicated

Taxes and other revenues: 11.5% (of GDP) (2023 est.)
note: central government tax revenue as a % of GDP
comparison ranking: 121

Current account balance: -$2.958 billion (2023 est.)
-$5.482 billion (2022 est.)
-$2.374 billion (2021 est.)
note: balance of payments - net trade and primary/secondary income in current dollars
comparison ranking: 159

Exports: $13.98 billion (2023 est.)
$11.986 billion (2022 est.)
$9.874 billion (2021 est.)
note: balance of payments - exports of goods and services in current dollars
comparison ranking: 100

Exports - partners: India 15%, UAE 14%, Uganda 12%, South Africa 10%, China 6% (2023)
note: top five export partners based on percentage share of exports

Exports - commodities: gold, refined petroleum, dried legumes, refined copper, coal (2023)
note: top five export commodities based on value in dollars

Imports: $16.059 billion (2023 est.)
$16.674 billion (2022 est.)
$11.61 billion (2021 est.)
note: balance of payments - imports of goods and services in current dollars
comparison ranking: 106

Imports - partners: China 32%, India 13%, UAE 9%, Saudi Arabia 5%, Japan 4% (2023)
note: top five import partners based on percentage share of imports

Imports - commodities: refined petroleum, plastics, garments, fertilizers, wheat (2023)
note: top five import commodities based on value in dollars

Reserves of foreign exchange and gold: $5.05 billion (2018 est.)
$5.888 billion (2017 est.)
$4.351 billion (2016 est.)
note: holdings of gold (year-end prices)/foreign exchange/special drawing rights in current dollars
comparison ranking: 100

Debt - external: $17.513 billion (2023 est.)
note: present value of external debt in current US dollars
comparison ranking: 37

Exchange rates: Tanzanian shillings (TZS) per US dollar -

Exchange rates: 2,597.9 (2024 est.)
2,383.043 (2023 est.)
2,303.034 (2022 est.)
2,297.764 (2021 est.)
2,294.146 (2020 est.)

ENERGY

Electricity access: *electrification - total population:* 45.8% (2022 est.)
electrification - urban areas: 74.7%
electrification - rural areas: 36%

Electricity: *installed generating capacity:* 1.818 million kW (2023 est.)
consumption: 9.109 billion kWh (2023 est.)
imports: 157.688 million kWh (2023 est.)
transmission/distribution losses: 2.039 billion kWh (2023 est.)
comparison rankings: installed generating capacity 122; consumption 108; imports 111; transmission/distribution losses 124

Electricity generation sources: *fossil fuels:* 74.5% of total installed capacity (2023 est.)
solar: 0.3% of total installed capacity (2023 est.)
hydroelectricity: 24.6% of total installed capacity (2023 est.)
biomass and waste: 0.7% of total installed capacity (2023 est.)

Coal: *production:* 2.341 million metric tons (2023 est.)
consumption: 740,000 metric tons (2023 est.)
exports: 1.602 million metric tons (2023 est.)
imports: 21 metric tons (2023 est.)
proven reserves: 1.41 billion metric tons (2023 est.)

Petroleum: *refined petroleum consumption:* 85,000 bbl/day (2023 est.)

Natural gas: *production:* 2.016 billion cubic meters (2023 est.)
consumption: 2.016 billion cubic meters (2023 est.)
proven reserves: 6.513 billion cubic meters (2021 est.)

Energy consumption per capita: 4.091 million Btu/person (2023 est.)
comparison ranking: 174

COMMUNICATIONS

Telephones - fixed lines: *total subscriptions:* 76,000 (2023 est.)
subscriptions per 100 inhabitants: (2023 est.) less than 1
comparison ranking: total subscriptions 144

Telephones - mobile cellular: *total subscriptions:* 70.2 million (2023 est.)
subscriptions per 100 inhabitants: 92 (2022 est.)
comparison ranking: total subscriptions 26

Broadcast media: about 45 TV stations, with 13 national that broadcast free-to-air TV; 196 radio stations, most operating at the district level, but also including 5 independent national stations and 1 state-owned national radio station; international broadcasts widely available through satellite TV; 3 major satellite TV providers (2020)

Internet country code: .tz

Internet users: *percent of population:* 29% (2023 est.)

Broadband - fixed subscriptions: *total:* 1.66 million (2023 est.)
subscriptions per 100 inhabitants: 2 (2023 est.)
comparison ranking: total 66

TRANSPORTATION

Civil aircraft registration country code prefix: 5H

Airports: 206 (2025)
comparison ranking: 31

Railways: *total:* 4,097 km (2022)
standard gauge: 421 km (2022)
narrow gauge: 969 km (2022) 1.067 m gauge
broad gauge: 2,707 km (2022) 1.000 m guage

Merchant marine: *total:* 381 (2023)
by type: bulk carrier 4, container ship 17, general cargo 170, oil tanker 58, other 132
comparison ranking: total 51

Ports: *total ports:* 8 (2024)
large: 0
medium: 1
small: 3
very small: 4
ports with oil terminals: 4
key ports: Chake Chake, Dar Es Salaam, Tanga, Zanzibar

MILITARY AND SECURITY

Military and security forces: Tanzania People's Defense Forces (TPDF or Jeshi la Wananchi la Tanzania, JWTZ): Land Forces, Naval Forces, Air Force, Nation Building Army (Jeshi la Kujenga Taifa, JKT), Reserve Forces

Ministry of Home Affairs: Tanzania Police Force (Jeshi la Polisi Tanzania) (2025)
note 1: the Nation Building Army (aka National Services) is a paramilitary organization under the Defense Forces that provides six months of military and vocational training to individuals as part of their two years of public service; after completion of training, some graduates join the regular Defense Forces while the remainder become part of the Reserves
note 2: the Tanzania Police Force includes the Police Field Force (aka Field Force Unit), a special police division with the responsibility for controlling unlawful demonstrations and riots

Military expenditures: 1.4% of GDP (2024 est.)
1.3% of GDP (2023 est.)
1.2% of GDP (2022 est.)
1.1% of GDP (2021 est.)
1.2% of GDP (2020 est.)

Military and security service personnel strengths: approximately 25,000 active Defense Forces (2025)

Military equipment inventories and acquisitions: the TPDF's inventory includes mostly Chinese and Russian/Soviet-era weapons and equipment (2024)

Military service age and obligation: 18-25 years of age for voluntary military service for men and women; 6-year commitment (2-year contracts afterwards); selective conscription for 2 years of public service (2024)

Military deployments: 520 Central African Republic (MINUSCA); more than 1,000 Democratic Republic of the Congo (MONUSCO and Southern African Development Community regional force); 125 Lebanon (UNIFIL); approximately 300 Mozambique (under bi-lateral agreement to assist with combatting an insurgency) (2025)

Military - note: the chief concerns of the Tanzania Defense Forces (TDPF) are maritime piracy and smuggling, border security, terrorism, animal poaching, and spillover from instability in neighboring countries, particularly Mozambique and the Democratic Republic of the Congo (DRC); it participates in multinational training exercises, regional peacekeeping deployments, and has ties with a variety of foreign militaries, including those of China, India, and the US; it has contributed troops to the UN's Force Intervention Brigade in the DRC; the TPDF also participated in the former Southern African Development Community intervention force in Mozambique, which assisted the Mozambique military in combating fighters affiliated with the Islamic State of Iraq and ash-Sham (ISIS); the regional force withdrew in 2024, but the TPDF continues to maintain troops in Mozambique as part of a separate bilateral security agreement; since 2020, the TPDF has reinforced the border with Mozambique following several cross-border attacks by ISIS fighters (2025)

TERRORISM

Terrorist group(s): Terrorist group(s): al-Shabaab; Islamic State of Iraq and ash-Sham (ISIS)
note: details about the history, aims, leadership, organization, areas of operation, tactics, targets, weapons, size, and sources of support of the group(s) appear(s) in Appendix T

TRANSNATIONAL ISSUES

Refugees and internally displaced persons: *refugees:* 218,123 (2024 est.)

IDPs: 75,117 (2024 est.)

THAILAND

INTRODUCTION

Background: Two unified Thai kingdoms emerged in the mid-13th century. The Sukhothai Kingdom, located in the south-central plains, gained its independence from the Khmer Empire to the east. By the late 13th century, Sukhothai's territory extended into present-day Burma and Laos. Sukhothai lasted until the mid-15th century. The Thai Lan Na Kingdom was established in the north with its capital at Chang Mai; the Burmese conquered Lan Na in the 16th century. The Ayutthaya Kingdom (14th-18th centuries) succeeded the Sukhothai and would become known as the Siamese Kingdom. During the Ayutthaya period, the Thai/Siamese peoples consolidated their hold on what is present-day central and north-central Thailand. Following a military defeat at the hands of the Burmese in 1767, the Siamese Kingdom rose to new heights under the military ruler TAKSIN, who defeated the Burmese occupiers and expanded the kingdom's territory into modern-day northern Thailand (formerly the Lan Na Kingdom), Cambodia, Laos, and the Malay Peninsula. In the mid-1800s, Western pressure led to Siam signing trade treaties that reduced the country's sovereignty and independence. In the 1890s and 1900s, the British and French forced the kingdom to cede Cambodian, Laotian, and Malay territories that had been under Siamese control.

Following a bloodless revolution in 1932 that led to the establishment of a constitutional monarchy, Thailand's political history was marked by a series of mostly bloodless coups with power concentrated among military and bureaucratic elites. Periods of civilian rule were unstable. The Cold War era saw a communist insurgency and the rise of strongman leaders. Thailand became a US treaty ally in 1954 after sending troops to Korea and later fighting alongside the US in Vietnam. In the 21st century, Thailand has experienced additional turmoil, including a military coup in 2006 that ousted then Prime Minister THAKSIN Chinnawat and large-scale street protests led by competing political factions in 2008-2010. In 2011, THAKSIN's youngest sister, YINGLAK Chinnawat, led the Puea Thai Party to an electoral win and assumed control of the government.

In 2014, after months of major anti-government protests in Bangkok, the Constitutional Court removed YINGLAK from office, and the Army, led by Gen. PRAYUT Chan-ocha, then staged a coup against the caretaker government. The military-affiliated National Council for Peace and Order (NCPO) ruled the country under PRAYUT for more than four years, drafting a new constitution that allowed the military to appoint the entire 250-member Senate and required a joint meeting of the House and Senate to select the prime minister – which effectively gave the military a veto on the selection. King PHUMIPHON Adunyadet passed away in 2016 after 70 years on the throne; his only son, WACHIRALONGKON (aka King RAMA X), formally ascended the throne in 2019. The same year, a long-delayed election allowed PRAYUT to continue his premiership, although the results were disputed and widely viewed as skewed in favor of the party aligned with the military. The country again experienced major anti-government protests in 2020. The reformist Move Forward Party won the most seats in the 2023 election but was unable to form a government, and Srettha THRAVISIN from the Pheu Thai Party replaced PRAYUT as prime minister after forming a coalition of moderate and conservative parties.

GEOGRAPHY

Location: Southeastern Asia, bordering the Andaman Sea and the Gulf of Thailand, southeast of Burma

Geographic coordinates: 15 00 N, 100 00 E

Map references: Southeast Asia

Area: *total:* 513,120 sq km
land: 510,890 sq km
water: 2,230 sq km
comparison ranking: total 53

Area - comparative: about three times the size of Florida; slightly more than twice the size of Wyoming

Land boundaries: *total:* 5,673 km
border countries (4): Burma 2,416 km; Cambodia 817 km; Laos 1,845 km; Malaysia 595 km

Coastline: 3,219 km

Maritime claims: *territorial sea:* 12 nm
exclusive economic zone: 200 nm
continental shelf: 200-m depth or to the depth of exploitation

Climate: tropical; rainy, warm, cloudy southwest monsoon (mid-May to September); dry, cool northeast monsoon (November to mid-March); southern isthmus always hot and humid

Terrain: central plain; Khorat Plateau in the east; mountains elsewhere

Elevation: *highest point:* Doi Inthanon 2,565 m
lowest point: Gulf of Thailand 0 m
mean elevation: 287 m

Natural resources: tin, rubber, natural gas, tungsten, tantalum, timber, lead, fish, gypsum, lignite, fluorite, arable land

Land use: *agricultural land:* 46% (2022 est.)
arable land: 33.6% (2022 est.)
permanent crops: 10.9% (2022 est.)
permanent pasture: 1.6% (2022 est.)
forest: 38.8% (2022 est.)
other: 15.2% (2022 est.)

Irrigated land: 64,150 sq km (2012)

Major lakes (area sq km): *salt water lake(s):* Thalesap Songkhla - 1,290 sq km

Major rivers (by length in km): Mae Nam Khong (Mekong) (shared with China [s], Burma, Laos, Cambodia, and Vietnam [m]) - 4,350 km; Salween (shared with China [s] and Burma [m]) - 3,060 km; Mun - 1,162 km
note: [s] after country name indicates river source; [m] after country name indicates river mouth

Major watersheds (area sq km): Indian Ocean drainage: Salween (271,914 sq km)

Pacific Ocean drainage: Mekong (805,604 sq km)

Population distribution: highest population density is found in and around Bangkok; significant population clusters throughout large parts of the country, particularly north and northeast of Bangkok and in the extreme southern region of the country

Natural hazards: land subsidence in Bangkok area resulting from the depletion of the water table; droughts

Geography - note: controls only land route from Asia to Malaysia and Singapore

PEOPLE AND SOCIETY

Population: *total:* 69,920,998 (2024 est.)
male: 34,065,311
female: 35,855,687
comparison rankings: total 20; male 20; female 20

Nationality: *noun:* Thai (singular and plural)
adjective: Thai

Ethnic groups: Thai 97.5%, Burmese 1.3%, other 1.1%, unspecified <0.1% (2015 est.)
note: data represent population by nationality

Languages: Thai (official) only 90.7%, Thai and other languages 6.4%, only other languages 2.9% (includes Malay, Burmese); English is a secondary language among the elite (2010 est.)
major-language sample(s):
สารานุกรมโลก - แหล่งข้อมูลพื้นฐานที่สำคัญ (Thai)
note: data represent population by language(s) spoken at home

Religions: Buddhist 92.5%, Muslim 5.4%, Christian 1.2%, other 0.9% (includes animist, Confucian, Hindu, Jewish, Sikh, and Taoist) (2021 est.)

Age structure: *0-14 years:* 15.8% (male 5,669,592/female 5,394,398)
15-64 years: 69% (male 23,681,528/female 24,597,535)
65 years and over: 15.1% (2024 est.) (male 4,714,191/female 5,863,754)

Dependency ratios: *total dependency ratio:* 44.8 (2024 est.)
youth dependency ratio: 22.9 (2024 est.)
elderly dependency ratio: 21.9 (2024 est.)
potential support ratio: 4.6 (2024 est.)

Median age: *total:* 41.5 years (2024 est.)
male: 40.2 years
female: 42.7 years
comparison ranking: total 49

Population growth rate: 0.17% (2024 est.)
comparison ranking: 180

Birth rate: 9.9 births/1,000 population (2024 est.)
comparison ranking: 189

Death rate: 8 deaths/1,000 population (2024 est.)
comparison ranking: 90

Net migration rate: -0.3 migrant(s)/1,000 population (2024 est.)
comparison ranking: 116

Population distribution: highest population density is found in and around Bangkok; significant population clusters throughout large parts of the country, particularly north and northeast of Bangkok and in the extreme southern region of the country

Urbanization: *urban population:* 53.6% of total population (2023)
rate of urbanization: 1.43% annual rate of change (2020-25 est.)

Major urban areas - population: 11.070 million BANGKOK (capital), 1.454 Chon Buri, 1.359 million Samut Prakan, 1.213 million Chiang Mai, 1.005 million Songkla, 1.001 million Nothaburi (2023)

Sex ratio: *at birth:* 1.05 male(s)/female
0-14 years: 1.05 male(s)/female
15-64 years: 0.96 male(s)/female
65 years and over: 0.8 male(s)/female
total population: 0.95 male(s)/female (2024 est.)

Mother's mean age at first birth: 23.3 years (2009 est.)

Maternal mortality ratio: 34 deaths/100,000 live births (2023 est.)
comparison ranking: 113

Infant mortality rate: *total:* 6.3 deaths/1,000 live births (2024 est.)
male: 6.9 deaths/1,000 live births
female: 5.6 deaths/1,000 live births
comparison ranking: total 165

Life expectancy at birth: *total population:* 78.2 years (2024 est.)
male: 75.2 years
female: 81.3 years
comparison ranking: total population 81

Total fertility rate: 1.54 children born/woman (2024 est.)
comparison ranking: 197

Gross reproduction rate: 0.75 (2024 est.)

Drinking water source: *improved: urban:* 100% of population (2022 est.)
rural: 100% of population (2022 est.)
total: 100% of population (2022 est.)
unimproved: urban: 0% of population (2022 est.)
rural: 0% of population (2022 est.)
total: 0% of population (2022 est.)

Health expenditure: 5.2% of GDP (2021)
16.1% of national budget (2022 est.)

Physician density: 0.54 physicians/1,000 population (2021)

Hospital bed density: 2.3 beds/1,000 population (2021 est.)

Sanitation facility access: *improved: urban:* 99.9% of population (2022 est.)
rural: 100% of population (2022 est.)
total: 100% of population (2022 est.)
unimproved: urban: 0.1% of population (2022 est.)
rural: 0% of population (2022 est.)
total: 0% of population (2022 est.)

Obesity - adult prevalence rate: 10% (2016)
comparison ranking: 140

Alcohol consumption per capita: *total:* 6.86 liters of pure alcohol (2019 est.)
beer: 1.85 liters of pure alcohol (2019 est.)
wine: 0.23 liters of pure alcohol (2019 est.)
spirits: 4.78 liters of pure alcohol (2019 est.)
other alcohols: 0 liters of pure alcohol (2019 est.)
comparison ranking: total 60

Tobacco use: *total:* 18.1% (2025 est.)
male: 36.1% (2025 est.)
female: 1.6% (2025 est.)
comparison ranking: total 83

Children under the age of 5 years underweight: 7.7% (2019)
comparison ranking: 57

Currently married women (ages 15-49): 60.8% (2023 est.)

Child marriage: *women married by age 15:* 5.5% (2022)
women married by age 18: 17% (2022)
men married by age 18: 5.8% (2022)

Education expenditure: 2.5% of GDP (2023 est.)
11.6% national budget (2023 est.)
comparison ranking: Education expenditure (% GDP) 171

Literacy: *total population:* 91.1% (2022 est.)
male: 90.7% (2022 est.)
female: 91.5% (2022 est.)

School life expectancy (primary to tertiary education): *total:* 16 years (2023 est.)
male: 16 years (2023 est.)
female: 16 years (2023 est.)

ENVIRONMENT

Environmental issues: air pollution from vehicle emissions; water pollution from organic and factory wastes; water scarcity; deforestation; soil erosion; illegal hunting; hazardous waste disposal

International environmental agreements: *party to:* Biodiversity, Climate Change, Climate Change-Kyoto Protocol, Climate Change-Paris Agreement, Comprehensive Nuclear Test Ban, Desertification, Endangered Species, Hazardous Wastes, Law of the Sea, Marine Life Conservation, Nuclear Test Ban, Ozone Layer Protection, Ship Pollution, Tropical Timber 2006, Wetlands
signed, but not ratified: none of the selected agreements

Climate: tropical; rainy, warm, cloudy southwest monsoon (mid-May to September); dry, cool northeast monsoon (November to mid-March); southern isthmus always hot and humid

Urbanization: *urban population:* 53.6% of total population (2023)
rate of urbanization: 1.43% annual rate of change (2020-25 est.)

Carbon dioxide emissions: 336.693 million metric tonnes of CO2 (2023 est.)
from coal and metallurgical coke: 79.928 million metric tonnes of CO2 (2023 est.)
from petroleum and other liquids: 160.931 million metric tonnes of CO2 (2023 est.)
from consumed natural gas: 95.834 million metric tonnes of CO2 (2023 est.)
comparison ranking: total emissions 18

Particulate matter emissions: 26.3 micrograms per cubic meter (2019 est.)

Methane emissions: *energy:* 708.8 kt (2022-2024 est.)
agriculture: 2,109.9 kt (2019-2021 est.)
waste: 635.8 kt (2019-2021 est.)
other: 57.9 kt (2019-2021 est.)

Waste and recycling: *municipal solid waste generated annually:* 26.853 million tons (2024 est.)
percent of municipal solid waste recycled: 40% (2022 est.)

Total water withdrawal: *municipal:* 2.739 billion cubic meters (2022 est.)
industrial: 2.777 billion cubic meters (2022 est.)
agricultural: 51.79 billion cubic meters (2022 est.)

Total renewable water resources: 438.61 billion cubic meters (2022 est.)

Geoparks: *total global geoparks and regional networks:* 2
global geoparks and regional networks: Khorat; Satun (2023)

GOVERNMENT

Country name: *conventional long form:* Kingdom of Thailand
conventional short form: Thailand
local long form: Ratcha Anachak Thai
local short form: Prathet Thai
former: Siam
etymology: the name means "Land of the Thai," referring to the local population; the people's name comes from the Thai word *tha*, meaning "to be free;" the former name of Siam comes from the Sanskrit word *syama*, meaning "dark"

Government type: constitutional monarchy

Capital: *name:* Bangkok
geographic coordinates: 13 45 N, 100 31 E
time difference: UTC+7 (12 hours ahead of Washington, DC, during Standard Time)
etymology: the name is from the Thai words *bang* (region) and *kok* (olive trees); the city's full ceremonial name holds the world record for longest place name, Krungthepmahanakhon amonrattanakosin mahintharayutthaya mahadilokphop noppharatratchathaniburirom udomratchaniwetmahasathan amonphimanawatansathit sakkathattiyawitsanukamprasit, which means "City of angels, great city of immortals, magnificent city of the nine gems, seat of the king, city of royal palaces, home of gods incarnate, erected by Vishvakarman at Indra's behest"

Administrative divisions: 76 provinces (*changwat*, singular and plural) and 1 municipality* (*maha nakhon*); Amnat Charoen, Ang Thong, Bueng Kan, Buri Ram, Chachoengsao, Chai Nat,

Chaiyaphum, Chanthaburi, Chiang Mai, Chiang Rai, Chon Buri, Chumphon, Kalasin, Kamphaeng Phet, Kanchanaburi, Khon Kaen, Krabi, Krung Thep* (Bangkok), Lampang, Lamphun, Loei, Lop Buri, Mae Hong Son, Maha Sarakham, Mukdahan, Nakhon Nayok, Nakhon Pathom, Nakhon Phanom, Nakhon Ratchasima, Nakhon Sawan, Nakhon Si Thammarat, Nan, Narathiwat, Nong Bua Lamphu, Nong Khai, Nonthaburi, Pathum Thani, Pattani, Phangnga, Phatthalung, Phayao, Phetchabun, Phetchaburi, Phichit, Phitsanulok, Phra Nakhon Si Ayutthaya, Phrae, Phuket, Prachin Buri, Prachuap Khiri Khan, Ranong, Ratchaburi, Rayong, Roi Et, Sa Kaeo, Sakon Nakhon, Samut Prakan, Samut Sakhon, Samut Songkhram, Saraburi, Satun, Sing Buri, Si Sa Ket, Songkhla, Sukhothai, Suphan Buri, Surat Thani, Surin, Tak, Trang, Trat, Ubon Ratchathani, Udon Thani, Uthai Thani, Uttaradit, Yala, Yasothon

Legal system: civil law system with common law influences

Constitution: *history:* many previous; latest drafted and presented 29 March 2016, approved by referendum 7 August 2016, signed into law by the king on 6 April 2017
amendment process: amendments require a majority vote in a joint session of the House and Senate and further require at least one fifth of opposition House members and one third of the Senate vote in favor; a national referendum is additionally required for certain amendments; all amendments require signature by the king

International law organization participation: has not submitted an ICJ jurisdiction declaration; non-party state to the ICCt

Citizenship: *citizenship by birth:* no
citizenship by descent only: at least one parent must be a citizen of Thailand
dual citizenship recognized: no
residency requirement for naturalization: 5 years

Suffrage: 18 years of age; universal and compulsory

Executive branch: *chief of state:* King WACHIRALONGKON; also spelled Vajiralongkorn (since 1 December 2016)
head of government: Prime Minister ANUTIN Charnvirakul (since 5 Sep 2025)
cabinet: Council of Ministers nominated by the prime minister, appointed by the king; a Privy Council advises the king
election/appointment process: the monarchy is hereditary; prime minister candidate approved by House of Representatives and appointed by the king

Legislative branch: *legislature name:* National Assembly (Rathhasapha)
legislative structure: bicameral

Legislative branch - lower chamber: *chamber name:* House of Representatives (Saphaphuthan Ratsadon)
number of seats: 500 (all directly elected)
electoral system: mixed system
scope of elections: full renewal
term in office: 4 years
most recent election date: 5/14/2023
parties elected and seats per party: Move Forward (151); Pheu Thai (141); Bhumjaithai (71); Palang Pracharath (40); United Thai Nation (36); Democrat Party (25); Other (36)
percentage of women in chamber: 19.6%
expected date of next election: May 2028

Legislative branch - upper chamber: *chamber name:* Senate (Wuthisapha)
number of seats: 200 (all indirectly elected)
scope of elections: full renewal
term in office: 5 years
most recent election date: 6/9/2024 to 6/26/2024
percentage of women in chamber: 22.5%
expected date of next election: June 2029
note: Senate members are indirectly elected from 20 eligible groups of professions, including agriculture, artists or athletes, business owners, education, employees or workers, independent professionals, industrialists, law and justice, mass communication, public health, science and technology, tourism-related professions, women, and elderly, disabled, or ethnic groups

Judicial branch: *highest court(s):* Supreme Court of Justice (consists of the court president, 6 vice presidents, 60-70 judges, and organized into 10 divisions); Constitutional Court (consists of the court president and 8 judges); Supreme Administrative Court (number of judges determined by Judicial Commission of the Administrative Courts)
judge selection and term of office: Supreme Court judges selected by the Judicial Commission of the Courts of Justice and approved by the monarch; judge term determined by the monarch; Constitutional Court justices - 3 judges drawn from the Supreme Court, 2 judges drawn from the Administrative Court, and 4 judge candidates selected by the Selective Committee for Judges of the Constitutional Court, and confirmed by the Senate; judges appointed by the monarch serve single 9-year terms; Supreme Administrative Court judges selected by the Judicial Commission of the Administrative Courts and appointed by the monarch; judges serve for life
subordinate courts: courts of first instance and appeals courts within both the judicial and administrative systems; military courts

Political parties: Bhumjaithai Party or BJT (aka Phumchai Thai Party or PJT; aka Thai Pride Party)
Chat Thai Phatthana Party (Thai Nation Development Party) or CTP
Move Forward Party or MFP (dissolved by order of the Constitutional Court, August 2024)
Palang Pracharat Party (People's State Power Party) or PPRP
Pheu (Puea) Thai Party (For Thais Party) or PTP
Prachachat Party or PCC
Prachathipat Party (Democrat Party) or DP
Thai Sang Thai Party
United Thai Nation (Ruam Thai Sang Chat) or UTN

Diplomatic representation in the US: *chief of mission:* Ambassador Dr. SURIYA Chindawongse (since 17 June 2024)
chancery: 1024 Wisconsin Avenue NW, Suite 401, Washington, DC 20007
telephone: [1] (202) 944-3600
FAX: [1] (202) 944-3611
email address and website: thai.wsn@thaiembdc.org
https://washingtondc.thaiembassy.org/en/index
consulate(s) general: Chicago, Los Angeles, New York

Diplomatic representation from the US: *chief of mission:* Ambassador Robert F. GODEC (since 7 October 2022)
embassy: 95 Wireless Road, Bangkok 10330
mailing address: 7200 Bangkok Place, Washington DC 20521-7200
telephone: [66] 2-205-4000
FAX: [66] 2-205-4103
email address and website: acsbkk@state.gov
https://th.usembassy.gov/
consulate(s) general: Chiang Mai

International organization participation: ADB, APEC, ARF, ASEAN, BIMSTEC, BIS, CD, CICA, CP, EAS, FAO, G-77, IAEA, IBRD, ICAO, ICC (national committees), ICRM, IDA, IFAD, IFC, IFRCS, IHO, ILO, IMF, IMO, IMSO, Interpol, IOC, IOM, IPU, ISO, ITSO, ITU, ITUC (NGOs), MIGA, NAM, OAS (observer), OIC (observer), OIF (observer), OPCW, OSCE (partner), PCA, PIF (partner), UN, UNAMID, UNCTAD, UNESCO, UNHCR, UNIDO, UNMOGIP, UNOCI, UNWTO, UPU, WCO, WFTU (NGOs), WHO, WIPO, WMO, WTO

Independence: 1238 (traditional founding date; never colonized)

National holiday: Birthday of King WACHIRALONGKON, 28 July (1952)

Flag: *description:* five horizontal bands of red (top), white, blue (double-width), white, and red
meaning: red stands for the nation and the blood of life, white for religion and the purity of Buddhism, and blue for the monarchy
note: similar to the flag of Costa Rica, but with the blue and red colors reversed

National symbol(s): garuda (mythical half-man, half-bird figure), elephant

National color(s): red, white, blue

National coat of arms: in 1911, King Vajiravudh (Rama VI) of Thailand officially adopted the Garuda as the national coat of arms and emblem; this mythological half-man, half-bird figure from the Hindu and Buddhist traditions is considered the *vahana* (vehicle) of the god Vishnu (Narayana) and was a symbol of royalty in Thailand for centuries

National anthem(s): *title:* "Phleng Chat Thai" (National Anthem of Thailand)
lyrics/music: Luang SARANUPRAPAN/Phra JENDURIYANG
history: music adopted 1934, lyrics adopted 1939; it is the law that citizens stand and show respect for nation when the anthem is heard; the anthem is played each day at 8:00 am and 6:00 pm when the flag is raised and lowered
title: "Phleng Sanlasoen Phra Barami" (A Salute to the Monarch)
lyrics/music: Narisara NUWATTIWONG and King VAJIRAVUDH/Pyotr SHCHUROVSKY
history: royal anthem, played in the presence of the royal family and during certain state ceremonies

National heritage: *total World Heritage Sites:* 8 (5 cultural, 3 natural)
selected World Heritage Site locales: Historic City of Ayutthaya (c); Historic Sukhothai and Associated Historic Towns (c); Thungyai-Huai Kha Khaeng Wildlife Sanctuaries (n); Ban Chiang Archaeological Site (c); Dong Phayayen-Khao Yai Forest Complex (n); Kaeng Krachan Forest Complex (n); The Ancient Town of Si Thep and its Associated Dvaravati Monuments (n); Phu Phrabat, a testimony to the Sīma stone tradition of the Dvaravati period (c)

ECONOMY

Economic overview: upper middle-income Southeast Asian economy; substantial infrastructure; major electronics, food, and automobile parts exporter;

globally used currency; extremely low unemployment, even amid COVID-19; ongoing Thailand 4.0 economic development

Real GDP (purchasing power parity): $1.558 trillion (2024 est.)
$1.519 trillion (2023 est.)
$1.489 trillion (2022 est.)
note: data in 2021 dollars
comparison ranking: 22

Real GDP growth rate: 2.5% (2024 est.)
2% (2023 est.)
2.6% (2022 est.)
note: annual GDP % growth based on constant local currency
comparison ranking: 138

Real GDP per capita: $21,700 (2024 est.)
$21,200 (2023 est.)
$20,800 (2022 est.)
note: data in 2021 dollars
comparison ranking: 99

GDP (official exchange rate): $526.411 billion (2024 est.)
note: data in current dollars at official exchange rate

Inflation rate (consumer prices): 1.4% (2024 est.)
8.5% (2023 est.)
-1.6% (2022 est.)
note: annual % change based on consumer prices
comparison ranking: 35

GDP - composition, by sector of origin: *agriculture:* 8.7% (2024 est.)
industry: 32.1% (2024 est.)
services: 59.2% (2024 est.)
note: figures may not total 100% due to non-allocated consumption not captured in sector-reported data
comparison rankings: agriculture 80; industry 43; services 96

GDP - composition, by end use: *household consumption:* 58.2% (2024 est.)
government consumption: 16.7% (2024 est.)
investment in fixed capital: 22.2% (2024 est.)
investment in inventories: -0.6% (2024 est.)
exports of goods and services: 70.1% (2024 est.)
imports of goods and services: -66.7% (2024 est.)
note: figures may not total 100% due to rounding or gaps in data collection

Agricultural products: sugarcane, rice, cassava, oil palm fruit, maize, rubber, tropical fruits, chicken, mangoes/guavas, fruits (2023)
note: top ten agricultural products based on tonnage

Industries: tourism, textiles and garments, agricultural processing, beverages, tobacco, cement, light manufacturing such as jewelry and electric appliances, computers and parts, integrated circuits, furniture, plastics, automobiles and automotive parts, agricultural machinery, air conditioning and refrigeration, ceramics, aluminum, chemical, environmental management, glass, granite and marble, leather, machinery and metal work, petrochemical, petroleum refining, pharmaceuticals, printing, pulp and paper, rubber, sugar, rice, fishing, cassava, world's second-largest tungsten producer and third-largest tin producer

Industrial production growth rate: 0.9% (2024 est.)
note: annual % change in industrial value added based on constant local currency
comparison ranking: 116

Labor force: 40.623 million (2024 est.)
note: number of people ages 15 or older who are employed or seeking work
comparison ranking: 16

Unemployment rate: 0.7% (2024 est.)
0.8% (2023 est.)
1% (2022 est.)
note: % of labor force seeking employment
comparison ranking: 4

Youth unemployment rate (ages 15-24): *total:* 4.3% (2024 est.)
male: 3.1% (2024 est.)
female: 6% (2024 est.)
note: % of labor force ages 15-24 seeking employment
comparison ranking: total 166

Population below poverty line: 5.4% (2022 est.)
note: % of population with income below national poverty line

Gini Index coefficient - distribution of family income: 33.5 (2023 est.)
note: index (0-100) of income distribution; higher values represent greater inequality
comparison ranking: 94

Average household expenditures: *on food:* 25.9% of household expenditures (2023 est.)
on alcohol and tobacco: 3% of household expenditures (2023 est.)

Household income or consumption by percentage share: *lowest 10%:* 3.4% (2023 est.)
highest 10%: 26.1% (2023 est.)
note: % share of income accruing to lowest and highest 10% of population

Remittances: 1.8% of GDP (2024 est.)
1.9% of GDP (2023 est.)
1.8% of GDP (2022 est.)
note: personal transfers and compensation between resident and non-resident individuals/households/entities

Budget: *revenues:* $102.84 billion (2023 est.)
expenditures: $114.521 billion (2023 est.)
note: central government revenues (excluding grants) and expenditures converted to US dollars at average official exchange rate for year indicated

Public debt: 61.1% of GDP (2023 est.)
note: central government debt as a % of GDP
comparison ranking: 77

Taxes and other revenues: 15.4% (of GDP) (2023 est.)
note: central government tax revenue as a % of GDP
comparison ranking: 89

Current account balance: $11.089 billion (2024 est.)
$7.412 billion (2023 est.)
-$17.162 billion (2022 est.)
note: balance of payments - net trade and primary/secondary income in current dollars
comparison ranking: 27

Exports: $369.191 billion (2024 est.)
$337.45 billion (2023 est.)
$324.111 billion (2022 est.)
note: balance of payments - exports of goods and services in current dollars
comparison ranking: 27

Exports - partners: USA 18%, China 13%, Japan 7%, Australia 4%, Singapore 4% (2023)
note: top five export partners based on percentage share of exports

Exports - commodities: machine parts, integrated circuits, trucks, cars, broadcasting equipment (2023)
note: top five export commodities based on value in dollars

Imports: $351.419 billion (2024 est.)
$327.008 billion (2023 est.)
$334.44 billion (2022 est.)
note: balance of payments - imports of goods and services in current dollars
comparison ranking: 27

Imports - partners: China 26%, Japan 11%, USA 7%, UAE 6%, Taiwan 5% (2023)
note: top five import partners based on percentage share of imports

Imports - commodities: crude petroleum, integrated circuits, natural gas, gold, vehicle parts/accessories (2023)
note: top five import commodities based on value in dollars

Reserves of foreign exchange and gold: $236.934 billion (2024 est.)
$224.47 billion (2023 est.)
$216.501 billion (2022 est.)
note: holdings of gold (year-end prices)/foreign exchange/special drawing rights in current dollars
comparison ranking: 16

Debt - external: $37.065 billion (2023 est.)
note: present value of external debt in current US dollars
comparison ranking: 23

Exchange rates: baht per US dollar -

Exchange rates: 35.294 (2024 est.)
34.802 (2023 est.)
35.061 (2022 est.)
31.977 (2021 est.)
31.294 (2020 est.)

ENERGY

Electricity access: *electrification - total population:* 99.9% (2022 est.)
electrification - urban areas: 100%
electrification - rural areas: 100%

Electricity: *installed generating capacity:* 55.971 million kW (2023 est.)
consumption: 215.281 billion kWh (2023 est.)
exports: 2.256 billion kWh (2023 est.)
imports: 35.805 billion kWh (2023 est.)
transmission/distribution losses: 14.44 billion kWh (2023 est.)
comparison rankings: installed generating capacity 27; consumption 22; exports 54; imports 4; transmission/distribution losses 186

Electricity generation sources: *fossil fuels:* 81.9% of total installed capacity (2023 est.)
solar: 2.7% of total installed capacity (2023 est.)
wind: 1.8% of total installed capacity (2023 est.)
hydroelectricity: 3.5% of total installed capacity (2023 est.)
biomass and waste: 10.1% of total installed capacity (2023 est.)

Coal: *production:* 12.812 million metric tons (2023 est.)
consumption: 42.371 million metric tons (2023 est.)
exports: 65,000 metric tons (2023 est.)
imports: 29.757 million metric tons (2023 est.)
proven reserves: 1.063 billion metric tons (2023 est.)

Petroleum: *total petroleum production:* 386,000 bbl/day (2023 est.)

refined petroleum consumption: 1.397 million bbl/day (2023 est.)
crude oil estimated reserves: 252.75 million barrels (2021 est.)

Natural gas: *production:* 29.614 billion cubic meters (2023 est.)
consumption: 52.351 billion cubic meters (2023 est.)
imports: 22.738 billion cubic meters (2023 est.)
proven reserves: 138.243 billion cubic meters (2021 est.)

Energy consumption per capita: 80.602 million Btu/person (2023 est.)
comparison ranking: 64

COMMUNICATIONS

Telephones - fixed lines: *total subscriptions:* 4.087 million (2023 est.)
subscriptions per 100 inhabitants: 6 (2023 est.)
comparison ranking: total subscriptions 33

Telephones - mobile cellular: *total subscriptions:* 121 million (2023 est.)
subscriptions per 100 inhabitants: 176 (2022 est.)
comparison ranking: total subscriptions 15

Broadcast media: 26 digital TV stations and 6 terrestrial TV stations broadcast nationally via relay stations, with 2 of the terrestrial stations military-owned and the other 4 state-owned or state-controlled; some leased to private enterprise; all required to broadcast government-produced news; multi-channel satellite and cable TV subscriptions available; radio frequencies allotted for over 500 government and commercial radio stations; many small community radio stations operate with low-power transmitters (2017)

Internet country code: .th

Internet users: *percent of population:* 90% (2023 est.)

Broadband - fixed subscriptions: *total:* 11.5 million (2023 est.)
subscriptions per 100 inhabitants: 16 (2023 est.)
comparison ranking: total 22

TRANSPORTATION

Civil aircraft registration country code prefix: HS

Airports: 105 (2025)
comparison ranking: 51

Heliports: 5 (2025)
comparison ranking: 104

Railways: *total:* 4,127 km (2017)
standard gauge: 84 km (2017) 1.435-m gauge (84 km electrified)
narrow gauge: 4,043 km (2017) 1.000-m gauge

Merchant marine: *total:* 884 (2023)
by type: bulk carrier 28, container ship 28, general cargo 88, oil tanker 251, other 489
comparison ranking: total 28

Ports: *total ports:* 21 (2024)
large: 1
medium: 2
small: 3
very small: 15
ports with oil terminals: 14
key ports: Bangkok, Laem Chabang, Pattani, Phuket, Sattahip, Si Racha

MILITARY AND SECURITY

Military and security forces: Royal Thai Armed Forces (RTARF): Royal Thai Army (RTA), Royal Thai Navy (RTN; includes Royal Thai Marine Corps), Royal Thai Air Force (RTAF)

Office of the Prime Minister: Royal Thai Police (2025)
note: official paramilitary forces in Thailand include the Thai Rangers (Thahan Phran or "Hunter Soldiers") under the Army; the Paramilitary Marines under the Navy; the Border Patrol Police (BPP) under the Royal Thai Police; the Volunteer Defense Corps (VDC or *O So*) and National Defense Volunteers (NDV), both under the Ministry of Interior; there are also several government-backed volunteer militias created to provide village security against insurgents in the Deep South or to assist government security forces

Military expenditures: 1.1% of GDP (2024 est.)
1.3% of GDP (2023 est.)
1.3% of GDP (2022 est.)
1.3% of GDP (2021 est.)
1.4% of GDP (2020 est.)

Military and security service personnel strengths: estimated 350,000 active-duty Armed Forces (250,000 Army; 70,000 Navy; 30,000 Air Force) (2025)

Military equipment inventories and acquisitions: the RTARF has a diverse array of foreign-supplied weapons and equipment, as well as some domestically produced items; in recent years, Thailand has received arms from a wide variety of countries, including China and the US; Thailand has a domestic defense industry, which produces such items as armored vehicles, artillery systems, naval vessels, unmanned aerial vehicles, and other military technologies (2024)

Military service age and obligation: 18 years of age for voluntary military service for men and women; 21 years of age for compulsory military service for men; men register at 18 years of age; volunteer service obligation may be as short as 6 or 12 months, depending on educational qualifications; conscript service obligation also varies by educational qualifications, but is typically 24 months (2024)
note: serving in the armed forces is a national duty of all Thai citizens; conscription was introduced in 1905; it includes women, however, only men over the age of 21 who have not gone through reserve training are conscripted; conscripts are chosen by lottery (on draft day, eligible draftees can request volunteer service, or they may choose to stay for the conscription lottery); approximately 100,000 men are drafted for military service each year

Military deployments: 280 South Sudan (UNMISS) (2024)

Military - note: the missions of the Royal Thai Armed Forces (RTARF) include defending the country's territory and sovereignty, protecting the monarchy, ensuring internal security, and responding to natural disasters; key areas of emphasis are disputed international borders and a low-level insurgency in the country's south; the military has historically had a large role in domestic politics and has attempted as many as 20 coups since the fall of absolute monarchy in 1932, the most recent being in 2014

in July 2025, following months of rising tensions, the RTARF and Cambodian military forces clashed in multiple locations along their disputed border; both sides blamed the other for provoking the five-day conflict, which included cross-border artillery shelling by both sides and air attacks by RTARF fighter aircraft and drones; since 2004, the RTARF and Thai paramilitary forces have combated a separatist insurgency in the southern Thailand provinces of Pattani, Yala, and Narathiwat, as well as parts of Songkhla; the insurgency is rooted in ethnic Malay nationalist resistance to Thai rule that followed the extension of Siamese sovereignty over the Patani Sultanate in the 18th century; the insurgency consists of several armed groups, the largest of which is the Barisan Revolusi Nasional-Koordinasi (BRN-C): insurgent attacks have largely involved bombings; since 2020, Thai officials have been negotiating with BRN, and has parallel talks with an umbrella organization, MARA Pattani, that claims to represent the insurgency groups (2025)

SPACE

Space agency/agencies: Geo-Informatics and Space Technology Development Agency (GISTDA; created in 2000 from the Thailand Remote Sensing Center that was established in 1979; GISTDA is under the Ministry of Higher Education, Science, Research and Innovation); National Space Policy Committee (NSPC; advisory body to the prime minister) (2025)

Space launch site(s): none; in 2023, announced intentions to build a spaceport with South Korean assistance (2025)

Space program overview: has an ambitious and growing national space program focused on the acquisition, production, and operation of satellites, as well as research and development of related space infrastructure, sciences, and technologies; operates communications and remote sensing (RS) satellites; manufactures scientific/research/testing cube satellites and developing the capabilities to produce RS satellites (has historically built satellites with foreign assistance); cooperates with a range of foreign space agencies and industries, including those of other ASEAN countries, China, France, India, the Netherlands, Pakistan, Russia, South Korea, and the US; founding member of the China-led Asia-Pacific Space Cooperation Organization (APSCO); has a growing space industry, including Southeast Asia's first dedicated satellite manufacturing facility, which opened in 2021 (2025)
note: further details about the key activities, programs, and milestones of the country's space program, as well as government spending estimates on the space sector, appear in the Space Programs reference guide

TRANSNATIONAL ISSUES

Refugees and internally displaced persons: *refugees:* 87,025 (2024 est.)

IDPs: 19 (2023 est.)
stateless persons: 612,524 (2024 est.)

Illicit drugs: USG identification: major precursor-chemical producer (2025)

TIMOR-LESTE

INTRODUCTION

Background: The island of Timor was actively involved in Southeast Asian trading networks for centuries, and by the 14th century, it exported sandalwood, slaves, honey, and wax. The sandalwood trade attracted the Portuguese, who arrived in the early 16th century; by mid-century, they had colonized the island, which was previously ruled by local chieftains. In 1859, Portugal ceded the western portion of the island to the Dutch. Imperial Japan occupied Portuguese Timor from 1942 to 1945, but Portugal resumed colonial authority after the Japanese defeat in World War II. The eastern part of Timor declared itself independent from Portugal on 28 November 1975, but Indonesian forces invaded and occupied the area nine days later. It was incorporated into Indonesia in 1976 as the province of Timor Timur (East Timor or Timor Leste). Indonesia conducted an unsuccessful pacification campaign in the province over the next two decades, during which as many as 250,000 people died.

In a UN-supervised referendum in 1999, an overwhelming majority of the people of Timor-Leste voted for independence from Indonesia. However, anti-independence Timorese militias – organized and supported by the Indonesian military – began a large-scale, scorched-earth campaign of retribution, killing approximately 1,400 Timorese and displacing nearly 500,000. Most of the country's infrastructure was destroyed, including homes, irrigation systems, water supply systems, schools, and most of the electrical grid. Australian-led peacekeeping troops eventually deployed to the country and ended the violence. In 2002, Timor-Leste was internationally recognized as an independent state.

In 2006, Australia and the UN had to step in again to stabilize the country, which allowed presidential and parliamentary elections to be conducted in 2007 in a largely peaceful atmosphere. In 2008, rebels staged an unsuccessful attack against the president and prime minister. Since that attack, Timor-Leste has made considerable progress in building stability and democratic institutions, holding a series of successful parliamentary and presidential elections since 2012. Nonetheless, weak and unstable political coalitions have led to periodic episodes of stalemate and crisis. The UN continues to provide assistance on economic development and strengthening governing institutions. Currently, Timor-Leste is one of the world's poorest nations, with an economy that relies heavily on energy resources in the Timor Sea.

GEOGRAPHY

Location: Southeastern Asia, northwest of Australia in the Lesser Sunda Islands at the eastern end of the Indonesian archipelago; note - Timor-Leste includes the eastern half of the island of Timor, the Oecussi (Ambeno) region on the northwest portion of the island of Timor, and the islands of Pulau Atauro and Pulau Jaco

Geographic coordinates: 8 50 S, 125 55 E

Map references: Southeast Asia

Area: *total:* 14,874 sq km
land: 14,874 sq km
water: 0 sq km
comparison ranking: total 159

Area - comparative: slightly larger than Connecticut; almost half the size of Maryland

Land boundaries: *total:* 253 km
border countries (1): Indonesia 253 km

Coastline: 706 km

Maritime claims: *territorial sea:* 12 nm
contiguous zone: 24 nm
exclusive fishing zone: 200 nm

Climate: tropical; hot, humid; distinct rainy and dry seasons

Terrain: mountainous

Elevation: *highest point:* Foho Tatamailau 2,963 m
lowest point: Timor Sea, Savu Sea, and Banda Sea 0 m

Natural resources: gold, petroleum, natural gas, manganese, marble

Land use: *agricultural land:* 23% (2022 est.)
arable land: 7.5% (2022 est.)
permanent crops: 5.4% (2022 est.)
permanent pasture: 10.1% (2022 est.)
forest: 61.8% (2022 est.)
other: 15.3% (2022 est.)

Irrigated land: 350 sq km (2012)

Population distribution: most of the population is concentrated in the western third of the country, particularly around Dili

Natural hazards: floods and landslides are common; earthquakes; tsunamis; tropical cyclones

Geography - note: the island of Timor is part of the Malay Archipelago and is the largest and easternmost of the Lesser Sunda Islands; the district of Oecussi is an exclave separated from Timor-Leste proper by Indonesia; Timor-Leste is the only Asian country located completely in the Southern Hemisphere

PEOPLE AND SOCIETY

Population: *total:* 1,506,909 (2024 est.)
male: 750,665
female: 756,244
comparison rankings: total 156; male 156; female 154

Nationality: *noun:* Timorese
adjective: Timorese

Ethnic groups: Austronesian (Malayo-Polynesian) (includes Tetun, Mambai, Tokodede, Galoli, Kemak, Baikeno), Melanesian-Papuan (includes Bunak, Fataluku, Bakasai), small Chinese minority

Languages: Tetun Prasa 30.6%, Mambai 16.6%, Makasai 10.5%, Tetun Terik 6.1%, Baikenu 5.9%, Kemak 5.8%, Bunak 5.5%, Tokodede 4%, Fataluku 3.5%, Waima'a 1.8%, Galoli 1.4%, Naueti 1.4%, Idate 1.2%, Midiki 1.2%, other 4.5% (2015 est.)
note: data represent population by mother tongue; Tetun and Portuguese are official languages; Indonesian and English are working languages; there are about 32 indigenous languages

Religions: Roman Catholic 97.6%, Protestant/Evangelical 2%, Muslim 0.2%, other 0.2% (2015 est.)

Age structure: *0-14 years:* 38.7% (male 299,929/female 283,416)
15-64 years: 56.8% (male 418,493/female 437,727)
65 years and over: 4.5% (2024 est.) (male 32,243/female 35,101)

Dependency ratios: *total dependency ratio:* 63.8 (2024 est.)
youth dependency ratio: 56.1 (2024 est.)
elderly dependency ratio: 7.7 (2024 est.)
potential support ratio: 13 (2024 est.)

Median age: *total:* 20.6 years (2024 est.)
male: 19.8 years
female: 21.3 years
comparison ranking: total 201

Population growth rate: 2.04% (2024 est.)
comparison ranking: 39

Birth rate: 29.7 births/1,000 population (2024 est.)
comparison ranking: 26

Death rate: 5.5 deaths/1,000 population (2024 est.)
comparison ranking: 180

Net migration rate: -3.8 migrant(s)/1,000 population (2024 est.)
comparison ranking: 192

Population distribution: most of the population is concentrated in the western third of the country, particularly around Dili

Urbanization: *urban population:* 32.5% of total population (2023)
rate of urbanization: 3.31% annual rate of change (2020-25 est.)

Major urban areas - population: 281,000 DILI (capital) (2018)

Sex ratio: *at birth:* 1.07 male(s)/female
0-14 years: 1.06 male(s)/female
15-64 years: 0.96 male(s)/female
65 years and over: 0.92 male(s)/female
total population: 0.99 male(s)/female (2024 est.)

Mother's mean age at first birth: 23 years (2016 est.)
note: data represents median age at first birth among women 25-49

Maternal mortality ratio: 192 deaths/100,000 live births (2023 est.)
comparison ranking: 39

Infant mortality rate: *total:* 32.2 deaths/1,000 live births (2024 est.)
male: 35.3 deaths/1,000 live births
female: 28.9 deaths/1,000 live births
comparison ranking: total 41

Life expectancy at birth: *total population:* 70.5 years (2024 est.)
male: 68.9 years
female: 72.3 years
comparison ranking: total population 174

Total fertility rate: 3.98 children born/woman (2024 est.)
comparison ranking: 24

Gross reproduction rate: 1.92 (2024 est.)

Drinking water source: *improved: urban:* 98.4% of population (2022 est.)
rural: 81.6% of population (2022 est.)
total: 87% of population (2022 est.)
unimproved: urban: 1.6% of population (2022 est.)
rural: 18.4% of population (2022 est.)
total: 13% of population (2022 est.)

Health expenditure: 11.4% of GDP (2021)
8.9% of national budget (2022 est.)

Physician density: 0.75 physicians/1,000 population (2020)

Sanitation facility access: *improved: urban:* 94.1% of population (2022 est.)
rural: 64% of population (2022 est.)
total: 73.7% of population (2022 est.)
unimproved: urban: 5.9% of population (2022 est.)
rural: 36% of population (2022 est.)
total: 26.3% of population (2022 est.)

Obesity - adult prevalence rate: 3.8% (2016)
comparison ranking: 190

Alcohol consumption per capita: *total:* 0.41 liters of pure alcohol (2019 est.)
beer: 0.27 liters of pure alcohol (2019 est.)
wine: 0.09 liters of pure alcohol (2019 est.)
spirits: 0.05 liters of pure alcohol (2019 est.)
other alcohols: 0 liters of pure alcohol (2019 est.)
comparison ranking: total 166

Tobacco use: *total:* 36.1% (2025 est.)
male: 62.6% (2025 est.)
female: 8.9% (2025 est.)
comparison ranking: total 7

Children under the age of 5 years underweight: 31.9% (2020)
comparison ranking: 3

Currently married women (ages 15-49): 55.9% (2023 est.)

Child marriage: *women married by age 15:* 2.6% (2016)
women married by age 18: 14.9% (2016)
men married by age 18: 1.2% (2016)

Education expenditure: 3% of GDP (2021 est.)
7.5% national budget (2021 est.)
comparison ranking: Education expenditure (% GDP) 150

Literacy: *total population:* 65.8% (2016 est.)
male: 72.2% (2016 est.)
female: 59.6% (2016 est.)

People - note: one of only two predominantly Christian nations in Southeast Asia, the other being the Philippines

ENVIRONMENT

Environmental issues: air pollution and deterioration of air quality; water quality, scarcity, and access; land and soil degradation; forest depletion; deforestation and soil erosion from slash-and-burn agriculture; loss of biodiversity

International environmental agreements: *party to:* Biodiversity, Climate Change, Climate Change-Kyoto Protocol, Climate Change-Paris Agreement, Desertification, Law of the Sea, Ozone Layer Protection
signed, but not ratified: Comprehensive Nuclear Test Ban

Climate: tropical; hot, humid; distinct rainy and dry seasons

Urbanization: *urban population:* 32.5% of total population (2023)
rate of urbanization: 3.31% annual rate of change (2020-25 est.)

Carbon dioxide emissions: 660,000 metric tonnes of CO2 (2023 est.)
from petroleum and other liquids: 660,000 metric tonnes of CO2 (2023 est.)
comparison ranking: total emissions 185

Particulate matter emissions: 20.4 micrograms per cubic meter (2019 est.)

Waste and recycling: *municipal solid waste generated annually:* 63,900 tons (2024 est.)
percent of municipal solid waste recycled: 13.5% (2022 est.)

Total water withdrawal: *municipal:* 99 million cubic meters (2022 est.)
industrial: 2 million cubic meters (2022 est.)
agricultural: 1.071 billion cubic meters (2022 est.)

Total renewable water resources: 8.215 billion cubic meters (2022 est.)

GOVERNMENT

Country name: *conventional long form:* Democratic Republic of Timor-Leste
conventional short form: Timor-Leste
local long form: Republika Demokratika Timor Lorosa'e (Tetum)/Republica Democratica de Timor-Leste (Portuguese)
local short form: Timor Lorosa'e (Tetum)/Timor-Leste (Portuguese)
former: East Timor, Portuguese Timor
etymology: the name partly derives from the Indonesian and Malay word *timur*, meaning "east;" *leste* is the Portuguese word for "east," so "Timor-Leste" literally means "Eastern-East"
note: pronounced TEE-mor LESS-tay

Government type: semi-presidential republic

Capital: *name:* Dili
geographic coordinates: 8 35 S, 125 36 E
time difference: UTC+9 (14 hours ahead of Washington, DC, during Standard Time)

Administrative divisions: 12 municipalities (*municipios*, singular - *municipio*) and 1 special adminstrative region* (*regiao administrativa especial*); Aileu, Ainaro, Baucau, Bobonaro (Maliana), Covalima (Suai), Dili, Ermera (Gleno), Lautem (Lospalos), Liquica, Manatuto, Manufahi (Same), Oe-Cusse Ambeno* (Pante Macassar), Viqueque
note: administrative divisions have the same names as their administrative centers; exceptions show the administrative center name in parentheses

Legal system: civil law system based on the Portuguese model

Constitution: *history:* drafted 2001, approved 22 March 2002, entered into force 20 May 2002
amendment process: proposed by Parliament and parliamentary groups; consideration of amendments requires at least four-fifths majority approval by Parliament; passage requires two-thirds majority vote by Parliament and promulgation by the president of the republic; passage of amendments to the republican form of government and the flag requires approval in a referendum

International law organization participation: accepts compulsory ICJ jurisdiction with reservations; accepts ICCt jurisdiction

Citizenship: *citizenship by birth:* no
citizenship by descent only: at least one parent must be a citizen of Timor-Leste
dual citizenship recognized: no
residency requirement for naturalization: 10 years

Suffrage: 17 years of age; universal

Executive branch: *chief of state:* President José RAMOS-HORTA (since 20 May 2022)
head of government: Prime Minister Kay Rala Xanana GUSMAO (since 1 July 2023)
cabinet: Council of Ministers; ministers proposed to the prime minister by the coalition in the Parliament and sworn in by the president
election/appointment process: president directly elected by absolute-majority popular vote in 2 rounds, if needed, for a 5-year term (eligible for a second term); following parliamentary elections, the president appoints the leader of the majority party or majority coalition as the prime minister
most recent election date: 19 March 2022, with a runoff on 19 April 2022
election results: *2022:* José RAMOS-HORTA elected president in second round - RAMOS-HORTA (CNRT) 62.1%, Francisco GUTERRES (FRETILIN) 37.9%
2017: Francisco GUTERRES elected president; Francisco GUTERRES (FRETILIN) 57.1%, António da CONCEICAO (PD) 32.5%, other 10.4%
expected date of next election: April 2027
note: the president is commander in chief of the military and can veto legislation, dissolve parliament, and call national elections

Legislative branch: *legislature name:* National Parliament
legislative structure: unicameral
number of seats: 65 (all directly elected)
electoral system: proportional representation
scope of elections: full renewal
term in office: 5 years
most recent election date: 5/21/2023
parties elected and seats per party: National Congress for the Reconstruction of Timor-Leste (CNRT) (31); Revolutionary Front for an independent East Timor (FRETILIN) (19); Democratic Party (PD) (6); Kmanek Haburas Unidade Nasional Timor Oan (KHUNTO) (5); People's Liberation Party (PLP) (4)
percentage of women in chamber: 35.4%
expected date of next election: May 2028

Judicial branch: *highest court(s):* Court of Appeals (consists of the court president and NA judges)
judge selection and term of office: court president appointed by the president of the republic from among the other court judges to serve a 4-year term; other court judges appointed - 1 by the Parliament and the others by the Supreme Council for the Judiciary, a body chaired by the court president and that includes mostly presidential and parliamentary appointees; other judges serve for life
subordinate courts: Court of Appeal; High Administrative, Tax, and Audit Court; district courts; magistrates' courts; military courts

Political parties: Democratic Party or PD

National Congress for Timorese Reconstruction or CNRT
National Unity of the Sons of Timor (Haburas Unidade Nasional Timor Oan or KHUNTO)
People's Liberation Party or PLP
Revolutionary Front of Independent Timor-Leste or FRETILIN

Diplomatic representation in the US: *chief of mission:* Ambassador José Luis GUTERRES (since 17 June 2024)
chancery: 4201 Connecticut Avenue NW, Suite 504, Washington, DC 20008
telephone: [1] (202) 966-3202

FAX: [1] (202) 966-3205
email address and website: info@timorlesteembassy.org

Diplomatic representation from the US: *chief of mission:* Ambassador (vacant); Chargé d'Affaires Bruce BEGNELL (since July 2025)
embassy: Avenida de Portugal, Praia dos Coqueiros, Dili
mailing address: 8250 Dili Place, Washington, DC 20521-8250
telephone: (670) 332-4684, (670) 330-2400

FAX: (670) 331-3206
email address and website: ConsDili@state.gov
https://tl.usembassy.gov/

International organization participation: ACP, ADB, AOSIS, ARF, ASEAN (observer), CPLP, EITI (compliant country), FAO, G-77, IBRD, ICAO, ICCt, ICRM, IDA, IFAD, IFC, IFRCS, ILO, IMF, IMO, Interpol, IOC, IOM, IPU, ITU, MIGA, NAM, OPCW, PIF (observer), UN, UNCTAD, UNESCO, UNIDO, Union Latina, UNWTO, UPU, WCO, WHO, WMO

Independence: 28 November 1975 (from Portugal); 20 May 2002 (from Indonesia)

National holiday: Restoration of Independence Day, 20 May (2002); Proclamation of Independence Day, 28 November (1975)

Flag: *description:* red with a black isosceles triangle (based on the left side) on a slightly longer yellow arrowhead that extends to the center of the flag; a white star is in the center of the black triangle
meaning: yellow stands for past colonialism, black for obscurantism that needs to be overcome, and red for the struggle for freedom; the white star represents peace and a guiding light

National symbol(s): Mount Ramelau

National color(s): red, yellow, black, white

National anthem(s): *title:* "Patria" (Fatherland)
lyrics/music: Fransisco Borja DA COSTA/Afonso DE ARAUJO
history: adopted 2002; the song was first used as an anthem when Timor-Leste declared its independence from Portugal in 1975; the lyricist, Francisco Borja DA COSTA, was killed in the Indonesian invasion just days after independence was declared

ECONOMY

Economic overview: lower middle-income Southeast Asian economy; government expenditures funded via oil fund drawdowns; endemic corruption undermines growth; foreign aid-dependent; wide-scale poverty, unemployment, and illiteracy

Real GDP (purchasing power parity): $5.863 billion (2024 est.)
$5.995 billion (2023 est.)
$7.322 billion (2022 est.)
note: data in 2021 dollars
comparison ranking: 178

Real GDP growth rate: -2.2% (2024 est.)
-18.1% (2023 est.)
-20.5% (2022 est.)
note: annual GDP % growth based on constant local currency
comparison ranking: 208

Real GDP per capita: $4,200 (2024 est.)
$4,300 (2023 est.)
$5,300 (2022 est.)
note: data in 2021 dollars
comparison ranking: 180

GDP (official exchange rate): $1.881 billion (2024 est.)
note: data in current dollars at official exchange rate

Inflation rate (consumer prices): 2.1% (2024 est.)
8.4% (2023 est.)
7% (2022 est.)
note: annual % change based on consumer prices
comparison ranking: 57

GDP - composition, by sector of origin: *agriculture:* 16.9% (2023 est.)
industry: 23.9% (2023 est.)
services: 61% (2023 est.)
note: figures may not total 100% due to non-allocated consumption not captured in sector-reported data
comparison rankings: agriculture 46; industry 100; services 80

GDP - composition, by end use: *household consumption:* 70% (2023 est.)
government consumption: 52.9% (2023 est.)
investment in fixed capital: 17.4% (2023 est.)
investment in inventories: 3.1% (2023 est.)
exports of goods and services: 22.9% (2023 est.)
imports of goods and services: -66.4% (2023 est.)
note: figures may not total 100% due to rounding or gaps in data collection

Agricultural products: maize, rice, coconuts, root vegetables, vegetables, cassava, other meats, pork, beans, coffee (2023)
note: top ten agricultural products based on tonnage

Industries: printing, soap manufacturing, handicrafts, woven cloth

Industrial production growth rate: -57% (2023 est.)
note: annual % change in industrial value added based on constant local currency
comparison ranking: 197

Labor force: 615,900 (2024 est.)
note: number of people ages 15 or older who are employed or seeking work
comparison ranking: 157

Unemployment rate: 1.7% (2024 est.)
1.6% (2023 est.)
1.6% (2022 est.)
note: % of labor force seeking employment
comparison ranking: 13

Youth unemployment rate (ages 15-24): *total:* 3.4% (2024 est.)
male: 3.2% (2024 est.)
female: 3.7% (2024 est.)
note: % of labor force ages 15-24 seeking employment
comparison ranking: total 176

Remittances: 11.7% of GDP (2024 est.)
9.3% of GDP (2023 est.)
5.1% of GDP (2022 est.)
note: personal transfers and compensation between resident and non-resident individuals/households/entities

Budget: *revenues:* $1.877 billion (2022 est.)
expenditures: $1.826 billion (2022 est.)
note: central government revenues (excluding grants) and expenditures converted to US dollars at average official exchange rate for year indicated

Taxes and other revenues: 21.6% (of GDP) (2022 est.)
note: central government tax revenue as a % of GDP
comparison ranking: 37

Current account balance: -$529.738 million (2024 est.)
-$177.336 million (2023 est.)
$408.059 million (2022 est.)
note: balance of payments - net trade and primary/secondary income in current dollars
comparison ranking: 109

Exports: $278.047 million (2024 est.)
$701.808 million (2023 est.)
$1.858 billion (2022 est.)
note: balance of payments - exports of goods and services in current dollars
comparison ranking: 199

Exports - partners: China 46%, Singapore 25%, Japan 15%, Indonesia 5%, USA 3% (2023)
note: top five export partners based on percentage share of exports

Exports - commodities: crude petroleum, natural gas, coffee, scrap iron, telephones (2023)
note: top five export commodities based on value in dollars

Imports: $1.197 billion (2024 est.)
$1.169 billion (2023 est.)
$1.286 billion (2022 est.)
note: balance of payments - imports of goods and services in current dollars
comparison ranking: 189

Imports - partners: Indonesia 34%, China 26%, Singapore 9%, Taiwan 5%, India 4% (2023)
note: top five import partners based on percentage share of imports

Imports - commodities: refined petroleum, rice, cars, plastic products, trucks (2023)
note: top five import commodities based on value in dollars

Reserves of foreign exchange and gold: $736.967 million (2024 est.)
$781.995 million (2023 est.)
$830.81 million (2022 est.)
note: holdings of gold (year-end prices)/foreign exchange/special drawing rights in current dollars
comparison ranking: 149

Debt - external: $238.042 million (2023 est.)
note: present value of external debt in current US dollars
comparison ranking: 120

Exchange rates: the US dollar is used

ENERGY

Electricity access: *electrification - total population:* 99.7% (2022 est.)
electrification - urban areas: 100%
electrification - rural areas: 100%

Electricity: *installed generating capacity:* 277,000 kW (2023 est.)
consumption: 411.519 million kWh (2023 est.)
transmission/distribution losses: 99.481 million kWh (2023 est.)

comparison rankings: installed generating capacity 167; consumption 178; transmission/distribution losses 45

Electricity generation sources: *fossil fuels:* 99.8% of total installed capacity (2023 est.)
solar: 0.2% of total installed capacity (2023 est.)

Coal: *imports:* 122,000 metric tons (2023 est.)

Petroleum: *total petroleum production:* 5,000 bbl/day (2023 est.)
refined petroleum consumption: 5,000 bbl/day (2023 est.)

Natural gas: *production:* 521.034 million cubic meters (2023 est.)
exports: 521.034 million cubic meters (2023 est.)

Energy consumption per capita: 6.825 million Btu/person (2023 est.)
comparison ranking: 163

COMMUNICATIONS

Telephones - fixed lines: *total subscriptions:* 2,000 (2023 est.)
subscriptions per 100 inhabitants: (2023 est.) less than 1
comparison ranking: total subscriptions 211

Telephones - mobile cellular: *total subscriptions:* 1.56 million (2023 est.)
subscriptions per 100 inhabitants: 110 (2022 est.)
comparison ranking: total subscriptions 158

Broadcast media: 7 TV stations (3 nationwide satellite coverage; 2 terrestrial coverage, mostly in Dili; 2 cable) and 21 radio stations (3 nationwide coverage) (2019)

Internet country code: .tl

Internet users: *percent of population:* 34% (2023 est.)

Broadband - fixed subscriptions: *total:* 0 (2023 est.)
subscriptions per 100 inhabitants: (2023 est.) less than 1
comparison ranking: total 212

TRANSPORTATION

Civil aircraft registration country code prefix: 4W

Airports: 11 (2025)
comparison ranking: 157

Heliports: 2 (2025)
comparison ranking: 140

Merchant marine: *total:* 1 (2023)
by type: other 1
comparison ranking: total 186

Ports: *total ports:* 1 (2024)
large: 0
medium: 0
small: 1
very small: 0
ports with oil terminals: 0
key ports: Dili

MILITARY AND SECURITY

Military and security forces: Timor-Leste Defense Force (Falintil-Forcas de Defesa de Timor-L'este, Falintil (F-FDTL)): Land Component, Air Force Component, Naval Component

Ministry of Interior: National Police of Timor-Leste (Polícia Nacional de Timor-Leste, PNTL) (2025)

Military expenditures: 2.5% of GDP (2024 est.)
2.5% of GDP (2023 est.)
1.4% of GDP (2022 est.)
1.2% of GDP (2021 est.)
1.8% of GDP (2020 est.)

Military and security service personnel strengths: approximately 2,000 Defense Forces (2025)

Military equipment inventories and acquisitions: the military is lightly armed and has a limited inventory consisting mostly of donated equipment from countries such as Australia, China, Portugal, South Korea, and the US (2024)

Military service age and obligation: 18 years of age for voluntary military service for men and women; compulsory service was authorized in 2020 for men and women aged 18-30 for 18 months of service, but the level of implementation is unclear (2023)

Military - note: the Timor-Leste Defense Force (F-FDTL) has both external defense and internal security roles; it also engages in national development missions, international peacekeeping, and regional security cooperation; the F-FDTL has ties with a variety of partners, including Australia, Brazil, Canada, China, Indonesia, Malaysia, New Zealand, the Philippines, Portugal, the UN, and the US (2025)

TOGO

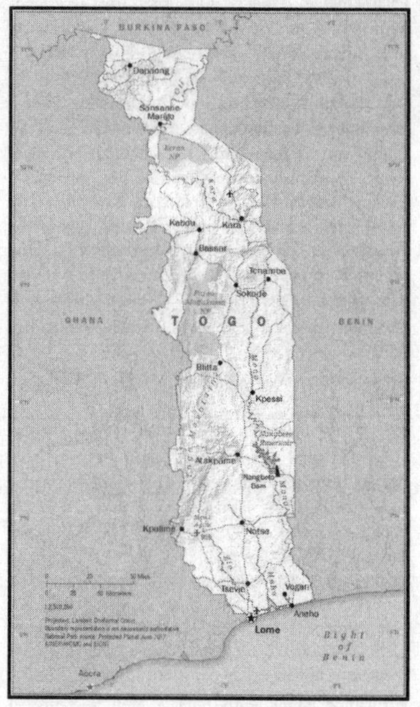

INTRODUCTION

Background: From the 11th to the 16th centuries, various ethnic groups settled the Togo region. From the 16th to the 18th centuries, the coastal region became a major trading center for enslaved people, and the surrounding region took on the name of "The Slave Coast." In 1884, Germany declared the area a protectorate called Togoland, which included present-day Togo. After World War I, colonial rule over Togo was transferred to France. French Togoland became Togo upon independence in 1960.

Gen. Gnassingbe EYADEMA, installed as military ruler in 1967, ruled Togo with a heavy hand for almost four decades. Despite the facade of multi-party elections instituted in the early 1990s, EYADEMA largely dominated the government. His Rally of the Togolese People (RPT) party has been in power almost continually since 1967, with its successor, the Union for the Republic, maintaining a majority of seats in today's legislature. Upon EYADEMA's death in 2005, the military installed his son, Faure GNASSINGBE, as president and then engineered his formal election two months later. Togo held its first relatively free and fair legislative elections in 2007. Since then, GNASSINGBE has started the country along a gradual path to democratic reform. Togo has held multiple presidential and legislative elections, and in 2019, the country held its first local elections in 32 years.

Despite those positive moves, political reconciliation has moved slowly, and the country experiences periodic outbursts of protests from frustrated citizens, leading to violence between security forces and protesters. Constitutional changes in 2019 to institute a runoff system in presidential elections and to establish term limits have done little to reduce the resentment many Togolese feel after more than 50 years of one-family rule. GNASSINGBE became eligible for his current fourth term and one additional fifth term under the new rules. The next presidential election is set for 2025.

GEOGRAPHY

Location: Western Africa, bordering the Bight of Benin, between Benin and Ghana

Geographic coordinates: 8 00 N, 1 10 E

Map references: Africa

Area: *total:* 56,785 sq km
land: 54,385 sq km
water: 2,400 sq km
comparison ranking: total 126

Area - comparative: slightly smaller than West Virginia

Land boundaries: *total:* 1,880 km
border countries (3): Benin 651 km; Burkina Faso 131 km; Ghana 1,098 km

Coastline: 56 km

Maritime claims: *territorial sea:* 30 nm
exclusive economic zone: 200 nm
note: the US does not recognize the territorial sea claim

Climate: tropical; hot, humid in south; semiarid in north

Terrain: gently rolling savanna in north; central hills; southern plateau; low coastal plain with extensive lagoons and marshes

Elevation: *highest point:* Mont Agou 986 m
lowest point: Atlantic Ocean 0 m
mean elevation: 236 m

Natural resources: phosphates, limestone, marble, arable land

Land use: *agricultural land:* 70.2% (2022 est.)
arable land: 48.7% (2022 est.)
permanent crops: 3.1% (2022 est.)
permanent pasture: 18.4% (2022 est.)
forest: 22.1% (2022 est.)
other: 7.6% (2022 est.)

Irrigated land: 70 sq km (2012)

Major watersheds (area sq km): Atlantic Ocean drainage: Volta (410,991 sq km)

Population distribution: one of the more densely populated African nations, with most of the population residing in rural communities; density is highest in the south on or near the Atlantic coast, as shown in this population distribution map

Natural hazards: hot, dry harmattan wind can reduce visibility in north during winter; periodic droughts

Geography - note: stretches through six distinct geographic regions; climate varies from tropical to savanna

PEOPLE AND SOCIETY

Population: *total:* 8,917,994 (2024 est.)
male: 4,395,271
female: 4,522,723
comparison rankings: total 101; male 101; female 100

Nationality: *noun:* Togolese (singular and plural)
adjective: Togolese

Ethnic groups: Adja-Ewe/Mina 42.4%, Kabye/Tem 25.9%, Para-Gourma/Akan 17.1%, Akposso/Akebu 4.1%, Ana-Ife 3.2%, other Togolese 1.7%, foreigners 5.2%, no response 0.4% (2013-14 est.)
note: Togo has an estimated 37 ethnic groups

Languages: French (official, language of commerce), Ewe and Mina (in the south), Kabye (sometimes spelled Kabiye) and Dagomba (in the north)

Religions: Christian 42.3%, folk religion 36.9%, Muslim 14%, Hindu <1%, Buddhist <1%, Jewish <1%, other <1%, none 6.2% (2020 est.)

Age structure: *0-14 years:* 38.7% (male 1,749,533/female 1,699,084)
15-64 years: 57% (male 2,486,142/female 2,597,914)
65 years and over: 4.3% (2024 est.) (male 159,596/female 225,725)

Dependency ratios: *total dependency ratio:* 75.4 (2024 est.)
youth dependency ratio: 67.8 (2024 est.)
elderly dependency ratio: 7.6 (2024 est.)
potential support ratio: 13.2 (2024 est.)

Median age: *total:* 20.7 years (2024 est.)
male: 19.9 years
female: 21.4 years
comparison ranking: total 199

Population growth rate: 2.41% (2024 est.)
comparison ranking: 21

Birth rate: 30.9 births/1,000 population (2024 est.)
comparison ranking: 23

Death rate: 5.1 deaths/1,000 population (2024 est.)
comparison ranking: 192

Net migration rate: -1.7 migrant(s)/1,000 population (2024 est.)
comparison ranking: 164

Population distribution: one of the more densely populated African nations, with most of the population residing in rural communities; density is highest in the south on or near the Atlantic coast, as shown in this population distribution map

Urbanization: *urban population:* 44.5% of total population (2023)
rate of urbanization: 3.6% annual rate of change (2020-25 est.)

Major urban areas - population: 1.982 million LOME (capital) (2023)

Sex ratio: *at birth:* 1.03 male(s)/female
0-14 years: 1.03 male(s)/female
15-64 years: 0.96 male(s)/female
65 years and over: 0.71 male(s)/female
total population: 0.97 male(s)/female (2024 est.)

Mother's mean age at first birth: 25 years (2017 est.)
note: data represents median age at first birth among women 25-29

Maternal mortality ratio: 349 deaths/100,000 live births (2023 est.)
comparison ranking: 23

Infant mortality rate: *total:* 38.4 deaths/1,000 live births (2024 est.)
male: 43 deaths/1,000 live births
female: 33.7 deaths/1,000 live births
comparison ranking: total 30

Life expectancy at birth: *total population:* 72.1 years (2024 est.)
male: 69.5 years
female: 74.7 years
comparison ranking: total population 165

Total fertility rate: 4.13 children born/woman (2024 est.)
comparison ranking: 20

Gross reproduction rate: 2.03 (2024 est.)

Drinking water source: *improved: urban:* 87% of population (2022 est.)
rural: 58.5% of population (2022 est.)
total: 71% of population (2022 est.)
unimproved: urban: 13% of population (2022 est.)
rural: 41.5% of population (2022 est.)
total: 29% of population (2022 est.)

Health expenditure: 5.6% of GDP (2021)
2.6% of national budget (2022 est.)

Physician density: 0.08 physicians/1,000 population (2022)

Hospital bed density: 0.6 beds/1,000 population (2019 est.)

Sanitation facility access: *improved: urban:* 82% of population (2022 est.)
rural: 19.2% of population (2022 est.)
total: 46.7% of population (2022 est.)
unimproved: urban: 18% of population (2022 est.)
rural: 80.8% of population (2022 est.)
total: 53.3% of population (2022 est.)

Obesity - adult prevalence rate: 8.4% (2016)
comparison ranking: 151

Alcohol consumption per capita: *total:* 1.4 liters of pure alcohol (2019 est.)
beer: 0.78 liters of pure alcohol (2019 est.)
wine: 0.09 liters of pure alcohol (2019 est.)
spirits: 0.2 liters of pure alcohol (2019 est.)
other alcohols: 0.33 liters of pure alcohol (2019 est.)
comparison ranking: total 141

Tobacco use: *total:* 5% (2025 est.)
male: 9.3% (2025 est.)
female: 0.7% (2025 est.)
comparison ranking: total 161

Children under the age of 5 years underweight: 15.2% (2017)
comparison ranking: 31

Currently married women (ages 15-49): 62% (2023 est.)

Child marriage: *women married by age 15:* 6.4% (2017)
women married by age 18: 24.8% (2017)
men married by age 18: 2.6% (2017)

Education expenditure: 4.1% of GDP (2023 est.)
11.6% national budget (2024 est.)
comparison ranking: Education expenditure (% GDP) 102

Literacy: *total population:* 72.6% (2022 est.)
male: 82.8% (2022 est.)
female: 63.7% (2022 est.)

School life expectancy (primary to tertiary education): *total:* 12 years (2017 est.)
male: 13 years (2017 est.)
female: 11 years (2017 est.)

ENVIRONMENT

Environmental issues: deforestation from slash-and-burn agriculture and the use of wood for fuel; very little rainforest still present and what remains is highly degraded; desertification; water pollution; air pollution in urban areas

International environmental agreements: *party to:* Biodiversity, Climate Change, Climate Change-Kyoto Protocol, Climate Change-Paris Agreement, Comprehensive Nuclear Test Ban, Desertification, Endangered Species, Hazardous Wastes, Law of the Sea, Nuclear Test Ban, Ozone Layer Protection, Ship Pollution, Tropical Timber 2006, Wetlands, Whaling
signed, but not ratified: none of the selected agreements

Climate: tropical; hot, humid in south; semiarid in north

Urbanization: *urban population:* 44.5% of total population (2023)
rate of urbanization: 3.6% annual rate of change (2020-25 est.)

Carbon dioxide emissions: 2.656 million metric tonnes of CO2 (2023 est.)
from coal and metallurgical coke: 372,000 metric tonnes of CO2 (2023 est.)
from petroleum and other liquids: 1.941 million metric tonnes of CO2 (2023 est.)
from consumed natural gas: 343,000 metric tonnes of CO2 (2023 est.)
comparison ranking: total emissions 154

Particulate matter emissions: 33.9 micrograms per cubic meter (2019 est.)

Methane emissions: *energy:* 43.3 kt (2022-2024 est.)
agriculture: 51.8 kt (2019-2021 est.)
waste: 31.3 kt (2019-2021 est.)
other: 10.4 kt (2019-2021 est.)

Waste and recycling: *municipal solid waste generated annually:* 1.109 million tons (2024 est.)
percent of municipal solid waste recycled: 3.5% (2022 est.)

Total water withdrawal: *municipal:* 140.7 million cubic meters (2022 est.)
industrial: 6.3 million cubic meters (2022 est.)
agricultural: 76 million cubic meters (2022 est.)

Total renewable water resources: 14.7 billion cubic meters (2022 est.)

GOVERNMENT

Country name: *conventional long form:* Togolese Republic
conventional short form: Togo
local long form: République Togolaise
local short form: none
former: French Togoland
etymology: the name derives from the town of Togodo (now Togoville) on the northern shore of Lake Togo; the town's name probably comes from the lake's name, which is composed of the Ewe words *to* ("water") and *go* ("shore")

Government type: presidential republic

Capital: *name:* Lome
geographic coordinates: 6 07 N, 1 13 E
time difference: UTC 0 (5 hours ahead of Washington, DC, during Standard Time)
etymology: the name comes from a local word meaning "little market"

Administrative divisions: 5 regions (*régions*, singular - *région*); Centrale, Kara, Maritime, Plateaux, Savanes

Legal system: customary law system

Constitution: *history:* several previous; latest adopted 27 September 1992, effective 14 October 1992; revised 6 May 2024
amendment process: proposed by the president of the republic or supported by at least one fifth of the National Assembly membership; passage requires four-fifths majority vote by the Assembly; a referendum is required if approved by only two-thirds majority of the Assembly or if requested by the president; constitutional articles on the republican and secular form of government cannot be amended

International law organization participation: accepts compulsory ICJ jurisdiction with reservations; non-party state to the ICCt

Citizenship: *citizenship by birth:* no
citizenship by descent only: at least one parent must be a citizen of Togo
dual citizenship recognized: yes
residency requirement for naturalization: 5 years

Suffrage: 18 years of age; universal

Executive branch: *chief of state:* President Jean-Lucien Kwassi Savi de TOVE (since 3 May 2025)
head of government: President of Council of Ministers Faure GNASSINGBE (since 3 May 2025)
cabinet: Council of Ministers appointed by the president on the advice of the president of the council of ministers
election/appointment process: president is appointed by the national assembly for one six-year term; the president of the council of ministers is the leader of the majority party in the national assembly and is confirmed by the Constitutional Court with no term limits
election results: *2020:* Faure GNASSINGBE reelected president; percent of vote - Faure GNASSINGBE (UNIR) 70.8%, Agbeyome KODJO (MPDD) 19.5%, Jean-Pierre FABRE (ANC) 4.7%, other 5%
2015: Faure GNASSINGBE reelected president; percent of vote - Faure GNASSINGBE (UNIR) 58.8%, Jean-Pierre FABRE (ANC) 35.2%, Tchaboure GOGUE (ADDI) 4%, other 2%
note: in May 2024, the President signed into law changes to the constitution that converted the presidential system to a parliamentary republic and created the President of Council of Ministers position

Legislative branch: *legislature name:* Parliament
legislative structure: bicameral
note: party lists are required to contain equal numbers of men and women

Legislative branch - lower chamber: *chamber name:* National Assembly (Assemblée nationale)
number of seats: 113 (all directly elected)
electoral system: proportional representation
scope of elections: full renewal
term in office: 6 years
most recent election date: 4/29/2024
parties elected and seats per party: Union for the Republic (UNIR) (108); Other (5)
percentage of women in chamber: 15%
expected date of next election: April 2030

Legislative branch - upper chamber: *chamber name:* Senate (Sénat)
number of seats: 61 (41 directly elected; 20 appointed)
scope of elections: full renewal
term in office: 6 years
most recent election date: 2/15/2025
parties elected and seats per party: Union for the Republic (UNIR) (34); Independents (3); Other (4)
percentage of women in chamber: 24.6%
expected date of next election: February 2031

Judicial branch: *highest court(s):* Supreme Court or Cour Suprême (organized into criminal and administrative chambers, each with a chamber president and advisors); Constitutional Court (consists of 9 judges, including the court president)
judge selection and term of office: Supreme Court president appointed by decree of the president of the republic on the proposal of the Supreme Council of the Magistracy, a 9-member judicial, advisory, and disciplinary body; other judicial appointments and judge tenure NA; Constitutional Court judges appointed by the National Assembly; judge tenure NA
subordinate courts: Court of Assizes (sessions court); Appeal Court; tribunals of first instance (divided into civil, commercial, and correctional chambers; Court of State Security; military tribunal

Political parties: Action Committee for Renewal or CAR
Alliance of Democrats for Integral Development or ADDI
Democratic Convention of African Peoples or CDPA
Democratic Forces for the Republic or FDR
National Alliance for Change or ANC
New Togolese Commitment
Pan-African National Party or PNP
Pan-African Patriotic Convergence or CPP
Patriotic Movement for Democracy and Development or MPDD
Socialist Pact for Renewal or PSR
The Togolese Party
Union of Forces for Change or UFC
Union for the Republic or UNIR

Diplomatic representation in the US: *chief of mission:* Ambassador Frédéric Edem HEGBE (since 24 April 2017)
chancery: 2208 Massachusetts Avenue NW, Washington, DC 20008
telephone: [1] (202) 234-4212
FAX: [1] (202) 232-3190
email address and website: embassyoftogo@hotmail.com
https://embassyoftogousa.com/

Diplomatic representation from the US: *chief of mission:* Ambassador (vacant); Chargé d'Affaires Richard C. MICHAELS (since June 2025)
embassy: Boulevard Eyadema
B.P. 852, Lomé
mailing address: 2300 Lome Place, Washington, DC 20521-2300
telephone: [228] 2261-5470
FAX: [228] 2261-5501
email address and website: consularLome@state.gov
https://tg.usembassy.gov/

International organization participation: ACP, AfDB, AIIB, AU, ECOWAS, EITI (compliant country), Entente, FAO, FZ, G-77, IAEA, IBRD, ICAO, ICRM, IDA, IDB, IFAD, IFC, IFRCS, ILO, IMF, IMO, Interpol, IOC, IOM, IPU, ISO (correspondent), ITSO, ITU, ITUC (NGOs), MIGA, MINURSO, NAM, OIC, OIF, OPCW, PCA, UN, UNAMID, UNCTAD, UNESCO, UNHCR, UNIDO, UNMIL, UNOCI, UNWTO, UPU, WADB (regional), WAEMU, WCO, WFTU (NGOs), WHO, WIPO, WMO, WTO

Independence: 27 April 1960 (from French-administered UN trusteeship)

National holiday: Independence Day, 27 April (1960)

Flag: *description:* five equal horizontal bands of green (top and bottom) alternating with yellow; a five-pointed white star on a red square is in the upper-left corner
meaning: the five horizontal stripes stand for the country's regions; red stands for the people's loyalty and patriotism; green for hope, fertility, and agriculture; yellow for mineral wealth and faith that hard work and strength will bring prosperity; the star symbolizes life, purity, peace, dignity, and national independence
history: uses the colors of the Pan-African movement

National symbol(s): lion

National color(s): green, yellow, red, white

National anthem(s): *title:* "Salut à toi, pays de nos aieux" (Hail to Thee, Land of Our Forefathers)
lyrics/music: Alex CASIMIR-DOSSEH
history: adopted 1960, restored 1992; anthem was replaced during one-party rule between 1979 and 1992

National heritage: *total World Heritage Sites:* 1 (cultural)
selected World Heritage Site locales: Koutammakou; the Land of the Batammariba

ECONOMY

Economic overview: low-income West African economy; primarily agrarian economy; has a deep-water port; growing international shipping locale; improving privatization and public budgeting transparency; key phosphate mining industry; extremely high rural poverty

Real GDP (purchasing power parity): $27.115 billion (2024 est.)
$25.75 billion (2023 est.)
$24.199 billion (2022 est.)
note: data in 2021 dollars
comparison ranking: 149

Real GDP growth rate: 5.3% (2024 est.)
6.4% (2023 est.)
5.8% (2022 est.)
note: annual GDP % growth based on constant local currency
comparison ranking: 34

Real GDP per capita: $2,800 (2024 est.)
$2,800 (2023 est.)
$2,700 (2022 est.)
note: data in 2021 dollars
comparison ranking: 199

GDP (official exchange rate): $9.926 billion (2024 est.)
note: data in current dollars at official exchange rate

Inflation rate (consumer prices): 2.9% (2024 est.)
5.3% (2023 est.)
7.6% (2022 est.)
note: annual % change based on consumer prices
comparison ranking: 88

GDP - composition, by sector of origin: *agriculture:* 18% (2024 est.)
industry: 20% (2024 est.)
services: 52% (2024 est.)
note: figures may not total 100% due to non-allocated consumption not captured in sector-reported data
comparison rankings: agriculture 40; industry 128; services 134

GDP - composition, by end use: *household consumption:* 78.3% (2024 est.)
government consumption: 13.1% (2024 est.)
investment in fixed capital: 22.3% (2024 est.)
investment in inventories: 0% (2024 est.)
exports of goods and services: 24.4% (2024 est.)
imports of goods and services: -38.1% (2024 est.)
note: figures may not total 100% due to rounding or gaps in data collection

Agricultural products: cassava, maize, yams, sorghum, soybeans, beans, rice, vegetables, oil palm fruit, cotton (2023)
note: top ten agricultural products based on tonnage

Industries: phosphate mining, agricultural processing, cement, handicrafts, textiles, beverages

Industrial production growth rate: 4.2% (2024 est.)
note: annual % change in industrial value added based on constant local currency
comparison ranking: 55

Labor force: 3.345 million (2024 est.)
note: number of people ages 15 or older who are employed or seeking work
comparison ranking: 102

Unemployment rate: 2% (2024 est.)
2% (2023 est.)
2% (2022 est.)
note: % of labor force seeking employment
comparison ranking: 15

Youth unemployment rate (ages 15-24): *total:* 3.4% (2024 est.)
male: 3.3% (2024 est.)
female: 3.5% (2024 est.)
note: % of labor force ages 15-24 seeking employment
comparison ranking: total 177

Population below poverty line: 45.5% (2018 est.)
note: % of population with income below national poverty line

Gini Index coefficient - distribution of family income: 37.9 (2021 est.)
note: index (0-100) of income distribution; higher values represent greater inequality
comparison ranking: 54

Household income or consumption by percentage share: *lowest 10%:* 2.8% (2021 est.)
highest 10%: 29.6% (2021 est.)
note: % share of income accruing to lowest and highest 10% of population

Remittances: 7.1% of GDP (2023 est.)
8% of GDP (2022 est.)
7.8% of GDP (2021 est.)
note: personal transfers and compensation between resident and non-resident individuals/households/entities

Budget: *revenues:* $1.801 billion (2023 est.)
expenditures: $2.407 billion (2023 est.)
note: central government revenues and expenses (excluding grants/extrabudgetary units/social security funds) converted to US dollars at average official exchange rate for year indicated

Taxes and other revenues: 14.8% (of GDP) (2023 est.)
note: central government tax revenue as a % of GDP
comparison ranking: 93

Current account balance: -$20.738 million (2020 est.)
-$55.444 million (2019 est.)
-$184.852 million (2018 est.)
note: balance of payments - net trade and primary/secondary income in current dollars
comparison ranking: 87

Exports: $1.722 billion (2020 est.)
$1.665 billion (2019 est.)
$1.703 billion (2018 est.)
note: balance of payments - exports of goods and services in current dollars
comparison ranking: 167

Exports - partners: UAE 40%, India 13%, Angola 13%, Burkina Faso 4%, Cote d'Ivoire 3% (2023)
note: top five export partners based on percentage share of exports

Exports - commodities: gold, refined petroleum, soybeans, phosphates, coconuts/brazil nuts/cashews (2023)
note: top five export commodities based on value in dollars

Imports: $2.389 billion (2020 est.)
$2.261 billion (2019 est.)
$2.329 billion (2018 est.)
note: balance of payments - imports of goods and services in current dollars
comparison ranking: 170

Imports - partners: China 26%, India 26%, Belgium 6%, Netherlands 6%, USA 3% (2023)
note: top five import partners based on percentage share of imports

Imports - commodities: refined petroleum, garments, rice, palm oil, motorcycles and cycles (2023)
note: top five import commodities based on value in dollars

Debt - external: $1.923 billion (2023 est.)
note: present value of external debt in current US dollars
comparison ranking: 95

Exchange rates: Communaute Financiere Africaine francs (XOF) per US dollar -

Exchange rates: 606.345 (2024 est.)
606.57 (2023 est.)
623.76 (2022 est.)
554.531 (2021 est.)
575.586 (2020 est.)

ENERGY

Electricity access: *electrification - total population:* 57.2% (2022 est.)
electrification - urban areas: 96.5%
electrification - rural areas: 25%

Electricity: *installed generating capacity:* 326,000 kW (2023 est.)
consumption: 1.815 billion kWh (2023 est.)
imports: 1.1 billion kWh (2023 est.)
transmission/distribution losses: 206.938 million kWh (2023 est.)
comparison rankings: installed generating capacity 162; consumption 151; imports 76; transmission/distribution losses 66

Electricity generation sources: *fossil fuels:* 79.3% of total installed capacity (2023 est.)
solar: 11.9% of total installed capacity (2023 est.)
hydroelectricity: 8.7% of total installed capacity (2023 est.)
biomass and waste: 0.1% of total installed capacity (2023 est.)

Coal: *consumption:* 163,000 metric tons (2023 est.)
exports: 10 metric tons (2023 est.)
imports: 163,000 metric tons (2023 est.)

Petroleum: *refined petroleum consumption:* 14,000 bbl/day (2023 est.)

Natural gas: *consumption:* 176.16 million cubic meters (2023 est.)
imports: 176.16 million cubic meters (2023 est.)

Energy consumption per capita: 4.538 million Btu/person (2023 est.)
comparison ranking: 171

COMMUNICATIONS

Telephones - fixed lines: *total subscriptions:* 67,000 (2023 est.)
subscriptions per 100 inhabitants: 1 (2023 est.) less than 1
comparison ranking: total subscriptions 148

Telephones - mobile cellular: *total subscriptions:* 7.05 million (2023 est.)
subscriptions per 100 inhabitants: 74 (2022 est.)
comparison ranking: total subscriptions 113

Broadcast media: 1 state-owned TV station with multiple transmission sites; five private local TV stations; cable TV available; state-owned radio network with two stations; several dozen private radio stations and a few community radio stations; transmissions of multiple international broadcasters available (2019)

Internet country code: .tg

Internet users: *percent of population:* 37% (2023 est.)

Broadband - fixed subscriptions: *total:* 114,000 (2023 est.)
subscriptions per 100 inhabitants: 1 (2023 est.)
comparison ranking: total 130

TRANSPORTATION

Civil aircraft registration country code prefix: 5V

Airports: 7 (2025)
comparison ranking: 172

Railways: *total:* 568 km (2014)
narrow gauge: 568 km (2014) 1.000-m gauge

Merchant marine: *total:* 397 (2023)
by type: bulk carrier 1, container ship 10, general cargo 250, oil tanker 56, other 80
comparison ranking: total 49

Ports: *total ports:* 2 (2024)
large: 0
medium: 1
small: 0
very small: 1
ports with oil terminals: 2
key ports: Kpeme, Lome

MILITARY AND SECURITY

Military and security forces: Togolese Armed Forces (Forces Armees Togolaise, FAT): Togolese Army, Togolese Navy, Togolese Air Force, National Gendarmerie (Gendarmerie Nationale Togolaise or GNT)

Ministry of Security and Civil Protection: Togolese Police (2025)
note: the Police and GNT are responsible for law enforcement and maintenance of order within the country; the GNT is also responsible for migration and border enforcement; the GNT falls under the Ministry of the Armed Forces but also reports to the Ministry of Security and Civil Protection on many matters involving law enforcement and internal security; in 2022, the Ministry of the Armed Forces was made part of the Office of the Presidency

Military expenditures: 2.2% of GDP (2024 est.)
3% of GDP (2023 est.)
4% of GDP (2022 est.)
2.8% of GDP (2021 est.)
2.8% of GDP (2020 est.)

Military and security service personnel strengths: estimated 20,000 active Armed Forces, including Gendarmerie (2025)

Military equipment inventories and acquisitions: the FAT has a small inventory of mostly older equipment originating from a variety of countries, including Brazil, Russia/former Soviet Union, Turkey, the US, and some European nations, particularly France (2024)

Military service age and obligation: 18 years of age for military service for men and women; 24-month service obligation; no conscription (2023)
note: as of 2022, about 7% of the military's personnel were women

Military - note: the responsibilities of the Togolese Armed Forces (FAT) included both external defense and internal security; the FAT's primary concerns are border security, terrorism, and maritime security; in recent years, it has boosted operations in the northern border region of the country to secure the frontier and prevent banditry, illicit smuggling, and infiltrations from Jama'at Nasr al-Islam wal Muslimin (JNIM), a coalition of al-Qa'ida-affiliated militant groups based in Mali that also operates in neighboring Burkina Faso; in 2022, the Togolese Government declared a state of emergency in the north following an attack by JNIM fighters on a Togolese military post that killed several soldiers; the Navy and Air Force have increased focus on combating piracy and smuggling in the Gulf of Guinea
since its creation in 1963, the Togolese military has had a history of involvement in the country's politics, including assassinations, coups, and a crackdown in 2005 that killed hundreds of civilians; over the past decade, it has made some efforts to reform and professionalize, which have included increasing its role in UN peacekeeping activities, participating in multinational exercises, and receiving training from foreign partners, particularly France and the US; in addition, Togo has established a regional peacekeeping training center for military and police in Lome (2025)

TERRORISM

Terrorist group(s): Terrorist group(s): Jama'at Nusrat al Islam wal Muslimeen (JNIM)
note: details about the history, aims, leadership, organization, areas of operation, tactics, targets, weapons, size, and sources of support of the group(s) appear(s) in Appendix T

TRANSNATIONAL ISSUES

Refugees and internally displaced persons: *refugees:* 48,756 (2024 est.)
IDPs: 18,429 (2024 est.)

TOKELAU

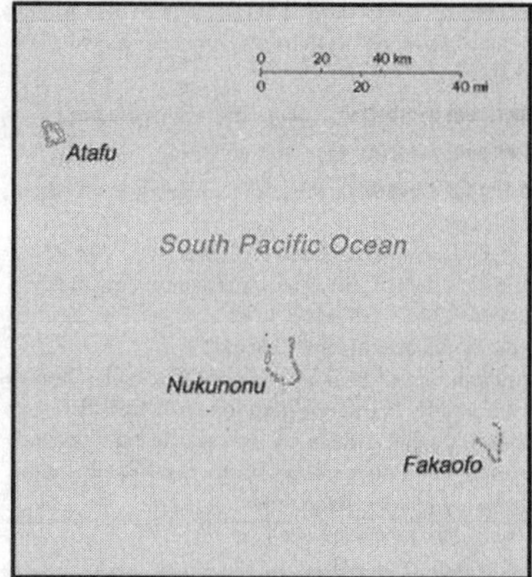

INTRODUCTION

Background: Tokelau is composed of three atolls (Fakaofo, Atafu, and Nukunonu), and it was first settled by Polynesians around A.D. 1000. The atolls operated relatively independently, but Fakaofo Atoll eventually subjugated the others. British explorers first saw the atolls in 1765 and 1791. Catholic and Protestant missionaries arrived in the 1840s and converted the population on the islands on which they landed.

In 1863 Peruvian slave raiders abducted many islanders, and roughly contemporary outbreaks of disease reduced the population to about 200. Settlers of diverse nationalities subsequently intermarried with Tokelauans. In the same period, local governance moved to a system based on a Council of Elders, which still exists today. British interest began in the late 1870s, and Tokelau became a British protectorate in 1889, and in 1916 under the name Union Group, Tokelau became part of the Gilbert and Ellice Islands Colony. In 1925, the UK placed Tokelau under New Zealand administration. The Tokelau Islands Act of 1948 formally transferred sovereignty from the UK to New Zealand, and Tokelauans were granted New Zealand citizenship. In 1979, the US relinquished its claim to Tokelau in the Treaty of Tokehega, and Tokelau relinquished its claim to Swains Island, which is part of American Samoa.

Economic opportunities in Tokelau are sparse, and about 80% of Tokelauans live in New Zealand. Tokelau held self-governance referendums in 2006 and 2007 in which more than 60% of voters chose free association with New Zealand; however, the referendums failed to achieve the two-thirds majority necessary to enact a status change.

GEOGRAPHY

Location: Oceania, group of three atolls in the South Pacific Ocean, about one-half of the way from Hawaii to New Zealand

Geographic coordinates: 9 00 S, 172 00 W

Map references: Oceania

Area: *total:* 12 sq km
land: 12 sq km
water: 0 sq km
comparison ranking: total 240

Area - comparative: about 17 times the size of the National Mall in Washington, D.C.

Land boundaries: *total:* 0 km

Coastline: 101 km

Maritime claims: *territorial sea:* 12 nm
exclusive economic zone: 200 nm

Climate: tropical; moderated by trade winds (April to November)

Terrain: low-lying coral atolls enclosing large lagoons

Elevation: *highest point:* unnamed location 5 m
lowest point: Pacific Ocean 0 m

Natural resources: fish

Land use: *agricultural land:* 60% (2022 est.)
arable land: 0% (2022 est.)
permanent crops: 60% (2022 est.)
permanent pasture: 0% (2022 est.)
forest: 0% (2022 est.)
other: 40% (2022 est.)

Irrigated land: 0 sq km (2022)

Population distribution: the small population is fairly evenly distributed among the three atolls

Natural hazards: lies in Pacific cyclone belt

Geography - note: consists of three atolls (Atafu, Fakaofo, Nukunonu), each with a lagoon surrounded by a number of reef-bound islets of varying length and rising to over 3 m (10 ft) above sea level

PEOPLE AND SOCIETY

Population: *total:* 2,453 (2024 est.)
male: 1,201 (2024 est.)
female: 1,252 (2024 est.)
comparison rankings: total 230; male 230; female 229

Nationality: *noun:* Tokelauan(s)
adjective: Tokelauan

Ethnic groups: Tokelauan 64.5%, part Tokelauan/Samoan 9.7%, part Tokelauan/Tuvaluan 2.8%, Tuvaluan 7.5%, Samoan 5.8%, other Pacific Islander 3.4%, other 5.6%, unspecified 0.8% (2016 est.)

Languages: Tokelauan 88.1% (a Polynesian language), English 48.6%, Samoan 26.7%, Tuvaluan 11.2%, Kiribati 1.5%, other 2.8%, none 2.8%, unspecified 0.8% (2016 ests.)
note: shares sum to more than 100% because some respondents gave more than one answer on the census

Religions: Congregational Christian Church 50.4%, Roman Catholic 38.7%, Presbyterian 5.9%, other Christian 4.2%, unspecified 0.8% (2016 est.)

Dependency ratios: *total dependency ratio:* 52.7 (2024)
youth dependency ratio: 40 (2024)
elderly dependency ratio: 12.6 (2024)
potential support ratio: 7.9 (2024)

Population growth rate: -0.01% (2019 est.)
comparison ranking: 197

Net migration rate: -3.84 migrant(s)/1,000 population (2021 est.)
comparison ranking: 194

Population distribution: the small population is fairly evenly distributed among the three atolls

Urbanization: *urban population:* 0% of total population (2023)
rate of urbanization: 0% annual rate of change (2020-25 est.)

Drinking water source: *improved:* rural: 99.7% of population (2022 est.)
total: 99.7% of population (2022 est.)
unimproved: rural: 0.3% of population (2022 est.)
total: 0.3% of population (2022 est.)

Physician density: 1.67 physicians/1,000 population (2021)

Sanitation facility access: *improved:* rural: 100% of population (2022 est.)
total: 100% of population (2022 est.)
unimproved: rural: 0% of population (2022 est.)
total: 0% of population (2022 est.)

Currently married women (ages 15-49): 52% (2023 est.)

ENVIRONMENT

Environmental issues: overfishing; damage to forest resources; pollution of freshwater and coastal waters from improper disposal of chemicals

Climate: tropical; moderated by trade winds (April to November)

Urbanization: *urban population:* 0% of total population (2023)
rate of urbanization: 0% annual rate of change (2020-25 est.)

GOVERNMENT

Country name: *conventional long form:* none
conventional short form: Tokelau
former: Union Islands, Tokelau Islands
etymology: the name comes from the Polynesian word *tokelau*, meaning "north wind;" the name "Tokelau Islands" was adopted in 1946, and the shortened form in 1976

Government type: parliamentary democracy under a constitutional monarchy

Dependency status: Tokelau is a non-self-governing territory of New Zealand and part of the Realm of New Zealand; Tokelau has its own political institutions, judicial system, public services (including telecommunications and shipping), and budget control

Capital: *time difference:* UTC+13 (18 hours ahead of Washington, DC during Standard Time)
note: there is no designated, official capital for Tokelau; the location of the capital rotates among the three atolls along with the head of government or Ulu o Tokelau

Administrative divisions: none (territory of New Zealand)

Legal system: common law system of New Zealand

Constitution: *history:* many previous; latest effective 1 January 1949 (Tokelau Act 1948 of New Zealand)
amendment process: proposed as a resolution by the General Fono; passage requires support by each village and approval by the General Fono
note: Tokelau is a non-self-governing territory and has been administered by New Zealand since 1926; Tokelau is considered "part of New Zealand" under the Tokelau Act 1948, and Tokelauans are New Zealand citizens; in the mid-2000s Tokelau held two referenda on becoming self-governing in free association with New Zealand; the first vote was held in February 2006 but narrowly missed the two-thirds majority required for a change of status, as did a second vote held in 2007; since the self-government referenda, Tokelau has put questions about its constitutional status on hold; it remains a territory of New Zealand but exercises a substantial degree of self-government

Citizenship: see New Zealand

Suffrage: 21 years of age; universal

Executive branch: *chief of state:* King CHARLES III (since 8 September 2022); represented by Governor-General of New Zealand Dame Cindy KIRO (since 21 September 2021); New Zealand is represented by Administrator Don HIGGINS (since June 2022)
head of government: (Ulu o Tokelau) Esera Fofō Filipo Tuisano TUISANO (since 17 March 2025)
cabinet: Council for the Ongoing Government of Tokelau (or Tokelau Council) functions as a cabinet; consists of 3 village leaders (Faipule) and 3 village mayors (Pulenuku)
election/appointment process: the monarchy is hereditary; governor general appointed by the monarch; administrator appointed by the Minister of Foreign Affairs and Trade in New Zealand; head of government chosen from the Council of Faipule to serve a 1-year term
note: the meeting place of the Tokelau Council and the head of government position rotates annually among the three atolls; this tradition has given rise to the somewhat misleading description that the capital rotates yearly between the three atolls, but Tokelau has no capital

Legislative branch: *legislature name:* General Fono (Fono Fakamua)
legislative structure: unicameral
number of seats: 20
electoral system: plurality/majority
scope of elections: full renewal
term in office: 3 years
most recent election date: 26 January 2023
parties elected and seats per party: independents (20)
percentage of women in chamber: 15%
expected date of next election: January 2026

Judicial branch: *highest court(s):* Court of Appeal (in New Zealand) (consists of the court president and 8 judges sitting in 3- or 5-judge panels, depending on the case)
judge selection and term of office: judges nominated by the Judicial Selection Committee and approved by three-quarters majority of the Parliament; judges serve for life
subordinate courts: High Court (in New Zealand); Council of Elders or Taupulega

Political parties: none

Diplomatic representation in the US: none (territory of New Zealand)

Diplomatic representation from the US: none (territory of New Zealand)

International organization participation: PIF (associate member), SPC, UNESCO (associate), UPU

Independence: none (territory of New Zealand)

National holiday: Waitangi Day, 6 February (1840)
note: Treaty of Waitangi established British sovereignty over New Zealand

Flag: *description:* a stylized yellow Tokelauan canoe on a dark blue field sails toward four white five-pointed stars on the left side
meaning: the stars are the Southern Cross constellation and represent the role of Christianity in Tokelauan culture; the stars and canoe together symbolize the country navigating into the future; yellow stands for happiness and peace, and blue for the ocean

National symbol(s): tuluma (fishing tackle box)

National color(s): blue, yellow, white

National anthem(s): *title:* "Viki O Tokelau" (Anthem of Tokelau)
lyrics/music: Eric Lemuelu FALIMA
history: adopted 2012; national contest was held to choose a local anthem
title: "God Defend New Zealand"
lyrics/music: Thomas BRACKEN [English], Thomas Henry SMITH [Maori]/John Joseph WOODS
history: official anthem, as a territory of New Zealand; played when no members of the royal family or the governor-general are present
title: "God Save the King"
lyrics/music: unknown
history: official anthem, as a territory of New Zealand; normally played only when a member of the royal family or the governor-general is present

ECONOMY

Economic overview: small New Zealand territorial island economy; labor force can work in New Zealand or Australia; significant remittances; largely solar-powered infrastructure; reliant on New Zealand funding; stamp, coin, and crafts producer

Real GDP (purchasing power parity): $7,711,583 (2017 est.)
note: data are in 2017 dollars.
comparison ranking: 221

Real GDP per capita: $6,004 (2017 est.)
$4,855 (2016 est.)
$4,292 (2015 est.)
note: data are in 2017 dollars
comparison ranking: 166

GDP (official exchange rate): $12.658 million (2017 est.)
note: data uses New Zealand Dollar (NZD) as the currency of exchange.

Inflation rate (consumer prices): 4% (2020 est.)
2.5% (2019 est.)
11% (2017 est.)
note: Tokelau notes that its wide inflation swings are due almost entirely to cigarette prices, a chief import.
comparison ranking: 124

Agricultural products: coconuts, root vegetables, tropical fruits, pork, bananas, eggs, chicken (2023)
note: top ten agricultural products based on tonnage

Industries: small-scale enterprises for copra production, woodworking, plaited craft goods; stamps, coins; fishing

Budget: *revenues:* $24,324,473 (2017 est.)
expenditures: $11,666,542 (2017 est.)

Exports - partners: Czechia 92%, Singapore 2%, Brazil 1%, South Africa 1%, Sri Lanka 1% (2023)
note: top five export partners based on percentage share of exports

Exports - commodities: cars, telephones, garments, iron fasteners, fabric (2023)
note: top five export commodities based on value in dollars

Imports - partners: Samoa 31%, Italy 23%, France 21%, Netherlands 16%, Germany 2% (2023)
note: top five import partners based on percentage share of imports

Imports - commodities: integrated circuits, stone processing machines, refined petroleum, gas turbines, plastic products (2023)
note: top five import commodities based on value in dollars

Exchange rates: New Zealand dollars (NZD) per US dollar -

Exchange rates: 1.652 (2024 est.)
1.628 (2023 est.)
1.577 (2022 est.)
1.414 (2021 est.)
1.542 (2020 est.)

COMMUNICATIONS

Telephones - fixed lines: *total subscriptions:* 300 (2010 est.)
subscriptions per 100 inhabitants: 22 (2010 est.)
comparison ranking: total subscriptions 219

Broadcast media: Sky TV access for about a third of the population; each atoll operates a radio service with shipping news and weather reports (2019)

Internet country code: .tk

Internet users: *percent of population:* 58.3% (2021 est.)

MILITARY AND SECURITY

Military - note: defense is the responsibility of New Zealand

TONGA

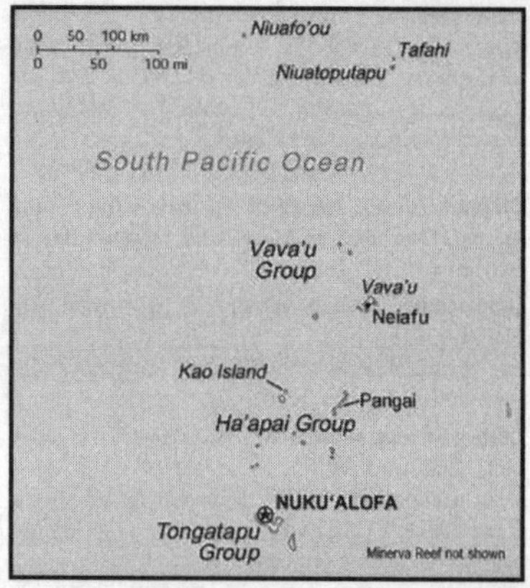

INTRODUCTION

Background: The first humans arrived in Tonga around 1000 B.C. The islands' politics were highly centralized under the Tu'i Tonga, or Tongan king, by A.D. 950, and by 1200, the Tu'i Tonga had expanded his influence throughout Polynesia and into Melanesia and Micronesia. The Tongan Empire began to decline in the 1300s, with civil wars, a military defeat to Samoa, and internal political strife. By the mid-1500s, some Tu'i Tongans were ethnic Samoan, and day-to-day administration of Tonga was transferred to a new position occupied by ethnic Tongans.

Dutch navigators explored the islands in the 1600s, followed by the British in the 1770s, who named them the Friendly Islands. Between 1799 and 1852 Tonga went through a period of war and disorder. In the 1830s, a low-ranking chief from Ha'apai began to consolidate control over the islands and was crowned King George TUPOU I in 1845, establishing the only still-extant Polynesian monarchy. During TUPOU's reign (1845–93), Tonga became a unified and independent country with a modern constitution (1875), legal code, and administrative structure. In separate treaties, Germany (1876), Great Britain (1879), and the US (1888) recognized Tonga's independence. His son and successor, King George TUPOU II, agreed to enter a protectorate agreement with the UK in 1900 after rival Tongan chiefs tried to overthrow him. As a protectorate, Tonga never completely lost its indigenous governance, but it did become more isolated and the social hierarchy became more stratified between a group of nobles and a large class of commoners. Today, about one third of parliamentary seats are reserved for nobles.

Tonga regained full control of domestic and foreign affairs and became a fully independent nation within the Commonwealth in 1970. A pro-democracy movement gained steam in the early 2000s, led by 'Akilisi POHIVA, and in 2006, riots broke out in Nuku'alofa to protest the lack of progress on reform. To appease the activists, in 2008, King George TUPOU V announced he was relinquishing most of his powers leading up to parliamentary elections in 2010 and henceforth most of the monarch's governmental decisions, except those relating to the judiciary, were to be made in consultation with the prime minister. The 2010 Legislative Assembly was called Tonga's first democratically elected Parliament. King George TUPOU V died in 2012 and was succeeded by his brother Crown Prince Tupouto'a Lavaka who ruled as George TUPOU VI. In 2015, 'Akalisi POHIVA became Tonga's first non-noble prime minister.

GEOGRAPHY

Location: Oceania, archipelago in the South Pacific Ocean, about two-thirds of the way from Hawaii to New Zealand

Geographic coordinates: 20 00 S, 175 00 W

Map references: Oceania

Area: *total:* 747 sq km
land: 717 sq km
water: 30 sq km
comparison ranking: total 189

Area - comparative: four times the size of Washington, D.C.

Land boundaries: *total:* 0 km

Coastline: 419 km

Maritime claims: *territorial sea:* 12 nm
exclusive economic zone: 200 nm
continental shelf: 200-m depth or to the depth of exploitation

Climate: tropical; modified by trade winds; warm season (December to May), cool season (May to December)

Terrain: mostly flat islands with limestone bedrock formed from uplifted coral formation; others have limestone overlying volcanic rock

Elevation: *highest point:* Kao Volcano on Kao Island 1,046 m
lowest point: Pacific Ocean 0 m

Natural resources: arable land, fish

Land use: *agricultural land:* 48.6% (2022 est.)
arable land: 27.8% (2022 est.)
permanent crops: 15.3% (2022 est.)

permanent pasture: 5.6% (2022 est.)
forest: 12.4% (2022 est.)
other: 39% (2022 est.)

Irrigated land: 0 sq km (2022)

Population distribution: over two thirds of the population lives on the island of Tongatapu; only 45 of the nation's 171 islands are occupied

Natural hazards: cyclones (October to April); earthquakes and volcanic activity on Fonuafo'ou
volcanism: moderate volcanic activity; Fonualei (180 m) has had frequent activity in recent years, and Niuafo'ou (260 m) has forced evacuations; other historically active volcanoes include Late and Tofua

Geography - note: the western islands (making up the Tongan Volcanic Arch) are all of volcanic origin; the eastern islands are nonvolcanic and are composed of coral limestone and sand

PEOPLE AND SOCIETY

Population: *total:* 104,889 (2024 est.)
male: 52,606
female: 52,283
comparison rankings: total 191; male 191; female 194

Nationality: *noun:* Tongan(s)
adjective: Tongan

Ethnic groups: Tongan 96.5%, other (European, Fijian, Samoan, Indian, Chinese, other Pacific Islander, other Asian, other) 3.5% (2021 est.)

Languages: Tongan only 85%, Tongan and other language 13.9%, Tongan not used at home 1.1% (2021 est.)
note: data represent language use at home of persons aged 5 and older

Religions: Protestant 63.9% (Free Wesleyan Church 34.2%, Free Church of Tonga 11.3%, Church of Tonga 6.8%, Seventh Day Adventist 2.5%, Assembly of God 2.5%, Tokaikolo/Maamafo'ou 1.5%, Constitutional Church of Tonga 1.2%, other Protestant 4%), Church of Jesus Christ 19.7%, Roman Catholic 13.7%, other 2.1%, none 0.6%, no answer 0.1% (2021 est.)

Age structure: *0-14 years:* 29.3% (male 15,627/ female 15,142)
15-64 years: 63.2% (male 33,445/female 32,867)
65 years and over: 7.4% (2024 est.) (male 3,534/ female 4,274)

Dependency ratios: *total dependency ratio:* 58.2 (2024 est.)
youth dependency ratio: 46.4 (2024 est.)
elderly dependency ratio: 11.8 (2024 est.)
potential support ratio: 8.5 (2024 est.)

Median age: *total:* 25.9 years (2024 est.)
male: 25.4 years
female: 26.4 years
comparison ranking: total 166

Population growth rate: -0.34% (2024 est.)
comparison ranking: 213

Birth rate: 19.7 births/1,000 population (2024 est.)
comparison ranking: 71

Death rate: 5 deaths/1,000 population (2024 est.)
comparison ranking: 195

Net migration rate: -18.1 migrant(s)/1,000 population (2024 est.)
comparison ranking: 227

Population distribution: over two thirds of the population lives on the island of Tongatapu; only 45 of the nation's 171 islands are occupied

Urbanization: *urban population:* 23.2% of total population (2023)
rate of urbanization: 0.99% annual rate of change (2020-25 est.)

Major urban areas - population: 23,000 NUKU'ALOFA (2018)

Sex ratio: *at birth:* 1.03 male(s)/female
0-14 years: 1.03 male(s)/female
15-64 years: 1.02 male(s)/female
65 years and over: 0.83 male(s)/female
total population: 1.01 male(s)/female (2024 est.)

Mother's mean age at first birth: 24.9 years (2012 est.)
note: data represents median age at first birth among women 25-49

Maternal mortality ratio: 67 deaths/100,000 live births (2023 est.)
comparison ranking: 82

Infant mortality rate: *total:* 11.8 deaths/1,000 live births (2024 est.)
male: 12.8 deaths/1,000 live births
female: 10.8 deaths/1,000 live births
comparison ranking: total 111

Life expectancy at birth: *total population:* 78 years (2024 est.)
male: 76.4 years
female: 79.7 years
comparison ranking: total population 84

Total fertility rate: 2.65 children born/woman (2024 est.)
comparison ranking: 62

Gross reproduction rate: 1.3 (2024 est.)

Drinking water source: *improved: urban:* 99.6% of population (2022 est.)
rural: 98.6% of population (2022 est.)
total: 98.8% of population (2022 est.)
unimproved: urban: 0.4% of population (2022 est.)
rural: 1.4% of population (2022 est.)
total: 1.2% of population (2022 est.)

Health expenditure: 6.3% of GDP (2021)
8.7% of national budget (2022 est.)

Physician density: 1.01 physicians/1,000 population (2021)

Sanitation facility access: *improved: urban:* 99.6% of population (2022 est.)
rural: 99.7% of population (2022 est.)
total: 99.6% of population (2022 est.)
unimproved: urban: 0.4% of population (2022 est.)
rural: 0.3% of population (2022 est.)
total: 0.4% of population (2022 est.)

Obesity - adult prevalence rate: 48.2% (2016)
comparison ranking: 7

Alcohol consumption per capita: *total:* 0.31 liters of pure alcohol (2019 est.)
beer: 0.03 liters of pure alcohol (2019 est.)
wine: 0.17 liters of pure alcohol (2019 est.)
spirits: 0.11 liters of pure alcohol (2019 est.)
other alcohols: 0 liters of pure alcohol (2019 est.)
comparison ranking: total 169

Tobacco use: *total:* 30.5% (2025 est.)
male: 46.1% (2025 est.)
female: 15.8% (2025 est.)
comparison ranking: total 19

Children under the age of 5 years underweight: 0.8% (2019)
comparison ranking: 111

Currently married women (ages 15-49): 54.9% (2023 est.)

Child marriage: *women married by age 15:* 0.4% (2019)
women married by age 18: 10.1% (2019)
men married by age 18: 2.8% (2019)

Education expenditure: 5.3% of GDP (2022 est.)
9.3% national budget (2024 est.)
comparison ranking: Education expenditure (% GDP) 53

Literacy: *total population:* 91.1% (2019 est.)
male: 83.8% (2019 est.)
female: 97.6% (2019 est.)

School life expectancy (primary to tertiary education): *total:* 18 years (2020 est.)
male: 16 years (2020 est.)
female: 19 years (2020 est.)

ENVIRONMENT

Environmental issues: deforestation from land being cleared for agriculture and settlement; soil exhaustion; water pollution due to salinization, sewage, and toxic chemicals from farming activities; coral reefs and marine populations threatened

International environmental agreements: *party to:* Biodiversity, Climate Change, Climate Change-Kyoto Protocol, Climate Change-Paris Agreement, Desertification, Endangered Species, Hazardous Wastes, Law of the Sea, Marine Dumping-London Convention, Marine Dumping-London Protocol, Marine Life Conservation, Nuclear Test Ban, Ozone Layer Protection, Ship Pollution
signed, but not ratified: none of the selected agreements

Climate: tropical; modified by trade winds; warm season (December to May), cool season (May to December)

Urbanization: *urban population:* 23.2% of total population (2023)
rate of urbanization: 0.99% annual rate of change (2020-25 est.)

Carbon dioxide emissions: 174,000 metric tonnes of CO_2 (2023 est.)
from petroleum and other liquids: 174,000 metric tonnes of CO_2 (2023 est.)
comparison ranking: total emissions 204

Particulate matter emissions: 7.4 micrograms per cubic meter (2019 est.)

Waste and recycling: *municipal solid waste generated annually:* 17,200 tons (2024 est.)
percent of municipal solid waste recycled: 12.2% (2022 est.)

GOVERNMENT

Country name: *conventional long form:* Kingdom of Tonga
conventional short form: Tonga
local long form: Pule'anga Fakatu'i 'o Tonga
local short form: Tonga
former: Friendly Islands
etymology: the name is of local origin and is said to mean "island;" the former name, the Friendly Islands, came from Captain James COOK in 1773, based on the welcome he received from the inhabitants

Government type: constitutional monarchy

Capital: *name:* Nuku'alofa
geographic coordinates: 21 08 S, 175 12 W
time difference: UTC+13 (18 hours ahead of Washington, DC, during Standard Time)
daylight saving time: +1hr, begins first Sunday in November; ends second Sunday in January
etymology: name is said to be composed of the local words *nuku*, meaning "residence or abode," and *alofa*, meaning "love;" it may also mean "the south," describing Tonga's position in relation to most other Polynesian islands

Administrative divisions: 5 island divisions; 'Eua, Ha'apai, Ongo Niua, Tongatapu, Vava'u

Legal system: English common law

Constitution: *history:* adopted 4 November 1875, revised 1988, 2016
amendment process: proposed by the Legislative Assembly; passage requires approval by the Assembly in each of three readings, the unanimous approval of the Privy Council (a high-level advisory body to the monarch), the Cabinet, and assent to by the monarch

International law organization participation: has not submitted an ICJ jurisdiction declaration; non-party state to the ICCt

Citizenship: *citizenship by birth:* no
citizenship by descent only: the father must be a citizen of Tonga; if a child is born out of wedlock, the mother must be a citizen of Tonga
dual citizenship recognized: yes
residency requirement for naturalization: 5 years

Suffrage: 21 years of age; universal

Executive branch: *chief of state:* King TUPOU VI (since 18 March 2012)
head of government: Prime Minister Aisake Valu EKE (since 22 January 2025)
cabinet: Cabinet nominated by the prime minister and appointed by the monarch
election/appointment process: the monarchy is hereditary; prime minister and deputy prime minister indirectly elected by the Legislative Assembly and appointed by the monarch
most recent election date: 24 December 2024
election results: *2024:* Aisake Valu EKE elected prime minsiter by the Legislative Assembly; Aisake Valu EKE (Independent) 16 votes, Viliami LATU (Independent) 8
2021: Siaosi SOVALENI elected prime minister by the Legislative Assembly; Siaosi SOVALENI 16 votes, Aisake EKE 10
note: a Privy Council advises the monarch

Legislative branch: *legislature name:* Legislative Assembly (Fale Alea)
legislative structure: unicameral
number of seats: 30 (17 directly elected; 9 indirectly elected)
electoral system: plurality/majority
scope of elections: full renewal
term in office: 4 years
most recent election date: 11/18/2021
percentage of women in chamber: 10%
expected date of next election: November 2025

Judicial branch: *highest court(s):* Court of Appeal (consists of the court president and a number of judges determined by the monarch)
judge selection and term of office: judge appointments and tenures made by the King in Privy Council and subject to consent of the Legislative Assembly
subordinate courts: Supreme Court; Magistrates' Courts; Land Courts
note: appeals beyond the Court of Appeal are brought before the King in Privy Council, the monarch's advisory organ that has both judicial and legislative powers

Political parties: Democratic Party of the Friendly Islands or DPFI or PTOA
Tonga People's Party (Paati 'a e Kakai 'o Tonga) or PAK or TPPI

Diplomatic representation in the US: *chief of mission:* Ambassador Viliana Va'inga TONE (since 20 April 2021)
chancery: 250 East 51st Street, New York, NY 10022
telephone: [1] (917) 369-1025

FAX: [1] (917) 369-1024
email address and website: tongaconsnot@gmail.com
consulate(s) general: San Francisco

Diplomatic representation from the US: *chief of mission:* Ambassador Marie DAMOUR (since 6 December 2022); note - Ambassador DAMOUR is based in the US Embassy in the Republic of Fiji and is accredited to Tonga as well as Kiribati, Nauru, and Tuvalu
embassy: although the US opened an embassy in Tonga on 9 May 2023, the US Ambassador to Fiji is accredited to Tonga while the Embassy is being staffed

International organization participation: ACP, ADB, AOSIS, C, FAO, G-77, IBRD, ICAO, ICRM, IDA, IFAD, IFC, IFRCS, IHO, IMF, IMO, IMSO, Interpol, IOC, IPU, ITU, ITUC (NGOs), OPCW, PIF, Sparteca, SPC, UN, UNCTAD, UNESCO, UNIDO, UPU, WCO, WHO, WIPO, WMO, WTO

Independence: 4 June 1970 (from UK protectorate status)

National holiday: Official birthday of King TUPOU VI, 4 July (1959)
note: the monarch's actual birthday is 12 July 1959, 4 July (2015) is the day the king was crowned; Constitution Day (National Day), 4 November (1875)

Flag: *description:* red with a red cross on a white rectangle in the upper-left corner
meaning: the cross stands for Christianity in Tonga, red for Christ's blood and sacrifice, and white for purity

National symbol(s): red cross on white field

Coat of arms of the Kingdom of Tonga: National color(s): red, white

National anthem(s): *title:* "Ko e fasi 'o e tu'i 'o e 'Otu Tonga" (Song of the King of the Tonga Islands)
lyrics/music: Uelingatoni Ngu TUPOUMALOHI/ Karl Gustavus SCHMITT
history: in use since 1874; more commonly known as "Fasi Fakafonua" (National Song)

ECONOMY

Economic overview: upper middle-income Pacific island economy; enormous diaspora and remittance reliance; key tourism and agricultural sectors; major fish exporter; rapidly growing Chinese infrastructure investments; rising methamphetamine hub

Real GDP (purchasing power parity): $740.082 million (2023 est.)
$724.972 million (2022 est.)
$742.114 million (2021 est.)
note: data in 2021 dollars
comparison ranking: 208

Real GDP growth rate: 2.1% (2023 est.)
-2.3% (2022 est.)
0.4% (2021 est.)
note: annual GDP % growth based on constant local currency
comparison ranking: 146

Real GDP per capita: $7,100 (2023 est.)
$6,900 (2022 est.)
$7,000 (2021 est.)
note: data in 2021 dollars
comparison ranking: 156

GDP (official exchange rate): $508.735 million (2023 est.)
note: data in current dollars at official exchange rate

Inflation rate (consumer prices): 3.2% (2024 est.)
6.4% (2023 est.)
11% (2022 est.)
note: annual % change based on consumer prices
comparison ranking: 101

GDP - composition, by sector of origin: *agriculture:* 17.5% (2023 est.)
industry: 13.5% (2023 est.)
services: 50.2% (2023 est.)
note: figures may not total 100% due to non-allocated consumption not captured in sector-reported data
comparison rankings: agriculture 42; industry 169; services 144

GDP - composition, by end use: *household consumption:* 107.6% (2023 est.)
government consumption: 29.1% (2023 est.)
investment in fixed capital: 27.3% (2023 est.)
investment in inventories: 0.3% (2023 est.)
exports of goods and services: 18.8% (2023 est.)
imports of goods and services: -75.4% (2023 est.)
note: figures may not total 100% due to rounding or gaps in data collection

Agricultural products: coconuts, pumpkins/squash, cassava, sweet potatoes, vegetables, yams, taro, root vegetables, plantains, lemons/limes (2023)
note: top ten agricultural products based on tonnage

Industries: tourism, construction, fishing

Industrial production growth rate: -11.1% (2023 est.)
note: annual % change in industrial value added based on constant local currency
comparison ranking: 187

Labor force: 34,800 (2024 est.)
note: number of people ages 15 or older who are employed or seeking work
comparison ranking: 189

Unemployment rate: 2.2% (2024 est.)
2.3% (2023 est.)
2.4% (2022 est.)
note: % of labor force seeking employment
comparison ranking: 16

Youth unemployment rate (ages 15-24): *total:* 6.3% (2024 est.)
male: 3.9% (2024 est.)
female: 10% (2024 est.)
note: % of labor force ages 15-24 seeking employment
comparison ranking: total 154

Population below poverty line: 20.6% (2021 est.)
note: % of population with income below national poverty line

Gini Index coefficient - distribution of family income: 27.1 (2021 est.)
note: index (0-100) of income distribution; higher values represent greater inequality
comparison ranking: 135

Household income or consumption by percentage share: *lowest 10%:* 4% (2021 est.)
highest 10%: 22% (2021 est.)
note: % share of income accruing to lowest and highest 10% of population

Remittances: 50% of GDP (2023 est.)
41.9% of GDP (2022 est.)
42% of GDP (2021 est.)
note: personal transfers and compensation between resident and non-resident individuals/households/entities

Budget: *revenues:* $276.025 million (2023 est.)
expenditures: $244.97 million (2023 est.)
note: central government revenues and expenses (excluding grants/extrabudgetary units/social security funds) converted to US dollars at average official exchange rate for year indicated

Public debt: 43.9% of GDP (2020 est.)
note: central government debt as a % of GDP
comparison ranking: 97

Taxes and other revenues: 23.8% (of GDP) (2023 est.)
note: central government tax revenue as a % of GDP
comparison ranking: 23

Current account balance: -$21.165 million (2024 est.)
-$30.087 million (2023 est.)
-$27.749 million (2022 est.)
note: balance of payments - net trade and primary/secondary income in current dollars
comparison ranking: 88

Exports: $119.511 million (2024 est.)
$95.345 million (2023 est.)
$59.926 million (2022 est.)
note: balance of payments - exports of goods and services in current dollars
comparison ranking: 207

Exports - partners: Guyana 17%, USA 17%, NZ 15%, Australia 15%, UAE 12% (2023)
note: top five export partners based on percentage share of exports

Exports - commodities: refined petroleum, gold, processed fruits and nuts, cassava, fish (2023)
note: top five export commodities based on value in dollars

Imports: $392.888 million (2024 est.)
$383.475 million (2023 est.)
$330.306 million (2022 est.)
note: balance of payments - imports of goods and services in current dollars
comparison ranking: 203

Imports - partners: Fiji 27%, NZ 24%, China 21%, Australia 8%, USA 5% (2023)
note: top five import partners based on percentage share of imports

Imports - commodities: refined petroleum, plastic products, poultry, cars, sheep and goat meat (2023)
note: top five import commodities based on value in dollars

Reserves of foreign exchange and gold: $377.299 million (2024 est.)
$396.53 million (2023 est.)
$375.564 million (2022 est.)
note: holdings of gold (year-end prices)/foreign exchange/special drawing rights in current dollars
comparison ranking: 166

Debt - external: $159.276 million (2023 est.)
note: present value of external debt in current US dollars
comparison ranking: 122

Exchange rates: pa'anga (TOP) per US dollar -

Exchange rates: 2.373 (2024 est.)
2.364 (2023 est.)
2.328 (2022 est.)
2.265 (2021 est.)
2.3 (2020 est.)

ENERGY

Electricity access: *electrification - total population:* 100% (2022 est.)

Electricity: *installed generating capacity:* 34,000 kW (2023 est.)
consumption: 67.01 million kWh (2023 est.)
transmission/distribution losses: 5.99 million kWh (2023 est.)
comparison rankings: installed generating capacity 200; consumption 202; transmission/distribution losses 11

Electricity generation sources: *fossil fuels:* 89% of total installed capacity (2023 est.)
solar: 9.6% of total installed capacity (2023 est.)
wind: 1.4% of total installed capacity (2023 est.)

Petroleum: *refined petroleum consumption:* 1,000 bbl/day (2023 est.)

Energy consumption per capita: 23.272 million Btu/person (2023 est.)
comparison ranking: 129

COMMUNICATIONS

Telephones - fixed lines: *total subscriptions:* 11,000 (2021 est.)
subscriptions per 100 inhabitants: 3 (2022 est.)
comparison ranking: total subscriptions 185

Telephones - mobile cellular: *total subscriptions:* 64,000 (2021 est.)
subscriptions per 100 inhabitants: 61 (2021 est.)
comparison ranking: total subscriptions 203

Broadcast media: 1 state-owned TV station and 3 privately owned TV stations; satellite and cable TV services available; 1 state-owned and 5 privately owned radio stations; Radio Australia available via satellite (2019)

Internet country code: .to

Internet users: *percent of population:* 59% (2023 est.)

Broadband - fixed subscriptions: *total:* 9,000 (2022 est.)
subscriptions per 100 inhabitants: 8 (2022 est.)
comparison ranking: total 187

TRANSPORTATION

Civil aircraft registration country code prefix: A3

Airports: 6 (2025)
comparison ranking: 175

Merchant marine: *total:* 29 (2023)
by type: container ship 1, general cargo 13, oil tanker 1, other 14
comparison ranking: total 136

Ports: *total ports:* 3 (2024)
large: 0
medium: 0
small: 0
very small: 3
ports with oil terminals: 0
key ports: Neiafu, Nuku Alofa, Pangai

MILITARY AND SECURITY

Military and security forces: His Majesty's Armed Forces Tonga (HMAF; aka Tonga Defense Services): Tonga Royal Guard, Tonga Land Force (Royal Tongan Marines), Tonga Navy, Air Wing

Ministry of Police and Fire Services: Tonga Police Force (2025)

Military expenditures: 1.8% of GDP (2024 est.)
1.6% of GDP (2023 est.)
1.6% of GDP (2022 est.)
1.5% of GDP (2021 est.)
2.1% of GDP (2020 est.)

Military and security service personnel strengths: approximately 600 active Armed Forces (2025)

Military equipment inventories and acquisitions: the military's inventory consists of light weapons, as well as some naval patrol vessels from Australia and a few US-origin aircraft (2024)

Military service age and obligation: voluntary military service for men and women 18-25; no conscription (2023)

Military - note: the military's primary missions are defending Tonga's sovereignty, providing maritime security, and protecting the King; it is also responsible for humanitarian assistance and disaster relief, search and rescue operations, monitoring against illegal fishing, and delivering supplies to the outer islands; the military has contributed limited numbers of personnel to multinational military operations in Afghanistan, Iraq, and the Solomon Islands; Australia, New Zealand, and the US are key partners Tonga has a "shiprider" agreement with the US, which allows local maritime law enforcement officers to embark on US Coast Guard (USCG) and US Navy (USN) vessels, including to board and search vessels suspected of violating laws or regulations within Tonga's designated exclusive economic zone (EEZ) or on the high seas
Tonga participated in World War I as part of the New Zealand Expeditionary Force, but the Tonga Defense Force (TDF) was not established until 1939 at the beginning of World War II; in 1943, New Zealand helped train about 2,000 Tongan troops who saw action in the Solomon Islands; the TDF was disbanded at the end of the war, but was reactivated in 1946 as the Tonga Defense Services (TDS); in 2013, the name of the TDS was changed to His Majesty's Armed Forces of Tonga (HMAF) (2025)

TRINIDAD AND TOBAGO

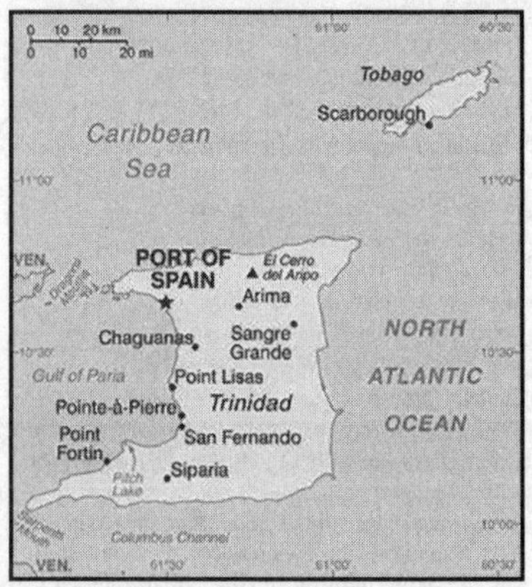

INTRODUCTION

Background: First colonized by the Spanish, Trinidad and Tobago came under British control in the early 19th century. The emancipation of enslaved people in 1834 disrupted the twin islands' sugar industry. Contract workers arriving from India between 1845 and 1917 augmented the labor force, which boosted sugar production as well as the cocoa industry. The discovery of oil on Trinidad in 1910 added another important export that remains the country's dominant industry. Trinidad and Tobago attained independence in 1962. The country is one of the most prosperous in the Caribbean, thanks largely to petroleum and natural gas production and processing. The government is struggling to reverse a surge in violent crime.

GEOGRAPHY

Location: Caribbean, islands between the Caribbean Sea and the North Atlantic Ocean, northeast of Venezuela

Geographic coordinates: 11 00 N, 61 00 W

Map references: Central America and the Caribbean

Area: *total:* 5,128 sq km
land: 5,128 sq km
water: 0 sq km
comparison ranking: total 173

Area - comparative: slightly smaller than Delaware

Land boundaries: *total:* 0 km

Coastline: 362 km

Maritime claims: *territorial sea:* 12 nm
contiguous zone: 24 nm
exclusive economic zone: 200 nm
continental shelf: 200 nm or to the outer edge of the continental margin
note: measured from claimed archipelagic baselines

Climate: tropical; rainy season (June to December)

Terrain: mostly plains with some hills and low mountains

Elevation: *highest point:* El Cerro del Aripo 940 m
lowest point: Caribbean Sea 0 m
mean elevation: 83 m

Natural resources: petroleum, natural gas, asphalt

Land use: *agricultural land:* 10.5% (2022 est.)
arable land: 4.9% (2022 est.)
permanent crops: 4.3% (2022 est.)
permanent pasture: 1.4% (2022 est.)
forest: 44.3% (2022 est.)
other: 45.2% (2022 est.)

Irrigated land: 70 sq km (2012)

Population distribution: population on Trinidad is concentrated in the western half of the island, on Tobago in the southern half

Natural hazards: outside usual path of hurricanes and other tropical storms

Geography - note: Pitch Lake, on Trinidad's southwestern coast, is the world's largest natural reservoir of asphalt

PEOPLE AND SOCIETY

Population: *total:* 1,408,966 (2024 est.)
male: 708,260
female: 700,706
comparison rankings: total 157; male 157; female 155

Nationality: *noun:* Trinidadian(s), Tobagonian(s)
adjective: Trinidadian, Tobagonian
note: Trinbagonian is used on occasion to describe a citizen of the country without specifying the island of origin

Ethnic groups: East Indian 35.4%, African descent 34.2%, mixed - other 15.3%, mixed - African/East Indian 7.7%, other 1.3%, unspecified 6.2% (2011 est.)

Languages: English (official), Trinidadian Creole English, Tobagonian Creole English, Caribbean Hindustani (a dialect of Hindi), Trinidadian Creole French, Spanish, Chinese

Religions: Protestant 32.1% (Pentecostal/Evangelical/Full Gospel 12%, Baptist 6.9%, Anglican 5.7%, Seventh Day Adventist 4.1%, Presbyterian/Congregational 2.5%, other Protestant 0.9%), Roman Catholic 21.6%, Hindu 18.2%, Muslim 5%, Jehovah's Witness 1.5%, other 8.4%, none 2.2%, unspecified 11.1% (2011 est.)

Age structure: *0-14 years:* 18.7% (male 134,508/female 129,180)
15-64 years: 67.2% (male 481,606/female 465,150)
65 years and over: 14.1% (2024 est.) (male 92,146/female 106,376)

Dependency ratios: *total dependency ratio:* 48.8 (2024 est.)
youth dependency ratio: 27.9 (2024 est.)
elderly dependency ratio: 21 (2024 est.)
potential support ratio: 4.8 (2024 est.)

Median age: *total:* 38.5 years (2024 est.)
male: 38 years
female: 39 years
comparison ranking: total 73

Population growth rate: 0.1% (2024 est.)
comparison ranking: 188

Birth rate: 10.5 births/1,000 population (2024 est.)
comparison ranking: 176

Death rate: 8.6 deaths/1,000 population (2024 est.)
comparison ranking: 71

Net migration rate: -0.9 migrant(s)/1,000 population (2024 est.)
comparison ranking: 142

Population distribution: population on Trinidad is concentrated in the western half of the island, on Tobago in the southern half

Urbanization: *urban population:* 53.4% of total population (2023)
rate of urbanization: 0.23% annual rate of change (2020-25 est.)

Major urban areas - population: 545,000 PORT-OF-SPAIN (capital) (2023)

Sex ratio: *at birth:* 1.04 male(s)/female
0-14 years: 1.04 male(s)/female
15-64 years: 1.04 male(s)/female
65 years and over: 0.87 male(s)/female
total population: 1.01 male(s)/female (2024 est.)

Maternal mortality ratio: 54 deaths/100,000 live births (2023 est.)
comparison ranking: 93

Infant mortality rate: *total:* 15.1 deaths/1,000 live births (2024 est.)
male: 17.1 deaths/1,000 live births
female: 13 deaths/1,000 live births
comparison ranking: total 94

Life expectancy at birth: *total population:* 76.5 years (2024 est.)
male: 74.6 years
female: 78.4 years
comparison ranking: total population 107

Total fertility rate: 1.63 children born/woman (2024 est.)
comparison ranking: 174

Gross reproduction rate: 0.8 (2024 est.)

Drinking water source: *improved:* total: 98.9% of population (2022 est.)
unimproved: total: 1.1% of population (2022 est.)

Health expenditure: 7% of GDP (2021)
10.9% of national budget (2022 est.)

Physician density: 4.16 physicians/1,000 population (2021)

Hospital bed density: 1.6 beds/1,000 population (2021 est.)

Sanitation facility access: *improved:* total: 99.9% of population (2022 est.)
unimproved: total: 0.1% of population (2022 est.)

Obesity - adult prevalence rate: 18.6% (2016)
comparison ranking: 117

Alcohol consumption per capita: *total:* 5.81 liters of pure alcohol (2019 est.)
beer: 2.92 liters of pure alcohol (2019 est.)
wine: 0.16 liters of pure alcohol (2019 est.)
spirits: 2.65 liters of pure alcohol (2019 est.)
other alcohols: 0.09 liters of pure alcohol (2019 est.)
comparison ranking: total 74

Currently married women (ages 15-49): 48.6% (2023 est.)

Child marriage: *women married by age 15:* 0.7% (2022)
women married by age 18: 4.2% (2022)

Education expenditure: 2.9% of GDP (2023 est.)
12.6% national budget (2025 est.)

comparison ranking: Education expenditure (% GDP) 159

Literacy: *female:* 93.8% (2022 est.)

ENVIRONMENT

Environmental issues: water pollution from agricultural chemicals, industrial wastes, and raw sewage; widespread pollution of waterways and coastal areas; illegal dumping; deforestation; soil erosion; fisheries and wildlife depletion

International environmental agreements: *party to:* Biodiversity, Climate Change, Climate Change-Kyoto Protocol, Climate Change-Paris Agreement, Comprehensive Nuclear Test Ban, Desertification, Endangered Species, Hazardous Wastes, Law of the Sea, Marine Dumping-London Protocol, Marine Life Conservation, Nuclear Test Ban, Ozone Layer Protection, Ship Pollution, Tropical Timber 2006, Wetlands
signed, but not ratified: none of the selected agreements

Climate: tropical; rainy season (June to December)

Urbanization: *urban population:* 53.4% of total population (2023)
rate of urbanization: 0.23% annual rate of change (2020-25 est.)

Carbon dioxide emissions: 33.629 million metric tonnes of CO2 (2023 est.)
from coal and metallurgical coke: 6,000 metric tonnes of CO2 (2023 est.)
from petroleum and other liquids: 3.634 million metric tonnes of CO2 (2023 est.)
from consumed natural gas: 29.989 million metric tonnes of CO2 (2023 est.)
comparison ranking: total emissions 68

Particulate matter emissions: 10.4 micrograms per cubic meter (2019 est.)

Methane emissions: *energy:* 160.3 kt (2022-2024 est.)
agriculture: 4.1 kt (2019-2021 est.)
waste: 59.1 kt (2019-2021 est.)
other: 6 kt (2019-2021 est.)

Waste and recycling: *municipal solid waste generated annually:* 727,900 tons (2024 est.)
percent of municipal solid waste recycled: 16.2% (2022 est.)

Total water withdrawal: *municipal:* 237.6 million cubic meters (2022 est.)
industrial: 128.9 million cubic meters (2022 est.)
agricultural: 16.7 million cubic meters (2022 est.)

Total renewable water resources: 3.84 billion cubic meters (2022 est.)

GOVERNMENT

Country name: *conventional long form:* Republic of Trinidad and Tobago
conventional short form: Trinidad and Tobago
etymology: explorer Christopher COLUMBUS named the larger island "La Isla de la Trinidad" (The Island of the Trinity) in 1498, possibly because of the three mountain peaks on the island; COLUMBUS may have gotten the name Tobago, spelled "tobaco" in Spanish, from the tobacco grown and smoked locally, or from its elongated cigar shape

Government type: parliamentary republic

Capital: *name:* Port of Spain
geographic coordinates: 10 39 N, 61 31 W
time difference: UTC-4 (1 hour ahead of Washington, DC, during Standard Time)
etymology: translation of the name the Spanish gave the town in 1595, Puerto de España; the name was anglicized after the British captured Trinidad in 1797

Administrative divisions: 9 regions, 3 boroughs, 2 cities, 1 ward
regions: Couva/Tabaquite/Talparo, Diego Martin, Mayaro/Rio Claro, Penal/Debe, Princes Town, Sangre Grande, San Juan/Laventille, Siparia, Tunapuna/Piarco
borough: Arima, Chaguanas, Point Fortin
cities: Port of Spain, San Fernando
ward: Tobago

Legal system: English common law; Supreme Court reviews legislative acts

Constitution: *history:* previous 1962; latest 1976
amendment process: proposed by Parliament; passage of amendments affecting constitutional provisions, such as human rights and freedoms or citizenship, requires at least two-thirds majority vote by the membership of both houses and assent of the president; passage of amendments, such as the powers and authorities of the executive, legislative, and judicial branches of government, and the procedure for amending the constitution, requires at least three-quarters majority vote by the House membership, two-thirds majority vote by the Senate membership, and assent of the president

International law organization participation: has not submitted an ICJ jurisdiction declaration; accepts ICCt jurisdiction

Citizenship: *citizenship by birth:* yes
citizenship by descent only: yes
dual citizenship recognized: yes
residency requirement for naturalization: 8 years

Suffrage: 18 years of age; universal

Executive branch: *chief of state:* President Christine KANGALOO (since 20 March 2023)
head of government: Prime Minister Kamla Susheila PERSAD-BISSESSAR (since 1 May 2025)
cabinet: Cabinet appointed from among members of Parliament
election/appointment process: president indirectly elected by an electoral college of selected Senate and House of Representatives members for a 5-year term (eligible for a second term); the president usually appoints the leader of the majority party in the House of Representatives as prime minister
most recent election date: 20 January 2023
election results: *2023:* Christine KANGALOO elected president by the electoral college on 20 January 2023; electoral college vote Christine KANGALOO (PNM) 48, Israel KHAN (UNC) 22
2018: Paula-Mae WEEKES (independent) elected president; ran unopposed and was elected without a vote; she was Trinidad and Tabago's first female head of state
expected date of next election: by February 2028

Legislative branch: *legislature name:* Parliament
legislative structure: bicameral
note: Tobago has a unicameral House of Assembly (19 seats; 15 assemblymen directly elected by simple majority vote and 4 appointed councilors - 3 on the advice of the chief secretary and 1 on the advice of the minority leader; members serve 4-year terms)

Legislative branch - lower chamber: *chamber name:* House of Representatives
number of seats: 42 (all directly elected)
electoral system: plurality/majority
scope of elections: full renewal
term in office: 5 years
most recent election date: 4/28/2025
parties elected and seats per party: United National Congress (UNC) (26); People's National Movement (PNM) (13); Other (2)
percentage of women in chamber: 23.8%
expected date of next election: April 2030

Legislative branch - upper chamber: *chamber name:* Senate
number of seats: 31 (all appointed)
scope of elections: full renewal
term in office: 5 years
most recent election date: 5/23/2025
percentage of women in chamber: 25.8%
expected date of next election: May 2030

Judicial branch: *highest court(s):* Supreme Court of the Judicature (consists of a chief justice for both the Court of Appeal with 12 judges and the High Court with 24 judges)
judge selection and term of office: Supreme Court chief justice appointed by the president after consultation with the prime minister and the parliamentary leader of the opposition; other judges appointed by the Judicial Legal Services Commission, headed by the chief justice and 5 members with judicial experience; all judges serve for life with mandatory retirement normally at age 65
subordinate courts: Courts of Summary Criminal Jurisdiction; Petty Civil Courts; Family Court
note: Trinidad and Tobago can file appeals beyond its Supreme Court to the Caribbean Court of Justice, with final appeal to the Judicial Committee of the Privy Council (in London)

Political parties: People's National Movement or PNM
United National Congress or UNC
Tobago People's Party or Tobago

Diplomatic representation in the US: *chief of mission:* Ambassador (vacant); Chargé d'Affaires Venessa RAMHIT-RAMROOP (since 4 June 2025)
chancery: 1708 Massachusetts Avenue NW, Washington, DC 20036-1975
telephone: [1] (202) 467-6490
FAX: [1] (202) 785-3130
email address and website: embdcinfo@foreign.gov.tt
https://foreign.gov.tt/missions-consuls/tt-missions-abroad/diplomatic-missions/embassy-washington-dc-us/
consulate(s) general: Miami, New York

Diplomatic representation from the US: *chief of mission:* Ambassador (vacant); Chargé d'Affaires Jenifer NEIDHART de ORTIZ (since January 2025)
embassy: 15 Queen's Park West, Port of Spain
mailing address: 3410 Port of Spain Place, Washington DC 20521-3410
telephone: (868) 622-6371
FAX: (868) 822-5905
email address and website: ptspas@state.gov
https://tt.usembassy.gov/

International organization participation: ACP, ACS, AOSIS, C, Caricom, CDB, CELAC, EITI (compliant country), FAO, G-24, G-77, IADB, IAEA, IBRD, ICAO, ICC (NGOs), ICCt, ICRM, IDA, IFAD, IFC, IFRCS, IHO, ILO, IMF, IMO, Interpol, IOC, IOM, IPU, ISO, ITSO, ITU, ITUC (NGOs), LAES, MIGA, NAM, OAS, OPANAL, OPCW, Pacific Alliance (observer), Paris Club (associate), UN, UNCTAD, UNESCO, UNIDO, UPU, WCO, WFTU (NGOs), WHO, WIPO, WMO, WTO

Independence: 31 August 1962 (from the UK)

National holiday: Independence Day, 31 August (1962)

Flag description: red with a white-edged black diagonal band from the upper left to the lower right
meaning: the colors represent the elements of earth, water, and fire; black also stands for the wealth of the land and the dedication of the people; white for the sea, the purity of the country's aspirations, and equality; red for the sun, the vitality of the land, and the people's courage and friendliness

National symbol(s): scarlet ibis (bird of Trinidad), cocrico (bird of Tobago), chaconia flower

National color(s): red, white, black

National coat of arms: designed in 1962, the coat of arms shows the scarlet ibis (national bird of Trinidad) and the cocrico (national bird of Tobago); they support a shield displaying two hummingbirds, because Trinidad is home to 18 species of the bird and is called the "Land of Hummingbirds;" three gold ships on a backdrop of national colors represent Christopher Columbus, who visited the islands; the three peaks in the lower left refer to Trinidad being named after the Holy Trinity and also represent a famous mountain; the image of a gold ship's wheel in front of a coconut palm was also used on the Great Seals of British Colonial Tobago; the gold helmet represents Queen Elizabeth II of England (ruler of the country at the time), and the national motto promotes harmony in diversity

National anthem(s): *title:* "Forged From the Love of Liberty"
lyrics/music: Patrick Stanislaus CASTAGNE
history: adopted 1962; song originally written as an anthem for the West Indies Federation; Trinidad and Tobago adopted it when the Federation dissolved

ECONOMY

Economic overview: high-income Caribbean economy; major hydrocarbon exporter; key tourism and finance sectors; high inflation and growing public debt; long foreign currency access delays; large foreign reserves and sovereign wealth fund

Real GDP (purchasing power parity): $43.362 billion (2024 est.)
$42.658 billion (2023 est.)
$42.058 billion (2022 est.)
note: data in 2021 dollars
comparison ranking: 137

Real GDP growth rate: 1.7% (2024 est.)
1.4% (2023 est.)
1.1% (2022 est.)
note: annual GDP % growth based on constant local currency
comparison ranking: 156

Real GDP per capita: $31,700 (2024 est.)
$31,200 (2023 est.)
$30,800 (2022 est.)
note: data in 2021 dollars
comparison ranking: 75

GDP (official exchange rate): $26.429 billion (2024 est.)
note: data in current dollars at official exchange rate

Inflation rate (consumer prices): 0.5% (2024 est.)
4.6% (2023 est.)
5.8% (2022 est.)
note: annual % change based on consumer prices
comparison ranking: 12

GDP - composition, by sector of origin: *agriculture:* 0.8% (2023 est.)
industry: 35% (2023 est.)
services: 59.9% (2023 est.)
note: figures may not total 100% due to non-allocated consumption not captured in sector-reported data
comparison rankings: agriculture 178; industry 34; services 89

GDP - composition, by end use: *household consumption:* 78.9% (2017 est.)
government consumption: 16.4% (2017 est.)
investment in fixed capital: 19.8% (2021 est.)
investment in inventories: 0% (2021 est.)
exports of goods and services: 45.4% (2017 est.)
imports of goods and services: -48.7% (2017 est.)

Agricultural products: chicken, fruits, coconuts, citrus fruits, maize, oranges, plantains, eggs, taro, mangoes/guavas (2023)
note: top ten agricultural products based on tonnage

Industries: petroleum and petroleum products, liquefied natural gas, methanol, ammonia, urea, steel products, beverages, food processing, cement, cotton textiles

Industrial production growth rate: -4.7% (2023 est.)
note: annual % change in industrial value added based on constant local currency
comparison ranking: 176

Labor force: 649,900 (2024 est.)
note: number of people ages 15 or older who are employed or seeking work
comparison ranking: 156

Unemployment rate: 4.6% (2024 est.)
4.3% (2023 est.)
4.4% (2022 est.)
note: % of labor force seeking employment
comparison ranking: 78

Youth unemployment rate (ages 15-24): *total:* 11.1% (2024 est.)
male: 10.3% (2024 est.)
female: 12% (2024 est.)
note: % of labor force ages 15-24 seeking employment
comparison ranking: total 112

Remittances: 0.8% of GDP (2024 est.)
0.8% of GDP (2023 est.)
0.7% of GDP (2022 est.)
note: personal transfers and compensation between resident and non-resident individuals/households/entities

Budget: *revenues:* $5.698 billion (2019 est.)
expenditures: $7.822 billion (2019 est.)
note: central government revenues (excluding grants) and expenses converted to US dollars at average official exchange rate for year indicated

Taxes and other revenues: 16.7% (of GDP) (2019 est.)
note: central government tax revenue as a % of GDP
comparison ranking: 80

Current account balance: $1.117 billion (2024 est.)
$2.948 billion (2023 est.)
$4.967 billion (2022 est.)
note: balance of payments - net trade and primary/secondary income in current dollars
comparison ranking: 57

Exports: $11.087 billion (2024 est.)
$11.545 billion (2023 est.)
$17.584 billion (2022 est.)
note: balance of payments - exports of goods and services in current dollars
comparison ranking: 114

Exports - partners: USA 28%, China 7%, Guyana 5%, Chile 5%, Netherlands 5% (2023)
note: top five export partners based on percentage share of exports

Exports - commodities: natural gas, alcohols, ammonia, crude petroleum, iron reductions (2023)
note: top five export commodities based on value in dollars

Imports: $10.19 billion (2024 est.)
$9.219 billion (2023 est.)
$10.968 billion (2022 est.)
note: balance of payments - imports of goods and services in current dollars
comparison ranking: 123

Imports - partners: USA 29%, Guyana 27%, China 8%, Brazil 4%, Canada 3% (2023)
note: top five import partners based on percentage share of imports

Imports - commodities: railway cargo containers, refined petroleum, cars, iron ore, excavation machinery (2023)
note: top five import commodities based on value in dollars

Reserves of foreign exchange and gold: $5.601 billion (2024 est.)
$6.256 billion (2023 est.)
$6.832 billion (2022 est.)
note: holdings of gold (year-end prices)/foreign exchange/special drawing rights in current dollars
comparison ranking: 93

Exchange rates: Trinidad and Tobago dollars (TTD) per US dollar -

Exchange rates: 6.75 (2024 est.)
6.75 (2023 est.)
6.754 (2022 est.)
6.759 (2021 est.)
6.751 (2020 est.)

ENERGY

Electricity access: *electrification - total population:* 100% (2022 est.)

Electricity: *installed generating capacity:* 2.139 million kW (2023 est.)
consumption: 9.001 billion kWh (2023 est.)
transmission/distribution losses: 492 million kWh (2023 est.)
comparison rankings: installed generating capacity 120; consumption 109; transmission/distribution losses 80

Electricity generation sources: *fossil fuels:* 99.9% of total installed capacity (2023 est.)
solar: 0.1% of total installed capacity (2023 est.)

Coal: *consumption:* 6 metric tons (2022 est.)
imports: 2,000 metric tons (2023 est.)

Petroleum: *total petroleum production:* 72,000 bbl/day (2023 est.)
refined petroleum consumption: 26,000 bbl/day (2023 est.)
crude oil estimated reserves: 242.982 million barrels (2021 est.)

Natural gas: *production:* 25.994 billion cubic meters (2023 est.)
consumption: 15.316 billion cubic meters (2023 est.)
exports: 10.737 billion cubic meters (2023 est.)
proven reserves: 298.063 billion cubic meters (2021 est.)

COMMUNICATIONS

Telephones - fixed lines: *total subscriptions:* 311,000 (2023 est.)
subscriptions per 100 inhabitants: 21 (2023 est.)
comparison ranking: total subscriptions 105

Telephones - mobile cellular: *total subscriptions:* 2.02 million (2023 est.)
subscriptions per 100 inhabitants: 131 (2022 est.)
comparison ranking: total subscriptions 151

Broadcast media: 6 free-to-air TV networks, 2 of which are state-owned; 24 subscription providers (cable and satellite); over 36 radio frequencies (2019)

Internet country code: .tt

Internet users: *percent of population:* 85% (2023 est.)

Broadband - fixed subscriptions: *total:* 404,000 (2023 est.)
subscriptions per 100 inhabitants: 27 (2023 est.)
comparison ranking: total 107

TRANSPORTATION

Civil aircraft registration country code prefix: 9Y

Airports: 3 (2025)
comparison ranking: 192

Merchant marine: *total:* 102 (2023)
by type: general cargo 1, other 101
comparison ranking: total 88

Ports: *total ports:* 10 (2024)
large: 0
medium: 1
small: 4
very small: 5
ports with oil terminals: 8
key ports: Galeota Point Terminal, Point Lisas Industrial Port, Point Lisas Port, Pointe-a-Pierre, Port of Spain

MILITARY AND SECURITY

Military and security forces: Trinidad and Tobago Defense Force (TTDF): Trinidad and Tobago Regiment (Army/Land Forces), Trinidad and Tobago Coast Guard, Trinidad and Tobago Air Guard, Trinidad and Tobago Defense Force Reserves
Trinidad and Tobago Police Service (TTPS) (2025)
note: the Ministry of National Security oversees both the TTDF and the TTPS

Military expenditures: 0.9% of GDP (2024 est.)
1% of GDP (2023 est.)
1% of GDP (2022 est.)
1% of GDP (2021 est.)
1% of GDP (2020 est.)

Military and security service personnel strengths: approximately 5,000 Defense Forces (2025)

Military equipment inventories and acquisitions: the TTDF's ground force inventory consists of light weapons, while the Coast Guard and Air Guard field mostly secondhand equipment from a mix of countries, including Australia, China, Italy, the Netherlands, the UK, and the US (2024)

Military service age and obligation: 18-25 years of age for voluntary military service for men and women (some age variations between services, reserves); no conscription (2024)

Military - note: the primary responsibilities of the Trinidad and Tobago Defense Force (TTDF) are conducting border and maritime security, assisting civil authorities in times of crisis or disaster, providing search and rescue services, port security, and supporting civil law enforcement, particularly in countering gang-related crime and trafficking of narcotics and other illicit goods; the Police Service maintains internal security (2025)

TERRORISM

Terrorist group(s): Terrorist group(s): Tren de Aragua (TdA)

TRANSNATIONAL ISSUES

Refugees and internally displaced persons: *refugees:* 24,134 (2024 est.)

TUNISIA

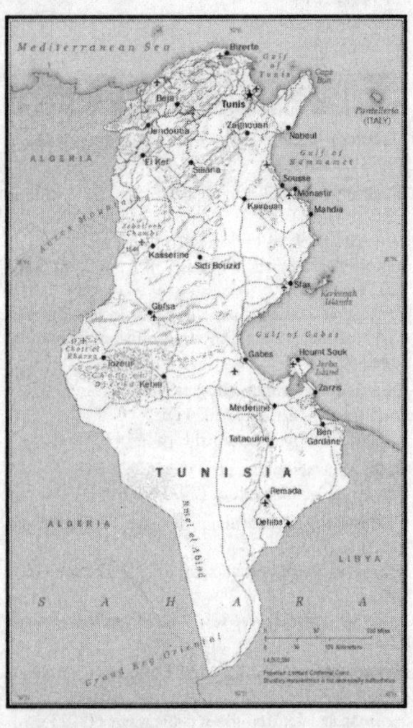

INTRODUCTION

Background: Many empires have controlled Tunisia, including the Phoenicians (as early as the 12 century B.C.), Carthaginians, Romans, Vandals, Byzantines, various Arab and Berber kingdoms, and Ottomans (16th to late-19th centuries). Rivalry between French and Italian interests in Tunisia culminated in a French invasion in 1881 and the creation of a protectorate. Agitation for independence in the decades after World War I finally convinced the French to recognize Tunisia as an independent state in 1956. The country's first president, Habib BOURGUIBA, established a strict one-party state. He dominated the country for 31 years, repressing Islamic fundamentalism and establishing rights for women. In 1987, Zine el Abidine BEN ALI replaced BOURGUIBA in a bloodless coup.

Street protests that began in Tunis in 2010 over high unemployment, corruption, widespread poverty, and high food prices escalated in 2011, culminating in rioting that led to hundreds of deaths and later became known as the start of the regional Arab Spring uprising. BEN ALI dismissed the government and fled the country, and a "national unity government" was formed. Elections for the new Constituent Assembly were held later that year, and human rights activist Moncef MARZOUKI was elected as interim president. The Assembly began drafting a new constitution in 2012 and, after several iterations and a months-long political crisis that stalled the transition, ratified the document in 2014. Parliamentary and presidential elections for a permanent government were held at the end of 2014. Beji CAID ESSEBSI was elected as the first president under the country's new constitution. After ESSEBSI's death in office in 2019, Kais SAIED was elected. SAIED's term, as well as that of Tunisia's 217-member parliament, was set to expire in 2024. However, in 2021, SAIED used the exceptional powers allowed under Tunisia's constitution to dismiss the prime minister and suspend the legislature. Tunisians approved a new constitution through public referendum in 2022, expanding presidential powers and creating a new bicameral legislature.

GEOGRAPHY

Location: Northern Africa, bordering the Mediterranean Sea, between Algeria and Libya

Geographic coordinates: 34 00 N, 9 00 E

Map references: Africa

Area: *total:* 163,610 sq km
land: 155,360 sq km
water: 8,250 sq km
comparison ranking: total 93

Area - comparative: slightly larger than Georgia

Land boundaries: *total:* 1,495 km
border countries (2): Algeria 1,034 km; Libya 461 km

Coastline: 1,148 km

Maritime claims: *territorial sea:* 12 nm
contiguous zone: 24 nm
exclusive economic zone: 12 nm

Climate: temperate in north with mild, rainy winters and hot, dry summers; desert in south

Terrain: mountains in north; hot, dry central plain; semiarid south merges into the Sahara

Elevation: *highest point:* Jebel ech Chambi 1,544 m
lowest point: Shatt al Gharsah -17 m
mean elevation: 246 m

Natural resources: petroleum, phosphates, iron ore, lead, zinc, salt

Land use: *agricultural land:* 62.4% (2022 est.)
arable land: 18.2% (2022 est.)
permanent crops: 13.6% (2022 est.)
permanent pasture: 30.6% (2022 est.)
forest: 4.5% (2022 est.)
other: 33% (2022 est.)

Irrigated land: 3,920 sq km (2013)

Major aquifers: North Western Sahara Aquifer System

Population distribution: the overwhelming majority of the population is located in the northern half of the country; the south remains largely underpopulated, as shown in this population distribution map

Natural hazards: flooding; earthquakes; droughts

Geography - note: strategic location in central Mediterranean

PEOPLE AND SOCIETY

Population: *total:* 12,048,847 (2024 est.)
male: 5,972,242
female: 6,076,605
comparison rankings: total 81; male 82; female 81

Nationality: *noun:* Tunisian(s)
adjective: Tunisian

Ethnic groups: Arab 98%, European 1%, Jewish and other 1%

Languages: Arabic (official, one of the languages of commerce), French (commerce), Tamazight
major-language sample(s):

كتاب حقائق العالم، أحسن كتاب تتعلم به المعلومات الأساسية

(Arabic)
The World Factbook, une source indispensable d'informations de base. (French)
note: despite having no official status, French plays a major role in the country and is spoken by about two thirds of the population

Religions: Muslim (official; Sunni) 99%, other (includes Christian, Jewish, Shia Muslim, and Baha'i) <1%

Age structure: *0-14 years:* 24.4% (male 1,516,871/ female 1,426,522)
15-64 years: 65.2% (male 3,861,731/female 3,990,802)
65 years and over: 10.4% (2024 est.) (male 593,640/ female 659,281)

Dependency ratios: *total dependency ratio:* 53.4 (2024 est.)
youth dependency ratio: 37.5 (2024 est.)
elderly dependency ratio: 16 (2024 est.)
potential support ratio: 6.3 (2024 est.)

Median age: *total:* 34.4 years (2024 est.)
male: 33.6 years
female: 35.1 years
comparison ranking: total 102

Population growth rate: 0.58% (2024 est.)
comparison ranking: 143

Birth rate: 13.5 births/1,000 population (2024 est.)
comparison ranking: 127

Death rate: 6.4 deaths/1,000 population (2024 est.)
comparison ranking: 143

Net migration rate: -1.3 migrant(s)/1,000 population (2024 est.)
comparison ranking: 154

Population distribution: the overwhelming majority of the population is located in the northern half of the country; the south remains largely underpopulated, as shown in this population distribution map

Urbanization: *urban population:* 70.5% of total population (2023)
rate of urbanization: 1.34% annual rate of change (2020-25 est.)

Major urban areas - population: 2.475 million TUNIS (capital) (2023)

Sex ratio: *at birth:* 1.06 male(s)/female
0-14 years: 1.06 male(s)/female
15-64 years: 0.97 male(s)/female
65 years and over: 0.9 male(s)/female
total population: 0.98 male(s)/female (2024 est.)

Maternal mortality ratio: 36 deaths/100,000 live births (2023 est.)
comparison ranking: 108

Infant mortality rate: *total:* 11.3 deaths/1,000 live births (2024 est.)
male: 12.7 deaths/1,000 live births
female: 9.8 deaths/1,000 live births
comparison ranking: total 119

Life expectancy at birth: *total population:* 77.3 years (2024 est.)
male: 75.7 years
female: 79.1 years
comparison ranking: total population 93

Total fertility rate: 1.93 children born/woman (2024 est.)
comparison ranking: 115

Gross reproduction rate: 0.94 (2024 est.)

Drinking water source: *improved: urban:* 98.8% of population (2022 est.)
rural: 93.4% of population (2022 est.)
total: 97.2% of population (2022 est.)
unimproved: urban: 1.2% of population (2022 est.)
rural: 6.6% of population (2022 est.)
total: 2.8% of population (2022 est.)

Health expenditure: 7% of GDP (2021)
11.2% of national budget (2022 est.)

Physician density: 1.32 physicians/1,000 population (2021)

Hospital bed density: 2.4 beds/1,000 population (2021 est.)

Sanitation facility access: *improved: urban:* 98.8% of population (2022 est.)
rural: 99.4% of population (2022 est.)
total: 99% of population (2022 est.)
unimproved: urban: 1.2% of population (2022 est.)
rural: 0.6% of population (2022 est.)
total: 1% of population (2022 est.)

Obesity - adult prevalence rate: 26.9% (2016)
comparison ranking: 40

Alcohol consumption per capita: *total:* 1.51 liters of pure alcohol (2019 est.)
beer: 0.99 liters of pure alcohol (2019 est.)
wine: 0.32 liters of pure alcohol (2019 est.)
spirits: 0.17 liters of pure alcohol (2019 est.)
other alcohols: 0.03 liters of pure alcohol (2019 est.)
comparison ranking: total 139

Tobacco use: *total:* 19% (2025 est.)
male: 37.6% (2025 est.)
female: 1.4% (2025 est.)
comparison ranking: total 76

Children under the age of 5 years underweight: 1.6% (2018)
comparison ranking: 103

Currently married women (ages 15-49): 53.9% (2023 est.)

Child marriage: *women married by age 15:* 0% (2018)
women married by age 18: 1.5% (2018)
men married by age 18: 0% (2018)

Education expenditure: 6.7% of GDP (2023 est.)
17.8% national budget (2024 est.)
comparison ranking: Education expenditure (% GDP) 20

Literacy: *total population:* 86.2% (2023 est.)
male: 92.7% (2023 est.)
female: 80.1% (2023 est.)

School life expectancy (primary to tertiary education): *total:* 14 years (2016 est.)
male: 14 years (2016 est.)
female: 15 years (2016 est.)

ENVIRONMENT

Environmental issues: toxic and hazardous waste disposal; water pollution from raw sewage; limited freshwater resources; deforestation; overgrazing; soil erosion; desertification

International environmental agreements: *party to:* Biodiversity, Climate Change, Climate Change-Kyoto Protocol, Climate Change-Paris Agreement, Comprehensive Nuclear Test Ban, Desertification, Endangered Species, Environmental Modification, Hazardous Wastes, Law of the Sea, Marine Dumping-London Convention, Nuclear Test Ban, Ozone Layer Protection, Ship Pollution, Wetlands
signed, but not ratified: Marine Life Conservation

Climate: temperate in north with mild, rainy winters and hot, dry summers; desert in south

Urbanization: *urban population:* 70.5% of total population (2023)
rate of urbanization: 1.34% annual rate of change (2020-25 est.)

Carbon dioxide emissions: 24.645 million metric tonnes of CO_2 (2023 est.)
from coal and metallurgical coke: 4,000 metric tonnes of CO_2 (2023 est.)
from petroleum and other liquids: 14.249 million metric tonnes of CO_2 (2023 est.)
from consumed natural gas: 10.392 million metric tonnes of CO_2 (2023 est.)
comparison ranking: total emissions 77

Particulate matter emissions: 26.5 micrograms per cubic meter (2019 est.)

Methane emissions: *energy:* 88 kt (2022-2024 est.)
agriculture: 94.5 kt (2019-2021 est.)
waste: 97.9 kt (2019-2021 est.)
other: 3 kt (2019-2021 est.)

Waste and recycling: *municipal solid waste generated annually:* 2.7 million tons (2024 est.)
percent of municipal solid waste recycled: 10.9% (2022 est.)

Total water withdrawal: *municipal:* 815.5 million cubic meters (2022 est.)
industrial: 61.9 million cubic meters (2022 est.)
agricultural: 2.71 billion cubic meters (2022 est.)

Total renewable water resources: 4.615 billion cubic meters (2022 est.)

GOVERNMENT

Country name: *conventional long form:* Republic of Tunisia
conventional short form: Tunisia
local long form: Al Jumhuriyah at Tunisiyah
local short form: Tunis

etymology: the country name derives from the capital city of Tunis

Government type: parliamentary republic

Capital: *name:* Tunis
geographic coordinates: 36 48 N, 10 11 E
time difference: UTC+1 (6 hours ahead of Washington, DC, during Standard Time)
etymology: the origin of the ancient name is unclear; it is sometimes associated with the name of the Phoenician goddess Tanith

Administrative divisions: 24 governorates (*wilayat*, singular - *wilayah*); Beja (Bajah), Ben Arous (Bin 'Arus), Bizerte (Banzart), Gabes (Qabis), Gafsa (Qafsah), Jendouba (Jundubah), Kairouan (Al Qayrawan), Kasserine (Al Qasrayn), Kebili (Qibili), Kef (Al Kaf), L'Ariana (Aryanah), Mahdia (Al Mahdiyah), Manouba (Manubah), Medenine (Madanin), Monastir (Al Munastir), Nabeul (Nabul), Sfax (Safaqis), Sidi Bouzid (Sidi Bu Zayd), Siliana (Silyanah), Sousse (Susah), Tataouine (Tatawin), Tozeur (Tawzar), Tunis, Zaghouan (Zaghwan)

Legal system: mixed system of civil law, based on the French civil code and Islamic (sharia) law; Supreme Court reviews some legislative acts in joint session

Constitution: *history:* several previous; latest draft published by the president 30 June 2022, approved by referendum 25 July 2022, and adopted 27 July 2022
amendment process: proposed by the president of the republic or one third of the Assembly of the Representatives of the People membership; following Constitutional Court review, approval to proceed requires an absolute majority vote in the Assembly, and final passage requires a two-thirds Assembly majority vote; the president can opt to submit an amendment to a referendum, which requires an absolute majority of votes cast for passage

International law organization participation: has not submitted an ICJ jurisdiction declaration; accepts ICCt jurisdiction

Citizenship: *citizenship by birth:* no
citizenship by descent only: at least one parent must be a citizen of Tunisia
dual citizenship recognized: yes
residency requirement for naturalization: 5 years

Suffrage: 18 years of age; universal except for active government security forces (including the police and the military), people with mental disabilities, people who have served more than three months in prison (criminal cases only), and people given a suspended sentence of more than six months

Executive branch: *chief of state:* President Kais SAIED (since 23 October 2019)
head of government: Prime Minister Sarra ZAAFRANI Zenzri (since 21 March 2025)
cabinet: prime minister appointed by the president; cabinet members appointed by the president in consultation with the prime minister
election/appointment process: president directly elected by absolute-majority popular vote in 2 rounds, if needed, for a 5-year term (eligible for a second term)
most recent election date: 6 October 2024
election results: *2024:* Kais SAIED reelected president in first round - Kais SAIED (independent) 90.7%, Ayachi ZAMMEL (Long Live Tunisia) 7.3%, Zouhair MAGHZAOUI (People's Movement) 2%
2019: Kais SAIED elected president in second round; percent of vote in first round - Kais SAIED (independent) 18.4%, Nabil KAROUI (Heart of Tunisia) 15.6%, Abdelfattah MOUROU (Nahda Movement) 12.9%, Abdelkrim ZBIDI (independent) 10.7%, Youssef CHAHED (Long Live Tunisia) 7.4%, Safi SAID (independent) 7.1%, Lotfi MRAIHI (Republican People's Union) 6.6%, other 21.3%; percent of vote in second round - Kais SAIED 72.7%, Nabil KAROUI 27.3%
expected date of next election: 2029
note: the president can dismiss any member of government on his own initiative or in consultation with the prime minister

Legislative branch: *legislative structure:* bicameral
note: in 2022, President SAIED issued a new electoral law that requires all legislative candidates to run as independents

Legislative branch - lower chamber: *chamber name:* Assembly of People's Representatives (Majlis Nawwab ash-Sha'ab)
number of seats: 161 (all directly elected)
electoral system: plurality/majority
scope of elections: full renewal
term in office: 5 years
most recent election date: 12/17/2022 to 1/29/2023
percentage of women in chamber: 15.8%
expected date of next election: December 2027

Legislative branch - upper chamber: *chamber name:* National Council of Regions and Districts
number of seats: 77 (all indirectly elected)
scope of elections: full renewal
term in office: 5 years
most recent election date: 4/19/2024
percentage of women in chamber: 13%
expected date of next election: April 2029

Judicial branch: *highest court(s):* Court of Cassation (consists of the first president, chamber presidents, and magistrates; organized into 27 civil and 11 criminal chambers)
judge selection and term of office: Supreme Court judges nominated by the Supreme Judicial Council, an independent 4-part body consisting mainly of elected judges and the remainder legal specialists; judge tenure based on terms of appointment; Constitutional Court (established in the 2014 and 2022 constitutions, but never implemented)
subordinate courts: Courts of Appeal; administrative courts; Court of Audit; Housing Court; courts of first instance; lower district courts; military courts
note: the Tunisian constitution of January 2014 called for the establishment of a constitutional court by the end of 2015, but the court was never formed; the new constitution of July 2022 calls for the establishment of a constitutional court consisting of 9 members appointed by presidential decree; members to include former senior judges of other courts

Political parties: Afek Tounes
Al Badil Al-Tounisi (The Tunisian Alternative)
Al-Amal Party
Call for Tunisia Party (Nidaa Tounes)
Current of Love (formerly the Popular Petition party)
Democratic Current
Democratic Patriots' Unified Party
Dignity Coalition or Al Karama Coalition
Ennahda Movement (The Renaissance)
Ettakatol Party
Free Destourian Party or PDL
Green Tunisia Party
Harakat Hak
Heart of Tunisia (Qalb Tounes)
July 25 Movement
Labor and Achievement Party
Long Live Tunisia (Tahya Tounes)
Movement of Socialist Democrats or MDS
National Coalition Party
National Salvation Front
New Carthage Party
Party of the Democratic Arab Vanguard
People's Movement
Republican Party (Al Joumhouri)
The Movement Party (Hizb Harak)
Third Republic Party
Tunisian Ba'ath Movement
Voice of the Republic
Workers' Party
note: President SAIED in 2022 issued a decree that forbids political parties' participation in legislative elections; although parties remain a facet of Tunisian political life, they have lost significant influence

Diplomatic representation in the US: *chief of mission:* Ambassador (vacant); Chargé d'Affaires Anis HAJRI (since 1 August 2025)
chancery: 1515 Massachusetts Avenue NW, Washington, DC 20005
telephone: [1] (202) 862-1850
FAX: [1] (202) 862-1858
email address and website: AT.Washington@Tunisiaembassy.org
https://www.tunisianembassy.org/

Diplomatic representation from the US: *chief of mission:* Ambassador Joey HOOD (since 2 February 2023)
embassy: Les Berges du Lac, 1053 Tunis
mailing address: 6360 Tunis Place, Washington DC 20521-6360
telephone: [216] 71-107-000
FAX: [216] 71-107-090
email address and website: tuniswebsitecontact@state.gov
https://tn.usembassy.gov/

International organization participation: ABEDA, AfDB, AFESD, AIIB, AMF, AMU, AU, BSEC (observer), CAEU, CD, EBRD, FAO, G-11, G-77, IAEA, IBRD, ICAO, ICC (national committees), ICCt, ICRM, IDA, IDB, IFAD, IFC, IFRCS, IHO, ILO, IMF, IMO, IMSO, Interpol, IOC, IOM, IPU, ISO, ITSO, ITU, ITUC (NGOs), LAS, MIGA, MONUSCO, NAM, OAS (observer), OIC, OIF, OPCW, OSCE (partner), UN, UNCTAD, UNESCO, UNHCR, UNIDO, UNOCI, UNOOSA, UNWTO, UPU, WCO, WFTU (NGOs), WHO, WIPO, WMO, WTO

Independence: 20 March 1956 (from France)

National holiday: Independence Day, 20 March (1956); Revolution and Youth Day, 14 January (2011)

Flag: *description:* red with a white disk in the center that displays a red crescent around a five-pointed red star
meaning: red stands for martyrs' blood shed the fight against oppression, and white for peace; the crescent and star are traditional symbols of Islam
history: resembles the Ottoman flag (red banner with white crescent and star), a reference to Tunisia's history as part of the Ottoman Empire

National symbol(s): red crescent moon and five-pointed star in a white circle

National color(s): red, white

National anthem(s): *title:* "Humat Al Hima" (Defenders of the Homeland)
lyrics/music: Mustafa Sadik AL-RAFII and Aboul-Qacem ECHEBBI/Mohamad Abdel WAHAB

history: adopted 1957, replaced 1958, restored 1987; Mohamad Abdel WAHAB also composed the music for the anthem of the United Arab Emirates

National heritage: *total World Heritage Sites:* 9 (8 cultural, 1 natural)
selected World Heritage Site locales: Amphitheatre of El Jem (c); Archaeological Site of Carthage (c); Medina of Tunis (c); Ichkeul National Park (n); Punic Town of Kerkuane (c); Kairouan (c); Medina of Sousse (c); Dougga / Thugga (c); Djerba: Testimony to a settlement pattern in an island territory (c)

ECONOMY

Economic overview: lower middle-income North African economy; drafting reforms for foreign lenders; high unemployment, especially for youth and women; hit hard by COVID-19; high public sector wages; high public debt; protectionist austerity measures; key EU trade partner

Real GDP (purchasing power parity): $156.086 billion (2024 est.)
$154.006 billion (2023 est.)
$153.945 billion (2022 est.)
note: data in 2021 dollars
comparison ranking: 82

Real GDP growth rate: 1.4% (2024 est.)
0% (2023 est.)
2.7% (2022 est.)
note: annual GDP % growth based on constant local currency
comparison ranking: 164

Real GDP per capita: $12,700 (2024 est.)
$12,600 (2023 est.)
$12,700 (2022 est.)
note: data in 2021 dollars
comparison ranking: 133

GDP (official exchange rate): $53.41 billion (2024 est.)
note: data in current dollars at official exchange rate

Inflation rate (consumer prices): 7.2% (2024 est.)
9.3% (2023 est.)
8.3% (2022 est.)
note: annual % change based on consumer prices
comparison ranking: 165

GDP - composition, by sector of origin: *agriculture:* 9.3% (2023 est.)
industry: 23.6% (2023 est.)
services: 62.1% (2023 est.)
note: figures may not total 100% due to non-allocated consumption not captured in sector-reported data
comparison rankings: agriculture 77; industry 102; services 75

GDP - composition, by end use: *household consumption:* 76.2% (2024 est.)
government consumption: 18.6% (2024 est.)
investment in fixed capital: 13.4% (2024 est.)
investment in inventories: 0% (2024 est.)
exports of goods and services: 48.4% (2024 est.)
imports of goods and services: -56.6% (2024 est.)
note: figures may not total 100% due to rounding or gaps in data collection

Agricultural products: milk, tomatoes, olives, onions, chillies/peppers, watermelons, potatoes, wheat, dates, oranges (2023)
note: top ten agricultural products based on tonnage

Industries: petroleum, mining (particularly phosphate, iron ore), tourism, textiles, footwear, agribusiness, beverages

Industrial production growth rate: -2.5% (2024 est.)
note: annual % change in industrial value added based on constant local currency
comparison ranking: 164

Labor force: 4.247 million (2024 est.)
note: number of people ages 15 or older who are employed or seeking work
comparison ranking: 95

Unemployment rate: 16.3% (2024 est.)
15.2% (2023 est.)
15.3% (2022 est.)
note: % of labor force seeking employment
comparison ranking: 176

Youth unemployment rate (ages 15-24): *total:* 40.1% (2024 est.)
male: 41.1% (2024 est.)
female: 37.6% (2024 est.)
note: % of labor force ages 15-24 seeking employment
comparison ranking: total 8

Population below poverty line: 16.6% (2021 est.)
note: % of population with income below national poverty line

Gini Index coefficient - distribution of family income: 33.7 (2021 est.)
note: index (0-100) of income distribution; higher values represent greater inequality
comparison ranking: 89

Average household expenditures: *on food:* 22.3% of household expenditures (2023 est.)
on alcohol and tobacco: 3.3% of household expenditures (2023 est.)

Household income or consumption by percentage share: *lowest 10%:* 3.1% (2021 est.)
highest 10%: 27% (2021 est.)
note: % share of income accruing to lowest and highest 10% of population

Remittances: 6% of GDP (2023 est.)
6.2% of GDP (2022 est.)
6.3% of GDP (2021 est.)
note: personal transfers and compensation between resident and non-resident individuals/households/entities

Budget: *revenues:* $10.866 billion (2019 est.)
expenditures: $12.375 billion (2019 est.)

Current account balance: -$1.111 billion (2023 est.)
-$3.969 billion (2022 est.)
-$2.77 billion (2021 est.)
note: balance of payments - net trade and primary/secondary income in current dollars
comparison ranking: 133

Exports: $19.732 billion (2023 est.)
$17.254 billion (2022 est.)
$14.054 billion (2021 est.)
note: balance of payments - exports of goods and services in current dollars
comparison ranking: 92

Exports - partners: France 22%, Italy 17%, Germany 13%, USA 4%, Libya 4% (2023)
note: top five export partners based on percentage share of exports

Exports - commodities: garments, insulated wire, olive oil, refined petroleum, crude petroleum (2023)
note: top five export commodities based on value in dollars

Imports: $21.953 billion (2023 est.)
$22.453 billion (2022 est.)
$18.178 billion (2021 est.)
note: balance of payments - imports of goods and services in current dollars
comparison ranking: 94

Imports - partners: Italy 13%, France 12%, China 10%, Russia 8%, Germany 7% (2023)
note: top five import partners based on percentage share of imports

Imports - commodities: refined petroleum, natural gas, plastic products, cars, plastics (2023)
note: top five import commodities based on value in dollars

Reserves of foreign exchange and gold: $9.344 billion (2024 est.)
$9.24 billion (2023 est.)
$8.094 billion (2022 est.)
note: holdings of gold (year-end prices)/foreign exchange/special drawing rights in current dollars
comparison ranking: 81

Debt - external: $21.212 billion (2023 est.)
note: present value of external debt in current US dollars
comparison ranking: 34

Exchange rates: Tunisian dinars (TND) per US dollar -

Exchange rates: 3.107 (2024 est.)
3.106 (2023 est.)
3.104 (2022 est.)
2.794 (2021 est.)
2.812 (2020 est.)

ENERGY

Electricity access: *electrification - total population:* 100% (2022 est.)
electrification - urban areas: 100%
electrification - rural areas: 99.7%

Electricity: *installed generating capacity:* 6.639 million kW (2023 est.)
consumption: 19.153 billion kWh (2023 est.)
exports: 80 million kWh (2023 est.)
imports: 2.576 billion kWh (2023 est.)
transmission/distribution losses: 4.629 billion kWh (2023 est.)
comparison rankings: installed generating capacity 80; consumption 79; exports 91; imports 63; transmission/distribution losses 159

Electricity generation sources: *fossil fuels:* 96.1% of total installed capacity (2023 est.)
solar: 2.3% of total installed capacity (2023 est.)
wind: 1.6% of total installed capacity (2023 est.)

Coal: *consumption:* 2,000 metric tons (2022 est.)
exports: 28 metric tons (2023 est.)
imports: 3,000 metric tons (2023 est.)

Petroleum: *total petroleum production:* 35,000 bbl/day (2023 est.)
refined petroleum consumption: 104,000 bbl/day (2023 est.)
crude oil estimated reserves: 425 million barrels (2021 est.)

Natural gas: *production:* 1.313 billion cubic meters (2023 est.)
consumption: 5.131 billion cubic meters (2023 est.)
imports: 3.887 billion cubic meters (2023 est.)
proven reserves: 65.129 billion cubic meters (2021 est.)

Energy consumption per capita: 33.754 million Btu/person (2023 est.)
comparison ranking: 111

COMMUNICATIONS

Telephones - fixed lines: *total subscriptions:* 1.863 million (2023 est.)

subscriptions per 100 inhabitants: 15 (2023 est.)
comparison ranking: total subscriptions 53

Telephones - mobile cellular: *total subscriptions:* 16.4 million (2023 est.)
subscriptions per 100 inhabitants: 129 (2022 est.)
comparison ranking: total subscriptions 69

Broadcast media: 2 state-owned TV stations; 10 private local TV stations; satellite TV service available; state-owned radio network with 2 stations; several dozen private radio stations and community radio stations; transmissions of multiple international broadcasters available (2019)

Internet country code: .tn

Internet users: *percent of population:* 72% (2023 est.)

Broadband - fixed subscriptions: *total:* 1.73 million (2023 est.)
subscriptions per 100 inhabitants: 14 (2023 est.)
comparison ranking: total 65

TRANSPORTATION

Civil aircraft registration country code prefix: TS

Airports: 14 (2025)
comparison ranking: 151

Heliports: 11 (2025)
comparison ranking: 73

Railways: *total:* 2,173 km (2014) (1,991 in use)
standard gauge: 471 km (2014) 1.435-m gauge
narrow gauge: 1,694 km (2014) 1.000-m gauge (65 km electrified)
dual gauge: 8 km (2014) 1.435-1.000-m gauge

Merchant marine: *total:* 72 (2023)
by type: container ship 1, general cargo 8, oil tanker 1, other 62
comparison ranking: total 107

Ports: *total ports:* 16 (2024)
large: 0
medium: 3
small: 7
very small: 6
ports with oil terminals: 10
key ports: Ashtart Oil Terminal, Banzart, Didon Terminal, Gabes, La Goulette, Menzel Bourguiba, Mersa Sfax, Sousse, Tazerka Oil Terminal, Tunis

MILITARY AND SECURITY

Military and security forces: Tunisian Armed Forces (Forces Armées Tunisiennes, FAT): Tunisian Army (includes Air Defense Force), Tunisian Navy, Tunisia Air Force

Ministry of Interior (MoI): Internal Security Forces (National Police, National Guard) (2025)
note: the National Police has primary responsibility for law enforcement in the major cities, while the National Guard (gendarmerie) oversees border security and patrols smaller towns and rural areas

Military expenditures: 2.5% of GDP (2024 est.)
2.5% of GDP (2023 est.)
2.7% of GDP (2022 est.)
3% of GDP (2021 est.)
3% of GDP (2020 est.)

Military and security service personnel strengths: approximately 35,000 active-duty Armed Forces (25,000 Army; 5,000 Navy; 5,000 Air Force) (2025)

Military equipment inventories and acquisitions: the Tunisian military's inventory consists mostly of older or second-hand equipment from a wide variety of suppliers, including Brazil, China, Turkey, and the US, as well as several European countries, such as France, Germany, and Italy (2024)

Military service age and obligation: 18-23 years of age for voluntary service for men and women; 20-23 years of age for compulsory (national) service for men with a 12-month service obligation; individuals engaged in higher education or vocational training programs prior to their military drafting are allowed to delay service until they have completed their programs (up to age 35); exemptions allowed for males considered to a family's sole provider (2023)
note: women have been allowed in the service since 1975 as volunteers; as of 2023, women constituted about 8% of the military and served in all three services

Military deployments: 775 Central African Republic (MINUSCA) (2024)

Military - note: the Tunisian Armed Forces (FAT) are responsible for territorial defense and internal security; operational areas of focus include counterterrorism and assisting with securing the border regions, particularly along the frontiers with Algerian and Libya
the FAT conducts bilateral and multinational training exercises with a variety of countries, including Algeria and other North African and Middle Eastern countries, France, and the US, as well as NATO; it also participates in UN peacekeeping operations; Tunisia has Major Non-NATO Ally (MNNA) status with the US, a designation under US law that provides foreign partners with certain benefits in the areas of defense trade and security cooperation (2025)

TERRORISM

Terrorist group(s): Terrorist group(s): Ansar al-Sharia in Tunisia; Islamic State of Iraq and ash-Sham (ISIS) network in Tunisia (known locally as Ajnad al-Khilafah or the Army of the Caliphate); al-Qa'ida in the Islamic Maghreb
note: details about the history, aims, leadership, organization, areas of operation, tactics, targets, weapons, size, and sources of support of the group(s) appear(s) in Appendix T

TRANSNATIONAL ISSUES

Refugees and internally displaced persons: *refugees:* 12,575 (2024 est.)

Trafficking in persons: *tier rating:* Tier 2 Watch List — the government did not demonstrate overall increasing efforts to eliminate trafficking compared with the previous reporting period, therefore Tunisia was downgraded to Tier 2 Watch List; for more details, go to: https://www.state.gov/reports/2025-trafficking-in-persons-report-174/

TURKEY (TURKIYE)

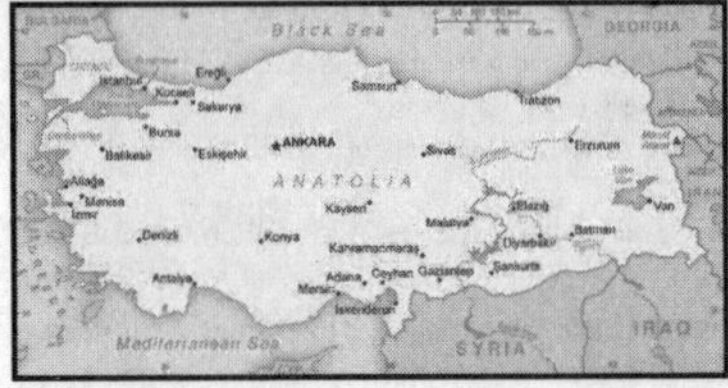

INTRODUCTION

Background: Modern Turkey was founded in 1923 from the remnants of the Ottoman Empire by reformer and national hero Mustafa KEMAL, known as Ataturk or "Father of the Turks." One-party rule ended in 1950, and periods of instability and military coups have since fractured the multiparty democracy, in 1960, 1971, 1980, 1997, and 2016.

Turkey joined the UN in 1945 and NATO in 1952. In 1963, Turkey became an associate member of the European Community; it began accession talks with the EU in 2005. Turkey intervened militarily on Cyprus in 1974 to prevent a Greek takeover of the island and has since acted as patron state to the "Turkish Republic of Northern Cyprus," which only Turkey recognizes. The Kurdistan Workers' Party (PKK), a US-designated terrorist organization, began a separatist insurgency in Turkey in 1984, and the struggle has long dominated the attention of Turkish security forces. In 2013, the Turkish Government and the PKK conducted negotiations aimed at ending the violence, but intense fighting resumed in 2015.

The Turkish Government conducted a referendum in 2017 in which voters approved constitutional amendments changing Turkey from a parliamentary to a presidential system.

GEOGRAPHY

Location: Southeastern Europe and Southwestern Asia (that portion of Turkey west of the Bosporus is geographically part of Europe), bordering the Black Sea, between Bulgaria and Georgia, and bordering the Aegean Sea and the Mediterranean Sea, between Greece and Syria

Geographic coordinates: 39 00 N, 35 00 E

Map references: Middle East

Area: *total:* 783,562 sq km
land: 769,632 sq km
water: 13,930 sq km
comparison ranking: total 38

Area - comparative: slightly larger than Texas

Land boundaries: *total:* 2,816 km
border countries (8): Armenia 311 km; Azerbaijan 17 km; Bulgaria 223 km; Georgia 273 km; Greece 192 km; Iran 534 km; Iraq 367 km; Syria 899 km

Coastline: 7,200 km

Maritime claims: *territorial sea:* 6 nm in the Aegean Sea
exclusive economic zone: in Black Sea only: to the maritime boundary agreed on with the former USSR
note: 12 nm in Black Sea and in Mediterranean Sea

Climate: temperate; hot, dry summers with mild, wet winters; harsher in interior

Terrain: high central plateau (Anatolia); narrow coastal plain; several mountain ranges

Elevation: *highest point:* Mount Ararat 5,137 m
lowest point: Mediterranean Sea 0 m
mean elevation: 1,132 m

Natural resources: coal, iron ore, copper, chromium, antimony, mercury, gold, barite, borate, celestite (strontium), emery, feldspar, limestone, magnesite, marble, perlite, pumice, pyrites (sulfur), clay, arable land, hydropower

Land use: *agricultural land:* 50% (2022 est.)
arable land: 26.2% (2022 est.)
permanent crops: 4.8% (2022 est.)
permanent pasture: 19% (2022 est.)
forest: 29.3% (2022 est.)
other: 20.7% (2022 est.)

Irrigated land: 52,150 sq km (2022)

Major lakes (area sq km): *fresh water lake(s):* Lake Beysehir - 650 sq km; Lake Egridir - 520 sq km
salt water lake(s): Lake Van - 3,740 sq km; Lake Tuz - 1,640 sq km;

Major rivers (by length in km): Euphrates river source (shared with Syria, Iran, and Iraq [m]) - 3,596 km; Tigris river source (shared with Syria, Iran, and Iraq [m]) - 1,950 km
note: [s] after country name indicates river source; [m] after country name indicates river mouth

Major watersheds (area sq km): Indian Ocean drainage: *(Persian Gulf)* Tigris and Euphrates (918,044 sq km)

Population distribution: the most densely populated area is found around the Bosporus in the northwest, where 20% of the population lives in Istanbul; with the exception of Ankara, urban centers remain small and scattered throughout the interior of Anatolia; an overall pattern of peripheral development exists, particularly along the Aegean Sea coast in the west, and the Tigris and Euphrates River systems in the southeast

Natural hazards: severe earthquakes, especially in northern Turkey, along an arc extending from the Sea of Marmara to Lake Van; landslides; flooding
volcanism: limited volcanic activity; the three historically active volcanoes (Ararat, Nemrut Dagi, and Tendurek Dagi) have not erupted since the 19th century or earlier

Geography - note: strategic location controlling the Turkish Straits (Bosporus, Sea of Marmara, Dardanelles) that link the Black and Aegean Seas; the 3% of Turkish territory north of the Straits lies in Europe and goes by the names of European Turkey, Eastern Thrace, or Turkish Thrace; the 97% of the country in Asia is referred to as Anatolia; Istanbul, which straddles the Bosporus, is the only metropolis in the world located on two continents; Mount Ararat, reputed to be the landing place of Noah's ark, is in the far-eastern part of the country

PEOPLE AND SOCIETY

Population: *total:* 84,119,531 (2024 est.)
male: 42,247,430
female: 41,872,101
comparison rankings: total 18; male 18; female 19

Nationality: *noun:* Turk(s)
adjective: Turkish

Ethnic groups: Turkish 70-75%, Kurdish 19%, other minorities 6-11% (2016 est.)

Languages: Turkish (official), Kurdish, other minority languages
major-language sample(s):
The World Factbook, temel bilgi edinmek için vazgeçilmez bir kaynak. (Turkish)

ڕاستییەکانی جیهان، باشترین سەرچاوەیە بۆ زانیارییە بنەڕەتییەکان (Kurdish)

Religions: Muslim 99.8% (mostly Sunni), other 0.2% (mostly Christians and Jews)

Age structure: *0-14 years:* 21.7% (male 9,358,711/ female 8,933,673)
15-64 years: 68.6% (male 29,219,389/female 28,494,315)
65 years and over: 9.6% (2024 est.) (male 3,669,330/ female 4,444,113)

Dependency ratios: *total dependency ratio:* 45.8 (2024 est.)
youth dependency ratio: 31.7 (2024 est.)
elderly dependency ratio: 14.1 (2024 est.)
potential support ratio: 7.1 (2024 est.)

Median age: *total:* 34 years (2024 est.)
male: 33.4 years
female: 34.6 years
comparison ranking: total 108

Population growth rate: 0.61% (2024 est.)
comparison ranking: 139

Birth rate: 13.8 births/1,000 population (2024 est.)
comparison ranking: 122

Death rate: 6.1 deaths/1,000 population (2024 est.)
comparison ranking: 151

Net migration rate: -1.5 migrant(s)/1,000 population (2024 est.)
comparison ranking: 156

Population distribution: the most densely populated area is found around the Bosporus in the northwest, where 20% of the population lives in Istanbul; with the exception of Ankara, urban centers remain small and scattered throughout the interior of Anatolia; an overall pattern of peripheral development exists, particularly along the Aegean Sea coast in the west, and the Tigris and Euphrates River systems in the southeast

Urbanization: *urban population:* 77.5% of total population (2023)
rate of urbanization: 1.11% annual rate of change (2020-25 est.)

Major urban areas - population: 15.848 million Istanbul, 5.397 million ANKARA (capital), 3.088 million Izmir, 2.086 million Bursa, 1.836 million Adana, 1.805 million Gaziantep (2023)

Sex ratio: *at birth:* 1.05 male(s)/female
0-14 years: 1.05 male(s)/female
15-64 years: 1.03 male(s)/female
65 years and over: 0.83 male(s)/female
total population: 1.01 male(s)/female (2024 est.)

Mother's mean age at first birth: 26.6 years (2020 est.)

Maternal mortality ratio: 15 deaths/100,000 live births (2023 est.)
comparison ranking: 135

Infant mortality rate: *total:* 18.4 deaths/1,000 live births (2024 est.)
male: 19.9 deaths/1,000 live births
female: 16.7 deaths/1,000 live births
comparison ranking: total 83

Life expectancy at birth: *total population:* 76.7 years (2024 est.)
male: 74.4 years
female: 79.2 years
comparison ranking: total population 103

Total fertility rate: 1.9 children born/woman (2024 est.)
comparison ranking: 119

Gross reproduction rate: 0.92 (2024 est.)

Drinking water source: *improved: urban:* 97.3% of population (2022 est.)
rural: 96% of population (2022 est.)
total: 97% of population (2022 est.)
unimproved: urban: 2.7% of population (2022 est.)
rural: 4% of population (2022 est.)
total: 3% of population (2022 est.)

Health expenditure: 4.6% of GDP (2021)
10% of national budget (2022 est.)

Physician density: 2.24 physicians/1,000 population (2022)

Hospital bed density: 3 beds/1,000 population (2020 est.)

Sanitation facility access: *improved: urban:* 99.8% of population (2022 est.)
rural: 98.7% of population (2022 est.)
total: 99.6% of population (2022 est.)
unimproved: urban: 0.2% of population (2022 est.)
rural: 1.3% of population (2022 est.)
total: 0.4% of population (2022 est.)

Obesity - adult prevalence rate: 32.1% (2016)
comparison ranking: 17

Alcohol consumption per capita: *total:* 1.18 liters of pure alcohol (2019 est.)
beer: 0.67 liters of pure alcohol (2019 est.)
wine: 0.16 liters of pure alcohol (2019 est.)
spirits: 0.35 liters of pure alcohol (2019 est.)
other alcohols: 0 liters of pure alcohol (2019 est.)
comparison ranking: total 147

Tobacco use: *total:* 30.1% (2025 est.)
male: 40.1% (2025 est.)
female: 20.1% (2025 est.)
comparison ranking: total 21

Children under the age of 5 years underweight: 1.5% (2018/19)
comparison ranking: 105

Currently married women (ages 15-49): 65.4% (2023 est.)

Child marriage: *women married by age 15:* 2% (2018)
women married by age 18: 14.7% (2018)

Education expenditure: 3.1% of GDP (2023 est.)
8.6% national budget (2023 est.)
comparison ranking: Education expenditure (% GDP) 149

Literacy: *total population:* 97% (2021 est.)
male: 99% (2021 est.)
female: 95% (2021 est.)

School life expectancy (primary to tertiary education): *total:* 20 years (2022 est.)
male: 20 years (2022 est.)
female: 20 years (2022 est.)

ENVIRONMENT

Environmental issues: water pollution from dumping of chemicals and detergents; air pollution, particularly in urban areas; deforestation; land degradation; conservation of biodiversity

International environmental agreements: *party to:* Air Pollution, Antarctic-Environmental Protection, Antarctic Treaty, Biodiversity, Climate Change, Climate Change-Kyoto Protocol, Comprehensive Nuclear Test Ban, Desertification, Endangered Species, Hazardous Wastes, Nuclear Test Ban, Ozone Layer Protection, Ship Pollution, Wetlands
signed, but not ratified: Climate Change-Paris Agreement, Environmental Modification

Climate: temperate; hot, dry summers with mild, wet winters; harsher in interior

Urbanization: *urban population:* 77.5% of total population (2023)
rate of urbanization: 1.11% annual rate of change (2020-25 est.)

Carbon dioxide emissions: 399.173 million metric tonnes of CO2 (2023 est.)
from coal and metallurgical coke: 155.26 million metric tonnes of CO2 (2023 est.)
from petroleum and other liquids: 147.211 million metric tonnes of CO2 (2023 est.)
from consumed natural gas: 96.703 million metric tonnes of CO2 (2023 est.)
comparison ranking: total emissions 15

Particulate matter emissions: 23.1 micrograms per cubic meter (2019 est.)

Waste and recycling: *municipal solid waste generated annually:* 35.374 million tons (2024 est.)
percent of municipal solid waste recycled: 32% (2022 est.)

Total water withdrawal: *municipal:* 7.144 billion cubic meters (2022)
industrial: 1.297 billion cubic meters (2022)
agricultural: 56.127 billion cubic meters (2022)

Total renewable water resources: 211.6 billion cubic meters (2022 est.)

Geoparks: *total global geoparks and regional networks:* 1
global geoparks and regional networks: Kula-Salihli (2023)

GOVERNMENT

Country name: *conventional long form:* Republic of Turkey
conventional short form: Turkey
local long form: Turkey Cumhuriyeti
local short form: Turkey
etymology: the name means "Land of the Turks"
note: Turkiye is an approved English short-form name for Turkey

Government type: presidential republic

Capital: *name:* Ankara
geographic coordinates: 39 56 N, 32 52 E
time difference: UTC+3 (8 hours ahead of Washington, DC, during Standard Time)
etymology: the name probably derives from the Indo-European root word *ang*, meaning "bend" and relating to the settlement's original location in a winding gorge; the city was referred to as Angora by the 13th century; the name was officially modified to Ankara in 1923 when the Republic of Turkey was founded

Administrative divisions: 81 provinces (*iller*, singular - *ili*); Adana, Adiyaman, Afyonkarahisar, Agri, Aksaray, Amasya, Ankara, Antalya, Ardahan, Artvin, Aydin, Balikesir, Bartin, Batman, Bayburt, Bilecik, Bingol, Bitlis, Bolu, Burdur, Bursa, Canakkale, Cankiri, Corum, Denizli, Diyarbakir, Duzce, Edirne, Elazig, Erzincan, Erzurum, Eskisehir, Gaziantep, Giresun, Gumushane, Hakkari, Hatay, Igdir, Isparta, Istanbul, Izmir (Smyrna), Kahramanmaras, Karabuk, Karaman, Kars, Kastamonu, Kayseri, Kilis, Kirikkale, Kirklareli, Kirsehir, Kocaeli, Konya, Kutahya, Malatya, Manisa, Mardin, Mersin, Mugla, Mus, Nevsehir, Nigde, Ordu, Osmaniye, Rize, Sakarya, Samsun, Sanliurfa, Siirt, Sinop, Sirnak, Sivas, Tekirdag, Tokat, Trabzon (Trebizond), Tunceli, Usak, Van, Yalova, Yozgat, Zonguldak

Legal system: civil law system based on various European systems, notably the Swiss civil code

Constitution: *history:* several previous; latest ratified 9 November 1982
amendment process: proposed by written consent of at least one third of Grand National Assembly (GNA) of Turkey (TBMM) members; adoption of draft amendments requires two debates in plenary TBMM session and three-fifths majority vote of all GNA members; the president of the republic can request TBMM reconsideration of the amendment and, if readopted by two-thirds majority TBMM vote, the president may submit the amendment to a referendum; passage by referendum requires absolute majority vote

International law organization participation: has not submitted an ICJ jurisdiction declaration; non-party state to the ICCt

Citizenship: *citizenship by birth:* no
citizenship by descent only: at least one parent must be a citizen of Turkey
dual citizenship recognized: yes, but requires prior permission from the government
residency requirement for naturalization: 5 years

Suffrage: 18 years of age; universal

Executive branch: *chief of state:* President Recep Tayyip ERDOGAN (since 28 August 2014)
head of government: President Recep Tayyip ERDOGAN (since 9 July 2018)
cabinet: Council of Ministers appointed by the president
election/appointment process: president directly elected by absolute-majority popular vote in 2 rounds, if needed, for a 5-year term (eligible for a second term)
most recent election date: 14 May 2023, with a runoff on 28 May 2023
election results: *2023:* Recep Tayyip ERDOGAN reelected president in second round - Recep Tayyip ERDOGAN (AKP) 52.2%, Kemal KILICDAROGLU (CHP) 47.8%
2018: Recep Tayyip ERDOGAN reelected president in first round - Recep Tayyip ERDOGAN (AKP) 52.6%, Muharrem INCE (CHP) 30.6%, Selahattin DEMIRTAS (HDP) 8.4%, Meral AKSENER (IYI) 7.3%, other 1.1%
expected date of next election: 2028

Legislative branch: *legislature name:* Grand National Assembly of Türkiye (Türkiye Büyük Millet Meclisi (T.B.M.M))
legislative structure: unicameral
number of seats: 600 (all directly elected)
electoral system: proportional representation
scope of elections: full renewal
term in office: 5 years
most recent election date: 5/14/2023
parties elected and seats per party: Justice and Development Party (AKP) (267); Republican People's Party (CHP) (130); Green and the Left Party of the Future (YSGP) (57); Nationalist Action Party (MHP) (50); Good Party (İyi Party) (44); Other (52)
percentage of women in chamber: 19.9%
expected date of next election: May 2028

Judicial branch: *highest court(s):* Constitutional Court or Anayasa Mahkemesi (consists of the president, 2 vice presidents, and 12 judges); Court of Cassation (consists of about 390 judges and is organized into civil and penal chambers); Council of State (organized into 15 divisions – 14 judicial and 1 consultative – each with a division head and at least 5 members)
judge selection and term of office: Constitutional Court members - 3 appointed by the Grand National Assembly and 12 by the president of the republic; court president and 2 deputy court presidents appointed from among its members for 4-year terms; judges serve 12-year, nonrenewable terms with mandatory retirement at age 65; Court of Cassation judges appointed by the Board of Judges and Prosecutors, a 13-member body of judicial officials; Court of Cassation judges serve until retirement at age 65; Council of State members appointed by the Board and by the president of the republic; members serve renewable, 4-year terms
subordinate courts: regional appeals courts; basic (first instance) courts; peace courts; aggravated crime courts; specialized courts, including administrative and audit

Political parties: Democracy and Progress Party or DEVA
Democrat Party or DP
Democratic Regions Party or DBP
Felicity Party (Saadet Party) or SP
Free Cause Party or HUDA PAR
Future Party (Gelecek Partisi) or GP
Good Party or IYI
Grand Unity Party or BBP
Justice and Development Party or AKP
Labor and Freedom Alliance (electoral alliance includes YSGP, HDP, TIP)
Nationalist Movement Party or MHP
New Welfare Party or YRP
Party of Greens and the Left Future or YSGP
People's Alliance (electoral alliance includes AKP, BBP, MHP, YRP)
Peoples' Democratic Party or HDP
Republican People's Party or CHP
Workers' Party of Turkey or TIP

Diplomatic representation in the US: *chief of mission:* Ambassador Sedat ÖNAL (since 17 June 2024)
chancery: 2525 Massachusetts Avenue NW, Washington, DC 20008
telephone: [1] (202) 612-6700
FAX: [1] (202) 612-6744
email address and website: embassy.washingtondc@mfa.gov.tr
T.C. Dışişleri Bakanlığı - Turkish Embassy In Washington, D.C. (mfa.gov.tr)
consulate(s) general: Boston, Chicago, Houston, Los Angeles, Miami, New York, San Francisco

Diplomatic representation from the US: *chief of mission:* Ambassador Thomas J. BARRACK (since 14 May 2025)
embassy: 1480 Sokak No. 1, Cukurambar Mahallesi, 06530 Cankaya, Ankara

mailing address: 7000 Ankara Place, Washington, DC 20512-7000
telephone: [90] (312) 294-0000
FAX: [90] (312) 467-0019
email address and website: Ankara-ACS@state.gov
https://tr.usembassy.gov/
consulate(s) general: Istanbul
consulate(s): Adana

International organization participation: ADB (nonregional member), Australia Group, BIS, BSEC, CBSS (observer), CD, CE, CERN (observer), CICA, CPLP (associate observer), D-8, EAPC, EBRD, ECO, EU (candidate country), FAO, FATF, G-20, IAEA, IBRD, ICAO, ICC (national committees), ICRM, IDA, IDB, IEA, IFAD, IFC, IFRCS, IHO, ILO, IMF, IMO, IMSO, Interpol, IOC, IOM, IPU, ISO, ITSO, ITU, ITUC (NGOs), MIGA, NATO, NEA, NSG, OAS (observer), OECD, OIC, OPCW, OSCE, Pacific Alliance (observer), Paris Club (associate), PCA, PIF (partner), SCO (dialogue member), SELEC, UN, UNCTAD, UNESCO, UNHCR, UNIDO, UNIFIL, UNOOSA, UNRWA, UNWTO, UPU, Wassenaar Arrangement, WCO, WFTU (NGOs), WHO, WIPO, WMO, WTO, ZC
note: Turkey is an EU candidate country and must complete accession criteria before being granted full membership

Independence: 29 October 1923 (republic proclaimed, succeeding the Ottoman Empire)

National holiday: Republic Day, 29 October (1923)

Flag: *description:* red with a vertical white crescent moon and five-pointed white star centered just outside the crescent's opening
meaning: the flag colors and designs closely resemble the Ottoman Empire's flag; the crescent moon and star serve as insignia for Turkic peoples; according to one interpretation, the flag represents the reflection of the moon and a star in a pool of blood of Turkish warriors

National symbol(s): vertical crescent moon with adjacent five-pointed star

National color(s): red, white

National anthem(s): *title:* "Istiklal Marsi" (The March of Independence)
lyrics/music: Mehmet Akif ERSOY/Zeki UNGOR
history: lyrics adopted 1921, music adopted 1932; the anthem's original music was adopted in 1924

National heritage: *total World Heritage Sites:* 22 (20 cultural, 2 mixed)
selected World Heritage Site locales: Archaeological Site of Troy (c); Ephesus (c); Diyarbakır Fortress and Hevsel Gardens Cultural Landscape (c); Hierapolis-Pamukkale (m); Göreme National Park and the Rock Sites of Cappadocia (m); Göbekli Tepe (c); Historic Areas of Istanbul (c); Selimiye Mosque and its Social Complex (c); Neolithic Site of Çatalhöyük (c); Bursa and Cumalıkızık: *the Birth of the Ottoman Empire (c); Gordion (c); Great Mosque and Hospital of Divriği (c); Hattusha:* the Hittite Capital (c); Nemrut Dağ (c); Xanthos-Letoon (c); City of Safranbolu (c); Pergamon and its Multi-Layered Cultural Landscape (c); Archaeological Site of Ani (c); Aphrodisias (c); Arslantepe Mound (c); Wooden Hypostyle Mosques of Medieval Anatolia (c); Turkmenistan (c); Sardis and the Lydian Tumuli of Bin Tepe (c)

ECONOMY

Economic overview: upper-middle-income, diversified Middle Eastern economy; industrializing economy that maintains large agricultural base; key energy, tourism, and construction sectors; high inflation, interest rates, and foreign debt pose risk to financial stability

Real GDP (purchasing power parity): $3.018 trillion (2024 est.)
$2.925 trillion (2023 est.)
$2.783 trillion (2022 est.)
note: data in 2021 dollars
comparison ranking: 12

Real GDP growth rate: 3.2% (2024 est.)
5.1% (2023 est.)
5.5% (2022 est.)
note: annual GDP % growth based on constant local currency
comparison ranking: 109

Real GDP per capita: $35,300 (2024 est.)
$34,300 (2023 est.)
$32,700 (2022 est.)
note: data in 2021 dollars
comparison ranking: 68

GDP (official exchange rate): $1.323 trillion (2024 est.)
note: data in current dollars at official exchange rate

Inflation rate (consumer prices): 58.5% (2024 est.)
53.9% (2023 est.)
72.3% (2022 est.)
note: annual % change based on consumer prices
comparison ranking: 206

GDP - composition, by sector of origin: *agriculture:* 5.6% (2024 est.)
industry: 25.9% (2024 est.)
services: 56.8% (2024 est.)
note: figures may not total 100% due to non-allocated consumption not captured in sector-reported data
comparison rankings: agriculture 107; industry 79; services 111

GDP - composition, by end use: *household consumption:* 59.4% (2024 est.)
government consumption: 14.7% (2024 est.)
investment in fixed capital: 31% (2024 est.)
investment in inventories: -5.5% (2024 est.)
exports of goods and services: 28% (2024 est.)
imports of goods and services: -27.8% (2024 est.)
note: figures may not total 100% due to rounding or gaps in data collection

Agricultural products: sugar beets, wheat, milk, tomatoes, barley, maize, potatoes, apples, grapes, watermelons (2023)
note: top ten agricultural products based on tonnage

Industries: textiles, food processing, automobiles, electronics, mining (coal, chromate, copper, boron), steel, petroleum, construction, lumber, paper

Industrial production growth rate: 2.2% (2024 est.)
note: annual % change in industrial value added based on constant local currency
comparison ranking: 94

Labor force: 36.081 million (2024 est.)
note: number of people ages 15 or older who are employed or seeking work
comparison ranking: 18

Unemployment rate: 8.5% (2024 est.)
9.4% (2023 est.)
10.5% (2022 est.)
note: % of labor force seeking employment
comparison ranking: 138

Youth unemployment rate (ages 15-24): *total:* 15.6% (2024 est.)
male: 12.4% (2024 est.)
female: 21.2% (2024 est.)
note: % of labor force ages 15-24 seeking employment
comparison ranking: total 75

Population below poverty line: 13.9% (2022 est.)
note: % of population with income below national poverty line

Gini Index coefficient - distribution of family income: 44.5 (2022 est.)
note: index (0-100) of income distribution; higher values represent greater inequality
comparison ranking: 20

Average household expenditures: *on food:* 22.8% of household expenditures (2023 est.)
on alcohol and tobacco: 2.3% of household expenditures (2023 est.)

Household income or consumption by percentage share: *lowest 10%:* 2.1% (2022 est.)
highest 10%: 35.2% (2022 est.)
note: % share of income accruing to lowest and highest 10% of population

Remittances: 0.1% of GDP (2024 est.)
0.1% of GDP (2023 est.)
0.1% of GDP (2022 est.)
note: personal transfers and compensation between resident and non-resident individuals/households/entities

Budget: *revenues:* $330.21 billion (2023 est.)
expenditures: $382.998 billion (2023 est.)
note: central government revenues (excluding grants) and expenditures converted to US dollars at average official exchange rate for year indicated

Public debt: 33.1% of GDP (2023 est.)
note: central government debt as a % of GDP
comparison ranking: 161

Taxes and other revenues: 18.5% (of GDP) (2023 est.)
note: central government tax revenue as a % of GDP
comparison ranking: 60

Current account balance: -$9.973 billion (2024 est.)
-$39.877 billion (2023 est.)
-$46.283 billion (2022 est.)
note: balance of payments - net trade and primary/secondary income in current dollars
comparison ranking: 182

Exports: $372.756 billion (2024 est.)
$357.588 billion (2023 est.)
$346.602 billion (2022 est.)
note: balance of payments - exports of goods and services in current dollars
comparison ranking: 26

Exports - partners: Germany 9%, USA 6%, UK 6%, UAE 5%, Iraq 5% (2023)
note: top five export partners based on percentage share of exports

Exports - commodities: garments, cars, gold, refined petroleum, vehicle parts/accessories (2023)
note: top five export commodities based on value in dollars

Imports: $367.022 billion (2024 est.)
$386.602 billion (2023 est.)
$383.7 billion (2022 est.)
note: balance of payments - imports of goods and services in current dollars
comparison ranking: 25

Imports - partners: China 13%, Russia 9%, Germany 9%, Switzerland 6%, USA 5% (2023)
note: top five import partners based on percentage share of imports

Imports - commodities: gold, refined petroleum, cars, plastics, natural gas (2023)
note: top five import commodities based on value in dollars

Reserves of foreign exchange and gold: $154.774 billion (2024 est.)
$140.868 billion (2023 est.)
$128.735 billion (2022 est.)
note: holdings of gold (year-end prices)/foreign exchange/special drawing rights in current dollars
comparison ranking: 22

Debt - external: $149.654 billion (2023 est.)
note: present value of external debt in current US dollars
comparison ranking: 6

Exchange rates: Turkish liras (TRY) per US dollar -

Exchange rates: 32.806 (2024 est.)
23.739 (2023 est.)
16.549 (2022 est.)
8.85 (2021 est.)
7.009 (2020 est.)

ENERGY

Electricity access: *electrification - total population:* 100% (2022 est.)

Electricity: *installed generating capacity:* 106.281 million kW (2023 est.)
consumption: 285.177 billion kWh (2023 est.)
exports: 1.993 billion kWh (2023 est.)
imports: 5.892 billion kWh (2023 est.)
transmission/distribution losses: 28.964 billion kWh (2023 est.)
comparison rankings: installed generating capacity 16; consumption 16; exports 60; imports 41; transmission/distribution losses 198

Electricity generation sources: *fossil fuels:* 57.1% of total installed capacity (2023 est.)
solar: 6.7% of total installed capacity (2023 est.)
wind: 10.9% of total installed capacity (2023 est.)
hydroelectricity: 19.9% of total installed capacity (2023 est.)
geothermal: 2.8% of total installed capacity (2023 est.)
biomass and waste: 2.6% of total installed capacity (2023 est.)

Nuclear energy: Number of nuclear reactors under construction: 4 (2025)

Coal: *production:* 82.534 million metric tons (2023 est.)
consumption: 124.183 million metric tons (2023 est.)
exports: 685,000 metric tons (2023 est.)
imports: 41.119 million metric tons (2023 est.)
proven reserves: 10.975 billion metric tons (2023 est.)

Petroleum: *total petroleum production:* 83,000 bbl/day (2023 est.)
refined petroleum consumption: 1.107 million bbl/day (2024 est.)
crude oil estimated reserves: 366 million barrels (2021 est.)

Natural gas: *production:* 807.281 million cubic meters (2023 est.)
consumption: 50.211 billion cubic meters (2023 est.)
exports: 896.281 million cubic meters (2023 est.)
imports: 50.484 billion cubic meters (2023 est.)
proven reserves: 3.794 billion cubic meters (2021 est.)

Energy consumption per capita: 70.521 million Btu/person (2023 est.)
comparison ranking: 71

COMMUNICATIONS

Telephones - fixed lines: *total subscriptions:* 9.926 million (2023 est.)
subscriptions per 100 inhabitants: 11 (2023 est.)
comparison ranking: total subscriptions 18

Telephones - mobile cellular: *total subscriptions:* 92.2 million (2023 est.)
subscriptions per 100 inhabitants: 106 (2022 est.)
comparison ranking: total subscriptions 19

Broadcast media: Turkish Radio and Television Corporation (TRT) operates multiple TV and radio networks and stations; multiple privately owned national TV stations and 567 private regional and local TV stations; multi-channel cable TV available; 1,007 private radio stations (2019)

Internet country code: .tr

Internet users: *percent of population:* 87% (2024 est.)

Broadband - fixed subscriptions: *total:* 19.6 million (2023 est.)
subscriptions per 100 inhabitants: 22 (2023 est.)
comparison ranking: total 14

TRANSPORTATION

Civil aircraft registration country code prefix: TC

Airports: 116 (2025)
comparison ranking: 46

Heliports: 240 (2025)
comparison ranking: 13

Railways: *total:* 11,497 km (2018)
standard gauge: 11,497 km (2018) 1.435-m gauge (1.435 km high speed train)

Merchant marine: *total:* 1,170 (2023)
by type: bulk carrier 43, container ship 43, general cargo 223, oil tanker 134, other 727
comparison ranking: total 22

Ports: *total ports:* 54 (2024)
large: 3
medium: 3
small: 6
very small: 42
ports with oil terminals: 28
key ports: Haydarpasa, Istanbul, Izmir, Mersin, Nemrut Limani Bay, Samsun

MILITARY AND SECURITY

Military and security forces: Turkish Armed Forces (TAF; Türk Silahlı Kuvvetleri, TSK): Turkish Land Forces (Türk Kara Kuvvetleri), Turkish Naval Forces (Türk Deniz Kuvvetleri; includes naval air and naval infantry), Turkish Air Forces (Türk Hava Kuvvetleri)

Ministry of Interior: Gendarmerie General Command (aka Gendarmerie of the Turkish Republic), Turkish Coast Guard Command, General Directorate of Security (National Police) (2025)
note: the Gendarmerie (Jandarma) is responsible for the maintenance of the public order in areas that fall outside the jurisdiction of police forces (generally in rural areas); in wartime, the Gendarmerie and Coast Guard would be placed under the operational control of the Land Forces and Naval Forces, respectively

Military expenditures: 2.3% of GDP (2025 est.)
2.1% of GDP (2024 est.)
1.5% of GDP (2023 est.)
1.4% of GDP (2022 est.)
1.6% of GDP (2021 est.)

Military and security service personnel strengths: approximately 495,000 active military personnel; approximately 150,000 Gendarmerie (2025)

Military equipment inventories and acquisitions: the military's inventory is comprised of domestically produced, European (particularly from Germany), and US weapons and equipment, as well as some Chinese, Russian, and South Korean acquisitions; it is a mix of older and modern weapons systems; Türkiye has a defense industry capable of producing a range of weapons systems for both export and internal use, including armored vehicles, naval vessels, and unmanned aerial vehicles/drones; Türkiye's defense industry also partners with other countries for defense production (2024)

Military service age and obligation: mandatory military service for men at age 20; service can be delayed if in university or in certain professions (researchers, professionals, and athletic, or those with artistic talents have the right to postpone military service until the age of 35); 6-12 months service; women may volunteer (2023)
note 1: after completing six months of service, if a conscripted soldier wants to and is suitable for extending his military service, he may do so for an additional six months in return for a monthly salary; all male Turkish citizens over the age of 20 are required to undergo a one month military training period, but they can obtain an exemption from the remaining 5 months of their mandatory service by paying a fee
note 2: as of 2021, women made up about 0.4% of the military's full-time personnel

Military deployments: approximately 200 Azerbaijan; approximately 250 Bosnia-Herzegovina (EUFOR); approximately 30,000 Cyprus; 325 Kosovo (NATO/KFOR); estimated 500 Libya; estimated 3,000 Qatar; estimated 1,000 Somalia (2025)
note: Turkey estimated to maintain several thousand military forces in both Iraq and Syria

Military - note: the responsibilities of the Turkish Armed Forces (TAF) include protecting the country's territory and sovereignty, participating in international peacekeeping operations, fulfilling Türkiye's military commitments to NATO, providing disaster/humanitarian relief and assistance to domestic law enforcement if requested by civil authorities, and supporting the country's overall national security interests; it also has overall responsibility for the security of Türkiye's borders; key areas of focus for the TAF are its operations in Syria, a protracted counterinsurgency campaign against the US-designated terrorist group the Kurdistan Worker's Party (PKK), territorial disputes with fellow NATO member Greece, regional conflicts, and threats from Islamic terrorist groups
Türkiye is active in international peacekeeping and other military/security operations under NATO and the UN, as well as under bilateral agreements with some countries, such as Azerbaijan, Libya, Somalia, and Qatar; Türkiye has been a member of NATO since 1952 and hosts the headquarters for a NATO Land Command and a Rapid Deployment Corps, multiple airbases for NATO and US aircraft, NATO air/missile defense systems, and training centers; the TAF is the second-largest military in NATO behind the US
the military traces its history back to 200 B.C., although the modern TAF was formed following the collapse of the Ottoman Empire at the conclusion of the Turkish War of Independence (1919-1923); the TAF traditionally has been viewed as the "guardian"

of Turkish politics, but its political role was diminished after the failed 2016 coup attempt; the military has a stake in Türkiye's economy through a holding company that is involved in the automotive, energy, finance, and logistics sectors, as well as iron and steel production (2025)

SPACE

Space agency/agencies: Turkish Space Agency (TUA; established 2018) (2025)

Space launch site(s): rocket test launch site on the Black Sea in Sinop Province; constructing a rocket launch facility in Somalia as of early 2025 (2025)

Space program overview: has an ambitious national space program with a focus on satellites, satellite components, software development, ground station technologies, and building up the country's space industries; manufactures and operates remote sensing and telecommunications satellites; in recent years has initiated a space launch vehicle (SLV) program with the goal of independently placing satellites into orbit and a probe on the Moon; has established relations with more than 25 foreign space agencies and corporations, including those of Azerbaijan, China, France, India, Japan, Kazakhstan, Pakistan, Russia, South Korea, Ukraine, and the US, as well as the European Space Agency; has state-owned rocket and satellite development companies, including some under the Ministry of Defense; also has a growing private space industry sector, and the Turkish Government has pledged to increase the country's share of the global space market (2025)
note: further details about the key activities, programs, and milestones of the country's space program, as well as government spending estimates on the space sector, appear in the Space Programs reference guide

TERRORISM

Terrorist group(s): Terrorist group(s): Islamic State of Iraq and ash-Sham (ISIS); Islamic Movement of Uzbekistan (IMU); Islamic Revolutionary Guard Corps (IRGC)/Qods Force; Kurdistan Workers' Party (PKK); al-Qa'ida; Revolutionary People's Liberation Party/Front (DHKP/C)
note: details about the history, aims, leadership, organization, areas of operation, tactics, targets, weapons, size, and sources of support of the group(s) appear(s) in Appendix T

TRANSNATIONAL ISSUES

Refugees and internally displaced persons: *refugees:* 3,094,818 (2024 est.)
IDPs: 538,105 (2024 est.)
stateless persons: 420 (2024 est.)

TURKMENISTAN

INTRODUCTION

Background: Present-day Turkmenistan has been at the crossroads of civilizations for centuries. Various Persian empires ruled the area in antiquity, and Alexander the Great, Muslim armies, the Mongols, Turkic warriors, and eventually the Russians conquered it. In medieval times, Merv (located in present-day Mary province) was one of the great cities of the Islamic world and an important stop on the Silk Road. Annexed by Russia in the late 1800s, Turkmen territories later figured prominently in the anti-Bolshevik resistance in Central Asia. In 1924, Turkmenistan became a Soviet republic; it achieved independence when the USSR dissolved in 1991.

President for Life Saparmurat NIYAZOV died in 2006, and Gurbanguly BERDIMUHAMEDOV, a deputy chairman under NIYAZOW, emerged as the country's new president. BERDIMUHAMEDOV won Turkmenistan's first multi-candidate presidential election in 2007, and again in 2012 and 2017 with over 97% of the vote in elections widely regarded as undemocratic. In 2022, BERDIMUHAMEDOV announced that he would step down from the presidency and called for an election to replace him. His son, Serdar BERDIMUHAMEDOV, won the ensuing election with 73% of the vote. Gurbanguly BERDIMUHAMEDOV, although no longer head of state, maintains an influential political position as head of the Halk Maslahaty (People's Council) and as National Leader of the Turkmen People, a title that provides additional privileges and immunity for him and his family. Since Gurbanguly BERDIMUHAMEDOV stepped down from the presidency, state-controlled media upgraded his honorific from Arkadag (protector) to Hero-Arkadag, and began referring to Serdar BERDIMUHAMEDOV as Arkadagly Serdar, which can be translated as "Serdar who has a protector to support him."

Turkmenistan has sought new export markets for its extensive hydrocarbon/natural gas reserves, which have yet to be fully exploited. Turkmenistan's reliance on gas exports has made the economy vulnerable to fluctuations in the global energy market, and economic hardships since the drop in energy prices in 2014 have led many citizens of Turkmenistan to emigrate, mostly to Turkey.

GEOGRAPHY

Location: Central Asia, bordering the Caspian Sea, between Iran and Kazakhstan

Geographic coordinates: 40 00 N, 60 00 E

Map references: Asia

Area: *total:* 488,100 sq km
land: 469,930 sq km
water: 18,170 sq km
comparison ranking: total 55

Area - comparative: slightly more than three times the size of Georgia; slightly larger than California

Land boundaries: *total:* 4,158 km
border countries (4): Afghanistan 804 km; Iran 1,148 km; Kazakhstan 413 km; Uzbekistan 1,793 km

Coastline: 0 km (landlocked)
note: Turkmenistan borders the Caspian Sea (1,768 km)

Maritime claims: none (landlocked)

Climate: subtropical desert

Terrain: flat-to-rolling sandy desert with dunes rising to mountains in the south; low mountains along border with Iran; borders Caspian Sea in west

Elevation: *highest point:* Gora Ayribaba 3,139 m
lowest point: Vpadina Akchanaya (Sarygamysh Koli is a lake in northern Turkmenistan with a water level that fluctuates above and below the elevation of Vpadina Akchanaya, the lake has dropped as low as -110 m) -81 m
mean elevation: 230 m

Natural resources: petroleum, natural gas, sulfur, salt

Land use: *agricultural land:* 84.3% (2022 est.)
arable land: 3.4% (2022 est.)
permanent crops: 0.1% (2022 est.)
permanent pasture: 80.8% (2022 est.)
forest: 8.8% (2022 est.)
other: 7% (2022 est.)

Irrigated land: 16,459 sq km (2012)

Major lakes (area sq km): *salt water lake(s):* Caspian Sea (shared with Iran, Azerbaijan, Russia, and Kazakhstan) - 374,000 sq km

Major rivers (by length in km): Amu Darya (shared with Tajikistan [s], Afghanistan, and Uzbekistan [m]) - 2,620 km
note: [s] after country name indicates river source; [m] after country name indicates river mouth

Major watersheds (area sq km): Internal (endorheic basin) drainage: *(Aral Sea basin)* Amu Darya (534,739 sq km)

Population distribution: the most densely populated areas are the southern, eastern, and northeastern oases; approximately 50% of the population lives in and around the capital of Ashgabat

Natural hazards: earthquakes; mudslides; droughts; dust storms; floods

Geography - note: landlocked; the western and central low-lying desolate portions of the country make up the great Garagum (Kara-Kum) desert, which occupies over 80% of the country; eastern part is plateau

PEOPLE AND SOCIETY

Population: *total:* 5,744,151 (2024 est.)
male: 2,842,870
female: 2,901,281
comparison rankings: total 116; male 116; female 116

Nationality: *noun:* Turkmenistani(s)
adjective: Turkmenistani

Ethnic groups: Turkmen 85%, Uzbek 5%, Russian 4%, other 6% (2003 est.)

Languages: Turkmen (official) 72%, Russian 12%, Uzbek 9%, other 7%
major-language sample(s):
Dünýä Faktlar Kitaby – esasy maglumatlaryň wajyp çeşmesidir (Turkmen)

Religions: Muslim 93%, Christian 6.4%, Buddhist <1%, folk religion <1%, Jewish <1%, other <1%, unspecified <1% (2020 est.)

Age structure: *0-14 years:* 24.5% (male 711,784/ female 692,967)
15-64 years: 68.6% (male 1,956,740/female 1,984,333)
65 years and over: 6.9% (2024 est.) (male 174,346/ female 223,981)

Dependency ratios: *total dependency ratio:* 45.8 (2024 est.)
youth dependency ratio: 35.6 (2024 est.)
elderly dependency ratio: 10.1 (2024 est.)
potential support ratio: 9.9 (2024 est.)

Median age: *total:* 31.2 years (2024 est.)
male: 30.7 years
female: 31.7 years
comparison ranking: total 128

Population growth rate: 0.92% (2024 est.)
comparison ranking: 101

Birth rate: 16.8 births/1,000 population (2024 est.)
comparison ranking: 93

Death rate: 6 deaths/1,000 population (2024 est.)
comparison ranking: 154

Net migration rate: -1.7 migrant(s)/1,000 population (2024 est.)
comparison ranking: 162

Population distribution: the most densely populated areas are the southern, eastern, and northeastern oases; approximately 50% of the population lives in and around the capital of Ashgabat

Urbanization: *urban population:* 54% of total population (2023)
rate of urbanization: 2.23% annual rate of change (2020-25 est.)

Major urban areas - population: 902,000 ASHGABAT (capital) (2023)

Sex ratio: *at birth:* 1.05 male(s)/female
0-14 years: 1.03 male(s)/female
15-64 years: 0.99 male(s)/female
65 years and over: 0.78 male(s)/female
total population: 0.98 male(s)/female (2024 est.)

Mother's mean age at first birth: 24.2 years (2019)

Maternal mortality ratio: 5 deaths/100,000 live births (2023 est.)
comparison ranking: 169

Infant mortality rate: *total:* 35.9 deaths/1,000 live births (2024 est.)
male: 43.6 deaths/1,000 live births
female: 27.7 deaths/1,000 live births
comparison ranking: total 34

Life expectancy at birth: *total population:* 72.4 years (2024 est.)
male: 69.4 years
female: 75.5 years
comparison ranking: total population 162

Total fertility rate: 2.02 children born/woman (2024 est.)
comparison ranking: 103

Gross reproduction rate: 0.99 (2024 est.)

Drinking water source: *improved: urban:* 100% of population (2022 est.)
rural: 100% of population (2022 est.)
total: 100% of population (2022 est.)
unimproved: urban: 0% of population (2022 est.)
rural: 0% of population (2022 est.)
total: 0% of population (2022 est.)

Health expenditure: 5.6% of GDP (2021)
8.5% of national budget (2022 est.)

Physician density: 1.93 physicians/1,000 population (2023)

Hospital bed density: 4 beds/1,000 population (2021 est.)

Sanitation facility access: *improved: urban:* 99.8% of population (2022 est.)
rural: 100% of population (2022 est.)
total: 99.9% of population (2022 est.)
unimproved: urban: 0.2% of population (2022 est.)
rural: 0% of population (2022 est.)
total: 0.1% of population (2022 est.)

Obesity - adult prevalence rate: 18.6% (2016)
comparison ranking: 116

Alcohol consumption per capita: *total:* 2.88 liters of pure alcohol (2019 est.)
beer: 0.65 liters of pure alcohol (2019 est.)
wine: 1.25 liters of pure alcohol (2019 est.)
spirits: 0.98 liters of pure alcohol (2019 est.)
other alcohols: 0 liters of pure alcohol (2019 est.)
comparison ranking: total 117

Tobacco use: *total:* 4.8% (2025 est.)
male: 9.4% (2025 est.)
female: 0.5% (2025 est.)
comparison ranking: total 162

Children under the age of 5 years underweight: 3.1% (2019)
comparison ranking: 78

Currently married women (ages 15-49): 64.3% (2023 est.)

Child marriage: *women married by age 15:* 0.2% (2019)
women married by age 18: 6.1% (2019)

Education expenditure: 2.7% of GDP (2023 est.)
20.5% national budget (2024 est.)
comparison ranking: Education expenditure (% GDP) 165

Literacy: *female:* 99.6% (2019 est.)

School life expectancy (primary to tertiary education): *total:* 13 years (2023 est.)
male: 12 years (2022 est.)
female: 12 years (2022 est.)

ENVIRONMENT

Environmental issues: soil and groundwater pollution from agricultural chemicals and pesticides; salination, waterlogging of soil due to poor irrigation methods; Caspian Sea pollution; river diversion for irrigation; soil erosion; desertification

International environmental agreements: *party to:* Biodiversity, Climate Change, Climate Change-Kyoto Protocol, Climate Change-Paris Agreement, Comprehensive Nuclear Test Ban, Desertification, Hazardous Wastes, Ozone Layer Protection, Ship Pollution, Wetlands
signed, but not ratified: none of the selected agreements

Climate: subtropical desert

Urbanization: *urban population:* 54% of total population (2023)
rate of urbanization: 2.23% annual rate of change (2020-25 est.)

Carbon dioxide emissions: 106.215 million metric tonnes of CO2 (2023 est.)
from coal and metallurgical coke: 100 metric tonnes of CO2 (2023 est.)
from petroleum and other liquids: 18.062 million metric tonnes of CO2 (2023 est.)
from consumed natural gas: 88.153 million metric tonnes of CO2 (2023 est.)
comparison ranking: total emissions 42

Particulate matter emissions: 28.1 micrograms per cubic meter (2019 est.)

Methane emissions: *energy:* 5,451.4 kt (2022-2024 est.)
agriculture: 294.9 kt (2019-2021 est.)
waste: 44.1 kt (2019-2021 est.)
other: 1.1 kt (2019-2021 est.)

Waste and recycling: *municipal solid waste generated annually:* 500,000 tons (2024 est.)
percent of municipal solid waste recycled: 15.3% (2022 est.)

Total water withdrawal: *municipal:* 453.5 million cubic meters (2022 est.)
industrial: 806.765 million cubic meters (2022 est.)
agricultural: 16.12 billion cubic meters (2022 est.)

Total renewable water resources: 24.765 billion cubic meters (2022 est.)

GOVERNMENT

Country name: *conventional long form:* none
conventional short form: Turkmenistan
local long form: none
local short form: Turkmenistan
former: Turkmen Soviet Socialist Republic
etymology: the suffix *-stan* means "land," so the country name means the "Land of the Turkmen [people];" the people's name means "Turk-like," from the Persian words *tork* and *mandan*, referring to their formerly nomadic lifestyle that differed from the settled Turks of Turkey

Government type: presidential republic; authoritarian

Capital: *name:* Ashgabat (Ashkhabad)
geographic coordinates: 37 57 N, 58 23 E
time difference: UTC+5 (10 hours ahead of Washington, DC, during Standard Time)
etymology: derived from the Turkmen words *ushq*, meaning "love," and *abad*, meaning "inhabited place" or "town;" the city was originally a military outpost built in 1881 that took its name from an ancient settlement on the site

Administrative divisions: *5 provinces (velayatlar, singular - velayat) and 1 independent city*:* Ahal Velayat (Arkadag), Ashgabat*, Balkan Velayat (Balkanabat), Dashoguz Velayat, Lebap Velayat (Turkmenabat), Mary Velayat
note: administrative divisions have the same names as their administrative centers; exceptions show the administrative center name in parentheses

Legal system: civil law system with Islamic (sharia) law influences

Constitution: *history:* several previous; latest adopted 14 September 2016
amendment process: proposed by the Assembly or Mejlis; passage requires two-thirds majority vote or absolute majority approval in a referendum

International law organization participation: has not submitted an ICJ jurisdiction declaration; non-party state to the ICCt

Citizenship: *citizenship by birth:* no
citizenship by descent only: at least one parent must be a citizen of Turkmenistan
dual citizenship recognized: yes

residency requirement for naturalization: 7 years

Suffrage: 18 years of age; universal

Executive branch: *chief of state:* President Serdar BERDIMUHAMEDOV (since 19 March 2022)
head of government: President Serdar BERDIMUHAMEDOV (since 19 March 2022)
cabinet: Cabinet of Ministers appointed by the president
election/appointment process: president directly elected by absolute-majority popular vote in 2 rounds, if needed, for a 7-year term (no term limits)
most recent election date: 12 March 2022
election results: *2022:* Serdar BERDIMUHAMEDOV elected president; percent of vote - Serdar BERDIMUHAMEDOV (DPT) 73%, Khydyr NUNNAYEV (independent) 11.1%, Agadzhan BEKMYRADOV (IAP) 7.2%, other 8.7%
2017: Gurbanguly BERDIMUHAMEDOV reelected president in the first round; percent of vote - Gurbanguly BERDIMUHAMEDOV (DPT) 97.7%, other 2.3%
expected date of next election: 2029
note: the president is both chief of state and head of government

Legislative branch: *legislature name:* Assembly (Mejlis)
legislative structure: unicameral
number of seats: 125 (all directly elected)
electoral system: plurality/majority
scope of elections: full renewal
term in office: 5 years
most recent election date: 3/26/2023
parties elected and seats per party: Democratic Party of Turkmenistan (DPT) (65); Groups of citizens of Turkmenistan (28); Agrarian Party (24); Party of Industrialists and Entrepreneurs (8)
percentage of women in chamber: 25.6%
expected date of next election: March 2028

Judicial branch: *highest court(s):* Supreme Court of Turkmenistan (consists of the court president and 21 associate judges and organized into civil, criminal, and military chambers)
judge selection and term of office: judges appointed by the president for 5-year terms
subordinate courts: High Commercial Court; appellate courts; provincial, district, and city courts; military courts

Political parties: Agrarian Party of Turkmenistan or APT
Democratic Party of Turkmenistan or DPT
Party of Industrialists and Entrepreneurs or PIE
note: all parties support President BERDIMUHAMEDOV; unofficial, small opposition movements exist abroad

Diplomatic representation in the US: *chief of mission:* Ambassador Meret ORAZOV (since 14 February 2001)
chancery: 2207 Massachusetts Avenue NW, Washington, DC 20008
telephone: [1] (202) 588-1500
FAX: [1] (202) 588-1500
email address and website: turkmenembassyus@verizon.net
https://usa.tmembassy.gov.tm/en

Diplomatic representation from the US: *chief of mission:* Ambassador Elizabeth ROOD (since 31 July 2024)
embassy: 9 1984 Street (formerly Pushkin Street), Ashgabat 744000
mailing address: 7070 Ashgabat Place, Washington, DC 20521-7070
telephone: [993] (12) 94-00-45
FAX: [993] (12) 94-26-14
email address and website: ConsularAshgab@state.gov
https://tm.usembassy.gov/

International organization participation: ADB, CIS (associate member, has not ratified the 1993 CIS charter although it participates in meetings and held the chairmanship of the CIS in 2012), EAPC, EBRD, ECO, FAO, G-77, IBRD, ICAO, ICRM, IDA, IDB, IFC, IFRCS, ILO, IMF, IMO, Interpol, IOC, IOM (observer), ISO (correspondent), ITU, MIGA, NAM, OIC, OPCW, OSCE, PFP, UN, UNCTAD, UNESCO, UNHCR, UNIDO, UNWTO, UPU, WCO, WFTU (NGOs), WHO, WIPO, WMO

Independence: 27 October 1991 (from the Soviet Union)

National holiday: Independence Day, 27 October (1991)

Flag: *description:* green field with a vertical red stripe near the left side; the stripe has five tribal *guls* (designs used in producing carpets) stacked above two crossed olive branches; five five-pointed white stars and a white crescent moon appear in the upper left corner of the main field
meaning: the green color and crescent moon stand for Islam, the five stars for the country's regions, and the guls for national identity

National symbol(s): Akhal-Teke horse

National color(s): green, white

National anthem(s): *title:* "Garaşsyz, Bitarap Türkmenistanyň" (Independent, Neutral, Turkmenistan State Anthem)
lyrics/music: collective/Veli MUKHATOV
history: adopted 1997; lyrics revised in 2008 to eliminate references to deceased President Saparmurat NYYAZOW

National heritage: *total World Heritage Sites:* 5 (4 cultural, 1 natural)
selected World Heritage Site locales: Ancient Merv (c); Kunya-Urgench (c); Parthian Fortresses of Nisa (c); Cold Winter Deserts of Turan (n); Silk Roads: Zarafshan-Karakum Corridor (c)

ECONOMY

Economic overview: upper middle-income Central Asian economy; has 10% of global natural gas reserves, exporting to Russia and China; natural resource rich; authoritarian and dominated by state-owned enterprises; major central-south Asian pipeline development

Real GDP (purchasing power parity): $134.555 billion (2024 est.)
$131.576 billion (2023 est.)
$123.778 billion (2022 est.)
note: data in 2017 dollars
comparison ranking: 89

Real GDP growth rate: 2.3% (2024 est.)
6.3% (2023 est.)
6.2% (2022 est.)
note: annual GDP % growth based on constant local currency
comparison ranking: 141

Real GDP per capita: $18,000 (2024 est.)
$17,900 (2023 est.)
$17,100 (2022 est.)
note: data in 2017 dollars
comparison ranking: 112

GDP (official exchange rate): $64.24 billion (2024 est.)
note: data in current dollars at official exchange rate

Inflation rate (consumer prices): 11.5% (2022 est.)
19.5% (2021 est.)
6.1% (2020 est.)
note: annual % change based on consumer prices
comparison ranking: 184

GDP - composition, by sector of origin: *agriculture:* 11.3% (2023 est.)
industry: 39.3% (2023 est.)
services: 49.4% (2023 est.)
note: figures may not total 100% due to non-allocated consumption not captured in sector-reported data
comparison rankings: agriculture 66; industry 22; services 149

Agricultural products: milk, wheat, potatoes, cotton, watermelons, tomatoes, grapes, barley, beef, lamb/mutton (2023)
note: top ten agricultural products based on tonnage

Industries: natural gas, oil, petroleum products, textiles, food processing

Labor force: 2.445 million (2024 est.)
note: number of people ages 15 or older who are employed or seeking work
comparison ranking: 122

Unemployment rate: 4.4% (2024 est.)
4.1% (2023 est.)
4.2% (2022 est.)
note: % of labor force seeking employment
comparison ranking: 73

Youth unemployment rate (ages 15-24): *total:* 9.6% (2024 est.)
male: 14.7% (2024 est.)
female: 6% (2024 est.)
note: % of labor force ages 15-24 seeking employment
comparison ranking: total 123

Average household expenditures: *on food:* 36.5% of household expenditures (2023 est.)
on alcohol and tobacco: 2.2% of household expenditures (2023 est.)

Remittances: 0% of GDP (2023 est.)
0% of GDP (2022 est.)
0% of GDP (2021 est.)
note: personal transfers and compensation between resident and non-resident individuals/households/entities

Budget: *revenues:* $5.954 billion (2019 est.)
expenditures: $6.134 billion (2019 est.)

Exports: $13.111 billion (2023 est.)
$14.67 billion (2022 est.)
$10.282 billion (2021 est.)
note: GDP expenditure basis - exports of goods and services in current dollars
comparison ranking: 104

Exports - partners: China 63%, Turkey 11%, Greece 7%, Uzbekistan 6%, Azerbaijan 4% (2023)
note: top five export partners based on percentage share of exports

Exports - commodities: natural gas, refined petroleum, fertilizers, crude petroleum, electricity (2023)
note: top five export commodities based on value in dollars

Imports: $7.563 billion (2023 est.)
$7.362 billion (2022 est.)
$6.25 billion (2021 est.)

note: GDP expenditure basis - imports of goods and services in current dollars
comparison ranking: 135

Imports - partners: Turkey 21%, UAE 21%, China 20%, Kazakhstan 8%, Germany 5% (2023)
note: top five import partners based on percentage share of imports

Imports - commodities: broadcasting equipment, cars, wheat, computers, iron pipes (2023)
note: top five import commodities based on value in dollars

Debt - external: $3.696 billion (2023 est.)
note: present value of external debt in current US dollars
comparison ranking: 78

Exchange rates: Turkmenistani manat (TMM) per US dollar -

Exchange rates: 4.125 (2017 est.)
3.5 (2016 est.)
3.5 (2015 est.)
3.5 (2014 est.)

ENERGY

Electricity access: *electrification - total population:* 100% (2022 est.)

Electricity: *installed generating capacity:* 6.512 million kW (2023 est.)
consumption: 21.526 billion kWh (2023 est.)
exports: 9 billion kWh (2023 est.)
transmission/distribution losses: 3.258 billion kWh (2023 est.)
comparison rankings: installed generating capacity 82; consumption 75; exports 26; transmission/distribution losses 145

Electricity generation sources: *fossil fuels:* 100% of total installed capacity (2023 est.)

Coal: *imports:* 200 metric tons (2023 est.)
proven reserves: 799.999 million metric tons (2023 est.)

Petroleum: *total petroleum production:* 272,000 bbl/day (2023 est.)
refined petroleum consumption: 152,000 bbl/day (2023 est.)
crude oil estimated reserves: 600 million barrels (2021 est.)

Natural gas: *production:* 84.277 billion cubic meters (2023 est.)
consumption: 44.936 billion cubic meters (2023 est.)
exports: 41.334 billion cubic meters (2023 est.)
proven reserves: 11.327 trillion cubic meters (2021 est.)

Energy consumption per capita: 261.142 million Btu/person (2023 est.)
comparison ranking: 11

COMMUNICATIONS

Telephones - fixed lines: *total subscriptions:* 802,000 (2021 est.)
subscriptions per 100 inhabitants: 10 (2022 est.)
comparison ranking: total subscriptions 76

Telephones - mobile cellular: *total subscriptions:* 6.25 million (2021 est.)
subscriptions per 100 inhabitants: 99 (2021 est.)
comparison ranking: total subscriptions 117

Broadcast media: state-controlled broadcast media; 7 state-owned TV and 4 state-owned radio networks; satellite dishes available for other broadcasts; officials sometimes limit access to satellite TV by removing satellite dishes

Internet country code: .tm

Internet users: *percent of population:* 21% (2017 est.)

Broadband - fixed subscriptions: *total:* 377,000 (2022 est.)
subscriptions per 100 inhabitants: 5 (2022 est.)
comparison ranking: total 108

TRANSPORTATION

Civil aircraft registration country code prefix: EZ

Airports: 23 (2025)
comparison ranking: 131

Heliports: 25 (2025)
comparison ranking: 51

Railways: *total:* 5,113 km (2017)
broad gauge: 5,113 km (2017) 1.520-m gauge

Merchant marine: *total:* 73 (2023)
by type: general cargo 6, oil tanker 8, other 59
comparison ranking: total 106

MILITARY AND SECURITY

Military and security forces: Armed Forces of Turkmenistan (aka Turkmen National Army): Ground Forces, Air Force, Navy

Ministry of Internal Affairs: Internal Troops, Turkmen (National) Police, Federal/State Border Guard Service (2024)

Military expenditures: 1.9% of GDP (2019 est.)
1.8% of GDP (2018 est.)
1.8% of GDP (2017 est.)
1.8% of GDP (2016 est.)
1.5% of GDP (2015 est.)

Military and security service personnel strengths: limited available information; estimated 35,000 active Armed Forces (2025)

Military equipment inventories and acquisitions: the military's inventory is comprised largely of Russian and Soviet-era weapons and equipment with smaller quantities of military systems from suppliers such as Brazil, China, Italy, and Turkey (2024)

Military service age and obligation: 18-27 years of age for compulsory military service for men and volunteer service for men and women; 24-month conscript service obligation (2025)

Military - note: the military is responsible for external defense and works closely with the Border Service on protecting the country's borders; areas of emphasis for the military include border security, competition on the Caspian Sea, regional stability, and military modernization; while Turkmenistan has a policy of permanent and "positive" neutrality and has declined to participate in post-Soviet military groupings such as the Collective Security Treaty Organization and the Shanghai Cooperation Organization, it has participated in multinational exercises and bilateral training with neighboring countries, including Russia and Uzbekistan; Turkmenistan joined NATO's Partnership for Peace program in 1994, but it does not offer any military forces to NATO-led operations (2025)

SPACE

Space agency/agencies: Turkmenistan National Space Agency (established 2011; transferred to the Space Department of the Ministry of Communications in 2019) (2025)

Space program overview: has a small space program focused on acquiring satellites and developing the infrastructure to build and operate satellites; particularly interested in communications and remote sensing satellites; has cooperated with the space agencies and/or space industries of France, Italy, Russia, South Korea, and the US (2025)
note: further details about the key activities, programs, and milestones of the country's space program, as well as government spending estimates on the space sector, appear in the Space Programs reference guide

TRANSNATIONAL ISSUES

Refugees and internally displaced persons: *refugees:* 3,409 (2024 est.)

Trafficking in persons: *tier rating:* Tier 2 Watch List — Turkmenistan does not fully meet the minimum standards for the elimination of trafficking but is making significant efforts to do so, therefore Turkmenistan was upgraded to Tier 2 Watch List; for more details, go to: https://www.state.gov/reports/2025-trafficking-in-persons-report/turkmenistan/

TURKS AND CAICOS ISLANDS

INTRODUCTION

Background: The islands were part of the UK's Jamaican colony until 1962, when they assumed the status of a separate Crown colony upon Jamaica's independence. The governor of The Bahamas oversaw affairs from 1965 to 1973. With Bahamian independence, the islands received a separate governor in 1973. Although independence was agreed upon for 1982, the policy was reversed, and the islands remain a British overseas territory. Grand Turk Island suffered extensive damage from Hurricane Maria in 2017.

GEOGRAPHY

Location: two island groups in the North Atlantic Ocean, southeast of The Bahamas, north of Haiti; note - although the Turks and Caicos Islands do not border the Caribbean Sea, geopolitically they are often designated as being Caribbean

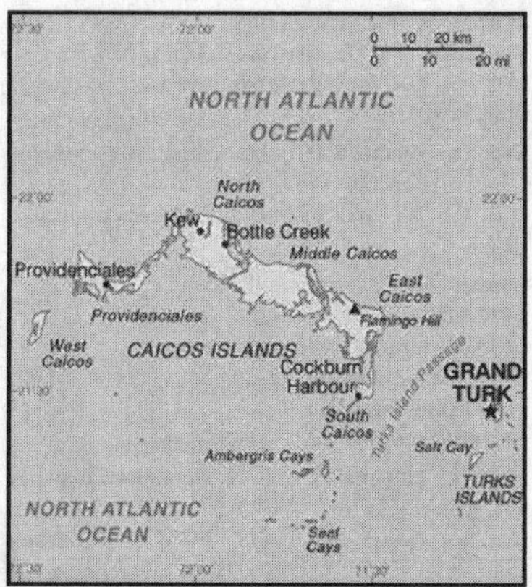

Geographic coordinates: 21 45 N, 71 35 W

Map references: Central America and the Caribbean

Area: *total:* 948 sq km
land: 948 sq km
water: 0 sq km
comparison ranking: total 185

Area - comparative: 2.5 times the size of Washington, D.C.

Land boundaries: *total:* 0 km

Coastline: 389 km

Maritime claims: *territorial sea:* 12 nm
exclusive fishing zone: 200 nm

Climate: tropical; marine; moderated by trade winds; sunny and relatively dry

Terrain: low, flat limestone; extensive marshes and mangrove swamps

Elevation: *highest point:* Blue Hill on Providenciales and Flamingo Hill on East Caicos 48 m
lowest point: Atlantic Ocean 0 m

Natural resources: spiny lobster, conch

Land use: *agricultural land:* 1.1% (2022 est.)
arable land: 1.1% (2022 est.)
permanent crops: 0% (2022 est.)
permanent pasture: 0% (2022 est.)
forest: 11.1% (2022 est.)
other: 87.9% (2022 est.)

Irrigated land: 0 sq km (2022)

Population distribution: eight of the thirty islands are inhabited; the island of Providenciales is the most populated, but the most densely populated is Grand Turk

Natural hazards: frequent hurricanes

Geography - note: include eight large islands and numerous smaller cays, islets, and reefs; only two of the Caicos Islands and six of the Turks group are inhabited

PEOPLE AND SOCIETY

Population: *total:* 60,439 (2024 est.)
male: 30,389
female: 30,050
comparison rankings: total 205; male 205; female 205

Nationality: *noun:* none
adjective: none

Ethnic groups: Black 87.6%, White 7.9%, mixed 2.5%, East Indian 1.3%, other 0.7% (2006 est.)

Languages: English (official)

Religions: Protestant 72.8% (Baptist 35.8%, Church of God 11.7%, Anglican 10%, Methodist 9.3%, Seventh Day Adventist 6%), Roman Catholic 11.4%, Jehovah's Witness 1.8%, other 14% (2006 est.)

Age structure: *0-14 years:* 20.4% (male 6,288/female 6,056)
15-64 years: 73.2% (male 22,232/female 22,011)
65 years and over: 6.4% (2024 est.) (male 1,869/female 1,983)

Dependency ratios: *total dependency ratio:* 36.6 (2024 est.)
youth dependency ratio: 27.9 (2024 est.)
elderly dependency ratio: 8.7 (2024 est.)
potential support ratio: 11.5 (2024 est.)

Median age: *total:* 36.3 years (2024 est.)
male: 36.5 years
female: 36.1 years
comparison ranking: total 93

Population growth rate: 1.77% (2024 est.)
comparison ranking: 49

Birth rate: 13 births/1,000 population (2024 est.)
comparison ranking: 133

Death rate: 3.6 deaths/1,000 population (2024 est.)
comparison ranking: 219

Net migration rate: 8.3 migrant(s)/1,000 population (2024 est.)
comparison ranking: 10

Population distribution: eight of the thirty islands are inhabited; the island of Providenciales is the most populated, but the most densely populated is Grand Turk

Urbanization: *urban population:* 94.2% of total population (2023)
rate of urbanization: 1.46% annual rate of change (2020-25 est.)

Major urban areas - population: 5,000 GRAND TURK (capital) (2018)

Sex ratio: *at birth:* 1.05 male(s)/female
0-14 years: 1.04 male(s)/female
15-64 years: 1.01 male(s)/female
65 years and over: 0.94 male(s)/female
total population: 1.01 male(s)/female (2024 est.)

Infant mortality rate: *total:* 11.1 deaths/1,000 live births (2024 est.)
male: 13.9 deaths/1,000 live births
female: 8.1 deaths/1,000 live births
comparison ranking: total 122

Life expectancy at birth: *total population:* 81.3 years (2024 est.)
male: 78.5 years
female: 84.1 years
comparison ranking: total population 44

Total fertility rate: 1.7 children born/woman (2024 est.)
comparison ranking: 164

Gross reproduction rate: 0.83 (2024 est.)

Drinking water source: *improved: urban:* 99.2% of population (2022 est.)
rural: 91.8% of population (2022 est.)
total: 98.8% of population (2022 est.)
unimproved: urban: 0.8% of population (2022 est.)
rural: 8.2% of population (2022 est.)
total: 1.2% of population (2022 est.)

Sanitation facility access: *improved: urban:* 98.8% of population (2022 est.)
rural: 97.7% of population (2022 est.)
total: 98.7% of population (2022 est.)
unimproved: urban: 1.2% of population (2022 est.)
rural: 2.3% of population (2022 est.)
total: 1.3% of population (2022 est.)

Children under the age of 5 years underweight: 0.4% (2019/20)
comparison ranking: 113

Currently married women (ages 15-49): 59.1% (2023 est.)

Child marriage: *women married by age 15:* 0% (2020)
women married by age 18: 23.3% (2020)
men married by age 18: 5.1% (2020)

Education expenditure: 3.1% of GDP (2023 est.)
8.7% national budget (2023 est.)
comparison ranking: Education expenditure (% GDP) 148

School life expectancy (primary to tertiary education): *total:* 14 years (2023 est.)
male: 15 years (2023 est.)
female: 14 years (2023 est.)

People - note: destination and transit point for illegal Haitian immigrants bound for the Bahamas and the US

ENVIRONMENT

Environmental issues: limited natural freshwater resources

Climate: tropical; marine; moderated by trade winds; sunny and relatively dry

Urbanization: *urban population:* 94.2% of total population (2023)
rate of urbanization: 1.46% annual rate of change (2020-25 est.)

Carbon dioxide emissions: 447,000 metric tonnes of CO2 (2023 est.)
from petroleum and other liquids: 447,000 metric tonnes of CO2 (2023 est.)
comparison ranking: total emissions 190

GOVERNMENT

Country name: *conventional long form:* none
conventional short form: Turks and Caicos Islands
abbreviation: TCA
etymology: the Turks Islands are named after the Turk's cap cactus, which is native to the islands and appears on the flag and coat of arms; the name Caicos may derive from *caya hico*, a phrase meaning "string of islands" in the Lucayan (Arawak) language, or from the Spanish word *cayo*, meaning "rock"

Government type: parliamentary democracy

Dependency status: overseas territory of the UK

Capital: *name:* Grand Turk (Cockburn Town)
geographic coordinates: 21 28 N, 71 08 W
time difference: UTC-5 (same time as Washington, DC, during Standard Time)
daylight saving time: +1hr, begins second Sunday in March; ends first Sunday in November
etymology: named after Sir Francis COCKBURN, who served as governor of the Bahamas from 1837 to 1844

Administrative divisions: none (overseas territory of the UK)

Legal system: mixed system of English common law and civil law

Constitution: *history:* several previous; latest signed 7 August 2012, effective 15 October 2012 (The Turks and Caicos Constitution Order 2011)

Citizenship: see United Kingdom

Suffrage: 18 years of age; universal

Executive branch: *chief of state:* King CHARLES III (since 8 September 2022); represented by Governor Dileeni Daniel-SELVARATNAM (since 29 June 2023)
head of government: Premier Washington MISICK (since 19 February 2021)
cabinet: Cabinet appointed by the governor from among members of the House of Assembly
election/appointment process: the monarch is hereditary; governor appointed by the monarch; following legislative elections, the governor appoints the leader of the majority party as the premier

Legislative branch: *legislature name:* House of Assembly
legislative structure: unicameral
number of seats: 21 (directly elected or appointed)
electoral system: mixed
scope of elections: full renewal
term in office: 4 years
most recent election date: 2/07/2025
parties elected and seats per party: PNP (16); PDM (2); independents (1)
percentage of women in chamber: 27.3%
expected date of next election: 2029

Judicial branch: *highest court(s):* Supreme Court (consists of the chief justice and other judges, as determined by the governor); Court of Appeal (consists of the court president and 2 justices)
judge selection and term of office: Supreme Court and Appeals Court judges appointed by the governor in accordance with the Judicial Service Commission, a 3-member body of high-level judicial officials; Supreme Court judges serve until mandatory retirement at age 65, but terms can be extended to age 70; Appeals Court judge tenure determined by individual terms of appointment
subordinate courts: magistrates' courts
note: appeals beyond the Supreme Court are referred to the Judicial Committee of the Privy Council (in London)

Political parties: People's Democratic Movement or PDM
Progressive National Party or PNP

Diplomatic representation in the US: none (overseas territory of the UK)

Diplomatic representation from the US: *embassy:* none (overseas territory of the UK)

International organization participation: Caricom (associate), CDB, Interpol (subbureau), UPU

Independence: none (overseas territory of the UK)

Flag: *description:* blue with the UK flag in the upper-left quadrant and the colonial shield centered on the right half of the flag; the shield is yellow and displays a conch shell, a spiny lobster, and Turk's cap cactus

National symbol(s): conch shell, Turk's cap cactus

National anthem(s): *title:* "This Land of Ours"
lyrics/music: Conrad HOWELL
history: serves as a local anthem
title: "God Save the King"
lyrics/music: unknown
history: official anthem, as a UK overseas territory

ECONOMY

Economic overview: British Caribbean island territorial economy; GDP and its tourism industry hit hard by COVID-19 disruptions; major biodiversity locale; US dollar user; fossil fuel dependent; negative trade balance; increasing unemployment

Real GDP (purchasing power parity): $1.554 billion (2024 est.)
$1.471 billion (2023 est.)
$1.293 billion (2022 est.)
note: data in 2021 dollars
comparison ranking: 201

Real GDP growth rate: 5.6% (2024 est.)
13.7% (2023 est.)
14.1% (2022 est.)
note: annual GDP % growth based on constant local currency
comparison ranking: 31

Real GDP per capita: $33,400 (2024 est.)
$31,800 (2023 est.)
$28,200 (2022 est.)
note: data in 2021 dollars
comparison ranking: 72

GDP (official exchange rate): $1.745 billion (2024 est.)
note: data in current dollars at official exchange rate

Inflation rate (consumer prices): 8.5% (2022 est.)
5% (2021 est.)
2.3% (2020 est.)
note: annual % change based on consumer prices
comparison ranking: 170

GDP - composition, by sector of origin: *agriculture:* 0.4% (2024 est.)
industry: 9.3% (2024 est.)
services: 72.6% (2024 est.)
note: figures may not total 100% due to non-allocated consumption not captured in sector-reported data
comparison rankings: agriculture 192; industry 192; services 27

Agricultural products: corn, beans, cassava (manioc, tapioca), citrus fruits; fish

Industries: tourism, offshore financial services

Industrial production growth rate: 9% (2024 est.)
note: annual % change in industrial value added based on constant local currency
comparison ranking: 17

Remittances: 0% of GDP (2023 est.)
0% of GDP (2022 est.)
0% of GDP (2021 est.)
note: personal transfers and compensation between resident and non-resident individuals/households/entities

Budget: *revenues:* $247.3 million (2017 est.)
expenditures: $224.3 million (2017 est.)

Current account balance: $172.709 million (2018 est.)
$35.016 million (2017 est.)
$247.081 million (2016 est.)
note: balance of payments - net trade and primary/secondary income in current dollars
comparison ranking: 71

Exports: $826.824 million (2018 est.)
$602.581 million (2017 est.)
$741.173 million (2016 est.)
note: balance of payments - exports of goods and services in current dollars
comparison ranking: 187

Exports - partners: Gabon 27%, USA 25%, Zimbabwe 17%, Czechia 8%, UAE 3% (2023)
note: top five export partners based on percentage share of exports

Exports - commodities: plastics, shellfish, carbonates, tobacco, garments (2023)
note: top five export commodities based on value in dollars

Imports: $544.219 million (2018 est.)
$484.842 million (2017 est.)
$438.041 million (2016 est.)
note: balance of payments - imports of goods and services in current dollars
comparison ranking: 200

Imports - partners: USA 73%, Dominican Republic 4%, Italy 3%, Japan 3%, China 2% (2023)
note: top five import partners based on percentage share of imports

Imports - commodities: refined petroleum, cars, aluminum structures, furniture, plastic products (2023)
note: top five import commodities based on value in dollars

Exchange rates: the US dollar is used

ENERGY

Electricity access: *electrification - total population:* 99.9% (2022 est.)
electrification - urban areas: 100%
electrification - rural areas: 100%

Electricity: *installed generating capacity:* 94,000 kW (2023 est.)
consumption: 252.088 million kWh (2023 est.)
transmission/distribution losses: 12.912 million kWh (2023 est.)
comparison rankings: installed generating capacity 187; consumption 186; transmission/distribution losses 20

Electricity generation sources: *fossil fuels:* 98.1% of total installed capacity (2023 est.)
solar: 1.9% of total installed capacity (2023 est.)

Petroleum: *refined petroleum consumption:* 3,000 bbl/day (2023 est.)

COMMUNICATIONS

Telephones - fixed lines: *total subscriptions:* 4,000 (2021 est.)
subscriptions per 100 inhabitants: 9 (2022 est.)
comparison ranking: total subscriptions 206

Telephones - mobile cellular: *total subscriptions:* 25,085 (2004 est.)
subscriptions per 100 inhabitants: 110 (2004 est.)
comparison ranking: total subscriptions 213

Broadcast media: no local terrestrial TV stations; broadcasts from the Bahamas, multi-channel cable, and satellite TV available; state-run radio network operates alongside private broadcasters, with a total of about 15 stations

Internet country code: .tc

Internet users: *percent of population:* 93.5% (2022)

TRANSPORTATION

Civil aircraft registration country code prefix: VQ-T

Airports: 9 (2025)
comparison ranking: 163

Merchant marine: *total:* 3 (2023)

by type: general cargo 1, other 2
comparison ranking: total 174

Ports: *total ports:* 3 (2024)
large: 0
medium: 0
small: 0
very small: 2
size unknown: 1
ports with oil terminals: 1
key ports: Cockburn Harbor, Grand Turk, Providenciales

MILITARY AND SECURITY

Military - note: defense is the responsibility of the UK

TRANSNATIONAL ISSUES

Refugees and internally displaced persons: *refugees:* 8 (2024 est.)

TUVALU

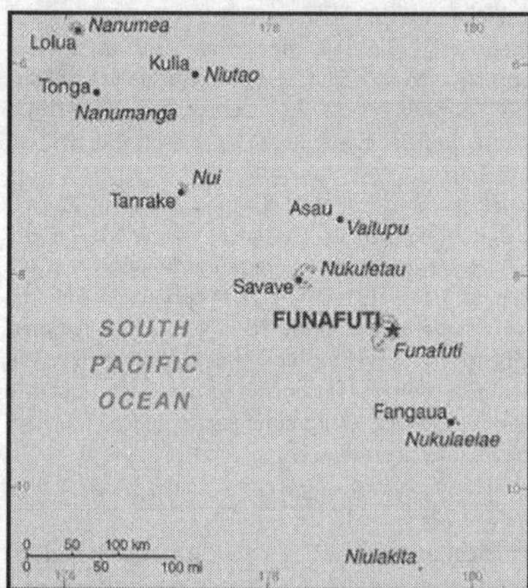

INTRODUCTION

Background: Voyagers from either Samoa or Tonga first populated Tuvalu in the first millennium A.D., and the islands provided a stepping-stone for various Polynesian communities that subsequently settled in Melanesia and Micronesia. Tuvalu eventually came under Samoan and Tongan spheres of influence, although proximity to Micronesia allowed some Micronesian communities to flourish in Tuvalu, in particular on Nui Atoll. In the late 1700s and early 1800s, a series of American, British, Dutch, and Russian ships visited the islands, which were named the Ellice Islands in 1819.

The UK declared a protectorate over islands in 1892 and merged them with the Micronesian Gilbert Islands. The Gilbert and Ellice Islands Protectorate became a colony in 1916. During World War II, the US set up military bases on a few islands, and in 1943, after Japan captured many of the northern Gilbert Islands, the UK transferred administration of the colony southward to Funafuti. After the war, Tarawa in the Gilbert Islands was once again made the colony's capital, and the center of power was firmly in the Gilbert Islands, including the colony's only secondary school. Amid growing tensions with the Gilbertese, Tuvaluans voted to secede from the colony in 1974, were granted self-rule in 1975, and gained independence in 1978 as Tuvalu. In 1979, the US relinquished its claims to the Tuvaluan islands in a treaty of friendship.

GEOGRAPHY

Location: Oceania, island group consisting of nine coral atolls in the South Pacific Ocean, about half way from Hawaii to Australia

Geographic coordinates: 8 00 S, 178 00 E

Map references: Oceania

Area: *total:* 26 sq km
land: 26 sq km
water: 0 sq km
comparison ranking: total 236

Area - comparative: about the size of Washington, D.C.

Land boundaries: *total:* 0 km

Coastline: 24 km

Maritime claims: *territorial sea:* 12 nm
contiguous zone: 24 nm
exclusive economic zone: 200 nm

Climate: tropical; moderated by easterly trade winds (March to November); westerly gales and heavy rain (November to March)

Terrain: low-lying and narrow coral atolls

Elevation: *highest point:* unnamed location 5 m
lowest point: Pacific Ocean 0 m
mean elevation: 2 m

Natural resources: fish, coconut (copra)

Land use: *agricultural land:* 60% (2022 est.)
arable land: 0% (2022 est.)
permanent crops: 60% (2022 est.)
permanent pasture: 0% (2022 est.)
forest: 33.3% (2022 est.)
other: 6.7% (2022 est.)

Irrigated land: 0 sq km (2022)

Population distribution: over half of the population resides on the atoll of Funafuti

Natural hazards: severe tropical storms are usually rare, but in 1997 there were three cyclones; low levels of islands make them sensitive to changes in sea level

Geography - note: one of the smallest and most remote countries on earth; six of the nine coral atolls – Nanumea, Nui, Vaitupu, Nukufetau, Funafuti, and Nukulaelae – have lagoons open to the ocean; Nanumaya and Niutao have landlocked lagoons; Niulakita does not have a lagoon

PEOPLE AND SOCIETY

Population: *total:* 11,733 (2024 est.)
male: 5,816
female: 5,917
comparison rankings: total 221; male 221; female 221

Nationality: *noun:* Tuvaluan(s)
adjective: Tuvaluan

Ethnic groups: Tuvaluan 97%, Tuvaluan/I-Kiribati 1.6%, Tuvaluan/other 0.8%, other 0.6% (2017 est.)

Languages: Tuvaluan (official), English (official), Samoan, Kiribati (on the island of Nui)

Religions: Protestant 92.7% (Congregational Christian Church of Tuvalu 85.9%, Brethren 2.8%, Seventh Day Adventist 2.5%, Assemblies of God 1.5%), Baha'i 1.5%, Jehovah's Witness 1.5%, other 3.9%, none or refused 0.4% (2017 est.)

Age structure: *0-14 years:* 29.2% (male 1,754/female 1,672)
15-64 years: 63.2% (male 3,736/female 3,675)
65 years and over: 7.6% (2024 est.) (male 326/female 570)

Dependency ratios: *total dependency ratio:* 58.3 (2024 est.)
youth dependency ratio: 46.2 (2024 est.)
elderly dependency ratio: 12.1 (2024 est.)
potential support ratio: 8.3 (2024 est.)

Median age: *total:* 27.8 years (2024 est.)
male: 26.8 years
female: 28.8 years
comparison ranking: total 155

Population growth rate: 0.78% (2024 est.)
comparison ranking: 112

Birth rate: 22 births/1,000 population (2024 est.)
comparison ranking: 55

Death rate: 7.8 deaths/1,000 population (2024 est.)
comparison ranking: 94

Net migration rate: -6.3 migrant(s)/1,000 population (2024 est.)
comparison ranking: 212

Population distribution: over half of the population resides on the atoll of Funafuti

Urbanization: *urban population:* 66.2% of total population (2023)
rate of urbanization: 2.08% annual rate of change (2020-25 est.)

Major urban areas - population: 7,000 FUNAFUTI (capital) (2018)

Sex ratio: *at birth:* 1.05 male(s)/female
0-14 years: 1.05 male(s)/female
15-64 years: 1.02 male(s)/female
65 years and over: 0.57 male(s)/female
total population: 0.98 male(s)/female (2024 est.)

Maternal mortality ratio: 170 deaths/100,000 live births (2023 est.)
comparison ranking: 46

Infant mortality rate: *total:* 27.8 deaths/1,000 live births (2024 est.)
male: 31.3 deaths/1,000 live births
female: 24 deaths/1,000 live births
comparison ranking: total 56

Life expectancy at birth: *total population:* 69 years (2024 est.)
male: 66.5 years
female: 71.6 years
comparison ranking: total population 184

Total fertility rate: 2.78 children born/woman (2024 est.)
comparison ranking: 55

Gross reproduction rate: 1.36 (2024 est.)

Drinking water source: *improved: urban:* 99% of population (2022 est.)
rural: 99.7% of population (2022 est.)
total: 99.3% of population (2022 est.)
unimproved: urban: 1% of population (2022 est.)
rural: 0.3% of population (2022 est.)
total: 0.7% of population (2022 est.)

Health expenditure: 20% of GDP (2021)
11.2% of national budget (2022 est.)

Physician density: 1.35 physicians/1,000 population (2020)

Sanitation facility access: *improved: urban:* 96.7% of population (2022 est.)
rural: 93.9% of population (2022 est.)
total: 95.8% of population (2022 est.)
unimproved: urban: 3.3% of population (2022 est.)
rural: 6.1% of population (2022 est.)
total: 4.2% of population (2022 est.)

Obesity - adult prevalence rate: 51.6% (2016)
comparison ranking: 5

Alcohol consumption per capita: *total:* 0.93 liters of pure alcohol (2019 est.)
beer: 0.01 liters of pure alcohol (2019 est.)
wine: 0.69 liters of pure alcohol (2019 est.)
spirits: 0.22 liters of pure alcohol (2019 est.)
other alcohols: 0 liters of pure alcohol (2019 est.)
comparison ranking: total 154

Tobacco use: *total:* 32.4% (2025 est.)
male: 46.2% (2025 est.)
female: 18.1% (2025 est.)
comparison ranking: total 16

Children under the age of 5 years underweight: 2.9% (2019/20)
comparison ranking: 81

Currently married women (ages 15-49): 66.1% (2023 est.)

Child marriage: *women married by age 15:* 0% (2020)
women married by age 18: 1.8% (2020)
men married by age 18: 1.7% (2020)

Education expenditure: 15.8% of GDP (2023 est.)
17% national budget (2024 est.)
comparison ranking: Education expenditure (% GDP) 2

ENVIRONMENT

Environmental issues: limited freshwater resources; beach erosion; deforestation; damage to coral reefs; rising sea levels

International environmental agreements: *party to:* Biodiversity, Climate Change, Climate Change-Kyoto Protocol, Climate Change-Paris Agreement, Desertification, Hazardous Wastes, Law of the Sea, Ozone Layer Protection, Ship Pollution, Whaling
signed, but not ratified: Comprehensive Nuclear Test Ban

Climate: tropical; moderated by easterly trade winds (March to November); westerly gales and heavy rain (November to March)

Urbanization: *urban population:* 66.2% of total population (2023)
rate of urbanization: 2.08% annual rate of change (2020-25 est.)

Particulate matter emissions: 6.8 micrograms per cubic meter (2019 est.)

Waste and recycling: *municipal solid waste generated annually:* 4,000 tons (2024 est.)

GOVERNMENT

Country name: *conventional long form:* none
conventional short form: Tuvalu
local long form: none
local short form: Tuvalu
former: Ellice Islands
etymology: the name in the local language means "group of eight" or "eight standing together," referring to eight of the country's nine islands; the remaining island, Nui, was left out of the original grouping because its inhabitants spoke a different language; the former name was given in honor of Canadian shipping company owner Alexander Ellice, who owned a ship that visited the islands in 1819

Government type: parliamentary democracy under a constitutional monarchy; a Commonwealth realm

Capital: *name:* Funafuti
geographic coordinates: 8 31 S, 179 13 E
time difference: UTC+12 (17 hours ahead of Washington, DC, during Standard Time)
etymology: the town has the same name as the island it is located on; the name may either come from the Polynesian word *futi* (banana) or the name Futi, one of the wives of a local ruler, with the word *funa* added as a feminine prefix
note: the capital is an atoll of 29 islets; administrative offices are in Vaiaku Village on Fongafale Islet

Administrative divisions: 7 island councils and 1 town council*; Funafuti*, Nanumaga, Nanumea, Niutao, Nui, Nukufetau, Nukulaelae, Vaitupu

Legal system: mixed system of English common law and local customary law

Constitution: *history:* previous 1978 (at independence); latest effective 1 October 1986
amendment process: proposed by the House of Assembly; passage requires at least two-thirds majority vote by the Assembly membership in the final reading

International law organization participation: has not submitted an ICJ jurisdiction declaration; non-party state to the ICCt

Citizenship: *citizenship by birth:* yes
citizenship by descent only: yes; for a child born abroad, at least one parent must be a citizen of Tuvalu
dual citizenship recognized: yes
residency requirement for naturalization: na

Suffrage: 18 years of age; universal

Executive branch: *chief of state:* King CHARLES III (since 8 September 2022); represented by Governor General Tofiga Vaevalu FALANI (since 29 August 2021)
head of government: Prime Minister Feleti Penitala TEO (since 27 February 2024)
cabinet: Cabinet members selected by the prime minister
election/appointment process: the monarchy is hereditary; governor general appointed by the monarch on recommendation of the prime minister and the parliament; prime minister and deputy prime minister elected by and from members of House of Assembly following parliamentary elections
election results: 2024: TEO was the only candidate nominated by the House of Assembly
2019: Kausea NATANO elected prime minister by House of Assembly; House of Assembly vote - 10 to 6

Legislative branch: *legislature name:* Parliament (Palamene)
legislative structure: unicameral
chamber name: Parliament of Tuvalu (Palamene o Tuvalu)
number of seats: 16 (all directly elected)
electoral system: plurality/majority
scope of elections: full renewal
term in office: 4 years
most recent election date: 1/26/2024
percentage of women in chamber: 0%
expected date of next election: January 2028

Judicial branch: *highest court(s):* Court of Appeal (consists of the chief justice and not less than 3 appeals judges); High Court (consists of the chief justice); appeals beyond the Court of Appeal are heard by the Judicial Committee of the Privy Council (in London)
judge selection and term of office: Court of Appeal judges appointed by the governor general on the advice of the Cabinet; judge tenure based on terms of appointment; High Court chief justice appointed by the governor general on the advice of the Cabinet; chief justice serves for life; other judges appointed by the governor general on the advice of the Cabinet after consultation with chief justice; judge tenure set by terms of appointment
subordinate courts: magistrates' courts; island courts; land courts

Political parties: *note:* no political parties, but members of parliament usually align in informal groupings

Diplomatic representation in the US: *chief of mission:* Ambassador Tapugao FALEFOU (since 19 April 2023); note - also Permanent Representative to UN
chancery: 685 Third Avenue, Suite 1104, New York, NY 10017
telephone: [1] (212) 490-0534
FAX: [1] (212) 808-4975
email address and website: tuvalumission.un@gmail.com
tuvalu.unmission@gov.tv
https://www.un.int/tuvalu/about
note: the Tuvalu Permanent Mission to the UN serves as the Embassy

Diplomatic representation from the US: *embassy:* the US does not have an embassy in Tuvalu; the US Ambassador to Fiji is accredited to Tuvalu

International organization participation: ACP, ADB, AOSIS, C, FAO, IBRD, IDA, IFAD, IFRCS (observer), ILO, IMF, IMO, IOC, ITU, OPCW, PIF, Sparteca, SPC, UN, UNCTAD, UNESCO, UNIDO, UPU, WHO, WIPO, WMO

Independence: 1 October 1978 (from the UK)

National holiday: Independence Day, 1 October (1978)

Flag: *description:* light blue with the UK flag in the upper-left quadrant; the right half of the flag has nine five-pointed yellow stars
meaning: the stars represent a map of the country, with each symbolizing an atoll in the ocean

National symbol(s): maneapa (native meeting house)

National color(s): light blue, yellow

National anthem(s): *title:* "Tuvalu mo te Atua" (Tuvalu for the Almighty)
lyrics/music: Afaese MANOA

history: adopted 1978; the anthem's name is also the nation's motto
title: "God Save the King"
lyrics/music: unknown
history: used since 1745

ECONOMY

Economic overview: upper middle-income Pacific island economy; extremely environmentally fragile; currency pegged to Australian dollar; large international aid recipient; subsistence agrarian sector; Te Kakeega sustainable development; domain name licensing incomes

Real GDP (purchasing power parity): $57.055 million (2023 est.)
$54.938 million (2022 est.)
$54.568 million (2021 est.)
note: data in 2021 dollars
comparison ranking: 219

Real GDP growth rate: 3.9% (2023 est.)
0.7% (2022 est.)
1.8% (2021 est.)
note: annual GDP % growth based on constant local currency
comparison ranking: 78

Real GDP per capita: $5,800 (2023 est.)
$5,500 (2022 est.)
$5,400 (2021 est.)
note: data in 2021 dollars
comparison ranking: 168

GDP (official exchange rate): $62.28 million (2023 est.)
note: data in current dollars at official exchange rate

Inflation rate (consumer prices): 11.5% (2022 est.)
6.2% (2021 est.)
1.9% (2020 est.)
note: annual % change based on consumer prices
comparison ranking: 183

GDP - composition, by sector of origin: *agriculture:* 15.9% (2015 est.)
industry: 7% (2015 est.)
services: 70% (2012 est.)
note: figures may not total 100% due to non-allocated consumption not captured in sector-reported data
comparison rankings: agriculture 53; industry 199; services 35

Agricultural products: coconuts, vegetables, tropical fruits, bananas, root vegetables, pork, chicken, eggs, pork fat, pork offal (2023)
note: top ten agricultural products based on tonnage

Industries: fishing

Remittances: 4.2% of GDP (2023 est.)
4.2% of GDP (2022 est.)
4.9% of GDP (2021 est.)
note: personal transfers and compensation between resident and non-resident individuals/households/entities

Budget: *revenues:* $87 million (2019 est.)
expenditures: $88 million (2019 est.)
note: revenue data include Official Development Assistance from Australia

Current account balance: $2.713 million (2022 est.)
$14.533 million (2021 est.)
$8.46 million (2020 est.)
note: balance of payments - net trade and primary/secondary income in current dollars
comparison ranking: 84

Exports: $2.232 million (2022 est.)
$2.745 million (2021 est.)
$3.089 million (2020 est.)
note: balance of payments - exports of goods and services in current dollars
comparison ranking: 213

Exports - partners: Thailand 88%, Japan 6%, Philippines 3%, Ireland 1%, USA 1% (2023)
note: top five export partners based on percentage share of exports

Exports - commodities: fish (2023)
note: top export commodities based on value in dollars over $500,000

Imports: $57.388 million (2022 est.)
$63.962 million (2021 est.)
$56.947 million (2020 est.)
note: balance of payments - imports of goods and services in current dollars
comparison ranking: 211

Imports - partners: China 42%, Fiji 24%, Japan 11%, Australia 11%, NZ 4% (2023)
note: top five import partners based on percentage share of imports

Imports - commodities: ships, refined petroleum, iron structures, fish, hand tools (2023)
note: top five import commodities based on value in dollars

Exchange rates: Tuvaluan dollars or Australian dollars (AUD) per US dollar -

Exchange rates: 1.515 (2024 est.)
1.505 (2023 est.)
1.442 (2022 est.)
1.331 (2021 est.)
1.453 (2020 est.)

ENERGY

Electricity access: *electrification - total population:* 100% (2022 est.)
electrification - urban areas: 100%
electrification - rural areas: 99.1%

COMMUNICATIONS

Telephones - fixed lines: *total subscriptions:* 2,000 (2021 est.)
subscriptions per 100 inhabitants: 21 (2022 est.)
comparison ranking: total subscriptions 214

Telephones - mobile cellular: *total subscriptions:* 9,000 (2021 est.)
subscriptions per 100 inhabitants: 80 (2021 est.)
comparison ranking: total subscriptions 220

Broadcast media: no TV stations; many households use satellite dishes to watch foreign TV; 1 state-owned radio station, Radio Tuvalu, includes relays from international broadcasters (2019)

Internet country code: .tv

Internet users: *percent of population:* 74% (2023 est.)

Broadband - fixed subscriptions: *total:* 0 (2022 est.)
subscriptions per 100 inhabitants: 5 (2022 est.)
comparison ranking: total 214

TRANSPORTATION

Civil aircraft registration country code prefix: T2

Airports: 1 (2025)
comparison ranking: 214

Merchant marine: *total:* 270 (2023)
by type: bulk carrier 21, container ship 3, general cargo 29, oil tanker 19, other 198
comparison ranking: total 61

Ports: *total ports:* 1 (2024)
large: 0
medium: 0
small: 0
very small: 1
ports with oil terminals: 1
key ports: Funafuti Atoll

MILITARY AND SECURITY

Military and security forces: no regular military forces; Tuvalu Police Force (2025)

Military - note: as part of the Falepili Union treaty between Australia and Tuvalu, which entered into force in August 2024, Australia committed to assist Tuvalu in response to a major natural disaster, health pandemic, or military aggression; Tuvalu pledged to mutually agree with Australia any partnership, arrangement, or engagement with any other State or entity on security and defense-related matters in Tuvalu

Tuvalu has a "shiprider" agreement with the US, which allows local maritime law enforcement officers to embark on US Coast Guard (USCG) and US Navy (USN) vessels, including to board and search vessels suspected of violating laws or regulations within Tuvalu's designated exclusive economic zone (EEZ) or on the high seas; "shiprider" agreements also enable USCG personnel and USN vessels with embarked USCG law enforcement personnel to work with host nations to protect critical regional resources (2025)

U

UGANDA

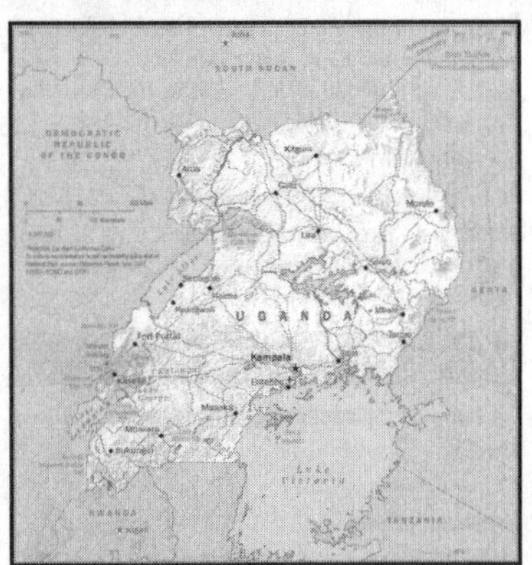

INTRODUCTION

Background: An ancient crossroads for various migrations, Uganda has as many as 65 ethnic groups that speak languages from three of Africa's four major linguistic families. As early as 1200, fertile soils and regular rainfall in the south fostered the formation of several large, centralized kingdoms, including Buganda, from which the country derives its name. Muslim traders from Egypt reached northern Uganda in the 1820s, and Swahili merchants from the Indian Ocean coast arrived in the south by the 1840s. The area attracted the attention of British explorers seeking the source of the Nile River in the 1860s, and this influence expanded in subsequent decades with the arrival of Christian missionaries and trade agreements; Uganda was declared a British protectorate in 1894. Buganda and other southern kingdoms negotiated agreements with Britain to secure privileges and a level of autonomy that were rare during the colonial period in Africa. Uganda's colonial boundaries grouped together a wide range of ethnic groups with different political systems and cultures, and the disparities between how Britain governed southern and northern areas compounded these differences, complicating efforts to establish a cohesive independent country.

Uganda gained independence in 1962 with one of the more developed economies and one of the strongest education systems in Sub-Saharan Africa, but it descended within a few years into political turmoil and internal conflict that lasted more than two decades. In 1966, Prime Minister Milton OBOTE suspended the constitution and violently deposed President Edward MUTESA, who was also the king of Buganda. Idi AMIN seized power in 1971 through a military coup and led the country into economic ruin and rampant mass atrocities that killed as many as 500,000 civilians. AMIN's annexation of Tanzanian territory in 1979 provoked Tanzania to invade Uganda, depose AMIN, and install a coalition government. In the aftermath, Uganda continued to experience atrocities, looting, and political instability and had four different heads of state between 1979 and 1980. OBOTE regained the presidency in 1980 through a controversial election that sparked renewed guerrilla warfare, killing as an estimated 300,000 civilians. Gen. Tito OKELLO seized power in a coup in 1985, but his rule was short-lived, with Yoweri MUSEVENI becoming president in 1986 after his insurgency captured the capital. MUSEVENI is widely credited with restoring relative stability and economic growth to Uganda but has resisted calls to leave office. In 2017, parliament removed presidential age limits, making it possible for MUSEVENI to remain in office for life.

GEOGRAPHY

Location: East-Central Africa, west of Kenya, east of the Democratic Republic of the Congo

Geographic coordinates: 1 00 N, 32 00 E

Map references: Africa

Area: *total:* 241,038 sq km
land: 197,100 sq km
water: 43,938 sq km
comparison ranking: total 81

Area - comparative: slightly more than two times the size of Pennsylvania; slightly smaller than Oregon

Land boundaries: *total:* 2,729 km
border countries (5): Democratic Republic of the Congo 877 km; Kenya 814 km; Rwanda 172 km; South Sudan 475 km; Tanzania 391 km

Coastline: 0 km (landlocked)

Maritime claims: none (landlocked)

Climate: tropical; generally rainy with two dry seasons (December to February, June to August); semiarid in northeast

Terrain: mostly plateau with rim of mountains

Elevation: *highest point:* Margherita Peak on Mount Stanley 5,110 m
lowest point: Albert Nile 614 m

Natural resources: copper, cobalt, hydropower, limestone, salt, arable land, gold

Land use: *agricultural land:* 71.9% (2022 est.)
arable land: 34.4% (2022 est.)
permanent crops: 11% (2022 est.)
permanent pasture: 26.5% (2022 est.)
forest: 11.2% (2022 est.)
other: 16.9% (2022 est.)

Irrigated land: 105 sq km (2013)

Major lakes (area sq km): *fresh water lake(s):* Lake Victoria (shared with Tanzania and Kenya) - 62,940 sq km; Lake Albert (shared with Democratic Republic of Congo) - 5,590 sq km; Lake Kyoga - 4,430 sq km; Lake Edward (shared with Democratic Republic of Congo) - 2,150 sq km

Major rivers (by length in km): Nile (shared with Rwanda [s], Tanzania, South Sudan, Sudan, and Egypt [m]) - 6,650 km
note: [s] after country name indicates river source; [m] after country name indicates river mouth

Major watersheds (area sq km): Atlantic Ocean drainage: Congo (3,730,881 sq km), *(Mediterranean Sea)* Nile (3,254,853 sq km)

Population distribution: population density is relatively high in comparison to other African nations; most of the population is concentrated in the central and southern parts of the country, particularly along the shores of Lake Victoria and Lake Albert; the northeast is least populated, as shown in this population distribution map

Natural hazards: droughts; floods; earthquakes; landslides; hailstorms

Geography - note: *landlocked; fertile, well-watered country with many lakes and rivers; Lake Victoria, the world's largest tropical lake and second-largest freshwater lake, is shared among three countries:* Kenya, Tanzania, and Uganda

PEOPLE AND SOCIETY

Population: *total:* 49,283,041 (2024 est.)
male: 24,040,560
female: 25,242,481
comparison rankings: total 31; male 31; female 30

Nationality: *noun:* Ugandan(s)
adjective: Ugandan

Ethnic groups: Baganda 16.5%, Banyankole 9.6%, Basoga 8.8%, Bakiga 7.1%, Iteso 7%, Langi 6.3%, Bagisu 4.9%, Acholi 4.4%, Lugbara 3.3%, other 32.1% (2014 est.)

Languages: English (official), Ganda or Luganda (most widely used of the Niger-Congo languages and the language used most often in the capital), other Niger-Congo languages, Nilo-Saharan languages, Swahili (official), Arabic

Religions: Protestant 45.1% (Anglican 32.0%, Pentecostal/Born Again/Evangelical 11.1%, Seventh Day Adventist 1.7%, Baptist.3%), Roman Catholic 39.3%, Muslim 13.7%, other 1.6%, none 0.2% (2014 est.)

Age structure: *0-14 years:* 47% (male 11,747,745/ female 11,427,932)
15-64 years: 50.6% (male 11,788,483/female 13,131,051)
65 years and over: 2.4% (2024 est.) (male 504,332/ female 683,498)

Dependency ratios: *total dependency ratio:* 97.8 (2024 est.)
youth dependency ratio: 93 (2024 est.)
elderly dependency ratio: 4.8 (2024 est.)
potential support ratio: 21 (2024 est.)

Median age: *total:* 16.2 years (2024 est.)
male: 15.5 years
female: 17.1 years
comparison ranking: total 228

Population growth rate: 3.18% (2024 est.)
comparison ranking: 6

Birth rate: 39.6 births/1,000 population (2024 est.)
comparison ranking: 5

Death rate: 4.7 deaths/1,000 population (2024 est.)
comparison ranking: 206

Net migration rate: -3.1 migrant(s)/1,000 population (2024 est.)
comparison ranking: 183

Population distribution: population density is relatively high in comparison to other African nations; most of the population is concentrated in the central and southern parts of the country, particularly along the shores of Lake Victoria and Lake Albert; the northeast is least populated, as shown in this population distribution map

Urbanization: *urban population:* 26.8% of total population (2023)

rate of urbanization: 5.41% annual rate of change (2020-25 est.)

Major urban areas - population: 3.846 million KAMPALA (capital) (2023)

Sex ratio: *at birth:* 1.03 male(s)/female
0-14 years: 1.03 male(s)/female
15-64 years: 0.9 male(s)/female
65 years and over: 0.74 male(s)/female
total population: 0.95 male(s)/female (2024 est.)

Mother's mean age at first birth: 19.4 years (2016 est.)
note: data represents median age at first birth among women 20-49

Maternal mortality ratio: 170 deaths/100,000 live births (2023 est.)
comparison ranking: 45

Infant mortality rate: *total:* 28.5 deaths/1,000 live births (2024 est.)
male: 31.8 deaths/1,000 live births
female: 25.1 deaths/1,000 live births
comparison ranking: total 53

Life expectancy at birth: *total population:* 69.7 years (2024 est.)
male: 67.5 years
female: 72 years
comparison ranking: total population 182

Total fertility rate: 5.17 children born/woman (2024 est.)
comparison ranking: 7

Gross reproduction rate: 2.55 (2024 est.)

Drinking water source: *improved:* *urban:* 80.3% of population (2022 est.)
rural: 51.8% of population (2022 est.)
total: 59.3% of population (2022 est.)
unimproved: *urban:* 19.7% of population (2022 est.)
rural: 48.2% of population (2022 est.)
total: 40.7% of population (2022 est.)

Health expenditure: 4.7% of GDP (2021)
4.9% of national budget (2022 est.)

Physician density: 0.19 physicians/1,000 population (2022)

Sanitation facility access: *improved:* *urban:* 67.1% of population (2022 est.)
rural: 27.9% of population (2022 est.)
total: 38.2% of population (2022 est.)
unimproved: *urban:* 32.9% of population (2022 est.)
rural: 72.1% of population (2022 est.)
total: 61.8% of population (2022 est.)

Obesity - adult prevalence rate: 5.3% (2016)
comparison ranking: 180

Alcohol consumption per capita: *total:* 6.82 liters of pure alcohol (2019 est.)
beer: 0.85 liters of pure alcohol (2019 est.)
wine: 0.01 liters of pure alcohol (2019 est.)
spirits: 0.5 liters of pure alcohol (2019 est.)
other alcohols: 5.46 liters of pure alcohol (2019 est.)
comparison ranking: total 61

Tobacco use: *total:* 4.5% (2025 est.)
male: 7.8% (2025 est.)
female: 1.5% (2025 est.)
comparison ranking: total 165

Children under the age of 5 years underweight: 7.6% (2019/20)
comparison ranking: 59

Currently married women (ages 15-49): 58.3% (2023 est.)

Child marriage: *women married by age 15:* 7.3% (2016)
women married by age 18: 34% (2016)
men married by age 18: 5.5% (2016)

Education expenditure: 2.6% of GDP (2022 est.)
8.5% national budget (2022 est.)
comparison ranking: Education expenditure (% GDP) 170

Literacy: *total population:* 69.1% (2016 est.)
male: 78.5% (2016 est.)
female: 61% (2016 est.)

School life expectancy (primary to tertiary education): *total:* 9 years (2016 est.)
male: 10 years (2016 est.)
female: 9 years (2016 est.)

ENVIRONMENT

Environmental issues: draining of wetlands for agricultural use; deforestation; overgrazing; soil erosion; water pollution from industrial discharge and water hyacinth infestation in Lake Victoria; widespread poaching

International environmental agreements: *party to:* Biodiversity, Climate Change, Climate Change-Kyoto Protocol, Climate Change-Paris Agreement, Comprehensive Nuclear Test Ban, Desertification, Endangered Species, Hazardous Wastes, Law of the Sea, Marine Life Conservation, Nuclear Test Ban, Ozone Layer Protection, Ship Pollution, Wetlands
signed, but not ratified: Environmental Modification

Climate: tropical; generally rainy with two dry seasons (December to February, June to August); semiarid in northeast

Urbanization: *urban population:* 26.8% of total population (2023)
rate of urbanization: 5.41% annual rate of change (2020-25 est.)

Carbon dioxide emissions: 6.354 million metric tonnes of CO2 (2023 est.)
from coal and metallurgical coke: -398 metric tonnes of CO2 (2023 est.)
from petroleum and other liquids: 6.354 million metric tonnes of CO2 (2023 est.)
comparison ranking: total emissions 129

Particulate matter emissions: 31.3 micrograms per cubic meter (2019 est.)

Waste and recycling: *municipal solid waste generated annually:* 7.045 million tons (2024 est.)
percent of municipal solid waste recycled: 24.1% (2022 est.)

Total water withdrawal: *municipal:* 328 million cubic meters (2022 est.)
industrial: 50 million cubic meters (2022 est.)
agricultural: 259 million cubic meters (2022 est.)

Total renewable water resources: 60.1 billion cubic meters (2022 est.)

GOVERNMENT

Country name: *conventional long form:* Republic of Uganda
conventional short form: Uganda
etymology: the name is derived from the Swahili word *u*, meaning "land" or "country," and the Ganda people; the origin of the Ganda name is unclear

Government type: presidential republic

Capital: *name:* Kampala
geographic coordinates: 0 19 N, 32 33 E
time difference: UTC+3 (8 hours ahead of Washington, DC, during Standard Time)
etymology: the name is said to come from an African antelope, the impala

Administrative divisions: 134 districts and 1 capital city*; Abim, Adjumani, Agago, Alebtong, Amolatar, Amudat, Amuria, Amuru, Apac, Arua, Budaka, Bududa, Bugiri, Bugweri, Buhweju, Buikwe, Bukedea, Bukomansimbi, Bukwo, Bulambuli, Buliisa, Bundibugyo, Bunyangabu, Bushenyi, Busia, Butaleja, Butambala, Butebo, Buvuma, Buyende, Dokolo, Gomba, Gulu, Hoima, Ibanda, Iganga, Isingiro, Jinja, Kaabong, Kabale, Kabarole, Kaberamaido, Kagadi, Kakumiro, Kalaki, Kalangala, Kaliro, Kalungu, Kampala*, Kamuli, Kamwenge, Kanungu, Kapchorwa, Kapelebyong, Karenga, Kasese, Kasanda, Katakwi, Kayunga, Kazo, Kibaale, Kiboga, Kibuku, Kikuube, Kiruhura, Kiryandongo, Kisoro, Kitagwenda, Kitgum, Koboko, Kole, Kotido, Kumi, Kwania, Kween, Kyankwanzi, Kyegegwa, Kyenjojo, Kyotera, Lamwo, Lira, Luuka, Luwero, Lwengo, Lyantonde, Madi-Okollo, Manafwa, Maracha, Masaka, Masindi, Mayuge, Mbale, Mbarara, Mitooma, Mityana, Moroto, Moyo, Mpigi, Mubende, Mukono, Nabilatuk, Nakapiripirit, Nakaseke, Nakasongola, Namayingo, Namisindwa, Namutumba, Napak, Nebbi, Ngora, Ntoroko, Ntungamo, Nwoya, Obongi, Omoro, Otuke, Oyam, Pader, Pakwach, Pallisa, Rakai, Rubanda, Rubirizi, Rukiga, Rukungiri, Rwampara, Sembabule, Serere, Sheema, Sironko, Soroti, Tororo, Wakiso, Yumbe, Zombo

Legal system: mixed system of English common law and customary law

Constitution: *history:* several previous; latest adopted 27 September 1995, promulgated 8 October 1995
amendment process: proposed by the National Assembly; passage requires at least two-thirds majority vote of the Assembly membership in the second and third readings; proposals affecting "entrenched clauses," including the sovereignty of the people, supremacy of the constitution, human rights and freedoms, the democratic and multiparty form of government, presidential term of office, independence of the judiciary, and the institutions of traditional or cultural leaders, also requires passage by referendum, ratification by at least two-thirds majority vote of district council members in at least two thirds of Uganda's districts, and assent of the president of the republic

International law organization participation: accepts compulsory ICJ jurisdiction; accepts ICCt jurisdiction

Citizenship: *citizenship by birth:* no
citizenship by descent only: at least one parent or grandparent must be a native-born citizen of Uganda
dual citizenship recognized: yes
residency requirement for naturalization: an aggregate of 20 years and continuously for the last 2 years prior to applying for citizenship

Suffrage: 18 years of age; universal

Executive branch: *chief of state:* President Yoweri Kaguta MUSEVENI (since 26 January 1986)
head of government: Prime Minister Robinah NABBANJA (since 14 June 2021)
cabinet: Cabinet appointed by the president from among elected members of Parliament or persons who qualify to be elected as members of Parliament
election/appointment process: president directly elected by absolute-majority popular vote in 2 rounds, if needed, for a 5-year term (no term limits)
most recent election date: 14 January 2021

election results: *2021*: Yoweri Kaguta MUSEVENI reelected president in the first round; percent of vote - Yoweri Kaguta MUSEVENI (NRM) 58.6%, Robert Kyagulanyi SSENTAMU (aka Bobi WINE) (NUP) 34.8%, Patrick Oboi AMURIAT (FDC) 3.2%, other 3.4%
2016: Yoweri Kaguta MUSEVENI reelected president in the first round; percent of vote - Yoweri Kaguta MUSEVENI (NRM) 60.6%, Kizza BESIGYE (FDC) 35.6%, other 3.8%
expected date of next election: 2026

Legislative branch: *legislature name*: Parliament
legislative structure: unicameral
number of seats: 529 (499 directly elected; 30 indirectly elected)
electoral system: plurality/majority
scope of elections: full renewal
term in office: 5 years
most recent election date: 1/14/2021 to 1/18/2021
parties elected and seats per party: National Resistance Movement (NRM) (336); National Unity Platform (NUP) (57); Forum for Democratic Change (FDC) (32); Independents (74); Other (30)
percentage of women in chamber: 34.1%
expected date of next election: January 2026

Judicial branch: *highest court(s)*: Supreme Court of Uganda (consists of the chief justice and at least 6 justices)
judge selection and term of office: justices appointed by the president of the republic in consultation with the Judicial Service Commission, an 8-member independent advisory body, and approved by the National Assembly; justices serve until mandatory retirement at age 70
subordinate courts: Court of Appeal (also acts as the Constitutional Court); High Court (includes 12 High Court Circuits and 8 High Court Divisions); Industrial Court; Chief Magistrate Grade One and Grade Two Courts throughout the country; qadhis courts; local council courts; family and children courts

Political parties: Democratic Party or DP
Forum for Democratic Change or FDC
Justice Forum or JEEMA
National Resistance Movement or NRM
National Unity Platform
People's Progressive Party or PPP
Uganda People's Congress or UPC

Diplomatic representation in the US: *chief of mission*: Ambassador Robie KAKONGE (since 12 December 2022)
chancery: 5911 16th Street NW, Washington, DC 20011
telephone: [1] (202) 726-7100
FAX: [1] (202) 726-1727
email address and website: washington@mofa.go.ug
https://washington.mofa.go.ug/

Diplomatic representation from the US: *chief of mission*: Ambassador William W. POPP (since 20 September 2023)
embassy: 1577 Ggaba Road, Kampala
mailing address: 2190 Kampala Place, Washington DC 20521-2190
telephone: [256] (0) 312-306-001
FAX: [256] (0) 414-259-794
email address and website: KampalaWebContact@state.gov
https://ug.usembassy.gov/

International organization participation: ACP, AfDB, ATMIS, AU, C, COMESA, EAC, EADB, FAO, G-77, IAEA, IBRD, ICAO, ICC (national committees), ICCt, IDA, IDB, IFAD, IFC, IFRCS, IGAD, ILO, IMF, IMO, Interpol, IOC, IOM, IPU, ISO (correspondent), ITC, ITSO, ITU, ITUC (NGOs), MIGA, NAM, OIC, OPCW, PCA, UN, UNCDF, UNCTAD, UNECA, UNDP, UNFPA, UNESCO, UNHCR, UNICEF, UNIDO, UNISFA, UNOCI, UNOPS, UNSOM, UNWTO, UPU, WCO, WFP, WFTU (NGOs), WHO, WIPO, WMO, WTO

Independence: 9 October 1962 (from the UK)

National holiday: Independence Day, 9 October (1962)

Flag: *description*: six equal horizontal bands of black (top), yellow, red, black, yellow, and red; a white disk is at the center and shows a grey crowned crane (the national symbol)
meaning: black stands for the African people, yellow for sunshine and vitality, and red for African brotherhood

National symbol(s): grey crowned crane

National color(s): black, yellow, red

National anthem(s): *title*: "O Uganda, Land of Beauty!"
lyrics/music: George Wilberforce KAKOMOA
history: adopted 1962; one of the shortest national anthems in the world

National heritage: *total World Heritage Sites*: 3 (1 cultural, 2 natural)
selected World Heritage Site locales: Bwindi Impenetrable National Park (n); Rwenzori Mountains National Park (n); Tombs of Buganda Kings at Kasubi (c)

ECONOMY

Economic overview: low-income, primarily agrarian East African economy; COVID-19 hurt economic growth and poverty reduction; lower oil prices threaten prior sector investments; endemic corruption; natural resource rich; high female labor force participation but undervalued

Real GDP (purchasing power parity): $144.137 billion (2024 est.)
$135.803 billion (2023 est.)
$128.923 billion (2022 est.)
note: data in 2021 dollars
comparison ranking: 84

Real GDP growth rate: 6.1% (2024 est.)
5.3% (2023 est.)
4.6% (2022 est.)
note: annual GDP % growth based on constant local currency
comparison ranking: 21

Real GDP per capita: $2,900 (2024 est.)
$2,800 (2023 est.)
$2,700 (2022 est.)
note: data in 2021 dollars
comparison ranking: 196

GDP (official exchange rate): $53.652 billion (2024 est.)
note: data in current dollars at official exchange rate

Inflation rate (consumer prices): 3.3% (2024 est.)
5.4% (2023 est.)
7.2% (2022 est.)
note: annual % change based on consumer prices
comparison ranking: 106

GDP - composition, by sector of origin: *agriculture*: 24.7% (2024 est.)
industry: 24.9% (2024 est.)
services: 43.1% (2024 est.)
note: figures may not total 100% due to non-allocated consumption not captured in sector-reported data
comparison rankings: agriculture 20; industry 90; services 183

GDP - composition, by end use: *household consumption*: 66.3% (2024 est.)
government consumption: 10% (2024 est.)
investment in fixed capital: 21.5% (2024 est.)
investment in inventories: 0.8% (2024 est.)
exports of goods and services: 16.9% (2024 est.)
imports of goods and services: -24.6% (2024 est.)
note: figures may not total 100% due to rounding or gaps in data collection

Agricultural products: plantains, sugarcane, milk, maize, cassava, sweet potatoes, vegetables, beans, potatoes, tea (2023)
note: top ten agricultural products based on tonnage

Industries: sugar processing, brewing, tobacco, cotton textiles; cement, steel production

Industrial production growth rate: 4.9% (2024 est.)
note: annual % change in industrial value added based on constant local currency
comparison ranking: 46

Labor force: 22.829 million (2024 est.)
note: number of people ages 15 or older who are employed or seeking work
comparison ranking: 31

Unemployment rate: 3% (2024 est.)
2.8% (2023 est.)
2.9% (2022 est.)
note: % of labor force seeking employment
comparison ranking: 39

Youth unemployment rate (ages 15-24): *total*: 4.5% (2024 est.)
male: 3.5% (2024 est.)
female: 5.5% (2024 est.)
note: % of labor force ages 15-24 seeking employment
comparison ranking: total 165

Population below poverty line: 20.3% (2019 est.)
note: % of population with income below national poverty line

Gini Index coefficient - distribution of family income: 42.7 (2019 est.)
note: index (0-100) of income distribution; higher values represent greater inequality
comparison ranking: 29

Average household expenditures: *on food*: 38.6% of household expenditures (2023 est.)
on alcohol and tobacco: 1.5% of household expenditures (2023 est.)

Household income or consumption by percentage share: *lowest 10%*: 2.4% (2019 est.)
highest 10%: 34.5% (2019 est.)
note: % share of income accruing to lowest and highest 10% of population

Remittances: 2.9% of GDP (2023 est.)
2.7% of GDP (2022 est.)
2.9% of GDP (2021 est.)
note: personal transfers and compensation between resident and non-resident individuals/households/entities

Budget: *revenues*: $7.616 billion (2023 est.)
expenditures: $10.043 billion (2023 est.)
note: central government revenues (excluding grants) and expenditures converted to US dollars at average official exchange rate for year indicated

Public debt: 53.1% of GDP (2023 est.)
note: central government debt as a % of GDP

comparison ranking: 92

Taxes and other revenues: 13% (of GDP) (2023 est.)
note: central government tax revenue as a % of GDP
comparison ranking: 106

Current account balance: -$3.766 billion (2023 est.)
-$4.064 billion (2022 est.)
-$3.605 billion (2021 est.)
note: balance of payments - net trade and primary/secondary income in current dollars
comparison ranking: 163

Exports: $9.084 billion (2023 est.)
$6.116 billion (2022 est.)
$6.231 billion (2021 est.)
note: balance of payments - exports of goods and services in current dollars
comparison ranking: 121

Exports - partners: India 21%, UAE 16%, Hong Kong 10%, South Sudan 8%, Kenya 6% (2023)
note: top five export partners based on percentage share of exports

Exports - commodities: gold, coffee, fish, refined petroleum, tobacco (2023)
note: top five export commodities based on value in dollars

Imports: $13.853 billion (2023 est.)
$11.079 billion (2022 est.)
$10.62 billion (2021 est.)
note: balance of payments - imports of goods and services in current dollars
comparison ranking: 109

Imports - partners: China 19%, UAE 12%, Tanzania 11%, India 10%, Kenya 7% (2023)
note: top five import partners based on percentage share of imports

Imports - commodities: refined petroleum, gold, plastics, packaged medicine, palm oil (2023)
note: top five import commodities based on value in dollars

Reserves of foreign exchange and gold: $3.359 billion (2018 est.)
$3.721 billion (2017 est.)
$3.098 billion (2016 est.)
note: holdings of gold (year-end prices)/foreign exchange/special drawing rights in current dollars
comparison ranking: 113

Debt - external: $10.469 billion (2023 est.)
note: present value of external debt in current US dollars
comparison ranking: 49

Exchange rates: Ugandan shillings (UGX) per US dollar -

Exchange rates: 3,757.263 (2024 est.)
3,726.14 (2023 est.)
3,689.817 (2022 est.)
3,587.052 (2021 est.)
3,718.249 (2020 est.)

ENERGY

Electricity access: *electrification - total population:* 47.1% (2022 est.)
electrification - urban areas: 72%
electrification - rural areas: 35.9%

Electricity: *installed generating capacity:* 1.452 million kW (2023 est.)
consumption: 4.254 billion kWh (2023 est.)
exports: 400.349 million kWh (2023 est.)
imports: 23.289 million kWh (2023 est.)
transmission/distribution losses: 1.116 billion kWh (2023 est.)
comparison rankings: installed generating capacity 128; consumption 134; exports 81; imports 121; transmission/distribution losses 104

Electricity generation sources: *fossil fuels:* 2.6% of total installed capacity (2023 est.)
solar: 2.6% of total installed capacity (2023 est.)
hydroelectricity: 86.6% of total installed capacity (2023 est.)
biomass and waste: 8.2% of total installed capacity (2023 est.)

Coal: *consumption:* 19 metric tons (2023 est.)
exports: 100 metric tons (2023 est.)
imports: 19 metric tons (2023 est.)
proven reserves: 799.999 million metric tons (2023 est.)

Petroleum: *refined petroleum consumption:* 44,000 bbl/day (2023 est.)
crude oil estimated reserves: 2.5 billion barrels (2021 est.)

Natural gas: *proven reserves:* 14.158 billion cubic meters (2021 est.)

Energy consumption per capita: 2.252 million Btu/person (2023 est.)
comparison ranking: 184

COMMUNICATIONS

Telephones - fixed lines: *total subscriptions:* 116,000 (2023 est.)
subscriptions per 100 inhabitants: (2023 est.) less than 1
comparison ranking: total subscriptions 133

Telephones - mobile cellular: *total subscriptions:* 42.1 million (2023 est.)
subscriptions per 100 inhabitants: 70 (2022 est.)
comparison ranking: total subscriptions 40

Broadcast media: public broadcaster, Uganda Broadcasting Corporation (UBC), operates radio and TV networks; 31 Free-To-Air (FTA) TV stations, 2 digital terrestrial TV stations, 3 cable TV stations, and 5 digital satellite TV stations; 258 FM stations

Internet country code: .ug

Internet users: *percent of population:* 15% (2023 est.)

Broadband - fixed subscriptions: *total:* 44,000 (2023 est.)
subscriptions per 100 inhabitants: (2023 est.) less than 1
comparison ranking: total 147

TRANSPORTATION

Civil aircraft registration country code prefix: 5X

Airports: 39 (2025)
comparison ranking: 106

Railways: *total:* 1,244 km (2014)
narrow gauge: 1,244 km (2014) 1.000-m gauge

MILITARY AND SECURITY

Military and security forces: Uganda People's Defense Force (UPDF): Land Force (includes marines), Air Force, Special Forces Command, Reserve Force

Ministry of Internal Affairs: Uganda Police Force (2025)
note 1: the Special Forces Command is a separate branch within the UPDF; it evolved from the former Presidential Guard Brigade and has continued to retain presidential protection duties in addition to its traditional missions, such as counterinsurgency
note 2: the Uganda Police Force includes air, field, territorial, and marine units, as well as a presidential guard force
note 3: in 2018, President MUSEVENI created a volunteer force of Local Defense Units under the military to beef up local security in designated parts of the country

Military expenditures: 2% of GDP (2023 est.)
2.2% of GDP (2022 est.)
2.5% of GDP (2021 est.)
2.5% of GDP (2020 est.)
1.7% of GDP (2019 est.)

Military and security service personnel strengths: approximately 45,000 active Defense Forces (2025)

Military equipment inventories and acquisitions: the UPDF's inventory is mix of older and some more modern weapons and equipment; it is comprised mostly of Russian/Soviet-era arms with smaller quantities of Chinese, Israeli, North Korean, South African, UK, US, and domestically-produced items; Uganda has a small defense industry that assembles or manufactures light armored vehicles and performs maintenance on some military equipment, including its Russian-made helicopters (2024)

Military service age and obligation: 18-22 years of age for voluntary military duty for men and women; 9-year service obligation (2025)

Military deployments: up to 5,000 Democratic Republic of Congo; up to 4,500 Somalia (African Union Support and Stabilization Mission in Somalia or AUSSOM) (2025)

Military - note: the responsibilities of the Uganda People's Defense Force (UPDF) include defending the sovereignty and territorial integrity of Uganda, assisting the civilian authorities in emergencies and natural disasters, contributing to regional security, participating in socio-economic development projects, conducting military diplomacy, and ensuring internal security, including civil unrest, internal insurgency, and terrorism; in recent years it has beefed up its presence along the borders with the Democratic Republic of the Congo and South Sudan; the UPDF participates in African and UN peacekeeping missions and is a key contributor to the East Africa Standby Force; the UPDF is constitutionally granted seats in parliament and is widely viewed as a key constituency for MUSEVENI; it has been used to break up rallies, raid opposition offices, and surveil rival candidates
the military traces its history back to the formation of the Uganda Rifles in 1895 under the British colonial government; the Uganda Rifles were merged with the Central Africa Regiment and the East Africa Rifles to form the King's African Rifles (KAR) in 1902, which participated in both world wars, as well as the Mau Mau rebellion in Kenya (1952-1960); in 1962, the Ugandan battalion of the KAR was transformed into the country's first military force, the Uganda Rifles, which was subsequently renamed the Uganda Army; the UPDF was established in 1995 from the former rebel National Resistance Army following the enactment of the 1995 Constitution of Uganda (2025)

TERRORISM

Terrorist group(s): Terrorist group(s): al-Shabaab; Islamic State of Iraq and ash-Sham - Democratic Republic of Congo (ISIS-DRC)

note: details about the history, aims, leadership, organization, areas of operation, tactics, targets, weapons, size, and sources of support of the group(s) appear(s) in Appendix T

TRANSNATIONAL ISSUES

Refugees and internally displaced persons: *refugees:* 1,796,597 (2024 est.)

IDPs: 22,209 (2024 est.)
stateless persons: 10,284 (2024 est.)

UKRAINE

INTRODUCTION

Background: Ukraine was the center of the first eastern Slavic state, Kyivan Rus, which was the largest and most powerful state in Europe during the 10th and 11th centuries. Weakened by internecine quarrels and Mongol invasions, Kyivan Rus was incorporated into the Grand Duchy of Lithuania and eventually into the Polish-Lithuanian Commonwealth. The cultural and religious legacy of Kyivan Rus laid the foundation for Ukrainian nationalism. A new Ukrainian state, the Cossack Hetmanate, was established during the mid-17th century after an uprising against the Poles. Despite continuous Muscovite pressure, the Hetmanate managed to remain autonomous for well over 100 years. During the latter part of the 18th century, the Russian Empire absorbed most Ukrainian territory. After czarist Russia collapsed in 1917, Ukraine – which has long been known as the region's "bread basket" for its agricultural production – achieved a short-lived period of independence (1917-20), but the country was reconquered and endured a Soviet rule that engineered two famines (1921-22 and 1932-33) in which over eight million died. In World War II, German and Soviet armies were responsible for seven to eight million more deaths. In 1986, a sudden power surge during a reactor-systems test at Ukraine's Chernobyl power station triggered the worst nuclear disaster in history, releasing massive amounts of radioactive material. Although Ukraine overwhelmingly voted for independence in 1991 as the Union of Soviet Socialist Republics (USSR) dissolved, democracy and prosperity remained elusive, with the legacy of state control, patronage politics, and endemic corruption stalling efforts at economic reform, privatization, and civil liberties.

In 2004 and 2005, a mass protest dubbed the "Orange Revolution" forced the authorities to overturn a presidential election and allow a new internationally monitored vote that swept into power a reformist slate under Viktor YUSHCHENKO. Rival Viktor YANUKOVYCH became prime minister in 2006 and was elected president in 2010. In 2012, Ukraine held legislative elections that Western observers widely criticized as corrupt. In 2013, YANUKOVYCH backtracked on a trade and cooperation agreement with the EU – in favor of closer economic ties with Russia – and then used force against protestors who supported the agreement, leading to a three-month protestor occupation of Kyiv's central square. The government's use of violence to break up the protest camp in 2014 led to multiple deaths, international condemnation, a failed political deal, and the president's abrupt departure for Russia. Pro-West President Petro POROSHENKO took office later that year; Volodymyr ZELENSKYY succeeded him in 2019.

Shortly after YANUKOVYCH's departure in 2014, Russian President Vladimir PUTIN ordered the invasion of Ukraine's Crimean Peninsula. In response, the UN passed a resolution confirming Ukraine's sovereignty and independence. In mid-2014, Russia began an armed conflict in two of Ukraine's eastern provinces. International efforts to end the conflict failed, and by 2022, more than 14,000 civilians were killed or wounded. On 24 February 2022, Russia escalated the conflict by invading the country on several fronts, in what has become the largest conventional military attack on a sovereign state in Europe since World War II. Russia made substantial gains in the early weeks of the invasion but underestimated Ukrainian resolve and combat capabilities. Despite Ukrainian resistance, Russia has laid claim to four Ukrainian oblasts – Donetsk, Kherson, Luhansk, and Zaporizhzhia – although none is fully under Russian control. The international community has not recognized the annexations. The invasion has also created Europe's largest refugee crisis since World War II, with over six million Ukrainian refugees recorded globally. It remains one of the two largest displacement crises worldwide (the other is the conflict in Syria). President ZELENSKYY has focused on boosting Ukrainian identity to unite the country behind the goals of ending the war through reclaiming territory and advancing Ukraine's candidacy for EU membership.

GEOGRAPHY

Location: Eastern Europe, bordering the Black Sea, between Poland, Belarus, Romania, and Moldova in the west and Russia in the east

Geographic coordinates: 49 00 N, 32 00 E

Map references: AsiaEurope

Area: *total:* 603,550 sq km
land: 579,330 sq km
water: 24,220 sq km
note: Russia annexed Crimea in 2014, an area of approximately 27,000 sq km (10,400 sq miles)
comparison ranking: total 48

Area - comparative: almost four times the size of Georgia; slightly smaller than Texas

almost four times the size of Georgia; slightly smaller than Texas: Land boundaries: *total:* 5,581 km
border countries (6): Belarus 1,111 km; Hungary 128 km; Moldova 1,202 km; Poland 498 km; Romania 601 km; Russia 1,944 km, Slovakia 97 km

Coastline: 2,782 km

Maritime claims: *territorial sea:* 12 nm
exclusive economic zone: 200 nm
continental shelf: 200 m or to the depth of exploitation

Climate: temperate continental; Mediterranean only on the southern Crimean coast; precipitation disproportionately distributed, highest in west and north, lesser in east and southeast; winters vary from cool along the Black Sea to cold farther inland; warm summers across the greater part of the country, hot in the south

Terrain: mostly fertile plains (steppes) and plateaus, with mountains found only in the west (the Carpathians) or in the extreme south of the Crimean Peninsula

Elevation: *highest point:* Hora Hoverla 2,061 m
lowest point: Black Sea 0 m
mean elevation: 175 m

Natural resources: iron ore, coal, manganese, natural gas, oil, salt, sulfur, graphite, titanium, magnesium, kaolin, nickel, mercury, timber, arable land

Land use: *agricultural land:* 71.3% (2022 est.)
arable land: 56.8% (2022 est.)
permanent crops: 1.5% (2022 est.)
permanent pasture: 13% (2022 est.)
forest: 16.7% (2022 est.)
other: 12% (2022 est.)

Irrigated land: 1,000 sq km (2022)

Major rivers (by length in km): Dunay (Danube) (shared with Germany [s], Austria, Slovakia, Hungary, Croatia, Serbia, Bulgaria, Moldova, and Romania [m]) - 2,888 km; Dnipro (Dnieper) river mouth (shared with Russia [s] and Belarus) - 2,287 km; Dnister (Dniester) river source and mouth (shared with Moldova) - 1,411 km; Vistula (shared with Poland [s/m] and Belarus) - 1,213 km
note: [s] after country name indicates river source; [m] after country name indicates river mouth

Major watersheds (area sq km): Atlantic Ocean drainage: *(Black Sea)* Danube (795,656 sq km), Don (458,694 sq km), Dnieper (533,966 sq km)

Population distribution: densest settlement in the eastern (Donbas) and western regions; notable concentrations in and around major urban areas of Kyiv, Kharkiv, Donets'k, Dnipropetrovs'k, and Odesa
note: the ongoing war with Russia has shifted significant portions of the population, particularly in the east

Natural hazards: occasional floods; occasional droughts

Geography - note: strategic position at the crossroads between Europe and Asia; second-largest country in Europe after Russia

PEOPLE AND SOCIETY

Population: *total:* 35,661,826 (2024 est.)
male: 17,510,149

female: 18,151,677
comparison rankings: total 43; male 44; female 42

Nationality: *noun:* Ukrainian(s)
adjective: Ukrainian

Ethnic groups: Ukrainian 77.8%, Russian 17.3%, Belarusian 0.6%, Moldovan 0.5%, Crimean Tatar 0.5%, Bulgarian 0.4%, Hungarian 0.3%, Romanian 0.3%, Polish 0.3%, Jewish 0.2%, other 1.8% (2001 est.)

Languages: Ukrainian (official) 67.5%, Russian (regional language) 29.6%, other (includes Crimean Tatar, Moldovan/Romanian, and Hungarian) 2.9% (2001 est.)
major-language sample(s):
Світова Книга Фактів – найкраще джерело базової інформації. (Ukrainian)

Religions: Orthodox (includes the Orthodox Church of Ukraine (OCU), Ukrainian Autocephalous Orthodox Church (UAOC), and the Ukrainian Orthodox - Moscow Patriarchate (UOC-MP)), Ukrainian Greek Catholic, Roman Catholic, Protestant, Muslim, Jewish (2013 est.)
note: Ukraine's population is overwhelmingly Christian; the vast majority - up to two thirds - identify themselves as Orthodox, but many do not specify a particular branch; the OCU and the UOC-MP each represent less than a quarter of the country's population, the Ukrainian Greek Catholic Church accounts for 8-10%, and the UAOC accounts for 1-2%; Muslim and Jewish adherents each compose less than 1% of the total population

Age structure: *0-14 years:* 12.3% (male 2,278,116/female 2,122,500)
15-64 years: 67.8% (male 12,784,928/female 11,376,460)
65 years and over: 19.9% (2024 est.) (male 2,447,105/female 4,652,717)

Dependency ratios: *total dependency ratio:* 47.6 (2024 est.)
youth dependency ratio: 18.2 (2024 est.)
elderly dependency ratio: 29.4 (2024 est.)
potential support ratio: 3.4 (2024 est.)
note: data include Crimea

Median age: *total:* 44.9 years (2024 est.)
male: 41.4 years
female: 49.2 years
comparison ranking: total 25

Population growth rate: 2.38% (2024 est.)
comparison ranking: 24

Birth rate: 6 births/1,000 population (2024 est.)
comparison ranking: 228

Death rate: 18.6 deaths/1,000 population (2024 est.)
comparison ranking: 1

Net migration rate: 36.5 migrant(s)/1,000 population (2024 est.)
comparison ranking: 1

Population distribution: densest settlement in the eastern (Donbas) and western regions; notable concentrations in and around major urban areas of Kyiv, Kharkiv, Donets'k, Dnipropetrovs'k, and Odesa
note: the ongoing war with Russia has shifted significant portions of the population, particularly in the east

Urbanization: *urban population:* 70.1% of total population (2023)
rate of urbanization: -0.27% annual rate of change (2020-25 est.)

Major urban areas - population: 3.017 million KYIV (capital), 1.421 million Kharkiv, 1.008 million Odesa, 942,000 Dnipropetrovsk, 888,000 Donetsk (2023)

Sex ratio: *at birth:* 1.06 male(s)/female
0-14 years: 1.07 male(s)/female
15-64 years: 1.12 male(s)/female
65 years and over: 0.53 male(s)/female
total population: 0.97 male(s)/female (2024 est.)

Mother's mean age at first birth: 26.2 years (2019 est.)

Maternal mortality ratio: 15 deaths/100,000 live births (2023 est.)
comparison ranking: 138

Infant mortality rate: *total:* 8.7 deaths/1,000 live births (2024 est.)
male: 9.7 deaths/1,000 live births
female: 7.6 deaths/1,000 live births
comparison ranking: total 141

Life expectancy at birth: *total population:* 70.5 years (2024 est.)
male: 65.4 years
female: 75.8 years
comparison ranking: total population 173

Total fertility rate: 1.22 children born/woman (2024 est.)
comparison ranking: 224

Gross reproduction rate: 0.59 (2024 est.)

Drinking water source: *improved: urban:* 90.8% of population (2022 est.)
rural: 100% of population (2022 est.)
total: 93.6% of population (2022 est.)
unimproved: urban: 9.2% of population (2022 est.)
rural: 0% of population (2022 est.)
total: 6.4% of population (2022 est.)

Health expenditure: 8% of GDP (2021)
10.6% of national budget (2021 est.)

Physician density: 3.53 physicians/1,000 population (2023)

Hospital bed density: 6.3 beds/1,000 population (2020 est.)

Sanitation facility access: *improved: urban:* 100% of population (2022 est.)
rural: 100% of population (2022 est.)
total: 100% of population (2022 est.)
unimproved: urban: 0% of population (2022 est.)
rural: 0% of population (2022 est.)
total: 0% of population (2022 est.)

Obesity - adult prevalence rate: 24.1% (2016)
comparison ranking: 61

Alcohol consumption per capita: *total:* 5.69 liters of pure alcohol (2019 est.)
beer: 2.44 liters of pure alcohol (2019 est.)
wine: 0.32 liters of pure alcohol (2019 est.)
spirits: 2.88 liters of pure alcohol (2019 est.)
other alcohols: 0.05 liters of pure alcohol (2019 est.)
comparison ranking: total 77

Tobacco use: *total:* 20.4% (2025 est.)
male: 35.5% (2025 est.)
female: 8% (2025 est.)
comparison ranking: total 66

Currently married women (ages 15-49): 61.6% (2023 est.)

Education expenditure: 5.9% of GDP (2022 est.)
8.5% national budget (2022 est.)
comparison ranking: Education expenditure (% GDP) 33

Literacy: *total population:* 100%
male: 100%
female: 100% (2021)

School life expectancy (primary to tertiary education): *total:* 13 years (2021 est.)
male: 13 years (2021 est.)
female: 14 years (2021 est.)

ENVIRONMENT

Environmental issues: air and water pollution; land degradation; solid waste management; biodiversity loss; deforestation; radiation contamination in the northeast from 1986 nuclear accident in Chornobyl'

International environmental agreements: *party to:* Air Pollution, Air Pollution-Nitrogen Oxides, Air Pollution-Sulphur 85, Antarctic-Environmental Protection, Antarctic-Marine Living Resources, Antarctic Treaty, Biodiversity, Climate Change, Climate Change-Kyoto Protocol, Climate Change-Paris Agreement, Comprehensive Nuclear Test Ban, Desertification, Endangered Species, Environmental Modification, Hazardous Wastes, Law of the Sea, Marine Dumping-London Convention, Nuclear Test Ban, Ozone Layer Protection, Ship Pollution, Wetlands
signed, but not ratified: Air Pollution-Heavy Metals, Air Pollution-Persistent Organic Pollutants, Air Pollution-Sulfur 94, Air Pollution-Volatile Organic Compounds

Climate: temperate continental; Mediterranean only on the southern Crimean coast; precipitation disproportionately distributed, highest in west and north, lesser in east and southeast; winters vary from cool along the Black Sea to cold farther inland; warm summers across the greater part of the country, hot in the south

Urbanization: *urban population:* 70.1% of total population (2023)
rate of urbanization: -0.27% annual rate of change (2020-25 est.)

Carbon dioxide emissions: 106.847 million metric tonnes of CO2 (2023 est.)
from coal and metallurgical coke: 45.512 million metric tonnes of CO2 (2023 est.)
from petroleum and other liquids: 24.488 million metric tonnes of CO2 (2023 est.)
from consumed natural gas: 36.847 million metric tonnes of CO2 (2023 est.)
comparison ranking: total emissions 41

Particulate matter emissions: 15.2 micrograms per cubic meter (2019 est.)

Methane emissions: *energy:* 1,003.4 kt (2022-2024 est.)
agriculture: 341.6 kt (2019-2021 est.)
waste: 409.2 kt (2019-2021 est.)
other: 70.9 kt (2019-2021 est.)

Waste and recycling: *municipal solid waste generated annually:* 15.242 million tons (2024 est.)
percent of municipal solid waste recycled: 4.5% (2022 est.)

Total water withdrawal: *municipal:* 1.66 billion cubic meters (2022)
industrial: 2.188 billion cubic meters (2022)
agricultural: 1.031 billion cubic meters (2022)

Total renewable water resources: 175.28 billion cubic meters (2022 est.)

GOVERNMENT

Country name: *conventional long form:* none
conventional short form: Ukraine
local long form: none

local short form: Ukraina
former: Ukrainian National Republic, Ukrainian State, Ukrainian Soviet Socialist Republic
etymology: the name derives from the Old East Slavic or Old Russian word *ukraina*, meaning "borderland," which was used to describe the area on medieval Russia's border at the time of the Tatar invasion in the 13th century

Government type: semi-presidential republic

Capital: *name:* Kyiv (Kiev is the transliteration from Russian)
geographic coordinates: 50 26 N, 30 31 E
time difference: UTC+2 (7 hours ahead of Washington, DC, during Standard Time)
daylight saving time: +1hr, begins last Sunday in March; ends last Sunday in October
etymology: the origin of the name is unclear; traditionally, the name comes from a Prince Kiy, who is said to have founded the city in the 9th century

Administrative divisions: 24 provinces (*oblasti*, singular - *oblast'*), 1 autonomous republic* (*avtonomna respublika*), and 2 municipalities** (*mista*, singular - *misto*) with oblast status; Cherkasy, Chernihiv, Chernivtsi, Crimea or Avtonomna Respublika Krym* (Simferopol), Dnipropetrovsk (Dnipro), Donetsk, Ivano-Frankivsk, Kharkiv, Kherson, Khmelnytskyi, Kirovohrad (Kropyvnytskyi), Kyiv**, Kyiv, Luhansk, Lviv, Mykolaiv, Odesa, Poltava, Rivne, Sevastopol**, Sumy, Ternopil, Vinnytsia, Volyn (Lutsk), Zakarpattia (Uzhhorod), Zaporizhzhia, Zhytomyr
note 1: administrative divisions have the same names as their administrative centers; exceptions show the administrative center name in parentheses
note 2: the United States does not recognize Russia's annexation or renaming of Ukraine's Autonomous Republic of Crimea and the municipality of Sevastopol; it similarly does not recognize the annexation of the Ukrainian oblasts Donetsk, Luhansk, Zaporizhzhia, and Kherson

Legal system: civil law system; judicial review of legislative acts

Constitution: *history:* several previous; latest adopted and ratified 28 June 1996
amendment process: proposed by the president of Ukraine or by at least one third of the Supreme Council members; adoption requires simple majority vote by the Council and at least two-thirds majority vote in its next regular session; adoption of proposals relating to general constitutional principles, elections, and amendment procedures requires two-thirds majority vote by the Council and approval in a referendum; constitutional articles on personal rights and freedoms, national independence, and territorial integrity cannot be amended

International law organization participation: has not submitted an ICJ jurisdiction declaration; non-party state to the ICCt

Citizenship: *citizenship by birth:* no
citizenship by descent only: at least one parent must be a citizen of Ukraine
dual citizenship recognized: no
residency requirement for naturalization: 5 years

Suffrage: 18 years of age; universal

Executive branch: *chief of state:* President Volodymyr ZELENSKYY (since 20 May 2019)
head of government: Prime Minister Yulia SVYRYDENKO (since 17 July 2025)
cabinet: Cabinet of Ministers nominated by the prime minister, approved by the Verkhovna Rada
election/appointment process: president directly elected by absolute-majority popular vote in 2 rounds, if needed, for a 5-year term (eligible for a second term); prime minister selected by the Verkhovna Rada
most recent election date: 31 March and 21 April 2019
election results: 2019: Volodymyr ZELENSKYY elected president in second round; percent of vote in first round - Volodymyr ZELENSKYY (Servant of the People) 30.2%, Petro POROSHENKO (BPP-Solidarity) 15.6%, Yuliya TYMOSHENKO (Fatherland) 13.4%, Yuriy BOYKO (Opposition Platform-For Life) 11.7%, 35 other candidates 29.1%; percent of vote in the second round - Volodymyr ZELENSKYY 73.2%, Petro POROSHENKO 24.5%, other 2.3%; Denys SHMYHAL (independent) elected prime minister; Verkhovna Rada vote - 291-59
2014: Petro POROSHENKO elected president in first round; percent of vote - Petro POROSHENKO (independent) 54.5%, Yuliya TYMOSHENKO (Fatherland) 12.9%, Oleh LYASHKO (Radical Party) 8.4%, other 24.2%; Volodymyr HROYSMAN (BPP) elected prime minister; Verkhovna Rada vote - 257-50
expected date of next election: scheduled for March/April 2024, but not held because Ukraine has been under martial law since February 2022
note: a National Security and Defense Council or NSDC was created in 1992 and tasked with developing national security policy on domestic and international matters and advising the president; a presidential administration helps draft presidential edicts and provides policy support to the president

Legislative branch: *legislature name:* Parliament (Verkhovna Rada)
legislative structure: unicameral
number of seats: 450 (all directly elected)
electoral system: mixed system
scope of elections: full renewal
term in office: 5 years
most recent election date: 7/21/2019
parties elected and seats per party: Servant of the People (254); Opposition Platform - For Life (43); Fatherland (26); European Solidarity (25); Independents (46); Other (30)
percentage of women in chamber: 21.2%
expected date of next election: May 2025
note 1: the next legislative election is expected to take place after the Russian-Ukrainian War ends
note 2: voting not held in Crimea and parts of two Russian-occupied eastern oblasts leaving 26 seats vacant; although this brings the total to 424 elected members (of 450 potential), article 83 of the constitution mandates that a parliamentary majority consists of 226 seats

Judicial branch: *highest court(s):* Supreme Court of Ukraine or SCU (consists of 100 judges, organized into civil, criminal, commercial and administrative chambers, and a grand chamber); Constitutional Court (consists of 18 justices); High Anti-Corruption Court (consists of 39 judges, including 12 in the Appeals Chamber)
judge selection and term of office: Supreme Court judges recommended by the High Qualification Commission of Judges (a 16-member state body responsible for judicial candidate testing and assessment and judicial administration), submitted to the High Council of Justice, a 21-member independent body of judicial officials; judges serve until mandatory retirement at age 65; High Anti-Corruption Court judges are selected by the same process, with one addition – a majority of a combined High Qualification Commission of Judges and a 6-member Public Council of International Experts must vote in favor of potential judges in order to recommend their nomination to the High Council of Justice; Constitutional Court justices appointed - 6 each by the president, the Congress of Judges, and the Verkhovna Rada; judges serve 9-year nonrenewable terms
subordinate courts: Courts of Appeal; district courts

Political parties: Batkivshchyna (Fatherland)
European Solidarity or YeS
Holos (Voice or Vote)
Opposition Bloc (formerly known as Opposition Bloc — Party for Peace and Development,
successor of the Industrial Party of Ukraine, and resulted from a schism in the original
Opposition Bloc in 2019; banned in court June 2022; ceased to exist in July 2022)
Opposition Bloc or OB (divided into Opposition Bloc - Party for Peace and Development and Opposition Platform - For Life in 2019; ceased to exist in July 2022)
Opposition Platform - For Life (resulted from a schism in the original Opposition Bloc in 2019; activities suspended by the National Security and Defense Council in March 2022; dissolved in April 2022)
Platform for Life and Peace
Radical Party or RPOL
Samopomich (Self Reliance)
Servant of the People
Svoboda (Freedom)

Diplomatic representation in the US: *chief of mission:* Ambassador Olha STEFANISHYNA (since 19 September 2025)
chancery: 3350 M Street NW, Washington, DC 20007
telephone: [1] (202) 349-2963
FAX: [1] (202) 333-0817
email address and website: emb_us@mfa.gov.ua
https://usa.mfa.gov.ua/en
consulate(s) general: Chicago, New York, San Francisco

Diplomatic representation from the US: *chief of mission:* Ambassador (vacant); Chargé d'Affaires Ambassador Julie S. DAVIS (since 5 May 2025)
embassy: 4 A. I. Igor Sikorsky Street, 04112 Kyiv
mailing address: 5850 Kyiv Place, Washington, DC 20521-5850
telephone: [380] (44) 521-5000
FAX: [380] (44) 521-5544
email address and website: kyivacs@state.gov
https://ua.usembassy.gov/

International organization participation: Australia Group, BSEC, CBSS (observer), CD, CE, CEI, CICA (observer), CIS (participating member, has not signed the 1993 CIS charter), EAEC (observer), EAPC, EBRD, FAO, GCTU, GUAM, IAEA, IBRD, ICAO, ICC (national committees), ICRM, IDA, IFC, IFRCS, IHO, ILO, IMF, IMO, IMSO, Interpol, IOC, IOM, IPU, ISO, ITU, ITUC (NGOs), LAIA (observer), MIGA, MONUSCO, NAM (observer), NSG, OAS (observer), OIF (observer), OPCW, OSCE, PCA, PFP, SELEC (observer), UN, UNCTAD, UNESCO, UNFICYP, UNIDO, UNISFA, UNMIL, UNMISS, UNOCI, UNOOSA, UNWTO, UPU, Wassenaar Arrangement, WCO, WFTU (NGOs), WHO, WIPO, WMO, WTO, ZC
note: Ukraine is an EU candidate country and must complete accession criteria before being granted full membership

Independence: *24 August 1991 (from the Soviet Union); notable earlier dates:* ca. 982 (VOLODYMYR I consolidates Kyivan Rus); 1199 (Principality (later Kingdom) of Ruthenia formed); 1648 (establishment of the Cossack Hetmanate); 22 January 1918 (from Soviet Russia)

National holiday: Independence Day, 24 August (1991)
note: 22 January 1918, the day Ukraine first declared its independence from Soviet Russia, is now celebrated as Unity Day

Flag: *description:* two equal horizontal bands of blue (top) and yellow
meaning: the colors date back to medieval heraldry, but they are sometimes said to represent grain fields under a blue sky

National symbol(s): tryzub (trident), sunflower

National color(s): blue, yellow

National anthem(s): *title:* "Shche ne vmerla Ukraina" (Ukraine Has Not Yet Perished)
lyrics/music: Paul CHUBYNSKYI/Mikhail VERBYTSKYI
history: music adopted 1991, lyrics adopted 2003; current version of the anthem is the first verse of CHUBYNSKYI's poem, plus the chorus

National heritage: *total World Heritage Sites:* 8 (7 cultural, 1 natural)
selected World Heritage Site locales: Kyiv: Saint Sophia Cathedral and Related Monastic Buildings, Kyiv Pechersk Lavra (c); Lviv Historic Center (c); Residence of Bukovinian and Dalmatian Metropolitans, Chernivtsi (c); Ancient City of Tauric Chersonese, Sevastopol (c); Wooden Tserkvas of the Carpathian Region (c); Ancient and Primeval Beech Forests of the Carpathians (n); Struve Geodetic Arc (c); The Historic Centre of Odesa (c)

ECONOMY

Economic overview: lower-middle-income, non-EU, Eastern European economy; key wheat and corn exporter; gradual recovery after 30% GDP contraction at start of war; damage to infrastructure and agriculture balanced by consumer and business resilience in western Ukraine; international aid has stabilized foreign exchange reserves, allowing managed currency float; continued progress on anti-corruption reforms

Real GDP (purchasing power parity): $577.583 billion (2024 est.)
$561.23 billion (2023 est.)
$531.796 billion (2022 est.)
note: data in 2021 dollars
comparison ranking: 46

Real GDP growth rate: 2.9% (2024 est.)
5.5% (2023 est.)
-28.8% (2022 est.)
note: annual GDP % growth based on constant local currency
comparison ranking: 119

Real GDP per capita: $16,300 (2024 est.)
$15,900 (2023 est.)
$13,800 (2022 est.)
note: data in 2021 dollars
comparison ranking: 119

GDP (official exchange rate): $190.741 billion (2024 est.)
note: data in current dollars at official exchange rate

Inflation rate (consumer prices): 6.5% (2024 est.)
12.8% (2023 est.)
20.2% (2022 est.)
note: annual % change based on consumer prices
comparison ranking: 159

GDP - composition, by sector of origin: *agriculture:* 7.1% (2024 est.)
industry: 19% (2024 est.)
services: 60.6% (2024 est.)
note: figures may not total 100% due to non-allocated consumption not captured in sector-reported data
comparison rankings: agriculture 91; industry 139; services 83

GDP - composition, by end use: *household consumption:* 62.4% (2024 est.)
government consumption: 37.9% (2024 est.)
investment in fixed capital: 18.9% (2024 est.)
investment in inventories: -0.3% (2024 est.)
exports of goods and services: 29.4% (2024 est.)
imports of goods and services: -48.3% (2024 est.)
note: figures may not total 100% due to rounding or gaps in data collection

Agricultural products: maize, wheat, potatoes, sugar beets, sunflower seeds, milk, barley, soybeans, rapeseed, tomatoes (2023)
note: top ten agricultural products based on tonnage

Industries: industrial machinery, ferrous and nonferrous metals, automotive and aircraft components, electronics, chemicals, textiles, mining, construction

Industrial production growth rate: 4.1% (2024 est.)
note: annual % change in industrial value added based on constant local currency
comparison ranking: 59

Labor force: 20.539 million (2021 est.)
note: number of people ages 15 or older who are employed or seeking work
comparison ranking: 34

Unemployment rate: 9.9% (2021 est.)
9.5% (2020 est.)
8.2% (2019 est.)
note: % of labor force seeking employment
comparison ranking: 147

Youth unemployment rate (ages 15-24): *total:* 19.1% (2021 est.)
male: 18.1% (2021 est.)
female: 20.4% (2021 est.)
note: % of labor force ages 15-24 seeking employment
comparison ranking: total 58

Population below poverty line: 1.6% (2020 est.)
note: % of population with income below national poverty line

Gini Index coefficient - distribution of family income: 25.6 (2020 est.)
note: index (0-100) of income distribution; higher values represent greater inequality
comparison ranking: 145

Average household expenditures: *on food:* 41.7% of household expenditures (2023 est.)
on alcohol and tobacco: 6.9% of household expenditures (2023 est.)

Household income or consumption by percentage share: *lowest 10%:* 4.3% (2020 est.)
highest 10%: 21.7% (2020 est.)
note: % share of income accruing to lowest and highest 10% of population

Remittances: 6.3% of GDP (2024 est.)
8.3% of GDP (2023 est.)
10.4% of GDP (2022 est.)
note: personal transfers and compensation between resident and non-resident individuals/households/entities

Budget: *revenues:* $86.185 billion (2023 est.)
expenditures: $121.657 billion (2023 est.)
note: central government revenues (excluding grants) and expenditures converted to US dollars at average official exchange rate for year indicated

Public debt: 58.7% of GDP (2020 est.)
note: central government debt as a % of GDP
comparison ranking: 79

Taxes and other revenues: 17.5% (of GDP) (2023 est.)
note: central government tax revenue as a % of GDP
comparison ranking: 73

Current account balance: -$13.749 billion (2024 est.)
-$9.564 billion (2023 est.)
$7.976 billion (2022 est.)
note: balance of payments - net trade and primary/secondary income in current dollars
comparison ranking: 185

Exports: $56.114 billion (2024 est.)
$51.28 billion (2023 est.)
$57.517 billion (2022 est.)
note: balance of payments - exports of goods and services in current dollars
comparison ranking: 66

Exports - partners: Poland 12%, Romania 9%, Turkey 7%, China 6%, Spain 6% (2023)
note: top five export partners based on percentage share of exports

Exports - commodities: corn, seed oils, wheat, iron ore, soybeans (2023)
note: top five export commodities based on value in dollars

Imports: $92.025 billion (2024 est.)
$89.159 billion (2023 est.)
$83.254 billion (2022 est.)
note: balance of payments - imports of goods and services in current dollars
comparison ranking: 48

Imports - partners: China 16%, Poland 14%, Germany 8%, Turkey 6%, USA 4% (2023)
note: top five import partners based on percentage share of imports

Imports - commodities: refined petroleum, cars, natural gas, packaged medicine, plastic products (2023)
note: top five import commodities based on value in dollars

Reserves of foreign exchange and gold: $43.781 billion (2024 est.)
$40.51 billion (2023 est.)
$28.506 billion (2022 est.)
note: holdings of gold (year-end prices)/foreign exchange/special drawing rights in current dollars
comparison ranking: 47

Debt - external: $90.003 billion (2023 est.)
note: present value of external debt in current US dollars
comparison ranking: 11

Exchange rates: hryvnia (UAH) per US dollar -

Exchange rates: 40.152 (2024 est.)
36.574 (2023 est.)
32.342 (2022 est.)
27.286 (2021 est.)
26.958 (2020 est.)

ENERGY

Electricity access: *electrification - total population:* 100% (2022 est.)

Electricity: *installed generating capacity:* 60.297 million kW (2023 est.)
consumption: 89.402 billion kWh (2023 est.)
exports: 6.1 billion kWh (2023 est.)
imports: 3.28 billion kWh (2023 est.)
transmission/distribution losses: 10.347 billion kWh (2023 est.)
comparison rankings: installed generating capacity 24; consumption 36; exports 37; imports 57; transmission/distribution losses 182

Electricity generation sources: *fossil fuels:* 32.9% of total installed capacity (2023 est.)
nuclear: 50.6% of total installed capacity (2023 est.)
solar: 4.5% of total installed capacity (2023 est.)
wind: 1% of total installed capacity (2023 est.)
hydroelectricity: 9.9% of total installed capacity (2023 est.)
biomass and waste: 1% of total installed capacity (2023 est.)

Nuclear energy: Number of operational nuclear reactors: 15 (2025)

Number of nuclear reactors under construction: 2 (2025)

Net capacity of operational nuclear reactors: 13.11GW (2025 est.)

Percent of total electricity production: 55% (2023 est.)

Number of nuclear reactors permanently shut down: 4 (2025)

Coal: *production:* 19.603 million metric tons (2023 est.)
consumption: 25.012 million metric tons (2023 est.)
exports: 32,000 metric tons (2023 est.)
imports: 5.442 million metric tons (2023 est.)
proven reserves: 34.375 billion metric tons (2023 est.)

Petroleum: *total petroleum production:* 3,000 bbl/day (2023 est.)
refined petroleum consumption: 192,000 bbl/day (2023 est.)
crude oil estimated reserves: 395 million barrels (2021 est.)

Natural gas: *production:* 17.681 billion cubic meters (2023 est.)
consumption: 19.705 billion cubic meters (2023 est.)
exports: 95.994 million cubic meters (2022 est.)
imports: 2.028 billion cubic meters (2023 est.)
proven reserves: 1.104 trillion cubic meters (2021 est.)

Energy consumption per capita: 57.856 million Btu/person (2023 est.)
comparison ranking: 85

COMMUNICATIONS

Telephones - fixed lines: *total subscriptions:* 1.434 million (2023 est.)
subscriptions per 100 inhabitants: 4 (2023 est.)
comparison ranking: total subscriptions 59

Telephones - mobile cellular: *total subscriptions:* 50.3 million (2023 est.)
subscriptions per 100 inhabitants: 135 (2021 est.)
comparison ranking: total subscriptions 36

Broadcast media: media landscape dominated by oligarch-owned news outlets; United News created for 24-hour news about the war with Russia, a joint effort from the Ukrainian public broadcaster and top commercial TV channels; Ukraine Radio's Suspilne and privately owned Radio NV are the national talk radio networks (2021)

Internet country code: .ua

Internet users: *percent of population:* 82% (2023 est.)

Broadband - fixed subscriptions: *total:* 8.07 million (2023 est.)
subscriptions per 100 inhabitants: 20 (2023 est.)
comparison ranking: total 28

TRANSPORTATION

Civil aircraft registration country code prefix: UR

Airports: 152 (2025)
comparison ranking: 35

Heliports: 44 (2025)
comparison ranking: 42

Railways: *total:* 21,733 km (2014)
standard gauge: 49 km (2014) 1.435-m gauge (49 km electrified)
broad gauge: 21,684 km (2014) 1.524-m gauge (9,250 km electrified)

Merchant marine: *total:* 410 (2023)
by type: container ship 1, general cargo 83, oil tanker 14, other 312
comparison ranking: total 48

Ports: *total ports:* 26 (2024)
large: 3
medium: 0
small: 8
very small: 15
ports with oil terminals: 8
key ports: Berdyansk, Dnipro-Buzkyy, Feodosiya, Illichivsk, Kerch, Kherson, Mariupol, Mykolayiv, Odesa, Sevastopol, Yuzhnyy

MILITARY AND SECURITY

Military and security forces: Armed Forces of Ukraine (AFU; Zbroyni Syly Ukrayiny or ZSU): Ground Forces, Naval Forces, Air Forces, Air Assault Forces, Marine Corps, Special Operations Forces, Unmanned Systems Forces, Territorial Defense Forces (Reserves)

Ministry of Internal Affairs: National Guard of Ukraine, State Border Guard Service of Ukraine (includes Maritime Border Guard or Sea Guard), National Police of Ukraine (2025)
note 1: combat units of the National Guard, National Police, and Border Guards come under the control of the Armed Forces in wartime.
note 2: the Territorial Defense Forces (TDF) were formally established in July 2021; the TDF evolved from former Territorial Defense Battalions and other volunteer militia and paramilitary units that were organized in 2014-2015 to fight Russian-backed separatists in the Donbas; in January 2022, the TDF was activated as a separate military branch
note 3: collectively, the AFU and the forces under the Ministry of Interior are known as the Defense Forces of Ukraine (DFU)

Military expenditures: 4% of GDP (2021 est.)
4.4% of GDP (2020 est.)
3.4% of GDP (2019 est.)
3.1% of GDP (2018 est.)
3.1% of GDP (2017 est.)
note: since Russia's invasion of the country in early 2022, annual defense spending has increased to more than 30% of GDP according to some estimates

Military and security service personnel strengths: estimated 850,000-1 million active Defense Forces (2025)
note: following the Russian invasion of Ukraine in February 2022, President ZELENSKY announced a general mobilization of the country; prior to the invasion, Ukraine had approximately 200,000 active Armed Forces troops, approximately 50,000 National Guard, and approximately 40,000 State Border Guard

Military equipment inventories and acquisitions: prior to the full-scale Russian invasion in February 2022, the Ukrainian military was equipped largely with Russian-origin and Soviet-era weapons systems; since the invasion, it has received considerable quantities of weapons, including Soviet-era and more modern Western systems, from European countries and the US; Ukraine also has a growing inventory of domestically produced weapons and equipment (2024)

Military service age and obligation: 18 years of age for voluntary service for men and women; 25 years of age for conscription for men; 18-24 months service obligation (2025)
note 1: conscription was abolished in 2012, but reintroduced in 2014; following the Russian invasion in 2022, all non-exempt men ages 18-60 were required to register with their local recruitment offices and undergo medical screening for possible service; the Territorial Defense Forces accept volunteers, 18-60 years of age
note 2: in February 2025, the military implemented a new option for volunteers age 18-24 to sign one-year contracts in return for higher wages, a signing bonus, exemption from mobilization for 12 months, and other social benefits
note 3: women have been able to volunteer for military service since 1993; as of 2024, nearly 70,000 women were serving in the armed forces in both uniformed and civilian positions
note 4: since 2015, the Ukrainian military has allowed foreigners and stateless persons, 18-45 (in special cases up to 60), to join on 3-5-year contracts, based on qualifications; following the 2022 Russian invasion, the military began accepting medically fit foreign volunteers on a larger scale into an International Legion

Military deployments: *note:* prior to the Russian invasion in 2022, Ukraine had committed about 500 troops to the Lithuania, Poland, and Ukraine joint military brigade (LITPOLUKRBRIG), which was established in 2014; the brigade is headquartered in Poland and is comprised of an international staff, three battalions, and specialized units; units affiliated with the multinational brigade remain within the structures of the armed forces of their respective countries until the brigade is activated for participation in an international operation

Military - note: the primary focus of the Ukrainian Armed Forces (UAF) is defense against Russian aggression; in February 2022, Russia launched a full-scale invasion of Ukraine in what is the largest conflict in Europe since the end of World War II in 1945; as of 2025, the front line of the fighting stretched about 1,000 kilometers (some 600 miles) north and south in eastern and southern Ukraine; Russia's forces have also launched missile and armed drone strikes throughout Ukraine, hitting critical infrastructure, including power, water, and heating facilities, as well as other civilian targets; Russia first invaded Ukraine in 2014, occupying Ukraine's province of Crimea and backing separatist forces in the Donbas region with arms, equipment, and training, as well as military personnel, although Moscow denied their presence prior to 2022; the UAF has received outside military assistance since the Russian

invasion, including equipment and training, chiefly from Europe and the US
Ukraine has a relationship with NATO dating back to the early 1990s, when Ukraine joined the North Atlantic Cooperation Council (1991) and the Partnership for Peace program (1994); the relationship intensified in the wake of the 2014 Russia-Ukraine conflict and Russian seizure of Crimea to include NATO support for Ukrainian military capabilities development and capacity-building; NATO and individual NATO countries further increased support to the Ukrainian military following Russia's 2022 invasion (2025)

SPACE

Space agency/agencies: State Space Agency of Ukraine (SSAU; established 1992 as the National Space Agency of Ukraine or NSAU and renamed in 2010) (2025)

Space program overview: Ukraine inherited a large and well-developed space program when it took over all of the former Soviet defense/space industry that was located on its territory upon the country's independence in 1991; the modern program includes the production of satellite/space launch vehicles (SLVs)/rocket carriers and their components, satellites, and satellite subcomponents; prior to the full scale Russian invasion in February 2022, Ukraine was producing more than 100 SLVs, SLV stages, or SLV engines annually, and since 1991, over 160 rockets and more than 370 spacecraft had been manufactured by Ukraine or produced with its participation; Ukraine cooperates with numerous foreign space agencies and industries, including those of Brazil, Canada, China, the European Space Agency (ESA), the EU, and their member states (particularly Italy and Poland), Japan, Kazakhstan, Russia (curtailed after 2014), Turkey, and the US; Ukraine's "space cluster," a region between the cities of Dnipro, Kharkiv, and Kyiv includes around 20 state-run space industries; in 2019, the Ukrainian Parliament began allowing private companies to engage in space endeavors, including launching rockets into space and allowing companies to negotiate with foreign companies without the state's approval (2025)
note 1: Dnipro, known as Ukraine's "Rocket City," was one of the Soviet Union's main centers for space, nuclear, and military industries and played a crucial role in the development and manufacture of both civilian and military rockets
note 2: further details about the key activities, programs, and milestones of the country's space program, as well as government spending estimates on the space sector, appear in the Space Programs reference guide

TRANSNATIONAL ISSUES

Refugees and internally displaced persons: *refugees:* 2,876 (2024 est.)

IDPs: 3,665,165 (2024 est.)
stateless persons: 10,910 (2024 est.)

UNITED ARAB EMIRATES

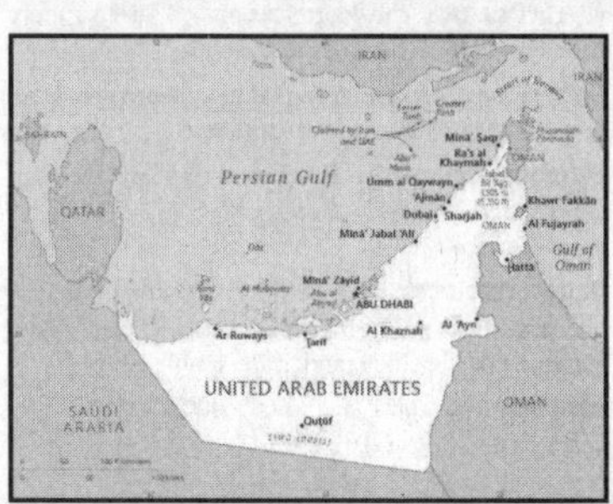

INTRODUCTION

Background: The Trucial States of the Persian Gulf coast granted the UK control of their defense and foreign affairs in 19th-century treaties. In 1971, six of these states – Abu Dhabi, 'Ajman, Al Fujayrah, Ash Shariqah, Dubayy, and Umm al Qaywayn – merged to form the United Arab Emirates (UAE). Ra's al Khaymah joined in 1972.

The UAE's per-capita GDP is on par with those of leading West European nations. For more than three decades, oil and global finance drove the UAE's economy. In 2008-09, the confluence of falling oil prices, collapsing real estate prices, and the international banking crisis hit the UAE especially hard. The UAE did not experience the "Arab Spring" unrest seen elsewhere in the Middle East in 2010-11, partly because of the government's multi-year, $1.6-billion infrastructure investment plan for the poorer northern emirates, and its aggressive pursuit of advocates for political reform.

The UAE in recent years has played a growing role in regional affairs. In addition to donating billions of dollars in economic aid to help stabilize Egypt, the UAE was one of the first countries to join the Defeat ISIS coalition, and to participate as a key partner in a Saudi-led military campaign in Yemen. In 2020, the UAE and Bahrain signed a peace agreement (the Abraham Accords) with Israel – brokered by the US – in Washington, D.C. The UAE and Bahrain thus became the third and fourth Middle Eastern countries, along with Egypt and Jordan, to recognize Israel.

GEOGRAPHY

Location: Middle East, bordering the Gulf of Oman and the Persian Gulf, between Oman and Saudi Arabia

Geographic coordinates: 24 00 N, 54 00 E

Map references: Middle East

Area: *total:* 83,600 sq km
land: 83,600 sq km
water: 0 sq km
comparison ranking: total 115

Area - comparative: slightly larger than South Carolina; slightly smaller than Maine

Land boundaries: *total:* 1,066 km
border countries (2): Oman 609 km; Saudi Arabia 457 km

Coastline: 1,318 km

Maritime claims: *territorial sea:* 12 nm
contiguous zone: 24 nm
exclusive economic zone: 200 nm
continental shelf: 200 nm or to the edge of the continental margin

Climate: desert; cooler in eastern mountains

Terrain: flat, barren coastal plain merging into rolling sand dunes of vast desert; mountains in east

Elevation: *highest point:* Jabal Bil 'Ays 1,905 m
lowest point: Persian Gulf 0 m
mean elevation: 149 m

Natural resources: petroleum, natural gas

Land use: *agricultural land:* 5.5% (2022 est.)
arable land: 0.7% (2022 est.)
permanent crops: 0.6% (2022 est.)
permanent pasture: 4.2% (2022 est.)
forest: 4.5% (2022 est.)
other: 90% (2022 est.)

Irrigated land: 940 sq km (2022)

Population distribution: population is heavily concentrated to the northeast on the Musandam Peninsula; the three largest emirates – Abu Dhabi, Dubai, and Sharjah – are home to nearly 85% of the population

Natural hazards: frequent sand and dust storms

Geography - note: strategic location along southern approaches to Strait of Hormuz, a transit point for crude oil; Abu Zaby (Abu Dhabi) and Dubayy (Dubai) together account for over 90% of UAE's area and two-thirds of the population

PEOPLE AND SOCIETY

Population: *total:* 10,032,213 (2024 est.)
male: 6,824,131
female: 3,208,082
comparison rankings: total 94; male 76; female 111

Nationality: *noun:* Emirati(s)
adjective: Emirati

Ethnic groups: Emirati 11.6%, South Asian 59.4% (includes Indian 38.2%, Bangladeshi 9.5%, Pakistani 9.4%, other 2.3%), Egyptian 10.2%, Filipino 6.1%, other 12.8% (2015 est.)
note: data represent the total population; as of 2019, immigrants make up about 87.9% of the total population, according to UN data

Languages: Arabic (official), English, Hindi, Malayalam, Urdu, Pashto, Tagalog, Persian
major-language sample(s):
كتاب حقائق العالم، المصدر الذي لا يمكن الاستغناء عنه للمعلومات الأساسية
(Arabic)

Religions: Muslim 74.5% (official) (Sunni 63.3%, Shia 6.7%, other 4.4%), Christian 12.9%, Hindu 6.2%, Buddhist 3.2%, agnostic 1.3%, other 1.9% (2020 est.)
note: data represent the total population; as of 2020, immigrants make up about 88.1% of the total population, according to UN data

Age structure: *0-14 years:* 16.4% (male 842,577/female 802,302)
15-64 years: 81.4% (male 5,812,470/female 2,353,750)
65 years and over: 2.2% (2024 est.) (male 169,084/female 52,030)

Dependency ratios: *total dependency ratio:* 22.9 (2024 est.)
youth dependency ratio: 20.1 (2024 est.)
elderly dependency ratio: 2.7 (2024 est.)
potential support ratio: 36.9 (2024 est.)

Median age: *total:* 35.8 years (2024 est.)
male: 38.1 years
female: 29.8 years
comparison ranking: total 95

Population growth rate: 0.6% (2024 est.)
comparison ranking: 140

Birth rate: 10.7 births/1,000 population (2024 est.)
comparison ranking: 174

Death rate: 1.7 deaths/1,000 population (2024 est.)
comparison ranking: 228

Net migration rate: -3.1 migrant(s)/1,000 population (2024 est.)
comparison ranking: 181

Population distribution: population is heavily concentrated to the northeast on the Musandam Peninsula; the three largest emirates – Abu Dhabi, Dubai, and Sharjah – are home to nearly 85% of the population

Urbanization: *urban population:* 87.8% of total population (2023)
rate of urbanization: 1.5% annual rate of change (2020-25 est.)

Major urban areas - population: 3.008 million Dubai, 1.831 million Sharjah, 1.567 million ABU DHABI (capital) (2023)

Sex ratio: *at birth:* 1.06 male(s)/female
0-14 years: 1.05 male(s)/female
15-64 years: 2.47 male(s)/female
65 years and over: 3.25 male(s)/female

UNITED KINGDOM

INTRODUCTION

Background: The United Kingdom of Great Britain and Northern Ireland was created when the Kingdoms of England and Scotland – which previously had been distinct states under a single monarchy – were joined under the 1707 Acts of Union. The island of Ireland was incorporated under the 1800 Acts of Union, while Wales had been part of the Kingdom of England since the 16th century. The United Kingdom has historically played a leading role in developing parliamentary democracy and in advancing literature and science. The 18th and 19th centuries saw the rapid expansion of the British Empire despite the loss of the Thirteen Colonies, and at its zenith in the early 20th century, the British Empire stretched over one fourth of the earth's surface. The first half of the 20th century saw two World Wars seriously deplete the UK's strength and the Irish Republic withdraw from the union. The second half witnessed the dismantling of the Empire and the UK rebuilding itself into a modern and prosperous European nation. As one of five permanent members of the UN Security Council and a founding member of NATO and the Commonwealth of Nations, the UK pursues a global approach to foreign policy. The devolved Scottish Parliament, the National Assembly for Wales, and the Northern Ireland Assembly were established in 1998.

The UK was an active member of the EU after its accession in 1973, although it chose to remain outside the Economic and Monetary Union. However, motivated in part by frustration at a remote bureaucracy in Brussels and massive migration into the country, UK citizens in 2016 voted by 52 to 48 percent to leave the EU. On 31 January 2020, the UK became the only country to depart the EU – a move known as "Brexit" – after prolonged negotiations on EU-UK economic and security relationships.

GEOGRAPHY

Location: Western Europe, islands - including the northern one-sixth of the island of Ireland - between the North Atlantic Ocean and the North Sea; northwest of France

Geographic coordinates: 54 00 N, 2 00 W

Map references: Europe

Area: *total:* 243,610 sq km
land: 241,930 sq km
water: 1,680 sq km
note 1: England covers 53% of the area, Scotland 32%, Wales 9%, and Northern Ireland 6%
note 2: includes Rockall and the Shetland Islands, which are part of Scotland
comparison ranking: total 80

Area - comparative: twice the size of Pennsylvania; slightly smaller than Oregon

Land boundaries: *total:* 499 km
border countries (1): Ireland 499 km

Coastline: 12,429 km

Maritime claims: *territorial sea:* 12 nm
continental shelf: as defined in continental shelf orders or in accordance with agreed upon boundaries
exclusive fishing zone: 200 nm

Climate: temperate; moderated by prevailing southwest winds over the North Atlantic Current; more than one-half of the days are overcast

Terrain: mostly rugged hills and low mountains; level to rolling plains in east and southeast

Elevation: *highest point:* Ben Nevis 1,345 m
lowest point: The Fens -4 m
mean elevation: 162 m

Natural resources: coal, petroleum, natural gas, iron ore, lead, zinc, gold, tin, limestone, salt, clay, chalk, gypsum, potash, silica sand, slate, arable land

Land use: *agricultural land:* 69.6% (2022 est.)
arable land: 24.8% (2022 est.)
permanent crops: 0.2% (2022 est.)
permanent pasture: 44.6% (2022 est.)
forest: 13.3% (2022 est.)
other: 17.2% (2022 est.)

Irrigated land: 718 sq km (2018)

Population distribution: the core of the population lies in and around London, with significant clusters found in central Britain around Manchester and Liverpool, in the Scottish lowlands between Edinburgh and Glasgow, in southern Wales in and around Cardiff, and in far-eastern Northern Ireland, centered on Belfast

Natural hazards: winter windstorms; floods

Geography - note: lies near vital North Atlantic sea lanes; only 35 km (22 mi) from France and linked by tunnel under the English Channel (the Channel Tunnel or Chunnel); because of heavily indented coastline, no location is more than 125 km (78 mi) from tidal waters

PEOPLE AND SOCIETY

Population: *total:* 68,459,055 (2024 est.)
male: 34,005,445
female: 34,453,610
comparison rankings: total 21; male 21; female 22

Nationality: *noun:* Briton(s), British (collective plural)
adjective: British

Ethnic groups: White 87.2%, Black/African/Caribbean/black British 3%, Asian/Asian British: Indian 2.3%, Asian/Asian British: Pakistani 1.9%, mixed 2%, other 3.7% (2011 est.)

Languages: English
note: the following are recognized regional languages: Scots (about 30% of the population of Scotland), Scottish Gaelic (about 60,000 speakers in Scotland), Welsh (about 20% of the population of Wales), Irish (about 10% of the population of Northern Ireland), Cornish (some 2,000 to 3,000 people in Cornwall) (2012 est.)

Religions: Christian (includes Anglican, Roman Catholic, Presbyterian, Methodist) 59.5%, Muslim 4.4%, Hindu 1.3%, other 2%, unspecified 7.2%, none 25.7% (2011 est.)

Age structure: *0-14 years:* 16.7% (male 5,872,937/female 5,592,665)
15-64 years: 63.9% (male 22,062,643/female 21,702,401)
65 years and over: 19.3% (2024 est.) (male 6,069,865/female 7,158,544)

Dependency ratios: *total dependency ratio:* 56.4 (2024 est.)
youth dependency ratio: 26.2 (2024 est.)
elderly dependency ratio: 30.2 (2024 est.)
potential support ratio: 3.3 (2024 est.)

Median age: *total:* 40.8 years (2024 est.)
male: 40.1 years
female: 41.5 years
comparison ranking: total 58

Population growth rate: 0.45% (2024 est.)
comparison ranking: 154

Birth rate: 10.8 births/1,000 population (2024 est.)
comparison ranking: 170

Death rate: 9.2 deaths/1,000 population (2024 est.)
comparison ranking: 53

Net migration rate: 2.9 migrant(s)/1,000 population (2024 est.)
comparison ranking: 39

Population distribution: the core of the population lies in and around London, with significant clusters found in central Britain around Manchester and Liverpool, in the Scottish lowlands between Edinburgh and Glasgow, in southern Wales in and around Cardiff, and in far-eastern Northern Ireland, centered on Belfast

Urbanization: *urban population:* 84.6% of total population (2023)
rate of urbanization: 0.8% annual rate of change (2020-25 est.)

Major urban areas - population: 9.648 million LONDON (capital), 2.791 million Manchester, 2.665 million Birmingham, 1.929 million West Yorkshire, 1.698 million Glasgow, 952,000 Southampton/Portsmouth (2023)

Sex ratio: *at birth:* 1.05 male(s)/female
0-14 years: 1.05 male(s)/female
15-64 years: 1.02 male(s)/female
65 years and over: 0.85 male(s)/female
total population: 0.99 male(s)/female (2024 est.)

Mother's mean age at first birth: 29 years (2018 est.)
note: data represents England and Wales only

Maternal mortality ratio: 8 deaths/100,000 live births (2023 est.)
comparison ranking: 155

Infant mortality rate: *total:* 3.8 deaths/1,000 live births (2024 est.)
male: 4.2 deaths/1,000 live births
female: 3.3 deaths/1,000 live births
comparison ranking: total 190

Life expectancy at birth: *total population:* 82.2 years (2024 est.)
male: 80.1 years
female: 84.4 years
comparison ranking: total population 33

Total fertility rate: 1.63 children born/woman (2024 est.)
comparison ranking: 177

Gross reproduction rate: 0.8 (2024 est.)

Drinking water source: *improved: urban:* 100% of population (2022 est.)
rural: 100% of population (2022 est.)
total: 100% of population (2022 est.)
unimproved: urban: 0% of population (2022 est.)
rural: 0% of population (2022 est.)
total: 0% of population (2022 est.)

Health expenditure: 11.3% of GDP (2022)
20.7% of national budget (2022 est.)

Physician density: 3.3 physicians/1,000 population (2023)

Hospital bed density: 2.4 beds/1,000 population (2021 est.)

Sanitation facility access: *improved: urban:* 99.8% of population (2022 est.)
rural: 99.8% of population (2022 est.)
total: 99.8% of population (2022 est.)
unimproved: urban: 0.2% of population (2022 est.)
rural: 0.2% of population (2022 est.)
total: 0.2% of population (2022 est.)

Obesity - adult prevalence rate: 27.8% (2016)
comparison ranking: 36

Alcohol consumption per capita: *total:* 9.8 liters of pure alcohol (2019 est.)
beer: 3.53 liters of pure alcohol (2019 est.)
wine: 3.3 liters of pure alcohol (2019 est.)
spirits: 2.35 liters of pure alcohol (2019 est.)
other alcohols: 0.61 liters of pure alcohol (2019 est.)
comparison ranking: total 24

Tobacco use: *total:* 11.5% (2025 est.)
male: 13.3% (2025 est.)
female: 9.8% (2025 est.)
comparison ranking: total 118

Currently married women (ages 15-49): 50.7% (2023 est.)

Child marriage: *women married by age 18:* 0% (2021)

Education expenditure: 4.9% of GDP (2022 est.)
10.6% national budget (2022 est.)
comparison ranking: Education expenditure (% GDP) 67

School life expectancy (primary to tertiary education): *total:* 18 years (2022 est.)
male: 17 years (2022 est.)
female: 18 years (2022 est.)

ENVIRONMENT

Environmental issues: air pollution in the London region; soil pollution from pesticides and heavy metals; decline in marine and coastal habitats from housing, tourism, and industry

International environmental agreements: *party to:* Air Pollution, Air Pollution-Heavy Metals, Air Pollution-Multi-effect Protocol, Air Pollution-Nitrogen Oxides, Air Pollution-Persistent Organic Pollutants, Air Pollution-Sulphur 94, Air Pollution-Volatile Organic Compounds, Antarctic-Environmental Protection, Antarctic-Marine Living Resources, Antarctic Seals, Antarctic Treaty, Biodiversity, Climate Change, Climate Change-Kyoto Protocol, Climate Change-Paris Agreement, Comprehensive Nuclear Test Ban, Desertification, Endangered Species, Environmental Modification, Hazardous Wastes, Law of the Sea, Marine Dumping-London Convention, Marine Dumping-London Protocol, Marine Life Conservation, Nuclear Test Ban, Ozone Layer Protection, Ship Pollution, Tropical Timber 2006, Wetlands, Whaling
signed, but not ratified: none of the selected agreements

Climate: temperate; moderated by prevailing southwest winds over the North Atlantic Current; more than one-half of the days are overcast

Urbanization: *urban population:* 84.6% of total population (2023)
rate of urbanization: 0.8% annual rate of change (2020-25 est.)

Carbon dioxide emissions: 340.94 million metric tonnes of CO2 (2023 est.)
from coal and metallurgical coke: 17.093 million metric tonnes of CO2 (2023 est.)
from petroleum and other liquids: 197.133 million metric tonnes of CO2 (2023 est.)
from consumed natural gas: 126.713 million metric tonnes of CO2 (2023 est.)
comparison ranking: total emissions 17

Particulate matter emissions: 7.8 micrograms per cubic meter (2019 est.)

Methane emissions: *energy:* 353.4 kt (2022-2024 est.)
agriculture: 1,030.2 kt (2019-2021 est.)
waste: 1,070.1 kt (2019-2021 est.)
other: 62 kt (2019-2021 est.)

Waste and recycling: *municipal solid waste generated annually:* 30.771 million tons (2024 est.)
percent of municipal solid waste recycled: 34.2% (2022 est.)

Total water withdrawal: *municipal:* 6.227 billion cubic meters (2022 est.)
industrial: 1.01 billion cubic meters (2022 est.)
agricultural: 1.183 billion cubic meters (2022 est.)

Total renewable water resources: 147 billion cubic meters (2022 est.)

Geoparks: *total global geoparks and regional networks:* 10 (2025)
global geoparks and regional networks: Arran; Black Country; Cuilcagh Lakelands (includes Ireland); English Riviera; Fforest Fawr; GeoMôn; Mourne Gullion Strangford; North Pennines AONB; North-West Highlands; Shetland (2025)

GOVERNMENT

Country name: *conventional long form:* United Kingdom of Great Britain and Northern Ireland; note - the island of Great Britain includes England, Scotland, and Wales
conventional short form: United Kingdom
abbreviation: UK
etymology: the name United Kingdom is self-descriptive; the name Britain probably derives from the Celtic word *pretani*, meaning "painted people;" the designation of Great Britain for England, Scotland, and Wales dates back to medieval times and was used to distinguish the island from Little Britain, or Brittany, in modern France; the name Ireland evolved from the Gaelic name Eriu, which is possibly

derived from the Old Celtic *iveriu*, meaning "good land"

Government type: parliamentary constitutional monarchy; a Commonwealth realm

Capital: *name:* London
geographic coordinates: 51 30 N, 0 05 W
time difference: UTC 0 (5 hours ahead of Washington, DC, during Standard Time)
daylight saving time: +1hr, begins last Sunday in March; ends last Sunday in October
time zone note: the time statements apply to the United Kingdom proper, not to its crown dependencies or overseas territories
etymology: the name derives from the Roman settlement of Londinium, established on the current site of London around A.D. 43; the original meaning of the name is uncertain

Administrative divisions: England: 24 two-tier counties, 32 London boroughs and 1 City of London or Greater London, 36 metropolitan districts, 59 unitary authorities (including 4 single-tier counties*)
two-tier counties: Cambridgeshire, Cumbria, Derbyshire, Devon, East Sussex, Essex, Gloucestershire, Hampshire, Hertfordshire, Kent, Lancashire, Leicestershire, Lincolnshire, Norfolk, North Yorkshire, Nottinghamshire, Oxfordshire, Somerset, Staffordshire, Suffolk, Surrey, Warwickshire, West Sussex, Worcestershire

London boroughs and City of London or Greater London: Barking and Dagenham, Barnet, Bexley, Brent, Bromley, Camden, Croydon, Ealing, Enfield, Greenwich, Hackney, Hammersmith and Fulham, Haringey, Harrow, Havering, Hillingdon, Hounslow, Islington, Kensington and Chelsea, Kingston upon Thames, Lambeth, Lewisham, City of London, Merton, Newham, Redbridge, Richmond upon Thames, Southwark, Sutton, Tower Hamlets, Waltham Forest, Wandsworth, Westminster
metropolitan districts: Barnsley, Birmingham, Bolton, Bradford, Bury, Calderdale, Coventry, Doncaster, Dudley, Gateshead, Kirklees, Knowlsey, Leeds, Liverpool, Manchester, Newcastle upon Tyne, North Tyneside, Oldham, Rochdale, Rotherham, Salford, Sandwell, Sefton, Sheffield, Solihull, South Tyneside, St. Helens, Stockport, Sunderland, Tameside, Trafford, Wakefield, Walsall, Wigan, Wirral, Wolverhampton
unitary authorities: Bath and North East Somerset; Bedford; Blackburn with Darwen; Blackpool; Bournemouth, Christchurch and Poole; Bracknell Forest; Brighton and Hove; City of Bristol; Buckinghamshire; Central Bedfordshire; Cheshire East; Cheshire West and Chester; Cornwall; Darlington; Derby; Dorset; Durham County*; East Riding of Yorkshire; Halton; Hartlepool; Herefordshire*; Isle of Wight*; Isles of Scilly; City of Kingston upon Hull; Leicester; Luton; Medway; Middlesbrough; Milton Keynes; North East Lincolnshire; North Lincolnshire; North Northamptonshire; North Somerset; Northumberland*; Nottingham; Peterborough; Plymouth; Portsmouth; Reading; Redcar and Cleveland; Rutland; Shropshire; Slough; South Gloucestershire; Southampton; Southend-on-Sea; Stockton-on-Tees; Stoke-on-Trent; Swindon; Telford and Wrekin; Thurrock; Torbay; Warrington; West Berkshire; West Northamptonshire; Wiltshire; Windsor and Maidenhead; Wokingham; York

Northern Ireland: 5 borough councils, 4 district councils, 2 city councils
borough councils: Antrim and Newtownabbey; Ards and North Down; Armagh City, Banbridge, and Craigavon; Causeway Coast and Glens; Mid and East Antrim
district councils: Derry City and Strabane; Fermanagh and Omagh; Mid Ulster; Newry, Murne, and Down
city councils: Belfast; Lisburn and Castlereagh

Scotland: 32 council areas
council areas: Aberdeen City, Aberdeenshire, Angus, Argyll and Bute, Clackmannanshire, Dumfries and Galloway, Dundee City, East Ayrshire, East Dunbartonshire, East Lothian, East Renfrewshire, City of Edinburgh, Eilean Siar (Western Isles), Falkirk, Fife, Glasgow City, Highland, Inverclyde, Midlothian, Moray, North Ayrshire, North Lanarkshire, Orkney Islands, Perth and Kinross, Renfrewshire, Shetland Islands, South Ayrshire, South Lanarkshire, Stirling, The Scottish Borders, West Dunbartonshire, West Lothian

Wales: 22 unitary authorities
unitary authorities: Blaenau Gwent, Bridgend, Caerphilly, Cardiff, Carmarthenshire, Ceredigion, Conwy, Denbighshire, Flintshire, Gwynedd, Isle of Anglesey, Merthyr Tydfil, Monmouthshire, Neath Port Talbot, Newport, Pembrokeshire, Powys, Rhondda Cynon Taff, Swansea, The Vale of Glamorgan, Torfaen, Wrexham

Dependent areas: Anguilla; Bermuda; British Indian Ocean Territory; British Virgin Islands; Cayman Islands; Falkland Islands; Gibraltar; Montserrat; Pitcairn Islands; Saint Helena, Ascension, and Tristan da Cunha; South Georgia and the South Sandwich Islands; Turks and Caicos Islands (12)

Legal system: common law system; has nonbinding judicial review of Acts of Parliament under the Human Rights Act of 1998

Constitution: *history:* uncoded; partly statutes, partly common law and practice
amendment process: proposed as a bill for an Act of Parliament by the government, by the House of Commons, or by the House of Lords; passage requires agreement by both houses and by the monarch (Royal Assent)

International law organization participation: accepts compulsory ICJ jurisdiction with reservations; accepts ICCt jurisdiction

Citizenship: *citizenship by birth:* no
citizenship by descent only: at least one parent must be a citizen of the United Kingdom
dual citizenship recognized: yes
residency requirement for naturalization: 5 years

Suffrage: 18 years of age; universal

Executive branch: *chief of state:* King CHARLES III (since 8 September 2022)
head of government: Prime Minister Keir STARMER (since 5 July 2024)
cabinet: Cabinet appointed by the prime minister
election/appointment process: the monarchy is hereditary; following legislative elections, the leader of the majority party or majority coalition usually becomes the prime minister
note 1: in addition to serving as the UK head of state, the British sovereign is the constitutional monarch for 14 additional Commonwealth countries (each referred to as a "Commonwealth realm")
note 2: King CHARLES III succeeded his mother, Queen ELIZABETH II, after serving as Prince of Wales (heir apparent) for over 64 years – the longest such tenure in British history

Legislative branch: *legislature name:* UK Parliament
legislative structure: bicameral

Legislative branch - lower chamber: *chamber name:* House of Commons
number of seats: 650 (all directly elected)
electoral system: plurality/majority
scope of elections: full renewal
term in office: 5 years
most recent election date: 7/4/2024
parties elected and seats per party: Labour Party (411); Conservative Party (121); Liberal Democrats (72); Other (46)
percentage of women in chamber: 40.5%
expected date of next election: July 2029

Legislative branch - upper chamber: *chamber name:* House of Lords
number of seats: 800 (all appointed)
parties elected and seats per party: Conservative Party (286); Labour Party (212); Liberal Democrats (76); Crossover (Independents) 180; other (6)
percentage of women in chamber: 31%
note: the number of total seats in the House of Lords does not include ineligible members or members on leave of absence

Judicial branch: *highest court(s):* Supreme Court (consists of 12 justices, including the court president and deputy president)
judge selection and term of office: judge candidates selected by an independent committee of several judicial commissions, then recommended to the prime minister, and appointed by the monarch; justices serve for life
subordinate courts: England and Wales: Court of Appeal (civil and criminal divisions); High Court; Crown Court; County Courts; Magistrates' Courts; Scotland: Court of Sessions; Sheriff Courts; High Court of Justiciary; tribunals; Northern Ireland: Court of Appeal in Northern Ireland; High Court; county courts; magistrates' courts; specialized tribunals

Political parties: Alliance Party or APNI (Northern Ireland)
Conservative and Unionist Party
Democratic Unionist Party or DUP (Northern Ireland)
Green Party of England and Wales or Greens
Labor (Labour) Party
Liberal Democrats (Lib Dems)
Party of Wales (Plaid Cymru)
Reform UK
Scottish National Party or SNP
Sinn Fein (Northern Ireland)
Social Democratic and Labor Party or SDLP (Northern Ireland)
Traditional Unionist Voice or TUV
UK Independence Party or UKIP
Ulster Unionist Party or UUP (Northern Ireland)
Workers Party of Great Britian

Diplomatic representation in the US: *chief of mission:* Ambassador (vacant); Chargé d'Affaires James ROSCOE (since 11 September 2025)
chancery: 3100 Massachusetts Avenue NW, Washington, DC 20008
telephone: [1] (202) 588-6500

FAX: [1] (202) 588-7870
email address and website: ukin.washington@fcdo.gov.uk
https://www.gov.uk/world/organisations/british-embassy-washington
consulate(s) general: Atlanta, Boston, Chicago, Houston, Los Angeles, Miami, New York, San Francisco

Diplomatic representation from the US: *chief of mission:* Ambassador Warren A. STEPHENS (since 21 May 2025)
embassy: 33 Nine Elms Lane, London, SW11 7US
mailing address: 8400 London Place, Washington DC 20521-8400
telephone: [44] (0) 20-7499-9000
FAX: [44] (0) 20-7891-3845
email address and website: SCSLondon@state.gov https://uk.usembassy.gov/
consulate(s) general: Belfast, Edinburgh

International organization participation: ADB (nonregional member), AfDB (nonregional member), Arctic Council (observer), Australia Group, BIS, C, CBSS (observer), CD, CDB, CE, CERN, EAPC, EBRD, ECB, EIB, EITI (implementing country), ESA, EU, FAO, FATF, G-5, G-7, G-8, G-10, G-20, IADB, IAEA, IBRD, ICAO, ICC (national committees), ICCt, ICRM, IDA, IEA, IFAD, IFC, IFRCS, IGAD (partners), IHO, ILO, IMF, IMO, IMSO, Interpol, IOC, IOM, IPU, ISO, ITSO, ITU, ITUC (NGOs), MIGA, MONUSCO, NATO, NEA, NSG, OAS (observer), OECD, OPCW, OSCE, Pacific Alliance (observer), Paris Club, PCA, PIF (partner), SELEC (observer), SICA (observer), UN, UNCTAD, UNESCO, UNFICYP, UNHCR, UNMISS, UNOOSA, UNRWA, UN Security Council (permanent), UNSOM, UPU, Wassenaar Arrangement, WCO, WHO, WIPO, WMO, WTO, ZC

Independence: *no official date of independence:* 927 (minor English kingdoms unite); 3 March 1284 (enactment of the Statute of Rhuddlan uniting England and Wales); 1536 (Act of Union incorporates England and Wales); 1 May 1707 (Acts of Union unite England, Scotland, and Wales as Great Britain); 1 January 1801 (Acts of Union unite Great Britain and Ireland as the United Kingdom of Great Britain and Ireland); 6 December 1921 (Anglo-Irish Treaty formalizes partition of Ireland; six counties become Northern Ireland and remain part of the UK); 12 April 1927 (Royal and Parliamentary Titles Act establishes current name of the United Kingdom of Great Britain and Northern Ireland)

National holiday: the UK does not celebrate one particular national holiday

Flag: *description:* blue field with the red cross of Saint George (patron saint of England) edged in white on top of the diagonal red cross of Saint Patrick (patron saint of Ireland), which is on top of the diagonal white cross of Saint Andrew (patron saint of Scotland)
history: the official name is the Union Flag, but commonly called the Union Jack; the design and colors have been the basis for a number of other flags

National symbol(s): lion (all of Britain); lion, Tudor rose, oak (England); lion, unicorn, thistle (Scotland); dragon, daffodil, leek (Wales); shamrock, flax (Northern Ireland)

National color(s): red, white, blue (all of Britain); red, white (England); blue, white (Scotland); red, white, green (Wales)

National anthem(s): *title:* "God Save the King"
lyrics/music: unknown
history: in use since 1745; by tradition, the song serves as both the national and royal anthem; it is known as either "God Save the Queen" or "God Save the King," depending on the gender of the reigning monarch; it also serves as the royal anthem for many Commonwealth nations

National heritage: *total World Heritage Sites:* 33 (28 cultural, 4 natural, 1 mixed); note - includes one site in Bermuda
selected World Heritage Site locales: Giant's Causeway and Causeway Coast (n); Ironbridge Gorge (c); Stonehenge, Avebury, and Associated Sites (c); Castles and Town Walls of King Edward in Gwynedd (c); Blenheim Palace (c); City of Bath (c); Tower of London (c); St Kilda (m); Maritime Greenwich (c); Old and New Towns of Edinburgh (c); Royal Botanic Gardens, Kew (c); The English Lake District (c)

ECONOMY

Economic overview: high-income, non-EU European economy; global financial center and dominant service sector; sluggish growth from stringent monetary policy, reduced business investment, low productivity and participation rates; fiscal austerity in face of high public debt

Real GDP (purchasing power parity): $3.636 trillion (2024 est.)
$3.596 trillion (2023 est.)
$3.582 trillion (2022 est.)
note: data in 2021 dollars
comparison ranking: 10

Real GDP growth rate: 1.1% (2024 est.)
0.4% (2023 est.)
4.8% (2022 est.)
note: annual GDP % growth based on constant local currency
comparison ranking: 174

Real GDP per capita: $52,500 (2024 est.)
$52,500 (2023 est.)
$53,000 (2022 est.)
note: data in 2021 dollars
comparison ranking: 38

GDP (official exchange rate): $3.644 trillion (2024 est.)
note: data in current dollars at official exchange rate

Inflation rate (consumer prices): 3.3% (2024 est.)
6.8% (2023 est.)
7.9% (2022 est.)
note: annual % change based on consumer prices
comparison ranking: 109

GDP - composition, by sector of origin: *agriculture:* 0.6% (2024 est.)
industry: 16.7% (2024 est.)
services: 72.8% (2024 est.)
note: figures may not total 100% due to non-allocated consumption not captured in sector-reported data
comparison rankings: agriculture 185; industry 157; services 26

GDP - composition, by end use: *household consumption:* 61.3% (2023 est.)
government consumption: 20.5% (2023 est.)
investment in fixed capital: 17.6% (2023 est.)
investment in inventories: -0.4% (2023 est.)
exports of goods and services: 32% (2023 est.)
imports of goods and services: -33.1% (2023 est.)
note: figures may not total 100% due to rounding or gaps in data collection

Agricultural products: milk, wheat, sugar beets, barley, potatoes, chicken, rapeseed, pork, beef, oats (2023)
note: top ten agricultural products based on tonnage

Industries: machine tools, electric power equipment, automation equipment, railroad equipment, shipbuilding, aircraft, motor vehicles and parts, electronics and communications equipment, metals, chemicals, coal, petroleum, paper and paper products, food processing, textiles, clothing, other consumer goods

Industrial production growth rate: -0.5% (2024 est.)
note: annual % change in industrial value added based on constant local currency
comparison ranking: 142

Labor force: 35.359 million (2024 est.)
note: number of people ages 15 or older who are employed or seeking work
comparison ranking: 19

Unemployment rate: 4.2% (2024 est.)
4% (2023 est.)
3.8% (2022 est.)
note: % of labor force seeking employment
comparison ranking: 69

Youth unemployment rate (ages 15-24): *total:* 12.4% (2024 est.)
male: 14.9% (2024 est.)
female: 9.7% (2024 est.)
note: % of labor force ages 15-24 seeking employment
comparison ranking: total 99

Population below poverty line: 18.6% (2017 est.)
note: % of population with income below national poverty line

Gini Index coefficient - distribution of family income: 32.4 (2021 est.)
note: index (0-100) of income distribution; higher values represent greater inequality
comparison ranking: 102

Average household expenditures: *on food:* 8.7% of household expenditures (2023 est.)
on alcohol and tobacco: 3% of household expenditures (2023 est.)

Household income or consumption by percentage share: *lowest 10%:* 3% (2021 est.)
highest 10%: 24.6% (2021 est.)
note: % share of income accruing to lowest and highest 10% of population

Remittances: 0.1% of GDP (2024 est.)
0.1% of GDP (2023 est.)
0.1% of GDP (2022 est.)
note: personal transfers and compensation between resident and non-resident individuals/households/entities

Budget: *revenues:* $1.211 trillion (2023 est.)
expenditures: $1.442 trillion (2023 est.)
note: central government revenues (excluding grants) and expenditures converted to US dollars at average official exchange rate for year indicated

Public debt: 138.6% of GDP (2023 est.)
note: central government debt as a % of GDP
comparison ranking: 5

Taxes and other revenues: 27.4% (of GDP) (2023 est.)
note: central government tax revenue as a % of GDP
comparison ranking: 7

Current account balance: -$96.634 billion (2024 est.)
-$118.354 billion (2023 est.)
-$70.962 billion (2022 est.)
note: balance of payments - net trade and primary/secondary income in current dollars
comparison ranking: 193

Exports: $1.117 trillion (2024 est.)
$1.078 trillion (2023 est.)
$1.041 trillion (2022 est.)
note: balance of payments - exports of goods and services in current dollars
comparison ranking: 4

Exports - partners: USA 14%, China 8%, Germany 8%, Netherlands 7%, Ireland 7% (2023)
note: top five export partners based on percentage share of exports

Exports - commodities: cars, gold, gas turbines, packaged medicine, crude petroleum (2023)
note: top five export commodities based on value in dollars

Imports: $1.158 trillion (2024 est.)
$1.114 trillion (2023 est.)
$1.1 trillion (2022 est.)
note: balance of payments - imports of goods and services in current dollars
comparison ranking: 4

Imports - partners: China 13%, USA 11%, Germany 10%, France 5%, Norway 4% (2023)
note: top five import partners based on percentage share of imports

Imports - commodities: cars, gold, crude petroleum, refined petroleum, natural gas (2023)
note: top five import commodities based on value in dollars

Reserves of foreign exchange and gold: $174.598 billion (2024 est.)
$177.915 billion (2023 est.)
$176.41 billion (2022 est.)
note: holdings of gold (year-end prices)/foreign exchange/special drawing rights in current dollars
comparison ranking: 20

Exchange rates: British pounds (GBP) per US dollar -

Exchange rates: 0.782 (2024 est.)
0.805 (2023 est.)
0.811 (2022 est.)
0.727 (2021 est.)
0.78 (2020 est.)

ENERGY

Electricity access: *electrification - total population:* 100% (2022 est.)
electrification - urban areas: 99.9%
electrification - rural areas: 100%

Electricity: *installed generating capacity:* 114.749 million kW (2023 est.)
consumption: 262.166 billion kWh (2023 est.)
exports: 9.449 billion kWh (2023 est.)
imports: 33.212 billion kWh (2023 est.)
transmission/distribution losses: 28.961 billion kWh (2023 est.)
comparison rankings: installed generating capacity 14; consumption 20; exports 25; imports 5; transmission/distribution losses 197

Electricity generation sources: *fossil fuels:* 36.2% of total installed capacity (2023 est.)
nuclear: 13.8% of total installed capacity (2023 est.)
solar: 4.9% of total installed capacity (2023 est.)
wind: 30.7% of total installed capacity (2023 est.)
hydroelectricity: 1.7% of total installed capacity (2023 est.)
biomass and waste: 12.6% of total installed capacity (2023 est.)

Nuclear energy: Number of operational nuclear reactors: 9 (2025)

Number of nuclear reactors under construction: 2 (2025)

Net capacity of operational nuclear reactors: 5.88GW (2025 est.)

Percent of total electricity production: 12.5% (2023 est.)

Number of nuclear reactors permanently shut down: 36 (2025)

Coal: *production:* 1.568 million metric tons (2023 est.)
consumption: 7.372 million metric tons (2023 est.)
exports: 981,000 metric tons (2023 est.)
imports: 6.633 million metric tons (2023 est.)
proven reserves: 26 million metric tons (2023 est.)

Petroleum: *total petroleum production:* 753,000 bbl/day (2023 est.)
refined petroleum consumption: 1.406 million bbl/day (2024 est.)
crude oil estimated reserves: 2.5 billion barrels (2021 est.)

Natural gas: *production:* 34.029 billion cubic meters (2023 est.)
consumption: 63.553 billion cubic meters (2023 est.)
exports: 15.842 billion cubic meters (2023 est.)
imports: 45.226 billion cubic meters (2023 est.)
proven reserves: 180.661 billion cubic meters (2021 est.)

Energy consumption per capita: 94.28 million Btu/person (2023 est.)
comparison ranking: 55

COMMUNICATIONS

Telephones - fixed lines: *total subscriptions:* 26.627 million (2023 est.)
subscriptions per 100 inhabitants: 39 (2023 est.)
comparison ranking: total subscriptions 8

Telephones - mobile cellular: *total subscriptions:* 84.3 million (2023 est.)
subscriptions per 100 inhabitants: 121 (2022 est.)
comparison ranking: total subscriptions 21

Broadcast media: public-service British Broadcasting Corporation (BBC) is the largest broadcasting company in the world; BBC operates multiple TV networks with regional and local TV; mixed system of public and commercial TV broadcasters along with satellite and cable systems provide access to hundreds of international TV stations; BBC operates multiple national, regional, and local radio networks with multiple transmission sites; large number of commercial and satellite radio stations available (2018)

Internet country code: .uk

Internet users: *percent of population:* 96% (2023 est.)

Broadband - fixed subscriptions: *total:* 28.2 million (2023 est.)
subscriptions per 100 inhabitants: 41 (2023 est.)
comparison ranking: total 9

TRANSPORTATION

Civil aircraft registration country code prefix: G

Airports: 1,057 (2025)
comparison ranking: 7

Heliports: 139 (2025)
comparison ranking: 20

Railways: *total:* 16,390 km (2020) 6,167 km electrified

Merchant marine: *total:* 868 (2023)
by type: bulk carrier 34, container ship 46, general cargo 62, oil tanker 13, other 713
note: includes Channel Islands (total fleet 2; general cargo 1, other 1); excludes Isle of Man
comparison ranking: total 29

Ports: *total ports:* 185 (2024)
large: 7
medium: 24
small: 67
very small: 86
size unknown: 1
ports with oil terminals: 67
key ports: Aberdeen, Barrow-in-Furness, Barry, Belfast, Blyth, Bristol, Cardiff, Dundee, Falmouth Harbour, Glasgow, Greenock, Grimsby, Immingham, Kingston-upon-Hull, Leith, Lerwick, Liverpool, London, Londonderry, Lyness, Manchester, Milford Haven, Newport, Peterhead, Plymouth, Portland Harbour, Portsmouth Harbour, Southampton, Sunderland, Teesport, Tynemouth

Transportation - note: begun in 1988 and completed in 1994, the Channel Tunnel (nicknamed the Chunnel) is a 50.5-km (31.4-mi) rail tunnel under the English Channel at the Strait of Dover; it runs from Folkestone, Kent, in England to Coquelles, Pas-de-Calais, in northern France and is the only fixed link between the island of Great Britain and mainland Europe

MILITARY AND SECURITY

Military and security forces: United Kingdom Armed Forces (aka British Armed Forces, aka His Majesty's Armed Forces): British Army, Royal Navy (includes Royal Marines), Royal Air Force (2025)

Military expenditures: 2.4% of GDP (2025 est.)
2.3% of GDP (2024 est.)
2.3% of GDP (2023 est.)
2.3% of GDP (2022 est.)
2.3% of GDP (2021 est.)

Military and security service personnel strengths: approximately 138,000 Regular Forces (75,000 Army including the Gurkhas; 32,000 Navy including the Royal Marines; 31,000 Air Force) (2025)
note: the military also maintains approximately 40-45,000 reserves and other personnel on active duty

Military equipment inventories and acquisitions: the inventory of the British military is comprised mostly of domestically produced weapons and equipment, with a smaller mix of some imported Western weapons systems, particularly from the US; the UK defense industry is capable of producing a wide variety of air, land, and sea weapons systems and is one of the world's top weapons suppliers; it also cooperates with other European countries and the US in the research and development of weapons systems (2025)

Military service age and obligation: some variations by service, but generally 16-36 years of age for enlisted (with parental consent under 18) and 18-29 for officers; minimum length of service 4 years; women serve in all military services including combat roles; conscription abolished in 1963 (2024)
note 1: women made up 11.7% of the military's full-time personnel in 2024
note 2: the British military allows Commonwealth nationals who are current UK residents and have been in the country for at least 5 years to apply; it also accepts Irish citizens
note 3: the British Army has continued the historic practice of recruiting Gurkhas from Nepal to serve in the Brigade of Gurkhas; the British began to recruit Nepalese citizens (Gurkhas) into the East India Company Army during the Anglo-Nepalese War (1814-1816); the Gurkhas subsequently were brought into the British Indian Army and by 1914,

there were 10 Gurkha regiments, collectively known as the Gurkha Brigade; following the partition of India in 1947, an agreement between Nepal, India, and Great Britain allowed for the transfer of the 10 regiments from the British Indian Army to the separate British and Indian armies; four of the regiments were transferred to the British Army, where they have since served continuously as the Brigade of Gurkhas

Military deployments: the British military has more than 8,000 personnel on permanent or long-term rotational deployments around the globe in support of NATO, UN, or other commitments and agreements; key deployments include approximately 1,000 in Brunei, approximately 2,500 in Cyprus (includes 250 for UNFICYP), approximately 900-1,000 in Estonia (NATO), over 1,000 in the Falkland Islands, 500-600 in Gibraltar, and more than 1,000 in the Middle East; its air and naval forces conduct missions on a global basis; the British military also participates in large scale NATO exercises, including providing some 16,000 personnel for the 6-month 2024 Steadfast Defender exercise (2024)

Military - note: the British military has a long history, a global presence, and a wide range of missions and responsibilities, including protecting the UK, its dependencies and territories, national interests, and values, preventing conflict, providing humanitarian assistance, participating in international peacekeeping, building relationships, and fulfilling the UK's alliance and treaty commitments; in addition to its role in the UN, the UK is a leading member of NATO

the UK is a member of the Five Power Defense Arrangements (FPDA), a series of mutual assistance agreements reached in 1971 embracing Australia, Malaysia, New Zealand, Singapore, and the UK; in 2014, the UK led the formation of the Joint Expeditionary Force (JEF), a pool of high-readiness military forces from the Baltic and Scandinavian countries intended to respond to a wide range of contingencies both in peacetime and in times of crisis or conflict; the UK military also has strong bilateral ties with a variety of foreign militaries, particularly the US, with which it has a mutual defense treaty; British and US military forces have routinely operated side-by-side across a wide range of operations; other close military relationships include Australia, France, Germany, and the Netherlands; in 2010, for example, France and the UK signed a declaration on defense and security cooperation that included greater military interoperability and a Combined Joint Expeditionary Force (CJEF), a deployable, combined Anglo-French military force for use in a range of crisis scenarios (2025)

SPACE

Space agency/agencies: UK Space Agency (UKSA; established in 2010) (2025)

note 1: the UKSA replaced the British National Space Center (BNSC; established in 1985); in 2025, the UK Government announced that the UKSA would be absorbed into the Department for Science, Innovation, and Technology (DSIT) as of April 2026

note 2: in 2021, the British formed the joint service UK Space Command under the Ministry of Defense for military space operations, space workforce, and space capabilities

Space launch site(s): Spaceport 1 (Outer Hebrides, Scotland); Spaceport Machrihanish (Argyll, Scotland); Glasgow Prestwick (South Ayrshire, Scotland); Spaceport Snowdonia (Gwynedd, Wales); SaxaVord UK Spaceport (Unst, Shetland Islands); Sutherland Spaceport (Sutherland, Scotland); Sutherland, Scotland (Cornwall Airport Newquay, Cornwall) (2024)

Space program overview: has a long-standing and comprehensive national space program; is active across all areas of the space sector outside of human space flight, including satellite launch vehicles (SLVs)/rockets and their components, space probes, satellites and satellite subcomponents, space sensors, spaceports, and various other space-related capabilities and technologies; is a founding member of the European Space Agency (ESA) and heavily involved in ESA programs; has bi-lateral relations with many ESA members and is a close partner of the US NASA; since 2016 has forged over 350 relationships with international organizations across nearly 50 countries; participates in international programs such as the International Space Station and the James Webb Space Telescope; has a large commercial space sector involved in the production of SLVs and their components, satellites, satellite subcomponents and sensors, and other space-related technologies; the UK has a space industrial plan, and the UKSA has provided funding to encourage and support commercial space projects (2025)

note: further details about the key activities, programs, and milestones of the country's space program, as well as government spending estimates on the space sector, appear in the Space Programs reference guide

TERRORISM

Terrorist group(s): Terrorist group(s): Continuity Irish Republican Army (CIRA); Islamic State of Iraq and ash-Sham (ISIS); al-Qa'ida; Real Irish Republican Army (RIRA)

note: details about the history, aims, leadership, organization, areas of operation, tactics, targets, weapons, size, and sources of support of the group(s) appear(s) in Appendix T

TRANSNATIONAL ISSUES

Refugees and internally displaced persons: *refugees:* 640,460 (2024 est.)

stateless persons: 4,672 (2024 est.)

Illicit drugs: USG identification: major precursor-chemical producer (2025)

UNITED STATES

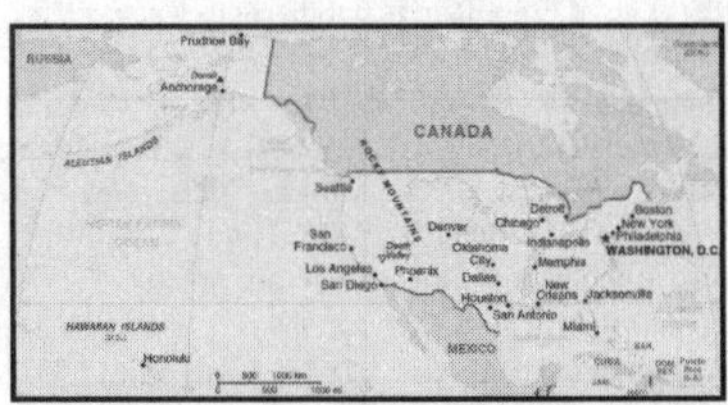

INTRODUCTION

Background: Thirteen of Britain's American colonies broke with the mother country in 1776 and were recognized as the new nation of the United States of America following the Treaty of Paris in 1783. During the 19th and 20th centuries, 37 new states were added as the nation expanded across the North American continent and acquired a number of overseas possessions. Two of the most traumatic experiences in the nation's history were the Civil War (1861-65), in which a northern Union of states defeated a secessionist Confederacy of 11 southern slave states, and the Great Depression of the 1930s, an economic downturn during which about a quarter of the labor force lost its jobs. Buoyed by victories in World Wars I and II and the end of the Cold War in 1991, the US remains the world's most powerful nation state. Since the end of World War II, the economy has achieved relatively steady growth, low unemployment, and rapid advances in technology.

GEOGRAPHY

Location: North America, bordering both the North Atlantic Ocean and the North Pacific Ocean, between Canada and Mexico

Geographic coordinates: 38 00 N, 97 00 W

Map references: North America

Area: *total:* 9,833,517 sq km

land: 9,147,593 sq km

water: 685,924 sq km

note: includes only the 50 states and District of Columbia, no overseas territories

comparison ranking: total 4

Area - comparative: about half the size of Russia; about three-tenths the size of Africa; about half the size of South America (or slightly larger than Brazil); slightly larger than China; more than twice the size of the European Union

Land boundaries: *total:* 12,002 km

border countries (2): Canada 8,891 km (including 2,475 km with Alaska); Mexico 3,111 km

note: US Naval Base at Guantanamo Bay, Cuba is leased by the US and is part of Cuba; the base boundary is 28.5 km

Coastline: 19,924 km

Maritime claims: *territorial sea:* 12 nm

contiguous zone: 24 nm

exclusive economic zone: 200 nm

continental shelf: not specified

Climate: mostly temperate, but tropical in Hawaii and Florida, arctic in Alaska, semiarid in the great plains west of the Mississippi River, and arid in the Great Basin of the southwest; low winter temperatures in the northwest are ameliorated occasionally in January and February by warm chinook winds from the eastern slopes of the Rocky Mountains

note: many consider Mount McKinley, the highest peak in the United States, to be the world's coldest mountain because of its combination of high elevation and its subarctic location at 63 degrees north latitude; permanent snow and ice cover over 75 percent of the mountain, and enormous glaciers, up to 45 miles long and 3,700 feet thick, spider out from its base in every direction; it is home to some of the world's coldest and most violent weather, where winds of over 150 miles per hour and temperatures of -93°F have been recorded.

Terrain: vast central plain, mountains in west, hills and low mountains in east; rugged mountains and broad river valleys in Alaska; rugged, volcanic topography in Hawaii

Elevation: *highest point:* Mount McKinley 6,190 m (highest point in North America)
lowest point: Death Valley (lowest point in North America) -86 m
mean elevation: 760 m
note 1: Mount McKinley is one of the most striking features on the entire planet; at 20,310 feet, it is the crowning peak of the Alaska Range and the highest mountain on North America; it towers three and one-half vertical miles above its base, making it a mile taller from base to summit than Mt. Everest; McKinley's base sits at about 2,000 feet above sea level and rises over three and one-half miles to its 20,310 foot summit; Everest begins on a 14,000-foot high plain, then summits at 29,028 feet
note 2: the peak of Mauna Kea (4,207 m above sea level) on the island of Hawaii rises about 10,200 m above the Pacific Ocean floor; by this measurement, it is the world's tallest mountain – higher than Mount Everest (8,850 m), which is recognized as the tallest mountain above sea level

Natural resources: coal, copper, lead, molybdenum, phosphates, rare earth elements, uranium, bauxite, gold, iron, mercury, nickel, potash, silver, tungsten, zinc, petroleum, natural gas, timber, arable land
note: the US has the world's largest coal reserves with 491 billion short tons accounting for 27% of the world's total

Land use: *agricultural land:* 45.1% (2022 est.)
arable land: 16.6% (2022 est.)
permanent crops: 0.3% (2022 est.)
permanent pasture: 28.2% (2022 est.)
forest: 33.9% (2022 est.)
other: 21% (2022 est.)

Irrigated land: 234,782 sq km (2017)

Major lakes (area sq km): *fresh water lake(s):* Michigan – 57,750 sq km; Superior* – 53,348 sq km; Huron* – 23,597 sq km; Erie* – 12,890 sq km; Ontario* – 9,220 sq km; Lake of the Woods – 4,350 sq km; Iliamna – 2,590 sq km; Okeechobee – 1,810 sq km; Belcharof – 1,190 sq km; Red – 1,170 sq km; Saint Clair – 1,113 sq km; Champlain – 1,100 sq km
note - Great Lakes* area shown as US waters
salt water lake(s): Great Salt – 4,360 sq km; Pontchartrain – 1,620 sq km; Selawik – 1,400 sq km; Salton Sea – 950 sq km

Major rivers (by length in km): Missouri - 3,768 km; Mississippi - 3,544 km; Yukon river mouth (shared with Canada [s]) - 3,190 km; Saint Lawrence (shared with Canada) - 3,058 km; Rio Grande river source (mouth shared with Mexico) - 3,057 km; Colorado river source (shared with Mexico [m]) - 2,333 km; Arkansas - 2,348 km; Columbia river mouth (shared with Canada [s]) - 2,250 km; Red - 2,188 km; Ohio - 2,102 km); Snake - 1,670 km
note: [s] after country name indicates river source; [m] after country name indicates river mouth

Major watersheds (area sq km): Atlantic Ocean drainage: *(Gulf of America)* Mississippi* (3,202,185 sq km); Rio Grande (607,965 sq km); *(Gulf of Saint Lawrence)* Saint Lawrence* (1,049,636 sq km total, US only 505,000 sq km)

Pacific Ocean drainage: Yukon* (847,620 sq km, US only 23,820 sq km); Colorado (703,148 sq km); Columbia* (657,501 sq km, US only 554,501 sq km)
note: watersheds shared with Canada shown with *

Major aquifers: Northern Great Plains Aquifer, Cambrian-Ordovician Aquifer System, Californian Central Valley Aquifer System, Ogallala Aquifer (High Plains), Atlantic and Gulf Coastal Plains Aquifer

Population distribution: large urban clusters are spread throughout the eastern half of the US (particularly the Great Lakes area, northeast, east, and southeast) and the western-tier states; mountainous areas such as the Rocky Mountains and Appalachians, deserts in the southwest, the dense boreal forests in the extreme north, and the central prairie states are less densely populated; Alaska's population is concentrated along its southern coast, particularly around Anchorage, and Hawaii's is centered on the island of Oahu

Natural hazards: tsunamis; volcanoes; earthquake activity around Pacific Basin; hurricanes along the Atlantic and Gulf of America coasts; tornadoes in the Midwest and Southeast; mud slides in California; forest fires in the west; flooding; permafrost in northern Alaska is a major impediment to development
volcanism: volcanic activity in the Hawaiian Islands, Western Alaska, the Pacific Northwest, and in the Northern Mariana Islands; Mauna Loa (4,170 m) in Hawaii and Mount Rainier (4,392 m) in Washington have been deemed Decade Volcanoes by the International Association of Volcanology and Chemistry of the Earth's Interior, worthy of study due to their explosive history and close proximity to human populations; Pavlof (2,519 m) is the most active volcano in Alaska's Aleutian Arc and poses a significant threat to intercontinental air travel; St. Helens (2,549 m), famous for the devastating 1980 eruption, remains active today; other historically active volcanoes are mostly concentrated in the Aleutian arc and Hawaii, including (in Alaska) Aniakchak, Augustine, Chiginagak, Fourpeaked, Iliamna, Katmai, Kupreanof, Martin, Novarupta, Redoubt, Spurr, Wrangell, Trident, Ugashik-Peulik, Ukinrek Maars, Veniaminof, (in Hawaii) Haleakala, Kilauea, Loihi, (in the Northern Mariana Islands) Anatahan, (in the Pacific Northwest) Mount Baker, and Mount Hood; see note 2 under "Geography - note"

Geography - note: *note 1:* world's third-largest country by size (after Russia and Canada) and by population (after China and India); Mt. McKinley is the highest point (6,190 m; 20,308 ft) in North America, and Death Valley is the lowest point (-86 m; -282 ft)
note 2: the western US coast and the southern coast of Alaska lie along the Ring of Fire, which is a belt bordering the Pacific Ocean that contains about 75% of the world's volcanoes and up to 90% of the world's earthquakes
note 3: the Aleutian Islands are a chain of volcanic islands that divide the Bering Sea (north) from the main Pacific Ocean (south); they extend about 1,800 km (1,118 mi) westward from the Alaskan Peninsula; the archipelago consists of 14 larger islands, 55 smaller islands, and hundreds of islets; there are 41 active volcanoes on the islands, which together form a large northern section of the Ring of Fire
note 4: Mammoth Cave, in west-central Kentucky, is the world's longest known cave system with more than 650 km (405 miles) of surveyed passageways, which is nearly twice as long as the second-longest cave system, the Sac Actun underwater cave in Mexico (see "Geography -note" under Mexico)
note 5: Kazumura Cave on the island of Hawaii is the world's longest and deepest lava-tube cave; it has been surveyed at 66 km (41 mi) long and 1,102 m (3,614 ft) deep
note 6: Bracken Cave outside San Antonio, Texas is the world's largest bat cave and the summer home to the largest colony of bats in the world; an estimated 20 million Mexican free-tailed bats roost in the cave from March to October, making it the world's largest known concentration of mammals

PEOPLE AND SOCIETY

Population: *total:* 341,963,408 (2024 est.)
male: 168,598,780
female: 173,364,628
comparison rankings: total 3; male 3; female 3

Nationality: *noun:* American(s)
adjective: American

Ethnic groups: White 61.6%, Black or African American 12.4%, Asian 6%, Indigenous and Alaska native 1.1%, Native Hawaiian and Other Pacific Islander 0.2%, other 8.4%, two or more races 10.2% (2020 est.)
note: a separate listing for Hispanic is not included because the US Census Bureau considers Hispanic to mean persons of Spanish/Hispanic/Latino origin including those of Mexican, Cuban, Puerto Rican, Dominican Republic, Spanish, and Central or South American origin living in the US who may be of any race or ethnic group (White, Black, Asian, etc.); an estimated 18.7% of the total US population is Hispanic as of 2020

Languages: English only (official) 78.2%, Spanish 13.4%, Chinese 1.1%, other 7.3% (2017 est.)
note: data represent the language spoken at home; English is the official national language as of March 2025, but English previously had official status in 32 of the 50 states; Hawaiian is an official language in the state of Hawaii, and 20 indigenous languages are official in Alaska

Religions: Protestant 46.5%, Roman Catholic 20.8%, Jewish 1.9%, Church of Jesus Christ 1.6%, other Christian 0.9%, Muslim 0.9%, Jehovah's Witness 0.8%, Buddhist 0.7%, Hindu 0.7%, other 1.8%, unaffiliated 22.8%, don't know/refused 0.6% (2014 est.)

Age structure: *0-14 years:* 18.1% (male 31,618,532/female 30,254,223)
15-64 years: 63.4% (male 108,553,822/female 108,182,491)
65 years and over: 18.5% (2024 est.) (male 28,426,426/female 34,927,914)

Dependency ratios: *total dependency ratio:* 55.4 (2024 est.)
youth dependency ratio: 27 (2024 est.)
elderly dependency ratio: 28.4 (2024 est.)
potential support ratio: 3.5 (2024 est.)

Median age: *total:* 38.9 years (2022 est.)
male: 37.8 years
female: 40 years
comparison ranking: total 69

Population growth rate: 0.67% (2024 est.)
comparison ranking: 131

Birth rate: 12.2 births/1,000 population (2024 est.)
comparison ranking: 145

Death rate: 8.5 deaths/1,000 population (2024 est.)
comparison ranking: 72

Net migration rate: 3 migrant(s)/1,000 population (2024 est.)
comparison ranking: 38

Population distribution: large urban clusters are spread throughout the eastern half of the US (particularly the Great Lakes area, northeast, east, and southeast) and the western-tier states; mountainous areas such as the Rocky Mountains and Appalachians, deserts in the southwest, the dense boreal forests in the extreme north, and the central prairie states are less densely populated; Alaska's population is concentrated along its southern coast, particularly around Anchorage, and Hawaii's is centered on the island of Oahu

Urbanization: *urban population:* 83.3% of total population (2023)
rate of urbanization: 0.96% annual rate of change (2020-25 est.)

Major urban areas - population: 18.937 million New York-Newark, 12.534 million Los Angeles-Long Beach-Santa Ana, 8.937 million Chicago, 6.707 million Houston, 6.574 million Dallas-Fort Worth, 5.490 million WASHINGTON, D.C. (capital) (2023)

Sex ratio: *at birth:* 1.05 male(s)/female
0-14 years: 1.05 male(s)/female
15-64 years: 1 male(s)/female
65 years and over: 0.81 male(s)/female
total population: 0.97 male(s)/female (2024 est.)

Mother's mean age at first birth: 27 years (2019 est.)

Maternal mortality ratio: 17 deaths/100,000 live births (2023 est.)
comparison ranking: 130

Infant mortality rate: *total:* 5.1 deaths/1,000 live births (2024 est.)
male: 5.4 deaths/1,000 live births
female: 4.7 deaths/1,000 live births
comparison ranking: total 173

Life expectancy at birth: *total population:* 80.9 years (2024 est.)
male: 78.7 years
female: 83.1 years
comparison ranking: total population 49

Total fertility rate: 1.84 children born/woman (2024 est.)
comparison ranking: 133

Gross reproduction rate: 0.9 (2024 est.)

Drinking water source: *improved: urban:* 100% of population (2022 est.)
rural: 100% of population (2022 est.)
total: 100% of population (2022 est.)
unimproved: urban: 0% of population (2022 est.)
rural: 0% of population (2022 est.)
total: 0% of population (2022 est.)

Health expenditure: 16.6% of GDP (2022)
24.7% of national budget (2022 est.)

Physician density: 3.68 physicians/1,000 population (2022)

Hospital bed density: 2.7 beds/1,000 population (2020 est.)

Sanitation facility access: *improved: urban:* 99.9% of population (2022 est.)
rural: 98.5% of population (2022 est.)
total: 99.6% of population (2022 est.)
unimproved: urban: 0.1% of population (2022 est.)
rural: 1.5% of population (2022 est.)
total: 0.4% of population (2022 est.)

Obesity - adult prevalence rate: 36.2% (2016)
comparison ranking: 12

Alcohol consumption per capita: *total:* 8.93 liters of pure alcohol (2019 est.)
beer: 3.97 liters of pure alcohol (2019 est.)
wine: 1.67 liters of pure alcohol (2019 est.)
spirits: 3.29 liters of pure alcohol (2019 est.)
other alcohols: 0 liters of pure alcohol (2019 est.)
comparison ranking: total 35

Tobacco use: *total:* 22.1% (2025 est.)
male: 27.7% (2025 est.)
female: 16.7% (2025 est.)
comparison ranking: total 52

Children under the age of 5 years underweight: 0.4% (2017/18)
comparison ranking: 115

Currently married women (ages 15-49): 51.9% (2023 est.)

Education expenditure: 5.4% of GDP (2022 est.)
14% national budget (2022 est.)
comparison ranking: Education expenditure (% GDP) 49

School life expectancy (primary to tertiary education): *total:* 16 years (2022 est.)
male: 15 years (2022 est.)
female: 17 years (2022 est.)

ENVIRONMENT

Environmental issues: air pollution; water pollution from runoff of pesticides and fertilizers; declining natural freshwater resources in the west; deforestation; mining; desertification; species conservation; invasive species

International environmental agreements: *party to:* Air Pollution, Air Pollution-Heavy Metals, Air Pollution-Multi-effect Protocol, Air Pollution-Nitrogen Oxides, Antarctic-Environmental Protection, Antarctic-Marine Living Resources, Antarctic Seals, Antarctic Treaty, Climate Change, Desertification, Endangered Species, Environmental Modification, Marine Dumping-London Convention, Marine Life Conservation, Nuclear Test Ban, Ozone Layer Protection, Ship Pollution, Tropical Timber 2006, Wetlands, Whaling
signed, but not ratified: Air Pollution-Persistent Organic Pollutants, Air Pollution-Volatile Organic Compounds, Biodiversity, Climate Change-Kyoto Protocol, Comprehensive Nuclear Test Ban, Hazardous Wastes, Marine Dumping-London Protocol

Climate: mostly temperate, but tropical in Hawaii and Florida, arctic in Alaska, semiarid in the great plains west of the Mississippi River, and arid in the Great Basin of the southwest; low winter temperatures in the northwest are ameliorated occasionally in January and February by warm chinook winds from the eastern slopes of the Rocky Mountains
note: many consider Mount McKinley, the highest peak in the United States, to be the world's coldest mountain because of its combination of high elevation and its subarctic location at 63 degrees north latitude; permanent snow and ice cover over 75 percent of the mountain, and enormous glaciers, up to 45 miles long and 3,700 feet thick, spider out from its base in every direction; it is home to some of the world's coldest and most violent weather, where winds of over 150 miles per hour and temperatures of -93°F have been recorded.

Urbanization: *urban population:* 83.3% of total population (2023)
rate of urbanization: 0.96% annual rate of change (2020-25 est.)

Carbon dioxide emissions: 4.795 billion metric tonnes of CO2 (2023 est.)
from coal and metallurgical coke: 777.302 million metric tonnes of CO2 (2023 est.)
from petroleum and other liquids: 2.258 billion metric tonnes of CO2 (2023 est.)
from consumed natural gas: 1.76 billion metric tonnes of CO2 (2023 est.)
comparison ranking: total emissions 2

Particulate matter emissions: 7.4 micrograms per cubic meter (2019 est.)

Methane emissions: *energy:* 20,500.6 kt (2022-2024 est.)
agriculture: 9,063.9 kt (2019-2021 est.)
waste: 4,974 kt (2019-2021 est.)
other: 758.6 kt (2019-2021 est.)

Waste and recycling: *municipal solid waste generated annually:* 265.225 million tons (2024 est.)
percent of municipal solid waste recycled: 14.8% (2022 est.)

Total water withdrawal: *municipal:* 58.39 billion cubic meters (2022 est.)
industrial: 209.7 billion cubic meters (2022 est.)
agricultural: 176.2 billion cubic meters (2022 est.)

Total renewable water resources: 3.069 trillion cubic meters (2022 est.)

GOVERNMENT

Country name: *conventional long form:* United States of America
conventional short form: United States
abbreviation: US or USA
etymology: the name America was first used in 1507 and is derived from the first name of Amerigo VESPUCCI (1454-1512), an Italian explorer, navigator, and cartographer; the name United States first appeared in a document subtitle during the discussions that led to the Declaration of Independence in 1776

Government type: constitutional federal republic

Capital: *name:* Washington, D.C.
geographic coordinates: 38 53 N, 77 02 W
time difference: UTC-5 (during Standard Time)
daylight saving time: +1hr, begins second Sunday in March; ends first Sunday in November; note - no DST for Hawaii and most of Arizona
time zone note: the 50 United States cover six time zones
etymology: named after George WASHINGTON (1732-1799), the first president of the United States

Administrative divisions: 50 states and 1 district*; Alabama, Alaska, Arizona, Arkansas, California, Colorado, Connecticut, Delaware, District of Columbia*, Florida, Georgia, Hawaii, Idaho, Illinois, Indiana, Iowa, Kansas, Kentucky, Louisiana, Maine, Maryland, Massachusetts, Michigan, Minnesota, Mississippi, Missouri, Montana, Nebraska, Nevada, New Hampshire, New Jersey, New Mexico, New York, North Carolina, North Dakota, Ohio, Oklahoma, Oregon, Pennsylvania, Rhode Island, South Carolina, South Dakota, Tennessee, Texas, Utah, Vermont, Virginia,

Washington, West Virginia, Wisconsin, Wyoming

Dependent areas: American Samoa, Baker Island, Guam, Howland Island, Jarvis Island, Johnston Atoll, Kingman Reef, Midway Islands, Navassa Island, Northern Mariana Islands, Palmyra Atoll, Puerto Rico, Virgin Islands, Wake Island (14)
note: from 18 July 1947 until 1 October 1994, the US administered the Trust Territory of the Pacific Islands; it entered into a political relationship with all four political entities: the Northern Mariana Islands is a commonwealth in political union with the US (effective 3 November 1986); the Republic of the Marshall Islands signed a Compact of Free Association with the US (effective 21 October 1986); the Federated States of Micronesia signed a Compact of Free Association with the US (effective 3 November 1986); Palau concluded a Compact of Free Association with the US (effective 1 October 1994)

Legal system: common law system based on English common law at the federal level; state legal systems based on common law, except Louisiana, where state law is based on Napoleonic civil code; judicial review of legislative acts

Constitution: *history:* previous 1781 (Articles of Confederation and Perpetual Union); latest drafted July - September 1787, submitted to the Congress of the Confederation 20 September 1787, submitted for states' ratification 28 September 1787, ratification completed by nine of the 13 states 21 June 1788, effective 4 March 1789
amendment process: proposed as a "joint resolution" by Congress, which requires a two-thirds majority vote in both the House of Representatives and the Senate or by a constitutional convention called for by at least two thirds of the state legislatures; passage requires ratification by three fourths of the state legislatures or passage in state-held constitutional conventions as specified by Congress; the US president has no role in the constitutional amendment process

International law organization participation: withdrew acceptance of compulsory ICJ jurisdiction in 2005; withdrew acceptance of ICCt jurisdiction in 2002

Citizenship: *citizenship by birth:* yes
citizenship by descent only: yes
dual citizenship recognized: no, but the US government acknowledges such situtations exist; US citizens are not encouraged to seek dual citizenship since it limits protection by the US
residency requirement for naturalization: 5 years

Suffrage: 18 years of age; universal

Executive branch: *chief of state:* President Donald J. TRUMP (since 20 January 2025)
head of government: President Donald J. TRUMP (since 20 January 2025)
cabinet: Cabinet appointed by the president, approved by the Senate
election/appointment process: president and vice president indirectly elected on the same ballot by the Electoral College of electors chosen from each state; president and vice president serve a 4-year term (eligible for a second term)
most recent election date: 5 November 2024
election results: 2024: Donald J. TRUMP elected president; electoral vote - Donald J. TRUMP (Republican Party) 312, Kamala HARRIS (Democratic Party) 226; percent of direct popular vote - Donald J. TRUMP 49.8%, Kamala HARRIS 48.3%, other 1.9%
2020: Joseph R. BIDEN, Jr. elected president; electoral vote - Joseph R. BIDEN, Jr. (Democratic Party) 306, Donald J. TRUMP (Republican Party) 232; percent of direct popular vote - Joseph R. BIDEN Jr. 51.3%, Donald J. TRUMP 46.9%, other 1.8%
expected date of next election: 7 November 2028
note: the president is both chief of state and head of government

Legislative branch: *legislature name:* Congress
legislative structure: bicameral
note: in addition to the regular members of the House of Representatives there are 6 non-voting delegates elected from the District of Columbia and the US territories of American Samoa, Guam, Puerto Rico, the Northern Mariana Islands, and the Virgin Islands; these are single seat constituencies directly elected by simple majority vote to serve a 2-year term (except for the resident commissioner of Puerto Rico who serves a 4-year term); the delegate can vote when serving on a committee and when the House meets as the Committee of the Whole House, but not when legislation is submitted for a "full floor" House vote; election of delegates last held on 8 November 2022 (next to be held on 3 November 2024)

Legislative branch - lower chamber: *chamber name:* House of Representatives
number of seats: 435 (all directly elected)
electoral system: plurality/majority
scope of elections: full renewal
term in office: 2 years
most recent election date: 11/5/2024
parties elected and seats per party: Republican Party (220); Democratic Party (215)
percentage of women in chamber: 29%
expected date of next election: November 2026

Legislative branch - upper chamber: *chamber name:* Senate
number of seats: 100 (all directly elected)
electoral system: plurality/majority
scope of elections: partial renewal
term in office: 6 years
most recent election date: 11/5/2024
parties elected and seats per party: Republican Party (15); Democratic Party (19)
percentage of women in chamber: 26%
expected date of next election: November 2026

Judicial branch: *highest court(s):* US Supreme Court (consists of 9 justices – the chief justice and 8 associate justices)
judge selection and term of office: president nominates and, with the advice and consent of the Senate, appoints Supreme Court justices; justices serve for life
subordinate courts: Courts of Appeal (includes the US Court of Appeal for the Federal District and 12 regional appeals courts); 94 federal district courts in 50 states and territories
note: the US court system consists of the federal court system and the state court systems; each court system is responsible for hearing certain types of cases, but neither is completely independent of the other, and the systems often interact

Political parties: Democratic Party
Green Party
Libertarian Party
Republican Party

International organization participation: ADB (nonregional member), AfDB (nonregional member), ANZUS, APEC, Arctic Council, ARF, ASEAN (dialogue partner), Australia Group, BIS, BSEC (observer), CBSS (observer), CD, CE (observer), CERN (observer), CICA (observer), CP, EAPC, EAS, EBRD, EITI (implementing country), FAO, FATF, G-5, G-7, G-8, G-10, G-20, IADB, IAEA, IBRD, ICAO, ICC (national committees), ICRM, IDA, IEA, IFAD, IFC, IFRCS, IGAD (partners), IHO, ILO, IMF, IMO, IMSO, Interpol, IOC, IOM, ISO, ITSO, ITU, ITUC (NGOs), MIGA, MINUSTAH, MONUSCO, NAFTA, NATO, NEA, NSG, OAS, OECD, OPCW, OSCE, Pacific Alliance (observer), Paris Club, PCA, PIF (partner), Quad, SAARC (observer), SELEC (observer), SICA (observer), SPC, UN, UNCTAD, UNESCO, UNHCR, UNHRC, UNITAR, UNMIL, UNMISS, UNOOSA, UNRWA, UN Security Council (permanent), UNTSO, UPU, USMCA, Wassenaar Arrangement, WCO, WHO, WIPO, WMO, WTO, ZC

Independence: 4 July 1776 (declared independence from Great Britain); 3 September 1783 (recognized by Great Britain)

National holiday: Independence Day, 4 July (1776)

Flag: *description:* 13 equal horizontal stripes of red (top and bottom) alternating with white; a blue rectangle in the upper-left corner has 50 five-pointed white stars, arranged in nine offset horizontal rows of six stars (top and bottom) alternating with rows of five stars
meaning: the stars represent the 50 states, and the stripes represent the 13 original colonies; blue stands for loyalty, devotion, truth, justice, and friendship; red for courage, zeal, and fervency; white for purity and rectitude of conduct
note 1: sometimes referred to by its nickname of "Old Glory"
note 2: the design and colors have been the basis for a number of other flags, including Chile, Liberia, Malaysia, and Puerto Rico

National symbol(s): bald eagle

National color(s): red, white, blue

National anthem(s): *title:* "The Star-Spangled Banner"
lyrics/music: Francis Scott KEY/John Stafford SMITH
history: adopted 1931; during the War of 1812, Francis Scott KEY witnessed the successful American defense of Baltimore's Fort McHenry against a British naval bombardment, later writing a poem about it that would become the US national anthem; the lyrics were set to the tune of "The Anacreontic Song;" there are four verses, but only the first verse is sung

National heritage: *total World Heritage Sites:* 26 (13 cultural, 12 natural, 1 mixed); note - includes one site in Puerto Rico
selected World Heritage Site locales: Yellowstone National Park (n); Grand Canyon National Park (n); Cahokia Mounds State Historic Site (c); Independence Hall (c); Statue of Liberty (c); Yosemite National Park (n); Papahānaumokuākea (m); Monumental Earthworks of Poverty Point (c); The 20th-Century Architecture of Frank Lloyd Wright (c); Mesa Verde National Park (c); Mammoth Cave National Park (n); Monticello and the University of Virginia in Charlottesville (c); Olympic National Park (n); Everglades National Park (n); Kluane / Wrangell-St. Elias / Glacier Bay / Tatshenshini-Alsek (n); Redwood National and State Parks (n); Great Smoky Mountains National Park (n); La Fortaleza and San Juan National Historic Site in Puerto Rico (c); Chaco Culture (c); Hawaii Volcanoes National Park (n); Taos Pueblo

(c); Carlsbad Caverns National Park (n); Waterton Glacier International Peace Park (n); Moravian Church Settlements (c); San Antonio Missions (c); Hopewell Ceremonial Earthworks (c)

ECONOMY

Economic overview: world's largest economy by nominal GDP; largest importer and second-largest exporter; home to leading financial exchanges and global reserve currency; high and growing public debt; inflation moderating but remains above pre-pandemic levels

Real GDP (purchasing power parity): $25.676 trillion (2024 est.)
$24.977 trillion (2023 est.)
$24.276 trillion (2022 est.)
note: data in 2021 dollars
comparison ranking: 2

Real GDP growth rate: 2.8% (2024 est.)
2.9% (2023 est.)
2.5% (2022 est.)
note: annual GDP % growth based on constant local currency
comparison ranking: 124

Real GDP per capita: $75,500 (2024 est.)
$74,200 (2023 est.)
$72,700 (2022 est.)
note: data in 2021 dollars
comparison ranking: 13

GDP (official exchange rate): $29.185 trillion (2024 est.)
note: data in current dollars at official exchange rate

Inflation rate (consumer prices): 2.9% (2024 est.)
4.1% (2023 est.)
8% (2022 est.)
note: annual % change based on consumer prices
comparison ranking: 87

GDP - composition, by sector of origin: *agriculture:* 0.9% (2024 est.)
industry: 17.3% (2024 est.)
services: 79.7% (2024 est.)
note: figures may not total 100% due to non-allocated consumption not captured in sector-reported data
comparison rankings: agriculture 177; industry 154; services 12

GDP - composition, by end use: *household consumption:* 67.9% (2024 est.)
government consumption: 13.4% (2024 est.)
investment in fixed capital: 21.6% (2024 est.)
investment in inventories: 0.1% (2024 est.)
exports of goods and services: 10.9% (2024 est.)
imports of goods and services: -14% (2024 est.)
note: figures may not total 100% due to rounding or gaps in data collection

Agricultural products: maize, soybeans, milk, wheat, sugar beets, sugarcane, potatoes, chicken, pork, tomatoes (2023)
note: top ten agricultural products based on tonnage

Industries: highly diversified, world leading, high-technology innovator, second-largest industrial output in the world; petroleum, steel, motor vehicles, aerospace, telecommunications, chemicals, electronics, food processing, consumer goods, lumber, mining

Industrial production growth rate: 3.25% (2021 est.)
note: annual % change in industrial value added based on constant local currency
comparison ranking: 76

Labor force: 174.174 million (2024 est.)
note: number of people ages 15 or older who are employed or seeking work
comparison ranking: 3

Unemployment rate: 4.2% (2024 est.)
3.7% (2023 est.)
3.7% (2022 est.)
note: % of labor force seeking employment
comparison ranking: 67

Youth unemployment rate (ages 15-24): *total:* 9.4% (2024 est.)
male: 10.4% (2024 est.)
female: 8.3% (2024 est.)
note: % of labor force ages 15-24 seeking employment
comparison ranking: total 128

Gini Index coefficient - distribution of family income: 41.8 (2023 est.)
note: index (0-100) of income distribution; higher values represent greater inequality
comparison ranking: 34

Average household expenditures: *on food:* 6.8% of household expenditures (2023 est.)
on alcohol and tobacco: 1.9% of household expenditures (2023 est.)

Household income or consumption by percentage share: *lowest 10%:* 1.8% (2023 est.)
highest 10%: 30.4% (2023 est.)
note: % share of income accruing to lowest and highest 10% of population

Remittances: 0% of GDP (2024 est.)
0% of GDP (2023 est.)
0% of GDP (2022 est.)
note: personal transfers and compensation between resident and non-resident individuals/households/entities

Budget: *revenues:* $4.877 trillion (2023 est.)
expenditures: $6.857 trillion (2023 est.)
note: central government revenues (excluding grants) and expenditures converted to US dollars at average official exchange rate for year indicated

Public debt: 114.8% of GDP (2023 est.)
note: central government debt as a % of GDP
comparison ranking: 12

Taxes and other revenues: 10.6% (of GDP) (2023 est.)
note: central government tax revenue as a % of GDP
comparison ranking: 126

Current account balance: -$1.134 trillion (2024 est.)
-$905.378 billion (2023 est.)
-$1.012 trillion (2022 est.)
note: balance of payments - net trade and primary/secondary income in current dollars
comparison ranking: 194

Exports: $3.191 trillion (2024 est.)
$3.072 trillion (2023 est.)
$3.039 trillion (2022 est.)
note: balance of payments - exports of goods and services in current dollars
comparison ranking: 2

Exports - partners: Canada 14%, Mexico 13%, China 8%, Germany 5%, Japan 4% (2023)
note: top five export partners based on percentage share of exports

Exports - commodities: crude petroleum, refined petroleum, natural gas, gas turbines, cars (2023)
note: top five export commodities based on value in dollars

Imports: $4.108 trillion (2024 est.)
$3.857 trillion (2023 est.)
$3.984 trillion (2022 est.)
note: balance of payments - imports of goods and services in current dollars
comparison ranking: 1

Imports - partners: Mexico 15%, China 15%, Canada 14%, Germany 5%, Japan 5% (2023)
note: top five import partners based on percentage share of imports

Imports - commodities: cars, crude petroleum, broadcasting equipment, computers, garments (2023)
note: top five import commodities based on value in dollars

Reserves of foreign exchange and gold: $910.037 billion (2024 est.)
$773.426 billion (2023 est.)
$706.644 billion (2022 est.)
note: holdings of gold (year-end prices)/foreign exchange/special drawing rights in current dollars
comparison ranking: 3

Exchange rates: British pounds per US dollar: 0.782 (2024 est.), 0.805 (2023 est.), 0.811 (2022 est.), 0.727 (2021 est.), 0.780 (2020 est.)

Canadian dollars per US dollar: 1.369 (2024 est.), 1.35 (2023 est.), 1.302 (2022 est.), 1.254 (2021 est.), 1.341 (2020 est.)

Chinese yuan per US dollar: 0.783 (2024 est.), 7.084 (2023 est.), 6.737 (2022 est.), 6.449 (2021 est.), 6.901 (2020 est.)
euros per US dollar: 0.924 (2024 est.), 0.925 (2023 est.), 0.950 (2022 est.), 0.845 (2021 est.), 0.876 (2020 est.)

Japanese yen per US dollar: 151.366 (2024 est.), 140.49 (2023 est.), 131.50 (2022 est.), 109.75 (2021 est.), 106.78 (2020 est.)
note 1: the following countries and territories use the US dollar officially as their legal tender: British Virgin Islands, Ecuador, El Salvador, Marshall Islands, Micronesia, Palau, Timor Leste, Turks and Caicos, and islands of the Caribbean Netherlands (Bonaire, Sint Eustatius, and Saba)
note 2: the following countries and territories use the US dollar as official legal tender alongside local currency: Bahamas, Barbados, Belize, and Panama

ENERGY

Electricity access: *electrification - total population:* 100% (2022 est.)

Electricity: *installed generating capacity:* 1.235 billion kW (2023 est.)
consumption: 4.085 trillion kWh (2023 est.)
exports: 19.87 billion kWh (2023 est.)
imports: 38.874 billion kWh (2023 est.)
transmission/distribution losses: 191.104 billion kWh (2023 est.)
comparison rankings: installed generating capacity 2; consumption 2; exports 14; imports 3; transmission/distribution losses 209

Electricity generation sources: *fossil fuels:* 58.9% of total installed capacity (2023 est.)
nuclear: 18.2% of total installed capacity (2023 est.)
solar: 5.6% of total installed capacity (2023 est.)
wind: 9.9% of total installed capacity (2023 est.)
hydroelectricity: 5.6% of total installed capacity (2023 est.)
geothermal: 0.4% of total installed capacity (2023 est.)

biomass and waste: 1.3% of total installed capacity (2023 est.)

Nuclear energy: Number of operational nuclear reactors: 94 (2025)

Net capacity of operational nuclear reactors: 96.95GW (2025 est.)

Percent of total electricity production: 18.5% (2023 est.)

Number of nuclear reactors permanently shut down: 41 (2025)

Coal: *production:* 534.234 million metric tons (2023 est.)
consumption: 495.156 million metric tons (2023 est.)
exports: 92.28 million metric tons (2023 est.)
imports: 3.825 million metric tons (2023 est.)
proven reserves: 247.883 billion metric tons (2023 est.)

Petroleum: *total petroleum production:* 20.953 million bbl/day (2023 est.)
refined petroleum consumption: 20.307 million bbl/day (2024 est.)
crude oil estimated reserves: 38.212 billion barrels (2021 est.)

Natural gas: *production:* 1.072 trillion cubic meters (2023 est.)
consumption: 920.47 billion cubic meters (2023 est.)
exports: 215.48 billion cubic meters (2023 est.)
imports: 82.917 billion cubic meters (2023 est.)
proven reserves: 13.402 trillion cubic meters (2021 est.)

Energy consumption per capita: 278.474 million Btu/person (2023 est.)
comparison ranking: 10

COMMUNICATIONS

Telephones - fixed lines: *total subscriptions:* 87.987 million (2023 est.)
subscriptions per 100 inhabitants: 26 (2023 est.)
comparison ranking: total subscriptions 2

Telephones - mobile cellular: *total subscriptions:* 386 million (2023 est.)
subscriptions per 100 inhabitants: 110 (2022 est.)
comparison ranking: total subscriptions 3

Broadcast media: 4 major terrestrial TV networks with affiliate stations, plus cable and satellite networks, independent stations, and a limited public broadcasting sector; thousands of TV stations broadcasting; multiple national radio networks with many affiliate stations; over 15,000 radio stations, most commercial; National Public Radio (NPR) has a network of about 900 member stations; satellite radio available (2018)

Internet country code: .us

Internet users: *percent of population:* 93% (2023 est.)

Broadband - fixed subscriptions: *total:* 131 million (2023 est.)
subscriptions per 100 inhabitants: 38 (2023 est.)
comparison ranking: total 2

TRANSPORTATION

Civil aircraft registration country code prefix: N

Airports: 16,116 (2025)
comparison ranking: 1

Heliports: 8,130 (2025)
comparison ranking: 1

Railways: *total:* 293,564.2 km (2014)
standard gauge: 293,564.2 km (2014) 1.435-m gauge

Merchant marine: *total:* 3,533 (2023)
by type: bulk carrier 4, container ship 60, general cargo 96, oil tanker 68, other 3,305
note - oceangoing self-propelled, cargo-carrying vessels of 1,000 gross tons and above
comparison ranking: total 7

Ports: *total ports:* 666 (2024)
large: 21
medium: 38
small: 132
very small: 475
ports with oil terminals: 204
key ports: Baltimore, Boston, Brooklyn, Buffalo, Chester, Cleveland, Detroit, Galveston, Houston, Los Angeles, Louisiana Offshore Oil Port (LOOP), Mobile, New Orleans, New York City, Norfolk, Oakland, Philadelphia, Portland, San Francisco, Seattle, Tri-City Port

MILITARY AND SECURITY

Military and security forces: United States Armed Forces (aka US Military): US Army (USA), US Navy (USN; includes US Marine Corps or USMC), US Air Force (USAF), US Space Force (USSF); US Coast Guard (USCG); National Guard (Army National Guard and Air National Guard) (2025)
note 1: the US Coast Guard is administered in peacetime by the Department of Homeland Security, but in wartime reports to the Navy
note 2: the Army National Guard and the Air National Guard are reserve components of their services and operate in part under state authority; the US military also maintains reserve forces for each branch
note 3: US law enforcement personnel include those of federal agencies, such as the Department of Homeland Security and Department of Justice, the 50 states, special jurisdictions, local sheriff's offices, and municipal, county, regional, and tribal police departments
note 4: some US states have "state defense forces" (SDFs), which are military units that operate under the sole authority of state governments; SDFs are authorized by state and federal law and are under the command of the governor of each state; most are organized as ground units, but air and naval units also exist

Military expenditures: 3.2% of GDP (2025 est.)
3.2% of GDP (2024 est.)
3.1% of GDP (2023 est.)
3.2% of GDP (2022 est.)
3.5% of GDP (2021 est.)

Military and security service personnel strengths: approximately 1.28 million active-duty Armed Forces (450,000 Army; 334,000 Navy; 317,000 Air Force; 10,000 Space Force; 168,000 Marine Corps); 42,000 Coast Guard) (2025)

Military equipment inventories and acquisitions: the US military's inventory is comprised almost entirely of domestically produced weapons systems (some assembled with foreign components) along with a smaller mix of imported equipment from a variety of countries such as Germany and the UK; the US defense industry is capable of designing, developing, maintaining, and producing the full spectrum of weapons systems; the US is the world's leading arms exporter (2024)

Military service age and obligation: 17 years of age (under 18 with parental consent) for voluntary service for men and women; maximum enlistment age 35 (Army), 42 (Air Force/Space Force), 41 (Navy), 28 (Marines), 41 (Coast Guard); 8-year service obligation, including 2-5 years active duty depending on the particular military service (2025)
note 1: the US military has been all-volunteer since 1973, but an act of Congress can reinstate the draft in case of a national emergency; males aged 18-25 must register with Selective Service
note 2: all military occupations and positions open to women; in 2022, women comprised 17.5% of the total US regular military personnel
note 3: non-citizens living permanently and legally in the US may join as enlisted personnel; they must have permission to work in the US, a high school diploma, and speak, read, and write English fluently; under the Compact of Free Association, citizens of the Federated States of Micronesia, the Republic of Palau, and the Republic of the Marshall Islands may volunteer

Military deployments: the US has more than 200,000 air, ground, and naval personnel deployed overseas on a permanent or a long-term rotational (typically 3-9 months) basis; key areas of deployment include approximately 5,000 in Africa, approximately 80,000 in Europe, approximately 10-15,000 in Southwest Asia, and more than 80,000 in East Asia (2024)

Military - note: the US military's primary missions are to deter potential enemies, provide for the defense of the US, its Territories, Commonwealths and possessions, and any areas occupied by the US, and to protect US national interests; its responsibilities are worldwide and include providing humanitarian assistance, participating in international military exercises and operations, conducting military diplomacy, and fulfilling the US's alliance and treaty commitments; the US has been a leading member of NATO since the Alliance's formation in 1949
the US military has a global presence; the separate services operate jointly under 11 regional or functionally based joint service "combatant" commands: Africa Command; Central Command, Cyber Command, European Command, Indo-Pacific Command, Northern Command, Southern Command, Space Command, Special Operations Command, Strategic Command, and Transportation Command
Congress officially created the US military in September 1789; the US Army was established in June 1775 as the Continental Army; after the declaration of independence in July 1776, the Continental Army and the militia in the service of Congress became known collectively as the Army of the United States; when Congress ordered the Continental Army to disband in 1784, it retained a small number of personnel that would form the nucleus of the 1st American Regiment for national service formed later that year; both the US Navy and the US Marines were also established in 1775, but the Navy fell into disuse after the Revolutionary War, and was reestablished by Congress in 1794; the first US military unit devoted exclusively to aviation began operations in 1913 as part of the US Army; the Army Air Corps (AAC) was the US military service dedicated to aerial warfare between 1926 and 1941; the AAC became the US Army Air Forces in 1941 and remained as a combat arm of the Army until the establishment of the US Air Force in 1947 (2025)

SPACE

Space agency/agencies: National Aeronautics and Space Administration (NASA; established 1958) (2025)
note: the National Reconnaissance Office (NRO; established in 1961) is responsible for designing, building, launching, and maintaining intelligence satellites; the US Space Command (USSPACECOM; established in 2019) is one of 11 unified combatant commands within the Department of Defense and is responsible for military operations in outer space, specifically all operations over 100 kilometers or 62 miles above mean sea level); the US Space Force (USSF; established 2019) is a branch of the US Armed Forces

Space launch site(s): has 20 government and commercial spaceports licensed by the Federal Aviation Administration spread across 10 states (Alabama, Alaska, California, Colorado, Florida, Georgia, New Mexico, Oklahoma, Texas, and Virginia) (2025)

Space program overview: has a large and comprehensive space program and is one of the world's top space powers; builds, launches, and operates space launch vehicles (SLVs)/rockets and the full spectrum of spacecraft, including interplanetary probes, manned craft, reusable rockets, satellites, space stations, and space planes; has an astronaut program and a corps of astronauts; researching and developing a broad range of other space-related technologies, such as advanced telecommunications and optics, navigational aids, propulsion, robotics, solar sails, and space-based manufacturing, repair, and refueling; has launched orbital or lander probes to the Sun and all the planets in the solar system, as well as to asteroids and beyond the solar system; has dozens of international missions and projects, including with Canada, Japan, Russia, South Korea, and the European Space Agency (ESA); as of October 2025, nearly 60 countries had signed onto the US-led Artemis Accords to enhance the governance of civil exploration and use of outer space, with the intention of advancing the Artemis Program, an international effort to establish a sustainable presence on the Moon and an onward human mission to Mars; the US commercial space industry is one of the world's largest and most capable and is active across the spectrum of US government space programs; US commercial companies conduct the majority of NASA and US military space launches (2025)
note: further details about the key activities, programs, and milestones of the country's space program, as well as government spending estimates on the space sector, appear in the Space Programs reference guide

TERRORISM

Terrorist group(s): Terrorist group(s): al-Qa'ida; Hizballah; Islamic Revolutionary Guard Corps (IRGC)/Qods Force; Islamic State of Iraq and ash-Sham (ISIS); La Mara Salvatruche (MS-13); Lashkar-e Tayyiba (LeT); Tren de Aragua (TdA)
note: details about the history, aims, leadership, organization, areas of operation, tactics, targets, weapons, size, and sources of support of the group(s) appear(s) in Appendix T

TRANSNATIONAL ISSUES

Refugees and internally displaced persons: *refugees:* 3,619,495 (2024 est.)

IDPs: 21,737 (2024 est.)

UNITED STATES PACIFIC ISLAND WILDLIFE REFUGES

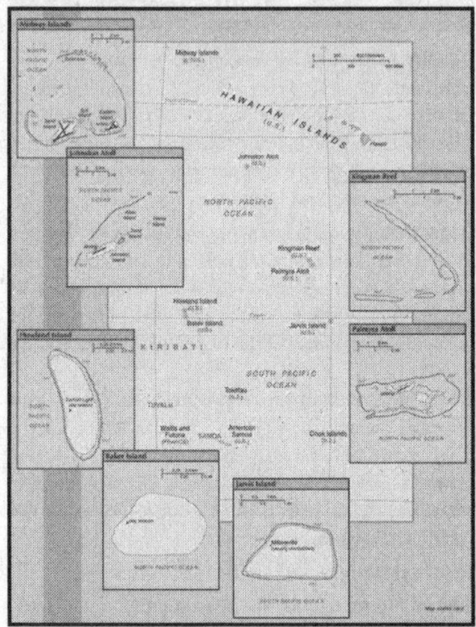

INTRODUCTION

Background: All of the following US Pacific Island territories except Midway Atoll constitute the Pacific Remote Islands National Wildlife Refuge (NWR) Complex and as such are managed by the Fish and Wildlife Service of the US Department of the Interior. Midway Atoll NWR has been included in a Refuge Complex with the Hawaiian Islands NWR and also designated as part of Papahanaumokuakea Marine National Monument. These remote refuges are the most widespread collection of marine- and terrestrial-life protected areas on the planet under a single country's jurisdiction. They sustain many endemic species including corals, fish, shellfish, marine mammals, seabirds, water birds, land birds, insects, and vegetation not found elsewhere.

Baker Island: The US took possession of the island in 1857. US and British companies mined its guano deposits during the second half of the 19th century. In 1935, a short-lived attempt at colonization began but was disrupted by World War II, and the island was thereafter abandoned. Baker Island was declared a National Wildlife Refuge in 1974.

Howland Island: The US discovered the island early in the 19th century and officially claimed it in 1857. Both US and British companies mined guano on the island until about 1890. Earhart Light, a day beacon near the middle of the west coast, was partially destroyed during World War II but subsequently rebuilt; it is named in memory of famed aviatrix Amelia EARHART. The US Department of the Interior administers the island as a National Wildlife Refuge.

Jarvis Island: First discovered by the British in 1821, the uninhabited island was annexed by the US in 1858 but abandoned in 1879 after tons of guano deposits were removed for use in producing fertilizer. The UK annexed the island in 1889 but never carried out plans for further exploitation. The US occupied and reclaimed the island in 1935. Abandoned after World War II, the island is currently a National Wildlife Refuge administered by the US Department of the Interior.

Johnston Atoll: Both the US and the Kingdom of Hawaii annexed Johnston Atoll in 1858, but it was the US that mined the guano deposits until the late 1880s. Johnston Atoll was designated a wildlife refuge in 1926. The US Navy took over the atoll in 1934, and the US Air Force assumed control in 1948. The site was used for high-altitude nuclear tests in the 1950s and 1960s, and until 2000, the atoll was maintained as a storage and disposal site for chemical weapons. Cleanup and closure of the weapons facility ended in 2005.

Kingman Reef: The US annexed Kingman Reef in 1922. Its sheltered lagoon served as a way station for flying boats on Hawaii-to-American Samoa flights during the late 1930s. There are no terrestrial plants on the reef, which is frequently awash, but it does support abundant and diverse marine fauna and flora. In 2001, the waters surrounding the reef out to 12 nm were designated a US National Wildlife Refuge.

Midway Islands: The US took formal possession of the Midway Islands in 1867. The laying of the trans-Pacific cable, which passed through the islands, brought the first residents in 1903. Between 1935 and 1947, Midway was used as a refueling stop for trans-Pacific flights. The US naval victory over a Japanese fleet off Midway in 1942 was one of the turning points of World War II. The islands continued to serve as a naval station until 1993. Today the islands are a US National Wildlife Refuge. The refuge was open to the public from 1996 to 2002 and again from 2008 to 2012, but it is now closed.

Palmyra Atoll: The Kingdom of Hawaii claimed the atoll in 1862, and the US included it among the Hawaiian Islands when it annexed the archipelago in 1898. The Hawaii Statehood Act of 1959 did not include Palmyra Atoll, which is now partly privately owned by the Nature Conservancy and partly US Government-owned and administered as a nature preserve. The lagoons and surrounding waters within the 12-nautical-mile US territorial seas were transferred to the US Fish and Wildlife Service and were designated a National Wildlife Refuge in 2001.

GEOGRAPHY

Location: Oceania

Baker Island: atoll in the North Pacific Ocean 3,390 km southwest of Honolulu, about halfway between Hawaii and Australia

Howland Island: island in the North Pacific Ocean 3,360 km southwest of Honolulu, about halfway between Hawaii and Australia

Jarvis Island: island in the South Pacific Ocean 2,415 km south of Honolulu, about halfway between Hawaii and Cook Islands

Johnston Atoll: atoll in the North Pacific Ocean 1,330 km southwest of Honolulu, about one-third of the way from Hawaii to the Marshall Islands

Kingman Reef: reef in the North Pacific Ocean 1,720 km south of Honolulu, about halfway between Hawaii and American Samoa

Midway Islands: atoll in the North Pacific Ocean 2,335 km northwest of Honolulu near the end of the Hawaiian Archipelago, about one-third of the way from Honolulu to Tokyo

Palmyra Atoll: atoll in the North Pacific Ocean 1,780 km south of Honolulu, about halfway between Hawaii and American Samoa

Geographic coordinates: Baker Island: 0 13 N, 176 28 W

Howland Island: 0 48 N, 176 38 W

Jarvis Island: 0 23 S, 160 01 W

Johnston Atoll: 16 45 N, 169 31 W

Kingman Reef: 6 23 N, 162 25 W

Midway Islands: 28 12 N, 177 22 W

Palmyra Atoll: 5 53 N, 162 05 W

Map references: Oceania

Area: *land:* 6,959.41 sq km (emergent land - 22.41 sq km; submerged - 6,937 sq km)

Baker Island: total - 129.1 sq km; emergent land - 2.1 sq km; submerged - 127 sq km

Howland Island: total - 138.6 sq km; emergent land - 2.6 sq km; submerged - 136 sq km

Jarvis Island: total - 152 sq km; emergent land - 5 sq km; submerged - 147 sq km

Johnston Atoll: total - 276.6 sq km; emergent land - 2.6 sq km; submerged - 274 sq km

Kingman Reef: total - 1,958.01 sq km; emergent land - 0.01 sq km; submerged - 1,958 sq km

Midway Islands: total - 2,355.2 sq km; emergent land - 6.2 sq km; submerged - 2,349 sq km

Palmyra Atoll: total - 1,949.9 sq km; emergent land - 3.9 sq km; submerged - 1,946 sq km

Area - comparative: Baker Island: about 2.5 times the size of the National Mall in Washington, D.C.

Howland Island: about three times the size of the National Mall in Washington, D.C.

Jarvis Island: about eight times the size of the National Mall in Washington, D.C.

Johnston Atoll: about 4.5 times the size of the National Mall in Washington, D.C.

Kingman Reef: a little more than 1.5 times the size of the National Mall in Washington, D.C.

Midway Islands: about nine times the size of the National Mall in Washington, D.C.

Palmyra Atoll: about 20 times the size of the National Mall in Washington, D.C.

Land boundaries: *total:* 0 km

Coastline: Baker Island: 4.8 km

Howland Island: 6.4 km

Jarvis Island: 8 km

Johnston Atoll: 34 km

Kingman Reef: 3 km

Midway Islands: 15 km

Palmyra Atoll: 14.5 km

Maritime claims: *territorial sea:* 12 nm
exclusive economic zone: 200 nm

Climate: Baker, Howland, and Jarvis Islands: equatorial; scant rainfall, constant wind, burning sun

Johnston Atoll and Kingman Reef: tropical, but generally dry; consistent northeast trade winds with little seasonal temperature variation

Midway Islands: subtropical with cool, moist winters (December to February) and warm, dry summers (May to October); moderated by prevailing easterly winds; most of the 107 cm of annual rainfall occurs during the winter

Palmyra Atoll: equatorial, hot; located within the low pressure area of the Intertropical Convergence Zone (ITCZ) where the northeast and southeast trade winds meet, it is extremely wet with between 400-500 cm of rainfall each year

Terrain: low and nearly flat sandy coral islands with narrow fringing reefs that have developed at the top of submerged volcanic mountains, which in most cases rise steeply from the ocean floor

Elevation: *highest point:* Baker Island, unnamed location 8 m; Howland Island, unnamed location 3 m; Jarvis Island, unnamed location 7 m; Johnston Atoll, Sand Island 10 m; Kingman Reef, unnamed location 2 m; Midway Islands, unnamed location less than 13 m; Palmyra Atoll, unnamed location 3 m
lowest point: Pacific Ocean 0 m

Natural resources: terrestrial and aquatic wildlife

Land use: *other:* 100% (2018 est.)

Natural hazards: Baker, Howland, and Jarvis Islands: the narrow fringing reef around the island poses a maritime hazard

Kingman Reef: wet or awash most of the time; maximum elevation of less than 2 m makes the reef a maritime hazard

Geography - note: Baker, Howland, and Jarvis Islands: scattered vegetation consisting of grasses, vines, and low-growing shrubs; primarily a nesting, roosting, and foraging habitat for seabirds, shorebirds, and marine wildlife; closed to the public

Johnston Atoll: Johnston Island and Sand Island are natural islands that have been expanded by coral dredging; North Island (Akau) and East Island (Hikina) are manmade islands formed from coral dredging; the egg-shaped reef is 34 km (21 mi) in circumference; closed to the public

Kingman Reef: barren coral atoll with deep interior lagoon; closed to the public

Midway Islands: a coral atoll managed as a National Wildlife Refuge and open to the public for wildlife observation and photography

Palmyra Atoll: high rainfall and lush vegetation make the environment of this atoll unique among the US Pacific Island territories; supports a large undisturbed stand of Pisonia beach forest

PEOPLE AND SOCIETY

Population: *note:* entry is only allowed through a Special Use Permit when the activity is deemed appropriate with purposes to the refuge establishment.

ENVIRONMENT

Environmental issues: Baker Island: no natural freshwater resources

Howland Island: no natural freshwater resources

Jarvis Island: no natural freshwater resources

Johnston Atoll: no natural freshwater resources; invasion of non-native species

Midway Islands: pollution from plastic; predominantly non-native plant species

Kingman Reef: none

Palmyra Atoll: none

Climate: Baker, Howland, and Jarvis Islands: equatorial; scant rainfall, constant wind, burning sun

Johnston Atoll and Kingman Reef: tropical, but generally dry; consistent northeast trade winds with little seasonal temperature variation

Midway Islands: subtropical with cool, moist winters (December to February) and warm, dry summers (May to October); moderated by prevailing easterly winds; most of the 107 cm of annual rainfall occurs during the winter

Palmyra Atoll: equatorial, hot; located within the low pressure area of the Intertropical Convergence Zone (ITCZ) where the northeast and southeast trade winds meet, it is extremely wet with between 400-500 cm of rainfall each year

Carbon dioxide emissions: 294,000 metric tonnes of CO2 (2023 est.)
from petroleum and other liquids: 294,000 metric tonnes of CO2 (2023 est.)
comparison ranking: total emissions 198

GOVERNMENT

Country name: *conventional long form:* none
conventional short form: Baker Island, Howland Island, Jarvis Island, Johnston Atoll, Kingman Reef, Midway Islands, Palmyra Atoll
etymology: self-descriptive name specifying the territories' affiliation and location

Dependency status: with the exception of Palmyra Atoll, the constituent islands are unincorporated, unorganized territories of the US; administered by the Fish and Wildlife Service of the US Department of the Interior as part of the National Wildlife Refuge System
note: Palmyra Atoll is part privately owned and part federally owned; the Office of Insular Affairs of the US Department of the Interior continues to administer nine excluded areas comprising certain tidal and submerged lands within the 12 nm territorial sea or within the lagoon

Legal system: the laws of the US apply

Diplomatic representation from the US: none (territories of the US)

Flag: the US flag is used

ENERGY

Coal: *imports:* 108,000 metric tons (2023 est.)

Petroleum: *refined petroleum consumption:* 2,000 bbl/day (2023 est.)

TRANSPORTATION

Airports: 2 (2025)
comparison ranking: 207

MILITARY AND SECURITY

Military - note: defense is the responsibility of the US

URUGUAY

INTRODUCTION

Background: The Spanish founded the city of Montevideo in modern-day Uruguay in 1726 as a military stronghold, and it soon became an important commercial center due to its natural harbor. Argentina initially claimed Uruguay, but Brazil annexed the country in 1821. Uruguay declared its independence in 1825 and secured its freedom in 1828 after a three-year struggle. The administrations of President Jose BATLLE in the early 20th century launched widespread political, social, and economic reforms that established a statist tradition. A violent Marxist urban guerrilla movement named the Tupamaros (or Movimiento de Liberación Nacional-Tupamaros) launched in the late 1960s and pushed Uruguay's president to cede control of the government to the military in 1973. By year-end, the rebels had been crushed, but the military continued to expand its hold over the government. Civilian rule was restored in 1985. In 2004, the left-of-center Frente Amplio (FA) Coalition won national elections that effectively ended 170 years of political control by the Colorado and National (Blanco) parties. The left-of-center coalition retained the presidency and control of both chambers of congress until 2019. Uruguay's political and labor conditions are among the freest on the South American continent.

GEOGRAPHY

Location: Southern South America, bordering the South Atlantic Ocean, between Argentina and Brazil

Geographic coordinates: 33 00 S, 56 00 W

Map references: South America

Area: *total:* 176,215 sq km
land: 175,015 sq km
water: 1,200 sq km
comparison ranking: total 91

Area - comparative: about the size of Virginia and West Virginia combined; slightly smaller than the state of
Washington

Land boundaries: *total:* 1,591 km
border countries (2): Argentina 541 km; Brazil 1,050 km

Coastline: 660 km

Maritime claims: *territorial sea:* 12 nm
contiguous zone: 24 nm
exclusive economic zone: 200 nm
continental shelf: 200 nm or the edge of continental margin

Climate: warm temperate; freezing temperatures almost unknown

Terrain: mostly rolling plains and low hills; fertile coastal lowland

Elevation: *highest point:* Cerro Catedral 514 m
lowest point: Atlantic Ocean 0 m
mean elevation: 109 m

Natural resources: arable land, hydropower, minor minerals, fish

Land use: *agricultural land:* 80.9% (2022 est.)
arable land: 12.1% (2022 est.)
permanent crops: 0.2% (2022 est.)
permanent pasture: 68.6% (2022 est.)
forest: 11.8% (2022 est.)
other: 7.3% (2022 est.)

Irrigated land: 2,230 sq km (2018)

Major lakes (area sq km): *salt water lake(s):* Lagoa Mirim (shared with Brazil) - 2,970 sq km

Major rivers (by length in km): Rio de la Plata/Parana river mouth (shared with Brazil [s], Argentina, Paraguay) - 4,880 km; Uruguay river mouth (shared with Brazil [s] and Argentina) - 1,610 km
note: [s] after country name indicates river source; [m] after country name indicates river mouth

Major aquifers: Guarani Aquifer System

Population distribution: most of the country's population resides in the southern half of the country; approximately 80% of the populace is urban; nearly half of the population lives in and around the capital of Montevideo

Natural hazards: seasonally high winds (the pampero is a chilly and occasional violent wind that blows north from the Argentine pampas), droughts, floods; because of the absence of mountains, which act as weather barriers, all locations are particularly vulnerable to rapid changes from weather fronts

Geography - note: second-smallest South American country (after Suriname); most of the low-lying landscape (three-quarters of the country) is grassland, ideal for cattle and sheep

PEOPLE AND SOCIETY

Population: *total:* 3,425,330 (2024 est.)
male: 1,660,132
female: 1,765,198
comparison rankings: total 133; male 135; female 133

Nationality: *noun:* Uruguayan(s)
adjective: Uruguayan

Ethnic groups: White 87.7%, Black 4.6%, Indigenous 2.4%, other 0.3%, none or unspecified 5% (2011 est.)
note: data represent primary ethnic identity

Languages: Spanish (official, Rioplatense is the most widely spoken dialect)
major-language sample(s):
La Libreta Informativa del Mundo, la fuente indispensable de información básica. (Spanish)

Religions: Roman Catholic 36.5%, Protestant 5% (Evangelical (non-specific) 4.6%, Adventist 0.2%, Protestant (non-specific) 0.3%), African American Cults/Umbanda 2.8%, Jehovah's Witness 0.6%, Church of Jesus Christ 0.2%, other 1%, Believer (not belonging to the church) 1.8%, agnostic 0.3%, atheist 1.3%, none 47.3%, unspecified 3.4%
Roman Catholic 42%, Protestant 15%, other 6%, agnostic 3%, atheist 10%, unspecified 24% (2023 est.)

Age structure: *0-14 years:* 18.9% (male 329,268/female 317,925)
15-64 years: 65.4% (male 1,112,622/female 1,128,418)
65 years and over: 15.7% (2024 est.) (male 218,242/female 318,855)

Dependency ratios: *total dependency ratio:* 49.1 (2024 est.)
youth dependency ratio: 26.9 (2024 est.)
elderly dependency ratio: 22.2 (2024 est.)
potential support ratio: 4.5 (2024 est.)

Median age: *total:* 36.5 years (2024 est.)
male: 34.9 years
female: 38.2 years
comparison ranking: total 89

Population growth rate: 0.26% (2024 est.)
comparison ranking: 170

Birth rate: 12.6 births/1,000 population (2024 est.)
comparison ranking: 136

Death rate: 9.1 deaths/1,000 population (2024 est.)
comparison ranking: 57

Net migration rate: -0.9 migrant(s)/1,000 population (2024 est.)
comparison ranking: 140

Population distribution: most of the country's population resides in the southern half of the country; approximately 80% of the populace is urban; nearly half of the population lives in and around the capital of Montevideo

Urbanization: *urban population:* 95.8% of total population (2023)
rate of urbanization: 0.4% annual rate of change (2020-25 est.)

Major urban areas - population: 1.774 million MONTEVIDEO (capital) (2023)

Sex ratio: *at birth:* 1.04 male(s)/female
0-14 years: 1.04 male(s)/female
15-64 years: 0.99 male(s)/female
65 years and over: 0.68 male(s)/female
total population: 0.94 male(s)/female (2024 est.)

Maternal mortality ratio: 15 deaths/100,000 live births (2023 est.)
comparison ranking: 136

Infant mortality rate: *total:* 8 deaths/1,000 live births (2024 est.)
male: 9.1 deaths/1,000 live births
female: 6.8 deaths/1,000 live births
comparison ranking: total 145

Life expectancy at birth: *total population:* 78.9 years (2024 est.)
male: 75.8 years
female: 82.1 years
comparison ranking: total population 70

Total fertility rate: 1.75 children born/woman (2024 est.)
comparison ranking: 149

Gross reproduction rate: 0.86 (2024 est.)

Drinking water source: *improved: urban:* 99.7% of population (2022 est.)
rural: 95.3% of population (2022 est.)
total: 99.5% of population (2022 est.)
unimproved: urban: 0.3% of population (2022 est.)
rural: 4.7% of population (2022 est.)
total: 0.5% of population (2022 est.)

Health expenditure: 9.4% of GDP (2021)
20.9% of national budget (2022 est.)

Physician density: 4.67 physicians/1,000 population (2022)

Hospital bed density: 2.5 beds/1,000 population (2021 est.)

Sanitation facility access: *improved: urban:* 99.3% of population (2022 est.)
rural: 100% of population (2022 est.)
total: 99.3% of population (2022 est.)
unimproved: urban: 0.7% of population (2022 est.)
rural: 0% of population (2022 est.)
total: 0.7% of population (2022 est.)

Obesity - adult prevalence rate: 27.9% (2016)
comparison ranking: 33

Alcohol consumption per capita: *total:* 5.42 liters of pure alcohol (2019 est.)
beer: 1.86 liters of pure alcohol (2019 est.)
wine: 2.86 liters of pure alcohol (2019 est.)
spirits: 0.71 liters of pure alcohol (2019 est.)
other alcohols: 0 liters of pure alcohol (2019 est.)
comparison ranking: total 82

Tobacco use: *total:* 18% (2025 est.)
male: 21.3% (2025 est.)
female: 14.9% (2025 est.)
comparison ranking: total 84

Children under the age of 5 years underweight: 1.8% (2018)
comparison ranking: 101

Currently married women (ages 15-49): 55.4% (2023 est.)

Education expenditure: 3.6% of GDP (2023 est.)
15.4% national budget (2023 est.)
comparison ranking: Education expenditure (% GDP) 125

Literacy: *total population:* 99% (2022 est.)
male: 99% (2022 est.)
female: 99% (2022 est.)

School life expectancy (primary to tertiary education): *total:* 18 years (2022 est.)
male: 16 years (2022 est.)
female: 19 years (2022 est.)

ENVIRONMENT

Environmental issues: water pollution from meat-packing, tannery industries; heavy metal pollution; inadequate solid and hazardous waste disposal; deforestation

International environmental agreements: *party to:* Antarctic-Environmental Protection, Antarctic-Marine Living Resources, Antarctic Treaty, Biodiversity, Climate Change, Climate Change-Kyoto Protocol, Climate Change-Paris Agreement, Comprehensive Nuclear Test Ban, Desertification, Endangered Species, Environmental Modification, Hazardous Wastes, Law of the Sea, Marine Dumping-London Protocol, Nuclear Test Ban, Ozone Layer Protection, Ship Pollution, Wetlands, Whaling
signed, but not ratified: Marine Dumping-London Convention, Marine Life Conservation

Climate: warm temperate; freezing temperatures almost unknown

Urbanization: *urban population:* 95.8% of total population (2023)
rate of urbanization: 0.4% annual rate of change (2020-25 est.)

Carbon dioxide emissions: 6.896 million metric tonnes of CO2 (2023 est.)
from coal and metallurgical coke: 39,000 metric tonnes of CO2 (2023 est.)
from petroleum and other liquids: 6.681 million metric tonnes of CO2 (2023 est.)
from consumed natural gas: 177,000 metric tonnes of CO2 (2023 est.)
comparison ranking: total emissions 124

Particulate matter emissions: 8.5 micrograms per cubic meter (2019 est.)

Methane emissions: *energy:* 18.1 kt (2022-2024 est.)
agriculture: 730.6 kt (2019-2021 est.)
waste: 115.4 kt (2019-2021 est.)
other: 2.8 kt (2019-2021 est.)

Waste and recycling: *municipal solid waste generated annually:* 1.26 million tons (2024 est.)
percent of municipal solid waste recycled: 24.8% (2022 est.)

Total water withdrawal: *municipal:* 424.428 million cubic meters (2022)
industrial: 603.701 million cubic meters (2022)
agricultural: 3.479 billion cubic meters (2022)

Total renewable water resources: 172.2 billion cubic meters (2022 est.)

Geoparks: *total global geoparks and regional networks:* 1
global geoparks and regional networks: Grutas del Palacio (2023)

GOVERNMENT

Country name: *conventional long form:* Oriental Republic of Uruguay
conventional short form: Uruguay
local long form: República Oriental del Uruguay
local short form: Uruguay
former: Banda Oriental, Cisplatine Province
etymology: name derives from the Uruguay River, which makes up the western border of the country; the river's name comes from the Guarani words *uru* (bird) and *guay* (tail)

Government type: presidential republic

Capital: *name:* Montevideo
geographic coordinates: 34 51 S, 56 10 W
time difference: UTC-3 (2 hours ahead of Washington, DC, during Standard Time)
etymology: the origin of the name is disputed but refers to a hill or mountain (*monte*); one theory combines the Spanish word *monte* (mountain) with the Latin *video* (I see)

Administrative divisions: 19 departments (*departamentos*, singular - *departamento*); Artigas, Canelones, Cerro Largo, Colonia, Durazno, Flores, Florida, Lavalleja, Maldonado, Montevideo, Paysandú, Rio Negro, Rivera, Rocha, Salto, San José, Soriano, Tacuarembó, Treinta y Tres

Legal system: civil law system based on the Spanish civil code

Constitution: *history:* several previous; latest approved by plebiscite 27 November 1966, effective 15 February 1967, reinstated in 1985 at the conclusion of military rule
amendment process: initiated by public petition of at least 10% of qualified voters, proposed by agreement of at least two fifths of the General Assembly membership, or by existing "constitutional laws" sanctioned by at least two thirds of the membership in both houses of the Assembly; proposals can also be submitted by senators, representatives, or by the executive power and require the formation of and approval in a national constituent convention; final passage by either method requires approval by absolute majority of votes cast in a referendum

International law organization participation: accepts compulsory ICJ jurisdiction; accepts ICCt jurisdiction

Citizenship: *citizenship by birth:* yes
citizenship by descent only: yes
dual citizenship recognized: yes
residency requirement for naturalization: 3-5 years

Suffrage: 18 years of age; universal and compulsory

Executive branch: *chief of state:* President Yamandú ORSI Martínez (since 1 March 2025)
head of government: President Yamandú ORSI Martínez (since 1 March 2025)
cabinet: Council of Ministers appointed by the president with approval of the General Assembly
election/appointment process: president and vice president directly elected on the same ballot by absolute-majority vote in 2 rounds, if needed, for a 5-year term (eligible for nonconsecutive terms)
most recent election date: 27 October 2024, with a runoff on 24 November 2024
election results: *2024:* Yamandú ORSI Martínez elected president in second round; percent of vote in first round - Yamandú ORSI Martínez (FA) 46.2%, Álvaro Luis DELGADO Ceretta (PN) 28.2%, Andrés OJEDA Ojeda Spitz (PC) 16.9%, other 8.7%; percent of vote in second round - Yamandú ORSI Martínez 52.1%, Álvaro Luis DELGADO Ceretta 47.9%
2019: Luis Alberto LACALLE POU elected president in second round; percent of vote in first round - Daniel MARTINEZ (FA) 40.7%, Luis Alberto LACALLE POU (PN) 29.7%, Ernesto TALVI (Colorado Party) 12.8%, Guido MANINI RIOS (Open Cabildo) 11.3%, other 5.5%; percent of vote in second round - Luis Alberto LACALLE POU 50.6%, Daniel MARTINEZ 49.4%
expected date of next election: 28 October 2029, with a runoff, if needed, on 25 November 2029
note: the president is both chief of state and head of government

Legislative branch: *legislature name:* General Assembly (Asamblea General)
legislative structure: bicameral

Legislative branch - lower chamber: *chamber name:* House of Representatives (Cámara de Representantes)
number of seats: 99 (all directly elected)
electoral system: proportional representation
scope of elections: full renewal
term in office: 5 years
most recent election date: 10/27/2024
parties elected and seats per party: Broad Front (FA) (48); National Party (PN) (29); Colorado Party (PC) (17); Other (5)
percentage of women in chamber: 31.3%

expected date of next election: October 2029

Legislative branch - upper chamber: *chamber name:* Senate (Cámara de Senadores)
number of seats: 31 (all directly elected)
electoral system: proportional representation
scope of elections: full renewal
term in office: 5 years
most recent election date: 10/27/2024
parties elected and seats per party: Broad Front (FA) (16); National Party (PN) (9); Colorado Party (PC) (5)
percentage of women in chamber: 32.3%
expected date of next election: October 2029

Judicial branch: *highest court(s):* Supreme Court of Justice (consists of 5 judges)
judge selection and term of office: judges nominated by the president and appointed by two-thirds vote in joint conference of the General Assembly; judges serve 10-year terms, with reelection possible after a lapse of 5 years following the previous term
subordinate courts: Courts of Appeal; District Courts (Juzgados Letrados); Peace Courts (Juzgados de Paz); Rural Courts (Juzgados Rurales)

Political parties: Broad Front or FA (Frente Amplio) - (a broad governing coalition that comprises 34 factions including Popular Participation Movement or MPP, Uruguay Assembly, Progressive Alliance, Broad Social Democratic Space, Socialist Party, Vertiente Artiguista, Christian Democratic Party, Big House, Communist Party, The Federal League, Fuerza Renovadora)
Colorado Party or PC (including Batllistas and Ciudadanos)
Intransigent Radical Ecologist Party (Partido Ecologista Radical Intransigente) or PERI
Independent Party
National Party or PN (including Todos (Everyone) and National Alliance)
Open Cabildo
Popular Unity

Diplomatic representation in the US: *chief of mission:* Ambassador Daniel CASTILLOS Gómez (since 5 September 2025)
chancery: 1913 I Street NW, Washington, DC 20006
telephone: [1] (202) 331-1313
FAX: [1] (202) 331-8142
email address and website: urueeuu@mrree.gub.uy
https://embassyofuruguay.us/
consulate(s) general: Miami, New York, San Francisco

Diplomatic representation from the US: *chief of mission:* Ambassador-designate Lou RINALDI (since September 2025)
embassy: Lauro Muller 1776, Montevideo 11200
mailing address: 3360 Montevideo Place, Washington DC 20521-3360
telephone: (+598) 1770-2000
FAX: [+598] 1770-2128
email address and website: MontevideoACS@state.gov
https://uy.usembassy.gov/

International organization participation: CAN (associate), CD, CELAC, FAO, G-77, IADB, IAEA, IBRD, ICAO, ICC (national committees), ICCt, ICRM, IDA, IFAD, IFC, IFRCS, IHO, ILO, IMF, IMO, Interpol, IOC, IOM, IPU, ISO, ITSO, ITU, LAES, LAIA, Mercosur, MIGA, MINUSTAH, MONUSCO, NAM (observer), OAS, OIF (observer), OPANAL, OPCW, Pacific Alliance (observer), PCA, SICA (observer), UN, UNASUR, UNCTAD, UNESCO, UNIDO, Union Latina, UNISFA, UNMOGIP, UNOCI, UNWTO, UPU, WCO, WFTU (NGOs), WHO, WIPO, WMO, WTO

Independence: 25 August 1825 (from Brazil)

National holiday: Independence Day, 25 August (1825)

Flag: *description:* nine equal horizontal stripes of white (top and bottom) alternating with blue; a white square in the upper-left corner has a yellow sun with a human face (outlined in black) known as the Sun of May, with 16 rays that alternate between triangular and wavy
meaning: the stripes represent the country's nine original departments; the sun refers to the legend of the sun breaking through the clouds on 25 May 1810 as independence was declared from Spain; the sun is said to be Inti, the Inca god of the sun
note: the banner was inspired by the national colors of Argentina and the design of the US flag

National symbol(s): Sun of May (a sun-with-face symbol)

National color(s): blue, white, yellow

National anthem(s): *title:* "Himno Nacional" (National Anthem of Uruguay)
lyrics/music: Francisco Esteban ACUNA de Figueroa/ Francisco Jose DEBALI
history: adopted 1848; the anthem is also known as "Orientales, la Patria o la tumba!" ("Uruguayans, the Fatherland or Death!"); it is the world's longest national anthem in terms of music (105 bars; almost five minutes); usually only the first verse and chorus are sung

National heritage: *total World Heritage Sites:* 3 (all cultural)
selected World Heritage Site locales: Historic City of Colonia del Sacramento; Fray Bentos Industrial Landscape; The work of engineer Eladio Dieste: Church of Atlántida

ECONOMY

Economic overview: high-income, export-oriented South American economy; South America's largest middle class; low socioeconomic inequality; growing homicide rates; growing Chinese and EU relations; 2019 Argentine recession hurt; key milk, beef, rice, and wool exporter

Real GDP (purchasing power parity): $108.502 billion (2024 est.)
$105.231 billion (2023 est.)
$104.456 billion (2022 est.)
note: data in 2021 dollars
comparison ranking: 95

Real GDP growth rate: 3.1% (2024 est.)
0.7% (2023 est.)
4.5% (2022 est.)
note: annual GDP % growth based on constant local currency
comparison ranking: 114

Real GDP per capita: $32,000 (2024 est.)
$31,100 (2023 est.)
$30,800 (2022 est.)
note: data in 2021 dollars
comparison ranking: 74

GDP (official exchange rate): $80.962 billion (2024 est.)
note: data in current dollars at official exchange rate

Inflation rate (consumer prices): 4.8% (2024 est.)
5.9% (2023 est.)
9.1% (2022 est.)
note: annual % change based on consumer prices
comparison ranking: 143

GDP - composition, by sector of origin: *agriculture:* 6.4% (2024 est.)
industry: 16.8% (2024 est.)
services: 65.3% (2024 est.)
note: figures may not total 100% due to non-allocated consumption not captured in sector-reported data
comparison rankings: agriculture 98; industry 155; services 56

GDP - composition, by end use: *household consumption:* 66.8% (2015 est.)
government consumption: 13.8% (2015 est.)
investment in fixed capital: 19.8% (2015 est.)
investment in inventories: -0.1% (2015 est.)
exports of goods and services: 22.5% (2015 est.)
imports of goods and services: -22.9% (2015 est.)
note: figures may not total 100% due to rounding or gaps in data collection

Agricultural products: milk, rice, wheat, barley, soybeans, beef, rapeseed, sugarcane, maize, beef offal (2023)
note: top ten agricultural products based on tonnage

Industries: food processing, electrical machinery, transportation equipment, petroleum products, textiles, chemicals, beverages

Industrial production growth rate: 4.4% (2024 est.)
note: annual % change in industrial value added based on constant local currency
comparison ranking: 53

Labor force: 1.768 million (2024 est.)
note: number of people ages 15 or older who are employed or seeking work
comparison ranking: 129

Unemployment rate: 8.5% (2024 est.)
8.4% (2023 est.)
7.9% (2022 est.)
note: % of labor force seeking employment
comparison ranking: 137

Youth unemployment rate (ages 15-24): *total:* 26.4% (2024 est.)
male: 23.5% (2024 est.)
female: 29.8% (2024 est.)
note: % of labor force ages 15-24 seeking employment
comparison ranking: total 30

Population below poverty line: 10.1% (2023 est.)
note: % of population with income below national poverty line

Gini Index coefficient - distribution of family income: 40.9 (2023 est.)
note: index (0-100) of income distribution; higher values represent greater inequality
comparison ranking: 36

Average household expenditures: *on food:* 18.7% of household expenditures (2023 est.)
on alcohol and tobacco: 1.2% of household expenditures (2023 est.)

Household income or consumption by percentage share: *lowest 10%:* 2.1% (2023 est.)
highest 10%: 30.8% (2023 est.)
note: % share of income accruing to lowest and highest 10% of population

Remittances: 0.2% of GDP (2024 est.)
0.2% of GDP (2023 est.)
0.2% of GDP (2022 est.)
note: personal transfers and compensation between resident and non-resident individuals/households/ entities

Budget: *revenues:* $27.781 billion (2023 est.)
expenditures: $17.808 billion (2023 est.)
note: central government revenues (excluding grants) and expenditures converted to US dollars at average official exchange rate for year indicated

Public debt: 62.4% of GDP (2023 est.)
note: central government debt as a % of GDP
comparison ranking: 71

Taxes and other revenues: 18.7% (of GDP) (2023 est.)
note: central government tax revenue as a % of GDP
comparison ranking: 58

Current account balance: -$821.38 million (2024 est.)
-$2.64 billion (2023 est.)
-$2.675 billion (2022 est.)
note: balance of payments - net trade and primary/secondary income in current dollars
comparison ranking: 122

Exports: $23.329 billion (2024 est.)
$21.946 billion (2023 est.)
$23.56 billion (2022 est.)
note: balance of payments - exports of goods and services in current dollars
comparison ranking: 89

Exports - partners: China 21%, Brazil 17%, USA 8%, Argentina 5%, Netherlands 5% (2023)
note: top five export partners based on percentage share of exports

Exports - commodities: wood pulp, beef, milk, rice, wood (2023)
note: top five export commodities based on value in dollars

Imports: $19.117 billion (2024 est.)
$19.259 billion (2023 est.)
$19.639 billion (2022 est.)
note: balance of payments - imports of goods and services in current dollars
comparison ranking: 96

Imports - partners: Brazil 22%, China 18%, Argentina 11%, USA 9%, Nigeria 4% (2023)
note: top five import partners based on percentage share of imports

Imports - commodities: crude petroleum, refined petroleum, cars, trucks, fertilizers (2023)
note: top five import commodities based on value in dollars

Reserves of foreign exchange and gold: $17.378 billion (2024 est.)
$16.257 billion (2023 est.)
$15.127 billion (2022 est.)
note: holdings of gold (year-end prices)/foreign exchange/special drawing rights in current dollars
comparison ranking: 67

Exchange rates: Uruguayan pesos (UYU) per US dollar -

Exchange rates: 40.213 (2024 est.)
38.824 (2023 est.)
41.171 (2022 est.)
43.555 (2021 est.)
42.013 (2020 est.)

ENERGY

Electricity access: *electrification - total population:* 100% (2022 est.)

Electricity: *installed generating capacity:* 5.682 million kW (2023 est.)
consumption: 9.826 billion kWh (2023 est.)
exports: 2 billion kWh (2023 est.)
imports: 84 million kWh (2023 est.)
transmission/distribution losses: 1.136 billion kWh (2023 est.)
comparison rankings: installed generating capacity 85; consumption 106; exports 59; imports 113; transmission/distribution losses 105

Electricity generation sources: *fossil fuels:* 8% of total installed capacity (2023 est.)
solar: 3.8% of total installed capacity (2023 est.)
wind: 37% of total installed capacity (2023 est.)
hydroelectricity: 27.3% of total installed capacity (2023 est.)
biomass and waste: 23.9% of total installed capacity (2023 est.)

Coal: *consumption:* 8,000 metric tons (2023 est.)
imports: 13,000 metric tons (2023 est.)

Petroleum: *total petroleum production:* 400 bbl/day (2023 est.)
refined petroleum consumption: 50,000 bbl/day (2023 est.)

Natural gas: *consumption:* 90.018 million cubic meters (2023 est.)
imports: 90.871 million cubic meters (2023 est.)

Energy consumption per capita: 45.755 million Btu/person (2023 est.)
comparison ranking: 98

COMMUNICATIONS

Telephones - fixed lines: *total subscriptions:* 1.205 million (2023 est.)
subscriptions per 100 inhabitants: 36 (2023 est.)
comparison ranking: total subscriptions 63

Telephones - mobile cellular: *total subscriptions:* 4.8 million (2023 est.)
subscriptions per 100 inhabitants: 139 (2022 est.)
comparison ranking: total subscriptions 128

Broadcast media: mix of privately owned and state-run broadcast media; over 100 commercial radio stations and about 20 TV channels; cable TV is available; many community radio and TV stations; adopted the hybrid Japanese/Brazilian HDTV standard (ISDB-T) in 2010 (2019)

Internet country code: .uy

Internet users: *percent of population:* 90% (2023 est.)

Broadband - fixed subscriptions: *total:* 1.1 million (2023 est.)
subscriptions per 100 inhabitants: 32 (2023 est.)
comparison ranking: total 78

TRANSPORTATION

Civil aircraft registration country code prefix: CX

Airports: 65 (2025)
comparison ranking: 75

Heliports: 4 (2025)
comparison ranking: 109

Railways: *total:* 1,673 km (2016) (operational; government claims overall length is 2,961 km)
standard gauge: 1,673 km (2016) 1.435-m gauge

Merchant marine: *total:* 58 (2023)
by type: container ship 1, general cargo 4, oil tanker 3, other 50
comparison ranking: total 115

Ports: *total ports:* 8 (2024)
large: 0
medium: 1
small: 1
very small: 6
ports with oil terminals: 2
key ports: Colonia, Fray Bentos, Jose Ignacio, La Paloma, Montevideo, Nueva Palmira, Paysandu, Puerto Sauce

MILITARY AND SECURITY

Military and security forces: Armed Forces of Uruguay (Fuerzas Armadas del Uruguay or FF.AA. del Uruguay): National Army, National Navy (includes Coast Guard (Prefectura Nacional Naval or PRENA)), Uruguayan Air Force

Ministry of Interior: National Police (2025)
note: the National Police includes the paramilitary National Republican Guard (Guardia Nacional Republicana)

Military expenditures: 2.1% of GDP (2024 est.)
2% of GDP (2023 est.)
2% of GDP (2022 est.)
2.3% of GDP (2021 est.)
2% of GDP (2020 est.)

Military and security service personnel strengths: approximately 23,000 active-duty Armed Forces (15,000 Army; 5,000 Navy; 3,000 Air Force) (2025)

Military equipment inventories and acquisitions: the military's inventory includes a variety of mostly older or second-hand equipment originating from a wide range of suppliers, including Brazil, Canada, the former Czechoslovakia, Germany, Portugal, Russia/former Soviet Union, South Korea, Spain, and the US (2024)

Military service age and obligation: 18-30 years of age (18-22 years of age for Navy) for voluntary military service for men and women; up to 40 years of age for specialists; enlistment is voluntary in peacetime, but the government has the authority to conscript in emergencies (2025)
note: as of 2023, women comprised nearly 20% of the active military

Military deployments: 600 Democratic Republic of the Congo (MONUSCO); 200 Golan Heights (UNDOF) (2024)

Military - note: the armed forces are responsible for defense of the country's independence, national sovereignty, and territorial integrity, as well as protecting strategic resources; it has some domestic responsibilities, including perimeter security for a number of prisons, border security, and providing humanitarian/disaster assistance; it also assists the Ministry of Interior in combating narcotics trafficking; the military participates in UN peacekeeping missions and multinational exercises with foreign partners; Uruguay traditionally has held security ties with Argentina, Brazil, Peru, and the US; since 2018, it has also signed defense cooperation agreements with China and Russia (2025)

TRANSNATIONAL ISSUES

Refugees and internally displaced persons: *refugees:* 32,149 (2024 est.)

IDPs: 33 (2024 est.)
stateless persons: 5 (2024 est.)

UZBEKISTAN

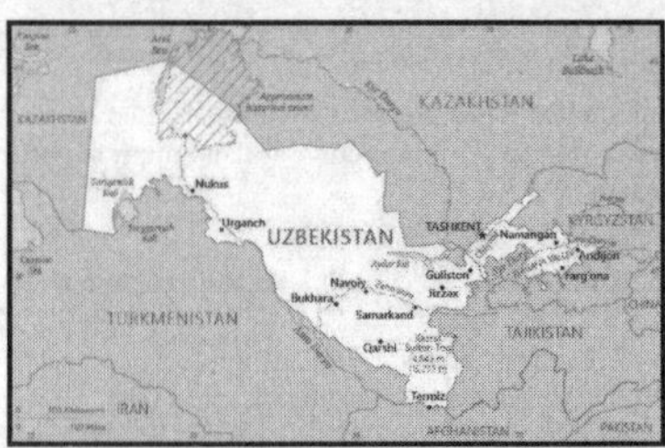

INTRODUCTION

Background: Uzbekistan is the geographic and population center of Central Asia, with a diverse economy and a relatively young population. Russia conquered and united the disparate territories of present-day Uzbekistan in the late 19th century. Stiff resistance to the Red Army after the Bolshevik Revolution was eventually suppressed and a socialist republic established in 1924. During the Soviet era, intensive production of "white gold" (cotton) and grain led to the overuse of agrochemicals and the depletion of water supplies, leaving the land degraded and the Aral Sea and certain rivers half-dry. Independent since the Union of Soviet Socialist Republics (USSR) dissolved in 1991, the country has diversified agricultural production while developing its mineral and petroleum export capacity and increasing its manufacturing base, although cotton remains a major part of its economy. Uzbekistan's first president, Islom KARIMOV, led Uzbekistan for 25 years until his death in 2016. His successor, former Prime Minister Shavkat MIRZIYOYEV, has improved relations with Uzbekistan's neighbors and introduced wide-ranging economic, judicial, and social reforms. MIRZIYOYEV was reelected in 2021 with 80% of the vote and again following a 2023 constitutional referendum with 87% of the vote.

GEOGRAPHY

Location: Central Asia, north of Turkmenistan, south of Kazakhstan

Geographic coordinates: 41 00 N, 64 00 E

Map references: Asia

Area: *total:* 447,400 sq km
land: 425,400 sq km
water: 22,000 sq km
comparison ranking: total 59

Area - comparative: about four times the size of Virginia; slightly larger than California

Land boundaries: *total:* 6,893 km
border countries (5): Afghanistan 144 km; Kazakhstan 2,330 km; Kyrgyzstan 1,314 km; Tajikistan 1,312 km; Turkmenistan 1,793 km

Coastline: 0 km (doubly landlocked)
note: Uzbekistan includes the southern portion of the Aral Sea with a 420 km shoreline

Maritime claims: none (doubly landlocked)

Climate: mostly mid-latitude desert, long, hot summers, mild winters; semiarid grassland in east

Terrain: mostly flat-to-rolling sandy desert with dunes; broad, flat intensely irrigated river valleys along course of Amu Darya, Syr Darya (Sirdaryo), and Zaravshan; Fergana Valley in east surrounded by mountainous Tajikistan and Kyrgyzstan; shrinking Aral Sea in west

Elevation: *highest point:* Xazrat Sulton Tog' 4,643 m
lowest point: Sariqamish Kuli -12 m

Natural resources: natural gas, petroleum, coal, gold, uranium, silver, copper, lead and zinc, tungsten, molybdenum

Land use: *agricultural land:* 58.1% (2022 est.)
arable land: 9.1% (2022 est.)
permanent crops: 1% (2022 est.)
permanent pasture: 47.9% (2022 est.)
forest: 8.5% (2022 est.)
other: 33.5% (2022 est.)

Irrigated land: 37,305 sq km (2022)

Major lakes (area sq km): *fresh water lake(s):* Aral Sea (shared with Kazakhstan) - largely dried up

Major rivers (by length in km): Syr Darya (shared with Kyrgyzstan [s], Tajikistan, and Kazakhstan [m]) - 3,078 km; Amu
Darya river mouth (shared with Tajikistan [s], Afghanistan, and Turkmenistan) - 2,620 km
note: [s] after country name indicates river source; [m] after country name indicates river mouth

Major watersheds (area sq km): Internal (endorheic basin) drainage: *(Aral Sea basin)* Amu Darya (534,739 sq km), Syr Darya (782,617 sq km)

Population distribution: most of the population is concentrated in the fertile Fergana Valley in the easternmost arm of the country; the south has significant clusters of people, but the central and western deserts are sparsely populated

Natural hazards: earthquakes; floods; landslides or mudslides; avalanches; droughts

Geography - note: along with Liechtenstein, one of the only two doubly landlocked countries in the world

PEOPLE AND SOCIETY

Population: *total:* 36,520,593 (2024 est.)
male: 18,324,813
female: 18,195,780
comparison rankings: total 42; male 41; female 41

Nationality: *noun:* Uzbekistani
adjective: Uzbekistani

Ethnic groups: Uzbek 83.8%, Tajik 4.8%, Kazakh 2.5%, Russian 2.3%, Karakalpak 2.2%, Tatar 1.5%, other 2.9% (2017 est.)

Languages: Uzbek (official) 74.3%, Russian 14.2%, Tajik 4.4%, other 7.1%
major-language sample(s):
Jahon faktlari kitobi, asosiy ma'lumotlar uchun zaruriy manba. (Uzbek)
note: in the semi-autonomous Republic of Karakalpakstan, both the Karakalpak language and Uzbek have official status

Religions: Muslim 88% (mostly Sunni), Eastern Orthodox 9%, other 3%

Age structure: *0-14 years:* 29.6% (male 5,597,947/female 5,213,403)
15-64 years: 63.7% (male 11,649,017/female 11,617,411)
65 years and over: 6.7% (2024 est.) (male 1,077,849/female 1,364,966)

Dependency ratios: *total dependency ratio:* 57 (2024 est.)
youth dependency ratio: 46.5 (2024 est.)
elderly dependency ratio: 10.5 (2024 est.)
potential support ratio: 9.5 (2024 est.)

Median age: *total:* 28.9 years (2024 est.)
male: 28.1 years
female: 29.8 years
comparison ranking: total 148

Population growth rate: 1.43% (2024 est.)
comparison ranking: 69

Birth rate: 20.5 births/1,000 population (2024 est.)
comparison ranking: 64

Death rate: 5.1 deaths/1,000 population (2024 est.)
comparison ranking: 190

Net migration rate: -1.1 migrant(s)/1,000 population (2024 est.)
comparison ranking: 149

Population distribution: most of the population is concentrated in the fertile Fergana Valley in the easternmost arm of the country; the south has significant clusters of people, but the central and western deserts are sparsely populated

Urbanization: *urban population:* 50.5% of total population (2023)
rate of urbanization: 1.25% annual rate of change (2020-25 est.)

Major urban areas - population: 2.603 million TASHKENT (capital) (2023)

Sex ratio: *at birth:* 1.08 male(s)/female
0-14 years: 1.07 male(s)/female
15-64 years: 1 male(s)/female
65 years and over: 0.79 male(s)/female
total population: 1.01 male(s)/female (2024 est.)

Mother's mean age at first birth: 23.7 years (2019 est.)

Maternal mortality ratio: 26 deaths/100,000 live births (2023 est.)
comparison ranking: 118

Infant mortality rate: *total:* 18.2 deaths/1,000 live births (2024 est.)
male: 21.1 deaths/1,000 live births
female: 15.1 deaths/1,000 live births
comparison ranking: total 85

Life expectancy at birth: *total population:* 76.2 years (2024 est.)
male: 73.6 years
female: 79 years
comparison ranking: total population 114

Total fertility rate: 2.76 children born/woman (2024 est.)
comparison ranking: 57

Gross reproduction rate: 1.33 (2024 est.)

Drinking water source: *improved:* *urban:* 98% of population (2022 est.)
rural: 95.2% of population (2022 est.)
total: 96.6% of population (2022 est.)
unimproved: *urban:* 2% of population (2022 est.)
rural: 4.8% of population (2022 est.)
total: 3.4% of population (2022 est.)

Health expenditure: 7.7% of GDP (2021)

7.1% of national budget (2022 est.)

Physician density: 2.81 physicians/1,000 population (2021)

Hospital bed density: 4.9 beds/1,000 population (2021 est.)

Sanitation facility access: *improved: urban:* 98.1% of population (2022 est.)
rural: 98.7% of population (2022 est.)
total: 98.4% of population (2022 est.)
unimproved: urban: 1.9% of population (2022 est.)
rural: 1.3% of population (2022 est.)
total: 1.6% of population (2022 est.)

Obesity - adult prevalence rate: 16.6% (2016)
comparison ranking: 123

Alcohol consumption per capita: *total:* 2.45 liters of pure alcohol (2019 est.)
beer: 0.18 liters of pure alcohol (2019 est.)
wine: 0.09 liters of pure alcohol (2019 est.)
spirits: 2.19 liters of pure alcohol (2019 est.)
other alcohols: 0 liters of pure alcohol (2019 est.)
comparison ranking: total 124

Tobacco use: *total:* 15.4% (2025 est.)
male: 30.2% (2025 est.)
female: 1% (2025 est.)
comparison ranking: total 102

Children under the age of 5 years underweight: 1.8% (2021)
comparison ranking: 99

Currently married women (ages 15-49): 68.6% (2023 est.)

Child marriage: *women married by age 15:* 0.2% (2022)
women married by age 18: 3.4% (2022)

Education expenditure: 5.5% of GDP (2023 est.)
21.6% national budget (2022 est.)
comparison ranking: Education expenditure (% GDP) 41

Literacy: *total population:* 100% (2022 est.)
male: 100% (2022 est.)
female: 100% (2022 est.)

School life expectancy (primary to tertiary education): *total:* 13 years (2024 est.)
male: 13 years (2024 est.)
female: 13 years (2024 est.)

ENVIRONMENT

Environmental issues: growing concentrations of chemical pesticides and natural salts in the shrinking Aral Sea; desertification; water pollution and soil salination from industrial wastes and the heavy use of fertilizers and pesticides; soil contamination from buried nuclear processing and agricultural chemicals

International environmental agreements: *party to:* Biodiversity, Climate Change, Climate Change-Kyoto Protocol, Climate Change-Paris Agreement, Comprehensive Nuclear Test Ban, Desertification, Endangered Species, Environmental Modification, Hazardous Wastes, Ozone Layer Protection, Wetlands
signed, but not ratified: none of the selected agreements

Climate: mostly mid-latitude desert, long, hot summers, mild winters; semiarid grassland in east

Urbanization: *urban population:* 50.5% of total population (2023)
rate of urbanization: 1.25% annual rate of change (2020-25 est.)

Carbon dioxide emissions: 110.992 million metric tonnes of CO2 (2023 est.)
from coal and metallurgical coke: 12.845 million metric tonnes of CO2 (2023 est.)
from petroleum and other liquids: 13.437 million metric tonnes of CO2 (2023 est.)
from consumed natural gas: 84.71 million metric tonnes of CO2 (2023 est.)
comparison ranking: total emissions 40

Particulate matter emissions: 46.6 micrograms per cubic meter (2019 est.)

Methane emissions: *energy:* 848.1 kt (2022-2024 est.)
agriculture: 868.1 kt (2019-2021 est.)
waste: 261.3 kt (2019-2021 est.)
other: 4.5 kt (2019-2021 est.)

Waste and recycling: *municipal solid waste generated annually:* 4 million tons (2024 est.)
percent of municipal solid waste recycled: 31.6% (2022 est.)

Total water withdrawal: *municipal:* 2.3 billion cubic meters (2022)
industrial: 1.2 billion cubic meters (2022)
agricultural: 41 billion cubic meters (2022)

Total renewable water resources: 48.87 billion cubic meters (2022 est.)

GOVERNMENT

Country name: *conventional long form:* Republic of Uzbekistan
conventional short form: Uzbekistan
local long form: O'zbekiston Respublikasi
local short form: O'zbekiston
former: Uzbek Soviet Socialist Republic
etymology: the name comes from the local people, the Uzbeks, whose name is said to have originated with Mongol leader Ghiyath ad-Din Muhammad UZBEK; the Persian suffix *-stan* means "country"

Government type: presidential republic; highly authoritarian

Capital: *name:* Tashkent (Toshkent)
geographic coordinates: 41 19 N, 69 15 E
time difference: UTC+5 (10 hours ahead of Washington, DC, during Standard Time)
etymology: the current name of the ancient city was first used in the 11th century and comes from the Sogdian (Turkic) words *tash* (stone) and *kent* (town); the city was first recorded in the 5th or 4th century B.C. with the name of Chach or Shash

Administrative divisions: 12 provinces (*viloyatlar*, singular - *viloyat*), 1 autonomous republic* (*avtonom respublikasi*), and 3 cities** (*shahar*); Andijon Viloyati, Buxoro Viloyati [Bukhara Province], Farg'ona Viloyati [Fergana Province], Jizzax Viloyati, Namangan Shahri, Namangan Viloyati, Navoiy Viloyati, Qashqadaryo Viloyati (Qarshi), Qoraqalpog'iston Respublikasi [Karakalpakstan Republic]* (Nukus), Samarqand Shahri [Samarkand City], Samarqand Viloyati [Samarkand Province], Sirdaryo Viloyati (Guliston), Surxondaryo Viloyati (Termiz), Toshkent Shahri [Tashkent City]**, Toshkent Viloyati [Nurafshon], Xorazm Viloyati (Urganch)
note: administrative divisions show the same names as their administrative centers; exceptions show the administrative center name in parentheses

Legal system: civil law system
note: in 2020, the criminal code, criminal procedure code, and code of administrative responsibility were reformed; a constitutional referendum in 2023 included additional criminal code reforms

Constitution: *history:* several previous; latest adopted 8 December 1992
amendment process: proposed by the Supreme Assembly or by referendum; passage requires two-thirds majority vote of both houses of the Assembly or passage in a referendum

International law organization participation: has not submitted an ICJ jurisdiction declaration; non-party state to the ICCt

Citizenship: *citizenship by birth:* no
citizenship by descent only: at least one parent must be a citizen of Uzbekistan
dual citizenship recognized: no
residency requirement for naturalization: 5 years

Suffrage: 18 years of age; universal

Executive branch: *chief of state:* President Shavkat MIRZIYOYEV (since 14 December 2016)
head of government: Prime Minister Abdulla ARIPOV (since 14 December 2016)
cabinet: Cabinet of Ministers appointed by the president with most requiring approval of the Senate chamber of the Supreme Assembly (Oliy Majlis)
election/appointment process: president directly elected by absolute-majority popular vote in 2 rounds, if needed, for a 7-year term (eligible for a second term); prime minister nominated by majority party in the Supreme Assembly but appointed along with the ministers and deputy ministers by the president
most recent election date: 9 July 2023
election results: *2023:* Shavkat MIRZIYOYEV reelected president in snap election; percent of vote - Shavkat MIRZIYOYEV (LDPU) 87.7%, Robaxon Maxmudova (Adolat) 4.5%, Ulugbek Inoyatov (PDP) 4%, Abdushukur Xamzayev (Ecological Party) 3.8%
2021: Shavkat MIRZIYOYEV reelected president in first round; percent of vote - Shavkat MIRZIYOYEV (LDPU) 80.3%, Maqsuda VORISOVA (PDP) 6.7%, Alisher QODIROV (National Revival Democratic Party) 5.5%, Narzullo OBLOMURODOV (Ecological Party) 4.1%, Bahrom ABDUHALIMOV (Adolat) 3.4%
expected date of next election: 2030

Legislative branch: *legislature name:* Supreme Assembly (Oliy Majlis)
legislative structure: bicameral

Legislative branch - lower chamber: *chamber name:* Legislative Chamber (Qonunchilik palatasi)
number of seats: 150 (all directly elected)
electoral system: mixed system
scope of elections: full renewal
term in office: 5 years
most recent election date: 10/27/2024
parties elected and seats per party: Movement of Entrepreneurs and Businesspeople - Liberal Democratic Party (UzLiDeP) (64); Milliy Tiklanish Democratic Party (O'zMTDP) (29); Social Democratic Party ("Adolat" SDP) (21); People's Democratic Party (XDP) (20); Ecological Party (O'EP) (16)
percentage of women in chamber: 38%
expected date of next election: October 2029

Legislative branch - upper chamber: *chamber name:* Senate (Senat)
number of seats: 65 (56 indirectly elected; 9 appointed)
scope of elections: full renewal
term in office: 5 years
most recent election date: 11/7/2024 to 11/12/2024
percentage of women in chamber: 24.6%

expected date of next election: November 2029

Judicial branch: *highest court(s):* Supreme Court (consists of 67 judges organized into administrative, civil, criminal, and economic sections); Constitutional Court (consists of 7 judges)
judge selection and term of office: judges of the highest courts nominated by the president and confirmed by the Senate of the Oliy Majlis; judges appointed for a single 10-year term; the court chairman and deputies appointed for 10-year terms without the right to reelection. (Article 132 of the constitution)
subordinate courts: regional, district, city, and town courts

Political parties: Ecological Party of Uzbekistan (O'zbekiston Ekologik Partivasi)
Justice (Adolat) Social Democratic Party of Uzbekistan
Liberal Democratic Party of Uzbekistan (O'zbekiston Liberal-Demokratik Partiyasi) or LDPU
National Revival Democratic Party of Uzbekistan (O'zbekiston Milliy Tiklanish Demokratik Partiyasi)
People's Democratic Party of Uzbekistan (Xalq Demokratik Partiyas) or PDP (formerly Communist Party)

Diplomatic representation in the US: *chief of mission:* Ambassador Furqat SIDIKOV (since 19 April 2023)
chancery: 1746 Massachusetts Avenue NW, Washington, DC 20036
telephone: [1] (202) 887-5300
FAX: [1] (202) 293-6804
email address and website: info.washington@mfa.uz
https://www.uzbekistan.org/
consulate(s) general: New York

Diplomatic representation from the US: *chief of mission:* Ambassador Jonathan HENICK (since 14 October 2022)
embassy: 3 Moyqorghon, 5th Block, Yunusobod District, 100093 Tashkent
mailing address: 7110 Tashkent Place, Washington DC 20521-7110
telephone: [998] 78-120-5450
FAX: [998] 78-120-6335
email address and website: ACSTashkent@state.gov
https://uz.usembassy.gov/

International organization participation: ADB, CICA, CIS, EAEU (observer), EAPC, EBRD, ECO, EEU (observer), FAO, IAEA, IBRD, ICAO, ICC (national committees), ICCt, ICRM, IDA, IDB, IFAD, IFC, IFRCS, ILO, IMF, Interpol, IOC, ISO, ITSO, ITU, MIGA, NAM, OIC, OPCW, OSCE, PFP, SCO, UN, UNCTAD, UNESCO, UNIDO, UNOOSA, UNWTO, UPU, WCO, WFTU (NGOs), WHO, WIPO, WMO, WTO (observer)

Independence: 1 September 1991 (from the Soviet Union)

National holiday: Independence Day, 1 September (1991)

Flag: *description:* three equal horizontal bands of blue (top), white, and green separated by narrow red stripes with a vertical white crescent moon and 12 five-pointed white stars in the left corner of the top band
meaning: blue stands for the Turkic peoples and the sky, white for peace and the striving for purity in thoughts and deeds, and green for nature and Islam; the red stripes represent the vital force of all living organisms; the crescent stands for Islam, and the 12 stars for the months and constellations of the Uzbek calendar

National symbol(s): khumo (mythical bird)

National color(s): blue, white, red, green

National anthem(s): *title:* "O'zbekiston Respublikasining Davlat Madhiyasi" (National Anthem of the Republic of Uzbekistan)
lyrics/music: Abdulla ARIPOV/Mutal BURHANOV
history: adopted 1992; after the fall of the Soviet Union, Uzbekistan kept the music of its Soviet-era anthem but adopted new lyrics

National heritage: *total World Heritage Sites:* 7 (5 cultural, 2 natural)
selected World Heritage Site locales: Itchan Kala (c); Historic Bukhara (c); Historic Shakhrisyabz (c); Samarkand - Crossroad of Cultures (c); Western Tien Shan (n); Cold Winter Deserts of Turan (n); Silk Roads: Zarafshan-Karakum Corridor (c)

ECONOMY

Economic overview: lower-middle income Central Asian economy; key exporter of natural gas, cotton, and gold; ongoing reform efforts to reduce state-owned sector dominance, attract foreign investment, and improve sustainability of cotton production

Real GDP (purchasing power parity): $379.989 billion (2024 est.)
$356.797 billion (2023 est.)
$335.678 billion (2022 est.)
note: data in 2021 dollars
comparison ranking: 57

Real GDP growth rate: 6.5% (2024 est.)
6.3% (2023 est.)
6% (2022 est.)
note: annual GDP % growth based on constant local currency
comparison ranking: 19

Real GDP per capita: $10,500 (2024 est.)
$10,000 (2023 est.)
$9,600 (2022 est.)
note: data in 2021 dollars
comparison ranking: 141

GDP (official exchange rate): $114.965 billion (2024 est.)
note: data in current dollars at official exchange rate

Inflation rate (consumer prices): 9.6% (2024 est.)
10% (2023 est.)
11.4% (2022 est.)
note: annual % change based on consumer prices
comparison ranking: 176

GDP - composition, by sector of origin: *agriculture:* 18.3% (2024 est.)
industry: 31.8% (2024 est.)
services: 45.2% (2024 est.)
note: figures may not total 100% due to non-allocated consumption not captured in sector-reported data
comparison rankings: agriculture 38; industry 45; services 173

GDP - composition, by end use: *household consumption:* 68% (2024 est.)
government consumption: 13.9% (2024 est.)
investment in fixed capital: 37.1% (2024 est.)
investment in inventories: -3.8% (2024 est.)
exports of goods and services: 22.8% (2024 est.)
imports of goods and services: -38% (2024 est.)
note: figures may not total 100% due to rounding or gaps in data collection

Agricultural products: milk, wheat, cotton, potatoes, carrots/turnips, tomatoes, grapes, watermelons, vegetables, apples (2023)
note: top ten agricultural products based on tonnage

Industries: textiles, food processing, machine building, metallurgy, mining, hydrocarbon extraction, chemicals

Industrial production growth rate: 7.2% (2024 est.)
note: annual % change in industrial value added based on constant local currency
comparison ranking: 23

Labor force: 13.974 million (2024 est.)
note: number of people ages 15 or older who are employed or seeking work
comparison ranking: 44

Unemployment rate: 4.5% (2024 est.)
4.5% (2023 est.)
4.5% (2022 est.)
note: % of labor force seeking employment
comparison ranking: 75

Youth unemployment rate (ages 15-24): *total:* 10.9% (2024 est.)
male: 7.2% (2024 est.)
female: 18.1% (2024 est.)
note: % of labor force ages 15-24 seeking employment
comparison ranking: total 113

Population below poverty line: 11% (2023 est.)
note: % of population with income below national poverty line

Gini Index coefficient - distribution of family income: 34.5 (2023 est.)
note: index (0-100) of income distribution; higher values represent greater inequality
comparison ranking: 80

Average household expenditures: *on food:* 46.3% of household expenditures (2023 est.)
on alcohol and tobacco: 3.2% of household expenditures (2023 est.)

Household income or consumption by percentage share: *lowest 10%:* 2.1% (2023 est.)
highest 10%: 25.3% (2023 est.)
note: % share of income accruing to lowest and highest 10% of population

Remittances: 14.4% of GDP (2024 est.)
13.8% of GDP (2023 est.)
17.2% of GDP (2022 est.)
note: personal transfers and compensation between resident and non-resident individuals/households/entities

Budget: *revenues:* $21.565 billion (2023 est.)
expenditures: $25.953 billion (2023 est.)
note: central government revenues (excluding grants) and expenditures converted to US dollars at average official exchange rate for year indicated

Taxes and other revenues: 11.5% (of GDP) (2023 est.)
note: central government tax revenue as a % of GDP
comparison ranking: 120

Current account balance: -$5.738 billion (2024 est.)
-$7.799 billion (2023 est.)
-$2.847 billion (2022 est.)
note: balance of payments - net trade and primary/secondary income in current dollars
comparison ranking: 177

Exports: $26.173 billion (2024 est.)
$25.05 billion (2023 est.)
$20.966 billion (2022 est.)

note: balance of payments - exports of goods and services in current dollars
comparison ranking: 87

Exports - partners: Switzerland 34%, Russia 12%, UK 11%, China 7%, Turkey 6% (2023)
note: top five export partners based on percentage share of exports

Exports - commodities: gold, cotton yarn, garments, fertilizers, fabric (2023)
note: top five export commodities based on value in dollars

Imports: $43.624 billion (2024 est.)
$42.646 billion (2023 est.)
$35.643 billion (2022 est.)
note: balance of payments - imports of goods and services in current dollars
comparison ranking: 71

Imports - partners: China 32%, Russia 17%, Kazakhstan 8%, S. Korea 6%, Turkey 5% (2023)
note: top five import partners based on percentage share of imports

Imports - commodities: cars, vehicle parts/accessories, packaged medicine, refined petroleum, aircraft (2023)
note: top five import commodities based on value in dollars

Reserves of foreign exchange and gold: $41.237 billion (2024 est.)
$34.558 billion (2023 est.)
$35.774 billion (2022 est.)
note: holdings of gold (year-end prices)/foreign exchange/special drawing rights in current dollars
comparison ranking: 51

Debt - external: $25.714 billion (2023 est.)
note: present value of external debt in current US dollars
comparison ranking: 30

Exchange rates: Uzbekistani soum (UZS) per US dollar -

Exchange rates: 12,652.287 (2024 est.)
11,734.833 (2023 est.)
11,050.145 (2022 est.)
10,609.464 (2021 est.)
10,054.261 (2020 est.)

ENERGY

Electricity access: *electrification - total population:* 100% (2022 est.)

Electricity: *installed generating capacity:* 17.901 million kW (2023 est.)
consumption: 75.753 billion kWh (2023 est.)
exports: 2.043 billion kWh (2023 est.)
imports: 4.977 billion kWh (2023 est.)
transmission/distribution losses: 3.433 billion kWh (2023 est.)
comparison rankings: installed generating capacity 53; consumption 42; exports 57; imports 46; transmission/distribution losses 148

Electricity generation sources: *fossil fuels:* 90.8% of total installed capacity (2023 est.)
solar: 0.6% of total installed capacity (2023 est.)
hydroelectricity: 8.7% of total installed capacity (2023 est.)

Coal: *production:* 6.379 million metric tons (2023 est.)
consumption: 8.941 million metric tons (2023 est.)
exports: 4,000 metric tons (2023 est.)
imports: 3.521 million metric tons (2023 est.)
proven reserves: 1.375 billion metric tons (2023 est.)

Petroleum: *total petroleum production:* 64,000 bbl/day (2023 est.)
refined petroleum consumption: 111,000 bbl/day (2023 est.)
crude oil estimated reserves: 594 million barrels (2021 est.)

Natural gas: *production:* 43.249 billion cubic meters (2023 est.)
consumption: 44.455 billion cubic meters (2023 est.)
exports: 1.308 billion cubic meters (2023 est.)
imports: 2.514 billion cubic meters (2023 est.)
proven reserves: 1.841 trillion cubic meters (2021 est.)

Energy consumption per capita: 55.305 million Btu/person (2023 est.)
comparison ranking: 89

COMMUNICATIONS

Telephones - fixed lines: *total subscriptions:* 6.147 million (2023 est.)
subscriptions per 100 inhabitants: 17 (2023 est.)
comparison ranking: total subscriptions 26

Telephones - mobile cellular: *total subscriptions:* 37.5 million (2023 est.)
subscriptions per 100 inhabitants: 103 (2022 est.)
comparison ranking: total subscriptions 43

Broadcast media: state-controlled media; 17 state-owned broadcasters, including 13 TV and 4 radio, with national service; about 20 privately owned TV stations, overseen by local officials, broadcast locally; privately owned TV stations required to lease transmitters from state-owned Republic TV and Radio Industry Corporation (2019)

Internet country code: .uz

Internet users: *percent of population:* 89% (2023 est.)

Broadband - fixed subscriptions: *total:* 10.8 million (2023 est.)
subscriptions per 100 inhabitants: 30 (2023 est.)
comparison ranking: total 24

TRANSPORTATION

Civil aircraft registration country code prefix: UK

Airports: 74 (2025)
comparison ranking: 69

Heliports: 3 (2025)
comparison ranking: 121

Railways: *total:* 4,642 km (2018)
broad gauge: 4,642 km (2018) 1.520-m gauge (1,684 km electrified)

MILITARY AND SECURITY

Military and security forces: Armed Forces of Uzbekistan: Army, Air and Air Defense Forces; National Guard

Ministry of Internal Affairs: Internal Security Troops, Border Guards, police (2024)
note 1: the National Guard is under the Defense Ministry, but is independent of the other military services; it is responsible for ensuring public order and the security of diplomatic missions, radio and television broadcasting, and other state entities
note 2: the State Security Service, whose chairperson reports directly to the president, is responsible for national security and intelligence matters, including terrorism, corruption, organized crime, border control, and narcotics

Military expenditures: 2.8% of GDP (2019 est.)
2.9% of GDP (2018 est.)
2.7% of GDP (2017 est.)
2.5% of GDP (2016 est.)
2.5% of GDP (2015 est.)

Military and security service personnel strengths: limited available information; estimated 50,000 active Armed Forces (2025)

Military equipment inventories and acquisitions: the Uzbek Armed Forces use mainly Russian or Soviet-era weapons and equipment with smaller quantities of items from suppliers such as China, Turkey, and the US; Uzbekistan has a small defense industry, which is involved in repairing and maintaining aircraft and armored vehicles, as well as producing light armored vehicles, unmanned aerial vehicles/drones, and other military items (2025)

Military service age and obligation: 18-27 years of age for compulsory military service for men; 12-month service obligation (those conscripted have the option of paying for a shorter service of one month while remaining in the reserves until the age of 27) (2024)
note: Uzbek citizens who have completed their service terms in the armed forces have privileges in employment and admission to higher educational institutions

Military - note: the military's responsibilities include ensuring the country's sovereignty and territorial integrity, securing its borders, and assisting with internal security; regional security and international terrorism are areas of concern; Uzbekistan joined the Russian-sponsored Collective Security Treaty Organization (CSTO) in the 1990s but withdrew in 1999; it returned in 2006 but left again in 2012; although not part of CSTO, Uzbekistan continues to maintain defense ties with Russia, including joint military exercises and defense industrial cooperation; it also has defense ties with other regional countries, including Azerbaijan, China, India, Kazakhstan, Pakistan, and Turkey; it is part of the Shanghai Cooperation Organization (SCO) and participates in SCO training exercises (2025)

SPACE

Space agency/agencies: Space Research and Technology Agency (UzCosmos or UzSpace; established 2019) (2025)
note: Uzcosmos operates under the Ministry of Digital Technologies

Space program overview: has a small but growing space effort focused on acquiring satellites and developing the country's space industries and technologies in key sectors, including cartography, data processing, environmental and disaster monitoring, land use, resource management, and telecommunications; developing a 10-year national space program; recognized for its astronomy program; member of international space organizations; cooperates with foreign space agencies or commercial companies from a variety of countries, including those of Canada, China, France, India, Israel, Japan, Kazakhstan, Russia, South Korea, Spain, Turkey, and UAE (2025)
note: further details about the key activities, programs, and milestones of the country's space program,

as well as government spending estimates on the space sector, appear in the Space Programs reference guide

TERRORISM

Terrorist group(s): Terrorist group(s): Islamic Jihad Union (IJU); Islamic Movement of Uzbekistan (IMU); Islamic State of Iraq and ash-Sham - Khorasan (ISIS-K)
note 1: these groups have typically been active in the area where the Uzbek, Kyrgyz, and Tajik borders converge and ill-defined and porous borders allow for the relatively free movement of people and illicit goods
note 2: details about the history, aims, leadership, organization, areas of operation, tactics, targets, weapons, size, and sources of support of the group(s) appear(s) in Appendix T

TRANSNATIONAL ISSUES

Refugees and internally displaced persons: *refugees:* 8,505 (2024 est.)
stateless persons: 20,000 (2024 est.)

VANUATU

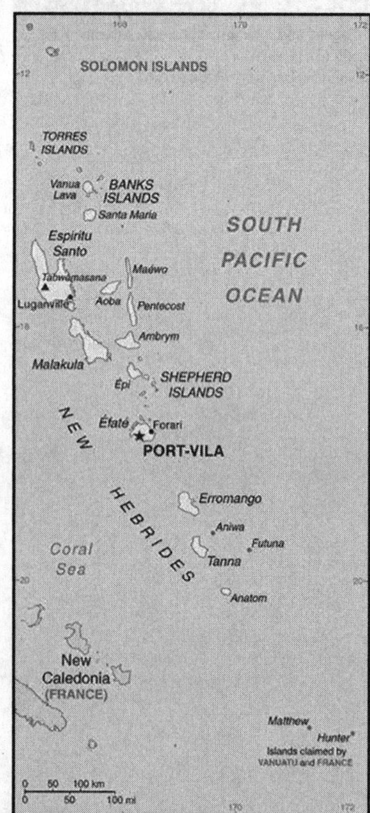

INTRODUCTION

Background: Austronesian speakers from the Solomon Islands first settled Vanuatu around 2000 B.C. By around 1000, localized chieftain systems began to develop on the islands. Around 1600, Melanesian Chief ROI MATA united some of the islands of modern-day Vanuatu under his rule. In 1606, a Portuguese explorer was the first European to see Vanuatu's Banks Islands and Espiritu Santo, setting up a short-lived settlement on the latter. The next European explorers arrived in the 1760s, and the islands – then known as the New Hebrides – were frequented by whalers in the 1800s. European interest in harvesting the islands' sandalwood trees caused conflict with the inhabitants. In the 1860s, European planters in Australia, Fiji, New Caledonia, and Samoa needed labor and kidnapped almost half the adult males on the islands to work as indentured servants.

With growing and overlapping interests in the islands, France and the UK agreed that the New Hebrides would be neutral in 1878 and established a joint naval commission in 1887. In 1906, the two countries created the UK-France condominium to jointly administer the islands, with separate laws, police forces, currencies, and education and health systems. The condominium arrangement was dysfunctional, and the UK used France's initial defeat in World War II to assert greater control over the islands. During the war, the US stationed up to 50,000 soldiers in Vanuatu. In 1945, they withdrew and sold their equipment, leading to the rise of political and religious movements known as "cargo cults," such as the John Frum movement.

The UK-France condominium was reestablished after World War II. The UK was interested in moving the condominium toward independence in the 1960s, but France was hesitant. Political parties agitating for independence began to form, largely divided along linguistic lines. France eventually relented, and elections were held in 1974, with independence granted to the newly named Vanuatu in 1980 under English-speaking Prime Minister Walter LINI. The Nagriamel Movement, with support from French-speaking landowners, then declared the island of Espiritu Santo independent from Vanuatu, but the short-lived state was dissolved 12 weeks later. Linguistic divisions have lessened over time, but highly fractious political parties have led to weak coalition governments that require support from both Anglophone and Francophone parties. Since 2008, prime ministers have been ousted more than a dozen times through no-confidence motions or temporary procedural issues.

GEOGRAPHY

Location: Oceania, group of islands in the South Pacific Ocean, about three-quarters of the way from Hawaii to Australia

Geographic coordinates: 16 00 S, 167 00 E

Map references: Oceania

Area: *total:* 12,189 sq km
land: 12,189 sq km
water: 0 sq km
note: includes more than 80 islands, about 65 of which are inhabited
comparison ranking: total 162

Area - comparative: slightly larger than Connecticut

Land boundaries: *total:* 0 km

Coastline: 2,528 km

Maritime claims: *territorial sea:* 12 nm
contiguous zone: 24 nm
exclusive economic zone: 200 nm
continental shelf: 200 nm or to the edge of the continental margin
note: measured from claimed archipelagic baselines

Climate: tropical; moderated by southeast trade winds from May to October; moderate rainfall from November to April; may be affected by cyclones from December to April

Terrain: mostly mountainous islands of volcanic origin; narrow coastal plains

Elevation: *highest point:* Tabwemasana 1,877 m
lowest point: Pacific Ocean 0 m

Natural resources: manganese, hardwood forests, fish

Land use: *agricultural land:* 15.3% (2022 est.)
arable land: 1.6% (2022 est.)
permanent crops: 10.3% (2022 est.)
permanent pasture: 3.4% (2022 est.)
forest: 36.3% (2022 est.)
other: 48.4% (2022 est.)

Irrigated land: 0 sq km (2022)

Population distribution: three quarters of the population lives in rural areas; the urban populace lives primarily in two cities, Port-Vila and Lugenville; the three largest islands – Espiritu Santo, Malakula, and Efate – accommodate over half of the populace

Natural hazards: tropical cyclones (January to April); volcanic activity; volcanism also causes minor earthquakes; tsunamis
volcanism: significant volcanic activity with multiple eruptions in recent years; Yasur (361 m), one of the world's most active volcanoes, has experienced continuous activity in recent centuries; other historically active volcanoes include Aoba, Ambrym, Epi, Gaua, Kuwae, Lopevi, Suretamatai, and Traitor's Head

Geography - note: a Y-shaped chain of four main islands and 80 smaller islands; several of the islands have active volcanoes, including several underwater volcanoes

PEOPLE AND SOCIETY

Population: *total:* 318,007 (2024 est.)
male: 157,932
female: 160,075
comparison rankings: total 179; male 179; female 179

Nationality: *noun:* Ni-Vanuatu (singular and plural)
adjective: Ni-Vanuatu

Ethnic groups: Ni-Vanuatu 99%, other 1% (European, Asian, other Melanesian, Polynesian, Micronesian, other) (2020 est.)

Languages: indigenous languages (more than 100) 82.6%, Bislama (official; creole) 14.5%, English (official) 2.1%, French (official) 0.8% (2020 est.)
note: data represent first language spoken for population aged 3 years and above

Religions: Protestant 39.9% (Presbyterian 27.2%, Seventh Day Adventist 14.8%, Anglican 12%, Churches of Christ 5%, Assemblies of God 4.9%, Neil Thomas Ministry/Inner Life Ministry 3.2%), Roman Catholic 12.1%, Apostolic 2.3%, Church of Jesus Christ 1.8%, customary beliefs (including Jon Frum cargo cult) 3.1%, other 12%, none 1.4%, unspecified 0.1% (2020 est.)

Age structure: *0-14 years:* 31.1% (male 50,584/female 48,475)
15-64 years: 63.8% (male 99,496/female 103,425)
65 years and over: 5% (2024 est.) (male 7,852/female 8,175)

Dependency ratios: *total dependency ratio:* 56.7 (2024 est.)
youth dependency ratio: 48.8 (2024 est.)
elderly dependency ratio: 7.9 (2024 est.)
potential support ratio: 12.7 (2024 est.)

Median age: *total:* 24.6 years (2024 est.)
male: 24.1 years
female: 25 years
comparison ranking: total 176

Population growth rate: 1.55% (2024 est.)
comparison ranking: 61

Birth rate: 20.8 births/1,000 population (2024 est.)
comparison ranking: 63

Death rate: 4 deaths/1,000 population (2024 est.)
comparison ranking: 215

Net migration rate: -1.3 migrant(s)/1,000 population (2024 est.)
comparison ranking: 153

Population distribution: three quarters of the population lives in rural areas; the urban populace lives primarily in two cities, Port-Vila and Lugenville; the three largest islands – Espiritu Santo, Malakula, and Efate – accommodate over half of the populace

Urbanization: *urban population:* 26% of total population (2023)
rate of urbanization: 2.55% annual rate of change (2020-25 est.)

Major urban areas - population: 53,000 PORT-VILA (capital) (2018)

Sex ratio: *at birth:* 1.05 male(s)/female
0-14 years: 1.04 male(s)/female
15-64 years: 0.96 male(s)/female
65 years and over: 0.96 male(s)/female
total population: 0.99 male(s)/female (2024 est.)

Maternal mortality ratio: 100 deaths/100,000 live births (2023 est.)
comparison ranking: 66

Infant mortality rate: *total:* 13.7 deaths/1,000 live births (2024 est.)
male: 15 deaths/1,000 live births
female: 12.3 deaths/1,000 live births
comparison ranking: total 103

Life expectancy at birth: *total population:* 75.7 years (2024 est.)
male: 74 years
female: 77.4 years
comparison ranking: total population 123

Total fertility rate: 2.53 children born/woman (2024 est.)
comparison ranking: 69

Gross reproduction rate: 1.23 (2024 est.)

Drinking water source: *improved: urban:* 99.2% of population (2022 est.)
rural: 88.6% of population (2022 est.)
total: 91.3% of population (2022 est.)
unimproved: urban: 0.8% of population (2022 est.)
rural: 11.4% of population (2022 est.)
total: 8.7% of population (2022 est.)

Health expenditure: 4.4% of GDP (2021)
3.9% of national budget (2022 est.)

Physician density: 0.16 physicians/1,000 population (2019)

Sanitation facility access: *improved: urban:* 94% of population (2022 est.)
rural: 66.9% of population (2022 est.)
total: 73.9% of population (2022 est.)
unimproved: urban: 6% of population (2022 est.)
rural: 33.1% of population (2022 est.)
total: 26.1% of population (2022 est.)

Obesity - adult prevalence rate: 25.2% (2016)
comparison ranking: 52

Alcohol consumption per capita: *total:* 1.6 liters of pure alcohol (2019 est.)
beer: 0.34 liters of pure alcohol (2019 est.)
wine: 0.39 liters of pure alcohol (2019 est.)
spirits: 0.87 liters of pure alcohol (2019 est.)
other alcohols: 0 liters of pure alcohol (2019 est.)
comparison ranking: total 136

Tobacco use: *total:* 17.8% (2020 est.)
male: 33% (2020 est.)
female: 2.6% (2020 est.)
comparison ranking: total 86

Currently married women (ages 15-49): 69.2% (2023 est.)

Education expenditure: 10.6% of GDP (2023 est.)
20.9% national budget (2023 est.)
comparison ranking: Education expenditure (% GDP) 4

Literacy: *total population:* 88% (2023 est.)
male: 87.7% (2023 est.)
female: 88.2% (2023 est.)

ENVIRONMENT

Environmental issues: water pollution; limited potable water; inadequate sanitation; deforestation

International environmental agreements: *party to:* Antarctic-Marine Living Resources, Biodiversity, Climate Change, Climate Change-Kyoto Protocol, Climate Change-Paris Agreement, Comprehensive Nuclear Test Ban, Desertification, Endangered Species, Hazardous Wastes, Law of the Sea, Marine Dumping-London Convention, Marine Dumping-London Protocol, Ozone Layer Protection, Ship Pollution, Wetlands
signed, but not ratified: none of the selected agreements

Climate: tropical; moderated by southeast trade winds from May to October; moderate rainfall from November to April; may be affected by cyclones from December to April

Urbanization: *urban population:* 26% of total population (2023)
rate of urbanization: 2.55% annual rate of change (2020-25 est.)

Carbon dioxide emissions: 292,000 metric tonnes of CO2 (2023 est.)
from petroleum and other liquids: 292,000 metric tonnes of CO2 (2023 est.)
comparison ranking: total emissions 200

Particulate matter emissions: 9.1 micrograms per cubic meter (2019 est.)

Waste and recycling: *municipal solid waste generated annually:* 70,200 tons (2024 est.)
percent of municipal solid waste recycled: 52.9% (2022 est.)

Total renewable water resources: 10 billion cubic meters (2022 est.)

GOVERNMENT

Country name: *conventional long form:* Republic of Vanuatu
conventional short form: Vanuatu
local long form: Ripablik blong Vanuatu
local short form: Vanuatu
former: New Hebrides
etymology: the name means "Our land forever" in several of the Austronesian languages spoken on the islands; the former name, New Hebrides, was given by Captain James COOK in 1774 because he thought they looked similar to the Hebrides islands off the coast of Scotland

Government type: parliamentary republic

Capital: *name:* Port-Vila (on Efate)
geographic coordinates: 17 44 S, 168 19 E
time difference: UTC+11 (16 hours ahead of Washington, DC, during Standard Time)
etymology: the local name of Vila is sometimes used alone for the the port town; its meaning is unknown

Administrative divisions: 6 provinces; Malampa, Penama, Sanma, Shefa, Tafea, Torba

Legal system: mixed system of English common law, French law, and customary law

Constitution: *history:* draft completed August 1979, finalized by constitution conference 19 September 1979, ratified by French and British Governments 23 October 1979, effective 30 July 1980 at independence
amendment process: proposed by the prime minister or by the Parliament membership; passage requires at least two-thirds majority vote by Parliament in special session with at least three fourths of the membership; passage of amendments affecting the national and official languages, or the electoral and parliamentary system also requires approval in a referendum

International law organization participation: has not submitted an ICJ jurisdiction declaration; accepts ICCt jurisdiction

Citizenship: *citizenship by birth:* no
citizenship by descent only: both parents must be citizens of Vanuatu; in the case of only one parent, it must be the father who is a citizen
dual citizenship recognized: no
residency requirement for naturalization: 10 years

Suffrage: 18 years of age; universal

Executive branch: *chief of state:* President Nikenike VUROBARAVU (since 23 July 2022)
head of government: Prime Minister Jotham NAPAT (since 11 February 2025)
cabinet: Council of Ministers appointed by the prime minister, responsible to Parliament
election/appointment process: president indirectly elected by an electoral college consisting of Parliament and presidents of the 6 provinces; national president serves a 5-year term; following legislative elections, the Parliament usually elects the leader of the majority party or majority coalition (who must also be a member of Parliament) as prime minister
most recent election date: 23 July 2022
election results: *2022:* Nikenike VUROBARAVU elected president in eighth round; electoral college vote - Nikenike VUROBARAVU (VP) 48 votes, Solas MOLISA (VP) 4 votes
expected date of next election: 2027
note: the National Council of Chiefs (Malvatu Mauri) is a formal advisory body of chiefs recognized by the country's constitution; it advises the government on matters of culture and language

Legislative branch: *legislature name:* Parliament
legislative structure: unicameral
number of seats: 52 (all directly elected)
electoral system: proportional representation
scope of elections: full renewal
term in office: 4 years
most recent election date: 1/16/2025
parties elected and seats per party: Leaders Party of Vanuatu (LPV) (9); Vanua'aku Pati (VP) (7); Iauko Group (IG) (6); Union of Moderate Parties (UMP) (6); Rural Development Party (RDP) (6); Graon mo Jastis Pati (Land and Justice Party, GJP) (5); Reunification Movement for Change (RMC) (5); Other (8)
percentage of women in chamber: 1.9%
expected date of next election: January 2029

Judicial branch: *highest court(s):* Court of Appeal (consists of 2 or more judges of the Supreme Court designated by the chief justice); Supreme Court (consists of the chief justice and 6 puisne judges – 3 local and 3 expatriate)

judge selection and term of office: Supreme Court chief justice appointed by the president after consultation with the prime minister and the leader of the opposition; other judges appointed by the president on the advice of the Judicial Service Commission, a 4-member advisory body; judges serve until the age of retirement
subordinate courts: Magistrates Courts; Island Courts

Political parties: Iauko Group (Eagle Party) or IG
Land and Justice Party (Graon mo Jastis Pati or GJP)
Leaders Party of Vanuatu or LPV
Rural Development Party or RDP
Reunification of Movement for Change or RMC
Union of Moderate Parties or UMP
Vanua'aku Pati (Our Land Party) or VP

Diplomatic representation in the US: *chief of mission:* Ambassador Odo TEVI (since 8 September 2017)
note - also Permanent Representative to the UN
chancery: 800 Second Avenue, Suite 400B, New York, NY 10017
telephone: [1] (212) 661-4303

FAX: [1] (212) 422-3427
email address and website: vanunmis@aol.com
https://www.un.int/vanuatu/
note: the Vanuatu Permanent Mission to the UN serves as the embassy

Diplomatic representation from the US: *chief of mission:* Ambassador Ann Marie YASTISHOCK (since 16 April 2024); note - also accredited to the Papua New Guinea and the Solomon Islands, based in Port Moresby, Papua New Guinea
embassy: Port Vila

International organization participation: ACP, ADB, AOSIS, C, FAO, G-77, IBRD, ICAO, ICRM, IDA, IFC, IFRCS, ILO, IMF, IMO, IMSO, IOC, IOM, ITU, ITUC (NGOs), MIGA, NAM, OAS (observer), OIF, OPCW, PIF, Sparteca, SPC, UN, UNCTAD, UNESCO, UNIDO, UNWTO, UPU, WCO, WFTU (NGOs), WHO, WIPO, WMO, WTO

Independence: 30 July 1980 (from France and the UK)

National holiday: Independence Day, 30 July (1980)

Flag: *description:* two equal horizontal bands of red (top) and green with a black isosceles triangle (based on the left side); a black-edged yellow stripe in the shape of a horizontal "Y" faces the left side and encloses the triangle; a boar's tusk in the triangle circles two crossed namele fern fronds, all in yellow
meaning: red stands for unity and the blood of men and boars, green for the richness of the islands, and black for the ni-Vanuatu people; the yellow "Y" reflects the islands' layout in the Pacific Ocean and symbolizes the light of the Gospel; the boar's tusk is a symbol of prosperity; the ferns represent peace
note: one of four national flags that reflect the shape of the country in the flag design; the others are Bosnia and Herzegovina, Brazil, and Eritrea

National symbol(s): boar's tusk with crossed fern fronds

National color(s): red, black, green, yellow

National anthem(s): *title:* "Yumi, Yumi, Yumi" (We, We, We)
lyrics/music: Francois Vincent AYSSAV
history: adopted 1980; the anthem is written in the native Bislama

National heritage: *total World Heritage Sites:* 1 (cultural)
selected World Heritage Site locales: Chief Roi Mata's Domain

ECONOMY

Economic overview: lower-middle income Pacific island economy; extremely reliant on subsistence agriculture and tourism; environmentally fragile; struggling post-pandemic and Tropical Cyclone Harold rebound; sizeable inflation; road infrastructure aid from Australia

Real GDP (purchasing power parity): $1.039 billion (2024 est.)
$999.162 million (2023 est.)
$1.009 billion (2022 est.)
note: data in 2021 dollars
comparison ranking: 207

Real GDP growth rate: 4% (2024 est.)
-1% (2023 est.)
5.2% (2022 est.)
note: annual GDP % growth based on constant local currency
comparison ranking: 74

Real GDP per capita: $3,200 (2024 est.)
$3,100 (2023 est.)
$3,200 (2022 est.)
note: data in 2021 dollars
comparison ranking: 192

GDP (official exchange rate): $1.161 billion (2024 est.)
note: data in current dollars at official exchange rate

Inflation rate (consumer prices): 11.2% (2023 est.)
6.7% (2022 est.)
2.3% (2021 est.)
note: annual % change based on consumer prices
comparison ranking: 182

GDP - composition, by sector of origin: *agriculture:* 24.9% (2022 est.)
industry: 7.5% (2022 est.)
services: 60.4% (2022 est.)
note: figures may not total 100% due to non-allocated consumption not captured in sector-reported data
comparison rankings: agriculture 19; industry 198; services 84

GDP - composition, by end use: *household consumption:* 77.2% (2022 est.)
government consumption: 23.9% (2022 est.)
investment in fixed capital: 38.8% (2022 est.)
investment in inventories: 0.4% (2022 est.)
exports of goods and services: 9.6% (2022 est.)
imports of goods and services: -55.5% (2022 est.)
note: figures may not total 100% due to rounding or gaps in data collection

Agricultural products: coconuts, oranges, yams, cabbages, taro, bananas, chillies/peppers, chestnuts, sweet potatoes, cassava (2023)
note: top ten agricultural products based on tonnage

Industries: food and fish freezing, wood processing, meat canning

Industrial production growth rate: -19.7% (2022 est.)
note: annual % change in industrial value added based on constant local currency
comparison ranking: 192

Labor force: 118,100 (2024 est.)
note: number of people ages 15 or older who are employed or seeking work
comparison ranking: 181

Unemployment rate: 5.1% (2024 est.)
5.1% (2023 est.)
5.2% (2022 est.)
note: % of labor force seeking employment
comparison ranking: 90

Youth unemployment rate (ages 15-24): *total:* 11.6% (2024 est.)
male: 9.6% (2024 est.)
female: 14% (2024 est.)
note: % of labor force ages 15-24 seeking employment
comparison ranking: total 108

Population below poverty line: 15.9% (2019 est.)
note: % of population with income below national poverty line

Gini Index coefficient - distribution of family income: 32.3 (2019 est.)
note: index (0-100) of income distribution; higher values represent greater inequality
comparison ranking: 105

Household income or consumption by percentage share: *lowest 10%:* 3% (2019 est.)
highest 10%: 24.7% (2019 est.)
note: % share of income accruing to lowest and highest 10% of population

Remittances: 12.9% of GDP (2023 est.)
19.2% of GDP (2022 est.)
20.3% of GDP (2021 est.)
note: personal transfers and compensation between resident and non-resident individuals/households/entities

Budget: *revenues:* $386.577 million (2023 est.)
expenditures: $378.659 million (2023 est.)
note: central government revenues and expenses (excluding grants/extrabudgetary units/social security funds) converted to US dollars at average official exchange rate for year indicated

Public debt: 71.7% of GDP (2023 est.)
note: central government debt as a % of GDP
comparison ranking: 54

Taxes and other revenues: 17.4% (of GDP) (2023 est.)
note: central government tax revenue as a % of GDP
comparison ranking: 74

Current account balance: -$127.432 million (2022 est.)
-$75.451 million (2021 est.)
-$57.858 million (2020 est.)
note: balance of payments - net trade and primary/secondary income in current dollars
comparison ranking: 97

Exports: $152.087 million (2022 est.)
$82.08 million (2021 est.)
$132.943 million (2020 est.)
note: balance of payments - exports of goods and services in current dollars
comparison ranking: 203

Exports - partners: Thailand 49%, Japan 19%, Cote d'Ivoire 10%, China 7%, USA 3% (2023)
note: top five export partners based on percentage share of exports

Exports - commodities: fish, ships, perfume plants, wood, copra (2023)
note: top five export commodities based on value in dollars

Imports: $579.347 million (2022 est.)
$520.391 million (2021 est.)
$438.373 million (2020 est.)
note: balance of payments - imports of goods and services in current dollars
comparison ranking: 198

Imports - partners: China 26%, Australia 15%, Angola 11%, Fiji 9%, NZ 8% (2023)
note: top five import partners based on percentage share of imports

Imports - commodities: refined petroleum, ships, plastic products, poultry, trucks (2023)
note: top five import commodities based on value in dollars

Reserves of foreign exchange and gold: $614.65 million (2024 est.)
$643.768 million (2023 est.)
$638.537 million (2022 est.)
note: holdings of gold (year-end prices)/foreign exchange/special drawing rights in current dollars
comparison ranking: 153

Debt - external: $299.746 million (2023 est.)
note: present value of external debt in current US dollars
comparison ranking: 117

Exchange rates: vatu (VUV) per US dollar -

Exchange rates: 119.167 (2024 est.)
119.112 (2023 est.)
115.354 (2022 est.)
109.452 (2021 est.)
115.38 (2020 est.)

ENERGY

Electricity access: *electrification - total population:* 70% (2022 est.)
electrification - urban areas: 97%
electrification - rural areas: 60.7%

Electricity: *installed generating capacity:* 39,000 kW (2023 est.)
consumption: 74.766 million kWh (2023 est.)
transmission/distribution losses: 5.264 million kWh (2023 est.)
comparison rankings: installed generating capacity 198; consumption 201; transmission/distribution losses 10

Electricity generation sources: *fossil fuels:* 74.9% of total installed capacity (2023 est.)
solar: 8.7% of total installed capacity (2023 est.)
wind: 5% of total installed capacity (2023 est.)
hydroelectricity: 11.2% of total installed capacity (2023 est.)
biomass and waste: 0.1% of total installed capacity (2023 est.)

Petroleum: *refined petroleum consumption:* 2,000 bbl/day (2023 est.)

Energy consumption per capita: 12.934 million Btu/person (2023 est.)
comparison ranking: 144

COMMUNICATIONS

Telephones - fixed lines: *total subscriptions:* 3,000 (2022 est.)
subscriptions per 100 inhabitants: 1 (2022 est.)
comparison ranking: total subscriptions 208

Telephones - mobile cellular: *total subscriptions:* 256,000 (2022 est.)
subscriptions per 100 inhabitants: 78 (2022 est.)
comparison ranking: total subscriptions 182

Broadcast media: 1 state-owned TV station; multi-channel pay TV available; state-owned Radio Vanuatu has 2 radio stations; 2 privately owned radio broadcasters; multiple international broadcasts available (2023)

Internet country code: .vu

Internet users: *percent of population:* 46% (2023 est.)

Broadband - fixed subscriptions: *total:* 4,000 (2022 est.)
subscriptions per 100 inhabitants: 1 (2022 est.)
comparison ranking: total 196

TRANSPORTATION

Civil aircraft registration country code prefix: YJ

Airports: 31 (2025)
comparison ranking: 120

Merchant marine: *total:* 338 (2023)
by type: bulk carrier 11, container ship 3, general cargo 101, other 223
comparison ranking: total 54

Ports: *total ports:* 3 (2024)
large: 0
medium: 0
small: 1
very small: 2
ports with oil terminals: 2
key ports: Forari Bay, Luganville, Port Vila

MILITARY AND SECURITY

Military and security forces: no regular military forces; Vanuatu Police Force (VPF) (2025)
note: the VPF includes the paramilitary Vanuatu Mobile Force (VMF) and Police Maritime Wing (VMW); the VMF has external security responsibilities

Military - note: the separate British and French police forces were unified in 1980 as the New Hebrides Constabulary, which was commanded by Ni-Vanuatu officers while retaining some British and French officers as advisors; the Constabulary was subsequently renamed the Vanuatu Police Force later in 1980
the Vanuatu Mobile Force has received training and other support from Australia, China, France, New Zealand, and the US
Vanuatu has a "shiprider" agreement with the US, which allows local maritime law enforcement officers to embark on US Coast Guard (USCG) and US Navy (USN) vessels, including to board and search vessels suspected of violating laws or regulations within Vanuatu's designated exclusive economic zone (EEZ) or on the high seas; "shiprider" agreements also enable USCG personnel and USN vessels with embarked USCG law enforcement personnel to work with host nations to protect critical regional resources (2025)

TRANSNATIONAL ISSUES

Refugees and internally displaced persons: IDPs: 2,336 (2024 est.)

Trafficking in persons: *tier rating:* Tier 2 Watch List — Vanuatu does not fully meet the minimum standards for the elimination of trafficking, but the government has devoted sufficient resources to a written plan that, if implemented, would constitute significant efforts to meet the minimum standards; therefore, Vanuatu was granted a waiver per the Trafficking Victims Protection Act from an otherwise required downgrade to Tier 3 and remained on Tier 2 Watch List for the third consecutive year; for more details, go to: https://www.state.gov/reports/2025-trafficking-in-persons-report/vanuatu/

VENEZUELA

INTRODUCTION

Background: Venezuela was one of three countries that emerged from the collapse of Gran Colombia in 1830, the others being Ecuador and New Granada (Colombia). For most of the first half of the 20th century, military strongmen ruled Venezuela and promoted the oil industry while allowing some social reforms. Democratically elected governments largely held sway until 1999, but Hugo CHAVEZ, who was president from 1999 to 2013, exercised authoritarian control over other branches of government. This trend continued in 2018 when Nicolas MADURO claimed the presidency for his second term in an election boycotted by most opposition parties and widely viewed as fraudulent. The legislative elections in 2020 were also seen as fraudulent, and most opposition parties and many international actors consider the resulting National Assembly illegitimate. In 2021, many opposition parties broke a three-year election boycott and participated in mayoral and gubernatorial elections, despite flawed conditions. As a result, the opposition more than doubled its representation at the mayoral level and retained four of 23 governorships. The 2021 regional elections marked the first time since 2006 that the EU was allowed to send an electoral observation mission to Venezuela.

MADURO has placed strong restrictions on free speech and the press. Since CHAVEZ, the ruling party has expanded the state's role in the economy through expropriations of major enterprises, strict currency exchange and price controls, and over-dependence on the petroleum industry for revenues. Years of economic mismanagement left Venezuela ill-prepared to weather the global drop in oil prices in 2014, sparking an economic decline that has resulted in reduced government social spending, shortages of basic goods, and high inflation. Worsened living conditions have prompted nearly 8 million Venezuelans to emigrate, mainly settling in nearby countries. The US imposed financial sanctions on MADURO and his representatives in 2017 and on sectors of the Venezuelan economy in 2018. Limited sanctions relief followed when the MADURO administration began making democratic and electoral concessions.

The government's mismanagement and lack of investment in infrastructure has also weakened the country's energy sector. Caracas has relaxed some

controls to mitigate the impact of its sustained economic crisis, such as allowing increased import flexibility for the private sector and the informal use of US dollars and other international currencies. Ongoing concerns include human rights abuses, rampant violent crime, political manipulation of the judicial and electoral systems, and corruption.

GEOGRAPHY

Location: Northern South America, bordering the Caribbean Sea and the North Atlantic Ocean, between Colombia and Guyana

Geographic coordinates: 8 00 N, 66 00 W

Map references: South America

Area: *total:* 912,050 sq km
land: 882,050 sq km
water: 30,000 sq km
comparison ranking: total 34

Area - comparative: almost six times the size of Georgia; slightly more than twice the size of California

Land boundaries: *total:* 5,267 km
border countries (3): Brazil 2,137 km; Colombia 2,341 km; Guyana 789 km

Coastline: 2,800 km

Maritime claims: *territorial sea:* 12 nm
contiguous zone: 15 nm
exclusive economic zone: 200 nm
continental shelf: 200-m depth or to the depth of exploitation

Climate: tropical; hot, humid; more moderate in highlands

Terrain: Andes Mountains and Maracaibo Lowlands in northwest; central plains (llanos); Guiana Highlands in southeast

Elevation: *highest point:* Pico Bolivar 4,978 m
lowest point: Caribbean Sea 0 m
mean elevation: 450 m

Natural resources: petroleum, natural gas, iron ore, gold, bauxite, other minerals, hydropower, diamonds

Land use: *agricultural land:* 24.4% (2022 est.)
arable land: 2.9% (2022 est.)
permanent crops: 0.8% (2022 est.)
permanent pasture: 20.6% (2022 est.)
forest: 52.3% (2022 est.)
other: 23.3% (2022 est.)

Irrigated land: 10,550 sq km (2012)

Major lakes (area sq km): *salt water lake(s):* Lago de Maracaibo - 13,010 sq km

Major rivers (by length in km): Rio Negro (shared with Colombia [s] and Brazil [m]) - 2,250 km; Orinoco river source and mouth (shared with Colombia) - 2,101 km
note: [s] after country name indicates river source; [m] after country name indicates river mouth

Major watersheds (area sq km): Atlantic Ocean drainage: Amazon (6,145,186 sq km), Orinoco (953,675 sq km)

Population distribution: most of the population is concentrated in the northern and western highlands along an eastern spur at the northern end of the Andes, an area that includes the capital of Caracas

Natural hazards: subject to floods, rockslides, mudslides; periodic droughts

Geography - note: *note 1:* the country lies on major sea and air routes linking North and South America
note 2: Venezuela has some of the most unique geology in the world; tepuis are the massive table-top mountains of the western Guiana Highlands that tend to be isolated and thus support unique endemic plant and animal species; their sheer cliffsides help create some of the most spectacular waterfalls in the world, including Angel Falls, the world's highest (979 m; 3,212 ft) that drops from Auyan Tepui

PEOPLE AND SOCIETY

Population: *total:* 31,250,306 (2024 est.)
male: 15,555,451
female: 15,694,855
comparison rankings: total 49; male 49; female 50

Nationality: *noun:* Venezuelan(s)
adjective: Venezuelan

Ethnic groups: unspecified Spanish, Italian, Portuguese, Arab, German, African, Indigenous

Languages: Spanish (official) 98.2%, indigenous 1.3%, Portuguese 0.1%, other 0.4% (2023 est.)
major-language sample(s):
La Libreta Informativa del Mundo, la fuente indispensable de información básica. (Spanish)

Religions: Roman Catholic 48.1%, Protestant 31.6% (Evangelical 31.4%, Adventist 0.2%), Jehovah's Witness 1.4%, African American/umbanda 0.7%, other 0.1%, believer 3.5%, agnostic 0.1%, atheist, 0.4%, none 13.6%, unspecified 0.6% (2023 est.)

Age structure: *0-14 years:* 25% (male 3,987,361/female 3,811,307)
15-64 years: 65.9% (male 10,264,353/female 10,330,376)
65 years and over: 9.1% (2024 est.) (male 1,303,737/female 1,553,172)

Dependency ratios: *total dependency ratio:* 51.7 (2024 est.)
youth dependency ratio: 37.9 (2024 est.)
elderly dependency ratio: 13.9 (2024 est.)
potential support ratio: 7.2 (2024 est.)

Median age: *total:* 31 years (2024 est.)
male: 30.3 years
female: 31.7 years
comparison ranking: total 129

Population growth rate: 2.34% (2024 est.)
comparison ranking: 27

Birth rate: 16.7 births/1,000 population (2024 est.)
comparison ranking: 94

Death rate: 6.5 deaths/1,000 population (2024 est.)
comparison ranking: 137

Net migration rate: 13.2 migrant(s)/1,000 population (2024 est.)
comparison ranking: 3

Population distribution: most of the population is concentrated in the northern and western highlands along an eastern spur at the northern end of the Andes, an area that includes the capital of Caracas

Urbanization: *urban population:* 88.4% of total population (2023)
rate of urbanization: 1.16% annual rate of change (2020-25 est.)

Major urban areas - population: 2.972 million CARACAS (capital), 2.368 million Maracaibo, 1.983 million Valencia, 1.254 million Barquisimeto, 1.243 million Maracay, 964,000 Ciudad Guayana (2023)

Sex ratio: *at birth:* 1.05 male(s)/female
0-14 years: 1.05 male(s)/female
15-64 years: 0.99 male(s)/female
65 years and over: 0.84 male(s)/female
total population: 0.99 male(s)/female (2024 est.)

Maternal mortality ratio: 227 deaths/100,000 live births (2023 est.)
comparison ranking: 36

Infant mortality rate: *total:* 13.9 deaths/1,000 live births (2024 est.)
male: 15.4 deaths/1,000 live births
female: 12.2 deaths/1,000 live births
comparison ranking: total 101

Life expectancy at birth: *total population:* 74.5 years (2024 est.)
male: 71.5 years
female: 77.7 years
comparison ranking: total population 142

Total fertility rate: 2.18 children born/woman (2024 est.)
comparison ranking: 87

Gross reproduction rate: 1.06 (2024 est.)

Drinking water source: *improved:* total: 93.3% of population (2022 est.)
unimproved: total: 6.7% of population (2022 est.)

Health expenditure: 4% of GDP (2021)
6% of national budget (2022 est.)

Physician density: 1.66 physicians/1,000 population (2017)

Hospital bed density: 1 beds/1,000 population (2020 est.)

Sanitation facility access: *improved:* total: 98.4% of population (2022 est.)
unimproved: total: 1.6% of population (2022 est.)

Obesity - adult prevalence rate: 25.6% (2016)
comparison ranking: 49

Alcohol consumption per capita: *total:* 2.51 liters of pure alcohol (2019 est.)
beer: 1.54 liters of pure alcohol (2019 est.)
wine: 0.01 liters of pure alcohol (2019 est.)
spirits: 0.92 liters of pure alcohol (2019 est.)
other alcohols: 0.03 liters of pure alcohol (2019 est.)
comparison ranking: total 123

Currently married women (ages 15-49): 51.5% (2023 est.)

Education expenditure: 1.3% of GDP (2017 est.)

0% national budget (2023 est.)
comparison ranking: Education expenditure (% GDP) 195

Literacy: *total population:* 97% (2016 est.)
male: 97% (2016 est.)
female: 97% (2016 est.)

ENVIRONMENT

Environmental issues: sewage pollution of Lago de Valencia; oil and urban pollution of Lago de Maracaibo; deforestation; soil degradation; urban and industrial pollution, especially along the Caribbean coast; threat to the rainforest ecosystem from mining operations

International environmental agreements: *party to:* Antarctic-Environmental Protection, Antarctic Treaty, Biodiversity, Climate Change, Climate Change-Kyoto Protocol, Climate Change-Paris Agreement, Comprehensive Nuclear Test Ban, Desertification, Endangered Species, Hazardous Wastes, Marine Life Conservation, Nuclear Test Ban, Ozone Layer Protection, Ship Pollution, Tropical Timber 2006, Wetlands
signed, but not ratified: none of the selected agreements

Climate: tropical; hot, humid; more moderate in highlands

Urbanization: *urban population:* 88.4% of total population (2023)
rate of urbanization: 1.16% annual rate of change (2020-25 est.)

Carbon dioxide emissions: 76.73 million metric tonnes of CO2 (2023 est.)
from coal and metallurgical coke: 179,000 metric tonnes of CO2 (2023 est.)
from petroleum and other liquids: 27.928 million metric tonnes of CO2 (2023 est.)
from consumed natural gas: 48.623 million metric tonnes of CO2 (2023 est.)
comparison ranking: total emissions 48

Particulate matter emissions: 16.1 micrograms per cubic meter (2019 est.)

Methane emissions: *energy:* 3,595.7 kt (2022-2024 est.)
agriculture: 1,007.8 kt (2019-2021 est.)
waste: 328.3 kt (2019-2021 est.)
other: 7 kt (2019-2021 est.)

Waste and recycling: *municipal solid waste generated annually:* 9.779 million tons (2024 est.)
percent of municipal solid waste recycled: 21.3% (2022 est.)

Total water withdrawal: *municipal:* 5.123 billion cubic meters (2022 est.)
industrial: 793.3 million cubic meters (2022 est.)
agricultural: 16.71 billion cubic meters (2022 est.)

Total renewable water resources: 1.325 trillion cubic meters (2022 est.)

GOVERNMENT

Country name: *conventional long form:* Bolivarian Republic of Venezuela
conventional short form: Venezuela
local long form: República Bolivariana de Venezuela
local short form: Venezuela
former: State of Venezuela, Republic of Venezuela, United States of Venezuela
etymology: in 1499, the stilt-houses built on Lake Maracaibo reminded explorers Alonso de OJEDA and Amerigo VESPUCCI of buildings in Venice, Italy, and they named the region "Venezuola," meaning "Little Venice"

Government type: federal presidential republic

Capital: *name:* Caracas
geographic coordinates: 10 29 N, 66 52 W
time difference: UTC-4 (1 hour ahead of Washington, DC, during Standard Time)
etymology: named for the Caracas tribe that originally settled in the area; the origin of their name is unknown

Administrative divisions: 23 states (*estados*, singular - *estado*), 1 capital district* (*distrito capital*), and 1 federal dependency** (*dependencia federal*); Amazonas, Anzoátegui, Apure, Aragua, Barinas, Bolivar, Carabobo, Cojedes, Delta Amacuro, Dependencias Federales (Federal Dependencies)**, Distrito Capital (Capital District)*, Falcon, Guárico, La Guairá, Lara, Merida, Miranda, Monagas, Nueva Esparta, Portuguesa, Sucre, Táchira, Trujillo, Yaracuy, Zulia
note: the federal dependency consists of 11 federally controlled island groups with a total of 72 individual islands

Legal system: civil law system based on the Spanish civil code

Constitution: *history:* many previous; latest adopted 15 December 1999, effective 30 December 1999
amendment process: proposed through agreement by at least 39% of the National Assembly membership, by the president of the republic in session with the cabinet of ministers, or by petition of at least 15% of registered voters; passage requires simple majority vote by the Assembly and simple majority approval in a referendum

International law organization participation: has not submitted an ICJ jurisdiction declaration; accepts ICCt jurisdiction

Citizenship: *citizenship by birth:* yes
citizenship by descent only: yes
dual citizenship recognized: yes
residency requirement for naturalization: 10 years; reduced to five years in the case of applicants from Spain, Portugal, Italy, or a Latin American or Caribbean country

Suffrage: 18 years of age; universal

Executive branch: *chief of state:* Notification Statement: the United States does not recognize Nicolas MADURO Moros as president of Venezuela President Nicolas MADURO Moros (since 19 April 2013)
head of government: President Nicolas MADURO Moros (since 19 April 2013)
cabinet: Council of Ministers appointed by the president
election/appointment process: president directly elected by simple-majority popular vote for a 6-year term (no term limits)
most recent election date: 28 July 2024
election results: *2024:* official results disputed; Nicolas MADURO Moros was declared the winner by the MADURO-controlled National Electoral Council; percent of vote - Nicolas MADURO Moros (PSUV) 52%, Edmundo GONZÁLEZ Urrutia (Independent) 43.2%, Luis Eduardo MARTÍNEZ (AD) 1.2%, other 3.6%
2018: Nicolas MADURO Moros reelected president; percent of vote - Nicolas MADURO
Moros (PSUV) 67.9%, Henri FALCON (AP) 20.9%, Javier BERTUCCI 10.8%
expected date of next election: 2030
note 1: the president is both chief of state and head of government
note 2: the United States recognizes that Edmundo GONZÁLEZ won the most votes in the 28 July 2024 presidential election because of overwhelming evidence, including more than 80% of the tally sheets received directly from polling stations that indicated GONZÁLEZ received the most votes by an insurmountable margin

Legislative branch: *legislature name:* National Assembly (Asamblea Nacional)
legislative structure: unicameral
number of seats: 277 (all directly elected)
electoral system: mixed system
scope of elections: full renewal
term in office: 5 years
most recent election date: 5/25/2025
percentage of women in chamber: 32.1%
expected date of next election: May 2030
note: in 2020, the National Electoral Council increased the number of seats in the National Assembly from 167 to 277 for the December 2020 election

Judicial branch: *highest court(s):* Supreme Tribunal of Justice (consists of 32 judges organized into constitutional, political-administrative, electoral, civil appeals, criminal appeals, and social divisions)
judge selection and term of office: judges proposed by the Committee of Judicial Postulation (an independent body of organizations dealing with legal issues and of the organs of citizen power) and appointed by the National Assembly; judges serve nonrenewable 12-year terms
subordinate courts: Superior or Appeals Courts (Tribunales Superiores); District Tribunals (Tribunales de Distrito); Courts of First Instance (Tribunales de Primera Instancia); Parish Courts (Tribunales de Parroquia); Justices of the Peace (Justicia de Paz) Network

Political parties: A New Era (Un Nuevo Tiempo) or UNT
Cambiemos Movimiento Ciudadano or CMC
Christian Democrats or COPEI (also known as the Social Christian Party)
Citizens Encounter or EC
Clear Accounts or CC
Coalition of parties loyal to Nicolas MADURO - Great Patriotic Pole or GPP
Coalition of opposition parties - Democratic Alliance (Alianza Democratica) (includes AD, EL CAMBIO, COPEI, CMC, and AP)
Come Venezuela (Vente Venezuela) or VV
Communist Party of Venezuela or PCV
Consenso en la Zona or Conenzo
Convergencia
Democratic Action or AD
Fatherland for All (Patria para Todos) or PPT
Fearless People's Alliance or ABP
Fuerza Vecinal or FV
Hope for Change (Esperanza por el Cambio) or EL CAMBIO
Justice First (Primero Justicia) or PJ
LAPIZ
Movement to Socialism (Movimiento al Socialismo) or MAS
Popular Will (Voluntad Popular) or VP
Progressive Advance (Avanzada Progresista) or AP
The Radical Cause or La Causa R
United Socialist Party of Venezuela or PSUV
Venezuela First (Primero Venezuela) or PV

Venezuelan Progressive Movement or MPV
Venezuela Project or PV

Diplomatic representation in the US: none
note: the embassy, which had been run by the Venezuelan political opposition, announced on 5 January 2023, that it had ended all embassy functions

Diplomatic representation from the US: *chief of mission:* Ambassador (vacant); Chargé d'Affaires John McNAMARA (since 1 February 2025); note - serves as the chief of mission of the Venezuela Affairs Unit, located in the US Embassy, Bogota
embassy: Venezuela Affairs Unit, US Embassy, Carrera 45 N. 24B-27, Bogota, Colombia
mailing address: 3140 Caracas Place, Washington DC 20521-3140
telephone: 1-888-407-4747
email address and website: ACSBogota@state.gov
https://ve.usembassy.gov/

International organization participation: ACS, Caricom (observer), CD, CDB, CELAC, FAO, G-15, G-24, G-77, IADB, IAEA, IBRD, ICAO, ICC (national committees), ICCt (signatory), ICRM, IDA, IFAD, IFC, IFRCS, IHO, ILO, IMF, IMO, IMSO, Interpol, IOC, IOM, IPU, ITSO, ITU, ITUC (NGOs), LAES, LAIA, LAS (observer), MIGA, NAM, OAS, OPANAL, OPCW, OPEC, PCA, Petrocaribe, UN, UNASUR, UNCTAD, UNESCO, UNHCR, UNHRC, UNIDO, Union Latina, UNOOSA, UNWTO, UPU, WCO, WFTU (NGOs), WHO, WIPO, WMO, WTO

Independence: 5 July 1811 (from Spain)

National holiday: Independence Day, 5 July (1811)

Flag: *description:* three equal horizontal bands of yellow (top), blue, and red, with the coat of arms on the left side of the yellow band and an arc of eight five-pointed white stars centered on the blue band
meaning: yellow stands for the riches of the land, blue for the courage of its people, and red for the blood shed in attaining independence
history: the flag retains the three equal horizontal bands and three main colors from the flag of Gran Colombia, the South American republic that broke up in 1830; in 2006, President Hugo CHAVEZ added the eighth star – the original seven stars represented the country's provinces that united in the war of independence – to match Simon Bolivar's flag from 1827 and to represent the historic province of Guayana

National symbol(s): troupial (bird)

National color(s): yellow, blue, red

National anthem(s): *title:* "Gloria al bravo pueblo" (Glory to the Brave People)
lyrics/music: Vicente SALIAS/Juan Jose LANDAETA
history: adopted 1881; lyrics were written in 1810; both SALIAS and LANDAETA were executed in 1814 during Venezuela's fight for independence

National heritage: *total World Heritage Sites:* 3 (2 cultural, 1 natural)
selected World Heritage Site locales: Coro and its Port (c); Canaima National Park (n);
Ciudad Universitaria de Caracas (c)

ECONOMY

Economic overview: South American economy; ongoing hyperinflation since mid-2010s; chaotic economy due to political corruption, infrastructure cuts, and human rights abuses; in debt default; oil exporter; hydropower consumer; rising Chinese relations

Real GDP (purchasing power parity): $110.943 billion (2023 est.)
$106.672 billion (2022 est.)
$98.768 billion (2021 est.)
note: data in 2015 dollars
comparison ranking: 93

Real GDP growth rate: -19.67% (2018 est.)
-14% (2017 est.)
-15.76% (2017 est.)
note: annual GDP % growth based on constant local currency
comparison ranking: 215

Real GDP per capita: $4,900 (2023 est.)
$4,600 (2022 est.)
$4,000 (2021 est.)
note: data in 2015 dollars
comparison ranking: 175

GDP (official exchange rate): $139.395 billion (2023 est.)
note: data in current dollars at official exchange rate

Inflation rate (consumer prices): 200.9% (2022 est.)
1,588.5% (2021 est.)
2,355.1% (2020 est.)
note: annual % change based on consumer prices
comparison ranking: 213

Agricultural products: milk, sugarcane, maize, rice, plantains, oil palm fruit, bananas, chicken, pineapples, potatoes (2023)
note: top ten agricultural products based on tonnage

Industries: agricultural products, livestock, raw materials, machinery and equipment, transport equipment, construction materials, medical equipment, pharmaceuticals, chemicals, iron and steel products, crude oil and petroleum products

Labor force: 11.136 million (2024 est.)
note: number of people ages 15 or older who are employed or seeking work
comparison ranking: 50

Unemployment rate: 5.5% (2024 est.)
5.5% (2023 est.)
5.8% (2022 est.)
note: % of labor force seeking employment
comparison ranking: 104

Youth unemployment rate (ages 15-24): *total:* 10.6% (2024 est.)
male: 9.3% (2024 est.)
female: 13.2% (2024 est.)
note: % of labor force ages 15-24 seeking employment
comparison ranking: total 115

Population below poverty line: 33.1% (2015 est.)
note: % of population with income below national poverty line

Average household expenditures: *on food:* 52% of household expenditures (2023 est.)
on alcohol and tobacco: 2.8% of household expenditures (2023 est.)

Budget: *revenues:* $30 million (2017 est.)
expenditures: $76 million (2017 est.)

Public debt: 38.9% of GDP (2017 est.)
note: data cover central government debt, as well as the debt of state-owned oil company PDVSA; the data include treasury debt held by foreign entities; the data include some debt issued by subnational entities, as well as intragovernmental debt; intragovernmental debt consists of treasury borrowings from surpluses in the social funds, such as for retirement, medical care, and unemployment; some debt instruments for the social funds are sold at public auctions
comparison ranking: 136

Current account balance: -$3.87 billion (2016 est.)
-$3.87 billion (2016 est.)
-$16.051 billion (2015 est.)
note: balance of payments - net trade and primary/secondary income in current dollars
comparison ranking: 164

Exports: $83.401 billion (2018 est.)
$93.485 billion (2017 est.)
$28.684 billion (2016 est.)
note: balance of payments - exports of goods and services in current dollars
comparison ranking: 53

Exports - partners: USA 50%, China 10%, Spain 9%, Brazil 6%, Turkey 5% (2023)
note: top five export partners based on percentage share of exports

Exports - commodities: crude petroleum, petroleum coke, scrap iron, alcohols, fertilizers (2023)
note: top five export commodities based on value in dollars

Imports: $18.432 billion (2018 est.)
$18.376 billion (2017 est.)
$25.81 billion (2016 est.)
note: balance of payments - imports of goods and services in current dollars
comparison ranking: 100

Imports - partners: China 35%, USA 24%, Brazil 12%, Colombia 7%, Turkey 4% (2023)
note: top five import partners based on percentage share of imports

Imports - commodities: refined petroleum, soybean meal, corn, plastic products, vehicle parts/accessories (2023)
note: top five import commodities based on value in dollars

Reserves of foreign exchange and gold: $9.794 billion (2017 est.)
$10.15 billion (2016 est.)
$15.625 billion (2015 est.)
note: holdings of gold (year-end prices)/foreign exchange/special drawing rights in current dollars
comparison ranking: 78

Exchange rates: bolivars (VEB) per US dollar -

Exchange rates: 9.975 (2017 est.)
9.257 (2016 est.)
6.284 (2015 est.)
6.284 (2014 est.)
6.048 (2013 est.)

ENERGY

Electricity access: *electrification - total population:* 100% (2022 est.)

Electricity: *installed generating capacity:* 33.493 million kW (2023 est.)
consumption: 56.493 billion kWh (2023 est.)
exports: 600 million kWh (2023 est.)
transmission/distribution losses: 25.849 billion kWh (2023 est.)
comparison rankings: installed generating capacity 35; consumption 49; exports 75; transmission/distribution losses 194

Electricity generation sources: *fossil fuels:* 21.6% of total installed capacity (2023 est.)

hydroelectricity: 78.3% of total installed capacity (2023 est.)

Coal: *production:* 149,000 metric tons (2023 est.)
consumption: 80,000 metric tons (2023 est.)
exports: 124,000 metric tons (2023 est.)
imports: 2,000 metric tons (2023 est.)
proven reserves: 730.999 million metric tons (2023 est.)

Petroleum: *total petroleum production:* 801,000 bbl/day (2023 est.)
refined petroleum consumption: 203,000 bbl/day (2023 est.)
crude oil estimated reserves: 303.806 billion barrels (2021 est.)

Natural gas: *production:* 23.873 billion cubic meters (2023 est.)
consumption: 23.873 billion cubic meters (2023 est.)
proven reserves: 5.674 trillion cubic meters (2021 est.)

Energy consumption per capita: 54.474 million Btu/person (2023 est.)
comparison ranking: 92

COMMUNICATIONS

Telephones - fixed lines: *total subscriptions:* 2.683 million (2022 est.)
subscriptions per 100 inhabitants: 10 (2022 est.)
comparison ranking: total subscriptions 41

Telephones - mobile cellular: *total subscriptions:* 18.8 million (2022 est.)
subscriptions per 100 inhabitants: 63 (2022 est.)
comparison ranking: total subscriptions 67

Broadcast media: mix of state-run and private broadcast media subject to high levels of control; 13 public service networks, 61 privately owned TV networks, 1 privately owned news channel with limited national coverage, and a Maduro-backed Pan-American channel; 3 Maduro-aligned radio networks control about 65 news stations and another 30 stations targeted at specific audiences; Maduro-sponsored community broadcasters include 235 radio stations and 44 TV stations; the number of private broadcast radio stations declining, but many remain (2021)

Internet country code: .ve

Internet users: *percent of population:* 62% (2017 est.)

Broadband - fixed subscriptions: *total:* 2.7 million (2022 est.)
subscriptions per 100 inhabitants: 10 (2022 est.)
comparison ranking: total 53

TRANSPORTATION

Civil aircraft registration country code prefix: YV

Airports: 509 (2025)
comparison ranking: 17

Heliports: 88 (2025)
comparison ranking: 28

Railways: *total:* 447 km (2014)
standard gauge: 447 km (2014) 1.435-m gauge (41.4 km electrified)

Merchant marine: *total:* 272 (2023)
by type: bulk carrier 3, container ship 1, general cargo 26, oil tanker 17, other 225
comparison ranking: total 60

Ports: *total ports:* 31 (2024)
large: 1
medium: 2
small: 11
very small: 17
ports with oil terminals: 21
key ports: Amuay (Bahia de Amuay), Bahia de Pertigalete, Ciudad Bolivar, Guanta, La Guaira, La Salina, Las Piedras, Maracaibo, Puerto Cabello, Puerto de Hierro, Puerto la Cruz, Puerto Miranda, Puerto Ordaz, Punta Cardon

MILITARY AND SECURITY

Military and security forces: Bolivarian National Armed Forces (Fuerza Armada Nacional Bolivariana, FANB): Bolivarian Army (Ejercito Bolivariano, EB), Bolivarian Navy (Armada Bolivariana, AB; includes marines, Coast Guard), Bolivarian Military Aviation (Aviacion Militar Bolivariana, AMB), Bolivarian Militia (Milicia Bolivariana), Bolivarian National Guard (Guardia Nacional Bolivaria, GNB), Presidential Honor Guard

Ministry of Interior, Justice, and Peace: Bolivarian National Police (Policía Nacional Bolivariana, PNB) (2025)
note 1: the Bolivarian Militia and the Presidential Honor Guard are considered special/ secondary components of the FANB; the Militia is composed of the Military Reserve and the Territorial Militia and is comprised of armed civilians who receive periodic training in exchange for a small stipend
note 2: the National Guard was made part of the FANB in 2007 and is responsible for maintaining public order, guarding the exterior of key government installations and prisons, conducting counter-narcotics operations, monitoring borders, and providing law enforcement in remote areas; it reports to both the Ministry of Defense and the Ministry of Interior, Justice, and Peace
note 3: the PNB is a federal force created by Hugo CHAVEZ in 2008 as a "preventative police force," separate from state and local ones; the PNB largely focuses on policing Caracas' Libertador municipality, patrolling Caracas-area highways, railways, and metro system, and protecting diplomatic missions; the PNB includes the Special Action Forces (Fuerzas de Acciones Especiales, FAES), a paramilitary unit created by President MADURO to bolster internal security after the 2017 anti-government protests

Military expenditures: 0.6% of GDP (2024 est.)
0.5% of GDP (2023 est.)
0.6% of GDP (2022 est.)
0.3% of GDP (2021 est.)
1.6% of GDP (2020 est.)

Military and security service personnel strengths: information varies; approximately 125-150,000 active Armed Forces; estimated 200,000 Bolivarian Militia (2025)

Military equipment inventories and acquisitions: the FANB inventory is comprised mostly of Russian/Soviet-era weapons and equipment; in recent years, it has acquired some material from China and Iran; it also has smaller quantities of older equipment from France, Germany, Spain, the UK, and the US (2024)
note: the US prohibited the sale or transfer of military arms or technology to Venezuela in 2006

Military service age and obligation: 18-30 (25 for women) for voluntary service; the minimum service obligation is 24-30 months; 17-39 for Militia service; all citizens of military service age (18-50) are obligated to register for military service and subject to military training (2025)

Military - note: the armed forces (FANB) are responsible for ensuring Venezuela's independence, sovereignty, and territorial integrity; they also have a domestic role, including assisting with maintaining internal security, conducting counter-narcotics missions, contributing to national socio-economic development, and providing disaster relief/humanitarian assistance; the military conducts internal security operations in large parts of the country and has been deployed against illegal armed groups operating in the Colombian border region and other areas to combat organized crime gangs involved in narcotics trafficking and illegal mining; it has ties with the militaries of China, Cuba, Iran, and Russia
the FANB has a role in the country's economy and political sectors; military officers hold key positions in state-owned companies, government ministries, and funding agencies; the FANB runs corporation involved in agriculture, banking, communications, energy, insurance, mining, and transportation (2025)

SPACE

Space agency/agencies: Bolivarian Agency for Space Activities (Agencia Bolivariana para Actividades Espaciales, ABAE; formed 2007) (2025)
note: the ABAE is under the Ministry of Science, Technology, and Innovation; it was originally known as the Venezuelan Space Center (CEV; created 2005)

Space program overview: has a small national program primarily focused on the acquisition of satellites and stimulating the country's science and technological capabilities; operates satellites and maintains two satellite ground control stations; participates in multinational space organizations, such as the Latin American and Caribbean Space Agency; closest bilateral partners are China and Russia; also has bilateral framework agreements for space cooperation with Argentina, Bolivia, Brazil, the US, and Uruguay (2025)
note: further details about the key activities, programs, and milestones of the country's space program, as well as government spending estimates on the space sector, appear in the Space Programs reference guide

TERRORISM

Terrorist group(s): Terrorist group(s): National Liberation Army (ELN); Revolutionary Armed Forces of Colombia-People's Army (FARC-EP); Segundo Marquetalia (SM); Tren de Aragua (TdA)
note: details about the history, aims, leadership, organization, areas of operation, tactics, targets, weapons, size, and sources of support of the group(s) appear(s) in Appendix T

TRANSNATIONAL ISSUES

Refugees and internally displaced persons: *refugees:* 20,911 (2024 est.)

IDPs: 2,338 (2024 est.)

Trafficking in persons: *tier rating:* Tier 3 — Venezuela does not fully meet the minimum standards for the elimination of trafficking and is not making any efforts to do so, therefore, Venezuela remained on Tier 3; for more details, go to: https://www.state.gov/reports/2025-trafficking-in-persons-report/venezuela/

Illicit drugs: USG identification: major illicit drug-producing and/or drug-transit country
major precursor-chemical producer (2025)

VIETNAM

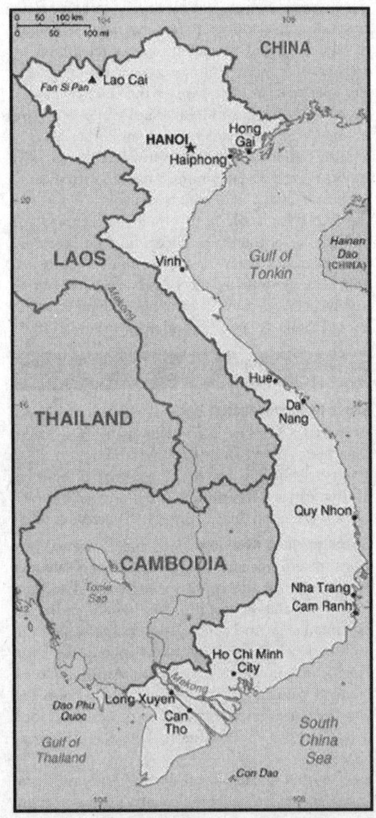

INTRODUCTION

Background: Vietnam's early history included periods of occupation by outside forces and eventual power consolidation under Vietnamese dynastic families. A succession of Han Chinese emperors ruled the area, which was centered on the Red River Valley, until approximately the 10th century. The Ly Dynasty (11th-13th century) created the first independent Vietnamese state, which was known as Dai Viet, and established their capital at Thang Long (Hanoi). Under the Tran Dynasty (13th-15th century), TRAN Hung Dao, one of Vietnam's national heroes, led Dai Viet forces to fight off Mongol invaders in 1279. After a brief Chinese occupation in the early 1400s, Vietnamese resistance leader LE Thai To made himself emperor and established the Le Dynasty, which lasted until the late 18th century despite decades of political turmoil, civil war, and division. During this period, Dai Viet expanded southward to the Central Highlands and Mekong Delta, reaching the approximate boundaries of modern-day Vietnam by the 1750s. Dai Viet suffered additional civil war and division in the latter half of the 18th century, but it was reunited and renamed Vietnam under Emperor NGUYEN Phuc Anh (aka Gia Long) in 1802.

France began its conquest of Vietnam in 1858 and made Vietnam part of French Indochina in 1887. Vietnam declared independence after World War II, but the French continued to rule until communist forces under Ho Chi MINH defeated them in 1954. Under the Geneva Accords of 1954, Vietnam was divided into the communist North and anti-communist South. Fighting erupted between the two governments shortly afterwards with the North supporting communist rebels in the South and eventually committing thousands of combat troops. The US provided to the South significant economic and military assistance, including large numbers of US military forces, which reached a peak strength of over 500,000 troops in 1968.

US combat forces were withdrawn following a cease-fire agreement in 1973. Two years later, North Vietnamese forces overran the South, reuniting the country under communist rule. The conflict, known as the Second Indochina War (1955-1975), devastated Vietnam, spilled over into the neighboring countries of Cambodia and Laos, and is estimated to have resulted in the deaths of up to 3 million Vietnamese civilians and soldiers. It also caused more than 58,000 US combat and non-combat deaths and created deep domestic divisions in the US.

Despite the return of peace, the country experienced little economic growth for over a decade because of its diplomatic isolation, leadership policies, and the persecution and mass exodus of citizens, many of them successful South Vietnamese merchants. However, since the enactment of Vietnam's "doi moi" (renovation) policy in 1986, the economy has seen strong growth, particularly in agricultural and industrial production, construction, exports, foreign investment, and tourism. Nevertheless, the Communist Party maintains tight political and social control of the country, and Vietnam faces many related challenges, such as rising income inequality and corruption.

GEOGRAPHY

Location: Southeastern Asia, bordering the Gulf of Thailand, Gulf of Tonkin, and South China Sea, as well as China, Laos, and Cambodia

Geographic coordinates: 16 10 N, 107 50 E

Map references: Southeast Asia

Area: *total:* 331,210 sq km
land: 310,070 sq km
water: 21,140 sq km
comparison ranking: total 67

Area - comparative: about three times the size of Tennessee; slightly larger than New Mexico

Land boundaries: *total:* 4,616 km
border countries (3): Cambodia 1,158 km; China 1,297 km; Laos 2,161 km

Coastline: 3,444 km (excludes islands)

Maritime claims: *territorial sea:* 12 nm
contiguous zone: 24 nm
exclusive economic zone: 200 nm
continental shelf: 200 nm or to the edge of the continental margin

Climate: tropical in south; monsoonal in north with hot, rainy season (May to September) and warm, dry season (October to March)

Terrain: low, flat delta in south and north; central highlands; hilly, mountainous in far north and northwest

Elevation: *highest point:* Fan Si Pan 3,144 m
lowest point: South China Sea 0 m
mean elevation: 398 m

Natural resources: antimony, phosphates, coal, manganese, rare earth elements, bauxite, chromate, offshore oil and gas deposits, timber, hydropower, arable land

Land use: *agricultural land:* 39.3% (2022 est.)
arable land: 21.5% (2022 est.)
permanent crops: 15.7% (2022 est.)
permanent pasture: 2% (2022 est.)
forest: 47.2% (2022 est.)
other: 13.5% (2022 est.)

Irrigated land: 46,000 sq km (2012)

Major rivers (by length in km): Sông Tiên Giang (Mekong) river mouth (shared with China [s], Burma, Laos, Thailand, Cambodia) - 4,350 km; Pearl river source (shared with China [m]) - 2,200 km; Red river mouth (shared with China [s]) - 1,149 km
note: [s] after country name indicates river source; [m] after country name indicates river mouth

Major watersheds (area sq km): Pacific Ocean drainage: Mekong (805,604 sq km)

Population distribution: though it has one of the highest population densities in the world, the population is not evenly dispersed; clustering is heaviest along the South China Sea and Gulf of Tonkin, with the Mekong Delta (in the south) and the Red River Valley (in the north) having the largest concentrations of people

Natural hazards: occasional typhoons (May to January) with extensive flooding, especially in the Mekong River delta

Geography - note: *note 1:* extending 1,650 km (1,025 mi) north to south, the country is only 50 km (31 mi) across at its narrowest point
note 2: Son Doong in Phong Nha-Ke Bang National Park is the world's largest cave (greatest cross-sectional area) and is the largest known cave passage in the world by volume at 38.5 million cu m (about 1.35 billion cu ft); it connects to Thoong cave, but not yet officially – when recognized, it will add an additional 1.6 million cu m; it is so massive that it contains its own jungle, underground river, and localized weather system, with clouds forming inside the cave and spewing from its exits

PEOPLE AND SOCIETY

Population: *total:* 105,758,975 (2024 est.)
male: 53,109,175
female: 52,649,800
comparison rankings: total 16; male 16; female 16

Nationality: *noun:* Vietnamese (singular and plural)
adjective: Vietnamese

Ethnic groups: Kinh (Viet) 85.3%, Tay 1.9%, Thai 1.9%, Muong 1.5%, Khmer 1.4%, Mong 1.4%, Nung 1.1%, other 5.5% (2019 est.)

note: 54 ethnic groups are recognized by the Vietnamese Government

Languages: Vietnamese (official); English (often as a second language); some French, Chinese, and Khmer; mountain-area languages (including Mon-Khmer and Malayo-Polynesian)
major-language sample(s):
Dữ kiện thế giới, là nguồn thông tin cơ bản không thể thiếu. (Vietnamese)

Religions: Catholic 6.1%, Buddhist 5.8%, Protestant 1%, other 0.8%, none 86.3% (2019 est.)
note: most Vietnamese are culturally Buddhist

Age structure: *0-14 years:* 23.2% (male 12,953,719/female 11,579,690)
15-64 years: 68.5% (male 36,591,845/female 35,887,201)
65 years and over: 8.3% (2024 est.) (male 3,563,611/female 5,182,909)

Dependency ratios: *total dependency ratio:* 45.9 (2024 est.)
youth dependency ratio: 33.8 (2024 est.)
elderly dependency ratio: 12.1 (2024 est.)
potential support ratio: 8.3 (2024 est.)

Median age: *total:* 33.1 years (2024 est.)
male: 32 years
female: 34.2 years
comparison ranking: total 113

Population growth rate: 0.89% (2024 est.)
comparison ranking: 102

Birth rate: 14.9 births/1,000 population (2024 est.)
comparison ranking: 111

Death rate: 5.8 deaths/1,000 population (2024 est.)
comparison ranking: 165

Net migration rate: -0.2 migrant(s)/1,000 population (2024 est.)
comparison ranking: 106

Population distribution: though it has one of the highest population densities in the world, the population is not evenly dispersed; clustering is heaviest along the South China Sea and Gulf of Tonkin, with the Mekong Delta (in the south) and the Red River Valley (in the north) having the largest concentrations of people

Urbanization: *urban population:* 39.5% of total population (2023)
rate of urbanization: 2.7% annual rate of change (2020-25 est.)

Major urban areas - population: 9.321 million Ho Chi Minh City, 5.253 million HANOI (capital), 1.865 million Can Tho, 1.423 million Hai Phong, 1.221 million Da Nang, 1.111 million Bien Hoa (2023)

Sex ratio: *at birth:* 1.1 male(s)/female
0-14 years: 1.12 male(s)/female
15-64 years: 1.02 male(s)/female
65 years and over: 0.69 male(s)/female
total population: 1.01 male(s)/female (2024 est.)

Maternal mortality ratio: 48 deaths/100,000 live births (2023 est.)
comparison ranking: 96

Infant mortality rate: *total:* 14.1 deaths/1,000 live births (2024 est.)
male: 14.4 deaths/1,000 live births
female: 13.7 deaths/1,000 live births
comparison ranking: total 99

Life expectancy at birth: *total population:* 76.1 years (2024 est.)
male: 73.5 years
female: 78.9 years
comparison ranking: total population 115

Total fertility rate: 2.03 children born/woman (2024 est.)
comparison ranking: 102

Gross reproduction rate: 0.96 (2024 est.)

Drinking water source: *improved: urban:* 99.1% of population (2022 est.)
rural: 97.2% of population (2022 est.)
total: 98% of population (2022 est.)
unimproved: urban: 0.9% of population (2022 est.)
rural: 2.8% of population (2022 est.)
total: 2% of population (2022 est.)

Health expenditure: 4.6% of GDP (2021)
10.7% of national budget (2022 est.)

Physician density: 1.11 physicians/1,000 population (2021)

Hospital bed density: 2.6 beds/1,000 population (2017 est.)

Sanitation facility access: *improved: urban:* 99.9% of population (2022 est.)
rural: 90.9% of population (2022 est.)
total: 94.4% of population (2022 est.)
unimproved: urban: 0.1% of population (2022 est.)
rural: 9.1% of population (2022 est.)
total: 5.6% of population (2022 est.)

Obesity - adult prevalence rate: 2.1% (2016)
comparison ranking: 192

Alcohol consumption per capita: *total:* 3.41 liters of pure alcohol (2019 est.)
beer: 3.18 liters of pure alcohol (2019 est.)
wine: 0.02 liters of pure alcohol (2019 est.)
spirits: 0.21 liters of pure alcohol (2019 est.)
other alcohols: 0 liters of pure alcohol (2019 est.) comparison ranking: total 105

Tobacco use: *total:* 22% (2025 est.)
male: 43.1% (2025 est.)
female: 2.1% (2025 est.)
comparison ranking: total 53

Children under the age of 5 years underweight: 11.6% (2020)
comparison ranking: 46

Currently married women (ages 15-49): 72.6% (2023 est.)

Child marriage: *women married by age 15:* 1.1% (2021)
women married by age 18: 14.6% (2021)
men married by age 18: 1.9% (2021)

Education expenditure: 2.9% of GDP (2022 est.)
15.4% national budget (2022 est.)
comparison ranking: Education expenditure (% GDP) 160

Literacy: *total population:* 96% (2022 est.)
male: 97% (2022 est.)
female: 95% (2022 est.)

School life expectancy (primary to tertiary education): *total:* 14 years (2022 est.)
male: 15 years (2022 est.)
female: 14 years (2022 est.)

ENVIRONMENT

Environmental issues: deforestation and soil degradation from logging and slash-and-burn agriculture; water pollution; overfishing; groundwater contamination limits potable water supply; air pollution

International environmental agreements: *party to:* Biodiversity, Climate Change, Climate Change-Kyoto Protocol, Climate Change-Paris Agreement, Comprehensive Nuclear Test Ban, Desertification, Endangered Species, Environmental Modification, Hazardous Wastes, Law of the Sea, Ozone Layer Protection, Ship Pollution, Tropical Timber 2006, Wetlands
signed, but not ratified: none of the selected agreements

Climate: tropical in south; monsoonal in north with hot, rainy season (May to September) and warm, dry season (October to March)

Urbanization: *urban population:* 39.5% of total population (2023)
rate of urbanization: 2.7% annual rate of change (2020-25 est.)

Carbon dioxide emissions: 305.404 million metric tonnes of CO2 (2023 est.)
from coal and metallurgical coke: 218.502 million metric tonnes of CO2 (2023 est.)
from petroleum and other liquids: 72.383 million metric tonnes of CO2 (2023 est.)
from consumed natural gas: 14.52 million metric tonnes of CO2 (2023 est.)
comparison ranking: total emissions 20

Particulate matter emissions: 20.9 micrograms per cubic meter (2019 est.)

Methane emissions: *energy:* 806.7 kt (2022-2024 est.)
agriculture: 2,146.3 kt (2019-2021 est.)
waste: 683.4 kt (2019-2021 est.)
other: 40.4 kt (2019-2021 est.)

Waste and recycling: *municipal solid waste generated annually:* 9.57 million tons (2024 est.)
percent of municipal solid waste recycled: 46% (2022 est.)

Total water withdrawal: *municipal:* 1.206 billion cubic meters (2022 est.)
industrial: 3.074 billion cubic meters (2022 est.)
agricultural: 77.75 billion cubic meters (2022 est.)

Total renewable water resources: 884.12 billion cubic meters (2022 est.)

Geoparks: *total global geoparks and regional networks:* 4 (2025)
global geoparks and regional networks: Dak Nong; Dong Van Karst Plateau; Lang Son;
Non nuoc Cao Bang (2025)

GOVERNMENT

Country name: *conventional long form:* Socialist Republic of Vietnam
conventional short form: Vietnam
local long form: Cong Hoa Xa Hoi Chu Nghia Viet Nam
local short form: Viet Nam
former: Democratic Republic of Vietnam (North Vietnam), Republic of Vietnam (South Vietnam)
abbreviation: SRV
etymology: the name translates as "Viet south;" *Viet* is an ethnic term of unknown origin that dates back to ancient times, and *nam* (south) refers to the country's location

Government type: communist party-led state

Capital: *name:* Hanoi (Ha Noi)
geographic coordinates: 21 02 N, 105 51 E
time difference: UTC+7 (12 hours ahead of Washington, DC, during Standard Time)
etymology: the name means "inside the river," from the Vietnamese words *ha* (river) and *noi* (inside), and refers to its location in a bend of the Red River

Administrative divisions: 58 provinces (*tinh*, singular and plural) and 5 municipalities (*thanh pho*, singular and plural)
provinces: An Giang, Bac Giang, Bac Kan, Bac Lieu, Bac Ninh, Ba Ria-Vung Tau, Ben Tre, Binh Dinh, Binh Duong, Binh Phuoc, Binh Thuan, Ca Mau, Cao Bang, Dak Lak, Dak Nong, Dien Bien, Dong Nai, Dong Thap, Gia Lai, Ha Giang, Ha Nam, Ha Tinh, Hai Duong, Hau Giang, Hoa Binh, Hung Yen, Khanh Hoa, Kien Giang, Kon Tum, Lai Chau, Lam Dong, Lang Son, Lao Cai, Long An, Nam Dinh, Nghe An, Ninh Binh, Ninh Thuan, Phu Tho, Phu Yen, Quang Binh, Quang Nam, Quang Ngai, Quang Ninh, Quang Tri, Soc Trang, Son La, Tay Ninh, Thai Binh, Thai Nguyen, Thanh Hoa, Thua Thien-Hue, Tien Giang, Tra Vinh, Tuyen Quang, Vinh Long, Vinh Phuc, Yen Bai
municipalities: Can Tho, Da Nang, Ha Noi (Hanoi), Hai Phong, Ho Chi Minh City (Saigon)

Legal system: civil law system with European influences

Constitution: *history:* several previous; latest adopted 28 November 2013, effective 1 January 2014
amendment process: proposed by the president, by the National Assembly's Standing Committee, or by at least two thirds of the National Assembly membership; a decision to draft an amendment requires approval by at least a two-thirds majority vote of the Assembly membership, followed by the formation of a constitutional drafting committee to write a draft and collect citizens' opinions; passage requires at least two-thirds majority of the Assembly membership; the Assembly can opt to conduct a referendum

International law organization participation: has not submitted an ICJ jurisdiction declaration; non-party state to the ICCt

Citizenship: *citizenship by birth:* no
citizenship by descent only: at least one parent must be a citizen of Vietnam
dual citizenship recognized: no
residency requirement for naturalization: 5 years

Suffrage: 18 years of age; universal

Executive branch: *chief of state:* President Luong CUONG (since 21 Oct 2024)
head of government: Prime Minister Pham Minh CHINH (since 26 July 2021)
cabinet: Cabinet proposed by the prime minister, confirmed by the National Assembly, and appointed by the president
election/appointment process: president indirectly elected by the National Assembly from among its members for a single 5-year term; prime minister recommended by the president and confirmed by the National Assembly; deputy prime ministers appointed by the president and confirmed by the National Assembly
note: in August 2024, To LAM was elected general secretary of the Central Committee of the Communist Party of Vietnam, the country's most powerful position

Legislative branch: *legislature name:* National Assembly (Quoc-Hoi)
legislative structure: unicameral
number of seats: 500 (all directly elected)
electoral system: plurality/majority
scope of elections: full renewal
term in office: 5 years
most recent election date: 5/23/2021
parties elected and seats per party: Communist Party (485); Other (14)
percentage of women in chamber: 31.4%
expected date of next election: May 2026

Judicial branch: *highest court(s):* Supreme People's Court (consists of the chief justice and 13 judges)
judge selection and term of office: chief justice elected by the National Assembly upon the recommendation of the president for a 5-year, renewable term; deputy chief justice appointed by the president from among the judges for a 5-year term; judges appointed by the president and confirmed by the National Assembly for 5-year terms
subordinate courts: High Courts (administrative, civil, criminal, economic, labor, family, juvenile); provincial courts; district courts; Military Court
note: the National Assembly Standing Committee can establish special tribunals on the recommendation of the chief justice

Political parties: Communist Party of Vietnam or CPV
note: other parties banned

Diplomatic representation in the US: *chief of mission:* Ambassador Nguyen Quoc DZUNG (since 19 April 2022)
chancery: 1233 20th Street NW, Suite 400, Washington, DC 20036
telephone: [1] (202) 861-0737
FAX: [1] (202) 861-0917
email address and website: vanphong@vietnamembassy.us
http://vietnamembassy-usa.org/
consulate(s) general: Houston, San Francisco
consulate(s): New York

Diplomatic representation from the US: *chief of mission:* Ambassador Marc KNAPPER (since 11 February 2022)
embassy: 7 Lang Ha Street, Hanoi
mailing address: 4550 Hanoi Place, Washington, DC 20521-4550
telephone: [84] (24) 3850-5000
FAX: [84] (24) 3850-5010
email address and website: ACShanoi@state.gov
https://vn.usembassy.gov/
consulate(s) general: Ho Chi Minh City

International organization participation: ADB, APEC, ARF, ASEAN, CICA, CP, EAS, FAO, G-77, IAEA, IBRD, ICAO, ICC (NGOs), ICRM, IDA, IFAD, IFC, IFRCS, ILO, IMF, IMO, IMSO, Interpol, IOC, IOM, IPU, ISO, ITSO, ITU, MIGA, NAM, OIF, OPCW, PCA, UN, UNCTAD, UNESCO, UNHRC, UNIDO, UNOOSA, UNWTO, UPU, WCO, WFTU (NGOs), WHO, WIPO, WMO, WTO (2024)

Independence: 2 September 1945 (from France)

National holiday: Independence Day (National Day), 2 September (1945)

Flag: *description:* red field with a five-pointed yellow star in the center
meaning: red stands for revolution and blood, and the five-pointed star for the five elements of the populace – peasants, workers, intellectuals, traders, and soldiers – that unite to build socialism

National symbol(s): five-pointed yellow star on a red field, lotus blossom

National color(s): red, yellow

National anthem(s): *title:* "Tien quan ca" (The Song of the Marching Troops)
lyrics/music: Nguyen Van CAO
history: adopted as the national anthem of the Democratic Republic of Vietnam in 1945; it became the national anthem of the unified Socialist Republic of Vietnam in 1976; only the first verse is used as the official anthem

National heritage: *total World Heritage Sites:* 9 (6 cultural, 2 natural, 1 mixed)
selected World Heritage Site locales: Complex of Hué Monuments (c); Ha Long Bay (n); Hoi An Ancient Town (c); My Son Sanctuary (c); Phong Nha-Ke Bang National Park (n); Imperial Citadel of Thang Long - Hanoi (c); Citadel of the Ho Dynasty (c); Trang An Landscape Complex (m); Yen Tu-Vinh Nghiem-Con Son, Kiep Bac Complex of Monuments and Landscapes (c)

ECONOMY

Economic overview: lower middle-income socialist East Asian economy; rapid economic growth since Đổi Mới reforms; strong investment and productivity growth; tourism and manufacturing hub; TPP signatory; declining poverty aside from ethnic minorities; systemic corruption

Real GDP (purchasing power parity): $1.456 trillion (2024 est.)
$1.359 trillion (2023 est.)
$1.294 trillion (2022 est.)
note: data in 2021 dollars
comparison ranking: 25

Real GDP growth rate: 7.1% (2024 est.)
5.1% (2023 est.)
8.5% (2022 est.)
note: annual GDP % growth based on constant local currency
comparison ranking: 16

Real GDP per capita: $14,400 (2024 est.)
$13,500 (2023 est.)
$13,000 (2022 est.)
note: data in 2021 dollars
comparison ranking: 127

GDP (official exchange rate): $476.388 billion (2024 est.)
note: data in current dollars at official exchange rate

Inflation rate (consumer prices): 3.6% (2024 est.)
3.3% (2023 est.)
3.2% (2022 est.)
note: annual % change based on consumer prices
comparison ranking: 116

GDP - composition, by sector of origin: *agriculture:* 11.9% (2024 est.)
industry: 37.6% (2024 est.)
services: 42.4% (2024 est.)
note: figures may not total 100% due to non-allocated consumption not captured in sector-reported data
comparison rankings: agriculture 65; industry 26; services 185

GDP - composition, by end use: *household consumption:* 54.3% (2023 est.)
government consumption: 8.8% (2023 est.)
investment in fixed capital: 30.1% (2023 est.)
investment in inventories: 1.5% (2023 est.)
exports of goods and services: 86.5% (2023 est.)
imports of goods and services: -78.4% (2023 est.)
note: figures may not total 100% due to rounding or gaps in data collection

Agricultural products: rice, vegetables, sugarcane, cassava, maize, pork, fruits, bananas, coconuts, coffee (2023)
note: top ten agricultural products based on tonnage

Industries: food processing, garments, shoes, machine-building; mining, coal, steel; cement, chemical fertilizer, glass, tires, oil, mobile phones

Industrial production growth rate: 8.2% (2024 est.)
note: annual % change in industrial value added based on constant local currency
comparison ranking: 19

Labor force: 57.133 million (2024 est.)
note: number of people ages 15 or older who are employed or seeking work
comparison ranking: 12

Unemployment rate: 1.5% (2024 est.)
1.7% (2023 est.)
1.6% (2022 est.)
note: % of labor force seeking employment
comparison ranking: 11

Youth unemployment rate (ages 15-24): *total:* 6.8% (2024 est.)
male: 7% (2024 est.)
female: 6.6% (2024 est.)
note: % of labor force ages 15-24 seeking employment
comparison ranking: total 148

Population below poverty line: 4.3% (2022 est.)
note: % of population with income below national poverty line

Gini Index coefficient - distribution of family income: 36.1 (2022 est.)
note: index (0-100) of income distribution; higher values represent greater inequality
comparison ranking: 66

Average household expenditures: *on food:* 34.9% of household expenditures (2023 est.)
on alcohol and tobacco: 1.9% of household expenditures (2023 est.)

Household income or consumption by percentage share: *lowest 10%:* 2.6% (2022 est.)
highest 10%: 28.1% (2022 est.)
note: % share of income accruing to lowest and highest 10% of population

Remittances: 3.2% of GDP (2023 est.)
3.2% of GDP (2022 est.)
3.5% of GDP (2021 est.)
note: personal transfers and compensation between resident and non-resident individuals/households/entities

Budget: *revenues:* $68.818 billion (2022 est.)
expenditures: $83.707 billion (2022 est.)
note: central government revenues and expenses (excluding grants/extrabudgetary units/social security funds) converted to US dollars at average official exchange rate for year indicated

Public debt: 58.5% of GDP (2017 est.)
note: official data; data cover general government debt and include debt instruments issued (or owned) by government entities other than the treasury; the data include treasury debt held by foreign entities; the data include debt issued by subnational entities, as well as intragovernmental debt; intragovernmental debt consists of treasury borrowings from surpluses in the social funds, such as for retirement, medical care, and unemployment; debt instruments for the social funds are not sold at public auctions
comparison ranking: 80

Current account balance: $28.047 billion (2024 est.)
$25.793 billion (2023 est.)
$1.402 billion (2022 est.)
note: balance of payments - net trade and primary/secondary income in current dollars
comparison ranking: 19

Exports: $429.383 billion (2024 est.)
$374.986 billion (2023 est.)
$385.241 billion (2022 est.)
note: balance of payments - exports of goods and services in current dollars
comparison ranking: 23

Exports - partners: USA 28%, China 20%, Japan 6%, Hong Kong 4%, Germany 3% (2023)
note: top five export partners based on percentage share of exports

Exports - commodities: broadcasting equipment, garments, integrated circuits, machine parts, footwear (2023)
note: top five export commodities based on value in dollars

Imports: $398.672 billion (2024 est.)
$339.785 billion (2023 est.)
$369.746 billion (2022 est.)
note: balance of payments - imports of goods and services in current dollars
comparison ranking: 22

Imports - partners: China 49%, Singapore 6%, Japan 6%, Hong Kong 5%, Taiwan 4% (2023)
note: top five import partners based on percentage share of imports

Imports - commodities: integrated circuits, broadcasting equipment, fabric, plastics, telephones (2023)
note: top five import commodities based on value in dollars

Reserves of foreign exchange and gold: $83.082 billion (2024 est.)
$92.238 billion (2023 est.)
$86.54 billion (2022 est.)
note: holdings of gold (year-end prices)/foreign exchange/special drawing rights in current dollars
comparison ranking: 31

Debt - external: $34.426 billion (2023 est.)
note: present value of external debt in current US dollars
comparison ranking: 25

Exchange rates: dong (VND) per US dollar -

Exchange rates: 24,164.886 (2024 est.)
23,787.319 (2023 est.)
23,271.212 (2022 est.)
23,159.783 (2021 est.)
23,208.368 (2020 est.)

ENERGY

Electricity access: *electrification - total population:* 100% (2022 est.)

Electricity: *installed generating capacity:* 85.725 million kW (2023 est.)
consumption: 277.501 billion kWh (2023 est.)
exports: 933.237 million kWh (2023 est.)
imports: 3.106 billion kWh (2023 est.)
transmission/distribution losses: 18.197 billion kWh (2023 est.)
comparison rankings: installed generating capacity 19; consumption 17; exports 71; imports 60; transmission/distribution losses 188

Electricity generation sources: *fossil fuels:* 50.6% of total installed capacity (2023 est.)
solar: 9.7% of total installed capacity (2023 est.)
wind: 4.2% of total installed capacity (2023 est.)
hydroelectricity: 34.3% of total installed capacity (2023 est.)
biomass and waste: 1.1% of total installed capacity (2023 est.)

Coal: *production:* 51.519 million metric tons (2023 est.)
consumption: 96.099 million metric tons (2023 est.)
exports: 815,000 metric tons (2023 est.)
imports: 43.637 million metric tons (2023 est.)
proven reserves: 3.116 billion metric tons (2023 est.)

Petroleum: *total petroleum production:* 187,000 bbl/day (2023 est.)
refined petroleum consumption: 544,000 bbl/day (2023 est.)
crude oil estimated reserves: 4.4 billion barrels (2021 est.)

Natural gas: *production:* 7.48 billion cubic meters (2023 est.)
consumption: 7.48 billion cubic meters (2023 est.)
proven reserves: 699.426 billion cubic meters (2021 est.)

Energy consumption per capita: 40.263 million Btu/person (2023 est.)
comparison ranking: 102

COMMUNICATIONS

Telephones - fixed lines: *total subscriptions:* 2.316 million (2023 est.)
subscriptions per 100 inhabitants: 2 (2023 est.)
comparison ranking: total subscriptions 46

Telephones - mobile cellular: *total subscriptions:* 131 million (2023 est.)
subscriptions per 100 inhabitants: 140 (2022 est.)
comparison ranking: total subscriptions 14

Broadcast media: state-controlled broadcast media, with oversight from the Ministry of Information and Communication (MIC); state-controlled national TV provider, Vietnam Television (VTV), has several channels with regional broadcasting centers; law limits access to satellite TV, but many access foreign programming via home satellite equipment; state-controlled Voice of Vietnam, the national radio broadcaster, broadcasts on several channels and is repeated on AM, FM, and shortwave stations (2018)

Internet country code: .vn

Internet users: *percent of population:* 78% (2023 est.)

Broadband - fixed subscriptions: *total:* 22.8 million (2023 est.)
subscriptions per 100 inhabitants: 23 (2023 est.)
comparison ranking: total 12

TRANSPORTATION

Civil aircraft registration country code prefix: VN

Airports: 36 (2025)
comparison ranking: 112

Heliports: 26 (2025)
comparison ranking: 50

Railways: *total:* 2,600 km (2014)
standard gauge: 178 km (2014) 1.435-m gauge; 253 km mixed gauge
narrow gauge: 2,169 km (2014) 1.000-m gauge

Merchant marine: *total:* 1,973 (2022)
by type: bulk carrier 117, container ship 45, general cargo 1,176, oil tanker 134, other 501
comparison ranking: total 13

Ports: *total ports:* 16 (2024)
large: 0
medium: 1
small: 6
very small: 9
ports with oil terminals: 12

key ports: Da Nang, Hai Phong, Nghe Tinh, Nha Trang, Thanh Ho Chi Minh, Vinh Cam Ranh, Vung Tau

MILITARY AND SECURITY

Military and security forces: People's Army of Vietnam (PAVN; aka Vietnam People's Army, VPA): Ground Forces (Army), Navy (includes naval infantry), Air Defense - Air Force, Vietnam Border Guard, Vietnam Coast Guard
Vietnam People's Ministry of Public Security; Vietnam Civil Defense Force (2025)
note 1: the People's Public Security Ministry is responsible for internal security and controls the national police, a special national security investigative agency, and other internal security units, including specialized riot police regiments
note 2: the Vietnam Coast Guard was established in 1998 as the Vietnam Marine Police and renamed in 2013; Vietnam established a civilian maritime self-defense force in 2010; the Vietnam Department of Fisheries Resources Surveillance (DFIRES; under the Ministry of Agriculture and Rural Development), established in 2013, is responsible for fisheries enforcement, aquatic conservation roles, and is designated as Vietnam's standing agency for combating illegal, unregulated, and unreported fishing; it is armed, allowed to use force if necessary, and works in tandem with the Vietnam Coast Guard
note 3: the PAVN is the military arm of the ruling Communist Party of Vietnam (CPV) and responsible to the Central Military Commission (CMC), the highest party organ on military policy; the CMC is led by the CPV General Secretary

Military expenditures: 1.8% of GDP (2023 est.)
2.3% of GDP (2022 est.)
2.3% of GDP (2021 est.)
2.4% of GDP (2020 est.)
2.3% of GDP (2019 est.)

Military and security service personnel strengths: approximately 450,000 active-duty People's Army of Vietnam (2025)

Military equipment inventories and acquisitions: the PAVN is armed largely with weapons and equipment from Russia and the former Soviet Union; in recent years, Vietnam has moved to diversify arms its arms suppliers and has acquired items from countries such as India, South Korea, and the US; Vietnam has a small defense industry involved in the manufacture of small arms, ground combat vehicles, and naval systems (2025)
note: the US lifted an embargo on arms sales to Vietnam in 2016

Military service age and obligation: 18 years of age for compulsory and voluntary military service for men and women (in practice only men are drafted); service obligation is between 24 (Army, Air Defense) and 36 (Navy and Air Force) months (2024)

Military deployments: 190 Abyei/South Sudan/Sudan (UNISFA) (2024)

Military - note: since withdrawing its military occupation forces from Cambodia in the late 1980s and the end of Soviet aid in 1991, Vietnam has practiced a non-aligned foreign policy and security doctrine known as the "Four Nos" (no alliances, no siding with one country against another, no foreign bases, and no using force in international relations); despite longstanding tensions with Beijing over maritime boundaries in the South China Sea, Vietnam puts a priority on stable relations with China, given its proximity, size, and status as Vietnam's largest trading partner
the responsibilities of the People's Army of Vietnam (PAVN) include protecting the country's independence, sovereignty, territorial integrity, and national interests, as well as assisting civilian authorities with natural disasters; in recent years, the PAVN has placed additional emphasis on protecting Vietnam's interests in the disputed South China Sea; the military is also involved in economic projects, such as electrical infrastructure, oil and gas services, hydroelectric projects, aviation and seaport services, telecommunications, and the shipbuilding industry, while military-owned factories and enterprises produce weapons and equipment (2025)

SPACE

Space agency/agencies: Vietnam National Space Center (VNSC; established 2011) (2025)
note: the VNSC is under the Vietnamese Academy of Science and Technology (VAST)

Space program overview: has a growing national space program focused on acquiring, operating, and exploiting satellites, as well as expanding domestic capabilities in satellites and associated sub-system production, space sciences, and technology applications; builds and operates communications and remote sensing satellites; conducting research and development on space science and applied space technologies, such as advanced optics and space data exploitation; has worked closely with Japan on its space program; cooperation has included funding, loans, training, technical expertise, and data sharing; has also established relationships with the space agencies or commercial space sectors of some European countries (such as France), India, and the US (2025)
note: further details about the key activities, programs, and milestones of the country's space program, as well as government spending estimates on the space sector, appear in the Space Programs reference guide

TRANSNATIONAL ISSUES

Refugees and internally displaced persons: *refugees:* 19 (2024 est.)

IDPs: 2,568 (2024 est.)
stateless persons: 20,590 (2024 est.)

VIRGIN ISLANDS

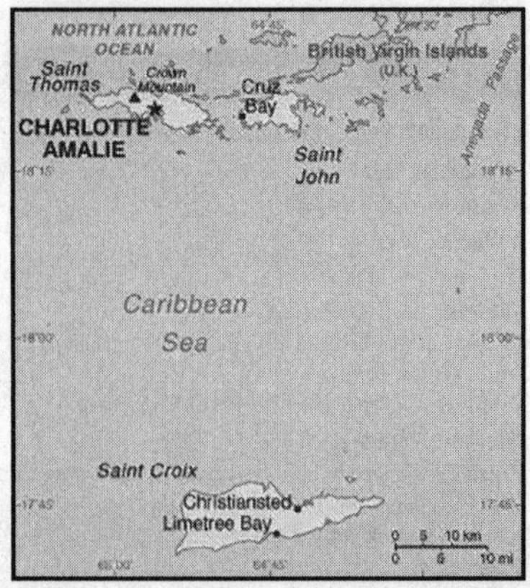

INTRODUCTION

Background: The Danes secured control over the southern Virgin Islands of Saint Thomas, Saint John, and Saint Croix during the 17th and early 18th centuries. Sugarcane, produced by African slave labor, drove the islands' economy during the 18th and early 19th centuries. In 1917, the US purchased the Danish holdings, which had been in economic decline since the abolition of slavery in 1848. In 2017, Hurricane Irma passed over the northern Virgin Islands of Saint Thomas and Saint John and inflicted severe damage to structures, roads, the airport on Saint Thomas, communications, and electricity. Less than two weeks later, Hurricane Maria passed over the island of Saint Croix in the southern Virgin Islands, inflicting considerable damage with heavy winds and flooding rains.

GEOGRAPHY

Location: Caribbean, islands between the Caribbean Sea and the North Atlantic Ocean, east of Puerto Rico

Geographic coordinates: 18 20 N, 64 50 W

Map references: Central America and the Caribbean

Area: *total:* 1,910 sq km
land: 346 sq km
water: 1,564 sq km
comparison ranking: total 181

Area - comparative: twice the size of Washington, D.C.

Land boundaries: *total:* 0 km

Coastline: 188 km

Maritime claims: *territorial sea:* 12 nm
exclusive economic zone: 200 nm

Climate: subtropical, tempered by easterly trade winds, relatively low humidity, little seasonal temperature variation; rainy season September to November

Terrain: mostly hilly to rugged and mountainous with little flat land

Elevation: *highest point:* Crown Mountain 474 m
lowest point: Caribbean Sea 0 m

Natural resources: pleasant climate, beaches foster tourism

Land use: *agricultural land:* 9.4% (2022 est.)
arable land: 2.6% (2022 est.)
permanent crops: 0.6% (2022 est.)
permanent pasture: 6.3% (2022 est.)

forest: 57.7% (2022 est.)
other: 32.8% (2022 est.)

Irrigated land: 1 sq km (2012)

Population distribution: overall population density throughout the islands is relatively low, but concentrations appear around Charlotte Amalie on St. Thomas and Christiansted on St. Croix

Natural hazards: several hurricanes in recent years; frequent and severe droughts and floods; occasional earthquakes

Geography - note: important location along the Anegada Passage, a key shipping lane for the Panama Canal; Saint Thomas has one of the best natural deepwater harbors in the Caribbean

PEOPLE AND SOCIETY

Population: *total:* 104,377 (2024 est.)
male: 49,520
female: 54,857
comparison rankings: total 192; male 195; female 191

Nationality: *noun:* Virgin Islander(s) (US citizens)
adjective: Virgin Islander

Ethnic groups: African-American or African descent 71.4%, White 13.3%, Indigenous 0.4%, Native Hawaiian and other Pacific Islander 0.1%, other 6.3%, mixed 7.5% (2020 est.)
note: 18.4% self-identify as Latino

Languages: English 71.6%, Spanish or Spanish Creole 17.2%, French or French Creole 8.6%, other 2.5% (2010 est.)

Religions: Protestant 65.5%, Roman Catholic 27.1%, other Christians 2.2%, other 1.5%, none 3.7% (2010 est.)

Age structure: *0-14 years:* 18.7% (male 9,983/female 9,547)
15-64 years: 59.8% (male 29,519/female 32,899)
65 years and over: 21.5% (2024 est.) (male 10,018/female 12,411)

Dependency ratios: *total dependency ratio:* 67.2 (2024 est.)
youth dependency ratio: 31.3 (2024 est.)
elderly dependency ratio: 35.9 (2024 est.)
potential support ratio: 2.8 (2024 est.)

Median age: *total:* 43 years (2024 est.)
male: 42.1 years
female: 43.9 years
comparison ranking: total 37

Population growth rate: -0.54% (2024 est.)
comparison ranking: 223

Birth rate: 11.1 births/1,000 population (2024 est.)
comparison ranking: 162

Death rate: 9.2 deaths/1,000 population (2024 est.)
comparison ranking: 52

Net migration rate: -7.3 migrant(s)/1,000 population (2024 est.)
comparison ranking: 218

Population distribution: overall population density throughout the islands is relatively low, but concentrations appear around Charlotte Amalie on St. Thomas and Christiansted on St. Croix

Urbanization: *urban population:* 96.2% of total population (2023)
rate of urbanization: -0.11% annual rate of change (2020-25 est.)

Major urban areas - population: 52,000 CHARLOTTE AMALIE (capital) (2018)

Sex ratio: *at birth:* 1.06 male(s)/female
0-14 years: 1.05 male(s)/female
15-64 years: 0.9 male(s)/female
65 years and over: 0.81 male(s)/female
total population: 0.9 male(s)/female (2024 est.)

Infant mortality rate: *total:* 7.3 deaths/1,000 live births (2024 est.)
male: 8.3 deaths/1,000 live births
female: 6.3 deaths/1,000 live births
comparison ranking: total 153

Life expectancy at birth: *total population:* 80.7 years (2024 est.)
male: 77.6 years
female: 84.1 years
comparison ranking: total population 51

Total fertility rate: 1.97 children born/woman (2024 est.)
comparison ranking: 108

Gross reproduction rate: 0.95 (2024 est.)

Sanitation facility access: *improved:* total: 99.1% of population (2022 est.)
unimproved: total: 0.9% of population (2022 est.)

Currently married women (ages 15-49): 27.4% (2023)

ENVIRONMENT

Environmental issues: lack of natural freshwater resources; protection of coral reefs; solid waste management; coastal development; increased boating and overfishing

Climate: subtropical, tempered by easterly trade winds, relatively low humidity, little seasonal temperature variation; rainy season September to November

Urbanization: *urban population:* 96.2% of total population (2023)
rate of urbanization: -0.11% annual rate of change (2020-25 est.)

Carbon dioxide emissions: 2.378 million metric tonnes of CO2 (2023 est.)
from petroleum and other liquids: 2.378 million metric tonnes of CO2 (2023 est.)
comparison ranking: total emissions 157

Waste and recycling: *municipal solid waste generated annually:* 146,500 tons (2024 est.)

GOVERNMENT

Country name: *conventional long form:* none
conventional short form: Virgin Islands
former: Danish West Indies
abbreviation: VI
etymology: in 1493, the islets, cays, and rocks around the major islands in the chain reminded explorer Christopher COLUMBUS of Saint Ursula and her 11,000 virgin followers (Santa Ursula y las Once Mil Virgenes), which over time was shortened to the Virgins (las Virgenes)

Government type: unincorporated organized territory of the US with local self-government; republican form of territorial government with separate executive, legislative, and judicial branches

Dependency status: unincorporated, organized territory of the US, with policy relations with the US federal government under the jurisdiction of the Office of Insular Affairs, US Department of the Interior

Capital: *name:* Charlotte Amalie
geographic coordinates: 18 21 N, 64 56 W
time difference: UTC-4 (1 hour ahead of Washington, DC, during Standard Time)
etymology: named in honor of Danish King CHRISTIAN V's wife, Charlotte AMALIE of Hesse-Kassel, after the colony was established in 1672

Administrative divisions: *none (territory of the US); there are no first-order administrative divisions as defined by the US government, but 3 islands are considered second-order:* Saint Croix, Saint John, Saint Thomas

Legal system: US common law

Constitution: *history:* 22 July 1954 - the Revised Organic Act of the Virgin Islands functions as a constitution for this US territory

Citizenship: see United States

Suffrage: 18 years of age; universal
note: island residents are US citizens but do not vote in US presidential elections

Executive branch: *chief of state:* President Donald J. TRUMP (since 20 January 2025)
head of government: Governor Albert BRYAN, Jr. (since 7 January 2019)
cabinet: Territorial Cabinet appointed by the governor and confirmed by the Senate
election/appointment process: president and vice president indirectly elected on the same ballot by an Electoral College of electors chosen from each state; president and vice president serve a 4-year term (eligible for a second term); under the US Constitution, residents of the Virgin Islands do not vote in elections for US president and vice president, but they can vote in the Democratic and Republican party presidential primary elections; governor and lieutenant governor directly elected on the same ballot by absolute majority vote in 2 rounds if needed for a 4-year term (eligible for a second term)
most recent election date: 8 November 2022
election results: 2022: Albert BRYAN, Jr. reelected governor; percent of vote - Albert BRYAN, Jr. (Democratic Party) 56%, Kurt VIALET (independent) 38%
2018: Albert BRYAN, Jr. elected governor in the second round; percent of vote in first round - Albert BRYAN, Jr. (Democratic Party) 38.1%, Kenneth MAPP (independent) 33.5%, Adlah "Foncie" DONASTORG, Jr. (independent) 16.5%, other 11.9%; percent of vote in second round - Albert BRYAN, Jr. (Democratic Party) 54.5%, Kenneth MAPP (independent) 45.2%, other 0.3%
expected date of next election: November 2026

Legislative branch: *note:* the Virgin Islands delegate to the US House of Representatives can vote when serving on a committee and when the House meets as the Committee of the Whole House, but not when legislation is submitted for a "full floor" House vote

Judicial branch: *highest court(s):* Supreme Court of the Virgin Islands (consists of the chief justice and 2 associate justices)
judge selection and term of office: justices appointed by the governor and confirmed by the Virgin Islands Senate; justices serve initial 10-year terms and upon reconfirmation, during the extent of good behavior; chief justice elected to position by peers for a 3-year term
subordinate courts: Superior Court (Territorial Court renamed in 2004); US Court of Appeals for the Third Circuit (has appellate jurisdiction over the District Court of the Virgin Islands; it is a territorial court and is not associated with a US federal judicial district); District Court of the Virgin Islands

Political parties: Democratic Party

Independent Citizens' Movement or ICM
Republican Party

Diplomatic representation in the US: none (territory of the US)

Diplomatic representation from the US: none (territory of the US)

International organization participation: AOSIS (observer), Interpol (subbureau), IOC, UPU, WFTU (NGOs)

Independence: none (territory of the US)

National holiday: Transfer Day (from Denmark to the US), 31 March (1917)

Flag: *description:* white field with a modified US coat of arms in the center between the large blue initials "V" and "I"; the coat of arms shows a yellow eagle holding an olive branch in its right talon and three arrows in its left, with a shield of seven red and six white vertical stripes below a blue panel
meaning: white is a symbol of purity, and the letters stand for the Virgin Islands

National anthem(s): *title:* "Virgin Islands March"
lyrics/music: multiple/Alton Augustus ADAMS, Sr.
history: adopted 1963; serves as a local anthem
title: "The Star-Spangled Banner"
lyrics/music: Francis Scott KEY/John Stafford SMITH
history: official anthem, as a US territory

ECONOMY

Economic overview: high-income, tourism-based American territorial economy; severe COVID-19 economic disruptions; major rum distillery; high public debt; sluggish reopening of large oil refinery; environmentally susceptible to hurricanes; many informal industries

Real GDP (purchasing power parity): $4.9 billion (2022 est.)
$4.965 billion (2021 est.)
$4.789 billion (2020 est.)
note: data in 2021 dollars
comparison ranking: 185

Real GDP growth rate: -1.3% (2022 est.)
3.7% (2021 est.)
-1.6% (2020 est.)
note: annual GDP % growth based on constant local currency
comparison ranking: 203

Real GDP per capita: $46,500 (2022 est.)
$46,900 (2021 est.)
$45,100 (2020 est.)
note: data in 2021 dollars
comparison ranking: 46

GDP (official exchange rate): $4.672 billion (2022 est.)
note: data in current dollars at official exchange rate

GDP - composition, by end use: *household consumption:* 68.9% (2022 est.)
government consumption: 34.4% (2022 est.)
investment in fixed capital: 7.5% (2016 est.)
investment in inventories: 15% (2016 est.)
exports of goods and services: 97.4% (2022 est.)
imports of goods and services: -108.3% (2022 est.)
note: figures may not total 100% due to rounding or gaps in data collection

Agricultural products: fruit, vegetables, sorghum; Senepol cattle

Industries: tourism, watch assembly, rum distilling, construction, pharmaceuticals, electronics

Labor force: 47,200 (2024 est.)
note: number of people ages 15 or older who are employed or seeking work
comparison ranking: 188

Unemployment rate: 12.1% (2024 est.)
12.4% (2023 est.)
13.1% (2022 est.)
note: % of labor force seeking employment
comparison ranking: 165

Youth unemployment rate (ages 15-24): *total:* 25.3% (2024 est.)
male: 22% (2024 est.)
female: 28.9% (2024 est.)
note: % of labor force ages 15-24 seeking employment
comparison ranking: total 33

Budget: *revenues:* $1.496 billion (2016 est.)
expenditures: $1.518 billion (2016 est.)

Exports: $4.549 billion (2022 est.)
$4.069 billion (2021 est.)
$1.62 billion (2020 est.)
note: GDP expenditure basis - exports of goods and services in current dollars
comparison ranking: 142

Exports - partners: Haiti 14%, Guadeloupe 7%, Malaysia 7%, Martinique 7%, Barbados 7%, British Virgin Islands 5% (2019)

Exports - commodities: refined petroleum, jewelry, recreational boats, watches, rum (2019)
top five export commodities based on value in dollars

Imports: $5.058 billion (2022 est.)
$4.057 billion (2021 est.)
$3.184 billion (2020 est.)
note: GDP expenditure basis - imports of goods and services in current dollars
comparison ranking: 152

Imports - partners: India 18%, Algeria 14%, South Korea 9%, Argentina 9%, Sweden 7%, Brazil 5% (2019)

Imports - commodities: refined petroleum, crude petroleum, rubber piping, jewelry, beer (2019)

Exchange rates: the US dollar is used

ENERGY

Electricity access: *electrification - total population:* 100% (2022 est.)

Electricity: *installed generating capacity:* 326,000 kW (2023 est.)
consumption: 618.819 million kWh (2023 est.)
transmission/distribution losses: 50.181 million kWh (2023 est.)
comparison rankings: installed generating capacity 161; consumption 169; transmission/distribution losses 38

Electricity generation sources: *fossil fuels:* 97.2% of total installed capacity (2023 est.)
solar: 2.8% of total installed capacity (2023 est.)

Coal: *exports:* 4 metric tons (2023 est.)

Petroleum: *refined petroleum consumption:* 16,000 bbl/day (2023 est.)

COMMUNICATIONS

Telephones - fixed lines: *total subscriptions:* 76,000 (2021 est.)
subscriptions per 100 inhabitants: 88 (2022 est.)
comparison ranking: total subscriptions 145

Telephones - mobile cellular: *total subscriptions:* 80,000 (2021 est.)
subscriptions per 100 inhabitants: 80 (2021 est.)
comparison ranking: total subscriptions 196

Broadcast media: about a dozen TV stations, including 1 public TV station; multi-channel cable and satellite TV available; 24 radio stations

Internet country code: .vi

Internet users: *percent of population:* 64% (2017 est.)

Broadband - fixed subscriptions: *total:* 9,000 (2022 est.)
subscriptions per 100 inhabitants: 10 (2022 est.)
comparison ranking: total 185

TRANSPORTATION

Airports: 2 (2025)
comparison ranking: 208

Heliports: 4 (2025)
comparison ranking: 112

Merchant marine: *total:* 2 (2023)
by type: general cargo 1, other 1
comparison ranking: total 177

Ports: *total ports:* 6 (2024)
large: 0
medium: 0
small: 3
very small: 3
ports with oil terminals: 3
key ports: Charlotte Amalie, Christiansted, Cruz Bay, Frederiksted, Limetree Bay, Port Alucroix

MILITARY AND SECURITY

Military and security forces: US Virgin Islands Police Department (VIPD); US Virgin Islands National Guard (VING) (2025)

Military - note: defense is the responsibility of the US

WAKE ISLAND

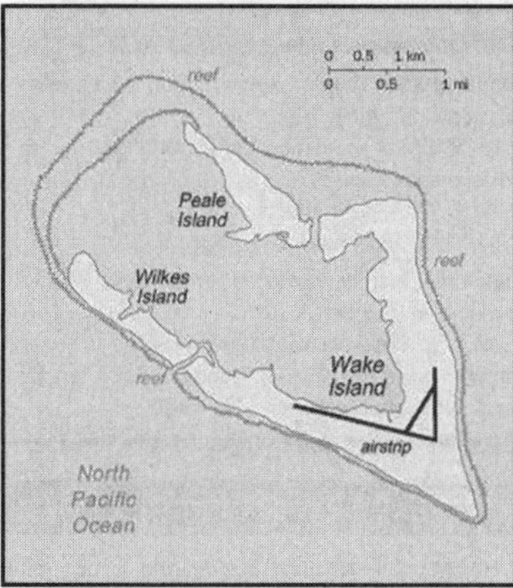

INTRODUCTION

Background: Early Micronesian and Polynesian settlers probably visited Wake Island, and oral legends tell of periodic voyages to the islands by people from the Marshall Islands. Wake Island was uninhabited when Spanish explorer Alvaro de Mendana de NEYRA became the first European to see it in 1568 and still had no inhabitants when English captain Samuel WAKE sailed by it in 1796. The United States Exploring Expedition visited the island in 1841, and the US annexed it in 1899 to use as a cable and refueling station for its newly acquired Pacific territories of Hawaii, the Philippines, and Guam. In the 1930s, Pan American Airways built facilities on Wake Island so that it could be used as a stopover for flights from the US to China. In 1941, the US began to install military assets on Wake Island, and Japan then captured the island and held it until the end of World War II. In 1946, commercial airlines resumed using Wake Island as a refueling stop.

In 1973, the Marshall Islands claimed Wake Island, based on the oral legends, although the US has not recognized these claims. In 1974, the US military took exclusive control of the island's airstrip and restricted visitors. In 1978, Bikini Islanders from the Marshall Islands, who were evacuated in the 1950s and 1960s because of US nuclear tests, considered rehoming on Wake Island, but the US military rejected that plan. Since the 1970s, the island has been important for missile defense testing. In 2009, Wake Island was included in the Pacific Remote Islands Marine National Monument.

GEOGRAPHY

Location: Oceania, atoll in the North Pacific Ocean, about two-thirds of the way from Hawaii to the Northern Mariana Islands

Geographic coordinates: 19 17 N, 166 39 E

Map references: Oceania

Area: *total:* 7 sq km
land: 6.5 sq km
water: 0 sq km
comparison ranking: total 242

Area - comparative: about 11 times the size of the National Mall in Washington, D.C.

Land boundaries: *total:* 0 km

Coastline: 19.3 km

Maritime claims: *territorial sea:* 12 nm
exclusive economic zone: 200 nm

Climate: tropical

Terrain: atoll of three low coral islands, Peale, Wake, and Wilkes, built up on an underwater volcano; central lagoon is former crater, islands are part of the rim

Elevation: *highest point:* unnamed location 8 m
lowest point: Pacific Ocean 0 m

Natural resources: none

Land use: *agricultural land:* 0% (2018 est.)
other: 100% (2018 est.)

Irrigated land: 0 sq km (2022)

Natural hazards: subject to occasional typhoons

Geography - note: strategic location in the North Pacific Ocean

PEOPLE AND SOCIETY

Population: *total:* no permanent inhabitants
note: personnel maintain and operate the airfield and weather station

ENVIRONMENT

Environmental issues: limited potable water; hazardous waste disposal

Climate: tropical

Carbon dioxide emissions: 1.214 million metric tonnes of CO_2 (2023 est.)
from petroleum and other liquids: 1.214 million metric tonnes of CO_2 (2023 est.)
comparison ranking: total emissions 169

GOVERNMENT

Country name: *conventional long form:* none
conventional short form: Wake Island
etymology: the name comes from one of two explorers who sighted the islands in the late 1700s; British Captain William WAKE visited in 1792, as did his relative, British Captain Samuel WAKE, in 1796, and sources disagree on which captain claimed the honor of naming the island

Dependency status: unincorporated, unorganized territory of the US; administered by the Department of the Interior; the 11th US Air Force currently conducts activities on the atoll, and it is managed from Pacific Air Force Support Center

Legal system: US common law

Citizenship: see United States

Independence: none (territory of the US)

Flag: the US flag is used

ENERGY

Electricity access: *electrification - total population:* 100% (2021)

Petroleum: *refined petroleum consumption:* 8,000 bbl/day (2023 est.)

COMMUNICATIONS

Broadcast media: US Armed Forces Radio and Television Service (AFRTS) provides satellite radio/TV broadcasts (2018)

TRANSPORTATION

Airports: 1 (2025)
comparison ranking: 226

Ports: *total ports:* 1 (2024)
large: 0
medium: 0
small: 0
very small: 1
ports with oil terminals: 1
key ports: Wake Island

MILITARY AND SECURITY

Military - note: defense is the responsibility of the US; the island serves as a trans-Pacific refueling stop for military aircraft and supports US Missile Defense Agency (MDA) testing activities; Wake is managed by the US Air Force (2025)

WALLIS AND FUTUNA

INTRODUCTION

Background: Around 800 B.C., the first settlers arrived on the islands of Wallis and Futuna, which are a natural midpoint between Fiji and Samoa. Around A.D. 1500, Tongans invaded Wallis, and a chiefdom system resembling Tonga's formal hierarchy developed on the island. Tongans attempted to settle Futuna but were repeatedly rebuffed. Samoans settled Futuna in the 1600s, and a slightly less centralized chiefdom system formed. Dutch explorers were the first Europeans to see the islands in 1616, followed intermittently by other Europeans, including British explorer Samuel WALLIS in 1767. French Catholic missionaries were the first Europeans to permanently settle Wallis and Futuna in 1837, and they converted most of the population of both islands by 1846. The missionaries and newly converted King LAVELUA of Uvea on Wallis asked France for a protectorate in 1842 following a local rebellion. France agreed, although the protectorate status would not be ratified

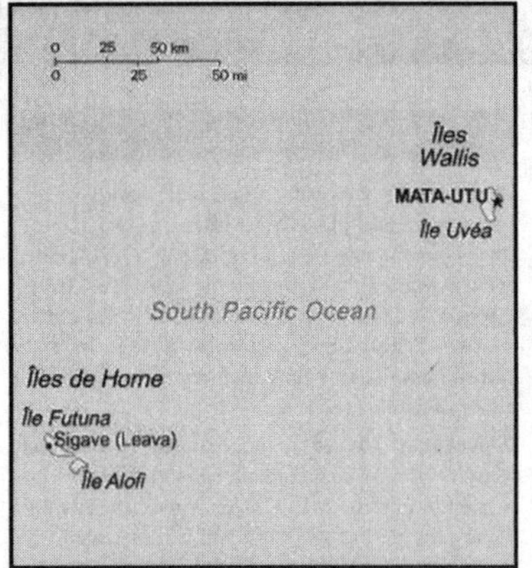

until 1887. In 1888, King MUSULAMU of Alo and King TAMOLE of Sigave, both on Futuna, signed a treaty establishing a French protectorate; the Wallis and Futuna protectorate was integrated into the territory of New Caledonia the same year. France renegotiated the terms of the protectorate with the territory's three kings in 1910, expanding French authority.

Wallis and Futuna was the only French colony to side with the Vichy regime during World War II, until the arrival of Free French and US troops in 1942. In 1959, inhabitants of the islands voted to separate from New Caledonia, becoming a French overseas territory in 1961. Despite the split, a significant Wallisian and Futunan community still lives in New Caledonia. In 2003, Wallis and Futuna became a French overseas collectivity. The islands joined the Pacific Islands Forum as an associate member in 2018, two years after France's other Pacific territories became full members of the organization.

GEOGRAPHY

Location: Oceania, islands in the South Pacific Ocean, about two-thirds of the way from Hawaii to New Zealand

Geographic coordinates: 13 18 S, 176 12 W

Map references: Oceania

Area: *total:* 142 sq km
land: 142 sq km
water: 0 sq km
note: includes Ile Uvea (Wallis Island), Ile Futuna (Futuna Island), Ile Alofi, and 20 islets
comparison ranking: total 221

Area - comparative: 1.5 times the size of Washington, D.C.

Land boundaries: *total:* 0 km

Coastline: 129 km

Maritime claims: *territorial sea:* 12 nm
exclusive economic zone: 200 nm

Climate: tropical; hot, rainy season (November to April); cool, dry season (May to October); rains 250-300 cm per year (80% humidity); average temperature 26.6 degrees Celsius

Terrain: volcanic origin; low hills

Elevation: *highest point:* Mont Singavi (on Futuna) 522 m
lowest point: Pacific Ocean 0 m

Natural resources: NEGL

Land use: *agricultural land:* 42.9% (2022 est.)
arable land: 7.1% (2022 est.)
permanent crops: 35.7% (2022 est.)
permanent pasture: 0% (2022 est.)
forest: 41.6% (2022 est.)
other: 15.5% (2022 est.)

Irrigated land: 0.6 sq km (2022)

Natural hazards: cyclones; tsunamis

Geography - note: both island groups have fringing reefs; Wallis contains several prominent crater lakes

PEOPLE AND SOCIETY

Population: *total:* 15,964 (2024 est.)
male: 8,201
female: 7,763
comparison rankings: total 220; male 220; female 220

Nationality: *noun:* Wallisian(s), Futunan(s), or Wallis and Futuna Islanders
adjective: Wallisian, Futunan, or Wallis and Futuna Islander

Ethnic groups: Polynesian

Languages: Wallisian (indigenous Polynesian language) 58.9%, Futunian 30.1%, French (official) 10.8%, other 0.2% (2003 est.)

Religions: Roman Catholic 99%, other 1%

Age structure: *0-14 years:* 19.8% (male 1,643/female 1,511)
15-64 years: 67.5% (male 5,535/female 5,247)
65 years and over: 12.7% (2024 est.) (male 1,023/female 1,005)

Dependency ratios: *total dependency ratio:* 48.1 (2024 est.)
youth dependency ratio: 29.3 (2024 est.)
elderly dependency ratio: 18.8 (2024 est.)
potential support ratio: 5.3 (2024 est.)

Median age: *total:* 36.3 years (2024 est.)
male: 35.5 years
female: 37.3 years
comparison ranking: total 92

Population growth rate: 0.22% (2024 est.)
comparison ranking: 174

Birth rate: 11.8 births/1,000 population (2024 est.)
comparison ranking: 151

Death rate: 6 deaths/1,000 population (2024 est.)
comparison ranking: 153

Net migration rate: -3.6 migrant(s)/1,000 population (2024 est.)
comparison ranking: 189

Urbanization: *urban population:* 0% of total population (2023)
rate of urbanization: 0% annual rate of change (2020-25 est.)

Major urban areas - population: 1,000 MATA-UTU (capital) (2018)

Sex ratio: *at birth:* 1.05 male(s)/female
0-14 years: 1.09 male(s)/female
15-64 years: 1.05 male(s)/female
65 years and over: 1.02 male(s)/female
total population: 1.06 male(s)/female (2024 est.)

Infant mortality rate: *total:* 3.9 deaths/1,000 live births (2024 est.)
male: 3.8 deaths/1,000 live births
female: 3.9 deaths/1,000 live births
comparison ranking: total 188

Life expectancy at birth: *total population:* 81.1 years (2024 est.)
male: 78.2 years
female: 84.2 years
comparison ranking: total population 45

Total fertility rate: 1.71 children born/woman (2024 est.)
comparison ranking: 160

Gross reproduction rate: 0.83 (2024 est.)

Drinking water source: *improved:* rural: 99.3% of population (2022 est.)
total: 99.3% of population (2022 est.)
unimproved: urban: NA
rural: 0.7% of population (2022 est.)
total: 0.7% of population (2022 est.)

Sanitation facility access: *improved:* rural: 94.2% of population (2022 est.)
total: 94.2% of population (2022 est.)
unimproved: rural: 5.8% of population (2022 est.)
total: 5.8% of population (2022 est.)

Currently married women (ages 15-49): 56% (2023)

ENVIRONMENT

Environmental issues: deforestation (only small portions of the original forests remain) due to wood as the main fuel source; soil erosion; lack of natural freshwater resources; lack of soil fertility on the islands of Uvea and Futuna

Climate: tropical; hot, rainy season (November to April); cool, dry season (May to October); rains 250-300 cm per year (80% humidity); average temperature 26.6 degrees Celsius

Urbanization: *urban population:* 0% of total population (2023)
rate of urbanization: 0% annual rate of change (2020-25 est.)

GOVERNMENT

Country name: *conventional long form:* Territory of the Wallis and Futuna Islands
conventional short form: Wallis and Futuna
local long form: Territoire des Iles Wallis et Futuna
local short form: Wallis et Futuna
former: Hoorn Islands is the former name of the Futuna Islands
etymology: Wallis Island is named after British Captain Samuel WALLIS, who visited in 1767; Futuna is a local name, and the meaning is unclear

Government type: parliamentary democracy (Territorial Assembly); overseas collectivity of France

Dependency status: overseas collectivity of France

Capital: *name:* Mata-Utu (on Ile Uvea)
geographic coordinates: 13 57 S, 171 56 W
time difference: UTC+12 (17 hours ahead of Washington, DC, during Standard Time)

Administrative divisions: 3 administrative precincts (*circonscriptions*, singular - *circonscription*) Alo, Sigave, Uvea

Legal system: French civil law

Constitution: *history:* 4 October 1958 (French Constitution)
amendment process: French constitution amendment procedures apply

Citizenship: see France

Suffrage: 18 years of age; universal

Executive branch: *chief of state:* President Emmanuel MACRON (since 14 May 2017); represented by Administrator Superior Blaise GOURTAY (since 1 August 2023)

head of government: President of the Territorial Assembly Munipoese MULI'AKA'AKA (since 20 March 2022)
cabinet: Council of the Territory appointed by the administrator superior on the advice of the Territorial Assembly
election/appointment process: French president elected by absolute-majority popular vote in 2 rounds, if needed, for a 5-year term (eligible for a second term); administrator superior appointed by the French president on the advice of the French Ministry of the Interior; the presidents of the Territorial Government and the Territorial Assembly elected by assembly members
note: there are 3 traditional kings with limited powers

Legislative branch: *legislature name:* Territorial Assembly (Assemblée territoriale)
legislative structure: unicameral
number of seats: 20 (directly elected)
electoral system: proportional representation
scope of elections: full renewal
term in office: 5 years
most recent election date: 3/20/2022
parties elected and seats per party: Ofa mo'oni ki tou fenua (2); Mauli fetokoniaki (2); 1 seat each from 16 other lists
note: 1 senator is indirectly elected to the French Senate by an electoral college for a 6-year term, and 1 deputy is directly elected to the French National Assembly for a 5-year term

Judicial branch: *highest court(s):* Court of Assizes or Cour d'Assizes (consists of 1 judge; court hears primarily serious criminal cases)
judge selection and term of office: NA
subordinate courts: courts of first instance; labor court
note 1: appeals beyond the Court of Assizes are heard before the Court of Appeal or Cour d'Appel (in Noumea, New Caledonia)
note 2: justice is generally administered under French law by the high administrator, but the 3 traditional kings administer customary law

Political parties: Left Radical Party or PRG (formerly Radical Socialist Party or PRS and the Left Radical Movement or MRG)
Lua Kae Tahi (Giscardians)
Rally for Wallis and Futuna-The Republicans (Rassemblement pour Wallis and Futuna) or RPWF-LR
Socialist Party or PS
Taumu'a Lelei
Union Pour la Democratie Francaise or UDF

Diplomatic representation in the US: none (overseas territory of France)

Diplomatic representation from the US: none (overseas collectivity of France)

International organization participation: PIF (observer), SPC, UPU

Independence: none (overseas collectivity of France)

National holiday: Fête de la Fédération, 14 July (1790)
note: often incorrectly referred to as Bastille Day, the celebration commemorates the storming of the Bastille prison on 14 July 1789 and the establishment of a constitutional monarchy; other names for the holiday are *la Fête nationale* (National Holiday) and *le Quatorze Juillet* (14th of July)

Flag: *description:* unofficial local flag has a red field with four white isosceles triangles in the middle; the apexes of the triangles are oriented inward and at right angles to each other; a small flag of France, outlined in white on two sides, is in the upper-left corner
meaning: the triangles represent the three native kings of the islands and the French administrator
history: the design is derived from a red flag with a white cross that French missionaries introduced in the 19th century
note: the flag of France is used for official occasions

National symbol(s): red saltire (Saint Andrew's Cross) on a white square on a red field

National color(s): red, white

National anthem(s): *title:* "La Marseillaise" (The Song of Marseille)
lyrics/music: Claude-Joseph ROUGET de Lisle
history: official anthem, as a French territory

ECONOMY

Economic overview: lower-middle-income, agrarian French dependency economy; heavily reliant on French subsidies; licenses fishing rights to Japan and South Korea; major remittances from New Caledonia; aging workforce; import-dependent; deforestation-fueled fragility

Agricultural products: coconuts, breadfruit, yams, taro, bananas; pigs, goats; fish

Industries: copra, handicrafts, fishing, lumber

Budget: *revenues:* $32.54 million (2015 est.)
expenditures: $34.18 million (2015 est.)

Exports - partners: Denmark 35%, Sweden 14%, Netherlands 14%, Pakistan 9%, Poland 7% (2023)
note: top five export partners based on percentage share of exports

Exports - commodities: seats (2023)
note: top export commodities based on value in dollars over $500,000

Imports - partners: Fiji 35%, France 32%, NZ 11%, Australia 6%, China 4% (2023)
note: top five import partners based on percentage share of imports

Imports - commodities: refined petroleum, prepared meat, poultry, iron pipe fittings, animal food (2023)

Exchange rates: Comptoirs Francais du Pacifique francs (XPF) per US dollar -

Exchange rates: 110.31 (2024 est.)
110.347 (2023 est.)
113.474 (2022 est.)
100.88 (2021 est.)
104.711 (2020 est.)

COMMUNICATIONS

Telephones - fixed lines: *total subscriptions:* 3,000 (2021 est.)
subscriptions per 100 inhabitants: 26 (2021 est.)
comparison ranking: total subscriptions 207

Telephones - mobile cellular: *total subscriptions:* 0 (2018)
subscriptions per 100 inhabitants: 0 (2019)
comparison ranking: total subscriptions 225

Broadcast media: publicly owned French Overseas Network (RFO), which broadcasts to France's overseas departments, collectivities, and territories, is carried on the RFO Wallis and Fortuna TV and radio stations (2019)

Internet country code: .wf

Internet users: *percent of population:* 45.8% (2021 est.)

TRANSPORTATION

Airports: 2 (2025)
comparison ranking: 197

Merchant marine: *total:* 1 (2023)
by type: general cargo 1
comparison ranking: total 183

Ports: *total ports:* 1 (2024)
large: 0
medium: 0
small: 0
very small: 1
ports with oil terminals: 0
key ports: Mata-Utu

MILITARY AND SECURITY

Military - note: defense is the responsibility of France

WEST BANK

INTRODUCTION

Background: The landlocked West Bank – the larger of the two Palestinian territories – is home to some three million Palestinians. Inhabited since at least the 15th century B.C., the area currently known as the West Bank has been dominated by a succession of different powers. In the early 16th century, it was incorporated into the Ottoman Empire. The West Bank fell to British forces during World War I, becoming part of the British Mandate of Palestine. After the 1948 Arab-Israeli War, Transjordan (later renamed Jordan) captured the West Bank and annexed it in 1950; Israel then captured it in the Six-Day War in 1967. Under the Oslo Accords – a series of agreements that were signed between 1993 and 1999 – Israel transferred to the newly created Palestinian Authority (PA) security and civilian responsibility for the many Palestinian-populated areas of the West Bank, as well as the Gaza Strip.

In addition to establishing the PA as an interim government, the Oslo Accords divided the West Bank into three areas, with one fully managed by the PA (Area A), another fully managed by Israel (Area C), and a third with shared control (Area B) until a permanent agreement could be reached between the Palestine Liberation Organization (PLO) and Israel. In 2000, a violent *intifada*, or uprising, began across the Palestinian territories, and in 2001, negotiations for a permanent agreement between the PLO

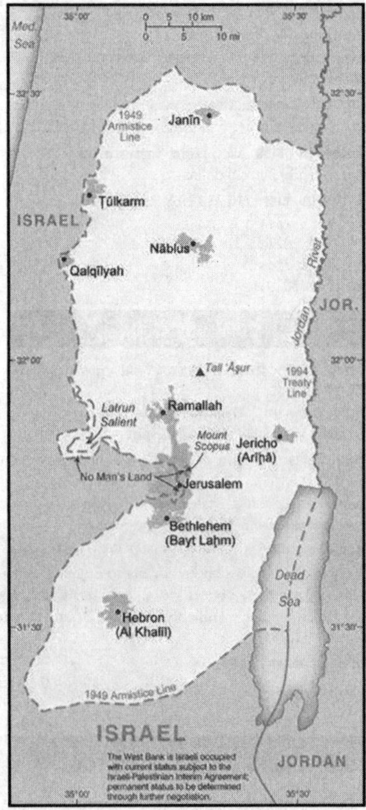

and Israel on final status issues stalled. Subsequent attempts to re-start direct negotiations have not resulted in progress toward determining final status of the area.

The PA last held national elections in 2006, when the Islamic Resistance Movement (HAMAS) won a majority of seats in the Palestinian Legislative Council (PLC). Fatah, the dominant Palestinian political faction in the West Bank, and HAMAS failed to maintain a unity government, leading to violent clashes between their respective supporters and to HAMAS's violent seizure of all PA military and governmental institutions in the Gaza Strip in 2007. In 2018, the Palestinian Constitutional Court dissolved the PLC. In recent years, Fatah and HAMAS have made several attempts at reconciliation, but the factions have been unable to implement agreements.

GEOGRAPHY

Location: Middle East, west of Jordan, east of Israel

Geographic coordinates: 32 00 N, 35 15 E

Map references: Middle East

Area: *total:* 5,860 sq km
land: 5,640 sq km
water: 220 sq km
note: includes West Bank, Latrun Salient, and the northwest quarter of the Dead Sea, but excludes Mt. Scopus; East Jerusalem and Jerusalem No Man's Land are also included only as a means of depicting the entire area occupied by Israel in 1967
comparison ranking: total 171

Area - comparative: slightly smaller than Delaware

Land boundaries: *total:* 478 km
border countries (2): Israel 330 km; Jordan 148 km

Coastline: 0 km (landlocked)

Maritime claims: none (landlocked)

Climate: temperate; temperature and precipitation vary with altitude, warm to hot summers, cool to mild winters

Terrain: mostly rugged, dissected upland in west, flat plains descending to Jordan River Valley to the east

Elevation: *highest point:* Khallat al Batrakh 1,020 m
lowest point: Dead Sea -431 m

Natural resources: arable land

Land use: *agricultural land:* 64.9% (2022 est.)
arable land: 7% (2022 est.)
permanent crops: 11.8% (2022 est.)
permanent pasture: 46.1% (2022 est.)
forest: 1.7% (2022 est.)
other: 33.4% (2022 est.)
note: includes Gaza Strip

Irrigated land: (2013) 151 sq km; note - includes Gaza Strip

Major lakes (area sq km): *salt water lake(s):* Dead Sea (shared with Jordan and Israel) - 1,020 sq km
note - endorheic hypersaline lake; 9.6 times saltier than the ocean; lake shore is 431 meters below sea level

Population distribution: the most populous Palestinian communities in the West Bank are located in the central ridge and western half of its territory; Jewish settlements are located throughout the West Bank, the most populous in the Seam Zone – between the 1949 Armistice Line and the separation barrier – and around Jerusalem

Natural hazards: droughts

Geography - note: landlocked; highlands are main recharge area for Israel's coastal aquifers (2017)

PEOPLE AND SOCIETY

Population: *total:* 3,243,369 (2024 est.)
male: 1,648,450
female: 1,594,919
note: approximately 468,300 Israeli settlers live in the West Bank (2022); approximately 236,600 Israeli settlers live in East Jerusalem (2021)
comparison rankings: total 135; male 136; female 136

Ethnic groups: Palestinian Arab, Jewish, other

Languages: Arabic, Hebrew (spoken by Israeli settlers and many Palestinians), English (widely understood)
major-language sample(s):

كتاب حقائق العالم، المصدر الذي لا يمكن الاستغناء عنه للمعلومات الأساسية

(Arabic)

Religions: Muslim 80-85% (predominantly Sunni), Jewish 12-14%, Christian 1-2.5% (mainly Greek Orthodox), other, unaffiliated, unspecified <1% (2012 est.)

Age structure: *0-14 years:* 36.7% (male 609,497/female 579,227)
15-64 years: 59.5% (male 979,719/female 949,746)
65 years and over: 3.9% (2024 est.) (male 59,234/female 65,946)

Dependency ratios: *total dependency ratio:* 68.1 (2024 est.)
youth dependency ratio: 61.6 (2024 est.)
elderly dependency ratio: 6.5 (2024 est.)
potential support ratio: 15.4 (2024 est.)

Median age: *total:* 21.9 years (2024 est.)
male: 21.6 years
female: 22.1 years
comparison ranking: total 189

Population growth rate: 2.07% (2024 est.)
comparison ranking: 37

Birth rate: 27.8 births/1,000 population (2024 est.)
comparison ranking: 32

Death rate: 3.3 deaths/1,000 population (2024 est.)
comparison ranking: 223

Net migration rate: -3.8 migrant(s)/1,000 population (2024 est.)
comparison ranking: 191

Population distribution: the most populous Palestinian communities in the West Bank are located in the central ridge and western half of its territory; Jewish settlements are located throughout the West Bank, the most populous in the Seam Zone – between the 1949 Armistice Line and the separation barrier – and around Jerusalem

Urbanization: *urban population:* 77.6% of total population (2023)
rate of urbanization: 2.85% annual rate of change (2020-25 est.)
note: data represent Gaza Strip and the West Bank

Sex ratio: *at birth:* 1.06 male(s)/female
0-14 years: 1.05 male(s)/female
15-64 years: 1.03 male(s)/female
65 years and over: 0.9 male(s)/female
total population: 1.03 male(s)/female (2024 est.)

Maternal mortality ratio: 16 deaths/100,000 live births (2023 est.)
note: data represent Gaza Strip and the West Bank
comparison ranking: 132

Infant mortality rate: *total:* 15.1 deaths/1,000 live births (2024 est.)
male: 17.5 deaths/1,000 live births
female: 12.6 deaths/1,000 live births comparison ranking: total 93

Life expectancy at birth: *total population:* 76.5 years (2024 est.)
male: 74.4 years
female: 78.8 years
comparison ranking: total population 108

Total fertility rate: *3.49 children born/woman (2024 est.) comparison ranking:* 34

Gross reproduction rate: 1.69 (2024 est.)

Drinking water source: *improved: urban:* 98% of population (2022 est.)
rural: 100% of population (2022 est.)
total: 98.4% of population (2022 est.)
unimproved: urban: 2% of population (2022 est.)
total: 1.6% of population (2022 est.)
note: includes Gaza Strip and the West Bank

Health expenditure: 13.5% of national budget (2022 est.)
note: includes Gaza Strip and the West Bank

Physician density: 3.25 physicians/1,000 population (2020)

Hospital bed density: 1.3 beds/1,000 population (2019 est.)

Sanitation facility access: *improved: urban:* 100% of population (2022 est.)
rural: 99% of population (2022 est.)
total: 99.8% of population (2022 est.)
unimproved: urban: 0% of population (2022 est.)

rural: 1% of population (2022 est.)
total: 0.2% of population (2022 est.)
note: includes Gaza Strip and the West Bank

Children under the age of 5 years underweight: 2.1% (2019/20)
note: estimate is for Gaza Strip and the West Bank
comparison ranking: 93

Currently married women (ages 15-49): 62.4% (2023 est.)
note: data includes Gaza and the West Bank

Child marriage: *women married by age 15:* 0.7% (2020)
women married by age 18: 13.4% (2020)
note: includes both the Gaza Strip and the West Bank

Education expenditure: 5.4% of GDP (2021 est.)
note: includes Gaza Strip and the West Bank
comparison ranking: Education expenditure (% GDP) 46

Literacy: *total population:* 98% (2022 est.)
male: 99% (2022 est.)
female: 97% (2022 est.)
note: estimates are for Gaza and the West Bank

School life expectancy (primary to tertiary education): *total:* 13 years (2023 est.)
male: 12 years (2023 est.)
female: 14 years (2023 est.)
note: data represent Gaza Strip and the West Bank

ENVIRONMENT

Environmental issues: adequacy of freshwater supply; sewage treatment

Climate: temperate; temperature and precipitation vary with altitude, warm to hot summers, cool to mild winters

Urbanization: *urban population:* 77.6% of total population (2023)
rate of urbanization: 2.85% annual rate of change (2020-25 est.)
note: data represent Gaza Strip and the West Bank

Carbon dioxide emissions: 3.913 million metric tonnes of CO_2 (2023 est.)
from petroleum and other liquids: 3.913 million metric tonnes of CO_2 (2023 est.)
note: includes the West Bank and the Gaza Strip
comparison ranking: total emissions 143

Particulate matter emissions: 31.3 micrograms per cubic meter (2019 est.)

Waste and recycling: *municipal solid waste generated annually:* 1.387 million tons (2024 est.)
note: data represent combined total from the Gaza Strip and the West Bank.

Total water withdrawal: *municipal:* 251 million cubic meters (2022)
industrial: 37 million cubic meters (2022)
agricultural: 158 million cubic meters (2022)
note: data represent combined total from the Gaza Strip and the West Bank.

Total renewable water resources: 837 million cubic meters (2022 est.)
note: data represent combined total from the Gaza Strip and the West Bank.

GOVERNMENT

Country name: *conventional long form:* none
conventional short form: West Bank
etymology: name refers to the location of the British Mandate of Palestine that was occupied and administered by Jordan in 1948, on the west bank of the Jordan River; the designation was retained after the 1967 Six-Day War and subsequent changes in administration

National heritage: *total World Heritage Sites:* 4 (all cultural)
selected World Heritage Site locales: Ancient Jericho/Tell es-Sultan; Birthplace of Jesus: Church of the Nativity and the Pilgrimage Route, Bethlehem; Hebron/Al-Khalil Old Town; Land of Olives and Vines – Cultural Landscape of Southern Jerusalem, Battir

ECONOMY

Real GDP (purchasing power parity): $20.339 billion (2024 est.)
$27.694 billion (2023 est.)
$29.016 billion (2022 est.)
note: data in 2021 dollars; entry includes West Bank and Gaza Strip
comparison ranking: 154

Real GDP growth rate: -26.6% (2024 est.)
-4.6% (2023 est.)
4.1% (2022 est.)
note: annual GDP % growth based on constant local currency; entry includes West Bank and Gaza Strip
comparison ranking: 216

Real GDP per capita: $3,800 (2024 est.)
$5,400 (2023 est.)
$5,800 (2022 est.)
note: data in 2021 dollars; entry includes West Bank and Gaza Strip
comparison ranking: 185

GDP (official exchange rate): $13.711 billion (2024 est.)
note: data in current dollars at official exchange rate; entry includes West Bank and Gaza Strip

Inflation rate (consumer prices): 53.7% (2024 est.)
5.9% (2023 est.)
3.7% (2022 est.)
note: annual % change based on consumer prices; entry includes West Bank and Gaza Strip comparison ranking: 204

GDP - composition, by sector of origin: *agriculture:* 5.7% (2022 est.)
industry: 17.4% (2022 est.)
services: 58.3% (2022 est.)
note: figures may not total 100% due to non-allocated consumption not captured in sector-reported data
comparison rankings: agriculture 105; industry 152; services 101

GDP - composition, by end use: *household consumption:* 95.5% (2024 est.)
government consumption: 20.7% (2024 est.)
investment in fixed capital: 24.7% (2023 est.)
investment in inventories: 1.7% (2024 est.)
exports of goods and services: 21% (2024 est.)
imports of goods and services: -60.3% (2024 est.)
note: figures may not total 100% due to rounding or gaps in data collection

Agricultural products: tomatoes, cucumbers, olives, poultry, milk, potatoes, sheep milk, eggplants, gourds

Industries: small-scale manufacturing, quarrying, textiles, soap, olive-wood carvings, and mother-of-pearl souvenirs

Industrial production growth rate: -32.2% (2024 est.)
note: annual % change in industrial value added based on constant local currency; entry includes West Bank and Gaza Strip
comparison ranking: 194

Labor force: 1.391 million (2022 est.)
note: number of people ages 15 or older who are employed or seeking work; entry includes West Bank and Gaza Strip
comparison ranking: 137

Unemployment rate: 24.5% (2022 est.)
26.4% (2021 est.)
25.9% (2020 est.)
note: % of labor force seeking employment; entry includes West Bank and Gaza Strip
comparison ranking: 186

Youth unemployment rate (ages 15-24): *total:* 36.1% (2022 est.)
male: 31.6% (2022 est.)
female: 56.6% (2022 est.)
note: % of labor force ages 15-24 seeking employment
comparison ranking: total 13

Population below poverty line: 29.2% (2016 est.)
note: % of population with income below national poverty line; entry includes West Bank and Gaza Strip

Gini Index coefficient - distribution of family income: 36.4 (2023 est.)
note: index (0-100) of income distribution; higher values represent greater inequality; entry includes West Bank and Gaza Strip
comparison ranking: 62

Household income or consumption by percentage share: *lowest 10%:* 2.5% (2023 est.)
highest 10%: 27.1% (2023 est.)
note: % share of income accruing to lowest and highest 10% of population; entry includes West Bank and Gaza Strip

Remittances: 5.4% of GDP (2024 est.)
18.2% of GDP (2023 est.)
24% of GDP (2022 est.)
note: personal transfers and compensation between resident and non-resident individuals/households/entities; entry includes West Bank and Gaza Strip

Budget: *revenues:* $1.409 billion (2021 est.)
expenditures: $1.499 billion (2021 est.)
note: central government revenues and expenditures (excluding grants and social security funds) converted to US dollars at average official exchange rate for year indicated

Taxes and other revenues: 21.5% (of GDP) (2021 est.)
note: central government tax revenue as a % of GDP; entry includes West Bank and Gaza Strip
comparison ranking: 39

Current account balance: -$2.899 billion (2024 est.)
-$2.895 billion (2023 est.)
-$2.037 billion (2022 est.)
note: balance of payments - net trade and primary/secondary income in current dollars; entry includes West Bank and Gaza Strip
comparison ranking: 157

Exports: $2.885 billion (2024 est.)
$3.413 billion (2023 est.)
$3.533 billion (2022 est.)
note: balance of payments - exports of goods and services in current dollars; entry includes West Bank and Gaza Strip
comparison ranking: 156

Exports - partners: Jordan 51%, Turkey 12%, UAE 8%, Saudi Arabia 5%, UK 4% (2023)

note: top five export partners based on percentage share of exports; entry includes the West Bank and the Gaza Strip

Exports - commodities: scrap iron, tropical fruits, olive oil, building stone, prepared meat (2023)
note: top five export commodities based on value in dollars; entry includes the West Bank and the Gaza Strip

Imports: $8.264 billion (2024 est.)
$11.637 billion (2023 est.)
$12.257 billion (2022 est.)
note: balance of payments - imports of goods and services in current dollars; entry includes West Bank and Gaza Strip
comparison ranking: 131

Imports - partners: Egypt 25%, Jordan 17%, China 8%, Germany 7%, UAE 7% (2023)
note: top five import partners based on percentage share of imports; entry includes the West Bank and the Gaza Strip

Imports - commodities: cement, raw sugar, cars, baked goods, perfumes (2023)
note: top five import commodities based on value in dollars; entry includes the West Bank and the Gaza Strip

Reserves of foreign exchange and gold: $1.328 billion (2024 est.)
$1.323 billion (2023 est.)
$896.9 million (2022 est.)
note: holdings of gold (year-end prices)/foreign exchange/special drawing rights in current dollars; entry includes West Bank and Gaza Strip
comparison ranking: 138

Exchange rates: new Israeli shekels (ILS) per US dollar -

Exchange rates: 3.7 (2024 est.)
3.67 (2023 est.)
3.36 (2022 est.)
3.23 (2021 est.)
3.442 (2020 est.)

ENERGY

Electricity access: *electrification - total population:* 100% (2022 est.)
note: includes the West Bank and the Gaza Strip

Electricity: *installed generating capacity:* 352,000 kW (2023 est.)
consumption: 6.956 billion kWh (2023 est.)
imports: 6.925 billion kWh (2023 est.)
transmission/distribution losses: 988 million kWh (2023 est.)
note: includes the West Bank and the Gaza Strip
comparison rankings: installed generating capacity 157; consumption 118; imports 37; transmission/distribution losses 97

Electricity generation sources: *fossil fuels:* 66.5% of total installed capacity (2023 est.)
solar: 33.5% of total installed capacity (2023 est.)
note: includes the West Bank and the Gaza Strip

Coal: *exports:* 1 metric tons (2023 est.)
note: includes the West Bank and the Gaza Strip

Petroleum: *refined petroleum consumption:* 29,000 bbl/day (2023 est.)
note: includes the West Bank and the Gaza Strip

Energy consumption per capita: 14.991 million Btu/person (2023 est.)
note: includes the West Bank and the Gaza Strip
comparison ranking: 140

COMMUNICATIONS

Telephones - fixed lines: *total subscriptions:* 384,000 (2023 est.)
subscriptions per 100 inhabitants: 7 (2023 est.)
note: entry includes the West Bank and the Gaza Strip
comparison ranking: total subscriptions 100

Telephones - mobile cellular: *total subscriptions:* 4.15 million (2023 est.)
subscriptions per 100 inhabitants: 78 (2021 est.)
note: entry includes the West Bank and the Gaza Strip
comparison ranking: total subscriptions 133

Broadcast media: the Palestinian Authority operates 1 TV and 1 radio station; about 20 private TV and 40 radio stations; Jordanian TV and satellite TV accessible

Internet country code: .ps
note: IANA has designated.ps for the West Bank, same as Gaza Strip

Internet users: *percent of population:* 87% (2023 est.)
note: includes the Gaza Strip

Broadband - fixed subscriptions: *total:* 431,000 (2023 est.)
subscriptions per 100 inhabitants: 8 (2023 est.)
note: includes the Gaza Strip
comparison ranking: total 104

TRANSPORTATION

Airports: 1 (2025)
comparison ranking: 211

Heliports: 2 (2025)
comparison ranking: 134

MILITARY AND SECURITY

Military and security forces: per the Oslo Accords, the Palestinian Authority (PA) is not permitted a conventional military but maintains security and police forces; PA security personnel have operated exclusively in the West Bank since HAMAS seized power in the Gaza Strip in 2007; PA forces include the Palestinian National Security Forces, Presidential Guard, Civil Police, Civil Defense, Preventive Security Organization, the General Intelligence Organization, and the Military Intelligence Organization (2024)
note: the National Security Forces conduct gendarmerie-style security operations in circumstances that exceed the capabilities of the Civil Police; it is the largest branch of the PA security services and acts as the internal Palestinian security force; the Presidential Guard protects facilities and provides dignitary protection; the Preventive Security Organization is responsible for internal intelligence gathering and investigations related to internal security cases, including political dissent

Military expenditures: not available

Military and security service personnel strengths: the PA police and security forces have approximately 28,000 active personnel, including about 11,500 National Security Forces (2024)

Military equipment inventories and acquisitions: the security services are lightly equipped with small arms, light weapons, and wheeled vehicles (2024)

Military - note: Palestinian Authority security forces maintain security control of 17.5% (called Area A) of the
West Bank, as agreed by the Palestine Liberation Organization and Israel in the Oslo Accords, although Israeli security forces frequently conducted security operations there; Israeli security forces maintain responsibility for the remaining 82.5% of the West Bank, including Area B (22.5%), where the Palestinian Authority has administrative control, and Area C (60%), where Israel maintains administrative control (2024)

TERRORISM

Terrorist group(s): Terrorist group(s): Al-Aqsa Martyrs Brigade; HAMAS; Palestine Islamic Jihad; Palestine Liberation Front; Popular Front for the Liberation of Palestine
note: details about the history, aims, leadership, organization, areas of operation, tactics, targets, weapons, size, and sources of support of the group(s) appear(s) in Appendix T

TRANSNATIONAL ISSUES

Refugees and internally displaced persons: IDPs: 2,032,011 (2024 est.)

WORLD

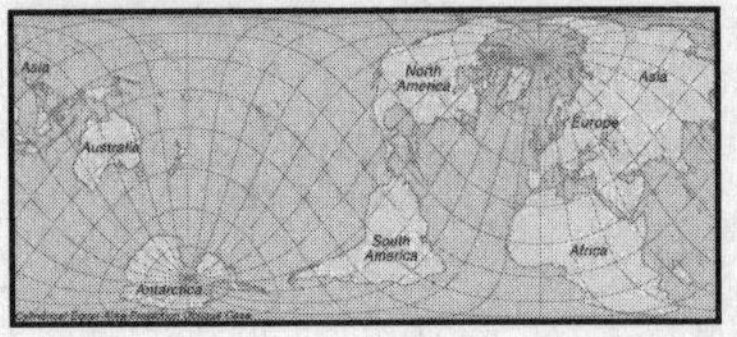

INTRODUCTION

Background: Globally, the 20th century was marked by: (a) two devastating World Wars; (b) the Great Depression of the 1930s; (c) the end of vast colonial empires; (d) rapid advances in science and technology; (e) the Cold War between the Western alliance and the Warsaw Pact nations; (f) a sharp rise in living standards in North America, Europe, and Japan; (g) increased concerns about environmental degradation including deforestation, energy and water shortages, declining biological diversity, and air pollution; and (h) the ultimate emergence of the US as the only world superpower. The planet's population continues to expand at a fast rate: from 1 billion in 1820 to 2 billion in 1930, 3 billion in 1960, 4 billion in

1974, 5 billion in 1987, 6 billion in 1999, 7 billion in 2012, and 8 billion in 2022. For the 21st century, the continued exponential growth in science and technology raises both hopes (e.g., advances in medicine and agriculture) and fears (e.g., development of even more lethal weapons of war).

GEOGRAPHY

Geographic overview: The surface of the Earth is approximately 70.9% water and 29.1% land. The water portion is the World Ocean, the single largest feature of the planet and one that connects all places on the globe. The continental landmasses divide this ocean into five major ocean basins, which are (in decreasing order of size) the Pacific, Atlantic, Indian, Southern, and Arctic. *The World Factbook* describes these five as oceans. Because of the major ocean currents and the effects of the major air masses above them, the Pacific and Atlantic Oceans are generally divided at the equator into the North and South Pacific Oceans and the North and South Atlantic Oceans, creating seven major water bodies – the so-called "Seven Seas."

About 97.5% of the Earth's water is saltwater. Of the 2.5% that is fresh, about two thirds is frozen, mostly locked up in mountain glaciers and the Antarctic ice sheets. If all the surface ice on earth fully melted, the sea level would rise about 70 m (230 ft).

Earth's land portion is divided into landmasses called continents. Different continental definitions are recognized in certain parts of the world, with some more heavily based on culture than physical geography.

Depending on the convention used, the number of continents can vary from five to seven. The most common classification recognizes seven, which are (from largest to smallest) Asia, Africa, North America, South America, Antarctica, Europe, and Australia. Asia and Europe are sometimes lumped together into a Eurasian continent, and North and South America are sometimes grouped as the Americas, with either usage resulting in a continent total of six (or five, if both are used).

North America is commonly understood to include Greenland and the Caribbean islands and to extend south to the Isthmus of Panama. The Ural Mountains and the Ural River are usually considered the easternmost part of Europe, the Caspian Sea is the limit to the southeast, and the Caucasus Mountains, the Black Sea, and the Mediterranean to the south. Asia usually incorporates all the islands of the Philippines, Malaysia, and Indonesia. The Pacific islands are often lumped with Australia and designated as Oceania or Australasia. Africa's northeast extremity is frequently delimited at the Isthmus of Suez, but for geopolitical purposes, the Egyptian Sinai Peninsula is often included as part of Africa.

In total, the United States recognizes 197 countries. Using the seven-continent model and grouping islands with adjacent continents, Africa has the most countries with 54. Europe has 49 countries and Asia 48, with five countries shared: Azerbaijan, Georgia, Kazakhstan, Russia, and Turkey. North America has 23, Oceania has 16, and South America has 12.

countries by continent: Africa (54): Algeria, Angola, Benin, Botswana, Burkina Faso, Burundi, Cabo Verde, Cameroon, Central African Republic, Chad, Comoros, Democratic Republic of the Congo, Republic of the Congo, Cote d'Ivoire, Djibouti, Egypt, Equatorial Guinea, Eritrea, Eswatini, Ethiopia, Gabon, The Gambia, Ghana, Guinea, Guinea-Bissau, Kenya, Lesotho, Liberia, Libya, Madagascar, Malawi, Mali, Mauritania, Mauritius, Morocco, Mozambique, Namibia, Niger, Nigeria, Rwanda, Sao Tome and Principe, Senegal, Seychelles, Sierra Leone, Somalia, South Africa, South Sudan, Sudan, Tanzania, Togo, Tunisia, Uganda, Zambia, Zimbabwe

Europe (49): Albania, Andorra, Austria, Azerbaijan*, Belarus, Belgium, Bosnia and Herzegovina, Bulgaria, Croatia, Czech Republic, Denmark, Estonia, Finland, France, Georgia*, Germany, Greece, Holy See (Vatican City), Hungary, Iceland, Ireland, Italy, Kazakhstan*, Kosovo, Latvia, Liechtenstein, Lithuania, Luxembourg, Malta, Moldova, Monaco, Montenegro, Netherlands, North Macedonia, Norway, Poland, Portugal, Romania, Russia*, San Marino, Serbia, Slovakia, Slovenia, Spain, Sweden, Switzerland, Turkey*, Ukraine, United Kingdom (* indicates part of the country is also in Asia)

Asia (48): Afghanistan, Armenia, Azerbaijan*, Bahrain, Bangladesh, Bhutan, Brunei, Burma, Cambodia, China, Cyprus, Georgia*, India, Indonesia, Iran, Iraq, Israel, Japan, Jordan, Kazakhstan*, North Korea, South Korea, Kuwait, Kyrgyzstan, Laos, Lebanon, Malaysia, Maldives, Mongolia, Nepal, Oman, Pakistan, Philippines, Qatar, Russia*, Saudi Arabia, Singapore, Sri Lanka, Syria, Tajikistan, Thailand, Timor-Leste, Turkey*, Turkmenistan, United Arab Emirates, Uzbekistan, Vietnam, Yemen (* indicates part of the country is also in Europe)

North America (23): Antigua and Barbuda, The Bahamas, Barbados, Belize, Canada, Costa Rica, Cuba, Dominica, Dominican Republic, El Salvador, Grenada, Guatemala, Haiti, Honduras, Jamaica, Mexico, Nicaragua, Panama, Saint Kitts and Nevis, Saint Lucia, Saint Vincent and the Grenadines, Trinidad and Tobago, United States

Oceania (16): Australia, Cook Islands, Fiji, Kiribati, Marshall Islands, Federated States of Micronesia, Nauru, New Zealand, Niue, Palau, Papua New Guinea, Samoa, Solomon Islands, Tonga, Tuvalu, Vanuatu

South America (12): Argentina, Bolivia, Brazil, Chile, Colombia, Ecuador, Guyana, Paraguay, Peru, Suriname, Uruguay, Venezuela

Three of the states described above – France, Netherlands, and the United Kingdom – consist of smaller political entities that are referred to as countries. France considers French Polynesia an overseas country; the Kingdom of the Netherlands refers to all four of its constituent parts (the Netherlands and the islands of Aruba, Curacao, and Sint Maarten) as countries; and the United Kingdom is composed of the countries of England, Wales, Scotland, and Northern Ireland.

the World from space: Earth is the only planet in the solar system to have water in its three states of matter: liquid (oceans, lakes, and rivers), solid (ice), and gas (water vapor in clouds). From a distance, Earth would be the brightest of the eight planets in the solar system because of the planet's water reflecting sunlight.

Earth has a slight equatorial bulge – a difference between its equatorial and polar diameters – because of the centrifugal force from the planet rotating on its axis. The equatorial diameter is 12,756 km, but the polar diameter is 12,714 km; the circumference at the equator is 40,075 km, and the polar circumference is 40,008 km.

Area: *total:* 510.072 million sq km
land: 148.94 million sq km
water: 361,899,999 sq km
note: 70.9% of the world's surface is water, 29.1% is land

Area - comparative: land area about 16 times the size of the US

Area - rankings: *top fifteen World Factbook entities ranked by size:* Pacific Ocean 155,557,000 sq km; Atlantic Ocean 76,762,000 sq km; Indian Ocean 68,556,000 sq km; Southern Ocean 20,327,000 sq km; Russia 17,098,242 sq km; Antarctica 14,200,000 sq km; Arctic Ocean 14,056,000 sq km; Canada 9,984,670 sq km; United States 9,826,675 sq km; China 9,596,960 sq km; Brazil 8,515,770 sq km; Australia 7,741,220 sq km; European Union 4,324,782 sq km; India 3,287,263 sq km; Argentina 2,780,400 sq km

top ten largest water bodies: Pacific Ocean 155,557,000 sq km; Atlantic Ocean 76,762,000 sq km; Indian Ocean 68,556,000 sq km; Southern Ocean 20,327,000 sq km; Arctic Ocean 14,056,000 sq km; Coral Sea 4,184,100 sq km; South China Sea 3,595,900 sq km; Caribbean Sea 2,834,000 sq km; Bering Sea 2,520,000 sq km; Mediterranean Sea 2,469,000 sq km

top ten largest landmasses: Asia 44,568,500 sq km; Africa 30,065,000 sq km; North America 24,473,000 sq km; South America 17,819,000 sq km; Antarctica 14,200,000 sq km; Europe 9,948,000 sq km; Australia 7,741,220 sq km; Greenland 2,166,086 sq km; New Guinea 785,753 sq km; Borneo 751,929 sq km

top ten largest islands: Greenland 2,166,086 sq km; New Guinea (Indonesia, Papua New Guinea) 785,753 sq km; Borneo (Brunei, Indonesia, Malaysia) 751,929 sq km; Madagascar 587,713 sq km; Baffin Island (Canada) 507,451 sq km; Sumatra (Indonesia) 472,784 sq km; Honshu (Japan) 227,963 sq km; Victoria Island (Canada) 217,291 sq km; Great Britain (United Kingdom) 209,331 sq km; Ellesmere Island (Canada) 196,236 sq km

top ten longest mountain ranges (land-based):* Andes (Venezuela, Colombia, Ecuador, Peru, Bolivia, Chile, Argentina) 7,000 km; Rocky Mountains (Canada, US) 4,830 km; Great Dividing Range (Australia) 3,700 km; Transantarctic Mountains (Antarctica) 3,500 km; Kunlun Mountains (China) 3,000 km; Ural Mountains (Russia, Kazakhstan) 2,640 km; Atlas Mountains (Morocco, Algeria, Tunisia) 2,500 km; Appalachian Mountains (Canada, US) 2,400 km; Himalayas (Pakistan, Afghanistan, India, China, Nepal, Bhutan) 2,300 km; Altai Mountains (Kazakhstan, Russia, Mongolia) 2,000 km

*lengths are approximate; if oceans are included, the Mid-Ocean Ridge is by far the longest mountain range at 40,389 km

top ten largest forested countries (sq km and percent of land): Russia 8,149,310 (49.8%); Brazil 4,935,380 (58.9%); Canada 3,470,690 (38.2%); United States 3,103,700 (33.9%); China 2,098,640 (22.3%); Democratic Republic of the Congo 1,522,670 (67.2%); Australia 1,250,590 (16.3%); Indonesia 903,250 (49.9%); Peru 738,054 (57.7%); India 708,600 (23.8%) (2016 est.)

top ten most densely forested countries (percent of land): Suriname (98.3%), Federated States of Micronesia (91.9%), Gabon (90%), Seychelles (88.4%), Palau (87.6%), Guyana (83.9%), Laos (82.1%), Solomon Islands (77.9%), Papua New Guinea (74.1%), Finland (73.1%) (2016 est.)

top ten largest (non-polar) deserts:* Sahara (Algeria, Chad, Egypt, Libya, Mali, Mauritania, Niger, Western Sahara, Sudan, Tunisia) 9,200,000 sq km; Arabian (Saudi Arabia, Iraq, Jordan, Kuwait, Oman, Qatar, United Arab Emirates, Yemen) 2,330,000 sq km;

Gobi (China, Mongolia) 1,295,000 sq km; Kalahari (Botswana, Namibia, South Africa) 900,000 sq km; Patagonian (Argentina) 673,000 sq km; Syrian (Syria, Iraq, Jordan, Saudi Arabia) 500,000 sq km; Chihuahuan (Mexico) 362,000 sq km; Kara-Kum (Turkmenistan) 350,000 sq km; Great Victoria (Australia) 348,750 sq km; Great Basin (United States) 343,169 sq km
*if the two polar deserts were included, they would rank first and second: Antarctic Desert 14,200,000 sq km and Arctic Desert 13,900,000 sq km
ten smallest independent countries: Holy See (Vatican City) 0.44 sq km; Monaco 2 sq km; Nauru 21 sq km; Tuvalu 26 sq km; San Marino 61 sq km; Liechtenstein 160 sq km; Marshall Islands 181 sq km; Cook Islands 236 sq km; Niue 260 sq km; Saint Kitts and Nevis 261 sq km

Land boundaries: the land boundaries in *The World Factbook* total 279,035.5 km (not counting shared boundaries twice), but the number is only an estimate because of the difficulty in precisely measuring natural features such as rivers
note 1: 46 nations and other areas are landlocked, these include: Afghanistan, Andorra, Armenia, Austria, Azerbaijan, Belarus, Bhutan, Bolivia, Botswana, Burkina Faso, Burundi, Central African Republic, Chad, Czechia, Eswatini, Ethiopia, Holy See (Vatican City), Hungary, Kazakhstan, Kosovo, Kyrgyzstan, Laos, Lesotho, Liechtenstein, Luxembourg, North Macedonia, Malawi, Mali, Moldova, Mongolia, Nepal, Niger, Paraguay, Rwanda, San Marino, Serbia, Slovakia, South Sudan, Switzerland, Tajikistan, Turkmenistan, Uganda, Uzbekistan, West Bank, Zambia, Zimbabwe; two of these, Liechtenstein and Uzbekistan, are doubly landlocked
note 2: worldwide, about one quarter of interior (non-coastal) borders are rivers; South America with 43% leads the continents, followed by North America with 32%, Africa with 30%, Europe with 23%, and Asia with 18%; Australia has no interior national river borders
note 3: two nations, China and Russia, each border 14 other countries

Coastline: 356,000 km
note: 95 nations and other entities are islands that border no other countries: American Samoa, Anguilla, Antigua and Barbuda, Aruba, Ashmore and Cartier Islands, The Bahamas, Bahrain, Baker Island, Barbados, Bermuda, Bouvet Island, British Indian Ocean Territory, British Virgin Islands, Cabo Verde, Cayman Islands, Christmas Island, Clipperton Island, Cocos (Keeling) Islands, Comoros, Cook Islands, Coral Sea Islands, Cuba, Curacao, Cyprus, Dominica, Falkland Islands (Islas Malvinas), Faroe Islands, Fiji, French Polynesia, French Southern and Antarctic Lands, Greenland, Grenada, Guam, Guernsey, Heard Island and McDonald Islands, Howland Island, Iceland, Isle of Man, Jamaica, Jan Mayen, Japan, Jarvis Island, Jersey, Johnston Atoll, Kingman Reef, Kiribati, Madagascar, Maldives, Malta, Marshall Islands, Mauritius, Mayotte, Federated States of Micronesia, Midway Islands, Montserrat, Nauru, Navassa Island, New Caledonia, New Zealand, Niue, Norfolk Island, Northern Mariana Islands, Palau, Palmyra Atoll, Paracel Islands, Philippines, Pitcairn Islands, Puerto Rico, Saint Barthelemy, Saint Helena, Saint Kitts and Nevis, Saint Lucia, Saint Pierre and Miquelon, Saint Vincent and the Grenadines, Samoa, Sao Tome and Principe, Seychelles, Singapore, Sint Maarten, Solomon Islands, South Georgia and the South Sandwich Islands, Spratly Islands, Sri Lanka, Svalbard, Taiwan, Tokelau, Tonga, Trinidad and Tobago, Turks and Caicos Islands, Tuvalu, Vanuatu, Virgin Islands, Wake Island, Wallis and Futuna

Maritime claims: *most countries make the following claims measured from the mean low-tide baseline as described in the 1982 UN Convention on the Law of the Sea:* territorial sea - 12 nm, contiguous zone - 24 nm, and exclusive economic zone - 200 nm; additional zones provide for exploitation of continental shelf resources and an exclusive fishing zone; boundary situations with neighboring states prevent many countries from extending their fishing or economic zones to a full 200 nm

Climate: a wide equatorial band of hot and humid tropical climates is bordered north and south by subtropical temperate zones that separate two large areas of cold and dry polar climates
ten driest places on Earth (average annual precipitation): McMurdo Dry Valleys, Antarctica 0 mm (0 in)
Arica, Chile 0.76 mm (0.03 in)
Al Kufrah, Libya 0.86 mm (0.03 in)
Aswan, Egypt 0.86 mm (0.03 in)
Luxor, Egypt 0.86 mm (0.03 in)
Ica, Peru 2.29 mm (0.09 in)
Wadi Halfa, Sudan 2.45 mm (0.1 in)
Iquique, Chile 5.08 mm (0.2 in)
Pelican Point, Namibia 8.13 mm (0.32 in)
El Arab (Aoulef), Algeria 12.19 mm (0.48 in)
ten wettest places on Earth (average annual precipitation): Mawsynram, India 11,871 mm (467.4 in)
Cherrapunji, India 11,777 mm (463.7 in)
Tutunendo, Colombia 11,770 mm (463.4 in)
Cropp River, New Zealand 11,516 mm (453.4 in)
San Antonia de Ureca, Equatorial Guinea 10,450 mm (411.4 in)
Debundsha, Cameroon 10,299 mm (405.5 in)
Big Bog, US (Hawaii) 10,272 mm (404.4 in)
Mt Waialeale, US (Hawaii) 9,763 mm (384.4 in)
Kukui, US (Hawaii) 9,293 mm (365.9 in)
Emeishan, China 8,169 mm (321.6 in)
ten coldest places on Earth (lowest average monthly temperature): Verkhoyansk, Russia (Siberia) -47°C (-53°F) January
Oymyakon, Russia (Siberia) -46°C (-52°F)
January Eureka, Canada -38.4°C (-37.1°F) February
Isachsen, Canada -36°C (-32.8°F) February
Alert, Canada -34°C (-28°F) February
Kap Morris Jesup, Greenland -34°C (-29°F) March
Cornwallis Island, Canada -33.5°C (-28.3°F) February
Cambridge Bay, Canada -33.5°C (28.3°F) February
Ilirnej, Russia -33°C (-28°F) January
Resolute, Canada -33°C (-27.4°F) February
ten hottest places on Earth (highest average monthly temperature): Death Valley, US (California) 39°C (101°F) July
Iranshahr, Iran 38.3°C (100.9°F) June
Ouallene, Algeria 38°C (100.4°F) July
Kuwait City, Kuwait 37.7°C (100°F) July
Medina, Saudi Arabia 36°C (97°F) July
Buckeye, US (Arizona) 34°C (93°F) July
Jazan, Saudi Arabia 33°C (91°F) June
Al Kufrah, Libya 31°C (87°F) July
Alice Springs, Australia 29°C (84°F) January
Tamanrasset, Algeria 29°C (84°F) June

Terrain: a compilation of terrain extremes can be found in the World elevation entry; the world's ocean floors also display wide variation, as explained in the bathymetry and major ocean currents entries under each of the five ocean entries (Arctic, Atlantic, Indian, Pacific, and Southern)
top ten world caves: compiled from Geography - note(s) under country entries
largest cave: Son Doong in Phong Nha-Ke Bang National Park, Vietnam, is the world's largest cave (greatest cross sectional area) and is the largest known cave passage by volume; it currently measures a total of 38.5 million cu m (about 1.35 billion cu ft); it connects to Thung cave, but not yet officially – when recognized, it will add an additional 1.6 million cu m in volume
largest ice cave: the Eisriesenwelt (Ice Giants World) inside the Hochkogel mountain near Werfen, Austria, is the world's largest and longest ice cave system at 42 km (26 mi)
longest cave: Mammoth Cave in west-central Kentucky is the world's longest known cave system with more than 650 km (405 mi) of surveyed passageways
longest salt cave: the Malham Cave in Mount Sodom in Israel is the world's longest salt cave at 10 km (6 mi); its survey is not complete, so its recorded length will eventually increase
longest underwater cave: the Sac Actun cave system in Mexico is the longest underwater cave in the world at 348 km (216 mi), and the second-longest cave worldwide
longest lava tube cave: Kazumura Cave on the island of Hawaii is the world's longest and deepest lava tube cave; it has been surveyed at 66 km (41 mi) long and 1,102 m (3,614 ft) deep
deepest cave: Veryovkina Cave in the country of Georgia is the world's deepest cave at 2,212 m (7,257 ft)
deepest underwater cave: the Hranice Abyss in Czechia is the world's deepest surveyed underwater cave at 404 m (1,325 ft); its survey is not complete, and it could be 800-1,200 m deep
largest cave chamber: the Miao Room in the Gebihe cave system in China's Ziyun Getu He Chuandong National Park has about 10.78 million cu m (380.7 million cu ft) of volume
largest bat cave: Bracken Cave outside San Antonio, Texas, is the world's largest bat cave; an estimated 20 million Mexican free-tailed bats roost in the cave from March to October, making it the world's largest known concentration of mammals
bonus "cave" - the world's largest sinkhole: the Xiaoxhai Tiankeng sinkhole in Chongqing Municipality, China is 660 m deep, with a volume of 130 million cu m

Elevation: *highest point:* Mount Everest 8,849 m
lowest point: Denman Glacier (Antarctica) more than -3,500 m (in the oceanic realm, Challenger Deep in the Mariana Trench is the lowest point, lying -10,924 m below the surface of the Pacific Ocean)
mean elevation: 840 m
top ten highest mountains (measured from sea level): Mount Everest (China-Nepal) 8,849 m; K2 (China-Pakistan) 8,611 m; Kanchenjunga (India-Nepal) 8,586 m; Lhotse (China-Nepal) 8,516 m; Makalu (China-Nepal) 8,485 m; Cho Oyu (China-Nepal) 8,188 m; Dhaulagiri (Nepal) 8,167 m; Manaslu (Nepal) 8,156 m; Nanga Parbat (Pakistan) 8,125 m; Annapurna (Nepal) 8,091 m;
note: Mauna Kea (United States) is the world's tallest mountain as measured from base to summit; the peak lies on the island of Hawaii, but its base begins more than 70 km offshore and at a depth of about 6,000 m; total height estimates range from 9,966 m to 10,203 m
top ten highest island peaks: Puncak Jaya (New Guinea) 4,884 m (Indonesia)*; Mauna Kea (Hawaii) 4,207 m

(United States); Gunung Kinabalu (Borneo) 4,095 m (Malaysia)*; Yu Shan (Taiwan) 3,952 (Taiwan)*; Mount Kerinci (Sumatra) 3,805 m (Indonesia); Mount Erebus (Ross Island) 3,794 (Antarctica); Mount Fuji (Honshu) 3,776 m (Japan)*; Mount Rinjani (Lombok) 3,726 m (Indonesia); Aoraki-Mount Cook (South Island) 3,724 m (New Zealand)*; Pico de Teide (Tenerife) 3,718 m (Spain)*
* indicates the highest peak for that *Factbook* entry
highest point on each continent: Asia - Mount Everest (China-Nepal) 8,849 m; South America - Cerro Aconcagua (Argentina) 6,960 m; North America - Mount McKinley (United States) 6,190 m; Africa - Kilimanjaro (Tanzania) 5,895 m; Europe - El'brus (Russia) 5,633 m; Antarctica - Vinson Massif 4,897 m; Australia - Mount Kosciuszko 2,229 m
highest capital on each continent: South America - La Paz (Bolivia) 3,640 m; Africa - Addis Ababa (Ethiopia) 2,355 m; Asia - Thimphu (Bhutan) 2,334 m; North America - Mexico City (Mexico) 2,240 m; Europe - Andorra la Vella (Andorra) 1,023 m; Australia - Canberra (Australia) 605 m
lowest point on each continent: Antarctica - Denman Glacier more than -3,500 m; Asia - Dead Sea (Israel-Jordan) -431 m; Africa - Lac Assal (Djibouti) -155 m; South America - Laguna del Carbon (Argentina) -105 m; North America - Death Valley (United States) -86 m; Europe - Caspian Sea (Azerbaijan-Kazakhstan-Russia) -28 m; Australia - Lake Eyre -15
lowest capital on each continent: Asia - Baku (Azerbaijan) -28 m; Europe - Amsterdam (Netherlands) -2 m; Africa - Banjul (Gambia); Bissau (Guinea-Bissau), Conakry (Guinea), Djibouti (Djibouti), Libreville (Gabon), Male (Maldives), Monrovia (Liberia), Tunis (Tunisia), Victoria (Seychelles) 0 m; North America - Basseterre (Saint Kitts and Nevis), Kingstown (Saint Vincent and the Grenadines), Panama City (Panama), Port of Spain (Trinidad and Tobago), Roseau (Dominica), Saint John's (Antigua and Barbuda), Santo Domingo (Dominican Republic) 0 m; South America - Georgetown (Guyana) 0 m; Australia - Canberra (Australia) 605 m

Land use: *agricultural land:* 38% (2022 est.)
arable land: 10.7% (2022 est.)
permanent crops: 1.5% (2022 est.)
permanent pasture: 25.8% (2022 est.)
forest: 30.6% (2022 est.)
other: 31.4% (2022 est.)

Irrigated land: 3,242,917 sq km (2012 est.)

Major lakes (area sq km): *top ten largest natural lakes:* Caspian Sea (Azerbaijan, Iran, Kazakhstan, Russia, Turkmenistan) 374,000 sq km; Lake Superior (Canada, United States) 82,100 sq km; Lake Victoria (Kenya, Tanzania, Uganda) 62,940 sq km; Lake Huron (Canada, United States) 59,600 sq km; Lake Michigan (United States) 57,750 sq km; Lake Tanganyika (Burundi, Democratic Republic of the Congo, Tanzania, Zambia) 32,000 sq km; Great Bear Lake (Canada) 31,328 sq km; Lake Baikal (Russia) 31,500 sq km; Lake Malawi (Malawi, Mozambique, Tanzania) 22,490 sq km; Great Slave Lake (Canada) 28,568 sq km
note 1: the areas of the lakes are subject to seasonal variation; only the Caspian Sea is saline, the rest are fresh water
note 2: Lakes Huron and Michigan are technically a single lake because the flow of water between the Straits of Mackinac that connects the two lakes keeps their water levels at near-equilibrium; combined, Lake Huron-Michigan is the largest freshwater lake by surface area in the world
note 3: if ranked by water volume, the Caspian Sea would still be first, but it would be followed Lakes Baikal, Tanganyika, Superior, and Malawi; Lake Superior contains more water than the other four North American Great Lakes (Erie, Huron, Michigan, Ontario) combined

Major rivers (by length in km): *top ten longest rivers:* Nile (Africa) 6,650 km; Amazon (South America) 6,436 km; Yangtze (Asia) 6,300 km; Mississippi-Missouri (North America) 6,275 km; Yenisey-Angara (Asia) 5,539 km; Huang He/Yellow (Asia) 5,464 km; Ob-Irtysh (Asia) 5,410 km; Congo (Africa) 4,700 km; Amur (Asia) 4,444 km; Lena (Asia) 4,400 km
note: there are 21 countries without rivers: three in Africa (Comoros, Djibouti, Libya), one in the Americas (Bahamas), eight in Asia (Bahrain, Kuwait, Maldives, Oman, Qatar, Saudi Arabia, United Arab Emirates, Yemen), three in Europe (Malta, Monaco, Holy See), and six in Oceania (Kiribati, Marshall Islands, Nauru, Niue, Tonga, Tuvalu); these countries also do not have natural lakes

Major watersheds (area sq km): a watershed is a drainage basin on an area of land where precipitation collects and drains off into a common outlet, such as into a river, bay, or other body of water; oceans ultimately take in the drainage from 83% of all land area; the remaining 17% of the land drains into internal (endorheic) basins

The World Factbook lists 51 watersheds across 102 countries: Asia - 18
Europe - 9
Africa - 9
North and Central America - 8
South America - 5
Australia - 2
all watersheds with an area of at least 500,000 sq km have been included, along with a number of smaller, regionally significant watersheds; together, these represent the surface hydrology water flows that are the world's primary sources of fresh water for individual consumption, industry, and agriculture

Major aquifers: aquifers are underground layers of water-bearing permeable rock formations; groundwater from aquifers can be extracted using a water well

The World Factbook lists 37 major aquifers across 52 countries: Africa - 13
Asia - 10
North America - 5
South America - 3
Europe - 4
Australia -2
these aquifers contain the bulk of the stored volume of groundwater; this represents more than 30% of the world's fresh water; in the US, groundwater is primarily used for irrigation; globally, 70% of the groundwater withdrawn is used for agriculture; groundwater also supplies almost half of all drinking water worldwide

Population distribution: six of the world's seven continents are widely and permanently inhabited; Asia is the most populous continent, with about 60% of the world's population (China and India together account for over 35%); Africa comes in second with over 15%, Europe has about 10%, North America 8%, South America almost 6%, and Oceania less than 1%; the harsh conditions on Antarctica prevent any permanent habitation

Natural hazards: large areas of the world are subject to severe weather and natural disasters (cyclones, earthquakes, landslides, tsunamis, volcanic eruptions, etc.)
volcanism: this is a driver and consequence of plate tectonics, the physical process reshaping the Earth's lithosphere; the world is home to more than 1,500 potentially active volcanoes, with over 500 of these erupting in recorded history; an estimated 500 million people live near volcanoes; associated dangers include lava flows, mud flows, pyroclastic flows, ash clouds, ash fall, ballistic projectiles, gas emissions, landslides, earthquakes, and tsunamis; in the 1990s, the International Association of Volcanology and Chemistry of the Earth's Interior created a list of 16 "Decade Volcanoes" with great potential for destruction: Avachinsky-Koryaksky (Russia), Colima (Mexico), Etna (Italy), Galeras (Colombia), Mauna Loa (US), Merapi (Indonesia), Nyiragongo (Democratic Republic of the Congo), Rainier (US), Sakurajima (Japan), Santa Maria (Guatemala), Santorini (Greece), Taal (Philippines), Teide (Spain), Ulawun (Papua New Guinea), Unzen (Japan), Vesuvius (Italy)
volcano statistics: countries with the most volcanoes: (Holocene Epoch, the past 12,000 years*): United States (162), Japan (122), Indonesia (120), Russia (117), Chile (91);
*roughly 1,350 volcanoes have erupted over this time period; about 40-50 eruptions are ongoing at any one time; the frequency of volcanoes has not increased
longest erupting volcano: Santa Maria volcano in Guatemala has been constantly erupting since 22 June 1922; the Yasur volcano on Tanna Island in Vanuatu has been in constant activity since Captain Cook observed it in 1774, but it is not cited due to lack of a clear start date; tephra stratigraphy and radiocarbon dating show that the Yasur activity may have begun ca. A.D. 1270
highest volcano (above sea level): Nevado Ojos del Salado (6,893 m; 22,615 ft) on the Chile-Argentina border is the world's highest volcano above sea level and the highest peak in Chile
highest volcano (from base): Mauna Kea (US) is the world's tallest mountain, measured from base to summit; the peak lies on the island of Hawaii, but its base begins more than 70 km (43 mi) offshore and at a depth of about 6,000 m; total height estimates range from 9,966 m to 10,203 m
earthquakes: the vast majority of earthquakes occur in three large zones; the *Circum-Pacific Belt* (known as the Ring of Fire) borders the Pacific and is the largest zone of volcanic and seismic activity, with about 90% of earthquakes (81% of the largest) and about 75% of active volcanoes; the belt extends northward from Chile along the South American coast, then through Central America, Mexico, the western US, southern Alaska, and the Aleutian Islands, to Japan, the Philippines, Papua New Guinea, the southwestern Pacific, and New Zealand; the *Alpide Belt* extends from Java to Sumatra, northward along the mountains of Burma, eastward through the Himalayas and the Mediterranean, and into the Atlantic Ocean, accounting for about 17% of the largest earthquakes; the third belt follows the long Mid-Atlantic Ridge

Wonders of the World: The Seven Wonders of the Ancient World: The conquests of Alexander the Great (r. 336-323 B.C.) in the fourth century B.C. fostered the spread of Greek culture to the lands around the eastern Mediterranean and much of the Middle East, ushering in what is today referred to as the Hellenistic Period (323-31 B.C.). Hellenistic sightseers compiled guidebooks with outstanding monuments in those parts of the world, including Persia, Egypt, and Babylon. Seven sites were usually emphasized since that number was considered magical, perfect, and complete. Not all wonders lists from ancient times agreed, but six sites consistently appeared (the Walls of Babylon sometimes substituted for the Lighthouse of Alexandria). The "classic" Seven Wonders most often cited are listed below.

1. *The Great Pyramid of Egypt:* The oldest of the Seven Wonders, the Great Pyramid, is the only one that remains largely intact. Commissioned by the Pharaoh Khufu (r. ca. 2589-2566 B.C.), it is the largest of the three pyramids at Giza. It served as the ruler's tomb and was built over a period of about 20 years, concluding around 2560 B.C. The pyramid is estimated to have been 146.5 m tall when completed and was the tallest man-made structure in the world for over 3,800 years (until the 14th century A.D.). Most of the original limestone casing stones that formed the outer smooth surface of the pyramid are gone. Today, the pyramid's height is about 139 m.

2. *The Hanging Gardens of Babylon:* This is the only one of the ancient Seven Wonders for which a definitive location has never been established. No surviving Babylonian texts mention the Gardens, nor have any archeological remains been discovered in today's Iraq. According to tradition, the gardens were a remarkable feat of engineering, with an ascending series of mud-brick-tiered gardens containing a variety of trees, shrubs, and vines that, when viewed from below, resembled a leafy green mountain. The Gardens are frequently attributed to the Neo-Babylonian King Nebuchadnezzar II (r. 605-562 B.C.), who may have had them built for his Median wife, Queen Amytis, because she missed the green hills and valleys of her homeland.

3. *The Temple of Artemis (Artemision) at Ephesus:* This Greek temple at Ephesus (3 km southwest of Selcuk in present-day western Turkey) was dedicated to the goddess Artemis and was completely rebuilt twice: once after a 7th century B.C. flood and then after a 356 B.C. act of arson. In its final form, it was judged to be one of the Seven Wonders and survived for 600 years. The building was composed entirely of marble, with massive dimensions reported to be 130 m by 69 m, and included 127 columns, each about 18 m tall. The temple was damaged in a Gothic raid in A.D. 268, and Christians finally closed it in the early-to-mid 5th century. The structure was dismantled in succeeding centuries, and today almost nothing of the temple remains.

4. *The Mausoleum of Halicarnassus:* Constructed in about 350 B.C., the Mausoleum of Halicarnassus was located on the site of the present-day city of Bodrum in southwestern Turkey. It was the tomb of Mausolus, a Persian ruler, and his wife – the term "mausoleum" is derived from his name. The structure stood about 45 m high and took about 20 years to complete. A series of earthquakes between the 12th and 15th centuries A.D. devastated the structure, which was the last of the original Seven Wonders to be destroyed.

5. *The Colossus of Rhodes:* This statue of the Greek sun god Helios, constructed at the entrance to Rhodes' harbor to celebrate the city's successful repulse of a siege, was made of iron tie bars to which brass or bronze plates were attached to form a skin. Contemporary descriptions list its height at about 70 cubits, or 33 m – approximately the same height as the Statue of Liberty (34 m) – which would make it the tallest statue in the ancient world. Completed in about 280 B.C., the monument stood for only about 54 years until it toppled in an earthquake in 226 B.C. The remains lay on the ground for over 800 years before finally being sold for scrap.

6. *The Lighthouse (Pharos) of Alexandria:* Completed around 275 B.C., the lighthouse stood on Pharos Island at the entrance to the Egyptian port city of Alexandria for about 1,600 years. Three earthquakes severely damaged it between A.D. 956 and 1323, when it was deactivated. The shape of the structure appeared on a number of ancient coins: a solid square base, which made up about half the height, supported an octagonal middle section and a cylindrical top. The height of the structure is thought to have been between 100 m (328 ft) and 140 m (459 ft). A mirror at its apex reflected sunlight during the day, and a fire burned at night.

7. *The Statue of Zeus at Olympia in Greece:* The giant seated statue of the king of the Greek gods in the sanctuary of Olympia was completed by the Greek sculptor Phidias in about 435 B.C. Roughly 13 m (43 ft) tall, it was constructed of ivory plates and gold panels on a wooden framework, and the god's throne was ornamented with ebony, ivory, gold, and precious stones. With the rise of Christianity, the sanctuary at Olympia fell into disuse; the details of the statue's final destruction are unknown.

note: The Lighthouse of Alexandria may have been the last of the wonders to be completed (ca. 275 B.C.), and the Colossus of Rhodes was the first to be destroyed in about 226 B.C., so the Seven Wonders existed at the same time for only about 50 years in the middle of the third century B.C.

The New Seven Wonders of the World: A private initiative to come up with a new list of seven of the world's wonders sprang up early in the new millennium. Worldwide balloting – via internet or telephone – included a list of 200 existing monuments. Over 100 million votes were reportedly cast over a period of several years, and the final list below was announced on 7 July 2007 (7-7-2007). The seven are inscribed as UNESCO World Heritage Sites.

1. *Chichen Itza, Yucatan, Mexico:* This archeological site includes the impressive remains of a large pre-Columbian Mayan city that flourished around A.D. 600-1100. Among the structures at the site are the massive Temple of the Warriors complex, an observatory (El Caracol), the Great Ball Court, and the Sacred Cenote (sinkhole) where offerings were made. The most famous building is the step-pyramid known as the Temple of Kukulcan that dominates the center of the site and serves as the symbol of Chichen Itza. The pyramidal structure is 24 m (79 ft) high; the crowning temple adds another 6 m (20 ft). Located in the dense jungles of Yucatan, it is one of the most visited tourist sites in Mexico.

2. *The Colosseum, Rome, Italy:* The Roman Emperor Vespasian began construction on the Colosseum in A.D. 72, and his son Titus completed it in A.D. 80, with Domitian (A.D. 81-96) making further modifications. The three emperors make up the Flavian Dynasty, and the structure is also known as the Flavian Amphitheater. It is estimated to have seated about 65 thousand spectators and was most famously used for gladiatorial contests and public spectacles. Earthquakes and thieves destroyed much of the original structure, but it remains an iconic symbol of Rome. The Colosseum is one of the most popular tourist attractions in the world.

3. *Christ the Redeemer Statue, Rio de Janeiro, Brazil:* Built between 1922 and 1931, the 30-m (98-ft) sculpture is reputed to be the largest Art Deco statue in the world. Its pedestal provides another 8 m (26 ft) in height, and the arms stretch out to 28 m (92 ft). Built of reinforced concrete and soapstone, the statue has become a cultural icon of both Rio and Brazil.

4. *Great Wall, China:* The name refers to a series of fortification systems that stretched across China's northern historical borders and served as protection against nomadic peoples. An archeological survey revealed that the wall and its associated branches measure 21,196 km (13,171 mi). The earliest of the walls date to the 7th century B.C.; stretches began to be linked in the 3rd century B.C., and successive dynasties added to or maintained sections of the walls. The best-known and best-preserved parts of the wall were built during the Ming Dynasty (1368-1644). The Great Wall is acknowledged as one of the most impressive architectural feats in history.

5. *Machu Picchu, Cuzco Region, Peru:* The Inca citadel of Machu Picchu, situated on a 2,430 m (7,972 ft) Andean mountain ridge, is now thought to have been erected as an estate for the Inca Emperor Pachacuti (r. 1438-1471) and may have also served as a religious sanctuary. Built between about 1450 and 1460, it was abandoned a century later, at the time of the Spanish conquest. It was built in the classic Inca style, using polished, fitted, dry-stone walls, and was home to about 750 people, mostly support staff to the nobility. The religious monuments include the Intiwatana, a carved ritual stone that was a kind of sundial and is referred to as "The Hitching Post of the Sun," the Torreon or Temple of the Sun, and the Intimachay, a sacred cave.

6. *Petra, Ma'an, Jordan:* Petra is believed to have been established in the 4th century B.C. as the capital of the Nabataean Kingdom, an entity that grew wealthy as the nexus of trade routes in the southern Levant. The Roman Empire annexed it in A.D. 106. The city is famous for its carved-rock architecture and water conduit system, which allowed the Nabataeans to create an artificial oasis. The city may have had a population of 20,000 at its peak in the first century A.D.

7. *Taj Mahal, Agra, Uttar Pradesh, India:* This ivory-white mausoleum was commissioned in 1632 by Shah Jahan (r. 1628-1658) as the final resting place for his favorite wife, Mumtaz Mahal. The building also houses the tomb of Shah Jahan himself. The Taj Mahal is the centerpiece of a 17-hectare (42-acre) complex that includes a guest house, a mosque, and formal gardens. The project was completed in 1653.

note: The Great Pyramid of Egypt, the only surviving wonder of the ancient seven, received honorary status on the New Seven Wonders list.

Geography - note: *note:* the Earth is now thought to be about 4.55 billion years old, about one-third of the 13.8-billion-year age estimated for the universe; the earliest widely accepted date for life appearing on Earth is 3.48 billion years ago

PEOPLE AND SOCIETY

Population: *total:* 8,057,236,243 (2024 est.)
male: 4,046,854,454
female: 4,010,381,789

Languages: *most-spoken language:* English 18.8%, Mandarin Chinese 13.8%, Hindi 7.5%, Spanish 6.9%, French 3.4%, Arabic 3.4%, Bengali 3.4%, Russian 3.2%, Portuguese 3.2%, Urdu 2.9% (2022 est.)
most-spoken first language: Mandarin Chinese 12.3%, Spanish 6%, English 5.1%, Arabic 5.1%, Hindi 3.5%, Bengali 3.3%, Portuguese 3%, Russian 2.1%,

Japanese 1.7%, Punjabi, Western 1.3%, Javanese 1.1% (2018 est.)
note 1: the six UN languages – Arabic, Chinese (Mandarin), English, French, Russian, and Spanish (Castilian) – are the mother tongue or second language of about 49.6% of the world's population (2022), and are the official languages in more than half the states in the world; some 400 languages have more than a million first-language speakers (2018)
note 2: all told, there are estimated to be 7,168 living languages spoken in the world (2023); approximately 80% of these languages are spoken by fewer than 100,000 people; about 150 languages are spoken by fewer than 10 people; communities that are isolated in mountainous regions often develop multiple languages – Papua New Guinea, for example, boasts about 840 separate languages (2018)
note 3: approximately 2,300 languages are spoken in Asia; 2,140, in Africa; 1,310 in the Pacific; 1,060 in the Americas; and 290 in Europe (2020)

Religions: Christian 31.1%, Muslim 24.9%, Hindu 15.2%, Buddhist 6.6%, folk religions 5.6%, Jewish <1%, other <1%, unaffiliated 15.6% (2020 est.)

Age structure: *0-14 years:* 24.5% (male 1,018,005,046/female 958,406,907)
15-64 years: 65.2% (male 2,658,595,672/female 2,592,930,538)
65 years and over: 10.3% (2024 est.) (male 370,253,736/female 459,044,344)

Dependency ratios: *total dependency ratio:* 53.4 (2024 est.)
youth dependency ratio: 37.7 (2024 est.)
elderly dependency ratio: 15.7 (2024 est.)
potential support ratio: 6.4 (2024 est.)

Median age: *total:* 31 years (2020 est.)
male: 30.3 years
female: 31.8 years

Population growth rate: 1.03% (2021 est.)
note: this rate results in about 154 net additions to the worldwide population every minute or 2.6 people every second

Birth rate: 17 births/1,000 population (2024 est.)
note: this rate results in about 260 worldwide births per minute or 4.3 births every second

Death rate: 7.9 deaths/1,000 population (2024 est.)
note: this rate results in about 121 worldwide deaths per minute or 2 deaths every second

Population distribution: six of the world's seven continents are widely and permanently inhabited; Asia is the most populous continent, with about 60% of the world's population (China and India together account for over 35%); Africa comes in second with over 15%, Europe has about 10%, North America 8%, South America almost 6%, and Oceania less than 1%; the harsh conditions on Antarctica prevent any permanent habitation

Urbanization: *urban population:* 57.5% of total population (2023)
rate of urbanization: 1.73% annual rate of change (2020-25 est.)

Major urban areas - population: *ten largest urban agglomerations:* Tokyo (Japan) - 37,393,000; New Delhi (India) - 30,291,000; Shanghai (China) - 27,058,000; Sao Paulo (Brazil) - 22,043,000; Mexico City (Mexico) - 21,782,000; Dhaka (Bangladesh) - 21,006,000; Cairo (Egypt) - 20,901,000; Beijing (China) - 20,463,000; Mumbai (India) - 20,411,000; Osaka (Japan) - 19,165,000 (2020)
ten largest urban agglomerations, by continent: Africa - Cairo (Egypt) - 20,901,000; Lagos (Nigeria) - 134,368,000; Kinshasha (DRC) - 14,342,000; Luanda (Angola) - 8,330,000; Dar Es Salaam (Tanzania) - 6,702,000; Khartoum (Sudan) - 5,829,000; Johannesburg (South Africa) - 5,783,000; Alexandria (Egypt) - 5,281,000; Abidjan (Cote d'Ivoire) - 5,203,000; Addis Ababa (Ethiopia) - 4,794,000
Asia - Tokyo (Japan) - 37,393,000; New Delhi (India) - 30,291,000; Shanghai (China) - 27,058,000; Dhaka (Bangladesh) - 21,006,000; Beijing (China) - 20,463,000; Mumbai (India) - 20,411,000; Osaka (Japan) - 19,165,000; Karachi (Pakistan) - 16,094,000; Chongqing (China) - 15,872,000; Istanbul (Turkey) - 15,190,000
Europe - Moscow (Russia) - 12,538,000; Paris (France) - 11,017,000; London (United Kingdom) - 9,304,000; Madrid (Spain) - 6,618,000; Barcelona (Spain) - 5,586,000, Saint Petersburg (Russia) - 5,468,000; Rome (Italy) - 4,257,000; Berlin (Germany) - 3,562,000; Athens (Greece) - 3,153,000; Milan (Italy) - 3,140,000
North America - Mexico City (Mexico) - 21,782,000; New York-Newark (United States) - 18,804,000; Los Angeles-Long Beach-Santa Ana (United States) - 12,447,000; Chicago (United States) - 8,865,000; Houston (United States) - 6,371,000; Dallas-Fort Worth (United States) - 6,301,000; Toronto (Canada) - 6,197,000; Miami (United States) - 6,122,000; Atlanta (United States) - 5,803,000; Philadelphia (United States) - 5,717,000
Oceania - Melbourne (Australia) - 4,968,000, Sydney (Australia) - 4,926,000; Brisbane (Australia) - 2,406,000; Perth (Australia) - 2,042,000; Auckland (New Zealand) - 1,607,000; Adelaide (Australia) - 1,336,000; Gold Coast-Tweed Head (Australia) - 699,000; Canberra (Australia) - 457,000; Newcastle-Maitland (Australia) - 450,000; Wellington (New Zealand) - 415,000
South America - Sao Paulo (Brazil) - 22,043,000; Buenos Aires (Argentina) - 15,154,000; Rio de Janeiro (Brazil) - 13,458,000; Bogota (Colombia) - 10,978,000; Lima (Peru) - 10,719,000; Santiago (Chile) - 6,767,000; Belo Horizonte (Brazil) - 6,084,000; Brasilia (Brazil) - 4,646,000; Porto Alegre (Brazil) - 4,137,000; Recife (Brazil) - 4,127,000 (2020)

Sex ratio: *at birth:* 1.05 male(s)/female
0-14 years: 1.05 male(s)/female
15-64 years: 1.03 male(s)/female
65 years and over: 0.81 male(s)/female
total population: 1.01 male(s)/female (2024 est.)

Maternal mortality ratio: 197 deaths/100,000 live births (2023 est.)

Infant mortality rate: *total:* 28.3 deaths/1,000 live births (2024 est.)

Life expectancy at birth: *total population:* 70.5 years (2020)
male: 68.4 years
female: 72.6 years

Total fertility rate: 2.42 children born/woman (2020 est.)

Drinking water source: *improved: urban:* 97.9% of population (2022 est.)
rural: 84% of population (2022 est.)
total: 91.8% of population (2022 est.)
unimproved: urban: 2.1% of population (2022 est.)
rural: 16% of population (2022 est.)
total: 8.2% of population (2022 est.)

Health expenditure: 10.4% of GDP (2021)

Sanitation facility access: *improved: urban:* 88.9% of population (2022 est.)
rural: 70.1% of population (2022 est.)
total: 80.8% of population (2022 est.)
unimproved: urban: 11.1% of population (2022 est.)
rural: 29.9% of population (2022 est.)
total: 19.2% of population (2022 est.)

Children under the age of 5 years underweight: 12.3% (2022)

Currently married women (ages 15-49): 66.2% (2023 est.)

Child marriage: *women married by age 15:* 4.3% (2023)
women married by age 18: 18.7% (2023)
men married by age 18: 2.7% (2022)

ENVIRONMENT

Environmental issues: large areas of the world are subject to overpopulation, industrial disasters, pollution (air, water, acid rain, toxic substances), loss of vegetation (overgrazing, deforestation, desertification), loss of biodiversity; soil degradation, soil depletion, erosion; ozone layer depletion; waste disposal; temperature change

World biomes: Types of biomes: A biome is a biogeographical designation describing a biological community of plants and animals that has formed in response to a physical environment and a shared regional climate. Biomes can extend over more than one continent. Different classification systems define different numbers of biomes. *The World Factbook* recognizes the following seven biomes used by NASA: tundra, coniferous forest, temperate deciduous forest, rainforest, grassland, shrubland, and desert.

Tundra biome: The tundra is the coldest of the biomes. It also receives low amounts of precipitation, making the tundra similar to a desert. Tundra comes from the Finnish word tunturia, meaning "treeless plain." Tundra is found in the regions just below the ice caps of the Arctic, extending across North America to Europe and to Siberia in Asia. Temperatures usually range between -40°C (-40 °F) and 18°C (64°F). The temperatures are so cold that there is a layer of permanently frozen ground below the surface, called permafrost. This permafrost is a defining characteristic of the tundra biome. In the tundra summers, the top layer of soil thaws only a few inches down, providing a growing surface for the roots of vegetation. This biome sees 150 to 250 mm (6 to 10 in) of rain per year. Vegetation in the tundra has adapted to the cold and the short growing season and consists of lichens, mosses, grasses, sedges, and shrubs, but almost no trees.

Coniferous forest biome: The coniferous forest is sandwiched between the tundra to the north and the deciduous forest to the south. Coniferous forest regions have long, cold, snowy winters; warm, humid summers; well-defined seasons; and at least four to six frost-free months. The average temperature in winter ranges from -40°C (-40°F) to 20°C (68°F). The average summer temperatures are usually around 10°C (50°F). 300 to 900 mm (12 to 35 in) of rain per year can be expected in this biome. Vegetation consists of trees that produce cones and needles, which are called coniferous-evergreen trees. Some needles remain on the trees all year long. Some of the more common conifers are spruces, pines, and firs.

Temperate deciduous forest biome: Temperate deciduous forests are located in the mid-latitude areas, which means that they are found between the polar regions and the tropics. The deciduous forest regions are exposed to warm and cold air masses, which cause this area to have four seasons. Hot summers and cold winters are typical. The average daily temperatures range between -30°C (-22°F) and 30°C (86°F), with a yearly average of 10°C (50°F). On average, this biome receives 750 to 1,500 mm (30 to 59 in) of rain per year. Vegetation includes broadleaf trees (oaks, maples, beeches), shrubs, perennial herbs, and mosses.

Rainforest biome: The rainforest biome remains warm all year and stay frost-free. The average daily temperatures range from 20°C (68°F) to 25°C (77°F). Rainforests receive the most yearly rainfall of all of the biomes, and a typical year sees 2,000 to 10,000 mm (79 to 394 in) of rain. Vegetation typically includes vines, palm trees, orchids, and ferns. There are two types of rainforests: tropical rainforests are found closer to the equator, and temperate rainforests are found farther north near coastal areas. The majority of common houseplants come from the rainforest.

Grassland biome: Grasslands are open, continuous, and fairly flat areas of grass. Found on every continent except Antarctica, they are often located between temperate forests at high latitudes and deserts at subtropical latitudes. Depending on latitude, the annual temperature range can be -20°C (-4°F) to 30°C (86°F). Grasslands receive around 500 to 900 mm (20 to 35 in) of rain per year. Tropical grasslands have dry and wet seasons that remain warm all the time. Temperate grasslands have cold winters and warm summers with some rain. Vegetation is dominated by grasses but can include sedges and rushes, along with some legumes (clover) and herbs. A few trees may be found in this biome along the streams, but not many due to the lack of rainfall.

Shrubland biome: Shrublands include chaparral, woodland, and savanna, and are composed of shrubs or short trees. Many shrubs thrive on steep, rocky slopes, but there is usually not enough rain to support tall trees. Shrublands are located in west coastal regions between 30° and 40° North and South latitude and are usually found on the borders of deserts and grasslands. The summers are hot and dry with temperatures up to 38°C (100°F). Winters are cool and moist, with temperatures around -1 °C (30°F). Annual rainfall in the shrublands varies greatly, but 200 to 1,000 mm (8 to 40 in) of rain per year can be expected. Vegetation includes aromatic herbs (sage, rosemary, thyme, oregano), shrubs, acacia, chamise, grasses. Plants have adapted to fire caused by frequent lightning strikes in the summer.

Desert biome: The most important characteristic of a desert biome is that it receives very little rainfall, usually about 250 mm (10 in) of rain per year. During the day, desert temperatures rise to an average of 38°C (100°F). At night, desert temperatures fall to an average of -4°C (about 25°F). Vegetation is sparse, consisting of cacti, small bushes, and short grasses. Perennials survive for several years by becoming dormant and flourishing when water is available. Annuals are referred to as ephemerals because some can complete an entire life cycle in weeks. Since desert conditions are so severe, the plants that live there need to adapt to compensate. Some, such as cacti, store water in their stems and use it very slowly, while others, like bushes, conserve water by growing few leaves or by having large root systems to gather water.

Climate: a wide equatorial band of hot and humid tropical climates is bordered north and south by subtropical temperate zones that separate two large areas of cold and dry polar climates
ten driest places on Earth (average annual precipitation): McMurdo Dry Valleys, Antarctica 0 mm (0 in)
Arica, Chile 0.76 mm (0.03 in)
Al Kufrah, Libya 0.86 mm (0.03 in)
Aswan, Egypt 0.86 mm (0.03 in)
Luxor, Egypt 0.86 mm (0.03 in)
Ica, Peru 2.29 mm (0.09 in)
Wadi Halfa, Sudan 2.45 mm (0.1 in)
Iquique, Chile 5.08 mm (0.2 in)
Pelican Point, Namibia 8.13 mm (0.32 in)
El Arab (Aoulef), Algeria 12.19 mm (0.48 in)
ten wettest places on Earth (average annual precipitation): Mawsynram, India 11,871 mm (467.4 in)
Cherrapunji, India 11,777 mm (463.7 in)
Tutunendo, Colombia 11,770 mm (463.4 in)
Cropp River, New Zealand 11,516 mm (453.4 in)
San Antonia de Ureca, Equatorial Guinea 10,450 mm (411.4 in)
Debundsha, Cameroon 10,299 mm (405.5 in)
Big Bog, US (Hawaii) 10,272 mm (404.4 in)
Mt Waialeale, US (Hawaii) 9,763 mm (384.4 in)
Kukui, US (Hawaii) 9,293 mm (365.9 in)
Emeishan, China 8,169 mm (321.6 in)
ten coldest places on Earth (lowest average monthly temperature): Verkhoyansk, Russia (Siberia) -47°C (-53°F) January
Oymyakon, Russia (Siberia) -46°C (-52°F) January
Eureka, Canada -38.4°C (-37.1°F) February
Isachsen, Canada -36°C (-32.8°F) February
Alert, Canada -34°C (-28°F) February
Kap Morris Jesup, Greenland -34°C (-29°F) March
Cornwallis Island, Canada -33.5°C (-28.3°F) February
Cambridge Bay, Canada -33.5°C (28.3°F) February
Ilirnej, Russia -33°C (-28°F) January
Resolute, Canada -33°C (-27.4°F) February
ten hottest places on Earth (highest average monthly temperature): Death Valley, US (California) 39°C (101°F) July
Iranshahr, Iran 38.3°C (100.9°F) June
Ouallene, Algeria 38°C (100.4°F) July
Kuwait City, Kuwait 37.7°C (100°F) July
Medina, Saudi Arabia 36°C (97°F) July
Buckeye, US (Arizona) 34°C (93°F) July
Jazan, Saudi Arabia 33°C (91°F) June
Al Kufrah, Libya 31°C (87°F) July
Alice Springs, Australia 29°C (84°F) January
Tamanrasset, Algeria 29°C (84°F) June

Urbanization: *urban population:* 57.5% of total population (2023)
rate of urbanization: 1.73% annual rate of change (2020-25 est.)

Carbon dioxide emissions: 37.079 billion metric tonnes of CO2 (2023 est.)
from coal and metallurgical coke: 16.652 billion metric tonnes of CO2 (2023 est.)
from petroleum and other liquids: 12.463 billion metric tonnes of CO2 (2023 est.)
from consumed natural gas: 7.964 billion metric tonnes of CO2 (2023 est.)

Total renewable water resources: 54 trillion cubic meters (2011 est.)

GOVERNMENT

Capital: *time difference:* there are 21 world entities (20 countries and 1 dependency) with multiple time zones: Australia, Brazil, Canada, Chile, Democratic Republic of Congo, Ecuador, France, Greenland (part of the Danish Kingdom), Indonesia, Kazakhstan, Kiribati, Mexico, Micronesia, Mongolia, Netherlands, New Zealand, Papua New Guinea, Portugal, Russia, Spain, United States
note 1: in some instances, the time zones pertain to portions of a country that lie overseas
note 2: in 1851, the British set their prime meridian (0° longitude) through the Royal Observatory at Greenwich, England; this meridian became the international standard in 1884 and thus the basis for the standard time zones of the world; today, GMT is officially known as Coordinated Universal Time (UTC) and is also referred to as "Zulu time"; UTC is the basis for all civil time, with the world divided into time zones expressed as positive or negative differences from UTC
note 3: each time zone is based on 15° starting from the prime meridian; in theory, there are 24 time zones based on the solar day, but there are now upward of 40 because of fractional hour offsets that adjust for various political and physical geographic realities; see the Standard Time Zones of the World map included with the World and Regional Maps
daylight saving time: some 67 countries – including most of the world's leading industrialized nations – use daylight savings time (DST) in at least a portion of the country; China, Japan, India, and Russia are major industrialized countries that do not use DST; Asia and Africa generally do not observe DST, and it is generally not observed near the equator, where sunrise and sunset times do not vary enough to justify it; some countries observe DST only in certain regions; only a minority of the world's population – about 20% – uses DST

Administrative divisions: 197 countries, 69 dependent areas and other entities

Dependent areas: Australia dependencies: Ashmore and Cartier Islands, Christmas Island, Cocos (Keeling) Islands, Coral Sea Islands, Heard Island and McDonald Islands, Norfolk Island (6)

France dependencies: Clipperton Island, French Polynesia, French Southern and Antarctic Lands, New Caledonia, Saint Barthelemy, Saint Martin, Saint Pierre and Miquelon, Wallis and Futuna (8)

New Zealand dependency: Tokelau (1)

Norway dependencies: Bouvet Island, Jan Mayen, Svalbard (3)

United Kingdom dependencies: Anguilla; Bermuda; British Indian Ocean Territory; British Virgin Islands; Cayman Islands; Falkland Islands; Gibraltar; Montserrat; Pitcairn Islands; Saint Helena, Ascension, and Tristan da Cunha; South Georgia and the South Sandwich Islands; Turks and Caicos Islands (12)

United States dependencies: American Samoa, Baker Island, Guam, Howland Island, Jarvis Island, Johnston Atoll, Kingman Reef, Midway Islands, Navassa Island, Northern Mariana Islands, Palmyra Atoll, Puerto Rico, Virgin Islands, Wake Island (14)

Legal system: *the legal systems of nearly all countries are modeled on elements of five main types:* civil law (including French law, the Napoleonic Code, Roman law, Roman-Dutch law, and Spanish law), common law (including English and US law), customary law, mixed or pluralistic law, and religious law (including Islamic sharia law); an additional type of legal system – international law – governs the conduct of independent nations in their relationships with one another

International law organization participation: all UN members are parties to the statute that established the

International Court of Justice (ICJ) or World Court; as of June 2025, 125 countries have also ratified or acceded to the Rome Statute of the International Criminal Court (ICCt), the treaty that established the ICCt (see the reference guide on International Organizations and Groups for differences between the ICJ and ICCt mandates)

Executive branch: *chief of state:* there are 27 countries with royal families in the world: *most are in Asia (13) and Europe (10), three are in Africa, and one in Oceania; monarchies by continent are as follows:* Asia (Bahrain, Bhutan, Brunei, Cambodia, Japan, Jordan, Kuwait, Malaysia, Oman, Qatar, Saudi Arabia, Thailand, United Arab Emirates); Europe (Belgium, Denmark, Liechtenstein, Luxembourg, Monaco, Netherlands, Norway, Spain, Sweden, United Kingdom); Africa (Eswatini, Lesotho, Morocco); Oceania (Tonga)
note 1: Andorra and the Holy See (Vatican) are also monarchies of a sort, but they are not ruled by royal houses; Andorra has two co-princes (the president of France and the bishop of Urgell) and the Holy See is ruled by an elected pope
note 2: the UK sovereign is also the monarch for the 14 Commonwealth countries (including Australia, Canada, Jamaica, New Zealand)

Legislative branch: 230 political entities have legislative bodies; of these, 144 are unicameral (a single "house") and 86 are bicameral (both upper and lower houses); 33 territories, possessions, or other special administrative units have their own governing bodies

Flag: a "World" flag does not exist, but the United Nations (UN) flag – adopted on 7 December 1946 – has sometimes been used to represent the entire planet; the flag displays the official UN emblem in white on a blue background; the emblem design shows a world map in an azimuthal equidistant projection centered on the North Pole, with the image flanked by two olive branches; blue was chosen to represent peace, in contrast to the red usually associated with war; the map projection includes all the continents except Antarctica
note 1: the flags of 12 nations – Austria, Botswana, Georgia, Jamaica, Japan, Laos, Latvia, Micronesia, Nigeria, North Macedonia, Switzerland, and Thailand – have no top or bottom and may be flown with either long edge on top
note 2: the most common colors found on national flags are as follows: red (~75%), white (~70%), and blue (~50%); these three colors are so prevalent that there are only two countries, Jamaica and Sri Lanka, that do not include one of them; the three next most popular colors are yellow/gold and green (both ~45%) and black (~30%)
note 3: flags composed of three colors are by far the most common type and, of those, the red-white-blue combination is the most widespread

United Nations flag: National anthem(s): *title:* almost every country has a national anthem (and Denmark and New Zealand have two); most anthems have lyrics, which are usually in the official language or the most common language of the country; countries with more than one official language sometimes offer several versions
note: the first anthem to be officially adopted (1795) was "La Marseillaise" (The Song of Marseille) of France; Japan claims to have the shortest anthem, "Kimigayo" (The Emperor's Reign), that consists of 11 measures; Japan's anthem has the world's oldest lyrics, dating to the 10th century or earlier; Greece has the anthem with the longest lyrics, "Ymnos eis tin Eleftherian" (Hymn to Liberty), with 158 stanzas; Uruguay has the anthem with the longest musical score, "Himno Nacional" (National Anthem of Uruguay), with 105 bars (almost five minutes)

National heritage: *total World Heritage Sites:* 1,223 (952 cultural, 231 natural, 40 mixed) (2024)
note: a summary of each country's UNESCO World Heritage sites can be found in the national heritage data field, under the Government category for the country

ECONOMY

Real GDP (purchasing power parity): $173.163 trillion (2024 est.)
$167.633 trillion (2023 est.)
$162.058 trillion (2022 est.)
note: data in 2021 dollars

Real GDP growth rate: 2.9% (2024 est.)
2.9% (2023 est.)
3.4% (2022 est.)
note: annual GDP % growth based on constant local currency

Real GDP per capita: $21,300 (2024 est.)
$20,800 (2023 est.)
$20,300 (2022 est.)
note: data in 2021 dollars

GDP (official exchange rate): $111.326 trillion (2024 est.)
note: data in current dollars at official exchange rate

Inflation rate (consumer prices): 3% (2024 est.)
5.9% (2023 est.)
7.9% (2022 est.)
note: annual % change based on consumer prices

GDP - composition, by sector of origin: *agriculture:* 4% (2024 est.)
industry: 26% (2024 est.)
services: 66.2% (2024 est.)
note: figures may not total 100% due to non-allocated consumption not captured in sector-reported data

GDP - composition, by end use: *household consumption:* 56.4% (2023 est.)
government consumption: 16.6% (2023 est.)
investment in fixed capital: 25.9% (2023 est.)
investment in inventories: 0.6% (2023 est.)
exports of goods and services: 29.1% (2023 est.)
imports of goods and services: -28.3% (2023 est.)
note: figures may not total 100% due to rounding or gaps in data collection

Agricultural products: the whole range of agricultural products
top ten agricultural products by global production tonnage: sugarcane, maize, rice, wheat, milk, oil palm fruit, potatoes, soybeans, cassava, vegetables (2023)

Industries: dominated by the onrush of technology, especially in computers, robotics, telecommunications, and medicines and medical equipment; most of these advances take place in OECD nations; only a small portion of non-OECD countries have succeeded in rapidly adjusting to these technological forces; the accelerated development of new technologies is complicating already grim environmental problems

Industrial production growth rate: 2.9% (2024 est.)
note: annual % change in industrial value added based on constant local currency

Labor force: 3.696 billion (2024 est.)
note: number of people ages 15 or older who are employed or seeking work

Unemployment rate: 4.9% (2024 est.)
5% (2023 est.)
5.3% (2022 est.)
note: % of labor force seeking employment

Youth unemployment rate (ages 15-24): *total:* 13.6% (2024 est.)
male: 13.2% (2024 est.)
female: 15.3% (2024 est.)
note: % of labor force ages 15-24 seeking employment

Remittances: 0.7% of GDP (2024 est.)
0.8% of GDP (2023 est.)
0.8% of GDP (2022 est.)
note: personal transfers and compensation between resident and non-resident individuals/households/entities

Budget: *revenues:* $21.68 trillion (2017 est.)
expenditures: $23.81 trillion (2017 est.)

Taxes and other revenues: 13.8% (of GDP) (2023 est.)
note: central government tax revenue as a % of GDP

Exports: $32.379 trillion (2024 est.)
$31.271 trillion (2023 est.)
$31.782 trillion (2022 est.)
note: balance of payments - exports of goods and services in current dollars

Exports - commodities: the whole range of industrial and agricultural goods and services
top ten commodities by share of world trade: crude petroleum, cars, refined petroleum, integrated circuits, broadcasting equipment, gold, natural gas, garments, vehicle parts/accessories, packaged medicine (2022)

Imports: $31.244 trillion (2024 est.)
$30.334 trillion (2023 est.)
$30.871 trillion (2022 est.)
note: balance of payments - imports of goods and services in current dollars

Imports - commodities: the whole range of industrial and agricultural goods and services
top ten - share of world trade: see listing for exports

ENERGY

Electricity access: *electrification - total population:* 91.4% (2022 est.)
electrification - urban areas: 97.7%
electrification - rural areas: 84%

Electricity: *installed generating capacity:* 9.08 billion kW (2023 est.)
consumption: 27.047 trillion kWh (2023 est.)
exports: 810.999 billion kWh (2023 est.)
imports: 804.542 billion kWh (2023 est.)
transmission/distribution losses: 2.053 trillion kWh (2023 est.)

Electricity generation sources: *fossil fuels:* 60.1% of total installed capacity (2023 est.)
nuclear: 9.2% of total installed capacity (2023 est.)
solar: 5.6% of total installed capacity (2023 est.)
wind: 8% of total installed capacity (2023 est.)
hydroelectricity: 14.4% of total installed capacity (2023 est.)
geothermal: 0.3% of total installed capacity (2023 est.)
biomass and waste: 2.4% of total installed capacity (2023 est.)

Nuclear energy: Number of operational nuclear reactors: 416 (2025)

Number of nuclear reactors under construction: 62 (2025)

Net capacity of operational nuclear reactors: 376.59GW (2025)

Number of nuclear reactors permanently shut down: 214 (2025)

Coal: *production:* 9.368 billion metric tons (2023 est.)
consumption: 9.382 billion metric tons (2023 est.)
exports: 1.494 billion metric tons (2023 est.)
imports: 1.507 billion metric tons (2023 est.)
proven reserves: 1.166 trillion metric tons (2023 est.)

Petroleum: *total petroleum production:* 99.887 million bbl/day (2023 est.)
refined petroleum consumption: 101.86 million bbl/day (2023 est.)
crude oil estimated reserves: 1.697 trillion barrels (2021 est.)

Natural gas: *production:* 4.143 trillion cubic meters (2023 est.)
consumption: 4.1 trillion cubic meters (2023 est.)
exports: 1.219 trillion cubic meters (2023 est.)
imports: 1.226 trillion cubic meters (2023 est.)
proven reserves: 206.683 trillion cubic meters (2021 est.)

Energy consumption per capita: 73.108 million Btu/person (2023 est.)

COMMUNICATIONS

Telephones - fixed lines: *total subscriptions:* 839.8 million (2024 est.)
subscriptions per 100 inhabitants: 11 (2023 est.)

Telephones - mobile cellular: *total subscriptions:* 9,144,200,000 (2024 est.)
subscriptions per 100 inhabitants: 112 (2024 est.)

Internet users: *percent of population:* 68% (2024 est.)
top ten countries by Internet usage (in millions): 854 China; 560 India; 293 United States; 171 Indonesia; 149 Brazil; 123 Nigeria; 119 Japan; 116 Russia; 96 Bangladesh; 88 Mexico (2023)

Broadband - fixed subscriptions: *total:* 1,495,600,000 (2023 est.)
subscriptions per 100 inhabitants: 18 (2022 est.)
note: the worldwide total of fixed broadband subscriptions has been higher than fixed telephony subscriptions since 2017

TRANSPORTATION

Airports: 47,242 (2025)

Heliports: 21,741 (2025)

Railways: *total:* 1,148,186 km (2013)

Merchant marine: *total:* 103,577 (2023)
by type: bulk carrier 13,141, container ship 5,815, general cargo 19,918, oil tanker 11,604, other 53,099

MILITARY AND SECURITY

Military expenditures: 2.4% of GDP (2024 est.)
2.3% of GDP (2023 est.)
2.2% of GDP (2022 est.)
2.2% of GDP (2021 est.)
2.3% of GDP (2020 est.)

Military and security service personnel strengths: approximately 20 million active-duty military personnel worldwide (2025)
note: the largest militaries in the world based on personnel numbers belong to China, India, the US, North Korea, and Russia

Military equipment inventories and acquisitions: the US is the world's leading arms exporter (2024)

Military deployments: as of mid-2025, there were approximately 68,000 personnel deployed on UN peacekeeping missions worldwide (2025)

TRANSNATIONAL ISSUES

Trafficking in persons: *tier rating:* Tier 2 Watch List: (25 countries) Algeria, Barbados, Bolivia, Brazil, Brunei, Burkina Faso, Cabo Verde, Democratic Republic of the Congo, Republic of Congo, Djibouti, Fiji, Hong Kong, Kyrgyzstan, Liberia, Maldives, Nepal, Niger, Rwanda, Saint Lucia, Solomon Islands, South Africa, Tunisia, Turkmenistan, Vanuatu, Zimbabwe (2025)

Tier 3: (20 countries) Afghanistan, Belarus, Burma, Cambodia, Chad, People's Republic of China, Cuba, Eritrea, Iran, Democratic People's Republic of Korea, Laos, Macau, Nicaragua, Papua New Guinea, Russia, Sint Maarten, South Sudan, Sudan, Syria, Venezuela (2025)

YEMEN

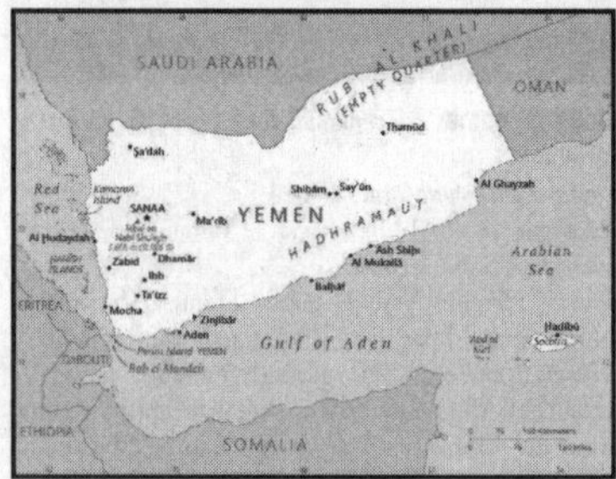

INTRODUCTION

Background: The Kingdom of Yemen (colloquially known as North Yemen) became independent from the Ottoman Empire in 1918 and in 1962 became the Yemen Arab Republic. The British, who had set up a protectorate area around the southern port of Aden in the 19th century, withdrew in 1967 from what became the People's Republic of Southern Yemen (colloquially known as South Yemen). Three years later, the southern government adopted a Marxist orientation and changed the country's name to the People's Democratic Republic of Yemen. The exodus of hundreds of thousands of Yemenis from the south to the north contributed to two decades of hostility between the states, which were formally unified as the Republic of Yemen in 1990. A southern secessionist movement and brief civil war in 1994 was quickly subdued. In 2000, Saudi Arabia and Yemen agreed to delineate their border. Fighting in the northwest between the government and the Houthis, a Zaydi Shia Muslim minority, continued intermittently from 2004 to 2010, and then again from 2014 to the present. The southern secessionist movement was revitalized in 2007.

Public rallies in Sana'a against then President Ali Abdallah SALIH – inspired by similar Arab Spring demonstrations in Tunisia and Egypt – slowly gained momentum in 2011, fueled by complaints over high unemployment, poor economic conditions, and corruption. Some protests resulted in violence, and the demonstrations spread to other major cities. The Gulf Cooperation Council (GCC) mediated the crisis with the GCC Initiative, an agreement in which the president would step down in exchange for immunity from prosecution. SALIH eventually agreed to step down and transfer some powers to Vice President Abd Rabuh Mansur HADI. After HADI's uncontested election victory in 2012, SALIH formally transferred all presidential powers. In accordance with the GCC Initiative, Yemen launched a National Dialogue Conference (NDC) in 2013 to discuss key constitutional, political, and social issues. HADI concluded the NDC in 2014 and planned to proceed with constitutional drafting, a constitutional referendum, and national elections.

The Houthis, perceiving their grievances were not addressed in the NDC, joined forces with SALIH and expanded their influence in northwestern Yemen, which culminated in a major offensive against military units and rival tribes and enabled their forces to overrun the capital, Sana'a, in 2014. In 2015, the Houthis surrounded key government facilities, prompting HADI and the cabinet to resign. HADI fled first to Aden – where he rescinded his resignation – and then to Oman before moving to Saudi Arabia and asking the GCC to intervene militarily in Yemen. Saudi Arabia assembled a coalition of Arab militaries and began airstrikes, and ground fighting continued through 2016. In 2016, the UN initiated peace talks that ended without agreement. Rising tensions between the Houthis and SALIH culminated in Houthi forces killing SALIH. In 2018, the Houthis and the Yemeni Government participated in UN-brokered peace talks, agreeing to a limited ceasefire and the establishment of a UN mission.

In 2019, Yemen's parliament convened for the first time since the conflict broke out in 2014. Violence then erupted between HADI's government and the pro-secessionist Southern Transitional Council (STC) in southern Yemen. HADI's government and the STC signed a power-sharing agreement to end the fighting, and in 2020, the signatories formed a new cabinet. In 2020 and 2021, fighting continued as the Houthis gained territory and also conducted regular UAV and missile attacks against targets in Saudi Arabia. In 2022, the UN brokered a temporary truce between the Houthis and the Saudi-led coalition. HADI and his vice-president resigned and were replaced by an eight-person Presidential Leadership Council. Although the truce formally expired in 2022, the parties nonetheless refrained from large-scale conflict through the end of 2023. Saudi Arabia, after the truce expired, continued to negotiate with the Yemeni Government and Houthis on a roadmap agreement that would include a permanent ceasefire and a peace process under UN auspices.

GEOGRAPHY

Location: Middle East, bordering the Arabian Sea, Gulf of Aden, and Red Sea, between Oman and Saudi Arabia

Geographic coordinates: 15 00 N, 48 00 E

Map references: Middle East

Area: *total:* 527,968 sq km
land: 527,968 sq km
water: 0 sq km
note: includes Perim, Socotra, the former Yemen Arab Republic (YAR or North Yemen), and the former People's Democratic Republic of Yemen (PDRY or South Yemen)
comparison ranking: total 52

Area - comparative: almost four times the size of Alabama; slightly larger than twice the size of Wyoming

Land boundaries: *total:* 1,601 km
border countries (2): Oman 294 km; Saudi Arabia 1,307 km

Coastline: 1,906 km

Maritime claims: *territorial sea:* 12 nm
contiguous zone: 24 nm
exclusive economic zone: 200 nm
continental shelf: 200 nm or to the edge of the continental margin

Climate: mostly desert; hot and humid along west coast; temperate in western mountains affected by seasonal monsoon; extraordinarily hot, dry, harsh desert in east

Terrain: narrow coastal plain backed by flat-topped hills and rugged mountains; dissected upland desert plains in center slope into the desert interior of the Arabian Peninsula

Elevation: *highest point:* Jabal an Nabi Shu'ayb 3,666 m
lowest point: Arabian Sea 0 m
mean elevation: 999 m

Natural resources: petroleum, fish, rock salt, marble; small deposits of coal, gold, lead, nickel, and copper; fertile soil in west

Land use: *agricultural land:* 44.4% (2022 est.)
arable land: 2.2% (2022 est.)
permanent crops: 0.6% (2022 est.)
permanent pasture: 41.7% (2022 est.)
forest: 1% (2022 est.)
other: 54.5% (2022 est.)

Irrigated land: 6,800 sq km (2012)

Population distribution: the vast majority of the population is found in the Asir Mountains (part of the larger Sarawat Mountain system), located in the far western region of the country

Natural hazards: sandstorms and dust storms in summer
volcanism: limited volcanic activity; Jebel at Tair (Jabal al-Tair, Jebel Teir, Jabal al-Tayr, Jazirat at-Tair) (244 m), which forms an island in the Red Sea, became active in 2007; other historically active volcanoes include Harra of Arhab, Harras of Dhamar, Harra es-Sawad, and Jebel Zubair, although many of these have not erupted in over a century

Geography - note: strategic location on Bab el Mandeb, the strait linking the Red Sea and the Gulf of Aden and one of world's most active shipping lanes

PEOPLE AND SOCIETY

Population: *total:* 32,140,443 (2024 est.)
male: 16,221,139
female: 15,919,304
comparison rankings: total 48; male 47; female 47

Nationality: *noun:* Yemeni(s)
adjective: Yemeni

Ethnic groups: predominantly Arab; but also Afro-Arab, South Asian, European

Languages: Arabic (official)
major-language sample(s):
كتاب حقائق العالم، المصدر الذي لا يمكن الاستغناء عنه للمعلومات الأساسية
(Arabic)
note: a distinct Socotri language is widely used on Socotra Island and Archipelago; Mahri is still fairly widely spoken in eastern Yemen

Religions: Muslim 99.1% (official; virtually all are citizens, an estimated 65% are Sunni and 35% are Shia), other 0.9% (includes Jewish, Baha'i, Hindu, and Christian; many are refugees or temporary foreign residents) (2020 est.)

Age structure: *0-14 years:* 34.4% (male 5,622,998/female 5,430,285)
15-64 years: 62.2% (male 10,112,603/female 9,865,805)
65 years and over: 3.4% (2024 est.) (male 485,538/female 623,214)

Dependency ratios: *total dependency ratio:* 71.3 (2024 est.)
youth dependency ratio: 66 (2024 est.)
elderly dependency ratio: 5.4 (2024 est.)
potential support ratio: 18.6 (2024 est.)

Median age: *total:* 22 years (2024 est.)
male: 21.9 years
female: 22.2 years
comparison ranking: total 188

Population growth rate: 1.78% (2024 est.)
comparison ranking: 48

Birth rate: 23.4 births/1,000 population (2024 est.)
comparison ranking: 49

Death rate: 5.5 deaths/1,000 population (2024 est.)
comparison ranking: 182

Net migration rate: -0.2 migrant(s)/1,000 population (2024 est.)
comparison ranking: 108

Population distribution: the vast majority of the population is found in the Asir Mountains (part of the larger Sarawat Mountain system), located in the far western region of the country

Urbanization: *urban population:* 39.8% of total population (2023)
rate of urbanization: 3.71% annual rate of change (2015-20 est.)

Major urban areas - population: 3.292 million SANAA (capital), 1.080 million Aden, 941,000 Taiz, 772,000 Ibb (2023)

Sex ratio: *at birth:* 1.05 male(s)/female
0-14 years: 1.04 male(s)/female
15-64 years: 1.03 male(s)/female
65 years and over: 0.78 male(s)/female
total population: 1.02 male(s)/female (2024 est.)

Mother's mean age at first birth: 20.8 years (2013 est.)
note: data represents median age at first birth among women 25-49

Maternal mortality ratio: 118 deaths/100,000 live births (2023 est.)
comparison ranking: 62

Infant mortality rate: *total:* 44.6 deaths/1,000 live births (2024 est.)
male: 49.9 deaths/1,000 live births
female: 39 deaths/1,000 live births
comparison ranking: total 26

Life expectancy at birth: *total population:* 68.2 years (2024 est.)
male: 65.8 years
female: 70.6 years
comparison ranking: total population 191

Total fertility rate: 2.82 children born/woman (2024 est.)
comparison ranking: 54

Gross reproduction rate: 1.37 (2024 est.)

Drinking water source: *improved:* *urban:* 77.2% of population (2022 est.)
rural: 51.8% of population (2022 est.)
total: 61.8% of population (2022 est.)
unimproved: *urban:* 22.8% of population (2022 est.)
rural: 48.2% of population (2022 est.)
total: 38.2% of population (2022 est.)

Health expenditure: 4.3% of GDP (2015)
2.5% of national budget (2022 est.)

Physician density: 0.1 physicians/1,000 population (2023)

Sanitation facility access: *improved:* *urban:* 83.1% of population (2022 est.)
rural: 44.8% of population (2022 est.)
total: 59.9% of population (2022 est.)
unimproved: *urban:* 16.9% of population (2022 est.)
rural: 55.2% of population (2022 est.)
total: 40.1% of population (2022 est.)

Obesity - adult prevalence rate: 17.1% (2016)
comparison ranking: 120

Alcohol consumption per capita: *total:* 0.02 liters of pure alcohol (2019 est.)
beer: 0.02 liters of pure alcohol (2019 est.)
wine: 0 liters of pure alcohol (2019 est.)
spirits: 0 liters of pure alcohol (2019 est.)
other alcohols: 0 liters of pure alcohol (2019 est.)
comparison ranking: total 182

Tobacco use: *total:* 20.2% (2025 est.)
male: 33.1% (2025 est.)
female: 7.3% (2025 est.)
comparison ranking: total 67

Currently married women (ages 15-49): 60.4% (2023 est.)

Child marriage: *women married by age 15:* 6.5% (2023)
women married by age 18: 29.6% (2023)

Literacy: *female:* 54.1% (2023 est.)

ENVIRONMENT

Environmental issues: limited natural freshwater resources; inadequate supplies of potable water; overgrazing; soil erosion; desertification

International environmental agreements: *party to:* Biodiversity, Climate Change, Climate Change-Kyoto Protocol, Desertification, Endangered Species, Environmental Modification, Hazardous Wastes, Law of the Sea, Marine Dumping-London Protocol, Nuclear Test Ban, Ozone Layer Protection, Wetlands
signed, but not ratified: Climate Change-Paris Agreement, Comprehensive Nuclear Test Ban

Climate: mostly desert; hot and humid along west coast; temperate in western mountains affected by seasonal monsoon; extraordinarily hot, dry, harsh desert in east

Urbanization: *urban population:* 39.8% of total population (2023)
rate of urbanization: 3.71% annual rate of change (2015-20 est.)

Carbon dioxide emissions: 8.193 million metric tonnes of CO_2 (2023 est.)
from coal and metallurgical coke: 93,000 metric tonnes of CO_2 (2023 est.)
from petroleum and other liquids: 8.08 million metric tonnes of CO_2 (2023 est.)
from consumed natural gas: 21,000 metric tonnes of CO_2 (2023 est.)
comparison ranking: total emissions 115

Particulate matter emissions: 43.9 micrograms per cubic meter (2019 est.)

Methane emissions: *energy:* 190.5 kt (2022-2024 est.)
agriculture: 192.2 kt (2019-2021 est.)
waste: 135.9 kt (2019-2021 est.)
other: 0.4 kt (2019-2021 est.)

Waste and recycling: *municipal solid waste generated annually:* 4.837 million tons (2024 est.)
percent of municipal solid waste recycled: 8% (2016 est.)

Total water withdrawal: *municipal:* 265 million cubic meters (2022 est.)
industrial: 65 million cubic meters (2022 est.)
agricultural: 3.235 billion cubic meters (2022 est.)

Total renewable water resources: 2.1 billion cubic meters (2022 est.)

GOVERNMENT

Country name: *conventional long form:* Republic of Yemen
conventional short form: Yemen
local long form: Al Jumhuriyah al Yamaniyah
local short form: Al Yaman
former: Yemen Arab Republic [Yemen (Sanaa) or North Yemen] and People's Democratic Republic of Yemen [Yemen (Aden) or South Yemen]
etymology: the name origin is unclear but may come from the Arabic word *al-yamin*, meaning "the right," as a reference to its geographic position in relation to Mecca

Government type: in transition

Capital: *name:* Sanaa
geographic coordinates: 15 21 N, 44 12 E
time difference: UTC+3 (8 hours ahead of Washington, DC, during Standard Time)
etymology: the name is reputed to mean "fortified place" in an ancient language

Administrative divisions: 22 governorates (*muhafazat*, singular - *muhafazah*); Abyan, 'Adan (Aden), Ad Dali', Al Bayda', Al Hudaydah, Al Jawf, Al Mahrah, Al Mahwit, Amanat al 'Asimah (Sanaa City), 'Amran, Arkhabil Suqutra (Socotra Archipelago), Dhamar, Hadramawt, Hajjah, Ibb, Lahij, Ma'rib, Raymah, Sa'dah, San'a' (Sanaa), Shabwah, Ta'izz

Legal system: mixed system of Islamic (sharia) law, Napoleonic law, English common law, and customary law

Constitution: *history:* adopted by referendum 16 May 1991 (following unification)

International law organization participation: has not submitted an ICJ jurisdiction declaration; non-party state to the ICCt

Citizenship: *citizenship by birth:* no
citizenship by descent only: the father must be a citizen of Yemen; if the father is unknown, the mother must be a citizen
dual citizenship recognized: no
residency requirement for naturalization: 10 years

Suffrage: 18 years of age; universal

Executive branch: *chief of state:* Presidential Leadership Council Chairperson Dr. Rashad Muhammad al-ALIMI (since 19 April 2022)
head of government: Prime Minister Salim Salih BIN BURAYK (since 9 May 2025)
cabinet: 24 members from northern and southern Yemen, with representatives from Yemen's major political parties
election/appointment process: formerly, the president was directly elected by absolute-majority popular vote in 2 rounds, if needed, for a 7-year term (eligible for a second term); vice president appointed by the president; prime minister appointed by the president
most recent election date: 21 February 2012
election results: *2012:* Abd Rabuh Mansur HADI (GPC) elected consensus president
note: on 7 April 2022, President Abd Rabuh Mansur HADI announced his abdication, the dismissal of Vice President ALI MUHSIN al-Ahmar and the formation of a Presidential Leadership Council, an eight-member body chaired by former minister Rashad AL-ALIMI; on 19 April 2022, the Council

was sworn in before Parliament and began assuming the responsibilities of the president and vice president and carrying out the political, security, and military duties of the government; in May 2025, Chairperson al-ALIMI made changes to his cabinet

Legislative branch: *legislature name:* Parliament (Majlis)
legislative structure: bicameral
note: the last legislative election occurred in 2003, and the six-year term for the House of Representatives expired in 2009. Ongoing instability, beginning in 2011, has since prevented new elections. A new Shura Council was appointed in 2021 and is currently chaired by Dr. Ahmed Obaid bin Dagher (as of Jan 2025).

Legislative branch - lower chamber: *chamber name:* House of Representatives (Majlis Annowab)
number of seats: 301 (all directly elected)
electoral system: plurality/majority
scope of elections: full renewal
term in office: 6 years
most recent election date: 4/27/2003
parties elected and seats per party: General People's Congress (GPC) (238); Yemeni Congregation for Reform (Islah) (46); Other (17)
percentage of women in chamber: 0%

Legislative branch - upper chamber: *chamber name:* Shura Council (Majlis Alshoora)
number of seats: 111 (all appointed)
scope of elections: full renewal
most recent election date: 4/28/2001
percentage of women in chamber: 1.1%
note: the Shura Council serves in an advisory role to the president; it has no legislative responsibilities

Judicial branch: *highest court(s):* Supreme Court (consists of the court president, 2 deputies, and nearly 50 judges; court organized into constitutional, civil, commercial, family, administrative, criminal, military, and appeals scrutiny divisions)
judge selection and term of office: judges appointed by the Supreme Judicial Council, which is chaired by the president of the republic and includes 10 high-ranking judicial officers; judges serve for life with mandatory retirement at age 65
subordinate courts: appeal courts; district or first instance courts; commercial courts

Political parties: General People's Congress or GPC (3 factions: pro-Hadi, pro-Houthi, pro-Salih)
Nasserist Unionist People's Organization
National Arab Socialist Ba'ath Party
Southern Transitional Council or STC
Yemeni Reform Grouping or Islah
Yemeni Socialist Party or YSP

Diplomatic representation in the US: *chief of mission:* Ambassador Abdulwahab Abdullah Ahmed AL-HAJRI (since 24 July 2025)
chancery: 2319 Wyoming Avenue NW, Washington, DC 20008
telephone: [1] (202) 965-4760
FAX: [1] (202) 337-2017
email address and website: Information@yemenembassy.org
https://www.yemenembassy.org/

Diplomatic representation from the US: *chief of mission:* Ambassador Steven H. FAGIN (since 1 June 2022); note - the embassy closed in March 2015; Yemen Affairs Unit currently operates out of US Embassy Riyadh
embassy: previously - Sa'awan Street, Sanaa
mailing address: 6330 Sanaa Place, Washington DC 20521-6330
telephone: US Embassy Riyadh [966] 11-488-3800 previously - [967] 1 755-2000
FAX: US Embassy Riyadh [966] 11-488-7360
email address and website: YemenEmergencyUSC@state.gov
https://ye.usembassy.gov/

International organization participation: AFESD, AMF, CAEU, CD, EITI (temporarily suspended), FAO, G-77, IAEA, IBRD, ICAO, ICRM, IDA, IDB, IFAD, IFC, IFRCS, ILO, IMF, IMO, IMSO, Interpol, IOC, IOM, IPU, ISO, ITSO, ITU, ITUC (NGOs), LAS, MIGA, MINURSO, MINUSMA, MONUSCO, NAM, OAS (observer), OIC, OPCW, UN, UNAMID, UNCTAD, UNESCO, UNHCR, UNIDO, UNISFA, UNMHA, UNMIL, UNMIS, UNOCI, UNVIM, UNWTO, UPU, WCO, WFTU (NGOs), WHO, WIPO, WMO, WTO

Independence: *22 May 1990 (Republic of Yemen established with the merger of the Yemen Arab Republic [Yemen (Sanaa) or North Yemen] and the People's Democratic Republic of Yemen [Yemen (Aden) or South Yemen]);*
notable earlier dates: 1 November 1918 (North Yemen independent from the Ottoman Empire), 27 September 1962 (North Yemen becomes republic), 30 November 1967 (South Yemen independent from the UK)

National holiday: Unification Day, 22 May (1990)

Flag: *description:* three equal horizontal bands of red (top), white, and black
meaning: the band colors come from the Arab Liberation flag and represent oppression (black) overcome through bloody struggle (red), to be replaced by a bright future (white)
note: similar to the flags of Iraq (Arabic inscription centered in the white band) and Egypt (heraldic eagle centered in the white band)

National symbol(s): golden eagle

National color(s): red, white, black

National anthem(s): *title:* "Al-qumhuriyatu l-muttahida" (United Republic)
lyrics/music: Abdullah Abdulwahab NOA'MAN/ Ayyoab Tarish ABSI
history: adopted 1990; the music first served as the anthem for South Yemen before unification with North Yemen in 1990

National heritage: *total World Heritage Sites:* 5 (4 cultural, 1 natural)
selected World Heritage Site locales: Old Walled City of Shibam (c); Old City of Sana'a (c); Historic Town of Zabid (c); Socotra Archipelago (n); Landmarks of the Ancient Kingdom of Saba, Marib (c)

ECONOMY

Economic overview: low-income Middle Eastern economy; infrastructure, trade, and economic institutions devastated by civil war; oil/gas-dependent but decreasing reserves; massive poverty, food insecurity, and unemployment; high inflation

Real GDP (purchasing power parity): $18.719 billion (2024 est.)
$18.908 billion (2023 est.)
$19.294 billion (2022 est.)
note: data in 2015 dollars
comparison ranking: 156

Real GDP growth rate: 0.8% (2018 est.)
-5.1% (2017 est.)
-9.4% (2016 est.)
note: annual GDP % growth based on constant local currency
comparison ranking: 184

Real GDP per capita: $200 (2024 est.)
$200 (2023 est.)
$300 (2022 est.)
note: data in 2015 dollars
comparison ranking: 219

GDP (official exchange rate): $8.278 billion (2024 est.)
note: data in current dollars at official exchange rate

Inflation rate (consumer prices): 29.1% (2022 est.)
26% (2021 est.)
19.6% (2020 est.)
note: annual % change based on consumer prices
comparison ranking: 198

GDP - composition, by sector of origin: *agriculture:* 28.7% (2018 est.)
industry: 25.4% (2018 est.)
services: 41.8% (2018 est.)
note: figures may not total 100% due to non-allocated consumption not captured in sector-reported data
comparison rankings: agriculture 14; industry 83; services 189

Agricultural products: mangoes/guavas, potatoes, milk, onions, spices, chicken, sorghum, watermelons, tomatoes, grapes (2023)
note: top ten agricultural products based on tonnage

Industries: crude oil production and petroleum refining; small-scale production of cotton textiles, leather goods; food processing; handicrafts; aluminum products; cement; commercial ship repair; natural gas production

Industrial production growth rate: -1.1% (2018 est.)
note: annual % change in industrial value added based on constant local currency
comparison ranking: 150

Labor force: 7.848 million (2024 est.)
note: number of people ages 15 or older who are employed or seeking work
comparison ranking: 65

Unemployment rate: 17.1% (2024 est.)
17.1% (2023 est.)
17.4% (2022 est.)
note: % of labor force seeking employment
comparison ranking: 177

Youth unemployment rate (ages 15-24): *total:* 32.4% (2024 est.)
male: 31.8% (2024 est.)
female: 38.4% (2024 est.)
note: % of labor force ages 15-24 seeking employment
comparison ranking: total 18

Remittances: 20.05% of GDP (2023 est.)
16.02% of GDP (2022 est.)
19.44% of GDP (2021 est.)
note: personal transfers and compensation between resident and non-resident individuals/households/ entities

Budget: *revenues:* $2.207 billion (2019 est.)
expenditures: $3.585 billion (2019 est.)

Current account balance: -$2.419 billion (2016 est.)
-$3.026 billion (2015 est.)
-$1.488 billion (2014 est.)
note: balance of payments - net trade and primary/ secondary income in current dollars
comparison ranking: 154

Exports: $384.5 million (2017 est.)

$938.469 million (2016 est.)
$1.867 billion (2015 est.)
note: balance of payments - exports of goods and services in current dollars
comparison ranking: 195

Exports - partners: UAE 28%, India 21%, Saudi Arabia 17%, Oman 7%, Malaysia 5% (2023)
note: top five export partners based on percentage share of exports

Exports - commodities: gold, fish, scrap iron, shellfish, industrial acids/oils/alcohols (2023)
note: top five export commodities based on value in dollars

Imports: $4.079 billion (2017 est.)
$8.256 billion (2016 est.)
$7.697 billion (2015 est.)
note: balance of payments - imports of goods and services in current dollars
comparison ranking: 157

Imports - partners: China 23%, UAE 15%, Saudi Arabia 11%, Turkey 8%, India 7% (2023)
note: top five import partners based on percentage share of imports

Imports - commodities: wheat, raw sugar, rice, iron bars, plastic products (2023)
note: top five import commodities based on value in dollars

Reserves of foreign exchange and gold: $1.251 billion (2022 est.)
$1.688 billion (2021 est.)
$969.613 million (2020 est.)
note: holdings of gold (year-end prices)/foreign exchange/special drawing rights in current dollars
comparison ranking: 141

Debt - external: $6.492 billion (2023 est.)
note: present value of external debt in current US dollars
comparison ranking: 63

Exchange rates: Yemeni rials (YER) per US dollar -

Exchange rates: 1,355.116 (2023 est.)
1,115.002 (2022 est.)
1,028.108 (2021 est.)
743.006 (2020 est.)
486.731 (2019 est.)

ENERGY

Electricity access: *electrification - total population:* 76% (2022 est.)
electrification - urban areas: 96.1%
electrification - rural areas: 65%

Electricity: *installed generating capacity:* 1.79 million kW (2023 est.)
consumption: 2.579 billion kWh (2023 est.)
transmission/distribution losses: 486.24 million kWh (2023 est.)
comparison rankings: installed generating capacity 124; consumption 147; transmission/distribution losses 79

Electricity generation sources: *fossil fuels:* 83% of total installed capacity (2023 est.)
solar: 17% of total installed capacity (2023 est.)

Coal: *consumption:* 27,000 metric tons (2023 est.)
imports: 36,000 metric tons (2023 est.)

Petroleum: *total petroleum production:* 15,000 bbl/day (2023 est.)
refined petroleum consumption: 58,000 bbl/day (2023 est.)
crude oil estimated reserves: 3 billion barrels (2021 est.)

Natural gas: *production:* 10.286 million cubic meters (2023 est.)
consumption: 10.286 million cubic meters (2023 est.)
proven reserves: 478.555 billion cubic meters (2021 est.)

Energy consumption per capita: 2.987 million Btu/person (2023 est.)
comparison ranking: 178

COMMUNICATIONS

Telephones - fixed lines: *total subscriptions:* 728,000 (2022 est.)
subscriptions per 100 inhabitants: 2 (2022 est.)
comparison ranking: total subscriptions 79

Telephones - mobile cellular: *total subscriptions:* 20 million (2023 est.)
subscriptions per 100 inhabitants: 46 (2021 est.)
comparison ranking: total subscriptions 65

Broadcast media: state-run TV with 2 stations; state-run radio with 2 national radio stations and 5 local stations; stations from Oman and Saudi Arabia can be accessed

Internet country code: .ye

Internet users: *percent of population:* 14% (2020 est.)

Broadband - fixed subscriptions: *total:* 486,000 (2022 est.)
subscriptions per 100 inhabitants: 1 (2022 est.)
comparison ranking: total 99

TRANSPORTATION

Civil aircraft registration country code prefix: 7O

Airports: 37 (2025)
comparison ranking: 107

Heliports: 6 (2025)
comparison ranking: 96

Merchant marine: *total:* 30 (2023)
by type: general cargo 2, oil tanker 1, other 27
comparison ranking: total 133

Ports: *total ports:* 10 (2024)
large: 1
medium: 2
small: 2
very small: 5
ports with oil terminals: 6
key ports: Aden, Al Ahmadi, Al Mukalla, Al Mukha, Ras Isa Marine Terminal

MILITARY AND SECURITY

Military and security forces: Yemeni Armed Forces: Yemeni National Army, Air Force and Air Defense, Navy and Coastal Defense Forces, Border Guard, Strategic Reserve Forces (includes Special Forces and Presidential Protection Brigades, which are under the Ministry of Defense but responsible to the president), Popular Committee Forces (aka Popular Resistance Forces; government-backed tribal militia)

Ministry of Interior: Security Forces, Emergency Forces, Counterterrorism Units (2025)
note 1: both Saudi Arabia and the United Arab Emirates have raised and continue to back tribal and regionally based irregular forces in Yemen
note 2: Houthi (alt Huthi; aka Ansarallah) forces include land, aerospace (air, missile), naval/coastal defense, presidential protection, special operations, internal security, and militia/tribal auxiliary components; a considerable portion–up to 70 percent by some estimates–of Yemen's military and security forces defected in whole or in part to former president SALAH and the Houthi opposition in 2011-2015

Military and security service personnel strengths: not available

Military equipment inventories and acquisitions: the Yemeni Government forces have an inventory consisting primarily of Russian and Soviet-era weapons and equipment
Houthi forces are armed largely with weapons seized from the Yemeni Government stockpiles, smuggled in from Iran, and manufactured copies of Iranian designs and pre-war Yemeni Government weapons, such as Chinese and Russian missiles (2024)

Military service age and obligation: 18 is the legal minimum age for voluntary military service; conscription abolished in 2001; 2-year service obligation (note - limited information since the start of the civil war in 2014) (2022)
note: as late as 2022, all parties to the ongoing conflict were implicated in child soldier recruitment and use; during the beginning of the truce in April 2022, the Houthis signed a plan with the UN to end the recruitment and use of child soldiers; Houthi leaders previously pledged to end the use of child soldiers in 2012, as did the Government of Yemen in 2014

Military - note: government forces under the Yemeni Ministry of Defense are responsible for both external and internal defense; their priorities are the Houthi separatists (aka Ansarallah, which has been designated a terrorist organization by the US), the terrorist groups al-Qa'ida in the Arabian Peninsula (AQAP) and the Islamic State of Iraq and ash-Sham in Yemen (ISIS-Yemen), and maritime security, particularly against arms smuggling; in 2022, the Yemeni Government and the Houthis signed a truce, halting most fighting and establishing humanitarian measures; the former front lines of conflict, in some areas mirroring Yemen's pre-unification borders, remain static; AQAP and ISIS-Yemen continue to be active in remote areas (2025)

TERRORISM

Terrorist group(s): Terrorist group(s): Ansarallah (Houthis); Hizballah; Islamic Revolutionary Guard Corps (IRGC)/Qods Force; Islamic State of Iraq and ash-Sham (ISIS) - Yemen; al-Qa'ida in the Arabian Peninsula (AQAP)
note: details about the history, aims, leadership, organization, areas of operation, tactics, targets, weapons, size, and sources of support of the group(s) appear(s) in Appendix T

TRANSNATIONAL ISSUES

Refugees and internally displaced persons: *refugees:* 60,921 (2024 est.)

IDPs: 4,795,983 (2024 est.)

Z

ZAMBIA

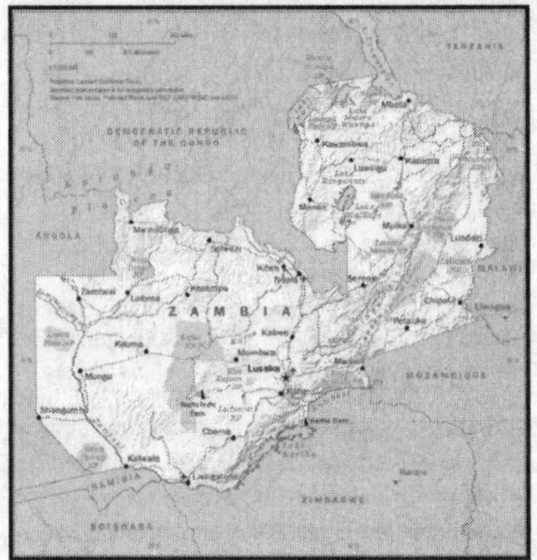

INTRODUCTION

Background: Bantu-speaking groups mainly from the Luba and Lunda Kingdoms in the Congo River Basin and from the Great Lakes region in East Africa settled in what is now Zambia beginning around A.D. 300, displacing and mixing with previous population groups in the region. The Mutapa Empire developed after the fall of Great Zimbabwe to the south in the 14th century and ruled the region, including large parts of Zambia, from the 14th to 17th century. The empire collapsed as a result of the growing slave trade and Portuguese incursions in the 16th and 17th centuries. The region was further influenced by migrants from the Zulu Kingdom to the south and the Luba and Lunda Kingdoms to the north, after invading colonial and African powers displaced local residents into the area around the Zambezi River, in what is now Zambia. In the 1880s, British companies began securing mineral and other economic concessions from local leaders. The companies eventually claimed control of the region and incorporated it as the protectorate of Northern Rhodesia in 1911. The UK took over administrative control from the British South Africa Company in 1924. During the 1920s and 1930s, advances in mining spurred British economic ventures and colonial settlement.

Northern Rhodesia's name was changed to Zambia upon independence from the UK in 1964, under independence leader and first President Kenneth KAUNDA. In the 1980s and 1990s, declining copper prices, economic mismanagement, and a prolonged drought hurt the economy. Elections in 1991 brought an end to one-party rule and propelled the Movement for Multiparty Democracy (MMD) into power. The subsequent vote in 1996, however, saw increasing harassment of opposition parties and abuse of state media and other resources. Administrative problems marked the election in 2001, with three parties filing a legal petition challenging the election of ruling party candidate Levy MWANAWASA. MWANAWASA was reelected in 2006 in an election that was deemed free and fair. Upon his death in 2008, he was succeeded by his vice president, Rupiah BANDA, who won a special presidential byelection later that year. BANDA and the MMD lost to Michael SATA and the Patriotic Front (PF) in the 2011 general elections. SATA, however, presided over a period of haphazard economic management and attempted to silence opposition to PF policies. SATA died in 2014 and was succeeded by his vice president, Guy SCOTT, who served as interim president until 2015, when Edgar LUNGU won the presidential byelection and completed SATA's term. LUNGU then won a full term in the 2016 presidential elections. Hakainde HICHILEMA was elected president in 2021.

GEOGRAPHY

Location: Southern Africa, east of Angola, south of the Democratic Republic of the Congo

Geographic coordinates: 15 00 S, 30 00 E

Map references: Africa

Area: *total:* 752,618 sq km
land: 743,398 sq km
water: 9,220 sq km
comparison ranking: total 40

Area - comparative: almost five times the size of Georgia; slightly larger than Texas

Land boundaries: *total:* 6,043.15 km
border countries (8): Angola 1,065 km; Botswana 0.15 km; Democratic Republic of the Congo 2,332 km; Malawi 847 km; Mozambique 439 km; Namibia 244 km; Tanzania 353 km; Zimbabwe 763 km

Coastline: 0 km (landlocked)

Maritime claims: none (landlocked)

Climate: tropical; modified by altitude; rainy season (October to April)

Terrain: mostly high plateau with some hills and mountains

Elevation: *highest point:* Mafinga Central 2,330 m
lowest point: Zambezi river 329 m
mean elevation: 1,138 m

Natural resources: copper, cobalt, zinc, lead, coal, emeralds, gold, silver, uranium, hydropower

Land use: *agricultural land:* 32.1% (2022 est.)
arable land: 5.1% (2022 est.)
permanent crops: 0.1% (2022 est.)
permanent pasture: 26.9% (2022 est.)
forest: 59.8% (2022 est.)
other: 8.2% (2022 est.)

Irrigated land: 1,560 sq km (2012)

Major lakes (area sq km): *fresh water lake(s):* Lake Tanganyika (shared with Democratic Republic of Congo, Tanzania, and Burundi) - 32,000 sq km; Lake Mweru (shared with Democratic Republic of Congo) - 4,350 sq km; Lake Bangweulu - 4,000-15,000 sq km seasonal variation

Major rivers (by length in km): Congo river source (shared with Angola, Republic of Congo, and Democratic Republic of Congo [m]) - 4,700 km; Zambezi river source (shared with Angola, Namibia, Botswana, Zimbabwe, and Mozambique [m]) - 2,740 km
note: [s] after country name indicates river source; [m] after country name indicates river mouth

Major watersheds (area sq km): Atlantic Ocean drainage: Congo (3,730,881 sq km)

Indian Ocean drainage: Zambezi (1,332,412 sq km)

Major aquifers: Upper Kalahari-Cuvelai-Upper Zambezi Basin

Population distribution: one of the highest levels of urbanization in Africa; high density in the central area, particularly around the cities of Lusaka, Ndola, Kitwe, and Mufulira, as shown in this population distribution map

Natural hazards: periodic drought; tropical storms (November to April)

Geography - note: landlocked; the Zambezi forms a natural river boundary with Zimbabwe; Lake Kariba on the Zambia-Zimbabwe border forms the world's largest reservoir by volume (180 cu km; 43 cu mi)

PEOPLE AND SOCIETY

Population: *total:* 20,799,116 (2024 est.)
male: 10,407,253
female: 10,391,863
comparison rankings: total 63; male 63; female 64

Nationality: *noun:* Zambian(s)
adjective: Zambian

Ethnic groups: Bemba 21%, Tonga 13.6%, Chewa 7.4%, Lozi 5.7%, Nsenga 5.3%, Tumbuka 4.4%, Ngoni 4%, Lala 3.1%, Kaonde 2.9%, Namwanga 2.8%, Lunda (north Western) 2.6%, Mambwe 2.5%, Luvale 2.2%, Lamba 2.1%, Ushi 1.9%, Lenje 1.6%, Bisa 1.6%, Mbunda 1.2%, other 13.8%, unspecified 0.4% (2010 est.)

Languages: Bemba 33.4%, Nyanja 14.7%, Tonga 11.4%, Lozi 5.5%, Chewa 4.5%, Nsenga 2.9%, Tumbuka 2.5%, Lunda (North Western) 1.9%, Kaonde 1.8%, Lala 1.8%, Lamba 1.8%, English (official) 1.7%, Luvale 1.5%, Mambwe 1.3%, Namwanga 1.2%, Lenje 1.1%, Bisa 1%, other 9.7%, unspecified 0.2% (2010 est.)
note: Zambia is said to have over 70 languages, although many of these may be considered dialects; all of Zambia's major languages are members of the Bantu family; Chewa and Nyanja are mutually intelligible dialects

Religions: Protestant 75.3%, Roman Catholic 20.2%, other 2.7% (includes Muslim, Buddhist, Hindu, and Baha'i), none 1.8% (2010 est.)

Age structure: *0-14 years:* 42.1% (male 4,418,980/female 4,337,187)
15-64 years: 55.1% (male 5,726,265/female 5,736,732)
65 years and over: 2.8% (2024 est.) (male 262,008/female 317,944)

Dependency ratios: *total dependency ratio:* 81.4 (2024 est.)
youth dependency ratio: 76.4 (2024 est.)
elderly dependency ratio: 5.1 (2024 est.)
potential support ratio: 19.8 (2024 est.)

Median age: *total:* 18.4 years (2024 est.)
male: 18.2 years
female: 18.6 years
comparison ranking: total 219

Population growth rate: 2.83% (2024 est.)
comparison ranking: 10

Birth rate: 34.1 births/1,000 population (2024 est.)
comparison ranking: 16

Death rate: 5.9 deaths/1,000 population (2024 est.)
comparison ranking: 160

Net migration rate: 0.1 migrant(s)/1,000 population (2024 est.)

comparison ranking: 76

Population distribution: one of the highest levels of urbanization in Africa; high density in the central area, particularly around the cities of Lusaka, Ndola, Kitwe, and Mufulira, as shown in this population distribution map

Urbanization: *urban population:* 46.3% of total population (2023)
rate of urbanization: 4.15% annual rate of change (2020-25 est.)

Major urban areas - population: 3.181 million LUSAKA (capital), 763,000 Kitwe (2023)

Sex ratio: *at birth:* 1.03 male(s)/female
0-14 years: 1.02 male(s)/female
15-64 years: 1 male(s)/female
65 years and over: 0.82 male(s)/female
total population: 1 male(s)/female (2024 est.)

Mother's mean age at first birth: 19.2 years (2018 est.)
note: data represents median age at first birth among women 20-49

Maternal mortality ratio: 85 deaths/100,000 live births (2023 est.)
comparison ranking: 69

Infant mortality rate: *total:* 35.6 deaths/1,000 live births (2024 est.)
male: 38.9 deaths/1,000 live births
female: 32.1 deaths/1,000 live births
comparison ranking: total 37

Life expectancy at birth: *total population:* 66.9 years (2024 est.)
male: 65.2 years
female: 68.7 years
comparison ranking: total population 199

Total fertility rate: 4.42 children born/woman (2024 est.)
comparison ranking: 18

Gross reproduction rate: 2.18 (2024 est.)

Drinking water source: *improved: urban:* 88.6% of population (2022 est.)
rural: 51.1% of population (2022 est.)
total: 68.2% of population (2022 est.)
unimproved: urban: 11.4% of population (2022 est.)
rural: 48.9% of population (2022 est.)
total: 31.8% of population (2022 est.)

Health expenditure: 6.6% of GDP (2021)
8.9% of national budget (2022 est.)

Physician density: 0.32 physicians/1,000 population (2022)

Sanitation facility access: *improved: urban:* 78.1% of population (2022 est.)
rural: 40.9% of population (2022 est.)
total: 57.9% of population (2022 est.)
unimproved: urban: 21.9% of population (2022 est.)
rural: 59.1% of population (2022 est.)
total: 42.1% of population (2022 est.)

Obesity - adult prevalence rate: 8.1% (2016)
comparison ranking: 155

Alcohol consumption per capita: *total:* 3.82 liters of pure alcohol (2019 est.)
beer: 1.26 liters of pure alcohol (2019 est.)
wine: 0.04 liters of pure alcohol (2019 est.)
spirits: 0.36 liters of pure alcohol (2019 est.)
other alcohols: 2.16 liters of pure alcohol (2019 est.)
comparison ranking: total 98

Tobacco use: *total:* 11.7% (2025 est.)
male: 21.4% (2025 est.)
female: 2.4% (2025 est.)

comparison ranking: total 116

Children under the age of 5 years underweight: 11.8% (2018/19)
comparison ranking: 42

Currently married women (ages 15-49): 53.3% (2023 est.)

Child marriage: *women married by age 15:* 5.2% (2018)
women married by age 18: 29% (2018)
men married by age 18: 2.8% (2018)

Education expenditure: 4.1% of GDP (2023 est.)
14.5% national budget (2025 est.)
comparison ranking: Education expenditure (% GDP) 101

Literacy: *total population:* 71.1% (2018 est.)
male: 81.7% (2018 est.)
female: 62.2% (2018 est.)

ENVIRONMENT

Environmental issues: air pollution and acid rain in the mineral extraction and refining region; chemical runoff into watersheds; loss of biodiversity; poaching; deforestation; soil erosion; desertification; lack of adequate water treatment

International environmental agreements: *party to:* Biodiversity, Climate Change, Climate Change-Kyoto Protocol, Climate Change-Paris Agreement, Comprehensive Nuclear Test Ban, Desertification, Endangered Species, Hazardous Wastes, Law of the Sea, Nuclear Test Ban, Ozone Layer Protection, Wetlands
signed, but not ratified: none of the selected agreements

Climate: tropical; modified by altitude; rainy season (October to April)

Urbanization: *urban population:* 46.3% of total population (2023)
rate of urbanization: 4.15% annual rate of change (2020-25 est.)

Carbon dioxide emissions: 9.877 million metric tonnes of CO2 (2023 est.)
from coal and metallurgical coke: 4.835 million metric tonnes of CO2 (2023 est.)
from petroleum and other liquids: 5.042 million metric tonnes of CO2 (2023 est.)
comparison ranking: total emissions 109

Particulate matter emissions: 16.1 micrograms per cubic meter (2019 est.)

Waste and recycling: *municipal solid waste generated annually:* 2.608 million tons (2024 est.)
percent of municipal solid waste recycled: 12.6% (2022 est.)

Total water withdrawal: *municipal:* 290 million cubic meters (2022 est.)
industrial: 130 million cubic meters (2022 est.)
agricultural: 1.152 billion cubic meters (2022 est.)

Total renewable water resources: 104.8 billion cubic meters (2022 est.)

GOVERNMENT

Country name: *conventional long form:* Republic of Zambia
conventional short form: Zambia
former: Northern Rhodesia
etymology: name is derived from the Zambezi River, which flows through the western part of the country and forms the southern border with Zimbabwe

Government type: presidential republic

Capital: *name:* Lusaka
geographic coordinates: 15 25 S, 28 17 E
time difference: UTC+2 (7 hours ahead of Washington, DC, during Standard Time)
etymology: named after a village with a headman (chief) called LUSAAKAS

Administrative divisions: 10 provinces; Central, Copperbelt, Eastern, Luapula, Lusaka, Muchinga, Northern, North-Western, Southern, Western

Legal system: mixed system of English common law and customary law

Constitution: *history:* several previous; latest adopted 24 August 1991, promulgated 30 August 1991
amendment process: proposed by the National Assembly; passage requires two-thirds majority vote by the Assembly in two separate readings at least 30 days apart; passage of amendments affecting fundamental rights and freedoms requires approval by at least one half of votes cast in a referendum prior to consideration and voting by the Assembly

International law organization participation: has not submitted an ICJ jurisdiction declaration; accepts ICCt jurisdiction

Citizenship: *citizenship by birth:* only if at least one parent is a citizen of Zambia
citizenship by descent only: yes, if at least one parent was a citizen of Zambia
dual citizenship recognized: yes
residency requirement for naturalization: 5 years for those with an ancestor who was a citizen of Zambia, otherwise 10 years residency is required

Suffrage: 18 years of age; universal

Executive branch: *chief of state:* President Hakainde HICHILEMA (since 24 August 2021)
head of government: President Hakainde HICHILEMA (since 24 August 2021)
cabinet: Cabinet appointed by president from among members of the National Assembly
election/appointment process: president directly elected by absolute-majority popular vote in 2 rounds, if needed, for a 5-year term (eligible for a second term)
most recent election date: 12 August 2021
election results: *2021:* Hakainde HICHILEMA elected president; percent of the vote - Hakainde HICHILEMA (UPND) 57.9%, Edgar LUNGU (PF) 37.3%, other 4.8%
2016: Edgar LUNGU reelected president; percent of vote - Edgar LUNGU (PF) 50.4%, Hakainde HICHILEMA (UPND) 47.6%, other 2%; note - the president is both chief of state and head of government
expected date of next election: 2026

Legislative branch: *legislature name:* National Assembly
legislative structure: unicameral
number of seats: 167 (156 directly elected; 8 appointed)
electoral system: plurality/majority
scope of elections: full renewal
term in office: 5 years
most recent election date: 8/12/2021
parties elected and seats per party: United Party for National Development (UPND) (82); Patriotic Front (PF) (60); Independents (13); Other (1)
percentage of women in chamber: 15%
expected date of next election: August 2026

Judicial branch: *highest court(s):* Supreme Court (consists of the chief justice, deputy chief justice, and at least 11 judges); Constitutional Court (consists of the court president, vice president, and 11 judges)

judge selection and term of office: Supreme Court and Constitutional Court judges appointed by the president of the republic upon the advice of the 9-member Judicial Service Commission, which is headed by the chief justice, and ratified by the National Assembly; judges normally serve until age 65
subordinate courts: Court of Appeal; High Court; Industrial Relations Court; subordinate courts (3 levels, based on upper limit of money involved); Small Claims Court; local courts (2 grades, based on upper limit of money involved)

Political parties: Alliance for Democracy and Development or ADD
Forum for Democracy and Development or FDD
Movement for Multiparty Democracy or MMD
Party of National Unity and Progress or PNUP
Patriotic Front or PF
United Party for National Development or UPND

Diplomatic representation in the US: *chief of mission:* Ambassador Chibamba KANYAMA (since 30 June 2023)
chancery: 2200 R Street NW, Washington, DC 20008
telephone: [1] (202) 234-4009

FAX: [1] (202) 332-0826
email address and website: info@zambiaembassy.org
https://www.zambiaembassy.org/

Diplomatic representation from the US: *chief of mission:* Ambassador Michael C. GONZALES (since 16 September 2022)
embassy: Eastern end of Kabulonga Road, Ibex Hill, Lusaka
mailing address: 2310 Lusaka Place, Washington DC 20521-2310
telephone: [260] (0) 211-357-000

FAX: [260] (0) 211-357-224
email address and website: ACSLusaka@state.gov
https://zm.usembassy.gov/

International organization participation: ACP, AfDB, AU, C, COMESA, EITI (compliant country), FAO, G-77, IAEA, IBRD, ICAO, ICCt, ICRM, IDA, IFAD, IFC, IFRCS, ILO, IMF, Interpol, IOC, IOM, IPU, ISO (correspondent), ITSO, ITU, ITUC (NGOs), MIGA, MONUSCO, NAM, OPCW, PCA, SADC, UN, UNCTAD, UNDOF, UNESCO, UNHCR, UNIDO, UNISFA, UNMIL, UNMISS, UNOCI, UNWTO, UPU, WCO, WHO, WIPO, WMO, WTO

Independence: 24 October 1964 (from the UK)

National holiday: Independence Day, 24 October (1964)

Flag: *description:* green field with a soaring orange eagle in the upper-right corner; a panel of three vertical bands is under the eagle, in red (left side), black, and orange
meaning: green stands for the country's natural resources and vegetation, red for the struggle for freedom, black for the people, and orange for the country's mineral wealth; the eagle represents the people's ability to rise above the nation's problems

National symbol(s): African fish eagle

National color(s): green, red, black, orange

National anthem(s): *title:* "Lumbanyeni Zambia" (Stand and Sing of Zambia, Proud and Free)
lyrics/music: multiple/Enoch Mankayi SONTONGA
history: adopted 1964; the melody, which comes from the popular song "God Bless Africa," a popular song and anthem in southern Africa

National heritage: *total World Heritage Sites:* 1 (natural)
selected World Heritage Site locales: Mosi-oa-Tunya/ Victoria Falls

ECONOMY

Economic overview: lower-middle-income sub-Saharan economy; regional hydroelectricity producer; trade ties and infrastructure investments from China; IMF assistance to restructure debt burden; one of youngest and fastest-growing labor forces; systemic corruption; extreme rural poverty

Real GDP (purchasing power parity): $79.207 billion (2024 est.)
$76.129 billion (2023 est.)
$72.251 billion (2022 est.)
note: data in 2021 dollars
comparison ranking: 106

Real GDP growth rate: 4% (2024 est.)
5.4% (2023 est.)
5.2% (2022 est.)
note: annual GDP % growth based on constant local currency
comparison ranking: 73

Real GDP per capita: $3,700 (2024 est.)
$3,700 (2023 est.)
$3,600 (2022 est.)
note: data in 2021 dollars
comparison ranking: 186

GDP (official exchange rate): $26.326 billion (2024 est.)
note: data in current dollars at official exchange rate

Inflation rate (consumer prices): 15% (2024 est.)
10.9% (2023 est.)
11% (2022 est.)
note: annual % change based on consumer prices
comparison ranking: 188

GDP - composition, by sector of origin: *agriculture:* 1.8% (2024 est.)
industry: 37.5% (2024 est.)
services: 55.1% (2024 est.)
note: figures may not total 100% due to non-allocated consumption not captured in sector-reported data
comparison rankings: agriculture 157; industry 28; services 122

GDP - composition, by end use: *household consumption:* 47.1% (2023 est.)
government consumption: 13.3% (2023 est.)
investment in fixed capital: 26.4% (2023 est.)
investment in inventories: 5% (2023 est.)
exports of goods and services: 40.8% (2023 est.)
imports of goods and services: -37.4% (2023 est.)
note: figures may not total 100% due to rounding or gaps in data collection

Agricultural products: sugarcane, cassava, maize, soybeans, milk, vegetables, wheat, groundnuts, sweet potatoes, beef (2023)
note: top ten agricultural products based on tonnage

Industries: copper mining and processing, emerald mining, construction, foodstuffs, beverages, chemicals, textiles, fertilizer, horticulture

Industrial production growth rate: 3.5% (2024 est.)
note: annual % change in industrial value added based on constant local currency
comparison ranking: 71

Labor force: 7.407 million (2024 est.)
note: number of people ages 15 or older who are employed or seeking work
comparison ranking: 67

Unemployment rate: 6% (2024 est.)
6% (2023 est.)
6% (2022 est.)
note: % of labor force seeking employment
comparison ranking: 113

Youth unemployment rate (ages 15-24): *total:* 9.9% (2024 est.)
male: 10.1% (2024 est.)
female: 9.6% (2024 est.)
note: % of labor force ages 15-24 seeking employment
comparison ranking: total 122

Population below poverty line: 60% (2022 est.)
note: % of population with income below national poverty line

Gini Index coefficient - distribution of family income: 51.5 (2022 est.)
note: index (0-100) of income distribution; higher values represent greater inequality
comparison ranking: 6

Household income or consumption by percentage share: *lowest 10%:* 1.5% (2022 est.)
highest 10%: 39.1% (2022 est.)
note: % share of income accruing to lowest and highest 10% of population

Remittances: 0.9% of GDP (2023 est.)
0.8% of GDP (2022 est.)
1.1% of GDP (2021 est.)
note: personal transfers and compensation between resident and non-resident individuals/households/ entities

Budget: *revenues:* $5.388 billion (2021 est.)
expenditures: $6.19 billion (2021 est.)
note: central government revenues and expenses (excluding grants/extrabudgetary units/ social security funds) converted to US dollars at average official exchange rate for year indicated

Public debt: 71.4% of GDP (2021 est.)
note: central government debt as a % of GDP
comparison ranking: 55

Taxes and other revenues: 16.8% (of GDP) (2021 est.)
note: central government tax revenue as a % of GDP
comparison ranking: 79

Current account balance: -$582.715 million (2023 est.)
$1.093 billion (2022 est.)
$2.63 billion (2021 est.)
note: balance of payments - net trade and primary/ secondary income in current dollars
comparison ranking: 110

Exports: $11.454 billion (2023 est.)
$12.444 billion (2022 est.)
$11.728 billion (2021 est.)
note: balance of payments - exports of goods and services in current dollars
comparison ranking: 113

Exports - partners: Switzerland 27%, China 15%, India 13%, UAE 12%, DRC 10% (2023)
note: top five export partners based on percentage share of exports

Exports - commodities: raw copper, refined copper, gold, precious stones, electricity (2023)
note: top five export commodities based on value in dollars

Imports: $10.854 billion (2023 est.)
$10.022 billion (2022 est.)
$7.691 billion (2021 est.)
note: balance of payments - imports of goods and services in current dollars
comparison ranking: 117

Imports - partners: South Africa 25%, China 15%, UAE 10%, India 5%, Japan 5% (2023)
note: top five import partners based on percentage share of imports

Imports - commodities: refined petroleum, fertilizers, trucks, sulphur, tractors (2023)
note: top five import commodities based on value in dollars

Reserves of foreign exchange and gold: $3.173 billion (2023 est.)
$2.968 billion (2022 est.)
$2.754 billion (2021 est.)
note: holdings of gold (year-end prices)/foreign exchange/special drawing rights in current dollars
comparison ranking: 117

Debt - external: $16.597 billion (2023 est.)
note: present value of external debt in current US dollars
comparison ranking: 38

Exchange rates: Zambian kwacha (ZMK) per US dollar -

Exchange rates: 26.166 (2024 est.)
20.212 (2023 est.)
16.938 (2022 est.)
20.018 (2021 est.)
18.344 (2020 est.)

ENERGY

Electricity access: *electrification - total population:* 47.8% (2022 est.)
electrification - urban areas: 87%
electrification - rural areas: 14.5%

Electricity: *installed generating capacity:* 3.986 million kW (2023 est.)
consumption: 14.399 billion kWh (2023 est.)
exports: 3 billion kWh (2023 est.)
imports: 180 million kWh (2023 est.)
transmission/distribution losses: 2.229 billion kWh (2023 est.)
comparison rankings: installed generating capacity 99; consumption 90; exports 50; imports 110; transmission/distribution losses 127

Electricity generation sources: *fossil fuels:* 11% of total installed capacity (2023 est.)
solar: 0.8% of total installed capacity (2023 est.)
hydroelectricity: 87.9% of total installed capacity (2023 est.)
biomass and waste: 0.4% of total installed capacity (2023 est.)

Coal: *production:* 2.091 million metric tons (2023 est.)
consumption: 2.081 million metric tons (2023 est.)
exports: 15,000 metric tons (2023 est.)
imports: 103,000 metric tons (2023 est.)
proven reserves: 945 million metric tons (2023 est.)

Petroleum: *refined petroleum consumption:* 34,000 bbl/day (2023 est.)

Energy consumption per capita: 8.265 million Btu/person (2023 est.)
comparison ranking: 158

COMMUNICATIONS

Telephones - fixed lines: *total subscriptions:* 81,000 (2023 est.)
subscriptions per 100 inhabitants: (2023 est.) less than 1
comparison ranking: total subscriptions 142

Telephones - mobile cellular: *total subscriptions:* 21.2 million (2023 est.)
subscriptions per 100 inhabitants: 99 (2022 est.)
comparison ranking: total subscriptions 63

Broadcast media: 47 state-controlled and private TV stations; state-owned Zambia National Broadcasting Corporation (ZNBC) has 2 TV channels, controls 1, and owns shares in 2 more; 137 radio stations, with 133 private and 4 state-owned (2019)

Internet country code: .zm

Internet users: *percent of population:* 33% (2023 est.)

Broadband - fixed subscriptions: *total:* 99,000 (2023 est.)
subscriptions per 100 inhabitants: (2023 est.) less than 1
comparison ranking: total 134

TRANSPORTATION

Civil aircraft registration country code prefix: 9J

Airports: 120 (2025)
comparison ranking: 44

Heliports: 4 (2025)
comparison ranking: 108

Railways: *total:* 3,126 km (2014)
narrow gauge: 3,126 km (2014) 1.067-m gauge
note: includes 1,860 km of the Tanzania-Zambia Railway Authority (TAZARA)

Merchant marine: *total:* 2 (2023)
by type: general cargo 1, oil tanker 1
comparison ranking: total 178

MILITARY AND SECURITY

Military and security forces: Zambia Defense Force (ZDF): Zambia Army, Zambia Air Force, Zambia National Service

Ministry of Home Affairs and Internal Security: Zambia Police (2025)
note 1: the Zambia National Service is a support organization that also does public work projects; its main objectives revolve around land development, agriculture, industries, youth skills training as well as arts, sports and culture; the ZDF also includes a Defense Force Medical Service
note 2: the Zambia Army comprises the Regular Force, the Home Guard, and the Territorial Reserve

Military expenditures: 1.3% of GDP (2024 est.)
1.3% of GDP (2023 est.)
1.1% of GDP (2022 est.)
1.1% of GDP (2021 est.)
1.2% of GDP (2020 est.)

Military and security service personnel strengths: approximately 16,000 active Defense Forces (2025)

Military equipment inventories and acquisitions: the ZDF's inventory is largely comprised of Chinese, Russian, and Soviet-era weapons and equipment along with smaller quantities of items–particularly aircraft–from such suppliers as Israel and the US (2024)

Military service age and obligation: 18-25 years of age (17 with parental consent) for voluntary military service for men and women; no conscription; 12-year enlistment period (7 years active, 5 in the Reserves) (2023)
note: Zambia had military conscription from 1975-1980

Military deployments: 930 Central African Republic (MINUSCA) (2024)

Military - note: the Zambia Defense Forces (ZDF) are responsible for territorial defense, border security, and providing support to African and UN peacekeeping operations; it also has some domestic security responsibilities in cases of national emergency and is involved in socio-economic support; in recent years, ZDF has been directed to assist in agricultural production; the ZDF is part of the Southern Africa Development Community (SADC) Standby Force and participates in multinational training exercises; it has received training assistance from China and the US
the ZDF traces its roots to the Northern Rhodesia Regiment, which was raised by the British colonial government to fight in World War II; the ZDF was established in 1964 from units of the dissolved Federation of Rhodesia and Nyasaland armed forces; it participated in a number of regional conflicts during the 1970s and 1980s; Zambia actively supported independence movements such as the Union for the Total Liberation of Angola (UNITA), the Zimbabwe African People's Union (ZAPU), the African National Congress of South Africa (ANC), and the South-West Africa People's Organization (SWAPO) (2025)

TRANSNATIONAL ISSUES

Refugees and internally displaced persons: *refugees:* 88,918 (2024 est.)

IDPs: 131,349 (2024 est.)

ZIMBABWE

INTRODUCTION

Background: The hunter-gatherer San people first inhabited the area that eventually became Zimbabwe. Farming communities migrated to the area around A.D. 500 during the Bantu expansion, and Shona-speaking societies began to develop in the Limpopo valley and Zimbabwean highlands around the 9th century. These societies traded with Arab merchants on the Indian Ocean coast and organized under the Kingdom of Mapungubwe in the 11th century. A series of powerful trade-oriented Shona states succeeded Mapungubwe, including the Kingdom of Zimbabwe (ca. 1220-1450), Kingdom of Mutapa (ca. 1450-1760), and the Rozwi Empire. The Rozwi Empire expelled Portuguese colonists from the Zimbabwean plateau, but the Ndebele clan of Zulu King MZILIKAZI eventually conquered the area in

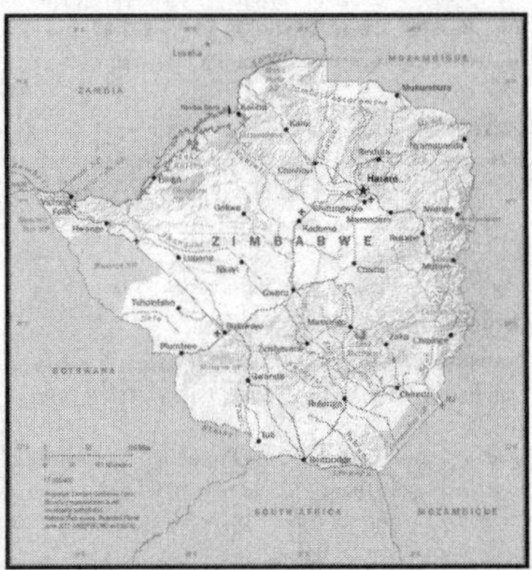

1838 during the era of conflict and population displacement known as the Mfecane.

In the 1880s, colonists arrived with the British South Africa Company (BSAC) and obtained a written concession for mining rights from Ndebele King LOBENGULA. The king later disavowed the concession and accused the BSAC agents of deceit. The BSAC annexed Mashonaland and then conquered Matabeleland during the First Matabele War of 1893-1894, establishing company rule over the territory. In 1923, the UK annexed BSAC holdings south of the Zambezi River, which became the British colony of Southern Rhodesia. The 1930 Land Apportionment Act restricted Black land ownership and established rules that would favor the White minority for decades. A new constitution in 1961 further cemented White minority rule.

In 1965, the government under White Prime Minister Ian SMITH unilaterally declared its independence from the UK. London did not recognize Rhodesia's independence and demanded more voting rights for the Black majority in the country. International diplomacy and an uprising by Black Zimbabweans led to biracial elections in 1979 and independence (as Zimbabwe) in 1980. Robert MUGABE, who led the uprising and became the nation's first prime minister, was the country's only ruler (as president since 1987) from independence until 2017. In the mid-1980s, the government tortured and killed thousands of civilians in a crackdown on dissent known as the Gukurahundi campaign. Economic mismanagement and chaotic implementation of land redistribution policies periodically crippled the economy. General elections in 2002, 2008, and 2013 were severely flawed and widely condemned but allowed MUGABE to remain president. In 2017, Vice President Emmerson MNANGAGWA became president after a military intervention that forced MUGABE to resign, and MNANGAGWA cemented power by sidelining rival Grace MUGABE (Robert MUGABE's wife). In 2018, MNANGAGWA won the presidential election, and he has maintained the government's long-standing practice of violently disrupting protests and politicizing institutions. Economic conditions remain dire under MNANGAGWA.

GEOGRAPHY

Location: Southern Africa, between South Africa and Zambia

Geographic coordinates: 20 00 S, 30 00 E

Map references: Africa

Area: *total:* 390,757 sq km
land: 386,847 sq km
water: 3,910 sq km
comparison ranking: total 62

Area - comparative: about four times the size of Indiana; slightly larger than Montana

Land boundaries: *total:* 3,229 km
border countries (4): Botswana 834 km; Mozambique 1,402 km; South Africa 230 km;
Zambia 763 km

Coastline: 0 km (landlocked)

Maritime claims: none (landlocked)

Climate: tropical; moderated by altitude; rainy season (November to March)

Terrain: mostly high plateau with higher central plateau (high veld); mountains in east

Elevation: *highest point:* Inyangani 2,592 m
lowest point: junction of the Runde and Save Rivers 162 m
mean elevation: 961 m

Natural resources: coal, chromium ore, asbestos, gold, nickel, copper, iron ore, vanadium, lithium, tin, platinum group metals

Land use: *agricultural land:* 39.5% (2022 est.)
arable land: 8.1% (2022 est.)
permanent crops: 0.2% (2022 est.)
permanent pasture: 31.3% (2022 est.)
forest: 44.9% (2022 est.)
other: 15.7% (2022 est.)

Irrigated land: 1,740 sq km (2012)

Major rivers (by length in km): Zambezi (shared with Zambia [s]), Angola, Namibia, Botswana, and Mozambique [m]) - 2,740 km; Limpopo (shared with South Africa [s], Botswana, and Mozambique [m]) - 1,800 km
note: [s] after country name indicates river source; [m] after country name indicates river mouth

Major watersheds (area sq km): Indian Ocean drainage: Zambezi (1,332,412 sq km)

Internal (endorheic basin) drainage: Okavango Basin (863,866 sq km)

Major aquifers: Upper Kalahari-Cuvelai-Upper Zambezi Basin

Population distribution: aside from major urban agglomerations in Harare and Bulawayo, population distribution is fairly even, with slightly greater overall numbers in the eastern half, as shown in this population distribution map

Natural hazards: recurring droughts; floods and severe storms are rare

Geography - note: landlocked; the Zambezi forms a natural river boundary with Zambia; in full flood (February-April), the massive Victoria Falls on the river forms the world's largest curtain of falling water; Lake Kariba on the Zambia-Zimbabwe border forms the world's largest reservoir by volume (180 cu km; 43 cu mi)

PEOPLE AND SOCIETY

Population: *total:* 17,150,352 (2024 est.)
male: 8,343,790
female: 8,806,562
comparison rankings: total 72; male 72; female 72

Nationality: *noun:* Zimbabwean(s)
adjective: Zimbabwean

Ethnic groups: African 99.6% (predominantly Shona; Ndebele is the second largest ethnic group), other (includes Caucasian, Asiatic, mixed race) 0.4% (2022 est.)

Languages: Shona (official, most widely spoken) 80.9%, Ndebele (official, second most widely spoken) 11.5%, English (official, traditionally used for official business) 0.3%, 13 minority languages (official; includes Chewa, Chibarwe, Kalanga, Koisan, Nambya, Ndau, Shangani, sign language, Sotho, Tonga, Tswana, Venda, and Xhosa) 7%, other 0.3% (2022 est.)
note: data represent population by mother tongue

Religions: Apostolic Sect 40.3%, Pentecostal 17%, Protestant 13.8%, other Christian 7.8%, Roman Catholic 6.4%, African traditionalist 5%, other 1.5% (includes Muslim, Jewish, Hindu), none 8.3% (2022 est.)

Age structure: *0-14 years:* 38.3% (male 3,315,075/female 3,254,643)
15-64 years: 57.8% (male 4,758,120/female 5,152,773)
65 years and over: 3.9% (2024 est.) (male 270,595/female 399,146)

Dependency ratios: *total dependency ratio:* 73 (2024 est.)
youth dependency ratio: 66.3 (2024 est.)
elderly dependency ratio: 6.8 (2024 est.)
potential support ratio: 14.8 (2024 est.)

Median age: *total:* 21.2 years (2024 est.)
male: 20.3 years
female: 22 years
comparison ranking: total 194

Population growth rate: 1.91% (2024 est.)
comparison ranking: 44

Birth rate: 28.8 births/1,000 population (2024 est.)
comparison ranking: 29

Death rate: 6.5 deaths/1,000 population (2024 est.)
comparison ranking: 136

Net migration rate: -3.2 migrant(s)/1,000 population (2024 est.)
comparison ranking: 184

Population distribution: aside from major urban agglomerations in Harare and Bulawayo, population distribution is fairly even, with slightly greater overall numbers in the eastern half, as shown in this population distribution map

Urbanization: *urban population:* 32.5% of total population (2023)
rate of urbanization: 2.41% annual rate of change (2020-25 est.)

Major urban areas - population: 1.578 million HARARE (capital) (2023)

Sex ratio: *at birth:* 1.03 male(s)/female
0-14 years: 1.02 male(s)/female
15-64 years: 0.92 male(s)/female
65 years and over: 0.68 male(s)/female
total population: 0.95 male(s)/female (2024 est.)

Mother's mean age at first birth: 20.3 years (2015 est.)
note: data represents median age at first birth among women 25-49

Maternal mortality ratio: 358 deaths/100,000 live births (2023 est.)
comparison ranking: 19

Infant mortality rate: *total:* 33.4 deaths/1,000 live births (2024 est.)
male: 37 deaths/1,000 live births
female: 29.6 deaths/1,000 live births
comparison ranking: total 39

Life expectancy at birth: *total population:* 67.2 years (2024 est.)
male: 65.6 years
female: 68.8 years
comparison ranking: total population 198

Total fertility rate: 3.47 children born/woman (2024 est.)
comparison ranking: 36

Gross reproduction rate: 1.71 (2024 est.)

Drinking water source: *improved: urban:* 92.8% of population (2022 est.)
rural: 47.7% of population (2022 est.)
total: 62.3% of population (2022 est.)
unimproved: urban: 7.2% of population (2022 est.)
rural: 52.3% of population (2022 est.)
total: 37.7% of population (2022 est.)

Health expenditure: 2.8% of GDP (2021)
5.2% of national budget (2022 est.)

Physician density: 0.14 physicians/1,000 population (2023)

Sanitation facility access: *improved: urban:* 97.5% of population (2022 est.)
rural: 50.3% of population (2022 est.)
total: 65.6% of population (2022 est.)
unimproved: urban: 2.5% of population (2022 est.)
rural: 49.7% of population (2022 est.)
total: 34.4% of population (2022 est.)

Obesity - adult prevalence rate: 15.5% (2016)
comparison ranking: 126

Alcohol consumption per capita: *total:* 3.11 liters of pure alcohol (2019 est.)
beer: 1.2 liters of pure alcohol (2019 est.)
wine: 0.05 liters of pure alcohol (2019 est.)
spirits: 0.39 liters of pure alcohol (2019 est.)
other alcohols: 1.47 liters of pure alcohol (2019 est.)
comparison ranking: total 110

Tobacco use: *total:* 8.4% (2025 est.)
male: 17.6% (2025 est.)
female: 0.7% (2025 est.)
comparison ranking: total 139

Children under the age of 5 years underweight: 9.7% (2019)
comparison ranking: 52

Currently married women (ages 15-49): 61.6% (2023 est.)

Child marriage: *women married by age 15:* 5.4% (2019)
women married by age 18: 33.7% (2019)
men married by age 18: 1.9% (2019)

Education expenditure: 0.4% of GDP (2023 est.)
17.9% national budget (2025 est.)
comparison ranking: Education expenditure (% GDP) 199

Literacy: *total population:* 93.2% (2019 est.)
male: 93.1% (2019 est.)
female: 93.4% (2019 est.)

ENVIRONMENT

Environmental issues: deforestation; soil erosion; land degradation; air and water pollution; poaching; toxic waste and heavy metal pollution from mining

International environmental agreements: *party to:* Biodiversity, Climate Change, Climate Change-Kyoto Protocol, Climate Change-Paris Agreement, Comprehensive Nuclear Test Ban, Desertification, Endangered Species, Hazardous Wastes, Law of the Sea, Ozone Layer Protection, Wetlands
signed, but not ratified: none of the selected agreements

Climate: tropical; moderated by altitude; rainy season (November to March)

Urbanization: *urban population:* 32.5% of total population (2023)
rate of urbanization: 2.41% annual rate of change (2020-25 est.)

Carbon dioxide emissions: 12.578 million metric tonnes of CO2 (2023 est.)
from coal and metallurgical coke: 7.629 million metric tonnes of CO2 (2023 est.)
from petroleum and other liquids: 4.949 million metric tonnes of CO2 (2023 est.)
comparison ranking: total emissions 101

Particulate matter emissions: 14.5 micrograms per cubic meter (2019 est.)

Waste and recycling: *municipal solid waste generated annually:* 1.45 million tons (2024 est.)
percent of municipal solid waste recycled: 21.8% (2022 est.)

Total water withdrawal: *municipal:* 547.078 million cubic meters (2022 est.)
industrial: 81.352 million cubic meters (2022 est.)
agricultural: 4.281 billion cubic meters (2022 est.)

Total renewable water resources: 20 billion cubic meters (2022 est.)

GOVERNMENT

Country name: *conventional long form:* Republic of Zimbabwe
conventional short form: Zimbabwe
former: Southern Rhodesia, Rhodesia, Zimbabwe-Rhodesia
etymology: takes its name from the Kingdom of Zimbabwe (13th-15th century) and its capital of Great Zimbabwe, which was built of stone; the name Zimbabwe comes from the Bantu phrase *zimba we bahwe*, meaning "houses of stones;" the former name, Rhodesia, was derived from the name of British colonial administrator Cecil RHODES

Government type: presidential republic

Capital: *name:* Harare
geographic coordinates: 17 49 S, 31 02 E
time difference: UTC+2 (7 hours ahead of Washington, DC, during Standard Time)
etymology: named after a village of Harare at the site of the present capital; the village name derived from a Shona chieftain, NE-HARAWA, whose name meant "he who does not sleep"

Administrative divisions: 8 provinces and 2 cities* with provincial status; Bulawayo*, Harare*, Manicaland, Mashonaland Central, Mashonaland East, Mashonaland West, Masvingo, Matabeleland North, Matabeleland South, Midlands

Legal system: mixed system of English common law, Roman-Dutch civil law, and customary law

Constitution: *history:* previous 1965 (at Rhodesian independence), 1979 (Lancaster House Agreement), 1980 (at Zimbabwean independence); latest final draft completed January 2013, approved by referendum 16 March 2013, approved by Parliament 9 May 2013, effective 22 May 2013
amendment process: proposed by the Senate or by the National Assembly; passage requires two-thirds majority vote by the membership of both houses of Parliament and assent of the president of the republic; amendments to constitutional chapters on fundamental human rights and freedoms and on agricultural lands also require approval by a majority of votes cast in a referendum

International law organization participation: has not submitted an ICJ jurisdiction declaration; non-party state to the ICCt

Citizenship: *citizenship by birth:* no
citizenship by descent only: the father must be a citizen of Zimbabwe; in the case of a child born out of wedlock, the mother must be a citizen
dual citizenship recognized: no
residency requirement for naturalization: 5 years

Suffrage: 18 years of age; universal

Executive branch: *chief of state:* President Emmerson Dambudzo MNANGAGWA (since 4 September 2023)
head of government: Vice President Constantino CHIWENGA (since 11 September 2023)
cabinet: Cabinet appointed by president, responsible to National Assembly
election/appointment process: each presidential candidate nominated with a nomination paper signed by at least 10 registered voters (at least 1 candidate from each province) and directly elected by absolute-majority popular vote in 2 rounds, if needed, for a 5-year term (no term limits); co-vice presidents drawn from party leadership
most recent election date: 23 August 2023
election results: *2023:* Emmerson MNANGAGWA reelected president in first round; percent of vote - Emmerson MNANGAGWA (ZANU-PF) 52.6%, Nelson CHAMISA (MDC-T) 44%, Wilbert MUBAIWA (NPC) 1.2%, other 2.2%
2018: Emmerson MNANGAGWA elected president in first round; percent of vote - Emmerson MNANGAGWA (ZANU-PF) 50.7%, Nelson CHAMISA (MDC-T) 44.4%, Thokozani KHUPE (MDC-N) 0.9%, other 4%
expected date of next election: 2028

Legislative branch: *legislature name:* Parliament
legislative structure: bicameral

Legislative branch - lower chamber: *chamber name:* National Assembly
number of seats: 280 (all directly elected)
electoral system: mixed system
scope of elections: full renewal
term in office: 5 years
most recent election date: 8/23/2023
parties elected and seats per party: ZANU-PF (175); Citizens Coalition for Change (CCC) (104)
percentage of women in chamber: 30.1%
expected date of next election: August 2028
note: 60 seats are reserved for women and 10 additional seats are reserved for candidates aged 21 - 35

Legislative branch - upper chamber: *chamber name:* Senate
number of seats: 80 (60 directly elected; 20 indirectly elected)
electoral system: proportional representation
scope of elections: full renewal
term in office: 5 years
most recent election date: 8/23/2023
parties elected and seats per party: ZANU-PF (33); Citizens Coalition for Change (CCC) (27)
percentage of women in chamber: 44.3%
expected date of next election: August 2028
note: 18 seats are reserved for the National Council Chiefs, and 2 reserved for members with disabilities

Judicial branch: *highest court(s):* Supreme Court (consists of the chief justice and 4 judges); Constitutional Court (consists of the chief and deputy chief justices and 9 judges)
judge selection and term of office: Supreme Court judges appointed by the president on recommendation of

the Judicial Service Commission, an independent body consisting of the chief justice, Public Service Commission chairman, attorney general, and 2-3 members appointed by the president; judges normally serve until age 65 but can elect to serve until age 70; Constitutional Court judge appointment NA; judges serve nonrenewable 15-year terms
subordinate courts: High Court; Labor Court; Administrative Court; regional magistrate courts; customary law courts; special courts

Political parties: Citizens Coalition for Change
Movement for Democratic Change or MDC-T
National People's Congress or NPC
Zimbabwe African National Union-Patriotic Front or ZANU-PF
Zimbabwe African Peoples Union or ZAPU

Diplomatic representation in the US: *chief of mission:* Ambassador (vacant); Chargé d'Affaires Sarah BHOROMA (since 12 November 2024)
chancery: 1608 New Hampshire Avenue NW, Washington, DC 20009
telephone: [1] (202) 332-7100

FAX: [1] (202) 483-9326
email address and website: general@zimembassydc.org
https://zimembassydc.org/

Diplomatic representation from the US: *chief of mission:* Ambassador Pamela M. TREMONT (since August 2024)
embassy: 2 Lorraine Drive, Bluffhill, Harare
mailing address: 2180 Harare Place, Washington DC 20521-2180
telephone: [263] 867-701-1000

FAX: [263] 24-233-4320
email address and website: consularharare@state.gov
https://zw.usembassy.gov/

International organization participation: ACP, AfDB, ATMIS, AU, COMESA, FAO, G-15, G-77, IAEA, IBRD, ICAO, ICRM, IDA, IFAD, IFC, IFRCS, ILO, IMF, IMO, Interpol, IOC, IOM, IPU, ISO, ITSO, ITU, ITUC (NGOs), MIGA, NAM, OPCW, PCA, SADC, UN, UNAMID, UNCTAD, UNESCO, UNIDO, UNISFA, UNMIL, UNMISS, UNOCI, UNSOM, UNWTO, UPU, WCO, WFTU (NGOs), WHO, WIPO, WMO, WTO

Independence: 18 April 1980 (from the UK)

National holiday: Independence Day, 18 April (1980)

Flag: *description:* seven equal horizontal bands of green (top), yellow, red, black, red, yellow, and green, with a white isosceles triangle edged in black based on the left side; in the middle of the triangle, a yellow bird is on top of a five-pointed red star
meaning: the bird represents the long history of the country; white stands for peace, green for agriculture, yellow for mineral wealth, red for the blood shed to achieve independence, and black for the people

National symbol(s): Zimbabwe bird symbol, African fish eagle, flame lily

National color(s): green, yellow, red, black, white

National anthem(s): *title:* "Kalibusiswe Ilizwe leZimbabwe" [Ndebele] "Simudzai Mureza WeZimbabwe" [Shona] (Blessed Be the Land of Zimbabwe)
lyrics/music: Solomon MUTSWAIRO/Fred Lecture CHANGUNDEGA
history: adopted 1994; lyrics in the country's three main languages were written by Zimbabwean poet and academic MUTSWAIRO

National heritage: *total World Heritage Sites:* 5 (3 cultural, 2 natural)
selected World Heritage Site locales: Mana Pools National Park, Sapi, and Chewore Safari Areas (n); Great Zimbabwe National Monument (c); Khami Ruins National Monument (c); Mosi-oa- Tunya/ Victoria Falls (n); Matobo Hills (c)

ECONOMY

Economic overview: low income Sub-Saharan economy; political instability and endemic corruption have prevented reforms and stalled debt restructuring; new Zimbabwe Gold (ZiG) currency latest effort to combat ongoing hyperinflation; reliant on natural resource extraction, agriculture and remittances

Real GDP (purchasing power parity): $57.391 billion (2024 est.)
$56.249 billion (2023 est.)
$53.399 billion (2022 est.)
note: data in 2021 dollars
comparison ranking: 120

Real GDP growth rate: 2% (2024 est.)
5.3% (2023 est.)
6.1% (2022 est.)
note: annual GDP % growth based on constant local currency
comparison ranking: 149

Real GDP per capita: $3,500 (2024 est.)
$3,400 (2023 est.)
$3,300 (2022 est.)
note: data in 2021 dollars
comparison ranking: 189

GDP (official exchange rate): $44.188 billion (2024 est.)
note: data in current dollars at official exchange rate

Inflation rate (consumer prices): 104.7% (2022 est.)
98.5% (2021 est.)
557.2% (2020 est.)
note: annual % change based on consumer prices
comparison ranking: 211

GDP - composition, by sector of origin: *agriculture:* 5.4% (2024 est.)
industry: 31.8% (2024 est.)
services: 55.8% (2024 est.)
note: figures may not total 100% due to non-allocated consumption not captured in sector-reported data
comparison rankings: agriculture 108; industry 44; services 118

GDP - composition, by end use: *household consumption:* 91.5% (2024 est.)
government consumption: 12.5% (2024 est.)
investment in fixed capital: 3.6% (2024 est.)
investment in inventories: 0.9% (2024 est.)
exports of goods and services: 22.1% (2024 est.)
imports of goods and services: -30.6% (2024 est.)
note: figures may not total 100% due to rounding or gaps in data collection

Agricultural products: sugarcane, beef, maize, cabbages, potatoes, tomatoes, milk, onions, bananas, wheat (2023)
note: top ten agricultural products based on tonnage

Industries: mining (coal, gold, platinum, copper, nickel, tin, diamonds, clay, numerous metallic and nonmetallic ores), steel, wood products, cement, chemicals, fertilizer, clothing and footwear, foodstuffs, beverages

Industrial production growth rate: 2.7% (2024 est.)
note: annual % change in industrial value added based on constant local currency
comparison ranking: 88

Labor force: 6.386 million (2024 est.)
note: number of people ages 15 or older who are employed or seeking work
comparison ranking: 74

Unemployment rate: 8.6% (2024 est.)
8.8% (2023 est.)
10.1% (2022 est.)
note: % of labor force seeking employment
comparison ranking: 140

Youth unemployment rate (ages 15-24): *total:* 14% (2024 est.)
male: 12.9% (2024 est.)
female: 15.4% (2024 est.)
note: % of labor force ages 15-24 seeking employment
comparison ranking: total 88

Population below poverty line: 38.3% (2019 est.)
note: % of population with income below national poverty line

Gini Index coefficient - distribution of family income: 50.3 (2020 est.)
note: index (0-100) of income distribution; higher values represent greater inequality comparison ranking: 10

Household income or consumption by percentage share: *lowest 10%:* 2.5% (2017 est.)
highest 10%: 34.8% (2017 est.)
note: % share of income accruing to lowest and highest 10% of population

Remittances: 9.4% of GDP (2023 est.)
9.4% of GDP (2022 est.)
9.4% of GDP (2021 est.)
note: personal transfers and compensation between resident and non-resident individuals/households/entities

Budget: *revenues:* $17 million (2018 est.)
expenditures: $23 million (2018 est.)

Taxes and other revenues: 7.2% (of GDP) (2018 est.)
note: central government tax revenue as a % of GDP
comparison ranking: 142

Current account balance: $133.877 million (2023 est.)
$304.966 million (2022 est.)
$348.215 million (2021 est.)
note: balance of payments - net trade and primary/secondary income in current dollars comparison ranking: 73

Exports: $7.603 billion (2023 est.)
$7.453 billion (2022 est.)
$6.575 billion (2021 est.)
note: balance of payments - exports of goods and services in current dollars
comparison ranking: 126

Exports - partners: UAE 45%, China 18%, South Africa 15%, Mozambique 4%, Hong Kong 2% (2023)
note: top five export partners based on percentage share of exports

Exports - commodities: gold, tobacco, nickel, minerals, diamonds (2023)
note: top five export commodities based on value in dollars

Imports: $10.293 billion (2023 est.)
$9.569 billion (2022 est.)
$8.104 billion (2021 est.)
note: balance of payments - imports of goods and services in current dollars
comparison ranking: 122

Imports - partners: South Africa 37%, China 15%, Bahamas, The 5%, Singapore 5%, UAE 4% (2023)
note: top five import partners based on percentage share of imports

Imports - commodities: refined petroleum, fertilizers, trucks, soybean oil, stone processing machines (2023)
note: top five import commodities based on value in dollars

Reserves of foreign exchange and gold: $484.973 million (2024 est.)
$115.53 million (2023 est.)
$598.622 million (2022 est.)
note: holdings of gold (year-end prices)/foreign exchange/special drawing rights in current dollars
comparison ranking: 161

Debt - external: $6.671 billion (2023 est.)
note: present value of external debt in current US dollars
comparison ranking: 62

Exchange rates: Zimbabwean dollars (ZWD) per US dollar -

Exchange rates: 3,266.332 (2024 est.)
3,509.172 (2023 est.)
374.954 (2022 est.)
88.552 (2021 est.)
51.329 (2020 est.)
note: ongoing hyperinflation rendered Zimbabwean dollar essentially worthless; introduction of Zimbabwe Gold (ZiG) as new currency effective April 2024

ENERGY

Electricity access: *electrification - total population:* 50.1% (2022 est.)
electrification - urban areas: 89%
electrification - rural areas: 33.7%

Electricity: *installed generating capacity:* 2.491 million kW (2023 est.)
consumption: 8.346 billion kWh (2023 est.)
exports: 395 million kWh (2023 est.)
imports: 2.297 billion kWh (2023 est.)
transmission/distribution losses: 1.864 billion kWh (2023 est.)
comparison rankings: installed generating capacity 114; consumption 113; exports 82; imports 65; transmission/distribution losses 121

Electricity generation sources: *fossil fuels:* 32.5% of total installed capacity (2023 est.)
solar: 0.4% of total installed capacity (2023 est.)
hydroelectricity: 65.7% of total installed capacity (2023 est.)
biomass and waste: 1.5% of total installed capacity (2023 est.)

Coal: *production:* 7.968 million metric tons (2023 est.)
consumption: 6.705 million metric tons (2023 est.)
exports: 984,000 metric tons (2023 est.)
imports: 71,000 metric tons (2023 est.)
proven reserves: 502 million metric tons (2023 est.)

Petroleum: *total petroleum production:* 800 bbl/day (2023 est.)
refined petroleum consumption: 34,000 bbl/day (2023 est.)

Energy consumption per capita: 10.855 million Btu/person (2023 est.)
comparison ranking: 147

COMMUNICATIONS

Telephones - fixed lines: *total subscriptions:* 310,000 (2023 est.)
subscriptions per 100 inhabitants: 2 (2023 est.)
comparison ranking: total subscriptions 106

Telephones - mobile cellular: *total subscriptions:* 15 million (2023 est.)
subscriptions per 100 inhabitants: 88 (2022 est.)
comparison ranking: total subscriptions 72

Broadcast media: government owns all local radio and TV stations; foreign shortwave broadcasts and satellite TV available; in rural areas, access to TV broadcasts is extremely limited; analog TV only, no digital service (2017)

Internet country code: .zw

Internet users: *percent of population:* 38% (2023 est.)

Broadband - fixed subscriptions: *total:* 269,000 (2023 est.)
subscriptions per 100 inhabitants: 2 (2023 est.)
comparison ranking: total 116

TRANSPORTATION

Civil aircraft registration country code prefix: Z

Airports: 144 (2025)
comparison ranking: 37

Heliports: 5 (2025)
comparison ranking: 101

Railways: *total:* 3,427 km (2014)
narrow gauge: 3,427 km (2014) 1.067-m gauge (313 km electrified)

MILITARY AND SECURITY

Military and security forces: Zimbabwe Defense Forces (ZDF): Zimbabwe National Army (ZNA), Air Force of Zimbabwe (AFZ)

Ministry of Home Affairs: Zimbabwe Republic Police (2025)

Military expenditures: 0.4% of GDP (2024 est.)
0.3% of GDP (2023 est.)
0.9% of GDP (2022 est.)
1.4% of GDP (2021 est.)
1% of GDP (2020 est.)

Military and security service personnel strengths: approximately 30,000 active Zimbabwe Defense Forces (2025)

Military equipment inventories and acquisitions: the ZDF inventory is comprised mostly of Russian/Soviet-era and Chinese armaments with smaller quantities of older or obsolescent material from countries such as Brazil, France, Italy, South Africa, the UK, and the US; since the early 2010s, Zimbabwe has been under an arms embargo from the EU, as well as targeted sanctions from Australia, Canada, New Zealand, the UK, and the US (2024)

Military service age and obligation: 18-22 years of age for voluntary military service for men and women (18-24 for officer cadets; 18-30 for technical/specialist personnel); no conscription (2023)

Military - note: the primary responsibilities of the Zimbabwe Defense Forces (ZDF) are protecting the country's sovereignty and territory and securing its borders; it also has a role in domestic security and socio-economic development projects and has continued to be active in the country's politics since the 2017 military-assisted political transition; the ZDF is part of the Southern Africa Development Community (SADC) Standby Force and provided troops for the SADC military deployment to Mozambique from 2021-2024; Zimbabwe has defense ties with China and Russia
the ZDF was formed after independence from the former Rhodesian Army and the two guerrilla forces that opposed it during the Rhodesian Civil War (aka "Bush War") of the 1970s, the Zimbabwe African National Liberation Army (ZANLA) and the Zimbabwe People's Revolutionary Army (ZIPRA); the ZDF intervened in the Mozambique Civil War (1983-1992), the Democratic Republic of Congo during the Second Congo War (1998-2003), and the Angolan Civil War (1975-2002) during the late 1990s (2025)

SPACE

Space agency/agencies: Zimbabwe National Geospatial and Space Agency (ZINGSA; established in 2019 and officially launched in 2021) (2025)
note: ZINGSA is under the Ministry of Higher and Tertiary Education, Science, and Technology Development

Space program overview: has a nascent program with the goal of utilizing space technologies in economic development, including remote sensing capabilities to assist with monitoring or managing agriculture and food security, climate change, disease outbreaks, environmental hazards and disasters, and natural resources, as well as weather forecasting; has cooperated with Japan and Russia (2025)
note: further details about the key activities, programs, and milestones of the country's space program, as well as government spending estimates on the space sector, appear in the Space Programs reference guide

TRANSNATIONAL ISSUES

Refugees and internally displaced persons: *refugees:* 22,432 (2024 est.)

IDPs: 32,675 (2024 est.)

Trafficking in persons: *tier rating:* Tier 2 Watch List—the government did not demonstrate overall increasing efforts to eliminate trafficking compared with the previous reporting period, therefore Zimbabwe remained on Tier 2 Watch List for the second consecutive year; for more details, go to: https://www.state.gov/reports/2025-trafficking-in-persons-report/zimbabwe/

APPENDIX A: ABBREVIATIONS

ABEDA	Arab Bank for Economic Development in Africa
ACP Group	African, Caribbean, and Pacific Group of States
ADB	Asian Development Bank
AfDB	African Development Bank
AFESD	Arab Fund for Economic and Social Development
AG	Australia Group
Air Pollution	Convention on Long-Range Transboundary Air Pollution
Air Pollution-Nitrogen Oxides	Protocol to the 1979 Convention on Long-Range Transboundary Air Pollution Concerning the Control of Emissions of Nitrogen Oxides or Their Transboundary Fluxes
Air Pollution-Persistent Organic Pollutants	Protocol to the 1979 Convention on Long-Range Transboundary Air Pollution on Persistent Organic Pollutants
Air Pollution-Sulphur 85	Protocol to the 1979 Convention on Long-Range Transboundary Air Pollution on the Reduction of Sulphur Emissions or Their Transboundary Fluxes by at Least 30%
Air Pollution-Sulphur 94	Protocol to the 1979 Convention on Long-Range Transboundary Air Pollution on Further Reduction of Sulphur Emissions
Air Pollution-Volatile Organic Compounds	Protocol to the 1979 Convention on Long-Range Transboundary Air Pollution Concerning the Control of Emissions of Volatile Organic Compounds or Their Transboundary Fluxes
AMF	Arab Monetary Fund
AMISOM	African Union Mission in Somalia
AMU	Arab Maghreb Union
Antarctic Marine Living Resources	Convention on the Conservation of Antarctic Marine Living Resources
Antarctic Seals	Convention for the Conservation of Antarctic Seals
Antarctic-Environmental Protocol	Protocol on Environmental Protection to the Antarctic Treaty
ANZUS	Australia-New Zealand-United States Security Treaty
AOSIS	Alliance of Small Island States
APEC	Asia-Pacific Economic Cooperation
Arabsat	Arab Satellite Communications Organization
ARF	ASEAN Regional Forum
ASEAN	Association of Southeast Asian Nations
ATMIS	African Union Transition Mission in Somalia
AU	African Union
Autodin	Automatic Digital Network
BA	Baltic Assembly
bbl/day	barrels per day
BCIE	Central American Bank for Economic Integration
BDEAC	Central African States Development Bank
Benelux	Benelux Union
BGN	United States Board on Geographic Names
BIMSTEC	Bay of Bengal Initiative for Multi-sectoral Technical and Economic Cooperation
BIS	Bank for International Settlements
BRICS	(Brazil, Russia, India, China, and South Africa)
BSEC	Black Sea Economic Cooperation Zone
°C	degree(s) Celsius, degree(s) centigrade
C	Commonwealth
CACM	Central American Common Market
CAEU	Council of Arab Economic Unity
CAN	Andean Community
Caricom	Caribbean Community and Common Market
CBSS	Council of the Baltic Sea States
CCC	Customs Cooperation Council
CD	Community of Democracies
CDB	Caribbean Development Bank
CE	Council of Europe
CEI	Central European Initiative
CELAC	Community of Latin America and Caribbean States
CEMA	Council for Mutual Economic Assistance
CEMAC	Economic and Monetary Community of Central Africa
CEPGL	Economic Community of the Great Lakes Countries
CERN	European Organization for Nuclear Research

CIA	Central Intelligence Agency
CICA	Conference of Interaction and Confidence-Building Measures in Asia
c.i.f.	cost, insurance, and freight
CIS	Commonwealth of Independent States
CITES	see Endangered Species
Climate Change	United Nations Framework Convention on Climate Change
Climate Change-Kyoto Protocol	Kyoto Protocol to the United Nations Framework Convention on Climate Change
COCOM	Coordinating Committee on Export Controls
COMESA	Common Market for Eastern and Southern Africa
Comsat	Communications Satellite Corporation
CP	Colombo Plan
CPLP	Comunidade dos Paises de Lingua Portuguesa
CSN	South American Community of Nations became UNASUL - Union of South American Nations
CSTO	Collective Security Treaty Organization
CTBTO	Preparatory Commission for the Nuclear-Test-Ban Treaty Organization
CY	calendar year
D-8	Developing Eight
Desertification	United Nations Convention to Combat Desertification in Those Countries Experiencing Serious Drought and/or Desertification, Particularly in Africa
DIA	United States Defense Intelligence Agency
DST	daylight savings time
EAC	East African Community
EADB	East African Development Bank
EAEC	Eurasian Economic Community
EAPC	Euro-Atlantic Partnership Council
EAS	East Asia Summit
EBRD	European Bank for Reconstruction and Development
EC	European Community OR European Commission
ECA	Economic Commission for Africa
ECB	European Central Bank
ECE	Economic Commission for Europe
ECLAC	Economic Commission for Latin America and the Caribbean
ECO	Economic Cooperation Organization
ECOMIG	ECOWAS Mission in The Gambia
ECOWAS	Economic Community of West African States
ECSC	European Coal and Steel Community OR Eastern Caribbean Supreme Court
EEC	European Economic Community
EEZ	exclusive economic zone
EFTA	European Free Trade Association
EIB	European Investment Bank
EITI	Extractive Industry Transparency Initiative
EMU	European Monetary Union
Endangered Species	Convention on the International Trade in Endangered Species of Wild Flora and Fauna (CITES)
Entente	Council of the Entente
Environmental Modification	Convention on the Prohibition of Military or Any Other Hostile Use of Environmental Modification Techniques
ESA	European Space Agency
ESCAP	Economic and Social Commission for Asia and the Pacific
est.	estimate
EU	European Union
EUFOR	European Union Force in Bosnia and Herzegovina
Euratom	European Atomic Energy Community
Eutelsat	European Telecommunications Satellite Organization
EUTM	European Union Training Mission (military force deployed to provide advice, operational training, and education to security forces in Bosnia-Herzegovina, Central African Republic, Mali, and Somalia)
°F	degree(s) Fahrenheit
FAO	Food and Agriculture Organization
FATF	Financial Action Task Force
f.o.b.	free on board

ft	foot
FttP	FttP: Fiber to the Home (FttP) is a pure fiber-optic cable connection running from an Internet Service Provider (ISP) directly to the user's home or business
FY	fiscal year
G-10	Group of 10
G-11	Group of 11
G-15	Group of 15
G-20	Group of 20
G-24	Group of 24
G-5	Group of 5
G-6	Group of 6
G-7	Group of 7
G-77	Group of 77
GCC	Gulf Cooperation Council
GCN	Global Caribbean Network
GCTU	General Confederation of Trade Unions
GDP	gross domestic product
GMT	Greenwich Mean Time
GNP	gross national product
GSM	global system for mobile cellular communications
GUAM	Organization for Democracy and Economic Development; acronym for member states - Georgia, Ukraine, Azerbaijan, Moldova
Hazardous Wastes	Basel Convention on the Control of Transboundary Movements of Hazardous Wastes and Their Disposal
IADB	Inter-American Development Bank
IAEA	International Atomic Energy Agency
IANA	Internet Assigned Numbers Authority
IBRD	International Bank for Reconstruction and Development (World Bank)
ICAO	International Civil Aviation Organization
ICC	International Chamber of Commerce
ICCt	International Criminal Court
ICJ	International Court of Justice (World Court)
ICRC	International Committee of the Red Cross
ICRM	International Red Cross and Red Crescent Movement
ICSID	International Center for Settlement of Investment Disputes
IDA	International Development Association
IDB	Islamic Development Bank
IDP	Internally Displaced Person
IEA	International Energy Agency
IFAD	International Fund for Agricultural Development
IFC	International Finance Corporation
IFRCS	International Federation of Red Cross and Red Crescent Societies
IGAD	Inter-Governmental Authority on Development
IHO	International Hydrographic Organization
ILO	International Labor Organization
IMF	International Monetary Fund
IMO	International Maritime Organization
IMSO	International Mobile Satellite Organization
in	inch
Inmarsat	International Maritime Satellite Organization
InOC	Indian Ocean Commission
Intelsat	International Telecommunications Satellite Organization
Interpol	International Criminal Police Organization
Intersputnik	International Organization of Space Communications
IOC	International Olympic Committee
IOM	International Organization for Migration
IPU	Inter-Parliamentary Union
ISO	International Organization for Standardization
ISP	Internet Service Provider
ITC	International Trade Center

ITSO International Telecommunications Satellite Organization
ITU International Telecommunication Union
ITUC International Trade Union Confederation, the successor to ICFTU (International Confederation of Free Trade Unions) and the WCL (World Confederation of Labor)
kg kilogram
kHz kilohertz
km kilometer
kW kilowatt
kWh kilowatt-hour
LAES Latin American and Caribbean Economic System
LAIA Latin American Integration Association
LAS League of Arab States
Law of the Sea United Nations Convention on the Law of the Sea (LOS)
LNG liquefied natural gas
LOS see Law of the Sea
m meter
Marine Dumping Convention on the Prevention of Marine Pollution by Dumping Wastes and Other Matter
Marine Life Conservation Convention on Fishing and Conservation of Living Resources of the High Seas
Medarabtel Middle East Telecommunications Project of the International Telecommunications Union
Mercosur Southern Cone Common Market
MFO Multinational Force & Observers--Sinai
MHz megahertz
mi mile
MIGA Multilateral Investment Guarantee Agency
MINURCAT United Nations Mission in the Central African Republic and Chad
MINURSO United Nations Mission for the Referendum in Western Sahara
MINUSCA United Nations Multidimensional Integrated Stabilization Mission in the Central African Republic
MINUSMA United Nations Multidimensional Integrated Stabilization Mission in Mali
MINUSTAH United Nations Stabilization Mission in Haiti
mm millimeter
MONUSCO United Nations Organization Stabilization Mission in the Democratic Republic of the Congo
mt metric ton
Mt. Mount
NA not available
NAFTA North American Free Trade Agreement
NAM Nonaligned Movement
NATO North Atlantic Treaty Organization
NC Nordic Council
NEA Nuclear Energy Agency
NEGL negligible
NGA National Geospatial-Intelligence Agency
NGO nongovernmental organization
NIB Nordic Investment Bank
nm nautical mile
NSG Nuclear Suppliers Group
Nuclear Test Ban Treaty Banning Nuclear Weapons Tests in the Atmosphere, in Outer Space, and Under Water
OAPEC Organization of Arab Petroleum Exporting Countries
OAS Organization of American States
OAU Organization of African Unity; see African Union
OECD Organization for Economic Cooperation and Development
OECS Organization of Eastern Caribbean States
OHCHR Office of the United Nations High Commissioner for Human Rights
OIC Organization of the Islamic Conference
OIF International Organization of the French-speaking World
OPANAL Agency for the Prohibition of Nuclear Weapons in Latin America and the Caribbean
OPCW Organization for the Prohibition of Chemical Weapons
OPEC Organization of Petroleum Exporting Countries
OSCE Organization for Security and Cooperation in Europe
Ozone Layer Protection Montreal Protocol on Substances That Deplete the Ozone Layer
PCA Permanent Court of Arbitration

PFP	Partnership for Peace
PIF	Pacific Islands Forum
PPP	purchasing power parity
Quad	Quadrilateral Security Dialogue
RG	Rio Group
SAARC	South Asian Association for Regional Cooperation
SACEP	South Asia Co-operative Environment Program
SACU	Southern African Customs Union
SADC	Southern African Development Community
SAFE	South African Far East Cable
SCO	Shanghai Cooperation Organization
SELEC	Convention of the Southeast European Law Enforcement Centers
SHF	super-high-frequency
Ship Pollution	Protocol of 1978 Relating to the International Convention for the Prevention of Pollution From Ships, 1973 (MARPOL)
SICA	Central American Integration System
Sparteca	South Pacific Regional Trade and Economic Cooperation Agreement
SPC	Secretariat of the Pacific Communities
SPF	South Pacific Forum
sq km	square kilometer
sq mi	square mile
TAT	Trans-Atlantic Telephone
Tropical Timber 83	International Tropical Timber Agreement, 1983
Tropical Timber 94	International Tropical Timber Agreement, 1994
UDEAC	Central African Customs and Economic Union
UHF	ultra-high-frequency
UN	United Nations
UNAMA	United Nations Assistance Mission in Afghanistan
UNAMID	African Union/United Nations Hybrid Operation in Darfur
UNASUR	Union of South American Nations
UNCLOS	United Nations Convention on the Law of the Sea, also known as LOS
UNCTAD	United Nations Conference on Trade and Development
UNDCP	United Nations Drug Control Program
UNDEF	United Nations Democracy Fund
UNDOF	United Nations Disengagement Observer Force
UNDP	United Nations Development Program
UNEP	United Nations Environment Program
UNESCO	United Nations Educational, Scientific, and Cultural Organization
UNFICYP	United Nations Peacekeeping Force in Cyprus
UNFPA	United Nations Population Fund
UNHCR	United Nations High Commissioner for Refugees
UNHRC	United Nations Human Rights Council
UNICEF	United Nations Children's Fund
UNIDO	United Nations Industrial Development Organization
UNIFIL	United Nations Interim Force in Lebanon
UNISFA	United Nations Interim Force for Abyei
UNITAR	United Nations Institute for Training and Research
UNMIK	United Nations Interim Administration Mission in Kosovo
UNMIL	United Nations Mission in Liberia
UNMIS	United Nations Mission in the Sudan
UNMISS	United Nations Mission in South Sudan
UNMIT	United Nations Integrated Mission in Timor-Leste
UNMOGIP	United Nations Military Observer Group in India and Pakistan
UNOCI	United Nations Operation in Cote d'Ivoire
UNODC	United Nations Office of Drugs and Crime
UNOPS	United Nations Office of Project Services
UNRWA	United Nations Relief and Works Agency for Palestine Refugees in the Near East
UNSC	United Nations Security Council
UNSOM	United Nations Assistance Mission in Somalia
UNTSO	United Nations Truce Supervision Organization
UNWTO	World Tourism Organization

UPU	Universal Postal Union
USG	United States Government
USSR	Union of Soviet Socialist Republics (Soviet Union); used for information dated before 25 December 1991
UTC	Coordinated Universal Time
VHF	very-high-frequency
VSAT	very small aperture terminal
WADB	West African Development Bank
WAEMU	West African Economic and Monetary Union
WCL	World Confederation of Labor
WCO	World Customs Organization
Wetlands	Convention on Wetlands of International Importance Especially As Waterfowl Habitat
WEU	Western European Union
WFP	World Food Program
WFTU	World Federation of Trade Unions
Whaling	International Convention for the Regulation of Whaling
WHO	World Health Organization
WIPO	World Intellectual Property Organization
WMO	World Meteorological Organization
WTO	World Trade Organization

APPENDIX B: INTERNATIONAL ORGANIZATIONS AND GROUPS

African Development Bank Group (AfDB)
address – Avenue Joseph Anoma, 01 BP 1387 Abidjan 01, Côte d'Ivoire
phone – 225 2720263900
website – www.afdb.org/en
established – 14 August 1963
effective – 10 September 1964
aim – help reduce poverty, improve living conditions for Africans, and mobilize resources for the continent's economic and social development
regional members – (54) Algeria, Angola, Benin, Botswana, Burkina Faso, Burundi, Cabo Verde, Cameroon, Central African Republic, Chad, Comoros, Democratic Republic of the Congo, Republic of the Congo, Cote d'Ivoire, Djibouti, Egypt, Equatorial Guinea, Eritrea, Eswatini, Ethiopia, Gabon, The Gambia, Ghana, Guinea, Guinea-Bissau, Kenya, Lesotho, Liberia, Libya, Madagascar, Malawi, Mali, Mauritania, Mauritius, Morocco, Mozambique, Namibia, Niger, Nigeria, Rwanda, Sao Tome and Principe, Senegal, Seychelles, Sierra Leone, Somalia, South Africa, South Sudan, Sudan, Tanzania, Togo, Tunisia, Uganda, Zambia, Zimbabwe
non-regional members – (28) Argentina, Austria, Belgium, Brazil, Canada, China, Denmark, Finland, France, Germany, India, Ireland, Italy, Japan, South Korea, Kuwait, Luxembourg, Netherlands, Norway, Portugal, Saudi Arabia, Spain, Sweden, Switzerland, Turkey (Turkiye), UAE (ADF member only), UK, US

African Union (AU)
note – replaces Organization of African Unity (OAU)
address – P.O. Box 3243, Roosvelt Street W21K19
Addis Ababa, Ethiopia
phone – 251 11 551 77 00
fax – 251 11 551 78 44
website – https://au.int/
established – 9 July 2002
aim – to achieve greater unity among African States; to defend states' integrity and independence; to accelerate political, social, and economic integration; to encourage international cooperation; to promote democratic principles and institutions
members – (55) Algeria, Angola, Benin, Botswana, Burkina Faso (suspended), Burundi, Cabo Verde, Cameroon, Central African Republic, Chad, Comoros, Democratic Republic of the Congo, Republic of the Congo, Cote d'Ivoire, Djibouti, Egypt, Equatorial Guinea, Eritrea, Eswatini, Ethiopia, Gabon (suspended), The Gambia, Ghana, Guinea (suspended), Guinea-Bissau, Kenya, Lesotho, Liberia, Libya, Madagascar, Malawi, Mali (suspended), Mauritania, Mauritius, Morocco, Mozambique, Namibia, Niger (suspended), Nigeria, Rwanda, Sahrawi Arab Democratic Republic (Western Sahara), Sao Tome and Principe, Senegal, Seychelles, Sierra Leone, Somalia, South Africa, South Sudan, Sudan (suspended), Tanzania, Togo, Tunisia, Uganda, Zambia, Zimbabwe

Agency for the Prohibition of Nuclear Weapons in Latin America and the Caribbean (OPANAL)
note – acronym from Organismo para la Proscripcion de las Armas Nucleares en la America Latina y el Caribe (OPANAL)
address – Milton #61, Colonia Anzures, Alcaldía Miguel Hidalgo
P. C. 11590, Mexico City, Mexico
phone – (52) 55 5255 2914
fax – (52) 55 5255 3748
email – info@opanal.org
website – https://www.opanal.org
established – 14 February 1967 under the Treaty of Tlatelolco
aim – maintain a nuclear-weapons-free zone in Latin America and the Caribbean and encourage peaceful uses of atomic energy and the global prohibition of nuclear weapons
members – (33) Antigua and Barbuda, Argentina, The Bahamas, Barbados, Belize, Bolivia, Brazil, Chile, Colombia, Costa Rica, Cuba, Dominica, Dominican Republic, Ecuador, El Salvador, Grenada, Guatemala, Guyana, Haiti, Honduras, Jamaica, Mexico, Nicaragua, Panama, Paraguay, Peru, Saint Kitts and Nevis, Saint Lucia, Saint Vincent and the Grenadines, Suriname, Trinidad and Tobago, Uruguay, Venezuela

Andean Community (CAN)
note – formerly known as the Andean Group (AG) and the Andean Common Market (Ancom)
address – Av. Paseo de la República 3895, San Isidro, Lima, Perú
phone – (511) 7016400
email – correspondencia@comunidadandina.org
website – http://www.comunidadandina.org/
established – 26 May 1969; present name established 1 October 1992
effective – 16 October 1969
aim – to achieve an integral, balanced, and autonomous development, through Andean integration, with projection towards a South American and Latin American integration
members – (4) Bolivia, Colombia, Ecuador, Peru
associate members – (5) Argentina, Brazil, Chile, Paraguay, Uruguay
observers – (2) Morocco, Spain, Turkey

Arab Bank for Economic Development in Africa (ABEDA)
note – also known as Banque Arabe de Développement Economique en Afrique (BADEA)
address – P. O. Box 2640 Khartoum - Sudan
phone – 249-1-83773646 /83773709
fax – 249-1-83770600/83770498
email – badea@badea.org
website – https://www.badea.org/

established – 18 February 1974
effective – 16 September 1974
aim – to strengthen economic, financial, and technical cooperation between Arab and African regions
members – (17) Algeria, Bahrain, Egypt, Iraq, Jordan, Kuwait, Lebanon, Libya, Mauritania, Morocco, Oman, Qatar, Saudi Arabia, Sudan, Syria, Tunisia, UAE; plus the Palestine Liberation Organization (not included in member count); note - these are all the members of the Arab League, excluding Comoros, Djibouti, Somalia, Yemen

Arab Fund for Economic and Social Development (AFESD)
address – P.O. Box 21923 SAFAT, 13080 Kuwait, State of Kuwait
phone – (965) 2495 9000
fax – (965) 249 593 90/91/92
email – HQ@ARABFUND.ORG
website – https://www.arabfund.org/
established – 16 May 1968
aim – to promote economic and social development projects in Arab countries
members – (21) Algeria, Bahrain, Comoros, Djibouti, Egypt, Iraq, Jordan, Kuwait, Lebanon, Libya, Mauritania, Morocco, Oman, Qatar, Saudi Arabia, Somalia, Sudan, Syria, Tunisia, UAE, Yemen; plus the Palestine Liberation Organization (not included in the member count)

Arab Maghreb Union (AMU)
address – 73, Rue Tensift, Agdal Rabat, Morocco
phone – 212 537 68 13 74/73/72/71
fax – 212 537 68 13 77
email – Sg.uma@maghrebarabe.org
website – https://maghrebarabe.org/
established – 17 February 1989
aim – to promote cooperation and integration among the Arab states of northern Africa
members – (5) Algeria, Libya, Mauritania, Morocco, Tunisia

Arab Monetary Fund (AMF)
address – Arab Monetary AMF Building, Corniche Street, Abu Dhabi, United Arab Emirates
phone – (971) (2) 6171400
fax – (971) (2) 6326454
website – https://www.amf.org.ae/en
established – 27 April 1976
effective – 2 February 1977
aim – to promote Arab cooperation, development, and integration in monetary and economic affairs
members – (21) Algeria, Bahrain, Comoros, Djibouti, Egypt, Iraq, Jordan, Kuwait, Lebanon, Libya, Mauritania, Morocco, Oman, Qatar, Saudi Arabia, Somalia, Sudan, Syria, Tunisia, UAE, Yemen; plus the Palestine Liberation Organization (not included in the member count)

Arctic Council
address – Arctic Council Secretariat, Fram Centre, Postboks 6606, Stakkevollan, 9296 Tromsø, Norway
email – acs@arctic-council.org
website – https://arctic-council.org/
established – 19 September 1996
aim – to address the common concerns and challenges faced by Arctic governments and the people of the Arctic; to protect the Arctic environment
members – (8) Canada, Denmark (Greenland, Faroe Islands), Finland, Iceland, Norway, Russia, Sweden, US
permanent participants – (6) Aleut International Association, Arctic Athabaskan Council, Gwich'in Council International, Inuit Circumpolar Conference, Russian Association of Indigenous People of the North, Saami Council
observers – (13) China, France, Germany, India, Italy, Japan, Netherlands, Poland, Singapore, South Korea, Spain, Switzerland, UK

ASEAN Regional Forum (ARF)
address – ARF Unit, ASEAN Secretariat, 70A Jalan Sisingamangaraja, Jakarta, Indonesia 12110
phone – (6221) 7262991; 7243372
fax – (6221) 7398234; 7243504
email – ARFUnit@asean.org
website – https://aseanregionalforum.asean.org
established – 25 July 1994
aim – to foster constructive dialogue and consultation on political and security issues of common interest and make significant contributions to efforts towards confidence-building and preventive diplomacy in the Asia-Pacific region
members – (27) Australia, Bangladesh, Brunei, Burma, Cambodia, Canada, China, EU, India, Indonesia, Japan, North Korea, South Korea, Laos, Malaysia, Mongolia, New Zealand, Pakistan, Papua New Guinea, Philippines, Russia, Singapore, Sri Lanka, Thailand, Timor-Leste, US, Vietnam

Asian Development Bank (ADB)
address – 6 ADB Avenue, Mandaluyong City 1550, Metro Manila, Philippines
phone – 63 2 8632 4444
fax – 63 2 8636 2444
website – https://www.adb.org/
established – 19 December 1966
aim – to achieve a prosperous, inclusive, resilient, and sustainable Asia and the Pacific, while sustaining efforts to eradicate extreme poverty
members – (50) Afghanistan, Armenia, Australia, Azerbaijan, Bangladesh, Bhutan, Brunei, Burma, Cambodia, China, Cook Islands, Fiji, Georgia, Hong Kong, India, Indonesia, Japan, Kazakhstan, Kiribati, South Korea, Kyrgyzstan, Laos, Malaysia, Maldives, Marshall Islands, Federated States of Micronesia, Mongolia, Nauru, Nepal, NZ, Niue, Pakistan, Palau, Papua New Guinea, Philippines, Samoa, Singapore, Solomon Islands, Sri Lanka, Taiwan, Tajikistan, Thailand, Timor-Leste, Tonga, Turkmenistan, Tuvalu, Uzbekistan, Vanuatu, Vietnam

non-regional members – (19) Austria, Belgium, Canada, Denmark, Finland, France, Germany, Ireland, Israel, Italy, Luxembourg, Netherlands, Norway, Portugal, Spain, Sweden, Switzerland, United Kingdom, United States

Asian Infrastructure Investment Bank (AIIB)

address – Tower A, Asia Financial Center, No.1 Tianchen East Road, Chaoyang District, Beijing 100101
phone – 86-10-8358-0000
fax – 86 (0)10-8358-0920
email – information@aiib.org
website – https://www.aiib.org/en/index.html
established – January 2016
aim – to improve social and economic outcomes in Asia
regional members (including prospective members) – (52) Afghanistan, Australia, Azerbaijan, Bahrain, Bangladesh, Brunei, Burma, Cambodia, China, Cook Islands, Cyprus, Fiji, Georgia, Hong Kong, India, Indonesia, Iran, Iraq, Israel, Jordan, Kazakhstan, Kuwait, Kyrgyzstan, Laos, Malaysia, Maldives, Mongolia, Nauru, Nepal, New Zealand, Oman, Pakistan, Papua New Guinea, Philippines, Qatar, Russia, Samoa, Saudi Arabia, Singapore, Solomon Islands, South Korea, Sri Lanka, Tajikistan, Thailand, Timor-Leste, Tonga, Turkey, UAE, Uzbekistan, Vanuatu, Vietnam; prospective- Lebanon
non-regional members (including prospective members) – (59) Algeria, Argentina, Austria, Belarus, Belgium, Benin, Brazil, Canada, Chile, Cote d'Ivoire, Croatia, Denmark, Ecuador, Egypt, Ethiopia, Finland, France, Germany, Ghana, Greece, Guinea, Hungary, Iceland, Ireland, Italy, Liberia, Luxembourg, Madagascar, Malta, Mauritania, Morocco, Netherlands, Norway, Peru, Poland, Portugal, Romania, Rwanda, Serbia, South Africa, Spain, Sudan, Sweden, Switzerland, Tanzania, Togo, Tunisia, United Kingdom, Uruguay; prospective - Bolivia, Colombia, Nigeria, Senegal, Venezuela

Asia-Pacific Economic Cooperation (APEC)

address – 35 Heng Mui Keng Terrace, Singapore 119616
phone – 65 6891 9600
fax – 65 6891 9690
email – info@apec.org
website – https://www.apec.org/
established – 7 November 1989
aim – to build a dynamic and harmonious Asia-Pacific community by championing free and open trade and investment, promoting and accelerating regional economic integration, encouraging economic and technical cooperation, enhancing human security, and facilitating a favorable and sustainable business environment
members – (21) Australia, Brunei, Canada, Chile, China, Hong Kong, Indonesia, Japan, Malaysia, Mexico, New Zealand, Papua New Guinea, Peru, Philippines, Russia, Singapore, South Korea, Taiwan, Thailand, US, Vietnam
observers – (3) Association of Southeast Asian Nations, Pacific Economic Cooperation Council, Pacific Islands Forum Secretariat

Association of Caribbean States (ACS)

address – 5-7 Sweet Briar Road, St. Clair, P.O. Box 660, Port of Spain, Trinidad and Tobago, West Indies
phone – 868 622 9575
fax – 868 622 1653
email – communications@acs-aec.org
website – www.acs-aec.org
established – 24 July 1994
aim – enhance political dialogue that allows members the opportunity to identify areas of common interest and concern that may be addressed at the regional level, and the solutions that can be found through cooperation
members – (25) Antigua and Barbuda, The Bahamas, Barbados, Belize, Colombia, Costa Rica, Cuba, Dominica, Dominican Republic, El Salvador, Grenada, Guatemala, Guyana, Haiti, Honduras, Jamaica, Mexico, Nicaragua, Panama, Saint Kitts and Nevis, Saint Lucia, Saint Vincent and the Grenadines, Suriname, Trinidad and Tobago, Venezuela
associate members – (10) Aruba, Bonaire, British Virgin Islands, Curacao, French Guiana, Guadeloupe, Martinique, Monserrat, Saba, Saint Barthelemy, Saint Martin, Sint Maarten, Sint Eustatius

Association of Southeast Asian Nations (ASEAN)

address – 70A Jalan Sisingamangaraja, Jakarta 12110
phone – (+6221)7262991, 7243372
fax – (+6221)7398234, 7243504
email – public@asean.org
website – https://asean.org/
established – 8 August 1967
aim – to encourage regional economic, social, and cultural cooperation among the non-Communist countries of Southeast Asia
members – (11) Brunei, Burma, Cambodia, Indonesia, Laos, Malaysia, Philippines, Singapore, Thailand, Timor-Leste, Vietnam
dialogue partners – (11) Australia, Canada, China, EU, India, Japan, South Korea, NZ, Russia, UK, US
observer – (1) Papua New Guinea

Australia Group (AG)

address – RG Casey Building, John McEwen Crescent, BARTON ACT 0221, Australia
phone – 61 2 6261 9399
fax – 61 2 6261 2151
email – wais_dfat@bigpond.com
website – https://www.dfat.gov.au/publications/minisite/theaustraliagroupnet/site/en/index.html
established – June 1985
aim – to consult on and coordinate export controls related to chemical and biological weapons

members – (43) Argentina, Australia, Austria, Belgium, Bulgaria, Canada, Croatia, Cyprus, Czechia, Denmark, Estonia, European Union, Finland, France, Germany, Greece, Hungary, Iceland, India, Ireland, Italy, Japan, South Korea, Latvia, Lithuania, Luxembourg, Malta, Mexico, Netherlands, New Zealand, Norway, Poland, Portugal, Romania, Slovakia, Slovenia, Spain, Sweden, Switzerland, Turkey (Turkiye), Ukraine, United Kingdom, United States

Baltic Assembly (BA)
address – Citadeles Street 2-616, Riga LV-1010, Latvia
phone – 371 67225178
website – https://www.baltasam.org/
established – 12 May 1990
effective – 8 November 1991
aim – to thoroughly discuss various cooperation issues between Baltic states
members – (3) Estonia, Latvia, Lithuania

Bank for International Settlements (BIS)
address – Centralbahnplatz 2, 4051 Basel, Switzerland
phone – (+41 61) 280 8080
fax – (+41 61) 280 9100 and (+41 61) 280 8100
website – https://www.bis.org/
established – 20 January 1930
effective – 17 March 1930
aim – to promote cooperation among central banks in international financial settlements
members – (63) Algeria, Argentina, Australia, Austria, Belgium, Bosnia and Herzegovina, Brazil, Bulgaria, Canada, Chile, China, Colombia, Croatia, Czechia, Denmark, Estonia, European Central Bank, Finland, France, Germany, Greece, Hong Kong, Hungary, Iceland, India, Indonesia, Ireland, Israel, Italy, Japan, South Korea, Kuwait, Latvia, Lithuania, Luxembourg, Malaysia, Mexico, Morocco, Netherlands, NZ, North Macedonia, Norway, Peru, Philippines, Poland, Portugal, Romania, Russia, Saudi Arabia, Serbia, Singapore, Slovakia, Slovenia, South Africa, Spain, Sweden, Switzerland, Thailand, Turkey (Turkiye), UAE, United Kingdom, United States, Vietnam; note - Montenegro has a separate central bank; its links with BIS are currently under review

Bay of Bengal Initiative for Multi-Sectoral Technical and Economic Cooperation (BIMSTEC)
address – House No-N.W.(I)-06, Road No-53,
Gulshan-02, Dhaka-1212, Bangladesh
phone – 880-2222290096-98
fax – 880-2222287565
email – communications@bimstec.org
website – https://bimstec.org/
established – 6 June 1997
aim – to foster socio-economic cooperation among members
members – (7) Bangladesh, Bhutan, Burma, India, Nepal, Sri Lanka, Thailand

Benelux Union (Benelux)
note – acronym from Belgium, Netherlands, and Luxembourg; was formerly known as Benelux Economic Union
address – Regentschapsstraat 39, 1000 Brussel
phone – (32) (0)2/519.38.11
fax – (32) (0)2/513.42.06
email – info@benelux.int
website – https://www.benelux.int/nl/
established – 3 February 1958
effective – 1 November 1960; changed names 17 June 2008
aim – to develop closer economic and legal cooperation and integration
members – (3) Belgium, Luxembourg, Netherlands

Black Sea Economic Cooperation Zone (BSEC)
address – Darüşşafaka Cad. Seba Center, İş Merkezi, No.45 Kat 3, Istinye 34460 Sarıyer-Istanbul, Turkey
phone – 90 212 229 63 30-35
fax – 90 212 229 63 36
email – info@bsec-organization.org
website – http://www.bsec-organization.org/
established – 25 June 1992
aim – to enhance regional stability through economic cooperation
members – (13) Albania, Armenia, Azerbaijan, Bulgaria, Georgia, Greece, Moldova, North Macedonia, Romania, Russia, Serbia, Turkey (Turkiye), Ukraine; note – North Macedonia is in the process of joining
observers – (16) Austria, EU, Commission on the Protection of the Black Sea Against Pollution, Croatia, Czechia, Egypt, Energy Charter Secretariat, Germany, Hungary, International Black Sea Club, Israel, Italy, Poland, Slovakia, Tunisia, United States

Caribbean Community and Common Market (Caricom)
address – Turkeyen Georgetown, Guyana
phone – 1(592) 222-0001
email – registry@caricom.org; communications@caricom.org
website – https://caricom.org/
established – 4 July 1973
effective – 1 August 1973

aim – to promote economic integration and development, especially among the less developed countries
members – (15) Antigua and Barbuda, The Bahamas, Barbados, Belize, Dominica, Grenada, Guyana, Haiti, Jamaica, Montserrat, Saint Kitts and Nevis, Saint Lucia, Saint Vincent and the Grenadines, Suriname, Trinidad and Tobago
associate members – (5) Anguilla, Bermuda, British Virgin Islands, Cayman Islands, Turks and Caicos Islands
observers – (8) Aruba, Colombia, Curacao, Dominican Republic, Mexico, Puerto Rico, Sint Maarten, Venezuela

Caribbean Development Bank (CDB)
address – PO Box 408, Wildey, St. Michael, Barbados, WI BB11000
phone – 246 539 1600
website – https://www.caribank.org/
established – 18 October 1969
effective – 26 January 1970
aim – to promote economic development and cooperation
borrowing members – (19) Anguilla, Antigua and Barbuda, The Bahamas, Barbados, Belize, British Virgin Islands, Cayman Islands, Dominica, Grenada, Guyana, Haiti, Jamaica, Montserrat, Saint Kitts and Nevis, Saint Lucia, Saint Vincent and the Grenadines, Suriname, Trinidad and Tobago, Turks and Caicos Islands
non-borrowing members – (9) Brazil, Canada, China, Colombia, Germany, Italy, Mexico, United Kingdom, Venezuela

Central African States Development Bank (BDEAC)
note – acronym from Banque de Developpement des Etats de l'Afrique Centrale
address – Boulevard Denis SASSOU N'GUESSO, B.P. 1177, Brazzaville, République du Congo
phone – (242) 04 426 83 00
fax – (242) 22 281 18 80
email – bdeac@bdeac.org
website – https://www.bdeac.org/
established – 3 December 1975
aim – to provide loans for economic development
members – (11) African Development Bank (AfDB), Cameroon, Central African States Bank (BEAC), Central African Republic, Chad, Republic of the Congo, Equatorial Guinea, France, Gabon, Kuwait, Libya

Central American Bank for Economic Integration (CABEI)
note – acronym from Banco Centroamericano de Integracion Economico
website – https://www.bcie.org/en/
established – 13 December 1960 signature of Articles of Agreement
effective – 31 May 1961 began operations
aim – to promote economic integration and development
members – (8) Belize, Costa Rica, Dominican Republic, El Salvador, Guatemala, Honduras, Nicaragua, Panama
nonregional members – (7) Argentina, Colombia, Cuba, South Korea, Mexico, Spain, Taiwan

Central American Integration System (SICA)
address – Final Bulevar Cancillería, Distrito El Espino, Ciudad Merliot, Antiguo Cuscatlán, La Libertad, El Salvador
phone – (503) 2248-8800 / 2248-6900
email – info@sica.int
website – https://www.sica.int/
established – 13 December 1991
effective – operational 1 February 1993
aim – to strengthen democracy; to set up a new model of regional security; to promote freedom; to achieve a regional system of welfare and economic and social justice; to attain economic unity and strengthen the area as an economic bloc; to act as a bloc in international matters
members – (7) Belize, Costa Rica, El Salvador, Guatemala, Honduras, Nicaragua, Panama
associate member – (1) Dominican Republic
regional observers – (9) Argentina, Brazil, Chile, Colombia, Ecuador, Mexico, Peru, US, Uruguay
extra-regional observers – (15) Australia, EU, France, Germany, Holy See, Italy, Japan, South Korea, Morocco, NZ, Qatar, Spain, Taiwan, Turkey (Turkiye), UK

Central European Initiative (CEI)
note – evolved from the Quadrilateral Initiative and the Hexagonal Initiative
address – Via Genova 9, 34121 Trieste, Italy
phone – 39 040 7786 777
fax – 39 040 360 640
email – cei@cei.int
website – https://www.cei.int/
established – 11 November 1989 as the Quadrilateral Initiative, 27 July 1991 became the Hexagonal Initiative, July 1992 its present name was adopted
aim – to form an economic and political cooperation group for the region between the Adriatic and the Baltic Seas
members – (18) Albania, Belarus, Bosnia and Herzegovina, Bulgaria, Croatia, Czechia, Hungary, Italy, Moldova, Montenegro, North Macedonia, Poland, Romania, Serbia, Slovakia, Slovenia, Ukraine

Collective Security Treaty Organization (CSTO)
address – 3/2, Sverchkov lane, Moscow, 101000, Russia
phone – 7 (495) 623-43-46; 7 (495) 621-37-86
email – odkb@gov.ru
website – https://en.odkb-csto.org/

established – 7 October 2002
aim – to coordinate military and political cooperation, to develop multilateral structures and mechanisms of cooperation for ensuring national security of the member states
members – (6) Armenia, Belarus, Kazakhstan, Kyrgyzstan, Russia, Tajikistan

Colombo Plan (CP)

address – 52, Ananda Coomaraswamy Mawatha, Colombo 3, Sri Lanka P.O Box 596
phone – 94 11 2576 322
fax – 94 11 2576 311
email – info@colombo-plan.org
website – https://colombo-plan.org/
established – May 1950 proposal was adopted; 1 July 1951 commenced full operations
aim – to promote economic and social development in Asia and the Pacific
members – (27) Afghanistan, Australia, Bangladesh, Bhutan, Brunei, Burma, Fiji, India, Indonesia, Iran, Japan, South Korea, Laos, Malaysia, Maldives, Mongolia, Nepal, NZ, Pakistan, Papua New Guinea, Philippines, Saudi Arabia, Singapore, Sri Lanka, Thailand, US, Vietnam

Common Market for Eastern and Southern Africa (COMESA)

note – formerly known as Preferential Trade Area for Eastern and Southern Africa (PTA)
address – COMESA Center, Ben Bella Road, P.O Box 30051, Lusaka, Zambia
phone – 260 211 229 725/32
email – info@comesa.int
website – https://www.comesa.int/
established – treaty signed 5 November 1993; treaty ratified 8 December 1994
aim – recognizing, promoting and protecting fundamental human rights, commitment to the principles of liberty and rule of law, maintaining peace and stability through the promotion and strengthening of good neighborliness, commitment to peaceful settlement of disputes among member states
members – (21) Burundi, Comoros, Democratic Republic of the Congo, Djibouti, Egypt, Eritrea, Eswatini, Ethiopia, Kenya, Libya, Madagascar, Malawi, Mauritius, Rwanda, Seychelles, Somalia, Sudan, Tunisia, Uganda, Zambia, Zimbabwe

Commonwealth (C)

note – also known as Commonwealth of Nations
address – Marlborough House, Pall Mall, London, SW1Y 5HX, United Kingdom
phone – 44 (0) 20 7747 6500
fax – 44 (0) 20 7930 0827
website – https://thecommonwealth.org/
established – 31 December 1931
aim – to foster multinational cooperation and assistance, as a voluntary association that evolved from the British Empire
members – (56) Antigua and Barbuda, Australia, The Bahamas, Bangladesh, Barbados, Belize, Botswana, Brunei, Cameroon, Canada, Cyprus, Dominica, Eswatini, Fiji, Gabon, The Gambia, Ghana, Grenada, Guyana, India, Jamaica, Kenya, Kiribati, Lesotho, Malawi, Malaysia, Maldives, Malta, Mauritius, Mozambique, Namibia, Nauru, NZ, Nigeria, Pakistan, Papua New Guinea, Rwanda, Saint Kitts and Nevis, Saint Lucia, Saint Vincent and the Grenadines, Samoa, Seychelles, Sierra Leone, Singapore, Solomon Islands, South Africa, Sri Lanka, Tanzania, Togo, Tonga, Trinidad and Tobago, Tuvalu, Uganda, UK, Vanuatu, Zambia
note 1 – on 7 December 2003, Zimbabwe withdrew its membership from the Commonwealth
note 2 – 15 of the Commonwealth countries are Commonwealth realms that share a common monarch: Antigua and Barbuda, Australia, The Bahamas, Belize, Canada, Grenada, Jamaica, NZ, Papua New Guinea, Saint Kitts and Nevis, Saint Lucia, Saint Vincent and the Grenadines, Solomon Islands, Tuvalu, UK

Commonwealth of Independent States (CIS)

address – 220030, Minsk, Kirov str., 17
phone – 37517 215-50-01
email – cr@cis,minsk.by
website – CIS Executive Committee
established – 8 December 1991
effective – 21 December 1991
aim – to coordinate intercommonwealth relations and to provide a mechanism for the orderly dissolution of the USSR
members – (9) Armenia, Azerbaijan, Belarus, Kazakhstan, Kyrgyzstan, Moldova, Russia, Tajikistan, Uzbekistan
associate member – (1) Turkmenistan; note – Georgia left the organization in 2009; Ukraine has not formally withdrawn from the organization but did formally end its participation in CIS statutory bodies in 2018

Community of Democracies (CD)

address – Aleje Ujazdowskie 41, 00-540 Warsaw, Poland
phone – 48-22-375-90-00
fax – 48-22-3195628
email – info@community-democracies.org
website – https://community-democracies.org/
established – 27 June 2000
aim – "to respect and uphold core democratic principles and practices" including free and fair elections, freedom of speech and expression, equal access to education, rule of law, and freedom of peaceful assembly
members – (106) Albania, Algeria, Argentina, Armenia, Australia, Austria, Azerbaijan, Bangladesh, Belgium, Belize, Benin, Bolivia, Bosnia and Herzegovina, Botswana, Brazil, Bulgaria, Burkina Faso, Cabo Verde, Canada, Chile, Colombia, Costa Rica, Croatia, Cyprus, Czechia, Denmark, Dominica, Dominican Republic, Ecuador, Egypt, El Salvador, Estonia, Finland, Georgia, Germany, Greece, Guatemala, Haiti, Hungary, Iceland, India, Indonesia, Ireland, Israel, Italy, Japan, Jordan, Kenya, South Korea, Kuwait, Latvia, Lesotho, Liechtenstein, Lithuania, Luxembourg,

Madagascar, Malawi, Mali, Malta, Mauritius, Mexico, Moldova, Monaco, Mongolia, Morocco, Mozambique, Namibia, Nepal, Netherlands, NZ, Nicaragua, Niger, Nigeria, North Macedonia, Norway, Panama, Papua New Guinea, Paraguay, Peru, Philippines, Poland, Portugal, Qatar, Romania, Russia, Saint Lucia, Sao Tome and Principe, Senegal, Seychelles, Slovakia, Slovenia, South Africa, Spain, Sri Lanka, Sweden, Switzerland, Tanzania, Thailand, Tunisia, Turkey (Turkiye), Ukraine, UK, US, Uruguay, Venezuela, Yemen

Comuinidade dos Paises de Lingua Portuguesa (CPLP)
address – Palácio Conde de Penafiel, Rua de S. Mamede (ao Caldas), nº 21
1100 – 533 Lisboa, Portugal
phone – 351 21 392 85 60
fax – 351 21 392 85 88
website – https://www.cplp.org/
established – 1996
aim – to establish a forum for friendship among Portuguese-speaking nations where Portuguese is an official language
members – (9) Angola, Brazil, Cabo Verde, Equatorial Guinea, Guinea-Bissau, Mozambique, Portugal, Sao Tome and Principe, Timor-Leste
associate observers – (32) Andorra, Argentina, Canada, Chile, Cote d'Ivoire, Czechia, European Public Law Organization, France, G7+, Georgia, Greece, Hungary, Ibero-American Summit, India, Ireland, Italy, Japan, Luxembourg, Mauritius, Namibia, Organization of Ibero-American States, Peru, Qatar, Romania, Senegal, Serbia, Slovakia, Spain, Turkey (Turkiye), UK, US, Uruguay

Conference of Interaction and Confidence-Building Measures in Asia (CICA)
address – 55/20, Mangilik Yel ave., Nur-Sultan, Republic of Kazakhstan
phone – 7 7172 576510
email – info@s-cica.kz
website – https://www.s-cica.org/
established – proposed 5 October 1992; established 14 September 1999
aim – promoting a multi-national forum for enhancing cooperation towards promoting peace, security, and stability in Asia
members – (26) Afghanistan, Azerbaijan, Bahrain, Bangladesh, Cambodia, China, Egypt, India, Iran, Iraq, Israel, Jordan, Kazakhstan, Kyrgyzstan, Mongolia, Pakistan, Qatar, South Korea, Russia, Sri Lanka, Tajikistan, Thailand, Turkey (Turkiye), UAE, Uzbekistan, Vietnam; plus the Palestine Liberation Organization (not included in member count)
observers – (14) Belarus, Indonesia, International Organization for Migration, Japan, Laos, League of Arab States, Malaysia, OSCE, Parliamentary Assembly of the Turkic Speaking Countries, Philippines, Turkmenistan, Ukraine, UN, US

Convention of the Southeast European Law Enforcement Center (SELEC)
note – successor to Southeast European Cooperative Initiative (SECI) formed in 1996 to help the Southeast European countries rebuild and stabilize through access to resources
address – Palace of Parliament, 10th floor 13 Septembrie Blvd., no. 1-5, Sector 5, 050711 Bucharest
phone – (+4 021) 303.60.09
fax – (+4 021) 303.60.77
email – secretariat@selec.org
website – https://www.selec.org/
established – 7 October 2011
aim – to provide support for member states and enhance coordination in preventing and combating crime in trans-border activity
members – (11) Albania, Bosnia and Herzegovina, Bulgaria, Greece, Hungary, Moldova, Montenegro, North Macedonia, Romania, Serbia, Turkey (Turkiye)
operational partners – (5) Interpol, Italy, Saudi Arabia, UK, US
observers – (20) Austria, Belarus, Belgium, Criminal Information Center to Combat Drugs, Czechia, EU Border Assistance Mission to Moldova and Ukraine (EUBAM), France, Georgia, Germany, International Organization for Migration (IOM), Israel, Japan, The Netherlands, Slovakia, Spain, Switzerland, Ukraine, United Nations Mission in Kosovo (UNMiK), United Nations Office on Drugs and Crime (UNODC), World Customs Organization (WCO)

Council of Europe (CE)
address – Avenue de l'Europe F-67075 Strasbourg Cedex, France
phone – 33 (0)3 88 41 20 00
website – https://www.coe.int/en/web/portal/home
established – 5 May 1949
effective – 3 August 1949
aim – to promote increased unity and quality of life in Europe
members – (47) Albania, Andorra, Armenia, Austria, Azerbaijan, Belgium, Bosnia and Herzegovina, Bulgaria, Croatia, Cyprus, Czechia, Denmark, Estonia, Finland, France, Georgia, Germany, Greece, Hungary, Iceland, Ireland, Italy, Latvia, Liechtenstein, Lithuania, Luxembourg, Malta, Moldova, Monaco, Montenegro, Netherlands, North Macedonia, Norway, Poland, Portugal, Romania, Russia, San Marino, Serbia, Slovakia, Slovenia, Spain, Sweden, Switzerland, Turkey (Turkiye), Ukraine, UK
observers – (6) Canada, Holy See, Israel, Japan, Mexico, US

Council of the Baltic Sea States (CBSS)
address – Momma Reenstiernas Palats, Wollmar Yxkullsgatan 23, 118 50 Stockholm, Sweden
phone – 46 8 440 19 20
email – cbss@cbss.org
website – https://cbss.org/
established – 6 March 1992
aim – to promote cooperation among the Baltic Sea states in the areas of aid to new democratic institutions, economic development, humanitarian aid, energy and the environment, cultural programs and education, and transportation and communication
members – (12) Denmark, Estonia, EU, Finland, Germany, Iceland, Latvia, Lithuania, Norway, Poland, Russia, Sweden
observers – (11) Belarus, France, Hungary, Italy, Netherlands, Romania, Slovakia, Spain, Ukraine, UK, US

Council of the Entente (Entente)
address – Conseil de l'Entente, 01 BP 3734 Abidjan 01
phone – 225 20 509 200
email – conseildelentente@conseildelentente.org
website – http://conseildelentente.org/
established – 29 May 1959
aim – to promote economic, social, and political coordination
members – (5) Benin, Burkina Faso, Cote d'Ivoire, Niger, Togo

Developing Eight (D-8)
address – Darüşşafaka Caddesi Seba Center, No: 45, Kat: 3 Istinye 34460, Sarıyer-Istanbul/Turkey
phone – 90 (212) 356 18 23; +90 (212) 356 18 24
fax – 90 (212) 356 18 29
email – secretariat@developing8.org; info@developing8.org
website – https://developing8.org/
established – 15 June 1997
aim – to improve developing countries' positions in the world economy, diversify and create new opportunities in trade relations, enhance participation in decision-making at the international level, provide better standards of living
members – (8) Bangladesh, Egypt, Indonesia, Iran, Malaysia, Nigeria, Pakistan, Turkey (Turkiye)

East African Community (EAC)
note – originally established in 1967, it was disbanded in 1977 and reestablished in 2000
address – EAC Close, Afrika Mashariki Road, P.O. Box 1096, Arusha, Tanzania
phone – 255 (0)27 216 2100
fax – 255 (0)27 216 2190
email – eac@eachq.org
website – https://www.eac.int/
established – 7 July 2000
aim – to establish a political and economic union among the countries
members – (8) Burundi, Democratic Republic of the Congo, Kenya, Rwanda, Somalia, South Sudan, Tanzania, Uganda

East African Development Bank (EADB)
address – EADB Building, Plot 4 Nile Avenue, Kampala, Uganda
phone – 256 417 112900/1/2, +256 414 673065, +256 312 230000
fax – 256-41-253585
email – enquiry@eadb.org
website – https://eadb.org/
established – 6 June 1967
effective – 1 December 1967
aim – to promote economic development
members – (4) Kenya, Rwanda, Tanzania, Uganda

East Asia Summit (EAS)
address – 70A Jalan Sisingamangaraja, Jakarta, Indonesia 12110
phone – 6221 7262991 ext. 291
fax – 6221 7398234
email – eas.admin@asean.org
website – https://eastasiasummit.asean.org/
established – 14 December 2005
aim – to promote cooperation in political and security issues; to promote development, financial stability, energy security, economic integration and growth; to eradicate poverty and narrow the development gap in East Asia, and to promote deeper cultural understanding
members – (18) Australia, Brunei, Burma, Cambodia, China, India, Indonesia, Japan, South Korea, Laos, Malaysia, NZ, Philippines, Russia, Singapore, Thailand, US, Vietnam

Economic and Monetary Community of Central Africa (CEMAC)
note – was formerly the Central African Customs and Economic Union (UDEAC)
address – CEMAC Building, Avenue des Martyrs, BP 969, Bangui – Central African Republic
email – cemac@cemac.int
website – https://www.cemac.int/
established – (UDEAC) 8 December 1964; (CEMAC) 16 March 1994
effective – (UDEAC) 1 January 1966; (CEMAC) June 1999
aim – to promote the establishment of a Central African Common Market
members – (11) Angola, Burundi, Cameroon, Central African Republic, Chad, Democratic Republic of the Congo, Republic of the Congo, Equatorial Guinea, Gabon, Sao Tome and Principe, Rwanda

Economic and Monetary Union (EMU)
note – an integral part of the European Union; also known as the European Economic and Monetary Union
address – European Central Bank, 60640 Frankfurt am Main, Germany
phone – 49 69 1344
website – European Central Bank – https://www.ecb.europa.eu/home/html/index.en.html
established – 1-2 December 1969 (proposed at summit conference of heads of government); 7 February 1992 (Maastricht Treaty signed)
aim – to promote a single market by creating a single currency, the euro

members – (27) Austria, Belgium, Bulgaria, Croatia, Cyprus, Czechia, Denmark, Estonia, Finland, France, Germany, Greece, Hungary, Ireland, Italy, Latvia, Lithuania, Luxembourg, Malta, Netherlands, Poland, Portugal, Romania, Slovakia, Slovenia, Spain, Sweden

Economic and Social Council (ECOSOC)
email – ecosocinfo@un.org
website – https://www.un.org/ecosoc/en/home
established – 26 June 1945
effective – 24 October 1945
aim – to coordinate the economic and social work of the UN; includes five regional commissions (Economic Commission for Africa, Economic Commission for Europe, Economic Commission for Latin America and the Caribbean, Economic and Social Commission for Asia and the Pacific, Economic and Social Commission for Western Asia) and nine functional commissions (Commission for Social Development, Commission on Human Rights, Commission on Narcotic Drugs, Commission on the Status of Women, Commission on Population and Development, Statistical Commission, Commission on Science and Technology for Development, Commission on Sustainable Development, and Commission on Crime Prevention and Criminal Justice)
members – (54) selected on a rotating basis from all regions

Economic Cooperation Organization (ECO)
address – No. 1, Golbou Alley, Kamranieh St., Tehran, Iran
Postal Code: 1951933114
phone – 98(21) 22831733-4 & 22292066
fax – 98(21) 22831732
email – registry@eco.int
website – https://www.eco.int/index.php
established – 27-29 January 1985
aim – to promote regional cooperation in trade, transportation, communications, tourism, cultural affairs, and economic development
members – (10) Afghanistan, Azerbaijan, Iran, Kazakhstan, Kyrgyzstan, Pakistan, Tajikistan, Turkey (Turkiye), Turkmenistan, Uzbekistan

European Bank for Reconstruction and Development (EBRD)
address – Five Bank Street, London, E14 4BG, United Kingdom
phone – 020 7338 6000
website – https://www.ebrd.com/home
established – 8-9 January 1990 (proposals made)
effective – 15 April 1991 (bank inaugurated)
aim – to facilitate the transition of seven centrally planned economies in Europe (Bulgaria, former Czechoslovakia, Hungary, Poland, Romania, former USSR, and former Yugoslavia) to market economies by committing 60% of its loans to privatization
members – (72) Albania, Armenia, Australia, Austria, Azerbaijan, Belarus, Belgium, Bosnia and Herzegovina, Bulgaria, Canada, China, Croatia, Cyprus, Czechia, Denmark, Egypt, Estonia, European Investment Bank (EIB), EU, Finland, France, Georgia, Germany, Greece, Hungary, Iceland, India, Ireland, Israel, Italy, Japan, Jordan, Kazakhstan, South Korea, Kosovo, Kyrgyzstan, Latvia, Lebanon, Libya, Liechtenstein, Lithuania, Luxembourg, Malta, Mexico, Moldova, Mongolia, Montenegro, Morocco, Netherlands, NZ, North Macedonia, Norway, Poland, Portugal, Romania, Russia, San Marino, Serbia, Slovakia, Slovenia, Spain, Sweden, Switzerland, Tajikistan, Tunisia, Turkey (Turkiye), Turkmenistan, Ukraine, UAE, UK, US, Uzbekistan

European Central Bank (ECB)
address – 60640 Frankfurt am Main, Germany
phone – 49 69 1344 0
website – https://www.ecb.europa.eu/home/html/index.en.html
established – 1 June 1998
aim – to administer the monetary policy of the EU eurozone member states
Euro area members – (19) Austria, Belgium, Cyprus, Estonia, Finland, France, Germany, Greece, Ireland, Italy, Latvia, Lithuania, Luxembourg, Malta, Netherlands, Portugal, Slovakia, Slovenia, Spain
non-Euro area members – (8) Bulgaria, Croatia, Czechia, Denmark, Hungary, Poland, Romania, Sweden

European Free Trade Association (EFTA)
address – Rue de Varembé, 9-11, 1211 Geneva 20, Switzerland
phone – 41 22 332 26 00
fax – 41 22 332 26 77
email – mail.gva@efta.int
address – Avenue des Arts 19H, 1000 Brussels, Belgium
phone – 32 2 286 17 11
email – mail.bxl@efta.int
website – https://www.efta.int/
established – 4 January 1960
effective – 3 May 1960
aim – to promote expansion of free trade
members – (4) Iceland, Liechtenstein, Norway, Switzerland

European Investment Bank (EIB)
address – 98-100, boulevard Konrad Adenauer, L-2950 Luxembourg
phone – 352 4379-22000
fax – 352 4379-62000
website – https://www.eib.org/en/index.htm
established – 25 March 1957

effective – 1 January 1958
aim – to promote economic development of the EU and its predecessors, the EEC and the EC
members – (27) Austria, Belgium, Bulgaria, Croatia, Cyprus, Czechia, Denmark, Estonia, Finland, France, Germany, Greece, Hungary, Ireland, Italy, Latvia, Lithuania, Luxembourg, Malta, Netherlands, Poland, Portugal, Romania, Slovakia, Slovenia, Spain, Sweden

European Organization for Nuclear Research (CERN)
note – acronym retained from the predecessor organization, Conseil Européenne pour la Recherche Nucléaire
address – Esplanade des Particules 1, P.O. Box, 1211 Geneva 23, Switzerland
phone – 41 (0) 22 76 784 84 or 41 (0) 22 76 776 76
email – cern.reception@cern.ch
website – https://home.cern/
established – 1 July 1953
effective – 29 September 1954
aim – to foster nuclear research for peaceful purposes only
members – (23) Austria, Belgium, Bulgaria, Czechia, Denmark, Finland, France, Germany, Greece, Hungary, Israel, Italy, Netherlands, Norway, Poland, Portugal, Romania, Serbia, Slovakia, Spain, Sweden, Switzerland, UK
associate members – (10) Croatia, Cyprus, Estonia, India, Latvia, Lithuania, Pakistan, Slovenia, Turkey (Turkiye), Ukraine
observers – (6) EU, Japan, Joint Institute for Nuclear Research (JINR), Russia, United Nations Educational, Scientific, and Cultural Organization (UNESCO), US

European Space Agency (ESA)
address – 24 rue du Général Bertrand, CS 30798, 75345 Paris CEDEX 7, France
phone – 33 1 53 69 76 54
fax – 33 1 53 69 75 60
website – https://www.esa.int/
established – 31 May 1975
aim – to promote peaceful cooperation in space research and technology
members – (22) Austria, Belgium, Czechia, Denmark, Estonia, Finland, France, Germany, Greece, Hungary, Ireland, Italy, Luxembourg, Netherlands, Norway, Poland, Portugal, Romania, Spain, Sweden, Switzerland, UK
associate member – (3) Slovenia, Latvia, Lithuania
cooperating states – (6) Bulgaria, Canada, Croatia, Cyprus, Malta, Slovakia

European Union (EU)
see European Union page

Financial Action Task Force (FATF)
address – 2, rue André Pascal, 75775 Paris Cedex 16 FRANCE
phone – 33 1 45 24 90 90
email – Contact@fatf-gafi.org
website – https://www.fatf-gafi.org/
established – initiated during the G-7 Summit in Paris in 1989
aim – to develop and promote policies to combat money laundering and terrorist financing
members – (39) Argentina, Australia, Austria, Belgium, Brazil, Canada, China, Denmark, EC, Finland, France, Germany, Greece, Gulf Cooperation Council, Hong Kong, Iceland, India, Ireland, Israel, Italy, Japan, South Korea, Luxembourg, Malaysia, Mexico, Netherlands (Aruba, Curacao, Sint Maarten), NZ, Norway, Portugal, Russia, Saudi Arabia, Singapore, South Africa, Spain, Sweden, Switzerland, Turkey (Turkiye), UK, US
observers – (1) Indonesia

Food and Agriculture Organization (FAO)
address – Viale delle Terme di Caracalla, 00153 Rome, Italy
phone – (+39) 06 57051
email – FAO-HQ@fao.org
website – https://www.fao.org/home/en
established – 16 October 1945
aim – to raise living standards and increase availability of agricultural products; a UN specialized agency
members – (195) includes all UN member countries except Liechtenstein; plus the Cook Islands, the EU, and Niue
associate members – (2) Faroe Islands, Tokelau

General Confederation of Trade Unions (GCTU)
address – Leninsky pr.,42, Moscow, Russia
phone – 7(495)938-7212
email – mail@vkp.ru
website – General Confederation of Trade Unions
established – 16 April 1992
aim – to consolidate trade-union actions to protect citizens' social and labor rights and interests, to help secure trade unions' rights and guarantees, and to strengthen international trade-union solidarity
members – (10) Armenia, Azerbaijan, Belarus, Georgia, Kazakhstan, Kyrgyzstan, Moldova, Russia, Tajikistan, Uzbekistan

Gulf Cooperation Council (GCC)
note – also known as the Cooperation Council for the Arab States of the Gulf
address – King Khaled Road, Riyadh, Saudi Arabia
phone – 966114827777
fax – 966114829089

email – Site@gccsg.org
website – https://www.gcc-sg.org/en-us/Pages/default.aspx
established – 25 May 1981
aim – to promote regional cooperation in economic, social, political, and military affairs
members – (6) Bahrain, Kuwait, Oman, Qatar, Saudi Arabia, UAE

Indian Ocean Commission (InOC)
address – Blue Tower, 3rd floor, rue de l'institut, 72201, Ebony, Mauritius
website – Home | Indian Ocean Commission
established – 21 December 1982
aim – to organize and promote regional cooperation in all sectors, especially economic
members – (5) Comoros, France (for Reunion), Madagascar, Mauritius, Seychelles
Inter-American Development Bank (IADB)
note – also known as Banco Interamericano de Desarrollo (BID)
address – 1300 New York Avenue, N.W., Washington, D.C. 20577, USA
phone – (202) 623-1000
fax – (202) 623-3096
website – https://www.iadb.org/en
established – 8 April 1959
effective – 30 December 1959
aim – to promote economic and social development in Latin America
members – (48) Argentina, Austria, The Bahamas, Barbados, Belgium, Belize, Bolivia, Brazil, Canada, Chile, China, Colombia, Costa Rica, Croatia, Denmark, Dominican Republic, Ecuador, El Salvador, Finland, France, Germany, Guatemala, Guyana, Haiti, Honduras, Israel, Italy, Jamaica, Japan, South Korea, Mexico, Netherlands, Nicaragua, Norway, Panama, Paraguay, Peru, Portugal, Slovenia, Spain, Suriname, Sweden, Switzerland, Trinidad and Tobago, UK, US, Uruguay, Venezuela

Inter-Governmental Authority on Development (IGAD)
note – formerly known as Inter-Governmental Authority on Drought and Development (IGADD)
address – Avenue Georges Clemenceau P.O. Box 2653 Djibouti, Republic of Djibouti
phone – 253-21354050
fax – 253-21356994
website – https://igad.int/
established – 15-16 January 1986 as the Inter-Governmental Authority on Drought and Development; revitalized 21 March 1996 as the Inter-Governmental Authority on Development
aim – to promote a social, economic, and scientific community among its members
members – (8) Djibouti, Eritrea, Ethiopia, Kenya, Somalia, South Sudan, Sudan, Uganda
partners – (34) African Development Bank, Australia, Austria, Belgium, Brazil, Canada, China, Czechia, Denmark, EC, Finland, FAO, France, Germany, Greece, India, Ireland, Italy, Japan, LAS, Luxembourg, Netherlands, New Zealand, Norway, Russia, Spain, Sweden, Switzerland, Turkey (Turkiye), UK, UN Development Program, US, World Bank, World Food Program

International Atomic Energy Agency (IAEA)
address – Vienna International Centre, PO Box 100
A-1400 Vienna, Austria
phone – 43 (1) 2600-0
fax – 43 (1) 2600-7
website – https://www.iaea.org/
established – 26 October 1956
effective – 29 July 1957
aim – to promote peaceful uses of atomic energy
members – (173) Afghanistan, Albania, Algeria, Angola, Antiqua and Barbuda, Argentina, Armenia, Australia, Austria, Azerbaijan,The Bahamas, Bahrain, Bangladesh, Barbados, Belarus, Belgium, Belize, Benin, Bolivia, Bosnia and Herzegovina, Botswana, Brazil, Brunei, Bulgaria, Burkina Faso, Burma, Burundi, Cambodia, Cameroon, Canada, Central African Republic, Chad, Chile, China, Colombia, Comoros, Democratic Republic of the Congo, Republic of the Congo, Costa Rica, Cote d'Ivoire, Croatia, Cuba, Cyprus, Czechia, Denmark, Djibouti, Dominica, Dominican Republic, Ecuador, Egypt, El Salvador, Eritrea, Estonia, Eswatini, Ethiopia, Fiji, Finland, France, Gabon, Georgia, Germany, Ghana, Greece, Guatemala, Guyana, Haiti, Holy See, Honduras, Hungary, Iceland, India, Indonesia, Iran, Iraq, Ireland, Israel, Italy, Jamaica, Japan, Jordan, Kazakhstan, Kenya, South Korea, Kuwait, Kyrgyzstan, Laos, Latvia, Lebanon, Lesotho, Liberia, Libya, Liechtenstein, Lithuania, Luxembourg, Madagascar, Malawi, Malaysia, Mali, Malta, Marshall Islands, Mauritania, Mauritius, Mexico, Moldova, Monaco, Mongolia, Montenegro, Morocco, Mozambique, Namibia, Nepal, Netherlands, NZ, Nicaragua, Niger, Nigeria, North Macedonia, Norway, Oman, Pakistan, Palau, Panama, Papua New Guinea, Paraguay, Peru, Philippines, Poland, Portugal, Qatar, Romania, Russia, Rwanda, Saint Lucia, Saint Vincent and the Grenadines, Samoa, San Marino, Saudi Arabia, Senegal, Serbia, Seychelles, Sierra Leone, Singapore, Slovakia, Slovenia, South Africa, Spain, Sri Lanka, Sudan, Sweden, Switzerland, Syria, Tajikistan, Tanzania, Thailand, Togo, Trinidad and Tobago, Tunisia, Turkey (Turkiye), Turkmenistan, Uganda, Ukraine, UAE, UK, US, Uruguay, Uzbekistan, Vanuatu, Venezuela, Vietnam, Yemen, Zambia, Zimbabwe; note – Cabo Verde, the Gambia, Guinea, and Tonga need to deposit the necessary legal instruments with the IAEA

International Bank for Reconstruction and Development (IBRD)
note – also known as the World Bank
address – 1818 H Street, NW Washington, DC 20433
phone – (202) 473-1000
website – https://www.worldbank.org/en/home
established – 22 July 1944
effective – 27 December 1945
aim – to provide economic development loans; a UN specialized agency
members – (189) includes all UN member countries except Andorra, Cuba, North Korea, Liechtenstein, Monaco; plus Kosovo

International Center for Settlement of Investment Disputes (ICSID)
address – 1818 H Street, NW, MSN C3-300, Washington DC 20433 – United States
phone – 202-458-1534
fax – 202-522-2615
email – ICSIDsecretariat@worldbank.org
website – International Centre for Settlement of Investment Disputes
established – 14 October 1966
aim – serve as a forum for investor-state dispute settlement in most international investment treaties and in numerous investment laws and contracts
member states – (158) includes all UN member countries except Andorra, Antigua and Barbuda, Bahrain, Bangladesh, Bhutan, Bolivia, Brazil, Burma, Croatia, Cuba, Cyprus, Czechia, Dominica, Eritrea, Honduras, India, Iran, Kiribati, Laos, Maldives, Marshall Islands, Monaco, Palau, Poland, South Africa, Suriname, Tajikistan, Turkmenistan, Tuvalu, Vanuatu

International Chamber of Commerce (ICC)
address – 33-43 avenue du Président Wilson, 75116 Paris, France
phone – 33 (0) 1 49 53 28 28
fax – 33 (0) 1 86 26 67 44
email – icc@iccwbo.org
website – https://iccwbo.org/
established – 1919
aim – to promote free trade and private enterprise and to represent business interests at national and international levels
countries with national committees – (90) Afghanistan, Albania, Argentina, Armenia, Australia, Austria, Bahrain, Bangladesh, Belgium, Bolivia, Brazil, Bulgaria, Burkina Faso, Canada, Chile, China, Colombia, Costa Rica, Croatia, Cuba, Cyprus, Czechia, Denmark, Dominican Republic, Ecuador, Egypt, Estonia, Finland, France, Georgia, Germany, Ghana, Greece, Guatemala, Hong Kong, India, Indonesia, Iran, Ireland, Italy, Japan, Jordan, Kenya, South Korea, Kuwait, Lebanon, Lithuania, Luxembourg, Macau, Malaysia, Mexico, Monaco, Morocco, Netherlands, NZ, Nigeria, North Macedonia, Norway, Pakistan, Panama, Paraguay, Peru, Poland, Portugal, Qatar, Romania, Russia, Saudi Arabia, Serbia, Singapore, Slovakia, Slovenia, South Africa, Spain, Sri Lanka, Sweden, Switzerland, Syria, Taiwan, Thailand, Turkey (Turkiye), Ukraine, UAE, UK, US, Uruguay, Venezuela

International Civil Aviation Organization (ICAO)
address – 999 Robert-Bourassa Boulevard, Montréal, Québec H3C 5H7, Canada
phone – 1 514-954-8219
fax – 1 514-954-6077
email – icaohq@icao.int
website – https://www.icao.int/Pages/default.aspx
established – 7 December 1944
effective – 4 April 1947
aim – to promote international cooperation in civil aviation; a UN specialized agency
members – (193) includes all UN member countries except Liechtenstein (192 total); plus Cook Islands

International Conference on the Great Lakes Region (ICGLR)
address – PO Box 7076, Bujumbura, Burundi, Boulevard du Japan, No 38
phone – +257 22 25 6824/25/27/29
fax – +257 22 25 6828
email – secretariat@icglr.org
website – https://icglr.org
established – 2006
effective – May 2007
aim – implementation of the Pact on Security, Stability, and Development in the Great Lakes Region, as well as other initiatives, in order to attain peace, security, stability, and development
members – (12): Angola, Burundi, Central African Republic, Democratic Republic of Congo, Republic of the Congo, Kenya, Rwanda, South Sudan, Sudan, Tanzania, Uganda, Zambia

International Court of Justice (ICJ)
note – also known as the World Court; primary judicial organ of the UN; superseded Permanent Court of International Justice (attached to the League of Nations)
address – Peace Palace, Carnegieplein 2, 2517 KJ The Hague, The Netherlands
phone – 31 70 302 23 23
email – information@icj-cij.org
website – https://www.icj-cij.org/en
established – 26 June 1945 with the signing of the UN Charter (inaugural sitting of the Court was on 18 April 1946)
aim – to settle disputes submitted by member states and to provide advice to UN organs and other international agencies
members – (15 judges) elected by the UN General Assembly and Security Council to represent all principal legal systems; judges elected to nine-year terms (eligible for two additional terms); elections held every three years for one third of the judges
jurisdiction – based on the principle of consent in contentious issues; countries provide declarations of consent to compulsory jurisdiction of the ICJ either with or without reservations (date in parentheses after each country is when the UN secretary-general received the declaration); Haiti, Luxembourg, Nicaragua, and Uruguay deposited declarations with the Permanent Court of International Justice prior to 1945, and these were later transferred to the ICJ
states accepting compulsory jurisdiction with reservations – (61) Australia (22 March 2002), Barbados (1 August 1980), Belgium (17 June 1958), Botswana (16 March 1970), Bulgaria (21 June 1992), Cambodia (19 September 1957), Canada (10 May 1994), Democratic Republic of the Congo (8 February 1989), Cote d'Ivoire (29 September 2001), Cyprus (3 September 2002), Denmark (10 December 1956), Djibouti (2 September 2005), Egypt (22 July 1957), Estonia (31 October 1991), Eswatini (26 May 1969), Finland (25 June 1958), The Gambia (22 June 1966), Germany (30 April 2008), Greece (10 January 1994), Guinea (4 December 1998), Honduras (6 June 1986), Hungary (22 October 1992), India (18 September

1974), Ireland (15 December 2011), Japan (9 July 2007), Italy (25 November 2014), Kenya (19 April 1965), Lesotho (6 September 2000), Liberia (20 March 1952), Liechtenstein (29 March 1950), Lithuania (26 September 2012), Madagascar (2 July 1992), Malawi (12 December 1966), Malta (2 September 1983), Marshall Islands (23 April 2013), Mauritius (23 September 1968), Mexico (28 October 1947), Netherlands (1 August 1956), New Zealand (23 September 1977), Nicaragua (24 September 1929), Nigeria (30 April 1998), Norway (25 June 1996), Pakistan (13 September 1960), Panama (25 October 1921), Peru (7 July 2003), Philippines (18 January 1972), Poland (25 March 1996), Portugal (25 February 2005), Romania (23 June 2015), Senegal (2 December 1985), Slovakia (28 May 2004), Somalia (11 April 1963), Spain (20 October 1990), Sudan (2 January 1958), Suriname (31 August 1987), Sweden (6 April 1957), Switzerland (28 July 1948), Timor-Leste (21 September 2012), Togo (25 October 1979), Uganda (3 October 1963), United Kingdom (5 July 2004)
states accepting compulsory jurisdiction without reservations – (12) Austria (19 May 1971), Cameroon (3 March 1994), Costa Rica (20 February 1973), Dominica (31 March 2006), Dominican Republic (30 September 1924), Equatorial Guinea (11 August 2017), Georgia (20 June 1995), Guinea-Bissau (7 August 1989), Haiti (4 October 1921), Luxembourg (15 September 1930), Paraguay (25 September 1996), Uruguay (28 January 1921)

International Criminal Court (ICCt)
address – Oude Waalsdorperweg 10, 2597 AK, The Hague, The Netherlands
phone – 31 (0)70 515 8515
fax – 31 (0)70 515 8555
website – https://www.icc-cpi.int/
established – 1 July 2002
aim – to hold all individuals and countries accountable to international laws of conduct; to specify international standards of conduct; to provide an important mechanism for implementing these standards; to ensure that perpetrators are brought to justice
members – 21 judges (three judges form the Presidency) and six judges each in the Pre-trial, Trial, and Appeals Divisions; judges elected by secret ballot by the Assembly of States Parties to the Rome Statute for nine-year terms (not eligible for reelection)
states accepting jurisdiction – (123) Afghanistan, Albania, Andorra, Antigua and Barbuda, Argentina, Australia, Austria, Bangladesh, Barbados, Belgium, Belize, Benin, Bolivia, Bosnia and Herzegovina, Botswana, Brazil, Bulgaria, Burkina Faso, Cabo Verde, Cambodia, Canada, Central African Republic, Chad, Chile, Colombia, Comoros, Democratic Republic of the Congo, Republic of the Congo, Cook Islands, Costa Rica, Cote d'Ivoire, Croatia, Cyprus, Czechia, Denmark, Djibouti, Dominica, Dominican Republic, Ecuador, El Salvador, Estonia, Fiji, Finland, France, Gabon, The Gambia, Georgia, Germany, Ghana, Greece, Grenada, Guatemala, Guinea, Guyana, Honduras, Hungary, Iceland, Ireland, Italy, Japan, Jordan, Kenya, Kiribati, South Korea, Latvia, Lesotho, Liberia, Liechtenstein, Lithuania, Luxembourg, Madagascar, Malawi, Maldives, Mali, Malta, Marshall Islands, Mauritius, Mexico, Moldova, Mongolia, Montenegro, Namibia, Nauru, Netherlands, NZ, Niger, Nigeria, North Macedonia, Norway, Panama, Paraguay, Peru, Poland, Portugal, Romania, Saint Kitts and Nevis, Saint Lucia, Saint Vincent and the Grenadines, Samoa, San Marino, Senegal, Serbia, Seychelles, Sierra Leone, Slovakia, Slovenia, South Africa, Spain, Suriname, Sweden, Switzerland, Tajikistan, Tanzania, Timor-Leste, Trinidad and Tobago, Tunisia, Uganda, UK, Uruguay, Vanuatu, Venezuela, Zambia, Palestine Liberation Organization

International Criminal Police Organization (Interpol)
address – 200, quai Charles de Gaulle, 69006 Lyon, France
fax – 33 4 72 44 71 63
website – https://www.interpol.int/en
established – September 1923 set up as the International Criminal Police Commission; 13 June 1956 constitution modified and present name adopted
aim – to promote international cooperation among police authorities in fighting crime
members – (193) Afghanistan, Albania, Algeria, Andorra, Angola, Antigua and Barbuda, Argentina, Armenia, Aruba, Australia, Austria, Azerbaijan, The Bahamas, Bahrain, Bangladesh, Barbados, Belarus, Belgium, Belize, Benin, Bhutan, Bolivia, Bosnia and Herzegovina, Botswana, Brazil, Brunei, Bulgaria, Burkina Faso, Burma, Burundi, Cabo Verde, Cambodia, Cameroon, Canada, Central African Republic, Chad, Chile, China, Colombia, Comoros, Democratic Republic of the Congo, Republic of the Congo, Costa Rica, Cote d'Ivoire, Croatia, Cuba, Curacao, Cyprus, Czechia, Denmark, Djibouti, Dominica, Dominican Republic, Ecuador, Egypt, El Salvador, Equatorial Guinea, Eritrea, Estonia, Eswatini, Ethiopia, Fiji, Finland, France, Gabon, The Gambia, Georgia, Germany, Ghana, Greece, Grenada, Guatemala, Guinea, Guinea-Bissau, Guyana, Haiti, Holy See, Honduras, Hungary, Iceland, India, Indonesia, Iran, Iraq, Ireland, Israel, Italy, Jamaica, Japan, Jordan, Kazakhstan, Kenya, Kiribati, South Korea, Kuwait, Kyrgyzstan, Laos, Latvia, Lebanon, Lesotho, Liberia, Libya, Liechtenstein, Lithuania, Luxembourg, Madagascar, Malawi, Malaysia, Maldives, Mali, Malta, Marshall Islands, Mauritania, Mauritius, Mexico, Moldova, Monaco, Mongolia, Montenegro, Morocco, Mozambique, Namibia, Nauru, Nepal, Netherlands, NZ, Nicaragua, Niger, Nigeria, North Macedonia, Norway, Oman, Pakistan, Panama, Papua New Guinea, Paraguay, Peru, Philippines, Poland, Portugal, Qatar, Romania, Russia, Rwanda, Saint Kitts and Nevis, Saint Lucia, Saint Vincent and the Grenadines, Samoa, San Marino, Sao Tome and Principe, Saudi Arabia, Senegal, Serbia, Seychelles, Sierra Leone, Singapore, Sint Maarten, Slovakia, Slovenia, Solomon Islands, Somalia, South Africa, South Sudan, Spain, Sri Lanka, Sudan, Suriname, Sweden, Switzerland, Syria, Tajikistan, Tanzania, Thailand, Timor-Leste, Togo, Tonga, Trinidad and Tobago, Tunisia, Turkey (Turkiye), Turkmenistan, Uganda, Ukraine, UAE, UK, US, Uruguay, Uzbekistan, Vanuatu, Venezuela, Vietnam, Yemen, Zambia, Zimbabwe; plus the Palestine Liberation Organization (not included in the member count)

International Development Association (IDA)
address – 1818 H Street, NW, Washington D.C. 29433, United States
website – https://ida.worldbank.org/en/home
established – 26 January 1960
effective – 24 September 1960
aim – to provide economic loans for low-income countries; UN specialized agency and IBRD affiliate
IDB-eligible countries – (74) Afghanistan, Bangladesh, Benin, Bhutan, Burkina Faso, Burma, Burundi, Cabo Verde, Cambodia, Cameroon, Central African Republic, Chad, Comoros, Democratic Republic of the Congo, Republic of the Congo, Cote d'Ivoire, Dominica, Djibouti, Eritrea, Ethiopia, Fiji, The Gambia, Ghana, Grenada, Guinea, Guinea-Bissau, Guyana, Haiti, Honduras, Kenya, Kiribati, Kosovo, Kyrgyzstan, Laos, Lesotho, Liberia, Madagascar, Malawi, Maldives, Mali, Marshall Islands, Mauritania, Federated States of Micronesia, Mozambique, Nepal, Nicaragua, Niger, Nigeria, Pakistan, Papua New Guinea, Rwanda, Saint Lucia, Saint Vincent and the Grenadines, Samoa, Sao Tome and Principe, Senegal, Sierra Leone, Solomon Islands, Somalia, South Sudan, Sudan, Syria, Tajikistan, Tanzania, Timor-Leste, Togo, Tonga, Tuvalu, Uganda, Uzbekistan, Vanuatu, Yemen, Zambia, Zimbabwe

International Energy Agency (IEA)
address – 9 rue de la Fédération, 75739 Paris Cedex 15, France
phone – 33 (0)1 40 57 65 00
fax – 33 (0)1 40 57 65 09
website – https://www.iea.org/
established – 15 November 1974
aim – to promote cooperation on energy matters, especially emergency oil sharing and relations between oil consumers and oil producers; established by the OECD
members – (30) Australia, Austria, Belgium, Canada, Czechia, Denmark, Estonia, Finland, France, Germany, Greece, Hungary, Ireland, Italy, Japan, South Korea, Luxembourg, Mexico, Netherlands, New Zealand, Norway, Poland, Portugal, Slovakia, Spain, Sweden, Switzerland, Turkey (Turkiye), UK, US

International Finance Corporation (IFC)
address – 2121 Pennsylvania Avenue, NW Washington, DC 20433
phone – (202) 473-1000
website – https://www.ifc.org/wps/wcm/connect/corp_ext_content/ifc_external_corporate_site/home
established – 25 May 1955
effective – 24 July 1956
aim – to support private enterprise in international economic development; a UN specialized agency and IBRD affiliate
members – (184) includes all UN member countries except Andorra, Brunei, Cuba, North Korea, Liechtenstein, Monaco, Nauru, Saint Vincent and the Grenadines, San Marino, Tuvalu; plus Kosovo

International Fund for Agricultural Development (IFAD)
address – Via Paolo di Dono, 44, 00142 Roma, ITALY
phone – 39-0654591
fax – 39-065043463
email – ifad@ifad.org
website – https://www.ifad.org/en/
established – November 1974
effective – 1977
aim – to promote agricultural development; a UN specialized agency
members – (177)
List A – (28 industrialized aid contributors) Austria, Belgium, Canada, Cyprus, Denmark, Estonia, Finland, France, Germany, Greece, Hungary, Iceland, Ireland, Israel, Italy, Japan, Luxembourg, Netherlands, NZ, Norway, Poland, Portugal, Russia, Spain, Sweden, Switzerland, UK, US
List B – (12 petroleum-exporting aid contributors) Algeria, Gabon, Indonesia, Iran, Iraq, Kuwait, Libya, Nigeria, Qatar, Saudi Arabia, UAE, Venezuela
List C – (137 potential aid recipients) Afghanistan, Albania, Angola, Antigua and Barbuda, Argentina, Armenia, Azerbaijan, Bahamas, Bangladesh, Barbados, Belize, Benin, Bhutan, Bolivia, Bosnia and Herzegovina, Botswana, Brazil, Burkina Faso, Burma, Burundi, Cabo Verde, Cambodia, Cameroon, Central African Republic, Chad, Chile, China, Colombia, Comoros, Democratic Republic of the Congo, Republic of the Congo, Cook Islands, Costa Rica, Cote d'Ivoire, Croatia, Cuba, Djibouti, Dominica, Dominican Republic, Ecuador, Egypt, El Salvador, Equatorial Guinea, Eritrea, Eswatini, Ethiopia, Fiji, Gambia, Georgia, Ghana, Grenada, Guatemala, Guinea, Guinea-Bissau, Guyana, Haiti, Honduras, India, Jamaica, Jordan, Kazakhstan, Kenya, Kiribati, North Korea, South Korea, Kyrgyzstan, Laos, Lebanon, Lesotho, Liberia, Madagascar, Malawi, Malayasia, Maldives, Mali, Malta, Marshall Islands, Mauritania, Mauritius, Mexico, Micronesia, Moldova, Mongolia, Montenegro, Morocco, Mozambique, Namibia, Nauru, Nepal, Nicaragua, Niger, Niue, North Macedonia, Oman, Pakistan, Palau, Panama, Papua New Guinea, Paraguay, Peru, Philippines, Romania, Rwanda, Saint Kitts and Nevis, Saint Lucia, Saint Vincent and the Grenadines, Samoa, Sao Tome and Principe, Senegal, Seychelles, Sierra Leone, Solomon Islands, Somalia, South Africa, South Sudan, Sri Lanka, Sudan, Suriname, Syria, Tajikistan, Tanzania, Thailand, Timor-Leste, Tonga, Togo, Trinidad and Tobago, Tunisia, Turkey (Turkiye), Tuvalu, Uganda, Uzbekistan, Vanuatu, Vietnam, Yemen, Zambia, Zimbabwe

International Hydrographic Organization (IHO)
note – name changed from International Hydrographic Bureau on 22 September 1970
address – 4b quai Antoine 1er, B.P. 445, MC 98011 MONACO CEDEX
phone – 377 93 10 81 00
email – info@iho.int
website – https://iho.int/
established – June 1919
effective – June 1921
aim – to train hydrographic surveyors and nautical cartographers to achieve standardization in nautical charts and electronic chart displays; to provide advice on nautical cartography and hydrography; to develop the sciences in the field of hydrography and techniques used for descriptive oceanography
members – (95) Algeria, Argentina, Australia, Bahrain, Bangladesh, Belgium, Brazil, Brunei, Bulgaria, Burma, Cameroon, Canada, Chile, China (including Hong Kong and Macau), Colombia, Democratic Republic of the Congo, Croatia, Cuba, Cyprus, Denmark, Dominican Republic, Ecuador, Egypt, Estonia, Fiji, Finland, France, Georgia, Germany, Ghana, Greece, Guatemala, Guyana, Iceland, India, Indonesia, Iran, Ireland, Italy, Jamaica, Japan, Kenya, North Korea, South Korea, Kuwait, Latvia, Lebanon, Malaysia, Malta, Mauritius, Mexico, Monaco, Montenegro, Morocco, Mozambique, Netherlands, NZ, Nigeria, Norway, Oman, Pakistan, Papua New Guinea, Peru, Philippines, Poland, Portugal, Qatar, Romania, Russia, Samoa, Saudi Arabia, Serbia, Seychelles, Singapore, Slovenia, Solomon Islands, South Africa, Spain, Sri Lanka, Suriname, Sweden, Syria, Thailand, Tonga, Trinidad and Tobago, Tunisia, Turkey (Turkiye), Ukraine, UAE, UK (including Anguilla, Bermuda, British Virgin Islands, Cayman Islands, Montserrat, and Turks and Caicos), US, Uruguay, Vanuatu, Venezuela, Vietnam
International Labor Organization (ILO)
address – 4 route des Morillons, CH-1211 Genève 22, Switzerland
phone – 41 (0) 22 799 6111
fax – 41 (0) 22 798 8685

email – ilo@ilo.org
website – https://www.ilo.org/global/lang--en/index.htm
established – 11 April 1919 became operative; 14 December 1946 affiliated with the UN
aim – to deal with world labor issues; a UN specialized agency
members – (187) includes all UN member countries except Andorra, Bhutan, North Korea, Liechtenstein, Federated States of Micronesia, Monaco, Nauru; includes the Cook Islands

International Maritime Organization (IMO)
note – name changed from Intergovernmental Maritime Consultative Organization (IMCO) on 22 May 1982
address – 4 Albert Embankment, London SE1 7SR, United Kingdom
phone – 44 (0) 20 7735 7611
fax – 44 (0) 20 7735 7611
email – info@imo.org
website – https://www.imo.org/
established – 6 March 1948 set up as the Inter-Governmental Maritime Consultative Organization
effective – 17 March 1958
aim – to deal with international maritime affairs; a UN specialized agency
members – (174) includes all UN member countries except Afghanistan, Andorra, Bhutan, Botswana, Burkina Faso, Burundi, Central African Republic, Chad, Eswatini, Kyrgyzstan, Laos, Lesotho, Liechtenstein, Mali, Federated States of Micronesia, Niger, Rwanda, South Sudan, Tajikistan, Uzbekistan; includes the Cook Islands
associate members – (3) Faroe Islands, Hong Kong, Macau

International Mobile Satellite Organization (IMSO)
address – 4 Albert Embankment, London SE1 7SR, United Kingdom
phone – 44 (0) 20 3970 1060
email – info@imso.org
website – https://imso.org/
established – 15 April 1999
aim – acts as watchdog over Inmarsat (International Maritime Satellite Organization), a private company, to make sure it follows ICAO standards and recommended practices; plays an active role in the development of international telecommunications policies
members – (104) Algeria, Antigua and Barbuda, Argentina, Australia, The Bahamas, Bahrain, Bangladesh, Belarus, Belgium, Bolivia, Bosnia and Herzegovina, Brazil, Brunei, Bulgaria, Cameroon, Canada, Chile, China, Colombia, Comoros, Cook Islands, Costa Rica, Croatia, Cuba, Cyprus, Czechia, Denmark, Ecuador, Egypt, Fiji, Finland, France, Gabon, Georgia, Germany, Ghana, Greece, Honduras, Hungary, Iceland, India, Indonesia, Iran, Iraq, Israel, Italy, Japan, Jordan, Kenya, North Korea, South Korea, Kuwait, Latvia, Lebanon, Liberia, Libya, Malaysia, Malta, Marshall Islands, Mauritius, Mexico, Monaco, Mongolia, Montenegro, Morocco, Mozambique, Netherlands, NZ, Nigeria, Norway, Oman, Pakistan, Palau, Panama, Peru, Philippines, Poland, Portugal, Qatar, Romania, Russia, Saudi Arabia, Senegal, Serbia, Singapore, Slovakia, South Africa, Spain, Sri Lanka, Sweden, Switzerland, Tanzania, Thailand, Tonga, Tunisia, Turkey (Turkiye), Ukraine, UAE, UK, US, Vanuatu, Venezuela, Vietnam, Yemen

International Monetary Fund (IMF)
address – 700 19th Street NW, Washington, D.C. 20431
address – 1900 Pennsylvania Ave NW, Washington, DC, 20431
phone – 1 (202) 623-7000
fax – 1 (202) 623-4661
email – publicaffairs@imf.org
website – https://www.imf.org/en/Home
established – 22 July 1944
effective – 27 December 1945
aim – to promote world monetary stability and economic development; a UN specialized agency
members – (190) includes all UN member countries except Cuba, North Korea, Liechtenstein, Monaco; plus Kosovo; note - includes the following dependencies or areas of special interest: China (Hong Kong and Macau), Netherlands (Aruba, Curacao, Sint Maarten), UK (Anguilla, Montserrat)

International Olympic Committee (IOC)
address – Maison Olympique, 1007 Lausanne, Switzerland
website – https://olympics.com/ioc
established – 23 June 1894
aim – to promote the Olympic ideals of excellence, friendship, and respect, and to administer the Olympic games
National Olympic Committees – (205) Afghanistan, Albania, Algeria, American Samoa, Andorra, Angola, Antigua and Barbuda, Argentina, Armenia, Aruba, Australia, Austria, Azerbaijan, The Bahamas, Bahrain, Bangladesh, Barbados, Belarus, Belgium, Belize, Benin, Bermuda, Bhutan, Bolivia, Bosnia and Herzegovina, Botswana, Brazil, British Virgin Islands, Brunei, Bulgaria, Burkina Faso, Burma, Burundi, Cabo Verde, Cambodia, Cameroon, Canada, Cayman Islands, Central African Republic, Chad, Chile, China, Colombia, Comoros, Democratic Republic of the Congo, Republic of the Congo, Cook Islands, Costa Rica, Cote d'Ivoire, Croatia, Cuba, Cyprus, Czechia, Denmark, Djibouti, Dominica, Dominican Republic, Ecuador, Egypt, El Salvador, Equatorial Guinea, Eritrea, Estonia, Eswatini, Ethiopia, Fiji, Finland, France, Gabon, The Gambia, Georgia, Germany, Ghana, Greece, Grenada, Guam, Guatemala, Guinea, Guinea-Bissau, Guyana, Haiti, Honduras, Hong Kong, Hungary, Iceland, India, Indonesia, Iran, Iraq, Ireland, Israel, Italy, Jamaica, Japan, Jordan, Kazakhstan, Kenya, Kiribati, North Korea, South Korea, Kosovo, Kuwait, Kyrgyzstan, Laos, Latvia, Lebanon, Lesotho, Liberia, Libya, Liechtenstein, Lithuania, Luxembourg, Madagascar, Malawi, Malaysia, Maldives, Mali, Malta, Marshall Islands, Mauritania, Mauritius, Mexico, Federated States of Micronesia, Moldova, Monaco, Mongolia, Montenegro, Morocco, Mozambique, Namibia, Nauru, Nepal, Netherlands, NZ, Nicaragua, Niger, Nigeria, North Macedonia, Norway, Oman, Pakistan, Palau, Panama, Papua New Guinea, Paraguay, Peru, Philippines, Poland, Portugal, Puerto Rico, Qatar, Romania, Russia, Rwanda, Saint Kitts and Nevis, Saint Lucia, Saint Vincent and the Grenadines, Samoa, San Marino, Sao Tome and Principe, Saudi Arabia, Senegal, Serbia, Seychelles, Sierra Leone, Singapore, Slovakia, Slovenia, Solomon Islands, Somalia, South Africa, South Sudan, Spain, Sri Lanka, Sudan, Suriname, Sweden, Switzerland,

Syria, Taiwan, Tajikistan, Tanzania, Thailand, Timor-Leste, Togo, Tonga, Trinidad and Tobago, Tunisia, Turkey (Turkiye), Turkmenistan, Tuvalu, Uganda, Ukraine, UAE, UK, US, Uruguay, Uzbekistan, Vanuatu, Venezuela, Vietnam, Virgin Islands, Yemen, Zambia, Zimbabwe; plus the Palestine Liberation Organization (not included in member count)

International Organization for Migration (IOM)

note – established as Provisional Intergovernmental Committee for the Movement of Migrants from Europe; renamed Intergovernmental Committee for European Migration (ICEM) on 15 November 1952; renamed Intergovernmental Committee for Migration (ICM) in November 1980; current name adopted 14 November 1989
address – 17 Route des Morillons, 1211 Geneva 19, Switzerland
phone – 41 22 717 9111 or 41.22.798 6150
email – hq@iom.int
website – https://www.iom.int/
established – 5 December 1951
aim – to facilitate orderly international emigration and immigration
members – (174) Afghanistan, Albania, Algeria, Angola, Antigua and Barbuda, Argentina, Armenia, Australia, Austria, Azerbaijan, The Bahamas, Bangladesh, Belarus, Belgium, Belize, Benin, Bolivia, Bosnia and Herzegovina, Botswana, Brazil, Bulgaria, Burkina Faso, Burma, Burundi, Cabo Verde, Cambodia, Cameroon, Canada, Central African Republic, Chad, Chile, China, Colombia, Comoros, Democratic Republic of the Congo, Republic of the Congo, Cook Islands, Costa Rica, Cote d'Ivoire, Croatia, Cuba, Cyprus, Czechia, Denmark, Djibouti, Dominica, Dominican Republic, Ecuador, Egypt, El Salvador, Eritrea, Estonia, Eswatini, Ethiopia, Fiji, Finland, France, Gabon, The Gambia, Georgia, Germany, Ghana, Greece, Grenada, Guatemala, Guinea, Guinea-Bissau, Guyana, Haiti, Holy See, Honduras, Hungary, Iceland, India, Iran, Ireland, Israel, Italy, Jamaica, Japan, Jordan, Kazakhstan, Kenya, Kiribati, South Korea, Kyrgyzstan, Laos, Latvia, Lesotho, Liberia, Libya, Lithuania, Luxembourg, Madagascar, Malawi, Maldives, Mali, Malta, Marshall Islands, Mauritania, Mauritius, Mexico, Federation of Micronesia, Moldova, Mongolia, Montenegro, Morocco, Mozambique, Namibia, Nauru, Nepal, Netherlands, NZ, Nicaragua, Niger, Nigeria, North Macedonia, Norway, Pakistan, Palau, Panama, Papua New Guinea, Paraguay, Peru, Philippines, Poland, Portugal, Romania, Russia, Rwanda, Saint Kitts and Nevis, Saint Lucia, Saint Vincent and the Grenadines, Samoa, Sao Tome and Principe, Senegal, Serbia, Seychelles, Sierra Leone, Slovakia, Slovenia, Solomon Islands, Somalia, South Africa, South Sudan, Spain, Sri Lanka, Sudan, Suriname, Sweden, Switzerland, Tajikistan, Tanzania, Thailand, Timor-Leste, Togo, Tonga, Trinidad and Tobago, Tunisia, Turkey (Turkiye), Turkmenistan, Tuvalu, Uganda, Ukraine, UK, US, Uruguay, Uzbekistan, Vanuatu, Venezuela, Vietnam, Yemen, Zambia, Zimbabwe
observers – (8) Bahrain, Bhutan, Indonesia, Kuwait, Malaysia, Qatar, San Marino, Saudi Arabia

International Organization for Standardization (ISO)

address – Chemin de Blandonnet 8, CP 401, 1214 Vernier, Geneva, Switzerland
phone – 41 22 749 01 11
email – central@iso.org
website – https://www.iso.org/home.html
established – February 1947
aim – to promote the development of international standards with a view to facilitating international exchange of goods and services and to developing cooperation in the sphere of intellectual, scientific, technological, and economic activity
members – (124 national standards organizations) Afghanistan, Algeria, Argentina, Armenia, Australia, Austria, Azerbaijan, Bahamas, Bahrain, Bangladesh, Barbados, Belarus, Belgium, Benin, Bolivia, Bosnia and Herzegovina, Botswana, Brazil, Bulgaria, Burkina Faso, Burundi, Cameroon, Canada, Chile, China, Colombia, Democratic Republic of the Congo, Costa Rica, Cote d'Ivoire, Croatia, Cuba, Cyprus, Czechia, Denmark, Dominican Republic, Ecuador, Egypt, El Salvador, Estonia, Ethiopia, Fiji, Finland, France, Gabon, Germany, Ghana, Greece, Hungary, Iceland, India, Indonesia, Iran, Iraq, Ireland, Israel, Italy, Jamaica, Japan, Jordan, Kazakhstan, Kenya, North Korea, South Korea, Kuwait, Latvia, Lebanon, Libya, Lithuania, Luxembourg, Malawi, Malaysia, Mali, Malta, Mauritius, Mexico, Mongolia, Montenegro, Morocco, Namibia, Nepal, Netherlands, NZ, Nigeria, North Macedonia, Norway, Oman, Pakistan, Panama, Peru, Philippines, Poland, Portugal, Qatar, Romania, Russia, Rwanda, Saint Lucia, Saudi Arabia, Senegal, Serbia, Singapore, Slovakia, Slovenia, South Africa, Spain, Sri Lanka, Sudan, Sweden, Switzerland, Syria, Tanzania, Thailand, Trinidad and Tobago, Tunisia, Turkey (Turkiye), Uganda, Ukraine, UAE, UK, US, Uruguay, Uzbekistan, Vietnam, Zimbabwe
correspondent members – (36) Albania, Angola, The Bahamas, Bhutan, Brunei, Burma, Cambodia, Chad, Dominica, Eritrea, Eswatini, The Gambia, Georgia, Guatemala, Guyana, Haiti, Honduras, Hong Kong, Kyrgyzstan, Laos, Macau, Madagascar, Mauritania, Moldova, Mozambique, Nicaragua, Niger, Papua New Guinea, Paraguay, Saint Kitts and Nevis, Seychelles, Sierra Leone, Tajikistan, Turkmenistan, Vanuatu, Zambia; plus the Palestine Liberation Organization (not included in member count)
subscriber members – (4) Antigua and Barbuda, Belize, Saint Vincent and the Grenadines, Sao Tome and Principe

International Organization of the French-speaking World (OIF)

note – name changed from Agency of Cultural and Technical Cooperation (ACCT) in 1997; also known as Organisation Internationale de la Francophonie
address – 19-21 avenue Bosquet, 75007 Paris, France
phone – (33) 1 44 37 33 25
fax – (33) 1 45 79 14 98
website – https://www.francophonie.org/
established – 20 March 1970
aim – founded around a common language to promote and spread the cultures of its members and to reinforce cultural and technical cooperation between them
members – (54) Albania, Andorra, Armenia, Belgium, Benin, Bulgaria, Burkina Faso, Burundi, Cabo Verde, Cambodia, Cameroon, Canada, Canada – New Brunswick, Canada - Quebec, Central African Republic, Chad, Comoros, Democratic Republic of Congo, Republic of Congo, Cote d'Ivoire, Djibouti, Dominica, Egypt, Equatorial Guinea, France, Gabon, Greece, Guinea, Guinea-Bissau, Haiti, Laos, Lebanon, Luxembourg, Madagascar, Mali, Mauritania, Mauritius, Moldova, Monaco, Morocco, Niger, North Macedonia, Romania, Rwanda, Saint Lucia, Sao Tome and Principe, Senegal, Seychelles, Switzerland, Togo, Tunisia, Vanuatu, Vietnam, Wallonia-Brussels
associate members – (7) Cyprus, Ghana, Kosovo, New Caledonia, Qatar, Serbia, UAE
observers – (27) Argentina, Austria, Bosnia and Herzegovina, Canada - Ontario, Costa Rica, Croatia, Czechia, Dominican Republic, Estonia, Gambia, Georgia, Hungary, Ireland, South Korea, Latvia, Lithuania, Lousiana, Malta, Mexico, Montenegro, Mozambique, Poland, Slovakia, Slovenia, Thailand, Ukraine, Uruguay

International Red Cross and Red Crescent Movement (ICRM)

address – 19 Avenue de la paix, 1202 Geneva, Switzerland
phone – 41 22 734 60 01
website – The International Red Cross and Red Crescent Movement | ICRC
established – 1928
aim – to promote worldwide humanitarian aid through the International Committee of the Red Cross (ICRC) in wartime, and International Federation of Red Cross and Red Crescent Societies (IFRCS; formerly League of Red Cross and Red Crescent Societies, or LORCS) in peacetime
members – (192) Afghanistan, Albania, Algeria, Andorra, Angola, Antigua and Barbuda, Argentina, Armenia, Australia, Austria, Azerbaijan, The Bahamas, Bahrain, Bangladesh, Barbados, Belarus, Belgium, Belize, Benin, Bolivia, Bosnia and Herzegovina, Botswana, Brazil, Brunei, Bulgaria, Burkina Faso, Burma, Burundi, Cabo Verde, Cambodia, Cameroon, Canada, Central African Republic, Chad, Chile, China, Colombia, Comoros, Democratic Republic of the Congo, Republic of the Congo, Cook Islands, Costa Rica, Cote d'Ivoire, Croatia, Cuba, Cyprus, Czechia, Denmark, Djibouti, Dominica, Dominican Republic, Ecuador, Egypt, El Salvador, Equatorial Guinea, Eritrea, Estonia, Eswatini, Ethiopia, Fiji, Finland, France, Gabon, The Gambia, Georgia, Germany, Ghana, Greece, Grenada, Guatemala, Guinea, Guinea-Bissau, Guyana, Haiti, Honduras, Hungary, Iceland, India, Indonesia, Iran, Iraq, Ireland, Israel, Italy, Jamaica, Japan, Jordan, Kazakhstan, Kenya, Kiribati, North Korea, South Korea, Kuwait, Kyrgyzstan, Laos, Latvia, Lebanon, Lesotho, Liberia, Libya, Liechtenstein, Lithuania, Luxembourg, Madagascar, Malawi, Malaysia, Maldives, Mali, Malta, Marshall Islands, Mauritania, Mauritius, Mexico, Federated States of Micronesia, Moldova, Monaco, Mongolia, Montenegro, Morocco, Mozambique, Namibia, Nepal, Netherlands, NZ, Nicaragua, Niger, Nigeria, North Macedonia, Norway, Pakistan, Palau, Panama, Papua New Guinea, Paraguay, Peru, Philippines, Poland, Portugal, Qatar, Romania, Russia, Rwanda, Saint Kitts and Nevis, Saint Lucia, Saint Vincent and the Grenadines, Samoa, San Marino, Sao Tome and Principe, Saudi Arabia, Senegal, Serbia, Seychelles, Sierra Leone, Singapore, Slovakia, Slovenia, Solomon Islands, Somalia, South Africa, South Sudan, Spain, Sri Lanka, Sudan, Suriname, Sweden, Switzerland, Syria, Tajikistan, Tanzania, Thailand, Timor-Leste, Togo, Tonga, Trinidad and Tobago, Tunisia, Turkey (Turkiye), Turkmenistan, Tuvalu, Uganda, Ukraine, UAE, UK, US, Uruguay, Uzbekistan, Vanuatu, Venezuela, Vietnam, Yemen, Zambia, Zimbabwe, plus the Palestine Liberation Organization

International Telecommunication Satellite Organization (ITSO)

address – 4400 Jenifer Street, NW, Suite #333, Washington, D.C. 20015
phone – 202 243 5096
email – itsomail@itso.int
website – https://itso.int/
established – August 1964
aim – to act as a watchdog over Intelsat, Ltd., a private company, to make sure it provides public telecommunication services on a global and nondiscriminatory basis
members – (149) Afghanistan, Algeria, Angola, Argentina, Armenia, Australia, Austria, Azerbaijan, The Bahamas, Bahrain, Bangladesh, Barbados, Belgium, Benin, Bhutan, Bolivia, Bosnia and Herzegovina, Botswana, Brazil, Brunei, Burkina Faso, Cabo Verde, Cameroon, Canada, Central African Republic, Chad, Chile, China, Colombia, Comoros, Democratic Republic of the Congo, Republic of the Congo, Costa Rica, Cote d'Ivoire, Croatia, Cuba, Cyprus, Czechia, Denmark, Dominican Republic, Ecuador, Egypt, El Salvador, Equatorial Guinea, Estonia, Eswatini, Ethiopia, Fiji, Finland, France, Gabon, The Gambia, Georgia, Germany, Ghana, Greece, Guatemala, Guinea, Guinea-Bissau, Haiti, Holy See, Honduras, Hungary, Iceland, India, Indonesia, Iran, Iraq, Ireland, Israel, Italy, Jamaica, Japan, Jordan, Kazakhstan, Kenya, North Korea, South Korea, Kuwait, Kyrgyzstan, Lebanon, Libya, Liechtenstein, Luxembourg, Madagascar, Malawi, Malaysia, Mali, Malta, Mauritania, Mauritius, Mexico, the Federated States of Micronesia, Monaco, Mongolia, Montenegro, Morocco, Mozambique, Namibia, Nepal, Netherlands, NZ, Nicaragua, Niger, Nigeria, Norway, Oman, Pakistan, Panama, Papua New Guinea, Paraguay, Peru, Philippines, Poland, Portugal, Qatar, Romania, Russia, Rwanda, Saudi Arabia, Senegal, Serbia, Singapore, Somalia, South Africa, Spain, Sri Lanka, Sudan, Sweden, Switzerland, Syria, Tajikistan, Tanzania, Thailand, Togo, Trinidad and Tobago, Tunisia, Turkey (Turkiye), Uganda, UAE, UK, US, Uruguay, Uzbekistan, Venezuela, Vietnam, Yemen, Zambia, Zimbabwe
International Telecommunication Union (ITU)
address – International Telecommunication Union (ITU), Place des Nations, 1211 Geneva 20 Switzerland
phone – 41 22 730 5111
fax – 41 22 733 7256
email – itumail@itu.int
website – https://www.itu.int/en/Pages/default.aspx
established – 17 May 1865 set up as the International Telegraph Union; 9 December 1932 adopted present name
effective – 1 January 1934; affiliated with the UN – 15 November 1947
aim – to deal with world telecommunications issues; a UN specialized agency
members – (193) includes all UN member countries except Palau (192 total); plus Holy See

International Trade Union Confederation (ITUC)

note – its predecessors were the International Confederation of Free Trade Unions (ICFTU) and the World Confederation of Labor (WCL)
address – Boulevard du Roi Albert II, 5, Bte 1, 1210 Brussels, Belgium
phone – 32 (0)2 224 0211
fax – 32 (0)2 201 5815
email – info@ituc-csi.org
website – https://www.ituc-csi.org/
established – 3 November 2006
aim – to promote the trade union movement
members – (332 affiliated organizations in 162 countries or territories and the Palestine Liberation Organization as of November 2019)
Afghanistan, Albania, Algeria, Angola, Antigua and Barbuda, Argentina, Armenia, Australia, Austria, Azerbaijan, Bahrain, Bangladesh, Barbados, Belarus, Belgium, Belize, Benin, Bermuda, Bonaire, Bosnia and Herzegovina, Botswana, Brazil, Bulgaria, Burkina Faso, Burma, Burundi, Cabo Verde, Cambodia, Cameroon, Canada, Central African Republic, Chad, Chile, Colombia, Comoros, Democratic Republic of the Congo, Republic of the Congo, Cook Islands, Costa Rica, Cote d'Ivoire, Croatia, Curacao, Cyprus, Czechia, Denmark, Djibouti, Dominica, Dominican Republic, Ecuador, Egypt, El Salvador, Eritrea, Estonia, Eswatini, Ethiopia, Fiji, Finland, France, French Polynesia, Gabon, Georgia, Germany, Ghana, Greece, Grenada, Guatemala, Guinea, Guinea-Bissau, Haiti, Honduras, Holy See, Hong Kong, Hungary, Iceland, India, Indonesia, Iraq, Ireland, Israel, Italy, Japan, Jordan, Kazakhstan, Kenya, Kiribati, South Korea, Kosovo, Kuwait, Latvia, Lesotho, Liberia, Liechtenstein, Lithuania, Luxembourg, Madagascar, Malawi, Malaysia, Mali, Malta, Mauritania, Mauritius, Mexico, Moldova, Mongolia, Montenegro, Morocco, Mozambique, Namibia, Nepal, Netherlands, New Caledonia, New Zealand, Nicaragua, Niger, Nigeria, North Macedonia, Norway, Oman, Pakistan, Panama,

Paraguay, Peru, Philippines, Poland, Portugal, Romania, Russia, Rwanda, Saint Lucia, Samoa, San Marino, Sao Tome and Principe, Senegal, Serbia, Sierra Leone, Singapore, Slovakia, Somalia, South Africa, Spain, Sri Lanka, Sudan, Suriname, Sweden, Switzerland, Taiwan, Tanzania, Thailand, Togo, Tonga, Trinidad and Tobago, Tunisia, Turkey (Turkiye), Uganda, Ukraine, UK, US, Vanuatu, Venezuela, Yemen, Zambia, Zimbabwe, Palestine Liberation Organization

Inter-Parliamentary Union (IPU)

address – 5, chemin du Pommier, Case postale 330, CH-1218 Le Grand-Saconnex, Geneva, Switzerland
phone – 41 22 919 41 50
fax – 41 22 919 41 60
email – postbox@ipu.org
website – https://www.ipu.org/
established – 1889
aim – fosters contacts among parliamentarians, considers and expresses views of international interest and concern with the purpose of bringing about action by parliaments and parliamentarians, contributes to the defense and promotion of human rights, contributes to better knowledge of representative institutions
members – (178) Afghanistan, Albania, Algeria, Andorra, Angola, Argentina, Armenia, Australia, Austria, Azerbaijan, Bahrain, Bangladesh, Belarus, Belgium, Benin, Bhutan, Bolivia, Bosnia and Herzegovina, Botswana, Brazil, Bulgaria, Burkina Faso, Burma, Burundi, Cabo Verde, Cambodia, Cameroon, Canada, Central African Republic (suspended), Chad, Chile, China, Colombia, Comoros, Democratic Republic of the Congo, Republic of the Congo (suspended), Costa Rica, Cote d'Ivoire, Croatia, Cuba, Cyprus, Czechia, Denmark, Djibouti, Dominican Republic, Ecuador, Egypt, El Salvador, Equatorial Guinea, Estonia, Eswatini, Ethiopia, Fiji, Finland, France, Gabon, The Gambia, Georgia, Germany, Ghana, Greece, Guatemala, Guinea, Guinea-Bissau, Guyana, Haiti (suspended), Honduras (suspended), Hungary, Iceland, India, Indonesia, Iran, Iraq, Ireland, Israel, Italy, Japan, Jordan, Kazakhstan, Kenya, North Korea, South Korea, Kuwait, Kyrgyzstan, Laos, Latvia, Lebanon, Lesotho, Libya, Liechtenstein, Lithuania, Luxembourg, Madagascar, Malawi, Malaysia, Maldives, Mali, Malta, Marshall Islands, Mauritania, Mauritius, Mexico, Federated States of Micronesia, Moldova, Monaco, Mongolia, Montenegro, Morocco, Mozambique, Namibia, Nepal, Netherlands, NZ, Nicaragua, Niger, Nigeria, North Macedonia, Norway, Oman, Pakistan, Palau, Panama, Papua New Guinea (suspended), Paraguay, Peru, Philippines, Poland, Portugal, Qatar, Romania, Russia, Rwanda, Saint Lucia, Saint Vincent and the Grenadines, Samoa, San Marino, Sao Tome and Principe, Saudi Arabia, Senegal, Serbia, Seychelles, Sierra Leone, Singapore, Slovakia, Slovenia, Somalia, South Africa, South Sudan, Spain, Sri Lanka, Sudan, Suriname, Sweden, Switzerland, Syria, Tanzania, Tajikistan, Thailand, Timor-Leste, Togo, Tonga, Trinidad and Tobago, Tunisia, Turkey (Turkiye), Turkmenistan, Tuvalu, Uganda, Ukraine, UAE, UK, Uruguay, Uzbekistan, Vanuatu, Venezuela, Vietnam, Yemen, Zambia, Zimbabwe; plus the Palestine Liberation Organization (not included in member count)
associate members – (13) Andean Parliament, Arab Parliament, Central American Parliament, East African Legislative Assembly, European Parliament, Interparliamentary Assembly of Member States of the Commonwealth of Independent States, Inter-Parliamentary Committee of the West African Economic and Monetary Union, Latin American and Caribbean Parliament, Parliament of the Central African Economic and Monetary Community, Parliament of the Economic Community of West African States, Parliamentary Assembly of La Francophonie, Parliamentary Assembly of the Black Sea Economic Cooperation, Parliamentary Assembly of the Council of Europe

Islamic Development Bank (IsDB)

address – 8111 King Khalid St., Al Nuzlah Al Yamania Dist. Unit No. 1, Jeddah 22332-2444, Kingdom of Saudi Arabia
phone – 966 12 6361400
fax – 966 126366871
email – info@isdb.org
website – https://www.isdb.org/
established – 15 December 1973 by declaration of intent
effective – 12 August 1974
aim – to promote Islamic economic aid and social development
members – (56) Afghanistan, Albania, Algeria, Azerbaijan, Bahrain, Bangladesh, Benin, Brunei, Burkina Faso, Cameroon, Chad, Comoros, Cote d'Ivoire, Djibouti, Egypt, Gabon, The Gambia, Guinea, Guinea-Bissau, Guyana, Indonesia, Iran, Iraq, Jordan, Kazakhstan, Kuwait, Kyrgyzstan, Lebanon, Libya, Malaysia, Maldives, Mali, Mauritania, Morocco, Mozambique, Niger, Nigeria, Oman, Pakistan, Qatar, Saudi Arabia, Senegal, Sierra Leone, Somalia, Sudan, Suriname, Syria, Tajikistan, Togo, Tunisia, Turkey (Turkiye), Turkmenistan, Uganda, UAE, Uzbekistan, Yemen; plus the Palestine Liberation Organization (not included in member count)

Lake Chad Basin Commission (LCBC)

address – Place de la Grande Armée, B.P. 727, N'Djamena, Chad
phone – 235 22 52 41 45 / 235 22 52 40 29
fax – 235 22 52 41 37
email – info@cblt.org
website – https://cblt.org/
established – 22 May 1964
aim – the management of the Lake Chad and its shared water resources, preservation of its ecosystems, and the promotion of regional integration, peace, security, and development
members – (6) Cameroon, Central African Republic, Chad, Libya, Niger, Nigeria
observers – (3) Democratic Republic of the Congo, Republic of the Congo, Egypt

Latin American and Caribbean Economic System (LAES)

note – also known as Sistema Economico Latinoamericana (SELA)
address – Avenida Francisco de Miranda, Caracas 1060, Miranda, Venezuela
phone – (58-212) 955 71 11
fax – (58-212) 951 52 92
email – sela_sp@sela.org / sela@sela.org
website – http://www.sela.org/en/
established – 17 October 1975
aim – to promote economic and social development through regional cooperation

members – (25) Argentina, The Bahamas, Barbados, Belize, Bolivia, Brazil, Chile, Colombia, Cuba, Dominican Republic, Ecuador, El Salvador, Guatemala, Guyana, Haiti, Honduras, Mexico, Nicaragua, Panama, Paraguay, Peru, Suriname, Trinidad and Tobago, Uruguay, Venezuela

Latin American Integration Association (LAIA)
note – also known as Asociacion Latinoamericana de Integracion (ALADI)
address – Cebollatí 1461, Barrio Palermo, Montevideo - Uruguay C.P. 11200
phone – (598) 24101121
email – sgaladi@aladi.org
website – https://www.aladi.org/sitioaladi/
established – 12 August 1980
effective – 18 March 1981
aim – to promote freer regional trade
members – (13) Argentina, Bolivia, Brazil, Chile, Colombia, Cuba, Ecuador, Mexico, Panama, Paraguay, Peru, Uruguay, Venezuela
observers – (26) China, Costa Rica, Dominican Republic, Economic Commission for Latin America and the Caribbean, El Salvador, European Commission, Guatemala, Honduras, Ibero-American General Secretariat, Inter-American Development Bank, Inter-American Institute for Cooperation on Agriculture, Italy, Japan, South Korea, Latin American Development Bank, Latin America Economic System, Nicaragua, Organizacion Panamericana de la Salud, Organization of American States, Portugal, Romania, Russia, Spain, Switzerland, Ukraine, United Nations Development Program

League of Arab States (LAS)
note – also known as Arab League (AL)
website – http://www.lasportal.org/Pages/Welcome.aspx
established – 22 March 1945
aim – to promote economic, social, political, and military cooperation
members – (21) Algeria, Bahrain, Comoros, Djibouti, Egypt, Iraq, Jordan, Kuwait, Lebanon, Libya (suspended), Mauritania, Morocco, Oman, Qatar, Saudi Arabia, Somalia, Sudan, Syria (suspended), Tunisia, UAE, Yemen; plus the Palestine Liberation Organization (not included in member count)
observers – (5) Armenia, Brazil, Eritrea, India, Venezuela

Multilateral Investment Guarantee Agency (MIGA)
address – 1818 H Street, NW, Washington, DC 20433
phone – 202.458.2538
fax – 202.522.0316
email – migainquiry@worldbank.org
website – https://www.miga.org/
established – 11 October 1985
effective – 12 April 1988
aim – encourages flow of foreign direct investment among member countries by offering investment insurance, consultation, and negotiation on conditions for foreign investment and technical assistance; a UN specialized agency
members – (182) includes all UN member countries except Andorra, Brunei, Cuba, Kiribati, North Korea, Liechtenstein, Marshall Islands, Monaco, Nauru, San Marino, Tonga, Tuvalu; plus Kosovo

Nordic Council (NC)
address – Ved Stranden 18, 1061 Copenhagen K, Denmark
phone – 45 33 96 04 00
email – nordisk-rad@norden.org
website – https://www.norden.org/en/nordic-council
established – 16 March 1952
effective – 12 February 1953
aim – to promote regional economic, cultural, and environmental cooperation
members – (8) Aland, Denmark, Faroe Islands, Finland, Greenland, Iceland, Norway, Sweden
observers – (1) Sami Parliamentary Council

Nordic Investment Bank (NIB)
address – Fabianinkatu 34, P.O. Box 249, FI-00171 Helsinki, Finland
phone – 358 10 618 001
fax – 358 10 618 0725
email – info@nib.int
website – https://www.nib.int/
established – 4 December 1975
effective – 1 June 1976
aim – to promote economic cooperation and development
members – (8) Denmark (including Faroe Islands and Greenland), Estonia, Finland (including Aland Islands), Iceland, Latvia, Lithuania, Norway, Sweden

North Atlantic Treaty Organization (NATO)
address – Boulevard Leopold III, Brussels, Belgium
website – https://www.nato.int/
established – 4 April 1949
aim – to promote mutual defense and cooperation
members – (32) Albania, Belgium, Bulgaria, Canada, Croatia, Czechia, Denmark, Estonia, Finland, France, Germany, Greece, Hungary, Iceland, Italy, Latvia, Lithuania, Luxembourg, Montenegro, Netherlands, North Macedonia, Norway, Poland, Portugal, Romania, Slovakia, Slovenia, Spain, Sweden, Turkey (Turkiye), UK, US

Nuclear Energy Agency (NEA)

note – also known as OECD Nuclear Energy Agency
mailing address – 2, rue André Pascal, 75775 Paris Cedex 16, France
visiting address – 46, quai Alphone Le Gallo, 92100 Boulogne-Billancourt, France
phone – 33 1 45 24 10 10
website – https://www.oecd-nea.org/
established – 1 February 1958
aim – to promote the peaceful uses of nuclear energy; associated with OECD
members – (34) Argentina, Australia, Austria, Belgium, Bulgaria, Canada, Czechia, Denmark, Finland, France, Germany, Greece, Hungary, Iceland, Ireland, Italy, Japan, South Korea, Luxembourg, Mexico, Netherlands, Norway, Poland, Portugal, Romania, Russia, Slovakia, Slovenia, Spain, Sweden, Switzerland, Turkey (Turkiye), UK, US
strategic partners – (2) China, India

Nuclear Suppliers Group (NSG)

note – also known as the London Suppliers Group or the London Group
website – https://www.nuclearsuppliersgroup.org/en/
established – 1974
effective – 1975
aim – to establish guidelines for exports of nuclear materials, processing equipment for uranium enrichment, and technical information to countries of proliferation concern and regions of conflict and instability
members – (48) Argentina, Australia, Austria, Belarus, Belgium, Brazil, Bulgaria, Canada, China, Croatia, Cyprus, Czechia, Denmark, Estonia, Finland, France, Germany, Greece, Hungary, Iceland, Ireland, Italy, Japan, Kazakhstan, South Korea, Latvia, Lithuania, Luxembourg, Malta, Mexico, Netherlands, NZ, Norway, Poland, Portugal, Romania, Russia, Serbia, Slovakia, Slovenia, South Africa, Spain, Sweden, Switzerland, Turkey (Turkiye), Ukraine, UK, US
observer – (2) Chairman of the Zangger Committee, European Commission (EU)

Organisation for Economic Cooperation and Development (OECD)

address – 2, rue André Pascal, 75016 Paris, France
website – https://www.oecd.org/
established – 14 December 1960
effective – 30 September 1961
aim – to promote economic cooperation and development
members – (38) Australia, Austria, Belgium, Canada, Chile, Colombia, Costa Rica, Czechia, Denmark, Estonia, Finland, France, Germany, Greece, Hungary, Iceland, Ireland, Israel, Italy, Japan, South Korea, Latvia, Lithuania, Luxembourg, Mexico, Netherlands, NZ, Norway, Poland, Portugal, Slovakia, Slovenia, Spain, Sweden, Switzerland, Turkey (Turkiye), UK, US
special member – (1) European Commission (EU)

Organization for Democracy and Economic Development (GUAM)

note – acronym standing for the member countries, Georgia, Ukraine, Azerbaijan, Moldova; formerly known as GUUAM before Uzbekistan withdrew on 5 May 2005
address – Sofiivska str 2-A 01001 Kyiv, Ukraine
phone – 380 44 206 37 37
fax – 380 44 206 30 06
email – secretariat@guam-organization.org
website – https://guam-organization.org/en/
established – 7 June 2001
aim – commits the countries to cooperation and assistance in social and economic development, the strengthening and broadening of trade and economic relations, and the development and effective use of transport and communications, highways, and related infrastructure crossing the boundaries of the member states
members – (4) Azerbaijan, Georgia, Moldova, Ukraine

Organization for Security and Cooperation in Europe (OSCE)

note – formerly the Conference on Security and Cooperation in Europe (CSCE), established 3 July 1975
address – Wallnerstrasse 6, 1010 Vienna, Austria
phone – 43 1 514 360
fax – 43 1 514 36 6996
email – pm@osce.org
website – https://www.osce.org/
established – 1 January 1995
aim – to foster the implementation of human rights, fundamental freedoms, democracy, and the rule of law; to act as an instrument of early warning, conflict prevention, and crisis management; and to serve as a framework for conventional arms control and confidence-building measures
members – (57) Albania, Andorra, Armenia, Austria, Azerbaijan, Belarus, Belgium, Bosnia and Herzegovina, Bulgaria, Canada, Croatia, Cyprus, Czechia, Denmark, Estonia, Finland, France, Georgia, Germany, Greece, Holy See, Hungary, Iceland, Ireland, Italy, Kazakhstan, Kyrgyzstan, Latvia, Liechtenstein, Lithuania, Luxembourg, Malta, Moldova, Monaco, Mongolia, Montenegro, Netherlands, North Macedonia, Norway, Poland, Portugal, Romania, Russia, San Marino, Serbia, Slovakia, Slovenia, Spain, Sweden, Switzerland, Tajikistan, Turkey (Turkiye), Turkmenistan, Ukraine, UK, US, Uzbekistan
partners for cooperation – (11) Afghanistan, Algeria, Australia, Egypt, Israel, Japan, Jordan, South Korea, Morocco, Thailand, Tunisia

Organization for the Prohibition of Chemical Weapons (OPCW)

address – Johan de Wittlaan 32, 2517 JR The Hague, The Netherlands
phone – 31 70 416 3300
fax – 31 70 306 3535

website – https://www.opcw.org/
established – 29 April 1997
aim – to enforce the Convention on the Prohibition of the Development, Production, Stockpiling, and Use of Chemical Weapons and on Their Destruction; to provide a forum for consultation and cooperation among the signatories of the Convention
members (countries or entities that have ratified the Convention) – (192) Afghanistan, Albania, Algeria, Andorra, Angola, Antigua and Barbuda, Argentina, Armenia, Australia, Austria, Azerbaijan, The Bahamas, Bahrain, Bangladesh, Barbados, Belarus, Belgium, Belize, Benin, Bhutan, Bolivia, Bosnia and Herzegovina, Botswana, Brazil, Brunei, Bulgaria, Burkina Faso, Burma, Burundi, Cabo Verde, Cambodia, Cameroon, Canada, Central African Republic, Chad, Chile, China, Colombia, Comoros, Democratic Republic of the Congo, Republic of the Congo, Cook Islands, Costa Rica, Cote d'Ivoire, Croatia, Cuba, Cyprus, Czechia, Denmark, Djibouti, Dominica, Dominican Republic, Ecuador, El Salvador, Equatorial Guinea, Eritrea, Estonia, Eswatini, Ethiopia, Fiji, Finland, France, Gabon, The Gambia, Georgia, Germany, Ghana, Greece, Grenada, Guatemala, Guinea, Guinea-Bissau, Guyana, Haiti, Holy See, Honduras, Hungary, Iceland, India, Indonesia, Iran, Iraq, Ireland, Italy, Jamaica, Japan, Jordan, Kazakhstan, Kenya, Kiribati, South Korea, Kuwait, Kyrgyzstan, Laos, Latvia, Lebanon, Lesotho, Liberia, Libya, Liechtenstein, Lithuania, Luxembourg, Madagascar, Malawi, Malaysia, Maldives, Mali, Malta, Marshall Islands, Mauritania, Mauritius, Mexico, Federated States of Micronesia, Moldova, Monaco, Mongolia, Montenegro, Morocco, Mozambique, Namibia, Nauru, Nepal, Netherlands, NZ, Nicaragua, Niger, Nigeria, Niue, North Macedonia, Norway, Oman, Pakistan, Palau, Panama, Papua New Guinea, Paraguay, Peru, Philippines, Poland, Portugal, Qatar, Romania, Russia, Rwanda, Saint Kitts and Nevis, Saint Lucia, Saint Vincent and the Grenadines, Samoa, San Marino, Sao Tome and Principe, Saudi Arabia, Senegal, Serbia, Seychelles, Sierra Leone, Singapore, Slovakia, Slovenia, Solomon Islands, Somalia, South Africa, Spain, Sri Lanka, Sudan, Suriname, Sweden, Switzerland, Syria, Tajikistan, Tanzania, Thailand, Timor-Leste, Togo, Tonga, Trinidad and Tobago, Tunisia, Turkey (Turkiye), Turkmenistan, Tuvalu, Uganda, Ukraine, UAE, UK, US, Uruguay, Uzbekistan, Vanuatu, Venezuela, Vietnam, Yemen, Zambia, Zimbabwe, Palestine Liberation Organization
signatory states (countries that have signed, but not ratified, the Convention) – (1) Israel

Organization of African, Caribbean, and Pacific States (OACPS)
address – Place Charles Rogier 16 1210 Saint-Josse-ten-Noode, Belgium
phone – 32 2 743 06 00
fax – 32 2 735 55 73
email – info@acp.int
website – http://www.acp.int/
established – 6 June 1975
aim – to manage their preferential economic and aid relationship with the EU and sustainable development of member states and their gradual integration into the global economy, which entails making poverty reduction a matter of priority and establishing a new, fairer, and more equitable world order
members – (79) Angola, Antigua and Barbuda, The Bahamas, Barbados, Belize, Benin, Botswana, Burkina Faso, Burundi, Cabo Verde, Cameroon, Central African Republic, Chad, Comoros, Democratic Republic of the Congo, Republic of the Congo, Cook Islands, Cote d'Ivoire, Cuba, Djibouti, Dominica, Dominican Republic, Equatorial Guinea, Eritrea, Eswatini, Ethiopia, Fiji, Gabon, The Gambia, Ghana, Grenada, Guinea, Guinea-Bissau, Guyana, Haiti, Jamaica, Kenya, Kiribati, Lesotho, Liberia, Madagascar, Malawi, Mali, Marshall Islands, Mauritania, Mauritius, Federated States of Micronesia, Mozambique, Namibia, Nauru, Niger, Nigeria, Niue, Palau, Papua New Guinea, Rwanda, Saint Kitts and Nevis, Saint Lucia, Saint Vincent and the Grenadines, Samoa, Sao Tome and Principe, Senegal, Seychelles, Sierra Leone, Solomon Islands, Somalia, South Africa, Sudan, Suriname, Tanzania, Timor-Leste, Togo, Tonga, Trinidad and Tobago, Tuvalu, Uganda, Vanuatu, Zambia, Zimbabwe

Organization of American States (OAS)
address – 17th Street and Constitution Ave., NW, Washington, DC, 20006-4499
phone – (202) 370 5000
fax – (202) 458 3967
website – https://www.oas.org/en/
established – 14 April 1890 as the International Union of American Republics; 30 April 1948 adopted present charter
effective – 13 December 1951
aim – to promote regional peace and security, as well as economic and social development
members – (35) Antigua and Barbuda, Argentina, The Bahamas, Barbados, Belize, Bolivia, Brazil, Canada, Chile, Colombia, Costa Rica, Cuba (suspended), Dominica, Dominican Republic, Ecuador, El Salvador, Grenada, Guatemala, Guyana, Haiti, Honduras, Jamaica, Mexico, Nicaragua, Panama, Paraguay, Peru, Saint Kitts and Nevis, Saint Lucia, Saint Vincent and the Grenadines, Suriname, Trinidad and Tobago, US, Uruguay, Venezuela
observers – (72) Albania, Algeria, Angola, Armenia, Austria, Azerbaijan, Bangladesh, Belgium, Benin, Bosnia and Herzegovina, Bulgaria, China, Croatia, Cyprus, Czechia, Denmark, Egypt, Equatorial Guinea, Estonia, EU, Finland, France, Georgia, Germany, Ghana, Greece, Holy See, Hungary, Iceland, India, Ireland, Israel, Italy, Japan, Kazakhstan, South Korea, Latvia, Lebanon, Liechtenstein, Lithuania, Luxembourg, Malta, Moldova, Monaco, Montenegro, Morocco, Netherlands, Nigeria, North Macedonia, Norway, Pakistan, Philippines, Poland, Portugal, Qatar, Romania, Russia, Saudi Arabia, Serbia, Slovakia, Slovenia, Spain, Sri Lanka, Sweden, Switzerland, Thailand, Tunisia, Turkey (Turkiye), Ukraine, UK, Vanuatu, Yemen

Organization of Arab Petroleum Exporting Countries (OAPEC)
address – P.O. Box 20501, Safat 13066, Kuwait
phone – (965) 24959000
email – oapec@oapecorg.org
website – https://www.oapecorg.org/Home
established – 9 January 1968
aim – to promote cooperation in the petroleum industry
members – (11) Algeria, Bahrain, Egypt, Iraq, Kuwait, Libya, Qatar, Saudi Arabia, Syria, Tunisia (suspended), UAE; note - Indonesia left OAPEC in 2008, returned again on 1 January 2016, and suspended its membership once again on 30 November 2016

Organization of Eastern Caribbean States (OECS)
address – Morne Fortune, P.O. Box 179, Castries, Saint Lucia
phone – 1 (758) 455-6327

fax – 1 758-452 2194
email – oecs@oecs.int
website – https://www.oecs.org/en/
established – 18 June 1981
effective – 4 July 1981
aim – to promote political, economic, and defense cooperation
protocol members – (7) Antigua and Barbuda, Dominica, Grenada, Montserrat, Saint Kitts and Nevis, Saint Lucia, Saint Vincent and the Grenadines
associate members – (4) Anguilla, British Virgin Islands, Guadeloupe, Martinique

Organization of Islamic Cooperation (OIC)

note – formerly the Organization of the Islamic Conference
address – P.O. Box 178, Jeddah 21411, Kingdom of Saudi Arabia
phone – (966)-12-6515222
fax – (966)-12-6512288
website – https://www.oic-oci.org/home/?lan=en
established – 22-25 September 1969
aim – to promote Islamic solidarity in economic, social, cultural, and political affairs
members – (56) Afghanistan, Albania, Algeria, Azerbaijan, Bahrain, Bangladesh, Benin, Brunei, Burkina Faso, Cameroon, Chad, Comoros, Cote d'Ivoire, Djibouti, Egypt, Gabon, The Gambia, Guinea, Guinea-Bissau, Guyana, Indonesia, Iran, Iraq, Jordan, Kazakhstan, Kuwait, Kyrgyzstan, Lebanon, Libya, Malaysia, Maldives, Mali, Mauritania, Morocco, Mozambique, Niger, Nigeria, Oman, Pakistan, Qatar, Saudi Arabia, Senegal, Sierra Leone, Somalia, Sudan, Suriname, Syria, Tajikistan, Togo, Tunisia, Turkey (Turkiye), Turkmenistan, Uganda, UAE, Uzbekistan, Yemen; plus the Palestine Liberation Organization (not included in member count)
observers – (12) AU, Bosnia and Herzegovina, Central African Republic, ECO, LAS, Moro National Liberation Front, NAM, Parliamentary Union of the OIC Member States, Russia, Thailand, Turkish Cypriot State, UN

Organization of Petroleum Exporting Countries (OPEC)

address – Helferstorferstrasse 17, A-1010, Vienna, Austria
website – https://www.opec.org/opec_web/en/
established – 14 September 1960
aim – to coordinate petroleum policies
members – (12) Algeria, Equatorial Guinea, Gabon, Iran, Iraq, Kuwait, Libya, Nigeria, Republic of the Congo, Saudi Arabia, UAE, Venezuela

Organization of Turkic States (OTS)

note – formerly known as the Cooperation Council of Turkic Speaking States - Turkic Council
address – Binbirdirek, Piyer Loti Cd. No.2, 34122 Fatih/İstanbul, Turkey (Türkiye)
phone – 90 212 283 16 44
fax – 90 212 283 16 86
website – www.turkicstates.org
established – 3 October 2009
email – info@turkicstates.org
aim – to enable multi-faceted cooperation among its member and observer states in more than 20 areas, ranging from economy to transport and customs, energy to agriculture, education to youth and sports, digitalization to justice and security, culture to tourism and health
members – (5) Azerbaijan, Kazakhstan, Kyrgyzstan, Turkey (Turkiye), Uzbekistan
observers – (3) Hungary, Turkmenistan, Cyprus (Turkish Republic of Northern Cyprus)

Pacific Community (SPC)

address – 95 Promenade Roger Laroque, BP D5, 98848 Noumea, New Caledonia
phone – 687 26 20 00
fax – 687 26 38 18
email – spc@spc.int
website – https://www.spc.int/
established – 6 February 1947
effective – 29 July 1948
aim – to serve island development in 22 Pacific countries; to develop technical assistance and professional, scientific, and research support; to build planning and management capability
members – (27) America Samoa, Australia, Cook Islands, Fiji, France, French Polynesia, Guam, Kiribati, Marshall Islands, Federated States of Micronesia, Nauru, New Caledonia, NZ, Niue, Northern Mariana Islands, Palau, Papua New Guinea, Pitcairn Islands, Samoa, Solomon Islands, Tokelau, Tonga, Tuvalu, US, Vanuatu, Wallis and Futuna

Pacific Islands Forum (PIF)

note – formerly known as South Pacific Forum (SPF); in 2000 changed its name to Pacific Islands Forum
address – Ratu Sukuna Road, Suva, Fiji
phone – (679) 331 2600
email – info@forumsec.org
website – https://www.forumsec.org/
established – 5 August 1971
aim – to promote regional cooperation in political matters
members – (18) Australia, Cook Islands, Fiji, French Polynesia, Kiribati, Marshall Islands, Federated States of Micronesia, Nauru, New Caledonia, NZ, Niue, Palau, Papua New Guinea, Samoa, Solomon Islands, Tonga, Tuvalu, Vanuatu
associate members – (1) Tokelau
partners – (18) Canada, China, Cuba, EU, France, Germany, India, Indonesia, Italy, Japan, South Korea, Malaysia, Philippines, Spain, Thailand, Turkey, UK, US

observers – (12) ACP Secretariat, American Samoa, Asia Development Bank, The Commonwealth Secretariat, Commonwealth of the Northern Marianas, Guam, International Organization for Migration, Timor-Leste, UN Secretariat, Wallis and Futuna, Western and Central Pacific Fisheries Commission, The World Bank

Paris Club
address – Direction générale du Trésor - 139, rue de Bercy - 75572 Paris Cedex 12, France
website – https://clubdeparis.org/
established – 1956
aim – to provide a forum for debtor countries to negotiate rescheduling of debt service payments or loans extended by governments or official agencies of participating countries; to help restore normal trade and project finance to debtor countries
members – (22) Australia, Austria, Belgium, Brazil, Canada, Denmark, Finland, France, Germany, Ireland, Israel, Italy, Japan, South Korea, Netherlands, Norway, Russia, Spain, Sweden, Switzerland, UK, US
ad hoc participants – (14) Abu Dhabi, Argentina, China, Czechia, India, Kuwait, Mexico, Morocco, NZ, Portugal, Saudi Arabia, South Africa, Trinidad and Tobago, Turkey (Turkiye)

Partnership for Peace (PFP)
website – NATO - Topic: Partnership for Peace programme
established – 10-11 January 1994
aim – to expand and intensify political and military cooperation throughout Europe; increase stability, diminish threats to peace, and build relationships by promoting the spirit of practical cooperation and commitment to democratic principles that underpin NATO; program under the auspices of NATO
members – (21) Armenia, Austria, Azerbaijan, Belarus, Bosnia and Herzegovina, Georgia, Ireland, Kazakhstan, Kyrgyzstan, Malta, Moldova, Russia, Serbia, Sweden, Switzerland, Tajikistan, Turkmenistan, Ukraine, Uzbekistan; note - a nation that becomes a member of NATO is no longer a member of PFP

Permanent Court of Arbitration (PCA)
address – Peace Palace, Carnegieplein 2, 2517 KJ The Hague, The Netherlands
phone – 31 70 302 4165
fax – 31 70 302 4167
email – bureau@pca-cpa.org
website – https://pca-cpa.org/en/home/
established – 29 July 1899
aim – to facilitate the settlement of international disputes
members – (121) Albania, Argentina, Australia, Austria, The Bahamas, Bahrain, Bangladesh, Belarus, Belgium, Belize, Benin, Bolivia, Brazil, Bulgaria, Burkina Faso, Cambodia, Cameroon, Canada, Chile, China, Colombia, Democratic Republic of the Congo, Costa Rica, Croatia, Cuba, Cyprus, Czechia, Denmark, Djibouti, Dominican Republic, Ecuador, Egypt, El Salvador, Eritrea, Estonia, Eswatini, Ethiopia, Fiji, Finland, France, Georgia, Germany, Greece, Guatemala, Guyana, Haiti, Honduras, Hungary, Iceland, India, Iran, Iraq, Ireland, Israel, Italy, Japan, Jordan, Kenya, South Korea, Kosovo, Kuwait, Kyrgyzstan, Laos, Latvia, Lebanon, Libya, Liechtenstein, Lithuania, Luxembourg, Madagascar, Malaysia, Malta, Mauritius, Mexico, Mongolia, Montenegro, Morocco, Netherlands, NZ, Nicaragua, Nigeria, North Macedonia, Norway, Pakistan, Panama, Paraguay, Peru, Philippines, Poland, Portugal, Qatar, Romania, Russia, Rwanda, Sao Tome and Principe, Saudi Arabia, Senegal, Serbia, Singapore, Slovakia, Slovenia, South Africa, Spain, Sri Lanka, Sudan, Suriname, Sweden, Switzerland, Thailand, Togo, Turkey (Turkiye), Uganda, Ukraine, UAE, UK, US, Uruguay, Venezuela, Vietnam, Zambia, Zimbabwe; plus the Palestine Liberation Organization (not included in member count)

Shanghai Cooperation Organization (SCO)
note – originally founded as the Shanghai 5 in 1996; changed its name to the Shanghai Cooperation Organization with the admission of Uzbekistan in 2001
address – Chaoyang District, Ritan road, 7, 100600, Beijing, China
phone – 86-10-65329807
fax – 86-10-65329808
email – sco@sectsco.org
website – http://eng.sectsco.org/
established – 15 June 2001
effective – 19 September 2003
aim – to combat terrorism, extremism, and separatism; to safeguard regional security through mutual trust, disarmament, and cooperative security; and to increase cooperation in political, trade, economic, scientific and technological, cultural, and educational fields
members – (8) China, India, Kazakhstan, Kyrgyzstan, Pakistan, Russia, Tajikistan, Uzbekistan
dialogue members – (6) Armenia, Azerbaijan, Cambodia, Nepal, Sri Lanka, Turkey (Turkiye)
observers – (4) Afghanistan, Belarus, Iran, Mongolia

South Asia Co-operative Environment Program (SACEP)
address – South Asia Co-operative Environment Programme (SACEP), 146/24A, Havelock Road, Colombo 05, Sri Lanka
phone – 94 11 2596443 / 2596442
fax – 94 11 2589369
email – info@sacep.org / secretariat@sacep.org
website – http://www.sacep.org/
established – 1982
aim – to promote regional cooperation in South Asia in the field of environment, both natural and human, and on issues of economic and social development; to support conservation and management of natural resources of the region
members – (8) Afghanistan, Bangladesh, Bhutan, India, Maldives, Nepal, Pakistan, Sri Lanka

South Asian Association for Regional Cooperation (SAARC)
address – G.P.O. Box 4222, Tridevi Sadak, Kathmandu, Nepal

phone – (977 1) 4221785, 4226350, 4231334
fax – (977 1) 4227033, 4223991
email – saarc@saarc-sec.org
website – https://www.saarc-sec.org/
established – 8 December 1985
aim – to promote economic, social, and cultural cooperation
members – (8) Afghanistan, Bangladesh, Bhutan, India, Maldives, Nepal, Pakistan, Sri Lanka
observers – (9) Australia, Burma, China, EU, Iran, Japan, South Korea, Mauritius, US

South Pacific Regional Trade and Economic Cooperation Agreement (Sparteca)
established – 1981
aim – to redress unequal trade relationships of Australia and New Zealand with small island economies in the Pacific region
members – (15) Australia, Cook Islands, Fiji, Kiribati, Marshall Islands, Federated States of Micronesia, Nauru, NZ, Niue, Papua New Guinea, Samoa, Solomon Islands, Tonga, Tuvalu, Vanuatu
Southern African Customs Union (SACU)
address – Corner Julius K. Nyerere and Feld Street, PBag 13285, Windhoek, Namibia, 9000
phone – 264 (61) 295 8000
fax – 264 (61) 245 611
email – info@sacu.int
website – https://sacu.int/
established – 11 December 1969
aim – to promote free trade and cooperation in customs matters
members – (5) Botswana, Eswatini, Lesotho, Namibia, South Africa

Southern African Development Community (SADC)
note – evolved from the Southern African Development Coordination Conference (SADCC), established on 1 April 1980
address – SADC House, Plot No. 54385, Central Business District, Private Bag 0095, Gaborone, Botswana
phone – 267 395 1863
fax – 267 397 2848, 267 318 1070
email – registry@sadc.int
website – https://www.sadc.int/
established – 17 August 1992
aim – to promote regional economic development and integration
members – (16) Angola, Botswana, Comoros, Democratic Republic of the Congo, Eswatini, Lesotho, Madagascar, Malawi, Mauritius, Mozambique, Namibia, Seychelles, South Africa, Tanzania, Zambia, Zimbabwe

United Nations Assistance Mission in Afghanistan (UNAMA)
note – gives civilian support only
address – Kabul, Afghanistan
website – https://unama.unmissions.org/
established – 28 March 2002
aim – to support the government of Afghanistan, in its attempt to improve security, governance, economic development, and regional cooperation; protect civilians and support efforts to support human rights

United Nations Children's Fund (UNICEF)
note – acronym retained from the predecessor organization, UN International Children's Emergency Fund
website – https://www.unicef.org/
established – 11 December 1946
aim – to help establish child health and welfare services
executive board members – (36) members states are elected to three-year terms by the UN's Economic and Social Council and regionally allocated: Africa (8 seats), Asia (7), Eastern Europe (4), Latin America and Caribbean (5) and Western Europe and others (12)

United Nations Conference on Trade and Development (UNCTAD)
address – Palais des Nations, 8-14, Av. de la Paix, 1211 Geneva 10, Switzerland
website – https://unctad.org/
established – 30 December 1964
aim – to promote international trade
members – (195) all UN members plus Holy See and the Palestine Liberation Organization

United Nations Development Program (UNDP)
website – https://www.undp.org/
established – 22 November 1965
aim – to provide technical assistance to stimulate economic and social development
executive board members – (36) selected on a rotating basis from all regions

United Nations Economic Commission for Africa (UNECA)
address – Menelik II Ave. P.O. Box 3001, Addis Ababa, Ethiopia
phone – 251-11-544-5000
fax – 251-11-551 4416
website – https://www.uneca.or
established – 1958

aim – promote the economic and social development of its member states, foster intra-regional integration, and promote international cooperation for Africa's development
members – (54) Algeria, Angola, Benin, Botswana, Burkina Faso, Burundi, Cabo Verde, Cameroon, Central African Republic, Chad, Comoros, Democratic Republic of the Congo, Republic of the Congo, Cote d'Ivoire, Djibouti, Egypt, Eritrea, Eswatini, Ethiopia, Equatorial Guinea, Gabon, Gambia, Ghana, Guinea, Guinea-Bissau, Kenya, Lesotho, Liberia, Libya, Madagascar, Malawi, Mali, Mauritania, Mauritius, Mozambique, Morocco, Namibia, Niger, Nigeria, Rwanda, Sao Tome and Principe, Senegal, Seychelles, Sierra Leone, Somalia, South Africa, South Sudan, Sudan, Tanzania, Togo, Tunisia, Uganda, Zambia, Zimbabwe

United Nations Educational, Scientific, and Cultural Organization (UNESCO)

address – 7 Pl. de Fontenoy-Unesco, 75007 Paris, France
website – https://www.unesco.org/en
established – 16 November 1945
effective – 4 November 1946
aim – to promote cooperation in education, science, and culture
members – (194) includes all UN member countries except Liechtenstein, as well as the Cook Islands and Niue; plus the Palestine Liberation Organization (not included in the member count)
associate members – (11) Anguilla, Aruba, British Virgin Islands, Cayman Islands, Curacao, Faroe Islands, Macau, Montserrat, New Caledonia, Sint Maarten, Tokelau

United Nations Environment Program (UNEP)

address – United Nations Avenue, Gigiri Nairobi, Kenya, P.O. Box 30552, 00100, Nairobi, Kenya
phone – 254 (0)20 762 1234
website – https://www.unep.org/
established – 15 December 1972
aim – to promote international cooperation on all environmental matters
members – (193) Environment Assembly includes all UN member states

United Nations General Assembly

website – https://www.un.org/en/ga/
established – 26 June 1945
effective – 24 October 1945
aim – to function as the primary deliberative organ of the UN
members – (193) all UN members are represented in the General Assembly

United Nations High Commissioner for Refugees (UNHCR)

address – Case Postale 2500, CH-1211 Geneva 2 Dépôt, Switzerland
phone – 41 22 739 8111
website – https://www.unhcr.org/en-us/
established – 3 December 1949
effective – 1 January 1951
aim – to ensure the humanitarian treatment of refugees and find permanent solutions to refugee problems
members (executive committee) – (110) Afghanistan, Algeria, Angola, Argentina, Armenia, Australia, Austria, Azerbaijan, Bangladesh, Belarus, Belgium, Benin, Brazil, Bulgaria, Burkina Faso, Cameroon, Canada, Chad, Chile, China, Colombia, Congo, Democratic Republic of the Congo, Costa Rica, Cote d'Ivoire, Croatia, Cyprus, Czechia, Denmark, Djibouti, Ecuador, Egypt, Estonia, Ethiopia, Fiji, Finland, France, Georgia, Germany, Ghana, Greece, Guatemala, Guinea, Holy See, Hungary, Iceland, India, Iran, Ireland, Israel, Italy, Japan, Jordan, Kenya, South Korea, Latvia, Lebanon, Lesotho, Lithuania, Luxembourg, Madagascar, Malawi, Mali, Malta, Mexico, Moldova, Montenegro, Morocco, Mozambique, Namibia, Netherlands, New Zealand, Nicaragua, Nigeria, North Macedonia, Norway, Pakistan, Paraguay, Peru, Philippines, Poland, Portugal, Republic of the Congo, Romania, Russia, Rwanda, Senegal, Serbia, Slovakia, Slovenia, Somalia, South Africa, Spain, Sudan, Sweden, Switzerland, Tanzania, Thailand, Togo, Tunisia, Turkey (Turkiye), Turkmenistan, Uganda, Uruguay, United Kingdom, United States, Venezuela, Yemen, Zambia, Zimbabwe

United Nations Human Rights Council (UNHRC)

address – Alais des Nations, CH 1211 Geneva 10, Switzerland
phone – 41 22 917 9220
website – https://www.ohchr.org/en/ohchr_homepage
established – 15 March 2006
effective – 19 June 2006
aim – strengthen the promotion and protection of human rights around the globe and address human rights violations
membershipzstates serve for three years; membership is based on equitable geographical distribution as follows:

1. African states: 13 seats
2. Asia-Pacific states: 13 seats
3. Latin American and Caribbean states: 8 seats
4. Western European and other states: 7 seats
5. Eastern European states: 6 seats

members – (47) Albania, Algeria, Bangladesh, Belgium, Benin, Bolivia, Brazil, Bulgaria, Burundi, Chile, China, Colombia, Costa Rica, Côte d'Ivoire, Cuba, Cyprus, Czechia, Democratic Republic of Congo, Dominican Republic, Ethiopia, France, Gambia, Georgia, Germany, Ghana, Iceland, Indonesia, Japan, Kenya, Kuwait, Kyrgyzstan, Malawi, Maldives, Marshall Islands, Mexico, Morocco, Netherlands, North Macedonia, Qatar, Romania, Spain, South Africa, South Korea, Sudan, Switzerland, Thailand, Vietnam (2025)

United Nations Industrial Development Organization (UNIDO)
address – Vienna International Centre, Wagramerstr. 5, P.O. Box 300, A-1400 Vienna, Austria
phone – 43 (1) 26026-0
fax – 43 (1) 2692669
website – https://www.unido.org/
established – 17 November 1966
effective – 1 January 1967
aim – UN specialized agency that promotes industrial development, especially among the members
members – (170) includes all UN member countries except Andorra, Australia, Belgium, Brunei, Canada, Denmark, Estonia, France, Greece, Iceland, Latvia, Liechtenstein, Lithuania, Nauru, NZ, Palau, Portugal, San Marino, Singapore, Slovakia, Solomon Islands, South Sudan, UK, US

United Nations Institute for Training and Research (UNITAR)
address – 7 bis, Avenue de la Paix, CH-1202 Geneva 2, Switzerland
phone – 41 22 917 8400
email – info@unitar.org
website – https://www.unitar.org/
established – 11 December 1963 adoption of the resolution establishing the Institute
effective – 24 March 1965
aim – to help the UN become more effective through training and research
members (Board of Trustees) – (14) Algeria, China, Fiji, Finland, Germany, Japan, India, Mexico, Nigeria, Russia, Sweden, Switzerland, UK, US; note - the UN Secretary General can appoint up to 30 members; trustees are eligible for a maximum of two consecutive, three-year terms

United Nations Office for Outer Space Affairs (UNOOSA)
address – Vienna International Centre, Wagramerstrasse 5, A-1220 Vienna
phone – 43-1 26060-84950
fax – 43-1 26060-5830
website – https://www.unoosa.org
established – 13 December 1958
aim – help all countries, especially developing countries, access and leverage the benefits of space to accelerate sustainable development through a variety of activities that cover all aspects related to space, from space law to space applications
members – (102) Albania, Algeria, Angola, Argentina, Armenia, Australia, Austria, Azerbaijan, Bahrain, Bangladesh, Belarus, Belgium, Benin, Bolivia, Brazil, Bulgaria, Burkina Faso, Cameroon, Canada, Chad, Chile, China, Colombia, Costa Rica, Cuba, Cyprus, Czechia, Denmark, Dominican Republic, Ecuador, Egypt, El Salvador, Ethiopia, Finland, France, Germany, Ghana, Guatemala, Greece, Hungary, India, Indonesia, Iran, Iraq, Israel, Italy, Japan, Jordan, Kazakhstan, Kenya, Kuwait, Lebanon, Libya, Luxembourg, Malaysia, Mauritius, Mexico, Mongolia, Morocco, Netherlands, New Zealand, Nicaragua, Niger, Nigeria, Norway, Oman, Pakistan, Panama, Paraguay, Peru, Philippines, Poland, Portugal, Qatar, Romania, Russia, Rwanda, Saudi Arabia, Senegal, Sierra Leone, Singapore, Slovakia, Slovenia, South Africa, South Korea, Spain, Sri Lanka, Sudan, Sweden, Switzerland, Syria, Thailand, Tunisia, Turkey (Turkiye), Ukraine, United Arab Emirates, United Kingdom, United States, Uruguay, Uzbekistan, Venezuela, Vietnam

United Nations Population Fund (UNFPA)
note – acronym retained from predecessor organization UN Fund for Population Activities
address – 605 Third Avenue, New York, NY 10158
website – https://www.unfpa.org/
established – 11 July 1967
aim – to assist both developed and developing countries in dealing with their population problems
members (executive board) – (36) selected on a rotating basis from all regions

United Nations Relief and Works Agency for Palestine Refugees in the Near East (UNRWA)
website – https://www.unrwa.org/
established – 8 December 1949
aim – to provide assistance to Palestinian refugees
members (advisory commission) – (28) Australia, Belgium, Brazil, Canada, Denmark, Egypt, Finland, France, Germany, India, Ireland, Italy, Japan, Jordan, Kuwait, Lebanon, Luxembourg, Netherlands, Norway, Qatar, Saudi Arabia, Spain, Sweden, Switzerland, Syria, Turkey (Turkiye), UAE, UK
observers (of the advisory commission) – (4) EU, League of Arab States, Organization of Islamic Cooperation, Palestine Liberation Organization

United Nations Research Institute for Social Development (UNRISD)
address – Palais des Nations, 1211 Geneva 10, Switzerland
phone – 41 (0)22 917 3060
fax – 41 (0)22 917 0650
email – info.unrisd@un.org
website – https://www.unrisd.org/
established – 1963
aim – to conduct research into the problems of economic development during different phases of economic growth
members (advisory commission) – no country members, but a Board of Directors currently consisting of a chairperson appointed by the UN Secretary General and 10 members confirmed by ECOSOC and a representative of the Secretary General

United Nations Secretariat
website – https://www.un.org/en/about-us/secretariat
established – 26 June 1945
effective – 24 October 1945

aim – to serve as the primary administrative organ of the UN; a Secretary General is appointed for a five-year term by the General Assembly on the recommendation of the Security Council
members - the UN Secretary General and staff

United Nations Security Council (UNSC)

website – https://www.un.org/securitycouncil/
established – 26 June 1945
effective – 24 October 1945
aim – to maintain international peace and security
permanent members – (5) China, France, Russia, UK, US
nonpermanent members – (10) elected for two-year terms by the UN General Assembly; end of term year in parentheses: Algeria (2025), Denmark (2026), Guyana (2025), Greece (2026), Pakistan (2026), Panama (2026), South Korea (2025), Sierra Leone (2025), Slovenia (2025), Somalia (2026)

United Nations Trusteeship Council

website – https://www.un.org/en/about-us/trusteeship-council
established – 26 June 1945
effective – 24 October 1945
aim – supervise the administration of the 11 UN trust territories; it formally suspended operations but was not dissolved on 1 November 1994, after the last UN Trust Territory became the Republic of Palau, a constitutional government in free association with the US
members – the five permanent members of the UN Security Council: China, France, Russia, UK, US

United Nations (UN)

address – 405 E 45th St, New York, NY 10017
website – United Nations
established – 26 June 1945
effective – 24 October 1945
aim – to maintain international peace and security and to promote cooperation involving economic, social, cultural, and humanitarian problems
constituent organizations – the UN is composed of six principal organs and numerous subordinate agencies and bodies as follows:

1) **Secretariat**
2) **General Assembly:** International Computing Center (ICC), International Trade Center (ITC), Joint United Nations Program on HIV/AIDS (UN-AIDS), Office of the United Nations High Commissioner for Refugees (UNHCR), United Nations Capital Development Fund (UNCDF), United Nations Center for Human Settlements (UN-Habitat), United Nations Children's Fund (UNICEF), United Nations Conference on Trade and Development (UNCTAD), United Nations Development Program (UNDP), United Nations Environment Program (UNEP), United Nations Institute for Disarmament Research (UNIDIR), United Nations Institute for Training and Research (UNITAR), United Nations Interregional Crime and Justice Research Institute (UNICRI), United Nations International Strategy for Disaster Reduction (UNISDR), United Nations Office on Drugs and Crime (UNODC), United Nations Population Fund (UNFPA), United Nations Office of Project Services (UNOPS), United Nations Relief and Works Agency for Palestine Refugees in the Near East (UNRWA), United Nations Research Institute for Social Development (UNRISD), United Nations System Staff College (UNSSC), United Nations University (UNU), United Nations Women, United Nations Volunteers (UNV), World Food Program (WFP)
3) **Security Council:** International Criminal Tribunal for the Former Yugoslavia (ICTY) (1995-2012), International Criminal Tribunal for Rwanda (ICTR) (1993-2012), United Nations Compensation Commission, United Nations Disengagement Observer Force (UNDOF), African Union/United Nations Hybrid Operation in Darfur (UNAMID), United Nations Assistance Mission in Afghanistan (UNAMA), United Nations Interim Administration Mission in Kosovo (UNMIK), United Nations Interim Force for Abyei (UNIFSA), United Nations Interim Force in Lebanon (UNIFIL), United Nations Mission in Liberia (UNMIL) (2003-2018), United Nations Military Observer Group in India and Pakistan (UNMOGIP), United Nations Multidimensional Integrated Stabilization Mission in Mali (MINUSMA), United Nations Operation in Cote d'Ivoire (UNOCI) (2004-2016), United Nations Mission for the Referendum in Western Sahara (MINURSO), United Nations Mission in South Sudan (UNMISS), United Nations Organization Stabilization Mission in the Democratic Republic of the Congo (MONUSCO), United Nations Peace-Keeping Force in Cyprus (UNFICYP), United Nations Stabilization Mission in Haiti (MINUSTAH); note – in 2017, transitioned into a smaller organization (MINUJUSTH), United Nations Multidimensional Integrated Stabilization Mission in the Central African Republic, and United Nations Truce Supervision Organization (UNTSO)
4) **Economic and Social Council (ECOSOC):** Commission for Social Development, Commission on Crime Prevention and Criminal Justice, Commission on Narcotics Drugs, Commission on Population and Development, Commission on Science and Technology for Development, Commission on Sustainable Development, Commission on the Status of Women, Economic and Social Commission for Asia and the Pacific (ESCAP), Economic and Social Commission for Western Asia (ESCWA), Economic Commission for Africa (ECA), Economic Commission for Europe (ECE), Economic Commission for Latin America and the Caribbean (ECLAC), Statistical Commission, Food and Agriculture Organization of the United Nations (FAO), International Atomic Energy Agency (IAEA), Preparatory Commission for the Nuclear-Test-Ban Treaty Organization (CTBTO), International Bank for Reconstruction and Development (IBRD), International Center for Secretariat of Investment Disputes (ICSID), International Civil Aviation Organization (ICAO), International Development Association (IDA), International Finance Corporation (IFC), International Fund for Agricultural Development (IFAD), International Labor Organization (ILO), International Maritime Organization (IMO), International Monetary Fund (IMF), International Telecommunication Union (ITU), Multilateral Investment Guarantee Agency (MIGA), Statistical Commission, United Nations Educational, Scientific, and Cultural Organization (UNESCO), United Nations Forum on Forests, United Nations Industrial Development Organization (UNIDO), Universal Postal Union (UPU), World Health Organization (WHO), World Intellectual Property Organization (WIPO), World Meteorological Organization (WMO), World Tourism Organization (UNWTO), and World Trade Organization (WTO), United Nations Office on Drugs and Crime (UNODC), World Bank Group (WBG), Statistical Commission, UN Forum on Forests
5) **Trusteeship Council** (inactive; no trusteeships at this time)
6) **International Court of Justice (ICJ)**

UN members – (193) Afghanistan, Albania, Algeria, Andorra, Angola, Antigua and Barbuda, Argentina, Armenia, Australia, Austria, Azerbaijan, The Bahamas, Bahrain, Bangladesh, Barbados, Belarus, Belgium, Belize, Benin, Bhutan, Bolivia, Bosnia and Herzegovina, Botswana, Brazil, Brunei, Bulgaria, Burkina Faso, Burma, Burundi, Cabo Verde, Cambodia, Cameroon, Canada, Central African Republic, Chad, Chile, China, Colombia,

Comoros, Democratic Republic of the Congo, Republic of the Congo, Costa Rica, Cote d'Ivoire, Croatia, Cuba, Cyprus, Czechia, Denmark, Djibouti, Dominica, Dominican Republic, Ecuador, Egypt, El Salvador, Equatorial Guinea, Eritrea, Estonia, Eswatini, Ethiopia, Fiji, Finland, France, Gabon, The Gambia, Georgia, Germany, Ghana, Greece, Grenada, Guatemala, Guinea, Guinea-Bissau, Guyana, Haiti, Honduras, Hungary, Iceland, India, Indonesia, Iran, Iraq, Ireland, Israel, Italy, Jamaica, Japan, Jordan, Kazakhstan, Kenya, Kiribati, North Korea, South Korea, Kuwait, Kyrgyzstan, Laos, Latvia, Lebanon, Lesotho, Liberia, Libya, Liechtenstein, Lithuania, Luxembourg, Madagascar, Malawi, Malaysia, Maldives, Mali, Malta, Marshall Islands, Mauritania, Mauritius, Mexico, Federated States of Micronesia, Moldova, Monaco, Mongolia, Montenegro, Morocco, Mozambique, Namibia, Nauru, Nepal, Netherlands, NZ, Nicaragua, Niger, Nigeria, North Macedonia, Norway, Oman, Pakistan, Palau, Panama, Papua New Guinea, Paraguay, Peru, Philippines, Poland, Portugal, Qatar, Romania, Russia, Rwanda, Saint Kitts and Nevis, Saint Lucia, Saint Vincent and the Grenadines, Samoa, San Marino, Sao Tome and Principe, Saudi Arabia, Senegal, Serbia, Seychelles, Sierra Leone, Singapore, Slovakia, Slovenia, Solomon Islands, Somalia, South Africa, South Sudan, Spain, Sri Lanka, Sudan, Suriname, Sweden, Switzerland, Syria, Tajikistan, Tanzania, Thailand, Timor-Leste, Togo, Tonga, Trinidad and Tobago, Tunisia, Turkey (Turkiye), Turkmenistan, Tuvalu, Uganda, Ukraine, UAE, UK, US, Uruguay, Uzbekistan, Vanuatu, Venezuela, Yemen, Zambia, Zimbabwe
observers – (1) Holy See; plus the Palestine Liberation Organization (not included in observer count)

United Nations University (UNU)
website – https://unu.edu/
established – 3 December 1973
aim – to conduct research in development, welfare, and human survival and to train scholars
members – 12 members of UNU Council and the Rector that are appointed by the UN Secretary General and the Director General of UNESCO, plus three *ex officio* members (the UN Secretary General, the UNESCO Director General, and the UNITAR Executive Director)

Universal Postal Union (UPU)
address – International Bureau, Weltpoststrasse 4, 3015 Berne, Switzerland
website – https://www.upu.int/en/home
established – 9 October 1874, affiliated with the UN 15 November 1947
effective – 1 July 1948
aim – to promote international postal cooperation; a UN specialized agency
members – (192) includes all UN member countries except Andorra, Marshall Islands, Federated States of Micronesia, Palau; plus Aruba, Curacao, Sint Maarten, the Holy See, and Overseas Territories of the UK; note - includes the following dependencies or areas of special interest: Australia (Norfolk Island), China (Hong Kong, Macau), Denmark (Faroe Islands, Greenland), France (French Guiana, French Polynesia including Clipperton Island, French Southern and Antarctic Lands, Guadeloupe, Martinique, Mayotte, New Caledonia, Reunion, Saint Barthelemy, Saint Martin, Saint Pierre and Miquelon, Bassas da India, Europe, Juan de Nova, Glorioso Islands, Tromelin, Wallis and Futuna), Netherlands (Aruba, Curacao, Sint Maarten), NZ (Cook Island, Niue, Tokelau), UK (Guernsey, Isle of Man, Jersey; Anguilla, Bermuda, British Indian Ocean Territory, British Virgin Islands, Cayman Islands, Falkland Islands, Gibraltar, Montserrat, Pitcairn Islands, Saint Helena, Ascension, and Tristan da Cunha, South Georgia and South Sandwich Islands, Turks and Caicos), US (American Samoa, Guam, Northern Mariana Islands, Puerto Rico, Virgin Islands)

Wassenaar Arrangement
note – successor to COCOM
address – Wassenaar Arrangement Secretariat, Vienna, Austria
phone – 43 1 960 03
email – secretariat@wassenaar.org
website – https://www.wassenaar.org/
established – 11-12 July 1996
aim – to contribute to regional and international security and stability by promoting transparency and greater responsibility in transfers of conventional arms and dual-use goods and technologies to prevent destabilising accumulations; to ensure, through members states' national policies, that transfers of these items do not contribute to the development or enhancement of military capabilities that undermine these goals, and are not diverted to support such capabilities; to prevent the acquisition of these items by terrorists
members – (42) Argentina, Australia, Austria, Belgium, Bulgaria, Canada, Croatia, Czechia, Denmark, Estonia, Finland, France, Germany, Greece, Hungary, India, Ireland, Italy, Japan, Latvia, Lithuania, Luxembourg, Malta, Mexico, Netherlands, New Zealand, Norway, Poland, Portugal, Romania, Russia, Slovakia, Slovenia, South Africa, South Korea, Spain, Sweden, Switzerland, Turkey (Turkiye), Ukraine, UK, US

West African Development Bank (WADB)
note – also known as Banque Ouest-Africaine de Développement (BOAD); a financial institution of WAEMU
address – 68, Avenue de la Libération, Lome, Togo
phone – (228) 22.21.59.06 / 22.21.42.44 / 22.21.01.13
fax – (228) 22.21.52.67 / 22.21.72.69
email – boadsiege@boad.org
website – https://www.boad.org/en/
established – 14 November 1973
aim – to promote regional economic development and integration
regional members – (8) Benin, Burkina Faso, Cote d'Ivoire, Guinea-Bissau, Mali, Niger, Senegal, Togo

West African Economic and Monetary Union (WAEMU)
note – also known as Union Economique et Monétaire Ouest Africaine (UEMOA)
address – 380 Avenue Professeur Joseph Ki-Zerbo 01 BP 543, Ouagadougou, Burkina Faso
phone – 226 25 31 88 73, 226 25 31 88 74, 226 25 31 88 75, 226 25 31 88 76
fax – 226 25 31 88 72
email – commission@uemoa.int
website – http://www.uemoa.int/en
established – 1 August 1994
aim – to increase competitiveness of members' economic markets; to create a common market
members – (8) Benin, Burkina Faso, Cote d'Ivoire, Guinea-Bissau, Mali, Niger, Senegal, Togo

World Bank Group

note – five institutions make up the World Bank Group: International Bank for Reconstruction and Development (IBRD), International Development Association (IDA), International Finance Corporation (IFC), Multilateral Investment Guarantee Agency (MIGA), International Center for Settlement of Investment Disputes (ICSID)
address – 1818 H Street, NW, Washington DC 20433 - United States
phone – 202-473-1000
email – starinitiative@worldbank.org
website – World Bank Group - International Development, Poverty and Sustainability
established – 4 July 1944
aim – end extreme poverty and boost shared prosperity on a livable planet
member states – (189) Afghanistan, Albania, Algeria, Andorra, Angola, Antigua and Barbuda, Argentina, Armenia, Australia, Austria, Azerbaijan, The Bahamas, Bahrain, Bangladesh, Barbados, Belarus, Belgium, Belize, Benin, Bhutan, Bolivia, Bosnia and Herzegovina, Botswana, Brazil, Brunei, Bulgaria, Burkina Faso, Burma, Burundi, Cabo Verde, Cambodia, Cameroon, Canada, Central African Republic, Chad, Chile, China, Colombia, Comoros, Democratic Republic of the Congo, Republic of the Congo, Costa Rica, Cote d'Ivoire, Croatia, Cuba, Cyprus, Czechia, Denmark, Djibouti, Dominica, Dominican Republic, Ecuador, Egypt, El Salvador, Equatorial Guinea, Eritrea, Estonia, Eswatini, Ethiopia, Fiji, Finland, France, Gabon, The Gambia, Georgia, Germany, Ghana, Greece, Grenada, Guatemala, Guinea, Guinea-Bissau, Guyana, Haiti, Honduras, Hungary, Iceland, India, Indonesia, Iran, Iraq, Ireland, Israel, Italy, Jamaica, Japan, Jordan, Kazakhstan, Kenya, Kiribati, North Korea, South Korea, Kuwait, Kyrgyzstan, Laos, Latvia, Lebanon, Lesotho, Liberia, Libya, Liechtenstein, Lithuania, Luxembourg, Madagascar, Malawi, Malaysia, Maldives, Mali, Malta, Marshall Islands, Mauritania, Mauritius, Mexico, Federated States of Micronesia, Moldova, Monaco, Mongolia, Montenegro, Morocco, Mozambique, Namibia, Nauru, Nepal, Netherlands, NZ, Nicaragua, Niger, Nigeria, North Macedonia, Norway, Oman, Pakistan, Palau, Panama, Papua New Guinea, Paraguay, Peru, Philippines, Poland, Portugal, Qatar, Romania, Russia, Rwanda, Saint Kitts and Nevis, Saint Lucia, Saint Vincent and the Grenadines, Samoa, San Marino, Sao Tome and Principe, Saudi Arabia, Senegal, Serbia, Seychelles, Sierra Leone, Singapore, Slovakia, Slovenia, Solomon Islands, Somalia, South Africa, South Sudan, Spain, Sri Lanka, Sudan, Suriname, Sweden, Switzerland, Syria, Tajikistan, Tanzania, Thailand, Timor-Leste, Togo, Tonga, Trinidad and Tobago, Tunisia, Turkey (Turkiye), Turkmenistan, Tuvalu, Uganda, Ukraine, UAE, UK, US, Uruguay, Uzbekistan, Vanuatu, Venezuela

World Customs Organization (WCO)

note – began as the Customs Cooperation Council (CCC)
website – http://www.wcoomd.org/
established – 15 December 1950
aim – to promote international cooperation in customs matters
members – (182) Afghanistan, Albania, Algeria, Andorra, Angola, Antigua and Barbuda, Argentina, Armenia, Australia, Austria, Azerbaijan, The Bahamas, Bahrain, Bangladesh, Barbados, Belarus, Belgium, Belize, Benin, Bermuda, Bhutan, Bolivia, Bosnia and Herzegovina, Botswana, Brazil, Brunei, Bulgaria, Burkina Faso, Burma, Burundi, Cabo Verde, Cambodia, Cameroon, Canada, Central African Republic, Chad, Chile, China, Colombia, Comoros, Democratic Republic of the Congo, Republic of the Congo, Costa Rica, Cote d'Ivoire, Croatia, Cuba, Curacao, Cyprus, Czechia, Denmark, Djibouti, Dominican Republic, EU, Ecuador, Egypt, El Salvador, Eritrea, Estonia, Eswatini, Ethiopia, Fiji, Finland, France, Gabon, The Gambia, Georgia, Germany, Ghana, Greece, Guatemala, Guinea, Guinea-Bissau, Guyana, Haiti, Honduras, Hong Kong, Hungary, Iceland, India, Indonesia, Iran, Iraq, Ireland, Israel, Italy, Jamaica, Japan, Jordan, Kazakhstan, Kenya, South Korea, Kosovo, Kuwait, Kyrgyzstan, Laos, Latvia, Lebanon, Lesotho, Liberia, Libya, Lithuania, Luxembourg, Macau, Madagascar, Malawi, Malaysia, Maldives, Mali, Malta, Mauritania, Mauritius, Mexico, Moldova, Mongolia, Montenegro, Morocco, Mozambique, Namibia, Nepal, Netherlands, NZ, Nicaragua, Niger, Nigeria, North Macedonia, Norway, Oman, Pakistan, Panama, Papua New Guinea, Paraguay, Peru, Philippines, Poland, Portugal, Qatar, Romania, Russia, Rwanda, Saint Lucia, Samoa, Sao Tome and Principe, Saudi Arabia, Senegal, Serbia, Seychelles, Sierra Leone, Singapore, Slovakia, Slovenia, Somalia, South Africa, South Sudan, Spain, Sri Lanka, Sudan, Sweden, Switzerland, Syria, Tajikistan, Tanzania, Thailand, Timor-Leste, Togo, Tonga, Trinidad and Tobago, Tunisia, Turkey (Turkiye), Turkmenistan, Uganda, Ukraine, UAE, UK, US, Uruguay, Uzbekistan, Vanuatu, Venezuela, Vietnam, Yemen, Zambia, Zimbabwe; plus the Palestine Liberation Organization (not included in the member count)

World Food Program (WFP)

address – Via Cesare Giulio Viola 68, Parco dei Medici, 00148 – Rome - Italy
phone – 39-06-65131
fax – 39-06-6590632
website – https://www.wfp.org/
established – 24 November 1961
aim – to provide food aid in support of economic development or disaster relief; an ECOSOC organization
members (Executive Board) – (36) selected on a rotating basis from all regions for a three-year term and eligible for reelection

World Health Organization (WHO)

address – Avenue Appia 20, 1211 Geneva, Switzerland
phone – 41 22 791 21 11
website – https://www.who.int/
established – 22 July 1946
effective – 7 April 1948
aim – to deal with health matters worldwide; a UN specialized agency
members – (194) includes all UN member countries except Liechtenstein; plus Cook Islands and Niue

World Intellectual Property Organization (WIPO)

address – 34, chemin des Colombettes, CH-1211 Geneva 20, Switzerland
website – https://www.wipo.int/portal/en/index.html
established – 14 July 1967
effective – 26 April 1970
aim – to furnish protection for literary, artistic, and scientific works; a UN specialized agency
members – (194) includes all UN member countries except Federated States of Micronesia, South Sudan; plus Cook Islands, Holy See, Niue

World Meteorological Organization (WMO)
address – 7 bis, avenue de la Paix, Case postale 2300, CH-1211 Geneva 2, Switzerland
phone – 41 (0) 22 730 81 11
fax – 41 (0) 22 730 81 81
email – wmo@wmo.int
website – https://public.wmo.int/en
established – 11 October 1947
effective – 4 April 1951
aim – to sponsor meteorological cooperation; a UN specialized agency
members – (193) includes all UN member countries except Equatorial Guinea, Grenada, Liechtenstein, Marshall Islands, Palau, Saint Kitts and Nevis, Saint Vincent and the Grenadines, San Marino (185 total); plus Cook Islands and Niue and 6 territories (British Caribbean Territories, French Polynesia, Hong Kong, Macau, Curacao and Sint Maarten [joint membership], New Caledonia)

World Tourism Organization (UNWTO)
address – Calle Poeta Joan Maragall 42, 28020 Madrid, Spain
phone – 34 91 567 8100
email – info@unwto.org
website – https://www.unwto.org/
established – 2 January 1975
aim – to promote tourism as a means of contributing to economic development, international understanding, and peace
members – (160) Afghanistan, Albania, Algeria, Andorra, Angola, Antiqua and Barbuda, Argentina, Armenia, Austria, Azerbaijan, The Bahamas, Bahrain, Bangladesh, Barbados, Belarus, Benin, Bhutan, Bolivia, Bosnia and Herzegovina, Botswana, Brazil, Brunei, Bulgaria, Burkina Faso, Burma, Burundi, Cabo Verde, Cambodia, Cameroon, Central African Republic, Chad, Chile, China, Colombia, Comoros, Democratic Republic of the Congo, Republic of the Congo, Costa Rica, Cote d'Ivoire, Croatia, Cuba, Cyprus, Czechia, Djibouti, Dominican Republic, Ecuador, Egypt, El Salvador, Equatorial Guinea, Eritrea, Eswatini, Ethiopia, Fiji, France, Gabon, The Gambia, Georgia, Germany, Ghana, Greece, Guatemala, Guinea, Guinea-Bissau, Haiti, Honduras, Hungary, India, Indonesia, Iran, Iraq, Israel, Italy, Jamaica, Japan, Jordan, Kazakhstan, Kenya, North Korea, South Korea, Kuwait, Kyrgyzstan, Laos, Lebanon, Lesotho, Liberia, Libya, Lithuania, Madagascar, Malawi, Malaysia, Maldives, Mali, Malta, Mauritania, Mauritius, Mexico, Moldova, Monaco, Mongolia, Montenegro, Morocco, Mozambique, Namibia, Nepal, Netherlands, Nicaragua, Niger, Nigeria, North Macedonia, Oman, Pakistan, Palau, Panama, Papua New Guinea, Paraguay, Peru, Philippines, Poland, Portugal, Qatar, Romania, Russia, Rwanda, Samoa, San Marino, Sao Tome and Principe, Saudi Arabia, Senegal, Serbia, Seychelles, Sierra Leone, Slovakia, Slovenia, Somalia, South Africa, Spain, Sri Lanka, Sudan, Switzerland, Syria, Tajikistan, Tanzania, Thailand, Timor-Leste, Togo, Trinidad and Tobago, Tunisia, Turkey (Turkiye), Turkmenistan, Uganda, Ukraine, UAE, Uruguay, Uzbekistan, Vanuatu, Venezuela, Vietnam, Yemen, Zambia, Zimbabwe
associate members – (6) Aruba, Flemish Community of Belgium, Hong Kong, Macau, Madeira Islands, Puerto Rico
observers – (1) Holy See, plus Palestine Liberation Organization (not included in the official count)

World Trade Organization (WTO)
note – succeeded General Agreement on Tariff and Trade (GATT)
address – Rue de Lausanne, 154, Case postale, 1211 Geneva 2, Switzerland
phone – 41 (0)22 739 51 11
email – enquiries@wto.org
website – https://www.wto.org/
established – 15 April 1994
effective – 1 January 1995
aim – to provide a forum to resolve trade conflicts between members and to carry on negotiations with the goal of further lowering and/or eliminating tariffs and other trade barriers
members – (166) Afghanistan, Albania, Angola, Antigua and Barbuda, Argentina, Armenia, Australia, Austria, Bahrain, Bangladesh, Barbados, Belgium, Belize, Benin, Bolivia, Botswana, Brazil, Brunei, Bulgaria, Burkina Faso, Burma, Burundi, Cabo Verde, Cambodia, Cameroon, Canada, Central African Republic, Chad, Chile, China, Colombia, Democratic Republic of the Congo, Republic of the Congo, Costa Rica, Cote d'Ivoire, Croatia, Cuba, Cyprus, Czechia, Denmark, Djibouti, Dominica, Dominican Republic, Ecuador, Egypt, El Salvador, Estonia, Eswatini, EU, Fiji, Finland, France, Gabon, The Gambia, Georgia, Germany, Ghana, Greece, Grenada, Guatemala, Guinea, Guinea-Bissau, Guyana, Haiti, Honduras, Hong Kong, Hungary, Iceland, India, Indonesia, Ireland, Israel, Italy, Jamaica, Japan, Jordan, Kazakhstan, Kenya, South Korea, Kuwait, Kyrgyzstan, Laos, Latvia, Lesotho, Liberia, Liechtenstein, Lithuania, Luxembourg, Macau, Madagascar, Malawi, Malaysia, Maldives, Mali, Malta, Mauritania, Mauritius, Mexico, Moldova, Mongolia, Montenegro, Morocco, Mozambique, Namibia, Nepal, Netherlands, NZ, Nicaragua, Niger, Nigeria, North Macedonia, Norway, Oman, Pakistan, Panama, Papua New Guinea, Paraguay, Peru, Philippines, Poland, Portugal, Qatar, Romania, Russia, Rwanda, Saint Kitts and Nevis, Saint Lucia, Saint Vincent and the Grenadines, Samoa, Saudi Arabia, Senegal, Seychelles, Sierra Leone, Singapore, Slovakia, Slovenia, Solomon Islands, South Africa, Spain, Sri Lanka, Suriname, Sweden, Switzerland, Chinese Taiwan, Tajikistan, Tanzania, Thailand, Timor-Leste, Togo, Tonga, Trinidad and Tobago, Tunisia, Turkey (Turkiye), Uganda, Ukraine, UAE, UK, US, Uruguay, Vanuatu, Venezuela, Vietnam, Yemen, Zambia, Zimbabwe
observers – (25) Algeria, Andorra, Azerbaijan, The Bahamas, Belarus, Bhutan, Bosnia and Herzegovina, Comoros, Curacao, Equatorial Guinea, Ethiopia, Holy See, Iran, Iraq, Lebanon, Libya, Sao Tome and Principe, Serbia, Somalia, South Sudan, Sudan, Syria, Timor-Leste, Turkmenistan, Uzbekistan; note – with the exception of the Holy See, an observer must start accession negotiations within five years of becoming an observer

Zangger Committee (ZC)
address – Fuhrichgasse 6A-1010 Vienna, Austria
website – http://zanggercommittee.org/
established – early 1970s
aim – to establish guidelines for the export control provisions of the Nonproliferation of Nuclear Weapons Treaty (NPT)
members – (39) Argentina, Australia, Austria, Belarus, Belgium, Bulgaria, Canada, China, Croatia, Czechia, Denmark, Finland, France, Germany, Greece, Hungary, Ireland, Italy, Japan, Kazakhstan, South Korea, Luxembourg, Netherlands, NZ, Norway, Poland, Portugal, Romania, Russia, Slovakia, Slovenia, South Africa, Spain, Sweden, Switzerland, Turkey (Turkiye), Ukraine, UK, US
observers – (1) EU (permanent observer)

APPENDIX C: SELECTED INTERNATIONAL ENVIRONMENTAL AGREEMENTS

Air Pollution
see Convention on Long-Range Transboundary Air Pollution

Air Pollution-Heavy Metals
see Protocol to the 1979 Convention on Long-Range Transboundary Air Pollution on Heavy Metals

Air Pollution-Nitrogen Oxides
see Protocol to the 1979 Convention on Long-Range Transboundary Air Pollution Concerning the Control of Emissions of Nitrogen Oxides or Their Transboundary Fluxes

Air Pollution-Persistent Organic Pollutants
see Protocol to the 1979 Convention on Long-Range Transboundary Air Pollution on Persistent Organic Pollutants

Air Pollution-Sulphur 85
see Protocol to the 1979 Convention on Long-Range Transboundary Air Pollution on the Reduction of Sulphur Emissions or Their Transboundary Fluxes by at least 30%

Air Pollution-Sulphur 94
see Protocol to the 1979 Convention on Long-Range Transboundary Air Pollution on Further Reduction of Sulphur Emissions

Air Pollution-Volatile Organic Compounds
see Protocol to the 1979 Convention on Long-Range Transboundary Air Pollution Concerning the Control of Emissions of Volatile Organic Compounds or Their Transboundary Fluxes

Antarctic - Environmental Protocol
see Protocol on Environmental Protection to the Antarctic Treaty

Antarctic Treaty
opened for signature – 1 December 1959
entered into force – 23 June 1961
objective – to ensure that Antarctica is used for peaceful purposes only (such as international cooperation in scientific research); to defer the question of territorial claims asserted by some nations and not recognized by others; to provide an international forum for management of the region; applies to land and ice shelves south of 60 degrees south latitude
parties – (53) Argentina, Australia, Austria, Belarus, Belgium, Brazil, Bulgaria, Canada, Chile, China, Colombia, Cuba, Czechia, Denmark, Ecuador, Estonia, Finland, France, Germany, Greece, Guatemala, Hungary, Iceland, India, Italy, Japan, Kazakhstan, North Korea, South Korea, Malaysia, Monaco, Mongolia, Netherlands, NZ, Norway, Pakistan, Papua New Guinea, Peru, Poland, Portugal, Romania, Russia, Slovakia, South Africa, Spain, Sweden, Switzerland, Turkey (Turkiye), Ukraine, UK, US, Uruguay, Venezuela

Basel Convention on the Control of Transboundary Movements of Hazardous Wastes and Their Disposal
note – abbreviated as Hazardous Wastes
opened for signature – 22 March 1989
entered into force – 5 May 1992
objective – to reduce transboundary movements of wastes subject to the Convention to a minimum consistent with the environmentally sound and efficient management of such wastes; to minimize the amount and toxicity of wastes generated and ensure their environmentally sound management as closely as possible to the source of generation; to assist LDCs in environmentally sound management of the hazardous and other wastes they generate
parties – (186 and the Palestine Liberation Organization) Afghanistan, Albania, Algeria, Andorra, Angola, Antigua and Barbuda, Argentina, Armenia, Australia, Austria, Azerbaijan, The Bahamas, Bahrain, Bangladesh, Barbados, Belarus, Belgium, Belize, Benin, Bhutan, Bolivia, Bosnia and Herzegovina, Botswana, Brazil, Brunei, Bulgaria, Burkina Faso, Burma, Burundi, Cambodia, Cameroon, Canada, Cape Verde, Central African Republic, Chad, Chile, China, Colombia, Comoros, Democratic Republic of the Congo, Republic of the Congo, Cook Islands, Costa Rica, Cote d'Ivoire, Croatia, Cuba, Cyprus, Czechia, Denmark, Djibouti, Dominica, Dominican Republic, Ecuador, Egypt, El Salvador, Equatorial Guinea, Eritrea, Estonia, Eswatini, Ethiopia, EU, Finland, France, Gabon, The Gambia, Georgia, Germany, Ghana, Greece, Guatemala, Guinea, Guinea-Bissau, Guyana, Haiti, Honduras, Hungary, Iceland, India, Indonesia, Iran, Iraq, Ireland, Israel, Italy, Jamaica, Japan, Jordan, Kazakhstan, Kenya, Kiribati, North Korea, South Korea, Kuwait, Kyrgyzstan, Latvia, Laos, Lebanon, Lesotho, Liberia, Libya, Liechtenstein, Lithuania, Luxembourg, Madagascar, Malawi, Malaysia, Maldives, Mali, Malta, Marshall Islands, Mauritania, Mauritius, Mexico, Federated States of Micronesia, Moldova, Monaco, Mongolia, Montenegro, Morocco, Mozambique, Namibia, Nauru, Nepal, Netherlands, NZ, Nicaragua, Niger, Nigeria, North Macedonia, Norway, Oman, Pakistan, Palau, Panama, Papua New Guinea, Paraguay, Peru, Philippines, Poland, Portugal, Qatar, Romania, Russia, Rwanda, Saint Kitts and Nevis, Saint Lucia, Saint Vincent and the Grenadines, Samoa, Sao Tome and Principe, Saudi Arabia, Senegal, Serbia, Seychelles, Sierra Leone, Singapore, Slovakia, Slovenia, Somalia, South Africa, Spain, Sri Lanka, Sudan, Suriname, Sweden, Switzerland, Syria, Tajikistan, Tanzania, Thailand, Togo, Tonga, Trinidad and Tobago, Tunisia, Turkey (Turkiye), Turkmenistan, Uganda, Ukraine, UAE, UK, Uruguay, Uzbekistan, Venezuela, Vietnam, Yemen, Zambia, Zimbabwe, Palestine Liberation Organization
countries that have signed, but not yet ratified – (1) US

Biodiversity
see Convention on Biological Diversity

Climate Change
see United Nations Framework Convention on Climate Change

Climate Change-Kyoto Protocol
see Kyoto Protocol to the United Nations Framework Convention on Climate Change

Climate Change-Paris Agreement
see Paris Agreement under the United Nations Framework Convention on Climate Change

Comprehensive Nuclear Test-Ban Treaty
note – abbreviated as CTBT
opened for signature – 24 September 1996
currently not in force – the CTBT will not formally enter into force until eight remaining "nuclear-capable states" sign and ratify the treaty; to date China, Egypt, Iran, Israel, and the United States have signed but not ratified the Treaty; India, North Korea, and Pakistan have not signed it
objective – bans all nuclear weapons test explosions, for both civilian and military purposes, in all environments
parties – (170) Afghanistan, Albania, Algeria, Andorra, Angola, Antigua and Barbuda, Argentina, Armenia, Australia, Austria, Azerbaijan, The Bahamas, Bahrain, Bangladesh, Barbados, Belarus, Belgium, Belize, Benin, Bolivia, Bosnia and Herzegovina, Botswana, Brazil, Brunei, Bulgaria, Burkina Faso, Burma, Burundi, Cabo Verde, Cambodia, Cameroon, Canada, Central African Republic, Chad, Chile, Colombia, Comoros, Democratic Republic of the Congo, Cook Islands, Costa Rica, Cote d'Ivoire, Croatia, Cuba, Cyprus, Czechia, Denmark, Djibouti, Dominican Republic, Ecuador, El Salvador, Eritrea, Estonia, Eswatini, Ethiopia, Fiji, Finland, France, Gabon, Georgia, Germany, Ghana, Greece, Grenada, Guatemala, Guinea, Guinea-Bissau, Guyana, Haiti, Holy See, Honduras, Hungary, Iceland, Indonesia, Iraq, Ireland, Italy, Jamaica, Japan, Jordan, Kazakhstan, Kenya, Kiribati, South Korea, Kuwait, Kyrgyzstan, Laos, Latvia, Lebanon, Lesotho, Liberia, Libya, Liechtenstein, Lithuania, Luxembourg, Madagascar, Malawi, Malaysia, Maldives, Mali, Malta, Marshall Islands, Mauritania, Mexico, Micronesia, Moldova, Monaco, Mongolia, Montenegro, Morocco, Mozambique, Namibia, Nauru, Netherlands, NZ, Nicaragua, Niger, Nigeria, Niue, North Macedoia, Norway, Oman, Palau, Panama, Paraguay, Peru, Philippines, Poland, Portugal, Qatar, Romania, Russia, Rwanda, Saint Kitts and Nevis, Saint Lucia, Saint Vincent and the Grenadines, Samoa, San Marino, Senegal, Serbia, Seychelles, Sierra Leone, Singapore, Slovakia, Slovenia, South Africa, Spain, Sudan, Suriname, Sweden, Switzerland, Tajikistan, Tanzania, Thailand, Timor-Leste, Togo, Trinidad and Tobago, Tunisia, Turkey (Turkiye), Turkmenistan, Uganda, Ukraine, UAE, UK, Uruguay, Uzbekistan, Vanuatu, Venezuela, Vietnam, Zambia, Zimbabwe
countries that have signed, but not ratified – (15) China, Egypt, Equatorial Guinea, The Gambia, Iran, Israel, Nepal, Papa New Guinea, Sao Tome and Principe, Solomon Islands, Sri Lanka, Timor-Leste, Tuvalu, United States, Yemen

Convention for the Conservation of Antarctic Seals
note – abbreviated as Antarctic Seals
opened for signature – 1 June 1972
entered into force – 11 March 1978
objective – to promote and achieve the protection, scientific study, and rational use of Antarctic seals; to maintain a satisfactory balance within the ecological system of Antarctica
parties – (17) Argentina, Australia, Belgium, Brazil, Canada, Chile, France, Germany, Italy, Japan, Norway, Pakistan, Poland, Russia, South Africa, UK, US
countries that have signed, but not yet ratified – (1) NZ

Convention on Biological Diversity
note – abbreviated as Biodiversity
opened for signature – 5 June 1992
entered into force – 29 December 1993
objective – to develop national strategies for the conservation and sustainable use of biological diversity and to address the fair and equitable sharing of benefits arising out of the utilization of genetic resources
parties – (195 and the Palestine Liberation Organization) Afghanistan, Albania, Algeria, Andorra, Angola, Antigua and Barbuda, Argentina, Armenia, Australia, Austria, Azerbaijan, The Bahamas, Bahrain, Bangladesh, Barbados, Belarus, Belgium, Belize, Benin, Bhutan, Bolivia, Bosnia and Herzegovina, Botswana, Brazil, Brunei, Bulgaria, Burkina Faso, Burma, Burundi, Cambodia, Cameroon, Canada, Cape Verde, Central African Republic, Chad, Chile, China, Colombia, Comoros, Democratic Republic of the Congo, Republic of the Congo, Cook Islands, Costa Rica, Cote d'Ivoire, Croatia, Cuba, Cyprus, Czechia, Denmark, Djibouti, Dominica, Dominican Republic, Ecuador, Egypt, El Salvador, Equatorial Guinea, Eritrea, Estonia, Eswatini, Ethiopia, EU, Fiji, Finland, France, Gabon, The Gambia, Georgia, Germany, Ghana, Greece, Grenada, Guatemala, Guinea, Guinea-Bissau, Guyana, Haiti, Honduras, Hungary, Iceland, India, Indonesia, Iran, Iraq, Ireland, Israel, Italy, Jamaica, Japan, Jordan, Kazakhstan, Kenya, Kiribati, North Korea, South Korea, Kuwait, Kyrgyzstan, Laos, Latvia, Lebanon, Lesotho, Liberia, Libya, Liechtenstein, Lithuania, Luxembourg, Madagascar, Malawi, Malaysia, Maldives, Mali, Malta, Marshall Islands, Mauritania, Mauritius, Mexico, Federated States of Micronesia, Moldova, Monaco, Mongolia, Montenegro, Morocco, Mozambique, Namibia, Nauru, Nepal, Netherlands, NZ, Nicaragua, Niger, Nigeria, Niue, North Macedonia, Norway, Oman, Pakistan, Palau, Panama, Papua New Guinea, Paraguay, Peru, Philippines, Poland, Portugal, Qatar, Romania, Russia, Rwanda, Saint Kitts and Nevis, Saint Lucia, Saint Vincent and the Grenadines, Samoa, San Marino, Sao Tome and Principe, Saudi Arabia, Senegal, Serbia, Seychelles, Sierra Leone, Singapore, Slovakia, Slovenia, Solomon Islands, Somalia, South Africa, South Sudan, Spain, Sri Lanka, Sudan, Suriname, Sweden, Switzerland, Syria, Tajikistan, Tanzania, Thailand, Timor-Leste, Togo, Tonga, Trinidad and Tobago, Tunisia, Turkey (Turkiye), Turkmenistan, Tuvalu, Uganda, Ukraine, UAE, UK, Uruguay, Uzbekistan, Vanuatu, Venezuela, Vietnam, Yemen, Zambia, Zimbabwe, Palestine Liberation Organization
countries that have signed, but not yet ratified – (1) US

Convention on Fishing and Conservation of Living Resources of the High Seas
note – abbreviated as Marine Life Conservation
opened for signature – 29 April 1958
entered into force – 20 March 1966
objective – to solve through international cooperation the problems involved in the conservation of living resources of the high seas, taking into consideration the effects of modern technology, the world's population needs, and the dangers of over-exploitation
parties – (39) Australia, Belgium, Bosnia and Herzegovina, Burkina Faso, Cambodia, Colombia, Republic of the Congo, Denmark, Dominican Republic, Fiji, Finland, France, Haiti, Jamaica, Kenya, Lesotho, Madagascar, Malawi, Malaysia, Mauritius, Mexico, Montenegro, Netherlands, Nigeria, Portugal, Senegal, Serbia, Sierra Leone, Solomon Islands, South Africa, Spain, Switzerland, Thailand, Tonga, Trinidad and Tobago, Uganda, UK, US, Venezuela

countries that have signed, but not yet ratified – (21) Afghanistan, Argentina, Bolivia, Canada, Costa Rica, Cuba, Ghana, Iceland, Indonesia, Iran, Ireland, Israel, Lebanon, Liberia, Nepal, NZ, Pakistan, Panama, Sri Lanka, Tunisia, Uruguay

Convention on Long-Range Transboundary Air Pollution
note 1 – abbreviated as Air Pollution
note 2 – also referred to as Long-Range Transboundary Air Pollution (LRTAP)
opened for signature – 13 November 1979
entered into force – 16 March 1983
objective – to protect the human environment against air pollution and, as far as possible, to gradually reduce and prevent air pollution, including long-range transboundary air pollution
parties – (51) Albania, Armenia, Austria, Azerbaijan, Belarus, Belgium, Bosnia and Herzegovina, Bulgaria, Canada, Croatia, Cyprus, Czechia, Denmark, Estonia, EU, Finland, France, Georgia, Germany, Greece, Hungary, Iceland, Ireland, Italy, Kazakhstan, Kyrgyzstan, Latvia, Liechtenstein, Lithuania, Luxembourg, Malta, Moldova, Monaco, Montenegro, Netherlands, North Macedonia, Norway, Poland, Portugal, Romania, Russia, Serbia, Slovakia, Slovenia, Spain, Sweden, Switzerland, Turkey (Turkiye), Ukraine, UK, US
countries that have signed, but not yet ratified – (2) Holy See, San Marino

Convention on the Conservation of Antarctic Marine Living Resources
note – abbreviated as Antarctic-Marine Living Resources
opened for signature – 5 May 1980
entered into force – 7 April 1982
objective – to safeguard the environment and protect the integrity of the ecosystem of the seas surrounding Antarctica, and to conserve Antarctic marine living resources
members – (25) Argentina, Australia, Belgium, Brazil, Chile, China, EU, France, Germany, India, Italy, Japan, South Korea, Namibia, NZ, Norway, Poland, Russia, South Africa, Spain, Sweden, Ukraine, UK, US, Uruguay
acceding states – (11) Bulgaria, Canada, Cook Islands, Finland, Greece, Mauritius, Netherlands, Pakistan, Panama, Peru, Vanuatu

Convention on the International Trade in Endangered Species of Wild Flora and Fauna (CITES)
note – abbreviated as Endangered Species
opened for signature – 3 March 1973
entered into force – 1 July 1975
objective – to protect certain endangered species from overexploitation by means of a system of import/export permits
parties – (183) Afghanistan, Albania, Algeria, Angola, Antigua and Barbuda, Argentina, Armenia, Australia, Austria, Azerbaijan, The Bahamas, Bahrain, Bangladesh, Barbados, Belarus, Belgium, Belize, Benin, Bhutan, Bolivia, Bosnia and Herzegovina, Botswana, Brazil, Brunei, Bulgaria, Burkina Faso, Burma, Burundi, Cambodia, Cameroon, Canada, Cape Verde, Central African Republic, Chad, Chile, China, Colombia, Comoros, Democratic Republic of the Congo, Republic of the Congo, Costa Rica, Cote d'Ivoire, Croatia, Cuba, Cyprus, Czechia, Denmark, Djibouti, Dominica, Dominican Republic, Ecuador, Egypt, El Salvador, Equatorial Guinea, Eritrea, Estonia, Eswatini, Ethiopia, EU, Fiji, Finland, France, Gabon, The Gambia, Georgia, Germany, Ghana, Greece, Grenada, Guatemala, Guinea, Guinea-Bissau, Guyana, Honduras, Hungary, Iceland, India, Indonesia, Iran, Iraq, Ireland, Israel, Italy, Jamaica, Japan, Jordan, Kazakhstan, Kenya, South Korea, Kuwait, Kyrgyzstan, Laos, Latvia, Lebanon, Lesotho, Liberia, Libya, Liechtenstein, Lithuania, Luxembourg, Madagascar, Malawi, Malaysia, Maldives, Mali, Malta, Mauritania, Mauritius, Mexico, Moldova, Monaco, Mongolia, Montenegro, Morocco, Mozambique, Namibia, Nepal, Netherlands, NZ, Nicaragua, Niger, Nigeria, North Macedonia, Norway, Oman, Palau, Pakistan, Panama, Papua New Guinea, Paraguay, Peru, Philippines, Poland, Portugal, Qatar, Romania, Russia, Rwanda, Saint Kitts and Nevis, Saint Lucia, Saint Vincent and the Grenadines, Samoa, San Marino, Sao Tome and Principe, Saudi Arabia, Senegal, Serbia, Seychelles, Sierra Leone, Singapore, Slovakia, Slovenia, Solomon Islands, Somalia, South Africa, Spain, Sri Lanka, Sudan, Suriname, Sweden, Switzerland, Syria, Tajikistan, Tanzania, Thailand, Togo, Tonga, Trinidad and Tobago, Tunisia, Turkey (Turkiye), Uganda, Ukraine, UAE, UK, US, Uruguay, Uzbekistan, Vanuatu, Venezuela, Vietnam, Yemen, Zambia, Zimbabwe

Convention on the Prevention of Marine Pollution by Dumping of Wastes and Other Matter, 1972 (London Convention)
note – abbreviated as Marine Dumping-London Convention
opened for signature – 29 December 1972
entered into force – 30 August 1975
objective – to promote effective control of all sources of marine pollution and to take all practicable steps to prevent pollution of the sea by dumping and to encourage regional agreements supplementary to the Convention
parties – (87) Afghanistan, Antigua and Barbuda, Argentina, Australia, Azerbaijan, Barbados, Belarus, Belgium, Benin, Bolivia, Brazil, Bulgaria, Canada, Cape Verde, Chile, China, Democratic Republic of the Congo, Costa Rica, Cote d'Ivoire, Croatia, Cuba, Cyprus, Denmark, Dominican Republic, Egypt, Equatorial Guinea, Finland, France, Gabon, Germany, Greece, Guatemala, Haiti, Honduras, Hungary, Iceland, Iran, Ireland, Italy, Jamaica, Japan, Jordan, Kenya, Kiribati, South Korea, Libya, Luxembourg, Malta, Mexico, Monaco, Montenegro, Morocco, Nauru, Netherlands, NZ, Nigeria, Norway, Oman, Pakistan, Panama, Papua New Guinea, Peru, Philippines, Poland, Portugal, Russia, Saint Lucia, Saint Vincent and the Grenadines, Serbia, Seychelles, Sierra Leon, Slovenia, Solomon Islands, South Africa, Spain, Suriname, Sweden, Switzerland, Syria, Tanzania, Tonga, Tunisia, Ukraine, UAE, UK, US, Vanuatu
associate members to the London Convention – (3) Faroe Islands, Hong Kong, Macau
countries that have signed, but not yet ratified – (3) Chad, Kuwait, Uruguay

Convention on the Prohibition of Military or Any Other Hostile Use of Environmental Modification Techniques
note – abbreviated as Environmental Modification
opened for signature – 18 May 1977
entered into force – 5 October 1978
objective – to prohibit the military or other hostile use of environmental modification techniques in order to further world peace and trust among nations
parties – (77 and the Palestine Liberation Organization) Afghanistan, Algeria, Antigua and Barbuda, Argentina, Armenia, Australia, Austria, Bangladesh, Belarus, Belgium, Benin, Brazil, Bulgaria, Canada, Cameroon, Cape Verde, Chile, China, Costa Rica, Cuba, Cyprus, Czechia, Denmark, Dominica, Egypt, Estonia, Finland, Germany, Ghana, Greece, Guatemala, Honduras, Hungary, India, Ireland, Italy, Japan, Kazakhstan, North Korea, South Korea, Kuwait, Kyrgyzstan, Laos, Lithuania, Malawi, Mauritius, Mongolia, Netherlands, NZ, Nicaragua, Niger, Norway,

Pakistan, Panama, Papua New Guinea, Poland, Romania, Russia, Saint Lucia, Saint Vincent and the Grenadines, Sao Tome and Principe, Slovakia, Slovenia, Solomon Islands, Spain, Sri Lanka, Sweden, Switzerland, Tajikistan, Tunisia, Ukraine, UK, US, Uruguay, Uzbekistan, Vietnam, Yemen, Palestine Liberation Organization
countries that have signed, but not yet ratified – (16) Bolivia, Democratic Republic of the Congo, Ethiopia, Holy See, Iceland, Iran, Iraq, Lebanon, Liberia, Luxembourg, Morocco, Portugal, Sierra Leone, Syria, Turkey (Turkiye), Uganda

Convention on Wetlands of International Importance Especially as Waterfowl Habitat (Ramsar)

note – abbreviated as Wetlands
opened for signature – 2 February 1971
entered into force – 21 December 1975
objective – to stem the progressive encroachment on and loss of wetlands now and in the future
parties – (170) Albania, Algeria, Andorra, Antigua and Barbuda, Argentina, Armenia, Australia, Austria, Azerbaijan, The Bahamas, Bahrain, Bangladesh, Barbados, Belarus, Belgium, Belize, Benin, Bhutan, Bolivia, Bosnia and Herzegovina, Botswana, Brazil, Bulgaria, Burkina Faso, Burma, Burundi, Cabo Verde, Cambodia, Cameroon, Canada, Central African Republic, Chad, Chile, China, Colombia, Comoros, Democratic Republic of the Congo, Republic of the Congo, Costa Rica, Cote d'Ivoire, Croatia, Cuba, Cyprus, Czechia, Denmark, Djibouti, Dominican Republic, Ecuador, Egypt, El Salvador, Equatorial Guinea, Estonia, Eswatini, Fiji, Finland, France, Gabon, The Gambia, Georgia, Germany, Ghana, Greece, Grenada, Guatemala, Guinea, Guinea-Bissau, Honduras, Hungary, Iceland, India, Indonesia, Iran, Iraq, Ireland, Israel, Italy, Jamaica, Japan, Jordan, Kazakhstan, Kenya, Kiribati, South Korea, Kyrgyzstan, Kuwait, Laos, Latvia, Lebanon, Lesotho, Liberia, Libya, Liechtenstein, Lithuania, Luxembourg, Madagascar, Malawi, Malaysia, Mali, Malta, Marshall Islands, Mauritania, Mauritius, Mexico, Moldova, Monaco, Mongolia, Montenegro, Morocco, Mozambique, Namibia, Nepal, Netherlands, NZ, Nicaragua, Niger, Nigeria, North Macedonia, Norway, Oman, Pakistan, Palau, Panama, Papua New Guinea, Paraguay, Peru, Philippines, Poland, Portugal, Romania, Russia, Rwanda, Saint Lucia, Samoa, Sao Tome and Principe, Senegal, Serbia, Seychelles, Sierra Leone, Slovakia, Slovenia, South Africa, South Sudan, Spain, Sri Lanka, Sudan, Suriname, Sweden, Switzerland, Syria, Tanzania, Tajikistan, Thailand, Togo, Trinidad and Tobago, Tunisia, Turkey (Turkiye), Turkmenistan, Uganda, Ukraine, UAE, UK, US, Uruguay, Uzbekistan, Venezuela, Vietnam, Yemen, Zambia, Zimbabwe

Desertification

see United Nations Convention to Combat Desertification in those Countries Experiencing Serious Drought and/or Desertification, Particularly in Africa

Endangered Species

see Convention on the International Trade in Endangered Species of Wild Flora and Fauna (CITES)

Environmental Modification

see Convention on the Prohibition of Military or Any Other Hostile Use of Environmental Modification Techniques

Hazardous Wastes

see Basel Convention on the Control of Transboundary Movements of Hazardous Wastes and Their Disposal

International Convention for the Regulation of Whaling

note – abbreviated as Whaling
opened for signature – 2 December 1946
entered into force – 10 November 1948
objective – to protect all species of whales from overhunting; to establish a system of international regulation for the whale fisheries to ensure proper conservation and development of whale stocks; to safeguard for future generations the great natural resources represented by whale stocks
parties – (89) Antigua and Barbuda, Argentina, Australia, Austria, Belgium, Belize, Benin, Brazil, Bulgaria, Cambodia, Cameroon, Chile, China, Colombia, Republic of the Congo, Costa Rica, Cote D'Ivoire, Croatia, Cyprus, Czechia, Denmark, Dominica, Dominican Republic, Ecuador, Eritrea, Estonia, Finland, France, Gabon, The Gambia, Germany, Ghana, Grenada, Guinea, Guinea-Bissau, Hungary, Iceland, India, Ireland, Israel, Italy, Japan, Kenya, Kiribati, South Korea, Laos, Liberia, Lithuania, Luxembourg, Mali, Marshall Islands, Mauritania, Mexico, Monaco, Mongolia, Morocco, Nauru, Netherlands, NZ, Nicaragua, Norway, Oman, Palau, Panama, Peru, Poland, Portugal, Romania, Russia, Saint Kitts and Nevis, Saint Lucia, Saint Vincent and the Grenadines, San Marino, Sao Tome and Principe, Senegal, Slovakia, Slovenia, Solomon Islands, South Africa, Spain, Suriname, Sweden, Switzerland, Tanzania, Togo, Tuvalu, UK, US, Uruguay

International Tropical Timber Agreement, 2006

note – abbreviated as Tropical Timber, 2006; ITTA, 2006; or ITTA3
opened for signature – 3 April 2006
entered into force – 7 December 2011; note - superseded the International Tropical Timber Agreement, 1994, which itself superseded the International Tropical Timber Agreement, 1983
objective – to promote the expansion and diversification of international trade in tropical timber from sustainably managed and legally harvested forests and to promote the sustainable management of tropical timber producing forests
parties – (74) Abania, Australia, Austria, Belgium, Benin, Brazil, Bulgaria, Burma, Cambodia, Cameroon, Central African Republic, China, Colombia, Democratic Republic of the Congo, Republic of the Congo, Costa Rica, Cote d'Ivoire, Croatia, Cyprus, Czechia, Denmark, Ecuador, Estonia, EU, Fiji, Finland, France, Gabon, Germany, Ghana, Greece, Guatemala, Guyana, Honduras, Hungary, India, Indonesia, Ireland, Italy, Japan, South Korea, Latvia, Liberia, Lithuania, Luxembourg, Madagascar, Malaysia, Mali, Malta, Mexico, Mozambique, Netherlands, NZ, Norway, Panama, Papua New Guinea, Peru, Philippines, Poland, Portugal, Romania, Slovakia, Slovenia, Spain, Suriname, Sweden, Switzerland, Thailand, Togo, Trinidad and Tobago, UK, US, Venezuela, Vietnam
countries that have signed, but not yet ratified – (2) Nigeria, Paraguay

Kyoto Protocol to the United Nations Framework Convention on Climate Change

note – abbreviated as Climate Change-Kyoto Protocol
opened for signature – 16 March 1998
entered into force – 16 February 2005

objective – to further reduce greenhouse gas emissions by enhancing the national programs of developed countries aimed at this goal and by establishing percentage reduction targets for the developed countries
parties – (192) Afghanistan, Albania, Algeria, Angola, Antigua and Barbuda, Argentina, Armenia, Australia, Austria, Azerbaijan, The Bahamas, Bahrain, Bangladesh, Barbados, Belarus, Belgium, Belize, Benin, Bhutan, Bolivia, Bosnia and Herzegovina, Botswana, Brazil, Brunei, Bulgaria, Burkina Faso, Burma, Burundi, Cabo Verde, Cambodia, Cameroon, Central African Republic, Chad, Chile, China, Colombia, Comoros, Democratic Republic of the Congo, Republic of the Congo, Cook Islands, Costa Rica, Cote d'Ivoire, Croatia, Cuba, Cyprus, Czechia, Denmark, Djibouti, Dominica, Dominican Republic, Ecuador, Egypt, El Salvador, Equatorial Guinea, Eritrea, Estonia, Eswatini, Ethiopia, EU, Fiji, Finland, France, Gabon, The Gambia, Georgia, Germany, Ghana, Greece, Grenada, Guatemala, Guinea, Guinea-Bissau, Guyana, Haiti, Honduras, Hungary, Iceland, India, Indonesia, Iran, Iraq, Ireland, Israel, Italy, Jamaica, Japan, Jordan, Kazakhstan, Kenya, Kiribati, North Korea, South Korea, Kuwait, Kyrgyzstan, Laos, Latvia, Lebanon, Lesotho, Liberia, Libya, Liechtenstein, Lithuania, Luxembourg, Madagascar, Malawi, Malaysia, Maldives, Mali, Malta, Marshall Islands, Mauritania, Mauritius, Mexico, Federated States of Micronesia, Moldova, Monaco, Mongolia, Montenegro, Morocco, Mozambique, Namibia, Nauru, Nepal, Netherlands, NZ, Nicaragua, Niger, Nigeria, Niue, North Macedonia, Norway, Oman, Pakistan, Palau, Panama, Papua New Guinea, Paraguay, Peru, Philippines, Poland, Portugal, Qatar, Romania, Russia, Rwanda, Saint Kitts and Nevis, Saint Lucia, Saint Vincent and the Grenadines, Samoa, San Marino, Sao Tome and Principe, Saudi Arabia, Senegal, Serbia, Seychelles, Sierra Leone, Singapore, Slovakia, Slovenia, Solomon Islands, Somalia, South Africa, Spain, Sri Lanka, Sudan, Suriname, Sweden, Switzerland, Syria, Tajikistan, Tanzania, Thailand, Timor-Leste, Togo, Tonga, Trinidad and Tobago, Tunisia, Turkey (Turkiye), Turkmenistan, Tuvalu, Uganda, Ukraine, UAE, UK, Uruguay, Uzbekistan, Vanuatu, Venezuela, Vietnam, Yemen, Zambia, Zimbabwe
countries that have signed, but not yet ratified - (1) US

Law of the Sea
see United Nations Convention on the Law of the Sea (LOS)

Marine Dumping-London Convention
see Convention on the Prevention of Marine Pollution by Dumping of Wastes and Other Matter, 1972 (London Convention)

Marine Dumping-London Protocol
see Protocol to the Convention on the Prevention of Marine Pollution by Dumping of Wastes and Other Matter, 1972 (London Convention)

Marine Life Conservation
see Convention on Fishing and Conservation of Living Resources of the High Seas

Montreal Protocol on Substances That Deplete the Ozone Layer
note – abbreviated as Ozone Layer Protection
opened for signature – 16 September 1987
entered into force – 1 January 1989
objective – to protect the ozone layer by controlling emissions of substances that deplete it
parties – (197 and the Palestine Liberation Organization) Afghanistan, Albania, Algeria, Andorra, Angola, Antigua and Barbuda, Argentina, Armenia, Australia, Austria, Azerbaijan, The Bahamas, Bahrain, Bangladesh, Barbados, Belarus, Belgium, Belize, Benin, Bhutan, Bolivia, Bosnia and Herzegovina, Botswana, Brazil, Brunei, Bulgaria, Burkina Faso, Burma, Burundi, Cambodia, Cameroon, Canada, Cape Verde, Central African Republic, Chad, Chile, China, Colombia, Comoros, Democratic Republic of the Congo, Republic of the Congo, Cook Islands, Costa Rica, Cote d'Ivoire, Croatia, Cuba, Cyprus, Czechia, Denmark, Djibouti, Dominica, Dominican Republic, Ecuador, Egypt, El Salvador, Equatorial Guinea, Eritrea, Estonia, Eswatini, Ethiopia, EU, Fiji, Finland, France, Gabon, The Gambia, Georgia, Germany, Ghana, Greece, Grenada, Guatemala, Guinea, Guinea-Bissau, Guyana, Haiti, Holy See, Honduras, Hungary, Iceland, India, Indonesia, Iran, Iraq, Ireland, Israel, Italy, Jamaica, Japan, Jordan, Kazakhstan, Kenya, Kiribati, North Korea, South Korea, Kuwait, Kyrgyzstan, Laos, Latvia, Lebanon, Lesotho, Liberia, Libya, Liechtenstein, Lithuania, Luxembourg, Madagascar, Malawi, Malaysia, Maldives, Mali, Malta, Marshall Islands, Mauritania, Mauritius, Mexico, Federated States of Micronesia, Moldova, Monaco, Mongolia, Montenegro, Morocco, Mozambique, Namibia, Nauru, Nepal, Netherlands, NZ, Nicaragua, Niger, Nigeria, Niue, North Macedonia, Norway, Oman, Pakistan, Palau, Panama, Papua New Guinea, Paraguay, Peru, Philippines, Poland, Portugal, Qatar, Romania, Russia, Rwanda, Saint Kitts and Nevis, Saint Lucia, Saint Vincent and the Grenadines, Samoa, San Marino, Sao Tome and Principe, Saudi Arabia, Senegal, Serbia, Seychelles, Sierra Leone, Singapore, Slovakia, Slovenia, Solomon Islands, Somalia, South Africa, South Sudan, Spain, Sri Lanka, Sudan, Suriname, Sweden, Switzerland, Syria, Tajikistan, Tanzania, Thailand, Timor-Leste, Togo, Tonga, Trinidad and Tobago, Tunisia, Turkey (Turkiye), Turkmenistan, Tuvalu, Uganda, Ukraine, UAE, UK, US, Uruguay, Uzbekistan, Vanuatu, Venezuela, Vietnam, Yemen, Zambia, Zimbabwe

Multi-effect Protocol
see Protocol to the 1979 Convention on Long-Range Transboundary Air Pollution to Abate Acidification, Eutrophication, and Ground-Level Ozone

Nuclear Test Ban
see Treaty Banning Nuclear Weapons Tests in the Atmosphere, in Outer Space, and Under Water

Ozone Layer Protection
see Montreal Protocol on Substances That Deplete the Ozone Layer

Paris Agreement under the United Nations Framework Convention on Climate Change
note – abbreviated as Paris Agreement
opened for signature – 22 April 2016
entered into force – 4 November 2016
objective – to improve upon and replace the Kyoto Protocol, an earlier international treaty designed to curb the release of greenhouse gases that contribute to global warming; the Paris Agreement's goal is to hold global average temperature increase to well below 2 degrees Celsius - preferably to 1.5 degrees Celsius - compared to pre-industrial levels and to achieve a climate neutral world by mid-century

parties – (189 and the Palestine Liberation Organization) Afghanistan, Albania, Algeria, Andorra, Angola, Antigua and Barbuda, Argentina, Armenia, Australia, Austria, Azerbaijan, The Bahamas, Bahrain, Bangladesh, Barbados, Belarus, Belgium, Belize, Benin, Bhutan, Bolivia, Bosnia and Herzegovina, Botswana, Brazil, Brunei, Bulgaria, Burkina Faso, Burma, Burundi, Cape Verde, Cambodia, Cameroon, Canada, Central African Republic, Chad, Chile, China, Colombia, Comoros, Democratic Republic of the Congo, Republic of the Congo, Cook Islands, Costa Rica, Cote d'Ivoire, Croatia, Cuba, Cyprus, Czechia, Denmark, Djibouti, Dominica, Dominican Republic, Ecuador, Egypt, El Salvador, Equatorial Guinea, Estonia, Eswatini, Ethiopia, EU, Fiji, Finland, France, Gabon, The Gambia, Georgia, Germany, Ghana, Greece, Grenada, Guatemala, Guinea, Guinea-Bissau, Guyana, Haiti, Honduras, Hungary, Iceland, India, Indonesia, Ireland, Israel, Italy, Jamaica, Japan, Jordan, Kazakhstan, Kenya, Kiribati, North Korea, South Korea, Kuwait, Kyrgyzstan, Laos, Latvia, Lebanon, Lesotho, Liberia, Liechtenstein, Lithuania, Luxembourg, Madagascar, Malawi, Malaysia, Maldives, Mali, Malta, Marshall Islands, Mauritania, Mauritius, Mexico, Federated States of Micronesia, Moldova, Monaco, Mongolia, Montenegro, Morocco, Mozambique, Namibia, Nauru, Nepal, Netherlands, NZ, Nicaragua, Niger, Nigeria, Niue, North Macedonia, Norway, Oman, Pakistan, Palau, Panama, Papua New Guinea, Paraguay, Peru, Philippines, Poland, Portugal, Qatar, Romania, Russia, Rwanda, Saint Kitts and Nevis, Saint Lucia, Saint Vincent and the Grenadines, Samoa, San Marino, Sao Tome and Principe, Saudi Arabia, Senegal, Serbia, Seychelles, Sierra Leone, Singapore, Slovakia, Slovenia, Solomon Islands, Somalia, South Africa, South Sudan, Spain, Sri Lanka, Sudan, Suriname, Sweden, Switzerland, Syria, Tajikistan, Tanzania, Thailand, Timor-Leste, Togo, Tonga, Trinidad and Tobago, Tunisia, Turkmenistan, Tuvalu, Uganda, Ukraine, UAE, UK, Uruguay, Uzbekistan, Vanuatu, Venezuela, Vietnam, Zambia, Zimbabwe, Palestine Liberation Organization
countries that have signed, but not ratified – (6) Eritrea, Iran, Iraq, Libya, Turkey, Yemen

Protocol of 1978 Relating to the International Convention for the Prevention of Pollution From Ships, 1973 (MARPOL)
note – abbreviated as Ship Pollution
opened for signature – 1 June 1978
entered into force – 2 October 1983
objective – to preserve the marine environment in an attempt to completely eliminate pollution by oil and other harmful substances and to minimize accidental spillage of such substances
parties – (158) Albania, Algeria, Angola, Antigua and Barbuda, Argentina, Australia, Austria, Azerbaijan, The Bahamas, Bahrain, Bangladesh, Barbados, Belarus, Belgium, Belize, Benin, Bolivia, Brazil, Brunei, Bulgaria, Burma, Cabo Verde, Cambodia, Cameroon, Canada, Chile, China, Colombia, Comoros, Republic of Congo, Cook Islands, Cote d'Ivoire, Croatia, Cuba, Cyprus, Czechia, Denmark, Djibouti, Dominica, Dominican Republic, Ecuador, Egypt, El Salvador, Equatorial Guinea, Estonia, Fiji, Finland, France, Gabon, The Gambia, Georgia, Germany, Ghana, Greece, Grenada, Guatemala, Guinea, Guinea-Bissau, Guyana, Honduras, Hungary, Iceland, India, Indonesia, Iran, Iraq, Ireland, Israel, Italy, Jamaica, Japan, Jordan, Kazakhstan, Kenya, Kiribati, North Korea, South Korea, Kuwait, Latvia, Lebanon, Liberia, Libya, Lithuania, Luxembourg, Madagascar, Malawi, Malaysia, Maldives, Malta, Marshall Islands, Mauritania, Mauritius, Mexico, Moldova, Monaco, Mongolia, Montenegro, Morocco, Mozambique, Namibia, Netherlands, NZ, Nicaragua, Nigeria, Niue, Norway, Oman, Pakistan, Palau, Panama, Papua New Guinea, Peru, Philippines, Poland, Portugal, Qatar, Romania, Russia, Saint Kitts and Nevis, Saint Lucia, Saint Vincent and the Grenadines, Samoa, Sao Tome and Principe, Saudi Arabia, Senegal, Serbia, Seychelles, Sierra Leone, Singapore, Slovakia, Slovenia, Solomon Islands, South Africa, Spain, Sri Lanka, Sudan, Suriname, Sweden, Switzerland, Syria, Tanzania, Thailand, Togo, Tonga, Trinidad and Tobago, Tunisia, Turkey (Turkiye), Turkmenistan, Tuvalu, Uganda, Ukraine, UAE, UK, US, Uruguay, Vanuatu, Venezuela, Vietnam

Protocol on Environmental Protection to the Antarctic Treaty
note – abbreviated as Antarctic-Environmental Protocol
opened for signature – 4 October 1991
entered into force – 14 January 1998
objective – to provide for comprehensive protection of the Antarctic environment and dependent and associated ecosystems; applies to the area covered by the Antarctic Treaty
parties – (41) Argentina, Australia, Belarus, Belgium, Brazil, Bulgaria, Canada, Chile, China, Columbia, Czechia, Ecuador, Finland, France, Germany, Greece, India, Italy, Japan, South Korea, Malaysia, Monaco, Netherlands, NZ, Norway, Pakistan, Peru, Poland, Portugal, Romania, Russia, South Africa, Spain, Sweden, Switzerland, Turkey (Turkiye), Ukraine, UK, US, Uruguay, Venezuela
countries that have signed, but not yet ratified – (5) Austria, Denmark, Hungary, North Korea, Slovakia

Protocol to the 1979 Convention on Long-Range Transboundary Air Pollution Concerning the Control of Emissions of Nitrogen Oxides or Their Transboundary Fluxes
note – abbreviated as Air Pollution-Nitrogen Oxides
opened for signature – 31 October 1988
entered into force – 14 February 1991
objective – to provide for the control or reduction of nitrogen oxide emissions and their transboundary fluxes
parties – (35) Albania, Austria, Belarus, Belgium, Bulgaria, Canada, Croatia, Cyprus, Czechia, Denmark, Estonia, EU, Finland, France, Germany, Greece, Hungary, Ireland, Italy, Liechtenstein, Lithuania, Luxembourg, Netherlands, North Macedonia, Norway, Poland, Russia, Slovakia, Slovenia, Spain, Sweden, Switzerland, Ukraine, UK, US

Protocol to the 1979 Convention on Long-Range Transboundary Air Pollution Concerning the Control of Emissions of Volatile Organic Compounds or Their Transboundary Fluxes
note – abbreviated as Air Pollution-Volatile Organic Compounds
opened for signature – 18 November 1991
entered into force – 29 September 1997
objective – to provide for the control and reduction of national emissions of volatile organic compounds in order to reduce their transboundary fluxes
parties – (24) Austria, Belgium, Bulgaria, Croatia, Czechia, Denmark, Estonia, Finland, France, Germany, Hungary, Italy, Liechtenstein, Lithuania, Luxembourg, Monaco, Netherlands, North Macedonia, Norway, Slovakia, Spain, Sweden, Switzerland, UK
countries that have signed, but not yet ratified – (6) Canada, EU, Greece, Portugal, Ukraine, US

Protocol to the 1979 Convention on Long-Range Transboundary Air Pollution on Further Reduction of Sulphur Emissions
note – abbreviated as Air Pollution-Sulphur 94
opened for signature – 14 June 1994
entered into force – 5 August 1998
objective – to provide for a further reduction in national sulfur emissions or transboundary fluxes on a regional basis within Europe

parties – (29) Austria, Belgium, Bulgaria, Canada, Croatia, Cyprus, Czechia, Denmark, EU, Finland, France, Germany, Greece, Hungary, Ireland, Italy, Liechtenstein, Lithuania, Luxembourg, Monaco, Netherlands, North Macedonia, Norway, Slovakia, Slovenia, Spain, Sweden, Switzerland, UK
countries that have signed, but not yet ratified – (3) Poland, Russia, Ukraine

Protocol to the 1979 Convention on Long-Range Transboundary Air Pollution on Heavy Metals
note – abbreviated as Air Pollution-Heavy Metals
opened for signature – 24 June 1998
entered into force – 29 December 2003
objective – to reduce emissions of the heavy metals cadmium, lead, and mercury from industrial sources, combustion processes, and waste incineration
parties – (34) Austria, Belgium, Bulgaria, Canada, Croatia, Cyprus, Czechia, Denmark, Estonia, EU, Finland, France, Germany, Hungary, Latvia, Liechtenstein, Lithuania, Luxembourg, Moldova, Monaco, Montenegro, Netherlands, North Macedonia, Norway, Portugal, Romania, Serbia, Slovakia, Slovenia, Spain, Sweden, Switzerland, UK, US
countries that have signed, but not yet ratified – (7) Armenia, Greece, Iceland, Ireland, Italy, Poland, Ukraine

Protocol to the 1979 Convention on Long-Range Transboundary Air Pollution on Persistent Organic Pollutants
note – abbreviated as Air Pollution-Persistent Organic Pollutants
opened for signature – 24 June 1998
entered into force – 23 October 2003
objective – to provide for the control, reduction, or elimination of discharges, emissions of persistent organic pollutants
parties – (34) Austria, Belgium, Bulgaria, Canada, Croatia, Cyprus, Czechia, Denmark, Estonia, EU, Finland, France, Germany, Hungary, Iceland, Ireland, Italy, Latvia, Liechtenstein, Lithuania, Luxembourg, Moldova, Montenegro, Netherlands, North Macedonia, Norway, Romania, Serbia, Slovakia, Slovenia, Spain, Sweden, Switzerland, UK
countries that have signed, but not yet ratified – (6) Armenia, Greece, Poland, Portugal, Ukraine, US

Protocol to the 1979 Convention on Long-Range Transboundary Air Pollution on the Reduction of Sulphur Emissions or Their Transboundary Fluxes by at Least 30%
note – abbreviated as Air Pollution-Sulphur 85
opened for signature – 8 July 1985
entered into force – 2 September 1987
objective – to provide for national reductions in sulfur emissions or transboundary fluxes by 30% of 1980 emission or transboundary flux levels by no later than 1993
parties – (25) Albania, Austria, Belarus, Belgium, Bulgaria, Canada, Czechia, Denmark, Estonia, Finland, France, Germany, Hungary, Italy, Liechtenstein, Lithuania, Luxembourg, Netherlands, North Macedonia, Norway, Russia, Slovakia, Sweden, Switzerland, Ukraine

Protocol to the 1979 Convention on Long-Range Transboundary Air Pollution to Abate Acidification, Eutrophication, and Ground-Level Ozone
note – abbreviated as Multi-effect Protocol
opened for signature – 30 November 1999
entered into force – 17 May 2005
objective – to reduce acidification, eutrophication, and ground-level ozone by setting emissions ceilings for sulphur dioxide, nitrogen oxides, volatile organic compounds, and ammonia
parties – (27) Belgium, Bulgaria, Canada, Croatia, Cyprus, Czechia, Denmark, EU, Finland, France, Germany, Hungary, Latvia, Lithuania, Luxembourg, Netherlands, North Macedonia, Norway, Portugal, Romania, Slovakia, Slovenia, Spain, Sweden, Switzerland, UK, US
countries that have signed, but not yet ratified – (8) Armenia, Austria, Greece, Ireland, Italy, Liechtenstein, Moldova, Poland

Protocol to the Convention on the Prevention of Marine Pollution by Dumping of Wastes and Other Matter, 1972 (London Convention)
note – abbreviated as Marine Dumping-London Protocol
opened for signature – 1 April 1997
entered into force – 24 March 2006
objective – prohibits all wastes for ocean disposal except those specifically identified; this "reverse list" ensures that the few materials that are permitted for ocean disposal are carefully evaluated and will not pose a danger to human health or the environment, and that there are not more feasible alternatives for their reuse or disposal
parties – (53) Angola, Antigua and Barbuda, Australia, Barbados, Belgium, Bulgaria, Canada, Chile, China, Republic of the Congo, Denmark, Egypt, Estonia, Finland, France, Guatemala, Georgia, Germany, Ghana, Guyana, Iceland, Ireland, Iran, Italy, Japan, Kenya, South Korea, Luxembourg, Madagascar, Marshall Islands, Mexico, Morocco, New Zealand, Netherlands, Nigera, Norway, Peru, Philippines, Saint Kitts and Nevis, Saudi Arabia, Sierra Leone, Slovenia, South Africa, Spain, Suriname, Sweden, Switzerland, Tonga, Trinidad and Tobago, United Kingdom, Uruguay, Vanuatu, Yemen
countries that have signed, but not yet ratified – (3) Argentina, Brazil, United States

Ship Pollution
see Protocol of 1978 Relating to the International Convention for the Prevention of Pollution From Ships, 1973 (MARPOL)

Treaty Banning Nuclear Weapon Tests in the Atmosphere, in Outer Space, and Under Water
note 1 – abbreviated as Nuclear Test Ban
note 2 – also referred to as Limited Nuclear Test-Ban Treaty (LTBT)
opened for signature – 5 August 1963
entered into force – 10 October 1963
objective – to ban nuclear weapons testing in the atmosphere, outer space, or under water
parties – (125) Afghanistan, Antigua and Barbuda, Argentina, Armenia, Australia, Austria, The Bahamas, Bangladesh, Belarus, Belgium, Benin, Bhutan, Bolivia, Bosnia and Herzegovina, Botswana, Brazil, Bulgaria, Burma, Cabo Verde, Canada, Central African Republic, Chad, Chile, Colombia, Democratic Republic of the Congo, Costa Rica, Cote d'Ivoire, Croatia, Cyprus, Czechia, Denmark, Dominican Republic, Ecuador, Egypt, El Salvador, Eswatini, Equatorial Guinea, Fiji, Finland, Gabon, The Gambia, Germany, Ghana, Greece, Guatemala, Guinea-Bissau, Honduras,

Hungary, Iceland, India, Indonesia, Iran, Iraq, Ireland, Israel, Italy, Jamaica, Japan, Jordan, Kenya, South Korea, Kuwait, Laos, Lebanon, Liberia, Libya, Luxembourg, Madagascar, Malawi, Malaysia, Malta, Mauritania, Mauritius, Mexico, Mongolia, Montenegro, Morocco, Nepal, Netherlands, NZ, Nicaragua, Niger, Nigeria, Norway, Pakistan, Panama, Papua New Guinea, Peru, Philippines, Poland, Romania, Russia, Rwanda, Samoa, San Marino, Senegal, Serbia, Seychelles, Sierra Leone, Singapore, Slovakia, Slovenia, South Africa, Spain, Sri Lanka, Sudan, Suriname, Sweden, Switzerland, Syria, Tanzania, Thailand, Togo, Tonga, Trinidad and Tobago, Tunisia, Turkey (Turkiye), Uganda, Ukraine, UK, US, Uruguay, Venezuela, Yemen, Zambia
countries that have signed, but not yet ratified – (10) Algeria, Burkina-Faso, Burundi, Cameroon, Ethiopia, Haiti, Mali, Paraguay, Portugal, Somalia

Tropical Timber, 2006
see International Tropical Timber Agreement, 2006

United Nations Convention on the Law of the Sea (LOS)
note – abbreviated as Law of the Sea
opened for signature – 10 December 1982
entered into force – 16 November 1994
objective – to provide a comprehensive legal regime for the sea and oceans
parties – (167 and the Palestine Liberation Organization) Albania, Algeria, Angola, Antigua and Barbuda, Argentina, Armenia, Australia, Austria, Azerbaijan, The Bahamas, Bahrain, Bangladesh, Barbados, Belarus, Belgium, Belize, Benin, Bolivia, Bosnia and Herzegovina, Botswana, Brazil, Brunei, Bulgaria, Burkina Faso, Burma, Cabo Verde, Cameroon, Canada, Chad, Chile, China, Comoros, Democratic Republic of the Congo, Republic of the Congo, Cook Islands, Costa Rica, Cote d'Ivoire, Croatia, Cuba, Cyprus, Czechia, Denmark, Djibouti, Dominica, Dominican Republic, Ecuador, Egypt, Equatorial Guinea, Estonia, Eswatini, EU, Fiji, Finland, France, Gabon, The Gambia, Georgia, Germany, Ghana, Greece, Grenada, Guatemala, Guinea, Guinea-Bissau, Guyana, Haiti, Honduras, Hungary, Iceland, India, Indonesia, Iraq, Ireland, Italy, Jamaica, Japan, Jordan, Kenya, Kiribati, South Korea, Kuwait, Laos, Latvia, Lebanon, Lesotho, Liberia, Lithuania, Luxembourg, Madagascar, Malawi, Malaysia, Maldives, Mali, Malta, Marshall Islands, Mauritania, Mauritius, Mexico, Federated States of Micronesia, Moldova, Monaco, Mongolia, Montenegro, Morocco, Mozambique, Namibia, Nauru, Nepal, Netherlands, NZ, Nicaragua, Niger, Nigeria, Niue, North Macedonia, Norway, Oman, Pakistan, Palau, Panama, Papua New Guinea, Paraguay, Philippines, Poland, Portugal, Qatar, Romania, Russia, Saint Kitts and Nevis, Saint Lucia, Saint Vincent and the Grenadines, Samoa, Sao Tome and Principe, Saudi Arabia, Senegal, Serbia, Seychelles, Sierra Leone, Singapore, Slovakia, Slovenia, Solomon Islands, Somalia, South Africa, Spain, Sri Lanka, Sudan, Suriname, Sweden, Switzerland, Tanzania, Thailand, Timor-Leste, Togo, Tonga, Trinidad and Tobago, Tunisia, Tuvalu, Uganda, Ukraine, UK, Uruguay, Vanuatu, Vietnam, Yemen, Zambia, Zimbabwe, Palestine Liberation Organization
countries that have signed, but not yet ratified – (14) Afghanistan, Bhutan, Burundi, Cambodia, Central African Republic, Colombia, El Salvador, Ethiopia, Iran, North Korea, Libya, Liechtenstein, Rwanda, UAE

United Nations Convention to Combat Desertification in Those Countries Experiencing Serious Drought and/or Desertification, Particularly in Africa
note – abbreviated as Desertification
opened for signature – 14 October 1994
entered into force – 26 December 1996
objective – to combat desertification and mitigate the effects of drought through an integrated framework that is consistent with Agenda 21, employing international cooperation and partnership arrangements, and effective action at all levels
parties – (196 and the Palestine Liberation Organization) Afghanistan, Albania, Algeria, Andorra, Angola, Antigua and Barbuda, Argentina, Armenia, Australia, Austria, Azerbaijan, The Bahamas, Bahrain, Bangladesh, Barbados, Belarus, Belgium, Belize, Benin, Bhutan, Bolivia, Bosnia and Herzegovina, Botswana, Brazil, Brunei, Bulgaria, Burkina Faso, Burma, Burundi, Cambodia, Cameroon, Canada, Cape Verde, Central African Republic, Chad, Chile, China, Colombia, Comoros, Democratic Republic of the Congo, Republic of the Congo, Cook Islands, Costa Rica, Cote d'Ivoire, Croatia, Cuba, Cyprus, Czechia, Denmark, Djibouti, Dominica, Dominican Republic, Ecuador, Egypt, El Salvador, Equatorial Guinea, Eritrea, Estonia, Eswatini, Ethiopia, EU, Fiji, Finland, France, Gabon, The Gambia, Georgia, Germany, Ghana, Greece, Grenada, Guatemala, Guinea, Guinea-Bissau, Guyana, Haiti, Honduras, Hungary, Iceland, India, Indonesia, Iran, Iraq, Ireland, Israel, Italy, Jamaica, Japan, Jordan, Kazakhstan, Kenya, Kiribati, North Korea, South Korea, Kuwait, Kyrgyzstan, Laos, Latvia, Lebanon, Lesotho, Liberia, Libya, Liechtenstein, Lithuania, Luxembourg, Madagascar, Malawi, Malaysia, Maldives, Mali, Malta, Marshall Islands, Mauritania, Mauritius, Mexico, Federated States of Micronesia, Moldova, Monaco, Mongolia, Montenegro, Morocco, Mozambique, Namibia, Nauru, Nepal, Netherlands, NZ, Nicaragua, Niger, Nigeria, Niue, North Macedonia, Norway, Oman, Pakistan, Palau, Panama, Papua New Guinea, Paraguay, Peru, Philippines, Poland, Portugal, Qatar, Romania, Russia, Rwanda, Saint Kitts and Nevis, Saint Lucia, Saint Vincent and the Grenadines, Samoa, San Marino, Sao Tome and Principe, Saudi Arabia, Senegal, Serbia, Seychelles, Sierra Leone, Singapore, Slovakia, Slovenia, Solomon Islands, Somalia, South Africa, South Sudan, Spain, Sri Lanka, Sudan, Suriname, Sweden, Switzerland, Syria, Tajikistan, Thailand, Tanzania, Timor-Leste, Togo, Tonga, Trinidad and Tobago, Tunisia, Turkey (Turkiye), Turkmenistan, Tuvalu, Uganda, Ukraine, UAE, UK, US, Uruguay, Uzbekistan, Vanutu, Venezuela, Vietnam, Yemen, Zambia, Zimbabwe

United Nations Framework Convention on Climate Change
note – abbreviated as Climate Change
opened for signature – 9 May 1992
entered into force – 21 March 1994
objective – to achieve stabilization of greenhouse gas concentrations in the atmosphere at a low enough level to prevent dangerous anthropogenic interference with the climate system
parties – (196 and the Palestine Liberation Organization) Afghanistan, Albania, Algeria, Andorra, Angola, Antigua and Barbuda, Argentina, Armenia, Australia, Austria, Azerbaijan, The Bahamas, Bahrain, Bangladesh, Barbados, Belarus, Belgium, Belize, Benin, Bhutan, Bolivia, Bosnia and Herzegovina, Botswana, Brazil, Brunei, Bulgaria, Burkina Faso, Burma, Burundi, Cambodia, Cameroon, Canada, Cape Verde, Central African Republic, Chad, Chile, China, Colombia, Comoros, Democratic Republic of the Congo, Republic of the Congo, Cook Islands, Costa Rica, Cote d'Ivoire, Croatia, Cuba, Cyprus, Czechia, Denmark, Djibouti, Dominica, Dominican Republic, Ecuador, Egypt, El Salvador, Equatorial Guinea, Eritrea, Estonia, Eswatini, Ethiopia, EU, Fiji, Finland, France, Gabon, The Gambia, Georgia, Germany, Ghana, Greece, Grenada, Guatemala, Guinea, Guinea-Bissau, Guyana, Haiti, Honduras, Hungary, Iceland, India, Indonesia, Iran, Iraq, Ireland, Israel, Italy, Jamaica, Japan, Jordan, Kazakhstan, Kenya, Kiribati, North Korea, South Korea, Kuwait, Kyrgyzstan, Laos, Latvia, Lebanon, Lesotho, Liberia, Libya, Liechtenstein, Lithuania, Luxembourg, Madagascar, Malawi, Malaysia, Maldives, Mali, Malta, Marshall Islands, Mauritania, Mauritius, Mexico, Federated States of

Micronesia, Moldova, Monaco, Mongolia, Montenegro, Morocco, Mozambique, Namibia, Nauru, Nepal, Netherlands, NZ, Nicaragua, Niger, Nigeria, Niue, North Macedonia, Norway, Oman, Pakistan, Palau, Panama, Papua New Guinea, Paraguay, Peru, Philippines, Poland, Portugal, Qatar, Romania, Russia, Rwanda, Saint Kitts and Nevis, Saint Lucia, Saint Vincent and the Grenadines, Samoa, San Marino, Sao Tome and Principe, Saudi Arabia, Senegal, Serbia, Seychelles, Sierra Leone, Singapore, Slovakia, Slovenia, Solomon Islands, Somalia, South Africa, South Sudan, Spain, Sri Lanka, Sudan, Suriname, Sweden, Switzerland, Syria, Tajikistan, Tanzania, Thailand, Timor-Leste, Togo, Tonga, Trinidad and Tobago, Tunisia, Turkey (Turkiye), Turkmenistan, Tuvalu, Uganda, Ukraine, UAE, UK, US, Uruguay, Uzbekistan, Vanuatu, Venezuela, Vietnam, Yemen, Zambia, Zimbabwe

Wetlands
see Convention on Wetlands of International Importance Especially As Waterfowl Habitat (Ramsar)

Whaling
see International Convention for the Regulation of Whaling

APPENDIX T: TERRORIST ORGANIZATIONS

This listing includes terrorist groups designated by the US State Department as Foreign Terrorist Organizations (FTOs), as well as an additional 10 non-designated, self-proclaimed branches and affiliates of the Islamic State of Iraq and ash-Sham (ISIS) FTO. The information provided includes details on each cited group's history, goals, leadership, organization, areas of operation, tactics, weapons, size, and sources of support.

Abdallah Azzam Brigades (AAB)

aka – AAB, Ziyad al-Jarrah Battalions of the Abdallah Azzam Brigades; Yusuf al-'Uyayri Battalions of the Abdallah Azzam Brigades; Marwan Hadid Brigades; Marwan Hadid Brigade; Abdullah Azzam Brigades in the Land of Al Sham
history – formed around 2005 as a Sunni jihadist group with ties to al-Qa'ida; named after the influential jihadist ideologue Abdallah Yusuf Azzam; formally announced its presence in a 2009 video statement while claiming responsibility for a rocket attack against Israel; involved in the Syrian War from 2013 until approximately 2018, typically fighting against Iranian-backed forces, particularly Hizballah; announced its dissolution in 2019 and has not claimed any subsequent attacks as of 2023
goals – rid the Middle East of Western influence, disrupt Israel's economy and its efforts to establish security, and erode Shia Muslim influence in Lebanon
leadership and organization – Sirajeddin ZURAYQAT (var: Surajuddin Zureiqat, Siraj al-Din Zreqat, Siraj al-Din Zuraiqat) was AAB's spiritual leader, spokesman, and commander; was divided into regionally based branches
areas of operation – primarily Lebanon; also active in Gaza and Syria
targets, tactics, and weapons – principal targets were Shia Muslims, the Shia terrorist group Hizballah, and Israel; was responsible for several car and suicide bombing attacks against Shia Muslims in Beirut, Lebanon, including twin suicide bombs that detonated outside the Iranian Embassy in Beirut, Lebanon—killing 22 and injuring at least 140; claimed responsibility for numerous rocket attacks against Israel and Lebanon; members were typically armed with small arms, light machine guns, grenades, rockets, and improvised explosive devices
strength – not available
financial and other support – primarily Lebanon; also active in Gaza and Syria
designation – placed on the US Department of State's list of Foreign Terrorist Organizations on 30 May 2012

Abu Sayyaf Group (ASG)

aka – al-Harakat al Islamiyya (the Islamic Movement); al-Harakat-ul al-Islamiyah; Bearer of the Sword; Father of the Executioner; Father of the Swordsman; International Harakatu'l Al-Islamia; Lucky 9; Islamic State in the Philippines; Mujahideen Commando Freedom Fighters
history – formed in 1991 when it split from the Moro Islamic Liberation Front; linked to al-Qa'ida in the 1990s and 2000s; in 2014, an ASG faction pledged allegiance to ISIS and in 2016 formed ISIS-East Asia's (ISIS-EA) branch in the Philippines; participated in the attack on Marawi City and the subsequent 5-month siege in 2017 alongside other ISIS-affiliated militants; ASG fighters affiliated with ISIS-EA were reportedly linked to suicide attacks in 2019 and 2020 in Jolo, Sulu province; continued to be active in 2025, but was assessed to be significantly weakened due to losses from counter-terrorism operations by Philippine security forces; in recent years, the group has focused on local violence and criminal activity, especially kidnap-for-ransom operations
goals – stated goal is to establish an independent Islamic state in the Muslim-majority provinces of the southern Philippines, although in practice, the group primarily uses terrorism for profit
leadership and organization – top leadership not available; loosely structured and family/clan/network-based; factions tend to coalesce around individual leaders
areas of operation – the southern Philippines, especially Basilan, Jolo, and Tawi-Tawi islands and their surrounding waters, as well as Mindanao; also has been active in Malaysia
targets, tactics, and weapons – targets military and security personnel, facilities, and checkpoints; also attacks civilian targets, such as churches, markets, and ferry boats; conducted the country's deadliest terrorist attack when it bombed a ferry boat in Manila Bay in 2004, killing 116 people; known for kidnapping civilians for ransom, particularly foreigners, and has killed hostages when ransoms were not paid; tactics include ambushes, assassinations, beheadings, car bombings, complex assaults involving dozens of fighters, and suicide bombings; has conducted acts of piracy in local waters; weapons include small arms, light and heavy machine guns, mortars, landmines, and improvised explosive devices
strength – assessed in 2023 to have less than 200 armed fighters
financial and other support – funded primarily through kidnapping-for-ransom operations and extortion; makes financial appeals on social media; may receive funding from external sources, including remittances from overseas Philippine workers and Middle East-based sympathizers; has received training and other assistance from other regional terrorist groups; has received weapons and ammunition from corrupt local government officials or through smuggling
designation – placed on the US Department of State's list of Foreign Terrorist Organizations on 8 October 1997

Al-Aqsa Martyrs Brigade (AAMB)

aka – al-Aqsa Martyrs Battalion; al-Aqsa Brigades; Martyr Yasser Arafat; Kata'ib Shuhada al-Aqsa; The Brigades; al-Aqsa Intifada Martyrs' Group; Martyrs of al-Aqsa Group
history – emerged at the outset of the second intifada in September 2000 as a loosely-organized armed wing of Yasser ARAFAT's Fatah faction in the West Bank; in 2002, some members splintered from Fatah while others remained loyal; the group carried out suicide attacks against Israeli targets between 2001-2007; following an agreement between Israel and the Palestinian Authority (PA) after the HAMAS takeover of Gaza in 2007, Israel pardoned some AAMB fighters in return for an agreement to disarm; after a trial period, those that disarmed were absorbed into PA security forces while those that refused were targeted by PA security forces; still others formed splinter groups such as the Al-Aqsa Martyrs Brigades-Nidal al-Amoudi Division and the Popular Resistance Committees in Gaza; some factions participated in operations against Israeli targets through the 2010s, including the "Stabbing Intifada" and periodic rocket attacks; publicly claimed that it participated in the October 2023 attack on Israel from Gaza and was active in 2024 against Israeli security and military forces in both Gaza and the West Bank
goals – drive Israeli military forces and settlers from Jerusalem, the West Bank, and the Gaza Strip and establish a Palestinian state
leadership and organization – not available; most of the group's original leaders have been captured or killed by Israel; typically has operated as a collection of loosely organized cells with their own leaders and independent operational agendas
areas of operation – Israel, Gaza, and the West Bank; has members in Palestinian refugee camps in Lebanon
targets, tactics, and weapons – targets Israeli military and security personnel and civilians; conducts military-style assaults, rocket attacks, bombings, ambushes, and suicide operations; claimed first female suicide bombing inside Israel in 2002 and a double bombing in Tel Aviv in 2003 that killed

more than 20 civilians; launched numerous rocket attacks against Israel in the 2010s; fighters typically armed with small arms, light and heavy machine guns, mortars, improvised explosive devices, rockets, and rocket propelled grenades
strength – estimated in 2023 to have a few hundred members
financial and other support – Iran has provided AAMB with funds and guidance, mostly through Hizballah facilitators; has cooperated with other terrorist groups throughout its existence, including HAMAS, the Popular Front for the Liberation of Palestine (PFLP), and Palestinian Islamic Jihad (PIJ)
designation –placed on the US Department of State's list of Foreign Terrorist Organizations on 27 March 2002

al-Ashtar Brigades (AAB)

aka – Saraya al-Ashtar; the military arm of the al-Wafa Islamic movement
history – is an Iranian-backed Shia militant group established in 2013 with the aim of overthrowing the ruling Sunni family in Bahrain; in 2018, formally adopted Iran's Islamic Revolutionary Guard Corps branding in its logo and flag and reaffirmed the group's loyalty to Tehran; active as of 2024
goals – seeks to overthrow Bahrain's monarchy; also seeks to expel US and other Western military forces from Bahrain
leadership and organization – Qassim Abdullah Ali AHMED (aka Qassim al Muamen); operates in cells
areas of operation – based in Bahrain; its leaders and some members are located in Iran
targets, tactics, and weapons – targets local security forces in Bahrain and has plotted to attack oil pipelines; promotes violence against the British, Saudi Arabian, and US governments; claimed a drone attack on Israel in 2024; methods include shootings and bombings; equipped with small arms, drones, explosives, including improvised explosive devices
strength – not available
funding and other support – receives funding, training, and weapons support from the Iranian Revolutionary Guard Corps; has also allied itself with Iranian-backed Iraqi Shia militants and with Lebanese Hizballah for financial and logistic support
designation – placed on the US Department of State's list of Foreign Terrorist Organizations on 11 July 2018

al-Mourabitoun

aka – Al-Murabitun; al-Mulathamun Battalion; al-Mulathamun Brigade; al-Muwaqqi'un bil-Dima; Those Signed in Blood Battalion (or Brigade); Signatories in Blood; Those who Sign in Blood; Witnesses in Blood; Signed-in-Blood Battalion; Masked Men Brigade; Khaled Abu al-Abbas Brigade; al-Mulathamun Masked Ones Brigade; al-Murabitoun; The "Sentinels" or "Guardians"
history – was part of al-Qa'ida in the Islamic Maghreb (AQIM) but split from AQIM in 2012 over leadership disputes; merged with the Mali-based Movement for Unity and Jihad in West Africa to form al-Murabitoun in August 2013; some members split from the group in mid-2015 and declared allegiance to the Islamic State, which acknowledged the pledge in October 2016, creating the Islamic State in the Greater Sahara; in late 2015, al-Mulathamun/al-Mourabitoun announced a re-merger with AQIM and in 2017, joined a coalition of al-Qa'ida-affiliated groups operating in the Sahel region known as Jama'at Nusrat al-Islam wal-Muslimin (JNIM); no incidents have been claimed or attributed to Al-Murabitoun since 2018 but Al-Murabitoun fighters likely continue to participate in attacks claimed by JNIM
goals – replace regional governments with an Islamic state; expel Western influence
leadership and organization – unclear; operates under the JNIM banner
areas of operation – Algeria, Burkina Faso, Libya, Mali, and Niger
targets, tactics, and weapons – primarily targets Western interests in the Sahel but also regional military forces, including Malian, French (until their withdrawal in 2022), and UN; known for high-profile attacks with small arms and explosives against civilian targets frequented or run by Westerners, including restaurants, hotels, mines, and energy facilities; in 2013, claimed responsibility for taking over 800 people hostage during a four-day siege at the Tiguentourine gas plant in southeastern Algeria, resulting in the deaths of 39 civilians; claimed responsibility for suicide car bombings at military bases in Niger and Mali, including one on a military camp in Gao, Mali in 2017 that killed at least 60 and wounded more than 100; armed with small arms, machine guns, landmines, mortars, and explosives, including ground and vehicle-borne improvised explosive devices
strength – not available; dated information suggests a few hundred
financial and other support – engages in kidnappings for ransom and smuggling activities; receives support through its connections to other terrorist organizations in the region; acquired weapons from Libya, battlefield captures, and seized stockpiles from local militaries
designation – placed on the US Department of State's list of Foreign Terrorist Organizations on 19 December 2013

al-Qa'ida (AQ)

aka – al-Qa'eda; al-Qaeda; Qa'idat al-Jihad (The Base for Jihad); formerly Qa'idat Ansar Allah (The Base of the Supporters of God); the Islamic Army; Islamic Salvation Foundation; The Base; The Group for the Preservation of the Holy Sites; The Islamic Army for the Liberation of the Holy Places; the World Islamic Front for Jihad Against Jews and Crusaders; the Usama Bin Ladin Network; the Usama Bin Ladin Organization; al-Jihad; the Jihad Group; Egyptian al-Jihad; Egyptian Islamic Jihad; New Jihad
history – formed under Usama BIN LADIN (UBL) circa 1988; helped finance, recruit, transport, and train fighters for the Afghan resistance against the former Soviet Union in the 1980s; in the 1990s, was based in Sudan and then Afghanistan, where it planned and staged attacks; merged with al-Jihad (Egyptian Islamic Jihad) in 2001; developed a reputation for carrying out large-scale, mass casualty attacks against civilians; after its 2001 attack on the US, it lost dozens of mid- and senior-level operatives to counterterrorism efforts, including UBL in May 2011, which disrupted operations although the group continued to recruit, plan, inspire, and conduct attacks as of 2025; has established affiliated organizations in the Middle East, Africa, and Asia, and its contemporary strength is primarily in these affiliates; tied to the Taliban in Afghanistan
goals – eject Western influence from the Islamic world, unite the worldwide Muslim community, overthrow governments perceived as un-Islamic, and ultimately, establish a pan-Islamic caliphate under a strict Salafi Muslim interpretation of sharia; direct, enable, and inspire individuals to conduct attacks, recruit, disseminate propaganda, and raise funds on behalf of the group around the world; destabilize local economies and governments by attacking security services, government targets, and civilian targets; maintain its traditional safe haven in Afghanistan; establish and maintain additional safehavens elsewhere
leadership and organization – has not formally acknowledged the 2022 death of its previous leader, Ayman al-ZAWAHIRI; Iran-based Sayf al-'Adl is reportedly the group's current de facto leader; has a leadership council ("majlis al-shura"); reportedly maintains branches for military, security, political, religious, financial, and media affairs; affiliates have separate emirs (leaders) and organizational structures that vary by region
areas of operation – based in South Asia with core members in Afghanistan, Iran, Pakistan; considers Afghanistan as an ideological and logistical hub to mobilize and recruit new fighters and rebuild its external operations capability; employs an affiliate or proxy model, which includes al-Qa'ida in the Arabian Peninsula (Yemen), al-Qa'ida in the Islamic Maghreb (North Africa and the Sahel), Hurras al-Din (Syria), al-Shabaab (Somalia), and al-Qa'ida in the Indian Subcontinent (Afghanistan, Bangladesh, India, and Pakistan); has supporters, sympathizers, and associates worldwide; maintains a strong online presence and individuals inspired by the group's ideology may conduct operations without direction from its central leadership; opportunistically enters (or secures the allegiance of participants in) local conflicts

targets, tactics, and weapons – considers its enemies to be Shia Muslims, US and Western interests, so-called "apostate" governments perceived to be supporting the US and the West, and the Islamic State of Iraq and ash-Sham (ISIS); leaders have encouraged followers to attack European, Israeli, NATO, Russian, and US targets, including military bases and forces; targets have included airplanes, embassies, hotels, military bases and forces, restaurants, ships, tourists sites, and trains; employs a combination of guerrilla warfare and terrorist tactics; known for use of suicide bombers, car bombs, explosive-laden boats, and airplanes; conducted the September 11, 2001 attacks on the US, which involved 19 operatives hijacking and crashing four US commercial jets—two into the World Trade Center in New York City, one into the Pentagon, and the last into a field in Shanksville, Pennsylvania—killing nearly 3,000 people
strength – as of 2024, it was estimated to have about 400 fighters in Afghanistan; the organization remained a focal point of inspiration for a worldwide network of affiliated groups and other sympathetic terrorist organizations
financial and other support –primarily depends on donations from like-minded supporters and from individuals, primarily in the Gulf States; uses social media platforms to solicit donations and has been channeled funds through cyberfinancing campaigns; has received some funds from kidnapping for ransom operations; historically has acquired money from funds diverted from Islamic charitable organizations; also recruits followers through social media
designation – placed on the US Department of State's list of Foreign Terrorist Organizations on 8 October 1999
note – has some ideological and tactical similarities with the Islamic State of Iraq and ash-Sham (ISIS) and the groups typically operate in the same conflict zones, but the relationship is mostly adversarial, and they compete for resources and recruits, and often clash militarily

al-Qa'ida in the Arabian Peninsula (AQAP)

aka – al-Qa'ida in the South Arabian Peninsula; al-Qa'ida in Yemen; al-Qa'ida of Jihad Organization in the Arabian Peninsula; al-Qa'ida Organization in the Arabian Peninsula; Tanzim Qa'idat al-Jihad fi Jazirat al-Arab; AQY; Ansar al-Shari'a; Sons of Abyan; Sons of Hadramawt; Sons of Hadramawt Committee; Civil Council of Hadramawt; National Hadramawt Council
history – formed in 2009 from a combination of al-Qa'ida members and locally focused jihadists; in subsequent years, claimed responsibility for numerous terrorist acts against both local and foreign targets, including an attempted attack on a US-bound commercial airliner in December 2009, a foiled plot to send explosive-laden packages to the US on cargo planes, and an attack on the Paris headquarters of a newspaper in 2015; the group took advantage of Yemen's civil war in 2014-15 to expand operations in the country, controlling a large portion of the southern part of the Yemen by 2016; after 2017, the group began losing territory, fighters, and leaders to internal dissensions, desertions, and casualties from clashes with Yemeni and international security forces, the Houthis, and the Islamic State of Iraq and ash-Sham (ISIS); nevertheless, as of 2025 the group continued to persist as a local and regional threat
goals – establish a caliphate guided by its interpretation of Islamic law; advocates the overthrow of the Saudi Arabian and Yemeni Governments, and follows al-Qa'ida's longstanding goal of attacking the US
leadership and organization – led by Saad bin Atef al-Awlaki (aka Abu al-Laith); has a leadership council ("majlis al-shura") comprised of lieutenant commanders who are responsible for overall political direction and military operations; organized in branches or wings for military operations, political, propaganda (recruitment), religious issues (for justifying attacks from a theological perspective while offering spiritual guidance), and security; typically operates in a decentralized manner that allows individual cells to operate independently
areas of operation – operates primarily in southern and central Yemen; probably has a limited presence in Saudi Arabia
targets, tactics, and weapons – attacks a wide variety of targets, including the Yemeni Government, forces affiliated with the United Arab Emirates and Saudi Arabia, the Houthis; Shia Muslims, and Western interests; specific targets have included business people, commercial airliners and cargo planes, embassies, diplomats, merchant ships, and oil facilities; regularly calls for attacks against Western interests and regional partners in the group's media releases; has waged open warfare with ISIS elements in Yemen since 2018; employs guerrilla-style and terrorist tactics, including ambushes, assassinations, bombings, complex assaults, snipers, and suicide attacks; equipped with small arms, machine guns, artillery, rockets, landmines, anti-tank missiles, armored combat vehicles, man-portable air defense systems (MANPADs), armed unmanned aerial vehicles (drones), and improvised explosive devices, including car bombs, road side bombs, and suicide vests
strength – estimated in 2025 to have 2-3,000 fighters
financial and other support – receives funding from theft, robberies, oil and gas revenue, kidnapping-for-ransom operations, and donations from like-minded supporters; has received report from the al-Shabaab terrorist group in Somalia; for nearly a year after seizing the city of Mukallah in April 2015, had access millions of dollars from port fees and funds stolen from the central bank; has seized weapons and equipment from the Yemeni military; recruits through social media, print, and digital means
designation – placed on the US Department of State's list of Foreign Terrorist Organizations on 19 January 2010

al-Qa'ida in the Indian Subcontinent (AQIS)

aka – al-Qaeda in the Indian Subcontinent; Qaedat al-Jihad in the Indian Subcontinent, Qaedat al-Jihad, Jamaat Qaidat al-Jihad fi'shibhi al-Qarrat al-Hindiya,
history – al-Qa'ida leader Ayman al-ZAWAHIRI announced AQIS's inception in a video address in September 2014; the group claimed responsibility for a September 2014 attack on a naval dockyard in Karachi in an attempt to seize a Pakistani warship; since the assault, the group has conducted a limited number of small attacks on civilians and some members fought in Afghanistan with the Taliban; AQIS suffered some losses to Indian counter-terrorism operations in 2020-2022; in 2021, the group released two propaganda videos specifically targeting India and Kashmir, and in 2022 threatened to conduct suicide bombings in several Indian cities; AWIS has ties to designated terrorist groups Lashkare Tayyiba (LeT) and Tehrik-e-Taliban Pakistan (TTP); active in 2025
goals – establish an Islamic caliphate in the Indian subcontinent; support the broader goals of al-Qai'da's central leadership
leadership and organization – Usama MAHMOOD (alt. Osama MEHMOOD; aka Abu Zar); has a shura council, which, like other AQ affiliates, probably includes subordinates and branches/wings for military/security, intelligence, religious, propaganda, political matters, and recruitment; reportedly has regional branches for Bangladesh, India, and Pakistan; Ansar al-Islam in Bangladesh has claimed to be the official wing of AQIS in Bangladesh
areas of operation – Afghanistan, Bangladesh, India, and Pakistan
targets, tactics, and weapons – military and security personnel, political parties, foreigners, foreign aid workers, academics, students, and secular bloggers; in 2023, AQIS published a booklet urging attacks against US diplomats and military personnel located overseas; has engaged in suicide bombings, small-arms attacks, ambushes, and assassinations; has used small arms and improvised explosive devices, as well as crude weapons such as machetes; claimed responsibility for the 2016 machete murders of two editors of a human rights magazine in Dhaka, Bangladesh
membership – estimated in 2024 to have up to 400 members
financial and other support – likely receives financial and material support from AQ senior leadership; also engages in kidnapping-for-ransom, extortion, and general criminal activity to raise funds
designation – placed on the US Department of State's list of Foreign Terrorist Organizations on 1 July 2016

al-Qa'ida in the Islamic Maghreb (AQIM)

aka – GSPC; Le Groupe Salafiste Pour la Predication et le Combat; Salafist Group for Preaching and Combat; Salafist Group for Call and Combat; Tanzim al-Qa'ida fi Bilad al-Maghrib al-Islamiya

history – formed in 1998 in Algeria under Hassan HATTAB, when he split from the Armed Islamic Group (GIA); was known as the Salafist Group for Preaching and Combat (GSPC) until rebranding itself as AQIM in September 2006; has since undergone various schisms and rapprochements; in 2011, a Mauritanian-led group broke away, calling itself the Movement for Unity and Jihad in West Africa (MUJWA); in 2012, the Veiled Men Battalion split off and rebranded itself the al-Mulathamun Battalion; al-Mulathamun and MUJWA merged to form al-Mourabitoun in 2013; in late 2015, AQIM reincorporated al-Murabitoun and in 2017, the Mali Branch of AQIM and al-Murabitoun joined the Mali-based al-Qa'ida coalition Jama'at Nasr al-Islam wal-Muslimin (JNIM); continued to be active through 2024 despite pressure from regional and international counterterrorism operations, particularly in using North Africa as a support zone for assisting JNIM operations in Mali and the Sahel, including operating transnational financial networks to move and share funds

goals – overthrow "apostate" African regimes and establish an Islamic state across all of North and West Africa; support the broader goals of al-Qai'da's central leadership

leadership and organization – Abu Obaida al-ANNABI (aka Abu Ubaydah Yusuf al-Anabi, Yazid Mubarak); has a shura council comprised of regional commanders and the heads of the political, military, judicial, and media committees; locally organized into "battalions" and "brigades," which may range in size from a few dozen to several hundred fighters at any given time

areas of operation – has historically operated in the coastal areas of northern Algeria and in Libya and Tunisia, but counterterrorism efforts have forced it largely into the Sahel region, including Mali; has claimed attacks in Algeria, Burkina Faso, Cote d'Ivoire, and Mali

targets, tactics, and weapons – targets local and international military and security forces using both terrorist and guerrilla warfare tactics; employs improvised explosive devices, suicide bombers, as well as light weapons, machine guns, mortars, rockets, and landmines; also attacks "soft" civilian targets such as hotels, resorts, and restaurants that cater to Westerners and tourists with small arms, explosives, and suicide bombers; known for assassinations and kidnappings

strength – estimated in 2023 to have up to 1,000 fighters

financial and other support – engages in kidnappings-for-ransom and other criminal activities, particularly extorting drug trafficking groups and others; arms largely acquired from Libyan stockpiles, battlefield captures, or via illicit regional arms markets

designation – GSPC was designated as a Foreign Terrorist Organization on 27 March 2002; the Department of State amended the GSPC designation on 20 February 2008, after the GSPC officially joined with al-Qa'ida in September 2006 and became AQIM

al-Shabaab (AS)

aka – the Harakat Shabaab al-Mujahidin (HSM); al-Shabab; Shabaab; the Youth; Mujahidin al-Shabaab Movement; Mujahideen Youth Movement; Mujahidin Youth Movement; al-Hijra, Al Hijra, Muslim Youth Center, MYC, Pumwani Muslim Youth, Pumwani Islamist Muslim Youth Center

history – descended from Al-Ittihad Al-Islami, a Somali terrorist group whose leaders fought in Afghanistan in the 1990s and formed circa 2003; has operated as a core al-Qa'ida affiliate since 2012; was the militant wing of the former Somali Islamic Courts Council that took over parts of Somalia in 2006; after 2006, engaged in an insurgency against the Government of Somalia and supporting foreign military forces and a campaign of violence against Somali civilians; responsible for numerous high-profile bombings and other attacks throughout Somalia resulting in thousands of civilian deaths; occupies or influences large areas of rural Somalia through coercion, control over local economies and commercial transit points; provides rudimentary government services in areas under its control, including rule of law through sharia courts, sharia-based institutions and schools, funding, services, security, and food; continued to conduct attacks in Somalia and engage in fighting with security forces into 2025

goals – discredit, destabilize, and overthrow the Federal Government of Somalia; establish Islamic rule in Somalia and the border regions of Somalia-Kenya and southern Ethiopia; drive out Western influence

leadership and organization – led by Ahmad DIRIYE (aka Abu UBEYDAH/UBAIDAH, Abu Ubaidah DIREYE, Ahmad UMAR) since September 2014; DIRIYE reportedly directs both an executive council and a shura (or consultative) council; the executive council runs the group's operations and is made up of committees, ministries, departments, or wings, including for finance, intelligence and security (Amniyat), media/propaganda, politics, education, judicial matters, religion, logistics, explosives (Sanaaca), and military operations (Jabhat), as well as regional commanders or shadow governors in areas that al-Shabaab controls; each regional division has sub-offices or wings, including for security and taxation; has shown the ability to mobilize and coordinate significant numbers of fighters for large-scale ground attacks; in 2024, had reportedly formed a pan-East African force of foreign fighters known as Muhajirin

areas of operation – primarily Somalia; has also conducted operations in Ethiopia, Kenya, and Uganda

targets, tactics, and weapons – targets Somali Government officials, military units, police, and civilians, international aid workers, journalists, foreign troops (including US, African Union), and neighboring countries contributing to military stabilization operations in Somalia, particularly Ethiopia, Kenya, and Uganda; attacks hotels, schools, military bases, police stations, shopping areas, and infrastructure, such as telecommunications towers; also targets the Islamic State faction operating in northern Somalia; combines insurgent/guerrilla and terrorist tactics, including assassinations, drive-by shootings, ambushes, suicide bombings, hostage taking, armed drone attacks, indiscriminate attacks on civilians, roadside improvised explosive devices (IEDs), mortar and rocket-propelled grenade (RPG) attacks, and complex ground assaults involving multiple suicide bombers, followed by an assault by members carrying small arms and explosives; in 2022 and 2023, for example, it conducted two ground assaults involving vehicle-mounted bombs and hundreds of militants on international military peacekeeper bases that killed more than 50 troops in each incident; has placed vehicle-mounted bombs in high-density urban areas, including attacks in Mogadishu in 2022, 2019, and 2017 that together killed over 700 civilians; typically armed with small arms, light and heavy machine guns, landmines, mortars, RPGs, IEDs, man-portable air defense systems, and unmanned aerial vehicles/drones

strength – estimated in 2025 to have 10,000-18,000 fighters

financial and other support – obtains funds primarily through extortion of businesses, taxation, and zakat (religious donations) collections from the local populations, robbery, illegal charcoal production and exports, and remittances and other money transfers from the Somali diaspora (although these funds are not always intended to support al-Shabaab members); estimated that the group generates \$100-\$150 million annually; probably receives training, arms, and bomb-making materials from other al-Qa'ida branches; has captured arms, ammunition, and other materiel from regional and Somali military forces; also purchases arms and ammunition through black markets; operates military training camps in areas it occupies

designation – placed on the US Department of State's list of Foreign Terrorist Organizations on 18 March 2008

Ansar al-Dine (AAD)

aka – Ansar Dine; Ansar al-Din; Ancar Dine; Ansar ul-Din; Ansar Eddine; Defenders of the Faith
history – formed in November 2011 as a Tuareg rebel group under Iyad Ag Ghali and in mid-2012 began an association with al-Qai'da in the Islamic Maghrib (AQIM), in part because of their shared desire to implement Islamic law in Mali; was among the terrorist groups to take over northern Mali following the March 2012 coup that toppled the Malian Government; proceeded to destroy UNESCO World Heritage sites and enforce a severe interpretation of Islam upon the civilian population living in the areas under their control; beginning in 2013, French and African military forces forced AAD and its allies out of the population centers they had seized, severely weakening AAD, although the group made a comeback in 2015-2016; in 2017, joined Jama'ah Nusrah al-Islam wal-Muslimin (Group for the Support of Islam and Muslims, JNIM), a coalition of al-Qa'ida-linked groups in Mali that formed the same year; active in 2024
goals – replace the Malian government with an Islamic state
leadership and organization – led by its founder Iyad Ag GHALI (aka Abu al-FADEL), who also leads JNIM; reportedly has regionally based branches; operates under the JNIM banner
areas of operation – Mali
targets, tactics, and weapons – targets Malian military and security forces, as well as supporting Russian security personnel; also targeted French and UN military troops prior to their departure in 2022 and 2023, respectively; uses a mix of insurgent/guerrilla warfare hit-and-run and terrorist tactics, including ambushes, complex ground assaults involving dozens of fighters, road side bombs, rocket attacks, assassinations, kidnappings, and car and suicide bombings; fighters are armed with small arms, light and heavy machine guns, rocket-propelled grenades, landmines, mortars, rockets, trucks mounting machine guns (aka "technicals"), and explosives, including improvised explosive devices
strength – not available
financial and other support – cooperates with and has received support from al-Qa'ida since its inception; also reportedly receives funds from foreign donors and through smuggling; has utilized arms and equipment captured from the Malian Army or received from former Libyan military stockpiles; has taken advantage of trans-Saharan smuggling routes to resupply from illicit markets in Libya and elsewhere in the region
designation – placed on the US Department of State's list of Foreign Terrorist Organizations on 22 March 2013

Ansar al-Islam (AAI)

aka – Ansar al-Sunna; Ansar al-Sunna Army; Devotees of Islam; Followers of Islam in Kurdistan; Helpers of Islam; Jaish Ansar al-Sunna; Jund al-Islam; Kurdish Taliban; Kurdistan Supporters of Islam; Partisans of Islam; Soldiers of God; Soldiers of Islam; Supporters of Islam in Kurdistan
history – founded in December 2001 with support from al-Qa'ida; originated in the Iraqi Kurdistan region with the merger of two Kurdish terrorist factions, Jund al-Islam and a splinter group of the Islamic Movement of Kurdistan; from 2003 to 2011, conducted attacks against a wide range of targets in Iraq, including government and security forces, as well as US and Coalition troops; in the summer of 2014, a faction of AAI pledged allegiance to ISIS and the two factions reportedly have fought each other; after 2014, most activity has been in Syria where AAI has fought against Syrian regime forces, although it claimed a bombing attack against members of a Shia militia in Iraq in late 2019; active in 2024
goals – expel Western interests from Iraq and, ultimately, establish an Iraqi state operating according to its interpretation of sharia; similar goals in Syria
leadership and organization – led by Amir Shaykh Abu Hashim Muhammad bin Abdul Rahman al-IBRAHIM; likely has a cell-based structure
areas of operation – Iraq and Syria
targets, tactics, and weapons – historically targeted Iraqi security and police forces, citizens, politicians, and Shia militia forces for assassinations, bombings, and executions; targets Syrian government forces and pro-Syrian regime militias with guerrilla-style hit-and-run assaults and terrorist attacks; equipped with small arms, light and heavy machine guns, rocket-propelled grenades, mortars, and explosives, including improvised explosive devices
strength – estimated in 2023 to have less than 300 fighters
financial and other support – receives assistance from a loose network of associates in Europe and the Middle East
designation – placed on the US Department of State's list of Foreign Terrorist Organizations on 22 March 2004

Ansar al-Shari'a groups in Libya (ASL)

aka – Ansar al-Shari'a in Benghazi (AAS-B); Ansar al-Sharia in Darnah (AAS-D); Ansar al-Shariah Brigade; Ansar al-Shari'a Brigade; Katibat Ansar al-Sharia in Benghazi; Ansar al-Shariah-Benghazi; Al-Raya Establishment for Media Production; Ansar al-Sharia; Soldiers of the Sharia; Ansar al-Shariah; Supporters of Islamic Law; Partisans of Islamic Law; Supporters of Islamic Law in Darnah, Ansar al-Sharia Brigade in Darnah; Ansar al-Sharia in Derna
history – consists of Ansar al-Shari'a in Benghazi (AAS-B) and Ansar al-Sharia in Darnah (AAS-D); AAS-B and AAS-D were formed in 2011 following the fall of the QADHAFI regime as Sunni Muslim Salafist armed groups with links to al-Qa'ida; at their peak in 2013, held territory and operated branches in Benghazi, Darnah, Sirte, Ajdabiya, and Nawfalia; promoted charitable work to gain popular support from local communities; in 2014, began fighting against the Libyan National Army (LNA) under General HIFTER and the Islamic State in Libya (ISIS-Libya) and by 2015 had lost most of their territory and suffered heavy losses; in May 2017, AAS-B announced its dissolution due to battle losses, as well as defections to ISIS-Libya; AAS-D's status as of 2023 was unclear
goals – a strict implementation of sharia in Libya
leadership and organization – not available
areas of operation – operated mostly in eastern Libya, particularly Benghazi and Darnah
targets, tactics, and weapons – targeted Libyan political and security officials and Westerners for kidnappings, executions, bombings, and assassinations; AAS-B participated in the 2012 attacks on US diplomatic facilities in Benghazi, for example; also conducted guerrilla warfare hit-and-run and terrorist attacks against Libyan security forces, LNA militias, and other terrorist groups using small arms and light weapons, rockets, mortars, anti-tank guided missiles, anti-aircraft artillery and missiles, improvised explosive devices and suicide bombings
strength – not available
financial and other support – obtained funds from al-Qa'ida in the Islamic Maghreb, witting and unwitting Islamic charities, donations from sympathizers, and criminal activities; raided Libyan military bases for weapons and ammunition
designation – AAS-B and AAS-D were placed on the US Department of State's list of Foreign Terrorist Organizations on 13 January 2014

Ansar al-Shari'a in Tunisia (AAS-T)

aka – Al-Qayrawan Media Foundation; Supporters of Islamic Law; Ansar al-Sharia in Tunisia; Ansar al-Shari'ah; Ansar al-Shari'ah in Tunisia; Ansar al-Sharia

history – formed in April 2011 as a Sunni Salafi-jihadist militant organization linked to al-Qa'ida; combined community service, proselytization, and violence to promote its ideology and goals; in 2014, multiple AAS-T leaders swore loyalty to the Islamic State and many left the group to fight in Syria; has not claimed any attacks in recent years, and its status is unclear
goals – expand its influence in Tunisia and, ultimately, replace the Tunisian Government with one operating according to Islamic law
leadership and organization – not available
areas of operation – headquartered in Tunisia; has also operated in Libya
targets, tactics, and weapons – attacked Tunisian military and security personnel; also targeted Tunisian politicians, religious sites, and groups and places representing Western influence, such as tourists and tourist sites; tactics included assassinations and bombings; also organized riots and violent demonstrations against the Tunisian government; members were typically armed with small arms, rocket-propelled grenades, and other light weapons, as well as explosives
strength – not available
financial and other support – not available
designation – placed on the US Department of State's list of Foreign Terrorist Organizations on 13 January 2014

Ansarallah

aka: Huthis; Houthis; Ansar Allah; Ansarullah; Partisans of God; Supporters of God; Huthi/Houthi group; Huthi/Houthi Movement
history – Ansarallah, commonly referred to as the Huthis (or Houthis), is a militant group comprised mostly of the Zaydi Shia Muslim minority, and it controls parts of northern and western Yemen; founded in 1992, the Huthis initially focused on religious and cultural revivalism but later shifted to political activism and nationalism; they subsequently launched an armed rebellion and fought intermittently with the government from 2004 to 2010, and then again from 2014 to the present; they also fought against a Saudi-led coalition that has backed the Yemeni Government and have controlled the capital Sanaa since late 2014; they oppose Israel and the US and align with the Iranian-led "axis of resistance," which includes the terrorist groups HAMAS and Hizballah; during the 2023-2025 Israel-HAMAS war, the Huthis provided military support to HAMAS, which included attacks on Israeli and Western targets; the group is known for its repressive conduct in areas under its control
goals – defend territories the group occupies; maintain economic, political, and social control over the population in occupied territories; topple the internationally-recognized Yemeni Government
leadership and organization – as of May 2025, Abdel-Malik AL-HOUTHI is the political leader; the group is organized into ministries; Muhammad Abdel Karim AL GHAMARI is chief of the armed forces, which include aerospace (air, missile), land, naval/coastal defense, presidential protection, special operations, internal security, and militia/tribal auxiliary forces
areas of operation – Yemen
targets, tactics, and weapons – has targeted Israel, US naval vessels, UAE-backed Yemeni security forces, the Yemeni Government, and prior to 2023, Saudi Arabia and the UAE; during the Israel-HAMAS War (2023-2025), the Huthis attacked commercial and military vessels in the Red Sea and other waterways, as well as Israel itself, with missiles and armed unmanned systems; has also conducted operations against elements of al-Qa'ida and the Islamic State terrorist groups present in Yemen; armed as a conventional military force with armored vehicles, anti-aircraft and anti-armor weapons, artillery, drones, ballistic missiles, cruise missiles (anti-ship and ground attack), land and naval mines, and other light and heavy weapons
strength – not available
financial and other support – receives material support from Iran and Russia; Iran's Islamic Revolutionary Guard Corps-Qods Force and Hizballah have provided arms, training, and financial assistance; also armed with weapons captured or seized from the Yemeni Government
designation – placed on the US Department of State's list of Foreign Terrorist Organizations on 25 February 2025

Army of Islam (AOI)

aka – Jaysh al-Islam; Jaish al-Islam; JAI
history – formed around 2005 as a Salafi Sunni Muslim splinter from HAMAS; subscribes to Salafist ideology of global jihad blended with the traditional model of armed Palestinian resistance; traditionally focused on attacking Israel and Egypt; in September 2015, ISIS claimed that the Army of Islam had pledged allegiance to ISIS and declared itself as part of the Islamic State's Sinai Province; it has not claimed responsibility for any attacks in recent years, but was considered active as of 2023
goals – establish a regional Islamic emirate
leadership and organization – led by Mumtaz DUGHMUSH; organization not available
areas of operation – Egypt, Gaza, Israel
targets, tactics, and weapons – has targeted the Egyptian and Israeli governments and their citizens, as well as American, British, and New Zealand citizens; has a history of conducting rocket attacks against Israel, kidnapping civilians, and attacking Christians; conducted a bombing attack on a Coptic Christian church in Egypt in 2011 that killed 25 and wounded 100; equipped with small arms, bombs, light and heavy machine guns, mortars, rockets, and improvised explosives devices
strength – not available
financial and other support – receives much of its funding from a variety of criminal activities in Gaza
designation – placed on the US Department of State's list of Foreign Terrorist Organizations on 19 May 2011

Asa'ib Ahl al-Haqq (AAH)

aka – Ahl al-Kahf; Band of the Righteous; Bands of Right; Islamic Shia Resistance in Iraq; Khazali Faction/Network; Khazali Special Groups Network; League of Righteousness
history – is an Iraqi Shia militia and political group that split off from Jaysh al-Mahdi in 2006; it fought against US military forces in Iraq from 2006 until the US withdrawal in 2011; following the rise of the Islamic State of Iraq and ash-Sham (ISIS) in 2013, the group fought alongside the Iraqi military as part of the Popular Mobilization Committee and Affiliated Forces (PMC or PMF) militia forces (aka Popular Mobilization Units or PMU) until ISIS's territorial defeat in 2017; fought in support of the ASAD regime in Syria from 2011 until at least 2017; in 2017, AAH's affiliated political party (Al Sadiqun Bloc) was approved by the Iraqi electoral commission to run in the national election; in 2018, Al Sadiqun joined the Al Fatah Alliance (Victory), a political coalition primarily comprised of parties affiliated with Iranian-backed Shia militias; in late 2019, it participated in an assault on the US Embassy compound in Baghdad; active as of 2024, including indirect fire attacks on US facilities in Iraq, typically using front names or proxy groups
goals – maintain a Shia-controlled government in Iraq, promote Iran's political and religious influence in Iraq, and expel the remaining US military presence
leadership and organization – led by Qays al-KHAZALI; maintains a paramilitary force inside the PMC/PMF that is divided into three brigades (the 41st, 42nd, and 43rd PMC brigades) representing geographic sectors of Iraq; reportedly models itself after Lebanese Hizballah

note – following the onset of the Hamas-Israel war in the Gaza Strip in October 2023, an umbrella group called the Islamic Resistance in Iraq (IRI or al-Haya al-Tansiqiya lil-Muqawama al-Iraqiya) announced its formation by claiming responsibility for an October 2023 failed drone strike on an US military base in northern Iraq; the IRI is a coalition of all Iran-backed Shiite militias operating in Iraq, including designated terrorist groups AAH and Kataib Hezbollah (KH), operating in solidarity with HAMAS in its war with Israel; since its establishment, the IRI has claimed responsibility for dozens of attacks on US elements in Iraq and Syria; it has also claimed responsibility for more than 100 attacks on Israel
area(s) of operation – based in Iraq; sent fighters to Syria during that country's civil war
targets, tactics, and weapons – targets foreign military forces, US interests, ISIS, and Sunni Muslims; from 2006 to 2011, claimed to have conducted more than 6,000 attacks against US and Coalition forces; carries out abductions, executions, and targeted killings of Sunni Muslims; has killed civilian protesters and used mass gatherings to protest domestic and international political decisions; fought as a paramilitary/irregular force in Syria and alongside the Iraqi military; armed with a variety of weapons, including small arms, machine guns, rocket-propelled grenades, mortars, rockets, artillery, armed unmanned aerial vehicles/drones, improvised explosive devices, and armored vehicles
strength – estimated in 2023 to have 10-15,000 members
financial and other support – receives funding, logistical support, training, and weapons from the Iranian Revolutionary Guard Force-Qods Force and Lebanese Hizballah; solicits donations online and through a pro-Iran television channel; also raises funds through legitimate business enterprises, as well as criminal activities, including kidnappings-for-ransom, smuggling, and taxing/extortion of economic activities in areas where the group is dominant; AAH's official status provides some members government salaries and access to state resources
designation – placed on the US Department of State's list of Foreign Terrorist Organizations on 10 January 2020

Asbat al-Ansar (AAA)

aka – Band of Helpers; Band of Partisans; League of Partisans; League of the Followers; God's Partisans; Gathering of Supporters; Partisan's League; Esbat al-Ansar; Isbat al-Ansar; Osbat al-Ansar; Usbat al-Ansar; Usbat ul-Ansar
history – emerged in the early 1990s in Lebanon under the late Shaykh Hisham SHRAID, a Palestinian refugee and preacher; until the 2000s, was known for assassinating Lebanese religious leaders and government officials, as well as bombing venues it deemed un-Islamic and representing Western influence, such as nightclubs, theaters, and liquor stores; from 2005 to 2011, some members fought against US and Coalition forces in Iraq; has links to al-Qa'ida and other Sunni terrorist groups; has not claimed responsibility for any attacks in recent years
goals – aims to thwart perceived anti-Islamic and pro-western influences in Lebanon
leadership and organization – not available
areas of operation – primary base of operations is the Ayn al-Hilwah Palestinian refugee camp near Sidon in southern Lebanon
targets, tactics, and weapons – until the mid-2000s, operatives conducted small-scale bombing and shooting attacks in Lebanon against Christian, secular, and Shia Muslim figures and institutions, elements of foreign influence inside the country, and Lebanese government officials, such as judges; has also plotted against foreign diplomatic targets; weapons include small arms, rocket-propelled grenades, and improvised explosive devices
strength – estimated in 2023 to have a few hundred members
financial resources – likely receives donations from sympathizers and through international Sunni extremist networks
designation – placed on the US Department of State's list of Foreign Terrorist Organizations on 27 March 2002

Balochistan Liberation Army (BLA)

aka – Baloch Liberation Army; Majeed Brigade
history – the Balochistan Liberation Army (BLA) is an ethno-nationalist militant organization seeking the independence of Pakistan's Balochistan province; while its origins go back to the 1960s, the modern BLA formed in the early 2000s amid growing discontent among the Baloch people over historical grievances, particularly perceptions of ethnic, economic, and political marginalization by the Pakistani Government; it consisted mostly of experienced fighters drawn from pre-existing Baloch militant groups and initially operated as a loosely-organized movement conducting a low-level insurgency before gradually becoming more structured
goals – establish an independent Baloch state encompassing majority-Baloch areas of Pakistan, as well as Afghanistan and Iran
leadership and organization – BLA is broken into two factions; the dominant Jeeyand faction (BLA-J) is led by Bashir Zeb BALOCH, while the Azad faction (BLA-A) is under Hyrbyair MARRI; BLA-J has special operational units such as the Majeed Brigade and the Fatah Squad, as well as intelligence and information wings; BLA works closely with other Baloch militant groups and is part of an umbrella group called Baluch Raaji Aaajohi e Sangar, or the Baloch National Freedom Front; other members include the Balochistan Republican Guard and the Balochistan Liberation Front
areas of operation – operates primarily in Balochistan and has conducted occasional attacks in Karachi, Sindh Province; allegedly has a training presence in southern Afghanistan and eastern Iran
targets, tactics, and weapons – targets Pakistani security forces, infrastructure, and civilians, including Chinese nationals and projects associated with the China-Pakistan Economic Corridor; specific targets since 2018 have included buses, government buildings, military checkpoints and convoys, railway stations, and trains, as well as the Pakistan Stock Exchange in Karachi and the Chinese consulate in Karachi; one of its deadliest operations was a series of coordinated attacks in 2024 that focused on key infrastructure, security checkpoints, and Chinese interests in Balochistan and killed dozens of people; tactics have included assassinations, bombings, complex and guerrilla-style attacks, hijackings, kidnappings, shootings, and suicide bombings; it is typically armed with small arms, light machine guns, grenades, improvised explosive devices, and other types of bombs
strength – not available
financial and other support – funding sources are diverse and reportedly include contributions from the Baloch diaspora and criminal activities such as extortion, kidnappings for ransom, and narcotics trafficking
designation – placed on the US Department of State's list of Foreign Terrorist Organizations on 11 August 2025

Barrio 18

designated as a Foreign Terrorist Organization on 23 September 2025; additional information to follow

Boko Haram (BH)

aka – Nigerian Taliban; Jama'atu Ahlus-Sunnah Lidda'Awati Wal Jihad; Jama'atu Ahlis Sunna Lidda'awati wal-Jihad; Jama'atu Ahlus-Sunnah (JAS); People Committed to the Prophet's Teachings for Propagation and Jihad; Sunni Group for Preaching and Jihad
history – formed in 2002 under the late Muslim cleric Mohammed YUSUF; in 2009, launched an insurgency and campaign of terror against the Nigerian Government, its security forces, and civilians and captured territory roughly the size of Belgium in northeastern Nigeria by 2015; in the subsequent years, the Nigerian military dislodged the group from almost all of the territory it previously controlled, although it continued to operate in Nigeria, as well as in Cameroon, Chad, and Niger; in 2015, the group declared allegiance to the Islamic State in Iraq and al-Sham (ISIS) and began calling itself ISIS in West Africa (ISIS-WA); following an ISIS decision regarding a change in leadership in 2016, the group split into two factions with one group continuing its activities under the original Boko Haram leader, Abubakar bin Muhammad SHEKAU, and the other

operating as ISIS-WA; the two groups subsequent engaged in significant fighting against each other; in recent years, Boko Haram has lost territory and suffered heavy casualties, including battlefield losses, defections to ISIS-WA, desertions, and surrenders to government forces; however, it continued conducting attacks and maintained a safehaven in northeast Nigeria as of 2025; since 2009, violence associated with Boko Haram and ISIS-WA has killed an estimated 40,000 people, mostly civilians, and displaced over 2 million
goals – establish an Islamic state in Nigeria based on Islamic law
leadership and organization – not available; some accounts have the group divided into two factions, each operating in separate areas with different leaders; previously, the group had a shura council and regionally based cells/commands, which operated with some autonomy; under the shura were departments for logistics, propaganda, training and education, finance, weapons procurement, recruitment, and legal/religious issues
areas of operation – primarily Nigeria, but also Cameroon, Chad, and Niger
targets, tactics, and weapons – targets tourists and other foreigners (particularly businessmen), wealthy civilians, and government leaders to kidnap for ransom or kill; conducts shootings and suicide bombing attacks against government buildings, military installations, police stations, schools, markets, places of worship and entertainment, and sometimes entire villages; has kidnapped thousands of civilians, including children, many of whom are either forced or indoctrinated into fighting with the group or conducting suicide bombings; some female captives are subjected to forced labor and sexual servitude; conducts an insurgency combining guerrilla warfare and terrorist tactics against military and security forces; uses small arms, light and heavy machine guns, landmines, mortars, rockets, armored vehicles, trucks mounted with machine guns (aka "technicals"), improvised explosive devices, car bombs, and suicide bombings;
strength – unclear; estimated in 2023 to have up to 2,000 members
financial and other support – largely self-financed through criminal activities such as looting, extortion, kidnapping-for-ransom, bank robberies, cattle rustling, and assassinations for hire; has seized vehicles, weapons, ammunition, and other supplies from the Nigerian and Nigerien militaries and has acquired other arms from the regional black market
designation – placed on the US Department of State's list of Foreign Terrorist Organizations on 14 November 2013

Communist Party of the Philippines/New People's Army (CPP/NPA)

aka – Communist Party of the Philippines; CPP; New People's Army; NPA; Bagong Hukbong Bayan or BHB; Communist Party of the Philippines-New People's Army-National Democratic Front or CPP-NPA-NDF
history – CPP formed in 1968, while the NPA, its armed/military wing, formed in 1969; since 1971, the NPA has waged a Maoist-based insurgency and terrorist campaign against the Philippine Government that has resulted in about 40,000 civilian and combatant deaths; from 2016 to 2019, several attempts were made to establish a cease-fire and peace deal between the CPP/NPA and the Philippine Government without success; talks typically broke down when each side accused the other of initiating attacks or violating cease-fires; in subsequent years, the CPP/NPA continued to carry out killings, raids, kidnappings, acts of extortion, and other forms of violence primarily directed against Philippine security forces; 2023 saw an estimated 250 fatalities amongst civilians, CPP/NPA fighters, and government security personnel; in November 2023, the CPP/NPA and the Philippine Government agreed to restart talks, but as of 2024 Philippine security forces continued to conduct operations against the group
goals – destabilize the Philippines' economy to inspire the populace to revolt; ultimately wants to overthrow the government and install a Maoist-based regime; opposes the US military and commercial presence in the Philippines
leadership and organization – unclear following the death of its long-time leader Jose Maria SISON in December 2022; highest leadership body is its 26-member Central Committee, which reported to SISON; organized in "fronts" or regions but operates in cells and platoons at the local level; overt political wing is known as the National Democratic Front
areas of operation – the Philippines; in 2023, the CPP claimed its armed wing was present in about 70 of the country's 82 provinces; however, its operations and clashes with government forces were occurring in only a few rural areas, including northern Mindanao, southern Luzon, and parts of the Visayas; some of the group's leaders, including its negotiating panel, live in exile in the Netherlands
targets, tactics, and weapons – targets military and security forces, government officials and facilities, local infrastructure (including power facilities, telecommunication towers, and bridges), foreign enterprises, and businesses that refuse to pay "revolutionary taxes"; follows a Maoist-inspired protracted guerrilla warfare strategy; uses a combination of guerrilla and terrorist tactics, including ambushes, assassinations, bombings, kidnapping of security personnel, and raids on military and security posts; also has attacked local infrastructure, plantations, mines, foreign enterprises, and US personnel and interests (has not attacked a US citizen or facility since 2001, however); employs small arms, light weapons, grenades, improvised explosive devices, and landmines; has employed city-based assassination squads at times
strength – estimated in 2024 to have about 1,500 full-time combatants (from a peak of about 25,000 armed members in the late 1980s)
financial and other support – raises funds through theft and extortion, including extracting "revolutionary taxes" from local businesses; probably also receives donations from sympathizers in the Philippines, Europe, and elsewhere; arms and ammunition largely stolen or captured from Philippine military and security forces or acquired on the black market
designation –placed on the US Department of State's list of Foreign Terrorist Organizations on 9 August 2002

Continuity Irish Republican Army (CIRA)

aka – Continuity Army Council; Continuity IRA; Republican Sinn Fein
history – terrorist splinter group that became operational in 1986 as the clandestine armed wing of Republican Sinn Fein, following its split from Sinn Fein; "Continuity" refers to the group's belief that it is carrying on the original goal of the Irish Republican Army (IRA) of forcing the British out of Northern Ireland; rejects ceasefires, weapons decommissioning, and all peace accords, including the Belfast Agreement and the 1998 Good Friday Agreement; cooperates with the larger Real IRA (RIRA), another US-designated terrorist group; in June 2017, released a statement claiming it would disband and decommission some of its arms over the following three months, describing the conflict as a "futile war"; however, some members claimed responsibility for several attacks or attempted attacks against the Police Service of Northern Ireland (PSNI) between 2019 and 2021; remained active as of 2023
goals – disrupt the Northern Ireland peace process, remove British rule in Northern Ireland and, ultimately, unify Ireland
leadership and organization – operations are guided by its Irish Continuity Army Council
areas of operation – UK and Republic of Ireland
targets, tactics, and weapons – targets have included civilians, British security forces, and police officers in Northern Ireland; has carried out assassinations, bombings, extortion operations, hijackings, and robberies; on occasion, has provided advance warning to police of its attacks; members are typically equipped with small arms and explosives
strength – estimated in 2023 to have fewer than 50 members
financial and other support – receives donations from local and international sympathizers, but the majority of funds are obtained through criminal activity, including bank robberies, extortion, and smuggling
designation – placed on the US Department of State's list of Foreign Terrorist Organizations on 13 July 2004

Gran Grif

aka – Gran Grif gang; Gran Grif de Savien; Savien gang; Baz Gran Grif; Big Claw Crew

history – Gran Grif is the largest criminal gang in Haiti's Artibonite department, an important rice growing region located between the capital Port-au-Prince and Cap-Haïtien, Haiti's main northern city; the gang was founded around 2016 by Prophane VICTOR, a former member of the country's Parliament who has been sanctioned for human rights violations by the US and UN and is currently in custody in Haiti; since 2022, the gang has been responsible for mass kidnappings and multiple massacres of civilians and self-defense group members in Artibonite, including an attack in October 2024 that killed more than 125 people in the town of Pont-Sondé, forcing more than 6,000 of its 10,000 residents to flee; the gang claimed it was retaliating for civilians allying with a local self-defense group and refusing to pay an extortion fee

goals – territorial control, particularly highways through the Artibonite region; gain political influence

leadership and organization – led by Luckson ELAN; probably cooperates with the designated terrorist alliance/group Viv Ansanm

area of operation – Haiti (primarily Artibonite Department)

targets, tactics, and weapons – targets civilians, journalists, self-defense groups, non-aligned criminal gangs, the Haitian Government, National Police, and Armed Forces, and the UN Multinational Security Support Mission force; tactics include beatings, destruction of property, forced displacements, kidnappings, harassment, hijackings, large-scale gun attacks, looting, murder, sexual violence, and stealing crops and livestock; armed with small arms, including military-grade weapons

strength – not available

financial and other support – criminal activities such as extortion, illegal highway tolls, kidnappings for ransom, and theft; ammunition and firearms mostly trafficked into Haiti

designation – placed on the US Department of State's list of Foreign Terrorist Organizations on 2 May 2025

Gulf Cartel

aka – Cártel de Golfo or CDG; Osiel Cardenas-Guillen Organization

history – transnational criminal organization based in northeast Mexico and originally founded in the 1930s to smuggle whiskey and other illicit commodities into the US; CDG expanded significantly in the 1980s through a deal with the Colombia-based Cali Cartel to control drug trafficking routes to the US; by the mid-1990s, it was reportedly earning billions of dollars in cash each year and had built a wide-reaching delivery network across the US; in recent years, the group has splintered into several rival factions, causing leadership voids and the loss of territory and influence; as of 2024, these factions continued to control significant areas of the US-Mexico border, primarily in Tamaulipas state, while profiting from the smuggling of migrants and illicit drugs into the US, as well as cash and guns back into Mexico; at the same time, the factions' control of key municipalities is threatened by its Tamaulipas State-based rival the Northeast Cartel (Zetas Cartel del Noreste or CDN)

leadership and organization – numerous former leaders have been arrested or killed

area(s) of operation – areas along the northeastern part of the US-Mexico border, particularly Tamaulipas state

tactics, targets, and weapons – engages in assassinations and murder of civilians, government officials, and police to intimidate and control territory; the group is involved in drug and arms trafficking, extortion, kidnapping, migrant smuggling, human trafficking, and other illicit activities

strength – not available

financial and other support – illicit activities

designation – placed on the US Department of State's list of Foreign Terrorist Organizations on 20 February 2025

HAMAS

aka – HAMAS is the acronym for Harakat al-Muqawama al-Islamiya (Islamic Resistance Movement); Izz al-Din al Qassam (Qassim) Battalions; Izz al-Din al Qassam (or Qassim) Brigades; Izz al-Din al Qassam (or Qassim) Forces; Students of Ayyash; Student of the Engineer; Yahya Ayyash Units

history – established in 1987 at the onset of the first Palestinian uprising, or Intifada, as an outgrowth of the Palestinian branch of the Muslim Brotherhood; prior to 2005 it conducted numerous attacks against Israel, including more than 50 suicide bombings; in addition, the group used a network of *Dawa* or social services that included charities, schools, clinics, youth camps, fundraising, and political activities to help build grassroots support amongst Palestinians in Gaza; HAMAS won the Palestinian Legislative Council elections in 2006, giving it control of significant Palestinian Authority (PA) ministries in Gaza; in 2007, the group expelled the PA and its dominant political faction Fatah in a violent takeover and has subsequently remained the de facto ruler of Gaza; it has also engaged in sporadic rocket attacks, border clashes, organized protests, and periodic targeted attacks against Israeli citizens, as well as significant conflicts with Israel in 2008-2009, 2012, 2014, and 2021; in October 2023, HAMAS conducted a surprise air and ground attack into Israel, which triggered a large Israeli military counteroffensive into Gaza

goals – ideology combines Palestinian nationalism with Islamic fundamentalism; seeks to maintain control of the Gaza Strip to facilitate Palestinian nationalist aims; the group's charter calls for establishing an Islamic Palestinian state in place of Israel and rejects all agreements made between the Palestine Liberation Organization and Israel

leadership and organization – not available; previous leader (Yahya SINWAR) killed in October 2024; has a shura council as its central consultative body; has smaller shura/executive committees to supervise political activities, military operations, social services, finances, and media relations; military wing (the 'Izz al-Din al-Qassam Brigades) organized into approximately six "brigades," special forces (Nukhba Special Forces), and various paramilitary units

areas of operation – has controlled Gaza since 2007 and has a presence in the West Bank; also has a presence in the Palestinian refugee camps in Lebanon and key regional capitals such as Doha, Qatar, and Cairo

targets, tactics, and weapons – targets Israeli military forces and civilians, as well as Islamic State and other Salafist armed group members based in Gaza; tactics include terrorist and hit-and-run/guerrilla-style operations, including ambushes, raids, suicide bombings, improvised explosive attacks, shootings, and rocket attacks; weapons include small arms, light and heavy machine guns, rockets (some with ranges of up to 200kms), mortars, rocket-propelled grenades, man-portable air defense systems, anti-tank missiles, armed unmanned aerial vehicles/drones, and improvised explosive devices (IEDs), including balloons armed with IEDs or designed to start fires; has also engaged in cyber espionage and computer network exploitation operations

strength – estimated 20-40,000 armed combatants prior to the start of the war with Israel in October 2023

financial and other support – the military wing receives funding, weapons, and training from Iran and procures additional weapons from the regional black market; weapons are typically supplied through tunnels under the border with Sinai and/or through maritime smuggling routes; also raises funds in some Gulf countries as well as through business taxation, donations from Palestinian expatriates, international investments, and through its own charity organizations

designation – placed on the US Department of State's list of Foreign Terrorist Organizations on 8 October 1997

Haqqani Network (HQN)

aka – Haqqani Taliban Network, Afghanistan Mujahidin
history – formed in the late 1980s during the then-Soviet Union's occupation of Afghanistan; founder, Jalaluddin HAQQANI, established a relationship with Usama BIN LADIN in the mid-1980s and joined the Taliban in 1995; the HAQQANI Network (HQN) helped the Taliban capture the capital, Kabul, in 1996; after the fall of the Taliban to US and allied forces in 2001, HAQQANI retreated to Pakistan where, under the leadership of his son, Sirajuddin HAQQANI (Jalaluddin HAQQANI reportedly died in 2018), HQN continued to conduct an insurgency in Afghanistan against the Afghan Government and its security forces, Afghan civilians, and foreign military forces; the insurgency continued until the collapse of the Afghan Government in August 2021; afterwards, HQN remained a semi-autonomous component of the Afghan Taliban and a close ally of al-Qa'ida; it cooperates with other regional terrorist groups, including the Islamic Movement of Uzbekistan and Lashkar e-Tayyiba; following the Taliban takeover of Afghanistan, HQN secured control of the de facto ministries of interior, intelligence, and immigration and largely controlled the country's internal security
goals – support the Taliban's rule in Afghanistan; prior to August 2021, expel foreign military forces from Afghanistan and replace the Afghan Government with an Islamic state operating according to a strict Salafi Muslim interpretation of sharia under the Afghan Taliban
leadership and organization – operational commander is Sirajuddin HAQQANI, who leads the group through its Peshawar Shura, which features both military and political wings and consists of Haqqani family members along with veteran commanders trusted by the family; during the insurgency, it operated under Taliban command and control but maintained significant autonomy and regional influence in its area of operations in southeast Afghanistan; beginning in 2015, HAQQANI was the deputy leader of the Afghan Taliban, and as of 2024 was the acting interior minister for the de facto Taliban government
areas of operation – Afghanistan
targets, tactics, and weapons – employed insurgency-type tactics, including coordinated small-arms assaults coupled with the use of mortars and rockets, rocket-propelled grenades, improvised explosive devices, suicide attacks, and car/truck bombs against Afghan Government security forces, US military, and other coalition troops; also targeted Afghan civilians and foreigners with kidnappings, bombings, and suicide attacks; attacked government buildings, hotels, embassies, markets, and schools; conducted some of Afghanistan's most deadly bombings, including truck bomb attacks in Kabul in 2017 and 2018 that killed more than 250 civilians; in 2019, conducted multiple attacks in Kabul that killed 100 people and injured more than 500; equipped with small arms, light and heavy machine guns, mortars, rockets, rocket-propelled grenades, and improvised explosive devices
strength – estimated in 2023 to have 3-5,000 fighters; during the insurgency against the Afghan Government, HQN's numbers fluctuated based on time of year and battlefield operations
financial and other support – in addition to the funding it received as part of the broader Afghan Taliban, HQN received some assistance from donors in Pakistan and the Gulf; most funds are from taxing local commerce, extortion, smuggling, kidnapping-for-ransom, and other licit and illicit business ventures; recruits, trains, raises funds, resupplies, and plans operations in the tribal areas of Pakistan; reportedly receives weapons smuggled in from Iran and Pakistan
designation – placed on the US Department of State's list of Foreign Terrorist Organizations on 19 September 2012

Harakat al-Nujaba

designated on 17 September 2025; additional information to follow

Harakat Ansar Allah al-Awfiya

designated on 17 September 2025; additional information to follow

Harakat Sawa'd Misr (HASM)

aka – HASM Movement; Arms of Egypt Movement; HASSAM; HASAM; Harakah Sawa'id Misr; Movement of Egypt's Arms
history – formed in 2015; the group is in part composed of alienated Muslim Brotherhood (MB) members who view violence rather than dialogue as a more effective means to overthrow the Egyptian Government and operate independent of MB; in 2016, the group claimed responsibility for the assassination of a senior Egyptian security official, as well as the attempted assassination of Egypt's former Grand Mufti; following a January 2017 shootout with Egyptian security forces in Cairo, HASM declared a jihad against the Egyptian Government; later in 2017, it claimed an ambush attack that killed more than 50 Egyptian security forces and an attack on Burma's embassy in Cairo; in January 2019, it conducted a car bomb attack targeting security forces in Giza, which it claimed killed or wounded 10 soldiers; in August of the same year, it was held responsible (but denied responsibility) for a car bomb attack on a government health institute in Cairo, killing at least 20 people and injuring dozens; continued to be active as of 2025
goals – overthrow the Egyptian Government and replace it with an Islamic regime
leadership and organization – Yahya al-Sayyid Ibrahim MUSA and Alaa Ali Mohammed al-SAMAHI (both based in Turkey); organization is not available, but probably operates in small, loosely connected cells and networks
areas of operation – Egypt (some leaders in Turkey)
targets, tactics, and weapons – primarily Egyptian security officials and other government-affiliated targets; typical attacks include ambushes, shootings, and bombings, including car bombings; employs improvised explosive devices and small arms
strength – not available
financial and other support – not available
designation – placed on the US Department of State's list of Foreign Terrorist Organizations on 14 January 2021

Harakat ul-Jihad-i-Islami (HUJI)

aka – Movement of Islamic Holy War; Harkat-ul-Jihad-al Islami; Harkat-al-Jihad-ul Islami; Harkat-ul-Jehad-al-Islami; Harakat ul Jihad-e-Islami; Harakat-ul Jihad Islami
history – formed in 1980 in Afghanistan to fight against the former Soviet Union; following the Soviet withdrawal in 1989, HUJI redirected its efforts to the cause of Muslims in the Indian state of Jammu and Kashmir; it also supplied fighters to the Taliban in Afghanistan to fight Afghan, Coalition, and US forces; HUJI has experienced internal splits, and a portion of the group aligned with al-Qa'ida; it has not publicly claimed any attacks since 2015, and the group's status was unclear as of 2023
goals – annexation of the state of Jammu and Kashmir into Pakistan and establishment of Islamic rule in Afghanistan, India, and Pakistan
leadership and organization – not available
areas of operation – Afghanistan, India, and Pakistan
targets, tactics, and weapons – targeted Pakistani military, security, and police personnel, as well as Indian security forces in the Kashmir region and Indian Government officials; also targeted Hindu and Western civilians; its most significant attack was the bombing of the New Delhi High Court in 2011, which killed 11 people and injured 76; attacks typically involved the use of small arms, grenades, and improvised explosive devices

strength – not available
financial and other support – not available
designation – placed on the US Department of State's list of Foreign Terrorist Organizations on 6 August 2010

Harakat ul-Jihad-i-Islami/Bangladesh (HUJI-B)
aka – Harakat ul Jihad e Islami Bangladesh; Harkatul Jihad al Islam; Harkatul Jihad; Harakat ul Jihad al Islami; Harkat ul Jihad al Islami; Harkat-ul-Jehad-al-Islami; Harakat ul Jihad Islami Bangladesh; Islami Dawat-e-Kafela; IDEK
history – formed in 1992 by a group of former Bangladeshi Afghan veterans wanting to establish Islamist rule in Bangladesh; HUJI-B leaders signed the February 1998 *fatwa* sponsored by Usama BIN LADEN that declared US civilians legitimate targets; in October 2005, Bangladeshi authorities banned the group; the group has connections to al-Qa'ida and Pakistani terrorist groups advocating similar objectives, including HUJI and Lashkar e-Tayyiba; its activities have waned in recent years but remained active as of 2023
goals – install an Islamic state in Bangladesh; draws inspiration from al-Qaida and the Afghan Taliban
leadership and organization – not available
areas of operation – Bangladesh and India
targets, tactics, and weapons – conducts low-level bombing attacks against Bangladeshi officials and Westerners; also targets activists, bloggers, academics, religious minorities, and political rallies; its most lethal attack occurred in 2004, when operatives lobbed grenades during a political rally in Dhaka, killing 24 and injuring about 400 others; attackers typically have used small arms, hand grenades, and various explosives, including petrol bombs and improvised explosive devices
strength – not available
financial and other support – funding comes from a variety of sources, including donations from sympathetic individuals and organizations and criminal activities such as piracy, smuggling, and arms running
designation – placed on the US Department of State's list of Foreign Terrorist Organizations on 5 March 2008

Harakat ul-Mujahidin (HUM)
aka – Harakat ul-Ansar; HUA; Jamiat ul-Ansar; JUA; al-Faran; al-Hadid; al-Hadith; Harakat ul-Mujahidin; Ansar ul Ummah
history – formed in 1985 under Maulana Fazlur Rahman KHALIL in the Pakistani state of Punjab as an anti-Soviet jihadist group that splintered from Harakat ul-Jihad-i-Islami (HUJI); HUM operated terrorist training camps in eastern Afghanistan until US air strikes destroyed them in 2001; a significant portion of the group defected to Jaysh-e-Mohammed after 2000; in 2003, it began using the name Jamiat ul-Ansar; Pakistan banned the group the same year; HUM is a long been an ally of al-Qa'ida and has links to other terrorist groups in the region, including Lashkar-e-Taiba, Jaish-e-Muhammad, and Lashkar-e-Jhangvi; the group has not claimed any attacks since 2017 but it reportedly remained active as of 2024
goals – annex the Indian Union Territory of Jammu and Kashmir into Pakistan
leadership and organization – Badr MUNIR has led the group since 2005; organization unavailable
areas of operation – operates primarily in Afghanistan and in the Indian state of Jammu and Kashmir; also operates in Muzaffarabad in Pakistan-administered Azad Kashmir and in other cities in Pakistan
targets, tactics, and weapons – conducted numerous attacks against Indian troops, government officials, and civilians in the state of Jammu and Kashmir, as well as in India's northeastern states, especially between 2005 and 2013; also attacked Western targets, such as the 2002 suicide car bombing of a bus carrying French workers in Karachi, Pakistan, that killed 15 and wounded 20; uses various attack methods, including suicide bombings, airplane hijackings, kidnappings, and assassinations; typically used small arms, grenades, and improvised explosive devices
strength – estimated in 2023 to have only a small number of cadres active
financial and other support – receives donations from wealthy supporters in Pakistan
designation – placed on the US Department of State's list of Foreign Terrorist Organizations on 8 October 1997

Hizballah
aka – the Party of God; Hezbollah; Islamic Jihad; Islamic Jihad Organization; Revolutionary Justice Organization; Organization of the Oppressed on Earth; Islamic Jihad for the Liberation of Palestine; Organization of Right Against Wrong; Ansar Allah; Followers of the Prophet Muhammed; Lebanese Hizballah; Lebanese Hezbollah; LH; Foreign Relations Department; External Security Organization; Foreign Action Unit; Hizballah International; Special Operations Branch; External Services Organization; External Security Organization of Hezbollah
history – formed in 1982 following the Israeli invasion of Lebanon as a Shia militant group that takes its ideological inspiration from the Iranian revolution and the teachings of the late Ayatollah KHOMEINI; it generally follows the religious guidance of the Iranian Supreme Leader; Hizballah is closely allied with Iran and the two often work together on shared initiatives, although it also acts independently in some cases; the group shared a close relationship with the former Syrian ASAD regime and provided assistance – including thousands of fighters – to regime forces in the Syrian civil war; since the early 1990s, Hizballah has evolved into a business and political enterprise and become a state within a state in Lebanon with strong influence in Lebanon's Shia community; it actively participates in Lebanon's political system and runs social programs, such as hospitals and schools; it has seats in Lebanon's parliament and has had members appointed to the Lebanese Government's ministries; the group's military capabilities have the characteristics of both a paramilitary and a conventional military force; Hizballah fought a month-long war with Israel in 2006; from 2019-2023, it engaged in periodic tit-for-tat hostile exchanges with Israel, typically involving Hizballah missile or rocket attacks, followed by Israeli air strikes; following the terrorist group HAMAS's attack on Israel in October 2023 and subsequent Israeli invasion of Gaza, Hizballah sought to demonstrate solidarity with HAMAS by launching barrages of missiles, rockets, and armed drones into northern Israel; Hizballah's actions triggered Israeli air and ground counterattacks; clashes continued into early 2025
goals – accrue military resources and political power and defend its position of strength in Lebanon; seeks to expel Western influence from Lebanon and the greater Middle East, destroy the state of Israel, and establish Islamic rule in Lebanon and the Palestinian territories
leadership and organization – Secretary General NAIM QASSEM; the secretary general historically has had two deputies and managed the organization through a seven-seat Shura Council with five subordinate specialized assemblies: the Executive, Judicial, Parliamentary, Political, and Jihad Councils; each assembly oversees several sub-entities that handle Hizballah's affairs in various sectors; for example, the Jihad/Military council reportedly has two wings, the Islamic Resistance (combat operations) and the Security Organ (external and internal security operations): Islamic Resistance is organized into territorial commands and units of infantry, artillery, rockets, coastal defense, and commandos/special forces (Unit 1800 or Radwan Force); Hizballah also has Lebanese militia "brigades" which serve as auxiliary forces; the Security Organ has two sub-branches: the Islamic Jihad Organization (External Security Organization, aka Unit 910) for external operations, including the group's international terrorist operations, recruitment, fundraising, intelligence gathering, and support to Shia militias abroad; and the Party Security Organ, which is responsible for internal security; has a youth movement known as the al-Mahdi Scouts
areas of operation – Lebanon; Syria; operatives and financiers have been arrested or detained in Africa, Asia, Europe, the Middle East, South America, and North America

targets, tactics, and weapons – targets include Israeli security forces, civilians, and interests, Jews, US and Western military forces, and other symbols of American/Western influence in the Middle East; in Syria, the group conducted operations against the foes of the Syrian ASAD regime, particularly those affiliated with the Islamic State and al-Qa'ida terrorist organizations; Hizballah historically has used a variety of guerrilla-style hit-and-run and terrorist tactics; some of its most devastating attacks involved the use of car/truck bombs, such as the 1983 attacks on the US Embassy, the US Marine barracks, and a French military base in Beirut, which killed over 300 civilians and military personnel; it has conducted attacks on Israeli and Jewish targets abroad, including bombings in Argentina in 1992 and 1994 which killed more than 100 and wounded more than 500 others; since the 2000s, Hizballah has developed elements of a more traditional state-like conventional military force and demonstrated considerable military capabilities; forces are equipped with small arms, light and heavy machineguns, mortars, landmines, improvised explosive devises, artillery, armored combat vehicles, rockets, antiaircraft guns, ballistic missiles, anti-ship cruise missiles, armed unmanned aerial vehicles/drones, man-portable air defense systems, and antitank guided missiles; prior to the 2023-2025 fighting with Israel, the group was estimated to have as many as 150,000 missiles and rockets of various types and ranges
strength – estimated in 2024 to have up to 50,000 armed combatants, divided between full-time and reserve personnel; in 2021, the group's leadership claimed the group had 100,000 trained fighters
financial and other support – receives most of its funding, training, and weapons, as well as political, diplomatic, and organizational aid, from Iran; Iran's annual financial backing to Hizballah – which has been estimated to be hundreds of millions of dollars annually – accounts for the overwhelming majority of the group's annual budget; the Syrian ASAD regime also furnished training, weapons, and diplomatic and political support; it also receives additional funding in the form of legal businesses, international criminal enterprises (including smuggling, narcotics trafficking, and money laundering), and donations from the Shia in Lebanon and Lebanese diaspora communities worldwide; Hizballah has developed a network of training camps in Lebanon
designation – placed on the US Department of State's list of Foreign Terrorist Organizations on 8 October 1997

Hizbul Mujahideen (HM)

aka – Hizb-ul-Mujahideen; Party of Mujahideen; Party of Holy Warriors
history – formed in 1989 and is one of the largest and oldest militant separatist groups fighting against Indian rule in the state of Jammu and Kashmir; HM reportedly operated in Afghanistan through the mid-1990s and trained alongside the Afghan Hizb-e-Islami Gulbuddin until the Taliban takeover; it is made up primarily of ethnic Kashmiris and has conducted operations jointly with other Kashmiri militant groups; HM was active as of 2023
goals – supports the liberation of the territory of Jammu and Kashmir from Indian control and its accession to Pakistan, although some cadres are pro-independence
leadership and organization – led by Syed SALAHUDDIN (aka Mohammad Yusuf SHAH); reportedly organized in five regionally-based divisions; probably operates in small loosely connected networks and cells
areas of operation – headquartered in Pakistan but conducts operations primarily in India, particularly the Indian Union Territory of Jammu and Kashmir
targets, tactics, and weapons – focuses attacks on Indian security forces and politicians in the state of Jammu and Kashmir; most attacks involved small arms and grenades, although it has also utilized improvised explosive devices, including vehicle-mounted
strength – estimated in 2023 to have up to 1,500 members
financial and other support – specific sources of support are not clear, but probably originate in Pakistan, as well as from local fundraising
designation – placed on the US Department of State's list of Foreign Terrorist Organizations on 17 August 2017

Hurras al-Din

aka – Tanzim Hurras al-Din; Tandhim Hurras al-Din; Hurras al-Deen; Houras al-Din; HAD; al-Qa'ida in Syria (AQS); Guardians of the Religion Organization; Sham al-Ribat
history – publicly announced itself in February 2018 as an al-Qa'ida affiliate after its members broke away from al-Nusrah Front (subsequently rebranded as Hayat Tahrir al-Sham, or HTS) because HTS publicly cut ties with al-Qa'ida; maintains allied or cooperative relationships with several extremist elements in Syria, including Jamaat Ansar al-Islam, the Turkestan Islamic Party (TIP), Sham al-Islam, and Ansar al-Tawhid; viewed as the leading force behind the "Incite the Believers" jihadist alliance in Syria, which conducts battlefield operations against Syrian Government forces in northern Syria; since 2020, has had a tense relationship HTS/al-Nusrah Front, which controls Syria's northwestern province of Iblib, that has involved assassinations, open clashes, competition for recruits, and arrests of its members by HTS; rejected the March 2020 Russian-Turkish ceasefire agreement in Idlib and continued conducting attacks on Russian, Syrian, and Turkish forces; a campaign by HTS to detain HAD members since 2020 hampered the group's ability to conduct operations and prompted some members to defect, while HAD itself became overshadowed by HTS; in January 2025, HAD released a statement announcing its own dissolution
goals – oust Syrian President Bashar al-ASAD's regime and replace it with a Sunni Islamic State; likely adheres to al-Qa'ida's chief objectives of neutralizing Israeli and US influence within the Middle East, specifically within the Levant
leadership and organization – led by Samir HIJAZI (aka Abu Hamamm al-Shami, Faruq al-Suri, Mohammed Abu Khalid al-Suri); has a shura council; as of 2020, claimed to be comprised of 16 jihadist factions; sub-structure not available, but operational units probably organized into cells and "battalions"
areas of operation – mostly in the Syrian provinces of Idlib and Latakia, with a small presence in Dara'a
targets, tactics, and weapons – primarily attacks Syrian Government and pro-regime forces; has also conducted armed assaults against Turkish and Russian military forces active in Syria; potentially responsible for the kidnapping of aid workers in northwestern Syria; has encouraged violent attacks against Israeli and Western targets in its propaganda releases; employs insurgent-type tactics; has conducted assassinations and car bombings; armed largely with small arms, bombs, explosives (including vehicle mounted improvised explosive devices), mortars, machine guns, and trucks mounting machine guns (aka "technicals")
strength – estimated in 2025 have approximately 2,000 fighters, including foreigners and associated armed factions
financial and other support – appeals for donations under the auspices of supporting its efforts against the Syrian Government; leverages social media platforms to call for financial assistance, public support, and recruits; active in training operatives at a number of unspecified training camps in Syria
designation – placed on the US Department of State's list of Foreign Terrorist Organizations on 5 September 2019

Indian Mujahedeen (IM)

aka – Indian Mujahidin; Islamic Security Force-Indian Mujahideen (ISF-IM)

history – formed as an ultra-conservative Islamic movement circa 2004 from remnants of the radical youth organization Students Islamic Movement of India; IM is responsible for dozens of bomb attacks throughout India since 2005 and the deaths of hundreds of civilians; it maintains ties to other terrorist entities including Pakistan-based Lashkar e-Tayyiba, Jaish-e-Mohammed, and Harakat ul-Jihad Islami; by 2016, IM was increasingly linked to the Islamic State of Iraq and ash-Sham (ISIS); that year, IM operatives were identified in an ISIS propaganda video threatening attacks on India, and an IM cell linked to ISIS was reportedly plotting attacks on multiple targets in India; Indian authorities have disrupted bombing plots by the group and apprehended dozens of suspected IM operatives; the group was active as of 2023 but has not publicly claimed any attacks in recent years
goals – establish Islamic rule in India; stated goal is to carry out terrorist operations against Indians for their perceived oppression of Muslims
leadership and organization – not available
areas of operation – India
targets, tactics, and weapons – known for carrying out multiple coordinated bombings in crowded areas against Indian and Western civilian and economic targets, including restaurants and commercial centers; in 2008, was responsible for 16 synchronized bomb blasts in crowded urban centers, including an attack in Delhi that killed 30 people and an attack at a local hospital in Ahmedabad that killed 38; in 2010, the group bombed a popular German bakery frequented by tourists in Pune, India, killing 17 and wounding more than 60 people; attackers typically have used improvised explosive devices
strength – not available
financial and other support – suspected of obtaining funding and support from other terrorist organizations, as well as from sources in Pakistan and the Middle East; IM leadership has been linked to general criminal activity, kidnapping, and extortion to raise funds
designation – placed on the US Department of State's list of Foreign Terrorist Organizations on 19 September 2011

Islamic Jihad Union (IJU)

aka – Islamic Jihad Group; IJG; Islomiy Jihod Ittihodi; al-Djihad al-Islami; Dzhamaat Modzhakhedov; Islamic Jihad Group of Uzbekistan; Jamiat al-Jihad al-Islami; Jamiyat; The Jamaat Mojahedin; The Kazakh Jama'at; The Libyan Society
history – emerged in 2002 as a splinter movement of the Islamic Movement of Uzbekistan (IMU) after internal splits over goals; originally known as the Islamic Jihad Group but was renamed Islamic Jihad Union in 2005; IJU was formed to overthrow the Government of Uzbekistan, but has been more active in Afghanistan and Syria; it pledged allegiance to the Afghan Taliban in 2015 and participated in Taliban attacks against the former Afghan Government; it continued to maintain a presence in Afghanistan following the 2021 Taliban takeover; IJU also participated in the Syrian conflict as part of a coalition of al-Qa'ida-linked terrorist groups
goals – overthrow the Uzbek Government and replace it with an Islamic state; support al-Qa'ida's overall goals
leadership and organization – Ilimbek MAMATOV; probably operates in a loose network of cells
areas of operation – Afghanistan, Syria, Türkiye, Uzbekistan, and Europe
targets, tactics, and weapons – targeted international and Afghan military and security forces in Afghanistan and Syrian regime forces using a variety of guerrilla warfare and terrorist tactics; targets in Uzbekistan included security checkpoints, law enforcement facilities, market places, and foreign embassies, often with suicide bombers; in 2007, German authorities disrupted an IJU cell planning to attack multiple targets in Germany with car bombs; fighters are armed with small arms, light and heavy machine guns, rocket-propelled grenades, antiaircraft weapons, and various explosives including improvised explosive devices and car bombs
strength – estimated in 2023 to have 200-250 members in Afghanistan
financial and other support – not available
designation – placed on the US Department of State's list of Foreign Terrorist Organizations on 17 June 2005

Islamic Movement of Uzbekistan (IMU)

aka – Islamic Party of Uzbekistan; Islamskaia partiia Turkestana;, byvshee Islamskoe dvizhenie Uzbekistana; Islamic Movement of Turkistan
history – established to overthrow the Uzbekistani government and establish an Islamic state but for much of its existence, IMU operated in northern Afghanistan and fought against international forces supporting the former Afghan Government; the group has long been allied to al-Qa'ida, the Afghan Taliban, and Tehrik-i-Taliban Pakistan, and frequently conducted joint operations with those organizations; in 2015, IMU leader Usman GHAZI publicly announced the group's shift of allegiance to ISIS and has since cooperated with the Islamic State's Khorasan Province; in 2016 a faction of IMU announced its continued commitment to the Taliban and al-Qa'ida, marking a split with GHAZI and the rest of the group; numerous IMU members, including possibly GHAZI, were subsequently reported to have been killed as a result of hostilities between ISIS and IMU's former Taliban allies; the group's operational tempo has decreased in recent years, but it was active as of 2024
goals – overthrow the Uzbek Government and establish an Islamic state
leadership and organization – Samatov MAMASOLI (aka Abu Ali); probably structured as a network of cells
areas of operation – Afghanistan, Pakistan, Syria, Türkiye, and Central Asia
targets, tactics, and weapons – targeted military and security forces and government facilities using guerrilla warfare and terrorist tactics, including ambushes, assassinations, ground assaults, indirect fire attacks, kidnappings, and suicide bombings; in 2010 the IMU claimed responsibility for an ambush that killed 25 Tajik troops in Tajikistan; in 2014, it claimed responsibility for an attack on Karachi's international airport that resulted in the deaths of at least 39 people, as well as a 2012 attack on a Pakistani prison that freed nearly 400 prisoners (both attacks conducted jointly with the Tehrik-i-Taliban Pakistan terrorist group); it also attacked government and allied foreign military forces in Afghanistan, as well as security forces in Pakistan; typically used small arms and light weapons, mortars, rockets, and various explosives, including car bombs and suicide vests
strength – estimated to have up to 500 fighters as of 2023
financial and other support – receives support from a large Uzbek diaspora, allied terrorist organizations, and sympathizers from Europe, Central and South Asia, and the Middle East; also engages in narcotics trafficking and conducts kidnappings for ransom
designation – placed on the US Department of State's list of Foreign Terrorist Organizations on 25 September 2000

Islamic Revolutionary Guard Corps (IRGC)/Qods Force

aka – Islamic Revolutionary Guards, Pasdaran (Guards), Revolutionary Guards, Sepah (Corps), Sepah-e Pasdaran-e Enghelab-e Eslami; Quds ("Jerusalem") Force
history – formed in May 1979 in the immediate aftermath of Shah Mohammad Reza PAHLAVI's fall, as leftists, nationalists, and Islamists jockeyed for power; while the interim prime minister controlled the government and state institutions, such as the army, followers of Ayatollah Ruhollah KHOMEINI organized counterweights, including the IRGC, to protect the Islamic revolution; the IRGC's command structure bypassed the elected president and went directly to KHOMEINI; the Iran-Iraq War (1980–88) transformed the IRGC into more of a conventional fighting force with its own ground, air, naval, and special forces, plus control over Iran's strategic missile and rocket forces; the IRGC is highly institutionalized and operates as a parallel military force to Iran's regular armed forces (Artesh); it is heavily involved in internal security and have significant influence in the political and economic spheres of Iranian society, as well as Iran's foreign policy; the IRGC's special operations forces are known as the Qods

Force which specializes in foreign missions, providing advice, funding, guidance, material support, training, and weapons to militants in countries such as Afghanistan, Bahrain, Lebanon, Iraq, Syria, and Yemen, as well as extremist groups, including al-Ashtar Brigades, Asa'ib Ahl al-Haqq, HAMAS, Hizballah, Kata'ib Hizballah, and Palestine Islamic Jihad
goals – protect Iran's Islamic revolution and the state; spread Iranian/Shia influence; provide internal security, including border control, law enforcement, and suppressing domestic opposition; influence Iran's politics, economy, and foreign policy
leadership and organization – commander of the IRGC not available; Brigadier General Ismail QAANI is the commander of the Qods Force; organized along the lines of a traditional conventional military force with Ground Forces, Navy (includes marines), Aerospace Force (includes the strategic missile forces), Cyber Command, Qods Force (special operations), and Basij Paramilitary Forces (aka Popular Mobilization Army); the IRGC ground forces are deployed throughout Iran in all 31 provinces and Tehran and include a broad mix of armored, infantry, mechanized, and commando units, which are postured to counter internal unrest or a ground invasion; the IRGC also has branches for intelligence, counterintelligence, and security; the Qods Force is reportedly divided into branches focusing on intelligence/espionage, finance, politics, sabotage, and special operations, as well as regionally-focused directorates; the Basij is a volunteer paramilitary group under the IRGC with local organizations across the country which augment internal security
areas of operation – headquartered in Tehran; active throughout Iran and the Middle East region, as well as Afghanistan, Gaza, Iraq, Lebanon, Syria, and Yemen; has a worldwide capability to commit attacks if Iranian leadership deems it appropriate; in recent years, Qods Force planning for terror attacks has been uncovered and disrupted in a number of countries worldwide, including Albania, Bahrain, Belgium, Bosnia, Bulgaria, Denmark, France, Germany, Kenya, Turkey, and the US
targets, tactics, and weapons – targets US, Israeli, Saudi, and UAE interests, as well as Iranian dissident groups; the IRGC is armed to fight as a conventional military force with typical ground, air, and naval platforms and weapons; the Qods Force conducts a wide-range of covert or terrorist-type attacks; it also has active and growing cyberwarfare capabilities; the IRGC/Qods Force also makes extensive use of proxy and partner forces such as Hizballah, Shia militias in Iraq, and the Houthis in Yemen; Iran has provided a wide range of arms to proxy/partner forces, including small arms, rockets, rocket-propelled grenades, air defense systems, coastal defense cruise missiles, improvised explosive devises (IEDs), anti-aircraft weapons, armor-piercing explosively formed projectiles, and armed unmanned aerial vehicles/drones
strength – IRGC: estimated in 2023 to have up to 190,000 personnel, including 5-15,000 in the Qods Force; Basij Paramilitary Forces: estimated 100,000 full-time, uniformed personnel; the Basij reportedly can mobilize several hundred thousand additional personnel when required
financial and other support – the IRGC receives a portion of the Iranian defense budget, by some estimates as much as 50%; IRGC-linked companies reportedly control up to 20% of Iran's economy; IRGC/Qods Forces also exert control over strategic industries, commercial services, and black-market enterprises, and have engaged in large-scale illicit finance schemes and money laundering
designation – placed on the US Department of State's list of Foreign Terrorist Organizations on 15 April 2019

Islamic State of Iraq and ash-Sham – Democratic Republic of the Congo (ISIS-DRC)

aka – Islamic State of Iraq and ash-Sham – Central Africa (ISIS-Central Africa); Islamic State - Central Africa; Islamic State's Central Africa Province (ISCAP); Wilayat (or Wilayah) Central Africa; Madina Tawheed wal Mujahideen ("the City of Monotheism and Holy Warriors"); Allied Democratic Forces (ADF)
history – first mentioned as "ISIS-Central Africa" in an August 2018 speech by then-ISIS leader al-BAGHDADI; claimed its first attack against the Democratic Republic of the Congo (DRC) military near the border with Uganda in April 2019; has its origins in the DRC-based militant group Allied Democratic Forces (ADF), which was founded in 1995 with the stated goal of overthrowing the Ugandan Government but shifted in the late 1990s to carrying out attacks against civilians, military forces, and UN peacekeepers in the DRC; many of ADF's early members came from Uganda's Salafist movement; online posts by some ADF members in 2016 and 2017 referred to their group as Madina Tawheed wal Mujahideen ("the City of Monotheism and Holy Warriors") and displayed an ISIS-like flag; in 2020 and 2022, it launched assaults on prisons in eastern DRC that resulted in the escape of approximately 2,000 prisoners, including several hundred ISIS/ADF fighters and sympathizers; in 2022, the group conducted its first suicide bombing in Goma and was openly engaging in combat with DRC and international military forces; continued to be active in 2025
goals – implement ISIS's strict interpretation of sharia and establish an Islamic state in central Africa
leadership and organization – Seka Musa BALUKU, who presides over a shura/executive council of senior leaders, including a military commander; military wing reportedly has sub-commanders for intelligence, operations, training, finances, logistics, and medical services
areas of operation – DRC, primarily in the Nord Kivu and Ituri provinces; also active in Uganda; has emerged as a regional conduit for facilitating funds transfers to ISIS cells in East Africa
targets, tactics, and weapons – Congolese civilians, particularly Christians, and military/security forces, as well as UN personnel; has attacked churches and schools; has a reputation for brutal violence against Congolese citizens and regional military forces, with attacks killing approximately 5,000 civilians between 2014 and 2021; methods include insurgent-type tactics, direct ground assaults, small-scale attacks, indiscriminate killings, ambushes, assassinations, kidnappings, and suicide bombings; uses small arms, machine guns, improvised explosive devices, rocket-propelled grenades, mortars, and unmanned aerial vehicles (UAVs)/drones
strength – assessed in 2024 to have up to 2,000 fighters
financial and other support – reportedly receives some funding from control of mines and the export of minerals, as wells as from ISIS-Core through a web of financial mechanisms running through Kenya, Somalia, South Africa and Uganda; arms include seized weapons and ammunition from the DRC military
designation – placed on the US Department of State's list of Foreign Terrorist Organizations on 10 March 2021

Islamic State of Iraq and ash-Sham – East Asia (ISIS-EA) in the Philippines

aka – ISIS in the Philippines (ISIS-P); ISIL Philippines; ISIL in the Philippines; IS Philippines (ISP); Islamic State in the Philippines; Islamic State in Iraq and Syria in Southeast Asia; ISIS-East Asia; IS-EA; Dawlah Islamiyah; Dawlatul Islamiyah Waliyatul Masrik; Dawlatul Islamiyah Waliyatul Mashriq; IS East Asia Division; ISIS Branch in the Philippines; ISIS "Philippines province"
history – Islamic militants in the Philippines initially pledged allegiance to ISIS in 2014, however the group officially formed in 2016 with now-deceased leader Isnilon HAPILON as the first amir; ISIS media claimed its first attack in the Philippines against Philippine soldiers on Mindanao Island in March 2016; in May 2017, ISIS-EA and fighters from associated jihadist groups stormed and captured the city of Marawi on Mindanao; five months of subsequent fighting for the city between the militants and the Philippine military resulted in nearly 900 militants and more than 160 Philippine soldiers killed; over 300,000 residents were forced to flee the area during the fighting; in 2018, the group conducted the first recorded suicide attack in the Philippines; ISIS-EA has since claimed several additional suicide and other high-profile bombings, including two suicide bombings undertaken by females within one hour of one another in August of 2020 in the capital of Sulu province and the 2023 bombing of a Catholic mass at a state university; remained active at low levels as of 2025
goals – create an Islamic state in the southern Philippines and across Southeast Asia adhering to ISIS's strict interpretation of sharia

leadership and organization – not available; Esmael Abdulmalik (aka Abu Turaife), the leader of Bangsamoro Islamic Freedom Fighters (BIFF), was touted by pro-ISIS media channels as the emir in 2024; is comprised of a decentralized, loose network of groups with varying levels of allegiance and ties to ISIS, including the Abu Sayaf Group (ASG), the Maute Group (aka Daulah Islamiyah Fi Ranao, Islamic State of Lanao, Abu Zacaria Group), Ansar al-Khilafah Philippines (AKP), and BIFF; these groups operate autonomously and maintain their own leaders and organizational structures
areas of operation – southern Philippines
targets, tactics, and weapons – targets Philippine security forces and non-Muslim civilians; has attacked government-related targets, military bases and security checkpoints, public transportation, churches, internet cafés, resorts, and street festivals; employs a mix of insurgent-type and terrorist tactics, including armed assaults, bombings, mortar attacks, and suicide attackers; weapons include small arms, improvised explosive devices, light and heavy machine guns, rocket-propelled grenades, mortars, and hand grenades
strength – estimated in 2025 to have 100-200 fighters
financial and other support – receives some financial assistance from ISIS-core, but mostly relies on criminal activities such as kidnappings for ransom and extortion; maintains training camps in remote areas under its control and acquires weapons through smuggling and captured or black market purchases of Philippine military arms; receives some media support from ISIS-core
designation – placed on the US Department of State's list of Foreign Terrorist Organizations on 28 February 2018

Islamic State of Iraq and ash-Sham – Mozambique (ISIS-M)

aka – Ansar al-Sunna; Helpers of Tradition; Ahl al-Sunna wal-Jamaa (ASWJ); Adherents to the Traditions and the Community; al-Shabaab in Mozambique; Islamic State Central Africa province; Wilayah Central Africa; Ansaar Kalimat Allah; Supporters of the Word of Allah, "Mashababos"
history – based on a domestic terrorist group known as Ansar al-Sunna (aka al-Shabaab, among other names) that has conducted an insurgency against the Mozambique Government since 2017; pledged allegiance to ISIS in 2018 and was acknowledged by ISIS as an affiliate in 2019; since 2017, violence associated with the group has led to the deaths of approximately 6,000 civilians, security force members, and suspected ISIS-M militants, and displaced approximately one million persons in northern Mozambique (as of 2025); the group was responsible for orchestrating a series of large-scale and sophisticated attacks resulting in the capture of the port of Mocimboa da Praia, Cabo Delgado Province in August 2020, which it held for a year; in March 2021, it seized the northern Mozambican town of Palma, holding it for four days while killing dozens of civilians and security personnel; in 2021-2022, several African countries sent military troops to assist the Mozambique Government's efforts to defeat the group; these military operations have resulted in setbacks to ISIS-M, including personnel losses and the destruction of some bases and training camps; nevertheless, the group continued to engage in low-intensity attacks in 2025
goals – implement ISIS's strict interpretation of sharia and establish an Islamic state
leadership and organization – led by Abu Yasir HASSAN; reportedly has regional commands; and operates mostly in semi-autonomous cells, although the group has shown the ability to mass fighters for specific attacks
areas of operation – northern Mozambique; primarily Cabo Delgado province; has conducted cross-border attacks in Tanzania
targets, tactics, and weapons – targets civilians, Mozambique military and security forces and other symbols of government authority, foreign private security contractors, and foreign military forces providing assistance to the Mozambique Government; specific targets have included army barracks, police stations, security checkpoints, government buildings, banks, churches, and gas stations; has captured entire villages and towns; attacks characterized by ambushes and complex assaults on military and security forces, murders of gas industry workers and contractors, indiscriminate killings of civilians, including women and children, beheadings, executions, kidnappings, and looting and burning out villages; has been accused of wholesale abductions of women and girls; armed with small arms, machine guns, improvised explosives (IEDs), mortars, and rocket-propelled grenades (RPG); has used motorboats to conduct raids on coastal villages
strength – as of 2025, was estimated to have 300-400 fighters
financial and other support – unclear; the group has targeted banks in some operations; the area's natural resources, including gas, gems, timber, and wildlife present opportunities for fund-raising; in addition, the group has taken control of food supplies in areas under its control and captured weapons from government security forces; has been accused of using child soldiers
designation – placed on the US Department of State's list of Foreign Terrorist Organizations on 10 March 2021

Islamic State of Iraq and ash-Sham – Sinai Province (ISIS-SP)

aka – Islamic State-Sinai Province (IS-SP); ISIS-Sinai Province; ISIS-Sinai; ISIL Sinai Province (ISIL-SP); The State of Sinai; Wilayat Sinai; Islamic State in the Sinai; Ansar Bayt al-Maqdes; Ansar Beit al-Maqdis (ABM); Jamaat Ansar Beit al-Maqdis; Jamaat Ansar Beit al-Maqdis fi Sinaa; Ansar Jerusalem; Supporters of Jerusalem; Supporters of the Holy Place; Allies of the Holy House
history – began as Ansar Bayt al-Maqdis (ABM), which rose to prominence in 2011 following the uprisings in Egypt; ABM was responsible for attacks against Egyptian and Israeli government and security elements and against tourists in Egypt; in November 2014, ABM officially declared allegiance to ISIS; it subsequently conducted a bloody insurgency against Egyptian security forces under the ISIS banner and become one of the most deadly of the ISIS affiliates; the Egyptian Government deployed thousands of military troops and other security personnel to the Sinai to suppress the insurgency; the group continued to be active as of 2025, although it was reported to be significantly weakened by Egyptian counter-terrorism efforts
goals – spread the Islamic caliphate by eliminating the Egyptian government, destroying Israel, and establishing an Islamic emirate in the Sinai
leadership and organization – current leader not available; reportedly has sections or branches for security, military affairs, bomb-making, and media operations
areas of operation – Egypt
targets, tactics, and weapons – typically targets Egyptian security forces, particularly checkpoints, convoys, and bases; conducts ambushes, assassinations, complex attacks involving dozens of attackers, car and suicide bombings, kidnappings, public executions, and road side bombings attacks; conducted large armed assaults on a military base in 2018 and on the Egyptian city of Sheikh Zuweid in 2014; also targets Egyptian Government facilities and officials, oil pipelines and other infrastructure, tourists, religious minorities, government-allied tribes, places of worship, and airliners; two of its most deadly attacks were the 2017 assault by suicide bombers and gunmen on an Egyptian Sufi mosque that killed more than 300 and the 2015 bombing of a Russian airliner from the Egyptian resort town of Sharm el-el-Sheikh, which killed all 231 on board; typically armed with small arms, light and heavy machine guns, rocket-propelled grenades, mortars, car bombs, and improvised explosive devices
strength – estimated in 2023 to have a few hundred members
financial and other support – receives funding from external actors, including core ISIS, and from smuggling; weapons reportedly are smuggled in from Gaza, Sudan, and Libya
designation – placed on the US Department of State's list of Foreign Terrorist Organizations on 9 April 2014

Islamic State of Iraq and ash-Sham – West Africa (ISIS-WA)

aka – Islamic State West Africa Province (ISWAP); Islamic State of Iraq and the Levant-West Africa (ISIL-WA); Islamic State of Iraq and Syria West Africa Province; ISIS West Africa Province; ISIS-West Africa (ISIS-WA); Wilayat Gharb Ifriqiyya
history – formed in 2015-2016 when a faction of Boko Haram broke off and pledged allegiance to ISIS; the split occurred primarily because of the indiscriminate violence Boko Haram inflicted on Muslims; in 2016, began waging an insurgency against the Nigerian Government, overrunning dozens of military bases and killing hundreds of soldiers; by 2019, reportedly controlled hundreds of square miles of territory in the Lake Chad region where it governed according to a strict interpretation of Islamic law and attempted to cultivate support among local civilians by focusing on filling gaps in governance; claimed additional attacks against Nigerian and regional military forces in 2021-2024; during the same period, it also engaged in fighting with Boko Haram and had reportedly far outstripped the group in size and capacity; since 2009, violence associated with Boko Haram and ISIS-WA had killed an estimated 40,000 people, mostly civilians, and displaced more than 2 million persons; as of early 2025, ISIS-W was recognized as the most active ISIS affiliate
goals – implement ISIS's strict interpretation of sharia and replace regional governments with an Islamic state
leadership and organization – not available; Abu Musab al-BARNAWI reportedly killed in 2021 by Nigerian military; has a shura council, as well as military and regional commanders/leaders; probably operates in small units and cells that mass for larger operations
areas of operation – Nigeria (primarily Borno and Yobe States) and the greater Lake Chad region (including the Diffa Region of Niger, the Far North Region in Cameroon, and areas of Chad near Lake Chad)
targets, tactics, and weapons – attacks security forces, state-sponsored civilian defense groups, government targets, infrastructure, and individuals who collaborate with the government; also targets aid workers, Christians, and members of Boko Haram; attacks military bases and mobile military columns; in 2018-2019, it overran more than 20 military bases in northeastern Nigeria, including one assault that resulted in the deaths of some 100 soldiers; in 2022, it claimed responsibility for an attack on a prison in Nigeria's capital Abuja which freed nearly 900 inmates including 60 of its members; employs ambushes, complex ground assaults, hit-and-run attacks, targeted killings, road side bombs, and kidnappings of security forces personnel; fighters typically equipped with small arms, light and heavy machine guns, vehicle mounted weapons, rocket-propelled grenades, mines, rockets, improvised explosive devices (including vehicle-mounted), armored vehicles (including tanks), and weaponized drones
strength – estimated in 2025 to have 8-12,000 active members
financial and other support – receives some funding from core ISIS and local sources, including kidnappings-for-ransom, other criminal activities, taxation, extortion, and some farming activities; utilizes captured vehicles, weapons, and ammunition from the Nigerian military; maintains training camps and publicly advertised a "Caliphate Cadet School" featuring children between 8-16 years old undergoing indoctrination and military-style training; has links to ISIS-Greater Sahara
designation – placed on the US Department of State's list of Foreign Terrorist Organizations on 28 February 2018

Islamic State of Iraq and ash-Sham in Bangladesh (ISB)

aka – ISIS-Bangladesh, Caliphate in Bangladesh; Caliphate's Soldiers in Bangladesh; Soldiers of the Caliphate in Bangladesh; Khalifa's Soldiers in Bengal; Islamic State Bangladesh; Islamic State in Bangladesh; Islamic State in Bengal; Dawlatul Islam Bengal; ISIB; Abu Jandal al-Bangali; Jammat-ul Mujahadeen-Bangladesh; JMB; Neo-JMB; New JMB
history – formed in 2014 out of ISIS's desire to expand to the Indian Subcontinent; the group describes itself as ISIS's official branch in Bangladesh and consists of individuals who defected from Jamaat-ul-Mujahideen Bangladesh and Jund at-Tawhid wal-Khilafah; ISIS-B has killed dozens in mostly smaller attacks, including a US citizen, and wounded more than 200 since its formation; the group was active as of 2023
goals – protect Muslims in Bangladesh from perceived injustices and, ultimately, establish an Islamic caliphate in the Indian subcontinent
leadership and organization – led by Mahadi Hasan Jon; probably operates in a cell-based network
areas of operation – operates in major cities throughout Bangladesh
targets and tactics – primarily targets military and security personnel but also activists, bloggers, academics, religious minorities, and foreigners (particularly Westerners); has attacked restaurants, places of worship, government buildings, and crowds of civilians, typically with small arms, grenades, and improvised explosives devices, including suicide bombers; most deadly attack was a 2016 armed assault on a bakery in Dhaka, where the attackers used small arms, grenades, and machetes to kill 24 people
strength – at least several dozen members as of 2023
financial and other support – has received some support from ISIS; other funding sources not available
designation – placed on the US Department of State's list of Foreign Terrorist Organizations on 28 February 2018

Islamic State of Iraq and ash-Sham in Libya (ISIS-L)

aka – ISIS-Libya, Islamic State-Libya; IS-Libya; Islamic State of Iraq and the Levant in Libya (ISIL-L); Wilayat Barqa; Wilayat Fezzan; Wilayat Tripolitania; Wilayat Tarablus; Wilayat al-Tarabulus; Desert Army; Jaysh al-Sahraa
history – formed in 2014 when then ISIS leader Abu Bakr al-BAGHDADI dispatched operatives from Syria to establish a branch; claimed responsibility for its first operation, a suicide attack on a hotel in Tripoli, in January 2015; from 2015 to 2016, it grew to as many as 6,000 fighters, established a stronghold in Sirte, and expanded operations into Libya's oil producing region; from late 2016 to 2017, the group was driven from Sirte into the desert by Libyan forces, with assistance from the US military, while suffering heavy losses in personnel; since 2018, ISIS-Libya has altered its strategy to what it described as a *nikayah* (war of attrition) of guerrilla warfare and traditional terrorist tactics with small bands of fighters operating out of ungoverned spaces in Libya; it claimed several small-scale attacks against local military and security services in 2020-2021 despite losses to government counterterrorism operations; although weakened, the group in 2025 retained some operational capability and was involved in providing logistics support to ISIS groups in the Sahel and in operational activities such as conducting kidnappings for ransom, including of traffickers
goals – prevent the formation of a reunified Libyan state, secure control over the country's oil resources and, ultimately, establish an Islamic caliphate in Libya
leadership and organization – leadership not available; reportedly operates in cells that are geographically dispersed
areas of operation – Libya; has some mobile desert camps in rural central and southern Libya and is assessed to retain an undetermined number of dormant cells in some coastal cities
targets, tactics, and weapons – targets military and security forces, oil infrastructure, and entities or individuals associated with Libya's competing governments; targets include oil facilities, security checkpoints and police stations, and symbolic state targets such as Libya's electoral commission headquarters and the Ministry of Foreign Affairs; also kidnaps local notables for potential prisoner exchanges or ransom; attacks typically are hit-and-run type and conducted with small arms and suicide bombers; weapons mostly include small arms, rocket-propelled grenades, mortars, light and heavy machine guns, landmines, and improvised explosive devices
strength – estimated in 2024 to have 300-500 fighters

financial and other support – ISIS core has provided ad hoc financial support; additional funding comes from arms smuggling, taxes on illicit trade routes, kidnappings for ransom, and external sources, such as enterprises run by sympathizers, especially in western Libya; has acquired weapons through captured Libyan military stockpiles and smuggling networks
designation – placed on the US Department of State's list of Foreign Terrorist Organizations on 20 May 2016

Islamic State of Iraq and ash-Sham in the Greater Sahara (ISIS-GS)

aka – ISIS in the Greater Sahara; Islamic State in the Greater Sahel; Islamic State of the Greater Sahel or ISGS; Islamic State's Sahel Province or ISSP; ISIS-Sahel; ISIS-Sahel Province; ISIS in the Islamic Sahel; ISIS in the Sahel or ISIS-Sahel
history – emerged in May 2015 when Adnan Abu Walid al-SAHRAWI and his followers split from the al-Qaida-affiliated group al-Murabitoun and pledged allegiance to ISIS; ISIS acknowledged the group in October 2016; subsequently began carrying out attacks in the Sahel region, including one on a joint US-Nigerien military force operating near the Mali-Niger border in October 2017; by February 2018, it was regularly clashing with French military forces and allied local militias operating under the French-sponsored counterterrorism operation known as Operation Barkhane, as well as Burkinabe, Malian, and Nigerien troops; attacks on Nigerien and Malian military bases in late 2019 killed 89 and 54 soldiers, respectively; by 2020, it was fighting with the local al-Qa'ida-aligned coalition known as Jama'at Nusrat al-Islam wal-Muslimin (JNIM) over territory, including control of gold extraction areas and access to buyers; in 2022, was elevated to an ISIS branch and changed its name to ISIS-Sahel; in February 2023, it ambushed a military convoy in northern Burkina Faso, killing more than 70 soldiers; as of 2025, the group had gained strength and ground and was attacking government security forces in Burkina Faso, Mali, and Niger, as well as engaging in periodic clashes with JNIM
goals – replace regional governments with an Islamic state; reportedly has not developed a cohesive, ideologically driven narrative but instead tries to adapt its message to what can garner the most support from local communities
leadership and organization – Mohamed Ibrahim al-Salem al-Shafi'i (aka Aba al-Saharawi or al-Sahrawi); probably operates in small, mobile, geographically dispersed cells or groups with varying levels of autonomy that consolidate for operations; as of 2025, the Nigeria-based Lakurawa group had reportedly pledged allegiance to ISIS-GS
areas of operation – Burkina Faso, Mali, Niger, and to a lesser extent Benin
targets, tactics, and weapons – targets local military and security forces, foreign/international military forces, civilians, ethnic groups, local government officials, humanitarian workers, schools, and entire villages; employs insurgency-type tactics against military and security forces, including ambushes, targeted killings, hit-and-run attacks, mortar attacks, road side bombs, car and truck bombs, suicide bombers, and direct assaults; weapons include assault rifles, light machine guns, motorcycles, trucks mounting machine guns (aka "technicals"), mortars, and improvised explosive devices (IEDs)
strength – estimated in 2024 to have up to 2-3,000 fighters
financial and other support – specific sources not available, but probably originates from smuggling activities, local donations and taxation, attacks on gold mines, kidnapping for ransom, theft, and from other groups operating in the region; most of its weapons probably originate from the black market or are captured after attacks on local security forces; engages in the smuggling of weapons, mostly from facilitation networks in southern Libya; has links with ISIS-West Africa
designation – placed on the US Department of State's list of Foreign Terrorist Organizations on 23 May 2018

Islamic State of Iraq and ash-Sham (ISIS)

aka – al-Qa'ida in Iraq; al-Qa'ida Group of Jihad in Iraq; al-Qa'ida Group of Jihad in the Land of the Two Rivers; al-Qa'ida in Mesopotamia; al-Qa'ida in the Land of the Two Rivers; al-Qa'ida of Jihad in Iraq; al-Qa'ida of Jihad Organization in the Land of the Two Rivers; al-Qa'ida of the Jihad in the Land of the Two Rivers; al-Tawhid; Jam'at al-Tawhid Wa'al-Jihad; Tanzeem Qa'idat al Jihad/Bilad al Raafidaini; Tanzim Qa'idat al-Jihad fi Bilad al-Rafidayn; The Monotheism and Jihad Group; The Organization Base of Jihad/Country of the Two Rivers; The Organization Base of Jihad/Mesopotamia; The Organization of al-Jihad's Base in Iraq; The Organization of al-Jihad's Base in the Land of the Two Rivers; The Organization of al-Jihad's Base of Operations in Iraq; The Organization of al-Jihad's Base of Operations in the Land of the Two Rivers; The Organization of Jihad's Base in the Country of the Two Rivers; al-Zarqawi Network; Islamic State of Iraq; Islamic State of Iraq and al-Sham; Islamic State of Iraq and Syria; ad-Dawla al-Islamiyya fi al-'Iraq wa-sh-Sham; Daesh; Dawla al Islamiya; Al-Furqan Establishment for Media Production; Islamic State; ISIL; ISIS; ISIS-Core; Amaq News Agency; Al Hayat Media Center; Al-Hayat Media Center; Al Hayat
history – formed in the 1990s under the name al-Tawhid wal-Jihad by Jordanian militant Abu Mus'ab al-ZARQAWI to oppose the presence of Western military forces in the Middle East and the West's support for, and the existence of, Israel; in late 2004, ZARQAWI pledged allegiance to al-Qa'ida (AQ) and the group became known as al-Qa'ida in Iraq (AQI); ZARQAWI led AQI against US and Coalition Forces in Iraq until his death in June 2006; in October 2006, AQI renamed itself the Islamic State in Iraq; in 2013, it adopted the moniker ISIS to express regional ambitions and expanded operations to Syria where it established control of a large portion of eastern Syria; in June 2014, then ISIS leader Abu Bakr al-BAGHDADI declared a worldwide Islamic caliphate with its capital in Raqqa, Syria; by 2015, ISIS held an area in Iraq and Syria with an estimated population of between 8 and 12 million, including the Iraqi city of Mosul; it imposed a brutal version of Islamic law in the areas under its control and became known for brutality against perceived enemies, its large contingent of foreign fighters, and a substantial social media presence; by the end of 2017, the group had lost control of its largest population centers in both Iraq and Syria, including Mosul and Raqqa, to US and allied military forces; ISIS lost its final piece of territory in Baghuz, Syria in March 2019; it has since transitioned to an insurgency, reverting to guerrilla warfare and more traditional terrorist tactics, developing sleeper cells, and assimilating into the broader population in Iraq and Syria where it continued to maintain a presence and conduct operations as of 2025
goals – replace the world order with a global Islamic state based in Iraq and Syria, expand its branches and networks globally, and rule according to ISIS's strict interpretation of Islamic law; in Iraq and Syria, it seeks to reestablish itself as a viable insurgency that is capable of seizing and controlling territory
leadership and organization – Abu Hafs al-Hashimi al-Quraishi (likely a nom de guerre) named leader in 2023 after predecessor killed; the top leader (emir) and a senior shura council determine the group's strategic direction and appoints the heads of provinces (*wilayat*); an "appointed (or delegated) committee" and up to 14 sub-bureaus or offices (*dawawin*) are reportedly charged with administrative duties, including security, explosives manufacturing, finances, religious matters, recruitment, military operations, training and education, media functions, resources and plunder, etc.; the group typically operates in small cells or groups in Iraq and Syria, but can organize in greater numbers for specific operations; outside of Iraq and Syria, ISIS-Core has adopted a flatter, more networked and decentralized structure, giving greater operational autonomy to its external branches, networks, and claimed provinces; ISIS-Core has relied on its General Directorate of Provinces (GDP) offices to provide funding and operational guidance for these branches, networks, and provinces; GDP offices include: the al-Furqan Office (West Africa and the Sahel); the Dhu al-Nurayn Office (North Africa and Sudan); al-Karrar Office (East, Central, and Southern Africa, and Yemen regions); the Afghanistan-based al-Siddiq Office (South, Central, and Southeast Asia); and the Iraq-based Bilad al-Rafidayn Office
areas of operation – ISIS-Core operations remain predominately in Iraq and Syria; ISIS has about 20 external branches, networks, or wilayat (provinces, governorates) in more than 20 countries: Algeria, Azerbaijan, Bangladesh, the Caucasus (Russia), Central Africa (the Democratic

Republic of the Congo, Mozambique), East Asia (Philippines, Indonesia), Greater Sahara (tri-border area of Burkina Faso, Mali, Niger), India, Libya, Khorasan (Afghanistan), Pakistan, Palestine (Israel), the Sahel (Mali), Sinai Peninsula (Egypt), Saudi Arabia, Somalia, Tunisia, Turkey, West Africa (northeastern Nigeria, southeastern Niger, northern Cameroon, areas of Chad around Lake Chad), and Yemen; local terrorist groups in other countries, such as Lebanon and Sudan, have pledged allegiance to ISIS; has supporters, sympathizers, and associates worldwide and has inspired or conducted attacks in Australia, Belgium, France, Germany, Iran, Maldives, Russia, Spain, Sri Lanka, Sweden, Tajikistan, Turkey, the UK, and the US; authorities in other countries, including, but not exclusive to, Austria, Brazil, Bulgaria, Canada, Greece, Israel, Italy, Jordan, Lebanon, Malaysia, and the Netherlands have arrested ISIS members or supporters or disrupted plots linked to ISIS; maintains a strong online presence and continuously calls for attacks against Western countries and their interests around the world; individuals inspired by its ideology may conduct operations without direction from the ISIS's central leadership
targets, tactics, and weapons – targets governments or groups that oppose its hardline Islamist ideology, including military forces and security services, government officials, perceived Sunni rivals, Westerners, and religious and ethnic minorities; typically targets security forces in Iraq and Syria, as well as tribal and civic leaders and other symbols of government; has also targeted infrastructure in Iraq, such as electrical towers; known for indiscriminate killings, mass executions, political assassinations, torture, kidnappings, rape and sexual slavery, forced marriages and religious conversions, conscripting children, publishing videos of beheadings, and using civilians as human shields; has engaged in the systematic destruction of antiquities, places of worship, monasteries, and other elements of the cultural heritage of ancient communities; attacks places of worship, shopping centers and markets, tourist sites, hotels, concert venues, restaurants, train stations, nightclubs, government buildings, and infrastructure targets; attacks on civilians typically involve the use of small arms, vehicle bombs, explosive vests, and ramming vehicles into crowds of people; employs insurgent/guerrilla-style hit-and-run, and terrorist attacks against military and security forces that include the use of ambushes, snipers, complex ground/military assaults, mortar and rocket attacks, road side bombs, and suicide devices; possesses a wide variety of weapons, including small arms, light and heavy machine guns, rocket-propelled grenades, mortars, rockets, man-portable air defense systems (MANPADS), anti-tank guided missiles, and a variety of improvised explosive devices, including unmanned aerial vehicles (UAVs) armed with explosives
strength – estimated in 2024 to have up to 7,000 members in Iraq and Syria
financial and other support – raises funds through ad hoc criminal activities, particularly extortion activities, kidnapping for ransom, robberies, and smuggling; also receives funds through private donations, crowd-sourcing, online humanitarian appeals, and investments in legitimate businesses; prior to 2019, received virtually of its funding from oil sales, taxation, and selling confiscated goods within areas it controlled in Iraq and Syria; the group currently holds no territory, which has significantly reduced its ability to generate, store, and transfer revenue, but it continues to generate some revenue from criminal activities through its clandestine networks and provides financial support and guidance to its network of global branches and affiliates; ISIS has armed itself with weapons it has captured, purchased through local arms trafficking networks, and produced on its own; also recruits members, supporters, and sympathizers online through social media platforms
designation – predecessor organization al-Qa'ida in Iraq (AQI) was placed on the US Department of State's list of Foreign Terrorist Organizations on 17 December 2004

Islamic State of Iraq and ash-Sham: self-proclaimed ISIS branches, networks, and provinces (non-FTO designated)
note: this appendix provides short descriptions of identified or self-proclaimed ISIS branches, networks, and provinces that have not been designated by the US State Department as Foreign Terrorist Organizations
Islamic State of Iraq and ash-Sham – Algeria: the Islamic State declared the establishment of a province in Algeria (Wilayat al-Jazair) in 2014; the group includes elements of a local terrorist organization known as Jund al-Khilafa; goal is to replace the Algerian Government with an Islamic state; targets security forces, local government figures, and Western interests; largely defunct due to pressure from Algerian security forces, although ISIS-Core claimed responsibility for a February 2020 attack on an Algerian military base near the border with Mali; the group historically maintained an operational and recruitment presence mostly in the northeastern part of the country
Islamic State of Iraq and ash-Sham network in Azerbaijan: *ISIS declared a new network in Azerbaijan in 2019; additional information not available*
Islamic State of Iraq and ash-Sham – Caucasus Province: ISIS-Caucasus Province (ISIS-CP; aka Wilayat Qawqaz) was announced in 2015; it grew out of the former al-Qa'ida-affiliated Islamic Emirate of the Caucasus, which suffered from losses to Russian counterterrorism operations, leadership disputes, and defections to ISIS; ISIS-CP claimed responsibility for its first attack against a Russian Army barracks in 2015 and additional attacks on local security forces in 2020, including a suicide bombing; in the 2020s, Russian security services have conducted multiple operations against suspected ISIS militants in the Caucasus; ISIS-CP operates in the North Caucasus area of the Russian Federation between the Black Sea and Caspian Sea; typically has conducted attacks against local security and military forces, as well as non-Muslim civilians, with small arms, improvised explosives, and knives
Islamic State of Iraq and ash-Sham – India: the Islamic State-India (aka ISI; Islamic State-Hind; Wilayah of Hind) was announced in 2019 when ISIS-Core claimed it restructured the group's Khorasan Province and created separate provinces for affiliated elements operating in India and Pakistan; the announcement followed an attack claimed by ISIS on Indian security forces in India-administered Kashmir; ISI is reportedly dominated by Kashmiri jihadists and has conducted several additional low-scale attacks targeting Indian security forces in Kashmir
Islamic State of Iraq and ash-Sham – East Asia networks in Indonesia: comprises a loose network of ISIS affiliates, cells, and supporters known locally as Jemaah Anshorut Daulau (JAD); JAD has the goal of replacing the Indonesian Government with an Islamic state and has attacked security forces and Christians, including a series of suicide bombings against three churches in 2018 that killed more than 30 civilians; JAD includes former members of the FTO-designated group Jemaah Ansharut Tauhid (JAT; aka Jemmah Ansharut Tauhid; Laskar 99), which disbanded in 2015 to join JAD (some members reportedly joined al-Qa'ida); in recent years, Indonesian security forces have disrupted several planned attacks by JAD and arrested numerous members
Islamic State of Iraq and ash-Sham – Pakistan: ISIS announced in 2019 that it restructured the group's Khorasan Province and created separate provinces for ISIS-affiliates operating in Pakistan and India; ISIS in Pakistan operates mostly in Balochistan and northern Sindh provinces and chiefly targets non-Muslims and the local Shia population, particularly the Hazaras; it claimed several attacks Baluchistan in 2020 and 2021; ISIS has claimed additional attacks in Pakistan, including a March 2022 suicide bombing on a Shia mosque in Peshawar that killed 64, but it is unclear if the attack was carried out by the Pakistan branch or ISIS-Khorasan
Islamic State of Iraq and ash-Sham – Somalia: formed in 2015-2016; it is a splinter group of al-Shabaab and reportedly founded by former al-Shabaab commander Abdulqadir MUMIN (alt. Abdul Qadir Mumin) in 2015-2016; the group operates primarily in the remote mountains of the Bari area of the semi-autonomous Puntland region and targets Somali Government and security forces, Puntland security forces, African Union peacekeepers, and al-Shabaab elements through low-level attacks using small arms and improvised explosive devices, as well as targeted assassinations; it has also employed unmanned aerial systems for reconnaissance and some explosive deployment; ISIS in Somalia has reportedly gained prominence as a financial support hub for other Islamic State affiliates in Africa; it was estimated in 2025 to have 600-800 fighters, many of which were foreigners from the region, North Africa, and the Arabian Peninsula

Islamic State of Iraq and ash-Sham cell in Sudan: *operational since 2019 and headed by Abu Bakr al-Iraqi who was under orders from ISIS core to establish a logistical and financial base in the Sudan; in 2024, the cell was assessed to have 100-200 members, who acted as facilitators for logistical movements and transactions*

Islamic State of Iraq and ash-Sham network in Tunisia: *a network of cells, supporters, and Islamic militant groups in Tunisia claiming allegiance to ISIS, including Jund al-Kilafah (JAK or "Soldiers of the Caliphate"); goal is to replace the Tunisian Government with an Islamic state and implement ISIS's strict interpretation of sharia; since 2015, the network has conducted periodic attacks against security forces and tourist sites frequented by Westerners, such as a resort in Sousse and a museum in Tunis; attacks have included suicide bombings, improvised explosive devices mounted on motorcycles, stabbings, targeted assassinations, and bank robberies; the network claimed an attack in 2021 that killed four soldiers and Tunisian security forces disrupted at least two terrorist cells linked to ISIS in 2022; the network is mostly active in the mountainous region along the border with Algeria, particularly the Chaambi Mountains near the city of Kasserine*

Islamic State of Iraq and ash-Sham – Turkey: publicly announced in 2019 when ISIS released a video of a group of fighters in Turkey pledging allegiance to then-ISIS leader al-BAGHDADI and declaring a new province (wilayat) in Turkey; the speaker threatened both Turkey and the US while the fighters in the video were armed with assault rifles, grenades, light machine guns, and rocket-propelled grenade launchers; Turkey served as a transit point for foreign fighters traveling to Syria to join the self-declared Islamic State (IS) caliphate and participate in the Syrian civil war; prior to the declaration of a province in Turkey, the Turkish government suspected ISIS of responsibility for numerous attacks, including suicide bombings at Ataturk Airport in June 2016 and at a wedding in August 2016, as well as a shooting at a nightclub in January 2017; following the collapse of the IS caliphate in 2019, ISIS continued to see Turkey as a transit hub for smuggling fighters, funding, supplies, and weapons into Syria; as of 2024, Turkish security forces continued to conduct counter-terrorism operations against ISIS and militants linked to the group

Islamic State of Iraq and ash-Sham – Yemen: publicly announced in 2015 after a self-proclaimed ISIS affiliate calling itself "Wilayat Sana'a" claimed responsibility for a mosque bombing in Yemen that killed approximately 140 people; goal is to replace the ruling Yemeni Government and the Houthi rival government with an Islamic state; after 2015, it carried out hundreds of attacks against Yemeni security forces, Yemeni Government facilities and personnel, Houthi forces, Shia Muslims, and the local al-Qa'ida affiliate (al-Qa'ida in the Arabian Peninsula or AQAP); attacks included suicide bombers, car/truck bombs, road side bombs, ambushes, armed ground assaults, kidnappings, and targeted assassinations; operational primarily in south and central Yemen; in recent years, the group reportedly has suffered heavy losses in fighting with AQAP and Houthi forces and experienced internal disputes and leadership problems; as of 2025, it was assessed to be degraded in capabilities and strength (estimated to have fewer than 100 fighters) and was minimally active

Islamic State of Iraq and ash-Sham-Khorasan Province (ISIS-K)

aka – Islamic State of Iraq and Syria-Khorasan; Islamic State in Iraq and the Levant-Khurasan (ISIL-K); Islamic State Khurasan (IS, ISK, ISISK); Islamic State of Iraq and Levant in Khorasan Province (ISKP); Islamic State's Khorasan Province; ISIL-Khorasan; Wilayat al-Khorasan; Wilayat Khurasan; ISIL's South Asia Branch; South Asian Chapter of ISIL

history – formed in 2015 primarily from former members of Tehrik-e Taliban Pakistan, the Afghan Taliban, and the Islamic Movement of Uzbekistan; ISIS-K frequently fought with the Afghan Taliban over control of territory and resources while conducting an insurgency against the Afghan Government and foreign military forces; the group suffered heavy losses of fighters, leaders, and territory to Afghan and US counterterrorism operations, as well as to the Taliban, but retained the ability to orchestrate attacks, recruit, and replenish leadership positions; since the fall of the Afghan Government to the Taliban and the US/Coalition military withdrawal in August 2021, ISIS-K has conducted dozens of attacks against the Taliban; since 2022, it has also claimed attacks against targets outside of Afghanistan, including in Pakistan, Russia, Tajikistan, and Uzbekistan; the group is assessed to be one of ISIS's most lethal branches and the most serious terrorist threat in Afghanistan, as well as the wider region

goals – portrays itself as the primary rival to the Taliban and seeks to portray the Taliban as incapable of providing security in the country; also seeks to undermine the relationship between the Taliban and neighboring countries; ultimately seeks to establish an Islamic caliphate in Afghanistan, Pakistan, and parts of Central Asia, including Iran

leadership and organization – reportedly continues to be Sanaullah GHAFARI (aka Shahab al-Muhajir); operates in small cells; ISIS restructured the Khorasan Province in May 2019, when it announced the creation of separate provinces for India and Pakistan

areas of operation – Afghanistan, Pakistan, and Central Asia (note - "Khorasan" is a historical region that encompassed northeastern Iran, southern Turkmenistan, and northern Afghanistan); in 2024, it claimed attacks in Afghanistan, Iran, Pakistan, Russia, and Turkey

targets, tactics, and weapons – targets the Taliban, the Haqqani Network, Shia Muslims (particularly the Hazaras community), followers of Sufi Islam, security and military personnel, and diplomatic and infrastructure targets; known for indiscriminate and large-scale attacks against civilians in Afghanistan and Pakistan; its targets have included Shia religious sites, neighborhoods, and other gathering places, diplomatic facilities in Kabul, an Afghan prison, Kabul airport, a voter registration center, a television station, a hospital, a concert hall, and an election rally; in 2022, it claimed responsibility for a suicide bombing attack on a Shia mosque in Pakistan that killed 63 persons, and in August 2021, it conducted a bombing attack on the Kabul Airport that killed 13 US military personnel and 169 Afghan civilians; in March 2024, it claimed responsibility for an attack on a Moscow concert hall that left more than 140 people dead; it has employed a variety of insurgent- and terrorist-type tactics, including ambushes, assassinations, hit-and-run attacks/raids/military-style assaults, roadside bombings and other improvised explosive device (IEDs) operations, mortar/rocket attacks, and suicide bombings; fighters are typically armed with small arms, light and heavy machine guns, mortars, rockets, and various IEDs, including car bombs, road side bombs, and suicide vests

strength – estimated in 2025 have approximately 2,000 fighters

financial and other support – ISIS-K receives periodic funding from ISIS-Core; additional funds come from illicit criminal commerce, donations (often through the use of cryptocurrencies), ransoms, taxes, and extortion on the local population and businesses

designation – placed on the US Department of State's list of Foreign Terrorist Organizations on 14 January 2016

Jaish-e-Mohammed (JeM)

aka – the Army of Mohammed; Mohammed's Army; Tehrik ul-Furqaan; Khuddam-ul-Islam; Khudamul Islam; Kuddam e Islami; Jaish-i-Mohammed

history – founded in 2000 by former senior Harakat ul-Mujahideen leader Masood AZHAR upon his release from prison in India; JeM subsequently claimed responsibility for multiple attacks in India-administered Kashmir, India, and Pakistan; after 2008, it fought US and Coalition forces in Afghanistan until the Taliban came to power in 2021; JeM maintains close relations with the Taliban and al-Qa'ida in Afghanistan; it has conducted several attacks against Indian security forces in Jammu and Kashmir since 2018, including a suicide bombing in the city of Pulwama that killed 40 security police in 2019; JeM was active as of 2025

goals – drive India from the disputed region of Kashmir and establish Pakistani sovereignty

leadership and organization – led by Maulana Mohammed Masood AZHAR Alvi (aka Wali Adam Isah), with his brother and deputy, Mufti Abdul Rauf AZHAR Alvi, as well as a seven-member executive committee

areas of operation – Indian and Pakistan

targets, tactics, and weapons – attacks Indian military, security, and government officials, personnel, bases, and buildings; periodically attacks Pakistani government and security personnel; attempted to assassinate former Pakistani President Pervez MUSHARRAF in 2003; has assaulted and kidnapped Christians and foreigners; typically employs small arms, light and heavy machine guns, rocket-propelled grenades, mines, improvised explosive devices, suicide bombers, and car bombs
strength – estimated in 2023 to have about 500 members
financial and other support – to avoid asset seizures by the Pakistani Government, JEM since 2007 has withdrawn funds from bank accounts and invested in legal businesses, such as commodity trading, real estate, and the production of consumer goods; also collects funds through donation requests, sometimes using charitable causes to solicit donations
designation – placed on the US Department of State's list of Foreign Terrorist Organizations on 26 December 2001

Jama'at Nusrat al-Islam wal-Muslimin (JNIM)

aka – Jamaat Nosrat al-Islam wal-Mouslimin; Group for the Support of Islam and Muslims; Group to Support Islam and Muslims; GSIM; GNIM; Nusrat al-Islam wal-Muslimeen
history – formed in 2017 when the Mali Branch of al-Qa'ida in the Islamic Maghreb (AQIM), al-Murabitoun, Ansar al-Dine, and the Macina Liberation Front (FLM; aka Katiba Macina or Macina Battalion/Brigade) agreed to work together as a coalition; describes itself as al-Qa'ida's official branch in Mali and has pledged allegiance to al-Qa'ida leader Ayman al-ZAWAHIRI and deceased AQIM emir Abdelmalek DROUKDEL; has conducted hundreds of attacks against local and international security troops, as well as some civilian targets, including a passenger boat in Mali in 2023; attempts to displace the authority of local governments in the areas where it operates, including providing services through its own self-described non-profit organizations, conflict arbitration, policing, and community dispute resolution; engaged in fighting over territory with the Islamic State of Iraq and ash-Sham in the Greater Sahara (ISIS-GS), although there have been periods of reported cooperation and local truces; the group continued to conduct attacks into 2025 and is recognized as one of al-Qa'ida's most active affiliates
goals – unite all terrorist groups in the Sahel, eliminate Western influence in the region, force out all international military forces, and establish an Islamic state centered on Mali
leadership and organization – led by Iyad ag Ghali (alt. Iyad Ag Ghaly; note - also the leader of Ansar al-Dine); JNIM portrays itself as broad alliance of jihadist groups; in recent years, it reportedly has developed from a loose coalition to a more developed formal structure with centralized leadership, regional commanders, and local commanders; has a dedicated media unit known as az-Zalaqah; coalition members and affiliates reportedly maintain their existing leadership and organizational structures
areas of operation – Benin, Burkina Faso, Côte d'Ivoire, Mali, Niger, and Togo
targets, tactics, and weapons – targets foreign and local military and security forces, as well as various non-state armed groups, including pro-government militias and rival jihadist militants; has attacked military bases and outposts, security checkpoints, patrols, and convoys; also targets other symbols of the government's authority, including local leaders, civil servants, schools, teachers, and infrastructure, such as bridges, as well as foreigners; typically employs insurgent-type tactics, including hit and run attacks, raids, and complex assaults, assassinations, kidnappings, ambushes, bombings, improvised explosive devises, and mortar attacks; typically employs small arms, machine guns, rocket-propelled grenades, improvised explosive devices (IEDs), armed drones, mortars, rockets, suicide bombers, and car bombs
strength – assessed in 2024 to have 5-6,000 fighters; in July 2024, it reportedly mustered more than 1,000 fighters in an attack on a Togolese military base
financial and other support – receives funding through kidnappings-for-ransom, cattle rustling, extortion, protection taxes on local residents, and from smugglers who pay a tax in exchange for safe transit through JNIM-controlled trafficking routes in Mali; has attacked gold mines in areas outside government control and used the profits to recruit new members and buy weapons; equipped with arms captured from local military forces and from the black market
designation – placed on the US Department of State's list of Foreign Terrorist Organizations on 6 September 2018

Jama'atu Ansarul Muslimina Fi Biladis-Sudan (Ansaru)

aka – Ansarul Muslimina Fi Biladis Sudan; Vanguards for the Protection of Muslims in Black Africa; JAMBS; Jama'atu Ansaril Muslimina Fi Biladis Sudan
history – formed in January 2012 as a breakaway faction of Boko Haram in the aftermath of a January 2012 Boko Haram attack in the city of Kano, Nigeria, that resulted in the deaths of at least 180 people, mostly Muslims; the Ansaru faction objected to Boko Haram's attacks on fellow Muslims and killing non-Muslims who posed no threat to Muslims; claimed a kidnapping in 2013 and did not claim any further attacks until claiming responsibility for several in 2020, including two attacks on the Nigerian Army that resulted in the deaths of more than 60 Nigerian soldiers; the group announced its reemergence in late 2019; in January 2022, the group publicly announced that it had pledged loyalty to al-Qa'ida in the Islamic Maghreb (AQIM); active as of 2025
goals – defend Muslims throughout Africa by fighting against the Nigerian Government and international interests; rid Nigeria of Western influence and establish an Islamic state in Nigeria
leadership and organization – reportedly led by Abu Usama ANSARI; previously was under Khalid al-BARNAWI until he was captured by the Nigerian Army in 2016; leads through a shura, but information on the group's organizational structure is otherwise not available
areas of operation – operates in the northwest and north central regions of Nigeria, particularly Kaduna State, including the Benin-Niger-Nigeria tri-border area; also has reportedly taken part in al-Qa'ida operations in the Sahel
targets, tactics, and weapons – targets Nigerian Government officials and security/military forces; also kidnaps and kills foreigners, especially Westerners and abducts individuals with ties to potential ransom payers; uses small arms, light weapons, and explosives to carry out coordinated attacks, including ambushes and hit-and-run assaults; reportedly cooperating with some armed gangs operating in northwest Nigeria, including providing weapons
strength – not available; has reportedly absorbed some former Boko Haram fighters
financial and other support – unclear, although some funding probably is generated from kidnappings for ransom and cattle rustling; the group reportedly received training and weapons from al-Qa'ida elements in Mali, as well as arms from smugglers operating in the Sahel
designation – placed on the US Department of State's list of Foreign Terrorist Organizations on 14 November 2013

Jaysh al Adl (Jundallah)

aka – Jeysh al-adl, Army of Justice; Jaish ul-Adl, Jaish al-Adl, Jaish Aladl, Jeish al-Adl; Jundullah; Jondullah; Jundollah; Jondollah; Jondallah; Army of God (God's Army); Baloch Peoples Resistance Movement (BPRM); People's Resistance Movement of Iran (PMRI); Jonbesh-i Moqavemat-i-Mardom-i Iran; Popular Resistance Movement of Iran; Soldiers of God; Fedayeen-e-Islam; Former Jundallah of Iran
history – formed in 2002 under the name Jundallah as an anti-Iranian Sunni Muslim armed group; founder and then-leader Abdulmalik RIGI was captured and executed by Iranian authorities in 2010; the group has engaged in numerous attacks on Iranian civilians, government officials, and

security personnel; Jundallah adopted the name Jaysh al Adl in 2012 and has since claimed responsibility for attacks under that name; it claimed multiple attacks against Iranian security forces in 2023 and 2024
goals – stated goals are to secure recognition of Balochi cultural, economic, and political rights from the Iranian government; procure greater autonomy for Balochis in Iran and Pakistan
leadership and organization – Abdolrahim Mullahzadeh (aka Salahuddin Farooqi); reportedly has branches based on regions of Iran and Pakistan where it is active
areas of operation – Afghanistan, Iran, and Pakistan; operates primarily in the province of Sistan va Baluchestan of southeastern Iran and the Baloch areas of Afghanistan and Pakistan
targets, tactics, and weapons – primarily targets Iranian security forces but also government officials and Shia civilians; attacks include ambushes, assassinations, assaults, car bombings, hit-and-run attacks, kidnappings, and suicide bombings; one of its most deadly attacks was a February 2019 suicide car bombing of a bus carrying Islamic Revolutionary Guard Corps personnel that killed 27; it also claimed an attack which killed 11 Iranian police officers in December 2023; weapons include small arms, light weapons, and various improvised explosive devices such as suicide vests and car bombs
strength – not available
financial and other support – not available
designation – placed on the US Department of State's list of Foreign Terrorist Organizations on 4 November 2010

Jaysh Rijal al-Tariq al Naqshabandi (JRTN)

aka – Jaysh Rijal al-Tariq al-Naqshabandi; Army of the Men of the Naqshbandi Order; Armed Men of the Naqshabandi Order; Naqshbandi Army; Naqshabandi Army; Men of the Army of al-Naqshbandia Way; Jaysh Rajal al-Tariqah al-Naqshbandia; JRTN; JRN; AMNO
history – emerged in December 2006 as an Arab secular Ba'athist nationalistic armed group in response to SADDAM Husayn's execution; consisted largely of Iraqi Sunni Muslims following Naqshabandi Sufi Islam ideals; between 2006 and the 2011 withdrawal of US forces from Iraq, claimed responsibility for numerous attacks on US bases and personnel; in 2014, elements joined forces with ISIS in opposition to the Iraqi government and assisted with the taking of Mosul, but fissures later emerged between the two factions; some elements splintered off, but the majority of JRTN was subsumed by ISIS; current status unavailable; has not claimed responsibility for any attacks since 2016
goals – end external influence in Iraq and, ultimately, overthrow the Iraqi Government to install a secular Ba'athist state within the internationally recognized borders of Iraq
leadership and organization – not available
areas of operation – Iraq
strength – not available
targets, tactics, and weapons – targeted Iraqi Government military and security forces and Iraqi Kurds who belong to any of the separatist Kurdish groups; also targeted US military personnel from 2006 to 2011; used small arms, light and heavy machine guns, artillery rockets, various improvised explosive devices, including roadside and vehicle-borne bombs
financial resources – received funding from former members of the SADDAM regime, major tribal figures in Iraq, and contributions from Gulf-based sympathizers
designation – placed on the US Department of State's list of Foreign Terrorist Organizations on 30 September 2015

Jemaah Islamiya (JI)

aka – Jemaa Islamiyah, Jema'a Islamiyah, Jemaa Islamiyya, Jema'a Islamiyya, Jemaa Islamiyyah, Jema'a Islamiyyah, Jemaah Islamiah, Jema'ah Islamiyah, Jemaah Islamiyyah, Jema'ah Islamiyyah, Jama'a Assalafiyah Lidda'wa Wal Jihad, Islamic Congregation, Salafi Group for Call and Holy War, Jemaah Islamia, al-Qa'ida Indonesia
history – has roots in the Darul Islam movement that emerged in Indonesia in the 1940s to resist the country's post-colonial government, which it viewed as too secular; JI's earliest efforts to organize date back to the late 1960s and early 1970s under co-founders Abu Bukar BA'ASYIR and Abdullah SUNGKAR; sent fighters to Afghanistan in the 1980s during the war with the Soviet Union; gained international notoriety in 2002 for the suicide bombing of a nightclub on the resort island of Bali that killed more than 200 people; in subsequent years, Indonesian authorities killed or captured several hundred JI operatives, including several senior leaders; however, JI remained active in recruiting and cultivating support through religious boarding schools, mosques, print publications, the internet, media outlets, and charitable organizations that are fronts for the organization; sent fighters to conflicts in Iraq, the Philippines, and Syria for training and battlefield experience while clandestinely building a paramilitary force; affiliated with al-Qa'ida and has ties with the Abu Sayaf Group in the Philippines; did not claim responsibility for any attacks between 2016 and 2024, although it remained active; in June 2024, senior JI leaders declared in a video that they were disbanding the organization, and a majority of the group's estimated 6,000 members reportedly supported the decision
goals – stated goal is to create an Islamic state comprising Malaysia, Singapore, Indonesia, and the southern Philippines
leadership and organization – current leadership not available; has a shura council, a paramilitary wing, and regional units known as *mantiqi*, which are responsible for administration and operations; each *mantiqi* is divided into smaller districts known as *wakalah*
areas of operation – operates throughout Indonesia; reportedly strongest in Java; has operated in the Philippines, Malaysia, and Singapore
targets, tactics, and weapons – targets Christians and Western interests, particularly tourist sites such as nightclubs and hotels; the majority of its victims have been civilians; attackers historically used small arms and improvised explosive devices, including car bombs and suicide vests
strength – estimated in 2024 to have up to 6,000 members
financial and other support – fundraises through membership donations and criminal and business activities, including cultivating palm oil plantations; has received financial, ideological, and logistical support from Middle Eastern contacts and illegitimate charities and organizations; collects cash remittances from Indonesians abroad; members have received weapons and explosives training in Afghanistan, Iraq, Pakistan, the Philippines, and Syria
designation – placed on the US Department of State's list of Foreign Terrorist Organizations on 23 October 2002

Kata'ib al-Imam Ali

designated on 17 September 2025; additional information to follow

Kata'ib Hizballah (KH)

aka – Hizballah Brigades; Hizballah Brigades in Iraq; Hizballah Brigades-Iraq; Kata'ib Hezbollah; Khata'ib Hezbollah; Khata'ib Hizballah; Khattab Hezballah; Hizballah Brigades-Iraq of the Islamic Resistance in Iraq; Islamic Resistance in Iraq; Kata'ib Hizballah Fi al-Iraq; Katibat Abu Fathel al-A'abas; Katibat Zayd Ebin Ali; Katibut Karbalah; Brigades (or Battalions) of the Party of God

history – formed in 2007 from several predecessor networks and former members of the Badr Organization as an Iraqi Shia militia and political organization; KH fought against US and Coalition forces from 2007 to 2011 and sent members to Syria to fight alongside Lebanese Hizballah and Syrian Government forces beginning in 2012; it fought in Iraq against the Islamic State of Iraq and ash-Sham (ISIS) as a member of the Popular Mobilization Committee and Affiliated Forces (PMC or PMF), an umbrella group of mostly Shia militia groups, and was accused of extrajudicial killings and abductions of Iraqi Sunni Muslims during this period; in 2018, its affiliated political party (Independent Popular Gathering) joined the Al Fatah (Victory) Alliance, a political coalition primarily comprised of parties affiliated with Iranian-backed Shia militias; in 2019 and early 2020, it conducted several attacks against US military bases and participated in an assault on the US Embassy in Baghdad; KH was also involved in attacking and abducting anti-government protesters in Baghdad; the organization continued to be active in 2025, including attacks on US forces, typically using front names or proxy groups to obfuscate its involvement in attacks; KH has strong ties to the Iranian Revolutionary Guard Corps (IRGC) and recognizes Ayatollah KHAMENEI, the Supreme Leader of Iran, as its spiritual leader
goals – overthrow the Iraqi Government to install a government based on Shia Muslim laws and precepts; eliminate US influence in Iraq
leadership and organization – led by a shura council, with individuals reportedly selected by the IRGC; secretary general of the council is Ahmad Mohsen Faraj al-HAMIDAWI (aka Abu Hussein, Abu Zalata, Abu Zeid); shura council members are responsible for special military operations, military/paramilitary forces, funding and logistics, civil affairs, media, social/cultural affairs, and administration; KH fighters comprise three brigades of the PMC's paramilitary forces (aka Popular Mobilization Forces, PMF), the 45th, 46th, and 47th
areas of operation – Iraq; participated in the Syrian civil war
targets, tactics, and weapons – targets ISIS fighters, Sunni Muslim civilians, rival Shia factions, and US personnel and interests; employs both guerrilla-style and terrorist tactics, including hit-and-run assaults, ambushes, mortar and rocket attacks, roadside bombs, car bombs, targeted killings/assassinations, sniping, and abductions; has been accused of torturing and executing Sunni civilians, as well as looting and burning Sunni homes; fighters are equipped with small arms, machine guns, rockets, mortars, man-portable air defense systems (MANPADs), improvised explosive devices, rocket-propelled grenades, anti-aircraft guns, artillery, recoilless rifles, light tactical vehicles (Humvees), truck-mounted weapons (aka "technicals"), armed unmanned aerial vehicles/drones, and armored vehicles
strength – estimated in 2023 to have as many as 30,000 members
financial and other support – receives funding, logistical support, intelligence, training, and weapons from the IRGC-Qods Force and Lebanese Hizballah; solicits donations online and through a pro-Iran television channel; also raises funds through criminal activities, including kidnappings-for-ransom, smuggling, and taxing/extortion of activities in areas where the group is dominant; it also has legitimate business enterprises, such as property holdings and investments
designation – placed on the US Department of State's list of Foreign Terrorist Organizations on 2 July 2009

Kata'ib Sayyid al-Shuhada

designated on 17 September 2025; additional information to follow

Kurdistan Workers Party (PKK)

aka – Kongra-Gel; the Kurdistan Freedom and Democracy Congress; the Freedom and Democracy Congress of Kurdistan; KADEK; Partiya Karkeran Kurdistan; the People's Defense Force; Halu Mesru Savunma Kuvveti; Kurdistan People's Congress; People's Congress of Kurdistan; KONGRAGEL, KGK
history – founded by Abdullah ÖCALAN in 1978 as a Marxist-Leninist separatist organization comprised primarily of Turkish Kurds; the PKK launched a rural campaign of violence in 1984 which expanded to include urban terrorism in the early 1990s; fighting with Turkish security forces peaked in the mid-1990s with an estimated 40,000 casualties, the destruction of thousands of villages in the largely Kurdish southeast and east of Turkey, and the displacement of hundreds of thousands of Kurds; following his capture in 1999, ÖCALAN ordered members to refrain from violence and requested dialogue with the Turkish government; PKK foreswore violence until 2004, when its militant wing took control, renounced the self-imposed cease-fire, and began conducting attacks from bases within Iraq; in 2009, the Turkish Government and the PKK resumed peace negotiations, but talks broke down after the PKK carried out an attack in July 2011 that left 13 Turkish soldiers dead; between 2012 and 2015, negotiations resumed but ultimately broke down owing partly to domestic political pressures and the war in Syria; clashes with Turkish security forces after 2015 occurred largely in the country's rural southeast, northern Iraq, and northern Syria, and are estimated to have caused the deaths of as many as 7,000 PKK members, Turkish security forces personnel, and civilians; in March 2025, the group announced a cease-fire with the Turkish Government and in May declared that it was disbanding
goals – advance Kurdish autonomy, political, and cultural rights in Türkiye, Iran, Iraq, and Syria, and ultimately, establish an independent Kurdish state centered in southeastern Türkiye
leadership and organization – ÖCALAN, currently serving life imprisonment in Türkiye, is still the group's leader and figurehead, but day-to-day affairs and operations are run by Murat KARAYILAN and a three-man Executive Committee; the armed wing of the PKK is called the People's Defense Force (Hêzên Parastina Gel or HPG)
areas of operation – located primarily in northern Iraq (headquartered in the Qandil Mountains) and southeastern Türkiye; also present in Iran, Syria, and Europe
targets, tactics, and weapons – primarily attacks Turkish Government personnel and security forces, including military patrols, convoys, security checkpoints, police stations, and government buildings; uses a mixture of guerrilla warfare and terrorist tactics, including armed assaults, hit-and-run attacks, kidnappings, grenade attacks, car bombs, remotely-detonated improvised explosive devices (IEDs), IED-equipped unmanned aerial vehicles (UAVs), and suicide bombers; for most of its history, the group has waged a rural insurgency, but the collapse of the peace process in 2015 led to a two-year campaign of urban violence before it resorted back to a rural-based insurgency; weapons include small arms, anti-tank weapons, machine guns, grenades, mortars, man-portable air defense systems (MANPADs), UAVs, and various IEDs
strength – estimated in 2023 to have 4-5,000 members
financial and other support – receives logistical and financial support from sympathizers among the Kurdish community in southeast Türkiye, Syria, Iraq, and Iran, as well as the Kurdish diaspora in Europe; additional sources of funding include criminal activity, such as narcotics smuggling and extortion
designation – placed on the US Department of State's list of Foreign Terrorist Organizations on 8 October 1997

La Mara Salvatrucha (MS-13)

history – a transnational network of loosely-affiliated criminal gangs that originated in the US in the 1980s but spread to Central America as individuals returned from the US; it has come under increasing pressure from law enforcement in countries such as El Salvador, which in 2022 instituted a widespread crackdown against MS-13 and other gangs under an emergency decree authorizing thousands of military troops to support the police

leadership and organization – not available; MS-13 is loosely structured with leaders in El Salvador providing strategic guidance which cells of gang members inconsistently adhere to
area(s) of operation – chiefly active in El Salvador, Guatemala, Honduras, Mexico, and the US; has appeared in some European countries such as Italy and Spain; largely urban-based
tactics, targets, and weapons – has a reputation for brutality and violence; attacks have included assassinations and the use of improvised explosive devices; engages in a wide range of criminal activities including extortion, drug smuggling, illegal gambling, gang wars, human trafficking, migrant smuggling, murder, and prostitution
strength – not available
financial and other support – extortion is reportedly the chief revenue stream; also makes money through other illicit activities
designation – placed on the US Department of State's list of Foreign Terrorist Organizations on 20 February 2025

Lashkar i Jhangvi (LJ)
aka – Lashkar-e-Jhangvi (LeJ), Lashkar-i-Jhangvi, Lashkar Jangvi, Army of the Jhangvi, Lashkar e Jhangvi al-Almi, LeJ al-Alami
history – formed around 1996 as a terrorist offshoot of the Sunni Deobandi sectarian group Sipah-i-Sahaba Pakistan; banned by the Pakistani Goverment in 2001 as part of an effort to rein in sectarian violence, causing many LJ members to seek refuge in Afghanistan with the Taliban, with whom the group had existing ties; after the collapse of the Taliban in Afghanistan, members became active in aiding other terrorists, providing them with safe houses, false identities, and protection in Pakistani cities; linked to al-Qa'ida and Tehrik-e Taliban Pakistan (TTP); since 2017, it has lost several senior leaders to Pakistani counter-terrorism operations; in 2020-21, the group reportedly split into factions with one faction pledging allegiance to TTP; LJ was active as of 2023, although it did not claim any attacks that year
goals – exterminate Shia Muslims and religious minorities; rid the region of Western influence and, ultimately, establish an Islamic state under sharia in Pakistan
leadership and organization – not available
areas of operation – Pakistan
targets, tactics, and weapons – targets Shia Muslims, Sufi Muslims, non-Muslims, and Westerners; has attacked buses, markets, mosques, political rallies, and other venues where non-Muslims congregate, as well as churches and hotels; has also conducted attacks on Pakistani officials and security personnel, including an attempted assassination of the Pakistani prime minister in 1999; tactics have included ambushes, suicide bombings, targeted killings, and vehicle bombings such as detonating a water tanker filled with explosives that killed or wounded more than 250 in Baluchistan, Pakistan in 2013; operatives typically armed with small arms and light weapons, grenades, improvised explosive devices, and suicide vests
strength – assessed in 2023 to have a few hundred members
financial and other support – funding comes from donors in Pakistan and the Middle East, particularly Saudi Arabia; engages in criminal activity to fund its activities, including extortion
designation – placed on the US Department of State's list of Foreign Terrorist Organizations on 30 January 2003

Lashkar-e Tayyiba (LeT)
aka – Jamaat-ud-Dawa, JuD; Lashkar-i-Taiba; al Mansooreen; Al Mansoorian; Army of the Pure; Army of the Pure and Righteous; Army of the Righteous; Lashkar e-Toiba; Paasban-e-Ahle-Hadis; Paasban-e-Kashmir; Paasban-i-Ahle-Hadith; Pasban-e-Ahle-Hadith; Pasban-e-Kashmir; Jama'at al-Dawa; Jamaat ud-Daawa; Jamaat ul-Dawah; Jamaat-ul-Dawa; Jama'at-i-Dawat; Jamaiat-ud-Dawa; Jama'at-ud-Da'awah; Jama'at-ud-Da'awa; Jamaati-ud-Dawa; Idara Khidmate-Khalq; Falah-i-Insaniat Foundation; FiF; Falah-e-Insaniat Foundation; FalaheInsaniyat; Falah-i-Insaniyat; Falah Insania; Welfare of Humanity; Humanitarian Welfare Foundation; Human Welfare Foundation; Al-Anfal Trust; Tehrik-e-Hurmat-e-Rasool; TehrikeTahafuz Qibla Awwal; Al-Muhammadia Students; Al-Muhammadia Students Pakistan; AMS; Tehreek-e-Azadi-e-Kashmir; Kashmir Freedom Movement; Tehreek Azadi Jammu and Kashmir; Tehreek-e-Azadi Jammu and Kashmir; TAJK; Movement for Freedom of Kashmir; Tehrik-i-Azadi-i Kashmir; Tehreek-e-Azadi-e-Kashmir; TEK; Kashmir Freedom Movement ;Milli Muslim League; Milli Muslim League Pakistan; MML
history – formed in the late 1980s as the armed wing of Markaz ud Dawa ul-Irshad (MDI), a Pakistan-based extremist organization and charity originally formed to oppose the Soviet presence in Afghanistan; LeT began attacking Indian troops and civilian targets in the state of Jammu and Kashmir in 1993; Pakistan banned the group in 2002, and it often operates under the guise of its charitable affiliates and other front organizations to avoid sanctions and has combined with other groups like Jaish-e-Muhammad and Hizbul Mujahideen to mount anti-India attacks; LeT is linked to al-Qa'ida and has reportedly provided refuge and training to al-Qa'ida members in Pakistan; the group provided support to the Afghan Taliban prior to the Taliban takeover in 2021; LeT continued to active as of 2025
goals – annex the Indian Union Territory of Jammu and Kashmir to Pakistan and foment an Islamic insurgency in India; oust Western and Indian influence in Afghanistan; enhance its recruitment networks and paramilitary training in South Asia; and, ultimately, install Islamic rule throughout South Asia
leadership and organization – led by Hafiz Mohammad SAEED (imprisoned in Pakistan since 2020); has a robust infrastructure in Pakistan with district offices and departments (or wings) overseeing finances, charities, politics/government, foreign affairs, media and propaganda, social welfare programs, military operations, external affairs, education/students, ulema (clerics), and the building of mosques and madrassas; has zone/regional commanders; typically conducts military/terrorist operations in cells; activities are coordinated through numerous front organizations, including charities; set up a political party, the Milli Muslim League, in 2017
areas of operation – Afghanistan, India, and Pakistan
targets, tactics, and weapons – primarily focuses on Indian military and security, government, and civilian targets; has participated in attacks against Western interests in Afghanistan and called for the killing of non-Muslims and Westerners worldwide; typical attacks include ambushes, bombings, grenade attacks, and hit-and-run raids; most notorious attack was the November 2008 operation against two luxury hotels, a Jewish center, a train station, and a café in Mumbai, India that killed 166 people, including six Americans, and injured more than 300; the attack was carried out by 10 gunmen armed with automatic weapons and grenades; operatives typically armed with assault rifles, explosives, grenades, IEDs, landmines, machine guns, mortars, and rocket-propelled grenades
strength – estimated in 2023 to have up to 5,000 members
financial and other support – collects donations in Pakistan and the Gulf, as well as from other donors in the Middle East and the West; raises funds in Pakistan through charities, legitimate businesses, farming, and taxation; focuses recruitment on Pakistani nationals, but also recruits internationally
designation – placed on the US Department of State's list of Foreign Terrorist Organizations on 26 December 2001

Liberation Tigers of Tamil Eelam (LTTE)
aka – Ellalan Force, Tamil Tigers

history – formed circa 1975 and began an armed campaign against the Sri Lankan government to establish a Tamil homeland in 1983; LTTE started out as a guerrilla force but developed considerable conventional military capabilities, including air, artillery, and naval; it employed an integrated insurgent strategy targeting primarily Sri Lanka's key installations and senior political and military leaders; LTTE established and administered a de facto state (Tamil Eelam) with Kilinochchi as its capital and provided state functions such as courts, a police force, a bank, a radio station (Voice of Tigers), a television station (National Television of Tamil Eelam), and boards for humanitarian assistance, health, and education; from 1983 until 2009, fighting between government forces and LTTE resulted in 300,000 internally displaced persons, a million Tamils leaving the country, and as many as 100,000 deaths; in early 2009, Sri Lankan forces captured the LTTE's key strongholds, including Kilinochchi, defeated the last LTTE fighting forces, killed its leader Velupillai PRABHAKARN, and declared military victory; approximately 12,000 members surrendered to Sri Lankan military forces; since its defeat, the LTTE's international network of sympathizers and financial support has persisted
goals – revive the movement to establish a Tamil homeland
leadership and organization – not available; prior to its defeat, the LTTE's structure included a central governing committee led by PRABHAKARAN that oversaw all of its activities; LTTE's military forces were conventionally organized into brigades and regiments of infantry, artillery, air defense, anti-tank, mortars, and security forces; the forces also included special units for naval (Sea Tigers), air (Air Tigers), and intelligence capabilities, as well as a unit of suicide bombers (Black Tigers)
areas of operation – was based in the northeastern part of Sri Lanka; since its defeat, supporters have been active in India, Malaysia, and Sri Lanka
targets, tactics, and weapons – targeted Sri Lankan Government, political, and security officials, and military forces, as well as transportation nodes and infrastructure; carried out a sustained military campaign against Sri Lankan military and security forces; employed a mix of conventional, guerrilla, and terrorist tactics, including ground assaults and numerous assassinations and suicide bombings; forces were armed with a variety of weapons, including small arms, machine guns, rocket-propelled grenades, anti-aircraft guns, anti-tank weapons, mortars, artillery, explosives, small naval craft, and light aircraft
strength – not available
financial and other support – financial network of support continued after the group's military defeat in 2009; employs charities as fronts to collect and divert funds for its activities
designation – placed on the US Department of State's list of Foreign Terrorist Organizations on 8 October 1997

Los Choneros

designated on 5 September 2025; additional information to follow

Los Lobos

designated on 5 September 2025; additional information to follow

National Liberation Army (ELN)

aka – Ejercito de Liberacion Nacional; ELN
history – Colombian Marxist-Leninist group formed in 1964; ELN reached its peak in the late 1990s, then suffered a marked period of decline, where it suffered from internal conflict and losses to both the Colombian security services and paramilitary forces that targeted leftist guerrilla groups; the group engaged in periodic negotiations with the Colombian Government throughout the 2000s and early 2010s while continuing to conduct attacks against security forces and the country's economic infrastructure; formal talks were started again in 2017 and continued into 2018; however, the government suspended the talks indefinitely following a January 2019 ELN car bomb attack on the National Police Academy in Bogota that killed 22 and wounded more than 80 others; ELN expanded its presence into some areas left by the FARC following that group's peace agreement with the Colombian Government in 2016, as well as neighboring Venezuela in order to escape Colombian security forces and exploit opportunities for illicit financing and recruitment; the group has also engaged in periodic fighting with FARC dissidents and other criminal groups over territory and drug trafficking routes, particularly near the Colombia-Venezuela border; peace talks with the Colombian Government in 2023 resulted in a 6-month cease-fire and then a year-long armistice in 2024; however, continued disputes with the Colombian Government and cease-fire violations, including attacks on infrastructure, civilians, and FARC dissidents, as well as an assault on a Colombian military base in September 2024, led to the suspension of talks
goals – defend Colombians who it believes to be victims of social, political, and economic injustices perpetrated by the Colombian government
leadership and organization – led by Eliecer Erlinto Chamorro (alt. Eliecer Herlinto Chamorro; aka "Antonio Garcia") since 2021; at the top of the organizational structure is the Central Command ("Comando Central" or COCE), which oversees all ELN political, military, financial, and international operations; under the COCE is a 23-member National Directorate that serves as the link between the COCE and the seven "War Fronts" (six regional and one urban-based front that operates in multiple large cities); each front has multiple subdivisions and subunits and operates with a significant degree of autonomy
areas of operation – Colombia and Venezuela
targets, tactics, and weapons – mostly attacks Colombia's military forces, security services, and economic infrastructure, in particular oil and gas pipelines and electricity pylons; typical tactics include mortaring police stations and military bases, placing explosive devices on pipelines, electric pylons, and near roads, and engaging in ambushes, roadblocks, and sniper attacks; conducts numerous kidnappings of civilians and members of the security services; in February 2022, it orchestrated an armed strike across significant portions of Colombia (as many as 10 departments) that included violent attacks and targeted killings, blocking highways, setting off explosions, burning vehicles, hanging the ELN flag on public buildings, and patrolling streets in villages and towns in areas where the group maintains a strong presence; fighters are equipped with small arms, rocket-propelled grenades, landmines, explosives, and mortars
strength – estimated in 2024 to have 5-6,000 members
financial and other support – draws funding from the narcotics trade, extortion of oil and gas companies, illegal mining (expansion into Venezuela has included taking control of mines, allowing the group to use the acquisition of gold and diamond deposits to help provide funding), and kidnapping-for-ransom payments
designation – placed on the US Department of State's list of Foreign Terrorist Organizations on 8 October 1997

New Generation Jalisco Cartel

aka – Cártel de Jalisco Nueva Generación or CJNG; New Generation Cartel of Jalisco
history – transnational criminal group that emerged in the 2009-2011 timeframe when the Milenio Cartel split up following a series of arrests, killings, and internal divisions; CJNG subsequently rose rapidly in prominence in drug trafficking, including cocaine, fentanyl, and methamphetamines, while engaging in aggressive and violent confrontations with Mexican Government security forces and rival drug-trafficking organizations (DTOs); by 2020, the Mexican Government recognized it as one of the most powerful drug DTOs in the country, as well as a top security threat

leadership and organization – assessed to operate under a business franchise model overseen by Rubin Nemesio OSEGUERA Cervantes (aka "El Mencho") and a small group of top-tier commanders that include his direct relatives and report directly to him; reportedly has a specialized unit dedicated to operating drones/unmanned aerial vehicles
area(s) of operation – named for the west-central Mexican state where it is based but has a presence in nearly every state in Mexico and contacts in a variety of countries, including Australia, Bolivia, Canada, China, Colombia, Peru, the US, and in Southeast Asia; most important foreign connections are assessed to be with drug trafficking groups in neighboring Guatemala, which help it control part of the cocaine and synthetic drug supply chain into Mexico and the US, as well as in Colombia, where the group's emissaries establish partnerships to gain access to cocaine supplies
tactics, targets, and weapons – known as one of the most violent groups in Mexican history; targets Mexican military and police, including assassination attempts on officials, such as Mexico City's public security secretary in 2020; claimed responsibility for the 2015 killing of 15 police officers in Jalisco; uses violence and intimidation against rival DTOs and local communities to expand its influence and territory, including homicides, forced disappearances, and mass murders; possesses military-grade weaponry, such as machine guns, rocket-propelled grenades, explosive-dropping drones, and improvised explosive devices (IEDs); known for its public relations campaigns and social media presence
strength – not available
financial and other support – generates revenue from illicit activities, including extortion, wildlife trafficking, and theft of natural resources such as minerals and oil
designation – placed on the US Department of State's list of Foreign Terrorist Organizations on 20 February 2025

New Michoacana Family, The

aka – La Nueva Familia Michoacana or LNFM
history – LNFM is one of the successors of the La Familia Michoacana, a powerful transnational criminal organization that splintered in the early 2010s; it has been accused of trafficking drugs such as cocaine, fentanyl, and methamphetamines into the US
leadership and organization – co-led by brothers Johnny HURTADO Olascoaga and Jose Alfredo HURTADO Olascoaga
area(s) of operation – based in Mexico's Pacific coast state of Michoacán but has operations in multiple other states, particularly in the country's south and around Mexico City
tactics, targets, and weapons – attacks Mexican officials and security forces, including one in 2022 that killed a town's mayor and 19 others and a 2021 incident that left 13 police officers dead; attacks have included drones and explosives; criminal activities also include extortion, migrant smuggling, human trafficking, illegal mining, kidnapping, and murder
strength – not available
financial and other support – criminal activities, particularly drug trafficking and extortion
designation – placed on the US Department of State's list of Foreign Terrorist Organizations on 20 February 2025

Northeast Cartel

aka – Cártel del Noreste or CDN; Los Zetas
history – transnational criminal organization that emerged in the 2010s from the remnants of another criminal group known as Los Zetas, which served as the armed enforcement wing for the Gulf Cartel; CDN's operations have centered on the Mexican city of Nuevo (New) Laredo, Tamaulipas State along the US-Mexico border, although the group has sought to expand southwards; since 2019, CDN has fought with other criminal and drug trafficking organizations over territory and drug trafficking routes, including the Gulf Cartel, the Sinaloa Cartel, and the New Generation Jalisco Cartel; the capture of former leader Juan Gerardo TREVINO-CHAVEZ (aka "el Huevo") by the Mexican Army in 2022 sparked an hours-long firefight and high levels of violence in Nuevo Laredo
leadership and organization – not available; several leaders have been arrested by Mexican authorities in recent years
area(s) of operation – based in northeastern Mexico, particularly Nuevo Laredo, but has used violence to exert control over large swaths of North Mexico, including along the US border
tactics, targets, and weapons – targets law enforcement, Mexican Army, and Mexican National Guard personnel, as well as members of rival drug-trafficking organizations (DTOs); involved in assassinations, kidnappings, and murders; also engaged in drug trafficking, extortion, migrant smuggling, human trafficking, kidnapping, theft, and other illicit activities
strength – not available
financial and other support – various illicit activities, including extortion of both illegal markets and certain legal businesses within its territory; primary source of income reportedly comes from taxing various groups that use the Nuevo Laredo (Mexico)-Laredo (US) border crossing, including drug traffickers and migrant smugglers
designation – placed on the US Department of State's list of Foreign Terrorist Organizations on 20 February 2025

Palestine Islamic Jihad (PIJ)

aka – PIJ-Shaqaqi Faction; PIJ-Shallah Faction; Islamic Jihad of Palestine; Islamic Jihad in Palestine; Abu Ghunaym Squad of the Hizballah Bayt al-Maqdis; Al-Quds Squads; Al-Quds Brigades; Saraya al-Quds; Al-Awdah Brigades; Harakat al-Jihad al-Islami al-Filastin
history – a Sunni Islamist group formed by militant Palestinians in Gaza in 1979 as an off-shoot of the Muslim Brotherhood in Egypt; draws inspiration from the Iranian revolution and receives support from Iran, Syria, and Lebanese Hizballah; PIJ is the smaller of the two main Palestinian militant groups in Gaza, the other being the ruling HAMAS group with which it cooperates, although the two have disagreed over strategy for confronting Israel; unlike HAMAS, PIJ refuses to negotiate with Israel and rejects a two-state solution; the group has been responsible for many attacks on Israeli targets since the 1990s including barrages of mortar and rocket strikes, and it participated with HAMAS in the October 2023 attack on Israel that triggered an Israeli counterattack on Gaza; in 2024, PIJ was engaged in fighting with the Israeli military inside Gaza
goals – committed to the destruction of Israel and to the creation of an Islamic state in historic Palestine, an area that covers present-day Israel, Gaza, and the West Bank
leadership and organization – led by Ziyad al-NAKHALLAH and an eight-member leadership council (al-Maktab al-Am or General Bureau); has a 15-member political council, which represents PIJ members in Gaza, the West Bank, Israeli prisons, and abroad; also has an armed wing, known as the al-Quds (Jerusalem) Brigades, which has subordinate regional military commands, "brigades," or "battalions" that are comprised of cells and smaller units
areas of operation – Israel, the Gaza Strip, and the West Bank; maintains a presence in Lebanon and Syria and offices in Tehran, Iran
targets, tactics, and weapons – targets Israeli civilians and military personnel; most attacks have been conducted with bombs/improvised explosive devices (IEDs), mortars, rockets, and small arms, although the group has also carried out abductions and suicide bombings; armed with small arms and light weapons, artillery rockets, man-portable air defense systems (MANPADs), mortars, armed unmanned aerial vehicles (aka drones), anti-tank guided missiles, rockets, and IEDs
strength – estimated in 2023 to have about 1,000 members

financial and other support – receives financial assistance, military training, and weapons primarily from Shia Muslim Iran in pursuit of their shared anti-Israel ideology; Hizballah provides safe harbor to PIJ leaders and representatives in Lebanon and probably facilitates Iran's support to PIJ; trains with HAMAS; maintains a tunnel network to smuggle goods, arms, and ammunition across borders
designation – placed on the US Department of State's list of Foreign Terrorist Organizations on 8 October 1997

Palestine Liberation Front – Abu Abbas Faction
aka – PLF; PLF-Abu Abbas; Palestine Liberation Front
history – initially founded in the 1960s and merged with several other Palestinian groups after the Six-Day War in 1967 but broke away in the late 1970s; the PLF split into pro-Palestinian Liberation Organization (PLO), pro-Syrian, and pro-Libyan factions by 1984 with the pro-PLO faction being led by Muhammad Zaydan (aka Abu Abbas); the PLF was suspected of supporting terrorism by other Palestinian groups against Israel in the 1990s; it claimed responsibility for small-scale attacks against Israeli military personnel and an Israeli civilian in 2008 and 2010; has not claimed any attacks since 2010 (as of late 2023)
goals – committed to establishing an independent Palestinian state
leadership and organization – led by Secretary General Dr. Wasil ABU YUSUF, a longtime member on the PLO's executive committee
areas of operation – maintains a presence in the Gaza Strip, Lebanon, Syria, and the West Bank
targets, tactics, and weapons – primarily targeted Israeli military and security personnel with occasional shootings and improvised explosive device (IED) attacks; weapons include small arms, artillery rockets, explosives, grenades, and mortars
strength – not available
financial and other support – not available
designation – placed on the US Department of State's list of Foreign Terrorist Organizations on 8 October 1997

Popular Front for the Liberation of Palestine – General Command (PFLP-GC)
aka – PFLP-GC, Al-Jibha Sha'biya lil-Tahrir Filistin-al-Qadiya al-Ama, Ahmed Jibril Militia
history – a Marxist-Nationalist and secular group that split from the Popular Front for the Liberation of Palestine (PFLP) in 1968, claiming it wanted to concentrate more on resistance and less on politics; carried out dozens of attacks in Europe and the Middle East during the 1970s and 1980s, including bombings of two Western airliners; was also was known for cross-border attacks into Israel using unusual means, such as hot-air balloons and motorized hang gliders; since the early 1990s, the group has supported Hizballah's attacks against Israel, trained members of other Palestinian terrorist groups, and smuggled weapons; between 2012-2015, it claimed responsibility for several rocket attacks against Israel and the bombing of a bus carrying civilians; after 2015, PFLP-GC fought alongside Syrian regime forces during the Syrian civil war; it claimed responsibility for firing rockets into Israel in 2021 and an attack on Israeli settlers in the West Bank in 2024; the PFLP-GC participated on the side of HAMAS and other Palestinian militant groups in fighting inside the Gaza Strip during the 2023-2025 Israel-HAMAS conflict
goals – destroy Israel and remove Western influence from the Middle East, ultimately establishing a Marxist Palestinian state
leadership and organization – Talal NAJI (elected leader in July 2021 after the death of Ahmad JIBRIL, the group's leader and founder); overall organization not available, but has a military wing known as the Jihad Jibril Brigades
areas of operation – Syria, Lebanon, Gaza Strip, and the West Bank
targets, tactics, and weapons – targets Israeli civilians and the military and what it perceives to be Israeli interests; also targeted paramilitary forces fighting against the Syrian ASAD regime; used innovative attack methods, including barometric bombs to destroy civilian aircraft and mail bombs, as well as hot-air balloons and motorized hang-gliders for cross-border attacks; also incorporates guerrilla tactics; weapons have typically included grenades, improvised explosive devices (IEDs), rockets, small arms, light machine guns, and suicide vests
strength – estimated in 2023 to have several hundred members
financial and other support – receives funds, logistical support, military training, and weapons from Iran and the Hizballah terrorist group; also received support from Syria prior to the fall of the ASAD regime; garners payments in exchange for providing training to other armed militant groups
designation – placed on the US Department of State's list of Foreign Terrorist Organizations on 8 October 1997

Popular Front for the Liberation of Palestine (PFLP)
aka – Halhul Gang; Halhul Squad; Palestinian Popular Resistance Forces; PPRF; Red Eagle Gang; Red Eagle Group; Red Eagles; Martyr Abu-Ali Mustafa Battalion
history – formed in December 1967 as an umbrella organization for Marxist and Arab nationalist groups after Israel seized the West Bank; became the second largest faction, and the main opposition force to Fatah within the Palestine Liberation Organization (PLO); earned a reputation for large-scale international attacks in the 1960s and 1970s, including high-profile hijackings of Israeli and Western aircraft; declined in the 1980s following the collapse of the Soviet Union which had been its chief benefactor, and with the emergence of non-PLO groups such as HAMAS and Palestine Islamic Jihad; increased its operational tempo in the 2000s, carrying out at least two suicide bombings and launching multiple joint operations with other Palestinian militant groups; conducted attacks in Israel in 2014 and 2017, which resulted in the deaths of several Israeli and US citizens; in 2020, Israeli security forces in the West Bank arrested approximately 50 members of a PFLP cell believed to be behind a string of deadly attacks in the area and seized weapons and bomb making materials; claimed two separate attacks in the West Bank in early 2023 and participated in the HAMAS-led attack on Israel in October 2023
goals – destroy the state of Israel and, ultimately, establish a secular, Marxist Palestinian state with Jerusalem as its capital
leadership and organization – official leader, General Secretary Ahmad SA'DAT, has been serving a 30-year prison sentence in Israel since 2006; Deputy Secretary General 'Abd-al-Rahim MALLUH (var: Abdul Rahim MALLOUH) oversees daily operations; MALLUH is also a member of the PLO's Executive Committee; has a Political Bureau and a military wing known as the Martyr Abu-Ali Mustafa Brigade
areas of operation – headquartered in the Gaza Strip; also operates in Israel, Lebanon, Syria, and the West Bank
targets, tactics, and weapons – primarily targets Israeli civilians and military personnel; tactics have included assassinations, bombings, including suicide bombings, mortar and rocket strikes, kidnappings, and small arms attacks; in 2014, two members with axes, guns, and knives attacked a synagogue in West Jerusalem, killing five, including three Americans; fighters typically equipped with small arms, light machine guns, artillery rockets, mortars, man-portable surface-to-air missiles, improvised weapons, and explosives, including improvised explosive devices and suicide vests
strength – not available
financial and other support – not available
designation – placed on the US Department of State's list of Foreign Terrorist Organizations on 8 October 1997

Real Irish Republican Army (RIRA)

aka – Real IRA; 32 County Sovereignty Committee; 32 County Sovereignty Movement; Irish Republican Prisoners Welfare Association; Real Oglaigh Na Heireann; Óglaigh na hÉireann (ÓNH); New Irish Republican Army (New IRA or NIRA)
established – formed in 1997 as the clandestine armed wing of the 32 County Sovereignty Movement, a political pressure group dedicated to removing British forces from Northern Ireland and unifying Ireland; claims to be the true descendent of the original Irish Republican Army; many members are former Provisional Irish Republican Army who left the organization after the group renewed its ceasefire in 1997 and brought experience in terrorist tactics and bomb-making to RIRA; has historically sought to disrupt the Northern Ireland peace process and did not participate in the September 2005 weapons decommissioning; despite internal rifts and calls by some jailed members, including the group's founder Michael "Mickey" McKEVITT, for a cease-fire and disbandment, RIRA pledged to continue conducting attacks; in 2012, RIRA merged with other small dissident republican groups to form the New IRA (NIRA); reportedly cooperates with the Continuity Irish Republican Army (CIRA); claimed responsibility or been suspected in numerous bombing attempts and shootings since 2012, including attacks or attempted attacks against police in 2021, 2022, and 2023; the Police Service of Northern Ireland (PSNI) disrupted a NIRA bomb plot to coincide with a visit to Belfast by the US President in 2023 and has made arrests of RIRA/NIRA members as recently as 2024
goals – disrupt the Northern Ireland peace process, remove British rule in Northern Ireland and, ultimately, unify Ireland
leadership and organization – current leadership not available; reportedly has a command structure similar to the former Provisional IRA, with an "Army Council" consisting of a chief of staff and directors for training, operations, finance, and publicity; rank-and-file members operate in secret cells
areas of operation – UK and the Republic of Ireland
targets, tactics, and weapons – primarily targets police and other security personnel; tactics typically involve shootings and low-impact bombing attacks; weapons include small arms, mortars, and explosives, including IEDs and car bombs
strength – estimated in 2023 to have approximately 100 active members
financial and other support – receives funding from money laundering, smuggling, and other criminal activities; suspected of receiving funds from sympathizers in the US; has attempted to buy weapons from gun dealers in the US and the Balkans
designation – placed on the US Department of State's list of Foreign Terrorist Organizations on 16 May 2001

Resistance Front, The (TRF)

aka: Kashmir Resistance
history: TRF is a proxy for Lashkar-e-Taiba (LeT), a US- and UN-designated terrorist group based in Pakistan; the group announced its existence in 2019 after India revoked the special autonomous status of the India-administered region of Jammu and Kashmir; the name is reportedly meant to suggest nationalist Kashmiri--as opposed to foreign-supported or religious-based--resistance to the Indian Government and deflect attention from LeT and other Pakistan-based terrorist groups active in Jammu and Kashmir; in 2023, the Indian Government designated the group a proxy of LeT and banned it; since claiming its first attack in October 2019, TRF has claimed responsibility for numerous others in Jammu and Kashmir, including an April 2025 attack that killed 26 civilians and sparked a short military conflict between India and Pakistan
goals: foment an insurgency in the Indian Union Territory of Jammu and Kashmir and ultimately annex the territory to Pakistan
leadership **and organization:** *reportedly founded and led by Sheikh Sajjad GUL; organization structure not available*
areas **of operation:** *Indian Union Territory of Jammu and Kashir*
targets, **tactics, and weapons:** *targets civilians, politicians, religious minority groups, security forces, and tourists; conducts insurgency-type operations, including ambushes, bombings, grenade attacks, targeted killings, and other small-scale attacks; largest attack was in April 2025, when five attackers armed with military-style assault rifles killed 26 civilians at a tourist site; weapons include small arms, light machine guns, grenades, improvised explosive devices, and other types of bombs*
strength: not available; composed of Kashmiri fighters; draws some members from LeT
financial **and other support:** *not available*
designation: placed on the US Department of State's list of Foreign Terrorist Organizations on 17 July 2025

Revolutionary Armed Forces of Colombia – People's Army (FARC-EP)

aka – Fuerzas Armadas Revolucionarias de Colombia – Ejercito del Pueblo; FARC dissidents FARC – EP ; Revolutionary Armed Forces of Colombia dissidents FARC – EP; FARC – D/FARC – EP; Grupo Armado Organizado Residual FARC – EP; GAO-R FARC – EP; Residual Organized Armed Group FARC – EP; Central General Staff (Estado Mayor Central or EMC or FARC-EMC)
history – in 2016, the former Revolutionary Armed Forces of Colombia (FARC) signed a peace deal in which about 13,000 fighters gave up their weapons in exchange for numerous concessions from the Colombian Government, including development programs for rural areas and the opportunity for former guerrilla leaders to participate in local politics and avoid time in prison; however, a group of approximately 1,000 FARC "dissidents," led by Nestor Gregorio VERA Fernandez, commander of the FARC 1st Front, refused to lay down their arms and returned to fighting, eventually adopting the name FARC-EP; in late 2019, the Colombian Government began conducting military operations against FARC-EP; despite peace talks and a months-long cease-fire with the Colombian Government in late 2023 that extended into 2024, the group was again conducting attacks and fighting with Colombian security forces as of 2025; the FARC-EP has also fought with a rival FARC dissident group and US-designated terrorist group, Segunda Marquetalia, over control of revenue and territory
goals – the former FARC sought to install a Marxist-Leninist regime in Colombia through a violent revolution; the group seeks to unite all FARC dissidents and leftist guerrilla groups in Colombia
leadership and organization – leader Nestor Gregorio VERA Fernandez (aka Ivan MORDISCO); reportedly organized similarly to the former FARC with regionally based commands and subordinate "fronts" or "blocs" and "mobile columns," although some information points to a more fragmented command and control structure based in large part on alliances with disparate ex-FARC members and groups, as well as criminal organizations
areas of operation – Colombia and Venezuela
targets, tactics, and weapons – attacks Colombian Government, military, and police targets, as well as civilians and critical infrastructure, such as oil pipelines; tactics include armed assaults, assassinations, bombings, extortion operations, and hostage-takings; weapons include small arms, grenades, landmines, machine guns, mortars, rocket propelled grenades, and explosives, including improvised explosive devices (IEDs)
strength – estimated to have as many as 3,500 members as of 2024
financial and other support – generates funds through narcotics trafficking, extortion, illegal mining (typically gold), and other illicit economies; collects taxes from locals in areas it occupies
designation – placed on the US Department of State's list of FTOs on 30 November 2021; the designation followed the revocation of the designation of the Revolutionary Forces of Colombia (FARC) as an FTO; note – the former FARC has a political party (Comunes or "Together") that holds seats in the Colombian Congress

Revolutionary People's Liberation Party/Front (DHKP/C)

aka – Dev Sol; Dev Sol Armed Revolutionary Units; Dev Sol Silahli Devrimci Birlikleri; Dev Sol SDB; Devrimci Halk Kurtulus Partisi/Cephesi; Devrimci Sol; Revolutionary Left
history – formed in Türkiye originally in 1978 as Devrimci Sol, or Dev Sol, a splinter faction of Dev Genc (Revolutionary Youth); renamed in 1994 after factional infighting; "Party" refers to the group's political activities and "Front" alludes to its militant operations; advocates a Marxist-Leninist ideology and opposes the US, NATO, and the Turkish establishment; reorganized after the death of its founder and leader Dursun KARATAS from cancer in 2008 and was reportedly in competition with the Kurdistan Workers' Party for influence in Türkiye; since the late 1980s has primarily targeted Turkish security and military officials; in the 1990s began to conduct attacks against foreign—including US—interests; activities have declined in recent years, but the group remained active into 2024 with periodic small-scale attacks while continuing to be targeted by Turkish security forces
goals – espouses a Marxist-Leninist ideology and seeks to overthrow the Turkish Government and rid Türkiye of "imperialist" foreign influences, such as NATO and the US
leadership and organization – current leadership not available; head of DHKP/C in Türkiye, Gulten MATUR, arrested by Turkish authorities in November 2022; reportedly operates in small, clandestine cells
areas of operation – Türkiye; has a presence in Europe, especially Germany and Greece; historically active in Syria
targets, tactics, and weapons – has targeted Turkish businessmen, civilians, police, politicians, and soldiers; has also attacked police and other government buildings, including an attempt to take a hostage in the Turkish Parliament in 2019 and a rocket attack against the Istanbul police headquarters in 2017; has also targeted foreign interests, especially US military and diplomatic personnel and facilities, such as opening fire on the US Consulate with small arms in 2015 and a suicide bombing attack against the US Embassy in 2013; typical tactics include assassinations, hostage taking, rocket attacks, suicide bombings, remotely detonated bombs, and car bombs; weapons include small arms, hand grenades, artillery rockets, and improvised explosive devices
strength – estimated to have several dozen members inside Türkiye in 2023; has a support network in Europe
financial and other support – finances its activities chiefly through donations and extortion; in Europe, it engages in fundraising, arms smuggling, and other criminal ventures to support its operations in Türkiye
designation – placed on the US Department of State's list of Foreign Terrorist Organizations on 8 October 1997

Revolutionary Struggle (RS)

aka – Epanastatikos Aghonas; EA
history – EA (or RS) is a Marxist extremist group that emerged in 2003 following the arrests of members of two other Greek Marxist groups, 17 November (17N) and Revolutionary People's Struggle; first gained notoriety when it claimed responsibility for the September 2003 bombings at the Athens Courthouse during the trials of 17N members; after 2003, EA conducted numerous attacks against Greek and US targets in Greece but conducted its last successful attack in 2014; Greek authorities arrested the group's leaders—husband and wife Nikolaos MAZIOTIS and Pola ROUPA--in 2014 and 2017, respectively; the arrests, along with follow-on arrests of other EA members, disrupted the group's ability to conduct operations, although its remaining members have been linked to other anarchist groups in Greece
goals – disrupt the influence of globalization and international capitalism on Greek society and, ultimately, overthrow the Greek Government
leadership and organization – not available
areas of operation – Greece, primarily in Athens and its suburbs
targets, tactics, and weapons – from 2003 to 2014, EA targeted Greek and US Government buildings, Greek police officers, the Athens Stock Exchange, and offices of major foreign corporations; EA was also linked to several Greek bank robberies, probably to help fund its operations; used small arms although most attacks involved explosives, including improvised explosive devices (IEDs), vehicle-borne IEDs, and parcel bombs; sometimes conducted attacks at night or in the early morning and called in bomb threats before attacks to limit casualties
strength – estimated to have fewer than two dozen members in 2023
financial and other support – unclear, but most likely supported itself through criminal activities, including bank robberies
designation – placed on the US Department of State's list of Foreign Terrorist Organizations on 18 May 2009

Segunda Marquetalia

aka – New Marquetalia; Second Marquetalia; La Nueva Marquetalia; FARC dissidents Segunda Marquetalia; Revolutionary Armed Forces of Colombia Dissidents Segunda Marquetalia; FARC-D Segunda Marquetalia; FARC-SM; Grupo Armado Organizado Residual Segunda Marquetalia; GAO-R Segunda Marquetalia;, Residual Organized Armed Group Segunda Marquetalia; Armed Organized Residual Group Segunda Marquetalia; note - "Marquetalia" is a reference to the town of Marquetalia, Colombia, that was the original stronghold of communist peasant militants who would later become the now former FARC
history – created in August 2019 by former commanders of the Revolutionary Armed Forces of Colombia (FARC) after they abandoned the 2016 peace accord between the FARC and the Colombian Government because of frustration over perceived lack of progress in implementing the terms of the accord; Segunda Marquetalia attempts to carry out the key functions of the state in the areas under its control, including taxation, security, and maintaining infrastructure; in July 2024, the group agreed to a unilateral cease-fire with the Colombian Government; however, it continued to fight with a rival FARC dissident group, FARC-People's Army (FARC-EP), over control of revenue and territory
goals – position itself as the natural successor of the former FARC and unite different groups that claim FARC heritage; the former FARC sought to install a Marxist-Leninist regime in Colombia through a violent revolution; the group seeks to unite or form alliances with armed leftist guerrilla organizations in Colombia, including ex-FARC members, the ELN (National Liberation Army), and the smaller EPL (People's Liberation Army)
leadership and organization – Luciano Marin ARANGO (aka Ivan MARQUEZ) (note - ARANGO was previously the FARC's second-in-command before demobilization, commander of the Caribbean bloc, and lead negotiator during the peace talks with the Colombian Government); has a central committee (aka central command), known as the National Directorate; claims to consist of a political wing (Partido Comunista Clandestino de Colombia or Clandestine Communist Party), as well as armed guerrilla forces and both armed and unarmed militia units; similar to the former FARC, it operates in "blocs" and "fronts"
areas of operation – Colombia and Venezuela
targets, tactics, and weapons – focuses most of its attacks on Colombian Government and military targets, as well as critical infrastructure, such as oil pipelines; also fights with rival FARC dissidents and other armed criminal groups; tactics have typically included armed assaults, assassinations, bombings, extortion operations, grenade and mortar attacks, and hostage takings; armed generally with small arms, grenades, improvised explosive devices, machine guns, and mortars
strength – estimated to have up to 2,000 members in 2024
financial and other support – funded primarily by involvement in illicit activity, including extortion, international drug trade, and illegal mining; collects taxes from locals in areas it occupies

designation – placed on the US Department of State's list of Foreign Terrorist Organizations on 30 November 2021; the designation followed the revocation of the designation of the Revolutionary Forces of Colombia (FARC) as an FTO; note – the former FARC has a political party (Comunes or "Together") that holds seats in the Colombian Congress

Shining Path (Sendero Luminoso, SL)

aka – Ejército Guerrillero Popular (People's Guerrilla Army); EGP; Ejército Popular de Liberación (People's Liberation Army); EPL; Partido Comunista del Peru (Communist Party of Peru); PCP; Partido Comunista del Peru en el Sendero Luminoso de Jose Carlos Mariategui (Communist Party of Peru on the Shining Path of Jose Carlos Mariategui); Socorro Popular del Peru (People's Aid of Peru); SPP; Militarizado Partido Comunista del Peru or MPCP; Militarized Communist Party of Peru; New Red Fraction (Nueva Fracción Roja – NFR; splinter group)
history – formed in the late 1960s as a breakaway faction of the Peruvian Communist Party by former university professor Abimael GUZMAN, whose teachings provided the basis of the group's militant Maoist doctrine; SL was one of the most ruthless terrorist groups in the Western Hemisphere at its height in the 1980s; the group conducted an insurgency against the Peruvian Government and waged a campaign of violence on civilians, particularly the rural peasantry, resulting in the deaths of an estimated 70,000 Peruvians between 1980 and 2000; in September 1992, Peruvian authorities captured GUZMAN, who died in prison in 2021; following his capture, SL's membership declined and the remnants split into two factions; by 2014, one faction had largely been eliminated, while the other continued to operate; SL continues to try to reinvent itself, organize, and proselytize, particularly amongst university students and in rural areas; in recent years, it has called itself the Militarized Communist Party of Peru (Militarizado Partido Comunista del Peru); SL's remnants remained active into 2024, although most of its operations were in support of narcotrafficking
goals – historically aimed to replace existing Peruvian institutions with a peasant revolutionary regime
leadership and organization – Victor Quispe PALOMINO (aka Comrade Jose); organization not available
areas of operation – Peru; most active in the Valley of the Apurimac, Ene, and Mantaro Rivers (VRAEM), a vast jungle area near the Andes mountains and home to most of Peru's coca cultivation and production
targets, tactics, and weapons – primary targets in recent years have been Peruvian soldiers and police personnel running counter-narcotics and counter-terrorism operations against the group; also abducts and kills civilians; killed 16 civilians in an attack on a village in May 2021; typically uses guerrilla style hit-and-run tactics, including grenade attacks and snipers; weapons include small arms and other light weapons, grenades, and other explosives, including improvised explosive devices
strength – estimated in 2023 to have less than 350 active members
financial resources – primarily funded by the illicit narcotics trade, including collecting taxes from drug trafficking organizations, providing security for traffickers, and growing coca to produce cocaine
designation – placed on the US Department of State's list of Foreign Terrorist Organizations on 8 October 1997

Sinaloa Cartel

aka – Cártel de Sinaloa; Mexican Federation; Pacific Cartel
history – recognized as one of the world's first and most powerful drug cartels; its primary focus is trafficking narcotics such as cocaine, fentanyl, and methamphetamine to the US; the Sinaloa Cartel traces its heritage back to the Guadalajara Cartel of the 1980s; the Cartel expanded its operations through the 1990s and 2000s in a campaign of violence against the Mexican Government and rival criminal organizations such as the Tijuana Cartel, as well as transactional alliances with other drug-trafficking organizations (DTOs), such as the Gulf Cartel and Milenio Cartel; it also established connections with Mexico's economic and political elite and penetrated the government and security forces, largely through bribery; the cartel has been targeted by the Mexican Government for years, and some of the group's senior leaders have been arrested and extradited to the US as recently as 2024
leadership and organization – does not have a hierarchical structure but rather a confederation of leaders typically linked by kinship or regional ties; operates as a network of cells and factions that may share resources, such as smuggling routes, contacts, and access to suppliers and money laundering networks; internal power struggles and fluctuating alliances have led to periodic clashes among the factions, which reportedly have armed wings to protect territories; operations in both Mexico and foreign countries are often outsourced to local partners
area(s) of operation – based in Sinaloa, Mexico, and operates across large parts of Mexico, particularly along the northwest Pacific coast and both the northern and southern borders; in 2024, was assessed to operate in 47 countries worldwide, including the US
tactics, targets, and weapons – targets security forces, civilians, and rival DTOs such as the New Generation Jalisco Cartel, using assassinations, executions, kidnapping, and murder; uses bribery and transactional alliances to spread its footprint and influence; has a reputation for using sophisticated smuggling techniques, including tunnels under the US-Mexico border; other criminal activities include extortion, migrant smuggling, money laundering, oil and mineral theft, prostitution, weapons trafficking, and wildlife trafficking
strength – not available
financial and other support – illicit activities; also profits from taxing migrant traffickers and some legal industries such as agriculture and fishing
designation – placed on the US Department of State's list of Foreign Terrorist Organizations on 20 February 2025

Tehrik-e-Taliban Pakistan (TTP)

aka – Pakistani Taliban; Tehreek-e-Taliban; Tehrik-e-Taliban; Tehrik-i-Taliban Pakistan; Tehrik-e Jihad Pakistan (TJP)
history – formed in 2007 to oppose Pakistani military efforts in the Federally Administered Tribal Areas (FATA) when previously disparate tribal militants agreed to cooperate and eventually coalesced under the leadership of now-deceased leader Baitullah MEHSUD (var. MAHSUD); TTP subsequently emerged as one of Pakistan's deadliest terrorist organizations; it was responsible for assaults on a Pakistani naval base in 2011, Karachi's international airport in 2014, and a military school in Peshawar that killed 150 people, mostly students, also in 2014; TTP entered into peace talks with the Pakistani Government in 2014, but the talks collapsed that same year; beginning around 2014, the group suffered from several years of internal conflict, fragmentation, public backlash for deadly attacks targeting civilians, and members defecting to ISIS's Khorasan branch in Afghanistan; however, beginning in 2020, several jihadist groups, including Jamat-ul-Ahrar (JuA), Hizb-ul-Ahrar (HuA), and the designated FTO Lashkar I Jhangvi (LJ), pledged allegiance to TTP (JuA and HuA had split off around 2014), while at the same time, the group increased the number of attacks in Pakistan; TTP conducted peace talks with the Pakistan Government accompanied by a cease-fire in 2021 but when the cease-fire ended in December 2021, the group further increased its operations, conducting hundreds of attacks in 2022-2024
goals – opposes Pakistani military efforts in Khyber Pakhtunkhwa province, the former tribal areas, and other areas of Pakistan; aims to push the Government of Pakistan out of Khyber Pakhtunkhwa province and establish Sharia by waging a terrorist campaign against the Pakistani military and state; note - TTP has ties to and draws ideological guidance from al-Qa'ida (AQ)

leadership and organization – led by Mufti Noor Wali MEHSUD (aka Abu Mansur Asim); has a shura council with two regional committees covering seven zones of operation; however, because TTP is a coalition of more than 15 groups, as well as tribal factions, operational levels of cooperation may vary
areas of operation – based primarily in eastern Afghanistan; conducts operations in Pakistan
targets, tactics, and weapons – targets Pakistani Government officials and military, security, and police personnel, as well as pro-government tribal elders, Shia Muslims, educational figures, the general civilian population, and Westerners; previously targeted US military personnel in Afghanistan; claimed responsibility for a failed 2010 attempt to detonate an explosive device in New York City's Times Square; suspected of involvement in the 2007 assassination of former Pakistani Prime Minister Benazir BHUTTO; has attacked an airport, buses, churches, government buildings, homes of Pakistani officials, markets, hotels, military bases and convoys, mosques, public gatherings, schools, security checkpoints, and entire neighborhoods of Shia Muslims; tactics typically have involved ambushes, hit-and-run raids, small arms attacks, complex military-style assaults, kidnappings, assassinations, suicide bombings, and grenade, mortar, and rocket attacks; weapons include small arms, light and heavy machine guns, mortars, rockets, rocket-propelled grenades, and explosives, including remotely detonated improvised explosive devices (IEDs), suicide vests, and car bombs
strength – estimated in 2025 to have approximately 6,000 fighters
financial and other support – primarily recruits from the former FATA and finances its operations through donations, extortion, kidnappings-for-ransom, natural resource extraction, and other criminal activity, including arms and narcotics trafficking; has received equipment, ideological guidance, training, and weapons from AQ in Afghanistan; the Afghan Taliban is also reported to have provided support to TTP, and Afghan Taliban rank and file and AQ members have reportedly assisted TTP forces in cross-border attacks
designation – placed on the US Department of State's list of Foreign Terrorist Organizations on 1 September 2010

Tren de Aragua (TdA)

aka – Aragua Train
history – transnational criminal organization that originated as a prison gang in the Tocorón prison in Aragua, Venezuela, in the 2010s; in 2023, 11,000 Venezuelan police and military personnel stormed the Tocorón prison to seize what was reportedly TdA's center of operations; however, the group's leadership escaped, and the organization expanded first in Venezuela and then regionally with the flow of migrants fleeing economic and social disorder; by 2023, it had established a transnational criminal network with loosely-organized cells and contacts in several South American countries, which were engaged in wide range of criminal activities; the group has been targeted by security forces across the region
leadership and organization – led by Héctor Rustherford GUERRERO Flores (aka El Niño Guerrero or the "Warrior Child"), Yohan Jose ROMERO (aka Johan Petrica), Larry ALVAREZ Nunez (aka Larry Changa); reportedly organized into cells, with unknown connections to GUERRERO or other leaders in Venezuela; factions in Chile and Peru reportedly operate under names such as the Gallegos, the Hijos de Dios, and Dinastía Alayón
area(s) of operation – chiefly active in Venezuelan diaspora communities in Bolivia, Colombia, Chile, Peru, and Venezuela, but also assessed to have a presence in Brazil, Panama, Trinidad and Tobago, and the US; largest presence remains in Venezuela
targets, tactics, weapons – targets law enforcement officers and local gangs to intimidate and expand control of territory and criminal enterprises; has clashed with the National Liberation Front (ELN) guerrilla/terrorist group along the Colombian-Venezuela border over control of illicit cross-border trafficking, such as contraband, drugs, and migrants; engages in criminal activities such as assassinations, bribery, cybercrime, debt bondage, extortion, human trafficking for sexual exploitation, illegal mining, migrant smuggling, money laundering, murders, and robberies
strength – estimated to have several thousand members, although it is unclear how many are part of copycat groups claiming affiliation
financial and other support – money laundering, extortion, trafficking of illicit goods, migrant smuggling, and contracted "service provider" for other transnational criminal organizations
designation – placed on the US Department of State's list of Foreign Terrorist Organizations on 20 February 2025

United Cartels

aka – Cárteles Unidos or CU; Tepalcatepec Cartel (Cartel de Tepalcatepec); The Grandfather Cartel (Cartel del Abuelo); Cartel de Los Reyes; La Resistencia
history – loose coalition of drug-trafficking organizations (DTOs) and some civilian self-defense groups that formed in the 2020 timeframe to combat the violent expansion of the New Generation Jalisco Cartel (Cartel Jalisco Nueva Generación – CJNG) into Mexico's state of Michoacán; organizations operating under the CU banner have changed over time, first appearing around 2010 to combat the expansion of Los Zetas criminal group in the states of Michoacán and Jalisco; the current coalition has been targeted by the Mexican Government for synthetic-drug trafficking, homicides, and extortion rackets in the agricultural sector
leadership and organization – coalition was reportedly initiated by Juan José Farías ÁLVAREZ (aka "El Abuelo"), the leader of the Cartel del Abuelo (aka Cartel de Tepalcatepec)
area(s) of operation – operates primarily in the Mexican states of Michoacán and Jalisco where it has been engaged in frequent violent clashes with the CJNG over drug trafficking routes and illicit economies
tactics, targets, and weapons – targets the CJNG and civilians; armed with military-grade weapons
strength – not available
financial and other support – drug trafficking, extortion
designation – placed on the US Department of State's list of Foreign Terrorist Organizations on 20 February 2025

Viv Ansanm

aka – Living Together; Vivre Ensemble
history – Viv Ansanm was formed in 2023 as a coalition of the two main criminal gang alliances operating primarily in and around Haiti's capital, Port-au-Prince, G-9 and G-Pép; in February 2024, Viv Ansanm launched a series of coordinated attacks targeting public institutions and prisons across the Port-au-Prince metropolitan area aimed at destabilizing the transitional government led by interim Prime Minister Ariel HENRY, who announced his resignation on 11 March; violence associated with gang turf wars subsequently largely ceased but coordinated gang efforts to seize and control government territory in Port-au-Prince and neighboring areas increased; since 2024, the gang coalition has forced the closure of the Port-au-Prince international airport and the cessation of commercial flights and has blockaded and taxed shipments to the capital's main shipping ports; it has also seized or forced the closure of businesses, hospitals, and schools
goals – consolidate control over Port-au-Prince; expand reach into additional provinces; gain political influence
leadership and organization – the spokesperson is Jimmy "Barbecue" CHERIZIER; the alliance may include more than 25 armed gangs/factions, including about half a dozen core constituent gangs such as 5 Seggon, Kraze Barye, and 400 Mawozo
area of operation – controls much of Port-au-Prince; has begun expanding territorial control into the remainder of Quest Department and the nearby departments of Artibonite and Centre

targets, tactics, and weapons – targets civilians, self-defense groups, journalists, non-aligned criminal gangs, the Haitian Government, National Police, and Armed Forces, and the UN Multinational Security Support Mission force; specific targets have included businesses, courthouses, customs offices, highways, infrastructure, neighborhoods, police stations, ports, and prisons; tactics include beatings, extortion, harassment, hijackings, kidnappings for ransom, destruction of property, forced displacements, large-scale gun attacks, looting, murder, sexual violence, and torture; equipped with small arms, including military-grade weapons
strength – not available
financial and other support – engages in criminal activities, including extortion, kidnappings for ransom, and theft; controls some businesses and infrastructure in Port-au-Prince; probably still receives some support from corrupt economic and political elite; ammunition and firearms mostly trafficked into Haiti
designation – placed on the US Department of State's list of Foreign Terrorist Organizations on 2 May 2025

REFERENCE MAPS

POLITICAL MAP OF ANTARCTIC REGION

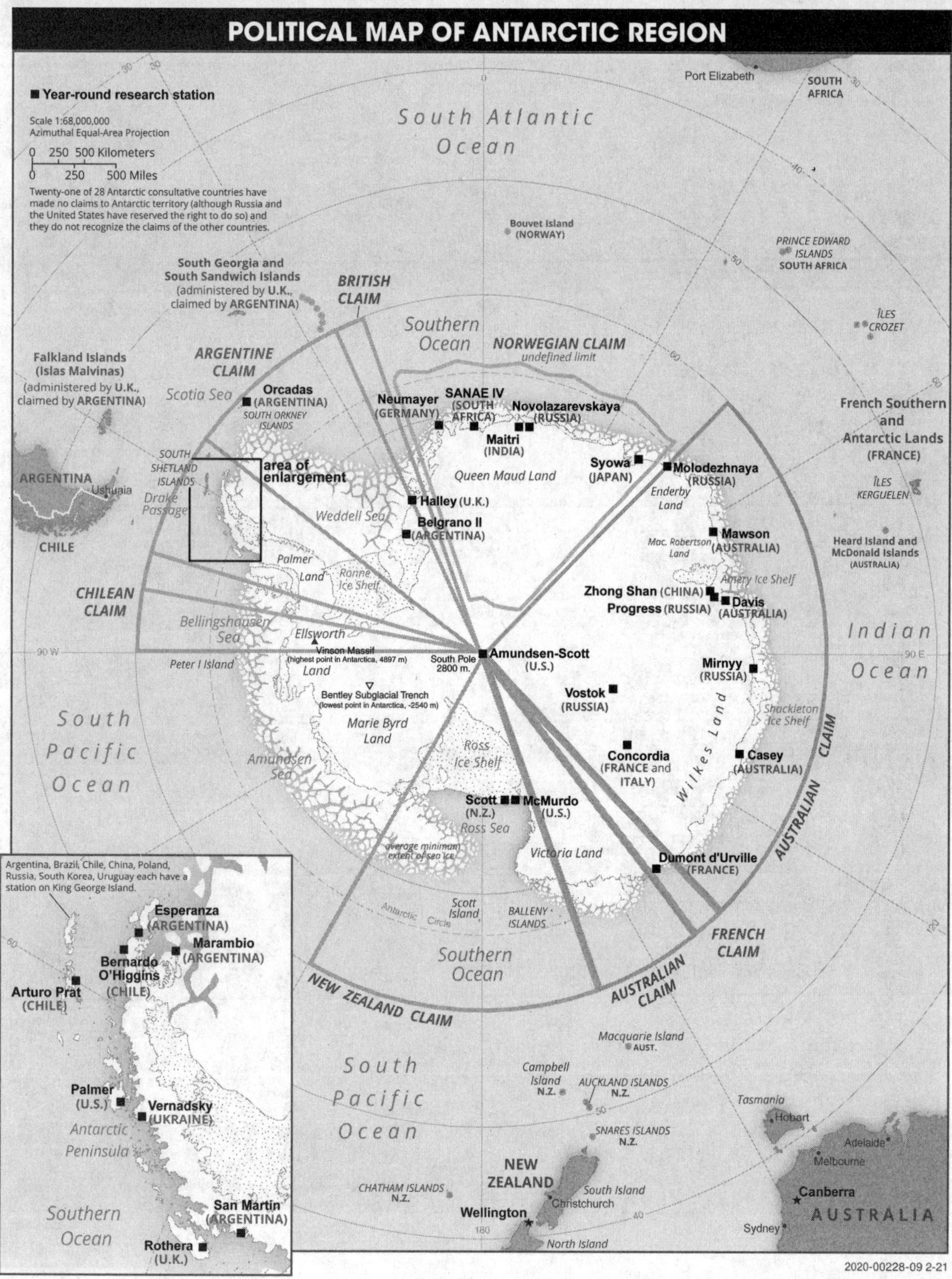

POLITICAL MAP OF ARCTIC REGION

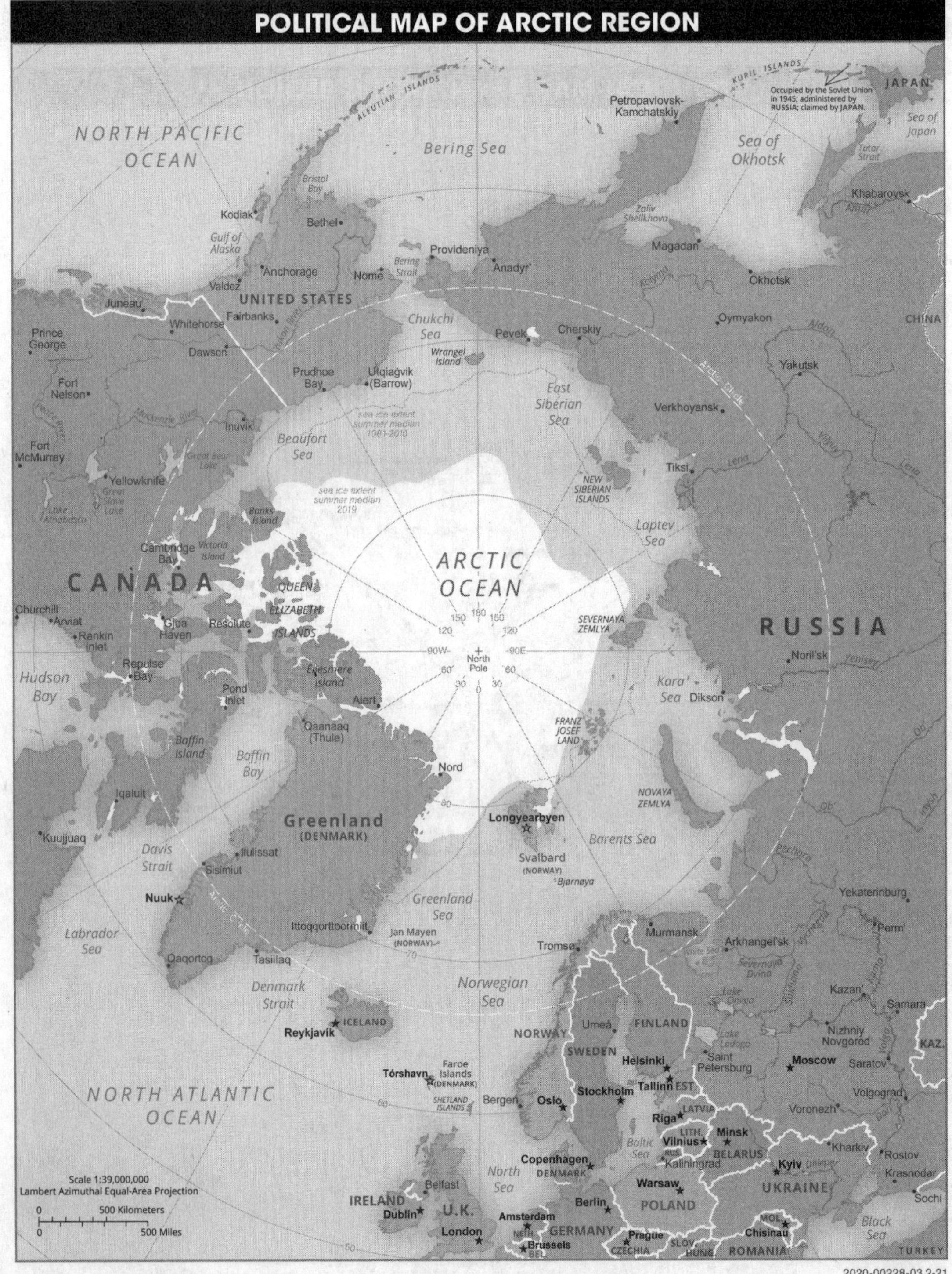

2020-00228-03 2-21

PHYSICAL MAP OF ARCTIC REGION

POLITICAL MAP OF AFRICA

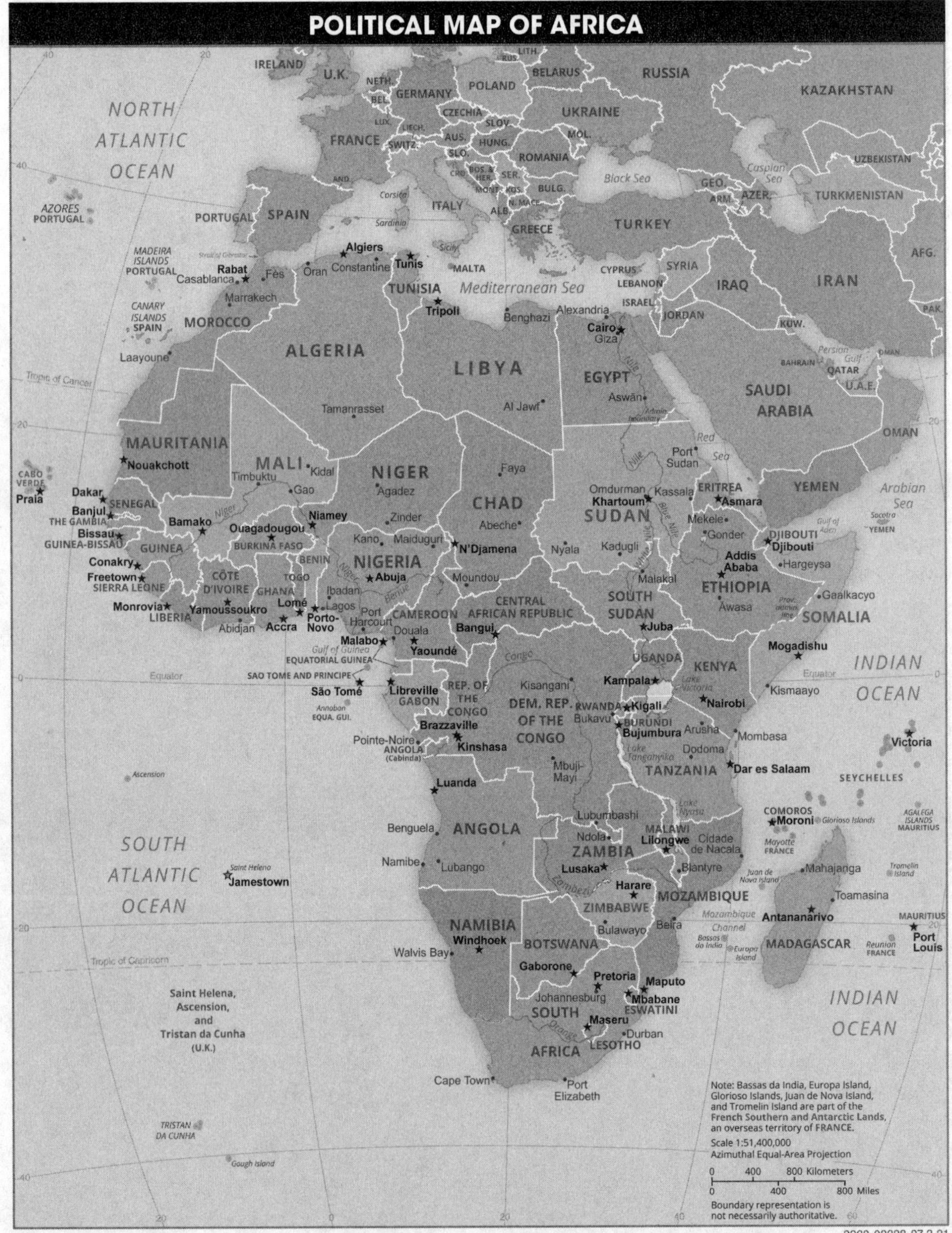

2020-00228-07 2-21

PHYSICAL MAP OF AFRICA

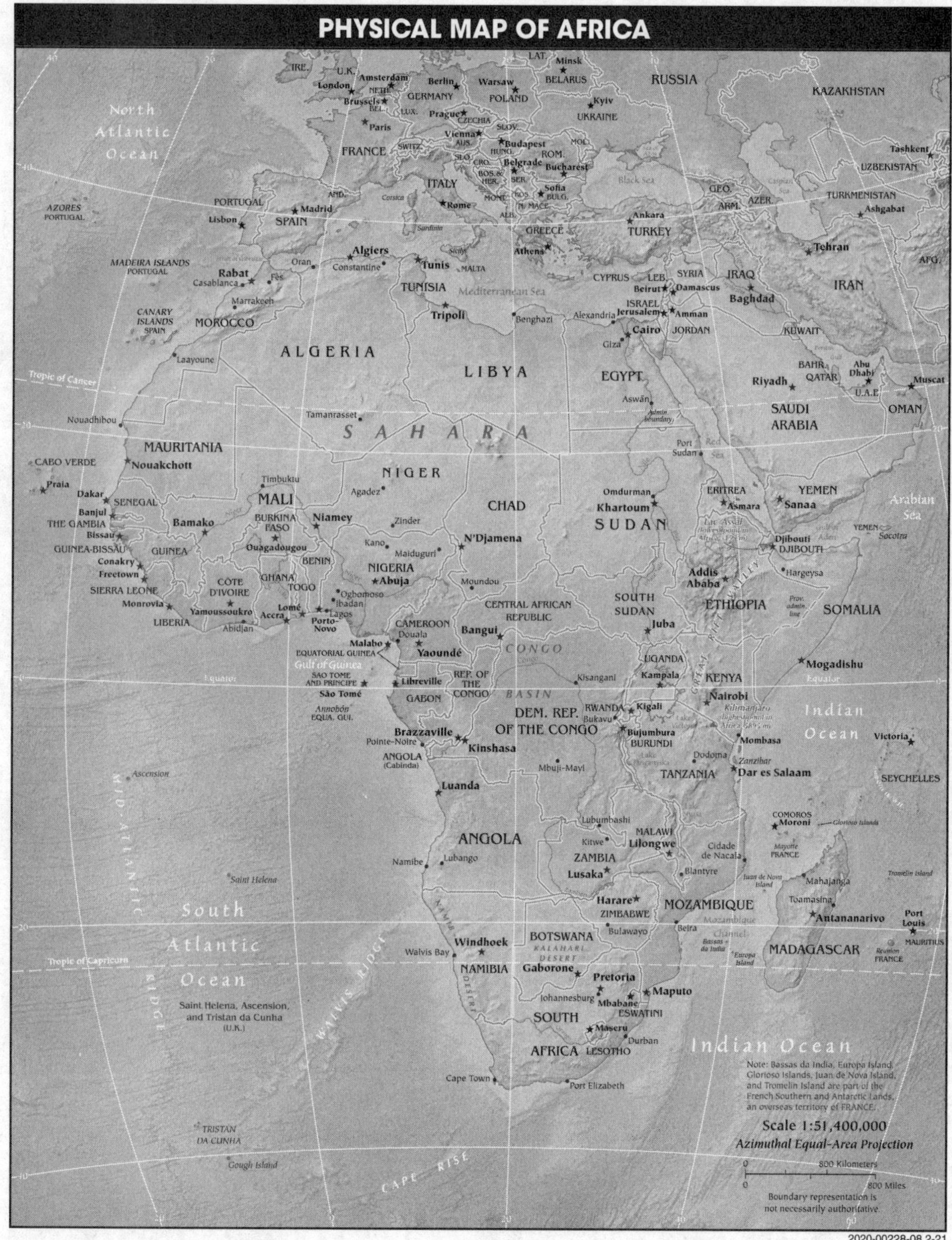

2020-00228-08 2-21

POLITICAL MAP OF ASIA

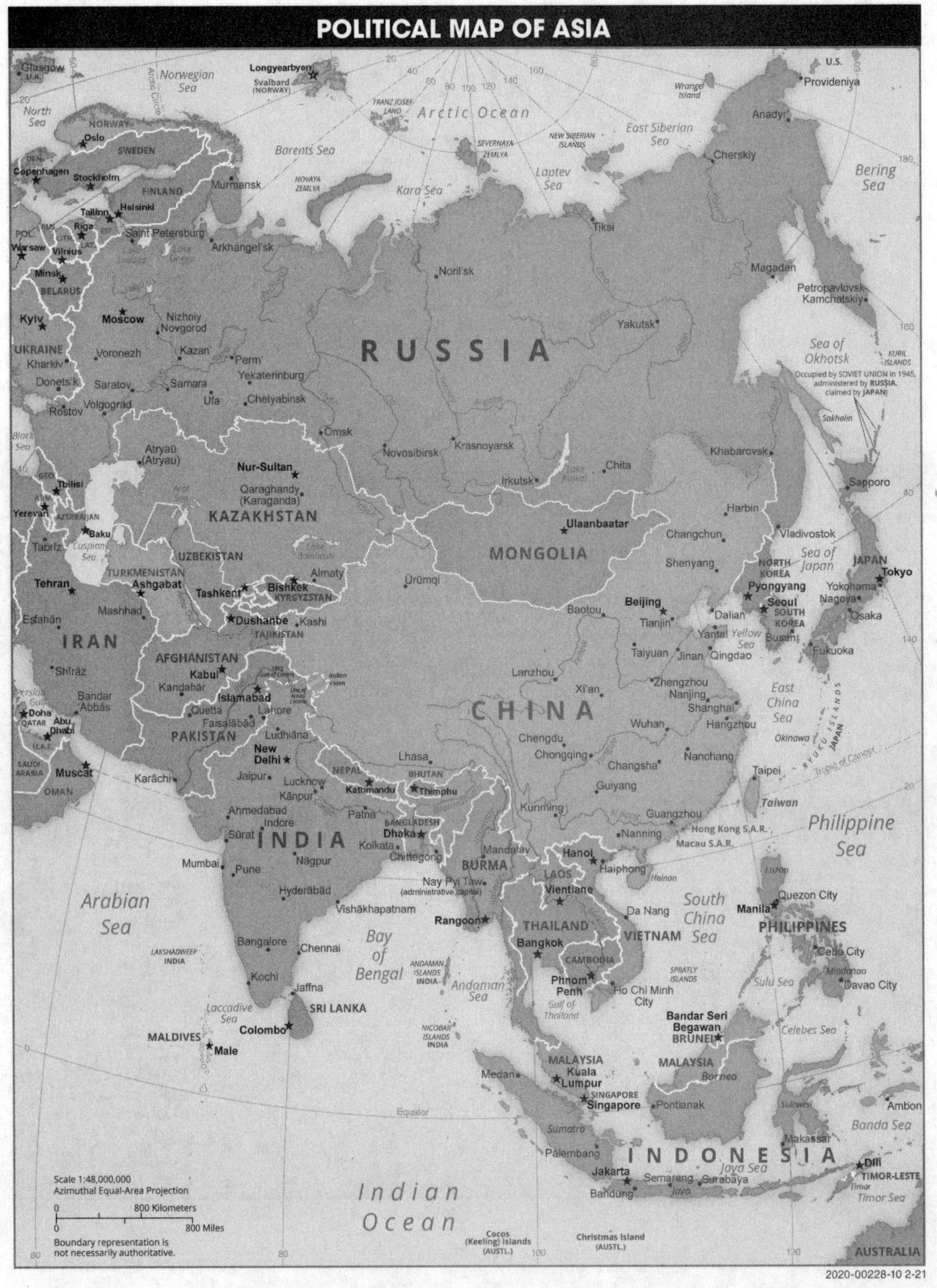

2020-00228-10 2-21

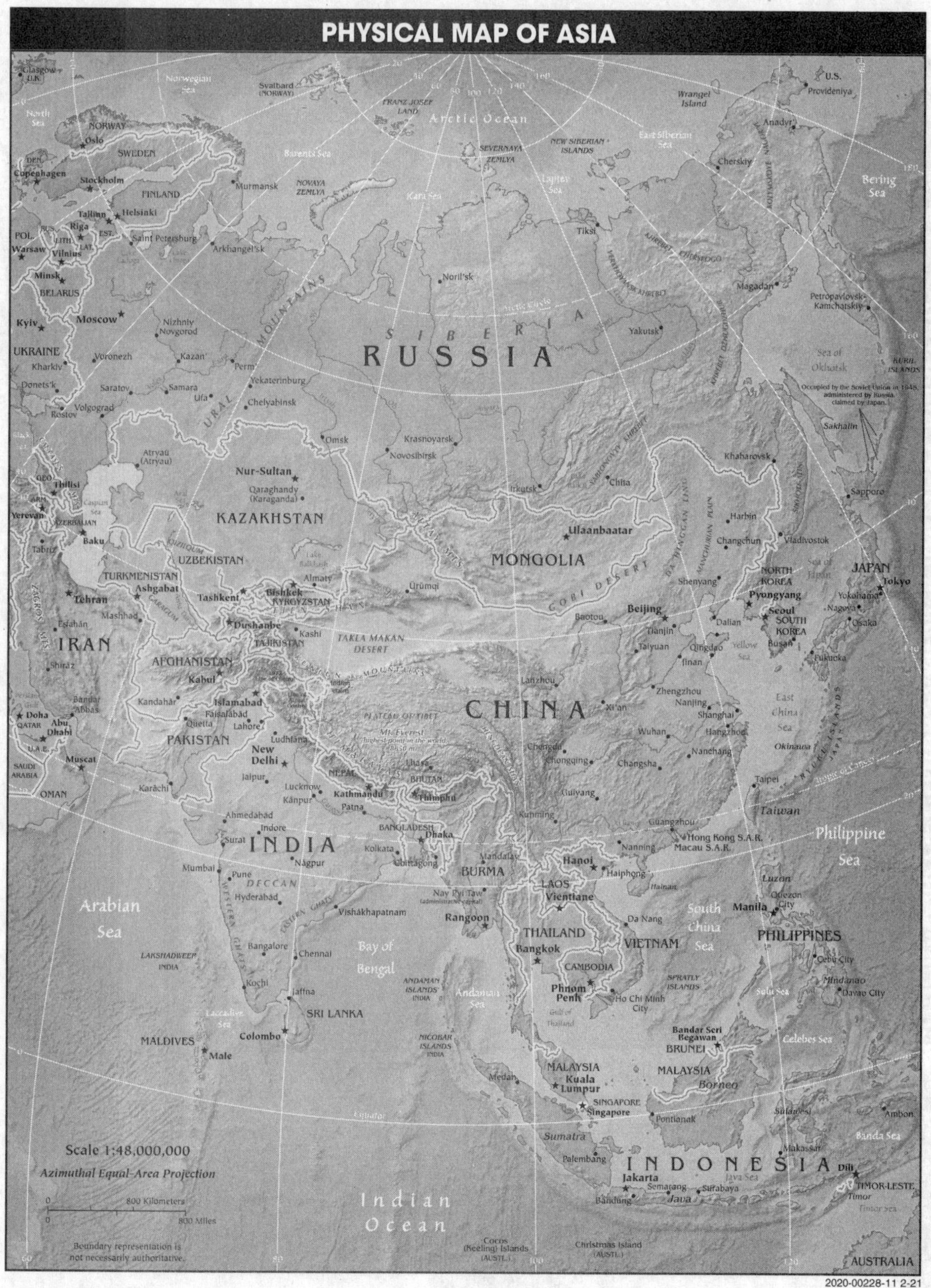

2020-00228-11 2-21

POLITICAL MAP OF CENTRAL AMERICA AND THE CARIBBEAN

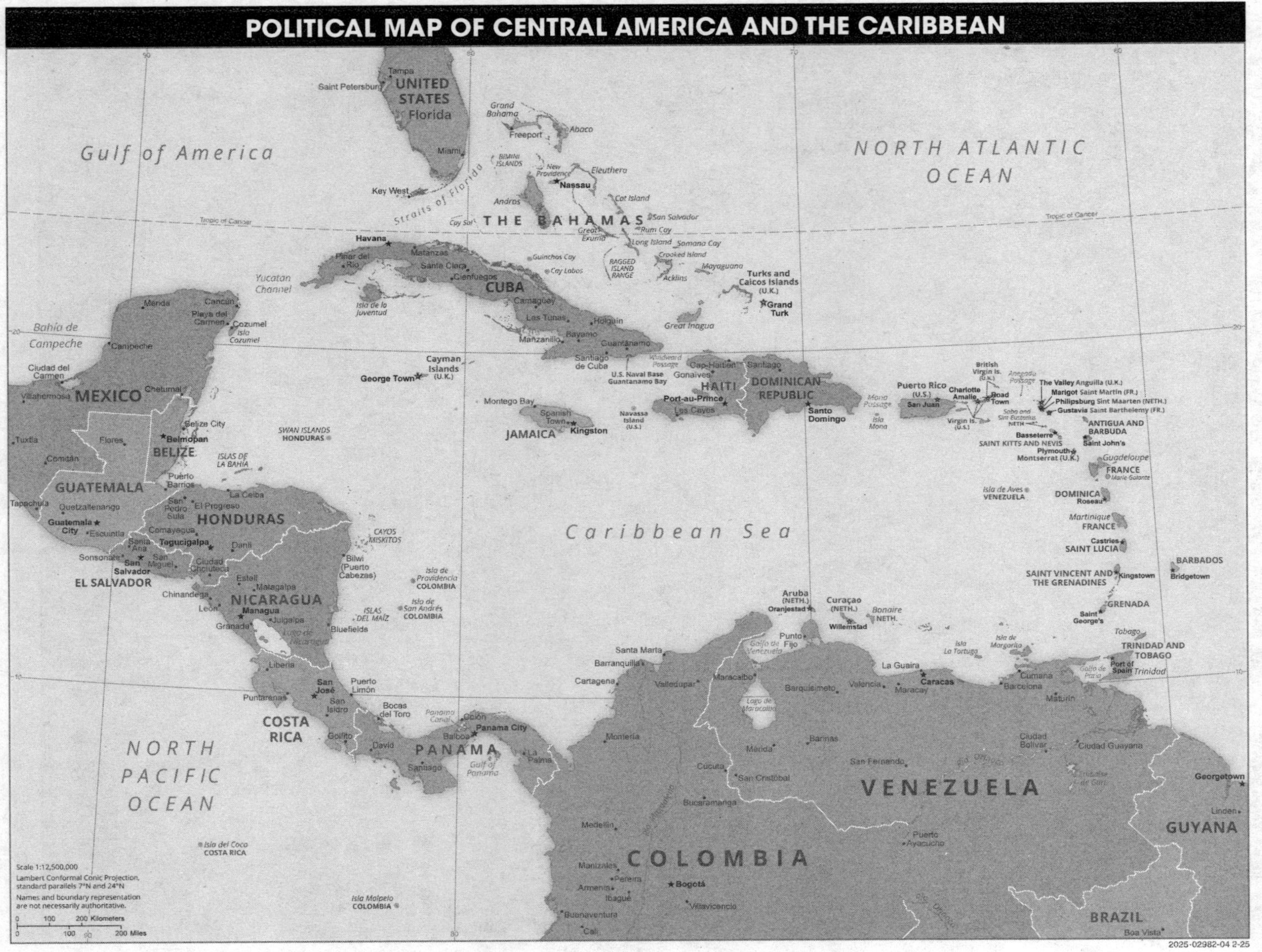

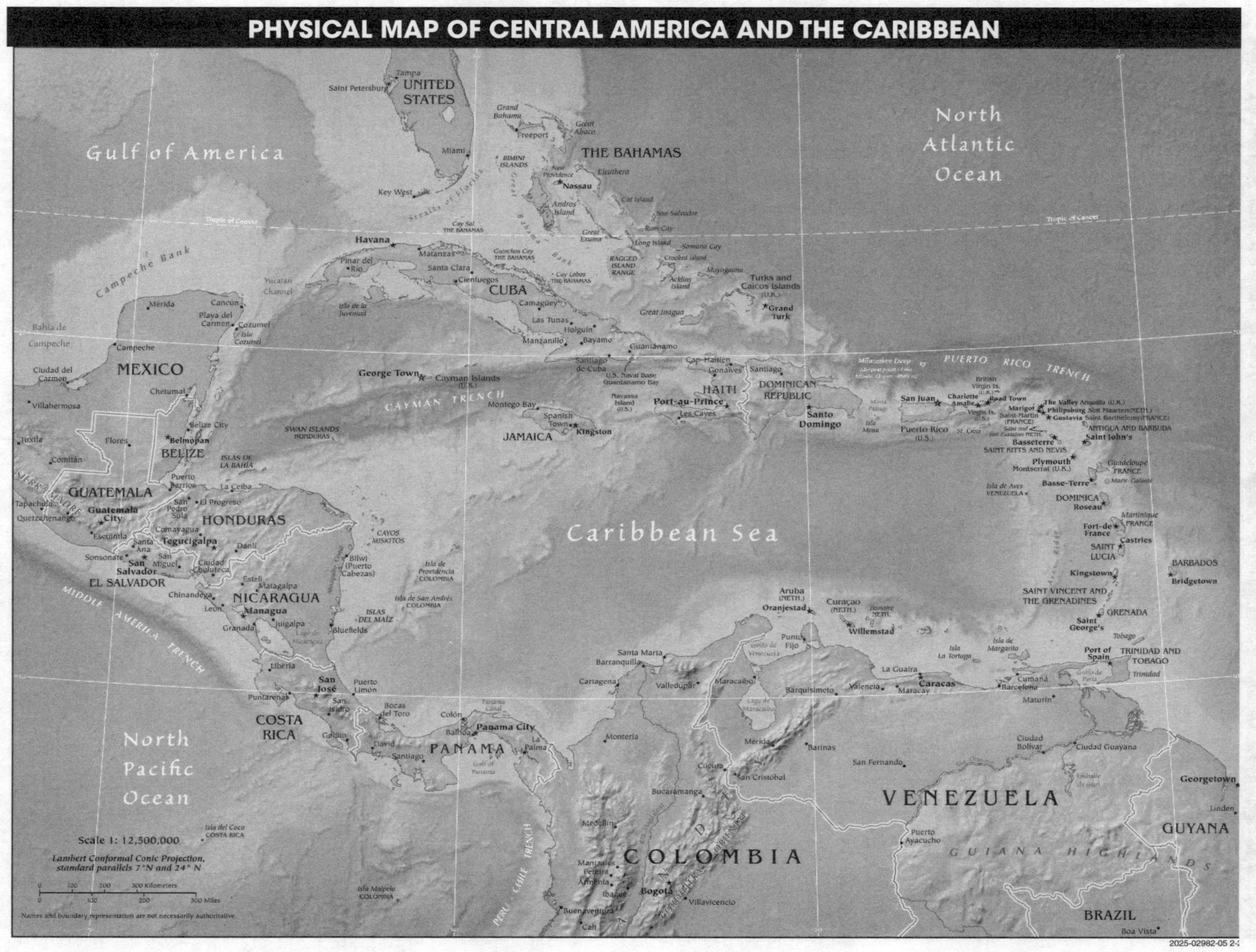
PHYSICAL MAP OF CENTRAL AMERICA AND THE CARIBBEAN
Gulf of America
North Atlantic Ocean
Caribbean Sea
North Pacific Ocean
UNITED STATES
Saint Petersburg
Tampa
Miami
Key West
Straits of Florida
Grand Bahama
Freeport
Great Abaco
BIMINI ISLANDS
THE BAHAMAS
New Providence
Nassau
Eleuthera
Andros Island
Cat Island
San Salvador
Great Exuma
Long Island
Rum Cay
Samana Cay
Crooked Island
Acklins Island
Mayaguana
Great Bahama Bank
RAGGED ISLAND RANGE
Great Inagua
Turks and Caicos Islands (U.K.)
Grand Turk
Cay Sal THE BAHAMAS
Havana
Matanzas
Pinar del Río
Santa Clara
Cienfuegos
CUBA
Isla de la Juventud
Camagüey
Las Tunas
Holguín
Manzanillo
Bayamo
Guantánamo
Santiago de Cuba
U.S. Naval Base Guantanamo Bay
Campeche Bank
Yucatan Channel
Mérida
Cancún
Playa del Carmen
Cozumel
Bahía de Campeche
Campeche
Ciudad del Carmen
MEXICO
Chetumal
Villahermosa
Tuxtla
Comitán
Belize City
Belmopan
BELIZE
Flores
GUATEMALA
Guatemala City
Quetzaltenango
Tapachula
Escuintla
Puerto Barrios
ISLAS DE LA BAHIA
La Ceiba
San Pedro Sula
El Progreso
HONDURAS
Comayagua
Tegucigalpa
Danlí
Santa Ana
Sonsonate
San Salvador
San Miguel
EL SALVADOR
Ciudad Choluteca
Estelí
Matagalpa
Chinandega
NICARAGUA
León
Managua
Granada
Juigalpa
Lago de Nicaragua
Bluefields
Bilwi (Puerto Cabezas)
CAYOS MISKITOS
ISLAS DEL MAIZ
Isla de Providencia COLOMBIA
Isla de San Andrés COLOMBIA
SWAN ISLANDS HONDURAS
Liberia
Puntarenas
San José
Puerto Limón
San Isidro
Golfito
COSTA RICA
Bocas del Toro
David
Santiago
Colón
Panama Canal
Balboa
Panama City
La Palma
PANAMA
Gulf of Panama
Isla del Coco COSTA RICA
Isla Malpelo COLOMBIA
MIDDLE AMERICA TRENCH
PERU-CHILE TRENCH
George Town
Cayman Islands (U.K.)
CAYMAN TRENCH
Montego Bay
Spanish Town
Kingston
JAMAICA
Navassa Island (U.S.)
Cap-Haïtien
Gonaïves
HAITI
Port-au-Prince
Les Cayes
Santiago
DOMINICAN REPUBLIC
Santo Domingo
Mona Passage
Isla Mona
PUERTO RICO TRENCH
Milwaukee Deep
San Juan
Puerto Rico (U.S.)
Charlotte Amalie
British Virgin Is. (U.K.)
Road Town
Virgin Is. (U.S.)
St. Croix
The Valley Anguilla (U.K.)
Marigot
Saint-Martin (FRANCE)
Philipsburg Sint Maarten (NETH.)
Gustavia Saint Barthelemy (FRANCE)
ANTIGUA AND BARBUDA
Saint John's
Basseterre
SAINT KITTS AND NEVIS
Plymouth
Montserrat (U.K.)
Guadeloupe FRANCE
Marie-Galante
Basse-Terre
Isla de Aves VENEZUELA
DOMINICA
Roseau
Martinique FRANCE
Fort-de-France
Castries
SAINT LUCIA
BARBADOS
Bridgetown
Kingstown
SAINT VINCENT AND THE GRENADINES
GRENADA
Saint George's
Tobago
TRINIDAD AND TOBAGO
Port of Spain
Trinidad
Gulf of Paria
Aruba (NETH.)
Oranjestad
Curaçao (NETH.)
Willemstad
Bonaire NETH.
Punto Fijo
Golfo de Venezuela
Isla La Tortuga
Isla de Margarita
Santa Marta
Barranquilla
Cartagena
Valledupar
Maracaibo
Lago de Maracaibo
Barquisimeto
Valencia
Maracay
La Guaira
Caracas
Barcelona
Cumaná
Maturín
Mérida
Barinas
Cúcuta
San Cristóbal
San Fernando
Ciudad Bolívar
Ciudad Guayana
Embalse de Guri
VENEZUELA
Puerto Ayacucho
GUIANA HIGHLANDS
Georgetown
Linden
GUYANA
BRAZIL
Boa Vista
Montería
Bucaramanga
Medellín
Manizales
Pereira
Armenia
Ibagué
Bogotá
Villavicencio
Buenaventura
Cali
COLOMBIA
ANDES
Tropic of Cancer
Scale 1: 12,500,000
Lambert Conformal Conic Projection, standard parallels 7°N and 24°N
0 100 200 300 Kilometers
0 100 200 300 Miles
Names and boundary representation are not necessarily authoritative.
2025-02982-05 2-2

POLITICAL MAP OF EUROPE

PHYSICAL MAP OF EUROPE

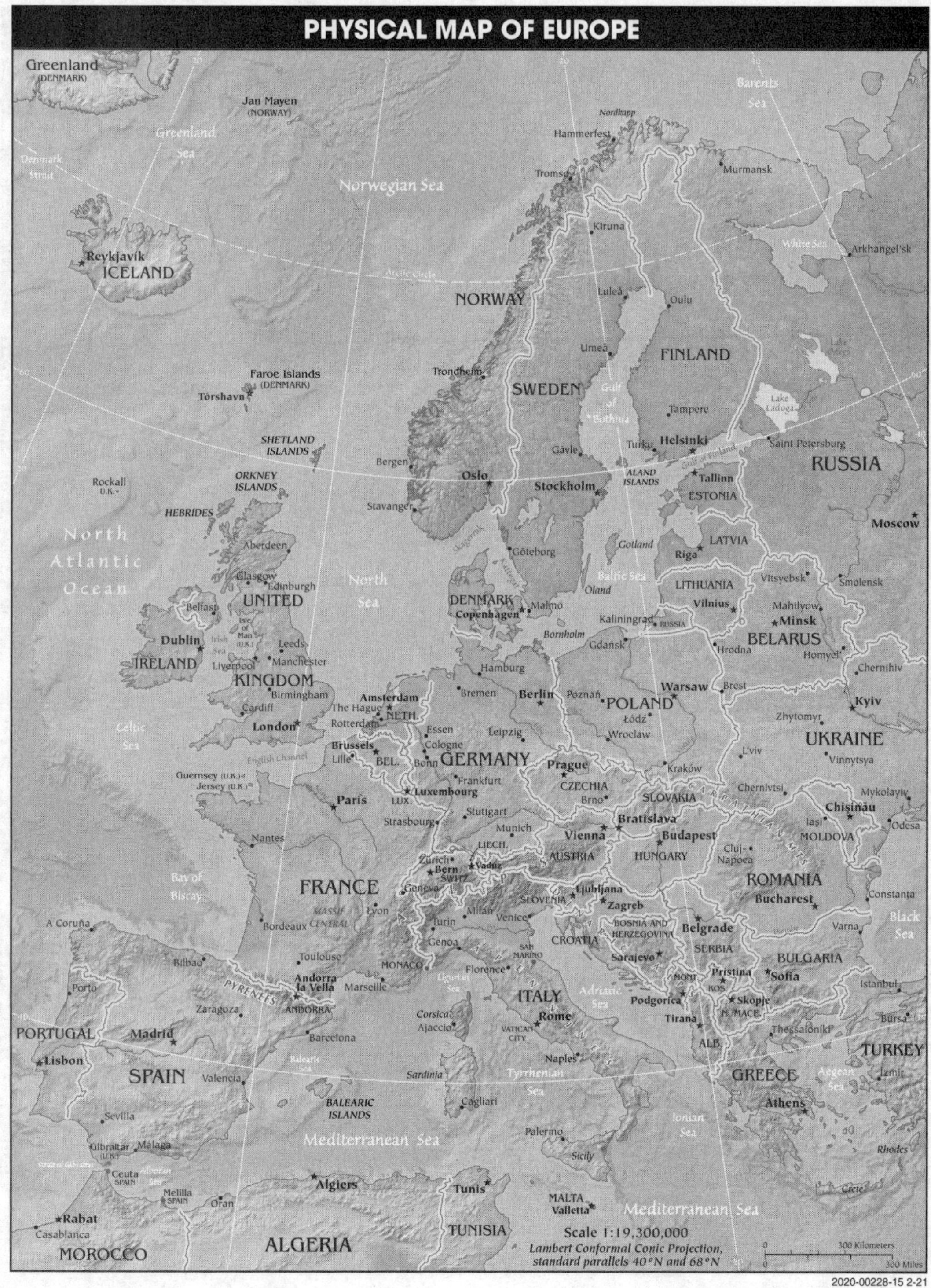

2020-00228-15 2-21

POLITICAL MAP OF MIDDLE EAST

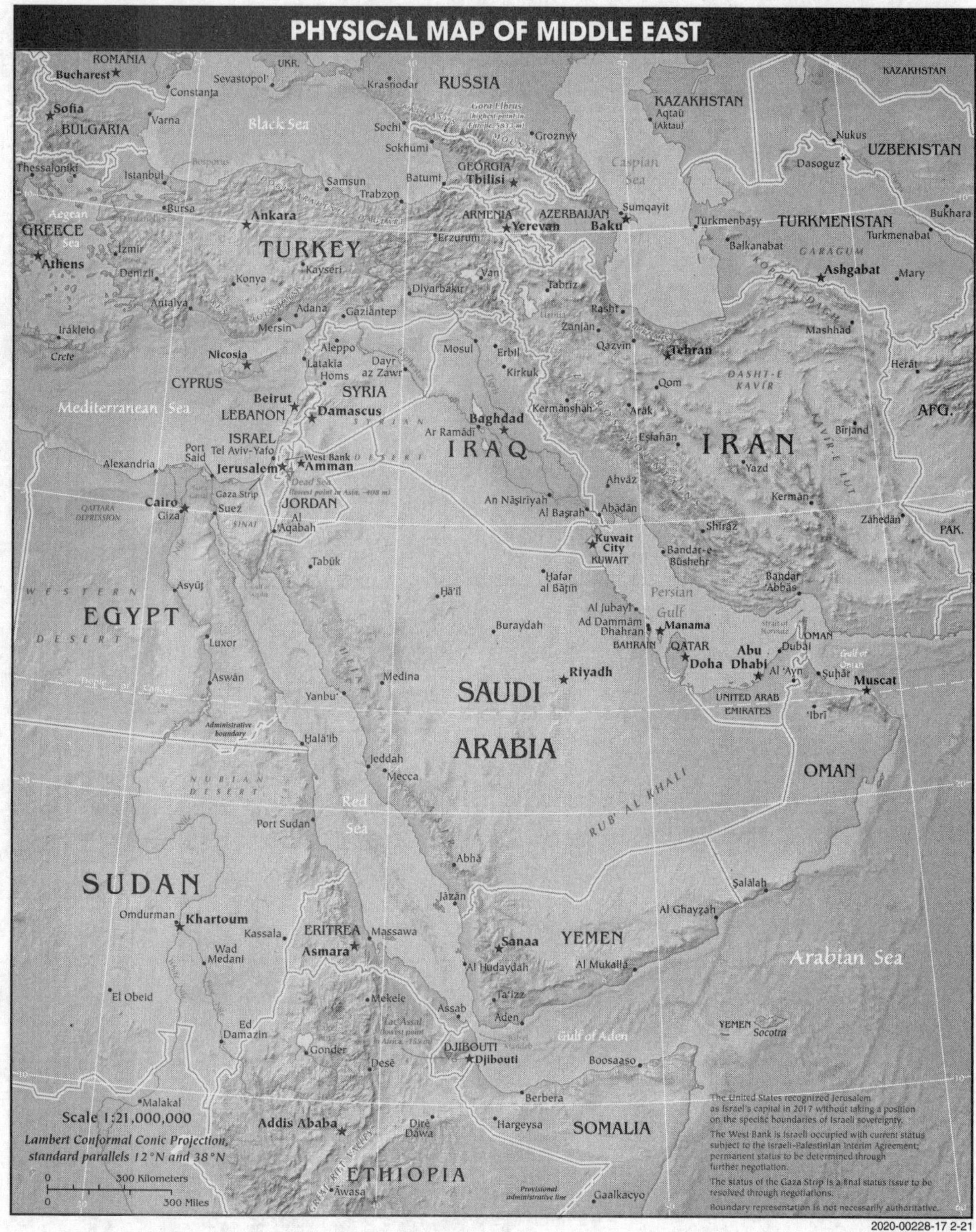
PHYSICAL MAP OF MIDDLE EAST
ROMANIA
Bucharest
UKR.
Sevastopol'
Krasnodar
RUSSIA
KAZAKHSTAN
Constanța
Sofia
BULGARIA
Varna
Black Sea
Sochi
Groznyy
KAZAKHSTAN
Aqtaū
(Aktau)
Nukus
UZBEKISTAN
Sokhumi
Thessaloníki
Istanbul
Bosporus
Samsun
Trabzon
Batumi
GEORGIA
Tbilisi
Caspian Sea
Dasoguz
Bursa
Ankara
ARMENIA
Yerevan
AZERBAIJAN
Baku
Sumqayit
Türkmenbaşy
TURKMENISTAN
Bukhara
Turkmenabat
Aegean Sea
GREECE
Athens
İzmir
TURKEY
Erzurum
Balkanabat
GARAGUM
Ashgabat
Mary
Denizli
Kayseri
Konya
Van
Tabrīz
Antalya
Adana
Gaziantep
Diyarbakır
Rasht
Mashhad
Iráklelo
Crete
Mersin
Zanjān
Qazvīn
Tehran
Nicosia
Aleppo
Latakia
Homs
Dayr az Zawr
Mosul
Erbīl
Kirkuk
Herāt
CYPRUS
SYRIA
Qom
DASHT-E KAVĪR
Beirut
LEBANON
Damascus
Kermānshāh
Arāk
AFG.
Mediterranean Sea
ISRAEL
Baghdad
Ar Ramādī
Eşfahān
IRAN
Bīrjand
Port Said
Tel Aviv-Yafo
West Bank
IRAQ
Alexandria
Jerusalem
Amman
Yazd
Dead Sea
(lowest point in Asia, -408 m)
Ahvāz
Gaza Strip
Cairo
Giza
Suez
JORDAN
An Nāşirīyah
Al Başrah
Abādān
Kermān
QATTARA DEPRESSION
SINAI
Al 'Aqabah
Kuwait City
KUWAIT
Shīrāz
Zāhedān
PAK.
Tabūk
Bandar-e Būshehr
Ḩafar al Bāţin
Bandar 'Abbās
WESTERN DESERT
Asyūţ
Ḩā'il
Persian Gulf
EGYPT
Al Jubayl
Ad Dammām
Dhahran
Manama
BAHRAIN
Buraydah
Strait of Hormuz
OMAN
Luxor
QATAR
Doha
Abu Dhabi
Dubai
Gulf of Oman
Aswān
Medina
Riyadh
Al 'Ayn
Şuḩār
Muscat
Tropic of Cancer
Yanbu'
SAUDI ARABIA
UNITED ARAB EMIRATES
'Ibrī
Administrative boundary
Ḩalā'ib
Jeddah
Mecca
OMAN
NUBIAN DESERT
Red Sea
RUB' AL KHALI
Port Sudan
Abhā
SUDAN
Şalālah
Jāzān
Al Ghayzah
Omdurman
Khartoum
Kassala
ERITREA
Massawa
Asmara
Sanaa
YEMEN
Arabian Sea
Wad Medani
Al Ḩudaydah
Al Mukallā
El Obeid
Mekele
Ta'izz
Assab
Aden
YEMEN
Socotra
Ed Damazin
Lac Assal
(lowest point in Africa, -155 m)
Gulf of Aden
Gonder
DJIBOUTI
Djibouti
Boosaaso
Desē
Malakal
Berbera
Scale 1:21,000,000
Lambert Conformal Conic Projection, standard parallels 12°N and 38°N
Addis Ababa
Dirē Dawa
Hargeysa
SOMALIA
ETHIOPIA
Āwasa
Provisional administrative line
Gaalkacyo
0 300 Kilometers
0 300 Miles
The United States recognized Jerusalem as Israel's capital in 2017 without taking a position on the specific boundaries of Israeli sovereignty.
The West Bank is Israeli occupied with current status subject to the Israeli-Palestinian Interim Agreement; permanent status to be determined through further negotiation.
The status of the Gaza Strip is a final status issue to be resolved through negotiations.
Boundary representation is not necessarily authoritative.
2020-00228-17 2-21

POLITICAL MAP OF NORTH AMERICA

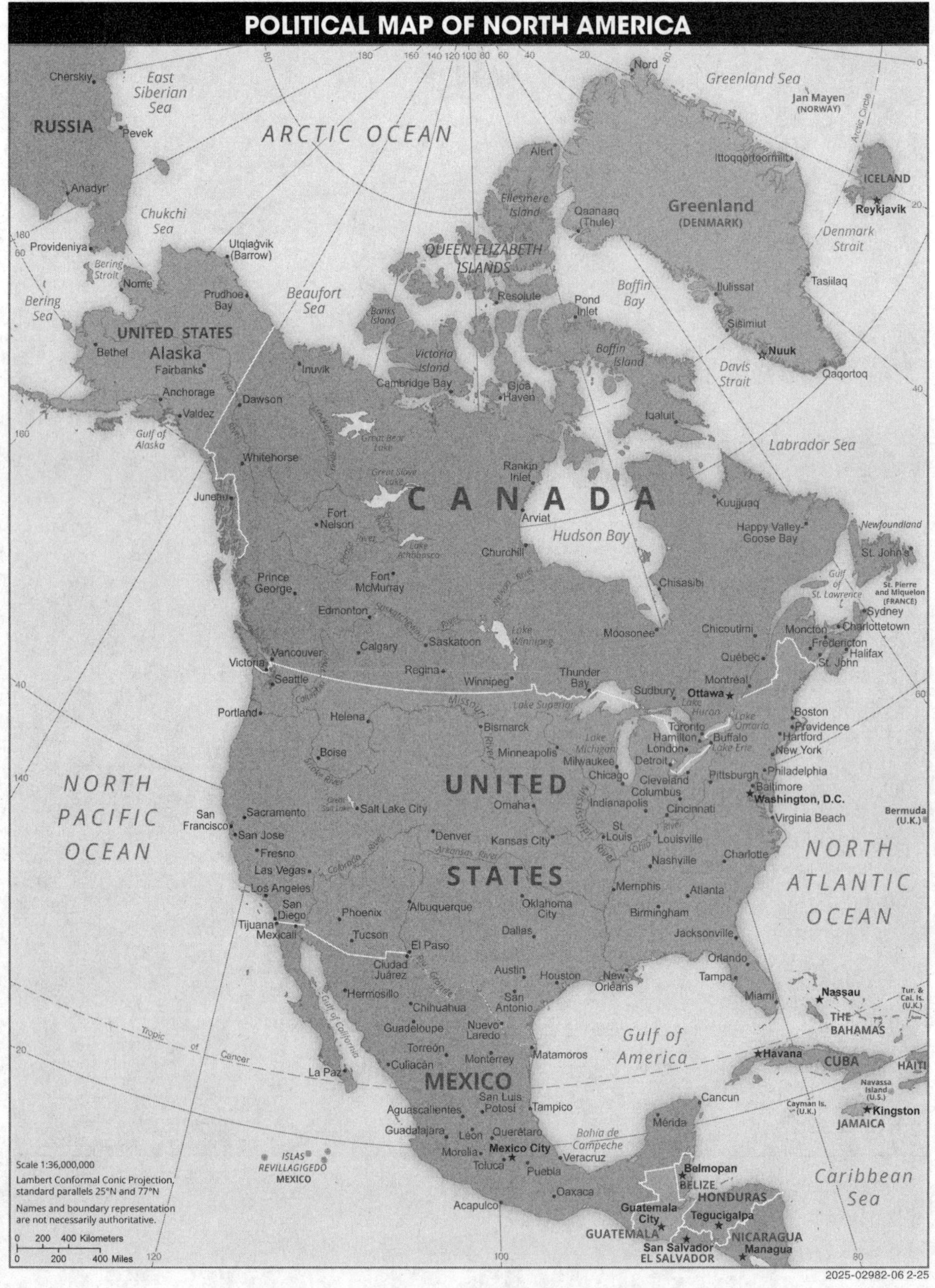

PHYSICAL MAP OF NORTH AMERICA

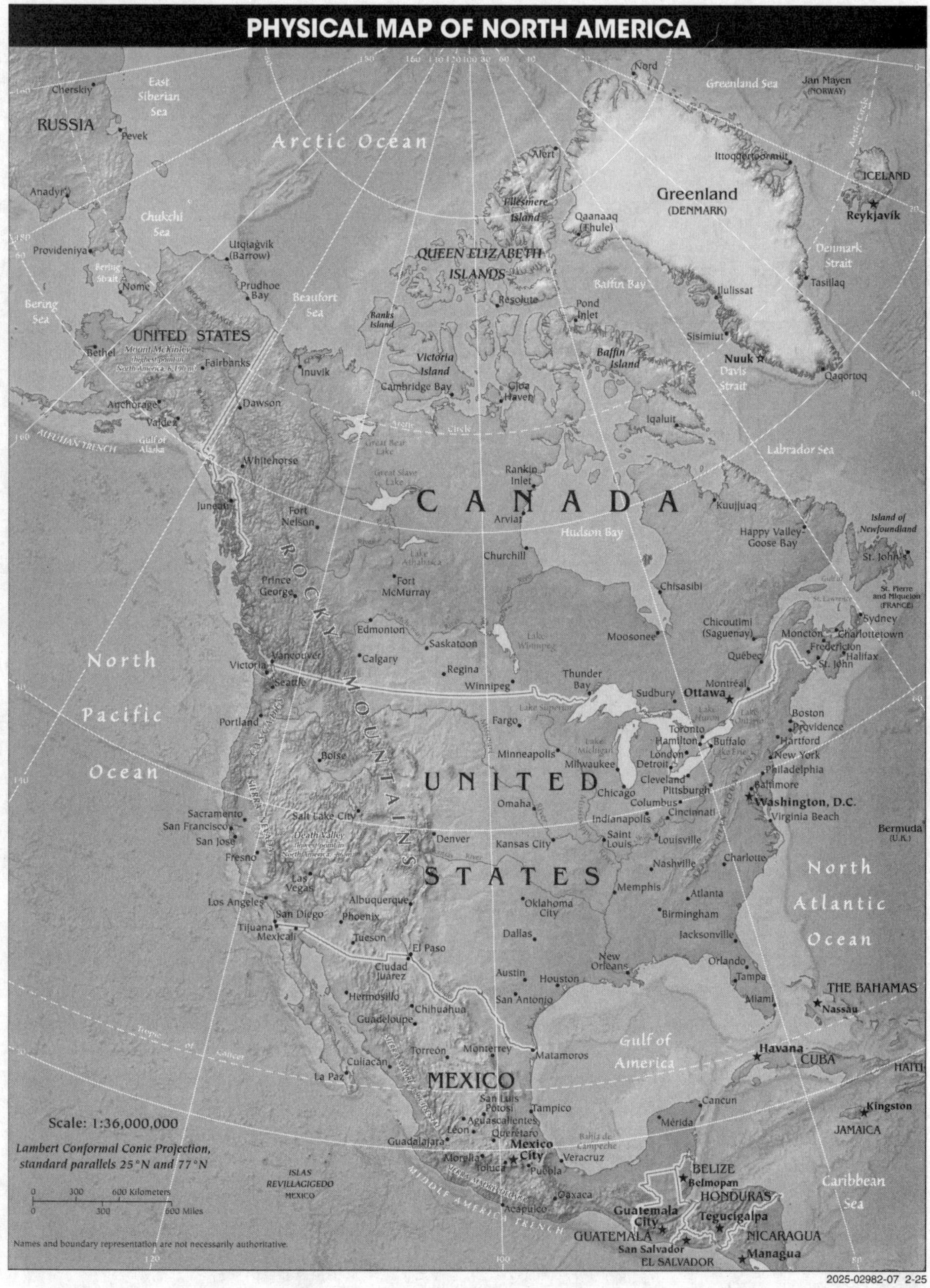

2025-02982-07 2-25

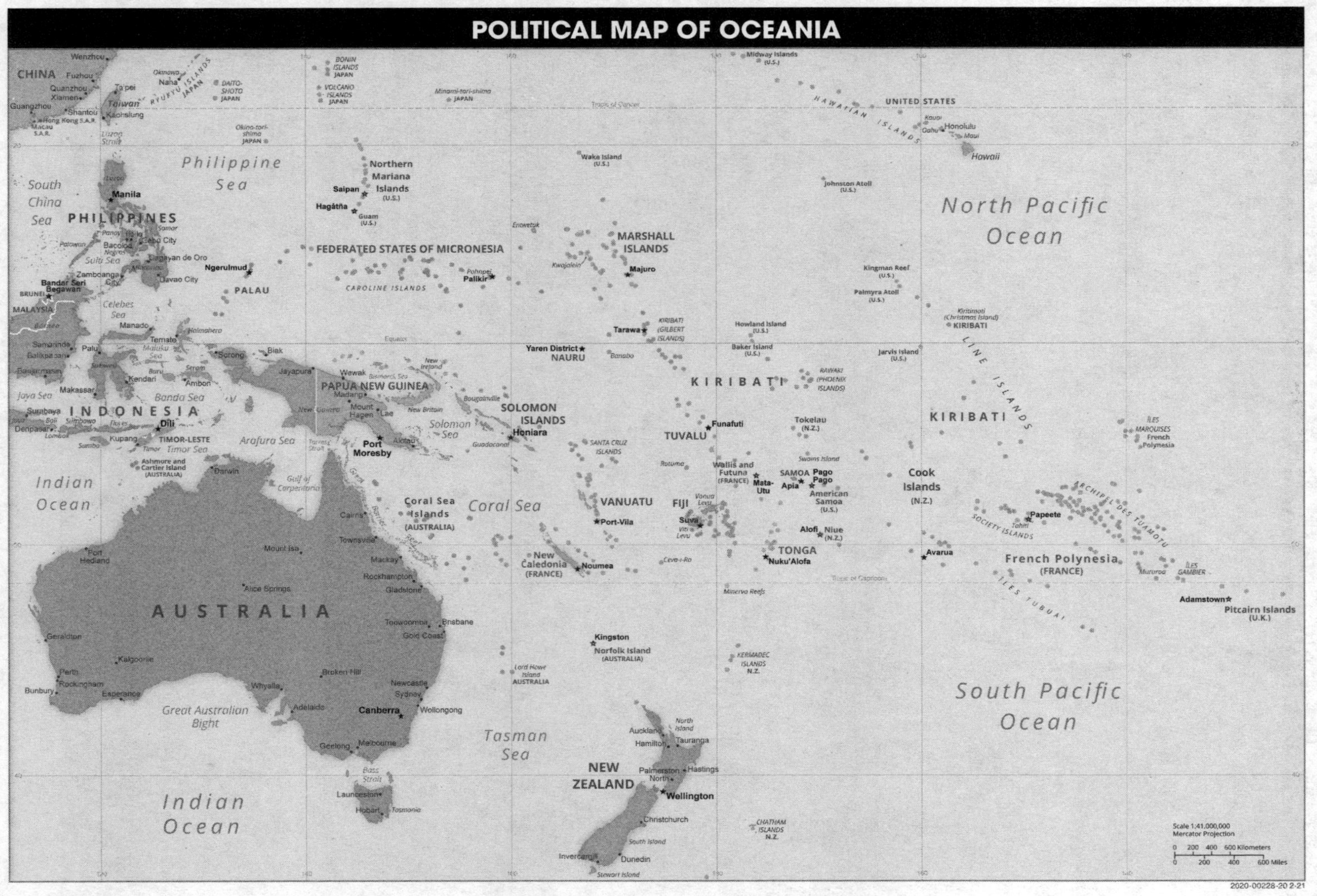
POLITICAL MAP OF OCEANIA
North Pacific Ocean
South Pacific Ocean
Indian Ocean
Philippine Sea
South China Sea
Coral Sea
Tasman Sea
Arafura Sea
Solomon Sea
Banda Sea
Celebes Sea
Timor Sea
Great Australian Bight
AUSTRALIA
NEW ZEALAND
PAPUA NEW GUINEA
INDONESIA
PHILIPPINES
CHINA
MALAYSIA
BRUNEI
FEDERATED STATES OF MICRONESIA
MARSHALL ISLANDS
KIRIBATI
SOLOMON ISLANDS
VANUATU
FIJI
TUVALU
TONGA
SAMOA
NAURU
PALAU
TIMOR-LESTE
UNITED STATES
Hawaii
French Polynesia (FRANCE)
Cook Islands (N.Z.)
New Caledonia (FRANCE)
Northern Mariana Islands (U.S.)
Pitcairn Islands (U.K.)
Norfolk Island (AUSTRALIA)
Wallis and Futuna (FRANCE)
American Samoa (U.S.)
Tokelau (N.Z.)
Niue (N.Z.)
Coral Sea Islands (AUSTRALIA)
Ashmore and Cartier Island (AUSTRALIA)
Guam (U.S.)
Wake Island (U.S.)
Midway Islands (U.S.)
Johnston Atoll (U.S.)
Kingman Reef (U.S.)
Palmyra Atoll (U.S.)
Howland Island (U.S.)
Baker Island (U.S.)
Jarvis Island (U.S.)
Canberra
Wellington
Port Moresby
Honiara
Port-Vila
Suva
Funafuti
Majuro
Tarawa
Palikir
Apia
Pago Pago
Nuku'Alofa
Yaren District
Ngerulmud
Manila
Dili
Hagåtña
Saipan
Noumea
Papeete
Avarua
Adamstown
Kingston
Mata-Utu
Alofi
Honolulu
Scale 1:41,000,000
Mercator Projection
2020-00228-20 2-21

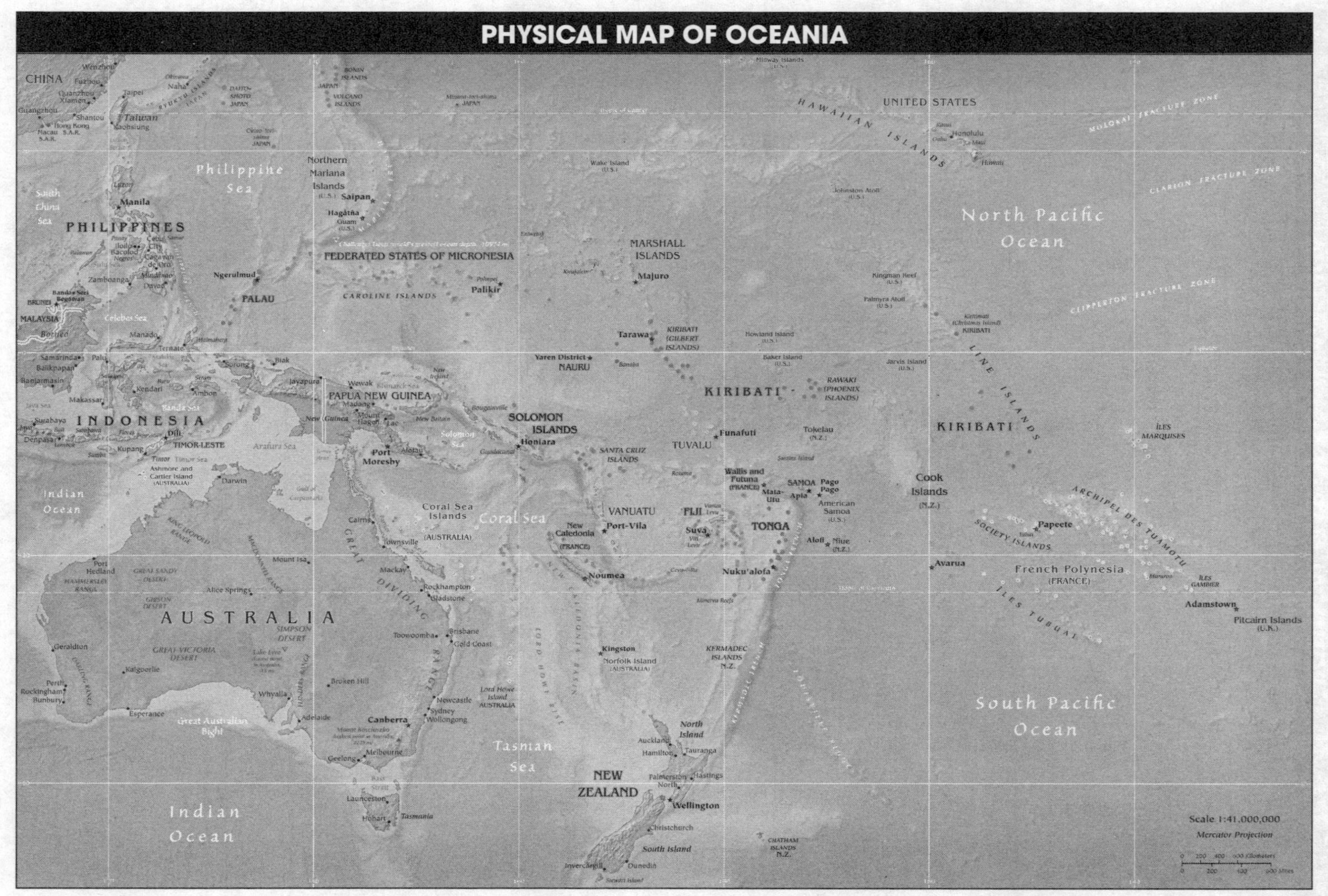
PHYSICAL MAP OF OCEANIA
North Pacific Ocean
South Pacific Ocean
Indian Ocean
Philippine Sea
Coral Sea
Tasman Sea
CHINA
PHILIPPINES
INDONESIA
AUSTRALIA
PAPUA NEW GUINEA
SOLOMON ISLANDS
FEDERATED STATES OF MICRONESIA
MARSHALL ISLANDS
PALAU
NAURU
KIRIBATI
TUVALU
VANUATU
FIJI
TONGA
SAMOA
NEW ZEALAND
UNITED STATES
HAWAIIAN ISLANDS
LINE ISLANDS
Cook Islands (N.Z.)
French Polynesia (FRANCE)
Pitcairn Islands (U.K.)
Manila
Ngerulmud
Palikir
Majuro
Tarawa
Honiara
Port Moresby
Port-Vila
Suva
Funafuti
Apia
Nuku'alofa
Noumea
Canberra
Wellington
Papeete
Adamstown
Scale 1:41,000,000
Mercator Projection

POLITICAL MAP OF SOUTH AMERICA

PHYSICAL MAP OF SOUTH AMERICA

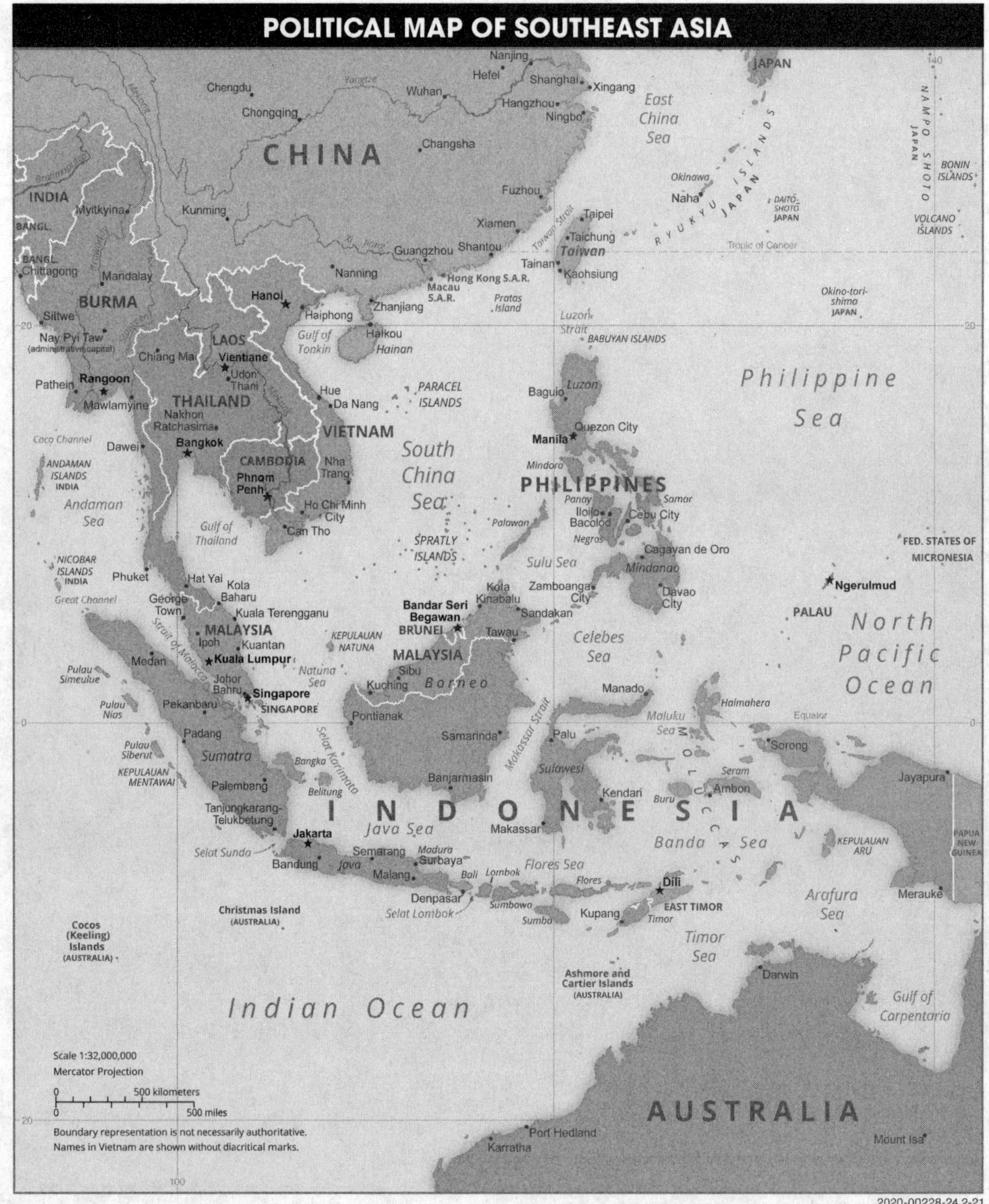
POLITICAL MAP OF SOUTHEAST ASIA
CHINA
Nanjing
Hefei
Shanghai
Xingang
Chengdu
Wuhan
Hangzhou
Ningbo
Chongqing
Changsha
East China Sea
JAPAN
NAMPO SHOTO JAPAN
BONIN ISLANDS
Okinawa
Naha
RYUKYU ISLANDS JAPAN
DAITO-SHOTO JAPAN
VOLCANO ISLANDS
Fuzhou
INDIA
Myitkyina
Kunming
BANGL.
Xiamen
Taipei
Taichung
Taiwan
Taiwan Strait
Tropic of Cancer
BANGL.
Chittagong
Mandalay
Guangzhou
Shantou
Tainan
Kaohsiung
Nanning
Hong Kong S.A.R.
Macau S.A.R.
Pratas Island
BURMA
Hanoi
Haiphong
Zhanjiang
Okino-tori-shima JAPAN
Sittwe
Nay Pyi Taw (administrative capital)
Luzon Strait
BABUYAN ISLANDS
Gulf of Tonkin
Haikou
Hainan
LAOS
Chiang Mai
Vientiane
Udon Thani
Pathein
Rangoon
Philippine Sea
Hue
Da Nang
PARACEL ISLANDS
Baguio
Luzon
Mawlamyine
THAILAND
Nakhon Ratchasima
VIETNAM
Quezon City
Manila
Coco Channel
Dawei
Bangkok
South China Sea
Mindoro
ANDAMAN ISLANDS INDIA
CAMBODIA
Phnom Penh
Nha Trang
PHILIPPINES
Samar
Panay
Andaman Sea
Ho Chi Minh City
Iloilo
Bacolod
Cebu City
Palawan
Gulf of Thailand
Can Tho
Negros
SPRATLY ISLANDS
Cagayan de Oro
FED. STATES OF MICRONESIA
NICOBAR ISLANDS INDIA
Phuket
Hat Yai
Kota Baharu
Sulu Sea
Mindanao
Great Channel
George Town
Kota Kinabalu
Zamboanga City
Davao City
Ngerulmud
Kuala Terengganu
Bandar Seri Begawan
Sandakan
PALAU
MALAYSIA
KEPULAUAN NATUNA
BRUNEI
Tawau
North Pacific Ocean
Ipoh
Kuantan
Strait of Malacca
Celebes Sea
Medan
Kuala Lumpur
MALAYSIA
Pulau Simeulue
Johor Bahru
Natuna Sea
Sibu
Manado
Kuching
Borneo
Halmahera
Singapore
SINGAPORE
Pulau Nias
Pekanbaru
Pontianak
Equator
Maluku Sea
Padang
Samarinda
Makassar Strait
Palu
Sorong
Pulau Siberut
Sumatra
Bangka
Selat Karimata
Sulawesi
Seram
Jayapura
KEPULAUAN MENTAWAI
Palembang
Belitung
Banjarmasin
Kendari
Ambon
Buru
MOLUCCAS
Tanjungkarang-Telukbetung
INDONESIA
Jakarta
Java Sea
Makassar
Banda Sea
PAPUA NEW GUINEA
KEPULAUAN ARU
Selat Sunda
Semarang
Madura
Surbaya
Bandung
Java
Malang
Bali
Lombok
Flores Sea
Flores
Dili
Denpasar
Selat Lombok
Sumbawa
EAST TIMOR
Arafura Sea
Merauke
Christmas Island (AUSTRALIA)
Sumba
Kupang
Timor
Cocos (Keeling) Islands (AUSTRALIA)
Timor Sea
Darwin
Ashmore and Cartier Islands (AUSTRALIA)
Gulf of Carpentaria
Indian Ocean
Scale 1:32,000,000
Mercator Projection
500 kilometers
500 miles
AUSTRALIA
Port Hedland
Karratha
Mount Isa
Boundary representation is not necessarily authoritative.
Names in Vietnam are shown without diacritical marks.
2020-00228-24 2-21

PHYSICAL MAP OF SOUTHEAST ASIA

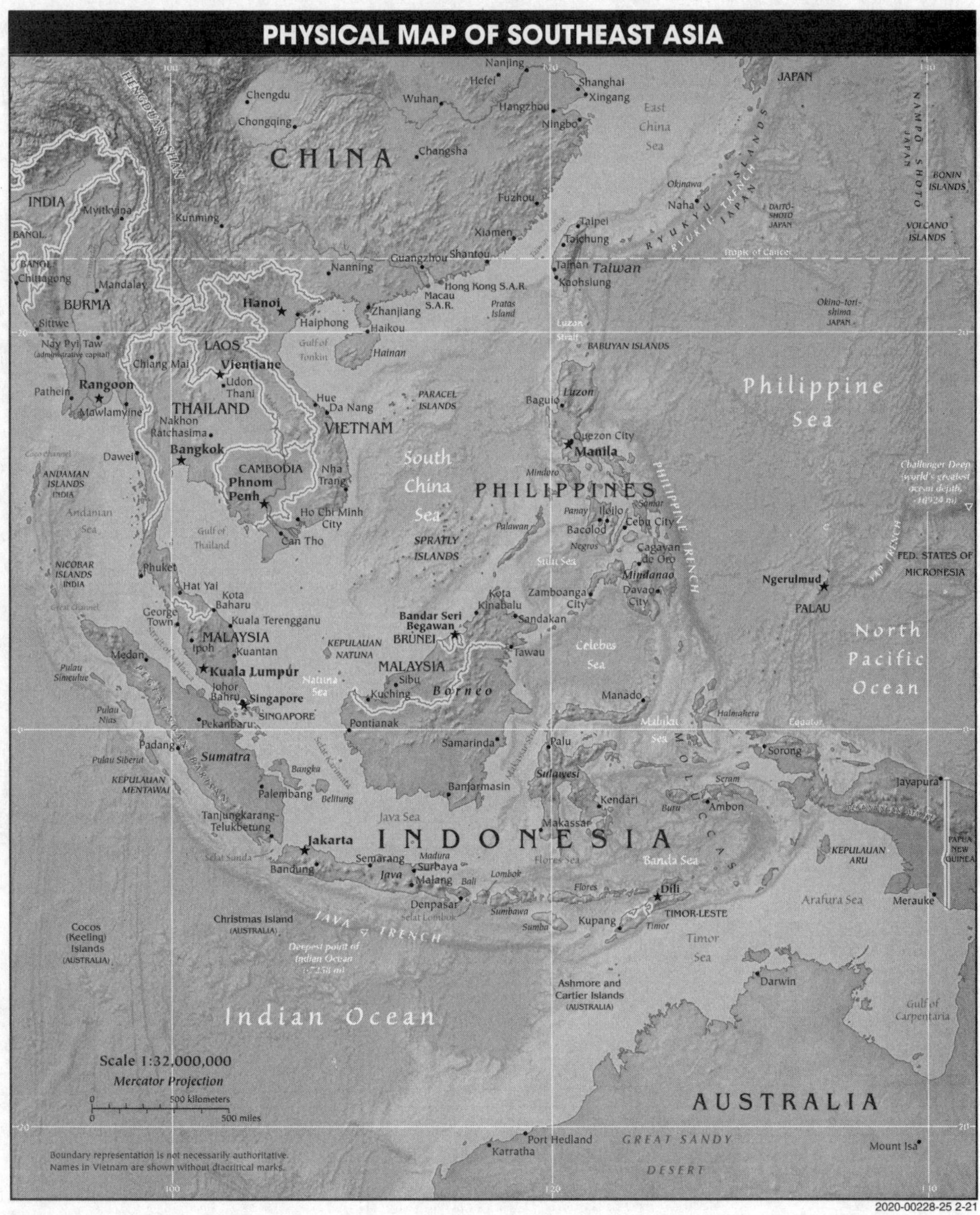

2020-00228-25 2-21

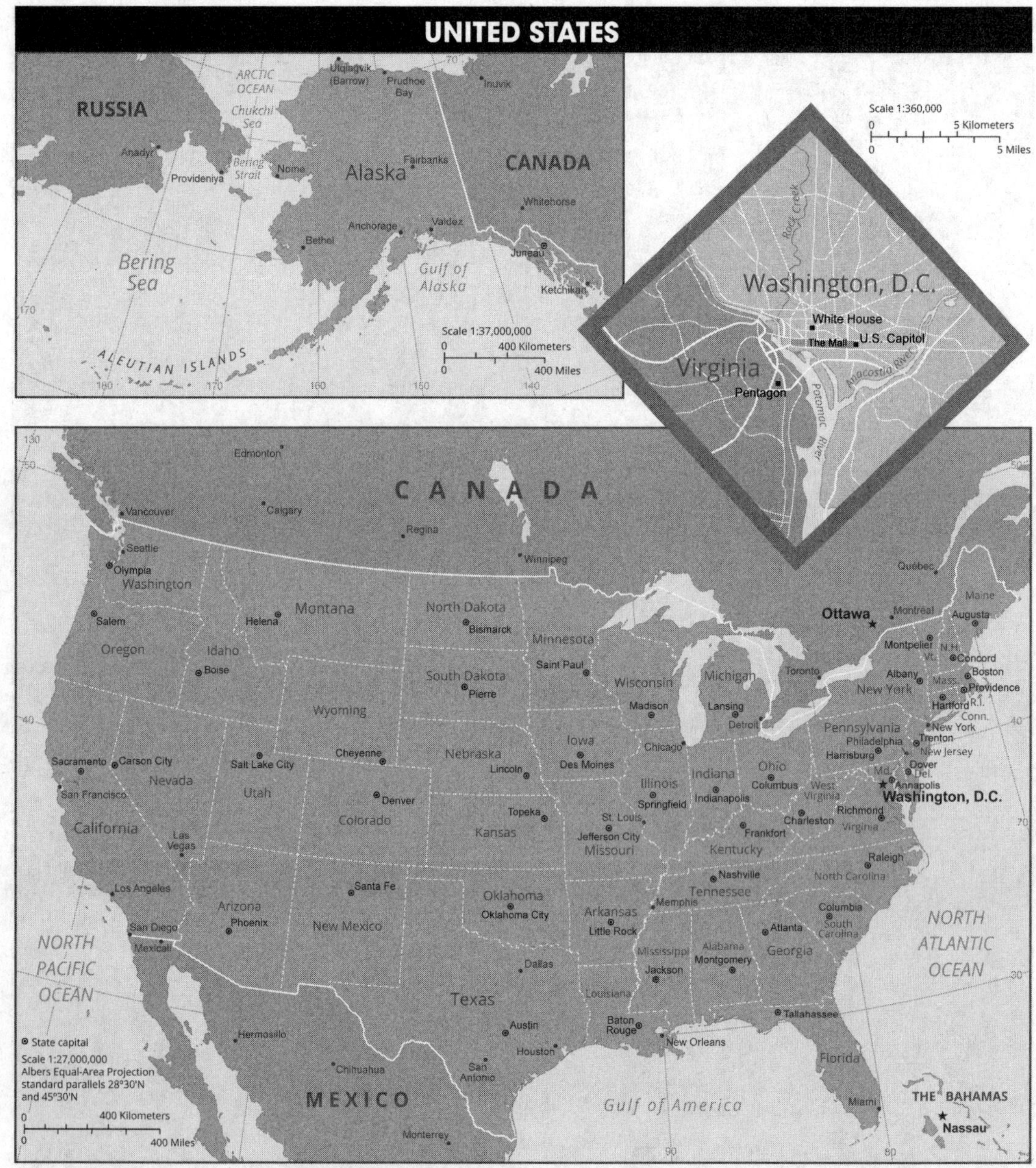

Names and boundary representation are not necessarily authoritative.

Midway Islands (U.S.)

NORTH PACIFIC OCEAN

NORTHWEST HAWAIIAN ISLANDS

Tropic of Cancer

Kauai
Hawaii
Honolulu
Oahu
Maui
Hawaii

Scale 1:34,000,000
0 400 Kilometers
0 400 Miles

2025-02982-08 3-25

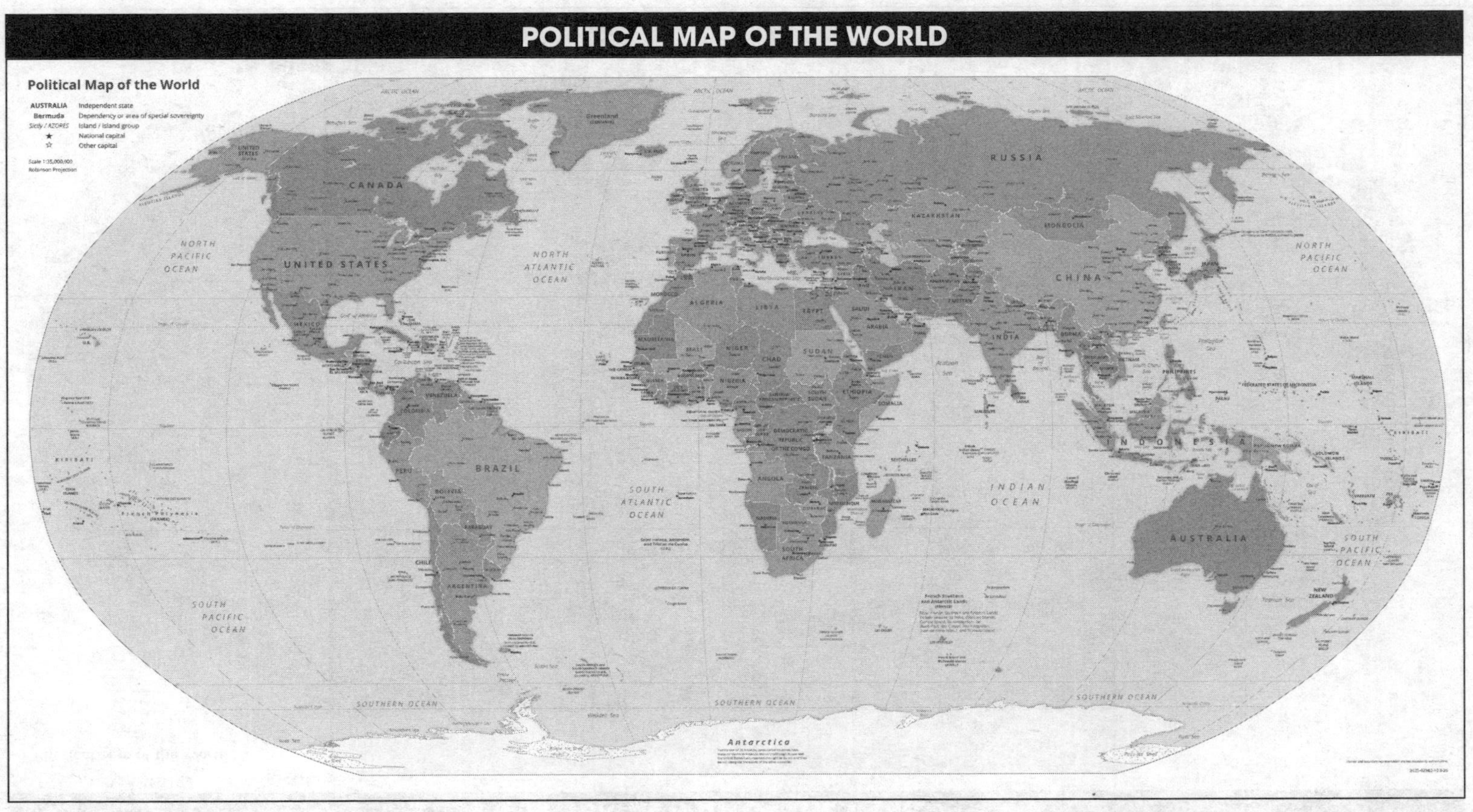

POLITICAL MAP OF THE WORLD
Political Map of the World
AUSTRALIA Independent state
Bermuda Dependency or area of special sovereignty
Sicily / AZORES Island / island group
National capital
Other capital
Scale 1:35,000,000
Robinson Projection
Greenland
CANADA
UNITED STATES
MEXICO
VENEZUELA
COLOMBIA
PERU
BRAZIL
BOLIVIA
PARAGUAY
CHILE
ARGENTINA
RUSSIA
KAZAKHSTAN
MONGOLIA
CHINA
INDIA
IRAN
SAUDI ARABIA
ALGERIA
LIBYA
EGYPT
MAURITANIA
MALI
NIGER
CHAD
SUDAN
SOUTH SUDAN
ETHIOPIA
SOMALIA
NIGERIA
DEMOCRATIC REPUBLIC OF THE CONGO
TANZANIA
ANGOLA
SOUTH AFRICA
PHILIPPINES
INDONESIA
AUSTRALIA
NEW ZEALAND
KIRIBATI
Antarctica
ARCTIC OCEAN
NORTH PACIFIC OCEAN
SOUTH PACIFIC OCEAN
NORTH ATLANTIC OCEAN
SOUTH ATLANTIC OCEAN
INDIAN OCEAN
SOUTHERN OCEAN

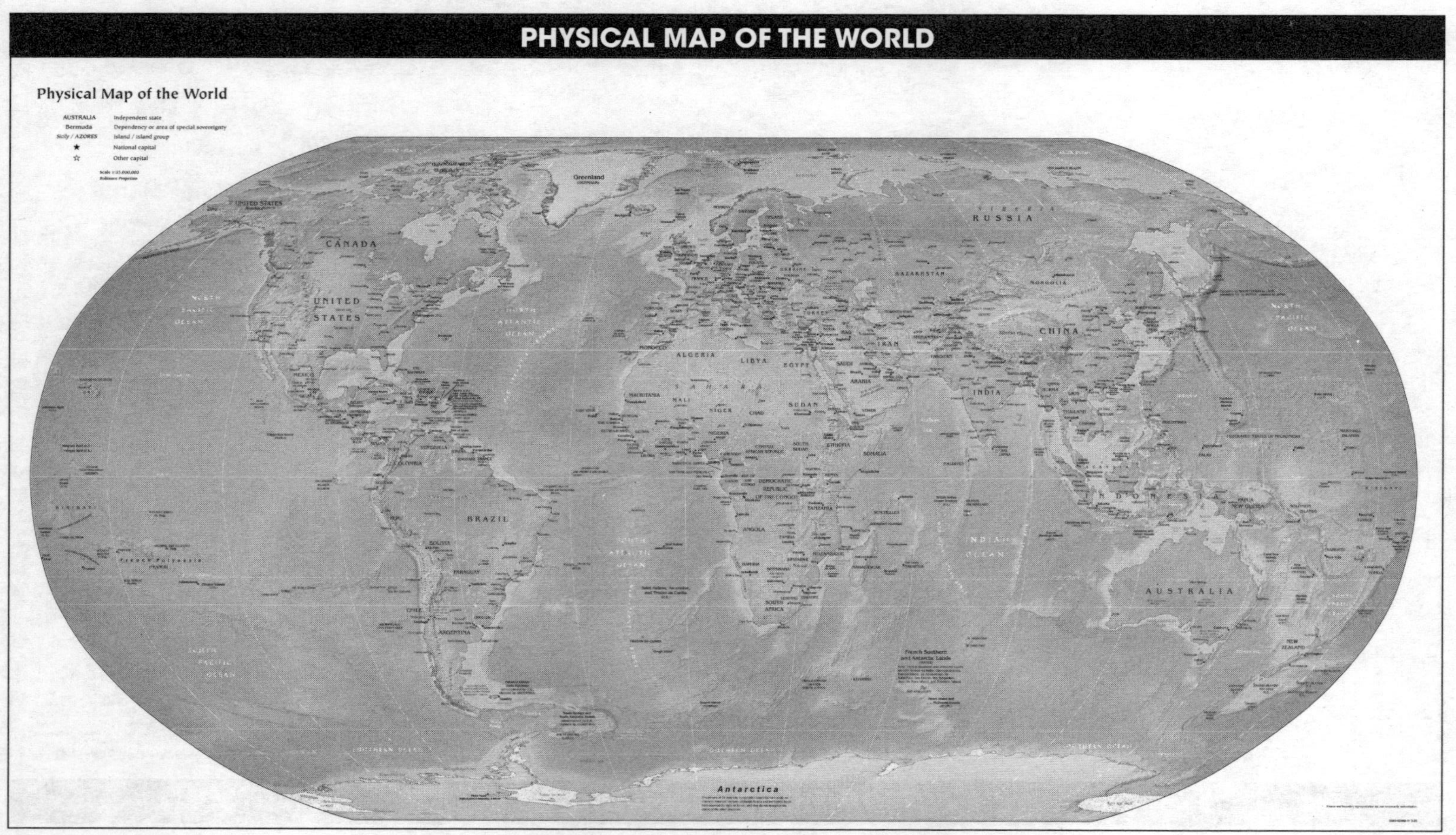
PHYSICAL MAP OF THE WORLD
Physical Map of the World
AUSTRALIA Independent state
Bermuda Dependency or area of special sovereignty
Sicily / AZORES Island / island group
★ National capital
☆ Other capital
Greenland
CANADA
UNITED STATES
NORTH PACIFIC OCEAN
NORTH ATLANTIC OCEAN
RUSSIA
KAZAKHSTAN
MONGOLIA
CHINA
IRAN
INDIA
ALGERIA
LIBYA
EGYPT
MAURITANIA
MALI
NIGER
CHAD
SUDAN
SOMALIA
DEMOCRATIC REPUBLIC OF THE CONGO
TANZANIA
ANGOLA
SOUTH AFRICA
BRAZIL
BOLIVIA
PARAGUAY
ARGENTINA
SOUTH ATLANTIC OCEAN
SOUTH PACIFIC OCEAN
INDIAN OCEAN
French Polynesia
INDONESIA
PAPUA NEW GUINEA
AUSTRALIA
NEW ZEALAND
French Southern and Antarctic Lands
SOUTHERN OCEAN
Antarctica

WORLD OCEANS

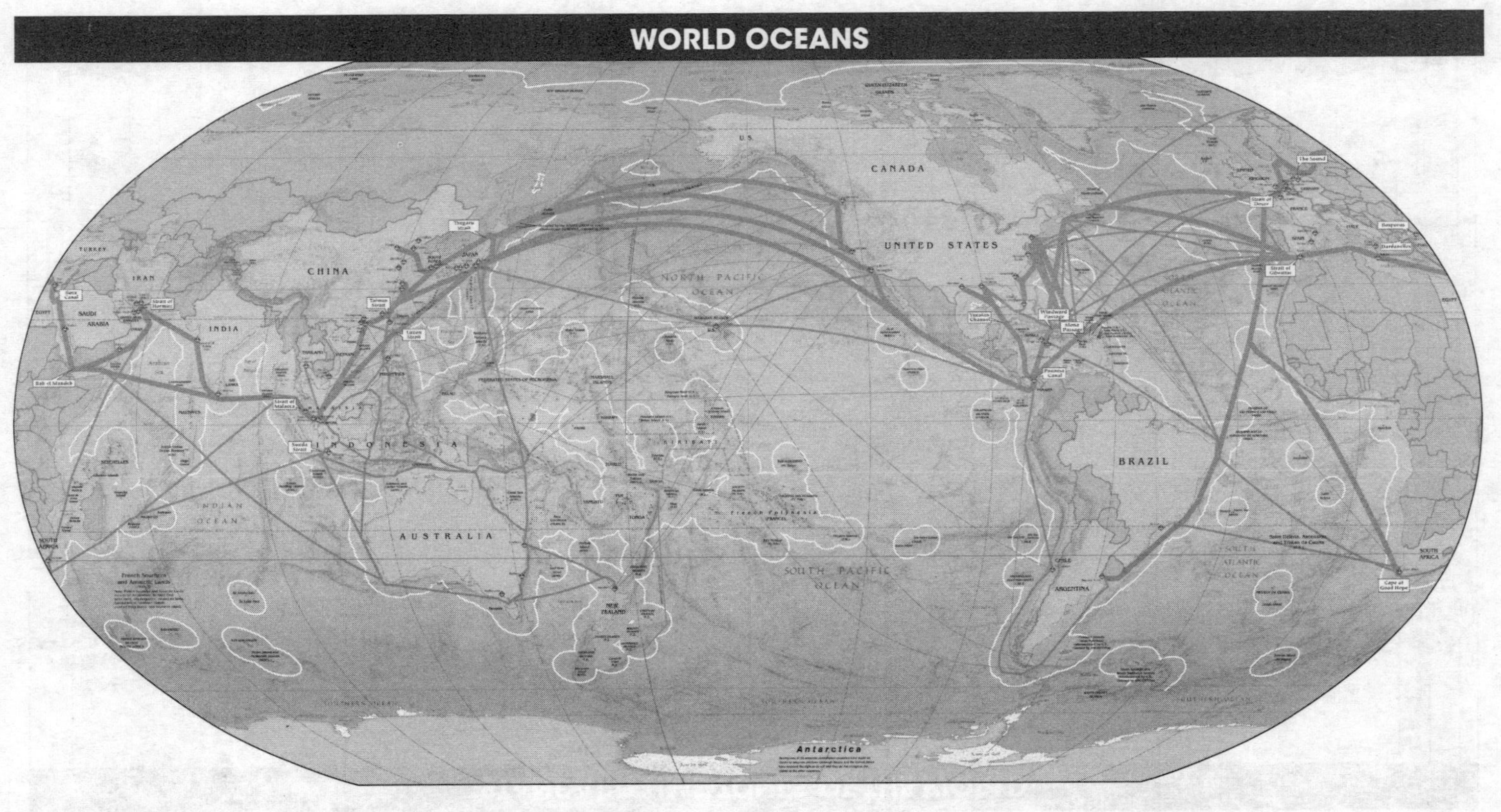

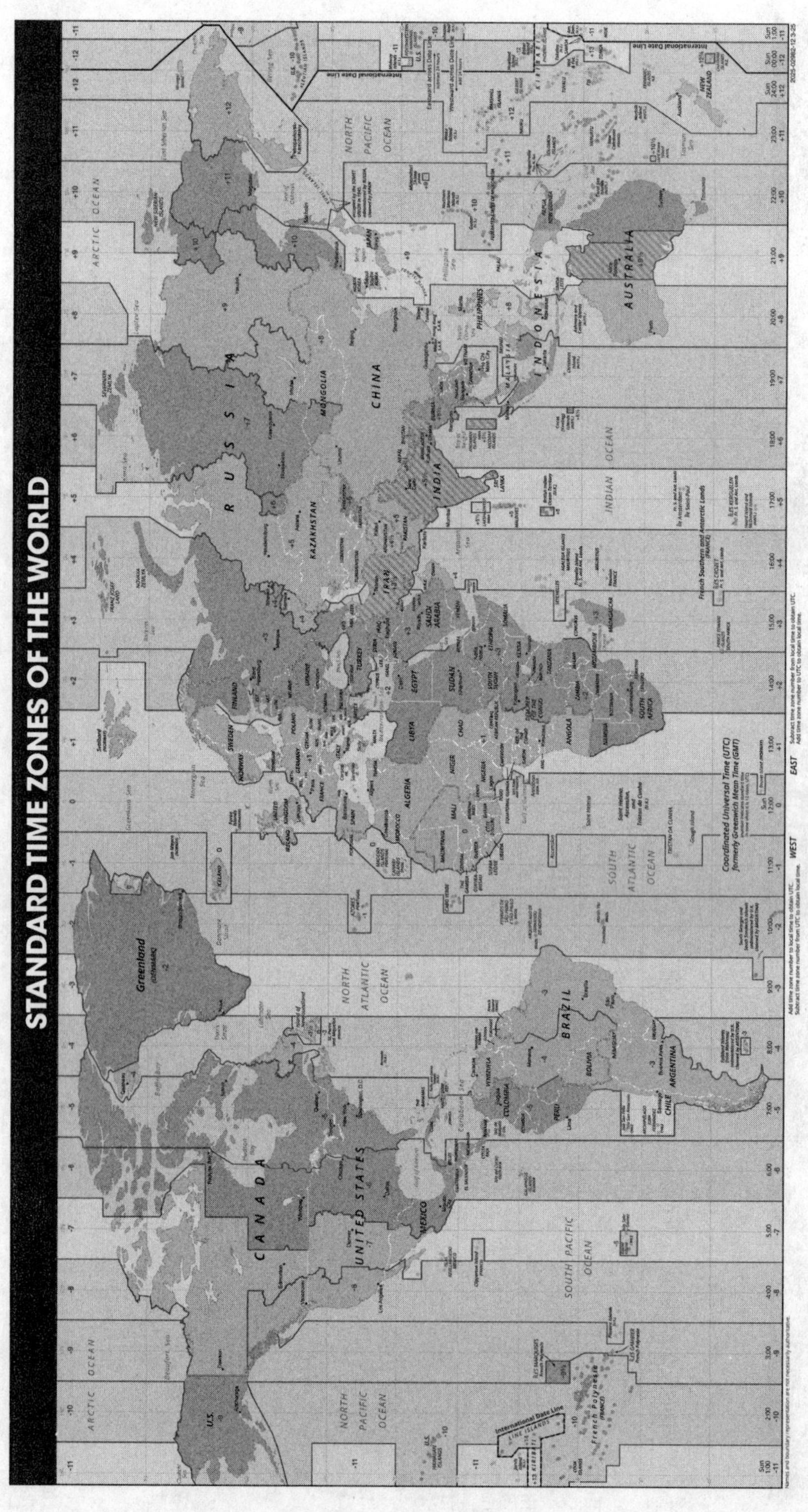
STANDARD TIME ZONES OF THE WORLD
ARCTIC OCEAN
NORTH PACIFIC OCEAN
SOUTH PACIFIC OCEAN
NORTH ATLANTIC OCEAN
SOUTH ATLANTIC OCEAN
INDIAN OCEAN
CANADA
UNITED STATES
MEXICO
Greenland
BRAZIL
ARGENTINA
RUSSIA
CHINA
INDIA
KAZAKHSTAN
MONGOLIA
INDONESIA
AUSTRALIA
ALGERIA
LIBYA
EGYPT
SUDAN
International Date Line
Coordinated Universal Time (UTC)
formerly Greenwich Mean Time (GMT)

NOTES

NOTES